Cookbook Writers

James Beard
Marian Burros
Julia Child
Craig Claiborne
M. F. K. Fisher
Pierre Franey
Jean D. Hewitt
Graham Kerr
Margaret Romagnoli
Raymond Sokolov
Jane Stern
. . . and more

Dance Critics

William Como
Arlene Croce
Edwin Denby
John Gruen
Deborah Jowitt
Marcia B. Siegel
Tobi Tobias
. . . and more

Dancers

George Balanchine
Christopher d'Amboise
Katherine Dunham
Margot Fonteyn
Jose Greco
Natalia Makarova
Peter Martins
Valery Panov
. . . and more

Diet Specialists

Stuart Berger
Jane Brody
Martin Katahn
Jean Nidetch
Nathan Pritikin
Lendon Smith
Herman Tarnower
Roy L. Walford
. . . and more

Drama Critics

Clive Barnes
Eric Bentley
Robert S. Brustein
Martin Esslin
Brendan Gill
Walter Kerr
Joseph Wood Krutch
John Simon
Stark Young
. . . and more

Economists

Alfred D. Chandler, Jr.
Martin S. Feldstein
Milton Friedman
John Kenneth Galbraith
L. St. Clare Grondona
Robert L. Heilbroner
Ursula Kathleen Hicks
Jean Monnet
Felix G. Rohatyn
Walt W. Rostow
Herbert A. Simon
Herbert Stein
James Tobin
Friedrich August von Hayek
Barbara Ward
. . . and more

Educators

J. D. Bernal
Joseph A. Califano, Jr.
Marva Collins
Robert Lyons Danly
Thomas Flanagan
Ronald Gross
Theodore M. Hesburgh
Jonathan Kozol
A. S. Neill
Neil Postman
Anne Rogovin
Richard B. Sewall
Norman R. Shapiro
Ellease Southerland
Daniel H. Yergin
. . . and more

Entrepreneurs

Walt Disney
Malcolm Forbes
J. Paul Getty
Mary Kay
Ray Kroc
Dan Lundberg
Ted Turner
. . . and more

Essayists

G. K. Chesterton
Bryan F. Griffin
Edward Hoagland
John McPhee
Joseph Mitchell
George Orwell
Calvin Trillin
E. B. White
Ellen Willis
Tom Wolfe
. . . and more

Explorers

Edwin E. Aldrin, Jr.
Michael Collins
Jacques Yves Cousteau
Thor Heyerdahl
Edmund Hillary
John Hunt
Peter Matthiessen
Alfred M. Worden
. . . and more

Feminists

Simone de Beauvoir
Susan Brownmiller
Andrea Dworkin
Barbara Ehrenreich
Betty Friedan
Germaine Greer
Kate Millet
Gloria Steinem
Rebecca West
. . . and more

Film Critics

Andre Bazin
Vincent Canby
Judith Crist
Roger Ebert
Pauline Kael
Stanley Kauffmann
Leonard Maltin
Harry Medved
Michael Medved
Rex Reed
Andrew Sarris
Richard Schickel
Gene Siskel
. . . and more

Folklorists

Roger Abrahams
Dan Ben-Amos
Jan Harold Brunvand
Richard M. Dorson
David King Dunaway
Alan Dundes
Barbara Kirshenblatt-Gimblett
Maria Leach
Alan Lomax
Stith Thompson
. . . and more

Gossip Columnists

Rona Barrett
Sheilah Graham
Hedda Hopper
Diana McLellan
Louella Parsons
Liz Smith
. . . and more

Historians

Herbert Aptheker
Jacques Benoist-Mechin
Anthony Blunt (art)
Daniel J. Boorstin
Fernand Braudel
Arthur Bryant
Bruce Catton
Kenneth Clark
Alessandra Comini
Merle Eugene Curti
Robert Darnton
David Brion Davis
Bern Dibner
Ariel Durant
Will Durant
Antonia Fraser
Peter Gay
Eugene D. Genovese
Richard Hofstadter
Hugh Honour (art)
Paul Horgan
Rhys L. Isaac
Emmanuel Le Roy Ladurie
Golo Mann
Thomas K. McCraw
Edmund Morgan
Thomas Pakenham
Erwin Panofsky (art)
Meyer Schapiro
Arthur Schlesinger, Jr.
C. V. Wedgwood
Theodore H. White
C. Vann Woodward
Louis Booker Wright
. . . and more

Horror and Occult Writers

Peter Benchley
William Peter Blatty
Edgar E. Cayce
John Coyne
Stephen King
Richard Burton Matheson
Ruth Shick Montgomery
Anne Rice
John Sand
John Saul
Jess Stearn
Whitley Strieber
. . . and more

Humorists

Roy Blount
Erma Bombeck
Art Buchwald
Peter De Vries
Ogden Nash
S. J. Perelman
James Stevenson
James Thurber
. . . and more

Jazz Artists

Louis Armstrong
Duke Ellington
Dizzy Gillespie
Benny Goodman
Charles Mingus
Art Taylor
Mel Torme
. . . and more

Lexicographers

Tana de Gamez
J. L. Dillard
Stuart Flexner
E. Arsenio Manuel
Leo C. Rosten
. . . and more

Literary Critics

M. H. Abrams
R. P. Blackmur

Literary Critics

(continued)

Harold Bloom
Cleanth Brooks
Malcolm Cowley
Jonathan Culler
David Daiches
Richard Ellmann
William Empson
Leslie A. Fiedler
Northrop Frye
Helen Gardner
Alfred Kazin
Frank Kermode
H. D. F. Kitto
F. R. Leavis
Q. D. Leavis
Percy Lubbock
John Crowe Ransom
I. A. Richards
Christopher Ricks
Lionel Trilling
Helen Hennessy Vendler
Rene Wellek
Edmund Wilson
W. K. Wimsatt, Jr.
. . . and more

Magazine and Journal Editors

Uri Avnery
Gray Davis Boone
Charles Brasch
Helen Gurley Brown
Tina Brown
Norman Cousins
Martha Foley
Tatyana Mamonova
Victoria Ocampo
William S. Schlamm
William Shawn
Jann S. Wenner
. . . and more

Media Figures and Celebrities

Alan Alda
Lauren Bacall
Joseph Bologna
Anita Bryant
George Burns
Rosalyn Carter
Dick Cavett
Charlie Chaplin
Sammy Davis, Jr.
Ruby Dee
Phil Donahue
Mike Douglas
Buddy Ebsen
Redd Foxx
Arlene Francis
David Frost
Chief Dan George
Julie Harris
Sterling Hayden
Charlton Heston
Bob Hope
Ann Jackson
Lady Bird Johnson
Angela Lansbury
Norman Lear
Shirley MacLaine
Mary Martin
Groucho Marx
Ed McMahon
Bette Midler
Roger George Moore
Nancy Davis Reagan
Robert Redford
Mister Rogers
Roy Rogers
Rosalind Russell
Margaret Truman
Liv Ullmann
Diana Dalziel Vreeland
John Wayne
Shelley Winters
. . . and more

Memoirists and Autobiographers

Quentin Crisp
Betty Ford
Helen Hanff
Billy Hayes
Nadezhda Mandelstam
Joyce Maynard
Veljko Micunovic
Richard Rodriguez
. . . and more

Military Scientists

Dwight D. Eisenhower
Basil Henry Liddell Hart
Daniel Lang
S. L. A. Marshall
John Cecil Masterman
C. Northcote Parkinson
William C. Westmoreland
Elmo Russell Zumwalt, Jr.
. . . and more

Music Critics

Lester Bangs
Robert Christgau
Jonathan Cott
Gary Giddins
Nat Hentoff
Greil Marcus
Dave Marsh
Hugues Panassie
Harold Schonberg
Nat Shapiro
Ritchie Yorke
. . . and more

Mystery and Suspense Writers

Edward S. Aarons
Eric Ambler
Gwendoline Williams Butler
James M. Cain
Agatha Christie
Mary Higgins Clark
Len Deighton
Ian Fleming
Ken Follet
Dick Francis
Sarah Gainham
Erle Stanley Gardner
John Edmund Gardner
Martha Grimes
Dashiell Hammett
Joseph Hansen
P. D. James
H. R. F. Keating
Harry Kemelman
William X. Kienzle
Emma Lathen
John le Carre
Elmore Leonard
Robert Ludlum
John D. MacDonald
Kenneth Millar
Margaret Millar
L. A. Morse
Bernard Newman
Ruth Rendell
Dorothy L. Sayers
Trevanian
. . . and more

Naturalists and Environmentalists

Cleveland Amory
Wendell Berry
Rachel Carson
Barry Commoner
Claude L. Fly
Euell Gibbons
Anne W. Simon
Victor Wolfgang Von Hagen
. . . and more

Novelists

Chinua Achebe
Alice Adams
Vassily Aksyonov
Jorge Amado
Kingsley Amis
Ivo Andric
Harriet Simpson Arnow
Miguel Angel Asturias
Margaret Atwood
James Baldwin
Djuna Barnes
John Barth
Donald Barthelme
Saul Bellow
Heinrich Boell
Jorge Luis Borges
Elizabeth Bowen
Anita Brookner
Pearl S. Buck
Anthony Burgess
Erskine Caldwell
Italo Calvino
Truman Capote
Angela Carter
Adolfo Bioy Casares
Louis-Ferdinand Celine
John Cheever
Julio Cortazar
Robertson Davies
Joan Didion
Isak Dinesen
Jose Donoso
John Dos Passos
Sergei Dovlatov
Margaret Drabble
Marguerite Duras
Lawrence Durrell
Ralph Ellison
William Faulkner
E. M. Forster
John Fowles
Ladislav Fuks
William Gaddis
Gabriel Garcia Marquez
Jean Genet
Jose Maria Gironella
Janusz Glowacki
Gail Godwin
William Golding
Nadine Gordimer
Mary Gordon
Guenter Grass
Shirley Ann Grau
Graham Greene
Jiri Grusa
Knut Hamsun
Peter Handke
Elizabeth Hardwick
John Hawkes
Joseph Heller
Ernest Hemingway

(continued on back endsheets)

Check the *Contemporary Authors* Cumulative Index to Locate Sketches on These and Thousands of Other Authors

Contemporary Authors®

ISSN 0010-7468

Contemporary Authors®

A Bio-Bibliographical Guide to Current Writers in Fiction, General Nonfiction, Poetry, Journalism, Drama, Motion Pictures, Television, and Other Fields

HAL MAY
SUSAN M. TROSKY
Editors

NANCY H. EVANS
LOUISE MOONEY
Associate Editors

LES STONE
Senior Writer

volume 124

Gale Research Inc. • Book Tower • Detroit, Michigan 48226

STAFF

Hal May and Susan M. Trosky, *Editors, Original Volumes*
Nancy H. Evans and Louise Mooney, *Associate Editors*
Les Stone, *Senior Writer*
Polly A. Vedder, *Senior Assistant Editor*
Christa Brelin, Thomas Kozikowski, Nancy Pear, Joanne M. Peters, and Elizabeth Thomas, *Assistant Editors and Writers*
Barbara K. Carlisle, Barbara A. Cicchetti, Carol Lynn DeKane, Janice E. Drane, Jeremy Kane, and Linda S. Smouse, *Assistant Editors*
Arlene True, *Sketchwriter*
Peter Benjaminson, Jean W. Ross, and Walter W. Ross, *Interviewers*
Diane L. Dupuis, Linda Hubbard, Renee A. Kingcaid, Frances Locher, Paulette Petrimoulx, Charles J. Rzepka, Alan Shucard, and Curtis Skinner, *Contributing Editors*
James G. Lesniak, *Index Coordinator*

Linda Metzger, *Senior Editor, Contemporary Authors*

Mary Rose Bonk, *Research Supervisor*
Alysa I. Hunton and David Esse Salamie, *Assistant Research Coordinators*
Reginald A. Carlton, Jane Cousins-Clegg, and Norma Sawaya, *Senior Research Assistants*
Aida M. Barse, Thomas P. Buckley, John P. Dodt, Shirelle Goss, Clare Kinsman, Timothy P. Loszewski, Andrew Guy Malonis, Sharon McGilvray, Shirley Seip, and Tracey Head Turbett, *Research Assistants*

Special recognition is given to the staff of Young People's Literature Department, Gale Research Inc.

Library of Congress Catalog Card Number 62-52046
ISBN 0-8103-1924-1
ISSN 0010-7468

Computerized photocomposition by
Typographics, Incorporated
Kansas City, Missouri

Contents

Authors and Media People
Featured in This Volume vii

Preface ix

Volume Update Chart xiii

Author Listings 1

Cumulative Index 493

Authors and Media People Featured in This Volume

Howard H. Baker, Jr. (American politician)—Baker served as U.S. senator from Tennessee from 1967 to 1985 and became President Ronald Reagan's White House chief of staff in 1987. In addition, he is the author of *No Margin for Error* and *What Must Be Done and How We Must Do It.*

Jean-Jacques Beineix (French filmmaker)—Renowned for both his dazzling style and his self-indulgent approach, Beineix wrote the screenplays for such provocative motion pictures as "Diva," "The Moon in the Gutter," and "Betty Blue."

Mongo Beti (African author)—Beti explores the encroachment of Western ways upon African civilization in such novels as *Remember Ruben, Perpetua and the Habit of Unhappiness,* and *Lament for an African Pol.* Critics regard him as "one of the most elegant and sophisticated of African writers."

Alvin Boretz (American writer)—Boretz is among television's most prolific writers, with an estimated one thousand scripts to his credit, many for such "Golden Age of Television" anthologies as "Playhouse 90" and "General Electric Theatre." (Sketch contains interview.)

Marcel Brion (French writer who died in 1984)—Said to have opened a wealth of cultural knowledge to the general reader, Brion published more than one hundred works of history, criticism, and fiction. *The Medici: A Great Florentine Family* and *Art of the Romantic Era* are among his writings.

Helen Caldicott (Australian-born pediatrician, activist, and author)—Caldicott, an antinuclear activist and co-author of *Nuclear Madness: What You Can Do!* and author of *Missile Envy: The Arms Race and Nuclear War,* was nominated for the Nobel Peace Prize in 1985. (Sketch contains interview.)

Anton Chekhov (Russian physician and writer who died in 1904)—Chekhov is considered the father of both the modern short story and the modern play. His masterpieces, the dramas "The Three Sisters," "The Cherry Orchard," "Uncle Vanya," and "The Seagull," influenced such playwrights as George Bernard Shaw, Tennessee Williams, and Arthur Miller.

Countee Cullen (American writer who died in 1946)—Deemed one of the brightest luminaries of the Harlem Renaissance, Cullen won widespread recognition when he published *Color,* his first and, say critics, his best book of poems. His belief that art transcends race was behind his goal of achieving colorblind artistic freedom.

Saul David (American film producer)—David produced several successful movies, including "Von Ryan's Express," "Our Man Flint," "Fantastic Voyage," and "Logan's Run," his best-known film. He also wrote the 1981 book *The Industry: Life in the Hollywood Fast Lane.*

Philip J. Davis (American mathematician)—In addition to his technical writings, Davis, professor of applied mathematics at Brown University, has produced books for general readers. One of these works, *The Mathematical Experience,* won an American Book Award in 1983.

Michael Ende (German writer)—Ende is the author of *The Neverending Story,* a critically acclaimed fantasy novel that was a best-selling book in West Germany for three years and was on best-seller lists in the United States and elsewhere. It was also adapted as a commercially successful movie.

Julius J. Epstein (American screenwriter)—Epstein co-authored the Academy Award-winning screenplay for the now classic film "Casablanca," starring Humphrey Bogart and Ingrid Bergman. "Arsenic and Old Lace" and "Reuben, Reuben" are among Epstein's numerous other films.

Stuart Evans (British novelist)—Evans's highly structured and intellectually demanding "Windmill Hill" novels have been praised for their wit and insight. According to the author, the five-volume series examines "the lack of resolve and intellectual conviction in Western liberal democracy." (Sketch contains interview.)

Veronica Geng (American writer)—Called "the cleverest *New Yorker* humorist to come along since Woody Allen," Geng practices the art of social satire. Twenty-nine of her "lethal" parodies, many first published in *New Yorker,* appear in her 1984 collection, *Partners.*

Andre Gide (French writer who died in 1951)—Gide's extensive body of work, written in a variety of genres, records the personal conflicts of the Nobel Prize-winning author. His reputation in the United States was secured by his novels *The Immoralist, Lafcadio's Adventures,* and *The Counterfeiters.*

Gary Hart (American politician and author)—A former U.S. senator whose campaign for the Democratic presidential nomination in 1988 was undermined by widely publicized allegations of marital infidelity, Hart has written two novels as well as the political works *Right From the Start* and *America Can Win.*

Jim Henson (American puppeteer)—Henson is the award-winning creator of the Muppets and, reputedly, the most successful puppeteer in history. The Muppets have appeared on such popular children's television shows as "Sesame Street" and "Fraggle Rock" and in several Muppet movies.

Florence Howe (American educator, publisher, and writer)—Howe's writings, including the 1984 collection of essays *Myths of Coeducation,* reflect the author's longtime advocacy of social and educational reform. She is the founder and president of Feminist Press. (Sketch contains interview.)

Gwyn Jones (Welsh scholar and writer)—Specializing in the history and legends of Celtic, Norse, English, and Welsh peoples, Jones edited *The Oxford Book of Welsh Verse in English,* translated *The Golden Cockerel Mabinogion* with Thomas Jones, and wrote *Kings, Beasts, and Heroes.*

Kinoshita Junji (Japanese playwright)—Kinoshita is deemed contemporary Japan's most notable playwright, and he is credited with bridging the gap between classical Japanese theater and the modern world. "Twilight Crane" and "Between God and Man: A Judgment on War Crimes" are among his works.

David Malouf (Australian writer)—Malouf, an Australian currently living in Italy, wrote the 1978 novel *An Imaginary Life,* which won the New South Wales Premier's Prize for fiction, and the novella *Fly Away Peter,* which received a Book of the Year Award in 1982.

Michael Martone (American educator and author)—An interest in the various aspects of celebrity led to Martone's critically acclaimed *Alive and Dead in Indiana,* a collection of short stories, each focusing on a fictional episode in the life of a famous, or infamous, real-life personality. (Sketch contains interview.)

Peyo (Belgian cartoonist)—Peyo is the pseudonym of cartoonist Pierre Culliford, creator of the tiny blue trolls known as Smurfs. These cartoon figures have been consistently popular since their first appearance in 1957, and they are the basis for Peyo's array of best-selling books and television shows.

Max Robinson (American broadcast journalist)—The first black journalist to anchor a prime-time national network news program, Robinson appeared on "ABC World News Tonight" from 1978 to 1983. He and co-anchors Frank Reynolds, Peter Jennings, and Barbara Walters were credited with bringing ABC's news ratings into parity with those of the other major networks. (Sketch contains interview.)

Rudy Rucker (American mathematician and author)—Rucker is the author of *Mind Tools* and *Infinity and the Mind* and other nonfiction works. He also writes science fiction novels, such as *Software* and *Master of Space and Time,* noted for their originality. (Sketch contains interview.)

Bob Shacochis (American writer)—Shacochis won the American Book Award for First Fiction in 1985 for his volume of short stories, *Easy in the Islands.* His second book is the novel *Swimming in the Volcano.* His writings have also been published in literary journals and other periodicals. (Sketch contains interview.)

Hugh Sidey (American journalist)—A correspondent and columnist for *Time* magazine since 1958, Sidey has covered the administrations of seven U.S. presidents and has written books on three of them: John F. Kennedy, Lyndon B. Johnson, and Gerald R. Ford.

Wallace Stevens (American poet who died in 1955)—Deemed by critic Harold Bloom as "the best and most representative American poet of our time," Stevens was known as a master stylist. Abstract and provocative, his canon includes the award-winning *Auroras of Autumn* and *The Collected Poems of Wallace Stevens.*

Patti Stren (Canadian author and illustrator of children's books)—*Hug Me,* Stren's self-illustrated best-seller about an affectionate porcupine, is popular with adults and children alike. Other well-received books by the author include *Mountain Rose* and *Bo, the Constrictor That Couldn't.*

Frank J. Sulloway (American scholar)—Sulloway's standing as a respected scholar in the history of science stems from his book *Freud, Biologist of the Mind: Beyond the Psychoanalytic Legend.* For his achievements in scholarship Sulloway was awarded the MacArthur Prize in 1984. (Sketch contains interview.)

Ted Tally (American playwright)—A successful young playwright, Tally is the author of several plays, all lauded by critics. "Terra Nova," a serious work about Antarctic explorer Robert Falcon Scott, is his best known; others are the comedies "Hooters," "Coming Attractions," and "Little Footsteps." (Sketch contains interview.)

Janelle Taylor (American romance novelist)—Taylor's best-selling "Ecstasy Saga" series was recognized at the 1983 Sioux National Celebration for its accurate portrayal of native Americans. Other award-winning historical romances by Taylor include *Golden Torment* and *First Love, Wild Love.* (Sketch contains interview.)

Askia Muhammad Abu Bakr el Toure (American poet)—A leader of the black aesthetic movement since the early 1960s, Toure has written volumes of essays and poems, notably *Songhai!* and *Juju: Magic Songs for the Black Nation.* He has also served as editor-at-large of the journal *Kitabu Cha Jua.*

Stansfield Turner (American naval officer and government official)—A career officer in the U.S. Navy, Turner served as director of the Central Intelligence Agency during Jimmy Carter's presidency. His memoir, *Secrecy and Democracy: The CIA in Transition,* was published in 1985. (Sketch contains interview.)

Preface

The more than 800 entries in *Contemporary Authors* (*CA*), Volume 124, bring to more than 90,000 the number of authors now represented in the *Contemporary Authors* series. *CA* includes nontechnical writers in all genres—fiction, nonfiction, poetry, drama, etc.—whose books are issued by commercial, risk publishers or by university presses. Authors of books published only by known vanity or author-subsidized firms are ordinarily not included. Since native language and nationality have no bearing on inclusion in *CA*, authors who write in languages other than English are included in *CA* if their works have been published in the United States or translated into English.

Although *CA* focuses primarily on authors of published books, the series also encompasses prominent persons in communications: newspaper and television reporters and correspondents, columnists, newspaper and magazine editors, photojournalists, syndicated cartoonists, screenwriters, television scriptwriters, and other media people.

Starting with Volume 104, the editors of *CA* began to broaden the series' scope to encompass authors deceased since 1900 whose works are still of interest to today's readers. (Previously, *CA* covered only living writers and authors deceased 1960 or later.) Since the great poets, novelists, short story writers, and playwrights of the early twentieth century are popular writers for study in today's high school and college curriculums, and since their writings continue to be analyzed by literary critics, these writers are in many ways as contemporary as the authors *CA* has featured up to this point.

Therefore, *CA* contains information on important authors who lived and wrote between 1900 and 1959. Numerous authors from this period, most of whom will receive longer treatment later, are represented in *CA* with short, succinct entries that summarize their lives and literary contributions. These brief entries are further explained in the section of the preface headed "Brief Entries."

Each volume of *CA* now also includes a limited number of full-length entries on authors deceased before 1960. Providing detailed commentary about writers' lives and literary achievements, these sketches in addition offer both a historical and contemporary review of the authors' critical reputations. The entries in this volume on Anton Chekhov, Countee Cullen, Andre Gide, and Wallace Stevens reflect the variety of early twentieth-century authors to be featured in future *CA* volumes.

No charge or obligation is attached to a *CA* listing. Authors are included in the series solely on the basis of the above criteria and their interest to *CA* users.

Compilation Methods

The editors make every effort to secure information directly from the authors through questionnaires and personal correspondence. If writers of special interest to *CA* users are deceased or fail to reply to requests for information, material is gathered from other reliable sources. Biographical dictionaries are checked (a task made easier through the use of Gale's *Biography and Genealogy Master Index* and other volumes in the "Gale Biographical Index Series"), as are bibliographical sources such as *Cumulative Book Index* and *The National Union Catalog*. Published interviews, feature stories, and book reviews are examined, and often material is supplied by the authors' publishers. All sketches, whether prepared from questionnaires or through extensive research, are sent to the biographees for review prior to publication. Sketches on recently deceased authors are sent to family members, agents, etc., if possible, for a similar review.

Format

CA is designed to present, clearly and concisely, biographical and bibliographical information in three kinds of listings: sketches, brief entries, and obituary notices. The series' easy-to-use format ensures that a reader needing specific information can quickly focus on the pertinent portion of an entry. Sketches, for instance, contain individual paragraphs with rubrics identifying addresses, memberships, and awards and honors. Furthermore, in sketch sections headed "Writings," the title of each book, play, and other published or unpublished work appears on a separate line, clearly distinguishing one title from another. This same convenient bibliographical presentation is featured in the "Biographical/Critical Sources" sections of sketches and brief entries and in the

"Obituaries and Other Sources" sections of obituary notices where individual book and periodical titles are also listed on separate lines. *CA* readers can therefore quickly scan these often-lengthy bibliographies to find the titles they need.

Brief Entries

CA users have indicated that having some information, however brief, on authors not yet in the series would be preferable to waiting until full-length sketches can be prepared as outlined above under "Compilation Methods." Since Volume 104, therefore, *CA* has included concise, condensed entries on both early twentieth-century and current writers who presently do not have sketches in *CA*. These short listings, identified by the heading "Brief Entry," highlight the authors' careers and writings and often provide a few sources where additional information can be found.

Brief entries are not intended to serve as sketches. Instead, they are designed to increase *CA*'s comprehensiveness and thus better serve *CA* users by providing pertinent information about a large number of authors, many of whom will be the subjects of full-length sketches in forthcoming volumes.

Informative Sidelights

Numerous *CA* sketches contain sidelights, which provide personal dimensions to the listings, supply information about the critical reception the authors' works have received, or both. Some authors presented in Volume 124 worked closely with *CA*'s editors to develop interesting, incisive sidelights. Professional storyteller Steve Sanfield, for example, describes his concern with "getting onto paper forgotten and vaguely remembered tales that still have the power to touch human hearts and minds."

CA's editors also compile sidelights when authors and media people of particular interest do not supply sidelights material or when demand for information about the critical reception accorded their writings is especially high. For instance, assistant editor and writer Elizabeth Thomas discusses the novels *Two Crimes, The Dead Girls,* and *The Lightning of August* in sidelights for deceased Mexican author Jorge Ibarguengoitia, and Australian writer David Malouf, who wrote the novel *An Imaginary Life,* is the subject of sidelights by assistant editor Carol Lynn DeKane.

We hope these sketches, as well as others with sidelights compiled by *CA*'s editors, provide informative and enjoyable reading.

Exclusive Interviews

CA provides exclusive, primary information on certain writers in the form of interviews. Prepared specifically for *CA,* the never-before-published conversations presented in the section of the sketch headed "*CA* Interview" give users the opportunity to learn the authors' thoughts, in depth, about their craft. Subjects chosen for interviews are, the editors feel, authors who hold special interest for *CA*'s readers.

Writers and journalists in this volume whose sketches include interviews are Alvin Boretz, Helen Caldicott, Stuart Evans, Florence Howe, Michael Martone, Max Robinson, Rudy Rucker, Bob Shacochis, Frank J. Sulloway, Ted Tally, Janelle Taylor, and Stansfield Turner.

Obituary Notices Make *CA* Timely and Comprehensive

To be as timely and comprehensive as possible, *CA* publishes obituary notices on deceased authors within the scope of the series. These notices provide date and place of birth and death, highlight the author's career and writings, and list other sources where additional biographical information and obituaries may be found. To distinguish them from full-length sketches, obituaries are identified with the heading "Obituary Notice."

CA includes obituary notices for writers who already have full-length entries in earlier *CA* volumes—48 percent of the obituary notices in this volume are for such authors—as well as for authors who do not yet have sketches in the series. Deceased writers of special interest currently represented only by obituary notices will be scheduled for full-length sketch treatment in forthcoming *CA* volumes.

Contemporary Authors New Revision Series

A major change in the preparation of *CA* revision volumes began with the first volume of *Contemporary Authors New Revision Series.* No longer are all of the sketches in a given *CA* volume updated and published together as a revision volume. Instead, entries from a number of volumes are assessed, and only those sketches requiring *significant change* are revised and published in a *New Revision Series* volume. This enables us to

provide *CA* users with updated information about active writers on a more timely basis and avoids printing entries in which there has been little or no change. As always, the most recent *CA* cumulative index continues to be the user's guide to the location of an individual author's revised listing.

Contemporary Authors Autobiography Series

Designed to complement the information in *CA* original and revision volumes, the *Contemporary Authors Autobiography Series* provides autobiographical essays written by important current authors. Each volume contains twenty to thirty specially commissioned autobiographies and is illustrated with numerous personal photographs supplied by the authors. The range of contemporary writers describing their lives and interests in the *Autobiography Series* encompasses authors such as Dannie Abse, Vance Bourjaily, Doris Grumbach, Elizabeth Forsythe Hailey, Marge Piercy, Frederik Pohl, Alan Sillitoe, William Stafford, Diane Wakoski, and Elie Wiesel. Though the information presented in the autobiographies is as varied and unique as the authors, common topics of discussion include their motivations for writing, the people and experiences that shaped their careers, the rewards they derive from their work, and their impressions of the current literary scene.

Autobiographies included in the *Contemporary Authors Autobiography Series* can be located through both the *CA* cumulative index and the *Contemporary Authors Autobiography Series* cumulative index, which lists not only personal names but also titles of works, geographical names, subjects, and schools of writing.

Contemporary Authors Bibliographical Series

The *Contemporary Authors Bibliographical Series* is a comprehensive survey of writings by and about the most important authors since World War II in the United States and abroad. Each volume concentrates on a specific genre and nationality and features approximately ten major writers. Volume 1, for instance, covers the American novelists James Baldwin, John Barth, Saul Bellow, John Cheever, Joseph Heller, Norman Mailer, Bernard Malamud, Carson McCullers, John Updike, and Eudora Welty. *Bibliographical Series* entries consist of three parts: a primary bibliography that lists works written by the author, a secondary bibliography that lists works about the author, and an analytical bibliographical essay that thoroughly discusses the merits and deficiencies of major critical and scholarly works. Complementing the information in other *CA* volumes, the *Bibliographical Series* is a new key to finding and evaluating information on the lives and writings of those authors who have attracted significant critical attention.

Each author's entry in the *Contemporary Authors Bibliographical Series* can be located through both the *CA* cumulative index and, beginning with Volume 2, the *Contemporary Authors Bibliographical Series* cumulative author index. A cumulative index to the critics discussed in the bibliographical essays also appears in each *Bibliographical Series* volume.

CA Numbering System

Occasionally questions arise about the *CA* numbering system. Despite numbers like "97-100" and "124," the entire *CA* series consists of only 84 physical volumes with the publication of *CA* Volume 124. The following information notes changes in the numbering system, as well as in cover design, to help users better understand the organization of the entire *CA* series.

_CA_ First Revisions

- 1-4R through 41-44R (11 books)
  Cover: Brown with black and gold trim.
  There will be no further *First Revisions* because revised entries are now being handled exclusively through the more efficient *New Revision Series* mentioned below.

_CA_ Original Volumes

- 45-48 through 97-100 (14 books)
  Cover: Brown with black and gold trim.
- 101 through 124 (24 books)
  Cover: Blue and black with orange bands.
  The same as previous *CA* original volumes but with a new, simplified numbering system and new cover design.

_CA_ New Revision Series

- *CANR*-1 through *CANR*-24 (24 books)
  Cover: Blue and black with green bands.
  Includes only sketches requiring extensive change; **sketches are taken from any previously published _CA_ volume.**

CA Permanent Series

- *CAP*-1 and *CAP*-2 (2 books)
  Cover: Brown with red and gold trim.
  There will be no further *Permanent Series* volumes because revised entries are now being handled exclusively through the more efficient *New Revision Series* mentioned above.

CA Autobiography Series

- *CAAS*-1 through *CAAS*-7 (7 books)
  Cover: Blue and black with pink and purple bands.
  Presents specially commissioned autobiographies by leading contemporary writers.

CA Bibliographical Series

- *CABS*-1 and *CABS*-2 (2 books)
  Cover: Blue and black with blue bands.
  Provides comprehensive bibliographical information on published works by and about major modern authors.

Retaining *CA* Volumes

As new volumes in the series are published, users often ask which *CA* volumes, if any, can be discarded. The Volume Update Chart on page xiii is designed to assist users in keeping their collections as complete as possible. All volumes in the left column of the chart should be retained to have the most complete, up-to-date coverage; volumes in the right column can be discarded if the appropriate replacements are held.

Cumulative Index Should Always Be Consulted

The key to locating an individual author's listing is the *CA* cumulative index bound into the back of alternate original volumes (and available separately as an offprint). Since the *CA* cumulative index provides access to *all* entries in the *CA* series, the latest cumulative index should always be consulted to find the specific volume containing an author's original or most recently revised sketch.

For the convenience of *CA* users, the *CA* cumulative index also includes references to all entries in these related Gale literary series: *Authors in the News, Children's Literature Review, Concise Dictionary of American Literary Biography, Contemporary Literary Criticism, Dictionary of Literary Biography, Short Story Criticism, Something About the Author, Something About the Author Autobiography Series, Twentieth-Century Literary Criticism,* and *Yesterday's Authors of Books for Children.*

Acknowledgments

The editors wish to thank Judith S. Baughman for her assistance with copy editing.

Suggestions Are Welcome

The editors welcome comments and suggestions from users on any aspects of the *CA* series. If readers would like to suggest authors whose entries should appear in future volumes of the series, they are cordially invited to write: The Editors, *Contemporary Authors,* Gale Research Inc., Book Tower, Detroit, MI 48226-1822; or call toll-free at 1-800-521-0707.

Volume Update Chart

IF YOU HAVE:	YOU MAY DISCARD:
1-4 First Revision (1967)	1 (1962) 2 (1963) 3 (1963) 4 (1963)
5-8 First Revision (1969)	5-6 (1963) 7-8 (1963)
Both 9-12 First Revision (1974) AND *Contemporary Authors Permanent Series,* Volume 1 (1975)	9-10 (1964) 11-12 (1965)
Both 13-16 First Revision (1975) AND *Contemporary Authors Permanent Series,* Volumes 1 and 2 (1975, 1978)	13-14 (1965) 15-16 (1966)
Both 17-20 First Revision (1976) AND *Contemporary Authors Permanent Series,* Volumes 1 and 2 (1975, 1978)	17-18 (1967) 19-20 (1968)
Both 21-24 First Revision (1977) AND *Contemporary Authors Permanent Series,* Volumes 1 and 2 (1975, 1978)	21-22 (1969) 23-24 (1970)
Both 25-28 First Revision (1977) AND *Contemporary Authors Permanent Series,* Volume 2 (1978)	25-28 (1971)
Both 29-32 First Revision (1978) AND *Contemporary Authors Permanent Series,* Volume 2 (1978)	29-32 (1972)
Both 33-36 First Revision (1978) AND *Contemporary Authors Permanent Series,* Volume 2 (1978)	33-36 (1973)
37-40 First Revision (1979)	37-40 (1973)
41-44 First Revision (1979)	41-44 (1974)
45-48 (1974) 49-52 (1975) ↓ ↓ 124 (1988)	NONE: These volumes will not be superseded by corresponding revised volumes. Individual entries from these and all other volumes appearing in the left column of this chart will be revised and included in the *New Revision Series.*
Volumes in the *Contemporary Authors New Revision Series*	NONE: The *New Revision Series* does not replace any single volume of *CA.* All volumes appearing in the left column of this chart must be retained to have information on all authors in the series.

Contemporary Authors

**Indicates that a listing has been compiled from secondary sources believed to be reliable but has not been personally verified for this edition by the author sketched.*

AARON, Stephen 1936-

PERSONAL: Born March 25, 1936, in New York, N.Y.; son of S. David (a salesman) and Sara (a bookkeeper; maiden name, Goldstein) Aaron. *Education:* Harvard University, B.A., 1957; City University of New York, Ph.D., 1979.

ADDRESSES: Office—53 East 82nd St., New York, N.Y. 10028.

CAREER: Wilbur Theater, Boston, Mass., founder and artistic director of Repertory Boston, 1958-59; Harvard University, Cambridge, Mass., lecturer in drama and assistant director of Loeb Drama Center, 1959-61; director of plays on and Off-Broadway, 1962-65; stage producer, 1962-74; New Theater Workshop, New York City, founder and artistic director, 1965-71; Group Relations Workshop, New York City, co-administrator, 1975; The Bridge, New York City, group therapist, 1975-76; New York Hospital, New York City, psychology intern at Payne Whitney Clinic, 1977-78; private practice of adolescent and adult psychotherapy in New York City, 1978—. Lecturer at New York University, 1962-65; visiting lecturer at Rutgers University, 1965-71; acting teacher at Juilliard School, 1969—. Interviewer for Kenwood Psychological Services, 1981—; adjunct supervisor for doctoral program in clinical psychology at City University of New York, 1984—.

AWARDS, HONORS: Knox fellow at Oxford University, 1958.

WRITINGS:

Stage Fright: Its Role in Acting, University of Chicago Press, 1986.

Contributor to psychology journals.

WORK IN PROGRESS: Freud on Stanislavsky; a psychoanalytic study of the process of acting.

BIOGRAPHICAL/CRITICAL SOURCES:

PERIODICALS

Atlantic Monthly, June, 1986.
Washington Post Book World, June 22, 1986.

* * *

ABBOTT, Lee K(ittredge) 1947-

PERSONAL: Born October 17, 1947, in Panama Canal Zone; son of Lee Kittredge (in the military) and Elaine (a housewife; maiden name, Kelly) Abbott; married Pamela Jo Dennis (a bookstore manager), December 20, 1969; children: Noel Lee-Kittredge (son), Kelly Glenn (son). *Education:* New Mexico State University, B.A., 1970, M.A., 1973; attended Columbia University, 1970; University of Arkansas, M.F.A., 1977.

ADDRESSES: Home—2571 Charney Rd., University Heights, Ohio 44118. *Office*—Department of English, Case Western Reserve University, 2040 Adelbert Rd., Cleveland, Ohio 44106. *Agent*—Elaine Markson, Elaine Markson Literary Agency, Inc., 44 Greenwich Ave., New York, N.Y. 10011.

CAREER: Case Western Reserve University, Cleveland, Ohio, assistant professor, 1977-82, associate professor, 1983-87, professor of English, 1987—. Visiting professor at Colorado College, 1984, and Washington University, St. Louis, Mo., 1985; Gladys Louise Fox Visiting Professor at Rice University, 1988.

MEMBER: Associated Writing Programs.

AWARDS, HONORS: Fellow of National Endowment for the Arts, 1979 and 1985; St. Lawrence Award for Fiction from *Fiction International,* 1981, for *The Heart Never Fits Its Wanting;* O. Henry Prize from Doubleday & Co., 1984, for "Living Alone in Iota"; Prize for Fiction from *Story Quarterly,* 1985, for "Youth on Mars"; National Magazine Award from Graduate School of Journalism at Columbia University, and Editors Choice Award from Wampeter-Doubleday, both 1986, both for "Time and Fear and Somehow Love"; Pushcart Prize from Pushcart Press, 1986, for "X."

WRITINGS:

The Heart Never Fits Its Wanting (stories), North American Review Press, 1980.
Love Is the Crooked Thing (stories), Algonquin Books, 1986.
Strangers in Paradise (stories), Putnam, 1987.

Work represented in anthologies, including *Best American Short Stories,* 1984 and 1987. Contributor to magazines, including *Atlantic, Epoch, Harper's, Georgia Review, Missouri Review,* and *Southern Review.*

WORK IN PROGRESS: The Lost History of Everything, stories, for Putnam.

SIDELIGHTS: All of Lee K. Abbott's story collections to date are set in New Mexico, but his stories vary widely. He writes about bank robbers, soldiers in Vietnam, college professors, and rock and roll bands, with a wit and style that prompted reviewer Amy Hempel to call him "something of a linguistic hellion." Hempel wrote in the *New York Times Book Review:* "Mr. Abbott's enthusiastic wordplay is a great deal of fun," yet when he "stows the be-bop speed rap for a little peace and quiet, he writes quietly powerful stories." Hempel particularly enjoyed "Having the Human Thing of Joy," the story of a man who discovers his wife's infidelity and reminisces about his mother, and "The Final Proof of Fate and Circumstance," a tale related by a father to his son, which ends the collection *Love Is the Crooked Thing*.

William Ferguson, also of the *New York Times Book Review,* described the characters of *Strangers in Paradise:* "We see them either at home, driven to various kinds of excess by the pressures of love and sports . . . , or confused and frightened abroad. . . . Plots tend to overlap, . . . as if several fields of force were being directed at a single invisible core of meaning, in a prose at once exuberant and inventive."

BIOGRAPHICAL/CRITICAL SOURCES:

PERIODICALS

New York Times Book Review, March 16, 1986, February 15, 1987.
Virginia Quarterly Review, autumn, 1986.

* * *

ABRAMS, Lawrence F.

PERSONAL: Education—Received B.S. and M.S.T.; candidate for Ed.S. in future studies.

CAREER: D. C. Everest Senior High School, Schofield, Wis., English teacher, 1969—. Photography teacher at University of Wisconsin—Madison and University of Wisconsin—Marathon. Member of board of directors of College for Kids.

MEMBER: Council for Wisconsin Writers (board member).

AWARDS, HONORS: Council for Wisconsin Writers, honorable mention in 1982 for *The Big Rigs,* third place in 1984 for *Throw It Out of Sight,* and second place in outdoor writing in 1985 for *Biking the Great Lakes Islands*.

WRITINGS:

(Photographer) Kathleen S. Abrams, *The Big Rigs: Trucks, Truckers, and Trucking* (juvenile), Messner, 1981.
Mysterious Powers of the Mind (juvenile), Messner, 1982.
Throw It Out of Sight! Building and Flying a Hand-Launched Glider (juvenile), Dillon, 1984.
Photography for Writers, Entwood, 1986.
(Illustrator) Beverly Butler Olson, *Maggie by My Side* (Junior Literary Guild selection), Dodd, 1987.

WITH WIFE, KATHLEEN S. ABRAMS

Logging and Lumbering (juvenile), Messner, 1980.
Successful Landlording, Structures Publishing, 1980, revised edition, Entwood, 1985.
One Hundred Years From Now (juvenile), Messner, 1983.
Exploring Wisconsin, Rand McNally, 1983.
Salvaging Old Barns and Houses: Tear It Down and Save the Pieces, Sterling Publications, 1983.
Biking the Great Lakes Islands: A Guide to Biking Seven Islands in the Great Lakes, Entwood, 1985.

Contributor of about 150 articles to magazines.

WORK IN PROGRESS: Illustrating *Alternative Careers* by Kathleen S. Abrams, for F. Watts.

SIDELIGHTS: Lawrence F. Abrams told *CA:* "I have an interest in nearly every subject, so my books and illustrations span a variety of topics. I enjoy providing useful information in a readable and entertaining form."

BIOGRAPHICAL/CRITICAL SOURCES:

PERIODICALS

Appraisal, fall, 1984.

* * *

ABRAMS, Mark 1906-

PERSONAL: Born April 27, 1906, in London, England; son of Abram (a shopkeeper) and Anna (a housewife; maiden name, Jackson) Abrams; married Una Strugnell (divorced, 1949); married Jean Bird (a housewife), March 21, 1952; children: (first marriage) Philip, Evelyn; (second marriage) Sarah Abrams Kearns. *Education:* London School of Economics and Political Science, London, B.Sc., 1927, Ph.D., 1929.

ADDRESSES: Home—12 Pelham Sq., Brighton BN1 4ET, England. *Office*—Institute of Gerontology, 552 King's Rd., London SW10 0VA, England.

CAREER: London Press Exchange, London, England, director, 1934-39; British Broadcasting Corp., London, director of Propaganda Analysis Unit, 1940-42; British Foreign Office, London, manager of political intelligence department, 1943-46; London Press Exchange, director, 1946-72; Research Officer at Institute of Gerontology, London; writer. Director of Social Science Research Council research unit, 1973-80. *Military service:* Supreme Headquarters of the Allied Expeditionary Force (SHAEF), 1944-46.

MEMBER: British Sociological Society, Social Research Association, American Gerontological Society, Civil Service Club.

AWARDS, HONORS: Helen Dinerman Award from American Association for Public Opinion Research, 1979; Gold Medal from British Market Research Society, 1983.

WRITINGS:

Money and the Trade Cycle, John Lane, 1930.
The Population of Great Britain, Allen & Unwin, 1945.
The Condition of the British People, 1911-1945, Gollancz, 1946.
Social Surveys and Social Action, Heinemann, 1951.
Must Labour Lose? Penguin, 1960.
(Editor with David Gerard and Noel Timms) *Values and Social Change in Britain,* Macmillan, 1985.
Britain's Elderly Population, Macmillan, 1987.
A Social Audit of Old Age, Macmillan, 1987.

Chairman of editorial board of *Patterns of Prejudice*.

SIDELIGHTS: Mark Abrams told *CA:* "I first became interested in gerontology when I was engaged to study the various conditions of the twelve thousand elderly people living in York, Yorkshire, England, in 1947. I am currently studying the economic, social, and health differences—which are substantial—between the 'younger elderly' (sixty-five to seventy-four) and the 'older elderly' (seventy-five and older)."

AVOCATIONAL INTERESTS: Documenting the decay of civilized standards in contemporary Britain, locating isolated villages in Greece to visit on holiday.

* * *

ADLER, B.
See ADLER, William

* * *

ADLER, William 1951-
(B. Adler)

PERSONAL: Born December 18, 1951, in Brooklyn, N.Y.; son of Marvin (a financial officer) and Esther (a bookkeeper; maiden name, Suskin) Adler; married Sara Moulton (a magazine editor), September 6, 1981; children: Ruth Moulton Adler. *Education:* Attended University of Michigan, 1969-71. *Politics:* Independent. *Religion:* "Lapsed Jew."

ADDRESSES: Home—New York, N.Y. *Office*—Rush Artist Management, 298 Elizabeth, New York, N.Y. 10012. *Agent*—Lori Perkins, Barbara Lowenstein Associates, Inc., 121 West 27th St., New York, N.Y. 10001.

CAREER: Sun, Ann Arbor, Mich., contributing music editor, 1973-76; WBCN-Radio, Boston, Mass., disc jockey, 1977; *Boston Herald,* Boston, pop music critic, 1978-80; free-lance writer in New York, N.Y., 1980-84; Rush Artist Management, New York City, director of publicity, 1984—.

WRITINGS:

UNDER NAME B. ADLER

Tougher Than Leather: The Authorized Biography of Run-DMC, New American Library, 1987.

Contributor to periodicals, including *Rolling Stone, People, Village Voice,* and *Daily News.*

WORK IN PROGRESS: Research for an extensive, novelistic account of the careers of "poet/revolutionary" John Sinclair and his associates during the 1960s.

SIDELIGHTS: William Adler told *CA:* "My enduring twin interests have been music and writing. I never understood how blessed I was to have grown up in Detroit in the sixties until I moved, in 1976, to Boston, where the citizens are the clear and pitiful victims of cultural deprivation. Detroit's culture, musical in particular, had an enormous impact upon me. From it I've been able to derive everything I've needed in the way of emotional, ethical, philosophical, and spiritual sustenance. As my friend John Sinclair has pointed out, there is a whole lifestyle implicit in the music of Afro-Americans—of which Detroit is a great capital.

"My writing is a modest form of repayment for all the nourishment I've received from the music and musicians I love—and a way of sustaining my endless researches. To paraphrase a song, my life was saved by rock 'n' roll—and by jazz, blues, and rhythm and blues.

"My first book, *Tougher Than Leather,* is a biography of some very popular young musicians, Run-DMC, whom I admire and with whom I've worked for the past three-and-one-half years."

AGUILERA MALTA, Demetrio 1909-

PERSONAL: Born May 24, 1909, in Guayaquil, Ecuador; son of Demetrio and Teresa (Malta) Aguilera; married Velia Marquez Ramos, September 17, 1957; children: Ciro, Adda de Manosalvas, Marlene de Davalos. *Education:* Attended the University of Guayaquil, 1928-29.

ADDRESSES: Home—Tercera Pocita 32, Mexico City 17, Mexico.

CAREER: Writer, 1930—. Worked as a newspaper reporter in Guayaquil, Ecuador; held several administrative and diplomatic posts with the government of Ecuador, including undersecretary of Education, 1937, charge d'affairs in Chile, 1948, and cultural attache in Brazil, 1949; visiting professor at numerous colleges and universities, including University of Mexico, University of Guatemala, University of Panama, University of Rio de Janeiro, Howard University, Scripps College, and University of California at Irvine.

MEMBER: Latin American Community of Writers, Pan American Union.

AWARDS, HONORS: Literary Merit Medal from the Republic of Ecuador; Cruzeiro do Sul award from Brazil.

WRITINGS:

NOVELS

Don Goyo, Editorial Cenit (Madrid), 1933, translation by John and Carolyn Brushwood published as *Don Goyo,* Humana, 1980.

C.Z. (Canal Zone): Los yanquis en Panama, Ediciones Ercilla (Santiago de Chile), 1935.

Madrid! Reportaje novelado de una retaguardia heroica (title means "Madrid! Novelized Report on a Heroic Rearguard"), Ediciones Ercilla (Santiago de Chile), 1937.

La isla virgen (title means "The Virgin Isle"), Vera & Cia (Guayaquil), 1942.

Una cruz en la Sierra Maestra (title means "A Cross in the Sierra Maestra"), Editorial Sophos (Buenos Aires), 1960.

La caballeresa del sol: El gran amor de Bolivar, Ediciones Guadarrama (Madrid), 1964, translation by Willis Knapp Jones published as *Manuela,* Southern Illinois University Press, 1967.

El Quijote de El Dorado: Orellana y el Rio de las Amazonas, (title means "The Quixote of Eldorado: Orellana and the Amazon River"), Ediciones Guadarrama (Madrid), 1964.

Un nuevo mar para el rey: Balboa, Anayansi, y el Oceano Pacifico (title means "A New Sea for the King: Balboa, Anayansi, and the Pacific Ocean"), Ediciones Guadarrama (Madrid), 1965.

Siete lunas y siete serpientes, Fondo de Cultura Economica (Mexico City), 1970, translation by Gregory Rabassa published as *Seven Serpents and Seven Moons,* University of Texas Press, 1979.

El secuestro del general (title means "The General's Kidnapping"), J. Mortiz (Mexico City), 1973, translation by Peter Earle published as *Babelandia,* Humana, 1985.

Jaguar, Editorial Grijalbo (Mexico City), 1977.

Requiem para el diablo (title means "Requiem for the Devil"), J. Mortiz (Mexico City), 1978.

PLAYS

Espana leal (title means "Loyalist Spain"; three-act), Talleres Graficos de Educacion (Quito), 1938.

Lazaro, published in *Revista del Colegio Nacional Vicente Rocafuerte,* Volume 18, number 53 (Guayaquil), 1941.

(With Willis Knapp Jones) *Sangre Azul* (three-act), Pan American Union (Washington, D.C.), 1948, translation by the authors published simultaneously in English as *Blue Blood.*

El tigre (title means "The Tiger"; one-act), Editorial Casa de la Cultura Ecuatoriana (Quito), 1956.

Trilogia ecuatoriana: Teatro breve (title means "Ecuadoran Trilogy: Short Plays"; contains "Honorarios" ["Honorariums"], "Dientes Blancos" ["White Teeth"], and "El tigre" ["The Tiger"]), Ediciones de Andrea (Mexico City), 1959.

Infierno negro (title means "Black Hell"; two-act), Universidad Veracruzana (Jalapa, Mexico), 1967.

Teatro completo (title means "Complete Plays"), Finisterre (Mexico City), 1970.

SHORT STORIES

(With Enrique Gil Gilbert and Joaquin Gallegos Lara) *Los que se van: Cuentos del cholo y del montuvio* (title means "Those Who Go Away: Stories of the *Cholo* and the Mountain"), Hispanoamerica, Zea y Paladines (Guayaquil), 1930.

(With Manuel Mejia Valera) *El cuento actual latinoamericano* (title means "The Contemporary Latin American Short Story"), Ediciones de Andrea (Mexico City), 1973.

Hechos y leyendas de nuestra America: Relatos hispanoamericanos (title means "Legends and Events of Our America: Stories of Hispanic America"), Departamento del Distrito Federal, Secretaria de Obras y Servicios (Mexico City), 1975.

NONFICTION

Leticia: Notas y comentarios de un periodista ecuatoriano (title means "Leticia: Notes and Commentary by an Ecuadoran Journalist"), Talleres Graficos Benedetti (Panama City), 1932.

(With Juan Aguilera Malta, Fausto Aguilera Malta, and Fernando Aguilera Malta) *Guayaquil 70: Metropoli dinamica* (title means "Guayaquil 70: Dynamic City"), Publicaciones Aguilera Malta (Guayaquil), 1970.

Contributor of articles and stories to newspapers and magazines and author of short pamphlets on political and historical topics.

SIDELIGHTS: Ecuadoran novelist and playwright Demetrio Aguilera Malta first attracted notice in 1930 with a collection of short stories he published in the anthology *Los que se van: Cuentos del cholo y del montuvio.* The book, co-authored with Joaquin Gallegos Lara and Enrique Gil Gilbert, was a kind of manifesto for the Grupo de Guayaquil, an assembly of young, socially conscious, realist writers intent on giving voice to the needs and aspirations of the country's neglected *cholos,* or peasants, of Ecuador's Guayas coastal region. Aguilera Malta's stories were acclaimed for their sensitive depiction of an often harsh and violent world, and they prepared the ground for his two major realist novels set in the Guayas region, *Don Goyo* and *La isla virgen.*

The protagonist of *Don Goyo* is a tough old *cholo* patriarch of mixed Spanish and Indian descent who fights a losing battle with powerful white men whose economic interests threaten to usurp *cholo* land and destroy the natives' harmonious relationship with nature. In death and defeat, Don Goyo takes on a legendary status, symbolizing the fate of the Indian in countless tragedies played out all over the Americas. In *La isla virgen,* set on a coastal island, this epochal conflict takes an unusual twist. Assisted by the powerful jungle and wild animals, the *cholos* succeed in beating back the forces of "progress," proving that the will of the virgin earth is stronger than that of man.

Aguilera Malta's interest in political and social themes is also reflected in his numerous historical novels. *Madrid!* is a semifictional account of the author's personal experience as a reporter with a Republican unit defending Madrid during the Spanish Civil War. *Una cruz en la Sierra Maestra* is set during the Cuban Revolution and forms the first volume of the author's "Episodios americanos" series on Latin American historical topics. Other titles in the series include *El Quijote de El Dorado* and *Un nuevo mar para el rey,* which imaginatively reconstruct the American adventures of the sixteenth-century Spanish explorers Francisco de Orellana and Vasco Nunez de Balboa. *La caballeresa del sol,* Aguilera Malta's most successful historical novel, is a portrait of Manuela Saenz de Thorne, the little-known military officer, political adviser, and mistress of nineteenth-century Latin American independence leader Simon Bolivar.

Aguilera Malta is also well known in his native country as a playwright whose numerous dramatic works cover a broad thematic and stylistic range. Among his best-received dramas are the realistic tragedy "Lazaro," about an idealistic schoolteacher; and *Infierno negro,* a highly expressionistic allegory on the subject of black oppression throughout history. The latter play is structured as a series of flashbacks in the appalling career of the late Horridus Nebus, who tried to solve the "black problem" in the mythical town of Nylonpolis by setting up a factory to make sausage of black flesh. Resurrected after his death and made to stand trial before black survivors, Horridus is condemned to live like his victims as a "wandering Negro" among white people, until such time as a black brotherhood is established. The play's surreal narrative is embellished on the stage with symbolic masks and a liturgical accompaniment of African music mixed with quotes from contemporary poets.

Surrealistic expressionism similarly characterizes Aguilera Malta's recent novels, notably *Siete lunas y siete serpientes,* published in the United States in 1979 as *Seven Moons and Seven Serpents.* Set in the mythical coastal city of Santoronton in an unnamed South American country, the narrative recalls the *cholo*-wilderness theme of the author's earliest work generalized into the timeless and universal struggle between the forces of good and evil. Moving back and forth in time, Aguilera Malta depicts the "magical-realist" foundations of the jungle village and the bizarre and complex relationships of its current inhabitants. The book's colorful characters include Father Candido, the village priest; his talkative companion; the Burned Christ, an effigy who occasionally comes down from his cross but refuses to interfere in human affairs; Candido's godson Candelario Mariscal, a marauding colonel with the power to turn himself into a crocodile; Crisostomo Chalena, a local entrepreneur who makes a pact with the Devil and seizes control of the town's water supply; and the sorcerer's daughter Dominga, who nightly fights off a serpent that threatens her virginity. Aguilera Malta's style mirrors this magical yet sensually concrete world with "rhythmic, onomatopoeic lyricism, earthy dialogue, and stream-of-consciousness technique molded into an admixture of African, Indian, and Christian myths," observed Clementine Rabassa in *Books Abroad.* The result, concluded *Washington Post Book World* reviewer Donald Yates, "is a multi-faceted allegory whose final reso-

lution points toward the affirmation of tolerance and forgiveness."

BIOGRAPHICAL/CRITICAL SOURCES:

PERIODICALS

Books Abroad, spring, 1971.
Times Literary Supplement, January 11, 1980.
Washington Post Book World, December 23, 1979.
World Literature Today, summer, 1965, spring, 1978, summer, 1979.*

—*Sketch by Curtis Skinner*

* * *

AJILVSGI, Geyata 1933-

PERSONAL: Name originally Peggy Ann Taylor; name legally changed in 1975; born July 27, 1933, in Titus County, Tex.; daughter of Thomas Jackson (a farmer) and Birdie (Harbor) Taylor; married Doyle Amerson (deceased); married James H. Yantis (divorced); children: (first marriage) Russell Doyle, Guy Victor, Carmen Zane. *Education:* Attended East Texas State University, 1971-72; University of Texas at Austin, 1973, and Southern Methodist University, 1977. *Religion:* "Native American."

ADDRESSES: Home—Hearne, Tex.

CAREER: Member of rare plant study team for Pineywoods Region of Texas Organization for Endangered Species, 1968-73; Espey, Huston & Associates, Inc., Austin, Tex., staff plant taxonomist, 1973-82; Texas A&M University, College Station, herbarium botanist, 1982-85; free-lance writer and photographer, 1985—. Botanical guide to the Big Thicket area of Texas, 1966-72; botanical researcher for Texas Research Foundation, 1968-73, and U.S. Fish and Wildlife Service, 1968-71.

MEMBER: Lepidopterists Society, Texas Organization for Endangered Species.

WRITINGS:

Wild Flowers of the Big Thicket: East Texas and Western Louisiana, Texas A&M University Press, 1979.
Wildflowers of Texas, Shearer, 1984.
Gardening for Butterflies in Texas, Texas Monthly Press, in press.
Common Butterflies of Texas, Texas Monthly Press, in press.

Author of "Naturalist Notebook," a column in *Mount Pleasant Tribune*. Contributor of articles and photographs to magazines and newspapers, including *Audubon, Outdoor World, Texas Parks and Wildlife,* and *Texas Highways.*

WORK IN PROGRESS: Wildflowers of the Rockies, completion expected in 1991.

* * *

ALBRIGHT, Horace M(arden) 1890-1987

PERSONAL: Born January 6, 1890, in Bishop, Calif.; died of heart failure, March 28, 1987, in Los Angeles, Calif.; son of George L. and Mary (Marden) Albright; married Grace Marian Noble, December 23, 1915 (died c. 1981); children: Robert (deceased), Marian (Mrs. Ross D. Schenck). *Education:* University of California, B.L., 1912; Georgetown University, LL.B., 1914.

CAREER: U.S. Department of the Interior, Washington, D.C., member of staff in office of the secretary of the interior, 1913-16, assistant attorney assigned to national park affairs, 1915-17; National Park Service, Washington, D.C., assistant director, 1917-19, acting director, 1917-18, assistant field director and superintendent of Yellowstone National Park, 1919-29, temporarily in charge of Yosemite National Park, 1927-28, director of National Park Service, 1929-33; U.S. Potash Co., general manager and director, 1933-56, vice-president, 1933-46, president, 1946-56. Member of National Capital Park and Planning Commission, 1929-33; member of Palisades Interstate Park Committee of New York and New Jersey, 1945-61; Resources for the Future, member of board of directors, chairman, 1952-61; member of National Parks Advisory Council, beginning in 1958; member of advisory council of National Outdoor Recreation Resources Review Committee, 1959-62; Pacific Tropical Botanical Garden, president, 1964-71, member of board of trustees. Member of board of directors of Grand Teton Lodge Co.; trustee of Colonial Williamsburg Foundation, 1934-58, and Jackson Hole Preserve, Inc., 1945-77; member of council of Save the Redwoods League; member of National Trust for Historic Preservation and Desert Protective Council. Regents Lecturer at University of California, Berkeley, 1961; member of board of trustees of Mills College, 1939-42 and 1951-59. Member of board of directors of North American Philips Co. and Philips Trust, 1953-61, and Arnold Bakers, 1956-61.

AWARDS, HONORS: Order of the Northern Star of Sweden, 1926; Pugsley Gold Medal from American Scenic and Historic Preservation Society, 1933; Conservation Award from U.S. Department of the Interior, 1952; Frances K. Hutchinson Medal from Garden Club of America, 1959; Theodore Roosevelt Medal for the Conservation of National Resources from Theodore Roosevelt Association, 1959; University of California established the Horace M. Albright Conservation Lecture Series, 1961; American Scenic and Historic Preservation Society established the Horace M. Albright Scenic Preservation Award; Audubon Medal; Gold Medal from Camp Fire Club of America, 1962; National Park Service established the Horace M. Albright Training Center at Grand Canyon National Park, 1963; Berkeley fellow, 1968; Distinguished Service Award from American Forestry Association, 1968; award from Cosmos Club, 1974; Neasham Medal for Historic Preservation from California Historical Society, 1976; Horace M. Albrey Medal, 1979; U.S. Medal of Freedom, 1980; John Muir Award from Sierra Club, 1986; honorary degrees from University of Montana, 1956, University of California, 1961, and University of New Mexico, 1962.

WRITINGS:

(With Frank J. Taylor) *"Oh, Ranger!" A Book About the National Parks,* Stanford University Press, 1928, revised edition, Dodd, 1946, reprinted, Chatham Press, 1972.
(With Robert Cahn) *The Birth of the National Park Service: The Founding Years, 1913-1933,* Howe Brothers, 1985.

Contributor to periodicals.

BIOGRAPHICAL/CRITICAL SOURCES:

PERIODICALS

Journal of American History, September, 1986.
Time, December 23, 1985.

OBITUARIES:

PERIODICALS

Los Angeles Times, March 29, 1987.

National Parks, May/June, 1987, July/August, 1987.
New York Times, March 29, 1987, April 7, 1987.
Washington Post, March 29, 1987.*

* * *

ALBUS, James Sacra 1935-

PERSONAL: Born May 4, 1935, in Louisville, Ky.; son of George Charles and Lucy Bell (Sacra) Albus. *Education:* Wheaton College, Wheaton, Ill., B.S., 1957; Ohio State University, M.S., 1958; University of Maryland at College Park, Ph.D., 1972.

ADDRESSES: Home—9520 West Stanhope Rd., Kensington, Md. 20895. *Office*—Robot Systems Division, Center for Manufacturing Engineering, National Bureau of Standards, Washington, D.C. 20234.

CAREER: National Aeronautics and Space Administration, Washington, D.C., electronics engineer at Goddard Space Flight Center, 1958-72; National Bureau of Standards, Washington, D.C., chief of Robot Systems Division at Center for Manufacturing Engineering, 1973—.

AWARDS, HONORS: National Aeronautics and Space Administration Invention Award in 1963, Sustained Superior Performance Award in 1968, Group Achievement Award in 1968, and Superior Achievement Award in 1970; Hugh L. Dryden Memorial fellow of National Space Club, 1967; fellow of Washington Academy of Sciences, 1973; U.S. Department of Commerce Silver Medal in 1975 and Gold Medal in 1987.

WRITINGS:

Brains, Behavior, and Robotics, McGraw, 1981.

Contributor to scientific journals.

* * *

ALCOSSER, Sandra (B.) 1944-

BRIEF ENTRY: Born February 3, 1944, in Washington, D.C. American educator, editor, essayist, short fiction writer, and poet. Alcosser has won significant critical acclaim with her first two volumes of poetry. *Each Bone a Prayer* (Charles Street Press, 1982) earned the 1980 National University Chapbook Award, and *A Fish to Feed All Hunger* (University Press of Virginia, 1986) garnered the 1984 Associated Writing Programs Award in poetry. In addition, Alcosser won the 1976 Dylan Thomas Poetry Award from the New School for Social Research and a 1987 COMBO Fellowship in Poetry from the San Diego Arts Council, among other honors. For an unpublished collection of short stories she received the 1986 P.E.N. Syndicated Fiction Project Award.

Alcosser began her academic career in 1982 as an instructor at Louisiana State University, later becoming an assistant professor there. In 1986 she became an associate professor of English at San Diego State University. She has contributed numerous poems and occasional essays and short fiction to magazines and literary journals, including *American Scholar, New Yorker, North American Review,* and *Poetry,* and much of her work is represented in poetry anthologies. Alcosser has also served on the editorial staffs of periodicals, including *Denver Quarterly, New Delta Review,* and *Cut Bank. Addresses: Home*—N.W. 5791 West County Line Rd., Florence, Mont. *Office*—Department of English and Comparative Literature, San Diego State University, San Diego, Calif. 92182.

BIOGRAPHICAL/CRITICAL SOURCES:

PERIODICALS

Bloomsbury Review, July/August, 1987.
Denver Quarterly, spring/summer, 1986.
Midwest Poetry Review, September, 1986.
Poetry, January, 1987.

* * *

ALEXANDER, R(obert) McNeill 1934-

PERSONAL: Born July 7, 1934, in Lisburn, Northern Ireland; son of Robert Priestley (an engineer) and Janet (an author; maiden name, McNeill) Alexander; married Ann Elizabeth Coulton (an adult education teacher), July 29, 1961; children: Jane Coulton, Robert Gordon. *Education:* Cambridge University, B.A., 1955, Ph.D., 1958, M.A., 1959; University of Wales, D.Sc., 1969.

ADDRESSES: Home—14 Moor Park Mount, Leeds LS6 4BU, England. *Office*—Department of Pure and Applied Zoology, University of Leeds, Leeds LS2 9JT, England.

CAREER: University of Wales, University College of North Wales, Bangor, assistant lecturer, 1958-61, lecturer, 1961-68, senior lecturer in zoology, 1968-69; University of Leeds, Leeds, England, professor of zoology, 1969—.

MEMBER: Royal Society (fellow), Society for Experimental Biology, Institute of Biology (fellow), American Society of Zoologists (honorary member), Zoological Society of London.

AWARDS, HONORS: Scientific Medal from Zoological Society of London, 1969; Linnean Medal from Linnean Society of London, 1979.

WRITINGS:

Functional Design in Fishes, Hutchinson, 1967, 3rd edition, 1974.
Animal Mechanics, Sidgwick & Jackson, 1968, 2nd edition, 1983.
Size and Shape, Edward Arnold, 1971.
The Chordates, Cambridge University Press, 1975, 2nd edition, 1981.
Biomechanics, Chapman & Hall, 1975.
(Editor with Geoffrey Goldspink) *Mechanics and Energetics of Animal Locomotion,* Chapman & Hall, 1977.
The Invertebrates, Cambridge University Press, 1979.
Locomotion of Animals, Blackie & Son, 1982.
Optima for Animals, Edward Arnold, 1982.
(Editor) *The Collins Encyclopaedia of Animal Biology,* Collins, 1986.
Elastic Mechanisms in Animal Movement, Cambridge University Press, 1988.
The Dynamics of Dinosaurs and Other Extinct Giants, Columbia University Press, 1988.

Contributor to scientific journals.

SIDELIGHTS: R. McNeill Alexander told *CA:* "My principle research interest is the mechanics of animal movement, especially walking and running of people and other large mammals, and of dinosaurs. My books treat animal structure and movement as problems in engineering."

ALLEGRO, John Marco 1923-1988 (Ian McGill)

OBITUARY NOTICE—See index for *CA* sketch: Born February 17, 1923, in London, England; died February 17, 1988, in Cheshire (one source says London), England. Educator, archaeologist, authority on Semitic texts, lecturer, and author. Allegro was a key member of the international team that deciphered the Dead Sea Scrolls in the early 1950s. The scrolls, found in caves near the Dead Sea in the late 1940s, included Old Testament manuscripts and ranged in date from 100 B.C. to the first century. Published in 1956, *The Dead Sea Scrolls* proved a commercial success and brought Allegro great public recognition as a formidable scholar of ancient writings. His acclaim, however, turned to notoriety in 1970 when he left his teaching post at the University of Manchester and published *The Sacred Mushroom and the Cross,* in which he contended that Judaism and Christianity derived from an ancient cult devoted to sex and the consumption of mushrooms. In his later years Allegro was also known for his intensely anti-Christian beliefs. Among his other books are *The Dead Sea Scrolls: A Reappraisal, Search in the Desert, The End of a Road,* and *The Dead Sea Scrolls and the Christian Myth*. In addition, Allegro wrote novels under the pseudonym Ian McGill.

OBITUARIES AND OTHER SOURCES:

PERIODICALS

Chicago Tribune, February 24, 1988.
Los Angeles Times, February 23, 1988.
New York Times, February 23, 1988.
Times (London), February 22, 1988.

* * *

ALLEN, Clabon Walter 1904-1987

OBITUARY NOTICE: Born December 28, 1904, in Perth, Western Australia; died December 11, 1987, in Canberra, Australia. Astronomer, educator, and author. Allen was an emeritus professor of astronomy at University College, London, whose research on the solar atmosphere provided valuable information on the relationships between the earth and the sun. Director of the London University observatory, Allen took part in five solar eclipse expeditions. In addition to contributing numerous articles to scientific journals, he wrote two books: *Astrophysical Quantities* and *Hiking from Early Canberra*.

OBITUARIES AND OTHER SOURCES:

BOOKS

The Blue Book: Leaders of the English-Speaking World, St. Martin's, 1976.
The Writer's Directory: 1986-1988, St. James Press, 1986.
Who's Who, 140th edition, St. Martin's, 1988.

PERIODICALS

Times (London), December 11, 1987.

* * *

ALLEY, Rewi 1897-1987

OBITUARY NOTICE—See index for *CA* sketch: Born December 2, 1897, in Springfield (some sources say Christchurch), New Zealand; immigrated to China, 1927; died after a stroke, December 20 (one source says December 27), 1987, in Beijing, China. Political activist, laborer, administrator, translator, and author. Alley was known for his dedication to the Communist cause in China. After immigrating to China in 1927, Alley allied himself with the Communists, and during the country's civil war he supplied Communist rebels with food and medical supplies. He also organized more than two thousand cooperative factories for the Communists and established a technical school. When the war ended in 1950 Alley continued to promote communism in his many writings. He also participated in activities of the Asian and Pacific Peace Liaison Committee. His influence diminished significantly during China's Cultural Revolution of the late 1960s, when nearly all foreigners were suspected of anticommunism. In 1985, almost ten years after the Cultural Revolution waned, Alley was named an honorary citizen of Gansu province, but he never received Chinese citizenship. His extensive literary canon contains such works as *The People Have Strength, Human China: A Diary, The Influence of the Thought of Mao Tse-tung, Some Chinese Children,* and *Travels in China*. Alley also wrote many volumes of poetry and translated Chinese verse into English.

OBITUARIES AND OTHER SOURCES:

BOOKS

Current Biography, H. W. Wilson, 1988.

PERIODICALS

Los Angeles Times, January 1, 1988.
New York Times, December 28, 1987.

* * *

ALLPORT, Susan 1950-

PERSONAL: Born July 5, 1950, in New Haven, Conn.; daughter of Alexander Wise (an administrator) and Jane (Raible) Allport; married David C. Howell (a designer), September 10, 1978; children: Liberty, Cecil. *Education:* Pitzer College, B.A., 1972; Tulane University of Louisiana, M.S., 1977. *Politics:* Democrat. *Religion:* None.

ADDRESSES: Home and office—333 Hook Rd., Katonah, N.Y. 10536. *Agent*—Virginia Barber, 353 West 21st St., New York, N.Y. 10011.

CAREER: Writer.

MEMBER: American Medical Writers Association, National Association of Science Writers.

WRITINGS:

Explorers of the Black Box: The Search for the Cellular Basis of Memory, Norton, 1986.

BIOGRAPHICAL/CRITICAL SOURCES:

PERIODICALS

Los Angeles Times, October 28, 1986.
Washington Post Book World, February 22, 1987.

* * *

ANDERSON, Emily 1891-1962

PERSONAL: Born March 17, 1891, in Galway, Ireland; died October 26, 1962, in London, England; daughter of Alexander Anderson (a university president). *Education:* Attended University of Berlin and University of Marburg.

CAREER: Teacher at Queen's College, in Barbados, and National University of Ireland, University College, Galway; employed by British Foreign Office until retirement in 1951. *Wartime service:* British War Office, Intelligence, 1940-43; served in the Middle East.

AWARDS, HONORS: Officer of the Order of the British Empire.

WRITINGS:

(Translator) Benedetto Croce, *Goethe,* Methuen, 1923.
(Editor, translator, and author of introduction and notes) *The Letters of Mozart and His Family,* three volumes, Macmillan, 1938, 2nd edition, St. Martin's, 1966, abridged edition published as *Mozart's Letters,* Penguin, 1956.
(Translator) Roland Tenschert, *Wolfgang Amadeus Mozart,* Karl Gordon, 1952.
(Editor and translator) *The Letters of Beethoven,* three volumes, St. Martin's, 1961.*

* * *

ANDERSON, R(oy) C(laude) 1931-
(Roy Anderson)

PERSONAL: Born December 23, 1931, in Cleethorpes, South Humberside, England.

ADDRESSES: The Mount, Hook Cross, Bickington, near Newton Abbot, Devonshire, England.

CAREER: Manager for Coach and Travel Organisation.

MEMBER: Chartered Institute of Transport (fellow).

WRITINGS:

The Tramways of Bournemouth and Poole, Light Railway Transport League, 1964.
The Tramways of East Anglia, Light Railway Transport League, 1969.
(With G.G.A. Frankis) *History of Royal Blue Express Services,* A. M. Kelley, 1970, 2nd edition, David & Charles, 1985.
(Wth J. M. Anderson) *Quicksilver: A Hundred Years of Coaching, 1750-1850,* David & Charles, 1973.
(With G.G.A. Frankis) *A History of Western National,* David & Charles, 1979.
A History of Crosville Motor Services, David & Charles, 1981.
(Under name Roy Anderson; with Gregory Fox) *A Pictorial Record of L.M.S. Architecture,* Oxford Publishing, 1981.
A History of Midland Red, David & Charles, 1984.
(Under name Roy Anderson) *The Markets and Fairs of England and Wales,* Bell & Hyman, 1985.

Contributor to transport journals.*

* * *

ANDERSON, Roy
See ANDERSON, R(oy) C(laude)

* * *

ANDREE, Robert G(erald) 1912-1987

OBITUARY NOTICE—See index for *CA* sketch: Born May 30, 1912, in Grand Rapids, Mich.; died November 1, 1987, in South Holland, Ill. Educator, administrator, editor, and author. Andree was a Rhodes scholar and Fulbright fellow whose career in education spanned fifty years and included administrative posts such as high school principal and school district superintendent. In 1965 he became professor of educational administration and curriculum at Southern Illinois University at Edwardsville. His writings include *Collective Negotiations: A Guide to School Board-Teacher Relations, America's Secondary Schools: To Tell It Like It Is, America's Elementary Schools: To Tell It Like It Is,* and *P/R in Public Schools.* Andree also co-edited *Collective Negotiations: A Symposium* and served on the editorial board of *Clearing House.*

OBITUARIES AND OTHER SOURCES:

PERIODICALS

Chicago Tribune, November 5, 1987.

* * *

ANDREWS, Eamonn 1922-1987

OBITUARY NOTICE—See index for *CA* sketch: Born December 19, 1922, in Dublin, Ireland; died of deterioration of the main heart muscle, November 5, 1987, in London, England. Radio and television broadcaster and author. Andrews achieved fame as host of the long-running British television programs "What's My Line?" and "This Is Your Life." He entered the broadcasting profession while still a teenager when he abandoned hopes of a boxing career and began covering the sport for Radio Eireann. Also a commentator on soccer and rugby matches, Andrews, in 1949, became the host of the radio program "Microphone Parade." By 1951 he was serving as moderator of the radio quiz show "Ignorance Is Bliss," contributing broadcasts to other radio programs, and providing commentary for televised boxing matches. That same year he assumed the role of chairman on the televised show "What's My Line?," and in 1955 he became the host of another popular television program, "This Is Your Life."

When his contract with the British Broadcasting Corporation expired in 1964, Andrews joined Independent Television and became host of one of the medium's first talk programs, "The Eamonn Andrews Show." In the late 1960s, Andrews was assigned to the news program "Today," which he hosted for ten years. Aside from his work as a broadcaster and program host, Andrews helped develop Irish television. His writings include a play, "The Moon Is Black," an autobiography, *This Is My Life,* and another nonfiction volume, *Surprise of Your Life.*

OBITUARIES AND OTHER SOURCES:

PERIODICALS

Chicago Tribune, November 8, 1987.
Los Angeles Times, November 6, 1987.
New York Times, November 7, 1987.
Times (London), November 6, 1987.

* * *

ANDREWS, Kevin 1924-

PERSONAL: Born January 20, 1924, in Peking, China; naturalized Greek citizen, 1975; son of Harold St. Clair Smallwood (a British Army officer) and Yvette Borup Andrews (a saleswoman); married Nancy Cummings de Foret (a poet), May 19, 1954 (separated, 1968); children: Corinna, Ioanna, Alexis. *Education:* Harvard University, B.A. (magna cum laude), 1947; graduate study at American School of Classical

Studies, Athens, 1947-51. *Politics:* "Decidedly left of center." *Religion:* Anglican.

ADDRESSES: Home—Trivonianou 69, 116 36 Athens, Greece.

CAREER: University and high school lecturer in the United States and Greece. *Military service:* U.S. Army, reconnaissance scout in 10th Mountain Infantry Division, 1943-45; clerk in Allied Military Government, 1945-46; served in Italy; received Bronze Star.

MEMBER: Writers Society (Athens).

WRITINGS:

Castles of the Morea, American School of Classical Studies at Athens, Princeton, N.J., 1953, reprinted, Hakkert, 1978.
The Flight of Ikaros, Houghton, 1959, revised edition, Penguin, 1984.
Cities of the World: Athens, A. S. Barnes, 1967.
First Will and Testament (poem), privately printed, 1974.
Athens Alive; or, The Practical Tourist's Companion to the Fall of Man, Hermes Publications, 1979.
Greece in the Dark, 1967-1974, Hakkert, 1980.
Byzantine Blues (verse satire), privately printed, 1980.
A Bomb to the Labyrinth (essays), Hakkert, in press.

Contributor to magazines and newspapers, including *New York Review of Books, Journal of the Hellenic Diaspora, Massachusetts Review,* London *Times, Times Literary Supplement,* and several others in Europe.

WORK IN PROGRESS: Whirlpools in a Tideless Sea, a novel about Anglo-Saxon expatriates in Greece.

SIDELIGHTS: "Born to expatriation," Kevin Andrews told *CA,* "and an alien in both lands of a divided inheritance, I found my permanent home—at the age of twenty-three—in a country so long spied upon, interfered with, and dictated to, that the outsider (settler or package tourist) is now less welcome there than perhaps anywhere on earth. This illogical choice of a homeland may have stemmed from an obscure, unshakeable affinity with a place that two thousand years of foreign domination have transformed into an outcast among nations—no matter how cosseted for its remoter history or wooed (not to say bulldozed) for the sake of geopolitics today.

"When the Civil War entered its third phase in 1947, it provided an extensive microcosm of the Cold War more recently begun. My own life, then, of pedantic application and unscholarly escapades generated a lasting commitment to this country and its people, and took form in a series of heterogeneous writings all on Greece. Finally, after the ordeal of the Colonels' Dictatorship, I became a naturalized Greek citizen in 1975.

"The study of this land's Dark Ages (essentially uninterrupted from the fourth century A.D. until at least the nineteenth, and in some quarters till the present day), together with the worm's eye view that one can only get here of other countries' Greek or East Mediterranean policy, have fused and colored my major interest and spur to writing. This is nothing so easily definable as one small Balkan country's politics, but rather the current history acting itself out—with international ramifications, echoing repetitions, and a very special clarity throughout the ages—on its defenseless but strategic soil.

"Because colorless or ill-constructed sentences don't deserve to be read, I am often reminded of Orwell's vision of political writing as possibly an art. It seldom is, but why should it not be? One can meditate on current history (if one is sufficiently involved and has the energy to clothe it in language) as extensively as on the ways of God. I do not see any great difference between history and fiction; the human material is the same in each."

"The writings of Kevin Andrews stand completely on their own and they are neglected at peril by anyone concerned with contemporary Greece," wrote Patrick Leigh Fermor in the *Times Literary Supplement*. The critic described *Castles of the Morea* as "a classic of scholarship," a result of the author's early travels, by foot, through the Peloponnesus. Andrews lived with shepherds and villagers and learned to love the mountains and their people in a way, according to Leigh Fermor, that few foreigners can.

Andrews's second book reflects his serious concern for the mountain people in the bloody wake of Greece's Occupation. Leigh Fermor wrote: "Intuition, desperate concern, strong literary gifts, poetic flair, a marvellous knack for decanting the Greek vernacular into English—all these skilfully interwoven strands turn *The Flight of Ikaros* . . . into one of the great and lasting books about Greece." And Louis MacNeice praised, in the London *Observer,* its "characters of full-blooded impact. . . . If you want some truth about Greece, here it is."

Times Literary Supplement reviewer Peter Green was equally impressed by *Cities of the World: Athens,* and he praised Andrews for his economical style and iconoclastic perspective on the Greek capital. "With gay impartiality he mows down romantic tourists and bureaucratic provincialism, the restored Stoa of Attilus and the Kolonaki bourgeoisie, all in one splendid, swiftly executed holocaust." What the author reveals is a lively history of the ancient and modern city, full of detail and accurate observation, opined Green. The stories in *Cities of the World* were described by the reviewer as collectors' items, and the book "as fresh and gleaming and original as a new-minted coin." Green concluded, "No lover (as opposed to flatterer) of Athens, no one who wants to penetrate behind either her ancient or her modern facade can afford to ignore it."

In 1979 Andrews published *Athens Alive*. In the foreword he wrote, "The collection is addressed to the general reader . . . but it is also aimed, with malice aforethought, in the direction of those earnest functionaries in the world's more active government agencies and business corporations who occasionally read books. . . ." The book reveals, through painstakingly collected primary sources (including Byzantine documents and the observations of early travelers in Greece), a passionate aspect of the author's perspective on Athens and its future. Andrews is a meticulous student of Athenian and Greek history, from the Roman conquest to the present day. He has been an eyewitness to the post-Occupation years, the Civil War of the 1940s, the Colonels' Dictatorship of 1967-74, and the encroachment of tourists and developers in his beloved city. "No review can adequately explore this Aladdin's cave," Leigh Fermor wrote of *Athens Alive* in the *Times Literary Supplement*. "One can only hope, by darting about inside it, to give some idea of its richness and variety."

BIOGRAPHICAL/CRITICAL SOURCES:

BOOKS

Andrews, Kevin, *Athens Alive; or, The Practical Tourist's Companion to the Fall of Man,* Hermes Publications, 1979.

PERIODICALS

Observer (London), March 1, 1959.
Times Literary Supplement, November 23, 1967, June 13, 1980.

* * *

ANGELINO, Marie
See GARBUTT, Janice (D.) Lovoos

* * *

ANSHEN, Melvin (Leon) 1912-

PERSONAL: Born July 2, 1912, in Boston, Mass.; son of Zalkend and Fanny (Kogan) Anshen; married Gertrude Lakson, September 14, 1936. *Education:* Harvard University, A.B., 1933, M.B.A., 1935, D.C.S., 1940.

ADDRESSES: Home—205 West End Ave., Apt. 17-C, New York, N.Y. 10023.

CAREER: Indiana University—Bloomington, began as assistant professor, became professor of industrial administration, 1937-51; Carnegie Institute of Technology (now Carnegie-Mellon University), Pittsburgh, Pa., professor of industrial administration, 1951-62; Columbia University, New York, N.Y., professor of business, 1962-81, Garrett Professor of Public Policy and Business Responsibility, 1972-81, professor emeritus, 1981—. Visiting lecturer at Harvard University, 1947; visiting professor at Stanford University, 1950. Director of research coordination staff of War Production Board, 1942-46; acting deputy administrator of program and requirements for Defense Production Administration, 1951.

WRITINGS:

(With Clare Wright Baker) *Modern Marketing,* McGraw, 1939.
An Introduction to Business, Macmillan, 1942, revised edition, 1949.
(With David Novick and W. C. Truppner) *Wartime Production Controls,* Columbia University Press, 1949, reprinted, Da Capo, 1976.
(With Francis Dunham Wormuth) *Private Enterprise and Public Policy,* Macmillan, 1954.
(Editor with George Leland Bach) *Management and Corporations, 1985,* McGraw, 1960.
(Editor and author of commentary) *Managing the Socially Responsible Corporation: The 1972-1973 Paul Garrett Lectures,* Macmillan, 1974.
Corporate Strategies for Social Performance, Macmillan, 1980.

* * *

ANZOVIN, Steven 1954-

PERSONAL: Born September 10, 1954, in Hartford, Conn.; son of Russell (a musician) and Beverly (a union official; maiden name, Gold) Anzovin; married Janet Podell (a writer), June 2, 1974; children: Rafael, Miriam. *Education:* Connecticut College, B.A. (cum laude), 1976; Pratt Institute, M.F.A., 1980. *Politics:* "Congenital Democrat." *Religion:* Jewish.

ADDRESSES: Home and office—156 Jane St., Englewood, N.J. 07631.

CAREER: Free-lance writer, editor, illustrator, and videographer, 1979—. Designer of video systems for Adwar Video Corp., 1980-81; associate of film production company, Smash Communications, Inc., 1981—. Associate editor at St. Martin's Press, 1981-83; development editor for Prentice-Hall, Inc., 1984-86.

WRITINGS:

(Associate editor) *The Annual Obituary 1981,* St. Martin's, 1982, 1982 edition, 1983.
(Editor) *The Problem of Immigration,* H. W. Wilson, 1985.
(Editor) *The Star Wars Defense,* H. W. Wilson, 1986.
(Editor) *Terrorism,* H. W. Wilson, 1986.
(Editor) *South Africa,* H. W. Wilson, 1987.
(Editor and contributor) *World Artists, 1980-1985,* H. W. Wilson, 1987.
(Editorial director) *Art in America's 1987-1988 Annual Guide to Galleries, Museums, and Artists,* Brant Publications, 1987, 1988-89 edition, 1988.
(With wife, Janet Podell) *It Hurts: A Parent's Guide to Children's Needs,* Bantam, 1987.
(Editor with J. Podell) *Speeches of the American Presidents,* H. W. Wilson, 1987.
Using Deluxe Paint II: Graphics for the Commodore Amiga and the Apple II GS, self-illustrated, Compute!, 1988.
(Editor with J. Podell) *The Soviet Union,* H. W. Wilson, 1988.
Compute!'s Quick and Easy Guide to HyperCard, self-illustrated, Compute!, 1988.
Exploring HyperCard, self-illustrated, Compute!, 1988.
(Editor with J. Podell and Joseph Nathan Kane) *Facts About the States,* H. W. Wilson, in press.

Also author of a book on producing desktop video with the Amiga computer for Scott, Foresman, 1988; editor with wife, Janet Podell, of a book on the U.S. Constitution for H. W. Wilson; associated with H. W. Wilson's *Facts About the Presidents.*

Contributor to *Video Age International.*

WORK IN PROGRESS: Research for a book on computer animation techniques for artists.

SIDELIGHTS: Steven Anzovin told *CA:* "I'm an information collater and provider—my only aim is to present the facts with as much clarity as the material allows. This creates some difficulties when I write about art and computers—with computers things are definite, clear, yes/no, on/off, while art cannot be discussed adequately without allusion, metaphor, and ambiguity."

* * *

ARENAS, Reinaldo 1943-

BRIEF ENTRY: Born July 16, 1943, in Holguin, Oriente, Cuba; immigrated to United States, 1980. Cuban educator, editor, and author. Arenas has earned worldwide recognition for his imaginative novels, short stories, and poems, which combine realistic situations with surrealistic images. His first published work, *Celestino antes del alba* (Union de Escritores, 1967), won an award from the Cuban Writers' Union in 1965. Translated in 1987 as *Singing From the Well* (Viking), the poetic novel exposes the harshness of rural life in Latin America. Arenas's subsequent works were banned in Cuba but enjoyed a generous acceptance elsewhere. *El mundo alucinante* (Diogenes, 1969), translated as *Hallucinations: Being an Account of the Life and Adventures of Friar Servando Teresa de Mier* (Harper, 1971), recounts the experiences of a rebellious Mexican monk, and *Otra vez el mar* (Argos, c. 1982), translated as *Farewell to the Sea* (Viking, 1986), comments on Cuba's restrictive government through the thoughts of two seaside

vacationers. Arenas's other writings include the short story collection *Termina el desfile* (Seix Barral, 1981) and the long poem *El Central* (Seix Barral, 1981; translated as *El Central: A Cuban Sugar Mill* [Avon Books, 1983]). Arenas has served on the editorial staffs of such magazines as *Caribbean Review, Unveiling Cuba, Mariel Magazine,* and *Noticias de Arte*. *Addresses: Home*—328 West 44th St., Apt. 63, New York, N.Y. 10036. *Agent*—Thomas Colchie Associates, Inc., 700 Fort Washington Ave., New York, N.Y. 10040.

BIOGRAPHICAL/CRITICAL SOURCES:

BOOKS

Contemporary Literary Criticism, Volume 41, Gale, 1987.
A Dictionary of Contemporary Latin American Authors, Center for Latin American Studies, Arizona State University, 1975.

PERIODICALS

Americas, September, 1981, January-February, 1982.
Globe and Mail (Toronto), June 21, 1986.
New York Times Book Review, August 29, 1971, November 24, 1985.
Times Literary Supplement, May 7, 1971.
Washington Post Book World, September 5, 1971.

* * *

ARLISS, Leslie 1901-1987

OBITUARY NOTICE: Surname originally Andrews; born in 1901 in London, England; died December 30, 1987, on the island of Jersey in the English Channel. Film director and producer, journalist, and screenwriter. Arliss appealed to the escapist longings of a war-torn generation, shooting melodramas such as "The Wicked Lady," "The Man in Gray," and "Love Story" for the Gainsborough movie company in the 1940s. His films helped to launch the careers of Margaret Lockwood, James Mason, Stewart Granger, and later, Joan Collins. After an early stint as a journalist in South Africa, Arliss turned to directing and writing for movies. His screenplays include "Tonight's the Night," "Orders Is Orders," and "Jack Ahoy." Following work on late-war propaganda films with J. B. Priestley, Arliss produced "Douglas Fairbanks Presents" and "The Buccaneers" for British television.

OBITUARIES AND OTHER SOURCES:

BOOKS

Halliwell's Filmgoer's Companion, 8th edition, Scribner, 1984.
The World Encyclopedia of Film, A. & W. Visual Library, 1972.

PERIODICALS

Los Angeles Times, January 5, 1988.
Times (London), January 2, 1988.
Washington Post, January 3, 1988.

* * *

ARMSTRONG, Leslie 1940-

PERSONAL: Born May 17, 1940, in Boston, Mass.; daughter of Sinclair Howard Armstrong (an internist) and Barbara Lewis Zinsser (a lawyer); married William Dudley Priester (a cardiologist), May 7, 1983; children: Vanessa Lale Cortesi, Sinclair Scott Smith, Helen Elizabeth. *Education:* Brown University, B.A., 1962; Columbia University, M.Arch., 1966. *Politics:* Independent. *Religion:* None.

ADDRESSES: Home—333 West 70th St., New York, N.Y. 10023. *Office*—Armstrong Cumming Architects, 118 West 22nd St., New York, N.Y. 10011.

CAREER: Armstrong/Childs Architects P.C., New York City, partner, 1973-77; Armstrong Childs Lang Associates (architects), New York City, partner, 1977-79; Leslie Armstrong Architect, New York City, proprietor, 1979-83; Armstrong Cumming Architects, New York City, partner, 1984—. Member of board of trustees of Robert College, Istanbul, Turkey.

MEMBER: American Institute of Architects, National Council of Architectural Registration Boards, U.S. Institute for Theatre Technology (member of board of directors, 1970-72), Architectural League, Municipal Arts Society.

AWARDS, HONORS: Sponsor's Award from U.S. Institute for Theatre Technology, 1976; design award from Baltimore, Md., chapter of American Institute of Architects, 1981, for Grand Opera House, Wilmington, Del.

WRITINGS:

The Little House, Collier Books, 1979.
(With Roger Morgan) *Space for Dance: An Architectural Design Guide,* Publishing Center for Cultural Resources, 1984.

SIDELIGHTS: Leslie Armstrong told *CA*: "The Little House concept was born in 1970 when two close friends and I were trying to figure out the absolute bare minimum house that each of them could build on their respective still-to-be-purchased plots of land near Wilmington, Delaware. C. Ray Smith, an architectural editor and critic, encouraged me to make drawings and models sufficiently detailed to qualify the Little House for a 1970 Progressive Architecture design award. We did not win anything, but we did have some fine ink drawings and little wood models to show for our efforts. Neither friend ever bought land, but they kept at me to find a format for making the Little House concept available to a wider audience—people like them.

"In the spring of 1978, my partners and I were working with a free-lance consultant to develop a brochure presenting the range of our capabilities as architects. In the course of showing her our work I took out the Little House drawings and models and told her its history. She was fascinated and decided the vehicle for the Little House was a book. And she promptly sold it to Collier.

"Although the *Little House* book is one step removed from a finished building, we took it into our office as we would a bona fide architectural commission and there treated it to the full range of consulting engineers and experts that any other project would enjoy. Once we had the architectural problems worked out, we set about turning the Little House building into a book about building the Little House.

"Since the book's publication, I have received many letters and photographs from builders and teachers who have used the book as a general residential design and construction textbook—the purpose to which I think it is best suited.

"*Space for Dance* was commissioned jointly in 1980 by the design arts and dance programs at the National Endowment of the Arts in response to the growth of dance as a performing art form and the absence of published technical criteria and information on the specific spatial and architectural needs of

dance. Roger Morgan, a theatre design consultant with whom I have worked on many performing arts projects, and I submitted our qualifications and were selected based on our prior experience and my already having one book under my belt. *Space for Dance* was well received because it addresses both verbally and graphically the needs of dance both on its own and side by side with other performing art forms with whom it may share a given facility."

BIOGRAPHICAL/CRITICAL SOURCES:

PERIODICALS

New York Times, May 3, 1979.

* * *

ASALS, Frederick (John) 1935-

PERSONAL: Born May 12, 1935, in Philadelphia, Pa.; son of Frederick and Frances (Burns) Asals; divorced; children: Katharine, Sarah, David. *Education:* College of William and Mary, B.A., 1957; Middlebury College, M.A., 1961; Brown University, Ph.D., 1967.

ADDRESSES: Office—New College, University of Toronto, Toronto, Ontario, Canada M5S 1A1.

CAREER: Brown University, Providence, R.I., instructor in English, 1967-68; University of Toronto, Toronto, Ontario, assistant professor, 1968-74, associate professor of English, 1974—.

MEMBER: Modern Language Association of America.

AWARDS, HONORS: Award for best book of explication from *Explicator,* 1982, for *Flannery O'Connor: The Imagination of Extremity.*

WRITINGS:

Flannery O'Connor: The Imagination of Extremity, University of Georgia Press, 1982.

Contributor to language and literature journals.

WORK IN PROGRESS: A study of the making of Malcolm Lowry's *Under the Volcano.*

BIOGRAPHICAL/CRITICAL SOURCES:

PERIODICALS

Times Literary Supplement, January 21, 1983.

* * *

ASHMOLE, Bernard 1894-1988

OBITUARY NOTICE—See index for *CA* sketch: Born June 22, 1894, in Ilford, England; died February 25, 1988. Museum curator, educator, and author. An authority on classical sculpture, Ashmole first worked as an assistant curator of coins at Oxford University's Ashmolean Museum (named for one of Ashmole's ancestors) in the mid-1920s; he then became director of the British School at Rome. In 1939 he began a nineteen-year association with the University of London as Yates Professor of Classical Archaeology, and during his last nine years at that post he also served as keeper of Greek and Roman antiquities at the British Museum. He subsequently accepted titled professorships at Oxford University and the University of Aberdeen, then withdrew from education in 1962 and concentrated on writing and research. Among his books are *Greek Sculpture and Painting,* written with J. D. Beazley, *Olympia: The Sculpture of the Temple of Zeus,* written with Nicholas Yalouris and Alison Frantz, and *Architect and Sculptor in Classical Greece.*

OBITUARIES AND OTHER SOURCES:

BOOKS

The International Who's Who, 51st edition, 1987.

PERIODICALS

Times (London), February 26, 1988.

B

BACHMAN, David C(hristian) 1934-

PERSONAL: Born April 11, 1934, in Peoria, Ill.; son of Leland Alvin and Elsie May (Springer) Bachman; married Betty June Foster, September 9, 1956; children: Lynne Allison, Laura Ailene. *Education:* Goshen College, B.A., 1958; Northwestern University, M.D., 1962. *Religion:* Presbyterian.

ADDRESSES: Home—242 County Rd., No. 12 B, Ridgway, Colo. 81432. *Office*—302 Second St., Ouray, Colo. 81427.

CAREER: Cook County Hospital, Chicago, Ill., intern, 1962-63; Northwestern University, Evanston, Ill., resident in orthopedic surgery, 1963-67; private practice of medicine as orthopedic surgeon, 1967-80; private practice of medicine in Ouray, Colo., 1982—. Medical officer of Ouray Mountain Rescue, 1980—; coroner of Ouray County, 1982—; Ouray County Emergency Management Board, captain, 1984-86, vice-chairman, 1986—; orthopedic consultant to Telluride Community Clinic. Past member of staff at Northwestern Memorial Hospital, Children's Memorial Hospital, and Grant Hospital, all in Chicago; Northwestern University, past director of Center for Sports Medicine, assistant professor, 1967-80; team physician for Chicago Bulls basketball team, 1967-80.

MEMBER: American Medical Association, American College of Sports Medicine, American Academy of Orthopaedic Surgery, American College of Surgeons, American Orthopedic Society for Sports Medicine, Clinical Orthopaedic Society, Phi Rho Sigma.

WRITINGS:

(With Marilyn Preston) *Dear Dr. Jock: The People's Guide to Sports and Fitness,* Dutton, 1980.

(With H. Bates Noble) *The Diet That Lets You Cheat,* Crown, 1983.

Author of "Dr. Jock," a weekly sports medicine column distributed by Chicago Tribune-New York Times Syndicate. Editor of *Sportsmedicine-Fitness Report,* 1981-82.

WORK IN PROGRESS: An oral history of Ouray County, Colorado.

SIDELIGHTS: David C. Bachman told *CA:* "I began writing about sports medicine before it became a popular topic. Sports medicine should be aimed at preventing illness and injury, but there was a dearth of information on the subject at the beginning. People still need to learn how to keep from hurting themselves.

"Living in western Colorado is a unique experience. I'm going to try to tell the story of what it has been and what it is like."

* * *

BAGGLEY, John (Samuel) 1940-

PERSONAL: Born February 21, 1940, in Alford, Lincolnshire, England; son of Samuel (a solicitor's clerk) and Edna Minnie (a teacher; maiden name, Parker) Baggley. *Education:* University of Durham, B.A. (with honors), 1962; studied at House of the Sacred Mission, 1962-66.

ADDRESSES: Home—St. Edburg's Vicarage, Victoria Rd., Bicester OX6 7PQ, England.

CAREER: Ordained Anglican priest, 1967; began as curate, became team vicar in Poplar Team Ministry in London, England, 1966-72; parish priest at Anglican church in London, 1972-82; St. Edbury's, Bicester, England, parish priest and team rector, 1982—.

WRITINGS:

Doors of Perception: Icons and Their Spiritual Significance, Mowbray, 1987.

WORK IN PROGRESS: Research on "the place of symbolism in Christianity and the ways in which symbolism and imagery form a nonverbal language to express some of the most important aspects of human experience."

SIDELIGHTS: John Baggley's book on religious icons has been welcomed by Anglican and Orthodox critics alike. A. M. Allchin related in the *Church Times* that *Doors of Perception* is "an admirable introduction to the subject for those who are approaching it for the first time. . . . There is something very moving about this book," which provides historical background, compares icons to the scriptures from which they are drawn, and examines the icon painters themselves. Basil Youdell wrote in the *Orthodox News:* "This is really a 'theological' book in the best sense—it is a book about Union with God and the kind of spirituality we need. . . . [Baggley] has really grasped what the Orthodox Christian faith is all about." The author's journey into spirituality inspired Stanley Young

to write in the *Oxford Diocesan:* "Those who follow him to the end of this journey will be immensely rewarded by the spiritual perception he brings to this study."

Baggley told *CA:* "*Doors of Perception* was written out of interest in both the impact of Eastern Orthodox churches on Western churches and society and in the relationship between the verbal and the visual in the Christian theological and spiritual tradition. My interest in the Orthodox church was sparked during my theological training, partly through having George Every as a tutor and partly through the visitors from the Eastern churches who came to the House of the Sacred Mission at Kelham. In 1964 I visited Mount Athos, the great Greek Orthodox monastic center in northern Greece, for the first time; that was like stepping into a different world, but one which seemed strangely complementary to the Western world with its very cerebral philosophical and theological ethos. I never lost interest in the Orthodox church, but my interest was renewed in the 1970s by having the opportunity to see good examples of medieval icons at the Temple Gallery in London and by getting to know the gallery's director, Richard Temple (who provided the appendix and most of the illustrations in *Doors of Perception*). This coincided with a time when I was working in a very mixed and multi-racial parish in East London, where there was an urgent need to accept and understand different patterns of religious experience; this seemed to spark further interest in icons, largely as a way of entering into a tradition of silent prayer and attentiveness. Icons seemed to appear in the West at a time when the visual mode of perception was becoming increasingly significant; churches and monasteries throughout Europe seem to welcome the holy icons of the Orthodox church as a valuable aid to prayer and thereby find in the icons a way of beginning to overcome some of the barriers that have existed between the Eastern and Western churches. While there are good examples of Christian painting and sculpture in the medieval West that are closely linked to a tradition of prayer and worship, the icon apparently gained an acceptance in the West today because it belongs to a very deep tradition of interior prayer and is in fact an externalization in painting or mosaic of profound theological and spiritual wisdom."

BIOGRAPHICAL/CRITICAL SOURCES:

PERIODICALS

Church Times, March 6, 1987.
Orthodox News, April, 1987.
Oxford Diocesan, April, 1987.
Times Literary Supplement, April 24, 1987.

* * *

BAILEY, Paul Dayton 1906-1987

OBITUARY NOTICE—See index for *CA* sketch: Born in 1906 in American Fork, Utah; died October 26, 1987, in Claremont, Calif. Publisher, editor, and author. Bailey was a prolific chronicler of the Mormon church and the American West. In 1941 he established Westernlore Press and named himself publisher and editor. The company published many of Bailey's books, including *Polygamy Was Better Than Monotony,* and *Holy Smoke: A Dissertation on the Utah War,* as well as several biographies. Some of his books, such as *For This My Glory: A Story of a Mormon Life* and *An Unnatural History of Death Valley: With Reflections on the Valley's Varmints, Virgins, Vandals, and Visionaries,* were published by other firms.

OBITUARIES AND OTHER SOURCES:

PERIODICALS

Los Angeles Times, November 1, 1987.

* * *

BAILLIE, Kate 1957-

PERSONAL: Born March 29, 1957, in Iserloehn, West Germany; daughter of J.R.E. (a brigadier general in the British Army) and Lettice Mary (Pumphrey) Hamilton-Baillie. *Education:* King's College, Cambridge, B.A. (with honors), 1978. *Politics:* Socialist. *Religion:* None.

ADDRESSES: Home—London, England.

CAREER: Conde Nast Publications, London, England, journalist, 1978-79; English language teacher in Paris, London, and Cairo, 1979-83; free-lance writer, 1984—.

MEMBER: Writers' Guild of Great Britain.

WRITINGS:

(With Tom Salmon and Andrew Sanger) *The Rough Guide to France,* Routledge & Kegan Paul, 1986.
(With Salmon) *The Rough Guide to Paris,* Routledge & Kegan Paul, 1987.
Coastline: Our Threatened Heritage, Kingfisher Books, 1987.
(Co-editor and contributor) *The Rough Guide to Brittany and Normandy,* Routledge & Kegan Paul, 1987.

Contributor to a travel book for women, *Half the Earth,* and to magazines and newspapers, including *Spare Rib, Time Out, Bad News, El Informador del Caribe, Al Ahaly,* and *Labour Herald.*

WORK IN PROGRESS: "Rainbow Keys," a story for five-to-ten-year-olds.

SIDELIGHTS: Kate Baillie told *CA:* "Truth and accuracy, clarity, rhythm and poetry, sensitivity to the associations of every word—these are some of the qualities I strive for in writing. Writing is always slow and painful, with rare moments of total absorption and fulfillment. Money is certainly no motivation: in fact, I need to be supported by another income to carry on. Working with a good editor is of vital importance. Talking to people, to anyone, provides the best groundwork research and is my main source of inspiration.

"I have traveled a fair bit. It has always been the conversations, new friendships, different views of the world, and the subtleties of other languages that I treasure more than landscapes, food, and so on. I speak tolerable French, basic German, and pidgin Arabic and Polish.

"The *Rough Guides* are only 'rough' in the sense that they are selective rather than comprehensive and are aimed at the low-budget traveler, though in fact the readership is very diverse both in age and income. What distinguishes the France and Paris books from other guides is their attitude and the range of information covered. We list tango clubs as well as opera houses and mention current politicians as well as ancient kings. Activities for children are given just as much prominence as details of Gothic architecture, and we don't treat established sights with awe and reverence unless they really deserve it. The idea is not just to inform but to provide a good, thought-provoking, and entertaining read."

BAINES, Frank 1915-1987

OBITUARY NOTICE: Born September 24, 1915, in London, England; died October 22, 1987. Author. As a boy, Baines ran away from school and set out on a series of adventures, upon which he would later base his books. The unconventional Baines was, among other things, an apprentice to Gusten Erikson on an Australia-bound Finnish bark, a Conservative Party agent, a monk in a Hindu monastery, a tea chest repairer, a gossip columnist, a ditch digger, a convict (he was jailed for refusing to pay mandatory insurance contributions to the British state health service), an actor in a film directed by Pier Paolo Pasolini, and an owner of an antiques business. His autobiographical works include *Look Towards the Sea, In Deep, Culture of Bacillus,* and *Officer Boy.*

OBITUARIES AND OTHER SOURCES:

PERIODICALS

Times (London), October 27, 1987.

* * *

BAKER, Howard H(enry), Jr. 1925-

PERSONAL: Born November 15, 1925, in Huntsville, Tenn.; son of Howard Henry (a politician) and Dora (Ladd) Baker; married Joy Dirksen, December 22, 1951; children: Darek Dirksen, Cynthia. *Education:* Undergraduate study at University of the South and Tulane University of Louisiana; University of Tennessee (now University of Tennessee at Knoxville), LL.B., 1949. *Politics:* Republican.

ADDRESSES: Home—Huntsville, Tenn. *Office*—c/o the White House, 1600 Pennsylvania Ave., Washington, D.C. 20500.

CAREER: Admitted to the Bar of the State of Tennessee; senior partner in Baker, Worthington, Barnett & Crossley (now Baker, Worthington, Crossley, Stansberry & Woolf), Knoxville, Tenn. U.S. Senate, Washington, D.C., senator from Tennessee, 1967-85, minority leader, 1977-81, majority leader, 1981-85; Vinson & Elkins, Washington D.C., senior partner, 1985—; White House chief of staff, 1987—. Director of American Telegraph and Telephone, Gannett Company, and MCA; chairman of the board of First National Bank, Oneida, Tenn.; member of advisory board of Merrill Lynch and board of trustees of Mayo Clinic. Has been a member of various senatorial committees, including the Select Committee on Presidential Campaign Activities (vice-chairman), Committee on Environment and Public Works, Committee on Foreign Relations, Committee on Rules and Administration, and the Select Committee on Intelligence (ex-officio). *Military service:* U.S. Naval Reserve, active duty, 1943-46; became lieutenant junior grade.

MEMBER: American Bar Association.

AWARDS, HONORS: Presidential Medal of Freedom, 1984.

WRITINGS:

No Margin for Error: America in the Eighties, foreword by Daniel Patrick Moynihan, Times Books, 1980.

What Must Be Done and How We Must Do It, Times Books, 1980.

Howard Baker's Washington: An Intimate Portrait of the Nation's Capital City, Norton, 1982.

SIDELIGHTS: When Howard H. Baker, Jr., was named White House chief of staff by President Ronald Reagan on February 27, 1987, his selection was applauded as a "superb and overdue step" by the *Christian Science Monitor*. Many felt that Baker, who came to the post already possessed of a distinguished political career, would help lend new credibility to a Reagan administration beleaguered by the Iran-*contra* scandal, in which funds from the sale of weapons to Iran were allegedly diverted to the resistance fighters in Nicaragua. He served three terms as U.S. senator from Tennessee and was minority leader of the U.S. Senate from 1977 to 1981 and majority leader from 1981 to 1985. Baker also made an unsuccessful bid for the office of U.S. president in 1980 and was reportedly gearing up to run again in 1988 when Reagan named him chief of staff. Praised for his ability to obtain compromises from opposing factions in the Senate, Baker first gained national exposure during the televised Senate Watergate hearings of the early 1970s, which investigated charges of wrongdoing by President Richard M. Nixon and members of his administration. He acquired a reputation for fairness and honesty at that time by tenaciously demanding, though he and President Nixon were both of the Republican party, "What did the President know and when did he know it?"

Baker was born into a political family. His paternal grandfather was a judge, his maternal grandmother the first woman county sheriff in Tennessee, and his father, Howard Baker, Sr., the U.S. representative from Tennessee's second congressional district from 1951 to 1964. Upon his father's death, Baker's stepmother took over the seat. Baker was quoted in an article by Stephen Rattner for the *New York Times* as saying "My father had a profound impact on me in a way I don't think I could ever explain."

From his earliest political acts, Baker has adopted the role of conciliator. He went to law school at the University of Tennessee, claiming that he meant to continue his undergraduate studies in engineering but the registration line for law was shorter, and became student body president on a platform of resolving differences between fraternity members and nonmembers. After receiving his LL.B. in 1949, Baker went to work with the law firm of Baker, Worthington, Barnett & Crossley, which his grandfather founded in 1885. He practiced criminal law, specializing in defending accused murderers. Baker also, in the words of Rattner, "dabbled in bank, coal, and real-estate deals that made millions."

In 1964, Baker was expected to run an easy race for the congressional seat in the House of Representatives that his father had occupied but instead chose a more challenging fight to replace Senator Estes Kefauver, who had also died. Baker's subsequent loss was at least partially due to the fact that Barry Goldwater headed the Republican ticket that year and suffered a landslide defeat at the hands of President Lyndon B. Johnson. He ran for the seat again, however, in 1966, this time for a full six-year term. The young politician took a more moderate stance in his second attempt, swaying traditionally Democratic voters and winning 35 percent of Tennessee's black vote, an unusual feat for a Republican. He won the election, becoming the first popularly elected Republican senator in the history of Tennessee.

Though his voting record during his eighteen years in the Senate was labeled "conservative" by Martin Tolchin in the *New York Times,* Baker has taken positions that range throughout the political spectrum. He voted for the Equal Rights Amendment, largely supported legislation to protect the environment—though he backed the Tellico Dam project in spite of its negative implications for the endangered snail darter—and

was one of only three Southern senators to vote for civil rights legislation in 1968. Baker cast one of the deciding votes needed to ratify the treaty ceding the Panama Canal back to Panama, and he supported it although criticized by many conservative members of his party. Jess Cook of the *Los Angeles Times* called the Republican senator's backing of the treaty "the most courageous and statesmanlike act of his career."

On the more conservative side, Baker has opposed busing and gun control, and though he generally favors an arms limitation agreement with the Soviet Union, he has supported the anti-balistic missile and was instrumental in the defeat of the Strategic Arms Limitation Treaty (SALT) during President Jimmy Carter's administration. Rattner reported Baker's reasoning against SALT: "With his ordered, precise mind, he mastered the technicalities and what he saw as the technical defects of the proposed treaty. At the top of his list was the provision allowing the Soviet Union to keep 308 SS-18 missiles, mammoth weapons with firepower equal to the entire United States arsenal. 'That is not equality,' he insisted." Summing up Baker's practice when facing an issue being decided in the Senate, Rattner wrote, "The . . . formula [is] simple: strike a responsible pose at the outset, seek the counsel of experts on both sides and then make a decision of conscience."

In 1973, Baker was named vice-chairman of the Select Committee on Presidential Campaign Activities (Senate Watergate Committee) by then minority leader Senator Hugh Scott of Pennsylvania. Baker's service as the ranking Republican on the committee was distinguished by his serious attitude toward the Watergate problem and his insistence on discovering President Nixon's role in the scandal. According to Rattner, Baker's participation in the televised hearings "[left] most Americans with the impression that he had nothing at heart but the interests of his country." The senator's professional way of phrasing his questions gave him credibility with Nixon supporters and opponents alike. Baker himself recognized the importance of his role in the Watergate investigation. Rattner quoted him as saying "nobody on that committee was more diligent in doing what I announced that I was going to do—that was, to follow the facts wherever they led. Remember, I started those hearings convinced Nixon was innocent. And it wasn't many days though until I realized that we had a quite different situation on our hands and I made that statement—that [it] was going to be painful; it was going to be difficult but Republicans were going to follow the inquiry wherever it led us and let the chips fall where they may. And I think we did that with a vengeance."

Besides leading to his selection as keynote speaker for the 1976 Republican convention because he was one of the few party members the Watergate scandal left with a positive public image, Baker's position on the Watergate committee was probably beneficial in his obtaining the minority leadership of the Senate. He had sought the post unsuccessfully twice before, but Scott's retirement left it vacant in 1977. Baker was considered a longshot going into the competition against Senator Robert Griffin of Michigan, but he won by a vote of nineteen to eighteen. The deciding factor, apparently, was that Baker was judged to be more articulate than Griffin. As Richard D. Lyons put it in a *New York Times* article, "considering the small number of Republicans in both chambers of Congress, the party believes it needs leaders who can act as effective spokesmen." Interestingly, when Baker became minority leader of the Senate, he occupied the same post his father-in-law, Senator Everett Dirksen of Illinois, had until his death in 1969. Baker married Dirksen's daughter, Joy, in 1951. Baker's new position in the Senate gave him a greater chance to exercise his ability to compromise, which he continued to do throughout his term as Republican leader. Tolchin asserted that Baker "made a career out of being a conciliator, bringing together disparate factions and cajoling them into agreements that led to legislation." When Ronald Reagan was elected president in 1980, enough Republicans were elected to the Senate to give them control of it, and Baker was then elected majority leader. He filled this powerful post with skill. In Tolchin's words, "Mr. Baker reconciled the liberal and conservative wings of his party and then reconciled the President's goals with those of the Senate Republicans. At the same time, he won the respect and affection of Democratic leaders of both the House and Senate." Tolchin quoted Democratic Senator Jim Sasser from Tennessee describing Baker: "He's a genius at finding the compromise point and pushing it through."

Baker took some of his attention from the Senate in order to run in the presidential election of 1980. He explained his desire to become president to Rattner, saying that the office of president of the United States is "the only place where you can identify problems and state them to the country and persuade people to follow you." The senator's campaign platform included an emphasis on foreign policy. Baker told Rattner that America needed to "signal that we intend to remain strong to protect our vital interests and that we're going to stop giving up a little at a time, whether it's in the Caribbean, whether it's in Africa, whether it's in the Middle East." Reagan, however, won the Republican nomination, and Baker returned to his senatorial duties.

Part of Baker's presidential campaign effort had been the publication of two books in 1980, one of which, *No Margin for Error: America in the Eighties,* was widely reviewed. In it he detailed more of his ideas for the presidency, including establishing presidential offices in the Capitol building to aid cooperation between the legislative and executive branch, and dividing the legislative year in two with the latter half solely dedicated to matters of budget. These concepts were hailed as "intriguing suggestions" by Cook and labeled "worth talking about" by Martin F. Nolan in the *Washington Post Book World.* Nolan, while lauding Baker as "genuinely intellectual," declared that his "tone is best when conversational rather than hortatory." Similarly, Cook observed, "those who have seen Baker in operation, or for that matter in this year's GOP [Grand Old Party, i.e., Republican] primary debates, know him as a warm, engaging fellow and a folksy storyteller. Thus the relative paucity of personal and anecdotal material in this volume is especially disappointing."

Baker's 1982 book, *Howard Baker's Washington: An Intimate Portrait of the Nation's Capital City,* combines aspects of his career with his favorite hobby, photography. Baker's photographs have been displayed in galleries throughout the country and published in national magazines. Tolchin remarked that the Republican leader "rarely is without his camera"and that during his last term as a senator "he took it to White House meetings, frequently photographing the President and Vice President as well as many of the staff members." Thus, *Howard Baker's Washington* includes photos of many Washington celebrities. In *Newsweek* Baker called his camera's viewfinder "the only place where I can reasonably aspire to perfection. I can *never* do that in politics [or] in the Congress."

In 1983 Baker announced that he would not seek a fourth senate term in 1984, immediately sparking rumors that he planned another presidential bid, either in 1984 if Reagan did

not seek re-election, or in 1988. After all, as *Time* reported, Baker had ended his 1980 campaign for the nation's highest office with the comment, "You have to be unemployed to run for President." When Baker had served out his third term, he became a senior partner in the Washington offices of Vinson & Elkins, a Houston-based law firm. By 1985, however, Godfrey Sperling was interviewing Baker for the *Christian Science Monitor* as a candidate for the 1988 presidential election "already deep in the preparatory stage of running." In the interview Baker favored a balanced budget amendment, "not to outlaw deficits, which is pie in the sky, but to make it at least less convenient for Congress to expand the deficit." He also spoke of his support for the Strategic Defense Initiative (SDI or Star Wars), a project which would theoretically explode enemy nuclear weapons before they could reach the atmosphere, saying "the whole idea that we are going to protect this country [without SDI] by threatening to incinerate the Soviet Union is repugnant." Baker summed up his forthcoming bid for president by proclaiming, "I know where I want to take the country."

Baker, however, felt it was his duty to abandon his presidential hopes when President Reagan asked him to become White House chief of staff in 1987. After Reagan accepted Donald Regan's resignation due to the then chief of staff's alleged involvement in the Iran-*contra* affair, the President's friend Paul Laxalt, former senator from Nevada, recommended that Baker fill the vacancy. Baker flew to the White House from a Florida retreat, and after a consultation period with the President and the First Lady, was heralded as the new chief of staff. *Time* hailed his appointment as "the most encouraging sign in months that Reagan is still capable of saving his Administration from the Iranscam quagmire," and quoted Baker as announcing, "I expect that there will be good things out of the last two years of the Reagan Administration. And I intend to help him."

AVOCATIONAL INTERESTS: Photography.

BIOGRAPHICAL/CRITICAL SOURCES:

PERIODICALS

Best Sellers, October, 1980.
Christian Science Monitor, August 20, 1985, March 2, 1987.
Los Angeles Times, August 22, 1980.
Newsweek, August 30, 1982, September 12, 1983.
New York Times, January 5, 1977, November 4, 1979, April 16, 1985, February 28, 1987, March 3, 1987, September 6, 1987.
Time, January 24, 1983, March 9, 1987, March 16, 1987.
Washington Post Book World, September 7, 1980.

—*Sketch by Elizabeth Thomas*

* * *

BAKR el TOURE, Askia Muhammad Abu
See TOURE, Askia Muhammad Abu Bakr el

* * *

BALDWIN, James (Arthur) 1924-1987

OBITUARY NOTICE—See index for *CA* sketch: Born August 2, 1924, in New York, N.Y.; died of stomach cancer, December 1, 1987, in St. Paul de Vence, France; buried at Ferncliff Cemetery in Ardsley, N.Y. Preacher, laborer, and author. An eloquent and passionate critic of racial discrimination, Baldwin is considered one of the most important writers to appear since World War II. The child of a Harlem minister, Baldwin began his own preaching career in Harlem as a young teenager. After experiencing a religious crisis, Baldwin left the church and moved to New York City's bohemian Greenwich Village, where he worked at menial jobs and wrote articles for publications such as *Nation* and *Commentary*. By the late 1940s Baldwin had become disgusted with American bigotry, and before the decade ended he moved to France. He made his literary debut in 1953 with *Go Tell It on the Mountain,* a novel about an adolescent coming to terms with his own religious and social convictions in an oppressive environment. This work, derived from Baldwin's own childhood experiences, showed him to be an intense, talented writer.

Baldwin's next work, the nonfiction *Notes of a Native Son,* brought him even greater acclaim as an articulate critic of bigotry and social inequality. Two more nonfiction volumes, *Nobody Knows My Name* and *The Fire Next Time,* confirmed his status, and by the early 1960s he ranked as a leading figure in contemporary literature. During the middle years of that decade Baldwin returned to the United States, where he became involved in the civil rights movement. But following the assassination of leading activist Martin Luther King, Jr., Baldwin began making periodic trips to France, and in 1974 he once again settled there. Among his later works is the novel *Harlem Quartet*—about jazz clubs of the 1950s—which earned the author the French-American Friendship Prize, one of his many literary awards.

OBITUARIES AND OTHER SOURCES:

BOOKS

The International Who's Who, 51st edition, Europa, 1987.

PERIODICALS

Chicago Tribune, December 2, 1987.
Los Angeles Times, December 2, 1987.
New York Times, December 2, 1987, December 9, 1987.
Times (London), December 2, 1987.
Washington Post, December 2, 1987.
USA Today, December 2, 1987.

* * *

BALLSTADT, Carl A. 1931-

PERSONAL: Born December 28, 1931, in Sault Ste. Marie, Ontario, Canada; son of Paul A. (a paper maker) and Hilda (Liedtke) Ballstadt; married Dorothy Copeland (a nurse), July 8, 1967; children: Kurt, Marnin (daughter). *Education:* University of Western Ontario, B.A., 1957, M.A., 1959; University of London, Ph.D., 1965. *Religion:* Lutheran.

ADDRESSES: Office—Department of English, McMaster University, 1280 Main St. W., Hamilton, Ontario, Canada L8S 4L1.

CAREER: Teacher at schools in Sault Ste. Marie, Ontario, 1953-60; University of Saskatchewan, Saskatoon, instructor, 1962-64, assistant professor of English, 1964-66; University of Guelph, Guelph, Ontario, assistant professor of English, 1966-76; McMaster University, Hamilton, Ontario, assistant professor, 1967-72, associate professor, 1972-85, professor of English, 1986—.

MEMBER: Bibliographical Society of Canada, Association for Canadian Studies, Canadian Association for American Studies.

WRITINGS:

The Search for English-Canadian Literature, University of Toronto Press, 1975.
Catharine Parr Traill and Her Works, ECW Press, 1983.
(Editor with Elizabeth Hopkins and Michael Peterman) *Susanna Moodie: Letters of a Lifetime,* University of Toronto Press, 1986.
(Editor) Susanna Moodie, *Roughing It in the Bush,* Carleton University Press, 1988.
(Editor) *Letters of Catharine Parr Traill,* University of Toronto Press, in press.

SIDELIGHTS: Carl A. Ballstadt told *CA:* "Canadian literature has 'come into its own' in the past two decades with the emergence of writers such as Margaret Atwood, Margaret Laurence, Alice Munro, and Timothy Findlay—writers whose work has commanded a good deal of attention in other parts of the world. But the work of these people often reflects their sense of a particular and fascinating Canadian past with which they can identify. Works by both Atwood and Laurence, for example, include a recognition of kindred spirits in Susanna Moodie and Catharine Parr Traill, two of our prominent nineteenth-century writers. And yet, there is still much that we do not know about Moodie and Traill. As is the case with so many early Canadian authors, their literature has been completely considered while their letters have been ignored, at least until recently.

"My own scholarship has been devoted to establishing a better basis for knowing ourselves by understanding how our colonial ancestors felt about emerging nationhood and about the status of literature and other modes of cultural expression in a colony or a new nation. My work began with a broad study of early critical materials concerning the desire for and the nature of literature in the British American colonies and the Canadian Confederation. The main discovery of that survey was the high degree to which nineteenth-century observations of Canadian literature anticipated and were consistent with those made by our twentieth-century writers and critics with respect to such matters as moderation in nationalism, an eclectic outlook, our experience of 'northernness,' and our cultural subordination to Britain and the United States.

"One other concern of those early critics was the process of transition from Old World to New World culture. Moodie and Traill offer a rich basis for the examination of that transition—hence, my interest in their lives and writings. Furthermore, the process of transition continues to be a major theme in Canadian literature."

BIOGRAPHICAL/CRITICAL SOURCES:

PERIODICALS

Globe and Mail (Toronto), February 8, 1986.

* * *

BALMUTH, Miriam S.

PERSONAL: Education—Cornell University, A.B., 1946; Ohio State University, M.A., 1950; Harvard University, Ph.D., 1964.

ADDRESSES: Office—Department of Classics, Tufts University, Medford, Mass. 02155.

CAREER: Faculty member teaching classics and archaeology at Tufts University, Medford, Mass.

WRITINGS:

(Editor with R. J. Rowland, Jr.) *Studies in Sardinian Archaeology,* University of Michigan Press, 1984.
(Editor) *Studies in Sardinian Archaeology II: Sardinia in the Mediterranean,* University of Michigan Press, 1986.

WORK IN PROGRESS: Editing *Studies in Sardinian Archaeology III: Nuragic Sardinia and the Mycenaean World* for British Archaeological Reports.*

* * *

BARKER, Sebastian 1945-

PERSONAL: Born April 16, 1945, in Gloucestershire, England; son of George Granville (an author) and Elizabeth (an author; maiden name, Smart) Barker; married Julie Rosalind Ellis, August 29, 1969 (divorced May 12, 1980); married Sally Louise Rouse (a teacher), March 29, 1986; children: (first marriage) Chloe Therese Katherine, Miranda Rose Korinne Faith. *Education:* Corpus Christi College, Oxford, M.A. (natural science), 1968; University of East Anglia, M.A. (English literature), 1970.

ADDRESSES: Home and office—22a Lawford Rd., London NW5 2LN, England.

CAREER: Writer. Writer in residence at South Hill Park Arts Centre, Stamford Arts Centre, Stamford College for Further Education, Grantham City Library, Spalding City Library, and Berkshire County Council, 1980-85; director or co-director of Bracknell Literature Festivals, Surrey Literature Festival, and Royal Berkshire Poetry Festival, 1980-85.

MEMBER: Poetry Society (general council), Oxford Union (life member).

AWARDS, HONORS: Arts Council grant,1976.

WRITINGS:

POETRY, EXCEPT AS NOTED

Poems, Cygnet Press, 1974.
The Dragon, Quill Books, 1976.
In the Rocks, Martin Brian & O'Keeffe, 1977.
Who Is Eddie Linden (documentary novel), Jay Landesman, 1979.
Epistles, Martin Brian & O'Keeffe, 1980.
A Fire in the Rain, Martin Brian & O'Keeffe, 1982.
A Nuclear Epiphany, Friday Night Fish Publications, 1984.
Boom, Free Man's Press Editions, 1985.
(Editor) Chirstopher Barker, *Portraits of Poets* (poetry and photography), Carcanet New Press, 1986.

WORK IN PROGRESS: The Autobiography of a Philosopher, based on the life and works of a nineteenth-century German philosopher.

SIDELIGHTS: Sebastain Barker told *CA:* "I put the essence of my life as I see it into my work. Each of my books is a completely separate conception. I do not allow myself duplication in a new book of original work done in a book already published. By holding fast to this principle, I want to bring the whole area of my unconscious motivation into the developing pattern of my work, as seen over a lifetime; and I am not so ingenuous that I think this can be done by writing sequel after sequel along the same track.

"I start from the premise that, in literature, I just don't believe a word of it. That is, I don't believe this myth, this story, this

set of characters, this set of words. I am deeply suspicious, then, of books that take their myths for granted, churn out the same old stories, and make up people who are clearly not people at all but figments of the collective literary imagination. In all such works, it seems to me, the unconscious powers of our time are really writing the books, and the authors themselves are the ventriloquist's dummies of the age. I am not implying this is a disgraceful thing to be by any means: often, as we can see on television, the ventriloquist's dummy is much more amusing and intelligent than the ventriloquist. All I am saying is that it is impossible for me to function as a writer in this way. I cannot believe in my words if I have not discovered them in the very pulse of my being.

"I am a poet writing in the English mystical tradition, who feels quite at home in all the forms and formlessnesses that have come down to our time. I admire genres both in poetry and in the rest of literature, but my talents within them, barring straightforward prose and a documentary approach, are pedestrian and derivative at best. In poetry, however, in my own field, I have a freedom and a discipline within that freedom which own no masters but which have lived and paid homage to many.

"In general, the subjects of my poems chose themselves. I have learned to let the important issues find their own way into my writing, noticing how it is the way I actually live that attracts them to me or makes them feel that my life is actually repellent to them.

"Poetry for me is the exploration of reality. It is not a side-issue in life, nor is it the pedantic mapping of the daily suburbs of social or private existence. It must always be facing the reality of what it has not yet done, otherwise as an art it has no conscience, and no art has so great a conscience as poetry, for no other art has the obstinacy of articulacy to contend with.

"My *Autobiography of a Philosopher* is unlike anything I have done before. But its genesis is the same as with all my poems: it comes out of the inescapable need something feels inside myself to get itself written. Each of my poems has been a spiritual necessity, something which, if I didn't do and didn't do as well as I could, would shame me in my own eyes and make it difficult, if not impossible, for me to live with myself. Each poem is a crisis and one which can only be solved satisfactorily by the sight and sound of each letter and punctuation mark set firmly in the shape of the finished poem. Poems that don't make it, don't make it in my experience because they are not enough of a crisis."

* * *

BARNES, Irston Roberts 1904-1988

OBITUARY NOTICE: Born February 14, 1904, in New Haven, Conn.; died of cancer, January 19, 1988, in Groton, Conn. Educator, economist, naturalist, and author. Barnes taught economics at Yale and Columbia universities, served as a government economist and division chief of the Federal Trade Commission, and was chairman of the Audubon Naturalist Society. In addition to writing "The Naturalist," a weekly column for the *Washington Post,* from 1951 to 1976, he authored *The Economics of Public Utilities Regulation.*

OBITUARIES AND OTHER SOURCES:

BOOKS

Who's Who in America, 44th edition, Marquis, 1986.

PERIODICALS

New York Times, January 22, 1988.
Washington Post, January 24, 1988.

* * *

BARNETT, Peter Herbert 1945-

PERSONAL: Born July 27, 1945, in Worcester, Mass.; son of Herbert P. (an artist) and Elizabeth (a musician; maiden name, Lettinger) Barnett; married Vivian Endicott (a museum curator), July 1, 1967; children: Sarah, Alexander. *Education:* Haverford College, B.A., 1966; Columbia University, Ph.D., 1970; Brooklyn College of the City University of New York, M.A., 1988.

ADDRESSES: Home—317 West 83rd St., New York, N.Y. 10024. *Office*—Department of Philosophy, John Jay College of Criminal Justice of the City University of New York, 444 56th St., New York, N.Y. 10019.

CAREER: Columbia University, New York, N.Y., assistant to dean of School of General Studies, 1968-69, director of admissions, 1969-70; Alice Lloyd College, Pippa Passes, Ky., assistant professor of philosophy and dean of students, 1970-71; John Jay College of Criminal Justice of the City University of New York, New York City, assistant professor, 1971-78, associate professor of philosophy, 1978—. Teaching and administrative fellow at Woodrow Wilson National Fellowship Foundation, 1970-71; faculty coordinator of Microcomputer Resources Laboratory, University Computer Center of the City University of New York, 1986-87.

MEMBER: International Society for the Study of Time, Association for Computing Machinery, New York Academy of Sciences, Haverford College Honor Society Founder's Club.

AWARDS, HONORS: Woodrow Wilson fellow, 1966-67.

WRITINGS:

Two Philosophical Experiments: Interrogations of Authority, Concentration in the Present, University Press of America, 1977.
Time Trap, Assembling Press, 1980.
Can You Tell Me How What You Are Doing Now Is to Do Something Philosophical, Assembling Press, 1980.
Tools of Thought: The Practical Basis of Formal Reasoning, Schenkman, 1981.
Reciprocal Encoding-Decoding Construction, Tony Zwicker, 1981-83.

Contributor to periodicals.

WORK IN PROGRESS: Thinking Without Surfaces: A Philosophical Experiment in Nonobjective Construction, to be published in the form of computer software; research on the philosophical issues of artifical intelligence.

SIDELIGHTS: Peter Herbert Barnett told *CA:* "The primary foci of my philosophical research and writing are the study of the nature of time, the present, and passage; and the search for new media of philosophical communication. These two themes have led to a series of experiments in graphic and textual interaction, which have taken the form of 'artists' books' rather than conventional philosophical texts. Cutouts, dovetails, strings, and interactive design elements characterize my publications since 1978.

"During the past four years I have engaged in intensive study of computer science for its applicability to my philosophical

research and, conversely, the application of my research to the development of artificial intelligence.''

* * *

BAROLINI, Teodolinda 1951-

PERSONAL: Born December 19, 1951, in Syracuse, N.Y.; daughter of Antonio (a poet and novelist) and Helen (a writer; maiden name, Mollica) Barolini; married Douglas G. Caverly (an investment manager), June 21, 1980. *Education:* Sarah Lawrence College, B.A., 1972; Columbia University, M.A., 1973, Ph.D., 1978.

ADDRESSES: Office—Department of French and Italian, New York University, 19 University Place, New York, N.Y. 10003.

CAREER: University of California, Berkeley, assistant professor of Italian, 1978-83; New York University, New York, N.Y., associate professor of Italian, 1983—.

MEMBER: American Association of Teachers of Italian, American Boccaccio Association, Dante Society of America (vice-president, 1983-86), Mediaeval Academy of America, Modern Language Association of America.

AWARDS, HONORS: Fellow of American Association of University Women, 1977-78, American Council of Learned Societies, 1981-82, and National Endowment for the Humanities, 1986-87; Howard R. Marraro Prize from Modern Language Association of America, 1986, for *Dante's Poets.*

WRITINGS:

(Contributor) *European Writers: The Middle Ages and the Renaissance,* Scribner, 1983.
Dante's Poets: Textuality and Truth in the ''Comedy,'' Princeton University Press, 1984.

Contributor of articles to journals, including *Italica* and *Romance Philology.*

WORK IN PROGRESS: Dante's Ulyssean Art: The Narrative Journey of the ''Commedia''; a monograph on the fifth canto of Dante's *Inferno.*

* * *

BARR, Margaret Scolari 1901-1987

OBITUARY NOTICE: Born in 1901 in Rome, Italy; immigrated to United States, 1925; died of colon cancer, December 30, 1987, in New York, N.Y. Art historian, educator, linguist, and author. A respected art historian, Barr was influential in the New York art community for about fifty years. She taught art history at the Spence School for thirty-seven of those years, became involved in efforts to help such artists as Jacques Lipchitz, Piet Mondrian, Max Ernst, Yves Tanguy, and Andre Masson escape from Europe during World War II, and assisted her husband, Alfred Barr, in his duties as director of the Museum of Modern Art. Scholars contend that without Barr's skills as an interpreter—she was fluent in four languages—her husband would have been unable to publish books on Pablo Picasso and Henri Matisse. Barr herself wrote *Medardo Rosso,* credited as the best work in English on the sculptor. In addition, she translated Matisse's *Notes of a Painter* into English. A chronology of her life with her husband was in progress at the time of her death.

OBITUARIES AND OTHER SOURCES:

PERIODICALS

New York Times, December 31, 1987.

* * *

BARTLETT, Amy 1949-

PERSONAL: Born March 18, 1949; daughter of Eliot Fitch (an artist) and Christine (Price) Bartlett. *Education:* Vassar College, A.B., 1972; New York University, M.A., 1985.

ADDRESSES: Home—500 East 77th St., Apt. 702, New York, N.Y. 10162.

CAREER: Harper & Row Publishers, Inc., New York City, manuscript reader, 1974-76; Farrar, Straus & Giroux, New York City, assistant editor, 1976-78; Crown Publishers, Inc., New York City, associate editor, 1978-79; tutor and writing workshop teacher for Literacy Volunteers, 1979-82; New York University, New York City, administrator of writing program, 1983-84; Poets House, New York City, director, 1984-85; free-lance writer, 1985—.

MEMBER: Poetry Society of America.

AWARDS, HONORS: Academy of American Poets Prize, 1983, for a collection of four poems, including ''Love With the Same Name''; National Poetry Series Award, 1984, for manuscript of *Afterwards.*

WRITINGS:

Afterwards (poems), Persea Books, 1985.

Contributor of poems to *Mudfish* and *Ironweed.*

WORK IN PROGRESS: Another collection of poems.

* * *

BARTON, Wayne 1944-

PERSONAL: Born May 23, 1944, in North Cowden, Tex.; son of John Samuel (an oil field worker) and Alene (a housewife; maiden name, Gurley) Barton; married Margaret Whisenand (a housewife), April 4, 1966; children: Charles, Kristin. *Education:* Texas Tech University, B.S., 1967. *Religion:* Presbyterian.

ADDRESSES: Home—2509 Emerson, Midland, Tex. 79705. *Agent*—Charles Neighbors, Inc., 7600 Blanco Rd., Suite 3607, San Antonio, Tex. 78216.

CAREER: Arco Oil & Gas Co., engineer in Roswell, N.M., Casper, Wyo., and Midland, Tex., 1967—. Editorial associate of Writer's Digest School of Short Fiction.

MEMBER: Society of Petroleum Engineers, Western Writers of America (member of board of directors, 1985-87).

AWARDS, HONORS: Western Writers of America Spur Award, 1981, for magazine article ''One Man's Code,'' Medicine Pipe Bearer Award, 1982, for *Ride Down the Wind.*

WRITINGS:

Ride Down the Wind (western novel), Doubleday, 1982.
Return to Phantom Hill (western novel), Doubleday, 1984.
(With Stan Williams) *Warhorse* (western novel), Pocket Books, 1988.
Live by the Gun (western novel), Pocket Books, 1988.

Author of "Bookmarks," a monthly column in *Roundup*. Contributor of articles and stories to magazines, including *Far West, Analog,* and *Empire*.

WORK IN PROGRESS: A historical novel set in Elizabethan times.

* * *

BASS, Thomas A. 1951-

PERSONAL: Born March 9, 1951, in Chagrin Falls, Ohio; son of Nathan Winthrop and Audrey (DeJong) Bass; married Roberta Lyles Krueger; children: Maude Catherine Bass-Krueger. *Education:* Univerity of Chicago, A.B., 1973; University of California, Ph.D., 1980.

ADDRESSES: Agent—Nat Sobel, Nat Sobel Associates, Inc., 146 East 19th St., New York, N.Y. 10003.

CAREER: Writer.

WRITINGS:

The Eudaemonic Pie, Houghton, 1985.

WORK IN PROGRESS: A book on science in Africa for Houghton, publication expected in 1988.

SIDELIGHTS: As a graduate student in California, Thomas A. Bass shared an old house with several other young men and women, many of them with strong backgrounds in physics and mathematics. In *The Eudaemonic Pie,* Bass tells what happened when the group decided they could use scientific knowledge to win large amounts of money by betting on roulette in Las Vegas, Nevada.

Bass and his friends knew that in roulette betting customarily continues after the ball has been released but before it has come to rest in one of the numbered slots of the roulette wheel. They reasoned that if they could observe the motion of the ball and the wheel, and use a computer to calculate the ball's likely destination, they could place their bets accordingly. Hoping to buy a large communal estate with the proceeds from their gambling, the group saw their goal as something nobler than money alone—a state of happiness-through-reason that the Greek philosopher Aristotle called eudaemonia. As the title of the book suggests, if Bass and his friends could find a recipe for the "eudaemonic pie" of happiness, they could all get a slice.

Surprisingly, research indicated that the group's strategy was legal, since they were improving their odds of winning at roulette without trying to change the outcome of the game. However, they surmised that casino managements would be angry with such efforts, so in addition to all the mathematical calculations and computer programming involved, the group had to develop electronic gear they could hide on their persons. One of their key pieces of equipment, for instance, turned out to be a computer hidden in a shoe.

Writing in the *New York Times,* Christopher Lehmann-Haupt said that Bass's story "is a veritable pinata of a book, which, when smashed by the reader's enthusiastic attention, showers down upon him everything from the history of useless roulette systems to the latest developments in chaos theory and their possible relevance to Darwinian evolution." Lehmann-Haupt praised the suspense of Bass's narrative and the relish with which the author recounts his activities.

Although Bass and his friends won some bets at smaller gambling houses, they eventually called off their attempts to win at the major casinos in Las Vegas, defeated by persistent problems with their electronic devices. Reviewers, though, considered the author's story of the project to be a success. "Bass has produced an exuberant and affecting work," wrote John Wilkes in the *Los Angeles Times Book Review,* noting that the author "has done the best job so far of capturing the marriage of technical imagination and the communal coziness that gave birth to Silicon Valley," the center of California's computer industry.

BIOGRAPHICAL/CRITICAL SOURCES:

PERIODICALS

Los Angeles Times Book Review, June 9, 1985.
New York Times, May 8, 1985.
New York Times Book Review, May 19, 1985.

* * *

BATMAN, Richard (Dale) 1932-

PERSONAL: Born September 24, 1932, in St. Louis, Mo.; son of Victor H. (a labor negotiator) and Erma (a teacher; maiden name, Dale) Batman; married Ann Harrington (an arts administrator), July 7, 1956; children: Dayle Houk, Denise Miles. *Education:* University of Colorado, B.A., 1954; Northwestern University, M.A. (film), 1959; University of Southern California, M.A. (history), 1962, Ph.D., 1965.

ADDRESSES: Home—8 Alderwood Way, San Rafael, Calif. 94901. *Agent*—Fred Hill, 2237 Union St., San Francisco, Calif. 94123.

CAREER: Mount San Antonio College, Walnut, Calif., instructor in U.S. history, 1964-67; San Francisco State University, San Francisco, Calif., assistant professor, 1967-72, associate professor, 1972-78, professor of history, 1978—. *Military service:* U.S. Army, 1955-56.

MEMBER: Western History Association, California Historical Society, Authors Guild.

WRITINGS:

American Ecclesiastes: The Stories of James Pattie, Harcourt, 1985, published as *James Pattie's West: The Dream and the Reality,* University of Oklahoma Press, 1986.
The Outer Coast, Harcourt, 1985.

Contributor to periodicals, including *California History Society Quarterly* and *Virginia Cavalcade*. Associate editor of *Journal of the West,* 1968-78; editorial consultant to *California History,* 1984—.

WORK IN PROGRESS: Editing a new edition of *The Personal Narratives of James Pattie,* for Mountain Press; a book about a twentieth-century trip through the American West and Mexico.

SIDELIGHTS: Richard Batman's first book, *American Ecclesiastes: The Stories of James Pattie,* examines *The Personal Narrative of James O. Pattie,* the lively autobiography of the nineteenth-century fur trapper. Pattie's narrative describes fights with Indians, romances, narrow escapes, starvation, and imprisonment, and has been the subject of some debate by historians out to prove or disprove it. According to Richard G. Lillard, writing in the *Los Angeles Times Book Review,* "Industrious researcher Richard Batman does a professional job of separating demonstrable fact and strong probability from innocent error and manifest fiction." Batman recognizes that most of the events did occur—even if Pattie was not always

the center of them—and asserts that the *Personal Narrative* "came out of a conflict between the real Pattie, an unimportant loser, and the man he wished he had been," reported Alvin M. Josephy, Jr., in the *New York Times Book Review*. The critic joined with Lillard in commending Batman's research and resourcefulness in unraveling the historical truth. Deeming the work "the first coherent retelling of [Pattie's] whole story," Josephy praised Batman's "rich tapestry of history, biography and other explanatory material" and concluded that the author "whets the appetite for another reading of the original, with the knowledge that its colorful characters, places and events will be even more vivid and interesting than before."

In *The Outer Coast* Batman tells the stories of a number of people who took part in California's early history—mariners, trappers, clergymen, and other eighteenth-century immigrants to the area. Assessed Gerald Haslam in the *Los Angeles Times Book Review,* "'The Outer Coast' surveys an interesting, not widely understood aspect of Western history, and Batman demonstrates his ability to digest considerable and varied research, then convert it into a readable text for non-specialists." Although Haslam expressed disappointment that Batman's writing is "strangely repetitive in places," he found the author's prose "generally crisp" and occasionally ironic. Critics such as Alan Ryan of the *Washington Post Book World* delighted in the "endlessly interesting" personalities portrayed. Applauded Ryan, "The great strength of Batman's book is that he never fails to keep in mind that his subjects were fallible human beings."

Batman told *CA:* "I began work on *American Ecclesiastes* strictly as a historian, using my research techniques and abilities in an attempt to check the validity of *The Personal Narrative of James O. Pattie*. I soon discovered, however, that the important thing was not so much the narrow issue of what was true and what wasn't but the more universal question of the effect this trip through the early American West was having on a young man's mind.

"Therefore I turned away from the straight historical approach of simply reciting facts and analyzing whether they were true or false. At the same time, however, I also rejected the idea of turning this into a wildly exciting but uncritical adventure narrative of life in the early West. Instead, I tried to combine these two worlds by maintaining historical integrity and also keeping the thread of adventure. But my main concern, throughout the book, was to develop and deepen the characterization of my main character, James Pattie. It was for that reason that I tried to develop two main themes—what actually happened and what Pattie claimed happened. I know of no better way to understand both people and the world in which they live than to develop the differences between what they see—or claim to see—and what everyone else sees—or claims to see.

"I feel that the approach of using the *Personal Narrative* to gain insight into Pattie and the world in which he lived was the proper one for this particular subject. I have not, however, tried to force it onto incompatible subjects, and in more recent work I have turned to a broader use of journals to convey the experiences of various people faced with the all-but-unknown world of the West. Yet I am still mainly interested not so much in raw facts as in conveying some understanding of what it felt like on a personal level to live in other times and places and to be involved in historic events, both large and small."

BIOGRAPHICAL/CRITICAL SOURCES:

PERIODICALS

Los Angeles Times Book Review, February 10, 1985, January 5, 1986.

New York Times Book Review, March 17, 1985, May 11, 1986.

Washington Post Book World, January 12, 1986.

* * *

BAUM, Louis 1948-

PERSONAL: Born March 15, 1948, in South Africa; son of Rudolf Josef (an accountant) and Heather (a florist; maiden name, Shulman) Baum; married Stephanie Goodman (a teacher), March 26, 1971 (divorced); children: Simon. *Education:* Received B.A. from University of Cape Town.

ADDRESSES: Home and office—London, England.

CAREER: Bookseller, London, England, editor, 1980—. Director of J. Whitaker & Sons and Standard Book Numbering Agency.

MEMBER: Groucho Club.

WRITINGS:

FOR CHILDREN

Juju and the Pirate, Andersen Press, 1983.
I Want to See the Moon, Bodley Head, 1984.
After Dark, Andersen Press, 1984.
Are We Nearly There? Bodley Head, 1986.

WORK IN PROGRESS: Children's books.

* * *

BECKER, Carol 1947-

PERSONAL: Born in 1947, in Brooklyn, N.Y.; daughter of George (an auctioneer) and Helen (a hairdresser; maiden name, Stislow) Becker. *Education:* State University of New York at Buffalo, B.A. (cum laude), 1964; University of California, San Diego, Ph.D., 1975.

ADDRESSES: Home—Chicago, Ill. *Office*—Department of Liberal Arts, School of the Art Institute of Chicago, Columbus Dr. at Jackson Blvd., Chicago, Ill. 60603. *Agent*—Jane Jordan Browne, Multimedia Product Development, Inc., 410 South Michigan Ave., Room 724, Chicago, Ill. 60605.

CAREER: San Diego State University, San Diego, Calif., lecturer in comparative literature, 1975-76; University of California, San Diego, La Jolla, assistant professor of English, 1976; *In These Times,* Chicago, Ill., staff writer and office manager, 1976-77; School of the Art Institute of Chicago, Chicago, assistant professor, 1978-83, associate professor of liberal arts, 1983—, chairperson of department, 1983-84, chairperson of Graduate Division, 1984—. Lecturer at Columbia College, Chicago, 1978, and Northeastern Illinois University, 1979; public speaker; journalist; guest on television and radio programs.

MEMBER: International Society of Political Psychology, Modern Language Association of America, National Women Studies Association.

WRITINGS:

The Invisible Drama: Women and the Anxiety of Change, Macmillan, 1987.

Contributor of articles, photographs, and reviews to magazines.

WORK IN PROGRESS: Two books, *Male Anxiety and the Fear of Female Authority* and *Women, Anxiety, and Creativity.*

SIDELIGHTS: Carol Becker told *CA:* "I have been particularly interested in the impact of the women's movement on American society. I am also interested in writing that is accessible to a mass readership, without losing complexity or a theoretical base.

"I decided to write *The Invisible Drama: Women and the Anxiety of Change* because, having spent many years in the women's movement, I was distressed to realize that women were not as free or as joyous about their newfound liberation as we had anticipated. In fact, it appeared that women were suffering greatly, even with their new positions of power and their new, more progressive personal relationships. I decided to find out why this was the case.

"I began carefully observing myself and all the women close to me. I then interviewed many women across the social strata, and from this compilation of material as well as my philosophical and psychological research into writings in the field I came up with a theory and a process that I thought would help women understand the deeper unconscious dilemmas that change had created in them. The book is a serious attempt to help women understand their situation in the belief that anxiety has a greater hold when its roots are left obscured or unknown. I wanted the book to be healing as well as challenging to women intellectually.

"I have spoken to myriad women's groups of all types about these issues and have found that although the particulars day to day may be different depending on economic and social status, the problems are remarkably similar at an emotional or psychological level. The book has received a great deal of positive response.

"My training is in literature and philosophy. I wrote a book that crosses philosophy, literature, sociology, and psychology. I am presently engaged in studying the creative process in women and its relationship to anxiety, and I am also interested in the issues of women and power. I have spent five years now in administrative positions and have observed women's interactions with me in these positions, men's interactions and resistances to women in positions of authority, and my own and other women's difficulties in these positions. I have therefore become interested in what holds women and the culture back on the creative, practical, psychological level."

BIOGRAPHICAL/CRITICAL SOURCES:

PERIODICALS

Chicago Tribune, February 1, 1987.

* * *

BEECHERT, Edward D. 1920-

PERSONAL: Born June 10, 1920, in Hawthorne, Calif.; son of Edward D. and Mary (Lynde) Beechert; married Alice Dewey, 1950; children: three. *Education:* University of California, Berkeley, A.B., 1947, M.A., 1950, Ph.D., 1957.

ADDRESSES: *Office*—Department of History, University of Hawaii at Manoa, 2530 Dole St., Honolulu, Hawaii 96822.

CAREER: Mexico City College, Mexico City, Mexico, instructor in history, 1953; Modesto Junior College, Modesto, Calif., instructor in history and economics, 1955-57; Ventura College, Ventura, Calif., instructor in history, 1957-60; California State University, Sacramento, assistant professor of social science, 1960-63; University of Hawaii at Hilo, assistant professor, 1963-64, associate professor of history, 1964-66; St. Mary's College of California, Moraga, associate professor of history, 1966-68; University of Hawaii at Manoa, Honolulu, associate professor, 1968-73, professor of history, 1973—, coordinator of Pacific Regional Oral History Program, 1970—. Member of staff of Institute of American History, at University of California, 1965.

MEMBER: Organization of American Historians, Economic History Association, Oral History Association.

AWARDS, HONORS: Grants from Samuel Mosher Foundation, 1956-57, Institute of American History, 1964, and National Endowment for the Humanities, 1977-78.

WRITINGS:

Writing the History of Hawaiian Trade Unions, University of Hawaii Press, 1967.

(With Bill Abbott) *The American Trade Union Movement,* Industrial Relations Center, University of Hawaii at Manoa, 1970.

(Editor) *The History of the Honolulu Typographical Union,* University of Hawaii Press, 1970.

Waipahu Plantation Village: A History, Parks Department, City of Honolulu, 1974.

The Filipino in the ILWU Philippines Study Association, University of Michigan Press, 1978.

Labor Relations in Hawaii, 1850-1937, University of California Press, 1980.

(Contributor) A. Graves and W. Albert, editors, *World Crisis in Sugar Production, 1914-1950,* University of East Anglia, 1983.

Honolulu Harbor: A Social History, University of South Carolina Press, 1988.

Contributor to periodicals, including *Oral History Review, Journal of American History,* and *International Journal of Oral History.*

WORK IN PROGRESS: A study, with Brij Lal, of plantation worker reactions to plantation labor systems in the major sugar producing areas of the world from 1850 to 1950, *Patterns of Resistance,* for University of Hawaii Press.

* * *

BEER, Jeanette (Mary Ayres)

PERSONAL: Born in Wellington, New Zealand; immigrated to United States, naturalized citizen; daughter of Alexander Samuel (a lawyer) and Una Doreen (a teacher; maiden name, Castle) Scott; married Colin Gordon Beer (a university professor), June 27, 1959; children: Stephen James Colin, Jeremy Michael Alexander. *Education:* Victoria University of Wellington, B.A., 1954, M.A. (with first class honors), 1955; University of Poitiers, Diplome d'etudes francaises, 1957; Oxford University, B.A., 1958, M.A. (with first class honors), 1962; Columbia University, Ph.D., 1967. *Religion:* Anglican.

ADDRESSES: *Home*—256 West Hudson Ave., Englewood, N.J. 07631. *Office*—Department of French, Purdue University, West Lafayette, Ind. 47907.

CAREER: Victoria University of Wellington, Wellington, New Zealand, assistant lecturer in French, 1956; lecturer at Uni-

versity of Montpellier, Montpellier, France, 1958-59; Oxford University, Oxford, England, Una Goodwin research fellow of St. Anne's College, Olwen Rhys memorial fellow and Commonwealth fellow of Lady Margaret Hall, 1959-60; University of Otago, Dunedin, New Zealand, lecturer in French, 1962-64; Barnard College, New York City, instructor in French, 1966-68; Fordham University, New York City, assistant professor, 1968-69, associate professor, 1969-76, professor of French, 1977-80, director of Medieval Studies Program, 1972-80; Purdue University, West Lafayette, Ind., professor of French, 1980—, head of department of foreign languages and literatures, 1980-83, fellow of Center for Humanistic Studies, 1986. Chairman of Inter-University Doctoral Consortium Project for Medieval and Renaissance Studies, 1979-80; National Endowment for the Humanities, member of national board of consultants, 1979—, assistant director of Division of Fellowships and Seminars, 1983-84; member of review panel of Indiana Committee for the Humanities, 1986. Broadcaster on WRVR-Radio and WFUV-Radio.

MEMBER: International Arthurian Society, International Courtly Literature Society, American Association of Teachers of French, American Comparative Literature Association, American Philological Association, Mediaeval Academy of America, Modern Language Association of America, Societe Rencesvals, Medieval Association of the Mid-West (member of council), Columbia University Graduate Faculties Alumni Association, Columbia University Medieval Seminar.

AWARDS, HONORS: National Endowment for the Humanities grant, 1973-80, fellowship, 1980; fellow of Indiana Committee for the Humanities, 1985; grant from American Philosophical Society, 1986.

WRITINGS:

Villehardouin: Epic Historian, Droz, 1968.
A Medieval Caesar, Droz, 1976.
Medieval Fables: Marie de France, A. H. & A. W. Reed (Wellington), 1981, Dodd, 1983.
Narrative Conventions of Truth in the Middle Ages, Droz, 1981.
"Master Richard's Bestiary of Love" and "Response," illustrations by Barry Moser, Penny Royal Press, 1985.

General editor of *Teaching Language Through Literature,* 1971—. Contributor to *Dictionary of the Middle Ages.* Contributor of articles and reviews to language and literature journals, including *New Zealand Journal of French Studies, Parergon, Romance Philology,* and *Mosaic.*

WORK IN PROGRESS: The French Language in the Middle Ages; a "diplomatic edition" of *Le Bestiaire d'amour;* editing *Medieval Translation.*

* * *

BEINEIX, Jean-Jacques 1946-

PERSONAL: Born October 8, 1946, in Paris, France. *Education:* Earned baccalaureat philosophie, 1966, and certificate in pre-medical studies, 1968.

ADDRESSES: Office—Cargo Films, 3 Rue Ernest Gouin, Paris 75017, France.

CAREER: Screenwriter and director. Worked as assistant to Jean Becker on television series "Les Saintes cheries," 1969, and as assistant to several film directors, including Rene Clement, Claude Berri, and Jerry Lewis; director of television commercials. Founded Cargo Films, 1984.

AWARDS, HONORS: First prize from Trouville Film Festival and nomination for Cesar for best short film from French Academy of Motion Picture Arts and Sciences, both 1977, both for "Le Chien de Monsieur Michel"; four Cesars, 1981, for "Diva"; first prize from Montreal Film Festival and nomination for best foreign-language film from American Academy of Motion Picture Arts and Sciences, both 1986, both for "Betty Blue."

WRITINGS:

SCREENPLAYS; AND DIRECTOR

(With Jean Van Hamme) "Diva" (adapted from the novel by Delacorta), Les Films Galaxie/Greenwich Film Production, 1981, released in the United States as "Diva," United Artists Classics, 1982.
(With Olivier Mergault) "La Lune dans le caniveau" (adapted from the novel *The Moon in the Gutter* by David Goodis), Gaumont/TFI Productions/SFPC/Opera Film Produzione, 1983, released in the United States as "The Moon in the Gutter," Triumph Films, 1983.
"Betty Blue" (adapted from the novel *37 Degres 2 le matin* by Philippe Djian), Constellation/Cargo Films, 1986, released in the United States as "Betty Blue," Alive Films, 1986.

Also screenwriter and director of short film "Le Chien de Monsieur Michel" (title means "The Dog of Mr. Michel"), 1977.

WORK IN PROGRESS: Directing the motion picture "Bats," adapted from Marc Behm's novel *The Ice Maiden.*

SIDELIGHTS: Jean-Jacques Beineix has gained considerable recognition—some might even say notoriety—in the 1980s for three films of wildly contrasting stature. For his first full-length film, 1981's "Diva," Beineix earned acclaim as a dazzling visual stylist, and while his grasp of narrative may have seemed tenuous and his sense of characterization merely superficial, his technical prowess enabled the film to succeed with both critics and audiences. With "The Moon in the Gutter," however, Beineix incurred almost universal scorn as a self-conscious, pretentious artist whose thematic use of color and technique rendered his work empty and even ridiculous. And with his third film, "Betty Blue," Beineix divided critics by tempering his technique to suit his alternately disturbing and amusing tale of love and madness. Detractors of "Betty Blue" objected to Beineix's seemingly haphazard approach to narrative and his perplexing shifts in tone, but reviewers favoring the work cited its frank, unabashed sexuality and surprising humor. Thus, in a mere six years Beineix has been hailed as a master and condemned as a pretender, dismissed as a naif and commended as a pioneer.

Beineix came to filmmaking as an assistant to a surprisingly diverse group of directors, including Rene Clement and Jerry Lewis, and he gained his initial directing experiences with television commercials. In 1977 he enjoyed success with his first short film, "Le Chien de Monsieur Michel," which won first prize at the Trouville Film Festival and was nominated for a Cesar (the French Academy Award). Impressed with Beineix's work, film producer Irene Silberman engaged him to write and direct an adaptation of Delacorta's quirky suspense novel *Diva.* The project then stalled, and Beineix had

to badger the hapless Silberman before she finally agreed to finance what became his first full-length film.

Upon release in 1981, "Diva" initially elicited only negative responses from French critics and drew few patrons. It remained in circulation, however, and slowly developed an extensive following over a period of several months. This gradual success prompted greater critical recognition: "Diva" was eventually acknowledged as one of the best French films of the year, and Beineix was hailed as a talented newcomer.

The actual plot of "Diva" centers on various characters' efforts to obtain two different audio cassette tapes. Most important of these characters is Jules, a delivery boy who secretly records a soprano's recital and is consequently pursued by two Taiwanese executives eager to use the illegal tape in blackmailing the singer—hitherto unrecorded—into signing a contract. Unbeknownst to Jules a second cassette, one bearing incriminating evidence against members of a drug and prostitution ring, has been hidden in his delivery bag by a woman who is then killed by hoodlums associated with the crime gang. These thugs then track Jules, as does a corrupt police official, Saporta, who is also implicated on the second tape. Jules, meanwhile, has befriended a Vietnamese girl, Alba, to whom he lends the concert tape. She, in turn, lends the tape to Gorodish, a Zen-influenced eccentric whose tranquil demeanor masks a penchant for intrigue and adventure. It is Gorodish who realizes the importance of the second tape and sells it to the despicable Saporta for a considerable sum. Eventually, however, the resourceful Gorodish is overwhelmed by the two thugs and Jules is forced to fend for himself during a violent climax that leaves several characters dead. In the closing sequence, Jules relinquishes the concert tape to the unsuspecting singer, who then hears her recorded voice for the first time. The Taiwanese had already withdrawn from the action, having earlier robbed Saporta of the second tape and assuming that they were actually obtaining the recital cassette.

With its twisted plot and oddball characters, "Diva" proved an entertaining mix of suspense and humor, violence and romance. But its critical success, and its immense popularity in France and the United States, derived essentially from Beineix's stylized visualization of Delacorta's novel. The film is full of bright colors and pop-art images: Jules's apartment, for instance, contains a melange of odd objects and dizzying effects, including an enormous wall in which an automobile appears to be roaring through the air and into the room; Gorodish's quarters, however, are entirely black, perhaps as counterpoint to the overwhelming visual chaos of Jules's home and of Paris itself.

Beineix's technical prowess also dazzled critics, particularly during an exhilarating chase sequence in which Jules flees from the thugs by speeding his scooter through the Paris subways and along stairways and escalators. And in the opening sequence, the camera slowly winds about a small auditorium as if in tempo with the soprano's opening aria. More than one critic noted that Beineix, in his first film, already possessed an impressive command of cinematic technique.

Not all critics, however, were entirely awed by Beineix's work. Vincent Canby, for instance, complained in the *New York Times* that the film's only assets were those pertaining to style. He charged that "Diva" was devoid of content. More typical, though, was David Ansen's *Newsweek* review hailing "Diva" as "an utterly stunning debut." He wrote, "You have only to watch ten minutes of . . . Beineix's flamboyantly seductive thriller, to know you are in the hands of a man born to make movies." And though he conceded that "Diva" was a rather superficial film, he added that it "demonstrates the depth of pleasure a shallow movie can provide" and attributed those pleasures to Beineix's "extravagant visual imagination."

Most critics claimed that Beineix's obsession with style led to folly in his next work, "The Moon in the Gutter." The film's plot, much simpler than that of "Diva," concerns Gerard, a despairing stevedore endlessly searching for the rapist who drove his sister to suicide. Haunting the streets and bars of an eerie port, Gerard initially suspects his own brother Frank, a filthy, despicable fellow given to drink and treachery. While stalking his brother, however, Gerard meets another vaguely suspicious fellow, the wealthy Newton Channing, who suffers his own secret guilt and also wallows in alcoholism. Gerard experiences immediate love for Newton's sister, Loretta, and much of the film then focuses on his attempt to flee from poverty and despair through his love for her. Their romance culminates in their nighttime drive to a fantastic castle perched on a cliff. Once inside, they exchange rings (actually halos removed from plastic madonnas) and vow eternal love. But from this episode, which may have been a dream, Gerard awakens in the bed of his father's lover—a fat, middle-aged loudmouth—and then stumbles into the bed of his own lover, the lusty Bella, who ultimately grows jealous of Loretta and, at Frank's behest, hires brutes to thrash Gerard. When Gerard discovers the scheme, he confronts his greasy brother, who then concedes that he may have raped their sister. Gerard then prepares to slash Frank, only to realize that his brother had spoken out of confusion and ignorance. Gerard then understands, too, that life with Loretta—and thus escape from the ghetto—is futile, and he returns home.

As even its detractors concede, a plot synopsis of "The Moon in the Gutter" yields only the slightest indication of its contents. More than "Diva," "The Moon in the Gutter" is a work of self-conscious stylization, one in which colors—particularly green and blood red—assume extraordinary thematic significance, and characters themselves become symbols, and thus archetypes. Moreover, the film's settings are contrived to create an air of artificiality, and Beineix has acknowledged that he intended the film as a fairy-tale melodrama of largely psychological dimensions. He told *Film Comment* that "The Moon in the Gutter" was a self-consciously cinematic exploration of the subconscious. "In my film," he declared, "the filmmaker reflects on his own art."

Unfortunately for Beineix, his obscure, highly stylized melodrama met with nearly universal vilification in both Europe and North America. At its Cannes Film Festival premiere "The Moon in the Gutter" was greeted with loud derision from spectators, many of whom stormed from the theatre as early as fifteen minutes into the screening. And upon commercial release in France the work was roundly condemned as an utter waste of talented performers, notably Gerard Depardieu and Nastassia Kinski, and of slightly more than three million dollars—an imposing sum in the French film industry. The film was subsequently rejected by the New York Film Festival and received only minimal distribution in the United States and Canada.

American reviewers were particularly vehement in assessing Beineix's film. The *Los Angeles Times*'s Kevin Thomas called "The Moon in the Gutter" "an homage to . . . Beineix's monumental self-indulgence," and the *Washington Post*'s Gary Arnold contended that the film was often "wildly ludicrous" and summarized it as a "cautionary disaster, the definitive

example of how to turn an exploitable little pretext for romantic melodrama into an elaborate excuse for embarrassment.'' Similarly, Gene Siskel, who wrote in the *Chicago Tribune* that Beineix's film was ''significantly bad,'' asserted that its failure ''serves as a lesson that a director can get carried away with style to the point that he makes a film that is all frosting and no cake.''

Among the few critics expressing any appreciation for ''The Moon in the Gutter'' were Tom Milne, writing in Britain's *Monthly Film Bulletin,* and Lawrence O'Toole, who reviewed the film in Canada's *Maclean's* magazine. Milne valued Beineix's attempt more than his actual achievement and conceded that the film occasionally lapsed into vulgarity and pretension, but he added that ''with all its faults . . . [it] shows a film-maker straining every nerve to make a *film.*'' More enthusiastic was O'Toole, who hailed ''The Moon in the Gutter'' as a ''surrealistic masterpiece'' and dismissed conventional means of analyzing it as inevitably futile. ''To take a surrealist piece . . . and apply ordinary, literal meanings to it is a complete waste of time,'' he alleged. For O'Toole, Beineix's ambitious work was a triumph of ''supreme style,'' and he speculated that it ''may still emerge as one of the most misperceived [films] ever made.''

In a 1987 *Film Comment* article, Beineix seemed gracious in accepting the largely negative response to ''The Moon in the Gutter.'' Like O'Toole, he considered his film ''a masterpiece,'' but he confessed that he may have entrusted too much thematic and narrative worth to the film's visuals. ''I thought the images would be strong enough to mesmerize audiences,'' he said. ''They weren't.'' In the same article he thanked his detractors for reminding him ''that there are rules'' and confessed that in his next film, ''Betty Blue,'' he had attempted to remain more faithful to structure and chronology. ''I can't commit suicide every time I make a movie,'' he stated. ''Even if I think of myself as subversive or rebellious, I know I have to give the audience a chance to understand what I do.''

With ''Betty Blue'' Beineix did, indeed, succeed in restoring his reputation both with filmgoers—at least those frequenting art houses—and with some of his detractors. The 1986 film details the often stormy relationship between a complacent handyman, Zorg, and his sexy lover, Betty. Zorg is a low-key fellow who had earlier written a long, complex—and consequently unpublished—novel. Betty is an earthy, unbalanced woman who—in various fits of ire—sets fire to a beachhouse, stabs an unruly restaurant customer with a fork, and slashes an unctuous literary critic with a comb. After several escapades, Betty blinds herself in one eye and is hospitalized, whereupon Zorg realizes that doctors will work to suppress her more vibrant, and volatile, personality traits. He then slips into the hospital while disguised as a woman and smothers his helpless lover. Upon returning home he resumes his literary career, having earlier learned that his novel, which had been tirelessly submitted by Betty to various publishers, had finally been accepted for publication.

Unlike either ''Diva,'' which had enjoyed mostly positive reviews, or ''The Moon in the Gutter,'' which was overwhelmingly condemned, ''Betty Blue'' earned many mixed reactions with critics praising Beineix's handling of specific elements—notably sexuality—but objecting to his seemingly haphazard sense of realism and dramatic chronology. *New Republic*'s Stanley Kauffmann, for instance, decried the film's overtly episodic nature and seeming spontaneity by noting, ''The fact that life is often improvised is no excuse: we demand more of art than of feckless life.'' And David Denby, reviewing ''Betty Blue'' in *New York,* charged Beineix with adopting ''a whimsical, slapdash attitude towards tragedy,'' but he admitted that the film also ''embraces all the good, free, generous pleasures.'' Critics more partial to the film praised its often free-wheeling and unpredictable plot and lauded Beineix's frank approach to sexuality. *Time*'s Richard Schickel was among those reviewers who welcomed the work's ''quirky incident and compassionate humor'' and contended that the film marked a new maturity in Beineix's artistry. Similarly, the *Village Voice*'s Andrew Sarris commended Beineix's direction, particularly his approach to the lovemaking sequences, and applauded the entire film as a surprisingly entertaining and provocative work. ''By never being timid about their lust,'' Sarris observed, ''the two lovers take us deep into their maddened psyches.'' Sarris deemed the film ''a compelling entertainment.''

Since restoring his reputation with ''Betty Blue,'' Beineix has found himself in demand in both Europe and America. ''They all want to sign me up and I want to resist them,'' he told Marcia Pally in *Film Comment.* Uncertain about his ability to negotiate in the business-oriented world of American film-making, Beineix also voiced his displeasure with persistent and aggressive industry hustlers. ''The phone never stops, and everyone is pushing,'' he complained. ''And I have to play games with all of them.'' But he added that he might work in the American industry if allowed to maintain control of his work. ''I want to choose the right script,'' he confided to Pally, ''and I have to be my own producer.'' With the surprising success of ''Betty Blue,'' it seems increasingly likely that an American company will eventually accede to Beineix's stipulations.

AVOCATIONAL INTERESTS: Mountain climbing, motorcycling, sailing.

BIOGRAPHICAL/CRITICAL SOURCES:

PERIODICALS

Chicago Tribune, September 9, 1983.
Film Comment, November-December, 1981, August, 1983, February, 1987.
Los Angeles Times, September 9, 1983.
Maclean's, September 19, 1983.
Monthly Film Bulletin, September, 1982, January, 1984.
New Republic, November 24, 1986.
Newsweek, April 19, 1982, September 19, 1983.
New York, September 12, 1983, November 17, 1986.
New Yorker, September 19, 1983.
New York Times, April 16, 1982, July 2, 1982, September 9, 1983.
Rolling Stone, April 29, 1982.
Time, April 26, 1982, January 19, 1987.
Village Voice, April 20, 1982, September 20, 1983, November 4, 1986.
Washington Post, September 9, 1983, September 13, 1983.

—Sketch by Les Stone

* * *

BELCHER, Jerry 1930-1987

OBITUARY NOTICE: Born April 29, 1930, in Kansas City, Mo.; died of cancer, September 5, 1987, in South Pasadena, Calif. Reporter, editor, and author. Belcher wrote for several northern California newspapers early in his career and was a reporter for the *Los Angeles Times* at the time of his death. A

first-rate newsman, he was winner of San Francisco Club press awards and co-winner of the 1985 *Los Angeles Times* Editorial Award for the best news story written under pressure. Belcher was a reporter for the *San Francisco Examiner* when Patricia Hearst, daughter of newspaper publisher Randolph Hearst, was kidnapped in 1974. He later co-authored a book about the Hearst crisis entitled *Patty/Tania*.

OBITUARIES AND OTHER SOURCES:

PERIODICALS

Los Angeles Times, September 6, 1987.

* * *

BELL, James Madison 1826-1902

PERSONAL: Born April 3, 1826, in Gallipolis, Ohio; died in 1902; married Louisiana Sanderline in 1847 (some sources say 1848); children: seven. *Education:* Attended schools in Cincinnati and Cleveland, Ohio.

CAREER: Plasterer, social activist, poet, and orator.

WRITINGS:

A Poem: Delivered August 1st, 1862 . . . at the Grand Festival to Commemorate the Emancipation of the Slaves in the British West Indian Isles, B. F. Sterett, 1862.

A Poem Entitled "The Day and the War," Delivered January 1, 1864, at Platt's Hall at the Celebration of the First Anniversary of President Lincoln's Emancipation Proclamation, Agnew & Deffebach, 1864.

An Anniversary Poem Entitled "The Progress of Liberty," Delivered January 1st, 1866 . . . at the Celebration of the Third Anniversary of President Lincoln's Proclamation, Agnew & Deffebach, 1866.

A Poem, Entitled "The Triumph of Liberty," Delivered April 7, 1870, at Detroit Opera House on the Occasion of the Fifteenth Amendment to the Constitution of the United States, Tunis Steam Printing, 1870.

The Poetical Works of James Madison Bell, introduction by B. W. Arnett, Wynkoop, Hallenbeck, Crawford, 1901.

"Modern Moses, or 'My Policy' Man" (poem), published in *Early Black Poets,* edited by William H. Robinson, W. C. Brown, 1969.

Also author of "Emancipation in the District of Columbia" and the poem "Andrew Jackson Swinging Around in a Circle." Poetry represented in anthologies, including *An Anthology of Verse by American Negroes,* edited by N. I. White and W. C. Jackson, 1924.

SIDELIGHTS: James Madison Bell was a poet known primarily for his writings and activism in support of the abolition of slavery during the American Civil War. A friend of abolitionist John Brown, Bell wrote and read poetry for antislavery rallies and took part in the oganization of Brown's 1859 raid on the arsenal at Harpers Ferry, West Virginia. Regarded as somewhat conventional, his writings are nonetheless respected for their inspirational qualities and their moral and political stands.

A plasterer throughout his life, Bell "mastered the literary traditions and poetic conventions of his day" despite receiving only a limited education, reported Keith E. Byerman in the *Dictionary of Literary Biography*. Observed Byerman, "Such mastery of convention was itself an argument for equality at a time when most whites, including many abolitionists, assumed that blacks were inherently incapable of acquiring even the rudiments of culture." Bell regularly used iambic tetrameter and both alternating rhyme and couplets in his poetry, and while his imagery and phrasing were considered conventional, his intent was often political rather than aesthetic. "It must be recognized that Bell was not as interested in the craftsmanship of his poetry as he was in the moral and political arguments that could be made through verse," asserted Byerman.

In addition to working as a plasterer and poet, Bell was involved in politics. During the 1870s he served as a county delegate of the Republican party, and in 1872 he was elected a delegate to the Republican National Convention. He gave speeches, read his poetry at commemorative gatherings, and supported various party candidates for many years. A number of his poems, in fact, were written to celebrate anniversaries of U.S. President Abraham Lincoln's Emancipation Proclamation or the freeing of slaves in the British West Indies. Concluded Byerman, Bell "adopted whatever techniques would facilitate his goal as a spokesman against slavery and for black rights." While the bulk of his work featured political themes, in later years Bell also used his poetry to promote Christianity, addressing subjects such as immortality, the nature of evil, and Protestant doctrine.

BIOGRAPHICAL/CRITICAL SOURCES:

BOOKS

Dictionary of Literary Biography, Volume 50: *Afro-American Writers Before the Harlem Renaissance,* Gale, 1986.*

* * *

BENJAMIN, Judy-Lynn
See del REY, Judy-Lynn

* * *

BENNETT, G. V.
See BENNETT, Gareth Vaughan

* * *

BENNETT, Gareth Vaughan 1929-1987
(G. V. Bennett)

OBITUARY NOTICE: Born in November, 1929; died c. December 7, 1987, in Oxford, England. Church historian, clergyman, educator, and author. An apprentice to Norman Sykes, the late dean of Winchester—one of England's foremost private schools—Bennett was considered a gifted church historian. Early in his career he was a lecturer in history at King's College in London and in 1956 was ordained to a curacy at Prittlewell, Essex, before becoming fellow, dean of divinity, and tutor at Oxford University's New College. As a member of the Crown Appointments Commission, Bennett was involved in the highest levels of church affairs. He wrote *White Kennett, 1660-1728: Bishop of Peterborough, The Tory Crisis in Church and State, 1688-1730,* and was widely assumed to be the author of the anonymous preface to the controversial 1987 edition of *Crockford's Clerical Directory.*

OBITUARIES AND OTHER SOURCES:

PERIODICALS

Times (London), December 9, 1987.

* * *

BENTON, John Frederic 1931-1988

OBITUARY NOTICE—See index for *CA* sketch: Born July 15, 1931, in Philadelphia, Pa.; died February 25, 1988, in Pasadena, Calif. Historian, educator, editor, and author. An authority on the Middle Ages, Benton sparked academic controversy in 1986 with his contention that the celebrated epistolary exchange between twelfth-century lovers Heloise and Abelard was generated entirely by the latter. He was, in addition, known for pioneering the application of image enhancement techniques—originally devised for use in space exploration—to the study of medieval manuscripts. In 1965 Benton joined the faculty of the California Institute of Technology, and in 1972 he held a Fulbright professorship at the University of Reims. For his various achievements Benton received a MacArthur Foundation fellowship in 1986. His writings include *Town Origins: The Evidence From Medieval England* and a contribution to the volume *The Meaning of Courtly Love*. He also edited such works as *Self and Society in Medieval France: The Memoirs of Abbot Guibert of Nogent* and, with Thomas N. Bisson, *Medieval Statecraft and the Perspectives of History: Essays by Joseph R. Strayer*.

OBITUARIES AND OTHER SOURCES:

BOOKS

Directory of American Scholars, Volume 1: *History,* 8th edition, Bowker, 1982.

PERIODICALS

Los Angeles Times, February 27, 1988.
Washington Post, March 1, 1988.

* * *

BENTON, Joseph Nelson, Jr. 1924-1988

OBITUARY NOTICE: Born September 16, 1924, in Danville, Va.; died of a heart attack, February 13, 1988, in Washington, D.C. Reporter and broadcast journalist. Benton enjoyed a distinguished career as a newsman with the Columbia Broadcasting System (CBS) for more than twenty years. During that time he covered the 1963 assassination of President John F. Kennedy, the Vietnam War, the space program, civil rights, and White House activities. He began at CBS in 1960, writing news stories in New York City. He soon became correspondent and bureau chief in New Orleans, Louisiana, and later in Chicago, Illinois. Following two years in Saigon, South Vietnam, he moved to Washington, where he served as a correspondent until his retirement in 1982. Benton anchored "The CBS Morning News" for a few years in the early 1970s and joined Baltimore's WMAR-TV news staff as an anchor after retiring from CBS.

OBITUARIES AND OTHER SOURCES:

BOOKS

Who's Who in America, 44th edition, Marquis, 1986.

PERIODICALS

Los Angeles Times, February 17, 1988.
Washington Post, February 14, 1988.

* * *

BERG, Barbara J.

PERSONAL: Born in Washington, D.C.; daughter of Samuel (a psychologist) and Matilda (a librarian; maiden name, Gruber) Goldberg; married Richard Berg, June 27, 1965 (divorced, 1970); married Arnold Schlanger (an attorney), September 12, 1971; children: Alison Gail, Andrew Ryan. *Education:* University of Rochester, A.B., 1968; Graduate School and University Center of the City University of New York, Ph.D., 1976.

ADDRESSES: Home—New York, N.Y. *Agent*—Georges Borchardt, Inc., 136 East 57th St., New York, N.Y. 10022.

CAREER: Taught history at Sarah Lawrence College, Bronxville, N.Y., 1976-78; Marymount Manhattan College, New York, N.Y., instructor in history, 1978-81; instructor in medicine and literature at Mount Sinai School of Medicine, New York, N.Y., 1982-85; adjunct professor of history at Bernard M. Baruch College of the City University of New York, 1986-87. Consultant to National Endowment for the Humanities, 1976-82, Children's Television Workshop, 1977-78, and Rockefeller Foundation, 1977-81. Member of the community board and lay member of the ethics committee of Mount Sinai Hospital, 1978—.

MEMBER: Authors Guild.

WRITINGS:

The Remembered Gate: Origins of American Feminism; The Woman and the City, 1800-1860, Oxford University Press, 1978.
Nothing to Cry About, Seaview, 1981.
The Crisis of the Working Mother: Resolving the Conflict Between Family and Work, Summit Books, 1986.

Contributor of articles to periodicals, including the Baltimore *Sun, Ms., New York Times Magazine, Parents' Magazine, Savvy,* and the *Washington Post.*

WORK IN PROGRESS: A historical novel set in New York City during the first half of the nineteenth century.

SIDELIGHTS: Barbara J. Berg focuses attention upon evolving roles of American women in *The Remembered Gate*. In the book, the author offers a historical account of the growth and development of a feminist consciousness, which she traces back to urban women of the early 1800s. According to reviewer Alden Whitman of the *New York Times,* Berg's research "leads her to draw a distinction between feminism and women's rights. Feminism, she declares, is a woman's 'freedom to decide her own destiny; freedom from sex-determined roles; freedom from society's oppressive restrictions; freedom to express her thoughts fully and convert them freely to action,'" whereas women's rights are "demands for 'particular privileges' such as the vote, equal education and job opportunities and equal access to public facilities."

In her next two books, *Nothing to Cry About* and *The Crisis of the Working Mother,* Berg addresses the hardships and complexities involved in motherhood. A career woman who had postponed childbearing until after the age of thirty, the author relates her own physical and emotional experiences of a late

miscarriage, a second infant's death shortly after its birth, an adoption, and finally the healthy delivery of her son in *Nothing to Cry About*. The book not only discusses the physical difficulties and the disappointment some pregnant women face but also the potential insensitivity of both society and the medical profession. One critic deemed the book "must reading" for women who postpone starting a family. Berg analyzes further struggles of motherhood in *The Crisis of the Working Mother,* a report on the consequences of guilt feelings among contemporary women who work outside the home and must leave their children in the care of others. Berg, according to *Los Angeles Times* critic Roselle M. Lewis, concluded that "working mothers act out their sense of guilt and loss in not being prime caretakers for their children" by spoiling their children, by becoming workaholics, and by developing feelings of jealousy toward their children's caretakers.

Berg told *CA:* "I hope that through my writing I am able to illuminate and give meaning to conflicts and difficulties women encounter in their lives. If something I've written has enabled someone to find a solution to a problem, I believe my work has been successful."

BIOGRAPHICAL/CRITICAL SOURCES:

PERIODICALS

Los Angeles Times, November 20, 1986.
New York Times, February 2, 1978.

* * *

BERGIN, Thomas Goddard 1904-1987

OBITUARY NOTICE—See index for *CA* sketch: Born November 17, 1904, in New Haven, Conn.; died October 30 (one source says October 31), 1987, in Madison, Conn. Educator, academic administrator, editor, translator, and author. Bergin was a longtime professor of Romance languages and an authority on the life and work of medieval Italian poet Dante Alighieri. Bergin spent most of his academic career at Yale University, where he was both Benjamin F. Barge Professor of Romance Languages and chairman of the department of Italian and Spanish throughout much of the 1950s. In 1958 he became Yale's Sterling Professor of Romance Languages. Among his books are *Cervantes: His Life, His Times, His Works; Dante: His Life, His Times, His Works;* and *Petrarch.* He also edited many volumes of medieval works, including his own translation of Dante's *Divine Comedy,* which includes *Inferno, Purgatory,* and *Paradise.*

OBITUARIES AND OTHER SOURCES:

BOOKS

Directory of American Scholars, Volume III: *Foreign Languages, Linguistics, and Philology,* Bowker, 1982.

PERIODICALS

New York Times, November 3, 1987.
Washington Post, November 4, 1987.

* * *

BERMAN, Edgar F(rank) 1915(?)-1987

OBITUARY NOTICE—See index for *CA* sketch: Born August 6, 1915 (some sources say 1919 or 1924), in Baltimore, Md.; died of a heart attack, November 25, 1987, in Baltimore, Md. Physician, consultant, administrator, journalist, and author. Berman was a physician whose wide-ranging skills and interests brought him both acclaim and notoriety. He began his medical career as a surgeon, and in 1950 he contributed greatly to the treatment of throat cancer by becoming the first doctor to implant a plastic esophagus into a human being. Seven years later, with a dog as his subject, he executed the first successful heart transplant. He subsequently worked in Africa with eminent physician and humanitarian Albert Schweitzer and participated in Tom Dooley's Medical International Cooperation Organization, serving as its president from 1959 to 1965. Through this organization Berman met Senator Hubert H. Humphrey, whom he served as an adviser on medicine when Humphrey became vice-president under President Lyndon Johnson.

During the 1960s Berman also worked as a consultant to federal agencies and served in the Democratic party's planning council of the national committee. In 1970, however, he was compelled to abandon his party activities after publicly commenting that women were poor leaders because of their "raging hormonal imbalances." Berman, who was also a gynecologist, generated further sexism in his 1982 book *The Compleat Chauvinist: A Survival Guide for the Bedeviled Male,* which featured chapters such as "The Brain That's Tame Lies Mainly in the Dame." Among his other writings are *The Unchanging Woman; Population and Politics; The Solid Gold Stethoscope;* and *Hubert: The Triumph and Tragedy of the Humphrey I Knew.* In addition, Berman wrote newspaper columns for the North American Newspaper Alliance syndicate.

OBITUARIES AND OTHER SOURCES:

BOOKS

Who's Who in America, 43rd edition, Marquis, 1984.

PERIODICALS

Chicago Tribune, November 28, 1987.
Los Angeles Times, November 28, 1987.
New York Times, November 26, 1987.
Times (London), November 28, 1987.

* * *

BERNSTEIN, John Andrew 1944-

PERSONAL: Born March 25, 1944, in Boston, Mass.; son of Melvin and Evelyn Bernstein. *Education:* Harvard University, A.B. (magna cum laude), 1966, A.M., 1967, Ph.D., 1970.

ADDRESSES: Home—103 Cheltenham Rd., Newark, Del. 19711. *Office*—Department of History, University of Delaware, Newark, Del. 19711.

CAREER: University of Delaware, Newark, assistant professor, 1970-79, associate professor of modern European intellectual history, 1979—.

MEMBER: Phi Beta Kappa.

WRITINGS:

(Editor) *Select Sermons of Benjamin Whichcote,* Scholars' Facsimiles & Reprints, 1977.
Shaftesbury, Rousseau, and Kant: An Introduction to the Conflict Between Aesthetic and Moral Values in Modern Thought, Fairleigh Dickinson University Press, 1980.
Nietzsche's Moral Philosophy, Fairleigh Dickinson University Press, 1987.

Contributor to history and theology journals.

WORK IN PROGRESS: Ideas of Progress.

* * *

BERNSTEIN, Michael Andre 1947-

PERSONAL: Born August 31, 1947, in Innsbruck, Austria; immigrated to Canada, 1956, naturalized citizen, 1956; son of John Vladimir (a diplomat) and Marion (Sklarz) Bernstein; married Jeanne Wolff von Amerongen (a clinical psychologist), November 3, 1980; children: Anna-Nora. *Education:* Princeton University, B.A., 1969; Oxford University, B.Litt., 1973, D.Phil., 1975.

ADDRESSES: Office—Department of Comparative Literature, University of California, Berkeley, Calif. 94720.

CAREER: University of California, Berkeley, assistant professor, 1975-81, associate professor, 1981-87, professor of English and comparative literature, 1987—.

AWARDS, HONORS: Danforth fellowship, 1969-75; fellowships from Association of Commonwealth Universities, 1969-73, Canada Council, 1973-75, American Council of Learned Societies, 1977-78 and 1981, and University of California, 1978-79.

WRITINGS:

The Tale of the Tribe: Ezra Pound and the Modern Verse Epic, Princeton University Press, 1980.

(Contributor) B. Hatlen, editor, *George Oppen: Man and Poet,* National Poetry Foundation/University of Maine Press, 1981.

Prima Della Rivoluzione (poems; title means "Before the Revolution"), National Poetry Foundation/University of Maine Press, 1984.

(Contributor) Marianne Korn, editor, *Ezra Pound and History,* National Poetry Foundation/University of Maine Press, 1985.

Contributor of numerous critical essays, poems, and reviews to American and European journals.

WORK IN PROGRESS: Talent and the Individual Tradition, publication expected in 1990; *The Abject Hero.*

SIDELIGHTS: Michael Andre Bernstein told *CA:* "I am interested in the relationship between history and literature and in the problems of representation in general."

BIOGRAPHICAL/CRITICAL SOURCES:

PERIODICALS

Times Literary Supplement, March 6, 1981.

* * *

BERRY, Geoffrey 1912-1988

OBITUARY NOTICE: Born May 13, 1912; died January 29, 1988, in Kendal, England. Environmentalist, accountant, photographer, and author. Berry's lifelong concern for the preservation and beautification of the countryside led him to abandon his career in accounting and accept the post of secretary of the Friends of the Lake District, an efficient conservation body in northwest England. Through his efforts, the Friends successfully restricted powerboats on three of the district's lakes and stopped the extraction of large quantities of water from two other northwestern lakes. He wrote *Across the Northern Hills, A Tale of Two Lakes,* and is co-author of *The Lake District: A Century of Conservation.* He contributed numerous articles to local newspapers and his photographs appear in Melvyn Bragg's *Land of the Lakes.*

OBITUARIES AND OTHER SOURCES:

PERIODICALS

Times (London), February 1, 1988.

* * *

BESSER, Joe 1907-1988

OBITUARY NOTICE: Born in 1907, in St. Louis, Mo.; died c. March 1 in 1988, in North Hollywood, Calif. Comedian, vaudevillian actor, and author. Besser is best remembered for creating the role of Joe with the famous comedy act "The Three Stooges." He joined the zany comic team's Moe Howard and Larry Fine in 1954, after the deaths of Shemp Howard and Curly Howard, both of whom had previously played the third stooge. Known for whining such lines as "Oooh, you crazy" and "Not so h-a-a-a-a-rd," Besser agreed to join the Stooges only after receiving assurance that he would not be subjected to the group's usual physical abuse.

Besser began his entertainment career at the age of ten, running errands for a music business in St. Louis, Missouri. He later toured with a magician, and made his vaudeville debut in the early 1920s. In his lifetime, Besser graced the stage, the airwaves, and the screen with his unique brand of humor. Besides playing Joe, he created the obnoxious character of Stinky on "The Abbott and Costello Show." With the unveiling of the Stooges' star on Hollywood's Walk of Fame in 1983, Besser declared his time spent as a Stooge "the happiest years" of his life in the business. He wrote two autobiographies in collaboration with other authors, entitled *Not Just a Stooge* and *Once a Stooge Always a Stooge.* Besser was found dead March 1, 1988, at his home in Hollywood, Calif.

OBITUARIES AND OTHER SOURCES:

BOOKS

Besser, Joe, and Jeff and Greg Lenberg, *Not Just a Stooge,* Excelsior Books, 1984.

Besser, Joe, and others, *Once a Stooge Always a Stooge,* Roundtable, 1987.

PERIODICALS

Chicago Tribune, March 6, 1988.
Los Angeles Times, March 2, 1988.
New York Times, March 2, 1988.
Washington Post, March 3, 1988.

* * *

BETI, Mongo
See BIYIDI, Alexandre

* * *

BEYERLIN, Walter W(ilhelm) 1929-

PERSONAL: Born June 23, 1929, in Reutlingen, Germany (now West Germany); son of Wilhelm and Emma (Braun) Beyerlin; married Astrid Gottfriedsen, April 15, 1966. *Education:* Attended University of Goettingen, 1952-53, Univer-

sity of Basel, 1953, and University of Edinburgh, 1955-56; University of Tuebingen, Th.D., 1956, Th.D. habil., 1960.

ADDRESSES: Home—Klosterbusch 10, D-4400 Muenster, Nordrhein-Westfalen, West Germany. *Office*—Universitaetsstrasse 13-17, D-4400 Muenster, West Germany.

CAREER: Ordained minister of Evangelical Lutheran church, 1954; *stiftsrepetent* in Tuebingen, West Germany, 1957-58; University of Tuebingen, Tuebingen, assistant, 1958-60, docent in theology, 1960-63; University of Kiel, Kiel, West Germany, ordinary professor and director of Theological Seminary, 1963-73; University of Muenster, Muenster, West Germany, ordinary professor and director of theological seminary, 1973—.

WRITINGS:

Die Kulttraditionen Israels in der Verkuendigung des Propheten Micha (title means "Israel's Cultic Traditions in Micah's Prophecy"), Vandenhoeck & Ruprecht, 1959.
Herkunft und Geschichte der Aeltesten Sinaitraditionen, Mohr-Siebeck, 1961, translation by Stanley Rudman published as *Origins and History of the Oldest Sinaitic Traditions,* Basil Blackwell, 1965.
(Translator) N. W. Porteous, *Das Danielbuch* (title means "The Book of Daniel"), Vandenhoeck & Ruprecht, 1962.
Die Rettung der Bedraengten in den Feindpsalmen der Einzelnen auf institutionelle Zusammenhaenge untersucht, Vandenhoeck & Ruprecht, 1970.
(Editor with Hellmut Brunner and others) *Religionsgeschichtliches Textbuch zum Alten Testament,* Vandenhoeck & Ruprecht, 1975, translation by John Bowden published as *Near Eastern Religious Texts Relating to the Old Testament,* Westminster, 1978.
Wir sind wie Traeumende: Studien zum 126 Psalm, Katholisches Bibelwerk, 1978, translation by Dinah Livingstone published as *We Are Like Dreamers: Studies in Psalm 126,* T. & T. Clark, 1982.
Werden und Wesen des 107 Psalms (title means "Growth and Nature of Psalm 107"), de Gruyter, 1978.
Der 52 Psalm: Studien zu seiner Einordnung, Kohlhammer, 1980.
Wider die Hybris des Geistes: Studien zum 131 Psalm, Katholisches Bibelwerk, 1982.
Weisheitlich-kultische Heilsordnung: Studien zum 15 Psalm, Neukirchener Verlag, 1985.
Weisheitliche Vergewisserung mit Bezug auf den Zionskult: Studien zum 125 Psalm, Vandenhoeck und Ruprecht, 1985.

Contributor to theology journals.

* * *

BIGGS, Bradley 1920-

PERSONAL: Born August 29, 1920, in Newark, N.J.; son of Bradley (a bottler) and Julia (a nurse; maiden name, DeFreece) Biggs; married Kunigunde Elsinger (a teacher), July 27, 1960; children: Bradley III, Carina, Siegfried Koschinski. *Education:* Attended Tennessee Agricultural and Industrial State University (now Tennessee State University), 1957, and University of Nevada, 1962-63; University of Maryland at College Park, B.A., 1964; graduate study at University of Southern California; Wesleyan University, M.A., 1969, M.A.T., 1973. *Politics:* Republican. *Religion:* Protestant.

ADDRESSES: Home—10093 Dahlia Ave., Palm Beach Gardens, Fla. 33410. *Office*—Office of the Assistant Vice-President for Administrative Affairs, Florida International University, North Miami Campus, 151st and Biscayne Blvd., North Miami, Fla. 33181.

CAREER: National Youth Administration, executive assistant to mayor of Newark, N.J., 1939; professional football player for New York Brown Bombers, 1939; U.S. Army, 1939-61, commissioned second lieutenant, 1942, combat duty in Korea, 1950-51, general staff officer in Germany, 1953-56, deputy chief of staff of 24th Infantry Division in Germany, 1958-60, retiring as lieutenant colonel; associated with the undergraduate division of University of Maryland, Munich, West Germany, 1961-64; associated with U.S. Army Education System, Germany, 1961-64; associated with U.S. Air Force Education System, France, 1964-66; Middlesex Community College, Middlesex, Conn., registrar, 1966-73; deputy commissioner of public works for the State of Connecticut, 1973-75; Middlesex Community College, associate professor of political science and dean of administration, 1975-76; South Central Community College, New Haven, Conn., administrative head, 1976; president of Biggs International Development Corp., 1976-77; Department of Health and Hospitals, Boston, Mass., director of police, 1977; Boston Housing Authority, Boston, administrator, 1978; Florida International University, North Miami, assistant director of Plant Division, 1980-83, assistant vice-president for administrative affairs, 1983—. Member of board of directors of Teenagers Organization for Productive Services, 1968-70, and Russell Library, 1973-74; Community Action Group for the Middletown Area, member of board of directors, 1968-72, vice-president of board, 1971-72; incorporator of Middlesex Memorial Hospital, 1970-71. Fellow of Wesleyan University, Middletown, 1961-70.

MEMBER: Alpha Sigma Lambda, Pi Sigma Alpha, Phi Alpha Theta.

AWARDS, HONORS: Military—Combat Infantry Badge, Bronze Star, Purple Heart.

WRITINGS:

Gavin, Shoe String, 1980.
The Triple Nickles, Shoe String, 1986.

WORK IN PROGRESS: Our Debt to Toussaint; Judicial Intervention Into Municipal Government; The Assassins: A Breed Extinct, a novel, for Delacroix Press; *The First Black Tankers,* for Shoe String; *Stand Up and Be Counted.*

SIDELIGHTS: During more than twenty years of active service in the armed forces, Bradley Biggs made more than 260 parachute jumps, 30 glider flights, and commanded the rifle company that spearheaded the assault on Yechon, the first U.S. victory in Korea. An officer in the Army's first black tank battalion, he went on to become the first black officer accepted for airborne duty in the U.S. Army and was one of the first black officers to be selected when the army was integrated after World War II. Biggs also became the first black executive officer and temporarily commanded an airborne armor heavy tank battalion.

Biggs told *CA:* "My book, *The Triple Nickles,* is the history of the only all-black parachute infantry battalion the world has ever known. This history opens a new, untold chapter in black social history. The high professional standards of the men of the 555th, their skill in airborne operations, fearlessness in testing new concepts, and effectiveness in training other service personnel marked them as black pioneers whose achievements had an impact on society far beyond the army. As the first regular army unit to be integrated, the 555th showed how this major goal could be achieved, without incident. The vision

of these men opened the way for the present-day, fully integrated military."

AVOCATIONAL INTERESTS: Scuba diving, fencing, archery, private flying, parachuting.

* * *

BINGHAM, Madeleine (Mary Ebel) 1912-1988 (Julia Mannering)

OBITUARY NOTICE—See index for *CA* sketch: Listed in some sources under title Baroness Madeleine Mary Ebel Clanmorris; born February 1, 1912, in London (one source says Sutton), England; died February 16, 1988. Author. Bingham produced a variety of writings, including the published play *The Man From the Ministry,* the semi-biographical tale *The Passionate Poet: A Romantic Story Based Upon Lord Byron's Loves and Adventures* (under the pseudonym Julia Mannering), and the biographies *Masks and Facades: Sir John Vanbrugh, the Man in His Setting* and *Henry Irving: The Greatest Victorian Actor.* She also contributed short stories to periodicals such as *Harper's* and *Vanity Fair.*

OBITUARIES AND OTHER SOURCES:

PERIODICALS

Times (London), February 19, 1988.

* * *

BISHOP, Ron 1922(?)-1988

OBITUARY NOTICE: Born c. 1922; died of complications resulting from a stroke, January 30, 1988, in Santa Monica, Calif. Professional athlete, laborer, television writer, and author. Beginning in 1958 Bishop wrote dozens of scripts for television series, often westerns such as "Gunsmoke," "Maverick," and "How the West Was Won." In 1973 he shared an Emmy nomination with co-author Robert Totten for "The Red Pony," based on the John Steinbeck story of the same name and broadcast on "Bell System Family Theatre." Bishop was a volunteer ambulance driver in Burma during World War II when he was pressed into service as leader of a platoon of British Army soldiers, and his battlefield heroics made him a member of the Order of the British Empire. When he returned to America he worked as a football player, wrestler, stevedore, and lumberjack before becoming established as a writer. Bishop also contributed to magazines, including *Atlantic Monthly, Field and Stream, Harper's, True,* and *Vogue.*

OBITUARIES AND OTHER SOURCES:

PERIODICALS

Los Angeles Times, February 5, 1988.

* * *

BIYIDI, Alexandre 1932- (Mongo Beti, Eza Boto)

PERSONAL: Professionally known as Mongo Beti; born June 30, 1932, in M'Balmayo (one source says Akometam), Cameroon; married; children: three. *Education:* Attended University of Aix-Marseille; received B.A. (with honors) from Sorbonne, University of Paris, M.A., 1966. *Politics:* Marxist.

ADDRESSES: Agent—Helena Strassova, Paris, France.

CAREER: Educator in Lamballe, France; secondary education instructor in classical Greek, Latin, and French literature in Rouen, France. Writer, 1953—.

AWARDS, HONORS: Sainte-Beuve Prize, 1948, for *Mission Accomplished,* and 1957, for *King Lazarus.*

WRITINGS:

NOVELS; UNDER PSEUDONYM MONGO BETI, EXCEPT AS NOTED:

(Under pseudonym Eza Boto) *Ville cruelle* (title means "Cruel City"), Editions Africaines, 1954.

Le Pauvre Christ de Bomba, Laffont, 1956, translation by Gerald Moore published as *The Poor Christ of Bomba,* Heinemann Educational [London], African Writers Series, 1971.

Mission terminee, Buchet Chastel/Correa, 1957, translation by Peter Green published as *Mission Accomplished,* Macmillan, 1958 (published in England as *Mission to Kala,* Muller, 1958), rewritten by John Davey and published as *Mission to Kala* (illustrated by Peter Edwards), Heinemann Educational, African Writers Series, 1964.

Le Roi miracule: Chronique des Essazam, Buchet Chastel/Correa, 1958, English translation published as *King Lazarus,* Muller [London], 1960, published as *King Lazarus: A Novel* (introduction by O. R. Dathorne), Macmillan/Collier, 1971.

Main basse sur le Cameroun: Autopsie d'une decolonisation (political essay; title means "The Plundering of Cameroon"), F. Maspero, 1972.

Remember Ruben (title in pidgin English), Buchet Chastel, 1973, translation by Gerald Moore published under the same title, Three Continents Press, 1980.

Perpetue et l'habitude du malheur, Buchet Chastel, 1974, translation by John Reed and Clive Wake published as *Perpetua and the Habit of Unhappiness,* Heinemann Educational, African Writers Series, 1978.

La Ruine presque cocasse d'un polichinelle: Remember Ruben deux, Harmattan, 1979, translation by Richard Bjornson published as *Lament for an African Pol,* Three Continents Press, 1985.

Les Deux Meres de Guillaume Ismael Dzewatama: Futur Camionneur, Buchet Chastel, 1982.

La Revanche de Guillaume Ismael Dzewatama, Buchet Chastel, 1984.

Founder in 1978 and editor of *Peuples noirs Peuples africains* (tribune of French-speaking black radicals). Contributor during the early 1960s to the anti-colonial journals *Tumultueux Cameroun* and *Revue camerounaise.*

SIDELIGHTS: Born in the Cameroon town of M'Balmayo and educated in French missionary schools and universities, Mongo Beti, as he prefers to be known, centers his novels on the encroachment of Western ideals, education, and religion upon African civilization. In particular, he laments the inability of European administrators and missionaries during the early twentieth century colonial rule to recognize the inherent value of existing African religions and beliefs, as well as the Africans' own inability to withstand European influence. Calling Beti "one of the most elegant and sophisticated of African writers," Eustace Palmer reflected in his book *The Growth of the African Novel* that "taken as a whole [Beti's work] probably gives the most thoroughgoing exposure to the stupidity of the imperialist attempt to devalue traditional education and religion and replace them by an inadequate western educational system and a hypocritical Christian religion."

In his first four novels, written from 1954 to 1958, Beti couches

his disdain for European imperialist advances and his own countrymen's gullibility in episodic tales combining comic farce and bitter satire. Thomas Cassirer pointed out in a *L'Esprit Createur* review that each of Beti's anti-imperialist novels features an "African village . . . situated at the meeting point between traditional communal life and a new awareness of imminent change." When European administrators and missionaries—sometimes well-meaning and sometimes corrupt, but always ignorant—arrive in an untouched African village, misunderstanding and chaos inevitably ensue. Beti emphasizes the absurdity of the misunderstandings, suggesting through satire the harm that befalls both the modern and traditional societies when their people attempt to impose conflicting values on one another.

While a student at Aix, Beti penned his first novel, *Ville cruelle*—which means "Cruel City"—under the pseudonym Eza Boto. He has since repudiated both the name and the novel, which is generally considered weak and melodramatic. Critics have noted, however, that this early effort displays much of the perceptive wit found in his later writings. Set in Tanga, the site of lumber mills and rail yards, the novel details the bewilderment and anger of African workers and their families at this unsolicited imposition of Western industrialization.

In *The Poor Christ of Bomba,* set in the colonial 1930s, comic irony arises when the well-meaning Reverend Father Superior Drumont sets out to convert the inhabitants of a bush village and save them from the greed and temptation that had corrupted Europeans, later to discover that the Africans had only embraced his religion hoping to learn the Europeans' secrets of material success. He also learns that the "sixa," a missionary house where African girls live for several months to learn the duties of a Christian wife, has become an agent not of Christian piety but of venereal disease. "Faced with this horrendous proof that he has unknowingly [perpetrated] the very corruption from which he tried to protect the Africans," Cassirer related, "Father Drumont returns to Europe in despair."

Father Drumont represents the type of missionary Beti treats sympathetically in his novels, according to Cassirer. "They are . . . the only ones who explicitly believe in a universal humanity that transcends barriers of race and culture," he explained. "Yet the missionaries' faith in universal humanity remains purely abstract because their primitivist view of the African leads them to treat him as a pure child of nature with no cultural identity of his own." A. C. Brench further described Beti's missionaries in *The Novelists' Inheritance in French Africa* as "the kind who want to do good for the Africans but, unfortunately for them, start from the premise that all Africans are unable to organize their lives unless helped by Europeans." This well-meaning denial of an inherent African culture and intellect is not only insulting to Africans, Brench suggested, but is harmful to both cultures, as the character Father Drumont learns. "The change that takes place in the Father is one of the most interesting features of the novel," Palmer found. Although not all missionaries are so enlightened during the course of their work, Palmer explained, with each discovery of a failed good intention "the Father seems to be gradually groping his way towards a realization of the validity of traditional life and culture."

The missionary in *King Lazarus,* Father Le Guen, is somewhat more zealous and uncompromising than Father Drumont of *The Poor Christ of Bomba*. Palmer noted, "Thematically, [*King Lazarus*] is similar to the earlier novels since it is also concerned with the exposure of the pretentiousness of an alien cultural and imperialist system which shows little respect for the traditional life and dignity of the people." In the novel, Father Le Guen persuades the polygamous tribal chief of the Essazam to convert to Christianity and give up all but one of his wives. The twenty-two former wives and their families, outraged at the breach of tribal custom as well as at the rudeness of turning the women out of their home, protest to the French colonial authorities. In the confrontation between the civil administration, the missionary, and the tribal chief, Beti exposes the vices of each party. The authorities, attempting to stop Father Le Guen from converting the chief, do not do so out of any respect for the tribal culture but for reasons of political expediency, Palmer pointed out. Father Le Guen believes his firm stand on Christianity and monogamy are for the best, but he ignores such thoughtful and practical considerations as where the now-homeless ex-wives will live. "His zeal might have been partly excused if the conversion to Christianity had made the chief a better man," Palmer maintained. "On the contrary, it seems to liberate the most repulsive impulses in him." Irony and comedy pervade in *King Lazarus* as in Beti's other works, but, according to Palmer, "its prevailing cynicism suggests the bitterness of a man who is probably fed up with most things."

Like *The Poor Christ of Bomba* and *King Lazarus,* Beti's *Mission Accomplished* "is a farce but, at the same time, there is bitterness and sorrow," judged Brench. Set in the 1950s—the last decade of colonial rule in Cameroon—the novel details the shortcomings of the colonial educational system. No whites appear in the novel, but European influence is introduced by the protagonist, Jean-Marie Medza, who returns to his village home after failing his exams at a French secondary school. He is immediately sent to Kala, a bush village, to retrieve the runaway wife of a distant relative. "Initially, he looks upon this mission as a means of parading his superior knowledge," Brench related, and the villagers reward him with food, animals, and the chief's daughter in marriage for the wisdom they believe he is teaching them. "Only later does he realize how inadequate his education and understanding of life really are," Brench remarked. "Jean-Marie appreciates more and more, as his stay lengthens, the positive qualities they have and which he has never been able to acquire."

Summarizing Beti's thesis in the novel, Palmer explained that "the formal classical education to which young francophones were exposed was ultimately valueless, since it alienated them from their roots in traditional society, taught them to consider the values of that society inferior to French ones and gave them little preparation for the life they were to lead."

An opponent of the French government in control of his country and, later, of the Yaounde regime in power, Beti left Cameroon before it achieved its independence in 1960. After settling in France, Beti became a teacher and for more than a decade gave up writing. In 1972, however, he composed a lengthy essay entitled *Main basse sur le Cameroun: Autopsie d'une decolonisation* (the title means "The Plundering of Cameroon"), criticizing the Yaounde regime for remaining under the control of the French after the country's formal liberation.

A series of novels soon followed, focusing more on the problems of modern, decolonized Cameroon than on the country during its colonization. Still containing elements of satire, the books assume a documentary-style narrative and approach cynicism more closely than Beti's previous works. In *Remember Ruben, Perpetua and the Habit of Unhappiness,* and *La-*

ment for an African Pol, Beti depicts the harsh aspects of life under the rule of Baba Toura, a tyrannical president of the United Republic of Cameroon after the country's independence. Wrote Robert P. Smith, Jr., in *World Literature Today,* "Toura's administration, which fosters famine, misery, persecution and corruption in the wake of African independence, is perpetuated by evil characters in the novels against whom heroic protagonists struggle constantly." Heroic inspiration arises from the memory of patriot Ruben Um Nyobe, leader of political opposition in Cameroon before its independence. Although Ruben himself never appears in the novels, tales of his valiant deeds and lofty ideals motivate oppressed villagers into revolutionary action.

Remember Ruben follows the life of a solitary, young boy renamed Mor-Zamba by the villagers who take him in, and a friend he makes, Abena. When Mor-Zamba is older his neighbors send him to a labor camp to prevent his marriage to the daughter of a prominent villager, and Abena goes after him. The men reunite eighteen years later, Abena having become a revolutionary and a hero, and Mor-Zamba having learned his true origin. Ben Okri of *New Statesman* praised the author's handling of "the relationship between individuals and a complex, clouded situation of emerging national politics," adding that "Beti's depiction of a colony's traumas, confusions and corruptions is vivid and masterly."

Again emphasizing the corruption of national politics through glimpses of the harshness of individual lives, Beti laments the slave-like conditions of the modern woman in contemporary Africa in his *Perpetua and the Habit of Unhappiness.* The novel focuses on the miserable marriage of the main character, Perpetua, to her husband, Edouard; the tender but doomed affair between Perpetua and her lover, Zeyang; and the true friendship between Perpetua and her companion, Anna-Marie. Robert P. Smith, Jr., writing in the *College Language Association Journal,* called the novel "a dramatic indictment of the ill-fated independence in [Beti's] native land dominated by corrupt dictatorial power, as well as a forceful denunciation of the disgraceful status of African women in such regimes." Smith praised Beti's treatment of modern-day Africa, saying the author wrote *Perpetua* "not to criticize the colonial past as was his custom, but to accuse the present period of independence and self-government, and to pave the way to a better future for Africa and Africans."

A novel that "no serious reader of African literature can afford to neglect," advised *Choice*'s N. F. Lazarus, Beti's *Lament for an African Pol* chronicles the activities of Mor-Zamba, who reappears from the novel *Remember Ruben* with two revolutionary friends to organize a resistance "against the despotic rule of a colonially sanctioned chief." According to Smith in *World Literature Today,* "the novel takes on a 'Robin Hood' atmosphere when the three resolute Rubenists set out on their long journey, robbing the rich and giving to the poor, outwitting the oppressors and conveying courage to the oppressed." Affirming that Beti's "storytelling technique remains vibrant and captivating," Smith noted that, as in *Perpetua,* "of particular interest is the author's sympathetic treatment of African women."

Again "studying marriage patterns and the evolving roles of women," Beti's 1982 novel, *Les Deux Meres de Guillaume Ismael Dzewatama: Futur Camionneur,* recounts "a curious love story, full of drama, harmonizing the political and literary," assessed Hal Wylie in a review of the book in *World Literature Today.* Wylie explained that, similar to Beti's other writings, *Les Deux Meres* "focuses on a unique family which nevertheless dramatizes the sad plight of a corrupt, dictatorial country like Beti's own Cameroon." The family in the novel consists of young Guillaume Ismael, his father, and Guillaume's two mothers—the father's first wife and his French mistress, whom he married to resolve a difficult situation. The double marriage solves nothing; instead, it prompts more confusion. Reflected Wylie, "Seeing the tensions from the point of view of the African boy and his good-hearted, idealistic but naive white mother throws into relief the melodrama and pathos of modern Africa and all its ironies."

Commenting on Beti's range of political and social statements and his episodic, satirical method of conveying them, Brench remarked: "Nothing is sacred: prejudices, passions, ideals, purity are all corrupted by Beti's unrelenting laughter and insistence on the physical nature of things. . . . Yet, behind all this there is this inexpressible sadness, as if a great deception had made life bitter and cynical humour was the only relief." Several critics have pointed to a statement about Cameroon made by the character Jean-Marie at the end of *Mission Accomplished,* calling it Beti's lament for the plight of the African people: "The tragedy which our nation is suffering today is that of a man left to his own devices in a world which does not belong to him, which he has not made and does not understand."

MEDIA ADAPTATIONS: Perpetua and the Habit of Unhappiness was adapted by Michael Etherton as a play by the same title; it was first produced in Zaria, Nigeria, in 1981.

BIOGRAPHICAL/CRITICAL SOURCES:

BOOKS

Brench, A. C., *The Novelists' Inheritance in French Africa: Writers From Senegal to Cameroon,* Oxford University Press, 1967.

Contemporary Literary Criticism, Volume 27, Gale, 1984.

Moore, Gerald, *Seven African Writers,* Oxford University Press, 1962.

Palmer, Eustace, *The Growth of the African Novel,* Heinemann Educational, 1979.

The Penguin Companion to Classical, Oriental, and African Literature, McGraw, 1969.

PERIODICALS

Choice, October, 1975, January, 1986.
College Language Association Journal, March, 1976.
Journal of Black Studies, December, 1976.
L'Esprit Createur, autumn, 1970.
Nation, October 11, 1965.
New Statesman, January 30, 1981.
Times Literary Supplement, May 15, 1969, October 29, 1971.
World Literature Today, winter, 1982, winter, 1984.*

—*Sketch by Christa Brelin*

*   *   *

BLACKMORE, Charles (David) 1957-

PERSONAL: Born July 5, 1957, in Bradford, England; son of Allan Wilson (an army officer) and June (Stevenson) Blackmore; married Tina King (an insurance broker), March 22, 1986; children: Oliver Charles Wilson. *Education:* University of Leeds, B.A. (with honors), 1978. *Religion:* Church of England.

ADDRESSES: Home—Forge Cottage, Kilmeston near Alves-

ford, Hertfordshire SO24 0NR, United Kingdom. *Agent*—Pilot Productions Ltd., 59 Charlotte St., London W1P 1LA, England.

CAREER: British Army, 1978—, served with Royal Green Jackets in Northern Ireland, 1979-80, the Far East, Cyprus, and England, 1980-81, Northern Ireland, 1981-82, Germany, 1982-83, and the Middle East, Canada, and Germany, 1983-85, attached to a Gurkha regiment in Hong Kong, 1985—; present rank, major.

MEMBER: Royal Geographical Society (fellow).

WRITINGS:

In the Footsteps of Lawrence of Arabia, Harrap, 1986.

WORK IN PROGRESS: A book "on retired ex-patriarchs in the Far East," especially in former British colonies, publication by Harrap expected in 1988.

SIDELIGHTS: A career officer in the British Army, Charles Blackmore was the leader of a small expedition of British soldiers who, in 1985, attempted to follow the path of the legendary T. E. Lawrence through Jordan. The group hired camels and native guides to accompany them on their thousand-mile journey. Blackmore's book, *In the Footsteps of Lawrence of Arabia,* records the expedition's daily activities and compares the men's experiences to those attributed to Lawrence's party more than seventy years ago.

Blackmore told *CA:* "My ten years in the British Army have been fascinating and varied enough to preclude any specific highlights, but my expeditions and extensive travels are perhaps noteworthy. In addition to the Lawrence expedition, I led a party of ten soldiers five hundred miles over the Galacian mountains of north Spain in the winter of 1982. Our aim was to commemorate the 175th anniversary of our regiment's actions in the Retreat to Corunna from the French. The expedition members were dressed in the uniforms of 1808, and the Spanish people adored it!

"Following that successful journey, I had the desire to travel in the desert. I had visited Jordan on an attachment to the Jordanian Army in 1981, and this fueled my interest in Lawrence. He was such a charismatic and enigmatic personality that the romantic in me wanted to try to penetrate the legend. Since boyhood I had been interested in him and his writing *The Seven Pillars of Wisdom*—an interest that stemmed directly from my grandfather, who had served in the desert near Lawrence during World War I. In my planning of a desert journey, the immediate convenience of 1985 being the year of the fiftieth anniversary of Lawrence's death gave me the idea to make it a commemorative journey.

"Our expedition was the first of its kind to ever retrace Lawrence's journeys authentically—that is, by camel. The difficulties encountered involved both the weather and the Bedouin tribesmen. The weather varied in extremes, and this became a daily test of physical endurance. The Bedouin, on the other hand, were the source of our mental hardship, until we understood how their minds worked. A key feature of my book is that it recounts the interactions between these seasoned desert warriors and the young, idealistic Englishmen seeking adventure on our expedition.

"The journey was a success, if only for having delved a little deeper behind the Lawrence myth and legend. My conclusions about him were modest—for I did not seek, as do others, to join the popular bandwagon of defaming popular British heroes. The rest is in my book."

AVOCATIONAL INTERESTS: Classical music, all outdoor sports, gliding, sailing, journalism.

BIOGRAPHICAL/CRITICAL SOURCES:

PERIODICALS

Times Literary Supplement, January 30, 1987.

*   *   *

BLAKE, Gerald H(enry) 1936-

PERSONAL: Born February 1, 1936, in Southampton, England; son of Geoffrey Thomas (a master mariner) and Grace (Dibben) Blake; married Brenda Jane Peach (a college lecturer), April 17, 1965; children: Robert, Carolyn, Julia. *Education:* St. Edmund Hall, Oxford, B.A. (with honors), 1960; Oxford University, M.A., 1960; University of Southampton, Ph.D., 1964.

ADDRESSES: Home—Principal's House, Collingwood College, University of Durham, Durham DH1 3LT, England. *Office*—Department of Geography, University of Durham, Durham DH1 3LE, England.

CAREER: St. John's College, Johannesburg, South Africa, schoolteacher, 1960-61; University of Durham, Durham, England, lecturer, 1964-75, reader, 1975—, principal of Collingwood College, 1987—. Justice of the peace for county of Durham, 1972—. *Military Service:* National Service, Gold Coast Regiment, 1954-56; became second lieutenant.

MEMBER: British Society for Middle Eastern Studies (fellow), Royal Geographical Society (fellow).

WRITINGS:

(With P. Beaumont and J. M. Wagstaff) *The Middle East: A Geographical Study,* Wiley, 1976, Fulton, 2nd edition, 1988.

(With A. D. Drysdale) *The Middle East and North Africa: Political Geography,* Oxford University Press, 1985.

(With J. C. Dewdney and J. K. Mitchell) *Cambridge Atlas of the Middle East and North Africa,* Cambridge University Press, 1987.

(Editor) *Maritime Boundaries and Ocean Resources,* Croom Helm, 1987.

WORK IN PROGRESS: Boundaries and Territory in Arabia and the Gulf: An Analysis and Guide to Primary Sources, a study of Arabian land and sea political boundaries, publication by Archive Editions expected in 1988.

SIDELIGHTS: Gerald H. Blake told *CA:* "The Middle East is one of the world's most vital regions, and one of the most misunderstood. My books have sought to highlight some of the geographical realities which underpin political events in the area. My latest research concerns the origins and evolution of land and maritime boundaries between states: while many are the product of an earlier imperial age, others remain to be drawn, especially at sea."

AVOCATIONAL INTERESTS: Travel, rowing, maritime museums.

*   *   *

BLANSHARD, Brand 1892-1987

OBITUARY NOTICE—See index for *CA* sketch: Born August 27, 1892, in Fredericksburg, Ohio; died after a long illness,

November 19 (one source says November 18), 1987, in New Haven, Conn. Philosopher, educator, academic administrator, editor, and author. Blanshard was known in his field as a staunch rationalist. He spent the final years of his teaching career at Yale University, where he was professor of philosophy from 1945 to 1961 and chairman of his department in the late 1940s and again in 1960. He wrote more than three hundred books and articles, including such works as *The Nature of Thought; On Philosophical Style; Reason and Goodness; Reason and Analysis;* and *Four Reasonable Men: Marcus Aurelius, John Stuart Mill, Ernest Renan, Henry Sidgwick.* Blanshard also edited the volume *Education in the Age of Science* and contributed to periodicals such as the *New York Times Book Review* and *Saturday Review.*

OBITUARIES AND OTHER SOURCES:

PERIODICALS

New York Times, November 21, 1987.
Times (London), December 3, 1987.
Washington Post, November 21, 1987.

* * *

BLISS, Dorothy E(lizabeth) 1916-1987

OBITUARY NOTICE—See index for *CA* sketch: Born February 13, 1916, in Cranston, R.I.; died of cancer, December 26, 1987, in Providence, R.I. Museum curator, educator, researcher, editor, and author. Bliss was curator of the American Museum of Natural History in New York City from 1967 to 1980. Prior to working at the museum she taught science at the Milton Academy in Massachusetts and worked as a researcher at Harvard University. She wrote *Shrimps, Lobsters, and Crabs: Their Fascinating Life Story* and contributed to such works as *The Physiology of Crustacea* and *The Biology of Crustacea.* In addition, she was editor in chief of the ten-volume *Biology of Crustacea.*

OBITUARIES AND OTHER SOURCES:

PERIODICALS

New York Times, January 2, 1988.

* * *

BLUM, Lawrence A. 1943-

PERSONAL: Born April 16, 1943, in Baltimore, Md.; son of Irving and Lois (Hoffberger) Blum; married Judith Smith (a college professor), June 22, 1975; children: Benjamin, Sarah, Laura. *Education:* Princeton University, A.B., 1964; Harvard University, M.A., 1965, Ph.D., 1974; attended Linacre College, Oxford, 1968-69. *Religion:* Jewish.

ADDRESSES: Home—149 Prospect St., Cambridge, Mass. 02139. *Office*—Department of Philosophy, University of Massachusetts, Harbor Campus, Boston, Mass. 02125.

CAREER: University of Massachusetts, Boston, assistant professor, 1973-80, associate professor of philosophy, 1980—. Visiting associate professor at University of California, Los Angeles, spring, 1984.

MEMBER: American Philsophical Association.

AWARDS, HONORS: Fellow of National Endowment for the Humanities, 1986-87.

WRITINGS:

Friendship, Altruism, and Morality, Routledge & Kegan Paul, 1980.

(With V. J. Seidler) *A Truer Liberty: Simone Weil and Marxism,* Routledge & Kegan Paul, in press.

CONTRIBUTOR

R. Kruschwitz and R. Roberts, *The Virtues: Contemporary Essays in Moral Character,* edited by Ken Kings, Wadsworth, 1987.

J. Kagan and S. Lamb, editors, *The Emergence of Morality in Young Children,* University of Chicago, 1988.

Contributor to philosophy journals.

SIDELIGHTS: In his book *Friendship, Altruism, and Morality,* Lawrence A. Blum argues that morality is as much a matter of emotion as rationality. This places him opposite great moral philosophers such as Immanuel Kant and more in line with classical thinkers like Aristotle. Blum asserts in particular that compassion, sympathy, and friendship are central moral phenomena neglected in Kantian-influenced traditions of morality.

BIOGRAPHICAL/CRITICAL SOURCES:

PERIODICALS

Boston, October, 1982.
Times Literary Supplement, February 20, 1981.

* * *

BOBO, Lawrence (Douglas) 1958-

PERSONAL: Born February 18, 1958, in Nashville, Tenn.; son of Joseph Randall (a physician) and Joyce (a teacher; maiden name, Cooper) Bobo. *Education:* Loyola Marymount University, B.A. (magna cum laude), 1979; University of Michigan, M.A., 1981, Ph.D., 1984. *Politics:* Democrat.

ADDRESSES: Home—1782 Fordem Ave., No. 303, Madison, Wis. 53704. *Office*—Department of Sociology, University of Wisconsin—Madison, 1180 Observatory Dr., Madison, Wis. 53706.

CAREER: University of Wisconsin—Madison, assistant professor of sociology, 1981—. Senior research consultant to National Research Council-National Academy of Science.

AWARDS, HONORS: Scholarly Achievement Award from North Central Sociological Association, 1986, for *Racial Attitudes in America: Trends and Interpretations.*

WRITINGS:

(With Howard Schuman and Charlotte Steeh) *Racial Attitudes in America: Trends and Interpretations,* Harvard University Press, 1985.

SIDELIGHTS: Lawrence Bobo told *CA:* "My principal research interests are racial attitudes and relations, black political participation, and the educational status of blacks. My work has aimed to identify the major dimensions, sociopsychological bases, and patterns of change in the racial attitudes of white and black Americans using nationally representative survey data and quantitative research techniques. The major concerns of my research include: work that theorizes and tests empirically ideas about the impact of competitive intergroup relations on black-white attitudes; analyses of patterns of change within major types of racial attitudes; examination of how

beliefs about the process of socioeconomic stratification influence support for policies such as affirmative action; an assessment of the extent and causes of black-white differences in perceptions of racial inequality; and the use of systematic experimentation within surveys to test hypotheses about racial attitudes. To varying degrees, all of this research sheds light on the complex dilemma of widespread support for racial equality and integration but substantial opposition to many of the policies that have been proposed as means to achieve such ends.

"I am beginning work on a National Science Foundation-funded project on political participation that focuses mainly on blacks, but also addresses black-white similarities and differences. Using 1987 data collected as part of this project and baseline data from a 1967 survey, the research will examine change in the forms (e.g., voting, campaign activity) and overall levels of black political participation as well as assess the effects of socioeconomic status, social location (e.g., Southern residence, living in areas with and without a history of machine politics), community involvement, and politically relevant psychological orientations on black political participation. My work for the National Research Council's Committee on the Status of Black Americans has involved preparation of a thorough review of the literature on racial attitudes and preparation of a synthetic monograph on the educational status of blacks. The latter emphasizes change since the 1940s with a special focus on trends in attainment, achievement, and school desegregation."

BIOGRAPHICAL/CRITICAL SOURCES:

PERIODICALS

Times Literary Supplement, June 13, 1986.

* * *

BOCHCO, Steven 1943-

BRIEF ENTRY: Born December 16, 1943. American television producer, editor, and writer. Bochco won outstanding popular and critical acclaim during the 1980s as executive producer, occasional writer, and co-creator, with Michael Kozoll, of the television series "Hill Street Blues." The police drama, which ran weekly on NBC (National Broadcasting Company) from 1981 to 1987, was described as innovative and realistic because of its large and varied cast, overlapping storylines, and often bewildering use of background noise and hand-held camera techniques. Although it initially received poor viewer ratings and mixed criticism, "Hill Street Blues" gained a loyal following and won twenty-six Emmy awards while Bochco co-produced the show, including six that Bochco received himself. For his work on the show, the producer/writer also won a George Foster Peabody Broadcasting Award, an Edgar Allan Poe Award, a Humanitas Prize, two Golden Globe awards, and three People's Choice awards. Bochco left the series in 1985 and became co-creator and executive producer of "L.A. Law," a hit television series that premiered on NBC in September of 1986. The show, about a successful Los Angeles law firm, garnered five Emmy awards in its first year, including an outstanding writing award for Bochco and co-author Terry Louise Fisher. Prior to his work with "Hill Street Blues" and "L.A. Law," Bochco produced, edited, and/or wrote scripts for earlier television series, including "Columbo"—for which he won two Emmy awards for writing—"Quincy," "Bay City Blues," "Delvecchio," and "Paris." *Addresses: Office*—Twentieth Century-Fox, 10201 West Pico Blvd., Los Angeles, Calif. 90035.

BIOGRAPHICAL/CRITICAL SOURCES:

BOOKS

Contemporary Literary Criticism, Volume 35, Gale, 1985.
Les Brown's Encyclopedia of Television, New York Zoetrope, 1982.
Who's Who in Television and Cable, Facts on File, 1983.

PERIODICALS

New York, September 15, 1986.
Rolling Stone, March 13, 1986.

* * *

BODECKER, N(iels) M(ogens) 1922-1988

OBITUARY NOTICE—See index for *CA* sketch: Born January 13, 1922, in Copenhagen, Denmark; immigrated to United States, 1952; died of cancer of the colon, February 1, 1988, in Hancock, N.H. Illustrator and author of children's books. Bodecker was perhaps best known as editor, illustrator, and translator of *It's Raining Said John Twaining,* a collection of Danish nursery rhymes that was named one of 1973's notable books by the American Library Association, the School Library Association, and the National Book League of the United Kingdom. Among Bodecker's other self-illustrated volumes are *Miss Jaster's Garden; Hurry, Hurry, Mary Dear! and Other Nonsense Poems;* and *A Person From Britain Whose Head Was the Shape of a Mitten, and Other Limericks.* Bodecker also illustrated children's books by other writers, including Edward Eager and Robert Kraus.

OBITUARIES AND OTHER SOURCES:

BOOKS

Twentieth-Century Children's Writers, 2nd edition, St. Martin's, 1983.

PERIODICALS

New York Times, February 3, 1988.
Publishers Weekly, February 26, 1988.

* * *

BOHLKE, L(andall) Brent 1942-1987

PERSONAL: Born December 29, 1942, in Hastings (one source said Kenesaw), Neb.; died of lung cancer, March 7, 1987, in New York, N.Y.; son of Wallace Russel and Waunetta Lavonne (Ernst) Bohlke; married Beverly Anne Plambeck, August 21, 1965; children: Saraugh, Susannah. *Education:* Hastings College, B.A., 1964; Seabury-Western Theological Seminary, M.Div., 1967; University of Nebraska—Lincoln, M.A., 1973, further graduate study, 1977-81.

CAREER: Ordained Episcopal priest, 1967; vicar of Episcopal churches in Seward, Neb., and York, Neb., both 1967-71; University of Nebraska—Lincoln, chaplain, 1971-81, instructor in English, 1974-81; Doane College, Crete, Neb., member of English faculty and chaplain; Church of St. John the Evangelist, Barrytown, N.Y., rector. Chaplain at Nebraska Women's Reformatory, York, 1967-71, and Bard College; pastor of Episcopal church in Crete. Chairman of department of Christian education, Diocese of Nebraska, 1967-72. Member of Seward Police-Community Relations Board, 1967-71; member of board of directors of Justice, Inc., 1972—.

WRITINGS:

(Editor) *Willa Cather in Person: Interviews, Speeches, and Letters,* University of Nebraska Press, 1987.

OBITUARIES:

PERIODICALS

Lincoln Journal, March 9, 1987.*

* * *

BOLAND, Bridget 1913-1988

OBITUARY NOTICE—See index for *CA* sketch: Born March 13, 1913, in London, England; died January 19, 1988. Author of plays, screenplays, novels, and nonfiction. Boland was probably best known for her published play *The Prisoner,* about a man's psychiatric degeneration from incarceration and interrogation. The play was adapted for film in 1955 and provided the basis for the popular 1960s television series of the same title. Boland's other publications include the play *Temple Folly* and the novels *The Wild Geese, Portrait of a Lady in Love,* and *Caterina.* She also produced the nonfiction volume *At My Mother's Knee* and wrote the screenplays for several motion pictures, including the 1956 adaptation of Leo Tolstoy's *War and Peace* and the 1969 film "Anne of the Thousand Days."

OBITUARIES AND OTHER SOURCES:

BOOKS

Who's Who, 139th edition, St. Martin's, 1987.

PERIODICALS

Times (London), January 27, 1988.

* * *

BOND, Charles R(ankin), Jr. 1915-

PERSONAL: Born April 22, 1915, in Dallas, Tex.; son of Charles Rankin (a painter) and Magnolia (a housewife; maiden name, Turner) Bond; married Doris Inez Walker (a housewife), September 14, 1942; children: Rebecca Bond Stuart, Cindy Bond Gilmer, Jeannie, Charles Rankin III. *Education:* Texas A & M University, B.S., 1949. *Religion:* Protestant.

ADDRESSES: Home—5305 Marsh Creek Dr., Austin, Tex. 78759.

CAREER: U.S. Air Force, career officer, 1938-68, became commander of 12th Air Force, retiring as major general. Volunteer with American Volunteer Group, the Flying Tigers, serving in China, 1941-42. Consultant to Texas Instruments, Inc.

MEMBER: Alzheimer's Disease and Related Disorders Association (member of local board of directors).

AWARDS, HONORS: Military—Distinguished Service Medal, Legion of Merit, British Distinguished Flying Cross, Thai Red Cross Medal, two Chinese medals, one Brazilian medal; trophy for outstanding achievement from Flying Tigers, 1972.

WRITINGS:

(With Terry Anderson) *A Flying Tiger's Diary,* Texas A & M University Press, 1984.

WORK IN PROGRESS: Research on Alzheimer's disease.

BOND, William Henry 1915-

PERSONAL: Born August 14, 1915, in York, Pa.; son of Walter Loucks and Ethel (Bossert) Bond; married Helen Elizabeth Lynch, December 6, 1943; children: Nancy Barbara, Sally Lynch. *Education:* Haverford College, A.B. (with honors), 1937; Harvard University, M.A., 1938, Ph.D., 1941.

ADDRESSES: Home—109 Valley Rd., Concord, Mass. 01742.

CAREER: Research fellow with Folger Shakespeare Library, 1941-42; Harvard University, Cambridge, Mass., assistant to librarian at Houghton Library, 1946-48, curator of manuscripts, 1948-64, librarian, 1965-82, lecturer at university, 1964-67, professor of bibliography, 1967-86, librarian and professor emeritus, 1986—. Assistant keeper of manuscripts at British Museum, 1952-53; Sandars Reader in Bibliography at Cambridge University, 1981-82. Member of board of trustees of Emerson Memorial Association, 1964—, Historic Deerfield, Inc., 1965—, and Concord Free Library, 1966-71. *Military service:* U.S. Naval Reserve, active duty, 1943-46; became first lieutenant.

MEMBER: Bibliographical Society of America (president, 1974-75), American Antiquarian Society (member of council), Bibliographical Society (England), Massachusetts Historical Society, Colonial Society of Massachusetts (president, 1984—), Johnsonians, Grolier Club, Club of Odd Volumes, Phi Beta Kappa.

AWARDS, HONORS: Senior Fulbright fellow, 1952-53; Guggenheim fellow, 1982-83.

WRITINGS:

EDITOR

Christopher Smart, *Jubilate Agno,* Harvard University Press, 1954.

Supplement to the Census of Medieval and Renaissance Manuscripts in the United States, Bibliographical Society of America, 1962.

The Houghton Library, 1942-1967, Harvard College Library, Harvard University, 1967.

Eighteenth Century Studies in Honor of Donald F. Hyde, Grolier Club, 1970.

William Alexander Jackson, *Records of a Bibliographer: Selected Papers,* Harvard University Press, 1981.

WORK IN PROGRESS: Revising Sandars Lectures at Cambridge University on the subject of Thomas Hollis.

* * *

BONNER, Terry Nelsen
See CASTORO, Laura A(nn)

* * *

BOOTH, Mark Haworth
See HAWORTH-BOOTH, Mark

* * *

BOOTHROYD, (John) Basil 1910-1988

OBITUARY NOTICE—See index for *CA* sketch: Born March 4, 1910, in Worksop, England; died February 27, 1988. Bank

clerk, broadcaster, editor, and author. Boothroyd was a long-time writer for the British humor magazine *Punch,* where he became known for producing well-crafted, wide-ranging humor. He began writing for the publication in 1938—after fifteen years as a bank clerk—and eventually collected many of his pieces in volumes such as *Home Guard Goings-on From "Punch"; or, The London Charivari, 1940-1941* and *Adastral Bodies From "Punch."* Boothroyd also broadcast humorous commentaries on British radio, and he published some of those writings in *Boothroyd at Bay: Some Radio Talks.* Among his other books are *Prince Philip: An Informal Biography* and *A Shoulder to Laugh On,* an autobiography.

OBITUARIES AND OTHER SOURCES:

BOOKS

Who's Who, 139th edition, St. Martin's, 1987.

PERIODICALS

Times (London), March 1, 1988.

* * *

BORETZ, Alvin 1919-

PERSONAL: Born June 15, 1919, in New York, N.Y.; son of Samuel (a tailor) and Mollie (a shopkeeper; maiden name, Milch) Boretz; married Lucille Garson, November 1, 1942; children: Jennifer Boretz Kahnweiler, Carrie. *Education:* Brooklyn College (now Brooklyn College of the City University of New York), B.A., 1942. *Politics:* Liberal. *Religion:* Jewish.

ADDRESSES: Home—Woodmere, N.Y. *Agent*—Creative Artists Agency, 1888 Century Park E., Los Angeles, Calif. 90067.

CAREER: Writer of scripts for stage, screen, radio, and television programs, including "The Alcoa Hour," "Armstrong Circle Theatre," "General Electric Theatre," "Playhouse 90," "ABC Afterschool Special," "CBS Children's Hour," "ABC Movie of the Week," and "NBC World Premiere Movie." *New York Evening Journal,* New York City, copy assistant, 1937; Modern Industrial Bank, New York City, credit analyst, 1937-42; free-lance radio scriptwriter, 1942-54; television scriptwriter, 1954—. Adjunct professor of screenwriting at Hofstra University and of communications at Adelphi University, both 1976-78; president of board of trustees of Hewlett-Woodmere Public Library, Long Island, N.Y. *Military service:* U.S. Army Air Force, 1942-45; became warrant officer.

MEMBER: Writers Guild of America (member of council, 1962-74; vice-president, 1969-71), Dramatists Guild, P.E.N. American Center.

AWARDS, HONORS: Ohio State Award from Institute for Education by Radio-Television, 1956, for radio play "Little Girl Lost"; Harcourt Brace Award for best television play, 1957, for "Trial of Poznan"; Godmothers' League Public Service Award, 1961, for "Armstrong Circle Theatre" television play "The Hidden World"; first prize from Family Service Association, 1963, for "Armstrong Circle Theatre" television play "Battle of Hearts"; Christopher Award, 1973, for children's drama "Follow the North Star," an "ABC Afterschool Special" presentation.

WRITINGS:

"Brass Target" (screenplay; based on the novel *The Algonquin Project* by Frederick Nolan), United Artists, 1978.

"Made in America" (two-act stage play), first produced in Los Angeles at Mark Taper Forum, February 11, 1984.

Author of many documentaries, several hundred radio plays, and more than one thousand television plays, including "The Blue Men," "The Desperate Season," "No License to Kill," "House of Cards," "Trial of Poznan," "The Hidden World," "Battle of Hearts," and "Follow the North Star," Also author of scripts for episodes of television series "The Defenders," "Dr. Kildare," "Medical Center," and "Kojak," among others.

SIDELIGHTS: Alvin Boretz is widely known as one of television's most prolific writers. With an estimated one thousand dramatic scripts and various awards to his credit, he is an industry veteran who contributed to such "Golden Age of Television" shows as "The Alcoa Hour," "Playhouse 90," and "General Electric Theatre." He also wrote scripts for episodes of a number of television series, including "Kojak" as well as the "ABC Afterschool Special" and "NBC World Premiere Movie." Before television became popular during the early 1950s, Boretz wrote for radio. In that medium the writer honed his language skills and developed a flair for writing dialogue. Additionally, he became noted for strong character development, a feature which—with the sensitive but forthright handling of themes such as divorce, suicide, and mental retardation—distinguishes Boretz's critically acclaimed work.

Contributing to a feature film project, Boretz wrote the screenplay for "Brass Target," a 1978 motion picture released by United Artists and starring Sophia Loren, John Cassavetes, and George Kennedy as U.S. Army General George S. Patton. Based on the novel *The Algonquin Project* by Frederick Nolan, the film suggests that Patton was assassinated in Germany by conspiring fellow officers who stole Nazi gold worth $2.5 million. After comparing the film to such predecessors as "The Great Escape" and "Day of the Jackal," Roger Ebert of the Chicago *Sun-Times* observed: "What sets [this] movie apart is that real care was lavished on" developing the characters' and the script's complexities. Commenting on the film's "bang-up job of re-creating the German-Swiss settings," an article in the *New York Post* declared, "you're willing to accept the whole thing as documentary. . . . 'Brass Target' moves fast, hits hard, and makes you believe a very tall story." Ebert concurred, asserting that "the movie earns its stripes."

One of Boretz's stage plays, "Made in America," made its debut in 1984 at the Mark Taper Forum in Los Angeles. It was described as "a big play, with no scarcity of themes" by theatre critic Dan Sullivan writing in the *Los Angeles Times.* Set in middle-class Boston, the play pivots around a blue-collar, second-generation Irish American who laments the deteriorating condition of his life and his country. "Boretz shows a good grasp of his characters and . . . where he wants to go with them," opined Sullivan, adding that each of the play's scenes offers a "fresh attempt" to convey the main character's general malaise. Noting Boretz's sometimes humorous dialogue in an otherwise serious play, Sullivan determined that "we may be dealing with an optimist here."

Boretz told *CA:* "As a boy I began frequenting downtown Brooklyn's first-run movie houses that also featured stage shows. That was enough to fire anyone's imagination, and I knew where my future lay. The Depression precluded full-time attendance at college so I switched to evening sessions and rummaged around for jobs—from usher to copy boy, to reporter, to credit investigator at a bank, and then into the U.S. Army

Air Force a few months after the bombing of Pearl Harbor at the onset of World War II.

"After my discharge from the army, I was still young enough and brave enough to try to make it as a dramatic writer. I managed to write a few radio plays and eventually was doing two or three a week. It was a marvelous training ground and gave me a love and respect for language that has helped me immeasurably. Writing in all three dramatic forms—television, movies, and the theatre—allows me to work on a limitless range of material, as most stories naturally fall into one medium more easily than the other two. For my thematic material I look for the affirmation in most people's struggles."

AVOCATIONAL INTERESTS: Squash; bicycling; a generous sampling of theatre, concerts, and museums; travel both at home and abroad; magazines, newspapers, and people, where "the ideas come from all and crowd each other out."

CA INTERVIEW

CA interviewed Alvin Boretz by telephone on May 28, 1986, at his home in Woodmere, New York.

CA: You started your career by writing radio plays. How did the first break happen, the foot in the door?

BORETZ: Let me start at the beginning. I had been on the high school newspaper. I was in college at night in Brooklyn, and I managed to get a job as a copyboy on the *New York* [*Evening*] *Journal*. I hoped to make my career as a reporter, but then the *New York American*—which was a morning paper—was merged into the *Journal,* and they fired five thousand people, of whom I was one. That was very disappointing to me. Then I got a job working in a bank for eighteen dollars a week. I hated every moment. I kept going to college at night, and I was writing all that time.

I was drafted in early 1942 and was in the Air Force for three-and-a-half years. I still wanted to write. Toward the end, I picked up *Variety* and I read all the names of people who were buying radio scripts. I called up a producer and said, "I'd like to write for your show." He said, "What have you written?" I told him I had written something in California—which I hadn't, but I didn't think he would check. I wrote a script for him and he liked it, and then people began to hear my work and they would call and offer me more work. So I began the very difficult life of a free-lance writer. I had a young family, and I had to beat the bushes for work. But I did more and more and I got better and better, and finally people knew me. When television began, I was right on the scene, because television began in New York and they went to people who had written for radio.

CA: And you've said that radio was a very good training ground for you.

BORETZ: Yes. I loved radio because it taught me language. I always liked language, but I really fell in love with it writing for radio. Through language, you were shaping everything—the place, the people. And every line of dialogue not only had to impart information and show characterization, at the same time it also had to be a good line in itself. Just the alliteration of the line, or the words you chose, would convey the emotion you were trying to get. So it was a great, great teacher. And I've always loved writing dialogue. I think it's one of my strengths.

Even the names of the people were important in radio. I remember a play with a landlady character who was very grasping, very gossipy, and she intruded into the lives of the people who boarded with her. She was like a leech. *Leech,* you know, gives you the feeling of something very slimy. So I called her Mrs. Meech. And every time you'd hear her name, almost in a subliminal way, you would get a reaction to that landlady. That's a tiny thing, but it's symbolic of what you could do with language. And you learned to be economical. People's attention spans are not very great, and you can't keep going on and on.

There were wonderful things done in radio, and some fine writers came out of radio. I had always wanted to be a dramatist, but as a young writer with a family, I didn't have a choice. I'd just come out of the war, and out of the Depression before that, and I didn't have the wherewithal to do exactly what I wanted to do. But going to television was great because the directors were all from the theatre. I worked with people like George Roy Hill, Frank Schaffner, Sidney Lumet, and Yul Brynner—who was a director at that time. The plays would be rehearsed down in an old ballroom on Second Avenue in New York. All the leading actors in Britain and America would come over to work on these shows: "The U.S. Steel Hour," "Armstrong Circle Theatre," "Studio One." It would be nothing to walk into the lobby and see [actors such as] Sir Cedric Hardwicke [and] Robert Morley, stars from Hollywood as well as from Broadway stage. It was a very, very exciting time.

CA: That must be why television drama was so fine in those days. It came right out of theatre.

BORETZ: It *was* theatre. You rehearsed for two or three weeks, and the writer was there, as he is when he's working on a play. If the actor was uncomfortable with something, or a scene didn't work, the writer was on hand to change it. In film and television now, it's the very rare exception to invite the writer to be on the set. I was fortunate to work with directors who would arrange for the studios to pay me to be on the set, because they had a tradition of considering the writer an important part of the show. There are a lot of directors now who get very upset when a writer comes on the sound stage. It's really endemic; it's been going on ever since the movies were created. The writer is the low man on the totem pole. Everybody agrees in private that he's very important, but when it comes to where he stands in the hierarchy, he's ignored. Even today, critics—when they review a show—will often forget to mention the writer.

CA: Do people sometimes ask for your advice on how to get started as a writer?

BORETZ: They do, and I say that there's no rule. You write something and then you bang on doors, and if you believe in yourself, it will someday happen to you. But you can't just sit there in a tweed jacket smoking a pipe and think that someone's going to think of you and call you up. I respect talent enormously, and I firmly believe that people with talent will make it. There are very few brilliant writers in this country who are sitting at home unknown. It just does not happen, because good talent is very rare and it shines by example, because it's so singular.

CA: In your television scripts, you've dealt with such things as suicide and mental retardation, and you've scoffed at the

notion that writers can't tell the truth about those and other serious problems on television. How well do you think television is dealing with the tough subjects now?

BORETZ: I think it's kind of tentative. They do the subjects, but the problem is that they kind of tiptoe around the edges. They really don't always get into the heart of the subject. That's not a blanket indictment. I think it depends on the individual show. If you get a good writer and a fine producer who's going to fight for this show, you'll get a good piece of work. But every writer gets kind of gun-shy. He has to be careful that he doesn't engage in self-censorship. My theory is to go for the jugular and then give ground in a very grudging way if you have to. Otherwise, you're not going to get on the air.

CA: Are there any topics you feel shouldn't be treated on television?

BORETZ: I would hope not. I feel that's based on the judgment and taste of the people doing the work. Like every other business, it's got its charlatans, its quick-buck operators, and to me it's a miracle that as much good work gets done as does. But that's because you've also got a lot of fine people working in it who know what they're doing. I have enormous respect for them, and when I see a good show, I get really excited.

CA: You've written for children. The plays "Follow the North Star" and "Summer Is Forever" were particularly well reviewed. Did you have special concerns and aims when you were writing for children?

BORETZ: I didn't know whether I could write for children or not. Then I began trying it. After I finished these plays and they were well received, I was talking about them with Gene Wilder, whom I met in my producer's office. I said, "I didn't know if I could write for kids." And he said, "The reason you did it well is because you wrote the truth." He said, "Writing truthfully for children is the whole secret." It's a funny thing. I've taught writing. You really can't teach writing. You can teach craft, the way to structure a show. But obviously you can't teach writing; that's innate in the individual. And I feel that all good writers work out of their own instincts and perceptions. The exciting thing about writing to me is that it always comes. I'm not saying it comes in a flash, but I seldom get stuck. If you're tuned in to what you're doing, if you're a creative individual, it always happens. Where it comes from, you don't know, but you have a hell of a time.

CA: You've written more than one thousand television scripts. Were most of them free-lance, or mainly commissioned?

BORETZ: After you're known as a writer, when people know they can get a professional job out of you, you get an audience. You can call them up and say, "Let me tell you an idea that I have." The networks are so anxious to get material that they are very open about listening to people. Of course, if they can count on an agent for screening, that's very helpful. I would say in answer to your question that my scripts have been half speculated and half commissioned. But things change very quickly in television and movies. They're always thinking that the next man coming on is better, so you're constantly having to prove yourself—not to yourself, but to them. Of course there *are* times when you have to prove yourself to yourself too, when you get beaten down. The egos in this business—particularly those of writers—are very weak, including my own. Every time you sit down to write a script, you say to yourself, My God, will I know how to do it? Even though you've been doing it all your adult life. But then you begin to work, and it all comes back. That's the fun of it.

The real point is that if you wait for your agent to get you work, or you wait for someone to call you, you're going to live a very precarious existence. You've got to be a self-starter. Whatever your agent gets for you, or a producer calls about, is a bonus. It's a very hard craft, and you've got to work at it. You can't expect people to give you things. Besides, if you're any good, you keep getting ideas all the time, and you want to do them.

CA: Ideas for television and movies seem to run in cycles. Certain types of shows are popular for a few years, and then something else comes along. Apart from the obvious sociological indicators, are there any reliable ways of predicting what new kind of show or script might work?

BORETZ: There's an old joke that the reason "60 Minutes" has such a large audience is because half the people watching are in the television business looking for ideas. As a matter of fact, practically once a month there's an idea that's taken from "60 Minutes" and becomes the "Movie of the Week." It happens constantly. This is a condition that goes back to the old days in the movies, when they wouldn't buy original material. They would only buy things that someone else had taken a chance on, like a produced play or a published book. That meant that someone else had put their money on the line and exercised their judgment. That's changed around in the movies. Now they're very willing to take chances on original material, which I think is healthy and good. But in television, they're comfortable with something that's proven its value elsewhere. And it is very cyclical. It can be that way in television because you get material on the air quickly. But in the movies, from the time the script is written, you're talking about a year-and-a-half to two years. If you try to write something that's popular when you start on it, you're liable to miss the boat.

What's happening in the movies now is the influence of the so-called youth market. I really don't understand that because every time an adult movie comes out and it's good, it does extremely well at the box office—like "Ordinary People" and "Terms of Endearment." But the studios still insist on making these horror movies and these kid movies, where boys are looking through peepholes at girls. It's terrible, because they're wasting the heart of what movies can be. I'm getting very nostalgic; I'm thinking the studio system of making movies wasn't so bad after all. Some wonderful movies came out of that.

CA: Does an idea of yours every start as a script for television and end up being written for stage or screen?

BORETZ: I do have a genesis like that, as a matter of fact. I had been working on "Playhouse 90," and it had ended. About five years later, they decided they were going to revive it and call it "CBS Playhouse." The first thing I wrote for it was a play I had always wanted to do about the hidden injuries of class in this country, in which a blue-collar worker in his forties feels he has wasted his life and that he failed to realize the promise of America. As the story develops he begins to understand that what he's done with his life is not so terrible. He's been a man who's just done the best he could.

That was going to be the fourth play done on the new show; Gene Hackman liked the script, and he was going to play the main character. Well, the first two or three shows they aired didn't get good ratings, and they decided not to continue with "CBS Playhouse." My heart has always been with the theatre, as I said earlier. About a year after this happened, I said, I like the idea of doing this play for the stage. But I'm not going to use that script, because you write differently for the stage than you do for television. I took that character and wrote a whole new play called "Made in America." It was the first play I'd written, and a year later, in August 1984, it was done at the Mark Taper Forum in Los Angeles. It got pretty good reviews—not sensational, because it was a work in progress and it had been advertised as such, but very encouraging. In the audience on opening night was the director-general of the Finnish State Theatre. He came over to me and said, "I'd like to do this play in Helsinki." And Gordon Davidson said he wanted to bring it back to the Forum, but I said there were things I wanted to do with it. Before I could leave California and get back to work on the play, I had some television offers that were very difficult to turn down, so those took some time. Now I'm getting back to writing the play, and I'm hopeful that nice things will happen with it.

That all came out of the fact that I have always treated television not as an offshoot of theatre, but I've tried to do the things that I would hope to write in theatre. I've never looked down on being a television writer, even though people always knock the medium. I think that, whatever you write, you get better and better. You always do the best you can, in a way, for yourself. Maybe it took me all those years to become the writer I always hoped to be, but I feel very much in command of myself and my material. The response I get tells me that none of the work has been wasted, that the long years of writing for radio and television have paid off. I think any good writer has a voice, and that voice takes a long time to shape. It doesn't happen overnight. It's hard to feel sorry for a new writer who has an overnight success—whatever that is—because success is success, and it's always wonderful to have. But then you have to sustain it. And if you really haven't got the experience and the knowledge, it's very hard to do. Writing is a tough business. But television to me has never, never been a waste of time. Not only have I made my living at it and brought up a family, but at the same time I have learned and learned and learned, and I've had a hell of a time.

CA: Do you watch a lot of television?

BORETZ: I don't watch the episodic shows at all unless it's something that gets a big huzzah; then I'm curious to see it. But I watch periodically. I'll watch something on the networks if someone tells me it's a good show or if the idea piques my interest. I watch a lot of the British imports; I find a lot of their work much more literate than ours, on a general basis.

CA: In the movie "Brass Target," you went beyond the novel it was based on—Frederick Nolan's The Algonquin Project*—to develop the theory that General George S. Patton was assassinated. Did you do original research for the movie?*

BORETZ: No. I went on the book and then took my own flight of fancy. But I had read a lot of things in previous years about Patton. There was a great deal of speculation, particularly when I was getting out of the Air Force. After the picture came out, I got the most extraordinary letter from a doctor who had been a captain in the Medical Corps. He had been in charge of a little medical station only ten miles away from where the actual accident happened, when Patton's car ran into the lorry across the road. He said that instead of the ambulance bringing Patton to his hospital for immediate treatment, he was taken over fifty or sixty miles toward Munich. He never could understand that. The whole area had been cordoned off; something was very much awry. He talked to other people, his suspicions began to arise, and he wrote his father about this in a letter. When the letter was received by his father, the censors had blocked out all that stuff about Patton.

I obviously didn't hit the truth, but I have the feeling that, together, the writer of the novel and I as a screenwriter came pretty close to what might have happened. It's a very interesting speculation. But the picture had a tough break. Roger Ebert, of the Chicago *Sun-Times,* gave it a good review. He called it things like a classy conspiracy thriller with a very literate script and good characters. But just as it opened in Chicago, the heavy snows hit and Mayor Jane Byrne didn't get the streets cleaned up. That was in 1978.

CA: You're also a book collector, I believe. Any special concentrations?

BORETZ: I concentrate on the Irish Renaissance. I used to collect O'Neill, but I don't any longer. Then I collected [Sean] O'Casey. What I'm concentrating on now is [John Millington] Synge, Lady [Isabella Augusta] Gregory, and [William Butler] Yeats. I also have what I feel is an outstanding collection of [James] Joyce. He's my main man because he was the greatest novelist of the century. As a subcollection, I've collected all the first printings of *Ulysses* in different languages. Wherever I go, I find them. When I was in Spain last year, I picked one up in Catalan!

CA: What's missing from stage, screen, or television that you'd like to see—and maybe like to write yourself?

BORETZ: Every writer has his own pet projects, things he wants to write about. A few years ago I ran across Robert Hayes, the fellow who started the Coalition for the Homeless. I wanted to write that story desperately. I thought it was very exciting and it would reach forty or fifty million people. I met Hayes—he's very shy—and we had a handshake deal. It took me two years to sell it, and then ABC's "Theatre of the Week" bought it. I called Hayes up to tell him, and he said, "Well, someone else has entered the picture." The agent Sam Cohn had come in with a movie deal for it, so Hayes left me high and dry. I was very disappointed because I thought it would be a very important show. It was going to be played by Gregg Harrison, who used to play the young doctor in "Trapper John, M.D." It was all set and everybody was very excited. I was just about to write the script when Hayes pulled out. That really hurt.

The problem with dealing with contemporary events in television is that everybody reads newspapers and magazines, and you're really competing with everybody else in the field if you grab those stories. The only way to preserve your individuality and originality is to create your own stories based on your own ideas.

CA: You've shown in your television scripts particularly a strong concern for serious personal and social problems. Would you like to comment on that?

BORETZ: I was an original founder of United Cerebral Palsy [UCP] because I had a cerebral palsy son. I'd like to read you something from the first annual report, which was published in 1950 with a foreword by President [Harry S.] Truman. There's a chapter called "A Dream Come True." It's about how doctors were trying to find out more about cerebral palsy, and it was very difficult. It said, "In New York City in 1946, there were enough local groups to form the New York State Association for Cerebral Palsy, which then became United Cerebral Palsy. Then one night in February, 1947, a brighter spotlight of hope fell in many still-darkened homes. It was a radio program, 'Love Is a Doctor,' a nationwide series exploring the unknown. The writer knew his subject. His heart was poured into the script that Alvin Boretz wrote, because every word he wrote was about his own son. So tremendous was the flood of inquiries that the sponsor, a copper manufacturing company, commissioned the writing and publication of a small informative pamphlet on cerebral palsy prepared by the writers of *Science Illustrated*. Swiftly now, more groups were formed throughout the nation. They corresponded with each other and discussed forming a united national front against a common enemy."

Not only was I a founder of UCP, but I feel that my story—the script that I wrote—played a tremendous part in helping UCP become a reality. And that's one of the reasons why, in later years, I would go to the problems of society to find a lot of my material. I felt that was part of my function as a writer. I've always felt very proud of that, and I feel very encouraged by it. It's one of the things that keeps you going in this terribly difficult business.

BIOGRAPHICAL/CRITICAL SOURCES:

PERIODICALS

Los Angeles Times, March 3, 1984.
New York Post, February 22, 1978.
New York Times, March 17, 1960, November 1, 1972, December 22, 1978.
Sun-Times (Chicago), December 26, 1978.
Variety, June 10, 1959, January 9, 1962, January 28, 1970, November 8, 1972.

—*Interview by Jean W. Ross*

* * *

BORGEN, Robert 1945-

PERSONAL: Born August 30, 1945, in Baltimore, Md.; son of Isadore Herbert (a lawyer) and Evelyn (a statistician; maiden name, Talmadge) Borgen; married Sophia Lee (a historian), August 18, 1979. *Education:* Antioch College, B.A., 1967; University of Michigan, M.A., 1969, Ph.D., 1978.

ADDRESSES: Office—Department of East Asian Language and Literature, University of Hawaii at Manoa, 2500 Campus Rd., Honolulu, Hawaii 96822.

CAREER: University of Virginia, Charlottesville, acting assistant professor of Japanese, 1975-77; University of Hawaii at Manoa, Honolulu, associate professor of Japanese, 1977—.

MEMBER: Association for Asian Studies.

AWARDS, HONORS: Research grants from Fulbright, National Endowment for the Humanities, Social Science Research Council, and Japan Foundation.

WRITINGS:

Sugawara no Michizane and the Early Heian Court, Harvard University Press, 1986.

Contributor of research articles to *Monumenta Nipponica.*

WORK IN PROGRESS: A study and translation of *Jojin's Diary: The Record of a Pilgrimage to the T'ien-t'ai and Wu-t'ai Mountains (1072-1073),* completion expected in 1989.

SIDELIGHTS: Robert Borgen told *CA:* "These days, Japan is fashionable, but the fashion is for contemporary affairs. My own interest is a throwback to the time when Americans were more likely to admire Japan's traditional arts and culture than its contemporary economy. My book, *Sugawara no Michizane and the Early Heian Court,* introduces the life and times of a ninth-century Japanese aristocrat, Sugawara no Michizane, who is one of the most familiar figures in early Japanese history. In Japan, he is famed as a literary figure who wrote principally in Chinese, a diplomat who proposed that Japan abandon relations with China, and a political figure who rose from relative obscurity to become the most powerful minister at court. He is best known, however, not for these real achievements but because he was slandered and died in exile after producing a last flurry of poems protesting his innocence. Subsequently, his angry ghost returned and hounded his mortal rivals to death. To placate him, he was posthumously pardoned, promoted, and finally deified. Even today, he is popularly worshiped as a patron saint of school entrance examinations.

"My book is, for better or worse, 'academic,' laced with footnotes and appended with a long list of Chinese characters to please the specialist. But it is not so technical as to lie beyond the grasp of anyone interested in early Japan. My parents read it without difficulty. I hope it will present an alternate view of the early Japanese court, one that is more accurate historically than the image created by reading the age's great literary masterpieces, such as *The Tale of Genji.*

"I chose to study Michizane in part because he is a colorful figure (my unofficial reason), and in part because he offered a means of evaluating the impact of Chinese culture on early Japan (my official reason). In the future, I hope to return to him and study the history of how he was worshiped. First, however, I have decided to further pursue early Japanese relations with China. My current project is a study and translation of the diary kept by a Japanese monk who traveled throughout China in 1072 and 1073, visiting Buddhist holy mountains and the imperial court. My draft translation is already over five hundred pages long and I have just begun work on writing out the annotation. When it is done, it should become my second book. Some of the diary is rather dull and will only interest specialists, but the journey as a whole, told in remarkable detail, was a great adventure, and I hope also to write it up in more accessible fashion to publish separately."

* * *

BOTO, Eza
See BIYIDI, Alexandre

* * *

BOURDIER, James A(aron) 1929-1987

OBITUARY NOTICE: Born February 28, 1929, in Opelousas, La.; died November 22, 1987, in Atlanta, Ga.; buried in Atlanta, Ga. Photojournalist. An award-winning, widely traveled

photographer, Bourdier took pictures in eighty-six countries over the course of his career. After a stint on the *Opelousas Daily World* Bourdier joined the Associated Press (AP) in 1961 and was soon based at its Miami bureau. While covering unrest in the Dominican Republic during the mid-1960s, Bourdier earned a Picture of the Year Award from the National Press Photographer's Association and the top prize of the AP Managing Editors Association for his photographs of a student being killed during a demonstration. He transferred to Saigon, South Vietnam (now Ho Chi Minh City, Vietnam) in 1970 as a news photo editor, but two years later he returned to his post in Miami, remaining until 1978. He subsequently served in Rome and Chicago. In 1985 Bourdier returned several times to Vietnam, releasing his photographs in the collection *Images of Vietnam*.

OBITUARIES AND OTHER SOURCES:

BOOKS

Who's Who in America, 41st edition, Marquis, 1980.

PERIODICALS

Chicago Tribune, November 25, 1987.

* * *

BOURNE, J(ohn) M. 1949-

PERSONAL: Born April 5, 1949, in Burslem, Staffordshire, England; son of Harold (a brickmaker) and Annie (a housewife; maiden name, Sheldon) Bourne; married Celena Barbara Pietralska (a housewife), July 16, 1977; children: Peter, Thomas. *Education:* University of Leicester, B.A. (with first class honors), 1970, Ph.D., 1976.

ADDRESSES: Home—33 Sir John's Rd., Selly Park, Birmingham B29 7EP, England. *Office*—School of History, University of Birmingham, Birmingham B15 2TT, England.

CAREER: Department of Health and Social Security, London, England, civil servant, 1970-72; Oxford University, Oxford, England, Fereday fellow of St. John's College, 1975-79; University of Birmingham, Birmingham, England, lecturer in modern history, 1979—.

MEMBER: Historical Association.

WRITINGS:

Patronage and Society in Nineteenth-Century England, Edward Arnold, 1986.

Georgian Tiverton, Devon and Cornwall Record Society, 1986.

Britain and the Great War, 1914-1918, Edward Arnold, in press.

WORK IN PROGRESS: Research on the middle class in nineteenth-century England.

SIDELIGHTS: In the *Times Literary Supplement,* David Cannadine described *Patronage and Society in Nineteenth-Century England* as a "pioneering, important and excellently written book." The subject of patronage has received little attention from historical researchers, yet, according to J. M. Bourne, it has had a significant impact throughout the course of British history. The author did not confine his studies to the formal, royal patronage practiced until the early part of the nineteenth century. He concentrated on the development of administrative patronage that came later, and the impact it made upon England's growing middle class. Bourne argued that, contrary to the views of its critics, patronage provided an efficient recruitment system for the kinds of officials required by the industrial revolution. His reviewer concluded: "Like all stimulating books, this makes us want to know more. In the language of the subject, it is a very good job indeed."

Bourne told *CA:* "My interest in patronage arose accidentally. I stumbled across it in the records of the British East India Company. Of course, I was aware of its existence before this time, but to the extent that I thought about it at all it was only to regard it as an antiquated survival from a corrupt past. I had to overcome this prejudice before I could make any progress in a real understanding of the subject, but once I had done so I became convinced that patronage in nineteenth-century England had been generally misunderstood and would remain so unless it was treated in a wider and more sympathetic context than that of a species of political corruption. The role of patronage was much greater than this and it has advantages as well as disadvantages and strengths as well as weaknesses in many areas of English life. Some of these I have tried to explore."

BIOGRAPHICAL/CRITICAL SOURCES:

PERIODICALS

Times Literary Supplement, June 27, 1986.

* * *

BOYINGTON, (Gregory) Pappy 1912-1988

OBITUARY NOTICE: Name originally Gregory Boyington; nicknamed "Pappy" by flyers under his command during World War II; nickname added to legal name c. 1962; born December 4, 1912, in Coeur d'Alene, Idaho; died of cancer, January 11, 1988, in Fresno, Calif.; buried in Arlington National Cemetery, Arlington, Va. Aviator and author. A renowned fighter pilot during World War II, Boyington shot down twenty-eight Japanese planes between 1941 and 1944, making him the fourth-best air ace of his day. He joined the U.S. Marines in 1936, became a pilot the next year and a flight instructor by 1941. That fall, while America was still a neutral nation, he left the Marines for an unofficial American squadron nicknamed the "Flying Tigers," which provided air defense for China in its fight against Japan. Boyington shot down six Japanese fighters within a year to become an ace.

In 1942, with America in the war, Boyington returned to the Marines but was relegated to administrative duties because of a leg injury. The next year he convinced his superiors to let him command a fighter squadron drawn largely from pilots other units had rejected, a group soon known as the "Black Sheep." Based in the South Pacific, they shot down dozens of Japanese planes, and Boyington, known for a colorful disregard of military formalities, became a celebrity. After he disappeared during a mission in 1944 he was awarded the Navy Cross and the Medal of Honor, and upon his release from a Japanese prison camp at the war's end, Americans welcomed him home as a hero. Plagued by alcoholism after he retired from the Marines in 1947, Boyington worked at odd jobs and made appearances at air shows. He titled his 1958 autobiography *Baa, Baa, Black Sheep,* and in the mid-1970s he was technical adviser to a television series based on the book.

OBITUARIES AND OTHER SOURCES:

BOOKS

Boyington, Pappy, *Baa, Baa, Black Sheep,* Putnam, 1958.

Medal of Honor Recipients: 1862-1978, U.S. Government Printing Office, 1979.
Webster's American Military Biographies, Merriam, 1978.

PERIODICALS

Chicago Tribune, January 12, 1988.
Los Angeles Times, January 12, 1988.
New York Times, January 12, 1988.
Washington Post, January 12, 1988.

* * *

BRADFORD, David F(rantz) 1939-

PERSONAL: Born January 8, 1939, in Cambridge, Mass.; son of Mark Waldo and Matilda (Frantz) Bradford; married Gunthild Klaerchen Huober, February 20, 1964; children: Theodore Huober, Catherine Louise. *Education:* Amherst College, B.A. (magna cum laude), 1960; Harvard University, M.S., 1962; graduate study, Churchill College, Cambridge, 1963-64; Stanford University, Ph.D., 1966.

ADDRESSES: Home—50 Pine St., Princeton, N.J. 08542. *Office*—Woodrow Wilson School of Public and International Affairs, Princeton University, Princeton, N.J. 08544.

CAREER: Office of the Secretary of Defense, Washington, D.C., economic consultant in Germany, England, and Washington, 1964-65; Princeton University, Princeton, N.J., assistant professor, 1966-71, associate professor, 1971-75, professor of economics and public affairs, 1975—, associate dean of Woodrow Wilson School of Public and International Affairs, 1974-75, 1978-80, and 1985—, acting dean, 1980 and 1987. Deputy assistant secretary for tax policy, U.S. Treasury Department, 1975-76; research associate and director of research in taxation, National Bureau of Economic Research, 1977—.

MEMBER: American Economic Association, National Tax Association, Econometric Society, Phi Beta Kappa.

AWARDS, HONORS: Woodrow Wilson fellow, 1960-61; Exceptional Service Award from U.S. Treasury Department, 1976; Fulbright fellow in Belgium, 1977.

WRITINGS:

(With U.S. Treasury Tax Policy staff) *Blueprints for Basic Tax Reform,* 2nd edition, Tax Analysts, 1984.
Untangling the Income Tax, Harvard University Press, 1986.

Contributor to journals.

WORK IN PROGRESS: Research on the theory and practice of taxation.

SIDELIGHTS: David F. Bradford told *CA:* "Most of my writing is in the form of technical articles. The first book I wrote was actually a government study, and I had a lot of help from a large professional staff. The next one, *Untangling the Income Tax,* was done on my own, but it still aims to be objective, that is, not to push my own policy preferences. The book deals with a subject that is at once arcane and immediate for millions of Americans. It is part text and part treatise, but it is supposed to interest the mythical educated lay person. If it works, its influence will show up in ten to twenty years, in the form of a much less complex tax system."

BRADLEY, Melanie (Rose) Choukas
See CHOUKAS-BRADLEY, Melanie (Rose)

* * *

BRAGGIN, Mary Vetterling
See VETTERLING-BRAGGIN, Mary (Katherine)

* * *

BRAND, Irene B. 1929-

PERSONAL: Born December 1, 1929, in Southside, W.Va.; daughter of Jabez Clarence (a farmer) and Margaret (a housewife; maiden name, Dalton) Beard; married Rodney P. Brand (a bank officer), April 7, 1956. *Education:* Marshall University, A.B., 1966, M.A., 1970. *Religion:* Baptist.

ADDRESSES: Home—2770 U.S. Route 35 S., Southside, W.Va. 25187.

CAREER: Point Pleasant Junior High School, Point Pleasant, W.Va., teacher of French and American history, 1966—.

MEMBER: Daughters of the American Revolution, Romance Writers of America, West Virginia Writers.

AWARDS, HONORS: Loving Cup Award from Blue Ridge Christian Writer's Conference, 1986, for *Where Morning Dawns.*

WRITINGS:

History of the Fifth Avenue Baptist Church, privately printed, 1972.
(Contributor) Vincie Alessi, editor, *Programs for Advent and Christmas,* Judson, 1981.
(Contributor) Alessi, editor, *Programs for Lent and Easter,* Judson, 1983.
Today's Women (nonfiction), Standard Publishing, 1984.
A Change of Heart (romance), Thomas Nelson, 1984.
Meet Mary and Martha (nonfiction), Standard Publishing, 1985.
A Mighty Flame (romance), Thomas Nelson, 1985.
Only a Clay Vessel (biography), McClain Printing, 1985.
Where Morning Dawns (romance), Zondervan, 1986.
Come Gentle Spring (romance), Zondervan, 1987.
Love Is the Key (romance), Zondervan, 1988.

Contributor to church publications.

WORK IN PROGRESS: Teen-age romance and young adult fiction.

SIDELIGHTS: Irene B. Brand told *CA:* "I wanted to write for as long as I can remember, and even as a child I tried my hand at a novel. I continued writing inconsequential things until about fifteen years ago when I started to consider myself a writer. From the first, I was successful at writing articles, plays, and program materials, but not until 1984 did I publish a book. I've had seven in print since that time.

"I'm a firm believer that it's necessary to write every day if one is to be successful as an author. While I don't sit down at the computer and 'type' each day, I always have a book in progress—research, thought, or actual writing. It's also important that an author read widely and consistently. The most difficult part of writing for me is the first draft. I like research, editing, and rewriting, but the initial writing takes all of my brain power.

"The writing of inspirational romances seemed the opportunity to provide a choice for readers who don't like sensual

romances but still prefer light reading. All of my writing reflects my fundamental Christian beliefs and daily life, although none of my characters are autobiographical.

"My book *A Mighty Flame,* set in England, was influenced by my husband's and my trips to Great Britain. Many of the incidents in the book were personal experiences. This is also true of the historical romances, as we've visited Roanoke Island, N.C., and have made several visits to Jamestown. My first romance, *A Change of Heart,* was set in Nebraska, my husband's native state, which we visit each year."

AVOCATIONAL INTERESTS: Travel (Europe, South America, Scandinavia, New Zealand).

* * *

BRANEGAN, James Augustus III 1950-

PERSONAL: Born June 6, 1950, in Philadelphia, Pa.; son of James Augustus, Jr., and Emmeline Elizabeth (McBurney) Branegan. *Education:* Cornell University, B.A., 1972; Northwestern University, M.S. in Journalism, 1973.

ADDRESSES: Home—2129 Florida Ave. N.W., Washington, D.C. 20008. *Office*—1050 Connecticut Ave. N.W., Suite 850, Washington, D.C. 20036.

CAREER/WRITINGS: Chicago Today, Chicago, Ill., reporter, 1973-74; *Chicago Tribune,* Chicago, reporter, 1974-81; Time, Inc., New York, N.Y., 1981—, began as correspondent for *Time* magazine in Chicago, became energy and environment correspondent in Washington, D.C., science and technical correspondent in Washington, D.C., chief economic correspondent in Washington, D.C.

MEMBER: National Association of Science Writers.

AWARDS, HONORS: Co-recipient of Pulitzer Prize in journalism for special local reporting, 1976.

* * *

BRANIGAN, Keith 1940-

PERSONAL: Born April 15, 1940, in Slough, Buckinghamshire, England; son of Arthur Allan (a clerk) and Constance Gladys (a homemaker; maiden name, Saunders) Branigan; married Kuabrat Sivadith, June 20, 1965; children: Alun, Holly, Tania. *Education:* University of Birmingham, B.A., 1963; Ph.D., 1966.

ADDRESSES: Home—Sheffield, England. *Office*—Department of Prehistory and Archaeology, University of Sheffield, Sheffield S10 2TN, England.

CAREER: University of Birmingham, Birmingham, England, research fellow, 1965-66; University of Bristol, Bristol, England, lecturer in archaeology, 1966-67; University of Sheffield, Sheffield, England, professor of prehistory and archaeology, 1976—. Director of Archaeology in Education; chairman of British Universities Archaeology Committee, 1980-86.

MEMBER: Prehistoric Society (vice-president, 1980-83), Society for the Promotion of Roman Studies, Society of Antiquaries of London (fellow).

WRITINGS:

Copper and Bronzeworking in Early Bronze Age Crete, P. Aestroem, 1968.

The Foundations of Palatial Crete: A Survey of Crete in the Early Bronze Age, Praeger, 1970.

The Tombs of Mesara: A Study of Funerary Architecture and Ritual in Southern Crete, 2800-1700 B.C., Duckworth, 1970.

Latimer: Belgic, Roman, Dark Age, and Early Modern Farm, Bristol Chess Valley Archaeological and Historical Society, 1971.

Town and Country: The Archaeology of Verulamium and the Roman Chilterns, Spurbooks, 1973.

Reconstructing the Past: A Basic Introduction to Archaeology, David & Charles, 1974.

Aegean Metalwork of the Early and Middle Bronze Ages, Clarendon Press, 1974.

Atlas of Ancient Civilizations, John Day, 1976.

Prehistoric Britain: An Illustrated Survey, Spurbooks, 1976.

(Editor with P. J. Fowler) *The Roman West Country: Classical Culture and Celtic Society,* David & Charles, 1976.

The Roman Villa in Southwest England, Moonraker Press, 1977.

Gatcombe: The Excavation and Study of a Romano-British Villa Estate, 1967-1976, British Archaeological Reports, 1978.

(Editor) *Rome and the Brigantes: The Impact of Rome on Northern England,* Department of Prehistory and Archaeology, University of Sheffield, 1980.

Roman Britain: Life in an Imperial Province, Reader's Digest Association, 1980.

(With Michael Vickers) *Hellas: The Civilizations of Ancient Greece,* McGraw, 1980.

(Editor) *Atlas of Archaeology,* St. Martin's, 1982.

Prehistory, Kingfisher, 1984.

The Catuvellauni, Alan Sutton, 1986.

General editor of series "Peoples of Roman Britain," Duckworth, 1973—.

WORK IN PROGRESS: Research on the occupation of caves in the Romano-British period.

SIDELIGHTS: Keith Branigan has been praised by critics for his ability to explain a difficult, technical, and often dry subject to the educated general reader. A. M. Snodgrass wrote in the *Times Literary Supplement,* "*Aegean Metalwork of the Early and Middle Bronze Ages* is the Plain Man's Guide to Aegean prehistory . . . a book which can be understood without wide background knowledge or preconceptions." It is a detailed book, nonetheless. The critic continues, "This is the modern approach at its best: let us see the *entire* picture of the evidence available."

Of *Town and Country,* the *Times Literary Supplement* reported: "The story-line is simple and uncluttered with the provisos that normally beset archaeological writing. It is a straightforward description of life among the upper echelons of Roman society."

Keith Branigan told *CA:* "By the age of eight I had decided I wanted to be an archaeologist. I never consciously worked toward it, but suddenly at the age of eighteen the opportunity was there in front of me and I grabbed it. It was the same, I suppose, with writing. I always enjoyed writing essays, and I had an English master who encouraged me, so when I was offered a contract to write a book I didn't hesitate a minute. I really enjoy writing, particularly those books that try to reach out and introduce new people to the sheer enjoyment of archaeology. But archaeology is one of the fastest moving subjects under the sun—so much new evidence every year, so

many new theories to read and digest—that it becomes increasingly difficult to keep up with it all *and* find time to write.

"My greatest thrill in archaeology was excavating an Early Minoan communal tomb (from about 2500 B.C.) in southern Crete in the early 1970s. Although it had been looted by modern tomb robbers there was much to learn from it about the fascinating people who had built and used it."

BIOGRAPHICAL/CRITICAL SOURCES:

PERIODICALS

Times Literary Supplement, October 12, 1973, January 10, 1975.

* * *

BRASNETT, Bertrand R(ippington) 1893-1988

OBITUARY NOTICE: Born January 22, 1893, in Marham, Norfolk, England; died February 6, 1988. Theologian, clergyman, educator, administrator, and author. Ordained a priest in 1918, Brasnett worked between the mid-1920s and the early 1940s in several posts in the Episcopal diocese of Edinburgh, Scotland. At the Theological College of the Scottish Episcopal Church he was vice-principal from 1925 until 1929, then principal and Pantonian Professor of Theology; at St. Mary's Cathedral he worked at various times as honorary chaplain, canon, and chancellor; and he served the bishop as examining chaplain. He left these posts around 1942 to go to Oxford, England, where he served briefly as select preacher at Oxford University before retiring. Brasnett wrote *The Suffering of the Impassible God, The Infinity of God,* and *God the Worshipful.*

OBITUARIES AND OTHER SOURCES:

BOOKS

Who's Who, 140th edition, St. Martin's, 1988.
Who Was Who Among English and European Authors, 1931-1949, Gale, 1978.

PERIODICALS

Times (London), February 11, 1988.

* * *

BRAUND, Hal
See BRAUND, Harold

* * *

BRAUND, Harold 1913-1988
(Hal Braund)

OBITUARY NOTICE—See index for *CA* sketch: Born November 26, 1913, in Ceylon; died after a long illness, February 18, 1988, in Coffs Harbour, New South Wales, Australia. Business manager, accountant, and author. A recipient of the Military Cross, Braund led Allied fighters in dangerous, Japanese-occupied northern Burma during World War II. After the war he worked in Pakistan as a general manager for Steel Brothers and in Australia as an accountant at Haileybury College. His writings include the books *Distinctly I Remember* and *Calling to Mind: Being Some Account of the First Hundred Years (1870-1970) of Steel Brothers & Co. Ltd.* Under the name Hal Braund he contributed light verse to magazines.

OBITUARIES AND OTHER SOURCES:

PERIODICALS

Times (London), February 19, 1988.

* * *

BRAYMAN, Harold 1900-1988

OBITUARY NOTICE—See index for *CA* sketch: Born March 10, 1900, in Middleburgh, N.Y.; died of heart failure, January 3, 1988, in Wilmington, Del. Educator, public relations director, journalist, and author. Brayman was director of public relations for the Du Pont Company from 1944 to 1965. Prior to joining Du Pont he taught at a New Jersey high school and wrote for various newspapers, including the *Philadelphia Evening Ledger* and the *Houston Chronicle.* At that time—the late 1930s and early 1940s—he also wrote a syndicated column, "The Daily Mirror of Washington." Brayman's books include *Corporate Management in a World of Politics; Developing a Philosophy for Business Action; A History of the Lincoln Club of Delaware* (written with A. O. H. Grier); and *The President Speaks . . . Off the Record.* In addition, he was editor of *Public Relations Journal* in 1956.

OBITUARIES AND OTHER SOURCES:

BOOKS

Who's Who in the World, 8th edition, Marquis, 1986.

PERIODICALS

New York Times, January 10, 1988.
Washington Post, January 7, 1988.

* * *

BREO, Dennis L. 1942-

PERSONAL: Born October 26, 1942, in Freeport, Ill.; son of Leon John and Susie (Sturtevant) Breo; married Barbara Arnold, August 24, 1968 (divorced November 1, 1973); married Suzanne Downs (in sales), August 29, 1981; children: (first marriage) David Christopher. *Education:* Northwestern University, B.S.J., 1964.

ADDRESSES: Home—4201 North Clarendon, Chicago, Ill. 60613. *Office*—*American Medical News,* American Medical Association, 535 North Dearborn St., Chicago, Ill. 60610. *Agent*—Gayle Benderoff, 1120 Park Ave., New York, N.Y. 10028.

CAREER: Freeport Journal-Standard, Freeport, Ill., reporter, 1963-66; American Medical Association, Chicago, Ill., special assignments editor of *American Medical News,* 1966—. *Military service:* Illinois National Guard, 1965-71.

MEMBER: American Association of Medical Society Executives, American Society of Association Executives, National Association of Science Writers, American Medical Writers Association, Sigma Delta Chi.

AWARDS, HONORS: Howard Blakeslee Award from American Heart Association, 1985, for a series of 1984 articles on the "Baby Fae" baboon-heart transplant; six Peter Lisagor Awards for Exemplary Journalism from Chicago Headliners Club; twenty-nine citations from American Society of Business Press Editors and International Association of Business Communicators.

WRITINGS:

(With Noel Keane) *The Surrogate Mother,* Everest House, 1981.
(With Robert S. Eliot) *Is It Worth Dying For? Stress Management Guide,* Bantam, 1984.
Extraordinary Care, Chicago Review Press, 1986.

Contributor to magazines, including *People, Reader's Digest,* and *TV Guide,* and newspapers. Contributing editor of *Chicago Tribune Sunday Magazine.*

WORK IN PROGRESS: Research for a book on AIDS.

SIDELIGHTS: Dennis L. Breo told *CA:* "I am a medical journalist who has traveled widely to provide eyewitness reportage on major medical stories and personalities. My first book, *The Surrogate Mother,* was an outgrowth of an assignment for the American Medical Association (AMA). In it I intended to capture the human drama as well as provide a broad overview of the emerging controversies surrounding the early surrogacy cases. My personal view, then and now, is that while surrogacy offers a revolutionary new hope to infertile couples, the legal, medical, moral, and psychological issues are so new that only time will tell how they will eventually be resolved. My second book, on stress, was motivated by the stress of deadline reporting and my co-author, Dr. Eliot's, personal experience. This world-renowned cardiologist had a stress-induced heart attack as he stood at a podium lecturing on how to prevent heart attacks!

"The third, *Extraordinary Care,* is an anthology of ten years of my AMA exclusive interviews with physicians to the rich and powerful and those who have been caught in major controversies. I was fortunate to obtain exclusive interviews with the physicians who cared for Adolf Hitler, Howard Hughes, Elvis Presley, the shah of Iran, Muhammad Ali, and President Reagan and Pope John Paul (after their 1981 shootings); to talk to newsmakers like the people behind the laetrile controversy, John Hinckley's psychiatrists, convicted Green Beret doctor-murderer Jeffrey MacDonald, Jani Adams, the falsely accused 'Death Angel' of Las Vegas, representative of the medical school on Grenada invaded by U.S. Marines, the surgeons behind the artificial heart and Baby Fae surgeries, and the doctor who refused medical school admission to Allan Bakke, setting off the historic 'reverse-bias' lawsuit; and to profile prominent physicians ranging from Gregory Hemingway, son of the novelist Ernest Hemingway, to transsexual tennis player Renee Richards, from John Rock, discoverer of the 'Pill,' to Story Musgrave, an astronaut who walked in space, from *Joy of Sex* author Alex Comfort to running guru George Sheehan, and from novelist Walker Percy to AMA's James H. Sammons."

In 1986 Breo was named one of the one hundred national finalists for the "Journalist-in-Space" competition sponsored by the National Aeronautics and Space Administration (NASA).

BIOGRAPHICAL/CRITICAL SOURCES:

PERIODICALS

Chicago Tribune, March 17, 1987, May 24, 1987.
Freeport Journal-Standard, June 23, 1979, May 30, 1984.
Gary Post-Tribune, June 21, 1987.

* * *

BRESLOW, Lou 1900(?)-1987

OBITUARY NOTICE: Born c. 1900 in Boston, Mass.; died of pneumonia, November 10 (one source says November 11), 1987, in Woodland Hills, Calif. Film actor, cameraman, and screenwriter. Over the course of fifty years Breslow wrote or helped to write more than one hundred screenplays, including the classic Marx Brothers comedies "Duck Soup" and "Horse Feathers." He achieved notoriety as the co-author, with Val Burton, of the 1951 farce "Bedtime for Bonzo." The film, which spotlighted then-actor Ronald Reagan as a professor in charge of a frisky chimpanzee, was revived years later when Reagan became president of the United States. Breslow worked in Hollywood as an extra and cameraman during the 1920s, later becoming a contract screenwriter for Paramount and Twentieth Century-Fox.

OBITUARIES AND OTHER SOURCES:

PERIODICALS

Los Angeles Times, November 14, 1987.
Washington Post, November 15, 1987.

* * *

BRETTELL, Richard (Robson) 1949-

PERSONAL: Born January 17, 1949, in Rochester, N.Y.; son of Herbert Robson and Ellen (Sackett) Brettell; married Caroline Bieler, June 9, 1973. *Education:* Yale University, B.A., 1971, Ph.D., 1977.

ADDRESSES: Home—3750 North Lake Shore Dr., Chicago Ill. 60613. *Office*—Art Institute of Chicago, South Michigan Ave. at East Adams, Chicago, Ill. 60603.

CAREER: University of Texas at Austin, assistant professor of art history and academic program director, 1976-80; Art Institute of Chicago, Chicago, Ill., Searle Curator of European Painting, 1980—. Adjunct professor at Northwestern University, 1984—; member of faculty at University of Chicago, 1983-84; lecturer at colleges, universities, and museums; member of J. Paul Getty Center for the History of Art, 1987—.

MEMBER: College Art Association of America (member of board of directors, 1986—), Society of Architectural Historians, American Association of Museums, Elizabethan Club, Phelps Association, Midwest Art History Association.

AWARDS, HONORS: Fellow of National Endowment for the Humanities, 1980; visiting fellow at J. Paul Getty Museum, 1985.

WRITINGS:

(With Christopher Lloyd) *A Catalogue of the Drawings by Camille Pissarro in the Ashmolean Museum,* Oxford University Press, 1980.
(With Caroline B. Brettell) *Painters and Peasants in the Nineteenth Century,* Skira Publications, 1983.
(With Nancy Keeler, Sydney Kilgore, and Roy Flukinger) *Paper and Light: The Calotype in Great Britain and France, 1839-1870,* David Godine, 1984.
(With Suzanne Folds McCullagh) *Degas in the Art Institute of Chicago,* Abrams, 1984.
(With Scott Schaefer, Sylvie Gache-Patin, and Francoise Heilbrun) *A Day in the Country: Impressionism and the French Landscape,* Abrams, 1984.
An Impressionist Legacy: The Collection of Sara Lee Corporation, Abbeville, 1986.
(With Steven Starling) *The Art of the Edge: European Frames, 1300-1900,* Art Institute of Chicago, 1986.

French Paintings of the Nineteenth Century: The Art Institute of Chicago, Volume I: *French Salon Artists, 1800-1900,* Volume II: *French Impressionists,* Volume III: *Post Impressionists,* Art Institute of Chicago, 1987.

Contributor to museum journals.

WORK IN PROGRESS: A major Paul Gauguin retrospective exhibition and catalogue, with Charles Stuckey and Francoise Cachin.

* * *

BRINSMEAD, Hesba Fay
See HUNGERFORD, Hesba (Fay) Brinsmead

* * *

BRION, Marcel 1895-1984

PERSONAL: Born November 21, 1895, in Marseilles, France; died October 23, 1984, in Paris, France; son of Raoul (a lawyer) and Jeanne (Berrin de Faultrier) Brion; married Liliane Guerry (a scientific research director), October 26, 1940; children: Patrick, Agnes. *Education:* Graduated from College Champittet and the Aix-en-Provence Faculty of Law.

CAREER: Lawyer in private practice, Marseilles, 1920-24; writer, 1925-84. *Military service:* French Army, 1914-18; received Croix de Guerre.

AWARDS, HONORS: Grand Prix de Litterature from the Academie Francaise, 1953; Prix des Ambassadeurs, 1955; Prix Litteraire de Monaco, 1956; elected to the Academie Francaise, 1964; named officer of the Legion d'honneur (France), commander of the Ordre du Merite (France), officer of the Crown of Italy, officer of the Order of Merit of Italy, and officer of the Order of Merit of the Federal Republic of Germany.

WRITINGS:

NONFICTION

Giotto, Editions Rieder, 1927.
La Vie d'Attila, Gallimard, 1928, revised edition, Club des Librairies de France, 1958, translation by Harold Ward and Richard Glaenzer published as *Attila, the Scourge of God,* R. M. McBride, 1929.
Gobineau, Cahiers du Sud, 1928.
Rudyard Kipling, [Paris], 1929.
Le Caprice espagnol, Gallimard, 1929.
Turner, Editions Rieder, 1929.
Bartolome de las Casas, "Father of the Indians," translated from the French by Coley B. Taylor, Dutton, 1929.
La Vie d'Alaric, Gallimard, 1930, translation by Frederick H. Martens published as *Alaric, the Goth,* R. M. McBride, 1930.
Pierre Puget, Plon, 1930.
La Vie des Huns, Gallimard, 1931, translation by Frederick H. Martens published as *The Story of the Huns,* R. M. McBride, 1931.
L'Aventureuse Reussite de Theodora, [Paris], 1934, translation by Warre Bradley Wells published as *Crowned Courtesan: The Tale of Theodora, Empress of Byzantium,* J. Long, 1936.
Fredegonde et Brunehaut, Editions de France, 1935.
Theodoric, roi des Ostrogoths, 454-526, Payot, 1935.
Laurent le magnifique, A. Michel, 1937.
La Resurrection des villes mortes, 2 volumes, Payot, 1937-38, revised edition, Plon, 1959, translation by Neil Mann published as *The World of Archaeology,* Macmillan, 1962, Volume I: *India, China, America,* Volume II: *Central Asia, Africa, the Near East.*
Bosch, [Paris], 1938.
Caterina Cornaro, regina di Cipro, Fratelli Treves, 1938, original French edition published as *Catherine Cornaro, reine de Chypre,* A. Michel, 1945.
Blanche de Castille, femme de Louis VIII, mere de Saint-Louis, 1188-1252, Editions de France, 1939.
Gruenewald, Plon, 1939.
Michel-Ange, A. Michel, 1939, revised edition published as *Michel-Ange, 1475-1564,* Club des Editeurs, 1960, translation by James Whitall published as *Michelangelo,* Greystone Press, 1940.
Les Amantes: Diotima, Marianna Alcoforado, Frederique Brion, Charlotte Stieglitz, Louise Labe, A. Michel, 1941.
La Reine Jeanne, R. Laffont, 1944.
Rembrandt, A. Michel, 1946.
Charles la Temeraire: Grand-duc d'Occident, Hachette, 1947, reprinted, J. Tallandier, 1977.
Lumiere de la Renaissance, R. Laffont, 1948.
Machiavel, A. Michel, 1948.
Savonarole, le heraut de Dieu, La Colombe, 1948.
Frederic II de Hohenstaufen, J. Tallandier, 1948.
De Cesar a Charlemagne, des origines a l'an 1000, Fayard, 1949.
(With Philippe Lefrancois, J. L. Vaudoyer, and Jean Desternes) *L'Italie,* Ode, 1949, published in English as *Italy,* Whittlesey House, 1950.
Goethe, A. Michel, 1949.
Les Mains dans la peinture, A. Michel, 1949.
(Editor) *Georges Rouault* (text in French, English, and German), E. S. Herrmann, 1950.
Leonard de Vinci, A. Michel, 1952, translation by Lucy Norton published as *Leonardo da Vinci,* Heinemann, 1955.
La Revolte des gladiateurs, Amiot-Dumont, 1952.
Le Pape et le prince: Les Borgia, Hachette, 1953.
Bayard, Hachette, 1953.
Schumann et l'ame romantique, A. Michel, 1954, translation by Geoffrey Sainsbury published as *Schumann and the Romantic Age,* Macmillan, 1956.
Histoire de l'Egypte, Fayard, 1954.
Mozart, Amiot-Dumont, 1955, revised and illustrated edition published by Club des Libraires de France, 1956.
Leonor Fini et son oeuvre, J. J. Pauvert, 1955.
Les Animaux, un grand theme de l'art, Horizons de France, 1955, translation by Frances Hogarth-Gaute published as *Animals in Art,* F. Watts, 1959.
Klee, A. Somogy, 1955.
La Bible dans l'art: Un Choix des plus belles oeuvres, peintures, sculptures, dessins, et miniatures inspires par l'Ancien Testament, Phaidon, 1956, translation by Lucy Norton and Elizabeth Osborne published simultaneously as *The Bible in Art: Miniatures, Paintings, Drawings, and Sculptures Inspired by the Old Testament.*
L'Ombrie: Couverture d'Yves Brayer, Arthaud, 1956.
Provence, translation by S. G. Colverson, Essential Books, 1956, original French edition published as *La Provence,* Arthaud, 1958.
Art abstrait, A. Michel, 1956.
La Peinture moderne de l'impressionnisme a l'art abstrait, D'Art Somogy, 1957, translation by Stuart Hood published as *Modern Painting, From Impressionism to Abstract Art,* Thames and Hudson, 1958.
(Contributor) *Art Since 1945,* Abrams, 1958.

(Author of introduction) *Raoul Dufy: Paintings and Watercolours,* translation of introduction by Lucy Norton, Phaidon, 1958.

(Editor) Jean Cocteau and others, *Leonard de Vinci,* Hachette, 1959.

Chagall, Somogy, 1959, translation by A. H. N. Molesworth published as *Chagall,* Abrams, 1962.

La Peinture allemande, P. Tisne, 1959, translation by W. J. Strachan published as *German Painting,* Universe Books, 1959.

(With Hermann Oldenberg) *Le Bouddha,* Part One: "La Vie historique" by Oldenburg, Part Two: "La Vie legendaire" by Brion, Club des Libraires de France (Paris), 1959.

Kandinsky, Somogy, 1960, English translation published by Abrams, 1962.

La Vie quotidienne a Vienne a l'epoque de Mozart et de Schubert, Hachette, 1960, translation by Jean Stewart published as *Daily Life in the Vienna of Mozart and Schubert,* Weidenfeld & Nicolson, 1961.

Ces Palais ou Dieu habite: L'Architecture religieuse de 1400 a 1800, Librairie Artheme A. Fayard, 1960.

Durer, l'homme et son oeuvre, Somogy, 1960, translation by James Cleugh published as *Durer, His Life and Work,* Tudor, 1960.

Pompeii and Herculaneum: The Glory and the Grief, photographs by Edwin Smith, translation by John Rosenberg, Crown, 1960, original French edition published as *Pompei et Herculanum,* A. Michel, 1962.

Art fantastique, A. Michel, 1961.

Paris, photographs by Willy Ronis and Roger Henrard, Arthaud, 1962, translation by Claire Eliane Engel published as *Paris in Color,* Rand McNally, 1964.

Frances Bott (text in French and German), Bodensee-Verlag, 1962.

Venise, photographs by Edwin Smith, A. Michel, 1962, translation by Neil Mann published as *Venice, the Masque of Italy,* Crown, 1962.

L'Allemagne romantique, A. Michel, Volume I, 1962, Volume II, 1963, Volume III: *Le Voyage initiatique,* 1977, Volume IV: *Le Voyage initiatique 2,* 1978.

L'Art romantique, Hachette, 1963, translation by David Carroll published as *Art of the Romantic Era: Romanticism, Classicism, Realism,* Praeger, 1966.

Vermeer, Editions Aimery Somogy, 1963, translation by Sally Marks published as *Vermeer,* Oldbourne Press, 1962.

(Editor) *Tamerlan,* A. Michel, 1963.

L'Age d'or de la peinture hollandaise, Meddens (Brussels), 1964.

(Contributor) *Rembrandt,* Hachette, 1965.

Discours de reception de Marcel Brion a l'Academie francaise et reponse de Rene Huyghe, A. Michel, 1965.

L'Oeil, l'esprit, et la main du peintre, Plon, 1966.

La Musique et l'amour, Hachette, 1967.

Peinture romantique, A. Michel, 1967.

De Pompeii a l'ile de Paques, Gautier-Languereau, 1967.

Discours de reception a l'Academie francaise et reponse de Marcel Brion, Grasset, 1967.

L'Art fantastique, L'Inter, 1968.

La Grande Aventure de la peinture religieuse: Le Sacre et sa representation, Perrin, 1968.

Le Siecle des Medicis, photographs by Wim Swaan and others, A. Michel, 1969, translation by Giles and Heather Cremonesi published as *The Medici: A Great Florentine Family,* Crown, 1969.

Le Louvre, musee des maitres, Editions Cercle d'art, 1970, translation by Matila Simon published as *Masterpieces of the Louvre,* Abrams, c. 1970.

Titien, Somogy, 1971.

Quatre Siecles de surrealisme: L'Art fantastique dans la gravure, P. Belfond, 1973.

Paul Cezanne, Plantyn/Delta/Kluwer, 1974, English translation published as *Cezanne,* Doubleday, 1974.

Guardi, H. Screpei, 1976.

Ernst Fuchs de Draeger, Draeger Editeur, 1977, English translation published as *Ernst Fuchs,* Abrams, c. 1983.

FICTION

Le Theatre des esprits (short stories), Editions de la librairie de l'universite, 1941.

Un Enfant de la terre et du ciel (novel), A. Michel, 1943.

Les Escales de la haute nuit (short stories), R. Laffont, 1942, reprinted, 1965.

Le Portrait de Belinda (short stories), R. Laffont, 1945.

La Chanson de l'oiseau etranger et autres contes (short stories), A. Michel, 1958.

La Ville de sable (novel), A. Michel, 1959.

La Folie Celadon (novel), A. Michel, 1963.

La Rose de cire (novel), A. Michel, 1964.

L'Enchanteur (novel), A. Michel, 1965.

De l'autre cote de la foret (novel), A. Michel, 1966.

Les Miroirs et les gouffres (novel), A. Michel, 1968.

L'Ombre d'un arbre mort (novel), A. Michel, 1970.

Les Escales de la haute nuit et autres nouvelles fantastiques (short stories), Verviers, Gerard, 1971.

Nous avons traverse la montagne (novel), A. Michel, 1972.

Chateau d'ombres (novel), A. Michel, 1974.

Le Fete de la Tour des Ames (novel), A. Michel, 1974.

Algues: Fragments d'un journal intime (novel), A. Michel, 1976.

Le Journal du visiteur (novel), A. Michel, 1980.

Le Chateau de la princesse Ilse (novel), A. Michel, 1981.

Contributor of short stories and articles to newspapers and magazines.

SIDELIGHTS: Prolific French author Marcel Brion pursued a broad range of literary interests in a career spanning seven decades. A longtime critic specializing in German and Italian literature for the Paris daily *Le Monde,* Brion wrote several books of literary criticism and published more than twenty of his own novels and short story collections. Brion also distinguished himself as an art critic and historian in numerous works on Renaissance and modernist painting, including full-scale studies of Michelangelo Buonarroti, Leonardo da Vinci, Johannes Vermeer, Rembrandt Harmensz van Rijn, Paul Cezanne, Paul Klee, Marc Chagall, and Wassily Kandinsky. In addition to his writings on literature and art, Brion produced numerous historical biographies on subjects as varied as Attila the Hun and the Medici family of Renaissance Florence. He also contributed texts to several popular archaeological and travel photography books, including *Pompeii and Herculaneum* and *Venice, the Masque of Italy*. Brion's vivacious, popular style—which the French termed *haute vulgarization,* or "high vulgarization"—was sometimes criticized by academic experts in the many different fields he explored, but his clear exposition and cogent insights have been credited with helping to make a wealth of cultural knowledge accessible to the general reader.

As a cultural historian, Brion was particularly interested in the German romantic movement of the late eighteenth and nineteenth centuries and the Italian Renaissance of the fifteenth

and sixteenth centuries. Among the author's principal works on romanticism—a literary and artistic sensibility that exalted individual creativity, freedom of form, and the primacy of the senses and emotions over reason and intellect—are his studies of poet Johann Wolfgang von Goethe and composer Robert Schumann and a four-volume work of literary criticism, *L'Allemagne romantique*. The third volume of this work, subtitled *Le Voyage initiatique,* compares the important Romantic theme of spiritual initiation, or the achievement of a transcendental experience that shatters mundane reality, in nineteenth-century literature to such modern German authors as Hermann Hesse. In his copiously illustrated *Art of the Romantic Era,* Brion looks at romanticism's influence on architecture, sculpture, and painting in Germany, other European countries, Russia, and the United States.

One of Brion's major books on the Italian Renaissance is *The Medici: A Great Florentine Family,* a cultural and political history featuring photographs by Wim Swaan. The Medici, originally a family of humble Tuscan farmers, rose to dominate the political and cultural life of the city-state of Florence in the fifteenth and sixteenth centuries by means of their powerful banking and merchant operations and remarkable political skill. While turning Florence's republican system of government into a kind of *de facto* monarchy, Cosimo de' Medici, his grandson Lorenzo "the Magnificent," and other family leaders also actively supported and nurtured many of the city's extraordinary artists, including Donatello, Lorenzo Ghiberti, Sandro Botticelli, and Michelangelo, and effectively transformed a provincial town into one of the cultural capitals of Europe. Brion discusses the art works reproduced in *The Medici* in the context of the prevailing artistic and intellectual climate and provides biographical sketches of the major artistic and political personalities of the day. Although the bulk of the volume is devoted to the dynamic Renaissance Medici, the narrative follows the family's fortunes from the time they were rulers of Florence until the mid-eighteenth century, when the city came under the domain of Empress Maria Teresa of Austria and when the last Medici, Archduchess Anna Maria Ludovica, bequeathed the family's vast art collection to the Florentine public.

Archaeological discovery underpins Brion's cultural history in *Pompeii and Herculaneum: The Glory and the Grief.* Drawing on the findings of two hundred years of archaeological excavations, the author attempts to recreate daily life in the first-century Italian cities before they were destroyed by the cataclysmic volcanic eruption of Mount Vesuvius in 79 A.D. The *Times Literary Supplement* described the oversized volume as "a work of quite scholarly popularization, adorned with beautiful photographs" by Edwin Smith and added, "Brion writes with charm and vivacity and knows how to make archaeological facts and artefacts come to life." Brion similarly used archaeological findings to illustrate everyday life in ancient societies in his two-volume survey of seminal world cultures, *The World of Archaeology*. Written in a lively and popular style, the work discusses the aim and techniques of modern archaeology, the important field discoveries of this century, and current theories about the beginnings of civilization in the Indus Valley, China, America, Central Asia, Africa, and the Near East.

Though better known as an art critic and cultural historian, Brion was also a successful writer of fiction. Many of his works display fantastic or surrealistic themes and imagery, as in his 1981 novel, *Le Chateau de la princesse Ilse*. The story, set in a small Swiss mountain village, turns on the relationship between a young girl, Ilse, and an unnamed adult narrator, both of whom are obsessed by castles. Reality and fantasy mingle as Ilse's descriptions of her trips to a mysterious castle in the nearby forest spark memories of castle dreams from the narrator's childhood. "Brion attempts to evoke in his readers a sense of wonder, to appeal to the fantasy of the child that dwells in the adult now preoccupied with utilitarian concerns," noted *French Review* critic Philip H. Solomon. Other notable works of fiction by Brion include the novel *La Rose de cire* and the short story collection *Les Escales de la haute nuit et autres nouvelles fantastiques*.

BIOGRAPHICAL/CRITICAL SOURCES:

PERIODICALS

French Review, October, 1982.
Guardian Weekly, February 13, 1977.
History Today, February, 1970.
Times (London), October 30, 1984.
Times Literary Supplement, November 13, 1969, March 29, 1974.
Washington Post, September 2, 1969.*

—*Sketch by Curtis Skinner*

* * *

BRITT, George (William Hughes) 1895-1988

OBITUARY NOTICE: Born October 5, 1895, in Millerburg, Ky.; died February 4, 1988, in Hightstown, N.J. Educator, editor, journalist, and author. Britt worked for fourteen years as a feature writer at the *New York World-Telegram* and the *New York Post,* and he was also employed by papers in Chicago, Oklahoma City, and Kansas City, Missouri. For more than fifteen years he taught newswriting at Columbia University. Britt wrote *The Fifth Column Is Here; Forty Years, Forty Millions: The Career of Frank A. Munsey;* and, with Heywood Broun, *Christians Only*. He also edited *Shoeleather and Printers' Ink, 1924-1974*.

OBITUARIES AND OTHER SOURCES:

BOOKS

American Authors and Books: 1640 to the Present Day, 3rd revised edition, Crown, 1972.

PERIODICALS

New York Times, February 7, 1988.

* * *

BROUN, Heywood Oren 1950(?)-1987
(Hob Broun)

OBITUARY NOTICE: Born c. 1950, in New York, N.Y.; died of asphyxiation, December 16 (one source says December 15), 1987, in Portland, Ore. Author. Paralyzed as the result of a spinal tumor several years before he died, Broun wrote by blowing air through a tube linked to the keyboard of a computer. He needed a respirator to breathe, and its failure caused his death. Broun was named after his father, well-known journalist Heywood Hale Broun, and sometimes adopted the first name Hob for his writings, which include the novels *Odditorium* and *Inner Tube* and a collection of short stories awaiting publication when he died.

OBITUARIES AND OTHER SOURCES:

PERIODICALS

New York Times, December 24, 1987.
Washington Post, December 28, 1987.

* * *

BROUN, Hob
See BROUN, Heywood Oren

* * *

BROWN, Judith K.

PERSONAL: Married Maurice F. Brown (a professor), 1957 (died); children: Frederick W. K., Mathilde Charlotte. *Education:* Cornell University, B.S., 1952; Harvard University, M.Ed., 1954, Ed.D., 1962; London Institute of Education, London, Certificate in Child Development, 1955; postdoctoral study at Radcliffe College, 1967-69.

ADDRESSES: Office—Department of Sociology and Anthropology, Oakland University, Rochester, Mich. 48063.

MEMBER: Association for Anthropology and Gerontology, American Anthropological Association (fellow), Current Anthropology (associate), Society for Psychological Anthropology, American Association of University Professors, Canadian Ethnology Society.

AWARDS, HONORS: Postdoctoral fellowship from Bunting Institute of Radcliffe College, 1967 and 1968; Oakland University faculty research grants, 1970 and 1981, and Educational Development Fund small grant award, 1982.

CAREER: Oakland University, Rochester, Mich., lecturer, 1964-66, assistant professor, 1969-75, associate professor, 1975-83, professor of anthropology, 1983—.

WRITINGS:

(Editor with Virginia Kerns) *In Her Prime: A New View of Middle-Aged Women,* Bergin & Garvey, 1985.

Contributor of articles to collections, including *Toward an Anthropology of Women,* Monthly Review Press, 1975; *Sex Differences: Social and Biological Perspectives,* Anchor Books, 1976; *Handbook of Cross-Cultural Human Development,* Garland, 1981. Contributor of articles and book reviews to scholarly journals, including *Current Anthropology, Ethos, Anthropos,* and *American Anthropologist.*

WORK IN PROGRESS: Research on relationships between mothers-in-law and daughters-in-law in various cultures.

BIOGRAPHICAL/CRITICAL SOURCES:

PERIODICALS

American Anthropologist, September, 1986.
Newsweek, February 14, 1983.

* * *

BROWN, Rebecca 1956-

PERSONAL: Born March 27, 1956, in San Diego, Calif.; daughter of Vergil Neal, Jr. (a military officer) and Barbara Ann (a social worker; maiden name, Wildman) Brown. *Education:* George Washington University, B.A. (with honors), 1978; University of Virginia, M.F.A., 1981. *Politics:* Liberal Democrat.

ADDRESSES: Home—Seattle, Wash., and London, England. *Agent*—Pamela Joseph, 12 Eresby House, Rutland Gate SW7 1BG London, England.

CAREER: Office worker, 1978-85; teacher and artist in residence in Washington, 1985-87; full-time writer, 1987—. Freelance journalist and editor; worked as carpenter and rock music critic.

MEMBER: Associated Writing Programs, Phi Beta Kappa.

AWARDS, HONORS: Artist in residence of Washington State Arts Commission, 1984-87.

WRITINGS:

The Evolution of Darkness (short stories), Brilliance Books, 1984.
The Haunted House (novel), Picador, 1986, Viking, 1987.
The Children's Crusade (novel), Picador, in press.

Work represented in anthologies, including *Mae West Is Dead,* Faber, 1983; *Passion Fruit,* Pandora, 1986. Contributor to magazines, including *Little Magazine, Rock Creek, Bridges, George Washington Review,* and *Bumbershoot,* and to newspapers, including *Seattle Times, Seattle Woman, Women's Review* (London), *Northwest Passage,* and *Lost Music Network.*

WORK IN PROGRESS: The Dogs of God, a novel, publication expected in 1990.

SIDELIGHTS: Rebecca Brown's first novel, *The Haunted House,* consists of three parts. The first is a reminiscence of Robin Daley's childhood and adolescence as the child of a Navy pilot. It is the story of move after move, to homes from which her father was absent more often than not. Eventually the narrator begins to invent fantasies to describe and glamorize her missing father. To reviewer Barbara Fisher Williamson of the *Washington Post,* this is the most fascinating part of the book: "In bright images and direct language, narrator Robin Daley tells of her early life, a life distorted by loss and sudden departure."

In the second part of the novel, distortion intrudes more sharply into the narrative as Robin's mother intervenes, now "famous and apparently free of the past, even to the point of denying she has any children," according to *Times Literary Supplement* critic Jeanette Winterson. In part three, the allegory of the haunted house becomes apparent. Robin and her female lover attempt to remodel the mother's house, and the home becomes a symbol for Robin's mind, in which reality has crumbled and from which escape seems impossible. Winterson wrote: "There is nothing tentative about Brown's writing; we believe her because she has a sure hand, because she can make something bizarre into something likely, and because it is our own fears we recognize and our own ability disastrously to re-invent." Deborah Moggach of the London *Sunday Times* praised Brown's "new voice—ripe and imaginative, often funny, and sliding craftily between fact and wishful fantasy."

Brown told *CA:* "I've always wanted to write and I always have. Both the short stories in *The Evolution of Darkness* and my first novel, *The Haunted House,* explore ideas about the betrayal of intimacy, especially the intimacies in families or between lovers. Though the surreal and fantastical elements in these books aren't autobiographical, I think of them as emotionally autobiographical: real late-night-sweating-blood kind of stuff. I get away from a bit of that in my third book, *The Children's Crusade.* It generated similarly passionate emotions, but getting some distance from my past (like leaving the

United States for Europe) has let me see some of my personal issues in terms of a bigger picture.

"The title, *The Children's Crusade,* and much of the metaphor and action is taken from that amazing incident in the late Middle Ages when a troop of kids marched off to re-conquer the Holy Lands for the Christian church. *The Children's Crusade* continues, like *The Evolution of Darkness* and *The Haunted House,* to explore the incredible power of family intimacies. But it also looks at how individuals are molded by the peculiar hysterias and mass movements of their society.

"I've also been researching and writing what I hope will be my next novel, *The Dogs of God.* I've been going to church a lot—high Anglican and high Roman Catholic—though I'm not a member of either. I've been reading Spanish and English mystics and walking around cloisters and convents and cathedrals and gasping at accounts of the medieval and Spanish Inquisitions.

"I've found the climate for my work as a writer much more amenable in England than in the United States, where I live during part of the year. I like working in London because it's easy for me to drop out socially for a while to write, and no one picks at me. Nevertheless, I'm glad I've been able to have a schedule of social stuff in Seattle, Washington, for a few months, working for the bulk of the year in London."

BIOGRAPHICAL/CRITICAL SOURCES:

PERIODICALS

Sunday Times (London), June 29, 1986.
Times Literary Supplement, August 1, 1986.
Washington Post, February 10, 1987.

* * *

BROWNING, Rufus P(utnam) 1934-

PERSONAL: Born March 16, 1934, in Cleveland, Ohio; son of Robert Hamilton (a physician) and Lucy (a pianist; maiden name, Beckett) Browning; married Patricia Jean Parker, April 28, 1956 (divorced); married Elizabeth Barkin, March 20, 1982; children: (first marriage) Marla, Ross Parker, Charles Mentzer, Mark Woods. *Education:* Oberlin College, A.B., 1954; Yale University, M.A., 1955, Ph.D., 1961.

ADDRESSES: Office—Department of Political Science, San Francisco State University, San Francisco, Calif. 94132.

CAREER: University of Wisconsin—Madison, assistant professor of political science, 1961-67; Michigan State University, East Lansing, associate professor of political science, 1967-73; San Francisco State University, San Francisco, Calif., professor of political science, 1974—, chairman of department, 1974-77. Senior research political scientist at Institute for Government Studies, University of California, Berkeley, 1976-81. *Military service:* U.S. Army, 1955-57.

MEMBER: American Political Science Association, American Society for Public Administration, Policy Studies Organization.

AWARDS, HONORS: Ford Foundation fellow, 1959-60; fellow of Social Science Research Council, 1960-61; grants from National Science Foundation, 1965-67, 1976-81, and American Council of Learned Societies, 1968, 1972.

WRITINGS:

(With Dale Rogers Marshall and David H. Tabb) *Protest Is Not Enough: The Struggle of Blacks and Hispanics for Equality in Urban Affairs,* University of California Press, 1984.

Contributor to political science journals.

WORK IN PROGRESS: An edited collection of original articles on minority politics in major U.S. cities, publication by Longman expected in 1989.

* * *

BROWNLOW, Cecil Alexander III 1926-1988

OBITUARY NOTICE: Born September 21, 1926, in Columbia (one source says Mount Pleasant), Tenn.; died of lung cancer, February 23, 1988, in Potomac, Md. Journalist. Brownlow worked for *Aviation Week and Space Technology* for more than twenty years, and in 1972 his writing and reporting garnered him both the James J. Strebig and Robert S. Ball awards of the Aviation/Space Writers Association. After training as a Navy pilot during the mid-1940s, Brown joined the International News Service in 1949, and he reported on the Korean War before he left for a job on the rewrite desk of the *New York Herald Tribune* in 1952. He joined *Aviation Week* three years later, serving as Washington bureau chief from 1956 to 1960 and national editor from 1964 until 1972, when he became executive editor. Brown left the magazine in 1977 and subsequently ran his own newspapers in New York's Hudson Valley. In 1981 he went to Washington, D.C., as an editor for the Flight Safety Foundation.

OBITUARIES AND OTHER SOURCES:

BOOKS

Who's Who in America, 40th edition, Marquis, 1978.

PERIODICALS

Washington Post, February 25, 1988.

* * *

BROWNSTEIN, Karen (Osney) 1944-

PERSONAL: Born May 19, 1944, in Madison, Wis.; daughter of Bert (a food company executive) and Lucille (a humorist; maiden name, Glass) Osney; married; children: two sons. *Education:* Barnard College, A.B., 1966; Northwestern University, M.A.T., 1977.

ADDRESSES: Home and Office—415 Lowell Ave., Palo Alto, Calif. 93401.

CAREER: Public relations consultant to nonprofit agencies, 1970-76; Our Stories/Ourselves Fiction Writing Workshops, Palo Alto, Calif., founder and teacher, 1977—. Vice-president for communications, Friends of Brain Tumor Research; member of board of directors, Stanford University Hillel Foundation.

MEMBER: Literary Guild.

WRITINGS:

Brainstorm, Macmillan, 1980.
Memorial Day (novel), Doubleday, 1983.
In a Certain Light (novel), Putnam, 1985.

Also author of television play, "Our Play's Last Act."

WORK IN PROGRESS: Film at Eleven, a novel about heroes, real and imagined; *Crash,* a novel about surviving; a film adaptation of *Memorial Day.*

SIDELIGHTS: Karen Brownstein commented to *CA:* "Playwright, biographer, and teacher Howard Teichmann was the mentor of my career from the beginning. His best advice was 'the only way to screw 'em is to go on writing.' I believe the wisest words on writing came from Cynthia Ozick who said, 'Writing is an act of courage.' I would amend that to say, writing is an act of courage performed with no witnesses."

* * *

BUISSERET, David 1934-

PERSONAL: Surname is pronounced "Bwee-se-*ray*"; born December 18, 1934, in Wight, England; immigrated to United States, 1980; son of Ralph (a teacher) and Margaret (Hill) Buisseret; married Patricia Connolly (a researcher), 1961; children: Timothy, Kate, Claire, Mark, Paul. *Education:* Corpus Christi College, Cambridge, B.A., 1958, Ph.D., 1961. *Politics:* "Tory Democrat." *Religion:* Roman Catholic.

ADDRESSES: Home—5126 Lunt Ave., Skokie, Ill. 60077. *Office*—Newberry Library, 60 West Walton, Chicago, Ill. 60610.

CAREER: University of the West Indies, Kingston, Jamaica, lecturer, 1964-72, reader, 1972-75, professor of history, 1975-80; Newberry Library, Chicago, Ill., research director, 1980—. Member of Jamaica National Trust Commission. *Military service:* British Army, 1953-55; became lieutenant. Royal Air Force Volunteer Reserve, pilot officer, 1955-61.

MEMBER: International Society for the History of Cartography, Royal Historical Society, French Historical Society, Society for Nautical Research, Association of Caribbean Historians, Chicago Maritime Society.

AWARDS, HONORS: Premiere medaille from Institut de France, 1972.

WRITINGS:

Sully, Allen & Unwin, 1968.
(With Michael Pawson) *Port Royal, Jamaica,* Oxford University Press, 1975.
(With Jack Tyndale-Biscoe) *Historic Jamaica From the Air,* Ginn & Co., 1975.
Historic Architecture of the Caribbean, Heinemann, 1980.
Henry IV, Allen & Unwin, 1984.

WORK IN PROGRESS: Editing the memoirs of Maximilien de Bethune, Duc de Sully; *Historic Illinois From the Air,* 1990; research on cartography of Renaissance Europe and cartography of the Spanish colonial empire.

SIDELIGHTS: David Buisseret told *CA:* "I have tried to write only about subjects and problems that interested me. This has meant that while I began as a historian of sixteenth-century France, I have been seduced into studying as well the history of the other places I have lived in, particularly Jamaica and the midwestern United States. I feel a strong need to understand my surroundings in space as well as in time, which is no doubt why I much enjoy trying to help scholars use the rich cartographic resources of the Newberry Library. My own major project, which I hope will one day become a book, aims to explain how Europeans, who in 1400 generally had not seen a map, by 1600 used them for a very wide variety of activities. I think this development is very important both for intellectual history and for understanding many other areas."

BIOGRAPHICAL/CRITICAL SOURCES:

PERIODICALS

Times Literary Supplement, September 28, 1984.

* * *

BUNGE, Nancy L(iddell) 1942-

PERSONAL: Born May 13, 1942, in La Crosse, Wis.; daughter of Jonathan Clement (a lawyer) and Anne (a teacher; maiden name, Gunn) Bunge. *Education:* Radcliffe College, A.B. (cum laude), 1964; University of Chicago, M.A., 1966; University of Wisconsin—Madison, Ph.D., 1970.

ADDRESSES: Home—401 Rampart Way, East Lansing, Mich. 48823. *Office*—Department of American Thought and Language, 295 East Bessey Hall, Michigan State University, East Lansing, Mich. 48824.

CAREER: George Washington University, Washington, D.C., instructor, 1968-70, assistant professor of American literature, 1970-73; Michigan State University, East Lansing, assistant professor, 1973-79, associate professor, 1979-84, professor of American thought and language, 1984—. Senior Fulbright lecturer in American literature and culture at University of Vienna, 1986-87.

MEMBER: Modern Language Association of America.

WRITINGS:

(Contributor) Hilbert H. Campbell and Charles E. Modlin, editors, *Sherwood Anderson: Centennial Studies,* Whitston, 1976.
(Contributor) David D. Anderson, editor, *Critical Essays on Sherwood Anderson,* G. K. Hall, 1981.
Finding the Words: Conversations With Writers Who Teach, Swallow Press/Ohio University Press, 1985.

WORK IN PROGRESS: The Writer and the University; a Jungian analysis of Nathaniel Hawthorne's fiction.

SIDELIGHTS: Nancy L. Bunge told *CA:* "In 1979, I set out to interview writers who teach because I hoped they could offer fresh perspectives on university education, particularly in the humanities. The fifty writers I've spoken with have given me far more than I expected. I've had some trouble distancing myself from their remarks and drawing my own conclusions because the people I interviewed were so kind, but I'm certain that no matter how many more writers I speak with or how critically I come to regard their statements, I'll always wish I could be as lively, honest, and generous as the poets and novelists who've spoken to me."

BIOGRAPHICAL/CRITICAL SOURCES:

PERIODICALS

Washington Post Book Review, February 3, 1985.

* * *

BUNGE, Robert Pierce 1930-

PERSONAL: Born September 24, 1930, in Oak Park, Ill.; son of George Herbert and Caroline Elizabeth (Pierce) Bunge; married Muriel Perlman, March 17, 1956; stepchildren: Harmon Berns, Hilary Berns. *Education:* University of Mexico,

B.A., 1950; Roosevelt University, M.A., 1973; DePaul University, Ph.D., 1982.

ADDRESSES: Home—6 Cherrywood Court, Vermillion, S.D. 57069. *Office*—Department of Modern Languages, University of South Dakota, University and Clark Sts., Vermillion, S.D. 57069.

CAREER: Teacher of adult evening classes at public schools in Maine Township and Park Ridge, Ill., 1962-74; DePaul University, Chicago, Ill., lecturer in philosophy, 1974-79; University of South Dakota, Vermillion, associate professor of Lakota (Sioux) language, 1979—. Lecturer at Roosevelt University, 1971, 1973, 1975, and 1977; director of Native American Plains Projects. Regional director of National Exchange Club; member of Vermillion City Council. *Military service:* U.S. Army, 1952-54; served in Pacific theater.

MEMBER: International Platform Association, American Philosophical Association, Theosophical Society, Siouan and Caddoan Linguistic Society, Rocky Mountain Language Society.

WRITINGS:

(Contributor) E. T. Paulson, editor, *Sioux Collections,* Institute of Indian Studies, University of South Dakota, 1982.
An American Urphilosophie: An American Philosophy, B.P. (Before Pragmatism), University Press of America, 1984.
Lakota Children's Dictionary and Coloring Book, Native American Plains Projects, Inc., 1986.
Dakota Children's Dictionary and Coloring Book, Native American Plains Projects, Inc., 1987.
Nakota Children's Dictionary and Coloring Book, Native American Plains Projects, Inc., 1988.

Contributor to magazines, including *Contemporary Philosophy, Listening, Intellect,* and *Ultimate Reality and Meaning.*

WORK IN PROGRESS: A complete trilogy of Sioux dialects; *Philosophy of the Teton Sioux,* a revision of *An American Urphilosophie;* a history of Indian life from the Indian point of view; translating *Lakota Tales,* originally written in Lakota by Eugene Buechel; a textbook on the Dakota language; a book on modern Indian psychology; an article on the farm life of the Iowa Indian, to be included in the book *Gunkholing in Iowa,* edited by Robert Sayre.

SIDELIGHTS: Robert Pierce Bunge is competent in twenty-two languages. He has taught Russian, Arabic, Spanish, French, Portuguese, German, Japanese, and both Mandarin and Cantonese Chinese. He currently teaches the Lakota language, as well as Russian, Spanish, and Chinese.

Bunge told *CA:* "My degree is in philosophy, specifically the philosophy of language. I had hoped to use my study of all the world philosophies, both of the majority and minority groups of peoples in the world, plus the languages I know, to gain a better grasp of the problems of mankind and make a contribution to advance—however slightly—man's peaceful progress. The nuclear holocaust—the destruction of the ecological order—I am convinced, are problems stemming from a lopsided philosophy of life, permeated not by science, but by 'scientism.' Therefore I have undertaken an in-depth study of relationships, a study of the various social orders of man—both advanced and primitive—relative to his total environment. I perceive this as my mission and my life's work. Additionally, I feel that philosophy, particularly ethics, is the tool with which to grapple with world problems and that language is both the vehicle to communicate possible solutions and, for me, the best key to the psyche of a people."

BIOGRAPHICAL/CRITICAL SOURCES:

PERIODICALS

Ultimate Reality and Meaning, June, 1987.

* * *

BURFORD, E(phraim) J(ohn) 1905-

PERSONAL: Born July 15, 1905, in London, England; married Anne de Bruss. *Education:* Attended school in London, England. *Politics:* Liberal. *Religion:* Agnostic.

ADDRESSES: Home—111 Addison House, Grove End Rd., London NW8 9EJ, England.

CAREER: Democrat/Die Demokraat, Johannesburg, South Africa, joint editor, c. 1946-49; commerce director of a London, England, export house, 1949-70; historical writer, 1970—.

WRITINGS:

Queen of the Bawds (biography), Neville Spearman, 1973.
The Orrible Synne, Calder & Boyars, 1973.
Bawds and Lodgings (history), P. Owen, 1975.
In the Clink: The History of the Clink Prison, New English Library, 1977.
(Editor) *A Pleasant Collection of Bawdy Ballads,* Penguin, 1982, reprinted as *Bawdy Verse: A Pleasant Collection,* 1983.
Wits, Wenchers, and Wantons: London's Low Life; Covent Garden in the Eighteenth Century, Salem House, 1986.
The Story of St. James's, London (tentative title), R. Hale, 1988.

WORK IN PROGRESS: A Biographical Dictionary of Nicknames of Eighteenth-Century Men and Women of Pleasure: The Whoremongers; a second collection of bawdy ballads; *The Romance of Old London Bridge.*

SIDELIGHTS: E. J. Burford told *CA:* "My particular interests are ancient history and archaeology, and the history of social and sexual *mores* in London. I have traveled extensively all over Europe, including the eastern bloc. Because of my interest in philology and languages I speak French, German, Afrikaans, and Spanish, as well as some Russian. I have also traveled throughout eastern and central Africa, having lived in South Africa for almost twenty years.

"I write of those aspects of London's history that most other historians tend to ignore. They believe that politics, economics, and, above all, the successions of kings and queens are more important than chronicling the lives and sufferings of the poor, indigent, and especially that mass of womenfolk compelled to sell their bodies for bread. By writing about prostitutes I try to expose the villainies of the groups who make profit from the degradation of these women and show that such activities have existed from ancient times. My books should serve as weapons in the hands of all who seek true emancipation of womankind."

BIOGRAPHICAL/CRITICAL SOURCES:

PERIODICALS

Spectator, October 27, 1973.

BURN, Duncan (Lyall) 1902-1988

OBITUARY NOTICE: Born August 10, 1902; died January 9, 1988. Economist, educator, journalist, and author. Industrial correspondent of the London *Times* from 1946 to 1962, Burn was known for his dissident views on British economic policy. At a time when public opinion in England often favored government intervention in industry, he regularly spoke out in favor of unhindered private enterprise. He also questioned Britain's nuclear energy program, most notably the prediction that it would result in less expensive power. In addition to his work in journalism, Burn was active in education and public policymaking. He was a lecturer in economic history at the University of Liverpool and Cambridge University before World War II, and visiting professor of economics at the University of Manchester from 1967 to 1969 and Bombay University during 1971. His government posts ranged from wartime service in the Ministry of Supply to specialist adviser for the House of Commons select committee on energy during the 1980s. Burn wrote *Economic History of Steelmaking, 1867-1939; The Steel Industry, 1939-1959; The Political Economy of Nuclear Energy;* and *Nuclear Power and the Energy Crisis: Politics and the Atomic Industry*. He both edited and contributed to *The Structure of British Industry*.

OBITUARIES AND OTHER SOURCES:

BOOKS

Who's Who, 139th edition, St. Martin's, 1987.

PERIODICALS

Times (London), January 13, 1988.

BURR, Samuel Engle, Jr. 1897-1987

OBITUARY NOTICE: Born December 6, 1897, in Bordentown, N.J.; died of pneumonia and meningitis, November 16, 1987, in Princeton, N.J. Educator, administrator, and author. Burr was a sixth-generation descendant of Aaron Burr, an American politician of the early nineteenth century whose fortunes waned after he killed political rival Alexander Hamilton in a duel and was later accused of treason. Samuel Burr, who sought to restore his ancestor's reputation, wrote several books about him and was a founder and president-general of the Aaron Burr Association. Burr was a high school teacher and administrator before World War II, and after wartime service in the U.S. Army he joined the staff of American University in Washington, D.C. He was a professor of education there from 1947 until 1968, during which time he also had administrative duties. Thereafter he was managing director of Burr Publications. Burr's writings include the books *Colonel Aaron Burr: The American Phoenix, Colonel Aaron Burr: The Misunderstood Man, Napoleon's Dossier on Aaron Burr, The Burr-Hamilton Duel and Related Matters, An Introduction to Progressive Education,* and *Small Town Merchant*.

OBITUARIES AND OTHER SOURCES:

BOOKS

Who's Who in the South and Southwest, 15th edition, Marquis, 1976.

PERIODICALS

New York Times, November 20, 1987.
Washington Post, November 19, 1987.

C

CAIN, T. G. S. 1944-

PERSONAL: Born May 9, 1944, in Bedfordshire, England; son of Thomas Henry William (a farmer) and Celia (Steven) Cain; married Hana Bobkova, August 29, 1968; children: Camilla, Miriam, Thomas. *Education:* Gonville and Caius College, Cambridge, B.A., 1966, Ph.D., 1970.

ADDRESSES: *Home*—53 Fern Ave., Newcastle upon Tyne NE2 2QU, England. *Office*—School of English, University of Newcastle upon Tyne, Newcastle upon Tyne NE1 7RU, England.

CAREER: University of Newcastle upon Tyne, Newcastle upon Tyne, England, lecturer in English, 1970—, head of School of English, 1982—. Visiting lecturer at University of Michigan, Dearborn, 1975, 1978.

WRITINGS:

Tolstoy, Elek, 1976.
(Editor with R.K.R. Thornton) Nicholas Hilliard, *Treatise Concerning the Arte of Limning,* Carcanet, 1981.
(Editor) *Jacobean and Caroline Poetry: An Anthology,* Methuen, 1981.
(Editor) *The Stuarts,* Methuen, 1986.
(Editor) Ben Jonson, *Poetaster,* Revels Plays, in press.

SIDELIGHTS: T.G.S. Cain told *CA:* "I have an interest in the interaction of European and English literature and the relationship between literature and the other arts."

BIOGRAPHICAL/CRITICAL SOURCES:

PERIODICALS

Times Literary Supplement, March 19, 1982.

* * *

CAINE, Lynn 1924(?)-1987

OBITUARY NOTICE: Born c. 1924 in New York, N.Y.; died of cancer, December 16, 1987, in New York, N.Y. Publicist, editorial secretary, and author. Caine wrote the 1974 best-seller *Widow,* which recounts her struggle to recover from the death of her husband and provide for their two small children. The book was adapted for television in 1976. Caine worked for many years in the publishing industry, beginning as an editorial secretary at New American Library and then becoming a publicist. She was director of publicity at Farrar, Straus & Giroux from 1955 to 1964, and subsequently publicity manager of the New York City office of Little, Brown & Company from 1967 to 1976. The success of *Widow* allowed her to retire from publishing and work full time as a free-lance writer and lecturer. Caine also wrote the nonfiction books *What Did I Do Wrong? Mothers, Children, Guilt; Lifelines;* and *Lynn Caine's Book for Widows,* which was scheduled for publication after her death.

OBITUARIES AND OTHER SOURCES:

BOOKS

The Author Speaks: Selected PW [*Publishers Weekly*] *Interviews, 1967-1976,* Bowker, 1977.
Caine, Lynn, *Widow,* Morrow, 1974.
Who's Who in America, 44th edition, Marquis, 1986.

PERIODICALS

New York Times, December 19, 1987.
Publishers Weekly, January 8, 1988.

* * *

CALDICOTT, Helen (Mary) 1938-

PERSONAL: Born August 8, 1938, in Melbourne, Victoria, Australia; daughter of Philip (a factory manager) and Mary Mona Enyd (an interior designer; maiden name, Coffey) Broinowski; married William Caldicott (a physician), December 8, 1962; children: Philip, Penny, William, Jr. *Education:* University of Adelaide, received B.S. (surgery), M.B. (medicine), 1961.

ADDRESSES: *Home*—45 Leonard St., Gloucester, Mass. 01930. *Office*—P.O. Box 348, Arlington, Mass. 02174.

CAREER: Royal Adelaide Hospital, Adelaide, South Australia, Australia, intern, 1961; general practice of medicine in South Australia, 1963-65; Children's Hospital Medical Center, Boston, Mass., fellow in nutrition, 1967-68; Adelaide Children's Hospital, Adelaide, intern, 1972, resident, 1973-74, founder and head of cystic fibrosis clinic, 1975-76; Children's Hospital Medical Center, fellow in cystic fibrosis, 1975-76, associate, 1977-80; activist and writer. Harvard University, Medical School, Cambridge, Mass., fellow in nutrition,

1966-68, instructor in pediatrics, 1977-80. Appeared in documentary films "Eight Minutes to Midnight: A Portrait of Dr. Helen Caldicott," Physicians for Social Responsibility, 1981, "If You Love This Planet," National Film Board of Canada, 1982, and "In Our Hands," Action for Nuclear Disarmament, 1982; guest on radio and television programs, including "The Merv Griffin Show," "Donahue," "The Today Show," "Good Morning, America," "60 Minutes," and "Nightline."

MEMBER: American Thoracic Society, Royal Australasian College of Physicians, Physicians for Social Responsibility (president, 1978-83; president emeritus, 1983—), Medical Campaign Against Nuclear War (founder), Women's Action for Nuclear Disarmament (founder), Women's Party for Survival (founder).

AWARDS, HONORS: Prize for clinical medicine from British Medical Association, 1960; award from Consumer Action Now, Margaret Mead Award from Environmental Defense Center, Thomas Merton Prize for Peace from Thomas Merton Society, and Humanist of the Year Award from Ethical Society of Boston, all 1980; Gandhi Peace Prize from Promoting Enduring Peace and SANE Peace Award from SANE Education Fund, both 1981; Humanist of the Year Award from American Association of Humanistic Psychology and Audubon "A" Award from Massachusetts Audubon Society, both 1982; Woman of the Year Award from Boston College, Peace Award from American Association of University Women, Humanitarian Award from Massachusetts Psychological Association, Elizabeth Blackwell Award from American Medical Women's Association, Abraham L. Sacher Award from Brandeis University, Ansel Adams Award from Second Biennial Fate of the Earth Conference, and Outstanding Writer Award from Massachusetts Bay Association of Writing Programs, all 1984; President's Award from Hofstra University, Integrity Award from John-Roger Foundation, Peace Medal Award from United Nations Association of Australia, and Nobel Peace Prize nomination, all 1985; International Year of Peace Award from Australian Government, 1986; numerous honorary degrees from institutions including Antioch University, Emmanuel College, Russell Sage College, State University of New York at Binghamton, University of Linkoeping (Linkoeping, Sweden), and University of Notre Dame.

WRITINGS:

(With Nancy Herrington and Nahum Stiskin) *Nuclear Madness: What You Can Do!* Autumn Press, 1978, new edition published as *Nuclear Madness: What You Can Do; With a New Chapter on Three Mile Island,* Bantam, 1980.

Missile Envy: The Arms Race and Nuclear War, Morrow, 1984.

SIDELIGHTS: Since her 1971 fight to stop France from testing nuclear weapons over the southern Pacific Ocean, Australian-born physician Helen Caldicott has become "probably the most effective antinuclear speaker" in America, averred Nobel Prize-winning biologist George Wald in a 1979 *Ms.* article. Caldicott's speeches on the health dangers posed by nuclear fallout helped convince many Australians to protest and end the testing; she later led the successful effort to halt uranium mining and exporting in that country also. After moving to the United States in 1977, Caldicott focused much of her energy on protesting against nuclear weapons, pushing for a freeze on the building of such weapons and urging all Americans to become involved in the debate over nuclear technology. In *Nuclear Madness: What You Can Do!,* written with Nancy Herrington and Nahum Stiskin, Caldicott stated: "I believe it imperative that the American public understand that nuclear power generation is neither safe, nor clean, nor cheap; that new initiatives are urgently required if we are to avoid nuclear catastrophe in a world armed to the teeth with atomic weapons; and that these initiatives must begin with awareness, concern, and action on the part of the individual citizen. . . . We must educate ourselves . . . then move powerfully as individuals accepting full responsibility for preserving our planet for our descendants."

Caldicott's own awareness of nuclear hazards stemmed in part from her experiences as a pediatrician. In treating patients stricken with cystic fibrosis and leukemia, she realized that even one radioactive particle could damage a cell or a gene, thus making such genetic diseases and cancers more likely. "I decided that promoting the elimination of nuclear weapons and power was part of practicing . . . real preventive medicine," she told *Ms.* The results of her decision included reviving the antinuclear organization Physicians for Social Responsibility and leaving her medical practice to devote more time to educating the public.

Concern for her children also motivated her to activism. Recounted Caldicott, "When my husband and I decided to have our first child, I had nightmares thinking that the baby would live to see the horrors that I'd read about as a girl." Reading scientific studies of nuclear issues helped solidify her opposition to the technology, showing how weapons tests and routine reactor operation produce substances that affect the entire food chain. Caldicott was particularly troubled to discover that children face the greatest dangers from radiation. Because children are still growing, their cells reproduce quickly; a radiation-damaged cell only reproduces more damaged—cancerous—cells.

From the beginning of her campaign for a nuclear-free world, Caldicott has focused on a personal approach to sharing what she has learned. As a physician and as a parent she addresses church groups, college students, hospital staffs, and labor unions. She reaches many through magazine and newspaper articles, and she speaks on radio and television news programs. Commented Wald in *Ms.*, "She has a gift for making the hard scientific facts meaningful to the public." Using blackboard drawings, Caldicott explains the technological and medical realities, and data collected from government reports and scientific studies fuel her arguments. Yet even while she conveys hard facts, Wald observed, "she doesn't hesitate to raise moral questions or display intense emotions about these matters that are life-threatening in the extreme." To critics against her emotional appeal, Caldicott offered her defense in a *Los Angeles Times* article: "This is a very emotional issue. . . . To be unemotional about the end of the world is sick."

Caldicott also spreads her message with her books, which have been deemed useful educational tools. In the *New York Times Book Review* Philip M. Boffey described *Nuclear Madness* as "a primer on the medical hazards of nuclear fission." The critic questioned some of Caldicott's assertions, but he acknowledged the book's "undeniable strengths," among them clarity, simplicity, dispassionate tone, and attention to neglected issues. For example, among the issues she discusses is the disposal of radioactive waste; she notes that "even if unbreakable, corrosion-resistant containers could be designed, any storage site on earth would have to be kept under constant surveillance by incorruptible guards, administered by moral politicians living in a stable, warless society, and left undisturbed by earthquakes, natural disasters, or other acts of God for no less than half a million years."

Missile Envy: The Arms Race and Nuclear War analyzes the intricacies of defense strategy and the capabilities of nuclear arsenals worldwide. Caldicott offers several explanations for the U.S.-U.S.S.R. arms race and suggests that human nature must change to prevent the annihilation of mankind. Taylor Branch, writing in the *New York Times Book Review,* faulted Caldicott's diagnosis as superficial and criticized her emotional leaps between denunciations and religious appeals, but the critic judged her arguments convincing regarding specific arms issues. "Caldicott is at her best," Branch reflected, "when she goes into the maw of the doomsday machine itself to describe the missile systems, nuclear warheads and military theories in their deadliest applications." Branch also hailed the author's contention that "the logical consequence of the preparation for nuclear war is nuclear war."

Through her writings and lectures Caldicott "has captured the hearts and minds of people around the world," stated scientist Freeman Dyson in *New Yorker*. "You cannot brush aside her message as the emotional outpouring of a fanatic. She speaks from a solid basis of medical experience." Her work has made countless people aware of the dangers, achieving notable successes in Australia, yet "the world of the warriors [nuclear defense advocates] goes on its way as if Dr. Caldicott didn't exist," asserted Dyson. In December of 1982 Caldicott won a small concession, a lengthy private meeting with U.S. President Ronald Reagan, but she left frustrated because Reagan was "not receptive at all to what I had to say," she recalled in *Missile Envy*. Explained Dyson, "There is prejudice and antipathy on both sides. The military establishment looks on the peace movement as a collection of ignorant people meddling in a business they do not understand, while the peace movement looks on the military establishment as a collection of misguided people protected by bureaucratic formality from all contact with human realities. Both these preconceptions create barriers to understanding." Reflecting on what she has achieved and what remains to be done, Caldicott urged again in *Missile Envy:* "It is time for people to rise to their full moral and spiritual height, to take the world on their shoulders like Atlas. . . . Think how much Americans could achieve by using . . . the democracy they have inherited from their forebears. All it takes is willpower and determination. . . . Think of what we are about to destroy."

CA INTERVIEW

CA interviewed Helen Caldicott by telephone on August 14, 1986, at her home in Gloucester, Massachusetts.

CA: Since you read Nevil Shute's On the Beach *as a teenager, you've been concerned about nuclear technology, and since the early 1970s you've been very actively involved in working against it. What do you see as the biggest hurdles in your work today?*

CALDICOTT: There are various hurdles. One is that living and eating and sleeping and dreaming nuclear war and nuclear power for the last fifteen years has taken a psychological and physical toll. I'm about to retire and go back to Australia. I had to keep on top of the literature, so I got to the point where I became terrified because I knew so much. Also, because Ronald Reagan has done an end run around our work, I don't see any political change that is significantly going to alter the present course toward annihilation. There are slow changes, and there is now a vast movement in this country which is more politically sophisticated and knowledgeable than it's ever been before. There are, I would estimate, ten to twenty million people in that condition. Things move slowly—human change always moves slowly—but I need a break.

CA: In 1980 you "left medicine to save lives," as the dean of a New York medical school put it. Will you go back to medicine now?

CALDICOTT: I don't know. I'm interested in maybe working in Australia with various organizations there in a medical fashion. I don't think I want to talk too much about it at the moment, but I'm thinking very hard now about what I want to do in Australia, which is in the curious position of not supporting its friend and ally and colleague New Zealand in its nuclear-free policy, but rather supporting the United States of America in its nuclear policy. It's becoming host to a huge number of American bases, including CIA [Central Intelligence Agency] bases, first-strike bases, Star Wars research, nuclear weapons in the harbors, and exporting uranium. I'm very interested now in the South Pacific area, particularly my own country.

CA: One of the ways you've spread your message is by writing books: Nuclear Madness, *first published in 1978, and* Missile Envy, *published in 1984. Did you find it hard to spend the necessary time alone for the writing after being so much with other people?*

CALDICOTT: No. *Nuclear Madness* I wrote in just a few months; it sort of spilled out of me. The same with *Missile Envy;* I wrote that in about four months. I had saved a large number of newspaper cuttings and books and articles, and I just correlated them and wrote it all down. I was full of the stuff. It was really with a sense of relief that I wrote both books. And I feel that if everybody in America read both *Nuclear Madness* and *Missile Envy,* the arms race would cease.

CA: On the first book, you had the assistance of Nancy Herrington and Nahum Stiskin. How did the collaboration work?

CALDICOTT: It was difficult. There were a lot of tensions. But out of it came an extraordinarily good book. I think often creative work is filled with tension. But I have to say that Nahum Stiskin always said that he wanted it to be the White Paper on the nuclear issue, and indeed it became that. It sold over two hundred thousand copies, and I think it's being used as a textbook in many colleges.

CA: Do you find more writers involved in the antinuclear movement now than ever before?

CALDICOTT: When I started in this country in 1976, there were virtually no books on the subject. I'm generalizing, but there were very few either on nuclear power or weapons. Now there's a surfeit. I get sent manuscripts and books all the time for comments on the covers. If you go to a normal bookshop you'll find shelves and shelves of books on the nuclear issue. The information is increasing all the time, and that's exciting.

CA: Have your own children become active against nuclear technology?

CALDICOTT: The two boys haven't. They know all about it, and the younger one says that when it happens, he wants to be standing on the roof of the Statehouse, right in the middle of the target. The older boy doesn't think about it but enjoys

life. Our middle child, the daughter, Penny, is in medical school, third year. She actually went to the Soviet Union two years ago with a group of medical students and took a lot of photographs. They were hosted by Russian medical students. Now she gives talks in Australia about the Soviet Union and about nuclear issues. She's lovely, young and fresh and optimistic, and she's become very popular as a speaker and has been written up in several articles in the Australian press. I'm very proud of her.

CA: You've been involved in the television documentary "Eight Minutes to Midnight" and a "Nova" segment dealing with the nuclear threat, among other films. How effectively do you think the productions for television touched the segment of the public that you wanted to reach with them?

CALDICOTT: They touched a few, but those films should have been on commercial television. It's obscene that the commercial stations don't play this stuff. NBC [National Broadcasting Company], as a subsidiary of RCA, has just been bought by General Electric, who not only makes nuclear power plants but is one of the largest producers of nuclear weapons and delivery missiles. ABC [American Broadcasting Companies] is involved with a right-wing corporation, and most of the advertisements that are bought to be played on commercial television are bought by corporations that manufacture weapons. Almost every corporation in this country now is involved in some way or other with the production of military goods, and it's not in their best interest for profit to educate the people about the realities of a nuclear world. So things are very tricky, and the fate of the earth rests in the hands of the media right now. It makes me sick, frankly sick, that very good shows don't get played. For instance, my film "If You Love This Planet," made by the Canadian Film Board, won an Academy Award but was banned by the U.S. Justice Department as foreign propaganda; that's never been played on commercial television. It's been played in Canada, and most Canadians recognize me when I go up there, which is a sort of barometer of the state of education of the people.

CA: Have any of the films been aired in England?

CALDICOTT: I don't know, but I know that "If You Love This Planet" has been translated into Japanese and played on Japanese TV. It was played in Sweden, where I got a huge response. It was played in Germany. It's been translated into Chinese, I think, and Spanish. Wherever I travel, I find that people have seen it before I get there.

CA: Meryl Streep was somehow involved with "Eight Minutes to Midnight," wasn't she?

CALDICOTT: She hosted an opening of it on Broadway, and we spoke together. She's been very supportive. She's got three children.

CA: Is the antinuclear movement becoming increasingly powerful in other countries? There seems to be a lot going on in Europe.

CALDICOTT: Yes. I think [the 1986 Soviet nuclear power plant accident at] Chernobyl has helped to educate Europe about the nuclear threat. You see, we're talking about the fact that America manipulates most countries in the world except the Soviet Union. For instance, in Holland 80 percent of the Dutch people didn't want the cruise missiles, but they got them anyway. America manipulates the politicians and the press and threatens the country with sanctions and other things. As we travel around Europe, it's really obscene to see what this country's doing—and throughout the world. It's happening in my country, certainly. They are threatening little New Zealand with trade sanctions. And really, it's all about manifest destiny and the profit motive of the multinational corporations. The multinational corporations run the government of this country. Everybody knows that. It's not really a free democracy at all. It could be if the people decided to use it as such, but they don't; they're lazy and apathetic. The Pentagon is used as a scaffolding for the multinationals to do what they want with impunity throughout the world. That includes South Africa, because there are very important minerals there that are necessary for weapons and that can only be gotten from South Africa. Hence the lack of sanctions. That's just a typical example, let alone the situation in Central and South America.

CA: Do you think we've learned anything in this country from the nuclear plant accident at Chernobyl?

CALDICOTT: Yes. I think there's deep concern now in the hearts and souls of most people. And I'm not castigating the American people; I'm castigating the powers-that-be that brainwash them.

CA: In Missile Envy *you associate the warmaking impulse predominantly with men and the peacemaking impulse largely with women, drawing also on psychologist Carl Jung's masculine and feminine principles, the animus and the anima. Has this point drawn particular criticism from readers?*

CALDICOTT: From a few men who are fairly sensitive about their maleness. But mostly people agree. In fact, last night [television talk-show host] Phil Donahue did a segment of his series "The Human Animal." He talked about testosterone being the main drive toward a man's aggressiveness, and I totally and heartily agree with that. He said that young boys are more aggressive than young girls, and they are. This has all been proven now.

CA: How large is WAND, the Women's Action for Nuclear Disarmament, which you founded?

CALDICOTT: It's got about twenty thousand members, and it's doing some very sophisticated political work. It's lobbying in Washington. We've just produced an excellent report about why the freeze failed. It cost $160,000 and it's published in a magazine called *Turnabout*. We did a national poll; we interviewed a hundred top members of the major national media to find out what happened there, and interviewed twenty members of the House and Senate. The media killed the freeze. They said it was a great movement, unique, huge, but the freeze wasn't a good idea. The media are not representing the people in this country, they're representing business interests. When the freeze got to Washington, the media interviewed the so-called specialists and the experts like Edward Teller, James Schlesinger, and Harold Brown. No one thought to interview the intellectual leaders of the freeze. When 80 percent of the population supports an idea, the leaders must be given legitimacy by the national press. Congress voted for the freeze because their constituents were clamoring for it, but they said it wasn't a good idea because the Russians would never accept it. In their ignorance they failed to note that the Russians had introduced it before the United Nations and in the Geneva negotiations.

CA: In 1978 you began reviving Physicians for Social Responsibility (PSR), which had been formed in 1962 but was no longer very active. You served as president of that organization from 1978 to 1983. Are you still very active in it?

CALDICOTT: No. There was a male power struggle. It's become a conservative, male-oriented organization like the American Medical Association, and they look backwards instead of forward. The present male leadership have no vision for the future. They've taken full credit for all the work I and many other people did and they claimed credit for the Nobel Prize. They are now rewriting the history of PSR according to their version, writing me out of it and writing out the other wonderful people who were involved. This happens a lot to women.

CA: Is there no way you can come back at them?

CALDICOTT: It's taken me a couple of years to get over it, and when I've attempted to present the true story, they've said "sour grapes." I think it's a win-lose situation. If you win, you're the victor; if you lose, you're shut out. It's the male power game. That's how soldiers work. But I'm coming out of it now. I think I'll write my biography, and I'll call it *An Aroused Woman*. I'll write everything down; I think it's terribly important for women to know this, because it happens to us all the time. The woman who started Mothers Against Drunk Driving, Candy Lightner, has just been removed by her male board because she doesn't have a college degree. It happens all the time. Women never get to top levels of management. It is symptomatic of the pathology in the society whereby the peacemakers, the nurturers, have no power and the men brutalize them. They also brutalize each other. Many men in power are primitive emotionally, and it's clear they may blow up the world unless we develop a means both to educate them and to make obsolete their continuous anachronistic power play. That's what I'm interested in now.

CA: Are there women's groups in this country that you would be interested in working in league with?

CALDICOTT: I think so, all the women's groups. But I have to go away and cogitate and mull things over. I find when my mind's clear and I'm able to read and think, ideas come to me.

CA: Do you feel the existing groups are doing worthy work?

CALDICOTT: Yes, but not big enough work. I think that the National Organization for Women is totally on the wrong track in begging the men for equal rights and talking about abortion. Women should be running for Congress and the Senate. There should be a constitutional amendment that says that of the two senators from each state, one must be a woman. That would be very important.

CA: What kind of speaking schedule have you been keeping lately?

CALDICOTT: I stopped about six weeks ago, but until then I was on the road almost constantly.

CA: Have your audiences been mostly very large groups?

CALDICOTT: Yes, and all sorts. Thirty thousand Methodist women, about twenty thousand Church of Christ women. I did the huge national convocation of Presbyterians and I've spoken to lots and lots of Catholics. In fact, I've got one more talk, and that's to the Archdiocese of Chicago. I've spoken to Episcopalians, Mennonites, Mormans, doctors and lawyers, merchants and chiefs.

CA: Do the churches have the right kind of clout to get involved and be useful to the movement?

CALDICOTT: They have the right kind of clout, but they tend to move slowly and they're cautious. I've had priests who've said to me, "Oh, I can't talk about that to my congregation, they're too conservative." I say to them, "What would Jesus do if he came back?"

CA: How would you advise people who are concerned but not knowledgeable on the subject of nuclear technology to go about becoming informed and involved?

CALDICOTT: To read my two books. And having done that to get a background, they should watch one of the network news shows each night, watch "Nightline," read the *New York Times* every day (though I feel it is becoming more and more right-wing) and also read *Nation* magazine, which is excellent.

CA: According to articles I've read, you enjoy sewing, knitting, cooking, gardening, playing the clarinet, even painting. Will you be able to get back to some of these activities now?

CALDICOTT: I'm doing them already. I'm having a lovely time.

CA: You've mentioned an autobiography. Do you have other books planned beyond that?

CALDICOTT: No. That seems to be the next logical one. I think it will be therapeutic for me, and I think it will be interesting to women, because I've done a lot. I'm really interested in the power of women. I'm interested in mobilizing the female population politically. It's time, *really* time.

CA: In Current Biography *you're described as a long-time atheist who has now come to be a "nonsectarian believer" in a "higher force." Could you comment on how you made that change in spite of the very gloomy facts you've been dealing with for so many years?*

CALDICOTT: I attended a series of seminars run by a group called the Creative Initiative Foundation, which has now turned into Beyond War. They had excellent teaching on how to have a good marriage and be good parents and develop personally, spiritually. They taught the teachings of Jesus, and also Eastern philosophy. They taught me how to meditate and pray. Being a scientific skeptic, I did it with some skepticism and tested it and found that it worked, and that there is a higher force that I can tap into. It's helped me enormously; it really has been a lifesaver in dealing with these most monumental problems that I talk about. And it's helped me in being able to release the outcome and being able to say, I'm not responsible for the earth personally; I'll do the best I can and be guided rather than feeling total responsibility, which I did for many years.

BIOGRAPHICAL/CRITICAL SOURCES:

BOOKS

Current Biography, H. W. Wilson, 1983.
Contemporary Issues Criticism, Volume 2, Gale, 1984.

PERIODICALS

Family Circle, May 18, 1982.
Harper's, March, 1985.
Los Angeles Times, June 27, 1984.
Ms., July, 1979, July, 1984.
New Yorker, February 6, 1984.
New York Times, May 25, 1979, August 18, 1985, June 2, 1986.
New York Times Book Review, August 26, 1979, July 29, 1984.
People, November 30, 1981.

—*Sketch by Polly A. Vedder*

—*Interview by Jean W. Ross*

* * *

CALDWELL, Ben(jamin) 1937-

PERSONAL: Born September 24, 1937, in New York, N.Y.

ADDRESSES: Office—P.O. Box 656, Morningside Station, New York, N.Y. 10026.

CAREER: Writer.

AWARDS, HONORS: Guggenheim fellowship for playwriting, 1970.

WRITINGS:

PLAYS

The Job (one-act; first produced in 1966; also produced as part of "What Is Going On"; see below); published in *Drama Review*, summer, 1968, published in *Black Identity*, edited by Francis E. Kearns, Holt, 1970, published in *Nommo: An Anthology of Modern African and Black American Literature*, edited by William H. Robinson, Macmillan, 1972.

Riot Sale; or, Dollar Psyche Fake-Out (first produced in 1966), published in *Drama Review*, summer, 1968, published in *Black Culture: Reading and Writing Black*, edited by Gloria M. Simmons and Helene D. Hutchinson, Holt, 1972.

Mission Accomplished (first produced in 1967), published in *Drama Review*, summer, 1968.

Prayer Meeting; or, The First Militant Minister (one-act; first produced as "Militant Preacher" in Newark, N.J., at Spirit House Theatre, April, 1967), Jihad, 1968, published in *Black Fire: An Anthlogy of Afro-American Writing*, edited by Le Roi Jones and Larry Neal, Morrow, 1968; published in *A Black Quartet: Four New Black Plays* (anthology of works by four playwrights; first produced Off-Broadway by Chelsea Theatre Center at Brooklyn Academy of Music, April 25, 1969), introduction by Clayton Riley, New American Library, 1970.

The King of Soul; or, The Devil and Otis Redding: A One-Act Musical Tragedy (first produced in 1968), published in *New Plays From the Black Theatre*, edited by Ed Bullins, Bantam, 1969.

Family Portrait; or, My Son, the Black Nationalist (one-act; produced as part of "What Is Going On"; see below), published in *New Plays From the Black Theatre*, edited by Ed Bullins, Bantam, 1969.

Top Secret; or, A Few Million After B.C. (first produced in Los Angeles, Calif., by Performing Arts Society in 1969; produced as part of "What Is Going On"; see below), published in *Drama Review*, summer, 1968.

Hypnotism (one-act), published in *Afro-Arts Anthology*, Jihad, 1969, published in *Black Culture: Reading and Writing Black*, edited by Gloria M. Simmons and Helene D. Hutchinson, Holt, 1972.

"Run Around" (one-act), first produced in New York City at Third World House, June, 1970.

All White Caste; After the Separation: A Slow-Paced One-Act Play (produced as part of "What Is Going On"; see below), published in *Black Drama Anthology*, edited by Woodie King, Jr., and Ronald Milner, New American Library, 1971.

An Obscene Play (for Adults Only), published in *Alafia*, winter, 1971.

The Wall (one-act), published in *Scripts*, May, 1972.

"What Is Going On," (program of short plays; contains "All White Caste," "Family Portrait," "Rights and Reasons," "The Job," "Top Secret"), first produced in New York City at New Federal Theatre, November 23, 1973.

"The World of Ben Caldwell: A Dramatized Examination of the Absurdity of the American Dream and Subsequent Reality," first produced in New York City at New Federal Theatre, April, 1982.

"Moms," first produced Off-Broadway at Astor Palace Theater, August 4, 1987.

Also author of "The Fanatic; or, Testifying" (one-act), "The Interview," "Recognition" (one-act), "Reverend Mac; or, God and Company," "Right Attitude; or, Is You Is or Is You Ain't a Revolutionary," "Un-Presidented; or, What Needs to Be Done" (one-act), and "Uptight or . . ."

OTHER

(With Askia Muhammad Toure) *Juju: Magic Songs for the Black Nation* (collection of poetry and prose), Third World Press, 1970.

SIDELIGHTS: Born in New York City's Harlem neighborhood, Ben Caldwell is known for short satirical plays that comment on the situation of black people in white-dominated America. He first came to prominence in the 1960s as the result of his association with LeRoi Jones (now known as Imamu Amiri Baraka), a major black playwright whose Spirit House Theatre premiered one of Caldwell's best-known works, "Prayer Meeting; or, The First Militant Minister" (originally titled "Militant Preacher"). In "Prayer Meeting," Caldwell uses a comic premise to dramatize the political message that black people must be willing to struggle actively for their rights and that they should not expect an easy accommodation with white society. The play shows a black minister as he returns home and prays for God's help in avoiding an angry reaction by members of his congregation to the death of a black teenager at the hands of the police. The minister does not realize that his arrival has interrupted a burglary in his own house. Remaining unseen by the minister, the burglar disdainfully responds to the man's prayer by claiming to be the voice of God. Berated into action by "God," the minister abandons his philosophy of nonconfrontation and resolves to lead his parishioners on City Hall. "Prayer Meeting" was presented Off-Broadway as part of the production "A Black Quartet," which also includes plays by Jones and two other prominent black playwrights, Ed Bullins and Ronald Milner. Reviewing

the "Quartet" for the *New York Times,* Clayton Riley praised Caldwell's play for its "beautifully delineated satiric focus."

In other plays Caldwell casts doubts on the motives of whites who claim to help black people. "Top Secret; or, A Few Million After B.C." shows white government leaders—silently attended by their black servants—trying to develop new ways to maintain their racial domination. The leaders decide that contraception, which promises blacks the freedom of an active sexual life without pregnancy, will actually aid the white power structure by limiting the size of the black population.

Two programs of Caldwell's short works have been presented at the New Federal Theatre in New York City. "What Is Going On" comprises five plays, including "Top Secret." "The World of Ben Caldwell" is a collection of skits and monologues, subtitled "A Dramatized Examination of the Absurdity of the American Dream and Subsequent Reality." Reviewing the latter show for the *Village Voice,* Stanley Crouch noted that "Caldwell's strong suit is a great ability to stitch together fabrics of rhetoric ranging from bureaucratic to black bottom barber shop."

BIOGRAPHICAL/CRITICAL SOURCES:

BOOKS

Dictionary of Literary Biography, Volume 38, *Afro-American Writers After 1955: Dramatists and Prose Writers,* Gale, 1985.

PERIODICALS

New York Times, August 3, 1969, November 28, 1973, April 10, 1982, August 9, 1987.
Players, February-March, 1976.
Village Voice, April 27, 1982.

* * *

CAMPBELL, Joseph 1904-1987

OBITUARY NOTICE—See index for *CA* sketch: Born March 26, 1904, in New York City; died after a brief illness, October 30 (one source says October 31), 1987, in Honolulu, Hawaii. Educator, mythologist, editor, and author. Campbell was known for his lifelong work on mythology and culture. He taught at Sarah Lawrence College from 1934 to 1972, and during those years he published such important works as *The Hero With a Thousand Faces,* an analysis of heroism as a reflection of culture that later inspired the "Star Wars" series of motion pictures, and the four-volume *Masks of God,* which traces the development of mythology in various cultures. Among Campbell's other writings are *A Skeleton Key to "Finnegans Wake"* (a collaboration with Henry Morton Robinson), *Myths to Live By,* and the multi-volume *Historical Atlas of World Mythology,* which was left incomplete at his death. He also edited many volumes, including the 1970 book *Myths, Dreams, and Religion.*

OBITUARIES AND OTHER SOURCES:

BOOKS

Who's Who in America, 44th edition, Marquis, 1986.

PERIODICALS

Chicago Tribune, November 5, 1987.
New York Times, November 3, 1987.
Time, November 16, 1987.
Washington Post, November 4, 1987.

CAMPION, Joan 1940-

PERSONAL: Birth-given name, Betty Anne Arner; name legally changed, c. 1978; born April 14, 1940, in Weissport, Pa.; daughter of George David (a delivery man) and Esther Louise (a store clerk; maiden name, Fairchild) Arner. *Education:* Cedar Crest College, B.A., 1961. *Politics:* Liberal Democrat. *Religion:* Roman Catholic.

ADDRESSES: P.O. Box 5106, Bethlehem, Pa. 18015.

CAREER: Worked as reporter and feature writer for *Lehighton Times-News,* Lehighton, Pa.; *Bethlehem Globe-Times,* Bethlehem, Pa., proofreader and free-lance feature writer, 1973-75; free-lance writer and editor, 1975—; free-lance music critic for *Bethlehem Globe-Times,* Bethlehem, Pa., 1984—. Member of Center for Independent Study, New Haven, Conn. Past member of local Democratic Committee.

MEMBER: Society for the History of Czechoslovak Jews, South Bethlehem Historical Society (founder).

AWARDS, HONORS: Grants from Memorial Foundation for Jewish Culture, 1979, and Simon Wiesenthal's Jewish Documentation Center, 1986.

WRITINGS:

In the Lion's Mouth: Gisi Fleischmann and the Jewish Fight for Survival, University Presses of America, 1987.

Contributor to newspapers and magazines, including *Prevention* and *Rotarian.*

WORK IN PROGRESS: Revising and completing a book for young people, set in Arthurian times.

SIDELIGHTS: Joan Campion told *CA:* "I think ethnic (racial, religious) hatreds will destroy us if we don't learn to eliminate them, and all the 'serious' writing I will ever do is bent on eradicating such prejudices. I still don't know of a better way to do this than to introduce readers to members of other cultures with whom they can identify and sympathize, as millions sympathized with German Jewish diarist Anne Frank, for example.

"To me, Gisi Fleischmann is just such a person, a very ordinary but very great heroic figure who rescued thousands from the Nazis. I happened to read a few pages about this woman before my first visit to Israel in 1978, and I could not get her out of my mind. I decided I would have to have a book about her at all costs. After searching for a long time, both in the United States and in Israel, I realized there was no such book. So I wrote one—not without much self-doubt and hesitation."

AVOCATIONAL INTERESTS: "I will go up in anything that flies; I have three cats; and I love walking and hiking. I also play several musical instruments—recorders, pennywhistle, electronic keyboard, and harmonica—and I especially love opera."

* * *

CANTELON, Philip L(ouis) 1940-

PERSONAL: Born November 7, 1940, in Fort Wayne, Ind.; son of Philip E. and Marie (Gehrke) Cantelon; married; children: Philip W. *Education:* Dartmouth College, A.B., 1962;

University of Michigan, A.M., 1963; Indiana University, Ph.D., 1971.

ADDRESSES: Office—History Associates, Inc., Historic Montrose School, 5721 Randolph Rd., Rockville, Md. 20852.

CAREER: History master at military school, 1963-65; Williams College, Williamstown, Mass., lecturer, 1968-69, assistant professor of history, 1969-77, director of oral history project, 1970-77; Kyushu University, Fukuoka, Japan, professor of American history and civilization, 1978-79; History Associates, Inc., Rockville, Md., president, 1980—. Senior Fulbright professor at U.S. Education Commission in Japan, 1978-79; professor at Seinan Gakuin University, 1978-79. Speechwriter and editor for Office of the Secretary of Housing and Urban Development, 1974-75; senior partner of C & W Associates, 1979—. Chairman of Montgomery County Historic Preservation Commission; member of board of directors of Peerless Rockville Historic Preservation Ltd., Montgomery County Historical Society, and National Center for the Study of History.

MEMBER: American Historical Association, Organization of American Historians, Oral History Association, Society for History in Federal Government, National Council on Public History, Society of American Archivists, Cosmos Club.

AWARDS, HONORS: Frederick Lieber Teaching Award from Indiana University.

WRITINGS:

(With Robert C. Williams) *Crisis Contained: The Department of Energy at Three Mile Island,* Southern Illinois University Press, 1982.

(Editor with Williams) *The American Atom: A Documentary History of Nuclear Policies From the Discovery of Fission to the Present, 1939-1984,* University of Pennsylvania Press, 1985.

Contributor to journals, including *American Heritage* and *Public Historian.*

* * *

CARPENTER, Kenneth J(ohn) 1923-

PERSONAL: Born May 17, 1923, in London, England; immigrated to United States, 1977; son of James F. (in commerce) and Dorothy (a teacher; maiden name, George) Carpenter; married Antonina Pecoraro, June 18, 1977. *Education:* Cambridge University, B.A., 1944, Ph.D., 1948, Sc.D., 1975.

ADDRESSES: Home—6201 Rockwell St., Oakland, Calif. 94618. *Office*—Department of Nutritional Science, University of California, Berkeley, Calif. 94720.

CAREER: Rowett Institute, Aberdeen, Scotland, scientific officer in nutrition, 1948-56; Cambridge University, Cambridge, England, lecturer, 1956-75, reader in nutrition, 1975-77, fellow of Sidney Sussex College, 1961-77; University of California, Berkeley, professor of experimental nutrition, 1977—, chairman of department of nutritional science, 1981-83. Royal Society fellow at Central Food Research Institute, Mysore, India, 1960.

MEMBER: American Association for the History of Medicine, American Institute of Nutrition, British Nutrition Society.

AWARDS, HONORS: Kellogg fellow at Harvard University, 1955-56.

WRITINGS:

Pellagra, Hutchinson Ross, 1981.

The History of Scurvy and Vitamin C, Cambridge University Press, 1986.

WORK IN PROGRESS: A history of ideas about dietary protein, publication expected in 1989.

SIDELIGHTS: Kenneth J. Carpenter told *CA:* "My interest is in the history of ideas and the diversity of cultural beliefs. I try to relate this to what I see in my professional work as a scientist in the field of nutrition."

BIOGRAPHICAL/CRITICAL SOURCES:

PERIODICALS

Nature, November 13, 1986.

New England Journal of Medicine, January 22, 1987.

Times Literary Supplement, November 7, 1986.

* * *

CARR, Mary Jane 1899-1988

OBITUARY NOTICE—See index for *CA* sketch: Born April 23, 1899, in Portland, Ore.; died January 4, 1988, in Portland, Ore. Journalist and author. Carr wrote the popular children's book *Children of the Covered Wagon,* which was adapted by Walt Disney film studios as "Westward Ho! The Wagons" in 1956. Prior to writing for children, Carr was an associate editor for the *Catholic Sentinel.* She left that publication and began writing for the *Oregonian,* where she produced serialized tales. Among her series was *Young Pioneers,* which she published as *Children of the Covered Wagon* in 1934. Her subsequent writings include *Young Mac of Fort Vancouver; Peggy and Paul and Laddy; Stranger at the Apple Ranch;* and the verse volume *Top of the Morning.*

OBITUARIES AND OTHER SOURCES:

BOOKS

American Catholic Who's Who, Volume 23: *1980-1981,* National Catholic News Service, 1979.

PERIODICALS

Los Angeles Times, January 7, 1988.

Washington Post, January 7, 1988.

* * *

CARRINGTON, Leonora 1917-

PERSONAL: Born in 1917, in Lancashire, England; married Renato Leduc (a cultural attache), 1941 (marriage ended); married Chiqui Weisz (a photographer); children: (second marriage) Gabriel, Pablo. *Education:* Studied art in Florence and Paris; attended Ozenfant Academy, London, 1937.

ADDRESSES: Home—Chihuahua 194, Colonia Roma, Mexico D.F.7.

CAREER: Surrealist painter and writer. Also sculptor; tapestry, stage set, and costume designer; and illustrator. Exhibitions of artwork held in Paris, New York City, and Mexico City; major retrospective in New York City and Austin, Tex., 1975-76. Commissioned muralist for National Museum of Anthropology, Mexico City, 1962. Works represented in permanent collection of Museum of National History, Mexico City.

WRITINGS:

(Translator) Andres Medina and Laurette Sejourne, *El mundo magico de los Mayas,* Museo Nacional de Antropologia, 1964.

Penelope (play; first produced in 1957), Gallimard, 1969.

En bas (autobiography), translation published as *Down Below,* Black Swan, 1972.

"Opus Sinistrus" (play), first produced in New York City at Theatre of Latin America, 1974.

Le Cornet acoustique (novel), Flammarion, 1974, translation published as *The Hearing Trumpet,* illustrations by son, Pablo Weisz-Carrington, St. Martin's, 1976.

La Dame ovale (short stories), illustrations by Max Ernst, translation by Rochelle Holt published as *The Oval Lady, and Other Stories: Six Surreal Stories,* Capra, 1975.

La Porte de pierre (novel), translation published as *The Stone Door,* St. Martin's, 1977.

Stories represented in *Anthology of Black Humor,* edited by Andre Breton. Contributor to surrealist reviews *VVV* and *View.*

SIDELIGHTS: In an article for *Ms.* Gloria Orenstein described the art of surrealist Leonora Carrington as "magical and poetic." A companion of German painter and sculptor Max Ernst in the years before World War II, Carrington frequented the Surrealist Group in Paris, adopting their credo "the imaginary becomes real." Her paintings convey a world in which the disturbing and the wondrous co-exist ("gentle menacing," one critic called it), filled with insect-like humans, mythical creatures, magic animals, and female symbols (most prevalently, the egg). Her writings, too, explore the intricate web between the real, the visionary, and man's spiritual enlightenment. "In both life and art," Orenstein observed, "Carrington continued to search for a connection between the macrocosm and the microcosm that would yield a vision of reality, both visible and invisible."

A gifted child born into an upper-class English family, Carrington met with frustrations in her private education until her imaginative nature and artistic ambitions were encouraged at an Italian boarding school when she was fifteen. There she learned to paint, visiting the great museums and studying the works of the masters. Although her parents objected to her career choice, Carrington eventually studied art with Amedee Ozenfant (a protege of Fernand Leger and Le Corbusier) in London. It was through the instructor that she came to meet Ernst.

Living together in the south of France, Carrington and Ernst attended Paris surrealist meetings and participated in artistic and literary events with such surrealist principals as Marcel Duchamp, Andre Breton, and Paul Eluard. Carrington exhibited her works at the International Surrealist Exhibition of 1938; Ernst illustrated her fantastic short stories. Because Ernst was a German citizen, the outbreak of World War II prompted his immigration to the United States in 1941. Carrington sought refuge in Spain, where she suffered a mental breakdown and was committed to a psychiatric hospital. She recalls the experience in the highly regarded autobiographical account *Down Below.* "The breakdown opened an inner universe of dream imagery," related Orenstein. "It was an intimate journal of her mental breakdown, and a document of human suffering transcended by artistic vision."

After her release from the sanatorium Carrington traveled to Portugal, where she met and married Mexican cultural attache Renato Leduc. The two settled in New York City, where the artist showed her work in surrealist exhibitions and wrote for surrealist literary reviews. In 1942 she and Leduc moved to Mexico, where the couple divorced and Carrington married Hungarian refugee and photographer Chiqui Weisz; there the pair remained, raising two sons. It was for Mexico City's National Museum of Anthropology that Carrington executed her best-known work in 1962, the enormous mural "El Mundo Magico de los Mayas." Orenstein elaborated: "Based upon intimate knowledge of the people of Chiapas (a state in southeast Mexico near the Yucatan) who are the descendants of the Mayas, the mural incorporates a depiction of the Mayan magical traditions into a poetic evocation of the Chiapas landscape. Here again Carrington's ability to unify the visionary and the real is dramatically clear." The artist is also credited with launching the women's liberation movement in Mexico in the early 1970s. As often expressed in her work, Carrington sees the mechanistic, aggressive male force as responsible for civilization's probable fate of nuclear annihilation; it is in the creative, altruistic female principle that she gleans humankind's salvation. "If women remain passive," she once stated, "I think there is very little hope for the survival of life on this earth."

In reviewing what has come to be considered a contemporary classic—Carrington's 1974 fantasy novel *The Hearing Trumpet—Times Literary Supplement* writer Gabriele Annan recognized a corresponding theme. Narrated by ninety-two-year-old Marian Leatherby, a new resident in an ominous retirement home, the story includes occult secrets, poisonings, a feminist uprising, mythical identities, and a search for the Holy Grail. "I am not sure I have got the plot absolutely right, and I may have misinterpreted some of the symbols," reported Annan. "But I am fairly certain that the novel is about the triumph of the unstructured, unaggressive, intuitive, spontaneous, sexy, female principle over the hierarchical, hieratic, ruthless, unimaginative, uncreative male one."

Calling *The Hearing Trumpet* "an unashamed and confident fantasy," Paddy Kitchen commented in the *Listener,* "I enjoyed the surreal home [Marian] is put into by her unloving son . . . but not so much the ensuing occult dramas and pursuit of the Holy Grail." *National Review* critic Ronald De Feo concurred; "the more whimsical and outrageous Miss Carrington grows . . . the less inspired and infectious her book seems," he wrote. "Unlike the fantasy of her paintings, the fantasy here too often comes across as arbitrary." Still, a reviewer for the *Atlantic* declared "this wildly fanciful rumpus in an old ladies' home . . . witty, mischievous, amusing reading." And Annan concluded: "Luckily the writing is as neat, dry and witty as the content is wild, woolly and portentous. Mrs. Leatherby's voice is the voice of an exemplary old lady, sedate, demure, and reasonable. It is the contrast between the language and what it says that gives the book its considerable charm."

The surrealist ambience that suffuses Carrington's second fantasy novel, *The Stone Door,* is evoked with odd characters, mystical journeys, and startling images; "[it] virtually obliges its reader to scan like a collage or patchwork its irregular pattern of truncated narratives studded with surprising similes and cultural reminders," *Times Literary Supplement* reviewer Jane Miller described. Not as successful as its predecessor, *The Stone Door* met with reservations like those expressed by Mary Hope in the *Spectator,* "This is for enthusiasts only: a surrealist novel whose images are fierce and compelling, but whose drift is obscure." "In spite of all its waywardness and intimations of profundity the novel is finally a good deal more

like a prettily embroidered sampler than some gravely worked cabbalistic banner,'' Miller agreed, ''for its eclectic, not to say magpie, snatching at bright detail and unexplained incident is controlled by a tastefulness and sense of design which are old-fashioned and charming rather than portentous.''

BIOGRAPHICAL/CRITICAL SOURCES:

PERIODICALS

Atlantic, October, 1976.
Listener, June 2, 1977.
Ms., August, 1974.
National Review, April 1, 1977.
New York Times Book Review, January 1, 1978.
Spectator, April 22, 1978.
Times Literary Supplement, May 27, 1977, April 28, 1978.*

—Sketch by Nancy Pear

* * *

CARTLEDGE, Paul 1947-

PERSONAL: Born March 24, 1947, in London, England; son of Marcus Raymond (a banker) and Margaret (Oakley) Cartledge; married Judith Portrait (a lawyer), July 21, 1976; children: Gabrielle. *Education:* Oxford University, B.A. (with first class honors), 1969, D.Phil., 1975.

ADDRESSES: Home—Cambridge, England. *Office*—Clare College, Cambridge University, Cambridge CB2 1TL, England.

CAREER: New University of Ulster, Coleraine, Northern Ireland, lecturer in classics, 1972-73; National University of Ireland, Trinity College, Dublin, lecturer in classics, 1973-78; University of Warwick, Coventry, England, lecturer in classical civilization, 1978-79; Cambridge University, Cambridge, England, lecturer in ancient history, 1979—, fellow and director of studies in classics at Clare College, 1981—.

MEMBER: Society for the Promotion of Hellenic Studies, Society of Antiquaries of London (fellow).

AWARDS, HONORS: Leverhulme grant, 1982.

WRITINGS:

Sparta and Lakonia: A Regional History, 1300-362 B.C., Routledge & Kegan Paul, 1979.
(Editor with F. D. Harvey, and contributor) *Crux: Essays in Greek History Presented to G. E. M. de Ste. Croix,* Duckworth, 1985.
Agesilaos and the Crisis of Sparta, Duckworth, 1987.
Classical Greece: A Social and Economic History, Dent, 1988.
(With A. J. S. Spawforth) *Hellenistic and Roman Sparta,* Routledge & Kegan Paul, 1988.

Contributor to classical studies journals and newspapers.

WORK IN PROGRESS: The Greeks, publication by Oxford University Press expected in 1990.

SIDELIGHTS: Paul Cartledge told *CA:* ''Though my professional preoccupation is with ancient Greece, the history I write has to be meaningful to people living in societies with radically different economic, social, religious, and political structures. Comparative study of contemporary non-Western societies and Mediterranean village communities is therefore vital to my work. Equally important is a sense of place: hence my extensive travel and archaeological field work in Greece, especially in the region around Sparta in the southern Peloponnese.''

Simon Hornblower wrote in the *Times Literary Supplement* that *Sparta and Lakonia* is, in many ways, the best book available on Sparta. According to its critic, the book is both a ''densely documented'' archaeological study and ''a vigorous political and social history of Classical Sparta.'' The author's ''major achievement,'' Hornblower concluded, ''is to bring out the importance of Sparta's *perioikoi,* that is, the members of the communities which were controlled by Sparta but were not reduced by her to serfdom.''

BIOGRAPHICAL/CRITICAL SOURCES:

PERIODICALS

Times Literary Supplement, February 15, 1980.

* * *

CASEY, Patrick
See THURMAN, Wallace (Henry)

* * *

CASTORO, Laura A(nn) 1948-
(Laura Parker; Terry Nelsen Bonner, pseudonym)

PERSONAL: Born September 18, 1948, in Fort Worth, Tex.; daughter of David Edward (a dentist) and Mary Dell (a teacher; maiden name, Guinn) Parker; married Christopher Castoro (in middle management), June 8, 1968; children: Theresa Marie, Anthony David, Christopher Michael. *Education:* Attended Howard University, 1966-68, and Texas A & I University, 1971-73. *Politics:* Independent. *Religion:* Roman Catholic.

ADDRESSES: Home and office—Plano, Tex. *Agent*—Denise Marcil, Denise Marcil Literary Agency, 316 West 82nd St., New York, N.Y. 10024.

CAREER: Writer, 1979—. Speaker at numerous conferences and workshops. Member of Higher Arts Council in Dallas, and Fort Worth, both 1981-85.

MEMBER: Greater Dallas Writers Association (co-founder, 1979).

WRITINGS:

UNDER NAME LAURA PARKER

Silks and Sabers (historical romance), Dell, 1980.
Jim Bridger: Mountain Man (western), Dell, 1981.
Kit Carson: Trapper King (western), Dell, 1982.
Emerald and Sapphire (historical romance), Pocket Books, 1983.
Until Love Is Enough (contemporary romance), Avon, 1983.
The Perfect Choice (romance), Silhouette, 1983.
Moth and Flame (historical romance), Pocket Books, 1984.
Dangerous Company (romantic suspense), Silhouette, 1984.
Rose of the Mists (historical romance), Warner Books, 1985.
A Rose in Splendor (historical romance), Warner Books, 1986.
The Secret Rose (historical romance), Warner Books, 1987.

OTHER

(Under pseudonym Terry Nelsen Bonner) *The Free Woman* (Australian saga), Dell, 1983.
(With David M. Bailey) *Careers in Computers* (young adult nonfiction), Messner, 1985.

WORK IN PROGRESS: Rebellious Angels, ''a story of a young American woman whose struggle to become a writer in the 1890s is won amid the high-society life of New York and the

decadent literary circles of London,'' publication expected in 1988.

SIDELIGHTS: Laura A. Castoro told *CA:* ''When I was growing up in Pine Bluff, Arkansas, I never had thoughts of becoming a writer. One day in the third grade I was elected secretary of my class. I was so excited that I showed the minutes of the first meeting to my father. He was happy for me but sent me back to recopy the notes because of spelling and punctuation errors. His exact words were, 'Anything worth doing is worth doing right.' After the third trip back to recopy the notes, I decided that I didn't want to be secretary of anything and I certainly didn't want to write for a living!

''Years later, when I began writing my first novel, my father's words came back to haunt me. Over the years my father had used that phrase so often in connection with any project I undertook that it had become second nature. My first book was written only for myself, but I found I was not satisfied with only guessing what people wore and ate. I went to the library to do research. Little did I know then that my book would later sell and be published.

''Now that I have thirteen published books to my credit, I still retain that desire for perfection that makes me write over and over again until I've done the best I can do. It's a special legacy from my father and I hope to pass it on to my three children.''

* * *

CATANZARITI, John 1942-

PERSONAL: Born June 1, 1942, in New York, N.Y.; son of Dominick and Rose Catanzariti; married Rosemary Bellofatto in 1965; children: Jason, Tracie. *Education:* Queens College of the City University of New York, B.A., 1964, M.A., 1973.

ADDRESSES: Office—''Papers of Thomas Jefferson,'' C-9-J Firestone Library, Princeton University, Princeton, N.J. 08544.

CAREER: Queens College of the City University of New York, Flushing, N.Y., associate editor, 1970-80, co-editor, 1980-81, editor and project director of ''Papers of Robert Morris,'' 1981-86; Princeton University, Princeton, N.J., senior research historian and editor of ''Papers of Thomas Jefferson,'' 1987—.

MEMBER: Organization of American Historians, Association for Documentary Editing, Institute of Early American History and Culture.

WRITINGS:

(Associate editor) *The Papers of Robert Morris, 1781-1784,* University of Pittsburgh Press, Volume I, 1973, Volume II, 1975, Volume III, 1977, Volume IV, 1978.
(Editor with E. James Ferguson) *The Papers of Robert Morris, 1781-1784,* University of Pittsburgh Press, Volume V, 1980, Volume VI, 1984, Volume VII, 1988.
(Editor) *The Papers of Thomas Jefferson,* Volume 24, Princeton University Press, in press.

* * *

CERMAK, Martin
See DUCHACEK, Ivo D(uka)

CESARA, Manda
See POEWE, Karla

* * *

CHAMBERS, James 1948-
(Jimmy Cliff)

BRIEF ENTRY: Professionally known as Jimmy Cliff; born in 1948 in St. Catherine (one source says St. James), Jamaica. Jamaican singer, actor, and songwriter. Jimmy Cliff was one of the first musicians to introduce reggae—a popular Jamaican combination of calypso and African music—to audiences outside the West Indies. When Cliff was fourteen he moved to Kingston, Jamaica, where his recordings became popular, and in 1965 the singer moved to England to further his career. Once there he encountered racial prejudice—a theme on which he began to base his songs—and musical rejection, which prompted him to modify reggae with more conservative music styles. Cliff's late 1960s album *Wonderful World, Beautiful People* (A & M) demonstrated the singer's break from strict reggae tradition and became his first worldwide hit. In 1972 Cliff starred in ''The Harder They Come,'' a movie about a rural Jamaican boy who, like Cliff, travels to Kingston to become a reggae star. Released in the United States in 1973, the film became a cult hit, as did the movie's title soundtrack. Cliff's other albums include *Unlimited, Music Maker, Struggling Man, Follow My Mind,* and *The Best of Jimmy Cliff.*

BIOGRAPHICAL/CRITICAL SOURCES:

BOOKS

Contemporary Literary Criticism, Volume 21, Gale, 1982.
Directory of Blacks in the Performing Arts, Scarecrow, 1978.
The Illustrated Encyclopedia of Rock, revised edition, Harmony Books, 1978.
Rock On: The Illustrated Encyclopedia of Rock n' Roll, Volume II: *The Modern Years, 1964-Present,* Crowell, 1978.

PERIODICALS

Crawdaddy, January, 1974, August, 1975.
Melody Maker, April 24, 1976.
Rolling Stone, September 27, 1973.

* * *

CHAMBERS, John W. 1933-

PERSONAL: Born September 29, 1933, in New York, N.Y.; son of Robert A. (a lawyer) and Jean (a writer; maiden name, Wheeler) Chambers; married Margaret Powell, 1960 (divorced, 1969); married Carole Griffith (an actress), 1969; children: (first marriage) Margaret Watson, John Powell. *Education:* Yale University, B.A., 1957; Columbia University, M.A., 1961. *Politics:* Independent. *Religion:* Protestant.

ADDRESSES: Home—109 Division Ave., Blue Point, N.Y. 11715. *Agent*—Joan Daves, 59 East 54th St., New York, N.Y. 10022.

CAREER: Schoolteacher in Washington, Conn., 1962-69; worked in odd jobs, did free-lance writing, 1969-71; Morrell & Co. (retail wine outlet), Nye, N.Y., began as salesman, became manager, 1971-85; Winebow, Inc. (wholesale wine distributors), New York, N.Y., sales representative, 1985—. *Military service:* U.S. Army, 1973-75.

WRITINGS:

JUVENILE NOVELS

Fritzi's Winter, Atheneum, 1979.
Finder, Atheneum, 1981.
Showdown at Apple Hill, Atheneum, 1982.
Footlight Summer, Atheneum, 1983.
Fire Island Forfeit, Atheneum, 1984.
The Colonel and Me, Atheneum, 1985.

Wine columnist for *Medical Tribune,* 1978-84. Contributor of articles and stories to magazines.

WORK IN PROGRESS: Tuxedo Tom, a story about a cat, set on Fire Island, completion expected in 1988; an adult mystery novel, completion expected in 1988; *Clambo's Revenge,* a juvenile mystery set on Fire Island.

SIDELIGHTS: John W. Chambers told *CA:* "My writing career developed as an outgrowth of storytelling to my children. *Fritzi's Winter* was written to be read aloud to them. Three of my books are set on Fire Island, a barrier beach off southern Long Island, where I have a summer house. Early horseback riding experiences led to *The Colonel and Me,* and two years of summer theater resulted in *Footlight Summer.*

"I consider my primary object as a juvenile writer is to entertain. I believe stories should be imaginative and well narrated, with good characterization, and they should be upbeat. My characters act morally without being goody-goody, but I face them with moral crises that require decisions. I consider myself a realist, not a naturalist. I am not inclined to write about abortion, rape, and similar subject matter. There is all too much of this on television, in the movies, and in the newspapers. I think juvenile literature should offer an alternative, and I endeavor to do so."

* * *

CHAR, Rene(-Emile) 1907-1988

OBITUARY NOTICE—See index for *CA* sketch: Born June 14, 1907, in L'Isle-sur-la-Sorgue, Vaucluse, France; died February 19, 1988, in Paris, France; buried in L'Isle-sur-la-Sorgue, Vaucluse, France. Military leader, translator, and author. Char was considered the greatest French poet of the twentieth century by such esteemed figures as writer Albert Camus and Prime Minister Jacques Chirac. During the first years of his career Char became a follower of Andre Breton's surrealist movement, and his poems from the early 1930s reflect that influence. Within a few years, however, Char broke with the surrealists and began producing poems dealing with Europe's increasingly pervasive fascism. During World War II, after participating in the French defeat at Alsace, he became a target of investigation by France's pro-Nazi Vichy government, which considered anyone with surrealist connections as a likely Communist and thus an enemy of the state. Char fled into the Alps, where he assumed command of a Free French Forces' parachute division. Although wounded in 1944, he remained active in the Resistance, and he eventually fought in the battles leading to the liberation of Provence. For his actions he received the Medal of the Resistance and the Cross of War.

After the war Char resumed his writing career to great acclaim, and he was subsequently named to the French Legion of Honor. His writings in English translation are *Leaves of Hypnos,* a war journal; *Hypnos Waking,* a selection of poetry and prose; and *Poems of Rene Char.* Among his many volumes in French are *Le Marteau sans maitre* (title means "Hammer Without a Master") and *La Nuit talismanic* (title means "The Talismanic Night"). Char also wrote plays and criticism.

OBITUARIES AND OTHER SOURCES:

BOOKS

The International Who's Who, 51st edition, Europa, 1987.

PERIODICALS

Chicago Tribune, February 21, 1988.
Los Angeles Times, February 21, 1988.
New York Times, February 21, 1988.
Times (London), February 22, 1988.
Washington Post, February 21, 1988.

* * *

CHASE, Philander D(ean) 1943-

PERSONAL: Born March 10, 1943, in Elkin, N.C.; son of Vern Warren and Marion (Wagner) Chase; married Jeanne Sheaffer (a teacher), September 18, 1971. *Education:* North Carolina State University, B.A., 1965; Duke University, M.A., 1968, Ph.D., 1973.

ADDRESSES: Home—223 Old Lynchburg Rd., Charlottesville, Va. 22903. *Office*—"Papers of George Washington," Alderman Library, University of Virginia, Charlottesville, Va. 22901.

CAREER: University of Virginia, Charlottesville, assistant editor of "Papers of George Washington," 1974—.

MEMBER: American Historical Association, Organization of American Historians, Association for Documentary Editing, Institute for Early American History and Culture, Southern Historical Association.

AWARDS, HONORS: Fellow of National Historic Publications and Records Commission, 1973-74; Phillip M. Hamer Award for documentary editing from Society of American Archivists, 1978, for *The Diaries of George Washington.*

WRITINGS:

(Assistant editor) *The Diaries of George Washington,* six volumes, University Press of Virginia, 1976-79.
(Assistant editor) *The Papers of George Washington: Colonial Series,* University Press of Virginia, Volume 1: *1748-August 1755,* 1982, Volume 2: *August 1755-April 1756,* 1982, Volume 3: *April-November 1756,* 1984, Volume 4: *November 1756-October 1757,* 1984, Volume 5: *October 1757-August 1758,* 1988, Volume 6: *August 1758-December 1760,* 1988.
(Editor) *The Papers of George Washington: Revolutionary War Series,* University Press of Virginia, Volume 1: *June-September 1775,* 1985, Volume 2: *September-December 1775,* 1987, Volume 3: *January-April 1776,* 1988.

Contributor to history journals.

* * *

CHEEKS, James E. 1930-

PERSONAL: Born July 6, 1930, in Cleveland, Ohio; son of Elmer Jay (an engineer) and Ella Mae (a social worker) Cheeks; children: Audrey Cheeks Wehba. *Education:* University of Chicago, B.A., 1950, J.D., 1954.

ADDRESSES: Home—64 East 94th St., New York, N.Y. 10128. *Office*—Research Institute of America, 90 Fifth Ave., New York, N.Y. 10128.

CAREER: Research Institute of America, New York, N.Y., editorial vice-president, 1976—. Adjunct professor at Pace University. Member of Bar of New York, Illinois, and U.S. Supreme Court. *Military service:* U.S. Army, 1954-56.

WRITINGS:

How Proper Planning Can Reduce Your Income Taxes, Pilot Books, 1971.

(With Sidney Kess) *A Practical Guide to Tax Planning,* TMI, 1974.

How to Compensate Executives, Dow Jones-Irwin, 1974, 3rd edition, 1982.

Keoghs: Keys to Security and Wealth, F. Watts, 1986.

* * *

CHEKHONTE, Antosha
See CHEKHOV, Anton (Pavlovich)

* * *

CHEKHOV, Anton (Pavlovich) 1860-1904
(A Man Without a Spleen, Antosha Chekhonte, My Brother's Brother, v)

PERSONAL: Middle name (patronymic) also transliterated as Pavlovitch; surname also transliterated as Cechov, Cekov, Cexov, Chehov, Chekhoff, Chekov, Tchehov, Tchekhof, Tchekhoff, Tchekhov, Tchekkof, Tchekoff; born January 16 (some sources say 17), 1860, in Taganrog, Russia (now U.S.S.R.); died of tuberculosis, July 2 (one source says July 1), 1904, in Badenweiler, Germany (now West Germany); buried in Moscow, U.S.S.R.; son of Pavel Yegorovitch (an owner of a grocery business) and Yevgeniya Yakovlevna (Morozov) Chekhov; married Olga Leonardovna Knipper (an actress), May 25, 1901. *Education:* University of Moscow, M.D., 1884.

CAREER: Physician and writer. Editor of the literary section of *Russkaya mysl,* 1903; founder of two rural schools.

MEMBER: Society of Russian Dramatic Writers and Opera Composers, Society for Lovers of Russian Literature (provisional president, 1903), Literary Fund.

AWARDS, HONORS: Pushkin Prize from the Division of Russian Language and Letters of the Academy of Sciences, 1888, for collection of stories, *V sumerkakh* (*In the Twilight*); elected Honorary Academician of the Pushkin Section of Belle Lettres of Academy of Sciences, 1899; awarded Order of St. Stanislav for work in the cause of national education, 1899; Griboedov Prize from the Society of Dramatic Writers and Opera Composers for *Tri syostry: Drama v chetyryokh deystviyakh* (*The Three Sisters: A Drama in Four Acts*).

WRITINGS:

PLAYS

"P'yessa bez nazvaniya (Platonov)" (one-act; written c. 1881); translation by John Cournos published as *That Worthless Fellow Platonov,* Dutton, 1930; translation by Basil Ashmore published as *A Play Without a Title (Platonov),* P. Nevill, 1952, published as *Don Juan (in the Russian Manner),* preface by Sir Desmond MacCarthy, P. Nevill, 1952, first produced in New York at the Minor Latham Drama Workshop, April 23, 1954; translation by Alex Szogyj published as *A Country Scandal (Platonov),* adaptation by Szogyj, Coward-McCann, 1960, first produced in New York at the Greenwich Mews Theater, May 5, 1960, published as *A Country Scandal: A Drama in Four Acts,* Samuel French, 1961; translation by Dmitri Makaroff published as *Platonov: An Abridged Version of an Untitled Play in Four Acts,* introduction by George Devine, Methuen, 1961; translation by David Magarshack published as *Platonov: A Play in Four Acts and Five Scenes,* Hill & Wang, 1964; translation by Michael Frayn published as *Wild Honey: The Untitled Play,* Methuen, 1984, first produced in London at the National Theater, 1984, produced on Broadway at the Virginia Theater, December 18, 1986.

O vrede tabaka: Stsena monolog (written c. 1886-1902), translation by Milka Petrovich published as *On the Harmful Effects of Tobacco,* adaptation by Boris Zupetz, pictures by Patrick Couratin, Quist, 1977.

"Ivanov: Drama v chetyryokh deystviyakh" (four-act), first produced in Moscow at the Korsh Theater, November 19, 1887; translation by Marian Fell published as *Ivanoff: A Play in Four Acts,* Brentanos, 1923; translation by Ariadne Nicolaeff published as *Ivanov: A Drama in Four Acts,* adaptation by John Gielgud, Theater Arts Books, 1966, first produced on Broadway at the Shubert Theater, May 3, 1966.

"Medved': Shutka v odnom deystvii" (one-act), first produced in Moscow at Korsh Theater, October, 1888; translation by Roy Temple House published as *A Bear,* Moods Publishing, 1909; translation by Hilmar Baukhage published as *The Boor: A Comedy in One Act,* Samuel French, 1915; translation by Eric Bentley published as *The Brute: A Joke in One Act,* Samuel French, 1956; published as *The Bear,* adapted by Joellen Bland, Denver Pioneer Drama Service, 1984.

"Predlozheniye: Shutka v odnom deystvii" (one-act; written c. 1888-89); translation by Baukhage and Barett H. Clark published as *A Marriage Proposal: Comedy in One Act,* Samuel French, 1914.

"Leshy: Komediya v chetyryokh deystviyakh" (four-act), first produced in Moscow at the Abramov Theater, November, 1889; translation by S. S. Koteliansky published as *The Wood Demon: A Comedy in Four Acts by Anton Tchehov,* Macmillan, 1926.

"Chayka: Komediya v chetyryokh deystviyakh" (four-act), first produced in St. Petersburg at the Alexandrine Theater, October 17, 1896; translation by Fred Eisemann published as *The Sea-gull,* R. G. Badger, 1913; translation by Julius West published as *The Sea-gull: A Play in Four Acts,* Hendersons, 1915; translation by Stark Young published as *The Sea Gull,* Scribner, 1939, first produced on Broadway at the Shubert Theater, March 28, 1938, reprinted as *The Sea Gull: A Drama in Four Acts,* Samuel French, 1950; translation by Magarshack published as *The Seagull: Produced by Stanislavsky,* edited and introduction by S. D. Balukhaty, Dobson, 1952; translation by David Iliffe published as *The Seagull: A Play,* Samuel French (London), 1953; translation by Bernard W. Sznycer published as *The Gull: A Comedy in Four Acts,* [New York], 1967, published in England as *The Gull,* Poets' and Painters' Press, 1974; translation by Jean-Claude Van Itallie published as *Anton Chekhov's The Sea Gull: A New Version,* Dramatists Play Service, 1974, published as *The*

Sea Gull: A Comedy in Four Acts, commentaries by William M. Hoffman and Daniel Seltzer, textual notes by Paul Schmidt, Harper & Row, 1977; translation by Ann Jellicoe published as *The Sea Gull,* edited by Henry Popkin, Avon, 1975; translation by David French published as *The Seagull,* Playwright's Co-op (Toronto), 1977, published as *The Seagull: A Play,* notes by Donna Orwin, General Paperbacks, 1978; translation by Thomas Kilroy published as *The Seagull,* Methuen, 1981; translation with introduction by Tania Alexander and Charles Sturridge published as *The Seagull: A Comedy in Four Acts,* Amber Lane Press, 1985; translation and introduction by Frayn published as *The Seagull: A Comedy in Four Acts,* Methuen, 1986.

"Dyadya Vanya: Stseny iz derevenskoy zhizni v chetyroykh deystviyakh" (four-act), first produced in Moscow at the Moscow Art Theater, October 26, 1899; translation by Jenny Covan published as *Uncle Vanya: A Comedy in Four Acts,* Brentanos, 1922; adaptation and translation by Rose Caylor published as *Uncle Vanya,* Covici, Friede, 1930; translation by Young published as *Uncle Vanya: Scenes From Village Life in Four Acts,* Samuel French, 1956; translation by Tyrone Guthrie and Leonid Kipnis published as *Uncle Vanya: Scenes From Country Life in Four Acts,* University of Minnesota Press, 1969; translation by Robert W. Corrigan published as *Uncle Vanya: An Authoritative Text Edition of a Great Play,* Avon, 1974; translation by John Murrell published as *Uncle Vanya: Scenes From Rural Life,* Theatrebooks (Toronto), 1978; translation by Pam Gems published as *Uncle Vanya,* introduction by Edward Braun, Methuen, 1979; translation by Van Itallie published as *Uncle Vanya: Scenes From Country Life in Four Acts,* Dramatists Play Service, 1980; translation and introduction by Frayn published as *Uncle Vanya: Scenes From Country Life in Four Acts,* Methuen, 1987.

"Tri syostry: Drama v chetyryokh deystviyakh" (four-act), first produced in Moscow at the Moscow Art Theater, January 21, 1901; translation by Covan published as *The Three Sisters: A Drama in Four Acts,* Brentanos, 1922; translation by Young published as *The Three Sisters: A Drama in Four Acts,* Samuel French, 1941; translation by Guthrie and Kipnis published as *The Three Sisters: An Authoritative Text Edition,* critical material selected and introduced by Popkin, Avon, 1965; translation and notes by Randell Jarrell published as *The Three Sisters,* Macmillan, 1969; translation by Moura Budberg published as *Three Sisters,* Davis-Poynter, 1971; translation by Van Itallie published as *Anton Chekhov's Three Sisters: A New English Version,* Dramatists Play Service, 1979; translation by Brian Friel published as *Anton Chekhov's Three Sisters: A Translation,* Gallery Books (Dublin), 1981; translation and introduction by Frayn published as *Three Sisters: A Drama in Four Acts,* Methuen, 1983; translation by Lanford Wilson published as *Three Sisters: A Play,* Dramatists Play Service, 1984, first produced in Hartford, Conn., at the Hartford Stage, 1984.

"Vishnyovy Sad: Komediya v chetyryokh deystriyakh" (four-act), first produced in Moscow at the Moscow Art Theater, January 17, 1904; translation and introduction by Max S. Mandell published as *The Cherry Garden: A Comedy in Four Acts,* C. G. Whaples, 1908; translation by Covan published as *The Cherry Orchard: A Comedy in Four Acts,* Brentanos, 1922; translation by Hubert Butler published as *The Cherry Orchard: A Play in Four Acts,* introduction by Guthrie, Baker International Play Bureau, 1934; translation by Irina Skariatina first produced as "The Cherry Orchard" on Broadway at the National Theater, January 25, 1944; translation by Young published as *The Cherry Orchard: A Drama in Four Acts,* [New York], 1947; published as *The Wistoria Trees,* adaptation by Joshua Logan, Random House, 1950, first produced on Broadway, 1950; published as *The Cherry Orchard,* Foreign Languages Publishing House (Moscow), 1956; translation by Gielgud published as *The Cherry Orchard: A Comedy in Four Acts,* introduction by Michel Saint-Denis, Theater Arts Books, 1963; translation by W. L. Goodman published as *The Cherry Orchard,* dialogue and adaptation by Henry S. Taylor, Ginn, 1964; published as *Chekhov's The Cherry Orchard,* edited by Herbert Goldstone, Allyn & Bacon, 1965; translation by Avrahm Yarmolinsky published as *The Cherry Orchard,* critical material selected and introduced by Popkin, Avon, 1965; translation by Guthrie and Kipnis published as *The Cherry Orchard: A Play in Four Acts,* University of Minnesota Press, 1965; translation by Van Itallie published as *The Cherry Orchard,* Dramatists Play Service, 1977, published as *The Cherry Orchard: A Comedy in Four Acts,* Grove Press, 1977, revised version, Dramatists Play Service, 1979; translation by Helen Rappaport published as *The Cherry Orchard,* new version by Trevor Griffiths, Pluto Press, 1978; translation and introduction by Frayn published as *The Cherry Orchard: A Comedy in Four Acts,* Methuen, 1978.

Chekhov published a collection of plays in 1897.

COLLECTED PLAYS IN ENGLISH TRANSLATION

Plays, translation and introduction by Marian Fell, first series, Scribner, 1912.

***Two Plays by Tchekhof: The Seagull* [and] *The Cherry Orchard,* translation, introduction and notes by George Calderon, G. Richards, 1912.**

Plays by Anton Tchekoff, translation and introduction by Julius West, second series, Scribner, 1916.

Plays From the Russian, translation by Constance Garnett, two volumes, Chatto & Windus, 1923.

The Plays of Anton Tchekov, translation by Garnett, preface by Eva Le Gallienne, Modern Library, 1930, University Microfilms, 1974.

Plays: The Seagull, The Cherry Orchard, On the High Road, The Wedding, The Proposal, The Anniversary, The Bear, The Three Sisters, woodcuts by Howard Simon, Three Sirens Press, 1935, published as *Plays,* Perma Giants, 1950.

The Cherry Orchard and Other Plays, woodcuts by Simon, Grosset & Dunlap, 1936.

Five Famous Plays, translations by West and Fell, Scribner, 1939.

Three Plays, translation by S. S. Koteliansky, Penguin (Harmondsworth), 1940.

The Plays of Anton Chekov: Nine Plays Including the Seagull . . . and Others, translation by Garnett, Caxton House, 1945.

Nine Plays, Grosset & Dunlap, 1946, published as *Nine Plays of Chekov: The Sea Gull, The Cherry Orchard, The Three Sisters, and Others,* 1963.

Six Famous Plays, translations by West and Fell, Scribner, 1949.

Four Short Plays, translation by West, Duckworth, 1950.

Plays, Doric Books, 1950.

Chekhov Plays, translation by Elisaveta Fen, Penguin, 1951.
The Seagull, Uncle Vania, The Bear, The Proposal, A Jubilee, translation by Fen, Penguin (Harmondsworth), 1953, published as *The Seagull and Other Plays,* 1954.
Best Plays, translation and introduction by Stark Young, Modern Library, 1956.
Three Plays: The Cherry Orchard, Three Sisters, Ivanov, translation and introduction by Fen, Penguin (Harmondsworth), 1956.
The Brute, and Other Farces, edited by Eric Bentley, translated by Bentley and Theodore Hoffman, Samuel French, 1958, Applause, 1985.
Four Great Plays, Bantam, 1958.
Plays, translation and introduction by Fen, Penguin, 1959.
Six Plays of Chekhov, translation and introduction by Robert W. Corrigan, foreword by Harold Clurman, Holt, 1962.
Chekhov: The Major Plays, translation by Ann Dunnigan, foreword by Robert Brustein, New American Library, 1964.
Uncle Vanya; The Cherry Orchard; and The Wood Demon, translated and edited by Ronald Hingley, Oxford University Press, 1964.
The Sea Gull [and] *The Tragedian in Spite of Himself,* translations by Fred Eisemann and Olive Frances Murphy, International Pocket Library, 1965.
Uncle Vanya, and The Cherry Orchard, translation by Hingley, Oxford University Press, 1965.
Ten Early Plays, translation and introduction by Alex Szogyi, Bantam, 1965.
Two Plays: The Cherry Orchard [and] *Three Sisters,* translation by Garnett, introduction by John Gielgud, illustrations by Lajos Szalay, Heritage Press, 1966.
Four Plays, translation, preface, afterwords, and notes by Szogyi, Washington Square Press, 1968.
Ivanov, The Seagull, and Three Sisters, translation by Hingley, Oxford University Press, 1968.
Four Plays, translation by David Magarshack, Hill & Wang, 1969.
Chekhov Plays, introduction and appreciation by Arnold B. McMillin, illustrated by Mette Ivers, Heron Books, 1969.
Eight Plays, translation by Fen, Franklin Library, 1976.
Anton Chekhov's Plays, translated and edited by Eugene Kerr Bristow, Norton, 1977.
Chekhov: Five Major Plays, translation and introduction by Hingley, Oxford University Press, 1977.
The Cherry Orchard and The Seagull, translation by Laurence Senelick, AHM Publishing, 1977.
Five Plays, translation and introduction by Hingley, Oxford University Press, 1980.
Two Plays: The Three Sisters; The Cherry Orchard, translation by Fen, illustrations by Elaine Raphael and Don Bolognese, Franklin Library, 1980.
Chekhov's Great Plays: A Critical Anthology, edited and introduced by Jean-Pierre Barricelli, New York University Press, 1981.

SHORT FICTION

Contributor, sometimes under the pseudonyms A Man Without a Spleen, Antosha Chekhonte, My Brother's Brother, or v, of more than four hundred short stories, including "An Anonymous Story," "Anyuta," "Ariadne," "At Christmas," "At Home," "An Awkward Business," "The Beauties," "The Beggar," "The Butterfly," "Concerning Love," "The Daughter of Albion," "The Death of a Government Official," "A Dreadful Night," "A Dreary Story," "Easter Night," "The Encounter," "Enemies," "Excellent People," "Fat and Thin," "Gooseberries," "Grisha," "Gusev," "A Hard Case," "Heartache," "The Huntsman," "In Exile," "In the Cart," "In the Ravine," "In Trouble," "The Malefactor," "A Marriageable Girl," "Mire," "The Misfortune," "Murder," "My Life," "My Wife," "The Name-Day Party," "New Villa," "On Official Business," "Oysters," "Peasant Women," "Peasants," "Revenge," "Romance With Double Bass," "Sergeant Prishibeyev," "Sleepy," "A Trifle From Life," "The Two Volodyas," "Typhus," "Vanka," "Verochka," "A Woman's Kingdom," "The Witch," "The Work of Art," to numerous periodicals, including *Budil'nik, Novoye vremya, Oskolki, Petersburgskaya gazeta, Russkaya mysl, Russkiye vedemosti, Severny vestnik, Strekoza,* and *Zhurnal dlya vsekh.*

Chekhov published a number of collections of his works during his lifetime, including: *Sbornik dlya detey* (title means "A Collection of Children's Stories"; 1883); *Pestrye rasskazy* (title means "Motley Tales"; 1886); *V sumerkakh* (title means "In the Twilight"; 1887); *Nevinnye rechi* (title means "Innocent Speeches"; 1887); *Rasskazy* (title means "Tales"; 1888); *Detvora* (title means "Children"; 1889); also an 1890 collection whose title has been translated as "Gloomy People" and an 1894 collection whose title has been translated as "Stories and Tales."

COLLECTED SHORT FICTION IN ENGLISH TRANSLATION

The Black Monk, and Other Stories, translation by R.E.C. Long, Duckworth, 1903, F. A. Stokes, 1915, reprinted, Books for Libraries Press, 1970.
The Kiss, and Other Stories, translation by Long, Duckworth, 1908, F. A. Stokes, 1916, reprinted, Books for Libraries Press, 1972.
Stories of Russian Life, translation by Marian Fell, Scribner, 1914.
The Bet, and Other Stories, translation by S. S. Koteliansky and J. M. Murry, J. W. Luce, 1915.
Russian Silhouettes: More Stories of Russian Life, translation by Fell, Scribner, 1915, reprinted, Books for Libraries Press, 1970.
The Steppe, and Other Stories, translation by Adeline Lister Kaye, F. A. Stokes, 1915, reprinted, Books for Libraries Press, 1970.
The House With the Mezzanine, and Other Stories, translation by Koteliansky and Gilbert Cannan, Scribner, 1917.
Rothschild's Fiddle, and Other Stories, Boni & Liveright, 1917, reprinted, Books for Libraries Press, 1970.
The Tales of Chekhov, translation by Garnett, two volumes, Macmillan, 1917, reprinted, Ecco Press, 1984—.
Nine Humorous Tales, translation by Isaac Goldberg and Henry T. Schnittkind, Stratford, 1918, 2nd edition, revised, Books for Libraries Press, 1970.
My Life, and Other Stories, translation by Koteliansky and Cannan, C. W. Daniel, 1920, reprinted, Books for Libraries Press, 1971.
The Grasshopper and Other Stories, translation and introduction by A. E. Chamot, McKay, 1926, reprinted, Books for Libraries Press, 1972.
The Shooting Party, translation by Chamot, Stanley Paul, 1926, McKay, 1927, revised by Julian Symons, Deutsch, 1986.
Select Tales of Tchehov, translation by Garnett, two volumes, Chatto & Windus, 1927, reprinted, Barnes & Noble, 1967-68.
Short Stories, translation by Garnett, introduction by Evelyn May Albright, Macmillan, 1928.

The Stories of Anton Tchekov, edited and introduced by Robert N. Linscott, Modern Library, 1932, published as *The Stories of Anton Chekhov,* 1959.
Tales From Tchekhov, translation by Garnett, Penguin, 1938.
My Life, translation by E. R. Schimanskaya, Staples, 1943, reprinted, University Microfilms, 1975.
Short Stories, translation by Chamot, Commodore Press, 1946.
The Beggar, and Other Stories, selected by J. I. Rodale, illustrations by George W. Rickey, Story Classics, 1949.
Selected Stories, translation by Garnett, Chatto & Windus, 1953.
The Woman in the Case, and Other Stories, translation by April FitzLyon and Kyril Zinovieff, introduction by Andrew G. Colin, Spearman & Calder, 1953, British Book Centre (New York), 1954.
Short Novels and Stories, translation by Ivy Litvinov, Foreign Languages Publishing House (Moscow), 1954.
Peasants, and Other Stories, selection and preface by Edmund Wilson, Doubleday, 1956, reprinted, Franklin Library, 1982.
Tales, State Press of Artistic Literature (Moscow), 1956.
Three Years, translation by Rose Prokofieva, Foreign Languages Publishing House (Moscow), 1958.
Great Stories, translation by Garnett, edited and introduced by David H. Greene, Dell, 1959.
Kashtanka, translation by Charles Dowsett, illustrations by William Stobbs, Oxford University Press (London), 1959, H. Z. Walck, 1961.
St. Peter's Day, and Other Tales, translation and introduction by Frances H. Jones, Capricorn Books, 1959.
Wife for Sale, translation by David Tutsev, J. Calder, 1959.
Early Stories, translation by Nora Gottlieb, Bodley Head, 1960, Doubleday, 1961.
Selected Stories, translation by Ann Dunnigan, foreword by Ernest J. Simmons, New American Library, 1960.
The Image of Chekhov: Forty Stories in the Order in Which They Were Written, translation and introduction by Robert Payne, Knopf, 1963.
Selected Stories, translation and introduction by Jessie Coulson, Oxford University Press, 1963.
Lady With Lapdog, and Other Stories, translation and introduction by David Magarshack, Penguin, 1964.
Late-blooming Flowers, and Other Stories, translation by I. C. Chertok and Jean Gardner, McGraw, 1964.
The Thief, and Other Tales, translation by Ursula Smith, Vantage, 1964.
Ward Six, and Other Stories, translation by Dunnigan, afterword by Rufus W. Mathewson, New American Library, 1965.
Shadows and Light: Nine Stories by Anton Chekhov, translated and selected by Miriam Morton, illustrations by Ann Grifalconi, Doubleday, 1968.
Stories, translation by Chamot and Garnett, introduction by Arnold B. McMillin, illustrations by Mette Ivers, Heron Books (Geneva), 1969.
The Wolf and The Mutt, translation by Guy Daniels, wood engravings by Stefan Martin, McGraw, 1971.
The Sinner From Toledo, and Other Stories, translation by Arnold Hinchliffe, Fairleigh Dickinson University Press, 1972.
The Short Stories of Anton Chekhov, selection and introduction by Helen Muchnic, illustrations by Lajos Szalay, Cardavon Press, 1973.
Seven Stories, translation and introduction by Ronald Hingley, Oxford University Press, 1974.
Short Stories, translation and introduction by Elisaveta Fen, aquatints by Nigel Lambourne, Folio Society, 1974.
Eleven Stories, translation and introduction by Hingley, Oxford University Press, 1975.
Chuckle With Chekhov: A Selection of Comic Stories, selected and translated by Harvey Pitcher and James Forsyth, Swallow House Books, 1975.
Anton Chekhov's Short Stories: Texts of the Stories, Backgrounds, Criticism, selected and edited by Ralph E. Matlaw, Norton, 1979.
Boys, translation by James Riordan, illustrations by Ruben Vardzigulyants, Progress, 1979.
White Star (juvenile), translation by Michelle MacGrath, illustrations by N. Charushin, Malysh, 1980.
Chekhov: The Early Stories, 1883-1888, selected and translated by Patrick Miles and J. Murray Pitcher, 1982, Macmillan, 1983.
The Kiss, and Other Stories, translation and introduction by Ronald Wilks, Penguin, 1982.
The Duel, and Other Stories, translation and introduction by Wilks, Penguin, 1984.
The Russian Master, and Other Stories, translation, introduction, and notes by Hingley, Oxford University Press, 1984.
The Black Monk, and Other Stories, Alan Sutton, 1985.
The Party, and Other Stories, translation and introduction by Wilks, Penguin, 1985.
The Fiancee, and Other Stories, translation and introduction by Wilks, Penguin (Harmondsworth), 1986.
The Shooting Party, University of Chicago Press, 1987.
Ward Number Six, and Other Stories, translation and introduction by Hingley, Oxford University Press, 1988.

CORRESPONDENCE

Letters of Anton Chekhov to His Family and Friends, translation by Garnett, Macmillan, 1920.
Letters on the Short Story, the Drama, and Other Literary Topics, selected and edited by Louis S. Friedland, Minton, Balch, 1924, reprinted, Dover, 1966.
The Life and Letters of Anton Tchekhov, edited with translation by S. S. Koteliansky and Philip Tomlinson, G. H. Doran, 1925, B. Blom, 1965.
The Letters of Anton Pavlovitch Tchehov to Olga Leonardovna Knipper, edited with translation by Garnett, G. H. Doran, 1925, B. Blom, 1966.
Selected Letters, edited with introduction by Lillian Hellman, translation by Sidonie K. Lederer, Farrar, Straus, 1955, 1984.
Letters of Anton Chekhov, translation by Michael Henry Heim and Simon Karlinsky with introduction, selection, and commentary by Karlinsky, Harper & Row, 1973, published as *Anton Chekhov's Life and Thought: Selected Letters and Commentary,* University of California Press, 1975.
Letters of Anton Chekhov, selected and edited by Avrahm Yarmolinsky, translation by Bernard Guilbert Guerney and Lynn Solotaroff, Viking, 1973.

OTHER

The Diary of Anton Tchehov, translation by S. S. Koteliansky and Katherine Mansfield, Atheneum, 1920.
Note-book of Anton Chekhov, translated by Koteliansky and Leonard Woolf, B. W. Heubsch, 1921; published with *Reminiscences of Anton Chekhov* (see below).
(With Maksim Gorky, Alexander Kuprin, and I. A. Bunin) *The Note-books of Anton Tchekhov* [with] *Reminiscences*

of Tchekhov by Maksim Gorky (the former by Chekhov, [also see above] the latter by Gorky, Kuprin, and Bunin), translation by Koteliansky and Woolf, Hogarth Press, 1921, reprinted, Folcroft Library Editions, 1973 (also see above).

Anton Tchekhov: Literary and Theatrical Reminiscences, translated and edited by Koteliansky, G. H. Doran, 1927, reprinted, Haskell House Publishers, 1974.

The Personal Papers of Anton Chekhov, translation by Constance Garnett, introduction by Matthew Josephson, Lear, 1948.

The Unknown Chekhov: Stories and Other Writings Hitherto Untranslated, translation and introduction by Yarmolinsky, Noonday Press, 1954, published as *The Unknown Chekhov: Stories and Other Writings,* Funk & Wagnalls, 1968.

The Island: A Journey to Sakhalin (nonfiction), translation by Luba and Michael Terpak, introduction by Robert Payne, Washington Square Press, 1967.

SELECTED WORKS

The Tales of Tchehov, translation by Constance Garnett, thirteen volumes, Macmillan, 1916-22, reprinted, Ecco Press, 1984—.

The Plays of Tchehov, translation by Garnett, two volumes, Chatto & Windus, 1922-23, reprinted, 1965-70.

The Works of Anton Chekhov, one volume, W. J. Black, 1929, published as *The Best Known Works of Anton Chekhov,* Blue Ribbon Books, 1936, reprinted, Books for Libraries Press, 1972.

Plays and Stories, translation by S. S. Koteliansky, Dent, 1937, Dutton, 1938, reprinted, with introduction by David Magarashack, Dutton, 1967.

The Portable Chekhov, edited and introduced by Avrahm Yarmolinsky, Viking, 1947, reprinted, Penguin, 1978.

Izbrannie proizvedeniya v trekh tomakh (title means "Selected Works"), three volumes, [Moscow], 1964.

Anton Chekhov—Plays and Stories, translation by Ann Dunnigan, International Collectors Library, 1965.

Selected Works in Two Volumes, translation by Ivy Litvinov, Progress, 1973.

Chekhov, selected and translated by Patrick Miles and Harvey Pitcher, Abacus, 1984.

COMPLETE WORKS

Polnoe sobranie sochinenii i pisem A. P. Chekhova (title means "Complete Works and Letters of A. P. Chekhov"), edited by S. D. Balukhatyi and others, twenty volumes, [Moscow], 1944-51.

The Oxford Chekhov, translated and edited by Ronald Hingley, Oxford University Press, nine volumes, 1964-75.

Polnoe sobranie sochinenii i pisem A. P. Chekhova (title means "Complete Works and Letters of A. P. Chekhov"), edited by N. F. Bel'chikov and others, thirty volumes, Gorky Institute of World Literature of the U.S.S.R. Academy of Sciences, 1974-83.

A. F. Marx published an eleven-volume complete edition of Chekhov's works from 1900 to 1903.

MEDIA ADAPTATIONS: Numerous Chekhov writings have been adapted for the stage and screen by other authors, including Joseph Buloff, Michael Chekhov, Maria Irene Fornes, Spalding Gray, John Guare, David Mamet, Michael O'Hara, Luba Kadison, Evrom Allen Mintz, Thomas Pasatieri, Harold Poppe, Mark Schweid, Wendy Wasserstein, Michael Weller, Robert Whittier, Samm-Art Williams, Avrahm Yarmolinsky, and Alek Zolin.

SIDELIGHTS: Anton Pavlovich Chekhov, considered the father of the modern short story and of the modern play, was born, the third of six children, in the Russian seaport town of Taganrog, near the Black Sea. Son of a grocer and grandson of a serf who had bought his family's freedom before emancipation, Chekhov was well-acquainted with the realities of nineteenth-century lower-middle-class and peasant life, an acquaintance that was reflected objectively and unsentimentally in his mature writings.

Chekhov's father, Pavel, was a religious zealot and family tyrant who terrorized Anton and his two older brothers, Alexander and Nicolai. Although the three younger children recalled a much less terrifying figure in Pavel, Chekhov remarked to Alexander in an 1889 letter reprinted in Avrahm Yarmolinsky's *Letters of Anton Chekhov,* "Despotism and lying mangled our childhood to such a degree that one feels queasy and fearful recalling it." The writer's mother, Yevgeniya, was an excellent storyteller, and Chekhov is supposed to have acquired his own gift for narrative and to have learned to read and write from her.

At the age of eight he was sent to the local grammar school, where he proved an average pupil. Rather reserved and undemonstrative, he nevertheless gained a reputation for satirical comments, for pranks, and for making up humorous nicknames for his teachers. He enjoyed playing in amateur theatricals and often attended performances at the provincial theater. As an adolescent he tried his hand at writing short "anecdotes," farcical or facetious stories, although he is also known to have written a serious long play at this time, "Fatherless," which he later destroyed.

The first real crisis in Chekhov's life occurred in 1875, when his father's business failed. Threatened with imprisonment for debt, Pavel left to find work in Moscow, where his two eldest sons were attending the university. Yevgeniya, left behind with Anton and the younger children, soon lost her house to a local bureaucrat who had posed as a family friend. She and the children departed for Moscow in July, 1876, leaving Anton in Taganrog to care for himself and finish school. The episode provided him with a theme—the loss of a home to a conniving middle-class upstart—that was to appear later in the short story "Tsvety zapozdalyie" ("Late-blooming Flowers," 1882), and to mature in his last play, "Vishnyovy Sad: Komediya v chetyryokh deystriyakh" ("The Cherry Orchard: A Comedy in Four Acts," 1904). The family struggled financially while Pavel looked for work, and Chekhov helped by selling off household goods and tutoring younger schoolboys in Taganrog. In 1877 Pavel found a position in a clothing warehouse, and in 1879 Chekhov passed his final exams and joined his family in Moscow, where he had obtained a scholarship to study medicine at Moscow University.

Chekhov was first prompted to write less by an urge toward artistic expression than by the immediate need to support his family. His earliest efforts at publication, after his move to Moscow, were directed at the lowbrow comic magazines that flourished during this period of political repression in Russia, when to speak directly and critically of the imperial government and its vast bureaucracy could doom a writer to the penal colony of Sakhalin Island in Siberia. But Chekhov, who was never politically motivated in his writings or committed in his personal views, was not in danger of provoking official ire. Although he believed strongly in artistic freedom and scientific

progress, "politically speaking," revealed Ronald Hingley in *A New Life of Anton Chekhov,* "he might as well have been living on the moon as in Imperial Russia." Chekhov had read and enjoyed the comic weeklies since his schoolboy days, was under no illusions about their literary standards, and simply sought the income they provided. His first published piece appeared in the St. Petersburg weekly *Strekoza* ("Dragonfly") in March, 1880. Many more items followed during the next three years in similar journals and under various pseudonyms, the most common being "Antosha Chekhonte," a nickname bestowed upon Chekhov some years before by his favorite grammar school teacher.

In 1882 Chekhov met Nicolas Leykin, the owner and publisher of *Oskolki* ("Fragments"), the finest of the St. Petersburg comic weeklies, to which he began submitting most of his better work. *Oskolki* was distinguished from the general run of comic periodicals by the firmness of Leykin's editorial control and his friendly acquaintance with the St. Petersburg censor, which allowed *Oskolki* to be a bit more outspoken than its competitors. Leykin insisted on very short items, no more than two and one-half pages, with a consistently comic tone throughout. While the young writer resisted the uniformly comic requirements, the restrictions on length proved salutory to Chekhov, who was to become the first modern master of a spare and economical prose style in fiction.

The years 1883 to 1885 were very productive for Chekhov, who was in desperate need of money; but in the general litter of tired jokes and farcical trivia that came from his pen at this time, only a few stories, still popular in Soviet Russia, stand out: "Smert' chinovnika" ("The Death of a Government Official," 1883), "Tolsty i tonki" ("Fat and Thin," 1883), "Doch Al'biona" ("The Daughter of Albion," 1883), "Khameleon" ("A Chameleon," 1884), "Ustritsy" ("Oysters," 1884), "Strashnaya noch" ("A Dreadful Night," 1884), "Yeger" ("The Huntsman," 1885), "Zloumyshlenniki" ("The Malefactors," 1885), "Neschastye" ("The Misfortune," 1885), and "Unter Prishibeyev" ("Sergeant Prishibeyev," 1885). To these early writings of quality must be added Chekhov's only attempt at a novel, the serialized *Drama na okhote* (*The Shooting Party,* 1884).

Making their first appearance among these brief vignettes and jokes are the themes that predominate in Chekhov's fiction: the obsequiousness and petty tyranny of government officials; the sufferings of the poor as well as their coarseness and vulgarity; the vagaries and unpredictability of feeling; the ironical misunderstandings, disillusionments, and cross-purposes that make up the human comedy in general. But Chekhov's art was also developing during the mid-1880s to embrace more serious themes—starvation in "Oysters," abandonment in "The Huntsman," remorse in "The Misfortune." The narrative began to identify more closely with a particular character's point of view and to show more atmosphere or mood by evoking through concrete details the emotions at work in a character's mind.

One of the earliest examples of what D. S. Mirsky in his *Modern Russian Literature* essay labeled "biography of a mood" appears in "The Huntsman," which presents a roving peasant who refuses to go home with his wife because he prefers the freedom of a sporting life—as a "shooter" for the local landowner—and cohabitation with another woman. Here, as so often in Chekhov's mature stories, there is no real plot, no dramatic emotional flare-up, only a moment of confrontation which radically condenses the life histories of both husband and wife. In this moment nothing changes in their relationship or promises to change. Details of the scene—the heat and stillness, the road stretched "taut as a thong"—reflect both the hopeless stagnation of the couple's marriage and the tension of this encounter.

Chekhov's interest in more serious writing found its first outlet in the newspaper *Petersburgskaya gazeta* ("The Petersburg Gazette"), to which, in 1885, he began sending stories that Leykin and other comic editors had rejected as unsuitably somber. Here Chekhov found no restrictions on length or tone. Soon after his first visit to St. Petersburg in December, 1885, he was invited to write for the most respected of the city papers, *Novoye vremya* ("New Times"), owned and edited by the conservative anti-Semite Alexis Suvorin, who insisted that Chekhov now publish under his own name. Chekhov was not particularly bothered by Suvorin's political views. Although the young writer was to receive harsh criticism from the left-wing intelligentsia for publishing with Suvorin, he was much more upset at having to abandon his pseudonym: still considering literature, even at this point, to be second in importance to medicine, he had hoped to reserve the use of his real name for future medical publications. "Besides medicine, my wife," he wrote Alexander in a letter printed in Yarmolinsky's collection, "I have also literature—my mistress."

By 1886, however, Chekhov was becoming a well-known writer in St. Petersburg. He had already published one collection of magazine stories in 1883 and another, *Pestrye rasskazy* (*Motley Tales*), was to appear in May. According to Ernest J. Simmons in *Chekhov: A Biography,* a letter reached Chekhov in March from D. V. Grigorovich, the dean of Russian letters, praising "Antosha Chekhonte"'s work as showing "real talent," which "sets you in the front rank among writers in the new generation." It was one of the few laudatory remarks on his writing by which the typically undemonstrative Chekhov seemed genuinely moved, and his appreciative reply to Grigorovich was uncharacteristically enthusiastic and effusive.

The years 1886 to 1887 were the most productive of Chekhov's career. Though he was still writing stories in an ironically comic vein, such as "Roman s kontrabasom" ("Romance With Double Bass," 1886), "Mest'" ("Revenge," 1886), and "Proizvedeniye iskusstva" ("The Work of Art," 1886), his more serious plots were becoming attenuated almost to the point of stasis. In addition, whle sounding a strong note of pathos, as in "Van'ka" ("Vanka," 1886), Chekhov maintained strict authorial detachment: "Grisha" ("Grisha," 1886), "Ved'ma" ("The Witch," 1886), "Svyatoy Noch'yu" ("Easter Night," 1886), "Toska" ("Heartache," 1886), "Verochka" (Verochka," 1887), and "Potseluy" ("The Kiss," 1887) all demonstrate Chekhov's growing ability to render life from within the minds of his characters through the registration of significant details and to portray experience without preaching or attitudinizing.

It was precisely for his refusal to pass judgment on even his most despicable characters—in stories like "Anyuta" ("Anyuta," 1886), "Zhiteyskaya meloch" ("A Trifle From Life," 1886), "Vragi" ("Enemies," 1887), and "Tina" ("Mire," 1886)—that Chekhov received his most negative criticism. Even his friend and countryhouse landlady, Mariya Kiselev, could not refrain from scolding him for "rummaging in a dung heap," to which he replied, as Yarmolinsky's collection shows, in a manner thoroughly compatible with his medical training and outlook: "To think that it is the duty of literature to pluck the pearl from the heap of villains is to deny literature itself. Lit-

erature is called artistic when it depicts life as it actually is. . . . A writer should be as objective as a chemist." As for trying to instruct his readers, which was the principle task of any great writer according to contemporary critics of Russian culture, he later wrote to Suvorin in a letter printed by Yarmolinsky, "You are confusing two concepts: *the solution of a problem* and *the correct posing of a question*. Only the second is obligatory for an artist." Granted Chekhov's strictures on authorial preaching, however, many stories from this period—for example, "Vstrecha" ("The Encounter," 1887), "Nishchy" ("The Beggar," 1887), "Beda" ("In Trouble," 1887), and "Khoroshyie lyudi" ("Excellent People," 1886)—show the unfortunate moralizing tendencies of Leo Tolstoy, who had by this time become an object of admiration for the young writer.

Despite the general brightening of the Chekhov family's monetary prospects throughout the 1880s, debts continued to mount, mostly due to the spendthrift habits of the older brothers, Alexander and Nicolai, debts which Anton undertook to pay. At the same time his health had been deteriorating since December, 1884, when he had suffered his first episode of bloody sputum and painful lungs, symptoms of the tuberculosis that was eventually to kill him. Though a doctor himself, having received his medical degree in the summer previous to his first attack, Chekhov spent most of his remaining years denying that there was anything seriously wrong with him. Nevertheless, by the summer of 1887, debt, ill health, and the prodigious effort of writing to keep pace with family expenses forced Chekhov to take a vacation trip to the Steppes and eastern Ukraine, including a visit to Taganrog.

The trip refreshed Chekhov's boyhood memories and provided material for his first publication in a serious literary, or so-called "thick," journal, *Severny vestnik* ("The Northern Herald"), in March, 1888. "Step'" ("The Steppe") tells the story of a nine-year-old boy's journey across the vast plains of southern Russia with his merchant uncle and a local priest. Considered too long, impressionistic, and plotless for the popular press, "The Steppe" marked Chekhov's entry into the ranks of the major Russian writers and the beginning of his artistic maturity. Later in 1888 he received the Pushkin Prize from the Division of Russian Language and Letters of the Academy of Sciences for his collection of stories, *V sumerkakh* (*In the Twilight*), published the previous year. Typically, he declared himself unimpressed. This collection and later ones—*Rasskazy* (*Tales,* 1888), *Detvora* (*Children,* 1889), and a collection whose title has been translated as "Gloomy People" (1890)—went through many editions.

Meanwhile, Chekhov had made his theatrical debut in the autumn of 1887 with the premiere of his four-act play, "Ivanov," at the Korsh Theater in Moscow. He had written two earlier one-act plays, neither of which had been produced, and a very long, melodramatic, four-act potboiler, "Platonov," which was neither produced nor published in his lifetime. In "Ivanov," a middle-aged landowner beset by debts and weary of marriage seeks an affair with a neighbor's daughter while his Jewish wife, Sara, rejected by her family for marrying a Gentile, is dying of tuberculosis. The play marks a great advance over the histrionics and verbosity of "Platonov" but shows little of Chekhov's later experimentation with understatement, anticlimax, and implied feeling. Audience and critical reaction was polarized: on the one hand, the play was very well made, so good, in fact, that Hingley in *A New Life of Anton Chekhov* deemed it superior to "Chayka: Komediya Chetyryokh deystviyakh" ("The Seagull: A Comedy in Four Acts"), Chekhov's first truly innovative contribution to modern drama. On the other hand, the playwright had refused to represent his hero's behavior in an unfavorable light and even showed the only character who denounces Ivanov, Sara's doctor, Lvov, to be self-righteous and narrow-minded. This constituted another instance in which Chekhov's objectivity violated the canons of Russian literary taste.

From 1888 to 1890 Chekhov continued to write for the theater. In addition to a new but poorly received four-act play, "Leshy" ("The Wood Demon," 1889), he wrote four one-act farces, "Medved'" ("The Bear"), "Predlozheniye" ("The Proposal"), "Tragic" ("A Tragic Role"), and "Svad'ba" ("The Wedding"), all quite successful. On January 31, 1889, *Ivanov* opened its St. Petersburg run at the Alexandrine Theater to extremely favorable reviews. But Chekhov, bending under the strain of overseeing rehearsals, advising his producers, and dealing with the press, was becoming morose and irritated at his success. He declared himself "bored" with "Ivanov" and contemptuous of theatrical people. In general, he was impatient with praise because it seldom matched his own highly critical self-estimation, while fame brought with it heightened public expectations and unsolicited advice. It also brought visitors, and even toward welcome visitors Chekhov often felt ambivalent. When alone with his family, as at his rented countryhouse in Babkino or in summer residences at Luka in the Ukraine, he longed for company and the excitement of city life. But he quickly grew tired of guests because they kept him away from his work.

After 1888 Chekhov's fiction diminished in quantity but increased in quality. He began trying to write longer stories without sacrificing conciseness. To the period from 1888 to 1890 belong such prized works as "Nepriyatnaya istoriya" ("An Awkward Business," 1888), "Krasavitsy" ("The Beauties," 1888), "Spat' khochetsya" ("Sleepy," 1888), and his two brilliant long stories, "Imeniny" ("The Name-Day Party," 1888) and "Skuchnaya istoriya" ("A Dreary Story," 1889).

These two works, along with "Sleepy" and "The Seizure," are among the finest instances of what Oliver Elton in *Chekhov: The Taylorian Lecture* called the "clinical study": stories drawing on Chekhov's medical expertise and depicting psychosomatic illness or the psychological effects of physical disease or distress. It was a form he had used in earlier stories such as "Oysters" and "Tif" ("Typhus," 1887) but had never before developed at such length or with such skill. In "The Name-Day Party" a pregnant wife, hurt and infuriated by her husband's failure to share his professional concerns with her, must cope with the added pressures of entertaining the guests at his name-day party. This superb study of the emotional effects of marital and social hypocrisy ends with a harrowing description of the wife's experience of miscarriage, which results from the day-long physical and mental strain. Chekhov claimed that many of his female readers attested to the accuracy of this story's description of labor pains, a description based on his clinical observations.

In "A Dreary Story" a dying medical professor, Nicolai Stepanovich, recounts at length his final months, his night fears and insomnia, his impatience with colleagues and weariness with family affairs. Alarmed by his own indifference to his daughter's elopement with a scoundrel and vulgarian, he registers that indifference as "a paralysis of the soul, a premature death," and discovers within himself only a bundle of peevish desires uninformed by any "general idea, or the god of a living

man." When his ward, Katya, a disillusioned actress who has been seduced and betrayed and who is beset by the advances of a new unwanted suitor, begs for Nicolai's advice, he cannot reply, leaving her bitterly disappointed. Having discovered the meaninglessness of life, the professor is now useless to the living.

Scholars have drawn numerous parallels between Chekhov and his protagonist in "A Dreary Story," particularly in the professor's pessimistic and cynical opinions on life, on the academic professions, and on the theater, despite Chekhov's own vigorous disclaimers to Suvorin, recorded by Simon Karlinsky in *Anton Chekhov's Life and Thought:* "If I present you with the professor's ideas, have confidence in me and don't look for Chekhovian ideas in them." In any case, the theme of life's meaninglessness recurs often in the writer's later work, along with a healthy scepticism—but never cynicism—toward the possible fulfillment of human hopes. It is far from true that, as Lev Shestov maintained in *Anton Tchekhov and Other Essays,* Chekhov was doing only one thing in his writing, "killing human hopes"; but it is a rare occasion in his fictive universe when expectations of happiness—especially in matters of the heart—are fulfilled. At the same time, Chekhov strongly believed in scientific and technological progress—slow though it might be in coming—and was a thoroughgoing pragmatist, like another character of his, Dr. Astrov, the conservationist and physician in "Dyadya Vanya: Stseny iz derevenskoy zhizni v chetyroykh deystviyakh" ("Uncle Vanya: Scenes From Country Life in Four Acts"). The author believed in doing one's best for today, letting tomorrow take care of itself, and remaining open to the joys of life, however vulnerable to subsequent disappointment such openness might leave one. Chekhov's least likeable characters are nearly always energetic and efficient but indifferent to deeper human feelings, or else so benumbed by suffering and privation as to have died emotionally, like the narrator of "A Dreary Story" or the Siberian ferryman, Semyon, of "V ssylke" ("In Exile," 1892).

By early 1890, Chekhov's spirits were low. His brother Nicolai had died the previous summer after a protracted bout of tuberculosis. In the autumn, "The Wood Demon" had been rejected by two theaters and had closed for good after three performances at a third. A projected novel had been abandoned after two years of intense work, and the liberal press was attacking him for his "unprincipled writing." On top of everything else, Chekhov was bored. In April, after months of preparation, he set off to visit the eastern Siberian penal colony of Sakhalin Island to take a census of its inhabitants, interview its officials, and write a report on conditions there. Though he cited scientific, humanitarian, and literary reasons for his unusual decision, and a vague desire to "pay off my debt to medicine," according to a letter printed by Yarmolinsky, Chekhov was motivated principally by the need for a radical change of scene.

The trip was arduous and hazardous, even for a healthy man: five thousand miles across the Siberian wilderness, three thousand by horse-drawn cart along the infamous *trakt,* the dirt road that spanned Siberia. On arrival, Chekhov observed and carefully recorded the misery of life on the five-hundred-mile-long island, conducting some 160 interviews a day. In October he sailed for Odessa by way of Vladivostok, Hong Kong, Singapore (which he found depressing), Ceylon (which he thought a paradise on earth), and Port Said, arriving December 1. Once in Moscow, he joined his family in their new lodgings on Malaya Dmitrovka Street. Material based on his eastern journey later appeared in "Gusev" ("Gusev," 1890), "In Exile" (1892), and "Ubiystvo" ("Murder," 1895).

From February to March of 1891, Chekhov worked on "Duel'" ("The Duel," 1891), a long story set in the Caucasus and depicting the antagonism between a young, Bohemian romantic and idealist, Layevsky, and a cold-blooded, hard-working, ambitious zoologist, von Koren, who has fanatical convictions about the need to "exterminate" social "drones" like Layevsky. Typically, their creator refuses to take sides in the dispute, although Layevsky reforms at the end. In March and April, Chekhov journeyed with Suvorin and his son to Italy and France, locales which appeared later in "Rasskaz neizvestnovo cheloveka" ("An Anonymous Story," 1893) and "Ariadna" ("Ariadne," 1895). That summer, he lived at Bogimovo in a mansion provided for the season by an admirer of his work. There he began a scholarly book, *Ostrov Sakhalin* (*Sakhalin Island*), finished "The Duel," and wrote "Baby" ("Peasant Women," 1891). In September he returned to Moscow where he spent the winter working on "An Anonymous Story," "Zhena" ("My Wife," 1892), and a work whose title is translated as "The Butterfly" (1892).

In March, 1892, Chekhov and his family moved to his newly purchased country estate at Melikhovo in Moscow District. Here they remained in residence until 1899, their longest—and happiest—stay in any one home. Chekhov the landowner was on good terms with the local peasants, treating their medical problems free of charge, paying for his own dispensary, financing and overseeing the building of schools, and organizing measures against the cholera epidemics of 1892 and 1893. His experiences greatly influenced his depiction of peasant life in such mature works as "Muzhiki" ("Peasants," 1897) and "V ovrage" ("In the Ravine," 1900), the former of which caused a furor when first published because Chekhov refused to sentimentalize or idealize his peasants in the accepted manner of such promoters of unsophisticated wisdom as Tolstoy and Fyodor Dostoevsky. At one point, "Peasants" even reads like an indictment of the peasantry for its brutality, greed, and sordidness. While the *narodniks,* or "peasant fanciers," of the liberal press excoriated Chekhov, the Marxists praised the story for its realistic portrayal of class conditions.

Dissatisfied, as ever, with staying in one location for too long, Chekhov made frequent trips to Moscow, St. Petersburg, and the south of Russia. Everywhere he went he was welcomed, praised, and celebrated with parties, but he felt rather distant from it all and soon wearied of the social round. At about this time Chekhov apparently took his first mistress, Lydia Yavorsky, an actress at Moscow's Korsh Theater. It was not a passionate affair. Chekhov had always manifested a somewhat fastidious attitude toward sex, commensurate with his generally stolid or passive temperament, and seemed to believe that unrestrained sexual activity contributed to senility. As Hingley delicately put it in *A New Life of Anton Chekhov,* "We are certainly entitled to deduce that he was somewhat undersexed." Chekhov's very brief "engagement" to his sister's Jewish friend, Dunya Efros, in January, 1886, is treated so lightly and ironically in his letters to his friend, Bilibin, as to lead Hingley in *A New Life* to regard it as a private joke.

Other women figured in Chekhov's life during the early 1890s, including Lydia ("Lika") Mizinov, another friend of his sister's whose intense love for him he reciprocated only as friendship, and Lydia Avilova, wife, mother, and minor writer, who, at their first meeting, managed to convince herself that Chekhov felt toward her a passionate, undying love that was stifled

only by guilt over her marital status. Mizonov finally turned her attentions to Chekhov's friend, the Ukrainian writer Ignatius Potapenko, a married man; Chekhov used the affair as a model for the relationship between Trigorin, the writer, and Nina, the aspiring actress, in "The Seagull," much to the chagrin of Mizinov and Potapenko. As for Avilova's allegations presented in her memoirs *Chekhov in My Life,* most modern scholars—with the exception of David Magarshack, who added an appendix to the 1970 reprint of *Chekhov: A Life* specifically to refute Ernest Simons's dismissal of Avilova's claims—see them as highly subjective interpretations unsubstantiated by corroborating evidence in Chekhov's notebooks and correspondence.

During his stay at Melikhovo, Chekhov began to publish more frequently in the liberal press, particularly in *Russkaya mysl* ("Russian Thought") and *Russkiye vedemosti* ("The Russian Gazette"). His trip to Sakhalin and the publication of a chapter on escapees in late 1891 were admired by left-wing critics and helped to patch up a quarrel between Chekhov and V. M. Lavrov, the editor of *Russkaya mysl.* After two years of hesitation over possible censorship, Chekhov sent Lavrov *Sakhalin Island,* minus the last four chapters, for serialized publication from October, 1893 to July, 1894. The entire work was printed in the journal during 1895. Chekhov's longest piece by far, it was hailed by liberals as a signal contribution to the movement for prison reform. Over the ensuing years *Russkaya mysl* was to publish "The Seagull," "Tri syostry: Drama v chetyryokh deystviyakh" ("The Three Sisters: A Drama in Four Acts"), and thirteen of Chekhov's finest stories, including "Palata No. 6" ("Ward Number Six," 1892), in which the irresponsible director of a decrepit insane asylum ends up committed to his own ward. According to W. H. Bruford in *Anton Chekhov,* Communist leader Vladimir Ilich Lenin, reading the story as an allegorical representation of a repressive society, later wrote, "When I had read this story to the end, I was filled with awe. I could not remain in my room and went out of doors. I felt as if I were locked up in a ward too."

"Ward Number Six" and a later story "Moya zhizn'" ("My Life," 1896), the account of a young man who defies his architect father to work as a common laborer, mark Chekhov's final experiments with the Tolstoyan philosophy of pacifistic resistence to evil. Tolstoy was still, however, a towering object of Chekhov's admiration because of his two great novels, *War and Peace* and *Anna Karenina,* the latter of which had influenced Chekhov's writing of "The Name-Day Party." In August, 1894, Chekhov visited Yasnaya Polyana, Tolstoy's family estate, and the two became good friends despite their divergent views on the role of literature and the arts.

Other outstanding works from Chekhov's Melikhovo period include a study of intellectual megalomania, "Chorny monakh" ("The Black Monk," 1894), "Babye tsarstvo" ("A Woman's Kingdom," 1894), "Volodya bol'shoy i Volodya malen'ki" ("The Two Volodyas," 1894), "Tri goda" ("Three Years," 1895), "Ariadne" (1895), "Skripka Rotshil'da" ("Rothschild's Fiddle," 1895), "Na podvode" ("In the Cart," 1897), "Vrodnom uglu" ("At Home," 1897), and the so-called "trilogy" of stories—one whose title has been translated as "A Hard Case" (1898), "Kryzhovnik" ("Gooseberries," 1898), and "O lyubvi" ("Concerning Love," 1898)—each of which is told by one narrator to characters who figure as narrators in the other two stories. All three stories focus on a failure to grasp the essential joys of life by not taking advantage of opportunities that come only once in a lifetime, for fear of making a mistake.

From October to November, 1895, Chekhov wrote "The Seagull," a play that deliberately flouts the stage conventions of nineteenth-century theater: it has no starring role, its dramatic action declines rather than builds with each act, and it eschews dramatic crises and the direct representation of powerful feelings. Yarmolinsky's *Letters* records the playwright's own assessment of his art in *The Seagull:* "I began it *forte* and wound it up *pianissimo*—contrary to all the precepts of dramatic art." As his first effort in a radically new form of dramatic composition, "The Seagull" reveals the full extent of Chekhov's originality. But the play is flawed by heavy-handed symbolism borrowed from the Norwegian dramatist Henrik Ibsen—the use of the dead seagull to represent hopes betrayed; and the work contains an ambivalence of tone that does not resolve itself, as it does in the later plays, into a perfect balance of opposites.While Donald Rayfield argued in *A Chekhov Companion* essay that the play is in many ways meant to be "farcical," critics are generally undecided about how seriously to take its subtitle, "A Comedy in Four Acts," since the work treats the ruin of a young woman's life and the suicide of the young man who once loved her.

"The Seagull"'s premiere on October 17, 1896, at the Alexandrine Theater in St. Petersburg was a complete disaster, due as much to the circumstances in which the play was produced as to its originality. Besides being underrehearsed, "The Seagull" was scheduled for the benefit night of a well-known comic actress, for whom there was no part in the play. Her assembled fans were displeased with what they felt was highbrow experimentation, and a riot ensued. Though later performances were well received, theater management decided to close the play after only five performances. Chekhov was devastated and swore never again to write plays. He was nevertheless devoting a great deal of effort to revising "The Wood Demon," the 1889 stage failure that eventually became the play "Uncle Vanya."

On the evening of March 22, 1897, Chekhov suffered a violent hemorrhage of the lungs while at dinner with Suvorin in Moscow. He was hospitalized for two weeks, during which time he suffered a second hemorrhage. He then had to acknowledge his illness. During the ensuing summer at Melikhovo, he stopped writing completely, cut back on all his activities, and his health began to improve.

For the winter of 1897 to 1898, Chekhov sought a climate favorable to his health, resuming his writing in Nice on the French Riviera. In France at this time controversy was stirred by the Dreyfus affair, in which military officer Alfred Dreyfus was wrongly tried and imprisoned for treason against France; Chekhov took an interest in the case, particularly after the publication of Emile Zola's "J'accuse," a defense of the court-martialed Jewish lieutenant. Support for Dreyfus also earned Chekhov's partisanship, which led to a break with his friend Suvorin, whose *Novoye vremya* was publishing vehemently anti-Semitic attacks on the Dreyfusards.

In Nice Chekhov was contacted by Vladimir Nemirovich-Danchenko, cofounder along with Constantin Stanislavsky of the new Moscow Art Theater, which was intended to stimulate public taste for the "new drama." Nemirovich-Danchenko was ecstatic about "The Seagull" and persuaded Chekhov to let him produce it as part of the troupe's first season. From that point on, Chekhov's activities as a dramatist and those of the Moscow Art Theater were intertwined. In September, 1898,

on his way to winter in Yalta, Chekhov attended rehearsals of his play and was introduced to the members of the new theater troupe, including Olga Knipper, the actress who later became his wife. On December 17, 1898, the Moscow Art Theater performed "The Seagull" for the first time since its disastrous premiere. At the end of the first act, after a stunned silence, the audience exploded into applause. At their insistence, a telegram was sent to Chekhov in Yalta to tell him of his success.

During Chekhov's stay in Yalta that winter he purchased land on which to build a new villa and bought a seaside cottage not far from the city. His stories from this time, such as "Novaya dacha" ("New Villa," 1898), and especially "Po delam sluzhby" ("On Official Business," 1898), show a growing awareness of the rift between the upper and lower classes and a new concern for social justice. It was at this time, perhaps not coincidently, that he became friends with a young writer of social conscience, Maksim Gorky. In early 1899 Chekhov was elected an Honorary Academician of the Pushkin Section of Belle Letters of the Academy of Sciences.

Chekhov divided his time between Melikhovo and Moscow during the spring and summer of 1899, helping the Maly Theater in its preparations for the Moscow premiere of "Uncle Vanya," which had been making the rounds of provincial theaters since its appearance two years before in Chekhov's collected plays. Except for its principal characters and central theme, "Uncle Vanya" is almost unrecognizable as a later version of "The Wood Demon." The play focuses on the Voynitsky household, plunged into turmoil by the sudden appearance of the now nearly senile Professor Serebryakov, the intellectual brother-in-law for whose benefit "Uncle" Vanya Voynitsky, to manage the family estate, has sacrificed his adult life. In representing this situation Chekhov fulfilled the promise of "The Seagull": he created a perfectly orchestrated tragicomedy of nuanced pauses, significant breakdowns and cross-purposes in conversation, elusively symbolic objects, and farcical violence, all pointing up the unrecoverable loss of a whole and meaningful life.

However, the play was much too ambiguous for the Theatrical and Literary Committee that administered the imperial theaters, of which the Maly was one. They voted to send "Uncle Vanya" back to its author for cuts and changes. Chekhov took the opportunity to withdraw the play and submit it to his new friends at the Moscow Art Theater, where it became the talk of the autumn season in Moscow after its first performance on October 26, 1899.

From October to December, 1899, Chekhov worked on his last group of stories—"Na Svyatkakh" ("At Christmas," 1899), "In the Ravine" (1900), and "Dama s sobachkoy" ("A Lady With a Pet Dog," 1889)—the last of which Virginia Llewellyn Smith, in *Anton Chekhov and the Lady With a Dog,* called "a summary of the entire topic" of "Chekhov's attitude to women and to love." Meanwhile, he and Olga Knipper had begun exchanging letters after her short visit to Chekhov's Yalta villa the previous April, when the Moscow Art Theater had made a Crimean tour. During the summer of 1900 the two became lovers, but only after Olga first made a point of securing the friendship of Chekhov's sister, Mariya, and the good will of the Chekhov household. By August Olga was playfully cajoling the writer in her letters from Moscow to marry her.

During October, 1900, Chekhov joined Olga in Moscow with the manuscript of "The Three Sisters," to which he had devoted nearly all his energies since the new year. In *The Hudson Review* Howard Moss described "The Three Sisters" as "the most musical of all of Chekhov's plays in construction, the one that depends most heavily on the repetition of motifs," and yet a play that is "seemingly artless." Charles J. Rzepka declared in his *Modern Language Studies* essay that *The Three Sisters* continually invokes "a world of art" larger than life while, like life itself, betraying no "sense of . . . a final cause" or "ultimate purpose." "The Three Sisters" was also the most difficult play, as it turned out, for Chekhov to complete to his satisfaction, and he was still revising it on his arrival in Moscow. Ominously, the Art Theater actors and producers felt it to be unplayable. Irritated, as much with Moscow in general as with the players, and feeling definitely uncomfortable with Olga's constant presence, Chekhov took a brief trip to St. Petersburg and then left for Nice; from there he sent back to Moscow revised versions of Acts III and IV and detailed stage directions for "The Three Sisters."

In general, Chekhov was unhappy with most of the Art Theater's productions of his plays because of Stanislavsky's tendency to overplay and underscore scenes that Chekhov had conceived as exquisitely understated and indirect. This clash of interpretative styles became very clear during rehearsals for "The Three Sisters," where the real tragedy appears not in such events as the killing of Irina's suitor, Tusenbach, by the ironical dandy, Solyoni, nor in the success of Natasha, the grasping and ruthless sister-in-law of the Prozoroffs, but in the agonizing stultification of three lives that are finally smothered under the weight of everyday occurrences. When "The Three Sisters" premiered on January 21, 1901, response was lackluster, criticism lukewarm. The public did not know how to receive the play. This news reached Chekhov as he was touring Italy.

Afer he returned to Yalta in early 1901, Olga increasingly pressured Chekhov to marry her. She did not want to spend time with him and his family in Yalta, living in his house and secretly joining him in his room at night. In May, Chekhov reluctantly agreed to matrimony and joined Olga in Moscow to exchange vows. His sister, Mariya, was bitterly hurt, even "nauseated," by the event, but while her year-old relationship with Olga was temporarily strained, the two ultimately resumed a friendship that endured for many years after Chekhov's death. Contemporary accounts suggest that the marriage itself was something less than blissful. I. N. Altshuller, Chekhov's Yalta doctor, felt the liaison was a disaster for Chekhov's health. Chekhov's friend, the writer I. A. Bunin, was even more negative, seeing Olga's theatrical milieu as alien and threatening to her husband's peace of mind. Chekhov spent most of his time in the south while Olga performed with the Art Theater in Moscow or on tour, so the two lived as much apart as together. Olga would often write Chekhov from Moscow, describing wild cast parties and the amorous advances of fellow actors, apparently in order to excite jealousy in her rather passive husband. Chekhov, on his part, would frequently excuse himself from joining her in Moscow or, when with her, contrive reasons to take brief journeys away from her.

During the summer of 1901, in Yalta, Chekhov began coughing up blood once more, and his declining health prompted him to make his will. When he went to Moscow in September, he immersed himself in more rehearsals of "The Three Sisters" for the new season, personally producing Act III. On September 21 he saw it performed, and for perhaps the first time in his life felt perfectly satisfied with the interpretation of one of his plays. He was applauded in two curtain calls after Act III.

The following winter Chekhov's health worsened, but he continued to write, sending "Arkhiyerey" ("The Bishop") to *Zhurnal dlya vsekh* ("Journal for Everyone") in February of 1902. Also that month Olga visited Chekhov in Yalta. In March she had a miscarriage, and for the next four months her health fluctuated drastically. By July she had recovered sufficiently to allow a six-week holiday for her and Chekhov at Stanislavsky's family estate, Lyubimovka. These were perhaps the happiest few weeks of the Chekhovs' married life: they enjoyed abundant food, drink, relaxation, good company, and, most important, good fishing. But Chekhov left Lyubimovka in mid-August without providing his wife with a sufficient explanation for his departure, and afterward he and Olga quarreled by letter for a month.

In August, too, Chekhov, along with his friend and fellow academician, Vladimir Korolenko, resigned from the Academy of Sciences in protest over the expulsion of Maksim Gorky, who had been elected the previous February. Czar Nicolas II, discovering that Gorky had a police record and was under surveillance in connection with recent student unrest, had expressed his "profound chagrin" at the younger writer's appointment. Chekhov's resignation had little effect on the Academy, but did much to bolster Chekhov's reputation with the liberal intelligentsia. Back in Yalta over the winter, separated from Olga for five months, Chekhov worked on his last story, "Nevesta" ("A Marriageable Girl," 1903), and set about writing the first draft of "The Cherry Orchard," which he had been pondering for two years. He finished it in October, 1902, and sent it to Moscow for rehearsal.

By this time Chekhov's health had seriously worsened. He was irritable and impatient with everyone and became furious at Stanislavsky's and Nemirovich-Danchenko's misinterpretations of his new play. Unwilling to leave the play's production in their hands, he journeyed to Moscow against the advice of Dr. Altshuller and threw himself into preparations and rehearsals for "The Cherry Orchard," revising and editing as he went along. It was obvious that he and Stanislavsky were working at cross-purposes once again. Chekhov had conceived the play as a comedy, a "farce," while Stanislavsky kept encumbering the staging with ponderous tragic nuance.

Indeed, "The Cherry Orchard" represents the perfect embodiment of that exquisite balance of tragedy and farce with which Chekhov so skillfully imbued his mature plays. This portrait of the economic exploitation of the Ranevskaya family—doomed devotees of a humane and life-loving tradition—by the middle-class, vulgarian Lopakhin conveys the major themes of Chekhov's career placed in unresolvable but organic tension: the intrinsic value of opening oneself up to the beauty of the world and the love of others, and the foolishness of such openness in the face of the inevitable destruction of beauty and love. When it premiered on January 17, 1904, as part of a "Jubilee Celebration" of its author's twenty-five years as a writer, "The Cherry Orchard" was an immediate success. Later, back in Yalta, Chekhov was pleased by news of the play's successful opening in St. Petersburg on April 2, even though he remained convinced that the company did not really understand the play.

In May, quite near death, Chekhov left Russia on his doctor's orders for a spa at Badenweiler, Germany, taking Olga with him. Through most of June his health seemed to improve, but on June 29 he suffered a heart attack. He recovered, only to suffer another attack the next day. In the early morning hours of July 2, 1904, he awoke choking and delirious but had enough presence of mind to send for a doctor. While awaiting the physician Olga prepared some crushed ice to place on her husband's chest, but Chekhov protested, "You don't put ice on an empty heart." When the doctor arrived, Chekhov revealed, "Ich sterbe" ("I am dying"). Taking a sip of champagne, which at that time was considered salutary for heart victims, he remarked that he hadn't drunk champagne for ages, then turned on his side and closed his eyes. Moments later he was dead. In an ironic twist that he might have appreciated, Chekhov's body, sent back to Russia in a refrigerator car, was enclosed in a box marked "oysters."

Chekhov's influence on the modern short story and the modern play was immense. Among his innovations were his economical husbanding of narrative resources, his concentration on character as mood rather than action, his impressionistic adoption of particular points of view, his dispensing with traditional plot, and, as Charles May declared in an essay collected in *A Chekhov Companion,* his use of atmosphere as "an ambiguous mixture of both external details and psychic projection." In all these regards Chekhov had an immediate and direct impact on such Western writers as James Joyce, Katherine Mansfield, and Sherwood Anderson; indirectly, most major authors of short stories in the twentieth century, including Katherine Anne Porter, Franz Kafka, Ernest Hemingway, Bernard Malamud, and Raymond Carver, are in his debt.

With respect to twentieth-century drama, few playwrights with so small an ouevre have wielded such vast influence over the course of literary history. With Ibsen and Strindberg, Chekhov pioneered what Magarshack in *Chekhov the Dramatist* called the "indirect action" play: he used understatement and broken conversation, off-stage events and absent characters as catalysts of tension, but retained a strict impression of realism. He went further than his contemporaries in his rejection of the classical Aristotelian plot-line, in which rising and falling action comprise an immediately recognizable climax, catastrophe, and denouement. In Chekhov's mature plays, realism extended to the strict coincidence of stage time with real time, so that it was the elapsed time between acts, sometimes extending over months or years, that showed the changes taking place in characters. Thus, as Martin Esslin pointed out in an essay appearing in *A Chekhov Companion,* "the relentless forward pressure of the traditional dramatic form was replaced by a method of narration in which it was the *discontinuity* of the images that told the story, by implying what had happened in the gaps between episodes." At the same time, Chekhov's realism was not a simple transcription of life but a highly structured portrait subtly held together by complex networks of verbal imagery, repeated sounds and phrases, ambiguously suggestive or simply enigmatic props—all of which made up what has come to be known as the "subtext" of a Chekhov play.

Among Western playwrights, George Bernard Shaw was the first to grasp Chekhov's intentions and techniques, and he modeled his own "Heartbreak House" (1919) on "The Cherry Orchard." Yet it was not until the mid-1920s that Chekhov caught on with English audiences, becoming one of the trio of major dramatists regularly performed in British playhouses, along with Ibsen and Shakespeare. His influence on English playwrights other than Shaw, up to and including Harold Pinter, has been less direct, but no less powerful. In American drama the notion of "subtext" that Chekhov originated informs many of the works of Tennessee Williams, Arthur Miller, Clifford Odets, and William Inge. Chekhov's methods also anticipate Bertolt Brecht's technique of "Vefreundungseffekt" ("estrangement") and Samuel Beckett's dramatic stasis

and derealization; although Kenneth Rexroth's contention in *Classics Revisited* that "Chekhov's is truly a theater of the absurd," may overstate the case, Richard Gilman nevertheless concurred with Rexroth in *The Making of Modern Drama*.

Perhaps the most puzzling aspect of Chekhov's canon is the diversity of responses it excites. Early portraits of the man and his work tended toward sentimentality: Gorky in *Reminiscences of Anton Chekhov* recalled the "quiet, deep sigh of a pure and human heart," and Nina Andronikova Toumanova in *Anton Chekhov: Voice of a Twilight Russia* described a "gentle soul . . . in desperate fear of life," taking refuge "in a queer world of silvery twilight and dark shadows." The modern portrait of Chekhov, while much more nuanced and complex, is also contradictory. In *Chekhov: The Evolution of His Art*, Donald Rayfield detected at least three different Chekhovs emerging from the critical canvas, "optimist, pessimist-decadent, [and] scientific impressionist"; in an essay appearing in *Chekhov: A Collection of Critical Essays*, John Gassner sees two figures: on the one hand, "an artist of half-lights, a laureate of well-marinated futility, and a master of tragic sensibility," and on the other, "a paragon of breezy extroversion."

Nearly all his commentators concur that Chekhov was a master ironist, but not all agree on just when he was being ironic. In "The Cherry Orchard," for instance, is the student Trofimov—"buoyant, enthusiastic, and filled with hope" about the progress of humanity—indeed "Chekhov's spokesman," as Ruth Davies contended in *The Great Books of Russia*? Or is he simply a "queer bird," as the character Madame Ranevskaya tells him, someone whose "talk," asserted Joseph Wood Krutch in *Modern Drama: A Definition and an Estimate*, "like that of nearly all Chekhov's characters, will never be anything but talk"? Does the cherry orchard itself symbolize, as Krutch insisted, "the grace and beauty of the past which is being sacrificed because it has no utilitarian value"? Or is it what Magarshack identified in *Chekhov the Dramatist* as "a purely aesthetic symbol" that expresses "the destruction of beauty by those who are utterly blind to it"? These are the kinds of questions excited by the enigma that was Chekhov—lyricist and realist, comedian and tragedian, ironist and progressive. Perhaps, in the end, as Hingley suggested in *A New Life of Anton Chekhov*, Chekhov was himself "that tantalizing phenomenon: a Chekhov character."

BIOGRAPHICAL/CRITICAL SOURCES:

BOOKS

Aiken, Conrad, *Collected Criticism*, Oxford University Press, 1968.

Avilova, Lydia, *Chekhov in My Life: A Love Story*, translation by David Magarshack, Greenwood Press, 1971.

Bitsili, Petr M., *Chekhov's Art: A Stylistic Analysis*, translation by T. W. Clyman and E. J. Cruise, Ardis Press, 1983.

Bruford, W. H., *Anton Chekhov*, Yale University Press, 1957.

Clyman, Toby W., editor, *A Chekhov Companion*, Greenwood Press, 1985.

Davies, Ruth, *The Great Books of Russia*, University of Oklahoma Press, 1968.

Elton, Oliver, *Chekhov: The Taylorian Lecture*, Clarendon Press, 1929.

Emeljanow, Victor, editor, *Chekhov: The Critical Heritage*, Routlege & Kegan Paul, 1981.

Gilman, Richard, *The Making of Modern Drama: A Study of Buchner, Ibsen, Strindberg, Chekhov, Pirandello, Brecht, Beckett, Handke*, Farrar, Straus, 1974.

Gorky, Maksim, Alexander Kuprin, and I. A. Bunin, *Reminiscences of Anton Chekhov*, translation by S. S. Koteliansky and Leonard Woolf, B. W. Huebsch, 1921.

Hahn, Beverly, *Chekhov: A Study of the Major Stories and Plays*, Cambridge University Press, 1977.

Hingley, Ronald, *Chekhov: A Biographical and Critical Study*, Oxford University Press, 1950.

Hingley, Ronald, *A New Life of Anton Chekhov*, Knopf, 1976.

Jackson, Robert Louis, editor, *Chekhov: A Collection of Critical Essays*, Prentice-Hall, 1967.

Karlinsky, Simon, editor, *Anton Chekhov's Life and Thought: Selected Letters and Commentary*, translation by Karlinsky and Michael Henry Heim, University of California Press, 1975.

Krutch, Joseph Wood, *"Modernism" in Modern Drama: A Definition and an Estimate*, Cornell University Press, 1953.

Lafitte, Sophie, *Chekhov: 1860-1904*, translation by M. Budberg and G. Latta, Angus & Robertson, 1974.

Magarshack, David, *Chekhov: A Life*, Greenwood Press, 1952, reprinted, 1970.

Magarshack, David, *Chekhov the Dramatist*, Hill & Wang, 1960.

Magarshack, David, *The Real Chekhov: An Introduction to Chekhov's Last Plays*, Allen & Unwin, 1972.

Mirsky, D. S., *Modern Russian Literature*, Oxford University Press, 1925.

Pitcher, Harvey, *The Chekhov Play: A New Interpretation*, Chatto & Windus, 1973.

Rayfield, Donald, *Chekhov: The Evolution of His Art*, Barnes & Noble, 1975.

Rexroth, Kenneth, *Classics Revisited*, Quadrangle Books, 1968.

Shestov, Lev, *Anton Tchekhov and Other Essays*, translation by S. S. Koteliansky and J. M. Murry, Maunsel, 1916, reprinted, University of Michigan Press, 1966.

Simmons, Ernest J., *Chekhov: A Biography*, University of Chicago Press, 1962.

Smith, Virginia Llewellyn, *Anton Chekhov and the Lady With a Dog*, Oxford University Press, 1973.

Stowall, Peter, *Literary Impressionism: James and Chekhov*, University of Georgia Press, 1980.

Styan, J. L., *Chekhov in Performance*, Cambridge University Press, 1971.

Toumanova, Nina Andronikova, *Anton Chekhov: Voice of Twilight Russia*, Columbia University Press, 1937.

Tulloch, John, *Chekhov: A Structuralist Study*, Macmillan, 1980.

Twentieth-Century Literary Criticism, Gale, Volume 3, 1980, Volume 10, 1983.

Valency, Maurice, *The Breaking String: The Plays of Anton Chekhov*, Oxford University Press, 1966.

Winner, Thomas G., *Chekhov and His Prose*, Holt, 1966.

Woolf, Virginia, *The Common Reader*, Harcourt, 1948.

Yarmolinsky, Avrahm, editor, *Letters of Anton Chekhov*, translation by Bernard Guilbert Guerney and Lynn Solotaroff, Viking, 1973.

PERIODICALS

Atlantic Monthly, July, 1951.

Modern Language Studies, number 14, 1984.*

—*Sidelights by Charles J. Rzepka*

* * *

CHOUKAS-BRADLEY, Melanie (Rose) 1952-

PERSONAL: Born August 20, 1952, in Jacksonville, N.C.;

daughter of Michael, Jr. (a college alumni affairs director) and Juanita (a public relations director; maiden name, Crosby) Choukas; married James Richard Bradley (now Choukas-Bradley; an attorney), June 21, 1975; children: Sophia Crane. *Education:* Attended Pierce College, Athens, Greece, 1971; University of Vermont, B.A., 1974; studied plant identification at U.S. Department of Agriculture Graduate School, 1978-79.

ADDRESSES: Home—Germantown, Md. *Agent*—Paul Bradley, Bradley-Goldstein Agency, 7 Lexington Ave., New York, N.Y. 10010.

CAREER: WBRL (radio station), Berlin, N.H., sales representative, 1975-76, reporter and copywriter, 1975-77, news director, 1977; Rosapepe & Associates (a public interest consulting firm), Alexandria, Va., writer, 1978; U.S. House of Representatives, Committee on Interstate and Foreign Commerce, Washington, D.C., research assistant to Subcommittee on Oversight and Investigations, 1978; free-lance researcher, writer, photographer, and lecturer, 1979—. Writing teacher at Coos County Learning Center (adult education), Berlin, N.H., 1975-76; guest on numerous television and radio programs.

MEMBER: Garden Writers Association of America, National Organization for Women, Authors Guild, Washington Independent Writers.

WRITINGS:

(With Polly Alexander) *City of Trees: The Complete Botanical and Historical Guide to the Trees of Washington, D.C.*, illustrated with own photographs and with drawings and photographs by Alexander, Acropolis Books, 1981, revised edition published as *City of Trees: The Complete Field Guide to the Trees of Washington, D.C.*, Johns Hopkins University Press, 1987.

Contributor of articles and photographs to periodicals, including *Georgetowner, Greek Accent, Hill Rag, Washington Gardener, Washingtonian,* and *Washington Post*.

WORK IN PROGRESS: A nonfiction book on a feminist theme, publication by Dutton expected in 1989.

SIDELIGHTS: While living in the Washington, D.C., area during the late 1970s, Melanie Choukas-Bradley became interested in the many different trees growing there. Unable to find a suitable guide to identifying them, she decided to write one, embarking with co-author Polly Alexander on several years of research that resulted in *City of Trees*. The book is "a splendid field guide," assessed Robert Louis Benson in the *Washington Post Book World:* "practical, botanically sound and filled with good stories." Nearly three hundred drawings of leaves and fruits help the layman tell one tree from another, and color photographs of flowering trees further assist the descriptive text. In addition to describing each tree's physical appearance, Choukas-Bradley provides historical notes about a number of them, observing, for example, that some trees planted by George Washington still grow and discussing both trees imported from other countries as well as those native to the United States. To promote both sales of her book and tree-viewing, Choukas-Bradley also devised a twenty-eight-riddle puzzle leading on a treasure hunt of Washington trees. Whoever correctly identifies all the trees in the riddles will win a scarlet oak acorn in fourteen-karat gold worth one thousand dollars.

Choukas-Bradley told *CA:* "I get depressed when writers get together and talk about their word processors. I'm probably one of the few writers in America who doesn't own one and never will. I *like* to cut and paste. Scotch tape and scissors fill me with optimism. This doesn't mean I'd like to go back to the days of quill and inkpot, but I do like to gaze out over the top of my IBM Selectric to fields filled with Queen Anne's lace and chicory. If I wanted to stare at a computer terminal all day, I'd go to work for an airline. I think we need less, not more, technology. Somehow I can't picture Colette with a word processor.

"I find that my writing is heavily influenced by the weather. I'm always prolific on a September day when the wind is from the west. I owe this to what I call the 'compost theory.' All summer I've languished in Maryland's heat and humidity, doing little more than dragging myself to air conditioned libraries (and staring over the typewriter at chicory). Then comes the first breeze of fall and my writing takes off. I haven't been wasting time, I've been *composting*. Snowstorms are also good but they end up requiring heavy editing. That gives me an excuse to go out to the hardware store as soon as the roads are cleared to buy more scotch tape."

AVOCATIONAL INTERESTS: Women's rights, environmental issues, nature, psychology.

BIOGRAPHICAL/CRITICAL SOURCES:

PERIODICALS

Christian Science Monitor, July 8, 1982.
Evening Sun (Baltimore), November 11, 1982.
Richmond News Leader, July 17, 1982.
Sunday Journal (Kankakee, Ill.), April 25, 1982.
Washington Post Book World, May 2, 1987.

* * *

CHRISTMAN, Luther (Parmalee) 1915-

PERSONAL: Born February 26, 1915, in Summit Hill, Pa.; son of Elmer and Elizabeth (Barnicott) Christman; married Dorothy Mary Black, December 5, 1939; children: Gary James, Judith Ann Kinney, Lillian Jane. *Education:* Pennsylvania Hospital School of Nursing for Men, Diploma, 1939; Temple University, B.S., 1948, Ed.M., 1952; Michigan State University, Ph.D., 1965. *Politics:* Democrat. *Religion:* Unitarian-Universalist.

ADDRESSES: Home—19141 Loomis St., Homewood, Ill. 60430. *Office*—College of Nursing, Rush University, 600 South Paulina St., Chicago, Ill. 60612; and Department of Nursing Affairs, Rush-Presbyterian-St. Luke's Medical Center, 1753 West Congress Parkway, Chicago, Ill. 60612.

CAREER: Pennsylvania Hospital, Philadelphia, private duty nurse and assistant head nurse, 1939-48; Cooper Hospital School of Nursing, Camden, N.J., instructor in nursing, 1948-53; Yankton State Hospital, Yankton, S.D., director of nursing, 1953-56; Michigan Department of Mental Health, Lansing, nursing consultant, 1956-63; University of Michigan, Ann Arbor, associate professor of psychiatric nursing, 1963-67, research associate at Institute of Social Research, 1964-67, and Bureau of Hospital Administration, 1965-67; Vanderbilt University, Nashville, Tenn., professor of nursing, dean of School of Nursing, professor of sociology, and director of nursing at university hospital, all 1967-72, member of board of directors of Center for Health Services, 1971-72; Rush University, Chicago, Ill., professor of nursing and sociology, dean of College of Nursing, and vice-president of nursing affairs, all 1972-87, John L. and Helen Kellogg Dean of College of Nursing, 1978-87, dean emeritus, 1987—.

Visiting professor at College of New South Wales, 1978, Nordic School of Public Health, Goteborg, Sweden, 1979, and University of Lund, 1981; lecturer at Jikei Medical College, 1984; member of visiting faculty at Case Western Reserve University, 1985. Rush-Presbyterian-St. Luke's Medical Center, member of attending staff, senior scientist, and vice-president of nursing affairs, 1972—; member of board of directors of Center for Nursing Ethics, 1977. National Commission for the Study of Nursing and Nursing Education, member of nursing panel, 1968-70, regional associate, 1972-73; member of White House Committee on Children and Youth, 1970; member of Institute of Medicine, National Academy of Science; Heart International, member of board of directors, 1978-83, chairman of board, 1982—; member of Veterans Administration Exchange of Medical Information Review Group, 1971-76; member of National Institute of Mental Health team to survey mental health facilities of Colorado, 1962, and Georgia, 1964; vice-president and member of executive committee of board of directors of National Academy of Health In-Service Education, 1970-72; member of national nursing panel of President's Commission for the Study of Ethical Problems in Medicine and Biomedical and Behavioral Research, 1981; member of professional and technical advisory committee of Joint Commission on Accreditation of Hospitals, 1983-87; chairman of nursing group, National Academies of Practice, 1984—. Member of Michigan Psychiatric Manpower Task Force, 1964; member of planning council of Michigan Health Facilities, 1965-67; member of Tennessee Board of Nursing, 1967-69; member of Virginia Governor's Committee on Nursing, 1968; member of nursing education committee of Tennessee Higher Education Commission, 1971-72; member of Illinois Implementation Commission on Nursing, 1972-76; Illinois Cancer Council, chairman of committee on cancer nursing, 1976-81, member of board of directors, 1980-82; member of board of directors of Westberg Institute, 1982-83; consultant to National Center for Health Services Research; consultant to Medicus Corp. *Military service:* U.S. Maritime Service, 1943-45; became pharmacist's mate first class.

MEMBER: American Association for the Advancement of Science (fellow), American Association for Cancer Education, American Association of Colleges of Nurses, American Nurses Association (member of National Commission on Nursing Services, 1980-84), National Male Nurses Association (member of executive board, 1979), American Association of Men in Nursing (past chairman of the board), American Sociological Association, Biomedical Engineering Society, Society for Applied Anthropology (fellow), Society for General Systems Research, American Academy of Nursing (fellow), Illinois Nurses Association (member of board of directors, 1977-79), New York Academy of Sciences, Alpha Omega Alpha (honorary member), Alpha Kappa Delta, Sigma Theta Tau.

AWARDS, HONORS: Fellow of Institute of Medicine of Chicago, 1974—; named outstanding male nurse in the nation by National Association of Male Nurses, 1975; Annual Luther Christman Award was established by National Association of Male Nurses, 1975; visiting fellow of New Zealand Nurses Educational and Research Foundation, 1978; certificate of appreciation from Veterans Administration, 1980; D.H.L. from Thomas Jefferson University, 1980; nursing award from Council of Specialists in Psychiatric and Mental Health, 1980; Edith Moore Copeland Founders Award for Creativity from Sigma Theta Tau, 1981; named distinguished practitioner by National Academies of Practice, 1985; Old Master Award from Purdue University, 1985.

WRITINGS:

(With Michael Counte) *Interpersonal Behavior and Health Care,* Westview, 1981.

(With Counte) *Hospital Organization and Health Care Delivery,* Westview, 1981.

CONTRIBUTOR

Lucile Broadwell and Zella Von Gremp, editors, *Practical Nursing,* Lippincott, 1959.

Betty S. Bergersen and others, editors, *Current Concepts in Clinical Nursing,* Mosby, Volume I, 1967, Volume II, 1969.

Bonnie Bullough and Vern Bullough, editors, *Issues in Nursing,* 2nd edition, Springer Publishing, 1971.

Edith P. Lewis, editor, *Clinical Nurse Specialist,* American Journal of Nursing, 1971.

Harry Gottesfeld, editor, *Controversies in Community Mental Health,* Behavioral Publications, 1972.

Joan R. Riehl and Joan W. McVay, editors, *The Clinical Nurse Specialist Interpretations,* Appleton, 1973.

Loretta Sue Bermosk and Raymond Corsini, editors, *Critical Incidents in Nursing,* Saunders, 1973.

(Author of foreword) H. H. Schaeffer and P. L. Martin, *Behavioral Therapy,* 2nd edition, McGraw, 1975.

Gladys Scipien, Martha Barnard, Marilyn Chard, and others, editors, *Comprehensive Pediatric Nursing,* McGraw, 1975.

Janet A. Williamson, editor, *Current Perspectives in Nursing Education: The Changing Scene,* Mosby, 1976.

(Author of foreword) Janet A. Williamson, editor, *Nurse's Guide to Drugs,* Intermed Communications, 1979.

Norma Chaska, editor, *The Nursing Professions: Views Through the Mist,* McGraw, 1978.

Michael J. Millman, editor, *Nursing Personnel and the Changing Health Care System,* Ballinger, 1978.

Lorrain Machan, editor, *The Practitioner/Teacher Role: Practice What You Teach,* Nursing Resources, 1980.

Marie S. Berger, Dorothy Elhart, Sharon C. Firsich, and others, editors, *Management for Nurses,* Mosby, 1980.

W. Gibson Wood and Merrill E. Elias, editors, *Alcoholism and Aging: Advances in Research,* CRC Press, 1982.

Barbara J. Brown and Peggy L. Chinn, editors, *Nursing Education: Practical Methods and Models,* Aspen Systems Corp., 1982.

(Author of foreword) *Camping Safety and Health Management Manual,* American Red Cross, 1983.

OTHER

Author of forewords for annually revised nurses' drug handbook, beginning 1981. Contributor of more than two hundred articles and reviews to professional journals.

Guest editor of *Nursing Clinics of North America,* 1966; member of editorial board of *Perspectives in Psychiatric Care,* 1963-70, *Journal of Nursing Administration,* 1970-83, *Nursing Forum,* 1970-73, *Health Care Organization and Administration,* 1974-76, *Community Mental Health Review,* 1975-82, *Nurse Educator,* 1976-83, *Nursing Administration Quarterly,* 1976, and "Abstracts of Health Care Management Studies," University of Michigan, 1978-80; clinical editor of *Perspectives in Psychiatric Care,* 1967-69.

WORK IN PROGRESS: Research on "the reorganization of care directly around the patient for effective management."

SIDELIGHTS: Luther Christman told *CA:* "I take the position that the nursing profession cannot be strong in every country

unless it is strong in all countries. I have organized a series of international conferences to find ways and strategies to improve the quality of nursing education, as well as the organization of nursing care. I also arranged for the development of a film, 'The Rush Model of Nursing,' which is being distributed both nationally and internationally. My primary goal is to develop professional interdependence to improve patient care.''

AVOCATIONAL INTERESTS: Horticulture, birdwatching, environmental conservation work.

BIOGRAPHICAL/CRITICAL SOURCES:

PERIODICALS

Nursing Digest, Volume VI, number 2, 1978.

* * *

CHUBIN, Barry 1943-

PERSONAL: Born April 11, 1943, in Shiraz, Iran; son of A. H. (a diplomat) and N. (a housewife) Chubin; married Haideh Amjadi (an economist), July 7, 1977; children: Yasmine. *Education:* Drake University, B.A., 1966; Northwestern University, M.Sc., 1968.

ADDRESSES: Home and office—Nice, France. *Agent*—John Farquharson Ltd., 250 West 57th St., New York, N.Y. 10107.

CAREER: Held various key positions at National Iranian Oil Co., Teheran, 1968-77; Delta Iran Engineering and Construction Co., Teheran, director, 1978-79; writer, 1979—.

WRITINGS:

The Feet of a Snake (novel), Arbor House, 1984.

WORK IN PROGRESS: The Thirteenth Chief Directorate (tentative title), a novel about Soviet intelligence activity in the U.S. political arena.

SIDELIGHTS: Barry Chubin told *CA:* ''In Iran, during my decade as a civil servant, I worked in the hub of the National Iranian Oil Company—International Affaires. It was the experience I gained there—in various key positions—coupled with the radically different perspectives held by many Iranians vis-a-vis the revolution that provided the background to my first novel, *The Feet of a Snake.*

''After the revolution there were not many job offers available for a former speechwriter of the deposed Shah—which was one of my responsibilities at the oil company pertaining to his statements regarding the energy sector. Thus, Henry David Thoreau notwithstanding, it was virtually sheer desperation that led me to embark on my first novel. Today it is my first love.

''True, I have enjoyed exceptional luck. *The Feet of a Snake* has been a best-seller in England, additional printings have been called for, the film option has been picked up, and it has had six foreign language editions and rave reviews on both sides of the Atlantic—all of which have been enormously gratifying, thrilling to the nth degree.

''And the high is addictive. More so when coupled with the sheer potency of the creative process, which is—given the magnitude of competition one is confronted with—ultimately all one should realistically expect. The rest is up to God (who may reside on Madison Avenue).''

BIOGRAPHICAL/CRITICAL SOURCES:

PERIODICALS

Best Sellers, July, 1984.
Citizen (Gloucester), June 22, 1984.
Guardian (London), May 11, 1984.
Mystery News, May/June, 1984.

* * *

CHURCH, Roy A. 1935-

PERSONAL: Born February 21, 1935, in Wellingborough, Northamptonshire, England; son of William Alfred (a shoe worker) and Lillian Gertrude (a seamstress; maiden name, Morris) Church; married Gwenllian Elizabeth Martin (a schoolteacher), October 10, 1959; children: Benjamin Martin, Joseph William, Thomas Henry, Naomi Elizabeth Mary. *Education:* University of Nottingham, B.A., 1957, Ph.D., 1961.

ADDRESSES: Home—363 Unthank Rd., Norwich, Norfolk, England. *Office*—University of East Anglia, Norwich, Norfolk NR4 7TJ, England.

CAREER Worked for British Broadcasting Corp., London, England, 1959-60; Purdue University, Lafayette, Ind., professor of economics, 1960-61; University of Washington, Seattle, professor of economics, 1961-62; University of British Columbia, Vancouver, professor of economics, 1962-63; University of Birmingham, Birmingham, England, lecturer, 1963-68, senior lecturer in economic history, 1968-72; University of East Anglia, Norwich, England, professor of economic history, 1972—, pro-vice-chancellor, 1986—. Member of Social Science Research Council Economic and Social History Committee, 1971-76, Business Archives Council, 1972-82, and Economic and Social Research Council Industry and Employment Committee, 1983-87.

MEMBER: Royal Historical Society (fellow), Economic History Society (member of council, 1970—).

AWARDS, HONORS: Wadsworth Prize for Business History from Business Archives Council, 1987, for *The History of the British Coal Industry,* Volume III: *1830-1913: Victorian Preeminence.*

WRITINGS:

Economic and Social Change in a Midland Town, 1815-1900: Victorian Nottingham, Cass, 1966.
Kenricks in Hardware: A Family Business, 1790-1965, David & Charles, 1969.
The Great Victorian Boom, 1850-1873, Macmillan, 1975.
Herbert Austin: The British Motor Car Industry to 1941, Europa, 1979.
The Dynamics of Victorian Business: Problems and Perspectives, Allen & Unwin, 1980.
The History of the British Coal Industry, Volume III: *1830-1913: Victorian Preeminence,* Oxford University Press, 1986.

Editor of *Economic History Review,* 1983—.

WORK IN PROGRESS: The Strike Propensity of British Coal Miners Since 1890; The Rise and Decline of the British Motor Industry, 1896-1986.

BIOGRAPHICAL/CRITICAL SOURCES:

PERIODICALS

Times Literary Supplement, January 9, 1987.

CHURCHILL, Allen 1911-1988

OBITUARY NOTICE—See index for *CA* sketch: Born November 1, 1911, in Flushing, N.Y.; died of pancreatic cancer, January 16, 1988, in New York, N.Y. Editor and author. Churchill was known for his many nonfiction volumes on American life in the early decades of the twentieth century. He began his literary career in the 1930s as editor of magazines such as *Stage* and *Town and Country*, then worked for the publishing company G. P. Putnam's & Sons in the early 1940s. After World War II, in which Churchill served as a staff member of the Army weekly *Yank*, he spent twelve years writing for magazines. But in the late 1950s he quit writing for periodicals and began producing books. His more notable publications include *The Improper Bohemians: A Re-Creation of Greenwich Village in Its Heyday*, about the intellectual climate in the famed Manhattan neighborhood from 1912 to the beginning of the Great Depression; *Park Row: Turn of the Century Newspaper Days*, an account of New York City's competing newspapers during the years of publishers Joseph Pulitzer and William Randolph Hearst; and *They Never Came Back: Eight People Who Vanished*, which describes the circumstances surrounding the mysterious disappearances of several well-known persons, including the writer Ambrose Bierce. Other books by Churchill include *The Year the World Went Mad: 1927* and *Hitler—The Fuehrer as Seen by Contemporaries*. Churchill also edited the volume *All in Fun: An Anthology of Humor*.

OBITUARIES AND OTHER SOURCES:

PERIODICALS

New York Times, January 18, 1988.

* * *

CLARK, Al C.
See GOINES, Donald

* * *

CLARK, Keith 1939-

PERSONAL: Born February 13, 1939, in Monroe, Wis.; son of Donald Joseph (a shoe salesman) and Lois Elizabeth (a housewife; maiden name, Bolender) Clark. *Education:* Capuchin Seminary of St. Mary, B.A., 1962; Fordham University, M.S., 1968; graduate study at Oxford University, 1984-85.

ADDRESSES: Home and office—St. Lawrence Seminary, 301 Church St., Mount Calvary, Wis. 53057. *Agent*—Hintz & Fitzgerald, 207 East Buffalo, No. 211, Milwaukee, Wis. 53202.

CAREER: Entered Capuchin Order (O.F.M. Cap.), 1958, ordained Roman Catholic priest, 1965; St. Felix Friary, Huntington, Ind., member of novitiate team, 1968-70, novice master and guardian, 1970-75; Capuchin Province of St. Joseph, Milwaukee, Wis., director of formation and continuing education, 1975-78; Province of St. Joseph, Detroit, Mich., personnel director, 1978-84; St. Lawrence Seminary, Mount Calvary, Wis., president, 1986—. Lecturer at Albert Cardinal Meyer Institute; preacher at retreats.

MEMBER: National Catholic Education Association, National Organization for Continuing Education for Roman Catholic Clergy.

WRITINGS:

Make Space, Make Symbols, Ave Maria Press, 1979.
An Experience of Celibacy, Ave Maria Press, 1981.
Being Sexual . . . and Celibate, Ave Maria Press, 1986.

WORK IN PROGRESS: A book on communication and intimacy.

* * *

CLARK, Septima Poinsette 1898-1987

OBITUARY NOTICE—See index for *CA* sketch: Born May 3, 1898, in Charleston, S.C.; died December 15, 1987, near Charleston, S.C. Educator, public official, administrator, social activist, and author. The child of a former slave, Clark devoted much of her life to civil rights activities. She worked as a schoolteacher from 1922 until 1956, when she was fired from a job in Charleston, South Carolina, after joining the National Association for the Advancement of Colored People (NAACP). She subsequently worked in Tennessee's Citizenship Schools as director of programs promoting literacy among blacks. In addition, she worked with civil-rights leader Martin Luther King, Jr., as teacher training supervisor of the Southern Christian Leadership Conference, and in 1974 she won a position on Charleston County's school board. For her achievements Clark received a Living Legacy Award from President Jimmy Carter in 1979. She wrote an autobiography, *Echo in My Soul*.

OBITUARIES AND OTHER SOURCES:

BOOKS

In Black and White, 3rd edition, Supplement, Gale, 1985.

PERIODICALS

Los Angeles Times, December 17, 1987.
New York Times, December 17, 1987.

* * *

CLATWORTHY, Nancy M(oore) K. 1924-

PERSONAL: Born March 17, 1924, in Muncie, Ind.; daughter of Will Carleton (a surgeon) and Edith (Pfaffenberger) Moore; married Everett H. Kruger, Jr., June 10, 1944 (divorced, 1960); married H. William Clatworthy, Jr. (a surgeon and university professor), December 31, 1961. *Education:* Smith College, A.B., 1945; Western Reserve (now Case Western Reserve) University, M.A., 1948; Ohio State University, Ph.D., 1955. *Religion:* Episcopalian.

ADDRESSES: Home—Fireside Farms, 6400 Dublin Rd., Delaware, Ohio 43015. *Office*—Department of Sociology, Ohio State University, South Oval Dr., Columbus, Ohio 43210.

CAREER: Ohio State University, Columbus, associate professor of sociology, 1959—. Research associate at Ohio Rehabilitation Center. Chairman of research board of Columbus Junior League, 1957-59.

MEMBER: American Sociological Association, National Council on Family Relations, North Central Sociological Association, Smith College Club (president, 1955-57 and 1979-81).

WRITINGS:

(With Jerome D. Folkman) *Marriage Has Many Faces*, C. E. Merrill, 1970.

(With Nona Glazer-Malbin) *Old Family/New Family,* Van Nostrand, 1975.

(With Clara Shaw Schuster and Shirley Smith Ashburn) *The Process of Human Development: A Holistic Approach,* Little, Brown, 1980.

Contributor to textbook on the family, for Little, Brown. Writer for television series "The Councilors," 1973-74.

WORK IN PROGRESS: Social Values, Ethics, and Moral Behavior; Marriage for a Day; revising *Marriage Has Many Faces.*

SIDELIGHTS: Nancy M. K. Clatworthy told *CA:* "Values have been a key interest in both my family life and business."

* * *

CLIFF, Jimmy
See CHAMBERS, James

* * *

CLINARD, Helen Hall 1931-

PERSONAL: Born March 9, 1931, in Oxford, N.C.; daughter of John Perry (a pharmacist) and Daisy (a lawyer; maiden name, Cooper) Hall; married William Wake Shelton, Jr. (a physician), August 21, 1954 (died, October, 1960); married David Elwood Clinard (an insurance consultant), December 28, 1961; children: Julia Horner Shelton, William Wake Shelton, Perry Hall Shelton, Anne Cooper Clinard. *Education:* Women's College of the University of North Carolina (now University of North Carolina at Greensboro), B.F.A., 1953.

ADDRESSES: Home and office—3290 High Cliffs Rd., Pfafftown, N.C. 27040.

CAREER: Art supervisor at public schools in Asheboro, N.C., 1953-54; art teacher at a private school in Winston-Salem, N.C., 1954-57; R. J. Reynolds Tobacco, Winston-Salem, computer programmer, 1961; Effectiveness Training Associates, Pasadena, Calif., instructor, 1972-76; Effective Training and Consulting, Winston-Salem, executive director, 1976—. Senior instructor for Effectiveness Training, Inc. of California, 1972-77; member of faculty at Wake Forest University and British Association for Commercial and Industrial Education. Director and executive vice-president of Winston-Salem Citizens for Fair Housing, 1968-70; director of Locust Street Summer Enrichment Program, 1969; co-chairman of volunteer tutorial program for public schools of Winston-Salem, 1970-73.

MEMBER: American Society for Training and Development (national chairperson of Human Resource Development Consultants Special Interest Group, 1979; president of Piedmont chapter, 1979; regional director of International Division, 1980-81), Association for the Benefit of Child Development (president, 1969-72, 1975-76).

AWARDS, HONORS: Named International Trainer of the Year by American Society for Training and Development, 1981.

WRITINGS:

Winning Ways to Succeed With People, Gulf Publishing, 1985.

Contributor to training and education journals, and training manuals.

SIDELIGHTS: Helen Hall Clinard told *CA:* "Despite tremendous advances in new technology, there has been a lack of progress in knowledge and skill about getting along with people. We can put men into space and transplant human organs, but we haven't learned to live productively and harmoniously with other nations or even within our own nation, organizations, and families. This discrepancy is not surprising when you contrast the vast quantities of money, time, and energy that go into research, development, and training in new technologies with the very limited resources that are devoted to developing and teaching skills for getting along with people. It is possible for people to learn these skills, but they must be learned consciously because they are not in common use and are not likely to be absorbed through exposure to others.

"Interpersonal communication skills education is in its infancy as a science. Too frequently it is dealt with in a vague, unorganized, and subjective manner. I have tried to present this subject in an objective, well-organized, logical, and specific way. All of the skills I teach and write about will not only enable the user to be more successful with other people, they will also be appreciated and helpful to the people with whom they are used. The skills are universally needed and can be used wherever people live or work together. They are all based on sincerity and respect for the other person which, I believe, is necessary for any effective long-term relationship.

"My first exposure to some of these skills was through Thomas Gordon's Parent Effectiveness Training. Since then I have taught thousands of parents, teachers, managers, and consultants the skills that will help them become more effective at work and at home. I also help organizations develop training programs for their employees, and I train their trainers to teach these programs. This work involves frequent trips to Ireland and England. I enjoy meeting and talking with people around the world about this very personal subject. I also especially appreciate the close relationships I have developed with my family and friends through the use of these skills.

"My pleasure is in helping others, and my hope is that some day these skills will be taught routinely in our public schools, as well as in universities and in special training programs for teachers, parents, health professionals, managers, diplomats, and especially those in public office whose abilities to communicate effectively with others affect the lives of all of us."

* * *

CLYDE, Leslie
See KIPPS, Harriet C(lyde)

* * *

COCKERELL, Sydney M(orris) 1906-1987

OBITUARY NOTICE: Born June 6, 1906, in London, England; died November 6, 1987. Bookbinder, papermaker, educator, and author. Renowned as an expert in the restoration and binding of antique books, Cockerell learned his craft as a partner of his father, Douglas, who owned a bindery. He took charge of the firm when his father died in 1946. Cockerell repaired many precious volumes in the collections of British museums and libraries, developing new techniques for the work which were later adopted throughout the industry. He shared his expertise as a visiting lecturer at the School of Library and Archive Studies at University College, London, from 1945 to 1976, and he flew to Florence, Italy, as a consultant in 1966 when a catastrophic flood damaged many priceless books there. Cockerell's book *Marbling Paper* went through several editions during his lifetime, and he manufactured such paper at

his firm. He received the Order of the British Empire in 1980. Cockerell wrote *The Repairing of Books,* revised and enlarged his father's volume *Bookbinding and the Care of Books,* and contributed to *The Calligrapher's Handbook* and the *Encyclopaedia Britannica*.

OBITUARIES AND OTHER SOURCES:

BOOKS

Who's Who, 139th edition, St. Martin's, 1987.
Who's Who in Art, 21st edition, Art Trade Press, 1984.

PERIODICALS

Times (London), November 10, 1987.

* * *

COLE, Jennifer
See ZACH, Cheryl (Byrd)

* * *

COLE, Richard Cargill 1926-

PERSONAL: Born April 16, 1926, in Kansas City, Kan.; son of Horace Richard (a postal official) and Iris Verner (a housewife; maiden name, Cargill) Cole; married Florence Adaline Mason (a housewife), June 27, 1956; children: Celia Elizabeth Cole Colkitt, Paul Richard. *Education:* Hamilton College, B.A., 1950; Yale University, M.A., 1951, Ph.D., 1955. *Politics:* Republican. *Religion:* Presbyterian.

ADDRESSES: Home—Route 1, Box 1790, Davidson, N.C. 28036. *Office*—Department of English, Davidson College, Davidson, N.C. 28036.

CAREER: Manlius School, Manlius, N.Y., English teacher, 1951-52; Yale University, New Haven, Conn., assistant to dean of freshman, 1953-54; University of Texas at Austin, instructor in English 1954-57; Radford College (now University), Radford, Va., associate professor, 1957-59, professor of English, 1959-61; Davidson College, Davidson, N.C., professor of English, 1961—. *Military service:* U.S. Army Air Force, 1944-46; served in Europe; became sergeant.

MEMBER: Modern Language Association of America, South Atlantic Modern Language Association.

AWARDS, HONORS: Grant from American Council of Learned Societies, 1975; Robert Warnock research fellow at Yale University, 1975-76.

WRITINGS:

Irish Booksellers and English Writers, 1740-1800, Mansell Publishing, 1986.
(Editor) *Robert Colvill's Atlanta and Savannah,* Scholars' Facsimiles and Reprints, 1987.
(Editor) *John Singleton's European Journal, 1815-1817,* Peter Lang Publishing, 1987.

Editor of "The Private Papers of James Boswell," Yale University, 1975—. Contributor to literature and philology journals.

WORK IN PROGRESS: Editing James Boswell's correspondence in the years 1766 to 1769, for McGraw.

SIDELIGHTS: The subject of Richard Cargill Cole's first book is eighteenth-century Irish booksellers and their contribution to the popularity of British authors. He concerned himself not with the publishers who reprinted authorized editions from the British mainland but with the pirates who produced cheap, unauthorized copies of British titles. Though they were the object of bitter complaints from the London publishing industry, these Irish entrepreneurs were responsible for popularizing the work of authors like Dr. Johnson, Boswell, Goldsmith, and Gibbon, by making their work affordable to a wide audience. Reviewer James Raven wrote in the *Times Literary Supplement:* "*Irish Booksellers and English Writers, 1740-1800* is an important contribution to the history of eighteenth-century publishing."

BIOGRAPHICAL/CRITICAL SOURCES:

PERIODICALS

Times Literary Supplement, January 2, 1987.

* * *

COLES, Alan 1927-

PERSONAL: Born in 1927 in London, England; son of Bernard Henry and Florence Emily (Masterman) Coles; married Gay Smyth Garrod (a research assistant), 1951; children: Deborah Gay Coles Lawrence.

ADDRESSES: Office—University College, University of Wales, Cardiff, Wales.

CAREER: Writer. Owner and editor of South Devon Chronicle Group, 1962-68; editor of *Bermuda Sun,* 1973-75. *Military service:* Royal Navy, writer.

WRITINGS:

Three Before Breakfast: A True and Dramatic Account of How a German U-boat Sank Three British Cruisers in One Desperate Hour, Kenneth Mason, 1979.
(With Ted Briggs) *Flagship "Hood": The Fate of Britain's Mightiest Warship* (nonfiction), R. Hale, 1985.

Also author of *Slaughter at Sea,* for R. Hale.

WORK IN PROGRESS: Research on the naval history of World Wars I and II.

* * *

COLTON, Timothy J. 1947-

PERSONAL: Born July 14, 1947, in Timmons, Ontario, Canada; son of James M. (a businessman) and Rose E. (a housewife; maiden name, Spooner) Colton; married Patricia Jean Comeau (a teacher), May 31, 1968; children: Patricia Anne, Kathrine Rose. *Education:* University of Toronto, B.A., 1968, M.A., 1970; Harvard University, Ph.D., 1974.

ADDRESSES: Home—107 Glenview Ave., Toronto, Ontario, Canada M4R 1R1. *Office*—Political Science Department, 100 Saint George St., University of Toronto, Toronto, Ontario, Canada M5S 1A1.

CAREER: University of Toronto, Toronto, Ontario, assistant professor, 1974-79, associate professor, 1979-82, professor of political science, 1982—.

MEMBER: Joint Committee on Soviet Studies of American Council of Learned Societies/Social Science Research Council, American Association for Advancement of Slavic Studies (member of board).

WRITINGS:

Commissars, Commanders, and Civilian Authority: The Structure of Soviet Military Politics, Harvard University Press, 1979.

Big Daddy: Frederick G. Gardiner and the Building of Metropolitan Toronto, University of Toronto Press, 1980.

The Dilemma of Reform in the Soviet Union, Council on Foreign Relations, 1984, revised and enlarged edition, 1986.

WORK IN PROGRESS: Further research in government and politics of Moscow, political change under Soviet leader Mikhail Gorbachev.

* * *

COLVILLE, John Rupert 1915-1987

OBITUARY NOTICE—See index for *CA* sketch: Born January 28, 1915; died November 19, 1987, in Broughton, England. Government secretary, diplomat, business administrator, and author. Colville was private secretary to British prime ministers Neville Chamberlain, Winston Churchill, and Clement Attlee. After working in the British Government's Foreign Office in the late 1930s, Colville served Chamberlain as Britain entered what some historians have called its "darkest hour"—the first years of World War II. When Churchill assumed power, he retained Colville and made him an integral part of the country's war cabinet. Colville temporarily left his secretarial post to serve as a pilot in the Royal Air Force, for which he flew forty combat missions. He returned to his position with Churchill shortly before the war ended.

When Clement Attlee succeeded Churchill in 1945, Colville briefly served the new prime minister, then resumed his diplomatic career in the Foreign Office. His work there was interrupted by two years as private secretary to the recently married Princess Elizabeth, after which he returned to government work as a counsellor in Spain. Churchill again assumed the prime ministership in 1951, whereupon Colville left his diplomatic post to become joint principal private secretary. He served under Churchill until 1955, then left government work entirely and became director of Hill Samuel & Company, where he remained until 1975. Colville's writings include *Man of Valour: The Life of Field Marshall the Viscount Gort; Footprints in Time,* a memoir; *The New Elizabethans; The Portrait of a General,* an account of his great-grandfather, Charles Colville; and *Winston Churchill and His Inner Circle* (published in England as *The Churchillians*).

OBITUARIES AND OTHER SOURCES:

BOOKS

Who's Who, 139th edition, St. Martin's, 1987.

PERIODICALS

Times (London), November 21, 1987.

Washington Post, November 23, 1987.

* * *

COMSTOCK, George Adolphe 1932-

PERSONAL: Born May 17, 1932, in Seattle, Wash.; son of George H. and Alma (Doweidt) Comstock. *Education:* University of Washington, Seattle, B.A., 1954; Stanford University, M.A., 1958, Ph.D., 1967.

ADDRESSES: Office—S. I. Newhouse School of Public Communications, Syracuse University, Syracuse, N.Y. 13244.

CAREER: New York University, New York, N.Y., assistant professor of journalism, 1967-68; RAND Corp., Santa Monica, Calif., social psychologist, 1968-70, senior social psychologist, 1972-77; National Institute of Mental Health, Bethesda, Md., social psychologist, 1970-72; Syracuse University, Syracuse, N.Y., professor of communication, 1977-79, S. I. Newhouse Professor of Public Communication, 1979—. Senior science adviser to U.S. Surgeon General's Scientific Advisory Committee on Television and Social Behavior, 1970-72. *Military service:* U.S. Air Force, 1955-57; became captain.

MEMBER: International Communication Association, American Sociological Association, American Association for Public Opinion Research, Association for Education in Journalism, Society for the Psychological Study of Social Issues.

WRITINGS:

(Editor with Eli Rubinstein and John Murray) *Television and Social Behavior,* U.S. Government Printing Office, 1972.

(With Steven Chaffee, Maxwell McCombs, and others) *Television and Human Behavior,* Columbia University Press, 1978, revised, in press.

Television in America, Sage Publications, 1980, revised, 1988.

(Editor) *Public Communication and Behavior,* Academic Press, Volume I, 1986, Volume II, 1987.

(Contributor) Arnold Goldstein and Steven Apter, editors, *Youth Violence: Programs and Prospects,* Pergamon, 1986.

(With Hae-Jung Paik) *Television and Children,* ERIC, 1987.

(Contributor) Stuart Oskamp, editor, *Social Psychology Annual,* Sage Publications, 1987.

SIDELIGHTS: George Adolphe Comstock told *CA:* "My personal philosophy has always been to do what you can, when you can, as well as you can. I believe that it has served me well and led to many enriching and rewarding experiences and to what I regard as a relatively successful career."

AVOCATIONAL INTERESTS: Contemporary fiction, gourmet cooking, travel, collecting Mexican folk art, Thoroughbred horse racing.

BIOGRAPHICAL/CRITICAL SOURCES:

PERIODICALS

Annals of the American Academy of Political and Social Science, March, 1981.

* * *

CONNERY, John (R.) 1913-1987

OBITUARY NOTICE: Born July 15, 1913, in Chicago, Ill.; died of heart failure, December 22, 1987, in Evanston, Ill. Theologian, educator, and author. Connery was a Roman Catholic priest known as an expert in the field of bioethics. Although opposed to abortion, he argued in the controversial case of Karen Quinlan that it was morally acceptable to remove a brain-damaged person from a respirator, since morality required the use of all ordinary means to preserve a life, but not extraordinary means. Connery joined the Jesuit religious order in the 1930s. He was a professor of moral theology at West Baden College from 1948 to 1960, later moving successively to Bellarmine School of Theology in 1967, Jesuit School of Theology in 1970, and Chicago's Loyola University in 1976. From 1960 to 1967 he was superior of the Chicago province of the Jesuits. Connery was corresponding editor of the Catholic magazine *America* from 1959 to 1970 and contributed to

various religious and professional journals. He wrote the book *Abortion: The Development of the Roman Catholic Perspective.*

OBITUARIES AND OTHER SOURCES:

BOOKS

American Catholic Who's Who, Volume 23: *1980-1981,* National Catholic News Service, 1979.

PERIODICALS

Chicago Tribune, December 25, 1987.
New York Times, December 26, 1987.

* * *

CONNIFF, Richard 1951-

PERSONAL: Born March 2, 1951, in Jersey City, N.J.; son of James C. G. (a writer) and Dorothy (a homemaker; maiden name, Donnelly) Conniff; married Karen Braeder (a homemaker), May 23, 1981; children: James, Benjamin. *Education:* Yale University, B.A., 1973. *Religion:* Roman Catholic.

ADDRESSES: Home—P.O. Box 64, Deep River, Conn. 06417. *Agent*—Robert Lescher, 155 East 71st St., New York, N.Y. 10021.

CAREER: Newark Star-Ledger, Newark, N.J., reporter, 1973-75; free-lance writer, 1975-79; *Next,* New York, N.Y., senior writer, 1979-81; free-lance writer, 1981-83; *Geo,* New York City, managing editor, 1983-85; free-lance writer, 1985—.

WRITINGS:

The Devil's Book of Verse: Masters of the Poison Pen From Ancient Times to the Present Day, Dodd, 1983.
(With Alen MacWeeney) *Irish Walls,* Stewart, Tabori, 1986.

Contributor to magazines and newspapers, including *Architectural Digest, Audubon, Smithsonian,* and *Time.*

WORK IN PROGRESS: A novel about the nineteenth-century ivory trade.

SIDELIGHTS: Richard Conniff told *CA:* "I'm interested in propagating audacious speech, speech that is often satirical and usually humorous. I'm also interested in exploring the connections between human beings and the natural world."

Conniff's first book, *The Devil's Book of Verse,* is a collection of nearly four hundred poems of rude invective and wit, which have delighted critics since the volume appeared in 1983. The contributors are as ancient as Catullus and as contemporary as Dorothy Parker, Ogden Nash, and John Updike. The subjects of the poison pen are as varied as their authors: sex, the family, politics, religion, lawyers, and children are just a few.

Though *The Devil's Book of Verse* was acclaimed by its reviewers, it was not so well received by the publisher's parent company, a publisher of Bibles. When the author was asked to remove two poems containing an offensive word, Conniff refused, and it appeared that the book might not be distributed at all. The author filed a lawsuit and enlisted the support of such groups as the International P.E.N. and the American Society of Authors and Journalists to fight what they described as an act of censorship. Finally the suit was settled and Conniff received the unsold copies of his book. He established the Deep River Book Company to distribute them and continued his career as a free-lance writer.

In 1986 *Irish Walls* was published. This book, illustrated by the photographs of Alen MacWeeney, developed from Conniff's belief that the thousands of miles of walls dividing Ireland reveal the underlying nature of the Irish landscape and the people who live in it. The volume was described by Harriet Choice in the *Chicago Tribune* as "a charming and unique travel book."

AVOCATIONAL INTERESTS: Ireland, architectural restoration, Americana, travel.

BIOGRAPHICAL/CRITICAL SOURCES:

PERIODICALS

Chicago Tribune, October 5, 1986.
Newsday, September 21, 1983.

* * *

CONOLLY, Violet 1901(?)-1988(?)

OBITUARY NOTICE: Born c. 1901 in Glasnevin, Ireland; died c. 1988. Specialist in Soviet studies and author. Conolly was considered an important expert on the far eastern region of the U.S.S.R. She worked for many years in the research department of the British Foreign Office and was also employed by Chatham House and the now-defunct League of Nations. Her works include *Soviet Economic Policy in the East: Turkey, Persia, Afghanistan, Mongolia and Tanu Tuva, Sin Kiang; Soviet Trade From the Pacific to the Levant, With an Economic Study of the Soviet Far Eastern Region; Soviet Tempo: A Journal of Travel in Russia; Beyond the Urals: Economic Developments in Soviet Asia;* and *Siberia Today and Tomorrow: A Study of Economic Resources, Problems, and Achievements.*

OBITUARIES AND OTHER SOURCES:

PERIODICALS

Times (London), January 13, 1988.

* * *

COOK, (Will) Mercer 1903-1987

OBITUARY NOTICE—See index for *CA* sketch: Born March 30, 1903, in Washington, D.C.; died of pneumonia, October 4, 1987, in Washington, D.C. Educator, administrator, diplomat, editor, translator, songwriter, and author. Cook was an American ambassador to the African nations Niger and Senegal in the mid-1960s. In accepting the diplomatic posts he interrupted his work at Howard University, where he had taught Romance languages since 1945. He resumed his career there in 1966, then retired in 1970. In addition to his duties as professor and diplomat, Cook was director of Africa's Congress for Cultural Freedom in the early 1960s and was an alternate delegate to the United Nations General Assembly in 1963. Cook wrote such works as *Five French Negro Authors* and *The Haitian Novel,* and he collaborated with Stephen Henderson on writing *The Militant Black Writer in Africa and the United States.* In addition, Cook produced English translations and collections of works by West Indian and African writers, including Leopold Senghor. He also wrote songs.

OBITUARIES AND OTHER SOURCES:

PERIODICALS

New York Times, October 7, 1987.
Washington Post, October 16, 1987.

COREY, Stephen 1948-

PERSONAL: Born August 30, 1948, in Buffalo, N.Y.; son of Dale B. (a certified public accountant) and Julienne (a homemaker and nurse; maiden name, Holmes) Corey; married Mary Gibson (a nurse), January 28, 1970; children: Heather Lynn, Miranda Dawn. *Education:* State University of New York at Binghamton, B.A., 1971, M.A., 1974; University of Florida, Ph.D., 1979.

ADDRESSES: Office—Georgia Review, University of Georgia, Athens, Ga. 30602.

CAREER: University of Florida, Gainesville, instructor in English, 1979-80; University of South Carolina—Columbia, assistant professor of English, 1980-83; University of Georgia, Athens, assistant editor of *Georgia Review,* 1983-85, associate editor, 1985—.

MEMBER: Poets and Writers, South Atlantic Modern Language Association.

AWARDS, HONORS: First Book Award from Water Mark Poets, 1981, for *The Last Magician;* Excellence Award from Winthrop College, 1981, for *The Last Magician;* award from Swallow's Tale Press, 1984, for *Synchronized Swimming;* fellow of Florida Arts Council, 1979-80, South Carolina Arts Council, 1981-82, and Georgia Arts Council, 1985-86.

WRITINGS:

Twelve (poems), Renaissance Press, 1978.
The Last Magician (poems), Water Mark Press, 1981.
Fighting Death (poems), State Street Press, 1983.
Gentle Iron Lace (poems), Press of the Night Owl, 1984.
Synchronized Swimming (poems), Swallow's Tale Press, 1985.
(Editor with Stanley W. Lindberg) *Necessary Fictions: Selected Stories From the Georgia Review,* University of Georgia Press, 1986.
(Editor with Lindberg) *Keener Sounds: Selected Poems From the Georgia Review,* University of Georgia Press, 1987.

Contributor of articles and reviews to periodicals. Editor of *Devil's Millhopper,* 1977-83.

WORK IN PROGRESS: To Keep From Drifting Away, poems.

BIOGRAPHICAL/CRITICAL SOURCES:

BOOKS

Swanson, Gayle and William B. Thesing, *Conversations With South Carolina Poets,* John F. Blair, 1986.

PERIODICALS

Atlantic Journal and Constitution, March 1, 1987.
Virginia Quarterly Review, spring, 1982.

* * *

COSTAS, Orlando E(nrique) 1942-1987

*OBITUARY NOTICE—*See index for *CA* sketch: Born June 15, 1942, in Ponce, Puerto Rico; immigrated to United States, 1954; died of stomach cancer, November 5, 1987, in Newton Centre, Mass. Theologian, educator, and author. An ordained Baptist minister, Costas served as pastor of a number of churches in Puerto Rico and the United States. The clergyman also taught at various universities and seminaries, including the University of Wisconsin—Milwaukee and Eastern Baptist Theological Seminary, where he was named Thormley B. Woods Professor of Missiology and director of Hispanic Studies in 1979. In 1984 he became academic dean of Andover Newton Theological School, an affiliate of the American Baptist Churches and the United Church of Christ. Among his numerous writings in English are *The Church and Its Mission: A Shattering Critique From the Third World, Theology of Crossroads in Contemporary Latin America, Out of the Depth: A Contextual Theology of Evangelism,* and *Liberating News! A Contextual Theology of Evangelization.* Costas, who was a co-founder of the newspaper *La Guardia,* also worked as editor of *Occasional Essays* and *Pastorialia* between 1977 and 1979.

OBITUARIES AND OTHER SOURCES:

PERIODICALS

New York Times, November 8, 1987.

* * *

COTTER, Joseph S., Sr.
See COTTER, Joseph Seamon, Sr.

* * *

COTTER, Joseph Seamon, Sr. 1861-1949
(Joseph S. Cotter, Sr.)

PERSONAL: Born February 2, 1861, in Bardstown, Ky.; died March 14, 1949; son of Micheil J. and Martha (Vaughn) Cotter; married Maria F. Cox (a teacher and principal), July 22, 1891; children: Florence Olivia (died in 1914), Joseph Seamon (died in 1919), Leonidas (died in 1900). *Education:* Attended school through third grade; attended night school in Louisville, Ky.

*ADDRESSES: Home—*Louisville, Ky.

CAREER: Worked odd jobs throughout childhood and adolescence, including ragpicking, serving as a teamster on a levee, distillery work, tobacco stemming, and prizefighting; taught school in Kentucky, 1885-89; Louisville Public Schools, Louisville, Ky., teacher at Western Colored School, 1889-93, founder and principal of Paul L. Dunbar School, 1893-1911, principal of Samuel Coleridge-Taylor School, 1911-42; retired, 1942-49. Elected to the Louisville Board of Education, 1938.

MEMBER: Author's League of America, National Association for the Advancement of Colored People, Story Tellers League, Kentucky Negro Educational Association, Louisville Colored Orphan's Home Society (past director).

WRITINGS—UNDER NAME JOSEPH S. COTTER, SR., EXCEPT AS NOTED:

POETRY, EXCEPT AS NOTED

A Rhyming (includes "The Bachelor," "Man Does Not Know," and "Description of a Kentucky School House"), New South Publishing, 1895.
Links of Friendship (includes "Answer to Dunbar's 'After a Visit,'" "Answer to Dunbar's 'A Choice,'" "Six in Deportment," "The Devil and the Higher Critics," "A Just Reward," and "Sequel to 'The Pied Piper of Hamelin'"), Bradley & Gilbert, 1898.
Caleb, the Degenerate; A Play in Four Acts: A Study of the Types, Customs, and Needs of the American Negro (poetic drama), Bradley & Gilbert, 1903, recent edition, AMS Press, 1973.

A White Song and a Black One (includes "A White Song," "A Black Song," "Grant and Lee," "Reporting the Sermon," "The Loafing Negro," "The Don't Care Negro," and "The Vicious Negro"), Bradley & Gilbert, 1909, recent edition, AMS Press, 1975.

Negro Tales (short stories; includes "Caleb," "Rodney," "Tesney, the Deceived," "Regnan's Anniversary," "A Rustic Comedy," "Kotchin' De Nines," and "Observation"), Cosmopolitan Press, 1912, recent edition, Mnemosyne Publishing, 1969.

(Under name Joseph Seamon Cotter, Sr.) *Collected Poems of Joseph S. Cotter, Sr.* (includes "Style," "Babe on Babe," "The Negro Preacher," "The Negro Woman," and "The Negro Child"), Henry Harrison, 1938, recent edition, Books for Libraries Press, 1971.

Sequel to "The Pied Piper of Hamelin," and Other Poems (includes "Sequel to 'The Pied Piper of Hamelin,'" "A Poem," "The Door-Sill," "My Lad," "Mr. Goody's Goat," "Johnny's Dream of Santa Claus," "The Race Welcomes Dr. W. E. B. Du Bois as Its Leader," "The Tragedy of Pete," "The Wooded Path," and "Christmas Turkey"), Henry Harrison, 1939.

(Under name Joseph Seamon Cotter, Sr.) *Negroes and Others at Work and Play* (poems and prose; includes "A Town Sketch," "Another Cinderella," "One Strange Night," "The Chastisement," "Caesar Driftwood," "The True Negro," "Walnut Street," "Fourth Avenue of Yesteryear," "Psalm of the Zoot-Suit," and "The A-Bomb"), Paebar, 1947.

SIDELIGHTS: Joseph Seamon Cotter, Sr., overcame a childhood filled with odd jobs that staved off poverty and became a respected educator and author. Best remembered for his poem "The Tragedy of Pete," and for *Caleb, the Degenerate,* only the second play by a black American to be published, he is praised for his proficiency in different verse styles. Equally comfortable with black dialect poems influenced by his friendship with poet Paul Laurence Dunbar and with the rhyme and meter of Italian sonnets and traditional English ballads, Cotter produced several volumes of poems and short stories during his lengthy career as a teacher, principal, and member of the school board in Louisville, Kentucky.

When Cotter's art deals with the problems blacks faced in his times, it usually approaches the race issue in a conciliatory manner, according to A. Russell Brooks in the *Dictionary of Literary Biography*. In his blank verse drama *Caleb, the Degenerate,* Cotter, like famed black educator Booker T. Washington, argues that blacks are less likely to advance through political activism than through hard work in the fields of industry. Through contrasting Caleb and his corruptor, minister-politician Rahab, with the virtuous Bishop and his daughter Olivia, who run an industrial school for blacks, Cotter makes his case. Rahab, in Brooks's words, "instills in [Caleb] the notion that the ideal gentleman eats and wears only what he has picked up, borrowed, or stolen." He also leads Caleb to murder his own father and sell the corpse to a medical student. Another character, Dude, is also under Rahab's influence at the beginning of *Caleb,* but by the play's end he has been swayed to the side of good by Bishop and Olivia.

"It is not known if [*Caleb*] was ever produced," Brooks reported; the play was perceived as poor closet drama by many critics. Despite its unsuitability for the stage and some "stilted" dialogue, however, Brooks claimed that "pleasant surprises await the persevering reader: for example, several passages written in imitation of [English poet] John Milton's use of the epic simile."

Cotter "used dialect effectively in relating humorous incidents and situations," lauded Brooks. His dialect poems include "Reporting the Sermon," which concerns a preacher who delivers a sermon on the evils of drink only to try and drain the last drops from a near-empty liquor bottle while its former possessors watch from behind some weeds. "Christmas Turkey" takes advantage of black dialect to add flair to the speaker's plot to bore his fellow diners with an account of the turkey's life so that they lose their appetites and leave the whole turkey to him. Cotter's famous "The Tragedy of Pete," the story of a black man who kills the drunk driver responsible for the death of his girlfriend, takes the form of a folk ballad. Another of his poems in ballad form, "The Bachelor," portrays a boy taunting an old man into telling the strange reason why he never married—while he was looking to see if an old abandoned cottage was truly inhabited by witches, a huge weight came down on his back, rendering him incapable of enjoying women. Cotter also wrote many poems for children, such as "Sequel to 'The Pied Piper of Hamelin,'" which Robert T. Kerlin announced in the *South Atlantic Quarterly* "surpasses the original—[English poet Robert] Browning's—that is, in rushing rhythms and ingenious rhymes."

Cotter's fiction, often judged inferior to his better poems, includes the story "Regnan's Anniversary." Depicting a man who is late for his wedding because he was chased into a pond by two rival gangs, "Regnan's Anniversary" and Cotter's "Kotchin' De Nines," about a man whose dreams of riches lead him to poverty, were praised by Brooks for their "natural dialogue and characters and unified plots." Though Cotter's own stories are not considered memorable, he "was widely known and loved for his promotion of . . . the story-telling contests which he initiated in the Louisville public libraries," revealed Brooks.

BIOGRAPHICAL/CRITICAL SOURCES:

BOOKS

Dictionary of Literary Biography, Volume 50: *Afro-American Writers Before the Harlem Renaissance,* Gale, 1986.

PERIODICALS

South Atlantic Quarterly, July, 1921.*

* * *

COTTON, (Thomas) Henry 1907-1987

OBITUARY NOTICE: Born January 26, 1907, in Holmes Chapel, Cheshire, England; died December 22, 1987, in London, England. Golfer and author. Considered the premier British golfer of his time, Cotton won the British Open in 1934, 1937, and 1948, as well as the national open tournaments of Germany, Italy, France, Belgium, and Czechoslovakia. He also played in the Ryder Cup competition three times, serving as team captain, and he designed numerous golf courses. Cotton was professional golf correspondent of *Golf Monthly* and wrote several books about his sport, including *My Swing, Study the Golf Game With Henry Cotton, Henry Cotton's Guide to Golf in the British Isles, Play Better Golf, Golf: A Pictorial History,* and *Thanks for the Game: The Best of Golf With Henry Cotton.*

OBITUARIES AND OTHER SOURCES:

BOOKS

The International Who's Who, 50th edition, Europa, 1986.
Who's Who, 139th edition, St. Martin's, 1987.

PERIODICALS

New York Times, December 25, 1987.
Washington Post, December 25, 1987.

* * *

COULSON, N. J.
See COULSON, Noel J(ames)

* * *

COULSON, Noel J(ames) 1928-1986
(N. J. Coulson)

PERSONAL: Born August 18, 1928, in Blackrod, Lancashire, England; died August 30, 1986; son of George Frederick and Marjorie Elizabeth Coulson; married Muriel Ivatts, 1951; children: two daughters. *Education:* Keble College, Oxford, M.A. (with first class honors).

CAREER: Called to the Bar at Gray's Inn, 1961; University of London, London School of Oriental and African Studies, London, England, lecturer, 1954-64, reader in Islamic law, 1964-65; Ahmadu Bello University, Zaria, Nigeria, dean of faculty of law, 1965-66; University of London, London School of Oriental and African Studies, professor of Oriental law, 1967-86, chairman of board of studies in laws, 1980-82, head of law department, 1981-86, dean of faculty of laws, 1984-86. Visiting professor at University of California, Los Angeles, 1961, 1977, University of Chicago, 1968, University of Pennsylvania, 1970, University of Utah, 1977, and Harvard University, 1979, 1984. *Military service:* Royal Air Force, intelligence officer in Parachute Regiment, 1950-52; served in Cyprus and the Suez Canal Zone; became lieutenant.

WRITINGS:

A History of Islamic Law, Edinburgh University Press, 1964.
Conflicts and Tension in Islamic Jurisprudence, University of Chicago Press, 1969.
(Under name N. J. Coulson) *Succession in the Muslim Family,* Cambridge University Press, 1971.
Commercial Law in the Gulf States: The Islamic Legal Tradition, Graham & Trotman, 1984.

Contributor to law and Islamic studies journals.

BIOGRAPHICAL/CRITICAL SOURCES:

PERIODICALS

Times (London), September 3, 1986.*

* * *

COUPER, Heather 1949-

PERSONAL: Surname is pronounced "Cooper"; born June 2, 1949, in Wallasey, England; daughter of George Elder (an airline pilot) and Anita (an administrator; maiden name, Taylor) Couper. *Education:* University of Leicester, B.S. (with honors), 1973; graduate study at Oxford University.

ADDRESSES: *Home*—55 Colomb St., London SE10 9EZ, England. *Agent*—David Higham Associates Ltd., 5-8 Lower John St., Golden Square, London W1R 4HA, England.

CAREER: University of Cambridge Observatories, Cambridge, England, research assistant, 1969-70; Old Royal Observatory, Greenwich, London, England, lecturer, 1977-83; full-time broadcaster and writer, 1983—. Chairman of the joint Department of Education and Science/British National Space Centre Working Group on Remote Sensing and chairman of the school curriculum, 1987—.

MEMBER: British Astronomical Association (president, 1984-86; vice-president, 1986—), Royal Astronomical Society (fellow; member of Education Committee), Junior Astronomical Society (president, 1987—), Royal Society of Arts (fellow).

AWARDS, HONORS: Special Award for series in engineering and technology from the New York Academy of Sciences, and Outstanding Science Book for Children from the American National Science Teachers Association, both 1978, both for *Space Frontiers;* Information Book Award from *Times Educational Supplement,* 1987, for *Galaxies and Quasars.*

WRITINGS:

Exploring Space, Octopus Books, 1980.
Space, the Final Frontier, Crescent, 1980.
(With Terence Murtagh) *Heavens Above,* F. Watts, 1981.
Journey Into Space, Grolier, 1984.
(With Ronald Alpiar) *Starfinder,* Century Communications, 1984.
Comets and Meteors, F. Watts, 1985.
The Planets, F. Watts, 1985.
The Stars, F. Watts, 1985.
(With Patrick Moore) *Halley's Comet Pop-Up Book,* Deans, 1985.
(With David Pelham) *The Universe: A Three-Dimensional Study,* Random House, 1985.

WITH NIGEL HENBEST

Space Frontiers (juvenile), edited by Christopher Cooper, Viking, 1978.
All About Space (juvenile), edited by Cooper, Marshall Cavendish, 1981, EMC Publishing, 1983.
The Restless Universe, Philip & Son, 1982.
Astronomy (juvenile), F. Watts, 1983.
Physics (juvenile), F. Watts, 1983.
The Planets, Pan, 1985, published as *New Worlds: In Search of the Planets,* Addison-Wesley, 1986.
The Sun, F. Watts, 1986.
The Moon, F. Watts, 1986.
Galaxies and Quasars, F. Watts, 1986.
Telescopes and Observatories, F. Watts, 1987.
Spaceprobes and Satellites, F. Watts, 1987.
The Stars, Pan, 1988.
Guide to the Galaxy, Cambridge University Press, in press.

OTHER

(With Henbest) "The Planets" (television script; based on Couper and Henbest's book of the same name), Moving Picture Company, 1986.
(Also presenter) "The Stars" (six-part television series; based on Couper and Henbest's book of the same name), Moving Picture Company, 1988.
(Also presenter and producer) "Secrets of the Stars" (script for star show), London Planetarium, 1988.

Columnist for *The Independent.* Contributor to encyclopedias, including *Encyclopaedia Brittanica, Encyclopedia of Astronomy and Space,* Crowell, 1976, and *Encyclopedia of Space Travel and Astronomy,* Octopus Books, 1979. Contributor to

periodicals, including *Popular Astronomy, New Scientist, Guardian, Cosmopolitan,* and the *Daily Mail.*

SIDELIGHTS: Through her numerous books, astronomy writer Heather Couper relays to the general reading public complex scientific information in what critics consider clear, understandable layman's terms. Three of her 1985 books, *New Worlds: In Search of the Planets, The Universe: A Three Dimensional Study,* and *Halley's Comet Pop-Up Book,* focus on a variety of galactic subjects. In *New Worlds,* Couper and coauthor Nigel Henbest provide updated information on the nine planets, gathered by space probes launched in the late 1970s and 1980s. The authors devote a chapter to each and provide historical data as well as new color photographs taken of the planets by the probes, including Voyager II's shots of the moon of Uranus. In *The Universe,* author Couper and designer David Pelham offer illustrations of the Solar System and explanations of the Big Bang Theory and the life cycle of stars.

The third book, *Halley's Comet Pop-Up Book,* was written expressly for the return of the comet to Earth's sight in March and April of 1986. In this book Couper and Patrick Moore provide astronomy buffs with the comet's history, advice on how to locate it, and information on the four space probes sent to explore it. The volume also contains diagrams and a three-dimensional telescope that shows views of the comet seen at various times during its approach toward Earth.

Couper told *CA:* "When I spotted a green shooting star at the age of eight I didn't realize it was to get me hooked on astronomy for life. Apart from a period in my teens when I was hotly in pursuit of stars of a different kind, I have been getting my inspiration from the heavens.

"I suppose I'm what you'd loosely call a 'scientific translator'; I earn my keep by turning numbers and jargon into everyday words. I did begin a career as a research astronomer myself, but I rapidly realized that my forte lay in communication rather than computation. But I do have a scientific background. That's why scientists (who may lack the time or the inclination to 'popularize') seem happy to feed me data to 'translate.' They don't even seem to mind my acting as an unofficial spokesman!

"Why stay with astronomy when there are other sciences so worthy of popularizing? I do so partly because I'm hooked, but also because astronomy is the one science that almost everyone has an interest in. Even now there are vestiges of that old hostility—or sometimes it's just plain indifference—towards science. Living, as we do, in an increasingly technological world, this kind of apathy is sad—even dangerous. I try to wake up most people's latent scientific interest via the wonder they feel when looking up at the night sky. I'm doing this increasingly through television (astronomy is such a visual subject, after all), and at the moment I'm just starting on my fourth U.K. television series. If someone watching feels, 'Well, if *she* understands it, then so can I,' then I'll have gotten the message across."

AVOCATIONAL INTERESTS: Gourmet vegetarian food, fine and homemade wine, baroque and classical music, theatre, parties, London in general, the English countryside, travel (United States and Europe, Australia and New Zealand, Columbia, and Sumatra).

BIOGRAPHICAL/CRITICAL SOURCES:

PERIODICALS

Boston Sunday Globe, September 29, 1985.
Daily Express (London), July 22, 1986.
Daily Mail (London), November 1, 1984, November 16, 1985.
Guardian (London), March 16, 1985, April 10, 1985.
New Zealand Listener, June 27, 1987.
Sunday Times (London), June 30, 1985, January 4, 1987.
Times (London), October 29, 1984.
Times Literary Supplement, November 29, 1985.

* * *

COWHERD, Raymond Gibson 1909-

PERSONAL: Born December 5, 1909, in Sedalia, Mo.; son of William S. and Margaret J. Cowherd; married, 1968; children: Patricia. *Education:* William Jewell College, A.B., 1933; Eastern Baptist Theological Seminary, B.D., 1936; University of Pennsylvania, A.M., 1936, Ph.D., 1940.

ADDRESSES: Home—804 West Market St., Bethlehem, Pa. 18018.

CAREER: University of Pennsylvania, Philadelphia, instructor in history, 1936-38; Kalamazoo College, Kalamazoo, Mich., assistant professor of history, 1944-46; Lehigh University, Bethlehem, Pa., began as assistant professor of history, 1946, professor emeritus, 1975—, chairman of department, 1967-68.

MEMBER: American Historical Association, American Academy of Political and Social Science, Academy of Political Science, Conference for British Studies.

AWARDS, HONORS: Grant from American Council of Learned Societies.

WRITINGS:

The Politics of English Dissent, New York University Press, 1956.

Political Economists and the English Poor Laws: A Historical Study of the Influence of Classical Economics on the Formulation of Social Welfare Policy, Ohio University Press, 1977.

Contributor to scholarly journals.

* * *

CRAIG, Denys
See STOLL, Dennis G(ray)

* * *

CRAIG, Pamela Tudor
See TUDOR-CRAIG, Pamela

* * *

CRAIG, Raymond C. 1928-

PERSONAL: Born July 20, 1928, in Independence, Mo.; son of Raymond L. (a businessman) and Edna (a housewife; maiden name, Forsha) Craig; married Mary Young (divorced September, 1983); children: Alice, Mary. *Education:* William Jewell College, A.B., 1950; Vanderbilt University, M.A., 1952; University of Illinois at Urbana-Champaign, Ph.D., 1983.

ADDRESSES: Home—3408 Woodfront Pl., Indianapolis, Ind. 46222. *Office*—Department of English, Marian College, 3200 North Cold Spring Rd., Indianapolis, Ind. 46222.

CAREER: U.S. Department of Defense, West Germany, intelligence analyst, 1955-60; Holt, Rinehart & Winston, New

York, N.Y., regional manager, 1961-68; D. C. Heath & Company, Boston, Mass., assistant to president, 1968-69; Macmillan Company, New York City, regional manager, became vice president, 1969-71; self-employed in San Francisco, Calif., 1971-75; Holt, Rinehart & Winston, New York City, regional manager, 1975-83; University of Illinois, Champaign, Ill., visiting assistant professor of English, 1981-83; Marian College, Indianapolis, Ind., associate professor of English, 1983—. *Military service:* U.S. Army, 1952-55; became sergeant.

MEMBER: Modern Language Association of America, National Council of Teachers of English.

WRITINGS:

The Humor of H. E. Taliaferro, University of Tennessee Press, 1987.

Contributor to *American Encyclopedia of Humor,* 1987.

* * *

CRAIG, Webster
See RUSSELL, Eric Frank

* * *

CRANDALL, Robert Warren 1940-

PERSONAL: Born February 28, 1940, in Akron, Ohio; son of Clarence L. (an engineer) and Elsie (a nurse; maiden name, Gingell) Crandall; married Maureen Sullivan (an economist), August 27, 1966; children: Margaret, James. *Education:* University of Cincinnati, A.B., 1962; Northwestern University, M.A., 1965, Ph.D., 1968.

ADDRESSES: Office—Department of Economics, Brookings Institution, Washington, D.C. 20036.

CAREER: Brookings Institution, Washington, D.C., Johnson research fellow, 1965-66; Massachusetts Institute of Technology, Cambridge, assistant professor, 1966-71, associate professor of economics, 1971-74; deputy director and acting director of U.S. Council on Wage and Price Stability, 1975-78; Brookings Institute, senior fellow, 1978—. Member of board of directors of Home Owners Warranty, Baltimore Life Insurance, and Economists, Inc.

MEMBER: American Economic Association.

WRITINGS:

The U.S. Steel Industry in Recurrent Crisis: Policy Options in a Competitive World, Brookings Institution, 1981.
(With Lester B. Lave) *The Scientific Basis of Health and Safety Regulation,* Brookings Institution, 1981.
Controlling Industrial Pollution, Brookings Institution, 1983.
(With Lester B. Lave, Theodore E. Keeler, and Howard K. Gruenspecht) *Regulating the Automobile,* Brookings Institution, 1986.
(With Donald Bennett) *Up From the Ashes: The Rise of the Steel Minimill in the United States,* Brookings Institution, 1986.
Deregulation and Divestiture in the U.S. Telephone Industry, Brookings Institution, 1988.

Contributor to business and economics journals.

* * *

CRAWFORD, Marion (Kirk) 1910(?)-1988

OBITUARY NOTICE: Born c. 1910 in Dunfermline, Scotland; died February 11, 1988, in Aberdeen, Scotland. Teacher, governess, and author. After Crawford graduated from Edinburgh University she became an English teacher and governess to children of the British aristocracy. From 1933 to 1950 she worked for the British royal family as governess of Princess Elizabeth, future Queen of England, and her sister Princess Margaret. Crawford's best-selling book about the experience, *The Little Princesses,* was disdained by the royal court and other British authority figures as a violation of privacy. Crawford also wrote *The Queen Mother.*

OBITUARIES AND OTHER SOURCFS:

PERIODICALS

Times (London), February 18, 1988.

* * *

CRISTY, Ann
See MITTERMEYER, Helen (Hayton Monteith)

* * *

CROFT, Julian (Charles Basset) 1941-

PERSONAL: Born May 31, 1941, in Newcastle, New South Wales, Australia; son of Jack (a clerk) and Florence (a homemaker; maiden name, Champion) Croft; married Loretta Ruth Amelia De Plevitz (a psychologist), October 23, 1967 (divorced); children: Laurence James. *Education:* University of Newcastle, B.A., 1960, and B.A. (with honors), 1964, both from University College, M.A. (with honors), 1967.

ADDRESSES: Home—3 Caroline Cres., Armidale, New South Wales 2350, Australia. *Office*—Department of English, University of New England, Armidale, New South Wales 2351, Australia.

CAREER: Australian Commonwealth Film Unit, Sydney, production assistant, 1961-62; University of Sierra Leone, Freetown, lecturer in English, 1968-70; University of New England, Armidale, Australia, senior lecturer in English, 1970—.

MEMBER: Australian Society of Authors, Association for the Study of Australian Literature (founder; treasurer, 1977-80; executive member, 1980-87).

AWARDS, HONORS: Commonwealth Poetry Prize from British Airways, 1985, for *Breakfasts in Shanghai.*

WRITINGS:

T. H. Jones, University of Wales Press, 1975.
(Editor with Don Dale-Jones) *The Collected Poems of T. Harri Jones,* Gwasg Gomer, 1976.
(Editor) Kenneth Slessor, *Backless Betty From Bondi,* Angus & Robertson, 1983.
Breakfasts in Shanghi (poems), Angus & Robertson, 1984.
Their Solitary Way (novel), Angus & Robertson, 1985.
(Editor) *The Portable Robert D. FitzGerald,* University of Queensland Press, 1987.

Also author, with John McCallum, of play "Eugenia Falleni." Co-editor of *Notes and Furphies,* 1978-87.

WORK IN PROGRESS: Develop and Print, a novel about the Australian documentary film industry, set in 1961; a critical study of the Australian novelist Joseph Furphy.

SIDELIGHTS: Julian Croft told *CA:* "I didn't think of myself as a writer until I was in my twenties. Music and film were

my passions. But the influence of the poet T. H. Jones, whose biography I wrote after he died at a tragically early age, convinced me that what I saw and what I heard could be united into one creation. Poetry is the only art in which the visual imagination, the music which surrounds us, and the ideas we play with in dreams and in waking can be united into one. I've written in many styles, and it took a long time for my own to develop, but I can't imagine a poetry without the undersong of music; hence much of my work is an interplay between formal metrical organization and the freedoms of the spoken voice.

"I have spent my past few years learning to be a white Australian (I'm fifth generation and fittingly from convict exiles—my great-great grandfather was transported for life for highway robbery in 1820) who does not look back to Europe for inspiration and solace. Living in West Africa in the late sixties cured me of that. The example of a colonized people who were proud of their own identity and capable of taking the colonial culture and transmuting it into something new impressed me greatly. I came back to Australia hoping I could do the same here. My poetry shows that exploration of my family roots and the assertion of some political independence in Australian attitudes.

"In my novel, which is really a novella, I show the collapse of a marriage between a Swiss woman and an Australian man during the late sixties and the early seventies. Their relationship is set off against the geopolitical crises of the time. The action takes place in Hong Kong at the start of the Cultural Revolution, Prague during the spring of 1968, Paris in the summer riots of the same year, Chile in the run-up to the election which brought Allende to power, West Africa during the Nigerian Civil War, Athens during the coup of 1967, and so on. The novel tries to show the collision of values between a progressive thinker of the sixties (the woman) and the conservative man, and to explore the notion of federation in marriage. The style is very elliptical and bare, and it uses a foregrounded symbolism to call attention to its own literariness. One of my main influences was the Swiss writer Max Frisch, whose *Stille* and *Homo Faber* I greatly admire.

"My recent play was written in response to the pressure put on sexual identity by the women's movement. The subject is the case of a famous Sydney transvestite (female) who lived as a man, married twice, and murdered her first wife. It is a shocking story, but it made a powerful music drama—a hybrid of an opera and a play."

BIOGRAPHICAL/CRITICAL SOURCES:

PERIODICALS

Times Literary Supplement, July 23, 1976, June 20, 1986.

* * *

CULLEN, Countee 1903-1946

PERSONAL: Birth-given name Countee LeRoy Porter; first name pronounced "Coun-tay"; born May 30, 1903, in Louisville, Ky. (some sources say New York, N.Y., or Baltimore, Md.); died of uremic poisoning, January 9, 1946, in New York, N.Y.; buried in Woodlawn Cemetery, New York, N.Y.; married Nina Yolande DuBois, April 9, 1928 (divorced, 1930); married Ida Mae Roberson, September 27, 1940. *Education:* New York University, B.A., 1925; Harvard University, M.A., 1926.

CAREER: Poet, columnist, editor, novelist, playwright, children's writer, and educator. Assistant editor and author of monthly column "The Dark Tower" for *Opportunity: Journal of Negro Life,* 1926-28; traveled back and forth between France and the United States, 1928-34; Frederick Douglass Junior High School, New York, N.Y., teacher of English, French, and creative writing, 1934-45.

MEMBER: New York Civic Club, Phi Beta Kappa, Alpha Delta Phi.

AWARDS, HONORS: Witter Bynner Prize for poetry for "Poems," John Reed Memorial Prize from *Poetry* magazine for "Threnody for a Brown Girl," Amy Spingarn Award from *Crisis* magazine for "Two Moods of Love," and second prize winner in *Palm* Poetry Contest for "Wisdom Cometh With the Years," all 1925; second prize winner in *Crisis* Poetry Contest, 1926, for "Thoughts in a Zoo"; Harmon Foundation Literary Award from National Association for the Advancement of Colored People (NAACP), 1927, for "distinguished achievement in literature by a Negro"; Guggenheim Foundation fellowship, France, 1928-30.

WRITINGS:

POETRY

Color (includes "Heritage," "Atlantic City Waiter," "Near White," "To a Brown Boy," "For a Lady I Know," "Yet Do I Marvel," "Incident," "The Shroud of Color," "Oh, for a Little While Be Kind," "Brown Boy to Brown Girl," and "Pagan Prayer"), Harper, 1925, reprinted, Arno Press, 1969.

Copper Sun (includes "If Love Be Staunch," "The Love Tree," "Nocturne,'" "Threnody for a Brown Girl," and "To Lovers of Earth: Fair Warning"), decorations by Charles Cullen, Harper, 1927.

(Editor) *Caroling Dusk: An Anthology of Verse by Negro Poets,* decorations by Aaron Douglas, Harper, 1927, reprinted, 1974.

The Black Christ, and Other Poems (includes "The Black Christ," "Song of Praise," "Works to My Love," "In the Midst of Life," "Self Criticism," "To Certain Critics," and "The Wish"), decorations by Charles Cullen, Harper, 1929, reprinted, University Microfilms, 1973.

The Medea, and Some Poems (includes translation of Euripides' play *Medea,* "Scottsboro, Too, Is Worth Its Song," "Medusa," "The Cat," "Only the Polished Skeleton," "Sleep," "After a Visit," and "To France"), Harper, 1935.

On These I Stand: An Anthology of the Best Poems of Countee Cullen (includes "Dear Friends and Gentle Hearts," "Christus natus est," and some previously unpublished poems), Harper, 1947.

OTHER

The Ballad of the Brown Girl: An Old Ballad Retold, illustrations and decorations by Charles Cullen, Harper, 1927.

(Author of introduction) Frank Ankenbrand and Isaac Benjamin, *The House of Vanity,* Leibman Press, 1928.

One Way to Heaven (novel), Harper, 1932, reprinted, AMS Press, 1975 (also see below).

(Contributor) Fred J. Ringel, editor, *America as Americans See It,* Harcourt, 1932.

The Lost Zoo (a Rhyme for the Young, but Not Too Young), illustrations by Charles Sebree, Harper, 1940, new edition, with illustrations by Joseph Low, Follett, 1969.

My Lives and How I Lost Them (juvenile; autobiography of fictional character Christopher Cat), drawings by Robert Reid Macguire, Harper, 1942, new edition, with illustrations by Rainey Bennett, Follett, 1971.

(With Owen Dodson) "The Third Fourth of July" (one-act play), published in *Theatre Arts,* 1946.

(With Arna Bontemps) "St. Louis Woman" (musical adaptation of Bontemps's novel *God Sends Sunday;* first produced at Martin Beck Theater in New York City, March 30, 1946), published in *Black Theatre,* edited by Lindsay Patterson, Dodd, 1971.

Also author of unpublished plays, including "Let the Day Perish" (with Waters Turpin), "The Spirit of Peace," and "Heaven's My Home" (an adaptation, with Harry Hamilton, of Cullen's novel, *One Way to Heaven*), and of book reviews.

Contributor to *Crisis, Phylon, Bookman, Harper's, American Mercury, Century, Nation, Poetry,* and other periodicals.

SIDELIGHTS: Countee Cullen was perhaps the most representative voice of the Harlem Renaissance. His life story is essentially a tale of youthful exuberance and talent—of a star that flashed across the Afro-American firmament and then sank toward the horizon. When his paternal grandmother and guardian died in 1918, the fifteen-year-old Countee LeRoy Porter was taken into the home of the Reverend Frederick A. Cullen, the pastor of Salem Methodist Episcopal Church, Harlem's largest congregation. There the young Countee entered the approximate center of black politics and culture in the United States and acquired both the name and awareness of the influential clergyman who was later elected president of the Harlem chapter of the National Association for the Advancement of Colored People (NAACP).

In view of America's racial climate during the 1920s, Harlem was scarcely a serene place, but it was an enormously stimulating milieu for Afro-American intellectuals. The high hopes of the black community for acceptance and equality had turned to disillusionment at the end of World War I, when returning black soldiers all too often experienced unemployment and were otherwise mistreated. Resentment pulsated through black urban centers like Harlem, which had burgeoned during the war as black workers migrated there to fill jobs temporarily vacated by the diversion of white laborers into the military. For the first time in Afro-American history, a black urban consciousness—conducive to the flowering of the arts—was developing. From Harlem, the largest of the new, densely populated black urban communities—in which Cullen was listening and learning—burst forth an outpouring of Afro-American arts known as the Harlem Renaissance.

While Cullen's informal education was shaped by his exposure to black ideas and yearnings, his formal education derived from almost totally white influences. This dichotomy heavily influenced his creative work and his criticism, particularly because he did extremely well at the white-dominated institutions he attended and won the approbation of white academia. In high school Cullen earned academic honors that in turn garnered him the posts of vice-president of his class and editor of the school newspaper, as well as prizes for poetry and oratory. His glory continued at New York University, where he obtained first or second prizes in a number of poetry contests, including the national Witter Bynner Contests for undergraduate poetry and contests sponsored by *Poetry* magazine. Harvard University's Irving Babbitt publicly lauded Cullen's "The Ballad of the Brown Girl," and in 1925—which proved a bumper year for the young man's harvest of literary prizes—Cullen graduated from New York University, was accepted into Harvard's masters program, and published his first volume of poetry, *Color*.

During the next four years Cullen reached his zenith. A celebrated young man about Harlem, he had in print by 1929 four books of his own poems and a collection of poetry he edited, *Caroling Dusk,* written by other Afro-Americans. His letters from Harvard to his Harlem friend Harold Jackman exuded self-satisfaction and sometimes the snide intolerance of the *enfant terrible*. The climax of those heady years may have come in 1928. That year Cullen was awarded a Guggenheim fellowship to write poetry in France, and he married Nina Yolande DuBois—the daughter of W. E. B. DuBois, a man who for decades was the acknowledged leader of the Afro-American intellectual community. Few social events in Harlem rivaled the magnitude of the latter event, and much of Harlem joined in the festivities that marked the joining of the Cullen and DuBois lineages, two of its most notable families.

Because of Cullen's success in both black and white cultures, and because of his romantic temperament, he formulated an aesthetic that embraced both cultures. He came to believe that art transcended race and that it could be used as a vehicle to minimize the distance between black and white peoples. When he chose as his models poet John Keats and—to a lesser extent—A. E. Housman, he did so not consciously to curry favor with white America but for four logical reasons: First, though there had been Afro-American poets, there was not yet an Afro-American poetic tradition—in any meaningful sense of the term—to draw upon. Second, the English poetic tradition was the one that was available to him—the one that had been taught to him in schools he attended. Third, he felt challenged to demonstrate that a black poet could excel within that traditional framework. And fourth, he felt absolutely free to choose as exemplars any poets in the world with whom he sensed a temperamental affinity (and he certainly had that affinity with Housman and, especially, Keats). In addition, he shared their romantic self-involvement; he had an ego that was sensitive to the slightest tremors and that needed expression to remain whole, and—like Keats—he had to believe in human perfectibility.

In poems such as "Heritage" and "Atlantic City Waiter," Cullen reflects the urge to hearken back to African arts—a phenomenon called "Negritude" that was one of the motifs of the Harlem Renaissance. The cornerstone of his aesthetic, however, was the call for black-American poets to work conservatively, as he did, within English conventions. In his 1927 foreword to *Caroling Dusk,* Cullen observed that "since theirs is . . . the heritage of the English language, their work will not present any serious abberation from poetic tendencies of their times." Braving the wrath of less moderate peers, he further stated that "negro poets, dependent as they are on the English language, may have more to gain from the rich background of English and American poetry than from any nebulous atavistic yearnings toward an African inheritance." Even the subtitle of the collection, *An Anthology of Verse by Negro Poets,* reflects his belief in the essential oneness of art; it implies no distinction between white poetry and black poetry, and it assumes there is only poetry, which in the case of *Caroling Dusk* is simply composed by Afro-American writers.

His dedication to oneness led Cullen to be cautious of any black writer's work that threatened to erect rather than pull down barricades between the races. Thus, in a February, 1926, "Dark Tower" column in which Cullen reviewed Langston

Hughes's *The Weary Blues,* Cullen pressed Hughes not to be a "racial artist" and to omit jazz rhythms from his poems. In a later column he prodded black writers to censor themselves by avoiding "some things, some truths of Negro life and thought . . . that all Negroes know, but take no pride in." For Cullen, showcasing unpleasant realities would "but strengthen the bitterness of our enemies" and thereby weaken the bridge of art between blacks and whites.

Such warnings, however, did not prevent the critic Cullen from praising black artists whenever he found their work meritorious, even when it was overtly racial. In another of his "Dark Tower" columns, he complimented Amy Spingarn's *Pride and Humility,* for example, even though he thought its "clearest notes" were to be heard "in those poems which have a racial framework." Since his primary criterion for judging a work was always aesthetic, Cullen applauded any poetry that appealed to him, without regard to the color of the writer. He had good things to say about Edna St. Vincent Millay, E. A. Robinson, and Robert Frost, but he was less favorable toward such avant garde poets as Amy Lowell, in whose work he found little "for the hungry heart to feed upon." Generally, three principles informed his criticism: First, he tended to be more attracted to romantic rather than unromantic poetry. Second, he was conservative in his tastes and therefore put off by experimentation such as that of Amy Lowell. Third, although he put special effort into trying to further the interests of black artists, he was governed by a keen sense of impartiality and a commitment to bringing the races into closer harmony.

A paradox exists, however, between Cullen's philosophy and writing. While he argued that racial poetry was a detriment to the color-blindness he craved, he was at the same time so affronted by the racial injustice in America that his own best verse—indeed most of his verse—gave voice to racial protest. In fact, the title of Cullen's 1925 collection, *Color,* was not chosen unintentionally, nor did Cullen include sections with that same title in later volumes by accident. Both early and late in his career he was, in spite of himself, largely a racial poet. This is evident throughout Cullen's works from the *Color* pieces and the introduction of racial violence into his 1927 *Ballad of a Brown Girl* to the poems that he selected for the posthumously published *On These I Stand,* of which substantially more than half are racial poems.

Of the six identifiable racial themes in Cullen's poetry, the first is Negritude, or Pan-African impulse, a pervasive element of the 1920s international black literary movement that scholar Arthur P. Davis in a 1953 *Phylon* essay called "the alien-and-exile theme." Specific examples of this motif in Cullen's poetry include his attribution of descent from African kings to the girl featured in his *Ballad of a Brown Girl* as well as the submerged pride exhibited by the waiter in the poem "Atlantic City Waiter" whose graceful movement resulted from "Ten thousand years on jungle clues." Probably the best-known illustration of the Pan-African impulse in Cullen's poetry is found in "Heritage," where the narrator realizes that although he must suppress his African heritage, he cannot ultimately surrender his black heart and mind to white civilization. "Heritage," like most of the Negritude poems of the Harlem Renaissance and like political expression such as Marcus Garvey's popular back-to-Africa movement, powerfully suggests the duality of the black psyche—the simultaneous allegiance to America and rage at her racial inequities.

Four similar themes recur in Cullen's poems, expressing other forms of racial bias. These include a kind of black chauvinism that prevailed at the time and that Cullen portrayed in both *Ballad of the Brown Girl* and *The Black Christ,* when in those works he judged that the passion of blacks was better than that of whites. Likewise, the poem "Near White" exemplifies the author's admonition against miscegenation, and in "To a Brown Boy" Cullen propounds a racially motivated affinity toward death as a preferred escape from racial frustration and outrage. Another poem, "For a Lady I Know," presents a satirical view of whites obliviously mistreating their black counterparts as it depicts blacks in heaven doing their "celestial chores" so that upper-class whites can remain in their heavenly beds.

Using a sixth motif, Cullen exhibits a direct expression of irrepressible anger at racial unfairness. His outcry is more muted than that of some other Harlem Renaissance poets—Hughes, for example, and Claude McKay—but that is a matter of Cullen's innate and learned gentility. Those who overlook his strong indictment of racism in American society miss the main thrust of Cullen's work. His poetry throbs with anger as in "Incident" when he recalls his personal response to being called "nigger" on a Baltimore bus, or in the selection "Yet Do I Marvel," in which Cullen identifies what he regards as God's most astonishing miscue—that he could "make a poet black, and bid him sing!" In addition to his own personal experiences, Cullen also focuses on public events. For instance, in "Scottsboro, Too, Is Worth Its Song," he upbraids American poets, who had championed the cause of white anarchists in the controversial Sacco-Vanzetti trials, for not defending the nine black youths indicted on charges of raping two white girls in a freight car passing through Scottsboro, Alabama, in 1931.

In *The Book of American Negro Poetry,* author James Weldon Johnson explained with acute sympathy Cullen's compulsion to write poetry that seems to fly in the face of his declarations against poetry of race. Johnson wrote: "Strangely, it is because Cullen revolts against . . . racial limitations—technical and spiritual—that the best of his poetry is motivated by race. He is always seeking to free himself and his art from these bonds. He never entirely escapes, but from the very fret and chafe he brings forth poetry that contains the quintessence of race consciousness."

Cullen, then, was a forceful but genteel protest poet; yet, he was much more. He was also consistent in his intention to write good traditional poetry for the social purpose of showing what common sense should have told white Americans but what they still demanded be proven to them—that blacks *could* write poetry and write it as well as anyone. To that end, much of Cullen's poetry deals with such universal subjects as faith and doubt, love, and mortality.

On the subject of religion, Cullen waywardly progressed from uncertainty to Christian acceptance. Early on he was given to irony and even defiance in moments of youthful skepticism. In "Heritage," for example, he observes that a black Christ could command his faith better than the white one. When he was twenty-four, he provided a third-person description of himself in which he commented that his "chief problem has been that of reconciling a Christian upbringing with a pagan inclination. His life so far has not convinced him that the problem is insoluble." But before very long, his grandmother Porter's influence and that of the Cullen rectory won out. Outrage over racial injustice notwithstanding, he had fairly well controlled the "pagan inclination" in favor of Christian orthodoxy by 1929, when he published *The Black Christ, and Other Poems*. In the opening of the book's narrative title poem,

the protagonist sings of embracing God in spite of certain earthly obstacles that he summarizes as "my country's shame." The speaker's brother has been beaten to death by a white lynch mob for an innocent relationship with a white woman; the narrator's resentment toward a savior who allows such evil to occur is overcome by his mother's proclamation of her unshakable faith, and any residue of doubt disappears when the murdered brother is resurrected. At the end the family is left to prosper in its piety. Furthermore, among the few previously unpublished poems that Cullen selected for inclusion in the posthumously published collection *On These I Stand* is one that confirms his continuing religious commitment as a way to cope with the injustices and disappointments of his life. Written during World War I, "Christus natus est" asserts that amid all the tragedy of war "The manger still / Outshines the throne" and that "Christ must and will / Come to his own."

To understand Cullen's treatment of love it is necessary first to examine the effete—weak or effeminate—quality of many of his love poems. David Levering Lewis, in *When Harlem Was in Vogue,* asserted that "impotence and death run through [Cullen's] poetry like dark threads, entangling his most affirmative lines." In general, Cullen's love poetry is clearly characterized not only by misgivings about women but also by a distrust of the emotion of heterosexual love. His "Medusa" and "The Cat," both contained in *The Medea, and Some Poems,* illustrate this vision of male-female relationships. In Cullen's version of the ancient myth, it is not the hideousness of Medusa that blinds the men who gaze upon her, but rather her beauty. So great is the destructive power of the attractive female that the narrator in "The Cat" imagines in the animal "A woman with thine eyes, satanic beast / Profound and cold as scythes to mow me down." Male lovers, on the other hand, are often portrayed as sickly with apprehension that a relationship is about to be ended either by a fickle partner or by death. In "If Love Be Staunch," for example, the speaker warns that love lasts no longer than "water stays in a sieve," and in "The Love Tree" Cullen portrays love as a crucifixion whereby future lovers may realize that "'Twas break of heart that made the love tree grow." What Lewis identified in Cullen's love poems as a "corroding suspicion of life cursed from birth" may have resulted from Cullen's alleged homosexuality.

Cullen's treatment of death in his writing was shaped by his early encounters with the deaths of his parents, brother, and grandmother, as well as by a premonition of his own premature demise. Running through his poems are a sense of the brevity of life and a romantic craving for the surcease of death. In "Nocturne" and "Works to My Love," death is readily accepted as a natural element of life. "Threnody for a Brown Girl" and "In the Midst of Life" portray even warmer feelings towards death as a welcome escape. And in poems such as "Only the Polished Skeleton" death is gratefully anticipated to bring relief from racial oppression: A stripped skeleton has no race; it can but "measure the worth of all it so despised." Looking forward to death, Cullen meanwhile accepted sleep as an effective surrogate. In the poem "Sleep" he portrays slumber as "lovelier" and "kinder" than any alternative. It is both a feline killer and gentle nourisher that suckles the sleeper: "though the suck be short 'tis good." In April, 1943, less than three years before he died of uremic poisoning, Cullen related in "Dear Friends and Gentle Hearts" that "blessedly this breath departs."

After 1929 Cullen's production of verse dropped off dramatically. It was limited to his translation of Euripides' play *Medea,* which appeared along with some new poems in his 1935 *Medea and Some Poems* and later with half a dozen previously unpublished pieces that were included in his posthumously published collection, *On These I Stand.* A complexity of reasons contributed to the dimming of his poetic star. The Harlem Renaissance required a white audience to sustain it, and as whites became preoccupied with their own tenuous situation during the Great Depression, they lost interest in the Afro-American arts. Also, Cullen's idealism about building a bridge of poetry between the races had been sorely tested by the time the 1920s ended. Moreover, he seemed affected by legitimate doubts concerning his growth as a poet. In "Self Criticism" he reflected whether he would go on singing a "failing note still vainly clinging / To the throat of the stricken swan." While his supporters continued to defend him on racial rather than literary grounds, his detractors gradually increased in numbers with the publication of each successive collection of his poetry. Harry Alan Potamkin, in a 1927 *New Republic* review of *Copper Sun,* found that Cullen had not really progressed since *Color* and that the poet had "capitalized on the fact of race." The reviewer concluded, in fact, that Cullen's poetry "begins and ends with a epithet skill." With the appearance of *The Black Christ, and Other Poems* in 1929, *Nation*'s Granville Hicks joined the chorus of critics expressing reservations and remarked that "in general, Mr. Cullen's talents do not seem to be developing as one might wish."

For a combination of causes, then, beginning in the early 1930s Cullen largely curtailed his poetic output and channeled his creative energy into other genres. He wrote a novel, *One Way to Heaven,* published in 1932, but its poor critical reception made it his only novel. The book reveals a flair for satire in its secondary plot, which centers around the Harlem salon of the irrepressible hostess Constancia Brandon; one particularly effective episode features a white intellectual bigot who is invited to read his tract, "The Menace of the Negro to Our American Civilization," to an audience of mainly black intellectuals. The novel itself, however, suffers from a fatal structural flaw. Cullen never successfully integrated the secondary plot—a takeoff on his own experience in Harlem intellectual circles—with the major story line, a melodrama in which itinerant con man Sam Lucas undergoes a fake religious conversion to edge his way into a Harlem congregation; marries and then cheats on his sweet young wife; and finally, on his death bed undergoes a change of heart. The characters in the main plot are generally based on stereotypes common in black-American folklore—the fast-talking trickster and the sagacious saintly old aunt, for example. Although Cullen displays some compassion toward them and a good deal of good-natured wit in dealing with the satirical figures, the two plots never adequately come together. As Rudolph Fisher said in a *New York Herald Tribune* review of *One Way to Heaven,* it was as if Cullen were "exhibiting a lovely pastel and cartoon on the same frame."

When thirty-one-year-old Cullen turned to teaching in 1934, he was determined to find some way other than literature to contribute to social change, but he did not abandon writing entirely. In 1935 he published his version of *Medea* (with the speeches and choral passages curiously attenuated) and collaborated with Harry Hamilton on "Heaven's My Home," a dramatic adaptation of *One Way to Heaven.* The play, which was never published, is actually more contrived than Cullen's novel, but unlike the original work "Heaven's My Home" manages to integrate the two plots by introducing a sexual relationship between the protagonists Lucas and Brandon.

Toward the end of his life, in the 1940s, Cullen was relatively successsful as a dramatist. With another collaborator, Owen Dodson, he worked on several projects, including "The Third Fourth of July," a one-act play printed in *Theatre Arts* in August, 1946. During this period Cullen rejected a professorship at Fisk University and instead remained in New York to work with Arna Bontemps on a dramatic version of her novel *God Sends Sunday*. Cullen, who suggested the adaptation, made this endeavor the center of his life, but the enterprise caused him much grief. By 1945 the play had become the musical "St. Louis Woman," and celebrated performer Lena Horne was expected to star in its Broadway and Hollywood productions. Then disaster struck. Walter White of the National Association for the Advancement of Colored People (NAACP) argued that the play, set in the black ghetto of St. Louis and featuring lower-class and seedy characters, was demeaning to blacks. Cullen was blamed for revealing the seamy side of black life, the very thing he had warned other black writers not to do. Many of Cullen's friends refused to defend him; some joined the attack, which was patently unjust. Admittedly, greed and criminality figure in the play, which focuses on the struggle between overbearing salon keeper-gambler Bigelow Brown and diminutive jockey Lil Augie for the affections of Della Greene, a hard-nosed and soft-hearted beauty. But as Cullen argued, the play really deals with human virtues—honor, love, decency, and loyalty. The controversy surrounding it wore on, however, until 1946. In March of that year, "St. Louis Woman" finally premiered on Broadway, featuring songs by Johnny Mercer and Harold Arlen such as "Come Rain, Come Shine" and making singer Pearl Bailey a star. Unfortunately, Cullen had died almost three months earlier and was to be remembered primarily for the poems he had written in his twenties—when he was one of Harlem's brightest luminaries.

The limitations of Cullen's poetry—such as its archaic and imitative ring, its occasional verbosity, and its tendency to sacrifice sense for conventional prosody—restricted his literary status to that of a minor poet with a real lyrical gift. But he was not guilty of the obsequious acceptance of white values for which 1960s black power poets such as Don Lee were to dismiss him. Cullen never compromised his integrity as a black man to gain advantage for himself. His primary goal was to bring America closer to racial harmony through his own art and that of his peers and ultimately to achieve complete and colorblind artistic freedom. As he defiantly proclaimed in "To Certain Critics" (published in *The Black Christ*), though some might call him a traitor to blacks, his program was too universal to be contained: "Never shall the clan / Confine my singing to its ways / Beyond the ways of man."

Probably more than any other writer of the Harlem Renaissance, Cullen carried out the intentions of black American intellectual leaders such as W. E. B. DuBois and James Weldon Johnson. These men had nothing but the highest praise for Cullen, for he was brilliantly practicing what they advocated, and he came close to embodying Alain Locke's "New Negro." "In a time," DuBois wrote in a 1928 *Crisis* essay, "when it is the vogue to make much of the Negro's aptitude for clownishness or to depict him objectively as a serio-comic figure, it is a fine and praiseworthy act for Mr. Cullen to show through the interpretation of his own subjectivity the inner workings of the Negro soul and mind." Johnson was pleased with Cullen's decision not to recognize "any limitation to 'racial' themes and forms." In Cullen's wish not to be "a negro poet," Johnson insisted, the writer was "not only within his right; he is right." As these authorities attest, to read Countee Cullen's work is to hear a voice as representative of the Harlem Renaissance as it is possible to find.

BIOGRAPHICAL/CRITICAL SOURCES:

BOOKS

Baker, Houston A., Jr., *A Many-Colored Coat of Dreams: The Poetry of Countee Cullen,* Broadside Press, 1974.

Bone, Robert, *The Negro Novel in America,* Yale University Press, 1965.

Bronz, Stephen H., *Roots of Racial Consciousness: The 1920s: Three Harlem Renaissance Authors,* Libra, 1964.

Davis, Arthur P., *From the Dark Tower: Afro-American Writers, 1900-1960,* Howard University Press, 1974.

Ferguson, Blanche E., *Countee Cullen and the Negro Renaissance,* Dodd, 1966.

Huggins, Nathan Irvin, *Harlem Renaissance,* Oxford, 1971.

Johnson, James Weldon, *The Book of American Negro Poetry,* Harcourt, 1922, revised edition, 1931, Harbrace, 1959.

Johnson, James Weldon, *Black Manhattan,* Knopf, 1930.

Lee, Don L., *Dynamite Voices I: Black Voices of the 1960s,* Broadside Press, 1971.

Littlejohn, David, *Black on White: A Critical Survey of Writing by American Negroes,* Viking, 1966.

Lewis, David Levering, *When Harlem Was in Vogue,* Knopf, 1981.

Locke, Alain, *Four Negro Poets,* Albert & Charles Boni, 1925.

Locke, Alain, *The New Negro, An Interpretation,* Albert & Charles Boni, 1925.

Margolies, Edward, *Native Sons: A Critical Study of Twentieth-Century Negro American Authors,* Lippincott, 1968.

Perry, Margaret, *A Bio-Bibliography of Countee P. Cullen, 1903-1946,* Greenwood, 1971.

Redding, J. Saunders, *To Make a Poet Black,* University of North Carolina Press, 1939.

Rosenblatt, Roger, *Black Fiction,* Harvard University Press, 1974.

Shucard, Alan, *Countee Cullen,* Twayne, 1984.

Singh, Amritjit, *The Novels of the Harlem Renaissance: Twelve Black Authors, 1923-1933,* Pennsylvania State University Press, 1976.

Wagner, Jean, *Black Poets of the United States: From Paul Laurence Dunbar to Langston Hughes,* University of Illinois Press, 1973.

PERIODICALS

Atlantic Monthly, No. 79, March, 1947.

College Language Association Journal, No. 13, 1970.

Crisis, No. 35, June, 1928.

Critique, No. 11, 1969.

Nation, March 12, 1930.

New Republic, No. 52, 1927.

New York Herald Tribune of Books, February 28, 1932.

Phylon, No. 14, 1953.*

—Sidelights by Alan Shucard

* * *

CULLIFORD, Pierre 1928- (Peyo)

PERSONAL: Born June 25, 1928, in Brussels, Belgium; son of a stockbroker; married wife, Nine, in 1951; children: Thierry (son), Veronique. *Education:* Attended Brussels Academy of the Fine Arts.

ADDRESSES: c/o Random House, Inc., 201 East 50th St., New York, N.Y. 10022.

CAREER: Author and illustrator of books for children; cartoonist. Worked for animation studio and for advertising agencies; gouacher; cartoonist for Belgian periodicals, including *La Derniere Heure,* the boy scout magazine *Mowgli,* the comic weekly *Spirou,* and the magazine *Bonnes Soirees,* 1947—. Creator of comic strips, including "Johan," 1947, "Pied Tendre," "Johan et Pirlouit," "Poussy," "Les Schtroumpfs," and "Benoit Brisefer."

WRITINGS:

"SMURF" BOOKS, IN ENGLISH TRANSLATION, UNDER PSEUDONYM PEYO

(With Yvan Delporte) *King Smurf,* Random House, 1977.
(With Delporte) *The Smurfette,* Hodder & Stoughton, 1978.
(With Delporte) *Smurphony in C* [and] *The Flying Smurf,* Hodder & Stoughton, 1978 (also see below).
(With Delporte) *The Smurfs and the Egg* [and] *The Hundredth Smurf,* Hodder & Stoughton, 1978 (also see below).
(With Delporte) *The Astrosmurf,* translated by Anthea Bell and Derek Hockridge, Random House, 1979.
The Smurfs and the Magic Flute, based on *La Flute a six schtroumpfs* by Delporte, translated by Bell, Hodder & Stoughton, 1979, Random House, 1983.
(With Delporte) *Romeo and Smurfette,* translated by Bell and Hockridge, Hodder & Stoughton, 1979 (also see below).
The Smurf's Apprentice, Hodder & Stoughton, 1979 (also see below).
The Smurf's Apprentice [and] (with Gos) *Smurftraps,* Hodder & Stoughton, 1979.
(With Delporte and Gos) *The Weather-Smurfing Machine* [and] (with Delporte) *Smurf Stories,* translated by Bell and Hockridge, Hodder & Stoughton, 1979 (also see below).
(With Delporte) *The Smurfic Games* [and] *Smurf of One and Smurf a Dozen of the Other,* translated by Bell and Hockridge, Hodder & Stoughton, 1980, Random House, 1984.
The Smurfs and the Howlibird, translated by Bell and Hockridge, Hodder & Stoughton Children's Books, 1980, Random House, 1983.
The Alien Smurf (based on original story by Delporte), S. Pemberton Pub., 1980, published as *The Fake Smurf,* Random House, 1981.
Smurf Cake, Random House, 1981.
A Smurf in the Air (based on original story by Delporte), Random House, 1981.
The Wandering Smurf (based on original story by Delporte), Random House, 1981.
A Little Smurf Bedtime Story, with pop-out pictures, Random House, 1982.
Rainy Day: A Smurf Book of Feelings, Random House, 1982.
Smurf on the Grow, with pop-out pictures, Random House, 1982.
The Smurf-Catching Trap, with pop-out pictures, Random House, 1982.
A Smurf Picnic, with pop-out pictures, Random House, 1982.
(With Delporte) *The Flying Smurf,* Random House, 1982.
(With Delporte and Gos) *The Weather-Smurfing Machine,* Random House, 1982.
Baker Smurf's Sniffy Book, Random House, 1982.
(With Delporte) *The Hundredth Smurf,* Random House, 1982.
(With Delporte) *Smurphony in C,* Random House, 1982.
Smurf Punch-Out Book, Random House, 1982.
The Wonderful World of Smurfs, Random House, 1982.
The Smurf ABC Book, Random House, 1983.
What Do Smurfs Do All Day? Beginner Books, 1983.
The Smurf Activity Book, illustrated by Rae P. Schwartz, translated by Bell and Hockridge, Random House, 1983.
Smurf Water Fun, Random House, 1983.
The Smurfs and Their Woodland Friends, Random House, 1983.
Coloring Magic With Painter Smurf, Random House, 1983.
(With Delporte) *"Romeo and Smurfette" and Twelve Other Smurfy Stories,* Random House, 1983.
The Smurf Year-Round Coloring Book, Random House, 1983.
Through the Seasons With Smurfette, Random House, 1983.
Baby Smurf's First Words, Random House, 1984.
(With Michel Matagne) *The Smurfs and the Miller,* Random House, 1984.
The Smurfs and the Toyshop, illustrated by Matagne, Random House, 1984.

"JOHAN ET PIRLOUIT" SERIES, IN FRENCH, UNDER PSEUDONYM PEYO

Le Chatiment de Basenhau, Dupuis, 1954.
Le Maitre de Roucybeuf, Dupuis, 1955.
Le Lutin du bois aux roches, Dupuis, 1956.
La Pierre de lune, Dupuis, 1957.
Le Serment des Vikings, Dupuis, 1958.
La Source des dieux, Dupuis, 1958.
La Fleche noire, Dupuis, 1959.
La Flute a six schtroumpfs, based on original story by Yvan Delporte, Dupuis, 1960.
Le Sire de Montresor, Dupuis, 1960.
La Guerre de sept fontaines, Dupuis, 1962.
L'Anneau de Castellac, Dupuis, 1963.
Le Pays maudit, Dupuis, 1964.
Le Sortilege de Maltrochu, Dupuis, 1970.

"SCHTROUMPFS" SERIES, IN FRENCH, UNDER PSEUDONYM PEYO

Histoires schtroumpfs, Dupuis, 1964.
Les Schtroumpfs noirs, Dupuis, 1964.
Le Schtroumpfissime, Dupuis, 1965.
La Schtroumpfette, Dupuis, 1967.
L'Oeuf et les schtroumpfs, Dupuis, 1968.
Les Schtroumpfs et le cracoucass, Dupuis, 1969.
Le Cosmoschtroumpf [and] *Le Schtroumpfleur de pluie,* Dupuis, 1970.
L'Apprenti schtroumpf, Dupuis, 1971.
Schtroumpf vert et vert schtroumpf: Jeux olympschtroumpfs, Dupuis, 1973.
La Soupe aux schtroumpfs, Dupuis, 1977.
Les Schtroumpfs olympiques, Paques schtroumpfantes [and] *Le Jardin des schtroumpfs,* Dupuis, 1983.
Le Bebe schtroumpf (includes "Le Schtroumpf bricoleur," "La Peinture schtroumpf," and "Une Fete schtroumpf"), Dupuis, 1984.

"MINI-SCHTROUMPFS" SERIES, IN FRENCH, UNDER PSEUDONYM PEYO

(With Yvan Delporte) *Le Gateau des schtroumpfs,* Dupuis, 1983.
(With Delporte) *La Schtroumpfette et la lune,* Dupuis, 1983.
(With Delporte) *Le Schtroumpf a l'envers,* Dupuis, 1983.
(With Delporte) *Le Schtroumpf qui vole,* Dupuis, 1983.
(With Delporte) *Le Schtroumpf vagabond,* Dupuis, 1983.
(With Delporte) *Le Schtroumpf et le turlusiphon,* Dupuis, 1983.
(With Delporte) *La Pluie et le beau schtroumpf,* Dupuis, 1983.

"TELESCHTROUMPFS" SERIES, IN FRENCH, UNDER PSEUDONYM PEYO

(With Yvan Delporte) *Super-Schtroumpfs,* Dupuis, 1983.
(With Delporte) *Gargamel la genereux,* Dupuis, 1983.
(With Delporte) *Le Farceur schtroumpf,* Dupuis, 1984.
(With Delporte) *Les Lunettes roses,* Dupuis, 1984.

OTHER "SCHTROUMPF" BOOKS, IN FRENCH, UNDER PSEUDONYM PEYO

Les Schtroumpfs et les jouets, illustrated by Matagne, Dupuis, 1969.
Les Schtroumpfs a la mer, Dupuis, 1983.
Les Schtroumpfs ont soif! Nathan, 1984.
La Bal des schtroumpfs, Nathan, 1984.
Que font les schtroumpfs toute la journee? Dupuis, 1984.
Le Roi des schtroumpfs, Nathan, 1984.

Also author, with Michel Matagne, of *Le Petit Canard des schtroumpfs* and *Le Moulin des schtroumpfs,* both Dupuis.

"BRISEFER" SERIES, IN FRENCH, UNDER PSEUDONYM PEYO

(With Francois Walthery) *Les Taxis rouges,* Dupuis, 1963.
(With Walthery) *Madame Adolphine,* Dupuis, 1966.
(With Walthery) *Les Douze Travaux de Benoit Brisefer,* Dupuis, 1968.
(With Walthery) *Tonton Placide,* Dupuis, 1969.
(With Walthery) *Le Cirque Bondoni,* Dupuis, 1971.
(With Albert Besteau) *Le Fetiche,* Dupuis, 1978.

Also author, with Walthery, of *Lady d'Olphine,* Dupuis.

OTHER WORKS IN FRENCH, UNDER PSEUDONYM PEYO

Ca, c'est Poussy, Dupuis, 1976.
Pour faire une flute, Dupuis, 1976.
(With Francois Walthery and Vicq) *Vous etes trop bon,* Dupuis, 1980.
(With Walthery and Gos) *Casse-tete chinois,* Dupuis, 1982.

SIDELIGHTS: Belgian cartoonist Pierre Culliford, who goes by the name Peyo, is best known as the creator of the *Schtroumpfs,* or, in English, the Smurfs. They were introduced in 1957 in one of Peyo's first comic strips for *Spirou* magazine, "Johan et Pirlouit." The strip centered on the adventures of a medieval page, Johan, and his bumbling companion Pirlouit, but the tiny blue trolls known as *Schtroumpfs* quickly captured the fancy of Peyo's French-speaking readers. So great was the demand for more *Schtroumpfs* stories that Peyo abandoned Johan and Pirlouit and focused on creating a strip populated almost solely by the *Schtroumpfs* and their devious enemy, the wizard Gargamel, and written in a sort of *Schtroumpf* jargon that utilizes the word "schtroumpf," or "smurf" in English translation, as a substitute for many verbs, adjectives, and nouns.

Since its inception, the world of the Smurfs has expanded tremendously to encompass an internationally best-selling series of books based on the original strips for *Spirou,* an animated feature film, a number of television specials, an extremely profitable line of Smurf toys, records, paper products, and clothing, and an Emmy-nominated television series produced by Hanna-Barbera that soared in the ratings to become the most popular children's television show in America.

Through the years, Peyo has remained at the head of his Smurf empire, continuing to draw and write for the books and the television shows—although he does engage numerous young cartoonists as apprentices to help with illustrations—supervising the animation of the Smurfs for both the movie "The Smurfs and the Magic Flute" and the television series and specials, and handling the business aspect of his enterprise as well. As Peyo commented in *Cahiers de la Bande Dessinee:* "I refuse to entrust my business to professionals who would either sell me a bill of goods, or neglect the quality for a larger profit. And on no account will I accept that. I want to supervise everything so that my little characters stay attractive and the same as they've always been."

He does, however, admit to being somewhat overwhelmed by his little creations, whose success has impinged on his time to pursue other projects and pastimes. With regard to his abandonment of "Johan et Pirlouit," for example, Peyo remarked: "I'm the first to regret it! I still have a very special feeling of tenderness for those two characters, but it's true that I'm a prisoner of the Smurfs' success. It's for them and not for 'Pirlouit' that the readers and publishers are asking. . . . Success dictated it! . . . Of course the day the Smurfs stop amusing me, I'll stop drawing them. But that day is yet to come. The Smurfs make up a sufficiently diversified community for me to create infinite possibilities of interesting situations."

Even so, Peyo dreams of one day reviving the "Johan et Pirlouit" strip, which is his favorite series, perhaps because he strongly identifies with the character Pirlouit. Peyo explained: "My friends tell me that of all the characters I've created, Pirlouit is the one who resembles me the most. I gladly admit it. Unconsciously, I endowed Pirlouit with my principal character traits." Moreover, Pirlouit was a successful character in his day. Introduced into the comic strip "Johan" as a secondary character, Pirlouit soon gained at least equal footing with the principal character Johan, a development that surprised his creator and served as a precursor to the later ascendency of the Smurfs. Recalled Peyo in 1983: "At the beginning, I thought Pirlouit would only survive the first episode, then I realized that the readers had quickly adopted him and that they would never forgive me if he suddenly disappeared. The same phenomenon occurred with the Smurfs, if not even in a stronger way." Peyo acknowledged, however, that the former popularity of "Johan et Pirlouit" could work against any attempt to revive the strip. "I know that 'Johan' and 'Pirlouit' have left good memories behind them," observed Peyo, "and if I started the series again I would be a little afraid of disappointing my readers. The more popular a character has been, the riskier his 'come back' is." Nonetheless, the Smurf television series has been extended by half an hour to allow for episodes concerning Pirlouit and Johan, and Peyo has a script in his drawer, ready for the time when he is "freed" by the Smurfs to devote several months to the revival of his favorite strip.

MEDIA ADAPTATIONS:

TELEVISION

"The Smurfs" special, NBC-TV, November 29, 1981.
"The Smurfs Springtime Special," NBC-TV, April 8, 1982.
"The Smurfs Christmas Special," NBC-TV, December 13, 1982.
"Evil Wizard Smurf-erized" special, NBC-TV, 1982.
"My Smurfy Valentine" special, NBC-TV, February 13, 1983.
"Smurfing in Sign Language," NBC-TV, December 24, 1983.
"The Smurfic Games," NBC-TV, May 20, 1984.
"Hefty and Wheelsmurfer," NBC-TV, October 13, 1984.
"Smurfily Ever After," NBC-TV, February 13, 1985.

"The Smurfs" weekly one-hour animated series, NBC-TV.

ANIMATED FILM

"La Flute a six schtroumpfs," released in the United States as "The Smurfs and the Magic Flute" by Belvision, 1975.

OTHER

Culliford's "Smurf" cartoons are featured on a line of merchandise that includes clothing, toys, records, and various novelty items.

BIOGRAPHICAL/CRITICAL SOURCES:

PERIODICALS

Cahiers de la Bande Dessinee, Number 12, 1971, Number 54, 1984.
People, September 27, 1982.*

* * *

CUSHMAN, Keith (Maxwell) 1942-

PERSONAL: Born December 23, 1942, in Jefferson City, Mo.; son of Jerome (a librarian and English professor) and Hanna (Trilinsky) Cushman; married wife, Judith Z. (a trade newspaper editor), March 16, 1969; children: Phoebe, Cameron Brett. *Education:* Harvard University, B.A., 1964; Princeton University, Ph.D., 1969. *Politics:* Democrat.

ADDRESSES: Home—3301 Madison Ave., Greensboro, N.C. 27403. *Office*—Department of English, University of North Carolina at Greensboro, Greensboro, N.C. 27412.

CAREER: University of Patna, Patna, India, Fulbright tutor in English, 1964-65; Chulalongkorn University, Bangkok, Thailand, lecturer in English, 1965-66; University of Chicago, Chicago, Ill., assistant professor of English, 1969-76; University of North Carolina at Greensboro, associate professor, 1976-83, professor of English, 1983—. Editor for Stone Management Consultants, 1976—.

MEMBER: D. H. Lawrence Society of North America (president, 1987—), Modern Language Association of America.

WRITINGS:

D. H. Lawrence at Work: The Emergence of the Prussian Officer Stories, University Press of Virginia, 1978.
(Contributor) Robert B. Partlow, editor, *D. H. Lawrence: The Man Who Lived,* Southern Illinois University Press, 1980.
(Editor with E. Claire Healey) *The Letters of D. H. Lawrence and Amy Lowell, 1914-1925,* Black Sparrow Press, 1985.
(Editor) D. H. Lawrence, *Memoir of Maurice Magnus,* Black Sparrow Press, 1987.
(Editor with Dennis Jackson) *D. H. Lawrence's Literary Heritage* (essays), UMI Research Press, in press.

WORK IN PROGRESS: D. H. Lawrence and the Brewsters, a book about Lawrence's friendship with two American expatriate painters from 1921 until his death in 1930.

SIDELIGHTS: Keith Cushman's *D. H. Lawrence at Work,* labeled an "earnest and useful" study by reviewer Jeffrey Meyers in the *Spectator,* focuses on the British author's work during the years between 1912 and 1915. Cushman pays particular attention to Lawrence's revisions of the short stories "The Shades of Spring," "The White Stocking," "The Thorn in the Flesh," "Odour of Chrysanthemums," "Daughters of the Vicar," and "The Prussian Officer." By examining the successive versions of these stories, according to Cushman, one can see stages in Lawrence's growth as a writer in terms of a higher level of emotional maturity and a greater ability to depict his beliefs precisely and clearly. Critiquing Cushman's work in the *Los Angeles Times Book Review,* John Halperin applauded his "great good sense and discriminating judgment" and concluded the book to be an "illuminating, intelligent, gentle probing of the secrets hidden in [Lawrence's] early manuscripts."

Cushman told *CA:* "The time I spend doing research on D. H. Lawrence remains ceaselessly fascinating. In recent years my perspective has shifted somewhat to include biographical as well as critical questions. I particularly value my friendships with other Lawrence scholars and the sense we are engaged in a common endeavor. My current project concerning Lawrence and his American friends the Brewsters is all the more exciting because I am in touch with the Brewsters' daughter Harwood, who is eager to help her parents become better known."

BIOGRAPHICAL/CRITICAL SOURCES:

PERIODICALS

Los Angeles Times Book Review, February 11, 1979.
Spectator, May 19, 1979.
Times Literary Supplement, December 7, 1979.

D

DABCOVICH, Lydia

ADDRESSES: Home—Brookline, Mass. *Office*—Art Institute of Boston, 700 Beacon St., Boston, Mass. 02159.

CAREER: Art Institute of Boston, Boston, Mass., teacher of illustration.

AWARDS, HONORS: There Once Was a Woman Who Married a Man was selected by the *New York Times* as one of the best illustrated children's books of 1978.

WRITINGS:

SELF-ILLUSTRATED CHILDREN'S BOOKS

Follow the River, Dutton, 1980.
Sleepy Bear, Dutton, 1982.
Mrs. Huggins and Her Hen Hannah, Dutton, 1985.

ILLUSTRATOR

Barbara Corcoran, *A Trick of Light,* Atheneum, 1972.
Marjorie Filley Stover, *Trail Boss in Pigtails,* Atheneum, 1972.
Jack London, *White Fang,* Heritage Press (Avon, Conn.), 1973.
Frank Emerson Andrews, *Nobody Comes to Dinner,* Little, Brown, 1976.
Norma Farber, *There Once Was a Woman Who Married a Man,* Addison-Wesley, 1978.
(With Charles Mikolaycak and Jim Arnosky) Richard Kennedy, *Delta Baby and Two Sea Songs,* Addison-Wesley, 1979.
Marjorie Lewis, *The Boy Who Would Be a Hero,* Coward, 1982.
Paul Fleischman, *The Animal Hedge,* Dutton, 1983.
Arielle North Olson, *Hurry Home, Grandma!* Dutton, 1984.
Deborah Hartley, *Up North in Winter,* Dutton, 1986.*

* * *

DAHLBERG, Arthur O.

ADDRESSES: Office—6 North Water St., Greenwich, Conn. 06830.

CAREER: Economic consultant and writer. Director of Visual Economics Laboratory at Columbia University, New York, N.Y.; employed by U.S. Economics Corp.

WRITINGS:

How to Save Free Enterprise, Devin-Adair, 1974.
How to Lower Interest Rates, Devin-Adair, 1983.

* * *

D'AMICO, John Francis 1947(?)-1987

OBITUARY NOTICE: Born c. 1947; died after a heart attack, December 8, 1987, in Jerusalem, Israel. Historian, educator, and author. D'Amico taught history at George Mason University beginning in 1980, specializing in the European eras of the Renaissance and Reformation. His book *Renaissance Humanism in Papal Rome: Humanists and Churchmen on the Eve of Reformation* won a 1983 award for best Italian history book from the American Catholic Historical Association. D'Amico also wrote *Theory and Practice in Renaissance Textual Criticism: Beatus Rhenanus Between Conjecture and History.*

OBITUARIES AND OTHER SOURCES:

PERIODICALS

Washington Post, December 12, 1987.

* * *

DANIELS, Kate 1953-

PERSONAL: Born July 2, 1953, in Richmond, Va.; daughter of Harry E. and Jean (Graham) Daniels; married Richard A. Jones III (a writer), 1978 (divorced, 1985); married Geoff Macdonald (a writer and a tennis professional), 1986; children: Samuel Graham Daniels Macdonald. *Education:* University of Virginia, B.A., 1975, M.A., 1977; Columbia University, M.F.A., 1980.

ADDRESSES: Home—Northampton, Mass. *Office*—Department of English, University of Massachusetts at Amherst, Amherst, Mass. 01002. *Agent*—Mary Evans, Virginia Barber Literary Agency, 353 West 21st St., New York, N.Y. 10011.

CAREER: University of Virginia, Charlottesville, lecturer in English, 1980-85; University of Massachusetts at Amherst, assistant professor of English, 1986—, Lilly Foundation teaching fellow, 1987-88. Editor and publisher, *Poetry East,* 1979—.

AWARDS, HONORS: Pushcart Prize for poetry from Pushcart Press, 1982; Agnes Lynch Starrett Poetry Prize from Univer-

sity of Pittsburgh, 1983; *Crazyhorse* Prize for poetry from University of Arkansas, 1983; fellowship from Mary Ingraham Bunting Institute, Harvard University, 1984-85, for literary biography of Muriel Rukeyser.

WRITINGS:

(Editor with Richard Jones) *Of Solitude and Silence: Writings on Robert Bly,* Beacon Press, 1982.
The White Wave (poetry), University of Pittsburgh Press, 1984.
Muriel Rukeyser: A Life of Poetry (literary biography), Random House, 1988.

Contributor of poems to periodicals, including *Virginia Quarterly Review, Massachusetts Review, New England Review, Pequod, Ironwood, Poetry Now,* and *Crazyhorse.*

Poetry editor, *Columbia: A Magazine of Poetry and Prose,* 1981-82; editor, *Scandinavian Review,* 1982-83.

WORK IN PROGRESS: The Niobe Poems, publication expected in 1988.

SIDELIGHTS: Kate Daniels worked as editor and publisher of the journal *Poetry East* beginning in 1979. Her first book, *Of Solitude and Silence: Writings on Robert Bly,* which Daniels edited with her *Poetry East* colleague Richard Jones, assembles tributes to and evaluations of the works of poet Bly, as well as poems, translations, and an essay by Bly himself.

A poet in her own right, Daniels has won the Agnes Lynch Starrett Poetry Prize and the Pushcart Prize for poetry. Reviewing her first published collection, *The White Wave,* James Hunter of the *Village Voice* declared, "There's spunk in these poems." Hunter observed: "Time and again [Daniels] reexamines lyric epiphany with the brute language, the cruel music of the everyday."

BIOGRAPHICAL/CRITICAL SOURCES:

PERIODICALS

Georgia Review, spring, 1985.
Hudson Review, winter, 1984.
Los Angeles Times Book Review, May 16, 1982.
Magill's Literary Annual, 1985.
New York Times Book Review, July 25, 1982.
North American Review, March 1985.
Silverfish Review, summer, 1986.
Village Voice, September 18, 1984.

* * *

DAVID, Ed
See WOHLMUTH, Ed

* * *

DAVID, Saul 1921-

PERSONAL: Born June 27, 1921, in New York, N.Y.; son of Chaim (a tailor) and Gishe (a tailor; maiden name, Marcus) David; married and divorced twice; children: Deborah (deceased), Rachel. *Education:* Attended Rhode Island School of Design, 1937-40. *Religion:* Jewish.

ADDRESSES: Home—Van Nuys, Calif. *Agent*—Roberta Pryor, International Creative Management, 40 West 57th St., New York, N.Y. 10019.

CAREER: Worked for FM radio stations and newspapers in York, Pa., and Port Huron, Mich.; Bantam Books, New York, N.Y., reader, 1950-57, editorial director, 1957-60; film producer, 1960—; writer. Executive story editor at Metro-Goldwyn-Mayer (MGM), 1972.

Producer of motion pictures, including "Von Ryan's Express," 1965, "Our Man Flint," 1966, "Fantastic Voyage," 1966, "In Like Flint," 1967, "Skullduggery," 1970, "Logan's Run," 1976, and "The Ravagers," 1979. *Military service:* U.S. Army, 1942-45; became sergeant.

WRITINGS:

(With William F. Nolan, Ben Roberts, and Ivan Goff) "Logan's Run" (pilot episode of television series, based on the novel of the same title by Nolan and George Clayton Johnson), CBS-TV, 1977.
The Industry: Life in the Hollywood Fast Lane, Times Books, 1981.

Also author of unproduced film scripts, including "Illegal Tender," "Boys' Rules," and "Tahm Gan Eden."

WORK IN PROGRESS: A novel, *Boys' Rules.*

SIDELIGHTS: As a producer—who supervises such aspects of filmmaking as budgeting, casting, filming schedules, and selection of screenwriters, directors, and locations—Saul David worked on a variety of motion pictures, including a string of successes in the 1960s and 1970s. He seemed to have a "golden touch," according to a *Detroit News* writer, but he also experienced the frustrations of American filmmaking. After leaving a flourishing editorial career in New York City, he endured years of broken contracts, actor disputes, and studio hassles in Hollywood. "Von Ryan's Express" was his first project, a war story about a group of American and British prisoners of war who hijack the train carrying them to Germany during World War II. Starring Frank Sinatra, the film was based on the best-selling David Westheimer novel of the same title; it received mixed reviews from critics but became a box-office success. Next came "Our Man Flint," a popular high-adventure spoof of James Bond movies that spawned a less-successful sequel, "In Like Flint." In between the two Flint pictures David produced the first of his science fiction films, "Fantastic Voyage," which won praise for its special effects depicting a trip through the inside of a human body. His next several productions also had science fiction premises, the best-known of which is "Logan's Run," set in a futuristic society that seems utopian but requires all its citizens to commit ritual suicide at age thirty.

In 1981 David wrote *The Industry: Life in the Hollywood Fast Lane,* a personal account of the reality behind the glamor—as the *Detroit News* critic commented, "that part of Hollywood that *isn't* all gods and goddesses." David devotes much of *The Industry* to his work on "Von Ryan's Express," the movie that introduced him to the inner workings of filmmaking. Specifically, noted Victoria Venker in the *Washington Post,* David "vividly describes, in several fascinating chapters, the behind-the-scenes hassles on 'Von Ryan's Express'—from Sinatra's demand that he be chauffeured to the set each morning in a helicopter to the nasty cables from the studio to keep the production on schedule." David encountered problems with his superiors at Twentieth Century-Fox from the beginning of the film's development. At that time studio head Darryl Zanuck ordered substantial changes in the screenplay written by David and Westheimer. Later the studio chose Sinatra for the lead, and the script, which portrayed a tough, by-the-book military officer, was rewritten again to suit Sinatra's offhand, anti-establishment image.

More difficulties arose during filming in Italy. Sinatra's insistence that director Mark Robson honor his pledge to keep the actor busy required Robson to postpone shots in which Sinatra did not appear, irritating Robson and eventually leading to an expensive hiatus for Sinatra so that Robson could film the bypassed sections. Furthermore, relations between Robson and David became strained as David attempted to uphold orders he received from the studio and Robson resisted most of his suggestions. Still, as *The Industry* attests, David proved himself equal to adversity on more than one occasion, winning a wardrobe disagreement with Sinatra and persuading the actor to do a scene he had earlier disputed. David, consequently, gained a reputation on the set as "the Guy Who Can Handle Sinatra." Additionally, David was able to arrange for the filming of the spectacular scenes of Rome, shot from a moving train, that reviewers such as Bosley Crowther of the *New York Times* found "stunning."

Problems within the microcosm of a production crew were accompanied by rough patches in David's career as a whole. While "Von Ryan's Express," "Our Man Flint," and "Fantastic Voyage" proved successful, David's contract with Twentieth Century-Fox as staff producer excluded him from the profits the films earned. Tentative deals made with other studios by his agents fell through under the pressure of bullying by Fox executives who didn't want to lose David before he produced the sequel to "Our Man Flint." When David's superiors cut several pivotal minutes from "In Like Flint" David had had enough. He revealed the story to the press and was promptly fired. He also vindicated himself by punctuating a Fox slogan displayed on a studio building that read "Think Twentieth"; with the aid of Tony Hope, Fox employee and son of comedian Bob Hope, it read "Think, Twentieth" instead.

From then on David moved from studio to studio, project to project. He worked briefly for ABC Features, then joined the Universal staff with "Skullduggery," which the latter at first supported and—after arguments about David's choice of actors and directors and numerous on-location problems—ultimately decried. David planned to sue Universal for its actions and was in turn sued by the studio for breach of contract and "various unspecified misdeeds," reports the producer. After three years of litigation David obtained a job with Metro-Goldwyn-Mayer (MGM) and ended up producing "Logan's Run." Later he made another science fiction movie, "The Ravagers," for Columbia.

According to reviewers, David's account in *The Industry* is accurate, his experiences typical of the movie business. In the *Chicago Tribune Book World* Larry McMurtry remarked that the book "describes confusion, caprice, and arrogance" and "confirms that it is virtually a miracle if a good film gets made." Opined Venker, David's years as a producer have "put him in a good position to make some fairly pointed observations about Hollywood"; she found David "particularly adept at describing all the insecurity and pain that underlie the glamor, money and success." Several writers lauded David's candor and humor in discussing the people and the intrigue of Hollywood, and a *Detroit News* critic summarized *The Industry* as an "excellent personal chronicle . . . a gem of a book."

David told *CA:* "I don't think anyone should offer wisdom unaccompanied by a cashier's check."

BIOGRAPHICAL/CRITICAL SOURCES:

BOOKS

David, Saul, *The Industry: Life in the Hollywood Fast Lane,* Times Books, 1981.

PERIODICALS

Chicago Tribune Book World, August 9, 1981.
Detroit News, September 6, 1981.
New York Times, June 24, 1965, January 26, 1966, September 8, 1966, March 16, 1967, March 12, 1970, June 24, 1976.
Publishers Weekly, August 21, 1981.
Washington Post, October 2, 1981.

—*Sketch by Polly A. Vedder*

* * *

DAVIES, Duncan (Sheppey) 1921-1987

PERSONAL: Born April 20, 1921, in Liverpool, Lancashire, England; died March 25, 1987; son of Duncan S. and Elsie Dana Davies; married Joan Ann Frimston, 1944; children: one son, three daughters. *Education:* Received B.Sc., M.A., C.Eng., and D.Phil. from Trinity College, Oxford.

CAREER: Imperial Chemical Industries, physical chemist in Dyestuffs Division, 1945-61, research director of General Chemicals Division, 1961-62, director of Petrochemical and Polymer Laboratory, 1962-67, deputy chairman of Mond Division in Runcorn Heath, England, 1967-69, general manager of research in London, England, 1969-77; British Department of Industry, scientist and chief engineer, 1977-82; BCRA Ltd., consulting technical director, 1982-84, chairman, beginning in 1984. Chairman of England's Science Research Council and Social Science Research Council, 1973-79; consulting technical director of Tate & Lyle, Unilever, and U.S. National Bureau of Standards; member of Science and Engineering Research Council, 1969-73 and 1977-82; member of Advisory Board for Research Councils, 1977-82; member of Swann Manpower Working Group, 1964-66, and Natural Environment Research Council advisory council on applied research and development, 1977-82; member of board of governors of Technical Change Centre, beginning in 1982. Visiting professor at Imperial College of Science and Technology, London, 1968-70, and University of York, 1983; visiting fellow of St. Cross College, Oxford, 1970; visiting professorial fellow of University of Wales, University College, Swansea, 1974-79; member of council of University of Liverpool, 1967-69, and Queen Elizabeth College, London, 1975-78.

AWARDS, HONORS: Castner Medal, 1967; D.Univ. from University of Stirling, 1975, and University of Surrey, 1980; D.Sc. from University of Bath, 1981, and Technion, 1982; Companion of the Bath, 1982.

WRITINGS:

(With M. Callum McCarthy) *Introduction to Technological Economics,* Wiley, 1967.
(With Tom Banfield and Ray Sheahan) *The Humane Technologist,* Oxford University Press, 1976.
(Editor) *Industrial Biotechnology in Europe: Issues in Public Policy,* Frances Pinter, 1986.

Also author, with D. M. Bathurst, of *Pictures and Words,* 1986. Contributor to scientific journals.

OBITUARIES:

PERIODICALS

Times (London), April 2, 1987.*

DAVIES, Joan 1934-
(Joan Lyngseth)

PERSONAL: Born January 29, 1934, in Rockglen, Saskatchewan, Canada; daughter of Arthur Davies and Emily Hague; married Delmar M. Lyngseth, July 29, 1957; children: Russell Blake. *Education:* Sheffield College of Commerce, Diploma, 1951; Carleton University, B.A. (with first class honors), 1962; University of Saskatchewan, B.A. (summa cum laude), 1961, M.A., 1963; doctoral study at Hertford College, Oxford, 1986—.

ADDRESSES: Home—477 Lisgar St., Ottawa, Ontario, Canada K1R 5H2. *Agent*—Nancy Colbert, Colbert Agency, 303 Davenport Rd., Toronto, Ontario, Canada M5R 1K5.

CAREER: South Yorkshire Times, Rotherham, Yorkshire, England, journalist, 1952-56; Government of Saskatchewan, Regina, information officer, 1957-59; Carleton University and Algonquin College, Ottawa, lecturer in English literature, 1965-70; free-lance writer, 1981—.

WRITINGS:

(Under name Joan Lyngseth) *Martin's Starwars* (juvenile), Borealis Press, 1978.

Wine and Wheat (autobiography), Western Producer Prairie Books, 1984.

Author of television scripts. Contributor of short stories to periodicals.

SIDELIGHTS: Joan Davies told *CA:* "*Wine and Wheat* is not autobiographical in the usual sense. It is rather the story of the vicissitude of two people, my parents, who by accidents of history spent their active years in two astonishingly different places: on a Saskatchewan prairie farm during the drought and depression of the late 1920s and early 1930s, and running a store in Sheffield, England, during World War II. After experiencing dust storms, grasshopper plagues, starving livestock, and extreme poverty in Canada, they returned to Sheffield to bombing raids, food shortages, and martial law restrictions. The story, thematically about the interrelation between time, place, and people, is theirs rather than my own.

"The book, like their experiences, was something of an accident. Two publishers had assumed a previous manuscript—the fictitious memoirs of a nurse—was autobiographical and rejected it when they learned it was fiction. After muttering evilly about voyeurism and the idiocy of rejecting a good manuscript because it was fictional, I turned to a facsimile of autobiography.

"The role of chance is rarely as simple as it appears. I married the first native Saskatchewanian I met and returned to the land of my birth by what appeared at the time to be purely chance. War in England, where I grew up, had provided no romance. But myriad tales of Saskatchewan had filled my childhood with romance, and the wonder of it all undoubtedly shaped my youthful romantic inclinations and my love of sharing stories with the world. Even my current studies might be related to the prairies of the 1930s. Good writing is often one of the benefits attendant on a good education. I am expecting my best storytelling to follow a stint at Oxford."

* * *

DAVIS, Archie K. 1911-

PERSONAL: Born January 22, 1911, in Winston-Salem, N.C.; son of Thomas W. (a physician) and Frances Adelaide (Conrad) Davis; married Mary Louise Haywood, May 12, 1938; children: Archie H., Louise Bahnson Davis Bennett, John Haywood, Thomas W. IV. *Education:* University of North Carolina at Chapel Hill, A.B., 1932, M.A., 1975. *Politics:* Democrat. *Religion:* Moravian.

ADDRESSES: Home—2828 Forest Dr., Winston-Salem, N.C. 27104. *Office*—P.O. Box 10689, Winston-Salem, N.C. 27108.

CAREER: Wachovia Bank & Trust Co., Winston-Salem, N.C., chairman of board of directors, 1956-74; Duke Endowment, chairman, 1976-82.

MEMBER: American Academy of Arts and Sciences (fellow), Phi Beta Kappa.

WRITINGS:

Boy Colonel of the Confederacy, University of North Carolina Press, 1985.

* * *

DAVIS, J. Morton 1929-

PERSONAL: Birth-given surname Davidowitz; born January 7, 1929, in New York, N.Y.; son of Morris and Sylvia (Mandel) Davidowitz; married Rosalind Selengut, September 24, 1949; children: Esti Davis Stahler, Ruki Davis Renov, Rivki, Laya. *Education:* Brooklyn College (now of the City University of New York), A.B. (magna cum laude), 1957; Harvard University, M.B.A. (with distinction), 1959. *Religion:* Jewish.

ADDRESSES: Home—7 Sutton Pl. S., Lawrence, N.Y. 11559. *Office*—D. H. Blair & Co., Inc., 44 Wall St., New York, N.Y. 10005.

CAREER: Shields & Co., New York City, account executive, 1959-62; D. H. Blair & Co., Inc., New York City, owner, chairman, and senior president, 1962—. Allied member of New York Stock Exchange and American Stock Exchange; president of D. H. Blair Securities Corp., 1967—, and Rivkalex Corp.; chairman of board of directors of Engex, Inc., Xoil Energy Resources, Inc. (also founder), and Xplor Energy, Inc.; chairman and president of Roundhill Capital and A Venture Capital SBIC Fund; member of board of directors of Satori Productions, Inc., and Westbank Enterprises, Inc. Lecturer at Brooklyn College of the City University of New York, New York University, Harvard University, Yeshiva University, Bard College, and University of California, Los Angeles; trustee of Yeshiva University, 1981—, and Graduate School of the City University of New York. Member of Independents, Republicans, and Democrats for Good Government.

MEMBER: Phi Beta Kappa, Harvard Club, Jockey Club, Racquet Club of Florida, Lawrence Tennis Club.

AWARDS, HONORS: Heritage Award from Yeshiva University, 1980; Covenant of Peace Award from Synagogue Council of America, 1983.

WRITINGS:

How to Make the Economy Succeed, Gardner Press, 1983.

Making America Work Again, Crown, 1983.

BIOGRAPHICAL/CRITICAL SOURCES:

PERIODICALS

Fortune, April 16, 1984.

DAVIS, Philip J. 1923-

PERSONAL: Born January 2, 1923, in Lawrence, Mass.; son of Frank and Annie (Shrager) Davis; married Hadassah Finkelstein (a historical writer), January 2, 1944; children: Abigail, Frank, Ernest, Joseph. *Education:* Harvard University, B.S., 1943, Ph.D., 1950.

ADDRESSES: Home—175 Freeman St., Providence, R.I. 02906. *Office*—Department of Applied Mathematics, Brown University, Providence, R.I. 02912.

CAREER: National Bureau of Standards, Washington, D.C., mathematician, 1952-58, chief of numerical analysis section, 1958-63; Brown University, Providence, R.I., professor of applied mathematics, 1963—.

MEMBER: Mathematical Association of America.

AWARDS, HONORS: Guggenheim fellow, 1956-57; math award from Washington Academy of Sciences, 1960; Chauvenet Prize from Mathematical Association of America, 1963; American Book Award from Association of American Publishers, 1983, for *The Mathematical Experience;* Lester R. Ford Prize from Mathematical Association of America, 1983; George Polya Prize from Mathematical Association of America, 1987.

WRITINGS:

The Lore of Large Numbers, Random House, 1961.
Interpolation and Approximation, Blaisdell Publishing, 1963.
The Mathematics of Matrices: A First Book of Matrix Theory and Linear Algebra, Blaisdell Publishing, 1965, 2nd edition, Xerox College Publishing, 1973.
(With Philip Rabinowitz) *Numerical Integration,* Blaisdell Publishing, 1967.
(With William G. Chinn) *3.1416 and All That* (essays), Simon & Schuster, 1969, 2nd edition, Birkhauser Boston, 1985.
The Schwarz Function and Its Applications (monograph), Mathematical Association of America, 1974.
(With Rabinowitz) *Methods of Numerical Integration,* Academic Press, 1975, 2nd edition, 1984.
Circulant Matrices, Wiley, 1979.
(With Reuben Hersh) *The Mathematical Experience,* introduction by Gian-Carlo Rota, Birkhauser Boston, 1981.
The Thread: A Mathematical Yarn, illustrations by Elisa M. Nazeley, Birkhauser Boston, 1983.
(With Hersh) *Descartes' Dream: The World According to Mathematics,* Harcourt, 1986.
(Editor with David Park) *No Way: The Nature of the Impossible,* W. H. Freeman, 1987.

SIDELIGHTS: In their award-winning *The Mathematical Experience* Philip J. Davis and Reuben Hersh describe, for general readers, the workings of the contemporary mathematical community. Looking at what mathematicians do and who they are, the authors focus on the science's most fundamental question: Do mathematical theorems and structures exist independent of the human mind? Exploring this timeless argument of discovery versus invention (with as many different labels), Davis and Hersh ultimately take the anthropocentric view: "Mathematics is a human invention. . . . These things we bring into the world . . . are mysterious to us, their creators. . . . [Mathematics is] the study of mental objects with reproducible properties." Thus, the mathematician's work—wrote Gian-Carlo Rota in the book's introduction—is "mostly a tangle of guesswork, analogy, wishful thinking and frustration."

While praising Davis and Hersh for discussing topics not usually found in books for general readers, *New York Review of Books* critic Martin Gardner took issue with their basic belief that "mathematics is a humanistic study." As a mathematical realist, the reviewer argued: "Why do mathematical theorems fit the universe so accurately that they have enormous explanatory and predictive power? . . . If mathematical concepts have no locus outside human culture, how has nature managed to produce such a boundless profusion of beautiful models of mathematical objects?" Gardner insisted that "mathematical progress, like scientific progress, mixes creativity with discovery"; he deemed the authors' stance more confusing than illuminating in explaining mathematics to a lay audience.

Reviewing *The Mathematical Experience* for the *Times Literary Supplement,* Roger Penrose confessed his Platonistic leanings as well. "How can it be that such childishly simple ingredients can have such power and unexpected application?" he similarly proposed. Still, his opposition to the views of Davis and Hersh did little to dampen his enthusiasm for their "sometimes witty . . . frequently instructive . . . compelling and stimulating" book; "it provides a remarkable opportunity for the general reader to peer into the minds and activities of those unfamiliar and often unworldly creatures, the professional working mathematicians," judged the critic. "Nothing quite like this book has been written about mathematics, and it may well become a sort of classic," a reviewer for the *New Yorker* agreed. And writing in *Harper's,* Hugh Kenner was heartened by the success of *The Mathematical Experience*—a "new *kind* of popular book" that indicates a reading public "with a fair capacity to ponder abstraction." "That's a powerful sign," the critic declared.

Davis and Hersh collaborated again to write *Descartes' Dream: The World According to Mathematics.* Reflecting on the increasing mathematization of the world since Rene Descartes ushered in the Age of Science with his methods of reason in the seventeenth century, the authors focus on the relationship that has evolved between man and the mathematics he has created. Today "we take it as a given that objective reality can be measured, counted, quantified and analyzed by the tools of mathematics," noted Lee Dembart in the *Los Angeles Times.* "But Davis and Hersh find the mathematization of reality both wrong and harmful. . . . Mathematics and science have no values; they must be tempered by humanism. . . . Reason, math and logic can do only so much. To follow them further is to invite catastrophe."

Assessing *Descartes' Dream* in the *New Statesman,* Peter Wilsher found Davis and Hersh "particularly good . . . on the application of mathematics to questions of social policy and its weaknesses when faced with the swirling complexity of real events and real people." Also a fan of the volume, Dembart remarked that "part of the pleasure of their book is the ease with which they convey complicated ideas, their masterful grasp of their material and the balanced tone of their argument"; the reviewer pronounced *Descartes' Dream* "just as wonderful" as the pair's first collaborative effort. *New York Times Book Review* critic Daniel Gorenstein, likewise, described the authors' approach as "speculative rather than analytical . . . more concerned with presenting diverse points of view than with attempting to reach definitive conclusions." The reviewer continued: "Mr. Davis and Mr. Hersh raise important questions about man's ability to adapt to an increasingly computerized world, but unfortunately their discussion is often too superficial or fragmented to give adequate guidance. Nevertheless, their book does provide an antidote to the

Cartesian view that mathematical and scientific knowledge will suffice to solve the central problems of human existence."

BIOGRAPHICAL/CRITICAL SOURCES:

PERIODICALS

Christian Science Monitor, May 14, 1982.
Globe and Mail (Toronto), April 11, 1987.
Harper's, October, 1981.
Los Angeles Times, November 11, 1986, July 21, 1987.
New Statesman, December 12, 1986.
New Yorker, March 9, 1981.
New York Review of Books, August 13, 1981.
New York Times Book Review, October 5, 1986.
Times Literary Supplement, May 14, 1982, February 13, 1987.

* * *

DAVIS, Sandra T. W. 1937-

PERSONAL: Born October 18, 1937, in Philadelphia, Pa.; daughter of Edward I. and Kate (Scolnick) Weisman; married Edward I. Davis (a project planner and administrator), June 18, 1961. *Education:* Temple University, B.S.Ed., 1959; University of Pennsylvania, M.A., 1961, Ph.D., 1968.

ADDRESSES: Home—750 Twin Rivers Dr. N., East Windsor, N.J. 08520. *Office*—American International Underwriters, 70 Pine St., 15th Floor, New York, N.Y. 10270.

CAREER: Sophia University, Tokyo, Japan, instructor in history, 1964-68; Old Dominion University, Norfolk, Va., assistant professor of history, 1968-69; Hunter College of the City University of New York, New York City, assistant professor of history, 1969-74; University of North Carolina at Charlotte, associate professor of history, 1974-76; independent researcher and consultant in Tokyo, 1977-80; CIGNA Corp., Philadelphia, Pa., market researcher and planning analyst, 1980-82; American International Group, New York City, manager of international research for corporate marketing research and development department, 1982-83, manager of research and development for American International Underwriters, 1983—. Lecturer at Far East Division of University of Maryland, 1967-68; visiting scholar at Sophia University, 1976-78.

MEMBER: Association for Asian Studies, American Marketing Association, Asia Society, Japan Society, International House of Japan.

AWARDS, HONORS: Japan Foundation fellowship, 1974-75.

WRITINGS:

Intellectual Change and Political Development in Early Modern Japan: Ono Azusa; A Case Study, Fairleigh Dickinson University Press, 1980.

(Editor with F. Hilary Conroy and Wayne Patterson, and contributor) *Japan in Transition,* Fairleigh Dickinson University Press, 1984.

Associated with *U.S. Export Opportunities to Japan,* 1978, and *U.S. Manufacturing Investment in Japan,* 1979. Contributor of about twenty articles to history and Asian studies journals.

SIDELIGHTS: Sandra T. W. Davis told *CA:* "*Intellectual Change and Political Development in Early Modern Japan* analyzes the career of Ono, one of the early Meiji intellectuals who studied in the United States and Great Britain and then applied Western political ideas to the Japanese scene. He was a founder—with Okuma Shigenobu—of the Rikken Kaishinto, one of the first political parties, and of Waseda University. He also wrote a major work on constitutional theory entitled *Kokken hanron,* which was influenced by the ideas of Jeremy Bentham and other British philosophers.

"I have moved from early Meiji political history to current trade and business problems. I now specialize in marketing studies on the Japanese and Asian markets. In my spare time I travel extensively in Asia."

* * *

DEBO, Angie 1890-1988

OBITUARY NOTICE—See index for *CA* sketch: Born January 30, 1890, in Beattie, Kan.; died February 21, 1988, in Enid, Okla. Historian, educator, editor, and author. Debo, who taught history at public schools and universities in Oklahoma and Texas, was called "the first lady of Oklahoma history." A prolific author, she published hundreds of articles and several books on the history of Oklahoma and the American Indian. For her highly acclaimed work Debo received a number of awards, including a 1987 Award for Scholarly Distinction from the American Historical Association and a Henry G. Bennett Distinguished Service Award from Oklahoma State University. In 1950 Debo was inducted into the Oklahoma Hall of Fame. Among her writings are *Oklahoma: Foot-Loose and Fancy-Free; And Still the Waters Run: The Betrayal of the Five Civilized Tribes; A History of the Indians of the United States; Geronimo: The Man, His Time, His Place;* and the award-winning *Rise and Fall of the Choctaw Republic.* As a columnist for the *Oklahoma City Times* from 1952 to 1954, Debo wrote "This Week in Oklahoma." Additionally, she edited such books as *History of the Choctaw* and was a contributor to *Encyclopedia Americana* and various periodicals.

OBITUARIES AND OTHER SOURCES:

BOOKS

Who's Who in America, 40th edition, Marquis, 1978.

PERIODICALS

Chicago Tribune, February 24, 1988.
Los Angeles Times, February 27, 1988.
New York Times, February 23, 1988.

* * *

DEGEN, Bruce 1945-

PERSONAL: Born June 14, 1945, in Brooklyn, N.Y.; son of Hyman and Molly Degen; married wife, Christine; children: Benjamin, Alexander. *Education:* Cooper Union, B.F.A., 1966; Pratt Institute, M.F.A., 1974.

ADDRESSES: Home—101 Clark St., Brooklyn, N.Y. 11201.

CAREER: Writing instructor and illustrator of books for children at School of Visual Arts, New York, N.Y.; worked as high school art teacher, opera scenery painter, advertising designer, and printmaker; director of artists' lithography studio in Israel, beginning in 1971; writer and illustrator.

MEMBER: Society of Children's Book Writers.

WRITINGS:

SELF-ILLUSTRATED CHILDREN'S BOOKS

Aunt Possum and the Pumpkin Man, Harper, 1977.
The Little Witch and the Riddle, Harper, 1980.

Jamberry, Harper, 1983.

ILLUSTRATOR

Malcolm Hall, *Forecast,* Coward, 1977.
Stephen Krensky, *A Big Day for Sceptres,* Atheneum, 1977.
Malcolm Hall, *Caricatures,* Coward, 1978.
Carol Chapman, *Ig Lives in a Cave,* Dutton, 1979.
Judy Delton, *Brimhall Turns to Magic,* Lothrop, 1979.
Marjorie Weinman Sharmat, *Mr. Jameson and Mr. Phillips,* Harper, 1979.
Claudia Louise Lewis, *Up and Down the River: Boat Poems,* Harper, 1979.
Jane Yolen, *Commander Toad in Space,* Coward, 1980.
Charlotte Herman, *My Mother Didn't Kiss Me Goodnight,* Dutton, 1980.
Donald J. Sobel, *Encyclopedia Brown's Second Record Book of Weird and Wonderful Facts,* Delacorte, 1981.
Clyde Robert Bulla, *Dandelion Hill,* Dutton, 1982.
Jane Yolen, *Commander Toad and the Planet of the Grapes,* Coward, 1982.
Joel L. Schwartz, *Upchuck Summer,* Delacorte, 1982.
Malcolm Hall, *Deadlines,* Coward, 1982.
Mary DeBall Kwitz, *Little Chick's Breakfast,* Harper, 1983.
Jane Yolen, *Commander Toad and the Big Black Hole,* Coward, 1983.
Lyn Littlefield Hoopes, *Daddy's Coming Home,* Harper, 1984.
Jane Yolen, *Commander Toad and the Dis-Asteroid,* Coward, 1985.
Joseph Slate, *Lonely Lula Cat,* Harper, 1985.
Bonnie Pryor, *Grandpa Bear,* Morrow, 1985.
Eleanor Coerr, *The Josefina Story Quilt,* Harper, 1986.
Jane Yolen, *Commander Toad and the Intergalactic Spy,* Coward, 1986.
Diane Stanley, *The Good-Luck Pencil,* Four Winds, 1986.
Bonnie Pryor, *Grandpa Bear's Christmas,* Morrow, 1986.
Nancy White Carlstrom, *Jesse Bear, What Will You Wear?* Macmillan, 1986.
Joanna Cole, *The Magic School Bus at the Waterworks,* Scholastic Inc., 1986.
Aileen Lucia Fisher, *When It Comes to Bugs: Poems,* Harper, 1986.
Larry Weinberg, *The Forgetful Bears Meet Mr. Memory,* Scholastic Inc., 1987.

WORK IN PROGRESS: Illustrating *The Magic School Bus Inside the Earth* by Joanna Cole, *Commander Toad and the Space Pirates,* by Jane Yolen, and *Better Not Get Wet, Jesse Bear,* by Nancy White Carlstrom; *Teddy Bear Towers,* for Harper.

SIDELIGHTS: Bruce Degen told *CA:* "After doing many different things in the field of art I decided to go back to the root of what made drawing fun for me as a child—children's books. I believe that good children's book art will delight the child, and this is the work of lasting interest. Being able to read to children, I can see by the children's candid reactions which elements truly communicate. Since I began, this work has involved me totally, and I hope I will be doing it as long as I can hold a pencil."

* * *

DEIGHTON, Lee C(ecil) 1906-1987

PERSONAL: Born October 7, 1906, in Seattle, Wash.; died following a brief illness, March 31, 1987; son of Cecil Harrison and Eva (Willcuts) Deighton; married Bethana Bucklin, September 2, 1933; children: Eve, Mark, Jane. *Education:* University of Minnesota, B.S., 1926.

CAREER: Director of Harcourt, Brace & Co. (now Harcourt Brace Jovanovich, Inc.), 1943-53; vice-president of Science Research Associates, 1954-56; Macmillan Publishing Co., Inc., New York, N.Y., vice-president of educational department, 1957-62, president, 1962-65, chairman of board of directors, 1965-70; Hardscrabble Press, Inc., president, beginning in 1973. President of American Educational Publishers Institute, 1967-68; senior vice-president of Crowell-Collier-Macmillan, Inc.

WRITINGS:

Vocabulary Development in the Classroom, Bureau of Publications, Teachers College, Columbia University, 1959.
(Editor in chief) *The Encyclopedia of Education,* ten volumes, Macmillan, 1971.
A Comparative Study of Spellings in Four Major Collegiate Dictionaries, Hardscrabble Press, 1972.
Handbook of American English Spelling, Van Nostrand, 1973.

Also author of *Sounds and Spellings, Words and Meanings, Basics of English,* and *Word Power.*

OBITUARIES:

PERIODICALS

Publishers Weekly, April 24, 1987.*

* * *

DeKOK, David (Paul) 1953-

PERSONAL: Surname is pronounced "De-*Cook*"; born July 17, 1953, in Holland, Mich.; son of Paul W. (a chemist) and Olga K. (a housewife; maiden name, Kilian) DeKok. *Education:* Hope College, B.A., 1975. *Religion:* Lutheran.

ADDRESSES: Home—423 Walnut St., Apt. 314, Harrisburg, Pa. 17101. *Office*—*Patriot,* 812 King Blvd., Harrisburg, Pa. 17101. *Agent*—Michael Steinberg, P.O. Box 274, Glencoe, Ill. 60022.

CAREER: News-Item, Shamokin, Pa., reporter, 1975-87; *Patriot,* Harrisburg, Pa., reporter, 1987—. Film consultant.

MEMBER: Society of Professional Journalists/Sigma Delta Chi (Central Pennsylvania chapter).

AWARDS, HONORS: Keystone Press Awards from Pennsylvania Newspaper Publishers Association, first place award in news series category, 1979, for stories about the mine fire in Centralia, Pa., first place award in feature story category, 1986, for story "Family's Dilemma: Illness, Loss of Jobs, Insensitive Bureaucracy," first place award in news story category, 1987, for story "Man Dead, Wife Hurt in Shooting"; first place award in public service category from Associated Press Managing Editors of Pennsylvania, 1981, for stories on the mine fire in Centralia.

WRITINGS:

Unseen Danger: A Tragedy of People, Government, and the Centralia Mine Fire, University of Pennsylvania Press, 1986.

WORK IN PROGRESS: A history of the German and American branches of a single family in the twentieth century and a novel about young men facing the draft.

SIDELIGHTS: David DeKok told *CA:* "My book *Unseen Danger* grew out of the reporting I did for the *News-Item,* a

small newspaper in Shamokin, Pennsylvania. The mine fire under Centralia, Pennsylvania, which is the topic of my book, was endlessly fascinating to me as a reporter. Writing factual, fair, but hard-hitting stories about Centralia's plight was the best way that I, as a concerned fellow human, could help the people there. I also hoped that my writing would make it more difficult for such a tragedy to occur again.

"I think that writing about environmental disasters like Centralia, particularly if done repeatedly, can be the catalyst that stirs an unconcerned bureaucracy to action. Even if it does not move the bureaucratic mountain, it may move elected officials to action, as it did in the case of Centralia."

BIOGRAPHICAL/CRITICAL SOURCES:

PERIODICALS

New York Times Book Review, January 4, 1987.

* * *

DELATUSH, Edith G. 1921-
(Edith DePaul, Alyssa Morgan, Edith St. George)

PERSONAL: Born November 21, 1921, in New York, N.Y.; daughter of Albert (a baker) and Freda (a housewife; maiden name, Von der Geest) Grieshammer; married George A. Delatush (a surgeon), June 2, 1943 (divorced, 1983); children: George A., Jr., Paul A. *Education:* Long Island College Hospital School of Nursing, R.N., 1942.

ADDRESSES: Home—200 Intracoastal Place, Apt. 104-B, Tequesta, Fla. 33469. *Agent*—Robin Kaigh Literary Agency, 300 East 54th St., New York, N.Y. 10022.

CAREER: Worked as registered nurse in New Jersey and Florida, 1960-79; writer, 1979—. Past commander of U.S. Coast Guard Auxiliary.

MEMBER: Romance Writers of America (coordinator for South Florida), Gold Coast Romance Writers (director).

WRITINGS—ROMANCE NOVELS:

Hand in Hand, Dell, 1985.
When Midnight Comes, Dell, 1985.
Burning Nights, Dell, 1986.
The Cape Cod Affair, Dell, 1986.
Tonight You're Mine, Dell, 1986.
The Best Revenge, Dell, 1987.

UNDER PSEUDONYM EDITH DePAUL

The Viscount's Witch, Dell, 1981.

UNDER PSEUDONYM ALYSSA MORGAN

Beckoning Heart, Dell, 1981.
Walk Beside Me, Friend, Dell, 1982.
Architect of Her Heart, Dell, 1982.
White Water Love, Dell, 1982.
No Other Love, Dell, 1983.

UNDER PSEUDONYM EDITH ST. GEORGE

Mountain Song, Silhouette, 1981.
West of the Moon, Silhouette, 1981.
Midnight Wine, Silhouette, 1981.
Dream Once More, Silhouette, 1982.
Delta River Magic, Silhouette, 1983.
Rose Colored Glass, Silhouette, 1983.
Color My Dream, Silhouette, 1984.
Velvet Is for Lovers, Silhouette, 1984.

WORK IN PROGRESS: Romance novels.

SIDELIGHTS: Edith G. Delatush told *CA:* "Today's romance genre is a far cry from the early one. The heroine is an independent thinker, who recognizes the fact that she can become more complete with the right man by her side. I was tired of the wars, the constant exposure of man's inhumanity to man that is fed us in the various mass media. I found this genre a joy to write, and, by the overwhelming popularity of this type of writing, women *and men* are proving this is what they want to read.

"The background for all my books is researched carefully and the sites visited so I can explore the full flavor of the area, whether it is Fiji, Egypt, Machu Picchu, or my home state."

BIOGRAPHICAL/CRITICAL SOURCES:

BOOKS

Falk, Kathryn, *Love's Leading Ladies,* Pinnacle Books, 1982.

PERIODICALS

P.M. Magazine of the Air, September, 1982.

* * *

del REY, Judy-Lynn 1943-1986
(Judy-Lynn Benjamin)

PERSONAL: Born January 26, 1943, in New York, N.Y.; died following a stroke, February 20, 1986, in New York, N.Y.; daughter of Zachary Harold and Norma Victoria (Breslau) Benjamin; married Lester del Rey (a writer and editor), March 21, 1971. *Education:* Hunter College of the City University of New York, B.A., 1965.

ADDRESSES: Home—310 East 46th St., Apt. 3M, New York, N.Y. 10017.

CAREER: Galaxy (science fiction magazine), New York City, began as editor's assistant, 1965, associate editor, 1966-69, managing editor, 1969-73; Random House, New York City, senior editor of Ballantine Books, 1973-77, vice-president of Ballantine Books, 1978-86, editor in chief of Del Rey Books, 1977-86, publisher of Del Rey Books, 1982-86.

AWARDS, HONORS: E. E. Smith Award from New England Science Fiction Association, 1970; named to Hunter College Hall of Fame, 1972.

WRITINGS:

(Editor under name Judy-Lynn Benjamin) *The Celtic Bull: Essays on James Joyce's Ulysses* (monograph), University of Tulsa, 1966.
(Editor) *Stellar Short Novels,* Ballantine, 1976.

Contributor to *World Book Encyclopedia,* 1972 and 1977. Editor of "Stellar" science fiction anthology series, Ballantine, 1974-81.

SIDELIGHTS: Founder and editor in chief of Del Rey Books, the science fiction imprint of Ballantine Books, Judy-Lynn del Rey was renowned for her ability to find and develop potential best-selling writers in her field. Among the successful books she introduced, Terry Brooks's first novel, *The Sword of Shannara,* and George Lucas's novel *Star Wars* figure prominently. Both earned best-seller status, helping to establish Ballantine/Del Rey as a leader in science fiction publishing. Since its

founding by del Rey and her husband, writer and editor Lester del Rey, the imprint has become "one of the most prestigious lines of science-fiction publications," reported Robert Coulson in his *Dictionary of Literary Biography* article about paperback science fiction.

After graduating from college in 1965, del Rey began her science fiction career by becoming an editor's assistant at *Galaxy* magazine; "my mother thought I should do *something*," she recounted in a *Publishers Weekly* interview. "I'd never even read the magazine." Under editor Frederik Pohl's tutelage, however, she learned much about science fiction, editing, and publishing, and she advanced to managing editor within four years.

Del Rey obtained an editorial post with Ballantine Books in 1973 when she approached the company with the rights to publish Arthur C. Clarke's *Rendezvous With Rama*—the first novel by the celebrated author of *2001: A Space Odyssey* since production of the film of the same title. She had been editing the book for serialization in *Galaxy*, and her move led to a multi-book contract between Clarke and Ballantine. Del Rey later increased Ballantine's schedule of science fiction publication from two books a month to six and oversaw a list including prominent authors such as Anne McCaffrey, Robert A. Heinlein, Isaac Asimov, and Piers Anthony. She also kept her eye on the short story field by editing for Ballantine the occasional "Stellar" anthologies of original science fiction stories by both established authors and new writers.

Del Rey Books took off with the publication of the tie-in novel for the movie "Star Wars," which del Rey had originally bought and published before the film's release. As the movie proceeded to break box-office records, the novel, reprinted with photographs from the film, became one of the fastest-selling books in publishing history. "Within three months," she told *Publishers Weekly*, "Del Rey was all over the best-seller lists." Under del Rey's leadership the imprint went on to publish the successful "Chronicles of Thomas Covenant" by first-novelist Stephen R. Donaldson, the "Belgariad" books of David Eddings, and Piers Anthony's popular "Incarnations of Immortality" series. In one seven-month period beginning in 1984, Del Rey had a new science fiction book on the *New York Times* best-seller list each month, of which 95 percent were paperback originals, developed personally by del Rey or by others under her direction. Observed one insider, "She's been right so many times she's the E. F. Hutton of publishing. When she talks, everybody listens." According to *Fantasy Review*, editor Charles N. Brown of the science fiction trade magazine *LOCUS* averred that del Rey "changed the industry by publishing the most commercially successful line of sf of all time."

BIOGRAPHICAL/CRITICAL SOURCES:

BOOKS

Dictionary of Literary Biography, Volume 8: *Twentieth-Century American Science Fiction Writers*, Gale, 1981.

PERIODICALS

Publishers Weekly, June 14, 1976, July 29, 1983, September 26, 1986.

OBITUARIES:

PERIODICALS

AB Bookman's Weekly, July 7, 1986.
Fantasy Review, March, 1986.
New York Times, February 22, 1986.
Publishers Weekly, March 7, 1986.
Washington Post, February 23, 1986.*

* * *

DEMAREST, Victoria Booth(-Clibborn) 1890-1982

PERSONAL: Born January 1, 1890, in Paris, France; immigrated to United States, 1918, naturalized citizen; died of heart failure, April 4, 1982, in St. Petersburg, Fla.; daughter of Arthur Sydney and Catherine (a Salvation Army pioneer) Booth-Clibborn; married Cornelius Agnew Demarest (an evangelist and church administrator), July 10, 1918 (died, 1959); children: six children and two stepchildren, including Victoria Beatrice (Mrs. Claxton Monro), Arthur Sydney, Evangeline, Cornelius. *Education:* Graduate of Paris Conservatory of Music.

CAREER: Ordained minister of Congregational Church (now United Church of Christ), 1949; preacher; leader of evangelistic missions; human relations counselor; author, playwright, and composer. Founder of America for God Crusade, Inc., 1935, and World Association of Mothers for Peace, Inc., 1946.

AWARDS, HONORS: D.D. degree.

WRITINGS:

The Holy Spirit: Companion Book to "Broken Lives" and "The Lily" (sermons), Demarest Book Concern, 1927.
Shade of His Hand, for the Comfort of the Sorrowing (poems and prose), Westminster, 1941.
What I Saw in Europe: A Challenge to Christians Everywhere, Vantage, 1953.
King David: A Drama, United Church Press, 1964.
Alive and Running: Devotions for Active People, Word Books, 1976.
A Violin, a Lily, and You, Valkyrie Press, 1976.
Sex and Spirit: God, Woman, and Ministry, Sacred Arts International, 1977, revised edition published as *God, Woman, and Ministry*, 1978.
The Greatest Week in History, Abingdon, 1982.

Author of hymn books and hymns, including "The Hymn of the Last Supper," "You Were a Working Man, My Lord," "Love Unconquerable," "The Shepherd's Psalm," and "Mary's Little Song"; composer of cantatas published by Boston Music Co. and sheet music published by Theodore Presser. Author of unpublished plays, including "King David and the Empty House," "The Devil and You," and "My Son Jesus."

OBITUARIES:

PERIODICALS

New York Times, April 6, 1982.*

* * *

DENNISON, Peter (John) 1942-

PERSONAL: Born August 18, 1942, in Wollongong, New South Wales, Australia. *Education:* University of Sydney, B.Mus., 1963; Oxford University, received M.A., D.Phil., 1970.

ADDRESSES: Home—156 Nicholson St., Fitzroy, Victoria 3065, Australia. *Office*—Faculty of Music, University of Melbourne, Parkville, Victoria 3052, Australia.

CAREER: Cambridge University, Cambridge, England, fellow of Clare College, director of music, and conductor of Cam-

bridge Philharmonic Orchestra and Choir, all 1971-75; University of Melbourne, Parkville, Australia, professor of music, 1975—. Chairman of board of directors of Melbourne Symphony Orchestra, 1985—.

MEMBER: Royal Music Association, Royal College of Organists (fellow).

WRITINGS:

Pelham Humfrey: Complete Church Music, two volumes, Stainer & Bell, 1972, revised edition, 1985.
Purcell: Ode on St. Cecilia's Day 1692, Novello, 1975.
(Editor) *The Richard Wagner Centenary in Australia,* University of Adelaide, 1985.
Pelham Humfrey, Oxford University Press, 1986.

Editor of *Locke: The Instrumental Music in the Tempest,* 1976; contributor to *Essays on English Music on Opera in Honour of Sir Jack Westrup,* 1976.

Contributor to music journals.

WORK IN PROGRESS: The Music of Elgar.

* * *

DePAUL, Edith
See DELATUSH, Edith G.

* * *

DePORTE, Anton W. 1928-

PERSONAL: Born November 1, 1928, in Oklahoma City, Okla. *Education:* University of Chicago, Ph.B., 1948, A.M., 1951, Ph.D., 1956; attended University of Paris, 1951-52.

ADDRESSES: Home—1221 Potomac St. N.W., Washington, D.C. 20007.

CAREER: U.S. Department of State, Washington, D.C., intelligence research specialist, 1955-66, chief of Region West and South Europe Division, 1966-70, deputy director of Office of Research and Analysis for Western Europe, 1970-72, member of planning and coordination staff, 1972-79, director of Office of Research for Western Europe, 1979-80. Visiting scholar at Institute of French Studies, New York University, 1982—.

AWARDS, HONORS: U.S. Department of State, Meritorious Honor Award, 1966, Superior Honor Award, 1970; fellow of Council on Foreign Relations, 1976-77.

WRITINGS:

(Contributor) Benedict V. Maciuika, editor, *Lithuania in the Last Thirty Years,* Human Relations Area Files, 1955.
De Gaulle's Foreign Policy, 1944-1946, Harvard University Press, 1968.
Europe Between the Superpowers: The Enduring Balance, Yale University Press, 1979.
Europe and the Superpower Balance, Foreign Policy, 1979.

WORK IN PROGRESS: A book on French society since World War II; research on U.S.-European relations.

BIOGRAPHICAL/CRITICAL SOURCES:

PERIODICALS

New Republic, June 30, 1979.
Times Literary Supplement, December 14, 1979.

Der HOVANESSIAN, Diana

PERSONAL: Born in Worcester, Mass.; daughter of John (a social worker) and Marian (Israelyan) Der Hovanessian; married James Dalley (separated); children: Maro, Sonia. *Education:* Received A.B. from Boston University; graduate study at Harvard University.

ADDRESSES: Home—2 Farrar St., Cambridge, Mass. 02138. *Agent*—Helen Rees, 308 Commonwealth Ave., Boston, Mass. 02115.

CAREER: Poet and lecturer, 1955—. Lecturer in American literature, poetry, and translation at various schools, including Boston University, Stetson University, Bard College, Columbia University, University of Connecticut, University of Pennsylvania, and Tempere University; conducts poetry workshops. Massachusetts Council of Arts and Humanities poet in the Massachusetts Schools, 1971—; member of board of directors of Armenian Museum, 1977-80, and member of the board of governors of Columbia University Translation Center, 1987—.

MEMBER: International P.E.N., Poetry Society of America, New England Poetry Club (member of board of directors, 1985—), Boston University Alumni Council (president, 1978—).

AWARDS, HONORS: St. Vartan Medal from Catholicosate of Beirut, Lebanon, 1970, for work in translations; Lyric Poetry award from the Poetry Society of America, 1977; translation grant from International P.E.N. and Columbia University, 1977; Jack Kolligian Award from National Association of Armenian Studies and Research, 1979, Boyan Humanities Award from Armenian Students Association, 1980, and A.R.S. Proodian Award from Armenian Relief Society, 1980, all for *Anthology of Armenian Poetry;* Barcelona Peace Prize from Phoenix Educational Corporation, 1985; van de Bovencamp-Erpf Award for excellence in literary translation from Columbia University Translation Center, 1986, for *Land of Fire;* numerous prizes from the World Order of Narrative Poets.

WRITINGS:

(Editor with Marzbed Margossian, and translator) *Anthology of Armenian Poetry,* Columbia University Press, 1979.
How to Choose Your Past (poetry), Ararat Press, 1979.
(Editor with Margossian, and translator) *Sacred Wrath: The Selected Poems of Vahan Tekeyan,* Ashod Press, 1982.
(Translator) *Come Sit Beside Me and Listen to Kouchag* (medieval poetry), Ashod Press, 1985.
(Editor with Margossian, and translator) Eghishe Charents, *Land of Fire,* Ardis, 1986.
(Translator) Gevorg Emin, *For You on New Year's Day,* introduction by Yevgeni Yevtushenko, Ohio University Press, 1986.
About Time (poetry), Ashod Press, 1987.

Also translator of Shen Mah's *The Bridge,* with Margossian. Contributor of poems and reviews to magazines and newspapers, including *American Scholar, Christian Science Monitor, American Poetry Review, Nation, New Republic, Partisan Review, Harper's,* and *Mademoiselle.* Member of editorial staff of *Young America, Young American Films,* and *Women's Wear Daily.*

WORK IN PROGRESS: Translations of Vahan Derian's *Coming to Terms,* Siamanto, Varoujan, and Vahakn Davtian; *Now*

I See It, a volume of shaped poems; *Songs of Bread, Songs of Salt.*

SIDELIGHTS: Diana Der Hovanessian told *CA:* "Because I live in the States, because I am an American, because I write in English I am called an American poet, but my Armenian ancestry speaks in a lot of what I say. And I have learned a great deal from the poetry I have translated. Not only has it been a window to the past but a wonderful new way of seeing and saying. Armenia is the perfect laboratory for anyone to study the history of poetry. Here in one place is a long unbroken chain of the art, from pagan days through the time of Christian hymns, from simple folk poems to the time of Turkish oppressions, when poetry with oblique messages had to provide the sense of history and pride to keep a people intact.

"In this history the reader discovers all the poets of the late nineteenth and early twentieth centuries have the same death date, 1915. Two hundred poets were the first to be rounded up and killed by the Turks at the outset of the Armenian genocide. No wonder in the little bit of land that is left to Armenians today poets and poetry are so revered, celebrated, and read. The Armenian subjects and the styles are similar to modern poetry world wide although there are probably more poems celebrating life and more love poems addressed to the land itself than elsewhere."

BIOGRAPHICAL/CRITICAL SOURCES:

PERIODICALS

Armenian Weekly, August 25, 1979.
Boston Globe, April 20, 1976.
Times Literary Supplement, January 18, 1980, January 2, 1987.

* * *

DERRIDA, Jacques 1930-

BRIEF ENTRY: Born in 1930 in El Biar, Algeria. French philosopher, educator, translator, and author. A philosophy teacher at Paris's Ecole Normale Superieure for more than twenty years, Derrida is famous for his controversial deconstruction strategy of literary criticism and philosophy. First presented in the introduction to his 1962 translation of Edmund Husserl's *Origin of Geometry,* for which Derrida won the Prix Cavailles, deconstructionism emphasizes the reader's role in extracting meaning from texts and the impossibility of determining absolute meaning. The strategy informs most of Derrida's major writings, which include *La Voix et le phenomene* (Presses Universitaires de France, 1967; translated as *Speech and Phenomena* [Northwestern University Press, 1973]), *L'Ecriture et la difference* (du Seuil, 1967; translated as *Writing and Difference* [University of Chicago Press, 1978]), *De la grammatologie* (Minuit, 1967; translated as *Of Grammatology* [Johns Hopkins University Press, 1976]), and *La Carte postale: De Socrate a Freud et au-dela* (Flammarion, 1980).

BIOGRAPHICAL/CRITICAL SOURCES:

BOOKS

Contemporary Literary Criticism, Volume 24, Gale, 1983.
Makers of Modern Culture, Facts on File, 1981.
Thinkers of the Twentieth Century, 2nd edition, St. James Press, 1987.
World Authors: 1975-1980, H. W. Wilson, 1985.

PERIODICALS

Los Angeles Times, March 11, 1982.
Los Angeles Times Book Review, July 7, 1985.
New Republic, April 16, 1977.
New York Review of Books, March 3, 1977.
New York Times Book Review, February 1, 1987.
Times Literary Supplement, February 15, 1968, July 4, 1980, September 30, 1983, December 5, 1986.

* * *

De SATGE, John (Cosmo) 1928-1984

PERSONAL: Born February 5, 1928, in Bexhill-on-Sea, England; died May 13, 1984, in Chichester, Sussex, England; married twice. *Education:* Christ Church, Oxford, M.A., 1955.

CAREER: Ordained Anglican priest; founding member of religious order, the Ecumenical Society of the Blessed Virgin Mary; Chichester Theological College, Chichester, England, vice-principal, until 1984.

WRITINGS:

Down to Earth: The New Protestant Vision of the Virgin Mary, Consortium Books, 1976.
Mary and the Christian Gospel, S.P.C.K., 1976.
Christ and the Human Prospect: The Unity of Existence Here and Hereafter, S.P.C.K., 1978.
Peter and the Single Church, S.P.C.K., 1981.
Mary's Place in the Christian Dialogue, St. Paul's, 1982.
(Translator) Jean Tillard, *The Bishop of Rome,* S.P.C.K., 1982.

CONTRIBUTOR

David M. Paton, editor, *The Parish Communion To-day: The Report of the 1962 Conference of Parish and People,* S.P.C.K., 1962.
E. L. Mascall and H. S. Box, editors, *The Blessed Virgin Mary: Essays by Anglican Writers,* Hilary House, 1963.
Les Sacrements d'initiation et les ministeres sacres, Fayard, 1974.

Contributor to theology journals.

OBITUARIES:

PERIODICALS

Times (London), May 19, 1984.*

* * *

Des PRES, Terrence 1939-1987

OBITUARY NOTICE—See index for *CA* sketch: Born December 26, 1939, in Effingham, Ill.; died November 16, 1987, in Hamilton, N.Y. Educator and author. Des Pres was affiliated with Colgate University, where he held the Crawshaw Chair in English Literature beginning in 1973. A specialist in Holocaust studies, he was the author of *The Survivor: An Anatomy of Life in the Death Camps.* Des Pres, who also wrote book reviews, contributed to various periodicals, including *Harper's* and *Partisan Review.* Before he died, he was working on a book on poetry and politics.

OBITUARIES AND OTHER SOURCES:

BOOKS

Directory of American Scholars, Volume II: *English, Speech, and Drama,* 8th edition, Bowker, 1982.

PERIODICALS

New York Times, November 18, 1987.

DEUTSCHER, Thomas (Brian) 1949-

PERSONAL: Born January 9, 1949, in Regina, Saskatchewan, Canada; son of Michael (a chartered accountant) and Etta (a homemaker; maiden name, Reinhart) Deutscher; married Marcella A. Schuck (a homemaker), 1971; children: Michael, Matthew, Thomas, Benjamin, Patrick, Mary Kathleen. *Education:* University of Saskatchewan, B.A., 1970, M.A., 1971; University of Toronto, Ph.D., 1978. *Religion:* Roman Catholic.

ADDRESSES: *Office*—St. Thomas More College, University of Saskatchewan, Saskatoon, Saskatchewan, Canada S7N 0W6.

CAREER: University of Saskatchewan, Saskatoon, assistant professor, 1978-84, associate professor of history, 1984—, dean of St. Thomas More College, 1985—.

MEMBER: Renaissance Society of America, American Catholic Historical Association.

WRITINGS:

(Associate editor) Peter G. Bietenholz, editor, *Contemporaries of Erasmus: A Biographical Register of the Renaissance and Reformation,* University of Toronto Press, Volume I: *A-E,* 1985, Volume II: *F-M,* 1986, Volume III: *N-Z,* 1987.

Contributor to *Journal of Ecclesiastical History*.

WORK IN PROGRESS: A study of the diocesan clergy of the northern Italian diocese of Novara, between the Council of Trent in 1563 and the end of the eighteenth century.

BIOGRAPHICAL/CRITICAL SOURCES:

PERIODICALS

Times Literary Supplement, February 28, 1986.

* * *

DEVAL, Gord 1930-

PERSONAL: Born January 18, 1930, in Winnipeg, Manitoba, Canada; son of Roy Ward Dickson (a television and radio producer) and Helene Faille (a homemaker); married first wife, Joan, June 30, 1951 (divorced); married Sheila Davidson; children: Ron, Randy, Connie, Wendy. *Education:* Attended University of Toronto, 1944-47. *Religion:* Protestant.

ADDRESSES: *Home and office*—23 Willowhurst Cres., Scarborough, Ontario, Canada M1R 3R7.

CAREER: Sporting goods salesman, 1950-62; insurance salesman, 1962-87; writer and film producer, 1987—. Guest on numerous radio and television programs; public speaker.

MEMBER: Toronto Sportsman's Association, Scarborough Fly and Bait Casting Association (president).

AWARDS, HONORS: Achievement awards from government of Ontario, including Special International Achievement in Sports, 1986; more than one hundred national and international casting titles, including All-Round Ontario and Canadian Champion, 1951-58, and Canadian, Regional U.S., North American, and British Commonwealth titles in all distance casting events, 1974-87; holder of three world, two North American, and twenty-two Canadian casting championship titles.

WRITINGS:

Fishin' Hats: A Collection of True Fish Stories, Simon & Pierre, 1983.

Fishin' Tales: A Collection of True Fish Stories, Simon & Pierre, 1984.

(Editor) *Life (and Death) in the "Yoonited States of Uhmurica",* cartoons by Ed Franklin, Simon & Pierre, 1984.

Take Me Fishin' Too, Daddy (Please), Simon & Pierre, 1985.

Free Food 'n Fun, General Publishing, 1987.

Casting About With Gord Deval, General Publishing, 1987.

Contributor to magazines and newspapers in the United States and Canada, including *Field and Stream, Outdoors Canada, Weekend,* and *Hunting and Fishing Canada*.

WORK IN PROGRESS: *Fishin's Easy,* publication expected in 1990; *The Last Great Lincoln* (novel), publication expected in 1990.

SIDELIGHTS: Gord Deval told *CA:* "The fishing stories in my books are one hundred percent true; there is no way I could fabricate such fascinating tales. I developed an early interest in fishing and casting through reading and meeting others (much older) interested in the sport, and I practiced . . . practiced . . . practiced. I also spent many hours working on, modifying, and redesigning the equipment.

"My interest in writing also developed when I was young: My father had me write a weekly essay on any topic I chose in order to collect my allowance. The amount of pocket money I received would be based on the marks the essays achieved after he read and corrected them. I enjoyed the challenge.

"Before editing *Life (and Death) in the 'Yoonited States of Uhmurica,'* I became intrigued by the number of bizarre items I would read—not in sensationalist 'rags' but in ordinary newspapers—that seemed to reflect life in the United States. Where but in the United States could a bank robber run out of a bank with his loot and promptly be mugged on the sidewalk? It happened in New York. I started to collect a file of such clippings and seven years later ended up with a drawer-full. What to do? Couldn't bring myself to throw them out so I approached a publisher and the book was born. Since *Uhmurica* was published I have collected enough clippings for a sequel, and I hope to interest a publisher with the project before too long."

BIOGRAPHICAL/CRITICAL SOURCES:

PERIODICALS

Globe and Mail (Toronto), March 3, 1984.

* * *

DIBBA, Ebou 1943-

PERSONAL: Given name is pronounced "*ee*-boo"; born August 10, 1943, in Banjul, Gambia; son of Babou and Oley (a housewife; maiden name, Jack) Dibba; married Tonia Evelyn May (a photographer); children: Ramatoulai, Mariama, Lamin. *Education:* University of Wales, University College of South Wales, Cardiff, B.A. (with honors), 1967; King's College, London, M.A., 1968. *Religion:* Muslim.

ADDRESSES: *Home*—Stables House, Castle Hill, Bletchingley, Surrey RH1 4LB, England. *Office*—Tandridge Adult Education Institute, Stychens Lane, Bletchingley, Surrey, England.

CAREER: Assistant teacher of English at school in Toulon, France, 1965-66; Latin and French tutor in Hatfield, England, 1967-68; North West Harringey Adult Education Centre, Muswell Hill, London, England, French tutor, 1972-74; Phoenix

Youth Club, London, England, youth worker, 1972-74; lecturer in modern languages and community education, 1974-78; Tandridge Adult Education Institute, Bletchingley, England, principal, 1979—. Member of British Association for Literacy in Development.

MEMBER: Association of Principals of Colleges, Commonwealth Institute for the Education of Adults, South East Arts Association.

WRITINGS:

The Marriage of Anansewa (nonfiction), Longman, 1978.
Olu and the Smugglers (juvenile), Longman, 1978.
The African Child (nonficton), Longman, 1980.
Chaff on the Wind (novel), Macmillan, 1986.
Fafa (tentative title; novel), Macmillan, in press.

SIDELIGHTS: Chaff on the Wind was praised warmly by critic Robert Brain of *Times Literary Supplement*. It is the story of two young men of Gambia who leave their rural villages for an urban life on the coast. The impact of the city upon these two very different personalities provides the reader with, according to Brain, "an unpretentious picture . . . of the West African coast in the 1930s." The critic was charmed by the colorful, sensuous setting that Ebou Dibba evoked for the Western reader, and by the variety of delightful characters who lived in this "shadowy world peopled by the relics of a more elegant European past."

Dibba told *CA:* "A love of the written word and a fascination with the beauty and transience of this world have been the prime sources of my motivation for writing. An interest in music (including drums and dancing) underpins all I do and feel. Africa and its mysteries, however, remain the abiding source from which I drink the water of inspiration.

"Although my writing is based on a real background, namely Gambia and its people, the substance and execution of that reality is fictional. I research the period I am writing first to make sure that customs and cultural, political, and social details are approximately right; thereafter I allow my imagination free range to produce something which I hope is at once fictional and familiar. This has not prevented some people from thinking they can identify characters in, say, *Chaff on the Wind*. Although it is the right of such people to see a work as they wish, it has not been my intention to use real people as characters in the book. The novel is certainly not autobiographical; that is one of the reasons it takes place in the 1930s.

"I left Gambia on a government scholarship to study in England and for no other reason. I find the Gambians gentle, articulate, intelligent, and adaptable. I am impressed by the fact that though they are from a small country (fewer than one million inhabitants), a number of Gambians seem able to work abroad and hold responsible and creative jobs ranging from acting and music (traditional and popular) to academic and administrative posts (as in certain departments and branches of the United Nations)."

BIOGRAPHICAL/CRITICAL SOURCES:

PERIODICALS

Times Literary Supplement, September 5, 1986.
West Africa, October 6, 1986.

* * *

DICKENS, Peter (Gerald Charles) 1917-1987

PERSONAL: Born June 4, 1917, in London, England; died May 25, 1987; son of Gerald (an admiral) and Pearl (Birch) Dickens; married Mary Blagrove, January 25, 1960; children: Carola Dickens Crocker, Marion Dickens Lloyd, Mark. *Education:* Attended Royal Naval College, Dartmouth, 1931-34.

CAREER: Royal Navy, career officer, 1931-64, commander of torpedo boat operations in World War II, fought at Dunkirk and Normandy, commander of a destroyer in the Mediterranean, captain of Chatham Naval Dockyard, retiring as captain.

AWARDS, HONORS: Military—Distinguished Service Order; Distinguished Service Cross; member of Order of the British Empire, 1942; mentioned in despatches.

WRITINGS:

H.M.S. Hesperus, Profile Publications, 1972.
Narvik: Battles in the Fjords, Naval Institute Press, 1974.
Night Action: MTB Flotilla at War, Naval Institute Press, 1974.
SAS, The Jungle Frontier: 22 Special Air Service Regiment in the Borneo Campaign, 1963-1966, Arms & Armour Press, 1983.

BIOGRAPHICAL/CRITICAL SOURCES:

BOOKS

Cooper, Bryan, *The Battle of the Torpedo Boats,* Macdonald & Co., 1970.
Scott, Peter, *The Battle of the Narrow Seas,* Country Life, 1945.
Scott, Peter, *The Eye of the Wind,* Hodder & Stoughton, 1961.

PERIODICALS

Times Literary Supplement, July 13, 1984.

OBITUARIES:

PERIODICALS

Times (London), May 26, 1987.*

* * *

DICKINS, A. S. M.
See DICKINS, Anthony (Stewart Mackay)

* * *

DICKINS, Anthony (Stewart Mackay) 1914-1987
(A. S. M. Dickins)

OBITUARY NOTICE: Born November 1, 1914; died after a long illness, November 26, 1987. Chess expert, musician, magazine founder, translator, and author. Talented in many fields, Dickens was prominent in the English literary world as a young man, helping to found the periodical *Poetry London*. He also performed as a pianist and organist. He spent time in India as secretary to the Maharajah of Bharnagar and published a highly regarded translation of poetry by Omar Khayyam in *London Magazine*. Later Dickins became known as an expert on chess problems, founding Q Press in 1967 to publish books on the subject. His works include *One Hundred Classics of the Chessboard* (with H. Ebert), *A Guide to Fairy Chess,* and *The Serieshelpmate* (with John M. Rice).

OBITUARIES AND OTHER SOURCES:

BOOKS

Golombek's Encyclopedia of Chess, Crown, 1977.

PERIODICALS

Times (London), November 30, 1987.

* * *

DIEFENDORF, Barbara B(oonstoppel) 1946-

PERSONAL: Born December 19, 1946, in Oakland, Calif.; married in 1972. *Education:* University of California, Berkeley, A.B., 1968, M.A., 1970, Ph.D., 1978.

ADDRESSES: Office—Department of History, Boston University, Boston, Mass. 02215.

CAREER: University of New Hampshire, Durham, assistant professor of humanities, 1979-80; Boston University, Boston, Mass., assistant professor, 1980-86, associate professor of history, 1986—.

MEMBER: American Historical Association, Renaissance Society of America, Society for French Historical Studies, Sixteenth Century Studies Conference, Society for Reformation Research.

AWARDS, HONORS: Fellow of National Endowment for the Humanities, 1983-84, and American Council of Learned Societies, 1987-88.

WRITINGS:

Paris City Councillors in the Sixteenth Century, Princeton University Press, 1983.

Contributor to history journals.

WORK IN PROGRESS: Religious Conflicts in Sixteenth-Century Paris.

BIOGRAPHICAL/CRITICAL SOURCES:

PERIODICALS

American Historical Review, February, 1984.
Times Literary Supplement, July 1, 1983.

* * *

DIEFENTHALER, Jon 1943-

PERSONAL: Born February 21, 1943, in Milwaukee, Wis.; son of Marlin George (a business executive) and Bernice (a teacher; maiden name, Scheiderer) Diefenthaler; married Linda Reineck (a consultant), December 30, 1967; children: Andrew, Katie, Lisa, Heidi. *Education:* Concordia Senior College, B.A., 1965; Concordia Seminary, M.Div., 1969; Washington University, St. Louis, M.A., 1970; University of Iowa, Ph.D., 1976. *Politics:* Independent.

ADDRESSES: Home—608 South Poplar Ave., Waynesboro, Va. 22980. *Office*—Bethany Lutheran Church, 100 Maple Ave., Waynesboro, Va. 22980.

CAREER: Ordained Lutheran minister, 1971; Concordia Theological Seminary, Springfield, Ill., assistant professor of historical theology, 1972-75; Bethany Lutheran Church, Waynesboro, Va., pastor, 1975—. Visiting professor at Lutheran Theological Seminary, Gettysburg, Pa., 1984-85.

MEMBER: American Society of Church History, American Historical Association, Organization of American Historians.

WRITINGS:

H. Richard Niebuhr: A Lifetime of Reflections on the Church and the World, Mercer University Press, 1986.

WORK IN PROGRESS: Editing an anthology of some of the occasional writings of H. Richard Niebuhr, for Mercer University Press; research on the historical development of Lutheranism in the southeastern United States.

SIDELIGHTS: Jon Diefenthaler told *CA:* "I am a clergyman and scholar, seeking to work in the field of American religious history in a way that relates to and aids interpretation of the church in which I am directly involved. My interest in Richard Niebuhr developed in connection with my work on a doctoral dissertation under Professor Sidney Mead at the University of Iowa. Persons familiar with the 'Niebuhr' name often confuse Richard with his brother Reinhold. Of the two brothers, Reinhold was the one who received the greater acclaim, flamboyantly championing the cause of justice in a society gripped by the Great Depression and for nearly four decades, assuming formal leadership roles in religious and political circles. Richard did not enjoy and so avoided this kind of limelight. Yet his insights were often more profound and his influence no less enduring.

"Still widely read are such major works of Richard Niebuhr as *Christ and Culture* and *The Social Sources of Denominationalism*. My approach to him is that of a historian, and my book examines his theological convictions in the light of his upbringing and early churchmanship in the comparatively small denomination of German immigrants known as the Evangelical Synod of North America. As crucial to the further development of these convictions, I emphasize Niebuhr's responses to the politics of World War II and the 'return to religion' fueled by the Cold War of the 1950s. At all points in his life, I see him struggling to determine and to express the church's proper relationship to the world. The Christian Gospel, as he saw it, compelled the Church to involve itself with the problems of secular society. But to bring about any real change, he felt it must at the same time remain true to the unique perspective provided by that Gospel. Every age has in fact faced a similar dilemma, and from Richard Niebuhr the Church of today has much to learn."

* * *

DINSDALE, Tim(othy Kay) 1924-1987

OBITUARY NOTICE—See index for *CA* sketch: Born September 27, 1924, in Aberyswyth, Wales; died December 14, 1987. Engineer, explorer, and author. For nearly thirty years Dinsdale had been tracking the legendary Loch Ness monster of Scotland. An aeronautical engineer by profession, he abandoned his twenty-year career developing and testing jet engines in 1959 to pursue the phenomenon affectionately known as "Nessie." In 1960 Dinsdale captured on film his sighting of what the Royal Air Force later determined was most likely an "animate" object. In between scouting ventures around the waters of Loch Ness and Loch Morar in his boat *Water Horse,* Dinsdale supported himself through lecturing and writing. He was the author of *Loch Ness Monster, The Story of the Loch Ness Monster, Project Water Horse, Man Beast,* and *Monster Hunt*—first published in England as *The Leviathans.*

OBITUARIES AND OTHER SOURCES:

BOOKS

The Writers Directory: 1986-1988, St. James Press, 1986.

PERIODICALS

Times (London), December 17, 1987.

DOGGETT, Rachel H. 1943-

PERSONAL: Born October 7, 1943, in Bellefonte, Pa.; married LeRoy E. Doggett, August 7, 1965. *Education:* University of Michigan, B.A., 1965; Catholic University of America, M.S.L.S., 1976.

ADDRESSES: Home—7001 Barkwater Court, Bethesda, Md. 20817. *Office*—Folger Shakespeare Library, 201 East Capitol St., Washington, D.C. 20003.

CAREER: Management trainee at Maritime Administration, 1965-66; Washington National Symphony, Washington, D.C., musical administrator, 1966-67; Folger Shakespeare Library, Washington, D.C., accessions librarian, 1967—.

MEMBER: Bibliographical Society of America, American Printing History Association, Smithsonian Institution, Friends of Music (member of steering committee), Bibliographical Society (London, England).

AWARDS, HONORS: Virginia LeMar Book Prize from Folger Shakespeare Library, 1978.

WRITINGS:

(Editor with Susan Jaskot and Robert Rand) *Time: The Greatest Innovator,* Folger Library, 1986.

* * *

DORFF, Elliot N. 1943-

PERSONAL: Born June 24, 1943, in Milwaukee, Wis.; son of Sol (a civil engineer) and Anne (a teacher; maiden name, Nelson) Dorff; married Marlynn Wertheimer; children: Tammy, Michael, Havi, Jonathan. *Education:* Columbia University, A.B. (summa cum laude), 1965, Ph.D., 1971; Jewish Theological Seminary of America, M.H.L., 1968, Rabbi, 1970.

ADDRESSES: Office—Department of Graduate Studies, University of Judaism, 15600 Mulholland Dr., Los Angeles, Calif. 90077.

CAREER: University of Judaism, Los Angeles, Calif., assistant professor, 1971-76, associate professor, 1976-85, professor of philosophy, 1985—, professor in residence at Camp Ramah, 1972—, dean of graduate studies, 1974—, provost, 1980—, coordinator of Earl Warren Institute of Ethics and Human Relations, 1984—. Lecturer at University of California, Los Angeles, 1974—, Fuller Theological Seminary, 1976, 1977, and University of Southern California, 1987; visiting associate professor at University of California, Irvine, 1976. Member of National Youth Commission, United Synagogue of America, 1971—; member of Conservative Movement Committee on Jewish Law and Standards, 1984—, and Commission on Conservative Philosophy, 1985—. Member of Board of Rabbis of Southern California. Member of board of directors of American Jewish Committee of Los Angeles, 1972-74, Hillel Council, 1974-76, and Jewish Family Service, 1985—; member of Los Angeles Priest-Rabbi Dialogue, 1974—; coordinator of Los Angeles Chevrah, 1982-85; member of Commission on Spirituality, Council on Jewish Life, Jewish Federation Council of Greater Los Angeles, 1983—; chairman of Jewish Hospice Commission, 1985—.

MEMBER: International Association of Jewish Lawyers and Jurists, Academy for Jewish Philosophy, American Academy of Religion, American Philosophical Association, Association of Jewish Studies (member of board of directors, 1982-85), Jewish Law Association, Rabbinical Assembly, Religious Education Association, Society for Values in Higher Education, Phi Beta Kappa.

WRITINGS:

Jewish Law and Modern Ideology, United Synagogue of America, 1970.

(With Sheldon Dorph and Victoria Kelman) *A First Course in Hebrew Bible Study,* Los Angeles Bureau of Jewish Education, 1977.

Conservative Judaism: Our Ancestors to Our Descendants, United Synagogue of America, 1977.

(With Arthur Rosett) *A Living Tree: The Roots and Growth of Jewish Law,* State University of New York Press, 1987.

CONTRIBUTOR

Helga Croner and Leon Klenicki, editors, *Issues in the Jewish-Christian Dialogue: Jewish Perspectives on Covenant, Mission, and Witness,* Paulist Press, 1979.

Stephen Garfinkel, editor, *Slow Down and Live: A Guide to Shabbat Observance and Enjoyment,* United Synagogue Youth, 1982.

Seymour Siegel and Elliot Gertel, editors, *God in the Teachings of Conservative Judaism,* Rabbinical Assembly, 1985.

The Poor Among Us: Jewish Tradition and Social Policy, American Jewish Committee, 1986.

Ronald L. Numbers and Darrel W. Amundsen, editors, *Caring and Curing: Health and Medicine in the Western Religious Traditions,* Macmillan, 1986.

Nuna Cardin, editor, *The Seminary Centennial Volume,* Jewish Theological Seminary of America, 1987.

Daniel Landes, editor, *Omnicide,* Simon Wiesenthal Center, Yeshiva University, 1988.

John Hick, editor, *Three Faiths: One God,* Macmillan, 1988.

WORK IN PROGRESS: "The Concept of God in the Conservative Movement," to be included in a book edited by Mordecai Waxman, publication by Rabbinical Assembly expected in 1988; "Honoring Aged Fathers and Mothers," for *Reconstructionist,* publication expected in 1988.

SIDELIGHTS: Elliot N. Dorff told *CA:* "*Conservative Judaism: Our Ancestors to Our Descendants,* although originally designed for teenagers, has been used for many adult education classes in synagogues as well as in university and seminary classes as an explanation of Conservative Judaism.

"*A Living Tree* grew out of the course in Jewish law that Arthur Rosett and I have taught at the University of California Law School since 1974. It has been used in typescript form in approximately ten law schools, although the book includes much explanatory material to make it understandable to those who have not had a background in Judaism or law.

"My interests in Jewish law are really part of my broader interests in Judaism and in the normative experience, whether the norm is expressed in morals (my dissertation topic), law, custom, or some other form."

* * *

DORFMAN, Ariel 1942-

BRIEF ENTRY: Born May 6, 1942, in Buenos Aires, Argentina; naturalized Chilean citizen, 1967. Chilean educator, journalist, and author. Dorfman, who has taught literature and international studies in Chile and the United States, is known

for his outspoken denunciations of Chilean dictator Augusto Pinochet. Exiled upon Pinochet's accession in 1973, Dorfman eventually settled in the United States, where he writes critical articles for American newspapers and expresses his country's anguish under oppression in fiction and nonfiction books. Among his writings are the essay collections *How to Read Donald Duck: Imperialist Ideology in the Disney Comic* (Idea Books, 1975), which he wrote with Armand Mattelart, and *The Empire's Old Clothes* (Pantheon, 1983), and the novels *Widows* (Pantheon, 1983) and *The Last Song of Manuel Sendero* (Penguin, 1987). *Addresses: Office*—International Studies, Duke University, Durham, N.C. 27706. *Agent*—Andrew Wiley, 250 West 57th St., Suite 2106, New York, N.Y. 10017.

BIOGRAPHICAL/CRITICAL SOURCES:

PERIODICALS

Chicago Tribune, March 18, 1987.
Los Angeles Times Book Review, June 12, 1983, April 5, 1987.
Nation, February 11, 1978, September 24, 1983, October 18, 1986.
New York Times Book Review, May 8, 1983, July 24, 1983, February 15, 1987.
Washington Post Book World, June 12, 1983, April 5, 1987.

* * *

DORSEY, Hebe 1925-1987

OBITUARY NOTICE: First name is pronounced "ay-bay"; born March 5, 1925, in Sousse, Tunisia; died of cancer, December 28 (some sources say December 27), 1987, in Neuilly-sur-Seine (one source says Paris), France; buried in France. Fashion writer and journalist. Dorsey was considered an innovator in fashion writing, reviewing fashion shows with the same critical eye another writer might apply to a play. She was based in Paris, and for about forty years she worked for the city's *International Herald Tribune,* beginning around 1950 when it was still the European edition of the now-defunct *New York Herald Tribune*. She became fashion editor in 1970. Dorsey also wrote for other publications, including a monthly column for the French edition of *Vogue* and articles on fashion and decorating for such periodicals as the *New York Times*. At her death she was scheduled to receive an award for international journalism from the Council of Fashion Designers of America. Dorsey compiled articles from the early days of the *Herald* in a collection titled *The Age of Opulence: The Belle Epoque in the Paris Herald, 1890-1914*.

OBITUARIES AND OTHER SOURCES:

BOOKS

World of Fashion: People, Places, Resources, Bowker, 1976.

PERIODICALS

Los Angeles Times, December 30, 1987.
Newsweek, January 11, 1988.
New York Times, December 29, 1987.
Washington Post, December 29, 1987.

* * *

DOUGLAS, Althea (Cleveland McCoy) 1926-

PERSONAL: Born December 25, 1926, in Moncton, New Brunswick, Canada; daughter of George E. (a railroad executive) and Nan (Chapman) McCoy; married J. Creighton Douglas (an executive), 1948. *Education:* McGill University, B.Sc., 1947, M.A., 1958; further graduate study at Carleton University, 1975-77.

ADDRESSES: Office—Althea Douglas Consultants, 64 Old Mill Rd., Toronto, Ontario, Canada M8X 1G8.

CAREER: McGill University, Montreal, Quebec, lecturer in English, 1947-59, research editor of "Burney Project," 1960-77, archivist of Penfield Collection at Neurological Institute, 1978-81; Althea Douglas Consultants, Toronto, Ontario, writer and editor, 1982—.

MEMBER: Association of Canadian Archivists, Association of Professional Genealogists (United States), Society of Genealogists (England), Ontario Genealogical Society, New Brunswick Genealogical Society, Toronto Area Archivists Group.

AWARDS, HONORS: Canada Council grants, 1961-64, 1965.

WRITINGS:

(With Joyce Hemlow and J. M. M. Burgess) *A Catalogue of the Burney Family Correspondence, 1749-1878,* New York Public Library and McGill Queens University Press, 1971.

The Journals and Letters of Fanny Burney (Madame d'Arblay), 1791-1840, Clarendon Press, (assistant editor) Volume I, 1972, (associate editor) Volume II, 1972, (assistant editor) Volume III, 1973, (research editor) Volume IV, 1973, (assistant editor and indexer) Volumes V-VI, 1975, (text editor) Volume VII, 1978, (assistant editor and indexer) Volume VIII, 1980, (text and research editor) Volumes IX-X, 1982, (assistant editor) Volumes XI-XII, 1982.

Contributor to history and genealogy magazines.

WORK IN PROGRESS: Editing *Diaries of Working Women, 1874, 1881, 1906, 1914;* contributing to a series of handbooks on genealogy and conservation, for the Ontario Genealogy Society.

SIDELIGHTS: Althea Douglas told *CA:* "Cataloging the Burney Papers, annotating Fanny Burney's journals and letters, and restoring many of her mutilated and edited manuscripts turned me into both an archivist and a genealogist. In Toronto I set up Althea Douglas Consultants, offering consulting services in both fields, as well as general editing and writing. In a number of published articles, I have tried to set down some of what we learned during that twenty-five-year project, but technical writing and editing have provided a profitable sideline.

"As I came to know Fanny Burney, I found myself in sharp disagreement with the critics who called her a 'prig' or a 'prude.' Though it is true that she always showed a concern for appearances and a sense of propriety, it never stopped her from doing highly unconventional things. She wrote successful novels in an age when many young women were forbidden even to read such works. She resigned a post in England's Court, giving up secure employment that few people of her lowly social position could even aspire to, yet she was granted a small lifetime pension by the Queen and retained her friendship. She then went off and married a French emigre who was a Catholic and, even worse, a 'constitutionalist'—a friend of the radical thinkers who had sought to achieve a constitutional monarchy in France. The Queen, however, continued to receive her at Court, and to pay her the pension.

"Fanny managed this by always behaving, superficially, in a most orthodox and proper manner. I found it quite delightful

to watch how, while presenting a non-threatening image to the established order, she managed to lead a remarkably unconventional life. Even her niece Charlotte Barrett—a very proper Victorian who, after Fanny's death, severely edited her journals—could not hide Fanny's spirit.

"About the time my colleagues and I finished the 'Burney Project,' I inherited several diaries kept by women relatives over short spans of time when they were 'working women,' two from the nineteenth century and two predating World War I. I originally transcribed them for the family. Then, as today, working outside the home did not exempt women from domestic chores, though they worked far longer hours than we do now. I feel these diaries could provide interesting basic material for researchers. Each needs to be placed in context, however, and that work keeps being delayed while I write service manuals and brochures for paying clients.

"The genealogy book is metamorphosing into a series of handbooks on both genealogical sources and conservation of artifacts, manuscripts, and photographs, part of a series proposed by the Ontario Genealogical Society."

* * *

DREYFUS, Kay 1942-

PERSONAL: Born May 26, 1942, in Ballarat, Victoria, Australia; daughter of Edward Frank (a musician) and Emily Gilbert (a musician; maiden name, Hornsby) Lucas; married George Dreyfus (a musician), November 4, 1968; children: Jonathan. *Education:* University of Melbourne, B.Mus., 1963, M.Mus., 1966, Ph.D., 1972.

ADDRESSES: Office—Grainger Museum, University of Melbourne, Parkville, Victoria 3052, Australia.

CAREER: University of Melbourne, Parkville, Victoria, Australia, curator of Grainger Museum, 1974—, research fellow, 1979-86, senior research fellow, 1987—. Member of UNESCO International Committee on Museums.

MEMBER: International Society of Musicologists, Musicological Society of Australia.

WRITINGS:

Percy Grainger's Kipling Settings, University of Western Australia Press, 1980.
(Editor) *Farthest North of Humanness: Letters of Percy Grainger, 1901-1914,* Macmillan, 1984.

SIDELIGHTS: Kay Dreyfus told *CA:* "My decision to edit a book of the letters of Percy Grainger arose directly out of my appointment as curator of the Grainger Museum at the University of Melbourne in 1974. Grainger was born in Australia in 1882 but lived abroad most of his life, first in Germany, from 1895 to 1900, then London, England, until 1914, then in the United States, where he became a citizen in 1917 and died in 1961. When I went to the museum I knew little more about him than most other people at that time: that he was a rather eccentric fellow who played the piano and composed a rather well-known piece called 'Country Gardens.' I, and most people, know a bit more about him now.

"It did not take me long to realize that the museum—which Grainger himself conceived, gave to the university, paid for, put his things in, and saw opened in 1939—was a unique cultural resource and that the collections were rich and resonant beyond the individual who had put them together. The letters were particularly fascinating for me as a writer: lively and well written, full of passion and enthusiasm and always reflecting the broader world of events and personalities. The letters were also written in a variety of languages other than English (though including English). These are published in translation. I liked the youthful letters, and since the Edwardian period, when Grainger lived in London, was also fascinating to me I decided to limit the first volume of his letters to that London period, from 1901 to 1914.

"As a concert pianist Grainger toured extensively in Britain and Europe, meeting or playing with many of the leading musical personalities of the day, commenting on the musical life as he observed it. He came twice to Australia during this period, and his responses to the country of his birth are of particular interest to Australian readers. He also made his triumphant public debut as a composer during this period. For me, the book was an act of faith in one of Australia's most interesting and idiosyncratic cultural figures. The letters are a form of cultural and social history as well as a completely uninhibited personal statement by a passionate and committed human being."

* * *

DUBITSKY, Cora Marie 1933-

PERSONAL: Surname originally Dubecki; surname changed by customs officials; born January 25, 1933, in Frackville, Pa.; daughter of Frank (a miner) and Sophia (a housewife; maiden name, Churko) Dubecki. *Education:* Notre Dame College of Maryland, B.A., 1963; Loyola University of Chicago, M.R.E., 1970; Indiana University—Bloomington, Ed.D., 1976. *Politics:* "Waiting for a third party for independent thinkers." *Religion:* Roman Catholic.

ADDRESSES: Home—3515 Washington Blvd., Arlington, Va. 22201. *Office*—American Catholic Lay Network, 3017 Fourth St. N.E., Washington, D.C. 20017.

CAREER: Teacher, 1950-70; St. Meinrad School of Theology, St. Meinrad, Ind., graduate assistant, 1970-74, associate professor of pastoral studies, 1974-82; Religious Education Institute, Fort Wayne, Ind., teacher trainer, 1983-84; administrator of human resources for Space Communications Co., 1985-87; American Catholic Lay Network, Washington, D.C., director, 1987—. Member of board of directors of Association of Professors of Education in Ministry, 1980-82.

MEMBER: Association of Professors in Ministry.

WRITINGS:

Building the Faith Community, Paulist Press, 1974.
The Kingdom of God: Challenge for Today's Christians, Sheed & Ward, 1987.
The American Bishops and the Old Testament Prophets, Mercury Press, 1988.

Contributor to religious education journals, including *Lumen Vitae, Journal of Religious Education,* and *Religious Teachers' Journal.*

SIDELIGHTS: Cora Marie Dubitsky told *CA:* "I enjoy developing new approaches to subjects and issues. *The Kingdom of God* presents an original method of interpretation, with schema based on psychologist Jean Piaget's stages of cognitive and moral development. I have also developed an original approach to the teaching of reading, and I would like to produce a videotape and workbook on the subject."

DUCHACEK, Ivo D(uka) 1913-1988
(Ivo Duka; Martin Cermak, a pseudonym)

OBITUARY NOTICE—See index for *CA* sketch: Born February 27, 1913, in Prostejov, Czechoslovakia; immigrated to United States, 1949, naturalized citizen; died of cancer of the pharynx, March 1, 1988, in Kent, Conn. Government official, educator, radio broadcaster, and author. As the pseudonymous Martin Cermak, Duchacek narrated the weekly commentary "Sunday Notebook" transmitted over the Voice of America—a radio service of the U.S. Information Agency—to Czechoslovakia. A refugee from that country following its Communist takeover in 1948, he concealed his true identity from his radio audience for the entire thirty-eight years he was in broadcasting.

Before he fled from his homeland in 1948, Duchacek was engaged in the government's diplomatic service and as a member of its Parliament; during the last year of World War II he served as liaison officer to the U.S. Army. After he arrived in the United States, Duchacek lectured and taught at a number of educational facilities, including Yale University and the City College of the City University of New York, where he received two teaching awards. Duchacek was the author or coauthor of several books, sometimes under the name Ivo Duka. Among them are *The Secret of Two Feathers, Martin and His Friend From Outer Space, Nations and Men, Rights and Liberties in the World Today, Power-Maps: Comparative Politics of Constitutions,* and *Conflict and Cooperation Among Nations,* with K. W. Thompson. Additionally, he contributed to various political science journals and other publications.

OBITUARIES AND OTHER SOURCES:

BOOKS

The Writers Directory: 1986-1988, St. James Press, 1986.

PERIODICALS

New York Times, March 3, 1988.

* * *

DUIS, Perry R. 1943-

PERSONAL: Born August 18, 1943, in Sterling, Ill.; son of Frank R. (a railroad machinist) and Pearl (a housewife; maiden name, Hemminger) Duis; married Cathlyn Schallhorn (a writer), October 1, 1976; children: Timothy. *Education:* Northwestern University, B.A., 1965; University of Chicago, M.A., 1966, Ph.D., 1970.

ADDRESSES: Office—Department of History, University of Illinois at Chicago Circle, Box 4348, Chicago, Ill. 60680.

CAREER: University of Illinois at Chicago Circle, Chicago, Ill., member of history faculty, 1971—.

WRITINGS:

Chicago: Creating New Traditions, Chicago Historical Society, 1976.
The Saloon: Public Drinking in Chicago and Boston, 1880-1920, University of Chicago Press, 1983.

* * *

DUKA, Ivo
See DUCHACEK, Ivo D(uka)

DUMKE, Edward J. 1946-

PERSONAL: Born March 10, 1946, in San Mateo, Calif.; son of Donald S. and Dorothy (Swett) Dumke. *Education:* San Francisco State College (now University), B.A. and Teaching Credential, 1969; Church Divinity School of the Pacific, M.Div., 1975.

ADDRESSES: Home—805 Barneson Ave., San Mateo, Calif. 94402.

CAREER: Ordained Episcopal minister, 1976; high school history teacher in San Mateo, Calif., 1969-71; Trinity Episcopal Cathedral, Sacramento, Calif., minister, 1976-78; minister in San Mateo, Calif., 1979-85; writer. National chairman of Committee for the Release of Patricia Hearst; director of St. Dorothy's Association; vice-president of Peninsula Halfway House.

WRITINGS:

The Serpent Beguiled Me and I Ate: A Heavenly Diet for Saints and Sinners, Doubleday, 1986.

WORK IN PROGRESS: A mystery novel.

SIDELIGHTS: According to *Los Angeles Times* reviewer Jonathan Kirsch, Edward J. Dumke's book "explores the most intimate reasons for overeating, and suggests an approach to eating that addresses our deepest spiritual needs." In *The Serpent Beguiled Me and I Ate,* Dumke postulates that, historically, the act of eating can be interpreted as an act of communion with the sacred, particularly from the Christian perspective. Kirsch quoted Dumke: "Dieting has become a new religion in American culture, and each new diet becomes a new cult with a new promise for salvation." The author presents a variety of diet plans, which are neither ridiculous nor dangerous, accompanied by spiritual meditations. The *Los Angeles Times* concluded: "Dumke's exceptional book is graced with authentic spiritual revelation and an uncompromising integrity."

BIOGRAPHICAL/CRITICAL SOURCES:

PERIODICALS

Los Angeles Times, September 21, 1986.

* * *

DUNBAR, Alice
See NELSON, Alice Ruth Moore Dunbar

* * *

DUNBAR, Alice Moore
See NELSON, Alice Ruth Moore Dunbar

* * *

DUNBAR, Paul Laurence 1872-1906

PERSONAL: Born June 27, 1872, in Dayton, Ohio; died of tuberculosis, February 9, 1906, in Dayton, Ohio; buried in Woodland Cemetery, Dayton, Ohio; son of Joshua (a former slave, soldier, and plasterer) and Matilda Glass (a former slave and laundress; maiden name, Burton) Dunbar; married Alice Ruth Moore (a writer and teacher), March 6, 1898 (separated, 1902). *Education:* Educated in Dayton, Ohio.

ADDRESSES: Home—219 North Summit St., Dayton, Ohio.

CAREER: Writer. Worked as elevator operator; editor of *Dayton Tattler* in Dayton, Ohio, 1890; court messenger, 1896; assistant clerk at Library of Congress in Washington, D.C., 1897-98.

WRITINGS:

POETRY

Oak and Ivy, Press of United Brethren Publishing House, 1893 (also see below).
Majors and Minors, Hadley & Hadley, 1896 (also see below).
Lyrics of Lowly Life (includes poems from *Oak and Ivy* and *Majors and Minors;* also see above), introduction by William Dean Howells, Dodd, 1896, reprinted, Arno, 1969.
Lyrics of the Hearthside, Dodd, 1899, reprinted, AMS Press, 1972.
Poems of Cabin and Field, Dodd, 1899, reprinted, AMS Press, 1972.
Candle-lightin' Time, Dodd, 1901, reprinted, AMS Press, 1972.
Lyrics of Love and Laughter, Dodd, 1903.
When Malindy Sings, Dodd, 1903, reprinted, AMS Press, 1972.
Li'l Gal, Dodd, 1904, reprinted, AMS Press, 1972.
Chris'mus Is a Comin', and Other Poems, Dodd, 1905.
Howdy, Honey, Howdy, Dodd, 1905, reprinted, AMS Press, 1972.
Lyrics of Sunshine and Shadow, Dodd, 1905, reprinted, AMS Press, 1972.
A Plantation Portrait, Dodd, 1905.
Joggin'erlong, Dodd, 1906, reprinted, Mnemosyne Publishing, 1969.
The Complete Poems of Paul Laurence Dunbar, Dodd, 1913, reprinted, 1980.
Speakin' o' Christmas, and Other Christmas and Special Poems, Dodd, 1914, reprinted, AMS Press, 1975.
Little Brown Baby: Poems for Young People, edited and with biographical sketch by Bertha Rodgers, illustrated by Erick Berry, Dodd, 1940, reprinted, 1966.
I Greet the Dawn: Poems, selected and with introduction by Ashley Bryan, Atheneum, 1978.

FICTION

The Uncalled (novel), Dodd, 1898, reprinted, AMS Press, 1972.
Folks From Dixie (short stories), Dodd, 1898, reprinted, Books for Libraries, 1969.
The Love of Landry (novel), Dodd, 1900, reprinted, Literature House, 1970.
The Strength of Gideon, and Other Stories, Dodd, 1900, reprinted, Arno, 1969.
The Fanatics (novel), Dodd, 1901, reprinted, Literature House, 1970.
The Sport of the Gods (novel), Dodd, 1902, reprinted, with introduction by Kenny J. Williams, 1981 (published in England as *The Jest of Fate: A Story of Negro Life,* Jarrold, 1902).
In Old Plantation Days (short stories), Dodd, 1903, reprinted, Negro Universities Press, 1969.
The Heart of the Happy Hollow (short stories), Dodd, 1904, reprinted, Books for Libraries, 1970.
The Best Stories of Paul Laurence Dunbar, edited and with introduction by Benjamin Brawley, Dodd, 1938.

PLAYS

"Uncle Eph's Christmas" (one-act musical), produced in 1900.

Also author of lyrics to songs in musical plays such as "In Dahomey."

OTHER

The Life and Works of Paul Laurence Dunbar, edited and with biography by Lida Keck Wiggins, J. L. Nichols, 1907, reprinted, Kraus Reprint, 1971.
The Letters of Paul and Alice Dunbar: A Private History (two volumes), edited by Eugene Wesley Metcalf, University Microfilms, 1974.
The Paul Laurence Dunbar Reader, edited by Jay Martin and Gossie H. Hudson, Dodd, 1975.

Author of lyrics to songs such as "Jes Lak White Folk," "Down De Lovers Lane: Plantation Croon," and "Who Knows."

Work represented in anthologies.

Contributor to periodicals, including *Bookman, Century, Detroit Free Press, Nation,* and *Saturday Evening Post.*

SIDELIGHTS: Paul Laurence Dunbar is widely acknowledged as the first important black poet in American literature. He enjoyed his greatest popularity in the early twentieth century following the publication of dialectic verse in collections such as *Majors and Minors* and *Lyrics of Lowly Life.* But the dialectic poems constitute only a small portion of Dunbar's canon, which is replete with novels, short stories, essays, and many poems in standard English. In its entirety, Dunbar's literary body has been acclaimed as an impressive representation of black life in turn-of-the-century America. As Dunbar's friend James Weldon Johnson noted in the preface to his *Book of American Poetry:* "Paul Laurence Dunbar stands out as the first poet from the Negro race in the United States to show a combined mastery over poetic material and poetic technique, to reveal innate literary distinction in what he wrote, and to maintain a high level of performance. He was the first to rise to a height from which he could take a perspective view of his own race. He was the first to see objectively its humor, its superstitions, its short-comings; the first to feel sympathetically its heart-wounds, its yearnings, its aspirations, and to voice them all in a purely literary form."

Dunbar began showing literary promise while still in high school in Dayton, Ohio, where he lived with his widowed mother. The only black in his class, he became class president and class poet. By 1889, two years before he graduated, he had already published poems in the *Dayton Herald* and worked as editor of the short-lived *Dayton Tattler,* a newspaper for blacks published by classmate Orville Wright, who later gained fame with brother Wilbur Wright as inventors of the airplane.

Dunbar aspired to a career in law, but his mother's meager financial situation precluded his university education. He consequently sought immediate employment with various Dayton businesses, including newspapers, only to be rejected because of his race. He finally settled for work as an elevator operator, a job that allowed him time to continue writing. At this time Dunbar produced articles, short stories, and poems, including several in the black-dialect style that later earned him fame.

In 1892 Dunbar was invited by one of his former teachers to address the Western Association of Writers then convening in Dayton. At the meeting Dunbar befriended James Newton Matthews, who subsequently praised Dunbar's work in a letter to an Illinois newspaper. Matthews's letter was eventually reprinted by newspapers throughout the country and thus brought Dunbar recognition outside Dayton. Among the readers of this

letter was poet James Whitcomb Riley, who then familiarized himself with Dunbar's work and wrote him a commendatory letter. Bolstered by the support of both Matthews and Riley, Dunbar decided to publish a collection of his poems. He obtained additional assistance from Orville Wright and then solicited a Dayton firm, United Brethren Publishing, that eventually printed the work, entitled *Oak and Ivy,* for a modest sum.

In *Oak and Ivy* Dunbar included his earliest dialect poems and many works in standard English. Among the latter is one of his most popular poems, "Sympathy," in which he expresses, in somber tone, the dismal plight of blacks in American society. In another standard English poem, "Ode to Ethiopia," he records the many accomplishments of black Americans and exhorts his fellow blacks to maintain their pride despite racial abuse. The popularity of these and other poems inspired Dunbar to devote himself more fully to writing.

Shortly after the publication of *Oak and Ivy* Dunbar was approached by attorney Charles A. Thatcher, an admirer sympathetic to Dunbar's financial strife, who offered to help finance Dunbar's college education. Dunbar, however, was greatly encouraged by sales of *Oak and Ivy* and so rejected Thatcher to pursue a literary career. Thatcher then applied himself to promoting Dunbar in nearby Toledo, Ohio, and helped him obtain work there reading his poetry at libraries and literary gatherings. Dunbar also found unexpected support from psychiatrist Henry A. Tobey, who helped distribute *Oak and Ivy* in Toledo and occasionally sent Dunbar much needed financial aid.

Tobey eventually teamed with Thatcher in publishing Dunbar's second verse collection, *Majors and Minors.* In this book Dunbar produced poems on a variety of themes and in several styles. He grouped the more ambitious poems, those written in standard English, under the heading "Majors," and he gathered the more superficial, dialect works as "Minors." Although Dunbar invested himself most fully in his standard poetry—which bore the influences of such poets as the English romantics and Americans such as Riley—it was the dialect verse that found greater favor with his predominantly white readership, and it was by virtue of these dialect poems that Dunbar gained increasing fame throughout the country. Instrumental to Dunbar's growing popularity was a highly positive, though extremely patronizing, review by eminent novelist William Dean Howells. Writing in *Harper's Weekly,* Howells praised Dunbar as "the first man of his color to study his race objectively" and commended the dialect poems as faithful representations of the black race.

Through Thatcher and Tobey, Dunbar met an agent and secured more public readings and a publishing contract. He then published *Lyrics of Lowly Life,* a poetry collection derived primarily from verse already featured in *Oak and Ivy* and *Majors and Minors.* This new volume sold impressively across America and established Dunbar as the nation's foremost black poet. On the strength of his recent acclaim Dunbar commenced a six-month reading tour of England. There he found publishers for a British edition of *Lyrics of Lowly Life* and befriended musician Samuel Coleridge-Taylor, with whom he then collaborated on the operetta "Dream Lovers."

When Dunbar returned to the United States in 1897 he obtained a clerkship at the Library of Congress in Washington, D.C. Soon afterwards he married fellow writer Alice Ruth Moore. Although his health suffered during the two years he lived in Washington, the period nonetheless proved fruitful for Dunbar. In 1898 he published his first short story collection, *Folks From Dixie,* in which he delineated the situation of blacks in both pre- and post-emancipation America. Although these tales, unlike some of his dialect verse, were often harsh examinations of racial prejudice, *Folks From Dixie* was well received upon publication.

Not so Dunbar's first novel, *The Uncalled,* which recalled Nathaniel Hawthorne's *The Scarlet Letter* in probing the spiritual predicament of a minister. Critics largely rejected *The Uncalled* as dull and unconvincing in its portrait of Frederick Brent, a pastor who had, in childhood, been abandoned by an alcoholic father and then raised by a zealously devout spinster, Hester Prime (Hawthorne's protagonist in *The Scarlet Letter* was named Hester Prine). After securing a pastor's post, Brent alienates church-goers by refusing to reproach an unwed mother. He resigns from his pastorship and departs for Cincinnati. After further misadventure—he ends his marriage engagement and encounters his father, now a wandering preacher—Brent finds fulfillment and happiness as minister in another congregation.

At the end of 1898, his health degenerating still further, Dunbar left the Library of Congress and commenced another reading tour. He published another verse collection, *Lyrics of the Hearthside,* and recovered any status he may have jeopardized with *The Uncalled.* In the spring of 1899, however, his health lapsed sufficiently to threaten his life. Ill with pneumonia, the already tubercular Dunbar was advised to rest in the mountains. He therefore moved to the Catskills in New York State, but he continued to write while recovering from his ailments.

In 1900, after a brief stay in Colorado, Dunbar returned to Washington, D.C. Shortly before his return he published another collection of tales, *The Strength of Gideon,* in which he continued to recount black life both before and after slavery. Reviewers at the time favored his pre-emancipation stories full of humor and sentiment, while ignoring more volatile accounts of abuse and injustice. More recently these latter stories have gained greater recognition from critics eager to substantiate Dunbar's opposition to racism.

Dunbar followed *The Strength of Gideon* with his second novel, *The Love of Landry,* about an ailing woman who arrives in Colorado for convalescence and finds true happiness with a cowboy. Like the earlier *Uncalled, The Love of Landry* was deemed unconvincing in its presentation of white characters and was dismissed as inferior to Dunbar's tales of blacks. Dunbar suffered further critical setback with his next novel, *The Fanatics,* about America at the beginning of the Civil War. Its central characters are from white families who differ in their North-South sympathies and spark a dispute in their Ohio community. *The Fanatics* was a commercial failure upon publication, and in the ensuing years it has continued to be regarded as a superficial, largely uncompelling work. Among the novel's many detractors is Robert Bone, who wrote in *The Negro in America* that Dunbar resorted to "caricature in his treatment of minor Negro characters" and that his stereotypic portraits of black characters only served to reinforce prejudice.

The Sport of the Gods, Dunbar's final novel, presents a far more critical and disturbing portrait of black America. The work centers on butler Berry Hamilton and his family. After Berry is wrongly charged with theft by his white employers, he is sentenced to ten years of prison labor. His remaining family—wife, son, and daughter—consequently find themselves targets of abuse in their southern community, and after being robbed by the local police they head north to Harlem. There they encounter further hardship and strife: the son be-

comes embroiled in the city's seamy nightlife and succumbs to alcoholism and crime; the naive daughter is exploited by fellow blacks and begins a questionable dancing career; and the mother, convinced that her husband's prison sentence has negated their marriage, weds an abusive profligate. A happy resolution is achieved only after Berry's accuser confesses, while dying, that his charge was fabricated, whereupon Berry is released from prison. He then travels north and finds his family in disarray. But the cruel second husband is then, conveniently, murdered, and the parental Hamiltons are reunited in matrimony.

Although its acclaim was hardly unanimous, *The Sport of the Gods* nonetheless earned substantial praise as a powerful novel of protest. By this time, however, Dunbar was experiencing considerable turmoil in his own life. Prior to writing *The Sport of the Gods* he had suffered another lapse of poor health, and he compounded his problems by resorting to alcohol. And after *The Sport of the Gods* appeared in 1902, Dunbar's marital situation—always troublesome—degenerated further due to his continued reliance on alcohol and to antagonism from his wife's parents.

Dunbar and his wife separated in 1902, but that separation only contributed to his continued physical and psychological decline. The next year, following a nervous breakdown and another bout of pneumonia, Dunbar managed to assemble another verse collection, *Lyrics of Love and Laughter*, and another short story collection, *In Old Plantation Days*. With *Lyrics of Love and Laughter* he confirmed his reputation as America's premier black poet. The volume contains both sentimental and somberly realistic expressions and depictions of black life, and it features both dialect and standard English verse. *In Old Plantation Days* is comprised of twenty-five stories set on a southern plantation during the days of slavery. Here Dunbar once again resorted to caricaturing his own race, portraying black slaves as faithful and obedient, slow-witted but good-natured workers appreciative of their benevolent white owners. Dunbar drew the ire of many critics for his stereotyped characters, and some of his detractors even alleged that he contributed to racist concepts while simultaneously disdaining such thinking.

If *In Old Plantation Days* was hardly a pioneering work, it was at least a lucrative publication and one that confirmed the preferences of much of Dunbar's public. With the short story collection *The Heart of Happy Hollow* he presented a greater variety of perspectives on aspects of black life in America, and he even included a tale on the moral folly of lynching. Dunbar followed *The Heart of Happy Hollow* with two more poetry collections, *Lyrics of Sunshine and Shadow* and *Howdy, Honey, Howdy,* both of which featured works from previous volumes.

Dunbar's health continued to decline even as he persisted in producing poems. But his reliance on alcohol to temper his chronic coughing only exacerbated his illness, and by the winter of 1905 he was fatally ill. He died on February 9, 1906, at age thirty-three.

In the years immediately following his death, Dunbar's standing as America's foremost black poet seemed assured, and his dialect poems were prized as supreme achievements in black American literature. In the ensuing decades, however, his reputation was damaged by scholars questioning the validity of his often stereotypic characterizations and his apparent unwillingness to sustain an anti-racist stance. Among his most vehement detractors from this period was Victor Lawson, whose *Dunbar Critically Examined* remains a provocative, if overly aggressive, study.

More recently Dunbar's stature has increased markedly. He is once again regarded as America's first great black poet, and his standard English poems are now, perhaps surprisingly, prized as his greatest achievements in verse. Contemporary champions include Addison Gayle, Jr., whose *Oak and Ivy: A Biography of Paul Laurence Dunbar,* is considered a key contribution to Dunbar studies, and black poet Nikki Giovanni, whose prose contribution to *A Singer in the Dawn: Reinterpretations of Paul Laurence Dunbar,* edited by Jay Martin, hails Dunbar as "a natural resource of our people." For Giovanni, as for other Dunbar scholars, his work constitutes both a history and a celebration of black life. "There is no poet, black or nonblack, who measures his achievement," she declared. "Even today. He wanted to be a writer and he wrote."

MEDIA ADAPTATIONS: Portions of Dunbar's work were adapted by Pauline Myers for the stage production "The World of My America: A One Woman Dramatization," and by Vinnette Carroll for the stage production "When Hell Freezes Over, I'll Skate."

BIOGRAPHICAL/CRITICAL SOURCES:

Bone, Robert, *Down Home: A History of Afro-American Short Fiction From Its Beginnings to the End of the Harlem Renaissance,* Putnam, 1975.

Brawley, Benjamin, *Paul Laurence Dunbar: Poet of His People,* University of North Carolina Press, 1936.

Brown, Sterling, *The Negro in American Fiction,* Associates in Negro Folk Education, 1937.

Cunningham, Virginia, *Paul Laurence Dunbar and His Song,* Dodd, 1947.

Dictionary of Literary Biography, Volume 51: *Afro-American Writers From the Harlem Renaissance to 1940,* Gale, 1987, Volume 54: *American Poets, 1880-1945, Third Series,* Gale, 1987.

DuBois, W. E. Burghardt, *The Gift of Black Folk: The Negro in the Making of America,* Stratford, 1924.

Gayle, Addison, Jr., *Oak and Ivy: A Biography of Paul Laurence Dunbar,* Anchor/Doubleday, 1971.

Gould, Jean, *That Dunbar Boy,* Dodd, 1958.

Johnson, James Weldon, editor, *The Book of American Negro Poetry,* Harcourt, 1922.

Lawson, Victor, *Dunbar Critically Examined,* Associated Publishers, 1941.

Loggins, Vernon, *The Negro Author: His Development in America to 1900,* Columbia University Press, 1931.

Martin, Jay, editor, *A Singer in the Dawn: Reinterpretations of Paul Laurence Dunbar,* Dodd, 1975.

Revell, Peter, *Paul Laurence Dunbar,* Twayne, 1979.

Twentieth-Century Literary Criticism, Gale, Volume 2, 1979, Volume 12, 1984.

Wagner, Jean, *Les Poetes negres des Etats-Unis,* Librairie Istra, 1963, translation by Kenneth Douglas published as *Black Poets of the United States: From Paul Laurence Dunbar to Langston Hughes,* University of Illinois Press, 1973.

Williams, Kenny J., *They Also Spoke: An Essay on Negro Literature in America,* Townsend Press, 1970.

PERIODICALS

American Literature, March, 1976.

American Scholar, spring, 1949.

CLA Journal, June, 1981.

Colored American Magazine, April, 1901, May, 1905.
Harper's Weekly, June 27, 1896.
Journal of Negro History, January, 1967.
Nation, June 23, 1926.
Ohio Historical Quarterly, April, 1958.
Phylon, March, 1959.
Poet Lore, spring, 1897.
Psychoanalytic Review, January, 1938.
Southern Workman, October, 1921.
Texas Quarterly, summer, 1971.*

—Sketch by Les Stone

* * *

DUNBAR-NELSON, Alice
See NELSON, Alice Ruth Moore Dunbar

* * *

DUNBAR-NELSON, Alice Moore
See NELSON, Alice Ruth Moore Dunbar

* * *

DUNCAN, Robert (Edward) 1919-1988
(Robert Edward Symmes)

OBITUARY NOTICE—See index for *CA* sketch: Name originally Edward Howard Duncan; born January 7, 1919, in Oakland, Calif.; died of a heart attack, February 3, 1988, in San Francisco, Calif. Editor and lyric poet. A prolific writer, Duncan is probably best remembered for his role in establishing the San Francisco Bay area as a hub of poetry in the United States. The diverse range of his work links him with various literary movements, particularly the romantics, the Beats, and the "Black Mountain School," which originated at a now defunct college of the same name in North Carolina. A self-described traditionalist, Duncan claimed that his work was aimed toward immediacy rather than originality; nonetheless, he distinguished his verse with a musical quality that proved unique.

Generally, his themes address the poet's individual response to his environment, but, specifically, Duncan's writing often focused on his own experiences as a homosexual. In addition, much of his verse deals with the very nature and creation of poetry. Commenting on his earlier works, some of which were published under the name Robert Edward Symmes, critics have named *The Opening of the Field, Roots and Branches,* and—to a lesser extent—*Bending the Bow* as most representative of his best poetry. Among his more than thirty other volumes are *Ground Work: Before the War, Ground Work II: In the Dark,* and *The Five Songs.* The recipient of a number of poetry prizes, Duncan also served as an editor of *Experimental Review, Phoenix,* and *Berkeley Miscellany* at the beginning of his career. A major collection of his manuscripts is archived in the Bancroft Library at the University of California, Berkeley. Duncan was the first recipient of the National Poetry Award.

OBITUARIES AND OTHER SOURCES:

BOOKS

Contemporary Literary Criticism, Volume 41, Gale, 1987.
Contemporary Poets, 4th edition, St. Martin's, 1985.
Dictionary of Literary Biography, Gale, Volume 5: *American Poets Since World War II,* 1980, Volume 16: *The Beats: Literary Bohemians in Postwar America,* 1983.
Paul, Sherman, *The Lost America of Love: Rereading Robert Creeley, Edward Dorn, and Robert Duncan,* Louisiana State University Press, 1981.

PERIODICALS

Los Angeles Times, February 4, 1988.
New York Times, February 4, 1988.
Times (London), February 11, 1988.

* * *

DUNHILL, Mary 1907(?)-1988

OBITUARY NOTICE: Born c. 1907; died February 24, 1988, in London, England. Corporate executive and author. Mary Dunhill was the daughter of Alfred Dunhill, founder of the English pipe and tobacco company that grew into a multinational corporation. She held a wide variety of jobs in the family firm beginning in the 1920s, and by 1944 she was a member of the corporate board. In 1961 she became chairman, and during her time in office the company received the Queen's Award to Industry three times. Dunhill took the title of president when she left the chairmanship in 1975. Her autobiography, *Our Family Business,* was published in 1979.

OBITUARIES AND OTHER SOURCES:

BOOKS

Dunhill, Mary, *Our Family Business,* Bodley Head, 1979.

PERIODICALS

Chicago Tribune, February 29, 1988.
Los Angeles Times, March 1, 1988.
Times (London), February 27, 1988.

* * *

DUNN, S. P.
See DUNN, Stephen P(orter)

* * *

DUNN, Stephen P(orter) 1928-
(S. P. Dunn)

PERSONAL: Born March 24, 1928, in Boston, Mass.; son of Leslie Clarence (a geneticist) and Louise (Porter) Dunn; married Ethel Deikman (a historian), October 6, 1956. *Education:* Columbia University, A.B., 1950, Ph.D., 1959.

ADDRESSES: Home and office—32 Highgate Rd., Berkeley, Calif. 94707.

CAREER: Fordham University, New York, N.Y., research associate on the U.S.S.R. at Institute for Contemporary Russian Studies, 1959-63; M. E. Sharpe, Inc. (publisher), Armonk, N.Y., editor, 1962-87. Translator of Russian ethnography for Arctic Institute of North America, 1960-65; research associate on the U.S.S.R. at Center for Slavic and East European Studies, University of California, Berkeley, 1964-68; lecturer at Monterey Institute of Foreign Studies (now Monterey Institute of International Studies), 1970-75; director of research at Highgate Road Social Science Research Station.

MEMBER: American Anthropological Association (fellow).

AWARDS, HONORS: Grants from National Science Foundation, 1962-65, Wenner-Gren Foundation for Anthropological Research, 1964-65, American Council of Learned Societies, 1966-67, 1970, and others.

WRITINGS:

(Under name S. P. Dunn) *Some Water Colors From Venice* (poems), Coalbin Press, 1956.
(With wife, Ethel Dunn) *The Peasants of Central Russia,* Holt, 1967, reprinted with new material, Waveland, 1988.
Sociology in the U.S.S.R., M. E. Sharpe, 1970.
Introduction to Soviet Ethnography, Highgate Road Social Science Research Station, 1975.
The Fall and Rise of the Asiatic Mode of Production, Routledge & Kegan Paul, 1983.

Contributor of more than one hundred articles and translations to periodicals. Contributing editor of *Station Relay;* past editor of *Soviet Sociology* and *Soviet Anthropology and Archaeology.*

WORK IN PROGRESS: Prolegomena to a General Theory of Religion.

* * *

DUNNING, Edward
See GILBERT, R(obert) A(ndrew)

* * *

DUNREA, Olivier Jean-Paul Dominique 1953-

PERSONAL: Name originally Clarence Miller, Jr.; surname pronounced "Dun-ray"; born September 22, 1953, in Virginia Beach, Va.; son of Clarence (a baker) and Marian (a homemaker; maiden name, Goodwin) Miller. *Education:* Attended University of Delaware, 1971-73; West Chester State College (now University), B.A., 1975; graduate study at Washington State University, 1975-76. *Politics:* None. *Religion:* None.

ADDRESSES: Home and office—214 Wendover St., Philadelphia, Pa. 19128.

CAREER: Worked variously as waiter, secretary, and management consultant; free-lance artist and actor in Philadelphia, Pa., San Francisco, Calif., and New York, N.Y., 1976-79; writer and illustrator, 1976—. Teacher of children's art and theatre; leader of workshops in makeup design, watercolor illustration, mask construction, movement and nonverbal communication, and model building. Work exhibited in shows in Philadelphia, Pa., and New York City.

MEMBER: Philadelphia Children's Reading Round Table.

AWARDS, HONORS: Cooper/Woods Award from English-Speaking Union, 1980; residency grant from National Endowment for the Arts and Delaware State Arts Council, 1981-83; Celebrating Literacy Award from International Reading Association, 1987.

WRITINGS:

Eddy B, Pigboy (for children), self-illustrated, Atheneum, 1983.
Ravena (for children), self-illustrated, Holiday House, 1984.
Fergus and Bridey (for children), self-illustrated, Holiday House, 1985.
Mogwogs on the March! (for children), self-illustrated, Holiday House, 1985.
Skara Brae: The Story of a Prehistoric Village (for children), self-illustrated, Holiday House, 1985.

WORK IN PROGRESS: Manuscripts on subjects including archaeology, farm life, prehistoric architecture, and castles, as well as further books about Ravena, pig books, and fantasy for young children.

SIDELIGHTS: Before his first book was published, Olivier Dunrea had sold seven manuscripts of fiction and nonfiction for children. Self-illustrated with ink and watercolor, his stories feature historical architecture and characters from folklore and are regarded as highly unusual. "He's doing a fanciful adaptation of a subject based in archaeology," Holiday House editor Margery Cuyler told Gary Soulsman in the Wilmington, Delaware, *Sunday News Journal.* "It's very original and his work shows a terrific feeling for color." Dunrea bases his books on his own research in northern Scotland and the Orkney and Shetland islands, using structures such as burial mounds, fortifications, and ancient settlements as settings. In *Ravena,* for example, the protagonist lives in a cairn, a mound of stones built to mark a grave. According to Philadelphia gallery manager Joan Lash, quoted in the *Philadelphia Inquirer,* "This is a promising artist."

Dunrea told *CA:* "The main influences in my work are archaeology, prehistoric architecture, and the folklore of Britain and Scandinavia. I am primarily interested in the Orkney and Shetland islands, the Outer Hebrides, and the Arran Islands west of Ireland. Stonework is my specialty. Architectural-style drawing is my favorite type of drawing—I am basically a frustrated architect. My own rural upbringing also provides lots of humorous and action-packed stories—*Eddy B, Pigboy,* for example."

BIOGRAPHICAL/CRITICAL SOURCES:

PERIODICALS

Philadelphia Inquirer, February 26, 1981, February 17, 1982.
Sunday News Journal (Wilmington), December 12, 1982.

* * *

DURAND, Loup 1933-

PERSONAL: Born September 18, 1933, in Flassans, France; son of Louis J. (an engineer) and Marie-Louise (Labadie) Durand; married Janine R. Dumas, March 11, 1961; children: Jean-Francois. *Education:* Received B.A. degrees in literature, law, and English from University of Paris; studied law in Saigon (now Ho Chi Minh City), Vietnam. *Politics:* "Depending on tax collectors." *Religion:* Catholic.

ADDRESSES: Home and Office—Bastide du Vieux-Moulin, 13320 Bouc Bel Air, France.

CAREER: Free-lance journalist, 1949-67; U.S. Information Service, Phnom Penh, Cambodia, interpreter and translator, 1958-61; Pressgroup, Paris, France, and Marseilles, France, editor in chief, 1967-70; full-time writer, 1970—.

AWARDS, HONORS: Prix du Quai des Orfevres, for *La Porte d'Or;* Prix du Roman d'Aventures; Prix du Suspense.

WRITINGS:

NOVELS

La Porte d'Or, Fayard, 1967.
Un Temps pour tuer, Fayard, 1968.
Pirates et barbaresques en Mediterranee, Aubanel, 1975.
Le Caid, Denoel, 1976.
"T.N.T." series, nine books, Laffont, 1978.
Jarai, Denoel, 1980, translation by Helen R. Lane published as *The Angkor Massacre,* Morrow, 1983.
La Gagne, Orban, 1980.

La Nuit des enfants rois, Orban, 1981.
La Porte de Kercabanac, Denoel, 1982.
Le Seigneur des tempetes, Denoel, 1983.

Also author of screenplays for the films "Nervose" and "Dancing," and of twenty television scripts; co-author of several novels.

WORK IN PROGRESS: A story about French explorers traveling the Rocky Mountain path of one of the author's ancestors who founded St. Louis, Missouri; a novel about sects; a script.

SIDELIGHTS: Loup Durand, whose thirty years of traveling have included seven spent in Cambodia, told *CA* that he began to write books "because it is the easiest way to earn money—saying enormous lies and staying home. I have the most sincere and deepest vocation for not taking myself seriously, but nevertheless did it one time when I wrote *The Angkor Massacre.*" Critics agree that the novel is a deadly serious, gripping account of events in Cambodia during its civil war in the 1960s and 1970s. "Adventure, politics, war, love, violence, suspense," ventured Paul Comeau in *World Literature Today,* "if these are the ingredients of a successful novel, [*The Angkor Massacre*] qualifies, since it contains them all." The turbulent history of the country mingles with the story, which involves a Frenchman, Lara, who has lived in Cambodia all his life, and the American he marries, Lisa, who has come to Vietnam in search of her brother, an army deserter. Lara brings Lisa and her brother to his homeland, where they must struggle for safety during a time of revolutionary upheaval.

Critics have praised Durand's skillful handling of the events in his novel. Wrote Comeau: "The reader is treated to an adventure 'film in words' liberally sprinkled with suspense-enhancing flashbacks." Jerome Doolittle declared in the *Washington Post* that "Durand has delivered exactly what he set out to deliver—a well-written, closely observed adventure story set in as exotic a locale as the world has to offer." He further determined that the book "hurtles to a jungle climax that should satisfy any adventure fan."

With the fates of the characters so wrapped up in the Cambodian revolution, moreover, the novel proves to be more than a simple adventure story, according to Jack Sullivan of the *New York Times Book Review.* Sullivan wrote: "Mr. Durand's subtle and commanding sense of place makes this novel considerably more than just another Far East thriller. Here Cambodia is a heartbreaking tragedy, not an occasion for exploitation."

BIOGRAPHICAL/CRITICAL SOURCES:

PERIODICALS

Los Angeles Times Book Review, May 22, 1983.
New York Times Book Review, April 10, 1983.
Washington Post, March 21, 1983.
World Literature Today, autumn, 1981.

E

EAMES, Andrew (John) 1958-

PERSONAL: Born July 9, 1958, in Brighton, England; son of Ronald Arthur (a doctor) and Margaret (a doctor; maiden name, MacLeod) Eames. *Education:* Cambridge University, B.A. (with honors), 1980.

ADDRESSES: Home—12A Glenfield Rd., Balham, London SW1Z 0HG, England.

CAREER: Free-lance journalist in Southeast Asia, 1980-83; features editor of an international transport paper, 1983-85; *Frontier* (magazine), London, England, editor, 1985-87; free-lance writer in London, 1987—. Photographer, with exhibitions in London.

WRITINGS:

Crossing the Shadow Line: Travels in South-East Asia, Hodder & Stoughton, 1986.

(Contributor) Merin Wexler, editor, *Great Britain,* Apa, 1986.

(Editor) *London,* Apa, in press.

Contributor of articles and photographs to magazines.

WORK IN PROGRESS: Mackinnon Kisstian, a novel about a missionary in Thailand.

SIDELIGHTS: Andrew Eames told *CA:* "I am a travel writer with a detailed knowledge of Southeast Asia, although nowadays I am moving into home news in the United Kingdom. My university thesis on Joseph Conrad provoked my first book, and my novel echoes some of Conrad's themes."

To John Ure of the *Times Literary Supplement, Crossing the Shadow Line* marks its author as "an observant traveller with a quick eye and ear . . . and a tolerance of the aberrations of those he encounters. He is frank about his own frustrations and the rapacious philosophy of his fellow travellers." The book describes Eames's two-year journey through Indonesia and Thailand to Nepal and India. His adventures provide clear comparisons to those of Lord Jim and other characters from the work of Joseph Conrad. In addition, Ure found that Eames's "comments on the antiseptic municipal regime in Singapore suggest that he has as sharp an eye for political and economic symptoms as he has for social ones."

BIOGRAPHICAL/CRITICAL SOURCES:

PERIODICALS

Times Literary Supplement, January 16, 1987.

* * *

EDELMAN, Marian Wright 1939-

PERSONAL: Born June 6, 1939, in Bennettsville, S.C.; daughter of Arthur J. and Maggie (Bowen) Wright; married Peter Benjamin Edelman, July 14, 1968; children: Joshua Robert, Jonah Martin, Ezra Benjamin. *Education:* Attended University of Paris and University of Geneva, 1958-59; Spelman College, B.A., 1960; Yale University, LL.B., 1963.

ADDRESSES: Office—Children's Defense Fund, 122 C St. N.W., Washington, D.C. 20001.

CAREER: National Association for the Advancement of Colored People (NAACP), Legal Defense and Education Fund, Inc., New York, N.Y., staff attorney, 1963-64, director of office in Jackson, Miss., 1964-68; partner of Washington Research Project of Southern Center for Public Policy, 1968-73; Children's Defense Fund, Washington, D.C., founder and president, 1973—. W. E. B. Du Bois Lecturer at Harvard University, 1986. Member of Lisle Fellowship's U.S.-U.S.S.R. Student Exchange, 1959; member of executive committee of Student Non-Violent Coordinating Committee (SNCC), 1961-63; member of Operation Crossroads Africa Project in Ivory Coast, 1962; congressional and federal agency liaison for Poor People's Campaign, summer, 1968; director of Harvard University's Center for Law and Education, 1971-73. Member of Presidential Commission on Americans Missing and Unaccounted for in Southeast Asia (Woodcock Commission), 1977, United States-South Africa Leadership Exchange Program, 1977, National Commission on the International Year of the Child, 1979, and President's Commission for a National Agenda for the Eighties, 1979; member of board of directors of Carnegie Council on Children, 1972-77, Aetna Life and Casualty Foundation, Citizens for Constitutional Concerns, U.S. Committee for UNICEF, and Legal Defense and Education Fund of the NAACP; member of board of trustees of Martin Luther King, Jr., Memorial Center, and Joint Center for Political Studies.

MEMBER: Council on Foreign Relations, Delta Sigma Theta (honorary member).

AWARDS, HONORS: Merrill scholar in Paris and Geneva, 1958-59; honorary fellow of Law School at University of Pennsylvania, 1969; Louise Waterman Wise Award, 1970; Presidential Citation from American Public Health Association, 1979; Outstanding Leadership Award from National Alliance of Black School Educators, 1979; Distinguished Service Award from National Association of Black Women Attorneys, 1979; National Award of Merit from National Council on Crime and Delinquency, 1979; named Washingtonian of the Year, 1979; Whitney M. Young Memorial Award from Washington Urban League, 1980; Professional Achievement Award from *Black Enterprise* magazine, 1980; Outstanding Leadership Achievement Award from National Women's Political Caucus and Black Caucus, 1980; Outstanding Community Service Award from National Hookup of Black Women, 1980; Woman of the Year Award from Big Sisters of America, 1980; Award of Recognition from American Academy of Pedodontics, 1981; Rockefeller Public Service Award, 1981; Gertrude Zimand Award from National Child Labor Committee, 1982; Florina Lasker Award from New York Civil Liberties Union, 1982; Anne Roe Award from Graduate School of Education at Harvard University, 1984; Roy Wilkins Civil Rights Award from National Association for the Advancement of Colored People, 1984; award from Women's Legal Defense Fund, 1985; Hubert H. Humphrey Award from Leadership Conference on Civil Rights, 1985; fellow of MacArthur Foundation, 1985; Grenville Clark Prize from Dartmouth College, 1986; Compostela Award of St. James Cathedral, 1987; more than thirty honorary degrees.

WRITINGS:

(Contributor) *Children Out of School in America,* Children's Defense, 1974.
(Contributor) Nathan B. Talbot, editor, *Raising Children in Modern America: Problems and Prospective Solutions,* Little, Brown, 1975.
(Contributor) David C. Warner, editor, *Toward New Human Rights: The Social Policies of the Kennedy and Johnson Administrations,* Lyndon B. Johnson School of Public Affairs, University of Texas at Austin, 1977.
Families in Peril: An Agenda for Social Change, Harvard University Press, 1987.

Principal author of *School Suspensions: Are They Helping Children?* 1975, and *Portrait of Inequality: Black and White Children in America,* 1980. Contributor to magazines.

SIDELIGHTS: Dubbed "the 101st Senator on children's issues" by Senator Edward Kennedy, Marian Wright Edelman left her law practice in 1968, just after the assassination of civil rights leader Martin Luther King, Jr., to work toward a better future for American children. She was the first black woman on the Mississippi bar and had been a civil rights lawyer with the National Association for the Advancement of Colored People. "Convinced she could achieve more as an advocate than as a litigant for the poor," wrote Nancy Traver in *Time,* Edelman moved to Washington, D.C., and began to apply her researching and rhetorical skills in Congress. She promotes her cause with facts about teen pregnancies, poverty, and infant mortality and—with her Children's Defense Fund—has managed to obtain budget increases for family and child health care and education programs. Her book, *Families in Peril: An Agenda for Social Change,* was judged "a powerful and necessary document" of the circumstances of children by *Washington Post* reviewer Jonathan Yardley, and it urges support for poor mothers and children of all races. In *Ms.* magazine Katherine Bouton described Edelman as "the nation's most effective lobbyist on behalf of children . . . an unparalleled strategist and pragmatist."

Edelman told *CA:* "I have been an advocate for disadvantaged Americans throughout my professional career. The Children's Defense Fund, which I have been privileged to direct, has become one of the nation's most active organizations concerned with a wide range of children's and family issues, especially those which most affect America's children: our poorest Americans.

"Founded in 1968 as the Washington Research Project, the Children's Defense Fund monitors and proposes improvements in federal, state, and local budgets, legislative and administrative policies in the areas of child and maternal health, education, child care, child welfare, adolescent pregnancy prevention, youth employment, and family support systems.

"In 1983 the Children's Defense Fund initiated a major long-term national campaign to prevent teenage pregnancy and provide positive life options for youth. Since then, we have launched a multimedia campaign that includes transit advertisements, posters, and television and radio public service announcements, a national prenatal care campaign, and Child Watch coalitions in more than seventy local communities in thirty states to combat teen pregnancy.

"The Children's Defense Fund also has been a leading advocate in Congress, state legislatures, and courts for children's rights. For example, our legal actions blocked out-of-state placement of hundreds of Louisiana children in Texas institutions, guaranteed access to special education programs for tens of thousands of Mississippi's children, and represented the interests of children and their families before numerous federal administrative agencies."

BIOGRAPHICAL/CRITICAL SOURCES:

PERIODICALS

Ebony, July, 1987.
Ms., July/August, 1987.
New York Times Book Review, June 7, 1987.
Time, March 23, 1987.
Washington Post, March 4, 1987.

* * *

EDWARDS, Eli
See McKAY, Festus Claudius

* * *

EDWARDS, Hazel (Eileen) 1945-

PERSONAL: Born September 21, 1945, in Melbourne, Australia; daughter of David (an engineer) and Hazel (a homemaker; maiden name, Abbot) Muir Moir; married Garnet George Edwards (a hospital manager), January 6, 1967; children: Kimberlea, Trevelyan. *Education:* Toorak Teachers College (now Victoria College), Trained Primary Teacher's Certificate, 1965; Monash University, B.A., 1971, B.Ed., 1974, M.Ed., 1980.

ADDRESSES: Home and office—28 Lana St., Blackburn S., 3130 Victoria, Australia. *Agent*—Curtis Brown (Australia) Pty., Ltd., P.O. Box 19, Paddington, 2021 New South Wales, Australia.

CAREER: Lecturer in English at Frankston and Toorak teachers' colleges, Malvern, Victoria, Australia, 1969-72; Council of Adult Education, Melbourne, Victoria, Australia, lecturer, 1973-85; free-lance writer and lecturer in women's issues, balancing multiple roles, and self-employment, 1986—. Member of Victoria College Council, 1982-86. Writer in residence in primary schools, 1982; conducts seminars and workshops for children and adults, 1987—.

MEMBER: Australian Society of Authors, Australian Writers Guild, Australian Journalists Association.

AWARDS, HONORS: There's a Hippopotamus on Our Roof Eating Cake was commended by the Australian Book Publishers Association Design Awards, 1980-81, and received a bronze medal at Leipzig International Book Fair, 1982; Literature Board grant, 1985, to complete research for an unpublished novel for teenagers, *Blue Light*.

WRITINGS:

NONFICTION

Women Returning to Study, Primary Education, 1975.
Houseworking: The Unsuperperson's Guide to Sharing the Load, Dove Communications, 1984.
(With Pam Chessell) *Being Your Own Boss,* Penguin, 1984.
Second Start: Challenge and Change in Mid Life, Penguin, 1987.
"Travelling On" (series), Council of Adult Education, 1988.

JUNIOR FICTION

General Store, Hodder, 1977.
Kendall, Min, and Temporary Fred, Hodder, 1980.
Mum on Wheels, Hodder, 1980.
Pancake Olympics, Rigby, 1981.
The Billycart Battle, Rigby, 1982.
Quirky the Ex, Rigby, 1982.
Mystery Twin, Hodder, 1983.
Skin Zip Me, Kangaroo Press, 1984.
Stupendous Speewah Antics, Edward Arnold, 1984.
The O Gang, Ashton Scholastic, 1985.
Storycraft (short stories), Harcourt, 1985.
Stowaway, Hodder, 1987.

PICTURE BOOKS

There's a Hippopotamus on Our Roof Eating Cake, illustrations by Deborah Niland, Hodder, 1980, Holiday House, 1986.
Honey the Hospital Dog, Buttercup Hodder, 1984.
The Imaginary Menagerie, illustrations by Rod Clement, Lothian, 1985.
Tolly Leaves Home, illustrations by Rosemary Wilson, Hodder, 1985.
Stickybeak, illustrations by Rosemary Wilson, Nelson, 1986.
Snail Mail, illustrations by Rod Clement, Collins, 1986.
Fish and Chips and Jaws, illustrations by Rae Dale, Nelson, 1987.
Grandma Zed, illustrations by Carolyn Johnston, Lothian, 1987.
The Hundreds and Thousands Kid, illustrations by Rosemary Wilson, Collins, 1988.

PLAY COLLECTIONS

Playing With Ideas, Nelson, 1980.
Playing With More Ideas, Nelson, 1981.
Primary Plays, Nelson, 1981.
More Primary Plays, Nelson, 1981.
Playpack 1, Nelson, 1983.
Enact 1, Longman Cheshire, 1983.
Enact 2, Longman Cheshire, 1984.
Workplays, Longman Cheshire, 1984.
Playpack 2, Nelson, 1984.
Playpack 3, Nelson, 1985.

CONTRIBUTOR

The Imagineers: Writing and Illustrating Children's Books, Alderman Harman Reading Time Publication, 1983.
Joe Goodman, *Win Some, Lose Some,* Collins, 1985.

Stories appear in "Flag" and "A.B.C. Listen and Read" series.

OTHER

Writing Better Essays, programmed by Brian and Vivienne Clarke, Educational Media, 1975.
(With Dorothy Enchaw) *Between Us,* Reinhold Australia, 1976.
(With V. Clarke) *Satire,* Educational Media, 1977.
(With V. Clarke) *Understanding the Novel,* Educational Media, 1977.
Australian Writers of Children's Literature, Educational Media, 1980.
Around Our Place (literacy series), Council of Adult Education, 1983.
Discussing Literature, Sorrett, 1980, 2nd edition, Longman Cheshire, 1984.
(With Pam Chessell) *Write Now 1,* Longman Cheshire, 1984.
(With Chessell) *Write Now 2,* Longman Cheshire, 1984.
(With Chessell) *Do Frogs Wear Jeans?* Longman Cheshire, 1985.
Coles Study Notes, "Tierra Lirra by the River," Lothian, 1985.
A Piece of My Mind (collection of fiction and nonfiction), Edward Arnold, 1986.
Do Elephants Ever Forget? Longman Cheshire, 1987.

Author of television script "I'm Going to Bed With Shakespeare." Reviewer of children's books for several newspapers.

WORK IN PROGRESS: "Water," a fiction series, for Harcourt; a sequel to *There's a Hippopotamus on Our Roof Eating Cake,* publication by Hodder expected in 1988.

MEDIA ADAPTATIONS: There's a Hippopotamus on Our Roof Eating Cake has been adapted for video by Box Hill, Technical and Further Education College, 1985.

* * *

EDWARDS, Lee R. 1942-

PERSONAL: Born April 30, 1942, in Brooklyn, N.Y.; daughter of David and Celia (Weintraub) Rosenblum; married Dallas Craig Edwards (a marine ecologist), June 19, 1964; children: one. *Education:* Swarthmore College, B.A., 1962; University of California, Berkeley, M.A., 1965; University of California, San Diego, Ph.D., 1969.

ADDRESSES: Home—R.F.D. 3, 8 Teawaddle Hill Rd., Amherst, Mass. 01002. *Office*—Department of English, University of Massachusetts at Amherst, Amherst, Mass. 01003.

CAREER: University of Massachusetts at Amherst, assistant professor, 1967-75, associate professor, 1975-80, professor of English and American literature, 1980—, associate dean of humanities and fine arts, 1983-85, professor of English and Women's Studies, 1987—, director of Women's Studies Program, 1987—.

MEMBER: Modern Language Association of America (Women's Caucus).

AWARDS, HONORS: Fellow of National Endowment for the Humanities, 1978.

WRITINGS:

(Contributor) Robert Elliott, editor, *Twentieth Century Interpretations of Moll Flanders,* Prentice-Hall, 1970.
(Editor) Charles Brockden Brown, *Alcuin,* Grossman, 1971.
(Editor with Arlyn Diamond) *American Voices, American Women,* Avon, 1973.
(Editor with Diamond) *The Authority of Experience: Essays in Feminist Criticism,* University of Massachusetts Press, 1977.
Psyche as Hero: Female Heroism and Fictional Form, Wesleyan University Press, 1984.

Contributor to literature journals. Editor of *Massachusetts Review,* 1974—.

WORK IN PROGRESS: A book tentatively titled *Pathograms and Schizo-texts: Writing Madly,* "which will study verbal materials produced by mad people, as well as literary narratives that attempt to re-present or re-produce insanity (especially schizophrenia)."

SIDELIGHTS: Lee R. Edwards told *CA:* "Since the beginning of my career, I have been particularly concerned with exploring the points at which fictional narratives and other social/cultural structures intersect, with the capacity of literature both to echo and to alter the surrounding world. *Psyche as Hero,* for example, considers what happens to the lives of women characters when novelists imagine their female protagonists as heroes rather than as heroines. My latest venture shifts the grounds of my investigation from social to psychological conventions. What I'm trying to find out is what, if any, is the relationship between the way(s) in which mad people experience their own madness and represent their own mental experiences and the ways in which insanity has been invoked, evoked, and/or incarnated in a variety of acceptably 'literary' texts."

The essays in *The Authority of Experience* were praised by Mary Ellmann in the *Times Literary Supplement* for their "lively discussion of female characters in men's writings. The contributors studied such authors as Chaucer, Shakespeare, Defoe, Camus, and Samuel Richardson. The selections reveal, according to Ellmann, "a willingness on the part of both male and female novelists to allow for the point of view of the other sex and to recognize variant interests."

BIOGRAPHICAL/CRITICAL SOURCES:

PERIDOCALS

Times Literary Supplement, April 15, 1977.

* * *

EDWARDS, S. W.
See SUBLETTE, Walter (Edwards)

* * *

EHRENBERG, Miriam

PERSONAL: Born in New York, N.Y.; married Otto Ehrenberg (a psychologist), 1956; children: Ingrid, Erica. *Education:* Received B.A. from Queens College (now of the City University of New York), M.A. from City University of New York, and Ph.D. from New School for Social Research.

ADDRESSES: Home—Sherman, Conn. *Office*—141 East 55th St., New York, N.Y. 10022.

CAREER: Private practice of psychology in New York, N.Y., 1970—. Assistant professor at City University of New York, 1972-74; director of psychotherapy for Spence-Chapin Services to Families and Children, 1974-84.

WRITINGS:

(With husband, Otto Ehrenberg) *The Psychotherapy Maze: A Consumer's Guide to Getting in and out of Therapy,* Holt, 1977, revised edition, Simon & Schuster, 1986.
(With O. Ehrenberg) *Optimum Brain Power,* Dodd, 1985.
(With O. Ehrenberg) *The Intimate Circle: Sexual Dynamics of Family Life,* Simon & Schuster, 1987.

SIDELIGHTS: Miriam Ehrenberg told *CA:* "I am interested in contemporary issues that affect personal well being, and the books I work on grow out of those concerns. In my practice as a psychologist, it became apparent that an underlying problem for many people is the limited concept they hold of their own possibilities. My writing has focused on trying both to dispel the cultural myths about people's capabilities and to provide concrete guidelines for developing underutilized potentials.

"The book on therapy, for example, demonstrates how people in therapy fall prey to the 'client trap' of having their legitimate concerns about therapy thrown back at them as proof of their neurotic doubt or hostility. This book also provides the information and tools needed to become a knowledgeable consumer of psychotherapy and to get the most out of the services contracted for.

"The book on intelligence traces the historical development of the myth about fixed intelligence and provides a step-by-step program for increasing intelligence, ranging from thinking exercises to obtaining necessary brain nutrients.

"The book on family sexuality shows how, despite the recent emphasis on sexual liberation, repressive attitudes still keep people from growing up comfortable with their sexuality and integrating it into their lives. This book provides a sex education program parents can use in the home and gives them concrete guidelines for understanding their own attitudes better and learning how to become more at ease with sexual issues.

"It has been very gratifying for me and my co-author/husband to know, through mail from readers, that we have helped people liberate themselves from self-restricting attitudes and lead more fulfilling lives."

* * *

EHRENBERG, Otto 1926-

PERSONAL: Born May 30, 1926, in Kassel, Germany (now West Germany); immigrated to the United States, 1937, naturalized citizen, 1942; son of Paul and Clara (Tillman) Ehrenberg; married Miriam Colbert (a psychologist), 1956; children: Ingrid, Erica. *Education:* University of Cincinnati, B.A., 1950; New School for Social Research, M.A., 1953; New York University, Ph.D., 1960; received diploma in psychotherapy and psychoanalysis from Adelphi University, 1967.

ADDRESSES: Home—Sherman, Conn. *Office*—141 East 55th St., New York, N.Y. 10022.

CAREER: Private practice of psychology in New York, N.Y., 1964—. Adjunct associate professor at City University of New

York, 1970-75; consultant to mental health agencies and business organizations, 1970—.

WRITINGS:

(With wife, Miriam Ehrenberg) *The Psychotherapy Maze: A Consumer's Guide to Getting in and out of Therapy,* Holt, 1977, revised edition, Simon & Schuster, 1986.
(With M. Ehrenberg) *Optimum Brain Power,* Dodd, 1985.
(With M. Ehrenberg) *The Intimate Circle: Sexual Dynamics of Family Life,* Simon & Schuster, 1987.

SIDELIGHTS: Otto Ehrenberg told *CA:* "Most of my writing supplements my work as a practicing psychologist by encouraging readers to make better use of their possibilities. *The Psychotherapy Maze* emphasizes that clients in psychotherapy not only have the right but the responsibility to evaluate the qualifications and capabilities of therapists as well as to take an active part in their psychotherapy, and it gives them the information they need to do just that. The traditional passive, accepting attitude towards psychotherapy is fundamentally counter-therapeutic, and it increases chances of abuse in psychotherapy. It has been gratifying to see in my practice an emerging trend toward a more critical and discriminating use of psychotherapy. The 1986 revision updates information about psychotherapy and is expanded to include discussion of the special issues encountered in psychotherapy by ethnic minorities, women, older people, and the gay-lesbian community.

"*Optimum Brain Power* is addressed to the myth that we are born with a fixed, inherited intelligence that cannot grow. This book defines intelligence as a capacity that develops as one uses it, and presents exercises in perception, thinking, and memory that help readers use the mind to its fullest potential. It is interesting to note that the first foreign translation appeared in Japan, a country that stresses intellectual achievement and whose children outperform their Western counterparts.

"Despite much talk about the sexual revolution in the 1960s and 1970s, there has been a conspicuous absence of greater tolerance toward the expression of sexual feelings within the American family. Most families are still unable to integrate normal sexuality into day-to-day life, resulting in family conflict and the inability of many children to make sex a happy, healthy part of life later on. In *The Intimate Circle* we describe four typical patterns of reacting to sexuality within the family and through many examples and interviews encourage parents to be more accepting of their children's essential sexuality."

* * *

EICHNER, Alfred S. 1937-1988

OBITUARY NOTICE—See index for *CA* sketch: Born March 23, 1937, in Washington, D.C.; died of a heart attack, February 10, 1988, in Closter, N.J. Economist, educator, editor, and author. A professor of economics at Rutgers University, Eichner became a prominent member of the influential post-Keynesian school of economics. As such he advocated government intervention as a means of regulating the U.S. economy and controlling unemployment. Between 1966 and 1980 Eichner taught at Columbia University and at the State University of New York College at Purchase. A member of the editorial board of *Journal of Post-Keynesian Economics,* he wrote or edited a number of books, including *A Guide to Post-Keynesian Economics, Why Economics Is Not Yet a Science,* and *The Macrodynamics of Advanced Market Economies.*

OBITUARIES AND OTHER SOURCES:

PERIODICALS

New York Times, February 13, 1988.

* * *

EISNER, Sigmund 1920-

PERSONAL: Born December 9, 1920, in Red Bank, N.J.; married Nancy Fereva (a librarian), June 15, 1949; children: six. *Education:* University of California, Berkeley, B.A., 1947, M.A., 1949; Columbia University, Ph.D., 1955.

ADDRESSES: Office—Department of English, University of Arizona, Tucson, Ariz. 95721.

CAREER: Oregon State College (now University), Corvallis, instructor, 1954-57, assistant professor of English, 1957-58; Dominican College of San Rafael, San Rafael, Calif., assistant professor, 1960-62, associate professor of English, 1962-66; University of Arizona, Tucson, associate professor, 1966-67, professor of English, 1967—. *Military service:* U.S. Army, 1942-46.

MEMBER: International Arthurian Society, Modern Language Association of America, Mediaeval Academy of America, National Council of Teachers of English, Medieval Association of the Pacific.

AWARDS, HONORS: Fulbright fellow in Ireland, 1958-59.

WRITINGS:

A Tale of Wonder: A Source Study of the Wife of Bath's Tale, John English, 1957.
The Tristan Legend: A Study in Sources, Northwestern University Press, 1969.
(Editor) Nicholas of Lynn, *Kalendarium,* Scolar Press, 1980.
(Contributor) Paul Ruggiers, editor, *The Variorum Chaucer,* University of Oklahoma Press, in press.

Contributor to scholarly journals and textbooks, including *Essays and Studies,* John Murray, 1976.

SIDELIGHTS: The Kalendarium of Nicholas of Lynn, written in 1386, was used by fourteenth-century English poet Geoffrey Chaucer as a resource for calculating time and understanding the astrology of his day. It reveals, according to *Times Literary Supplement* reviewer T. A. Shippey, "the appalling complexity of medieval science . . . and gives a clear picture of one aspect of medieval thought, interpreted only just enough to make it readily accessible."

Sigmund Eisner told *CA:* "I had so many bad teachers and read so many difficult books when I was in school, and even in college, that I always hoped I could do better. Now, I suppose, I am inspiring others in the same way."

BIOGRAPHICAL/CRITICAL SOURCES:

PERIODICALS

Times Literary Supplement, February 27, 1981.

* * *

EISS, Harry Edwin 1950-

PERSONAL: Surname rhymes with "lease"; born May 17, 1950, in Minneapolis, Minn.; son of Harry Earl (a printer) and Helen (a nurse; maiden name, Holmgren) Eiss; married Betty Palm (a bookkeeper); children: Meghan, Israel, Angela, Jared,

Ryan. *Education:* University of Minnesota, B.A. (English) and B.A. (humanities), both 1975; Mankato State University, M.S., 1976; University of North Dakota, Ph.D., 1982.

ADDRESSES: Office—Department of English, Eastern Michigan University, Ypsilanti, Mich. 48197.

CAREER: Northern Montana College, Havre, instructor, 1982-83, assistant professor, 1983-87; Eastern Michigan University, Ypsilanti, assistant professor of English, 1987—. Member of Montana Committee for the Humanities, 1985-87, and Montana State Reading Council; public speaker.

MEMBER: International Research Society for Children's Literature, Smithsonian Institution, American Academy of Arts and Sciences, Modern Language Association of America, Society for the Study of Myth and Tradition, American Culture Association, Popular Culture Association, National Council of Teachers of English, Advocates for Children's Literature, Coda: Poets and Writers, Children's Literature Association, Society of Children's Book Writers, National Puzzler's League.

WRITINGS:

Dictionary of Language Games, Puzzles, Amusements, Greenwood Press, 1986.
Dictionary of Mathematical Games, Puzzles, and Amusements, Greenwood Press, in press.
Literature for Young People on War and Peace (bibliography), Greenwood Press, in press.

Work represented in anthologies, including *Our Twentieth Century's Greatest Poets,* edited by Cole and Campbell, World of Poetry, 1982; *Today's Greatest Poems,* edited by Cole and Campbell, World of Poetry, 1983; *Our Western World's Greatest Poems,* edited by Cole and Campbell, World of Poetry, 1983. Contributor of poems and articles to magazines.

WORK IN PROGRESS: Child of the Lake, a novel.

SIDELIGHTS: Harry Edwin Eiss told *CA:* "I am interested in current peace movements, especially groups that are against nuclear weapons. My views on nuclear war and arms build-up are simply that, when looked at closely, they make no moral or military sense. They are being used by politicians and big businesses to further political and economic goals. Unfortunately, the United States is spending so much money on national defense that it is draining itself of all the economic, social, educational, and most every other kind of growth it could be making.

"I am also concerned about current U.S. policies in such places as Nicaragua. I have a strong attraction to all of the humanities and arts, and I find a need to explore philosophy. When I feel like letting my mind rest, I enjoy watching sports."

* * *

el ROPO, Smokestack
See PERRY, Charles

* * *

ELSTON, Robert 1934-1987

OBITUARY NOTICE: Name originally Robert Gornel Finkelstein; born May 29, 1934, in New York, N.Y.; died of a pulmonary embolism related to acquired immune deficiency syndrome (AIDS), December 10, 1987, in the Netherlands. Actor, director, producer, educator, and playwright. Elston's acting credits range from leading roles in such Broadway productions as "Spoon River Anthology" and "Vivat! Vivat! Regina" to regular appearances in the daytime television programs "Love of Life" and "As the World Turns." He also appeared in dozens of television commercials. Elston taught acting at Herbert Berghof Studios in New York City from 1964 until 1975, when he helped establish the American Renaissance Theatre. There he continued to teach and also produced and directed plays. Elston's writings include the plays "After Many a Summer," adapted from the works of Anton Chekov; "Run Children Run," with co-author Harvey Keith; and the one-man shows "Portrait of a Man" and "Notes." He also wrote the book for a musical, "Murder at the Gaiety."

OBITUARIES AND OTHER SOURCES:

BOOKS

Contemporary Theatre, Film, and Television, Volume 1, Gale, 1984.
Notable Names in the American Theatre, James White, 1976.

PERIODICALS

New York Times, December 29, 1987.

* * *

el-TOURE, Askia Muhammad Abu Bakr
See TOURE, Askia Muhammad Abu Bakr el

* * *

EMPRINGHAM, Antoinette F(leur) 1939-
(Toni Empringham)

PERSONAL: Born September 5, 1939, in Los Angeles, Calif.; daughter of James (a nutritionist) and Margarita (a secretary; maiden name, Feliz) Empringham. *Education:* University of Southern California, B.A. (cum laude), 1961, M.A., 1968, Ph.D., 1974.

ADDRESSES: Office—Department of English, El Camino College, Torrance, Calif. 90506. *Agent*—Judy M. Semler, 17221 East 17th St., Santa Ana, Calif. 92701.

CAREER: El Camino College, Torrance, Calif., professor of English, 1974—.

MEMBER: Modern Language Association of America.

WRITINGS:

(Editor under name Toni Empringham) *Fiesta in Aztlan: Anthology of Chicano Poetry,* Capra Press, 1982.

Also author of novel *Healing,* as yet unpublished.

SIDELIGHTS: Toni Empringham told *CA:* "I write to answer the voice that has always lived with me inside my head. I also write to satisfy and to bring closure to situations and characters that begin as fragments and end up whole only when I transfer them, translate them, and therefore make them real."

* * *

EMPRINGHAM, Toni
See EMPRINGHAM, Antoinette F(leur)

* * *

ENDE, Michael 1930(?)-

PERSONAL: Born c. 1930 in Garmisch-Partenkirchen, Ba-

varia, Germany (now West Germany); son of Edgar (a painter) and Luise (a physiotherapist); married Ingeborg Hoffman (an actress). *Education:* Attended the Otto Falckenburg actor's school, beginning in 1947.

ADDRESSES: Home—near Rome, Italy.

CAREER: Writer of satiric sketches for cabarets and film; theater critic for radio in Munich, West Germany; writer, 1961—.

AWARDS, HONORS: Buxtehuder Bulle (West Germany), Wilhelm-Hauff-Preis (West Germany), Premio Europeo "Provincia di Trento" (Italy), and International Janusz Korczak Prize (Poland), all for *The Neverending Story*.

WRITINGS:

FICTION

Jim Knopf und Lukas der Lokomotivfuehrer, illustrations by F. J. Tripp, Thienemann, 1961, translation with illustrations by Maurice S. Dodd published as *Jim Button and Luke the Engine-Driver,* Harrap (London), 1963.

Jim Knopf und die Wilde 13, illustrations by F. J. Tripp, Thienemann, 1964.

Das Schnurpsenbuch, illustrations by Siegfried Wagner, Thienemann, 1969.

Tranquilla Trampeltreu, die beharrliche Schildkroete, illustrations by Marie-Luise Pricken, Thienemann, 1972, revised and enlarged edition with illustrations by Manfred Schlueter, 1982.

Momo, Thienemann, 1973, translation by Frances Lobb published as *The Grey Gentleman,* Burke (London), 1974, translation by J. Maxwell Brownjohn published as *Momo,* Doubleday, 1985.

Das Kleine Lumpenkasperle, illustrations by Roswitha Quadflieg, Urachhaus, 1975.

(Editor with Irmela Breuder) *Bei uns zu Hans anderswo,* Thienemann, 1976.

Das Traumfresserchen, illustrations by Annegart Fuchshuber, Thienemann, 1978, translation by Gwen Marsh published as *The Dream-Eater,* illustrations by Fuchshuber, Dent (London), 1978.

Die unendliche Geschichte: Von A bis Z, Thienemann, 1979, translation by Ralph Manheim with illustrations by Roswitha Quadflieg published as *The Neverending Story,* Doubleday, 1983.

Die Schattennauhmaschine, illustrations by Binette Schroeder, Thienemann, 1982.

Das Gauklermaechen: Ein Spiel in sieben Bildern sowie einem Vor- und Nachspeil, Weitbrecht, 1982.

Der Spiegel im Spiegel: Ein Labyrinth, Weitbrecht, 1984, translation by J. Maxwell Brownjohn published as *Mirror in the Mirror: A Labyrinth,* Viking, 1986.

Filemon Faltenreich, illustrations by Christoph Hessel, Thienemann, 1984.

(And illustrator) *Der Goggolori: Eine bairische Maer,* Weitbrecht, 1984.

NONFICTION

(With Joerg Krichbaum) *Die Archaeologie der Dunkelheit: Gesprach uber Kunst und das Werk des Malers Edgar Ende,* Weitbrecht, 1985.

SIDELIGHTS: West German fantasy writer Michael Ende won international acclaim for his novel *The Neverending Story,* which became a best-seller in West Germany, the United States, and other countries in the early 1980s. Originally published and marketed as a children's book, Ende's fairy tale about a boy who comes under the magical thrall of an antique book he reads captured the imaginations of adult readers as an allegory for the decline of creative fantasy in the modern world. In *The Neverending Story* and *Momo,* another best-selling fable for all ages, Ende subtly probes such philosophical and moral themes as the relation between reality and the imagination and the meaning of love in a narrative context of high adventure and inventive whimsy.

The unlikely hero of *The Neverending Story* is a chubby ten-year-old boy named Bastian Balthazar Bux. On quarrelsome terms with his father and harassed by his schoolmates, Bastian seeks refuge one day in an antiquarian bookstore, where he discovers a mysterious old tome bound in silk and printed in red and green ink titled *The Neverending Story*. The intrigued Bastian smuggles the book out of the shop and repairs to a hideout in the attic of his school, where he is soon avidly absorbed in the story about a magical realm called Fantastica.

Taking the form of a book within a book, Ende's narrative alternates between Bastian's thoughts and the story the boy is reading, using red and green ink to distinguish between the two. Fantastica at first appears to be a fairly conventional fairy tale realm, ruled by the Childlike Empress and inhabited by elves, dragons, giant snakes, and a wicked sorceress. It turns out, however, that this world is threatened by the mysterious Nothingness that has surfaced in pockets all over the kingdom and that extinguishes existence wherever it appears. A young warrior named Artreyu sets out to rescue the Childlike Empress as oblivion invades her Ivory Tower palace.

Midway through his reading, Bastian is suddenly transported to Fantastica himself when he shouts a warning to Artreyu that the storybook hero heeds. Once inside the magical realm, the boy discovers that it is he, a human being who believes in dreams, who must rescue the empress and deliver Fantastica from Nothingness. He learns that the inhabitants, events, and even geography of the kingdom are determined by outside imaginations and that Fantastica is vanishing because of a lack of dreamers to recreate it.

Reluctantly pressed into service, Bastian must surmount numerous challenges to reach the Ivory Tower that have more to do with self-discovery than with the physical courage often celebrated in mythology. As Bastian develops confidence and a sense of self-esteem, he begins to recreate the world around him. His god-like powers soon go to his head, however, and he must ultimately battle his way out of an egotistical world of his own making and back to reality by discovering the transcending power of love. Fantastica is thus rescued and left free for another imagination to dream up again in the neverending creative cycle of fantasy and myth.

Reviewers of *The Neverending Story* in the United States generally applauded Ende's suspenseful plotting and inventive imagination but differed on whether the book worked effectively as a moral allegory for adults. In response to this mixed critical stance the author remarked wryly to *People*'s Logan Bentley: "You can enter the literary salon from prison, from the insane asylum, from a whorehouse—everywhere but from the children's room." Among the skeptical critics was *Newsday*'s Dan Cryer, who judged the novel "bereft of psychological insight or depth of characterization. It seems geared more to 'Star Wars' viewers than Tolkien readers. Anyone over 12 who gushes over this book ought to be kept in at recess." Somtow Sucharitkul of the *Washington Post Book World,* on the other hand, found *The Neverending Story* philosophically intriguing. "If there is a single subject with which all great

fantasies deal, it must of necessity be the nature of reality," the critic wrote. "At its best, *The Neverending Story* is a profound examination of these unanswerable questions. . . . It's an oasis in the desert of big-budget fantasy publishing, and for once delivers far more than it promises."

First popularized for the adult market by participants in the West German peace movement, *The Neverending Story* became a blockbusting best-seller in West Germany with virtually no promotion or advertising. The novel topped fiction sales for three years and remained on West German best-sellers lists for an astounding five years. Translated into twenty-five languages, *The Neverending Story* was published in Yugoslavia and the Soviet Union and became a best-seller in Spain, Italy, Japan, and the United States, where it was a Book-of-the-Month Club alternate selection. The novel also inspired a 1984 film of the same title directed by Wolfgang Petersen. The $25 million production featured extraordinary special effects and was a popular success in the United States and West Germany, but the screenplay's many departures from the novel provoked Ende to withdraw his name from the credits.

The Neverending Story's remarkable success prompted Ende's German publisher, Thienemann, to reissue the author's fantasy novel *Momo*, which was first published as a children's book in West Germany in 1973. When the new edition reached the number two spot on the West German best-seller list in 1981, *Momo* was also published abroad for the adult market. The protagonist of the book is a young waif named Momo who lives in the ruins of an ancient amphitheatre in a large city in contemporary Europe. Momo is a pure and innocent creature who whiles away the time playing carefree games of fantasy with other children. She also possesses the unusual gift of listening to others and helping them to understand and accept their past experiences.

Momo's idyllic world is threatened by the mysterious appearance of a phalanx of "men in gray" who gradually take control of the city. These sinister figures, it transpires, control the Timesaving Bank and set out to convince people that they are wasting their time by engaging in playful activity. The citizens are told to spend their time working instead, allowing the men in gray to steal the hours once spent in play and accumulate them like capital in their bank. Momo and her fantasy world represent a threat to the time thieves, but she escapes their clutches by following a magical tortoise to a place called Nowhere House, where she meets a mystical timekeeper named Professer Secundus Minutus Hora. Hora ultimately destroys the time-thieves by stopping all clocks in a "timequake" and life returns to an unhurried pace, proving the moral that "time is life itself, and life resides in the human heart."

Ende contributed his own humorous drawings to *Momo* that highlight "a visual quality to the prose," critic Francis Levy observed in the *New York Times Book Review*. But, Levy added, "it is the author's absurd logic" and "artful brand of surreal satire" that "really brings 'Momo' to life." Natalie Babbitt concurred in the *Washington Post Book World:* "There is real ingenuity to [the novel's] imaginative force. Professor Hora's discourses on time may raise a lot of questions. . . . But they are thought-provoking just the same. And the conception and shapes of its fantasy devices are charmingly fresh."

In *Mirror in the Mirror*, published in the United States in 1986, Ende mixed verbal and visual surrealism in an unusual format. The book consists of reproductions of drawings and etchings by Ende's father, the surrealist painter Edgar Ende, with accompanying stories written by Ende. "The drawings are illustrated by a text that in turn is illustrated by those very same drawings: this mirrored structure reflects the title of the book and Ende's never-ending vision of the world," observed Toronto *Globe and Mail* reviewer Alberto Manguel. "The reader goes from the words to the drawings and back to the words, collecting images on the way." Although at first no overall structure seems evident in the book, an oddly shapeless design emerges at the end, the critic noted. In Manguel's opinion, Ende accomplishes in *Mirror in the Mirror* what novelist Nathaniel Hawthorne once deemed impossible: "To write a dream, which shall resemble the real course of a dream, with all its inconsistency, its eccentricities and aimlessness—with nevertheless a leading idea running through the whole."

BIOGRAPHICAL/CRITICAL SOURCES:

BOOKS

Contemporary Literary Criticism, Volume 31, Gale, 1985.

PERIODICALS

Globe and Mail (Toronto), September 27, 1986.
Los Angeles Times Book Review, March 17, 1985.
Newsday, October 20, 1983.
Newsweek, November 14, 1983.
New York Times Book Review, November 6, 1983, February 17, 1985.
People, August 27, 1984.
Times Literary Supplement, November 25, 1983.
Washington Post Book World, October 16, 1983, March 17, 1985.*

—*Sketch by Curtis Skinner*

* * *

ENGEL, J. Ronald 1936-

PERSONAL: Born March 17, 1936, in Baltimore, Md.; son of John A. (an accountant) and Beatrice (a housewife; maiden name, McGee) Engel; married Joan Helen Gibb (a teacher and writer), September 7, 1957; children: John Mark, Kirsten Helene. *Education:* Johns Hopkins University, B.A., 1958; Lombard College, B.D., 1964; University of Chicago, M.A., 1971, Ph.D., 1977. *Politics:* Democrat.

ADDRESSES: Home—5530 South Shore Dr., Chicago, Ill. 60637. *Office*—Meadville/Lombard Theological School, 5701 South Woodlawn Ave., Chicago, Ill. 60637.

CAREER: Ordained Unitarian-Universalist minister; minister of Unitarian-Universalist church in Chicago, Ill., 1965-68; Meadville/Lombard Theological School, Chicago, assistant professor, 1970-77, associate professor, 1977-83, professor of social ethics, 1983—. Lecturer at University of Chicago, 1978—.

MEMBER: American Academy of Religion, American Society for Environmental History, Society of Christian Ethics, American Studies Association, Collegium: Association for Liberal Religious Studies (chairman, 1974-75).

AWARDS, HONORS: Melcher Book Award from Unitarian-Universalist Association, and award from Geographic Society of Chicago, both 1984, for *Sacred Sands*.

WRITINGS:

(Contributor) Philip Hefner and W. Widick Schroeder, editors, *Belonging and Alienation: Religious Foundations for the*

Human Future, Center for the Scientific Study of Religion, 1976.
(Contributor) W. Widick Schroeder and Gibson Winter, editors, *Belief and Ethics: Essays in Ethics, the Human Sciences, and Ministry in Honor of W. Alvin Pitcher,* Center for the Scientific Study of Religion, 1978.
(Contributor) Robert C. Schultz and J. Donald Hughes, editors, *Ecological Consciousness: Essays From the Earthday X Colloquium, University of Denver, April 21-24, 1980,* University Press of America, 1981.
Sacred Sands: The Struggle for Community in the Indiana Dunes, Wesleyan University Press, 1983.
(Contributor) Charles Amjad-Ali and W. Alvin Pitcher, editors, *Liberation and Ethics: Essays in Religious Social Ethics in Honor of Gibson Winter,* Center for the Scientific Study of Religion, 1985.
Ethics, Culture, and Sustainable Development, Cambridge University Press, 1988.

Contributor to theology journals.

WORK IN PROGRESS: Research on environmental ethics and world faiths; research on democratic faith in America.

SIDELIGHTS: Sacred Sands by J. Ronald Engel has been praised as a history, not only of the Indiana Dunes, but of the social, political, and scientific movements that were born there. The Dunes pageant of 1917 introduced a liturgical movement, or a civil religion, that was centered in the Dunes. One of the goals of the movement was the environmental and ecological production of the area, which survives as the Indiana National Dunes Seashore. Eugene Kennedy wrote in the *Chicago Tribune,* "Professor Engel does a thorough job of presenting a story that is now largely unknown . . . by most residents of the Midwest." He referred to the work as a "pleasant and splendid book."

Engel told *CA:* "The motivation for my writing, as well as my academic research and teaching, is rooted in my conviction that a new world faith (variously called the 'religion of democracy' and 'ecological' or 'evolutionary humanism') has arisen in the modern world. To give that faith definition and institutionalization is an important task. In *Sacred Sands,* I show the interplay between the models of scientific research that established the science of ecology in America through field studies in the Dunes, and the symbols of the progressive reform movement and artistic renaissance centered in Chicago and focused on the Dunes as a 'sacred landscape.'"

BIOGRAPHICAL/CRITICAL SOURCES:

PERIODICALS

Chicago Tribune, January 30, 1983.

* * *

EPSTEIN, Julius J. 1909-

PERSONAL: Born August 22, 1909, in New York, N.Y.; son of Henry (a livery stable proprietor) and Sarah (a housewife; maiden name, Gronenberg) Epstein; married Frances Sage (an actress), April 30, 1936 (divorced, 1945); married Ann Lazlo, October 1, 1949. *Education:* Attended Pennsylvania State College (now University), 1928-31.

ADDRESSES: Home—Los Angeles, Calif. *Office*—10556 Fontewelle Way, Los Angeles, Calif. 90077.

CAREER: Grew up in lower East Side of New York City; during college years became captain of boxing team; worked in radio publicity field briefly; moved to Hollywood, Calif., in 1933 and began career as screenwriter and playwright. Producer of motion pictures, including "Mr. Skeffington," 1944, "Take a Giant Step," 1959, "Light in the Piazza," 1962, "Any Wednesday," 1966, and "Pete 'n' Tillie," 1972.

MEMBER: Dramatists Guild, Screen Writers Guild.

AWARDS, HONORS: Intercollegiate Boxing Championship, 1929; Academy Award nomination from Academy of Motion Picture Arts and Sciences, 1938, for screenplay "Four Daughters," and 1984, for screenplay "Reuben, Reuben"; won Academy Award, 1943, for screenplay "Casablanca"; Laurel Award from Screen Writers Guild, 1955.

WRITINGS:

SCREENPLAYS

"Living on Velvet," Warner Bros., 1935.
(With brother, Philip G. Epstein, and Jerry Wald) "In Caliente," Warner Bros., 1935.
"Broadway Gondolier," Warner Bros., 1935.
"Little Big Shot," Warner Bros., 1935.
"I Live for Love," Warner Bros., 1935.
(With P. G. Epstein) "Stars Over Broadway," Warner Bros., 1935.
(With Wald) "Sons o' Gun," Warner Bros., 1936.
(With Margaret Le Vino) "Confession" (adapted from the German film "Mazurka"), Warner Bros., 1937.
(With Lenore Coffee) "Four Daughters," Warner Bros., 1938, remade as "Young at Heart," Warner Bros., 1954.
(With Milton Krims and Rowland Leigh) "Secrets of an Actress," Warner Bros., 1938.
(With P. G. Epstein) "Daughters Courageous," Warner Bros., 1939.
(With P. G. Epstein and Maurice Hanline) "Four Wives," Warner Bros., 1939.
(With P. G. Epstein) "Saturday's Children," Warner Bros., 1940.
(With P. G. Epstein) "No Time for Comedy" (adapted from S. N. Behrman's play of the same title), Warner Bros., 1940.
(With P. G. Epstein) "Strawberry Blonde," Warner Bros., 1941.
(With P. G. Epstein and Earl Baldwin) "Honeymoon for Three," Warner Bros., 1941.
(With P. G. Epstein) "The Man Who Came to Dinner" (adapted from George S. Kaufman and Moss Hart's play of the same title), Warner Bros., 1941.
(With P. G. Epstein and Avery Stephen Morehouse) "The Male Animal," Warner Bros., 1942.
(With P. G. Epstein and Howard Koch) "Casablanca" (adapted from Murray Bennet and Joan Allison's play "Everybody Comes to Rick's"), Warner Bros., 1943, published as *Casablanca: Script and Legend,* Overlook Press, 1973.
(With P. G. Epstein) "Mr. Skeffington," Warner Bros., 1944.
(With P. G. Epstein) "Arsenic and Old Lace" (adapted from Joseph Kesserling's play of the same title), Warner Bros., 1944.
(With P. G. Epstein, Charles Hoffman, and Catherine Turney) "One More Tomorrow," Warner Bros., 1946.
(With P. G. Epstein) "Romance on the High Seas," Warner Bros., 1948.
(With Valentine Davies and George Seaton) "Chicken Every Sunday" (adapted from Epstein's play based on Rosemary Taylor's novel of the same title), Twentieth Century-Fox, 1948.

(With P. G. Epstein) "My Foolish Heart" (adapted from J. D. Salinger's short story "Uncle Wiggily in Connecticut"), RKO, 1949.
(With P. G. Epstein) "Take Care of My Little Girl," Twentieth Century-Fox, 1951.
(With P. G. Epstein) "Forever Female," Paramount, 1954.
(With P. G. Epstein and Richard L. Brooks) "The Last Time I Saw Paris," Metro-Goldwyn-Mayer, 1954.
"The Tender Trap," Metro-Goldwyn-Mayer, 1955.
"Kiss Them for Me," Twentieth Century-Fox, 1957.
(With P. G. Epstein) "The Brothers Karamazov" (adapted from Fyodor Dostoyevsky's novel of the same title), Metro-Goldwyn-Mayer, 1958.
"Tall Story," Warner Bros., 1959.
(With Louis S. Peterson) "Take a Giant Step," United Artists, 1959.
"Fanny," Warner Bros., 1961.
"Light in the Piazza," Metro-Goldwyn-Mayer, 1962.
"Send Me No Flowers," Universal, 1964.
"Return From the Ashes," United Artists, 1965.
"Any Wednesday," Warner Bros., 1966.
"Pete 'n' Tillie" (adapted from Peter De Vries's novel *Witch's Milk*), Universal, 1972.
"Once Is Not Enough," Paramount, 1975.
(With Herbert Asmodi, James Hamilton, and Walter Kelley) "Cross of Iron," Avco Embassy Pictures, 1976.
(With Alan Mandel, Max Shulman, and Charles Shyer) "House Calls," Universal, 1978.
"Reuben, Reuben" (adapted from De Vries's novel of the same title), Twentieth Century-Fox, 1983.

PLAYS

(With P. G. Epstein) "And Stars Remain," first produced in New York at Guild Theatre, October 12, 1936.
(With P. G. Epstein) "Rufus and His Wife," first produced in Suffern, N.Y., at County Theatre, September 1, 1941.
(With P. G. Epstein) "Chicken Every Sunday" adapted from Rosemary Taylor's novel of the same title), first produced on Broadway at Henry Miller's Theatre, April 5, 1944.
(With P. G. Epstein) "That's the Ticket," first produced in Philadelphia at Shubert Theatre, September 24, 1948.
"But Seriously . . ." (two-act), first produced on Broadway at Henry Miller's Theatre, February 27, 1969.

TELEVISION

"The Pirate" (adapted from Harold Robbin's novel of the same title), Columbia Broadcasting System, 1978.

SIDELIGHTS: Julius J. Epstein has earned both recognition and admiration for his accomplishments in the motion picture industry. Although, like most screenwriters, he has ghostwritten his share of films, Epstein has received credit for more than forty screenplays in fifty years of writing. The most popular of his films, "Casablanca" (1943), is considered a classic by film critics and movie fans for its dazzling combination of foreign spies and sophisticated romance. The award-winning movie, which Epstein co-authored with his twin brother, Philip G. Epstein, and Howard Koch, helped him establish his reputation as a composer of realistic and snappy dialogue. Fay Kanin, a screenwriter and past president of the Motion Picture Academy, praised Epstein in a *New York Times* interview as "more than just a writer of good dialogue. He's a good constructionist. His stories have good bones."

Epstein's film career began in 1933, two years after he graduated from Pennsylvania State College (now University), when he arrived in Hollywood and immediately set to work on Warner Brothers' "Twenty Million Sweethearts" (1934), for which he received no screen credit. After writing and collaborating on various detective films, some credited and some not, Epstein achieved success with the screenplay of "Four Daughters" (1938), which he composed with Lenore Coffee. Both writers received Academy Award nominations for the musical, which involves the romantic adventures of four sisters. With two of the movie's follow-ups, "Daughters Courageous" (1939) and "Four Wives" (1939), Epstein and his brother began their long-standing partnership in screenwriting.

The Epsteins developed a prolific reputation in the film industry during their years with Warner Brothers, lasting until 1948. Their collaborations include adaptations of George S. Kaufman and Moss Hart's play "The Man Who Came to Dinner" (1941)—"a series of funny wisecracks and cleverly chosen metaphors," according to *Commonweal*'s Philip T. Hartung—and Joseph Kesserling's "Arsenic and Old Lace" (1944), in which two charming old ladies invite gentlemen into their home and kill them, hiding the bodies in the basement.

The brothers' longest-lasting success, "Casablanca," received two Academy Awards, including one for the screenplay, shared by the Epsteins and co-author Koch. Ironically, the movie was adapted from a Broadway failure, "Everybody Comes to Rick's" by Murray Bennet and Joan Allison. Humphrey Bogart starred in the film as Rick Blaine, a cynical American who runs a cafe in Casablanca, the Moroccan city through which European refugees often traveled to reach America during World War II. Wrote Hartung, "To Rick's cafe come all of Casablanca's adventurers, seekers, spies and police"—and Rick's former lover, played by Ingrid Bergman. Pleading for Rick's forgiveness for having left him years earlier, she asks his help in arranging the escape of her and her husband, a Czech publisher pursued by the Germans. The movie provides its audience the "tense thrill of a strange foreign place in which gather all types of unconventional people," Hartung related.

Despite its awards and the lofty status it attained among black-and-white films, "Casablanca" received only mediocre reviews when it first appeared. Although "the script is good" and it is "a moving and exciting film," acknowledged Hartung, "'Casablanca' is not by any means a first rate film." Critic Manny Farber of *New Republic* maintained in a 1942 review that "'Casablanca' is as ineffectual as a Collier's short story," though with a fine cast and a few key scenes "it is a pleasure of sorts." Such criticism did not hinder the movie from winning the hearts of its viewers, however, observed Aljean Harmetz in the *New York Times,* and it "went on to become one of the best-known Hollywood classics." Hal Wallis, who produced the film, told Harmetz the clever dialogue was one reason moviegoers cherish "Casablanca." He recalled that the Epsteins "came up with wonderful dialogue, bright lines, little punchy lines" for the movie, such as "Round up the usual suspects" and "Here's looking at you, kid."

Epstein and his brother had less success when they adapted J. D. Salinger's short story "Uncle Wiggily in Connecticut" as "My Foolish Heart" (1949) after leaving Warner Brothers. Depicting the breakdown of a woman after the death of her soldier husband, the film was found sensitive but too sentimental by critics. Salinger subsequently refused to allow any of his other works to be adapted into movies.

The four plays the brothers co-authored and the one Julius Epstein wrote alone suffered equally disappointing receptions.

Two of the plays, "Chicken Every Sunday" (1944) and "But Seriously . . ." (1969), the latter written by Julius Epstein, made it to Broadway, but they were not considered memorable. As *Cue*'s Marilyn Stasio said of "But Seriously . . . ," which closed after four performances, the play "presents an ardent apologia for mediocrity."

The brothers nevertheless prospered in the film industry, although they never matched the success they had achieved with "Casablanca." Their final collaborations, "Forever Female" (1954), "The Last Time I Saw Paris" (1954), and "The Brothers Karamazov" (1958), were released after Philip's death in 1952. Julius Epstein continued to write screenplays, winning accolades in 1961 for "Fanny," which he based on French playwright Marcel Pagnol's trilogy, "Marius," "Fanny," and "Cesare." In the movie, a woman who becomes pregnant by a soldier marries an older man, later to be reunited with her lover.

Epstein, who informed *Los Angeles Times* interviewer Lawrence Christon he is "one of the great aficionados of [novelist] Peter De Vries," first adapted one of De Vries's books, *Witch's Milk,* into "Pete 'n' Tillie" in 1972. Pauline Kael described the movie in *New Yorker* as "a nice picture . . . about decent people trying to live their lives somewhat rationally." The story concerns two sensible adults, played by Walter Matthau and Carol Burnett, who fall in love, marry, and have a child who dies at age nine from leukemia. Kael praised Epstein's portrayal of Pete as a "charming, waggish reprobate" and his interpretation of Tillie as "innocuously pleasant and the most straightforward of heroines." Commenting on a particularly touching scene, she observed that "it is apparent that Epstein carries the secrets of forties movies' heartbreak in his pockets." Although Stanley Kauffmann of *New Republic* felt, as did other critics, that "after the boy's death the script goes phony," he agreed that the film is "an amusing, moving sentimental comedy." He added, "The dialogue is churlishly bright, and the wisecracks stay on this side of human possibility."

Six years later Epstein teamed up with screenwriters Alan Mandel, Max Shulman, and Charles Shyer to compose Epstein's biggest box-office success, "House Calls" (1978). The comedy follows the offbeat romance of a lecherous doctor, played by Walter Matthau, and a scheming divorcee, played by Glenda Jackson—"an odd couple if ever there was one," according to Janet Maslin of the *New York Times*. Despite its outstanding success with audiences, "House Calls" received mixed reviews from critics. Maslin complained in her review of the mismatched sweethearts and the fluctuating plot, which she said "turns too sentimental too soon. One minute these lovers are talking good, solid horse sense about their relationship; the next minute they're mired in mush." Audience approval exceeded critics' reservations, however, for the movie spawned a three-year prime-time television series by the same name.

Epstein penned his next script alone, adapting another of De Vries's novels for the screen. In the words of *New Republic*'s Kauffmann, "Reuben, Reuben" (1983) is "essentially a character study" focusing on the freeloading habits of a dried-up poet in a New England town. Critic Vincent Canby described the main character, Gowan McGland, in a *New York Times* review as "an epic mess of underemployed talent. . . . [He] looks like the human manifestation of a hangover." Surviving on liquor, charm, and stolen waiters' tips, the disheveled but articulate has-been is "a wonderfully engaging character," Canby averred. Through his main character, wrote Lawrence Christon in a *Los Angeles Times* review, Epstein "fulfills the conventional notion of the poet as a boozing, lecherous wreck, and [he] rewards us with language as sparkling as a brook."

Epstein's witty dialogue in "Reuben, Reuben" won considerable admiration from critics, including Canby, who observed that "Mr. Epstein clearly has a fondness for Mr. De Vries's language. The 'Reuben, Reuben' screenplay is full of—without being overstuffed with—good lines. It has the kind of appreciation for the oddness of words you seldom find in films." David Ansen of *Newsweek* commended Epstein's clever presentation of the novel's "verbal wit and sly suburban satire," and Kauffmann called the dialogue "wry, bitter, [and] well wrought."

"I love good dialogue," Epstein once told *New York Times* interviewer Harmetz. This quality is perhaps the reason for the outstanding reputation Epstein has earned among his colleagues, Harmetz ventured, and has made the veteran screenwriter "a quintessential example of the breed."

MEDIA ADAPTATIONS: "House Calls" (television series), Columbia Broadcasting System, 1979-82.

BIOGRAPHICAL/CRITICAL SOURCES:

BOOKS

Dictionary of Literary Biography, Volume 26, *American Screenwriters,* Gale, 1984.

PERIODICALS

Commonweal, January 6, 1942, December 11, 1942.
Cue, March 8, 1969.
Los Angeles Times, December 18, 1983.
Maclean's, January 23, 1984.
New Republic, January 12, 1942, December 14, 1942, January 20, 1973, January 30, 1984.
Newsweek, January 2, 1984.
New Yorker, January 3, 1942, March 8, 1969, December 30, 1972.
New York Times, March 15, 1978, January 19, 1983, February 5, 1984.
Time, January 2, 1984.
Variety, March 5, 1969.

—Sketch by Christa Brelin

* * *

ESZTERHAS, Joe
See ESZTERHAS, Joseph A.

* * *

ESZTERHAS, Joseph A.
(Joe Eszterhas)

BRIEF ENTRY: Born in Csakanydoroszlo, Hungary; immigrated to United States. American journalist, screenwriter, and author. Beginning with the 1978 film "F.I.S.T.," for which he wrote the original story and co-authored the screenplay with star Sylvester Stallone, Eszterhas has written screenplays for numerous successful motion pictures. He launched his writing career in 1970, applying his firsthand knowledge of the shootings at a Kent State University protest demonstration to *Thirteen Seconds: Confrontation at Kent State* (Dodd, 1970), which he wrote with Michael D. Roberts. He later contributed regularly to *Rolling Stone* magazine. Eszterhas's other writings include the nonfiction books *Charlie Simpson's Apocalypse*

(Random House, 1974) and *Nark!* (Straight Arrow, 1974) and screenplays for "Flashdance" (Paramount, 1983), "Jagged Edge" (Columbia Pictures, 1985), and "Big Shots" (20th Century-Fox, 1987). *Addresses: Agent*—Rosalie Swedlin, Creative Artists Agency, 1888 Century Park E., Suite 1400, Los Angeles, Calif. 90067.

BIOGRAPHICAL/CRITICAL SOURCES:

PERIODICALS

Chicago Tribune, April 18, 1983, October 7, 1985, October 2, 1987.
Esquire, May 9, 1978.
Los Angeles Times, April 15, 1983, October 4, 1985, October 2, 1987.
Newsweek, January 14, 1974, October 12, 1987.
New York Times, April 15, 1983, October 4, 1985, October 2, 1987.

* * *

ETTIN, Andrew V(ogel) 1943-

PERSONAL: Born April 9, 1943, in Jersey City, N.J.; son of Morris and Cecil L. Ettin; married Johanna Logan, September 21, 1968 (divorced in February, 1987); married Carole Maxwell Stuart (a physician), May 16, 1987; children: Anna Katherine; Emily Katherine Stuart (stepdaughter). *Education:* Rutgers University, B.A., 1966; Washington University, St. Louis, Mo., 1967, Ph.D., 1972.

ADDRESSES: Home—3635 Stimpson Dr., Pfafftown, N.C. 27040. *Office*—Department of English, Wake Forest University, Winston-Salem, N.C. 27109.

CAREER: Cornell University, Ithaca, N.Y., assistant professor of English, 1970-77; Wake Forest University, Winston-Salem, N.C., assistant professor, 1977-79, associate professor of English, 1979—. Soloist with Piedmont Opera Theatre.

MEMBER: Modern Language Association of America, Milton Society, Spenser Society.

WRITINGS:

Literature and the Pastoral, Yale University Press, 1983.

WORK IN PROGRESS: A book on Nadine Gordimer, completion expected in 1989.

SIDELIGHTS: Andrew V. Ettin's acclaimed study *Literature and the Pastoral* examines the pastoral genre throughout history as it appears in a wide variety of works. Using a topical rather than chronological approach, Ettin "keeps us aware of how pervasive pastoral has been within literary tradition," asserted Herbert S. Lindenberger in *Wake Forest.* In addition to discussing recognized pastoral writers such as John Milton, Edmund Spenser, and Vergil, Ettin shows pastoral passages from such diverse writers as George Orwell, William Shakespeare, and Flannery O'Connor. The book is "remarkably appealing," remarked Lindenberger, and is "written with clarity and elegance." Concurring, a *Canadian Literature* reviewer summarized the work as "a substantial scholarly and literary achievement."

Ettin told *CA* that his scholarly interests embrace feminism, South African writing, and Judaism. He added, "The tension between tradition and change engrosses me, in my life and work. In the pastoral book, for instance, I was trying to understand how a genre can remain recognizable and yet be reshaped over time and space, as well as through the hands of artists using it for their own purposes. I was also exploring how literature so blatantly fictive was also about life and living—indeed, sometimes in absolutely topical ways. So it is in a different sense with Nadine Gordimer's work: the continuing commitment to her country of South Africa, her dissection of its injustices and oppressiveness. These different impulses, held together by her sense of the complexity of history and human need, move in very compelling and stylistically evolving fiction toward reshaping not a genre but a nation.

"Perhaps this is overschematizing, but I see the same elements at work in my active involvement with the two movements that have meant the most to my work: feminism and progressive Judaism. In them I find revisioning and redefining traditions, making something new out of what we know of the old. Involvement here also means commitment to both, a conversation with each, a conversation of utmost importance between the two, and it means action in my living and my writing. Increasingly I need to join my life and my work, to write and teach about that which most animates my passions, intellect, and convictions 'for the relief of the body and the reconstruction of the mind' (Adrienne Rich's phrase)."

BIOGRAPHICAL/CRITICAL SOURCES:

PERIODICALS

Canadian Literature, autumn, 1985.
Wake Forest, January, 1986.

* * *

EUSTIS, O. B.
See EUSTIS, Orville B.

* * *

EUSTIS, Orville B. 1913-1986
(O. B. Eustis)

PERSONAL: Born February 8, 1913, in Greenville, Miss.; died of a heart attack, August 11, 1986; son of Herbert Lee (a cotton broker and farmer) and Lola Belle (a housewife; maiden name, Finlay) Eustis; married Evelyn Varney (a registered nurse), in February, 1938 (deceased); children: Helen, Sam, Geneva Eustis French. *Education:* University of the South, B.S. (with honors), 1935. *Politics:* Republican. *Religion:* Episcopalian.

ADDRESSES: Home—13500 Lachine Dr., Route 1, Lachine, Mich. 49753; and c/o Geneva Eustis French, 309 Eagle Dr., Alpena, Mich. 49707.

CAREER: U.S. Gypsum Co., Chicago, Ill., began as millhand, became foreman in Greenville, Miss., 1935-36, assistant to divisional production manager in Chicago, 1936-38, quality superintendent and fabrications superintendent in Lisbon Falls, Me., 1938-40, night superintendent in St. Joseph, Mo., 1940-41, quality superintendent, hardboard superintendent, and board mill superintendent in Greenville, 1941-43, mill manager in Lisbon Falls, 1943-48, production engineer in Chicago and production manager of insulation division, 1948-53; Oregon Fibre Products Co., Pilot Rock, general manager, 1953-57; Atibiti Corp., Alpena, Mich., mill manager in Birmingham, Mich., 1957-63, vice-president of development, 1963-69, control superintendent in Alpena, 1969-78; writer and consultant, 1978-86. Vice-president and director of Thunder Bay River Watershed Council.

MEMBER: National Audubon Society, Phi Beta Kappa, Alpena Sportsmen's Club (past president).

AWARDS, HONORS: Fellow of Alpena Community College, 1973.

WRITINGS:

Notes From the North Country, University of Michigan Press, 1983.

Author of "OBE's Diary," a weekly column in four Michigan newspapers. Contributor to *Field and Stream.*

SIDELIGHTS: Orville B. Eustis told *CA:* "I had an uncle whose farm adjoined ours; he was an inveterate hunter and fisherman. To him I owe my lifelong love of the outdoors. My father did not hunt, but he was a birdwatcher long before it became popular. My mother encouraged hunting and fishing, and she cooked whatever I brought home. Close association with fine professors at the University of the South and ten thousand acres of university domain in which to wander gave me an insatiable curiosity and never-ending awe at the world around me.

"Management in the forest products industry requires a working knowledge of forestry and logging. To build and operate a fifty-million-dollar plant, a person must be able to plan for a perpetual wood supply. He becomes a conservationist by necessity. This kind of work was right down my alley, and I loved it. It gave me many opportunities to be outdoors. I worked, hunted, fished, and studied the outdoors all across the country, and I kept notes on my sightings and experiences.

"After a heart attack in 1969, I tried writing. I sold my first attempt to *Field and Stream.* In January, 1970, I began writing a weekly outdoor column, 'OBE's Diary,' for the *Alpena News,* and it later appeared in as many as twelve outstate newspapers. My book, *Notes From the North Country,* is a collection of my columns arranged in diary form for a twelve-month period."

BIOGRAPHICAL/CRITICAL SOURCES:

PERIODICALS

Detroit News, May 24, 1984.

[Death information provided by daughter, Geneva Eustis French]

* * *

EVANS, George Ewart 1909-1988(?)

OBITUARY NOTICE—See index for *CA* sketch: Born April 1, 1909, in Abercynon, Glamorganshire, Wales; died c. January, 1988. Historian, educator, and author. Regarded as a pioneer of oral history in England, Evans worked to preserve the rich cultural heritage eclipsed by that country's move toward industrialization. Drawing from various recollections shared by neighbors and ordinary working people, he published a number of books featuring the historical background that influenced the agricultural life-style once prevalent among British farming communities, among them *The Pattern Under the Plough: Aspects of the Folk-life of East Anglia* and two studies of the history and lore of farm horses and horsemen entitled *The Horse in the Furrow* and *Horse Power and Magic.* A former teacher, Evans turned his attention to writing and lecturing full time in 1948, when his hearing diminished. His other writings include the short novel *Voices of the Children; Where Beards Wag All: The Relevance of the Oral Tradition;* the classic *Ask the Fellows Who Cut the Hay;* and short stories, scripts for radio and film, and verse.

OBITUARIES AND OTHER SOURCES:

BOOKS

Evans, George Ewart, *The Strength of the Hills: An Autobiography,* illustrations by David Gentleman, Faber, 1983.

The Oxford Companion to Literature of Wales, Oxford University Press, 1986.

Who's Who, 139th edition, St. Martin's, 1987.

PERIODICALS

Times (London), January 13, 1988.

* * *

EVANS, Stuart 1934-

PERSONAL: Born October 20, 1934, in Swansea, Wales; son of T. Gomer (a schoolmaster) and Hetty (a homemaker; maiden name, Williams) Evans; married Kathleen Bridget Treacy (a radio producer), December 31, 1960. *Education:* Jesus College, Oxford, M.A. (with honors), 1956.

ADDRESSES: *Home*—124 Bedford Court Mansions, Bedford Sq., London W.C.1, England. *Agent*—David Higham Associates, 5-8 Lower John St., London W.1, England.

CAREER: Writer. Brunel College of Advanced Technology, London, England, lecturer in English and communicative studies, 1961-66; British Broadcasting Corporation, London, radio producer, 1966-84. *Military service:* Royal Navy, 1957-60; became instructor lieutenant.

MEMBER: Yr Academi Gymreig, Marylebone Cricket Club.

AWARDS, HONORS: Newdigate Prize for verse from Oxford University, 1955, for *Elegy for the Death of a Clown;* prize from Welsh Arts Council, 1978, for *The Caves of Alienation.*

WRITINGS:

"WINDMILL HILL" NOVELS

Centres of Ritual, Hutchinson, 1978.
Occupational Debris, Hutchinson, 1979.
Temporary Hearths, Hutchinson, 1982.
Houses on the Site, Hutchinson, 1984.
Seasonal Tribal Feasts, Hutchinson, 1987.

OTHER

Elegy for the Death of a Clown (poetry), Fantasy Press, 1955.
Imaginary Gardens With Real Toads (poetry), Phoenix Pamphlet Poets, 1972.
Meritocrats (novel), Hutchinson, 1974.
The Gardens of the Casino (novel), Hutchinson, 1976.
The Caves of Alienation (novel), Hutchinson, 1977.
The Function of the Fool (poetry), Hutchinson, 1977.
(Editor) *The Story Inside* (short stories), Hutchinson Education, 1977.

Contributor to periodicals, including *Books and Bookmen, Independent,* and London *Times.*

WORK IN PROGRESS: A novel tentatively titled *Piano Quintet;* a comic novel set in Wales during World War II; several other novels, including a psychological thriller and a trilogy; critical studies of Wallace Stevens and Mario Vargas Llosa.

SIDELIGHTS: Stuart Evans is known for his intellectually demanding, highly structured novels, notably the "Windmill Hill"

series of five works on apathy among the elite of contemporary Britain. Although most readily recognized for these and other novels, Evans began his literary career as a poet, and he won the prestigious Newdigate Prize from Oxford University for his student verse *Elegy for the Death of a Clown*. He subsequently published the modest verse work *Imaginary Gardens With Real Toads* in 1972. But by that time his thoughts were already turning to fiction, and in 1974 he produced his first novel, *Meritocrats*. This multifaceted satire focuses on moral duplicity among supposedly prim bourgeois intellectuals. Myrna Blumberg, reviewing *Meritocrats* in the London *Times*, expressed amazement at Evans's ambitious narrative strategy, which featured first-person accounts from each of the five principals, and she commended him for his refreshing work. ''I am astonished that this is Stuart Evans's first novel,'' she declared. ''It is witty, resourceful and brilliant.''

In his next published novel, *The Gardens of the Casino*, Evans extended his range by adopting an even more complex scheme incorporating allusions and quotations from other sources. *The Gardens of the Casino* details the interactions of a few dull and largely unsympathetic characters, including a suicidal artist, his unfaithful wife, her artist lover, and an American writer with a mania for precision and historical contexts. Evans's actual work is in marked contrast to those of his fictitious American novelist, for *The Gardens of the Casino* is impressively self-contained and void of contextual dependence.

Evans told *CA* that the autonomous nature of *The Gardens of the Casino* rendered it his ''purest'' work. Some critics, however, complained that the novel's self-containment and its complex form—featuring multiple perspectives and occasionally unattributed conversations and thoughts—resulted in confusion and even tedium. Writing in the *Times Literary Supplement*, David Wilson was among those reviewers who questioned Evans's elucidation of fiction-as-its-own reality, but he nonetheless acknowledged him as ''an intelligent, imaginative, skilful writer.''

In 1977 Evans published *The Caves of Alienation*, a complex philosophical novel about a despairing writer. Like the preceding novels, *The Caves of Alienation*, which was actually written before *The Gardens of the Casino* but temporarily lost, derives from obscure discourses and excerpts from invented media sources and several literary genres. In writing this novel, Evans adhered to his literary principle of creating the excerpted works *in their entirety* before extracting specific passages from them for the actual work. Among the receptive critics of Evans's third published work was John Mellors, who wrote in the *Listener* that *The Caves of Alienation* was ''stimulating and satisfying.'' Mellors added that Evans's interests in form and technique never compromised his skills as a storyteller. ''*The Caves of Alienation*,'' Mellors wrote, ''has a strong narrative content.''

After publishing his first three novels and a poetry collection (*The Function of the Fool*), Evans commenced his ambitious ''Windmill Hill'' series of five novels. ''The aim of the sequence,'' he told *CA*, ''is to examine the lack of resolve and intellectual conviction in Western liberal democracy as exemplified in various aspects of contemporary British life.'' In the series' first work, *Centres of Ritual*, Evans focuses his attention on the Highgate Group, a band of uninspired intellectuals whose dissatisfaction with the status quo results in little activity besides the mouthing of empty rhetoric. Unlike Evans's previous novels, *Centres of Ritual* is situated in a particular place and time—Britain from mid-1976 to mid-1977—and makes repeated references to actual occurrences. But like the other novels it unfolds through a complex collage of obscure conversations and excerpts from various fictitious writings—specifically: journals, correspondence, and a manuscript generated by a character chronicling the behavior of his peers.

Critical reception to the first portion of the ''Windmill Hill'' series was mixed, with critics decrying Evans's dependence on his glib wit and technique while applauding his ambition. John Mellors, for instance, charged that Evans's complex narrative strategy was inefficient in portraying certain characters, but he added that *Centres of Ritual* was ''an ambitious, complex novel'' and praised Evans's wit and insights. ''It is not often,'' Mellors concluded, ''that one gets such a stylish and entertaining novel of ideas.''

In his next work, *Occupational Debris*, Evans continued to chart the failings of Britain's intellectual elite by returning to one of his preferred narrative devices: an author's suicide. Here five other writers attempt to fathom the self-generated demise of their mentor, and as in previous works Evans employs shifting perspectives and quotes from material produced by the various characters within the work. *Occupational Debris* prompted critics to compare Evans's work to that of Iris Murdoch and C. P. Snow. *New Statesman*'s Valentine Cunningham, for example, charged Evans with failing to duplicate Murdoch's ''intellectual touch,'' while the *Listener*'s John Mellors declared that Evans was ''a more stylish and versatile writer than Snow.''

Temporary Hearths, the centerpiece of the ''Windmill Hill'' series, attends to the disillusionment of several middle-aged leftists: former radicals who have compromised the political ideals of their early years and now indulge themselves in sexual exploits. The *Listener*'s Mellors found *Temporary Hearths* an exhilarating portrait of the apathetic left, and the *Spectator*'s Barbara Trapido cited the novel's extensive dialogue as ''clever, epigrammatic and politically astute.'' She also acknowledged Evans's familiar ''kaleidoscopic flair with style'' and asserted that his novel was ''full of brilliance.''

In the fourth volume, *House on the Site*, Evans explores still another aspect of disillusion and despair among Britain's intellectual elite. The novel is concerned with isolationism, and its leading characters comprise a carefully contrived neighborhood in which inhabitants are selected for their compatibility but inevitably succumb to guilt over their escapist attitudes. A plot outline only hints at the philosophical complexity of this tale, which addresses notions of social interaction and philanthropic obligation and explores the psychological repercussions of apathy. As Isabel Raphael noted in the London *Times*, *Houses on the Site* is a ''deeply serious book.''

The concluding volume, *Seasonal Tribal Feasts*, offers a more contrasting perspective than previous entries, with the despair of academic intellectuals juxtaposed with the hopes of a young woman and an ambitious academician. The relationship between these two engaging characters never leads to extended romance, however, and the novel closes with the dismal implication that the promise of youth inevitably degenerates into the disillusion of middle age. In the London *Times*, Gillian Greenwood acknowledged the technical complexity of Evans's novel—which is, of course, replete with extensive use of material generated by various characters within the work—but added that, for all his formal feats, Evans had nonetheless fashioned a novel that was compelling and insightful. She declared that *Seasonal Tribal Feasts* contained ''convincing flesh

and blood'' and added that the novel's virtue as a highly convincing work made it a ''remarkable'' one.

Evans's achievements as both an innovator and keen observer have sometimes rendered him a difficult subject for readers accustomed to more superficial fare. But he has nonetheless gained impressive distinction for the complexity and compelling nature of his insights into the shortcomings of Britain's intellectuals. Perhaps most important in this respect is Evans's notion that the disillusion felt by Britain's leading thinkers is a direct result of their own social and political failings. ''Serious men and women have betrayed values which are unpopular or uncomfortable,'' he told *CA*. ''In so doing they have betrayed not only the society to which they are responsible but also themselves.'' To date, Evans's works have been ignored by American publishing, which often considers the commercial risk unfavorable for writing deemed specifically British. It is likely, however, that his books will hold considerable relevance for readers interested in the continued development of the modern novel or the plight of today's intellectual.

CA INTERVIEW

CA interviewed Stuart Evans by telephone on July 18, 1986, at his home in London.

CA: You began with poetry, winning the Newdigate Prize at Oxford in 1955. What sparked your interest in writing fiction?

EVANS: I'd been writing poetry since I was about fourteen, and not very good, most of it. I was quite surprised to win the Newdigate Prize, and then I became more afire with writing verse. But I'd always intended to write novels as well. I had experimented with fiction and prose before I won the Newdigate Prize. And I had intended to write drama too, but that I've abandoned completely.

CA: Your character Michael Dorf, in Houses on the Site, *says that poetry is ''the most advanced form of showing off as well as being the most feasible form of deception.'' Does his statement reflect any part of your feeling?*

EVANS: It did when I was writing *Houses on the Site,* because I became a little bit skeptical about the attitude of British poets. I've always admired American poets much more than I've admired British poets—this is the honest truth. My favorite poets are Wallace Stevens and Marianne Moore. I thought we were getting increasingly narcissistic with poetry readings and all the fuss and baloney that goes on around the British poetry circle. So it was slightly tongue-in-cheek, my writing that; but I did, up to a point, mean it. And at that time, I thought that my own verse was really very self-centered and didn't reflect anything else other than my private celebrations and grouses. And then, I don't know what happened, but I suddenly got a new lease of life, as it were, and began to have confidence in what I was writing again, and to see that I could write in a more dispassionate way.

CA: Poetry gave you the idea and some of the forms for structuring your novels tightly. How else do you think it has carried over into your fiction?

EVANS: Very little, in fact. But nearly all the novels are based upon poetic forms. The first three were not so tightly structured. *Meritocrats* was roughly based on poetic forms, *The Gardens of the Casino* less so, although that became more and more structured as I went on. *The Caves of Alienation* was much more of a sprawl. Of the Windmill Hill sequence, the first, *Centres of Ritual,* and the one I finished earlier this year, *Seasonal Tribal Feasts,* have exactly the same form but in reverse. It's based on the sestina. I invented the forms for the second and fourth, but they also are mirror images of each other in terms of construction. The middle one, *Temporary Hearths,* has its own structure that mirrors itself. There's a central section, and everything on either side of that balances completely. This is clearly a poetic device. Otherwise, I wouldn't have thought that there was very much carryover from the writing of poetry into the writing of prose.

CA: In an article in the London Times *Philip Howard spoke of the diagrams and tables you'd done for the Windmill Hill novels. Could you tell me more about that practice?*

EVANS: Whenever I've finished a book, my wife buys me a new set of colored pencils to encourage me to write the next one. *Meritocrats* was very much planned out with themes and characters and so on done in different colored pencils. *Gardens of the Casino* I started off completely without anything at all. The reason for that was that the third novel, *Caves of Alienation,* was most of it written, and I lost it.

CA: How did it happen, exactly?

EVANS: I worked at BBC-Radio in those days, and I took it in to an editing channel and left it there. I didn't *know* where I'd left it; it was very careless of me. The briefcase also contained poems and heaven knows what else. The studio manager with whom I was working was going on that particular day to Paris, so he gave it to one of his friends and said, ''Will you see that this gets back to Stuart Evans?'' The friend put it into a locker and then forgot about it. I got home and found that I didn't have my briefcase. I thought I might have left it in a taxi or whatever. I asked the police, and I asked at Broadcasting House if anybody had handed it in, and no, nobody had. My wife was away at the time, and I felt immensely miserable. But then I thought, the only thing to do is forget about that book; I'll just have to dredge it all up again. It had been quite carefully planned. I thought, I'll just start writing this book *Gardens of the Casino,* which was something that had been interesting me.

I had a drink with my wife the next day at lunch time—she'd just come home—and she was much more upset about it than I was; I'd become reconciled to it by then. She said, ''What are you going to do about it?'' and I said, ''I'm going to start a new book tomorrow.'' That's how *Gardens of the Casino* came into being. At first it wasn't planned at all; it just found its own way. Then as it got on I thought, this book needs discipline. So I did some planning on it.

The ''Windmill Hill'' sequence was planned in complete detail with different colored inks and different charts right from the very beginning. Mainly it is the order of the characters at first, and it is a question of ordering the material after that. Then there are notes about allusive material—what the characters are reading, the music they're listening to. In each of the books there is some particular tune which is fairly significant. In *Centres of Ritual* it's ''Blue Champagne.'' In the last one it's ''Lil' Darlin'.'' I can remember with the help of the charts how to work these references into the dialogue and that kind of thing. The next book I'm going to write will be very difficult indeed, and I'm not quite sure even how to start the charts!

CA: Your first novel, Meritocrats, *has lovely echoes of other writers. Were any of them intended as tributes to writers who inspired you to write?*

EVANS: Apart from [James] Joyce, which was an impudence on my part, all the others were straightforward parodies—of C. P. Snow, Iris Murdoch, Graham Greene, [Marcel] Proust, and [Alain] Robbe-Grillet. Joyce was an impertinence; he's the author that I admire most in the world.

CA: Do the very serious concerns of your novels and their careful planning preclude any presence of emotion at their conception? Do they begin solely in ideas?

EVANS: Meritocrats did, certainly. I first started thinking about it when I came to live in London after leaving the navy. I worked as a lecturer and met a lot of very smart people who always professed the most deep ethical and political concerns and whose private lives were—well, not necessarily a debauch, but the next best thing. These were publicly extremely respectable people. I decided to introduce into such a typical bunch of characters (who are entirely fictional; they're not based on anybody that I ever knew) two genuinely Dionysiac figures who were going to create as much havoc as they possibly could. That is how *Meritocrats* grew. I'm an only child myself, but I was interested in the brother-sister love theme because I'd been working on the [tragic drama trilogy] *Oresteia* of Aeschylus, and I was interested in the relationship between Electra and Orestes. I developed that theme not for any sensational reason but because I thought it was a good sort of focus for the whole book. It also gave the boy some reason for his violent action at the end.

CA: Often your novels contain pieces of other novels, as well as letters, scripts, reviews, poems. Can you tell me something about the genesis of this method in your work?

EVANS: In the second novel, *The Gardens of the Casino,* one of the central figures, Gervase Wright, was a novelist and poet and broadcaster. I thought I'd have to give some account of the kind of book he wrote in order to make him convincing. When it came to *The Caves of Alienation,* if people were going to write criticism about Michael Caradock, then they had to have something to write criticism about. The essays that occur in that book are fragmentary. Although I'd done a lot of work on people like Camus and Stevens, I didn't write long essays on them and just publish fragments in the book; I used fragments from the work that I'd already done on these people. But I wrote all the novels that Caradock wrote, completely, which took a long time. In *Occasional Debris,* the novelist is called Jack Maddox. That is, I think, my favorite book. I didn't write all the novels that Maddox is said to have written, but I planned them all as carefully as I would plan one of my own books. And I hope one day to write them.

CA: Would they stand as separate books, then?

EVANS: They would stand as separate books, yes. Maddox is not writing in any sequence at all; he's just writing one-off books, and I think there are about seven. But obviously I've got other things that I want to do myself first. I'm hoping to reserve Maddox's novels for about ten years or so.

CA: There are often writers in your books, and many looks at the way fiction is made and the motives for making it. Do you mean sometimes to say that talent is misspent and fiction is badly served?

EVANS: Not really; I don't think so. I think fiction is best served, as far as I know, in Latin America, where people like Mario Vargas Llosa, Gabriel Garcia Marquez, Manuel Puig, and Carlos Fuentes, up to a point, all seem to have immense opportunities for experiment. I think the Spanish-speaking people are very much more alert to demanding fiction than we are in this country. I think this also applies in the United States. I'm occasionally given books by American writers to review, and I'm always impressed by the vitality and the genuine questing zeal of the writers. In this country, with one or two notable exceptions—John Fowles being one—I feel that writers are on the whole fairly complacent, and the critics are quite content to have it this way because it's less work for them. There are some younger writers here who are very good. I think Graham Swift is very good indeed. He's a conventional writer, but he has an original outlook.

CA: In Temporary Hearths *you open and close with the interior monologue of the kidnapped man, and there are some pieces of that inside the story as well. Was this meant only to set the book clearly in a time when terrorism is common, or was there more behind it?*

EVANS: To set the atmosphere of terrorism was one of the reasons. At the time, if you remember, a lot of politicians around the world were being kidnapped and held by these little terrorist cells. What I also wanted to do was contrast the quite serious but relatively trivial worries and concerns of the other characters with those of this man who was there in this terrible room being reviled and mocked and tortured by the seven people who were holding him. I wanted to make the contrast between somebody who is in genuine danger and suffering very real and complete fear and utter humilation with the self-absorption of the other characters—even the Jack Maddox figure, who is a very angry man indeed, and angry with the society that he lives in. There is the significance of the *seven,* because the *Seven Against Thebes* and the *Epigoni* occur in the book. Also, it was a metaphor for the way that the left nowadays works as opposed to the sort of relatively liberal left of the book's main characters.

CA: There are many references in your books to actual current events and politics that set them specifically in a historical context. Do you think of how they'll be read years in the future?

EVANS: I've been taken to task for this by two reviewers. They say the books will need extensive footnotes in only a few years' time. I don't think it particularly matters. I don't ever mind, when I'm reviewing books, if I have to go and look something up in order to get the exact context of some reference or other. I think it gives it a particular flavor of the time. Take [Anthony] Trollope, for example. I'm not comparing myself to Trollope—I'm not that good by any means—but if you read his work, you find all kinds of contemporary references which only add to your pleasure in the work eventually, it seems to me. I would like to believe that readers apply themselves and read with a certain amount of dedication. And usually anybody who gets very far with one of my books has got dedication!

My next book is going to be out in February [1987], and the one I'm writing now is completely different. It's a comedy.

It's not formally adventurous at all, just a complete change from anything I've been writing. I'm sort of taking a holiday. But the one after that will not rely on contemporary references at all.

CA: Would you comment on the connection you see between archaeology and fiction that plays through the "Windmill Hill" novels?

EVANS: Yes. This started off because I was thinking about a novel which was based upon the various megalithic avenues dotted about northwestern Europe—in Brittany, here in Wiltshire and up to a point Dorset, and as you go south in France also there are a couple of others. The work was about a group of people who in a totally arcane way associated these sites with their own dreams of domination and a kind of anarchic view of the world. I was reading about this and came across the Windmill Hill site. My wife and I went down to look at it. There's very little there at the moment, but there are the Avebury circles, which are very impressive. You can't see much of Windmill Hill because they've cultivated over the ground, which was once excavated in the 1920's. I read everything I could about it and came across this statement in an essay by an archaeologist called Stuart Piggott: "The occupational debris implies temporary hearths and there is no evidence of permanent houses on the site." So there you've got three titles. Then I looked the site up in the *Encyclopaedia Britannica*. It was only a tiny entry, but it said that it seemed a site for centres of ritual and for seasonal tribal feasts. That's how my book titles came about.

The archaeological connection came through ordinary dinner conversation, when somebody was talking about archaeology in connection with the kind of trivial object that we get these days and think, oh, that'll be useful if I want to put flowers in it, or whatever. You keep some entirely trivial ephemeral object and maybe later you look at it and wonder, what on earth is this about? I'm looking around the room I'm sitting in now and imagining how it would be if it all fell to pieces and years from now someone were digging it up and wondering what an awful lot of the things were and what they were used for and why. It seemed to me that there was room in fiction for this kind of archaeological exploration of the society that we live in as we live in it, rather than retrospectively.

I've never particularly enjoyed the historical novels written in our own time. I admire the research that goes into them, the great detail and the care, but I've never particularly enjoyed them. And I thought it would be an interesting exercise to look at the society that we live in—particularly the kind of political, moral, and ethical attitudes that we have—in the context of our own time. I see the novelist, as indeed does a Canadian writer, Janette Turner Hospital, who wrote a book called *Borderline,* very much as an archaeologist who's digging things out and examining them and thinking, now what on earth does that mean? This can go too far. I recently read a novel I have to review which is based on catastrophe theory, and that is examining everything in such detail that it becomes very tedious indeed, and very irritating. In my case, it was a matter of digging it all out and holding it up for other people to make up their minds about what the significance or archaeological relevance was.

CA: Your books aren't readily accessible in the United States, I'm sorry to say. Are there any plans to start publishing them here in the future?

EVANS: I would like to very much. Various reasons have been given to my agent for not doing them there. One is that they're too British and would therefore not be of wide interest in the United States. Another reason, which I find unconvincing, is that they're too difficult. I think some of your writers are just as demanding and complicated as I am. For example, there are very good writers such as Gilbert Sorrentino and Joyce Carol Oates, and I think they are very demanding—and very, very rewarding as well. My agent is hoping that after *Seasonal Tribal Feasts* is published, he might be able to sell the whole "Windmill Hill" sequence. According to him, that happened with Anthony Powell, who had great difficulty getting published there until his Dance to the Music of Time sequence was entirely finished.

CA: You seem to have a most satisfactory writer-publisher relationship with Hutchinson. What's made it work well?

EVANS: A very good editor, a very sympathetic and pleasant man who cares a great deal about literature. He is responsible for all the literary fiction that Hutchinson turns out.

CA: Often in the British review periodicals several books will be lumped together in a treatment by a single reviewer under one heading. How do you feel about this practice?

EVANS: The *Times Literary Supplement* doesn't do this. But I'm afraid I have to be one of the people who does it for the London *Times,* because I review regularly for them. You're sent, at worst, twelve to fourteen books, and of course some of them are very demanding and you have to read them very carefully. Others, of course, you can just nip through. I would prefer on the whole just to have two, and many more words than we're allowed to have on the *Times*. I also review for *Books and Bookmen*. There they never send you more than two novels—usually pretty close in theme—and they give you a lot more words, something like a thousand to twelve hundred. I find that more satisfactory as a reviewer. But I never mind being one of the authors lumped together with a lot of other people.

CA: You worked as a BBC producer from 1966 to 1984. Do you feel the radio work has contributed something of value to the fiction writing?

EVANS: I did find radio techniques of great assistance, yes.

CA: Are you interested in doing any television writing?

EVANS: I'm interested in television writing, but not all that deeply, because I don't think I can write drama very well. I know people say that I write reasonable dialogue, but I've never been able to write it in a dramatic context; it has to be in the context of fiction. I'm also very interested in the cinema, so I'm interested in applying, insofar as they do apply, film techniques to the novel as well.

CA: You seem to be working on some stage of various projects at any given time. Does that ever make for problems, or can you keep it all going easily?

EVANS: I think it goes rather easily. There's no trouble at all in writing verse and novel and something else at the same time. Reviewing does get in the way. If you are being fair to the person you're reviewing, of course you have to give the work a lot of attention, and that takes quite a lot of time.

Occasionally I have to give a lecture or something like that. At one time I did it off the top of my head, but lately I've become increasingly diffident about it, so I worry a great deal and do lots of drafts. The odd jobs come along which get in the way of the writing, but, touch wood, I've never suffered from writer's block.

CA: Is there still a trilogy somewhere beyond the comic novel?

EVANS: It's three novels hence. There's the comic book, which is really a sort of holiday, as I've said. And then there's one which is going to be very difficult. Its structure will be based on musical rather than poetic forms and there are a lot of problems. There's one after that set in Greece, where my wife and I spent the best part of a year a couple of years ago. I did a lot of research for it there. It's contemporary in the sense that it's set in our own age, but it doesn't depend on current events. The trilogy comes after that, and it's going to take a lot of work, especially in the research involved.

BIOGRAPHICAL/CRITICAL SOURCES:

PERIODICALS

Listener, April 29, 1976, March 17, 1977, May 11, 1978, August 16, 1979, June 3, 1982, October 11, 1984.
New Statesman, April 30, 1976, June 29, 1979.
Spectator, March 12, 1977, May 12, 1982.
Times (London), December 12, 1974, May 3, 1982, May 20, 1982, August 30, 1984, February 9, 1987.
Times Literary Supplement, May 28, 1978, August 18, 1978, June 25, 1982, November 9, 1984.

—Sketch by Les Stone

—Interview by Jean W. Ross

* * *

EVERSON, David H. 1941-

PERSONAL: Surname is pronounced *Ee*-ver-son; born September 2, 1941, in Rochester, Minn.; son of Ralph H. (a boilermaker) and Margaret (a nurse; maiden name, Krueger) Everson; married Judith Leas (a college teacher); children: Christopher Jason. *Education:* Indiana State University, B.S., 1963, M.A., 1964; Indiana University—Bloomington, Ph.D., 1969.

ADDRESSES: Home—2328 East Lake, Springfield, Ill. 62707. *Office*—PAC 470, Legislative Studies Center, Sangamon State University, Springfield, Ill. 62708.

CAREER: Southern Illinois University, Carbondale, instructor, 1967-69, assistant professor of political science, 1969-70; Sangamon State University, Springfield, Ill., associate professor, 1970-80, professor of political science, 1981—. Affiliated with Illinois Legislative Studies Center, 1973—.

MEMBER: American Political Science Association, Midwest Political Science Association.

AWARDS, HONORS: Fellow of National Endowment for the Humanities, 1976-77.

WRITINGS:

(With Joann P. Paine) *An Introduction to Systematic Political Science,* Dorsey, 1973.
American Political Parties, New Viewpoints, 1980.
Public Opinion and Interest Groups in American Politics, F. Watts, 1982.
(Editor with Paul T. David) *The Presidential Election and Transition, 1980-1981,* Southern Illinois Press, 1983.
Recount (mystery novel), Ballantine, 1987.
Rebound (mystery novel), Ballantine, 1988.

Contributor to political science periodicals.

BIOGRAPHICAL/CRITICAL SOURCES:

PERIODICALS

Annals of the American Academy of Political and Social Science, September, 1980.

* * *

EWEN, Elizabeth 1943-

PERSONAL: Born November 12, 1943, in New York; daughter of Roger (a historian) and Frances (a poet; maiden name, Campanile) Wunderlich; married Stuart Ewen (a professor), October, 1966; children: Paul, Sam. *Education:* University of Wisconsin, B.A., 1965; State University of New York at Stony Brook, Ph.D., 1979.

ADDRESSES: Office—Department of American Studies, State University of New York, State University College at Old Westbury, Box 210, Old Westbury, N.Y. 11568.

CAREER: Affiliated with State University of New York, State University College at Old Westbury, beginning in 1974, became professor of American studies.

AWARDS, HONORS: State University of New York Chancellery Award for excellence in teaching, 1977.

WRITINGS:

Channels of Desire: Mass Images and the Shaping of American Consciousness, McGraw, 1982.
Immigrant Women in the Land of Dollars: Life and Culture on the Lower East Side, 1890-1925, Monthly Review Press, 1985.

WORK IN PROGRESS: Research on the history of the suburbs through the eyes of women, 1945 to the present.

* * *

EYVINDSON, Peter (Knowles) 1946-

PERSONAL: Surname is pronounced *Ay*-vind-son; born January 20, 1946, in Carberry, Manitoba, Canada; son of Kjartan (a carpenter) and Mary (a teacher; maiden name, Bailey) Eyvindson; married Linda Davis (a teacher), May 10, 1969; children: Kristoffer, Konrad, Kyle. *Education:* University of Manitoba, B.A., 1967, B.Ed., 1971. *Religion:* Christian.

ADDRESSES: Home—Box 51, Clavet, Saskatchewan, Canada S0K 0Y0.

CAREER: Schoolteacher in Melita, Manitoba, 1969-73; schoolteacher and librarian in Snow Lake, Manitoba, 1974-80; Clavet Comprehensive School, Clavet, Saskatchewan, teacher and librarian, 1980-84; professional storyteller, 1984—.

WRITINGS:

Kyle's Bath (juvenile), Pemmican Publications, 1984.
Old Enough (juvenile), Pemmican Publications, 1986.
The Wish Wind, Pemmican Publications, 1987.

SIDELIGHTS: "As a teacher, librarian, and storyteller," Peter Eyvindson told *CA,* "I became acutely aware of the finely

crafted work that authors of children's books must use to make their stories effective. Favorite authors like Judith Viorst, Charlotte Zolotow, and Shel Silverstein have had something significant to say to us all—children and adults—but they have managed to use children's picture books as vehicles that portray their thoughts.''

Eyvindson and his wife have spent their teaching years in the rural areas of Manitoba and Saskatchewan, where sources of entertainment for children are often meager. The author honed his storytelling skills in small schools, aided by hand-sewn props. Since he became a professional storyteller, Eyvindson has entertained some forty thousand children per year in Alberta, Manitoba, and Saskatchewan. The growth in recent years of the Canadian juvenile market has allowed the author to increase his repertoire of Canadian stories. His own work has been based on the experiences of his own children.

BIOGRAPHICAL/CRITICAL SOURCES:

PERIODICALS

Western Producer, July 17, 1986.

F

FABIAN, Ruth
See QUIGLEY, Aileen

* * *

FAIRWEATHER, Janet (Anne) 1945-

PERSONAL: Born October 4, 1945, in Coleford, Gloucestershire, England; daughter of William Henry (in business) and Anne (Popplewell) Fairweather. *Education:* Bedford College, London, B.A., 1967, Ph.D., 1977; McMaster University, M.A., 1972.

ADDRESSES: Home—Cambridge, England. *Office*—Faculty of Classics, Cambridge University, Sidgwick Ave., Cambridge, England.

CAREER: University of British Columbia, Vancouver, lecturer in classics, 1971-72; Cambridge University, Cambridge, England, research fellow of Girton College, 1973-76, free-lance teacher of classics, 1977—.

MEMBER: Society for the Promotion of Roman Studies, Classical Association.

WRITINGS:

Seneca the Elder, Cambridge University Press, 1981.

Contributor of articles on Roman poetry and ancient biographies to classical journals, including *Ancient Society* and *Classical Quarterly*.

SIDELIGHTS: Janet Fairweather told *CA:* "Since 1976 I have been obliged to work as a free-lancer, owing to the scarcity of university posts in my field and especially to the unwillingness of appointment boards to consider candidates over the age of thirty for junior posts. I am deeply troubled by the near-destruction of my own academic career, and those of others of my generation, by recent stringent economies and a hostility toward the arts disciplines in the universities. Free-lancing is not a satisfactory compromise: commercialism and scholarship will not mix."

As her first major project on a classical scholar, Fairweather chose to study the lesser-known Seneca: the father of the philosopher and dramatist, whose sole surviving work is an anthology of rhetorical exercises, reminiscences about Roman men of letters, and critical remarks. Her goal was to present not only a portrait and analysis of the anthologist himself but a broader consideration of the literary trends of the time in which he and his more famous son lived. The author's book, *Seneca the Elder,* was appreciated by *Times Literary Supplement* critic Miriam Griffin. The reviewer enjoyed Fairweather's view of Seneca as "an admirer of modern literary developments" and praised her analysis of his literary criticism "as descriptive, rather than theoretical or legislative." Griffin wrote: "The book is a notable contribution to the study of Latin literature, rhetoric and education."

BIOGRAPHICAL/CRITICAL SOURCES:

PERIODICALS

Times Literary Supplement, August 14, 1981.

* * *

FALK, S(tephen) J(ohn) 1942-
(Toby Falk)

PERSONAL: Born July 6, 1942, in Warminster, Wiltshire, England; son of John (a physician) and Katharine (Hellet) Falk; married Gael Hayter, 1984; children: Tamarind. *Education:* King's College, Cambridge, M.A., 1964.

ADDRESSES: Home—Place Farm, Place Farm Rd., Bletchingley, Surrey RH1 4QR, England.

CAREER: Sotheby's, London, England, cataloger of oriental manuscripts in miniatures, 1965-73; free-lance consultant on Indian and Persian miniature painting, 1973—.

WRITINGS:

Qajar Paintings, Faber & Faber, 1972.
(Contributor; under name Toby Falk) *Persian and Mughal Art,* Colnaghi Gallery, 1976.
(Contributor; under name Toby Falk) *Indian Painting,* Colnaghi Gallery, 1978.
(Under name Toby Falk; with Simon Digby) *Paintings From Mughal India,* Colnaghi Gallery, 1979.
(Under name Toby Falk; with Mildred Archer) *Indian Miniatures in the India Office Library,* Sotheby Parke Bernet, 1981.
(Editor; under name Toby Falk) *Treasures of Islam,* Philip Wilson, 1986.

WORK IN PROGRESS: A book, with Mildred Archer, on the Fraser brothers in India.

SIDELIGHTS: Indian Miniatures in the India Office Library was welcomed by critics as one of the first serious studies of Indian painting. The collection of the India Office Library is an important one, much of which was sold to the library by collector Richard Johnson in the year 1807. Authors Toby Falk and Mildred Archer were congratulated, not only for their well-organized descriptions, but for their discussion notes on the more important paintings. Andrew Topsfield wrote in the *Times Literary Supplement:* "In a field of study in which woolly dilettantism has been more common than rigorous scholarship, this book is a conspicuously solid contribution."

BIOGRAPHICAL/CRITICAL SOURCES:

PERIODICALS

Times Literary Supplement, August 6, 1982.

* * *

FALK, Toby
See FALK, S(tephen) J(ohn)

* * *

FEDUCCIA, (John) Alan 1943-

PERSONAL: Born April 25, 1943, in Mobile, Ala.; son of Joseph Charles (a lawyer and judge) and Mary Emily Feduccia; married Olivia Taylor. *Education:* Louisiana State University, B.S., 1965; University of Michigan, M.A., 1966, Ph.D., 1969.

ADDRESSES: Office—Department of Biology, University of North Carolina at Chapel Hill, Chapel Hill, N.C. 27514.

CAREER: University of Michigan, Ann Arbor, lecturer in zoology, 1969; Southern Methodist University, Dallas, Tex., assistant professor of biology, 1969-71; University of North Carolina at Chapel Hill, assistant professor, 1971-74, associate professor, 1974-79, professor of biology, 1979—, associate chairmen of department, 1982—. Research associate in vertebrate zoology at Smithsonian Institution, 1978-86.

MEMBER: American Ornithological Union (fellow), American Association for the Advancement of Science, Society for the Study of Evolution, Society of Vertebrate Paleontology, Sigma Xi.

WRITINGS:

The Structure and Evolution of Vertebrates, Norton, 1975.
(With Theodore W. Torrey) *Morphogenesis of the Vertebrates,* Wiley, 1979.
The Age of Birds, Harvard University Press, 1980.
Catesby's Birds of Colonial America, University of North Carolina Press, 1985.

Contributor of more than eighty scientific articles to periodicals, including *Evolution, Nature,* and *Science.*

SIDELIGHTS: Alan Feduccia told *CA:* "In 1976, just as the debate in the issue of 'hot-blooded dinosaurs' had reached its peak, I was national program chairman for the ninety-fourth annual meeting of the American Ornithologists' Union, and I organized and convened a symposium entitled 'The Ancestors and Origin of Birds,' which focused my attention on these important issues in avian evolution. What were the actual reptilian ancestors of birds? Did birds evolve flight as ground-dwelling, cursorial creatures that in some way began to fly, or did they evolve flight and feathers as arboreal forms that used the cheap expediency of gravity?

"I had already published several short papers on the hot-blooded dinosaur controversy—in fact, these were among the first counterarguments to the hypothesis that the dinosaurs were indeed endothermic. My interest was, of course, primarily from the standpoint of where birds fitted into the picture, because if birds were derived from feathered endothermic dinosaurs then the cursorial theory for the evolution of flight must be the most parsimonious. Critical to this question was whether or not the first known bird, the archaeopteryx, was earthbound, as proposed by John Ostrom, using its feathered wings to catch insects, or a flying form, probably having evolved its feathers in an aerodynamic context. My studies of these problems resulted in two discoveries that established beyond any reasonable doubt that the archaeopteryx was at least a glider and possibly capable of some powered flight, thus casting substantial doubt on the cursorial theory for the origin of avian flight.

"These were tremendously important discoveries for me, because for sometime I had been planning a major synthesis on avian evolution. The last book on the evolution of birds had been written in 1926 and the time was right. With the innumerable discoveries of fossil birds during the past fifty years, as well as the new critical information on the evolution of perching birds, the stage was set for such a synthesis. But the nagging questions that would prevent such a true synthesis concerned the questions shrouding the first bird, the archaeopteryx. Thus my studies of the archaeopteryx cleared the way for such a book, and in the fall of 1978 I wrote most of the manuscript of *The Age of Birds* while on leave at the Smithsonian's National Museum of Natural History."

* * *

FEINTUCH, Burt H. 1949-

PERSONAL: Born May 29, 1949, in Jersey City, N.J.; son of Stanley M. (an executive) and Janice (a teacher; maiden name, Albert) Feintuch; married Maxene Young (a teacher); children: Sophie. *Education:* Pennsylvania State University, B.A., 1971; University of Pennsylvania, M.A., 1972, Ph.D., 1975.

ADDRESSES: Home—1340 State St., Bowling Green, Ky. 42101. *Office*—Programs in Folk Studies, Western Kentucky University, Bowling Green, Ky. 42101.

CAREER: Western Kentucky University, Bowling Green, assistant professor, 1975-80, associate professor, 1980-85, professor of folk studies, 1985—.

MEMBER: American Folklore Society.

AWARDS, HONORS: Grants from National Endowment for the Arts, 1977, National Endowment for the Humanities, 1986, and American Council of Learned Societies, 1987.

WRITINGS:

Kentucky Folkmusic: An Annotated Bibliography, University Press of Kentucky, 1985.
(Editor and contributor) *The Conservation of Culture: Folklorists and the Public Sector,* University Press of Kentucky, 1988.

WORK IN PROGRESS: Research on regional musical revival in England.

FERGUSON, Charles W. 1901-1987 (Hilton Gregory)

OBITUARY NOTICE—See index for *CA* sketch: Born August 23, 1901, in Quanah, Tex.; died after a long illness, December 11 (one source says December 12), 1987, in Ossining, N.Y. Clergyman, publisher, editor, and author. Ferguson spent thirty-four years on the staff of *Reader's Digest,* from which he retired as senior editor in 1968. An ordained Methodist minister, he became religous editor of the George H. Doran publishing house and later served as president of Round Table Press for two years. Among the dozen books Ferguson wrote are the best-selling *Naked to Mine Enemies: The Life of Cardinal Wolsey,* the novel *Pigskin,* and the nonfiction works *A Is for Advent, Getting to Know the U.S.A.,* and *The Male Attitude.* A contributor to periodicals such as *Bookman, Harper's,* and *Saturday Review,* Ferguson sometimes published under the pseudonym Hilton Gregory.

OBITUARIES AND OTHER SOURCES:

BOOKS

Who's Who in America, 39th edition, Marquis, 1976.

PERIODICALS

New York Times, December 20, 1987.
Publishers Weekly, January 15, 1988.

* * *

FERRARINI, Elizabeth M. 1948-

PERSONAL: Born September 8, 1948, in Cambridge, Mass.; daughter of Bruno (a carpenter) and Alice (a housewife; maiden name, Ianuzzi) Ferrarini. *Education:* Suffolk University, B.S. (magna cum laude), 1982. *Politics:* Democrat. *Religion:* Roman Catholic.

ADDRESSES: Home and office—P.O. Box 16, Newton Upper Falls, Mass. 02164. *Agent*—Gerard Van der Leun, 464 Mill Hill Rd., Southport, Conn. 06490.

CAREER: Free-lance writer, 1980-86; Leading Edge World Trade, Needham, Mass., consulting editor of *Light* magazine, 1986-87; free-lance writer, 1987—. Market researcher for American Telephone and Telegraph and for Temple, Barker & Sloan. Teacher of business writing at Northeastern University.

MEMBER: Association for Women in Computing, Boston Computer Society.

AWARDS, HONORS: Best Computer Book Award from Computer Press Association, 1985, for *Infomania.*

WRITINGS:

Confessions of an Infomaniac, Sybex, 1984.
Infomania: The Guide to Essential Electronic Services, Houghton, 1985.

Contributor to magazines, including *Cosmopolitan, ComputerWorld, PC Week,* and *Penthouse.*

WORK IN PROGRESS: A book on competitive intelligence; producing a video documentary about the survival of a local pond.

SIDELIGHTS: "Writing is something you do alone," Elizabeth M. Ferrarini told *CA.* "Seek out the best teachers and critics. Look for constructive criticism. Learn to turn rejection into reward. If you really want to write, don't be afraid to take any type of employment that gives you a paycheck and free time to write. I still do temporary secretarial work on occasion."

BIOGRAPHICAL/CRITICAL SOURCES:

PERIODICALS

Boston Business Journal, February 25, 1985.
Boston Globe, June 10, 1983.
InfoWorld, September 23, 1983.
Los Angeles Times, December 5, 1983.
PC, October 30, 1984.
San Francisco Chronicle, August 15, 1984.

* * *

FERRY, W(illiam) Hawkins 1914(?)-1988

OBITUARY NOTICE—See index for *CA* sketch: Born November 18, 1914 (one source says 1913), in Detroit, Mich.; died of cardiac arrest, January 27, 1988, in Grosse Pointe Shores, Mich. Business executive, patron of the arts, historian, and author. Ferry devoted much of his life to preserving and supporting the Detroit Institute of Arts (DIA). An authority on architectural history and a collector of twentieth-century art, he became honorary curator of architecture in 1943. Later Ferry served as chairman of the museum's Metropolitan Art Association, Friends of Modern Art, and Advisory Board for Historic Landmarks and Districts of the City of Detroit. In 1960 he was named a trustee of the Founders Society of Detroit Institute of Arts, which his grandfather helped establish.

In addition, Ferry was affiliated with his father's business, D. M. Ferry, Jr., Trustee Corporation, beginning in 1942. There he advanced from treasurer to secretary and vice-president. Ferry, who taught art history at Wayne University (now Wayne State University) between 1946 and 1948, also wrote a number of articles and books on local architecture and art. These include *The Buildings of Detroit: A History* and *The Legacy of Albert Kahn,* a monograph co-authored with Walter B. Sanders on the work of the industrial architect who designed the Ford Motor Company's River Rouge plant in Detroit.

OBITUARIES AND OTHER SOURCES:

PERIODICALS

New York Times, January 28, 1988.

* * *

FIELD, Hartry H(amlin) 1946-

PERSONAL: Born November 30, 1946, in Boston, Mass.; son of Donald T. (a lawyer) and Adelaide (an editor; maiden name, Anderson) Field; children: Elizabeth. *Education:* University of Wisconsin—Madison, B.A., 1967; Harvard University, M.A., 1968, Ph.D., 1972.

ADDRESSES: Office—School of Philosophy, University of Southern California, Los Angeles, Calif. 90089.

CAREER: Princeton University, Princeton, N.J., assistant professor of philosophy, 1970-76; University of Southern California, Los Angeles, associate professor, 1976-81, professor of philosophy, 1981—.

MEMBER: American Philosophical Association, Philosophy of Science Association.

AWARDS, HONORS: Grants from National Endowment for the Humanities, 1972-73, and National Science Foundation, 1979-80 and 1982; Guggenheim fellowship, 1979-80; Lakatos Award, 1986.

WRITINGS:

Science Without Numbers: A Defence of Nominalism, Basil Blackwell, 1980.

Contributor to philosophy journals.

WORK IN PROGRESS: Research on the philosophy of logic, the philosophy of space and time, and theories of truth and of the content of mental states.

SIDELIGHTS: Hartry H. Field told *CA:* "A general theme throughout my work is the development of a scientific metaphysics and an account of the place of thought, reasoning, and values within such a metaphysics."

Hartry's goal in *The Science of Mind,* according to *Times Literary Supplement* critic Geoffrey Hunter, is to demolish the traditional argument that the existence of mathematical entities is necessary to an understanding of the physical world and to the science of physics. Field's view, Hunter wrote, is "that there is no need to postulate mathematical entities, or to regard mathematical claims about them as true, in order to pursue science." The author believes that, though mathematics provides convenient symbols for working with physical theories and concepts, the same scientific conclusions can be reached without the use of numbers. Even if numbers are used, he adds, it is not necessary to assume that the mathematical theories are true. They work equally well when mathematical entities are treated as fictions.

BIOGRAPHICAL/CRITICAL SOURCES:

PERIODICALS

Times Literary Supplement, February 20, 1981.

*   *   *

FIFIELD, William 1916-1987

*OBITUARY NOTICE—*See index for *CA* sketch: Born April 5, 1916, in Chicago, Ill.; died December 14, 1987, in Rancho Palos Verdes, Calif. Business agent, scriptwriter, and author. A free-lance writer who traveled extensively throughout his life, Fifield worked intermittently in radio and television and as an international representative for Bordeaux Wines between 1937 and 1958. Among his writings are more than one hundred radio and television plays, three novels, the biographical *Modigliani,* a collection of interviews titled *In Search of Genius,* and the *Encyclopaedia of Wines and Spirits,* written with Alexis Lichine. The recipient of an O. Henry Memorial Award for best short story, Fifield also contributed short fiction to various anthologies and to periodicals such as *Paris Review, Harper's,* and *Argosy.*

OBITUARIES AND OTHER SOURCES:

BOOKS

The Writers Directory: 1982-1984, Gale, 1981.

PERIODICALS

New York Times, December 17, 1987.

FISCHER, John Martin 1952-

PERSONAL: Born December 26, 1952, in Cleveland, Ohio; son of Joseph (a physician) and Armeda (Schutte) Fischer. *Education:* Stanford University, B.A., 1975, M.A., 1975; Cornell University, M.A., 1981, Ph.D., 1982.

*ADDRESSES: Office—*Department of Philosophy, P.O. Box 3650, Yale Station, Yale University, New Haven, Conn. 06520.

CAREER: Yale University, New Haven, Conn., assistant professor, 1981-85, associate professor of philosophy, 1985—.

WRITINGS:

(Editor) *Moral Responsibility,* Cornell University Press, 1986.

WORK IN PROGRESS: Control: Free Will and Moral Responsibility.

SIDELIGHTS: John Martin Fischer told *CA:* "I am working on a book that explores the concept of control and its relationship to such notions as freedom and moral responsibility. The concept of control is important to traditional questions about human freedom and moral responsibility."

*   *   *

FISHER, Dominic (Mayne Maitland) 1953-

PERSONAL: Born May 4, 1953, in Frome, Somerset, England; son of Noel Martin (an artist, architect, and designer) and Joan (Maitland) Fisher; married Christine Robin Lindop (an author and teacher), July 2, 1982. *Education:* University of Wales, University College of Wales, Aberystwyth, B.A. (with honors), 1974, Post Graduate Certificate in Education, 1976. *Politics:* "Dark pink with green stripes."

*ADDRESSES: Home and office—*70 St. Paul's Rd., Clifton, Bristol BS8 1LP, England.

CAREER: Teacher of English as a foreign language in Turkey, Spain, and Great Britain.

MEMBER: West of England Language Teachers Association.

AWARDS, HONORS: Second prize from York Penguin poetry competition, 1984, for "The City Museum"; first prize from Bristol Poems Competition, 1986, for "Watersheds."

WRITINGS:

(With wife, Christine Lindop) *Discover Britain,* Cambridge University Press, 1985, revised edition, in press.
(With Alan Jenkins, Peter McDonald, Jo Shapcott, and others) *New Chatto Poets* (anthology), Chatto & Windus, 1986.

Also author of English language teaching material.

Contributor to periodicals, including *Times Literary Supplement, Iron.*

WORK IN PROGRESS: A collection of poems, *Macaroons.*

SIDELIGHTS: Dominic Fisher told *CA:* "I am interested in language and those who use it; by occupation I am a teacher of English as a foreign language and a writer of English language teaching material, and my greatest interest is in writing poetry. My occupation, and the opportunities for travel it has afforded, have had, I believe, a formative effect on my poetry. It was not until I returned to the United Kingdom in 1982, after three years abroad, that I wrote anything that began to satisfy me. Recent poetry has involved the theme of life in the

modern city. It is, in part, a reaction to what I perceive to be the present stultifying economic and political climate.''

* * *

FISHER, George W. 1910(?)-1987

OBITUARY NOTICE: Born c. 1910; died after a long illness, December 9, 1987. Publicist, broadcaster, and journalist. Fisher was known for his writings about the entertainment world. His gossip column about Hollywood stars appeared in the *Los Angeles Evening News, Radio Mirror,* and *Modern Screen.* In addition, he was entertainment editor of the *Hollywood Citizen-News* beginning in 1973. Fisher began his career as a copy boy for the *San Francisco Examiner* at the age of fifteen, and three years later he was broadcasting news for the paper on radio station KYA. He was a broadcaster at several southern California radio stations over the course of thirty-three years. When Fisher retired from reporting, he formed the company George Fisher Public Relations. In 1986 he received the Diamond Circle Award.

OBITUARIES AND OTHER SOURCES:

PERIODICALS

Los Angeles Times, December 11, 1987.

* * *

FISHER, Rudolph 1897-1934

PERSONAL: Born May 9, 1897, in Washington, D.C.; died of a chronic intestinal ailment, December 26, 1934. *Education:* Brown University, B.A. (with honors), 1919, M.A., 1920; Howard University, earned degree (summa cum laude); further study at Columbia University.

ADDRESSES: Home—New York, N.Y.

CAREER: Physician and writer. Roentgenologist with Department of Health in New York, N.Y.; teacher.

MEMBER: Phi Beta Kappa, Sigma Psi, Delta Sigma Rho.

AWARDS, HONORS: Spingarn Prize, 1925, for ''High Yaller.''

WRITINGS:

NOVELS

The Walls of Jericho, Knopf, 1928, reprinted with preface by William Robinson, Jr., Arno Press/New York Times, 1969.

The Conjure-Man Dies: A Mystery Tale of Dark Harlem, Covici, Friede, 1932, reprinted with introduction by Stanley Ellin, Arno Press/New York Times, 1971 (also see below).

SHORT STORIES

''The City of Refuge'' in *Atlantic Monthly,* February, 1925; anthologized in *American Negro Short Stories,* edited by John Henrik Clark, Hill & Wang, 1966; and in *Black Literature in America,* edited by Houston A. Baker, Jr., McGraw, 1971.

''Ringtail'' in *Atlantic Monthly,* May, 1925.

''High Yaller'' in two parts in *Crisis,* October, 1925, November, 1925; anthologized in *Cavalcade: Negro American Writing From 1760 to the Present,* edited by Arthur P. Davis and Saunders Redding, Houghton, 1971.

''The Promised Land'' in *Atlantic Monthly,* January, 1927.

''The Backslider'' in *McClure's,* August, 1927.

''Blades of Steel'' in *Atlantic Monthly,* August, 1927; anthologized in *Anthology of American Negro Literature,* edited by Victor F. Calverton, Modern Library, 1929.

''Fire by Night'' in *McClure's,* December, 1927.

''Common Meter'' in *Baltimore Afro-American,* February, 1930; anthologized in *Best Short Stories by Afro-American Writers,* edited by Nick Aaron Ford and H. L. Faggett, Meador Publishing, 1950; and in *Black Voices: An Anthology of Afro-American Literature,* edited by Abraham Chapman, Mentor Books, 1968.

''Dust'' in *Opportunity,* February, 1931.

''Ezekiel'' in *Junior Red Cross News,* March, 1932.

''Ezekiel Learns'' in *Junior Red Cross News,* February, 1933.

''Guardian of the Law'' in *Opportunity,* March, 1933.

''Miss Cynthie'' in *Story,* June, 1933; anthologized in *The Best Short Stories by Negro Writers,* edited by Langston Hughes, Little, Brown, 1967; in *Dark Symphony: Negro Literature in America,* edited by James A. Emanuel and Theodore L. Gross, Free Press, 1968; and in *On Being Black: Writings by Afro-Americans From Frederick Douglass to the Present,* edited by Charles T. Davis and Daniel Walden, Fawcett, 1970.

''John Archer's Nose'' in *Metropolitan,* January, 1935.

Also author of unpublished stories ''Across the Airshaft'' and ''The Lindy Hop'' held at Brown University Archives.

OTHER

''Conjur Man Dies'' (play; adapted by Fisher from his novel *The Conjure-Man Dies: A Mystery Tale of Dark Harlem;* also see above), first produced c. 1936.

Contributor of nonfiction to periodicals, including *American Mercury, Survey Graphic Number,* and—with Earl B. McKinley—*Journal of Infectious Diseases.* Contributor of book reviews to *Book League Monthly* and *New York Herald Tribune Books.*

SIDELIGHTS: Rudolph Fisher was among the writers who sparked interest in black literature during the Harlem Renaissance of the 1920s. Within that group, he was notable for addressing the conditions of Harlem blacks and for adopting an incisively satiric approach in depicting that community. For these reasons, Fisher is widely regarded as one of the first writers to provide significant insights into the urban black society, and he is respected for both the realistic and humorous aspects of his short stories and novels. As Leonard J. Deutsch wrote in a 1979 issue of *Phylon:* ''Fisher was an insider who scratched deeply. The stories reveal his love for the people of Harlem and the diversity of talents they represent. They also help us to understand the quality of life of Harlem during the Renaissance period.''

Unlike the blacks that frequently populated his fiction, Fisher was sophisticated and extensively educated. He was born in Washington, D.C., and received his early education in New York and Rhode Island. He earned both undergraduate and graduate degrees from Brown University, where he distinguished himself for his academic prowess. He subsequently pursued a medical education at Howard University, from which he graduated with further honors, and at Columbia University.

It was during his time in medical school that Fisher published his first story, ''The City of Refuge,'' in the *Atlantic Monthly.* Abjuring the stereotypical portraiture that fellow blacks Claude McKay and Jean Toomer had appropriated from leading white writers, Fisher presented fully developed, sympathetic black characters. In ''The City of Refuge'' he recounted the expe-

riences of King Solomon Gillis, a naive out-of-towner who arrives enthusiastically in Harlem only to find himself exploited by his fellow blacks. This story, which Edward J. O'Brien selected for inclusion in the volume *Best Short Stories of 1925,* readily established Fisher as an iconoclast within the budding Harlem Renaissance.

Fisher quickly followed "The City of Refuge" with three more tales: "High Yaller," "Ringtail," and "The South Lingers On." In "High Yaller" he continued exploring exploitation and antagonism within the black community by focusing on a light-skinned black's predicament among abusive peers. As Arthur P. Davis noted in his volume *From the Dark Tower,* prejudice among blacks was a prevalent theme in Fisher's work. "Fisher . . . does not overplay the issue," Davis observed, "but he does not ignore or sidestep it." In "Ringtail" Fisher mined the same theme, only this time focusing on the abuses endured by a West Indian from Native Americans. A more humorous approach was taken by Fisher in "The South Lingers On," where he depicts Harlem as an extension of the South. Notable among the tale's five vignettes is the concluding portion, in which a transplanted Southern black regresses while attending a tent revival. As Davis noted in *From the Dark Tower,* the character "has not lost as much of his Southern upbringing as he had thought."

The more violent aspects of Harlem life are addressed by Fisher in tales such as "Blades of Steel" and "The Promised Land," both published in 1927. In "Blades of Steel" a gambler named Eight-Ball undoes the unsavory Dirty Cozzens by means of a clever, and grisly, trick with a razor. "The Promised Land," like other Fisher stories, deals with the plight of Southern blacks in the unfamiliar and unfriendly Harlem environs. Here a grandmother vainly attempts to reconcile two grandsons. Her efforts are futile, though, and one fellow eventually kills the other. Writing of "The Promised Land" in his book *Down Home,* Robert A. Bone noted Harlem's destructive effect on the unity of Southern blacks in Fisher's works. "Divisiveness," Bone wrote, "is the price the black community must pay to enter in the promised land."

Fisher's next important work is probably *The Walls of Jericho,* his satiric novel about a wealthy black's shattering experiences in a white portion of New York City. The novel's protagonist is Fred Merrit, a prosperous lawyer who moves into a strictly white neighborhood and consequently finds himself ostracized by both whites and blacks. Merrit, however, delights in distressing whites, and is only distressed by his own fellow blacks' reactions to his move. Unfortunately for Merrit, it is the antagonism he has generated within the black community that eventually undermines his life when a fellow black, hostile to Merrit's actions, torches his home.

The tone of *The Walls of Jericho* is largely satirical, with Fisher mocking aspiring blacks, out-of-towners, and—of course—righteous whites. When *The Walls of Jericho* was first published in 1928, reviewers focused on the work's humorous perspective. A critic for *Crisis* declared that Fisher's novel was "finely worked out with a delicate knowledge of human reactions." The critic added, however, that secondary characters were only "moderately funny" and speculated that Fisher's humor might mask his cynicism. "Perhaps he really laughs at all life and believes nothing," the reviewer considered. More impressed was a critic for the *Times Literary Supplement* who reported that *The Walls of Jericho* was "a sympathetic and extraordinarily impressive account" of black life. The reviewer added that Fisher "holds the reader's attention from the first to last" and that the tale is told "with unfailing and pungent humor."

Fisher followed *The Walls of Jericho* with "Common Meter," which appeared in the *Baltimore Afro-American* in 1930. "Common Meter" tells of two jazz musicians—drumming bandleader Bus Williams, who celebrates his music's strong ties to black culture; and light-skinned trumpeter Fess Baxter, who merely uses jazz as a forum for self-promotion and social climbing. The two musicians are rivals for the affections of a young woman, Jean. At a ballroom show, where the musicians' respective bands are engaged in a contest for "the jazz championship of the world," the loathsome Fess attempts to sabotage Bus's performance by slashing his drums. Jean then realizes that Bus possesses greater integrity and self-awareness, and she rescues his band by leading everyone—musicians and audience—in a foot stomping session that sustains the music's rhythm. Afterwards she rewards Bus with her love and the championship trophy.

In *Down Home,* Bone found "Common Meter" to be Fisher's reminder to fellow blacks of their heritage and rightful pride of achievement. "At bottom," wrote Bone, "Fisher is warning the black community to guard itself against a certain kind of spiritual loss. Don't abandon your ancestral ways when you move to the big city; don't discard the authentic blues idiom for the shallow, trivial, flashy, meretricious values of the urban world." Similarly, Thomas Friedman wrote in *Studies in Black Literature* that "Common Meter" was a superb example of black positivism. He declared: "By fully fifty years, Fisher anticipates the notion of 'Black is beautiful,' and uses the blackness of a man's skin to indicate his goodness. . . . As such, "Common Meter" is a valuable source for those who look for early indications of the change in Black consciousness and for those who search literature for positive uses of the color black."

In 1932 Fisher published his second novel, *The Conjure-Man Dies.* This quasi-supernatural mystery concerns the efforts of two sleuths—police sergeant Perry Dart and physician John Archer—to fathom the possible demise of N'Gana Frimbo, an African king who indulges in fortune-telling in his capacity as a Harlem psychiatrist. *The Conjure-Man Dies* is remarkable in that it is probably the first American mystery novel entirely populated by black characters. In the *New York Times Book Review,* Isaac Anderson described Fisher's novel as an entertaining and enlightening volume. Anderson cited the work's "lively picture of Harlem" and praised Fisher's skills as a comedic writer. Hugh M. Gloster, in his 1948 volume *Negro Voices in American Fiction,* also noted the novel's humor as well as its strengths as a mystery. He called *The Conjure-Man Dies* "a refreshing creation."

Fisher apparently found great pleasure in recording the antics of sleuths Dart and Archer, and he had intentions of writing at least two more novels featuring the characters. Unfortunately he was able to write the pair in only one more work, the short story "John Archer's Nose," before his untimely death in 1934. The story, appraised by Deutsch in his *Phylon* essay, amusingly details the devastating effect of superstition in the black community. Deutsch deemed the tale "supremely clever and witty."

Of Fisher's last works, the most important is probably "Miss Cynthie," his often-anthologized tale of a grandmother's initial disappointment, and eventual pride, in her grandson's suc-

cess as a musician. Like many of Fisher's previous tales, "Miss Cynthie" contrasts the values of Southern traditionalists and Northern blacks. Also consistent with Fisher's prior writings, "Miss Cynthie" uses music as a device for exploring these different values. In *Down Home,* Bone called "Miss Cynthie" "the best of Fisher's stories," and he noted that the story constituted an artistic breakthrough for Fisher. "Having given us a gallery of static characters," Bone contended, "he suddenly discovers how to *interiorize* his dramatic conflicts, so that his characters have an opportunity to grow."

"Miss Cynthie" and "John Archer's Nose" proved to be Fisher's last published works. His final writing was an adaptation, for the stage, of *The Conjure-Man Dies.* The play was produced in 1936, four years after Fisher's death. In the ensuing decades, his stature as a key black writer waned. In the early 1960s, however, critical interest in his work was revived, and today he is recognized as a unique and innovative artist.

BIOGRAPHICAL/CRITICAL SOURCES:

BOOKS

Abrahamson, Doris E., *Negro Playwrights in the American Theatre, 1925-1959,* Columbia University Press, 1969.
Bone, Robert A., *Down Home: A History of Afro-American Short Fiction From Its Beginnings to the End of the Harlem Renaissance,* Putnam, 1975.
Bone, Robert A., *The Negro Novel in America,* Yale University Press, 1965.
Bontemps, Arna, editor, *The Harlem Renaissance Remembered,* Dodd, 1972.
Brawley, Benjamin, *The Negro Genius: A New Appraisal of the Achievement of the American Negro in Literature and the Fine Arts,* Biblo & Tannen, 1937.
Brown, Sterling, *The Negro in American Fiction: Negro Poetry and Drama,* Arno Press, 1969.
Dictionary of Literary Biography, Volume 52: *Afro-American Writers From the Harlem Renaissance to 1940,* Gale, 1987.
Emanuel, James A. and Theodore L. Gross, editors, *Dark Symphony: Negro Literature in America,* Free Press, 1968.
Gayle, Addison, Jr., *The Way of the New World: The Black Novel in America,* Anchor Press/Doubleday, 1975.
Gross, Theodore L., *The Heroic Ideal in American Literature,* Free Press, 1971.
Hill, Herbert, editor, *Anger and Beyond,* Harper, 1966.
Huggins, Nathan Irvin, *Harlem Renaissance,* Oxford University Press, 1971.
Littlejohn, David, *Black on White: A Critical Survey of the Writings by Negroes,* Viking, 1966.
Twentieth-Century Literary Criticism, Volume 11, Gale, 1983.

PERIODICALS

Afro-American, August 11, 1928.
Amsterdam News, August 10, 1932.
Cleveland Open Shelf, December, 1928.
Crisis, November, 1928, September, 1932, July 1971.
New York Evening Post, July 30, 1932.
New York Herald Tribune, August 26, 1928, August 14, 1932.
New York Times, March 12, 1936.
New York Times Book Review, July 31, 1932.
Philadelphia Tribune, September 29, 1932.
Phylon, June, 1979.
Pittsburgh Courier, September 24, 1932.
Saturday Review of Literature, September 8, 1928, August 13, 1932.
Spectator, August 25, 1928.
Studies in Black Literature, spring, 1976.
Times Literary Supplement, September 6, 1928.*

—*Sketch by Les Stone*

* * *

FISHER, Sidney Thomson 1908-

PERSONAL: Born August 8, 1908, in Edmonton, Alberta, Canada; son of Frederick Thomson (in business) and Sarah (a teacher; maiden name, Boddy) Fisher; married Harriet Hall (a homemaker), August 14, 1952; children: Geoffrey Ernout, Sidney Harriet. *Education:* Attended University of Alberta, 1924-28; University of Toronto, B.A.Sc., 1930; McGill University, M.Sc., 1936. *Politics:* Liberal. *Religion:* None.

ADDRESSES: Home—400 Prince Arthur St. W., Apt. 5, Montreal, Quebec, Canada H2X 1T2.

CAREER: Northern Electric Co. Ltd. (Bell System), Montreal, Quebec, Canada, development engineer, 1929-40; F. T. Fisher's Sons Ltd., Montreal, consulting engineer, 1945-47; Radio Engineering Products Ltd., Montreal, high-technological electronics engineer, 1948-73; writer. *Military service:* Royal Canadian Air Force, squadron leader, 1940-45.

MEMBER: University Club (Montreal), University of Toronto Faculty Club, Royal St. Lawrence Yacht Club (Montreal).

AWARDS, HONORS: D.C.L. from McGill University, 1966; LL.D. from University of Toronto, 1969; officer of the Order of Canada, 1977.

WRITINGS:

The Merchant-Millers of the Humber Valley, NC Press Ltd., 1986.

Contributor of several hundred articles of literary and scientific nature to periodicals, including *Times Literary Supplement, Shakespeare Quarterly, Harvard Business Review,* and *Environment.*

WORK IN PROGRESS: Shakespeare's Emendations and Notes, for University of Toronto Press; *Shakespeare's London,* for NC Press Ltd.; *Shakespeare's Humor; Energy.*

SIDELIGHTS: Sidney Thomson Fisher told *CA:* "I began writing at fourteen or fifteen, and the subjects I then chose have lasted a lifetime: science, music, and Shakespeare. I am primarily an innovator, although my *Merchant-Millers of the Humber Valley* is local history and an exercise in filial piety. It details the career of my great-grandfather, Thomas Fisher, who was a Humber Miller. In 1973 I donated what was then the most important Shakespeare collection in the world in private hands to the University of Toronto, which named their rare book library the Thomas Fisher Library. As well as the Shakespeare Collection, I donated to the University of Toronto about sixty-five hundred Wenceslaus Hollar etchings, the third largest collection in the world and the only considerable one in America."

BIOGRAPHICAL/CRITICAL SOURCES:

PERIODICALS

Globe and Mail (Toronto), January 31, 1987.

* * *

FITZGERALD, Merni Ingrassia 1955-

PERSONAL: Born February 24, 1955, in Milwaukee, Wis.;

daughter of Anthony F. (a government employee) and Eleanor M. (a homemaker) Ingrassia; married David Fitzgerald, March 20, 1976 (divorced, 1986); children: Toni Marie, Jaimi Michelle. *Education:* James Madison University, B.S., 1976.

ADDRESSES: Home—236 Irving St., Falls Church, Va. 22046. *Office*—Fairfax County Park Authority, 4030 Hummer Rd., Annandale, Va. 22003.

CAREER: U.S. Peace Corps, Washington, D.C., assistant to press officer, 1983-86; Fairfax Country Park Authority, Annandale, Va., public information officer, 1986—. Outstanding child advocate of Virginia Division for Children, 1984; member of Virginia Governor's Overall Advisory Council on the Needs of Handicapped Persons; member of boards of directors of Falls Church Cable Access Corp. and Girl Scout Council of the Nation's Capital; member of Falls Church Community Education Advisory Commission. Brownie Girl Scout Leader, 1977—.

MEMBER: National Association of County Information Officers, Northern Virginia Press Club.

WRITINGS:

The Peace Corps Today (juvenile), Dodd, 1986.
Voice of America (juvenile), Dodd, 1987.

SIDELIGHTS: Merni Ingrassia Fitzgerald told *CA:* "My father was a journalist with his own sports column in the *Milwaukee Sentinel* for many years. I grew up thinking that a writer was a wonderful thing to be. When I worked in the public affairs office of the Peace Corps, children would write to us inquiring about the Peace Corps. There were no materials for children or teenagers, and it became apparent that a whole generation of children were unaware that the Peace Corps was alive and doing very well. The need was there, and using my many years of experience working with children, I wrote a book for children in grades four and up about the Peace Corps. My second book, also for children, is about another government agency, the Voice of America (VOA). Adults and children are not familiar with this government radio station for a simple reason—VOA does not promote itself in this country. I write in my 'extra' time, as I have a full-time job that keeps me very busy. I write on my dining room table, keeping my notes and drafts in a gold suitcase that inhabits the room for the duration."

* * *

FLEMMONS, Jerry 1936-

PERSONAL: Born January 14, 1936, in Stephenville, Tex.; son of Howard and Myrle (Hudgens) Flemmons; divorced, 1982; children: Christopher. *Education:* John Tarleton Agricultural College (now Tarleton State University), A.S., 1957; East Texas State College (now University), B.S., 1959, M.S., 1961.

ADDRESSES: Home—3716 Bryce Ave., Fort Worth, Tex. 76107. *Office—Star-Telegram,* 400 West Seventh St., Fort Worth, Tex. 76102.

CAREER: Star Telegram, Fort Worth, Tex., reporter, 1963-65, columnist and feature writer, 1965-68, travel editor, 1968—. Presenter of syndicated daily radio program; member of board of directors of Tarrant County Lighthouse for the Blind; consultant to Fort Worth Productions. *Military service:* U.S. Army Reserve, 1960-65.

MEMBER: Society of American Travel Writers (member of board of directors; vice-president, 1968-76), Sigma Delta Chi (member of board of directors, 1970-74).

AWARDS, HONORS: Pulitzer Prize nominations, 1979, for stories on a tornado in Wichita Falls, and 1983, for a retrospective analysis of the assassination of John F. Kennedy; named best writer and reporter in Texas by Headliner Club of Austin, 1979; National Headliners Club Award for best creative use of radio, 1980, for the final episode of "The Adventures of the Fort Worth Strangers," a simulated baseball game; Henry Bradshaw Sweepstakes Award, 1982 and 1987; National Book Award from Chicago Geographic Society, 1982, for *Texas;* Frank Johnson National Travel Writing Award from the city of Las Vegas, 1982, for best American story about Las Vegas; award from Headliner Club of Austin, 1983, for analysis of Kennedy's assassination; Mid-Western Sweepstakes Award, 1983, and best travel article awards, 1985 and 1986, from Society of American Travel Writers.

WRITINGS:

Fodor's Caribbean Guide, Fodor, 1978.
Amon: The Life of Amon G. Carter, Jenkins Publishing, 1978.
Texas, Rand McNally, 1982.
Cowboys, Plowboys and Slanted Pigs, Texas Christian University Press, 1984.
"O Dammit!" (two-act play), first produced at East Texas State University, Commerce, Texas, December, 1985.

Contributor to magazines and newspapers in the United States and abroad, including *Redbook, Better Homes and Gardens, Travel and Leisure,* and *Ford Times.* Contributing editor of *Southern Living.*

WORK IN PROGRESS: Revising *Amon;* collecting the writings of nineteenth-century Texas journalist William Brann.

SIDELIGHTS: Jerry Flemmons has traveled to more than one hundred foreign countries during the course of his career. He has journeyed by elephant and moped, dogsled and hot air balloon, by whatever means of transportation he needs to gather material for his travel stories. *Southern Living* has called him the most experienced travel writer in the South.

In Texas, Flemmons covered the assassination of President John F. Kennedy and the subsequent trial of Jack Ruby. He was one of the six reporters who served as pallbearers for accused assassin Lee Harvey Oswald. As a foreign correspondent, he covered the Vietnam war and reported from other locations in Southeast Asia.

Jerry Flemmons told *CA:* "I discovered a long time ago that I can't do anything but write, not for lack of any other ability but more because I am a compulsive scribbler. Beyond my regular work as a writer on travel destinations, I write on whatever interests me and on what I think should be preserved. I first wrote the biography of Amon Carter as a master's degree thesis and then expanded it into a book because Carter's career in Texas was the prototype for all those blustering, swaggering, and bombastic Texans we see portrayed in fictional literature, whether movies, novels, or television. That his 'playing cowboy' was only a pose for outsiders who believed all Texans acted that way is not important. He more than anyone else invented that character for twentieth-century purveyors of cliched Texans—the Urban Cowboy is only a yuppie Amon Carter.

"The character in my play, 'O Dammit!,' William Cowper Brann, was publisher of the *Iconoclast,* a magazine created in

smallish Waco, Texas, between 1894 and 1898. It had, by all accounts, the largest readership of any magazine in America, with subscriptions in at least twenty foreign countries. Brann was, as one reviewer called him, a mean Mark Twain—sarcastic, biting, blunt, and funny, with a style that ranged from classic intellectualism to gutter slang. He attacked everything, from politics to religion, the latter an affront to local Baptists. He was shot in the back while walking in downtown Waco, April 1, 1898—and immediately forgotten. The play has put his style on stage.

"I don't know if I have a career highlight, though the Kennedy assassination is memorable. I have been writing for newspapers, for money, since I was fourteen and expect to be doing it when I am ninety-four. I have had more fun in the last twenty-five years than most people do in an entire lifetime, and I see no end to the experiences. Tomorrow still is going to be the best day of my life, and I expect to scribble a few words about it."

* * *

FLETCHER, Ian 1920-

BRIEF ENTRY: Born August 22, 1920, in London, England. British librarian, educator, translator, editor, biographer, playwright, and poet. Fletcher was a children's librarian in the London borough of Lewisham from 1946 to 1955 before becoming an assistant lecturer in English literature at the University of Reading. He left that school as a professor in 1982 to teach at Arizona State University. His writings include the poetic works *Orisons, Picaresque and Metaphysical* (Editions Poetry, 1947) and *Motets: Twenty-one Poems* (University of Reading, 1962); the critical biographies *Beaumont and Fletcher* (Longman, 1967) and *Swinburne* (Longman, 1972); and the drama "A Passion Play" (first produced in 1943). Fletcher edited numerous works, including *Decadence of the 1890s* (Edward Arnold, 1979) and *British Poetry and Prose: 1870-1905* (Oxford University Press, 1987). He also translated selections from famous Italian poets for publication in his anthology *The Lover's Martyrdom: Translations From the Italian of Dante, Guarini, Tasso, and Marino, With Original Texts* (Fantasy Press, 1957). *Addresses: Home*—8 Warwick Rd., Reading, Berkshire, England.

BIOGRAPHICAL/CRITICAL SOURCES:

BOOKS

Contemporary Poets, 4th edition, St. Martin's, 1985.
International Who's Who in Poetry, 5th edition, Melrose, 1977.
The Writers Directory: 1986-1988, St. James Press, 1986.

PERIODICALS

Listener, June 22, 1967.
New Statesman, June 9, 1967.
Times Literary Supplement, January 11, 1980, October 2, 1981, July 6, 1984, July 3, 1987.

* * *

FLETCHER, John C(aldwell) 1931-

PERSONAL: Born November 1, 1931, in Bryan, Tex.; son of Robert Capers (an Episcopal priest) and Estelle Collins (Caldwell) Fletcher; married Adele Davis Woodall (a real estate agent), September 4, 1954; children: John Caldwell, Page Moss, Adele Davis. *Education:* University of the South, B.A., 1953; Virginia Theological Seminary, M.Div. (cum laude), 1956; attended University of Heidelberg, 1957; Union Theological Seminary, New York, N.Y., Ph.D., 1969. *Politics:* Democrat.

ADDRESSES: Home—203 Vassar Pl., Alexandria, Va. 22314. *Office*—National Institutes of Health, Bldg. 10, Room 1C150, Bethesda, Md. 20205.

CAREER: Ordained Episcopal priest, 1957; St. Luke's Episcopal Church, Mountain Brook, Ala., curate, 1957-60; Robert E. Lee Memorial Church, Lexington, Va., rector, 1960-64; Midtown Medical Center, New York, N.Y., chaplain, 1964-66; Virginia Theological Seminary, associate professor of church and society, 1966-71; Interfaith Metropolitan (Inter/Met) Seminary, Washington, D.C., director, 1971—, president, 1975-77. Assistant for bioethics at Warren G. Magnuson Clinical Center, National Institutes of Health, 1977—; associate for theological education at Alban Institute, Washington, D.C., 1977-83; project manager for Seminary Futures Project, 1979-83; project director at Hastings Center, 1979-82; member of genetic review board and advisory committee for Maternal and Child Health Program, Public Health Service, 1980-81; adjunct associate professor in department of community and family medicine at Georgetown University School of Medicine, 1983—; visiting scholar at University of Oslo Institute of Medical Genetics, 1984. Lecturer. *Military service:* Alabama Air National Guard, medical assistant, 1948-50.

MEMBER: Institute of Society, Ethics and Life Sciences (founding fellow; member of board of directors, 1980—), Society of Christian Ethics, Council of College Preachers (vice-chairman), Kennedy Institute of Ethics (senior fellow), Washington Academy of Medicine.

AWARDS, HONORS: Fulbright scholar, 1956-57.

WRITINGS:

(Translator) Dietrich Bonhoeffer, *Creation and Fall,* Macmillan, 1959.
(With Celia A. Hahn) *Inter/Met: Bold Experiment in Theological Education,* Alban Institute (Washington, D.C.), 1977.
Coping With Genetic Disorders: A Guide for Clergy and Parents, Harper, 1982.
The Future of Protestant Seminaries, Alban Institute, 1983.

Contributor of chapters in medical-ethical literature and articles to professional journals, including *New England Journal of Medicine*. Associate editor, *Encyclopedia of Bioethics,* 1975-78.

WORK IN PROGRESS: A book based on research in "comparative ethics" that will compare approaches to ethical problems in human genetics among medical geneticists in nineteen nations, for Springer-Verlag (Heidelberg).

SIDELIGHTS: In *Coping With Genetic Disorders* bioethicist John C. Fletcher examines the moral and medical, spiritual and scientific aspects of genetic disease. Besides presenting an overview of genetic fundamentals, the author shares his own experiences as a genetic counselor and outlines the clergy's role in meeting the medical-ethical questions that doctors, patients, and families face today. In addition, Fletcher addresses the problem of theodicy (how an all-good and merciful God can allow moral or natural evil), seeking a resolution for himself as well as for the anguished parents he counsels; the author arrives at "a view of evolution where God doesn't determine everything, but where God is not indifferent to evolution."

New Catholic World reviewer William F. Maestri called *Coping With Genetic Disorders* "a solid book that deserves a wide

readership.'' Commending its ''very helpful glossary of terms,'' he found the book ''well-footnoted with excellent resources for further reading.'' Philip Reilly concurred in the *Hastings Center Report,* noting that ''*Coping With Genetic Disorders* is ambitious, provocative, and enriched by Fletcher's willingness to share intensely personal meditations on the sorrows caused by genetic disease.'' And Sandy Rovner, writing in the *Washington Post,* deemed Fletcher's investigation an ''eloquent book'' with ''glimpses into the considerable and lucid thought processes of an insightful and caring spirit.'' ''It should be required reading for any health professional, clinical or research,'' the critic remarked, ''or for any patient or potential patient, family and friends, as well as for Fletcher's colleagues to whom it is aimed.''

Fletcher told *CA:* ''I am a minister by background with a lifelong interest in science and medicine, but since the 1960s I have tried to serve medicine as a bioethicist and the ministry by actively promoting change in theological education. I am an 'applied' bioethicist by choice, preferring to work 'in the trenches' with physicians and scientists. I am probably too heterodox in my religious beliefs to succeed full time in the ministry, but I see myself as a loyal member of the Protestant persuasion of the Episcopal church. I abhor intellectual dishonesty and the shallowness of most thinking and action in religious circles, but I will not put the need to be ultimately accountable aside, because I know that it is a genuine human need.

''I am sure that a lot of my motivation to be a minister and to work in science and medicine stems from the fact that both of my parents are deaf. My father is a retired missionary to the deaf, greatly helped by my mother's creativity and hard work to be a very effective worker with the deaf communities in the South at a time before there were public programs. I have three sisters who are also high achievers: Louise, an actress, won an Oscar for 'One Flew Over the Cuckoo's Nest'; Roberta teaches first grade in a rural school in Gloucester, Virginia; and Georgianna works for a large trade association in northern Virginia. I feel lucky to have a close family. I try to write about applied human genetics in a way that will resonate with traditional values about the family and yet yield new advances in diagnosis and treatment that promise liberation from biological imprisonment. Most Americans are scared of the whole area of genetics, largely because they have religiously inspired fears. I make it my business to try to think clearly about religion and human biology, so as to try to help others do the same.

''My personal philosophy is that responsibility is the highest achievement for a human being, and that each situation can be saved from meaninglessness by the search for responsibility.''

BIOGRAPHICAL/CRITICAL SOURCES:

PERIODICALS

Hastings Center Report, October, 1983.
New Catholic World, May/June, 1983.
Washington Post, February 18, 1983.

* * *

FONTANA, Biancamaria 1952-

PERSONAL: Born September 10, 1952, in Milan, Italy; daughter of Giuseppe (a manager) and Luciana (a manager; maiden name, Garrone) Fontana. *Education:* Universita degli Studi-Milan, Ph.D. (philosophy), 1974; Cambridge University, Ph.D. (history), 1983.

ADDRESSES: Home—31 Station Rd., Swavesey, Cambridgeshire CB4 5QJ, England. *Office*—King's College, Cambridge University, Cambridge CB2 1ST, England.

CAREER: Fondazione l'Einaudi, Turin, Italy, fellow in the history of ideas, 1977-79; Cambridge University, Cambridge, England, fellow of King's College, 1979-84; free-lance writer and translator, 1984-86; University of Edinburgh, Edinburgh, Scotland, visiting fellow at the Institute for Advanced Study, 1986; European University Institute, Florence, Italy, fellow, 1986-87; writer.

MEMBER: Societe B. Constant.

WRITINGS:

I Principi di Economic Politica di J. S. Mill (title means ''Principles of Political Economy''), two volumes, Utet, 1983.
Rethinking the Politics of Commercial Society: The Edinburgh Review, 1802-1832, Cambridge University Press, 1985.
The Political Writings of Benjamin Constant, Cambridge University Press, 1987.

WORK IN PROGRESS: The Liberty of the Moderns: A Study of Benjamin Constant's Political Thought.

SIDELIGHTS: Reviewer Peter Mandler informed readers of the *Times Literary Supplement* that Biancamaria Fontana's book, *Rethinking the Politics of Commercial Society,* represents ''a major contribution to a crucial historical project.'' Fontana's book is a study of the Scottish philosophers of the *Edinburgh Review* and their reaction to the French Revolution and its aftermath. The author contends that the revolution and the Napoleonic wars forced these Scotsmen to relocate in London, the capital of the empire, where they could play an active role in guiding Great Britain's politicians and lawmakers. She emphasizes that their efforts to reform the political system were eminently successful. For this, the critic wrote, ''she demonstrates a [broad] appreciation of what mattered in early nineteenth-century politics'' and an unusually shrewd ''grasp of the Edinburgh point of view.''

BIOGRAPHICAL/CRITICAL SOURCES:

PERIODICALS

Times Literary Supplement, May 2, 1986.

* * *

FORBES-ROBERTSON, Diana
See SHEEAN, Diana

* * *

FORD, Edmund Brisco 1901-1988

OBITUARY NOTICE—See index for *CA* sketch: Born April 23, 1901, in Papcastle, Cumberland, England; died January 22, 1988. Geneticist, educator, and author. A retired professor and former director of the genetics laboratory at Oxford University, Ford originated the scientific process known as ecological genetics and expanded the study of evolution. Through experimentation and field research mainly with butterflies and moths, he supported Darwin's theory of natural selection and demonstrated that a species' survival depends on its adaptability to the environment. Ford's highly esteemed work re-

sulted in a number of scientific innovations, among them the discovery of genetic polymorphism—a condition of variation within genes that accounts for such traits as susceptibility to disease. For outstanding contributions to the genetic theory of evolution, Ford received the Darwin Medal from the Royal Society of London in 1954. Additionally, he was one of the first scientists elected a fellow at All Souls College since the seventeenth century. Ford's writings include *Evolution Studied by Observation and Experiment, Understanding Genetics, Taking Genetics Into the Countryside,* and the 1945 best-seller *Butterflies.*

OBITUARIES AND OTHER SOURCES:

BOOKS

McGraw-Hill Modern Scientists and Engineers, McGraw, 1980.
Who's Who, 139th edition, St. Martin's, 1987.

PERIODICALS

Times (London), January 23, 1988.

* * *

FORDHAM, Frieda 1903-1988

OBITUARY NOTICE: Name originally Winefride Rothwell; born February 23, 1903, in Salford, Manchester, England; died January 7, 1988. Analytical psychologist and author. Fordham is best known as the author of *An Introduction to Jung's Psychology,* an authoritative text prefaced by the Swiss psychologist Carl Jung. Fordham, a psychiatric social worker, became interested in Jungian theory through her husband, a child psychologist whom she met while both were working at a child guidance clinic in London. She also was an adviser for the radio program for children, "Listen With Mother."

OBITUARIES AND OTHER SOURCES:

PERIODICALS

Times (London), January 18, 1988.

* * *

FORTEN, Charlotte
See GRIMKE, Charlotte L(ottie) Forten

* * *

FOURNET, Jean-Claude 1932-

PERSONAL: Born June 15, 1932; son of Pierre and Odile (Jouan) Fournet; married Arlette Belet, September 13, 1962; children: Marion, Julie, Pauline, Thomas. *Education:* Attended University Louis Pasteur and Lycee Janson de Sailly. *Religion:* Catholic.

ADDRESSES: Home—54 boulevard Maillot, 92200 Neuilly-sur-Seine, France. *Office*—Regidee, 30 rue des Acacias, 75017 Paris, France.

CAREER: Executive director of Publicis (advertising agency), 1954-70; Regidee (advertising and publishing company), Paris, France, owner, 1971—. *Military service:* French Army.

WRITINGS:

Trains: Jouets et modeles; La Collection du comte A. Giansanti Coluzzi et l'integrale Figurex, S. Godin, 1982, translation by Narisa Levy published as *The Trains on Avenue de Rumine,* edited by Allen Levy, Marshall Cavendish, 1982.

Contributor of articles to French periodicals.

WORK IN PROGRESS: A book on toy cars in the A. Giansanti collection; a book on toy armies in the Forbes collection.

* * *

FRANK, Katherine

PERSONAL: Education—University of Illinois at Chicago, B.A., 1972; University of Iowa, Ph.D., 1979.

ADDRESSES: Office—Department of English and European Languages, Bayero University, P.M.B. 3011, Kano, Nigeria. *Agent*—Jennifer Kavanagh, 39 Camden Park Rd., London NW1 9AX, England.

CAREER: University of Sierra Leone, Freetown, lecturer, 1980-83; Bayero University, Kano, Nigeria, senior lecturer, 1984—. Free-lance journalist.

MEMBER: Modern Language Association of America, Women in Nigeria, Bronte Society.

WRITINGS:

A Voyager Out: The Life of Mary Kingsley, Houghton, 1986.
Divide the Desolation (biography of Charlotte and Emily Bronte), Houghton, in press.

Contributor of articles and book reviews to periodicals, including *Miami Herald.*

WORK IN PROGRESS: A book on Arab women, publication expected in 1990.

SIDELIGHTS: Mary Kingsley, who *New York Times Book Review* critic Elinor Langer described as a "profoundly searching spirit," is the subject of Katherine Frank's "mature and satisfying" biography *A Voyager Out: The Life of Mary Kingsley.* After living the life of a homebound and dutiful daughter for the first thirty years of her life, Mary Kingsley, upon the death of her parents in 1892, sought freedom and adventure; she became an African explorer. She was "a most unlikely heroine," remarked Langer, as Kingsley's two major journeys to West Africa between 1893 and 1896 found the Victorian spinster paddling through swamps of the French Congo, climbing mountains, and living among Africans in tropical rain forests. Kingsley's exploits led her to write two books as well as to become a celebrated speaker in the select world of London's political and literary salons. But "she never fully fitted into life in England again, after that first trip [to Africa]," commented *Washington Post Book World* reviewer William Boyd. Kingsley acquired a great attachment and comforting oneness with Africa, and she considered it her home. Mary Kingsley was one of the "great travelers of history [and] different from all the scientists, explorers and tourists," maintained Boyd, because the most important aspect of her explorations was that she "traveled to find herself." She died of typhoid at the age of thirty-seven, during Africa's Boer War, while nursing prisoners of war near Cape Town.

It is Mary Kingsley's extraordinary life and the mysterious and alluring setting of Africa, Boyd noted, that Katherine Frank so aptly focuses upon in her "fascinating" book, *A Voyager Out.* "At its end," wrote Boyd, "one has come some way towards understanding the complexities of the unique person Mary Kingsley surely was." Elinor Langer further com-

mented, "Wisely, the author's emphasis is less on Kingsley's contributions to African scholarship, however important, than it is on her human experience." Katherine Frank has lived in West Africa herself for seven years, and Langer observed that "it is obvious from her writing . . . that the landscape that refreshed Kingsley refreshes her too." Although *Chicago Tribune* reporter Patrick Reardon claimed that Frank's "obvious affection and regard for her subject" is a minor drawback in that it "pushes Frank, unnecessarily, to explain away some of Kingsley's quirks," he conceded that "it animates Frank to tell the story of a complex and often hidden life with straightforward strength and clarity."

Frank told *CA:* "I think that 'biographizing' (an endeavor someone once accused me of comitting) is in a very real sense an act of self-preservation. Our own lives become enriched and endurable when we're allowed to live others' whether in the act of writing or reading about them, in biographies or fiction. I am drawn to the lives of women with whom I feel some sort of affinity or kinship, and women whose lives I find exotic, dangerous, unfathomable. I write, then, of people who wrest me out of the familiar historical/cultural world I am an accidental product of, and who entice me to *travel* through time and space: backwards into the nineteenth century and geographically to West Africa, Yorkshire, the Middle East. I wholeheartedly endorse Bernard Malamud's fictional biographer of D. H. Lawrence in the novel *Dubin's Lives* when Malamud makes Dubin say, 'Everybody's life is mine unlived. One writes lives [s]he can't live. To live forever is a human hunger.'"

BIOGRAPHICAL/CRITICAL SOURCES:

PERIODICALS

Chicago Tribune, September 19, 1986.
New York Times Book Review, November 30, 1986.
Washington Post Book World, December 21, 1986.

* * *

FRANKFURTER, Felix 1882-1965

BRIEF ENTRY: Born November 15, 1882, in Vienna, Austria; immigrated to United States, 1894; died of a heart attack, February 22, 1965. American attorney, civil servant, educator, associate justice of the Supreme Court, and author. A founder of the American Civil Liberties Union (ACLU) in the 1920s, Frankfurter spent a brief time in private law practice before he was appointed to assist Henry L. Stimson, U.S. Attorney for the Southern District of New York, in 1906. When Stimson became Secretary of War in 1911, Frankfurter followed him to Washington, D.C., to serve as law officer of the War Department's bureau of insular affairs. This led to positions within the adminstrations of U.S. presidents Theodore Roosevelt and Woodrow Wilson. Meanwhile, in 1914 Frankfurter became a professor at Harvard Law School, a duty he held until 1939. While still teaching law, he was a highly influential friend of U.S. President Franklin D. Roosevelt and recommended many of his students to posts in the president's administration; these young Harvard lawyers were instrumental in shaping the policies of Roosevelt's New Deal. In 1939, after the death of Justice Benjamin N. Cardozo, Roosevelt appointed Frankfurter as a replacement on the U.S. Supreme Court.

Frankfurter's record as an associate justice of the Supreme Court was varied. An adamant champion of Americans' right to privacy, he nevertheless in 1940 supported a Pennsylvania school district's authority to deny free education to children of Jehovah's Witnesses who refused to salute the American flag because of religious beliefs. Later, he played an important role in the landmark 1955 Supreme Court decision that began desegregation in American schools.

Some of Frankfurter's writings have been influential in shaping public opinion, especially his account of the trial and execution of anarchists Nicola Sacco and Bartolomeo Vanzetti, *The Case of Sacco and Vanzetti: A Critical Analysis for Lawyers and Laymen* (1927). His other books include *The Business of the Supreme Court: A Study in the Federal Judicial System* (1927), *The Commerce Clause Under Marshall, Taney, and Waite* (1937), *Mr. Justice Holmes and the Supreme Court* (1938) and the posthumously published *Of Law and Life and Other Things That Matter* (1969) and *From the Diaries of Felix Frankfurter* (1975). *Addresses: Home*—192 Brattle St., Cambridge, Mass.

BIOGRAPHICAL/CRITICAL SOURCES:

BOOKS

Current Biography, H. W. Wilson, 1957, April, 1965.
Frankfurter, Felix, *From the Diaries of Felix Frankfurter,* Norton, 1975.
Kurland, Philip B., *Mr. Justice Frankfurter and the Constitution,* University of Chicago Press, 1971.
Mendelson, Wallace, editor, *Felix Frankfurter, the Judge,* Reynal, 1964.
Thomas, Helen Shirley, *Felix Frankfurter: Scholar on the Bench,* Johns Hopkins University Press, 1960.

PERIODICALS

Atlantic, March, 1964.
New Republic, November 18, 1957, March 6, 1965.
Newsweek, June 4, 1956, September 10, 1962, March 8, 1965.
New York Times Book Review, August 31, 1975.
Time, June 27, 1960, March 5, 1965.

* * *

FRANKLIN, Bob 1949-

PERSONAL: Born June 21, 1949, in Birmingham, England; son of Arthur Elijah (a factory worker) and Olive (a homemaker; maiden name, Jackson) Franklin; married Annie Dimmock (a community worker) in August, 1975. *Education:* University of Hull, B.A. (with honors), 1973, Ph.D., 1981. *Politics:* Socialist. *Religion:* "Non-theist."

ADDRESSES: Office—Centre for Television Research, University of Leeds, Leeds LS2 9JT, England.

CAREER: Professional drummer, 1966-68; University of York, York, England, lecturer in politics, 1976-78; Newcastle Polytechnic, Newcastle upon Tyne, England, lecturer in politics, 1978-85; University of Leeds, Leeds, England, research fellow in political communication at Centre for Television Research, 1985—. Educational broadcaster for BBC-Radio, 1980-81.

MEMBER: Political Studies Association.

WRITINGS:

(Editor and contributor) *The Rights of Children,* Basil Blackwell, 1986.
(Contributor) T. Jeffs and M. Smith, editors, *Youth in a Divided Society,* Macmillan, 1988.

WORK IN PROGRESS: Research on the local press in Britain, local government public relations, and "ageism" and the dimensions of age and power in British society.

SIDELIGHTS: Bob Franklin told *CA:* "Children suffer from an almost total lack of meaningful decision-making in British society. Since young people are denied a voice of their own, I decided that someone should try to articulate their legitimate claim to rights. This prompted me to produce *The Rights of Children.* Age, much like class, race, and gender, structures the life chances of individuals.

"The responses to the book have been predictably hostile. The case for giving children a greater say in their affairs, which was outlined in the book, was too frequently dismissed as ridiculous rather than seriously considered or refuted; reviews tended toward the dismissive rather than the reasoned. This is disappointing. Many of the contributors are working with children in a number of settings as teachers, social workers, counselors, and so forth and outlined a number of practical procedures and proposals which, if implemented, would give children greater autonomy. We tend to treat children and the elderly (who are often considered to be returning to childhood) as stupid, weak, irrational people incapable of making their own decisions. The young and old exhibit other similarities: both are subject to physical abuse in the home.

"My other area of academic interest lies in the field of media studies; my particular concern here is with local political communication. My recent publications include studies of local government public relations activities and the attempts by central government to control local publicity initiatives through the Local Government Act of 1986."

BIOGRAPHICAL/CRITICAL SOURCES:

PERIODICALS

Times Literary Supplement, October 31, 1986.

* * *

FRASER, Flora 1958-

PERSONAL: Born October 30, 1958, in London, England; daughter of Hugh (a member of parliament) and Antonia (a writer; maiden name, Pakenham) Fraser; married Robert Powell-Jones (a barrister), March 29, 1980. *Education:* Attended Wadham College, Oxford, 1977-81. *Religion:* Roman Catholic.

ADDRESSES: Home—12 Hereford Mansions, London W2 5BA, England. *Agent*—Anne McDermid, Curtis Brown, 162-168 Regent St., London W1R 5TA, England.

CAREER: Full-time writer, 1981—.

WRITINGS:

Double Portrait, Fontana, 1983.
Maud: The Diaries of Maud Berkeley, introduction by grandmother, Elizabeth Longford, Secker & Warburg, 1985, published as *Maud: The Illustrated Diary of a Victorian Woman,* Chronicle Books, 1987.
Beloved Emma: The Life of Emma Lady Hamilton, Weidenfeld & Nicolson, 1986, published as *Emma, Lady Hamilton,* Knopf, 1987.
The English Gentlewoman, Barrie & Jenkins, 1987.

WORK IN PROGRESS: Regency Riot: The Trial of Queen Caroline, for Weidenfeld & Nicolson.

SIDELIGHTS: Continuing the literary tradition set forth by her grandmother, Lady Elizabeth Longford, and her mother, Lady Antonia Fraser, Flora Fraser explores the life and historical significance of a prominent British figure in *Beloved Emma: The Life of Emma Lady Hamilton.* "Longford books have always been concerned with History's Big Figures," noted Fiona MacCarthy in a *Times* review of the book. "[The] technique of summing up a certain period in history in terms of a single, central, nationally charismatic and politically influential lifespan" is evident in Fraser's biography, MacCarthy continued, adding that Emma "is a terrific subject. . . . [Her] marriage to Sir William, British minister at Naples, and liaison with Lord Nelson, the Hero of England, place her near enough to centre for the formula to work."

The book traces Emma's advancement from her childhood as a blacksmith's daughter, through her Pygmalion-like relations with the prominent British men who admired her, to her achievement of greatness in her marriage to Sir William Hamilton and subsequent affair with Lord Nelson. "What is remarkable about Emma," observed Roy Porter in the *Times Literary Supplement,* "is that she rose but was never made to suffer for it." Indeed, she seemed well-suited for the position she earned, Porter added, noting that upon her marriage to Sir William, Emma discovered "how well her naturally exuberant energies and generosities with people blossomed when given a stage for greatness."

Bettelou Peterson of the *Detroit Free Press* noted that Fraser's "readable work is well-documented and objective." And MacCarthy, complimenting not only Fraser's sensitivity but also her careful attention to detail, described her as "a researcher of the old school, dogged, thorough, returning to her base with an enormous haul of facts." Such a researcher is necessary, according to Porter, to understand and adequately portray Emma, "an exceedingly complex creature." *Beloved Emma,* concluded Ruth Clements in the Toronto *Globe and Mail,* "will probably reign as the definitive biography of Lady Hamilton."

Fraser told *CA:* "I owe a good deal to my mother and grandmother, who employed me during school and university holidays as a researcher. I learnt the rules of that most enjoyable pursuit, historical research, from them. And I learnt that, if you are bored writing something, the reader will tire of it pages earlier. So cut it!"

BIOGRAPHICAL/CRITICAL SOURCES:

PERIODICALS

Detroit Free Press, July 17, 1987.
Globe and Mail (Toronto), May 2, 1987.
New York Times Book Review, June 14, 1987.
Spectator, December 6, 1986.
Times (London), October 2, 1986, October 23, 1987.
Times Literary Supplement, December 5, 1986.
Washington Post Book World, May 31, 1987.

* * *

FREEMAN, Bjorn
See PRATNEY, William Alfred

* * *

FRIED, Eunice

PERSONAL: Surname is pronounced "freed"; born in Bridge-

port, Conn.; divorced, 1976; children: Jonathan. *Education:* Received B.A., University of Connecticut.

ADDRESSES: Home and office—85 Fourth Ave., Apt. 2KK, New York, N.Y. 10003. *Agent*—Julian Bach, 747 Third Ave., New York, N.Y. 10017.

CAREER: Travel, wine, and food writer, 1965—.

MEMBER: Wine Writers Circle (New York; founding member, 1974; chairman, 1977-81).

WRITINGS:

What Every Woman Should Know About Wine, Doubleday, 1974.

Burgundy: The Country, the Wines, the People, Harper, 1986.

Author of column on wine in *Black Enterprise,* 1981—. Frequent contributor to periodicals, including *Harper's Bazaar, Elle,* and *Connoisseur.*

SIDELIGHTS: Eunice Fried's *Burgundy: The Country, the Wines, the People* looks at wine making and selling by small-plot peasant vintners in France's Burgundy wine country—a tradition that spans at least sixteen centuries. Spending nearly a year there, the author discusses different aspects of the region's wine business, including its history, modern changes, the grape life-cycle, barrelmaking, and especially the people who produce the most celebrated wines. Deeming *Burgundy* "enjoyable" in a review for the *New York Times,* Frank J. Prial felt that Fried's chronicle of Burgundian villages and vineyards captures "just how it is." "Fried's greatest success is in connecting the process of making and selling wine with the daily lives of the Burgundians who do it," *Washington Post* critic Charles Monaghan concurred. "It is a rare accomplishment and I can't think of another book that even comes close to achieving this goal." And though the reviewer did regret the author's "failure to put Burgundy in the context of wine production in France and the world," he nonetheless concluded, "The wine-lover can learn much from Fried's book."

Fried told *CA:* "My writing centers largely on wine, food, travel, and profiles of people in these fields, and on cultural subjects."

BIOGRAPHICAL/CRITICAL SOURCES:

PERIODICALS

New York Times, December 17, 1986.
New York Times Book Review, December 8, 1974.
Washington Post, August 6, 1986.

* * *

FRIEDBERG, Joan Brest 1927-

PERSONAL: Born May 7, 1927, in Boston, Mass.; daughter of Aaron Philip (a poultry farmer) and Lillian (a homemaker and librarian; maiden name, Markell) Brest; married Simeon A. Friedberg (professor of physics), September 4, 1950; children: Elizabeth Friedberg McCoy, Aaron, Susan Friedberg Kalson. *Education:* Bryn Mawr College, A.B., 1948; University of Pittsburgh, M.A., 1964, Ph.D., 1972. *Politics:* Democrat. *Religion:* Jewish.

ADDRESSES: Home—1220 South Negley Ave., Pittsburgh, Pa. 15217. *Office*—Beginning With Books, The Carnegie Library of Pittsburgh, Homewood Branch, 7101 Hamilton Ave., Pittsburgh, Pa. 15208. *Agent*—Kendra Bersamin, BookStop, 67 Meadow View Rd., Orinda, Calif. 94563.

CAREER: R. R. Bowker Co., New York, N.Y., advertising and production assistant, 1948-50; Irene Kaufmann Settlement House, Pittsburgh, Pa., teacher, 1950-51; University of Pittsburgh, Pittsburgh, instructor, 1972-76, assistant professor of English, 1976-79; Carriage House Children's Center, Pittsburgh, teacher, 1979—. Co-director of Beginning With Books, Pittsburgh, 1984—.

MEMBER: Children's Literature Association, Bryn Mawr College Club of Western Pennsylvania (former secretary and president).

WRITINGS:

(With June B. Mullins and Adelaide W. Sukiennek) *Accept Me as I Am: Best Books of Juvenile Nonfiction on Impairments and Disabilities,* Bowker, 1985.

Contributor to *Cricket* magazine.

* * *

FROEHLICH, Gustav 1902-1987

OBITUARY NOTICE: Born March 21, 1902, in Hanover, Germany (now West Germany); died December 22, 1987. Actor, director, and author. In his sixty-year film career, Froehlich directed or acted in more than one hundred movies. Originally a stage actor, Froehlich left the theater after garnering praise for his role in Fritz Lang's "Metropolis," a 1926 science fiction film. He went on to appear in many movies, including "Asphalt," "Gitta Discovers Her Heart," and the 1933 film "The Rakoczy March," which he also directed. When the Nazis rose to power Froehlich continued to direct movies—they found his subject matter inoffensive—but he was prohibited from making them for a short while during World War II because of a disagreement over technique. During the 1960s Froehlich began acting in television films, and more recently he played in the serial "The Laurents." He published his autobiography, *My Life as a Film Hero—Those Were the Days,* in 1983.

OBITUARIES AND OTHER SOURCES:

PERIODICALS

Times (London), January 2, 1988.

* * *

FROHLICH, Gustav
See FROEHLICH, Gustav

G

GALE, Patrick (Evelyn Hugh Sadler) 1962-

PERSONAL: Born January 31, 1962, in Newport, Isle of Wight, England; son of Michael Sadler (a senior civil servant) and Philippa Jean (a homemaker; maiden name, Ennion) Gale. *Education:* New College, Oxford, B.A., 1983. *Politics:* Socialist. *Religion:* Church of England.

ADDRESSES: Agent—A. P. Watt, 24-26 Bedford Row, London WC1R 4HL, England.

CAREER: Writer. Has worked variously as a bone-sorter, cook, waiter, typist, and singer, 1979-85.

WRITINGS:

The Aerodynamics of Pork (novel), Abacus, 1985, Dutton, 1987.
Ease (novel), Abacus, 1985, Dutton, 1986.
Kansas in August (novel), Century, 1987, Dutton, 1988.
Facing the Tank (novel), Hutchinson, 1987.

Work represented in short story collections, including *Whitbread Stories One,* Hamish Hamilton, 1985, and *20 Under 35,* Hodder & Stoughton, 1987.

Reviewer for *Plays and Players,* 1985, and *London Daily News,* 1987. Regular contributor of book reviews to *Literary Review, Gay Times,* and *London Daily Telegraph.*

WORK IN PROGRESS: Little Bits of Baby, a novel; an article on Mozart's piano sonatas for *The Mozart Compendium,* edited by H. C. Robbins Landon, for Thames & Hudson; researching angels and the figure of the winged humanoid.

SIDELIGHTS: Domina Tey, a successful English playwright bent on experiencing life beyond her privileged existence, is the protagonist of Patrick Gale's early novel *Ease*. Temporarily engaging a room in a seedy London tenement, the dramatist senses a bold new play in her colorful lodgingmates and insinuates herself, unidentified, into their lives; yet unwittingly, Domina's manipulations lead to tragedy. "She . . . discovers that life beyond the literary world is serious stuff," wrote Polly Morrice in the *New York Times Book Review,* "and that people are more than talking puppets to be manipulated through three acts of witty dialogue."

While dissatisfied that the novel's tragic denouement leaves Domina "virtually unchanged," Morrice commended Gale's "agreeable boldness" and "ability to plot compactly." London *Times* critic Gillian Greenwood praised the novel's wit: "[*Ease*] is an accomplished high camp comedy with a cash of satire," she stated; "it's all rather enjoyable, and Mr. Gale's polished phrasing is a delight." And calling the author "a young British novelist whose gifts, and insights, are notable," Jonathan Yardley related in the *Washington Post:* "Patrick Gale writes with the understated fluency that is the hallmark of contemporary British fiction, and with the irony that usually accompanies it. Like William Boyd and Martin Amis, he skillfully blends the light and the dark, moving unobtrusively from comedy to drama without losing narrative momentum or integrity. It's a performance that arouses eager expectations for his next novel."

In *The Aerodynamics of Pork* Gale looks at the uncertainties of love and lust in modern life. At large in London is a burglar who steals the dire public prophecies of astrologers and prognosticators in order to thwart future cataclysmic events; against this backdrop, Gale explores the love relationships of two homosexuals, a pair of lesbians, and a beautiful virgin with a hysterical pregnancy. "It is a novel about love and sex in the new age, with all the complexities and ambiguities the age brings with it," described Yardley, "not the least of them being the looming sense that the age can come to a speedy end at scarcely a moment's notice."

Assessing *The Aerodynamics of Pork* in the *Los Angeles Times Book Review,* Richard Eder enjoyed Gale's "playful flourishes." "Playful, that is, until he turns sentimental and lush," determined the critic, referring to the central character's homosexual romance; Eder decided that "at its heart" Gale's fey tale is "righteous and didactic." Yardley, likewise, admitted that "'The Aerodynamics of Pork' . . .is not quite the success that 'Ease' . . . was." Still, the reviewer found plenty in the novel to admire. "Gale is a clever, original writer with a sharp eye for social comedy and an equally sharp ear for dialogue," wrote Yardley. "[He] is also a kind observer of the human comedy. For all the foolishness his characters are inclined to do and say, he likes them all the same, with the result that they become real people."

Unorthodox sexual relationships reappear in a third Gale novel, *Kansas in August*. An aspiring male dancer named Hilary and his psychiatrist sister share a lover; Hilary's frustrated attempts to adopt an abandoned baby he rescues and a traffic accident

that crushes the performer's legs provide the story's emotional grist. In a review for the *Times Literary Supplement* Mark Casserley noted that, while the inner conflicts of Gale's characters "fail to grip," their passage through "the chaotic, rubbish-filled, violent streets of London . . . is the most effective thing in his book." Writing in the London *Times,* John Nicholson commented, "The author . . . introduce[s] us to a surprisingly wide variety of human types and foibles" with "wry wit."

More lavish in their praise of *Kansas in August* were Stephen Fry in his review for the *Listener* and Maureen Freely in hers for the *Observer.* "*Kansas in August* is not a book to be slammed, damned, or panned," wrote Fry. "It is the work of an accomplished writer. . . . The characters, thankfully, are not bright young things, but mournfully marginal. The corny resolutions, the camp comforts, and the glittering escape of the great musical that are suggested in the title resonate distantly and with some irony throughout the book. . . . Gale's style is spare and disengaged from the pitiful melancholy of the drama." "Patrick Gale, on the strength of this modern, excellect, and sympathetic novel," predicted Fry, "seems to me to be bound for greatness." Freely called *Kansas in August* "Gale's best book this year" (a tongue-in-cheek comment on the publishing quirk that had Gale's first three novels appear in less than a year), explaining that "the writing is more controlled, the characters have more depth." Moreover, concluded Freely, "one is left with a suspicion that he is still skating on the surface of his talent."

Gale told *CA:* "Writing is at once an addiction and a livelihood. But music (I play the piano, harpsichord, cello, and tenor viol) has always come a close second. Other major interests: cookery, death, and cinema."

BIOGRAPHICAL/CRITICAL SOURCES:

PERIODICALS

Blitz Magazine, July, 1987.
Listener, May 21, 1987.
Los Angeles Times Book Review, July 19, 1987, March 27, 1988.
New York Times Book Review, December 14, 1986.
Observer, May 10, 1987.
Times (London), August 21, 1986, May 7, 1987.
Times Literary Supplement, July 24, 1987.
Washington Post, November 5, 1986, July 15, 1987.

* * *

GARBUTT, Janice (D.) Lovoos (Janice Lovoos; Marie Angelino, a pseudonym)

PERSONAL: The name Lovoos is pronounced *Loe*-vus; born in Dubuque, Iowa; daughter of Edmund Julius (a merchandise manager) and Hattie (a housewife; maiden name, Bals) Beck; married Frederic Doyle Penney (an artist, designer, and author; divorced); married Thor Lovoos (a film studio camera technician), 1950 (deceased); married Bernard Garbutt (an artist and animator of Disney cartoons, an author and illustrator of children's books); children: (first marriage) Edmund Freeman. *Education:* Attended Chouinard School of Art (now California Institute of Arts). *Politics:* Democrat. *Religion:* Christian Scientist.

ADDRESSES: Home and office—3357 P. Monte Hermoso, Laguna Hills, Calif. 92653. *Agent*—Sally Wecksler, 170 West End Ave., New York, N.Y. 10023.

CAREER: Artist and designer. Instructor at Chouinard School of Art (now California Institute of the Arts), 1947-48. Member of BMI Workshop, 1980.

MEMBER: American Society of Composers, Authors, and Publishers, Authors Guild, Dramatists Guild of America.

AWARDS, HONORS: Award from Southern Book Competition, 1973, for *Frederic Whitaker: Life and Work;* James A. Marshall Award from University of Michigan, 1980, for producing the musical "Simon's Towers."

WRITINGS:

UNDER NAME JANICE LOVOOS

(With Carlton Ball) *Making Pottery Without a Wheel,* Reinhold, 1965.
Design Is a Dandelion (self-illustrated juvenile), Golden Gate Junior Books, 1965.
(With Felice Paramore) *Modern Mosaic Techniques,* Watson-Guptill, 1967.
Frederic Whitaker: Life and Work, Northland Press, 1971.
Sculpting in Clay, Tab Books, 1982.
(With son, Edmund F. Penney) *Millard Sheets: One-Man Renaissance,* Northland Press, 1983.

Also author of monographs, including *Robert Ortlieb/Sculpture, Millard Sheets: Six Decades of Painting,* 1983, and *Two From California: Joan Irving/Rex Brandt,* 1984.

Contributor of more than five hundred articles to magazines and newspapers, including *American Artist* (under pseudonym Marie Angelino), *Los Angeles Times, Christian Science Monitor, Southwest Art, Charm, Parade,* and *Westways.*

WORK IN PROGRESS: Friendships: Ariel and Will Durant, publication expected in 1989; *Mary and Grace,* personal anecdotes about artists Mary Garden and Grace Moore; a revised edition of *Making Pottery Without a Wheel.*

SIDELIGHTS: "My career has been so varied," Janice Lovoos Garbutt told *CA,* "it is almost impossible to categorize. The many things I have done, no matter how irrelevant they seemed at the time, have been useful to me in one way or another.

"My formal art training at Chouinard School of Art included life drawing and painting with F. Tolles Chamberlain, design with Patti Patterson, and commercial design with Nelbert Chouinard and Vernon Caldwell. This began three days after graduation from high school and ended two years later, when I married Frederic Doyle Penney.

"I had already joined the work force as a designer of rugs and textiles while I was still in high school. Frederic and I quickly built a national reputation for our designs of unusual lampshades and small accessories. We exported to Japan, Australia, and Germany, and distributed our work to stores throughout the United States.

"About that time we joined the California Watercolor Society and often exhibited our work at the Los Angeles County Museum of Art, the California Art Club, and elsewhere. When we were divorced in the mid-thirties I began to write. I sold my first article to *American Artist,* creating an association that has endured through the years.

"During the war years (the forties) I did promotional writing and publicity for two international companies connected with the fabric and dress textile business. These contacts introduced

me to people in many walks of life that were new to me: famous designers, the press, all the personalities concerned with the glamorous world of fashion. During this period I also designed textiles, upholstery fabrics, and worked on special promotional advertising.

"In 1947 I was one of two fashion editors and writers selected to join the press conference funded by the San Francisco apparel business, to go to Paris and present California-made clothes. All this time, I was also painting, making friends with artists, most of whom have become famous and also remained friends through the years.

"In 1950, when I married Thor Lovoos, a camera technician with Goldwyn Studios, I began to make friends with people in the film business. I edited a magazine of entertainment and interviewed personalities such as Duke Ellington, Nat Cole, and all the good singers and bandleaders of that time. I also ghosted columns on entertainment for a well-known West Coast columnist.

"By 1980 Thor Lovoos had died, and I married Bernard Garbutt, writer and illustrator of many children's books, also known through his work as an artist and animator for Disney, especially for his work on 'Snow White' and 'Bambi.' By this time I had also written profiles of many artists. I have been told by a museum librarian that I have had five hundred articles published. Since the seventies I have more or less concentrated on art and artists, primarily the painters who comprise the California School.

"In 1980 I became a member of Lehman Engle's famous BMI Workshop and produced a musical with writer and composer Elizabeth Surace. 'Simon's Towers' is a musical legend based on the life of Simon Rodia, creator of the Watts Towers. This show won for us the James A. Marshall Award from the University of Michigan. I also wrote lyrics for Dr. Isaac Van Grove, former director of the Chicago Lyric Opera. Together we produced five one-act operas which have been produced many times by university groups in the South and Southwest.

"People remark on my enduring health and energy, and an enthusiasm that never quits. When asked, I can only say that I really do not believe in age. I do not discuss or consider it when venturing out on a new sea of fancy. I work some part of every day at creative ideas, and I long for more time to realize them."

BIOGRAPHICAL/CRITICAL SOURCES:

BOOKS

McClelland, Gordon and Jay Last, *The California Style,* Hillcrest Press, 1985.

* * *

GARDNER, Mary 1936-

PERSONAL: Born August 19, 1936, in Stevens Point, Wis.; daughter of Glen Edward (a bookkeeper) and Marguerite (a housewife and teacher; maiden name, Day) Braatz; married Russell Gardner, Jr. (a psychiatrist and professor), June 25, 1960; children: Rebecca Gardner Westphal, Martha, Ben. *Education:* Attended University of Freiburg, 1957-58; Wisconsin State University (now University of Wisconsin)—Stevens Point, B.S., 1959; University of Chicago, M.A., 1961; further graduate study at Graduate Center of the City University of New York, 1968-69.

ADDRESSES: Home—921 Blume Dr., Galveston, Tex. 77551. *Agent*—Diana Finch, Ellen Levine Literary Agency, Inc., 432 Park Ave. S., Suite 1205, New York, N.Y. 10016.

CAREER: Wayne State University, Detroit, Mich., lecturer in English, 1962-63; Hunter College of the City University of New York, New York, N.Y., lecturer in English, 1963-66; Montgomery Junior College, Rockville, Md., lecturer in English, 1966-68; Fairleigh Dickinson University, Teaneck, N.J., lecturer in English, 1969-70 and 1972-74; North Dakota State University, Fargo, lecturer in English, 1975-80; Moorhead State University, Moorhead, Minn., lecturer at New Center for Multidisciplinary Studies, 1980-84; Texas A & M University at Galveston, lecturer in English, 1984—.

AWARDS, HONORS: Scholar of German Academic Exchange Service, 1957-58; Woodrow Wilson fellow, 1960-61; Danforth fellow, 1968-69.

WRITINGS:

Keeping Warm (novel), Atheneum, 1987.

WORK IN PROGRESS: A novel set in the Midwest.

SIDELIGHTS: Mary Gardner told *CA:* "I began writing *Keeping Warm* while I was with my husband on his sabbatical in Philadelphia. Maybe I had reached the age of 'writing readiness,' as one of my friends calls it. Who knows? Now that I've had a legitimate identity change, writing seems completely natural to me. I seem to spend my non-writing time much as always: extensive unofficial involvement with many different people, housework, reading just about anything (but not romances, mysteries, or science fiction)."

Keeping Warm was described by Taffy Cannon of the *Los Angeles Times* as "such a fundamental American female fantasy that it's astonishing nobody's written this book before." It is the story of a widowed English teacher, who meets the man of her dreams, a country and western singer and songwriter. Their escapades, during a whirlwind relationship, embody all the qualities of fantasy unleashed. The result, Chris Goodrich reported in the *New York Times Book Review,* is irresistible charm. "Mrs. Gardner manages," Goodrich wrote, "to create a genuine and complex relationship between these two innocents." The critic praised her for an "uncommonly engaging" first novel: "Mary Gardner's instincts as an author are right on track."

BIOGRAPHICAL/CRITICAL SOURCES:

PERIODICALS

Los Angeles Times, February 12, 1987.
New York Times Book Review, January 18, 1987.

* * *

GARFIELD, Sydney 1916(?)-1988

OBITUARY NOTICE: Born c. 1916; died in a traffic accident, January 3, 1988. Dentist and author. Garfield is remembered as the author of the best-selling book *Teeth Teeth Teeth,* which explores the history and folklore of dentistry. He originally studied to be an aerospace engineer but changed career directions after he moved from New York City and enrolled in the University of Southern California Dental School. Garfield practiced dentistry in Beverly Hills, serving celebrities as well as animals—he once made a set of dentures for a chimpanzee.

OBITUARIES AND OTHER SOURCES:

PERIODICALS

Los Angeles Times, January 9, 1988.

* * *

GARNER, Helen 1942-

BRIEF ENTRY: Born November 7, 1942, in Geelong, Victoria, Australia. Australian educator, journalist, and author. Garner taught secondary school in Melbourne, Australia, from 1966 until 1972, when she was dismissed for having answered students' questions about sexuality. She has served as a theater critic for the Australian *National Times* and as a feature writer for the Melbourne *Age* beginning in 1985. Her first novel, *Monkey Grip* (McPhee Gribble, 1977), about a drug addict and the woman who loved him, won a National Book Council Award. Much of her fiction is set in the subculture of Melbourne and deals with drug abuse, music, sexual relationships, and communal living. Garner's writings also include *Honour, and Other People's Children: Two Stories* (McPhee Gribble, 1980); *Moving Out* (Nelson, 1983), a screenplay novelization she wrote with Jennifer Giles; *The Children's Bach* (McPhee Gribble, 1984); and a collection of short stories titled *Postcards From Surfers* (McPhee Gribble, 1986). *Addresses: Home*—849 Drummond St., North Carlton, Victoria 3054, Australia.

BIOGRAPHICAL/CRITICAL SOURCES:

BOOKS

Contemporary Novelists, 4th edition, St. Martin's, 1986.
The Oxford Companion to Australian Literature, Oxford University Press (Melbourne), 1985.

PERIODICALS

Los Angeles Times Book Review, October 18, 1981.
New York Times Book Review, April 4, 1982, December 7, 1986.
Times Literary Supplement, January 18, 1980, December 3, 1987.
Washington Post Book World, May 2, 1982, August 3, 1986.

* * *

GARVEY, Marcus (Moziah, Jr.) 1887-1940

PERSONAL: Middle name cited in some sources as Mosiah; born August 17, 1887, in St. Anne's Bay, Jamaica; died after two strokes, June 10, 1940, in London, England; buried at St. Mary's Cemetery, Kensal Green, London, England; son of Marcus Moziah (a stone mason) and Sarah Jane (Richardson) Garvey; married Amy Ashwood (a secretary), December, 1919 (divorced, June 15, 1922); married Amy Jacques (a secretary), July, 1922; children: Marcus Jacques, Julius Winston. *Education:* Attended Birkbeck College (London), 1912.

ADDRESSES: Home—London, England.

CAREER: Activist. Worked as printer's apprentice in Jamaica, c. 1901; foreman at printing company in Kingston, Jamaica, c. 1904; employee at Jamaican government printing office, c. 1910; worked on banana plantations in Costa Rica, c. 1912; printer for *African Times and Orient Review,* c. 1913; lecturer in United States and England; political candidate in Jamaica in 1930s. Founded Universal Negro Improvement Association and African Communities League, both 1914; Black Star Line and Negro Factories Corporation, both 1919; African Orthodox Church, Negro Political Union, and Black Cross Navigation and Trading Company, all 1924. Publisher of *Negro World* in New York, N.Y., 1918-33, and *Black Man* in London, England, 1934.

WRITINGS:

The Philosophy and Opinions of Marcus Garvey; or, Africa for the Africans, edited by wife, Amy Jacques Garvey, Universal Publishing House, Volume 1, 1923, Volume 2, 1925; reprinted, Cass, 1967; with preface by William Loren Katz, Arno Press, Volume 1, 1968, Volume 2, 1969.
The Tragedy of White Injustice (poetry), privately printed, 1927, reprinted, Haskell House, 1972.
Garvey and Garveyism, edited by wife, Amy Jacques Garvey, [Kingston, Jamaica], 1963.
Marcus Garvey and the Vision of Africa, edited by wife, Amy Jacques Garvey, and John H. Clarke, Random House, 1974.
Collected Papers and Documents, edited by E.U. Essien-Udom, Africana Modern Libraries Series, 1974.
(With Lumumba and Malcolm X) *The Black Handbook: 100 and More Quotes by Garvey, Lumumba, and Malcolm X,* edited by Shawna Maglangbayan, Third World Press, 1975.
More Philosophy and Opinions of Marcus Garvey, edited by wife, Amy Jacques Garvey, and E.U. Essien-Udom, Africana Modern Libraries Series, 1977.
The Poetical Works of Marcus Garvey, Majority Press, 1983.
The Marcus Garvey and Universal Negro Improvement Association Papers, edited by Robert A. Hill, University of California Press, Volume 1: *1826-August 1919,* 1983, Volume 2: *August 27, 1919-August 31, 1920,* 1983, Volume 3: *September 1920-August 1921,* 1984, Volume 4: *September 1, 1921-September 2, 1922,* 1985, Volume 5: *September 1922-August 1924,* 1987.
Message to the People: The Course of African Philosophy, edited by Tony Martin, Majority Press, 1986.

Also author of *Black Power in America,* edited by wife, Amy Jacques Garvey, 1968.

Contributor to periodicals, including *Africa Times and Orient Review, Black Man, Current History,* and *Negro World.*

SIDELIGHTS: Marcus Garvey was probably the most prominent black-rights champion of his era. As founder of the Universal Negro Improvement Association (UNIA) he led a movement promoting greater unity for blacks throughout the world. This movement, which counted more than eight million followers at its zenith, was the key force in the back-to-Africa cause that influenced black politics and social activism in the second and third decades of the twentieth century. In addition, Garvey promoted black-oriented businesses, notably the Black Star Line of ships for transporting blacks desiring a return to Africa. He also established *Negro World* and *Black Man,* two periodicals for black readers, and he devoted much of his energies to furthering the political union of blacks from all parts of the world. These various ambitions and enterprises rendered Garvey one of the most influential and, in some quarters, notorious blacks, one tirelessly dedicated to sparking greater achievements in black culture.

Garvey was born in 1887 in British-ruled Jamaica. In his youth he read voraciously, but his family's impoverished living circumstances compelled him to end his formal studies and begin working as a printer's apprentice. After moving to the Jamaican capital, Kingston, Garvey became foreman of a printing

company. But his employment there ended after he organized a workers' strike for increased wages. He subsequently worked at another printing office, then moved to Costa Rica and briefly labored on a banana plantation. During this period—around 1912—Garvey grew increasingly incensed at the abuse of Jamaicans working abroad. Formal complaint proved futile, and Garvey, who had earlier experienced similar prejudice while leading the failed printers' strike, began doubting the workability of black-white relations.

After leaving Costa Rica, Garvey traveled to London, England, where he made his initial acquaintance with Africans. Among the many blacks he befriended in London was Egyptian nationalist Duse Mohammed Ali, a staunch advocate of African independence. Duse published *African Times and Orient Review,* and he enlisted Garvey's services as a printer for the periodical. While working for Duse's publication Garvey read extensively on African history. He was particularly impressed with J. E. Casely Hayford's *Ethiopia Unbound,* which called for African unity, and with Booker T. Washington's autobiography *Up From Slavery,* in which Washington articulated his rise from slavery to an esteemed rank in American letters. It was the latter work that exerted the most notable influence on Garvey, and after reading it he pledged himself to Ali's cause of African unity.

In 1914 Garvey returned to Jamaica and, with the aid of several friends, formed UNIA and its coordinating body, the African Communities League. The UNIA, which consumed much of Garvey's energies for the next several years, was designed to promote black unity through education and commerce. Garvey's first project with UNIA was the founding of a trades school in Jamaica. But the project, modeled after Booker T. Washington's Tuskegee Institute in Alabama, failed to develop, whereupon Garvey decided to meet with Washington in America and study the institute there.

Unfortunately, Garvey's projected trades school was further set back when Washington died before Garvey could meet him. Garvey thus found himself an outsider without contacts when he finally arrived in New York City in 1916. Undaunted, Garvey eventually befriended American blacks through three years of traveling and speaking before church congregations and community organizations. In 1918 he gained greater access to America's black populace through his weekly newspaper *Negro World,* which regularly featured his own appeals and justifications for a united African state. The following year, encouraged by the sizable readership of *Negro World,* Garvey established UNIA offices in New York City, where UNIA world headquarters quickly gained recognition as the center of the back-to-Africa movement. In addition, UNIA branches were established in several other metropolitan areas with substantial black populations.

By 1920 the UNIA counted impressive membership from around the world. At its first convention, held in New York City's Harlem district at the UNIA's Liberty Hall, approximately 25,000 delegates convened to address black issues. In his speeches Garvey called for greater emphasis on the black perspective in all areas of life. He implied the existence of a black deity and fostered the notion of black—specifically African—aesthetic standards. He also presented a revisionist historical outlook, one recognizing the innumerable, and previously ignored, accomplishments of blacks throughout time. In his most ambitious proposal, Garvey championed the creation of a united black nation. To facilitate the formation of such a state, Garvey had already established the Black Star Line for transporting blacks from the United States. This shipping business was, in turn, only one of several ventures—including a grocery-store chain, a publishing house, and restaurants—intended by Garvey to further black economic independence by serving blacks exclusively.

Garvey's then daring business plans, together with his more ambitious concept of a united black nation, powerfully impressed delegates at the UNIA convention. These delegates eventually founded a quasi-exile government, the Empire of Africa, and declared Garvey its provisional president. Garvey, in turn, appeared in public sporting colorful military regalia while accompanied by the renegade government's other officers—bearing titles such as the Knights of the Nile and the Dukes of the Niger—in similar garb. To further the creation of his exiled state, Garvey negotiated with Liberia's leaders in a vain effort to obtain land for colonization. He also appealed to the League of Nations in a similarly futile attempt to win control of Germany's former colonies in Africa.

But as Garvey's popularity and influence rose among like-minded blacks, so his notoriety grew among individuals, including resentful blacks, who disagreed with him. By 1919 he had already been the target of one assassination attempt, and by 1920 his publication *Negro World* was outlawed in Britain and France. He also met with increasing opposition from some American blacks, notably leaders of the comparably conservative National Association for the Advancement of Colored People (NAACP), which Garvey had rejected as elitist and unsympathetic to the plight of blacks outside the United States. In addition, Garvey outraged many black artists by dismissing the Harlem Renaissance of black arts as a mediocre cultural movement.

By 1921, one year after the UNIA convention, American opposition to Garvey and his organization had grown further. When Garvey attempted to return to the United States after touring Central America, his reentry visa was withheld for four months by the U.S. State Department. When he finally arrived back in the United States, Garvey applied for U.S. citizenship and began modifying his philosophy. But his new proposals only succeeded in further alienating American blacks, many of whom were particularly outraged by his distinctions of racial purity and his bizarre contention that American blacks provoked persecution because of their supposedly mediocre achievements. At this time the UNIA began losing supporters worldwide.

As Garvey's stature suffered, so did the economic stability of his organization. The Black Star Line, which had been sustained by stock sales, had obtained outmoded and unsuitable steamships and was absorbing a disastrous portion of the UNIA's funds. Garvey attempted to avert financial catastrophe by soliciting investors through the U.S. mail. This maneuver caused the demise of Garvey's organization, for American law enforcers, acting on information received from the NAACP, charged Garvey with mail fraud. Serving as his own legal counsel, Garvey attempted to refute the charges in court. An investigation of the UNIA's records, however, disclosed that Garvey had long been financially exploited by his own followers within the organization and by those brokers with whom he had worked on the Black Star Line. Unable to establish his economic credibility, Garvey nonetheless fought the legal charge, seizing his trial as a forum for proclaiming his radical beliefs.

As a result of his unorthodox legal defense, Garvey was unable to refute the mail fraud charge, although testimony and records

established that he was an honest, though incompetent, businessman. In addition, his courtroom behavior offended jurors, and he consequently received a fine and a five-year prison sentence, though his codefendants were acquitted. Almost immediately after being sentenced Garvey was free on bail, and the UNIA raised further funds by selling stocks for a second shipping line, the Black Cross Navigation and Trading Company. But adversity continued to plague Garvey. The new shipping line proved another economic liability, and hopes for the back-to-Africa action fell when Liberia withdrew from negotiations with UNIA and arrested the organization's delegates.

In 1925, after the Supreme Court rejected an appeal, Garvey began serving his prison term. His wife and other UNIA officials tried to sustain the organization, and they found continued support from blacks convinced that Garvey was unjustly tried. The organization prospered further when American authorities commuted Garvey's remaining sentence and deported him to Jamaica. There he organized another impressive convention and founded the radical Jamaican Peoples Party, which called for independence from Britain and proposed several problack reforms. The world economic Depression, however, was already damaging the Jamaican economy and compelling Jamaican blacks to devote themselves to considerations more immediate than Garvey's ambitious designs. After his political candidacy failed, Garvey left Jamaica in 1935 and resettled in England. He subsequently commenced publication of a modest periodical, *Black Man,* and founded the School of African Philosophy, a mail-correspondence institution. In the late 1930s he organized a series of annual UNIA conventions in Canada. These conventions were only modest gatherings compared to earlier UNIA events, and they served as further indication of Garvey's lessening influence.

Garvey's health also declined at this time. By the late 1930s the asthmatic Garvey had twice endured pneumonia, and in 1940 he became partially paralyzed after a stroke. A second stroke proved fatal that June.

After Garvey's death the UNIA disbanded. Garvey, however, continues to be remembered as an inspirational force in black culture. In the 1960s, with the civil-rights movement and radical black organizations, his thoughts on black aesthetics and black nationalism held considerable relevance, and in a broader context he is respected as a galvanizing leader whose actions prompted greater international awareness of black culture in the first half of the twentieth century.

As a writer, Garvey is represented by several volumes containing works for the periodicals *Negro World* and *Black Man* and for the UNIA. *The Philosophy of Marcus Garvey,* his most prominent publication in his own lifetime, was reprinted in the late 1960s, and his writings for the UNIA have been published in several volumes by the University of California Press since 1983. Of the first two volumes in this series, *New York Times Book Review* critic Eric Foner found much to recommend. He called *The Marcus Garvey and Universal Negro Improvement Association Papers* "important records of the Afro-American experience." The series, Foner concluded, "lays the groundwork for a long overdue reassessment of Marcus Garvey and the legacy of racial pride, nationalism and concern with Africa he bequeathed to today's black community."

BIOGRAPHICAL/CRITICAL SOURCES:

BOOKS

Burkett, Randall K., *Black Redemption: Churchmen Speak for the Garvey Movement,* Temple University Press, 1978.

Cronon, Edmund David, *Black Moses: The Story of Marcus Garvey and the Universal Negro Improvement Association,* foreword by John Hope, University of Wisconsin Press, 1955.

Edwards, Adolph, *Marcus Garvey,* New Beacon, 1967.

Fax, Elton C., *Garvey: The Story of a Pioneer Black Nationalist,* foreword by John Henrik Clarke, Haskell House, 1969.

James, Cyril Lionel Robert, *A History of Pan-African Nationalism,* Dodd, 1972.

Martin, Tony, *Marcus Garvey, Hero,* Majority Press, 1984.

Martin, Tony, *Race First: The Ideological and Organizational Struggles of Marcus Garvey and the Universal Negro Improvement Association,* Greenwood Press, 1976.

Stein, Judith, *The World of Marcus Garvey: Race and Classism in Modern Society,* Louisiana State University Press, 1986.

Vincent, Theodore G., *Black Power and the Garvey Movement,* Ramparts, 1971.

PERIODICALS

Black Scholar, December, 1973.
Current History, September, 1923.
Essence, November, 1986.
Los Angeles Times Book Review, March 25, 1984.
Negro History Bulletin, October, 1962, November, 1974.
New Republic, October 29, 1984.
New York Times Book Review, February 5, 1984.

OBITUARIES:

PERIODICALS

New York Times, June 12, 1940.*

—*Sketch by Les Stone*

* * *

GATES, Doris 1901-1987

OBITUARY NOTICE—See index for *CA* sketch: Born November 26, 1901, in Mountain View, Calif.; died September 3, 1987, in Carmel, Calif. Librarian, educator, and author. Gates is perhaps best remembered for her Newbery Award-winning juvenile novel *Blue Willow,* which critics hailed as an innovative and valuable addition to the body of literature for young people. A former children's librarian and college instructor, she wrote several other books for children featuring such favorite topics as horses and Greek mythology. These include *Little Vic, A Morgan for Melinda, Lord of the Sky: Zeus,* and *Sensible Kate.*

OBITUARIES AND OTHER SOURCES:

BOOKS

Dictionary of Literary Biography, Volume 22: *American Writers for Children, 1900-1960,* Gale, 1983.

Twentieth-Century Children's Writers, 2nd edition, St. Martin's, 1983.

PERIODICALS

School Library Journal, December, 1987.

* * *

GATHERIDGE, R. Edward
See WILSON, Robert (Edward)

GELMAN, Mitch(ell Barry) 1962-

PERSONAL: Born March 21, 1962, in New York, N.Y.; son of Stephen M. (a journalist) and Rita (a writer; maiden name, Golden) Gelman. *Education:* Attended London School of Economics and Political Science, 1982-83; University of California, Berkeley, B.A. (with highest honors), 1985; attended National University of Singapore, 1985-86.

ADDRESSES: Home—New York, N.Y.

CAREER: Journalist. Part-time reporter for *Los Angeles Herald Examiner,* 1981, and *Time* magazine's London bureau, 1982-83; staff member of opinion section of *New York Newsday,* New York, N.Y., 1986—.

MEMBER: Phi Beta Kappa.

WRITINGS:

Great Quarterbacks of Pro Football, Scholastic Book Services, 1981.

THE "PLAY IT YOUR WAY" SERIES

Can You Win the Pennant? Pocket Books, 1983.
Pro Football Showdown, Pocket Books, 1983.
Super Bowl Sunday, Pocket Books, 1984.
World Series Pressure, Pocket Books, 1984.
Opening Day, Pocket Books, 1985.
Defending Champions, Pocket Books, 1985.

SIDELIGHTS: Mitch Gelman told *CA:* "I'm glad to be a working journalist back in New York after spending ten years living and traveling in the United States, Europe, and Asia."

* * *

GENG, Veronica 1941-

PERSONAL: Born January 10, 1941, in Atlanta, Ga.; daughter of Charles Emil and Rosina (Butter) Geng. *Education:* Received B.A. from University of Pennsylvania.

ADDRESSES: Agent—Andrew Wylie, 250 West 57th St., Suite 2331, New York, N.Y. 10019.

CAREER: Writer. *New Yorker,* New York, N.Y., fiction editor, 1977-82. Movie critic for *Soho News,* 1980-81.

WRITINGS:

Guess Who? A Cavalcade of Famous Americans (for young people), illustrations by Huntley Brown, Platt, 1969.
(Editor) *In a Fit of Laughter: An Anthology of Modern Humor* (for young people), introduction by Steve Allen, Platt, 1969.
(Editor with Barbara Creaturo) *Cosmopolitan's Hangup Handbook,* Cosmopolitan Books, 1971.
Partners (satire collection), Harper, 1984.

Regular contributor to *New Yorker.*

SIDELIGHTS: Called "the cleverest *New Yorker* humorist to come along since Woody Allen" by *National Review* contributor Terry Teachout, Veronica Geng exhibits her talent for social satire in *Partners,* a collection of twenty-nine parodies—many first appearing in the *New Yorker.* Using contemporary rhetoric to lampoon current mores and popular culture, Geng comments on such emblems of our age as the how-to book, the tell-all memoir, and the politician's newsletter. "Her strength is mimicking other styles," observed Ellen Stein, reviewing *Partners* for *Ms.* "[Geng] hoists her subjects on their own non sequiturs," Grace Lichtenstein agreed in the *Washington Post.* "She has what all real satirists have: an ear with perfect pitch."

Writing in the *New York Times,* Christopher Lehmann-Haupt determined that "the wit of many of the . . . pieces in 'Partners' . . . begins with the author's unlikely coupling of subjects." "Often," he continued, "these are as pungent in conception as they are in execution"; "Record Review," for example, "is a deft parody of a hip discographer with nothing less than the Watergate tapes as its subject." In the critique for the *Los Angeles Times Book Review* Elaine Kendall advanced a similar evaluation. "Though Geng is extremely particular about targets, she's wonderfully eclectic, impaling the innocuous with the same skillful glee she lavishes on the truly evil and pernicious," stated the reviewer. "Where she does this in the same brief essay, the effect is particularly hilarious."

While noting in Geng's satiric pieces "a particularly *New Yorker* brand of humor that is as dry and smooth as a good martini," Stein regretfully pointed out that "we rarely, if ever, hear Geng's own voice." "Geng's style is particularly opaque, never revealing the author's attitude toward her subjects other than a general amusement at society's foibles," elaborated the reviewer. "Personally, I prefer my satire a bit more Swiftian, where one senses the passion and moral outrage beneath the stance of ironic detachment." Lichtenstein, too, admitted that Geng's pastiches reveal "no new sensibility" or convey "no great political thrust." "Still, 'Partners' is fun," decided the critic, deeming its stylish, daring sendups "first-class."

To *Newsweek* reviewer Ron Givens it is "Geng's beautifully calibrated sense of style," particularly, that distinguishes her from other parody writers. While "mak[ing] you laugh out loud," the critic related, "[Geng] has refined her wit to the point where it's, well, erudite. . . . [It's] just right for educated funny bones." And Lehmann-Haupt maintained that Geng's clever burlesques slyly achieve their satiric ends. "Miss Geng is lethal," he wrote. "She wields what Mary Wortley Montagu once called 'a polished razor keen' that wounds 'with a touch that's scarcely felt or seen.'"

BIOGRAPHICAL/CRITICAL SOURCES:

PERIODICALS

Antioch Review, winter, 1985.
Christian Science Monitor, November 1, 1985.
Los Angeles Times Book Review, August 26, 1984.
Ms., October, 1984.
National Review, September 20, 1985.
Newsweek, September 17, 1984.
New York Times, July 6, 1984.
New York Times Book Review, July 15, 1984.
Washington Post, September 4, 1984.

* * *

GERSTEIN, Arnold A. 1940-

PERSONAL: Born November 20, 1940, in Kilgore, Tex.; son of Joseph (a rabbi) and Natalie (a medical technologist) Gerstein; married first wife, Lenore, December 27, 1964 (divorced September, 1979); married Cheryl Godfrey, January, 1983; children: Dylan, Daniella, Aaron. *Education:* Hebrew University of Jerusalem, B.A., 1963; University of Minnesota, M.A., 1966, Ph.D., 1972. *Religion:* Jewish.

ADDRESSES: Home—P.O. Box 371, White Pigeon, Mich. 49099.

CAREER: Western Michigan University, Kalamazoo, assistant professor, 1969-83, associate professor of humanities, 1983—. Participant in Heartlight Center-Spiritual Light Center for Wholistic Education.

WRITINGS:

(Translator) Nathan Rotenstreich, *Basic Problems of Marx's Philosophy,* Bobbs-Merrill, 1965.

(With James Reagan) *Win-Win: Approaches to Conflict Resolution at Home, in Business, Between Groups, and Across Cultures,* Peregrine Smith, 1986.

(Translator) Hugo Bergman, *The Philosophy of the Dialogue From Kierkegaard to Buber,* Blue Owl Press, 1987.

WORK IN PROGRESS: The Power of Unconditional Love, publication expected in 1988; *The Story of Heartlight Center: A Spiritual Center for Wholistic Education,* publication expected in 1989.

SIDELIGHTS: Arnold A. Gerstein told *CA:* "My work as a translator was a special gift to two philosophy teachers who inspired my life in Jerusalem from 1962 to 1964, and to Martin Buber, whom I met in 1958. My work on conflict resolution stemmed from work we did in Israel and a dream of ours, of peace between Arabs and Jews to be implemented through grassroots activity, including the workshop approach.

"James Reagan and I went to Israel to see if members of various peace and reconciliation groups as well as therapists and teachers wanted to learn conflict resolution skills from us. We did not want to resolve conflict for them. Our experience in Israel did in part inspire us to write the book *Win-Win* because it became so obvious how tired and burned out people were of win-lose and lose-lose situations in their lives. They were ready for a new step forwa.d no matter how risky it seemed. We were invited to speak to many groups and individuals about our approach to conflict resolution which involved the use of teaching people win-win principles in very concrete ways that could be immediately applied. Avoiding conflict was stressed as much as maneuvering in a conflict that was not avoided and should not be. Recently my approach emphasizes neutralizing extreme positionality through unconditional love and concern for the underlying needs of all individuals in the conflict situation.

"My involvement in Heartlight Center, a spiritual community and educational center, has provided me with deep understanding of what lies beyond the personality structure that conditions us so strongly. There is a deep desire for coming together as one, a desire for unity within diversity. This is realized by letting go of the self-seeking aspirations of the individual and thinking in terms of the whole, of what would benefit the whole and be an expression of selflessness and love. Once we look beyond our judgments of how things should be, an energy of love and caring that unifies people is created. Our uniquenesses still emerge strongly without sacrificing the harmony that naturally exists between people who view one another nonjudgmentally. At this time I am working with other spiritual communities to share what we have in common, to be resources to one another, and to learn whatever we can to further the reality of peace and brotherhood on this planet. Heartlight Center has a particular contribution to make, not a special or superior one in any sense. Its contribution is the teaching of oneness and divine unconditional love as a realizable fact which provides an answer for the education of our children and the restructuring of our society at every level. Among other things we have developed an elementary school to begin to make this vision a reality."

* * *

GHOSH, Dipali 1945-

PERSONAL: Born November 27, 1945, in Calcutta, India; daughter of Rajkumar and Mukherjee; married Amalendu Ghosh (an accountant), January 31, 1975. *Education:* Bombay University, B.A., 1967; Shreemati Nathibai Damodar Thackersey Women's University, B.A., 1967; Shreemati Nathibai Damodar Thackersey Women's University, B.Lib.Sc., 1968; Polytechnic of North London, postgraduate diploma in librarianship, 1980. *Religion:* Hindu.

ADDRESSES: Home—7 Henley Court, Aerodrome Rd., Watford Way, London NW4 4SR, England. *Office*—British Library, 14 Store St., London WC1E 7DG, England.

CAREER: Bombay Labour Institute, Bombay, India, librarian, 1968; Government Institute of Printing Technology, Bombay, librarian, 1968-70; Victoria Jubilee Technical Institute, Bombay, assistant librarian, 1970-75; British Library, Department of Oriental Collections, London, England, in various posts, 1975-85, curator, 1986—.

WRITINGS:

Translations of Bengali Works Into English, Mansell, 1986.

WORK IN PROGRESS: Editing, with Adrian Hale, *Union Catalogue of Serials From South Asia in Western Languages in British Libraries.*

SIDELIGHTS: Dipali Ghosh told *CA:* "I have compiled the bibliography *Translations of Bengali Works Into English* for the readers who cannot read the original language but who are interested to know about Bengali literature. It is also a source for orientalists, research workers, and librarians. There are many Bengali children in Western countries who are not aware of Bengali literature and are not able to read Bengali, and for them my bibliography would be quite useful. As a professional librarian, I feel it is my duty to let people know the resources in which they can find information."

* * *

GIBBON, (William) Monk 1896-1987

OBITUARY NOTICE—See index for *CA* sketch: Born December 15, 1896, in Dublin, Ireland; died October 29, 1987, in Dublin, Ireland. Author. Gibbon wrote several volumes of poetry, a number of books on travel, and an assortment of biographical works. He is by far best known, however, for his controversial study *The Masterpiece and the Man: Yeats as I Knew Him,* which caused a furor with its unflattering account of the renowned poet William Butler Yeats. Gibbon's diverse range of other writings includes *The Tremulous String: Poems in Prose; The Tales of Hoffman: A Study of the Film; The Rhine and Its Castles; An Intruder at the Ballet;* and various autobiographical publications, such as *The Seals* and *The Brahms Waltz.*

OBITUARIES AND OTHER SOURCES:

BOOKS

Contemporary Poets, 3rd edition, St. Martin's, 1980.
Dictionary of Irish Literature, Greenwood Press, 1979.

Who's Who, 139th edition, St. Martin's, 1987.

PERIODICALS

Times (London), October 30, 1987.

* * *

GIBBONS, Felton L(ewis) 1929-

PERSONAL: Born April 27, 1929, in Wilkinsburg, Pa.; son of George Rison (an executive) and Helen (a chemist; maiden name, Maxfield) Gibbons; married Mary Elizabeth Weitzel (an art historian), November 15, 1952 (divorced, 1978); children: David Scott, Elizabeth Patterson. *Education:* Yale University, B.A., 1951; Harvard University, M.A., 1957, Ph.D., 1961.

ADDRESSES: *Home and Office*—R.F.D.1, Box 418, Hopewell, N.J. 08525. *Agent*—Barbara Kouts, Spitzer Agency, 788 Ninth Ave., New York, N.Y. 10019.

CAREER: Princeton University, Princeton, N.J., instructor, 1960-64, assistant professor, 1964-68, associate professor of art history, 1968-82, Arthur Scribner Bicentennial Preceptor, 1965-68, director of graduate studies, assistant director of Art Museum, 1962-64, curator of drawings, 1966-70; independent historian and writer, 1982—. Member of faculty at New School for Social Research, spring, 1982, 1983; public speaker on art and art history. Local administrator of Committee to Rescue Italian Art in Florence, 1967-68. *Military service:* U.S. Naval Reserve, active duty, 1951-54; served in Pacific theater, including Korea; became lieutenant junior grade; received five battle stars.

MEMBER: College Art Association of America, Renaissance Society of America, Phi Beta Kappa.

AWARDS, HONORS: Fulbright scholar in Italy, 1964-65; fellow at Villa i Tatti, 1967-68, 1970-71.

WRITINGS:

Dosso and Battista Dossi: Court Painters at Ferrara, Princeton University Press, 1968.

Catalogue of Italian Drawings in the Art Museum, two volumes, Princeton University Press, 1977.

(With Deborah Strom) *History of Birdwatching in America* (tentative title), Norton, 1988.

Contributor of about thirty articles to art and history journals.

WORK IN PROGRESS: Research on "American environmentalism"; research on the relationship between nature writing and art in America.

SIDELIGHTS: Felton L. Gibbons told *CA:* "I inherited, from both parents, an interest in the outdoors and the workings of nature. I was an occasional birdwatcher, but for many years I was more involved with art history, which confined me mostly to the library and classroom. Five years ago I realized that man's vandalism of nature meant that outdoor life was being lost to us. I became a refugee from the New Jersey suburbs and moved to an ancient, rundown, rockstrewn, and troublesome farm, rich in bird and wildlife, rather remarkably located in the middle of our most populous state. I also took up birdwatching more intensively. I have pursued it throughout the United States and in Europe, especially England and Scotland.

"I am hardly an expert 'birder,' certainly not the obsessed six-hundred-species type (though I have seen more than five hundred), but I find birds revealing and ever-present clues to nature's mechanisms and the relations of these to man. Birds are not just subject to ecology, but are also teachers of that vital and distressing discipline. My interest in what's happening in nature, along with my training as a historian, led me and my co-author Deborah Strom to write a book on the history of birding. The literature on birding is large enough, but most of it is either scientific or consists of anecdotes about travel and lucky sightings. A serious history seemed to be needed, a history that would present this widespread avocation in the context of other American cultural accomplishments."

* * *

GIDE, Andre (Paul Guillaume) 1869-1951

PERSONAL: Born November 22 (one source says November 21), 1869, in Paris, France; died of pneumonia, February 19, 1951, in Paris, France; buried in Cuverville-en-Caux, Normandy, France; son of Paul (a professor) and Juliette (Rondeaux) Gide; married cousin, Madeleine Rondeaux, in 1895; children: (with Elisabeth van Rysselberghe) Catherine. *Education:* Educated privately and in public schools in Paris, France.

CAREER: Novelist, playwright, essayist, diarist, and translator. Co-founder of *La Nouvelle Revue francaise* in 1909 and of *L'Arche,* a literary magazine in North Africa; literary critic for *La Revue blanche*. Mayor of La Roque, a commune in Normandy, France, 1896; juror in Rouen, France, 1912; special envoy of the Colonial Ministry in Africa, 1925-26. Worked with the Red Cross and, later, in a convalescent home for soldiers, and became director of the Foyer Franco-Belge during World War I. Traveled extensively in Europe and Africa.

MEMBER: Royal Society of London (elected honorary fellow, 1924), American Academy of Arts and Letters (elected honorary corresponding member, 1950).

AWARDS, HONORS: Goethe Medal, 1932; honorary doctorate in letters from University of Oxford, 1947; Nobel Prize in literature from Nobel Foundation, 1947; Goethe Plaque from the city of Frankfort on the Main, 1949.

WRITINGS:

NOVELS; NOVELLAS

Le Voyage d'Urien, Librairie de l'Art Independant, 1893, second edition, with new preface by Gide, 1894, Editions de la Nouvelle Revue Francaise, 1929; translation with introduction and notes by Wade Baskin published as *Urien's Voyage,* Philosophical Library, 1964.

Paludes (satire), Librairie de l'Art Independant, 1895, Gallimard, 1936, reprinted, 1973; published with *Le Promethee mal enchaine* (see below) in *Marshlands* [and] *Prometheus Misbound: Two Satires,* translation by George D. Painter, New Directions Publishing, 1953, McGraw, 1965.

Le Promethee mal enchaine (satire), Mercure, 1899, new edition, Gallimard, 1925, reprinted, 1966; translation by Lilian Rothermere published as *Prometheus Illbound,* Chatto & Windus, 1919; published with *Paludes* (see above) in *Marshlands* [and] *Prometheus Misbound: Two Satires,* translation by George D. Painter, New Directions Publishing, 1953, McGraw, 1965.

L'Immoraliste, Mercure, 1902, reprinted, 1973, edited by Elaine Marks and Richard Tedeschi, Macmillan, 1963, edited by J. C. Davies, with English introduction and notes, Harrap (London), 1974; translation by Dorothy Bussy published as *The Immoralist,* Knopf, 1930, reprinted, 1961; translation by Richard Howard published as *The Immoralist,*

with introduction and afterword by Albert J. Guerard, Knopf, 1970, Modern Library, 1983.

La Porte etroite, Mercure, 1909, revised edition, 1959, reprinted, 1967, with preface by Jean Paulhan, Imprimerie Nationale, 1958, edited by M. Shackleton, Harrap, 1958, Heath (Boston), 1962, with illustrations by Laurent Pizzotti, Cercle du Bibliophile, 1969; translation by Dorothy Bussy published as *Strait Is the Gate,* Knopf, 1924, Robert Bentley, 1980.

Isabelle, Gallimard, 1911, reprinted, 1973, edited with introduction, notes, and vocabulary by Elsie Pell, F. S. Crofts (New York), 1947; translation by Dorothy Bussy published as *Isabelle,* Knopf, 1968; translation by Bussy published with *La Symphonie pastorale* (see below) in *Two Symphonies: Isabelle* [and] *The Pastoral Symphony,* Knopf, 1931, Vintage Trade, 1977 (published in England as *La Symphonie pastorale* [and] *Isabelle,* Penguin Books [Harmondsworth], 1963, reprinted, 1984).

Les Caves du Vatican: Sotie (satire), Gallimard, 1914, reprinted, 1974, Macmillan (New York), c. 1956, published as *Les Caves du Vatican,* edited and introduced by F. J. Jones, University of London Press, 1961, reprinted, 1970; translation by Dorothy Bussy published as *The Vatican Swindle,* Knopf, 1925, published as *Lafcadio's Adventures,* Knopf, 1928, Robert Bentley, 1980 (published in England as *The Vatican Cellars,* Cassell, 1952, Penguin Books [Harmondsworth], 1959, reprinted, 1976); adapted by Gide as *Les Caves du Vatican: Farce en trois actes et dix-neuf tableaux* (see *PLAYS* below).

La Symphonie pastorale, Editions de la Nouvelle Revue Francaise, 1919, Gallimard, 1972, edited by M. Shackleton, Harrap (London), 1951, reprinted, 1964, edited by Justin O'Brien and M. Shackleton, Heath (Boston), 1954, with notes by Rene-Marill Alberes, Gallimard, 1966, edited by Claude Martin, Lettres Modernes, 1970; translation by Dorothy Bussy published as *The Pastoral Symphony,* Knopf, 1968; translation by Bussy published with *Isabelle* (see above) in *Two Symphonies: Isabelle* [and] *The Pastoral Symphony,* Knopf, 1931, Vintage Trade, 1977 (published in England as *La Symphonie pastorale* [and] *Isabelle,* Penguin Books [Harmondsworth], 1963, reprinted, 1984).

Les Faux-Monnayeurs, Gallimard, 1926, reprinted, 1967, edited by J. C. Davies, with introduction and notes in English, Methuen Educational, 1986; translation by Dorothy Bussy published as *The Counterfeiters,* Knopf, 1927, with introduction by Raymond Weaver, Modern Library, c. 1931, Penguin Books (Harmondsworth), 1966, reprinted, 1982 (also published in England as *The Coiners,* Cassell, 1950, Digit Books, 1961); translation by Bussy published with *Le Journal des Faux-Monnayeurs* (translated and annotated by Justin O'Brien; see *AUTOBIOGRAPHY; JOURNALS,* below) in *The Counterfeiters* [with] *Journal of "The Counterfeiters,"* Knopf, 1951, Vintage Trade, 1973.

L'Ecole des femmes, Gallimard, 1929, translation by Dorothy Bussy published as *The School for Wives,* Knopf, 1929; published in *L'Ecole des femmes* [suivi de] *Robert* [et de] *Genevieve,* Gallimard, 1944, reprinted, 1973, translation by Bussy published as *The School for Wives, Robert,* [and] *Genevieve; or, The Unfinished Confidence,* Knopf, 1950, Robert Bentley, 1980 (also see below).

Robert: Supplement a "L'Ecole des femmes," Gallimard, 1929; published in *L'Ecole des femmes* [suivi de] *Robert* [et de] *Genevieve,* Gallimard, 1944, reprinted, 1973, translation by Dorothy Bussy published as *The School for Wives, Robert,* [and] *Genevieve; or, The Unfinished Confidence,* Knopf, 1950, Robert Bentley, 1980 (also see above).

Genevieve; ou, La Confidence inachevee, Gallimard, 1936; published in *L'Ecole des femmes* [suivi de] *Robert* [et de] *Genevieve,* Gallimard, 1944, reprinted, 1973, translation by Dorothy Bussy published as *The School for Wives, Robert,* [and] *Genevieve; or, The Unfinished Confidence,* Knopf, 1950, Robert Bentley, 1980 (also see above).

Thesee, Pantheon, 1946, Gallimard, 1946, reprinted, 1966; translation by John Russell published as *Theseus,* New Directions Publishing, 1949; published with *Oedipe* (see *PLAYS,* below) in *Two Legends: Oedipus* [and] *Theseus,* translation by Russell, Knopf, 1950, Vintage Trade, 1958 (published in England as *Oedipus* [and] *Theseus,* Secker & Warburg, 1950).

LYRICAL WORKS IN VERSE AND PROSE

Les Cahiers d'Andre Walter (title means "The Notebooks of Andre Walter"), Librairie de l'Art Independant, 1891; translation of first half with introduction by Wade Baskin published as *The White Notebook,* Philosophical Library, c. 1964; translation with introduction and notes by Baskin published as *The Notebooks of Andre Walter,* Philosophical Library, 1968, reprinted, P. Owen, 1986; published with *Les Poesies d'Andre Walter* (see below) in *Andre Walter: Cahiers et poesies,* Les Oeuvres Representatives, 1930, new edition, Gallimard, 1952.

Le Traite du Narcisse: Theorie du symbole (title means "Treatise of the Narcissus: Theory of the Symbol"), Librairie de l'Art Independant, 1891; translation by Dorothy Bussy published as "Narcissus" in *The Return of the Prodigal, Preceded by Five Other Treatises; With "Saul," a Drama in Five Acts,* Secker & Warburg, 1953 (see *COLLECTED WORKS,* below).

Les Poesies d'Andre Walter (title means "The Poems of Andre Walter"), Librairie de l'Art Independent, 1892; published with *Les Cahiers d'Andre Walter* (see above) in *Andre Walter: Cahiers et poesies,* Les Oeuvres Representatives, 1930, new edition, Gallimard, 1952.

La Tentative Amoureuse; ou, Le Traite du vain desir (title means "The Attempt at Love; or, The Treatise of Vain Desire"), Librairie de l'Art Independant, 1893; translation by Dorothy Bussy published as "The Lover's Attempt" in *The Return of the Prodigal, Preceded by Five Other Treatises; With "Saul," a Drama in Five Acts,* Secker & Warburg, 1953 (see *COLLECTED WORKS,* below).

Les Nourritures terrestres, Mercure, 1897, Gallimard, 1944; translation by Dorothy Bussy published with *Les Nouvelles Nourritures* (see below) as *The Fruits of the Earth,* Knopf, 1949 (published in England as *Fruits of the Earth,* Secker & Warburg, 1962, published as *Fruits of the Earth* [and] *Later Fruits of the Earth,* Penguin Books in association with Secker & Warburg, 1970, reprinted, 1982); published in *Les Nourritures terrestres* [et] *Les Nouvelles Nourritures,* Club des Libraires de France, 1956, Gallimard, 1958, reprinted, 1981 (also see below).

Les Nouvelles Nourritures, Gallimard, 1935; translation by Dorothy Bussy published with *Les Nourritures terrestres* (see above) as *The Fruits of the Earth,* Knopf, 1949 (published in England as *Fruits of the Earth,* Secker & Warburg, 1962, published as *Fruits of the Earth* [and] *Later Fruits of the Earth,* Penguin Books in association with Secker & Warburg, 1970, reprinted, 1982); published in *Les Nourritures terrestres* [et] *Les Nouvelles Nourritures,*

Club des Libraires de France, 1956, Gallimard, 1958, reprinted, 1981 (also see above).

PLAYS

"Philoctete," first performed privately, April 3, 1919; read in Paris, France, at Comedie des Champs-Elysees, October 16, 1937; published in *Philoctete; Le Traite du Narcisse; La Tentative Amoureuse; El Hadj,* Mercure, 1899 (also see *COLLECTED WORKS*, below); translation by Jackson Mathews published as "Philoctetes" in *My Theater: Five Plays and an Essay,* Knopf, 1952 (see *COLLECTED WORKS*, below); translation by Dorothy Bussy published as "Philoctetes" in *The Return of the Prodigal, Preceded by Five Other Treatises; With "Saul," a Drama in Five Acts,* Secker & Warburg, 1953 (see *COLLECTED WORKS*, below).

Le Roi Candaule (first produced in Paris, France, at Nouveau Theatre, May 9, 1901), Editions de la Revue Blanche, 1901, Gallimard, 1930; translation by Jackson Mathews published as "King Candaules" in *My Theater: Five Plays and an Essay,* Knopf, 1952 (see *COLLECTED WORKS*, below).

Saul: Drame en cinq actes (five-act play; first produced in Paris, France, at Theatre du Vieux-Colombier, June 16, 1922), Mercure, 1903, enlarged edition, with preface by Gide, 1904, Gallimard, 1969; translation by Jackson Mathews published as "Saul" in *My Theater: Five Plays and an Essay,* Knopf, 1952 (see *COLLECTED WORKS*, below); translation by Dorothy Bussy published as "Saul" in *Return of the Prodigal, Preceded by Five Other Treatises; With "Saul," a Drama in Five Acts,* Secker & Warburg, 1953 (see *COLLECTED WORKS*, below).

Le Retour de l'enfant prodigue (first produced in Monte Carlo, Monaco, at Theatre de Monte-Carlo, December 4, 1928; produced in Paris, France, at Theatre de l'Avenue, February 23, 1933; text first published in *Vers et Prose,* 1907), Bibliotheque de l'Occident, 1909; translation by Aldyth Thain published as *The Return of the Prodigal Son,* Utah State University Press, 1960; enlarged edition published as *Le Retour de l'enfant prodigue, precede de cinq autres traites,* Gallimard, 1932, reprinted, 1967 (see *COLLECTED WORKS*, below); translation by Dorothy Bussy published as "The Return of the Prodigal" in *The Return of the Prodigal, Preceded by Five Other Treatises; With "Saul," a Drama in Five Acts,* Secker & Warburg, 1953 (see *COLLECTED WORKS*, below).

Bethsabe (first published in *L'Ermitage,* 1903), Bibliotheque de l'Occident, 1912; translation by Jackson Mathews published as "Bathsheba" in *My Theater: Five Plays and an Essay,* Knopf, 1952 (see *COLLECTED WORKS*, below); translation by Dorothy Bussy published as "Bathsheba" in *The Return of the Prodigal, Preceded by Five Other Treatises; With "Saul," a Drama in Five Acts,* Secker & Warburg, 1953 (see *COLLECTED WORKS*, below).

Oedipe: Drame en trois actes (three-act play; first produced in Antwerp, Belgium, at Cercle Artistique, December 10, 1931; produced in Paris, France, at Theatre de l'Avenue, February 18, 1932), Gallimard, 1931, L'Arche (Paris), 1959; published with *Thesee* (see *NOVELS; NOVELLAS*, above), in *Two Legends: Oedipus* [and] *Theseus,* translation by John Russell, Knopf, 1950, Vintage Trade, 1958 (published in England as *Oedipus* [and] *Theseus,* Secker & Warburg, 1950).

Persephone (first produced in Paris, France, at l'Opera, April 30, 1934), Gallimard, 1934; translation by Samuel Putnam published as *Persephone,* Gotham Book Mart, 1949; translation by Jackson Mathews published as "Persephone" in *My Theater: Five Plays and an Essay,* Knopf, 1952 (see *COLLECTED WORKS*, below); adapted by Gide as *Persephone: Melodrame en trois tableaux d'Andre Gide* (opera libretto), music composed by Igor Fedorovich Stravinski, Boosey & Hawkes, 1950.

"Le Treizieme Arbre" (title means "The Thirteenth Tree"; one-act farce), first produced in Marseilles, France, at Rideau Gris, May 8, 1935; produced in Paris, France, at Theatre Charles de Rochefort, January 13, 1939.

Le Retour (title means "The Return"), Ides et Calendes, 1946.

(With Jean-Louis Barrault) *Le Proces: Piece tiree du roman de Kafka* (dramatization of Franz Kafka's novel *Der Prozess;* first produced October 10, 1947; English translation produced in New York City at Bouwerie Lane Theater, November, 1987), Gallimard, 1947; translation and adaptation by Jacqueline and Frank Sundstrom published as *The Trial,* Secker & Warburg, 1950; translation by Leon Katz and Joseph Katz published as *The Trial: A Dramatization Based on Franz Kafka's Novel,* Schocken, 1964.

Robert; ou, L'Interet general (title means "Robert; or, The General Interest"; five-act play; first produced in Tunis, Tunisia, at Theatre Municipal, April 30, 1946), Ides et Calendes (Neuchatel), 1949.

Les Caves du Vatican: Farce en trois actes et dix-neuf tableaux (three-act play; first produced in Montreux, Switzerland, at Societe des Belles-Lettres, December 9, 1933; revised script produced in Paris, France, at the Comedie-Francaise, December 13, 1950), Ides et Calendes, 1948, Gallimard, 1950.

ESSAYS; CRITICISM

Reflexions sur quelques points de litterature et de morale, Mercure, 1897.

Pretextes: Reflexions sur quelques points de litterature et de morale (collection of essays), Mercure, 1903, enlarged edition, 1913, reprinted, 1957; selections translated by Angelo P. Bertocci and others published with selections from *Nouveaux Pretextes* (see below) and *Incidences* (see below) in *Pretexts: Reflections on Literature and Morality,* selected, edited, and introduced by Justin O'Brien, Meridian Books, 1959, Books for Libraries Press, 1971; published with *Nouveaux Pretextes* (see below) in *Pretextes* [suivi de] *Nouveaux Pretextes: Reflexions sur quelques points de litterature et de morale,* Mercure, 1963.

Oscar Wilde: In memoriam (souvenirs) [and] *Le "De profundis,"* Mercure, 1910, reprinted, 1925; translation from the original French manuscript with introduction, notes, and bibliography by Stuart Mason published as *Oscar Wilde: A Study,* The Hollywell Press (Oxford), 1905; translation by Bernard Frechtman published as *Oscar Wilde: In Memoriam (Reminiscences)* [and] *De Profundis,* Philosophical Library, 1949 (published in England as *Oscar Wilde,* Kimber, 1951); translation by Lucy Gordon published as *Oscar Wilde: A Study,* Gordon Press, 1975.

Dostoievsky, d'apres sa correspondance, Figuiere, 1911.

Nouveaux Pretextes: Reflections sur quelques points de litterature et de morale (title means "Further Pretexts"), Mercure, 1911, reprinted, 1930; selections translated by Angelo P. Bertocci and others published with selections from *Pretextes* (see above) and *Incidences* (see below) in *Pretexts: Reflections on Literature and Morality,* selected, edited, and introduced by Justin O'Brien, Meridian Books, 1959, Books for Libraries Press, 1971; pub-

lished with *Pretextes* (see above) in *Pretextes* [suivi de] *Nouveaux Pretextes: Reflexions sur quelques points de litterature et de morale,* Mercure, 1963.

Souvenirs de la cour d'assises, Gallimard, 1914, Editions de la Nouvelle Revue Francaise, 1924; translation by Philip A. Wilkins published as *Recollections of the Assize Court,* Century Hutchinson (London and Melbourne), 1941.

Dostoievsky: Articles et causeries (criticism), Plon, 1923, Gallimard, 1964, reprinted, 1981; anonymous translation published as *Dostoevsky,* introduction by Arnold Bennett, Dent & Sons (London and Toronto), 1925, Knopf, 1926, new edition, New Directions Publishing, 1949, with new introduction by Albert J. Guerard, 1961, Greenwood Press (Westport), 1979.

Incidences, Editions de la Nouvelle Revue Francaise, 1924; selections translated by Angelo P. Bertocci and others published with selections from *Pretextes* (see above) and *Nouveaux Pretextes* (see above) in *Pretexts: Reflections on Literature and Morality,* selected, edited, and introduced by Justin O'Brien, Meridian Books, 1959, Books for Libraries Press, 1971.

Corydon (dialogues; first printed privately as *C.R.D.N.,* Imprimerie Ste. Catherine [Bruges], 1911, enlarged edition printed privately as *Corydon,* 1920), Gallimard, 1924, enlarged edition, 1929, reprinted, 1981; translation by Hugh Gibb published as *Corydon,* with comment on the book's second dialogue by Frank Beach, Farrar, Straus, 1950, Octagon (New York), 1977; translation by P.B. published as *Corydon: Four Socratic Dialogues,* Secker & Warburg, 1952; translation with introduction by Richard Howard published as *Corydon,* Farrar, Straus, 1983.

Caracteres, [Paris], c. 1925.

Un Esprit non prevenu (title means "An Unprejudiced Mind"), Editions Kra, 1929.

Essai sur Montaigne, Editions de la Pleiade, 1929; translation by Stephen H. Guest and Trevor E. Blewitt published as *Montaigne: An Essay in Two Parts,* Liveright, 1929.

Le Sequestree de Poitiers (title means "The Prisoner of Poitiers"), Gallimard, 1930.

L'Affaire Redureau [suivie de] *Faits divers* (first title means "The Redureau Case"), Gallimard, 1930.

Notes sur Chopin, Revue Internationale de Musique (Brussels), 1938, L'Arche (Paris), 1948; translation by Bernard Frechtman published as *Notes on Chopin,* Philosophical Library, 1949, Greenwood Press (Westport), 1978.

L'Evolution du theatre, edited and introduced by Carl Wildman, Editions de l'Universite de Manchester, 1939; translation by Jackson Mathews published as "The Evolution of the Theater" in *My Theater: Five Plays and an Essay,* Knopf, 1952 (see COLLECTED WORKS, below).

Interviews imaginaires, Gallimard, 1942, expanded edition published as *Interviews imaginaires; La Delivrance de Tunis; Pages de Journal, mai 1943,* Pantheon, 1943; translation of expanded edition by Malcolm Cowley published as *Imaginary Interviews,* Knopf, 1944.

Attendu que . . . (title means "Considering That . . ."), Charlot, 1943.

L'Enseignement de Poussin, Le Divan, 1945.

Paul Valery, Domat, 1947.

Poetique, Ides et Calendes, 1947.

Eloges (title means "Praises"), Ides et Calendes, 1948.

Rencontres (title means "Encounters"), Ides et Calendes, 1948.

Prefaces (title means "Prefaces"), Ides et Calendes, 1948.

Feuillets d'automne, precedes de quelques recents ecrits, Mercure, 1949, reprinted, 1971; translation by Elsie Pell published as *Autumn Leaves,* Philosophical Library, 1950.

Litterature engagee (title means "Committed Literature"; collection of works, including *Robert; ou, L'Interet general*), texts collected and edited by Yvonne Davet, Gallimard, 1950.

TRAVEL ESSAYS

Amyntas [with] *Mopsus, Feuilles de route, De Biskra a Touggourt, Le Renoncement au Voyage* (description of Algerian travels), Mercure, 1906, new edition, Gallimard, 1937; translation with illustrations by Villiers David published as *Amyntas,* Joe Lane, 1958, Dufour, 1961.

Dindiki, Editions de la Lampe d'Aladdin, 1927.

Voyage au Congo: Carnets de route, Gallimard, 1927, reprinted, 1956; translation by Dorothy Bussy published with *Le Retour du Tchad* (see below) as *Travels in the Congo,* Knopf, 1929, Penguin Books (Harmondsworth), 1986; published with *Le Retour du Tchad* (see below) in *Voyage au Congo* [suivi de] *Le Retour du Tchad: Carnets de route,* Gallimard, 1981.

Le Retour du Tchad; suite du "Voyage au Congo": Carnets de route (title means "Return From Chad"), Gallimard, 1928, published as *Le Retour du Tchad: Carnets de route,* 1963; translation by Dorothy Bussy published with *Voyage au Congo* (see above) in *Travels in the Congo,* Knopf, 1929, Penguin Books (Harmondsworth), 1986; published with *Voyage au Congo* (see above) in *Voyage au Congo* [suivi de] *Le Retour du Tchad: Carnets de route,* Gallimard, 1981.

Retour de l'U.R.S.S., Gallimard, 1936; translation by Dorothy Bussy published as *Return From the U.S.S.R.,* Knopf, 1937, McGraw, 1964 (published in England as *Back From the U.S.S.R.,* Secker & Warburg, 1937); published with *Retouches a mon "Retour de l'U.R.S.S."* (see below) in *Retour de l'U.R.S.S.* [suivi de] *Retouches a mon "Retour de l'U.R.S.S.,"* Gallimard, 1950, reprinted, 1978.

Retouches a mon "Retour de l'U.R.S.S." (title means "Revisions to My 'Return From the U.S.S.R.'"), Gallimard, 1973; translation by Dorothy Bussy published as *Afterthoughts: A Sequel to "Back From the U.S.S.R.,"* Secker & Warburg, 1937, published as *Afterthoughts on the U.S.S.R.,* Dial (New York), 1938; published with *Retour de l'U.R.S.S.* (see above) in *Retour de l'U.R.S.S.* [suivi de] *Retouches a mon "Retour de l'U.R.S.S.,"* Gallimard, 1950, reprinted, 1978.

AUTOBIOGRAPHY; JOURNALS

Si le grain ne meurt (autobiography; first part printed privately, Imprimerie Ste. Catherine, 1920, second part printed privately, 1921), Gallimard, 1926, reprinted, 1966; translation by Dorothy Bussy published as *If It Die: An Autobiography,* Random House, c. 1935, reprinted, c. 1963 (published in England as *If It Die,* Secker & Warburg, 1950, Penguin Books [Harmondsworth] in association with Secker & Warburg, 1982).

Numquid et tu? (meditations; first printed privately, Imprimerie Ste. Catherine, 1922), La Pleiade/J. Schiffrin (Paris), 1926.

Le Journal des Faux-Monnayeurs (journal of progress on the novel *Les Faux-Monnayeurs*), Editions Eos, 1926, Gallimard, 1934, reprinted, 1967; translation with notes by Justin O'Brien published as *Logbook of "The Coiners,"* Cassell (London), 1952; translation by O'Brien published with *Les Faux-Monnayeurs* (translated by Dorothy Bussy; see NOVELS, NOVELLAS, above) in *The Counterfeiters* [with]

Journal of "The Counterfeiters," Knopf, 1951, Vintage Trade, 1973.

Pages de Journal, 1929-1932, Gallimard, 1934, reprinted, 1943.

Nouvelles Pages de Journal, 1932-1935, Gallimard, 1936.

Journal, 1889-1939, La Pleiade/Editions de la Nouvelle Revue Francaise, 1939, La Pleiade/Gallimard, 1948, reprinted, 1970.

Pages de Journal, Charlot, 1944.

Pages de Journal, 1939-1942, edited by Jacques Schiffrin, Pantheon, 1944, enlarged edition published as *Journal, 1939-1942,* Gallimard, 1946.

Et nunc manet in te, Ides et Calendes, 1947, translation by Keene Wallis published as *The Secret Drama of My Life: Et nunc manet in te,* Boar's Head, 1951; enlarged edition published as *Et nunc manet in te* [suivi de] *Journal intime,* Ides et Calendes, 1951, translation with notes by Justin O'Brien published as *Madeleine (Et nunc manet in te),* Knopf, 1952, Bantam (New York), 1968 (published in England as *Et nunc manet in te* [and] *Intimate Journal,* Secker & Warburg, 1952).

Journal (collection of journals, 1889-1949), Gallimard, 1948-54, reprinted, 1965-66.

Journal, 1942-1949, Gallimard, 1950.

Ainsi soit-il; ou, Les Jeux sont faits (memoir), Gallimard, 1952, translation with introduction and notes by Justin O'Brien published as *So Be It; or The Chips Are Down (Ainsi soit-il; ou, Les Jeux sont faits),* Knopf, 1959.

Journal, 1939-1949; Souvenirs (collection of journals and other works), La Pleiade/Gallimard, 1954.

Journal (extracts), selected and edited by Lucien Adjadji, preface by Pierre de Boisdeffre, Didier Editions, c. 1970.

CORRESPONDENCE

Lettres, Editions de la Lampe d'Aladdin, 1930.

Lettres a Christian Beck, Editions de l'Altitude (Brussels), 1946.

(With Francis Jammes) *Correspondance, 1893-1938,* preface and notes by Robert Mallet, Gallimard, 1948.

(With Marcel Proust) *Lettres a Andre Gide,* Ides et Calendes, 1949.

(With Paul Claudel) *Correspondance, 1899-1926,* introduction and notes by Robert Mallet, Gallimard, 1949, translation with preface by John Russel published as *The Correspondence, 1899-1926, Between Paul Claudel and Andre Gide,* Pantheon, 1952, Beacon Press, 1964.

(With Charles Du Bos) *Lettres de Charles Du Bos et reponses d'Andre Gide,* Correa, 1950.

(With Paul Claudel, Aldous Huxley, and others) *Lettres inedites sur l'inquietude modern,* introductory comment by Pierre Angel, Editions Universelles, 1951.

(With Rainer Maria Rilke) *Correspondance, 1909-1926,* edited and introduced by Renee Lange, Correa, 1952.

(With Simone Manye) *Lettres a un sculpteur; precedees d'une lettre de Madame Andre Gide,* M. Sautier, 1952.

(With Eugene Dabit) *Eugene Dabit et Andre Gide; avec 18 lettres inedites d'Andre Gide,* compiled by Maurice Dubourg, M. Pernette, 1953.

(With Rainer Maria Rilke and Emile Verhaeren) *Correspondance inedite,* edited by Carlo Bronne, Messein, 1955.

(With Paul Valery) *Correspondance, 1890-1942,* preface and notes by Robert Mallet, Gallimard, 1955, reprinted, 1973, abridged translation by June Guicharnaud published as *Self-portraits: The Gide/Valery Letters, 1890-1942,* edited by Mallet, University of Chicago Press, 1966.

(With Charles Pierre Peguy) *Correspondance: Andre Gide [et] Peguy,* compiled by Alfred Saffrey, l'Amitie Charles Peguy (Paris), 1958.

(With Marcel Jouhandeau) *Correspondance avec Andre Gide,* M. Sautier, 1958.

(With Edmund William Gosse) *The Correspondence of Andre Gide and Edmund Gosse, 1904-1928,* translated, edited, introduced, and annotated by Linette F. Brugmans, New York University Press, 1959, Greenwood Press (Westport), 1977.

(With Andre Suares) *Correspondance, 1908-1920,* preface and notes by Sidney D. Braun, Gallimard, 1963.

(With Arnold Bennett) *Correspondance Andre Gide-Arnold Bennett: Vingt Ans d'amitie litteraire, 1911-1931,* edited, introduced, and annotated by Linette F. Brugmans, Droz (Geneva), 1964.

(With Andre Rouveyre) *Correspondance, 1909-1951,* edited and annotated by Claude Martin, Mercure, 1967.

(With Roger Martin du Gard) *Correspondance, 1913-1951,* two volumes, introduction by Jean Delay, Gallimard, 1968.

(With Francois Mauriac) *Correspondance Andre Gide-Francois Mauriac, 1912-1950,* edited and annotated by Jacqueline Morton, Gallimard, 1971.

(With Jean Cocteau) *Jean Cocteau and Andre Gide: An Abrasive Friendship* (bilingual edition), compiled by Arthur King Peters, Rutgers University Press, 1973.

(With Charles Brunard) *Correspondance avec Andre Gide [et] Souvenirs,* Pensee Universelle, 1974.

(With Albert Mockel) *Correspondance, 1891-1938,* edited and annotated by Gustave Vanwelkenhuyzen, Droz (Geneva), 1975.

(With Henri Gheon) *Correspondance: Henri Gheon, Andre Gide,* compiled by Jean Tipy, introduction and notes by Anne-Marie Moulenes and Tipy, Gallimard, c. 1976.

(With Jules Romains) *Correspondance Andre Gide-Jules Romains: L'Individu et l'unanime,* compiled by Claude Martin, Flammarion, 1976.

(With Jacques-Emile Blanche) *Correspondance Andre Gide/Jacques-Emile Blanche, 1892-1939,* compiled and annotated by Georges-Paul Collet, Gallimard, c. 1979.

(With Dorothy Bussy) *Correspondance Andre Gide-Dorothy Bussy,* edited and annotated by Richard Tedeschi and Jean Lambert, Gallimard, c. 1979-c. 1982; translation of selections published as *Selected Letters of Andre Gide and Dorothy Bussy,* edited by Tedeschi, introduced by Lambert, Oxford University Press, 1983.

(With Justin O'Brien) *Andre Gide-Justin O'Brien: Correspondance, 1937-1951,* edited and annotated by Jacqueline Morton, Universite Lyon II, Centre d'Etudes Gidiennes, 1979.

(With Gabrielle Vulliez and Paul Claudel) *La Tristesse d'un automne sans ete: Correspondance de Gabrielle Vulliez avec Andre Gide et Paul Claudel, 1927-1931,* compiled by Wanda Vulliez, Universite Lyon II, Centre d'Etudes Gidiennes, 1981.

(With Francois-Paul Alibert) *Correspondance, 1907-1950,* edited and annotated by Claude Martin, Presses Universitaires de Lyon, 1982.

(With Jean Giono) *Correspondance, 1929-1940,* edited and annotated by Roland Bourneuf and Jacques Cotnam, Universite Lyon II, Centre d'Etuded Gidiennes, 1983.

(With Jef Last) *Andre Gide-Jef Last: Correspondance, 1934-1950,* edited and annotated by C. J. Greshoff, Presses Universitaires de Lyon, c. 1985.

TRANSLATOR INTO FRENCH

Joseph Conrad, *Typhon,* Editions de la Nouvelle Revue Francaise, 1918, Gallimard, 1966.

(With others) Walt Whitman, *Oeuvres choisies,* Editions de la Nouvelle Revue Francaise, 1918.

William Shakespeare, *Antoine et Cleopatre,* Lucien Vogel, 1921.

William Blake, *La Mariage du ciel et de l'enfer,* Claude Aveline, 1923, Corti, 1965.

Shakespeare, *Hamlet* (produced October 17, 1946), bilingual edition, edited by Jacques Schiffrin, Pantheon, 1945, with preface by Justin O'Brien, Beacon Press, 1964.

Johann Wolfgang von Goethe, *Promethee,* H. Jonquieres, 1950.

(With Helene du Pasquier; and author of introduction) Rabindranath Tagore, *L'Offrande lyrique* [and] *La Corbeille de fruits,* the former translated by Gide, the latter translated by du Pasquier, Gallimard, 1963, reprinted, 1971.

Also translator of Tagore's *Amal et la lettre du roi.*

OTHER

Lettres a Angele, 1898-1899 (first published serially in *L'Ermitage,* 1898, 1899, 1900), Mercure, 1900.

Decouvrons Henri Michaux, Gallimard, 1941.

Jeunesse, Ides et Calendes, 1945.

Souvenirs litteraires et problemes actuels: Allocution et conference prononcees a Beyrouth en avril 1946; avec deux presentations de G. Bounoure, Les Lettres Francaises (Beirut), 1946.

(With Marie Henri Beyle) *Lamiel: Roman de Stendhal* [*precede de*] *En relisant "Lamiel,"* the former by Beyle, the latter by Gide, Editions du Livre Francais, 1947.

(Editor) *Anthologie de la poesie francaise* (collection of French poetry), Pantheon, 1949, Gallimard, 1966.

L'Esprit createur, Bruce Publishing, 1961.

(Author of introduction) Johann Wolfgang von Goethe, *Theatre,* Gallimard, 1964.

(With others) *The God That Failed,* Bantam (New York), 1965.

Entretiens avec Jean Amrouche (sound recording of radio interview), Disques Ades, c. 1970.

(Contributor) *Andre Gide, Karl Gjellerup,* [and] *Paul Heyse* (collection of works and speeches), A. Gregory, 1971.

(Author of preface) Hermann Hesse, *Le Voyage en Orient,* translated from the German into French by Jean Lambert, Calmann-Levy, 1972.

L'Arbitraire, Herne, 1972.

Le Recit de Michel, edited and annotated by Claude Martin, Ides et Calendes, 1972.

Soiree Andre Gide (includes *Oedipe*), Comedie Francaise, 1978.

COLLECTED WORKS

Philoctete; Le Traite du Narcisse; La Tentative amoureuse; El Hadj (includes "El Hadj; ou, Le Traite du faux prophete" [title means "El Hadj; or, The Treatise of the False Prophet"]), Mercure, 1899.

Morceaux choisis (title means "Selections"; collection of previously published and unpublished works), Editions de la Nouvelle Revue Francaise, 1921.

Pages choisies (collection of previously published and unpublished works), Georges Cres, 1921, with biographical and literary notes by Pierre Lafille, Hachette, 1964.

Divers: Caracteres; Un Esprit non prevenu; Dictees; Lettres (title means "Miscellany"), Gallimard, 1931.

Le Retour de l'enfant prodigue, precede de cinq autres traites: Le Traite du Narcisse, La Tentative Amoureuse, El Hadj, Philoctete, Bethsabe, Gallimard, 1932, reprinted, 1967, produced as sound recording, Crane Memorial Library (Vancouver), 1972; translation by Dorothy Bussy published as *The Return of the Prodigal, Preceded by Five Other Treatises; With "Saul," a Drama in Five Acts* (contains "Narcissus," "The Lover's Attempt," "El Hadj," "Philoctetes," "Bathsheba," "The Return of the Prodigal," "Saul"), Secker & Warburg, 1953.

Theatre (contains *Saul, Le Roi Candaule, Oedipe, Persephone, Le Treizieme Arbre*), Gallimard, 1942, reprinted, 1981.

Recits, roman, soties (collection of prose and poetry), Gallimard, 1948.

My Theater: Five Plays and an Essay (contains "Saul," "Bathsheba," "Philoctetes," "King Candaules," "Persephone," "The Evolution of the Theater"), translation by Jackson Mathews, Knopf, 1952.

Poesie; Journal; Souvenirs (collection of lyrical and autobiographical works), Gallimard, 1952.

Ne jugez pas; Souvenirs de la cour d'assises; L'Affaire Redureau; La Sequestree de Poitiers, Gallimard, c. 1957, reprinted, 1969.

Romans, recits, et soties: Ouevres lyriques (collection of works, including *Le Voyage d'Urien, Paludes, La Porte etroite, La Symphonie pastorale, Les Faux-Monnayeurs, Le Journal des Faux-Monnayeurs, Le Traite du Narcisse, El Hadj*), edited with notes and bibliography by Yvonne Davet and Jean-Jacques Thierry, introduction by Maurice Nadeau, La Pleiade/Gallimard, 1958, reprinted, 1975.

Oeuvres (collection of journals and lyrical works), Gallimard, 1960.

COMPLETE WORKS

Oeuvres completes, fifteen volumes, edited by Louis Martin-Chauffier, Gallimard and Editions de la Nouvelle Revue Francaise, 1932-39.

Theatre complet, eight volumes, Ides et Calendes, 1947-49.

The Journals of Andre Gide, four volumes, selected, edited, translated, introduced, and annotated by Justin O'Brien, Knopf, 1947-51 (published in England as *Journals,* Secker & Warburg, 1948-55, and as *Journals, 1889-1949,* Penguin Books [Harmondsworth], 1967, reprinted, 1984), published as *The Journals of Andre Gide, 1889-1949,* Vintage Trade, 1956.

MEDIA ADAPTATIONS

La Symphonie pastorale was adapted into a motion picture script of the same title by Pierre Bost and Jean Aurenche and published by Nouvelle Edition, with a preface by J. Delannoy, in 1948; the book was adapted into a play in three acts and published by F. De Wolfe & Robert Stone in 1954.

L'Immoraliste was adapted into a play titled *Andre Gide's "The Immoralist"* by Ruth and Augustus Goetz and published by Dramatists Play Service (New York) in 1962.

SIDELIGHTS: As a master of prose narrative, occasional dramatist and translator, literary critic (particularly of Fyodor Dostoevsky), letter writer, essayist, and diarist, Andre Gide provided twentieth-century French literature with one of its most intriguing examples of the man of letters. Gide continued the tradition of reflection on culture—its books and its institutions—established by the sixteenth-century essayist Michel de Montaigne, who had introduced the record of the self as a subject for serious literature in France. Inasmuch as it reflects the complex personality behind it, Gide's work enlarges this

permission to take the self as subject. Inasmuch as that personality is ironic, however, the record of the self is deliberately subverted. While Gide lent the authorial pronoun "I" to any number of heroes and heroines in his narratives, he simultaneously cast aspersions on their credibility; while he recorded in his voluminous *Journal* the activities and thought of an eighty-year lifetime, he refused to recognize his authentic portrait in anything he had written if it were considered separately from the self-examinations in the rest of his works. "Hardly a day goes by that I don't put everything back into question," he wrote in his *Journal* in 1922. Each volume was intended to challenge itself, what had preceded it, and what could conceivably follow it. This characteristic, according to Daniel Moutote in his *Cahiers Andre Gide* essay, is what makes Gide's work "essentially modern": the "perpetual renewal of the values by which one lives."

Gide's earliest works participate in what is generally known as the symbolist aesthetic. A literary and philosophical movement determined to break the hold of realism and rationalism on French poetry through the use of suggestion and allusive, emotionally charged language, symbolism was an important training element for the writers of Gide's generation who, as young men in their twenties, were just beginning to establish their careers during the last decade of the nineteenth century in France. The high seriousness of the movement, its goal of revolutionizing French literature, and its circle of intellectuals who gathered weekly in the living room of the master poet Stephane Mallarme to discuss the future of poetry appealed to the young Gide, who, like many of his companions at that time, thought of himself primarily as a poet and intellectual. Of rigorous Protestant stock, Gide approached his writing as a highly moral interrogation of the conventions of morality, as a labor in service of ideas created by the intellect first and the imagination second: "Imagination (with me)," he wrote in his *Journal* in the 1890s, "rarely precedes the idea; it's the latter, and not at all the former, that excites me. . . . For me, the idea of a work often precedes its *imagination* by several years."

By "imagination," Gide meant the actual elaboration of a work with plot, characters, and other elements that would bring the "idea" to life. For most of Gide's writing, the "idea" required a long maturation before its "imagination." Though he was accustomed by inclination and exercise to the written expression of ideas, Gide did not necessarily think of himself as one who wrote easily. His *Journal* through the years records the occasional bouts of nervous agitation that preceded the creation of new works; the procrastination, false starts, and abandoned projects; his complaints of scratchy pens, crooked tables, forgotten notebooks, inconsiderate visitors, and reluctant sentences that often made the work of writing difficult; and above all his frustration at wishing to say *everything* at once and having, necessarily, to say only part at a time. In an article reprinted in *Gide: A Collection of Critical Essays,* Alain Girard pointed out that the published *Journal* is not the complete private diary of its author, who admittedly tore out or withheld parts of it. Nevertheless, the *Journal* faithfully records the importance Gide gave to sincerity and truthfulness to the self as moral values mediating between culturally defined notions of good and evil. It is also clear to what extent sincerity and obligation to the self required the author's discipline and effort of will: "Certainly I could have been more easily a naturalist, doctor or pianist . . . than a writer," Gide wrote in his *Journal* in 1910, "but I can bring more diverse qualities to this career; the others would have been more exclusive; but it's to this one that I must bring the most willpower."

Gide's pseudonymic *Cahiers d'Andre Walter* (*The Notebook of Andre Walter*), a confessional work presented as a journal published posthumously, marked in 1891 Gide's entry into literary Paris. *Les Poesies d'Andre Walter* ("The Poems of Andre Walter") was published in 1892. In 1910, Gide remarked in his *Journal* that his present undertaking, *Corydon,* was his first work in twenty years to restore to him the "feeling of indispensability" that had dictated *Andre Walter*. Again in his 1924 *Journal* Gide recalled his earliest prose experiment: "I began to write before knowing French very well—and especially: before knowing how to use it well. But I was bursting. . . . At that time, I thought I could bend the language to my purposes." From the beginning, however, the French classical tradition of the word in obedience to the idea dominated Gide's concept of style; the tone and language of each work had to be perfectly suited to the subject being dealt with. He defined the beauty of a work in terms of the harmony of its composition and the exactitude and rigorousness of its style, writing, for example, in undated *Journal* notes this defense of the lack of imagery in *Andre Walter:* "Beginning with my *Notebooks of Andre Walter* I practiced a style that aimed toward a more secret and more essential beauty. . . . I wanted this language 'poorer' still, more strict, more refined, judging that the only purpose of ornamentation is to hide one's faults and that only thoughts insufficiently beautiful in themselves should fear perfect nudity [of style]."

Jacques Riviere, Gide's friend and collaborator on the *Nouvelle Revue francaise,* considered *Andre Walter* typical of the early Gide. Riviere wrote in his *Etudes* that the work's disparate passages are related among themselves only as phases in the "unity of the soul where everything takes place." Such concern to recount the multitudinous phases of the soul is easily attributable to the influence of symbolism in its contemplative mode, in which, for the writer, "living" meant specifically "watching oneself live." In a *Journal* entry for June 23, 1891, Gide remarked that he was "becoming Walter once again and so much the better"; Andre Walter is thus recognizable as a barely disguised but idealized fictional double for the real Andre, who could "watch himself live" within the fictionalized journal. Jean Delay wrote in *La Jeunesse d'Andre Gide* that the hero of the *Notebooks* represented Gide's "first experiment with the double," Gide the young author "transferr[ing] his own conflicts onto Andre Walter, exaggerating them and amplifying them to the crisis point." Throughout his works, Gide demonstrated an affinity for this literary form of the fictionalized diary; he was attracted by the technical problems of a genre that simultaneously limits, by its obligatory first-person point of view, and expands by its definition as "private writing," the kinds of things the supposed diarist can plausibly say about himself and the persons and events around him.

Gide's short *Traite du Narcisse: Theorie du symbole* ("Treatise of Narcissus: Theory of the Symbol") was his first work published in his own name and also appeared in 1891; it represented his attempt to synthesize the aesthetics of the symbolist movement. Inspired largely by a philosophical idealism the symbolists had derived from the German philosopher Arthur Schopenhauer, the "Narcissus" is mythico-religious in tone and willfully obscure in the symbolist manner. Jean-Jacques Thierry noted in his "Notice" for the Pleiade edition of the work that it was enthusiastically received as a type of artistic credo by some among Gide's circle of budding symbolists. In

similar fashion, Gide intended *Le Voyage d'Urien* (*Urien's Voyage,* 1893) to provide the movement—whose adherents until then had been producing mostly poetry, plays, and manifestos—with its exemplary novel. In the *Voyage,* Gide used imaginative landscapes as symbols of emotional states, announcing in his preface to the 1894 edition, cited by Thierry in the Pleiade edition, that "there is no emotion, however singular or new it might appear, that does not have *all its equivalents* in nature." However, according to Thierry, Gide's friend the poet Paul Valery suggested that with its overworked landscape symbolism, the book ran rather "hot" and "cold." *Urien's Voyage* is as dated—or outdated—by its style and its allegorical structure as Gide's other fable from this period, *La Tentative Amoureuse; ou, Le Traite du vain desir* ("The Attempt at Love; or, The Treatise of Vain Desire"). Years later, Gide briefly exempted the *Voyage* from the group of his works that had, he said in his *Journal* for August, 1910, originated in a "profound need to write [them]."

This statement was not, however, meant as a repudiation of his symbolist novel or of his other early writings. In this same *Journal* entry, Gide insisted that none of his early works deserved to be disavowed, provided that his readers not judge them in the same way as they judged his more mature works. And the *Voyage* itself could reveal, he added, to "anyone who knows how to read it," a good deal about its author. In fact, the early works announce many of the themes that figure in varying configurations throughout Gide's canon: sexual desire and renunciation, the conflicting demands of freedom and discipline, and, most evidently, the aesthetic approach—or belief in the value of art for its own sake—that Gide eventually insisted upon as the only valid criterion by which his works be judged. More than the themes, however, these creations herald many of the technical features by which the mature works are distinguished.

The journal form is only one manifestation of the preference for the first-person point of view that also dominates Gide's later narrative fiction, much of which he characterized not as "novels" but as "recits," or "accounts," stories spoken or written by first-person narrators about themselves and directed at specific audiences of listeners or readers. Gide's skill as narrator is evident in his ability to suggest multiple perspectives on the events recounted while remaining technically within the limits implied by the first-person point of view. One of these means of suggestion is the *mise en abyme,* a process of mirroring one story within another for which the play-within-a-play in William Shakespeare's *Hamlet* serves as the classic example. Gide understood the *mise en abyme* as a dramatization of the subject of the work within the experiences of the characters themselves; one of his favorite uses of this device eventually was to represent within the work a character/novelist writing or planning to write a novel on the exact subject as the novel (by Gide) in which the character appears. Still in his symbolist phase, however, and reflecting on *Andre Walter,* the *Narcissus,* and *The Attempt at Love* in his *Journal* for 1893, Gide considered the *mise en abyme* the most effective way to convey the essence of the "typical psychological novel"—that is, the influence of the story upon the storyteller, or, in terms closer to Gide's own willfully philosophical ones, the reaction of what is imagined upon the imagining subject.

In 1893 Gide left France for an extended tour of North Africa with his friend the painter Paul-Albert Laurens; he returned to North Africa for his wedding trip in the late fall and winter of 1895-96. Gide's discovery of the exotic beauty of the desert world and Arabic culture proved epoch-making: for the first time, he was surrounded by palpable "Orient," with its invitation to freedom and sensuality, as opposed to the "Occident," within whose culture had been formed his Protestant conscience that preached discipline, self-denial, and the repression of natural instincts. More specifically, the experiences of his African trips, which included time spent in the company of Irish playwright and poet Oscar Wilde, provoked in Gide the recognition of his own homosexuality. Recording his intense personal conflict through a freedom of expression he increasingly permitted himself, Gide made homosexuality the focal point, if not the metaphor, for a larger opposition between the individual and the cultural and religious institutions surrounding him.

In the 1890s, Gide's attack on culture took the more limited form of the rejection of symbolism. According to Maria van Rysselberghe in her *Cahiers de la petite dame,* he retained a preoccupation with form as the "greatest merit" of the symbolist aesthetic, but the artificiality and self-conscious literariness of the works it produced now became abundantly clear to the young writer seduced by the vastness of the North African landscape. In *Paludes* (*Marshlands,* 1895), Gide deftly satirized the Parisian literary salons he had previously frequented as he recounted the misadventures of an author who has announced to his friends that he is writing a book called—*Marshlands.* Although *Marshlands,* like Gide's earlier works, had a relatively limited circulation, it was recognized by his circle as a successful evocation of a particular literary and social climate. On May 12, 1900, the poet Paul Claudel wrote Gide a letter, cited by Thierry in the Pleiade edition of *Marshlands,* that described the book as "the most complete document we have on that special stifling and stagnant atmosphere we breathed in from 1885 to 1900." A completely different atmosphere is conveyed by the overtly allegorical "El Hadj; ou, Le Traite du faux prophete" ("El Hadj; or, The Treatise of the False Prophet"), completed in 1896. Instead of the salon, Gide here evoked the African desert, with abundant reference to the Old Testament and, as Yvonne Davet has observed in her Pleiade edition commentary, the definite influence of oriental literature.

Gide was, in fact, attempting to exorcise a feeling of personal stagnation and suffocation; he wrote in a *Journal* entry for August, 1894, that *Marshlands* seemed to him "the work of a sick man," his first African trip having been for him a physical convalescence as well as an intellectual and spiritual turning point. However, he also recognized that the difficulty he was having writing *Marshlands* was a sign of his physical and moral recovery. Of easier inspiration, because closer to his present state of mind, was the unabashedly lyrical work he had already begun and would publish after his wedding trip, *Les Nourritures terrestres* (*The Fruits of the Earth,* 1897). If *Marshlands* is "voluntarily limited," *The Fruits of the Earth,* a collection of prose, songs, and maxims addressed to the fictional "Nathanael," celebrates the response of all the senses to nature and desire, resolving all moral questions into a joyous pantheism that encourages Nathanael "not to wish to find God anywhere other than everywhere." By its final exhortation—"And now, Nathanael, throw aside my book"—the work substitutes for the intellectual refinements of symbolism their exact opposite; "life," a panorama of limitless possibilities, is pronounced superior to the static, limiting, fossilizing "book."

Later, when the post-war generation had "discovered" him as a moral influence, Gide insisted that his *Fruits of the Earth* had encouraged his readers to do nothing more than realize and heed the promptings of their own natures. Yet however

revolutionary, the work in its day did not reach a wide reading public; it was, he told himself, too new, too original for that. To Gide himself, *The Fruits of the Earth* always represented a high-water mark in his literary production. In the personal shorthand of the *Journal,* the book serves as a lifelong metaphor for exaltation and joy, for the lyrical response to life. Correcting proofs for the 1927 edition, Gide wrote in his 1926 *Journal,* "all things considered, [this book] is what it was supposed to be, and well done. . . . I read in it permission to become—and almost the announcement of my books that followed, of what I became." In 1931, again in his *Journal,* he pronounced *The Fruits of the Earth* "the most spontaneous, the most sincere" of all his books.

Gide's first major narrative work, *L'Immoraliste* (*The Immoralist,* 1902) is flanked, on one side, by a short novel and a group of plays, and on the other, by a period of depression and difficulty during which Gide reworked much of his old material and wrote and rewrote *La Porte etroite* (*Strait Is the Gate*), which, in 1909, brought him his first real success. In 1899, the short novel *Le Promethee mal enchaine* (*Prometheus Misbound*) introduced what would be Gide's major theme of the "gratuitous act"; the play *Philoctete* ("Philoctetes") was published in the same year, followed by a second play, *Le Roi Candaule* ("King Candaules"), in 1901 and a third, *Saul,* in 1903. Although they met with little critical success and are not considered major works, Gide's plays from this period are, according to Germaine Bree in *Andre Gide: L'Insaisissable Protee,* so original as to bear little resemblance to classical, naturalist, or symbolist theater. Rather, with their "ambiguity unresolved by the denouement" and Gide's evocation of a "special world in which language and gesture approach an encoded language," Bree declared, they "opened the way" for French theater as Sartre and Camus would develop it after World War II. During this period between *The Immoralist* and *Strait Is the Gate* there also appeared, to little critical fanfare, *Pretextes* (*Pretexts,* 1903), a collection of articles and short pieces; the evocative *Amyntas* (1906), that Gide in his 1910 *Journal* called his "most perfect" work to date; and *Le Retour de l'enfant prodigue* (*The Return of the Prodigal Son,* 1909)—a parable on the themes of *The Fruits of the Earth*—that Gide completed, contrary to his usual practice, within just three weeks during the winter of 1907, partly because, he explained in his *Journal* at the time, "I was tired of not writing any more and all the other subjects I have within me presented too many difficulties to be dealt with right away." His most important contribution to literature during this interim, however, turned out to be not a written work but the literary journal and publishing house he co-founded in 1909. With its goal of publishing the best of contemporary writing (of course, including Gide's), the history of the *Nouvelle Revue francaise* became, in the words of Gide's biographer Pierre de Boisdeffre in his *Cahiers Andre Gide* essay, "the history of all of French literature from the 1910's to the 1950's."

In *La Maturite d'Andre Gide de Paludes a l'Immoraliste,* Claude Martin called *The Immoralist* chronologically the first of Gide's "novels" actually to merit that label, since it was the first written "objectively," according to Gide's own later definition of objectivity as "'the novelist's permission to borrow the "I" of another.'" Although *Andre Walter, Urien's Voyage, Prometheus Misbound,* and *The Immoralist* had all been originally published as "novels," Gide eventually withdrew that tag from them, preferring to characterize as a "novel" only one of his works, *Les Faux-Monnayeurs* (*The Counterfeiters,* 1926); to *The Immoralist* reverted the description "recit." *Strait Is the Gate* and *Isabelle* (1911) were also reclassified as recits; Gide fretted in his 1910 *Journal* about the latter's "overly nuanced" quality and, by van Rysselberghe's account, labeled this short narrative his "least important work," one written as an exercise. The writer called *Les Caves du Vatican* (*Lafcadio's Adventures,* 1914), a longer and more complex narrative, a "sotie" or farce.

Although their publication dates span more than a decade, *The Immoralist, Strait Is the Gate,* and *Lafcadio's Adventures* were roughly contemporaneous in conception and were intended, despite the apparent contradictions among their themes, styles, and moral perspectives, to stand as complementary works that simultaneously rather than successively represented their author's thought. Irritated by his critics' failure to grasp the complementary nature of his first two recits, Gide specified in his *Journal* for 1912 that *Strait Is the Gate* was "a twin to *The Immoralist*" and added that "the two subjects grew up concurrently in my thought, the excess in one finding a tacit authorization in the excess of the other." After Gide wrote *Lafcadio's Adventures,* he wrote of the three books in his 1914 *Journal:* "If I could have, I would have written [these three books] *together*. I could not have written *The Immoralist* if I had not known I would also write *Strait Is the Gate,* and I needed to have written the one and the other to be able to allow myself *Lafcadio's Adventures*."

The Immoralist is recounted by the young Michel, whose convalescence from serious illness during his wedding trip to North Africa has converted him from a man formed by culture to one formed by nature; his "immorality" consists of his subsequent attempts, resulting finally in the death of his wife, to free himself from the restrictions imposed upon him by his education and his position in society. Yet as Lucie Delarue-Mardrus observed in her 1902 *La Revue blanche* assessment, Michel is "*not* the Immoralist. He is only *an effort towards immoralism,* or rather, . . . the eternal uncatechized, who demands lessons and examples from all and everyone." Of much different stuff, at first glance, is the rarefied Christian atmosphere of *Strait Is the Gate,* in which Jerome and Alissa continually defer and finally renounce their marriage plans in the name of a higher and more virtuous spiritual love. Despite Gide's denial in the 1951 *Et nunc manet in te* (*Madeleine*) that he had used his wife as any more than a point of departure for the characterization of Alissa, the work is often considered a fictionalized account of his courtship of his cousin Madeleine Rondeaux (their marriage, in fact, remained unconsummated). Finally, *Lafcadio's Adventures* is an extended dramatization, within a comical parody of the omniscent, realist novel, of Gide's concept of the "gratuitous act"; the hero, Lafcadio, is as equally capable of disinterested good as of disinterested evil and is morally susceptible—to the point of inflicting penknife wounds on his thigh—only to his perceived failings towards himself. In her *Cahiers Andre Gide* essay, Marguerite Yourcenar praised *Lafcadio's Adventures* as one of the few truly successful picaresque novels, a "novel of fantasy and adventure," marked by a light and spritely "rhythm" that calls to mind "certain pieces by Mozart."

In 1931, when his *Journal* and even his correspondence were being widely published, Gide reflected in the *Journal* that "the absence of echo"—or critical attention—for his earliest works had been the true guarantee of their value; writing for future readers, he said, he had written for timelessness. Pierre de Boisdeffre estimated in his *Vie d'Andre Gide, 1869-1951* that *The Immoralist* had had "only a handful" of reviewers, and Gide himself pessimistically predicted in his 1902 *Journal* that

an edition of only three hundred copies would be sufficient to meet demand; however, Claude Martin has documented in *La Maturite d'Andre Gide* the fairly extensive critical "echo" the book received in 1902 and 1903, pointing out that Gide was upset not that his book wasn't being read, but that it wasn't being read *well*. Among the flurry of articles about *The Immoralist,* Martin cites an essay by Marcel Drouin (Gide's brother-in-law writing under the pseudonym "Michel Arnauld") in *La Revue blanche* of November, 1902, an essay that constituted the authorized response to what Gide perceived as his readers' errors. Drouin wrote that the book would give rise to fewer misconceptions if "more people knew how to read, within the lines and between the lines, then reread, then reflect on their reading" of this book in which "the antithesis is next to the thesis, the objection with the argument, . . . united in the same soul and the single life [of the protagonist]." Among the false perceptions attending the book was one that attributed its derivation, suggested by its title, from Friedrich Nietzsche's "immoralism." Gide himself later insisted in his *Journal* for 1922 that his recit had not been so much "influenced" as "confirmed" by Nietzsche, whom he had discovered only after beginning to write the book; on the other hand, the *Journal* for 1905 records his satisfaction that at least one perceptive reader had praised him for having, with his protagonist Michel, peered through "the cracks in culture." An anecdote in the 1915 *Journal* relates that the novelist Paul Bourget demanded to know, in confidence, whether Michel was or was not a "practicing pederast." Replying coyly that his narrator was most aptly described as "a homosexual who does not yet recognize himself," Gide thus preserved the intended ambiguity of his protagonist's sexual portrait.

An article on Gide by the British critic Edmund Gosse in the September, 1909, *Contemporary Review* launched the success of *Strait Is the Gate*. Gide's often-quoted elation that "*Strait Is the Gate* is selling!" was no doubt seconded by the delicious irony of having to bring out a hasty second edition after his publisher had already destroyed the plates from the first. Begun in 1894 as the "Mort de Mlle Claire" ("The Death of Mademoiselle Claire"), the work was finished in October, 1908 (an event Gide commemorated, for unexplained reasons, by shaving off his mustache). The book, Gide thought, was rather well done, although he wrote in his *Journal* for 1909 that he preferred the final section, "Alissa's Journal," to those written in Jerome's name: "flaccid prose" for a "flaccid character." It is also true, however, that his success made him suspicious: as Jean-Jacques Thierry noted in the Pleiade edition, Gide wrote specifically of *Strait Is the Gate* and *The Pastoral Symphony,* "I believe that those of my works that reached the public most quickly are the least innovative."

In fact, *Strait Is the Gate*'s drama of renunciation and mysticism, pushed to its limits in the character of Alissa, did not win for Gide whole-hearted endorsement in either Catholic or Protestant circles. In the Pleiade edition, Thierry recorded Gide's responses to the uproar from both sides over the work: the Catholic poet Paul Claudel wrote him an "astonishing" letter, according to Gide, "denouncing the heresy of Protestantism in this . . . love of the good independent of the promised reward," while his Protestant readers "refused to recognize my heroine as Protestant." Gide's dissatisfaction with his critics after publication of *Strait Is the Gate* and again after that of *Lafcadio's Adventures* was sharp and profound: "I'm afraid I shall soon have to fight against a false image they're already drawing of me," he wrote in his *Journal* for October, 1910, "a monster to which they give my name, and that they're erecting in my stead, and that is ugly and frighteningly stupid." As Gide would sardonically recall in the *Journal* for 1937, this "absurd fear of being found at fault by the *pure*" had for a time almost prevented him from writing. (In 1952, the Roman Catholic church did, in fact, officially condemn all of Gide's writings.) Meanwhile, in his 1913 *Journal* he labeled his production up to the time of *Lafcadio's Adventures* incomplete, only partially representative of him, and, in his 1914 *Journal* he called it "negative . . . the reverse side of my heart and my mind," compared with what he had yet to write. If he refused to classify his narratives as "novels," he continued in an outburst against his critics in the 1914 *Journal,* his reason was that "I have up till now written only *ironic*—or, if you prefer, critical—books."

Gide's sensitivity to the critical reaction aroused by his works is well documented. Charles Du Bos described in *Le Dialogue avec Andre Gide* the author's "fear of and passion for compromising himself"; according to an entry in Gide's 1922 *Journal,* Madeleine Gide wrote to her husband in January of that year: "What very much disturbs me is the nasty campaign begun against you . . . if you were invulnerable, I wouldn't worry. But you are vulnerable, and you know it, and I know it." It was precisely by his refusal to choose a definitive ethical position within his works that Gide rendered himself most vulnerable to critical attack by partisan thinkers and keepers of public morality. He, in fact, repeatedly provoked such attacks, as demonstrated by this comment about *Strait Is the Gate,* which Thierry quotes in his "Notice" to the Pleiade edition: "It's to the gratuitousness of the work of art that the Protestant remains refractory; he wants the work to have meaning, instruction, usefulness." By his term "gratuitousness," Gide suggested the function of his works *as* art, proposing with his heroes and heroines—"against whom [I] cannot side any more than [I] set them up as exemplary"—not solutions, but enigmas and stimuli to his readers' reflection. The Catholic critic Henri Massis, a principal adversary whose articles always appeared, Gide complained in his *Journal* for 1921, the very day the writer's books went on sale, refused in his *Jugements* to accept an argument from aesthetic grounds in defense of moral nonpartisanship; for Massis, Gide's "classicism" and the "gratuitousness of [his] art" were simply code words for hypocrisy, moral turpitude, and evasion of responsibility.

As he had for the *Immoralist,* Gide responded to attacks of this nature by affirming, first, that his intention had never been to "influence," and, second, that anyone who attributed this intention to him wasn't reading him properly. In Massis's case, misreading involved misquoting—"Curious, this inability of Massis to quote a text exactly or without falsifying its meaning," he observed ruefully in his 1931 *Journal;* more seriously, as Gide protested in a 1921 entry, the critic interpreted the novelist's fictional characters as spokesmen for their creator. The basis of Gide's objection was thus the extreme *literality* with which his opponents tended to read his work, mistaking art as doctrine and direly envisaging an army of Gide disciples who would interpret his works as strict blueprints for anarchy. With the exception of *The Fruits of the Earth,* Gide eventually insisted, all of his works had to be read "ironically" or "critically," and even in this book, he wrote in his *Journal* for 1926, "there is, for whoever consents to read well and without prejudice, the critique of the book within the book itself, as it should be." In a 1950 letter to Pierre Lafille, a letter quoted by Lafille in his *Cahiers Andre Gide* essay, Gide wrote, "You have admirably noted that in each of my books there coexist and are juxtaposed, at one and the

same time, the depiction of a psychological state and the critique of that very state.'' Jean Hytier, in *Andre Gide,* explained this irony as a play of sympathy and antipathy, identification and distance, skillfully balanced in the recits: ''By sympathy, [Gide] makes these *first persons singular* speak with an accent of truth unequaled in French fiction; . . . by antipathy, he maintains all his reserve, marks the distances which separate him from his creatures. . . . Readers let themselves be carried away, and react naively to the story they are being told, . . . but [Gide] also intends the reader to withdraw his identification, either by the story's end, or . . . as it is being told.'' The characters themselves are the first victims of Gide's irony, for as Germaine Bree aptly observed in a 1951 *Yale French Studies* essay, they ''are rather like players who, in a football game, persist in playing basket ball, with the conviction that that is the game being played.''

Moutote contended that Gide's difficulties with his critics represented the ''drama of an avant-garde thinker'' who had to wait for the public to catch up with him. In moments of equanimity, Gide would show himself resigned to the wait and confident of its results; writing in his *Journal* in 1921, he declared: ''I would have stopped writing long ago if I were not convinced that those to come will discover in my writings what those today refuse to see, and what I know, however, I have put in them. . . . I will let my books patiently choose their readers; the small number of today will be the opinion-makers of tomorrow.'' ''Being out of step with his time,'' he summarized in the 1937 *Journal,* ''is what gives an artist his reason for being. . . . He opposes, he initiates.'' Even during the campaigns against him, Gide appreciated that bad press was better than no press at all, remarking wryly in a 1924 *Journal* entry that the ''diabolical uproar'' of Massis and his clan ''made me more famous in three months than my books . . . in thirty years.'' In fairness to Massis, however, it must be recognized that this critic was right about Gide's refusal to be pinned down by any single one of his books: ''If anyone thinks that in my latest work he has finally grasped what I am like,'' Gide wrote in his 1909 *Journal,* ''let him think again: it's always from my last-born that I am the most different.''

As if in reaction to his increasing notoriety, Gide's *Journal* for the years preceding World War I records his sense that, approaching his fortieth birthday, he had not yet said the most important of what he wanted to say. ''If I died today,'' he wrote in May of 1910, ''my entire opus would disappear in favor of *Strait Is the Gate,* that's the only [work] that would be given any consideration.'' Two years later he again lamented in the *Journal,* ''If I were to disappear now, no one could suspect, from what I've written, the better things I have yet to say. By what boldness, by what presumption of a long life, have I still kept the most important for the end?''

One of the works Gide counted as the most important at this time was *Corydon,* his treatise on homosexuality; a first private edition of twelve copies had been circulated among friends in 1911. Intending with this work to defend ''coldly, deliberately,'' the complete naturalness of homosexual love, Gide wanted, as he wrote in undated *Journal* notes, ''not to solicit pity [but] to DISTURB''; he had not, however, sought a larger public for his defense. During the war he had more serious reason to question not only the wisdom of publishing *Corydon,* but also the nature of his entire philosophical orientation. In the 1912 *Journal* he had written, ''Catholicism is unacceptable. Protestantism is intolerable. And I feel myself to be profoundly Christian.'' But with the conversion to Catholicism of several of his friends—Francis Jammes, Paul Claudel, and Henri Gheon—Gide felt pressure brought upon him to convert in his turn. A series of prayers and commentaries on Bible passages, the short work *Numquid et tu?* is his record of this spiritual crisis, from which he emerged in 1916 unconverted and evolving toward the agnosticism he would succinctly express in the 1927 *Journal:* ''I am an unbeliever. I will never be impious.'' Moreover, he had fallen in love with young Marc Allegret.

Although Gide had discussed in his *Journal* of 1910 a work with the provisional title ''L'Aveugle'' (''The Blind One'') and had already spoken of such a work to Paul Laurens as early as 1893, it was not until 1918 that he wrote the story of the domestic and religious crisis experienced by a Swiss pastor who falls in love with the blind girl he adopts. This short narrative, published in 1919 as *La Symphonie pastorale* (*The Pastoral Symphony*), both reflects Gide's long meditation on Christianity and its factions and heralds the serious marital crisis provoked by his relationship with Allegret. When Gide left for a stay in England with Marc in 1918, Madeleine burned her entire collection of his letters. Gide was devastated—as much, it appears, by the loss of the record he had hoped to leave posterity as by this announcement of his wife's spiritual and emotional withdrawal from him.

In his Pleiade edition commentary, Thierry recorded Gide's conviction that *The Pastoral Symphony* represented the liquidation of '' 'my last debt to the past,' '' since up to that point—and he was fifty in 1919—'' 'I hadn't written a single book that hadn't been conceived before I was thirty.' '' Charles Du Bos estimated in his *Approximations* that the *Symphony* resolved with ''a most perfect mastery'' the problem of ''the murkiness of the content transparent beneath the clarity of the form''; Jacques Riviere praised Gide for ''having shown the underside of a psychology that is unaware of itself.'' Gide himself explained, in various notes cited by Thierry, that his ''critique'' in the *Symphony* was directed against the danger of ''the free interpretation of the Scriptures'' and against the kind of self-deception, ''a form of lie told to oneself,'' to which the pastor falls prey.

It is not precisely true, however, that with *The Pastoral Symphony* Gide had acquitted himself of his debt to his past. During the war he had begun writing his memoirs, intending once again to speak out honestly about himself, since, as he wrote in his *Journal* in 1917, ''not a day goes by that I don't ask myself: if suddenly, today, in an hour, right now, I had to leave everthing, what would remain, what would appear, of everything I had to say?'' Naturally, such considerations led back to the matter of *Corydon;* Gide returned to the treatise in 1918, although he now lamented in his *Journal* that he was writing ''out of season'' and no longer ''out of need,'' for he had long since devised a ''practical solution'' to the problems he was describing. The 1920 edition of *Corydon* was once again private, limited to a mere twenty-one copies. Among those who read the work in this edition was the novelist Marcel Proust, obsessively engaged in populating his own massive work, *Remembrance of Things Past,* with a richly colorful and variously perverse homosexual crew. As Bernard Fay recalled in *Les Precieux,* Proust called *Corydon* ''quite a grotesque book . . . that, far from serving his cause, renders it completely heinous''; to Gide he counseled, according to an entry in the 1921 *Journal,* ''You can tell everything, . . . but on condition that you never say *I.*''

''It's when I can say 'I,' speaking in another's name, that I speak the best,'' Gide had told Maria van Rysselberghe in

1919 about *The Pastoral Symphony*. In *Corydon: Four Socratic Dialogues,* it is Corydon himself who, ostensibly gathering notes for a book on the subject, takes on the defense of pederasty; he bases his arguments on observations from the natural world as well as on the history and morals of ancient Greece. The truest notes in *Corydon* resound, however, less in the philosophical arguments advanced than in Corydon's outspoken opposition to society's condemnation of those outside its sexual norms. Contrary to the outcry Gide had anticipated, the publication of *Corydon* in 1924 met with only silence from the critics; van Rysselberghe, who wrote in her *Cahiers de la petite dame* that it had "disappointed almost everybody," explained that those who weren't shocked found it "unworthy of [Gide's] talent," that those who were shocked wouldn't talk about it, and that those in whose name Gide had meant to speak apparently found little to identify with in his particular case. Having written in his 1922 *Journal* about Freud and Freudianism, "I've been doing this without knowing it for ten years, fifteen years," Gide provided perhaps the most accurate appraisal of *Corydon*'s significance as psychoanalytic process. He declared in his *Journal* for 1933, "It's precisely when one refuses to grant any importance to the sexual question that it threatens to take on too much. [This question] ceased to bother me from the day I decided to consider it up front, to truly deal with it. *Corydon,* far from attesting to an obsession, . . . is the pledge of a deliverance. And who can say how many, with one stroke, this little book also *delivered*?"

A happier critical fate attended the memoirs, published in 1926 as *Si le grain ne meurt* (*If It Die*), and recounting Gide's life up to his engagement to Madeleine in 1895. A number of Gide's friends, who were in a position to judge the completed work against his expressed desire for clarity and sincerity, expressed either their disappointment at his excessive discretion or their opinion that too great a concern for clarity had vastly oversimplified Gide's portrait of himself. For Du Bos in the *Dialogue, If It Die* was long on preparation and short on revelation, finally only "caricatural" of a "Gide larger, fuller, more moving, I was going to say than his entire work, in any case than this rasping and grating sketch." More perceptively, however, Gide's friend Jacques Raverat acknowledged—as Gide approvingly noted in his *Journal* for 1920—that the only way to have a full portrait of the author was to read all of Gide's works at the same time, since "all the states that, for artistic reasons, you depict as successive can be simultaneous with you." Gide's biographers, particularly Jean Delay, have drawn attention to the numerous inaccuracies and omissions in Gide's recollections of his past in this work; tantalizingly related to both autobiography and fiction (Gide's own and fiction as a genre), however, *If It Die* has been regarded as a masterpiece of the genre called "literary autobiography" by C. D. E. Tolton in his *Andre Gide and the Art of Autobiography*.

In 1919 Gide began his early sketches for *The Counterfeiters,* explaining to van Rysselberghe that what he had in mind was "a work, a novel that would make people say: 'Ah yes! we understand why he claimed not to have written any before this.'" Besides countering the image left in the public mind by *Corydon, The Counterfeiters* was to leave behind the "monographs" of the recits in favor of multiplicity and counterpoint: "I conceive of the novel in the same manner as Dostoevsky, [as] a struggle between points of view," he told van Rysselberghe in a 1919 interview. Still working on the book in 1923, he wrote at that time in his *Journal,* "What I want a novel to be? an intersection—a rendez-vous of problems." From its inception, the notion of "journal" was integral to this work. To help keep track of his uncharacteristically broad range of material ("there's enough here to feed half a dozen novels," he observed in the 1921 *Journal*), Gide kept a special journal detailing his plans for and progress on the novel; the resulting *Journal des Faux-Monnayeurs* (*Journal of "The Counterfeiters"*) is Gide's record of, in Thierry's description, "the architecture of the novel [that shows] not a plot as it develops but a novel as it is being written." In addition, a fictional journal kept within the novel by the character Édouard (in preparation for *his* novel, also entitled *The Counterfeiters*) is the means by which Gide intended to decenter his narrative focus and make of *The Counterfeiters* "the critique of the novel . . . in general," as he explained to van Rysselberghe: "There isn't one center to my novel, there are two, as in an ellipse: the events on the one hand and their reaction in 'Edouard.' Ordinarily, when one writes a novel, one either starts with the characters and makes up events to develop them, or starts with the events and creates characters as needed to explain them. But 'Edouard,' who holds the psychological strings of a series of beings who confide in him, rather than writing a novel, dreams of making them act in reality, and he doesn't succeed in substantiating the characters by the events. These characters give him events, that he can't do anything with! and *that* becomes part of the subject."

The elaborate self-reflective structure of *The Counterfeiters*—its orchestration modeled in part, according to the 1924 *Journal,* on that of a J.S. Bach fugue—has assured its place within the modernist critique of the realist novel. In an article excerpted in *Gide: A Collection of Critical Essays,* novelist Francois Mauriac pronounced the work "by and large, . . . a failure," excepting "the pulsating vein of Edouard's *Journal,*" which was for Mauriac a token of Gide's commanding presence in the novel; on the other hand, David Littlejohn stated in his introduction to *Gide: A Collection of Critical Essays* that the 1927 American publication of *The Counterfeiters* assured Gide's reputation as a major novelist. Littlejohn added that "few important French writers of the twenties and thirties failed to comment on the Gide phenomenon; and outside of France his work was accorded the attention due that of an international master. . . . Every analysis of the 'New Novel' had to find room for *Les Faux-Monnayeurs*." On the evidence of his 1927 *Journal,* Gide was much more pleased with his American reviews than with his French ones; he considered the latter to be partisan and argumentative compared to the former. Writing for *La Revue de Paris* in 1927, Albert Thibaudet damned the novel with faint praise. Calling the work "monstrously intelligent" and "intelligently monstrous," as well as "the novel of novels and the novelist's novel," Thibaudet judged it worthy of "professional admiration" yet warned that it was too "non-conformist" to be wished success: "a public in conformity to this non-conformity, a public docile to Gide's perverse suggestions, that would concern me," he cautioned. From Claude-Edmonde Magny, author of the *Histoire du roman francais deput 1918,* however, came much less qualified admiration: he wrote that this "novel about the novelistic fantastic" and French literature's "most authentic novel about adolescence" was "eminently *readable,* and even fascinating for the reader left indifferent by the question of the pure novel or the gratuitous act." If anything, its "impression of the inexhaustible," its absence of finality and closure, Magny continued, made this novel more "real" than the "realist" novels it critiqued.

Gide's instructions to himself in his 1921 *Journal* to "distance myself from realism" in this book implied exactly such op-

position to the traditional novel; he intended to eliminate the "neutral parts" in favor of a greater appeal to his readers' imaginations and protested that his refusal to flatter the public's expectations of how novels should be written did not make him any less a novelist. "How easy it would have been for me to curry favor with the majority," Gide reflected in his 1929 *Journal,* "by writing *The Counterfeiters* like standard novels, describing the places and the people, analysing the emotions, explaining the situations, displaying on the surface everything I hide between the lines, and catering to the reader's laziness"; he added in an entry for 1930, "I only write for those who understand at a hint." He objected again in his 1931 *Journal* to critics' charges that he hadn't written a standard novel because he hadn't known how to: "What would be easier than to write a novel like the others! Very simply, I am loathe to, and can't bring myself any more than [Paul] Valery to write, 'The marquise went out at five o'clock,' or, . . . still more compromisingly, 'X. wondered for a long time whether. . . .'" A year after *The Counterfeiters* appeared in France, Gide remarked in the *Journal* that its public reception was running true to form: "[My] most recent [book] is only liked by those who hadn't yet liked the others, and all the readers the previous books have won for me declare they 'like this book much less.' I've gotten used to it." As well he should have, in light of his own precept recorded in the *Journal* for 1922: "Never take advantage, for any new work, of the momentum gained by the preceding one. By the same token, win for each new work a new public."

The Counterfeiters was, by Gide's admission in a 1928 entry, written for Marc Allegret, "to conquer his attention, his esteem," just as Gide's wife had been the dominant influence and the intended audience for the previous works. *The Counterfeiters* in press, Gide left with Marc on an extended tour of the Congo, the first of many voyages he would undertake and write about during the final third of his life. "All the long trips I haven't taken are like remorse within me," van Rysselberghe overheard him say before this departure, "traveling seems to me almost a duty, a kind of piety; I think the Good Lord must not be very happy with the way we honor Him, He must think, 'What! I gave them all that and look how little they make of it!'" Gide's *Voyage au Congo* (*Travels in the Congo,* 1927) and *Retour du Tchad* ("Return From Chad," 1928) have been presented in support of a social conscience that had first surfaced in his 1914 *Souvenirs de la cour d'assises* (*Recollections of the Assize Court*) before largely disappearing from the intervening works; Gide's descriptions in the *Travels* of the economic exploitation of French equatorial Africa led to a public debate on colonialism upon his return to Paris. Similarly, his observations on his trip to Moscow as an honored guest at Maxim Gorki's funeral, the 1936 *Retour de l'U.R.S.S.* (*Return From the U.S.S.R.*) and its 1937 supplement, *Retouches a mon "Retour de l'U.R.S.S."* (*Afterthoughts on the U.S.S.R.*), sharply critiqued the Soviet system and announced Gide's estrangement from the Communist movement, which he had supported financially and ideologically during the early 1930s.

Although *Les Nouvelles Nourritures* (*Later Fruits of the Earth,* 1935) is a work that Gide had been anticipating writing since the 1920s, Pierre de Boisdeffre has characterized it in *Metamorphoses de la litterature* as Gide's "Marxist Gospel"; a volume of letters, articles, and speeches from 1930 to 1938 grouped under the title *Litterature engagee* ("Committed Literature") records Gide's flirtation with Communism, including the eminently forgettable play *Robert; ou, L'Interet general* ("Robert; or, The General Interest"), of which the Moscow debut was hastily canceled after the apostasy of the *Return From the U.S.S.R.* Like Catholicism, Marxism ultimately proved too doctrinaire for Gide; despite their differing principles—the first, he judged, preaching charity and ignoring justice, the second announcing justice at the expense of love—their doctrinal similarity is brought out in this objection to Marx's writing in his *Journal* for summer, 1937: "It's the Latin Mass. Where one doesn't understand, one bows down."

Finally, a trio of recits from this period was also intended to respond to social issues. *L'Ecole des femmes* (*The School for Wives*) in 1929, *Robert* in 1929, and *Genevieve* in 1936 present the complex portrait of a courtship and marriage judged from the respective viewpoints of the fiancee become wife and mother, the husband, and ultimately the daughter. Through these three figures Gide intended, according to a *Journal* entry for 1930, "to meet head-on the whole question of feminism." Yet even Albert J. Guerard who, in his *Andre Gide,* had judged *The Immoralist* "one of the greatest realistic novels of the century" and parts of *The Counterfeiters* and *Lafcadio's Adventures* "among the triumphs of modern anti-realism," had to admit that "surely few important novelists have written books as superficial and as dull as *L'École des femmes, Robert,* and *Genevieve.*" It would appear that Gide agreed with Guerard. Arthur E. Babcock calls attention in his *Portraits of Artists: Reflexivity in Gidean Fiction, 1902-1946* to a 1947 letter in which Gide explained to Guerard, "My *School for Wives,* or at least the third part (*Genevieve*), is of all my books (and by far) the most painfully written. . . . At the time I was poisoned by the social question. Let's let it drop."

Gide's final works returned to what had always been for him a fertile source, equal to Christianity in imaginative possibility and moral instruction: Greek mythology. His version of *Oedipe* (*Oedipus,* 1931), which added, he said in his 1932 *Journal,* "jokes, trivialities and incongruities" to Sophocles' classic text, seemed to him a dramatization of the tragic "struggle between individualism and submission to religious authority"; his intention, he wrote in a *Journal* entry for 1933, was to evoke not terror and pity—the aims of the original Greek tragedy—but reflection. Evaluating his *Oedipus* in his 1931 *Journal,* he envisioned as a separate work a "decisive meeting" between the mythological king Theseus, whose life he had long wanted to write, and Oedipus, "each measuring himself against the other and illuminating, each under cover of the other, their two lives"; the meeting takes place near the end of Gide's final recit, his "testament" *Thesee* (*Theseus,* 1946), which Claude Martin called, in *Andre Gide par lui-meme,* "at the evening of his life, . . . an intelligent extract of his wisdom."

Gide's contributions to contemporary literature were publicly recognized during the last years of his life: an honorary fellow of the Royal Society of London since 1924, he was awarded both an honorary doctorate from the University of Oxford and the Nobel Prize in literature in 1947. His intimate writings continued to his death: *Et nunc manet in te* (*Madeleine*), published in 1951, is a poignant memorial to his wife, who had died in 1938; it completes the image Gide wished to leave of himself by including those previously unpublished pages of his *Journal* in which he discussed his relationship with "Emmanuele"/Madeleine. *Ainsi soit-il; ou, Les Jeux sont faits* (*So Be It; or, The Chips Are Down*) ends six days before Gide's death in 1951. Jean Delay considered this last work, along with *Andre Walter,* "aesthetically the least successful" and "psychologically the most interesting, [*Andre Walter*] because the twenty-year-old poet does not yet know how to create art,

[*So Be It*] because the octogenarian, sensing death approach, disdains to create it and allows his pen to run free." Gide's final work concluded with a characteristic refusal to conclude—writing or, as it turned out, living: "No! I can't affirm that with the end of this notebook, all will be closed; that it will be over. Maybe I will want to add something more.... At the last minute, add something more." *So Be It* was published posthumously in 1952.

BIOGRAPHICAL/CRITICAL SOURCES:

BOOKS

Arland, Marcel, and Jean Mouton, editors, *Entretiens sur Andre Gide,* Mouton, 1967.
Babcock, Arthur E., *Portraits of Artists: Reflexivity in Gidean Fiction, 1902-1946,* French Literature Publications, 1982.
Boisdeffre, Pierre de, *Metamorphoses de la litterature,* Alsatia, 1950, excerpted in *Les Critiques de notre temps et Gide,* edited by Michel Raimond, Garnier, 1971.
Boisdeffre, Pierre de, *Vie d'Andre Gide, 1869-1951: Essai de biographie critique,* Hachette, 1970.
Bree, Germaine, *Andre Gide: L'Insaisissable Protee,* Belles-Lettres, 1953, English revision and translation published as *Andre Gide,* Rutgers University Press, 1963; excerpted in *Les Critiques de notre temps et Gide,* edited by Michel Raimond, Garnier, 1971.
Cahiers Andre Gide, Gallimard, 1969—.
Cordle, Thomas, *Andre Gide,* Twayne, 1969.
Davet, Yvonne, editor, *Litterature engagee,* by Andre Gide, Gallimard, 1950.
Davet, Yvonne and Jean-Jacques Thierry, editors and authors of notes, *Romans, recits, et soties: Oeuvres lyriques,* texts by Andre Gide, La Pleiade/Gallimard, 1958.
Delay, Jean, *La Jeunesse d'Andre Gide,* two volumes, Gallimard, 1956, translation by June Guicharnaud published as *The Youth of Andre Gide,* University of Chicago Press, 1963.
Dictionary of Literary Biography, Volume 65: *French Novelists, 1900-1930,* Gale, 1988.
Du Bos, Charles, *Approximations,* Fayard, 1965, excerpted in *Les Critiques de notre temps et Gide,* edited by Michel Raimond, Garnier, 1971.
Du Bos, Charles, *Le Dialogue avec Andre Gide,* Correa, 1947, excerpted in *Les Critiques de notre temps et Gide,* edited by Michel Raimond, Garnier, 1971.
Fay, Bernard, *Les Precieux,* Perrin, 1966.
Fowlie, Wallace, *Andre Gide: His Life and Art,* Macmillan, 1965.
Gide, Andre, *Journal, 1889-1939,* La Pleiade/Gallimard, 1948.
Gide, Andre, *Journal, 1939-1949; Souvenirs,* La Pleiade/Gallimard, 1954.
Gide, Andre, *The Journals of Andre Gide,* four volumes, selected, edited, translated, introduced, and annotated by Justin O'Brien, Knopf, 1947-51.
Guerard, Albert J., *Andre Gide,* Harvard University Press (Cambridge), 1969.
Hytier, Jean, *Andre Gide,* Charlot, 1945, translation by R. Howard excerpted in *Gide: A Collection of Critical Essays,* edited by David Littlejohn, Prentice-Hall, 1970.
Ireland, G. W., *Gide: A Study of His Creative Writings,* Oxford University Press, 1970.
Littlejohn, David, *The Andre Gide Reader,* Knopf, 1971.
Littlejohn, David, editor and author of introduction, *Gide: A Collection of Critical Essays,* Prentice-Hall, 1970.
Magny, Claude-Edmonde, *Histoire du roman francais depuis 1918,* Seuil, 1950, excerpted in *Les Critiques de notre temps et Gide,* edited by Michel Raimond, Garnier, 1971.
Martin, Claude, *Andre Gide par lui-meme,* Seuil, 1964, excerpted in *Les Critiques de notre temps et Gide,* edited by Michel Raimond, Garnier, 1971.
Martin, Claude, *La Maturite d'Andre Gide: De "Paludes" a "L'Immoraliste,"* Klincksieck, 1977.
Martin du Gard, Roger, *Recollections of Andre Gide,* translation by John Russell, Viking, 1953.
Massis, Henri, *Jugements,* Plon, 1924.
Mauriac, Claude, *Conversations With Andre Gide,* translation by Michael Lebeck, Braziller, 1965.
Mauriac, Francois, *Memoires Interieurs,* translation by G. Hopkins, Eyre & Spottiswoode, 1960, excerpted in *Gide: A Collection of Critical Essays,* edited by David Littlejohn, Prentice-Hall, 1970.
O'Brien, Justin, *Index detaille des quinze volumes de l'Edition Gallimard des "Oeuvres completes" d'Andre Gide,* Pretexte, 1954.
O'Brien, Justin, *Portrait of Andre Gide,* Knopf, 1953.
Painter, George D., *Andre Gide: A Critical Biography,* Atheneum, 1968.
Raimond, Michel, editor, *Les Critiques de notre temps et Gide,* Garnier, 1971.
Riviere, Jacques, *Etudes,* Gallimard, 1944, excerpted in *Les Critiques de notre temps et Gide,* edited by Michel Raimond, Garnier, 1971.
Rysselberghe, Maria van, *Les Cahiers de la petite dame: Notes pour l'histoire authentique d'Andre Gide,* Gallimard, 1973.
Tolton, C. D. E., *Andre Gide and the Art of Autobiography: A Study of "Si le grain ne meurt,"* Macmillan (Toronto), 1975.
Twentieth-Century Literary Criticism, Gale, Volume 5, 1981, Volume 12, 1984.

PERIODICALS

Contemporary Review, September, 1909.
New York Times, December 27, 1983, November 3, 1987.
New York Times Book Review, October 2, 1983.
Perspectives on Contemporary Literature, number 8, 1982.
Revue blanche, July 15, 1902, November 15, 1902.
Revue de Paris, August 15, 1927.
Times Literary Supplement, June 26, 1981, March 7, 1986.
Yale French Studies, number 7, 1951.*

—*Sidelights by Renee A. Kingcaid*

* * *

GILBERT, R(obert) A(ndrew) 1942- (Edward Dunning)

PERSONAL: Born October 6, 1942, in Bristol, England; son of Rupert (an aircraft engineer) and Eileen Hilda (Crick) Gilbert; married Patricia Kathleen Linnell (an antiquarian bookseller), June 20, 1970; children: Nicholas Jerome, Matthew Robert, William Patrick, Laura Elizabeth Kathleen, Melissa Catherine. *Education:* University of Bristol, B.A. (with honors), 1964. *Politics:* Liberal. *Religion:* Anglican.

ADDRESSES: Home—4 Julius Rd., Bishopston, Bristol BS7 8EU, England.

CAREER: Antiquarian bookseller in Bristol, England, 1966—. Publishing consultant. Trustee of Yarker Library Trust and Hermetic Research Trust.

MEMBER: Churches' Fellowship for Psychical and Spiritual Studies (organizer of Southwest Region, 1981-84), Society of Authors.

WRITINGS:

A. E. Waite: A Bibliography, Thorsons, 1983.
The Golden Dawn: Twilight of the Magicians, Aquarian Press, 1983.
(Editor) *The Magical Mason: Hermetic Writings of W. Wynn Westcott,* Aquarian Press, 1983.
(Editor) *The Sorcerer and His Apprentice: Hermetic Writings of S. L. McGregor Mathers and J. W. Brodie Innes,* Aquarian Press, 1983.
The Golden Dawn Companion, Aquarian Press, 1986.
(Editor with Michael A. Cox) *The Oxford Book of English Ghost Stories,* Oxford University Press, 1986.
A. E. Waite: Magician of Many Parts, Crucible, 1987.
(With W. N. Birks) *The Treasure of Montsegur,* Crucible, 1987.
(Editor) *Hermetic Papers of A. E. Waite,* Aquarian Press, 1987.
(Editor under pseudonym Edward Dunning) *Selected Masonic Writings of A. E. Waite,* Aquarian Press, 1987.
The Western Hermetic Tradition, Aquarian Press, 1988.
Ritual: Its Meaning and Purpose, Dryad Press, 1988.

Contributor of articles and reviews to magazines and newspapers, including *Ars Quatuor Coronatorum, Christian Parapsychologist, Pegasus, Pendragon,* and *Yeats Annual.*

WORK IN PROGRESS: Freemasonry: An Illustrated History of the Craft Worldwide, with John Hamill; editing, with Godfrey Brangham and Roger Dobson, *Selected Letters of Arthur Machen; The Golden Dawn Scrapbook.*

SIDELIGHTS: R. A. Gilbert told *CA:* "My aim has been (and is) to promote those elements within the esoteric traditions of Western Europe and of the Judeo-Christian tradition which have been unjustly neglected on account of their presumed unorthodoxy. I wish to demonstrate their compatibility with orthodox Christianity. In addition, I continue to work on the questions of the nature and communication of mystical experience, the distribution of life within the universe, and the religious implications of cosmology. I give frequent lectures on all of these topics and on related areas of research, with the aim of encouraging audiences and readers to move away from their preconceptions and their tendency to cling to cherished, false beliefs. For instance, it has proved an extraordinarily difficult task to convince entrenched academics (despite documentary evidence) that Charles Williams *was* greatly influenced by the mystic A. E. Waite. The blindness of the self-righteous academic is a disease most difficult to cure."

BIOGRAPHICAL/CRITICAL SOURCES:

PERIODICALS

Times Literary Supplement, November 21, 1986.

* * *

GILLER, Robert M(aynard) 1942-

PERSONAL: Born September 14, 1942, in Chicago, Ill.; son of Edward M. and Lillian (Katz) Giller. *Education:* University of Illinois at Urbana-Champaign, completed three-year program, 1963, M.D., 1967; postdoctoral study at Columbia University, beginning in 1980.

ADDRESSES: Office—960 Park Ave., New York, N.Y. 10028. *Agent*—Al Lowman, 14 East 60th St., New York, N.Y. 10022.

CAREER: University of Illinois at Urbana-Champaign, intern, 1967-68; Cornell University, Ithaca, N.Y., resident in internal medicine at university hospital, 1968-69; private practice of (preventive) medicine in New York, N.Y., 1974—. Member of faculty at New School for Social Research, 1975—. *Military service:* U.S. Army, Medical Corps, 1969-71.

MEMBER: International Academy of Preventive Medicine, American College of Preventive Medicine (fellow), American Academy of Family Physicians, American College of Sports Medicine, American Medical Association, American Public Health Association.

AWARDS, HONORS: Physician's Recognition Award from American Medical Association, 1979, 1982, 1985, and 1988.

WRITINGS:

A Guide for Health, privately published, 1982.
(With Kathy Matthews) *Medical Makeover: The Revolutionary, No-Willpower Program for Lifetime Health,* Morrow, 1986.

SIDELIGHTS: Robert M. Giller has treated film stars, professional athletes, and performers—people in some of the twentieth century's most stressful occupations. His book *Medical Makeover* explains the physician's unique method for reducing the symptoms of stress. Giller believes that stress produces biochemical changes in the body, and that these chemical changes result in tiredness, irritability, fatigue, headaches, insomnia, and other stress-related symptoms. His program includes changing the body's chemical reactions by the use of vitamins and minerals, treating stress-related behavior patterns as one would treat addictions, and gradually teaching the patient to alter his stress-related responses.

BIOGRAPHICAL/CRITICAL SOURCES:

PERIODICALS

Health, November, 1986.

* * *

GILMOUR, Robin 1943-

PERSONAL: Born June 17, 1943, in Hamilton, Scotland; son of William (a doctor) and Agnes (Bell) Gilmour; married Elizabeth Simpson, December 29, 1969; children: Susannah, Lucy, Jonathan, Richard. *Education:* St. John's College, Cambridge, M.A., 1964; University of Edinburgh, Ph.D., 1969.

ADDRESSES: Home—9 Brighton Pl., Aberdeen AB1 6RT, Scotland. *Office*—Department of English, University of Aberdeen, Aberdeen, Scotland.

CAREER: New University of Ulster, Coleraine, Northern Ireland, lecturer in English, 1969-73; University of Aberdeen, Aberdeen, Scotland, lecturer, 1973-84, senior lecturer in English, 1984—.

WRITINGS:

The Idea of the Gentleman in the Victorian Novel, Allen & Unwin, 1981.
Thackeray: "Vanity Fair," Edward Arnold, 1982.
(Editor) Anthony Trollope, *Barchester Towers,* Penguin, 1983.
(Editor) Anthony Trollope, *The Warden,* Penguin, 1984.
The Novel in the Victorian Age: A Modern Introduction, Edward Arnold, 1986.

WORK IN PROGRESS: The Intellectual and Cultural Context of the Victorian Age, 1830-1890, for the Longman "Literature in English" series; general editorship of Edward Arnold's

"Modern Fiction" series; preparing the *David Copperfield* volume for the Allen & Unwin "Dickens Companions" series.

SIDELIGHTS: Robin Gilmour told *CA:* "I suppose my interest in Victorian literature comes from the fact that I had a rather Victorian childhood—the only child of not-so-young parents, brought up in a large (though modern) house, processed through the still Victorian (in my day) British private school system. I feel a strong affinity with the Victorians in their struggle to come to terms with modernity in the shape of secularization and the industrial and democratic revolutions, believing that the modern world began there and that we're all still sorting through the moral, spiritual, and intellectual agenda they left us. I became fascinated by the contradictions in their responses to these issues; hence my book on the idea of the gentleman, a concept which the Victorians tried to moralize and make into an ideal of secular integrity. They succeeded in this to a large extent, but the idea also, perhaps inevitably, remained trammeled by the realities of money, class, and the myriad exclusions of a hierarchical society.

"I've now written two books on the Victorian novel—three if one counts the little study of *Vanity Fair,* and I don't think I shall write any more, beyond articles one is invited to write. My interests are now in two main areas: intellectual history (hence the Longman book above) and more particularly the borderline between it and imaginative literature, including the late-Victorian and Edwardian agnostic temperament as reflected in fiction and autobiography; the other is the fiction of the British Empire in the twentieth century, post-Kipling and Conrad, about which I may write a volume for my Modern Fiction series.

"As this indicates, I see myself as a rather traditional kind of critic, but I don't feel apologetic about this, believing that the present deconstructive moment is a lunacy and a betrayal that will pass. Nor do I subscribe to any particular 'ism,' holding to unfashionable notions of individuality and disinterestedness."

BIOGRAPHICAL/CRITICAL SOURCES:

PERIODICALS

Times Literary Supplement, November 27, 1981.

* * *

GLASGOW, Jack
See LARSON, Doran

* * *

GLASSIE, Henry H(aywood) 1914-1987

OBITUARY NOTICE: Born May 24, 1914, in Chevy Chase, Md.; died of cardiac arrest, December 26, 1987, in Washington, D.C. Attorney, art gallery owner, and author. After practicing law for more than twelve years in New York City and Washington, D.C., in 1949 Glassie co-founded the firm Glassie, Pewett, Dudley, Beebe & Shanks, based in the District of Columbia. During World War II he had served with the U.S. Navy in the Philippines, then acted as chief counsel of the House of Representatives procurement committee for a year. Glassie specialized professionally in real estate development, restoring a number of historic buildings in the nation's capital, and he wrote a book on the subject, *Victorian Houses in Washington.* He also owned and operated the Montrose Galleries in Bethesda, Maryland, with his wife, and wrote *The Capital Image: Painters in Washington, 1800-1915* with Andrew J. Cosentino.

OBITUARIES AND OTHER SOURCES:

BOOKS

Who's Who in America, 42nd edition, Marquis, 1982.

PERIODICALS

Washington Post, December 29, 1987.

* * *

GODFREY, Peter 1917-

PERSONAL: Born September 8, 1917, in Vereeniging, South Africa; son of Louis (an entrepreneur) and Bessie (a housewife; maiden name, Gluckman) Godfrey; married Nina Cowan (an office consultant), July 3, 1941; children: Dennis Etien, Ronald Marcus. *Education:* University of the Witwatersrand, B.A. (literature), 1938; University of South Africa, B.A. (psychology; with honors), 1942.

ADDRESSES: Home—3 Ribblesdale, Roman Road, Dorking, Surrey RH4 3EX, England.

CAREER: Positions with various newspapers and magazines in South Africa, including editorships of anti-apartheid weekly, *Cape Standard,* and magazine *Spotlight* in Capetown and Johannesburg, 1933-61; *Drum,* London, England, editor in chief of East, Central, and West African editions, 1961-63; Odhams Press Ltd., London, subeditor of *Daily Herald* and *Sun,* 1963-69; IPC Business Press, London, chief subeditor of *Industry Week,* 1970; Clerical and Administrative Workers' Union, Wimbledon, England, public relations officer, 1970-71; *Times,* London, England, subeditor of "Business News," 1971-81; free-lance writer, 1981—. *Military service:* South African Army, Counter Intelligence, 1939-43.

MEMBER: Crime Writers Association (past member of council), Mystery Writers of America.

AWARDS, HONORS: Ellery Queen Short Story Award from *Ellery Queen's Mystery Magazine* in 1948 for "The Lady and the Dragon," in 1949 for "The Newtonian Egg," and in 1953 for "Hail and Farewell."

WRITINGS:

Death Under the Table (short stories), South African Scientific Publishers, 1954.

"Four O'Clock Noon" (three-act play), first produced in Johannesburg, South Africa, at Library Theatre, 1961.

Work represented in anthologies, including *John Creasey's Crime Collection,* St. Martin's, 1978-86; *Ellery Queen's Scenes of the Crime,* Dial; *Best Detective Stories of the Year,* Dutton, 1978, 1980. Contributor of more than two thousand stories to periodicals.

WORK IN PROGRESS: A novel, *The Erika Road,* about an international spy; an autobiography, *My Life With Malkhamowitz;* various crime novels.

SIDELIGHTS: Peter Godfrey's first play was written when he was fifteen years old, and he penned his first short story, which has an atomic theme, shortly after the first atomic bomb was exploded over Hiroshima. His novella, "Wanton Murder," was adapted into the film "The Girl in Black Stockings," starring Anne Bancroft. Godfrey's radio plays have been performed all over the world.

GOINES, Donald 1937(?)-1974
(Al C. Clark)

PERSONAL: Born December 15, 1937 (some sources indicate 1935 or 1936), in Detroit, Mich.; died of gunshot wounds, October 21, 1974, in Highland Park, Mich.; married (common law) Shirley Sailor; children: nine, including Donna and Camille from common-law marriage. *Education:* Educated in Detroit, Mich.

ADDRESSES: *Home*—Highland Park, Mich.

CAREER: Writer and convicted criminal. *Military service:* U.S. Air Force, 1951-54; served in Japan during Korean War.

WRITINGS—NOVELS; PUBLISHED BY HOLLOWAY HOUSE:

Dopefiend: The Story of a Black Junkie, 1971.
Whoreson: The Story of a Ghetto Pimp, 1972.
Black Gangster, 1972.
Street Players, 1973.
White Man's Justice, Black Man's Grief, 1973.
Black Girl Lost, 1973.
(Under pseudonym Al C. Clark) *Cry Revenge!* 1974.
Eldorado Red, 1974.
Swamp Man, 1974.
Never Die Alone, 1974.
Daddy Cool, 1974.
Inner City Hoodlum, 1975.

UNDER PSEUDONYM AL C. CLARK; "KENYATTA" SERIES

Crime Partners, 1974.
Death List, 1974.
Kenyatta's Escape, 1974.
Kenyatta's Last Hit, 1975.

SIDELIGHTS: Donald Goines was known for his grim novels about drug users and prostitutes in Detroit, Michigan. He was born in Detroit in 1937 and attended Catholic schools there, proving himself an earnest and cooperative student. In his mid-teens, however, he abruptly left school and joined the Air Force. In joining the service he lied about his age, an act that may account for the later discrepancy regarding his actual birthdate. During the Korean War, Goines was stationed in Japan. There he became a frequent drug user, and when he returned home in 1955 he was a heroin addict.

For the next fifteen years Goines supported his drug habit by pimping, robbing, and smuggling. For his crimes he was arrested fifteen times, and he served seven prison terms. While in jail—where he apparently remained free of heroin addiction—he was introduced to the writings of Robert "Iceberg Slim" Beck, a pimp-novelist who enjoyed substantial popularity among inmate readers. Inspired by Slim's *Trick Baby,* Goines—who had earlier attempted to write westerns—produced *Whoreson: The Story of a Ghetto Pimp,* a semiautobiographical novel about a pimp and his clashes with other seedy criminals. The world of *Whoreson* is an unsparing one where weakness or error inevitably leads to death. It is, perhaps, the raw, unyielding vision of *Whoreson* that made it popular with inmates whose opinions Goines solicited. Upon the advice of one particularly enthusiastic convict, Goines sent *Whoreson* to Iceberg Slim's publisher, the California-based Holloway House. The company, which specialized in black literature, readily accepted Goines's manuscript and requested additional works. Though still in prison, Goines quickly produced *Dopefiend: The Story of a Black Junkie,* which became his first published work. In *Dopefiend* he presented a graphic account of the drug addict's sordid life, tracing the degeneration of two middle-class blacks. In a *Village Voice* assessment of Goines's writings, Michael Covino described *Dopefiend* as a "relentless" depiction of loathsome and disgusting individuals. Particularly memorable is Porky, a vicious drug dealer first presented examining a pornographic magazine amid bloody squalor while a desperate addict jabs a syringe into her groin. *Dopefiend* abounds in such repellent situations: In one episode a pimp taunts a syphilitic prostitute, threatening to incorporate her into a sex show featuring animals; another passage details Porky's plan for killing two addicts who had robbed him. For Covino, the unsettling *Dopefiend* was "Goines's best book."

With advances from Holloway House for both *Dopefiend* and *Whoreson,* Goines could afford to concentrate on writing after he left prison in 1970. But by 1971 he had resumed drug use, and he consequently wrote only in the mornings, then spent the rest of each day indulging his heroin habit. In 1972 he nonetheless published a third novel, *Black Gangster,* about a cynical hoodlum who establishes a civil-rights organization as a front for prostitution and extortion. After publishing this novel, Goines moved to Los Angeles for greater access to Holloway House and to the nearby film industry, which he hoped to interest in his works.

In 1973 Goines published three more novels, including *White Man's Justice, Black Man's Grief,* an indictment of the American judicial system he termed racist. The novel tells of two inmates who conspire to commit a burglary after leaving prison. When one inmate is freed, he attempts the crime unassisted and kills a witness. Upon apprehension the killer names his black co-conspirator as the mastermind of the robbery and thus his accomplice in murder. The black convict is then tried and sentenced for murder even though he was in prison when the crime transpired.

Goines wrote eight more novels in 1974, including several works under the name of his friend Al C. Clark. Four of Goines's novels as Clark feature the ambitious militant Kenyatta, who rises from small-time hoodlum to leader of a two-thousand-member organization. With his military gang, Kenyatta hopes to eliminate all white police officers and rid the black ghetto of drugs and prostitution. Through considerable violence, he nearly succeeds. But in *Kenyatta's Last Hit*—the final work in a series that also features *Crime Partners, Death List,* and *Kenyatta's Escape*—he is killed while plotting the murder of a wealthy Los Angeles businessman dealing drugs.

Before writing *Kenyatta's Last Hit,* Goines returned to Detroit, having apparently disliked vast, unfamiliar Los Angeles. He settled with his common-law wife in nearby Highland Park. They were murdered there in October, 1974. Police suspected that robbery was the motive behind the slayings, though there were indications that Goines had once again involved himself in drug use.

In the years following his death Goines's novels continued to prove profitable for Holloway House, which reprinted his entire canon and reported total sales surpassing five million copies. Critical recognition, however, has been minimal. Mainstream publications ignore Goines's work, and more offbeat periodicals and literary journals rarely acknowledge his achievements. Covino's article in the *Village Voice* may promote greater recognition of Goines's talents as "a writer of unmediated raw realism, a chronicler of the black ghetto."

BIOGRAPHICAL/CRITICAL SOURCES:

BOOKS

Authors in the News, Volume 1, Gale, 1976.
Dictionary of Literary Biography, Volume 33: *Afro-American Fiction Writers After 1955,* Gale, 1984.
Stone, Eddie, *Donald Writes No More: A Biography of Donald Goines,* Holloway House, 1974.

PERIODICALS

Detroit Free Press, November 28, 1974.
Detroit News, November 15, 1974.
MELUS, summer, 1984.
Village Voice, August 4, 1987.*

—*Sketch by Les Stone*

* * *

GOLDBERG, Dorothy K(urgans) 1909(?)-1988

OBITUARY NOTICE—See index for *CA* sketch: Born c. 1909 in St. Louis, Mo.; died of lung cancer, February 13, 1988, in New York, N.Y. Social activist, artist, and author. Goldberg, who was married to former U.S. Supreme Court Justice Arthur Goldberg, was well known for her community service involvement. In particular, she established a number of education and employment programs in Washington, D.C., during the 1960s and organized such groups as Citizens for Public Education and Friends of the Juvenile Court. Goldberg also founded Widening Horizons, an employment assistance program for the disadvantaged. For her efforts she was honored by the commissioners of Washington, D.C., who designated December 9, 1965, "Dorothy Goldberg Day." An accomplished artist and speaker, Goldberg lectured around the United States on various issues involving women, the individual, and the United Nations. Her writings include *The Creative Woman,* the autobiographical *A Private View of a Public Life,* and a children's story titled "Lola and the Moving Stairs."

OBITUARIES AND OTHER SOURCES:

PERIODICALS

Chicago Tribune, February 15, 1988.
Los Angeles Times, February 17, 1988.
Washington Post, February 14, 1988.

* * *

GOLDBERGER, Nancy Rule 1937-

PERSONAL: Born October 25, 1937, in Canton, Ga.; daughter of James C. (a teacher) and Virginia (a teacher; maiden name, Doss) Rule; married Peter Israel (a publisher), February 4, 1956 (divorced, 1964); married Leo Goldberger (a professor), August 20, 1969; children: (second marriage) Jessica. *Education:* New York University, B.A., 1960, Ph.D., 1966.

ADDRESSES: Home—RFD 1, Box 34, Housatonic, Mass. 02136. *Office*—100 Bleecker St., New York, N.Y. 10012.

CAREER: Simon's Rock of Bard College, Great Barrington, Mass., director of evaluation, 1973-82; Austen Riggs Center, Stockbridge, Mass., psychologist, 1982-85; Fielding Institute, Santa Barbara, Calif., member of psychology faculty, 1986—. Consultant to book publishers, college faculties, and women's organizations. Vice-president of Berkshire Country Day School, 1977-86. Member of board of trustees of Women's Services Center in Pittsfield, Mass.

MEMBER: American Psychological Association.

WRITINGS:

(With Mary Field Belenky, Blythe McVicker Clinchy, and Jill Mattuck Tarule) *Women's Ways of Knowing: The Development of Self, Voice, and Mind,* Basic Books, 1986.

Contributor of articles to psychology and education journals, including *Review of Personality and Social Psychology, Journal of Experimental Research in Personality, Journal of Education,* and *Liberal Education.*

WORK IN PROGRESS: Women and Authority; a novel.

SIDELIGHTS: Nancy Rule Goldberger and her three co-authors examine the development of women's knowledge in their 1986 book, *Women's Ways of Knowing.* Their analysis, patterned after a study that focuses primarily on male undergraduates at Harvard University, delineates the ways in which women view their knowledge about themselves and the world. The results, according to *New York Times Book Review* contributor Sara Neustadtl, indicate that women's intellectual growth processes differ greatly from men's and may actually be hampered, not aided, by the present education system.

Based on interviews with 135 women of all ages and backgrounds, the study points to five basic "perspectives" women have toward their own knowledge. They range from the first, in which women lack the confidence and power to manage their lives, to the fifth category, in which women successfully combine intuition with intellect to master their environment. "By indirection," wrote Diane Kovacs in the *Los Angeles Times Book Review,* the study "illuminates how women can find that fifth way, their own voice and, with their voice, power." Kovacs added that the most interesting part of the book was the section in which the authors explore the "societal implications for women finding self, voice and mind," resulting in, among other things, the altering of family patterns and revamping of the male-dominated education system. Similarly, Neustadtl claimed that perhaps the most important finding brought to light in the study was that "women who function at the 'highest' level of intellectual development get there in spite of, and not because of, education" in an academic system dominated by male values. And praising the book as "remarkably clear and interesting to read," Naomi Black, writing in the *Globe and Mail,* concluded that *Women's Way of Knowing* "is probably the most important new study of the situation of women."

Goldberger told *CA:* "One of the most gratifying outcomes of our work on *Women's Ways of Knowing* has been the positive response from such diverse readers as individual women who have told us that they "found themselves on the pages," educational administrators, feminist scholars, and women in philanthropy, communication, law, and business. We wanted to write a book that avoided the gender, race, and class bias that characterizes human developmental research. We also wanted to avoid highly technical, academic language that tends to exclude the average reader. I think we have succeeded.

"I plan to continue my explorations of women's ways of knowing by turning to what is, for me, a new modality for saying what I know—that is, fiction."

AVOCATIONAL INTERESTS: Travel, nature, ethnic cooking.

BIOGRAPHICAL/CRITICAL SOURCES:

PERIODICALS

Globe and Mail (Toronto), April 18, 1987.

Los Angeles Times Book Review, September 7, 1986.
New York Times Book Review, October 5, 1986.

* * *

GOLDENBAUM, Sally 1941-
(Natalie Stone, a joint pseudonym)

PERSONAL: Born November 18, 1941, in Manitowoc, Wis.; daughter of Armin Louis (a shipbuilder) and Frances Arlene (Hussey) Pitz; married Donald M. Goldenbaum (a director of a business institute), September 27, 1969; children: Todd, Aria, Daniel. *Education:* Fontbonne College, B.A. (cum laude), 1965; attended University of Notre Dame, 1966; Indiana University—Bloomington, M.A., 1970.

ADDRESSES: Home and office—5300 West 67th, Prairie Village, Kan. 66208. *Agent*—Andrea Cirillo, Jane Rotrosen Agency, 318 East 51st St., New York, N.Y. 10022.

CAREER: Roman Catholic nun, 1960-67; teacher of Latin and religion at Roman Catholic high school in St. Louis, Mo., 1965-67; WQED-TV, Pittsburgh, Pa., public relations writer, 1968-69; writer for instructional television in Bloomington, Ind., 1969-71; editor of linguistic workbooks for Laidlaw Educational Publications, 1971-72; Rockhurst College, Kansas City, Mo., adjunct professor of philosophy, 1973-74; writer, 1974—. Creative writing teacher at Johnson County Community College. Member of board of directors of Kansas City Children's Center for the Visually Handicapped.

MEMBER: Romance Writers of America.

AWARDS, HONORS: Woodrow Wilson fellow, 1965.

WRITINGS:

ROMANCE NOVELS

(With Adrienne Staff) *What's a Nice Girl . . . ?* Bantam, 1985.
(With Adrienne Staff) *Banjo Man,* Bantam, 1986.
(With Adrienne Staff) *Crescendo,* Bantam, 1986.
(With Adrienne Staff) *Kevin's Story,* Bantam, 1986.
A Dream to Cling To, Bantam, 1987.
The Baron, Bantam, 1988.
Honeymoon Hotel, Silhouette, 1988.
Chantilly Lace, Silhouette, in press.

WITH ADRIENNE STAFF UNDER JOINT PSEUDONYM NATALIE STONE

Double Play, Dell, 1983.
Blue Ridge Autumn, Dell, 1984.
Summer Fling, Dell, 1984.
Sky Gypsy, Dell, 1985.
Words From the Heart, Dell, 1985.
With a Little Love, Dell, 1986.

SIDELIGHTS: Sally Goldenbaum told *CA:* "After moving to Kansas City, I fell into a job teaching English at a community college and met a fellow teacher, a misplaced New Yorker, who also wanted to write. Lacking the discipline necessary to finish a work of fiction individually, we decided to write a book together, primarily to see if we could do it. Romance novels seemed a likely genre for a co-authored book and that was the beginning of the Natalie Stone books for Dell. We then wrote several for Bantam, at which point my co-author moved to Florida and our writing was done long-distance.

"Writing together was great fun. We combined and elaborated on experiences (she, a nice Jewish girl from New York, and I, an ex-nun from a small Wisconsin town!), played with them, added whimsy and humor and came up with stories we hoped brought pleasure and joy to our readers. Naturally one of our books was about a Jewish lass from New York City who ended up in Kansas City (*What's a Nice Girl . . . ?*) and another told the tale of a sweet Irish woman who leaves the convent and comes of age (*Banjo Man*). Other stories evolved from things we read in the paper, people we met, and a lot of brainstorming as we sat at a small round table in our favorite French bakery. When we hit snags, we'd buy a six-pack of beer, rent a movie, and adjourn to one or the other's house for the afternoon (and inevitably ideas came from those hours), or we'd take off for a fine arts theater and watch old Alfred Hitchcock movies.

"But all good things end, I guess, and after Adrienne moved to Florida and we labored through two books long-distance, I began writing alone. It's not nearly as much fun—I don't laugh the same way or eat as many French pastries—but solo writing brings its own joys and a whole new kind of satisfaction. I can work more diligently on my individual style, and my characters have more freedom to change than when they were subject to a lengthy outline.

"In addition to writing romance books under contract, I am working on a larger novel on the side. My writing, plus keeping up with my family, teaching creative writing, and giving occasional talks and workshops on writing, fills my days. The creative writing classes provide a wonderful balance to writing. It's a nurturing process and brings with it great satisfaction. It is exciting to see ideas germinate, then take larger form, and to provide some of the encouragement and guidance that help transform the ideas into honest writing. Each class I teach teaches me, and I always walk away with new writing energy."

* * *

GOODWIN, (Trevor) Noel 1927-

PERSONAL: Born December 25, 1927, in Fowey, England; son of Arthur Daniel (a master mariner) and Blanche (Stephens) Goodwin; married Gladys Marshall Clapham, 1954 (divorced, 1960); married Anne Mason, November 23, 1963; children: Richard Mason Myers (stepson). *Education:* University of London, B.A., 1948; attended University of Aix-en-Provence, 1949-51.

ADDRESSES: Home—76 Skeena Hill, London SW18 5PN, England.

CAREER: News Chronicle, London, England, assistant music critic, 1952-54; *Manchester Guardian,* Manchester, England, assistant music critic, 1954-55; *Daily Express,* London, music and dance critic, 1956-78; free-lance critic, writer, and broadcaster, 1978—. Creator and presenter of music programs for BBC-Radio. Calouste Gulbenkian Foundation, member of dance advisory panel, 1972-76, member of National Enquiry Into Dance Education and Training in Britain, 1975-80; member of drama and dance advisory committee of British Council, 1973-88; Arts Council of Great Britain, member of council, 1973-81, chairman of Dance Advisory Panel and deputy chairman of Music Advisory Panel, 1979-81; trustee and director of Creative Dance Artists Trust's International Dance Course for Professional Choreographers and Composers, 1975—. *Military service:* British Army, Royal Army Education Corps, 1946-48; became captain.

MEMBER: Critics Circle (president, 1977; member of council and joint trustee).

AWARDS, HONORS: Santa Cruz Literary Prize from Anglo-Spanish Literary Society, 1973, for essay "Zarzuelas and Their History."

WRITINGS:

London Symphony: Portrait of an Orchestra, Naldrett Press, 1954.

A Ballet for Scotland, Canongate, 1979.

(Associate editor and contributor) Horst Koegler, *Concise Oxford Dictionary of Ballet,* Oxford University Press, 1982, revised edition, 1987.

(With Geraint Evans) *Sir Geraint Evans: A Knight at the Opera,* M. Joseph, 1984.

Contributor to *Encyclopaedia Britannica, American New Grove Dictionary of Music and Musicians, Encyclopedia of Opera, Dictionary of Composers, Cambridge Encyclopedia of Russia and the Soviet Union, New Oxford Companion to Music, Pipers Enzyklopaedie des Musiktheaters,* and *International Encyclopedia of Dance.* Contributor to music journals and newspapers. Executive editor of *Music and Musicians,* 1963-71; editor of *Royal Opera and Royal Ballet Yearbooks,* 1978-80; *Dance and Dancers,* contributing music editor, 1957—, associate editor, 1972—; area editor of *New Grove Dictionary of Music and Musicians,* 1981; overseas news editor of *Opera,* 1985—.

WORK IN PROGRESS: A history of the relationship between music and dance, for Dance Books.

SIDELIGHTS: Noel Goodwin told *CA:* "Direction of my work since 1978 has been largely in response to whatever has come my way—primarily reviews of performances and gramophone records for newspapers and magazines, but with special interest in expository writing in form of program notes for opera, ballet, and concerts or liners for gramophone records. All this is still continuing.

"The discussion of the function of music in performances of classical ballet and modern dance led me to take the initiative in planning and obtaining necessary support to establish International Dance Course for Professional Choreographers and Composers, then unique of its kind in the world, but since followed in Australia, Canada (and I think Israel), and considered for Jacob's Pillow in the United States. The purpose is not to 'teach' how to make dances, but to encourage creative collaboration at the highest professional level between the two disciplines. The writing in progress is partly intended to develop this, but within the context of overall history of music for theatrical dancing, perhaps finding value as a textbook for students.

"An early experience of zarzuela performances in Spain led to my interest in Spanish music generally and its history, as well as its diversity beyond the regional Andalucian style usually associated with that country."

* * *

GORDON, Jeffie Ross
See TESSLER, Stephanie Gordon

* * *

GOULD, Philip 1925-

PERSONAL: Born August 16, 1925, in Chicago, Ill.; son of Frank E. (a real estate manager) and Anne (a housewife; maiden name, Kilday) Gould; married Marion Laird (a housewife), 1960; children: Michael, Constance, Philip L. *Education:* Loyola University of Chicago, Ph.B., 1948.

ADDRESSES: Home—2628 Jefferson Park Circle, Charlottesville, Va. 22903.

CAREER: United Press (now United Press International), reporter and editor in New York, N.Y., Pittsburgh, Pa., and Cleveland, Ohio, 1948-50; WOR-Radio, New York City, radio news writer, 1950-51; National Broadcasting Company, New York City, radio news writer, 1951-52; free-lance writer in New York City, 1952-54; Radio Free Europe, New York City and Munich, West Germany, news editor, 1954-59; National Broadcasting Company, Chicago, Ill., radio news writer, 1960-61; United States Information Agency, writer and editor in Washington, D.C., 1961-63, information officer and press attache in India, Israel, Morocco, Netherlands, U.S.S.R., and United States, 1963-76, writer and editor in Washington, D.C., 1976-86; free-lance writer, 1986—. *Military service:* U.S. Army Air Forces, 1943-46; became sergeant.

WRITINGS:

Kitty Collins (novel), Algonquin Books, 1986.

Contributor of stories and reviews to periodicals, including *Collier's, Woman's Day,* and *Virginia Quarterly Review.*

WORK IN PROGRESS: A novel.

SIDELIGHTS: Philip Gould told *CA:* "The two heroines of *Kitty Collins* are a young, disadvantaged white girl who becomes an accomplished jazz pianist and singer, and Roberta Wilkins, an older black musician who teaches her to play and gives her a temporary home when Kitty's mother abandons her. A musical Roman Catholic nun and a musical Irish-American family with whom she also lives for a while contribute other major influences to the building of her character and career. The time is the 1940s and the settings are Chicago, New York, and Paris."

* * *

GRABAR, Oleg 1929-

PERSONAL: Born November 23, 1929, in Strasbourg, France; immigrated to United States, 1948, naturalized citizen, 1960; son of Andre and Julie (Ivanova) Grabar; married Terry Ann Harris, June 9, 1951; children: Nicolas Howard, Anne Louise. *Education:* Harvard University, B.A. (magna cum laude), 1950; University of Paris, Licence d'Histoire, 1950; Princeton University, Ph.D., 1955.

ADDRESSES: Home—37 Wolf Pine Way, Concord, Mass. 01742. *Office*—Department of Islamic Art, Harvard University, Cambridge, Mass. 02138.

CAREER: University of Michigan, Ann Arbor, instructor, 1954-55, assistant professor, 1955-59, associate professor, 1959-64, professor of Islamic art, 1964-69; Harvard University, Cambridge, Mass., professor of fine arts, 1969-79, Aga Khan Professor of Islamic Art, 1979—. American School of Oriental Research, director in Jerusalem and Jordan, 1960-61, vice-president, 1968—; director of Michigan-Harvard excavations in Syria, 1964-71.

MEMBER: College Art Association of America (director, 1968-72, 1981-85), Archaeological Institute of America, Mediaeval Academy of America, American Academy of Arts and Sci-

ences (councilman, 1982-86), Middle Eastern Studies Association, German Archaeological Institute.

WRITINGS:

Coinage of Tulunids, American Numismatic Society, 1957.
Persian Art Before and After the Mongol Conquest, University of Michigan Museum of Art, 1959.
Islamic Architecture and Its Decoration, Faber & Faber, 1967.
Sasanian Silver: Late Antique and Early Medieval Arts of Luxury From Iran, Univeristy of Michigan Museum of Art, 1967.
The Formation of Islamic Art, Yale University Press, 1973, revised and enlarged edition, 1987.
The Alhambra, Harvard University Press, 1978.
City in the Desert, Harvard University Press, 1978.
(With Sheila Blair) *Epic Images and Contemporary History,* University of Chicago Press, 1980.
(Editor) *Muqarnas: An Annual on Islamic Art and Literature,* Yale University Press, Volume I, 1983, Volume II, 1984.
The Illustrations of the Maqamat, University of Chicago Press, 1984.
(With Richard Ettinghausen) *The Art and Architecture of Islam, 650-1250,* Penguin, 1987.

Contributor to scholarly journals. Editor of *Arts Orientalis,* 1957-71.

WORK IN PROGRESS: A monograph; research on Islamic monuments in Sicily.

BIOGRAPHICAL/CRITICAL SOURCES:

PERIODICALS

Los Angeles Times Book Review, March 13, 1988.
Washington Post Book World, February 14, 1988.

* * *

GREEN, Smith Wendell 1917(?)-1987

OBITUARY NOTICE: Born c. 1917; died December 19, 1987, in Los Angeles, Calif. Journalist. Green worked as a reporter and political writer for the *Los Angeles Sentinel* and the *California Eagle* and owned the Afro-American News Bureau in Los Angeles. He was the first black elected president of Los Angeles City College's Associated Men's Students club, and during World War II he trained at Tuskegee Institute with the 369th Air Squadron, an all-black flying unit.

OBITUARIES AND OTHER SOURCES:

PERIODICALS

Los Angeles Times, December 25, 1987.

* * *

GREENBERG, Kenneth S. 1947-

PERSONAL: Born November 2, 1947; son of Samuel M. and Roslyn (Zimmerman) Greenberg; married Judith Leah Guttman (a professor of law), June 15, 1969; children: Laura, Amy, Lisa. *Education:* Cornell University, B.A., 1968; Columbia University, M.A., 1970; University of Wisconsin—Madison, Ph.D., 1976.

ADDRESSES: Office—Department of History, Suffolk University, Beacon Hill, Boston, Mass. 02108.

CAREER: Alfred University, Alfred, N.Y., assistant professor of American history, 1975-77; University of Massachusetts, Boston, visiting lecturer in history, 1977-78; Suffolk University, Boston, assistant professor, 1978-82, associate professor, 1982-87, professor of American history, 1987—. Harvard University, visiting scholar in American history, 1977-78, Charles Warren fellow, 1988.

MEMBER: American Historical Association, Organization of American Historians, Southern Historical Association.

AWARDS, HONORS: Fellow of National Endowment for the Humanities, 1988.

WRITINGS:

Masters and Statesmen: The Political Culture of American Slavery, Johns Hopkins University Press, 1985.

Contributor of articles and reviews to history journals.

WORK IN PROGRESS: A history of American duels.

* * *

GREENE, Lorenzo Johnston 1899-1988

OBITUARY NOTICE: Born November 16, 1899, in Ansonia, Conn.; died January 24, 1988, in Jefferson City, Mo. Human rights activist, educator, and author. Greene was a leader of the civil rights movement during its early days in Missouri, and he supported the founding of that state's Human Rights Commission during the 1950s. Because of his deep concern for human life, he was named to three presidential commissions—on housing, youth, and human rights—by Presidents Herbert Hoover, Dwight D. Eisenhower, and Lyndon B. Johnson. A professor at Lincoln University for thirty-nine years, Greene was chairman of the social science department at the time of his retirement in 1972. He was considered an authority on black American history and wrote extensively on such topics as the American Civil War and desegregation in the South. His works include *The Negro in Colonial New England, 1620-1776* and *Negro Wage Earner* as well as numerous articles published in scholarly journals.

OBITUARIES AND OTHER SOURCES:

BOOKS

Directory of American Scholars, Volume I: *History,* 7th edition, Bowker, 1978.
Who's Who Among Black Americans, 5th edition, Who's Who Among Black Americans, 1988.

PERIODICALS

Chicago Tribune, January 28, 1988.
Los Angeles Times, January 27, 1988.
New York Times, January 27, 1988.
Times (London), January 30, 1988.
Washington Post, January 28, 1988.

* * *

GREENE, Owen (John) 1954-

PERSONAL: Born November 5, 1954, in Chelmsford, England; son of Ieaun John (a teacher) and Hilda (a teacher; maiden name, Young) Greene; married Barbara Pearce (an administrator), October 25, 1986. *Education:* University of Bristol, B.Sc., 1976; doctoral study at Imperial College of Science and Technology, London, 1978-81.

ADDRESSES: Office—Faculty of Science, Open University, Milton Keynes MK7 6AA, England; School of Peace Studies, University of Bradford, Bradford BD7 1DP, England.

CAREER: Lecturer at College of Further Education, London, England, 1981-82; Open University, Milton Keynes, England, research fellow, 1982-86; University of Bradford, Bradford, England, lecturer in Peace Studies, 1986—. Member of Alternative Defence Commission; Scientists Against Nuclear Arms, research coordinator, 1982-85, national secretary, 1985—; member of steering committee of Defence Information Groups and Verification Technology Information Centre.

MEMBER: International Institute for Strategic Studies, British International Studies Association, Royal United Services Institute, Pugwash.

WRITINGS:

(With Barry Rubin, Neil Turok, Philip Webber, and Greane Wilkinson) *London After the Bomb,* Oxford University Press, 1982.
Europe's Folly, Campaign for Nuclear Disarmament, 1983.
(With Stan Openshaw and Philip Steadman) *Doomsday: Britain After Nuclear Attack,* Basil Blackwell, 1984.
(With Mike Pentz and Christopher Meredith) *Nuclear Winter: A New Dimension to the Nuclear Debate,* SANA, 1984.
(With Ian Percival and Irene Ridge) *Nuclear Winter: The Evidence and the Risk,* Polity Press, 1985.
(With Alternative Defence Commission) *After the Bomb,* Granada, 1985.
(With Oliver Penrose and Gordon Dyer) *Nuclear Weapons Technology,* Open University Press, 1986.
Nuclear Arms Control and Disarmament, Open University Press, 1986.
(With Alternative Defence Commission) *The Politics of Nuclear Disarmament,* Paladin, 1987.
(With Hugh Miall, Scila McLean, and Clive Ponting) *Do It Yourself Minister: Implementing a Non-Nuclear Defence Policy,* Oxford Research Group, 1987.
(Editor and contributor) *Defence and Policy Making,* Brassey's, 1988.

WORK IN PROGRESS: Research on the effects of war, nuclear strategy, alternative defence, and arms control.

SIDELIGHTS: Owen Greene told *CA:* "I first became involved in research on nuclear issues in 1980 after the onset of the 'Second Cold War' and the decisions to deploy International Nuclear Forces in Europe and upgrade civil defense. At the time I was carrying out research in theoretical physics, and so it was natural for my activities on nuclear issues to focus on technical questions relating to weapon systems, verification, and the potential consequences of war. My work on these issues has continued since 1980 and has had a significant political impact in the United Kingdom. Over the last three years I have been involved in a series of scientific meetings and analyses to assess and develop research on 'nuclear winter' through the Special Committee on Problems of the Environment. There is now strong evidence that a nuclear war could cause a climatic catastrophe: scientists who deny this are now in a small minority.

"Over the last few years I have given increased attention to Britain and the overall security policy of the North Atlantic Treaty Organization (NATO). It seems to me that the policies are dangerously unbalanced. They are aimed at maximizing deterrence against deliberate attack at the cost of crisis stability and of failing to tackle problems that could lead to a crisis. Thus I have been concerned with possible reforms in British and NATO defense policy. At the core of these reforms is a reliance on *conventional* deterrence to guard against any attack by the countries of the Warsaw Pact (the Soviet-bloc equivalent to NATO), combined with a shift towards more manifestly 'defensive' military postures and a withdrawal of theater nuclear weapons. The present NATO policy is sustained by a myth of overwhelming Warsaw Pact conventional superiority and by a desire to avoid uncomfortable questions within NATO. I have also carried out a series of research projects on the technical and political issues associated with implementing reforms or nuclear disarmament measures."

* * *

GREENSPAN, Emily 1953-

PERSONAL: Born July 22, 1953, in Boston, Mass.; daughter of Charles (an attorney) and Taube (an art historian; maiden name, Gargill) Greenspan; married Howard Kelting, 1984; children: Lily. *Education:* Vassar College, B.A., 1975.

ADDRESSES: *Home*—59 West 71st St., New York, N.Y. 10023. *Agent*—Wendy Lipkind, 225 East 57th St., New York, N.Y. 10022.

CAREER: Professional figure skater with International Holiday on Ice, 1975-76; *New York* (magazine), New York City, administrative assistant, 1976-77; assistant to writer Gail Sheehy, New York City, 1977-79; *Self* (magazine), New York City, staff writer, 1980-81. Free-lance writer, 1976—.

MEMBER: Authors Guild.

WRITINGS:

Little Winners: Inside the World of the Child Sports Star, Little, Brown, 1983.

Contributor to periodicals, including *Child, Cosmopolitan, Gentleman's Quarterly, Good Housekeeping, Mademoiselle, Ms., New York, New York Times Magazine, Parents, Seventeen, Travel and Leisure,* and *Us.*

SIDELIGHTS: In *Little Winners: Inside the World of the Child Sports Star,* Emily Greenspan examines the stresses and rewards that intensive sports training brings to the lives of child athletes and their families. As a promising figure skater, Greenspan had begun intensive training by the time she was ten years old. "I felt considerable pressure from myself, my parents and my coach," she admitted in a *New York Times Magazine* article, and, "considering the time and money my parents had invested, I felt guilty about expressing my anxieties." Her early experiences, in addition to interviews with others involved in competitive sports, became the basis of her book.

Greenspan observes that children are being introduced to competitive sports earlier than ever, increasing the risk of injury and growth problems and subjecting them to high stress before they are mature enough to handle it. Often, she asserts, children are pushed not because they want to pursue sports but because the parents enjoy the thrill of their child's success. Nonetheless, Greenspan is aware of the benefits of such training and achievement. "I had the opportunity," she wrote in the *New York Times Magazine,* "to develop a love of music and movement, some degree of discipline, close friendships, early experience with winning and losing and a feeling—when I walked into school late and my classmates turned in admiration—that I was special." In the *New York Times* she remarked, "I think it's wonderful to introduce sports, recreational activity to kids at an early age," but she cautioned that parents should "analyze themselves and their own ambitions

very carefully." Concluded Greenspan, "It would be helpful to balance [competitive sports] with family recreational activities, such as camping, hiking, bicycling, so that the kids don't feel that the affection of the parents in a sporting context rests solely with whether they win or lose."

Greenspan told *CA:* "Writing is perhaps the loneliest profession—especially when one is a single female. It is also—except for the lucky best-seller—not a very profitable vocation. But the opportunity it provides for learning, both about areas of interest and about oneself in the process, compensates for the hardships. I was impelled to write *Little Winners* because I was a child athlete myself, and certain questions about the experience still nagged at me twenty years later. I wanted to speak to athletes, parents, and coaches and learn what they were going through. It was easy to become absorbed in the material, because it meant so much to me. Writing does that—it provides a vehicle for reflection and an outlet for curiosity."

AVOCATIONAL INTERESTS: Piano, painting (watercolors).

BIOGRAPHICAL/CRITICAL SOURCES:

PERIODICALS

Ms., January, 1984.
New York Times, September 25, 1983.
New York Times Magazine, April 26, 1981, August 28, 1983.

* * *

GREGORY, Hilton
See FERGUSON, Charles W.

* * *

GRIMKE, Angelina (Emily) Weld 1880-1958

PERSONAL: Born February 27, 1880, in Boston, Mass.; died after a long illness, June 10, 1958, in New York, N.Y.; daughter of Archibald Henry (a lawyer, diplomat, publisher, and writer) and Sarah Eliza (a writer; maiden name, Stanley) Grimke. *Education:* Boston Normal School of Gymnastics, earned degree, 1902; attended Harvard University, 1904-10.

ADDRESSES: Home—New York, N.Y.

CAREER: Writer. Taught at schools in Washington, D.C., beginning in 1902.

WRITINGS:

Rachel (three-act play; first produced in Washington, D.C., at the Myrtilla Miner Normal School, March 3, 1916; produced in New York City at the Neighborhood Playhouse, April 26, 1917), Cornhill, 1920, reprinted, McGrath, 1969.

Poetry represented in anthologies such as *Negro Poets and Their Poems* (includes Grimke's "Dawn," "A Winter Twilight," "The Puppet-Player," "The Want of You," "El Belso," "At the Spring Dawn," and "To Keep the Memory of Charlotte Forten Grimke"), edited by Robert T. Kerlin, Associated Publishers, 1923; and *Caroling Dusk* (includes Grimke's "Hushed By the Hands of Sleep," "Greenness," "The Eyes of My Regret," "Grass Fingers," "Surrender," "The Ways O' Men," "Tenebris," "When the Green Lies Over the Earth," "A Mona Lisa," "Paradox," "Your Hands," "I Weep," "For the Candle Light," "Dusk," and "A Winter Twilight"), edited by Countee Cullen, Harper, 1927. Other anthologies featuring Grimke's verse include *Black and White: An Anthology of Washington Verse,* edited by J. C. Byars, Jr., Crane Press, 1927; *The Negro Caravan,* edited by Sterling A. Brown and others, Dryden Press, 1941; *The Poetry of the Negro, 1746-1949,* edited by Langston Hughes and Arna Bontemps, Doubleday, 1949; *American Negro Poetry,* edited by Arna Bontemps, Hill & Wang, 1963; *Black Writers of America,* edited by Richard K. Barksdale and Keneth Kinnamon, Macmillan, 1972; *The New Negro Renaissance: An Anthology,* co-edited by Michael W. Peplow, Holt, 1975; and *Black Sister: Poetry by Black American Women, 1746-1980,* Indiana University Press, 1981.

Contributor to periodicals, including *Birth Control Review, Boston Globe, Boston Pilot, Boston Transcript, Carolina, Crisis, Norfolk County Gazette,* and *Opportunity.*

SIDELIGHTS: Angelina Weld Grimke was a playwright and poet who produced her finest work—personal lyrics—during the Harlem Renaissance of the 1920s. Unlike many of her literary peers, Grimke came from an intellectual background. Her father was Archibald Grimke, a lawyer, writer, and publisher who championed black rights and served as vice-president of the National Association for the Advancement of Colored People (NAACP). Her mother was also a writer, but her influence was limited, for she abandoned the family in the late 1880s and never returned. Grimke was close to her father, though, and with his encouragement she attended prestigious liberal schools such as the Cushing Academy in Massachusetts. She graduated from the Boston Normal School of Gymnastics in 1902 and then moved to Washington, D.C., where she spent much of her career teaching high-school English.

By the time Grimke arrived in Washington, D.C., she had already published poems in both the *Norfolk County Gazette* and the *Boston Transcript.* Among these early works was a salutation to a nonagenarian relative. More daring was "Beware Les He Awakes!," her 1902 publication in which she warned of the revenge that might be sought eventually by persecuted blacks.

In 1909, seven years after she moved to Washington, D.C., Grimke produced her first extensively anthologized poem, "El Beso," which lyrically reflects on aspects of love. Throughout the next several years she wrote her greatest poems and gained recognition for her sensitive approach to subjects ranging from the social to the romantic. Unlike many Harlem Renaissance writers, however, Grimke avoided sensationalizing the plight of American blacks, and her social perspective is inevitably poignant. In her popular poem "The Black Finger" she stressed hope for the future of blacks by writing of a cypress tree that extends like a black finger into the air, and in "Written for the Fiftieth Anniversary Celebration at Dunbar High School" she assured slavery's descendants that a more promising world lay ahead. Other poems on race, however, offer a gloomier view. "Trees," for instance, describes a nature scene replete with dangling lynching victim, and "At April" notes the additional disappointment that will someday beset black children when they reach adulthood.

Although Grimke wrote compellingly about blacks, her preferred theme was love. Notable works on this theme include "When the Green Lies Over the Earth," "Greenness," "Grass Fingers," and "To Clarissa Scott Delany," poems in which love and the memory of love are elucidated through often pastoral imagery. In "When the Green Lies Over the Earth" springtime and the budding flowers and trees remind the poet of a former loved one, and in the elegiac "To Clarissa Scott

Delany'' Grimke mourns a dead woman whose finer qualities are perceived to endure even as nature endures.

In these and other poems Grimke also displays remarkable skill as an imagist. Works such as ''Dawn'' and ''A Winter Twilight'' reflect her melancholy state through brief descriptions of dim evenings, bleak fields, and pale stars. The four-line ''Dawn,'' with its compact rendering of a gray world and a distant hermit-thrush, is notably compelling in this regard. And in ''At the Spring Dawn'' Grimke portrays a vividly colored field in which silence is broken by a single bird darting against the sun.

Aside from poetry, Grimke wrote ''Rachel,'' a play sponsored by the NAACP in 1916. ''Rachel'' is about a young woman living with her brother and her mother in a New York City tenement. Early in the play Rachel and her brother are informed by their mother that their father had been killed years earlier by a lynching mob. Rachel's brother, Tom, responds with anger, but Rachel reacts by considering the bleak future she envisions for black children who will someday face cruel, and often violent, persecution. In the second act, set four years later, Tom tries to find work as a menial laborer and expresses bitter resentment toward America's racially prejudiced society. Rachel, meanwhile, learns of abuses endured by a withdrawn neighborhood girl and by a little boy, Jimmy, whom Rachel adopted after his parents died from chicken pox. The third, and final, act features Rachel distressed by her failure to soothe Jimmy, who has recurring nightmares. Rachel eventually receives a marriage proposal, but she rejects it, choosing to care for already existing black children rather than bring her own into an unfair world. Rarely performed in the ensuing decades, ''Rachel'' is nonetheless remembered as one of the first American plays written by and for blacks.

Another of Grimke's few non-verse works, the short story ''The Closing Door,'' shares with ''Rachel'' a bleak perspective on the bearing of black children in a racist society. In ''The Closing Door'' a woman learns that her brother has been killed by a lynching mob. She is consequently devastated, and after giving birth she becomes insane and kills the child. This story, oddly enough, was first published in *Birth Control Review*.

In her lifetime Grimke was a prominent poet, and her work was included in many key anthologies, including Countee Cullen's *Caroling Dusk* and Langston Hughes and Arna Bontemps's *Poetry of the Negro, 1746-1949*. But in the years since her death in 1958 she has been ignored by most literary critics, though the few that do consider her writings have valued her as a substantial and surprisingly sophisticated artist from a key time in the history of black American literature.

BIOGRAPHICAL/CRITICAL SOURCES:

BOOKS

Dictionary of Literary Biography, Gale, Volume 50: *Afro-American Writers Before the Harlem Renaissance*, 1986, Volume 54: *American Poets, 1880-1945, Third Series*, 1987.

PERIODICALS

Black World, April, 1976.
CLA Journal, June, 1977.
Conditions: Five, 1979.
Drama Critique, spring, 1964.*

—*Sketch by Les Stone*

GRIMKE, Charlotte L(ottie) Forten 1837(?)-1914 (Charlotte Forten; Miss C. L. F., Lottie, pseudonyms)

PERSONAL: Born August 17, 1837 (some sources say 1838), in Philadelphia, Pa.; died of a cerebral embolism, July 23, 1914, in Washington, D.C.; buried in Harmony Cemetery, Washington, D.C.; daughter of Robert Bridges (a sailmaker and abolitionist) and Mary Virginia (Wood) Forten; married Francis James Grimke (a Presbyterian minister and abolitionist), December 19, 1878; children: Theodora Cornelia (died in infancy). *Education:* State Normal School at Salem, teaching certificate, 1856.

CAREER: Epes Grammar School, Salem, Mass., teacher, 1856-58, 1860-61; Port Royal Relief Association and Freedman's Aid Society, St. Helena Island, S.C., teacher, 1862; Sumner High School, Washington, D.C., assistant to principal, 1871-72. Clerk for the Federal Treasury Department.

MEMBER: Salem Female Anti-Slavery Society.

WRITINGS:

(Translator, under pseudonym Miss C. L. F.) Emilie Erckmann and Alexander Chatrian, *Madame Therese; or, The Volunteers of '92*, Scribner, 1869.

Journal, edited with introduction and notes by Ray Allen Billington, Dryden Press, 1953, published as *A Free Negro in the Slave Era: The Journal of Charlotte L. Forten*, Collier, 1961 (published in England as *The Journal of Charlotte Forten: A Free Negro in the Slave Era*, Collier-Macmillan, 1967).

(Under name Charlotte Forten) *Life on the Sea Islands* (first published in *Atlantic Monthly*, May-June, 1864), reprinted in *Two Black Teachers During the Civil War: Mary S. Peake, the Colored Teacher at Fortress Monroe, by Lewis C. Lockenwood* [and] *Life on the Sea Islands by Charlotte Forten*, edited by W. L. Katz, Arno Press, 1969.

Poems represented in anthologies, including *The Rising Sun*, A. G. Brown, *Negro Poets and Their Poems*, Associated Publishing, 1935, *Life and Writings of the Grimke Family*, privately printed, 1951, *An Anthology of American Negro Literature*, and *Cavalcade*, Houghton, 1971.

Contributor of poems and essays to periodicals, sometimes under the pseudonyms Lottie or Miss C. L. F., including *Atlantic Monthly, New England Magazine, Liberator, National Anti-Slavery Standard, The Dunbar Speaker and Entertainer*, and *Christian Register*.

SIDELIGHTS: Charlotte L. Forten Grimke is known for her *Journal*, written between 1854 and 1864, that provided details of the abolitionist movement prior to and during the American Civil War. Grimke was born into a well-to-do Philadelphia, Pennsylvania, family. Her grandfather, James Forten, was a second generation freedman and the owner of a prosperous sailmaking business. He was also a nationally known advocate of the abolition of slavery. After Grimke's mother's death Grimke lived at his home and later with her uncle, Robert Purvis, whose estate offered a forum for abolitionist thinkers of the day and a haven for runaway slaves. Grimke was privately tutored while living in Philadelphia so she would not have to attend the segregated schools; but in 1854, when she moved to Salem, Massachusetts, to live with abolitionist Charles Lenox Remond and his wife, she enrolled in the integrated Salem Grammar School. She began her journal at the Remond home and often wrote of the progress of the Negroes' fight for

liberation and of her contact with the leading reformers of the day, including John Greenleaf Whittier, Wendell Phillips, and William Lloyd Garrison.

Racial awareness and the abolitionist movement were foremost in Grimke's mind. She wrote in her diary about the injustice of discrimination and how it affected her world view. She wrote of runaway slaves being hounded by mobs and captured slaves dragged through streets, and preferred Salem to Philadelphia because of the indignities blacks suffered in Pennsylvania. There, for example, she and her family were barred from restaurants, museums, theaters, and lectures and were forced to occupy segregated sections on public transportation. Neither was Grimke accepted wholeheartedly in Salem. She writes of one of her schoolmates: "There is one young girl and only one—Miss [Sarah] B[rown] who I believe thoroughly and heartily appreciates anti-slavery,—*radical* anti-slavery, and has no prejudice against color. I wonder that every colored person is not a misanthrope. Surely we have everything to make us hate mankind." She continued to relate an incident where she was snubbed on the street by white girls who were friendly to her in the classroom. "These are but trifles, certainly, to the great, public wrongs which we as a people are obliged to endure. . . . 'How long oh! how long must we continue to suffer—to endure?' Conscience answers it is wrong, it is ignoble to despair; let us labor earnestly and faithfully to acquire knowledge, to break down the barriers of prejudice and oppression."

Grimke's resentment prompted her driving ambition to prove herself as intelligent and as capable of improvement as whites. She was determined to study and learn all that she could in order to be a living example of the capabilities of black people. She was an outstanding student who taught herself French, German, and Latin and attended literary and political lectures. During a single year her diary shows that she read over one hundred books, ranging from the classics to contemporary poetry, that included works by Charles Dickens and Ralph Waldo Emerson.

Yet she was never satisfied with her progress. On Tuesday, June 15, 1858, Grimke wrote: "Have been under-going a thorough self-examination. The result is a mingled feeling of sorrow, shame and self-contempt. Have realized more deeply and bitterly than ever in my life my own ignorance and folly. Not only am I without the gifts of Nature,—wit, beauty and talent; without the accomplishments which nearly every one of my age, whom I know, possesses; but I am not even *intelligent*. And for *this* there is not the *shadow* of an excuse. Have had many advantages of late years; and it is entirely owning to my own want of energy, perseverance and application, that I have not improved them."

Upon graduation from the Salem Normal School, Grimke took a teaching position at Epes Grammar School in Salem and became the first Negro in Massachusetts to instruct whites. She was accepted by her students, their parents, her colleagues, and the school board, but poor health forced her to resign in March, 1858. She fought recurring tuberculosis for the next three years then returned to teaching. With a letter of reference from John Greenleaf Whittier, Grimke petitioned the Boston Educational Commission in August 1862 to send her as a volunteer for the Port Royal Experiment, an educational endeavor taking place on a group of Confederate islands off the coast of South Carolina that the Union forces occupied in 1861. The influx of the Northern army prompted the slave-holding plantation owners of the islands to flee and leave behind rich cotton fields and eight thousand illiterate slaves. To Northern liberals this evacuation provided the opportunity to prove the worth of the black man: that he could be educated, trained as a soldier, and be a useful citizen. Under Northern supervision an extensive program of educational, medical, and material aid was inaugurated.

Grimke arrived at St. Helena Island in October 1862 to teach at a small school, determined to show her race was capable of great accomplishments. There she wrote: "Let our motto . . . be 'Excelsior' and we cannot fail to make some improvement." Additionally, she sought to inspire her students of the Port Royal Experiment "with courage and ambition (of a noble sort,) and a high purpose." She was fascinated by their musical abilities, their religious services, and the language that the newly freed blacks spoke—Gullah, a combination of African languages. She was also as interested in the soldiers' progress as her students'. She was elated that field workers became soldiers to defend their freedom against the Confederate army: "They say the black soldiers fought the rebels bravely;— . . . I can think of nothing but this reg[iment]. How proud of it I am!" Grimke sent Whittier an essay on the project, "Life on the Sea Islands," and he had it published in two parts in the *Atlantic Monthly* in May and June of 1864. The challenge of the experiment gave her great satisfaction, especially when her students progressed in their studies, but the work and the environment were physically and emotionally draining. She endured warfare, ill health, heat, and flea infestation but returned to Philadelphia in May of 1864.

For the next decade Grimke wrote poetry and prose and taught. In 1877 she met Francis Grimke, the son of a slave and a plantation owner and the nephew of the well known feminists and abolitionists Sarah and Angelina Grimke. Enslaved as a youth, he went on to graduate as valedictorian of his class from Lincoln College and earned a degree in theology from Princeton University after he was freed. They married in 1878 and settled in Washington, D.C, where they led socially and culturally active lives.

BIOGRAPHICAL/CRITICAL SOURCES:

BOOKS

Cooper, Anna Julia, *Life and Writings of the Grimke Family,* privately printed, 1951, New York Public Library, 1974.

Dictionary of Literary Biography, Volume 50: *Afro-American Writers Before the Harlem Renaissance,* Gale, 1986.

Douty, Esther M., *Charlotte Forten, Free Black Teacher,* Garrard, 1971.

Forten, Charlotte L., *Journal,* edited with notes, by Ray Allen Billington, Dryden Press, 1953.

Longsworth, Polly, *Charlotte Forten, Black and Free,* Crowell, 1970.

Twentieth-Century Literary Criticism, Volume 16, Gale, 1985.

PERIODICALS

Negro History Bulletin, January, 1947.

New York Times Book Review, April 12, 1953.*

—Sketch by Carol Lynn DeKane

* * *

GRINNELL, Isabel Hoopes 1899(?)-1988

OBITUARY NOTICE: Born c. 1899; died February 23, 1988, in Bethesda, Md. Art curator and author. Grinnell joined the staff of the Metropolitan Museum in 1919, eventually becom-

ing assistant curator of Greek and Roman art before she left in 1932. Her books include a study of ancient architecture, *Greek Temples*.

OBITUARIES AND OTHER SOURCES:

PERIODICALS

New York Times, February 26, 1988.

* * *

GROSSMAN, Vasily (Semenovich) 1905-1964

BRIEF ENTRY: Given name sometimes transliterated as Vasilii or Vassili; born in 1905 in Berdichev, Russia (now U.S.S.R.); died following a long illness, September 14, 1964, in Moscow, U.S.S.R. Russian engineer, journalist, and author. Grossman spent several years as an industrial safety engineer before becoming a writer. He was a reporter for the Soviet Defense Ministry newspaper *Krasnaya zvezda* during World War II and drew on his wartime experiences in writing the novels *The People Immortal* (1943) and the posthumously published *Life and Fate* (1986). Grossman's work grew increasingly critical of the Soviet Government, and many of his books were banned in the Soviet Union and had to be smuggled to Western publishers. His other writings include *Stephan Kol'chugin* (1937), *Za pravoe delo* (1955), and *Forever Flowing* (1972). Grossman also co-edited *The Black Book* (c. 1981), an account of Nazi persecution of Jews in the Soviet Union during World War II.

BIOGRAPHICAL/CRITICAL SOURCES:

BOOKS

Cassell's Encyclopaedia of World Literature, revised and enlarged edition, Morrow, 1973.
Contemporary Literary Criticism, Volume 41, Gale, 1987.
Everyman's Dictionary of European Writers, Dutton, 1968.

PERIODICALS

Los Angeles Times Book Review, March 30, 1986.
New York Times, September 18, 1964, April 1, 1972, May 12, 1982.
New York Times Book Review, March 26, 1972, March 9, 1986.
Times Literary Supplement, February 23, 1973, November 22, 1985.

* * *

GRUNFELD, Frederic V(olker) 1929-1987

OBITUARY NOTICE—See index for *CA* sketch: Born June 2, 1929, in Berlin, Germany; immigrated to United States, 1939, naturalized citizen, 1944; died of a heart attack, December 9, 1987, in Barcelona, Spain. Radio announcer, journalist, and author. For thirty years Grunfeld served as a cultural correspondent in Europe. As such he was alternately employed by a number of periodicals, most notably *Reporter* and *Horizon*. Previously Grunfeld spent five years as a commentator for WQXR-Radio in New York City. Writing on a wide range of topics, he published several books, among them *The Hitler File: A Social History of Germany and the Nazis, 1918-1945, Prophets Without Honour: A Background to Freud, Kafka, Einstein, and Their World*, and a biography of the French sculptor Auguste Rodin that was nominated for a Pulitzer Prize. Grunfeld also contributed a number of publications to the Time-Life series of books and held editorial posts with the journals *Queen* and *Connoisseur*.

OBITUARIES AND OTHER SOURCES:

BOOKS

The Writers Directory: 1986-1988, St. James Press, 1986.

PERIODICALS

New York Times, December 11, 1987.
Times (London), December 14, 1987.
Washington Post, December 14, 1987.

* * *

GUTCH, John 1905-1988

OBITUARY NOTICE: Born July 12, 1905; died February 11, 1988. Colonial administrator and author. After joining the British Colonial Administrative Service in 1928, Gutch was stationed in the Gold Coast as an assistant district commissioner. He transferred to Palestine (now Israel) in 1936, then was appointed chief secretary of British Guiana in 1950 and served as the country's acting governor during its campaign for independence. In 1955 Gutch was named high commissioner for the Western Pacific with the Gilbert and Ellice Islands Colony and the British Solomon Islands Protectorate under his jurisdiction. Gutch retired from the Colonial Administrative Service in 1961 and then worked for British Electric Traction for eight years. His books include *Martyr of the Islands: The Life and Death of John Coleridge Patteson*, a biography of the first bishop of Melanesia; *Beyond the Reefs: The Life of John Williams, Missionary;* and an autobiography, *Colonial Servant*. He was made a member of the Order of the British Empire in 1947 and knighted ten years later.

OBITUARIES AND OTHER SOURCES:

BOOKS

Who's Who, 140th edition, St. Martin's, 1988.

PERIODICALS

Times (London), February 13, 1988.

* * *

GUTMAN, Kellie O. 1952-

PERSONAL: Born August 1, 1952, in Sacramento, Calif.; daughter of Robert Joseph (a chemist) and Rita (O'Grady) O'Connor; married Richard J. S. Gutman (an audiovisual producer, designer, and writer), August 18, 1974; children: Lucy O'Connor. *Education:* Attended University of California, Santa Cruz, 1970-72; Boston University, B.S., 1975. *Politics:* Democrat. *Religion:* Roman Catholic.

ADDRESSES: Home and office—Slide Factor, 75 Gardner St., West Roxbury, Mass. 02132.

CAREER: Teacher at school for multiply handicapped, deaf, and language-impaired children in Framingham, Mass., 1977-82; Slide Factor, West Roxbury, Mass., producer of audiovisual presentations, 1982—.

WRITINGS:

(With husband, Richard J. S. Gutman) *John Wilkes Booth Himself,* Hired Hand Press, 1979.

(With R.J.S. Gutman) *The Summer Camp Memory Book,* Crown, 1983.

SIDELIGHTS: Kellie O. Gutman told *CA:* "*John Wilkes Booth Himself* grew out of my husband's and my interest in Booth and his assassination of U.S. President Abraham Lincoln. It is a collection of all the known photographs of him, the actor and assassin. *The Summer Camp Memory Book,* although not a children's book, would delight anyone who went to summer camp as a child. It is a historical look and a present-day look at the experience of spending a summer at camp."

H

HAAKONSSEN, Knud 1947-

PERSONAL: Given name is pronounced ''Ca-*nute*''; born July 9, 1947, in Tingsted, Denmark; son of Helmer Daniel (a laborer) and Laura Eline (a shopkeeper; maiden name, Marquardsen) Haakonssen; married Lis Soerensen (a high school teacher), June 26, 1968 (divorced, 1986); married Lisbeth Mary Gurholt, January, 1987; children: (first marriage) Eric Christoph. *Education:* University of Copenhagen, M.A., 1972; University of Edinburgh, Ph.D., 1978.

ADDRESSES: Home—9 Patey St., Campbell, Australian Capital Territory 2601, Australia. *Office*—History of Ideas Unit, Research School of Social Sciences, Australian National University, P.O. Box 4, Canberra, Australian Capital Territory 2601, Australia.

CAREER: Monash University, Melbourne, Australia, senior tutor in philosophy, 1976-79; Victoria University of Wellington, Wellington, New Zealand, lecturer in political theory, 1979-82; Australian National University, Canberra, visiting fellow at History of Ideas Unit, 1981-82, research fellow, 1982-85, senior research fellow in the history of ideas, 1985—. Visiting professor at University of New Brunswick, 1984; visiting fellow at University of Aarhms, 1985, and University of Edinburgh, 1986.

MEMBER: Australian Association of Philosophy, Australian Political Studies Association, Australian Society of Legal Philosophy, Royal Institute of Philosophy, British Society for Eighteenth-Century Studies, Hume Society, Conference for the Study of Political Thought, Lessing Akademie, Deutsche Gesellschaft fuer die Erforschung des Achtzehnten Jahrhunderts.

WRITINGS:

The Science of a Legislator: The Natural Jurisprudence of David Hume and Adam Smith, Cambridge University Press, 1981.

(Editor) *The Liberal Tradition,* Center for Independent Studies, 1987.

(Editor) Thomas Reid, *Practical Ethics; Being Lectures and Papers on Natural Theology, Self-Government, Natural Jurisprudence, and the Law of Nations,* Princeton University Press, 1988.

Also translator into Danish of T. S. Kuhn's *The Structure of Scientific Revolutions,* Bertrand Russell's *Problems of Philosophy,* and selections of K. R. Popper's *Kritisk Rationalisme.* Contributor to history and political science journals.

WORK IN PROGRESS: A book on eighteenth-century theories of natural law; contributing to a book on philosophers John Locke, Adam Smith, and John Stuart Mill.

* * *

HABER, Carole R. 1951-

PERSONAL: Born May 24, 1951, in New York; daughter of Stanley B. (an attorney and certified public accountant) and Bernice (an attorney and certified public accountant; maiden name, Kraditor) Haber; married Peter M. Rothstein (in computer software business), May 17, 1981; children: Noah A. *Education:* Washington University, St. Louis, Mo., B.A., 1973; University of Pennsylvania, Ph.D., 1979.

ADDRESSES: Home—2033 Beverly Dr., Charlotte, N.C. 28207. *Office*—Department of History, University of North Carolina at Charlotte, Charlotte, N.C. 28223.

CAREER: University of North Carolina at Charlotte, assistant professor of history, 1979—.

MEMBER: American Studies Association, Organization of American Historians, American Association for the History of Medicine, Phi Beta Kappa.

WRITINGS:

Beyond Sixty-five: The Dilemma of Old Age in America's Past, Cambridge University Press, 1983.

Contributor to history and gerontology journals.

WORK IN PROGRESS: A book on the research that has been conducted on the history of aging, for Indiana University Press.

SIDELIGHTS: Carole R. Haber told *CA:* ''I hope that my work adds a historical perspective to the problems facing the elderly in America. It is my belief that the issues that beset the old today are not new; they were shaped by the social and economic forces of the nineteenth century. Before gerontologists can address and solve these questions properly, they must understand their historical roots and derivation.''

HAFEMEISTER, David W(alter) 1934-

PERSONAL: Born July 1, 1934, in Chicago, Ill.; son of Lester D. (a businessman) and Alma D. (a housewife; maiden name, Schmidt) Hafemeister; married Gina Rohlander (a weaver), 1961; children: Andrew, Jason, Heidi. *Education:* Northwestern University, B.S.M.E., 1957; University of Illinois at Urbana-Champaign, M.S., 1960, Ph.D., 1964.

ADDRESSES: Home—553 Serrano, San Luis Obispo, Calif. 93401. *Office*—Department of Physics, California Polytechnic State University, San Luis Obispo, Calif. 93407.

CAREER: Argonne National Laboratory, Argonne, Ill., Particle Accelerator Division, mechanical engineer, 1957-58; Los Alamos Scientific Laboratory, Los Alamos, N. M., physicist and research fellow in physics division, 1964-66; Carnegie-Mellon University, Pittsburgh, Pa., assistant professor of physics, 1966-69; California Polytechnic State University, San Luis Obispo, assistant professor, 1969-72, associate professor of physics, 1972—. Science adviser to U.S. Senator John Glenn, 1975-77; special assistant to undersecretary of state, 1977-78. Visiting scientist at Massachusetts Institute of Technology, 1983-84; visiting scientist at Lawrence Berkeley National Laboratory, 1985-86.

MEMBER: American Association for the Advancement of Science, American Physical Society.

AWARDS, HONORS: Scientific Congressional fellow, 1975-76; fellow of American Association for the Advancement of Science at Office of Strategic Nuclear Policy, U.S. Department of State, 1987—.

WRITINGS:

(With Anthony Buffa and Ronald Brown) *Physics for Modern Architecture,* Paladin, 1983.
(Editor with Dietrich Schroeer) *Physics and Technology of the Nuclear Arms Race,* American Institute of Physics, 1983.
(Editor with Henry Kelly and Barbara Levi) *Energy Sources: Conservation and Renewables,* American Institute of Physics, 1985.
(Editor with Kosta Tsipis and Penny Janeway) *Arms Control Verification: The Technologies That Make It Possible,* Pergamon, 1986.
Science and Society "Tests," El Corale, 1988.

SIDELIGHTS: David W. Hafemeister's fourth book, *Arms Control Verification: The Technologies That Make It Possible,* is, according to critic Paul Bracken, "a work that gives the educated public insight into the arcane world of the technologies that underlie assessments of whether or not states are living up to the agreements they enter into." *Arms Control Verification* is concerned, not so much with the question of whether an arms control agreement is being violated, but whether such an agreement can be verified by modern technology. Some of the book's contributors are disturbed by the development of such weapons as the cruise missile, the Stealth bomber, and the new, ultra-quiet submarines, which may be all but impossible to detect. Others consider the difficulty of accurately monitoring nuclear tests. Still other contributors pointed out that the monitoring devices themselves are capable of being used in an active, hostile manner. Bracken concluded in his *Washington Post Book World* review: "Overall this book is an important contribution to the understanding of arms control and national security because it throws light on obscure areas of technology."

Hafemeister told *CA:* "In several areas I remain optimistic that improved technologies can monitor arms control treaties. For example, by calibrating nuclear test sites with nuclear explosions it should be possible to measure the difference between test sites and thus improve the monitoring of the Threshold Test Ban Treaty. By employing remote, unattended seismic stations in the Soviet Union, it should be possible to reduce the threshold below 150 kilotons to the region of 1 to 10 kilotons. In the area of Strategic Arms Reduction Treaty or Strategic Arms Limitation Treaty, the advances in mobile missiles and cruise missiles present more difficult challenges than the silos of the past, but by using cooperative means, along with advances in electronics and optics, some of these difficulties can be overcome.

"In my view, science and technology are the driving forces of history, much more so than pan-nationalism and varying economics systems. If we don't look at the implications of these technologies, then we shouldn't be surprised if some negative results surface to haunt us. Our goal should be to refrain from those technologies that can make a bad situation worse."

BIOGRAPHICAL/CRITICAL SOURCES:

PERIODICALS

Washington Post Book World, June 22, 1986.

* * *

HAGGIE, Paul 1949-

PERSONAL: Born August 30, 1949, in England; son of George Henry (a company director) and Eva (a housewife; maiden name, Hawke) Haggie; married Deborah Frazer (a housewife), January 6, 1979; children: James. *Education:* Victoria University of Manchester, B.A., 1971, Ph.D., 1974.

ADDRESSES: Home—London, England. *Office*—Foreign and Commonwealth Office, King Charles St., London SW1A 2AH, England.

CAREER: Foreign and Commonwealth Office, London, England, third and second secretary, 1974-76, second and first secretary at British embassy in Bangkok, Thailand, 1976-80, first secretary in London, 1980-82, and Islamabad, 1982—.

MEMBER: Royal Bangkok Sports Club.

WRITINGS:

Britannia at Bay: The Defence of the British Empire Against Japan, 1931-1941, Oxford University Press, 1981.

Contributor to history and military journals.

WORK IN PROGRESS: Research on the careers of the Kelly brothers, who were both British admirals, for the Naval Records Society.

SIDELIGHTS: Paul Haggie told *CA:* "As an academic manque, who was diverted at an early stage into a diplomatic career, I still hanker occasionally for a return to teaching and research. Meanwhile I enjoy the built-in variety offered by the Foreign Service and the very broad outlook on life that it fosters."

BIOGRAPHICAL/CRITICAL SOURCES:

PERIODICALS

American Historical Review, April, 1982.
Observer, March 22, 1981.

Times Literary Supplement, June 12, 1981.
Virginia Quarterly Review, winter, 1982.

* * *

HAIG, Alexander M(eigs), Jr. 1924-

BRIEF ENTRY: Born December 2, 1924, in Philadelphia, Pa. American army officer, government official, business executive, and author. Haig, a retired four-star general, served as U.S. secretary of state for eighteen months during 1981 and 1982. A graduate of the U.S. Military Academy at West Point and of Georgetown University, Haig became a staff officer at the Pentagon in 1962 and, after a tour of duty in Vietnam, he was appointed in 1969 as senior military assistant to National Security Council adviser Henry A. Kissinger. In 1973 President Richard M. Nixon made Haig army vice-chief of staff, and later that year he was named White House chief of staff. Following the Watergate scandal and Nixon's resignation in 1974, President Gerald R. Ford designated Haig supreme allied commander of NATO forces in Europe, a post that won Haig wide respect. The recipient of a number of military honors, including the Department of Defense Distinguished Service Medal, Haig resigned from military service in 1979 and became president of United Technologies Corporation, a major defense contractor.

In December, 1980, President-elect Ronald Reagan named Haig as his choice for U.S. secretary of state, and on January 21, 1981, the appointment was confirmed by the Senate. In the months that followed, Haig helped formulate a foreign policy emphasizing U.S. opposition to Soviet expansion in Europe and Asia and was involved in a series of complex policy matters ranging from Middle Eastern affairs to the war between Great Britain and Argentina over the Falkland Islands. Conflicts with members of the president's staff and frustration over the administration's foreign policy prompted Haig's resignation on June 25, 1982. Haig's book *Caveat: Realism, Reagan, and Foreign Policy,* an account of his experiences as secretary of state, was published by Macmillan in 1984. *Addresses: Home*—6041 Crimson Ct., Bethesda, Md. 20817. *Office*—1155 15th St. N.W., Suite 800, Washington, D. C. 20005.

BIOGRAPHICAL/CRITICAL SOURCES:

BOOKS

Current Biography, H. W. Wilson, 1987.
Political Profiles: The Nixon/Ford Years, Facts on File, 1979.
Who's Who in American Politics, 11th edition, Bowker, 1987.

PERIODICALS

Atlantic Monthly, March, 1981.
New York Times, May 31, 1981, April 18, 1984.
Time, December 29, 1980, March 16, 1981.
Times Literary Supplement, May 25, 1984.
Washington Post Book World, May 13, 1984.

* * *

HAIGHT, M. R. 1938-

PERSONAL: Born February 28, 1938, in Los Angeles, Calif.; daughter of George Emory (a film producer) and Justine Whittimore (an actress and writer; maiden name, Chase) Haight; married R. D. A. Savage, c. 1962 (divorced, 1965). *Education:* St. Anne's College, Oxford, B.A., 1961, M.A. and B.Phil., both 1965; University of California, Berkeley, M.A., 1964. *Religion:* None.

ADDRESSES: Home—Glasgow, Scotland. *Office*—Department of Philosophy, University of Glasgow, Glasgow G12 8QQ, Scotland.

CAREER: University of Glasgow, Glasgow, Scotland, lecturer in philosophy, 1966—. Visiting professor at University of Wisconsin, 1986-87.

MEMBER: Aristotelian Society, Mind Association, British Society of Aesthetics, Scots Philosophical Association.

AWARDS, HONORS: Woodrow Wilson fellow, 1961-62.

WRITINGS:

A Study of Self-Deception, Humanities, 1980.
(Contributor) Mike W. Martin, editor, *Self-Deception and Self-Understanding,* University Press of Kansas, 1985.

Contributor of articles and reviews to philosophy journals.

WORK IN PROGRESS: Gunddh: A Study in Personal Identity; a collection of logic puzzles.

AVOCATIONAL INTERESTS: Cartooning and illustration.

* * *

HALLETT, Judith Peller 1944-

PERSONAL: Born April 4, 1944, in Chicago, Ill.; daughter of Leonard (an engineer) and Celia (in business; maiden name, Stern) Peller; married Mark Hallett (a neurologist), June 26, 1966; children: Nicholas Leonard, Victoria Claire. *Education:* Wellesley College, A.B., 1966; Harvard University, M.A., 1967, Ph.D., 1971. *Politics:* Democrat. *Religion:* Jewish.

ADDRESSES: Home—5147 Westbard Ave., Bethesda, Md. 20816. *Office*—Department of Classics, University of Maryland at College Park, College Park, Md. 20742.

CAREER: Clark University, Worcester, Mass., lecturer, 1972-73, assistant professor of classics, 1973-74; Boston University, Boston, Mass., assistant professor of classical studies, 1974-82; Brandeis University, Waltham, Mass., assistant professor of humanities, 1982-83; University of Maryland at College Park, associate professor of classics, 1983—. Member of Institute for Classical Studies, London, England, 1975-76.

MEMBER: American Philological Association, Association of Ancient Historians, Women's Classical Caucus (co-chair, 1987).

AWARDS, HONORS: Blegen visiting scholar at Vassar College, 1980; Fellowship for College Teachers, National Endowment for the Humanities, 1986-87.

WRITINGS:

Fathers and Daughters in Roman Society: Women in the Elite Family, Princeton University Press, 1984.

Contributor to classical studies and philology journals. Assistant editor of *Classical World,* 1980—.

WORK IN PROGRESS: Editing, translating into English, and writing literary commentary for the Latin work, *Priapea,* publication expected in 1989 or 1990.

SIDELIGHTS: Judith Peller Hallett told *CA* how she came to specialize in classical studies: "Five inspiring years of Latin in high school; antipathy to concentrating in subjects with massive numbers of majors such as English, history, and sociology; and compatibility with the interdisciplinary focus of classics as it was taught at Wellesley College. But I might well

have lost heart with the discipline during my years of graduate study (as the subject was there presented in a narrow and heavily linguistic manner) had the women's movement not come along to awaken my interest in uncovering and re-covering the women of classical antiquity.

"My study of the Roman elite family, which focuses on the father-daughter relationship as the most extensively elaborated male-female family tie, was prompted by the appalling neglect of male-female blood relationships (and obsession with male-female marital and sexual ties) on the part of earlier scholars. My sources, of course, are almost exclusively male, as practically nothing survives from ancient women themselves. But my earlier interest in such fields as English, history, and sociology served me well in applying comparative evidence and methods to my evidence—which enabled me to ask new questions and thereby illuminate classical Roman notions of female and male familial roles."

* * *

HAMILTON, Walter 1908-1988

OBITUARY NOTICE—See index for *CA* sketch: Born February 10, 1908, in London, England; died February 8, 1988. Educator, administrator, translator, and editor. Hamilton served in various teaching and administrative capacities at British schools including Cambridge University, from which he retired in 1978 as an honorary fellow of Trinity College. He intermittently accepted positions as master or headmaster of a number of private secondary schools for boys as well, and in 1972 he was named a fellow of Eton College. A scholar of the classics, Hamilton published three translations of Plato's works and co-edited *The Later Roman Empire* by historian Ammianus Marcellinus. Additionally, he edited the journal *Classical Quarterly* for one year.

OBITUARIES AND OTHER SOURCES:

BOOKS

Who's Who, 139th edition, St. Martin's, 1987.

PERIODICALS

Times (London), February 10, 1988.

* * *

HAMSON, C. J.
See HAMSON, Charles John

* * *

HAMSON, Charles John 1905-1987
(C. J. Hamson)

OBITUARY NOTICE: Born November 23, 1905; died November 14, 1987. Attorney, educator, editor, and author. A professor of comparative law at the University of Cambridge from 1953 to 1973, Hamson was educated at Cambridge University's Trinity College and at Harvard Law School. He was called to the Bar in 1929 but chose an academic career over practicing law. When World War II broke out he served in the British Army, was captured in Crete in 1941, and spent the rest of the war as a prisoner in Germany. Hamson returned to Cambridge after the war—having been elected a fellow of Trinity College in 1934—and was appointed reader, then professor of comparative law in 1953. He became a judge three years later and was selected as a Queen's Counsel in 1975. Hamson was editor of the *Cambridge Law Journal* from 1955 to 1974 and the author of a book on French law that was translated into French. He also wrote articles on legal topics.

OBITUARIES AND OTHER SOURCES:

BOOKS

Who's Who, 140th edition, St. Martin's, 1988.

PERIODICALS

Times (London), November 17, 1987.

* * *

HANDL, Irene 1902(?)-1987

OBITUARY NOTICE—See index for *CA* sketch: Born December 27 (one source says December 26), 1902 (some sources say 1901 or 1912), in London, England; died after a short illness, November 29, 1987, in London, England. Actress and author. Handl captured the hearts and attention of her countrymen with her endearing portrayals of such characters as a maid, a charwoman, or an eccentric old lady. An award-winning comedienne, she was featured in numerous films and the television series "Never Say Die" and "For the Love of Ada." She performed what was perhaps her best role as the disapproving wife of the late actor Peter Sellers in the film "I'm All Right, Jack,"and she also appeared in the title role in the West End production of "Goodnight Mrs. Puffin." She published her first novel, *The Sioux,* when she was about sixty-three. It was reprinted as *The Green and Purple Dream* in 1973, the same year a sequel, *The Gold Tip Pfitzer,* appeared.

OBITUARIES AND OTHER SOURCES:

BOOKS

Who's Who in the Theatre: A Biographical Record of the Contemporary Stage, 17th edition, Gale, 1981.

PERIODICALS

Chicago Tribune, December 2, 1987.
New York Times, November 30, 1987.
Times (London), November 30, 1987.

* * *

HARASYMIW, Bohdan 1936-

PERSONAL: Born August 30, 1936, in Saskatchewan, Canada; son of Dmytro and Maria (Kobak) Harasymiw; married Elaine Louise Verchomin (a teacher), May 14, 1966; children: Larissa Theodora, Peter Myroslav. *Education:* Queen's University, Kingston, Ontario, B.A., 1962; University of Alberta, M.A., 1965; University of Toronto, Ph.D., 1970.

ADDRESSES: Home—4616 148th St., Edmonton, Alberta, Canada T6H 5N5. *Office*—Department of Political Science, University of Calgary, 2500 University Ave. N.W., Calgary, Alberta, Canada T2N 1N4.

CAREER: Lecturer in political science at Waterloo Lutheran University, 1968-69; University of Calgary, Calgary, Alberta, assistant professor, 1969-75, associate professor, 1975-85, professor of political science, 1985—. *Military service:* Royal Canadian Navy, 1955-61.

MEMBER: Canadian Association of Slavists (president), Canadian Political Science Association, American Political Science Association, American Association for the Advancement of Slavic Studies.

WRITINGS:

Political Elite Recruitment in the Soviet Union, Macmillan, 1984.

The Soviet Party Official, Macmillan, in press.

SIDELIGHTS: Bohdan Harasymiw told *CA:* "I became interested in the Soviet Union during my youth when the Cold War was at its height. My first book deals with the processes through which people are drawn from Soviet society into the political elite, or *nomenklatura.* I discovered that social status clearly propels individuals into the party regardless of the leaders' concern for its proletarian character. Beyond that point, however, other criteria than status come into effect. This creates the possibility of conflict between those excluded from elite positions and those admitted, since status inconsistency is a common source of dissatisfaction: people who have achieved high social status, whether through education, occupational prestige, or money, expect to enjoy commensurate political status as well. As the Soviet society moves into the post-industrial phase this conflict is likely to be aggravated unless the traditional pattern of elite recruitment—long apprenticeship, preference for workers and peasants in social origin—is altered."

BIOGRAPHICAL/CRITICAL SOURCES:

PERIODICALS

Times Literary Supplement, February 8, 1985.

* * *

HARDY, Dennis 1941-

PERSONAL: Born June 26, 1941, in Brighton, England; son of Harry and Violet (Abdela) Hardy; married Bronwen Bone (a librarian), April 3, 1964; children: Rowan, Gemma, Alexis. *Education:* University of Exeter, B.A., 1962, M.A., 1969; University of London, Diploma in Town Planning, 1967.

ADDRESSES: Home—65 Weald Rd., Brentwood, Essex CM14 4TN, England. *Office*—School of Geography and Planning, Middlesex Polytechnic, Queensway, Enfield, Middlesex EN3 4SF, England.

CAREER: Middlesex County Council, London, England, planning officer, 1963-65; Greater London Council, London, England, planning officer, 1965-68; Middlesex Polytechnic, Enfield, England, lecturer in planning, 1968—, head of School of Geography and Planning, 1984—. Vice-chairman of Brentwood Civic Society, 1968-73; convener of Brentwood Campaign for Nuclear Disarmament, 1980-82. Member of editorial board of Town and Country Planning, 1987—.

MEMBER: Royal Town Planning Institute (fellow).

AWARDS, HONORS: Angel Literary Award from Angel Hotel, 1985, for *Arcadia for All.*

WRITINGS:

Alternative Communities in Nineteenth-Century England, Longman, 1979.

(With Colin Wood) *Arcadia for All: The Legacy of a Makeshift Landscape,* Mansell, 1984.

Goodnight Campers: The History of the British Holiday Camp, Mansell, 1986.

WORK IN PROGRESS: An official history of the Town and Country Planning Association, an "organization that started in 1899 to campaign for garden cities and is still actively involved with environmental issues."

SIDELIGHTS: Arcadia for All, according to Andrew Saint of the *Times Literary Supplement,* is a sensitive and detailed study of the "plotlands" that sprang up in various parts of England before and after World War I. The plotlands were tiny parcels of rural land on which disenfranchised city dwellers built primitive dwellings without municipal services or any discernible plan. They were despised by most of the greater population as eyesores that ruined the ever-shrinking British countryside, and after World War II most communities took legal steps to rid themselves of the variegated shantytowns or to establish stringent planning acts and dwelling codes to force compliance with more aesthetic tastes. Dennis Hardy and his co-author, however, argue a more positive view of the plotlands, namely that they served to ease the lot of the landless, often working-class, urban population and fostered individuality, creativity, and a freedom of the spirit. Saint called *Arcadia for All* a work of "consummate delicacy, skill and fairness," and a "sparkling, original and thoughtful book . . . in the modern, resurgent [William] Morris tradition." Concluded Saint, "It amounts to a parable about tolerance."

Hardy told *CA:* "One book can lead to another. From an initial publication on utopian communities (*Alternative Communities in Nineteenth-Century England*), I was led to research a more practical (but in some ways no less idealistic) kind of experiment, known in England as the 'plotlands.' In many ways, it is an American type of landscape, where settlements have grown up on a plot-by-plot basis, typically without any overall planning. But in England, with a much higher degree of planning, this kind of development is the exception rather than the rule. With Colin Ward I looked at a variety of plotland communities—many around London and along the southeastern coastline—typified by their ramshackle, makeshift appearance. Their heyday was the 1920's and 1930's, but there are still plenty of relics from a colorful phase of activity. Converted railway carriages, tumbledown shacks, and converted beach huts stand as testimony to a period when the poor and bohemians forced their way into the property market to live 'the simple life.'

"For years the plotlands have been reviled, largely by planners and public health inspectors and by self-styled custodians of the landscape who recoiled at the thought of an 'urban invasion.' We acknowledged these fears but discovered another side of the story—one of hope and opportunity for poor families who were able to find their own place 'in the sun.' An especially enjoyable part of the research was to interview some of these early pioneers and to share their memories and scrapbooks.

"In the course of this work, often on highly marginal land outside the main towns and protected areas of the countryside, we also came across many examples of a peculiarly British institution, the holiday camp. This is a miniature holiday resort that offers its own entertainments as well as accommodation. As with plotlands, holiday camps have never been far from controversy. A common criticism is that they are too regimented, with the largest camps receiving as many as twelve thousand visitors weekly. They have become something of a cultural joke, and yet, as with the plotlands, we discovered another dimension. Far from being associated solely with 'low taste' and regimentation, the holiday camps started as relatively small ventures, many with strong educational and political motives. We found that for the people who have spent a holiday in a camp (and as much as one quarter of the British

population has), the memories are fond rather than bitter. A conclusion of *Goodnight Campers* (named after a song commonly sung by campers at the end of the day) was to note what ordinary people think about their own experience and to recognize that holiday camps, for all their failings, have indeed offered social opportunities for many. Annual holidays with pay only entered the statute books in 1938, and since then holiday camps have played an important part in the British holiday scene.''

BIOGRAPHICAL/CRITICAL SOURCES:

PERIODICALS

Times Literary Supplement, October 26, 1984.

* * *

HARRIS, Alex(ander Eisemann) 1949-

PERSONAL: Born July 20, 1949, in Atlanta, Ga.; son of Arthur L. Harris (a businessman) and Helen Eisemann Alexander (an actress); married Margaret Sartor (a photographer, designer, and teacher), December 18, 1982. *Education:* Yale University, B.A., 1971.

ADDRESSES: Home—(September to May) 4604 Erwin Rd., Durham, N.C. 27705; (June to August) El Valle Route, Box 1, Chamisal, N.M. 87521. *Office*—Center for Documentary Photography, Duke University, 4875 Duke Station, Durham, N.C. 27706.

CAREER: Duke University, Durham, N.C., lecturer in documentary photography, 1975-79, director of Center for Documentary Photography, 1980—, professor of the practice of public policy and documentary photography, 1987—. Lecturer at University of North Carolina at Chapel Hill, 1975-79; conducted lectures on documentary photography at numerous colleges, museums, and photography centers; workshop leader. Photographer, with solo and group exhibitions, 1972—; work represented in permanent collections, including those at the Museum of Modern Art, Santa Fe Museum of Fine Arts, International Center of Photography, and National Museum of Natural History; guest curator of photographic exhibitions at International Center of Photography.

AWARDS, HONORS: Rockefeller Foundation fellow, 1977-78; Guggenheim fellow, 1979-80; grants from National Endowment for the Arts, 1981-82, and National Endowment for the Humanities, 1982, 1984; Lyndhurst Prize from Lyndhurst Foundation, 1984-87; Elliot Porter Purchase Award from New Mexico Council on Photography, 1985.

WRITINGS:

EDITOR AND AUTHOR OF INTRODUCTION, EXCEPT AS NOTED

Paul Kwilecki, *Understandings: Photographs of Decatur County, Georgia,* University of North Carolina Press, 1982.
William Bamberger, *Durham County Photographs,* Center for Documentary Photography, 1983.
(With wife, Margaret Sartor) *Gertrude Blom: Bearing Witness,* University of North Carolina Press, 1984.
(Associate editor with M. Sartor) Omar Badsha, editor, *South Africa: The Cordoned Heart,* Norton, 1986.
A World Unsuspected: Portraits of Southern Childhood, University of North Carolina Press, 1987.
(With Marvin Hoshino) Helen Levitt, *In the Street,* introduction by Robert Coles, University of North Carolina Press, 1987.

PHOTOGRAPHER

Robert Coles, *The Old Ones of New Mexico,* University of New Mexico Press, 1973.
Robert Coles, *The Last and First Eskimos,* New York Graphic Society, 1978.

Contributor of photographs to *Photography Within the Humanities, I Shall Save One Land Unvisited, The Essential Landscape,* and *Handbook of North American Indians,* Volume V: *The Arctic.*

OTHER

Contributor of articles and photographs to magazines and newspapers, including *New York Times Sunday Magazine, Washington Post Magazine, American Poetry Review, Humanities, Impact,* and *New Mexico.*

WORK IN PROGRESS: In Their Own Image, a photographic book on northern New Mexico, publication expected in 1989; *Villager,* photographs and text, with William de Buys, publication expected in 1989.

SIDELIGHTS: Alex Harris told *CA:* ``I am a photographer who has edited several books and written about issues in documentary photography and photography in the humanities. My most recent book, *A World Unsuspected,* involves eleven southern novelists of the post-war generation, each using family photographs as a catalyst for writing down childhood memories. I wrote an introduction to the book, in which I explored the relationship between photographs and memory and tried to expand our notion of the term 'documentary.'

``As a photographer, I have lived for a year-and-a-half (over a period of six years) with Alaskan Eskimos, and for the last fifteen years I have lived on and off in a northern New Mexican Hispanic village. My photographic work has focused on these two areas. Two photographic books have been published, and I am in the process of putting together two more.

``As the director of the Center for Documentary Photography at Duke University, I have had the opportunity to publish and write about the work of other documentary photographers. In each case, these photographers have had a kind of symbiotic relationship to their 'subjects'—a long-term commitment to the people and places they document. For example, Paul Kwilecki spent more than twenty-five years documenting his home country in south Georgia, and Gertrude Blom spent more than forty years photographing the Lacondon Maya who inhabit the last great rain forest of southern Mexico. My wife and I also traveled to South Africa in 1985, to help bring together the work of a multiracial group of twenty South African documentary photographers.''

BIOGRAPHICAL/CRITICAL SOURCES:

PERIODICALS

Chicago Tribune, September 30, 1987.
New York Times Book Review, October 11, 1987.

* * *

HARRIS, Marvin 1927-

PERSONAL: Born August 18, 1927, in Brooklyn, N.Y.; son of Irving and Sadie (Newman) Harris; married Madeline Grove, January 25, 1953; children: Robert Eric (deceased), Susan Lynn. *Education:* Columbia University, A.B., 1949, Ph.D., 1953.

ADDRESSES: Home—1511 North West 38th St., Gainesville, Fla. 32611. *Office*—Department of Anthropology, University of Florida, Gainesville, Fla. 32611.

CAREER: Columbia University, New York, N.Y., member of faculty, 1952—, assistant professor, 1953-59, associate professor, 1959-63, professor of anthropology, beginning in 1963, chairman of anthropology department, 1963-66; University of Florida, Gainesville, Fla., graduate research professor of anthropology, 1981—. Technical adviser to the Ministry of Education in Brazil, 1953; Ford Foundation fellow, 1956-57; executive secretary of the Columbia-Cornell-Harvard-Illinois Summer Field Studies Program, 1960-66; lecturer at Foreign Service Institute, 1966—. *Military service:* U.S. Army Air Forces, 1945-47.

MEMBER: American Anthropological Association, American Academy of Arts and Sciences.

AWARDS, HONORS: National Science Foundation grant, 1966-67.

WRITINGS:

Town and Country in Brazil, Columbia University Press, 1956.

Portugal's African "Wards": A First-Hand Report on Labor and Education in Mocambique, American Committee on Africa, 1958.

(With Charles Wagley) *Minorities in the New World: Six Case Studies,* Columbia University Press, 1958.

The Economy Has No Surplus? Bobbs-Merrill, c. 1960.

The Nature of Cultural Things, Random House, 1964.

Patterns of Race in the Americas, Walker, 1964.

The Rise of Anthropological Theory: A History of Theories of Culture, Harper, 1968.

(Editor, with Morton Fried and Robert Murphy) *War: The Anthropology of Armed Conflict and Aggression,* American Museum of Natural History Press, 1968.

Culture, Man, and Nature: An Introduction to General Anthropology, Crowell, 1971, reprinted as *Culture, People, Nature: An Introduction to General Anthropology,* Crowell, 1975.

Cows, Pigs, Wars, and Witches: The Riddles of Culture, Random House, 1974.

Cannibals and Kings: The Origins of Cultures, Random House, 1977.

Cultural Materialism: The Struggle for a Science of Culture, Random House, 1979.

America Now: The Anthropology of a Changing Culture, Simon & Schuster, 1981, revised edition published as *Why Nothing Works: The Anthropology of Daily Life,* Simon & Schuster, 1987.

Cultural Anthropology, Harper, 1983.

Good to Eat: Riddles of Food and Culture, Simon & Schuster, 1986.

(With Eric B. Ross) *Death, Sex, and Fertility: Population Regulation in Preindustrial and Developing Societies,* Columbia University Press, 1987.

(With Eric B. Ross) *Food and Evolution: Toward a Theory of Human Food Habits,* Temple University Press, 1987.

The Sacred Cow and the Abominable Pig: Riddles of Food and Culture, Simon & Schuster, 1987.

SIDELIGHTS: A well-known and controversial anthropologist, Marvin Harris addresses such topics as the Jewish ban on eating pork, the Hindu reverence for cattle, cannibalism, sexism, and war and attempts to explain them in his books as natural and logical results of the economic conditions affecting certain groups of people. "In each case," asserted Phoebe Adams in an *Atlantic Monthly* review of Harris's 1974 *Cows, Pigs, Wars, and Witches: The Riddles of Culture,* "he has discovered practical reasons for the conduct in question." In *Cows, Pigs, Wars, and Witches* and *The Sacred Cow and the Abominable Pig: Riddles of Food and Culture,* Harris explains that in the Middle East—home to the early Hebrews—raising pigs was economically impractical: The animals' only value was the meat they provided, and since they ate the same foods as humans they were expensive to keep. Grazing animals such as sheep, goats, and cattle, on the other hand, provided wool, milk, and labor in addition to protein, and since they ate grass they did not compete with their owners for food. Nevertheless, Harris maintains, pork remained a tasty temptation, so a manufactured "divine intervention" was necessary to keep the Hebrew nomads from raising the pigs and ruining themselves economically.

Similarly, in *Good to Eat: Riddles of Food and Culture,* Harris writes that the Hindu ban on slaughtering and eating cattle arose as a means of protecting Indian farmers. Harris contends that the labor, milk, and offspring cattle produced were—and still are—more valuable to Indians than was their meat. Explaining this in an interview with Carol Tavris in *Psychology Today,* Harris said, "Westerners think that Indians would rather starve than eat their cows. What they don't understand is that they will starve if they *do* eat their cows. . . . During droughts and famines in India, farmers who succumb to the temptation to kill their cows seal their [own] doom; for when the rains come they will be unable to plow their fields." Thus, the Hindu ban on killing cattle ensures farmers of their means of subsistence. Praising the book as "marvelously readable," Richard Flaste affirmed in the *New York Times Book Review* that "Mr. Harris's thesis . . . [gives] 'Good to Eat' the cohesion of argument rather than letting it stand as a kind of litany of insights about food preferences."

In *Cannibals and Kings: The Origins of Cultures,* Harris again offers his "urgent theory about the nature of man and the reason that human cultures take so many different shapes," according to a critic in the *New Yorker.* Writing "with clarity, charm, and pithiness," Harris explains—among other things—that cannibalism and war arose in some cultures because of the struggle for food in overpopulated regions, that female infanticide increased because of overpopulation and male supremacy, and that males achieved supremacy because there were more of them and they made better warriors than women did.

While some critics were impressed by the variety of topics Harris addresses, others, such as the *New York Times*'s John Leonard, doubted Harris's ability to cover them all adequately in one book. "He wants to explain everything from the Industrial Revolution to why Chinese don't like milk," Leonard complained in his review. "There is, in fact, too much crammed in this short, contentious . . . book." Some critics also questioned the thoroughness of Harris's research, believing his conclusions too simple. Refuting Harris's claim that the Aztecs practiced their elaborate ritual of human sacrifice simply because of a need for animal protein, Marshall Sahlins asserted in the *New York Review of Books* that "it takes a heroic act of utilitarian faith to conclude that this sacrificial system was a way the Aztecs had for getting some meat." While acknowledging the controversy Harris's deterministic theories spawned, reviewers nevertheless praised the originality of his ideas. Leonard, for example, termed the book "exciting," and Robert Lekachman, writing in the *Washington Post Book World,*

called the author's "magisterial interpretation of the rise and fall of human cultures and societies . . . fascinating."

Harris explains his means of reaching the conclusions he does in his 1974 *Cultural Materialism: The Struggle for a Science of Culture*. In the book, explained reviewer William Lederer in the *Chicago Tribune Book World,* "Harris proposes that he and his followers possess the best approach, or as he would say, the best 'research strategy' to understanding the similarities and differences among societies and cultures." Named after a movement the author founded, the book *Cultural Materialism,* in the words of Ashley Montagu in *Psychology Today,* "is designed to do no less than put the discipline [contemporary anthropology] on a more scientific footing. To that task Harris addresses himself with unselfconscious self-assurance." After reviewing and critiquing other widely accepted strategies in anthropology, Harris offers his own, which, according to James Sloan Allen in the *Saturday Review,* maintains that "all ideas and behavior arise from the tensions between human beings and their material environment." Separating the thoughts and behaviors of the members of a given society, Harris determines their influence on one another; the interaction between the two under certain material conditions determines how the society's culture will evolve.

"Previously, Mr. Harris has used cultural materialism to explain remote and exotic societies and customs," Robert Lekachman commented in the *New York Times Book Review,* but "he takes the unusual step [in *America Now: The Anthropology of a Changing Culture*] of applying his methods to his own society." Revised and reprinted in 1987 as *Why Nothing Works: The Anthropology of Daily Life,* Harris's "remarkably concise, angry outcry at the current condition of America" addresses topics ranging from defective appliances to the conditions creating a dependent welfare underclass, according to Lekachman. While some critics complained that, as in his other works, Harris attempts to cover too broad an area and thus resorts to making unconvincing generalizations, others praised the book as a comprehensive study of modern conditions in the United States.

Describing Harris's propositions, Allen G. Weakland of the *National Review* explained that the author does not feel America reached "its present state via a *chain* of events. Rather, our problems developed in 'cobweb' fashion—intricate patterns interlaced into a complicated whole." For example, *Why Nothing Works* proposes that a preponderance of low-quality goods have flooded the U.S. market chiefly because business executives today are devoted more to cost-effectiveness and upward mobility than to product quality. A minority underclass has developed that will likely remain due to the entrance of women into the work force, who, according to Harris, are more likely to be hired for most jobs than are their male minority counterparts. Accusing big business and government bureaucracy of perpetuating America's social and economic ills, Lekachman concluded, "Harris offers radical decentralization of economic activity as the only hope" for the country's recovery. "What [Harris] has to say," declared Don G. Campbell in the *Los Angeles Times,* "is important, valid and—idealistic or not—his solutions to the trend toward economic concentration . . . are challenging and, from this corner, workable."

BIOGRAPHICAL/CRITICAL SOURCES:

PERIODICALS

Atlantic Monthly, September, 1968, June, 1974.
Chicago Tribune Book World, August 5, 1979.
Los Angeles Times, November 10, 1981.
Nation, January 23, 1982.
National Review, December 25, 1981.
New Yorker, October 31, 1977.
New York Review of Books, October 10, 1968, November 23, 1978.
New York Times, October 20, 1977, December 31, 1985.
New York Times Book Review, October 30, 1977, September 9, 1979, January 31, 1982, January 5, 1986.
Psychology Today, January, 1975, June, 1979.
Saturday Review, November 10, 1979.
Washington Post Book World, November 6, 1977.

—*Sketch by Christa Brelin*

* * *

HARRISON, Eric George William Warde 1893-1987

OBITUARY NOTICE: Born March 23, 1893; died December 20, 1987. Military officer and author. Harrison fought in both world wars during his distinguished thirty-three-year career with the British military. In 1913 he was commissioned with the Royal Artillery, then saw action in France and Belgium during World War I. Harrison later served in Baltistan, British Lahaul, Chamba, and India, and during World War II he fought in North Africa and Italy. He retired from the service in 1946 as a major-general. Harrison was also a world-class athlete, representing Great Britain as a hurdler in the 1924 Olympics, and he played Rugby for the national team in 1919 and for the Army in 1920. An avid huntsman and gardener, Harrison's books include *Riding, To Own a Dog,* and his memoirs, *Gunners, Game, and Gardens.*

OBITUARIES AND OTHER SOURCES:

BOOKS

Who's Who, 140th edition, St. Martin's, 1988.

PERIODICALS

Times (London), December 22, 1987.

* * *

HARRISON, Francis Llewelyn 1905-1987 (Frank Llewelyn Harrison)

OBITUARY NOTICE: Some sources spell middle name Llewellyn; born September 29, 1905, in Dublin, Ireland; died in 1987. Musicologist, educator, editor, and author. A leading authority on medieval English music, Harrison was best known for his three-volume *Eton Choirbook,* an important collection of previously inaccessible Tudor church hymns. In 1935 Harrison traveled to Canada where he became professor of music at Queen's University, Kingston. He also taught for a year at Colgate University and at Washington University in St. Louis before returning to England in 1950 and taking a position at Oxford, where he eventually became senior research fellow. Harrison retired from there twenty years later and then became professor of ethnomusicology at the University of Amsterdam. His many works include the *Collins Music Encyclopaedia,* with J. A. Westrup; *Music in Medieval Europe,* which became a standard musicology textbook; *European Musical Instruments,* with his wife, J. Rimmer; *English Church Music in the Fourteenth Century;* and *Time, Place and Music.* He was general editor of the series "Early English Church Music" and editor of *Polyphonic Music of the Fourteenth Century.*

OBITUARIES AND OTHER SOURCES:

BOOKS

International Authors and Writers Who's Who, 9th edition, [and] *International Who's Who in Poetry,* 6th edition, Melrose, 1982.

Who's Who, 140th edition, St. Martin's, 1988.

PERIODICALS

Times (London), January 1, 1988.

* * *

HARRISON, Frank Llewelyn
See HARRISON, Francis Llewelyn

* * *

HART, Gary (Warren) 1936(?)-

PERSONAL: Surname originally Hartpence; surname legally changed, 1961; born November 28, 1936 (some sources say 1937), in Ottawa, Kan.; son of Carl (a farmer and salesman) and Nina Hartpence; married Oletha Ludwig (a teacher), 1958; children: Andrea, John. *Education:* Bethany Nazarene College, B.A., 1958; Yale University, B.D., 1961, LL.B., 1964. *Politics:* Democrat.

ADDRESSES: Home—Kittredge, Colo. *Office*—Washington, D.C.

CAREER: Admitted to bar, 1964. U.S. Department of Justice, Washington, D.C., 1964-66, began as appellate attorney, became special assistant to Secretary Stewart Udall of U.S. Department of Interior; private practice of law in Denver, Colo., 1967-70; national director of U.S. Senator George S. McGovern's presidential campaign, 1970-72; private practice of law in Denver, 1972-74; U.S. Senate, Washington, D.C., Democratic senator from Colorado, 1975-86, founder and first chairman of Environmental Study Conference, 1975, conglomerates adviser for Strategic Arms Limitation Talks (SALT II), 1977, adviser to United Nations Special Session on Disarmament, 1978, chairman of National Committee on Air Quality, 1978-81, founder of Conglomerates Military Reform Caucus, 1981; candidate for Democratic party's presidential nomination in 1984 and 1988 elections; private practice of law in Denver, 1987—; lecturer. Instructor in environmental resources at University of Colorado, 1967-70; consultant to National Water Commission and Public Land Review Commission, 1967-70; campaign organizer for Robert F. Kennedy, 1968; organizer of Democratic party's Reform Commission in Colorado, c. 1968; former member of board of commissioners of Denver Urban Renewal Authority and Park Hill Action Committee; member of board of visitors of U.S. Air Force Academy, 1975—, chairman, 1978-80. *Military service:* U.S. Naval Reserve, 1980.

WRITINGS:

Right From the Start: A Chronicle of the McGovern Campaign, Quadrangle, 1973.

(With William S. Cohen) *The Double Man* (novel), Macmillan, 1985.

The Strategies of Zeus (novel), Morrow, 1986.

(With William S. Lind) *America Can Win,* Adler & Adler, 1986.

Contributor to periodicals, including *New York Times.*

WORK IN PROGRESS: An autobiography, *One Man's Luck; Stepping Stones Across an Era: The Unfinished Story of a Generation.*

SIDELIGHTS: Gary Hart is probably the most notorious liberal politician to gain national prominence in the 1980s. Since announcing his candidacy for the Democratic party's presidential election in 1984—a candidacy in which Hart explicitly emphasized his policies instead of his personality—he has, paradoxically, been assessed extensively on the basis of his personal life. During the 1984 campaign he was subjected by the media to keen scrutiny and psychological speculation after it was disclosed that he had changed both his surname and his birthdate. At that time rumors already circulated concerning his alleged philandering. Ultimately, however, his candidacy was substantially undone on political grounds when opponent Walter Mondale ridiculed Hart's political philosophy—one calling for "new ideas"—as mere rhetoric.

In the ensuing years Hart worked to substantiate his reputation as an issues-oriented candidate by publishing *America Can Win,* an explication of his perspective on America's social and economic situations. He also softened his image as an aloof and enigmatic figure by occasionally discussing his past and his private life, and he revealed another aspect of himself by publishing two spy thrillers, *The Double Man* and *The Strategies of Zeus.* These various accomplishments enabled Hart to realize a position as the leading candidate for his party's nomination in the 1988 presidential election. But in mid-1987 allegations of sexual indiscretion once again threatened to undermine Hart's political aspirations. These rumors led to increased media attention and disclosures that, in turn, led to scandal and Hart's sudden withdrawal from the presidential race.

Although Hart achieved prominence for his politics, his background is in religion and philosophy. His father was a farmer who "drifted from job to job" according to *Time,* and his mother was a strict Christian who imposed a rigid code on her children; Hart was not allowed to smoke cigarettes or drink alcohol, nor was he allowed to dance or attend movies. In 1954 Hart enrolled at Bethany Nazarene College with intentions of studying for the ministry. At Bethany he was heavily influenced by Professor J. Prescott Johnson, who introduced him to the writings of nineteenth-century religious philosopher Soren Kierkegaard. According to Johnson, Hart was greatly influenced by Kierkegaard's work, notably his explication of the "either/or" proposition calling for either total commitment or detachment regarding causes and personal beliefs. Hart finished his studies at Bethany in 1961, but by that time his interests were turning away from specifically religious subjects. He nonetheless enrolled in Yale University's divinity school, but after graduating in 1961 he abandoned aspirations to the ministry and enrolled at Yale's law school, from which he graduated in 1964.

Upon completing his law studies Hart accepted a position as attorney for the U.S. Department of Justice. He subsequently worked in the Department of the Interior, then moved to Colorado to teach and work as an attorney and a consultant. After U.S. Senator Robert F. Kennedy began campaigning for the Democratic party's 1968 presidential nomination, Hart became increasingly active in the party, and even after the candidate's assassination Hart continued to work for other party members.

In late 1968 Hart proved instrumental in organizing the Democratic party's Reform Commission in Colorado. At this time he befriended U.S. Senator George S. McGovern, who would

become the party's presidential candidate in the 1972 election. Hart served as McGovern's campaign manager during that campaign, and his shrewd and innovative tactics were greatly responsible for McGovern's success. Perhaps foremost among Hart's contributions was his ability to correctly assess the strength of the party's liberal faction. He counseled McGovern to confirm his controversial, adamantly liberal positions on America's military and social programs. Hart also showed considerable expertise in his manipulation of McGovern's supporters within the party and in his ability to sustain McGovern's candidacy despite a seemingly constant monetary deficiency. To counter this severe lack of funds, Hart devised mail-order solicitations in which supporters were invited to contribute regular donations on a monthly basis. But though Hart's efforts enabled McGovern to win the Democratic party's nomination, they were ineffective in helping him secure the presidency from Republican incumbent Richard M. Nixon. In *Right From the Start: A Chronicle of the McGovern Campaign,* Hart attributed McGovern's defeat to the remote nature of the party's liberalism, and he described the entire experience as obvious and absurd, tragic and comic.

Following McGovern's loss, Hart returned to his law practice in Denver and wrote *Right From the Start.* In 1973 he commenced his own political career by pursuing the Democratic party's nomination for the U.S. Senate seat held by conservative Republican Peter H. Dominick. Hart won the election by an 18 percent margin, and in 1975 he assumed his new post in Washington, D.C.

In his first term Hart steadily established himself as a leading proponent of liberal causes. He proposed increases in education funding and supported national health legislation and government aid. In addition he advocated extensive revision of the nation's tax structure and urged a reduction in the country's considerable military budget.

Hart won reelection in 1981, but by that time his ambitions had shifted to the presidency. He announced his candidacy in 1982, two years before the actual election, and intensified his espousal of the liberal perspective. To many observers, Hart sought to portray himself as a pioneering innovator in American politics, one whose campaign was explicitly directed at ideas instead of image, and his slogan, "We need new ideas," came to summarize his campaign strategy. About his personality and past Hart spoke little. "I'm a private man," he contended. Nevertheless, it was discovered that Hart had changed his name from Hartpence, misrepresented his birthdate by one year, and twice altered his signature. These curious actions, which Hart only vaguely explained, were minimized by him as harmless and inconsequential. "I don't think they're issues with the people," he stated in *Time,* "though they seem to be the issues with reporters."

Allegations of sexual misconduct also circulated during Hart's first campaign. Rumors of sexual indiscretion apparently distressed staff members, although Hart dismissed such talk as mere gossip and lies. Some associates, however, later revealed an awareness of his questionable activities, and reporters eventually noted—during the 1987 scandal—that there was a general awareness among members of the press that Hart was sexually active outside his marriage.

Hart's 1984 candidacy, however, was probably most damaged by opponent Walter Mondale's ability to mock the validity of Hart's political image and his platform. Borrowing a phrase from a popular television commercial, Mondale appraised Hart's policies and asked, "Where's the beef?" With that question, posed during a nationally televised debate, Mondale succeeded in prompting skepticism regarding Hart's political enterprise, and throughout the remainder of the campaign he continued to question Hart's self-appointed role as a new leader in American politics. Mondale eventually won the Democratic party's nomination, but he lost the 1984 election to incumbent Republican Ronald Reagan.

After completing his second term in the Senate, Hart withdrew from campaign politics and turned to writing. He worked to bolster his reputation as an innovative liberal by delineating his policies in *America Can Win,* his book written with William S. Lind, and several position papers. In these writings Hart introduced his Strategic Investment Initiative, an ambitious socioeconomic program designed to promote improved education and technological development through federal investment initiatives provided to state and local governments. These initiatives, in turn, would fund expanded school years and compensatory programs for the underprivileged and would provide capital for recovering businesses and industries. Among Hart's other policies were plans to modify welfare spending and to increase the federal tax rate. Consistent with liberal policies, Hart opposed an increase in the military budget.

In the mid-1980s Hart also published two political thrillers, *The Double Man* and *The Strategies of Zeus.* Both novels concern dashing, dedicated political officials, and both works feature pointed comparisons of American and Soviet attitudes. *The Double Man,* which Hart wrote with William S. Cohen while both men were senators, was probably the more praised of the two books. It concerns a rather naive senator who discovers that a Soviet agent is manipulating terrorists to thwart key capitalists. Margaret Cannon, who reviewed *The Double Man* for the Toronto *Globe and Mail,* declared that Hart and Cohen "know their politics and philosophy, and readers won't be bored."

Hart worked without collaborators on *The Strategies of Zeus,* contending that the novel's commercial reception would serve as an "acid test" for his viability as a writer. Like Hart's earlier novel, *The Strategies of Zeus* centers on political intrigue—specifically, a plot centering on weapons negotiations—and weighs notions of patriotism and honor against those of pleasure and profit. But Hart intended the work to be instructive as well as entertaining, and he revealed that he had even considered complementing his actual narrative with essays on arms control and nuclear weapons. He told the *Washington Post* that the book, in addition to its purposes as an "acid test" and an educational adventure, would function as a vehicle for creating greater rapport with the American public. The *Post*'s Paul Taylor reported that Hart intended "to use the novel's publication as an excuse to start talking more about himself." Taylor added, though, that Hart acknowledged his own inability to discuss his past and private life.

It was questionable conduct in Hart's private life that nearly sabotaged his bid for the Democratic party's nomination in the 1988 presidential election. In early 1987 Hart showed surprising political strength—despite enormous debts from the 1984 campaign and a conspicuous lack of peer support—and was the favored candidate. In May, however, reports indicated that Hart was involved with a model, eventually identified as Donna Rice. Angered, Hart denied the rumors and challenged reporters to track his activities. The *Miami Herald* accepted Hart's challenge, and on May 5 the newspaper published evidence revealing Hart's ties with Rice. As Hart continued to vehemently deny that he had compromised his marriage through

his relationship with Rice, indications of other sexual indiscretions circulated in the press. As unfavorable publicity increasingly threatened his campaign, Hart suddenly withdrew from the race. The *Washington Post,* which reportedly possessed evidence of Hart's philandering, consequently abandoned plans to publish their findings.

Then, in a startling move in mid-December, 1987, Hart announced that he was reentering the 1988 Democratic presidential race. "There is no shame in losing, only in quitting," he declared. Addressing a cheering crowd of supporters in New Hampshire, Hart explained, "My family—Lee, John, and Andrea—understands the difficulties ahead. They are totally behind this step because we believe in ourselves and the American people."

His decision prompted a barrage of queries into his motives for renewing the presidential campaign. Some political strategists argued that he sought federal matching funds for campaign debts, including more than $1 million still owed from his 1984 bid for the Democratic presidential nomination. Others claimed that despite the humiliation of his earlier withdrawal, Hart retained a loyal political following and considerable political appeal. That following proved insubstantial, however, and in March, 1988, Hart ended his candidacy.

AVOCATIONAL INTERESTS: Reading, sculpting.

BIOGRAPHICAL/CRITICAL SOURCES:

BOOKS

Hart, Gary, *Right From the Start: A Chronicle of the McGovern Campaign,* Quadrangle, 1973.

PERIODICALS

Ann Arbor News, October 5, 1987.
Chicago Tribune, May 4, 1987, May 5, 1987, May 6, 1987, May 7, 1987, May 8, 1987, May 9, 1987, May 10, 1987, June 8, 1987, August 24, 1987, December 16, 1987, December 17, 1987, December 20, 1987, December 21, 1987, December 22, 1987, December 30, 1987, March 12, 1988.
Detroit News, May 5, 1985.
Globe and Mail (Toronto), July 20, 1985, December 12, 1987.
Los Angeles Times, June 27, 1985, May 5, 1987, May 6, 1987, May 7, 1987, May 8, 1987, May 9, 1987, May 10, 1987, June 17, 1987, August 26, 1987, September 9, 1987, September 10, 1987, December 16, 1987, December 17, 1987, December 18, 1987, December 21, 1987, February 13, 1988.
Miami Herald, May 3, 1987, May 4, 1987.
New Republic, May 18, 1987.
Newsweek, May 6, 1985, May 18, 1987.
New York Times, January 25, 1987, May 4, 1987, May 5, 1987, May 6, 1987, May 7, 1987, May 8, 1987, May 9, 1987, May 10, 1987, December 16, 1987, December 17, 1987, December 18, 1987, December 20, 1987, December 21, 1987, December 25, 1987, March 12, 1988.
New York Times Book Review, May 5, 1985, June 8, 1986, January 25, 1987.
New York Times Magazine, May 3, 1987.
People, June 15, 1987.
Time, March 26, 1984, September 21, 1987.
Washington Post, December 7, 1986, April 13, 1987, May 5, 1987, May 6, 1987, May 7, 1987, May 8, 1987, May 9, 1987, May 10, 1987, September 9, 1987, September 10, 1987, September 27, 1987, December 16, 1987, December 17, 1987, December 18, 1987, December 19, 1987, December 22, 1987, December 24, 1987, March 4, 1988.
Washington Post Book World, April 7, 1985, May 4, 1986, December 28, 1986.
Washington Post Magazine, July 12, 1987.*

—*Sketch by Les Stone*

* * *

HAU'OFA, Epeli 1939-

PERSONAL: Born December 7, 1939, in Papua New Guinea; son of missionaries; married wife, Barbara, 1966. *Education:* Attended University of New England, 1961-64, and McGill University, 1965-68; Australian National University, Ph.D., 1975.

ADDRESSES: Office—School of Social and Economic Development, University of the South Pacific, P.O. Box 1168, Suva, Fiji.

CAREER: University of Papua New Guinea, Port Moresby, senior tutor in sociology, 1968-70; University of the South Pacific, Suva, Fiji, research fellow, 1975-77; University of New South Wales, Kensington, Australia, visiting fellow, 1977; deputy private secretary to the King of Tonga, with office in Nuku'alofa, 1978-81; University of the South Pacific, director of Rural Development Centre in Nuku'alofa, 1981-83, reader in sociology, 1983—. Visiting fellow at Centre for Pacific Studies, University of Auckland, 1985; consultant to World Bank and Asian Development Bank.

WRITINGS:

Our Crowded Islands, Institute of Pacific Studies, University of the South Pacific, 1977.
Corned Beef and Tapioca: A Report on the Food Distribution Systems in Tonga, Development Studies Centre, Australian National University, 1979.
Mekeo: Inequality and Ambivalence in the Village Society, Australian National University Press, 1981.
Tales of the Tikongs (stories), Longman Paul, 1983.
Kisses in the Nederends, Penguin, 1987.

Co-founder and co-editor of *Faikava.*

SIDELIGHTS: Epeli Hau'ofa's fiction reflects a highly developed sense of the comic. The stories that comprise the *Tales of the Tikongs* describe the foibles and gentle follies of life on an imaginary South Pacific island so small it cannot be found on a map without the use of a microscope. Though Hau'ofa seems to admire the skills of the small-time swindler, his work becomes satirical when his targets are organized religion and government, or other institutions that victimize the simple people of the South Pacific. His stories have been compared favorably to the more serious social commentaries that followed the independence and development of the Third World.

* * *

HAVILAND, Virginia 1911-1988

OBITUARY NOTICE—See index for *CA* sketch: Born May 21 (one source says May 11), 1911, in Rochester, N.Y.; died of a stroke, January 6, 1988, in Washington, D.C. Librarian and author of children's books. Haviland devoted much of her life to promoting and improving the quality of juvenile literature. Her career began at the Boston Public Library, where she subsequently worked as reader's adviser for children until join-

ing the Library of Congress in 1963. As director of the Children's Books Section there Haviland reorganized the division into its present form now called the Children's Literature Center. In addition to her library functions, she served as president of the Children's Services Division of the American Library Association. Haviland wrote *Legends of North America* and *The Open-Hearted Audience* and edited sixteen titles in the "Favorite Fairy Tales" series published by Little, Brown between 1959 and 1973. She also contributed reviews on children's books to various periodicals, among them the *Washington Post* and *Horn Book.* For her overall contribution to children's literature, Haviland received the Catholic Library Association's Regina Medal and an award from Grolier Publishing.

OBITUARIES AND OTHER SOURCES:

BOOKS

Who's Who in America, 42nd edition, Marquis, 1982.

PERIODICALS

New York Times, January 9, 1988.
School Library Journal, February, 1988.
Washington Post, January 8, 1988.

* * *

HAWORTH-BOOTH, Mark 1944-

PERSONAL: Surname is pronounced "*Hay*-worth"; born August 20, 1944, in Westow, Yorkshire, England; son of Anthony Brough (a contractor and journalist) and Eva (a housewife; maiden name, Holm) Haworth-Booth; married Rosemary Joanna Miles (a curator), July 19, 1979; children: Emily, Alice. *Education:* Cambridge University, English tripos, 1966; University of Edinburgh, Post Graduate Diploma in Fine Art, 1969. *Religion:* Church of England.

ADDRESSES: Office—Department of Prints, Drawings, and Photographs, Victoria and Albert Museum, South Kensington, London SW7 2RL, England.

CAREER: City Art Gallery, Manchester, England, assistant keeper, 1969-70; Victoria and Albert Museum, London, England, assistant keeper of circulation, 1970-77, curator of photographs, 1977—.

WRITINGS:

E. McKnight Kauffer: A Designer and His Public, Gordon Fraser, 1979.
Donald McCullin, Collins Sons, 1982.
(With Brian Coe) *A Guide to Early Photographic Processes,* Victoria and Albert Museum, 1983.
(Editor) *The Golden Age of British Photography, 1839-1900,* Aperture, 1984.
(With David Miller) *Bill Brandt: Behind the Camera,* Aperture, 1985.

Contributor of poems to magazines, including *Spectator, New Statesman,* and *London Magazine.*

WORK IN PROGRESS: An exhibition and book "which attempt to anatomize the photographic medium as practiced in the 1980s," publication by the Victoria and Albert Museum expected in 1989; research on the photography of the 1850s.

SIDELIGHTS: Mark Haworth-Booth's *E. McKnight Kauffer: A Designer and His Public* is both a biography and a critique of the modernist advertising designer's social concerns. Celina Fox wrote in the *Times Literary Supplement:* "Mr. Haworth-Booth's book is imaginatively conceived and meticulously executed."

A Guide to Early Photographic Processes is a step-by-step guide for identifying the photographic processes used from 1840 to 1914. It should enable the reader to distinguish among five types of negative, three types of transparency, and twenty-seven types of print. Critic Colin Ford told readers of the *Times Literary Supplement* that Haworth-Booth's illustrations "are always revealing, excellently printed" to achieve "a better 'feel' of the processes than usual."

Haworth-Booth also edited the acclaimed *Golden Age of British Photography, 1839-1900,* which studies the work of photographic pioneers of the Victorian era, including William Henry Fox Talbot, who invented calotype, Roger Fenton, who covered the Crimean War with his photographs, and Julia Margaret Cameron, who is famous for her portrait studies. A reviewer in *New Yorker* declared that the "large and faithful-looking reproductions of these early calotypes and albumen, carbon, and platinum prints are stunning."

Haworth-Booth told *CA:* "The Victoria and Albert Museum holds the national collection of the art of photography in the United Kingdom. As curator, I am responsible for looking after a collection of three hundred thousand photographs and for adding new acquisitions, mounting exhibitions, and editing and writing books bringing this collection to new audiences in Great Britain, the United States, and elsewhere.

"I am interested in photography of the 1850s because the medium was then in its pristine heyday and exploring roles which later became characteristic of the medium. Looking at the pioneering days is a good way to crystallize new ideas about the nature of photography—such as, for example, the interesting relationship between photography and detection (made explicit in the writings of Charles Dickens)."

BIOGRAPHICAL/CRITICAL SOURCES:

PERIODICALS

New Yorker, November 26, 1984.
Times Literary Supplement, January 25, 1980, June 24, 1983.

* * *

HAYES, Bartlett (Harding, Jr.) 1904-1988

OBITUARY NOTICE—See index for *CA* sketch: Born August 5, 1904, in Andover, Mass.; died of congestive heart failure, February 14, 1988, in Peterboro, N.H. Educator, administrator, and author. Hayes served as director of the Addison Gallery of American Art at Phillips Academy for nearly thirty years. During that time he held a concurrent position as chairman of the school's art department. In addition, he assumed a major role in both the implementation of a visual arts program and the establishment of studio art courses, whereby the Addison Gallery's art collection became an integral part of classroom study at Phillips Academy. He also helped generate funds to build the new Art Center that opened there in 1963. After leaving his posts at the Phillips Academy and Addison Gallery, Hayes continued his interest in art through affiliations with the Smithsonian Institution, the Boston Museum of Fine Arts, and other organizations. Among his publications are *The Layman's Guide to Modern Art* and *Tradition Becomes Innovation: Modern Religious Architecture in America.*

OBITUARIES AND OTHER SOURCES:

BOOKS

Directory of American Scholars, Volume I: *History,* 8th edition, Bowker, 1982.

PERIODICALS

New York Times, February 16, 1988.

* * *

HEGESIPPUS
See SCHONFIELD, Hugh J(oseph)

* * *

HELION, Jean 1904-1987

OBITUARY NOTICE: Born April 21, 1904, in Couterne, Normandy, France; died of pneumonia, October 27, 1987 (one source says October 28), in Paris, France. Artist and author. An architectural draftsman who taught himself painting, Helion was active in the abstractionist movement in Paris during the 1930s. His canvases, featuring pastel-colored mechanical figures in rhythmic sequences, were first exhibited in Paris in 1927 and subsequently shown in New York and other American cities. Helion immigrated to the United States and was in the process of becoming an American citizen when World War II broke out. He returned to France to fight the Nazis, was captured by them, and spent nearly two years in a German prison camp. He escaped and returned to America, where he wrote *They Shall Not Have Me,* a book about his wartime activities. Helion's experiences during the war changed his philosophy on art, and he took to representational painting, because, as he stated in a *Time* interview quoted by the *New York Times,* "A man who has been locked up for a few years knows the value of reality." Helion's later paintings feature mundane subjects—umbrellas, watermelons, bowls of soup—as symbols of everyday life. He also lectured on painting technique and wrote exhibition catalogs.

OBITUARIES AND OTHER SOURCES:

BOOKS

Current Biography, H. W. Wilson, 1943, January, 1988.
The International Who's Who, 51st edition, Europa, 1987.

PERIODICALS

Los Angeles Times, October 29, 1987.
New York Times, October 30, 1987.

* * *

HELLER, David 1957-

PERSONAL: Born November 11, 1957, in Bridgeport, Conn.; son of Marcus and Blanche Heller. *Education:* Harvard University, B.A. (summa cum laude), 1979; University of Michigan, M.A., 1982, Ph.D., 1984. *Politics:* Independent. *Religion:* "Ecumenical."

ADDRESSES: Home—17 Durham St., Apt. 4F, Boston, Mass. 02115. *Agent*—Doe Coover, 168 Grove St., Medford, Mass. 02155.

CAREER: Writer.

MEMBER: American Psychological Association, P.E.N. New England, Phi Beta Kappa, Harvard Alumni Association, University of Michigan Alumni Association.

AWARDS, HONORS: White House fellow finalist, 1985; Roothbert Humanities Fellowship, 1985; *Power in Psychotherapeutic Practice* was chosen as a Macmillan Behavioral Sciences Book Club Selection, 1985.

WRITINGS:

Power in Psychotherapeutic Practice, Macmillan, 1985.
(With Dan Goleman) *The Pleasures of Psychology,* New American Library, 1986.
The Children's God, University of Chicago Press, 1986.
Dear God: Children's Letters to God, Doubleday, 1987.
Talking to Your Child About God, Bantam, in press.

Author of column on children and religion, syndicated by Religious News Service. Contributor to magazines, including *Psychology Today* and *Working Mother,* and to newspapers, including *Boston Herald, Sun* (Baltimore), *Washington Times, Sun-Times* (Chicago), *Miami Herald,* and *Newsday.*

WORK IN PROGRESS: The Story of Matt and Allison, a children's book about God, with Elizabeth Sobrero; *The Soul of a Man.*

SIDELIGHTS: David Heller told *CA:* "I am interested in the cultivation of spiritual values in popular culture. I would like to contribute to that in some meaningful and influential way."

The Children's God is derived from forty interviews of children, conducted by psychologist David Heller in Ann Arbor, Michigan. He interviewed boys and girls, aged four to twelve, of several religious faiths and concluded that sex, age, and religious orientation influence a child's perspective of God.

Heller added: "My own religious views are my motivation and source of guidance in all my writing. I believe in a great and uncategorizable God who is beyond religion and science, a God who is visible only with keen perception and personalized imagery—the tools of the human heart."

BIOGRAPHICAL/CRITICAL SOURCES:

PERIODICALS

Psychology Today, December, 1985.
Washington Post Book World, July 13, 1986.

* * *

HELLER, John 1896(?)-1987

OBITUARY NOTICE: Born c. 1896; died of pneumonia, December 7, 1987, in Tarrytown, N.Y. Candy manufacturer and author. Heller, who immigrated to the United States in 1940, established the Heller Candy company in New York City. He wrote a number of books, including *Memoir of a Reluctant Capitalist.*

OBITUARIES AND OTHER SOURCES:

PERIODICALS

New York Times, December 12, 1987.

* * *

HELMS, Jesse (Alexander, Jr.) 1921-

BRIEF ENTRY: Born October 18, 1921, in Monroe, N.C. American politician, business executive, television and radio commentator, journalist, and author. Helms has served as a U.S. senator from North Carolina since 1973. A staunch conservative who attracted a wide following, Helms became one

of the most influential senators in the early 1980s during the administration of President Ronald Reagan. In 1981 Helms introduced a controversial bill in the Senate that proposed outlawing abortion at any time during a pregnancy. The bill declared that human life, as protected by the U.S. Constitution, begins at the moment of conception. Helms also sponsored bills to permit prayer in public schools, prohibit the busing of students solely for integration, and require a balanced federal budget. In 1981 he became chairman of the Senate Committee on Agriculture, Nutrition, and Forestry.

Earlier in his career Helms had served as city editor of the North Carolina *Raleigh Times* and spent four years as a member of the Raleigh City Council. For twelve years prior to his election to the U.S. Senate in 1972, he was executive vice-president of the Capital Broadcasting Company, operator of WRAL-TV, radio station WRAL, and the Tobacco Radio Network. During that time Helms wrote and televised strongly conservative commentaries. His writings include *Where Free Men Shall Stand: A Sobering Look at the Supertaxing, Superspending, Superbureaucracy in Washington* (Zondervan, 1976) and *''A Lot of Human Beings Have Been Born Bums'': Twenty Years of the Words of Senator No* (Carolina Independent Publications, 1984), edited by Grace Nordhoff and illustrated by Michael Kuczynski. The senator also contributed to *The Defense of America: From Assured Destruction to Assured Survival* (Texas Policy Institute, 1983), edited by Albion Knight and David S. Sullivan. *Addresses: Home*—1513 Caswell St., Raleigh, N. C. 27608. *Office*—409 Dirksen Senate Office Bldg., Washington, D. C. 20510.

BIOGRAPHICAL/CRITICAL SOURCES:

BOOKS

Current Biography, H. W. Wilson, 1979.
Political Profiles: The Nixon/Ford Years, Facts on File, 1979.
Who's Who in American Politics, 11th edition, Bowker, 1987.

PERIODICALS

Newsweek, January 3, 1983, January 10, 1983, October 31, 1983, September 17, 1984, November 19, 1984.
Time, October 31, 1983, April 30, 1984, September 24, 1984.
U.S. News and World Report, November 15, 1982, August 29, 1983, October 15, 1984, November 19, 1984.
Village Voice, September 4, 1984.

* * *

HENBEST, Nigel 1951-

PERSONAL: Born May 6, 1951, in Manchester, Lancashire, England; son of Harold Bernard (a professor) and Rosalind Eve Skone (a psychiatrist; maiden name, James) Henbest. *Education:* University of Leicester, B.S. (with first class honors), 1972; Cambridge University, M.S., 1975.

ADDRESSES: Home and office—55 Colomb St., London SE10 9EZ, England.

CAREER: University of Leicester, Leicester, England, research assistant at Mount Etna, Sicily 1976–77; *New Scientist,* London, England, astronomy consultant, 1980—; Royal Greenwich Observatory, Sussex, England, consultant, 1982-85; British Astronomical Association, London, editor, 1985-87. Broadcaster on British radio and British Broadcasting Corporation World Service.

MEMBER: British Astronomical Association, Royal Astronomical Society, Association of British Science Writers.

AWARDS, HONORS: Special award for a series on engineering and technology from the New York Academy of Sciences, 1978, for *Space Frontiers.*

WRITINGS:

The Exploding Universe, Macmillan, 1979.
Spotter's Guide to the Night Sky (juvenile), illustrations by Michael Roffe, Mayflower, 1979.
Mysteries of the Universe, Van Nostrand, 1981 (published in England as *The Mysterious Universe,* Ebury Press, 1981).
(With Michael Marten) *The New Astronomy,* Cambridge University Press, 1983.
(Editor) *Observing the Universe,* Blackwell, 1984.
Comets, Stars, Planets, Admiral, 1985.
Halley's Comet, New Science Publications, 1985.

WITH HEATHER COUPER

Space Frontiers (juvenile), edited by Christopher Cooper, Viking, 1978.
All About Space (juvenile), edited by Cooper, Marshall Cavendish, 1981, EMC Publishing, 1983.
The Restless Universe, Philip & Son, 1982.
Astronomy (juvenile), F. Watts, 1983.
Physics (juvenile), F. Watts, 1983.
The Planets, Pan Books, 1985, published as *New Worlds: In Search of Planets,* Addison-Wesley, 1986.
The Sun, F. Watts, 1986.
The Moon, F. Watts, 1986.
Galaxies and Quasars, F. Watts, 1986.
Telescopes and Observatories, F. Watts, 1987.
Spaceprobes and Satellites, F. Watts, 1987.
Guide to the Galaxy, Cambridge University Press, 1988.
The Stars, Pan Books, 1988.

TELEVISION SCRIPTS

(With G. Jones) ''IRAS: The Infrared Eye,'' British Broadcasting Corporation (BBC-TV), 1985.
(Consultant) ''Halley's Comet,'' BBC-TV, 1986.
(With Couper) ''The Planets'' (based on Couper and Henbest's book of the same name), Moving Picture Company, 1986.

OTHER

Columnist for *The Independent* and *New Scientist.*

Contributor to encyclopedias, including *Encyclopaedia Britannica, Encyclopedia of Astronomy and Space,* and *Encyclopedia of Space Travel and Astronomy.* Also contributor to periodicals, including *Sunday Times, Guardian, Popular Astronomy, Astronomy, Christian Science Monitor,* and *Newton.*

SIDELIGHTS: Considered clear and understandable by critics, Nigel Henbest's books fill a literary black hole by guiding the reader through many of the most important achievements in astronomy and science in the past twenty-five years. In *The Exploding Universe,* Henbest provides a synopsis of the most outstanding developments in the sciences, from cosmology to physics, in the 1970's. Henbest and co-author Heather Couper, in *New Worlds: In Search of the Planets,* provide new information about the planets gathered by the fleet of interplanetary spaceprobes sent out during the 1980's and update current information in language understandable to the general reading public.

In *Observing the Universe,* Henbest compiles a selection of astronomical articles by acknowledged authorities which appeared in *New Scientist* from 1980 to 1983. The focus of this book is on observational techniques—optical and radio tele-

scopes, highly sophisticated spaceprobes, devices to detect gravity waves—but also includes historical articles, works on radio astronomy, and a piece on cosmic chemistry. *The New Astronomy* also concentrates on observational techniques and provides depictions of new findings gathered by radio, infrared, ultraviolet, X-ray, and gamma ray exploration of space. Colin Ronan, writing for the *Times Literary Supplement,* claimed that Henbest's *New Astronomy* is "the first [book] to present and explain 'new astronomy' to a wide public—[and] deserves every success."

Henbest told *CA:* "Astronomy is one of the few areas of science that the average person finds fascinating. By writing about the sky, its beauty and its mysteries, an author can not only grip his audience, but also impart—in a most gentle way—an understanding of how science and scientists work.

"When I began my career as an author, I was doing research at Cambridge, under the then Astronomer Royal. As a research scientist, I was learning more and more—about less and less! In my case, that meant the exploding gases from a supernova that went off over four hundred years ago.

"At the same time, there were very few people with a professional background who could—or who wanted to—explain astronomy to the public. So I moved into the field, and (somewhat to my surprise) found a virtually unlimited market for astronomy titles."

AVOCATIONAL INTERESTS: Travel, good and homemade wine, vegetarian food, and music.

BIOGRAPHICAL/CRITICAL SOURCES:

PERIODICALS

Times Literary Supplement, February 17, 1984.

* * *

HENDERSON, Linda Dalrymple 1948-

PERSONAL: Born January 22, 1948, in Warren, Pa.; daughter of Donald D. (an engineer) and Elizabeth (a teacher of mathematics; maiden name, Phillips) Dalrymple; married George Ervin Henderson (an attorney), August 22, 1970; children: Andrew Dalrymple, Elizabeth Yoe. *Education:* Dickinson College, A.B. (summa cum laude), 1969; Yale University, M.Phil., 1972, Ph.D., 1975.

ADDRESSES: Home—Austin, Tex. *Office*—Department of Art, University of Texas at Austin, Austin, Tex. 78712.

CAREER: Museum of Fine Arts, Houston, Tex, associate curator, 1974-76, curator, 1976-77; University of Texas at Austin, assistant professor, 1978-84, associate professor of art history, 1984—.

MEMBER: International Society of the Arts, Sciences, and Technology, College Art Association of America, Phi Beta Kappa, Phi Kappa Phi.

AWARDS, HONORS: Vasari Award from Dallas Museum, 1983, for *The Fourth Dimension and Non-Euclidian Geometry in Modern Art;* Phi Kappa Phi Faculty Scholar Award, 1985.

WRITINGS:

The Fourth Dimension and Non-Euclidian Geometry in Modern Art, Princeton University Press, 1983.

Contributor to art journals. Guest editor of *Art Journal,* spring, 1987.

WORK IN PROGRESS: A book that will examine the impact of mysticism and occultism on art and theory in France and America in the early years of the twentieth century, publication expected in about 1990.

SIDELIGHTS: Linda Dalrymple Henderson told *CA:* "My research focuses on modernism in the early twentieth century, a period in which a variety of artistic styles rapidly succeeded one another and the notion of totally abstract art was born. I believe these developments must be seen in the context of the radical redefinitions of reality and of the self that occurred in the late nineteenth and early twentieth centuries. My 1983 book, *The Fourth Dimension and Non-Euclidean Geometry in Modern Art,* examines the way in which new ideas about the nature of space (i.e., four-dimensional space and curved, non-Euclidean spaces) encouraged artists to turn away from the three-dimensional visual world as the arbiter of their art and to make bold formal innovations. For artists before World War I, such as the French cubists, these ideas had nothing to do with Albert Einstein's theory of relativity, which was popularized widely only after 1919.

"Currently, I am exploring other aspects of the new paradigms of reality and self in the early twentieth century and the way in which these changes encouraged an openness toward mystical and occult ideas among early modern artists as well as writers and musicians. The discovery of X rays, for example, offered artists a completely new image of reality that was applauded equally by scientists and by occultists who linked X rays to clairvoyant vision. Indeed, the line between the 'hard' sciences and mysticism and occultism was much less clear at the turn of the century than it is now. Thus, the psychologists who offered new information about the complexity of the perceiving self in this period, which preceded the popularization of Sigmund Freud after World War I, were often involved in psychical research and even spiritualism. I see my work, then, as an effort to recover some of the lost intellectual context of the early twentieth century, a context that has been mistakenly oversimplified by the many authors who cite Einstein and Freud as the major determinants of modern thought."

BIOGRAPHICAL/CRITICAL SOURCES:

PERIODICALS

Times Literary Supplement, December 30, 1983.

* * *

HENFIL
See SOUZA FILHO, Henrique de

* * *

HENSON, James Maury 1936-
(Jim Henson)

PERSONAL: Known professionally as Jim Henson; born September 24, 1936, in Greenville, Miss.; son of Paul Ransom (an agronomist) and Elizabeth Marcella (Brown) Henson; married Jane Anne Nebel (a puppeteer and business executive), May 28, 1959; children: Lisa Marie, Cheryl Lee, Brian David, John Paul, Heather Beth. *Education:* University of Maryland, B.A., 1960.

ADDRESSES: Office—Henson Associates, 117 East 69th St., New York, N.Y. 10021.

CAREER: Puppeteer; creator of the Muppets (puppets), 1954; co-founder and president of Henson Associates (television and

film production company), New York, N.Y., and London, England, 1957—. Producer of "Sam and Friends" (daily program) for WRC-TV, Washington, D.C., 1955-61; guest performer on television programs, including "The Ed Sullivan Show," "Today," "The Tonight Show," and "The Jimmy Dean Show"; creator and puppeteer of Muppet segments for "Sesame Street" television series, beginning in 1969; producer, writer, and performer for "The Muppet Show" series for Independent Television Corp., 1976-81; producer and director of "Fraggle Rock" series for Home Box Office, 1983-87; executive producer of "Muppet Babies" animated series for Columbia Broadcasting System (CBS-TV), 1984—; executive producer of "Fraggle Rock" animated series for National Broadcasting Company (NBC-TV); producer of more than two hundred television commercials.

Producer and director of television specials, including "Muppets on Puppets," 1968, "The Muppets Go Hollywood," 1979, "Of Muppets and Men," 1981, "The Muppets Go to the Movies," 1981, "The Fantastic Miss Piggy Show," 1982, "The Storyteller," 1987, "The Tale of the Bunny Picnic," 1987, and "Down at Fraggle Rock: Behind the Scenes," 1987.

Producer and/or director of motion pictures, including "The Muppet Movie," 1979, "The Great Muppet Caper," 1981, "The Dark Crystal," 1982, "Muppets Take Manhattan," 1984, and "Labyrinth," 1986. Puppeteer for motion picture "Follow That Bird," 1985. Producer of short films, including "Time Piece," 1965, "Run, Run," 1967, "Organized Brain," 1968, and "Final Speech," 1975.

Performer, as Muppet characters, on sound recordings, including "The Muppet Show" album, 1977, "The Muppet Show II," Arista, 1978, "The Muppet Movie," Atlantic, 1979, "A Christmas Together," RCA, 1979, "The Great Muppet Caper," Atlantic, 1981, "A Rocky Mountain Holiday," RCA, 1983, "The Muppets Take Manhattan," Warner, 1984, "Silly Songs," IJE, 1984, and "Presenting Fraggle Rock," CBS Records, 1987.

MEMBER: Puppeteers of America (president, 1962-63), American Federation of Television and Radio Artists (AFTRA), National Academy of Television Arts and Sciences, Directors Guild of America, American Film Institute, American Center of Union Internationale de la Marionette (president of board of directors, 1974-80; president emeritus, 1980—), Henson Foundation (president), Writers Guild, Screen Actors Guild.

AWARDS, HONORS: Seventeen Emmy Awards from the National Academy of Television Arts and Sciences, including those for "Sam and Friends" (best local entertainment program), 1958; for "Sesame Street" (outstanding individual achievement in children's programming), 1973-74 and 1975-76; for "The Muppet Show" (outstanding comedy-variety or music series), 1978; for "The Muppet Show With Carol Burnett" segment (outstanding writing in a variety, music, or comedy program), 1980-81; and for "The Storyteller—'Hans My Hedgehog'" (outstanding children's program), 1987.

Oscar nomination from the Academy of Motion Picture Arts and Sciences, 1965, for "Time Piece" (best live action short subject); award for outstanding children's show of the year from National Education Television, 1968, for the special, "Muppets on Puppets"; Entertainer of the Year Award from the American Guild of Variety Artists, 1976; eight Grammy Awards from the National Academy of Recording Arts and Sciences, including those for "The Muppet Show" album, 1979, and for best children's record, 1981. Citation from the Film Advisory Board, 1979, for "The Muppet Movie"; three George Foster Peabody Awards for excellence in television broadcasting, including one in 1979; awards for best television script of the year from the Writers Guild, 1979 and 1980, for "The Muppet Show"; First Founders Award from National Academy of Television Arts and Sciences, 1981; President's Fellow Award from Rhode Island School of Design, 1982; International Emmy from the International Council of the National Academy of Television Arts and Sciences, 1983, for the "Fraggle Rock" series; two Oscars from the British Academy of Television Arts; Award for Cablecasting Excellence, 1984, for "Fraggle Rock"; Humanitas Prize from the Human Family Educational and Cultural Institute, 1985; special recommendation from Central Council for Children's Welfare in Japan for "Fraggle Rock" series, 1987.

WRITINGS:

(And producer and director) "Time Piece" (screenplay), Contemporary Films, 1965.

(Co-author; and producer and director) "The Cube" (teleplay), broadcast by NBC-TV, 1969.

The Muppet Show Book, Abrams, 1978.

WORK IN PROGRESS: Another Muppet movie; five "non-Muppet" projects.

SIDELIGHTS: Jim Henson is widely regarded as the most successful puppeteer in history. Through the mediums of television and film, Henson's "Muppets"—distinctively furry, wide-mouthed, and pop-eyed creatures that are a cross between a puppet and a marionette—have become familiar to hundreds of millions of people around the world. Along with such Muppet stars as Big Bird, Kermit the Frog, Miss Piggy, and Oscar the Grouch, Henson has also created many other imaginative creatures for television and motion pictures. His films "The Dark Crystal" and "Labyrinth," considered milestones in celluloid monster making, combine traditional puppetry techniques with remote-control electronics to animate an assortment of bizarre beings.

Henson is the first puppeteer to adapt his craft exclusively to the visual requirements of television and film. Getting his start in puppetry while still in high school, he turned professional as a college freshman when a Washington, D.C., television station gave him his own five-minute-long late-night show called "Sam and His Friends." Henson first came to national attention in the late 1950s by making a series of television commercials for dog food, using one of his first Muppets, Rowlf the Dog. In designing Rowlf and his early sidekick Kermit the Frog, Henson rejected the painted wood construction of most puppets and marionettes of the time as insufficiently expressive for the all-seeing eye of television. Instead, he crafted his creatures out of flexible, fabric-covered foam rubber, giving them supple bodies and huge mouths that helped them convey a broad range of emotions. By the mid-1960s Henson and Rowlf were being featured on the "Jimmy Dean," "Tonight," and "Ed Sullivan" shows, and in 1968 the puppeteer broadcast his first special, "Muppets on Puppets," for National Educational Television.

The Muppets soon reached superstardom when they moved to "Sesame Street," the innovative children's television show that made its nationwide debut on educational stations in November, 1969. Produced by the nonprofit Children's Television Workshop, "Sesame Street" successfully adapted the flashy imagery and quick pacing of television commercials to teach preschoolers about letters, numbers, and social values. Joining

a regular cast of children and adults, the Muppets enlivened the show with their unpredictable antics and endeared themselves to audiences of all ages with their sharply etched and humanly fallible personalities. By the early 1970s an estimated six million of the three- to five-year-olds in the United States were regularly watching "Sesame Street," which was only a fraction of the show's total audience.

"Sesame Street" introduced many now-famous Muppets, including Ernie and Bert, two argumentative friends; Oscar the Grouch, a shaggy misanthrope who lives in a garbage can; the Cookie Monster, a wild being consumed by his lust for cookies; and Big Bird, an eight-foot-tall canary with the mind of a young child. Though Henson designed and built the Muppets, their individual characters were developed by a loose-knit creative team that also included puppeteer Frank Oz, chief writer Jerry Juhl, and the show's producer, Jon Stone. Henson and Oz acted as "Sesame Street"'s principal puppeteers, with Henson animating and speaking for Kermit, Rowlf, and Ernie, among others, and Oz personifying Bert, Cookie Monster, and the easygoing Grover.

The huge success of "Sesame Street" primed audiences for Henson's first weekly television program, "The Muppet Show," a syndicated half-hour series that premiered in September, 1976. Produced in England by Henson, in partnership with Lew Grade of the Independent Television Corporation, "The Muppet Show" was an instant hit that rapidly rose to become the top syndicated television show in the United States and the most popular first-run program in the world. At the height of its phenomenal success, approximately 250 million adults and children were watching the show in one hundred different countries. Henson drew again on the talents of Oz and Juhl to help him create a new crew of popular Muppets for the show, including Fozzie Bear; the rock musician Dr. Teeth and his drummer, Animal, a boisterous Muppet given to shouting demands like "Woman!" at odd intervals; and Oz's most outstanding character, the egotistical but sensitive Miss Piggy—the world's only porcine bathing beauty. "The Muppet Show" also featured frequent guest appearances by human celebrities who engaged in good-humored banter with the Muppets, usually on the losing side.

"The Muppet Show" was still going strong in 1981, but Henson decided to end the series that year to pursue new challenges. By then his humble cloth puppets had spawned a New York City-based business enterprise, Henson Associates, whose activities included licensing scores of children's books and records on Muppet themes, producing industrial films starring the Muppets, and merchandising a host of minor spin-off products, ranging from Big Bird lunch pails to Kermit coffee mugs. In 1983, Henson launched a new puppet show called "Fraggle Rock" that aired on the Home Box Office cable television network in the United States and was also seen in ninety other countries. "Fraggle Rock" featured a new family of Henson characters—fun-loving Fraggles, tiny mechanical workaholics called Doozers, and seven-foot giants known as Gorgs—to make a lighthearted point about the need for social cooperation and tolerance. During the following year, Henson produced the Emmy Award-winning show "Muppet Babies" for the Columbia Broadcasting Service (CBS-TV), airing on Saturday mornings and showing the Muppets in their infancy. In 1987 Henson's next Saturday morning series appeared—the animated "Fraggle Rock." The same year, the first of eight specials for the National Broadcasting Corporation (NBC-TV) began airing. Titled "The Storyteller," the productions are based on European folktales and involve human actors and the use of animatronic creatures instead of Muppets.

Increasingly, though, Henson turned to film because it afforded opportunities for expanding the technical limitations of puppetry and for exploring more sophisticated themes. He produced his first full-length feature film, "The Muppet Movie," in 1979, scoring a major hit with both young and mature audiences. A satire on the American fast-food industry and the lure of show-business fame, the film featured Kermit as a talented swamp singer who sets out on a cross-country trip to make his name in Hollywood. Along the way he encounters a variety of other Muppets—including the amorous Miss Piggy—and narrowly escapes the clutches of Doc Hopper, the owner of a chain of frog legs restaurants who wants to force Kermit to pose in ads for him. "The Muppet Movie" boasted some impressive feats in puppeteering, including the opening scene showing Kermit strumming a banjo on his swamp log, which Henson animated from an air-tight tank below the water, and a sequence depicting the amiable frog riding a bicycle. Two later Muppet films, "The Great Muppet Caper" in 1981 and "The Muppets Take Manhattan" in 1984, continued the Kermit-Miss Piggy love story with new madcap adventures and were also critical and commercial successes.

While maintaining an active association with the Muppets, Henson also created two extraordinary fantasy films: "The Dark Crystal" (1982) and "Labyrinth" (1986). "The Dark Crystal," conceptualized by Henson and directed by Henson and Frank Oz, features no human characters at all but rather an assortment of fantastic beings designed by the English fantasy artist Brian Froud and animated by puppetry, electronics, and special effects. The twenty-six million dollar film is set in the mythical past, with marauding, vulture-like creatures called the Skeksis plotting to get possession of a magic crystal that will allow them to tyrannize the world. They are opposed by the benevolent, armadillo-shaped Mystics and the planet's only surviving humanoids, a boy and a girl known as Gelflings. Even critics who found "The Dark Crystal"'s narrative unexceptional were dazzled by Henson's animation techniques and visual effects, and the film also proved to be a strong commercial success, grossing over fifty million dollars at the box office.

"Labyrinth" is a still more ambitious fantasy film collaboration, this time directed by Henson and produced by George Lucas (of "Star Wars" fame), who also served as story consultant. Lighter in tone than "The Dark Crystal," "Labyrinth" features a human heroine and villain and an imaginative assortment of animated monsters, gnomes, and elves. Its plot revolves around a fifteen-year-old girl who must learn the secrets of a magical labyrinth so that she can rescue her baby brother from his goblin kidnappers and their king, played by popular singer David Bowie. The labyrinth's ingeniously made, mechanically assisted inhabitants include the Wild Things—birdlike creatures with huge eyeballs—and Hoggle, a friendly gnome with an oversized head.

Henson and his team spent two years developing these odd beasts, who, as *New York Times* film critic Nina Darnton observed, "are not cold, automated electronic marvels, but fantastic humanoid creatures inhabiting a newly created world who mirror our own foibles, and so can move us and make us laugh." Darnton deemed "Labyrinth" a "remarkable achievement" and praised Henson for expanding the "possibilities of imaginative fantasy that can be transferred to the screen."

MEDIA ADAPTATIONS: Henson's Muppets have been the basis for hundreds of books for children, including *Sweet Dreams on Sesame Street,* Random, 1983; *You Are the Star of a Muppet Adventure,* by Ellen Weiss, Random, 1983; and *Muppet Babies at the Circus,* Random, 1985.

BIOGRAPHICAL/CRITICAL SOURCES:

BOOKS

Finch, Christopher, *Of Muppets and Men: The Making of the Muppet Show,* Knopf, 1981.
Henson Associates, *The Art of the Muppets: A Retrospective Look At Twenty-five Years of Muppet Magic,* Bantam, 1980.

PERIODICALS

Advertising Age, October 17, 1983.
American Cinema, December, 1982.
Chicago Tribune, June 30, 1986.
Films in Review, January, 1983.
Fortune, February 4, 1985.
Newsweek, December 27, 1982.
New York Times, December 22, 1974, June 22, 1979, December 15, 1980, May 20, 1981, June 26, 1981, December 17, 1982, July 13, 1984, September 15, 1985, June 27, 1986.
New York Times Magazine, June 10, 1979.
People, January 17, 1983, February 6, 1986, February 2, 1987.
School Library Journal, September, 1984.
Time, January 3, 1984, July 7, 1986.
USA Today, January 17, 1986.

—*Sketch by Curtis Skinner*

* * *

HENSON, Jim
See HENSON, James Maury

* * *

HERRMANN, Richard K. 1952-

PERSONAL: Born October 16, 1952, in Cleveland, Ohio; son of Robert and Betty Herrmann. *Education:* University of Pittsburgh, Ph.D., 1981.

ADDRESSES: *Office*—Department of Political Science, 154 North Oval Mall, Ohio State University, Columbus, Ohio 43210.

CAREER: Associated with Ohio State University, Columbus, 1981—.

MEMBER: International Society of Political Psychologists, International Studies Association, American Political Science Association.

WRITINGS:

Perceptions and Behavior in Soviet Foreign Policy, University of Pittsburgh Press, 1985.

Contributor to political science journals.

WORK IN PROGRESS: A book on Soviet policy in the Middle East and toward Islam in general, publication expected in 1989.

* * *

HICKS, Roger W(illiam) 1950-
(Roger Sutherland)

PERSONAL: Born June 15, 1950, in Cornwall, England; immigrated to the United States, 1987; son of William George (a naval officer) and D. Beryl (a teacher; maiden name, Reynolds) Hicks; married Catherine A. Milne (an artist and songwriter), January 7, 1977 (divorced, 1980); married Frances E. Schultz (a writer, photographer, and lecturer in theater studies), June 24, 1982. *Education:* University of Birmingham, LL.B., 1973. *Religion:* Buddhist.

ADDRESSES: *Agent*—Doreen Montgomery, Rupert Crew Ltd., 1A King's Mews, London WC1N 2JA, England.

CAREER: Teacher of art, English, history, and citizenship at schools in Gillingham, Kent, and Bristol, England, 1973-77; photographer, 1976—; free-lance writer, 1981—. Photographer's assistant in London, England, 1974-76; director of a public relations company.

MEMBER: Mensa.

WRITINGS:

The Snapshot Book, Colour Library Books, 1982, reprinted as *Your Guide to Better Photography,* 1984.
Techniques of Pin-up Photography, Colour Library Books, 1982.
Techniques of Colour Photography: The Creative Art, Colour Library Books, 1982.
Classic Cars: Jaguar, Colour Library Books, 1983.
Practical Glamour Photography, Quarto, 1984.
The Book of Calendar Girl Photography, Doubleday, 1984.
(With Ngakpa Chogyam) *Great Ocean: An Authorised Biography of His Holiness, the Dalai Lama,* Element Books, 1984.
A History of the 35mm Still Camera, Focal Press, 1984.
Motorcycle Touring in Europe, Collins, 1985.
(With Ray Daffurn) *Pictures That Sell,* Collins, 1985.
V-Twin: The Classic Motorcycle, Blandford, 1985.
(Under pseudonym Roger Sutherland) *Comet Catastrophe,* Javelin Books, 1985.
The Medium Format Handbook, Blandford, 1986.
Classic American Cars, Colour Library Books, 1986.
(With wife, Frances Schultz) *Long Stays in America,* David & Charles, 1986.
The Art of Holiday Photography, Fotobank Books, 1986.
(With Colin Glanfield) *Creative Colour Photography,* Colour Library Books, 1986.
The Traveller's Book of Colour Photography, W. H. Smith, 1986.
(With Schultz) *Long Stays in Portugal,* David & Charles, 1987.
(Author and photographer) *The 35mm Panorama,* David & Charles, 1987, Sterling, 1987.
Portrait Photography, Blandford, 1987.

WORK IN PROGRESS: *Tibet and the Tibetan People,* for Element Books; *Police Cars,* for Bishopsgate Press; *Photography for Fun and Profit,* for David & Charles; *The Railway Traveller at Home and Abroad,* for Kingfisher Books.

SIDELIGHTS: Roger W. Hicks told *CA:* "My first published works were poems which appeared in the 1960s; my first *paid* published work was a short story in 1974. When I was in my late twenties I became a full-time writer, working first for a company that produced self-instructional audiovisual material, and then I helped to set up the Contract Communications Division of International Computers Ltd.

"Since 1981 I have been a full-time free lance. At first, I was fairly uncritical about the kind of work I accepted. I regarded the first few years as an apprenticeship, a time to learn the

craft of writing, and I am profoundly grateful to those publishers (especially Colour Library Books) who paid me to learn. Now I try to be more selective, unless the bank manager or the tax man is banging at my door. For the last few years, I have been saying that I hope to learn to write by the time I am forty, which will be in 1990. With any luck I will be ahead of schedule.

"When I talk about learning to become a writer, I'm really talking about fiction. The main requirements of nonfiction are rather less demanding: you need to be able to research your subject, to construct a good working plan, and to make the subject interesting. With fiction, on the other hand, you are denied the support of a ready-made subject. You still need to research the background, but what you are really concerned with is *people,* and learning about people takes time. I don't think it's possible to write good fiction until you have a fair amount of experience in different fields. I have done all the usual things, like being a truckdriver, a beach guard, and so forth, and I have traveled as extensively as I could in Europe, the United States, and India.

"On a more basic level, 'learning to write' means something else. It means mastering the craft, making words do what you want them to do, and acquiring the discipline necessary to get those words down on paper *reliably*. I don't think that a writer who fails to deliver because he is drunk for weeks on end or shacked up with his latest paramour, or because he decides to 'discover himself' in a monastery, is entitled to be called a professional. If you want to take time off for this sort of thing, fine, but make sure that the delivery date on your contract is far enough away to allow for this.

"Although I have produced a few potboilers, I have always tried to write about things that interest me. I am extremely fortunate that I don't need hobbies. I get paid for doing the things I like to do, for instance writing, photography, travel, and motorcycling. I have also been interested in Tibet and matters Tibetan for many years, and I have had the great good fortune to meet His Holiness the Dalai Lama on a number of occasions, both when I was researching his biography and subsequently.

"My favorite among my own books to date is *The 35mm Panorama*. Not only did I enjoy writing it, but the book contains more than a hundred of my pictures, which were taken on three continents. My wife, Frances Schultz, is as keen on travel, photography, and writing as I am, and indeed she prefers to work with me rather than in her original field, which was theater. A good number of her pictures also appear in *The 35mm Panorama*.

"This brings me rather neatly to the present moment. As I write these words, I am a few weeks from moving from the United Kingdom to Los Angeles. My wife and I met there and, since her background in theater and mine in writing are now converging naturally, we want to work together on movie scripts. Los Angeles is obviously the place to do this. We shall continue to work on other books, both in the United States and the United Kingdom, but we hope that we can work in the cinema within the next few years."

* * *

HILL, John L. 1960-

PERSONAL: Born February 29, 1960, in Chicago, Ill.; adopted son of Ronald D. (an insurance executive) and Vilma Sada (a housewife) White; married Ana Maria Guedea (a paralegal), August 16, 1986. *Education:* Northern Illinois University, B.A., 1982, M.A., 1985; graduate study at Georgetown University, 1985—.

ADDRESSES: Home—8403 16th St., No. 107, Silver Spring, Md. 20910. *Office—Georgetown Journal of Legal Ethics,* 25 E St. N.W., Washington, D.C. 20001.

CAREER: Professional Services Corp., Chicago, Ill., speech writer, 1981-82; Northern Illinois University, DeKalb, instructor in philosophy, 1984-85; *Georgetown Journal of Legal Ethics,* Washington, D.C., articles editor, 1987—. Member of Law Students in Court.

MEMBER: Phi Sigma Tau (president, 1983-85).

WRITINGS:

The Enlightened Society, Theosophical Publishing, 1987.

WORK IN PROGRESS: The Ethical Implications of Prenatal Screening for Incurable Genetic Conditions; research on the legal and ethical implications of surrogate motherhood; research on freedom and determinism in Anglo-American jurisprudence.

SIDELIGHTS: John L. Hill told *CA:* "I was born legally blind, but I believe I have largely overcome this handicap. I was adopted at a few weeks of age. I am grateful both to my adopted parents, for their kindness, and to my natural mother, wherever she may be, for the courage it must have taken to bring me into this world alone.

"My current interests fall into three areas: philosophy of law, ethics, and bioethics. My curiosity in these areas covers issues in punishment, the concept of responsibility, the question of freedom and determinism, and international human rights. In bioethics I am concerned about the issues of abortion, euthanasia, genetic engineering, and eugenics (the sterilization of the mentally retarded). In general, I seek to combine an academic interest in philosophy and law to analyze these issues.

"Another practical interest is law, particularly its use in defending and upholding the rights of the underprivileged. I enjoy courtroom advocacy, particularly when it is applied successfully to meet these ends.

"I also believe that a dynamic outer life should be matched by a fulfilling inner life. I practice yoga and meditation daily, with the hope of becoming a more wise, compassionate, and loving human being. *The Enlightened Society* is the product of both an academic and a personal interest in this pursuit."

* * *

HILL, Ralph Nading 1917-1987

OBITUARY NOTICE—See index for *CA* sketch: Born September 19, 1917, in Burlington, Vt.; died of a stroke, December 10, 1987, in Burlington, Vt. Historian, editor, and author. Hill joined *Vermont Life* magazine as a senior editor in 1951 and later served on its advisory board. A lifetime resident of Vermont, he devoted his career to preserving and recording various aspects of that state's history. Hill wrote or edited a number of books, including *Robert Fulton and the Steamboat, Yankee Kingdom: Vermont and New Hampshire,* and *The College on the Hill: A Dartmouth Chronicle*.

OBITUARIES AND OTHER SOURCES:

PERIODICALS

New York Times, December 12, 1987.

* * *

HILVERT, John (Peter Paul) 1945-

PERSONAL: Born June 10, 1945, in Budapest, Hungary; son of George David and Catherine (Schueck) Hilvert; married Christine Mary Stuckey, May 29, 1971 (divorced July 8, 1982); married Linda Christine Bruce (a psychologist), January 23, 1983; children: (first marriage) Daniel Raoul, Alexandra Gretchen; (second marriage) Alan George, James John. *Education:* University of Sydney, B.A., 1968; Macquarie University, M.A., 1980, further graduate study, 1981-84. *Politics:* "No affiliation." *Religion:* Agnostic.

ADDRESSES: *Home*—103 Miller St., O'Connor, Australian Capital Territory 2601, Australia. *Office*—Department of Communications, Benjamin Offices, Belconnen, Australian Capital Territory 2617, Australia.

CAREER: Market and Audience Research, Sydney, Australia, research executive, 1969-73; Australian Government, Canberra, Australia, policy research executive, 1973-87. Chairman of Welfare Rights Centre, 1983-85.

MEMBER: Australian Clerical Officers Association.

WRITINGS:

Blue Pencil Warriors: Censorship and Propaganda in World War II, University of Queensland Press, 1984.

WORK IN PROGRESS: Research on communication and media developments, both national and international.

SIDELIGHTS: John Hilvert told *CA:* "I have incredible respect and admiration for anyone who writes books. I stumbled into my first book. My next one, if there is one, shall be less accident-prone and more an act of consciousness. I suspect that books of the future will be available through videotext data bases. Perhaps writing styles will need to accommodate and explore these technological developments."

In *Blue Pencil Warriors,* Hilvert explains that wartime censorship in Australia was implemented originally to protect national security. It was not long, however, before information embarrassing to Australia was suppressed, and news that presented the country in a favorable light, particularly to its valuable ally, the United States, was edited to enhance its effectiveness. Political messages emerged, and the line between censorship and propaganda disappeared. Virtually all of the print media became involved in the censorship process, and some Australian journalists pursued their goals with enthusiasm and pleasure. Michael Davie wrote in the *Times Literary Supplement,* "John Hilvert's book gives a careful account of censorship and propaganda in Australia during the Second World War, but the muddles and distortions of purpose it describes have parallels far outside Australia."

BIOGRAPHICAL/CRITICAL SOURCES:

PERIODICALS

Times Literary Supplement, August 10, 1984.

HINXMAN, Margaret 1924-

PERSONAL: Born October 8, 1924, in London, England; daughter of Charles Alfred (a railwayman) and Alice (a housewife; maiden name, Wood) Hinxman. *Education:* Attended girls' school in London, England. *Politics:* Liberal. *Religion:* Protestant.

ADDRESSES: *Home*—Worthing, Sussex, England. *Agent*—Mary Irvine, 11 Upland Park Rd., Oxford OX2 7RU, England.

CAREER: *Time and Tide,* London, England, feature writer and film critic, 1946-50; *Picturegoer,* London, feature writer and film critic, 1951-60; *Daily Cinema,* London, feature writer and film critic, 1960-67; *Sunday Telegraph,* London, feature writer and film critic, 1967-74; *Daily Mail,* London, feature writer and film critic, 1974-84; free-lance writer, 1984—. Feature writer and film critic for *Queen,* 1965-67, and *Woman,* 1965-74. *Military service:* Women's Royal Naval Service (WRENS), 1941-46.

AWARDS, HONORS: British Press Award, 1978, for film critic of the year.

WRITINGS:

(Editor with Roger Manvell, John Gillett, and David Robinson) *International Encyclopedia of Film,* M. Joseph, 1972.
(With Susan d'Arcy) *The Films of Dirk Bogarde,* Literary Services and Production, 1974.
End of a Good Woman (novel), Collins, 1976.
One Way Cemetery (novel), Collins, 1977.
The Telephone Never Tells (novel), Collins, 1982.
The Corpse Now Arriving (novel), Collins, 1983.
The Night They Murdered Chelsea (novel), Dodd, 1984.
The Boy From Nowhere (novel), Collins, 1985.
The Sound of Murder (novel), Collins, 1986.

Contributor to periodicals, including *Woman's Realm.*

WORK IN PROGRESS: A thriller set in Sussex, publication expected in 1988; a thriller set in the United States, publication expected in 1989; research for a novel about the early days of cinema.

SIDELIGHTS: Margaret Hinxman told *CA:* "We were a working class family with great pride, instilled in us by my magnificent mother, who taught her four children that nothing was unattainable. That was pretty inspiring at a time when class barriers in my country seemed impregnable! In a very positive sense, I was a child of the cinema, and my early ambition was in some way to be part of the cinema. I also knew I wanted to write. The two aims came together soon after I left the WRENS at the end of the war, when I had the luck to become a film critic. Until I retired from journalism in 1984, all my working life was spent writing about films.

"It was my galvanizing agent, Mary Irvine, who pressured me into writing fiction in my spare time: first, a series of short stories for the weekly *Woman's Realm,* then novels. At least, I started to write a 'straight' novel, but with a will of its own it turned into a mystery and, cursed or blessed with a devious mind, I realized my special bent was as a writer of crime fiction. I think my passion for, and hopefully knowledge of, the cinema has been a help. Crisp editing, tension, natural dialogue are qualities that contribute to a good thriller, as well as a good film.

"I use a good deal of show business material in my books, as well as the countryside and ambience of the area in which I

live. I think the only theme that crops up in all my work is 'faces': the faces people present to the world, even their friends and family, and the person who exists privately and secretly underneath the face. Graham Greene, Raymond Chandler, Ross MacDonald, Margaret Millar, Simon Brett, and Alison Lurie are just some of my idols, apart from the classical giants. But I admire practically all authors who are published. Even if their work is rubbish, it's damned hard and lonely work. A writer just lives for those wonderfully exhilarating moments when everything goes well.''

BIOGRAPHICAL/CRITICAL SOURCES:

PERIODICALS

Theatre Print Programme, May, 1982.

* * *

HIPPISLEY COXE, Antony D(acres) 1912-1988 (Charles Lacy)

OBITUARY NOTICE—See index for *CA* sketch: Born March 21, 1912, in London, England; died January 28, 1988. Circus aficionado, business adviser, media representative, editor, and author. Hippisley Coxe became internationally known as an authority on the circus. Attesting to his expertise are his many books on the subject, most notably *Seat at the Circus*—first published in 1951. Among his other publications are *The Book of the Sausage, Performance and Politics in Popular Drama, Haunted Britain, Just Cats,* and a number of pamphlets—one of which appeared under the name Charles Lacy. A man of multiple interests, Hippisley Coxe pursued a wide range of occupations, which included editorial, media, publicity, and advisory work. At the time of his death, Hippisley Coxe was preparing a circus exhibition titled ''Grand Parade,'' which was to be presented at London's Theatre Museum, where his collection of circus material is archived.

OBITUARIES AND OTHER SOURCES:

PERIODICALS

Times (London), January 30, 1988.

* * *

HISSEY, Jane (Elizabeth) 1952-

PERSONAL: Born September 1, 1952, in Norfolk, England; daughter of Richard Reeve (a naval officer) and Shelagh (Smith) Colls; married Ivan Hissey (a graphic designer), August 1, 1979; children: Owen James, Alison Julia. *Education:* Attended Great Yarmouth College of Art, 1969-70; Brighton College of Art and Design, B.A., 1974.

ADDRESSES: Home—Hassocks, Sussex, England. *Agent*—c/o Century Hutchinson Childrens Books Ltd., Brookmount House, 62-65 Chandos Place, Covent Garden, London WC2N 4NW, England.

CAREER: Worthing Sixth Form College, Sussex, England, art teacher, 1974-80; illustrator and designer, 1980—.

WRITINGS:

Old Bear (self-illustrated children's book), Philomel, 1986.
Little Bear's Trousers (self-illustrated children's book), Philomel, 1987.

WORK IN PROGRESS: Writing and illustrating another children's book, publication by Century Hutchinson expected in 1989.

SIDELIGHTS: Jane Hissey told *CA:* ''After I produced a number of greeting cards and a large, full-color calendar, I was approached by Century Hutchinson to write and illustrate a children's book. The idea appealed to me, because I am able to fit the work into the evenings. This leaves me free in the daytime to be with my children.

''I work in colored pencils in a realistic style; concentrating on accurate representation of form and texture, the well-worn toys that I portray in my children's books lend themselves to this technique. I feel that children enjoy detail and my books bring toys to life in a matter-of-fact way, familiar to children. Everyday objects are portrayed in ordinary settings—the action alone being unexpected!''

* * *

HITE, Molly 1947-

PERSONAL: Born June 26, 1947, in Seattle, Wash.; daughter of F. Herbert and Patricia G. Hite; married Gerard H. Cox; children: Joshua, Molly Amanda. *Education:* Seattle University, B.A. (summa cum laude), 1974; University of Washington, Seattle, Ph.D., 1981.

ADDRESSES: Home—117 Stewart Ave., Ithaca, N.Y. 14850. *Office*—Department of English, Cornell University, Ithaca, N.Y. 14853.

CAREER: Cornell University, Ithaca, N.Y., assistant professor of English, 1982—.

AWARDS, HONORS: Fellow of American Council of Learned Societies, 1984.

WRITINGS:

Ideas of Order in the Novels of Thomas Pynchon, Ohio State University Press, 1982.
Class Porn (novel), Crossing Press, 1987.
(Contributor) *Contemporary Authors New Revision Series,* Volume 22, Gale, 1987.

Contributor of articles and reviews to magazines.

WORK IN PROGRESS: The Other Side of the Story: Structures and Strategies of Recent Feminist Narratives.

* * *

HODGKINSON, Liz 1943-

PERSONAL: Born September 26, 1943, in St. Neots, England; daughter of George and Mabel (a businesswoman; maiden name, Grey) Garrett; married Neville Hodgkinson (a journalist), August 14, 1965; children: Tom, William. *Education:* University of Durham, B.A. (with honors), 1966. *Religion:* None.

ADDRESSES: Home—59 Petersham Rd., Richmond, Surrey, England. *Agent*—Maggie Noach, 21 Redan St., London W.14, England.

CAREER: Schoolteacher in South Shields, England, 1966-67, and Sunderland, England, 1967; journalist, 1968-78; free-lance writer, 1978—.

WRITINGS:

The Working Woman's Guide, Thorsons, 1985.
(Editor) *Bhagwan: The God That Failed,* Caliban, 1986.
Addictions, Thorsons, 1986.
Sex Is Not Compulsory, Columbus, 1986.
(With Derek Bryce-Smith) *The Zinc Solution,* Hutchinson, 1986.

Smile Therapy, Macdonald & Co., 1987.
Bodyshock: The Truth About Changing Sex, Columbus, 1987.
Unholy Matrimony, Columbus, 1987.
The Alexander Technique, Piatkus, 1988.

WORK IN PROGRESS: Novels.

SIDELIGHTS: Liz Hodgkinson told CA: "My book *Sex Is Not Compulsory* attracted worldwide media interest. It was the result of my growing conviction that sex is not, as has been commonly assumed, necessary to our lives. This put me in the peculiar position of being considered an expert on the subject of sexual and other relationships. Otherwise I am a feminist and vegetarian, interested in all avant-garde ideas."

Hodgkinson observed the behavior of monks and nuns, as well as non-religious celibates, and decided that sex is neither physically nor mentally necessary for good health. In fact, she pointed out some of the physical hazards of sex, including high blood pressure and heart failure, as well as venereal disease. The author claims that sex surveys reveal a declining frequency of sex that is proportional to the length of a relationship, and she asserts that this decrease in sexual desire is a normal and correct part of the aging process. Hodgkinson believes that celibate people lead longer and happier lives than people who are caught up in the stressful and continuous search for sexual fulfillment. She concludes that celibacy allows a person the time and freedom to pursue creative and imaginative activities without distraction.

Hodgkinson commented further: "My first book, *The Working Woman's Guide,* was written in the belief that all women should have the opportunity to make an individual career for themselves and that these days life as a wife and mother cannot be considered enough, although it may be an ingredient. It also puts forward the idea that all women should expect to be self-supporting financially, all their lives, and should never expect that a man will provide for them. In our present age, this is a dangerous assumption. Women should not be dependent and passive creatures, but should fulfill their own potential and never live vicarious, power-behind-the-throne lives.

"My second book, *Addictions,* is a practical guide to exactly what addictions are, how they start, why people become addicted, and why some people choose one drug over another. Also included in the book are interviews with addicts of various kinds, descriptions of self-help groups and organizations, and an explanation of the psychology of addiction, plus advice on how to free oneself from unwanted dependency on a habit-forming substance or activity.

"*Bhagwan: The God That Failed,* is the autobiographical account of Hugh Milne, the guru Bhagwan Rajneesh's former bodyguard, which I adapted for publication in book form. It explains why so many people became involved in the cult and what it offered, and it tells what Bhagwan was like as a person. The book traces the rise and fall of the Orange People, as they were called, from a small flat in Bombay, India, to huge premises in Poona, India, and later to Oregon, where Bhagwan amassed more than ninety Rolls Royce automobiles and became involved in litigation over land use and illegal entry to the country.

"My other books include *The Zinc Solution,* written with a well-respected British professor of chemistry, that explains why the trace element zinc is so important for the human body, mind, and emotions. Another book, *Smile Therapy,* draws on recent research into the therapeutic value of smiling and laughter and explains exactly what smiling and laughter are, and why they are so important to health and well-being. *Smile Therapy* also analyzes sense of humor, what is meant by wit, and the dangers of taking oneself too seriously.

"Finally, *Bodyshock: The Truth About Changing Sex* is, I believe, the first popular account of the phenomenon of transexualism, something that has intrigued and fascinated people for years. Many case histories are presented and the book describes at length the legal, medical, hormonal, and biological implications of sex change. The book also asks what the sex-change phenomenon tells us about the true differences between the sexes. This account is intended to be impartial and objective, but at the same time sympathetic to the plight of those who genuinely feel they were born into the wrong kind of body."

BIOGRAPHICAL/CRITICAL SOURCES:

PERIODICALS

Times (London), September 12, 1986.

* * *

HODGKISS, A(lan) G(eoffrey) 1921-

PERSONAL: Born June 19, 1921, in Newton-le-Willows, Lancashire, England; son of Robert (a porter) and Fanny (a homemaker; maiden name, Winstanley) Hodgkiss; married Helen Margaret Freestone, March 31, 1951 (died April 10, 1983); married June Margaret Till (a lecturer), June 23, 1984; children: Catherine Helen Greaves, Robert James. *Education:* Attended Wigan and District Mining and Technical College, 1937.

ADDRESSES: Home—25 Burnham Rd., Allerton, Liverpool L18 6JU, England.

CAREER: Warrington Rural District Council, Warrington, England, surveying assistant, 1939-46; University of Liverpool, Liverpool, England, principal experimental officer, 1946-83; writer. *Military service:* Royal Engineers, 1943-46; became sergeant.

MEMBER: British Cartographic Society (founding member), Society of University Cartographers (founding member), Friends of the Royal Liverpool Philharmonic Orchestra.

AWARDS, HONORS: Wallis Award from Society of University Cartographers, 1979, for monograph on cartographic facsimiles; honorary M.A. from University of Liverpool, 1983.

WRITINGS:

Maps for Books and Theses, self-illustrated, Pica Press, 1970.
(Editor with J. A. Patmore) *Merseyside in Maps,* Longmans, Green, 1970.
Discovering Antique Maps, Shire Publications, 1971.
Understanding Maps, Dawson & Sons, 1981.
(Editor with W.T.S. Gould) *Resources of Merseyside,* Liverpool University Press, 1982.
(With Andrew Tatham) *Keyguide to Information Sources in Cartography,* Facts on File, 1986.
(With J. J. Bagley) *Lancashire: A History of the County Palatine in Early Maps,* N. Richardson, 1986.

Editor of *SUC Bulletin* (Society of University Cartographers), 1964-73; contributing editor of *Canadian Cartographer,* 1965-73.

SIDELIGHTS: A. G. Hodgkiss told *CA:* "My books have the approach of a professional, practicing cartographer, which is

unusual, as most works on cartography are written by academics or curators of map collections."

AVOCATIONAL INTERESTS: Travel, India, music.

* * *

HOGAN, Lawrence D(aniel) 1944-

PERSONAL: Born June 1, 1944, in Stamford, Conn.; son of Lawrence D. (a fireman) and Mary Veronica (a bookkeeper and clerk; maiden name, Marino) Hogan; married Sara (Sally) Herzog (a YMCA program director), August 24, 1968; children: Rebecca, Matthew, Elizabeth. *Education:* Fairfield University, B.A., 1966; University of Connecticut, M.A., 1967; graduate study at North Carolina Central University, 1969; Indiana University, Ph.D., 1978; postdoctoral study at William Patterson College of New Jersey, 1978, New School for Social Research, 1979, Columbia University, 1979, Rutgers University, 1982, and Atlanta University, 1983.

ADDRESSES: Home—20 Rainier Rd., Fanwood, N.J. 07023. *Office*—Department of History, Union College, 1033 Springfield Ave., Cranford, N.J. 07016.

CAREER: Central Catholic High School, Norwalk, Conn., English and history teacher, 1967-70; Indiana University—Bloomington, associate instructor in history, 1970-75; DePauw University, Greencastle, Ind., lecturer in history, 1975; Indiana University at South Bend, instructor in history, 1977; Union College, Cranford, N.J., professor of history, 1977—.

Visiting professor of American studies at University of Notre Dame, 1986-87; public speaker at conferences and seminars. Member of Union College committees, including College Publications Committee, 1979, Black Organization of Students (adviser), 1979—, Middle States Evaluation Committee for Continuing Education (chairman, 1980-81), Advisory Board for Senior Citizen Center, 1980—, Community Education/Humanities Project (director, 1981-85), New Jersey Council for Senior Citizen Education (founding member), 1982—. Board member of Suburban Symphony Society of New Jersey, 1981-84. Publicity director for Area Five New Jersey Special Olympics, 1982-85.

MEMBER: American Historical Association, Organization of American Historians, American Association of University Professors, Community College Humanities Association, American Society for Baseball Research.

AWARDS, HONORS: Grants from National Endowment for the Humanities, 1979, 1980, 1981, and 1982; grants from Union County Cultural and Heritage Commission and New Jersey Committee for the Humanities, 1983, for program "Before You Can Say Jackie Robinson: Black Baseball in New Jersey in the Era of the Color Line, 1885-1950"; grants from New Jersey Committee for the Humanities and the New Jersey Historical Society for production of video documentary and from New Jersey Department of Higher Education for photo and memorabilia travel exhibit, accompanying teachers' guide, and catalog on black baseball, all titled "Before You Can Say Jackie Robinson: Black Baseball in America in the Era of the Color Line, 1885-1950."

WRITINGS:

A Black National News Service: The Associated Negro Press and Claude Barnett, 1919-1940, Fairleigh Dickinson University Press, 1984.

Contributor of articles on history and contemporary events to periodicals, including *Commonweal, Newsday, New York Times, Midstream, San Diego Union, Examiner* (San Francisco), and *American Visions.*

WORK IN PROGRESS: A book, *Before You Can Say Jackie Robinson: Black Baseball in America in the Era of the Color Line, 1885-1950;* a video documentary, "Black on White: The Black Press Reports America From Behind the Veil."

SIDELIGHTS: Lawrence D. Hogan told *CA:* "*A Black National News Service: The Associated Negro Press and Claude Barnett* deals with an especially fruitful period for Afro-American journalism. The years from the 1910s to the 1940s saw the birth and growth to phenomenal heights of newspapers that became national and international reporting instruments. These journals, including the Chicago *Defender,* the Pittsburgh *Courier,* and the Baltimore *Afro-American,* both shaped and reflected the rich communal life of black Americans.

"*A Black National News Service* is an in-depth study of a news instrument that operated at the heart of this black fourth estate. Founded in 1919 in Chicago by Claude Barnett and patterned after the Associated Press and United Press International, the Associated Negro Press (ANP) served Afro-American journalism as a national and international news gathering instrument through the mid-1960s. Its editors drew on the reporting of a full- and part-time staff to put together a twice-weekly news packet that went out to a membership of more than one hundred papers, including the major national and regional black journals. Barnett strove to make ANP an integral part of the black press establishment it served, thus sharing in and shaping the influence the papers enjoyed.

"Barnett's Associated Negro Press represents the highest development of an idea, which first surfaced in the post-Civil War decades, that the black press and people needed and would support a cooperative national news service. ANP's story offers an informative perspective from which to view the history of twentieth-century Afro-American journalism.

"In recent years my attention—my fancy—has been captured by the history of black baseball—the old Negro leagues. And why not, when one gets to listen to the likes of John 'Buck' O'Neil, who played first base for the Kansas City Monarchs through the 1930s and 1940s, tell us what it was like to play baseball in leagues where, to use the evocative title of Robert Peterson's 1970 classic study of Negro baseball, 'only the ball was white.' O'Neil said: 'There is nothing like getting your body to react to all the things one has to do on the ball field. It's as good as music; it's as good as sex. Waste no tears for me. I didn't come along too early. I was right on time.' I have had an incredibly wonderful time getting myself 'on time' with Negro league baseball and a group of veteran baseball players—Negro leaguers in their seventies, eighties, and nineties—who are unique figures in American sports history—and whom I now number among my personal friends."

BIOGRAPHICAL/CRITICAL SOURCES:

PERIODICALS

Star-Ledger (Newark), February 23, 1984.

* * *

HOLBURN, James 1900-1988

OBITUARY NOTICE: Born December 1, 1900, in Glasgow, Scotland; died in 1988. Journalist. A leading foreign corre-

spondent for the London *Times* for twenty years, Holburn took his first newspaper job in 1920 as a subeditor at the *Glasgow Herald*. He stayed with that newspaper for fourteen years before joining the staff of the *Times*. In 1935 the *Times* sent Holburn to Berlin as an assistant correspondent; he then served in Moscow and Ankara before becoming war correspondent in the Middle East in 1941. Afterward Holburn worked in Delhi, India, in New York City at the United Nations Headquarters, and in Cairo, Egypt, as Middle East correspondent. In 1955 he returned to the *Glasgow Herald* as editor and remained in that post until he retired in 1965. Holburn also contributed articles to numerous other periodicals.

OBITUARIES AND OTHER SOURCES:

BOOKS

Who Was Who Among English and European Authors, 1931-1949, Gale, 1978.
Who's Who, 140th edition, St. Martin's, 1988.

PERIODICALS

Times (London), March 1, 1988.

* * *

HOLDSWORTH, Christopher (John) 1931-

PERSONAL: Born January 29, 1931, in Bolton, Lancashire, England; son of James Oliver (a farmer) and Catherine (a housewife; maiden name, Theakston) Holdsworth; married Juliet Clutterbuck, August 19, 1957 (divorced, 1976); children: Robert Edmund. *Education:* Cambridge University, B.A., 1953, M.A., 1956, Ph.D., 1960. *Religion:* Society of Friends (Quakers).

ADDRESSES: Home—5 Pennsylvania Park, Exeter EX4 6HB, England. *Office*—Department of History and Archaeology, University of Exeter, Exeter EX4 4QH, England.

CAREER: University of London, University College, London, England, assistant lecturer, 1956, lecturer, 1959-67, senior lecturer, 1967-73, reader in medieval history, 1973-77; University of Exeter, Exeter, England, professor of medieval history, 1977—, head of department of history and archaeology, 1984—. Joseph Rowntree Charitable Trust, trustee, 1957—, chairman, 1980—.

MEMBER: Royal Historical Society (member of council, 1982-85), Society of Antiquaries.

WRITINGS:

Rufford Charters, four volumes, Thoroton Society, 1972-81.
(Editor with Diana Greenway and Jane Sayers) *Tradition and Change: Essays in Honour of Marjorie Chibnall,* Cambridge University Press, 1985.
Steps in a Large Room: A Quaker Explores the Monastic Tradition, Quaker Home Service, 1985.
(Editor) *Domesday Essays,* University of Exeter, 1986.
(Editor with T. P. Wiseman) *The Inheritance of Historiography,* University of Exeter, 1986.

Contributor to history journals.

WORK IN PROGRESS: Saint Bernard, completion expected in 1989.

SIDELIGHTS: Christopher Holdsworth told *CA:* "My interest in history was sparked by David Knowles and Marjorie Chibnall when I was a student at Cambridge, although I had gained a lot from being at a private school in York and from being brought up in a medieval farm house.

"I chose for my doctorate to work on the writings of English Cistercians in the late twelfth century, and in some ways I have never gotten away from them and their world. Editing a huge corpus of charters taught me more about social and economic history, and my present book on Saint Bernard will, I hope, bring together the insights that I have gained over thirty years. *Domesday Essays* contains lectures given in Exeter to mark the nine hundreth anniversary and have a mainly regional interest.

"Having spent much of my professional life around monasticism, it was almost inevitable that when I was invited to give a public lecture at the annual meeting of British Quakers that I chose to reflect on it from a very personal point of view. It is a tribute to what I have gained from other Christians over the years."

AVOCATIONAL INTERESTS: Playing cello and piano, travel.

* * *

HOLLAND, Elizabeth (Anne) 1928-

PERSONAL: Born January 11, 1928, in Farnborough, Hampshire, England; daughter of John Charles Francis (a major general) and Annie Christabel (Brunyate) Holland. *Education:* Attended University of Manitoba, 1943-44; University of Edinburgh, M.A. (with honors), 1949; University of London, B.Sc., 1970. *Religion:* Anglican.

ADDRESSES: Home and office—16 Prior Park Buildings, Bath, Avon BA2 4NP, England. *Agent*—A. M. Heath & Co., Ltd., 40-42 William IV St., London WC2N 4DD, England.

CAREER: International Missionary Council, London, England, research assistant, 1951-53; Boswall House (missionary residence), Edinburgh, Scotland, assistant warden, 1955-63; part-time lecturer in economics and history at Bath College of Further Education in Bath, and in Bristol, England, 1965-74; founder and director of Survey of Old Bath, 1980—; writer.

MEMBER: Bath History Research Group.

WRITINGS:

A Separate Person (novel), Macmillan (London), 1962.
The House in the North (novel), Macmillan (London), 1963.
The House by the Sea (novel), Chatto & Windus, 1965.
The Adding Up (novel), Chatto & Windus, 1968.
(With Robert Giddings) *J.R.R. Tolkien: The Shores of Middle-Earth* (literary criticism), Junction Books, 1981.

Editor of *New Tolkien Newsletter,* 1980—; editor of *The Road,* 1983—.

WORK IN PROGRESS: A literary study, *The Secret World of Touchstone, Fool of Arden; Bath History,* Volume II: *Town Guilds and Town Governments: A Study of the Old Guildhall of Bath.*

SIDELIGHTS: Elizabeth Holland told *CA:* "My work on British writer J.R.R. Tolkien has been called controversial, but to me it is the obvious commentary on Tolkien by someone from his own background."

Holland added: "I founded the Survey of Old Bath, a historical research venture, after making a complete genealogy of the

Chapmans, one of the leading families of Old Bath. (My father's mother, Lady Holland, was a Chapman.) My aim is to recreate the Tudor and Stuart cities of Bath—and, if possible, the medieval—which are usually ignored in favor of the Romans and Georgians. We work from original documents found chiefly in the Bath Record Office or city archives. We have now completed a scale map of Stuart Bath and are working to prepare it for publication.''

BIOGRAPHICAL/CRITICAL SOURCES:

PERIODICALS

New Statesman, October 30, 1981.

* * *

HOLLAND, William E. 1940-

PERSONAL: Born September 16, 1940, in Kearney, Neb.; son of John E. (a carpenter) and Frances (a homemaker; maiden name, Shimonek) Holland; married Judith Petersen (a homemaker), 1963; children: Lisa, Cynthia. *Education:* University of Nebraska at Lincoln, B.Sc. (civil engineering), 1963; Oxford University, B.A. (English), 1965; Stanford University, Ph.D., 1971, J.D., 1974.

ADDRESSES: Home—8107 Molokai Dr., Omaha, Neb. 68128. *Office*—1650 Farnam St., Omaha, Neb. 68102. *Agent*—Rhoda Weyr, 322 Central Park W., New York, N.Y. 10025.

CAREER: Kutak, Rock & Campbell (law firm), Omaha, Neb., partner, 1974—. *Military service:* U.S. Army, 1965-68, served as helicopter pilot; became captain; received Bronze Star and Air Medal.

WRITINGS:

Let a Soldier Die (novel), Delacorte, 1984.

SIDELIGHTS: Former Vietnam helicopter pilot William E. Holland weaves a tale of war and conscience in his first novel, *Let a Soldier Die*. He tells the story of an American helicopter gunship ace in Vietnam who grapples with staggering guilt after he mistakenly attacks American troops. Increasingly unable to reconcile himself to the death and destruction he wages in the name of war, ''[the pilot] is haunted by a dream of peace and beauty which grows stronger as it grows more unattainable,'' described Stephen Goodwin in the *Washington Post Book World.* ''This war novel, in fact, might also be described as an Army novel,'' the reviewer continued. ''The enemy, most often seen from a safe height, is a comfortable abstraction. . . . Questions of right and wrong, life and death, are beside the point so long as the Army goes about its business.'' It is no place for a man of conscience.

Judging *Let a Soldier Die* a ''strong first novel,'' Goodwin related: ''The flying scenes . . . will make you grab hold of the arms of your chair. The risk and thrill of flight are described in absolutely convincing detail.'' In addition, *Los Angeles Times* contributor David Stevenson observed that ''Holland somehow manages to successfully resurrect'' the stock characters and situations of the war novel genre. ''If there are no genuinely new war stories, there are new wars with sad variations and extrapolations on familiar themes of pain and death,'' elaborated the reviewer. ''What makes [Holland's] version effective is a portrayal of tactical and moral complications particular to Vietnam . . . hypocrisy, bleakness and futile heroism.''

BIOGRAPHICAL/CRITICAL SOURCES:

PERIODICALS

Los Angeles Times, January 17, 1985.
Washington Post Book World, October 28, 1984.

* * *

HOLT, Elizabeth B(asye) G(ilmore) 1906(?)-1987

PERSONAL: Born c. 1906 in San Francisco, Calif.; died of cancer, January 26, 1987, in Washington, D.C.; married James B. Holt (a foreign service officer); children: Elizabeth Holt Muench, John A., Peter G. *Education:* Graduate of University of Wisconsin—Madison, 1928; Radcliffe College, M.A., 1930; University of Munich, Ph.D., 1934; studied at Kunsthistorisches Institut.

CAREER: Duke University, Durham, N.C., member of art history faculty, beginning in 1934; Michigan State University, East Lansing, teacher of art history; member of faculty at Talladega College, American University, and Boston University.

AWARDS, HONORS: Freedom Bell Award from city of Berlin, Germany; Guggenheim fellow, 1980; honorary degrees from Syracuse University, 1983, and University of St. Andrews, 1985.

WRITINGS:

(Editor) *Literary Sources of Art History: An Anthology of Texts From Theophilus to Goethe,* Princeton University Press, 1947, revised edition published as *A Documentary History of Art,* Doubleday, Volume I: *The Middle Ages and the Renaissance,* 1958, Volume II: *Michelangelo and the Mannerists: The Baroque and the Eighteenth Century,* 1958, Volume III: *From the Classicists to the Impressionists: A Documentary History of Art and Architecture in the Nineteenth Century,* New York University Press, 1966.

(Editor) *The Emerging Role of Exhibitions and Critics,* Anchor, Volume I: *The Triumph of Art for the Public, 1785-1848,* 1979, Volume II: *The Art of All Nations, 1850-1873,* 1981.

BIOGRAPHICAL/CRITICAL SOURCES:

PERIODICALS

Boston Globe, January 30, 1987.
New York Times, January 28, 1987.*

* * *

HOOPER, Hedley Colwill 1919-
(Peter Hooper)

PERSONAL: Born May 19, 1919, in London, England; son of Ernest (a farmer) and Alice (Lee) Hooper. *Education:* University of New Zealand, B.A., 1946.

ADDRESSES: Home—369 Milton Rd., Paroa, Greymouth, New Zealand.

CAREER: Greymouth High School, Greymouth, New Zealand, head of English department, 1946-64; Westland High School, Hokitika, New Zealand, deputy principal, 1966-77; writer, 1977—. Bookseller, Greymouth, 1964-65. *Military service:* Royal New Zealand Air Force, 1942-45.

MEMBER: International P.E.N., Royal New Zealand Forest and Bird Society, Thoreau Society.

AWARDS, HONORS: Prose award from International P.E.N., 1980, for *A Song in the Forest;* grant from New Zealand Literary Fund, 1981; New Zealand Book Award in fiction, 1986, for *People of the Long Water*.

WRITINGS:

UNDER PSEUDONYM PETER HOOPER

A Map of Morning and Other Poems, Pegasus Press, 1964.
Journey Towards an Elegy and Other Poems, Nag's Head Press, 1969.
The Mind of Bones (poems), Inter-Media, 1971.
Earth Marriage (poems), Young & Waddington, 1972.
Profiles in Monochrome (poems), Aspect Press, 1974.
Selected Poems, McIndoe, 1977.
A Song in the Forest (novel), McIndoe, 1979.
The Goat Paddock and Other Stories, McIndoe, 1981.
Our Forests Ourselves (essays), McIndoe, 1981.
(Editor) *Winter Skies,* West Coast Writers Group, 1983.
(Editor and contributor) *Saturday Afternoons,* Longacres Press, 1984.
People of the Long Water (novel), McIndoe, 1985.
Time and the Forest (novel), McIndoe, 1986.

Work represented in anthologies, including *Acts of Resistance,* edited by Pat White; *Levity Brevity Bite,* edited by Peter Payne.

WORK IN PROGRESS: A novel, *Portraits of the Artist's Wife*.

SIDELIGHTS: Hedley Colwill Hooper told *CA:* "My interests are mainly intellectual and artistic, but I have spent most of my life in small, rural communities as a teacher, bookseller, and writer. Recent influences on my writing include holistic ideas in all fields, Taoism, and the new physics. I regard U.S. foreign policies as threats to world peace and strongly support New Zealand's antinuclear stance.

"From boyhood, imaginative writing has been one of my life's chief pleasures, kept alive throughout depression, war, and a busy conventional teaching career in rural isolation by poetry (personal, reflective, and lyrical-realistic), short stories, book reviewing, and endless drafts of more ambitious work.

"I'm lucky that ten years after retiring from teaching, I continue to be absorbed in full-time writing. To date, my most substantial project, the trilogy of 'Forest People' novels, after several printings, steadily gains widening recognition and readership. In depicting survival groups in a post-catastrophe New Zealand continuing into the future, the work weaves together myth, legend, poetry, spiritual, and temporal values drawn from contemporary New Zealand life. I've been concerned to portray mankind's endless struggles towards a possible hard-won reconciliation with self and the natural world. Even against today's frightful threat to the planet, I'd call myself soberly optimistic that life will prevail."

AVOCATIONAL INTERESTS: Travel (Europe, Kenya).

* * *

HOOPER, Peter
See HOOPER, Hedley Colwill

* * *

HOPF, Alice
See HOPF, Alice (Martha) L(ightner)

* * *

HOPF, Alice (Martha) L(ightner) 1904-1988
(Alice Hopf, A. M. Lightner, Alice Lightner)

OBITUARY NOTICE—See index for *CA* sketch: Born October 11, 1904, in Detroit, Mich.; died February 3, 1988, in Upper Black Eddy, Bucks County, Pa. Clerical worker, naturalist, and author. Hopf, who worked as a secretary and published under various names, wrote numerous science fiction and nature books for children. Her success and popularity among students and teachers alike derived from her skill in providing stimulating and informative reading that was easily comprehended by young people. Among Hopf's nonfiction writings are *Wild Traveler: The Story of a Coyote,* the award-winning *Misunderstood Animals,* and *Wild Cousins of the Cat*. Her fiction includes such titles as *The Rock of Three Planets* and *The Space Gypsies*. Additionally, Hopf was the author of a number of uncollected short stories, which she contributed to various periodicals.

OBITUARIES AND OTHER SOURCES:

BOOKS

Twentieth-Century Science Fiction Writers, 2nd edition, St. James Press, 1986.

PERIODICALS

New York Times, March 11, 1988.

* * *

HOUGH, Judy Taylor 1932-
(Judy Taylor)

PERSONAL: Surname rhymes with "plow"; born August 12, 1932, in Murton, Swansea, Wales; adopted daughter of Gladys Spicer Taylor (a teacher); married Richard Hough (a writer), June 7, 1980. *Education:* Educated until the age of sixteen in the United Kingdom.

ADDRESSES: Home and office—31 Meadowbank, Primrose Hill, London NW3 1AY, England.

CAREER: Bodley Head, London, England, specialist in children's books, 1951-84, director, 1967-84, deputy managing director, 1971-80; Chatto, Bodley Head & Jonathan Cape, London, director, 1973-80; Penguin Books, London, Beatrix Potter consultant, 1981—; associate director of Weston Woods Institute, 1984—.

MEMBER: Publishers Association (chairman of children's book group, 1969-72; member of council, 1972-78).

AWARDS, HONORS: Named a member of the Order of the British Empire for services to children's literature, 1971.

WRITINGS—ALL UNDER NAME JUDY TAYLOR:

My First Year: A Beatrix Potter Baby Book, Warne, 1983.
Beatrix Potter: Artist, Storyteller, and Countrywoman, illustrations by Beatrix Potter, Warne, 1987.
"That Naughty Rabbit": Beatrix Potter and "Peter Rabbit," Warne, 1987.

"SOPHIE AND JACK" SERIES; FOR CHILDREN

Sophie and Jack, illustrations by Susan Ganter, Bodley Head, 1982, Philomel Books, 1983.
. . . *Help Out,* illustrations by Ganter, Bodley Head, 1983, Philomel Books, 1984.
. . . *in the Snow,* illustrations by Ganter, Bodley Head, 1984.

"DUDLEY DORMOUSE" SERIES; FOR CHILDREN

Dudley Goes Flying, illustrations by Peter Cross, Putnam, 1986.
. . . and the Monster, illustrations by Cross, Putnam, 1986.
. . . in a Jam, illustrations by Cross, Putnam, 1987.
. . . and the Strawberry Shake, illustrations by Cross, Putnam, 1987.

Also author of *Dudley Bakes a Cake,* illustrations by Cross.

WORK IN PROGRESS: Compiling, with Elizabeth Battrich, Anne S. Hobbs, and Irene J. Whalley, *Beatrix Potter: 1866-1943,* an exhibition catalog; editing *Selected Letters of Beatrix Potter,* publication by Warne expected in 1989 or 1990.

SIDELIGHTS: Judy Taylor Hough told *CA:* "I've worked in the children's book field all my life, first as an editor and publisher, now as a writer. My interest in Beatrix Potter began at my mother's knee and continued through my collecting early children's books and my love of England's Lake District where I was at boarding school. Now I'm inextricably involved!"

AVOCATIONAL INTERESTS: Collecting early children's books, gardening.

* * *

HOUSTON, Beverle (Ann) 1936-1988

OBITUARY NOTICE—See index for *CA* sketch: Born December 23, 1936, in Reading, Pa.; died of cancer, February 27, 1988, in Los Angeles, Calif. Educator and author. Houston taught English and film studies in California secondary schools and colleges during most of her career. With Martha Kinder she wrote *Close-Up: A Critical Perspective on Film* and *Self and Cinema: A Transformalist Perspective*. She also contributed articles and reviews to literature and film journals. During the 1970s Houston served briefly as contributing editor of *Women and Film* and editor of *Quarterly Review of Film Studies*.

OBITUARIES AND OTHER SOURCES:

PERIODICALS

Los Angeles Times, March 2, 1988.

* * *

HOWARD, Deborah (Janet) 1946-

PERSONAL: Born February 26, 1946, in London, England; daughter of Thomas Were (a chemical manufacturer) and Isobel (in public service; maiden name, Brewer) Howard; married Malcolm Longair (an astronomer), September 26, 1975; children: Mark, Sarah. *Education:* Newnham College, Cambridge, B.A. (with first class honors), 1968; Courtauld Institute of Art, London, M.A. (with distinction), 1969, Ph.D., 1973.

ADDRESSES: Home—Edinburgh, Scotland. *Office*—Department of Architecture, University of Edinburgh, 20 Chambers St., Edinburgh EH1 1JZ, Scotland.

CAREER: Cambridge University, Clare Hall, Cambridge, England, Leverhulme fellow, 1972-73; University of London, University College, London, England, lecturer in art history, 1973-76; part-time lecturer at Cambridge, London, and Edinburgh universities, 1976-82; Edinburgh University, Edinburgh, Scotland, lecturer in architecture, 1982—. Temporary lecturer at Yale University, 1977 and 1980; member of Royal Fine Art Commission for Scotland.

MEMBER: National Trust, Scottish Wildlife Trust, Architectural Heritage Society of Scotland (member of cases panel and member of local and national executive committees), Friends of Scottish Monuments, Society of Architectural Historians, Society for Renaissance Studies, College Art Association, Association of Art Historians, Society of Antiquaries of London (fellow).

WRITINGS:

Jacopo Sansovino: Architecture and Patronage in Renaissance Venice, Yale University Press, 1975, revised edition, 1987.
The Architectural History of Venice, Batsford, 1980, Holmes & Meier, 1981, revised edition, Batsford, 1987.

Contributor of articles and book reviews to periodicals, including *Burlington* and *Journal of the Society of Architectural Historians*. Editor of the journal of the Architectural Heritage Society of Scotland.

WORK IN PROGRESS: Research in Venetian art and architecture.

SIDELIGHTS: In *Jacopo Sansovino: Architecture and Patronage in Renaissance Venice* Deborah Howard discusses the various civic, ecclesiastical, and aristocratic bodies that sponsored Venetian building in the sixteenth century. The life and architecture of Sansovino, a sculptor and architect who built for all the patron groups, serve to illustrate the workings of the patronage system. According to Anthony Blunt of the *Times Literary Supplement,* Howard's examination of how patrons' needs affected Sansovino's art "will interest equally the social historian and the student of architecture." The critic commended Howard's detailed research and imaginative treatment of material, judging it "a fascinating book, full of information and very readable."

Howard's next book, *The Architectural History of Venice,* chronicles Venetian building over a span of thirteen centuries, focusing on the most notable edifices rather than those most typical of their age. Howard also includes comments on building materials, modes of travel, explanations of structure, and historical context helpful to visitors. Altogether, observed Bruce Boucher in another *Times Literary Supplement* review, the author conveys a remarkable amount of information in a balanced, brief account. Boucher downplayed his only criticism of the work—that its focus on facts at times presents a "denatured" view of the city—and hailed it as "the best concise introduction to Venetian architecture in English."

Howard told *CA:* "I have recently been appointed a member of the Royal Fine Art Commission for Scotland, a small body of experts appointed by Royal Warrant to protect Scotland's artistic patrimony. I am a member of the cases panel of the Architectural Heritage Society of Scotland, which has the statutory right to report on all planning applications relating to 'listed' or historic buildings. In addition, I am the editor of their journal and a member of their local and national executive committees. Edinburgh is exceptionally rich in historic architecture, still preserving its medieval city as well as the remarkable Georgian 'New Town.' It is a dignified and civilized city in an exceptional natural setting, very much worth protecting in my view. I am also an enthusiastic supporter of efforts to preserve Scotland's countryside and wildlife. On a different line, I am involved in trying to improve the opportunities for women in academic life. I am the women's group representative of the local Association of University Teachers.

"Writing has now become a luxury, owing to the competition from my university teaching job, two small children, a peri-

patetic husband, and a big garden. Nonetheless, I still manage to maintain a steady output of articles and book reviews.''

AVOCATIONAL INTERESTS: Photography, music, gardening, hill-walking.

BIOGRAPHICAL/CRITICAL SOURCES:

PERIODICALS

New Statesman, May 1, 1981.
Times Literary Supplement, February 27, 1976, December 11, 1981.

* * *

HOWE, Florence 1929-

PERSONAL: Born March 17, 1929, in New York, N.Y.; daughter of Samuel (a taxi driver) and Frances (a bookkeeper; maiden name, Stilly) Rosenfeld; married third husband, Paul Lauter (a professor), in 1967 (divorced, 1987). *Education:* Hunter College, A.B., 1950; Smith College, A.M., 1951; graduate study at University of Wisconsin (now University of Wisconsin—Madison), 1951-54.

ADDRESSES: Home—201 East 87th St., Apt. 11 D, New York, N.Y. 10128. *Office*—Feminist Press, 311 East 94th St., New York, N.Y. 10128; and Department of English, City College of the City University of New York, 138th St. and Convent Ave., New York, N.Y. 10031.

CAREER: Hofstra College (now University), Hempstead, N.Y., instructor in English, 1954-57; Queens College of the City of New York (now Queens College of the City University of New York), Flushing, N.Y., lecturer in English, 1956-57; Goucher College, Towson, Md., assistant professor of English, 1960-71; Feminist Press, Old Westbury, N.Y., founder and president, 1970—, co-director, 1982-86, director, 1986—; State University of New York College at Old Westbury, Old Westbury, professor of humanities and American studies, 1971-87, coordinator of women's studies, 1971-74, chairperson of American studies, 1975-76; City College of the City University of New York, New York City, professor of English, 1987—.

Teacher at Freedom School in Jackson, Miss., summer, 1964; director of Project in the Teaching of Poetry for Goucher College and Baltimore Public Schools, 1967-71; visiting professor at colleges and universities in the United States and abroad, including University of Utah, 1973 and 1975, University of Washington, summer, 1974, Free University of Berlin, summer, 1978, Oberlin College, fall, 1978, Denison University, spring, 1979, University of Alabama, summer, 1979, and City University of New York, 1986-87; faculty exchange scholar at State University of New York, 1975; scholar in residence at Miami University, 1978; Drushal Distinguished Professor at College of Wooster, spring, 1980; U.S. delegate to UNESCO World Conference on Teaching and Research About Women, 1980; organizer, chairperson, and lecturer at conferences on women in the United States and abroad; has served as advisory board member to education institutes and organizations, including Teachers and Writers Collaborative, Center for Self-Reliant Education, and University of Arizona's Southwest Institute for Research on Women. Executive committee member of board of directors of the National Council for Research on Women, 1983-85.

MEMBER: Modern Language Association of America (chairperson of commission on the status of women, 1969-71, and of division of women's studies, 1978-83; second vice-president, 1971; first vice-president, 1972; president, 1973), National Women's Studies Association (founding member), Phi Beta Kappa.

AWARDS, HONORS: National Endowment for the Humanities research fellowship, 1971-73; elected to Hunter College Hall of Fame, 1973; Ford Foundation fellowship for the study of women in society, 1974-75; Fulbright Scholar Award to India, 1977; honorary D.H.L. from New England College, 1977, Skidmore College, 1979, and DePauw University, 1987; Mellon fellowship from Wellesley College, 1979; Mina P. Shaughnessy Medal from Modern Language Association of America, 1982-83; travel and lecture grant to Japan, India, and West Germany from U.S. Department of State, 1983.

WRITINGS:

(With husband Paul Lauter) *The Conspiracy of the Young,* World, 1970.
Seven Years Later: Women's Studies Programs in 1976: A Report of the National Advisory Council on Women's Educational Programs, The Council, 1977.
(With Lauter) *The Impact of Women's Studies on the Curriculum and the Disciplines* (monograph), National Institute of Education, 1980.
Myths of Coeducation: Selected Essays, 1964-1983, Indiana University Press, 1984.

EDITOR

Female Studies II: An Anthology of Sixty-six Syllabi and Bibliographies (monograph), Know, Inc. (Pittsburgh, Pa.), 1970.
(With Carol Ahlum) *Female Studies III: An Anthology of Fifty-four Syllabi and Bibliographies* (monograph), Know, Inc. 1971.
(With Ellen Bass, and author of introduction) *No More Masks! An Anthology of Poems by Women,* Anchor Press, 1973.
(And contributor) *Women and the Power to Change,* McGraw, 1975.
(And author of introduction with Nancy Hoffman) *Women Working: An Anthology of Stories and Poems,* Feminist Press, 1979.
(With Suzanne Howard and Mary Jo Boehm Strauss, and author of introduction) *Everywoman's Guide to Colleges and Universities,* Feminist Press, 1982.
(With Marsha Saxton) *With Wings: An Anthology of Literature by and About Women With Disabilities,* Feminist Press, 1987.
(With John Farragher) *Women and Higher Education: In Celebration of Mount Holyoke's 175th Birthday,* Norton, 1987.

Editor of phonograph record *Tough Poems for Tough People,* Caedmon, 1972.

Editor, *Women's Studies Quarterly,* 1972-82; member of editorial board of *Women's Studies: An Interdisciplinary Journal,* 1971—, *SIGNS: Women in Culture and Society,* 1974-80, *Journal of Education,* 1976—, *Correspondence of Lydia Marie Child,* 1977-81, and *Research in the Humanities,* 1977—, State University of New York Press, 1977-80.

CONTRIBUTOR

Nancy Larrick, editor, *Somebody Turned on a Tap in These Kids: Poetry and Young People Today,* Delacorte, 1971.
Louis Kampf and Lauter, editors, *The Politics of Literature,* Pantheon, 1972.
Alice S. Rossi and Anne Calderwood, editors, *Academic Women on the Move,* Russel Sage, 1973.

(Author of introduction) Nancy Frazier and Myra Sadker, *Sexism in School and Society,* Harper, 1973.

Jean Ramage Leppaluoto and others, editors, *Women on the Move: A Feminist Perspective,* Know, Inc., 1973.

Judith Stacey, Susan Bereaud, and Joan Daniels, editors, *And Jill Came Tumbling After: Sexism in American Education,* Dell, 1974.

(Author of introduction) Tamar Berkowitz, Jean Mangi, and Jane Williamson, editors, *Who's Who and Where in Women's Studies,* Feminist Press, 1974.

(Author of afterword) Agnes Smedley, *Portraits of Chinese Women in Revolution,* edited by Jan MacKinnon and Steve MacKinnon, Feminist Press, 1976.

Judith Stiehm, editor, *The Frontiers of Knowledge,* University of Southern California Press, 1976.

Contributor of numerous articles and essays to periodicals, including *American Scholar, College English, Colloquy, Contemporary Literature, English Record, Harvard Educational Review, Kansas Teacher, Liberal Education, Ms., Nation, New York Times, Phi Delta Kappan, PMLA, Radical Teacher, Saturday Review,* and *Today's Education.*

WORK IN PROGRESS: Editing and contributing to *Tradition and the Talents of Women,* for Illinois University Press; *Women and Revolution: Literary and Political Essays* and *Who Learns? Who Teaches? Essays in the Experience of Teaching,* both for Indiana University Press.

SIDELIGHTS: Feminist Florence Howe is a longtime advocate of educational and social reform. A professor of English at the City College of the City University of New York and a past president of the Modern Language Association, she is also a respected scholar and historian. For much of her career, however, Howe has been an outspoken critic of the academic system, arguing that the college curriculum is biased in favor of men and should be expanded to include courses that address the activities and interests of women. To this end, she has lectured widely and written extensively about the need to institute courses in women's studies as a basic part of the college curriculum. In addition, Howe is founder and publisher of the Feminist Press, an editing and publishing concern that, according to Joseph Duffy in the *New York Times Book Review,* "has, perhaps more than any other institution, helped to recover and make available a legacy of writing by and about women in American history and scholarship."

Howe's interest in feminist educational reform was influenced by her involvement in the civil rights movement of the 1960s. In her 1984 collection of essays, *Myths of Coeducation,* Howe explains that her experience as a Freedom School teacher in Mississippi during the summer of 1964 changed her life and set her on a path of social and educational activism. As one of several hundred volunteers recruited from the racially mixed, campus-based civil rights organization Student Nonviolent Coordinating Committee (SNCC), Howe worked with black children and teenagers in the schools, leading discussions and activities that examined the status of blacks in American society. The stated purpose of the Freedom Schools, reports Howe in her essay "Mississippi's Freedom Schools: The Politics of Education," included in *Myths of Coeducation: Selected Essays, 1964-1983,* was "to provide an educational experience for students which will make it possible for them to challenge the myths of our society, to perceive more clearly its realities, and to find alternatives, and ultimately, new directions for action." The SNCC, aware that schools for black children were inferior and served only to perpetuate the subordination of blacks in society, hoped that the program would encourage participants to view themselves more positively, to register to vote, and to enroll in previously all-white segregated schools—in short, to demand the rights guaranteed to all citizens but granted only to whites. Through this experience, Howe came to view educational reform as a necessary first step in effecting social reform. For, she asserts in her essay, "our schools are political grounds in which our students begin to learn about society's rules" and "if we wish to alter our students and our society, we must alter our schools."

Howe applied the lessons she learned from her summer in Mississippi to her fight for educational reform for women. As an assistant professor at an all-women's college during the 1960s, Howe had already begun to incorporate literature for women into her English courses, and as the women's movement spread through campuses in the late 1960s and early 1970s, she increasingly wrote and lectured on feminist issues. She determined that, like the black students in the Freedom Schools of the 1960s, women needed to begin questioning and challenging the assumptions of a society—and an educational system—that viewed them as subordinate to men. She was particularly concerned with the status of women in higher education. Noting that women's achievements fell noticeably behind men's on the university level, Howe argued that the college curriculum is geared toward men because of its male-centered perspective in such areas as literature, history, sociology, and psychology. "The implicit curricular message to women students is thus simple," writes Howe in an essay in *Myths of Coeducation,* "men work, write, and make history, psychology, theology: women get married, have babies, and rear them."

In order to alter what she considers an unfairly structured educational system, Howe, like many other feminists, has advocated the inclusion of women's studies into the college curriculum. An interdisciplinary program comprised of such courses as women's literature, health, economics, and history, women's studies has proliferated on campuses since the 1970s. Howe describes women's studies as "the educational arm of the women's movement," and she hopes that such programs will not only increase the number of women in higher education, but will transform the male-centered curriculum to one that also represents women and minorities. The impact of such a change, Howe asserts, will not only raise women's status in the university, but in the society at large. Additionally, she notes, courses that focus on women "begin to restore a lost feminist history and culture, a tradition and an ancestry necessary for human dignity."

Indeed, Howe's abiding concern for restoring the lost scholarship of women is reflected in her founding of the Feminist Press in 1970. Dedicated to publishing works by women authors of the past and present, the Feminist Press is a nonprofit, tax-exempt educational organization whose aim, writes Howe in a note from the publisher in the press's catalog, is "to change the education of girls and boys, women and men, through the publication of new kinds of books that would be educational for both teachers and students." She adds, "we are especially eager to reach teachers and students, and thus add to the classroom the 'lost' literature and history of women." As publisher, Howe also edits and has been president of Feminist Press since its founding. Additionally, Howe conceived and co-edited *Everywoman's Guide to Colleges and Universities,* a survey of the opportunities and services available to women at nearly six hundred institutions.

Throughout her more than thirty-year career, Howe has demonstrated an unwavering commitment to education and scholarship. As a teacher, writer, editor, and publisher, she has worked to reform those institutions that traditionally have excluded women from their ranks. Her contributions in the field of women's studies and feminist scholarship remain unparalleled and have made her a unique and valuable voice in the American feminist movement.

CA INTERVIEW

CA interviewed Florence Howe by telephone on June 18, 1986, at her office at the Feminist Press in New York City.

CA: You have been, as American Women Writers *says, "a national leader in the field of women's studies and one of its best informed historians," doing your work not only in the classroom but also as editor, publisher, writer, and lecturer. Do you still think of yourself, in all of these pursuits, chiefly as a teacher?*

HOWE: Yes.

CA: One of your primary long-term goals in women's studies has been to get women's history and literature integrated into the basic curriculum. To what extent do you see that happening now?

HOWE: To a surprising extent, especially in American literature and in American history. Books by and about women writers are being used more frequently in traditional American literature courses, for one thing. For another, though we haven't done a survey, we have at least an impression from talking with hundreds of faculty members that many English departments now have at least one course called "American Women Writers," and some departments have six or seven. But it's the initial introductory courses and some of the major courses that I was always most concerned about.

CA: Can you envision a time when women's lives and histories will be so truly integrated into the standard curriculum that the need for separate programs of women's studies would be eliminated?

HOWE: I don't see any way in which they will be eliminated. In part this is because, no matter what we do, we still have a two-thousand-year written history of separation, and that has made for very different patterns in men's and women's lives. So even though some of the curriculum will be comparative, some of it will be and should be separate. For example, [Samuel Taylor] Coleridge and [William] Wordsworth are approximately the same age as Jane Austen, and they lived in the same small country in Western Europe at the same time, and yet they led very different lives. It would be rather strange to see them in the same course, even if they wrote in the same genre. Finally, Elizabeth Barrett Browning and Emily Dickinson have more in common with Jane Austen than do Wordsworth and Coleridge. So my sense is that whatever happens, we will be teaching some courses in the tradition.

The same kind of comparison is true in this country. Willa Cather is certainly a daughter of Sarah Orne Jewett, and she needs to be seen in that line of writers. There are several dozen women writers who read each other, and not only United States writers; women in this country read writers in English wherever they were. They wrote to and about each other and out of their streams—as did male writers. We always took for granted that, as T. S. Eliot told us in "Tradition and the Individual Talent," male writers wrote to and for each other. So did women writers. I think we'll have those separate histories therefore. As for history *qua* history, in the classroom and the textbook, I think we're going to continue to have separate and together histories. And I don't see any reason not to. I think it's quite interesting.

CA: In the introduction to No More Masks!, *published in 1973, you spoke of the "new breed of conscious feminist scholars—historians and literary critics—who must review and restore our literature." Are there special difficulties in finding and restoring that literature?*

HOWE: Not really, unless you count the quantity as a special difficulty. I find it wonderful and even amusing. No one predicted how much there was, and there are vast amounts. Some presses are now talking about one hundred women novelists *before* Jane Austen, which is very startling. At the Feminist Press we continue to publish what we believe is of high literary quality. We're very choosy. There's lots and lots to choose from.

CA: Besides high literary quality, are there other criteria you apply in deciding what works to publish?

HOWE: Availability. That is, the context needs to be still important to a contemporary audience. Usability in the college classroom is very important to us because we publish forever and not for a single year or a couple of years. And availability means to us not only the classroom but the trade bookstore.

CA: Are there new writers—female or male—whose work you particularly admire for its treatment of women?

HOWE: I wouldn't say the ones I admire are new, but they are wonderful. Grace Paley and Tillie Olsen are among my favorites, as are Paule Marshall, Toni Morrison, and Alice Walker.

CA: Some of those are black writers, of course. In the introduction to No More Masks! *you wrote of black poetry: "The black tradition is distinctive, and only in the recent poems of young white women have we begun to feel something of its effects." Do you think that influence has increased since 1973?*

HOWE: Oh, yes, even on white male writers in general. At the time I wrote that, I don't think it had crossed the consciousness of many males that black women writers were so important to us. I think it's quite obvious that everyone is aware of how important black women writers are now in the United States.

CA: Your ambition to be a teacher was fostered by your mother, but your work in that direction was for a long time shaped and swayed largely by traditional male-oriented beliefs and social conditions. Do you see young women today making choices as if they were bound by the same strictures, despite some very real strides toward independence we've made in the last two decades?

HOWE: Some are clearly affected by what's happened in the last twenty years. Others, depending on where they've gone to school and the kinds of courses they've had, might be me back in the fifties. The picture is very mixed, interestingly

mixed. In fact, the latter kind, if they go on to graduate school or if they go to work, can't help but bump into their other kind, so that I think the prognosis is relatively cheerful. We have four interns here at the Feminist Press. They're from Wesleyan, Hunter, University of Massachusetts at Amherst, and Cornell. And they all chose us. They could have gone to other places. They are very sparkling, bright; they've all had women's studies and they really know our books. They are all twenty years old, more or less, and delightful. I wasn't so bright at that age.

CA: Do you find women in higher positions in colleges and universities being more supportive of women in lesser positions now than was the case when Women and the Power to Change *was published in 1975?*

HOWE: Oh yes, I think so. I think people still complain because they expect *all* women to be supportive of other women, and they're not. But I think there are more who are, and who are conscious of why they should be.

CA: From 1969 to 1971 you were first chairperson for the Modern Language Association's Commission on the Status of Women. Since that time you've served in other important capacities in the MLA [Modern Language Association], including a term as president in 1973. What kind of progression have you observed in that organization's attitudes toward women in academic positions and the teaching of women's studies?

HOWE: The new executive director of MLA is a woman, Phyllis Franklin. That's the first time in the history of the association. I was the first woman president in modern times; there had been two, I believe, in the first twenty years of the century and then none until 1973. Since then, I think men and women have had about the same number of years as president. Besides the fact that there's a female executive editor now for the first time, I think the board of directors and the editorial board of *PMLA* continue to have at least a fair representation of women, 40 to 60 percent.

CA: Since 1977 you've been an international spokesperson for women's studies. How does the situation with women's studies in other countries compare with that in ours?

HOWE: Very favorably in some places, and just getting started in others. I can think of few countries in the world in which there isn't some degree of enthusiasm and at least some beginning. At the World Conference on the United Nations Decade for Women in Nairobi [Kenya] last summer we did twenty sessions called "Women's Studies International." These were workshops and panels. And we had requests from women in Paraguay and from Uruguay and Uganda for assistance in starting women's studies programs in those countries. Those were the most astonishing to me. There are very active women's studies programs in the Sudan already, at the National University at Khartoum, and in countries like Japan, for example. In India, to name another, there are very, very active women's studies associations, national associations of academics, and many programs.

CA: You've written about how your own consciousness as a teacher was changed by your experience as a Freedom School teacher in Mississippi in 1964. Do you have what could be called a specific philosophy of teaching?

HOWE: Probably, but I don't know how to express it briefly. I think it would have to do with enabling students to understand their history, their identities, and to learn therefore from their strengths and abilities. Somehow to convince students that they have the power to learn is probably the first job of the teacher.

CA: That Mississippi experience also paved the way for your feminist consciousness, you've said, which was somewhat more delayed because of your dedication to the civil rights movement and the anti-Vietnam War movement.

HOWE: And also because of the ignorant way in which I was educated. That is, I knew nothing about women's history. I didn't even think in terms of women *having* any particular history, never thought about gender as an item that was a factor. I certainly thought about class and race, but not gender, although when I was a little kid my theme song to my mother constantly was, "Why do I have to do this and Jackie [my kid brother] doesn't?" And when she said, "Because you're a girl and he's a boy," I would always say, "Unfair" and she would say, "Well, who said anything had to be fair?" But very explicitly men did certain things and women did others because it was an Orthodox Jewish household. And my mother was a slave to all that, even though the reason she wanted me to be a teacher was that *she* had not been allowed to be a teacher because teachers were men, not women. My rabbi grandfather could not imagine a woman as a teacher.

CA: Looking back on the civil rights and anti-Vietnam War movements, do you think they were particularly good training for the women's movement?

HOWE: Yes, they were essential. We know that the nineteenth-century women's movements did not spring out of nowhere. They sprang out of great religious revival and out of the abolitionist movement. That's where women got their training and their ideas for activism. No movements spring out of themselves. Movements always learn from other movements. They learn even simple things, like how to do a mailing. Even the idea of having a movement has come from somewhere.

CA: In the preface to Myths of Coeducation *you referred to the young woman you taught in Mississippi who became your daughter. Did you actually adopt her?*

HOWE: Yes, informally. Her parents handed her to me, blessed her and blessed me, and we went off together for many years. Her parents are now dead and she has two children. She's a lawyer and lives with her lawyer husband in Stockton, California. Her two children are a boy, who is named Jackie after her favorite sister Jacqueline, and a girl, who's named Florence after me. The girl is five and the boy is ten. It's lovely.

CA: In your writing you've referred several times to the unfinished Ph.D. From this vantage point it doesn't seem to have handicapped your career. How do you feel about it now?

HOWE: I should have done it. It has and it hasn't handicapped my career. When people have wanted to avoid hiring me, they have pointed to that. Although I'm not overwhelmed with grief about it, I feel I was misguided in general and I'm sorry I didn't finish it for many different reasons, not the least of which is that I was on to a very good thing in relation to *Mrs. Dalloway* very early, long before the revival of interest in

Virginia Woolf. No one has done what I was trying to do. It's still in a drawer, and I may do it in my sixtieth year.

CA: Leaving alone the question of how you can possibly do everything you do, I'll just ask how your time is divided now among your professional activities.

HOWE: Mainly I'm at the press. I'm the president, and now that my partner, Maxine McCants, has left, I'm the full-time director and publisher.

CA: What about teaching? Are you doing any now?

HOWE: I'm not doing any classroom teaching right now. I do some lecturing and some workshops, and of course those are really teaching.

CA: As founder, president, and chief administrator of the press, what do you feel proudest of in its work since the beginning?

HOWE: What we started talking about early in this interview, the rediscovery of lost women writers.

CA: Do you see, by and large, a healthy self-concept among the women you're in contact with now?

HOWE: Indeed. One could always want more, but compared to what I remember of myself, compared to what I remember even of Goucher students in the early sixties, before the women's movement, these are women with a purpose and with a sense of their own futures as working persons and their efforts—difficult, still quite difficult—to balance a personal life and professional life.

CA: What do you feel is the most urgent priority in education today with regard to women?

HOWE: Ah, there are many. One is still dealing with that whole question of the male bias of the curriculum. We've made a start, but a start is hardly the whole curriculum. We have miles and miles to go.

BIOGRAPHICAL/CRITICAL SOURCES:

BOOKS

Howe, Florence, *Myths of Coeducation: Selected Essays, 1964-1983*, Indiana University Press, 1984.

PERIODICALS

The Feminist Press Catalog, 1987-88.
Ms., September, 1973, September, 1979.
New York Times, December 31, 1970.
New York Times Book Review, February 24, 1985.
Virginia Quarterly Review, spring, 1976.

—*Sketch by Paulette Petrimoulx*

—*Interview by Jean W. Ross*

* * *

HOWE, George Frederick 1901-1988

OBITUARY NOTICE: Born July 1, 1901, in Burlington (one source says Charlotte), Vt.; died of cancer, January 18, 1988, in Washington, D.C. Historian, educator, editor, and author. Howe taught history at the University of Cincinnati for nineteen years before embarking on a career as a government historian. A researcher with the Army's Historical Branch beginning in 1946, Howe joined the staff of the National Security Agency (NSA) eight years later as its senior historian. While serving in that post he wrote and supervised the writing of official Army historical works. In 1971 he was presented with the NSA's meritorious civilian service award and also retired, but he continued to work on government projects over the next twelve years. He was a founder of the Society of American Historians and a member of the editorial board and executive committee of the Mississippi Valley Historical Association. His books include *Chester Arthur: A Quarter-Century of Machine Politics* and *Northwest Africa: Seizing the Initiative in the West,* part of the U.S. Army's official history of World War II. He was also editor and co-author of *American Historical Association's Guide to Historical Literature.*

OBITUARIES AND OTHER SOURCES:

BOOKS

Directory of American Scholars, Volume I: *History,* 6th edition, Bowker, 1974.
Ohio Authors and Their Books: Biographical Data and Selective Bibliographies for Ohio Authors, Native and Resident, 1796-1950, World Publishing, 1962.

PERIODICALS

New York Times, January 26, 1988.
Washington Post, January 21, 1988.

* * *

HOYLE, Peter 1939-

PERSONAL: Born October 25, 1939, in Accrington, England; son of Fred (a textiles foreman) and Alice (a confectioner; maiden name, Haworth) Hoyle; married Dorothy Hamstead, September 28, 1963 (divorced, July, 1983); married Barbara Croop (a librarian), October 22, 1983; children: Richard, Judith. *Education:* Liverpool University, B.A. (with honors), 1962; Manchester School of Librarianship, chartered Library Association associate, 1966.

ADDRESSES: Home—19 Hexham Ave., Bolton, Lancashire BL1 5PP, England. *Agent*—Maggie Noach Literary Agency, 21 Redan St., London WI4 0AB, England.

CAREER: Lancashire County Libraries, Preston, England, assistant librarian, 1964-66; Bolton Public Libraries, Bolton, England, cataloger, 1966-74, acquisitions librarian, 1974-83; cataloger at Lancashire Polytechnic Library, 1983—.

AWARDS, HONORS: North West Arts Bursary, 1984.

WRITINGS:

The Man in the Iron Mask (novel), Carcanet, 1984.
Brantwood: The Story of an Obsession (novel), Carcanet, 1986.

WORK IN PROGRESS: Death of a Photographer, a novel; *Camera Lucida and Other Stories;* a novel set in a partly rural, partly industrial area of Lancashire in the 1950s.

SIDELIGHTS: The narrator of Peter Hoyle's first novel, *The Man in the Iron Mask,* is a contemporary loser whose lackluster existence is stirred by the arrival of a madman in the apartment upstairs. His neighbor is convinced that he is Louis XIV's imprisoned twin from Alexandre Dumas's *Man in the Iron Mask;* at first beguiled by the elegant fantasy, the narrator eventually attempts to shatter it, revealing vestiges of his own madness. "The distinctions between retainer and would-

be prisoner," judged John Melmouth in the *Times Literary Supplement,* "are winsomely dismantled."

In his second novel, *Brantwood: The Story of an Obsession,* Hoyle again looks at literary mania. Its young narrator visits John Ruskin's Victorian gothic retreat in order to chronicle the late philosopher's delusory last years; Brantwood's dark atmosphere, in turn, draws the biographer into a world of hallucination and the supernatural. "The reader is not always reassured that the delusions are delusions, and several mysteries—including the central mystery of Ruskin's madness—remain unsolved," noted Lindsay Duguid in a *Times Literary Supplement* critique. "The narrator's predicament is genuinely moving, and at the same time we are invited to admire in a more detached way the neat dovetailing of Ruskinian notions with the lives of his unbelieving biographers," the writer continued. "*Brantwood*'s *grand guignol* flourishes create an appropriate *frisson,* and the book is never less than enjoyable, humorous and humane."

Hoyle told *CA:* "Until 1980 I wrote only short stories. These gradually approached novella length. My first novel, *The Man in the Iron Mask,* was primarily concerned with the desire to live in a fictive world that is imaginatively satisfying rather than in the real world, a theme popular with late nineteenth-century symbolists and renegade naturalists who rejected reality for a dream world of their own. Until I was in my late thirties I had never read the Dumas novel or seen either the 1929 or the 1939 film adaptations, but once, for several weeks in childhood, I looked forward to borrowing a comic containing the story of the James Whale film version from a schoolmate who could never find it. More than twenty-five years later, writing the novel was in a sense an extension of what I imagined the story and the film might be like—the romanticized seventeenth-century atmosphere I projected myself into contrasting with the shabby urban industrial background against which my grandiose fantasies were taking place. My interest in the character of the legendary Man in the Iron Mask and a certain amount of background reading were grafted on to these very durable childhood recollections and fantasies."

BIOGRAPHICAL/CRITICAL SOURCES:

PERIODICALS

Times Literary Supplement, April 27, 1984, October 3, 1986.

* * *

HSU Ying 1935-

PERSONAL: Name is pronounced "Syu Ing"; born December 16, 1935, in Shanghai, China; daughter of Jing-An Hsu (a farmer) and Yong-fen Gu (a homemaker); married Bao-fa Tao (a broadcast correspondent), September 2, 1961; children: Dong Tao (son). *Education:* Foreign Languages Institute, Beijing, China, B.A., 1958; University of Utah, certification for teaching English as second language, 1982, M.Ed., 1985.

ADDRESSES: Home—1958 Browning Ave., Salt Lake City, Utah, 84108; and English Section, Foreign Language Press, People's Republic of China. *Office*—Department of Languages, University of Utah, Salt Lake City, Utah 84112.

CAREER: University of Utah, Salt Lake City, associate instructor in Chinese, 1980—, teaching assistant in elementary education studies, 1984—.

WRITINGS:

(Translator) *The Proud General,* Foreign Languages Press, 1960.

(With J. Marvin Brown) *Speaking Chinese in China,* Yale University Press, 1983.

WORK IN PROGRESS: An English/Chinese and Chinese/English business dictionary; a storybook for English-speaking students' extensive reading; preparing two more volumes of the conversational textbook *Speaking Chinese in China.*

SIDELIGHTS: Hsu Ying told *CA:* "I am interested in teaching the Chinese language to English-speaking people, in preparing textbooks for learning Chinese, and in writing about my four-year stay in the United States, comparing and contrasting the similarities and differences in education, culture, clothing, food, housing, and transportation between America and the People's Republic of China—my home country."

* * *

HUBBARD, Edward (Horton) 1937-

PERSONAL: Born July 2, 1937, in Birkenhead, England; son of John Horton (a bank manager) and Ellen G. (Dobie) Hubbard. *Education:* Attended University of Liverpool, 1955-62; Victoria University of Manchester, M.A., 1974. *Religion:* Church of England.

ADDRESSES: Home—88 Osmaston Rd., Prenton, Birkenhead L42 8LP, England.

CAREER: Architectural historian and writer. Member of Chester and Liverpool Diocesan Advisory Committees for the Care of Churches.

MEMBER: Society of Architectural Historians of Great Britain, Royal Archaeological Institute, Victorian Society, Society of Antiquaries (fellow).

WRITINGS:

(With Nikolaus Pevsner) *Cheshire,* Penguin, 1971.
Clwyd, Penguin, 1986.
(With John Vaughan) *Liverpool,* Victorian Society, 1986.

WORK IN PROGRESS: Architectural Patronage of the First Viscount Leverhulme, including the Port Sunlight Model Village; *John Douglas of Chester, Architect.*

SIDELIGHTS: Edward Hubbard told *CA:* "I have a life-long enthusiasm for buildings. I studied architecture at the University of Liverpool, but found that I was not suited to the practice of the art. I turned to architectural history and was awarded a Master of Arts degree for a thesis on the work of the architect John Douglas of Chester. I was disabled by serious illness in 1985, but I continue my research and writing as far as this limitation permits.

"I aim to provide detailed and scholarly information and, at the same time, communicate something of the enjoyment to be derived from understanding and appreciating architecture and the building environment within their historical contexts."

AVOCATIONAL INTERESTS: Music (especially opera), collecting books.

BIOGRAPHICAL/CRITICAL SOURCES:

PERIODICALS

Times Literary Supplement, June 27, 1986.

HUBBARD, J(ake) T(imothy) W(illiam) 1935-

PERSONAL: Born May 23, 1935, in London, England; son of Walter Glover (a master printer) and Ada Moubray (Rolland) Hubbard; married Susan Schwartz Long (a writer and university instructor), June, 1979; children: Stephanie, Rufus John, Katherine, Clare. *Education:* Attended Pembroke College, Cambridge, 1955-56; Queen's University at Kingston, B.A. (with honors), 1960; Columbia University, M.Sc., 1961. *Religion:* Anglican.

ADDRESSES: Office—S. I. Newhouse School of Public Communications, Syracuse University, Syracuse, N.Y. 13210.

CAREER: Reporter for *Winnipeg Free Press* and *Toronto Telegram,* 1958-60; *National Geographic,* Washington, D.C., staff writer, 1961; *Business Week,* New York City, staff writer and assistant editor, 1961-63; *Newsweek,* New York City, associate editor, 1963-65; University of Missouri, Columbia, associate professor of journalism, 1965-69; Syracuse University, Syracuse, N.Y., professor of magazine journalism, 1969—, chairman of magazine department, 1969—. President and co-founder of Quadrant Research Associates (editorial consultant firm). *Military service:* British Army, 1953-55; became lieutenant.

MEMBER: Half Crown Club (founding member), Antique Boat Museum, Save the River.

WRITINGS:

Banking in Mid-America, Public Affairs Press, 1969.
(Contributor) *Bicentennial History of the United States,* U.S. News and World Report, 1975.
Magazine Editing: How to Acquire the Skills You Need to Win a Job and Succeed in the Magazine Business, Prentice-Hall, 1982.
The Race: An Inside Account of What It's Like to Compete in the Observer Singlehanded Transatlantic Race From Plymouth, England, to Newport, Rhode Island (Dolphin Book Club Main Selection), Norton, 1986.

Contributor to periodicals, including *Newsweek, Business Week, National Geographic,* and *SAIL.*

WORK IN PROGRESS: A textbook on writing magazine articles; "a series of police procedural murder mysteries."

SIDELIGHTS: J. T. W. Hubbard told *CA:* "I grew up in a cottage on the east coast of England where I came to love the vagaries of the weather, the flow of the tides, and the life of the sailor. In the spring of 1984 I entered my home-finished cutter, *Johan Lloyde,* in the Observer Singlehanded Transatlantic Race (OSTAR). Under the rules, each contestant must sail his or her boat alone, without use of the engine, from Plymouth, England, to Newport, Rhode Island. Of the ninety-two boats that started, only sixty-four arrived in Newport. The others did not make it due to such mishaps as dismasting, capsizing, collision, whale attack, personal injury, and simple failure of nerve. I fought my share of gales and grappled with boarders in a brief stop at the mysterious Azorean isle of Flores in my forty-two day voyage to Newport. But it was the quirky personalities of my fellow entrants that intrigued me most. I became fascinated by the psychological and the mythic dimensions of this Homeric contest and wrote the story of my experiences in a book that eventually became *The Race.*"

OSTAR is staged every four years with competitors ranging from paid professional sailors backed by large corporations to amateurs like Hubbard, a journalism professor at Syracuse University, who built his own thirty-two-foot cutter. Larry Martz, writing for *Newsweek,* commended Hubbard's "engaging, witty account" of his six-week-long transatlantic sail and added that *The Race* is "well told, often funny and honest."

Andrew Mershon, writing for the *Oregonian,* called *The Race* a "rollicking good tale" while *Book Locker,* which goes to the 200,000 members of Boat Owners Association of America, described Hubbard as "undoubtedly the best writer ever to chronicle a major offshore race . . . his account of his crossing is both funny and philosophical." Les Galloway, writing in the San Francisco *Examiner,* likened *The Race* to the works of Joshua Slocum and Jack London, and noted that it is "an extremely well-written and paced book that can be read like a novel by those not interested in the technical side of ocean racing."

AVOCATIONAL INTERESTS: Cross-country skiing, boat building, history of navigation, colonial history.

BIOGRAPHICAL/CRITICAL SOURCES:

PERIODICALS

Book Locker, fall, 1986.
Newsweek, November 17, 1986.
Oregonian, September 16, 1986.
Examiner (San Francisco), January 22, 1987.

* * *

HUDSON, James R. 1933-

PERSONAL: Born January 28, 1933, in Cleveland, Ohio; son of Alfred Lee and Esther (Madigan) Hudson. *Education:* Columbia College, B.A., 1958; University of Michigan, M.A., 1960, Ph.D., 1965.

ADDRESSES; Home—638 Chestnut St., Lancaster, Pa. 17603. *Office*—Department of Behavioral Sciences, Pennsylvania State University, Capitol Campus, Middletown, Pa. 17057.

CAREER: Russell Sage Foundation, New York, N.Y., research associate, 1963-64; Bryn Mawr College, Bryn Mawr, Pa., research associate, 1964-66; University of California at Berkeley, interviewer-consultant, 1966; State University of New York at Stony Brook, assistant professor, 1966-72; Pennsylvania State University at Harrisburg, Middletown, associate professor, 1972-87, professor of social science and sociology, 1987—. Consultant to the University of California School of Criminology, 1966, and to the New York school system, 1967; volunteer consultant to the U.S. Commission on Civil Rights, 1966, and to the Philadelphia Fellowship Commission on Civil Rights, 1968-69. *Military service:* U.S. Army, special agent for the counterintelligence corps, 1956-59.

MEMBER: American Sociological Association, Eastern Sociological Society, Midwest Sociological Society, Pennsylvania Sociological Society.

WRITINGS:

(With William Haber and Louis A. Ferman) *The Impact of Technological Change: The American Experience,* W. E. Upjohn Institute, 1963.
(Editor) *Social Welfare Agencies: Internal and External Dimensions,* Practitioneers Press, 1980.

The Unanticipated City: Loft Conversions in Lower Manhattan, University of Massachusetts Press, 1988.

WORK IN PROGRESS: A text, tentatively titled *Cities, Suburbs, and Society,* on urban society that combines the theoretical perspectives of human ecology and social psychology.

SIDELIGHTS: James R. Hudson told *CA:* "I am very interested in the future of older cities. The central question for me is whether their rich history and architecture can be combined with a contemporary social organization that embraces, but does not enshrine the past and, at the same time, is economically and socially progressive."

* * *

HUGHES, John 1950(?)-

BRIEF ENTRY: American film director and producer, screenwriter, editor, and author. Hughes was described by Michael London in the *Los Angeles Times* as "arguably Hollywood's hottest writer and perhaps its least known success story." *New York Times* contributor Thomas O'Connor concurred, complimenting Hughes's "striking affinity for the nuances of contemporary adolescent style, speech, music and, above all, emotional concerns" and dubbed the screenwriter "the auteur of the youth-film genre, the man whose pictures take kids seriously and still make money."

Hughes began his writing career by selling jokes to established comedians such as Rodney Dangerfield, Henny Youngman, and Rip Taylor. At twenty-two he joined a Chicago advertising agency, and for the next seven years he worked as an advertising copywriter in Chicago. In 1979 Hughes turned to free-lance writing and editing for *National Lampoon* magazine. Commissioned by the publication to turn one of his most successful story contributions into a screenplay, Hughes produced "National Lampoon's Vacation," a 1983 box office triumph. A second 1983 winning original screenplay was his "Mr. Mom." In 1984 Hughes made his directorial debut with "Sixteen Candles," and since then the list of his scripts-turned-into-film successes has included "The Breakfast Club" (1985), "Weird Science" (1985), "Pretty in Pink" (1986), and "Ferris Bueller's Day Off" (1986), all of which Hughes both wrote and directed. *Addresses: Office*—Paramount Studios, 5555 Melrose Ave., Bldg. C, Rm. 201, Los Angeles, Calif. 90038. *Agent*—Bill Haber, Creative Artists Agency, Inc., 1888 Century Pk. E., Los Angeles, Calif. 90067.

BIOGRAPHICAL/CRITICAL SOURCES:

BOOKS

International Motion Picture Almanac, Quigley, 1987.

PERIODICALS

American Film, May, 1986.
Chicago Tribune, July 29, 1983, February 15, 1985, March 12, 1986, June 11, 1986, February 27, 1987.
Los Angeles Times, November 23, 1983, May 4, 1984, February 15, 1985, September 11, 1986, February 27, 1987, April 7, 1987.
Newsweek, August 12, 1985, March 17, 1986, June 16, 1986.
New York Times, August 26, 1983, May 4, 1984, February 15, 1985, August 2, 1985, March 9, 1986, June 11, 1986, February 27, 1987, March 15, 1987.
Time, March 3, 1986, June 23, 1986, March 9, 1987.

HUGHES, Russell Meriwether 1898(?)-1988 (La Meri)

OBITUARY NOTICE: Known professionally as La Meri; born in May, 1898 (one source says in 1900), in Louisville, Ky.; died January 7, 1988, in San Antonio, Tex. Dancer, dance ethnologist, educator, and author. Hughes is best remembered as a leading authority on ethnic dance; she performed throughout the world at the height of her career during the 1920s and 1930s. In San Antonio, Texas, Hughes received her first formal training, studying Mexican and Spanish folk dance and ballet, and made her professional debut, performing to silent movie prologues. Her major dance works include "Krishna Gopala," a 1940 presentation; a starring role in a vaudevillian revue that played on Broadway in 1949, "A Night in Spain"; and she choreographed an Indian classical dance rendition of the ballet "Swan Lake."

In 1940 Hughes co-founded the New York School of Natya, where she taught and performed with her ensemble, the Five Natyas. She expanded the school into the Ethnologic Dance Center two years later, and it remained an important training ground for ethnic dance until it closed in 1956. Hughes also taught at the Juilliard School of Dance and at various universities across the nation. When she retired in 1970 she founded Ethnic Dance Arts in Hyannis, Massachusetts, where she presented a yearly festival and awards. Under her professional name, La Meri, Hughes wrote numerous books on dance, including *Dance as an Art-Form, The Gesture Language of the Hindu Dance,* and *Spanish Dancing.* She also produced an autobiography, *Dance Out the Answer,* as well as the poetry collections *Mexican Moonlight, Poems of the Plains,* and *The Star Roper.*

OBITUARIES AND OTHER SOURCES:

BOOKS

Who Was Who Among North American Authors, 1921-1939, Gale, 1976.

PERIODICALS

New York Times, January 21, 1988.

* * *

HUMBER, William 1949-

PERSONAL: Born September 9, 1949, in Toronto, Ontario, Canada; son of Alfred and Betty (Westlake) Humber; married Catherine McConkey (a teacher), August 10, 1974; children: Bradley, Darryl, Karen. *Education:* University of Toronto, B.A. (with honors), 1972; York University, M.Environmental Studies, 1975. *Religion:* Anglican.

ADDRESSES: Home—15 Beech Ave., Bowmanville, Ontario, Canada L1C 3A1. *Office*—Seneca College, 1750 Finch Ave. E., Willowdale, Ontario, Canada M2J 2X5.

CAREER: Seneca College, Toronto, Ontario, program coordinator of continuing education, 1977-83, chairman of continuing education, 1983—. Public participation officer for North Pickering Project, 1974-76; president of Visual Arts Centre of Newcastle, 1975-76; member of Newcastle Community Services Planning Board, 1983-86.

MEMBER: North American Society for Sports History, Canadian Association for Sports Heritage, Society of American Baseball Research (secretary, 1982-83), British Society for Sports History.

AWARDS, HONORS: Fellow of Central Mortgage and Housing Corp., 1973.

WRITINGS:

Cheering for the Home Team: The Story of Baseball in Canada, Boston Mills Press, 1983.
Freewheeling: The Story of Bicycling in Canada, Boston Mills Press, 1986.

Television and radio writer. Contributor to *Canadian Encyclopedia.* Contributor to magazines, including *Horizon Canada, Athletics,* and *Innings.*

WORK IN PROGRESS: The 1928 Olympic Games, completion expected in 1988; *The History of Track and Field in Canada,* completion expected in 1989; *Early Winter Sports in Canada,* completion expected in 1990.

SIDELIGHTS: Bill Humber told *CA:* "I am interested in the study of sports, not as a record of trivia and numbers (though I say that not disparagingly, for I believe the *Baseball Encyclopedia,* for instance, is a significant existential statement about the worth of men's lives), but as a means of exploring a people's culture through storytelling. In making public presentations on this theme, I make use of theater, music, photography, and so on. I yearn for a return to the organized lyceum movement, with venues throughout North America where I could share my tales, but for now books and magazine articles will suffice."

In *Freewheeling,* Humber proposes that the introduction of the bicycle to the Canadian public revolutionized Victorian society and had an even greater impact than the development of the railway. Humber claims that the humble bicycle was the first form of transportation that even poor people could afford. It freed the urban family from the confines of the city and released rural workers from the isolated Canadian farm. Its influence spread, in the late nineteenth century, to the wide, open spaces of western Canada and even to the Yukon gold fields. Humber reports that the popularity of the bicycle led to the creation of machine shops and factories that paved the way for modern Canadian industry. To Oliver Bertin, a reviewer for the *Globe and Mail:* "Perhaps the best part of Humber's book is the wealth of fascinating photographs that bring Victorian Canada to life in a manner that is rarely seen."

BIOGRAPHICAL/CRITICAL SOURCES:

PERIODICALS

Globe and Mail (Toronto), December 13, 1986.

* * *

HUMEZ, Jean McMahon 1944-

PERSONAL: Born October 13, 1944, in Brookline, Mass.; daughter of Howard O. (a physicist) and Lucile (a writer; maiden name, Nelson) McMahon; married Paul Alexander Humez (a writer); children: Thomas A., Nancy McMahon Swanborn. *Education:* Bennington College, B.A., 1966; Yale University, M.Phil., 1969, Ph.D., 1971.

ADDRESSES: Home—151 Elm, Somerville, Mass. 02144. *Office*—Program of Women's Studies, University of Massachusetts, Harbor Campus, Boston, Mass. 02125.

CAREER: Boston University, Boston, Mass., assistant professor of English, 1970-75; University of Massachusetts, Harbor Campus, Boston, assistant professor, 1975-82, associate professor of women's studies, 1982—.

WRITINGS:

(Editor) *Gifts of Power: The Writings of Rebecca Jackson, Black Visionary, Shaker Eldress,* University of Massachusetts Press, 1981.
Mother's First-Born Children: Writings by and About Shaker Women, Indiana University Press, in press.

* * *

HUMMEL, Madeline
See MOORE, Madeline (Roberta)

* * *

HUNGERFORD, Hesba (Fay) Brinsmead 1922-
(Hesba Fay Brinsmead)

PERSONAL: Born March 15, 1922, in Bilpin, Australia; daughter of Edward Keneln Guy (a sawmill worker) and May (Lambert) Hungerford; married Reginald Henry Brinsmead (an opal miner), February 11, 1943; children: Bernard Hungerford, Ken Hungerford. *Education:* Attended a teachers college. *Politics:* "A swinging voter." *Religion:* Christian.

ADDRESSES: Home—Shamara Rd., Terranora, New South Wales 2486, Australia.

CAREER: Governess during World War II; teacher in New South Wales and Tasmania, Australia, 1943-46; writer, 1960—. Teacher of speech to deaf children, 1946.

MEMBER: Australian Society of Authors.

AWARDS, HONORS: Children's Book of the Year Award from Austrailian Children's Book Council, 1964, for *Pastures of the Blue Crane,* and 1976, for *Longtime Passing;* Mary Gilmore Award from Mary Gilmore Society, 1964, for *Pastures of the Blue Crane;* Elizabethan Award from Elizabethan Society, England, for *Isle of the Sea Horse.*

WRITINGS:

I Will Not Say the Day Is Done, Alternative, 1983.

JUVENILE; UNDER NAME HESBA FAY BRINSMEAD

Pastures of the Blue Crane, Oxford University Press, 1965.
Season of the Bear, Oxford University Press, 1966.
Beat of the City, Oxford University Press, 1967.
Isle of the Sea Horse, Oxford University Press, 1968.
Listen to the Wind, Oxford University Press, 1969.
Who Calls From Afar? Oxford University Press, 1969.
The Wind Harp, Cassell, 1974.
The Ballad of Benny Perhaps, Cassell, 1977.
Once There Was a Swagman, Oxford University Press, 1979.
High Dive, Hodder & Stoughton, 1979.
Free Is Lonely, Hodder & Stoughton, 1979.
The Honey Forest, Hodder & Stoughton, 1979.
Time for Tarquinea, Hodder & Stoughton, 1981.
***The Sand Forest,* Angus & Robertson, 1985.**
***Someplace Beautiful,* Hodder & Stoughton, 1986.**
***When We Come to the Ferry,* Hodder & Stoughton, 1988.**

Also author of *Echo in the Wilderness, Longtime Passing, Longtime Dreaming, Christmas at Longtime,* and *The Beggar of Assisi.*

WORK IN PROGRESS: A Drink of Wild Water, for Angus & Robertson; a collection of Celtic myths.

SIDELIGHTS: Hesba Brinsmead Hungerford told *CA:* "A writer cannot help writing. It is a matter of water finding its level.

It is important that one writes in order to earn one's bread, however, for writing is only satisfying when it is on a professional level. Otherwise there is no yardstick for measuring one's worth at a vocation. Some people think writers should write for the sake of art, but these are professional teachers, doctors, bank managers, and so on. I write for love *and* money!''

AVOCATIONAL INTERESTS: Training Alsatian dogs, bushwalking.

BIOGRAPHICAL/CRITICAL SOURCES:

BOOKS

McVitty, Walter, *Innocence and Experience,* Thomas Nelson, 1981.
Townsend, John Rowe, *A Sense of Story,* Longman, 1971.

* * *

HUNT, John P(aul) 1915-1988

OBITUARY NOTICE—See index for *CA* sketch: Born July 1, 1915, in Kalona, Iowa; died of an apparent pulmonary embolism, February 6, 1988, in Panorama City, Calif. Government official, journalist, and author. Hunt worked for newspapers, including the *Hollywood Citizen News* and *Los Angeles Mirror-News,* in Iowa and California during the 1940s and 1950s. He then served as press secretary for Los Angeles County District Attorney William McKesson and Los Angeles mayor Sam Yorty. Subsequent posts included community relations director of the Los Angeles Zoo and area economic coordinator for the City of Los Angeles. Hunt was the author of *A World Full of Animals* and of articles contributed to popular periodicals.

OBITUARIES AND OTHER SOURCES:

PERIODICALS

Los Angeles Times, February 11, 1988.

* * *

HUNTER, Clark

PERSONAL: Born in Paisley, Scotland; son of John (a master cooper) and Sarah (Goudie) Hunter; married Mary Anderson, September 8, 1948; children: Sally Hunter McMillan. *Education:* Attended Paisley College of Technology and Glasgow and West of Scotland Commercial College (now Strathclyde University). *Politics:* Apolitical.

ADDRESSES: Home and office—Holmdale, 27 Thornly Park Ave., Paisley PA2 7SD, Scotland.

CAREER: Director and chairman of various manufacturing firms in Scotland, products including steel drums, wooden barrels, scotch whiskey, and medicinal items. Active in National Health Service.

MEMBER: Paisley Chamber of Commerce (president), Paisley Rotary Club (president).

WRITINGS:

Let Burns Speak, J. & J. Cook, 1961.
The Life and Letters of Alexander Wilson, American Philosophical Society, 1983.

Also author of *John Heaviside Clark* and *The Poems of Alexander Wilson*. Contributor to periodicals, including *Scotland's Magazine*.

WORK IN PROGRESS: Researching the Scottish ancestry of U.S. president Ronald Reagan.

SIDELIGHTS: Clark Hunter's *The Life and Letters of Alexander Wilson* is a detailed look at the short life (1766 to 1813) and lengthy correspondences of Scottish-born American ornithologist Alexander Wilson. A contemporary of the great American bird artist John James Audubon, Wilson is considered the superior zoolist, his nine-volume *American Ornithology* recognized as a classic in its field. Hunter includes nearly three hundred pages of letters written by the scientist, poet, and educator to family and friends in the biography, many reflecting Wilson's years of rigorous field work.

Hunter told *CA:* ''I am primarily a bibliophile and book collector. My interests are catholic, including visual arts and sport. My collection is concentrated upon Robert Burns, Alexander Wilson, James Boswell, R. B. Cunninghame Graham, Hugh MacDiarmid, and other selected Scottish individuals and areas.''

BIOGRAPHICAL/CRITICAL SOURCES:

PERIODICALS

Times Literary Supplement, May 11, 1984.

* * *

HURD, Clement (G.) 1908-1988

OBITUARY NOTICE—See index for *CA* sketch: Born January 12, 1908, in New York, N.Y.; died of Alzheimer's and Parkinson's diseases, February 5, 1988, in San Francisco, Calif. Artist, illustrator, and author. Hurd was best known as an illustrator of children's books, particularly *Goodnight Moon* and *The Runaway Bunny,* two classics for the very young written by Margaret Wise Brown. He wrote *Town, Country, The Race, The Merry Chase,* and *Run, Run, Run*. Among the other children's books Hurd illustrated were more than forty written by his wife, Edith Thacher Hurd, including an ''I Can Read'' series for Harper & Row. Before pursuing an illustrator's career, Hurd studied painting in Paris and worked as a free-lance designer in New York City.

OBITUARIES AND OTHER SOURCES:

PERIODICALS

Los Angeles Times, February 10, 1988.
New York Times, February 10, 1988.
Publishers Weekly, February 26, 1988.
Washington Post, February 8, 1988.

* * *

HUTCHINSON, Joseph (Burtt) 1902-1988

OBITUARY NOTICE—See index for *CA* sketch: Born March 21, 1902, in Burton Latimer, Northamptonshire, England; died January 16, 1988. Scientist, educator, and author. Hutchinson won recognition for his work on the genetics and evolution of cotton and other crop plants. Early in his career Hutchinson worked as a geneticist and botanist for plant industries in Trinidad, India, and Africa. In 1957 he became a professor of agriculture at Cambridge University, a post he retained until his retirement in 1969 as professor emeritus. Among his publications are several standard texts in the agricultural field, including *Application of Genetics to Cotton Improvement, Farming and Food Supply: Interdependence of Countryside and Town,* and *The Challenge of the Third World*. Hutchinson edited *Essays on Crop Plant Evolution; Population and Food*

Supply: Essays on Human Need and Agricultural Prospects; and *Evolutionary Studies in World Crops: Diversity and Change in the Indian Subcontinent.*

OBITUARIES AND OTHER SOURCES:

BOOKS

Who's Who, 139th edition, St. Martin's, 1987.

PERIODICALS

Times (London), January 19, 1988.

* * *

HYLAND, Douglas K(irk) S(amuel) 1949-

PERSONAL: Born October 7, 1949, in Salem, Mass.; son of Samuel F. and Patricia E. Hyland; married Alice R. Merrill (a university professor), November 23, 1981; children: Samuel Irenee, Octavia duPont, Cassandra A. *Education:* University of Pennsylvania, B.A., 1971; University of Delaware, M.A., 1975, Ph.D., 1980.

ADDRESSES: Home—3000 Dundee Circle, Birmingham, Ala. 35213. *Office*—Birmingham Museum of Art, 2000 Eighth Ave. N., Birmingham, Ala. 35203.

CAREER: University of Kansas, Lawrence, professor of art history and curator of European and American painting, sculpture, and decorative arts at Spencer Museum, 1979-82; Memphis Brooks Museum of Art, Memphis, Tenn., director, 1982-84; Birmingham Museum of Art, Birmingham, Ala., director, 1984—. Visiting professor at Southwestern at Memphis, 1982-84.

MEMBER: American Association of Museums, College Art Association of America.

AWARDS, HONORS: Kress Smithsonian fellow, 1978-79.

WRITINGS:

Lorenzo Bartolini and Italian Influences on American Sculptors in Florence, Garland Publishing, 1985.

Author of exhibition catalogs.

I

IBARGUENGOITIA, Jorge 1928-1983

PERSONAL: Born in 1928 in Guanajuato, Mexico; married; died in an airplane crash, November 27, 1983, near Madrid, Spain.

CAREER: Playwright, 1953-83; novelist, 1963-83. Columnist for *Excelsior* in Mexico. Teacher of Spanish literature at various universities.

AWARDS, HONORS: Award from the Casa de las Americas, 1963, for *El atentado;* John Simon Guggenheim Memorial Fellowship from the John Simon Guggenheim Memorial Foundation, 1969; National Prize for a novel from the Mexican National Institute of Fine Arts.

WRITINGS:

(With Osvaldo Dragun) *Milagro en el mercado viejo* [and] *El atentado* (plays; the former by Dragon, the latter by Ibarguengoitia; also see below), Casa de las Americas, 1963.

Clotilde, El viaje, y El pajaro (play; contains "Clotilde en su casa," three acts; "El viaje superficial," four acts; and "Pajaro en mano," three acts), Universidad Veracruzana, 1964.

Los relampagos de agosto (novel), Casa de las Americas, 1964, published as *Los relampagos de agosto: Memorias de un general mexicano,* Ediciones de la flor, 1973, translation by Irene del Corral published as *The Lightning of August,* Avon Bard, 1986.

La ley de Herodes y otros cuentos (short stories; contains "El episodio cinematografico," "La ley de Herodes," "La mujer que no," "What Became of Pampa Hash?" "Manos muertas," "Cuento del canario," "Las pinzas," "Los tres muertos," "Mis embargos," "La vela perpetua," "Conversaciones con Bloomsbury," "Falta de espiritu Scout," and "Quien se lleva a Blanca?"), Mortiz, 1967.

Maten al leon (novel), Mortiz, 1969.

(Author of introduction) Leopoldo Alas, *La regenta,* Porrua, 1972.

Viajes en la America ignota (articles first published in *Excelsior*), Mortiz, 1972.

Estas ruinas que ves, Novaro, 1975.

Salvese quien pueda (articles first published in *Excelsior*), Novaro, 1975.

Las muertas (novel), Mortiz, 1977, translation by Asa Zatz published as *The Dead Girls,* Avon, 1983.

El atentado (three-act play; also see above), Mortiz, 1978.

Dos crimenes (novel), Mortiz, 1979, translation by Zatz published as *Two Crimes,* David Godine, 1984.

Los conspiradores, Argas Vergara, 1981.

Los pasos de Lopez, Ediciones Oceano, 1982.

Also author of several other plays.

SIDELIGHTS: Jorge Ibarguengoitia, a prize-winning novelist and playwright, was known throughout his native Mexico for his satiric treatment of Mexican social behavior and government. In addition to publishing plays, novels, and short stories, he served as a columnist for the Mexican newspaper *Excelsior* for eight years. Praised as "a politically committed writer" by reviewer Michele Slung in the *Washington Post Book World,* Ibarguengoitia was on his way to attend a congress on Hispanic culture in Bogota, Colombia, when the Avianca 747 aircraft in which he was traveling crashed in heavy fog. Reviewing Ibarguengoitia's third book in English translation, *The Lightning of August,* critic Ariel Dorfman mourned in the *New York Times Book Review,* "I wish it were possible to look forward to new works by this subtle, precise novelist."

El atentado, Ibarguengoitia's best-known play, is a "thinly disguised" dramatization of the 1928 assassination of Mexican President-elect Alvaro Obregon, according to Sam L. Slick reviewing in *World Literature Today*. The piece's action rises out of opposition between the Catholic church and the Mexican Government. Act one concerns the re-emergence of General Borges (Obregon's fictional counterpart) on the Mexican political scene and includes the Catholic bombing attempt on the Mexican Chamber of Deputies. Act two focuses on Pepe, a character based on Jose Toral, Obregon's assassin. Pepe's murder of Borges is depicted on stage, as is Pepe's capture and questioning. The assassin is also subjected to an interview with Vidal Sanchez, a likeness of then Mexican President Plutarco Elias Calles. Act three presents Pepe's trial, ending with Sanchez's reconciliation with the Catholic church as a result of Borges's death. Because of its controversial, political nature, *El atentado* was not performed in Mexico until thirteen years after its writing, in spite of its winning an award from the Casa de las Americas in 1963. Slick concluded, "*El atentado* . . . is significant in Mexican letters, for it honestly and courageously scrutinizes the marrow of national consciousness."

The Dead Girls, Ibarguengoitia's first novel in English translation, is also based on real events. "One of the best-written Mexican novels of recent vintage," in Slick's opinion, the book builds on the foundation of the Poquianchi case. The two Poquianchi sisters ran a prostitution ring during the 1950s and 1960s. They were arrested in 1964, after the discovery of women's bodies buried on the grounds of one of their brothels. But, as Ibarguengoitia says of *The Dead Girls* in its preface, "Some of the events described herein are real. All of the characters are imaginary." "His treatment of the villains and victims," observed Slick, "add[s] a human dimension to an otherwise pathetic cast of assassins and child prostitutes." In the novel, brothel owners Serafina and Archangela Baladro enjoy great success until a morals act is passed and surprisingly enforced by a provincial governor. The Baladros close two of their brothels "and retreat with their prize whores to the ostensibly padlocked [third, the] Casino del Danzo," related critic Laura Furman in the *Washington Post Book World.* Confined together with no opportunity to do business, the relationship between the Baladros and their prostitutes deteriorates. Some of the women rebel against their imprisonment within the casino; some are killed and secretly buried. As Furman explained, "the twists and turns of spiraling morality, presented without comment or judgment, form another plot line in this compelling book." Told from many different viewpoints and simulating police reports given by the principles in the case, "*The Dead Girls* is all the more effective for treating its grotesqueries in a cool and lucid tone," judged Nicholas Rankin of the *Times Literary Supplement.* The novel, lauded Furman, is "a beautifully wrought story" and "a brilliant, cool look at the forms and the tolls that power may take."

Ibarguengoitia's next work to be translated to English was *Two Crimes. Two Crimes* concerns Marcos Gonzales, described by John Sutherland in *Listener* as "a political radical in the evening, a minor civil servant by day," and by Jules Koslow in the *New York Times Book Review* as "a crafty antihero with a larcenous heart." Marcos gets into trouble with the Mexican authorities when he gives shelter to a terrorist—the government then suspects Marcos in the burning of a department store. He flees, heading for his family home in the small town of Muerdago. There he becomes embroiled in various plots by relatives to ingratiate themselves with a rich uncle, to be written into his will and then murder him. From the idealism of his former political activities, Marcos "soon reverts, without any great sense of irony, to the *macho* ethic and petit-bourgeois opportunism" of the "provincial" town, reviewer Savkar Altinel interpreted in the *Times Literary Supplement.* Employing what Altinel labeled "the conventions of bedroom farce," Ibarguengoitia further complicates Marcos's situation by having his protagonist seduce a mother and her daughter simultaneously. Called "a beautifully imagined and structured tale" by Slung, *Two Crimes* "seems a simple invitation to fun and frolic," declared Elizabeth Hanly, critiquing in the *Voice Literary Supplement,* but "prob[es] the dark side of experience, caressing it until secrets are delivered up." According to Slung, "Ibarguengoitia . . . lets no one off the hook, even though he seems to have some affection for even the rogues and deadbeats among his characters."

The Lightning of August's translation into English was heralded by Dorfman as making more accessible the "first satire" of the Mexican Revolution. Narrated by Major General Lupe Arroyo, *Lightning* centers on a group of incompetent generals, Arroyo included, who are striving for power. In their efforts they execute the wrong people and shell the wrong villages. Arroyo stands out from his fellow power-grabbers, however, in that he does not pretend to be acting out of idealism and is honest with his audience. Commenting on the book's somewhat madcap tone, Dorfman cautioned that "it is only after the laughter has subsided that we realize with a chill that the humor has enticed us into accepting on their own terms the characters' cold, almost matter-of-fact violence."

Another of Ibarguengoitia's novels, *Maten al leon,* was praised as "swift-moving" and "suspense-filled" by Edward M. Malinak in *Books Abroad. Maten* explores the nature of political dictatorship, featuring despot Don Manuel Belaunzaran of Arepa. Conspiracies to overthrow Belaunzaran are depicted, as are the consequences of these attempts on Arepa's people. Noting its "vivid picturesque detail," Malinak labeled *Maten al leon* an "outstanding literary contribution."

BIOGRAPHICAL/CRITICAL SOURCES:

BOOKS

Ibarguengoitia, Jorge, *The Dead Girls,* translated by Asa Zatz, Avon, 1983.

PERIODICALS

Books Abroad, summer, 1970.
Listener, August 9, 1984.
New York Times Book Review, September 23, 1984, February 23, 1986.
Times Literary Supplement, March 18, 1984, August 10, 1984.
Voice Literary Supplement, December, 1984.
Washington Post Book World, February 25, 1983, September 16, 1984.
World Literature Today, winter, 1979, summer, 1979, winter, 1981.

OBITUARIES

Review, January-May, 1984.*

—*Sketch by Elizabeth Thomas*

* * *

ILSON, Robert (Frederick) 1937-

PERSONAL: Born May 10, 1937, in New York, N.Y.; son of Frederick (a manufacturer) and Cynthia Sandra (an actress; maiden name, Etkin) Ilson; children: Sophia Frances. *Education:* New York University, B.A., 1955; Columbia University, M.A., 1959; University of London, Ph.D., 1971.

ADDRESSES: Home—58 Antrim Mansions, Antrim Rd., London N.W.3, England. *Office*—University College, University of London, Gower St., London W.C.1, England.

CAREER: Fulbright lecturer in English at various universities in Medellin, Colombia, 1966-68; research assistant for Survey of English Usage, 1971-74; Longman Group Ltd., Harlow, England, managing editor of dictionary and reference books department, 1974-78, managing editor of *Longman Dictionary of Contemporary English,* 1978; worked on various reference projects, 1979-80; University of London, Institute of Education, London, England, lecturer in English as a second language, 1980-82; University of London, University College, London, honorary research fellow and associate director of Survey of English Usage, 1981—.

MEMBER: International Association of Applied Linguistics (convenor of Commission on Lexicography and Lexicology), European Association for Lexicography (member of executive

board), Dictionary Society of North America, British Association for Applied Linguistics, British Fulbright Scholars' Association.

WRITINGS:

(Editor with Wolf-Dietrich Bald) *Studies in English Usage,* Lang, 1977.
(General editor) *The Second Barnhart Dictionary of New English,* Barnhart, 1980.
(Editor) *Dictionaries, Lexicography, and Language Learning,* Pergamon, 1985.
(Editor) *Lexicography: An Emerging International Profession,* Manchester University Press, 1986.
(With Morton Benson and Evelyn Benson) *Lexicographic Description of English,* John Benjamins, 1986.
(With Morton Benson and Evelyn Benson) *The BBI Combinatory Dictionary of English: A Guide to Word Combinations,* John Benjamins, 1986.
(Editor) *A Spectrum of Lexicography: Papers From AILA Brussels 1984,* John Benjamins, 1987.

Founder and editor of *How,* 1966—; editor of *EURALEX Bulletin,* 1984—, and *International Journal of Lexicography,* 1988—; member of editorial board of *New Oxford English Dictionary.*

SIDELIGHTS: Robert Ilson told *CA:* "I have done many things and when I was invited to become a lexicographer I jumped at the chance, because I thought that everything I'd ever done and every piece of information I knew would come in handy. I was right.

"Lexicography is great fun. It makes you realize that a *great white* is not just something bigger than a *large white,* or a *gunship* something bigger than a *gunboat.* It makes you understand how it was possible for someone to say of Charlie Chaplin: 'Charlie was a *great* golfer—and a *good* one.' It makes you wonder whether you can *mastermind* something good (like a medical breakthrough) or only something bad (like a bank heist), and wonder why one organization I belong to is called the 'International Association *of* Applied Linguistics' and another the 'British Association *for* Applied Linguistics.'

"Furthermore, lexicography is of use. Whenever I think it may be only a trivial pursuit, I recall the television program I saw about two people who sued a hospital for negligence. Before they went to court they spent six months with medical dictionaries so that they wouldn't be bamboozled by the terminology. Perhaps dictionaries can contribute to the process of demystification."

ILTINGER, Paula 1944-

PERSONAL: Born February 17, 1944, in Lima, Ohio; daughter of Francis (a businessman) and Bess (a dancer; maiden name, Cruickshank) Folkes; married G. Iltinger (an attorney), June 12, 1968; children: Esther, Ryan. *Education:* Attended public schools in Ohio. *Politics:* Republican. *Religion:* Protestant.

ADDRESSES: Home—8330 Lochdale, Dearborn Heights, Mich. 48127.

CAREER: Writer. Worked at day-care center in Plymouth, Mich., 1972-74, and as secretary at Joe Terry Services in Spitzburg, Ohio, 1979.

MEMBER: Daughters of Justice, Great Lakes Writers Cooperative.

AWARDS, HONORS: Award for community service from Dearborn Mothers and Women, 1986.

WRITINGS:

POETRY

Spring, Having Been, Shelling Press, 1967.
Nuance and Fervor, Brittanicus & Cramer, 1972.
True Nuns in Solitude, Albright Chapbooks, 1973.
An Eloquence Unspoken, privately printed, 1977.
An Eloquence Unheard, privately printed, 1977.

JUVENILE

Lord Bright Rightness and the Courage Mobile, Tots 'n Tops, 1984.
The Way From Spain, Tots 'n Tops, 1985.
Truth Through the Ages, Tots 'n Tops, 1986.

WORK IN PROGRESS: A collection of poems.

SIDELIGHTS: Paula Iltinger told *CA:* "I write for myself and for those readers who delight in small things and seemingly slight observations and reflections. I suppose I enjoy writing poetry the most, but I have found the market for childrens' books to be more lucrative, and so have devoted more of my energy to producing books in that field. I have found that producing these books is quite rewarding, but my first love remains poetry."

* * *

IMRIE, Richard
See PRESSBURGER, Emeric

J

JACKMAN, Robert W(illiam) 1946-

PERSONAL: Born October 31, 1946, in Oamaru, New Zealand; immigrated to the United States, 1968, naturalized citizen, 1980; son of David S. (a teacher) and Helen (a teacher; maiden name, Murray) Jackman; married Mary R. Peretz (a professor), September 10, 1968; children: Rachael, Saul. *Education:* University of Auckland, B.A., 1968; University of Wisconsin—Madison, M.A., 1970, Ph.D., 1972.

ADDRESSES: Home—Ann Arbor, Mich. *Office*—Department of Political Science, 313 South Kedzie Hall, Michigan State University, East Lansing, Mich. 48824.

CAREER: Michigan State University, East Lansing, assistant professor, 1972-75, associate professor, 1975-80, professor of political science, 1980—. Fellow at Center for Advanced Study in the Behavioral Sciences, Stanford, Calif., 1986-87.

AWARDS, HONORS: Guggenheim fellow, 1980-81; Distinguished Faculty Award from Michigan State University, 1988.

WRITINGS:

Politics and Social Equality: A Comparative Analysis, Wiley, 1975.

(With wife, Mary R. Jackman) *Class Awareness in the United States,* University of California Press, 1983.

WORK IN PROGRESS: A book on national political development, publication expected in 1989.

* * *

JACKSON, Donald (Dean) 1919-1987

OBITUARY NOTICE—See index for *CA* sketch: Born June 10, 1919, in Glenwood, Iowa; died of cancer of the prostate, December 9, 1987, in Colorado Springs, Colo. Publishing executive, educator, editor, and author. Jackson won recognition as a writer and editor in the field of American history. He was editor at the University of Illinois Press from 1948 to 1966, and from 1966 to 1968 he was associate director. In 1968 Jackson became professor of history at the University of Virginia and editor of *The Papers of George Washington,* posts he held until his retirement in 1978. Among Jackson's many publications are *Custer's Gold: The U.S. Cavalry Expedition of 1874, George Washington and the War of Independence,* and *Thomas Jefferson and the Stony Mountains.* Jackson edited *Black Hawk: An Autobiography, Letters of the Lewis and Clark Expedition, The Journals of Zebulon Montgomery Pike,* and other scholarly works. He also contributed articles to professional journals.

OBITUARIES AND OTHER SOURCES:

BOOKS

Directory of American Scholars, Volume I: *History,* 8th edition, Bowker, 1982.

PERIODICALS

New York Times, December 11, 1987.

Publishers Weekly, January 15, 1988.

* * *

JACKSON, Stanley W(ebber) 1920-

PERSONAL: Born November 17, 1920, in Montreal, Quebec, Canada; immigrated to the United States, naturalized citizen; son of Clarence Stanley and Ada Doris (a housewife; maiden name, Webber) Jackson; married Joan Katherine Currie, August 12, 1946. *Education:* McGill University, B.Com., 1941, M.D., C.M., 1950; graduate of Seattle Psychoanalytic Training Center and San Francisco Psychoanalytic Institute.

ADDRESSES: Home—72 Downs Rd., Bethany, Conn. 06525. *Office*—202 Connecticut Mental Health Center, Yale University, New Haven, Conn. 06520.

CAREER: Yale University, New Haven, Conn., professor of psychiatry and history of medicine and director of Outpatient Services at Connecticut Mental Health Center, 1964—. Past president of Western New England Institute for Psychoanalysis. *Military service:* Royal Canadian Air Force, navigator, 1941-45.

MEMBER: International Psychoanalytic Association, American Psychiatric Association, American Psychoanalytic Association, American Historical Association, American Association for the History of Medicine (member of council), Western New England Psychoanalytic Society (past president), Connecticut Psychiatric Society.

AWARDS, HONORS: M.A. from Yale University, 1975.

WRITINGS:

Melancholia and Depression: From Hippocratic Times to Modern Times, Yale University Press, 1987.

Contributor of articles and reviews to medical and history journals.

WORK IN PROGRESS: A history of psychological treatments.

BIOGRAPHICAL/CRITICAL SOURCES:

PERIODICALS

New York Times Book Review, April 5, 1987.
Times Literary Supplement, September 4, 1987.

* * *

JAMES, Thelma Gray 1899-1988

OBITUARY NOTICE—See index for *CA* sketch: Born May 30, 1899, in Detroit, Mich.; died January 23, 1988, in Detroit, Mich. Educator, editor, and author. James was a professor at Wayne State University for more than four decades and a leader in the establishment of the university's Urban Folklore Archives. James also served as president of state and national societies in folklore and as associate editor of the *Journal of American Folklore.* Her earliest teaching experiences were in the primary grades. James was the author of *Literature of the World,* a 1963 publication, and co-editor of *World Neighbors.* Her pioneering work in urban folklore earned her several awards.

OBITUARIES AND OTHER SOURCES:

BOOKS

Directory of American Scholars, Volume III: *Foreign Languages, Linguistics, and Philology,* 7th edition, Bowker, 1978.

PERIODICALS

Detroit Free Press, January 26, 1988.

* * *

JAY, Elisabeth 1947-

PERSONAL: Born February 8, 1947, in London, England; daughter of Brian Cyril (a clerk in holy orders) and Grace Amelia (Hogg) Aldis; married Richard Jay (a university lecturer), September 5, 1970 (separated, 1984); children: Anna Kate, Hugo William Aldis. *Education:* St. Anne's College, Oxford, B.A., 1969, M.Phil., 1971, D.Phil., 1975. *Religion:* Church of England.

ADDRESSES: Home—36 Millwood End, Long Hanborough, Oxfordshire OX7 2BY, England. *Office*—Westminster College, North Hinksey, Oxford, England.

CAREER: Westminster College, Oxford, England, lecturer, 1975-80, senior lecturer in English, 1981—. Tutor at Queen's University, Belfast, Northern Ireland, 1977-78; visiting professor at Ball State University, spring, 1984 and 1987-88.

AWARDS, HONORS: M.A. from Oxford University, 1975.

WRITINGS:

The Religion of the Heart: Anglican Evangelicalism and the Nineteenth Century Novel, Clarendon Press, 1979.
(Editor) *The Evangelical and Oxford Movements,* Cambridge University Press, 1983.
Faith and Doubt in Victorian Britain, Macmillan, 1986.
(Editor with husband, Richard Jay) *The Critics of Capitalism: Victorian Reactions to Political Economy,* Cambridge University Press, 1986.
(Editor and author of introduction) *The Journal of John Wesley: A Selection,* Oxford University Press, 1987.
(Editor) *The Autobiography of Mrs. M. O. W. Oliphant: A New and Full Text,* Oxford University Press, in press.

WORK IN PROGRESS: A critical study of the work of Mrs. M. O. W. Oliphant, publication by Clarendon Press expected in 1991.

SIDELIGHTS: In writing *The Religion of the Heart,* Elisabeth Jay has, according to *Times Literary Supplement* critic Owen Chadwick, undertaken a tedious, demanding subject, that of the Victorian religious novel. The result, he commented, is "a useful contribution to the study of an oddly elusive frame of mind." Chadwick particularly appreciated the author's historical account of American evangelicalism and the insight the book provides on the attitudes and spiritual beliefs of such authors as Mrs. Guyton, who wrote *Thornycroft Hall.* Jay's history also explains the decline of evangelicalism, which resulted ultimately in the demise of the nineteenth-century religious novel.

Brian Martin, another *Times Literary Supplement* reviewer, also praised Jay's work as a religious historian. He described *The Evangelical and Oxford Movements* as a stimulating collection, which "provokes arguments and invites questions." Martin found the editor's selections "valuable for students. . . . They are well chosen and show the conflict in belief between the Evangelicals and the Tractorians." The collection presents, in one volume, a highly diverse and otherwise inaccessible group of essays.

Jay told *CA:* "My initial work on nineteenth-century Anglican Evangelicalism was generated by an interest in discovering the roots of a belief and a mode of life that had informed my own upbringing. The further work on nineteenth-century religion grew from a conviction that religious movements develop and change in tension with competing beliefs and ideologies. The eclectic concerns of nineteenth-century novels make them a particularly rich field in which to work as one's own critical interests shift.

"Mrs. Oliphant, my current preoccupation, presents both a fascinating range of literary achievement: autobiographer, biographer, essayist, and novelist; and a life whose constant juggling of the concerns of work and single parenting is of immediate relevance to many twentieth-century readers. For me writing provides a space where I can discover what it is that I really think and justifies and refuels my teaching."

BIOGRAPHICAL/CRITICAL SOURCES:

PERIODICALS

Times Literary Supplement, February 15, 1980, May 13, 1983.

* * *

JENKINS, Hal
See JENKINS, Harold L.

* * *

JENKINS, Harold L. 1909(?)-1987
(Hal Jenkins)

OBITUARY NOTICE: Born c. 1909 in Dickinson, N.D.; died

of congestive heart failure, December 20, 1987, in Rockville, Md. A reporter with Ohio newspapers for nine years before joining the U.S. Agriculture Department's Soil Conservation Service (SCS), Jenkins began his thirty-year tenure with that agency in 1939 as an associate public information specialist in Dayton, Ohio. Sixteen years later he was named head of the SCS current information division in Washington, D.C., and retired from that post in 1969. Jenkins wrote *A Valley Renewed: The History of the Muskingum Watershed Conservancy District* under the name Hal Jenkins. He also founded and edited a newsletter for the Association of Retired Soil Conservation Service Employees.

OBITUARIES AND OTHER SOURCES:

PERIODICALS

Washington Post, December 23, 1987.

* * *

JENNINGS, Coleman A(lonzo) 1933-

PERSONAL: Born November 21, 1933, in Granger, Tex.; son of Vaudra R. and Elsie (Fox) Jennings; married Lola Hanawalt, 1961, children: Coleman Charles, Adrienne Elise. *Education:* University of Texas at Austin, B.F.A., 1958, M.F.A., 1961; New York University, Ed.D., 1974.

ADDRESSES: Office—Department of Drama, University of Texas at Austin, Austin, Tex. 78712.

CAREER: High school drama and history teacher in Austin, Tex., 1960-61; Midland Community Theatre, Midland, Tex., children's theatre director and teacher of creative drama, 1961-63; University of Texas at Austin, drama faculty, 1963—, chairman of department, 1981—, founder and director of Summer Theatre Pizazz, 1965—. Guest assistant professor at University of Illinois at Urbana-Champaign, summers, 1963-64; visiting assistant professor at New York University, summers, 1968, 1971; visiting lecturer at University of Arkansas at Little Rock, 1978, Trinity University and University of Texas at San Antonio, both 1980. Technical director at Chase Barn Playhouse, Whitefield, N.H., summers, 1956-57; technician and assistant manager of Off-Broadway productions, 1958-59; member of staff at Dallas Theatre Center, 1960. Member of U.S. Commission for UNESCO, 1969-75, member of its executive committee, 1973-75; U.S. representative to Jamaican UNESCO Cultural and Conservation Conference, 1970; member of National Conference on Theatre Education for Public Schools, 1977; member of executive committee of Education Program, National Endowment for the Arts, 1980. Chairman of Creative Drama Curriculum Committee of Texas Education Agency, 1969-72; member of Texas Alliance for Arts Education, 1978; member of theater panel of Texas Commission on the Arts and Humanities, 1978-80; judge of local drama contests. Member of executive committee of Winifred Ward Memorial Scholarship Fund, 1975; member of advisory board of Creative Theatre Unlimited, 1986—; consultant to Rockefeller Foundation and Performing Arts Repertory Theatre of New York City. *Military service:* U.S. Army, ground control radar operator, 1953-55; served in Europe.

MEMBER: International Association of Theatre for Children and Youth (member of executive committee, 1978-80), Children's Theatre Association of America (vice-president, 1973-75; president, 1975-77), Children's Theatre Conference of America (member of board of governors, 1965-68), American Theatre Association, National Educational Theatre Association, American Association of Theatre for Youth, Southwest Theatre Conference, Texas Educational Theatre Association (chairman of Creative Drama Curriculum Committee, 1965-70; member of board of directors, 1984-86), Texas Non-Profit Theatre Association.

AWARDS, HONORS: Charlotte Chorpenning National Award from Children's Theatre Association of America, 1962, for work at Midland Community Theatre, and 1965, for international exhibit "Children's Theatre in America"; grants from Texas Commission on the Arts and Humanities, 1975 and 1977; Founders Award from Texas Educational Theatre Association, 1986.

WRITINGS:

The Honorable Urashima Taro (play), Dramatic Publishing, 1972.

(Author of introduction) *Yankee Doodle,* Anchorage Press, 1975.

Learning Partners: Reading and Creative Dynamics, Texas Education Agency, 1976.

(Author of preface and contributor) *Go Adventuring: A Celebration of Winifred Ward, America's First Lady of Drama for Children,* Anchorage Press, 1977.

(Author of biography and play analyses) *Six Plays by Aurand Harris,* University of Texas Press, 1977.

I Didn't Know That: A Play for Youth Created Through Improvisations, American Theatre Association, 1978.

(With Lola Jennings) *Creative Drama in the Elementary School,* Texas Education Agency, 1978.

(Editor with Aurand Harris) *Plays Children Love: A Treasury of Contemporary and Classic Plays for Children,* Doubleday, 1981.

(Editor with Gretta Berghammer) *Theatre for Youth: Twelve Plays With Mature Themes,* University of Texas Press, 1986.

(Editor with Harris) *Plays Children Love, Volume II: A Treasury of Twenty Contemporary and Classic Plays for Children,* St. Martin's, 1988.

Contributor of articles and reviews to periodicals. Editor of *Children's Theatre Review,* 1965-67.

WORK IN PROGRESS: Children's Theatre Productions of the Federal Theatre of the W.P.A.; Graduate Research: Creative Drama and Theatre for Youth, a computerized databank of theses and dissertations written in the United States, from 1923 to the present; research on child actors, the child audience, and child performers of the nineteenth century on the English-speaking, adult stage.

BIOGRAPHICAL/CRITICAL SOURCES:

Fanfare, February, 1984.

* * *

JENTLESON, Bruce W. 1951-

PERSONAL: Born June 26, 1951, in New York, N.Y.; son of Theodore (a salesman) and Elaine (Rosenfield) Jentleson; married Barbara Cooney (a special education teacher), July 14, 1979; children: Adam James, Katherine Laura. *Education:* Cornell University, B.A. (cum laude), 1973, M.A., 1981, Ph.D., 1983; London School of Economics and Political Science, London, M.Sc., 1975.

ADDRESSES: Office—Department of Political Science, University of California, Davis, Calif. 95616.

CAREER: University of California, Davis, assistant professor of political science, 1983—. International affairs fellow of Council on Foreign Relations, 1987-88.

MEMBER: International Studies Association, American Political Science Association.

AWARDS, HONORS: Harold Lasswell Award from American Political Science Association, 1985, for "Pipeline Politics: The Alliance and Domestic Politics of American Economic Coercion Against the Soviet Union."

WRITINGS:

Pipeline Politics: The Complex Political Economy of East-West Energy Trade, Cornell University Press, 1986.

CONTRIBUTOR

Robert J. Lieben, editor, *Will Europe Fight for Oil?* Praeger, 1983.

Steven L. Spiegel, Mark Heller, and Jacob Goldberg, editors, *Soviet-American Competition in the Middle East,* Lexington Books, 1987.

Walter Goldstein, editor, *Dealing With the Soviets: NATO and the Northern Flank,* Pergamon-Brassey, 1987.

Contributor to political science journals.

WORK IN PROGRESS: A book on U.S. foreign policy toward Third World revolutions.

SIDELIGHTS: Bruce W. Jentleson told *CA:* "I am a strong believer in both the value of university education and the importance of political involvement. The challenge for a professor is to stimulate students to think and to help them develop analytic and writing skills, rather than just to memorize material. The challenge for a public official, especially one involved in foreign policy, is to help make this a safer and better world."

* * *

JERMAIN, Clive 1966(?)-1988

OBITUARY NOTICE: Born c. 1966; died of spinal cancer, March 2, 1988. Playwright. Jermain, who had been plagued by back pain since he was a young boy, had cancer of the spine; he was seventeen when he was told that he had only a short time to live. Feeling that he needed to leave something for posterity, he wrote an autobiographical play, "The Best Years of Your Life," which the British Broadcasting Corporation produced on television in 1986. Jermain's illness inspired establishment of the Search '88 Cancer Trust, an organization that raises money for cancer charities.

OBITUARIES AND OTHER SOURCES:

PERIODICALS

Times (London), March 3, 1988.

* * *

JOHNSON, Fenton 1888-1958

PERSONAL: Born May 7, 1888, in Chicago, Ill.; died September 17, 1958; son of Elijah H. and Jesse (Taylor) Johnson; married. *Education:* Attended University of Chicago, Northwestern University, and Columbia University, c. 1913.

CAREER: State University, Louisville, Ky., English teacher, c. 1912; writer for Eastern Press Association in New York City; acting dramatic editor of *New York News; Champion* (magazine), Chicago, Ill., editor, 1916-17; *Favorite Magazine,* Chicago, founder, 1918, editor, 1918-20; worked for Federal Writers' Project (Works Progress Administration) in Chicago during the 1930s. Founder of Reconciliation Movement (for racial cooperation), New York City, 1919-20.

MEMBER: Authors' League of America, Alpha Phi Alpha.

WRITINGS:

A Little Dreaming (poems), Peterson Linotyping Co. (Chicago), 1913, reprint, McGrath, 1969.

Visions of the Dusk (poems), privately printed (New York), 1915, facsimile edition, Books for Libraries, 1971.

Songs of the Soil (poems), privately printed (New York), 1916, reprint, AMS press, 1975.

For the Highest Good (essays), Favorite Magazine (Chicago), 1920, reprint, McGrath, 1969.

Tales of Darkest America (short stories), Favorite Magazine, 1920, facsimile edition, Books for Libraries, 1971.

Also author of unpublished poem collections "African Nights" and "The Daily Grind: 42 WPA Poems"; author of plays produced at Pekin Theater in Chicago, Ill., c. 1907. Work represented in anthologies, including *The New Poetry: An Anthology of Twentieth-Century Verse in English,* edited by Harriet Monroe and Alice Corbin Henderson, Macmillan, 1923; *An Anthology of American Poetry: Lyric America, 1630-1930,* edited by Alfred Kreymborg, Tudor, 1930; *The Book of American Negro Poetry,* edited by James Weldon Johnson, Harcourt, 1922, enlarged edition, 1931; *The Poetry of the Negro, 1746-1949,* edited by Langston Hughes and Arna Bontemps, Doubleday, 1949; *American Negro Poetry,* edited by Bontemps, Hill & Wang, 1963, revised edition, 1974; and *Blackamerican Literature, 1760-Present,* edited by Ruth Miller, Glencoe Press, 1971. Contributor to periodicals, including *Poetry: A Magazine of Verse, Others, Crisis, Favorite Magazine,* and *Liberator.*

SIDELIGHTS: In her *Dictionary of Literary Biography* entry for early twentieth-century poet Fenton Johnson, Shirley Lumpkin described Johnson's literary career as "a downward spiral." The only child in a middle-class black family living in Chicago, Johnson was able to indulge his interest in drama and poetry; some of his plays were produced at the Pekin Theater when he was nineteen and his first poetry collection was published soon after. The privately-printed volume was well received, its generous patrons financing two more collections of poems as well as Johnson's matriculation at the Pulitzer School of Journalism at Columbia University. But while Johnson wrote for the Eastern Press Association for a time, his real ambitions lay in exploring the boundaries of literature. He founded several literary publications, the most notable being *Favorite Magazine;* it folded after two years, however, typifying Johnson's lifelong struggle "to obtain a foothold in literature." Widespread recognition continued to elude the writer and his self-published final two books—essay and short story collections—added little to his reputation. After 1920 Johnson's work appeared in print largely through the interest of others, finding its way into an occasional anthology or literary magazine. He spent the remaining three decades of his life in literary obscurity.

Scholars agree that Johnson's failure to capture the literary imagination of his time was due, in part, to the age of transition in which he lived. Rural blacks were migrating to American cities, igniting an era of intense racism; "serious literary

men of color," wrote J. Saunders Redding in *To Make a Poet Black,* "found it hard to go beyond the limits of popular concept and to destroy the picture of themselves as it had been purposefully created in the mind of white America." Johnson's active literary years followed the reign of popular Negro dialect poet Paul Laurence Dunbar and presaged new black writers Claude McKay, Jean Toomer, Langston Hughes, and Countee Cullen. Ironically, the dozen or so poems through which Johnson's reputation survives were written after the poet's youthful successes, when poverty and obscurity prompted him to abandon his celebratory lyric and dialect styles for free verse depictions of urban despair and racial hopelessness.

According to Lumpkin, Johnson's first book of verse—*A Little Dreaming*—is marked by "Victorian/romantic diction, which was characteristic of the popular public 'cultivated' Anglo-American poetry of the early twentieth century." James P. Hutchinson judged the volume artificial and imitative in a *Studies in Black Literature* article, writing, "It is evident . . . that . . . Johnson sacrifices his own experience and tradition for that line of disembodied, sentimental and lyric verse written in a style which deservedly became outmoded." But while exploring the traditional poetic subjects of love, birth, death, grief, and gladness in *A Little Dreaming,* informed Lumpkin, Johnson also praises "the beauty of Afro-Americans"; "conceiving of himself and his poetry in such archaic, cliched, pseudoromantic terms in 1913 did not . . . mean that Johnson saw himself as separate from other black people." And the atypical theme of one poem in the collection, "The Plaint of the Factory Child," anticipates the writer's later, more powerful verse.

In his second poetry volume, *Visions of the Dusk,* "Johnson exchanges the lyric tradition for the Negro dialect tradition," observed Hutchinson, with "the subject matter . . . largely the portrayal of Negro life in America." Using the popular plantation-dialect style—with its gross misspellings and naive misuses of English representing black speech—for much of his verse, Johnson also experimented with poetic versions of Negro spirituals. "Neither dialect nor transcriptions of folk spirituals, Johnson's poetic imitations use rhythmical arrangements, imagery, and repetition to catch the patterns of the spirituals successfully enough to interest many future anthologists and editors," Lumpkin reported. "Fenton Johnson's spiritual poems . . . were the first genuinely powerful attempts to communicate some of the essence of spirituals in purely literary form."

The poetry collection *Songs of the Soil* contains more of the same; judging Johnson's nondialect verse superior, Lumpkin explained that the poet "did not discover the limitations of plantation dialect until later in his career." Still, "Johnson never used it to maintain plantation stereotypes," the critic stated. "It [was] never an evocation of the 'good old days of slavery'. . . . Nor were his speakers ever the foolish, sentimental, or undignified caricatures associated with minstrel characterizations of blacks." Lumpkin continued: "[Johnson's] linguistic styles might be imitative and reflective of the tastes of his age, but his attitudes and ideas are not sentimental nor are they molded by the stereotypical expectation of a white audience."

While the six short stories that comprise Johnson's *Tales of Darkest America* are largely dismissed as undistinguished, the collection does introduce the new theme of the Negro in the city. "The most memorable sketch, 'A Woman of Good Cheer,' succeeds because it treats the discrepancy between the uncomplicated life of the rural Negro and the destruction apparent in the urban experience of Blacks," wrote Hutchinson. "This latter theme is, fortunately, the subject of most of Johnson's [later] poems." Beset by professional failures and financial ruin, the writer expressed his weariness and despair in free verse that employed the stylistic innovations pioneered by Chicago "golden era" poets Vachel Lindsay, Edgar Lee Masters, and Carl Sandburg; Redding noted that "it is probably through Fenton Johnson that the influence of [these] midwestern poets . . . first touched Negro writers." Conveying a nihilistic view of life rarely encountered before in Afro-American verse (as in his best-known poem "Tired"), Johnson is regarded by some as one of the first black revolutionary poets. But to label his as such "is to engage in critical distortion," declared Hutchinson, maintaining that a survey of Johnson's literary output reveals a sentimental lyricist whose bleak free verse is atypical. Calling the writer "a minor poet . . . who responded, somewhat tardily, to the spirit of the times among the black urban poor," Lumpkin agreed, but added: "Considering the times during which he tried to make his way as a poet who sang of his people, times which included the most virulent expression of racial hatred and the Great Depression, and considering his own reversal of fortune, it seems remarkable that Johnson was able to write even a handful of living poems, poems that continue to strike the hearts of poets and readers."

BIOGRAPHICAL/CRITICAL SOURCES:

BOOKS

Brown, Sterling A., *Negro Poetry and Drama,* Associates in Negro Folk Education (Washington, D.C.), 1937.

Brown, Sterling A., Arthur Davis, and Ulysses Lee, editors, *The Negro Caravan,* Dryden, 1941.

Chapman, Abraham, editor, *Black Voices,* New American Library, 1968.

Cullen, Countee, editor, *Caroling Dusk: An Anthology of Verse by Negro Poets,* Harper, 1927.

Dictionary of Literary Biography, Volume 45: *American Poets, 1880-1945,* Gale, 1986.

Gibson, Donald B., editor, *Modern Black Poets: A Collection of Critical Essays,* Prentice-Hall, 1973.

Gloster, Hugh, *Negro Voices in American Fiction,* University of North Carolina Press, 1948, Russell, 1968.

Hayden, Robert, editor and author of introduction, *Kaleidoscope: Poems by American Negro Poets,* Harcourt, 1967.

Johnson, James Weldon, *The Book of American Negro Poetry,* Harcourt, 1922, reprint, 1969.

Kerlin, Robert T., *Negro Poets and Their Poems,* Associated Publishers, 1923, revised third edition, 1935.

Redding, J. Saunders, *To Make A Poet Black,* University of North Carolina Press, 1939, McGrath, 1968.

Redmond, Eugene B., *Drumvoices: The Mission of Afro-American Poetry, A Critical History,* Anchor/Doubleday, 1976.

Wagner, Jean, *Black Poets of the United States From Paul Laurence Dunbar to Langston Hughes,* translated by Kenneth Douglas, University of Illinois Press, 1973.

White, Newman Ivey and Walter Clinton Jackson, editors, *An Anthology of Verse by American Negroes,* Trinity College Press, 1924, Moore, 1968.

PERIODICALS

American Review of Reviews, January, 1914.

Crisis, volume 7, 1914, volume 12, 1916.

Literary World (London), April 2, 1914.

Poetry: A Magazine of Verse, volume 12, 1918.

Studies in Black Literature, autumn, 1976.*

—Sketch by Nancy Pear

* * *

JOHNSON, Penelope D(elafield) 1938-

PERSONAL: Born March 2, 1938, in New York, N.Y.; daughter of Richard (an attorney) and Margaret (an administrator; maiden name, Gade) Delafield; married Rollin M. Johnson (an orthopedic surgeon), December 19, 1957; children: R. Wade, Katherine L. *Education:* Yale University, B.A. (summa cum laude), 1973, M.Phil., 1976, Ph.D., 1979.

ADDRESSES: Office—Department of History, New York University, New York, N.Y. 10003.

CAREER: Yale University, New Haven, Conn., lecturer in history, 1977; New York University, New York, N.Y., assistant professor, 1979-86, associate professor of history, 1986—.

MEMBER: American Historical Association, Mediaeval Academy of America, Centre Europeen de Recherches sur les Congregations et Ordres Religieux, New England Historical Association, Berkshire Conference of Women Historians, Societe Archeologique, Scientifique, et Litteraire du Vendomois, Phi Beta Kappa.

AWARDS, HONORS: Grant from National Endowment for the Humanities, 1981; fellow of American Council of Learned Societies, 1981, and Rockefeller Foundation, 1985.

WRITINGS:

Prayer, Patronage, and Power: The Abbey of la Trinite, Vendome, 1032-1187 (monograph), New York University Press, 1981.

(Editor) *Selected Reading Lists and Course Outlines From American Colleges and Universities: Medieval History,* Markus Wiener, 1983.

Contributor to *Westminster Dictionary of Christian Spirituality.* Contributor of articles and reviews to history and religious studies journals.

WORK IN PROGRESS: Women and the Monastic Life in Medieval France, completion expected in 1989.

SIDELIGHTS: Penelope D. Johnson's *Prayer, Patronage, and Power* was described in the *Times Literary Supplement* as "an attractive, learned and lively book." Critic C. N. L. Brooke noted that the book emphasizes the ways in which the history of the abbey and its abbots "reflected and illuminated the religious and secular movements of the age." The author provides background material on the colorful, powerful warriors who surrounded and supported the abbey with their patronage, as well as the abbots themselves and the community in which they lived and worshiped. Brooke concluded his review: "The final impression of the book is that a great deal of firsthand, enthusiastic and skilled research has been presented with a light touch and a clear and penetrating insight."

BIOGRAPHICAL/CRITICAL SOURCES:

PERIODICALS

Times Literary Supplement, April 16, 1982.

* * *

JOHNSON, Thomas Herbert 1902-1985

PERSONAL: Born April 27, 1902, in Bradford, Vt.; died January 3, 1985; son of Herbert T. (an adjutant general) and Myra (a housewife; maiden name, Burbeck) Johnson; married Catherine Rice (in real estate), September 11, 1934; children: Laura Bradley, Thomas. *Education:* Williams College, A.B., 1926; Harvard University, A.M., 1929, Ph.D., 1934. *Religion:* Congregationalist.

ADDRESSES: c/o Ms. Laura J. Waterman, East Corinth, Vt. 05040.

CAREER: Rutgers University, New Brunswick, N.J., instructor, 1928-29; Williams College, Williamstown, Mass., instructor in English, 1929-31; Hackley School, Terrytown, N.Y., teacher, 1931-37; Lawrenceville School, Lawrenceville, N.J., teacher of English, 1937-72, chairman of department, 1944-67. Lecturer at Rutgers University, 1930-32, University of Iowa, 1936, New School for Social Research, 1943-44, Columbia University, 1948, and Harvard University, 1950; Chautauqua lecturer, 1937; visiting professor at University of Copenhagen, 1951-52, and University of Pennsylvania, 1958-59; Berg Professor at New York University, 1959-60. American literature bibliographer for Modern Language Association of America, 1943-47; nonfiction judge of National Book Awards, 1959.

MEMBER: Society of American Historians (fellow), American Studies Association (fellow), Bibliographical Society of America, Modern Language Association of America, Colonial Society of Massachusetts, Delta Upsilon, Century Club, Grolier Club.

AWARDS, HONORS: L.H.D. from Williams College, 1949; Guggenheim fellow, 1951-52; Litt.D. from Marlboro College, 1955, and Rutgers University, 1956; Chapbook Award, 1956; Litt.D. from Middlebury College, 1967.

WRITINGS:

(With Clarence H. Faust) *Jonathan Edwards,* Hill & Wang, 1935, reprinted, Telegraph Books, 1981.

(Editor with Perry Miller) *The Puritans,* American Book Co., 1938, revised edition, two volumes, Harper, 1963.

(Editor) Edward Taylor, *The Poetical Works,* Rockland Editions, 1939, reprinted, Princeton University Press, 1966.

(Editor and author of notes) *Men of Tomorrow: Nine Leaders Discuss the Problems of American Youth,* Putnam, 1942, reprinted, Books for Libraries, 1971.

(Editor and author of notes) *Return to Freedom: The Affairs of Our Time and Their Impact Upon Youth,* Putnam, 1944, reprinted, Books for Libraries, 1970.

(Editor and author of notes) *A Man's Reach: Some Choices Facing Youth Today,* Putnam, 1947.

(Editor with Robert E. Spiller, Willard Thorp, and Henry Seidel Canby) *Literary History of the United States,* Macmillan, 1948, revised edition, Macmillan, 1953.

(Editor and author of notes) *In Defense of Democracy,* Putnam, 1949.

Emily Dickinson: An Interpretive Biography, Belknap Press of Harvard University Press, 1955.

(Editor) *The Letters of Emily Dickinson,* three volumes, Belknap Press of Harvard University Press, 1958.

(Editor) *The Poems of Emily Dickinson,* three volumes, Belknap Press of Harvard University Press, 1963.

The Oxford Companion to American History, Oxford University Press, 1966.

(Editor) *The Complete Poems of Emily Dickinson,* Faber, 1970.

(Editor) *Emily Dickinson: Selected Letters,* Belknap Press of Harvard University Press, 1971.

Also author of *The Printed Writings of Jonathan Edwards, 1703-1738,* and editor of *Final Harvest: Emily Dickinson's Poems*. Contributor to *Encyclopaedia Britannica*.

SIDELIGHTS: Thomas Herbert Johnson's daughter, Laura Johnson Waterman, told *CA:* "I would say that my father had two focuses in his life: his teaching and his scholarship. Everything he wrote reflects these two lifelong commitments.

"It is hard for me to say which came first for him, but perhaps the teaching had the edge. He was devoted to it, especially at the secondary level where I believe he felt young minds could best be caught and shaped. He edited three books which express his strong involvement with teaching and youth.

"As for his scholarship, it seems all of a piece to me. He was born in the Connecticut River Valley and by coincidence the poets he focused on most deeply were all Connecticut River Valley born, too. He listed his religion as 'Congregationalist,' but that is soft. He was a Calvinist deep down. This explains for me his abiding attachment for the colonial poets which is reflected in his early work. Emily Dickinson, who is not a colonial poet but who was a Connecticut River Valley native, came to him in his later years. But then, one has to work up to Dickinson."

[Sketch confirmed by Thomas Herbert Johnson's daughter, Laura Johnson Waterman.]

* * *

JONES, Gwen 1951(?)-1988

OBITUARY NOTICE: Born c. 1951; died of cancer, February 6, 1988, in Pasadena, Calif. Journalist. Jones was one of the first black fashion editors of a major American newspaper. She held that position at the *Los Angeles Herald Examiner* from 1979 until she died in 1988. Beginning her career in journalism with Fairchild Publications, Jones worked for the company in Chicago, New York City, and Los Angeles; she then became associate editor of its *Men's Wear* magazine. She was also editor of *MBM, the Modern Magazine for Black Men* and a contributing editor to *Essence*. In 1984 Jones was named outstanding woman of the year by the Legal Defense Fund of the National Association for the Advancement of Colored People, as well as selected as one of the ten best dressed women in Los Angeles by the *Los Angeles Business Journal*. She taught at the Los Angeles Trade and Technical College and worked as a reporter on the syndicated television show "America" in 1984 and 1985.

OBITUARIES AND OTHER SOURCES:

PERIODICALS

Chicago Tribune, February 10, 1988.
Los Angeles Times, February 8, 1988.

* * *

JONES, Gwyn 1907-

PERSONAL: Born May 24, 1907, in Blackwood, Monmouthshire (now Gwent), Wales; son of George Henry (a miner) and Lily Florence (a teacher and midwife; maiden name, Nethercott) Jones; married Alice Reese in 1928 (died in 1979); married Mair Sivell in 1979. *Education:* University College Cardiff, University of Wales, B.A. (with first class honors), 1927, M.A. (with distinction), 1929.

ADDRESSES: Home—Castle Cottage, Sea View Place, Aberystwyth, Dyfed, Wales, United Kingdom.

CAREER: Grammar school teacher in Wigan, England, 1929-32, and Manchester, England, 1932-35; University of Wales, Cardiff, lecturer, 1935-40, and professor of English language and literature at University College Cardiff, 1965-75, fellow, 1980, Rendel Professor of English Language and Literature at University College of Wales, 1940-65, fellow, 1987. Lecturer. Fellow at Institut International des Arts et des Lettres, 1960; Ida Beam Visiting Professor at Iowa University, 1982. Founder and director of Penmark Press, Cardiff, 1939-60. Chairman of Welsh Arts Council, 1957-67; member of Arts Council of Great Britain.

MEMBER: Viking Society for Northern Research (honorary life member; president, 1951-52).

AWARDS, HONORS: Knight of the Order of the Falcon (Iceland), 1963, received Commander's Cross, 1987; elected member of Icelandic Community in North America, 1964; Commander of the Order of the British Empire, 1965; award from Welsh Arts Council, 1973; Christian Gauss Award from Phi Beta Kappa, 1973, for *Kings, Beasts, and Heroes;* Gwyn Jones Annual Lecture established in his honor by University College Cardiff and Welsh Arts Council, 1977; Steward of the Viking Kingdom of York, 1977-84; D.Litt. from University of Wales, 1977, University of Nottingham, 1978, and University of Southampton, 1983.

WRITINGS:

(Translator from the Norwegian and author of introduction and notes) *The Vatnsdalers' Saga,* Princeton University Press, 1944, reprinted, 1973.

(Translator from the Welsh with Thomas Jones) *The Golden Cockerel Mabinogion,* illustrations by Dorothea Braby, Golden Cockerel Press, 1948, published as *The Mabinogion,* Dutton, 1949, revised with enlarged introduction by G. Jones and T. Jones, 1974, special edition, illustrations by Jeff Thomas, Dent, 1976, illustrations by Alun Lee, Dragon's Dream, 1982.

(Author of postscript) Alun Lewis, *In the Green Tree,* illustrations by Braby, Golden Cockerel Press, 1952.

(Translator) *Sir Gawain and the Green Knight,* illustrations by Braby, Golden Cockerel Press, 1952.

(Reteller) *Welsh Legends and Folk-Tales,* illustrations by Joan Kiddell-Monroe, Oxford University Press, 1955.

(Reteller) *Scandinavian Legends and Folk-Tales,* illustrations by Kiddell-Monroe, Oxford University Press, 1956.

(Translator from the Old Icelandic and author of introduction and notes) *Egil's Saga,* American-Scandinavian Foundation and Syracuse University Press, 1960.

(Author of introduction) *Arthurian Chronicles,* Dent, 1962.

(Author of introduction) *Geoffrey of Monmouth: History of the Kings of Britain,* Dent, 1963.

The Norse Atlantic Saga: Being the Norse Voyages of Discovery and Settlement to Iceland, Greenland, America, Oxford University Press, 1964, 2nd edition, enlarged, published as *The Norse Atlantic Saga: Being the Norse Voyages of Discovery and Settlement to Iceland, Greenland, and North America,* 1986.

A History of the Vikings, Oxford University Press, 1968, revised edition, 1984.

Kings, Beasts, and Heroes, Oxford University Press, 1972.

FICTION

Richard Savage (novel), Viking, 1935.

Times Like These (novel), Gollancz, 1936.
The Nine-Days' Wonder (novel), Gollancz, 1937.
Garland of Bays (novel), Macmillan, 1938.
The Buttercup Field, and Other Stories, Penmark Press, 1945.
The Green Island (novella), engravings by John Petts, Golden Cockerel Press, 1946.
The Still Waters, and Other Stories, Davies, 1948.
The Flowers Beneath the Scythe (novel), Dent, 1952.
Shepherd's Hey, and Other Stories, Staples Press, 1953.
The Walk Home (novel), Dent, 1962, Norton, 1963.
Selected Short Stories (contains "The Buttercup Field," "All on a Summer's Day," "Guto Fewel," "Shacki Thomas," "Kittens," "Ora Pro Boscis," "All We Like Sheep," "A Man After God's Own Heart," "A White Birthday," "Four in a Valley," "The Brute Creation," "The Still Waters," "Their Bonds Are Loosed From Above," and "The Green Island"), Oxford University Press, 1974.

EDITOR

(And translator and author of introduction and notes) *Four Icelandic Sagas,* Princeton University Press, 1935, reprinted, University Microfilms, 1972.
(With E. M. Silvanus) *Narrative Poems for Schools,* three volumes, Rivingtons, 1935.
Prose [and] *Poems of Six Centuries,* two volumes, Rivingtons, 1935-36.
Welsh Short Stories, by E. Tegla Davies, Rhys Davies, Caradoc Evans . . . [and others], Penguin Books, 1940.
Salmacis and Hermaphroditus, Golden Cockerel Press, 1951.
William Browne, *Circe and Ulysses: The Inner Temple Masque,* Golden Cockerel Press, 1954.
(And author of introduction) *Welsh Short Stories,* Oxford University Press, 1956.
(And author of introduction) *Songs and Poems of John Dryden,* illustrations by Lavinia Blythe, Golden Cockerel Press, 1957.
The Metamorphoses of Publius Ovidius Naso, Golden Cockerel Press, 1958.
William Shakespeare, *Poems and Sonnets,* Golden Cockerel Press, 1960.
(And translator) *Eirik the Red, and Other Icelandic Sagas,* Oxford University Press, 1961, reprinted with introduction, 1972.
(With Islwyn Ffowc Elis, and author of introduction) *Twenty-five Welsh Stories,* Oxford University Press, 1971.
The Oxford Book of Welsh Verse in English, Oxford University Press, 1977.
(With Michael Quinn) *Fountains of Praise: University College Cardiff, 1883-1983,* University College Cardiff Press, 1983.

Founder and editor of *Welsh Review,* 1939-48.

OTHER

Author of "Being and Belonging," speech given on British Broadcasting Corporation Wales Annual Radio Lecture, November 14, 1977. Contributor to journals, including *American-Scandinavian Review, Beaver, Geographical Magazine, Life and Letters Today, Modern Language Review, Planet, Poetry Wales, Saga-Book,* and *Y Gymmrodor*.

WORK IN PROGRESS: Moving Gently Through Modern Welsh and Medieval Norse Pastures.

SIDELIGHTS: A dual emphasis on history and literature marks the writings of Gwyn Jones, a noted Welsh scholar and storyteller. Widely acclaimed, his books include studies of the history and legends of the Norse and Celtic peoples, fiction based on Welsh and English history, and editions of Welsh, English, and Norse literature. He has earned particular praise for promoting Anglo-Welsh literature—written in English by Welshmen—as an editor, lecturer, and journalist. Asserted Glyn Jones in the *Dictionary of Literary Biography,* Gwyn Jones's "contribution to the literature of his country in [English] has been varied, prolific, and of an impressively high standard."

History serves as the foundation of much of Jones's writing, and histories have been among his most highly regarded works. His *Norse Atlantic Saga,* describing the various sea journeys and colonies of the Vikings, combines "the virtues of a first-rate story with those of mature and accurate scholarship," according to the *Times Literary Supplement*. Drawing on his visits to archaeological excavations in Greenland as well as new translations of Old Norse sources, Jones presents a detailed account, vivid and "intricately argued," of Viking voyages to Iceland, Greenland, and North America. Evidencing Jones's "deep love of the Northern landscape and way of life," *The Norse Atlantic Saga* "combines passion and scholarship with rare skill." The revised edition, which takes into account a number of advances in the field, was described as "an impressive and enthralling study" in the same journal.

A History of the Vikings, which covers a wide range of Norse activities and culture, received praise as "a tremendous achievement" from Werner Wiskari of the *New York Times*. Acknowledging the many contradictions among ancient sources, Jones examines Viking exploration, religion, art, trade, raiding, and politics with the aid of archaeology, art history, philology, and religious history. Meticulously fitting legend and fact together, he builds "a vivid and living picture of the Viking adventure," said a *Times Literary Supplement* reviewer. Remarked Robert Conquest in *New Statesman,* Jones "has deployed a mass of material in a manner as readable as it is instructive." Critics also admired the author's objective approach and deft synthesis of diverse sources. Echoing the opinions of several reviewers, a writer for the *Virginia Quarterly Review* summarized the book as "a masterpiece of scholarship and execution."

In *Kings, Beasts, and Heroes,* reported the *Times Literary Supplement,* Jones explores "an exciting idea," studying three written folktales from different cultures and eras. Jones's texts are the Anglo-Saxon *Beowulf,* the Welsh *Culhwch and Olwen,* and the Norse *Saga of Hrolf Kraki,* and he focuses on investigating what kind of story each is—epic, saga, or romance—what it is about, how it is told, and how well it is told. By juxtaposing them, commented the critic, "you should find out a lot about what was likely to happen to the same kind of material in these three different cultures at these three different periods, and so about the nature of the three genres themselves." The critic appraised Jones's qualifications for tackling this promising enterprise: "Not only has he the Celtic gift for words . . . , he knows his texts inside-out, and is thoroughly at home in their different-flavoured worlds." As a result, related the reviewer, Jones reveals the "foundations and structure of medieval literary narrative."

Jones's fiction, drawing on more recent history, has impressed critics with good characterization, description, and historical accuracy. For example, his first novel, *Richard Savage,* centers on an actual eighteenth-century poet and displays Jones's "profound knowledge and understanding of the society and the literature of eighteenth-century England," according to Glyn Jones. Claiming to be the illegitimate son of an earl and a countess, Savage pursues his claim among the upper classes

and experiences as well the world of criminals and prostitutes in Jones's chronicle. *Times Like These,* judged a "fine and sensitive novel" and "one of the most accurate accounts in fiction" of working-class Wales during the early twentieth century, features a "splendid" characterization in Oliver Biesty, a proud and honorable coal miner. Jones sympathetically describes the miners' strike of 1926 and the hardships of Biesty's life and struggle for fair working conditions. Like *Richard Savage,* Jones's later novel *Garland of Bays* portrays a historical figure, the Elizabethan writer Robert Greene, and Jones's knowledge of the period again provides a "vivid and convincing background," judged Glyn Jones.

In the fourteen years between *Garland of Bays* and his next full-length novel, *The Flowers Beneath the Scythe,* Jones wrote a number of short stories, which demonstrate his shift toward specifically Welsh history and further show his talent for characterization and description. Welsh towns, villages, and farms are his settings and Welsh miners and country folk are his protagonists, observed Glyn Jones. The critic commented, "A kind of lyricism and a humor of character, of situation, and of expression are more evident in the short stories than in the novels, as are the author's tenderness and compassion and his pity for the duped and the wronged." He "has written stories in a variety of moods," elaborated a *Times Literary Supplement* writer, "and his eloquent prose has graced them all."

Characterization figures strongly in *The Flowers Beneath the Scythe,* as Jones chronicles the life of a young Welsh heiress during the two world wars. Chris Powell, who lost her first husband in World War I, marries again and witnesses the economic decline between the wars, the rise of fascism, and the onset of World War II, in which her second husband is killed. "In Chris," suggested Glyn Jones, the author "has produced one of his most impressive and sympathetic figures, warm, courageous, and infinitely loving"—a character emblematic of Jones's treatment of women. The book is also notable, stated Glyn Jones, for describing "the manner in which sensitive and caring people thought, felt, and acted when faced with the agonizing dilemmas of the period, especially the choice between pacifism and patriotism."

In addition to fiction and history, Jones has published highly regarded translations and editions of other author's works, often in the field of Welsh literature. With Thomas Jones, for instance, he produced "what is probably the most accurate and scholarly translation of the medieval Welsh tales known as the *Mabinogion,*" recalled Glyn Jones. The volume has been credited with reviving world interest in the stories and is regarded as a classic work. His editions of Welsh literature also include three collections of Welsh short stories and *The Oxford Book of Welsh Verse in English,* which is designed to "acquaint the English-language reader with the Welsh poetic achievement from its beginnings in the Heroic Age of Britain to the present day," recounted Russell Davies in the *Times Literary Supplement*. Jones edited, with Michael Quinn, the "stylish literary symposium" *Fountains of Praise,* which marked the centennial of Jones's alma mater, University College Cardiff, and was founder and editor of the periodical *Welsh Review*. Among Jones's other editions and translations are volumes of Scandinavian folktales and longer sagas and the works of writers such as William Shakespeare and John Dryden.

Jones told *CA:* "The short story is a literary genre that has always appeared congenial to the emotional needs, technical preoccupations, and social function of Welsh authors. Our poetry, from the Heroic Age to R. Williams Parry and Dylan Thomas, is best known for its lyrical nature and immediacy, and the short story is its prose counterpart. It certainly suits my own broodings over the grief and pain as well as the farce and joy attendant upon the human and animal creation.

"As a man who reads Homer, Tolstoy, and the Bible in English I have never doubted the value of translations. Translation itself is a task, craft, art as pleasurable as it is demanding. Perfect—or should I say almost perfect?—translations require substantially less genius but equal judgment and frequently more pains than their originals, but the translator's reward is immense. Creation in Language A is the first miracle; recreation in Language B is the second. And for a translator it is Language B that counts.

"Every scholar, whatever his discipline, needs history. And every student of early times needs to know where that history comes from. Chronicle, hagiography, kings' lives and the gests of nations, heroic poetry—whence and wherefore, and what are they worth? You are very quickly involved in 'history' soi-disant, historical tradition, legendary history, legend and fable and folktale, and the surviving repositories of mythology. In every sense of the word this is a wondrous field of study and interest. You are in at the dawn of religion, the shaping of nations and empires, the world's literatures oral and written, and the entire multifarious story of mankind. You are also in at your own personal genesis as thinker, believer, student, and creator. You gain much knowledge of yourself as your own mythmaker. And how should an artist exist without some such nourisher of his ego, some such impulse to achievement?"

BIOGRAPHICAL/CRITICAL SOURCES:

BOOKS

Dictionary of Literary Biography, Volume 15: *British Novelists, 1930-1959,* Gale, 1983.

Jones, Glyn and John Rowlands, *Profiles: A Visitors' Guide to Writing in Twentieth-Century Wales,* Gomer, 1980.

Price, Cecil, *Gwyn Jones,* University of Wales Press, 1976.

PERIODICALS

Atlantic Monthly, November, 1968, October, 1972.

New Statesman, December 20, 1968.

New Yorker, August 16, 1969.

New York Times, February 5, 1969.

Times Literary Supplement, June 1, 1956, September 30, 1960, March 12, 1964, November 21, 1968, March 27, 1969, October 6, 1972, March 4, 1977, March 2, 1984, October 10, 1986.

Virginia Quarterly Review, spring, 1969.

—*Sketch by Polly A. Vedder*

* * *

JONES, James T. 1948-

PERSONAL: Born April 5, 1948, in Decatur, Ill.; son of Marion Francis (a salesman) and Jean Elizabeth (a clerk; maiden name, Williamson) Jones; married Kimberly Ann Dulin (an attorney), February 8, 1957. *Education:* Eastern Illinois University, B.A., 1971, M.A. (with distinction), 1973; Southern Illinois University at Carbondale, Ph.D., 1980.

ADDRESSES: Home—Route 1, Box 356, Strafford, Mo. 65757. *Office*—Department of English, Southwest Missouri State University, 901 South National, Springfield, Mo. 65804.

CAREER: Millikin University, Decatur, Ill., instructor in English, 1980-83; Southwest Missouri State University, Springfield, assistant professor, 1983-87, associate professor of English, 1987—.

MEMBER: Modern Language Association of America, American Civil Liberties Union (Southwest Missouri chapter; president, 1986-87).

WRITINGS:

Wayward Skeptic: The Theories of R. P. Blackmur, University of Illinois Press, 1986.
(Editor) *Uncollected Essays of R. P. Blackmur,* University of Illinois Press, in press.

WORK IN PROGRESS: Editing an anthology, *The Theories of American New Criticism;* research on T. S. Eliot, New Criticism, modern and postmodern poetry.

SIDELIGHTS: James T. Jones told *CA:* "Despite prevailing Platonic prejudices that make it difficult to write books about literary critics, I was attracted to Blackmur by the difficulty of his style. I wanted to understand the purpose of a criticism that rivaled or surpassed its object in difficulty. The title of my first book, *Wayward Skeptic,* comes from Santayana, who believed that the human mind is wrenched from solipsism by the confrontation with meaning, resulting in what he called 'animal faith,' a brutally opportunistic sort of belief. I found a similar process in Blackmur, who admired Santayana's philosophy from a very early age.

"Blackmur's favorite adjective to describe the ideal state of literary criticism is the word *provisional.* By that he means that critical judgments should remain fluid and open to change. At the same time, however, he creates such a vivid sense of the living meaning of literature by his intense engagement with specific texts that momentarily, at least, his judgment is hypostatized. His ability to undercut himself and his pronouncements achieves, in a very preliminary way, exactly the state of self-contradiction that many deconstructionists now conceive for literature.

"My reading of Blackmur has led me to the belief that American New Criticism has much more to offer, in a theoretical sense, than connoisseurs of European methodology are willing to admit. Furthermore, I think that we are now distant enough from the origins of New Criticism to be able to look at it objectively and to use it as part of the foundation for future theoretical developments."

* * *

JONES-JACKSON, Pat
See JONES-JACKSON, Patricia

* * *

JONES-JACKSON, Patricia 1946-1986
(Pat Jones-Jackson)

OBITUARY NOTICE: Born in 1946; died of injuries suffered in an automobile accident, June 30, 1986, on Johns Island, S.C. While a doctoral student in linguistics at the University of Michigan, Jones-Jackson traveled to the Sea Islands, an archipelago off the southern Atlantic coast of the United States, to study the Gullah language. She researched that language, a mixture of various African dialects, while living on the islands, on and off, for thirteen years. She also traveled to West Africa to study the origins of Gullah. While an associate professor at Howard University, Jones-Jackson proposed an article to *National Geographic* on Gullah and the Sea Islands for the magazine. She died in a car accident on one of the islands while on the assignment. Her books include the posthumously published *When Roots Die,* a work about the Gullah language.

OBITUARIES AND OTHER SOURCES:

PERIODICALS

National Geographic, December, 1987.

* * *

JORDAN, Neil 1950(?)-

BRIEF ENTRY: Born in 1950 (some sources say 1951) in Sligo, Ireland. Irish film director, screenwriter, short story writer, and novelist. Regarded by some critics as one of the most original new talents of the 1980s, the award-winning writer Jordan is most noted for his rich, imaginative, and unique works. The author's first story collection, *Night in Tunisia and Other Stories* (Co-op Books [Dublin], 1976)—winner of the *Guardian* Fiction Prize in 1979—relates the frustrations and spiritual numbness suffered by characters living in contemporary Ireland. Also set in Ireland are Jordan's novels *The Past* (Braziller, 1980), which portrays a nameless narrator whose search to discover his parentage evokes the secrets and significance of the past, and *Dream of the Beast* (Chatto & Windus, 1983), a poetic fantasy describing an advertising man who transforms into the creature he has imagined for an ad campaign.

Jordan has demonstrated diverse themes in the film genre as well, writing and directing such movies as the 1982 thriller "Angel" (released in 1985 as "Danny Boy") and "The Company of Wolves" (1985), a fantasy based on a story by English novelist Angela Carter. For the latter production, Jordan was named best director by the British Critics Circle. He has perhaps gained most attention, however, as co-author and director of the critically acclaimed 1986 film "Mona Lisa," the novelization of which was published by Faber & Faber the same year. An unusual love story set in London, the film generated universal approval for its surrealistic tone and spirited, lurid romance.

BIOGRAPHICAL/CRITICAL SOURCES:

BOOKS

A Biographical Dictionary of Irish Writers, St. Martin's, 1985.
Contemporary Novelists, 4th edition, St. Martin's, 1986.
Dictionary of Irish Literature, Greenwood Press, 1979.

PERIODICALS

Chicago Tribune, April 22, 1985.
Los Angeles Times, November 19, 1980, April 19, 1985, June 20, 1985.
New York Times, April 19, 1985.
Times (London), September 6, 1986.
Times Literary Supplement, November 14, 1980, November 11, 1983.

* * *

JOSEFSBERG, Milt 1911-1987

OBITUARY NOTICE—See index for *CA* sketch: Born June 29, 1911, in New York, N.Y.; died after suffering a stroke, De-

cember 14, 1987, in Burbank, Calif. Television producer and author. Dubbed the maven of comedy by his contemporaries, Josefsberg won acclaim for his comedy writing for radio and television. Among his clients were celebrities Bob Hope, Jack Benny, Milton Berle, and Lucille Ball. A three-time Emmy Award nominee, Josefsberg won the coveted prize in 1978 for best comedy series for his work as a producer on the television program "All in the Family." Before taking up comedy writing for a living Josefsberg was a Broadway press agent. He also spent two years as a programming executive for the National Broadcasting Company. Josefsberg was the author of *The Jack Benny Show: The Life and Times of America's Best Loved Entertainer, Comedy Writing for Television and Hollywood,* and numerous television scripts.

OBITUARIES AND OTHER SOURCES:

PERIODICALS

Los Angeles Times, December 16, 1987.
Washington Post, December 18, 1987.

* * *

JOSKOW, Paul L. 1947-

PERSONAL: Born in 1947, in New York, N.Y.; son of Jules (an economist) and Charlotte (a housewife; maiden name, Epstein) Joskow; married Barbara Z. Chasen (a teacher), September 9, 1978; children: Suzanne Zoe. *Education:* Cornell University, B.A. (with distinction), 1968; Yale University, M.Phil., 1971, Ph.D., 1972.

ADDRESSES: Home—7 Chilton St., Brookline, Mass. 02146. *Office*—Department of Economics, Massachusetts Institute of Technology, 17 Massachusetts Ave., Cambridge, Mass. 02139.

CAREER: Massachusetts Institute of Technology, Cambridge, assistant professor, 1972-75, associate professor, 1975-78, professor of economics, 1978—. Visiting professor at Harvard University, 1979-80; Joel Dean Lecturer at Oberlin College, 1983; fellow at Center for Advanced Study in the Behavioral Sciences, Stanford, Calif., 1985-86. Member of Massachusetts Energy Facilities Siting Task Force, 1974, and Economic Task Force of National Commission for Review of Antitrust Laws, 1978; member of Regulatory Research Advisory Board of American Enterprise Institute for Public Policy Research, 1978—; public member of Administrative Conference of the United States, 1980-82; member of advisory council of Electric Power Research Institute, 1980-84, and advisory board of Sloan Foundation, 1984—; member of Economic Research Coordinating Group of New England Council, 1981-83; consultant to RAND Corp., National Science Foundation, and Organization for Economic Cooperation and Development. Member of Brookline Historical District Commission, 1981-83. *Military service:* U.S. Army Reserve, 1969-75; became staff sergeant.

MEMBER: American Economic Association, Econometric Society, National Economic Research Association, Phi Beta Kappa.

AWARDS, HONORS: Woodrow Wilson fellow.

WRITINGS:

(With Martin Baughman and Dilip Kamat) *Electric Power in the United States: Models and Policy Analysis,* MIT Press, 1979.
Controlling Hospital Costs: The Role of Government Regulation, MIT Press, 1981.
(With Richard Schmalensee) *Markets for Power: An Analysis of Electric Utility Deregulation,* MIT Press, 1983.

CONTRIBUTOR

Charles J. Cicchetti and John J. Jurewitz, editors, *Studies in Electric Utility Regulation,* Ballinger, 1975.
Werner Sichel, editor, *Public Utility Ratemaking in an Energy Conscious Environment,* Westview, 1979.
Mancur Olsen, editor, *A New Approach to the Economics of Health Care,* American Enterprise Institute for Public Policy Research, 1981.
Gary Fromm, editor, *Studies in Public Regulation,* MIT Press, 1981.
Michael A. Crew, editor, *Regulatory Reform and Public Utilities,* Lexington Books, 1982.
Gregory A. Daneke, editor, *Energy, Economics, and the Environment,* Lexington Books, 1982.
Eli Noam, editor, *Telecommunications Today and Tomorrow,* Harcourt, 1983.
Jerry A. Hausman and David A. Wise, editors, *Social Experimentation,* University of Chicago Press, 1985.
Franklin M. Fisher, editor, *Antitrust and Regulation: Essays in Memory of John McGowan,* MIT Press, 1985.

Contributor of more than forty articles and reviews to scholarly journals. *Bell Journal of Economics,* associate editor, 1976-77 and 1979-83, co-editor, 1977-78; associate editor of *RAND Journal of Economics,* 1984-85; member of editorial board of *Land Economics,* 1975-80, *Journal of Economic Behavior and Organization,* 1980—, *Energy Journal,* 1981—, and *Journal of Law, Economics, and Organization,* 1984—.

WORK IN PROGRESS: Research on industrial organization, government regulation, and "theory of the firm."

* * *

JOYCE, Bill
See JOYCE, William

* * *

JOYCE, William 1959(?)-
(Bill Joyce)

PERSONAL: Born c. 1959. *Education:* Graduated from Southern Methodist University.

ADDRESSES: Home—Shreveport, La.

CAREER: Illustrator and writer.

WRITINGS:

(Illustrator) Catherine Gray and James Gray, *Tammy and the Gigantic Fish* (juvenile), Harper, 1983.
(Illustrator, under name Bill Joyce) Marianna Mayer, *My First Book of Nursery Tales: Five Favorite Bedtime Stories,* Random House, 1983.
(Illustrator) Bethany Roberts, *Waiting-for-Spring Stories* (juvenile), Harper, 1984.
George Shrinks (self-illustrated juvenile), Harper, 1985.

Contributor of illustrations to periodicals.*

* * *

JOYNT, Carey Bonthron 1924-

PERSONAL: Born January 7, 1924, in Hensall, Ontario, Can-

ada; immigrated to the United States, 1948, naturalized citizen, 1958; son of Thomas Cleveland and Florence (Bonthron) Joynt; married Anne Wilson Morgan, August 21, 1948; children: David Morgan. *Education:* University of Western Ontario, B.A., 1945, M.A., 1948; Clark University, Ph.D., 1951. *Religion:* Presbyterian.

ADDRESSES: Home—1415 Oakwood Dr., Bethlehem, Pa. 18017. *Office*—Department of International Relations, Lehigh University, Bethlehem, Pa. 18015.

CAREER: Lehigh University, Bethlehem, Pa., assistant professor, 1951-56, associate professor, 1956-60, professor of international relations and chairman of department, 1956-74, Monro J. Rathbone Professor, 1975—. Member of Council on Church and Society of the United Presbyterian Church, 1969-73.

MEMBER: American Political Science Association, Institute for Strategic Studies.

AWARDS, HONORS: Ford Foundation fellow, 1957-58; fellow of American Council of Learned Societies, 1960; Guggenheim fellow, 1963; R. R. and E. C. Hillman Award from Lehigh University, 1970, for contributions to the university.

WRITINGS:

(With Percy E. Corbett) *Theory and Reality in World Politics,* University of Pittsburgh Press, 1978.
(With J. E. Hare) *Ethics and International Affairs,* Macmillan, 1982.
Decisions for War, Scholarly Journal, in press.

Contributor to political science journals.

SIDELIGHTS: Carey Bonthron Joynt told *CA:* "I am intensely interested in how to inject religious and ethical values into the making of high policy. The present urgent search for solutions to the nuclear dilemma is only one example of the desperate need for such a venture."

* * *

JUDGE, Harry George 1928-

PERSONAL: Born August 1, 1928, in England; son of George Arthur and Winifred Mary Judge; married Elizabeth Mary Patrick, 1956; children: Simon Patrick, Hilary Susan, Emma Margaret. *Education:* Brasenose College, Oxford, M.A., 1955; University of London, Ph.D., 1958.

ADDRESSES: Home—2 Upland Park Rd., Oxford, England. *Office*—Department of Educational Studies, Oxford University, 15 Norham Gardens, Oxford, England.

CAREER: Assistant master at grammar schools, 1954-59; Cumberland Lodge, Windsor, England, director of studies, 1959-62; headmaster of grammar school in Banbury, England, 1962-67, principal, 1967-73; Oxford University, Oxford, England, director of department of educational studies and fellow of Brasenose College, 1973—, tutor for admissions, 1980—. Visiting professor at Massachusetts Institute of Technology, 1977 and 1980-82, and Carnegie-Mellon University, 1984-86; visiting scholar at Harvard University, 1984-86; member of Public Schools Commission, 1966-70, James Committee of Inquiry Into Teacher Training, 1971-72, and Oxford Education Committee, 1982—; chairman of School Broadcasting Council, 1977-81, and Royal College of Nursing Committee on Nursing Education, 1984.

WRITINGS:

Louis XIV, Longman, 1965.
School Is Not Yet Dead, Longman, 1974.
American Graduate Schools of Education: A View From Abroad, Ford Foundation, 1982.
A Generation of Schooling: English Secondary Schools Since 1944, Oxford University Press, 1985.

General editor of *The Oxford Illustrated Encyclopedia,* 1985—. Contributor to education and history journals.

WORK IN PROGRESS: A study of the American high school; *British Educational Policy in the Twentieth Century.*

SIDELIGHTS: A Generation of Schooling provides a survey of development and change in the English school system from a unique personal perspective. The experiences of the author and his family breathe life into a complex string of events that previously have been regarded as complex and confusing. According to *Times Literary Supplement* reviewer John Mackay, Harry Judge "charts his course with clarity and restraint. . . . He is always seeking to be objective, is never partisan or strident, and is prepared to acknowledge the weaknesses, exaggerations and illogicalities of those who agree with his conclusion as well as those who do not."

BIOGRAPHICAL/CRITICAL SOURCES:

PERIODICALS

Times Literary Supplement, January 25, 1985.

* * *

JUNG, Leo 1892-1987

OBITUARY NOTICE: Born June 20, 1892, in Ung Brod, Moravia (now Czechoslovakia; some sources say Hungary or Slavonski Brod, Yugoslavia); died following a heart attack, December 19, 1987, in New York, N.Y. Rabbi, talmudic scholar, translator, editor, and author. Extremely active in the Jewish community for more than sixty years, Jung was editor of *The Jewish Library,* a six-volume encyclopedia of Jewish culture and religion. He was ordained a rabbi in Berlin in 1920 and came to the United States later that year to lead a congregation in Cleveland, Ohio. Jung moved to New York City two years later to become rabbi at the Jewish Center in Manhattan, and he held that position until retiring as rabbi emeritus in 1977. In addition, he was a professor of ethics at Yeshiva University beginning in 1931. During that year he also helped found the Jewish Braille Institute, where he worked with other rabbis and biblical scholars on a Braille edition of the Hebrew Scriptures, which was finally published in 1950. A member of several religious, cultural, and community organizations, Jung helped bring more than nine thousand European refugees to the United States following World War II. *Judaism in a Changing World, Toward Sinai, Living Judaism, Fallen Angels,* and *Essentials of Judaism* are among his writings. He also translated the Talmud.

OBITUARIES AND OTHER SOURCES:

BOOKS

Who's Who in American Jewry, Standard Who's Who, 1980.
Who's Who in World Jewry: A Biographical Dictionary of Outstanding Jews, Olive Books of Israel, 1978.

PERIODICALS

Chicago Tribune, December 22, 1987.

Los Angeles Times, December 22, 1987.
New York Times, December 21, 1987.
Washington Post, December 21, 1987.

*   *   *

JURGELA, Constantine R. 1904-1988

OBITUARY NOTICE: Born June 22, 1904, in Elizabeth, N.J.; died following a stroke, February 29, 1988, in Bethesda, Md. Attorney, translator, and author. Jurgela, who was head of the Lithuanian section of the Voice of America radio service for twenty-three years, was born in the United States but traveled to Lithuania in 1914 with his parents. He fought with the Lithuanian forces in a war for independence from the Soviet Union in 1919, then worked with the Lithuanian foreign ministry. Jurgela returned to the United States in 1924 and earned a law degree from Brooklyn Law School. He later practiced law in New York City, where he also served as director of the Lithuanian-American Information Center. In 1951 he began his long tenure with the Voice of America in Washington, D.C. Jurgela wrote many magazine articles and books about Lithuania, including *Lithuania in a Twin Teutonic Clutch, History of the Lithuanian Nation, Lithuania: The Outpost of Freedom,* and translated a number of works from Lithuanian into English.

OBITUARIES AND OTHER SOURCES:

BOOKS

American Catholic Who's Who, Volume 23: *1980-81,* National Catholic News Service, 1979.

PERIODICALS

Washington Post, March 2, 1988.

*   *   *

JWAIDEH, Nizar 1933(?)-1988

OBITUARY NOTICE: Born c. 1933; died of pancreatic cancer, January 20, 1988, in Washington, D.C. Administrator, journalist, and editor. Jwaideh served as foreign correspondent for the Associated Press from 1953 to 1960, then became foreign and national editor for Chicago *Sun-Times* and diplomatic editor for *U.S. News and World Report*. In 1981 he joined the Arab League Mission in Washington as director of public affairs. Jwaideh was also editor of *Arab Perspectives* magazine.

OBITUARIES AND OTHER SOURCES:

PERIODICALS

New York Times, January 24, 1988.

K

KARAS, Joza 1926-

PERSONAL: Given name is pronounced ''*Yo*-zha''; born May 3, 1926, in Warsaw, Poland; immigrated to the United States, 1954, naturalized citizen, 1958; son of Frantisek (a government official) and Marie (a teacher; maiden name, Rajda) Karas; married Milada Javora, October 24, 1953 (died September 8, 1974); married Anne Killackey (a reading consultant), February 14, 1976; children: Francis, Henry, Michael, Joan, Joseph, Alexander. *Education:* State Conservatory of Music, Prague, Czechoslovakia, Absolutorium, 1949; University of Hartford, M.Mus., 1957.

ADDRESSES: Home—212 Duncaster Rd., Bloomfield, Conn. 06002. *Office*—University of Hartford, 200 Bloomfield Ave., West Hartford, Conn. 06117.

CAREER: University of Hartford, West Hartford, Conn., violin instructor, 1955—. Violinist with Hartford Symphony, 1955—; founder and leader of Karas String Quartet.

MEMBER: American Federation of Musicians, Czechoslovak Society of Arts and Sciences in America.

AWARDS, HONORS: Official citation from General Assembly of the State of Connecticut, 1985, for *Music in Terezin, 1941-1945*.

WRITINGS:

Music in Terezin, 1941-1945, Beaufort Books (New York, N.Y.), 1985.

Contributor to music journals.

WORK IN PROGRESS: The Adventures of Joe Deepick, an autobiographical novel, completion expected in 1988.

SIDELIGHTS: Joza Karas was raised in Czechoslovakia and has lived in Germany, Colombia, and Canada. His travels have taken him to Israel, England, Romania, and Italy, and his languages include Czech, German, French, Spanish, and Latin.

Music in Terezin is the author's tribute to those talented Jewish composers and performers who were imprisoned in the Nazi concentration camp, Terezin, in Czechoslovakia. Unlike the other camps that were established by the Nazis during World War II, Terezin encouraged creativity and provided its inmates with musical instruments. The Germans not only sponsored daily performances of original works, but they also filmed a number of concerts for posterity. Since most of the musicians who found themselves in Terezin were later transferred to other concentration camps and killed, the camp at Terezin provided a valuable repository for the final contributions of some of the most remarkable Jewish musicians of the decade.

Karas told *CA:* ''I became interested in the research of the musical activities in the Terezin concentration camp in 1970. I realized that the entire history of the Holocaust had been researched and described in countless publications, but, for some unknown reason, this very interesting aspect of the Jewish tragedy was never explored, except for some minor inaccurate references in various books and articles. Through musical acquaintances in Prague, I made contact with several survivors of Terezin, who provided me with valuable information and also with names of other survivors, mainly from the ranks of musicians. During fifteen years of work, I was able to assemble a wealth of taped interviews, documents, artwork pertaining to the musical life in Terezin, and more than fifty original compositions written there.''

BIOGRAPHICAL/CRITICAL SOURCES:

PERIODICALS

Jewish Quarterly, Volume 33, number 2, 1986.
New York Times Book Review, April 28, 1985.
Sun (Baltimore), May 19, 1985.

* * *

KASULIS, T(homas) P(atrick) 1948-

PERSONAL: Surname is pronounced ''Ka-*soo*-lis''; born March 5, 1948, in Bridgeport, Conn.; son of Joseph J. (in business) and Albina (Checkanauskas) Kasulis; married Ellen Sponheimer (a writing specialist), June 5, 1970; children: Telemachus, Matthias, Benedict. *Education:* Yale University, B.A., 1970, M.Ph., 1972, Ph.D., 1975; University of Hawaii at Manoa, M.A., 1973. *Religion:* Roman Catholic.

ADDRESSES: Home—712 Chapple Ave., Ashland, Wis. 54806. *Office*—Department of Philosophy and Religion, Northland College, Ashland, Wis. 54086.

CAREER: University of Hawaii at Manoa, Honolulu, assistant professor of philosophy, 1975-80; Northland College, Ash-

land, Wis., associate professor, 1980-86, professor of philosophy and religion, 1986—, chairman of humanities division, 1984—. Mellon faculty fellow in humanities at Harvard University, 1979-80.

MEMBER: American Philosophical Association, Society for Asian and Comparative Philosophy, American Academy of Religion, Society for Values in Higher Education, Association for Asian Studies.

AWARDS, HONORS: Grants from Japanese Government Gift Fund, 1976, and American Council of Learned Societies, 1977; fellow of Japan Foundation, 1982.

WRITINGS:

Zen Action/Zen Person, University Press of Hawaii, 1981.

Contributor to philosophy and religious studies journals.

WORK IN PROGRESS: A book on the development of traditional Japanese values and modes of thought, including their impact on contemporary society, publication expected in 1989.

SIDELIGHTS: T. P. Kasulis told *CA:* "My primary concern as a scholar is to understand and articulate the relationships among culture, religion, philosophy, and values. How does 'tradition' influence contemporary societies' views of modernity? What role does and should religion play in today's technological world? How is the thinking of people today related to the values of cultural heritages going back centuries or even millennia? What hidden cultural assumption do we Westerners make about the nature of thought, objectivity, and modes of knowing? Are these same assumptions operative in non-Western technological societies such as Japan?

"My working assumption is that the logical form of thinking is essentially the same in all societies, but that various factors—historical, social, geographic, linguistic—have influenced thinkers of different cultural orientations to focus on different aspects of human experience. What is of paradigmatic philosophical concern in one country is, therefore, not necessarily of critical importance to the thinkers in another country. Each culture's intellectual tradition has tended to develop its own distinctive methodologies and terminologies suitable to its own particular concerns.

"The current level of interaction among the nations of the world and the increasing awareness of common economic, political, social, and moral problems require of us a deeper philosophical understanding of culture itself. Through such an understanding, we can better learn how to be true to our own traditions, yet tolerant and understanding—even respectful—of other traditions. By understanding our differences as well as our similarities, the thinkers and planners of divergent traditions can better learn from each other. In this regard, at least, my work may have some practical as well as theoretical benefit."

BIOGRAPHICAL/CRITICAL SOURCES:

PERIODICALS

Times Literary Supplement, October 30, 1981.

* * *

KATZ, Arthur M. 1942-

PERSONAL: Born May 23, 1942, in New York, N.Y.; son of Morris and Margaret (Holub) Katz; married Sima Rae Osdoby; children: Dara Elizabeth Osdoby Katz, Margaret Catherine Osdoby Katz. *Education:* City College of the City University of New York, B.S. (with honors), 1964; University of Rochester, Ph.D., 1969; Massachusetts Institute of Technology, M.S., 1974.

ADDRESSES: Home—2 Stevenage Circle, Rockville, Md. 20850.

CAREER: Wellesley College, Wellesley, Mass., assistant professor of chemistry, 1969-70; Harvard University, Cambridge, Mass., teaching fellow, 1971-72; scientist and administrator at U.S. Atomic Energy Commission, U.S. Energy Research and Development Administration, and U.S. Department of Energy, 1974-78; U. S. Department of Energy, Washington, D.C., scientist in Division of Regional Assessments, 1978-80, branch chief in Office of Safeguards and Security, 1980-83, branch chief in Office of Fusion Energy, 1984—. Member of Great Boston Committee on the Transportation Crisis and Joint Regional Transportation Committee, Boston Metropolitan Region, 1970-74; consultant to Joint Committee on Defense Production, U.S. Congress, 1976-79; tutor at University of Maryland, 1981.

MEMBER: American Chemical Society, American Association for the Advancement of Science, New Mark Commons Homes Association (president, 1982-84), Sigma Xi.

AWARDS, HONORS: Superior Achievement Award from U.S. Department of Energy, 1981.

WRITINGS:

Life After Nuclear War: The Economic and Social Impacts of Nuclear Attacks on the United States, Ballinger, 1981.

(Contributor with S. R. Osdoby) *Tre minuti a mezzanotte,* Editori Riunti, 1984.

Contributor to scientific journals.

WORK IN PROGRESS: Who Do I See—Me! (tentative title), about a child who has to come to terms with an irreversible congenital defect; "The Effects of Nuclear War on Human Society," to be published in *War: The Psychological Dimension,* edited by Betty Glad.

SIDELIGHTS: Arthur M. Katz told *CA:* "I felt strongly the full implications of nuclear war were being understated because the economic, social, and psychological effects of such a war, which were difficult to quantify, were being ignored and needed to be effectively presented to the public and policy makers. That is why I was willing to stick through the ten years it took to develop *Life After Nuclear War.* I have taken the opportunity to update my book with a chapter incorporating some of the lessons and insights from the nuclear-winter controversy and the accident at the Chernobyl nuclear reactor in the Soviet Union, and I am presently exploring possible routes to publication.

"In contrast to the grandiose horrors of nuclear war, I've been working on a children's book about the feelings and perceptions of a child with a serious and only partially resolvable medical problem. The motivation is personal—living through this experience with two remarkable people, my daughters. However, I've learned children's publishers are even more demanding and specialized than publishers of adult books."

* * *

KEAVENEY, Arthur 1951-

PERSONAL: Surname is pronounced "*Key*-van-ee"; born July 8, 1951, in Galway, Ireland; son of Michael (a train driver)

and Nuala (Scully) Keaveney; married Jennifer Downing (a careers information officer), August 23, 1980. *Education:* National University of Ireland, University College, Galway, B.A., 1972, M.A., 1975; University of Hull, Ph.D., 1978.

ADDRESSES: Home—Canterbury, Kent, England. *Office*—Darwin College, University of Kent at Canterbury, Canterbury CT2 7NY, England.

CAREER: University of Wales, University College of Wales, Aberystwyth, postdoctoral fellow, 1978-79; University of Kent at Canterbury, Canterbury, England, lecturer in classics, 1979—.

MEMBER: International Plutarch Society, Society for the Promotion of Roman Studies, American Philological Association, Societa degli Storici Europei.

WRITINGS:

(Contributor) Carl Deroux, editor, *Studies in Latin Literature and Roman History,* Volume III, Latomus, 1983.
Sulla: The Last Republican, Croom Helm, 1983.
Rome and the Unification of Italy, Croom Helm, 1987.

Contributor of more than thirty articles and reviews to classical studies and history journals.

WORK IN PROGRESS: A biography of Lucullus, publication expected in 1990.

SIDELIGHTS: "Having as my twin interests the classical languages and history in general," Arthur Keaveney told *CA,* "I have naturally gravitated towards the area of ancient history. My particular field is the Roman Republic and its constitution, but I also have a strong interest in the Greek writers Herodotus and Plutarch.

"My book *Sulla: The Last Republican* is the result of a fascination, stretching back to my school days, with one of the most colorful and controversial characters in Roman history. Indeed, Sulla's glittering career is such to suggest that, if epics should ever return to fashion, he would make an ideal subject for a movie. In his own day Sulla certainly aroused strong passions and, as a glance at the scholarly literature will show, he is still capable, on occasion, of doing so today. No full biography had appeared for many years, and I felt it opportune to try and present a balanced assessment of the man which, while not attempting to play down the more unpleasant aspects of his career, would draw attention to his very real and solid merits.

"*Rome and the Unification of Italy* is of a different order. It examines the attempts of the people of Italy to gain parity with their Roman overlords and try to explain why these attempts were made. When their repeated demands for citizenship were refused, the Italians at last made war on Rome itself. In the end they were defeated, but not before they had wrung from the Romans the concessions they sought. Italy was now politically united and was to remain so until the fall of the Roman Empire. In the future I hope to return to biography to examine the career of another comparatively neglected figure, Lucullus."

BIOGRAPHICAL/CRITICAL SOURCES:

PERIODICALS

Times Literary Supplement, November 18, 1983, February 5-11, 1988.

KEERY, Sam 1929-

PERSONAL: Born November 20, 1929, in Lisburn, Northern Ireland; son of Sam (a shoemaker) and Margaret (McCaughey) Keery. *Education:* Attended high school in Lisburn, Northern Ireland.

ADDRESSES: Home—23 Parkgate Cres., Hadley Wood, Barnet, Hertfordshire, England.

CAREER: Writer.

WRITINGS:

The Last Romantic Out of Belfast (novel), Blackstaff Press, 1984.
The Streets of Laredo (stories), J. Cape, 1986.

WORK IN PROGRESS: A novel entitled *The Demise of a Man of Letters,* "about a Belfast man dying of drink in a London hospital on Christmas day. The treatment is humorous despite the theme."

SIDELIGHTS: Sam Keery told *CA:* "I grew up in Lisburn, on the outskirts of Belfast within the Protestant community. After leaving school at the age of eighteen, I worked in linen mills. When I was twenty-one, I left Northern Ireland to knock around Australia for two years in every variety of jobs. Then I went to London, where I have been ever since.

"I wrote a story at age fifteen and sent it to J. B. Priestley, who was encouraging. Three years later I gave up writing, because so many others were doing it that I wondered if it might just be a phase of growing up that we all go through. At thirty-six I resumed writing, but only as a very private pastime, and with only a vague thought of publication 'someday.' Over the years a lot of material accumulated, and this has provided the basis for two books."

Keery's novel, *The Last Romantic Out of Belfast,* is a story of childhood and coming of age in Northern Ireland in the 1940s. The book was described in the *Times Literary Supplement* as a series of vignettes from the life of a Protestant boy who spent his time in the streets of Belfast, exposed to and resistant to all the conservative ideologies of his day. Of the author, critic Patricia Craig wrote: "It says much for the quality of his sensibility that his approach, far from being constricting, makes for subtlety and vividness."

The Streets of Laredo is a collection of twenty-two stories, described by Craig in a later *Times Literary Supplement* review: "Some very short, all briskly written, and all affording glimpses into somewhat unsatisfactory and routine-ridden lives." She praised Keery for his economical and exuberant style: the stories "contain a good deal of savour, including some tongue-in-cheek echoes of *Dubliners*... and much sharpness of observation."

BIOGRAPHICAL/CRITICAL SOURCES:

PERIODICALS

Belfast Review, June, 1984.
Irish Press, July 28, 1984.
Observer (London), June 24, 1984, December 14, 1986.
Times Literary Supplement, August 10, 1984, September 26, 1986.

* * *

KEETON, William T(insley) 1933-1980

PERSONAL: Born February 3, 1933, in Roanoke, Va.; died

of heart failure, August 17, 1980, in Ithaca, N.Y.; son of William Ivie and Doris (Tinsley) Keeton; married Barbara Sue Borcutt, August 9, 1958; children: Lynn Sue, Nancy Lee, William Scott. *Education:* University of Chicago, B.A., 1952, B.S., 1954; Virginia Polytechnic Institute and State University, M.S., 1956; Cornell University, Ph.D., 1958.

CAREER: Radford College, Radford, Va., instructor in microbiology, 1956; Cornell University, Ithaca, N.Y., assistant professor, 1958-59, associate professor, 1959-69, professor of biology, 1969-76, Liberty Hyde Professor, 1977-80, chairman of department of neurobiology, 1970-76, member of board of directors of Ornithology Laboratory, 1971-77, member of board of trustees of the university. Guest professor at Max-Planck Institute of Physiology, 1972-73; instructor in Pisa, Italy, 1977, and at University of Konstanz, 1978-79. President of Periculum Corp.

WRITINGS:

Biological Science, Norton, 1966, 3rd edition, 1980, abridged edition published as *Elements of Biological Science,* Norton, 1969, 2nd edition, 1973, laboratory guide (with Michael W. Dabney and Robert E. Zollinhofer) and instructor's guide, both 1968.
(Co-author) *Biology in the Laboratory,* with instructor's manual, Norton, 1970.
(Editor with Klaus Schmidt-Verlag) *Animal Migration, Navigation, and Homing,* Springer-Verlag, 1978.

Contributor to scientific journals.

BIOGRAPHICAL/CRITICAL SOURCES:

PERIODICALS

New York Times, August 21, 1980.*

* * *

KELLEY, Mary 1943-

PERSONAL: Born June 12, 1943, in Missoula, Mont.; daughter of George and June Bremer; married Robert Eaton Kelley (a writer), 1967. *Education:* Mount Holyoke College, B.A., 1965; New York University, M.A., 1970; University of Iowa, Ph.D., 1974.

ADDRESSES: Office—Department of History, Dartmouth College, Hanover, N.H. 03755.

CAREER: Time, New York City, researcher and reporter, 1965-70; Herbert H. Lehman College of the City University of New York, New York City, assistant professor of American history, 1974-76; University of North Carolina, Charlotte, assistant professor of history, 1976-77; Dartmouth College, Hanover, N.H., assistant professor, 1977-83, associate professor of history, 1983—.

MEMBER: American Historical Association, Organization of American Historians, American Studies Association.

WRITINGS:

(Editor and contributor) *Women, Identity, and Vocation in American History,* G. K. Hall, 1979.
Private Woman, Public Stage: Literary Domesticity in Nineteenth-Century America, Oxford University Press, 1984.
(Editor and author of introduction) Catharine Maria Sedgwick, *Hope Leslie; or, Early Times in the Massachusetts,* Rutgers University Press, 1987.
(Co-author) *The Limits of Sisterhood: The Beecher Sisters on Women's Rights and Woman's Sphere,* University of North Carolina Press, 1988.

Contributor to history and women's studies journals. Member of editorial board of *Journal of American History* and *Legacy,* 1984—, and *American Quarterly,* 1985—.

* * *

KENNEDY, Harold J. 1915(?)-1988

OBITUARY NOTICE: Born c. 1915 in Holyoke, Mass.; died of cardiac arrest, January 10, 1988, in New York, N.Y. Director, actor, producer, lecturer, playwright, and author. Known as a theatrical jack-of-all-trades, Kennedy spent the 1940s and 1950s writing, directing, and producing light, entertaining plays for summer stock theater companies, always including himself in a comic role. His best-known play, "A Goose for the Gander," became Gloria Swanson's Broadway debut in 1945. Kennedy was most successful, however, as director of works by other writers, and in 1966 he received the Chicago *Daily News* Critics Award for his direction of "A Man for All Seasons." He also appeared in several films and television programs and was a popular lecturer on the theater. His book, *No Pickle, No Performance: An Irreverent Theatrical Excursion From Tallulah to Travolta,* recounts his experiences in the entertainment business.

OBITUARIES AND OTHER SOURCES

BOOKS

Notable Names in the American Theatre, James White, 1976.
Who's Who in the Theatre: A Biographical Record of the Contemporary Stage, 17th edition, Gale, 1981.

PERIODICALS

New York Times, January 15, 1988.

* * *

KENYATTA, Jomo 1891(?)-1978

PERSONAL: Name originally Kamau wa Ngengi; baptized as Johnstone Kamau, 1914; known subsequently as Johnstone Kenyatta and Jomo Kenyatta; born c. October 20 in 1891 (some sources say 1889, 1890, 1893, 1897, or 1898), in Ichaweri (some sources say Ngenda), British East Africa Protectorate (now Kenya); died August 21 (some sources say August 22), 1978, in Mombasa, Kenya; son of Muigai (a small farmer and herdsman) and Wambui; married Grace Wahu, November 28, 1922; married Edna Grace Clarke (a schoolteacher and governess), May 11, 1942; married third wife, Grace; married fourth wife, Ngina; children: (first marriage) Peter Mugai, Margaret Wambui; (second marriage) Peter Magana; (third marriage) Jane Wambui; (fourth marriage) Uhuru, Muhoho, Nyokabi (some sources say a total of four sons and four daughters). *Education:* Attended Woodbroke College, 1931-32; studied in Moscow, U.S.S.R., c. 1932; attended London School of Economics and Political Science, c. 1936.

CAREER: Courier for sisal company in Nairobi, British East Africa Protectorate (became Kenya, 1920), c. 1915; interpreter for Supreme Court in Nairobi, 1919; stores clerk and water meter reader for city of Nairobi, 1922-28; Kikuyu Central Association, general secretary beginning in 1928, envoy in London, England, beginning in 1929; University of London, London, England, assistant in phonetics at School of Oriental and

African Studies, beginning in 1933; farm worker in England and lecturer for British Army and Workers' Educational Association, c. 1939-45; Independent Teachers' College, Githunguri, Kenya, vice-principal, 1946-47, principal, beginning in 1947; president of Kenya African Union (political party), beginning in 1947; imprisoned at Lokitaung, Kenya, 1953-59; detained in Lodwar, Kenya, 1959-61, and Marlal, Kenya, 1961; president of Kenya African National Union (political party), beginning in 1961; Government of Kenya, Nairobi, member of Legislative Council representing Fort Hall, beginning in 1962, minister of state for constitutional affairs and economic planning, 1962-63, prime minister and minister for internal security and defense, 1963-64, president, 1964-78. Helped organize fifth Pan-African Congress in Manchester, England, 1945; co-founder of Organization of African Unity. Actor in film "Sanders of the River," 1935.

MEMBER: International African Friends of Abyssinia (co-founder and honorary secretary), International African Service Bureau.

AWARDS, HONORS: Knight of Grace in Order of St. John of Jerusalem, 1972; Order of Golden Ark from World Wildlife Fund, 1974. Honorary fellow of London School of Economics and Political Science; honorary doctorates from Victoria University of Manchester and University of East Africa.

WRITINGS:

(Contributor) Nancy Cunard, editor, *Negro Anthology,* privately printed, 1934.

Facing Mount Kenya: The Tribal Life of the Gikuyu, introduction by Bronislaw Malinowski, Secker & Warburg, 1938, Vintage, 1962, AMS Press, 1978.

(With Lilias E. Armstrong) *The Phonetic and Tonal Structure of Kikuyu,* Oxford University Press, 1940.

My People of Kikuyu and the Life of Chief Wangombe, United Society for Christian Literature, 1942, Oxford University Press, 1966.

Kenya: The Land of Conflict, Panaf Service, 1945, International African Service Bureau, 1971.

Harambee! The Prime Minister of Kenya's Speeches, 1963-1964, From the Attainment of Internal Self-Government to the Threshold of the Kenya Republic, foreword by Malcolm MacDonald, edited by Anthony Cullen, Oxford University Press, 1964.

Suffering Without Bitterness: The Founding of the Kenya Nation, East African Publishing House, 1968.

The Challenge of Uhuru: The Progress of Kenya, 1968 to 1970; Selected and Prefaced Extracts From the Public Speeches of Jomo Kenyatta, President of the Republic of Kenya, East African Publishing House, 1971.

Founder and editor of *Muigwithania,* 1928-30. Contributor to periodicals, including *Daily Worker, Labour Monthly, Manchester Guardian, Negro Worker,* and *Sunday Worker.*

SIDELIGHTS: Jomo Kenyatta led the newly independent African nation of Kenya from 1964 until his death in 1978. He grew up in a traditional African culture as a member of Kenya's largest ethnic group, the Kikuyu. (His exact age is a matter of conjecture because the Kikuyu classified themselves by age-group, ignoring an individual's birthday.) Son of a small farmer and herdsman, Kenyatta saw firsthand how black Africans suffered when white settlers took over their land. As a young man Kenyatta moved to the capital city of Nairobi, where he held a succession of minor jobs. In 1928 he became general secretary of the Kikuyu Central Association (KCA), which sought to improve the living conditions of the Kikuyu under British rule, and as part of his job he traveled widely among his people. The periodical he edited for the association, *Muigwithania,* is believed to be the first black journal in Kenya. The next year Kenyatta went to England as a KCA representative, lobbying successfully for independent Kikuyu schools and unsuccessfully for land reform.

Kenyatta spent most of the next seventeen years in England, promoting the cause of black Kenyans in a wide variety of forums. He wrote letters to the Colonial Office and articles for British periodicals, joined Pan-African groups such as the International African Service Bureau, and lobbied influential guests at London cocktail parties. He commiserated with black activists such as Paul Robeson, famous American singer and actor; W. E. B. Du Bois, a leader of America's National Association for the Advancement of Colored People; and Kwame Nkrumah, future president of Ghana. Traveling widely in Europe, Kenyatta studied for several months at an institute in Moscow that hoped to inspire Communist revolutionaries. (When he later became president of Kenya, however, he declared his country unsuitable for communism.) Some of Kenyatta's political concerns are summarized in the short work *Kenya: Land of Conflict.*

Although Kenyatta never earned a bachelor's degree, he became a graduate student in anthropology at the London School of Economics and Political Science in the mid-1930s, turning a series of papers he wrote about Kikuyu culture into the book *Facing Mount Kenya.* The work uses the format and terminology of a Western scholarly study, devoting chapters to religion, education, sexual practices, and land ownership. But *Facing Mount Kenya* is also a defense of Kenyatta's African background, for it suggests that European influence had harmed the Kikuyu, whose culture at its most untouched was as worthy of respect as that of Europe. In the *New York Times Book Review,* John Barkham said that Kenyatta's eagerness to defend his people had compromised his work, but the *Times Literary Supplement* praised the book as "very readable and highly instructive," noting that Kenyatta had maintained professional standards and had stated his opinions with "due restraint." *Facing Mount Kenya* has been reprinted several times since it first appeared, and in 1953 *Christian Science Monitor* reviewer Marian Sorenson suggested that the book remained a useful background source for understanding black complaints against colonial rule.

Kenyatta returned to Kenya in 1946 and was elected president of a prominent political party, the Kenya African Union. He championed a reform program that included voting rights for blacks, an end to racial discrimination, and a more equitable distribution of land. At the same time, however, a black clandestine movement known as the Mau Mau began efforts to force the British from Kenya, murdering a small number of white settlers and many blacks suspected of collaborating with the white regime. British authorities, already concerned by Kenyatta's political prominence, became convinced that he was involved with the Mau Mau despite his public repudiation of its violence. Arrested in 1952, Kenyatta was tried and sentenced to prison as a Mau Mau organizer. Many sources cast doubt on the state's case against him.

As opposition to the colonial regime continued, the British resigned themselves to Kenya's eventual independence. Kenyatta, who remained highly popular while in prison and detention, was released from exile in a remote province in 1961. He was soon elected president of Kenya's largest political party,

the Kenya African National Union, and led his country to independence in 1964. Kenyatta's national agenda, which included giving blacks a more balanced share of the Kenyan economy and creating a sense of social unity, is reflected in *Harambee*, a collection of his speeches. The book was named for Kenyatta's political rallying cry—Swahili for "let us all pull together!"

Although Kenyatta insisted that Kenya become a one-party state and suppressed rivals to his personal rule, his political philosophy was notably pragmatic. Certain speeches in *Suffering Without Bitterness* outline Kenyatta's doctrine of "African socialism"—an eclectic mixture of individual initiative and concern for the common good. Assessing Kenyatta's career in *New Times*, Charles Mohr wrote that the Kenyan leader's "admirers and critics alike had come to see him as perhaps the leading exponent in Africa of moderate politics [and] laissez-faire economics." Kenyatta allowed nonblacks to remain and contribute their skills to the new country. The economy prospered, and with government encouragement blacks increasingly entered the fields of business and large-scale farming, helping to create Africa's largest black middle class. The press was "nearly free," as Kenneth Labich and James Pringle wrote in *Newsweek*. Kenyatta remained interested in Pan-Africanism, helping to found the Organization of African Unity and a short-lived common market with the neighboring states of Uganda and Tanzania.

Although Kenyatta faced recurrent political discontent—including complaints that he countenanced nepotism and official corruption—when he died in 1978 commentators generally held that he was a great asset to his country and would be difficult to replace. "The Kenya he governed," Mohr asserted, "is today one of the most . . . free societies on the continent."

BIOGRAPHICAL/CRITICAL SOURCES:

BOOKS

Arnold, Guy, *Kenyatta and the Politics of Kenya*, Dent, 1974.
Murray-Brown, Jeremy, *Kenyatta*, Allen & Unwin, 1972, Dutton, 1973, 2nd edition, Allen & Unwin, 1979.

PERIODICALS

Christian Science Monitor, August 27, 1953.
New York Times, August 22, 1978.
New York Times Book Review, September 6, 1953.
Times Literary Supplement, March 11, 1939.

OBITUARIES:

PERIODICALS

Newsweek, September 4, 1978.
New Times, September 18, 1978.
New York Times, November 6, 1978.
Time, September 4, 1978.*

—*Sketch by Thomas Kozikowski*

* * *

KEPPLER, Victor 1904-1987

OBITUARY NOTICE: Born September 30, 1904, in New York, N.Y.; died December 1, 1987, in New York, N.Y. Photographer and author. Though self-taught, Keppler established himself as one of New York's leading commercial photographers during the 1930s. He won considerable recognition in advertising for incorporating realistic settings and natural lighting found in photo-journalism and the stylized geometric patterns associated with cubism. Keppler received several awards, including the Photographers Hall of Fame Award in 1970. He also founded and was director of the Famous Photographers School in Westport, Connecticut, and wrote a number of books on photography, including *The Eighth Art: A Life of Color Photography; Commercial Photography; Your Future in Photography;* and *Man + Camera: A Photographic Autobiography.*

OBITUARIES AND OTHER SOURCES:

BOOKS

Contemporary Photographers, 2nd edition, St. James Press, 1988.

PERIODICALS

Infinity, August, 1971.
Modern Photography, September, 1978.
New York Times, December 3, 1987.

* * *

KIELL, Paul J(acob) 1930-

PERSONAL: Born October 8, 1930, in Newark, N.J. *Education:* Washington and Jefferson College, B.A., 1952; Chicago Medical School (now University of Health Sciences—Chicago Medical School), M.D., 1956.

ADDRESSES: 501 Lenox Ave., Westfield, N.J. 07090.

CAREER: Beth Israel Hospital, Newark, N.J., intern, 1956-57; Veterans Administration Hospital, Lyons, N.J., resident in psychiatry, 1957-59; Georgetown University, University Hospital, Washington, D.C., resident in psychiatry, 1961-62; private practice of psychiatry, 1962-65; Muhlenberg Hospital, Plainfield, N.J., psychiatrist, 1965-71; private practice of psychiatry, 1971—. *Military service:* U.S. Air Force, 1959-61; became captain.

WRITINGS:

(With Joseph S. Frelinghuysen) *Keep Your Heart Running: A Graduated Total Health and Fitness Program for People of All Ages*, Winchester Press, 1976.
(With Frelinghuysen) *The Complete Guide to Physical Fitness*, Stoeger Publishing, 1976.*

* * *

KIES, Cosette (Nell) 1936-

PERSONAL: Born September 2, 1936, in Platteville, Wis.; daughter of Guerdon and Gertrude (Pitts) Kies. *Education:* Wisconsin State College (now University of Wisconsin)—Platteville, B.S. (cum laude), 1957; University of Wisconsin—Madison, M.A. (art history), 1961, M.A. (library science), 1962; Columbia University, D.L.S., 1977.

ADDRESSES: *Home*—1507 Longwood Dr., Sycamore, Ill. 60178. *Office*—Department of Library and Information Studies, Northern Illinois University, DeKalb, Ill. 60115.

CAREER: University of Nebraska—Lincoln, senior assistant librarian, 1963-67; professional assistant for the American Library Association, 1968-69; consultant to the Illinois State Library, 1969-71; Ferguson Library, Stamford, Conn., assistant director, 1971-74; Vanderbilt University, George Peabody College for Teachers, Nashville, Tenn., associate professor of library and information science, 1974-83; Universidade Federal de Minas Gerais, Minas Gerais, Brazil, senior Fulbright

lecturer in library science, 1979-80; Northern Illinois University, DeKalb, professor of library and information studies, 1983—, chairperson of department, 1983—.

MEMBER: American Library Association, Women's National Book Association (president of Nashville chapter, 1981-83), American Association for State and Local History, Illinois Library Association.

WRITINGS:

Problems in Library Public Relations, Bowker, 1974.
Projecting a Positive Image Through Public Relations, American Library Association, 1979.
(Editor) *The Literary Allusions Cookbook,* Women's National Book Association, 1982.
The Occult in the Western World: An Annotated Bibliography, Shoe String, 1986.
Marketing and Public Relations for Libraries, Scarecrow, 1987.
Supernatural Fiction for Teens: Five Hundred Good Paperbacks to Read for Wonderment, Fear, and Fun, Libraries Unlimited, 1987.

Contributor of articles and reviews to library journals.

* * *

KILLIAN, James R(hyne), Jr. 1904-1988

OBITUARY NOTICE—See index for *CA* sketch: Born July 24, 1904, in Blacksburg, S.C.; died of a heart ailment, January 29, 1988, in Cambridge, Mass. Government official, educator, administrator, science adviser, editor, and author. Killian served both academia and government during his lengthy career. He was president of Massachusetts Institute of Technology (MIT) from 1949 to 1959, corporate chairman from 1959 to 1971, and honorary chairman following his retirement in 1971. Concomitantly, from 1957 to 1959 Killian served as U.S. President Dwight D. Eisenhower's special assistant for science and technology. As such Killian became chief architect of the country's space program, laying the groundwork for the establishment of the National Aeronautics and Space Administration (NASA).

Prior to his tenure as president of MIT, Killian held other administrative posts at the institute and was editor of *Technology Review,* a scientific journal published at MIT. During the 1960s and 1970s he served as chairman of the Carnegie Commission on Educational Television and of the Corporation for Public Broadcasting. Killian was a member of the boards of many organizations and won numerous awards and honors, including thirty-nine honorary degrees. His writings include *Sputnik, Scientists, and Eisenhower* and *Moments of Vision: The Stroboscopic Revolution in Photography,* which he co-authored, and articles contributed to various periodicals.

OBITUARIES AND OTHER SOURCES:

BOOKS

American Men and Women of Science: The Physical and Biological Sciences, 16th edition, Bowker, 1986.
Current Biography, H. W. Wilson, 1959, March, 1988.

PERIODICALS

New York Times, January 31, 1988.
Washington Post, January 31, 1988.

KIMMEL, Margaret Mary 1938-

PERSONAL: Born May 12, 1938, in Gary, Ind. *Education:* Rosary College, B.A., 1960, M.L.S., 1963.

CAREER: Gary Public Library, Gary, Ind., children's librarian, 1960-62; Enoch Pratt Free Library, Baltimore, Md., children's librarian, beginning in 1963; affiliated with Beveridge School Library in Gary; instructor at College of Librarianship Wales and Simmons College. Free-lance writer, Science Research Associates, 1961-62.

MEMBER: American Library Association, Indiana Library Association, Maryland Library Association.

AWARDS, HONORS: Magic in the Mist was selected for the Children's Book Showcase, 1976.

WRITINGS:

Magic in the Mist (juvenile fiction), illustrations by Trina Schart Hyman, McElderry Book, 1975.
(Editor with Thomas J. Galvin and Brenda H. White) *Excellence in School Media Programs,* American Library Association, 1980.
(With Elizabeth Segel) *For Reading Out Loud! A Guide to Sharing Books With Children,* foreword by Betsy Byars, Delacorte, 1983.*

* * *

KIMMENS, Andrew C(harles) 1942-

PERSONAL: Born January 13, 1942, in Meriden, Conn.; son of S. H. (a certified public accountant) and Alice D. Kimmens. *Education:* Dartmouth College, B.A., 1964; attended Jesus College, Oxford, 1964-65; Princeton University, M.A., 1967, Ph.D., 1969.

ADDRESSES: Home—659 Washington St., New York, N.Y. 10014.

CAREER: Jesus College, Oxford, Oxford, England, lecturer in English literature and language, 1967-68; Anthony Blond Ltd. (book publisher), London, England, reference editor, 1968-70, senior editor, 1970-73; free-lance writer, editor, and indexer, 1973-78; Arete Publishing Co., Princeton, N.J., managing editor, 1978-82; Facts on File Publications, New York, N.Y., general editor, 1983—.

WRITINGS:

(Editor) *Tales of the Ginseng,* Morrow, 1975.
(Editor) *Tales of Hashish,* Morrow, 1977.
(Editor) *The Stowe Psalter,* University of Toronto Press, 1980.
(Editor) *The Federal Deficit,* H. W. Wilson, 1985.
(Editor) *The United States and Nicaragua,* H. W. Wilson, 1987.

General editor of *Handbooks to the Modern World,* Facts on File, 1983—.

WORK IN PROGRESS: A biographical directory of world political leaders, publication by Macmillan expected in 1990.

SIDELIGHTS: Andrew C. Kimmens told *CA:* "Reference books last; with appropriate, periodic revision, well-conceived works of reference may prove useful to generations of scholars, students, and specialists, as well as interested general readers. Such books always require a great deal of planning and preparation, but they reward the careful compiler with the satisfaction of seeing accurate information and informed opinion generally available."

KING, Alec Hyatt
See KING, Alexander Hyatt

* * *

KING, Alexander Hyatt 1911-
(Alec Hyatt King)

PERSONAL: Born July 8, 1911, in Beckenham, Kent, England; son of Thomas Hyatt (in business) and Mabel Jessie (Brayne) King; married Evelyn Mary Davies (a lecturer in history of fine art), May 15, 1943; children: David Hyatt, Edmund Mervyn Bellamy. *Education:* King's College, Cambridge, B.A. (with first class honors), 1933, M.A., 1945.

ADDRESSES: Home—37 Pier Ave., Southwold, Suffolk 1P18 6BU, England.

CAREER: British Museum, London, England, assistant cataloger of Department of Printed Books, 1934-41, assistant keeper, 1941-59, deputy keeper, 1959-74, superintendent of Music Room, 1944-74; British Library, London, deputy keeper and music librarian, 1974-76. Sandars Reader in Bibliography at Cambridge University, 1962. Honorary secretary of British Union Catalogue of Early Music, 1948-57; chairman of executive committee of British Institute of Recorded Sound, 1951-62; vice-chairman of joint committee of International Association of Music Librarians and International Musicological Society, 1961-76; trustee of Hinrichsen Foundation, 1976-83.

MEMBER: International Association of Music Libraries (president, 1955-59), Bibliographical Society, Royal Musical Association (president, 1974-78), Royal Philharmonic Society (honorary librarian, 1969-82), German Mozart Society.

AWARDS, HONORS: D.Univ. from University of York, 1978; D.Mus. from University of St. Andrews, 1981.

WRITINGS:

UNDER NAME ALEC HYATT KING

Chamber Music, Max Parrish, 1948.
Handel's Messiah, Trustees of the British Museum, 1951.
(Contributor of illustrations) Alfred Einstein, *Short History of Music,* Cassell, 1953.
Mozart in Retrospect: Studies in Criticism and Bibliography, Oxford University Press, 1955, 2nd edition, 1956, revised edition, 1970.
Henry Purcell, 1659(?)-1695: George Frederic Handel, 1685-1959, Trustees of the British Museum, 1959.
Some British Collectors of Music, c. 1600-1960, Cambridge University Press, 1963.
Four Hundred Years of Music Printing, Trustees of the British Museum, 1964.
(Editor with Monica Carolan) *Letters of Mozart and His Family,* 2nd edition, Macmillan, 1966.
Handel and His Autographs, Trustees of the British Museum, 1967.
Mozart Chamber Music, BBC Publications, 1968, revised edition, 1986.
Mozart: A Biography With a Survey of Books, Editions, and Recordings, Clive Bingley, 1970.
Mozart Wind and String Concertos, BBC Publications, 1978, revised edition, 1986.
Printed Music in the British Museum: An Account of the Collections, the Catalogues, and Their Formation Up to 1920, Clive Bingley, 1979.
A Wealth of Music in the Collections of the British Library (Reference Division) and the British Museum, Clive Bingley, 1983.
A Mozart Legacy: Aspects of the British Library Collections, British Library Publications, 1984.
Musical Pursuits: Selected Essays, **British Library Publications, 1987.**

Series editor of "Concertgoers Companions," 1969-77, and "Auction Catalogues of Music: A Series of Facsimiles," 1973-77. Contributor to music journals. Editor of proceedings of the Royal Musical Association, 1952-57.

SIDELIGHTS: Alec Hyatt King told *CA:* "My career, both during my service in the British Museum and British Library and since my retirement in 1976, has been focused on three broad areas: to make known the British Museum music collections in general through the publication of books and articles and by the mounting of exhibitions with catalogs; to publish the results of my special researches into Mozart's bibliography and music, the study of music collecting, music printing, and particular areas of musical history; and to service, in various capacities, the institutions and societies with which I have long been associated, nationally and internationally."

BIOGRAPHICAL/CRITICAL SOURCES:

BOOKS

Neighbour, Oliver, editor, *Music and Bibliography: Essays in Honour of Alec Hyatt King,* Clive Bingley, 1980.

* * *

KINGSBURY, Donald (MacDonald) 1929-

PERSONAL: Born February 12, 1929, in San Francisco, Calif.; immigrated to Canada, 1948, naturalized citizen, 1955; son of Hector Macdonald (a mining engineer) and Laura (Barker) Kingsbury; married Mireille Fortier in 1950 (divorced in 1960); children: Dani Hector, Joel Fortier. *Education:* McGill University, B.Sc., 1956, M.Sc., 1960.

ADDRESSES: Home—1563 Ducharme Ave., Montreal, Quebec, Canada H2V 1G4. *Agent*—Eleanor Wood, 432 Park Ave. S., Suite 1205, New York, N.Y. 10016.

CAREER: McGill University, Montreal, Quebec, lecturer in mathematics, 1956-86; writer, 1986—.

MEMBER: Science Fiction Writers of America.

AWARDS, HONORS: Hugo award nominations from World Science Fiction Society for best novella, 1980, for "The Moon Goddess and the Son," and for best novel, 1982, for *Courtship Rite;* Compton Crook Award for best first novel from Balticon (science fiction convention) and Locus Award for best first novel from *Locus* magazine, both 1983, both for *Courtship Rite.*

WRITINGS:

"Ghost Town" (short story), published in *Astounding Science Fiction,* June, 1952.
Courtship Rite (science fiction novel), Timescape, 1982 (published in London as *Geta,* Panther, 1984).
The Moon Goddess and the Son (science fiction novel; first

published as a novella in *Analog Science Fiction/Science Fact,* December, 1979), Baen Books, 1986.

Work represented in anthologies, including *The Best Science Fiction of the Year 8* and *The Best Science Fiction Novellas of the Year 1,* both edited by Terry Carr, Ballantine, 1979; and *The Best Science Fiction Novellas of the Year 2,* edited by Carr, Ballantine, 1980.

Contributor to periodicals, including *Analog Science Fiction/Science Fact* and *Astounding Science Fiction.*

WORK IN PROGRESS: Novels in the *Courtship Rite* background, including *Godship's Night* and *The Finger Pointing Solward;* a novel in the *Moon Goddess* background, *The Gilgamesh Station;* a mathematical model of learning.

SIDELIGHTS: Considered a promising writer of technical science fiction, Donald Kingsbury began publishing short stories in the 1950s and produced his first full-length work in 1982. *Courtship Rite,* his Locus Award-winning debut novel, depicts the harsh planet Geta on which most native life forms are poisonous to human colonists; the people rely on eight imported "sacred" staples, genetic engineering of local "profane" plants and insects, and cannibalism during famine, evolving a complex system of rituals and customs. The formal eating of enemies, friends and relatives, criminals, and the genetically inferior has become part of their society. Group marriage within a strong clan culture developed as a response to the harsh environment. Observed H. Bruce Franklin in the *Washington Post Book World,* "Some of this is obviously meant to shock our sensibilities." Kingsbury's plot centers on the intrigues that ensue when one ruling family is advised to court an influential heretic for political reasons, ultimately deciding to test her worthiness by a challenge likely to cause her death. According to Franklin, this "society of tyrants and cannibals is offered to us as a charming fantasy of elegance and sexual freedom in which we may indulge as an alternative to our own history." Other critics have commended the author's handling of a complex plot and compared *Courtship Rite* favorably to the long visionary writings of Frank Herbert, author of the popular "Dune" series.

Kingsbury told *CA:* "*Courtship Rite* is the first of a series of novels in which I will examine the thesis of what might happen when a human culture arises that does not consider the human form as we know it to be sacred. The species of Homo sapiens is only a transitional form. There are many stories to be told about the transformation.

"In many ways I consider myself to be a visionary. I don't claim to predict the future, but I am not interested in worlds that are not possible. I like my science to be accurate and that includes my sociology. My stories do not include such pseudosciences as mental telepathy, which I consider to have no relevance to human destiny. Designing new kinds of humans, new governments, and odd cultures is my favorite sport. In *The Moon Goddess and the Son* I've tried to give historical roots to my future. Man's destiny is in space, but his roots are in the earth. History fascinates me because it says so much about what we will become."

BIOGRAPHICAL/CRITICAL SOURCES:

PERIODICALS

Analog Science Fiction/Science Fact, April, 1978.
Financial Post, December 1, 1984.
Washington Post Book World, July 25, 1982.

KINGSLAND, Sharon E. 1951-

PERSONAL: Born April 5, 1951, in Toronto, Ontario, Canada; immigrated to United States, 1981; daughter of Keith and Helen Kingsland; married Paul M. Romney (a historian), January 12, 1984. *Education:* University of Toronto, B.Sc., 1973, M.A., 1977, Ph.D., 1981.

ADDRESSES: Home—319 Birkwood Pl., Baltimore, Md. 21218. *Office*—Department of History of Science, Johns Hopkins University, 34th and Charles Sts., Baltimore, Md. 21218.

CAREER: Johns Hopkins University, Baltimore, Md., assistant professor, 1981-86, associate professor of history of science, 1986—.

MEMBER: American Historical Association, American Society of Zoologists, History of Science Society.

WRITINGS:

Modeling Nature: Episodes in the History of Population Ecology, University of Chicago Press, 1985.

WORK IN PROGRESS: A history of American genetics and evolutionary biology.

SIDELIGHTS: Sharon E. Kingsland told *CA:* "My interest in the history of science began with my awareness that the language of science conditions the way we ask questions about the world and the answers we will accept. *Modeling Nature* deals with the use of mathematical reasoning in biology and traces how the introduction of this new language changed the science of population ecology in the twentieth century. Being convinced that history is always relevant to today—if only we would draw the lessons from it—I hope that my book will speak to the modern ecologist who is grappling with these problems. Above all, I believe history is created by *people,* and in writing about science I have tried to convey a vivid impression of the individuals who have shaped our modern scientific world in this particular field."

BIOGRAPHICAL/CRITICAL SOURCES:

PERIODICALS

Times Literary Supplement, January 16, 1987.

* * *

KINKEAD-WEEKES, Mark 1931-

PERSONAL: Born April 26, 1931, in Pretoria, South Africa; son of Alfred Bernard and Vida May (Kinkead) Weekes; married Margaret Joan Irvine, March 31, 1959; children: Paul, Timothy Guy. *Education:* University of Capetown, B.A., 1951; Brasenose College, Oxford, M.A., 1954. *Religion:* Church of England.

ADDRESSES: Home—5 Albion Place, Ramsgate, Kent, England. *Office*—Rutherford College, University of Kent at Canterbury, Canterbury, Kent, England.

CAREER: University of Edinburgh, Edinburgh, Scotland, 1956-65, began as assistant lecturer, became lecturer in English; University of Kent at Canterbury, Canterbury, England, lecturer, beginning in 1965, became senior lecturer, professor of English literature, 1974—, pro vice-chancellor, 1974-78.

MEMBER: Royal Commonwealth Society, Association of University Teachers.

AWARDS, HONORS: Rhodes scholar, 1952-54; British Academy grant, 1977.

WRITINGS:

(With Ian Gregor) *William Golding: A Critical Study,* Faber, 1967, 2nd edition, 1984.

(Editor and contributor) *Twentieth Century Interpretations of "The Rainbow": A Collection of Critical Essays,* Prentice-Hall, 1971.

Samuel Richardson: Dramatic Novelist, Cornell University Press, 1973.

(Editor) D. H. Lawrence, *The Rainbow,* Cambridge University Press, 1988.

Contributor to literature journals.

WORK IN PROGRESS: A three-volume biography of D. H. Lawrence, with John Worthen and David Ellis, publication by Cambridge University Press expected in 1990-93.

SIDELIGHTS: Written with Ian Gregor, Mark Kinkead-Weekes's first book, *William Golding: A Critical Study,* is "easily the best study of Mr. Golding's art," according to Denis Donoghue of the *New York Review of Books.* Examining the symbolism, patterns, and mythic nature of Golding's novels, including *Lord of the Flies* and *The Inheritors,* the authors offer insight into his ambiguities and development. Some critics found the authors' method overparticular and undercritical, but Donoghue expressed a prevailing sentiment, writing that the book is "bound to become a standard work."

Kinkead-Weekes's *Samuel Richardson: Dramatic Novelist* is "an excellent study" of the eighteenth-century writer, asserted a *Times Literary Supplement* critic. Presenting a broad perspective on Richardson's output, Kinkead-Weekes open-mindedly discusses both the author's strengths and weaknesses. He also shows the limitations of narrow interpretations of Richardson's achievements. Observed the *Times Literary Supplement,* "This well-written and well-argued book, so full of critical perceptions and intelligent comments, lifts the discussion of Richardson's fiction on to a new plane."

Kinkead-Weekes told *CA:* "I have always been interested in exploratory writers, whose imagination takes them beyond their 'knowing'. I also have a lively interest in African and West Indian literatures in English, have written on Africa and West Indian fiction, and intend to do more of this in the future."

BIOGRAPHICAL/CRITICAL SOURCES:

PERIODICALS

Listener, June 22, 1967.
New Statesman, June 2, 1967.
New York Review of Books, December 7, 1967.
Times Literary Supplement, June 1, 1967, January 25, 1974.

* * *

KINNAIRD, John (William) 1924-1980

PERSONAL: Born December 5, 1924, in Nelsonville, N.Y.; died of cancer, May 24, 1980, in College Park, Md.; married Joan Kennedy, 1960; children: John, Stephen. *Education:* University of California, Berkeley, B.A., 1944; Columbia University, M.A., 1949, Ph.D., 1959.

CAREER: Bucknell University, Lewisburg, Pa., instructor in English, 1949-51; Rutgers University, New Brunswick, N.J., instructor in English, 1956; City College (now of City University of New York), New York, N.Y., lecturer in English, 1958-59; Vassar College, Poughkeepsie, N.Y., assistant professor of English, 1959-65; University of Maryland at College Park, began as associate professor, 1965, became professor of English. Lecturer at Hunter College (now of City University of New York), 1956; member of Ford Foundation Seminar on College Teaching, 1957; instructor at Adelphi College (now University), 1957-58. Reporter for *Newburgh News,* Newburgh, N.Y. *Military service:* U.S. Army, Office of Strategic Services, 1943-46; served in China-Burma-India theater.

AWARDS, HONORS: Fulbright fellow at Oxford University, 1953-55; grant from American Council of Learned Societies, 1965.

WRITINGS:

William Hazlitt, Critic of Power, Columbia University Press, 1978.

Reader's Guide to Olaf Stapledon, Starmont House, 1985.

Contributor to literature journals and *Partisan Review.*

BIOGRAPHICAL/CRITICAL SOURCES:

PERIODICALS

New York Times, May 26, 1980.
Washington Post, May 26, 1980.*

* * *

KINOSHITA Junji 1914-

PERSONAL: Born August 2, 1914, in Tokyo, Japan; son of Yahachiro (a government official) and Mie (a housewife; maiden name, Sassa) Kinoshita. *Education:* University of Tokyo, M.A., 1939.

ADDRESSES: Home—2-23-4 Mukoga-oka, Bunkyo-ku, Tokyo, Japan. *Agent*—Orion Press, 58 1-chome, Kanda Jimbocho, Chiyoda-ku, Tokyo 101, Japan.

CAREER: Hosei University, Tokyo, Japan, lecturer in English, 1939-43; Meiji University, Tokyo, professor of dramaturgy, 1946-63; playwright.

MEMBER: International Theatre Institute, P.E.N., Japan Literature Society, Japan Drama Society.

AWARDS, HONORS: Kishida Prize for Drama, 1947, for "Furo"; Mainichi Press Drama Award, 1949, for "Yuzuru"; Sankei Award for Children's Books and Publications, 1959, for *Nihon minwa sen;* Mainichi Press Book Award, 1959, for *Dorama no sekai,* and 1965, for *Mugen kido;* Yomiuri Literature Prize from Yomiuri Shimbun, 1978, for "Shigosen no matsuri," and 1984, for *Zenbu uma no hanashi;* Asahi Press Award, 1986, for "the long elaborating works in the field of drama from 'Yuzuru' to 'Shigosen no matsuri.'"

WRITINGS:

FULL-LENGTH PLAYS

"Yamanami" (three-act; title means "Over the Mountain Range"), first produced in Tokyo, Japan, at Mitsukoshi Theatre, 1949.

"Kaeru shoten" (three-act; title means "The Ascension of a Frog"), first produced in Tokyo at Mitsukoshi Theatre, 1952.

"Furo" (five-act; title means "Turbulent Waves"), first produced in Tokyo at First Insurance Hall, 1953.

"Onnyoro Seisuiki" (four-act; title means "The Rise and Fall of Onnyoro"), first produced as a modern drama in Tokyo at Chiyoda Public Hall, 1957; produced as a Kabuki play in Tokyo at Shinbashi Enbujo Theatre, 1960.

"Otto to yobareru Nihonjin" (three-act; title means "A Japanese Called Otto"), first produced in Osaka, Japan, at Sankei Hall, 1962.

"Okinawa" (three-act), first produced in Tokyo at Sabo Hall, 1963.

"Fuyu no Jidai" (three-act; title means "In the Age of Winter"), first produced in Tokyo at Toyoko Hall, 1964.

"Shiroi yoru no utage" (three-act; title means "Banquet in the White Night"), first produced in Tokyo at Sabo Hall, 1967.

"Kami to hito to no aida" (seven-act play in two parts), part one first produced as "Shinpan" (three-act; title means "The Judgment") in Nagoya, Japan, at Meitetsu Hall, 1970; part two first produced as "Natsu Nanpo no Romansu" (four-act; title means "Summer: A Romance on the South Sea") in Tokyo at Season Theatre, 1987; translation by Eric J. Gangloff published as *Between God and Man: A Judgment on War Crimes; A Play in Two Parts,* University of Washington Press, 1979.

"Shigosen no matsuri" (four-act; title means "The Meridian Rite"), first produced in Tokyo at National Theatre, 1978.

OTHER PLAYS

"Hikoichi-banashi" (title means "A Story of Hikoichi"), first produced in 1946.

"Hata no oto" (title means "The Sound of the Loom"), first produced in 1947.

"Sannen-ne Taro" (title means "Taro Who Slept for Three Years"), first produced in 1947.

"Kurai hibana" (title means "Dark Spark"), first produced in 1950.

"Yuzuru" (one-act; first produced in 1948), translation by A. C. Scott published as "Twilight Crane" in *Playbook: Five Plays for a New Theatre,* New Directions, 1956; translation by Takeshi Kurahashi published as *Twilight of a Crane,* Mirai-Sha, 1958.

"Sammyaku" (title means "Mountain Range"), first produced in 1959.

"Kikimimi zukin" (title means "The Magic Hearing Cap"), first produced in 1947.

Kinoshita Junji sakuhin shu (title means "Plays by Kinoshita Junji"), eight volumes, Miraisha, 1962-71.

Omon Tota: A Folktale Play, translated by George Marshall Murphy, University Microfilms, 1979.

Kinoshita Junji shu (title means "Collected Works of Kinoshita Junji"), sixteen volumes, Iwanami, 1988—.

Also author of a play collection, *Minwagekishu,* 1952; author of plays for radio and television.

ESSAYS AND CRITICISM

Kinoshita Junji hyoron-shu (title means "Critical Essays by Junji Kinoshita"), twelve volumes, Miraisha, 1972—.

Gikyoku no Nihongo (title means "The Japanese Language as Dramatic Dialogue"), Chuo Koronsha, 1982.

Also author of *Watashitachi no Shakespeare* (title means "Our Shakespeare"), 1953, *Engeki no dento to minwa* (title means "Dramatic Tradition and the Folktale"), 1956, *Geijutsu to shakai eno me* (title means "Opinions on the Arts and Society"), 1956, *Dorama no sekai* (title means "A Dramatist's Trip Around the World"), 1959, *Nihon ga Nihon de aru tame ni wa* (title means "Japan and the Japanese"), 1965, *Dorama to no taiwa* (title means "Dialogue With Drama"), 1968, *Zuiso Shakespeare* (title means "On Shakespeare"), 1969, *To Be or Not to Be,* 1972, *Shakespeare no sekai* (title means "The World of Shakespeare"), 1973, *Bokyaku ni tsuite* (title means "On Our Forgetfulness"), 1974, *Unmei no kochiragawa* (title means "This Side of Fate"), 1976, *Rekishi ni tsuite* (title means "On History"), 1976, *Koten o yakusu* (title means "On Translating the Japanese Classics"), 1978, *Ryokaku* (title means "The Vast Firmament"), 1980, *Rakutenteki Nihonjin* (title means "The Japanese and Their Foolish Optimism"), 1980, *Dorama ga naritatsu toki* (title means "The Moment When Drama Is Born"), 1981, *Dorama ni miru unmei* (title means "'Fate' in the Drama"), 1984, *Zenbu uma no hanashi* (title means "Stories All About the Horse"), 1984, *Heikemonogatari,* 1985, and *Giron shinokoshita koto* (title means "Discussions Left Undiscussed"), 1986.

OTHER

(Translator) *Kinoshita Junji yaku Shakespeare* (fifteen plays by William Shakespeare), eight volumes, Kodansha, 1988—.

Author of fiction, including *Ryu ga mieru toki,* 1978; the novels *Mugen kido* (title means "The Endless Track"), 1965, *Korekushon* (title means "On Horse Books Collection"), 1981, and *Hongo* (title means "Hongo, My Native Place"), 1983; and the short story collection *Yumemi kozo,* 1967.

Also author of *Engeki no honshitsu,* 1951, *Shingeki e no michi,* 1957, *Nihon minwa sen* (for children; title means "From the Japanese Folk Tales"), c. 1959, *Furui kuni atarashii geijutsu,* 1961, *Warashibe choja,* 1964, *Shimpojumu, Okinawa,* 1968, *Yama no seikurabe,* 1968, *Nitchu no genten kara,* 1972, *Kinoshita Junji, Nakamura Shin'ichiro,* 1974, *Gikyokuron,* 1977, and *Nakae Chomin no sekai,* 1977.

Editor, with Yonezo Hamamura, of *Kabuki, no, bunraku,* 1954; editor of *Nihon no minwa,* 1960; editor, with Hiroshi Noma and Rokuro Hidaka, of *Chishikijin no shiso to kodo,* 1964. Compiler with Shiro Okakura of *Yamamoto Yasue butai shashin shu* (two volumes), 1960; compiler with Miyao Ohara and Yoshie Hotta of *Nihon gembaku shishu,* 1970.

Translator into Japanese of works by Somerset Maugham.

WORK IN PROGRESS: A play based on the double-composed fantastic theme found only in the No play.

SIDELIGHTS: Hailed as the most notable playwright in modern Japanese theatre, Kinoshita Junji combines elements of traditional or classical Japanese drama with Western realism in plays based on Japanese folktales and historical and modern events. A student of Elizabethan drama, and specifically the works of William Shakespeare, he has sought ways of integrating classical writings—Western and Japanese—with modern themes and styles. He is often credited with bridging the gap between classical Japanese theatre and the modern world.

"Yuzuru," first produced in 1949, is among Kinoshita's best known early plays, an example of the many works he based on Japanese folktales. In the play, which was translated as *Twilight Crane* and *Twilight of a Crane,* a magical bird takes human form, weds the farmer who freed her from a snare, and gives him wealth by making fine cloth from her feathers. Enticed by greedy friends, the farmer soon makes her weave incessantly and breaks a promise to her; returning to her natural shape, the crane finally abandons him. The play proved popular and was adapted for No and Kabuki theatre as well as opera; it has been translated into more than ten languages and produced in the United States, Russia, and Europe.

Kinoshita maintains an interest in modern society as well as ancient legend, exemplified by "Kami to hito to no aida,"

which was translated as *Between God and Man: A Judgment on War Crimes*. Written in two parts, the play recreates Allied war crimes trials in Tokyo, Japan, from 1946 to 1948 in the first part and the 1950s trial of a Japanese private in the second part. Observed Emiko Sakurai in a *World Literature Today* review, the work "poses such ethical questions as the right of the victor to punish the vanquished when both sides have committed the same sins." Kinoshita uses techniques from both Japanese comic theatre and the theatre of the absurd to examine the nature of guilt, the definition of war crime, and the absurdity of existence, producing an effect Sakurai deemed "profound."

In "Shigosen no matsuri" Kinoshita's concerns with ancient and modern subjects, literatures, and dramatic styles come together to portray Japan at a critical historical moment, ostensibly the late 1100s but also suggesting the 1980s. Based on the thirteenth-century epic *Heike monogatari*, the play describes a power struggle between two families that set the course of several centuries of Japanese history. As in traditional No drama, individual characters and a chorus often finish each other's speeches, blurring the distinction between specific and general viewpoints and allowing the characters to see themselves in historical perspective. Adding to the play's past-present ambiguity, Kinoshita juxtaposes modern and ancient language, sometimes taking dialogue verbatim from the original tale. The playwright also draws on the Japanese traditions of Kyogen and Kabuki theatre as well as elements of Shakespearean, modern Japanese, and realistic Western drama. According to Brian Powell of the *Times Literary Supplement*, "Shigosen no matsuri" is "one of the most successful attempts in recent years to blend *no* and modern drama." Noting the acclaim the play received when it was produced at Japan's National Theatre, Powell reported that the Japanese critics were "unanimous in hailing a new form of drama that built on tradition rather than rejecting it."

AVOCATIONAL INTERESTS: Horseback riding.

BIOGRAPHICAL/CRITICAL SOURCES:

PERIODICALS

Times Literary Supplement, October 30, 1981.
World Literature Today, spring, 1980.

* * *

KIPPS, Harriet C(lyde) 1926-
(Leslie Clyde)

PERSONAL: Born August 20, 1926, in Metuchen, N.J.; daughter of Stephen Valentine (a marine engineer) and Della Pearl (a housewife; maiden name, Clyde) Clyde; married Charles Harrison Kipps, October 19, 1946 (deceased); children: Charles Harrison, Jr., Virginia Lee, Glenn Harold. *Education:* Rutgers University, B.A. (audited), 1948; graduate study at Cranston University; also attended Northern Virginia Community College. *Politics:* Nonpartisan. *Religion:* Baptist.

ADDRESSES: Office—Four-One-One, 7304 Beverly St., Annandale, Va. 22003.

CAREER: Rutgers University, New Brunswick, N.J., part-time research associate, 1946-57; *Salem Times-Register*, Salem, Va., principal editor, 1957-67; University Research Corp., Washington, D.C., training specialist, 1967; National Education Association, Washington, D.C., information specialist, 1967-69; Four-One-One, Annandale, Va., president, 1969—. Expert on organizational relations at U.S. Department of Housing and Urban Development, 1969-70; information associate at National Center for Voluntary Action, 1970-75; research associate at CPI Associates, 1975-77; director of National Clearinghouse on Voluntary Action, 1979-82; director of division of information exchange of ACTION Office of Volunteer Liaison, 1982-85. Development director of Old Dominion Candies, 1963-65; member of board of directors and staff liaison of Total Action Against Poverty (TAAP), 1965-67; consultant with Small World Associates. Officer of Annandale Civic Association; youth development officer of Parent Teacher Association; youth activities director of Fairlington Parents Without Partners; fund-raising coordinator of Annandale Boys' Clubs; workshop director.

MEMBER: International Platform Association, National School Volunteer Program, Mensa.

AWARDS, HONORS: White House Commendation for volunteer service, 1984; Volunteer Activist Award from Volunteer Clearinghouse of the Nation's Capital, 1984; academic excellence award for English and math, Raritan Township Schools; play selection award from Roanoke Valley Seven-University Selection Board.

WRITINGS:

"Your Roots Are Showing" (one-act play), first produced at Roanoke Valley Seven-University Drama Festival, Andrew Lewis Theatre, Salem, Va., 1966.
(Editor) Helga Roth and others, *University/Community Relations*, Temple University, 1972.
(Contributor) *Helping the Volunteer Get Started*, National Center for Voluntary Action, 1973.
(Editor) *Community Resource Directory*, Gale, 1982, 2nd edition, 1984.
Volunteerism and Youth: A Drug Abuse Deterrent, National Association for Human Development, 1987.
Music Therapy, Volunteer World, 1988.
Rhyme Therapy, Volunteer World, 1988.

"CHILDREN AND VOLUNTEERING" SERIES FOR YOUNG PEOPLE; UNDER PSEUDONYM LESLIE CLYDE; FICTION, EXCEPT AS NOTED

Volunteers! Who Are They? (nonfiction), Four-One-One, 1984.
Super Volunteers! Little Red Hen, 1985.
The Haunted House, Little Red Hen, 1985.
A Trip to the City, Little Red Hen, 1985.
Drugs at Millbrook, Little Red Hen, 1985.
The Magic Go-cart, Little Red Hen, 1985.
Vandalism at Millbrook, Little Red Hen, 1985.
Tina Whitefeather, Little Red Hen, 1985.
A Trip to the Mountains, Little Red Hen, 1985.
The Golden Paintbrush, Little Red Hen, 1985.
The New Americans, Little Red Hen, 1985.
The Super Duper Club, Little Red Hen, 1985.
Timid Timmy Comes Through, Little Red Hen, 1985.
The Power of Study, Little Red Hen, 1985.
"Lard Bucket" Wins Big, Little Red Hen, 1985.
All That Glitters, Little Red Hen, 1985.
The Hospice, Little Red Hen, 1985.
The Sharks Lose Their Bite, Little Red Hen, 1985.

WORK IN PROGRESS: Community Resource Tie Line, 3rd edition, an information bank on management and training in volunteerism; "Billy's Eyes," a television play about children with acquired immune deficiency syndrome (AIDS); *A Letter Killeth*, a story about World War II; *Black Armor: The Be-*

trayal, a novel centering on the "quota system" of the early 1970s and how it affected personal lives.

SIDELIGHTS: Harriet C. Kipps told *CA:* "Volunteerism always has been part of my life to some degree, but in recent years it has become a full-time occupation, not only because I write books and develop tools for this country (and some foreign nations), but also because of my work as a direct-service volunteer. In addition to the satisfaction that comes from volunteering, I am sure that my books and tools are better because of my firsthand experience. I feel strongly about youth volunteerism as a deterrent to drug abuse. I have seen hard evidence of this."

* * *

KITCHENER, Richard Frank 1941-

PERSONAL: Born May 28, 1941, in Covina, Calif.; son of Frank and Gussie (Farmer) Kitchener; married Karen Strohm (a teacher), September 21, 1965; children: Gregory, Brian. *Education:* California State University, Los Angeles, B.A., 1963, M.A., 1967; University of Minnesota—Twin Cities, Ph.D., 1970.

ADDRESSES: Home—1419 Ash Dr., Fort Collins, Colo. 80521. *Office*—Department of Philosophy, Colorado State University, Fort Collins, Colo. 80523.

CAREER: Colorado State University, Fort Collins, assistant professor, 1970-76, associate professor, 1976-79, professor of philosophy, 1980—. Director of Endowment for Applied Philosophy.

MEMBER: American Philosophical Association, American Psychological Association.

WRITINGS:

Piaget's Theory of Knowledge: Genetic Epistemology and Scientific Reason, Yale University Press, 1985.

Contributor to philosophy journals. Editor of *New Ideas in Psychology.*

* * *

KITUOMBA
See ODAGA, Asenath (Bole)

* * *

KLEINER, Art 1954-

PERSONAL: Born March 18, 1954, in New York, N.Y.; son of Julius (an educator) and Irene (an educator) Kleiner. *Education:* State University of New York at Albany, B.A., 1975; University of California, Berkeley, M.A., 1979.

ADDRESSES: Home—New York, N.Y. *Office*—I.A.F., P.O. Box 232, Old Chelsea Station, New York, N.Y. 10016. *Agent*—F. Joseph Spieler, 410 West 24th St., New York, N.Y. 10011.

CAREER: Point Foundation, Sausalito, Calif., editor, writer, and project organizer of Whole Earth, 1980-85; New York University, New York, N.Y., adjunct professor in Interactive Telecommunications Program, 1986—. Forum host of CompuServe Information Service, Columbus, Ohio, 1983—; consultant to Electronic Information Exchange System.

MEMBER: National Writers Union, Electronic Networking Association.

WRITINGS:

A Look Inside Robots (juvenile), Raintree Publishers, 1982.
(Editor with Stewart Brand) *News That Stayed News: Ten Years of CoEvolution Quarterly,* North Point Press, 1986.
The Mirror on the Desktop: A Personal Guide to Getting the Best Use From Your Personal Computer, H. P. Publishing, in press.

Contributor to magazines and newspapers, including *Aperture* and *New York Times Sunday Magazine.* Past editor of *CoEvolution Quarterly* and *Whole Earth Software Review.*

WORK IN PROGRESS: In My Brother's Country, a novel; a book on the culture of marketing.

* * *

KLINGELHOFER, E(dwin) L(ewis) 1920-

PERSONAL: Born October 4, 1920, in Buffalo, N.Y.; son of Benjamin Carl (in business) and Winifred (a housewife; maiden name, Townson) Klingelhofer; married Jean Elizabeth Merrick (a librarian), January 31, 1946; children: Anne Elizabeth, Jon Merrick. *Education:* State University of New York at Buffalo, B.S., 1946; University of Iowa, Ph.D., 1953.

ADDRESSES: P.O. Box 329, North San Juan, Calif. 95960.

CAREER: California State University, Sacramento, assistant professor, 1953-56, associate professor, 1956-61, professor of psychology, 1961-76; free-lance writer and consultant in psychology, 1976—. Visiting professor at University of East Africa, 1965-67; visiting research psychologist at University of California, Berkeley, 1970-72; senior Fulbright lecturer at University of Malawi, 1974-75. *Military service:* U.S. Army, 1942-46; became captain.

MEMBER: International African Institute, American Association for the Advancement of Science, American Psychological Association, American Association for Higher Education, African Studies Association, Western Psychological Association, Sigma Xi.

AWARDS, HONORS: Distinguished Community Service Award from city of Sacramento, California, 1970.

WRITINGS:

Human Behavior in Africa, Greenwood Press, 1972.
Educational Characteristics and Needs of New Students, Center for Research and Development in Higher Education, University of California, Berkeley, 1972.
(With M. Eric Gershwin) *Asthma: Stop Suffering, Start Living,* Addison-Wesley, 1987.
Coping With Grown Children, Humana, 1988.
(With Gershwin) *Conquering Your Child's Allergies,* Addison-Wesley, 1988.

WORK IN PROGRESS: Research on the effectiveness of asthma self-management programs.

SIDELIGHTS: E. L. Klingelhofer told *CA:* "One of my earliest memories is that of wanting to be a writer, but force of circumstance prevented me from doing it. In 1976 I decided that if I was to begin, I had to do it then. I've spent ten years learning the trade, and they have been the best, happiest ones of my life."

KNOBLAUCH, C(yril) H. 1945-

PERSONAL: Surname is pronounced "*Knob*-lock"; born October 5, 1945, in Minneapolis, Minn.; son of Cyril H. and Helen I. Knoblauch; married Lil Borop Brannon (a university professor), July 14, 1984. *Education:* College of St. Thomas, B.A., 1967; Brown University, M.A., 1969, Ph.D., 1973.

ADDRESSES: Home—7 Hawthorne Ave., Albany, N.Y. 12203. *Office*—Department of English, State University of New York at Albany, Albany, N.Y. 12222.

CAREER: Brown University, Providence, R.I., instructor in English, 1972-74; Columbia University, New York City, assistant professor of English, 1974-79; New York University, New York City, assistant professor of English, 1979-82; State University of New York at Albany, Albany, associate professor of English, 1982—. *Military service:* U.S. Army, 1969-71; became sergeant.

MEMBER: Modern Language Association of America, National Council of Teachers of English.

WRITINGS:

(With A. D. Van Nostrand) *Functional Writing,* Houghton, 1978.
(With Van Nostrand) *The Process of Writing: Discovery and Control,* Houghton, 1982.
(With wife, Lil Brannon) *Rhetorical Traditions and the Teaching of Writing,* Boynton Cook, 1984.

Also author of a book on contemporary rhetorical theory and modern philosophy, for Boynton Cook, in press.

Contributor to literature and composition journals.

BIOGRAPHICAL/CRITICAL SOURCES:

PERIODICALS

New York Times, July 27, 1984.

* * *

KNOTT, Kim 1955-

PERSONAL: Born May 25, 1955, in Watford, England; daughter of Len and Kay (Clarke) Knott. *Education:* University of Leeds, B.A. (with honors), 1976, M.A., 1977, Ph.D., 1982.

ADDRESSES: Home—Leeds, England. *Office*—Department of Theology and Religious Studies, University of Leeds, Leeds LS2 9JT, England.

CAREER: University of Leeds, Leeds, England, research fellow in religious studies, 1981—. Tutor at Open University, 1982-86.

WRITINGS:

Hinduism in Leeds, University of Leeds, 1986.
My Sweet Lord: The Hare Krishna Movement, Aquarian Press, 1986.

WORK IN PROGRESS: Research on South Asian religions in Britain, religion in the media, and new religious movements.

* * *

KOHN, Howard 1947-

PERSONAL: Born August 11, 1947, in Bay City, Mich.; son of Frederick John (a farmer) and Clara (a farmer; maiden name, Buchhage) Kohn; married Kathleen Weir, October 13, 1967 (divorced); married Diana Romanchuk (an editor), November 15, 1974; children: Elizabeth Anne. *Education:* University of Michigan, B.A. (cum laude), 1969. *Politics:* Independent.

ADDRESSES: Home—16 Jefferson Ave., Takoma Park, Md. 20912. *Office*—930 F St. N.W., Suite 300, Washington, D.C. 20004. *Agent*—The Robbins Office, 2 Dag Hammarskjold Plaza, 866 Second Ave., New York, N.Y. 10017.

CAREER: Bay City Times, Bay City, Mich., sportswriter, 1965-68; *Detroit Free Press,* Detroit, Mich., reporter, 1970-73; *Rolling Stone,* San Francisco, Calif., and New York, N.Y., senior editor, 1975-81; Center for Investigative Reporting, Washington, D.C., Washington director, beginning in 1981. Commissioner of San Francisco Media Softball League; director of Musicians United for Safe Energy; member of Disarmament Advisory Board.

MEMBER: Investigative Reporters and Editors, Media Alliance.

AWARDS, HONORS: Associated Press Sweepstakes Award, 1971, for a series of investigative articles in the *Detroit Free Press;* Associated Press second place award, 1972, for an autobiographical feature in the *Detroit Free Press;* Paul Tobenkin Memorial Award from Columbia Journalism School, United Press International Gold Medallion, and Associated Press Sweepstakes Award, all 1973, all for a series of investigative articles in the *Detroit Free Press;* Detroit Press Club award for news, 1974, for a series of investigative articles in the *Detroit Free Press;* Time, Inc. fellowship for nonfiction from Bread Loaf Writers' Conference, 1982, for *Who Killed Karen Silkwood?;* Laurel Award from *Columbia Journalism Review,* 1984, for an article in *Esquire.*

WRITINGS:

(Author, with David Shaber and David Weir, of screen story) Shaber, "Rollover" (screenplay), Warner Bros., 1981.
Who Killed Karen Silkwood? (nonfiction), Summit Books, 1981.

Also author of *Dark Circle* and *The Last Farmers.* Work represented in anthologies, including *The Silent Bomb: A Guide to the Nuclear Energy Controversy* and *Stalking the Feature Story.* Contributor of articles to periodicals, including *Rolling Stone, Esquire, Reader's Digest, Mother Jones, New Times,* and *Nation.* Editor of *Periodical Lunch.*

SIDELIGHTS: A former newspaper reporter and magazine editor, Howard Kohn has won several awards for his investigative reporting. While an editor at *Rolling Stone* Kohn wrote investigative reports on Israel's alleged nuclear arsenal, the existence of which is denied by the Israeli Government, and on events surrounding the kidnapping of publishing heiress Patty Hearst. His *Rolling Stone* reports on the mysterious 1974 death of Karen Silkwood became the basis of Kohn's 1981 book, *Who Killed Karen Silkwood?*

Silkwood had been an employee of the Kerr-McGee Corporation, manufacturers of radioactive plutonium-based fuel rods for nuclear reactors, and had worked in its Oklahoma City-area facility. As union shop steward she had alleged that workers at the plant were being exposed unnecessarily to harmful radiation and she had lobbied for improvements in working conditions. As she became more outspoken, Silkwood was

repeatedly contaminated by plutonium in a series of suspicious incidents viewed by some to be deliberate. One night when she was driving to meet a newspaper reporter supposedly to furnish him with documents that proved Kerr-McGee's criminal negligence, her car ran off the road and Silkwood died. No documents were found at the accident site, and the automobile accident's cause was never determined. In 1979 a federal jury ordered Kerr-McGee to pay Silkwood's estate $10.5 million, finding the corporation to have been negligent in her plutonium contamination; two years later the decision was overturned on appeal.

Kohn spent six years investigating the circumstances of Silkwood's life and death before writing *Who Killed Karen Silkwood?* According to the *Washington Post*'s James Conaway, Kohn attempts in the book to "enshrine" Silkwood as a "heroine to all those opposed to developing nuclear power." Conaway noted, as did other reviewers, that Kohn does not answer the question posed in his book's title; that after his six-year investigation, the facts still remain unclear. Pete Hamill, writing in the *New York Times Book Review,* faulted Kohn for inventing dialogue and thoughts for people in the book, although Kohn advises readers in his foreword that "the dialogue and conversational tics should not be taken as absolutely literal." Hamill nonetheless concluded that Kohn, a writer "with much talent, . . . was not well served by editors who allowed him such luxuries in a nonfiction book."

Other critics were more tolerant of Kohn's style. A *Time* reviewer insisted that, without establishing that anyone actually killed Karen Silkwood, Kohn nonetheless "proves beyond any reasonable doubt that many people had reasons for wanting Silkwood dead." And Sharon Ditman, writing in the *Los Angeles Times Book Review,* cited *Who Killed Karen Silkwood?* as "perhaps the most complete recounting" among many published treatments of the affair. Ditman deemed Kohn's research "quite thorough," his presentation "convincing and believable," and the story ultimately "fascinating."

Kohn told *CA:* "I grew up on an old-fashioned farm, milking cows by hand, hoeing, baling hay, chopping wood, and I left it behind as soon as I could. But there is something that farmers have, a sense of order and time and, above all, perseverance, and any writer worth a lick must have it too. It can even be said that farmers and writers, almost alone among contemporary Americans, live as they always have—giving up certain comforts for the sake of having their own way."

BIOGRAPHICAL/CRITICAL SOURCES:

PERIODICALS

Los Angeles Times Book Review, January 10, 1982.
New York Times Book Review, December 13, 1981, June 6, 1982.
Time, December 7, 1981.
Washington Post, December 1, 1981.

* * *

KORNBLUH, Marvin 1927-1987

OBITUARY NOTICE: Born in 1927 in Brooklyn, N. Y.; died after a heart attack, August 15, 1987, in Washington, D.C. Businessman, administrator, information systems analyst, educator, and author. Kornbluh began his career in information sciences as a systems analyst at the Pentagon during the mid-1950s. He later joined the Congressional Research Service at the Library of Congress, specializing in futures methodology, strategic planning, and information systems development. Kornbluh also established his own management training business and taught courses in management and information systems at the University of Maryland. He wrote *The Effective Executive and the Systems Challenge* and *How to Manage Financial Systems.*

OBITUARIES AND OTHER SOURCES:

BOOKS

The Future: A Guide to Information Sources, 2nd edition, World Future Society, 1979.

PERIODICALS

Washington Post, August 19, 1987.

* * *

KRAMER, Larry 1935-

BRIEF ENTRY: Born in 1935 in Bridgeport, Conn. American movie producer, playwright, screenwriter, and novelist. Larry Kramer is best known for his controversial works dealing with the lifestyles of homosexual males. His novel *Faggots* (Random House, 1978), which a number of critics found to be an offensive and sensationalized account, explicitly portrays members of New York's homosexual subculture indulging in a lifestyle of promiscuous sex. Kramer eventually gleaned critical approval with a later work also dealing with the gay community: his 1985 stage drama *The Normal Heart,* the novelization of which was published by New American Library the same year. The play—described by critics as angry, didactic, and polemic in tone—was one of the first to document the frustrating history of acquired immune deficiency syndrome (AIDS). For its attempt to inform the American public about the growing AIDS epidemic, while accusing the media and public officials of ignoring the gravity of the disease, *The Normal Heart* was hailed as a realistic and powerful drama dealing with universal concerns. Kramer also wrote and produced the 1969 movie adaptation of D. H. Lawrence's *Women in Love,* as well as the scripts for such productions as "Lost Horizon" (1971) and "A Sea Change" (1972). He was a founder of the Gay Men's Health Crisis in New York City. *Addresses: Home*—2 Fifth Ave. No. 32, New York, N.Y. 10011.

BIOGRAPHICAL/CRITICAL SOURCES:

BOOKS

Contemporary Literary Criticism, Volume 42, Gale, 1987.
International Motion Picture Almanac, Quigley, 1987.

PERIODICALS

Chicago Tribune, January 15, 1979, April 11, 1985, May 6, 1985.
Los Angeles Times, December 5, 1985, December 13, 1985.
New York Times, April 22, 1985, June 15, 1986.
New York Times Book Review, January 14, 1979.
Times (London), March 27, 1986.

KUIST, J(ames) M(arquis) 1935-

PERSONAL: Born April 21, 1935, in White Plains, N.Y.; son of Howard Tillman (a professor) and Leone (a housewife; maiden name, Marquis) Kuist; married Gisela Elvira Fiedler (a housewife), June 25, 1960; children: Christopher James. *Education:* Davidson College, A.B., 1957; Duke University, M.A., 1959, Ph.D., 1965.

ADDRESSES: Home—2205 West Hemlock Rd., Milwaukee, Wis. 53209. *Office*—Department of English, University of Wisconsin—Milwaukee, Milwaukee, Wis. 53201.

CAREER: College of William and Mary, Williamsburg, Va., instructor in English, 1959-61; University of North Carolina at Chapel Hill, instructor in English, 1964-65; University of Western Ontario, London, assistant professor of English, 1965-67; University of Wisconsin—Milwaukee, assistant professor, 1967-69, associate professor, 1969-78, professor of English, 1978—, chairman of department, 1982-85. Member of Milwaukee Symphony Chorus.

MEMBER: Modern Language Association of America, American Society for Eighteenth Century Studies, Johnson Society.

AWARDS, HONORS: National Endowment for the Humanities, younger humanist fellow, 1972-73, research tools grant, 1978-79.

WRITINGS:

(Editor) *Cursory Observations on the Poems Attributed to Thomas Rowley,* Augustan Reprint, 1966.
The Works of John Nichols: An Introduction, Kraus Reprint, 1968.
The Nichols File of the Gentleman's Magazine, University of Wisconsin Press, 1982.

Contributor to literature journals.

WORK IN PROGRESS: Opening the Mind: The History and Function of "The Gentleman's Magazine" (tentative title), completion expected in 1990; *Nichols and Family* (tentative title), a biographical study of John Nichols (1745-1826) and his successors, completion expected in 1995.

SIDELIGHTS: J. M. Kuist has focused his writing to date upon the *Gentleman's Magazine,* which was founded by Edward Cave in 1731. By the time the magazine came into the hands of the scholar John Nichols, it had become what reviewer Brian Vickers called "one of the great institutions of British culture." The magazine was a digest of news and feature articles culled from at least two hundred London periodicals, and, as such, it represented an enormous range of contemporary opinion. Under the editorship of John Nichols, the *Gentleman's Magazine* doubled in size to accommodate an ever-increasing correspondence section. Britain's leading writers contributed to the periodical, often under as many as a hundred pseudonyms. The Nichols File is a voluminous record of these contributions, in which a conscientious attempt was made to identify the authors of the pseudonymous pieces. Kuist's book *The Nichols File of the Gentleman's Magazine* provides the reader with an extensive index to the file. Vickers wrote in the *Times Literary Supplement:* "The material presented here is of great intrinsic interest, and the file as a whole constitutes an important literary discovery." He added that the book "provides a solid base for Professor Kuist's future research, which one can look forward to with some impatience."

Kuist told *CA:* "I started writing about the *Gentleman's Magazine* because of its historical importance both as the original 'magazine' and as a permanent storehouse of information. In writing about it, I became its reader, going from one monthly number to the next and finding, as one may in reading the successive issues of *Time* or *Harper's* today, that the *Gentleman's* gave me a sense of life unfolding in a real world. I have assembled most of the facts I will need to reconstruct the publishing history of this magazine. Chiefly, though, I want to lead my readers into an understanding of two deeply interrelated conditions that the existence of the *Gentleman's Magazine* created when it appeared in the eighteenth and nineteenth centuries: the informing pleasure its contemporary readers felt in exploring their world in its pages and the creative energy that contributing writers experienced as they took the opportunity to write for publication.

"Between 1750 and 1830 hundreds of men and women published their work in the *Gentleman's*. The editors did not pay for work they did not solicit, but they set aside half of each monthly issue for essays and notes and poems from the public at large. The manuscripts of such contributed work, along with correspondence such writers had with the editors, have been preserved in surprising quantities, and I have been able to follow episodes in the lives of numerous individuals for whom the articulation of ideas and opinions in the magazine became the enabling events in their intellectual experience. For me, cultural history emerges from the pages of the *Gentleman's Magazine* as a practically endless series of interwoven personal narratives, a documentary record with very human attributes. My interest in the Nichols family, which owned and produced the magazine during most of that era, is perhaps inseparable from my interest in the magazine, for the whole family—including wives and children, through three generations—took part in the publishing enterprise, orchestrated the affairs of the magazine, and shared intellectual preoccupations. I want to tell their story, too."

BIOGRAPHICAL/CRITICAL SOURCES:

PERIODICALS

Times Literary Supplement, January 7, 1983.

* * *

KURTIS, Bill
See KURTIS, William Horton

* * *

KURTIS, William Horton 1940-
(Bill Kurtis)

BRIEF ENTRY: Professionally known as Bill Kurtis; born September 21, 1940, in Pensacola, Fla. American broadcast journalist and author. Kurtis is an award-winning reporter widely recognized for his three-year stint as co-anchor of the television broadcast "CBS Morning News" beginning in 1982. He began his journalism career in 1966 at station WBBM-TV—the Columbia Broadcasting System (CBS) affiliate in Chicago—and joined the station again in 1985 as reporter and anchorman. He also worked as a news correspondent for CBS News in Los Angeles. Kurtis's numerous awards include an Emmy for his in-depth documentary on the harmful effects of

the deadly herbicide Agent Orange used during the Vietnam War, as well as a 1975 Press Club award for his reporting on the plight of Saigon children orphaned by American servicemen. His book *Bill Kurtis on Assignment* (Rand McNally, 1983) is a behind-the-scenes look into his coverage of these stories and others in such vital areas of the world as Iran, El Salvador, and Africa. *Addresses: Home*—547 West Fullerton, Chicago, Ill.; and 125 Stratton Rd., New Rochelle, N.Y. *Office*—WBBM-TV, 630 North McClurg Ct., Chicago, Ill. 60611. *Agent*—Robert Gottlieb, William Morris Agency, 1350 Avenue of the Americas, New York, N.Y. 10019.

BIOGRAPHICAL/CRITICAL SOURCES:

BOOKS

Who's Who in America, 44th edition, Marquis, 1986.

PERIODICALS

Publishers Weekly, November 25, 1983.

L

LaBIER, Douglas 1944-

PERSONAL: Surname is pronounced "La-*beer*"; born March 7, 1944, in Albany, N.Y.; son of Horace and Florence LaBier; married, 1966 (divorced, 1973); married Pearlbea Steiner, July 12, 1975; children: Michael, Sarah, Peter. *Education:* Union College, Schenectady, N.Y., B.A. (with honors), 1965; State University of New York at Buffalo, Ph.D., 1969; postdoctoral study at National Institute of Mental Health, 1969-70; Washington School of Psychiatry, certificate in psychoanalysis, 1977.

ADDRESSES: *Home*—3210 Davenport St. N.W., Washington, D.C. 20008. *Office*—Project on Adult Lives, 1636 Connecticut Ave. N.W., Suite 400, Washington, D.C. 20009. *Agent*—Candida Donadio & Associates, 231 West 22nd St., New York, N.Y. 10011.

CAREER: National Institute of Mental Health, Washington, D.C., supervisory psychologist, 1970-73; Project on Technology, Work, and Character, Washington, D.C., senior fellow, 1977-87; Project on Adult Lives, Washington, D.C., director, 1987—. Private practice of psychotherapy and psychoanalysis in Washington, D.C., 1970—; member of faculty at Washington School of Psychiatry, 1979—. Lecturer; consultant to business and government.

MEMBER: International Society of Political Psychology, National Writers Union, Authors Guild, American Psychological Association, American Anthropological Association, Psychologist-Psychoanalyst Practitioners, American Historical Association, Sigma Xi.

WRITINGS:

Modern Madness: The Emotional Fallout of Success, Addison-Wesley, 1986.

Contributor to periodicals, including *Fortune* and *Washington Post.*

WORK IN PROGRESS: Reclaiming the Promise, "a new vision of adult lives, based on research on people who have developed an integration of career success and personal fulfillment."

SIDELIGHTS: Douglas LaBier's patients are young, urban professionals. His first book, *Modern Madness,* is critical of the high-pressure, bureaucratic world in which these people work. The author describes the modern corporate milieu as intensely political, insecure, power-oriented, and stifling to the creative imagination. Its victims are often normal but anxious, depressed, and troubled young men and women; or, they are destructively competitive, fiercely aggressive executives, who appear to be quite happy in the corporate world. According to LaBier, this latter group is less emotionally healthy than the one which, at least, is concerned about what reviewer Lyn Emmerman called "the distorted demands of their jobs," the "office's climate of dog-eat-dog, creative tension." The critic reported in the *Chicago Tribune* that "LaBier is at his best when he sheds new light on [these] emotional struggles."

LaBier told *CA:* "My work as a writer has arisen from my interest in the possibilities for open-ended development in adulthood. I have become critical of the view of adult life, common to our culture, which accepts a sense of resignation and despair regarding change as equivalent to mature adulthood. I have been attempting to integrate the point of view of the Zen tradition into a practice of adult life for those in modern, urban, professional culture."

BIOGRAPHICAL/CRITICAL SOURCES:

PERIODICALS

Chicago Tribune, August 27, 1986, October 19, 1986.
Los Angeles Times, November 21, 1986.
New York Times, August 24, 1986.
Vogue, September, 1986.
Washington Post, June 2, 1982, May 8, 1985.

* * *

LACY, Charles
See HIPPISLEY COXE, Antony D(acres)

* * *

LADNER, Joyce A(nn) 1943-

PERSONAL: Born October 12, 1943, in Waynesboro, Miss.; married Walter Carrington. *Education:* Tougaloo College, B.A., 1964; Washington University, 1966, Ph.D., 1968; postdoctoral research at University of Dar es Salaam, Tanzania.

ADDRESSES: *Office*—Department of Sociology, Hunter College of the City University of New York, 695 Park Ave., New York, N.Y. 10021.

CAREER: Southern Illinois University, Edwardsville, assistant professor and curriculum specialist, 1968-69; affiliated with Wesleyan University, Middletown, Conn., 1969-70; University of Dar es Salaam, Dar es Salaam, Tanzania, research associate, 1970-71; Howard University, Washington, D.C., associate professor of sociology, 1971-76; Hunter College of the City University of New York, New York City, member of faculty of sociology, beginning in 1976.

MEMBER: American Sociological Association (member of board of directors), National Institute of Mental Health (review committee member of Minority Center), Social Science Research Council (fellow), Society for the Study of Social Problems, Caucus of Black Sociologists (member of board of directors), Association for the Study of Afro-American Life and History, Institute of the Black World (senior research fellow, 1969-71), Twenty-first Century Foundation (member of board of directors).

AWARDS, HONORS: Recipient of first fellowship from Black Women's Community Development Foundation, 1970-71, for study "Involvement of Tanzanian Women in Nation Building"; Russell Sage Foundation grant, 1972-73; Cummins Engine Foundation grant, 1972-73.

WRITINGS:

Tomorrow's Tomorrow: The Black Woman, Doubleday, 1971.

(Editor) *The Death of White Sociology* (collection of essays), Random House, 1973.

Mixed Families: Adopting Across Racial Boundaries, Doubleday, 1977.

Contributor to anthologies and to newspapers and periodicals. Contributing editor to *Black Scholar* and *Journal of Black Studies and Research.*

SIDELIGHTS: Sociologist Joyce A. Ladner has centered her twenty years of research and teachings on intergroup relations and minority issues in America. In her first work, *Tomorrow's Tomorrow: The Black Woman,* Ladner examines the lives of black women and the forces that mold their self-perceptions. Her findings are the result of interviews with more than thirty black adolescent girls from a St. Louis, Missouri, ghetto. The girls, in the words of Toni Cade Bambara in *Black World,* "speak on and live out what it means to grow up Black and female in a country that regards neither with any special fondness."

Analyzing her observations in the context of the black people's troubled history in America—"a society infamous for the lack of understanding and sympathy between the races," commented Susan E. Burke in *Best Sellers*—Ladner found the girls' aspirations refreshingly optimistic and their self-images surprisingly positive. Consequently, stated Bambara, *Tomorrow's Tomorrow* focuses not on "the weakness of the Black community . . . or on the crippling effects of racism . . . but rather on the intricate network of influences (familial, peer, societal, etc.) that bombard the young girl [and on] the counters and strategems she devises to get over from day to day—her inner strength." Dispelling the popular notion of low self-esteem among poor black women, noted Burke, Ladner found that "most of the girls [she interviewed] have the determination to 'make something' of themselves, and self-hatred is practically non-existent."

Ladner relates the inner strength of black women to their position in a society that holds different values from those of the white middle class. Because of differing cultural views of sexual morality, for example, an unmarried, pregnant black woman is less likely to be shunned or chastised than is an unmarried, pregnant white woman. Carol L. Adams, writing in the *American Journal of Sociology,* cited illegitimacy as a "concept viewed as inappropriate when studying the black community." Adams explained Ladner's perception "that the low-income black community holds an inherent value that no child can be 'illegal.' The child is seen as having the right to exist and [as] representing the fulfillment of womanhood, thus neither the mother nor the child is degraded and stigmatized."

Adams praised Ladner's "notion that black women are now serving as role models for white women who are beginning to question such things as the institution of marriage, the concept of illegitimacy, and the general moral code traditionally associated with this society." Although some critics accused Ladner's survey as being unscientific and thus inconclusive, Burke affirmed that "her observations are both valid and important," and Bambara called the study "a solid piece of scholarship . . . moving and vital and eminently sensible."

Ladner's 1977 *Mixed Families: Adopting Across Racial Boundaries* is "an interesting, well-balanced study" of transracial adoption, according to Diane A. Parente in *Best Sellers.* Transracial adoption became a popular trend in America during the late 1960s when white couples, eager to adopt but discouraged by a shortage of white infants available, were strongly encouraged by adoption agencies to take in "hard to place" minority children. During an era of civil rights activity, such an undertaking was also considered an important step in promoting interracial harmony. In the early 1970s, however, the trend slowed when an opposing philosophy arose, strongly supported by the National Association of Black Social Workers, maintaining that black children needed to grow up in black families to develop a positive self-image and a strong sense of identity.

Attempting to resolve the debate, Ladner interviewed 136 adoptive families to find out how they were coping with the personal and societal pressures they encountered. "Both sides of the controversy are objectively presented" in *Mixed Families,* determined Parente, adding that the "truth, apparently, lies somewhere in the middle." Some black adoptees—children and adults alike—and their white parents agree that it would have been better to have placed the black children with black parents, while other families maintain that the adoption helped them gain an irreplaceable understanding of racial differences and similarities. The author herself concludes that although efforts should be made to avoid unnecessary trauma by placing children with families of their own ancestry, transracial adoptions are preferable to institutional or foster care.

Ladner emphasizes the importance of parental understanding and patience, whatever the race of the adoptive parents and their adopted children. As David C. Anderson concluded in *New York Times Book Review:* "Relations between parent and child aren't supposed to be perfect; instead, they are richly complicated, molded by imponderable forces great and small. Our task, as parents, is only to manage the complexity as best we can." For mixed families, Ladner points out in her book this involves maintaining "a balanced view and not [erring] too much in either direction"—neither denying the child's blackness nor attempting, as a white parent, to become black by rejecting whiteness.

Marti Wilson of *Black Scholar* remarked that "the strength of *Mixed Families* is in the fact that it approaches the question of integration from a new perspective, and heightens the level

of dialogue on the subject of cross racial adoptions." And Parente asserted that in *Mixed Families* "the author provides a realistic glimpse of American racial attitudes and their day-to-day effects on all concerned."

BIOGRAPHICAL/CRITICAL SOURCES:

BOOKS

Contemporary Issues Criticism, Volume 1, Gale, 1982.
Ladner, Joyce A., *Mixed Families: Adopting Across Racial Boundaries,* Doubleday, 1977.

PERIODICALS

American Journal of Sociology, September, 1972.
Best Sellers, August, 1971, October, 1977.
Black World, October, 1971.
Black Scholar, November/December, 1979.
New York Times Book Review, August 14, 1977.*

—Sketch by Christa Brelin

* * *

LAMB, Charles M(oody) 1945-

PERSONAL: Born March 1, 1945, in Murfreesboro, Tenn.; son of Edward Clay and Opal (Tune) Lamb; married Candie McKay, June, 1973 (divorced). *Education:* Middle Tennessee State University, B.S. (with highest honors), 1967; University of Alabama, M.A., 1970, Ph.D., 1974. *Politics:* Democrat. *Religion:* Presbyterian.

ADDRESSES: Home—125 Westfield Rd., Eggertsville, N.Y. 14226. *Office*—Department of Political Science, 520 Park Hall, State University of New York at Buffalo, Buffalo, N.Y. 14260.

CAREER: George Washington University, Washington, D.C., research scientist in Program of Policy Studies in Science and Technology, 1973-75; U.S. Commission on Civil Rights, Washington, D.C., equal opportunity specialist in Office of Federal Civil Rights Enforcement, 1975-77; State University of New York at Buffalo, assistant professor, 1977-84, associate professor of political science, 1984—. Director of undergraduate studies in political science, 1987. Cataloger in Manuscript Division of Library of Congress, summer, 1966; administrative specialist in Office of Policy Analysis, National Aeronautics and Space Administration, summer, 1971; consultant to U.S. Congressional Office of Technology Assessment. *Military service:* U.S. Army, 1972; became lieutenant.

MEMBER: American Political Science Association (chairperson of Roundtable on Judicial Conflict and Consensus, 1982; chairperson of Panel on Affirmative Action in Employment, 1984; member of executive committee of Section on Law, Courts, and Judicial Process, 1984-86; chairperson of Panel on New Perspectives on the Supreme Court, 1985), Law and Society Association, Leadership Conference on Civil Rights, Policy Studies Organization, Housing Opportunities Made Equal, Midwest Political Science Association, Southern Political Science Association (chairperson of Panel on Jurimetrics, 1976), Northeastern Political Science Association (chairperson of Panel on Perspectives From Ethology for the Study of Political Behavior, 1983; member of executive council, 1983-85), New York State Political Science Association (chairperson of Section for Public Law and Judicial Politics, 1982-84; member of executive council, 1982-87; vice-president, 1984-85; president, 1985-86), Common Cause, Pi Sigma Alpha, Pi Gamma Mu, Pi Sigma Beta.

AWARDS, HONORS: Grants from U.S. Office of Technology Assessment, 1974-75, and National Science Foundation, 1974-75; Outstanding Academic Book Award from *Choice,* 1983, for *Supreme Court Activism and Restraint;* Outstanding Service Award from New York State Political Science Association, 1986.

WRITINGS:

Trends in State and Federal Land Use Law Relating to Inventories, Monitoring, and Evaluation (monograph), National Technical Information Service, 1974.
Land Use Politics and Law in the 1970s (monograph), Program of Policy Studies in Science and Technology, George Washington University, 1975.
(Editor with Stephen C. Halpern, and contributor) *Supreme Court Activism and Restraint,* Lexington Books, 1982.
(Editor with Charles S. Bullock III, and contributor) *Implementation of Civil Rights Policy,* Brooks/Cole, 1984.
(Editor with Sheldon Goldman, and contributor) *Judicial Conflict and Consensus: Behavioral Studies of American Appellate Courts,* University Press of Kentucky, 1986.
(Editor with Stephen C. Halpern, and contributor) *The Burger Court: Political and Judicial Profiles,* 1988.

Associate editor of newsletter of Section on Law, Courts, and Judicial Process, American Political Science Association, 1985-88.

CONTRIBUTOR

An Assessment of Information Systems Capabilities Required to Support U.S. Materials Policy Decisions, U.S. Government Printing Office, 1976.
The Federal Civil Rights Enforcement Effort: To Preserve, Protect, and Defend the Constitution, U.S. Government Printing Office, 1977.
Charles Bulmer and John C. Carmichael, editors, *Employment and Labor-Relations Policy,* Lexington Books, 1980.
Tinsley E. Yarbrough, editor, *The Reagan Administration and Human Rights,* Praeger, 1985.
Sheldon Goldman and Austin Sarat, editors, *American Court Systems,* 2nd edition, W. H. Freeman, 1988.

Contributor to *Encyclopedia of the American Judicial System: Studies of the Principal Institutions and Processes of Law.* Contributor of articles and reviews to political science and law journals, including *Annals of the American Academy of Political and Social Science.*

WORK IN PROGRESS: The Federal Government and Fair Housing; Warren Burger and Criminal Justice: Judicial Philosophy and Behavior; editing, with Stephen C. Halpern, *American Civil Liberties: Bridging the Gap Between Case Law and Politics.*

BIOGRAPHICAL/CRITICAL SOURCES:

PERIODICALS

American Political Science Review, December, 1982, June, 1985, June, 1987.
Journal of Politics, May, 1983.
Political Science Quarterly, spring, 1984.

* * *

La MERI
See HUGHES, Russell Meriwether

LANDORF, Joyce 1932-

PERSONAL: Born February 2, 1932, in Saginaw, Mich.; daughter of Clifford A. (a minister) and Marion (Uzon) Miller; children: Richard B., Laurie Landorf Jacob. *Religion:* Christian. *Education:* Attended Pasadena Community Playhouse; received A.A., Pasadena City College.

ADDRESSES: Office—Joyce Landorf Ministry, P.O. Box 2067, Del Mar, Calif. 92014.

CAREER: Author, columnist, public speaker, conference leader, and singer. Performed at U.S. Army bases in Okinawa, Japan, Korea, Laos, and the United States on behalf of the chaplins' division of the Pentagon, 1968, 1970, and 1971; director of Joyce Landorf Ministry, Del Mar, Calif.

AWARDS, HONORS: Honorary major general of the U.S. Army; *I Came to Love You Late* named fiction book of the year by *Campus Life,* 1977; Gold Medallion Award from Evangelical Christian Publishers Association, 1977, for *I Came to Love You Late;* President's Award from Christian Film Distributors Association, 1981, for "His Stubborn Love" film series; honorary doctorate of humanities from Azusa-Pacific University, 1984.

WRITINGS:

Let's Have a Banquet; or, Will One Dollar and Thirty-six Cents Be Enough, Zondervan, 1968.
His Stubborn Love, Zondervan, 1971.
Fragrance of Beauty, Victor, 1973.
The Richest Lady in Town, Zondervan, 1973.
For These Fragile Times, Victor, 1974.
Mix Butter With Love: A Cookbook for the Daughter-in-Law, Harvest Home, 1974.
Mourning Song, Revell, 1974.
Tough and Tender: What Every Woman Wants in a Man, Revell, 1975, revised edition, 1981.
But as for Me and My Family, Victor, 1976.
"Joyce, I Feel Like I Know You": Based on Letters and Conversations About Life's Pressure Points, Victor, 1976.
I Came to Love You Late, Revell, 1977.
The High Cost of Growing, Nelson, 1978, published as *I'm Still Growing,* 1983.
Joseph, Revell, 1981.
Change Points: When We Need Him Most, Revell, 1981.
Irregular People, Word, Inc., 1983.
He Began With Eve, Word, Inc., 1983.
Balcony People, Word, Inc., 1984.
Monday Through Saturday, Word, Inc., 1984.
Silent September, Word, Inc., 1984.

FILMS

"His Stubborn Love" (a six-film seminar; adapted from book of same title [also see above]), Word, Inc., 1981.

OTHER

Also author of sound recordings, including some adapted from own books and one from film series "His Stubborn Love" (also see above).

WORK IN PROGRESS: Babies, Butterflies, and Promises, the fourth book of an eight-part series, for Word, Inc.

BIOGRAPHICAL/CRITICAL SOURCES:

BOOKS

Authors in the News, Volume I, Gale, 1976.

PERIODICALS

Seattle Post-Intelligencer, January 14, 1975.

[Sketch verified by personal executive secretary, Joanne A. Kroon]

* * *

LANGBEIN, John H(arriss) 1941-

PERSONAL: Born November 17, 1941, in Washington, D.C.; son of I. L. (a lawyer) and M. V. (a statistician; maiden name, Harriss) Langbein; married Kirsti M. Hiekka (a legal administrator), June 24, 1973; children: Christopher H., Julia L., Anne K. *Education:* Columbia University, A.B., 1964; Harvard University, LL.B. (magna cum laude), 1968; Trinity Hall, Cambridge, LL.B. (with first class honors), 1969, Ph.D., 1971. *Politics:* Republican. *Religion:* Episcopalian.

ADDRESSES: Office—School of Law, University of Chicago, 1111 East 60th St., Chicago, Ill. 60637.

CAREER: Admitted to the Bar of the District of Columbia, 1968, of Inner Temple, 1969, and of Florida, 1970; University of Chicago, Chicago, Ill., assistant professor, 1971-73, associate professor, 1973-74, professor, 1974-80, Max Pam Professor of American and Foreign Law, 1980—. Visiting scholar at Max Planck Institute for European Legal History, Frankfurt, West Germany, 1969-70, 1977, and Max Planck Institute for Criminal Law, Freiburg, West Germany, 1973; visiting fellow at All Soul's College, Oxford, 1977; visiting professor at University of Michigan Law School, 1976, and Stanford University Law School, 1985-86.

MEMBER: International Academy of Comparative Law, International Academy of Estate and Trust Law, International Association of Procedural Law, American Academy of Arts and Sciences, American Association for the Comparative Study of Law, American Bar Association, American College of Probate Counsel, American Historical Association, American Society for Legal History, Selden Society, Gesellschaft fuer Rechtsvergleichung.

AWARDS, HONORS: Yorke Prize from Cambridge University, 1974, for *Prosecuting Crime in the Renaissance.*

WRITINGS:

Prosecuting Crime in the Renaissance: England, Germany, France, Harvard University Press, 1974.
Torture and the Law of Proof: Europe and England in the Ancien Regime, University of Chicago Press, 1977.
Comparative Criminal Procedure: Germany, West Publishing, 1977.
(Author of introduction) William Blackstone, *Commentaries on the Laws of England,* Volume III (reprint), University of Chicago Press, 1979.
(With Lawrence Waggoner) *Selected Statutes on Trusts and Estates,* Foundation Press, 1987.

Contributor to law journals.

BIOGRAPHICAL/CRITICAL SOURCES:

PERIODICALS

Times Literary Supplement, September 20, 1974, February 17, 1978.

LARKIN, Sarah
See LOENING, Sarah (Elizabeth) Larkin

* * *

LaROUCHE, Lyndon H(ermyle), Jr. 1922-

BRIEF ENTRY: Born September 8, 1922, in Rochester, N.H. American business consultant, lecturer, politician, editor, and author. Although Lyndon LaRouche is known for his ultraconservative political stance, he began his political career in 1948 as a member of the leftist Trotskyite Social Workers. During the 1970s his views underwent a drastic change and he formed his own right-wing organization, National Democratic Policy Committee (NDPC), which eventually claimed thirty thousand members. LaRouche ran for president several times, and in 1984 he gained national attention and notoriety when he and other NDPC members entered state and local Democratic primaries across the country. Several LaRouche candidates won, causing considerable controversy and prompting the Democratic Party to deny any affiliation with the LaRouche Democrats. LaRouche also founded and served as contributing editor of *Executive Intelligence Review*. He wrote several books, including *The Power of Reason: A Kind of Autobiography* (New Benjamin Franklin House, 1979), *Basic Economics for Conservative Democrats* (New Benjamin Franklin House, 1980), *The Ugly Truth About Milton Friedman* (New Benjamin Franklin House, c. 1980), *What Every Conservative Should Know About Communism* (New Benjamin Franklin House, 1980), *Why Revival of "SALT" Won't Stop War* (New Benjamin Franklin House, 1980), and *A Program for America: The LaRouche Democratic Campaign* (LaRouche Democratic Campaign, 1985). *Addresses: Home*—304 West 58th St., New York, N.Y. 10019.

BIOGRAPHICAL/CRITICAL SOURCES:

BOOKS

LaRouche, Lyndon H., Jr., *The Power of Reason: A Kind of Autobiography,* New Benjamin Franklin House, 1979.
Who's Who in American Politics, 9th edition, Bowker, 1983.

PERIODICALS

New Republic, February 6, 1984, November 19, 1984, April 14, 1986.
Newsweek, April 16, 1984, March 31, 1986, April 7, 1986.
New York Times, March 24, 1986, March 30, 1986, April 1, 1986, April 3, 1986.

* * *

LARSON, Doran 1957-
(Jack Glasgow)

PERSONAL: Born March 12, 1957, in Solana Beach, Calif.; son of Eric (in Federal Aviation Administration) and Lola (Roach) Larson. *Education:* University of California, Santa Cruz, B.A., 1980; State University of New York at Buffalo, M.A., 1985, graduate study, 1985—. *Politics:* "Democratic Socialist."

ADDRESSES: Agent—Eileen Fallon, Barbara Lowenstein Associates, Inc., 250 West 57th St., No. 714, New York, N.Y. 10107.

CAREER: Writer and teacher. President of Students in Solidarity With the Peoples of Latin America, 1986.

WRITINGS:

(Under pseudonym Jack Glasgow) *The Big Deal* (young adult novel), Bantam, 1985.

WORK IN PROGRESS: Maundy Thursday, a murder mystery set in San Francisco, Calif.; "a study of the nature and creation of masculine identity as it relates to the use of women as indexes of male value."

SIDELIGHTS: Doran Larson told *CA:* "Whether in fiction or nonfiction, I am constantly concerned with the nature of and investment of political power structures in gender relations. At the personal, community, national, or international level, I believe the bases of inequality and conflict lie in our narrow acceptance of conventional roles as men and women. So it is these structures I try to explore in all my writing."

* * *

LASKI, Marghanita 1915-1988
(Sarah Russell)

OBITUARY NOTICE—See index for *CA* sketch: Born October 24, 1915, in London, England; died after a brief illness, February 6, 1988, in Dublin, Ireland. Broadcaster, journalist, critic, and author. Laski was best known for her novels, biographical criticism, and abundant lexicographical contributions. Her novels include *Love on the Supertax, The Victorian Chaise-Longue,* and *Little Boy Lost,* which Paramount released as a 1953 movie starring Bing Crosby. Her second novel, *To Bed With Grand Music,* was published under the pseudonym Sarah Russell. Laski's critical work included books on English authors Jane Austen, George Eliot, and Rudyard Kipling and two studies of religious and aesthetic experience, *Ecstasy* and *Everyday Ecstasy.* Laski also edited juvenile anthologies, contributed articles and reviews to periodicals, including the *London Times* and *Vogue,* and supplied a quarter of a million quotations to *Oxford English Dictionary* supplements. Widely known as a radio broadcaster, Laski was one of the original panelists on the television program "What's My Line?"

OBITUARIES AND OTHER SOURCES:

BOOKS

Who's Who, 139th edition, St. Martin's, 1987.

PERIODICALS

Chicago Tribune, February 9, 1988.
Detroit Free Press, February 8, 1988.
New York Times, February 9, 1988.
Times (London), February 8, 1988.
Washington Post, February 10, 1988.

* * *

LAWRENCE, Elizabeth L. 1904-1985

PERSONAL: Born May 27, 1904, in Marietta, Ga.; died June 11, 1985, in Annapolis, Md.; daughter of Samuel and Elizabeth (Bradenbaugh) Lawrence. *Education:* Graduate of Barnard College; North Carolina State College (now University), B.S., 1930.

CAREER: Writer, 1942-59; *Charlotte Observer,* Charlotte, N.C., garden columnist, 1959-75; writer, 1975-85. Lecturer.

AWARDS, HONORS: Numerous horticultural awards.

WRITINGS:

A Southern Garden: A Handbook for the Middle South, University of North Carolina Press, 1942, revised edition, 1967.
The Little Bulbs: A Tale of Two Gardens, Criterion Books, 1957, reprinted, Duke University Press, 1986.
Gardens in Winter, Harper, 1961.
Lob's Wood, Cincinnati Nature Conservancy, 1971.
(Author of introduction) Gertrude Jekyll, *The Gardener's Essential Gertrude Jekyll,* Breslich & Foss, 1983.
Gardening for Love: The Market Bulletins, Duke University Press, 1987.

Contributor to magazines.

BIOGRAPHICAL/CRITICAL SOURCES:

PERIODICALS

New York Times Book Review, October 11, 1987.
Washington Post Book World, April 26, 1987.*

* * *

LAWRENCE, Peter 1921-1988

OBITUARY NOTICE: Born September 11, 1921, in Duxbury, Lancashire, England; died in 1988 in Sydney, New South Wales, Australia. Anthropologist, educator, poet, and author. Lawrence was an authority on New Guinea's "cargo" cults whose members prayed to their gods for such things as refrigerators, wireless radios, and canned food and believed, for example, that airplanes were messengers from their deities and their dead ancestors. He wrote a book, *Road Belong Cargo,* based on his research and experiences with the cults. Lawrence taught anthropology at several Australian universities and eventually became the chair of anthropology at Sydney University. He also wrote Byronic verse and published a poem in that style entitled "Don Juan in Melanesia."

OBITUARIES AND OTHER SOURCES:

BOOKS

International Authors and Writers Who's Who, 9th edition, [and] *Who's Who in Poetry,* 6th edition, Melrose, 1982.
Who's Who in the World, 4th edition, Marquis, 1978.

PERIODICALS

Times (London), March 2, 1988.

* * *

LAY, Shawn 1953-

PERSONAL: Born December 12, 1953, in Raceland, La.; son of Johnny G. (a lawyer) and Virginia (a housewife; maiden name, Lee) Lay; married Imelda Sibala (a housewife), January 7, 1983; children: Alexander, Lawrence. *Education:* University of Texas at El Paso, B.A., 1980, M.A., 1984; graduate study at Vanderbilt University, 1985—. *Religion:* Roman Catholic.

ADDRESSES: Home—1410 25th Ave., No. 912, Nashville, Tenn. 37212. *Office*—Department of History, Vanderbilt University, Nashville, Tenn. 37235.

CAREER: University of Texas at El Paso, lecturer in history, 1980-85; Vanderbilt University, Nashville, Tenn., teaching fellow, 1985—. *Military service:* U.S. Navy, electronics technician, 1972-78.

MEMBER: Association of Borderlands Scholars.

AWARDS, HONORS: C. L. Sonnichsen Publication Award from Texas Western Press, 1984, and Southwest Book Award from Border Regional Library Association, 1986, both for *War, Revolution, and the Ku Klux Klan.*

WRITINGS:

War, Revolution, and the Ku Klux Klan: A Study of Intolerance in a Border City, Texas Western Press, 1985.

WORK IN PROGRESS: Research on the metamorphosis of southern progressivism during the 1920s.

SIDELIGHTS: Shawn Lay told *CA:* "My book, *War, Revolution, and the Ku Klux Klan,* examines the Ku Klux Klan in El Paso, Texas, a community whose population in the 1920s was over 60 percent Hispanic and Roman Catholic. While the Klan of the 1920s is popularly viewed as having been an exceedingly violent and reactionary organization, I argue in the volume that the KKK in El Paso primarily served as a medium of progressive civic action for residents who were legitimately concerned over a variety of serious social problems. While El Paso was (and is) in many ways a unique American city, my findings are quite similar to those of a number of other Klan scholars." In the *New Mexico Historical Review,* Charles C. Alexander described Lay's book as "an exceedingly thorough monograph, one of the best studies in Klan history up to now."

Lay added: "Currently I am continuing my work on the social developments of the 1920s and studying for my doctorate under the eminent historian Dewey W. Grantham. It is my hope that I will be a professional historian whose work is equally appealing to scholars and the general reading public."

BIOGRAPHICAL/CRITICAL SOURCES:

PERIODICALS

Journal of American History, September, 1987.
Journal of Southern History, February, 1987.
New Mexico Historical Review, January, 1987.
Western Historical Quarterly, January, 1987.

* * *

LEA, John Sedgwick 1910(?)-1987

OBITUARY NOTICE: Born c. 1910 in Syracuse, N.Y.; died of cancer, November 17, 1987, in Washington, D.C. Administrator and editor. Lea joined the Smithsonian Institution as an editor and assistant chief of the editorial and publications division in 1950. After retiring in the mid-1970s he became a part-time research reports editor with the National Geographic Society.

OBITUARIES AND OTHER SOURCES:

PERIODICALS

Washington Post, November 19, 1987.

* * *

LEAF, Margaret P. 1909(?)-1988

OBITUARY NOTICE: Born c. 1909, in East Orange, N.J.; died of cancer, February 24, 1988, in Rockville, Md. Administrator, social activist, and author. Leaf was an executive in the home-building business but spent much of her time on children's causes. While living in Connecticut during the 1940s, for example, she participated in efforts to bring disadvantaged

children into mainstream school programs and also volunteered in programs to aid Hungarian refugees. She is probably best remembered, however, as the widow of Munro Leaf, the author of the famous children's book *The Story of Ferdinand the Bull,* which has been translated into more than sixty languages and has sold more than 2.5 million copies. It was also made into a Walt Disney cartoon. During the 1960s she and her husband became part of the U.S. State Department's cultural exchange program, traveling abroad and discussing children's books. They visited several countries, including India, Japan, and the Soviet Union. She wrote a children's book entitled *Eyes of the Dragon*.

OBITUARIES AND OTHER SOURCES:

PERIODICALS

Washington Post, February 27, 1988.

* * *

LEARY, David E. 1945-

PERSONAL: Born May 5, 1945, in Los Angeles, Calif.; son of Thomas G. and Betty (Elliott) Leary; married Marjorie Bates, June 11, 1972; children: Emily, Elizabeth, Matthew. *Education:* San Luis Rey College, B.A., 1968; San Jose State College (now University), M.A., 1971; University of Chicago, Ph.D., 1977.

ADDRESSES: Home—6 Croghan Lane, Durham, N.H. 03824. *Office*—Department of Psychology, University of New Hampshire, Durham, N.H. 03824.

CAREER: University of New Hampshire, Durham, assistant professor, 1977-81, associate professor, 1981-87, professor of psychology, history, and humanities, 1987—, chairperson of department of psychology, 1987—. Fellow at Center for Advanced Study in the Behavioral Sciences, Stanford, Calif., 1982-83.

MEMBER: American Psychological Association (fellow; past president of Division of the History of Psychology), Cheiron Society, History of Science Society, American Historical Association, Society for the History of Science in America.

AWARDS, HONORS: Grants from National Endowment for the Humanities, 1979, 1982-83, History of Psychology Foundation, 1980, National Science Foundation, 1980-82, 1982-83, and Mellon Foundation, 1986; PSP Award from Association of American Publishers, 1985, for *A Century of Psychology as Science*.

WRITINGS:

(Editor with Sigmund Koch) *A Century of Psychology as Science,* McGraw, 1985.

Contributor to periodicals, including *Journal of the History of Ideas, Journal of General Psychology, American Psychological Association Monitor,* and *American Psychologist*.

WORK IN PROGRESS: Research on the role of metaphor and rhetoric in the history of psychology; research on the historical relations between psychology and the humanities, especially philosophy, religion, literature, and the arts.

SIDELIGHTS: David E. Leary told *CA:* "I am deeply concerned to understand the influence of the humanities upon psychology, and the influence of psychology upon the humanities. Since many people think of science as independent of the larger culture in which it exists, most of the reciprocal influence between psychology and the humanities has been overlooked. Much of this influence has been positive and has contributed to the advancement of both science and culture. However, some of it has had or threatens to have unfortunate consequences—as for instance when psychologists utilize fruitful metaphors drawn from the larger culture, but do so in a simpleminded, reductionistic way. The result is often the creation of psychological myths, promulgated to the public at large as supposedly factual descriptions of psychological phenomena.

"For example, when cognitive psychologists claim that the human mind *is* a computer rather than *like* a computer, they present an oversimplified view of the mind, which suggests and endorses an oversimplified approach to human problem solving. Similarly, when social psychologists speak about human interactions, without qualification, as essentially 'exchanges' in which each actor seeks to maximize 'benefits' and minimize 'costs,' they unwittingly legitimate and reinforce a cultural ideology that might otherwise be subjected to critical scrutiny. No doubt, many people in our culture have been socialized to 'think like a computer' and to approach social situations with a 'market mentality,' but this does not mean that a rationalistic, cost/benefit mentality is an inevitable characteristic of the human condition. To suggest that human mentality or human behavior just *is* that way, and by implication that it *must* be that way, is to corroborate rather than analyze and assess particular patterns of thought and behavior.

"The cumulative effect of broadcasting such convictions as 'the human mind is but a machine' and 'human behavior is always self-interested' can be detected in the transformation of private self-images and in the formulation of many public policies. Although these convictions have been around for a very long time, beginning well before the advent of modern psychology, their endorsement by psychological science has added significant ballast in their favor.

"In summary, although I believe that psychology has the potential to enlighten and enliven us about the human condition, it can also contribute towards the creation of an image of what it means to be human—and thus toward changes in the realities of human life—that I find distasteful at best, and morally repugnant at worst. I hope that my own teaching and writing will encourage the critical examination and discussion of such matters. *A Century of Psychology as Science,* while having a broader and more diverse set of purposes, contributes to this examination and discussion."

* * *

LEE, Philip J. 1932-

PERSONAL: Born April 24, 1932, in Nashville, Tenn.; son of Philip J. (a railroad executive) and Sara (a housewife; maiden name, Joyner) Lee; married Roberta Williams (a university instructor and writer of children's books), September 13, 1958; children: Sarah Joyner, Philip J. III, Susan Williams, Walter Williams. *Education:* Davidson College, B.Sc., 1954; graduate study at Princeton Theological Seminary; Harvard University, S.T.B., 1957. *Politics:* New Democrat.

ADDRESSES: Home—395 Beaconsfield Cres., Saint John, New Brunswick, Canada E2M 2H7. *Office*—Church of St. John and St. Stephen, 101 Coburg St., Saint John, New Brunswick, Canada E2L 3J8.

CAREER: Student minister to Protestant parish in New York, N.Y., 1955-56; ordained Presbyterian minister, 1957; pastor

of Presbyterian church in Brooksville, Fla., 1957-60; University of North Carolina at Chapel Hill, chaplain to students, 1960-61; pastor of Presbyterian church in Boyds, Md., 1961-69; Church of St. John and St. Stephen, Saint John, New Brunswick, minister, 1969—. Moderator of Presbytery of Saint John and Synod of the Atlantic Provinces; chair of General Assembly Committee on International Affairs of Presbyterian Church in Canada. Founding co-director of Hospice; member of board of directors of Centracare; founding director of Church of St. John and St. Stephen Home, Inc.

MEMBER: Karl Barth Society of North America, Canadian Theological Society, St. Andrew's Society (chaplain).

AWARDS, HONORS: Honorary doctorate from Presbyterian College, Montreal, Quebec, 1987.

WRITINGS:

Against the Protestant Gnostics, Oxford University Press, 1987.

Contributor to theology journals and other magazines, including *Fiddlehead.*

SIDELIGHTS: Philip J. Lee told *CA* that his work and writing has been heavily influenced by the writings of Max Weber, Karl Barth, and Paul Lehmann. "*Against the Protestant Gnostics,*" he added, "was largely the result of my experience in the parish ministry. I was struck by the similarity between an overspiritualized, otherworldly heresy in the early church and a similar phenomenon within contemporary North American Protestantism."

AVOCATIONAL INTERESTS: Fishing, canoeing, cross-country skiing.

* * *

LEIGH, Eugene
See SELTZER, Leon E(ugene)

* * *

LEIGH, Ralph Alexander 1915-1987

OBITUARY NOTICE: Born January 6, 1915, in London, England; died December 22, 1987. Educator and editor. Considered one of England's outstanding scholars of seventeenth- and eighteenth-century French literature and thought, Leigh is remembered for editing the highly acclaimed *Correspondence complete de Jean-Jacques Rousseau.* Published in several volumes, his work brought him international recognition. Leigh taught at University of Edinburgh from 1944 to 1951, became a fellow of Trinity College in 1952, and was professor of French at the University of Cambridge from 1973 to 1982.

OBITUARIES AND OTHER SOURCES:

PERIODICALS

Times (London), December 23, 1987.

* * *

LEVINE, David O(scar) 1955-

PERSONAL: Born August 16, 1955, in Middletown, N.Y.; son of Jacques (in business) and Florence (in business) Levine; married Sherrie Zacharius (a chemist), July 12, 1981; children: Aaron. *Education:* University of Pennsylvania, B.A., 1976; Harvard University, A.M., 1978, Ph.D., 1981.

ADDRESSES: Home—10347 Tennessee Ave., Los Angeles, Calif. 90064. *Office*—Touch American History, 4201 Via Marina, Marina del Rey, Calif., 90292.

CAREER: University of California, Los Angeles, lecturer in history, 1981-87; Touch American History, Marina del Rey, Calif., executive director, 1986—. Research associate for Sloan Commission on Government and Higher Education, 1978-79; issues director for California Democratic Party, 1983-85.

MEMBER: American Historical Association, American Studies Association.

WRITINGS:

The American College and the Culture of Aspiration, 1915-1940, Cornell University Press, 1986.

WORK IN PROGRESS: An intellectual biography of David Riesman.

SIDELIGHTS: David O. Levine told *CA:* "I wrote *The American College and the Culture of Aspiration, 1915-1940* because I believe Americans—including professional educators and historians—know too little about the recent history of higher education. Despite the critical role higher education plays as an economic and social institution in American life, we fail generally to examine the economic, social, and political implications of the structure of higher education and even of individual policy-making and curricula decisions. By chronicling the impact of World War I, the creation of business programs, the establishment of admission quotas, the formation of junior colleges, and the effort to provide work-study programs during the Depression, I sought to show that higher education is a prism through which one can examine the often conflicting values and dreams in American society. More specifically, I examined the gap between rhetoric and reality: If we are a 'culture of aspiration,' then how successful are we at encouraging Americans to aspire to higher status? Educational rhetoric and policies demonstrate all too clearly that Americans are ambivalent about democracy and the preservation of existing social prerogatives.

"This same concern with the lack of historical perspective led me to assume my position with Touch American History. Touch American History has been created to establish innovative projects which stimulate interest in, and knowledge of, American history, particularly among young people. Our first program was the Commemoration of the Bicentennial of the United States Constitution at the Los Angeles County Museum in the summer of 1987. Now we are designing a self-contained 'museum on wheels' that will tour the United States. Our projects seek to be entertaining as well as educational.

"In the future I hope to return to my study of the life and work of David Riesman, the noted author of the classic *The Lonely Crowd.* Riesman is one of the key intellectual figures in the social sciences in this century. As a lawyer, sociologist, and educator, Riesman sheds a great deal of light on many of the social and intellectual currents of modern American life."

* * *

LEVINE, Sol 1914-1987

OBITUARY NOTICE—See index for *CA* sketch: Born November 16, 1914, in Bentleyville, Pa.; died of a brain tumor, December 5, 1987, in Arlington, Va. Engineer and author. Levine spent much of his career as an engineer with government and industry. He also wrote several books, including

Your Future in Electronic Engineering, Appointment in the Sky: The Story of Project Gemini, Your Future in NASA, and *Mathematics Handbook.*

OBITUARIES AND OTHER SOURCES:

PERIODICALS

Washington Post, December 10, 1987.

* * *

LEWIS, John D(onald) 1905-1988

OBITUARY NOTICE—See index for *CA* sketch: Born October 6, 1905, in Paterson, N.J.; died of cardiac arrest, January 23, 1988, in Oberlin, Ohio. Educator and author. Lewis was a faculty member of Oberlin College for nearly four decades, serving as professor of government from 1948 to 1972 and department chairman from 1953 to 1970. He also taught at the University of Wisconsin, Case Western Reserve and Pennsylvania State universities, and Colorado College during his career. Lewis's writings include *The Genossenschaft-Theory of Otto von Gierke* and, with Oscar Jaszi, *Against the Tyrant: The Tradition and Theory of Tyrranicide.* Lewis edited *Anti-Federalists Versus Federalists: Selected Documents,* co-edited *Democracy Is Different* and *The Study of Comparative Government,* and contributed articles to numerous periodicals.

OBITUARIES AND OTHER SOURCES:

BOOKS

Who's Who in the Midwest, 19th edition, Marquis, 1984.

PERIODICALS

New York Times, January 29, 1988.

* * *

LEYDA, Jay 1910-1988

OBITUARY NOTICE—See index for *CA* sketch: Born February 12, 1910, in Detroit, Mich.; died of heart failure, February 15, 1988, in New York, N.Y. Film historian, educator, editor, and author. Leyda studied filmmaking with Soviet director Sergei Eisenstein in Moscow before beginning a lifelong career as a film historian and teacher of cinema. During the 1940s he was technical adviser on Russian subjects for Hollywood studios and in the 1960s and 1970s he taught at Yale University and York University in Toronto. In 1973 he joined New York University, where he held the Pinewood Chair of Cinema until his death. Leyda was also author of *Kino: A History of the Russian and Soviet Film, Films Beget Films, Dianying—Electric Shadows: An Account of Films and the Film Audience in China, An Index to the Creative Work of Alexander Dovzhenko,* and *An Index to the Creative Work of V. E. Pudovkin.* In addition, he translated Eisenstein's theoretical works and wrote or edited books about American literary figures Herman Melville and Emily Dickinson, Russian composers Modest Petrovich Mussorgsky and Sergei Rachmaninoff, and early American and Soviet cinema.

OBITUARIES AND OTHER SOURCES:

PERIODICALS

New York Times, February 18, 1988.

LICHTMAN, Allan J. 1947-

PERSONAL: Born April 14, 1947, in Brooklyn, N.Y.; son of Emanuel (an optometrist) and Gertrude (a bookkeeper; maiden name, Cohen) Lichtman; married Sheila Bradford (a computer consultant), May 18, 1980; children: Kara. *Education:* Brandeis University, B.A., 1967; Harvard University, Ph.D., 1973.

ADDRESSES: Home—9219 Villa Dr., Bethesda, Md. 20817. *Office*—Department of History, American University, 4400 Massachusetts Ave. N.W., Washington, D.C. 20016.

CAREER: American University, Washington, D.C., member of faculty of history, 1973—, associate dean of College of Arts and Sciences, 1985—. Sherman Fairchild Distinguished Visiting Scholar at California Institute of Technology, 1980-81. Expert witness on qualitative analysis of political history for U.S. Department of Justice Lawyers' Committee for Civil Rights Under Law.

MEMBER: American Historical Association, Organization of American Historians, Social Science History Association.

AWARDS, HONORS: National age-group champion of three-thousand-meter steeplechase, 1979; named top speaker of National Platform Association, 1983-84.

WRITINGS:

(With Valerie French) *Historians and the Living Past: The Theory and Practice of Historical Study,* AHM Publishing, 1978.

(With Laura Langbein) *Ecological Inference,* Sage Publications, 1978.

Your Family History: How to Use Oral History, Personal Family Archives, and Public Documents to Discover Your Heritage, Vintage Book, 1978.

Prejudice and the Old Politics: The Presidential Election of 1928, University of North Carolina Press, 1979.

(Editor with Joan R. Challinor) *Kin and Communities: Families in America,* foreword by S. Dillon Ripley, introduction by Wilton S. Dillon, Smithsonian Institution Press, 1979.

Contributor to history and law journals.

WORK IN PROGRESS: Three books, *Political Prediction: The Logic of American Elections, American Political History: American Elections, 1880-1950,* and *The American Political World,* completion expected in 1989; *Lobbying: The Hidden World of Tommy the Cork, Washington's First Modern Lobbyist,* completion expected in 1990.

SIDELIGHTS: Allan J. Lichtman told *CA:* "I have sought in my work to integrate elements of humanistic and scientific study. My efforts have been designed both to recapture the contemporary meaning of past events and to analyze trends that may not have been apparent to historical protagonists. I have also sought to develop general theories of American politics and to test them by reference to historical data and to verifiable predictions of future events. My book on the logic of American elections develops and explains a new system for predicting election results without polls."

BIOGRAPHICAL/CRITICAL SOURCES:

PERIODICALS

American Historical Review, April, 1980.
Commonweal, June 6, 1980.

Washingtonian, November, 1986.
Washington Post, March 28, 1982, January 1, 1984.

* * *

LIGHTNER, A. M.
See HOPF, Alice (Martha) L(ightner)

* * *

LIGHTNER, Alice
See HOPF, Alice (Martha) L(ightner)

* * *

LINDLEY, Erica
See QUIGLEY, Aileen

* * *

LINEN, James A., III 1912-1988

OBITUARY NOTICE: Born June 20, 1912, in Waverly, Pa.; died February 1, 1988, in Greenwich, Conn. Business consultant and publisher. Linen began his publishing career in 1934 when he was hired as an office boy by Henry Luce, the founder of the Time publishing empire. He became an advertising salesman—after failing a writing test at Time—and went on to become the advertising manager of *Life* magazine in 1938. After serving in the armed forces during World War II as a psychological warfare specialist, Linen returned home in 1945 expecting to work again for *Life*. Instead Luce promoted him to publisher of *Time* magazine, a position he held for fifteen years, and in 1960 he became president of the parent company, Time, Inc. During Linen's tenure the Luce publishing empire expanded into book publishing, films, and learning systems. After suffering a stroke in 1969, Linen stepped down as president but continued as chairman of the executive committee. Though confined to a wheelchair, he remained active and traveled worldwide as an international business consultant, specializing in gathering heads of state, international developers, and business leaders for meetings concerning the development of their countries' economies.

OBITUARIES AND OTHER SOURCES:

BOOKS

The International Who's Who, 51st edition, Europa, 1987.
The International Year Book and Statesmen's Who's Who, Kelly's Directories, 1981.

PERIODICALS

New York Times, February 2, 1988.

* * *

LISIO, Donald J(ohn) 1934-

PERSONAL: Born May 27, 1934, in Oak Park, Ill.; son of Anthony and Dorothy (LoCelso) Lisio; married Suzanne Marie Swanson, April 22, 1958; children: Denise Anne, Stephen Anthony. *Education:* Knox College, B.A., 1956; Ohio University, M.A., 1958; University of Wisconsin, Ph.D., 1965. *Religion:* Episcopalian.

ADDRESSES: Home—4203 Twin Ridge Ct. S.E., Cedar Rapids, Iowa 52403. *Office*—Department of History, Coe College, 1220 First Ave. N.E., Cedar Rapids, Iowa 52402.

CAREER: University of Maryland, College Park, Md., member of faculty in overseas division, 1958-60; Coe College, Cedar Rapids, Iowa, assistant professor, 1964-69, associate professor, 1969-74, professor, 1974—, Henrietta Arnold Professor of History, 1980—, chairman of department, 1973-81. Member of the executive committee, Cedar Rapids Committee for Historic Preservation, 1975. *Military service:* U.S. Army, 1958-60.

MEMBER: American Historical Association, Organization of American Historians, American Association of University Professors, American Civil Liberties Union.

AWARDS, HONORS: William F. Vilas research fellow at the University of Wisconsin, 1963-64; National Endowment for the Humanities younger scholar fellow, 1969-70, research fellow, 1984-85; American Council of Learned Societies grantee, 1971-72, senior fellow, 1977-78.

WRITINGS:

The President and Protest: Hoover, Conspiracy, and the Bonus Riot, University of Missouri Press, 1974.
Hoover, Blacks, and Lily-Whites: A Study of Southern Strategies, University of North Carolina Press, 1986.
(Contributor) *The War Generation,* Kennikat, 1975.

Contributor to historical journals.

WORK IN PROGRESS: Hoover and the Disarmament Between the Wars: 1927-1933.

* * *

LITTLE, Alan M(acNaughton) G(ordon) 1901-1987

OBITUARY NOTICE: Born October 13, 1901, in Great Crosby, Lancashire, England; immigrated to United States in the late 1920s; died of cardiorespiratory arrest, November 22, 1987, in Washington, D.C. Government official, educator, and author. Little attended Yale University and earned his doctorate in classical languages and literature. He taught at Yale University, Harvard University, and Hobart College before World War II, whereupon he served with the United States Office of Strategic Services. In 1945 he joined the U.S. State Department and became a press attache with the American Embassy in Moscow, then joined the State Department's Foreign Service Institute as a professor, eventually serving as a department head in the school of foreign affairs. Little wrote several books, including *Myth and Society in Attic Drama, Roman Perspective Painting and the Ancient State, A Roman Bridal Drama at the Villa of the Mysteries,* and *Decor, Drama, and Design in Roman Painting*. In recognition for his cultural work, he received an award from the Italian government.

OBITUARIES AND OTHER SOURCES:

BOOKS

International Authors and Writers Who's Who, 9th edition, [and] *International Who's Who in Poetry,* 6th edition, Melrose, 1982.

PERIODICALS

Washington Post, December 5, 1987.

* * *

LOBEL, Arnold Stark 1933-1987

OBITUARY NOTICE—See index for *CA* sketch: Born May 22,

1933, in Los Angeles, Calif.; died of cardiac arrest, December 4, 1987, in New York, N.Y. Children's book illustrator and author best known for his four stories about a frog and a toad who share many adventures. Lobel illustrated nearly one hundred children's books, many of which he also wrote. Among the latter are *Mouse Tales, A Treeful of Pigs, Uncle Elephant, Ming Lo Moves the Mountain,* and the "Frog and Toad" series. Lobel's awards and honors include a 1971 Caldecott Honor Book award for *Frog and Toad Are Friends,* a 1973 Newbery Honor Book award for *Frog and Toad Together,* and a 1981 Caldecott Medal for *Fables,* a collection of animal tales.

OBITUARIES AND OTHER SOURCES:

BOOKS

Twentieth-Century Children's Writers, 2nd edition, St. Martin's, 1983.

PERIODICALS

New York Times, December 7, 1987.
School Library Journal, January, 1988.

* * *

LOCKE, Alain (Le Roy) 1886-1954

PERSONAL: Born September 13, 1886, in Philadelphia, Pa.; died following a long illness, June 9 (some sources say June 10), 1954, in New York, N.Y.; son of Pliny I. (a schoolteacher) and Mary (a schoolteacher; maiden name, Hawkins) Locke. *Education:* Harvard University, B.A. (with honors), 1907, Ph.D., 1918; Oxford University, B.Litt., 1910; graduate study at University of Berlin, 1910-11. *Religion:* Episcopalian.

ADDRESSES: Home—1326 R St. N.W., Washington, D.C.

CAREER: Howard University, Washington, D.C., assistant professor, 1912-17, professor of philosophy, 1917-53, chairman of philosophy department, 1918-53. Exchange professor at Fisk University, 1927-28; Inter-American Exchange Professor in Haiti, 1943; visiting professor at University of Wisconsin, 1945-46, and at The New School for Social Research, 1947.

MEMBER: International Institute of African Languages and Culture, American Negro Academy, American Philosophical Association, League of American Writers, Associates in Negro Folk Education (former secretary-editor), Conference on Science, Philosophy, and Religion (founding member), Society for Historical Research, Phi Beta Kappa, Phi Beta Sigma (honorary member), Theta Sigma, Sigma Pi Phi, Academie des Sciences Colonailes (corresponding member), Sociedad de Estudios Afro-Cubanos (honorary fellow), National Order of Honor and Merit (Haiti).

AWARDS, HONORS: Rhodes scholar, 1907-10; named to 1942 Honor Roll of Race Relations.

WRITINGS:

(Editor) *The New Negro: An Interpretation* (anthology), illustrations by Winold Reiss, A. & C. Boni, 1925, reprinted, with preface by Robert Hayden, Atheneum, 1970.
(Editor) *Four Negro Poets,* Simon & Schuster, 1927.
(Editor with Montgomery Gregory) *Plays of Negro Life: A Source-Book of Native American Drama,* illustrations by Aaron Douglas, Harper, 1927, Negro University Press, 1970.
The Negro in America (bibliography), American Library Association, 1933.
The Negro and His Music, Associates in Negro Folk Education, 1936, Kennikat, 1968, also published with *Negro Art: Past and Present,* Arno Press, 1969 (also see below).
Negro Art: Past and Present, Associates in Negro Folk Education, 1936, also published with *The Negro and His Music,* Arno Press, 1969 (also see below).
(Editor and annotator) *The Negro in Art: A Pictorial Record of the Negro Artist and of the Negro Theme in Art,* Associates in Negro Folk Education, 1940, Hacker Art Books, 1971.
(Editor with Bernhard J. Stern) *When Peoples Meet: A Study in Race and Culture Contacts,* Committee on Workshops, Progressive Education Association, 1942, revised edition, Hinds, Hayden & Eldredge, 1946.
Le Role du Negre dans la culture des Ameriques, Impr. de l'Etat, 1943.
The Negro and His Music [and] *Negro Art: Past and Present,* Arno Press, 1969.

Also author of *Race Contacts and Inter-Racial Relations,* 1916; *The Problem of Classification in Theory of Value,* 1918; *The Negro in American Literature,* 1929; and *Frederick Douglass: A Biography of Anti-Slavery,* 1935. Works represented in anthologies, including *The Black Aesthetic* and *Theatre: Essays on the Arts of the Theatre.*

Contributor to reference books and periodicals, including *Britannica Book of the Year, Harlem: A Forum of Negro Life, Phylon, Opportunity, Nation, Annals of the American Academy of Political and Social Science, Modern Quarterly, Theatre Arts, Carolina Magazine,* and *Crisis.* Edited a special Harlem issue of *Survey Graphic,* 1925, and the "Bronze Booklet" series of studies on Negro cultural achievements.

SIDELIGHTS: Alain Locke virtually brought about the Harlem Renaissance, a period of great literary and artistic activity originating in New York City during the 1920s, by compiling an anthology of the most outstanding Negro poetry and prose of the early twentieth century, *The New Negro: An Interpretation.* Because of the high literary merit of the works in the anthology, critics were forced to take black writing seriously. *The New Negro* also served as a unifying link for struggling black authors who previously thought that they were alone in their literary endeavors. Exposed to other writers' works and able to study different forms and themes, a generation of black authors were inspired by *The New Negro.*

Locke also urged Negroes to seek inspiration and take pride in their rich cultural heritage. In *The Negro in Art: A Pictorial Record of the Negro Artist and of the Negro Theme in Art* Locke stressed that the black man should look to the works of his African ancestors for subject matter, methods, and motifs to apply to modern painting and sculpture. The first section of *The Negro in Art* provides examples of seventeenth- to twentieth-century art works by Negroes, mostly American. The second section contains illustrations of black subjects in art; and the third part deals with the influence of African art on modern painting and sculpture.

Locke first became aware of the need to promote African culture while touring the American South for six months in 1911. He witnessed prejudice and discrimination, and realized that the black literati and artists could hold the key to easier race relations. He felt that by setting high standards for themselves and using their talents to gain the respect of the whites, blacks would cast aside their self-doubt, become more confident, and

would think of themselves as equal to whites. Locke's 1916 social study, *Race Contacts and Inter-Racial Relations,* grew out of his experiences in the South. He was also interested in interactions between majority and minority groups on a national and international level. On that subject Locke edited, with Bernhard J. Stern, *When Peoples Meet: A Study in Race and Culture Contacts* and wrote, while an Inter-American Exchange Professor in Haiti, *Le Role du Negre dans la culture des Ameriques,* about blacks in American society.

BIOGRAPHICAL/CRITICAL SOURCES:

BOOKS

Butcher, Margaret J., *The Negro in American Culture: Based on Materials Left by Alain Locke,* Knopf, 1956.

Dictionary of Literary Biography, Volume 51: *Afro-American Writers From the Harlem Renaissance to 1940,* Gale, 1987.*

* * *

LOCKE, Ralph P(aul) 1949-

PERSONAL: Born March 9, 1949, in Boston, Mass.; son of Merle I. and Doris (Tobis) Locke; married Lona M. Farhi, May 26, 1979; children: Martha Deborah, Susannah Felicia. *Education:* Harvard University, B.A., 1970; University of Chicago, M.A., 1974, Ph.D., 1980.

ADDRESSES: Home—Rochester, N.Y. *Office*—Department of Musicology, Eastman School of Music, University of Rochester, 26 Gibbs St., Rochester, N.Y. 14604.

CAREER: University of Rochester, Eastman School of Music, Rochester, N.Y., instructor, 1975-80, assistant professor, 1980-84, associate professor of musicology, 1984—.

MEMBER: American Musicological Society (member of council, 1985-87), Societe Francaise de Musicologie, Association Nationale Hector Berlioz.

AWARDS, HONORS: Grant from Deutscher Akademischer Austauschdienst, 1970; French government exchange fellow, 1974, and Bourse d'Ete, 1976; "Best Article of a Bibliographic Nature" award from Music Library Association, 1982, for "New Schumann Material in Upstate New York"; American Council of Learned Societies research fellowship, 1984.

WRITINGS:

(Contributor) Jon Finson and R. Larry Todd, editors, *Mendelssohn and Schumann,* Duke University Press, 1984.

Music, Musicians, and the Saint-Simonians, University of Chicago Press, 1986.

(Contributor) Peter A. Bloom, editor, *Music in Paris in the 1830s,* Pendragon Press, 1987.

Contributor to *New Harvard Dictionary of Music, New Grove Dictionary of Music, New Grove Dictionary of American Music,* and *Encyclopaedia Britannica.* Contributor of articles and reviews to music journals.

WORK IN PROGRESS: Research on musical exoticism from Rameau to Messiaen, text-music relations in the settings of Emily Dickinson's poems, musical life in Paris from 1789 to 1851, musical patronage in turn-of-the-century Boston (especially that of Isabella Stewart Gardner), and the Walton viola concerto.

SIDELIGHTS: Ralph P. Locke told *CA:* "My research focuses in varying ways on the relationship between music and society. In my book on the Saint-Simonians I sought to reveal the intricate and previously unknown ties that connected this major social movement of the 1830s to the music and musicians of its day, including Berlioz, Felicien David, Halevy, Liszt, and Mendelssohn. My current work on musical exoticism broadens the focus to include a wide range of composers—Rameau, Mozart, Chopin, Bizet, Verdi, Debussy, among others—and a number of intriguing issues touching on the ways in which musical portrayals of distant lands, especially the Middle East, contributed to the cultural self-definition of the Western European. And, since we are in many ways the heirs of that European, my study carries some implications for understanding some present day matters: the hidden messages in 'high culture,' the Western view of the non-Western world, and—most basic and important to me—the meanings that music, that supposedly abstract and pure art, transmits from composer and performer to listener."

* * *

LOCKHART, Freda Bruce 1909-1987

OBITUARY NOTICE: Born April 13, 1909; died November 7, 1987. Actress, film critic, columnist, and author. Lockhart studied theater at the Royal Academy of Music in the 1920s and made her stage debut in 1927. She appeared in the West End and on Broadway playing supporting roles, but was best known as an understudy to English actress Gertrude Lawrence. In 1935 Lockhart retired from the stage and began a new career as a film critic, writing for *Film Weekly, Daily Sketch,* and *Tatler.* She also wrote a film column for more than twenty years that appeared first in *Woman* and later in *Catholic Herald,* which named her Catholic Woman of the Year when she retired. Lockhart suffered from multiple sclerosis much of her life, prompting her to write a book, *London for the Disabled,* which proved influential in changing the public perspective of and improving facilities for the handicapped.

OBITUARIES AND OTHER SOURCES:

PERIODICALS

Times (London), November 9, 1987.

* * *

LOENING, Sarah (Elizabeth) Larkin 1896-1988 (Sarah Larkin)

OBITUARY NOTICE—See index for *CA* sketch: Born December 9, 1896, in Nutley, N.J.; died February 1, 1988, in Southampton, Long Island, N. Y. Author. Loening wrote more than ten books, many of them under the pseudonym Sarah Larkin. Titles include the narrative poems *Three Rivers: A Tale of New France, The Trevals: A Tale of Quebec,* and *Joan of Arc,* and prose works *Dimo, The Gift of Life,* and *Vignettes of a Life.* Loening also founded the Biblical Gardens at the Cathedral of St. John the Divine in Manhattan.

OBITUARIES AND OTHER SOURCES:

BOOKS

Who's Who of American Women, 15th edition, Marquis, 1986.

PERIODICALS

New York Times, February 5, 1988.

LOEWENSTEIN, Joseph 1952-

PERSONAL: Born October 20, 1952, in Charleston, W.Va.; son of Stanley M. (in business) and Jean Sinclair (an educational psychologist; maiden name, Foster) Loewenstein. *Education:* Wesleyan University, Middletown, Conn., B.A. (summa cum laude), 1974; Columbia University, M.A., 1975; graduate study at Warburg Institute, London, 1975-76; Yale University, M.A., 1978, Ph.D., 1982.

ADDRESSES: Office—Department of English, Box 1122, Washington University, Lindell-Skinker Blvd., St. Louis, Mo. 63130.

CAREER: Wesleyan University, Middletown, Conn., visiting instructor in English, 1980-81; Washington University, St. Louis, Mo., assistant professor, 1981-86, associate professor of English, 1986—.

MEMBER: Modern Language Association of America (regional delegate, 1985-88), Phi Beta Kappa.

WRITINGS:

Responsive Readings: Versions of Echo in Pastoral, Epic, and the Jonsonian Masque, Yale University Press, 1984.

WORK IN PROGRESS: The Matter of Authority, a history of ideas on the intellectual property in Renaissance art and literature, law and politics, publication expected in 1989.

* * *

LOGAN, John (Burton) 1923-1987

OBITUARY NOTICE—See index for *CA* sketch: Born January 23, 1923, in Red Oak, Iowa; died of a heart ailment and complications from gall bladder surgery, November 6, 1987, in San Francisco, Calif. Educator, editor, and author. Logan was a critically admired but little-known poet who edited several national poetry magazines, including *Critic* and *Nation.* He was also founder and editor of the Chicago-based poetry magazine *Choice.* From 1966 to 1985 Logan was an English professor at the State University of New York at Buffalo. Other teaching assignments included posts at Notre Dame University and San Francisco State College. Among Logan's many publications were the poetry collections *The Zig Zag Walk: Poems 1963 to 1968, The Anonymous Lover: New Poems, Only the Dreamer Can Change the Dream,* the play *Of Poems, Youth, and Spring,* and the autobiographical novel *The House That Jack Built; or, a Portrait of the Artist as a Sad Sensualist.* His *Collected Poems* was published in 1988 by Boa Editions. Logan also contributed fiction and criticism to periodicals.

OBITUARIES AND OTHER SOURCES:

BOOKS

Contemporary Poets, 4th edition, St. Martin's, 1985.

PERIODICALS

Chicago Tribune, November 9, 1987.
Los Angeles Times, November 10, 1987.
New York Times, November 10, 1987.

* * *

LOMBARD, Lawrence Brian 1944-

PERSONAL: Born November 24, 1944, in New York, N.Y.; son of Maurice (a podiatrist) and Martha (Simons) Lombard; married Marjorie Levy (a French teacher), August 28, 1966. *Education:* Cornell University, A.B., 1965; Stanford University, Ph.D., 1974.

ADDRESSES: Office—Department of Philosophy, 794 MacKenzie, Wayne State University, 5950 Cass Ave., Detroit, Mich. 48202.

CAREER: Wayne State University, Detroit, Mich., assistant professor, 1969-79, associate professor, 1979-87, professor of philosophy, 1987—.

MEMBER: American Philosophical Association, American Association of University Professors.

WRITINGS:

(Contributor) E. Le Pore and B. McLaughlin, editors, *Action and Events,* Basil Blackwell, 1985.
Events: A Metaphysical Study, Routledge & Kegan Paul, 1986.

Contributor to philosophy journals.

SIDELIGHTS: Lawrence Brian Lombard told *CA:* "My book, *Events,* presents a theory about events that construes them to be particulars; it embodies an attempt to take seriously the idea that events are the changes that objects undergo when they change. The theory is about what events really are, when they are identical, what properties they have essentially, and what relations they bear to entities of other kinds.

"In addition, the book contains an account of what philosophers are up to when they provide reasons for thinking that objects belonging to metaphysically interesting kinds exist. It also gives an account of the role of criteria of identity in such reasons (for example, distinct physical objects cannot be in the same place at the same time) and an account of what criteria of identity must be like in order to play such a role. The book also contains a discussion of some of the principal competing theories of events."

* * *

LOPATIN, Judy 1954-

PERSONAL: Surname is pronounced "Lo-*pay*-tin"; born October 5, 1954, in Detroit, Mich.; daughter of Irving (an architect) and Dorothy (a clinical social worker; maiden name, Simon) Lopatin. *Education:* University of Michigan, A.B., 1976; Columbia University, M.F.A., 1979.

ADDRESSES: Home—601 West 110th St., New York, N.Y. 10025. *Office*—Fiction Collective, Department of English, Brooklyn College of the City University of New York, Brooklyn, N.Y. 11210. *Agent*—Alison Bond Literary Agency, 171 West 79th St., New York, N.Y. 10024.

CAREER: Free-lance editor, 1979—. Editorial associate of Foundation Center, New York, N.Y., 1981-83.

MEMBER: Editorial Freelancers Association, Associated Writing Programs, Fiction Collective (member of editorial board, 1987), Authors Guild, Phi Beta Kappa.

WRITINGS:

Modern Romances (stories), Fiction Collective, 1986.

Contributor of stories to magazines, including *Benzene, Diana's Almanac, Mississippi Review, Shiny International,* and *Zone,* and newspapers.

WORK IN PROGRESS: Public Kissing, a collection of stories.

SIDELIGHTS: Judy Lopatin's first collection of short stories, according to James Marcus of the *New York Times Book Review,* "trains a quirky, agile intelligence on the New York-Paris axis, locating romance in hospitals, opium dens, law firms, movie theaters." The selections represent a variety of genres, ranging from the detective-fiction style of "The Real Life of Viviane Romance" to the pulp-romance overtones of "Trixie Taylor, Hospital Nurse." In a *Village Voice* review, Margo Mifflin reported: "Lopatin spins tales of yearning, paranoia, psychic powers, dark pasts, and personal mythologies." Her female characters, the critic added, are imaginative and compelling, self-sufficient and refreshing. Concluded Mifflin, "Her writing is rich in detail, bursting with thought, and spattered with fascinating cult trivia."

BIOGRAPHICAL/CRITICAL SOURCES:

PERIODICALS

New York Times Book Review, November 16, 1986.
Village Voice, November 18, 1986.

* * *

LOPEZ-REY (y ARROJO), Manuel 1902-1987

OBITUARY NOTICE—See index for *CA* sketch: Born September 30, 1902, in Madrid, Spain; died in 1987. Criminologist, lawyer, educator, editor, and author. Lopez-Rey won international recognition for his expertise in criminal law and criminology. For nearly two decades he worked for the United Nations in the fields of crime prevention, criminal justice, and penology. Earlier in his career Lopez-Rey was a county judge and director general of prisons in Spain as well as a professor of criminal law at universities in Spain, Bolivia, Chile, Argentina, and Peru. A prolific author, he wrote and edited many books, including *Crime: An Analytical Appraisal, Youth and Crime in Contemporary and Future Society, General Overview of Capital Punishment as a Legal Sanction, Criminal Justice and Criminology: An Inventory,* and *Guide to United Nations Criminal Policy.* Lopez-Rey also contributed more than one hundred articles to university and government publications and to criminology and sociology journals.

OBITUARIES AND OTHER SOURCES:

BOOKS

Who's Who in the World, 8th edition, Marquis, 1986.

PERIODICALS

Times (London), December 17, 1987.

* * *

LORENZ, Lee (Sharp) 1932-

BRIEF ENTRY: Born October 17, 1932, in Hackensack, N.J. American musician, commercial artist, illustrator, animator, cartoonist, editor, and author. Known primarily for his witty and sophisticated cartoons, *New Yorker* staff cartoonist and art editor Lee Lorenz also writes and illustrates children's books. Two stories are based on Geoffrey Chaucer's *Canterbury Tales*—"The Reeve's Tale" became *Scornful Simkin* (Prentice-Hall, 1980) and "The Miller's Tale" became *Pinchpenny John* (Prentice-Hall, 1981). Lorenz received a New Jersey Authors Award in 1983 for an original work for children, *Hugo and the Space Dog* (Prentice-Hall, 1983). He also wrote and illustrated adult books such as *Here It Comes: A Collection of Cartoons* (Bobbs-Merrill, 1968), *Now Look What You've Done* (Pantheon, 1977), and *Real Dogs Don't Eat Leftovers: A Guide to All That Is Truly Canine* (Long Shadow Books, 1983), a spin-off on the best-selling *Real Men Don't Eat Quiche: A Guidebook to All That Is Truly Masculine* (Pocket Books, 1982), which he illustrated for author Bruce Feirstein. Lorenz is also a professional coronetist. *Addresses: Home*—P.O. Box 131, Easton, Conn. 06612. *Office*—c/o *New Yorker,* New York, N.Y. 10036.

BIOGRAPHICAL/CRITICAL SOURCES:

BOOKS

World Encyclopedia of Cartoons, Chelsea House, 1980.

PERIODICALS

Christian Science Monitor, November 29, 1968.
New York Times Book Review, June 20, 1982, May 29, 1983, July 14, 1985.
Publisher's Weekly, October 3, 1980, April 3, 1981, November 6, 1981, April 2, 1982, May 7, 1982, January 21, 1983, September 2, 1983.

* * *

LOTTIE
See GRIMKE, Charlotte L(ottie) Forten

* * *

LOVETT, A(lbert) W(inston) 1944-

PERSONAL: Born December 16, 1944, in Abingdon, England; son of Edward (an insurance agent) and Agustina (Castroverde) Lovett. *Education:* Cambridge University, B.A., 1965, Ph.D., 1969. *Politics:* Social Democrat "Owenite." *Religion:* Deist.

ADDRESSES: Home—26 Coney Hill Rd., West Wickham, Kent BR4 9BX, England. *Office*—Department of History, University College, Dublin-4, Ireland.

CAREER: University of Newcastle upon Tyne, Newcastle upon Tyne, England, Sir James Knott Research Fellow, 1969-70; University College, Dublin, Ireland, assistant lecturer, 1970-76, college lecturer, 1976-87, reader, 1987—.

MEMBER: Royal Historical Society (fellow).

WRITINGS:

Philip II and Mateo Vazquez de Leca: The Government of Spain, 1572-1592, Droz (Geneva), 1977.
Europe, 1453-1610, Educational Company of Ireland Ltd., 1979.
Early Habsburg Spain, 1517-1598, Oxford University Press, 1986.

WORK IN PROGRESS: Research on the economic and monetary history of early modern Europe, 1450-1750.

SIDELIGHTS: A. W. Lovett told *CA:* "I was drawn to the writing of European history because I regard the continent as forming a single whole in spite of any political divisions. This unity stretches back to the Roman Empire and has persisted throughout the last two thousand years. This cultural integrity may reappear once again in a political form should the European Common Market result in the amalgamation of the European states that have signed the Treaty of Rome. I am a committed European; and to that extent I write a partisan version of history.

"In terms of my commitment to history as a discipline, I think that history has lost its way as a popular subject. Professional historians have sought ever remoter areas of historical experience in which to carry out their research. This search for novelty may be explained by the difficulties of promotion in a shrinking profession. Unfortunately, it leads directly to irrelevance and a justified indifference on the part of the general public. Professional historians have also abandoned the art of clarity in their writing. Instead, each subdivision within the discipline has evolved a jargon of its own, understandable only to a small group of initiates. This too has alienated the general reader. Unless those who practice history restore elegance and style to their rightful place as among the most important qualities to be cultivated by the professional, then history as a major subject is doomed to a terminal decline."

BIOGRAPHICAL/CRITICAL SOURCES:

PERIODICALS

*Times Literary Supplement,*March 13, 1987.

* * *

LOVOOS, Janice
See GARBUTT, Janice (D.) Lovoos

* * *

LOWER, Arthur R(eginald) M(arsden) 1889-1988

OBITUARY NOTICE—See index for *CA* sketch: Born August 12, 1889, in Barrie, Ontario, Canada; died January 7, 1988. Historian, educator, and author. Lower was an award-winning chronicler of Canadian history and a popular teacher at Canadian universities. His best known work, *From Colony to Nation: A History of Canada,* won the 1947 Governor-General's Literary Award and is considered a standard college reference text. Other books by Lower include *This Most Famous Stream: The Liberal Democratic Way of Life, Canadians in the Making: A Social History of Canada, History and Myth, A Pattern for History,* and two autobiographical works, *Unconventional Voyages* and *My First Seventy-five Years.* Lower also contributed articles and essays to books and periodicals in Canada and the United States.

OBITUARIES AND OTHER SOURCES:

BOOKS

The Canadian Who's Who, Volume XXII, University of Toronto Press, 1987.

PERIODICALS

Times (London), January 11, 1988.

* * *

LUBER, Philip 1948-

PERSONAL: Born February 9, 1948, in Philadelphia, Pa.; son of Bernard Jay and Ruth (Rudolph) Luber; married Cynthia Mate, June 18, 1977. *Education:* Tufts University, B.S., 1970; Temple University, M.A., 1977; University of Texas at Austin, Ph.D., 1981.

ADDRESSES: Agent—Alice Fried Martell, Martell Agency, 555 Fifth Ave., New York, N.Y. 10017.

CAREER: McLean Hospital, Belmont, Mass., psychologist, 1980-86; writer, 1986—.

MEMBER: Authors Guild, Mystery Writers of America.

WRITINGS:

Deadly Convictions, Warner Books, 1986.

* * *

LUISADA, Aldo A(ugusto) 1901-1987

OBITUARY NOTICE: Born June 26, 1901, in Florence, Italy; immigrated to United States, 1939; naturalized U.S. citizen, 1944; died November 20, 1987, in Chicago, Ill. Physician, scientist, educator, editor, and author. Luisada earned his medical degree in 1924 and during the 1930s taught at Royal University in Ferrara, Italy, where he was a full professor. Luisada later taught at Tufts University medical school where he also pursued a research career conducting studies on heart disease. In 1949 Luisada accepted simultaneous positions at Chicago Medical School as a teaching professor and at Chicago's Mt. Sinai Hospital as chairman of cardiovascular medicine. In 1971 Luisada was appointed distinguished professor of physiology and medicine at Chicago Medical School and from 1971 until 1983 he also served as the director of Oak Forest Hospital's cardiology department. Luisada was best known for his heart transplant research and for studies in reducing strain on cardiac patients. His work in cardiology eventually earned him a Morris Parker Award for research. Luisada also contributed over four hundred articles to professional and medical journals, served as editor in chief of *Cardiology,* and wrote several books, including *Hypotension, Pulmonary Edema, Sounds of the Diseased Heart,* and *The Heart Sounds.*

OBITUARIES AND OTHER SOURCES:

BOOKS

American Men and Women of Science: The Physical and Biological Sciences, 16th edition, Bowker, 1986.
Who's Who in America, 44th edition, Marquis, 1986.

PERIODICALS

Chicago Tribune, November 28, 1987.

* * *

LYLE, Albert Walter 1944-
(Sparky Lyle)

PERSONAL: Born July 22, 1944, in Du Bois, Pa.; son of Albert (a house remodeling contractor) and Margaret (a housewife; maiden name, Overturf) Lyle; married Judy Ann Fusco in 1967 (divorced April, 1977); married Mary Fontaine Massey (a stewardess), April 29, 1977; children: (first marriage) Dane, Shane; (second marriage) Scott Garrett. *Education:* Attended public schools in Reynoldsville, Pa. *Religion:* Protestant.

ADDRESSES: Home—17 Signal Hill Dr., Voorhees, N.J. 08043. *Office*—c/o Miller Brewing, 3939 West Highland Blvd., Milwaukee, Wis. 53201.

CAREER: Pitcher for various minor league baseball teams in Bluefield, W.Va., Fox Cities, Wis., Winston-Salem, N.C., Pittsfield, Mass., and Toronto, Ontario, 1964-67; Boston Red Sox, Boston, Mass, pitcher, 1967-72; New York Yankees, New York, N.Y., relief pitcher, 1972-78; Texas Rangers, Arlington, relief pitcher, 1979-80; Philadelphia Phillies, Philadelphia, Pa., relief pitcher, 1980-82. Appeared in radio and television commercials.

MEMBER: Screen Actors Guild, Major League Baseball Players Association, Elks Club.

AWARDS, HONORS: Cy Young Award from the Baseball Writers Association of America, 1977.

WRITINGS:

(Under name Sparky Lyle; with Peter Golenbock) *The Bronx Zoo,* Crown, 1979.

SIDELIGHTS: Albert Walter Lyle, known as "Sparky" Lyle to myriads of sports fans, became the first relief pitcher in the American League to win baseball's coveted Cy Young Award in 1977. That year, with his fastball and devastating slider, the left-hander was indispensable to the New York Yankees in taking the Eastern division title, the American League pennant, and the world championship. His book about life with the New York Yankees, *The Bronx Zoo,* became a best-seller.

Lyle was initially signed to play professional baseball by the Baltimore Orioles and pitched for two of their minor league farm clubs until 1965, when he was drafted by the Boston Red Sox. Again he pitched for some minor league affiliates, but was called up to the majors in the middle of the 1967 season. Lyle appeared in twenty-three games for the Red Sox and boasted a 2.30 earned run average (ERA), helping the team to the American League pennant. Because of a strained ligament in his pitching arm, however, Lyle was unable to participate in the 1967 World Series; the Red Sox were beaten by the St. Louis Cardinals. Lyle played four more seasons with the Red Sox, but Ralph Houk, then manager of the New York Yankees, had his eye on the young reliever. Houk was impressed by Lyle's ability to best both right- and left-handed batters, and by his self-confidence. Houk and the Yankees finally managed to acquire Lyle for the 1972 season when the Red Sox traded him for Danny Cater, a sorely needed first baseman.

In a seven-year stint that was highlighted by the Yankee's 1977 world championship and his winning the Cy Young Award, Lyle gave many great performances on the mound. He was happy there, having revered Yankee Stadium as a child. The pitching ace confessed to Carol Kleiman in the *Chicago Tribune,* "I loved that pinstriped [Yankee] uniform. Something about that uniform does make you play better. Something about that stadium." And play better he did, achieving a record-setting thirty-five saves in 1972, and a miniscule ERA of 1.66 in 1974—his career bests in each category. In 1977, during regular season play, Lyle made a record-breaking seventy-two appearances on the mound, came up with twenty-six saves, and led the American League with an ERA of 2.17—a figure which would have been an even more impressive 1.79 except for one bad game against the Boston Red Sox in which he allowed his opponents six runs in one and one-third innings.

His 1977 post-season record was also superb. Accustomed to the pressures of coming in to pitch in game-threatening situations, Lyle performed his relief duties in four of the five playoff games against the Kansas City Royals, winning the crucial last two. In the first game of the World Series, Lyle gave up a hit to one of the Los Angeles Dodgers that tied the game in the ninth inning, but then proceeded to mow down eleven Dodgers in a row. The Yankees, who hung on to win the game, eventually won the series by a margin of four games to two.

But even though his ace reliever won the Cy Young Award, Yankees owner George Steinbrenner felt he needed more of the same and signed up-and-coming relief pitchers Richard "Goose" Gossage and Rawly Eastwick. Lyle feared he would not see enough action in this situation to stay in good pitching form. His apprehensions proved valid, and at his own request he was traded to the Texas Rangers after the 1978 baseball season. Lyle later joined the Philadelphia Phillies in 1980.

In addition to allowing Lyle a backdrop for his pitching prowess, the New York Yankees provided him with the material for his bestseller, *The Bronx Zoo.* The book chronicles the author's experience with the Yankees, focusing on the 1977 championship season. Depicted on its pages are some of the quirky personalities who populated the New York ball club in the late seventies—Steinbrenner, super-star slugger Reggie Jackson, fiery-tempered ex-manager Billy Martin, and others. Lyle relates the times outfielder Lou Piniella used his bat on water coolers and light bulbs after striking out, among other anecdotes. As Phil Berger reported in the *New York Times Book Review,* "Lyle's account . . . is barbed, vulgar, and frequently funny." Except for a few of what he considered flaws, such as the left-hander's tendency to stress "the inadequacy of his six-figure salary," Berger found *The Bronx Zoo* "a lively entertainment."

In creating *The Bronx Zoo,* Lyle worked closely with his co-author, Peter Golenbock. The two men spent two or three afternoons a week together, with Golenbock asking questions and taping Lyle's answers. Lyle found the entire writing process difficult and troublesome. He was initially supposed to talk into a tape recorder unassisted, but, as the pitcher confessed to Judy Klemesrud in the *New York Times Book Review,* he "got mike-fright." Lyle also confided to Klemesrud that he "waited until the very last day to read the galleys, and [he] only read them because [he] had to." He summed up the total experience of being a best-selling author—including having to promote his book—to Kleiman thus: "It was awful." Lyle further explained that he did not like to "mess around with anything that interferes with playing baseball."

AVOCATIONAL INTERESTS: Astronomy, photography, history, collecting old canes, listening to jazz.

BIOGRAPHICAL/CRITICAL SOURCES:

BOOKS

Lyle, Sparky, and Peter Golenbock, *The Bronx Zoo,* Crown, 1979.

PERIODICALS

Chicago Tribune, August 21, 1979.
New York Times Book Review, April 29, 1979, May 13, 1979.
Village Voice, April 16, 1979.

—*Sketch by Elizabeth Thomas*

* * *

LYLE, Sparky
See LYLE, Albert Walter

* * *

LYNCH, David 1946-

BRIEF ENTRY: Born January 20, 1946, in Missoula, Mont. American film producer, director, and screenwriter. Regarded by many in the film business as a gifted artist, David Lynch directed and wrote (or co-authored) all of his films. He first gained attention in 1978 with "Eraserhead," a nightmarish

vision of America's industrial wasteland. It subsequently became a cult classic. In 1980 he received not only critical acclaim but two Oscar nominations for best director and best screenwriter for "The Elephant Man," based on the popular Broadway play. Lynch then adapted Frank Herbert's best-selling science fiction novel, *Dune,* to the screen. Released in 1984, the film "Dune" received mixed reviews and fared poorly at the box office. But Lynch's next effort, the 1986 film "Blue Velvet," was a financial success. A surreal blend of murder mystery, melodramatic romance, and comedy spiced with sexual naivete and kinkiness, the controversial film earned him another Oscar nomination for best director. While a fellow at the American Film Institute in Los Angeles in 1970, Lynch also made a thirty-four-minute, 16-mm color film entitled "The Grandmother." *Addresses: Office*—c/o De Laurentiis Entertainment, 720 Fifth Ave., New York, N.Y. 10019. *Agent*—c/o Rick Nicita, Creative Artists Agency, 1888 Century Park E., Los Angeles, Calif. 90067.

BIOGRAPHICAL/CRITICAL SOURCES:

BOOKS

Current Biography, H. W. Wilson, 1987.
Magill's Survey of Cinema, Volume II, Salem, 1981.

PERIODICALS

Los Angeles Times, December 14, 1984, September 19, 1986, September 23, 1986, September 26, 1986.
New York Times, May 1, 1979, May 28, 1984, November 16, 1984, December 14, 1984, September 19, 1986, October 11, 1986.
Rolling Stone, November 13, 1980, December 6, 1984.

*　　*　　*

LYNGSETH, Joan
See DAVIES, Joan

M

MABBOTT, John David 1898-1988

OBITUARY NOTICE—See index for *CA* sketch: Born November 18, 1898, in Duns, Scotland; died January 26, 1988. Educator and author. Mabbott, who was a fellow and lecturer in philosophy at Oxford University's St. John's College from 1924 to 1963, served as its president from 1963 to 1969. He wrote *The State and the Citizen, An Introduction to Ethics,* and *John Locke* and contributed to philosophical periodicals.

OBITUARIES AND OTHER SOURCES:

BOOKS

Who's Who, 139th edition, St. Martin's, 1987.

PERIODICALS

Times (London), January 28, 1988.

* * *

MacBRIDE, Sean 1904-1988

OBITUARY NOTICE: Born January 26, 1904, in Paris, France; died of pneumonia, January 15, 1988, in Dublin, Ireland. Lawyer, politician, statesman, social activist, journalist, and author. An Irish revolutionary, MacBride nevertheless won both the Nobel Peace Prize in 1974 and the Lenin Peace Prize in 1977 for his crusading efforts for nuclear disarmament and human rights. As a teenager MacBride joined the Irish Republican Army (IRA), an underground organization formed to drive the British out of Northern Ireland and thus unite the island into a single nation. At the age of twenty-four he became the IRA's chief of staff. During his tenure with the revolutionary movement, MacBride worked as a journalist and earned a law degree from National University in Dublin. In 1937 he joined the Irish bar and resigned from the IRA. MacBride went on to become a dedicated human rights advocate and one of Dublin's most successful trial lawyers. Though strongly opposed to the IRA's escalating campaign of violence, he often defended IRA suspects to expose the harsh conditions they endured in Irish jails.

MacBride continued the battle for human rights throughout his life, helping to found Amnesty International, the human rights monitoring organization. He also chaired the International Peace Bureau based in Geneva, Switzerland, devoting himself to worldwide nuclear disarmament, and was secretary general of the International Commission of Jurists from 1963 to 1970. MacBride served as the Irish foreign minister from 1948 to 1951 and as an Assistant Secretary General of the United Nations and United Nations Commissioner for Namibia from 1973 to 1976. MacBride wrote *Our People—Our Money* and *A Message to the Irish People*.

OBITUARIES AND OTHER SOURCES:

BOOKS

Current Biography, H. W. Wilson, 1949.
Who's Who, 140th edition, St. Martin's, 1988.

PERIODICALS

Chicago Tribune, January 16, 1988.
Los Angeles Times, January 16, 1988.
New York Times, January 16, 1988.
Washington Post, January 16, 1988.

* * *

MacEWEN, Gwendolyn (Margaret) 1941-1987

OBITUARY NOTICE—See index for *CA* sketch: Born September 1, 1941, in Toronto, Ontario, Canada; died November 30, 1987, in Toronto, Ontario, Canada. Educator, poet, and author. MacEwen, who was writer in residence at the University of Western Ontario and at the University of Toronto during the 1980s, was best known for her poetry. Collections of her poems include *Selah, The Shadow-Maker, The Armies of the Moon, The Fire-Eaters, Afterworlds,* and *Dragon Sandwiches,* a volume of poetry for children. MacEwen also wrote *King of Egypt, King of Dreams: A Novel, Noman's Land: Stories,* several documentaries, verse dramas, and radio plays. She was a translator of Greek poetry and a contributor to numerous anthologies and literary magazines.

OBITUARIES AND OTHER SOURCES:

PERIODICALS

Times (London), December 3, 1987.

MACKEY, William Wellington 1937-

PERSONAL: Born May 28, 1937, in Miami, Fla.; son of Milton and Doris Louise (Baso) Mackey. *Education:* Southern University (now Southern University and Agricultural and Mechanical College System), B.A., 1959; University of Minnesota, M.Ed., 1964.

CAREER: Playwright. Worked variously as a high school teacher, physical therapist, waiter, and bellhop; writer-in-residence at La Mama Experimental Theatre Club, New York, N.Y., 1971-72, and at Clark Center, New York City, 1973; visiting professor and writer-in-residence at Southern University (now Southern University and Agricultural and Mechanical College System), Baton Rouge, La., 1972.

AWARDS, HONORS: Rockefeller Foundation Playwright's Grant, 1972, to begin work on play "Love Me, Love Me, Daddy, or I Swear I'm Gonna Kill You."

WRITINGS:

PLAYS

Behold! Cometh the Vanderkellans! (three-act; first produced in Denver at Eden Theatrical Workshop, November 12, 1965; produced Off-Broadway at Theatre De Lys, March 31, 1971), Azazel Books, 1966.

"A Requiem for Brother X," first produced in Chicago at Chicago Hull House Parkway Theatre, 1968; produced Off-Off Broadway at Players Workshop, January 5, 1973.

"Billy Noname," first produced Off-Broadway at Truck and Warehouse Theatre, March 2, 1970.

"Family Meeting," first produced Off-Broadway at La Mama Experimental Theatre Club, January 28, 1972.

"Saga" (five-act musical), first produced in Miami at Cultural Arts Center of the Model Cities Program, 1976.

"Love Me, Love Me, Daddy, or I Swear I'm Gonna Kill You," first produced in New York City at American Folk Theatre, 1982.

Also author of "Death of Charlie Blackman" and "Homeboys." Work represented in anthologies, including *New Black Playwrights,* edited by William Couch, Jr., Avon, 1970, and *Black Drama Anthology,* edited by Woodie King and Ron Milner, New American Library, 1972.

SIDELIGHTS: Playwright William Wellington Mackey has won acclaim for his ability to portray, within the turmoil of a single representative family, the political struggles of the black people in America. Mackey's first production, "Behold! Cometh the Vanderkellans!" equates the disintegration of a well-established black family with the social upheaval in 1960s America, when racial perspectives were changing radically. The drama takes place during a family reunion in the fine home of the president of a prestigious southern black college. One by one, family members expose one another's vices and their own previously hidden fears and prejudices, causing their hypocritical family structure to break down. "The children are revealed as a whore, a homosexual, and an Uncle Tom; the parents' marriage is a sham," recounted critic Michele Gerrig in *Show Business*. In addition, Gerrig continued, "as the conflicts within the home are heightened, they are paralleled by student unrest and rioting outside," demonstrating the exposure of vices and prejudices in the American community. In his "unsettling" and "tense drama," Gerrig ventured, "William Wellington Mackey shows us, in microcosm, the agony of a race in transition."

In "Family Meeting," which was first produced Off-Broadway in 1972, Mackey again portrays radical social transformations of values in the breakdown of a black middle-class family. The dialogue in "Family Meeting" is more surrealistic than in "Behold!" however, and is carried principally by the young male protagonist. In a violent monologue the young man questions traditional beliefs and opinions about his race, delving into perplexing areas such as madness and death, portrayed by his white self and black self. The boy's personal confusion, according to reviewers, represents the turmoil that results from white values being forced upon black people.

"A Requiem for Brother X" was inspired by the sudden death in 1965 of black American religious and political leader Malcolm X. As in his other plays, Mackey examines the black community by focusing on a family gathering, but this time the characters are ghetto residents. While in "Behold!" and "Family Meeting" Mackey portrays the black middle-class members as destroying themselves with their own hypocrisy and greed, in "Requiem" he shows the poorer blacks as being trapped and ruined by external forces.

BIOGRAPHICAL/CRITICAL SOURCES:

BOOKS

Dictionary of Literary Biography, Volume 38: *Afro-American Writers After 1955: Dramatists and Prose Writers,* Gale, 1985.

PERIODICALS

Black World, April, 1975.
Negro Digest, April, 1967.
Show Business, April 8, 1971.
Variety, April 21, 1971.*

* * *

MACKINTOSH, N(icholas) J(ohn) 1935-

PERSONAL: Born July 9, 1935, in London, England; son of Ian and Daphne (Cochrane) Mackintosh; married Janet Ann Scott, July 16, 1960 (divorced); married Bundy Wilson, September 23, 1978; children: (first marriage) Alasdair, Lucy; (second marriage) Duncan, Douglas. *Education:* Magdalen College, Oxford, B.A., 1960, M.A., 1963, D.Phil., 1963.

ADDRESSES: Office—Department of Experimental Psychology, Cambridge University, Downing St., Cambridge CB2 3EB, England.

CAREER: Oxford University, Oxford, England, lecturer in psychology, 1965-67, research fellow of Lincoln College, 1966-67; Dalhousie University, Halifax, Nova Scotia, research professor of psychology, 1967-73; University of Sussex, Sussex, England, professor of psychology, 1973-81; Cambridge University, Cambridge, England, professor of experimental psychology and professorial fellow of King's College, 1981—. Visiting professor at University of Pennsylvania, 1965-66, University of Hawaii, 1972-73, and Bryn Mawr College, 1977.

MEMBER: Royal Society (fellow), British Psychological Society, Experimental Psychology Society.

WRITINGS:

(Editor with W. K. Honig) *Fundamental Issues in Associative Learning,* Dalhousie University Press, 1969.

(With N. S. Sutherland) *Mechanisms of Animal Discrimination Learning,* Academic Press, 1971.

The Psychology of Animal Learning, Academic Press, 1974.
Conditioning and Associative Learning, Oxford University Press, 1983.

Contributor to psychology journals; book reviewer for periodicals. Editor of *Quarterly Journal of Experimental Psychology,* 1977-87.

WORK IN PROGRESS: Intelligence and Intelligence Testing.

* * *

MACKINTOSH, Prudence 1944-

PERSONAL: Born September 25, 1944, in Texarkana, Tex.; daughter of John Quincy (a newspaper editor) and Ruth (a newspaper reporter and women's editor; maiden name, Burgadine) Mahaffey; married John A. Mackintosh (an attorney), June 6, 1966; children: Jack, Drew, William. *Education:* University of Texas at Austin, B.A., 1966. *Religion:* Episcopalian.

ADDRESSES: Home and office—3312 Beverly, Dallas, Tex. 75205. *Agent*—Wendy Weil, 747 Third Avenue, New York, N.Y. 10017.

CAREER: Junior high school English teacher in Austin, Tex., 1966-69; Hockaday School, Dallas, Tex., English teacher, 1969-70; writer, 1972—. Member of board of directors of Friends of the Dallas Public Library; member of advisory council of St. Philip's Episcopal School.

MEMBER: Authors Guild, Texas Institute of Letters, Charter 100 Club.

AWARDS, HONORS: Penney-Missouri Award from the University of Missouri School of Journalism, 1976, for article "Tube or Not Tube"; Allman fellow at Hockaday School, 1987; Outstanding Young Alumni Award from the University of Texas, 1981.

WRITINGS:

Thundering Sneakers (nonfiction), Doubleday, 1981.
Retreads (nonfiction), Doubleday, 1985.

Contributing editor of *Texas Monthly.*

WORK IN PROGRESS: Several magazine pieces.

SIDELIGHTS: Prudence Mackintosh told *CA:* "No one would recommend the newsroom of a daily newspaper as an ideal day care center, but since both of my parents worked for the *Texarkana Gazette and Daily News,* I spent my after-school hours amid the half-empty coffee cups, cigarette butts, chewed pencils, and general grime indigenous to newspaper offices in the 1940s and 1950s. I counted my daddy's reporters, who had neither the time nor the inclination to alter their conversations because a child was present, as my best friends. I fetched Eskimo pies for them and drank cokes on their coffee breaks at the old Grim Hotel across the street from the *Gazette* offices. I heard language I should never have heard, giggled at jokes I didn't understand, learned to recognize proofreading symbols and sons of bitches, pored over musty newspapers to read about the war I'd missed, drew pictures with big, black pencils on newsprint, and took junior high school sports scores over the telephone. Everything of interest in a small, east Texas town came through the doors of that newsroom. I met entertainers, every campaigning American president from Harry S. Truman through John F. Kennedy, inventors, preachers, crackpots, and clubwomen. Undoubtedly I complained, as all children do, that I was bored.

"In addition to being surrounded from birth by people who considered writing a basic motor skill, I logged an enormous number of hours at the First Baptist Church, which was also just a block from the *Gazette* offices. Aside from the spiritual benefits and the 'blood-washed' hymns I experienced, the Southern Baptists saw to it that I memorized huge amounts of the King James Bible. No one who writes can regret having majestic cadences like 'Blessed is the man who walketh not in the counsel of the ungodly. . .' indelibly imprinted on his brain at an early age.

"Perhaps my strongest motivation to write came from the fact that my family has never been comfortable with long-distance telephoning. We are letter writers. Early on I learned to validate life by putting it on paper for someone else. I still feel that I haven't entirely lived something until I've written about it. The living and the writing are enhanced in the process."

BIOGRAPHICAL/CRITICAL SOURCES:

PERIODICALS

Houston Post, February 15, 1981.

* * *

MacLAREN, Sherrill M. 1939-

PERSONAL: Born February 5, 1939, in Winnipeg, Manitoba, Canada; daughter of Ockie (an artist) and Maxwell (a writer; maiden name, Dennistoun) McBean; married Woody MacLaren (in business), May 17, 1962; children: Nicole, Michelle, Douglas, Monique. *Education:* University of British Columbia, R.N., 1956, B.Sc.N., 1962. *Politics:* "Capitalist." *Religion:* Anglican.

ADDRESSES: Home and office—Vancouver, British Columbia, Canada. *Agent*—Colbert Agency, 303 Davenport Rd., Toronto, Ontario, Canada M5R 1K5.

CAREER: Vancouver General Hospital, Vancouver, British Columbia, registered nurse, 1961; homemaker, 1962-77; writer, 1977—. Director of Brentwood College School.

WRITINGS:

Braehead: Three Founding Families in Nineteenth-Century Canada (nonfiction historical saga), McClelland & Stewart, 1986.
Canadian Women in Power, Seal Brooks, in press.

Writer for CBC-Radio, 1977-82. Contributor to magazines, including *Reader's Digest, Skyword,* and *Westworld.*

SIDELIGHTS: Sherrill M. MacLaren told *CA:* "I began writing in 1977 from the perspective of a former nurse. My concerns stemmed from the explosion of medical technology and the related questions about quality of life, informed consent, and the right to die—that is, the field of bioethics. From there I branched into areas of broader interest, for instance, scuba diving and the need for marine parks. My inspiration for *Braehead,* a true saga of six generations in Canada and Wyoming, was the opportunity to encapsulate one hundred years of documented history into a personal story for a broad readership."

BIOGRAPHICAL/CRITICAL SOURCES:

PERIODICALS

Maclean's, June 30, 1986.

MAIS, Roger 1905-1955

PERSONAL: Born August 11, 1905, in Kingston, Jamaica; died of cancer, June 21, 1955, in Kingston, Jamaica. *Education:* Attended public schools in the Blue Mountains, Jamaica.

CAREER: Writer. Worked variously as a civil servant, painter, farmer, photographer, and journalist for the *Daily Gleaner* and *Public Opinion*.

WRITINGS:

And Most of All Man (short stories and verse), City Printery (Kingston, Jamaica), 1939.

Face and Other Stories (short stories and verse), Universal Printery, 1942.

"The Potter's Field" (play), first published in *Public Opinion*, December 23, 1950.

Atalanta at Calydon (play), J. Cape, 1950.

Come Love, Come Death, Hutchinson, 1951.

The Hills Were Joyful Together, J. Cape, 1953, reprinted, with introduction by Daphne Morris, Heinemann, 1981 (also see below).

(And illustrator) *Brother Man,* J. Cape, 1954, reprinted, with introduction by Edward Brathwaite, Heinemann, 1974 (also see below).

Black Lightning, J. Cape, 1955, reprinted, with introduction by Jean D'Costa, Heinemann, 1983 (also see below).

The Three Novels of Roger Mais (contains *The Hills Were Joyful Together, Brother Man,* and *Black Lightning*), introduction by Norman W. Manley, J. Cape, 1966 (also see above).

Listen, The Wind, and Other Stories, Longman, c. 1986.

Also author of other plays, such as "Hurricane," "Masks and Paper Hats," and "The First Sacrifice."

WORK IN PROGRESS: A fourth novel.

SIDELIGHTS: Roger Mais, "the spokesman of emergent Jamaica," according to Jean D'Costa in her 1978 critique on Mais, is known primarily for his three novels of social protest. Among the first Jamaican novels to realistically examine that country's squalid urban conditions, *The Hills Were Joyful Together, Brother Man,* and *Black Lightning* greatly influenced the development of West Indian literature. Despite his middle-class upbringing in Jamaica's Blue Mountains, Mais empathized with the less fortunate urban slum dwellers and, as a writer, remained "fiercely dedicated to the exposure of social ills in [mid-twentieth-century] Jamaica," wrote D'Costa.

Of the three novels, *The Hills* provides the most explicit portrait of Caribbean slum life. Set in a ghetto in Kingston, Jamaica, *The Hills* examines the lives of three groups of black lower-class people. "Violence and misery is their common lot," observed reviewer Karina Williamson in the *Journal of Commonwealth Literature*. *The Hills*'s subject matter disturbed many members of Jamaican society, according to Jean Creary, who explained in *The Islands in Between* that Mais's readers were "thrown straight into a world everyone in Jamaica knew existed, and yet which the middle classes were united in a conspiracy of silence to ignore and reject." She found, however, that "within and behind this human underworld lies beauty and pattern." In one particularly acclaimed passage, Williamson wrote, Mais describes the ghetto community's "common capacity for gaiety and goodwill" during a beach celebration. In other instances he depicts sympathy and loyalty between characters despite their misfortunes, indicating that personal integrity can withstand even the most hostile environment. "Mais's attitude . . . is ultimately neither cynical nor defeatist," Williamson explained, asserting that it is the author's balanced perspective that accounts for the novel's literary merit. "The book has its grave weaknesses," Creary admitted, citing wordiness and melodrama, but it succeeds because the author's "weaknesses come from the same source where lies his strength—from his innocent and yet potent awareness of himself and of his environment."

Mais's second novel, *Brother Man,* focuses on Rastafarianism, a Caribbean religious movement in which members seek a return of blacks to Africa. For some of their rituals, which include smoking marijuana—though shunning alcohol—and refusing to cut their hair, Rastafarians were "feared, despised, and rejected" during the 1940s and 1950s, explained Edward Brathwaite in his 1974 introduction to Mais's novel. The protagonist of *Brother Man* is a peaceful Rastafarian leader named John Power or "Bra Man," whose life resembles that of Jesus Christ. "In many ways," wrote Oscar R. Dathorne in *Studies in the Novel,* "the parallel between Christ and Bra Man is followed almost too carefully." Most critics agreed that the novel's credibility weakens whenever Bra Man becomes too Christ-like, healing the sick and teaching in parables, for example. Dathorne added, however, that "in spite of all this, Bra Man is convincing, not only as a messianic Christ-figure but as a person."

Reviewers praised Mais's refinement in *Brother Man* of a complex linguistic technique he had introduced in *The Hills*. Combining the figurative language of the King James Bible with the words and syntax of Jamaican Creole, Mais developed an elaborate writing style that enhanced his allegorical narratives. This style, according to Creary, is especially effective in descriptions of Bra Man, "Mais's vision of the reincarnate Christ. . . . This Gospel Presence fuses with Mais's writing in the rhythmical, Biblical prose." Dathorne agreed, explaining that "the language helps to identify Bra Man, and the rhythm of the Bible is reserved for him."

Black Lightning, Mais's third novel, is a biblical allegory like *Brother Man*. Unlike Mais's first two novels, however, *Black Lightning* skirts social issues, focusing instead on the solitary artist. Set in the Jamaican countryside, the novel follows the progress a sculptor, Jake, makes on a statue he is carving of the biblical hero Samson. "As it takes shape," Creary noted, "the figure of Samson becomes increasingly identified with Jake himself." Initially perceiving himself as strong and independent, the artist begins fashioning his work after his own self-image. After his wife leaves him, Jake becomes more aware of his dependence on her and begins molding his statue into the image of a weaker man. "The finished work Jake contemptuously reveals . . . is not Samson in his prime, but the blinded Samson, a figure of ruined strength leaning on a little boy," related Kenneth Ramchand in *The West Indian Novel and Its Background*. Like Samson, Jake is eventually blinded and, in despair, he kills himself.

Although Mais's first two novels received greater popular and critical acclaim upon their publication, Ramchand believes that the author's third book is his most powerful one. "The work has been virtually disregarded in the West Indies," the critic pointed out, "but I would like to contend that it is in *Black Lightning* that Mais's art and understanding are in greatest harmony, and that it is upon this . . . novel that his reputation must rest." Williamson also lauded *Black Lightning*'s artistic merit and its contribution to Caribbean literature: "*Black*

Lightning, more than either of Mais's other novels, seems to me a landmark in the development of the West Indian novel.''

A supporter of the Jamaican nationalist movement of the 1930s and 1940s, Mais was imprisoned in 1944 for an essay he wrote, titled ''Now We Know,'' attacking English colonialism. Already the author of two short story collections, *And Most of All Man* and *Face and Other Stories,* Mais began writing his first novel during his six months in prison. Published nine years later, *The Hills Were Joyful Together* was quickly followed by *Brother Man* and *Black Lightning*. The author traveled to Europe in 1951 in search of a more accommodating artistic climate, but he returned to his homeland three years later, suffering from cancer. He died in Kingston in 1955, the year his third novel was published, leaving a fourth novel incomplete.

BIOGRAPHICAL/CRITICAL SOURCES:

BOOKS

D'Costa, Jean, *Roger Mais: ''The Hills Were Joyful Together'' and ''Brother Man,''* Longman, 1978.
James, Louis, editor, *The Islands in Between: Essays on West Indian Literature,* Oxford University Press, 1968.
Mais, Roger, *Brother Man,* introduction by Edward Brathwaite, Heinemann, 1974.
Moore, Gerald, *The Chosen Tongue: English Writings in the Tropical World,* Harper, 1969.
Ramchand, Kenneth, *The West Indian Novel and Its Background,* Barnes & Noble, 1970.
Twentieth-Century Literary Criticism, Volume 8, Gale, 1982.

PERIODICALS

Black Images, summer, 1972.
Journal of Commonwealth Literature, December, 1966.
Studies in the Novel, summer, 1972.*

—*Sketch by Christa Brelin*

* * *

MAJKA, Linda C. 1947-

PERSONAL: Surname is pronounced ''*My*-kah''; born September 27, 1947, in Washington, D.C.; daughter of Basil L. (a budget officer) and Lillian (a housewife; maiden name, Adams) Cafeo; married Theo J. Majka (a college professor), March 30, 1970. *Education:* College of William and Mary, B.A., 1969; University of California, Santa Barbara, M.A., 1973, Ph.D., 1978.

ADDRESSES: Home—Dayton, Ohio. *Office*—Department of Sociology and Anthropology, University of Dayton, 300 College Park Ave., Dayton, Ohio 45469.

CAREER: Portland State University, Portland, Ore., assistant professor of sociology, 1975-80; University of Dayton, Dayton, Ohio, assistant professor, beginning in 1981, became associate professor of sociology. Visiting associate professor at Antioch College, 1987-88.

MEMBER: Sociologists for Women in Society, Society for the Study of Social Problems.

WRITINGS:

(With husband, Theo J. Majka) *Farm Workers, Agribusiness, and the State,* Temple University Press, 1983.
(Editor with Patricia Voydanoff, and contributor) *Families and Economic Distress,* Sage Publications, 1988.

Contributor of articles and reviews to sociology journals, including *Contemporary Sociology* and *Society.*

SIDELIGHTS: In their 1983 book, *Farm Workers, Agribusiness, and the State,* Linda C. Majka and her husband vividly describe the attempts of migratory farm workers to unionize and the violence oftentimes associated with their efforts. Concentrating on the history of labor relations in California and the role of the state government in controlling farm worker conflict and insurgency, the authors analyze the success and failure of various forms of government intervention, such as the California Agriculture Labor Relations Act (ALRA) that was passed in 1975 to mediate existing farm labor-capital opposition. *Farm Workers, Agribusiness, and the State* is a ''sophisticated social history and political sociology of agrarian class relations from the late 1800s to the present,'' wrote Frederick H. Buttel in *Contemporary Sociology*. Similarly, *Rural Sociology* reviewer Max. J. Pferrer assessed that the Majkas' book represents ''one of the most comprehensive treatments of agricultural labor history in California.''

BIOGRAPHICAL/CRITICAL SOURCES:

PERIODICALS

Contemporary Sociology, January, 1984.
Rural Sociology, spring, 1984.

* * *

MAKOWER, Joel 1952-

PERSONAL: Born February 19, 1952, in Oakland, Calif.; son of Theodore and Frances Makower. *Education:* University of California, Berkeley, B.A., 1975.

ADDRESSES: Office—Tilden Press, 1001 Connecticut Ave. N.W., Washington, D.C. 20036.

CAREER: Free-lance journalist, 1975-81; Tilden Press, Washington, D.C., president, 1981—.

WRITINGS:

Office Hazards, Tilden Press, 1981.
Personal Computers A to Z, Doubleday, 1984.
(With Edward Murray) *Everybody's Computer Fix-It Book,* Doubleday, 1985.
Boom! Talkin' About Our Generation, Contemporary Books, 1985.
The Map Catalog, Vintage, 1986.
(Editor with Alan Green) *Instant Information,* Prentice-Hall, 1987.
(With John E. Merriam) *Trend Watching,* Amacom, 1988.
How to Buy a Used Car/How to Sell a Used Car, Perigee, 1988.

Author of column in *Washington Star,* 1979-81. Contributor to periodicals, including *Association Executive, Philadelphia, Washington Post,* and to airline magazines. Contributing editor of *Washingtonian,* 1977-82.

* * *

MALIK, Charles Habib 1906-1987

OBITUARY NOTICE—See index for *CA* sketch: Born February 11, 1906, in Btirram, Al-Koura, Lebanon; died after a long illness, December 28, 1987, in East Beirut, Lebanon. Politician, diplomat, educator, editor, and author. Malik, a retired foreign minister of Lebanon, pursued a career in poli-

tics and diplomacy for forty years. From 1945 to 1955 he served as diplomat at the United Nations and, for the last two of those years, as ambassador to the United States. In 1958 and 1959 Malik was president of the United Nations General Assembly. He also taught philosophy at the American University of Beirut for many years beginning in 1937. Malik wrote several books, including *Problem of Asia, Problem of Coexistence, Man in the Struggle for Peace,* and *The Wonder of Being*. In addition, he edited *God and Man in Contemporary Christian Thought* and *God and Man in Contemporary Islamic Thought* and contributed several hundred articles to numerous books and periodicals. A frequent lecturer in the United States and abroad, Malik received more than fifty honorary degrees from American and European universities as well as other awards and honors.

OBITUARIES AND OTHER SOURCES:

BOOKS

Current Biography, H. W. Wilson, 1988.
The International Who's Who, 51st edition, Europa, 1987.

PERIODICALS

Los Angeles Times, January 1, 1988.
Newsweek, January 11, 1988.
New York Times, December 29, 1987.
Washington Post, December 29, 1987.

* * *

MALLIOL, William
See McINENLY, William T(homas)

* * *

MALLORY, Kenneth 1945-

PERSONAL: Born March 22, 1945, in Boston, Mass.; son of G. Kenneth (a pathologist) and Carol (Fisher) Mallory; married Margaret Thompson (an English teacher), September 19, 1978. *Education:* Harvard University, B.A., 1967; also attended University of Massachusetts at Amherst and University of California. *Politics:* Independent.

ADDRESSES: Home—372 Charles River Rd., Watertown, Mass. 02172. *Office*—New England Aquarium, Central Wharf, Boston, Mass. 02110.

CAREER: MIT Press, Cambridge, Mass., sales representative, 1971-74; assistant marketing director of Earthwatch, 1974-75; Marine Aquarist Publications, Marlboro, Mass., editor, 1977-78; New England Aquarium, Boston, Mass., writer, print supervisor, and editor, 1979—.

MEMBER: National Association of Science Writers.

WRITINGS:

(Editor with Les Kaufman) *The Last Extinction,* MIT Press, 1986.

Contributor of articles and photographs to magazines, including *Oceans, Sea Frontiers,* and *International Wildlife*. Editor of *Marine Aquarium Review* and *Marine Aquarist,* both 1977-78, and *Aquasphere,* 1979—.

WORK IN PROGRESS: When the Camel Hurt God, on the Rendille nomads of Kenya; *White Sapana,* on initiation into the Pokot—a camel and oxen herding tribe of Kenya; *Edward Sylvester Morse,* a biography; *The Challenge of Hydroponics.*

SIDELIGHTS: The Last Extinction is a collection of essays by six scientists, all of whom believe that the natural world is facing a mass extinction, the like of which has not occurred for millions of years. It will not be a part of the natural extinction process, by which life forms evolve and improve over time. It will be cataclysmic, the authors claim, and it will be caused by the human species. Man's desire for food and other natural resources has already decimated large portions of the earth. The pressing need for energy, as well as the toxic wastes created by technological innovation, threaten the natural habitats that remain.

David M. Graber wrote in the *Los Angeles Times Book Review* that it is still possible to avert natural catastrophe, and that the purpose of Kenneth Mallory's book "is to help stimulate effective conservation" by pointing "out realistic alternative conservation strategies that can work to preserve at least a portion of our living heritage." In the *New York Times Book Review,* critic Dorion Sagan commented: "The value of the book lies in its deeply felt portrayal of the rapidly diminishing diversity of Earth's life." Species are disappearing before they even acquire scientific names, and many of the world's most beloved and interesting creatures are in danger of becoming "no more than museum pieces."

BIOGRAPHICAL/CRITICAL SOURCES:

PERIODICALS

Los Angeles Times Book Review, October 19, 1986.
New York Times Book Review, November 30, 1986.

* * *

MALOUF, (George Joseph) David 1934-

PERSONAL: Surname is pronounced "Ma-*louf*"; born March 20, 1934, in Brisbane, Queensland, Australia; son of George and Welcome (Mendoza) Malouf. *Education:* University of Queensland, B.A. (with honors), 1954. *Politics:* Socialist.

ADDRESSES: Home—Via Oberdan, Campagnatico, Grosseto, Italy. *Agent*—Curtis Brown Ltd., 162-168 Regent St., London W1R 5TA, England; and 27 Union St., Paddington, New South Wales 2021, Australia.

CAREER: University of Queensland, Brisbane, Australia, assistant lecturer in English, 1955-57; St. Anselm's College, Birkenhead, Cheshire, England, schoolmaster, 1962-68; University of Sydney, Sydney, Australia, lecturer in English, 1968-77; writer. Member of the Literature Board of the Australia Council, 1972-74.

AWARDS, HONORS: Grace Leven Prize for Poetry and Australian Literature Society Gold Medal, both 1974, and James Cook University of North Queensland Award from the Foundation for Australian Literary Studies, 1975, all for *Neighbours in a Thicket;* Australian Council fellowship, 1978; New South Wales Premier's Fiction Award, 1979, for *An Imaginary Life; The Age* Book of the Year Award and *The Age* award for fiction, both 1982, both for *Fly Away Peter;* Victorian Premier's Award, 1985, for *Antipodes;* New South Wales Premier's award for drama, 1987, for *Blood Relations.*

WRITINGS:

(Contributor) *Four Poets: David Malouf, Don Maynard, Judith Green, Rodney Hall,* Cheshires, 1962.

Bicycle and Other Poems, University of Queensland Press, 1970, published as *The Year of the Foxes and Other Poems,* Braziller, 1979.

(Co-editor) *We Took Their Orders and Are Dead: An Anti-War Anthology,* Ure Smith, 1971.
Neighbours in a Thicket: Poems, University of Queensland Press, 1974.
Johnno (novel), University of Queensland Press, 1975, Braziller, 1978.
(Editor) *Gesture of a Hand* (anthology), Holt (New South Wales), 1975.
Poems, 1975-1976, Prism (Sydney), 1976.
An Imaginary Life (novel), Braziller, 1978.
(With Katharine Brisbane and R. F. Brissenden) *New Currents in Australian Writing,* Angus & Robertson, 1978.
Wild Lemons (poems), Angus & Robertson, 1980.
First Things Last (poems), University of Queensland Press, 1981.
Selected Poems, Angus & Robertson, 1981.
Child's Play [and] *The Bread of Time to Come* (novellas), Braziller, 1981, *The Bread of Time to Come* published as *Fly Away Peter,* Chatto & Windus, 1982.
Child's Play (novella) [and] *Eustace* (short story) [and] *The Prowler* (short story), Chatto & Windus, 1982.
Harland's Half Acre (novel), Knopf, 1984.
Twelve Edmondstone Street (memoir), Chatto & Windus, 1985.
Antipodes (short stories), Chatto & Windus, 1985.
Blood Relations (play), Currency Press, 1988.

Contributor to periodicals, including *New York Review of Books, Poetry Australia, Southerly, Sydney Morning Herald,* and *The Australian.*

SIDELIGHTS: A prize-winning poet before he published his first novel, David Malouf was born and raised in Australia and now resides in Italy. Critics agree that Malouf writes as comfortably about cosmopolitan Europe as he does about his childhood home, and the author's favored themes and literary devices also traverse his poetry and prose. Reviewers have praised the vivid, sensuous descriptions and evocative settings of his works, throughout which Malouf weaves an awareness of the distinct cultures and the diverse characters within them. Malouf often interfuses the past, present, and future to create an all-inclusive, multidirectional point of reference, is interested in dualities that repel and compel, and searches for perfect unities with nature.

Fleur Adcock commented in a *Times Literary Supplement* review of Malouf's 1980 poetry collection, *First Things Last,* that Malouf "has a strong visual consciousness with a sense of joyful absorption in the natural world which makes the overworked word 'celebration' irresistible." Malouf revels in nature's various forms—from paradisical gardens to wilderness, from life in the ocean to wild lemon trees—in attempts to harmonize with nature. For example, in "The Crab Feast" the poet searches for crabs so that he can ingest, embody, and join with them. Music harmonizes with nature as well; and in the poem "An die Musik," man, music, and nature integrate: "We might have known it always: music / is the landscape we move through in our dreams," Adcock quoted the poet.

In *First Things Last* Malouf also experiments with time, creating a present contemporaneous with the past and future. As Adcock explained: "In an elegy for his father he writes of the dead being buried in the living and looking out through their eyes, as do the not yet born." And in the poem "Deception Bay" Malouf writes of his ancestors viewing the future through the eyes of the present generation. Malouf also experiments with prose-poetry and other free verse forms, yet he generally emphasizes his content more than technique. Critics have called his poetry mature, elegant, fine, and lavish, and lauded Malouf for his sensitivity and emotion. Adcock concluded that "Malouf's powerful imagination allows a certain amount of surrealism. . . . [He] can be playful . . . but he is a serious poet concerned with serious things."

Malouf's first novel, *Johnno,* was published in 1975. Reviewing the work for the *Times Literary Supplement,* Frank Pike commended the author for his resonant depiction of place and atmosphere: Malouf creates "an unaffected and densely detailed evocation of a particular way of life at a particular time; urban, unspectacular." According to Pike, the novel commences "with a convincing account, finely written without fine writing, of childhood and early adolescence" in suburban Brisbane during World War II. The story follows the rocky friendship of the honorable but impressionable narrator, Dante, and Johnno, an intriguing, disturbed, fatherless youth. Dante is attracted to Johnno's fondness for carousing and heavy drinking and tries unsuccessfully to mimic his behavior. After Johnno departs for the Congo the youths meet again in Paris, but by now the narrator is more wary of his old hero's unstable behavior. Afterward in Australia, Dante receives news of Johnno's drowning death, an event that confirms Dante's early suspicions that Johnno was suicidal. Dante then receives an angst-ridden note from Johnno written previous to his death, in which he cites Dante's emotional indifference and restraint as reasons for his suicide.

In 1979 Malouf was awarded the New South Wales Premier's prize for fiction for his second novel, *An Imaginary Life,* a fictionalized account of the ancient Roman poet Ovid's mature life. From the sketchy information available on the Roman's later years, Malouf created a life for the poet as he imagined it to have transpired after Ovid was exiled from Rome in 8 A.D. The circumstances which led to Ovid's banishment are unclear. Many historians hold that the poet was banished as punishment for ridiculing the Emperor Augustus's wife Livia in his just-completed epic poem "Metamorphoses," others believe he was exiled for arranging a lovers' tryst for Augustus's granddaughter Julia, and still more suppose Ovid's writing of the intemperate "Art of Love" at a time when Augustus was calling for virtue in Roman society is a reason. Nonetheless, Malouf fills in the blanks to create what Katha Pollitt, writing for the *New York Times Book Review,* deemed "an extraordinary novel" and "a work of unusual intelligence and imagination, at once sensuous and quirky, full of surprising images and intriguing insights."

Malouf depicts an aging Ovid who was once at the heart of pleasure-seeking Roman society but is now forced to the desolate reaches of the known world. At Tomis, a grim village of one hundred huts in modern Romania on the Black Sea, the barren land supports vegetation the poet cannot even identify. Malouf makes such a setting seemingly tangible in *An Imaginary Life,* prompting Pollitt to comment: "Mr. Malouf's [prose] is indeed fine: a spare yet evocative English that captures both the bleak monochromes of Tomis and the sunny humanized landscape of Ovid's remembered Italy, without ever losing the distinctive voice, now caustic, now dreamlike, in which Ovid tells his own story." Neither does he recognize the barbaric language of the inhabitants, nor do they understand Latin or the extravagance to which Ovid was accustomed in Rome. Kate Eldred, writing for *New Republic,* asserted: "Malouf shows us the mind of a great wordsmith struck dumb in his surroundings trying to adjust to a new life." Abandoned, isolated, and understandably less exuberant than when in Rome, Ovid becomes fixated with and prepares for death.

After a year in Tomis Ovid acquiesces and learns the language of the barbarians; yet he plants a garden in an attempt to tame the wilderness surrounding him. Four years pass, and Ovid spies a wild child in the woods who appears to have been raised by wolves and persuades the reluctant villagers to catch the boy. In the wolf-child Ovid sees the embodiment of man and nature and hopes to tame the wildness in him by teaching him to communicate. But in the process roles are reversed and teacher becomes pupil: Ovid learns to imitate the sounds of the wild and know the world through his senses, and subsequently rejects Roman volatility and frivolity. With the child's help the poet undergoes his last metamorphosis, regaining the communion with nature that he had lost in his youth.

Carole Horn, reviewing the novel for the *Washington Post,* pointed out that "the story works on emotional and philosophical planes. Malouf maintains a fine consistency of tone, and his language is hauntingly lovely." Pollitt agreed, stating that *An Imaginary Life* is "one of those rare books you end up underlining and copying out into notebooks and reading out loud to your friends." Eldred, impressed with Malouf's manipulation of time, remarked that the author "interplays the historical present, [which is] clumsy in English, with a narrative present and an anecdotal past tense, interweaving them so gracefully that the techniques aren't obvious, only the aftertaste of grandeur in certain passages, of a facile rhythm in others."

Harland's Half Acre, Malouf's 1984 novel, also garnered critical praise. It opens with protagonist Frank Harland living with his brothers and bemused father at Killarney, the remainder of what was once an expansive farm in the Australian countryside. Jim Crace, reviewing for *Times Literary Supplement,* commended Malouf for his polished descriptions: the "opening chapters are . . . stunningly artful evocations of Queensland and Queenslanders. The Harland acres ('lush country but of the green, subtropical kind, with sawmills in untidy paddocks') are squandered with 'extravagant folly' through drink, gambling, debt and neglect." Hearing fantastic tales of the glory of Killarney spun by his father, Frank dreams to restore the farm to its original grandeur as a gift to his family.

Talented at drawing, he travels to Brisbane and studies art, sending back to the farm most of his meager income earned by selling paintings. Frank eventually becomes famous, prospers, and slowly buys back the lands that once were part of Killarney. He also paints canvases of the farm, immortalizing it by his art. Jonathan Yardley in *Book World* called *Harland's Half Acre* "a rewarding book . . . long on intelligence and feeling" and commended the author for writing "a meditation on the subtle, mysterious relationship between life and art. . . . He has written it with great sensitivity."

Malouf's 1982 novella, *Fly Away Peter,* for which he won the Book of the Year Award and a fiction award from the Australian literary journal *The Age,* also commences in Australia. After spending twelve years in England, protagonist Ashley Crowther returns to a one-thousand-acre plantation he inherited in his native Queensland, unsure of what to do with it or his future. Already inhabiting this land is Jim Saddler, a young man who is content with a simple existence among nature observing the numerous species of birds that migrate to the swamps there. Ashley decides to make the estate a wildlife reserve and hires Jim to manage it. They befriend a nature photographer, Imogen Harcourt, and the three settle into a serene life until World War I disrupts the calm.

The men enlist and at the front encounter the horrors of war. "The scenes in the trenches," wrote Alan Brownjohn in the *Times Literary Supplement,* "are much the finest in *Fly Away Peter:* men passing down the slope from fields where peasants continue to till the ground and birds continue to sing, to enter that labyrinth of mud, rats and twitching bodies from which they will never return, or never return the same." Ashley, far removed from the individualistic living practiced at the plantation, becomes disillusioned, concluding that men are as cogs in machines—indistinct and replaceable. Imogen, still in Australia, thinks the fighting is absurd and senseless and concludes that a purpose is not necessary in life. David Guy in *Book World* wrote: "She understands that the life of men should be as Jim's once was, like the life that the birds lead. 'A life wasn't *for* anything. It simply was.'" And Jim reacts to the war by cultivating a tranquil plot of land in an attempt to reclaim the innocence he left behind in Australia.

Malouf made Italy the setting for his 1982 novella *Child's Play,* a first-person narrative told by a young terrorist preparing to assassinate an internationally acclaimed author. *Times Literary Supplement* reviewer Peter Kemp described the work as "surreally hard-edged," adding that "the world *Child's Play* projects is one where details have a hallucinatory vividness and patterns stand out with stark clarity: only significance remains creepily opaque." Guy stressed that Malouf's depiction of the brilliant, influential writer is "masterful" and that Malouf again employs the concept of a simultaneous past, present, and future. Guy explained that in his preparation the terrorist envisions the near and distant future and his own place in history: "Already he sees the photographs of the piazza where the assassination will take place as those of a historic site; he imagines it in newsprint and news photograph, media which distort and deaden an event but also in some ways create it; he sees himself as the hand of fate toward which a life's work has been leading, as a figure in the writer's biography." *Child's Play* prompted the critic to conclude: "Malouf is something of a primitive narrator, rough around the edges, but he is also a deeply serious writer, not to be taken up lightly . . . [and] a genuine artist."

The two short stories bound with *Child's Play,* "Eustace" and "The Prowler," take place in Australia. They, like *Child's Play* and *Johnno,* focus on society's fascination with elusive, sordid characters and demonstrate the author's preoccupation with the interaction of opposites. "Conformity, community, security are repeatedly set against anarchy, loneliness, danger," Peter Kemp observed in the *Times Literary Supplement.* "Obsessively, [Malouf's] work juxtaposes order and disturbance, light and dark. Those positives and negatives can unexpectedly change places. And always in Malouf's stories the powerful attraction between seemingly opposed poles is used to generate some shock effects." Also focusing on disparities is Malouf's 1985 collection of thirteen short stories, *Antipodes.* The tales follow new Australian immigrants and the problems they encounter in their attempts to assimilate into a new culture, and examine the tribulations of Australians in Europe as well.

Malouf told *CA:* "I write out of a strong sense of time and place, a past that is continuously present, and of continuities within change. Wholeness is what I see myself as being concerned with—which means, of course, disruption. As an Australian I am especially concerned with what is unique to that place, but as it is also seen from within a whole culture of which ours is a dialect—that is, my work frequently shifts

back and forth, as I do, between Queensland and Europe, and attempts to hold the hemispheres in a single view.''

BIOGRAPHICAL/CRITICAL SOURCES:

BOOKS

Malouf, David, *First Things Last,* University of Queensland Press, 1981.
Malouf, David, *Fly Away Peter,* Chatto & Windus, 1982.
Malouf, David, *Harland's Half Acre,* Knopf, 1984.

PERIODICALS

New Republic, May 13, 1978.
New York Times, July 14, 1978.
New York Times Book Review, April 23, 1978.
Times (London), June 17, 1982, January 31, 1985.
Times Literary Supplement, April 9, 1976, September 22, 1978, January 29, 1982, May 21, 1982, October 15, 1982, June 15, 1984, February 8, 1985.
Washington Post, May 12, 1978, September 26, 1984.
Washington Post Book World, May 2, 1982.

—*Sketch by Carol Lynn DeKane*

* * *

MALTA, Demetrio Aguilera
See AGUILERA MALTA, Demetrio

* * *

MAMOULIAN, Rouben (Zachary) 1897-1987

OBITUARY NOTICE—See index for *CA* sketch: Born October 8, 1897, in Tiflis, Caucasus, Russia (now U.S.S.R.); immigrated to United States, 1923, naturalized citizen, 1930; died December 4, 1987, in Los Angeles, Calif. Producer, director, and author. Mamoulian was one of stage and screen's foremost innovators, directing the critically acclaimed early talkie ''Applause'' in 1929, the famous 1932 version of ''Dr. Jekyll and Mr. Hyde'' with Fredric March in the dual title roles, the 1935 George Gershwin musical ''Porgy and Bess,'' and the 1935 premier Technicolor film, ''Becky Sharp.''

Mamoulian's stage credits included the landmark 1927 Broadway drama ''Porgy,'' Eugene O'Neill's ''Marco Millions'' in 1928, and Rodgers and Hammerstein's 1940s hit musicals ''Oklahoma!'' and ''Carousel.'' Mamoulian collaborated as a writer on several Broadway productions, and in 1965 he published *Hamlet: A New Version*. He also contributed articles to books and periodicals in his field. The recipient of numerous awards for his service to the motion picture industry, Mamoulian was the last surviving founder of the Directors Guild of America.

OBITUARIES AND OTHER SOURCES:

BOOKS

The International Who's Who, 51st edition, Europa, 1987.

PERIODICALS

Chicago Tribune, December 7, 1987.
Los Angeles Times, December 8, 1987.
New York Times, December 7, 1987.
Times (London), December 8, 1987.

* * *

MANDEL, Sheila 1930(?)-1987

OBITUARY NOTICE: Born c. 1930 in Barre, Vt.; died of lung cancer, December 10, 1987, in New York, N.Y. Administrator, editor, and author. Mandel was a *Life* magazine editor from 1957 to 1972. In 1978 she began work as the director of public affairs for Manpower Demonstration Research Corporation located in New York City. She and her husband Paul Mandel wrote a novel, *The Black Ship*.

OBITUARIES AND OTHER SOURCES:

PERIODICALS

New York Times, December 12, 1987.

* * *

MANDRAKE, Ethel Belle
See THURMAN, Wallace (Henry)

* * *

MANGANIELLO, Dominic 1951-

PERSONAL: Born November 4, 1951, in Cimitile, Italy; son of Francesco (a cook) and Lucia (a housewife; maiden name, Vacchiano) Manganiello; married Angelina (a homemaker; maiden name, Manganiello), 1979; children: Francesco, Lucia, Miriam. *Education:* McGill University, B.A., 1974; Oxford University, D.Phil., 1978. *Religion:* Roman Catholic.

ADDRESSES: Office—Department of English, University of Ottawa, Ottawa, Ontario, Canada K1N 6N5.

CAREER: Universite Laval, Montreal, Quebec, lecturer in English, 1978-79; University of Ottawa, Ottawa, Ontario, assistant professor, 1979-84, associate professor of English literature, 1984—.

WRITINGS:

Joyce's Politics, Routledge & Kegan Paul, 1980.
T. S. Eliot and Dante, Macmillan, in press.

SIDELIGHTS: Dominic Manganiello told *CA:* ''I wrote *Joyce's Politics* with a view to challenge the received wisdom that Joyce had no politics. Joyce shaped his artistic consciousness, the evidence showed, with reference to the following political determinants: pacifist anarchism and socialism, Irish nationalism, religious heresy, and philosophical egoism.

''The writing of *T. S. Eliot and Dante* took me on an altogether different plane. In his literary and social criticism, as well as in his verse, Eliot had perhaps paid Dante the finest tribute by a major writer of this century. I proposed, therefore, to demonstrate the truth of Ezra Pound's statement, that Eliot's was 'the true Dantescan voice' of the modern world, in its literary, philosophical, and theological dimensions. Eliot, more than any modern writer, understood Dante's total vision as relevant for the present time. In making more real to us the old verities of the *Divine Comedy,* then, Eliot's works unite the medieval and modern worlds in a unique way and validate Dante's vision both as fiction and as 'metafiction.'''

* * *

MANKIEWICZ, Thomas F. 1942-
(Tom Mankiewicz)

BRIEF ENTRY: Some sources spell surname Mankiewitz; professionally known as Tom Mankiewicz; born June 1, 1942,

in Los Angeles, Calif. American producer, director, and screenwriter. Although he earned the sobriquet "the Noel Coward of the action-adventure" from *Washington Post* critic Paul Attanasio for his work on the script of the medieval fantasy film "Ladyhawke" (Warner Bros., 1985), Mankiewicz is better known as one of Hollywood's leading "script doctors." He rewrote the screenplays for such features, prior to their release, as "The Eagle Has Landed" (Columbia, 1976), "The Cassandra Crossing" (Avco Embassy, 1977), and "Superman" (Warner Bros., 1978). He contributed to the popular "James Bond" series of spy films, rewriting "Diamonds Are Forever" (United Artists, 1971) and "The Spy Who Loved Me" (United Artists, 1977). He also created the original scripts for the Bond features "Live and Let Die" (United Artists, 1973) and "The Man With the Golden Gun" (United Artists, 1974). Mankiewicz co-produced and wrote the screenplay for "Mother, Jugs and Speed" (Twentieth Century-Fox, 1976), and made his directorial debut with the film "Dragnet 1987" (Universal, 1987), a parody of the 1950s television series, which he scripted with Dan Aykroyd and Alan Zweibel. Additionally, Mankiewicz has written for television and the stage; he co-authored the script for the pilot episode of the series "Hart to Hart"—as well as directed twelve of its early episodes—and wrote the book for the Broadway musical "Georgy" (1970), based on the film "Georgy Girl" (Columbia, 1966). *Addresses: Agent*—c/o Creative Artists Agency, 1888 Century Park E., Suite 1400, Los Angeles, Calif. 90067.

BIOGRAPHICAL/CRITICAL SOURCES:

BOOKS

International Motion Picture Almanac, Quigley, 1988.
Who's Who in the Motion Picture Industry, fifth edition, 1986.

PERIODICALS

Chicago Tribune, June 26, 1987.
Los Angeles Times, March 22, 1987, June 26, 1987.
New York Times, February 27, 1970, June 28, 1973, December 19, 1974, May 27, 1976, February 10, 1977, December 15, 1978, April 12, 1985, June 26, 1987.
Washington Post, March 3, 1985, April 15, 1985, June 27, 1987.

* * *

MANKIEWICZ, Tom
See MANKIEWICZ, Thomas F.

* * *

MANN, Richard G(eorge) 1949-

PERSONAL: Born July 26, 1949, in Derby, Conn.; son of George Harvey (in construction business) and Alberta (Jonah) Mann; married Jill Zoodsma (an administrator), September 3, 1971. *Education:* Kalamazoo College, B.A., 1971; University of Minnesota, M.A., 1974; New York University, Ph.D., 1982.

ADDRESSES: Home—Eugene, Ore. *Office*—Department of Art History, University of Oregon, Eugene, Ore. 97403.

CAREER: Frick Art Reference Library, New York, N.Y., researcher, 1982; University of Canterbury, Christchurch, New Zealand, lecturer, 1983; Rhodes College, Memphis, Tenn., assistant professor, 1984-85; State University of New York College at Purchase, assistant professor, 1985-87; University of Oregon, Eugene, assistant professor, 1987—.

MEMBER: College Art Association of America.

AWARDS, HONORS: Received research grant from National Endowment for the Humanities, 1985.

WRITINGS:

El Greco and His Patrons, Cambridge University Press, 1986.

WORK IN PROGRESS: With Jonathan Brown, *Systematic Catalogue of Spanish Paintings,* for National Gallery of Art/Cambridge University Press.

SIDELIGHTS: Richard G. Mann told *CA:* "In my books I try to convey my enthusiasm about works of art and explain the circumstances which fostered their creation."

AVOCATIONAL INTERESTS: Travel, mountain walking, and languages: Spanish, Catalan, French, German, Italian.

BIOGRAPHICAL/CRITICAL SOURCES:

PERIODICALS

Times Literary Supplement, May 23, 1986.

* * *

MANNERING, Julia
See BINGHAM, Madeleine (Mary Ebel)

* * *

MANNING, Frederic 1887(?)-1935 (Private 19022)

BRIEF ENTRY: Some sources spell given name Frederick; born c. 1887 in Point Piper (some sources say Sydney), Australia; immigrated to England, 1902 (one source says 1898); died following a bout with pneumonia, February 22, 1935, in London, England. Australian critic, poet, and writer. Manning's novel *Her Privates We* (1930), loosely based on his experiences as a foot soldier in France during World War I, was lauded by a *Times Literary Supplement* reviewer as "probably the best and honestest description of life in the ranks during the Great War that has yet appeared in English." Written under the pseudonym Private 19022—Manning's identity was not revealed until after his death—*Her Privates We* is an insightful, unsensationalized account of the battles at the French fronts on the Somme and Ancre rivers as seen through the eyes of the common soldier fighting in the trenches. Manning's other works, written under his name, include the verse narrative set in sixth-century France, *The Vigil of Brunhild* (1907); *Scenes and Portraits* (1909), a collection of six dialogues between the author and historical figures such as the ancient Greek playwright Euripedes and the sixteenth-century English politician Thomas Cromwell; *Eidola* (1917), a collection of war poems; and a biography of a British naval shipbuilder, *The Life of Sir William White* (1923).

BIOGRAPHICAL/CRITICAL SOURCES:

BOOKS

Klein, Holger, *The First World War in Fiction: A Collection of Critical Essays,* Macmillan (London), 1976, Barnes & Noble, 1977.
Longman Companion to Twentieth Century Literature, Longman, 1970.
Twentieth-Century Literary Criticism, Volume 25, Gale, 1988.

PERIODICALS

New York Times Book Review, October 23, 1977, October 12, 1986.

Times Literary Supplement, November 15, 1923, January 16, 1930, August 19, 1977.

* * *

MANOGARAN, Chelvadurai 1935-

PERSONAL: Born August 1, 1935, in Kuala Lumpur, Malaysia; immigrated to the United States, 1966, naturalized citizen, 1976; son of K. Chelvadurai (an insurance executive) Manogaran and Packiaratnam (a housewife) Thambippillai; married Santhanathevi Thambinayagam (a teacher); children: Shakila, Anita. *Education:* University of Ceylon, B.A., 1960; Clark University, M.A., 1968; Southern Illinois University at Carbondale, Ph.D., 1972. *Religion:* Hindu.

ADDRESSES: *Home*—2114 Grand Prix Dr., Racine, Wis. 53406. *Office*—Department of Geography, University of Wisconsin—Parkside, P.O. Box 2000, Kenosha, Wis. 53141.

CAREER: Jaffna College, Jaffna, Sri Lanka, lecturer in geography, 1960-66; University of Wisconsin—Parkside, Kenosha, assistant professor, 1970-74, associate professor of geography, 1975-86, associate professor of geography and international studies, 1986—. Member of county committee and regional commission to eliminate air and water pollution.

MEMBER: Association of American Geographers.

WRITINGS:

Ethnic Conflict and Reconciliation in Sri Lanka, University Press of Hawaii, 1987.

SIDELIGHTS: Chelvadurai Manogaran told *CA:* "I was motivated to write *Ethnic Conflict and Reconciliation in Sri Lanka* because I am deeply concerned about the economic, social, and political problems that face my community—Tamil—and the nation of Sri Lanka. The theme of this book is to show that the long-standing grievances of the Sinhalese people concerning language rights, status of Buddhism, employment and education opportunities, and political control of the nation have been resolved in their favor by the Sinhalese-dominated government and that the Tamils have been reduced to an oppressed minority. It is also shown that Sinhalese extremists are unwilling to recognize that Tamils have been alienated through discrimination and that their attitude towards the Tamils has greatly affected the ability of the Sinhalese and Tamils of the moderate persuasion to negotiate a political settlement of the ethnic problem.

"I have used my expertise on world affairs and my specialized training as a geographer to anaylyze topics relating to the nature and depth of ethnic conflict, the position of the Tamils in this conflict, efforts that have been made in the direction of reconciliation, why reconciliations have failed in the past, and what are the prospects of lasting peace in Sri Lanka. I believe that a lasting political settlement can be achieved by resolving the issues of demarcating the boundaries of the Tamil linguistic province, of permanently merging the northern province and a major portion of the eastern province, where Tamil-speaking people are dominant, and of devolving substantial legislative and executive powers to the proposed provincial council of the Tamil linguistic province."

MANVELL, (Arnold) Roger 1909-1987

OBITUARY NOTICE—See index for *CA* sketch: Born October 10, 1909, in Leicester, England; died November 30, 1987. Television executive, broadcaster, educator, and author. Manvell was best known as a film scholar and prolific author who served twelve years as director of the British Film Academy. He was also a regular broadcaster for the British Broadcasting Corporation, appeared on television in many countries, served on juries of international film festivals, and lectured widely. He joined Boston University's College of Communications in 1975 and was named a professor in 1982. Manvell's first book, *Film,* became the standard text in its field. Other works by Manvell include *On the Air, The Animated Film, The Living Screen, Film and the Second World War,* the novels *The Dreamers* and *The Passion,* and studies of filmmakers Ingmar Bergman and Charles Chaplin. He also collaborated on the early volumes of the classic *History of the British Film.* A student of Nazi Germany history, Manvell wrote a television play and a book on the plot to assassinate Adolf Hitler, and he was co-author of the biographies of several leading Nazis.

OBITUARIES AND OTHER SOURCES:

BOOKS

Who's Who, 139th edition, St. Martin's, 1987.

PERIODICALS

Los Angeles Times, December 4, 1987.

Times (London), December 2, 1987.

* * *

MAN WITHOUT a SPLEEN, A
See CHEKHOV, Anton (Pavlovich)

* * *

MARAVICH, Pete(r Press) 1947(?)-1988

OBITUARY NOTICE: Born June 22, 1947 (one source says 1948), in Aliquippa, Pa.; died of a heart attack, January 5, 1988, in Pasadena, Calif. Professional basketball player and author. Known for his flamboyant playing style and nicknamed "Pistol Pete" for his scoring ability, Maravich was considered one of the greatest athletes to ever play basketball. In three seasons at Louisiana State University, Maravich amassed 3,667 points—averaging forty-four per game—to reach a National Collegiate Athletic Association record. His best game was during the 1969-70 season when he scored sixty-nine points against Alabama. Maravich went on to play ten years of professional basketball with the Atlanta Hawks, the New Orleans and Utah Jazz, and the Boston Celtics. He won the National Basketball Association's scoring championship in 1977, averaging thirty-one points per game but never quite achieved the over-all career greatness predicted. In 1978 Maravich suffered a knee injury which eventually led to his retirement from the game in 1980. He wrote his autobiography, *Heir to a Dream,* in 1987.

OBITUARIES AND OTHER SOURCES:

BOOKS

Who's Who in America, 41st edition, Marquis, 1980.

PERIODICALS

Chicago Tribune, January 6, 1988.

Detroit Free Press, January 6, 1988.
Los Angeles Times, January 6, 1988.
New York Times, February 6, 1984, January 6, 1988.
Washington Post, January 6, 1988.

* * *

MARCUS, George E. 1946-

PERSONAL: Born October 17, 1946, in Pittsburgh, Pa.; son of Samuel C. and Rose (Shriber) Marcus; married Patricia Seed (a historian), June 21, 1984; children: Rachel Abigail. *Education:* Yale University, B.A. (magna cum laude), 1968; graduate study at Cambridge University, 1968-69; Harvard University, Ph.D., 1976.

ADDRESSES: Home—8211 Lorrie Dr., Houston, Tex. 77025. *Office*—Department of Anthropology, Rice University, Box 1892, Houston, Tex. 77251.

CAREER: Rice University, Houston, Tex., assistant professor, 1975-80, associate professor, 1980-85, professor of anthropology, 1985—, chairman of department, 1980—. Senior fellow in communications at East-West Institute, 1981; visiting member of School of Social Science, Institute for Advanced Study, Princeton, N.J., 1982-83. *Military service:* U.S. Army, 1969-71.

MEMBER: Phi Beta Kappa.

WRITINGS:

The Nobility and the Chiefly Tradition in the Modern Kingdom of Tonga, University Press of Hawaii, 1980.
(Editor) *Elites: Ethnographic Issues,* University of New Mexico Press, 1983.
(With Michael Fischer) *Anthropology as Cultural Critique: An Experimental Moment in the Human Sciences,* University of Chicago Press, 1986.
(Editor with James Clifford, and contributor) *Writing Culture: The Politics and Poetics of Ethnography,* University of California Press, 1986.
Families in the Grip of Wealth: Dynasties and the Dynastic Idea in American Culture, Harvard University Press, in press.

Co-editor of series "New Directions in Anthropological Writing," University of Wisconsin Press. Editor of *Cultural Anthropology,* 1986—.

SIDELIGHTS: George E. Marcus told *CA:* "My initial project in anthropology was a field study of contemporary nobles and chiefs of the Kingdom of Tonga, and I have continued this sort of interest with more current field work and research on the legacies and strategies of perpetuation among established elites of wealth, talent, and power in various American and European settings. Specifically, in the United States, I am concerned with elite self-images of superiority, first in an ideologically pervasive liberal era, and now in a widely perceived era of national decline.

"During my earlier research project, the process of turning notes, memories, and data into a series of academic writings preoccupied me for several years. My temperamental resistance to writing conventional ethnography and my introduction to recent techniques of literary criticism led me to a critique of anthropology from the perspective of its rhetoric and writing strategies. Out of this, in turn, came my effort to rethink the purposes of anthropological writing itself as a form of cultural criticism. Trying to revive certain long-standing but underdeveloped critical tendencies in anthropology by connecting them to a modernist tradition of critical thought in the West, I have tried to think of innovative, if not experimental, strategies for writing ethnography. Most of these strategies involve working back and forth between contexts of intellectual and academic debates and analogous contexts in the 'real life' of those who become subjects in ethnographic research, where versions of these same debates in very different idioms and for different purposes are also conducted.

"Rather than being privileged above or outside the world of one's subjects, academic discourse and concerns become comparable and equivalent to those of subjects. The demotion of the scientific gaze in relation to its distanced object, without establishing a total context of subjectivity, makes possible the exposure of the processes by which knowledge is produced in the human sciences at the same time that it is being presented as knowledge. In short, I am interested in the various ways of realizing the practice of a cultural hermeneutics in the framework of a now thoroughly critiqued tradition of ethnographic writing in anthropology. My recent theoretical work has been devoted to both this practice and this critique, and my hope is that this work has been registered in the way that I am writing about elites in decline."

BIOGRAPHICAL/CRITICAL SOURCES:

PERIODICALS

Times Literary Supplement, February 27, 1987.
Washington Post Book World, May 4, 1986.

* * *

MARLIN, John Tepper 1942-

PERSONAL: Born March 1, 1942, in Washington, D.C.; son of Ervin Ross (a federal government and United Nations official) and Hilda (a writer and artist; maiden name, van Stockum) Marlin; married Alice Rose Tepper (a nonprofit executive), September 25, 1971; children: John Joseph, Caroline Alice. *Education:* Harvard University, A.B. (cum laude), 1962; Oxford University, B.A., 1965, M.A., 1969; George Washington University, Ph.D., 1968.

ADDRESSES: Home—360 West 22nd St., New York, N.Y. 10011. *Office*—Council on Municipal Performance, 55 West 44th St., New York, N.Y. 10011.

CAREER: Federal Reserve Board, Washington, D.C., financial economist, 1964-66; Small Business Administration, Washington, D.C., financial economist, 1966-67; Federal Deposit Insurance Corp., Washington, D.C., financial economist, 1967-69; Bernard M. Baruch College of the City University of New York, New York City, assistant professor of economics and finance, 1969-73; Council on Municipal Performance, New York City, founder and president, 1973—. Vice-president of National Civic League, 1987—.

MEMBER: American Economic Association (life member), Financial Management Association (life member), Municipal Analysts Group of New York, Harvard Club of New York, City Club of New York, International House of Japan.

WRITINGS:

(With Gordon Milde and Lois Dean) *Let's Go: Guide to Europe,* Harvard Student Agencies, 1961.
The Wealth of Cities, Council on Municipal Performance, 1974.
(With James T. Avery) *The Book of American City Rankings,* Facts on File, 1983.

(Editor) *Contracting Municipal Services,* Wiley, 1984.
(With Immanuel Ness and Stephen T. Collins) *The Book of World City Rankings,* Free Press, 1986.
Cities of Opportunity, MasterMedia, 1988.

Editor of *National Civil Review* and *The Privatization Report;* founding editor of *Journal of Financial Education,* 1972-73.

SIDELIGHTS: John Tepper Marlin told *CA:* "My interest in cities dates back to 1961, when I worked on the first edition of the *Let's Go* guide to Europe. I grew up in half a dozen cities abroad and have always been interested in what makes them tick or stop ticking. In 1972 I started a nonprofit organization to rate government performance, the Council on Municipal Performance. In 1987 it became a division of the National Civic League, the new name of a group founded by Theodore Roosevelt and others in 1894. We are getting the word out that civics is not passe and that America must realize that its governance requires civic initiative to make government work.

"In our cities books we don't come up with an overall ranking for urban areas the way some other well-publicized books have done (the one that rated Pittsburgh as the most livable city, for example). We don't think that that is defensible. Instead, we rank on a number of different factors and let people make up their own minds. We are looking for long-term predictive factors, and small business growth and civic initiative are the two we zero in on. And in *Cities of Opportunity* we take a narrower focus; we are less interested in quality of life than in prospects for employment and prosperity. The overall value of these books is that they help people focus on their own personal future and provide data benchmarks against which to assure their own aspirations, thereby making their lifetime decision making easier and more effective."

* * *

MARSHALL, Megan 1954-

PERSONAL: Born June 8, 1954, in Oakland, Calif.; daughter of Woodbridge (a city planner) and Elva (a book designer; maiden name, Spiess) Marshall; married John Sedgwick (a writer), July 19, 1980; children: Sara Marshall Sedgwick. *Education:* Attended Bennington College, 1971-73; Harvard University, B.A., 1977.

ADDRESSES: Home and office—54 Rutland Sq., Boston, Mass. 02118. *Agent*—John Brockman, 2307 Broadway, New York, N.Y. 10024.

CAREER: Beacon Press, Boston, Mass., subsidiary rights manager, 1979-80; *Boston Review,* Cambridge, Mass., associate editor, 1981; Harvard University, Cambridge, advanced journalism teacher for summer writing program, 1982—.

MEMBER: Authors Guild, Writers Union, New England Writers for Survival, Phi Beta Kappa.

AWARDS, HONORS: Harvard Monthly award for most promising student writer in Harvard graduating class of 1977.

WRITINGS:

The Cost of Loving: Women and the New Fear of Intimacy, Putnam, 1984.

Author of column for *New Age Journal;* contributing editor, *Boston Review;* contributor to *New Republic, Working Woman,* and *Boston Globe Magazine.*

SIDELIGHTS: Megan Marshall's *The Cost of Loving: Women and the New Fear of Intimacy* looks at how the feminist movement of the early 1960s—with its cry for female independence and self-sufficiency—has affected today's generation of young women. Talking with forty single working women from the ages of twenty-six to thirty-seven, the author reveals that loneliness and confusion frequently accompany a professional lifestyle; "[the women] share . . . shock and disillusionment at the myth that failed," *Washington Post* reviewer Daphne Abeel elaborated, "that is, that economic independence and some opportunity to achieve equality in a man's world bring happiness." Although noting that the survey is "unscientific and largely undocumented" and its interviewees "far from representative of the population of women in our society as a whole," Abeel assessed, "what this book does provide is a current commentary." The critic added: "To give this short book its due, it does strike a chord and, undoubtedly, will be read by the generation to which it is directed with empathy and recognition."

Marshall told *CA:* "I've written about women's history, literature, and contemporary issues; education; American history and literature; Latin American fiction; classical music. I play classical piano and baroque harpsichord."

BIOGRAPHICAL/CRITICAL SOURCES:

PERIODICALS

Boston Globe, April 10, 1984.
Los Angeles Times, June 14, 1984.
USA Today, September 12, 1984.
Washington Post, July 7, 1984.

* * *

MARTER, Joan M. 1946-

PERSONAL: Born August 13, 1946, in Philadelphia, Pa.; daughter of Anthony and Rita (DiMascio) Mastrangelo; married Walter Marter (a broadcasting company director), November, 1967; children: Julia. *Education:* Temple University, B.A. (magna cum laude), 1968; University of Delaware, M.A., 1970, Ph.D., 1974.

ADDRESSES: Office—Department of Art History, Rutgers University, New Brunswick, N.J. 08903.

CAREER: Sweet Briar College, Sweet Briar, Va., assistant professor of art history, 1974-77; Rutgers University, New Brunswick, N.J., associate professor of art history, 1977—. Guest curator at Pennsylvania Academy of the Fine Arts, 1976, and at Detroit Institute of Arts and Metropolitan Museum of Art, 1982-83.

MEMBER: International Association of Art Critics (member of executive board of American section), College Art Association of America, Women's Caucus for Art.

AWARDS, HONORS: Chester Dale fellow at National Gallery of Art, 1973-74; Charles Montgomery Prize from Decorative Arts Society of Society of Architectural Historians, 1983, for *Design in America: The Cranbrook Vision.*

WRITINGS:

(With R. Boyle and F. Goodyear) *In This Academy,* Pennsylvania Academy of the Fine Arts, 1976.
Jose de Rivera Constructions, Tallier, 1980.
(With R. J. Clark and David DeLong) *Design in America: The Cranbrook Vision,* Abrams, 1983.

Contributor to art journals.

WORK IN PROGRESS: A book on American sculpture since 1930.

*   *   *

MARTIN, Lee Nicholson 1916(?)-1987

OBITUARY NOTICE: Born c. 1916, in Kellogg, Idaho; died of cancer, November 19, 1987, in Washington, D.C. Journalist. Martin began her career at the Tacoma, Washington, *News-Tribune,* then joined the Associated Press in Copenhagen, Denmark, in 1939. She returned to the United States when Nazi Germany occupied Denmark in 1940, and worked for *Time, Newsweek,* and the Office of War Information. After World War II, Martin joined her journalist husband, Robert P. Martin, in China. When the Communists took control of China in 1949, she left for Japan, where her husband joined her a year later. Both Martins became staff members of *U.S. News* in 1953. As a reporter Martin concentrated on economic and business issues, but also covered politics and general topics. Her assignments sent her throughout East Asia, including Indonesia and Vietnam. Martin retired from journalism when she and her husband returned to the United States in 1965.

OBITUARIES AND OTHER SOURCES:

PERIODICALS

Washington Post, November 20, 1987.

*   *   *

MARTIN, Luther H(oward), Jr. 1937-

PERSONAL: Born June 1, 1937, in Richmond, Va.; son of Luther Howard and Mary (McKay) Martin; married Ann Pherigo (divorced, 1971); married Rux Smyth (an editor), June 30, 1973; children: (first marriage) Brendan A., (second marriage) Hilary M. *Education:* Western Maryland College, B.A., 1959; Drew University, M.Div., 1962, S.T.M., 1963; Claremont Graduate School, Ph.D., 1972.

*ADDRESSES: Home—*Underhill Center, Vt. 05490. *Office—*Department of Religion, University of Vermont, 481 Main St., Burlington, Vt. 05405.

CAREER: University of Vermont, Burlington, instructor, 1967-71, assistant professor, 1971-76, associate professor, 1976-87, professor of religion, 1987—, chairman of department, 1978—.

MEMBER: North American Association for the Study of Religion (executive secretary), American Academy of Religion, Society for Values in Higher Education (fellow), Society of Biblical Literature.

WRITINGS:

(Editor with James Boss) *Essays on Jung and the Study of Religion,* University Press of America, 1986.

Hellenistic Religions: An Introduction, Oxford University Press, 1987.

(Editor with Huck Gutman and Patrick H. Hutton) *Technologies of the Self: A Seminar With Michel Foucault,* University of Massachusetts Press, 1988.

Co-editor of *Historical Reflections/Reflexions Historiques.*

SIDELIGHTS: Luther H. Martin, Jr., told *CA:* "My specialty is theory and method in the study of religion, especially as it is applied to the study of Hellenistic religions. I enjoy travel that is related to this study and have spent time in Europe, the Middle East, and the South Pacific."

*   *   *

MARTIN, Richard 1946-

PERSONAL: Born in 1946, in Bryn Mawr, Pa.; son of Frank H., Jr. (a banker) and Margaret (Dever) Martin. *Education:* Swarthmore College, B.A., 1967; Columbia University, M.A., 1969, M.Phil., 1971.

*ADDRESSES: Home—*235 East 22nd St., Apt. 9R, New York, N.Y. 10010. *Office—*Shirley Goodman Resource Center, Fashion Institute of Technology, 227 West 27th St., New York, N.Y. 10001.

CAREER: William Paterson College, Wayne, N.J., instructor in art history, 1972-73; Fashion Institute of Technology, New York, N.Y., instructor, 1973-76, assistant professor, 1976-80, associate professor, 1980-84, professor of art history, 1984—, executive director of Shirley Goodman Resource Center, 1980—. Adjunct professor at New York University, 1977—; member of adjunct faculty at School of Visual Arts, 1975-80; member of faculty at New School for Social Research, 1977, 1982.

WRITINGS:

Fashion and Surrealism, Rizzoli International, 1987.

Jocks and Nerds, Rizzoli International, in press.

Contributor to magazines, including *Art Journal* and *Dialogue.* Editor of *Arts,* 1974—, and *Dress,* 1984—.

WORK IN PROGRESS: The Artists of Fashion, publication expected in 1989.

BIOGRAPHICAL/CRITICAL SOURCES:

PERIODICALS

Avenue, February, 1987.

*   *   *

MARTIN, Susan Ehrlich 1940-

PERSONAL: Born July 15, 1940, in Philadelphia, Pa.; daughter of Matthew B. and Harriet (Weiler) Ehrlich; married Malcolm A. Martin (a research scientist), August 18, 1964; children: Daniel B., David A. *Education:* Swarthmore College, B.A., 1962; University of Rochester, M.S., 1964; American University, Ph.D., 1977.

*ADDRESSES: Home—*6408 Crane Ter., Bethesda, Md. 20034. *Office—*Police Foundation, 1001 22nd St. N.W., Washington, D.C. 20037.

CAREER: High school social studies teacher in Hayattsville, Md., 1964-67; National Institute of Mental Health, Bethesda, Md., social science analyst at Center for the Study of Metropolitan Problems, 1968-69; National Research Council, Washington, D.C., study director for Committee on Research on Law Enforcement and the Administration of Justice, 1977-82; Police Foundation, Washington, D.C., project director, 1983—. Consultant to Women's Equity Action League Fund, 1978, and to National Research Council, 1987—.

MEMBER: American Sociological Association, Society for the Study of Social Problems, Sociologists for Women in Society, Law and Society Association, American Society of Criminology.

AWARDS, HONORS: Candace Rogers Memorial Award from Eastern Sociological Society, 1974, for graduate student paper "The Washington Area Women's Center: A Case Study in Organizational Growth and Change."

WRITINGS:

"Breaking and Entering": Policewomen on Patrol, University of California Press, 1980.
(Editor with Lee B. Sechrest and Robin Rediner) *New Directions in the Rehabilitation of Criminal Offenders,* National Academy Press, 1981.
(Editor with Alfred Blumstein, Jacqueline Cohen, and Michael Tonry) *Research on Sentencing: The Search for Reform,* Volumes I and II, National Academy Press, 1983.

Contributor to criminology and law journals.

WORK IN PROGRESS: A report of the status of women in police work, publication by Police Foundation expected in 1988.

* * *

MARTINDALE, Charles (Anthony) 1949-

PERSONAL: Born May 1, 1949, in Cambridge, England; son of Michael George (an administrator) and Pauline Goulding (a housewife; maiden name, Brown) Martindale; married Michelle Anne Levy (a teacher), September 1, 1976. *Education:* Wadham College, Oxford, B.Phil., 1974. *Religion:* Church of England.

ADDRESSES: Office—Department of Classical and Medieval Studies, University of Sussex, Falmer, Sussex BN1 9QN, England.

CAREER: University of Sussex, Falmer, England, lecturer in classical and medieval studies, 1974-88; University of Bristol, Bristol, England, lecturer in classics, 1988—.

MEMBER: Classical Association (president of Sussex branch, 1981-87), Sussex Association of Classical Teachers (president, 1982-87).

WRITINGS:

(Editor) *Virgil and His Influence: Bimillennial Studies,* Bristol Classical Press, 1984.
John Milton and the Transformation of Ancient Epic, Croom Helm, 1986.
(Editor) *Ovid Renewed,* Cambridge University Press, 1988.

Contributor to literature and classical studies journals.

WORK IN PROGRESS: A book on Shakespeare and the classics, publication by Croom Helm expected in 1993.

SIDELIGHTS: Charles Martindale told *CA:* "I believe in the promotion of classical studies as part of a cultural continuum in the West. My special interests are the influence of ancient poetry on English poetry before 1800 and translation.

"Classics continue to decline in the schools, and stressing their wider links with European culture is a useful way of demonstrating their continued significance and vitality. I would regard this decline as a cultural disaster, cutting us off from our roots.

"Although he was not a learned man, William Shakespeare had probably received part of a grammar school education based on the study of Latin, and his works are permeated by the classical influence (mythology, Roman history, Greek romance material, and so forth). His work thus demonstrates how widespread that influence was. English poets such as William Butler Yeats and T. S. Eliot continued to be influenced by the classics. The English poetic tradition would be a completely different thing without them."

* * *

MARTONE, Michael 1955-

PERSONAL: Born August 22, 1955, in Fort Wayne, Ind.; son of Anthony (a telephone company switchman) and Patricia (a teacher and public school assistant superintendent; maiden name, Payne) Martone; married Theresa Pappas (a poet), April 3, 1984. *Education:* Attended Butler University, 1973-76; Indiana University, A.B., 1977; Johns Hopkins University, M.A., 1979.

ADDRESSES: Home—1116 North Second, Ames, Iowa 50010. *Office*—Iowa State University of Science and Technology, 203 Ross Hall, Ames, Iowa 50011. *Agent*—Sallie Gouverneur, 10 Bleeker St., New York, N.Y. 10012.

CAREER: Worked in a hotel, 1977-78; Johns Hopkins University, Baltimore, Md., instructor in writing seminars, 1979-80; Iowa State University of Science and Technology, Ames, assistant professor, 1980-83, associate professor of English, 1983—. Teacher in various creative writing programs. Program director of Fort Wayne Fine Arts Foundation, 1977-78.

AWARDS, HONORS: Myrtle Armstrong Fiction Award from Indiana University, 1977, for "Story Problems," a short story; Pushcart Prize from Pushcart Press, 1980-81, 1983-84, and 1985-86, for "Schliemann in Indianapolis," "Whistler's Father," "Highlights," and "Alfred Kinsey, Alone After an Interview, Dreams of Indiana"; mention, *Best American Short Stories 1981,* for "The Life You Save May Be Mine"; Creative Writing Fellowship Grant for Fiction from National Endowment for the Arts, 1983; stories "March of Dimes" and "A Short, Short Story Complete on These Two Pages," chosen for syndication, 1983 and 1984, by the P.E.N. and National Endowment for the Arts Syndicated Fiction Project; mention, *Best American Essays of 1986,* for "Pulling Things Back to Earth"; Margaret Jones Fiction Award from *Black Ice,* 1987, for "Lucky One in America."

WRITINGS:

At a Loss (poems), Windless Orchard, 1977.
Alive and Dead in Indiana (short stories), Knopf, 1984.
Return to Powers (prose poems), Windless Orchard, 1985.
Safety Patrol (short stories), Johns Hopkins University Press, 1988.

CONTRIBUTOR

F. Richard Thomas, editor, *The Landlocked Heart: Poems From Indiana,* Indiana Writers Press/Indiana University, 1980.
Hortense Calisher and Shannon Ravenel, editors, *Best American Short Stories 1981,* Houghton, 1981.
Guy Daniels and Leslie W. Hedley, editors, *Fiction Eighty-four: A New Anthology of Innovative Writing,* Exile Press, 1985.
Allen Woodman, editor, *Stories About How Things Fall Apart and What's Left When They Do,* Word Beat, 1985.
Best American Essays of 1986, Ticknor & Fields, 1986.

Editor of *Poet and Critic.* Publisher with wife, Theresa Pappas, of Story County Books.

Contributor of short stories and articles to periodicals, including *Antaeus, Antioch Review, Ascent, Aura, Benzene, Denver Quarterly, Indiana Review, Indiana Writes, Iowa Review, Life, Minnesota Review, Mississippi Valley Review, Northwest Review, Pig Iron, Shenandoah, Seems* and *Windless Orchard.*

WORK IN PROGRESS: Collection of essays, tentatively titled *Young Farmers in Love;* collection of short stories, tentatively titled *Safety Patrol.*

SIDELIGHTS: Michael Martone, a native of Indiana, published his first book of short stories in 1984. Written as monologues, each story in *Alive and Dead in Indiana* is a fictional narrative by or about a public figure with some connection to the author's home state. Among the motifs that bind the collection together are Martone's interest in the American past and his concern with various aspects of celebrity.

Some stories are narrated by a famous person. Set in the 1950s, "Pieces" is the account of an aspiring fried chicken entrepreneur who tells how he picked up a young hitchhiker as he drove around Indiana promoting his new product. The narrator's fame as Colonel Sanders still awaits him. In a story set still further in the past, notorious bank robber John Dillinger sits in the darkness of a movie theatre, watching a crime film while pondering his life. Only the reader knows that he will be shot down when he leaves the show.

Other stories view a well-known person through the memories of a narrator who once knew the celebrity but who has been left behind in obscurity. Film star James Dean, for instance, is recalled by his high school drama teacher, and poet Ezra Pound, who taught at Indiana's Wabash College early in his career, is remembered by a fraternity housemother he once took back to his room for the night.

Martone's concern with evoking memories of the past and with using fiction to discuss the lives of real people permeates the story "Whistler's Father," sometimes called the most complex tale in the collection. The narrator is a teenage boy who works at a historical re-creation of the frontier fort that eventually grew into the city of Fort Wayne. To make the past come alive, members of the staff pretend to be real people who were present at the fort in the summer of 1816, and the narrator's job is to play the part of sixteen-year-old George Washington Whistler, son of the fort's commander and father-to-be of the famous painter James Abbott McNeill Whistler. While the teenage narrator speaks, he blends his own life with the life of the long-dead character he plays, talking about both himself and George Whistler in the first person. As Jonathan Penner noted in the *New York Times Book Review,* Martone's story involves a delicate interplay of illusion and reality. "George Washington Whistler, we know, is historical, the narrator an illusion; yet within the world of the story, the opposite is true. It is a lovely reversal of the usual relationship between actor and role; a fictional boy pretending to be a real one."

Critics applauded *Alive and Dead in Indiana* as evidence of Martone's literary skill. Peter S. Prescott of *Newsweek* found the stories "very short, very fine, exceedingly complex." *Los Angeles Times* contributor Carolyn See pronounced Martone's work "elegant," and she felt that in writing about his home state, the author had found a way to evoke the reality of the country as a whole. "Just understand that place, and how we all make up stories about things, and you will understand America, its past and its future."

Martone told *CA:* "If writing is making choices, then all writing is about region. A story has limits, borders. It is a neighborhood, a state. The essential drama of the country is between the national wish of expansion and the specific nature of our lives and our stories."

CA INTERVIEW

CA interviewed Michael Martone by telephone on August 8, 1986, at his home in Ames, Iowa.

CA: Alive and Dead in Indiana *is the most unusual collection of short stories, all having to do with well-known people who had some connection to Indiana but are otherwise unrelated to each other. How did the idea evolve, and how did you find the people on whom the stories center?*

MARTONE: I read Max Apple's book *The Oranging of America.* And there was a scene too in Thomas Pynchon's *Gravity's Rainbow* where Slothrop comes up on a porch and there's Mickey Rooney. So I thought I'd like to use real people. But one thing that disturbed me in Apple's book and in Pynchon's book was that real people, especially famous people, were being used in a cartoon sort of way, especially for satire. I thought I'd like to use them differently. Another thing is that I grew up in Fort Wayne, Indiana. Fort Wayne is the birthplace of Edith Hamilton, who wrote the book *Mythology.* My mom was an English teacher, and she taught that book every year. So I grew up with these Greek myths written by this woman from my town. I liked myths. The third thing was that I went to Johns Hopkins University, and when I was there, I was writing stories in an unremarkable, contemporary way. I started to write some things about Fort Wayne mainly out of homesickness—it was the first time, really, that I'd been out of my home state in my life.

All these things combined and I thought, I'll write something about Alfred Kinsey away from home and have him think about a part of Indiana that was special to me and also have it all be about love. The Kinsey story was the first story that a lot of my fellow students liked, and the first one in which I didn't feel that I was really working hard to tell a story. That got me thinking: if it was that easy, and if it was that successful, maybe there's something in it for other stories. Then it wasn't hard for me to begin thinking of other people.

Once I thought of the book as a whole, right after the Kinsey story, I began choosing people who had several things in common. I wanted monologues, and I wanted them to be in some way about love, to have some sort of love-song properties to them. And I also wanted people who were well known but not known completely. Alfred Kinsey is a good example there; everyone knows of his sex research, but very few people know that he was an insect biologist. I began looking for people who were famous for one thing, keeping in mind Andy Warhol's saying that we're all going to be famous for fifteen minutes. My idea then was to take these people and, by not treating them as satire (not making fun of Alfred Kinsey for what he did, for example) but treating them seriously, I hoped to make them human again, to bring them back from the brink of being famous. To make James Dean not James Dean, but a high school student again—even though all that's made up. Even though I was telling myths, what I wanted to do was make these made-up lives real in a weird way.

CA: Writing fiction about real people has been done a lot in recent years, but not in the short story form. Was that a particularly intriguing challenge?

MARTONE: Yes. I not only wanted to make these people *people* instead of using them ironically for shock value—the way I saw real people being used in fiction most of the time—I also wanted to talk about being left behind. I started writing as a poet, and got interested in the short story. I always thought of short stories as being more like poems than like short novels, though I think it's widely held that short stories are more like novels. So when I approach short stories, I think of them as poems. I stopped writing poems because, when I would have my poems criticized, people would always talk about where the end-stop was. One day I just let the typewriter ding, and that's where I ended my line. I don't think of the stories much differently from the way I was thinking when I was writing "poems." That's why I chose that form.

CA: I think one of the most distinctive things about your stories is that the voice in most of them hits the reader absolutely head-on. It's as if nothing comes between the words and their impact; there's no mental filtering process necessary. Is this an effect that comes from doing poetry first?

MARTONE: Maybe from doing poetry first, but there's another factor. I think the story that reveals most about the method is the James Dean story, because it's about interpretation and about speeches. When I was in high school, I was thinking about the Greeks and reading *The Odyssey* and *The Iliad* and even [ancient Greek historian] Thucydides. I loved all that stuff. Thucydides, you know, tells his stories through speeches, especially long, extended speeches, monologues. I think maybe that's what comes through in my stories. We forget that in a lot of first-person tales the speaker is driven to speak, like Coleridge's ancient mariner. With my stories, that's what I kept thinking, that this is a driven speech, that the speaker is someone who really has to tell this story. The speech teacher in the James Dean story is talking about giving speeches or doing interpretations on the stage, and that's what I kept thinking of while I was writing.

CA: "Whistler's Father," the most complex of the stories in the book, is set in a fort between the St. Mary's and St. Joe rivers that is preserved as a historical site. Does that spot have some personal meaning for you?

MARTONE: There is a fort truly there—that isn't made up—and it does have a lot to do personally with me. I know that I'll probably continue to write about that city, at least, if not Indiana. I really like Indiana, especially Fort Wayne. One reason is that it's virgin turf. It would be tough to be a Southern writer; certain things have been gone over a lot. One thing that's sort of interesting about the Midwest is that people write it off as *not* being interesting, and in a way it's pretty easy to make it interesting because so few people visit it and know it. In the story called "Pieces," Colonel Sanders says something about how right near Fort Wayne there's a continental divide. Unlike the one in the big mountains out West, the continental divide in Fort Wayne is only a matter of ten feet. On one side of town, the water flows eventually into the Atlantic Ocean; on the other side, it flows eventually into the Gulf of Mexico. It's such a subtle continental divide. I think that's a real challenge for a writer. That's not personal, but on a metaphorical level it's interesting to me. In its Chamber of Commerce literature, Indiana calls itself the crossroads of America, and it really is. It's a fascinating place to me. In "Whistler's Father" I threw in as much as I could—things I was saving. It was the last story written, and I was really pleased that it worked as well as it did.

CA: Does your family go way back in Indiana?

MARTONE: There were two migrations of my family through Indiana, one the traditional east to west, and one from south to north, as the people from the south left the farms and went to Gary and Detroit to work in the auto factories. Half of my family comes from Kentucky. And, you know, people forget that most of southern Indiana was on the Confederate side in the Civil War. It's a long state, and Fort Wayne, being up in the northeast corner, is a long way from the southern part of it. I ask the students out here in Iowa where the Midwest is, and they always think that Ohio and Indiana are not part of it. They define a Midwestern state as mainly agricultural, because that's what Iowa is. I always defined Indiana as the predominant Midwestern state because it's half industry and half agriculture. Partly I think the Midwest is an interesting place because nobody really knows where it is, and everybody wants to be from there. Nobody wants to actually *live* there, but so many people like saying, "Oh, yeah, I grew up in the Midwest."

CA: With the implication that they did well in spite of it?

MARTONE: Yeah. Or that they're bringing with them those good American values, so they can be trusted in places like New York and Los Angeles.

CA: For years writers spoke of having to "pay" for a published collection of stories by promising and delivering a novel to their publisher, and new writers had a very difficult if not impossible time getting a collection published. Did you have any trouble getting yours published?

MARTONE: Gordon Lish was my editor, and probably most everybody who has worked with him has a sort of love-hate relationship with him. On the positive side, of all the editors I know, only Gordon reads literary magazines. Years before I actually met him, he saw the Alfred Kinsey story in the *Iowa Review,* and he wrote a note to say he liked it. When I met him, I had only written four of the stories. I showed those to him and he said, "I want to publish your book." Gordon is really known for that. He sees one paragraph and says he'll take your book. Gordon likes to think of himself as a discoverer; most of his authors are young people that he has found and groomed. That's what he did with me, so in a way it was incredibly easy and I was incredibly lucky. He just came out here to give a little lecture and read, and he said to the writers here, "Send me your stuff." We all did, and all of a sudden I had a contract. It happened on April Fools' Day of 1982. Not only was I unknown—I'd never had stories published in any of the major magazines—but I didn't even have the book written. And a contract for short stories was amazing. When I was finishing up the stories, there were several times when it didn't look like it was going to work. Gordon has a reputation for getting really excited about something, but then his excitement, in the afternoon light, will wane. I think the excitement is really genuine and important, but often he gets writers so excited that when the letdown comes, it's a bigger letdown than it should be. That's just the way he is.

The one big problem the book did have was legal problems. It was actually in galleys, with a story which was probably

one of the better stories in the book called "Highlights." It's about Mark Spitz, the swimmer, who narrates the story. All of a sudden, the lawyers at Knopf got real nervous about invasion of privacy and said, "We can't publish this story." That opened up a whole new chapter. Because I was trying to talk about the use of fame and the use of real people, it was essential that Mark Spitz be narrating this story. And the lawyers were using nonfiction tests on works of fiction. So it was very weird, but finally the fallout was that they couldn't publish that story. And I did have to go to talk to Mrs. Nall, who narrates the James Dean story. She had to give her permission for us to use it. I'll tell you how closely they were looking at the fiction. There was a line in the Colonel Sanders story where Mrs. Sanders said, "Good-bye. Take care of yourself." The lawyer said, "Can you substantiate that she said this?" I said, "No, I can't." That wasn't essential, but in the Spitz story and the James Dean story, it was essential to have them the way they were written. Would Mark Spitz have ever *seen* the story? That was the crisis of the book, and it almost didn't get published.

Knopf had rights to look at the second book, and I wrote a second book of stories. I think the implication was that I should have written a novel. But I think of myself as a short story writer. It doesn't follow, then, that if I just keep adding words, I'll be a novelist. Knopf turned down their option on it.

CA: So it's still making the rounds?

MARTONE: Yeah, it's been going around for about a year. What happened with *Alive and Dead* was interesting. It was pretty well reviewed, but in the current market it's hard to place, so it never went into paperback sales. I think the people who read it liked it, but it just didn't find its niche. So it was hard afterward to build on it. I was really pleased with it, and sort of pleased that the critics couldn't pin me down, though I think that hurt as far as the business side. But since it was all such a big surprise getting it published anyway, and especially after all the legal problems, everything was cream as far as I was concerned. I paid back my advance and made a little bit of money and got good reviews, so it was all fine with me.

CA: Speaking of reviews, I noticed that it was reviewed in the Los Angeles Times *and the* West Coast Review of Books. *Did someone at Knopf make sure the book was visible on the West Coast?*

MARTONE: Yes. I think that's one thing that Knopf is very good at doing. Their name does pack a lot of punch. I remember a review from San Francisco that was done by a historian, interestingly enough, and he reviewed the book as history. The funny thing was that it wasn't reviewed very well in the state where I live. Another funny thing is what happened in the *New York Times Book Review*. The reviewer, Jonathan Penner, had been given the galleys that included the Spitz story, and in his review he had talked most about that story. When the book came out and the Spitz story wasn't in it, everybody panicked. I was in Europe at the time this happened, and so was Penner. Here's the politics of the situation. Knopf wanted my book to get into the *New York Times,* so they asked the paper to cut out all references to the Spitz story, which the newspaper went ahead and did—even without Penner's OK. When we got back from Europe, the review had come out. We read it, and I said to my wife, "Something's missing here." And there was. It's a curious episode in my life, this whole business.

CA: How early did you start writing?

MARTONE: I guess it was my senior year in high school.

CA: And after Indiana University, where you took an A.B. degree in English, you went to Johns Hopkins for an M.A. in fiction writing. What do you feel are the pros and cons of going directly into a writing school as opposed to working away from the academic environment for a while first?

MARTONE: I did work a year in between. I graduated in '77 from Indiana University and then took a year off and worked in a hotel. I think there is an advantage to work, because I really wanted to get out of the hotel after a year of working nights! It also gave me time to prepare a good manuscript. I tell my [undergraduate] students here, if you want to go back, take a year off. And don't try to do the [graduate school] applications while you're also trying to finish your work here. Then too, the applications now cost a lot. So the time working gives them a chance to raise a little money.

I wouldn't say that working is needed to experience the world to write better fiction. My fiction has to do mainly with things that actually happened before I was even alive. I feel it's wrong to think that there's a definite program of how you become a writer in this country. I'm in the business; I give out degrees here too. But I think a lot of people feel that you have to win *these* awards, you have to go to *these* conferences, you have to study at *these* places, and then you'll get all the baggage tags that will make you a writer in this country. I tell my students that that's one possible way, but it's not *the* way to make you a writer. You can find your own way. When I was at Hopkins, I don't think Hopkins really had the reputation it seems to have acquired since then. John Barth was only recently there, and only a few of his students were beginning to publish at that time. So I suggest that it's sometimes good maybe to go to a place that doesn't have the reputation and be part of *making* its reputation.

CA: Does the Writers' Workshop at the University of Iowa take away young writers you might otherwise get at Iowa State?

MARTONE: We sort of sneak in the back door here. The legislature controls the state universities, and when people are looking to cut budgets, overlapping of services doesn't happen. We can't give an M.F.A. degree, so we give an M.A. instead here. And we have a very small program because their program is so large and famous. I think, though, that we teach undergraduate writing and contemporary literature far better than Iowa does, to students who aren't necessarily going to be writers. That's what we pride ourselves on. I also think we have a very good graduate fellowship, a free ride and lots of money to come here. But only a few people do that. It's a good program to come to if you just want to write. Iowa's far better in making connections. You meet 120 other writers there every year. So there's really hardly any overlap—except the official name for Iowa is the State University of Iowa, and our name is Iowa State University, so sometimes we get people who think they've made it into the famous workshop and we have to ask them, "Now, are you sure you want to come *here*?"

CA: Do you find, in the combination of teaching and writing, that the two activities are more mutually enriching than distracting?

MARTONE: I guess it depends on the day you ask. But I really do enjoy teaching, and I really enjoy teaching undergraduates, especially students who aren't going to be writers. I enjoy the students from farms, people who are going into business, because I like giving them permission to tell stories. Maybe it's Midwestern, maybe it's not, but it seems like here in the Midwest those young students in their very short lives have been told that their lives aren't worth much, that if they were really important, they wouldn't be here. Often the whole message from their schools, from television, from the books they read is that real life is happening somewhere else. I don't think it's necessarily just in Iowa; I think throughout the culture somebody's profiting from people's unhappiness, whether it be cosmetics companies or cola companies. I tell the students that only two percent of the people now live on farms, so it's a pretty rare experience. You've done things and you'll do things that hardly anyone else has done, and that's interesting intrinsically to people who are not on farms.

With the graduate students, since we're such a small program, it's more personal; we have more tutorials. I like teaching that way because the teaching isn't coupled so much with making people's careers as it would be at a pure graduate program. And I think it really has contributed to my writing, because now I'm working on a book of nonfiction about young farmers. I've loved going around this state and discovering it. Indiana's the state that was bred in the bone, you know, but Iowa is the sort of state that I've invented and discovered as I've been here.

I teach a course in contemporary rural literature now. That's been a real joy, and I think very fruitful to my own work. We had a farm film festival. We have field trips: we went to McDonald's and to a local cafe to see how food was prepared. And I go out and work on people's farms. I couldn't have done that without having a teaching job. It's fun; I really like it.

CA: Is it too early to tell more about the nonfiction book?

MARTONE: For now I am calling it *Young Farmers in Love.* It is a group of essays about young farmers—a hog farmer, a dairyman, a woman who raises sheep, a truck farmer, one of the only potato farmers in the state. I am looking to tell good stories, seeking to avoid the obvious and over-reported current farm crisis. These men and women are my age and doing a job that is incredibly difficult—their actions and gestures are at once both intensely real and richly symbolic. It is a book about place too. And I think I can never get too far away from writing about place.

BIOGRAPHICAL/CRITICAL SOURCES:

PERIODICALS

Los Angeles Times, July 16, 1984.
Newsweek, May 28, 1984.
New York Times Book Review, June 17, 1984, March 6, 1988.
West Coast Review of Books, September-October, 1984.

—Interview by Jean W. Ross

* * *

MARZOLF, Marion Tuttle 1930-

PERSONAL: Born July 6, 1930, in Greenville, Mich.; daughter of Stuart K. and Signe M. (Johnson) Tuttle; married Kingsbury Marzolf, May 7, 1953. *Education:* Michigan State University, B.A., 1952; University of Michigan, M.A., 1963, Ph.D., 1972.

ADDRESSES: Home—1420 Granger St., Ann Arbor, Mich. 48104. *Office*—Department of Communication, University of Michigan, Ann Arbor, Mich. 48109.

CAREER: Wallace-Lindeman, Grand Rapids, Mich., advertising copywriter, 1952-53; *Biloxi Bulletin,* Biloxi, Miss., reporter, 1953-54; *Washington Post,* Washington, D.C., reporter and assistant, 1955-57; *National Geographic,* Washington, D.C., editorial layout assistant, 1957-63; Eastern Michigan University, Ypsilanti, lecturer in journalism, 1964-68; University of Michigan, Ann Arbor, lecturer, 1967-73, assistant professor, 1973-78, associate professor of journalism, 1978—, associate chairman of department of communication, 1987—. Copy editor on city desk of *Ann Arbor News,* 1973.

MEMBER: American Studies Association, Association for Education in Journalism and Mass Communications, Immigration History Society, Society for the Advancement of Scandinavian Studies, Danish-American Historical Society, Women in Communications, Detroit Women Writers.

AWARDS, HONORS: Outstanding achievement award for leadership from Status of Women Committee of Association for Education in Journalism and Mass Communications, 1982.

WRITINGS:

Up From the Footnote: A History of Women Journalists, Hastings House, 1977.
The Danish-Language Press in America, Arno, 1979.

WORK IN PROGRESS: Early Critics of the Modern Urban American Press, publication expected in 1989; a book to cover the years from 1880 to 1947.

SIDELIGHTS: Marion Tuttle Marzolf told *CA:* "My research has been motivated by an interest in the unsung and unnoticed in American journalism history. First I wrote about the immigrant press in a dissertation that became a book. Then I studied the women who were so overlooked by mainstream history that I found them mentioned mostly in footnotes. Now I am concerned with the criticism and critics who have been noticed, but not studied."

* * *

MASSON, Andre (Aime Rene) 1896-1987

OBITUARY NOTICE: Born January 4, 1896, in Balagny-sur-Therain, Oise, France; died October 28, 1987, in Paris, France. Painter, graphic artist, illustrator, costume and set designer, and author. One of the last important exponents of surrealism, Masson referred to himself as an instinctive painter; he was known primarily for developing the creative technique of automatic writing, a spontaneous linear expression said to originate from the unconscious mind. In such a work, for example, Masson might draw patterns with glue, sprinkle them with sand, and then squeeze tubes of colored paint directly on the canvas or even spread on paint with his hands. Characteristically he worked in series and usually incorporated one or all of his favorite themes: eroticism, metamorphosis, and mortality. One of his best known series, painted during the 1930s, features the mythological Minotaur. The artist received several awards for his works, including the Grand Prix National des Arts in 1954 (one source says 1955) and the Sao Paulo Biennial Prize in 1963. Masson also became involved in the theater

and designed both costumes and sets for the 1933 production of the ballet, "Les Presages." He illustrated others' books, and wrote several of his own, including *The Pleasures of Painting, La Pieuvre, Memorandum, Bestiaire, Metamorphoses,* and *Le Vagabond du surrealisme.*

OBITUARIES AND OTHER SOURCES:

BOOKS

Contemporary Artists, 2nd edition, St. Martin's, 1983.
Current Biography, H. W. Wilson, 1974.
The International Who's Who, 51st edition, Europa, 1987.

PERIODICALS

Chicago Tribune, October 30, 1987.
Los Angeles Times, October 29, 1987.
New York Times, October 29, 1987.
Time, November 9, 1987.
Times (London), October 29, 1987.

* * *

MATHEUS, John F(rederick) 1887-1983

PERSONAL: Born September 10, 1887, in Keyser, W.Va.; died February 19, 1983; son of John William (a bank messenger and tannery worker) and Mary Susan (Brown) Matheus; married Maude A. Roberts, September 1, 1909 (died in 1965); married Ellen Turner Gordon, July 31, 1973. *Education:* Western Reserve University (now part of Case Western Reserve University), A.B. (cum laude), 1910; Columbia University, A.M., 1921; graduate study at the Sorbonne, Paris, summer 1925, and at University of Chicago, 1927.

ADDRESSES: Home—Charleston, W.Va.

CAREER: Florida Agricultural and Mechanical College (now University), Tallahassee, teacher of Latin, 1911-13, professor of modern languages, 1913-22; Department of Romance Languages at West Virginia State College (West Virginia Collegiate Institute from 1915 to 1929), Institute, professor and head of department, 1922-53, professor emeritus, beginning in 1953; professor of foreign languages at Maryland State College, 1953-54; Dilliard University, New Orleans, La., professor of Romance languages, 1954-57; Morris Brown College, Atlanta, Ga., associate professor of German and Spanish, 1958-59; Texas Southern University, Houston, assistant professor of foreign languages and literatures, 1959-61. Visiting professor at Hampton Institute, 1961-62, and at Kentucky State College (now University), 1962. Served U.S. League of Nations commission to investigate slavery in Liberia, c. 1930; director of teaching English in Haiti for Inter-American Educational Foundation, 1945-46; consultant to Lexicographic Board. Plays featured at a festival in Cleveland, Ohio.

MEMBER: American Association of University Professors, College Language Association (treasurer, beginning in 1942), American Association of Teachers of French (president of West Virginia chapter, 1949-50), Modern Language Teachers' Association (president of West Virginia chapter, 1952-53), American Association of Teachers of Spanish and Portuguese, American Academy of Language Research, West Virginia Association of Higher Education, Alpha Pi Alpha, Sigma Pi Phi, Sigma Delta Pi, among others.

AWARDS, HONORS: "Fog" received first prize in *Opportunity* short story contest, 1925; "Swamp Moccasin" received first prize in *Crisis* short story contest, 1926; award for best review of the year from *Journal of Negro History,* 1936; awarded "Officier de l'Ordre Nationale 'Honneur et Merite'" from Haitian Government.

WRITINGS:

SHORT STORIES

A Collection of Short Stories, edited by Leonard A. Slade, Jr., privately printed, 1974.

Author of "Fog," "Clay," "Swamp Moccasin," "Anthropoi," and twenty other stories.

DRAMA

"Tambour" (one-act play), first produced in Boston, 1929.
(Librettist) *Ouanga!* (opera in three acts; first produced in South Bend, Indiana, June, 1949), music by Clarence Cameron White, privately printed by White, 1939.

Also author of plays "'Cruiter," "Ti Yette," "Black Damp," and "Guitar."

OTHER

(Editor with W. Napoleon Rivers) *Dumas' Georges: An Intermediate French Reader* (based on novel by Alexandre Dumas pere), Associated Publishing, 1936.
(Contributor) Therman B. O'Daniel, editor, *Langston Hughes: Black Genius; A Critical Evaluation,* Morrow, 1971.

Work represented in numerous anthologies, including *Anthology of American Negro Literature,* 1929, *The New Negro: An Interpretation,* 1970, *Caroling Dusk: An Anthology of Verse by Negro Poets,* 1974, and *Plays and Pageants From the Life of the Negro,* 1979.

Contributor of poetry, short stories, articles, and book reviews to periodicals, including *Opportunity, Crisis, Journal of Negro History, Modern Language Journal, Carolina Magazine,* and *Negro Digest.*

Contributing editor to *Color.*

SIDELIGHTS: A professor of Romance languages, John F. Matheus wrote poetry, plays, and short stories. The latter genre, however, proved most successful for him critically and resulted in his privately printed volume of fiction, *A Collection of Short Stories.* Regarded as a humanist, Matheus infused most of his work with themes revealing the racial prejudices prevalent in the South and suggesting Christian understanding and reconciliation as an effective means of countering the evils of humanity. In his contest-winning 1925 "Fog," for example, he illustrates that "ignorance is thick and impenetrable, but, like a fog, it can be replaced by the clear light of understanding," according to a profile in *Dictionary of Literary Biography.* Similarly, other stories—and especially his plays—focus on the hardships, humiliation, and exploitation characteristic of Negro life during his day. Allegedly too reliant on cliches and exaggerated language, Matheus nonetheless conveyed the true spirit and history of his race and thus distinguished his writing as authentic Afro-American literature.

AVOCATIONAL INTERESTS: Travel (Europe, Cuba, Haiti, Africa, Mexico, Canada, and South America).

BIOGRAPHICAL/CRITICAL SOURCES:

BOOKS

Bardolph, Richard, *The Negro Vanguard,* Rinehart, 1959.

Bond, Frederick W., *The Negro and the Drama: The Direct and Indirect Contribution Which the American Negro Has Made to Drama and the Legitimate Stage,* McGrath, 1969.
Brawley, Benjamin Griffith, *The Negro Genius: A New Appraisal of the Achievement of the American Negro in Literature and the Fine Arts,* Biblo & Tannen, 1966.
Dictionary of Literary Biography, Volume 51: *Afro-American Writers From the Harlem Renaissance to 1940,* Gale, 1987.*

* * *

MATOSSIAN, Nouritza 1945-

PERSONAL: Born April 24, 1945, in Nicosia, Cyprus; daughter of Hagop (an industrialist) and Satenig (Nersessian) Matossian; married Rolf Gehlhaar (a composer), June 6, 1976; children: Hagop Fritz, Vahakn Wolfram. *Education:* Bedford College, London, B.Phil. (with honors), 1968. *Religion:* Armenian Orthodox.

ADDRESSES: Home and office—12 Glenilla Rd., London NW3 4AS, England. *Agent*—Deborah Rogers Ltd., 49 Blenheim Cres., London W11 2EF, England.

CAREER: Free-lance writer, guest lecturer, broadcaster, and interviewer, 1968—.

WRITINGS:

Xenakis, Kahn & Averill, 1986, Taplinger, 1987, translation from original manuscript published in French as *Iannis Xenakis,* Fayard, 1981.

Contributor to periodicals, including *Observer, Vogue, Harpers and Queen, Independent, USA Today, Music and Musicians,* and *Tempo.*

WORK IN PROGRESS: Research on the history of her Armenian family in Anatolia and Cyprus; research for a book on abstract expressionist painters; research on music, both classical and modern composers.

SIDELIGHTS: Nouritza Matossian reported that her interest in "new music" grew out of a thesis on Chomskyan linguistic analysis of different periods of music, as well as her "concern with the apparent break in language between classical and new music." She interviewed many musicians, including Iannis Xenakis, and "attempted a new form of biography/study of Xenakis by relating his thoughts, feelings, ideas, music, architecture, and philosophy with events from his life.

"Now," the author concluded, "I am more interested in fictional biography or novels based on the lives of real people."

BIOGRAPHICAL/CRITICAL SOURCES:

PERIODICALS

New Yorker, December 1, 1986.

* * *

MATSON, Albert Thomas 1915(?)-1987

OBITUARY NOTICE: Historian and author. A self-taught authority in the field of East African history, Matson devoted most of his time to the study of Kenya. His interest in the topic began in 1944 when he became a health inspector for the Kenyan Colonial Service and was asked by the Nandi District Council to write a history of the Nandi people. His efforts were eventually published as *Nandi Resistance to British Rule.* Publication of a second volume was forthcoming at the time of his death. Matson also contributed numerous articles to *Kenya Weekly News.*

OBITUARIES AND OTHER SOURCES:

PERIODICALS

Times (London), November 10, 1987.

* * *

MAY, Elaine 1932-

BRIEF ENTRY: Born April 21, 1932, in Philadelphia, Pa. American comedienne, actress, director, and playwright. Fame first came to May when she and Mike Nichols were performing improvisational sketches at supper clubs and cabarets in Chicago and New York. Highly successful, the comedians moved to Broadway, then toured the United States with a show billed as "An Evening With Mike Nichols and Elaine May" (1960). The pair recorded a comedy album of the same title and made numerous guest appearances on various television programs, including "The Jack Paar Show" and "Laugh-In." After parting with Nichols in 1961 May took to playwriting. She acted in the first full-length play that she wrote, "A Matter of Position" (first produced in 1962), and authored other off-Broadway presentations such as *Not Enough Rope* (Samuel French, 1964; first produced in 1962) and *Adaptation* (Dramatists Play Service, 1971; first produced in 1969), a one-act television game show parody that she also directed.

May then began writing for films. She wrote the screenplay for "Such Good Friends" (Paramount, 1971), but withdrew her name from the credits because she disapproved of its production. Next she wrote, directed, and starred in "A New Leaf" (Paramount, 1971), a screwball comedy she adapted from a short story by Jack Ritchie. The following year she directed the melodrama "The Heartbreak Kid" (Twentieth Century-Fox, 1972), which Vincent Canby of the *New York Times* declared "an unequivocal hit." Then May collaborated with Warren Beatty to write the script for the 1978 box-office smash "Heaven Can Wait" (Paramount)—a remake of the 1941 film "Here Comes Mr. Jordan." She also worked with Beatty on the script of "Reds" (Paramount, 1981), and did rewrite work on "Tootsie" (Columbia, 1982), the blockbuster about an unemployed actor, played by Dustin Hoffman, who disguises himself as a woman in order to win an acting job. May again worked with Beatty on "Ishtar" (Columbia, 1987), writing the screenplay and directing the story of two untalented, middle-aged songwriters—played by Beatty and Hoffman—in search of success. *Addresses: Office*—Directors Guild of America, 7950 West Sunset Blvd., Los Angeles, Calif. 90046. *Agent*—Dramatists Play Service, 440 Park Ave. S., New York, N.Y. 10016.

BIOGRAPHICAL/CRITICAL SOURCES:

BOOKS

Contemporary Dramatists, St. James Press, 1977.
Contemporary Literary Criticism, Volume 16, Gale, 1981.
Dictionary of Literary Biography, Volume 44: *American Screenwriters, Second Series,* Gale, 1986.
Who's Who in the Theatre: A Biographical Record of the Contemporary Stage, 17th edition, Gale, 1981.

PERIODICALS

Newsweek, December 27, 1976.

New York Times, October 10, 1960, March 14, 1971, April 25, 1971, December 18, 1972, June 28, 1978, April 11, 1987, May 15, 1987.

* * *

MAY, Stephen 1946-

PERSONAL: Born September 10, 1946, in Toronto, Ontario, Canada; immigrated to United States, 1957, naturalized citizen, 1970; son of Thomas J. (a sales manager) and Claire (a housewife; maiden name, Thompson) May; married Caroline Casteel (a business manager), October 13, 1972. *Education:* El Camino College, A.A., 1970; California State University, Carson, B.A. (cum laude), 1975, M.A. (magna cum laude), 1977.

ADDRESSES: Home and office—610 Country Dr., Monument, Colo. 80132. *Agent*—Rhoda Weyr, Rhoda Weyr Agency, 216 Vance St., Chapel Hill, N.C. 27514.

CAREER: Pan American World Airways, Los Angeles, Calif., passenger service representative, 1970-76; Pikes Peak College, Colorado Springs, Colo., instructor in English and humanities, 1978—. Adjunct professor at St. Francis College, Joliet, Ill., 1982, 1984, and 1986; guest lecturer at Colorado College, 1986. *Military service:* U.S. Army, 1964-67.

WRITINGS:

Pilgrimage (nonfiction), Ohio University Press, 1986.
(Author of introduction) Marshall Sprague, *Newport in the Rockies,* Ohio University Press, 1987.
Intruders in the Dust (nonfiction), Algonquin Books of Chapel Hill, 1988.

Feature writer, columnist, and contributing editor, *Southwest Art,* 1984—. Contributor to magazines and newspapers, including *Western Art Digest.*

WORK IN PROGRESS: The Lions of London, a novel based on the lives of painters Joseph Turner and John Constable and the development of the English romantic landscape school, publication expected in 1988.

SIDELIGHTS: Stephen May told *CA:* "The English language is such a wonderfully flexible medium for expression that it enables a writer to paint his or her picture of the world aided by an extra set of brushes or new box of paints. It is this flexibility and range that I try to cultivate in my work. I endeavor to vary—in each of my books, articles, or even prefaces—the subject, mood, pace, approach, and style, so that I am not writing in a redundant way or affecting a particular voice. A predictable writer is a dull (or dead) one. He or she should keep in reserve as many tricks, strategies, and devices as a veteran pitcher keeps sliders and curve balls, or as a spouse plans menus.

"*Pilgrimage* is essentially influenced by the Victorian travel writers who discovered history, people, wild landscapes, odds and ends, and a good deal of themselves in their journeys and rambles throughout the world.

"I have always been interested in Southwest culture—art, literature, landscape, and life-style. My second book, *Intruders in the Dust,* is an attempt to portray the lives of six artists against the backdrop of the 150-year exploration and settlement of the West. It begins in 1837 when Alfred Jacob Miller marched to the Rockies with a fur expedition, traces the development of the scenic school of painting (Thomas Moran), includes a demented romantic (Ralph Blakelock), explains the rise and fall of the Taos school (Joseph Sharp and Victor Higgins), and concludes in modern times with the New Mexico rambles and observations of Georgia O'Keeffe.

"Many writers have influenced me; as a matter of fact, *all* good writing moves me. If I had to single out those writers who were significant in my development, I would choose Charles Dickens for journalistic observation and characters, Joseph Conrad and Robert Louis Stevenson for description, H. E. Bates for style, Ernest Hemingway for his terseness and objectivity, Albert Camus for his lyrical essays, Franz Kafka for subject matter, R. F. Delderfield for historical settings and characters, John Fowles for his style, characters, and settings, and D. H. Lawrence for his authorial power. Also worth mentioning is the art criticism of John Canaday and Kenneth Clark. Both of these writers could enthrall a reader with their command of language as much as they could interpret clearly and intelligently the works of art and lives of artists they considered.

"I continue to travel extensively, but my favorite spots—the ones I go to for both research and relaxation—are England, Scotland, Ireland, Italy, Mexico, and the American Southwest.

"I like to teach writing about as much as I like the act of writing itself. Teaching writing frees me from the desk, allows me to see the frustrations and joys of young writers, gives me a chance to meet students and discuss strategies—in short, it puts me in touch with people again, which is what this game is all about."

BIOGRAPHICAL/CRITICAL SOURCES:

PERIODICALS

Denver Post, February 8, 1987.
Rocky Mountain News, March 25, 1987.

* * *

MAYES, Herbert R(aymond) 1900-1987

OBITUARY NOTICE—See index for *CA* sketch: Born August 11, 1900, in New York, N.Y.; died of pneumonia, October 30, 1987, in New York, N.Y. Publishing company executive, editor, and author. Mayes enjoyed a long and distinguished career as one of the nation's top magazine editors at *Good Housekeeping* and *McCall's.* Before heading *Good Housekeeping* he served as managing editor of *American Druggist* and editor of *Pictorial Review.* Mayes became managing editor of *Good Housekeeping* in 1937 and editor in 1938. He left *Good Housekeeping* in 1958 to join its main competitor, *McCall's.* Mayes retired as president and chief executive of the McCall Corporation in 1965. He was the author of the controversial *Alger: A Biography Without a Hero,* a study of Horatio Alger, Jr., and the memoir, *Magazine Maze: A Prejudiced Perspective.* He also edited *Editor's Choice,* a collection of short stories, and the two-volume *An Editor's Treasury: A Continuing Anthology of Prose, Verse, and Literary Curiosa.*

OBITUARIES AND OTHER SOURCES:

BOOKS

Who's Who in America, 44th edition, Marquis, 1986.

PERIODICALS

Los Angeles Times, November 4, 1987.

New York Times, November 1, 1987.
Washington Post, November 2, 1987.

* * *

McCALLUM, Ian R(obert) M(ore) 1919-1987

OBITUARY NOTICE—See index for *CA* sketch: Born November 28, 1919, in London, England; died October 29, 1987. Museum official, editor, and author. McCallum was associate editor of *Architects' Journal* from 1944 to 1949, executive editor of *Architecture Review* from 1949 to 1959, and director of the American Museum in Britain, near Bath, England, beginning in 1959. He was also author of *A Guide to Modern Buildings in London* and *Architecture USA* and editor of *Physical Planning: The Groundwork of a New Technique*.

OBITUARIES AND OTHER SOURCES:

PERIODICALS

Times (London), November 6, 1987.

* * *

McDONALD, Alan (Patrick) 1949-

PERSONAL: Born January 6, 1949, in Leeds, England; son of Harold (a local government officer) and Joyce Linney (a housewife; maiden name, Martin) McDonald; married, April 5, 1974 (divorced, 1980). *Education:* Trinity College, Cambridge, B.A. (with honors), 1970. *Politics:* Labour. *Religion:* None.

ADDRESSES: Home—16 Knowle Rd., Leeds LS4 2JF, England. *Agent*—MBA Literary Agents Ltd., 45 Fitzroy St., London W1P 5HR, England.

CAREER: Housing administrator for various organizations in England, 1973-80; writer.

AWARDS, HONORS: Oddfellows Social Concern Book Award, 1986, for *The Weller Way.*

WRITINGS:

The Weller Way: The Story of the Weller Streets Housing Cooperative, Faber, 1986.

Author of detective novels, of 1986 play "Heads Held High," of radio plays for the British Broadcasting Corp., and of episodes for the television series "Brookside."

SIDELIGHTS: Alan McDonald told *CA* that he has "always wanted to write both entertaining and intelligent work for a popular audience." His 1986 book, *The Weller Way,* is a study of the cooperative housing project "Weller Streets" constructed in Liverpool between 1977 and 1982. What distinguishes this building enterprise from similar housing developments in England is that it was virtually "conceived, designed, and built," reported Andrew Saint in the *Times Literary Supplement,* by its tenants—inexperienced men and women who were frustrated by their unsuccessful attempts to find decent living quarters in Liverpool. McDonald's book exposes the five-year struggle these determined people encountered with contractors, banks, architects, and government officials who tried to foil construction of the Weller Street cooperative.

BIOGRAPHICAL/CRITICAL SOURCES:

PERIODICALS

Times Literary Supplement, June 20, 1986.

McDONALD, (Duncan) Peter 1962-

PERSONAL: Born January 22, 1962, in Belfast, Northern Ireland; son of Duncan and Louise (Gibson) McDonald. *Education:* Oxford University, B.A. (with first class honors), 1983, D.Phil., 1986.

ADDRESSES: Office—Christ Church, Oxford University, St. Aldate's, Oxford OX1 1DP, England.

CAREER: Oxford University, Oxford, England, research lecturer in English at Christ Church, 1986—.

AWARDS, HONORS: E. C. Gregory Award for Poetry, 1987.

WRITINGS:

"Light" (play), first produced in Edinburgh, Scotland, in 1984.
(With Alan Jenkins, Jo Shapcott, Dominic Fisher, and others) *New Chatto Poets,* Chatto & Windus, 1986.

Also author of poetry volume *Consequences;* co-author of *Trio Poetry 3,* for Blackstaff Press.

Contributor to magazines, including *Poetry Review, Review of English Studies, North,* and *Irish Review*. Co-editor of *Oxford Poetry,* 1983-85.

WORK IN PROGRESS: A book of poetry, tentatively titled *Long Distance Information;* a critical study of the work of Louis MacNeice.

SIDELIGHTS: Peter McDonald told *CA:* "I am a poet, born and brought up in Belfast, now living and working in England. I still return to Belfast regularly and take an active interest in Irish affairs, though I am neither Loyalist nor Republican. I believe that the unprejudiced study of Anglo-Irish literature (at which I try to earn my living) might be worthwhile, in the long term at least."

AVOCATIONAL INTERESTS: Travel (especially in Italy), good wine, music of the 1970s.

* * *

McEWAN, Jenny 1951-

PERSONAL: Born December 18, 1951, in Barnet, England; daughter of J. James and Olga Bennett; married Malcolm McEwan (a barrister-at-law), July 10, 1976. *Education:* Exeter College, Oxford, L.L.B. (first class honors), 1973, B.C.L., 1975.

ADDRESSES: Home—Sunnyside, Moss Hall Lane, Rushton, Tarporley, Cheshire CW6 9BB, England. *Office*—Department of Law, University of Keele, Staffordshire ST5 5BG, England.

CAREER: Victoria University of Manchester, Manchester, England, lecturer in law, 1975-87; University of Keele, Staffordshire, England, senior lecturer in law, 1987—.

MEMBER: Society of Public Teachers of Law, Howard League for Penal Reform.

WRITINGS:

(With St. John Robilliard) *Police Powers and the Individual,* Basil Blackwell, 1986.
Evidence: The Modern Law, Basil Blackwell, 1988.

Contributor of articles to legal periodicals.

SIDELIGHTS: Jenny McEwan told *CA:* "I regard it as important that analysis of criminal law and related areas is placed in social and philosophical context. I wish to examine rules

relating to evidence and proceedings in court without omitting their effect on participants. Also I am interested in questioning whether procedures are designed to discover truth or whether the aim is different. I believe that many of the problems facing vulnerable prosecution witnesses, particularly children and rape complainants, stem from the adversarial nature of the criminal trial."

* * *

McGILL, Ian
See ALLEGRO, John Marco

* * *

McINENLY, William T(homas) 1932-
(William Malliol)

PERSONAL: Born November 20, 1932, in London, England; immigrated to United States, 1958, naturalized citizen, 1969; son of Theodore William (an engineer) and Lois Louise (a ballet dancer; maiden name, Carroll) McInenly; common law marriage to Christine A. Joseph, August 12, 1972 (marriage ended, February 2, 1984). *Education:* Oxford University, B.A., 1958; Princeton University, M.A., 1959; Columbia University, Ph.D., 1977. *Politics:* Nonpolitical, "but a capitalist." *Religion:* Church of England.

ADDRESSES: Home—1314 Oxford Place, Charlottesville, Va. 22905. *Office*—Money Market Directories, Inc., 300 East Market St., Charlottesville, Va. 22901.

CAREER: Cheshire Academy, Cheshire, Conn., English teacher, 1959-61; Prentice-Hall, Inc., Englewood Cliffs, N.J., advertising copywriter, 1961-62; A. B. McDonald & Co., Tahiti, ship's captain, 1962-64; Money Market Directories, Inc., New York, N.Y., and Charlottesville, Va., editor, 1970—. Has worked as an advertising manager, research director, marketing director, salesman, and telemarketing director. *Military service:* U.S. Marine Corps, 1950-53; served in Korea; became sergeant; received three Purple Hearts. French Foreign Legion, 1954-55; served in Algerian War. Royal Air Force, 1956-58; became lieutenant.

AWARDS, HONORS: MacDowell Residence for *A Sense of Dark,* 1968-69.

WRITINGS:

(Under pseudonym William Malliol) *A Sense of Dark,* Atheneum, 1968.
(Under Malliol pseudonym) *Slave,* Norton, 1986.

Contributor to film scripts, including work on "Jeremiah Johnson" and "Tai-Pan," and author of short stories and articles.

WORK IN PROGRESS: A novel, *When the Wind Blows,* for Norton.

SIDELIGHTS: William T. McInenly, under the pseudonym William Malliol, wrote his first novel, *A Sense of Dark,* about a young British-born U.S. Marine's search for God in the midst of the Korean War. Josh Greenfeld, writing for the *New York Times Book Review,* commended *A Sense of Dark,* noting that although McInenly "supplies enough blood and brutality to stock a year of prime-time television," none of the violence is gratuitous: it is necessary for the development of the theme. Greenfeld added that McInenly's "writing style is equally red and raw, but at the same time powerful and stark."

McInenly's hero, Brian "Kamikaze" Locke, came to Korea to devote himself to death. From a series of flashbacks it becomes evident that Locke has been made impervious to feeling by a number of senseless, violent deaths: his father was killed by an Irish Republican Army ambush, his uncle in the air war with Germany, his mother and childhood playmate in the blitzkrieg, and his girlfriend in a freak horseback riding accident. Consequently Locke adopts a twisted, albeit logical and convincing, Christian-soldier mentality: he decides that since "God wants people in heaven. . . . God kills them." Thus, "God causes wars to create death." Hence, Locke believes he is a minister of Christ by acting as a deputy of death; by killing he sends men to heaven while he awaits his own end. But during a respite in a hospital he gains the new insight that "Death is death. It doesn't have to be heaven." No longer obsessed by death, Locke decides to live. But he is sent to the Ratcastle, a grisly and suicidal outpost where ironically he meets his final fate.

McInenly's second novel, also written as William Malliol, is *Slave. Slave* is the saga of Hadi Abbabba Guwah, a man born into a tribe of cannibals in West Africa who undergoes a series of adventures and escapades before finding a life of civility among the Arabs of North Africa many years later. Forced to learn self-sufficiency and self-preservation at an early age after his parents' deaths, Hadi longs to better himself but is captured by Moslem slave traders. He escapes from his master and treks across the Sahara, performing menial chores for a band of robber Bedouins, assisting the Berbers in a clash with the French Foreign Legion, then joining the Legion as a medical assistant, cook, and mapmaker. Hadi is narcissistic, faint-hearted, and duplicitous, yet sensible enough to take advantage of his opportunities. He does eventually achieve the status to which he has always aspired. He becomes a wealthy government official and lives in a villa on the Mediterranean coast, and eventually buys a wife, only to discover that she is a lesbian. She dies in childbirth after bearing twin boys.

McInenly told *CA:* "I forced myself to learn to write, but these days it's fun and I like it. I have no real specific book I think important. Once it is done, it's dead. But I now take writing very seriously. I consider the male-female relationship vital, but I have not yet gotten to it. But I will. Give me time, please."

AVOCATIONAL INTERESTS: Oil painting, travel.

BIOGRAPHICAL/CRITICAL SOURCES:

BOOKS

Malliol, William, *A Sense of Dark,* Atheneum, 1968.

PERIODICALS

New York Times, July 10, 1968.
New York Times Book Review, August 4, 1968.

* * *

McKAY, Claude
See McKAY, Festus Claudius

* * *

McKAY, Festus Claudius 1889-1948
(Claude McKay; Eli Edwards, pseudonym)

PERSONAL: Born September 15, 1889 (some sources say 1890), in Sunny Ville (some sources say Clarendon), Jamaica, British

West Indies (now Jamaica); immigrated to United States, 1912; naturalized U.S. citizen, 1940; died of heart failure, May 22, 1948, in Chicago, Ill.; buried at Calvary Cemetery, Woodside, N.Y.; son of Thomas Francis (a farmer) and Anne Elizabeth (a farmer; maiden name, Edwards) McKay; married Eulalie Imelda Edwards, July 30, 1914 (divorced); children: Ruth Hope. *Education:* Attended Tuskegee Normal & Industrial Institute, 1912, and Kansas State College, 1912-14. *Religion:* Roman Catholic.

ADDRESSES: Home—Chicago, Ill.

CAREER: Writer. Worked as cabinetmaker's apprentice and wheelwright; constable at Jamaican Constabulary, Kingston, 1909; longshoreman, porter, bartender, and waiter, 1910-14; restaurateur, 1914; writer for *Pearsons Magazine,* 1918, and *Workers' Dreadnought* in London, England, 1919; associate editor of *Liberator,* 1921; American Workers representative at Third International in Moscow, U.S.S.R., 1922; artist's model in mid-1920s; worked for Rex Ingram's film studio in Nice, France, c. 1926; shipyard worker, c. 1941.

AWARDS, HONORS: Medal from Jamaican Institute of Arts and Sciences, c. 1912; Harmon Foundation Award for distinguished literary achievement from the National Association for the Advancement of Colored People (NAACP), 1929, for *Harlem Shadows* and *Home to Harlem;* award from James Weldon Johnson Literary Guild, 1937.

WRITINGS:

UNDER NAME CLAUDE McKAY, EXCEPT AS NOTED

Songs of Jamaica (poetry), introduction by Walter Jekyll, Gardner, 1912, reprinted, Mnemosyne Publications, 1969 (also see below).

Constab Ballads (poetry), Watts, 1912 (also see below).

Spring in New Hampshire, and Other Poems, Richards, 1920.

Harlem Shadows: The Poems of Claude McKay, introduction by Max Eastman, Harcourt, 1922.

Home to Harlem (novel), Harper, 1928, reprinted, Pocket Books, 1965.

Banjo, a Story Without a Plot (novel), Harper, 1929, reprinted, Harcourt, 1970.

Gingertown (short stories), Harper, 1932.

Banana Bottom (novel), Harper, 1933, reprinted, Chatham, 1970.

A Long Way From Home (autobiography), Furman, 1937, reprinted, Arno Press, 1969.

Harlem: Negro Metropolis (nonfiction), Dutton, 1940, reprinted, Harcourt, 1968.

Selected Poems, introduction by John Dewey, biographical note by Max Eastman, Bookman, 1953.

The Passion of Claude McKay: Selected Poetry and Prose, 1912-1948, edited by Wayne F. Cooper, Schocken, 1973.

The Dialectic Poetry of Claude McKay (contains *Songs of Jamaica* and *Constab Ballads;* also see above), edited by Wayne F. Cooper, Books for Libraries Press, 1972.

Trial by Lynching: Stories About Negro Life in North America, re-translated into English from Russian-language version by Robert Winter, edited by Alan L. McLeod, preface by H. H. Anniah Gowda, Centre for Commonwealth Literature and Research, University of Mysore, 1977.

The Negroes in America, re-translated into English from Russian-language version by Robert Winter, edited by Alan L. McLeod, Kennikat, 1977.

Work represented in anthologies.

Contributor to periodicals, including *Workers' Dreadnought, Negro World, Catholic Worker, Ebony, Epistle, Interracial Review, Jewish Frontier, Nation, Seven Arts* (under pseudonym Eli Edwards), *New York Herald Tribune Books,* and *Phylon.*

SIDELIGHTS: Claude McKay was a key figure in the Harlem Renaissance, a prominent literary movement of the 1920s. His work ranged from vernacular verse celebrating peasant life in Jamaica to fairly militant poems challenging white authority in America, and from generally straightforward tales of black life in both Jamaica and America to more philosophically ambitious fiction addressing instinctual/intellectual duality, which McKay found central to the black individual's efforts to cope in a racist society. Consistent in his various writings is his disdain for racism and the sense that bigotry's implicit stupidity renders its adherents pitiable as well as loathsome. As Arthur D. Drayton wrote in his essay "Claude McKay's Human Pity" (included by editor Ulli Beier in the volume *Introduction to African Literature*): "McKay does not seek to hide his bitterness. But having preserved his vision as poet and his status as a human being, he can transcend bitterness. In seeing . . . the significance of the Negro for mankind as a whole, he is at once protesting as a Negro and uttering a cry for the race of mankind as a member of that race. His human pity was the foundation that made all this possible."

McKay was born in Sunny Ville, Jamaica, in 1889. The son of peasant farmers, he was infused with racial pride and a great sense of black heritage. His early literary interests, though, were in English poetry. Under the tutelage of his brother, schoolteacher Uriah Theophilus McKay, and a neighboring Englishman, Walter Jekyll, McKay studied the British masters—including John Milton, Alexander Pope, and the later romantics—and European philosophers such as eminent pessimist Arthur Schopenhauer, whose works Jekyll was then translating from German into English. It was Jekyll who advised aspiring poet McKay to cease mimicking the English poets and begin producing verse in Jamaican dialect.

At age seventeen McKay departed from Sunny Ville to apprentice as a woodworker in Brown's Town. But he studied there only briefly before leaving to work as a constable in the Jamaican capital, Kingston. In Kingston he experienced and encountered extensive racism, probably for the first time in his life. His native Sunny Ville was predominantly populated by blacks, but in substantially white Kingston blacks were considered inferior and capable of only menial tasks. McKay quickly grew disgusted with the city's bigoted society, and within one year he returned home to Sunny Ville.

During his brief stays in Brown's Town and Kingston McKay continued writing poetry, and once back in Sunny Ville, with Jekyll's encouragement, he published the verse collections *Songs of Jamaica* and *Constab Ballads* in London in 1912. In these two volumes McKay portrays opposing aspects of black life in Jamaica. *Songs of Jamaica* presents an almost celebratory portrait of peasant life, with poems addressing subjects such as the peaceful death of McKay's mother and the black people's ties to the Jamaican land. *Constab Ballads,* however, presents a substantially bleaker perspective on the plight of Jamaican blacks and contains several poems explicitly critical of life in urban Kingston. Writing in *The Negro Novel in America,* Robert Bone noted the differing sentiments of the two collections, but he also contended that the volumes share a sense of directness and refreshing candor. He wrote: "These first two volumes are already marked by a sharpness of vision, an inborn realism, and a freshness which provides a pleasing con-

trast with the conventionality which, at this time, prevails among the black poets of the United States."

For *Songs of Jamaica* McKay received an award and stipend from the Jamaican Institute of Arts and Sciences. He used the money to finance a trip to America, and in 1912 he arrived in South Carolina. He then traveled to Alabama and enrolled at the Tuskegee Institute, where he studied for approximately two months before transferring to Kansas State College. In 1914 he left school entirely for New York City and worked various menial jobs. As in Kingston, McKay encountered racism in New York City, and that racism compelled him to continue writing poetry.

In 1917, under the pseudonym Eli Edwards, McKay published two poems in the periodical *Seven Arts*. His verses were discovered by critic Frank Harris, who then included some of McKay's other poems in *Pearson's Magazine*. Among McKay's most famous poems from this period is "To the White Fiends," a vitriolic challenge to white oppressors and bigots. A few years later McKay befriended Max Eastman, Communist sympathizer and editor of the magazine *Liberator*. McKay published more poems in Eastman's magazine, notably the inspirational "If We Must Die," which defended black rights and threatened retaliation for prejudice and abuse. "Like men we'll face the murderous, cowardly pack," McKay wrote, "Pressed to the wall, dying, but fighting back!" In *Black Poets of the United States,* Jean Wagner noted that "If We Must Die" transcends specifics of race and is widely prized as an inspiration to persecuted people throughout the world. "Along with the will to resistance of black Americans that it expresses," Wagner wrote, "it voices also the will of oppressed people of every age who, whatever their race and wherever their region, are fighting with their backs against the wall to win their freedom."

Upon publication of "If We Must Die" McKay commenced two years of travel and work abroad. He spent part of 1919 in Holland and Belgium, then moved to London and worked on the periodical *Workers' Dreadnought*. In 1920 he published his third verse collection, *Spring in New Hampshire,* which was notable for containing "Harlem Shadows," a poem about the plight of black prostitutes in the degrading urban environment. McKay used this poem, which symbolically presents the degradation of the entire black race, as the title for a subsequent collection.

McKay returned to the United States in 1921 and involved himself in various social causes. The next year he published *Harlem Shadows,* a collection from previous volumes and periodicals publications. This work contains many of his most acclaimed poems—including "If We Must Die"—and assured his stature as a leading member of the literary movement referred to as the Harlem Renaissance. He capitalized on his acclaim by redoubling his efforts on behalf of blacks and laborers: he became involved in the Universal Negro Improvement Association and produced several articles for its publication, *Negro World,* and he traveled to the Soviet Union, which he had previously visited with Eastman, and attended the Communist party's Fourth Congress.

Eventually McKay went to Paris, where he developed a severe respiratory infection and supported himself intermittently by working as an artist's model. His infection eventually necessitated his hospitalization, but after recovering he resumed traveling, and for the next eleven years he toured Europe and portions of northern Africa. During this period he also published three novels and a short story collection. The first novel, *Home to Harlem,* may be his most recognized title. Published in 1928, it concerns a black soldier—Jake—who abruptly abandons his military duties and returns home to Harlem. Jake represents, in rather overt fashion, the instinctual aspect of the individual, and his ability to remain true to his feelings enables him to find happiness with a former prostitute, Felice. Juxtaposed with Jake's behavior is that of Ray, an aspiring writer burdened with despair. His sense of bleakness derives largely from his intellectualized perspective, and it eventually compels him to leave alien, racist America for his homeland of Haiti.

In *The Negro Novel in America,* Robert Bone wrote that the predominantly instinctual Jake and the intellectual Ray "represent different ways of rebelling against Western civilization." Bone added, however, that McKay was not entirely successful in articulating his protagonists' relationships in white society. He declared that *Home to Harlem* was "unable to develop its primary conflict" and thus "bogs down in the secondary contrast between Jake and Ray."

Despite thematic flaws, *Home to Harlem*—with its sordid, occasionally harrowing scenes of ghetto life—proved extremely popular, and it gained recognition as the first commercially successful novel by a black writer. McKay quickly followed it with *Banjo,* a novel about a black vagabond living in the French port of Marseilles. Like Jake from *Home to Harlem,* protagonist Banjo embodies the largely instinctual way of living, though he is considerably more enterprising and quick-witted than the earlier character. Ray, the intellectual from *Home to Harlem,* also appears in *Banjo*. His plight is that of many struggling artists who are compelled by social circumstances to support themselves with conventional employment. Both Banjo and Ray are perpetually dissatisfied and disturbed by their limited roles in white society, and by the end of the novel the men are prepared to depart from Marseilles.

Banjo failed to match the acclaim and commercial success of *Home to Harlem,* but it confirmed McKay's reputation as a serious, provocative artist. In his third novel, *Banana Bottom,* he presented a more incisive exploration of his principal theme, the black individual's quest for cultural identity in a white society. *Banana Bottom* recounts the experiences of a Jamaican peasant girl, Bita, who is rescued by white missionaries after suffering a rape. Bita's new providers try to impose their cultural values on her by introducing her to organized Christianity and the British educational system. Their actions culminate in a horribly bungled attempt to arrange Bita's marriage to an aspiring minister. The prospective groom is exposed as a sexual aberrant, whereupon Bita flees white society. She eventually finds happiness and fulfillment among the black peasants.

Critics agree that *Banana Bottom* is McKay's most skillful delineation of the black individual's predicament in white society. Unfortunately, the novel's thematic worth was largely ignored when the book first appeared in 1933. Its positive reviews then were related to McKay's extraordinary evocation of the Jamaican tropics and his mastery of melodrama. In the ensuing years, though, *Banana Bottom* has gained increasing acknowledgement as McKay's finest fiction and the culmination of his efforts to articulate his own tension and unease through the novel.

McKay's other noteworthy publication during his final years abroad was *Gingertown,* a collection of twelve short stories. Six of the tales are devoted to Harlem life, and they reveal McKay's preoccupation with black exploitation and humiliation. Other tales are set in Jamaica and even in North Africa,

McKay's last foreign home before he returned to the United States in the mid-1930s. Once back in Harlem he began an autobiographical work, *A Long Way From Home,* in which he related his own problems as a black individual in a white society.

By the late 1930s McKay had developed a keen interest in Catholicism. Through Ellen Tarry, who wrote children's books, he became active in Harlem's Friendship House. His newfound religious interest, together with his observations and experiences at the Friendship House, inspired his essay collection, *Harlem: Negro Metropolis.* Like *Banjo, Banana Bottom,* and *Gingertown, Harlem: Negro Metropolis* failed to spark much interest from a reading public that was already tiring of literature by and about blacks. With his reputation already waning, McKay moved to Chicago and worked as a teacher for a Catholic organization. By the mid-1940s his health had deteriorated. He endured several illnesses throughout his last years and eventually died of heart failure in May, 1948.

In the years immediately following his death McKay's reputation continued to decline as critics found him conventional and somewhat shallow. Recently, however, McKay has gained recognition for his intense commitment to expressing the predicament of his fellow blacks, and he is now admired for devoting his art and life to social protest. As Robert A. Smith wrote in his *Phylon* publication "Claude McKay: An Essay in Criticism": "Although he was frequently concerned with the race problem, his style is basically lucid. One feels disinclined to believe that the medium which he chose was too small, or too large for his message. He has been heard."

BIOGRAPHICAL/CRITICAL SOURCES:

BOOKS

Barton, Rebecca Chalmers, *Witnesses for Freedom: Negro Americans in Autobiography,* Harper, 1948.
Beier, Ulli, editor, *Introduction to African Literature: An Anthology of Critical Writing From "Black Orpheus,"* Longmans, 1967.
Bone, Robert, *The Negro Novel in America,* Yale University Press, 1958.
Brawley, Benjamin, *The Negro Genius: A New Appraisal of the Achievement of the American Negro in Literature and the Fine Arts,* Dodd, 1937.
Bronze, Stephen, *Roots of Negro Consciousness, the 1920's: Three Harlem Renaissance Authors,* Libra, 1964.
Dictionary of Literary Biography, Gale, Volume 4: *American Writers in Paris, 1920-1939,* 1980, Volume 45: *American Poets, 1880-1945, First Series,* 1986, Volume 51: *Afro-American Writers From the Harlem Renaissance to 1940,* 1987.
Emanuel, James A., and Theodore L. Gross, *Dark Symphony: Negro Literature in America,* Free Press, 1968.
Fullinwider, S. P., *The Mind and Mood of Black America: 20th Century Thought,* Dorsey, 1969.
Gayle, Addison, Jr., *Claude McKay: The Black Poet at War,* Broadside, 1972.
Giles, James R., *Claude McKay,* Hall, 1976.
Gloster, Hugh M., *Negro Voices in American Fiction,* University of North Carolina Press, 1948.
Huggins, Nathan, *Harlem Renaissance,* Oxford University Press, 1971.
Hughes, Carl Milton, *The Negro Novelist: 1940-1950,* Citadel, 1953.
Kent, George E., *Blackness and the Adventure of Western Culture,* Third World Press, 1972.
Ramchand, Kenneth, *The West Indian Novel and Its Background,* Barnes & Noble, 1970.
Twentieth-Century Literary Criticism, Volume 7, Gale, 1982.
Wagner, Jean, *Les Poetes negres des Etats-Unis,* Librairies Istra, 1962, translation by Kenneth Douglas published as *Black Poets of the United States: From Paul Laurence Dunbar to Langston Hughes,* University of Illinois Press, 1973.

PERIODICALS

America, July 3, 1943.
Black Orpheus, June, 1965.
Bookman, April, 1928, February, 1930.
CLA Journal, March, 1972, June, 1973, December, 1975, March, 1980.
Crisis, June, 1928.
Extension, September, 1946.
Phylon, fall, 1948, fall, 1964.
New York Post, May 22, 1937.
Race, July, 1967.
Studies in Black Literature, summer, 1972.*

—*Sketch by Les Stone*

* * *

McMAHON, Joseph H(enry) 1930-1987

OBITUARY NOTICE—See index for *CA* sketch: Born October 21, 1930, in New York, N.Y.; died following a heart attack, November 12, 1987, in Middletown, Conn. Educator and author. McMahon began his career in French literature as an instructor at Yale University in 1960. He rose to the rank of associate professor there before joining the faculty of Wesleyan University in 1968, becoming that institution's Hollis Professor of Romance Languages and Literatures in 1982. McMahon's writings include *The Imagination of Jean Genet* and *Humans Being: The World of Jean-Paul Sartre.*

OBITUARIES AND OTHER SOURCES:

BOOKS

International Authors and Writers Who's Who, 10th edition, International Biographical Centre, 1986.
Who's Who in America, 44th edition, Marquis, 1986.
The Writers Directory: 1986-1988, St. James Press, 1986.

PERIODICALS

New York Times, November 15, 1987.

* * *

McNEIL, Art 1944-

PERSONAL: Born February 13, 1944, in Owen Sound, Ontario, Canada; son of Clifton Evan and Lucy (Lyons) McNeil; married Judith (a secretary treasurer), May 23, 1964; children: Debora, Karen. *Education:* Attended Royal Canadian School of Military Engineering, 1960-63; Whitworth College, M.A./A.B.S., 1983.

ADDRESSES: Office—The Achieve Group, 6315 Shawson Dr., Suite 7, Mississauga, Ontario, Canada L5T 1J2.

CAREER: Bell Canada, Toronto, Ontario, district marketing manager, 1970-74; Edmonton Telephones, Edmonton, Alberta, director of sales and marketing, 1974-78; The Achieve Group, Toronto, chief executive officer, 1978—. *Military ser-*

vice: Royal Canadian Engineers, 1960-64; Canadian Army, Militia, 1969-72; held rank of lieutenant.

WRITINGS:

"I" of the Hurricane: Creating Corporate Energy, Stoddard Publications, 1987.
VIP: Vision Integrated Performance, Key Porter Books, 1987.

SIDELIGHTS: According to David Climenhaga, a reviewer for the Toronto *Globe and Mail,* Art McNeil's first book contains practical information for corporate managers who want to stimulate human energy and creativity in the business environment. The author emphasizes the human element in today's corporation, stressing, for instance, the value of conversation as a replacement for written communications. The book contains formulas aimed at the creation of corporate energy and the fulfillment of human potential.

Art McNeil told *CA:* "My books and public speaking engagements are to executive teams and deal with leadership: developing a strategic context and creating behavior alignment at all levels of the organization. I wrote the books because of demands from CEOs [chief executive officers] who wanted my leadership model to cascade down their organization. *"I" of the Hurricane* has notes in the margin from five CEOs who read the manuscript—so you are reading with five other people. Also, one-fourth of the book is 'Executive Scrimmages,' designed to help people move from 'know' to 'do.'

"To lead implies a place to go or way of being that does not exist. Great leaders develop a vision of the preferred future and then signal their intent to move toward it—they 'walk their talk.'"

BIOGRAPHICAL/CRITICAL SOURCES:

PERIODICALS

Globe and Mail (Toronto), March 28, 1987, April 4, 1987.

* * *

McNICOLL, Alan (Wedel Ramsay) 1908-1987

OBITUARY NOTICE: Born April 3, 1908; died in 1987 in Canberra, Australia. Naval officer, diplomat, and poet. McNicoll joined the Royal Australian Navy at age sixteen as a cadet, eventually rising to vice-admiral and Australian chief of naval staff in 1965. He was involved in plans to test British atomic capabilities off the Australian coast in 1952 and was later responsible for equipping the Australian navy with modern weaponry. McNicoll served as Australia's first ambassador to Turkey from 1968 to 1973. He also published a translation of selected works by early Roman poet Horace, *Odes of Horace,* and a volume of original verse titled *Sea Voices.*

OBITUARIES AND OTHER SOURCES:

BOOKS

The Blue Book: Leaders of the English-Speaking World, St. Martin's, 1976.
Who's Who, 140th edition, St. Martin's, 1988.

PERIODICALS

Times (London), November 26, 1987.

* * *

MEANS, Gardiner C(oit) 1896-1988

OBITUARY NOTICE: Born in 1896 in Windham, Conn.; died of complications from a stroke, February 15, 1988, in Vienna, Va. Economist, economic analyst and consultant, and author. Means is best remembered as the originator of the theory of administered prices. His work influenced President Franklin D. Roosevelt's New Deal policies of the 1930s and President John F. Kennedy's confrontation with U.S. steel manufacturers in 1962. According to Means's theories, corporate industrial giants set and hold prices, disregarding fluctuations in demand, and then maintain profit levels by decreasing production and thus reducing costs when demand falls. Means wrote and co-authored several books, including *The Modern Corporation and Private Property, The Holding Company: Its Public Significance and Its Regulation, The Structure of the American Economy, The Corporate Revolution in America, Pricing Power and the Public Interest: A Study Based on Steel,* and *The Roots of Inflation.*

OBITUARIES AND OTHER SOURCES:

BOOKS

International Encyclopedia of the Social Sciences, Volume 18: Biographical Supplement, Free Press, 1979.
Who's Who in Economics: A Biographical Dictionary of Major Economists, 1700-1981, MIT Press, 1983.

PERIODICALS

Chicago Tribune, February 19, 1988.
Los Angeles Times, February 19, 1988.
New York Times, February 18, 1988.
Washington Post, February 17, 1988.

* * *

MEENAN, James F(rancis) 1910-1987

PERSONAL: Born in 1910 in Dublin, Ireland; died in 1987, in Dublin, Ireland; son of James Nahor (a physician) and Mary Elizabeth (Cleary) Meenan; married Annette Mahony, 1945; children: Veronica, Ann, Nicola. *Education:* National University of Ireland, University College, Dublin, M.A., 1932; studied at King's Inn, Dublin, 1930-33.

CAREER: Attorney, 1935-41; National University of Ireland, University College, Dublin, lecturer, 1936-61, professor of political economy and dean of faculty of commerce, 1961-80. Member of board of directors of Bank of Ireland and Maguire & Peterson.

WRITINGS:

The Italian Corporative System, Cork University Press, 1944.
Centenary History of the Literary and Historical Society of University College, Dublin, 1855-1955, Kerryman, 1956.
(Editor with David A. Webb) *A View of Ireland: Twelve Essays on Different Aspects of Irish Life and the Irish Countryside,* British Association for the Advancement of Science, 1957.
The Irish Economy Since 1922, Liverpool University Press, 1970.
George O'Brien: A Biographical Memoir, Gill & Macmillan, 1980.
(Editor with Desmond Clarke) *The Royal Dublin Society, 1731-1981,* Gill & Macmillan, 1981.
The Economic and Social State of the Nation: A Series of Public Lectures, Economic and Social Research Institute (Dublin), 1982.

Irish correspondent for *Economist.* Contributor to periodicals.

BIOGRAPHICAL/CRITICAL SOURCES:

PERIODICALS

Times Literary Supplement, January 30, 1981.

OBITUARIES:

PERIODICALS

Times (London), May 27, 1987.*

* * *

MEISLER, Richard 1940-

PERSONAL: Born March 3, 1940, in New York, N.Y.; son of Simon (a lawyer) and Rose (a teacher; maiden name, Kaver) Meisler; married Miriam Horowitz (a molecular biologist), December 22, 1962; children: Joshua, Daniel. *Education:* Antioch College, A.B., 1960; graduate study at Columbia University, 1960-63, Ph.D., 1966. *Politics:* "Unashamed liberal."

ADDRESSES: Home—1203 Gardner, Ann Arbor, Mich. 48104.

CAREER: Antioch College, Yellow Springs, Ohio, professor and administrator of first year program, 1963-69; State University of New York at Buffalo, administrator of the independent degree program, 1969-77; University of Michigan, Ann Arbor, Mich., lecturer in English, 1977—; writer, 1977—.

WRITINGS:

Trying Freedom: A Case for Liberating Education, Harcourt, 1984.

WORK IN PROGRESS: Two books, *Prison Semester* and *Images of Love and Lust.*

SIDELIGHTS: Described by *Washington Post* columnist Colman McCarthy as a gifted teacher and "a writer with intensity," Richard Meisler recounts his teaching experiences while at Antioch College and the State University of New York at Buffalo in his first book, *Trying Freedom: A Case for Liberating Education.* Considering himself to be temperamentally conventional, Meisler, according to reviewer McCarthy, nonetheless established and administered nontraditional academic programs—no schedules, no curriculum, no grades. Designed primarily to eliminate learning restrictions imposed by structured methods of teaching, Meisler's programs allowed students to create a personalized educational plan while working in conjunction with an adviser-teacher. Written evaluations replaced grades. His intention, wrote McCarthy, was "to blast away the authoritarianism that ruins education." The critic concluded that Meisler's "writing here does not put him 'on the side of kids' against the allegedly corrupt establishment. It puts him beyond sides, to a territory in higher education that truly is higher."

BIOGRAPHICAL/CRITICAL SOURCES:

PERIODICALS

Los Angeles Times, May 24, 1984.
Washington Post, July 20, 1984.

* * *

MENDEL, Arthur P(aul) 1927-1988

OBITUARY NOTICE—See index for *CA* sketch: Born July 17, 1927, in Chicago, Ill.; died February 28, 1988, in La Jolla, Calif. Educator, translator, editor, and author. Mendel taught history at institutions including Roosevelt University and New York University before joining the University of Michigan in the early 1960s. There he specialized in Russian and Middle East affairs, becoming a full professor. Mendel translated and edited *Short Stories of Tolstoy* and edited publications such as *Essential Works of Marxism, The Twentieth Century,* and *The Extraordinary Decade: Political Memoirs of Pavel Nikolaevich Miliukov, 1905-1917.* He also compiled the memoirs of early kibbutz settlers and the writings of other kibbutz members for the volume *Hagshama! Autobiography of the Kibbutz.* Mendel's own writings include *Dilemmas of Progress in Tsarist Russia.*

OBITUARIES AND OTHER SOURCES:

BOOKS

Directory of American Scholars, Volume I: *History,* 8th edition, Bowker, 1982.

PERIODICALS

Detroit Free Press, March 3, 1988.

* * *

MENDELS, Ora 1936-

PERSONAL: Born October 12, 1936, in Jerusalem, Israel; immigrated to United States, naturalized citizen; daughter of Wilfred (a surgeon) and Gertrude (Janower) Kark; married Joseph Mendels (a psychiatrist), January 8, 1959; children: Gilla, Charles, David. *Education:* Received B.A. from University of the Witwatersrand.

ADDRESSES: Home and office—Philadelphia, Pa. *Agent*—Ray Lincoln Literary Agency, 4 Surrey Rd., Melrose Park, Pa. 19126.

CAREER: Reporter, columnist, and editor in South Africa, 1947-63; writer.

WRITINGS:

Mandela's Children (novel), Little, Brown, 1987.

WORK IN PROGRESS: Another novel set in South Africa; a novel set in the Untied States and the Middle East.

* * *

MENG, John J(oseph) 1906-1988

OBITUARY NOTICE: Born December 12, 1906, in Cleveland, Ohio; died of heart failure, February 15, 1988, in Jackson, Miss. Administrator, educator, historian, and author. Meng was a professor of history at several universities during the 1930s and 1940s, then moved into administrative positions beginning in the 1950s. He served as president of Hunter College from 1960 to 1966, was executive vice-president of Fordham University from 1966 to 1969, and assumed the presidency of Marymount College from 1969 to 1973. An authority on Franco-American relations during the American and French revolutions, Meng was in great demand as a lecturer after his retirement in 1973, particularly in association with activities concerning the bicentennial celebrations of those revolutions. He wrote many books dealing primarily with academic affairs and history, including *Despatches and Instructions of Conrad Alexandre Gerard, 1778-1780; Guide to Materials for American History in the Libraries and Archives of Paris;* and *American History for Catholic High Schools.* He was the co-author of *Christianity and America.*

OBITUARIES AND OTHER SOURCES:

BOOKS

Current Biography, H. W. Wilson, 1961.

PERIODICALS

New York Times, February 17, 1988.
Washington Post, February 18, 1988.

* * *

MERICK, Wendell S. 1928(?)-1988

OBITUARY NOTICE: Born c. 1928; died of a liver ailment, February 11, 1988, in Bethesda, Md. Editor and journalist. As a foreign correspondent for United Press International, Merick traveled back and forth between Asia and the United States. He began his career in 1949 with the United Press wire service in Detroit. The press service then assigned him to Tokyo, Japan, where he covered the Korean war, and he spent seven years as a bureau chief in Hong Kong. Returning to the United States in 1960, Merick worked as an editor and columnist with the *Boston Traveler.* After three years he returned to Asia, where he worked for British newspapers and the American Broadcasting Company's radio network before being named Saigon bureau chief of *U.S. News & World Report* in 1966. The journalist reported from Vietnam and Australia, then returned to the United States again in 1976. Before retiring in 1983, he covered the Pentagon and worked for *U.S. News*'s book division.

OBITUARIES AND OTHER SOURCES:

PERIODICALS

Washington Post, February 15, 1988.

* * *

MIDDLETON, Michael (Humfrey) 1917-

PERSONAL: Born December 1, 1917, in London, England; son of Humfrey (a surveyor) and L. Irene (in publishing; maiden name, Tillard) Middleton; married Julie Harrison, April 10, 1954; children: Humfrey Hugo Sebastian, Kate Augusta Middleton Ellison, Rose Irene. *Education:* Attended school in Canterbury, England.

ADDRESSES: Home—46 Holland Park Ave., London W11 3QY, England. *Agent*—John Johnson Ltd., 45-47 Clerkenwell Green, London EC1R 0HT, England.

CAREER: Picture Post, London, England, assistant editor and art director, 1949-53; *Lilliput,* London, editor, 1953-54; *House and Garden,* London, editor, 1955-57; Civic Trust, London, deputy director, 1957-69, director, 1969-86; writer, lecturer, consultant, 1986—. Director-general for the United Kingdom, European Architectural Heritage Year, 1975; member of United Kingdom Commission for UNESCO, 1976-78.

MEMBER: Royal Institute of British Architects (honorary fellow), Society of Registered Designers (fellow), Landscape Institute (honorary fellow).

AWARDS, HONORS: John Grierson Award for best short film from British Federation of Film Societies, 1971, for "A Future for the Past"; Silver Wheat-Ear Trophy from Seventh Berlin International Film Festival, First Prize from Fourth Festival of Architectural Films and Eleventh Congress International Union of Architects, Premier Award from British and Scientific Film Association Construction Films Competition, and Silver Award from British Industrial Film Festival, all 1972, all for "A Future for the Past"; Commander of Order of the British Empire, 1975; "Europa Nostra" received the premier award in the United Kingdom Heritage Year Film Awards, 1975; Pro Merito Medal from Council of Europe, 1976.

WRITINGS:

Group Practice in Design, Architectural Press, 1967.
"A Future for the Past" (film), broadcast by British Broadcasting Corp. (BBC-TV), 1971.
Man Made the Town, St. Martin's, 1987.

Author of film "Europa Nostra," released in 1975. Contributor to *Dictionnaire de la peinture moderne, Dictionnaire de la sculpture moderne,* and *Histoire illustree de la peinture.* Contributor to magazines and newspapers in England and abroad. Art critic for *Spectator,* 1946-56.

SIDELIGHTS: Michael Middleton told *CA:* "Throughout my life, my interests have centered on the visual and the verbal. I have sought to bring together aspects of the fine and applied arts, architecture, and environmental design and to communicate them to a wider, nonspecialized audience or readership without bringing a hot flush of embarrassment to the cheeks of the specialist. I see environmental quality not as an optional dollop of cream on the cake but as fundamental to the economic and social well-being of communities and nations.

"I have had the good fortune to be able to travel widely (throughout Western Europe, through some thirty of the United States, in South Africa, Singapore, and Indonesia), mostly to give papers at conferences and to universities and other groups. I have also served as a consultant on environmental problems. I have seen how great a need there is for a greater sharing of experience in this field. *Man Made the Town* is an attempt, in a modest way, to do this.

"The book seeks to give a coherent overview, without too much professional jibber-jabber, of what it is that gives towns and cities their character, how things go wrong, some of the questions that have to be asked, and the kind of things that *can* be done to improve and enliven the urban scene if only we set our minds to it. In other words, it aims to give a more rounded picture, a better overall context into which to slot particular issues when they arise, than more highly specialized studies—dealing only with particular social and demographic problems, this or that building type, transportation alternatives, or whatever—can hope to do. Environmental quality, the quality of urban life, stems from the interrelationship of many factors. It seems to me important that we keep the overall picture and potential in mind, lest we get bogged down in secondary matters and lose sight of the real vision."

* * *

MILLER, Mary
See NORTHCOTT, (William) Cecil

* * *

MILLER, Raymond W(iley) 1895-1988

OBITUARY NOTICE: Born January 21, 1895, in San Jose, Calif.; died of a lung ailment, February 18, 1988, in Silver Spring, Md. Farmer, public relations executive, business consultant, lecturer, and author. Founder of the Public Relations Society of America and director of the Food and Agriculture

Organization (FAO) of the United Nations, Miller was best known for his public relations and consulting skills. Owner of an eighty-acre walnut farm since 1919, Miller became interested in agencies designed to aid farmers. He joined the San Joaquin County Farm Bureau, serving as its president from 1930 to 1931, whereupon it became the largest county farm bureau in the nation. He eventually became vice-president of the California Walnut Growers Association (now Diamond Walnut Growers) in 1933.

In publicizing these organizations, Miller developed his public relations skills, and he soon served as president of the Public Relations Society of America, the American Institute of Cooperation, and Public Relations Research Associates. He was also a consultant to North American businesses, government agencies, and foreign universities, as well as a lecturer in public relations and world affairs at the Harvard University Graduate School of Business Administration from 1948 to 1964. As a consultant to the FAO during the late 1940s and early 1950s Miller traveled extensively, promoting the organization's purpose of raising living standards, increasing food production, and improving nutrition habits. Among Miller's books are *Keepers of the Corporate Conscience, Can Capitalism Compete?, Communism, Capitalism, Cooperation, A Conservative Looks at Cooperatives, Balancing Food and People,* and *Monsignor Ligutti: The Pope's County Agent.*

OBITUARIES AND OTHER SOURCES:

BOOKS

The International Year Book and Statesmen's Who's Who, Thomas Skinner Directories, 1982.

The National Cyclopedia of American Biography, Volume N-63, James White, 1984.

PERIODICALS

Washington Post, February 21, 1988.

* * *

MINTER, William 1942-

PERSONAL: Born September 22, 1942, in Washington, D.C.; son of David R. and Mary Sue (Wootton) Minter; children: Samuel. *Education:* University of Arizona, B.A. (with high distinction), 1963; attended University of Ibadan, 1961-62; Union Theological Seminary, M.Div. (cum laude), 1966; University of Wisconsin—Madison, M.A., 1971, Ph.D., 1973.

ADDRESSES: Home—1839 Newton St. N.W., Washington, D.C. 20010. *Agent*—Gail Ross, 918 16th St. N.W., Washington, D.C. 20010.

CAREER: High school teacher and curriculum developer for Mozambique Liberation Front secondary school in Dar es Salaam, Tazania, 1966-68, Bagamoyo, Tanzania, 1974-75, and Ribaue, Mozambique, 1975-76; Africa News Service, Durham, N.C., research director and staff writer, 1976-82, contributing editor, 1982—. Free-lance computer programmer; visiting lecturer at University of North Carolina at Chapel Hill, spring, 1977.

MEMBER: Phi Beta Kappa, Phi Kappa Phi.

AWARDS, HONORS: Grant from National Endowment for the Humanities, 1978; Moody grant from Lyndon B. Johnson Library, 1982; Social Science Research Council grant, 1983.

WRITINGS:

Imperial Network and External Dependency: The Case of Angola, Sage Publications, 1972, revised edition, Monthly Review Press, 1973.

Portuguese Africa and the West, Penguin, 1972.

(With Laurence Shoup) *Imperial Brain Trust: The Council on Foreign Relations and United States Foreign Policy,* Monthly Review Press, 1977.

King Solomon's Mines Revisited: Western Interests and the Burdened History of Southern Africa, Basic Books, 1986.

CONTRIBUTOR

Bruce Douglass, editor, *Reflections on Protest,* John Knox, 1968.

George Daniels, editor, *Southern Africa: A Time for Change,* Friendship Press, 1969.

David Wiley and Allen Isaacman, editors, *Southern Africa: Society, Economy, and Liberation,* Michigan State University Press, 1982.

Nzongola-Ntalaja, editor, *The Crisis in Zaire: Myths and Realities,* Africa World Press, 1986.

Phyllis Johnson and David Martin, editors, *Destructive Engagement: Southern Africa at War,* Zimbabwe Publishing House, 1986.

Contributor to *Collier's Encyclopedia Year Book* and *Funk & Wagnalls Encyclopedia Year Book.* Contributor to periodicals, including *Third World Quarterly, Africa News, Southern Africa, Foreign Policy, Christianity and Crisis,* and *TransAfrica Forum.*

WORK IN PROGRESS: Research on Southern Africa, international relations, and Central America.

SIDELIGHTS: William Minter speaks Portuguese and "a smattering of Swahili." He reads Spanish, French, German, Dutch, and Afrikaans.

Minter told *CA:* "In my writing I have always walked the borderline between academic writing and popularization. I have been concerned both with accuracy and with reaching the broadest possible audience for serious writing on political and social issues. I am concerned that my writing serves to mobilize people around issues of human rights and social justice, and that has determined in large part what I write about. But I also believe that interest is not served by sloganeering, rhetoric, or jargon but by making an honest attempt to understand what is going on.

"On southern Africa in particular, on which most of my writing has been concentrated, I am convinced that most Americans fail to understand the depth of repression of the racial and colonial systems there and the extent to which the United States government and businesses are complicit in continuing that injustice. Racism, cold war ideology, and simple ignorance help maintain the United States as a society on the side of repression and injustice in much of the world, including southern Africa and Central America. Most Americans, if they could penetrate behind the disinformation or lack of information they are generally exposed to, would not agree with what is being done in their name."

* * *

Miss C. L. F.
See GRIMKE, Charlotte L(ottie) Forten

MITCHELL, Andrew W. 1953-

PERSONAL: Born February 15, 1953, in St. Helier, Jersey, Channel Islands; son of William Haemish (a farmer) and Ann (a housewife; maiden name, Shettle) Mitchell. *Education:* University of Bristol, honours degree, 1975. *Religion:* Church of England.

ADDRESSES: Home and office—182 Elsley Rd., London SW11 5LQ, England. *Agent*—June Hall, 19 College Cross, London N.1, England.

CAREER: Tsavo Research Centre, Voi, Kenya, research assistant, 1974; Scientific Exploration Society, London, England, project researcher, 1976-78; Operation Drake, London, scientific coordinator, 1979-80; free-lance television writer and researcher, 1980-84; BBC-TV, London, television producer in London and Bristol, England, 1984-86; free-lance television writer, producer, and presenter, 1986—.

MEMBER: Royal Geographical Society (fellow), Scientific Exploration Society (member of council), Fauna and Flora Preservation Society, Jersey Wildlife Preservation Trust.

WRITINGS:

Operation Drake: Voyage of Discovery, Severn House, 1981.
The Young Naturalist, Usborne Publishing, 1984.
The Enchanted Canopy: A Journey of Discovery to the Last Unexplored Frontier, The Roof of the World's Rainforests, Macmillan, 1986.
The Enchanted Islands, Collins, in press.

WORK IN PROGRESS: A major book about nature and man in the South Pacific, publication by Collins expected in 1989.

SIDELIGHTS: "I began life as a fascinated child naturalist," Andrew W. Mitchell told *CA,* "evolved into a zoologist and aspiring explorer, and now find myself as a television producer and broadcaster in the business of 'Planet P.R.' My books are an extension of this. I am passionately interested in and concerned about our dependence on the natural world, and therefore I seek to alert all to the way in which man is an animal, too, and relies upon nature for his survival. This explains my numerous expeditions to the tropics to census anything from hippos and crocodiles to life in the tropical rain forest canopy, and most recently to study the relationship between and colonization of the Pacific islands by nature and man."

Mitchell's expeditions began shortly after he earned his university degree in zoology. He has surveyed elephant migration patterns, observed the animal behavior in Tsavo National Park in Kenya, and counted crocodiles along the Tana River. In 1978 the author joined the Royal Geographical Society's Mulu expedition in Borneo, and this provided his introduction to the tropical rain forest.

For two years Mitchell served as the scientific coordinator of Operation Drake. From his headquarters on the brigantine *Eye of the Wind,* he managed biological, medical, and archaeological projects all over the world. In Panama and other tropical countries, the scientist suspended unique, aerial walkways throughout the rain forests. These allowed him the rare opportunity to study the lives and behavior of animals who spent their entire lives high above the ground. One of the results of his work is his book *The Enchanted Canopy.*

Critics have described the author as a natural communicator and his book as a lavishly illustrated, enjoyable introduction to life in the rain forests. Mitchell was able to study and photograph animals and plants that few scientists had ever seen, much less studied. The wonders he encountered convinced the author that "the inaccessible crowns of giant rain forest trees remain nature's last frontier, and are likely to reveal more about life on earth than any other environment on the planet." Mitchell determined that the public must be made to understand the desperate need for increased conservation efforts all over the world. *The Enchanted Canopy* represents a part of his contribution to this effort. Critic Catherine Caufield wrote in the *Los Angeles Times Book Review:* "This is a book that cries out to be made into a television program. . . . The stories that Mitchell collected would be breathtaking on film."

Since 1982 Mitchell has worked as a television producer. He was associated with David Attenborough's "The Living Planet," with "The Living Isles," and with "The Amateur Naturalist," a product of the author's mentor, Gerald Durrell.

BIOGRAPHICAL/CRITICAL SOURCES:

PERIODICALS

Australian, July 1, 1987.
Daily Mail, January 8, 1987.
Los Angeles Times Book Review, November 16, 1986.
New Yorker, March 23, 1987.
Observer, December 14, 1986.
Today, December 8, 1986.

* * *

MITTERMEYER, Helen (Hayton Monteith) 1930- (Hayton Monteith; Ann Cristy, Danielle Paul, pseudonyms)

PERSONAL: Born April 30, 1930, in Rochester, N.Y.; daughter of William (a builder) and Mary Margaret (a homemaker; maiden name, McMahon) Monteith; married Waldemar B. Mittermeyer (an engineer), June 21, 1952; children: Paul, Ann, Daniel, Cristine. *Education:* Attended University of Rochester, Nazareth College at Rochester, and Miss McCarthy's Business School. *Politics:* "A caring American who votes." *Religion:* "A believer in good."

ADDRESSES: Home—Rochester, N.Y. *Agent*—Phillipa Brophy, The Sterling Lord Agency, Inc., 660 Madison Ave., New York, N.Y. 10021.

CAREER: Writer. Swimming instructor for the retarded; works with the blind and hearing impaired; makes speeches on writing.

MEMBER: Romance Writers of America, Beaumont Writers, Genesee Writers, Algonquin West, Church and Garden Club (president, 1969-70), District Federation of Garden Clubs, Weather or Not Garden Club.

AWARDS, HONORS: Reviewer's Choice Award from *Romantic Times,* 1984, for *Homecoming.*

WRITINGS:

Surrender, Bantam, 1983.
Brief Delight, Bantam, 1983.
Unexpected Sunrise, Bantam, 1984.
Vortex, Bantam, 1984.
(Under pseudonym Danielle Paul) *Chameleon,* Harlequin, 1984.
Tempest, Bantam, 1985.
Kismet, Bantam, 1987.
Ablaze, Bantam, in press.

UNDER NAME HAYTON MONTEITH

To Love a Stranger, Dell, 1982.
Relentless Love, Dell, 1982.
Jinx Lady, Dell, 1982.
Lovers' Knot, Dell, 1984.
Pilgrim Soul, Dell, 1984.
Lotus Blossom, Dell, 1985.
Endless Obsession, Dell, 1986.
Desert Princess, Dell, 1986.
Silver Love, Dell, 1987.
Sapphire Heart, Dell, 1987.
Brief Encounter (tentative title), Dell, in press.

UNDER PSEUDONYM ANN CRISTY

From the Torrid Past, Jove, 1982.
Torn Asunder, Jove, 1982.
Enthralled, Jove, 1983.
Tread Softly, Jove, 1983.
No Gentle Possession, Jove, 1984.
Homecoming, Jove, 1984.
Mystique, Jove, 1984.

WORK IN PROGRESS: Currently working on three books, one of which will run about 150,000 words; *Stolen Scenes,* a mainstream novel.

SIDELIGHTS: Helen Mittermeyer told *CA:* "I have been writing since the age of six with time out for marriage and children. Life has been great, if at times harrowing and downright tough. Writing is all there is for the part of me that's me. The rest belongs to my family.

"What drives me in my writing? The beast that whips us all: the desire to paint the world with words. If I have a deep abiding belief about romance writing, it's this: There is nothing sexier on earth than a compassionate man or woman. Giving of self is the greatest gift, and it reaps the most rewards. It is this type of human being who intrigues and fascinates me, who pushes me onward to probe and dig at the character of such protagonists. Such people are never dull; they are magnets to those around them. My pen will never stop seeking them out and sketching them."

* * *

MIZENER, Arthur (Moore) 1907-1988

OBITUARY NOTICE—See index for *CA* sketch: Born September 3, 1907, in Erie, Pa.; died of congestive heart failure, February 11, 1988, in Bristol, R.I. Educator, editor, and author. Mizener will be best remembered for the acclaimed *The Far Side of Paradise,* his 1951 biography of American Jazz Age author F. Scott Fitzgerald. Credited with renewing interest in its subject, the profile was the first account of Fitzgerald's life to be published. Mizener taught English at Yale University, Wells College, and Carleton College before becoming Cornell University's Mellon Foundation Professor of English in 1951. He retired from teaching in 1975. The scholar edited several books, including *Reading for Writing* and *Modern Short Stories: The Uses of Imagination.* Mizener's own writings include *The Sense of Life in the Modern Novel, The Saddest Story: A Biography of Ford Madox Ford,* and *Scott Fitzgerald and His World.*

OBITUARIES AND OTHER SOURCES:

BOOKS

The International Who's Who, 51st edition, Europa, 1987.

PERIODICALS

Los Angeles Times, February 17, 1988.
New York Times, February 15, 1988.
Times (London), February 15, 1988.
Washington Post, February 18, 1988.

* * *

MODGIL, Celia 1937-

PERSONAL: Born December 5, 1937, in Kent, England; daughter of Victor Ernest (a local government officer) and Lilian Comfort (a housewife; maiden name, Stubbs) Scaplehorn; married Sohan Modgil (a university teacher of educational research and development), January 31, 1975; children: Gita, Ramayana, Kush Luv, Radha. *Education:* University of London, teacher's certificate, 1959, diploma in education, 1968; University of Surrey, M.Phil., 1975; King's College, London, Ph.D., 1980. *Religion:* Hindu.

ADDRESSES: Home—Kush Luv, 87 Burfield Rd., Old Windsor, Berkshire SL4 2LR, England. *Office*—Goldsmiths' College, University of London, New Cross, London SE14 6NW, England.

CAREER: Teacher at infants' school in Kent, England, 1959-63, and primary school in Kent, 1963-65; head of infants' department at primary school in Kent, 1965-67; University of London, Goldsmiths' College, London, England, lecturer, 1967-72, senior lecturer in education and educational psychology, 1972—.

WRITINGS:

WITH HUSBAND, SOHAN MODGIL

Piagetan Research: A Handbook of Recent Studies, National Foundation for Educational Research, 1974.
Piagetan Research: An Appreciation and Theory of Cognitive Development and Sensorimotor Intelligence, National Foundation for Educational Research, 1976.
Experimental Validation of Conservation and the Child's Conception of Space, National Foundation for Educational Research, 1976.
The Growth of Logic: Concrete and Formal Operations, National Foundation for Educational Research, 1976.
School Curriculum and Test Development, National Foundation for Educational Research, 1976.
Personality, Socialization, and Emotionality and Reasoning Among Handicapped Children, National Foundation for Educational Research, 1976.
Cognitive-Developmental Approach to Morality, National Foundation for Educational Research, 1976.
Training Techniques, National Foundation for Educational Research, 1976.
Cross-Cultural Studies, National Foundation for Educational Research, 1976.

EDITOR; WITH HUSBAND, SOHAN MODGIL

Toward a Theory of Psychological Development, National Foundation for Educational Research, 1980.
Jean Piaget: Consensus and Controversy, Praeger, 1982.
(And Geoffrey Brown) *Jean Piaget: An Interdisciplinary Critique,* Routledge & Kegan Paul, 1983.
Lawrence Kohlberg: Consensus and Controversy, Falmer, 1986.
Hans Eysenck: Consensus and Controversy, Falmer, 1986.
(And G. Verma and K. Malik) *Multicultural Education: The Interminable Debate,* Falmer, 1986.

Noam Chomsky: Consensus and Controversy, Falmer, 1987.
Arthur Jensen: Consensus and Controversy, Falmer, 1987.
B. F. Skinner: Consensus and Controversy, Falmer, 1987.
Conception and Child-Birth Reborn: Consensus and Controversy, Falmer, 1988.
Pre-Natal, Neonatal, and Infant Competence: Consensus and Controversy, Falmer, 1988.
Early Childhood to Puberty: Consensus and Controversy, Falmer, 1988.
Adolescence, Generation Under Pressure: Consensus and Controversy, Falmer, 1988.
Young Adulthood: Consensus and Controversy, Falmer, 1988.
Middle Age: Consensus and Controversy, Falmer, 1988.
Aging and Bereavement: Consensus and Controversy, Falmer, 1988.
(And Jonathan Clark) *Anthony Giddens: Consensus and Controversy; Two Types of Science,* Falmer, in press.
(And Clark) *John Goldthorpe: Consensus and Controversy; Two Types of Science,* Falmer, in press.
(And Clark) *Daniel Bell: Consensus and Controversy; Two Types of Science,* Falmer, in press.
(And Clark) *Robert K. Merton: Consensus and Controversy; Two Types of Science,* Falmer, in press.
(And Clark) *Ralf Dahrendorf: Consensus and Controversy; Two Types of Science,* Falmer, in press.

Co-editor of Falmer series "Falmer International Master-Minds Challenged: Psychology Series," 1986-87, "The Seven Ages of Man," 1988, and "Falmer International Master-Minds Challenged: Sociology Series," 1989-90.

WORK IN PROGRESS: Editing, with husband Sohan Modgil, *Special Education: The Integration Debate, Pupil Diversity, Development and Learning, Class Management and Control, Pupil Performance,* and series "Falmer Seminar Papers," all to be published by Falmer in 1991.

* * *

MODGIL, Sohan (Lal) 1938-

PERSONAL: Born December 21, 1938, in Uganda; son of Piyare Lal (an engineering surveyor) and Diwarki (a housewife; maiden name, Rajaram) Modgil; married Celia Scaplehorn (a lecturer in education and educational psychology), January 31, 1975; children: Gita, Ramayana, Kush Luv, Radha. *Education:* Government Teachers Training College, Nairobi, Kenya, Teachers Certificate (with first class honors), 1958; University of Durham, A.E., 1961; graduate study at University of Newcastle-upon-Tyne, 1965; Institute of Education, London, Diploma in Education, 1968; Victoria University of Manchester, M.A., 1969; attended University of Geneva, 1970; King's College, London, Ph.D., 1974. *Religion:* Hindu.

ADDRESSES: Home—Kush Luv, 87 Burfield Rd., Old Windsor, Berkshire SL4 2LR, England. *Office*—Faculty of Education, Brighton Polytechnic, Falmer, Brighton, Sussex, England.

CAREER: Teacher at primary schools in Nairobi, Kenya, 1959-62, and South Shields, England, 1962-66; Stamford House Remand Home and Classifying Centre, London, England, psychological tester and remedial teacher, 1966-68; teacher at residential school for "maladjusted" boys, 1968-71; Borough of Barnet, Child Guidance Clinic, London, educational psychologist, 1971-73; North East London Polytechnic, London, lecturer, 1973-75, senior lecturer in psychology of education, 1975-80; Brighton Polytechnic, Falmer, England, reader in educational research and development, 1980—.

AWARDS, HONORS: Commonwealth scholar of Kenya Ministry of Education, 1960.

WRITINGS:

WITH WIFE, CELIA MODGIL

Piagetan Research: A Handbook of Recent Studies, National Foundation for Educational Research, 1974.
Piagetan Research: An Appreciation and Theory of Cognitive Development and Sensorimotor Intelligence, National Foundation for Educational Research, 1976.
Experimental Validation of Conservation and the Child's Conception of Space, National Foundation for Educational Research, 1976.
The Growth of Logic: Concrete and Formal Operations, National Foundation for Educational Research, 1976.
School Curriculum and Test Development, National Foundation for Educational Research, 1976.
Personality, Socialization, and Emotionality and Reasoning Among Handicapped Children, National Foundation for Educational Research, 1976.
Cognitive-Developmental Approach to Morality, National Foundation for Educational Research, 1976.
Training Techniques, National Foundation for Educational Research, 1976.
Cross-Cultural Studies, National Foundation for Educational Research, 1976.

EDITOR WITH WIFE, CELIA MODGIL

Toward a Theory of Psychological Development, National Foundation for Educational Research, 1980.
Jean Piaget: Consensus and Controversy, Praeger, 1982.
(And Geoffrey Brown) *Jean Piaget: An Interdisciplinary Critique,* Routledge & Kegan Paul, 1983.
Lawrence Kohlberg: Consensus and Controversy, Falmer, 1986.
Hans Eysenck: Consensus and Controversy, Falmer, 1986.
(And G. Verma and K. Malik) *Multicultural Education: The Interminable Debate,* Falmer, 1986.
Noam Chomsky: Consensus and Controversy, Falmer, 1987.
Arthur Jensen: Consensus and Controversy, Falmer, 1987.
B. F. Skinner: Consensus and Controversy, Falmer, 1987.
Conception and Child-Birth Reborn: Consensus and Controversy, Falmer, 1988.
Pre-Natal, Neonatal and Infant Competence: Consensus and Controversy, Falmer, 1988.
Early Childhood to Puberty: Consensus and Controversy, Falmer, 1988.
Adolescence, Generation Under Pressure: Consensus and Controversy, Falmer, 1988.
Young Adulthood: Consensus and Controversy, Falmer, 1988.
Middle Age: Consensus and Controversy, Falmer, 1988.
Aging and Bereavement: Consensus and Controversy, Falmer, 1988.
(And Jonathan Clark) *Anthony Giddens: Consensus and Controversy; Two Types of Science,* Falmer, in press.
(And Clark) *John Goldthorpe: Consensus and Controversy; Two Types of Science,* Falmer, in press.
(And Clark) *Daniel Bell: Consensus and Controversy; Two Types of Science,* Falmer, in press.
(And Clark) *Robert K. Merton: Consensus and Controversy; Two Types of Science,* Falmer, in press.
(And Clark) *Ralf Dahrendorf: Consensus and Controversy; Two Types of Science,* Falmer, in press.

Co-editor of Falmer series "Falmer International Master-Minds Challenged: Psychology Series," 1986-87, "The Seven Ages of Man," 1988, and "Falmer International Master-Minds Challenged: Sociology Series," 1989-90.

WORK IN PROGRESS: Editing with wife, Celia Modgil, *Special Education: The Integration Debate, Pupil Diversity, Development and Learning, Class Management and Control, Pupil Performance,* and series "Falmer Seminar Papers," all for Falmer, 1991.

* * *

MONSON, Karen Ann 1945-1988

*OBITUARY NOTICE—*See index for *CA* sketch: Born March 25, 1945, in New Haven, Conn.; died of complications arising from cirrhosis of the liver, January 30, 1988, in Long Branch, N.J. Music critic and author. Monson served as the music critic for several periodicals, including the *Los Angeles Times,* the *Los Angeles Herald-Examiner,* the Baltimore *Sun,* and the now-defunct *Chicago Daily News.* She also directed Arizona State University's Louise Lincoln Kerr Cultural Center, and was an accomplished flutist. Monson received a Peabody Award in 1975 for a radio series she helped prepare on composer Igor Stravinsky as well as a Deems Taylor Award from the American Society of Composers, Authors, and Publishers in 1977. She also authored two biographies of musical figures, *Alban Berg* and *Alma Mahler: Muse to Genius.*

OBITUARIES AND OTHER SOURCES:

PERIODICALS

Chicago Tribune, February 3, 1988.
Los Angeles Times, February 2, 1988.
New York Times, February 1, 1988.

* * *

MONTEITH, Hayton
See MITTERMEYER, Helen (Hayton Monteith)

* * *

MOORE, Alice Ruth
See NELSON, Alice Ruth Moore Dunbar

* * *

MOORE, Colleen 1902(?)-1988

OBITUARY NOTICE: Name originally Kathleen Morrison; born August 19, 1902 (some sources say 1900 or 1903), in Port Huron, Mich.; died of cancer, January 25 (one source says January 26), 1988, in Paso Robles, Calif. Actress, business woman, and author. An originator of the famed 1920s "flapper" look of boyish bobbed hair and short skirts, silent screen star Colleen Moore was most noted for the flamboyant style she contributed to her films. The actress began her career in Hollywood at the age of fifteen, and, upon cutting her long, curly hair into a short bob, Moore became instantly popular appearing in the 1923 film "Flaming Youth;" her hairstyle and clothes were subsequently imitated by women across America. She soon became one of Hollywood's highest paid actresses, appearing in more than fifty films, including the silent "Ella Cinders," "So Big," and "Lilac Time," and later sound pictures such as "The Power and the Glory," which Moore considered her favorite. Abandoning her film career in 1937, Moore became avid in managing and making money from the stockmarket, and she eventually joined her third husband's prestigious New York brokerage firm. Her books include *The Enchanted Castle, Silent Star* (an autobiography), *Colleen Moore's Doll House,* and *How Women Can Make Money in the Stock Market.*

OBITUARIES AND OTHER SOURCES:

BOOKS

Who's Who in Hollywood, 1900-1976, Arlington House, 1976.
Who's Who of American Women, 6th edition, Marquis, 1970.

PERIODICALS

Chicago Times, January 31, 1988.
Los Angeles Times, January 26, 1988.
New York Times, January 27, 1988.
Times (London), January 28, 1988.
Washington Post, January 28, 1988.

* * *

MOORE, Madeline (Roberta) 1934-
(Madeline Hummel)

PERSONAL: Born December 23, 1934, in Lake Charles, La.; daughter of George H. (a business executive) and Clara Nell (a teacher; maiden name, McAdams) Moore; divorced; children: Diane Whipple, Susan Bellinger, Rebecca Hummel-Moore. *Education:* University of Texas, B.S., 1962, Ph.D., 1970. *Politics:* Democrat.

*ADDRESSES: Home—*641 14th St., San Francisco, Calif. 94114. *Office—*Kresge College, University of California, Santa Cruz, Calif. 95064.

CAREER: University of California, Santa Cruz, lecturer, 1971-72, assistant professor, 1973-79, associate professor of English literature, 1979-88. University of Sussex, visiting lecturer in English literature, 1980-81. Djerassi Foundation, Woodside, Calif., writer in residence, 1985.

MEMBER: Modern Language Association of America, Virginia Woolf Society (trustee and charter member, 1976-88), Friends of the Commission on the Status of Women (president of San Francisco chapter).

WRITINGS:

(Contributor) Ralph Freeman, editor, *Virginia Woolf: Revaluation and Continuity,* University of California Press, 1980.
(Contributor) Jane Marcus, editor, *New Feminist Essays on Virginia Woolf,* Macmillan, 1981.
The Short Season Between Two Silences: The Mystical and the Political in the Novels of Virginia Woolf, Allen & Unwin, 1984.

Contributor, sometimes under name Madeline Hummel, of articles and reviews to professional journals, including *Twentieth Century Literature, Women's Studies,* and *Texas Studies in Literature and Language.*

WORK IN PROGRESS: The Red Rocking Horse, a novel, completion expected in 1990.

SIDELIGHTS: Madeline Moore told *CA:* "When I wrote *The Short Season Between Two Silences,* I wanted to analyze Virginia Woolf's fiction in light of the most comprehensive possible understanding of her life, including her political and philosophical beliefs. As I write my own first novel, I find that

tranquility and trust in the depths of my spiritual resources make it possible for me to work well."

BIOGRAPHICAL/CRITICAL SOURCES:

PERIODICALS

Modern Fiction Studies, summer, 1985.
Notes and Queries, December, 1985.
Times Literary Supplement, August 10, 1984.

* * *

MOORHEAD, James H(owell) 1947-

PERSONAL: Born January 16, 1947, in Harrisburg, Pa.; son of Robert Blair (an electrician) and Tina (a homemaker; maiden name, Deaver) Moorhead; married Cynthia Stephens (a homemaker), April 5, 1969; children: Evan, Stefan. *Education:* Westminster College, New Wilmington, Pa., B.A., 1968; Princeton Theological Seminary, M.Div., 1971; Yale University, M.Phil, 1973, Ph.D., 1975. *Politics:* Democrat. *Religion:* Presbyterian.

ADDRESSES: Home—135 Clover Lane, Princeton, N.J. 08540. *Office*—Princeton Theological Seminary, CN 821, Princeton, N.J. 08542.

CAREER: North Carolina State University, Raleigh, assistant professor, 1975-80, associate professor of religion, 1980-84; Princeton Theological Seminary, Princeton, N.J., associate professor, 1984-86, professor of American church history, 1986—.

MEMBER: American Academy of Religion, American Society of Church History, American Historical Association, Organization of American Historians.

AWARDS, HONORS: Brewer Prize from American Society for Church History, 1976, for manuscript of *American Apocalypse;* fellow of National Endowment for the Humanities, 1981-82.

WRITINGS:

American Apocalypse: Yankee Protestants and the Civil War, 1860-1869, Yale University Press, 1978.

Contributor to religious and historical periodicals.

WORK IN PROGRESS: A study of Protestant views of eschatological themes in nineteenth-century America.

SIDELIGHTS: Focusing on the era of the American Civil War, *American Apocalypse* by James H. Moorhead discusses the extent to which some Protestants in the North viewed that conflict in biblical terms. As in the description of the end of the world in the Book of the Apocalypse, the Civil War was seen as a definitive battle between good and evil, in which God would assure victory by the North over the South and its immoral practice of slavery. Writing in the *New York Times,* Alden Whitman noted that "Moorhead has made a significant contribution not only to the intellectual history of the Civil War, but also to the general history of American thought."

BIOGRAPHICAL/CRITICAL SOURCES:

PERIODICALS

New York Times, May 26, 1978.

MORAN, Barbara B. 1944-

PERSONAL: Born July 8, 1944, in Columbus, Miss.; daughter of Robert Theron and Joan Brown Burns; married Joseph J. Moran (a psychologist), September 4, 1965; children: J. Michael, Brian Matthew. *Education:* Mount Holyoke College, A.B., 1966; Emory University, M.Ln., 1973; State University of New York at Buffalo, Ph.D., 1982.

ADDRESSES: Home—1307 LeClair St., Chapel Hill, N.C. 27514. *Office*—School of Library Science, University of North Carolina at Chapel Hill, Chapel Hill, N.C. 27514.

CAREER: Head of library and director of audiovisual service at school in Buffalo, N.Y., 1974-78; State University of New York at Buffalo, library intern, 1979-80; University of North Carolina at Chapel Hill, associate professor and assistant dean of library science, 1981—, member of Institute for Research in the Social Sciences, 1981—.

MEMBER: American Library Association, American Association of University Professors, Association for the Study of Higher Education, Association for Library and Information Science Education, Popular Culture Association, North Carolina Library Association, Beta Phi Mu.

AWARDS, HONORS: Grant from Council of Library Resources, 1985.

WRITINGS:

(Contributor) Fred Schroeder, editor, *Twentieth Century Popular Culture in Museums and Libraries,* Bowling Green University, 1980.
Academic Libraries: The Changing Knowledge Centers of Colleges and Universities, Association for the Study of Higher Education, 1984.
(Contributor) Marcia Tuttle and Jean G. Cook, editors, *Advances in Serials Management,* Jai Press, 1986.
(With Robert D. Stueart) *Library Management,* 3rd edition, Libraries Unlimited, 1987.

Contributor to library journals. Advisory editor of *Journal of Popular Literature,* 1985—.

WORK IN PROGRESS: Contributing to *Personnel Administration in Libraries,* edited by Sheila Creth, for Neal Schuman.

* * *

MORANTZ, Regina Markell
See MORANTZ-SANCHEZ, Regina (Ann) Markell

* * *

MORANTZ-SANCHEZ, Regina (Ann) Markell 1943-
(Regina Markell Morantz)

PERSONAL: Born August 28, 1943, in Brooklyn, N.Y.; daughter of Maxwell M. (in business) and Rosalind (a housewife, maiden name, Rosenberg) Markell; married Robert A. Morantz, June 27, 1965 (divorced, 1978); married George J. Sanchez (a historian), June 2, 1984; children: (first marriage) Alison, Jessica; (second marriage) Adam Max. *Education:* Barnard College, B.A., 1965; Columbia University, M.A., 1966, Ph.D., 1971. *Politics:* Democrat. *Religion:* Jewish.

ADDRESSES: Home—4400 Tomahawk Rd., Prairie Village, Kan. 66208. *Office*—Department of History, 2007 Wescoe, University of Kansas, Lawrence, Kan. 66045.

CAREER: Queens College of the City University of New York, New York, N.Y., instructor in history, 1967; C. W. Post

College of Long Island University, Greenvale, N.Y., assistant professor of history, 1971-73; University of Kansas, Lawrence, assistant professor, 1975-80, associate professor, 1981-85, professor of history, 1986—. Academic consultant for Women in Medicine Oral History Project, Medical College of Pennsylvania, 1975-78. Member of Coordinating Committee on Women in the Historical Profession.

MEMBER: American Historical Association, American Association for the History of Medicine, American Studies Association, Association of Jewish Studies, Organization for American Historians, Women's Studies Association.

AWARDS, HONORS: Grant from American Council of Learned Societies, 1974; grants from National Endowment for the Humanities, 1975, 1981, and 1987; grant from National Library of Medicine, 1976-78; Charles Warren Fellowship, 1983; Outstanding Woman Teacher Award from University of Kansas, 1986; prize for best book on women in science from History of Science Society, 1986, for *Sympathy and Science.*

WRITINGS:

(Under name Regina Markell Morantz; editor with Cynthia Stodola Pomerleau and Carol Hansen Fenichel) *In Her Own Words: Oral Histories of Women Physicians,* Greenwood Press, 1982.

Sympathy and Science: Women Physicians in American Medicine, Oxford University Press, 1985.

Forty oral autobiographies of physicians, published by Medical College of Pennsylvania, c. 1978.

WORK IN PROGRESS: "A social history of a spectacular nineteenth-century libel trial between a woman surgeon and the Brooklyn *Eagle* newspaper, *Conduct Unbecoming of a Woman,* for Princeton University Press; a history of marriage in the United States."

SIDELIGHTS: In her second book, *Sympathy and Science,* Regina Markell Morantz-Sanchez "brings a historical perspective on medicine" to contemporary controversies surrounding gender and science, observed Linda Gordon in the *New York Times Book Review.* Women physicians established their own schools in the nineteenth century, writes Morantz-Sanchez, and they were gradually admitted to many male institutions as well. For lack of financial support and other reasons, however, the women's colleges perished, and by the early twentieth century women physicians began to lose ground in the profession. "They are struggling back into medicine now," noted Gordon, though "the full measure of their influence has yet to be taken." The reviewer praised Morantz-Sanchez's analysis as "the first study to examine these events in the proper context."

Gordon noted the perceived difference between "masculine" emphasis on laboratory medicine and "feminine" concern for holistic healing, explaining that "Morantz-Sanchez acknowledges these poles but insists on a more complex history." The reviewer asserted: "We need both kinds of medicine. [*Sympathy and Science*] suggests that sex equality in medicine might yet contribute to a better balance."

Morantz-Sanchez told *CA:* "I learned two important things in graduate school. One was a respect for the complexity of the past. The other was that women have, until recently, been generally absent from the historical record. I have intended my work to be a contribution toward redressing the imbalance while not losing sight of the complexity of human events."

BIOGRAPHICAL/CRITICAL SOURCES:

PERIODICALS

New York Times Book Review, January 12, 1986.

* * *

MORE, Jasper 1907-1987

OBITUARY NOTICE—See index for *CA* sketch: Born July 31, 1907, in London, England; died October 28, 1987. Attorney, politician, and author. More practiced law from 1930 to 1939, when he entered the Ministry of Economic Warfare at the outbreak of World War II. He served with the Allied Commission in Italy during the latter part of the war. A Conservative, More was elected to the British House of Commons in 1960 and served for nineteen years. During his terms in Parliament, his duties included compiling reports of the House of Commons proceedings to Queen Elizabeth II. More wrote *The Saving of Income Tax, Surtax, and Death Duties, The Land of Italy, The Mediterranean, The Land of Egypt,* and the autobiographical *A Tale of Two Houses.*

OBITUARIES AND OTHER SOURCES:

BOOKS

Who's Who, 139th edition, St. Martin's, 1987

PERIODICALS

Times (London), October 30, 1987.

* * *

MOREHOUSE, Thomas A(lvin) 1937-

PERSONAL: Born May 26, 1937, in Minneapolis, Minn.; son of Sierl Alvin and Helen (Hill) Morehouse; married Karen M. Bornfleth, September 4, 1959 (divorced, 1976); married Dolores E. Sauberlich (a purchasing agent), June 3, 1978; children: Stephanie L. McBride, Julia K., David J. *Education:* Harvard University, A.B., 1960; University of Minnesota, M.A.P.A., 1961, Ph.D., 1968.

ADDRESSES: Home—3900 Amber Bay Loop, Anchorage, Alaska 99515. *Office*—School of Business and Public Affairs, University of Alaska, Anchorage, 3211 Providence Dr., Anchorage, Alaska 99508.

CAREER: U.S. Housing & Home Finance Agency, Washington, D.C., program analyst in metropolitan development, 1963-65; U.S. Department of Housing & Urban Development, Washington, D.C., program officer, 1965-67; University of Alaska, Anchorage, assistant professor, 1967-69, associate professor, 1969-74, professor of political science at Institute of Social and Economic Resources, 1974—, associate dean of public affairs, 1986—. Deputy director of Division Policy Development, Governor's Office, State of Alaska, 1975-76; president of board of directors of Independent Public Television, Inc., 1985—.

MEMBER: American Political Science Association, American Society for Public Administration, American Association for the Advancement of Science (president of arctic division, 1986-87), Academy of Political Science, Union of Concerned Scientists, Western Regional Science Association (member of board of directors), Association for Politics and the Life Sciences.

WRITINGS:

(With David Kresge and George Rogers) *Issues in Alaska Development,* University of Washington Press, 1978.
(With Gerald A. McBeath) *The Dynamics of Alaska Native Self-Government,* University Press of America, 1980.
(With McBeath and Linda Leask) *Alaska's Urban and Rural Governments,* University Press of America, 1984.
(Editor and contributor) *Alaska Resources Development,* Westview Press, 1984.
(With McBeath) *Alaska State Government and Politics,* University of Alaska Press, 1987.

Contributor of articles to periodicals, including *Polar Record, Public Administration Review,* and *State Government.*

SIDELIGHTS: Thomas A. Morehouse told *CA:* "My writings largely document my research projects, teaching assignments, and preoccupation with Alaskan politics, government, and public policy issues. I have been lucky to find a spot in the world where I can create intellectual puzzles that relate to people's concerns, and then help to resolve them or at least to influence thinking about how to approach and cope with them."

* * *

MORGAN, Alyssa
See DELATUSH, Edith G.

* * *

MORRISON, William R(obert) 1942-

PERSONAL: Born January 26, 1942, in Hamilton, Ontario, Canada; son of W. Robert (a judge) and Elizabeth (Ward) Morrison; married Kathleen Harrop, August 15, 1969 (divorced, 1973); married Linda Deacon, May 1, 1976; children: Catherine, John, Claire, Ruth. *Education:* McMaster University, B.A., 1963, M.A., 1964; University of Western Ontario, Ph.D., 1973.

ADDRESSES: Home—6 Magnacca Cres., Brandon, Manitoba, Canada R7B 2N9. *Office*—Department of History, Brandon University, Brandon, Manitoba, Canada R7A 6A9.

CAREER: Brandon University, Brandon, Manitoba, lecturer, 1969-73, assistant professor, 1973-75, associate professor, 1975-85, professor of history, 1985—.

MEMBER: Canadian Historical Association.

WRITINGS:

A Survey of the History and Claims of the Native Peoples of Northern Canada, Department of Indian Affairs, 1985.
Showing the Flag: The Mounted Police and Canadian Sovereignty in the North, 1894-1925, University of British Columbia Press, 1987.
(With K. S. Coates) *Land of the Midnight Sun: A History of the Yukon Territory,* Hurtig, 1988.
(With K. S. Coates) *Taking the North Down With Her: The Sinking of the "Princess Sophia,"* University of British Columbia Press, 1988.

Editor of *Northern History Newsletter;* book review editor for *Northern Review.*

WORK IN PROGRESS: With K. S. Coates, *The Army of Occupation: A Social History of the Alaska Highway.*

SIDELIGHTS: William R. Morrison told *CA:* "I am interested in the Canadian North—in its history and future, particularly in relation to the governments of Canada and the United States, and its native people. It seems to me that too much northern history has been written from the outside looking in, that is, from a southern point of view. My research colleague, K. S. Coates, and I have attempted to rectify this in our work. Thus our forthcoming book, *The Army of Occupation,* is a history of the Alaska Highway from a northern perspective—virtually everything written on the subject up until now has been oriented toward diplomacy or military history. We hope to alter this perspective."

* * *

MORTON, A(rthur) L(eslie) 1903-1987

OBITUARY NOTICE—See index for *CA* sketch: Born July 4, 1903, in Hengrave, Bury Saint Edmunds, Suffolk, England; died October 23, 1987. Editor, journalist, and author. Morton was a member of the British Communist Party and served on the staff of the *Daily Worker.* He edited the book, *Political Writings of William Morris,* and his numerous writings include *A People's History of England, The English Utopia, The Matter of Britain: The Arthurian Cycle and the Development of Feudal Society, The World of the Ranters, Freedom in Arms,* and *Collected Poems.* Morton was also a contributor to such publications as *Criterion, Listener,* and *Marxism Today.* He received an honorary doctorate from Rostock University in 1975.

OBITUARIES AND OTHER SOURCES:

BOOKS

International Authors and Writers Who's Who, 10th edition, International Biographical Centre, 1986.

PERIODICALS

Times (London), November 4, 1987.

* * *

MORTON, Joseph
See RICHMOND, Al

* * *

MORWOOD, James 1943-

PERSONAL: Born November 25, 1943, in Belfast, Northern Ireland; son of James Bryan (a doctor) and Kathleen (a housewife; maiden name, Weldon) Morwood. *Education:* Attended Cambridge University.

ADDRESSES: Home—3 Gayton House, Grove Hill, Harrow on the Hill, Middlesex HA1 3HF, England.

CAREER: Harrow School, Harrow on the Hill, England, Vaughan Librarian, 1973-85, became teacher of classics, head of classics program, 1979—. Director of Joint Association of Classical Teachers Summer School in Ancient Greece.

WRITINGS:

(With Maurice Balme) *Cupid and Psyche,* Oxford University Press, 1976.
The Life and Works of Richard Brinsley Sheridan, Scottish Academic Press, 1985.
(With Maurice Balme) *Oxford Latin Course,* three volumes, with instructor's guide, Oxford University Press, in press.

Contributor to philology and classical studies journals.

MOSS, Roger 1951-

PERSONAL: Born June 28, 1951, in Cheltenham, England; son of George Ernest (in Royal Air Force) and Muriel Ethel (Pye) Moss; married Susan Purdie, 1974 (separated, 1987); children: Nicholas Cory Peters (stepson). *Education:* University of Sussex, B.A., 1973, D.Phil., 1982.

ADDRESSES: Office—Department of Literature, University of Essex, Colchester, England. *Agent*—Radala & Associates, 17 Avenue Mansions, Finchley Rd., London N.W.3, England.

CAREER: University of Essex, Colchester, England, lecturer in literature, 1977—.

WRITINGS:

The Game of the Pink Pagoda (novel), Collins, 1986, Ballantine, 1987.

Contributor of articles and reviews to academic periodicals.

WORK IN PROGRESS: A novel; a long, "quasi-historical romance"; a "semi-academic" book on writing and the problems associated with it.

BIOGRAPHICAL/CRITICAL SOURCES:

PERIODICALS

Times Literary Supplement, August 15, 1986.

* * *

MUNRO, Duncan H.
See RUSSELL, Eric Frank

* * *

MUNSON, James (Edward Bradbury) 1944-

PERSONAL: Born April 20, 1944, in San Antonio, Tex.; son of Jacob Rescomb (a civil servant) and Vera Susan Elizabeth (a nurse; maiden name, Bradbury) Munson. *Education:* Baylor University, B.A. (cum laude), 1966; Oxford University, M.A. (with honors), 1973, D. Phil., 1974. *Politics:* Conservative ("High Tory"). *Religion:* Church of England.

ADDRESSES: Home and office—27 Middle Way, Summertown, Oxford OX2 7LG, England.

CAREER: Teacher at Oxford University, Oxford, England, and at University of London, London, England, 1969-76; features editor at *Christian World,* 1978-79. Member of National Trust of England and Wales, and of Friends of York Minster and Wells Cathedral; consultant to Farmington Institute.

MEMBER: Society of Authors.

WRITINGS:

(Editor) *Echoes of the Great War: The Diary of the Reverend Andrew Clark, 1914-1919,* Oxford University Press, 1985.
(With Richard Hullen) *Queen Victoria: A Portrait,* BBC Publications, 1987.
After the Deluge: Essays Towards the Desecularization of the Church, S.P.C.K., 1987.

Author of more than twenty-five television and radio scripts for British Broadcasting Corp.

WORK IN PROGRESS: Editing a collection of travel pieces written about America from 1859 to 1960, for University of Chicago Press.

SIDELIGHTS: James Munson told *CA:* "My work is confined to historical writings, with an occasional foray into literary history. I hope to work on the reactions of Western travelers to Russia, and I am interested in religious history from the 'High Church' viewpoint. Occasionally I write on the British monarchy and the southern Confederacy. I am interested in the interplay between Great Britain and America, especially in language, speech, and customs."

* * *

MURPHY, Charles J(ohn) V(incent) 1904-1987

OBITUARY NOTICE: Born in 1904 in Newton, Mass.; died of lung cancer, December 29, 1987, in Grafton, Vt. Journalist and author. Murphy is best known for his journalistic work with Time Incorporated as well as for his biographies on the Duke and Duchess of Windsor and British statesman Winston Churchill. Murphy began his journalistic career working for the Associated Press in New York City in 1925; he later wrote for the United Press International in New York, the *New York Evening Post,* and the *New York World* before becoming a free-lance writer in 1930. In 1936 he began his association with Time Incorporated, where he later became a senior writer for *Life* magazine and served *Fortune* magazine as Washington bureau chief specializing in defense and intelligence related coverage. He served in the latter capacity for fourteen years, until his retirement in 1966. As a biographer, Murphy was noted for writing *Struggle: The Life and Exploits of Commander Richard E. Byrd* and co-authoring *The Lives of Winston Churchill* and *The Windsor Story,* an account of the lives of the duke and duchess spent in exile. He is also the author of the children's books *Little Toot* and *Hercules and Loop.*

OBITUARIES AND OTHER SOURCES:

PERIODICALS

New York Times, January 1, 1988.
Washington Post, December 31, 1987.

* * *

MURPHY, Vi 1924(?)-1987

OBITUARY NOTICE: Born c. 1924; died of lymphoid cancer, November 29, 1987, in Bakersfield, Calif. Journalist. A newspaper reporter for thirty years, Murphy is remembered as one of the first journalists to be jailed after refusing to reveal a source. She began her career in Colorado, writing for such publications as the *Denver Post* and the *Gazette Telegraph.* In 1960, after writing a series of articles on corruption in the Colorado Springs judicial system, the journalist was called to court and asked to reveal the sources and documentation for her story. Murphy refused and was imprisoned for thirty days for contempt of court. She later worked for newspapers in Iowa and Illinois before writing for the *San Diego Union,* where she remained from 1969 until her retirement in 1976.

OBITUARIES AND OTHER SOURCES:

PERIODICALS

Los Angeles Times, December 2, 1987.
New York Times, December 6, 1987.

MURRAY, Joan 1943-

PERSONAL: Born August 12, 1943, in New York, N.Y.; daughter of Sidney (a physician) and Lucia Grace (a nurse; maiden name, de Castro) Charlat; married W. Ross Murray (an attorney), June 20, 1959; children: Laura, Victoria, Adam. *Education:* University of Toronto, B.A. (with honors), 1965, doctoral study, 1967-68; Columbia University, M.A., 1966.

ADDRESSES: Home—400 St. John St. W., Whitby, Ontario, Canada L1N 1N7. *Office*—Robert McLaughlin Gallery, Civic Centre, Oshawa, Ontario, Canada L1H 3Z3.

CAREER: Art Gallery of Ontario, Toronto, research curator, 1969, curator of Canadian art, 1970-73, acting chief curator, 1973; Robert McLaughlin Gallery, Oshawa, Ontario, director, 1974—. Visiting lecturer at York University, 1970-71; lecturer at Scarborough College, 1975-76, and museums and art galleries. Commentator on radio programs; co-host of "Arts National," on CBC-FM Radio, 1976-79; art critic on "Metro Morning," on CBL-Radio, 1977-78. Fellow of Bethune College, York University, 1974-82; judge and juror of art competitions; member of Postage Stamp Design Advisory Committee, 1973-78. Member of board of directors of Canadian Conference of the Arts, 1975-76, and Ontario Heritage Foundation, 1975-78; member of advisory council of Women's Cultural Centre, 1975-77, and Bata Shoe Museum Foundation, 1980—; member of art advisory panel of National Museums of Canada, 1987.

MEMBER: Canadian Art Museums Directors Organization, Canadian Museums Association (member of council, 1974-76), Ontario Association of Art Galleries (member of executive council, 1974-76).

AWARDS, HONORS: First prize in poetry from *Mademoiselle,* 1964; first prize in short story category from Canadian Broadcasting Corp., 1965, for "Plum Duff and the Walnut Tree"; Woodrow Wilson fellow, 1965; Canada Council fellow, 1965.

WRITINGS:

(Author of preface) S. Britton Osler, editor, *Court Houses in Ontario,* Carswell, 1979.

(Contributor) Anna Porter and Marjorie Harris, editors, *Farewell to the Seventies,* Thomas Nelson, 1979.

(With Robert Fulford) *The Beginning of Vision: The Drawings of Lawren S. Harris,* Douglas & McIntyre, 1982.

Letters Home, 1859-1906: The Letters of William Blair Bruce, Penumbra Press, 1982.

(Author of preface) Gordon Law, *Mythy Poems,* Maracle Press, 1982.

(Author of introduction) Kim Ondaatje, *Small Churches of Canada,* Lester and Orpen Dennys, 1982.

Kurelek's Vision of Canada, Hurtig, 1983.

The Best of the Group of Seven, Hurtig, 1984.

Daffodils in Winter: The Life and Letters of Pegi Nicol MacLeod, Penumbra Press, 1984.

The Last Buffalo: The Story of Frederick Arthur Verner, Pagurian Press, 1984.

The Best of Tom Thomson, Hurtig, 1986.

The Best Contemporary Canadian Art, Hurtig, 1987.

Work represented in anthologies, including *Landmarks of Canadian Art,* edited by Peter Mellen, McClelland & Stewart, 1978. Contributor of stories and articles to magazines and newspapers, including *Maclean's, Descant, Canadian Art, Canadian Reader, Vie des arts, Artpost, Canada Crafts, Inprint,* and *Art Impressions.*

Art editor of *Canadian Forum,* 1970-74; contributing editor of *Canadian Art,* 1984-86; member of editorial board of *Journal of Canadian Studies,* 1987—.

WORK IN PROGRESS: "A catalogue raisonne of Tom Thomson," for University of Toronto Press; research on Canadian women's art.

SIDELIGHTS: Joan Murray told *CA:* "I am particularly interested in Islamic art, medieval art, the life histories of art dealers, and the techniques of art. I paint and have had six shows."

* * *

MY BROTHER'S BROTHER
See CHEKHOV, Anton (Pavlovich)

N

NAAMANI, Israel T(arkow) 1913(?)-

PERSONAL: Born November 3, 1913 (some sources say 1912), in Zhitomir, Russia (now U.S.S.R.); immigrated to United States, 1929, naturalized citizen, 1937; son of Peter and Sarah (Sherif) Tarkow; married Zehava Rabichow, June 30, 1940; children: Roanete (Mrs. E. A. Goldman), Aviv. *Education:* Crane Junior College, A.A., 1933; Marquette University, Ph.B., 1935; graduate study at University of Chicago, 1937, 1939; Indiana University—Bloomington, M.A., 1942, Ph.D., 1945.

CAREER: B'nai Israel Schools, Chicago, Ill., director, 1944-46; Jewish Education Society, San Francisco, Calif., executive director, 1946-48; Bureau of Jewish Education, Louisville, Ky., executive director, 1948-66. University of Louisville, lecturer, 1949-59, associate professor, 1959-64, professor of political science, beginning in 1964, Distinguished Professor of Social Science, beginning in 1975, appointed chairman of department, 1971; professorial lecturer at Indiana University—Bloomington; director of workshops in Israel. President of Midwest Council of Jewish Educators, 1954-56; vice-president of National Council for Jewish Education, 1958-60.

MEMBER: Middle East Institute (fellow), Middle East Studies Association (fellow), American Political Science Association, American Jewish Historical Society, American Historical Society, National Association of Professors of Hebrew in Higher Learning (president, 1963-65).

WRITINGS:

The Abandonment of Splendid Isolation by Great Britain, publisher not known, 1946.

(Editor with David Rudavsky) *Doron: Hebraic Studies,* National Association of Professors of Hebrew in American Institutions of Higher Learning, 1965.

Nefilim Bamaarav (in Hebrew), publisher not known, 1968.

(Editor with Rudavsky and Abraham I. Katsh) *Israel Through the Eyes of Its Leaders: An Annotated Reader,* Meorot, 1971, revised edition published as *Israel, Its Politics and Philosophy: An Annotated Reader,* Behrman, 1974.

Israel: A Profile, Praeger, 1972.

The State of Israel, Behrman, 1980.

Contributor to scholarly journals. Contributing editor of *Encyclopedia Judaica,* 1971. Editor of *Omer,* 1951-55, *Igereth,* beginning in 1959, and *Hebrew Studies,* beginning in 1971; member of editorial board of *Hebrew Abstracts* and *Sheviley Hahinuch.**

*   *   *

NAIMY, Mikhail 1889-1988

OBITUARY NOTICE: Surname sometimes transliterated Nu'aimah' or Nu'ayma; born November 17, 1889, in Biskinta, Lebanon; died after developing pneumonia, February 28, 1988, in East Beirut, Lebanon. Philosopher, poet, essayist, dramatist, novelist, and biographer. Noted as one of Lebanon's major literary figures, Naimy began his career as a writer in the United States, where he lived for twenty-one years. The Lebanese-born author studied in a Russian missionary school in Jerusalem, attended high school in Moscow, and, upon immigrating to the United States in 1911, earned a law degree from Washington State University. After serving in the U.S. Army in France during World War I, Naimy began his writing career in 1919 and soon became close friends with Lebanese philosopher and writer Khalil Gibran. In 1932, shortly after Gibran's death, Naimy returned permanently to Lebanon and subsequently wrote the philosopher's biography, *Jibran Khalil Jibran,* which was later published in English as *Khalil Gibran.* Naimy wrote in both Arabic and English, and among his other works—which include drama, verse, novels, essays, and stories—are *Al-Aba' wa'l-banun, Hams al-jufun, Liqa, Akabir,* and the English-language *Book of Mirdad, a Lighthouse and a Haven.*

OBITUARIES AND OTHER SOURCES:

BOOKS

Cassell's Encyclopaedia of World Literature, revised and enlarged edition, Morrow, 1973.

Dictionary of Oriental Literatures, Volume III: *West Africa and North Africa,* Basic Books, 1974.

PERIODICALS

Chicago Times, March 2, 1988, March 6, 1988.

Los Angeles Times, March 2, 1988.

New York Times, March 1, 1988.

NAMBA, Toshio 1910-1987

OBITUARY NOTICE: Born in 1910; died in 1987 in Tokyo, Japan. Educator and author. Namba is best remembered as an authority on Scottish poet Robert Burns and for his Japanese translations of the poet's work. His avid scholarly interest led him to be appointed honorary president of the International Burns Federation in 1982. Namba was also director of the Japan-Scotland Society and was an unofficial ambassador between Japan and Scotland. His books include *Poetry of Robert Burns: Nature and Life, Study of Scottish and English Songs,* and *Study of Robert Burns's Poetry*.

OBITUARIES AND OTHER SOURCES:

PERIODICALS

Times (London), November 12, 1987.

* * *

NAVA, Michael 1954-

PERSONAL: Born September 16, 1954, in Stockton, Calif. *Education:* Colorado College, B.A., 1976; Stanford University, J.D., 1981.

ADDRESSES: Home—6537 Moore Dr., Los Angeles, Calif. 90048. *Office*—California Court of Appeal, 3580 Wilshire Blvd., Suite 400, Los Angeles, Calif. 90021.

CAREER: City of Los Angeles, Calif., deputy city attorney, 1981-84; private practice of law in Los Angeles, 1984-86; California Court of Appeal, Los Angeles, research attorney, 1986—.

WRITINGS:

The Little Death (novel), Alyson Publications, 1986.
Goldenboy (novel), Alyson Publications, in press.

WORK IN PROGRESS: A novel, *The New Age*.

SIDELIGHTS: Michael Nava told *CA:* "All any writer has to write about is his or her experience of the world. As a gay man—of Mexican descent, no less—my challenge as a writer is to convey the value of my experience without preaching or apologizing. Writing mysteries, I work with the familiar and am able to insert the unfamiliar."

* * *

NEAL, Helen Keating 1907-1987

PERSONAL: Born September 20, 1907, in Boston, Mass.; died of cancer and kidney failure, May 8, 1987, in Portsmouth, R.I.; daughter of Clarence Richard and Eva (Keating) Neal; married Joseph W. Still, August 20, 1954 (divorced June, 1960). *Education:* Attended University of Southern California, 1930-32.

CAREER: Safety Services Publications, Washington, D.C., editor, 1938-41; American Red Cross, assistant editor of safety publications, 1941-42, assistant to director of public information for North Atlantic area, 1942-44; Denhard, Pfeiffer & Wells, advertising copy writer, 1945-47; American Red Cross, national chief of advertising, 1948-51, assistant director of Office of Volunteers, 1951-59; National Health Council, public information specialist, 1960-62; National Institutes of Health, public information specialist, 1962-77. Organizer of Price Commission Speakers Bureau.

AWARDS, HONORS: White House Distinguished Honor Award, 1972; medical book of the year award from mid-Atlantic chapter of American Medical Writers Association, for *The Politics of Pain*.

WRITINGS:

(Editor) *Better Communications for Better Health,* Columbia University Press, 1962.
The Politics of Pain, McGraw, 1978.
Low Vision: What You Can Do to Preserve—and Even Enhance—Your Usable Sight, Simon & Schuster, 1987.

Also author of *The Foundation,* a novel.

Contributor to magazines, including *Science Digest, New York,* and *Publishers Weekly*.

BIOGRAPHICAL/CRITICAL SOURCES:

PERIODICALS

Boston Globe, May 13, 1987.
Washington Post, May 12, 1987, January 5, 1988.
Washington Times, May 13, 1987.*

* * *

NELSON, Alice Ruth Moore Dunbar 1875-1935 (Alice Dunbar, Alice Moore Dunbar, Alice Dunbar-Nelson, Alice Moore Dunbar-Nelson, Alice Ruth Moore)

PERSONAL: Born July 19, 1875, in New Orleans, La.; died September 18, 1935, in Philadelphia, Pa.; daughter of Joseph (a seaman) and Patricia (a seamstress; maiden name, Wright) Moore; married Paul Laurence Dunbar (a writer), March 8, 1898 (separated, 1902; died, 1906); married Henry Arthur Callis (a teacher), January, 1910 (divorced, 1911); married Robert J. Nelson (a journalist), April, 1916. *Education:* Attended Straight University, c. 1890; Cornell University, M.A.; postgraduate study at Pennsylvania School of Industrial Art and University of Pennsylvania.

CAREER: Writer. Worked as a teacher at schools in New Orleans, La., 1892-96, New York City, 1897, and Wilmington, Del., 1902-20, and at various black colleges. Co-founder of White Rose Mission (became White Rose House for Girls), in New York City, and of Industrial School for Colored Girls in Delaware; volunteer worker for Circle for Negro War Relief, 1918; member of field staff of Women's Committee on the Council of Defense; also member of Delaware's State Republican Committee, 1920; executive secretary for American Friends Interracial Peace Committee, 1928-31.

WRITINGS:

(Under name Alice Ruth Moore) *Violets, and Other Tales,* Monthly Review Press, 1895.
(Under name Alice Dunbar) *The Goodness of St. Rocque, and Other Stories,* Dodd, 1899.
(Editor, under name Alice Moore Dunbar) *Masterpieces of Negro Eloquence: The Best Speeches Delivered by the Negro From the Days of Slavery to the Present Time,* Douglass, 1914.
(Editor and contributor, under name Alice Moore Dunbar-Nelson) *The Dunbar Speaker and Entertainer,* J. L. Nichols, 1920.
(Under name Alice Dunbar-Nelson) *Give Us Each Day: The Diary of Alice Dunbar-Nelson,* edited and with introduction by Gloria T. Hull, Norton, 1984.

Work represented in anthologies, including *Negro Poets and Their Poems,* edited by Robert T. Kerlin, Associated Publishers, 1923, and *Caroling Dusk,* edited by Countee Cullen, Harper, 1927.

Author of unpublished novels "This Lofty Oak" and "Confessions of a Lazy Woman."

Author—probably under name Alice Moore Dunbar-Nelson—of column "Une Femme dit" in *Pittsburgh Courier,* 1926 and 1930, and of column "As in a Looking Glass" in *Washington Eagle,* 1926-30.

Contributor, often under name variations, to periodicals, including *A.M.E. Church Review, Crisis, Daily Crusader, Education,* Wilmington *Journal Every Evening, Journal of Negro History, Leslie's Weekly, Messenger, Saturday Evening Mail, Smart Set, Southern Workman,* and *Opportunity*. Founder and co-editor of *Wilmington Weekly,* 1920.

SIDELIGHTS: Alice Ruth Moore Dunbar Nelson was probably the first black woman to distinguish herself in American literature. She was a versatile writer who produced short stories, poems, and a wide range of criticism, and she was also a staunch supporter of black rights, devoting herself—both in public and private—to furthering the causes of racial equality and world peace. Nelson is thus considered an important figure not only for her literary achievements but for her work in sociopolitical forums. It is her impressive array of accomplishments and efforts that has prompted writers such as *Ms.* reviewer Carolyn Heilbrun to hail her as "gifted and ambitious."

Nelson was born Alice Ruth Moore in 1875. In New Orleans she readily distinguished herself scholastically, and by age fifteen she had enrolled at the city's Straight University. There she trained for a teaching career but also studied nursing and stenography. In addition she played in local music groups—classical and popular—and edited the women's page of a black fraternity publication. Many of her experiences and observations inspired her first work, *Violets, and Other Tales,* which she published in 1895 after commencing her teaching career in New Orleans.

Violets, and Other Tales, which contains poems and essays in addition to short stories, at times focuses on the melancholic aspects of life and love. In the title story, a young woman gives her beloved a bouquet of violets and dies soon afterward. Later her married sweetheart happens upon the flowers but is unable to recall how he obtained them, whereupon his unsympathetic wife pitches the withered flowers into the fireplace flames. Also notable, though less characteristic of the collection, is "The Woman," an engaging essay supporting female independence and women's careers.

Soon after the publication of *Violets, and Other Tales* Nelson moved to Massachusetts with her family. She then began corresponding with Paul Laurence Dunbar, an increasingly famous writer who had reportedly become infatuated with Nelson upon spotting her photograph in a Boston periodical. Nelson and Dunbar corresponded for two years before actually meeting in early 1897 as he prepared to undertake a reading tour of England. They became formally engaged during their brief encounter and secretly wed the next spring. In the interim Nelson taught in New York City and helped establish its White Rose Mission in Harlem.

While married to Dunbar, Nelson completed *The Goodness of St. Rocque, and Other Stories,* fourteen tales of Creole life in New Orleans. The collection is remembered for its vivid portraits of admirable individuals overcoming unfavorable circumstances. Among the noteworthy tales in the volume is the title work, in which a Creole woman resorts to both voodoo and Catholic ritual in an ultimately successful attempt to regain the love of a dashing fellow.

In 1902 Nelson and Dunbar separated. Nelson then traveled to Delaware and began teaching at both high school and college levels. For the next eighteen years Nelson lived and taught in Delaware. Dunbar died in 1906, and four years later Nelson married a fellow teacher. That marriage ended in 1911, however, and five years later she married again, this time to journalist Robert J. Nelson, with whom she remained for the rest of her life.

During this often turbulent period Nelson continued her literary career. She contributed short stories and poems to various periodicals and edited the volumes *Masterpieces of Negro Eloquence* and *The Dunbar Speaker and Entertainer,* which were principally intended for students. Included in the latter are some of her own writings, notably "I Sit and Sew," a poem in which she expressed her irritation at the general denigration of women's potential for contribution during the years of World War I. Dissatisfied with merely complaining, Nelson demonstrated her own usefulness by serving with the Circle of Negro War Relief in 1918 and then joining the Women's Commission on the Council of Defense, through which she organized relief efforts by black women in Southern states.

In the 1920s Nelson increased her involvement in social causes and politics. She supervised the activities of black women in Delaware's State Republican Committee in 1920 and executed similar responsibilities for the Democratic Party in New York City four years later. Toward the close of the decade she also served as executive secretary for the American Friends Interracial Peace Committee. But even during this period of political involvement she continued her writing career by appearing as a columnist in the *Pittsburgh Courier* and the *Washington Eagle* and by publishing poems and stories in periodicals such as the *Messenger* and *Crisis*. Her productivity remained steady until the end of the 1920s, when she published only one article in 1928 and another one in 1929. A 1932 article for Wilmington's *Journal Every Evening* became her only piece from that decade. She died three years later.

Although Nelson is sometimes considered merely a peripheral figure in the Harlem Renaissance of black literature, she is nonetheless esteemed for her daring advocacy of equal rights for women and blacks and for the consistently high quality of her poetry and prose. The distinguishing aspects—simplicity, precision, incisiveness—of her fiction and essays were also evident in her posthumously published *Give Us Each Day: The Diary of Alice Dunbar-Nelson*. Brent Staples, writing in the *New York Times Book Review,* recommended the diary for its insights into both the suffrage and black rights movements, observing that the work "lets us inside what was then a thriving national network of black women's social groups." Staples also contended that throughout the diary Nelson maintains "an entertaining haughtiness" that seemed essential to her self-esteem. He called the posthumous work "a valuable contribution to women's letters."

BIOGRAPHICAL/CRITICAL SOURCES:

BOOKS

Bone, Robert, *Down Home: A History of Afro-American Short Fiction From Its Beginnings to the End of the Harlem Renaissance,* Putnam, 1975.

Brawley, Benjamin, *Paul Laurence Dunbar: Poet of His People,* University of North Carolina Press, 1936.
Dictionary of Literary Biography, Volume 50: *Afro-American Writers From the Harlem Renaissance to 1940,* Gale, 1987.
Dunbar-Nelson, Alice, *Give Us Each Day: The Diary of Alice Dunbar-Nelson,* edited and with introduction by Gloria T. Hull, Norton, 1985.

PERIODICALS

CLA Journal, March, 1976.
Ms., June, 1985.
New York Times Book Review, April 14, 1985.*

—*Sketch by Les Stone*

* * *

NELSON, Ralph 1916-1987

OBITUARY NOTICE—See index for *CA* sketch: Born August 12, 1916, in New York (one source says Long Island City), N.Y.; died of cancer, December 21, 1987, in Santa Monica, Calif. Actor, director, producer, and playwright. Nelson will be best remembered as the director of the 1956 television drama "Requiem for a Heavyweight," for which he received an Emmy Award, and of the 1963 motion picture "Lilies of the Field," which garnered him an Oscar nomination. Overcoming a delinquent adolescence during which he was frequently arrested for vagrancy and suspicion of burglary in several states, Nelson began his stage-acting career in Los Angeles in the 1930s. He soon turned to writing and had some of his plays produced on Broadway in the 1940s, including "Mail Call" and "The Wind is Ninety." He then became an important figure in the so-called "golden age of television" of the 1950s, beginning as the director of the series "Mama" (also known as "I Remember Mama") and directing several dramas for series such as "Playhouse 90" and "General Electric Theater." Through Rainbow Productions, a company he founded in 1959, Nelson produced motion pictures such as "Father Goose" and "Charly." His last directorial work was done in 1979 on the television sequel to "Lilies" titled "Christmas, Lilies of the Field." Nelson's other writing credits include the play "Angels Weep" and the screenplays "The Man in the Funny Suit," "Flight of the Doves," and "The Wrath of God."

OBITUARIES AND OTHER SOURCES:

BOOKS

Who's Who in America, 43rd edition, Marquis, 1984.

PERIODICALS

Chicago Tribune, December 25, 1987.
Los Angeles Times, December 23, 1987.
Newsweek, January 4, 1988.
New York Times, December 25, 1987.
Washington Post, December 24, 1987.

* * *

NEWSON, Tony 1953-

PERSONAL: Born August 26, 1953, in Thetford, England; son of Thomas (a farmer) and Annie (Mickleburgh) Newson. *Education:* University of Birmingham, B.A. (with honors), 1974.

ADDRESSES: Home—2 Sawston Close, Radbrook Green, Shrewsbury, Shropshire SY3 6AY, England. *Office*—Shropshire Information Service, 1A Castle Gates, Shrewsbury SY1 2AQ, England.

CAREER: Oxford Polytechnic, Oxford, England, assistant librarian, 1976-78; University of Birmingham, Birmingham, England, librarian at Joint Centre for Regional, Urban, and Local Government Studies, 1978-83; Shropshire Information Service, Shrewsbury, England, senior librarian, 1983-87; principal reference and information librarian of Oxfordshire Libraries, 1987—. Member of Housing Management Information Working Party; member of management committee of Shrewsbury and Central Shropshire Citizens Advice Bureau.

MEMBER: Library Association (associate).

WRITINGS:

(With Philip Potter) *Housing Policy in Britain: An Information Sourcebook,* Mansell, 1984.
Housing Policy: An International Bibliography, Mansell, 1986.

Contributor to *Countryside Planning Yearbook.* Contributor to magazines.

WORK IN PROGRESS: Work related to parliamentary sources of housing information and the privatization of local authority services.

SIDELIGHTS: Tony Newson told *CA:* "The International Year of Shelter for the Homeless has focused attention on housing problems throughout the world. The 1987 general election and subsequent policy innovations in the United Kingdom have kept housing issues in the forefront of public debate. My work is aimed at making people aware of what sources are available to study housing policy and to campaign for free access to information needed for efficient and effective policy-making."

* * *

NEWTON, Peter A(nthony) 1935-1987

OBITUARY NOTICE: Born in 1935 in Leicester, England; died in 1987. Iconographer, historian, educator, and author. Newton is most noted for his expertise in medieval stained glass. An educator at York University in Kings Manor, England, he was instrumental in establishing the school's department of medieval studies, which became one of the leading centers for graduate research in England. Newton was a reader in history of art at London's Courtauld Institute of Art and in 1965 became Mellon Lecturer in British Mediaeval Art at York. He also served as academic adviser to the York Glazier's Trust, as such lending his skills in the field of glass conservation to help restore stained glass in various churches. His major publication is *The County of Oxford: A Catalogue of Medieval Stained Glass.*

OBITUARIES AND OTHER SOURCES:

PERIODICALS

Times (London), November 24, 1987.

* * *

NICKERSON, Jane Soames (Bon) 1900-1988

OBITUARY NOTICE—See index for *CA* sketch: Born in 1900; died January 10, 1988, in Long Island, N.Y. Secretary, translator, journalist, and author. Nickerson served as a secretary to author Hilaire Belloc beginning in the 1930s. Her duties in this post included much historical research. She was also the Paris correspondent for the London *Times,* and translated works

such as *The Origins of the First World War* and *The Political and Social Doctrine of Fascism*. Nickerson's own writings include *The Coast of Barbary*, reprinted as *A Short History of North Africa, From Pre-Roman Times to the Present: Libya, Tunisia, Algeria, Morocco; Homage to Malthus;* and *The English Press*.

OBITUARIES AND OTHER SOURCES:

PERIODICALS

New York Times, January 13, 1988.
Times (London), February 9, 1988.

* * *

NILL, Michael 1942-

PERSONAL: Born July 5, 1942, in Pittsburgh, Pa.; son of John George and Mildred M. (Bruner) Nill. *Education:* Fordham College (now University), B.A., 1966; Johns Hopkins University, M.A., 1968; University of Texas at Austin, Ph.D, 1981.

ADDRESSES: Home—74 Higgins Court, Baton Rouge, La. 70808. *Office*—Episcopal High School, 3200 Woodland Ridge Blvd., Baton Rouge, La. 70816.

CAREER: Grok Books, Austin, Tex., owner and manager, 1970-73; One Hundred Flowers Bookstore, Cambridge, Mass., owner and manager, 1973-75; *Liberation*, New York, N.Y., editor, 1975-77; Greenhill School, Dallas, Tex., teacher of classics, 1981-84; Episcopal High School, Baton Rouge, La., teacher, head of department of classics and dean of studies, 1984—. Co-chairman of Louisiana Junior Classical League.

MEMBER: American Philological Association, American Classical Association, Classical Association of the Midwest and South, Southern Humanities Conference.

AWARDS, HONORS: Fellow of Council for Basic Education, 1986.

WRITINGS:

Morality and Self-Interest in Protagoras, Antiphon, and Democritus, E. J. Brill, 1985.

Contributor of articles and reviews to magazines, including *Radical Therapist* and *One Hundred Flowers Review*.

WORK IN PROGRESS: A history of the teaching of Latin, Greek, and classical literature in U.S. education; research on Aristotle's *Poetics*.

SIDELIGHTS: Michael Nill told *CA:* "I have always been excited by Greek and Latin literature because of their emphasis on values and questions of the good life. It's tragic that so few are familiar with these writings, not just because they have shaped many of our own ideas, but also because they confront us with otherness and force us to become aware of, challenge, and perhaps even change our own assumptions and values. For example, we tend to see the good life in terms of externals like power, money, and physical comfort; and so we're willing to act immorally to procure these goods if we think we can get away with it. However, as I argue in my book, Greek thinking advanced to the position that morality and self-interest are compatible, that inner (spiritual and mental) goods are of the greatest value, and that a self-interested pursuit of such goods could never lead to immoral action, even if we were sure we could escape punishment in this world and the next. It is not that I think the compatibility of morality and self-interest can be proved philosophically, but that the attempt to do so raises central questions about life—and this kind of focus would do much to diminish the unfortunate influence of such contemporary value-setters as fundamentalists, the amoral, and the rich and famous.

"In my next project, a history of classical education in the United States, I hope to provide a reasoned defense of the study of classics. Of course, in comparison with earlier times, the role of classics in education is peripheral. There are a number of reasons for this, but classicists have to take part of the blame because of their emphasis on narrow scholarship and language drills and their failure to engage students in a stimulating and critical dialogue between ancient and modern attitudes."

* * *

NOOTEBOOM, Cees 1933-

BRIEF ENTRY: Surname is pronounced "*Noh*-te-bohm"; born July 31, 1933, in The Hague, Netherlands. Dutch playwright, poet, travel writer, and author. Though Nooteboom is still relatively unknown in the United States, he is regarded as one of the Netherlands's foremost writers. There he has published several volumes of poetry, five novels, two plays, and a number of travel books. He is also a regular contributor to the Dutch periodicals *Avenue* and *Elsevier's Magazine*. The winner of Mobil Oil Company's Pegasus Prize for Literature, Nooteboom's 1983 novel, *Rituals* (Louisiana State University Press), was the first of his fiction to appear in English translation. Its U.S. debut stirred mixed critical reaction but overall generated enthusiasm for a new talent. Subsequent writings in English include Nooteboom's *A Song of Truth and Semblance* (Louisiana State University Press, 1984), *Unbuilt Netherlands* (Rizzoli International, 1985), and *In the Dutch Mountains* (Louisiana State University Press, 1987). Considered an authority on Spain—where he lives part of the year—Nooteboom also produced an hour-long film on the pilgrimage to Santiago de Compostela, a commune located in a northwest province of the country. Additionally, a book on Spain titled *The Burning Vision* is forthcoming.

BIOGRAPHICAL/CRITICAL SOURCES:

PERIODICALS

New York Times Book Review, October 11, 1987.
San Francisco Chronicle, August 12, 1983.
Times Literary Supplement, December 28, 1984, January 8-14, 1988.
Washington Post Book World, June 26, 1983.

* * *

NORDTVEDT, Matilda 1926-

PERSONAL: Born November 27, 1926, in Bellingham, Wash.; daughter of Sven (a mill worker) and Ethel (a homemaker; maiden name, Hansen) Kivley; married Tom Nordtvedt (a pastor and real estate agent), April 29, 1949; children: Tim, Joel, Mark. *Education:* Attended Prairie Bible Institute. *Religion:* Lutheran Brethren.

ADDRESSES: Home—718 124th St. S.W., No. 82, Everett, Wash. 98204.

CAREER: Teacher and missionary in Japan, 1951-59; freelance writer, 1962—.

MEMBER: Washington Christian Writers' Fellowship.

AWARDS, HONORS: Special recognition award from Warm Beach Christian Writers and Speakers Conference, 1984.

WRITINGS:

All Things, Even Frisky (juvenile), Moody, 1973.
Take a Break (juvenile), Moody, 1973.
The Vanishing Act and Other Stories (juvenile), Moody, 1974.
Defeating Despair and Depression, Moody, 1975, reprinted as *How to Overcome Depression,* 1986.
Fat Alfie and the Feather Caper (juvenile), Moody, 1975.
No Longer a Nobody (juvenile), Moody, 1976.
Jeff and the Case of the Missing Uncle, Moody, 1978.
Living Beyond Depression, Bethany House, 1978.
(With Pearl Steinkuehler) *Showers of Blessing,* Moody, 1980.
(With Steinkuehler) *Something Old, Something New,* Moody, 1981.
(With Steinkuehler) *Something Borrowed, Something Blue,* Moody, 1981.
Daddy Isn't Coming Home (juvenile), Zondervan, 1981.
(With Steinkuehler) *Women's Programs for Every Season,* Moody, 1982.
(With Steinkuehler) *Ideas for Junior High Leaders,* Moody, 1983.
(With Steinkuehler) *Programs for Special Occasions,* Moody, 1984.
The Family Idea Book, Moody, 1984.
Ladybugs, Bees, and Butterfly Trees (juvenile), Bethany House, 1985.
Pilgrim Boy (juvenile), A Beka Books, 1987.
Secret in the Maple (juvenile), A Beka Books, 1987.
Read and Think Skill Sheets (juvenile), A Beka Books, 1987.

Author of family life column and another column entitled "One Mother to Another," both for *Gospel Herald.* Contributor of more than two thousand articles and stories to magazines.

WORK IN PROGRESS: Church school curriculum material.

SIDELIGHTS: Matilda Nordtvedt, whose books have been translated into Norwegian, Spanish, Portuguese, French, and Finnish, told *CA* that she is especially interested in Bible study and related Christian subjects.

Nordtvedt added: "I have wanted to write since I made my first attempts as a little girl. Living in Japan for eight years intensified that desire, although I was much too busy with missionary work and mothering three small sons to get serious about it then. I realize now that I not only needed more time in order to write, but I needed to grow more in my understanding, to find some answers for myself before I could teach others. I found those answers in the Bible and in a personal relationship with Jesus Christ and have tried to present them in my writings both for adults and for children.

"Most of the ideas for my stories and books have come from my Bible study. Of course, I have received ideas from other books and articles as well as from my own experiences, my family, and other people. Being a pastor's wife for many years has brought me into contact with a great variety of people and their problems.

"Early in my writing career I tried to diversify instead of specialize. I write fiction and nonfiction. I write feature articles, columns, fillers, puzzles, and curriculum. I write inspirational books as well as how-to books. And my children's books include fiction, historical fiction, and rhyme. Each new area I tried opened up other opportunities, and one writing endeavor led to another. I love trying something different.

"My greatest joy in writing has come from letters and telephone calls expressing readers' appreciation for help and encouragement received from what I have written. I was particularly thrilled and excited to discover—through my sister, strangely enough—that the children of a kidnapped Colombian missionary were given hope and encouragement by reading my first book, *All Things, Even Frisky,* in which a young boy named Billy is kidnapped. Because God took care of Billy in my story, the missionary's frightened children were comforted that God would also take care of their Daddy. After a most harrowing experience of being held prisoner by terrorists in the jungle, the children's father and his fellow missionaries were released unharmed."

* * *

NORMAN, Lloyd (Henry) 1913-1987

OBITUARY NOTICE—See index for *CA* sketch: Born November 25, 1913, in Aurora, Ontario, Canada; immigrated to United States c. 1916; died of a heart attack, November 12, 1987, in Tampa, Fla.; buried in King David Memorial Garden, Falls Church, Va. Social worker and journalist. Norman spent most of his long journalistic career covering the United States Defense Department, reporting events such as atomic bomb tests, the 1957 nonstop around-the-world journey of three B52 bomber planes, and the discovery of incorrect intelligence estimates of enemy infiltration during the Vietnam War. After a brief stint as a social worker, Norman became a reporter for the Chicago City News Bureau. He then signed on with the *Chicago Tribune,* beginning as a financial reporter; he was later assigned to Washington, D.C., to cover defense issues. In 1958 Norman left the *Tribune* to serve as the Pentagon correspondent for *Newsweek.* He retired in 1978.

OBITUARIES AND OTHER SOURCES:

PERIODICALS

Chicago Tribune, November 17, 1987.
Newsweek, November 23, 1987.
Washington Post, November 14, 1987.

* * *

NORMAN, Theodore 1910-1987

PERSONAL: Born March 12, 1910, in Cambridge, Mass.; died of cancer, May 14, 1987, in New York, N.Y.; son of Henry (a doctor) and Manya (a housewife; maiden name, Golden) Norman; married Jane M. Posner (an art education consultant), December 22, 1935; children: Alice Norman Mandel, Lucy Norman Friedman. *Education:* Harvard University, A.B., 1930, A.M., 1932, Ph.D., 1939.

CAREER: Harvard University, Cambridge, Mass., instructor in economics, 1935-38; U.S. Department of Agriculture, Washington, D.C., economist, 1938-47; Brookings Institution, Washington, D.C., economist, 1947-48; Council of Jewish Federations, New York, N.Y., researcher, 1948-49; New York Association of New Americans, New York City, assistant director, 1949-50; Baron de Hirsch Fund, New York City, managing director, 1950-77. Economist for Senate Civil Liberties Commission, 1939-40.

WRITINGS:

(With Edwin F. Dummeier and Richard B. Heflebower) *Economics: With Application to Agriculture,* 3rd edition, McGraw, 1950.

(With wife, Jane Norman) *Traveler's Guide to Europe's Art,* Channel Press, 1959, revised edition, Appleton, 1965.
(With J. Norman) *Wonderful Places to Take Children,* Channel Press, 1962.
(With J. Norman) *Traveler's Guide to America's Art,* Meredith Press, 1968.
An Outstretched Arm: A History of the Jewish Colonization Association, Routledge & Kegan Paul, 1985.

BIOGRAPHICAL/CRITICAL SOURCES:

PERIODICALS

New York Times, May 15, 1987.
Times Literary Supplement, November 8, 1985.*

* * *

NORTHCOTT, (William) Cecil 1902-1987 (Mary Miller, Arthur Temple)

OBITUARY NOTICE—See index for *CA* sketch: Born April 5, 1902, in Buckfast, Devonshire, England; died November 10, 1987. Clergyman, editor, journalist, and author. An ordained Congregationalist minister, Northcott is best remembered as the editorial secretary of the United Society for Christian Literature, a post he assumed in 1952. He was also involved with many other religious organizations, including the London Missionary Society and the United Council for Missionary Education, and served as an editor for Lutterworth Press. Affiliated with religious periodicals such as *Congregational Monthly* and *Christian Century,* Northcott served as the church's correspondent for the London *Daily Telegraph.* Occasionally using the pseudonym Arthur Temple, he wrote numerous books on religious subjects, including *Who Claims the World?: An Attempt to Present the Case for the Christian Missionary Enterprise; No Strangers Here: Meditations on the Gospel and the Church in the World;* and *Religious Liberty.* Northcott was also greatly interested in the exploration of Africa, and penned the biographies *Robert Moffat: Pioneer in Africa* and *David Livingstone: His Triumph, Decline, and Fall.* He authored religious works for children, under the pseudonym Mary Miller, including *Jesus, the Good Shepherd.*

OBITUARIES AND OTHER SOURCES:

BOOKS

Who's Who, 139th edition, St. Martin's, 1987.

PERIODICALS

Times (London), November 12, 1987.

* * *

NOTLEY, Alice 1945-

BRIEF ENTRY: Born November 8, 1945, in Bisbee, Ariz. American poet and author. Notley's award-winning poetry is known for its sensitive treatment of the nuances in personal relationships. Her work, which allegedly serves as a testament to the legacy of poet William Carlos Williams, addresses various aspects in the expanse of American culture and features Notley's creative experimentation with poetic form—especially free verse. According to Peter Schjeldahl in the *New York Times Book Review,* "Notley is easily the most authentic and effective poet . . . to emerge" from the so-called "New York School" in several years. Among the numerous collections of verse that she has published are *Incidentals in the Day World* (Angel Hair Books, 1973), *When I Was Alive* (Vehicle Editions, 1980), *Waltzing Matilda* (Kulchur Foundation, 1981), *Margaret and Dusty* (Coffee House Press, 1985), and *How Spring Comes* (Toothpaste Press, 1981), which received a 1982 San Francisco Poetry Center Book Award. In addition to her poems, Notley wrote a short autobiography entitled *Tell Me Again* (Am Here Books, 1982) and the impressionistic stage play "Anne's White Glove" (first produced at La Mama E.T.C., 1985). *Addresses: Home and office*—101 St. Marks Pl., No. 12A, New York, N.Y. 10009.

BIOGRAPHICAL/CRITICAL SOURCES:

BOOKS

Contemporary Poets, 4th edition, St. Martin's, 1985.

PERIODICALS

New York Times, April 19, 1985.
New York Times Book Review, January 17, 1982.

* * *

NOVITSKI, Joseph (W. D.) 1940-

PERSONAL: Born April 20, 1940, in Manila, Philippines; son of Francis J. (a businessman) and Mary (a painter; maiden name, Daniels) Novitski; married Isabel Helena Montero, August 31, 1968 (died July 4, 1978); married Paula Cassady (a teacher), September 2, 1978; children: Alexandra, Nicholas. *Education:* Yale University, B.A., 1961; attended Johns Hopkins School for Advanced International Studies, Bologna, Italy, 1964-65. *Politics:* "Skeptical independent."

ADDRESSES: Home—Apartado Aereo 26759, Bogota, Colombia. *Office*—5730 Southwest 74th St., Miami, Fla. 33143. *Agent*—Wendy Lipkind Agency, 225 East 57th St., New York, N.Y. 10022.

CAREER: Associated Press, New York City, correspondent in New York, Bogota, Colombia, and Brazil, 1965-68; *New York Times,* New York City, correspondent in South America, 1968-73; *Washington Post,* Washington, D.C., reporter, 1973-75; Las Amalias (producers of cut flowers), Bogota, director, 1975-87, managing director, 1987—. Owner and operator of Wine Creek Ranch and Vineyards, Healdsburg, Calif., 1977-85; director of Sonoma County Farm Bureau, 1979-85. *Military service:* U.S. Naval Reserve, 1957-72, active duty, 1961-63; became lieutenant.

MEMBER: Yale Club of New York City, Elizabethan Club.

WRITINGS:

A Vineyard Year, photographs by Nick Pavloff, Chronicle Books, 1983.
Wind Star: The Building of a Sailship (nonfiction), Macmillan, 1987.

WORK IN PROGRESS: An inquiry into the social uses of honor; a novel; a play; four short stories.

SIDELIGHTS: Joseph Novitski told *CA:* "My books are taken from what I know—farming and sea-going under sail. I was born in Asia and have lived and worked on all of the other continents except Australia and Antarctica. I have spent more than half my life in Latin America, and I speak fluent Spanish and Portuguese. This does not help me, however, to feel at home in the United States. Nonetheless, being an outsider everywhere helps that part of a writer which needs to be the easily engaged observer. I hope I'm right in thinking that the sense of surprise at the ordinary which every writer needs is

sharpened by being a steady stranger. I do find myself wholly at home among words on a page.

"I think I fail at Mario Vargas Llosa's definition of the author as a reverse strip tease artist who starts on the stage naked and dresses himself in full view of the audience. I am not enough of a performer. Vargas once was, but now he has grown so natural that one never senses the footlights. He and I grew up in the same towns in Peru—Lima and Piura—about four years apart, and if I had it to do over again, when people asked what I wanted to grow up to be I would know enough to answer: 'Mario Vargas.'"

* * *

NUDEL, Adele Rice 1927-

PERSONAL: Born August 26, 1927, in Baltimore, Md.; daughter of Maurice (a congressional press secretary) and Jean (Klawonsky) Rice; married David Nudel (a social worker and photographer), May 17, 1967; children: Lisa Potash, Marc Potash. *Education:* Antioch College, M.A., 1974.

ADDRESSES: *Home*—6004 Pimlico Rd., Baltimore, Md. 21209. *Office*—Widowed Person's Service, Sinai Hospital, 2401 West Belvedere Ave., Baltimore, Md. 21215. *Agent*—Joe Rhodes, Rhodes Literary Agency, Inc., 140 West End Ave., New York, N.Y. 10023.

CAREER: Sinai Hospital, Baltimore, Md., director of Widowed Person's Services, 1981—. Private practice as grief counselor; gives writing workshops.

WRITINGS:

For the Woman Over Fifty, Taplinger, 1978.
Starting Over: Help for Young Widows and Widowers, Dodd, 1987.

Author of short stories.

WORK IN PROGRESS: Short stories.

SIDELIGHTS: Adele Rice Nudel told *CA:* "I, like most writers, need to write. It is necessary to my emotional survival."

Nudel's book *Starting Over* is intended for a relatively neglected segment of the population: men and women who were widowed at the age of forty-five or younger. The author addresses the issues that are unique to young people who have lost a mate. These include dreams unrealized, plans cut short, children to raise alone, or children never born, as well as society's casual attitudes that life goes on and youth heals quickly. Nudel covers the financial hardships faced by young widows, and the trauma of having to make an abrupt foray into the job market. She covers the problems of dating and remarriage, which are different for a widowed person than a victim of divorce.

BIOGRAPHICAL/CRITICAL SOURCES:

PERIODICALS

New York Times, February 11, 1987.

O

O'BRIEN, Richard 1942-

PERSONAL: Born in 1942.

CAREER: Playwright, screenwriter, actor, and novelist.

WRITINGS:

(With Richard Hartley) *The Rocky Horror Show: A Musical* (play, adapted from O'Brien's novel *They Came From Denton High*), first produced in London and New York in 1973, Samuel French, 1983.

(With Jim Sharman) "The Rocky Horror Picture Show" (screenplay, adapted from the play "The Rocky Horror Show: A Musical" by O'Brien and Hartley; also see above), Twentieth Century-Fox, 1975.

"T. Zee" (play), music by Hartley; based on characters by Edgar Rice Burroughs, first produced in 1976.

"Disaster" (play), music by Hartley, first produced in 1978.

Also author of novel *They Came From Denton High,* 1977 television play "A Hymn From Jim," and 1981 motion picture "Shock Treatment."

SIDELIGHTS: Richard O'Brien wrote, with Richard Hartley and Jim Sharman, what many consider the epitome of cult films. "The Rocky Horror Picture Show," which runs weekends at midnight in cinemas around the world, is known for attracting a loyal and enthusiastic crowd at virtually every showing. Based on O'Brien's novel *They Came From Denton High,* a stage version of the story, entitled "The Rocky Horror Show," was first produced in London and New York in 1973. A "near-perfect late-night diversion," according to reviewer W. Stephen Gilbert in *Plays and Players,* the rock musical was described variously as satirical, cheerful, obscene, clever, and camp. Accurately, Clive Barnes predicted in his 1973 *New York Times* review that, with the play's "wit and cant, I suspect that this is the kind of show that, modestly produced, might do rather well in New York."

The show did succeed in New York, and in 1975 it was adapted for the screen as "The Rocky Horror Picture Show." Although "Rocky Horror"'s satiric digs at horror shows, sexual convention, and glitter rock did not appeal to mainstream movie audiences, late-night moviegoers welcomed the musical farce when theaters relegated it to midnight showings on weekends. As Bill Henkin recounts in his *"Rocky Horror Picture Show" Book,* "Every Friday and Saturday night, as the witching hour approaches, thousands of people across the United States, Canada, and the rest of the world line up to buy their tickets for *The Rocky Horror Picture Show*. . . . Such devotional behavior has occurred in the past, but never in movie history have the proportions been so huge, the audience so devout, or the duration so long."

Summing up the movie's plot, *Newsweek* reviewers described "Rocky Horror" as "a rather bizarre film about transvestites that impels people to dress in drag and act as if they were stark-raving mad." The main transvestite and "the joy of *The Rocky Horror Picture Show,*" according to Henkin, is Dr. Frank N. Furter, who has temporarily brought to Earth his Gothic castle, along with assorted ghoulish inhabitants, from his native planet of Transexual in the galaxy of Transylvania. Into the castle, at night, during a thunderstorm, on a dead-end road in the woods, stumble the recently engaged innocents, Brad Majors and Janet Weiss. They have been looking for their former science teacher, Dr. Everett Scott, who eventually appears in search of his nephew, Eddie. Also running around in the castle are Rocky Horror, Frank's muscular monster, and Riff Raff and Magenta, Frank's mutinous and incestuous servants.

Frank, a "hero-villain of mythic proportions," is the center of the show as he leads the characters through their rather unusual adventures, according to Henkin. "In a simple, stylized manner," the critic explains, "Frank is a study in contrasts. He is a ruthless master who has no qualms about committing murder, . . . serving Dr. Scott's roasted nephew to him for dinner, or seducing both a male and a female virgin in a single night." Every social taboo, from incest to cannibalism, is lampooned in "Rocky Horror." Even so, maintained *Horizon*'s Nora Sayre, the "movie can't be classified as decadent." According to Henkin, "The gay, straight, bi, and incestuous sexuality is so totally parodied that any 'message' of sexual liberation is incidental. The film is much more a hybrid fantasy of social decadence plugged straight into the brainstem of an extroverted culture. . . . And since the show is by no means confined to the screen, our responses are pure catharsis."

Audience response to the show—a production in itself—receives as much comment by movie critics as does the film's plot. *Newsweek*'s reviewers suggested that "the young fans" are merely following the movie's "infantile exhortation to 'Give yourself over to total pleasure'"; other critics point to Dr.

Frank N. Furter's motto: "Don't dream it—be it." Whatever their reasons, "Rocky Horror" devotees, many of whom boast of having seen the film hundreds of times, faithfully act out scenes in their seats and in the aisles as the movie progresses—and often with remarkable talent, according to D. Keith Mano of *National Review*. When "a really fine Dr. Frank N. Furter singalike stood in his small flashlit pool," he commented, "well, I found myself watching him, not the film." The more dedicated followers often perform the entire movie—in costume and with props—as a skit beside the movie screen, while the remaining fans participate at various intervals by squirting each other with squirtguns during a thunderstorm, throwing rice after a wedding scene, and pelting one another with warmed bread during an after-dinner toast, for example. During one beloved song, "The Time Warp," veteran members of a typical audience jump to the aisles to dance along with the characters on screen, while newcomers watch the performance with either delight or bewilderment. Audience members also speak to the movie's characters, usually in unison, as if to give them stage directions, encouragement, or abuse. "At times," observed Sayre, "it seems as if the script is being rewritten. The heroine is advised to 'Smile if you're horny'—and she positively beams. Even the props are obedient: when dozens of voices demand a coil of rope—'Rope, please!'—it promptly appears on the screen, and they shriek, 'Thank you!' All in all, they seem to control the movie . . . and that's one of the charms ["Rocky Horror"] has for its adherents."

Sayre and Henkin are among many reviewers with high praise for "Rocky Horror"'s successful blend of satire, naughtiness, and absurdity. "The film's appeal may be broader than anyone outside the phenomenon realizes," Henkin ventured. "Richard O'Brien succeeded in writing a script, lyrics, and music that *can* be enjoyed by any ten-year-old, and yet retains an appeal for adults after multiple screenings."

O'Brien and collaborator Hartley, encouraged by the success of "The Rocky Horror Show," wrote two subsequent musical plays during the 1970s. "T. Zee," whose main character parodies Edgar Rice Burrough's Tarzan, was described by *Variety* reviewer Hawk as "a camp spoof much along the lines of [the authors'] previous 'Rocky Horror Show.'" According to Hawk, the play "pokes fun at numerous comic-strip genres without worrying in the least about a consistent plot line or the likes." Although some reviewers, including *Melody Maker*'s Allan Jones, criticized the play as "chaotic" and lacking substance, Hawk praised the production as "inoffensive, confused fun."

Their next musical, "Disaster," mocks disaster movies such as producer Irwin Allen's "The Poseidon Adventure." In the spoof, recounted Irving Wardle in the London *Times*, "O'Brien assembles a party . . . including a hawkish American senator, a hippie oceanographer and his Woodstock-generation wife, a pirouetting black photographer, and an alcoholic doctor of divinity" on "a pair of Caribbean islands menaced by the impending collision of two gigantic icebergs." Wardle expressed disappointment in the play's omitting the anticipated "climax in which the icebergs do or do not collide," and also in the failure of the "gifted mid-Atlantic parodist," O'Brien, to create a musical to emulate his overwhelmingly successful "Rocky Horror Show."

MEDIA ADAPTATIONS: "The Rocky Horror Picture Show" was adapted by Richard J. Anobile as *The Official Rocky Horror Picture Show Movie Novel,* for A & W Visual Library, c. 1980.

BIOGRAPHICAL/CRITICAL SOURCES:

BOOKS

Contemporary Literary Criticism, Volume 17, Gale, 1981.
Henkin, Bill, *The "Rocky Horror Picture Show" Book,* Hawthorn Books, 1979.

PERIODICALS

Horizon, September, 1979.
Melody Maker, August 21, 1976.
National Review, November 24, 1978.
Newsweek, July 17, 1978.
Plays and Players, August, 1973.
Times (London), July 7, 1978.
Variety, August 18, 1976.*

—*Sketch by Christa Brelin*

* * *

O'CONNOR, Jane 1947-

PERSONAL: Born December 30, 1947, in New York, N.Y.; daughter of Norman and Dovie (Brandt) Abramson; married Jim O'Connor; children: two sons. *Education:* Smith College, B.A., 1969.

ADDRESSES: New York, N.Y.

CAREER: Random House, New York, N.Y., executive editor of "Books for Young Readers" series, 1968—.

AWARDS, HONORS: Award from New York Academy of Sciences, 1981, for *Magic in the Movies;* Nebraska Golden Sower Award from Nebraska Library Association, 1982, for *Yours Till Niagara Falls.*

WRITINGS:

CHILDREN'S BOOKS

Yours Till Niagara Falls, Hastings House, 1979.
(With Katy Hall) *Magic in the Movies: The Story of Special Effects,* Doubleday, 1980.
Just Good Friends, Harper, 1983.
(With Joyce Milton) *The Dandee Diamond Mystery,* Scholastic Inc., 1983.
(With Milton) *The Amazing Bubble Gum Caper,* Scholastic Inc., 1984.
(With husband, Jim O'Connor) *The Magic Top Mystery,* Scholastic Inc., 1984.
The Care Bears' Party Cookbook, Random House, 1985.
Lulu and the Witch Baby, Harper, 1986.
The Teeny Tiny Woman, Random House, 1986.
Lulu Goes to Witch School, Harper, 1987.
Sir Small, Random House, 1988.
(With O'Connor) *The Ghost in Tent Nineteen,* Random House, 1988.

WORK IN PROGRESS: The Amazing Adventures of Super Cluck, with Robert O'Connor, for Harper.

* * *

ODAGA, Asenath (Bole) 1937- (Kituomba)

PERSONAL: Born July 5, 1937, in Rarieda, Kenya; daughter of Blasto Akumu Aum (a farmer and catechist) and Patricia Abuya Abok (a farmer); married James Charles Odaga (a manager), January 27, 1957; children: Odhiambo Odongo, Akelo,

Adhiambo, Awnor. *Education:* Attended Kikuyu Teacher Training College, 1955-56; University of Nairobi, B.A. (with honors), 1974, Dip.Ed., 1974, M.A., 1981. *Religion:* Protestant.

ADDRESSES: Home and office—P.O. Box 1743, Kisumu, Kenya.

CAREER: Church Missionary Society's Teacher Training College, Ngiya, Kenya, teacher, 1957-58; teacher at Kambare School, 1957-58; Butere Girls School, Kahamega, Kenya, teacher, 1959-60; Nyakach Girls School, Kisumu district, Kenya, headmistress, 1961-63; Kenya Railways, Nairobi, Kenya, assistant secretary, 1964; Kenya Dairy Board, Nairobi, assistant secretary, 1965-68; Kenya Library Services, Nairobi, secretary, 1968; *East African Standard,* Nairobi, advertising assistant, 1969-70; Kerr Downey and Selby Safaris, Nairobi, advertising and office manager, 1969-70; Christian Churches Educational Association, Nairobi, assistant director of curriculum and development program, 1974-75; Institute of African Studies, University of Nairobi, Nairobi, research fellow, 1976-81; free-lance researcher, writer, and editor, 1982—. Manager of Thu Tinda Bookshop, 1982—, and Lake Publishers and Enterprises, 1982—; affiliated with Odaga & Associates (consulting firm), 1984—. Chairman of the board of governors of Nyakach Girls High School; member of Museum Management Committee, Kisumu, 1984—, and vice-chairman, 1984—.

MEMBER: Writers' Association of Kenya (founding member and secretary, 1978-87), Kenya Association of University Women (chairman of Kisumu chapter, 1983-87), Kenya Business and Professional Women's Club (past chairman), Rarieda Women's Group, Akala Women's Group (patron).

AWARDS, HONORS: Best Story award from *Voice of Women* magazine, 1967, for a short story, "The Suitor," and an unpublished play, "Three Brides in an Hour."

WRITINGS:

JUVENILE

The Secret of Monkey the Rock, illustrated by William Agutu, Thomas Nelson, 1966.
Jande's Ambition, illustrated by Adrienne Moore, East African Publishing, 1966.
The Diamond Ring, illustrated by A. Moore, East African Publishing, 1967.
The Hare's Blanket and Other Tales, illustrated by A. Moore, East African Publishing, 1967.
The Angry Flames, illustrated by A. Moore, East African Publishing, 1968.
Sweets and Sugar Cane, illustrated by Beryl Moore, East African Publishing, 1969.
The Villager's Son, illustrated by Shyam Varma, Heinemann Educational (London), 1971.
Kip on the Farm, illustrated by B. Moore, East African Publishing, 1972.
(Editor, with David Kirui and David Crippen) *God, Myself, and Others,* Evangel, 1976.
Kip at the Coast, illustrated by Gay Galsworthy, Evans, 1977.
Kip Goes to the City, illustrated by Galsworthy, Evans, 1977.
Poko Nyar Mugumba (title means "Poko Mugumba's Daughter"), illustrated by Sophia Ojienda, Foundation, 1978.
Thu Tinda: Stories From Kenya, Uzima, 1980.
The Two Friends (folktales), illustrated by Barrack Omondi, Bookwise (Nairobi), 1981.
Kenyan Folk Tales, illustrated by Margaret Humphries, Humphries (Caithness, Scotland), 1981.
(With Kenneth Cripwell) *Look and Write Book One,* Thomas Nelson, 1982.
(With Crimpwell) *Look and Learn Book Two,* Thomas Nelson, 1982.
My Home Book One, Lake Publishers (Kisumu), 1983.
Odilo Nungo Piny Kirom (title means "Ogilo, the Arms Can't Embrace the Earth's Waist"), illustrated by H. Kirui-koske, Heinemann Educational (London), 1983.
Nyamgondho Whod Ombare (title means "'Nyamgondho, the Son of Ombare' and Other Stories"), illustrated by Joseph Odaga, Lake Publishers, 1986.
Munde and His Friends, illustrated by Peter Odaga, Lake Publishers, 1987.
The Rag Ball, illustrated by J. Odaga, Lake Publishers, 1987.
Munde Goes to the Market, illustrated by P. Odaga, Lake Publishers, 1987.
Weche Sigendi gi Timbe Luo Moko (title means "Stories and Some Customs of the Luo"), Lake Publishers, 1987.
Story Time (folktales), Lake Publishers, 1987.

OTHER

Nyathini Koa e Nyuolne Nyaka Higni Adek (title means "Your Child From Birth to Age Three"), Evangel, 1976.
"Miaha" (five-act; title means "The Bride"), first produced in Nairobi, 1981.
(With S. Kichamu Akivaga) *Oral Literature: A School Certificate Course,* Heinemann Educational (Nairobi), 1982.
Simbi Nyaima (four-act; title means "The Sunken Village"; first produced in Kisumu, 1982), Lake Publishers, 1983.
Nyamgondho (four-act), first produced in Kisumu, 1983.
Yesterday's Today: The Study of Oral Literature, Lake Publishers, 1984.
The Shade Changes (fiction), Lake Publishers, 1984.
The Storm, Lake Publishers, 1985.
Literature for Children and Young People in Kenya, Kenya Literature Bureau (Nairobi), 1985.
Between the Years (fiction), Lake Publishers, 1987.
A Bridge in Time (fiction), Lake Publishers, 1987.
The Silver Cup (fiction), Lake Publishers, 1987.
Riana's Choice (short stories), Lake Publishers, 1987.
A Taste of Life, Lake Publishers, 1988.
Love Potion and Other Stories, Lake Publishers, 1988.
A Reed on the Roof, Block Ten, With Other Stories, Lake Publishers, 1988.

Member of editorial committee of Western Kenya branch of Wildlife Society. Contributor, sometimes under the name Kituomba, to periodicals, including *Women's Mirror* and *Viva.*

WORK IN PROGRESS: A Luo-English, English-Luo dictionary; a book on Juogi beliefs among the Abasuba of Rusinga Island; a book on Luo oral literature.

SIDELIGHTS: Asenath Odaga commented: "I'm basically a storyteller to both children and adults. And like any other artist, I strive to attain perfection through deeper perception and clear insights into the experiences of life and daily events that go on around me, because it's from some of these common banalities that I draw and fashion some of my writing. I realize that together with all those who possess this creative ability, we have in a small way, in all humility, become co-creators with our gods. In the foregoing realization lies my sensitivity (akin to religion) and profound feelings against injustices meted on others through negation of some of the universal human values on account of race (as in the case in South Africa): creed, gender, and culture.

"What I'm driving at is that art (literature) has several functions apart from providing entertainment. At least this has always been the case in most African societies where art, including literature, was never indulged in just for art's sake, or purely for its aesthetic and entertainment values, but always had several other functions in society."

AVOCATIONAL INTERESTS: Reading, photography, music, cooking, walking, painting, collecting traditional costumes and other artifacts of Kenyan people.

* * *

O'DEA, Agnes C. 1911-

PERSONAL: Born April 24, 1911, in St. John's, Newfoundland (now a province of Canada); daughter of John Vincent and Mary J. (Coady) O'Dea. *Education:* University of Toronto, B.A., 1931, B.L.Sc., 1940; attended Rutgers University, 1961. *Religion:* Roman Catholic.

ADDRESSES: Home—69 LeMarchant Rd., St. John's, Newfoundland, Canada A1C 2G9.

CAREER: Gosling Memorial Library, St. John's, Newfoundland, assistant librarian, 1934-39; Toronto Public Library, Toronto, Ontario, assistant branch librarian, 1940-49; Ontario Research Foundation, Toronto, assistant librarian, 1949-52; Memorial University of Newfoundland, St. John's, reference librarian, 1952-55, research librarian in department of history, 1955-60, cataloger, 1962-64, head of Centre for Newfoundland Studies, 1964-76.

MEMBER: Bibliographical Society of Canada, Atlantic Provinces Library Association, Newfoundland Historical Society, Newfoundland Library Association, Imperial Order of the Daughters of Canada.

AWARDS, HONORS: Certificate of Merit from Canadian Historical Association, 1976; Heritage Award from Newfoundland Historical Society, 1977; Merit Award from Atlantic Provinces Library Association, 1980; LL.D. from Memorial University of Newfoundland, 1987; Tremaine Medal from Bibliographic Society of Canada, 1987.

WRITINGS:

(Compiler) *Bibliography of Newfoundland,* two volumes, University of Toronto Press, 1986.

SIDELIGHTS: Agnes O'Dea told *CA:* "I first became interested in Newfoundland when I was assistant librarian at the St. John's Public Library in the 1930s. Many years later, to complement the research required in establishing a Newfoundland archive, I was commissioned to compile a Newfoundland bibliography. It was only six years after Newfoundland's union with Canada, and since bibliographies relating to Canada had not previously included Newfoundland, and the larger libraries had not as yet collected a great deal of material relating to the province, it was felt that such a bibliography would make a decided contribution to Canadiana.

"The first volume lists books in whole or in part relevant to this region—provincial and federal government documents as well as those of other countries, atlases and maps when accompanied by text, published collections of photographs or drawings, independently paged periodical articles, literary works by Newfoundlanders, some sheet music, a few film shorts and motion pictures, and theses and royal commission reports. Volume two consists mainly of author, title, and subject indexes."

OPPENHEIM, S(aul) Chesterfield 1897-1988

OBITUARY NOTICE: Born January 16, 1897, in New York, N.Y.; died of cardiac arrest, January 29, 1988, in Silver Spring, Md. Attorney, legal adviser, educator, and author. Oppenheim is most noted for his expertise in antitrust, patent, trademark, and copyright law. He taught law for twenty-five years at George Washington University before joining the law school faculty at the University of Michigan in 1953, where he was named professor emeritus upon his retirement in 1965. Active throughout his career in antitrust concerns, he was chairman of the American Bar Association's antitrust law section, co-chairman for the Attorney General's National Committee to Study Anti-Trust Laws from 1953 to 1955, and a consultant on research for the Patent, Trademark and Copyright Research Institute at George Washington University from 1957 to 1972. Additionally, he served as counsel to the Washington, D.C., law firm Howrey & Simon from 1970 to 1983, as editor of the Little, Brown and Company's "Trade Regulation Series," and as a founder of the Bureau of National Affairs' advisory board of "The Anti-Trust and Trade Regulation Report." Oppenheim's publications include *Cases on Trade Regulation, Cases on Federal Anti-Trust Laws, Lawyers Robinson-Patman Act Sourcebook,* and *Unfair Trade Practices and Consumer Protection: Cases and Comments.*

OBITUARIES AND OTHER SOURCES:

BOOKS

Directory of American Scholars, Volume IV: *Philosophy, Religion, and Law,* 6th edition, Bowker, 1974.
Who's Who in American Law, 2nd edition, Marquis, 1979.

PERIODICALS

Washington Post, February 1, 1988.

* * *

ORSBORN, Carol 1948-

PERSONAL: Born February 6, 1948, in Chicago, Ill.; daughter of Lloyd and Mae (Kaplan) Matzkin; married Daniel Edward Orsborn (a public relations executive), June 16, 1970; children: Grant, Jody. *Education:* Attended University of California, Berkeley, B.A., 1966-70.

ADDRESSES: Home—Mill Valley, Calif. *Office*—Orsborn Group, 1728 Union St., San Francisco, Calif. 94123. *Agent*—John Brockman Associates, Inc., 2307 Broadway, New York, N.Y. 10024.

CAREER: Orsborn Group (public relations firm), San Francisco, Calif., founder and president, 1971—. Founder of Superwomen's Anonymous, 1986.

MEMBER: Phi Beta Kappa.

WRITINGS:

Enough Is Enough: Exploding the Myth of Having It All, Putnam, 1986.

SIDELIGHTS: Carol Orsborn told *CA:* "I consider myself to be a spiritual activist, using writing as a tool to wake up my peers to an expanded vision of what is possible for ourselves. I believe that the how-to genre of contemporary mass market

literature has mass hypnotized us into believing that coping is the ideal, to be reached by overcoming deep-seated psychological barriers. I founded my organization to make the point that we deserve more than 'to hold our own in a battle.' To do so requires making concrete changes in the way we live, the way we work, the way we buy products, and the way we talk to one another.

"I believe that my book was the expression of a quiet revolution well under way in homes and workplaces throughout the world. Over thirty thousand members of my organization have taken a stand, freeing themselves from the struggle to have, do, and be 'it all.' I call on women to 'live their own lives.' As such, there is no single 'correct' solution. Instead, I present *Enough Is Enough* as a guide to personal liberation from the superwoman myth. The book's underlying message is that women take the time to disengage from the pace and demands that have kept them too busy to be conscious of their real needs and desires as human beings. I believe that once women take the time for themselves, their own common sense kicks in to help light the way to true liberation. By providing one role model, I hope to make the way a bit easier for my fellow travelers."

BIOGRAPHICAL/CRITICAL SOURCES:

PERIODICALS

Chicago Tribune, December 8, 1986.

* * *

OWEN, David E(lystan) 1912-1987

PERSONAL: Born February 27, 1912, in Kingston on Thames, England; died April 9, 1987; son of John Griffith and Gertrude (Heaten) Owen; married Pearl Jennings, April 2, 1936; children: one son, one daughter. *Education:* King's College, London, B.Sc. (with first class honors), 1933, Ph.D., 1935.

CAREER: Liverpool Museum, Liverpool, England, keeper of geology, 1935-47; Leeds City Museum, Leeds, England, director, 1947-57; Manchester Museum, Manchester, England, director, 1957-76. Founder at Boat Museum, Ellesmere Port, England, and volunteer worker there until 1987; founding member of North-West Museums and Art Galleries Service. *Military service:* British Army, Royal Artillery, 1939-45; became major.

AWARDS, HONORS: Commander of Order of the British Empire, 1972.

WRITINGS:

The Story of Mersey and Deeside Rocks, G. Philip & Son, 1939.

(With T. A. Hume) *Kirkstall Abbey Excavation,* Thoresby Society, 1951-55.

Handbook for Museum Curators, Museums Association, 1954.

Kirkstall Abbey: A History, E. J. Arnold, 1955.

Water Highways, Phoenix House, 1967.

Water Rallies, Dent, 1969.

Water Byways, David & Charles, 1973.

Canals to Manchester, Manchester University Press, 1977.

Cheshire Waterways: Clapham via Lancaster, Dalesman, 1979.

The Manchester Ship Canal, Manchester University Press, 1983.

Exploring England by Canal, David & Charles, 1986.

Also author of *Staffordshire Waterways,* 1986.

Contributor to geology, paleontology, and archaeology journals.

BIOGRAPHICAL/CRITICAL SOURCES:

PERIODICALS

Times (London), April 23, 1987.*

* * *

OWENS, Edgar (Leonard) 1924-1987

OBITUARY NOTICE: Born November 20, 1924, in Altoona, Pa.; died of complications from emphysema, December 2, 1987. Government expert, program specialist, and author. Owens is most noted for his contributions to such government organizations as the Agency for International Development (AID) and Appropriate Technology International (ATI). After serving in the Army Air Forces in the Pacific during World War II, Owens worked for the North Atlantic Treaty Organization (NATO) in Paris in the early 1950s. Later that decade he worked for foreign assistance programs. Beginning his association with AID when it was created in 1961, he became a rural development and appropriate technology specialist, taking assignments in Pakistan, Thailand, and Vietnam. He helped organize the program development organization ATI and was its senior adviser for eight years after retiring from AID in 1977. His book *Development Reconsidered: Bridging the Gap Between Government and People* was published in 1972.

OBITUARIES AND OTHER SOURCES:

PERIODICALS

Washington Post, December 4, 1987.

P

PADEN, William D(oremus, Jr.) 1941-

PERSONAL: Born June 20, 1941, in Lawrence, Kan.; son of William Doremus (a professor) and Dagmar (Parr) Paden; married Frances Freeman (a professor), June 27, 1973; children: Catherine, William. *Education:* Yale University, B.A., 1963, Ph.D., 1971; University of Illinois at Urbana-Champaign, M.A., 1966.

ADDRESSES: Home—1604 Lincoln St., Evanston, Ill. 60201. *Office*—Department of French, Northwestern University, 633 Clark St., Evanston, Ill. 60201.

CAREER: Northwestern University, Evanston, Ill., instructor, 1968-71, assistant professor, 1971-74, associate professor, 1974-81, professor of French and Italian, 1981—.

MEMBER: International Courtly Literature Society, Mediaeval Academy of America, Modern Language Association of America, Societe Guilhem IX (president, 1985—).

AWARDS, HONORS: Fellow of National Endowment for the Humanities, 1976-77, 1987-88.

WRITINGS:

(Contributor) Giose Rimanelli and Kenneth John Atchity, editors, *Italian Literature: Roots and Branches,* Yale University Press, 1976.

(Editor with Tilde Sankovitch and Patricia H. Stablein) *The Poems of the Troubadour: Bertran de Born,* University of California Press, 1986.

(Editor) *The Medieval Pastourelle* (anthology), Garland Publishing, 1988.

An Introduction to Old Occitan, Modern Language Association of America, in press.

Contributor to literature and philosophy journals.

* * *

PAKULA, Alan J(ay) 1928-

BRIEF ENTRY: Born April 7, 1928, in New York, N.Y. American motion picture producer, director, and screenwriter. Pakula's reputation as a filmmaker derives mainly from his ability to elicit exceptional performances from the stars cast in his pictures. This natural rapport with actors, together with his technical acumen, affords him widespread critical acclaim throughout the motion picture industry. The majority of moviegoers, however, seem only vaguely aware of his personal identity and fail to associate Pakula's name with his screen credits. This is due partially to the filmmaker's relative anonymity among the general public and partially to the diverse range of genres and styles featured in his work. Pakula is especially noted for his creative depiction of psychological elements enhanced by various audio and visual effects.

Since beginning his career as a producer with "Fear Strikes Out," a 1957 screenplay based on the life of baseball player Jim Piersall, Pakula has produced and/or directed at least a dozen successful films. Among them are "Love With the Proper Stranger" (1963), "Up the Down Staircase" (1967), "Klute" (1971), "Starting Over" (1979), and the Academy Award-winning "To Kill a Mockingbird" (1963). Following an eleven-year collaboration with "Fear Strikes Out" director Robert Mulligan, Pakula initially combined his producing skills with directing in a solo effort "The Sterile Cuckoo"—an offbeat 1969 romantic comedy starring Liza Minnelli. Critics generally voiced enthusiasm for the film, and he continued directing (while sometimes also producing) a number of popular motion pictures, including the 1976 box-office smash "All the President's Men"—which garnered Pakula an Academy Award nomination for best director. In addition to his producing and directing work, the filmmaker wrote the screenplay for "Sophie's Choice" (1982), which received nominations for best screen adaptation from both the Academy of Motion Picture Arts and Sciences and the Writers Guild of America. *Addresses: Office*—Pakula Productions, 330 West 58th St., Suite 5H, New York, N.Y. 10019. *Agent*—William Morris Agency, 151 El Camino Dr., Beverly Hills, Calif. 90212.

BIOGRAPHICAL/CRITICAL SOURCES:

BOOKS

Contemporary Theatre, Film, and Television, Volume 1, Gale, 1984.

Current Biography, H. W. Wilson, 1980.

PERIODICALS

New York Post, April 15, 1976.

New York Times, June 3, 1977, November 21, 1982.

PALAMOUNTAIN, Joseph Cornwall, Jr. 1920-1987

OBITUARY NOTICE—See index for *CA* sketch: Born November 26, 1920, in West Newton, Mass.; died of cardiac arrest, November 23, 1987, in Saratoga Springs, N.Y. Educator, college administrator, editor, and author. Palamountain was the president of Skidmore College for twenty-two years beginning in 1965. Previous to his term at Skidmore, he taught government at Harvard and Wesleyan universities. He helped edit *American National Government: Policy and Politics* and *Issues and Perspectives in American Government,* and edited two series on American government for the Scott, Foresman publishing company. Palamountain's additional writings include *The Politics of Distribution* and the third edition of *Government and the American Economy.*

OBITUARIES AND OTHER SOURCES:

BOOKS

Who's Who in America, 44th edition, Marquis, 1986.

PERIODICALS

New York Times, November 25, 1987.

* * *

PANIN, Dimitri (Mikhailovich) 1911-1987

OBITUARY NOTICE: Born in 1911; died November 18, 1987, in Paris, France. Engineer, physicist, scientific researcher, and author. One of the many scientists imprisoned by Russian leader Joseph Stalin in the 1940s, Panin was the model for the character Sologdin in Russian novelist Aleksander Solzhenitsyn's book *The First Circle*. In captivity for sixteen years, Panin endured the first part of his detention in the rugged labor camps of Soviet central Asia before being sent to the prison research center near Moscow. It is said that he endured so much suffering that he evenutally became immune to pain and was, hence, able to work unfalteringly on important scientific projects. Author Solzhenitsyn—who was himself an inmate of the prison and Panin's comrade—was allegedly so impressed with Panin's ability to ignore pain that he recounted the scientist's courage and their relationship in his 1965 novel. Panin was released from the prison in 1956 and immigrated to France in 1972. His own experiences in the camps are recorded in his 1976 work *The Notebooks of Sologdin*.

OBITUARIES AND OTHER SOURCES:

PERIODICALS

Times (London), November 20, 1987.

* * *

PARASOL, Peter
See STEVENS, Wallace

* * *

PARKER, (Herbert) John (Harvey) 1906-1987

OBITUARY NOTICE—See index for *CA* sketch: Born July 15, 1906, in Bristol, England; died November 24, 1987. Politician, editor, and author. Parker will be best remembered as a longtime member of the British Parliament for the Labour party. One of his most important deeds was to introduce the Legitimacy Act of 1959, which made legitimate the children of bigamous marriages in which one partner was proven ignorant of the spouse's previous marriage. Parker was also a member of the socialist Fabian Society, and he once met Soviet premier Josef Stalin while abroad. He edited a series of Yugoslavian novels in English translation, and his writings include *Public Enterprise, Democratic Sweden, Modern Turkey, Forty-two Days in the Soviet Union, Labour Marches On,* and *Harold Wilson: A Pictorial Biography*. His memoir, *Father of the House: Fifty Years in Politics,* was published in 1982.

OBITUARIES AND OTHER SOURCES:

BOOKS

Who's Who, 139th edition, St. Martin's, 1987.

PERIODICALS

Times (London), November 25, 1987.

* * *

PARKER, Laura
See CASTORO, Laura A(nn)

* * *

PARQUE, Richard (Anthony) 1935-

PERSONAL: Surname is pronounced "Par-*kay*"; born August 10, 1935, in Los Angeles, Calif.; son of Joe (a musician) and Helen Margaret (a teaching assistant; maiden name, Muto) Parque; married Vo Thi Lan (a designer), May 1, 1975; children: Kenneth, Phat, James. *Education:* California State University, Los Angeles, B.A., 1958, M.A., 1966, California State teaching credential, 1966; graduate study at University of Redlands, 1966. *Religion:* Christian.

ADDRESSES: Home—P.O. Box 327, Verdugo City, Calif. 91046. *Agent*—Siegel & Siegel Ltd., West 83rd St., New York, N.Y. 10024.

CAREER: Yucaipa High School, Yucaipa, Calif., science teacher, 1961-66; California State University System, Long Beach, Calif., instructor and science education adviser, 1966-68; McDonnell Douglas Astronautics Co., Huntington Beach, Calif., professional development and training administrator, 1968-71; Parque Consulting Associates, Downey, Calif., president and principal consultant, 1971-77 and 1979—; Ralph M. Parsons Co. (engineering), Pasadena, Calif., corporate director of education and training, 1977-78; Rockwell International, Downey, senior technical writer, 1978—. Teacher at the University of the West Indies, 1966; adjunct faculty member at San Diego State University, 1966-68, University of California, Irvine, 1972-73, California State University, Los Angeles, 1980, and University of California, Los Angeles, 1982. Free-lance writer for Research Associates of Los Angeles, 1980-82. *Military service:* U.S. Marine Corps, Marine Band and infantry, 1958-61; became sergeant.

MEMBER: American Society for Training and Development, National Management Association, National Science Teachers Association, Professional and Organizational Development Network in Higher Education, Consultants Network, National Writers Club, Academy of American Poets, Authors Guild, California Teachers Association, National Audubon Society, International Trumpet Guild.

AWARDS, HONORS: Science teaching award from National Aeronautics and Space Administration, 1966; special recognition from Colorado State University for Vietnam war novels.

WRITINGS:

Sweet Vietnam, Zebra Books, 1984.
Hellbound, Zebra Books, 1985.
Firefight, Zebra Books, 1986.
Flight of the Phantom, Zebra Books, 1987.
John's Dream, Zebra Books, 1987.
A Distant Thunder, Zebra Books, 1988.
The Search for Druzhnaya I, Zebra Books, 1988.

Author of poems appearing in poetry journals and anthologies. Self-syndicated column appeared in *Los Angeles Herald Examiner, Los Angeles Daily News,* and *Oregonian.* Also contributor of articles to periodicals, including *Soldier of Fortune, New Breed,* and *Manage.*

SIDELIGHTS: Richard Parque told *CA:* "My Marine Corps experience, enchantment with Oriental femininity (my wife is Vietnamese), and admiration for those who overcome great odds to excel have been my motivations to write. Add to that the freedom of expression that comes with writing and the need to clarify my personal thoughts and those of mankind, mix in a professional writer friend who encouraged me to begin writing, a supportive wife (who is an important source of information for my novels) and family, and you have the ingredients that launched an author.

"My novels are written to evoke emotion and to prick the mind to look deeper into the reserves that we have within ourselves to overcome crises. Central to this theme is the need to achieve and the desire to make our lives count. Many of my books are set in Vietnam, because the war there was so highly personalized to the extent that the only meaning was in the individual engagement and in the intense struggle to survive that took place for each person, mentally as well as physically. A different kind of hero came out of that war.

"Also, the Vietnam War produced many colorful and interesting characters, the kind that go into the making of memorable novels. There is a plethora of available plots, from a young second lieutenant trying to rationalize his involvement in a war no one supports to the clash between East/West cultures when a Marine falls in love with a Saigon prostitute, to the deadly games of espionage played all the way from Washington to Hanoi.

"My works contain large doses of adventure, danger, and romance, as well as allegory, poignancy, understatement, and other literary characteristics, particularly the emphasis of theme. It is my belief that the reader should be entertained as well as given an opportunity to exercise his/her mind. Therefore, my writing can be at the same time fun, exciting, lyrical, and educational."

AVOCATIONAL INTERESTS: Playing and teaching classical trumpet, reading and collecting master works of music and literature, studying natural history and science, backpacking, fishing.

BIOGRAPHICAL/CRITICAL SOURCES:

PERIODICALS

Glendale News-Press, October 14, 1984.
Insight, August 24, 1987.
Richmond Times-Dispatch, November 3, 1986.

* * *

PARTINGTON, Martin 1944-

PERSONAL: Born March 5, 1944, in Maidstone, England; son of Thomas P. (a teacher) and Mary (a violin teacher; maiden name, Jelly) Partington; married Marcia Carol Leavey, June, 1969 (divorced, 1973); married Daphne Isobel Mansell (an author), October 21, 1978; children: Daniel, Adam, Hannah. *Education:* Cambridge University, B.A., 1965, LL.B., 1966.

ADDRESSES: Office—Faculty of Law, University of Bristol, Bristol, England.

CAREER: University of Bristol, Bristol, England, assistant lecturer, 1966-69; University of Warwick, Coventry, England, assistant lecturer, 1969-73; University of London, London School of Economics and Political Science, London, England, lecturer in law, 1973-80; Brunel University, Uxbridge, Middlesex, England, professor of law and dean of faculty of social sciences, 1980-87; University of Bristol, Bristol, professor of law, 1987—.

WRITINGS:

Claim in Time (nonfiction), Frances Pinter, 1978, 2nd edition, Legal Action Group, 1988.
Landlord and Tenant (nonfiction), Weidenfeld & Nicolson, 1975, 2nd edition, 1980.
(With Andrew Arden) *Housing Law* (nonfiction), Sweet & Maxwell, 1983, 2nd edition, in press.
Cases and Materials in Housing Law, Sweet & Maxwell, 1988.

General editor of *Anglo-American Law Review.* Contributor of articles to periodicals and books.

SIDELIGHTS: Martin Partington told *CA:* "My primary objective has been to throw light on areas of law hitherto neglected by scholars and practitioners. Housing law affects everyone as the government attempts to regulate relationships between landlords and tenants or mortgagors and mortgagees, yet practitioners have not always grasped the full significance of the law. Similarly, social security law—the subject of *Claim in Time*—affects huge numbers of people in society, is very complex, and yet has also been ignored by both practitioners and scholars. The importance of studying law affecting the poor is as great as the study of law affecting the affluent."

AVOCATIONAL INTERESTS: Music (playing violin), gardening, walking, travel.

* * *

PASCOE, Elaine 1946-

PERSONAL: Born August 24, 1946, in New Rochelle, N.Y.; daughter of Clifford N. (a businessman) and Dorothy (a writer and editor; maiden name, Palmer) Pascoe; married Thomas J. Sedito, June 10, 1967 (divorced in August, 1975); children: Carey. *Education:* Western Connecticut State University, B.A. (summa cum laude), 1977; Manhattanville College, M.A., 1986.

ADDRESSES: c/o Westport Publishing Group, P.O. Box 149, Westport, Conn. 06881.

CAREER: White Plains Reporter and Dispatch, White Plains, N.Y., staff writer, 1977-78; *Practical Horseman,* Unionville, Pa., contributing editor, 1978-84, senior editor, 1984—. Member of editorial staff of *New Book of Knowledge,* Grolier, Inc., 1978-83. Member of adjunct faculty at Western Connecticut State University, 1986-87.

MEMBER: Women in Communications.

AWARDS, HONORS: Citation of Outstanding Merit from National Council for the Social Studies, 1986, for *Racial Prejudice.*

WRITINGS:

Racial Prejudice (young adult), F. Watts, 1985.
The Horse Owner's Preventive Maintenance Handbook, Scribner, 1986.
South Africa: Troubled Land (young adult), F. Watts, 1987.

Contributor to *New Book of Knowledge, Encyclopedia Americana Annual, Science Annual,* and *Academic American Encyclopedia.* Contributor of articles and photographs to magazines and newspapers, including *County Life. Performance Horseman,* contributing editor, 1982-84, senior editor, 1984—.

WORK IN PROGRESS: "Various short pieces and a historical book, as yet untitled, dealing with events in the 1800s."

SIDELIGHTS: Elaine Pascoe told *CA:* "In this video age, complex events are often reported in a way that isolates and oversimplifies them—and thus renders them meaningless. Young people in particular seem to lack the background and knowledge necessary to understand important developments taking place around them. Thus writing for young adults is both challenging and rewarding: the background must be filled in so that the reader can put the picture in perspective; then, one hopes, understanding comes. It was this hope that led me to write about racial prejudice and, as a natural outgrowth of that, South Africa, where prejudice of the most vicious sort has made the future look dim indeed.

"I've written about horses out of quite another motive: fondness for these delightful, elegant creatures. In writing *The Horse Owner's Preventive Maintenance Handbook,* I sought to fill a hole with a book that would tell not how to buy or ride a horse, and not how to patch it up when it became lame or sick, but how to keep a horse happy, healthy, and performing soundly for years."

* * *

PAUL, Danielle
See MITTERMEYER, Helen (Hayton Monteith)

* * *

p'BITEK, Okot 1931-1982

PERSONAL: Born in 1931 in Gulu, Uganda; died July 19, 1982; son of a schoolteacher; married twice. *Education:* Attended King's College, Budo; Government Training College, Mbarara, teaching certificate; Bristol University, certificate of education; University College of Wales, LL.B.; Institute of Social Anthropology, Oxford, B.Litt, 1963.

CAREER: Taught school in the area of Gulu, Uganda, and played on the Ugandan national soccer team in the mid-1950s; Makerere University, Kampala, Uganda, lecturer in sociology, 1964; Uganda National Theater and Uganda National Cultural Center, Kampala, director, 1966-68; University of Iowa, Iowa City, fellow of international writing program, 1969-70, writer in residence, 1971; University of Nairobi, Nairobi, Kenya, senior research fellow at Institute of African Studies and lecturer in sociology and literature, 1971-78; University of Ife, Ife, Nigeria, professor, 1978-82; Makerere University, Kampala, professor of creative writing, 1982; writer. Visiting lecturer at University of Texas, 1969. Founder of the Gulu Arts Festival, 1966, and the Kisumu Arts Festival, 1968.

AWARDS, HONORS: Jomo Kenyatta Prize for Literature from the Kenya Publishers Association, for *Two Songs,* 1972.

WRITINGS:

POETIC NOVELS

Song of Lawino: A Lament, East African Publishing, 1966, Meridian Books, 1969 (also see below).
Song of Ocol, East African Publishing, 1970 (also see below).
Song of a Prisoner, introduction by Edward Blishen, illustrations by E. Okechukwu Odita, Third Press, 1971 (also see below).
Two Songs: Song of Prisoner [and] Song of Malaya, illustrations by Trixi Lerbs, East African Publishing, 1971 (also see above).
Song of Lawino and Song of Ocol, introduction by G. A. Heron, illustrations by Frank Horley, East African Publishing, 1972 (also see above).

OTHER

Lak tar miyo kinyero wi lobo? (novel; title means "Are Your Teeth White? Then Laugh!"), Eagle Press, 1953.
African Religions in Western Scholarship, East African Literature Bureau, 1970.
Religion of the Central Luo, East African Literature, 1971.
Africa's Cultural Revolution (essays), introduction by Ngugi wa Thiong'o, Macmillan Books for Africa, 1973.
(Compiler and translator) *The Horn of My Love* (folk songs), Heinemann Educational Books, 1974.
(Compiler and translator) *Hare and Hornbill* (folktales), Heinemann Educational Books, 1978.

Contributor to periodicals, including *Transition.*

SIDELIGHTS: Eulogized as "Uganda's best known poet" in his London *Times* obituary, Okot p'Bitek had a distinguished career in the fields of sport, education, and the arts. While serving as a teacher in his native Uganda during the 1950s he played on the country's national soccer team, going to the 1956 Summer Olympic Games in London, England. P'Bitek stayed in Great Britain to obtain degrees from several universities before returning to Uganda to teach at the college level. He published his first book, *Lak tar miyo kinyero wi lobo?* (title means "Are Your Teeth White? Then Laugh!"), in 1953 but it was the 1966 publication of his *Song of Lawino* that brought p'Bitek his first real acclaim. In the same year, p'Bitek was named director of the Uganda National Theater and Cultural Center. In this post he founded the successful Gulu Arts Festival, a celebration of the traditional oral history, dance, and other arts of his ancestral Acholi people. Due to political pressures, however, p'Bitek was forced from his directorship after two years. He moved to Kenya, where, with the exception of visits to universities in the United States, he remained throughout the reign of Ugandan dictator Idi Amin. After founding the Kisumu Arts Festival in Kenya and later serving as a professor in Nigeria, p'Bitek eventually returned to Makerere University in Kampala, Uganda. He was a professor of creative writing there when he died in 1982.

P'Bitek sought, in his role as cultural director and author, to prevent native African culture from being swallowed up by the influences of Western ideas and arts. He was particularly interested in preserving the customs of his native Acholi. While serving as director for the Uganda National Theater and Cultural Center, p'Bitek proclaimed in an interview with Robert Serumaga which appeared in *African Writers Talking:* "The major challenge I think is to find what might be Uganda's contribution to world culture. . . . [W]e should, I think, look into the village and see what the Ugandans—the proper Ugandans—not the people who have been to school, have read—

and see what they do in the village, and see if we cannot find some root there, and build on this.'' He further explained to Serumago his feelings about the influence of Western culture on his own: ''I am not against having plays from England, from other parts of the world, we should have this, but I'm very concerned that whatever we do should have a basic starting point, and this should be Uganda, and then, of course, Africa, and then we can expand afterwards.''

Song of Lawino, p'Bitek's most famous work, takes as its central issue the defense of Acholi tradition against the encroachment of Western cultural influences. Originally composed by p'Bitek in the Acholi (sometimes known as Lwo or Luo) language, he translated *Song of Lawino* into English before its publication. He put the English words to traditional Acholi verse patterns, however, and the result was pleasing to many critics. A reviewer in the *Times Literary Supplement* lauded p'Bitek's creation thus: ''In rewriting his poem in English he has chosen a strong, simple idiom which preserves the sharpness and frankness of [its] imagery, a structure of short, free verses which flow swiftly and easily, and an uncondescending offer of all that is local and specific in the original.''

Categorized as a poetic novel, *Song of Lawino* is narrated by an Acholi woman named Lawino who tells an audience her life story in the form of an Acholi song. Her main complaint is against her husband Ocol, who neglects her because of her adherence to Acholi ways. Ocol, in contrast, tries to become as westernized as possible, rejecting his culture as backward and crude. His negative feelings toward his background are further symbolized by his preferring his mistress, Clementina, over Lawino. Clementina is thoroughly westernized, from her name to her high-heeled shoes. Lawino tells us that her rival straightens her hair, uses lipstick, and ''dusts powder on her face / And it looks so pale; / She resembles the wizard / Getting ready for the midnight dance.'' Lawino speaks disdainfully of what she perceives as unnatural behavior on the part of her husband and his mistress; in favorable opposition to this she praises the life of her village. Most critics agree that Lawino's loving descriptions of the simple Acholi rural activities and rituals leave the reader with no doubt as to whose side the author takes. As reported in the *Times Literary Supplement,* ''It is Lawino's voice that we need to hear, reminding us of the human reality behind glib rejections of the backward, the primitive, the 'bush people.''' P'Bitek later wrote *Song of Ocol,* which purports to offer Lawino's husband's defense, but most reviewers concurred in believing that Ocol's words merely confirm Lawino's condemnation of him. Another *Times Literary Supplement* critic judged that *Song of Ocol* ''savo[rs] too much of a conscientious attempt to give a voice to an essentially dull, pompous, and vindictive husband.''

P'Bitek's next poetic novels, published as *Two Songs: Song of Prisoner* [*and*] *Song of Malaya,* together won him the Kenya Publishers Association's Jomo Kenyatta Prize in 1972. *Song of Prisoner* relates the thoughts, both hopeful and despairing, of a political prisoner, and, according to the *Times Literary Supplement,* ''its imagery has much of the freshness and inventive energy of Okot's best work.'' The narrator describes his cell as a cold, imprisoning woman and relates his feelings of betrayal, his fears of his lover's unfaithfulness, and his daydreams of merrymaking. *Song of Malaya* is written in the persona of a prostitute and tells of the abuses she suffers. Judged slightly sentimental by some critics, the prose poem discusses, among other things, the irony in the fact that prostitutes are often rounded up and jailed by men who were their patrons the previous evening.

In his later years, p'Bitek's literary efforts turned primarily to translation. He published *The Horn of My Love,* a collection of Acholi folksongs in both Acholi and English translation, in 1974, and *Hare and Hornbill,* a collection of African folktales, in 1978. In *The Horn of My Love,* declared reviewer Gerald Moore in the *Times Literary Supplement,* ''p'Bitek argues the case for African poetry as poetry, as an art to be enjoyed, rather than as ethnographic material to be eviscerated.'' The book contains ceremonial songs about death, ancient Acholi chiefs, and love and courtship. *Hare and Hornbill,* according to Robert L. Berner critiquing in *World Literature Today,* is divided roughly in half between tales of humans and tales of animals, including one about a hare seducing his mother-in-law. ''P'Bitek is particularly qualified to deal with these tales,'' Berner proclaimed, and ''reveals a thorough understanding of African folk materials.''

BIOGRAPHICAL/CRITICAL SOURCES:

BOOKS

p'Bitek, Okot, *Song of Lawino: A Lament,* East African Publishing, 1966.

Pieterse, Cosmo, and Dennis Duerden, editors, *African Writers Talking,* Africana Publishing, 1972.

PERIODICALS

Times Literary Supplement, February 16, 1967, November 5, 1971, February 21, 1975.

World Literature Today, summer, 1979.

OBITUARIES:

PERIODICALS

Times (London), July 23, 1982.*

—Sketch by Elizabeth Thomas

* * *

PEACOCKE, Christopher 1950-

PERSONAL: Born May 22, 1950, in Birmingham, England; son of Arthur and Rosemary Peacocke; married Teresa Anne Rosen (a barrister), January, 1980. *Education:* Oxford University, M.A., 1971, B.Phil., 1974, D.Phil., 1979.

ADDRESSES: *Office*—Department of Philosophy, King's College, University of London, London WC2R 2LS, England.

CAREER: Oxford University, Oxford, England, fellow of All Souls College, 1975-79, fellow of New College, 1979-85; University of London, King's College, London, England, Susan Stebbing Professor of Philosophy, 1985—. Visiting professor at University of California, Berkeley, 1975-76, University of Michigan, 1978, University of California, Los Angeles, 1981, and Australian National University, 1981; fellow at Center for Advanced Study in the Behavioral Sciences, Palo Alto, Calif., 1983-84; visiting research associate at Stanford University's Center for the Study of Language and Information, 1984.

WRITINGS:

Holistic Explanation: Action, Space, Interpretation, Oxford University Press, 1979.

Sense and Content: Experience, Thought, and Their Relations, Oxford University Press, 1983.

Thoughts: An Essay on Content, Basil Blackwell, 1986.

Contributor to philosophy journals.

WORK IN PROGRESS: Research on the theory of meaning and truth; and on psychological exploration, in particular exploration involving the notion of context.

SIDELIGHTS: Christopher Peacocke's books have been described as difficult and complex writings on difficult and complex topics, intended for the elucidation of professional philosophers who are well-versed in their own and related fields. Stephen Stich declared in the *Times Literary Supplement* that Peacocke's views on holistic explanation are "defended with vigorous and often inventive argument, much of it tightly compressed and highly abstract," subtle and interesting. The author's second book was hailed by Avishai Margalit, also in the *Times Literary Supplement,* as ingenious and insightful.

BIOGRAPHICAL/CRITICAL SOURCES:

PERIODICALS

Times Literary Supplement, June 27, 1980, May 18, 1984.

* * *

PEAKE, C(harles) H. 1920(?)-1988

OBITUARY NOTICE: Born c. 1920 in London, England; died January 18, 1988. Educator and author. Peake was a well-known scholar of twentieth-century Irish author James Joyce as well as a specialist in eighteenth-century literature. While being trained as a teacher, Peake read English at London's Birbeck College. He then joined the staff of the University of London, serving first at University College and later at Queen Mary College. He retired from the university as professor emeritus in 1985. Peake's research on English satirist Jonathan Swift led to his 1960 article "Swift and Passions," which was published in *Modern Language Review,* and to a work later represented in David Vieth's 1984 *Essential Articles for the Study of Jonathan Swift's Poetry.* Also a probe into eighteenth-century literature is Peake's *Poetry of Landscape and the Night.* The author's most extensive research, however, concentrated on James Joyce and resulted in his critically acclaimed *James Joyce: The Citizen and the Artist.* The work, which investigates Joyce's book *Ulysses,* was praised by one critic in the late 1970s as the best critical analysis of the Joyce novel to date.

OBITUARIES AND OTHER SOURCES:

PERIODICALS

Times (London), January 25, 1988.

* * *

PELLY, David F. 1948-

PERSONAL: Born June 19, 1948, in Toronto, Ontario, Canada; son of John K. and Joan (Fraser) Pelly. *Education:* Royal Military College of Canada, B.Sc., 1970; additional study at University of Grenoble, 1977; University of Toronto, B.A., 1981.

ADDRESSES: Home—R.R. 1, Castleton, Ontario, Canada K0K 1M0.

CAREER: Royal Canadian Navy, 1966-76, served on destroyers and submarines in the Mediterranean Sea, Caribbean Sea, Pacific Ocean, and North Atlantic Ocean, leaving service as lieutenant commander; free-lance writer, 1976—.

MEMBER: Periodical Writers Association of Canada, Royal Geographical Society (fellow).

AWARDS, HONORS: Canada Council grants, 1978 and 1983; first prize from Canadian Historical Writing Contest, sponsored by Canada Packers, 1979, for "The Commonwealth Air Training Plan."

WRITINGS:

Expedition: An Arctic Journey Through History on George Back's River, Betelgeuse Books, 1981.

(With Ruth Annaqtussi Tulurialik) *Qikaaluktut: Images of Inuit Life,* Oxford University Press, 1986.

(Contributor) James Raffan, editor, *Wild Waters: Canoeing Canada's Wilderness Rivers,* Key Porter Books, 1986.

Contributor to *Historical Atlas of Canada.* Contributor of about fifty articles to magazines, including *Canadian Geographic, Northwest Explorer, Nature Canada, Caribou News, Canada Journal,* and *Sailing Canada.*

WORK IN PROGRESS: A textbook on the Inuit, publication by Grolier expected in 1988; a study of "Canadian-African aid relationships and the implicit cross-cultural communication, particularly with Lesotho," publication by Village Aid expected in 1988.

SIDELIGHTS: David F. Pelly told *CA:* "Much of my writing is based on my interests in the wilderness and other cultures. My focus on the Arctic and the Inuit, of course, brings these two areas of interest together. I first went to the Arctic as a wilderness canoeist—it is, after all, the ultimate Canadian wilderness. In time I came to know the land and then its people, but the two are (I now know) inextricably linked.

"Ruth Tulurialik asked me if I would help her put together a book of her drawings, and *Qikaaluktut* grew from there. We met while I was 'visiting' Baker Lake, an Inuit community in the Northwest Territories. I first arrived there in a canoe at the end of a fifty-two-day expedition across the barren lands. Over the past six years I've spent approximately half my time in the Arctic, traveling widely, much of it in the wilderness areas, by canoe in summer and sled in winter."

BIOGRAPHICAL/CRITICAL SOURCES:

PERIODICALS

Globe and Mail (Toronto), March 29, 1986.

* * *

PERISTIANY, John G(eorge) 1911-1987

OBITUARY NOTICE—See index for *CA* sketch: Born September 4, 1911, in Athens, Greece; died October 27, 1987, in Paris, France. Educator and author. Peristiany served as a lecturer in social anthropology at the University of London and at Cambridge and Oxford universities. He conducted extensive studies on the Kipsigis and Pokot peoples of Kenya, and on the notions of honor, respect, pride, and shame in Mediterranean cultures. Peristiany also served as the UNESCO Professor of Sociology at the Social Sciences Centre in Athens, Greece, beginning in 1960. His writings include *The Social Institutions of the Kipsigis* and *Further Studies in Honour and Shame,* and he served as editor for *Honor and Shame, Contributions to Mediterranean Sociology, Mediterranean Kinship,* and *Mediterranean Family Structures.*

OBITUARIES AND OTHER SOURCES:

PERIODICALS

Times (London), November 4, 1987.

* * *

PERKINS, Hugh V(ictor) 1918-1988

OBITUARY NOTICE—See index for *CA* sketch: Born June 9, 1918, in Toledo, Ohio; died following a stroke, February 10, 1988, in Madras, India. Educator and author. An expert in the field of child study, Perkins taught in public schools in Ohio before arriving at the University of Maryland as an assistant professor of human development in 1948. He taught at that institution for thirty-five years, retiring as a professor in 1983. Perkins's writings include *Research Evaluating a Child Study Program, Human Development and Learning,* and *Human Development.*

OBITUARIES AND OTHER SOURCES:

PERIODICALS

Washington Post, February 16, 1988.

* * *

PERRY, Charles 1941-
(Smokestack el Ropo, Elmo Rooney)

PERSONAL: Born August 5, 1941, in Los Angeles, Calif.; son of Douglas Brill (in sales) and Mary Elizabeth (a housewife; maiden name, Corbaley) Perry. *Education:* Attended Princeton University, 1959-61; attended Middle East Center for Arab Studies, Shimlan, Lebanon, 1962-63; University of California, Berkeley, A.B., 1963.

ADDRESSES: Office—12912 El Dorado Ave., Sylmar, Calif. 91342.

CAREER: University of California, Berkeley, animal caretaker, 1964-67; *Rolling Stone,* New York, N.Y., associate editor, 1968-76; *California* (a biweekly magazine), Los Angeles, Calif., contributing editor, 1979; writer. Sponsor of Los Angeles Garlic Week, 1983.

MEMBER: American Institute of Wine and Food, Lovers of the Stinking Rose (former Los Angeles chapter head).

WRITINGS:

(Editor under name Smokestack el Ropo) *Bedside Reader,* Straight Arrow, 1972.
The Haight-Ashbury: A History, Random House, 1984.

Author of column for *Los Angeles Times,* 1984. Correspondent, *The Cook's Magazine,* 1984. Contributor of articles to periodicals, including *Petits Propos Culinaires.*

WORK IN PROGRESS: Research on Near Eastern food history, including the general history of western Asian breads and grain-based foods, and the history of cookery in Iran, central Asia, Iraq/Persian Gulf, Syria/Nejd, Egypt, and Maghrib; translations of thirteenth-century Arabic cookbooks *Al-Wuslah al-Habib* and *Kitab al-At'imah al-mu'tadah.*

SIDELIGHTS: Charles Perry lived in the San Francisco Bay area of California before becoming a *Rolling Stone* associate editor in 1968. For *Rolling Stone* Perry sometimes wrote under the name Elmo Rooney; under another pseudonym, Smokestack el Ropo, he edited the book *Bedside Reader.* Written under his real name, Perry's *The Haight-Ashbury: A History* chronologically examines events that occurred in the mid-1960s in the district of San Francisco centered on the intersection of the streets Haight and Ashbury. Between 1965 and 1967 the Haight-Ashbury was the seat of youth counterculture—"the so-called Children's Crusade," Herbert Gold explained in the *New York Times Book Review,* "based on a mixture of rock and roll, drugs, liberated sex, funny clothes, underground publication, antiwar agitation, [and] communal experiments . . . [and featuring an] unparalleled blend of idealism, opportunism, [and] goofiness." According to Gold, Perry describes "the events, personalities, conflicts and vagrant notions that characterized the beginning of a turbulent national experience," and "his presentation recreates the times." A *New Yorker* critic concurred, deeming Perry a "trustworthy guide" through the neighborhood and the era.

Perry told *CA:* "I was a wholehearted, uncalculating participant in the Haight-Ashbury event with no thought of being a journalist, and I have long wished to set the record straight. I decided to be a writer at age eleven out of pure—and perhaps peculiar—desire to repay the Republic of Letters for the pleasure reading had given me; but advice from well-meaning elders that there's no way to make a living as a writer long dissuaded me from doing so. I've had a deep interest in the languages of Asia, especially western and central Asia, since I was thirteen. This led to interest in Asian food and food history, which led to my unexpected career as a food writer."

BIOGRAPHICAL/CRITICAL SOURCES:

PERIODICALS

Los Angeles Times, July 22, 1984.
Los Angeles Times Book Review, October 13, 1985.
Nation, September 15, 1984.
New Yorker, September 3, 1984.
New York Times, July 10, 1984.
New York Times Book Review, August 12, 1984.
Voice Literary Supplement, November, 1985.
Washington Post Book World, September 29, 1985.

* * *

PERRY, Susan
See PERRY, Susan M.

* * *

PERRY, Susan M. 1950-
(Susan Perry)

PERSONAL: Born May 1, 1950, in Cleveland, Ohio; daughter of William A. and Joyce (Hatfield-Cribb) Perry; married Jim Dawson (a reporter), October 1, 1977; children: Erin Dawson, Dylan Dawson. *Education:* Attended University of Wisconsin—Madison, 1968-70; American University, B.A., 1973.

ADDRESSES: Home and Office—3537 South Colfax Ave., Minneapolis, Minn. 55408. *Agent*—Heide Lange, Sanford J. Greenburger Associates, Inc., 55 Fifth Ave., New York, N.Y. 10022.

CAREER: Free-lance writer, 1973-77 and 1979—; Center for Science in the Public Interest, Washington, D.C., editor, 1977-78; Time-Life Books, Inc., Alexandria, Va., writer and editor, 1978-79. Teacher in Department of Continuing Education for Women at University of Minnesota.

MEMBER: Minnesota Scriptworks.

AWARDS, HONORS: American Health Book Award, 1985, for *Nightmare: Women and the Dalkon Shield.*

WRITINGS:

UNDER NAME SUSAN PERRY, EXCEPT AS NOTED

(Editor) *Michelangelo: Drawings,* Control Data Publications, 1982.
(Editor) *Raphael: Drawings,* 3M Publications, 1983.
(Editor) *Cezanne: Drawings,* 3M Publications, 1984.
(Under name Susan M. Perry, with Lisa Bellini) *Lean and Green Diet,* Avon, 1985.
(With husband, Jim Dawson) *Nightmare: Women and the Dalkon Shield,* Macmillan, 1985.
(With Dawson) *Your Body Rhythms,* Rawson Associates, 1987.

Contributor to Time-Life Books.

SIDELIGHTS: Susan M. Perry, who told *CA* her major professional interests include health and women's issues, focuses on both topics in *Nightmare: Women and the Dalkon Shield,* which she co-authored with her husband, Jim Dawson. The Dalkon Shield, a form of intrauterine device (IUD), was marketed by the A. H. Robins Company from 1970 to 1974 as a birth control method superior to other IUDs and even birth control pills. Upon thorough investigation, however, the shield was proven less effective than other forms of IUDs and twice as dangerous. Out of more than two million women who had the devices implanted, more than ninety thousand have suffered severe complications because of them, including miscarriages, sterility, and death. The extreme risk associated with the Dalkon Shields led to their official recall in 1984.

Researched from court documents and government transcripts, *Nightmare* recounts how "the inventors and manufacturers of the shield ignored, explained away and even covered up the medical realities of the device," promoting the IUD even after they were aware of its potential danger, wrote Rona Cherry in *New York Times Book Review.* The authors chronicle some of the individual tragedies caused by the deceit, and "they tell this incredible story in a straightforward, journalistic way," judged *Washington Post Book World* critic Robin Marantz Henig. In conclusion, Henig wrote, "*Nightmare* tries to focus on the personal consequences of impersonal acts."

BIOGRAPHICAL/CRITICAL SOURCES:

PERIODICALS

New York Times Book Review, September 22, 1985.
Washington Post Book World, November 17, 1985.

* * *

PERSICHETTI, Vincent 1915-1987

OBITUARY NOTICE: Born June 6, 1915, in Philadelphia, Pa.; died of lung cancer, August 14 (one source says August 13), 1987, in Philadelphia, Pa. Educator, composer, and author. A prolific composer of symphonies, sonatas, and chamber and choral music, as well as pieces for bands and solo instruments, Persichetti is noted for his largely conservative repertory combining classical, romantic, and modernist elements. The composer began his forty-year association with New York City's Juilliard School of Music in 1947, becoming chairman of the composition department in 1967 and chairman of the literature and materials department in 1970. Persichetti's compositions have been performed by orchestras across the country, and in 1973 the artist was commissioned by the Presidential Inaugural Committee to write a piece, "A Lincoln Address," for President Richard M. Nixon's second inaugural concert. Along with more than 150 musical works, including an opera, "The Sibyl," Persichetti was co-author of the monograph *William Schuman* and wrote the book *Twentieth-Century Harmony.*

OBITUARIES AND OTHER SOURCES:

BOOKS

Composium Directory of New Music, Crystal Musicworks, 1982-83.

PERIODICALS

Los Angeles Times, August 15, 1987.
Newsweek, August 24, 1987.
New York Times, August 15, 1987.
Washington Post, August 17, 1987.

* * *

PERTWEE, Michael (Henry Roland) 1916-

BRIEF ENTRY: Born April 24, 1916, in London, England. British playwright, film and television writer, journalist, and author. Although he began his career as a journalist, Pertwee soon became a highly productive author of plays and screenplays. He wrote several plays with his father, Roland Pertwee, including *The Paragon* (English Theatre Guild, 1948; first produced in 1948) and *The Baby-Sitters* (Samuel French, 1955). He also wrote the stage farces *She's Done It Again!* (English Theatre Guild, 1970; first produced in 1969) and *Don't Just Lie There, Say Something!* (Samuel French, 1973; first produced in 1971). Pertwee began writing scripts for motion pictures in 1939 and for television in 1950. Two teleplays he wrote about the popular Leslie Charteris detective, The Saint, were adapted by Fleming Lee for the book *Leslie Charteris' The Saint Abroad* (Doubleday, 1969). Pertwee's autobiography, *Name Dropping* (Frewin, 1974), was seen by reviewers as a light, entertaining work with abundant anecdotes about show business personalities. *Addresses: Home*—34 Aylestone Ave., London NW6 7AA, England.

BIOGRAPHICAL/CRITICAL SOURCES:

BOOKS

The Author's and Writer's Who's Who, 6th edition, reprinted, Burke's Peerage, 1971.
International Motion Picture Almanac, Quigley, 1988.
Pertwee, Michael, *Name Dropping,* Frewin, 1974.
Who's Who in the Theatre: A Biographical Record of the Contemporary Stage, 17th edition, Gale, 1981.
The Writers Directory: 1984-1986, St. James Press, 1983.

PERIODICALS

Books and Bookmen, January, 1975.

* * *

PESTELLI, Giorgio 1938-

PERSONAL: Born May 26, 1938, in Turin, Italy; son of Leo (a philologist) and Giuseppina (Perrachio) Pestelli; married Anna Claudia Vinca, September 20, 1967; children: Luisa, Carlo. *Religion:* Catholic. *Education:* Turin Conservatory, diploma, 1961; University of Turin, arts degree, 1964.

ADDRESSES: Home—Via Provana 7, Turin, Italy 10123.

CAREER: University of Turin, Turin, Italy, assistant lecturer, 1964-69, lecturer, 1969-77, professor of music, 1977—; Radio Audizioni Italiana, Turin, artistic director of symphonic orchestra, 1982-85. *Military service:* Brigata Alpina "Taurinense," 1965-66; became sergeant.

WRITINGS:

Le Sonate di Domenico Scarlatti, Giappichelli, 1967.

(Contributor) Alberto Basso and Guglielmo Barblan, editors, *Storia dell'opera,* Unione Tipogra Pica Editrice Torinese, 1976.

L'eta di Mozart e di Beethoven, Edizioni Di Torino, 1979, translation by Eric Cross published as *The Age of Mozart and Beethoven,* Cambridge University Press, 1984.

(Contributor) Stanley Sadie, editor, *New Grove Dictionary of Music and Musicians,* Macmillan, 1980.

Beethoven a Torino e in Piemonte nell'Ottocento, Edizioni Di Torino, 1982.

Di tanti palpiti-Cromeche musicali, 1972-1986 (collection of music reviews), Studio Tesi, 1986.

(Editor with Lorenzo Biaconi) *Storia dell'opera italiane,* Volumes I-VI, Edizioni di Torino, 1987.

Contributor to "Biblioteca Historiae Musicae Cultores" series. Also contributor of music reviews to *La Stampa* and of articles to journals in his field.

WORK IN PROGRESS: Research on music of the nineteenth century.

SIDELIGHTS: Giorgio Pestelli told *CA:* "All my interests in history and criticism concern musical performance. While playing Domenico Scarlatti's sonatas I felt the desire to suggest a chronological order of this big corpus. My *Sonate di Domenico Scarlatti* resulted. I have always studied and played the music of composers Wolfgang Amadeus Mozart and Ludwig van Beethoven, and my book *The Age of Mozart and Beethoven* grew out of my interest in them."

BIOGRAPHICAL/CRITICAL SOURCES:

PERIODICALS

Times Literary Supplement, April 27, 1984.

* * *

PEYO
See CULLIFORD, Pierre

* * *

PHILLIPS, Edward O. 1931-

PERSONAL: Born November 26, 1931, in Montreal, Quebec, Canada; son of A. Lovell and Dorothy S. Phillips. *Education:* McGill University, B.A., 1953; University of Montreal, Ll.L., 1956; Harvard University, A.M.T., 1957; Boston University, M.A., 1962; Montreal Museum of Fine Arts School of Art and Design, Diploma, 1968.

ADDRESSES: Home—Montreal, Quebec, Canada.

CAREER: English teacher at high school in Boston, Mass., 1958-61, and at elementary, junior high, and high school in Montreal, Quebec, 1962-65; artist, with solo and group exhibitions in Quebec, Ontario, and elsewhere, 1969-74; writer, 1974—.

MEMBER: International P.E.N., Writers Union of Canada, Canadian Authors Association, Crime Writers of Canada, Union des Ecrivains Quebecois.

AWARDS, HONORS: First prize for fiction from *Cross-Canada Writers Quarterly,* 1983, for "Why Don't You Sit Over Here?"; Arthur Ellis Award for fiction from Crime Writers of Canada, 1986, for *Buried on Sunday.*

WRITINGS:

Sunday's Child (novel), McClelland & Stewart, 1981.

Where There's a Will (novel), McClelland & Stewart, 1984.

Buried on Sunday (novel), McClelland & Stewart, 1986.

Contributor of stories to magazines, including *Matrix, Quarry, Rubicon, Saturday Night,* and *University of Windsor Review,* and of articles to the Montreal *Gazette.*

WORK IN PROGRESS: Hope Springs Eternal, completion expected in 1988.

SIDELIGHTS: Edward O. Phillips's first novel, *Sunday's Child,* is "a satiric romp in the finest picaresque mold," assessed Nancy Wigston in the Toronto *Globe and Mail.* Focusing on Geoffry Chadwick, a witty fifty-year-old homosexual who accidentally kills a thieving hustler, it is "savagely funny," Wigston observed, yet it also "takes a serious look at affectionate relations." Concluded Wigston, "*Sunday's Child* is masterful, original, and absolutely Canadian."

Where There's a Will, Phillips's next book, is "a murderously polite, utterly engaging comedy of manners," wrote Wigston. The critic praised Phillips for "his ability to shape living eccentrics out of material that in other hands would remain mere cardboard," for his irony, and for presenting an insightful glimpse of the Canadian people. Wigston found the novel "a worthy heir" to *Sunday's Child.*

In *Buried on Sunday,* Phillips details further adventures of Geoffry Chadwick. Three bank robbers hide out at a lake resort, holding the residents hostage, and the results, remarked Douglas Hill in the *Globe and Mail,* "are not at all predictable, and great fun." Hill lauded Phillips's characterization and his "stylish, witty prose."

BIOGRAPHICAL/CRITICAL SOURCES:

PERIODICALS

Gazette (Montreal), March 31, 1984, June 27, 1987.

Globe and Mail (Toronto), October 31, 1981, April 21, 1984, June 14, 1986, May 23, 1987.

* * *

PIATIGORSKY, Alexander 1929-

PERSONAL: Born January 30, 1929, in Moscow, U.S.S.R.; son of Moissey (a metallurgist) and Sarah (a teacher of German; maiden name, Zubin) Piatigorsky; married Elvira Popova, February 11, 1968; children: Galina, Maxim, Ilya, Veronica, Anna. *Education:* University of Msocow, Diploma in History of Philosophy, 1952; Academy of Sciences of the U.S.S.R., Ph.D., 1961. *Politics:* "Totally apolitical." *Religion:* Buddhist.

ADDRESSES: Home—46 Caterham Rd., Lewisham, London S.E.13, England. *Office*—Department of History, London School of Oriental and African Studies, University of London, Malet St., London WC1E 7HP, England. *Agent*—Andrew Nu-

renberg, 45-47 Clerkenwell Green, London EC1R 0HT, England.

CAREER: High school history teacher in Stalingrad (now Volvograd), U.S.S.R., 1952-55; Academy of Sciences of the U.S.S.R., Moscow, research fellow at Institute of Oriental Studies, 1956-68; University of Moscow, Moscow, part-time lecturer in Indian philosophy, 1969-73; University of London, London School of Oriental and African Studies, London, England, lecturer in ancient history of South Asia, 1975—. Visiting professor at University of Konstanz, 1975.

MEMBER: Royal Asiatic Society.

WRITINGS:

(Editor with Philip Denwood) *Buddhist Studies,* Curzon Press, 1983.

The Buddhist Philosophy of Thought: Essays in Interpretation, Curzon Press, 1984.

Contributor to philosophy journals.

WORK IN PROGRESS: Research on "some nonspecific problems of the phenomenology of religion."

SIDELIGHTS: In *The Buddhist Philosophy of Thought,* Alexander Piatigorsky makes clear his preference for the lessons of the early Buddhist teachers and disagrees with modern interpreters of the philosophy. Concentrating on the *dharmas*—states of consciousness—in the early text of the *Dhammasangani* and on the concepts of sentience, thought, and consciousness, Piatigorsky supports his complex thesis with numerous charts and tables. He contends that Buddhism is not simply another philosophy, but a metaphilosophy that embraces and stands above all others. Furthermore, Piatigorsky disputes the claim that the mind of Western man cannot fully comprehend Buddhism.

BIOGRAPHICAL/CRITICAL SOURCES:

PERIODICALS

Times Literary Supplement, May 4, 1984.

* * *

PILEGGI, Nicholas 1933-

PERSONAL: Born February 22, 1933, in New York, N.Y.; son of Nick and Susan (Defaslo) Pileggi. *Education:* Attended Long Island University.

ADDRESSES: *Agent*—Sterling Lord, 660 Madison Ave., New York, N.Y. 10021.

CAREER: Associated Press, New York City, reporter, 1956-68; *New York* (magazine), New York City, contributing editor, 1968—.

MEMBER: P.E.N., Players.

AWARDS, HONORS: Awards from New York State Bar Association and Detective Association.

WRITINGS:

Blye, Private Eye (nonfiction), Playboy Press, 1976.

Wiseguy: Life in a Mafia Family, (nonfiction), Simon & Schuster, 1985.

Contributor to periodicals, including *Esquire, Saturday Evening Post, New York Times,* and *Life.*

SIDELIGHTS: In his first book, *Blye, Private Eye,* Nicholas Pileggi focuses on the work of real-life private detective Irwin Blye. Pileggi's aim is to debunk the aura of glamour surrounding Blye's profession created by the fictional exploits of private-eye characters like Sam Spade and Philip Marlowe. As Andrew C. J. Bergman pointed out in the *New York Times Book Review,* "slinky temptresses do not drop by [Blye's] office . . . and his life is not packed with, or even occasionally punctuated by adventure and carnage, libidinous or otherwise." Instead Pileggi relates that Blye is a family man who has far more frequent need of various legal forms than of guns. With the right papers, Blye can gather information about anyone who pays taxes, owns a car, or receives a telephone bill. His cases concern everything from compiling evidence to clear accused criminals to assembling facts for clients contemplating divorce, and he is often involved in taking depositions for attorneys. Though Pileggi convinced reviewers that detective work is not as exciting as it is often portrayed in fiction, many of them found *Blye, Private Eye* interesting. Bergman reported that "Pileggi is an alert observer and a deft writer, capable of creating large effects with small strokes," and concluded that the book is "a virtual primer on detection."

Pileggi's next book, *Wiseguy: Life in a Mafia Family,* explores the life of organized crime figure Henry Hill. In a series of phone conversations and meetings, Hill, who as a member of the U.S. government's Witness Protection Program now lives under a newly fabricated identity, told Pileggi of his escapades under various crime bosses. In the words of Vincent Patrick, reviewing *Wiseguy* in the *New York Times Book Review,* "Mr. Pileggi molds Mr. Hill's life story into an absolutely engrossing book that rings with authenticity." Hill began working at the age of eleven for Paul Vario, allegedly a member of the Lucchese crime family, and became involved in illegal gambling, arson, and counterfeiting. He later became acquainted with James (Jimmy the Gent) Burke, and claims to have given Burke the tip that helped him plan the 1978 six-million-dollar robbery of the Lufthansa airline. Hill ended up testifying against Burke, who contracted the ten murders that followed the theft because he did not want to share the takings. For protection Hill was given a new identity and allowed to start a new life, but according to Pileggi, Hill misses his life as a criminal. As Walter Clemons concluded in *Newsweek,* "One believes the book because Henry Hill is unrepentant. Pileggi has done a terrific job of reporting, without moralizing."

BIOGRAPHICAL/CRITICAL SOURCES:

PERIODICALS

Publishers Weekly, February 7, 1986.
Newsweek, February 10, 1986.
New York Times, January 16, 1986.
New York Times Book Review, February 27, 1977, January 26, 1986.
Time, March 28, 1977, March 3, 1986.
Washington Post Book World, January 19, 1986.

* * *

PINSDORF, Marion K(atheryn) 1932-

PERSONAL: Born June 22, 1932, in Teaneck, N.J.; daughter of Charles W. (a carpenter) and Katheryn S. (a homemaker; maiden name, Green) Pinsdorf; married William C. Kelly (a newspaper executive), October 10, 1959 (divorced). *Education:* Drew University, B.A. (cum laude), 1954; New York University, M.A., 1967, Ph.D., 1976. *Religion:* Methodist.

ADDRESSES: Home—114 Leonia Ave., Leonia, N.J. 07605. *Agent*—Julian Bach Literary Agency, Inc., 747 Third Ave., New York, N.Y. 10017.

CAREER: Record, Hackensack, N.J., political reporter and editor of women's department, 1948-61; high school public relations teacher in New Milford, N.J., 1961-62; *Good Housekeeping,* New York City, associate copy editor and creator of "You and Your Diet" section, 1962-64; Borden, Inc., New York City, communications specialist, 1964-69; Hill & Knowlton, Inc. (international public relations counselors), New York City, vice-president, 1970-77; Textron, Inc., Providence, R.I., vice-president of corporate relations, 1977-80; INA Corp., Philadelphia, Pa., vice-president of corporate communications, 1980-82; Amfac, Inc., Honolulu, Hawaii, member of board of directors, 1982—. Director of financial communications for Smithkline Beckman Corp., 1982-83. Adjunct assistant professor at Brown University, 1979—; lecturer at Arizona State University; member of board of trustees of Drew University, 1977-81. President of board of trustees of Leonia Public Library, 1973-77.

MEMBER: American Historical Association, Public Relations Society of America, Financial Women's Association, Rhode Island Historical Society.

AWARDS, HONORS: D.Sc. from Nichols College, 1952.

WRITINGS:

(Contributor) *Critical Issues in Public Relations,* Prentice-Hall, 1975.
Communicating When Your Company Is Under Siege: Surviving Public Crises, Lexington Books, 1987.
Germans as Entrepreneurs in Brazil South, Fritz Lang, 1988.

Contributor of articles and reviews to periodicals, including *Times of the Americas.* Member of editorial advisory board of *Public Relations Quarterly.*

WORK IN PROGRESS: Corporate Cautionary Tales, "semifictional short pieces," publication expected in 1988; a general business book, publication expected in 1989.

SIDELIGHTS: Marion K. Pinsdorf told *CA:* "I entered journalism at the age of fifteen, driven by a thirsty mind and the need to finance my college education. The immediacy and pragmatism of journalism complemented my academic study of history. My corporate management positions, writing, and university teaching are a natural progression and outgrowth of that basis.

"I wrote *Communicating When Your Company Is Under Siege* first because I was asked and second because I felt my rather unique blending of journalist, historian, and corporate executive would help corporations communicate more effectively. The response has been most rewarding. One manager wrote to me that he felt the shock of recognition on every page. I considered that high praise indeed. As a consultant at Hill & Knowlton I advised many companies under siege—experiencing rapid acquisitions, merger and tender threats, and unexpected, drastic market shifts. As an officer myself, I survived the intense media attention created by corporate upheaval.

"In my experience, it is not difficult for a woman to be appointed or elected a corporate officer—surely not to handle the responsibilities. The difficulty is avoiding treatment as an invisible person and coming to power from different sources than male colleagues. It is difficult for a woman to have more street smarts than traditional corporate executives.

"Just as I was beginning graduate work in history, I visited Brazil and was captivated by this large, vital nation whose history, wars, problems, and promises I knew little about. I discovered a branch of my family that had pioneered businesses in Corumba, Mato Grosso, Brazil. I specialized in ties between the two countries that continue to intrigue me most—Brazil and Germany. The rigors of the German historical method, augmented by the fact-gathering of the Annales School, are good discipline for management decision making and are an antidote to wishful thinking or an incomplete database. Also, history has taught me to expect the unexpected; change comes in often surprising clusters rather than linearly or cyclically. Rather than effete background, I consider history a valuable management tool and surely a source of personal perspective and enrichment."

*　*　*

PODELL, Janet 1954-

PERSONAL: Born January 4, 1954, in Ithaca, N.Y.; daughter of Lawrence (a sociologist) and Diane (a librarian; maiden name, Kopperman) Podell; married Steven Anzovin (a writer and editor), June 2, 1974; children: Rafael, Miriam. *Education:* Trinity College, Hartford, Conn., B.A., 1975; Brown University, A.M., 1978. *Religion:* Jewish.

ADDRESSES: Home and office—156 Jane St., Englewood, N.J. 07631.

CAREER: Johnson Reprint Corp., New York, N.Y., secretary, 1978-79; free-lance writer, rewriter, copywriter, and editor, 1979—. Co-founder of Children and Parents in Hospitals, 1985.

MEMBER: Editorial Freelancers Association.

WRITINGS:

(Associate editor) *The Annual Obituary 1980,* St. Martin's, 1981.
(Editor) *The Annual Obituary,* St. Martin's, 1981 edition, 1982, 1982 edition, 1983.
(Editor) *Sports in America,* H. W. Wilson, 1986.
(Associate editor) *Art in America's 1987-88 Annual Guide to Galleries, Museums, and Artists,* Brant Publications, 1987, 1988-89 edition, 1988.
(Editor) *Rock Music in America,* H. W. Wilson, 1987.
(With husband, Steven Anzovin) *It Hurts: A Parent's Guide to Children's Needs,* Bantam, 1987.
(Editor with Anzovin) *Speeches of the American Presidents,* H. W. Wilson, 1987.
(Compiler) *1987 Survey of Bergen County (N.J.) Hospitals,* Children and Parents in Hospitals, 1987.
(Editor) *Religious Diversity in America,* H. W. Wilson, 1988.
(Editor with Anzovin) *The Soviet Union,* H. W. Wilson, 1988.
(Editor with Anzovin and Joseph Nathan Kane) *Facts About the States,* H. W. Wilson, in press.

Also editor with Anzovin of a book on the U.S. Constitution for H. W. Wilson; associated with H. W. Wilson's *Facts About the Presidents.*

Contributor to periodicals.

SIDELIGHTS: Janet Podell told *CA:* "I became a professional writer and editor for two reasons: first, because I have a talent for it; second, because it is a job that can be done at home, allowing me to do another, more important job: full-time mothering. I have been pregnant or nursing a child for seven

of the eight years that I've been free-lancing. My husband does the same kind of work I do, and we function as a team, sometimes collaborating, sometimes taking turns at the eternal game of 'beat the deadline.'

"Most of our output has been work for hire—that is, free-lance projects done in various fields for various publishers. Lately we have been fortunate enough to win book contracts of our own. Our anthology of presidential speeches had its start when we were doing research for the revised edition of the reference book *Facts About the Presidents* and realized that no such collection existed. This project, and many others to which we've contributed, required us to learn a lot about a subject in a relatively short time. In that sense, our work is really an extension of the old habit of reading and learning that both of us developed in childhood. What we did then was read for fun. What we do now is read for fun and profit."

* * *

POEWE, Karla 1941- (Manda Cesara)

PERSONAL: Surname is pronounced "*Po*-va"; born January 25, 1941, in Koenigsberg, Germany; daughter of Hugo and Olga (Schulz) Poewe; married November 16, 1940; children: Gudrun, Karla. *Education:* University of Toronto, B.A. (with honors), 1967; attended New York University, 1969; University of New Mexico, Ph.D., 1976. *Politics:* "Liberal conservative or conservative liberal." *Religion:* Lutheran.

ADDRESSES: Home—P.O. Box 3880, High River, Alberta, Canada T0L 1B0. *Office*—Department of Anthropology, University of Lethbridge, Lethbridge, Alberta, Canada T1K 3M4.

CAREER: University of Toronto, Toronto, Ontario, assistant professor of anthropology, 1976-77; University of Lethbridge, Lethbridge, Alberta, assistant professor, 1977-80, associate professor, 1980-84, professor of anthropology, 1984—. Research affiliate of Institute for African Studies at University of Zambia and Scientific Society of Windhoek, Namibia, 1973—; guest lecturer at University of Maryland at College Park, 1976; visiting fellow at Calgary Institute for the Humanities, 1986.

MEMBER: American Anthropological Association, South West Africa Scientific Society.

AWARDS, HONORS: Grant for Zambia from International Development Research Centre, 1972-75; grant from Society Science and Humanities Research Council of Canada, 1981-82, for research in Namibia; grants from Human Sciences Research Council of Pretoria and University of Zululand, 1987, for research in South Africa; grant from Secretary of State of Canada, 1987-88, for research on German-Canadians who were children in Germany during World War II.

WRITINGS:

(Contributor) Linda S. Cordell and Stephen Beckerman, editors, *The Versatility of Kinship: Studies in Anthropology,* Academic Press, 1980.

Matrilineal Ideology: Male-Female Dynamics in Luapula, Zambia, Academic Press, 1981.

(Under pseudonym Manda Cesara) *Reflections of a Woman Anthropologist: No Hiding Place,* Academic Press, 1982.

The Nambian Herero: A History of Their Psychosocial Disintegration and Survival, Edwin Mellen Press, 1985.

(With Irving Hexham) *Understanding Cults and New Religions,* Eerdmans, 1986.

Childhood in Germany During World War II: The Story of a Little Girl, Edwin Mellen Press, 1988.

Contributor to anthropology journals.

WORK IN PROGRESS: The Cultural Implications of Charismatic Christianity: Canada, America, and South Africa, with Irving Hexham, publication expected in 1990; *Renewed Charismatic Churches in South Africa,* a study of the socio-cultural implications of charismatic Christianity in South Africa.

SIDELIGHTS: Karla Poewe told *CA:* "I was born in Prussia in 1941. My family was bombed out and fled to Werdau, where we lived in refugee camps. At the age of five I moved to live with my grandmother near Hamburg, and I was later joined there by my mother and sister. In 1953 I immigrated to Toronto, where I received my public and high school education. In 1962 I became a stewardess with Trans Canada Airlines, and a year later I entered the University of Toronto.

"For my doctoral research, I undertook fieldwork in the Luapula Valley of Zambia, and I lived among the people I studied. My second major research project was in the black township of Katutura and on the Herero reserves in Namibia. I grew up with a fascination for Africa and Africans. Currently I am inspired by the spirituality of blacks, whites, and Indians in South Africa. It is a country in change. Herein it ought to be assisted, not shunned. Throughout my teaching career, my students and I have also conducted life history interviews with men and women in the area where we live.

"I am now exploring the condition of dislocation which, I feel, characterizes, not only the life experiences of post-colonials, but also my own. Writing anthropology in a critical and literary mode, I tend to focus on the experiential and the universal. Surviving extreme conditions and coming to terms with my German past motivated me to write *Reflections of a Woman Anthropologist* and *Childhood in Germany During World War II.*

"*Reflections of a Woman Anthropologist* was written under a pseudonym because it is very personal. For that matter all people and places mentioned in the text were given pseudonyms to protect their respective identities. Nevertheless, its subtitle, *No Hiding Place,* holds, because it was meant to address the tendency of some women to, as it were, 'hide' behind men, psychiatrists, and other helping institutions. It was time for them to leave those places of hiding, to look out at an exciting—if somewhat unjust—world, and to see therein a lively reflection of self. More importantly, however, *Reflections* suggests a theory of understanding that incorporates within one structure the researcher and those being researched. Beyond that, it argues that anthropology should aim, simultaneously, to understand and explain. All of my subsequent work is an effort to transcend these dualities."

* * *

POLLACK, Merrill S. 1924-1988

OBITUARY NOTICE—See index for *CA* sketch: Born July 24, 1924, in Middle Village, Long Island, N.Y.; died of a stroke, February 14, 1988, in Parkersberg, W.Va. Journalist, editor, and author. Pollack worked as a reporter on the staffs of the *Bronx Home News* and *New York Post* in the late 1940s before serving as an associate editor for publications such as *Promenade* and *Saturday Evening Post.* In 1963 he became senior editor for the publishing company Simon & Schuster; he later worked for W. W. Norton & Company as well as for Viking

Press. Pollack went into farming in 1974; at that time he also established Seneca Books, Incorporated. His writings include *How to Cope With. . ., O Is for Overkill,* and the children's works *Shem and Doon* and *Phaethon.*

OBITUARIES AND OTHER SOURCES:

PERIODICALS

Publishers Weekly, March 11, 1988.

* * *

POPE, Joya 1943-

PERSONAL: Born November 29, 1943, in Rochester, N.Y.; daughter of Robert M. (a biochemist and professor) and Kathryn F. (a biochemist and medical school dean) Fink; married Robert W. Pope, 1970 (divorced); children: Maya. *Education:* University of California, Los Angeles, B.A., 1969; Holistic Life University, Counseling Certificate, 1978. *Politics:* "Usually liberal."

ADDRESSES: Home—San Mateo, Calif.

CAREER: Nutritional consultant, 1979-84; psychic channel and consultant, 1985—.

WRITINGS:

(Contributor) Kate Warwick-Smith, editor, *The Michael Game,* Michael Digest Group, 1986.
The World According to Michael: An Old Soul's Guide to the Universe, Sage Publications, 1987.
Michael on Men and Women, Sage Publications, 1988.

Author of "Michael Views the News," a current events column in *Michael Connection.*

SIDELIGHTS: Joya Pope told *CA:* "Michael is the name of a group of souls who have completed their earth plane lessons and are now teaching—through channels—from the causal plane. The material Michael has been transmitting, through a growing number of channels, not only satisfies my hungry mind but throws the issues that arise in my life into a clear, objective light. My growth is now less bumpy than it has ever been.

"One of my reasons for writing is to share the basics of this information about life on this planet so that others may also experience more ease of growth. Writing about Michael, and channeling, seem to put me on track with my life purpose.

"Though I used to wade through serious books, what I enjoy these days are novels. In writing *The World According to Michael* my aim was to create a book that had sparkling language and clear ideas—a heavy metaphysical tome would not be my style. *Michael on Men and Women* reflects Michael's message that male and female are played out in a very unique way on this planet."

* * *

PORGES, Paul Peter 1927-

PERSONAL: Born February 7, 1927, in Vienna, Austria; immigrated to the United States, 1947, naturalized citizen, 1952; son of Gustav (a businessman) and Jeanette Porges; married Lucie Eisenstab (a fashion designer), 1951; children: Claudia M. Porges Holland, Vivette V. Porges Schorr. *Education:* Ecole des Beaux Arts, Geneva, Switzerland, equivalent of B.F.A., 1947; School of Visual Arts, B.F.A., 1977.

ADDRESSES: Home—New York, N.Y. *Office*—41 Union Sq., New York, N.Y. 10003.

CAREER: Free-lance cartoonist and graphic humorist, 1952—. Member of faculty at School of Visual Arts. *Military service:* U.S. Army, 1950-52.

MEMBER: Cartoonists Association (member of executive committee).

WRITINGS:

Mad How Not to Do It (cartoons), Warner Books, 1981.
Mad Cheap Shots (cartoons), Warner Books, 1984.
Mad Lobsters (cartoons), Warner Books, 1986.

Contributor of articles to *Signature* and cartoons to a wide variety of periodicals, including *Playboy, Saturday Evening Post, New Yorker, New York Times,* and *Mad.*

WORK IN PROGRESS: A comedy film script; a syndicated comic strip with Sam Gross.

SIDELIGHTS: Paul Peter Porges told *CA:* "My main interest is humor and the extension of cartoons into humor reporting on such topics as travel, leisure, sports, life-styles, and parenting."

* * *

PORTER, Bruce 1938-

PERSONAL: Born August 30, 1938, in Harrison, N.Y.; son of G. D. and A. K. Porter; married Lorna Devereux Scott (a psychiatric social worker), September 15, 1962; children: Nell, Alexandra. *Education:* Hamilton College, B.A., 1959; Columbia University, M.S. (cum laude), 1962.

ADDRESSES: Home—New York, N.Y. *Office*—Journalism Program, Brooklyn College of the City University of New York, 2308 Boylan Hall, Brooklyn, N.Y. 11210. *Agent*—International Creative Management, 40 West 57th St., New York, N.Y. 10019.

CAREER: U.S. Fish and Wildlife Service, Washington, D.C., game warden in the Aleutian Islands, 1959; *Hartford Courant,* Hartford, Conn., copy editor, 1960; *Waterbury Republican,* Waterbury, Conn., police reporter, 1961; *Providence Journal,* Providence, R.I., reporter, 1962-65; *New York World Telegram and Sun,* New York City, reporter, 1965-66; *New York Post,* New York City, reporter, 1966-67; *Newsweek,* New York City, writer and editor, 1967-73; Brooklyn College of the City University of New York, Brooklyn, N.Y., associate professor, 1973-75, professor of English, 1975—, director of journalism program. Adjunct professor at Columbia University, 1976—. Consultant to Ford Foundation and Edna McConnell Clark Foundation.

AWARDS, HONORS: Associated Press Managing Editors Award, 1964, for series on slum housing; Charles Stewart Mott Award for Distinguished Education Reporting from Education Writers Association, 1975, for magazine article "It Was a Good School to Integrate"; Unity Award in Media from Lincoln University, 1976, for magazine article.

WRITINGS:

(With Robert Curvin) *Blackout Looting!* Wiley, 1979.
(With Marvin Dunn) *The Miami Riot: Crossing the Bounds,* Heath, 1984.
(With Timothy Ferris) *The Practice of Journalism: A Guide to Reporting and Writing the News,* Prentice-Hall, 1987.

Work represented in anthologies, including *America's Troubles,* edited by T. E. Freeman and J. F. Kurz, Prentice-Hall, 1972; and *Problems of Today's World,* edited by E. F. Perry and S. N. Perry, Little, Brown, 1978.

Contributor to magazines and newspapers, including *Connoisseur, Ms., Playboy, Police, Psychology Today,* and *Saturday Review.*

WORK IN PROGRESS: One Hour at the Diner, nonfiction.

SIDELIGHTS: Bruce Porter's first book, *Blackout Looting!* is the result of an investigation, sponsored by the Ford Foundation, of the chaotic looting that occurred during a major power failure in New York City during the summer of 1977. The authors of the study were highly critical of official reports from the New York City mayor's office, which blamed the rioting on relatively well-to-do people and denied the impact of poverty and unemployment on the events of the summer. Porter and his co-author reconstructed in detail the events of the night in question and determined that the looting occurred in three distinct stages. The earlier looting they blamed on professional criminals. The middle stage was implemented by youth gangs looking for fun. The final stage, which did not begin until nearly midnight, involved the working-class people who were cited in the mayor's controversial report. Since the police did not begin making arrests until the third stage, Porter and Curvin asserted, police reports and official analyses neglected the participation of professional thieves and disadvantaged youth in the looting and provided unbalanced, misleading conclusions about the city's economic and political problems.

BIOGRAPHICAL/CRITICAL SOURCES:

PERIODICALS

New York Times, July 3, 1979.

* * *

POWER, Francis C. 1909(?)-1987

OBITUARY NOTICE: Born c. 1909; died after a heart attack, November 28, 1987, in Leesburg, Va. Architect, historian, and author. Spending fifty years of his life in the Washington, D.C., area, Power worked as an architect, taking a special interest in the history of stone architecture, before turning to a career in writing. His novel *The Encounter* was published in 1950 and reprinted in 1984.

OBITUARIES AND OTHER SOURCES:

PERIODICALS

Washington Post, December 1, 1987.

* * *

PRATNEY, William Alfred 1944-
(Winkie Pratney; Bjorn Freeman, a pseudonym)

PERSONAL: Born August 3, 1944, in Otahuhu, New Zealand; son of William (an athlete) and Lynne Ruth (in business; maiden name, Pennington) Pratney; married Faeona Rees-Thomas (a nurse and homemaker), March 3, 1968; children: Billy-David Anthony. *Education:* Attended Auckland University, 1963, and Central Bible College, 1966. *Religion:* Christian.

ADDRESSES: Box 215, Manurewa, South Auckland, New Zealand. *Office*—Box 876, Lindale, Tex. 75771.

CAREER: Youth for Christ, Auckland, New Zealand, director, 1964-65; itinerant public speaker in North America and New Zealand, 1965-68, and in the United States, Europe, and Australia, 1968-76; Communication Foundation, founder, president, and director in Manurewa, New Zealand, 1976-87, and Lindale, Tex., 1983-87. Counseling director of Teen Challenge, Detroit, Mich., 1968; international public speaker at conferences and on television and radio, 1984—. Member of board of reference of Agape Force International, America for Jesus, Genesis Training Center of Heritage College, Lifegate, and Sovereign World Publishing International.

MEMBER: New Zealand Microcomputer Association, Manurewa Lawn Tennis Club.

WRITINGS:

UNDER NAME WINKIE PRATNEY

Doorways to Discipleship, Communication Foundation, 1963, Bethany Fellowship, 1975.

Youth Aflame! A Manual for Discipleship, Communication Foundation, 1967, Bethany House, 1983.

Five Speak Out on Change, Gospel Publishing House, 1969.

Creation or Evolution: A Christian View of Science, Haven of Rest, 1971.

A Handbook for Followers of Jesus, Bethany Fellowship, 1977.

Star Wars, Star Trek, and Twenty-first Century Saints, Bible Voice, 1979.

El joven y su dios (title means "The Young [Man] and His God"), Edit Betania, 1982.

El joven y su mundo (title means "The Young [Man] and His World"), Edit Betania, 1982.

El joven y sus amigos (title means "The Young [Man] and His Friends"), Edit Betania, 1982.

El joven y sus dilemas (title means "The Young [Man] and His Problems"), Edit Betania, 1982.

Revival: Principles to Change the World, Whitaker House, 1983.

Devil Take the Youngest, edited by Bill Keith, Huntington House, 1985.

Divinity, Volume 1: *The Nature and Character of God,* Bethany House, 1988.

Deceived! A Study of Contemporary Cultural Deception, Bethany House, in press.

Author of monographs, tracts, study guides, and Christian television programs. Contributor of articles and columns to religious periodicals in Canada, England, New Zealand, and the United States.

WORK IN PROGRESS: Divinity, Volume 2: *The Nature and Character of Man* and Volume 3: *The Nature and Character of Salvation,* both for Bethany House; *Dark Wave, Bright Star: The New Consciousness,* and *Communication: The Lost Tools of Learning,* publication of both expected in 1989; under pseudonym Bjorn Freeman, *The Coming of the Dreamer,* a science fiction novel that "may first appear as a movie," publication expected in 1990.

SIDELIGHTS: Winkie Pratney told *CA:* "I hate writing. Any writer can knock out a dozen or more things they would rather do than write. No doubt one of the reasons God left the apostle Paul in jail is that it was the only way He could get the Bible finished. What person in their right mind enjoys sitting in front of a pad or a keyboard eight to twelve hours a day? Show me a writer and I will show you some sort of madman.

"Whatever my faults and failings, one is not the illusion that

I am even some kind of good—let alone great—writer. I am one of the world's internationally unknown authors. I do write. I write a lot. I do not claim to like it. I write under duress; I write by periodically dragging myself kicking and screaming to a keyboard; but I write because of the pile of letters from hurting, questioning, and needy young people that comes in each week, because of the faces I see sometimes coming back at night. I write because it is the best way I know to put into another mind and heart things undeservedly found, astonishing answers in wisdom drawn from another world. I write to explain, to embarrass the merely religious into holy activity, to shape the stuff of the spirit from which young dreams and visions are forged.

"Now, reading I like. I am an inveterate reader—the breakfast-Wheaties-packet, empty-matchbook-cover, label-blowing-in-the-wind variety. Leaving me in a library for relaxation is like enrolling an addict in a cocaine factory for rehabilitation. Given open options, I would like nothing better than browsing through the thoughts and words of others much more brilliant, talented, and moving than I perhaps can ever be. But I still write. Not for money, because while there are lots of pleasant and simple ways to make a living, telling the truth is not one of them. Nor for popularity, because my line of work historically tends to lead more to encounters with lions and catacombs than lionization and best-seller catalogs. When God wanted to talk to people, he gave us his son and a book. Since I love both, what choice do I have? I give back in gratitude to his world the offering of my own life and pen."

BIOGRAPHICAL/CRITICAL SOURCES:

PERIODICALS

Christian Life, February, 1985.
Communicate, April, 1985.
Decision, February, 1970.
Foreward Edge, Fall, 1987.
Grapevine, March, 1985.
Impact, April-May, 1980.
Keystone, February-April, 1981.
People of Destiny, January-February, 1986, March-April, 1987.
Reach Out, May, 1979.
Tidewater Chronicle, May, 1983.

* * *

PRATNEY, Winkie
See PRATNEY, William Alfred

* * *

PRENDERGAST, Alan 1956-

PERSONAL: Born September 18, 1956, in Denver, Colo.; son of Edmund Thomas (a dentist) and Yvonne (a teacher; maiden name, Saliba) Prendergast. *Education:* Colorado College, B.A., 1978.

ADDRESSES: Agent—Gwen Edelman Agency, 352 West 21st St., New York, N.Y. 10011.

CAREER: Gralla Publications, New York, N.Y., acquisitions research manager, 1978-79; *Rocky Mountain,* Denver, Colo., senior editor, 1980-82; writer, 1982—.

WRITINGS:

The Poison Tree: A True Story of Family Violence and Revenge, Putnam, 1986.

Work represented in anthologies, including *Writers of the Purple Sage: An Anthology of Recent Western Writing,* edited by Russell Martin and Marc Barasch, Viking. Contributor to magazines and newspapers, including *Rolling Stone, USA Today,* and *Video.*

SIDELIGHTS: The Poison Tree is the story of the Jahnke family of Cheyenne, Wyoming. Two teenaged children, Richard and Deborah Jahnke, ambushed their father late one night, and the boy shot and killed him. The trial of the youngsters revealed a tale of repeated abuse and conflicting emotions, and this tale is related in Alan Prendergast's book. Janet Cawley wrote in the *Chicago Tribune:* "There is a quality to the narrative that makes it hard to put down." The reviewer reported that Prendergast covered the story well, from the night of the murder to the teenagers' eventual release from the state facilities where they had been held.

BIOGRAPHICAL/CRITICAL SOURCES:

PERIODICALS

Chicago Tribune, June 13, 1986.

* * *

PRESSBURGER, Emeric 1902-1988
(Richard Imrie)

OBITUARY NOTICE—See index for *CA* sketch: Name originally Imre Pressburger; born December 5, 1902, in Miskolc, Hungary (now Romania); immigrated to England; died of bronchial pneumonia, February 5, 1988, in Saxstead, England. Producer, director, screenwriter, and novelist. Pressburger is best remembered as a partner in one of Britain's most famous motion picture production teams. In collaboration with Michael Powell, he wrote, produced, and directed many popular films of the 1940s and 1950s, including the classic ballet epic "The Red Shoes." Before settling in England, Pressburger served as a writer in the script department of Germany's UFA film company until he fled after the Nazi regime came to power. His other screen credits include "The Invaders," an Oscar-winning 1941 film about Nazis hiding in Canada during World War II, "Colonel Blimp," and, under the pseudonym Richard Imrie, "Operation Crossbow." Pressburger wrote the novels *Killing a Mouse on Sunday* (reprinted as *Behold a Pale Horse*), and *The Glass Pearls.* With Powell he also penned *The Red Shoes,* a novelization of their best-known film.

OBITUARIES AND OTHER SOURCES:

BOOKS

The International Who's Who, 49th edition, Europa, 1985.

PERIODICALS

Chicago Tribune, February 9, 1988.
Los Angeles Times, February 7, 1988.
New York Times, February 6, 1988.
Times (London), February 6, 1988.
Washington Post, February 8, 1988.

PRIVATE 19022
See MANNING, Frederic

* * *

PUCK, Wolfgang 1949-

PERSONAL: Born January 8, 1949, in St. Veit, Austria; immigrated to United States, 1973; son of Josef and Maria Puck; married Barbara Lazaroff (a designer), May 20, 1983. *Education:* Attended school in Villach, Austria.

ADDRESSES: Office—Spago, 8795 Sunset Blvd., Los Angeles, Calif. 90069. *Agent*—Maureen Lasher, 1210 Tellem Dr., Pacific Palisades, Calif. 90272.

CAREER: Apprentice at L'Ousteau de Baumaniere (restaurant), Les Baux, France; affiliated with Hotel de Paris, Monaco, and Maxim's, Paris, France; co-owner and chef at Ma Maison, Los Angeles, Calif.; Spago, Los Angeles, owner and chef, 1972—. Owner of Chinois on Main; culinary consultant.

WRITINGS:

Modern French Cooking for the American Kitchen, Houghton, 1980.

The Wolfgang Puck Cookbook: Recipes From Spago, Chinois, and Points East and West (self-illustrated), Random House, 1986.

"Cooking With Wolfgang Puck" (instructional video), Warner Home Video, 1987.

* * *

PURCELL, Gillis Philip 1904-1987

OBITUARY NOTICE: Born November 25, 1904, in Brandon, Manitoba, Canada; died November 16, 1987, in Toronto, Ontario, Canada. Journalist. A longtime Canadian newspaperman, Purcell spent forty-one years with the Canadian Press. He began his journalistic career working as a reporter for such papers as the *Herald* in Hanna, Alberta, and the *Border Cities Star* in Windsor, Ontario. Joining the Canadian Press in 1928, Purcell served as its press correspondent with the First Overseas Contingent of the Canadian Army from 1939 to 1940 before becoming its general manager in 1945. In 1967 the journalist received the National Press Club of Canada's Award for Excellence.

OBITUARIES AND OTHER SOURCES:

BOOKS

The Canadian Who's Who, Volume V, University of Toronto Press, 1970.

PERIODICALS

New York Times, November 18, 1987.

* * *

PURDUE, A(rthur) W(illiam) 1941-
(Bill Purdue)

PERSONAL: Born January 29, 1941, in North Shields, England; son of William Henry (a policeman) and Jessie (a librarian; maiden name, Borthwick) Purdue; married Marie Therese Conte-Helm (a lecturer in Japanese studies), August 28, 1979; children: Jessica Jane. *Education:* King's College, London, B.A. (with honors), 1962; University of Newcastle Upon Tyne, M.Letters, 1974. *Politics:* Conservative.

ADDRESSES: Home—Old Rectory, Allendale, Near Hexham, Northumberland NE47 9DA, England. *Office*—North Region, Open University, Regent Centre, Gosforth, Newcastle Upon Tyne, England.

CAREER: Newcastle Upon Tyne Polytechnic, Newcastle Upon Tyne, England, 1967-76, began as lecturer, became senior lecturer in history; Open University, North Region, Newcastle Upon Tyne, staff tutor in history, 1976—. *Military service:* Royal Navy, 1964-67; held rank of instructor lieutenant.

MEMBER: Historical Association, Social History Society, Literary and Philosophical Society of Newcastle Upon Tyne.

WRITINGS:

WITH J. M. GOLBY

The Civilisation of the Crowd: Popular Culture in England, 1750-1900, Schocken, 1984.

The Making of the Modern Christmas, University of Georgia Press, 1986.

The Monarchy and British Society, 1760-Present, Batsford, 1988.

OTHER

Author of instructional material and media programs, under name Bill Purdue. Contributor of articles and reviews to periodicals, including *Northern History, New Society, Country Life, International Review of Society History,* and *Asia.*

SIDELIGHTS: In *The Making of the Modern Christmas,* A. W. Purdue and co-author J. M. Golby state that Christmas, as it is celebrated today, is a Victorian, secular holiday, a celebration of "family, community, and nation" not limited to members of a Christian faith. Before Victorian times Christmas was celebrated, if at all, as a religious feast. Jonathan Yardley of the *Washington Post Book World* found the volume to be "very much a celebratory book. Its illustrations are numerous and delightful. . . . The book's text is forthright but affectionate."

Purdue told *CA:* "My main interests lie in the field of modern British history. Though I enjoy writing for an academic readership, I also write for a more general audience. It seems important to me that history does not become a subject for academic specialists only. Although my own specialty is British history, I am also interested in American history (my wife is a U.S. citizen) and the history of the Far East.

"*The Civilisation of the Crowd* and *The Making of the Modern Christmas* had their genesis in work that J. M. Golby and I did in the production of an Open University course on popular culture. We contributed history units to this course and considered the course to be of high academic value but became increasingly dissatisfied with what we considered to be a Marxist domination of the field of study. *The Civilisation of the Crowd* is a challenge to Marxist and neo-Marxist interpretations of the history of English popular culture, which have been put forward by American as well as British writers, and a reas-

sessment that highlights the positive and beneficial impact of a free economy on popular culture.

"In our research into popular culture, we were struck by the way in which the celebration of Christmas had become in the nineteenth century so important and so central to British and American culture. Our purpose in writing *The Making of Modern Christmas* was to produce an accessible and readable book that would nevertheless raise important and serious questions as to the development and nature of the modern Christmas."

BIOGRAPHICAL/CRITICAL SOURCES:

PERIODICALS

Washington Post Book World, December 7, 1986.

*   *   *

PURDUE, Bill
See PURDUE, A(rthur) W(illiam)

Q-R

QOBOZA, Percy 1938-1988

OBITUARY NOTICE: Born January 17, 1938, in Johannesburg, South Africa; died after a heart attack, January 17, 1988, in Johannesburg, South Africa. Editor and journalist. A prominent black journalist in South Africa, Qoboza was a strong opponent of his nation's apartheid policy, which separates the black majority from the smaller—though economically and politically empowered—white population. The noted editor of controversial anti-apartheid publications began his career working for the *World* in 1963, becoming its editor in 1974. The government closed the paper in 1977, and Qoboza was subsequently jailed without charge for more than five months. He then served as editor of the *Post,* which was also shut down by the government in 1980, whereupon the journalist came to the United States as a guest editor of the *Washington Star*. Returning to his own country, he became editor, in 1985, of the Johannesburg-based *City Press,* which gained the largest circulation of South African black-readership newspapers. For his journalistic performance Qoboza was awarded the Golden Pen of Freedom from the International Federation of Newspaper Proprietors. He also received honorary doctorates from Tufts University and Amherst College and was a Nieman fellow at Harvard University from 1975 to 1976.

OBITUARIES AND OTHER SOURCES:

PERIODICALS

Chicago Tribune, January 19, 1988.
Los Angeles Times, January 18, 1988.
New York Times, January 18, 1988.
Times (London), January 19, 1988, January 25, 1988.
Washington Post, January 18, 1988.

* * *

QUIGLEY, Aileen 1930-
(Ruth Fabian, Erica Lindley)

PERSONAL: Born in 1930 in Luton, England. *Education:* Attended University of Hull; received B.A. from University of London.

CAREER: Writer, including work on British Broadcasting Corp. programs "Morning Story" and "Woman's Hour."

MEMBER: Society of Authors.

WRITINGS:

Child of Fire, R. Hale, 1971.
King's Pawn, R. Hale, 1971.
Bloodstone, R. Hale, 1972.
Rose Brocade, R. Hale, 1972.
A Devil in Holy Orders, R. Hale, 1973.
(Under pseudonym Ruth Fabian) *A Scent of Violets,* R. Hale, 1973.
King Bastard: The Story of William the Conqueror, R. Hale, 1973.
Court Cadenza, R. Hale, 1974.
Empress to the Eagle, R. Hale, 1975.

Contributor to magazines, including *My Weekly* and *Woman's Day*.

UNDER PSEUDONYM ERICA LINDLEY

Shadow of Dungeon Wood, R. Hale, 1972.
The Brackenroyd Inheritance, New American Library, 1975.
The Devil in Crystal, New American Library, 1977.
Belladonna, New American Library, 1978.
Harvest of Destiny, New American Library, 1979.

* * *

RADIN, Ruth Yaffe 1938-

PERSONAL: Born October 8, 1938, in Hartford, Conn.; daughter of Simon M. and Molly A. Yaffe; married Shelden H. Radin (a professor), June, 1960; children: two daughters, one son. *Education:* Hartford College for Women, A.A., 1958; Connecticut College for Women (now Connecticut College), B.A., 1960; Southern Connecticut State College, M.S., 1963. *Religion:* Jewish.

CAREER: Elementary schoolteacher in Meriden, Conn., 1960-63, and Bethlehem, Pa., 1963-66; Congregation Keneseth Israel, Allentown, Pa., librarian, 1982—. Certified reading specialist, 1980—; writer.

AWARDS, HONORS: A Winter Place was named a "notable book" by the American Library Association in 1982.

WRITINGS:

JUVENILES

A Winter Place, Little, Brown, 1982.

Tac's Island, Macmillan, 1986.
Tac's Turn, Macmillan, 1987.
High in the Mountains, Macmillan, in press.

* * *

RAMIS, Harold (Allen) 1944-

BRIEF ENTRY: Born November 21, 1944, in Chicago, Ill. American actor, director, producer, editor, and scriptwriter. An alumnus of Chicago's influential Second City comedy troupe, Ramis has helped to write the screenplays for a string of hit motion picture comedies, including "National Lampoon's Animal House" (Universal, 1978), "Meatballs" (Paramount, 1979), "Caddyshack" (Orion, 1980), "Stripes" (Columbia, 1981), "Ghostbusters" (Columbia, 1984), and "Back to School" (Orion, 1986). His films are noted for their broad, physical humor and their appeal to one of the industry's key markets—teenagers and young adults. Ramis was an associate editor at *Playboy* magazine from 1968 until 1970, when he became an actor and writer for Second City. Four years later he transferred to the "National Lampoon Show" in New York City, but he resumed his duties for Second City in 1976, working on their television comedy series, "SCTV." Since the immense success of "Animal House" in 1978 Ramis has been principally involved with films. In addition to screenwriting he directed "Caddyshack," "National Lampoon's Vacation" (Warner Bros., 1983), and "Club Paradise" (Warner Bros., 1985), and produced both "Back to School" and an ABC television special titled "The Rodney Dangerfield Show." *Addresses: Agent*—Jack Rapke, Creative Artists Agency, 1888 Century Park E., Suite 1400, Los Angeles, Calif. 90067.

BIOGRAPHICAL/CRITICAL SOURCES:

BOOKS

Contemporary Theatre, Film, and Television, Volume 2, Gale, 1986.
Who's Who in America, 44th edition, Marquis, 1986.

PERIODICALS

Chicago Tribune, July 8, 1986.
Los Angeles Times, April 23, 1983.
Washington Post, September 5, 1984.

* * *

RAMSAY, J(ames) A(rthur) 1909-1988

OBITUARY NOTICE: Born September 6, 1909; died February 5, 1988. Scientist, educator, editor, and author. For his zoological and scientific research, Ramsay was considered one of the foremost experimental biologists of his time. In 1952 he became joint editor of the *Journal of Experimental Biology.* He later served as a reader in comparative physiology at Cambridge University before becoming professor of the same subject there in 1969. His research was published in papers, and his books include *Physiological Approach to the Lower Animals, The Experimental Basis of Modern Biology,* and *A Guide to Thermodynamics.*

OBITUARIES AND OTHER SOURCES:

BOOKS

Who's Who, 139th edition, St. Martin's, 1987.

PERIODICALS

Times (London), February 6, 1988.

RAMSEY, (Robert) Paul 1913-1988

OBITUARY NOTICE—See index for *CA* sketch: Born December 10, 1913, in Mendenhall, Miss.; died of a heart attack, February 29, 1988, in Princeton, N.J. Theologian, educator, and author. The author of the widely used seminary text *Basic Christian Ethics,* Ramsey was an expert participant in debates concerning the ethics of war, abortion, euthanasia, and genetic engineering. An opponent of situational ethics, he spent most of his academic career as a professor of religion at Princeton University, but taught previously at Millsaps College and Garrett Biblical Institute (now Garrett Theological Seminary). Ramsey's other writings include *War and the Christian Conscience, Life or Death: Ethics and Options, Fabricated Man, The Patient as Person,* and *Ethics at the Edges of Life.* He spent his last years working on a complete edition of the writings of eighteenth-century American Calvinist preacher Jonathan Edwards.

OBITUARIES AND OTHER SOURCES:

BOOKS

Directory of American Scholars, Volume IV: *Philosophy, Religion, and Law,* 8th edition, Bowker, 1982.

PERIODICALS

New York Times, March 2, 1988.
Washington Post, March 12, 1988.

* * *

RAMSEY, Russell W. 1935-

PERSONAL: Born May 29, 1935, in Sandusky, Ohio; son of Russell A. (an attorney) and Louise (a homemaker; maiden name, Wilcox) Ramsey; married Linda Stevens, April 12, 1958 (divorced December 21, 1976); married Roberta Smith (a professor and writer), September 4, 1977; children: Lyndall E., Sarah W., Elizabeth B., J. Carl Smith, Randall R. Smith, Russell R. *Education:* U.S. Military Academy, B.S., 1957; attended Florida State University extension program in Panama Canal Zone, 1960-62; University of Southern Mississippi, M.A., 1963; University of Florida, Ph.D., 1970, postdoctoral study, 1971-74; graduated from U.S. Army Command and General Staff College, 1983. *Politics:* "Domestic liberal—foreign policy conservative." *Religion:* Presbyterian.

ADDRESSES: Home—1808 Dawson Rd., Albany, Ga., 31707. *Office*—Air Command and Staff College, Room 245, Maxwell Air Force Base, Montgomery, Ala. 36112. *Agent*—Mary Jane Ross, 85 Sunset Lane, Tenafly, N.J. 07670.

CAREER: U.S. Army, Infantry, commissioned second lieutenant, 1957, instructor in counterinsurgency at School of the Americas, Panama Canal Zone, 1960-62, company commander at Ft. Benning, Ga., and An Khe, South Vietnam (now Vietnam), 1964-66, assistant professor of military science in Reserve Officer Training Corps (ROTC) program at University of Florida, Gainesville, 1966-69, leaving service as major; Alachua County Public Schools, Gainesville, founder and director of Mountain Top School for Social Adjustment, 1970-1972, founder and principal of Lincoln Vocational High School, 1972-74, founder and principal of Alternative School for Disturbed Adolescents, 1974-79; Job Corps, founder and director

of center in Gainesville, 1979-81, director of center in Albany, Ga., 1981-84; U.S. Army Reserve, commissioned major, 1980, assigned to faculty Armed Forces Staff College, Norfolk, Va., 1980-84, and to Joint Chiefs of Staff, Pentagon, Washington, D.C., 1985-88; Albany State College, Albany, Ga., assistant professor of criminal justice, 1985-87; Air Command and Staff College, Maxwell Air Force Base, Montgomery, Ala., professor of national security affairs, 1987—. Gainesville city commission, chairman of citizens' advisory committee, 1971-72, elected member of commission, 1973-76; member of Alachua County Detention Board, 1973-77; adjunct professor at Nova University, 1977-81, and Central Florida Community College, 1978-80; member of board of directors of Liberty House for Abused Women, Albany, Ga., 1985-87. Guest lecturer at U.S. military educational institutions. Consultant to federal, state, and local governments.

AWARDS, HONORS—Military: Bronze Star; Department of Defense Meritorious Service Medal; Air Medal; Distinguished Unit Citation; Meritorious Service Medal; Army Commendation Medal with Oak Leaf Cluster. Civilian: National Endowment for the Humanities honors scholar, 1977; holder of four age group records in U.S. Masters Swimming Competition, Georgia.

MEMBER: American Association of School Administrators, American Legion, Veterans of Foreign Wars, Reserve Officers Association, Association of Graduates of U.S. Military Academy, Fellowship of Christian Athletes, Albany Writers Guild (founder and president, 1986-87), Albany Kiwanis Club, Phi Alpha Theta, Phi Delta Kappa.

WRITINGS:

The Common Wildlife of Panama, Mount Hope Press, 1960.
Some Keys to the Vietnam Puzzle (annotated bibliography), University of Florida Research Libraries, 1968.
Peasant Revolution, 1950-1954, Carlton, 1969.
The Modern Violence in Colombia, 1964-1965, University Microfilms, 1970.
(Contributor) *Community Involvement in the Problems of Neglected and Delinquent Youth,* School Board of Alachua County and Florida State Department of Education, 1971.
(Contributor) Steve Collings, *Mountain Top,* Alachua County Public Schools, 1972.
Survey and Bibliography of La Violencia in Colombia, University of Florida Research Libraries, 1974.
(Editor) *Zarpazo, the Bandit* (diary), University of Alabama Press, 1977.
(Contributor) Southwest Regional Center for Community Education Development, *Community Education Resources Handbook,* Arizona State University, 1977.
(Contributor) Rex E. Schmid and others, *Contemporary Issues in Special Education,* McGraw, 1977.
(Editor, contributor, and translator) *Civil-Military Relations in Colombia, 1964-1965* (essays), Regents Press, 1978.
A Lady, A Champion (novel), Tyndale, 1985.
A Lady, A Healer (novel), Winston-Derek, 1986.
(And narrator) "Dougherty County Crime Control System" (television script), WALB-TV, 1986.
A Lady, A Peacemaker (novel), Branden Press, 1987.
God's Joyful Runner: The Biography of Eric Liddell (biography), Bridge Publishing, 1987.
From Mount Olympus to Calvary (biographies), Bridge Publishing, 1988.
An Officer and a Lady (novel), Tyndale, in press.

Contributor of numerous articles to periodicals, including newspapers and military, educational, and Latin American studies journals. Member of editorial staff of *Latin American Research Review,* 1967-73.

SIDELIGHTS: Russell W. Ramsey has written a series of books that combine a concern for Christian morality with an admiration for the self-discipline and dedication of amateur athletics. Ramsey found an embodiment of these ideals in Eric Liddell, subject of his biography *God's Joyful Runner.* Liddell, whose life story formed the basis of the popular 1981 film "Chariots of Fire," was a devout Christian who left behind the fame he won as an Olympic runner to become a missionary in China. The biography was approved by the Liddell family.

Inspired by Liddell's life story, Ramsey created a series of novels featuring the character Angela Weber, who as a teenager aspires to become a prize-winning swimmer and diver. The first novel, *A Lady, A Champion,* shows the heroine growing up in Sandusky, Ohio, during the 1930s—the time and place of Ramsey's own youth. Inculcated with the ideals of small-town America, Angela overcomes pain and adversity to become an Olympic gold medalist. Along the way she meets Eric Liddell, who reinforces her religious faith by reminding the young athlete that her most important goal is not an Olympic crown but the crown that awaits her in heaven if she follows the will of God. The *Georgia Kiwanian* praised the book as "inspiring" and "uplifting."

In subsequent volumes, Angela puts her Christian ideals into practice by helping others. In *A Lady, A Healer,* she becomes both a coach of the U.S. Olympic team and a coach of young handicapped athletes; in *A Lady, A Peacemaker,* she uses international athletic competition as a forum for promoting world peace. An editorial in the *Sandusky Register* lauded Ramsey for his efforts to restore moral values to literature, concluding, "As our own children wander through their lives, what will they find when they reach back for values? They could do a lot worse than to find Russ Ramsey."

Ramsey told *CA:* "I am creating a body of credible hero literature in America. My goal is to supplant the pseudo-sophistication of the post-Watergate era with a body of Americana that is genuinely inspirational. My heroes and heroines get hurt, they trip and fall, but they persevere. In the end, my characters—fictional and actual—are the greatness of America."

Ramsey added: "I am an unabashed Christian who respects all faiths."

AVOCATIONAL INTERESTS: "I am a swimmer, a runner, and a reader; I speak Spanish and write bilingually for publication; I do community service."

BIOGRAPHICAL/CRITICAL SOURCES:

PERIODICALS

Albany Herald (Albany, Ga.), May 28, 1984, November 6, 1985.
Albany Sunday Herald (Albany, Ga.), June 23, 1985, December 8, 1985.
Georgia Kiwanian, June, 1985.
Journal (Lorain, Ohio), September 1, 1985.
Kiwanis Magazine, May, 1987.
Sandusky Register (Sandusky, Ohio), June 30, 1985, August 19, 1985, August 25, 1985, May 31, 1987.
Sunday, January-March, 1986.

RANGEL, Carlos 1929-1988

OBITUARY NOTICE—See index for *CA* sketch: Born September 17, 1929, in Caracas, Venezuela; died of an apparent suicide, January 14 (one source says January 21), 1988. Educator, journalist, television producer and host, and author. Rangel will be best remembered as the producer and co-host of the popular Venezuelan television interview program "Buenos Dias," beginning in 1961. Previously he had taught at New York University and at the University of Caracas. Considered one of Latin America's most eminent conservative thinkers, Rangel spoke out against blaming the United States for the problems of Third World countries in his books, which included *The Latin Americans* and *Third World Ideology*. He also served as managing editor of the weekly *Memento*, as contributing editor of *Newsweek International*, and as associate editor of *World Paper*.

OBITUARIES AND OTHER SOURCES:

PERIODICALS

Chicago Tribune, January 18, 1988.
Los Angeles Times, January 17, 1988.
New York Times, January 28, 1988.

* * *

RANKI, Gyoergy 1930-1988

OBITUARY NOTICE: First name also transliterated Gyorgy; born August 4, 1930, in Budapest, Hungary; died February 19, 1988, in Budapest, Hungary. Historian, educator, and author. Ranki was best known as an authority on the economic history of Eastern Europe, and his analysis of underdevelopment and economic growth in that region associated him with the Hungarian reform movement. After joining the Communist party in 1947 and graduating from the Karl Marx Economic University, he joined the staff of the Institute of Historical Research of the Hungarian Academy of Sciences in 1953, eventually becoming its director in 1986. He was also a professor at the University of Debrecen in 1964 and a professor at Indiana University, where he held the chair of Hungarian studies beginning in 1982. Among his books are the 1961 Kossuth Prize-winner *Development of the Manufacturing Industry in Hungary: 1900-1944, Hungary: A Century of Economic Development, Economic Development in East Central Europe in the Nineteenth and Twentieth Centuries, The European Periphery and Industrialization: 1780-1914*, and *Economy and Foreign Policy: The Struggle of the Great Powers for Hegemony in the Danube Valley, 1919-1939*.

OBITUARIES AND OTHER SOURCES:

BOOKS

The International Who's Who, 51st edition, Europa, 1987.

PERIODICALS

Times (London), February 25, 1988.

* * *

RAPHAELSON, Elliot 1937-

PERSONAL: Born June 1, 1937, in Worcester, Mass.; son of Harry and Sarah Raphaelson; married Arline Markel (a contract specialist), July 15, 1962; children: Debra, Mark. *Education:* Clark University, A.B., 1959; Carnegie-Mellon University, M.S., 1961.

ADDRESSES: Home—5 Baron Court, Englishtown, N.J. 07726. *Office*—Chase Manhattan Bank, 33 Maiden Lane, 17th floor, New York, N.Y. 10081.

CAREER: General Electric Co., Binghamton, N.Y., computer programmer, 1961-63; Operations Research, Inc., Silver Spring, Md., systems analyst, 1963-66; Wakefern Food Corp., Elizabeth, N.J., manager of systems planning, 1966-69; CGA Computer Associates, East Orange, N.J., vice-president of technology, 1969-73; Chase Manhattan Bank, second vice-president, 1973—. Member of faculty at New School for Social Research; past member of faculty at Rutgers University and Carnegie-Mellon University; lecturer in finance, investments, and personal financial planning.

MEMBER: Data Processing Management Association.

WRITINGS:

Planning Your Financial Future, Wiley, 1982.

Contributor to business and computer science journals, popular magazines, and newspapers, including *Vogue, Town and Country, Working Woman, Self*, and *Working Mothers*.

WORK IN PROGRESS: A book on annuities.

SIDELIGHTS: Elliot Raphaelson told *CA:* "My writings emphasize a clear and concise style, and I try to write as much as possible for the layman. I try to write on subjects about which it is not easy for the consumer to get easy-to-understand information, and those for which, because of the vested interest of the sellers of financial products, it is important that the consumer understand the motives and biases of these sellers."

* * *

RATZAN, Scott C. 1962-

PERSONAL: Born October 21, 1962, in Hollywood, Calif.; son of Jerome J. (a physician) and Dawne (a teacher; maiden name, Levine) Ratzan. *Education:* Occidental College, A.B. (with highest honors), 1983; attended University of Chicago, 1983-85; Emerson College, M.A., 1986; Harvard University, M.P.A., 1987; University of Southern California, M.D., 1988.

ADDRESSES: Home—17350 Sunset Blvd., Suite 203C, Pacific Palisades, Calif. 90272; and 32144 Agoura Rd., Westlake Village, Calif. 91361. *Agent*—Michael Hamilburg, Mitchell J. Hamilburg Agency, 292 La Cienega Blvd., Suite 212, Beverly Hills, Calif. 90211.

CAREER: Westlake Community Hospital, Westlake, Calif., laboratory technician, 1978-81; University of Wisconsin—Madison, National Endowment for the Humanities Seminar research assistant, 1983; Massachusetts Institute of Technology News Study Group, Cambridge, research assistant, 1983-84; Democratic National Convention, San Francisco, Calif., research assistant, 1984; Emerson College, Boston, Mass., instructor in communication studies, guest researcher for News Study Group, 1985—. Executive director of Distinguished Physicians of America, Los Angeles, Calif., 1987—; speechwriter and communications consultant.

MEMBER: Outstanding Young Men of America, Phi Sigma Kappa, Town Hall Club of California, Harvard Club of Southern California.

AWARDS, HONORS: Outstanding National Speaker Award from Delta Sigma Rho-Tau Kappa Alpha, and Norman Freestone Outstanding Speaker Award from Occidental College Department of Resources, both 1982.

WRITINGS:

(With J. Gregory Payne) *The 1982 California Gubernatorial Campaign: A Special Kind of Journalism,* National Academy of Television Arts and Sciences, 1986.
(With Payne) *Tom Bradley: The Impossible Dream,* Roundtable, 1986.
"The Army Needs a Few Good Men" (television script), not yet produced.

Contributor to *California Journal* and *Los Angeles.*

WORK IN PROGRESS: Not Bad for a Kid With Rickets: The Life Story of Jose Feliciano, with Payne, publication expected in 1988; *Save Your Life: A Comprehensive Health Prolongation Plan.*

SIDELIGHTS: Scott C. Ratzan told *CA:* "One of the most positive traits of Los Angeles's mayor Tom Bradley is his desire and strong will never to give up. I was impressed with this when I worked with him as a speechwriter in the 1982 gubernatorial campaign. I was fascinated by this black sharecropper's rise from the fields of Texas to heading the nation's second largest city and his uncanny confidence that the American dream is still attainable for those with the hard work and dedication required to see it through. My work on singer Jose Feliciano is similar to that on Bradley in that all of my writing is geared toward documenting dreams of people who have overcome handicaps or obstacles through a will and tenacity to reach beyond what most would be satisfied with. My schooling in medicine, communication, and government enables me to understand these handicaps more intensely and to work toward the betterment of society and the community of which I am an active part. So it is with a sense and passion for justice and fairness that my writings seek to point out that one's dreams are not fantasy but merely previews of what can be with fortitude and determination."

* * *

RAUNIKAR, Robert 1931-

PERSONAL: Born June 13, 1931, in McAlester, Okla.; son of Ed and Frances (a homemaker; maiden name, Videgar) Raunikar; married Mary Angelum Leggett (a homemaker), December 20, 1958; children: Robert Austin, Jane Manning, Frank Edwin. *Education:* Attended Eastern Oklahoma State College, 1949-50; Oklahoma State University, B.S., 1956, M.S., 1958; North Carolina State University, Ph.D., 1963.

ADDRESSES: Home—937 Springer Dr., Griffin, Ga. *Office*—Department of Agricultural Economics, Georgia Experiment Station, Griffin, Ga. 30223-1797.

CAREER: University of Georgia, Georgia Experiment Station, Griffin, assistant professor, 1962-69, associate professor, 1969-77, professor of agricultural economics, 1977—. *Military service:* U.S. Air Force, 1951-55; became staff sergeant.

MEMBER: International Agricultural Economics Association, American Agricultural Economics Association (member of editorial council, 1974-77), Southern Agricultural Economics Association, Northeastern Agricultural Economics Council, Agricultural Economics Association of Georgia, Pi Gamma Mu, Gamma Sigma Delta.

WRITINGS:

(Contributor) Oral Capps, Jr., and Benjamin Senauer, editors, *Food Demand Analysis: Implications for the Future,* Virginia Polytechnic and State University, 1986.
(Editor with Chung-Liang Huang) *Food Demand Analysis: Problems, Issues, and Empirical Evidence,* Iowa State University Press, 1987.

Contributor to professional journals.

WORK IN PROGRESS: Continuing research on food demand and consumption behavior.

SIDELIGHTS: Robert Raunikar told *CA:* "My work has involved full-time research in the area of food demand and consumption behavior with emphasis on deriving the relationship of economic and socio-demographic factors to food consumption. The book on food demand analysis was initiated as a result of the need to compile information on demand analysis involving twenty-eight contributing authors. The compilation of information is intended to bring together most of the work that had been done, hence providing the current state of knowledge on the subject matter. Generally, food demand analysis as presented in the book provides information on the economic theory and data, and a presentation of applications and findings based on partial and complete demand systems. The book also addresses issues on nutritional adequacy of food and the effects of public nutrition policy."

* * *

RAY, H(enrietta) Cordelia 1849(?)-1916

PERSONAL: Born in 1849 (some sources say 1850); died January 5, 1916, in New York, N.Y.; daughter of Charles Bennett (an editor and clergyman) and Charlotte Augusta (Burrough) Ray; unmarried. *Education:* Studied Greek, Latin, French, and German at Sauveneur School of Languages; University of the City of New York (now New York University), M.A., 1891.

ADDRESSES: Home—Woodside, Long Island, N.Y.

CAREER: Educator, poet, and author. Taught in New York public school system for about thirty years, beginning around 1868 at the Colored American Grammar School in Manhattan. Private tutor in music, mathematics, and languages.

WRITINGS:

(With sister, Florence T. Ray) *Sketch of the Life of the Rev. Charles B. Ray* (biography; includes sonnet "To Our Father"), J. J. Little & Co., 1887.
Lincoln: Written for the Occasion of the Unveiling of the Freedmen's Monument in Memory of Abraham Lincoln, April 14, 1876, J. J. Little & Co., 1893.
Sonnets (poetry; includes "To My Mother," "Niobe," "Life," "Aspiration," "Incompleteness," "Self-Mastery," "Two Musicians," and "The Poet's Ministrants"), J. J. Little & Co., 1893.
Poems (collection), Grafton Press, 1910.

Contributor of verse to periodicals.

SIDELIGHTS: A New York schoolteacher by profession, H. Cordelia Ray distinguished herself as one of the few nineteenth-century black women to earn recognition for her literary achievements. In particular, she is best remembered for her poetry, in which she demonstrated her skill in poetic form and technique. Additionally, Ray found favor with critics who were impressed with the genteel quality, versatility, and idealism characteristic of her verse. Writing on familiar themes such as human emotions, nature, and the arts, as well as personal experiences of life and self, she published two volumes containing more than 150 of her poems.

Ray first attracted public attention for her poetry in 1876, when her lengthy poem "Lincoln: Written for the Occasion of the Unveiling of the Freedmen's Monument in Memory of Abraham Lincoln" was recited at a public celebration commemorating the anniversary of the former president's death. Though widely circulated the rhymed testimonial, which had been commissioned especially for the event, remained unpublished until 1893. Six years earlier *Sketch of the Life of the Rev. Charles B. Ray* appeared. A short biography written with her elder sister, Florence, the work served as a tribute to Ray's father and contained the sonnet "To Our Father," a solo effort by the younger daughter.

In addition to the poems she contributed to various periodicals, Ray produced two collections of her work. The first, *Sonnets,* debuted in 1893—the same year *Lincoln* was published. A much larger volume, *Poems,* appeared in 1910. It contains 145 pieces and is dedicated to Ray's sister and lifelong companion, Florence. The poems, like those in *Sonnets,* are for the most part variations on a modest range of themes. What distinguishes Ray's work, say critics, is the masterful execution of poetic form and technique for which she was best known. Especially noteworthy in the latter collection are some innovative ballads that elude the conventions of more traditional verse.

Nothing more of Ray's poetry was published after *Poems.* Described as a shy and reclusive woman, she gradually faded into obscurity following her death in 1916. According to a profile in *Dictionary of Literary Biography,* writer Hallie Quinn Brown observed: "Among a generation of brainy New York women, she was probably the most accomplished, yet outside her immediate circle the least known."

BIOGRAPHICAL/CRITICAL SOURCES:

BOOKS

Brown, Hallie Quinn, editor, *Homespun Heroines and Other Women of Distinction,* Aldine, 1926.

Dictionary of Literary Biography, Volume 50: *Afro-American Writers Before the Harlem Renaissance,* Gale, 1986.

Sherman, Joan R., *Invisible Poets: Afro-Americans of the Nineteenth Century,* University of Illinois Press, 1974.*

* * *

REDDING, (Jay) Saunders 1906-1988

OBITUARY NOTICE—See index for *CA* sketch: Born October 13, 1906, in Wilmington, Del.; died of heart failure, March 2, 1988, in Ithaca, N.Y. Educator and author. When Redding went to Brown University as a visiting professor in 1949 he became the first black member of an Ivy League university faculty. He taught at many other institutions, including Morehouse College, Southern University, and Hampton Institute before settling at Cornell University in 1970. Redding was also a member of the Haverford Group, a circle of black intellectuals concerned with fighting racial isolation. He wrote several well-received books—fiction, non-fiction, and autobiography—about the black experience in America, including *To Make a Poet Black, No Day of Triumph, Stranger and Alone, They Came in Chains: Americans From Africa, On Being Negro in America,* and *The Lonesome Road.*

OBITUARIES AND OTHER SOURCES:

BOOKS

Who's Who in America, 44th edition, Marquis, 1986.

PERIODICALS

New York Times, March 5, 1988.

* * *

REES, (Margaret) Una 1920-

PERSONAL: Born October 24, 1920, in Macclesfield, Cheshire, England; daughter of Henry Edwin (an engineer) and Winifred (a teacher; maiden name, Davies) Apps; married David Rees (a university lecturer), March 29, 1951; children: Mary Elizabeth, Hugh David. *Education:* University of Leeds, B.A. (with honors), 1941, Ph.D., 1944.

ADDRESSES: Home—27 Beechcroft Rd., Oxford, England.

CAREER: University of Wales, University College of North Wales, Bangor, lecturer in history, 1946-52; writer.

WRITINGS:

The Cartulary of Shrewsbury Abbey, National Library of Wales, 1975.

The Cartulary of Haughmond Abbey, University of Wales Press, 1985.

WORK IN PROGRESS: Research on thirteenth-century wool merchants of Shropshire; research on the charters of Lilleshall Abbey.

* * *

REICH, John Theodore 1906-1988

OBITUARY NOTICE: Given name originally Johannes; born September 30, 1906, in Vienna, Austria; died February 9, 1988, in Sarasota, Fla. Theater and television producer and director, educator, translator, and author. Head of production for fifteen years at Chicago's Goodman Theater and School of Drama, Reich is noted for substantially improving the institution's quality and creative development. He was a producer for theaters in Vienna, Austria, before immigrating to the United States, where he taught drama and theater at colleges and universities. He worked as an independent producer from 1951 until 1957 when he was chosen to become head of production at the Goodman Theatre, which was then an adjunct of the Art Institute of Chicago. Within the first three years of his term, he succeeded in substantially increasing the number of subscribers to the theater while recruiting professional artists to act with the student company.

In 1959 Reich was one of ten American directors to receive a ten thousand dollar grant from the Ford Foundation, which he used to further improve the Goodman. The following year he was named Chicago Theater Man of the Year. In guiding the theater towards professionalism, the director was praised for his varied repertory drawn from both European and American literature. He left the Goodman in 1972 to work in resident theaters throughout the country. Reich also produced and directed various television programs for the Columbia Broadcasting System during the 1940s and early 1950s. Among his writings are adaptations of plays, such as Johann Friedrich von Schiller's *Mary Stuart* and Arthur Schnitzler's *Comedy of Words,* as well as *The Salzburg Everyman* and several translations, including Friedrich Duerrenmatt's *The Accident.*

OBITUARIES AND OTHER SOURCES:

BOOKS

The International Who's Who, 51st edition, Europa, 1987.

Notable Names in the American Theatre, James White, 1976.

PERIODICALS

Chicago Tribune, February 11, 1988.

* * *

REID, Donald (Matthew) 1952-

PERSONAL: Born November 22, 1952, in Cambridge, Mass.; son of Robert Clark (a professor) and Anna Marie (a botanist; maiden name, Murphy) Reid; married Holly Virginia Russell (a graphic designer), August 26, 1980. *Education:* Wesleyan University, Middletown, Conn., B.A., 1974; Stanford University, M.A., 1975, Ph.D., 1981.

ADDRESSES: Home—Chapel Hill, N.C. *Office*—Department of History, University of North Carolina at Chapel Hill, Chapel Hill, N.C. 27514.

CAREER: University of North Carolina at Chapel Hill, assistant professor, 1981-86, associate professor of history, 1986—.

MEMBER: American Historical Association, Society for French Historical Studies.

AWARDS, HONORS: William Koren, Jr., Prize from Society for French Historical Studies, 1986, for "Industrial Paternalism: Discourse and Practice in Nineteenth-Century French Mining and Metallurgy."

WRITINGS:

The Miners of Decazeville: A Genealogy of Deindustrialization, Harvard University Press, 1985.

A Social History of France Since 1880, Methuen, in press.

Contributor to history journals.

WORK IN PROGRESS: The Sewers and Sewermen of Paris, and *Fathers Without Sons: Industrial Paternalism in Nineteenth-Century France,* for University of California Press.

* * *

REISER, Morton F(rancis) 1919-

PERSONAL: Born August 2, 1919, in Cincinnati, Ohio; son of Sigmund and Mary (Roth) Reiser; married Jane Lomas, March 18, 1945 (divorced); married Lynn B. Whisnant (a physician), December 19, 1976; children: (first marriage) David E., Barbara, Linda. *Education:* University of Cincinnati, B.S., 1940, M.D., 1943; New York Psychoanalytic Institute, graduated, 1960.

ADDRESSES: Home—99 Blake Rd., Hamden, Conn. 06517. *Office*—25 Park St., New Haven, Conn. 06519.

CAREER: King's County Hospital, Brooklyn, N.Y., intern, 1944; Cincinnati General Hospital, Cincinnati, Ohio, resident, 1944-50; private practice of psychiatry in Cincinnati, 1947-52, Washington, D.C., 1954-55, and New York, N.Y., 1955-69; Yale University, New Haven, Conn., professor of psychiatry, 1969, Charles B. G. Murphy Professor, 1978-86, chairman of department of psychiatry at Medical School, 1969-86. Cincinnati General Hospital, fellow in psychiatry, 1947-50, instructor, 1949-50, assistant professor, 1950-52; member of faculty at University of Cincinnati, 1949-52, and Washington School of Psychiatry, 1953-55; Yeshiva University, Albert Einstein College of Medicine, associate professor, 1955-58, professor, 1958-69, director of research in psychiatry, 1958-65; professorial lecturer at State University of New York Downstate Medical Center, 1959-65; member of faculty at Western New England Institute of Psychoanalysis, 1969—; past member of board of trustees and assistant lecturer at New York Psychoanalytic Institute. Diplomate of American Board of Psychiatry and Neurology; research psychiatrist in Neuropsychiatric Division of Walter Reed Army Institute of Research, 1954-55; visiting psychiatrist at Bronx Municipal Hospital, 1954-69; attending physician and chief of Division of Psychiatry at Montefiore Hospital and Medical Center, 1965-69; past member of staff at Christian R. Holmes Hospital. Committee member of World Health Organization, 1963; member of professional advisory committee of Jerusalem Mental Health Center, 1972—; chairman of clinical program projects review committee of National Institute of Mental Health, 1973-74; member of Josiah Macy, Jr. Foundation's Commission on the Present Condition and Future of Academic Psychiatry, 1977; member of study group, Center for Advanced Psychoanalytic Studies, Princeton, N.J. *Military service:* U.S. Army, 1952-54; became captain.

MEMBER: International Psycho-Analytical Association, International College of Psychosomatic Medicine (president, 1975), World Psychiatric Association, American College of Psychiatrists (fellow), American Psychiatric Association (fellow), American Society for Clinical Investigation, American Psychosomatic Association (president, 1960-61), American Federation for Clinical Research, American Association of Chairmen of Departments of Psychiatry (member of executive committee, 1971—; president, 1975-76), Academy of Behavioral Medicine Research (member of executive council, 1978), American Psychoanalytic Association (president, 1982-84), Association for the Psychophysiological Study of Sleep, Psychiatric Research Society, A. Graeme Mitchell Undergraduate Pediatric Society, American Association for the Advancement of Science (fellow), American Medical Association, Sigma Xi, Alpha Omega Alpha, Phi Eta Sigma, Pi Kappa Epsilon.

WRITINGS:

(Editor) *American Handbook of Psychiatry,* Volume IV: *Organic Conditions and Psychosomatic Medicine,* Basic Books, 1975.

Organic Disorders and Psychosomatic Medicine, Basic Books, 1976.

(With Hoyle Leigh) *The Patient: Biological, Psychological, and Social Dimensions of Medical Practice,* Plenum, 1980, revised edition, 1985.

Mind, Brain, Body: Toward a Convergence of Psychoanalysis and Neurobiology, Basic Books, 1985.

Double Code, Single File: Memory, Memories, and the Brain, Basic Books, 1988.

Contributor of more than one hundred articles to medical and scientific journals. Editor in chief of *Psychosomatic Medicine,* 1962-72; member of editorial board of *AMA Archive of General Psychiatry,* American Medical Association, 1961-71.

SIDELIGHTS: In *Mind, Brain, Body* Morton F. Reiser explores recent neurobiological research on memory networks in the brain. He examines Freud's theory of anxiety, according to which a person who experiences anxiety in a moment of danger will, if the situation recurs in the future, experience the same anxiety as a danger signal, enabling the person to take defensive, precautionary action. Morton's goal is to relate neurobiological research to the study and practice of psychoanalysis. B. A. Farrell wrote in the *New York Review of Books:* "I believe that the suggestions Reiser discusses here will prove interesting and stimulating to workers in the field." He added

that the author draws "the attention of the ordinary reader . . . to findings that help to clarify some of the confusion surrounding the psychoanalytic view of the mind; and thereby [he opens] the eyes of the skeptic to ways in which analytic theory may be brought within the scope of scientific inquiry."

In the *New York Times Book Review,* Richard M. Restak commented: "Dr. Reiser approaches neurobiology as a potential source for the biological underpinnings to psychoanalytic theory. . . . His goal is to discover ways of chemically regulating or altering the brain to restore or maintain its normal functions. His discussion of the stress response is cogent, well reasoned and a pleasure to read."

BIOGRAPHICAL/CRITICAL SOURCES:

PERIODICALS

New York Review of Books, July 18, 1985.
New York Times Book Review, January 20, 1985.

* * *

REYBOLD, Malcolm 1911(?)-1988

OBITUARY NOTICE: Born c. 1911 in Atlanta, Ga.; died January 7, 1988, on Long Island, N.Y. Advertising executive, publisher, and author. Reybold began his career in advertising working as director of marketing for Foote Cone & Belding and then as an associate director of marketing for J. Walter Thompson Company and McCann-Erickson. Turning to a career in publishing, he joined F. W. Dodge, a division of the publishing company McGraw-Hill, eventually retiring as publisher in 1965. Reybold's book, *The Inspector's Opinion: The Chappaquiddick Incident,* was published in 1975.

OBITUARIES AND OTHER SOURCES:

PERIODICALS

New York Times, January 15, 1988.

* * *

REYNOLDS, David S(pencer) 1948-

PERSONAL: Born August 30, 1948, in Providence, R.I.; son of Paul R. (in business) and Adelaide (an artist) Reynolds; married Suzanne Nalbantian (a professor of comparative literature), July 23, 1983; children: Aline Elizabeth. *Education:* Amherst College, B.A., 1970; University of California, Berkeley, Ph.D., 1979.

ADDRESSES: Home—16 Linden Lane, Old Westbury, N.Y. 11568. *Office*—Department of English, Rutgers University, Camden, N.J. 08102.

CAREER: Northwestern University, Evanston, Ill., assistant professor of English and American studies, 1980-86; Rutgers University, Camden, N.J., assistant professor and director of Whitman studies, 1986—. Visiting associate professor at Barnard College, 1983-84; visiting adjunct professor at New York University, 1986 and 1987.

MEMBER: Modern Language Association of America, Organization of American Historians, Institute for Early American History and Culture, P.E.N. American Center.

WRITINGS:

Faith in Fiction: The Emergence of Religious Literature in America, Harvard University Press, 1981.
George Lippard, G. K. Hall, 1982.
George Lippard, Prophet of Protest: Writings of an American Radical, Peter Lang, 1986.
Beneath the American Renaissance: The Subversive Imagination in the Age of Emerson and Melville, Knopf, 1988.

Contributor to literature journals.

SIDELIGHTS: David S. Reynolds told *CA:* "The study of literature was for years spoiled by too narrow a concern with a handful of canonized works, which were usually placed in a cultural vacuum. Of late, literary study has profited from canon revision and new historical methodologies, but much remains to be done to recapture the literary post in its fullness. Enlightened literary history can be written only after comprehensive research into a broad range of forgotten social and imaginative texts by writers of various geographical regions and different social groups. Such research shows that great literature is time-specific and culture-specific at the same time that it is universal. Far from being *detached* from society and history, literature is, to a large degree, *produced* by society and history.

"My own research began as an adventure into uncharted territories of nineteenth-century American popular literature. Having sampled the total range of American popular writing of the pre-Civil War period, I then reassessed the works of seven familiar authors—Ralph Waldo Emerson, Henry David Thoreau, Nathaniel Hawthorne, Herman Melville, Walt Whitman, Emily Dickinson, and Edgar Allan Poe—from a fresh historical perspective."

BIOGRAPHICAL/CRITICAL SOURCES:

PERIODICALS

Times Literary Supplement, January 22, 1982.

* * *

RIBEIRO, Aileen 1944-

PERSONAL: Born April 15, 1944; married Robert Ribeiro (a lawyer). *Education:* King's College, London, B.A., 1965; Courtauld Institute of Art, London, M.A., 1971, Ph.D., 1975.

ADDRESSES: Office—Courtauld Institute of Art, University of London, 20 Portman Square, London W1H 0BE, England.

CAREER: Courtauld Institute of Art, London, England, lecturer and head of history of dress department, 1971—. Governor of the Pasold Textile Fund, London.

WRITINGS:

A Visual History of Costume: The Eighteenth Century, Batsford, 1983.
The Dress Worn at Masquerades in England, 1730 to 1790, and Its Relation to Fancy Dress in Portraiture, Garland Publishing, 1984.
Dress in Eighteenth-Century Europe, 1715-1789, Batsford, 1984.
Dress and Morality, Batsford, 1986.
The Female Face, Tate Gallery, 1987.
(Contributor) *Franz Xaver Winterhalter and the Courts of Europe, 1830-1870,* National Portrait Gallery (London), 1987.
Dress and the French Revolution, Batsford, 1988.

Editor of costume accessories series and visual history of costume series, both published by Batsford. Contributor to periodicals, including *Times* (London), *Connoisseur, History Today, Apollo, Burlington Magazine, Connaissance des Arts,* and *Vogue.*

SIDELIGHTS: Aileen Ribeiro is an art historian specializing in the history of dress who "has taken the study of eighteenth-century dress several strides on in recent years," in the opinion of Pat Rogers of the *Times Literary Supplement.* Another *Times Literary Supplement* reviewer, Celina Fox, echoed Rogers, calling Ribeiro's *Dress in Eighteenth-Century Europe, 1715-1789* "an important book, certainly the most scholarly account of eighteenth-century dress ever to have been published," and praised its "richness of documentary evidence." In this work, Ribeiro focuses on fashion in Europe during the eighteenth century, or the "age of elegance," beginning with the ornate baroque dress of the early decades and concluding with the uncomplicated dress of the years prior to the French Revolution. She also assesses the role fashion played in society and the economy, eighteenth-century attitudes toward dress, and the relationship between fashion and social class.

According to Ribeiro in *Dress in Eighteenth-Century Europe,* the eighteenth-century upper classes often adopted certain forms of dress as an outward sign of their social standing. The Italian nobility wore black; in Russia the Empress Elizabeth demanded the women of her entourage to shave their heads and wear black wigs; and in France Madame de Pompadour required that her guests wear gray. Yet with all its attention to beautiful clothing, the "age of elegance" had its myths, which Ribeiro dispels. She acknowledges that the styles of dress of the working classes and poor dated back to the Middle Ages in some cases and were put together strictly for usefulness and economy. Ribeiro also found that many people devised ingenious methods to conceal the physical signs, such as pock-marked skin and rotting teeth, of poor hygiene and diet. The author provides evidence that one woman dyed her teeth black so that they'd appear to be lacquered. Even people most meticulous about their appearance failed to bathe regularly, and clothing—especially silks, which were almost impossible to clean—decayed in areas of heavy perspiration.

Ribeiro's second book, *The Dress Worn at Masquerades in England, 1730 to 1790, and Its Relation to Fancy Dress in Portraiture,* studies theatrical garb and costumes worn by men, women, and children during the greater part of the eighteenth century. Rogers was enthusiastic about Ribeiro's historic fashion discoveries that she presents in this work: "First, she has brought together an immense amount of pictorial evidence, which shows the prevalence of the stock motifs in fashionable dress more clearly than ever before. . . . Second, Ribeiro advances our knowledge of the role played by pattern books. . . . In addition, Ribeiro advances our knowledge of the role played by drapery painters," whose works influenced later generations of artists who portrayed subjects in flowing costumes.

AVOCATIONAL INTERESTS: Art and image in eighteenth-century portraiture in Europe, costume and caricature.

BIOGRAPHICAL/CRITICAL SOURCES:

PERIODICALS

Costume, Number 20, 1986, Number 21, 1987.
Literary Review, May, 1985, January, 1987.
Times Literary Supplement, February 22, 1985, January 10, 1986.

* * *

RICH, Paul B(enjamin) 1950-

PERSONAL: Born March 25, 1950, in Colchester, Essex, England; son of Charles A. and Clare (Young) Rich. *Education:* University of Sussex, B.A., 1972; University of York, B.Phil., 1973; University of Warwick, Ph.D., 1980. *Religion:* Church of England.

ADDRESSES: Home—4 Gleeson Dr., Warwick, Warwickshire CV34 5VA, England. *Office*—University of Warwick, Coventry CV4 7AL, England.

CAREER: University of the Witwatersrand, Johannesburg, South Africa, lecturer in political studies, 1974-76; University of Cape Town, Rondebosch, South Africa, lecturer in politics, 1976-77; Aston University, Birmingham, England, research fellow for Centre for Research in Ethnic Relations, 1980-84; University of Warwick, Coventry, England, research fellow, 1984-85, lecturer in politics, 1987—. Visiting lecturer at University of Bristol, 1986-87.

MEMBER: International Society for the Study of European Ideas, American Historical Association, Political Studies Association.

AWARDS, HONORS: Personal research grant from the British Academy, 1985; research fellowship from the Lee Lulme Trust, 1986-87.

WRITINGS:

White Power and the Liberal Conscience: Racial Segregation and South African Liberalism: 1921-1960, Manchester University Press, 1984.
Race and Empire in British Politics, Cambridge University Press, 1986.
(Editor with Zig Layton-Henry) *Race, Government, and Politics in Britain,* Macmillan, 1986.

WORK IN PROGRESS: Ruined Eden: The Politics of British Nationalism, a study of Anglo-American policy towards South Africa since 1945.

SIDELIGHTS: Paul B. Rich told *CA:* "I was motivated to understand the dynamics of racism in modern societies through seeing the plight of the black population in South Africa. I am interested also in the question of how liberal democratic values can be maintained in Western societies and in exploring the literary dimensions of cultural rootlessness in contemporary South African writing."

AVOCATIONAL INTERESTS: Skiing, squash, photography, travel, cinema, gardening, music.

BIOGRAPHICAL/CRITICAL SOURCES:

PERIODICALS

Times Literary Supplement, July 6, 1984.

* * *

RICHARDSON, Willis 1889-1977

PERSONAL: Born November 5, 1889, in Wilmington, North Carolina; died November 8, 1977; son of Willis Wilder and Agnes Ann (Harper) Richardson; married Mary Ellen Jones, September 1 (one source says September 3), 1914; children: Jean Paula, Shirley Antonella, Noel Justine. *Education:* Graduated from high school in Washington, D.C.

CAREER: U.S. Bureau of Engraving and Printing, Washington, D.C., clerk, 1911-54; playwright, 1920-77. Director, drama historian, teacher at institutions including Morgan College (now Morgan State University), director of Little Theatre group in Washington, D.C.

MEMBER: National Association for the Advancement of Colored People, Dramatists Guild, Harlem Cultural Council.

AWARDS, HONORS: First prize in *Crisis* Contest Awards, 1925, for "The Broken Banjo," and 1926, for "The Bootblack Lover"; honorable mention in *Opportunity* Contest Awards, 1925, for "Fall of the Conjurer"; Amy Spingarn Prize for drama, 1925 and 1926; Public School Prize, 1926, for "The King's Dilemma"; Edith Schwarb Cup from Yale University Theatre, 1928.

WRITINGS:

PLAYS

"The Deacon's Awakening: A Play in One Act" (first produced in St. Paul, Minn., in 1921), published in *Crisis,* November, 1920.
"The King's Dilemma" (one-act for children; first produced in Washington, D.C., May, 1926), published in *Brownies' Book,* December, 1920.
"The Gypsy's Finger Ring" (one-act for children), published in *Brownies' Book,* March, 1921.
"The Children's Treasure" (one-act for children), published in *Brownies' Book,* June, 1921.
"The Dragon's Tooth" (one-act for children), published in *Brownies' Book,* October, 1921.
"The Chip Woman's Fortune" (one-act), first produced in Chicago, January 29, 1923; produced on Broadway at Frazee Theatre, May 15, 1923.
"Mortgaged," first produced in Washington, D.C., at Howard University, March 29, 1924.
"Compromise" (one-act), first produced in Cleveland at Karamu House, February 26, 1925; produced in New York, May 3, 1926.
"The Broken Banjo" (first produced in New York, August 1, 1925), published in *Crisis,* February, 1926, and March, 1926.
"The Idle Head" (one-act), published in *Carolina,* April, 1927.
"The Flight of the Natives" (one-act; first produced in Washington, D.C., May 7, 1927), published in *Carolina,* April, 1927.
(Editor and contributor) *Plays and Pageants From the Life of the Negro* (twelve plays, including "The Black Horseman," "The House of Sham," and "The King's Dilemma" [all by Richardson]), Associated Publishers, 1930, reprinted, Roth Publishing, 1980.
"The Black Horseman," first produced in Baltimore, October 12, 1931.
(Editor with May Miller, and contributor) *Negro History in Thirteen Plays* (includes the one-acts "Antonio Maceo," "Attucks, the Martyr," "The Elder Dumas," "In Menelik's Court," and "Near Calvary" [all by Richardson]), Associated Publishers, 1935.
"Miss or Mrs.," first produced in Washington, D.C., May 5, 1941.
The King's Dilemma, and Other Plays for Children: Episodes of Hope and Dream (includes "The Dragon's Tooth," "The Gypsy's Finger Ring," "The King's Dilemma," "Man of Magic," "Near Calvary," and "The New Santa Claus"), Exposition Press, 1956.

Also author of one-act plays *Alimony Rastus,* Willis N. Bugbee, early 1920s, *A Ghost of the Past,* Paine Publishing, early 1920s, "Rooms for Rent," 1926, "Bold Lover," "The Brown Boy," "The Curse of the Shell Road Witch," and "The Dark Haven"; the three-act plays "Fall of the Conjurer," "The Bootblack Lover," and a version of "The Chip Woman's Fortune"; and of plays "The Peacock's Feather," 1928, "The Amateur Prostitute," "Chase," "The Danse Calinda," "Hope of the Lonely," "Imp of the Devil," "The Jail Bird," "Joy Rider," "The Man Who Married a Young Wife," "The New Generation," "The Nude Siren," "A Pillar of the Church," "The Rider of the Dream," and "The Visiting Lady."

OTHER

Echoes From the Negro Soul (poetry), Alamo Printing, 1926.

Contributor to periodicals, including *Carolina, Crisis,* and *Opportunity.*

Work represented in anthologies, including *The New Negro: An Interpretation,* edited by Alain Locke, Boni, 1925; *Plays of Negro Life: A Source-book of Native American Drama,* edited by Alain Locke and Montgomery Gregory, Harper, 1927; *Fifty More Contemporary One-Act Plays,* edited by Frank Shay, Appleton, 1928; *Readings From Negro Authors,* edited by Otelia Cromwell, Eva B. Dykes, and Lorenzo D. Turner, Harcourt, 1931; *American Literature by Negro Authors,* edited by Herman Dreer, Macmillan, 1950; *Anthology of the American Negro in the Theatre: A Critical Approach,* edited by Lindsay Patterson, Publishers Company, 1967; *Black Drama in America: An Anthology,* edited by Darwin T. Turner, Fawcett, 1971; *Black Writers of America,* edited by Richard Barksdale and Keneth Kinnamon, Macmillan, 1972; *Black Theatre, U.S.A.: Forty-five Plays by Black Americans,* edited by James V. Hatch with Ted Shine, Free Press, 1974; *The New Negro Renaissance,* edited by Arthur P. Davis and Michael Peplow, Holt, 1975.

SIDELIGHTS: Willis Richardson, the first black playwright to have a nonmusical play produced on Broadway, is remembered for his contributions to black theatre. Widely considered a pioneer, he dared to write serious plays about all levels of black life at a time when white playwrights wrote about stereotypical "darkies" and other black playwrights confined themselves to propaganda plays showing how blacks were victimized by whites. According to Bernard L. Peterson, Jr., writing in *Black World,* Richardson was "the first to make a significant contribution to both the quantity and the quality of serious Black American drama."

Among Richardson's first writings were his plays for children, which often dramatize lives of black heroes or use fairy-tale techniques to promote charity, equality, and brotherhood. Several were published in the monthly magazine *Brownies' Book* or later appeared in his collection *The King's Dilemma, and Other Plays for Children: Episodes of Hope and Dream.* "The King's Dilemma," a one-act play, traces the beginnings of democracy in a kingdom whose prince chooses to befriend a black boy, despite the king's opposition. Popular among schoolchildren, the play won the Public School Prize in 1926. "The Children's Treasure" takes a contemporary subject, a poor person facing eviction, and shows how five children help by contributing their own savings toward their neighbor's rent. In other plays Richardson tells of heroic and prominent blacks in history such as former slave Crispus Attucks, who was among the first to die in the American Revolution, Emperor Menelik of Abyssinia, and King Massinissa of East Numidia.

"The Chip Woman's Fortune," one of Richardson's best known works for adults, is famous as the first serious black play to appear on Broadway. Noted Peterson, "Black playwrights had previously been represented on The Great White Way by musical comedies and revues, but never before by a serious drama, albeit a one-act play." Presented on the same bill as Oscar

Wilde's "Salome," Richardson's play portrays Aunt Nancy, an old woman who supports herself by tending a man's invalid wife and collecting chips of wood and coal for fuel. When the man, Silas, faces losing his job and the Victrola he has not yet paid off, he asks Nancy to use her money to help him, but she has saved it for her son, Jim. Claiming the money Nancy has saved, Jim ultimately gives some of it to Silas for having provided for his mother.

Observed Peterson, "Most of [Richardson's] plays were attempts at realistic treatment of Black life (both contemporary and historical) on such a variety of themes as manhood and bravery; suffering under white tyranny . . . ; the problems of the urban family; . . . the social strivings of the middle class; Black exploitation of other Blacks, and many other relevant subjects." The playwright worked to preserve for history an image of blacks more comprehensive than that portrayed by white writers, capturing the "richness, diversity, and beauty of his race," described Patsy B. Perry in the *Dictionary of Literary Biography*. Through his plays and critical writings, his advocacy of black theatre, and his conviction that black drama should excel on the same merits as any other drama, Richardson did much to bring black artistry forward and promote the best characteristics of his, and all, people. Concluded Peterson, "Willis Richardson has tried to show us 'the soul of a people, and the soul of this people is truly worth showing.'"

BIOGRAPHICAL/CRITICAL SOURCES:

BOOKS

Dictionary of Literary Biography, Volume 51: *Afro-American Writers From the Harlem Renaissance to 1940,* Gale, 1987.

PERIODICALS

Black World, April, 1975.*

* * *

RICHMAN, Robert (Maxwell) 1914-1987

OBITUARY NOTICE: Born December 22, 1914, in Connersville, Ind.; died after a stroke, November 10, 1987, in Myrtle Beach, S.C. Administrator, educator, editor, and author. Richman is most noted as founder and director of Washington, D.C.'s Institute of Contemporary Arts, a cultural and educational organization that hosted hundreds of artistic performances, exhibitions, and lectures. An instructor at the University of Michigan from 1938 to 1945, Richman developed his philosophy that art and humanities should be incorporated into contemporary culture. He subsequently opened the nonprofit Institute of Contemporary Arts in 1947, which brought to the public readings from poets T. S. Eliot and Robert Frost, exhibitions of works by artist Joan Miro and architect Frank Lloyd Wright, and lectures from physicist Harold Urey and philosopher Paul Weiss, among many others. Foundation support ended in less than twenty years, and the institute closed in 1964. Richman was also the literature and arts editor of *New Republic* magazine from 1951 to 1954, and he edited the book *The Arts at Mid-Century*. Among his writings are *Colours of Darkness, Abstract Art in Indian America, The Endangered Phoenix, Seamusic Seascapes,* and *This Eloquent Geology*.

OBITUARIES AND OTHER SOURCES:

BOOKS

Who's Who in America, 43rd edition, Marquis, 1984.
Who's Who in American Art, 15th edition, Bowker, 1982.

PERIODICALS

Washington Post, November 13, 1987.

* * *

RICHMOND, Al 1913-1987 (Joseph Morton)

OBITUARY NOTICE—See index for *CA* sketch: Surname originally Richman, legally changed in 1947; born November 17, 1913, in London, England; immigrated to United States, 1922, naturalized citizen, 1943; died of pneumonia, November 6, 1987, in San Francisco, Calif. Journalist, editor, and author. Richmond is best remembered as one of fourteen American Communist Party members tried for violating the Smith Act—an antisubversion law later declared unconstitutional—by Senator Joseph McCarthy during his campaign against communism in the 1950s. Richmond was found guilty of conspiracy to teach and advocate the violent overthrow of the federal government and served one year in prison. At the time of his arrest Richmond was editor of the *Daily People's World,* an outspoken leftist newspaper he helped found in 1938. Previously, he served as a reporter for the New York communist periodical *Daily Worker*. Richmond wrote pamphlets against McCarthy under the pseudonym Joseph Morton, and he was the author of the autobiographical *A Long View From the Left: Memoirs of an American Revolutionary* published in 1973.

OBITUARIES AND OTHER SOURCES:

PERIODICALS

Chicago Tribune, November 10, 1987.
Los Angeles Times, November 9, 1987.
New York Times, November 9, 1987.
Washington Post, November 9, 1987.

* * *

RIFBJERG, Klaus (Thorvald) 1931-

BRIEF ENTRY: Surname is pronounced "*Riff*-berg"; born December 15, 1931, in Copenhagen, Denmark. Danish editor, poet, playwright, screenwriter, and author. Rifbjerg was hailed as "the best-known and most influential contemporary writer in Denmark" by Charlotte Schiander Gray in *Books Abroad*. He has written dozens of works, including novels, plays, screenplays, and collections of poetry and short stories, and his reputation for experimentation and nonconformity has added to his fame. According to Gray, Rifbjerg frequently writes about "the identity problem—the origin of the human being, his formative stages and his further development into adulthood." The theme predominates in two of the author's most popular works—the novel *Den kroniske uskyld* (title means "The Chronic Innocence"; Schoenberg, 1958), and the play *Udviklinger* (Gyldendal, 1965; first produced in 1965; translated as *Developments* in *Modern Nordic Plays: Denmark* [Universitetsforlaget, 1974]). His poetry collection *Konfrontation* (title means "Confrontation"; Schoenberg, 1960), stresses an openness to immediate, sensory experience, and is considered an important work of the Danish modernist movement. Rifbjerg has received several major literary awards, including the Nordic Council Prize for the novel *Anna (jeg) Anna* (Gyldendal, 1969; translated as *Anna, I, Anna* [Curbstone Press, 1982]). He has reviewed books, films, and plays for Danish periodicals, and he helped edit the influential literary magazine *Vindrosen* from 1959 to 1964. Additional works by Rifbjerg that have been translated into English include *Selected Poems*

(Curbstone Press, 1976) and the novel *Witness to the Future* (Fjord, 1987). *Addresses: Home*—Toldbodgade 73, DK-1253 Copenhagen, Denmark.

BIOGRAPHICAL/CRITICAL SOURCES:

BOOKS

Encyclopedia of World Literature in the Twentieth Century, Supplement, Ungar, 1975.
International Authors and Writers Who's Who, 9th edition, [and] *International Who's Who in Poetry,* 6th edition, Melrose, 1982.
The International Who's Who, 51st edition, Europa, 1987.
World Authors: 1970-1975, H. W. Wilson, 1980.

PERIODICALS

Books Abroad, winter, 1975.

* * *

RIOLS, Noreen 1926-

PERSONAL: Born May 9, 1926, in Malta; daughter of Richard Henry Pyke and Nora (Weild) Baxter; married Jacques Riols (a public relations executive), August 14, 1959; children: Olivier, Herve, Marie-France (Mrs. Herve Charles), Yves-Michel, Christopher. *Education:* St. Thomas's Hospital School of Nursing, London, England, S.R.N., 1955. *Politics:* None. *Religion:* Anglican.

ADDRESSES: Home—La Grange, rue Pierre Bourdan, 78160 Marly-le-roi, France.

CAREER: British Broadcasting Corp., London, England, acting writing secretariat in French Service, 1945-51; Opera Mundi Press Agency, Paris, France, assistant to head of English section, 1956-57; Organization for Economic Cooperation and Development, Paris, personal assistant to head of division, 1957-59; free-lance writer, 1959—.

MEMBER: Fellowship of Christian Writers.

AWARDS, HONORS: Poetry Society Bronze Medal for verse-speaking, 1943, Silver Medal for verse-speaking, 1944.

WRITINGS:

Eye of the Storm, Hodder & Stoughton, 1983, Ballantine, 1985.
Abortion: A Woman's Birthright? Hodder & Stoughton, 1986.
Only the Best, Hodder & Stoughton, 1987.

Writer for British Broadcasting Corporation program "Woman's Hour," 1972-81. Author of "Letter From Paris," a semimonthly feature in *Challenge*. Contributor to magazines, including *Christian Woman, Decision, Family, Power for Living,* and *Today*.

WORK IN PROGRESS: A Christian book, tentatively titled *Leaves From a Nurse's Notebook,* dealing with "the unsolvable problem of pain and loss and how one comes to terms with it, and with accepting that there are some questions that will never be answered this side of heaven."

SIDELIGHTS: Noreen Riols told *CA:* "My husband is French and I am English. We have lived in France since 1956, and we are both bilingual. Since I became a Christian, I try to use my writing gift to spread my faith. I also use it for my speaking at women's lunches and dinners, more so since my first book was published, and I have been invited to England, Holland, Belgium, and France.

"*Eye of the Storm* is a family story, showing my walk till I met Jesus. *Abortion: A Woman's Birthright?* simply tells what an abortion, even one advised by the medical profession, can do to a woman. It shows how the ramifications go far deeper than any physician ever explains and how, in my case and, I am sure, in the cases of many other women, the depression, guilt, and self-loathing that result can be worse than any post-natal depression. The book tells how forgiveness can only be found in Jesus with, ultimately, the possibility of being able to forgive oneself.

"*Only the Best* happened because I was tired of the second-class treatment of young women who stayed at home and looked after their husbands and families and didn't, as the media says, 'work.' So I wrote showing just what an effect a mother can have on her growing family and how, if one is seeking earthly immortality, it is not in winning Wimbledon, playing on Broadway, or being prime minister that one will get it. Earthly fame is ephemeral, but by nurturing and caring for a family, the ideals and values a mother instills into her children, for good or bad, positive or negative, will live on. I traced a thread right back to my great-grandmother, down to our own grandchildren, showing how this influence is passed on.

"I think the real value, if there is one, to my books is the fact that my work was first published at the unheard-of age of fifty-seven, the second a month before my sixtieth birthday, and the third two days before my sixty-first. I think this is a real encouragement to the older woman who has raised her family and now has time on her hands and is wondering just what to do with the rest of her life. The media keeps telling us that if we haven't done everything we want to do, achieved our ambitions by the time we're thirty-five we might as well give up, as it's too late. I hope I've proved the contrary. I imagine my books reflect my personal values, views, and experiences completely. The only message I can give to the Christian reader, or rather to the non-Christian reader or searcher is that this wonderful experience happened to me, and I'm no one special, so it could happen to you. All you have to do is to open your heart and ask Jesus to come in."

* * *

RITVO, Harriet 1946-

PERSONAL: Born September 19, 1946, in Cambridge, Mass.; daughter of Martin (a lawyer) and Zelma (a scientist; maiden name, Weiss) Ritvo. *Education:* Harvard University, A.B., 1968, Ph.D., 1975; attended Cambridge University, 1968-69.

ADDRESSES: Office—14N-333, Massachusetts Institute of Technology, 77 Massachusetts Ave., Cambridge, Mass. 02139.

CAREER: American Academy of Arts and Sciences, Cambridge, Mass., editor and staff associate, 1976-79; Massachusetts Institute of Technology, Cambridge, assistant professor, 1980-85, associate professor, 1985—.

AWARDS, HONORS: Fellowships from the Yale Center for British Art, 1984, and Stanford Humanities Center, 1985-86.

WRITINGS:

The Animal Estate: The English and Other Creatures in the Victorian Age, Harvard University Press, 1987.

Contributor of numerous essays and reviews to periodicals.

BIOGRAPHICAL/CRITICAL SOURCES:

PERIODICALS

Animals, November/December, 1987.
Chicago Tribune, October 7, 1987.
New York Times Book Review, October 11, 1987.
Times Higher Education Supplement, October 13, 1987.

* * *

RIVERS, Larry 1923-

PERSONAL: Original name, Yitzroch Loiza Grossberg; born August 17, 1923, in New York, N.Y.; son of Shiah (a plumber and trucking company owner) and Sonya (a housewife; maiden name, Hochberg) Grossberg; married Augusta Burger, 1945 (divorced); married Clarice Price, 1961 (divorced); children: (first marriage) Steven; (second marriage) Gwynne, Emma. *Education:* Attended Juilliard School of Music, 1944-45; attended Hans Hofmann's School of Fine Arts, 1947-48; New York University, B.F.A., 1951.

ADDRESSES: Home—404 East 14th St., New York, N.Y. 10009. *Agent*—Marlborough Gallery, Inc., 40 West 57th St., New York, N.Y. 10021.

CAREER: Saxophonist with jazz bands playing at Catskill resorts, 1940-42; saxophonist with the Shep Fields, Jerry Wald, and Johnny Morris jazz big bands, 1943-47; painter and sculptor, 1948—. One-man shows include those at Jane Street Gallery, New York City, 1949, Tibor de nagy Gallery, New York City, 1951-54 and 1956-62, Stable Gallery, New York City, 1954, Dwan Gallery, Los Angeles, Calif., 1961 and 1963, Martha Jackson Gallery, New York City, 1961, Galerie Rive Droit, Paris, France, 1962, Gimpel Fils Gallery, London, England, 1962, 1964, and 1976-77, Rose Art Museum, Brandeis University, Waltham, Mass., 1965, Pasadena Art Museum, Pasadena, Calif., 1965, Jewish Museum, New York City, 1965 and 1984, Detroit Institute of Arts, Detroit, Mich., 1965, Minneapolis Institute of Arts, Minneapolis, Minn., 1966, Art Institute of Chicago, Chicago, Ill., 1970, Marlborough Gallery, New York City, 1970, 1973-74, 1977, 1979, 1982, 1986, and 1988, Heath Gallery, Atlanta, Ga., 1971, Palais des Beaux-Arts, Brussels, Belgium, 1973, Olympia Galleries, Philadelphia, Pa., 1975, Bodley Gallery, New York City, 1977, Robert Miller Gallery, New York City, 1977, ACA Galleries, New York City, 1978, Museo de Arte Contemporaneo, Caracas, Venezuela, 1980, Kestner-Gesellschaft, Hanover, Germany, 1980, Staatliche Kunsthalle, Berlin, Germany, 1981, Kunstuerein, Munich, Germany, 1981, Galerie Biderman, Munich, 1981, Kunsthalle, Tuebingen, Germany, 1981, Hirshhorn Museum and Sculpture Garden, Washington, D.C., 1982, Elaine Horwich Gallery, Phoenix, Ariz., 1983, Guild Hall Museum, East Hampton, N.Y., 1983, and Lowe Art Museum, Coral Gables, Fla., 1983.

Work exhibited in group shows, including "Talent 1950," Kootz Gallery, New York City, 1950, Vanguard Gallery, Paris, France, 1953, "Annual Exhibition," Whitney Museum of American Art, New York City, 1954, 1958, 1960-61, 1963, and 1966, American Federation of Arts traveling exhibition, 1954-55, "Biennial Exhibition," Corcoran Gallery of Art, Washington, D.C., 1955, "U.S. Painting: Some Recent Directions," Stable Gallery, New York City, 1955, "Twelve Americans," Museum of Modern Art, New York City, 1956, "Fourth Biennial," Museum of Modern Art, Sao Paulo, Brazil, 1956, "Business Buys American Art," Whitney Museum of American Art, New York City, 1960, "Second Inter-American Paintings and Prints Biennial," Mexico City, Mexico, 1960, Seattle World's Fair, Seattle, Wash., 1962, Pennsylvania Academy of Fine Arts, Philadelphia, Pa., 1963, "Between the Fairs," Whitney Museum of American Art, New York City, 1964, "Painting and Sculpture of a Decade '54-'64," Tate Gallery, London, England, 1964, "Documenta III," Kassel, West Germany, 1964, "Art of the United States, 1670-1966," Whitney Museum of American Art, New York City, 1966, "First Flint Invitational," Flint Institute of Arts, Flint, Mich., 1966, John Herron Art Institute, Indianapolis, Ind., 1966, San Francisco Museum of Art, San Francisco, Calif., 1966, "Two Decades of American Painting," Museum of Modern Art, New York City, 1967, "Documenta IV," Kassel, Germany, 1968, and Art Institute of Chicago, Chicago, Ill., 1980, Minneapolis Institute of Arts, Minneapolis, Minn., 1980, La Jolla Museum of Art, La Jolla, Calif., 1980, Brooklyn Museum, Brooklyn, N.Y., 1980-81, Whitney Museum of American Art, New York City, 1981-82.

Work represented in permanent collections, including those at Brooklyn Museum, Brooklyn, N.Y., Whitney Museum of American Art, New York City, Museum of Modern Art, New York City, Metropolitan Museum of Art, New York City, Corcoran Gallery of Art, Washington, D.C., Rhode Island School of Design, Providence, R.I., North Carolina Museum of Art, Raleigh, N.C., Art Institute of Chicago, Chicago, Ill., Hirshhorn Museum and Sculpture Garden, Washington, D.C., and Tate Gallery, London, England.

Artist-in-residence at Slade School of Fine Art, London, England, 1964, and at Maryland Institute College of Art; taught at University of California at Santa Barbara, 1972. Designer of sets for musical and stage productions, including "Try! Try!" (1952), "The Slave" (1964), "The Toilet" (1964), and "Oedipus Rex" (1966). Tenor saxophonist with the Upper Bohemian Six jazz combo during the 1960s; tenor saxophonist and leader of seven-piece ensemble, the East 13th Street Band, 1979—.

Producer of films, including (with Pierre Gaisseau) "Africa and I," broadcast by the National Broadcasting Company, 1968, and "Tits," 1970. Actor in commercial and art films, including "Mounting Tension," 1950, "A Day in the Life of a Cleaning Woman," 1953, "Pull My Daisy," 1959, "Round Trip," 1967, and "Lovesick," 1982. Actor in stage productions, including "The Tinguely Machine; or, The Love Suicide of Kalucka." Contestant on Columbia Broadcasting System television quiz show "The $64,000 Question," 1957, won $32,000 for answering questions about contemporary art. *Military service:* U.S. Army Air Corps, 1942-43.

MEMBER: National Academy of Design.

AWARDS, HONORS: Biennial Exhibition Third Prize from Corcoran Gallery of Art, 1955, for painting "Self-Figure"; awards from arts festivals in Spoleto, Italy, and Newport, R.I.

WRITINGS:

(Illustrator) *Stones* (lithographic suite), Universal Limited Art Editions, 1959.

(Illustrator) Kenneth Koch, *When the Sun Tries to Go On* (poems), Black Sparrow Press, 1969.

(Illustrator) *The Donkey and the Darling,* Universal Limited Art Editions, 1977.

(With Carol Brightman) *Drawings and Digressions,* C. N. Potter, 1979.

Also author of "Kenneth Koch, A Tragedy," with Frank O'Hara, a play as yet neither published nor produced. Con-

tributor to periodicals, including the *New York Times Book Review, Artforum, Art News, Art in America, Horizons,* and *Seventeen.*

SIDELIGHTS: The iconoclastic painter, sculptor, and draftsman Larry Rivers defies classification. His work ranges stylistically from abstraction to hyper-realism, juxtaposes historical and personal themes, and appropriates imagery from a variety of sources ranging from Master paintings to cigarette packages. A ceaseless experimenter, Rivers occupies an important place in modern American art history as a transitional figure who combined the passion of the abstract expressionist movement of the 1950s with the realism, wit, and interest in commercial imagery that came to identify the Pop artists of the sixties. The few constants in Rivers's ever-evolving art are his masterly draftsmanship, innovative melding of abstract and figurative forms, and irrepressible drive to wrest the sublime from the banal.

Rivers began his career in the arts as a professional jazz saxophonist and only started painting and drawing when he was twenty-two years old. He quickly showed talent and, guided by painter friends he met through his music, began studying at the New York art school of famed abstractionist painter Hans Hofmann in 1947. Rivers experienced an artistic breakthrough the following year when he attended the Museum of Modern Art's retrospective of works by the great French post-impressionist Pierre Bonnard. He rapidly executed a series of paintings of domestic interiors in Bonnard's style, which were exhibited at his first one-man show at the Jane Street Gallery in 1949 and favorably reviewed by the influential critic Clement Greenberg for their command of color and exceptionally coherent composition. Rivers attracted further notice in 1950, when Greenberg and fellow critic Meyer Schapiro included him in the Kootz Gallery's "Talent 1950" show devoted to the work of promising young artists.

Rivers took up painting full time in 1950 and soon began associating with artists working in the abstract expressionist style, or what later became known as the New York School of the 1950s. At the Cedar Bar, a Greenwich Village watering hole for the artistic and literary avant-garde, he mingled with the "action painters" Willem de Kooning and Jackson Pollock and the poets John Ashbery and Frank O'Hara, the last of whom became his long-time artistic confidant and collaborator.

Although the abstract expressionists deeply influenced Rivers's style, he retained an interest in representation and never became part of the New York School. In 1953, he broke radically from the movement by painting "Washington Crosses the Delaware," a work that shocked and enraged the Cedar Bar crowd because of its historical references, appropriated imagery (from the nineteenth-century Emanuel Leutze work of the same title), and pictorial style. Rivers built a tension between these representational elements and the abstract qualities of his fragmented images, flattened space, and turbulent patches of pure paint in a manner that was to characterize his mature work. When the Museum of Modern Art bought the painting for its permanent collection in 1955, Rivers had arrived as a distinctive visionary on the New York art scene.

Rivers explored numerous other styles and media in the 1950s while exhibiting his work annually at the Tibor de nagy Gallery in Manhattan. Already highly regarded as a draftsman, he developed a pencil portrait style notable for its technical mastery of line and blurring use of erasure for expressionistic effect. The artist also devoted much of his painting to the human face and figure during this period, executing the 1955 "Double Portrait of Berdie" among other major works. A scrupulously exact nude study of Rivers's mother-in-law, the portrait roused considerable controversy in an art world still dominated by abstraction and helped inspire new interest in figurative realism. Rivers also sculpted in plaster/cement and welded steel during the 1950s and worked with Frank O'Hara on the *Stones* series of verse lithographs that *New York Times Book Review* critic Peter Schjeldahl termed "probably the most sparkling poet-painter collaboration ever."

In the early 1960s, Rivers anticipated the Pop Art movement by introducing commercial images from cigarette packages, French money, and playing cards into his work. One of the artist's favorite subjects during this period was the Dutch Masters cigar box, which featured a reproduction of a Rembrandt painting and earned Rivers the facetious title of the "Old Master of Dutch Masters cigars." Although he had subject matter and wit in common with the Pop artists of the later sixties, Rivers's aesthetic sensibility differed profoundly from such painters as Roy Lichtenstein and Andy Warhol, and he was never considered part of the Pop movement. Where Pop artists took a mockingly deadpan approach to commercial imagery and emphasized formal relationships, Rivers transformed these visual cliches with expressionist variations, often blurring lines or subverting space with overlays of transparent color. He seemed driven to probe the mysterious underside, or metaphysical essence, of every commonplace thing, often to comic effect.

This sensibility was also evident in the "Vocabulary Lesson" paintings Rivers started in 1962. These works featured an expressionistically painted nude figure of a woman with various parts of her body labeled by stenciled words and arrows. The artist appeared to be exploring the uses and limits of language in defining objective reality, a concern later shared by the Conceptual Art movement. Rivers's growing reputation as an intellectual maverick and stylistic innovator during these years earned him exhibition space at New York's prestigious Marlborough Gallery, and in 1965 the Jewish Museum mounted the first major retrospective of his work. The museum show featured the artist's monumental construction "A History of the Russian Revolution: From Marx to Mayakovsky," which was inspired by Rivers's reading of the Isaac Deutscher biography of Leon Trotsky. Rivers dubbed the thirty-three-foot-long work—which includes thirty individual paintings on canvas, a poem, and an actual machine gun, among other components—"the greatest painting-sculpture-mixed media of the twentieth century, or the stupidest."

Rivers continued to restlessly explore new modes of artistic expression from the late 1960s to the early eighties. Among other projects, he created sets for a New York staging of works by the playwright LeRoi Jones and the sets and costumes for a Metropolitan Opera production of Igor Stravinsky's oratorio "Oedipus Rex." Rivers also made a television film on Africa that was aired by the National Broadcasting Company in 1968, worked in videotape, illustrated books, and experimented with both modern airbrush technology and traditional Japanese pictorial techniques in his painting. In addition, the artist accepted numerous commissions for historical works during this period, the most ambitious of which was his multi-paneled "History of Matzoh (The Story of the Jewish People)," executed from 1982 to 1985. The massive work, shown at the Jewish Museum in 1985, depicted the joys and agonies of three thousand years of cultural history with detailed drawings emerging from an abstract background that resembled matzo, unleavened bread.

In recent years Rivers has turned to montage and relief in such mixed-media works as "Public and Private," exhibited at the Marlborough Gallery in October, 1986. His new technique consists in mounting cut-outs of painted canvas on foamboard carved to give it relief. Thematically, Rivers has continued to show an interest in the personalization of public imagery, or the interplay between individual and social consciousness.

"Public and Private," for example, juxtaposes such potent cultural and political symbols as Fred Astaire, Malcolm X, Fidel Castro, and a 1957 Chevy with painted snapshots of his mother-in-law and his house in Southampton. The images overlap and emerge from one another with a fluid spontaneity that suggests stream of consciousness. In other recent works, such as his 1985 "Duck Farm Relief," based on a well-known photograph by Roman Vishniac, Rivers directly appropriates his images from other artists. He explained to Ruth Bass in an October, 1986, *Art News* article that he is "not very good at making up things," and feels no compunction about taking good images where he can find them. "It's as if an orange starts to complain to me that I copied him without the orange's permission," Rivers remarked of critics who accuse him of stealing. "In other words, most of the world, I feel, is for one's taking. I don't have that much regard or respect for anything, myself included."

Rivers discusses his art and times with "incredible candor" in his book *Drawings and Digressions,* according to *New York Times Book Review* critic Peter Schjeldahl. The volume contains more than three hundred reproductions of Rivers's drawings annotated with the artist's remarks about his subjects, drawing technique, and philosophy of life and art. The drawings include many portraits of Rivers's family, friends, and acquaintances from New York's literary and artistic avant-garde, yielding a text Schjeldahl judged "as revealing and entertaining as any in the literature of artists talking. It is a document, full of slightly scandalous anecdote, that tells of survival in the New York art world—and at its maddest edges, where artistic and personal ambition, esthetics and career tactics, art and life mingle in a social milieu that is a hall of distorting mirrors." Reproductions of Rivers's work are also found in a 1970 monograph by Sam Hunter and in Helen A. Harrison's 1984 biographical and critical study, both of which bear the title *Larry Rivers.*

BIOGRAPHICAL/CRITICAL SOURCES:

BOOKS

Harrison, Helen A., *Larry Rivers,* Harper, 1984.
Hunter, Sam, *Larry Rivers,* Abrams, 1970, revised edition, 1971.
Nordness, Lee, editor, *Art USA Now,* Viking, 1963.
Rivers, Larry and Carol Brightman, *Drawings and Digressions,* C. N. Potter, 1979.
Rosenberg, Harold, *The Anxious Object: Art Today and Its Audience,* Horizon Press, 1964, University of Chicago Press, 1982.

PERIODICALS

Art in America, December, 1983, May, 1985, September, 1985.
Art News, November, 1977, May, 1983, October, 1986.
Arts, November, 1979.
Artsmagazine, February, 1971.
Inter/View, October, 1972.
Life, October, 1958.
New York Times, October 24, 1986.
New York Times Book Review, November 11, 1979.
New York Times Magazine, February 13, 1966.
Saturday Review, September 3, 1955.
Sports Illustrated, December 23, 1985.
Time, February 8, 1971.

—*Sketch by Curtis Skinner*

* * *

RIZZO, Mario 1948-

PERSONAL: Born July 6, 1948, in New York, N.Y. *Education:* Fordham University, A.B., 1970; University of Chicago, M.A., 1973, Ph.D., 1977.

ADDRESSES: *Office*—Department of Economics, New York University, Washington Sq., New York, N.Y. 10003.

CAREER: New York University, New York, N.Y., professor of economics, 1978—. Adjunct scholar at Cato Institute.

MEMBER: Phi Beta Kappa.

WRITINGS:

(With Gerald O'Driscoll) *The Economics of Time and Ignorance,* Basil Blackwell, 1983.

WORK IN PROGRESS: Economic Analysis of Law; Theories of Probabilistic Causation; Methodological Problems of Economics.

BIOGRAPHICAL/CRITICAL SOURCES:

PERIODICALS

Times Literary Supplement, October 11, 1985.

* * *

ROBERTSON, John (Charles) 1951-

PERSONAL: Born September 28, 1951, in Dundee, Scotland; son of Lewis F. and Elspeth (Badenoch) Robertson; married Maxine L. Berg (a historian), September 24, 1977; children: Frances, Gabriel (daughters). *Education:* Wadham College, Oxford, M.A., 1972; Christ Church, Oxford, D.Phil., 1981.

ADDRESSES: *Home*—34 Southmoor Rd., Oxford OX2 6RD, England.

CAREER: Oxford University, Oxford, England, research lecturer at Christ Church, 1975-80, fellow and tutor at St. Hugh's College and lecturer in modern history, 1980—.

MEMBER: Royal Historical Society (fellow), Scottish History Society.

WRITINGS:

(Contributor) Istvan Hont and Michael Ignatieff, editors, *Wealth and Virtue: Political Economy in the Scottish Enlightenment,* Cambridge University Press, 1983.
The Scottish Enlightenment and the Militia Issue, John Donald, 1985.

WORK IN PROGRESS: Research on the Scottish and Neapolitan enlightenments; research on universal monarchy.

SIDELIGHTS: The Scottish Enlightenment and the Militia Issue was welcomed by critics such as Bruce Lenman of the *Times Literary Supplement,* who opined, "John Robertson is to be congratulated on finding a topic which is both fresh and important." The English Standing Army Controversy of the years 1697 to 1698 aired sharply contrasting views regarding

whether a country should be defended by an army of mercenary professional soldiers or by a militia raised from its free adult male population. In his contribution to the debate, Scottish patriot Andre Fletcher asked why Scotland, which did not unite with England until 1707, was not entitled to a militia of its own. Robertson's study examines the positions of Scots from Fletcher to the leading figures of the Scottish Enlightenment, David Hume, Adam Ferguson, and Adam Smith. Asserted Lenman, "Robertson's book will be the standard work on its theme for a long time."

Robertson told *CA:* "On one side were Ferguson and his friends among the moderate clerical literati, who emphasized the value of campaigning for a national militia as an expression of national spirit. On the other were Hume and Smith, who followed Fletcher in giving more emphasis to the likely institutional effects of a militia. Drawing out the implications of Hume's and Smith's arguments, I concluded that the supporters of a militia treated the issue as an opportunity to assert their national identity without having to take institutional responsibility within Scotland—a pattern of noisy irresponsibility that has often been seen since in Scottish politics.

"My current research on Scotland and Naples is intended to show how smaller, 'provincial' nations could become major cultural and intellectual centers. It reflects a conviction that decentralization and pluralism are essential to political and intellectual vitality."

BIOGRAPHICAL/CRITICAL SOURCES:

PERIODICALS

Times Higher Education Supplement, April 26, 1985.
Times Literary Supplement, April 5, 1985.

* * *

ROBESON, Paul (Leroy Bustill) 1898-1976

PERSONAL: Surname is pronounced "*Robe*-son"; born April 9, 1898, in Princeton, N.J.; died after suffering a stroke, January 23, 1976, in Philadelphia, Pa.; son of William Drew (a clergyman) and Maria Louisa (a schoolteacher; maiden name, Bustill) Robeson; married Eslanda Cardozo Goode, August 17, 1921 (died, December, 1965); children: Paul Jr. *Education:* Rutgers College (now University), A.B., 1919; Columbia University, LL.B., 1923.

CAREER: Admitted to the Bar of New York; employed in a law firm, 1923; actor in plays, including "Simon the Cyrenian," 1921, "All God's Chillun Got Wings," 1924, "Othello," 1930 and 1943, and "Toussaint L'Ouverture," 1936; actor in films, including "Body and Soul," 1924, "The Emperor Jones," 1933, "Sanders of the River," 1935, and "Show Boat," 1936; singer in concert performances, for recordings, and in musical productions, including "Show Boat," 1928.

MEMBER: National Maritime Union (honorary member), Council on African Affairs (co-founder), Joint Anti-Fascist Refugee Committee, Committee to Aid China, Phi Beta Kappa, Alpha Phi Alpha, Sigma Tau Delta.

AWARDS, HONORS: Badge of Veterans of Abraham Lincoln Brigade, 1939; Donaldson Award for outstanding lead performance, 1944, for "Othello"; medal from American Academy of Arts and Letters, 1944, for good diction on the stage; Spingarn Medal from National Association for the Advancement of Colored People, 1944; Champion of African Freedom Award from National Church of Nigeria, 1950; Afro-American Newspapers Award, 1950; Stalin Peace Prize from U.S.S.R., 1952; German Peace Medal from East Germany, 1960; Ira Aldridge Award from Association for the Study of Afro-American Life and History, 1970; Civil Liberties Award from American Civil Liberties Union, 1970; Duke Ellington Medal from Yale University, 1972; Whitney M. Young, Jr., National Memorial Award from Urban League of Greater New York, 1972. Honorary degrees from Rutgers University, 1932 and 1973, Hamilton College, 1940, Morehouse College, 1943, Howard University, 1945, Moscow State Conservatory, 1959, and Humboldt University, 1960.

WRITINGS:

Here I Stand (autobiography), Othello Associates (New York), 1958.

COLLECTIONS

(Contributor) *Paul Robeson: The Great Forerunner,* Freedomways, 1971, new edition, Dodd, 1978, enlarged, 1985.

Paul Robeson: Tributes, Selected Writings, compiled and edited by Roberta Yancy Dent with the assistance of Marilyn Robeson and Paul Robeson, Jr., The Archives (New York), 1976.

Paul Robeson Speaks: Writings, Speeches, Interviews, 1918-1974, edited with an introduction by Philip S. Foner, Brunner, 1978.

Columnist for *People's Voice* during 1940s; editor and columnist for *Freedom,* c. 1951-55. Contributor to periodicals, including *African Observer, Afro-American, American Dialog, American Scholar, Daily Worker, Freedomways, Jewish Life, Masses and Mainstream, Messenger, National Guardian, New Statesman and Nation, New World Review, New York Age, Opportunity, Spectator,* and *Worker.*

SIDELIGHTS: Paul Robeson was one of America's most prominent black performers before his career was destroyed as a result of his controversial political positions, which ranged from promotion of racial equality to admiration for the Soviet Union. Though he became famous for his singing and acting, Robeson displayed a remarkable range of talents from an early age. As the third black student to attend Rutgers College, he distinguished himself academically and athletically, becoming a member of the Phi Beta Kappa honor society and an all-American football player. Robeson subsequently earned a law degree from Columbia University but soon became dissatisfied with the opportunities available to blacks in the legal profession. He turned to the theater and, although he had never intended to become a professional actor, appeared successfully in productions in New York City and London. In 1924 he joined the Provincetown Players, which was associated with playwright Eugene O'Neill, and attracted widespread critical attention with lead roles in two O'Neill plays—"The Emperor Jones" and "All God's Chillun Got Wings," a groundbreaking, controversial work about interracial marriage.

By the 1930s Robeson was a prosperous actor and singer of international stature. His stage credits included the title role in William Shakespeare's tragedy "Othello" and Joe in the musical "Show Boat," for which he sang the highly popular melody "Ol' Man River." Acclaimed for his singing voice, Robeson made numerous recordings and gave concerts in America and Europe that ranged from black spirituals to opera. He also appeared in several feature films, including adaptations of "The Emperor Jones" and "Show Boat."

As Robeson visited Europe to give performances, he increasingly identified with its political left. In England he was ex-

posed to socialism by playwright George Bernard Shaw and adherents of the country's Labour party. He met African nationalists Jomo Kenyatta and Kwame Nkrumah, and eventually co-founded the anticolonial Council on African Affairs. Robeson was deeply affected during a trip in 1934 when he was harassed by racist officials in Nazi Germany but was welcomed in the Communist Soviet Union. He became convinced that the Soviet Union, thanks to its political system, had conquered racism.

Robeson soon made his political concerns a part of his performing career. He lent his talents to a variety of political causes, singing to raise money for Jewish refugees from the Nazis and entertaining antifascist troops during the Spanish Civil War. Disillusioned with the limited roles available to blacks in film, Robeson announced in 1939 that he would curtail his movie acting. As Loften Mitchell later quoted him in the *New York Times:* "The industry was not prepared to permit me to portray the life or express the living interests, hopes and aspirations of the struggling people from whom I come. You bet they will never let me play a part in a film in which a Negro is on top."

During the 1930s and early 1940s, Robeson's political outspokenness was no impediment to his popularity. In 1943, for instance, he was received enthusiastically by theater audiences when he became the first black actor to play Othello on Broadway with a white supporting cast. The production's long run set a Broadway record for a Shakespeare play, and Robeson garnered a Donaldson Award for outstanding lead performance and a photo story in *Life* magazine. As Roger M. Williams observed in *American Heritage,* Robeson "was . . . being hailed as America's leading Negro."

But Robeson's fortunes changed with the end of World War II, when the wartime alliance of the United States and the Soviet Union deteriorated into mistrust and hostility. Many feared a war between the two former allies, and a resurgent political right wing in America often equated the advocacy of liberal or left-wing causes with disloyalty to the United States. Robeson continued to openly espouse the concerns of the political left, announcing in 1947 that he would take a two-year break from performing in order to fight racism in America and campaigning the next year for Progressive presidential candidate Henry Wallace. In a controversial 1949 speech at the World Peace Congress in Paris, quoted by Williams, Robeson said that it was "unthinkable that American Negroes could go to war on behalf of those who have oppressed us for generations against the Soviet Union, which in one generation has raised our people to full human dignity." Right-wing hostility to Robeson erupted into violence later that year when the singer gave two concerts in Peekskill, New York, and political opponents harassed and assaulted the audience.

In the next few years Robeson's career disintegrated. He found few opportunities to perform, saw his income plummet, and lost access to his European audience when the U.S. Government barred him from traveling abroad because he would not sign an anti-communist loyalty oath. During this period of ostracism Robeson wrote his autobiography, *Here I Stand,* which is not only an account of his life but a discussion of his political views and how they developed. He offers a social and political agenda for black people, urging them to become aware of their African heritage and contending that the civil rights struggle should be a mass movement of the black community, independent of white leadership. In the *New York Times Book Review* Sterling Stuckey wrote that *Here I Stand* "appears to be addressed primarily to ordinary black people and only secondarily to intellectuals. It is as though, while taking it up, one is listening more than reading, hearing Robeson's own words as his personality, unaffected, generous, full of humanity, comes forth from the pages."

In 1958, the year *Here I Stand* was published, Robeson was once again allowed to go abroad—on a related case the Supreme Court agreed with Robeson's contention that Americans cannot be denied the right to travel because of their political views. He soon became ill, however, and spent the rest of his life in virtual seclusion in the United States, an obscure figure to many younger Americans. In the 1970s Robeson repeatedly failed to attend the tributes organized in his honor, including a celebration of his seventy-fifth birthday at New York City's Carnegie Hall that included such prominent guests as Coretta Scott King, widow of slain civil rights leader Martin Luther King, Jr. As reported by Laurie Johnston in the *New York Times,* Mrs. King told the gathering that Robeson "had been 'buried alive' because, earlier than her husband, he had 'tapped the same wells of latent militancy' among blacks." Robeson died in 1976, a few weeks after suffering a stroke.

BIOGRAPHICAL/CRITICAL SOURCES:

BOOKS

Davis, Lenwood G., *A Paul Robeson Research Guide: A Selected, Annotated Bibliography,* Greenwood Press, 1982.

Editors of *Freedomways, Paul Robeson: The Great Forerunner,* enlarged edition, Dodd, 1985.

Gilliam, Dorothy Butler, *Paul Robeson: All-American,* New Republic Books, 1976.

Hoyt, Edwin P., *Paul Robeson: The American Othello,* World Publishing, 1967.

Robeson, Susan, *The Whole World in His Hands: A Pictorial Biography of Paul Robeson,* Citadel, 1981.

PERIODICALS

American Heritage, April, 1976.
Black World, July, 1972.
Life, November 22, 1943.
New York Times, August 6, 1972, April 16, 1973.
New York Times Book Review, October 21, 1973.
Times Literary Supplement, September 5, 1958.
West Coast Review of Books, January, 1979.

OBITUARIES:

PERIODICALS

Nation, February 7, 1976.
Newsweek, February 2, 1976.
New York Times, January 24, 1976.
Time, February 2, 1976.*

—*Sketch by Thomas Kozikowski*

* * *

ROBILLIARD, St. John Anthony 1953-

PERSONAL: Born September 17, 1953, in Guernsey, Channel Islands, England; son of Lemuel John (a fruit grower) and Eileen Dorothy (a writer and musician; maiden name, Connors) Robilliard. *Education:* Emmanuel College, Cambridge, M.A., 1975, LL.B., 1976; L'Universite de Caen, Certificat d'Etudes Juridiques Francaises et Normands, 1987.

ADDRESSES: Home—Le Foulon, St. Peter Port, Guernsey, Channel Islands, England. *Office*—Nigel Harris & Partners, Oak Walk, St. Peter, Jersey, Channel Islands, England.

CAREER: Victoria University of Manchester, Manchester, England, lecturer in law, 1976-87; Nigel Harris & Partners (law firm), Jersey, Channel Islands, England, lawyer, 1987—.

MEMBER: Society of Public Teachers of Law, Old Elizabethans Association, Guernsey Yacht Club, Cambridge University Liberal Club.

WRITINGS:

Jersey's Housing Control Law, Nuffield Foundation and British Academy, 1984.
Religion and the Law: Religious Liberty in Modern English Law, Manchester University Press, 1984.
Guernsey's Housing Control Law, Nuffield Foundation, 1985.
(With Jenny McEwan) *Police Powers and the Individual,* Basil Blackwell, 1986.
(Contributor) *Constitutions of Dependencies and Special Sovereignties,* Oceana, 1986.

Contributor to law journals and religious magazines.

WORK IN PROGRESS: Politics and the Law.

SIDELIGHTS: St. John Anthony Robilliard told *CA:* "I am a civil libertarian of the old school. My objective is the production of public law for an informed readership, wider than mere lawyers and academics. As a follower of John Stuart Mill, I take a restrictive view of laws that attempt to 'make people good' and that favor particular groups for whatever motive. English law has failed to get fully to grips with many of the real issues of religious liberty, while the United Kingdom law on race relations contains long-term seeds of unfairness for certain sections of the community."

BIOGRAPHICAL/CRITICAL SOURCES:

PERIODICALS

Times Literary Supplement, July 13, 1984.

* * *

ROBINSON, Max (C.) 1939-

PERSONAL: Born May 1, 1939, in Richmond, Va.; son of Maxie Cleveland and Doris (Jones) Robinson; married Beverly Hamilton; children: Mark, Maureen, Michael, Malik. *Education:* Attended Oberlin College, 1957-58, and Indiana University, 1959-60.

ADDRESSES: Home—Chicago, Ill.

CAREER/WRITINGS: WTOV-TV, Norfolk, Va., news announcer, 1959; WTOP-TV, Washington, D.C., correspondent and cameraman, 1965, anchorman, 1969-78; WRC-TV, Washington, correspondent, 1965-69; American Broadcasting Co., New York, N.Y., anchorman of "ABC World News Tonight" in Chicago, Ill., 1978-83; associated with WMAQ-TV in Chicago, beginning in 1983. Associate professor of communicative arts at Federal City College, 1968-72; journalist in residence at College of William and Mary, 1981. *Military service:* U.S. Air Force, 1959-60.

AWARDS, HONORS: Journalist of the Year award from Capital Press Club, 1967; award from National Education Association, 1966; Regional Emmy awards from National Academy of Television Arts and Sciences, both 1967, both for documentary "The Other Washington"; award from Ohio State University, 1967; awarded Star of Africa by the president of Liberia, 1972; outstanding news reporting award from the District of Columbia Chamber of Commerce, 1978; communication and leadership awards from Toastmasters International, 1978, Chicago State University, 1979, and Congress of National Black Churches, 1979; named honorary citizen of Indianapolis, Ind., 1978, Houston, Tex., 1978, Cincinnati, Ohio, 1979, Atlanta, Ga., 1979, and Gary, Ind., 1979; Max Robinson Day decreed in Washington, D.C., 1978, Richmond, Va., 1978, and Atlanta, Ga., 1981; LL.D. from North Carolina Agricultural and Technical State University, 1979; National Media Award from Capital Press Club, 1979; Litt.D. from Atlanta University, 1980, and Virginia University, 1981; National Emmy Award, 1981, for 1980 election coverage; honorary degree in public service from Voorhees College, 1981; D.Litt. from Virginia State University, 1981; Excellence in Journalism award from College of William and Mary, 1981; Drum Major for Justice Award from Martin Luther King, Jr., Memorial, 1981; recognition awards from National Association of Black Journalists, National Association of Media Women, and Detroit, Michigan, City Council, all 1981.

MEMBER: Society of Collegiate Journalists (honorary), Sigma Delta Chi.

WORK IN PROGRESS: An autobiographical work.

SIDELIGHTS: In 1979 *Ebony* described award-winning black television journalist Max Robinson as a "booming baritone" with an "extraordinary ability to understand people, [and] to analyze the news." The plaudits were in response to Robinson's work as one of four anchors of "ABC World News Tonight," which he joined in 1978 to become the first black to anchor a prime-time national network news program.

Robinson took up a career in broadcast journalism around 1959—a time when few, if any, blacks held positions in the field. He began as a voice-over news announcer for WTOV-TV in Norfolk, Virginia, and soon after he went to Washington, D.C., where he worked for stations WRC-TV and WTOP-TV. He had been anchoring the latter's "Eyewitness News" since 1969 when ABC selected him as anchorman of their national news desk in Chicago, Illinois. Together with "ABC World News Tonight" desk anchors Frank Reynolds in Washington, Peter Jennings in London, and Barbara Walters in New York City, Robinson is credited with helping to bring the evening news program's ratings to parity with those of the other major networks. Following Reynolds's death in 1983 Robinson left ABC and joined Chicago station WMAQ-TV.

CA INTERVIEW

CA interviewed Max Robinson by telephone at his apartment in Chicago, Illinois, August 21, 1986.

CA: Did you lose your first job in broadcast news because you refused to hide the fact that you were black?

ROBINSON: That was at WTOV in Norfolk, Virginia, around 1959. I was staying a short time with an aunt, and I saw this job listed in the paper under "Help Wanted—Male." They had two listings in the paper in those days: "Help Wanted—Male" and "Help Wanted—Male—C," which meant "colored." But the way I was raised was to go for what I wanted and never to assume that I couldn't get it. So I applied for the job, pretty much knowing that it was for whites.

I went in for the audition and the owner courteously auditioned me. They called back five finalists and I was one of them. They gave me a job two nights a week working as sort of a manager/announcer and doing news. I would do the news as a voice-over. A slide that read "News" was what you'd see on your TV set.

One day I decided—I had relatives in the area—that I'd do it like they did in the big time and let people see me when I did the news. I had them take down the slide, since I was in charge of the station when I was on. Apparently they got a bunch of phone calls from people who weren't ready for color television. The owner just couldn't deal with the pressure. He was very apologetic and felt terrible about it. That was the end of my TV career for that period of time.

CA: Did the other people who delivered the news on the other nights do it in back of a slide too?

ROBINSON: Yes.

CA: So it was the same treatment for everybody, right?

ROBINSON: Right. I'm fond of saying that my vanity got me.

CA: What was the next step in your broadcast career?

ROBINSON: I went to Washington, D.C., around February, 1965, and applied for what they called a training program at WTOP-Channel 5. I waited for a couple of months, which I spent working as a furniture salesman, and then was offered a job at WTOP as a floor director/trainee and took it, at $50 a week.

A month or so later, the news director supposedly wandered through the studio—actually, he was looking for me because he had heard about me—and just casually chatted with me for a while about my interests. I had been interested in news all the while, but the only job I could get was the one I had. He suggested I drop up some time to talk to him. And I dropped up the next day, deciding not to be coy. He talked with me about another trainee job. At that time WTOP found it convenient to have a lot of jobs listed as trainee jobs so that they could pay you less, but it was fine with me because I got a chance to do the work. So I became a cameraman/reporter/trainee. They reduced the salary for that job to $50 a week. It was the same salary I was making in my other job, but they were paying the other cameramen/reporters $75 a week. Nevertheless, it was an opportunity and I didn't quibble.

After I had worked as a cameraman/reporter for a while, they promoted me to full-time reporter. But they had me doing traffic reports, which was not satisfactory at all. Around that time, the people at WRC-TV, also in Washington, came looking for me. I went over there and did an audition and they hired me, after I'd been at WTOP less than a year.

CA: Things were rough for you at WRC, weren't they?

ROBINSON: They were very difficult, probably because I was their first [black]. And all of us who are first have to take the blows at the beginning. I can remember walking down the halls and speaking to people who would look right through me. It was hateful at times . . . I've been the first too often, quite frankly. We firsts ought to get extra pay.

CA: How did that sort of racism affect your career at WRC?

ROBINSON: The news director there admitted that I had the talent for being an anchor, but he said that Washington wasn't ready for a black anchor. I told him I thought that was his opinion, not Washington's. And I left, after three and one-half years, with less than good feelings. And when I went to talk to the people at TOP—I understood that they wanted to talk to me—one of my stipulations was that I wanted an opportunity to anchor, because I thought I was good at it. So WTOP gave me the opportunity I was denied at WRC. And within two years, I was the Number One anchor in Washington.

CA: So I guess you were right about the kind of anchor Washington wanted.

ROBINSON: Not only Washington but the country generally. The people are a lot more ready for many things than some of the people who call themselves leaders give them credit for.

CA: Was WTOP where you and Gordon Peterson were co-anchors?

ROBINSON: Right.

CA: Did you two get along well?

ROBINSON: Very.

CA: Any problems, not with personalities, but with co-anchoring? I imagine coordination might be a problem, for instance.

ROBINSON: We worked extremely well together and I think Gordon would say the same thing. I've had other partners, but I've never had one better than Gordon.

CA: Is it true that, at that time anyway, WTOP's executives didn't want to stake everything on a black anchor such as yourself, but wanted to hedge their bets by teaming you with a white anchor such as Peterson?

ROBINSON: I think the problems of race in America are reflected in television, although I must point out that I did work as a solo anchor for two years at WTOP on the eleven o'clock show after I had teamed with Gordon.

CA: You left WTOP to move to Chicago to work for ABC there. Chicago is known for giving out-of-town news personalities a rough time. Did they make it rough on you?

ROBINSON: Yeah. It was almost like, "What are you doing coming to our town?" Especially the anchorpeople in town. One, Bill Kurtis, was quoted as saying, "I don't know how well he will relate in the wheat fields of Kansas," and I never figured out what that meant. Another anchor said, "When you come to Chicago, be humble." Really dumb things, thinly veiled racist statements. As much as I could I just ignored them. I know the citizenry of Chicago accepted me. Chicago's a bit more insular than a lot of other places, but once they accept you, they accept you.

CA: Aside from that insularity you experienced, what other differences did you notice between working in D.C. and working in Chicago?

ROBINSON: Well, quite frankly, I think I always did and still do consider D.C. my home. I got my start there and there was

always a kind of support there I couldn't expect anywhere else. It was more than just Max Robinson the television journalist and the viewers. It was almost like family. I'd get into cabs in Washington and the drivers would adamantly refuse to take any money. They didn't do that in Chicago.

CA: You were part of ABC's national anchor system in Chicago, weren't you?

ROBINSON: Yes. They called it several things. At one point it was even called a floating anchor, which is a contradiction in terms. But what they did in effect was, instead of having a dual national anchor or a single national anchor, they went to three. I think they did it because whereas at the local level you can have one black and one white, they decided at the network level to have at least two white people with the one black. I really believe that.

CA: What did you think of the system aside from that aspect of it?

ROBINSON: Even though at times I had questions about the rationale for it, I think it worked amazingly well. It freed me up to do a lot of traveling, and coming out of, various places in the country when the news dictated it. Also, I think our show was paced better than the other two evening news shows and I think our ratings reflected that. ABC had never been competitive in ratings terms before this program, but our show was competitive.

CA: At that time you were heading the domestic desk, you worked as a correspondent, and you were one of three anchors.

ROBINSON: Yes, but the jobs were really very compatible. I worked terribly hard, but that's generally true in network. I traveled a lot. The most challenging thing about my role at ABC during those days was that I was on the road at least twice a week. And every day, I was anchoring. Some days, when the viewers would see me coming out of Chicago the whole week, I'd often do out-of-town stories between shows, flying back to Chicago just in time to anchor. Or I'd anchor the show from wherever the event happened to be.

CA: ABC News and Sports President Roone Arledge was said to have proposed at that time that of the three anchors in the ABC system—Frank Reynolds, Peter Jennings, and you—Reynolds be made the first among equals. Did that ever happen? What was your reaction?

ROBINSON: The expression was used, as I remember, after the meetings. But what they wanted was a focus. They felt that with Frank, Peter, Max, and no one being the focal point, it created a problem. That was their judgment. What was my reaction? I accepted it. But I'm as competitive as the next person.

CA: You made a speech at Smith College in which you talked about being excluded from the coverage of the Iranian hostage homecoming and of Reagan's inauguration. What did you blame that exclusion on?

ROBINSON: The fact is, that except for Royal Kennedy, there were no blacks on the air at those times. They came behind what I said about that and said that's not true, Hal Walker was. But Hal Walker was on the air *after* I complained at Smith College, which was after the inauguration. I also complained about the treatment of Ulrich Hayes, who was the U.S. ambassador to Algeria, and who happened to be black. He was one of the key people involved in gaining the release of the hostages. When they were released, they came through a reception line and he was shown greeting them, with his wife, but he was never identified. I complained about that publicly. I also complained to the people at ABC. And their response was, "Well, you can't know everything."

Well, I've noticed how we become invisible at times to certain reporters, and it's always been galling to us. So it was a matter of my talking to the students at Smith College about things I felt we had to address, to resolve, and to confront. It was not an angry speech. It was a speech that said, "Let's face up to the problems we have." As part of the speech, I talked about the problems of racism at the networks, including mine, but the speech covered America. It was not focused, except for a very small passage, on network news. The speech started, in fact, with Smith College and some of the problems I had found on that campus as represented to me by black students when I got there.

CA: Why were black reporters excluded from the hostage homecoming and the inauguration coverage?

ROBINSON: I think there were some emotional things happening in our country at that time. I think first of all there was relief when the hostages were released. But it was relief mixed with a kind of embarrassment that this powerful country had been treated in that fashion. With Ronald Reagan coming into office, the country was obviously swinging toward the right. There were quite a few powerful emotions going, and I think that psychologically this was triggering some reactions in newsrooms across the country.

We've seen it happen before. If black reporters did not have to worry about eating every day, you'd find out a lot of things that have happened that all of us compare notes on. It's too consistent to be by accident. I remember when two black prisoners took over a cell block in Washington and held quite a few whites hostages. We, the black broadcast journalists, noticed that assignments involving coverage of this didn't come our way. Why were they excluding us? Because this story had a kind of emotional weight where people at that particular time felt uneasy at dealing with us.

At WTOP I managed to raise this issue to the point of talking about this. And especially with Jim Snyder, the news director there. Even though in the early days we had our battles, we came to respect each other because we were finally able to communicate. Sometimes, initially, it was hostile, but it was honest. That's among the reasons why WTOP was the best place I ever worked, because we had an understanding: I wasn't trying to save my job by not saying some things that were hurtful to me. And not just me. I'm a believer that that's the only way to get out of this mess we've been in: honest communication. Sometimes it will not be pleasant for the other person, but at least by having it out there we can deal with it.

CA: Do you think TV now treats black anchors and reporters fairly?

ROBINSON: Well, I certainly think things have improved, because I remember when I came into this business, Hal Walker and I are fond of saying, we could have had a meeting of all the blacks in television news in a phone booth, because Hal and I could get in a phone booth, so obviously things have

improved in many ways. A lot of improvement is still required, let me hasten to add.

But I'm disappointed in TV coverage in general, not just the stories that deal with black people. In general, I think television news has not improved. Technically, it's better: we can take minicams out on the street. But in terms of the kinds of things we cover, I'm very disappointed in what I see. I think the race for ratings has taken over the business and that's very sad.

CA: What would you like to see covered that isn't covered now?

ROBINSON: First of all, we could be asking, are we covering the community or are we just covering things we think will titillate people? Yellow journalism is just rampant on TV, all for the sake of ratings. I think they'd do *anything* for the sake of ratings. I have very little respect for some of the people in this business, and that has not always been true. I don't know what the answer is. Obviously, ratings are the best thing we can figure out at this time, but I'm not exactly pleased with companies like Magid having the kind of influence they have on newsrooms in America. Magid Associates is a market research firm specializing in advising TV stations on improving the appeal of their newscasts. The firm usually recommends short news items delivered in among banter between the newspeople. I shudder when I realize the kind of impact they have.

CA: Do you think public television does a better job of reporting the news than commercial television does?

ROBINSON: Yes. I think the MacNeil-Lehrer show is a better show than network television news shows. But I think it's a different kind of show. I don't think you could take the network shows and have all of them do what MacNeil-Lehrer does. I think CNN [Cable News Network] is also making a stab, but I think they could use their time more wisely rather than rehashing and rehashing. I think we need to be more reflective. I think all of us in this business need to take time out to sit down and really seriously question how we are doing what we do, make assessments on how well we are doing it and how better we can do it, not with a view toward ratings but with a view toward truly serving the American people. We rarely do that. In the twenty-one years I was active in the business, I think I can remember maybe two or three times we sat down and talked about what we do. That's sad. And I think that's one of the fundamental problems.

To be fair, though, I think television news is a very difficult business. And I admire a lot of us in the business, particularly reporters and producers, who work very hard and have a lot of things to do and deadlines to meet. It's hard to be everything. I admire what we do in the business. At ABC you don't know how often we went down to the wire. We played on the edge constantly. And it was amazing that we could get the show on the air the way we did. So as critical as I may be at times, I'm also aware of the wonderful things that are done in television, particularly network television.

CA: Do you think the country would have been better off if TV had never been invented?

ROBINSON: No. I think that on balance it's a blessing. But it's a blessing we haven't utilized nearly well enough.

CA: What did you win your Emmy and National Education Association (NEA) award for?

ROBINSON: I won two regional Emmys and one national Emmy. The two regional Emmys were for "The Other Washington," a documentary I did on Anacostia, a kind of forgotten area of Washington, D.C. The National Emmy was for election coverage in 1980. The NEA award was a long time ago. It may have been just generally for the work I was doing in Washington.

CA: Why did you leave ABC?

ROBINSON: Well, when Frank [Reynolds] died, they took the opportunity to install Peter [Jennings] as the solo anchor. It didn't leave me very much to do. And since I had always said I'd never be one of those by the door, I was really trying to find something else to do when this job at WMAQ in Chicago came along and I took that opportunity.

CA: You're working on a book. What is it going to be about?

ROBINSON: It will touch on some of my years in the business.

CA: When do you think you'll have it finished?

ROBINSON: I haven't really set a deadline. My agents wanted to go ahead and get a publisher lined up. I may eventually do that if I find I'm not progressing as well as I want to, in order to give myself deadlines. The problem I'm having is that for the better part of my working career I've had deadlines set by the exigencies of the business and now I'm finding I have to set my own and that adjustment is taking a little bit. But I'm glad to have had this time out of the television business. My brain is waking up after years of enforced slumber.

CA: Are you going to go back into TV in one form or another?

ROBINSON: I would expect that I would do some things in television. I'm trying to work out a format for a show I want to do maybe ten times a year.

CA: Would it be news?

ROBINSON: It wouldn't be strictly news, but it would incorporate some aspects of the business, including news. But it probably would be unlike any television show you've seen.

BIOGRAPHICAL/CRITICAL SOURCES:

PERIODICALS

Detroit Free Press, July 9, 1978.
Ebony, January, 1979, August, 1979, August, 1983.
Variety, February 22, 1984, July 10, 1985.
Washington Post, December 31, 1987.*

—*Interview by Peter Benjaminson*

* * *

RODD, Kathleen Tennant 1912-1988
(Kylie Tennant)

OBITUARY NOTICE—See index for *CA* sketch: Born March

12, 1912, in Manly (one source says Sydney), New South Wales, Australia; died February 28, 1988, in Sydney, Australia. Editor and author. A full-time writer except for a ten-year stint as an editor and advisor for the Macmillan publishing firm, Rodd was one of Australia's best known authors of realistic fiction. All of her work was published under the name Kylie Tennant, including her first novel, *Tiburon,* which won the S. H. Prior Memorial Prize for best Australian novel in 1935. *The Battlers,* Rodd's most famous work, won the Australian Literary Society's Gold Medal in 1941. She also penned a number of nonfiction and juvenile books, such as *Australia: Her Story* and *All the Proud Tribesmen,* about the Australian Aborigines, which won a Children's Book Award in 1960. Rodd's other works include *Foveaux* and *The Joyful Condemned,* which was later expanded and retitled *Tell Morning This.*

OBITUARIES AND OTHER SOURCES:

BOOKS

Contemporary Novelists, St. Martin's, 1986.

PERIODICALS

Times (London), March 10, 1988.

* * *

RODGERS, Daniel T(racy) 1942-

PERSONAL: Born September 29, 1942, in Darby, Pa.; son of Oliver Eliot (a mechanical engineer) and Dorothy (Welch) Rodgers; married Irene Elizabeth Wylie, 1971; children: Peter, Dwight. *Education:* Brown University, A.B. and Sc.B., 1965; Yale University, Ph.D., 1973.

ADDRESSES: Office—Department of History, Princeton University, Princeton, N.J. 08544.

CAREER: University of Wisconsin—Madison, instructor, 1971-73, assistant professor, 1973-78, associate professor of history, 1978-80; Princeton University, Princeton, N.J., associate professor, 1980-86, professor of history, 1986—. Fulbright lecturer at University of Frankfurt, Frankfurt, West Germany, 1983-84.

MEMBER: American Historical Association.

AWARDS, HONORS: American Council of Learned Societies fellowship, 1976; Mellon fellow at Aspen Institute for Humanistic Studies, 1977; Frederick Jackson Turner Award from Organization of American Historians, 1978, for *The Work Ethic in Industrial America, 1850-1920;* Chancellor's Award for Excellence in Teaching, 1978; National Endowment for the Humanities fellowship, 1987-88.

WRITINGS:

The Work Ethic in Industrial America, 1850-1920, University of Chicago Press, 1978.
Contested Truths: Keywords in American Politics Since Independence, Basic Books, 1987.

Contributor of articles to *Journal of Interdisciplinary History, Journal of Social History,* and *Reviews in American History.*

WORK IN PROGRESS: "A book-length investigation of the transatlantic roots of the American welfare state in its formative years from the 1880s through the New Deal."

SIDELIGHTS: In *The Work Ethic in Industrial America, 1850-1920* Daniel T. Rodgers examines how America's work ethic evolved in accord with the changing needs of its capitalist economy. By the end of the nineteenth century the dignity of labor waned as spending habits—rather than earning habits—became the primary focus of an economy that required innumerable consumers for its wealth of factory goods; industrialization demanded a kind of "schizoid" existence, with "the same human being [devoting] eight hours to virtuously attentive work and the succeeding third of the day to resolutely frivolous expenditure," *New York Times Book Review* critic Robert Lekachman observed. Judging *The Work Ethic in Industrial America* an "elegant exercise in intellectual history," the reviewer decided that "Mr. Rodgers's book cries for a sequel." In a critique for *Nation* Milton Cantor, likewise, found the author's "consistently engaging and illuminating study . . . elegantly presented." "A subtle account of the hallowed and changing work ethic . . . is a subject well worth the talent of a historian of such detachment, knowledge and judiciousness," concluded the reviewer.

Rodgers told *CA:* "My work is intellectual history written (I like to think) at the junctures where ideas and social experience meet—where the constructions in our heads take on power and urgency."

BIOGRAPHICAL/CRITICAL SOURCES:

PERIODICALS

Nation, September 8, 1979.
New York Times Book Review, March 19, 1978, January 6, 1980.

* * *

ROES, Nicholas A. 1952-

PERSONAL: Born December 26, 1952, in Jersey City, N.J.; son of Nicholas R. (in advertising) and Mimi (a homemaker; maiden name, Maresca) Roes; married Nancy Bennett (a controller), November 26, 1977. *Education:* University of Bridgeport, B.S., 1974, M.A., 1983.

ADDRESSES: Home—Hackensack, N.J. *Office*—Nicholas A. Roes Associates, P.O. Box 205, Saddle River, N.J. 07458. *Agent*—Raines & Raines, 71 Park Ave., No. 4A, New York, N.Y. 10016.

CAREER: Free-lance writer, 1974—. Director of investment counseling firm of Nicholas A. Roes Associates, 1977—; director of investor relations for *Gambling Times,* 1984—.

MEMBER: International Association of Financial Planners, Edpress.

WRITINGS:

Helping Children Watch TV, Teacher Update, 1980.
America's Lowest Cost Colleges, Freundlich Books, 1985.
Wall Street Casino Guidebook: Investing Handbook for Winning on Wall Street, NAR Productions, 1988.

Author of "Investment Column," syndicated by NAR Productions, and "Wall Street Casino," a column in *Gambling Times*. Contributor to magazines, including *Arizona*. Editor of *Teacher Update* and *Investment Column Quarterly*.

SIDELIGHTS: Nicholas A. Roes told *CA:* "Most of my work consists of practical information in everyday language for everyday people. I enjoy using contrary hooks (i.e., college doesn't have to cost a lot, television viewing can be beneficial to children, you are your own best investment adviser), and I learn more from writing for others than I ever would from just reading.

"Writing has led to other successful businesses, but the writing was always most important. Because of many reader requests, I've taken a stab at investment counseling. But I greatly prefer doing a simple column that is helpful to many to constructing a complex investment plan for just one person.

"My 'Wall Street Casino' column offers advice on ways 'players' can manage their investments. I cover the rules of the investment game and how to come out a winner. *America's Lowest Cost Colleges* is now in its ninth edition. It's curious that people will clip coupons and compare prices when buying a bar of soap—but they don't really comparison shop for an important investment like college. When it comes to an education, expensive is not necessarily better."

* * *

ROGAN, Barbara 1951-

PERSONAL: Born June 7, 1951, in New York, N.Y.; daughter of David R. (in sales) and Eleanor (in sales; maiden name, Riemer) Rogan; married Benjamin Kadishson (a musician), August 17, 1980; children: Jonathan Rogan Kadishson, Daniel Rogan Kadishson. *Education:* St. John's College, Annapolis, Md., and Santa Fe, N.M., B.A., 1973.

ADDRESSES: Home—1548 Remsen Ave., New York, N.Y. 11236. *Agent*—Joy Harris, The Lantz Office, 888 Seventh Ave., New York, N.Y. 10016.

CAREER: Barbara Rogan Literary Agency, New York, N.Y., and Tel Aviv, Israel, director, 1975—. Member of board of directors of Jerusalem International Book Fair, 1980—.

WRITINGS:

Changing States (novel), Doubleday, 1981.
Golani's Angel (novel), Domino Press (Israel), 1985.
Cafe Nevo (novel), Atheneum, 1987.

WORK IN PROGRESS: A novel.

SIDELIGHTS: Zara—the daughter of Holocaust survivors, born in America but raised on a kibbutz—is the protagonist of Barbara Rogan's first novel, *Changing States*. Troubled by the militarism that saturates her environment, the young woman renounces her Jewish homeland after an Arab boyfriend is framed by the military and killed; Zara resumes her search for identity in travels through Europe and America. "Miss Rogan's depiction of this odyssey is both colourful and sharp," noted Holly Eley, admiring the author's descriptive talents in a review for the *Times Literary Supplement*. The critic did, however, wish that Rogan had focused more on "the political realities of contemporary Israel" and less on "Zara's unflagging self-analysis." Writing in the *New York Times Book Review*, Eleanor Foa Dienstag agreed; "Rogan . . . is scathing on the subject of macho-militarist native Israelis," remarked the reviewer, "and I wish she had explored more deeply the moral and political issues she raises about contemporary Israel." Still, Dienstag found the novel "exceptionally evocative of character and place," adding that "the author is a shrewd observer and passionate writer."

Rogan told *CA:* "For the past twelve years I have lived in Israel, where all of my novels are set. They are all political and touch in some way on Arab-Israeli relations. Two of my books include major characters who are Holocaust survivors and children of survivors. I am interested in the way traumas experienced by parents are relived by their children. In addition to fluent Hebrew I have reasonable competence in French, and I've traveled widely throughout Europe."

BIOGRAPHICAL/CRITICAL SOURCES:

PERIODICALS

New York Times Book Review, September 13, 1981.
Times Literary Supplement, April 24, 1981.

* * *

ROLL, Richard J(effrey) 1952-

PERSONAL: Born May 18, 1952, in New York, N.Y.; son of Irwin C. (an executive) and Marilyn W. (a community service counselor) Roll. *Education:* Brown University, B.A., 1974; Harvard University, M.B.A., 1977.

ADDRESSES: Office—Partnership Equitier Corporation, 575 Madison Ave., New York, N.Y. 10022.

CAREER: National Homes Journal, Lowell, Mass., assistant director of marketing, 1974-75; Citibank, New York City, product manager, 1977-78; Today's Communications, Inc., New York City, vice-president and publisher, 1978-79; Financial Marketing Corp. of America, Inc., New York City, president, 1979-86; Partnership Equitier Corp., New York City, chairman, 1987—. President of Best Years Resources, Inc., 1979-82; publisher of Sunday supplement for *Best Years Guide*, 1980-82. Trustee of John T. Lewis Memorial Scholarship Fund, Columbia University, 1978—. Member of advisory board of *Senior Summary*, 1979—. Private real estate investor and developer.

MEMBER: International Society of Pre-Retirement Planners, Harvard Club, Brown University Club, Uptown Racquet Club.

WRITINGS:

(With Hugh Downs) *The Best Years Book: How to Plan for Fulfillment, Security, and Happiness in the Retirement Years*, Delacorte, 1980.
(With G. Douglas Young) *Getting Yours: Financial Success Strategies for Young Professionals in a Tougher Era*, Putnam, 1982.

Contributor to financial, banking, and pre-retirement journals.

SIDELIGHTS: Richard Roll told *CA:* "Both of my books struck a responsive chord among their audiences by offering cogent

strategies for successful living. *The Best Years Book* was developed out of a recognition that the problems of aging are predictable, can be identified, and can be substantially avoided through good planning. But all of us only grow old once and don't have an opportunity therefore to learn from the experience. So the book was created as a sort of 'Whole Earth Catalog' of everything you need to know to plan for a healthy, prosperous, fulfilling later stage of life. We interviewed older and retired people in all kinds of situations across the United States to get their insights. The book is also an encyclopedic guide to financial planning for retirement, housing, lifestyle, keeping healthy and fit, and marital issues.

"*Getting Yours* is an incredibly smart book, for which my coauthor deserves most of the credit. While its prescriptions must be modified for the current low-inflationary era (or breathing spell), I have made a lot of money personally following the strategies in the book, in everything from financial investments to art and real estate. It offers the ambitious but inexperienced reader sophisticated insights into how things really work in a form that is easy to read and digest. I'm very proud of the book and have received a good deal of positive response from readers. Many more people could benefit from it."

* * *

ROLL, Samuel 1942-

PERSONAL: Born December 21, 1942, in Medellin, Colombia; immigrated to the United States, 1947, naturalized citizen, 1958; son of Jaime Hirsch (a businessman) and Bertha (a housewife; maiden name, Agudelo) Roll; married Elizabeth Ruth Jaffe (a psychologist), January 4, 1968; children: Julia, Eric. *Education:* Louisiana State University, B.A., 1964; Pennsylvania State University, M.S., 1967, Ph.D., 1968.

ADDRESSES: Home—1616 San Patricio S.W., Albuquerque, N.M. 87104. *Office*—Department of Psychology, University of New Mexico, Albuquerque, N.M. 87131.

CAREER: Pittsburgh Child Guidance Center, Pittsburgh, Pa., intern, 1967-68; Yale University, New Haven, Conn., clinical postdoctoral fellow, 1968-70; University of New Mexico, Albuquerque, assistant professor, 1970-74, associate professor, 1974-80, professor of psychology, 1980—, associate professor of psychiatry, 1980—, visiting professor of law, 1983, faculty director of Student Crisis Center, 1970-72. Diplomate of American Board of Professional Psychology and American Board of Forensic Psychology; member of professional specialty staff at Vista Sandia Psychiatric Hospital, 1972-77; visiting professor at University of Antioquia, 1975; director of postgraduate training in psychological assessment and child psychotherapy at Plan Nuevo Leon, Monterrey, Mexico, 1976-77; faculty member at Instituto de Salud Mental, Monterrey. Member of New Mexico State Board of Psychological Examiners, 1978-79; expert in civil and criminal forensic psychology, 1973—; member of advisory council of Vista Larga Therapeutic School, 1972-80; member of board of directors of Teaching Home of New Mexico Society for Autistic Children, 1978-79; member of advisory board of local Junior League; consultant to Justice Department of the Navajo Nation, State Department of Vocational Rehabilitation, and Indian Health Service.

MEMBER: Sociedad Interamericana de Psicologia, American Psychological Association, American Psychology-Law Society, American College of Forensic Psychology (member of board of directors, 1983—), Society of Personality Assessment (fellow), New Mexico Psychological Association (member of board of directors, 1973-76), Sigma Xi.

AWARDS, HONORS: Outstanding Professor Award from Las Campanas, 1974; Fulbright scholar, 1975.

WRITINGS:

(Contributor) M. R. Nason, Jaysuno Abramovich, and D. Cvitanovic, editors, *Tres problemas universitarios* (title means "Three University Problems"), University of New Mexico Press, 1975.
(Contributor) Richard H. Dana, editor, *Human Services for Cultural Minorities,* University Park Press, 1981.
(With Leverett Millen) *Soloman's Mothers: A Study of Mourning,* Research Press, 1986.
(With Theodora M. Abel and Rhoda Metraux) *Culture and Psychotherapy,* University of New Mexico Press, 1986.

Contributor of articles and reviews to psychology journals. Member of editorial board of *Journal of Forensic Psychology,* 1984-86.

WORK IN PROGRESS: A Guide to the Interpretation of Dreams in Therapy, completion expected in 1989; research on the mourning process in people with Acquired Immune Deficiency Syndrome (AIDS).

SIDELIGHTS: Samuel Roll has worked with the Quechua Indians of Puno, Peru, with the laboring and middle class Colombian in Medellin, with Mexicans in Mexico City and Monterrey, and with native Americans and members of Hispanic cultures in the United States.

* * *

RONALD, Ann 1939-

PERSONAL: Born October 9, 1939, in Seattle, Wash.; daughter of James Q. (a certified public accountant) and Cleo (Keller) Ronald. *Education:* Whitman College, B.A., 1961; University of Colorado, M.A., 1966; Northwestern University, Ph.D., 1970.

ADDRESSES: Office—Department of English, University of Nevada, Reno, Nev. 89557.

CAREER: University of Nevada, Reno, assistant professor, 1970-77, associate professor, 1977-82, professor of English, 1982—, chairman of department, 1985—.

MEMBER: Modern Language Association of America, Western Literature Association (president, 1984).

WRITINGS:

Zane Grey, Boise University Press, 1975.
Functions of Setting in the Novel, Arno, 1980.
The New West of Edward Abbey, University of New Mexico Press, 1982.
(Editor) *Words for the Wild: The Sierra Club Trailside Reader,* Sierra Books, 1987.

WORK IN PROGRESS: Research on contemporary American nature writing.

ROONEY, Elmo
See PERRY, Charles

* * *

ROSEMAN, Ellen Barbara 1947-

PERSONAL: Born July 24, 1947, in Montreal, Quebec, Canada; daughter of David and Constance Doris (Ginsberg) Roseman; married Edward Trapunski, June 9, 1974; children: Charles Benjamin, Richard Marc. *Education:* McGill University, B.A. (with honors), 1968; University of Toronto, M.A., 1969.

ADDRESSES: Home—175 Cottingham St., Toronto, Ontario, Canada M4V 1C4. *Office—Globe and Mail,* 444 Front St. W., Toronto, Ontario, Canada M5V 2S9. *Agent*—Nancy Colbert, 303 Davenport Rd., Toronto, Ontario, Canada.

CAREER: Maclean-Hunter Ltd., Toronto, Ontario, assistant editor, 1969-72; *Financial Post,* Toronto, reporter, 1972-73; *Toronto Star,* Toronto, reporter, 1973-75; *Globe and Mail,* Toronto, consumer columnist, 1975—. Member of Centre for Investigative Journalism.

MEMBER: Association of Canadian Television and Radio Artists, Southern Ontario Newspaper Guild.

AWARDS, HONORS: Kenneth R. Wilson Award from Business Press Editors Association, 1972.

WRITINGS:

Consumer, Beware! New Press, 1976.
(With Phil Edmonston) *Canadian Consumer's Survival Book,* General Publishing, 1977.
(With Colleen Darragh) *Canadian Parents' Sourcebook,* Doubleday Canada, 1986.

* * *

ROSENBAUM, Alan S(helby) 1941-

PERSONAL: Born August 27, 1941, in Rochester, N.Y.; married in 1974; children: three. *Education:* State University of New York at Buffalo, B.A., 1965, M.A., 1967, Ph.D., 1974.

ADDRESSES: Office—Department of Philosophy, Cleveland State University, 1983 East 24th St., Cleveland, Ohio 44115.

CAREER: Cleveland State University, Cleveland, Ohio, assistant professor, 1975-81, associate professor of philosophy, 1981—.

MEMBER: American Philosophical Association.

WRITINGS:

(Editor and contributor) *The Philosophy of Human Rights: International Perspectives,* Greenwood Press, 1980.
Coercion and Human Autonomy, Greenwood Press, 1986.
Constitutionalism: The Philosophical Dimension, Greenwood Press, in press.

Contributor to philosophy journals.

* * *

ROSSMAN, Marlene L. 1948-

PERSONAL: Born July 4, 1948, in Brooklyn, N.Y.; daughter of David (an accountant) and Anne (Stolz) Rossman; married Elliot Silverman (a lawyer), June 29, 1980. *Education:* Pace University, B.A., 1972, M.B.A., 1982; New York University, M.A., 1974.

ADDRESSES: Office—Rossman, Graham Associates, 201 East 17th St., New York, N.Y. 10003.

CAREER: City University of New York, New York City, adjunct professor of English and communications, 1973-76; Wingate English Academy, New York City, managing director, 1976-80; Rossman, Graham Associates (marketing, sales, and business planners), New York City, partner, 1980—. Adjunct professor at New York University, 1984-86, and Pace University, 1986—. Member of Women in Business Committee of Overseas Education Fund; member of steering committee of Women's Funding Coalition; member of National Women's Economic Alliance.

MEMBER: American Association of University Professors, Financial Women's Association (member of board of directors and chairperson of Professional Development Committee), Omicron Delta Epsilon.

WRITINGS:

The International Businesswoman: A Guide to Success in the Global Marketplace, Praeger, 1986.

Contributor to marketing and business journals, including *Marketing News.*

SIDELIGHTS: Marlene L. Rossman told *CA:* "I was inspired to write my book when, in 1984, I was giving a speech about my career as a marketing consultant. I was besieged with questions by women. These women had many of the same questions about the business world and its rigors that I had when I began. In order to help pave the way for other young career women, I decided to write a 'how-to' book."

BIOGRAPHICAL/CRITICAL SOURCES:

PERIODICALS

Times (London), October 6, 1986.

* * *

ROSTAND, Jean 1894-1977

BRIEF ENTRY: Born October 30, 1894, in Paris, France; died September 3, 1977. French scientist and author. Rostand was known for his expertise in genetics, entomology, herpetology, evolutionary theory, and embryology. The son of French dramatist Edmond Rostand (best known for "Cyrano de Bergerac"), he studied at the Faculty of Science in Paris and subsequently distinguished himself in social causes and creative literary endeavors as well as in science. In 1959 Rostand was named to the French Academy and was awarded the Kalinga Prize from UNESCO for his work in popularizing science. Also, he was eventually recognized as honorary president of France's movements devoted to peace and free expression. Among his many writings, which include fiction and philosophical and sociological essays, are the science books *Adventures Before Birth* (1936), *Life, the Great Adventure* (1956), *The Orion Book of Evolution* (1961), and *The Substance of Man* (1962). *Addresses: Home*—29 rue Pradier, 92 Ville d'Avray, Paris, France.

BIOGRAPHICAL/CRITICAL SOURCES:

BOOKS

Current Biography, H. W. Wilson, 1954, January, 1978.

The International Who's Who, 41st edition, Europa, 1977.

The Oxford Companion to French Literature, reprinted with corrections, Clarendon Press, 1966.

* * *

ROTIMI, E. G. O.
See ROTIMI, (Emmanuel Gladstone) Ola(wale)

* * *

ROTIMI, (Emmanuel Gladstone) Ola(wale) 1938(?)-
(E. G. O. Rotimi, Olawale Rotimi)

PERSONAL: Born c. 1938 in Sapele, Nigeria; son of Samuel Enitan and Dorcas Oruene (Addo) Rotimi; married Hazel Mae Gaudreau in 1965; children: Enitan, Oruene, Biodun Ola, Jr., Bankole. *Education:* Boston University, B.F.A., 1963; Yale University, M.F.A., 1966.

ADDRESSES: Home—Lagos, Nigeria. *Office*—Department of Creative Arts, University of Port Harcourt, P.M.B. 5323, Port Harcourt, Rivers State, Nigeria.

CAREER: University of Ife, Ife, Oyo State, Nigeria, research fellow, 1966-75, acting head of Department of Dramatic Arts, 1975-77; University of Port Harcourt, Port Harcourt, Rivers State, Nigeria, head of Department of Creative Arts and arts director, 1977—; playwright. Director of plays, including his own "The Gods Are Not to Blame," 1968, "The Prodigal," 1969, and "Holding Talks," 1970, Adegoke Durojaiye's "Gbe-Ku-de," 1969, and Aime Cesaire's "La Tragedie d'Henri Christophe," 1971.

MEMBER: African Writers Association, Association of Nigerian Authors, Society of Nigerian Theatre Artists.

AWARDS, HONORS: "Our Husband Has Gone Mad Again" was selected by Yale University as the major play of the year, 1966; first prize in international playwriting competition sponsored by *African Arts* magazine, 1969, for "The Gods Are Not to Blame"; first prize in Oxford University Press playwriting competition, 1969, for "Our Husband Has Gone Mad Again"; first prize at fourth Nigerian National Festival of the Arts, 1974, for creation and direction of dance-drama "And Man Brought the First Woman."

WRITINGS:

PLAYS

"To Stir the God of Iron" (three-act), first produced in Boston at Boston University Drama School, 1963.

Our Husband Has Gone Mad Again: A Comedy (three-act), first produced in New Haven, Conn., at Yale University Drama School, 1966, Oxford University Press, 1976.

The Gods Are Not to Blame (three-act; based on Sophocles' *Oedipus Rex*), first produced in Ife, Nigeria, at Ori Olokun Cultural Centre of the Institute of African Studies, University of Ife, 1968, Oxford University Press, 1971.

Kurunmi: An Historical Tragedy (three-act), first produced in Ife at second Ife Festival of the Arts, 1969, Oxford University Press, 1971.

"The Prodigal" (dance-drama), first produced in Ife at second Ife Festival of the Arts, 1969.

Holding Talks: An Absurdist Drama, first produced at the University of Ife, 1970, Oxford University Press, 1977.

Ovonramwen Nogbaisi: An Historical Tragedy in English (three-act), first produced in Ife at fourth Ife Festival of the Arts, 1971, Oxford University Press and Ethiope Publishing, 1977.

If, first produced at the University of Port Harcourt, 1979, Heinemann Educational Books, 1983.

"Hopes of the Living Dead," first produced at the University of Port Harcourt, 1984.

"Everyone His/Her Own Problem," first broadcast on British Broadcasting Corporation (BBC) African Theatre, London, 1987.

OTHER

(Contributor) Bruce King, editor, *Introduction to Nigerian Literature,* Evans Publications (London), 1971.

(Contributor) S. O. Biobaku, editor, *The Living Culture of Nigeria,* Thomas Nelson, 1976.

WORK IN PROGRESS: A Dictionary of Nigerian Pidgin English; In Praise of Poverty, a collection of original short stories on the psycho-emotional resilience of the poor in an uncaring society.

SIDELIGHTS: One of the most successful Nigerian playwrights writing in English, Ola Rotimi effectively conveys to both Nigerian and foreign audiences the culture and concerns of the African peoples. He specifically addresses the historical and political problems of Nigeria in a bold, sweeping style that, critics say, engrosses audiences in his productions.

Set in Nigeria, Rotimi's first play, "To Stir the God of Iron," was performed in 1963 by the Afro-American Dramatic Society of Boston University while Rotimi was a student there. Rotimi's next play, "Our Husband Has Gone Mad Again"—a politico-domestic comedy—was performed in 1966 at Yale University, where it was named the major play of the year.

After earning his master's of fine arts degree in 1966 from Yale University, Rotimi returned to Nigeria to take up a research fellowship at the University of Ife. While there he composed his highly successful "The Gods Are Not to Blame," based on Greek philosopher Sophocles' "Oedipus Rex," which he directed first at the Ori Olokun Cultural Centre in Ife in 1968 and later at London's Drum Arts Centre in 1978. "The Gods Are Not to Blame" is considered remarkable in its use of broken verse and powerful African imagery.

At the second Ife Festival of the Arts in 1969, Rotimi presented "Kurunmi" and "The Prodigal." "Kurunmi," considered one of his best works, is an epic play about the nineteenth-century Ijaiye War and a biting commentary on the Nigerian Civil War. In "Holding Talks," a 1970 absurdist drama, Rotimi exposes the irrationality of man's obsession with "talking" in situations that clearly demand action. "Ovonramwen Nogbaisi," produced in 1971 at the fourth Ife Festival of the Arts, indicts British imperialism for its role in the downfall of the Benin Empire, a highly organized kingdom in West Africa overtaken by the British in 1897. Provoked by Nigeria's socio-political inequities, Rotimi composed "If," a 1979 play that concerns the predicament of ordinary contemporary Nigerians trying to cope with adverse social and political circumstances following the war. "Hopes of the Living Dead," which premiered in 1984 to widespread critical acclaim and has since been revived twice, uses the historic rebellion of lepers against the British colonial administration in Nigeria at the turn of the century as a metaphor to articulate the striving and aspirations of the ordinary peoples of present-day Nigeria. Rotimi's radio play, "Everyone His/Her Own Problem," broadcast over the British Broadcasting Corporation's overseas service in 1987, recounts the universal preoc-

cupation of man grappling with personal problems of one kind or another.

Rotimi commented: "A play—for that matter, any work of art—must aim at transcending the purlieus of sheer aesthetics. Ultimate fulfillment comes to the artist when he realizes his work is being seriously discussed, that references or lessons are being drawn, that interpretations are being argued over, that new meanings are being adduced and rationalized, that topical analogies are being discovered. This, to my mind, is the enduring value, the consummation of the artistic expression. My creative passion as a playwright is for an accessible people's theatre informed by that which also impels it—namely, the spasms of the socio-political tendons of Africa yesterday, today, and tomorrow. As a director, my pictorial trademark is a preference for a convoluting concourse of juxtaposed, variegated happenings: a conjuration of the rhythm and agitations of existence in these (African) parts of our universe."

BIOGRAPHICAL/CRITICAL SOURCES:

BOOKS

Jones, Eldred, editor, *African Literature Today,* Heinemann Educational Books, 1982.

Ogungbesan, Kola, editor, *New West African Literature,* Heinemann Educational Books, 1979.

PERIODICALS

Bulletin of Black Theatre, winter, 1972.

* * *

ROTIMI, Olawale
See ROTIMI, (Emmanuel Gladstone) Ola(wale)

* * *

ROUSSIN, Andre (Jean Paul Marie) 1911-1987

OBITUARY NOTICE: Born January 22, 1911, in Marseilles, France; died November 3, 1987. Actor and playwright. Roussin joined Le Rideau Gris theater company after a brief career in journalism, and performed plays in Paris during World War II. He began writing plays in the 1940s, and his first, "Am-Stram-Gram," was produced in 1943 at the Athenee in Paris. He later enjoyed considerable success during the 1950s and 1960s in both Paris and London, with plays such as "The Little Hut"—which was translated into English by Nancy Mitford and established his reputation in Great Britain when it appeared at the Lyric Theater—and "Les Oeufs de l'autruche," and "On ne sait jamais." In April, 1973, he was elected to the Academie Francaise.

OBITUARIES AND OTHER SOURCES:

BOOKS

The International Who's Who, 51st edition, Europa, 1987.

Notable Names in the American Theatre, James White, 1976.

PERIODICALS

Times (London), November 7, 1987.

* * *

ROWAN, Andrew N(icholas) 1946-

PERSONAL: Born May 14, 1946, in Bulawayo, Rhodesia (now Zimbabwe); son of Albertus N. (a scientist) and Mary (a scientist; maiden name, Skaife) Rowan; married Kathleen Zuroski (a certified public accountant), August 29, 1981; children: Jennifer Katherine, Andrea Margaret. *Education:* University of Cape Town, B.Sc., 1968; Oxford University, B.A., 1971, D.Phil., 1975.

ADDRESSES: Home—Wellesley, Mass. *Office*—Tufts University School of Veterinary Medicine, 203 Harrison Ave., Boston, Mass. 02111.

CAREER: Pergamon Press, Oxford, England, editor, 1975-76; Fund for the Replacement of Animals in Medical Experiments (FRAME), London, England, scientific administrator, 1976-78; Institute for the Study of Animal Problems, Washington, D.C., associate director, 1978-82; Tufts University, Boston, Mass., assistant dean of new programs for School of Veterinary Medicine, 1983—. Member of advisory board of Johns Hopkins Center for Alternatives to Animal Testing, 1981—; consultant to Delta Society (human/animal/environment study), 1984—. *Military service:* South African Army, 1964.

MEMBER: American Association for the Advancement of Science, Lab Animal Science Association, Tissue Culture Association, Scientists Center for Animal Welfare.

AWARDS, HONORS: Rhodes scholar, 1968; Wankel Prize from German Animal Protection Society (Munich), 1979, for work promoting animal welfare.

WRITINGS:

(Editor) *Use of Alternatives in Drug Research,* Macmillan, 1980.

Of Mice, Models, and Men: A Critical Evaluation of Animal Research, State University of New York Press, 1984.

Contributor to scientific and animal publications. Founding editor, *International Journal for the Study of Animal Problems,* 1980-82, and Delta Society journal *Anthrozooes,* 1987—. Member of editorial board, *Journal of Medical Primatology,* 1979—.

WORK IN PROGRESS: The ethics of animal research; the history of veterinary medicine in Massachusetts; an animal welfare directory.

SIDELIGHTS: In *Of Mice, Models, and Men: A Critical Evaluation of Animal Research* Andrew N. Rowan looks at the state of animal experimentation in America. Examining case studies that illustrate its effectiveness and failures, the author finds "far too many cases where a little more thought would have resulted in a lot less animal suffering." The author advocates reform measures that include improved ethics instruction for animal researchers, more funds for developing alternatives to the use of animals in experiments, and ethics review boards at scientific institutions. "Rowan is not content to condemn," observed Stephen Clark in a review for the *Times Literary Supplement.* "He . . . provides clear guidelines which would, while allowing more animal experimentation than strict 'animal rightists' would like, cut down on the suffering and distress involved."

Finding *Of Mice, Models, and Men* "more reformist than radical, but with a sympathetic understanding of the radical case for 'animal rights,'" Clark determined, "it is a major strength of Rowan's indictment that he is not afraid to acknowledge that animal welfare enthusiasts often behave as badly . . . as scientists." The critic deemed the book "a model of what such studies should be," adding, "it is very much to be hoped that researchers will . . . adopt his practical suggestions [and] . . .

moral philosophers . . . take account of the practicalities he discusses.'' Writing in the *New York Review of Books*, Peter Singer also commended Rowan's balanced appraisal of a controversial subject and determined that ''his book is on the whole valuable and constructive.''

Rowan told *CA:* ''I am interested in man's relationship with animals and nature, searching for the real reasons behind our paradoxical attitudes toward them. This interesting intellectual problem also has very important implications in directing human civilization and our ability to live in harmony with nature.''

BIOGRAPHICAL/CRITICAL SOURCES:

PERIODICALS

New York Review of Books, January 17, 1985.
Times Literary Supplement, June 1, 1984.

* * *

ROWLAND, Judith 1944-

PERSONAL: Born May 12, 1944, in San Diego, Calif.; daughter of Alan L. (a physician) and Marjorie (Golden) Rowland; married Steven Mark Golbus (a physician); children: Kirstin Katherine, Justin Charles Wied. *Education:* Attended University of Padua, 1963; University of California, Berkeley, B.A., 1964; California Western School of Law, J.D., 1969.

ADDRESSES: Office—California Center on Victimology, 2404 Broadway, San Diego, Calif. 92102. *Agent*—Elaine Markson, 44 Greenwich Ave., New York, N.Y. 10011.

CAREER: Partner in private law practice in San Diego, Calif., 1970-72; San Diego County, deputy district attorney, 1972-81; Rowland, Garcia & Associates (law office), San Diego, consultant, 1984—; California Center on Victimology, San Diego, director of legal services for Crime Victims Legal Clinic, 1985—.

MEMBER: American Bar Association, National Organization for Victim Assistance, Authors Guild of America, California Bar Association, California Trial Lawyers Association, San Diego Bar Association, San Diego Trial Lawyers Association.

WRITINGS:

The Ultimate Violation: Rape Trauma Syndrome—An Answer for Victims, Justice in the Courtroom, Doubleday, 1985.

Contributor to *New Woman*.

WORK IN PROGRESS: Illusions of Justice: A Story of Crime Victims in America.

SIDELIGHTS: Former San Diego deputy district attorney Judith Rowland discusses the prosecution of rape cases in California in *The Ultimate Violation*. Recounting four trials in which she used a victim's post-rape behavior (Rape Trauma Syndrome) to prove a lack of consent, Rowland details her frustrating attempts to reform a system that wrongfully equates nonresistance with assent. Calling Rowland's ''forceful and agonizing look at what passes for justice for rape survivors'' a ''page-turning narrative,'' Shelley Neiderbach noted in *Ms.*, ''She invites the reader into the process—as witness—by incorporating court transcripts into the text and by elucidating the legal complications and psychological complexities.'' Deeming *The Ultimate Violation* ''an accessible and fascinating saga,'' Sheila James Kuehl made a similar observation in a critique for the *Los Angeles Times Book Review*. ''Rowland's treatment of the subject matter is novelistic,'' she remarked, ''presenting the kinds of victories for victims that make movie audiences cheer.''

Rowland told *CA:* ''The driving motivation behind my professional efforts is the victims' rights movement—as a lawyer, I want to be a strong and effective voice for victims of crime. I speak Italian, French, and Spanish fluently, and have lived a year in Paris and one in Padua, Italy. I was a founding partner in the first all-woman law firm in California and am the founder of the first legal clinic for victims of crime in the United States.''

BIOGRAPHICAL/CRITICAL SOURCES:

PERIODICALS

Los Angeles Times Book Review, August 25, 1985.
Ms., August 14, 1985.
New York Times Book Review, March 17, 1985.

* * *

RUAS, Charles (Edward) 1938-

PERSONAL: Born November 14, 1938, in Tientsin, China (now People's Republic of China); came to United States, 1951; son of Charles Edward (a civil engineer) and Erika Johanna (an editor for the United Nations; maiden name, Kunert) Ruas; married Agneta Danielsson, June 15, 1966 (divorced, 1975); children: Alexander Charles Edward. *Education:* Princeton University, B.A., 1960, Ph.D., 1965; Sorbonne, University of Paris, certificate in French literature, 1964.

ADDRESSES: Home—347 West Broadway, New York, N.Y. 10013. *Agent*—Irene Skolnick, Wallace & Sheil Agency, 177 East 70th St., New York, N.Y. 10021.

CAREER: New York University, New York City, instructor in Romance languages and literature, 1966-67; Columbia University, New York City, assistant professor of Romance languages and literature, 1968-75; WBAI (Radio Pacifica), New York City, arts director and host of interview program ''Writers in Performance,'' 1975-79; Arts in New York (pilot arts program for public television), New York City, co-producer, 1977-79; Public Broadcasting Service, New York City, producer of documentary program ''Dan Flavin: Bright White or Daylight,'' 1980; New York arts correspondent for National Public Radio (NPR), 1981-83; full-time free-lance writer, 1983—.

MEMBER: P.E.N. International.

AWARDS, HONORS: Danforth fellowship, 1962; Fulbright fellowship, 1965; grants from New York Council on the Arts, 1977-79, and National Endowment for the Arts (NEA), 1978.

WRITINGS:

(Contributor) Bill Henderson, editor, *The Art of Literary Publishing*, Pushcart, 1980.
Writers at Work, sixth series, edited by George Plimpton, Viking, 1984.
Conversations With American Writers, Knopf, 1985.
(Translator) Michel Foucault, *Death and the Labyrinth: The Life and Works of Raymond Roussel*, Doubleday, 1986.

Contributing editor, *Soho News*, 1980—. Contributor to *Paris Review* and *New York Times Book Review*.

WORK IN PROGRESS: Entering the Dream: The Children Written About in Classic Children's Literature, a history of the influence of creative parents on their children and a look

at the impact of books in which children appear as characters (*Alice in Wonderland, Peter Pan, The Wind in the Willows, Winnie the Pooh*); *Home Leave,* a fictional account of a transatlantic childhood.

SIDELIGHTS: Charles Ruas's *Conversations With American Writers* is a collection of fourteen dialogues with contemporary American writers like Normal Mailer, Gore Vidal, E. L. Doctorow, and Eudora Welty. Springing from interviews he conducted as an arts director for a New York City radio station and his print interviews for periodicals, the conversations focus on the artists at work—how and why they write. "The result is a mixture of biography, literary history, entertainment, and marginal notation on the authors' writings which tends to reinforce the ideas and style we perceive in their work," described Linda Barrett Osborne in a review for the *Washington Post Book World.* "The authors . . . speak openly about themselves within the conventions of the literary interview."

Examining Ruas's interviewing style in *Time,* R. Z. Sheppard determined, "Ruas . . . has selected and edited wisely. He thumps for no school of thought or critical trend. . . . What remains is not agreed-upon styles but individual voices." *Los Angeles Times Book Review* critic Ralph Sipper, too, commended Ruas's "gentle probing" and "thoughtful colloquies"; "clearly, writers respond to him," remarked the reviewer. And writing in the *New York Times Book Review,* Jonathan Cott maintained that "if one wanted to choose a surrogate interviewer to pose the questions 'one always wanted to ask' an admired author, one could find no better person than Charles Ruas." The critic explained, "Mr. Ruas displays the essential qualities of any first-rate interviewer: a thorough knowledge of, an irrepressible curiosity about, a profound sympathy for and a respectful but unceremonious directness toward the authors and the works at hand, enabling him to connect with and convey a remarkable sense of a writer's personal and artistic style and being."

Ruas told *CA:* "I was born in Tientsin, China, where my grandfather settled after the Boxer Rebellion. As French colonials, my family was driven out in 1946 when the Communists took over the north of China. My childhood was international, with much travel between France and the United States. I grew up in the United Nations community in Queens, New York, where I attended the local schools; I was chosen by United Nations Secretary-General Tryguie Lee to be the flag bearer at the cornerstone-laying ceremony of the United Nations headquarters building.

"I attended Princeton University, where I studied creative writing with R. P. Blackmur, and it was he who forced me into my first conversation with an American writer by arranging a conference for me with William Faulkner, who was then giving a seminar on his work at Princeton. I was the editor of the *Nassau Literary Magazine* in my junior year, and it was then that I began publishing short stories heavily influenced by my reading of Henry James. I specialized in French and English literature and received a Danforth fellowship to continue specialization in French. I then spent a year at the Sorbonne on a Fulbright fellowship, doing research for my doctoral dissertation. I wrote on the Duc de St. Simon because he was the major influence on the works of Balzac and Proust.

"In addition, during the course of my Fulbright year, I hitchhiked over every inch of Europe from France to Greece. As soon as I began teaching I used the summers to continue this exploration—from living in Ibiza to taking friends on an expedition through the Sahara. Thinking a desert ought to be all sand, we crossed thousands of miles of brushland waiting to arrive at the dunes. At Colomb-Bechard, the French atomic testing station, the Foreign Legion turned us back because we were all suffering from dehydration.

"It was while teaching at Columbia University that I became arts director at WBAI (Radio Pacifica) during the Vietnam War years. I used the station as a public platform to present my involvement with the arts, from painting to performance and avant-garde music. I concentrated especially on bringing innovative fiction and poetry before the public. As a result of this work I was given National Endowment for the Arts and New York Council on the Arts grants to work out models for all arts programming for public television. The product was a sample documentary on the work of Dan Flavin, the artist who works in fluorescent lights.

"*Conversations With American Writers* developed from this background. I was asked to structure my *Paris Review, Soho News,* and *New York Times Book Review* profiles and interviews into a book. I drew upon my previous work to attempt the portrayal of three decades of American fiction writers: those who began publishing immediately after World War II; those who began in the sixties; and those who first appeared in print during the seventies. In the individual interviews I attempt to present the full scope of the life of writing—which includes the work, the personality of the writer, the society in which he works—all within a historical perspective. (I translated Michel Foucault's study of Raymond Roussel because it attempts to analyze the forces that shape both the life and the work of the writer.) Coming from a background that includes China, Europe, and the United States, I have a relativistic point of view which looks at the individual artist in the context of his culture as a whole."

BIOGRAPHICAL/CRITICAL SOURCES:

PERIODICALS

Los Angeles Times Book Review, February 3, 1985, February 2, 1986.
New York Times Book Review, January 13, 1985.
Time, December 24, 1984.
Washington Post Book World, February 3, 1985.

* * *

RUCKER, Rudolf v(on) B(itter) 1946-
(Rudy Rucker)

PERSONAL: Born March 22, 1946, in Louisville, Ky.; son of Embry Cobb (an Episcopal priest) and Marianne (a homemaker; maiden name, von Bitter) Rucker; married Sylvia Bogsch (a teacher), June 24, 1967; children: Georgia, Rudolf, Jr., Isabel. *Education:* Swarthmore College, B.A., 1967; Rutgers University, M.A., 1969, Ph.D., 1973. *Religion:* Episcopalian.

ADDRESSES: Home—Los Gatos, Calif. *Office*—Department of Mathematics, San Jose State University, San Jose, Calif. 95192. *Agent*—Susan Protter, 110 West 40th St., New York, N.Y. 10018.

CAREER: State University of New York College at Geneseo, assistant professor of mathematics, 1972-78; University of Heidelberg, Heidelberg, West Germany, von Humboldt research fellow, 1978-80; Randolph-Macon Woman's College, Lynchburg, Va., associate professor of mathematics, 1980-82; free-lance writer, 1982-86; San Jose State University, San

Jose, Calif., associate professor of mathematics and computer science, 1986—.

MEMBER: American Mathematical Society, Science Fiction Writers of America (SFWA), Honorable Order of the Kentucky Colonels, and Church of the SubGenius.

AWARDS, HONORS: Philip K. Dick Memorial Award for best American original paperback book of the year from Philip K. Dick Society, 1982, for *Software.*

WRITINGS:

Geometry, Relativity, and the Fourth Dimension (nonfiction), Dover, 1977.

(Editor) *Speculations on the Fourth Dimension: Selected Writings of Charles H. Hinton,* Dover, 1980.

UNDER NAME RUDY RUCKER

White Light; or, What Is Cantor's Continuum Problem? (novel), Ace Books, 1980.

Spacetime Donuts (novel), Ace Books, 1981.

Infinity and the Mind: The Science and Philosophy of the Infinite (nonfiction), Birkhaeuser, 1982.

Software (novel), Ace Books, 1982.

The Fifty-seventh Franz Kafka (short stories; includes "The Man Who Ate Himself," "Inertia," "The Jack Kerouac Disembodied School of Poetics," and "The Indian Rope Trick Explained"), Ace Books, 1983.

The Sex Sphere (novel), Ace Books, 1983.

Light Fuse and Get Away (poems), Carp, 1983.

The Fourth Dimension: Toward a Geometry of Higher Reality (nonfiction), foreword by Martin Gardner, illustrations by David Povilaitis, Houghton, 1984.

Master of Space and Time (novel), Bluejay Books, 1984.

"Monument to the Third International" (short story), in *Magazine of Fantasy and Science Fiction,* December, 1984.

The Secret of Life (novel), Bluejay Books, 1985.

Mind Tools: The Five Levels of Mathematical Reality (nonfiction), Houghton, 1987.

(Editor and contributor) *Mathenauts: Tales of Mathematical Wonder* (short stories; includes "Message Found in a Copy of Flatland"), Arbor House, 1987.

Wetware (novel), Avon, 1988.

The Hollow Earth (novel), Avon, in press.

Contributor to periodicals, including *PKDS Bulletin, SFWA Bulletin,* and *Washington Post Book World.*

SIDELIGHTS: Rudolf v. B. Rucker, who exercises his curiosity about mathematics in both fiction and nonfiction, "blends the vulgarity of underground comics with some of the hardest ideas in philosophy and physics," asserted Charles Platt in the *Washington Post Book World.* "He also writes elegantly and captures the subtlety of human relationships in a realistic context." Sometimes credited with popularizing his subject, Rucker brings humor and originality to his technical studies of infinity, the fourth dimension, and mathematic thought as well as his science fiction stories. According to Michael Dirda, writing in the *Washington Post Book World,* "Rucker is an artist well worth discovering, reading, and keeping up with."

Much of Rucker's writing is science fiction with a mathematical foundation; his novel *White Light; or, What Is Cantor's Continuum Problem?* features a mathematician trying to solve a problem regarding degrees of infinity. Rucker mixes black comedy, satire, religion, drugs, and metaphysics in the story of the mathematician's adventures in other worlds and dimensions. Reviewing the book for the *Times Literary Supplement,* Andrew Hislop deemed *White Light* amusing and educational but judged that "for the layman there are too many dimensions—or at least the vital one is missing." He felt the book lacked "the sustained dramatic force of the best science fiction." Thomas M. Disch of the *Magazine of Fantasy and Science Fiction,* on the other hand, admired Rucker's unusual use of pure mathematics as the basis for an alien world, concluding that "*White Light* is a good, intelligent, powerful novel, and [an] auspicious debut in the sf field."

The novels *Spacetime Donuts* and *The Sex Sphere* also include mathematical concepts. In *Spacetime Donuts* Rucker experiments with the geometry of space, his use of math rendering a potentially trite plot "thoroughly original," according to Peter Nicholls in the *Washington Post Book World.* Depicting a utopia in which drugs and three-dimensional television entertain humanity while a computer rules, the story contains the idea that if a person shrinks enough he becomes gigantic. Nicholls described it as "a racy and entertaining tale, cheerfully full of bad language and bad taste." *The Sex Sphere* focuses on a highly sexual multidimensional alien trapped in a three-dimensional world. Charles Platt, in a *Washington Post Book World* review, hailed *The Sex Sphere* as "an example of science fiction's noble tradition of exploring eccentric ideas for their own sake, regardless of their commercial potential."

Some of Rucker's science fiction departs somewhat from his math orientation. *Software,* for instance, examines the implications of artificial intelligence in robots. Having achieved a measure of equality with humans, self-replicating robots seek to dominate men by taping their brain patterns and promising to immortalize this "software." *The Master of Space and Time* centers on a scientist who invents a machine that for two hours enables him to travel through time, visit other universes, and grant wishes. The book's humor prompted critics to compare Rucker with mathematician-writer Lewis Carroll. John Sladek described it in the *Washington Post Book World* as "a retelling of the old three-wishes fable," adding that "what makes it new here is that each wish is really a chance at absolute mastery of space and time . . . , that the wisher is well aware of the history of three-wishes fables, and that the author knows how to have fun with all of this."

In *The Secret of Life* Rucker concentrates more on characterization and less on mathematics, reported Pascal J. Thomas in *Fantasy Review.* Rucker's story revolves around a 1960s teenager who believes he is an alien in disguise. He remembers nothing from before the age of ten, possesses strange powers, and thinks he is on Earth to learn the secret of life. Mused Thomas, instead of relying on "his mathematical bag of tricks" Rucker depicts the youth in depth. The novel "loses some of Rucker's originality," Thomas observed, "while developing more traditional writing qualities." Tom Easton of *Analog Science Fiction/Science Fact* elaborated: "With *The Secret of Life* Rucker makes a bid to be the J. D. Salinger of the 1980s. His meat, as in *Catcher in the Rye,* is the pain of growing up, of coming to terms with reality, of fitting in. And he handles it well, in the process showing those of us who need showing that SF has all the potential of the mainstream, and is besides better suited to modern times."

Rucker's nonfiction, dealing with many of the same topics as his fiction, endeavors to make mathematical and scientific concepts accessible to the lay reader. Whereas *White Light* addresses infinity in a fictional setting, *Infinity and the Mind: The Science and Philosophy of the Infinite* shows the real calculations, paradoxes, and logic of serious inquiry into the sub-

ject. Easton felt the material would be difficult for the nonmathematician, who might question its relevance, but acknowledged that it "is beautiful for the hobbyist of numbers."

The Fourth Dimension: Toward a Geometry of Higher Reality explains the complexities of its subject "in the most painless possible way," marveled Sladek. Rucker uses well-known analogies to introduce his discussion, relating how a three-dimensional object would look as it passed through a two-dimensional world, for example, and extending the analogy to a four-dimensional object in a three-dimensional world. He explores his own variations as well, imagining a spherical two-dimensional world and a door between parallel two-dimensional worlds. Throughout, appraised Timothy Ferris in the *New York Times Book Review,* the work serves to "enhance rather than diminish our curiosity." The critic judged it "an invigorating book, a short but spirited slalom for the mind."

Showing how mathematics studies the world in terms of numbers, space, logic, infinity, and information, *Mind Tools: The Five Levels of Mathematical Reality* is "about thinking," in Sladek's opinion. In addition to mathematical thought, Rucker comments on transcendental meditation, archetypes, and Chinese philosophy, earning high marks for originality from *Los Angeles Times* reviewer Lee Dembart. Both Dembart and Sladek, however, deemed the book hard to follow and questioned the relevance of some of its parts. Dembart explained that "some of it is crystal clear, and some of it is opaque, and the two are inextricably interlaced." At least, Sladek allowed, Rucker "does not talk about mathematics in a boring classroom manner." George Johnson of the *New York Times Book Review* found the book "fascinating" and "dazzling," concluding that Rucker "provides an interesting and rigorous argument for his belief that there will never be an explanation for the universe that is any less complex than the universe itself."

"I don't think you can know where modern commercial SF writing has gotten to if you don't know about Rucker," wrote Algis Budrys in the *Magazine of Fantasy and Science Fiction.* Blending imaginative ideas reminiscent of H. G. Wells with humor and mathematical whimsy recalling Lewis Carroll, Rucker has carved his own niche in the realms of speculative fiction and popular science. In Platt's opinion, his writing is "science fiction as it should be: authoritative and tightly linked with our real lives and our real future." While some critics find Rucker's books occasionally superficial or unfinished, his energy and sense of fun often compensate. "If they sometimes feel as though Rucker made them up as he went along," remarked Dirda, "these loose and baggy books nonetheless sparkle with deadpan wit and a natural storyteller's flair."

Rucker told *CA:* "I view myself as a 'transrealist', using science fiction tools to get at deep archetypal truths. The idea is that the tools of science fiction serve as concrete symbols for subtextual realities. My novels *The Secret of Life, White Light,* and *The Sex Sphere* form a kind of transreal autobiographical trilogy covering my life between the ages of seventeen and thirty-four.

"I work back and forth between science fiction and science writing, sometimes using science fiction for thought experiments. My math research gives me ideas for stories, and my stories serve as laboratory tests for some of my ideas. Eventually I hope to get all my books, journals, letters, and so forth on a gigabyte laser disk, along with software that allows the reader to interrupt at any time and say, for example, 'Can you give me the science on that, Rudy?' or 'What was going on in your life when you wrote that?' or 'Where else do you mention Donald Duck?'"

CA INTERVIEW

CA interviewed Rudy Rucker by telephone on October 23, 1986, at his home in Los Gatos, California.

CA: There's a fine symbiotic relationship between your books on mathematics and your science fiction. How did it evolve?

RUCKER: A lot of my life I've been employed as a mathematics professor. It's natural for me to care a lot about mathematics. But also I've always been interested in developing the other half of my brain, as it were. The right half is the half that dreams tales, and the left half does proofs. I like to work back and forth between them. What I like best is to get interested in some weird idea and do a math book about it to break the ground, and then go back and use what I found out with proofs in my SF [science fiction]. I use the science fiction as a thought experiment, so I can look at something weird and say, What if it were really an experiential thing? The two main themes I've written about are infinity and higher dimensions.

CA: You said in the introduction to Infinity and the Mind *that you were writing it for the average reader. Do you find that the books on math attract a lot of general readers?*

RUCKER: Infinity and the Mind is certainly my hardest book, but over the years it's probably had the best sales. It has to be hard, given the subject matter, but people appreciate the effort that I've gone to make it understandable.

CA: Do the two readerships overlap; are there readers who like both the science fiction and the math?

RUCKER: I think the overlap is growing. People are finally realizing that I've done both these different things, and they're beginning to see my work as a unity. There was a period—I think it's over—when mathematicians were very uptight, and my science fiction was not something they would read. And on the other side, science fiction people were just wanting their little stories and not reading the math. But it's blending across the lines now, and my standing as a writer is improving. It's like in the game Go, where two groupings link up to encircle a large area.

CA: Math once had a rather bad reputation among people who were more interested in literature. Is that going away?

RUCKER: There's some improvement, but the two areas certainly are very different. As I say, it's almost like a right brain-left brain split. My feeling is that since we *do* each have both brains, it's nice to use them both.

CA: We're early given the idea that if we're good on one side of the brain, we're not good on the other.

RUCKER: That's it, yes. Particularly if you have siblings. Parents sometimes will apportion out to children what they're allowed to be good at. They'll say, "Your brother's good in science, and you're going to be good in art."

CA: Were you a science fiction reader early?

RUCKER: I read it a lot when I was a kid. There's an old joke about the Golden Age of Science Fiction: that's when you're thirteen. I definitely went through that. I grew up in Louisville [Kentucky], and there was maybe one shelf of science fiction in the library. I read it all and really liked it. Then when I got to college in the late sixties and on into the early seventies, I lost touch with science fiction. Looking back, that was kind of a dead period in science fiction. In the mid sixties there was what they called a New Wave movement, but that petered out, and the field really just did nothing all through the seventies—like so many things. But then at the beginning of the eighties I got back into SF, and it began getting very exciting again. There's a lot going on in science fiction. There are a lot of younger writers who are pretty influential now; they call themselves the cyberpunks. I'm the father of the cyberpunks.

CA: Then you mix with other science fiction writers a lot?

RUCKER: Yes, and over the years that's given me a lot of pleasure. The world of academia—less so now, but particularly back in the seventies, when I was getting into it—was very closed. There weren't enough jobs. If you told somebody, "I'm writing a book on infinity," it threatened them. There was so much competition; they didn't want any more. But I'd go and talk to science fiction writers, and if I said, "Hi, I'm a new science fiction writer," they'd say, "Great! I hope you write something really weird!" So I've had a lot of friends in the science fiction world. Just moving out to California—well, anywhere—you can meet science fiction writers easily. It's like being in a trade in the Middle Ages. I can go anywhere and I'll look up the local science fiction writers and they're glad to see me. They're very nice. In science fiction, there's some objectivity because there's the market, the dollar. If your book is decent, people will buy it. In small-time academia, it's all on somebody's say-so whether or not you can be a teacher or whether you can do research. But now I've plunged back into academia.

CA: Are you teaching full time again?

RUCKER: Yes. I'm teaching computer science at San Jose State. I had four years off; the last four years I was free-lancing in Lynchburg, Virginia. I did five books in four years, and I was getting maybe a little burned out. Also, the money wasn't coming quite fast enough; I have three kids just starting to go to college. So suddenly I'm back into academia. But it's really nice out here. It's a state school and it's all totally objective.

CA: Does the schedule make it difficult for you to write, or do you have a good mixture of writing and teaching?

RUCKER: I'm heading toward an ideal mix. I've only been here about three months, and it's really not fine-tuned yet. The way it is now, I can write on Tuesdays and Thursdays. I can see that it would take me a long time to finish a novel. I'm working on something right now, but I can't really be sure yet how it's going to work because I'm just getting started.

CA: How do you think computers are affecting the study of math?

RUCKER: They're having a tremendous effect on it. That's in fact one of the reasons I wanted to come back and teach computer science. I really want to master it. It's like ruler and compass constructions were for the Greeks. We've got these incredible machines, and there are gorgeous things being done: fractal graphics, cellular automata, chaotic graphics. You can just fill the screen up with these gorgeous colored things. Mathematics is becoming more empirical; people can make a conjecture and then run the program through a million computation steps and have something to look at. If you've coded it properly, you can summarize a million steps in one picture. It's great! Mathematics is going to go through an explosion.

CA: It sounds as if math could become more fun with these developments, because there's something to see, some visible proof.

RUCKER: Yeah. Not having that was something that always bothered me. I wrote a science fiction story about it once. If all musicians could do was write down scores like composers, they'd get very little publicity. But there's this wondrous thing, the orchestra, that turns the music symbols into sensations so the average person can get something out of it and have an opinion of it. Mathematics has always been lacking that. We've had the wonderful scores, but we haven't had an orchestra that could play them. Eventually the computer can become sort of an orchestra to play mathematics for the average person.

CA: It's very interesting how your math books really get beyond math and into philosophy.

RUCKER: Mathematics is a very rich and exact language. There's an immense vocabulary for certain rarefied concepts—like infinity. You can write a whole book about the different views of infinity in mathematics. Math is particularly good at things that are very abstract. When you get to a certain level of abstraction, you're further removed from the physical plane of immediate need and gratification; you're getting closer, as close as we can get, to ultimate reality. So mathematics is certainly very efficacious on the road to metaphysics.

CA: Has Infinity and the Mind *provoked a lot of response?*

RUCKER: I've gotten a lot of mail on that one. I guess on the average I get a letter a week on it. Of course, now I've moved and nobody knows where I live anymore! I used to show the letters to my wife and say, "Another nut heard from." But a lot of them were great. People really come out of the woodwork when you write about infinity.

CA: All kinds of people, or mainly scientific types?

RUCKER: All kinds of people, including artists. The first fan letter I ever got was after *White Light* came out. I'd just moved back to America—we'd been in Germany. And so I get this letter from Leavenworth Prison. Somebody had gotten the book from the prison library. What he'd done was to smear the sole of his foot with ink and jump on a piece of paper. He had this wrinkle that was shaped like a pentagram, and he wanted me to coauthor a book about this star wrinkle on his foot. I'm thinking, I spent years perfecting this intellectual feast, and here some convict puts ink on his foot and jumps on a piece of paper, and he thinks we're at the same level.

CA: That's truly funny—but maybe it wasn't funny to you.

RUCKER: It was, but I was glad he wrote me in care of the publisher.

CA: Have you heard from many people in other countries about the books?

RUCKER: Oh sure. They've been translated in just about every country.

CA: How do you feel about the way your books have been reviewed? Do you think reviewers have treated you fairly in both fields you write in?

RUCKER: The reviews I've gotten have by and large been good. I got one bad review for *The Sex Sphere,* but that was to be expected. It was deliberately an extremely radical book. But I certainly don't think I've gotten the recognition I would like. I've written twelve books and I'm broke! That doesn't seem right sometimes. My books are just a little bit different, to the point that they haven't caught on the way I imagined they would. It takes a lifetime anyhow. When you start out writing, you think you're going to do one book and be an overnight sensation. But what's the rush? I think in the long run I'll probably get a lot of recognitiion. After I'm safely dead.

CA: Do you like to shake people up with the science fiction, make them look at things in a new way?

RUCKER: Absolutely. Don't forget, I'm a beatnik sixties radical. I quoted Patti Smith in *White Light:* "Within the context of neo-rock we must seize and rend the veil of smoke which man calls order." That's cyberpunk.

CA: What do you enjoy reading?

RUCKER: I like some of the new science fiction; Lew Shiner's *Frontera* was good. I like Edgar Allan Poe; I've been reading his collected works. I still dip into [William] Burroughs and [Jack] Kerouac. I read *Scientific American* and math books. I used to read *Nugget* every month, in Lynchburg.

CA: You're working, you've said elsewhere, on a book called This Hollow Earth, *which you described as a historical science fiction novel. That description seems paradoxical on the surface. Can you talk about the book?*

RUCKER: There's an old theory that the earth is hollow, that there's a sun inside and people there. I've always liked that. Actually, in Poe's only novel, *The Narrative of Arthur Gordon Pym,* they get to the entrance to the hollow earth and Poe loses it; the book stops. My ancestors lived near Edgar Allan Poe in the 1830s, in Richmond, Virginia. I want to go back through time mentally and write a story set in the 1830s about a guy who hooks up with Poe. The guy and Poe make a journey to the inside of the Hollow Earth. I'm just starting.

CA: Beyond that, are there new kinds of things you'd like to write, and maybe new areas of math you'd like to explore?

RUCKER: I just finished a book called *Mind Tools,* on the history of mathematics from the viewpoint of information. I'd like to do a book on what I call unified information theory. I want to find out a lot about information theory. That's my main interest these days, information, chaos, fractals, cellular automata—it's great, being a scholar. You can always come back and there's always another mountain to climb. It's good exercise.

BIOGRAPHICAL/CRITICAL SOURCES:

PERIODICALS

Analog Science Fiction/Science Fact, June, 1982, September, 1982, March, 1983, April, 1985, May, 1985, December, 1985.
Chicago Tribune Book World, June 30, 1985.
Fantasy Review, January, 1985, September, 1985.
Los Angeles Times, May 26, 1987.
Los Angeles Times Book Review, April 21, 1985, October 6, 1985.
Magazine of Fantasy and Science Fiction, July, 1981, June, 1982, October, 1983, December, 1984.
New York Times Book Review, December 2, 1984, March 10, 1985, April 19, 1987.
SF and Fantasy Review, April, 1984.
Stardate, Volume 3, number 4, 1987.
Times Literary Supplement, November 28, 1980.
Washington Post, April 6, 1987.
Washington Post Book World, January 24, 1982, March 28, 1982, December 25, 1983, February 24, 1985, June 30, 1985, December 22, 1985, July 26, 1987.

—Sketch by Polly A. Vedder

—Interview by Jean W. Ross

* * *

RUCKER, Rudy
See RUCKER, Rudolf v(on) B(itter)

* * *

RUDDY, T(homas) Michael 1946-

PERSONAL: Born July 17, 1946, in Kansas City, Kan.; son of John Paul (a railroad car inspector) and Mary (a registered nurse; maiden name, Ronnau) Ruddy; married Eileen Downing (a preschool teacher), June 6, 1970; children: Joshua, Sarah, Noah. *Education:* Rockhurst College, A.B., 1968; Creighton University, M.A., 1970; Kent State University, Ph.D., 1973. *Politics:* Independent. *Religion:* Roman Catholic.

ADDRESSES: Home—4249 Shenandoah, St. Louis, Mo. 63110. *Office*—Department of History, St. Louis University, 221 North Grand Blvd., St. Louis, Mo. 63103.

CAREER: Creighton University, Omaha, Neb., instructor in history, summer, 1970; Kent State University, Kent, Ohio, assistant professor of history, 1973-77; St. Louis University, St. Louis, Mo., assistant professor, 1977-80, associate professor, 1980-87, professor of history, 1987—, director of university honors program, 1986—. Senior Fulbright lecturer in Joensuu, Finland, 1983-84. District historian of St. Louis District of Army Corps of Engineers, 1979—; St. Louis district director of National History Day Program.

MEMBER: Organization of American Historians, Society for Historians of American Foreign Relations.

WRITINGS:

(Contributor) Jules Davids, editor, *Perspectives in American Diplomacy,* Arno, 1976.
(Contributor) Harry T. Parker, editor, *Problems in European History,* Moore Publishing, 1979.
The Cautious Diplomat: Charles E. Bohlen and the Soviet Union, 1929-1969, Kent State University Press, 1986.

Contributor to *Encyclopedia of Russian and Soviet History* and *Encyclopedia Americana*. Also contributor to history journals.

WORK IN PROGRESS: A history of the political controversy surrounding the Meramec River Reservoir in Missouri, publication by U.S. Army, Corps of Engineers, expected in 1988; research on cold war relations between the United States and the neutral nations Sweden and Finland.

SIDELIGHTS: T. Michael Ruddy told *CA:* "I am interested in studying the history of Soviet-American relations in order to dispel the myths that surround these superpowers. My research into the career of Charles E. Bohlen, a realistic and informed analyst of Soviet-American relations and former ambassador to the Soviet Union and France, has led me to seek a realistic and less ideologically focused perspective on the Cold War. While living and teaching in Finland as a Fulbright scholar I became intrigued with the smaller nations which are as much a part of the Cold War as the superpowers, but obviously see the world and the threats differently from the great powers. Examining the perspective of smaller, neutral nations like Sweden and Finland illuminates both the perspective and the narrow focus of the larger powers."

* * *

RUPP, E. G.
See RUPP, E(rnest) Gordon

* * *

RUPP, E(rnest) Gordon 1910-1986
(E. G. Rupp, Gordon Rupp)

PERSONAL: Born January 7, 1910, in London, England; died December 19, 1986; married Marjorie Hibbard, 1938; children: one son. *Education:* King's College, London, B.A.; Wesley House, Cambridge, M.A., B.D., 1946, D.D., 1955; attended University of Strasbourg and University of Basel.

CAREER: Ordained Methodist minister, 1934; worked for a furniture dealer and a bank; itinerant minister to Methodist students, 1937-38; Methodist minister in Chislehurst, England, 1938-46; Richmond Theological College, Richmond, England, tutor in church history, 1947-52; Cambridge University, Cambridge, England, lecturer in divinity, 1952-56; Victoria University of Manchester, Manchester, England, professor of ecclesiastical history, 1956-67; Cambridge University, Dixie Professor of Ecclesiastical History, 1968-77, professor emeritus, 1977-86, fellow of Emmanuel College, 1968-77, honorary fellow, 1983, principal of Wesley House, 1967-74. Birkbeck Lecturer at Trinity College, Cambridge, 1947; president of Methodist Conference, 1968-69; member of central committee of World Council of Churches, 1969; Protestant observer at Second Vatican Council.

AWARDS, HONORS: Honorary fellow of Fitzwilliam College, Cambridge, 1969, and King's College, London, 1969; D.D. from University of Aberdeen and Victoria University of Manchester, 1979; Dr.Theol. from University of Paris.

WRITINGS:

Is This a Christian Country? Sheldon Press, 1941.
Martin Luther, Hitler's Cause. . .or Cure? In Reply to Peter F. Wiener, Lutterworth, 1945.
Studies in the Making of the English Protestant Tradition: Mainly in the Reign of Henry VIII, Cambridge University Press, 1947.
Luther's Progress to the Diet of Worms, 1521, S.C.M. Press, 1951, Harper, 1964.
Principalities and Powers: Studies in the Christian Conflict in History, Abingdon-Cokesbury, 1952, abridged edition, Epworth, 1965.
The Righteousness of God: Luther Studies, Hodder & Stoughton, 1953, Philosophical Library, 1954.
Thomas Jackson, Methodist Patriarch, Epworth, 1954.
Six Makers of English Religion, 1500-1700, Harper, 1957.
Protestant Catholicity: Two Lectures, Epworth, 1960.
Consideration Re-Considered: An Examination of "The Church of England and the Methodist Church," Epworth, 1964.
Last Things First (lectures), Fortress, 1964.
(Editor with Rupert Davis and A. Raymond George) *A History of the Methodist Church in Great Britain,* Epworth, Volume I, 1965, Volume II, 1978, Volume III, 1983.
The Old Reformation and the New, Fortress, 1967.
(Editor with F. F. Bruce) *Holy Book and Holy Tradition,* Eerdmans, 1968.
(Editor and translator, with A. N. Marlow, Philip S. Watson, and Benjamin Drewery) *Luther and Erasmus: Free Will and Salvation,* Westminster, 1969.
Patterns of Reformation, Fortress, 1969.
(Editor with Benjamin Drewery) *Martin Luther,* St. Martin's, 1970.
I Seek My Brethren: Bishop George Bell and the German Churches, Epworth, 1975.
Just Men: Historical Pieces, Epworth, 1977.
The Sixty Plus, and Other Sermons, Fount Paperbacks, 1978.
Thomas More: The King's Good Servant, Collins, 1978.
The People Called Methodist: Reflections on Our Origin, Our Experience, Our Discipleship, and Our Mission, Discipleship Resources, 1984.
Religion in England, 1688-1791, Clarendon Press, 1986.

Contributor to periodicals, sometimes under names E. G. Rupp and Gordon Rupp.

BIOGRAPHICAL/CRITICAL SOURCES:

BOOKS

Brooks, Peter, editor, *Christian Spirituality: Essays in Honour of Gordon Rupp,* S.C.M. Press, 1975.

PERIODICALS

Times Literary Supplement, July 7, 1966, April 30, 1970, April 1, 1983, December 22, 1986.*

* * *

RUPP, Gordon
See RUPP, E(rnest) Gordon

* * *

RUPPERSBURG, Hugh Michael 1950-

PERSONAL: Surname is pronounced "*Roo*-purz-burg"; born March 1, 1950, in Atlanta, Ga.; son of Hugh (a sales representative) and Margaret (a homemaker; maiden name, Caruthers) Ruppersburg; married Patricia Smith (a jeweler), June 4, 1978; children: Michael, Charles. *Education:* University of Georgia, A.B., 1972; University of South Carolina, M.A., 1974, Ph.D., 1978.

ADDRESSES: Home—5798 Barnett Shoals Rd., Athens, Ga. 30609. *Office*—Department of English, Park Hall, University of Georgia, Athens, Ga. 30602.

CAREER: University of Georgia, Athens, instructor, 1977-79, assistant professor, 1979-84, associate professor of English, 1984—.

MEMBER: National Council of Teachers of English, Modern Language Association of America, Popular Culture Association of America, Popular Culture Association of the South, South Central Modern Language Association, South Atlantic Modern Language Association, Society for the Study of Southern Literature, Philological Association of the Carolinas.

WRITINGS:

Voice and Eye in Faulkner's Fiction, University of Georgia Press, 1983.
Reading Faulkner's "Light in August": A Line-by-Line Glossary, Explication, and Commentary, University Press of Mississippi, 1988.

Contributor to *Dictionary of Literary Biography,* Gale. Also contributor to *Journal of American Culture, Journal of Popular Culture and Television, Mississippi Quarterly, South Atlantic Review, South Central Review,* and *Southern Humanities Review.*

WORK IN PROGRESS: Robert Penn Warren's American Vision.

SIDELIGHTS: Hugh Michael Ruppersburg told *CA:* "I am interested in Robert Penn Warren and William Faulkner as American, not Southern, writers. Their regional background may account for certain traits and attitudes in their work. To a large extent it provided them with a subject for their writings. Beyond that their Southernness, for me, is only incidental. They are both great writers of the Western world.

"Practically all of my published writing has been academic. Literary criticism is suffering now a state of catastrophic flux. By questioning the authority of the written word, it threatens to abolish itself and with it all literature. The writing I do may be, by contemporary standards, anachronistic. It gives me a small degree of satisfaction, and that is all one can ask."

* * *

RUSSELL, Eric Frank 1905-1978 (Webster Craig, Duncan H. Munro)

PERSONAL: Born January 6, 1905, in Camberley, Surrey, England; died February 28, 1978; son of an army instructor; married wife, Ellen, in 1930; children: Erica. *Education:* Attended military schools in England and abroad.

CAREER: Worked variously as switchboard operator, quantity surveyor, and draftsman; technical representative for steel and engineering firms in Liverpool, England, in 1930s; writer, 1937-78. *Military service:* King's Regiment, 1922-26. Royal Air Force, 1941-45.

MEMBER: Science Fiction Writers of America, British Interplanetary Society (founding member).

AWARDS, HONORS: Science Fiction Achievement Award ("Hugo") for best short story from World Science Fiction Society, 1955, for "Allamagoosa."

WRITINGS:

"The Saga of Pelican West" (novelette), in *Astounding Stories,* February, 1937.
Sinister Barrier (novel; first published serially in *Unknown,* March, 1939), World's Work, 1943, revised edition, Fantasy Press, 1948, reprinted, Del Rey, 1986.
Dreadful Sanctuary (novel; first published serially in *Astounding Science-Fiction, 1948*), Fantasy Press, 1951, revised edition, Lancer Books, 1963.
Sentinels From Space (novel; first published as *The Star Watchers* in 1951), Bouregy & Curl, 1953.
Deep Space (stories), Fantasy Press, 1954, abridged edition published as *Selections From Deep Space,* Bantam, 1955.
Men, Martians, and Machines (stories; includes "Jay Score" and "Symbiotica"), Dennis Dobson, 1955, reprinted, Robson Books, 1985, Roy Publishers, 1956, reprinted with introduction by George Zebrowski and foreword by Isaac Asimov, Crown, 1984.
Three to Conquer (novel), Avalon Books, 1956, reprinted, Del Rey, 1986.
Great World Mysteries (nonfiction), Roy Publishers, 1957.
Wasp (novel), Avalon Books, 1957, enlarged edition, Dennis Dobson, 1958, reprinted with introduction by Jack Chalker, Del Rey, 1986.
Six Worlds Yonder (stories) [and] *The Space Willies* (novel expanded from story "Plus X," first published in *Astounding Science-Fiction,* 1956), Ace Books, 1958 (also see below).
Next of Kin (enlarged edition of *The Space Willies*), Dennis Dobson, 1959, edited and abridged edition, University of London Press, 1964.
Far Stars (short stories), Dennis Dobson, 1961.
Dark Tides (stories), Dennis Dobson, 1962.
The Great Explosion (novel; incorporates short novel ". . .And Then There Were None," first published in *Astounding Science-Fiction,* 1951), Dodd, 1962.
The Rabble Rousers, Regency Books, 1963.
With a Strange Device (novel), Dennis Dobson, 1964, published as *The Mindwarpers,* Lancer Books, 1965.
Somewhere a Voice (stories), Dennis Dobson, 1965, Ace Books, 1966, published as *Somewhere a Voice, and Other Stories,* Penguin, 1968.
Like Nothing on Earth (contains "Hobbyist," "The Mechanical Mice," "Into Your Tent I'll Creep," "Nothing New," "Exposure," and "Ultima Thule"), Dennis Dobson, 1975.
The Best of Eric Frank Russell (contains "Mana," "Jay Score," "Homo Saps," "Metamorphosite," "Hobbyist," "Late Night Final," "Dear Devil," "Fast Falls the Eventide," "I am Nothing," "Weak Spot," "Allamagoosa," "Into Your Tent I'll Creep," and "Study in Still Life"), edited with introduction by Alan Dean Foster, Ballantine, 1978.

Author of short stories, sometimes under the pseudonyms Webster Craig and Duncan H. Munro, including "Vampire From the Void," "I, Spy!" and "First Person Singular." Work represented in anthologies, including *Four for the Future,* edited by Groff Conklin, Pyramid Books, c. 1959; and *Exiles: Three Novellas,* edited by Ben Bova, St. Martin's, 1978. Contributor to periodicals, including *Astounding, Fantasy, Tales of Wonder,* and *Unknown.*

SIDELIGHTS: Noted for his humor as well as his imagination, Eric Frank Russell began to write science fiction novels and short stories in the late 1930s, remaining popular for more than thirty years. Taut plotting and serious consideration of subjects such as sanity, racial intolerance, and emotional themes characterize his work. *Sinister Barrier,* which depicts an Earth owned and exploited by an alien race that causes and feeds on human suffering, was deemed highly imaginative and is among

Russell's best-remembered novels. Humor dominates the Hugo Award-winning short story "Allamagoosa," a lampoon of bureaucracy, and colors much of his other work—Russell's wisecracking style, in fact, overshadowed his British heritage and led some readers to consider him as American as his U.S. contemporaries.

BIOGRAPHICAL/CRITICAL SOURCES:

BOOKS

Moskowitz, Sam, *Seekers of Tomorrow,* World, 1966.*

* * *

RUSSELL, Sarah
See LASKI, Marghanita

* * *

RYAN, Allan A(ndrew), Jr. 1945-

PERSONAL: Born July 3, 1945, in Cambridge, Mass.; son of Allan Andrew (a certified public accountant) and Anne (a homemaker; maiden name, Conway) Ryan; married Nancy Foote (a homemaker), June 30, 1978; children: Elisabeth, Andrew. *Education:* Dartmouth College, A.B., 1966; University of Minnesota, J.D. (magna cum laude), 1970.

ADDRESSES: Office—1350 Massachusetts Ave., Suite 980, Cambridge, Mass. 02138. *Agent*—Muriel Nellis, 3539 Albermarle St. N.W., Washington, D.C. 20008.

CAREER: Law clerk for U.S. Supreme Court Justice Byron R. White in Washington, D.C., 1970-71; admitted to Bar of District of Columbia, 1972; associate of Williams, Connolly & Califano, Washington, D.C., 1974-77; U.S. Department of Justice, Washington, D.C., assistant to solicitor general, 1977-80, director of Office of Special Investigations (OSI), 1980-83, special assistant to attorney general, 1983; private law practice in Washington, D.C., 1983-85; Harvard University, Cambridge, Mass., attorney in Office of General Counsel, 1985—. Member of board of directors of Facing History and Ourselves National Foundation, Inc., 1985—. *Military service:* U.S. Marine Corps, 1971-74; became captain.

MEMBER: American Bar Association, District of Columbia Bar Association, Boston Bar Association.

WRITINGS:

Klaus Barbie and the U.S. Government, Government Publishing Office, 1983.
Quiet Neighbors: Prosecuting Nazi War Criminals in America, Harcourt, 1984.

WORK IN PROGRESS: Researching judicial resolution of international human rights violations.

SIDELIGHTS: From 1980 to 1983 Allan A. Ryan, Jr., directed a special Justice Department unit established to prosecute former Nazi collaborators living in the United States. *Quiet Neighbors: Prosecuting Nazi War Criminals in America* is his account of the deportation cases waged by the Office of Special Investigations (OSI); it is also a detailed and angry look at three decades of national policy that allowed Nazi war criminals to seamlessly enter the country and become citizens, enjoying the staunch protections of the American judicial system. Beginning with the postwar Displaced Persons Act, which favored—through ethnic and occupational quotas—Nazi collaborators over their victims, the author explores how American anti-Semitism and anti-communism led to official and public attitudes of apathy and neglect regarding the Holocaust. (The Immigration and Naturalization Service bungled most of its deportation cases.) "Tolerance of Nazis thus became not so much a policy as the inevitable result of an absence of policy," observed Art Seidenbaum in the *Los Angeles Times Book Review;* "the book documents the belated efforts of an embarrassed nation." "*Quiet Neighbors* is Ryan's account of the government's better-late-than-never efforts at bringing a few ex-Nazis to a little bit of justice," *Village Voice* critic Wendy Kaminer reiterated. "Ryan's purpose is not to review, once again, tales of the Holocaust or to examine the nature of evil. *Quiet Neighbors* is . . . primarily a story of America, of law, bureaucratic incompetence and 30 years of public indifference to genocide."

While judging Ryan's national indictment "excessively broad," Ralph Blumenthal commented in a critique for the *New York Times Book Review,* "Mr. Ryan is at his best narrating some of the harrowing cases prosecuted by the Office of Special Investigations." Kaminer, too, found "the passages recounting trial testimony of survivors, hard to read and impossible not to, . . . the most compelling in the book." The reviewer commended the author's narrative skills, stating: "He tells it like the good, fairminded prosecutor he probably was—with a sense of outrage, tempered by lawyerly objectivity, respect for the facts, and the ability to marshal them persuasively; like most good trial lawyers, he's a good storyteller." And deeming *Quiet Neighbors* "as immediate as newspaper headlines," Seidenbaum also praised Ryan's affecting account. "The stories [he] tells are riveting and real," wrote the critic. "The narrative is, by turns, sarcastic, intense, blisteringly critical. Ryan is, at times, editorial, preachy and a touch patronizing. . . . This book is an impassioned documentary of an ultimate irony: how a nation committed to freedom, that conquered the Nazis for that precious right, allowed those very persons the freedom that they had denied so many millions of others."

Ryan told *CA:* "*Quiet Neighbors* was, among other things, a refutation of the popular but false belief that Nazi war criminals entered the United States with the assistance of intelligence agencies. The truth is, unfortunately, more shocking: They entered as the beneficiaries of one of the most publicly debated, openly administered policies of postwar America. They are with us still."

BIOGRAPHICAL/CRITICAL SOURCES:

PERIODICALS

Globe and Mail (Toronto), June 1, 1985.
Los Angeles Times Book Review, December 2, 1984.
New York Times Book Review, November 11, 1984.
Village Voice, December 4, 1984.
Washington Post Book World, December 30, 1984.

* * *

RYGA, George 1932-1987

OBITUARY NOTICE—See index for *CA* sketch: Born July 27,

1932, in Deep Creek, Alberta, Canada; died November 18, 1987, in Summerland, British Columbia, Canada. Playwright and novelist. One of Canada's best known playwrights, Ryga will be best remembered for his 1967 play "The Ecstasy of Rita Joe," which sympathetically depicted the alienation of a young native American girl. His other plays include "Grass and Wild Strawberries," "Captives of the Faceless Drummer," and "Indian." Ryga also wrote the novel *Night Desk* and a travel book on China during its Cultural Revolution, *Beyond the Crimson Morning*.

OBITUARIES AND OTHER SOURCES:

BOOKS

Who's Who in Canadian Literature: 1985-1986, Reference Press, 1985.

PERIODICALS

Times (London), November 28, 1987.

S

SABLOSKY, Irving L. 1924-

PERSONAL: Born March 5, 1924, in Indianapolis, Ind.; son of David L. (in business) and Minnie (a housewife; maiden name, Rosner) Sablosky; married Miriam Miller, June 13, 1946 (divorced, August, 1954); married Patricia Breen, August 14, 1955 (died November 9, 1980); married Juliet Antunes (a foreign service officer), January 24, 1983; children: Harriet Ann Sablosky Phillippi, Nina Sablosky Freije, Michael B., Mairi B. Sablosky Rothman, Lia B., John W. *Education:* Indiana University—Bloomington, B.Mus. (with honors), 1947; graduate study at University of Chicago, 1963-64.

ADDRESSES: Home—6500 Kenhowe Dr., Bethesda, Md. 20817.

CAREER: Chicago Daily News, Chicago, Ill., music critic, 1947-57; U.S. Information Agency, Washington, D.C., foreign service officer, 1957-80, served in Seoul, Korea, 1958-60, Cebu, the Philippines, 1960-63, Hamburg, West Germany, 1965-68, cultural attache in Bangkok, Thailand, 1971-73, and in London, England, 1976-79; writer, 1980—. Lecturer in music at DePaul University, 1950-52. *Military service:* U.S. Army, 1943-45; served in European theater; received Purple Heart.

AWARDS, HONORS: Grant from Fromm Music Foundation, 1955-56.

WRITINGS:

American Music, University of Chicago Press, 1969.
What They Heard: Music in America, 1852-1881, Louisiana State University Press, 1986.

Author and narrator of ''Music Now—and Then,'' a series broadcast by National Educational Radio. Contributor to history journals and newspapers.

WORK IN PROGRESS: An updated final chapter for a new Spanish edition of *American Music,* distribution in Mexico and Latin America expected in 1988.

SIDELIGHTS: Irving L. Sablosky told *CA:* ''The problem of how to write about music has haunted me most of my life. It is one thing to write about musicians, or music history, or musical taste or performance; it is another to write about music itself, not in technical-analytical terms but in a way that will describe what a listener hears and experiences. Little of such writing exists (I think of some by Robert Schumann in the last century, some by Paul Rosenfeld in ours). It was partly because I came to see little possibility of accomplishing any such thing in the context of a daily newspaper that I left off being a music critic in Chicago. The foreign service offered a career in which I thought I would have an opportunity to explore music of other cultures and to explain something of our own. Though music was not central to my work with the U.S. Information Agency, my interest in music was something I could share with many I met and worked with overseas. In talking about our music to audiences in other countries, I believe I was able to convey something vital and real about American society and culture.

''It seems to me that lectures and radio programs are particularly effective media for dealing with music because one can support verbal descriptions with examples of the music itself. In the radio programs from the Fromm Foundation, 'Music Now—and Then,' I was able to use this approach to make some connections between music of our time and more familiar music of the past, and I look back on that series as a highlight of my career.''

* * *

SACKS, Peter
See SACKS, Peter M.

* * *

SACKS, Peter M. 1950-
(Peter Sacks)

PERSONAL: Born July 15, 1950, in Port Elizabeth, South Africa; immigrated to United States, 1970, naturalized citizen, 1983; son of Samuel (a doctor) and Esther (Gordon) Sacks; married Barbara Kassel (a painter), January 8, 1980. *Education:* Princeton University, A.B. (summa cum laude), 1973; Oxford University, M.Phil., 1976; Yale University, Ph.D., 1980.

ADDRESSES: Home—3519 Newland Rd., Baltimore, Md. 21218. *Office*—Department of English, Johns Hopkins University, 34th and Charles Sts., Baltimore, Md. 21218.

CAREER: Johns Hopkins University, Baltimore, Md., assistant professor, 1980-86, associate professor of English, 1986—, member of writing seminars department.

AWARDS, HONORS: Christian Gauss Award from Phi Beta Kappa, 1985, for *The English Elegy.*

WRITINGS:

The English Elegy: Studies in the Genre From Spenser to Yeats, Johns Hopkins University Press, 1985.
(Under name Peter Sacks) *In These Mountains* (poems), Macmillan, 1986.

Contributor of articles and poems to periodicals, including *Antioch Review, Boulevard, Georgia Review, New Republic, New Yorker, Partisan Review, Tikkun, TriQuarterly,* and *Yale Review.*

WORK IN PROGRESS: A book of poems; works of literary criticism, especially on contemporary American poetry; a book of travel writing; a book on figurative (representational) painting.

SIDELIGHTS: Peter M. Sacks told *CA:* "I was raised in South Africa. I am now an expatriate, but I am still caught up in that country's history. My work in poetry has usually sought to balance an openness to physical beauty on the one hand against historical suffering on the other.

"In scholarship, I was drawn to the genre of elegy, from the Renaissance to the present. While my chronological focus is now narrowing toward the twentieth century, my interests are widening within the field of poetry at large. Questions of the relationship between individual writers and cultural codes are of particular interest to me.

"Expatriation and the impulse to travel are still uppermost and have led to journeys through such regions as the Amazon, the Andes and Himalayas, Morocco, Namibia, and southern Mexico. Another strong interest is in writing about painting, primarily on representational painting of the last two centuries."

BIOGRAPHICAL/CRITICAL SOURCES:

PERIODICALS

Baltimore Sun, July 20, 1986.
Hudson Review, spring, 1987.
Virginia Quarterly Review, autumn, 1986.
Washington Post Book World, May 3, 1987.

* * *

SAGAN, Eli 1927-

PERSONAL: Born March 3, 1927, in Summit, N.J.; son of George (in manufacturing) and Esther (a homemaker; maiden name, Gooen) Sagan; married Frimi Giller (a teacher), August 7, 1949; children: Miriam, Rachel, Susannah, Daniel. *Education:* Harvard University, B.A., 1948. *Politics:* "Radical Democrat."

ADDRESSES: Home and office—153 Dwight Pl., Englewood, N.J. 07631.

CAREER: New York Girl Coat Co., New York, N.Y., vice-president, 1950-66, president, 1966-75; New England Conservatory of Music, Boston, Mass., instructor in humanities, 1971-76; University of California, Berkeley, guest lecturer in sociology, 1981-86; New School for Social Research, New York City, special lecturer, 1986—. Director of chamber music series at Art Center of Northern New Jersey, 1960-78; member of board of directors of Elizabeth Morrow School, 1970-74, Englewood School for Boys, 1971-73. Organizer of "Senators for Peace and New Priorities" rally, 1970, and rally for George McGovern, 1972, both in Madison Square Garden; delegate to Democratic National Convention, 1972; member of Businessmen for McCarthy and Business Men and Women for McGovern.

MEMBER: Fund for New Priorities in America (co-founder, 1969), Council for a Liveable World (member of board of directors, 1972—; treasurer, 1974-80).

AWARDS, HONORS: "I had the honor of being the only person cited twice on the Richard Nixon/John Dean 'Enemies List' in 1972."

WRITINGS:

Cannibalism: Human Aggression and Cultural Form, Harper, 1974.
(Contributor) Harry M. Johnson, editor, *Religious Change and Continuity,* Jossey-Bass, 1979.
The Lust to Annihilate: A Psychoanalytic Study of Violence in Ancient Greek Culture, Psychohistory Press, 1979.
At the Dawn of Tyranny: The Origins of Individualism, Political Oppression, and the State, Knopf, 1985.
Freud, Women, and Morality: The Psychology of Good and Evil, Basic Books, 1988.

WORK IN PROGRESS: Polis, Power, and Paranoia: The Origins of Democracy and Its Perversions in Ancient Greece.

SIDELIGHTS: In *At the Dawn of Tyranny: The Origins of Individualism, Political Oppression, and the State* Eli Sagan explores the stage in humankind's social development that lies between the tribal band society of hunter-gatherers and ancient civilizations like Egypt and Mesopotamia. Termed "complex society" by the author, this middle stage was the first expression of social cohesion not based on kinship; marking the beginnings of the state, such societies starkly exhibited the best and the worst of civilized life: politics, law, fine arts; poverty, social oppression, tyranny. Looking at a number of complex societies, Sagan "wants to know why civilization emerges in such a tyrannical and destructive form," assessed Andrew Bard Schmookler in the *New York Times Book Review.* Perceiving historical change as a reflection of humankind's psychological development, the author proposes that "the fear and anxiety caused by separation from the kin could only be handled . . . by the invention of class oppression"; that "along the developmental path of individuation . . . we have done some terrible things."

Writing that Sagan "is persuasive that these kingdoms provide a key to understanding forces that work more subtly in our own societies," Schmookler determined that the author's psychoanalytic explanation of history lends *At the Dawn of Tyranny* "its strengths—and its weaknesses." "[It] blinds him to the possible role of nonpsychological forces in cultural change," observed the critic; by viewing "history's nightmares as the responsibility of humankind in general" the author misses "how the workings of power can enable the pathological few to impose their will and their ways on the many." Still, Schmookler maintained that "psychological insights like Mr. Sagan's are indispensable to a complete historical understanding"; "as in his previous excellent and undeservedly neglected books," the reviewer continued, "Mr. Sagan is particularly adept at bringing us to confront the heart of human darkness." Deeming *At the Dawn of Tyranny* "rich in substance and humane in spirit," Schmookler concluded: "Whatever the shortcomings of his

explanatory framework . . . Mr. Sagan offers us a stimulating inquiry undertaken with intellectual courage and integrity." In a critique for the *Los Angeles Times Book Review* David M. Hayano concurred: "This is an adventurous work of broad sweep, posing more numerous and more difficult questions than it can legitimately answer."

Sagan told *CA:* "I am, essentially, a psychoanalytic sociologist interested in morality and the human capacity for destruction. In addition, I am fundamentally concerned with problems of social, cultural, and moral development. My concern for morality, my political activism, and my writing are all of a piece."

BIOGRAPHICAL/CRITICAL SOURCES:

PERIODICALS

Los Angeles Times Book Review, July 28, 1985.
New York Times Book Review, June 30, 1985.

* * *

ST. GEORGE, Edith
See DELATUSH, Edith G.

* * *

SANFIELD, Steve 1937-

PERSONAL: Born August 3, 1937, in Cambridge, Mass.; son of Harold S. (in business) and Rose (a housewife; maiden name, Silverman) Sanfield; married Jacqueline Bellon (an artist), February 4, 1969 (divorced, 1977); married Sarah Ruth Sparks (a teacher), September 6, 1985; children: Aaron. *Education:* University of Massachusetts at Amherst, B.A., 1958.

ADDRESSES: Home—22000 Lost River Rd., Nevada City, Calif. 95959.

CAREER: CBS-Radio News, Los Angeles, Calif., news editor, 1959-61; gardener, 1967-71; Midnight Movies Underground Cinema 12, Nevada City, Calif., promotional director, 1972-82; writer and storyteller, 1982—. Affiliated with California Poets in the Schools Program, 1975-77; storyteller in residence of California Arts Council, 1977-80; member of board of directors of American Storytelling Resource, 1978-82; North Columbia Schoolhouse Cultural Center, member of board of directors, 1981—, president, 1983-86; founder and artistic director of Sierra Storytelling Festival, 1985—; storytelling consultant to Educational Media Association and Centrum Foundation.

MEMBER: Society of Children's Book Writers, National Association for the Preservation and Perpetuation of Storytellers.

AWARDS, HONORS: First prize in Haiku Zasshi Zo annual haiku contest, 1985; award for a nonfiction work in progress, 1987, from the Society of Children's Book Writers.

WRITINGS:

Water Before and Water After (poems), Blackberry, 1974.
Backlog: A Cycle of Hoops From the Sierra Foothills (poems), Tooth of Time Books, 1975.
A Fall From Grace (poems), Aldebaran Review, 1976.
Wandering (poems), Shaman Drum, 1977.
The Confounding: A Paiute Tale to Be Told Aloud, Larkspur Press, 1980.
(Translator) Kage, *Only the Ashes* (poems), Tooth of Time Books, 1981.
A New Way (poems), Tooth of Time Books, 1983.
Forty Days and Forty Nights (poems), Plain View Press, 1983.
(With Dale Pendell) *Chasing the Cranes* (poems), Exiled-in-America Press, 1985.
A Natural Man: The True Story of John Henry (juvenile), David R. Godine, 1986.
He Smiled to Himself (poems), Shakti Press, in press.

Associate editor of *Kuksu: A Journal of Backcountry Writing,* 1974-78; contributing editor of *Zero: Contemporary Buddhist Life and Thought,* 1978-81.

WORK IN PROGRESS: Collected Hoops, poems; *The Adventures of High John the Conqueror,* stories.

SIDELIGHTS: Steve Sanfield told *CA:* "It was my work as a poet in the schools that led me to become a professional storyteller. My objective was not to get children to write 'great' poetry (I know of few adults who are capable of that), but rather to expose them to the joys of hearing and reading it. What I found was that most children weren't too interested in poetry, and what they enjoyed most was narrative poetry. I began to bring more narratives to them and discovered the children had a deep-seated need for stories, real stories. I began to introduce more and more of those until most of my time in the classroom was taken up in the telling of tales.

"Under the sponsorship of the California Arts Council, I became the first full-time storyteller in residence in the United States, and I held that position for three years. Since then I've told stories and given workshops at schools, universities, conferences, and festivals throughout the United States. In order to bring the magic and wonder and mystery of storytelling to my own community, from which I draw so much nourishment, I organized a Winter Tales Series in 1981. It has become so much a part of the cultural life of the San Juan Ridge that it continues to be a focal point of winters here in the mountains, and three years ago we had our first Sierra Storytelling Festival. This three-day event brings together the best storytellers and listeners in the West.

"All this telling has had a dramatic effect on my writing, and though poesy remains my first love, much of my energy is now devoted to finding, researching, developing, and finally getting onto paper forgotten and vaguely remembered tales that still have the power to touch human hearts and minds."

MEDIA ADAPTATIONS: Sanfield has made storytelling cassettes, "Singing Up the Mountains," released by Nita, Inc., in 1981, and "Could This Be Paradise," released by Backlog in 1984.

BIOGRAPHICAL/CRITICAL SOURCES:

BOOKS

Haifetz, Harold, editor, *Zen and Hasidism,* Quest Books, 1978.

PERIODICALS

Christian Science Monitor, March 13, 1987.
Los Angeles Times Book Review, March 1, 1987.
New Age Journal, December, 1984.
New York Times Book Review, December 28, 1986.
Sierra Heritage, summer, 1985.

* * *

SAUNDERS, James (Arthur) 1925-

BRIEF ENTRY: Born January 8, 1925, in London, England.

British educator and author. Saunders is a playwright known for both his absurdist comedies and his humanist dramas. He produced his first plays while working as a chemistry teacher, but in 1963 he left education to devote himself exclusively to playwriting. By that time Saunders had already gained recognition for his 1962 production *Next Time I'll Sing to You* (Random House, 1963), an absurdist comedy about various individuals enacting events in the life of an actual hermit. In the ensuing years Saunders increasingly distinguished himself as a master of self-consciously theatrical satire. Among his many other comedies is *The Borage Pigeon Affair* (Deutsch, 1970; first produced in 1969), which concerns a television crew documenting two village councillors disputing the merits of pigeons. In the 1970s Saunders adopted a more serious tone in works such as "Games" (published in *Games and After Liverpool,* Samuel French, 1973; first produced in 1971), in which characters rehearse a production about the American slaughter of Vietnamese villagers at My Lai, and "Squat" (1973), where an eviction was debated as it occurred, with the actual eviction participants on stage and in the audience. In 1977 Saunders enjoyed his greatest commercial success with *Bodies* (Amber Lane, 1979), an absurdist perspective on infidelity. *Addresses: Home*—24 St. Stephens Gardens, East Twickenham, Middlesex TW1 2LS, England. *Agent*—c/o Margaret Ramsey, 14A Goodwin's Court, London WC2, England.

BIOGRAPHICAL/CRITICAL SOURCES:

BOOKS

Crowell's Handbook of Contemporary Drama, Crowell, 1971.
Dictionary of Literary Biography, Volume 13: *British Dramatists Since World War II,* Gale, 1982.
The Encyclopedia of World Theatre, Scribner, 1977.

* * *

SAWIN, Martica 1927-

PERSONAL: Born January 22, 1929, in New York, N.Y.; daughter of Herman D. (a textile executive) and Martica (Sturges) Ruhm; married David M. Sawin (divorced); children: Martica Sawin Douglas, Maggy Sawin Wolf, Eugenia. *Education:* University of Iowa, B.A., 1950; Columbia University, M.A., 1968.

ADDRESSES: Office—Department of Art History, Parsons School of Design, 66 Fifth Ave., New York, N.Y. 10011.

CAREER: Arts, New York City, editor and contributor, 1952-63; Hunter College of the City University of New York, New York City, lecturer in art history, 1964-67; Parsons School of Design, New York City, member of art history faculty, 1967—, chairman of department, 1967-85, founder of "Parsons in Paris." Guest curator of exhibitions; member of board of directors of Rockland Center for the Arts; member of Rockland County Percent for Art in Public Places Commission and Friends of the Collection of the Portland Museum of Art. Member of Clarkstown Democratic Committee; member of board of trustees of Rockland Country Day School.

MEMBER: International Art Critics Association, College Art Association of America.

WRITINGS:

Wolf Kahn, Landscape Painter, Taplinger, 1981.
(Contributor) Paul Schimmel, editor, *The Interpretive Link,* Newport Harbor Museum, 1986.
(Contributor) Germaine Viatte, editor, *La Planete affolee* (title means "The Planet Gone Mad"), Flammarion, 1986.

Contributor of more than one hundred articles to art journals.

WORK IN PROGRESS: The Surrealist Incursion, "an account of the arrival in the United States during World War II of ten painters and poets belonging to the Surrealist group, pre-war Europe's last avant garde, and the way their presence altered the course of American art."

SIDELIGHTS: Martica Sawin told *CA:* "If I had the courage, tenacity, and creative resources to be a painter myself, there would be no need to write about art. It is my way of expressing my gratitude for what artists contribute to the excitement and glory of human experience. Along the way I try to probe for the genesis of the art work in the multiple stimuli that act on the individual psyche, all the while believing that it is the nature of art to elude absolute definition."

* * *

SAXTON, Mark 1914-1988

OBITUARY NOTICE—See index for *CA* sketch: Born November 28, 1914, in Mineola, N.Y.; died of an apparent heart attack, January 7, 1988, in New York, N.Y. Editor and author. Saxton served as an editor for New York City publishing firms such as Farrar & Rinehart, William Sloane Associates, and McGraw-Hill before settling at Harvard University Press for a number of years. When he left Harvard in 1968 he helped found the Gambit, Incorporated, publishing company in Boston. In 1980 Saxton returned to New York City as a free-lance editor. Saxon's novels include *Danger Road, The Broken Circle, Paper Chase,* and three books set in the imaginary kingdom of Islandia—*The Islar, The Two Kingdoms,* and *Havoc in Islandia.*

OBITUARIES AND OTHER SOURCES:

BOOKS

Who's Who in America, 44th edition, Marquis, 1986.

PERIODICALS

New York Times, January 13, 1988.
Publishers Weekly, February 5, 1988.

* * *

SCALA, James 1934-

PERSONAL: Born September 16, 1934, in Ramsey, N.J.; son of Louis (a bank teller) and Lorene (a teacher; maiden name, Hendrickson) Scala; married Nancy Peters (a homemaker), June 15, 1957; children: James, Gregory, Nancy, Kimberly. *Education:* Columbia University, A.B., 1960; Cornell University, Ph.D., 1964; postdoctoral study at Harvard University, 1967. *Politics:* Republican.

ADDRESSES: Home and office—44 Los Arabis Circle, Lafayette, Calif. 94549. *Agent*—Al Zuckerman, Writer's House, 21 West 26th St., New York, N.Y. 10010.

CAREER: Miami Valley Laboratories, Cincinnati, Ohio, staff scientist, 1964-66; Owens Illinois, Inc., Toledo, Ohio, director of fundamental research, 1966-71; Thomas J. Lipton, Inc., Englewood Cliffs, N.J., director of nutrition, 1971-75; General Foods Corp., Tarrytown, N.Y., director of health sciences, 1975-78; Shaklee Corp., San Francisco, Calif., senior vice-president, 1978-87; free-lance writer, 1987—. Professo-

rial lecturer at Georgetown University; instructor at University of California, Berkeley; fellow of American College of Nutrition. Member of sports medicine council of U.S. Olympic Ski Team; public speaker on drug abuse; Epcot adviser to Walt Disney. Patron of San Francisco Symphony. *Military service:* U.S. Air Force, 1953-56.

MEMBER: American Institute of Nutrition, Society of Cell Biology, American Dietetic Association, American Chemical Society, British Nutrition Society, Astronomical Society (member of board of directors), Sigma Xi.

AWARDS, HONORS: Distinguished scholar at University of Miami, Coral Gables, Fla., 1975-76.

WRITINGS:

Nutritional Determinants in Athletic Performance, Bull, 1982.
Making the Vitamin Connection, Harper, 1985.
The Arthritis Relief Diet, New American Library, 1987.
High Blood Pressure Control Without Drugs, New American Library, 1988.

Author of video script "The Nature of Nutrition." Contributor of more than fifty papers to scientific journals.

WORK IN PROGRESS: Human Longevity.

SIDELIGHTS: James Scala told *CA:* "I have spent some thirty years in education, research, and management. The most rewarding moments came when I was helping people understand themselves and their health. More importantly, I felt most fulfilled when I could help people improve their health through diet. I decided to make that my next career, and I now consider myself a full-time writer and lecturer on health and nutrition.

"Having traveled extensively as a speaker and scientist, I have concluded that people everywhere want a long, healthy life that is free of serious health problems. I want to do as much as I can to help them achieve that objective, and that has become the goal of my career."

AVOCATIONAL INTERESTS: "The forty-seven-foot cruising ketch, *LaScala,* is my source of relaxation and inspiration. Before my sun sinks close to the horizon, Nancy and I intend to take *LaScala* and search for the perfect anchorage in warm, tropical waters and get to know folks in all ports of call."

BIOGRAPHICAL/CRITICAL SOURCES:

PERIODICALS

Arizona Daily Star, November 8, 1986.
Chicago Sun-Times, July 16, 1987.
Sunday Express (London), July 26, 1987.
Times (London), July 26, 1987.
U.S.A. Today, November 11, 1986.

* * *

SCHATELL, Brian

PERSONAL: Education—Graduate of Parsons School of Design.

ADDRESSES: Home—Hoboken, N.J.

CAREER: Parsons School of Design, New York, N.Y., teacher of children's book illustration.

WRITINGS:

SELF-ILLUSTRATED BOOKS FOR JUVENILES

Farmer Goff and His Turkey Sam, Lippincott, 1982.
Midge and Fred, Lippincott, 1983.
Sam's No Dummy, Farmer Goff, Lippincott, 1984.
The McGoonys Have a Party, Lippincott, 1985.

ILLUSTRATOR

Vicki Cobb, *Lots of Rot,* Lippincott, 1981.
Vicki Cobb, *Fuzz Does It!* Lippincott, 1982.
Vicki Cobb, *Gobs of Goo,* Lippincott, 1983.
Juli Barbato, *From Bed to Bus,* Macmillan, 1985.
Juli Barbato, *Mom's Night Out,* Macmillan, 1985.*

* * *

SCHLOSSMAN, Beryl 1955-

PERSONAL: Born June 19, 1955, in New York, N.Y.; daughter of Irwin and Lin Schlossman. *Education:* Cornell University, B.A. (magna cum laude), 1976; University of Paris VII, Diploma d'Etudes approfondies, 1978, Doctorat de troisieme cycle, 1981; Johns Hopkins University, Ph.D., 1987.

ADDRESSES: Office—Department of Modern Languages, Emory University, Atlanta, Ga. 30322.

CAREER: Emory University, Atlanta, Ga., assistant professor of French, 1987—.

MEMBER: Modern Language Association of America, South Atlantic Modern Language Association, Phi Beta Kappa.

AWARDS, HONORS: Fulbright fellow in France, 1976-77.

WRITINGS:

Joyce's Catholic Comedy of Language, University of Wisconsin Press, 1985.

Contributor to literature journals.

WORK IN PROGRESS: The Allegory of Conversion: Self-Portraits and Fictions in Flaubert and Proust; two books of poetry.

* * *

SCHOFIELD, Mary Anne 1948-

PERSONAL: Born May 5, 1948, in Lancaster, Pa.; daughter of Albert M. (a business executive) and Anne M. (a homemaker) Schofield. *Education:* Rosemont College, A.B. (magna cum laude), 1970; Bryn Mawr College, M.A., 1971; University of Delaware, Ph.D., 1979.

ADDRESSES: Office—Department of English, St. Bonaventure University, St. Bonaventure, N.Y. 14778.

CAREER: University of Delaware, Newark, instructor in English, 1977-78; Villanova University, Villanova, Pa., assistant professor of English, 1979-80; St. Bonaventure University, St. Bonaventure, N.Y., assistant professor, 1980-83, associate professor, 1983-87, professor of English, 1987—. Assistant director of public relations for Chilton Book Co.; consultant to Plasser-Thaurer Corp.

MEMBER: American Society for Eighteenth-Century Studies, Popular Culture Association, Modern Language Association of America, Northeast American Society for Eighteenth-Century Studies (vice-president; president), Northeast Modern Language Association, Northeast Victorian Studies Association.

WRITINGS:

Quiet Rebellion: The Fictional Heroines of Eliza Haywood, University Press of America, 1981.

(Editor) *Four Novels by Eliza Haywood,* Scholars' Facsimiles and Reprints, 1982.
Eliza Haywood, G. K. Hall, 1985.
(Editor) *Masquerade Novels of Eliza Haywood,* Scholars' Facsimiles and Reprints, 1985.
(Editor) Sarah Fielding, *The Cry,* Scholars' Facsimiles and Reprints, 1985.
(Editor with Cecelia Macheski) *Fetter'd or Free? British Women Novelists, 1670-1815,* Ohio University Press, 1986.

Contributor to literature journals. Editor of *Barbara Pym Newsletter*.

WORK IN PROGRESS: Masquerade and Romance in Eighteenth-Century Feminine Fiction, publication expected in 1990; *Curtain Calls: Eighteenth-Century Women and the Theatre,* publication expected in 1990; *Cooking by the Book: Food in Literature and Culture,* publication expected in 1990.

SIDELIGHTS: Mary Anne Schofield told *CA:* "Eliza Haywood is the most popular and prolific—with sixty-odd novels—of eighteenth-century women writers. She is concerned with the predominant 'woman questions' of the eighteenth century, and her novels treat these issues in the subtext."

* * *

SCHONFIELD, Hugh J(oseph) 1901-1988 (Hegesippus)

OBITUARY NOTICE—See index for *CA* sketch: Born May 17, 1901, in London, England; died following a short illness, January 24, 1988, in London, England. Editor and author. Schonfield was best known for his controversial 1965 best-seller, *The Passover Plot: New Light on the History of Jesus,* which made the claim that Jesus arranged to be drugged for his crucifixion in order to appear dead, and planned to be taken down from the cross early by Joseph of Arimathea. Fascinated by Christianity, Schonfield dedicated his life to trying to demystify many of the religion's most sacred mysteries. He edited several books, including *Authentic Photography of Christ.* Occasionally using the pseudonym Hegesippus, he produced further works on the early Christians, such as *Saints Against Caesar: The Rise and Reactions of the First Christian Community, Those Incredible Christians,* and *The Pentecost Revolution.* In 1985 Schonfield published a translation of the New Testament considered controversial for its radical reinterpretation of Christian history.

OBITUARIES AND OTHER SOURCES:

BOOKS

International Authors and Writers Who's Who, 10th edition, International Biographical Centre, 1986.

PERIODICALS

Chicago Tribune, January 29, 1988.
New York Times, January 28, 1988.
Times (London), January 26, 1988.
Washington Post, January 28, 1988.

* * *

SCHRAMM, Wilbur (Lang) 1907-1987

OBITUARY NOTICE—See index for *CA* sketch: Born August 5, 1907; died December 27, 1987, in Honolulu, Hawaii. Educator, editor, journalist, and author. Schramm, who taught at institutions such as the University of Iowa, University of Illinois at Urbana-Champaign, and Stanford University, was an authority on mass communications. He began his career as a journalist and worked variously for the *Marietta Daily Herald,* the *Boston Herald,* and Associated Press before accepting his first teaching position in 1935. His extensive research in mass communications informed a number of his books, including *Responsibility in Mass Communication, The Story of Human Communication: From Painted Cane to Micro-Chip,* and *Circulation of News in the Third World,* which he wrote with L. Erwin Atwood. Schramm also edited *Communications in Modern Society* and *Quality in Instructional Television,* among other books.

OBITUARIES AND OTHER SOURCES:

PERIODICALS

New York Times, January 1, 1988.

* * *

SCHRECK, Alan (Edward) 1951-

PERSONAL: Born December 7, 1951, in Rochester, N.Y.; son of Karl Joseph (an industrial engineer) and Irene (a homemaker; maiden name, Varga) Schreck; married Nancy Elizabeth Pflug (a homemaker), May 15, 1982; children: Paul Alan, Jeanne Elizabeth, Mark Joseph. *Education:* University of Notre Dame, B.A., 1973; University of St. Michael's College, Toronto, Ontario, M.A., 1975, Ph.D., 1979. *Religion:* Roman Catholic.

ADDRESSES: Office—Department of Theology, Franciscan University of Steubenville, Franciscan Way, Steubenville, Ohio 43952.

CAREER: Franciscan University of Steubenville, Steubenville, Ohio, assistant professor, 1978-82, associate professor of theology, 1982—.

MEMBER: Catholic Theological Alliance.

WRITINGS:

Catholic and Christian: An Explanation of Commonly Misunderstood Catholic Beliefs, Servant Publications, 1984.
The Compact History of the Catholic Church, Servant Publications, 1987.
Basics of the Faith: A Catholic Catechism, Servant Publications, 1987.

SIDELIGHTS: Alan Schreck told *CA:* "My teaching at the Franciscan University of Steubenville has been the most formative influence on my writing. This university has been blessed with a vibrant environment of Christian faith among students and faculty alike. My writings on the Catholic Christian faith have been inspired and influenced by this faith community."

* * *

SCHREIBER, Ted
See SCHREIBER, V. Theodore

* * *

SCHREIBER, V. Theodore 1905-1986 (Ted Schreiber)

PERSONAL: Born December 4, 1905, in Kersey, Pa.; died November 12, 1986, in Huntingdon, Pa.; buried in Germany

Valley Cemetery; son of Henry and Mae (Diamond) Schreiber; married Margaretta Smith Walker, February 11, 1949; children: Adrian H.; (stepchildren) Edward W. Walker, Kay E. Walker Cummings, Dorothy J. Walker Claycomb, Paul R. Walker. *Education:* Central State Normal School (now Lock Haven State College), graduated, 1923; received M.A. from Pennsylvania State University; further graduate study at University of Mexico.

CAREER: Teacher of earth sciences, c. 1950-53; Rothrock High School, Mifflin County, Pa., teacher of earth sciences, c. 1953-71; substitute teacher, 1971-86. Lecturer on dinosaurs, fossils, and earth history. Member of Huntingdon County Democratic Committee.

WRITINGS:

(Editor) Roland T. Bird, *Bones for Barnum Brown: Adventures of a Dinosaur Hunter,* Texas Christian University Press, 1985.

Columnist for *Valley Log*. Contributor to magazines, including *Arizona Highways*.*

* * *

SCHUMAN, Howard 1928-

PERSONAL: Born March 16, 1928, in Cincinnati, Ohio; son of Robert A. and Esther (Bohn) Schuman; married Josephine Miles, September 1, 1951; children: Marc, Elisabeth, David. *Education:* Attended University of Chicago, 1947-48; Antioch College, A.B., 1953; Trinity University, M.S., 1956; Harvard University, Ph.D., 1961.

ADDRESSES: Home—1306 Kensington St., Ann Arbor, Mich. 48104.

CAREER: Harvard University, Cambridge, Mass., research associate, 1961-64; University of Michigan, Ann Arbor, assistant professor, 1964-67, associate professor, 1967-71, professor of sociology, 1971—, chairman of department, 1970-73, director of Detroit Area Study, 1965-71, faculty associate of Survey Research Center, 1967-74, program director, 1974-82, director of center, 1982-87. *Military service:* U.S. Army, 1954-56.

MEMBER: American Sociological Association, American Association for Public Opinion Research, American Association for the Advancement of Science.

WRITINGS:

Economic Development and Individual Change: A Social-Psychological Study of the Comilla Experiment in Pakistan, foreword by Alex Inkeles, Center for International Affairs, Harvard University, 1967.
(With Angus Campbell) *Racial Attitudes in Fifteen American Cities,* Institute for Social Research, University of Michigan, 1968.
(With Barry Gruenberg) *The Impact of City on Racial Attitudes,* Institute for Social Research, University of Michigan, 1970.
(With Otis Dudley Duncan and Beverly Duncan) *Social Change in a Metropolitan Community,* Russell Sage Foundation, c. 1973.
(With Shirley Hatchett) *Black Racial Attitudes: Trends and Complexities,* Institute for Social Research, University of Michigan, 1974.
(With Jean M. Converse) *Conversations at Random: Survey Research as Interviewers See It,* illustrations by Elizabeth E. Converse, Wiley, 1974.
(With Stanley Presser) *Questions and Answers in Attitude Surveys: Experiments on Question Form, Wording, and Context,* Academic Press, c. 1981.
(With Charlotte Steeth and Lawrence Bobo) *Racial Attitudes in America,* Harvard University Press, 1985.

Editor of *Public Opinion Quarterly.*

* * *

SCOTT, Helen G. 1915(?)-1987

OBITUARY NOTICE: Born c. 1915 in New York; died of a heart attack, November 20, 1987, in Paris, France. Translator and author. A close associate of French filmmaker Francois Truffaut, with whom she wrote *Hitchcock,* a book about the famous British motion picture director, Scott was a key advocate of New Wave film in the United States. She worked with such directors as Robert Benton, Jean-Luc Godard, and Milos Forman, and wrote the English language subtitles for such films as ''Jean de Florette'' and ''Manon of the Spring.'' As a young woman growing up in Paris, Scott became involved in broadcasting for the Free French during World War II and later served as press attache for Chief Justice Robert Jackson at the Nuremburg war trials. She was named Chevalier des Arts et des Lettres in 1986.

OBITUARIES AND OTHER SOURCES:

PERIODICALS

New York Times, November 24, 1987.

* * *

SCOTT, Hilda 1915-

PERSONAL: Born August 9, 1915, in New York, N.Y.; daughter of Leroy (a novelist) and Miriam (a psychologist; maiden name, Finn) Scott; married Herbert Lass (a journalist), April 22, 1938; children: Joseph, Andrew. *Education:* Vassar College, B.A. (cum laude), 1936.

ADDRESSES: Home—79 Martin St., Cambridge, Mass. 02138.

CAREER: Time, Inc., New York, N.Y., interviewer and researcher, 1938-49; journalist in Prague, Czechoslovakia, 1949-73; *Medical Tribune* (U.S. weekly), Prague, Central European correspondent, 1961-73; Arbeitsgemeinschaft fuer Lebensniveauvergleiche (Working Group on the Quality of Life), Vienna, Austria, associate researcher, 1973-80; full-time writer, 1980—. Helped organize first International Women's Day ceremonies for the United Nations Industrial Development Organization (UNIDO), 1978. Guest lecturer at educational institutions, including Yale University, Smith College, Wellesley College, Mount Holyoke College, and the universities of Toronto, Amsterdam, Rome, and Massachusetts at Amherst.

MEMBER: National Writers Union, Alliance for Independent Scholars (Cambridge).

WRITINGS:

Does Socialism Liberate Women? Experiences From Eastern Europe, Beacon Press, 1974, published as *Women and Socialism,* Allison & Busby, 1976.
(Contributor) Jean Lipman-Blumen and Jessie Bernard, editors, *Social Policy and Sex Roles,* Sage Publications, 1979.

(Editor with Margrit Eichler) *Women in Futures Research,* Pergamon, 1982.

Sweden's "Right to Be Human" Sex-Role Equality: The Goal and the Reality, M. E. Sharpe, 1982.

Working Your Way to the Bottom: The Feminization of Poverty, Pandora Press, 1984.

(Contributor) S. Acker, J. Megarry, S. Nisbet, and E. Hoyle, editors, *World Yearbook of Education 1984: Women and Education,* Kogan Page, 1984.

(With Juliet F. Brudney) *Forced Out: Why Veteran Employees Are Driven From Their Careers—and What They Can Do,* Simon & Schuster, 1987.

Contributor of articles and reviews to periodicals, including *Women's Studies International Forum, Working Woman, Working Mother, Resources for Feminist Research, Social Policy, In These Times,* and London *Guardian*. Contributing editor for annotated bibliography of Austrian publications on women in industrial relations, Austrian Federal Ministry of Science and Research, 1978. Guest editor for "Women in Politics" issue of *International Journal of Sociology,* fall, 1978.

WORK IN PROGRESS: Continuing research on women and the future of work.

SIDELIGHTS: Hilda Scott told *CA:* "My twin interests, social policy and the status of women in industrial society, had their origin in a family environment where poverty and social justice were perpetual concerns. The critical influence in my life was the thirty years I spent in Europe. I can best describe those years as a perpetual postgraduate education, forcing me to adapt to unfamiliar cultures. In Czechoslovakia I experienced the last years of Soviet leader Joseph Stalin's reign, the halting period of de-Stalinization culminating in the dramatic 'Prague Spring' experiment in democratic socialism, and its finale in the mid-twentieth-century Soviet invasion.

"In Austria I was able to finish my first book, *Does Socialism Liberate Women?,* based on material I had been collecting since the 1950s. Several study trips to Sweden resulted in a second book on that country's official sex-role equality program, *Sweden's 'Right to Be Human.'* A third book, *Working Your Way to the Bottom,* deals with the feminization of poverty in its international dimension.

"The search for a solution to the problems women encounter worldwide has focused my attention on the need for a redefinition of work to incorporate the enormous productivity of the informal, unpaid sector, particularly the unpaid work done by women. This is at present a major field of interest. My hopes are directed less toward ideologies and political parties and more in the direction of alternative movements that recognize the present period as one of crisis and transition and that are engaged in an open-ended search for answers. I consider the women's movement to be one of these."

Hilda Scott's analysis of Eastern European socialism in her first book, *Does Socialism Liberate Women?,* "combines the personal touch—the complaints of neighbor women about their aching backs and wayward children—with an overall view and theory," according to Eleanor M. Wheeler. The author, wrote Wheeler in *Nation,* "pays tribute to socialist health services, free and equal education, day-care centers, the right to jobs, equal property rights, generous maternity leave, easy divorce and abortion" in her praise for socialist means of liberating women. "But she calls for a developed theory of women's role," the reviewer added, "even under socialism." Pointing out the mistaken socialist belief that "the liberation of women would come automatically as private property and financial exploitation disappeared," Wheeler noted, Scott calls for a reorganization of the family structure to balance child care equally between the mother and father, with financial support from the government.

In another study on the economic condition of women, *Working Your Way to the Bottom: The Feminization of Poverty,* Scott "shows that women's work is universally concentrated in low-paying jobs—clerical, service, and manufacturing—and is more vulnerable to unemployment, with women's earnings invariaby less than men's," observed Muriel Haynes in *Ms.* Noting that "90 percent of the unpaid work in the world is done by women," wrote Haynes, the author "synthesizes ideas from a wide range of social thinkers, not all of them feminists," and asks: "What if this unpaid work—the kind of labor performed in the home and in other kinds of social service—could be 'paid for' in benefits: health insurance, old-age pensions, or access to a variety of facilities? . . . Visionary? Radical? Certainly," affirmed the reviewer, "but so once was democracy."

For *Forced Out: Why Veteran Employees Are Driven From Their Careers—and What They Can Do,* Scott and co-author Juliet F. Brudney interviewed more than one hundred job-seekers over fifty years old. Many of these men and women, wrote Peter Baida in the *New York Times Book Review,* "were the victims of layoffs specifically aimed at older workers—so-called voluntary early-retirement schemes that offered not so much a golden handshake as a golden shove." Scott and *Boston Globe* columnist Brudney offer "straightforward and sensible" tips, Baida commended, "about resumes, placement services, career agencies, networking, job fairs and legal remedies."

BIOGRAPHICAL/CRITICAL SOURCES:

PERIODICALS

Economic and Industrial Democracy, Volume 4, 1983.

Guardian (London), May 15, 1982, November 21, 1984.

Ms., May, 1985.

Nation, November 8, 1975.

New Republic, December 14, 1974.

New York Times Book Review, May 19, 1985, October 25, 1987.

Resources for Feminist Research, November, 1985.

Sociology and Social Research, October, 1976.

Women's Review of Books, April, 1985.

* * *

SCOTT, R(obert) B(algarnie) Y(oung) 1899-1987

OBITUARY NOTICE: Born July 16, 1899, in Toronto, Ontario, Canada; died November 1, 1987, in Toronto, Ontario, Canada. Educator, Old Testament scholar, and author. Scott began his academic career as a teacher at Union College in Vancouver and after several interim positions became the first Danforth Professor of Religion at Princeton University in 1955. His books include *The Relevance of the Prophets, Treasures From Judean Caves,* and *The Psalms as Christian Praise.* Scott received the Province of Quebec Literary Prize in 1946 and was made a fellow of the Royal Society of Canada in 1955.

OBITUARIES AND OTHER SOURCES:

BOOKS

American Authors and Books: 1640 to the Present Day, 3rd revised edition, Crown, 1972.

The Canadian Who's Who, Volume XXII, University of Toronto Press, 1987.

PERIODICALS

New York Times, November 1, 1987.

* * *

SELTZER, Leon E(ugene) 1918-1988
(Eugene Leigh)

OBITUARY NOTICE—See index for *CA* sketch: Born August 14, 1918, in Auburn, Me.; died of cardio-respiratory arrest, January 11, 1988, in Stanford, Calif. Publisher, attorney, editor, and author. Esteemed for his knowledge of copyright, Seltzer worked as an editor and publisher as well as a copyright lawyer. After beginning his career as an editor for Columbia University Press, he went on to become director of Stanford University Press, where he worked for nearly thirty years. Seltzer's book, *Exemptions and Fair Use in Copyright: The Exclusive Rights Tensions in the Copyright Act of 1976,* is regarded as a major work in the field. He also edited *The Columbia Lippincott Gazetteer of the World* and contributed stories, essays, and verse to magazines, sometimes under the pseudonym Eugene Leigh.

OBITUARIES AND OTHER SOURCES:

BOOKS

Who's Who in America, 44th edition, Marquis, 1986.

PERIODICALS

Publishers Weekly, January 29, 1988.

* * *

SEROKA, James H. 1950-
(Jim Seroka)

PERSONAL: Born March 5, 1950, in Detroit, Mich.; son of Henry (a realtor) and Mary (a homemaker; maiden name, Wyoral) Seroka; married Carolyn White (a social worker), June 29, 1970; children: Mihail, Maritsa. *Education:* University of Michigan, B.A., 1970; attended American University, 1970-71; Michigan State University, M.A., 1972, Ph.D., 1976.

ADDRESSES: Home—2003 Meadow Lane, Carbondale, Ill. 62901. *Office*—Department of Political Science, 3139 Faner Hall, Southern Illinois University, Carbondale, Ill. 62901.

CAREER: U.S. Department of Labor, Washington, D.C., manpower planning analyst, 1970-71; Michigan State University, East Lansing, instructor in political science, 1971-76; University of North Carolina at Greensboro, visiting assistant professor of political science, 1976-77; Appalachian State University, Boone, N.C., assistant professor of political science and assistant director of Appalachian Regional Bureau of Governments, 1977-79; Southern Illinois University, Carbondale, assistant professor, 1979-81, associate professor, 1981-87, professor of political science, 1987—, director of Rural and Small Town Administrative Project, 1980-85, director of Master of Public Affairs Program, 1987—. University of Belgrade, researcher and member of political science faculty, 1974, exchange professor of U.S. National Academy of Sciences, 1981, senior exchange professor, 1986; instructor at Lansing Community College, 1976; member of faculty at Randolph Technical Institute, 1976, 1977; instructor at Illinois Executive Development Academy, 1980, 1981; lecturer at University of Split, University of Nis, and Yugoslav Academy of Law and Political Science. Research associate at Russian and East European Studies Center, University of Illinois at Urbana-Champaign, 1977, 1978, 1982, 1985; member of U.S. State Department Scholar Diplomat Seminar on European Studies, 1979; interviewed on Yugoslav television; consultant to ABC-TV News.

MEMBER: International Personnel Management Association, International Political Science Association, International Studies Association, American Society for Public Administration (chairman of local development committee, 1980-82; local chapter president, 1982-83), American Political Science Association, Policy Studies Organization, Academy of Political Science, Rural Sociological Association, American Association for the Advancement of Slavic Studies, Community Development Society, Midwest Political Science Association, Southern Political Science Association, Southwestern Political Science Association, Western Political Science Association, Western Social Science Association.

AWARDS, HONORS: Grants from American Council of Learned Societies (for Yugoslavia), 1973, 1983, Ford Foundation (for Yugoslavia), 1974, National Endowment for the Humanities, 1979, 1984, 1987, National Academy of Sciences and Yugoslav Academy of Arts and Sciences, 1981, U.S. Office of Personnel Management, 1980-82, National Science Foundation, 1980-83, International Research and Exchanges Board, 1982-83, 1986, and Wilson Center, 1985; outstanding academic book of the year award from *Choice,* 1987, for *Political Organizations in Socialist Yugoslavia.*

WRITINGS:

UNDER NAME JIM SEROKA

(Contributor) Charles Bulmer and John Carmichael, editors, *Employment and Labor Relations Policy,* Heath, 1980.
(Editor with Maurice D. Simon, and contributor) *Developed Socialism in the Soviet Bloc: Political Theory vs. Political Reality,* Westview, 1982.
(Contributor) Gale Stokes, editor, *Nationalism in the Balkans,* Garland Publishing, 1984.
(With Rados Smiljkovic) *Political Organizations in Socialist Yugoslavia,* Duke University Press, 1986.
(Editor and contributor) *Rural Public Administration: Problems and Prospects,* Greenwood Press, 1986.

Contributor of articles and reviews to Slavic studies, political science, public administration, social science, and community development journals.

WORK IN PROGRESS: Rural Public Administration: Contrast With Urban Administration, publication expected in 1989.

* * *

SEROKA, Jim
See SEROKA, James H.

* * *

SEYDEL, Mildred Woolley 1890(?)-1988
(Mildred Seydell)

OBITUARY NOTICE—See index for *CA* sketch: Born c. 1890 in Atlanta, Ga.; died February 20, 1988. Publisher, editor, journalist, and author. Seydel covered important news events worldwide, notably the trial of John Scopes, who was indicted

for teaching evolution. She began her career in journalism in 1921, writing a column for the Charleston *Gazette,* and went on to contribute stories to newspapers published by the Hearst organization. Her columns included an interview with Italian dictator Benito Mussolini. Seydel also wrote books, among them *Secret Fathers, Chins Up, Come Along to Belgium,* and *Keep the Courage,* and she edited *Poetry Profile of Belgium,* which was published by her own firm, the Mildred Seydell Publishing Company, whose name reflects the name she used professionally.

OBITUARIES AND OTHER SOURCES:

BOOKS

Who's Who in America, 42nd edition, Marquis, 1982.

PERIODICALS

Chicago Tribune, February 22, 1988.

* * *

SEYDELL, Mildred
See SEYDEL, Mildred Woolley

* * *

SHACOCHIS, Bob
See SHACOCHIS, Robert G.

* * *

SHACOCHIS, Robert G. 1951-
(Bob Shacochis)

PERSONAL: Surname pronounced "Sha-*coach*-is"; born September 9, 1951, in West Pittston, Pa.; son of John P. (a civil servant) and Helen (a medical secretary; maiden name, Levonoski) Shacochis; married Barbara Petersen in 1976. *Education:* University of Missouri—Columbia, B.A., 1973, M.A., 1979; University of Iowa, M.F.A., 1982.

ADDRESSES: Home—Tallahassee, Fla. *Agent*—Gail Hochman, Brandt & Brandt Literary Agents, Inc., 1501 Broadway, New York, N.Y. 10036.

CAREER: Peace Corps, St. Vincent, Barbados, and St. Kitts, West Indies, agricultural journalist, 1975-76; *Palm Beach Evening Times,* Palm Beach, Fla., reporter, 1980; University of Missouri—Columbia, visiting lecturer in English, 1984-85; University of Iowa, Iowa City, visiting lecturer in English, 1985-86.

MEMBER: Poets and Writers.

AWARDS, HONORS: Literary fellowship from the National Endowment for the Arts, 1982, for fiction writing; best new contributor in fiction award from *Playboy,* 1982, for "Lord Short Shoe Wants the Monkey"; James Michener Award from Iowa Writers Workshop, 1983, for *Easy in the Islands;* Pushcart Prize from Pushcart Press, 1985, for "Hot Day on the Gold Coast"; scholarship and fellowship from Bread Loaf Writers Conference, 1983 and 1985, for fiction writing; the American Book Award for First Fiction from the Association of American Publishers, 1985, for *Easy in the Islands;* Best Stories From the South award, 1986, for "Where Pelham Fell."

WRITINGS:

UNDER NAME BOB SHACOCHIS

Easy in the Islands (short stories), Crown, 1985.

Swimming in the Volcano (novel), Crown, in press.

Work represented in anthologies, including *Pushcart X,* Pushcart Press, 1985. Contributor to periodicals, including *Esquire, Playboy, Chicago, Paris Review, Iowa Review, Missouri Review, Saturday Review, Black Warrior Review, Vogue, Harper's,* and *Tendril.* Fiction editor of *Missouri Review.*

WORK IN PROGRESS: A second collection of short stories.

SIDELIGHTS: Chosen from among several hundred works to receive the American Book Award for First Fiction, Bob Shacochis's 1985 collection of short stories, *Easy in the Islands,* explores life in maritime southern Florida and the Caribbean. Stephen Goodwin in the *Washington Post* called Shacochis's work "a stunning first book" and commended the author for his masterful portrayal of life in the tropics: "Shacochis evokes the islands, the flora and fauna, the rhythm of the language, the feel of the air and the presence of the sea. In the best stories, the details transport the readers to a foreign place and even more foreign way of life." In his Caribbean tales Shacochis mixes the dark and seedy elements of native society with the mythic characteristics of a tourist paradise. Thus he writes of hotels that are deteriorating and calypso singers who are vain and scheming, industrious fishermen as well as drug smugglers and poachers. Shacochis's stories are not, according to *Times Literary Supplement* critic Jim Crace, about "yachts and launches of moneyed America, but the ocean-going equivalents of pick-ups and campers—ketches, smacks and skiffs smelling of 'canvas, turpentine, machine oil and mold.'"

Time's Paul Gray echoed Crace, noting that the author depicts the regional differences of the islands without masking their unpleasant realities. "Shacochis shows a keen awareness of lush disparities," the reviewer remarked, offering as an example Shacochis's contrast of an island marketplace, "'the air luscious with the smells of spices, of frying coconut oil and garlic and cumin, the scents of frangipani and lime,'" with a slum area, "where everything 'smelled like rotting fruit and kerosene, urine and garlic.'" Shacochis further captures Caribbean life with the use of native dialect, which *Los Angeles Times* reviewer Elaine Kendall described as an "unlikely mixture of eighteenth-century English gentility and twentieth-century mainland crudity."

Inspiration for *Easy in the Islands* and Shacochis's island wisdom came from his adventures in the Caribbean as a wanderer and later as a member of the Peace Corps. With the Peace Corps, Shacochis was first stationed on the island of St. Vincent as a journalist with the Ministry of Agriculture. As part of his duties he kept a log, from which came the material for "The Pelican," a story about a young American anthropologist named Bowen who encounters pelican hunters who have a truckload of dead and half-dead birds. Out of pity, Bowen tries unsuccessfully to kill the suffering pelicans with his dull pocketknife, to the amusement of the hardened natives. "Dead Reckoning" is based on the author's ten-day trip to Florida through a storm in a sailboat, that Shacochis, in a *Publishers Weekly* interview, recalled was "like being at war."

"Shacochis not only offers some beguiling tropical tours," noted Gray, "he also shows how living in Eden can be considerably harder than jetting into and out of it." The title story, "Easy in the Islands," tells of the tribulations of Tillman, an American trying to manage a run-down tourist hotel that he inherited from his father. His difficulties with the tourists and staff escalate when his mother unexpectedly dies while visiting. Suspecting foul play, the authorities forbid Tillman to

bury the body and he is forced to keep the corpse in a freezer at the hotel. Thus he loses his guests and his staff and the bartender tries to shoot him. Impressed with the novelty of Shacochis's plots, Kendall noted that "this tale provides a splendid showcase for the author's satirical gifts, at full stretch is his demonstration of the ways in which island attitudes conspire to turn a well-meaning innkeeper into a desperado."

Other stories in *Easy in the Islands* include "Hot Day on the Gold Coast," which Crace deemed "richly comic," involving an overweight drug pusher out for a jog who ends up smuggling Haitian aliens into Florida. In "Lord Short Shoe Wants the Monkey" two men attempt to swap a woman's sexual favors for a monkey. And "Mundo's Sign," "the most extraordinary story" of the collection and "a marvelous tale that ranks with the best of [Joseph] Conrad and [Ernest] Hemingway," according to Goodwin, tells of a native fisherman who has had an erotic dream and interprets it to mean that he must kill a large turtle with his spear gun. He hunts and kills the turtle, only to argue with another fisherman claiming to have netted it before Mundo shot it.

Most of the nine tales of *Easy in the Islands* served as Shacochis's master's thesis at the University of Iowa, with five subsequently appearing in *Playboy* or *Esquire* and the rest in literary periodicals. Gray admired both the literary and general public appeal of the stories: "That parlay of the slick and scholarly is unusual, particularly for a beginning writer. . . . Shacochis has had the commercial prudence to learn and write about an uncommonly fascinating part of the hemisphere. Better still, his talent seems much more than a match for the subjects at his hand." Crace found "the writer's evident and infectiously romantic intimacy with the ocean where even the sail-ropes 'hum freedom'" appealing and maintained that Shacochis "has identified the maritime equivalent of the 'open highway' central to the white male American dream of 'breaking loose.'"

Shacochis's literary concerns are not limited to Caribbean fiction. For a nonfiction piece in *Harper's* entitled "An Island Between Seasons: The Task of Reimagining Haiti," Shacochis traveled to Haiti, the most economically depressed country of the Western Hemisphere, to study the nation in the year after President-for-Life Jean-Claude "Baby Doc" Duvalier stepped down in February, 1986, after a popular uprising. Also for *Harper's* he wrote "Yesterday's Revolution: Grenada, Mr. Reagan, and the Hangman," an account of the events that led to the U.S. military intervention on the tiny island-nation in 1983. Shacochis's additional writings include "Where Pelham Fell," a short story that appeared in *Esquire* concerning a retired colonel in modern Virginia who reassembles the bones of Civil War soldiers who were never given a proper burial. And *Chicago* published Shacochis's story about a victim of Alzheimer's disease, "Celebrations of the New World"—the story with which he gained admission to the University of Iowa Writers Workshop.

CA INTERVIEW

CA interviewed Bob Shacochis by telephone on November 14, 1986, at his home in Buxton, South Carolina.

CA: You started out to be a journalist but, after a series of island adventures both good and bad, decided to write fiction instead. Was the journalism background helpful when you began doing the fiction?

SHACOCHIS: It was helpful in a sort of contrary way. It motivated me to commit myself to a form of writing that I had previously been intimidated by but knew I wanted to do more than anything else. It looked like I was going to have to pay some dues as a journalist that I wasn't particularly willing to pay; it was going to be tedious and I wasn't destined to get the sort of assignments in writing that I wanted. So by default the change forced me to commit myself, to motivate myself to write fiction as a way out of what I felt was a smaller box for my work and for my life. I'd always wanted to write fiction but hadn't the slightest idea what a fiction writer's habits looked like. The easiest decision in the beginning was to be a journalist, and it took me a while to realize that it wasn't a bad decision, but it really wasn't the choice I wanted to make, and I had to grow up a bit before I was going to make the decision I could stick with. But I've always liked journalism. In fact, I thought of fiction writing as a way to establish a reputation that would eventually allow me to do the nonfiction that I longed to do. And that's happened, as a matter of fact. For instance, the *New York Times* sent me to Haiti in May to write about the revolution there. That didn't work out, but *Harper's* has bought the piece, and I'm engaged right now in doing a rewrite for them. I'm really gratified by the opportunity.

I was a teenage writer when all the New Journalists were becoming vogue, and they inspired me. Fiction writing at that time, in the late sixties and early seventies, had become extremely experimental and inaccessible; it was possible to establish a reputation simply by fooling around. I admired the writing that had gone on before that, the black humorists. The linguistic energy and thematic concerns of the New Journalists seemed to fit right in there. At the time I went to journalism school, people like Tom Wolfe and Gay Talese and Gail Sheehy seemed to have more scope and more excitement in their work than the people who were writing fiction. But when I tried to write that way in journalism school, I was treated like a bushfire. Teachers tried very hard to rein me in; they considered my work pretentious. But that was OK. It was part of a whole package of change going on in writing and in American culture.

CA: Did your material fall naturally into short stories, or did you make a conscious decision to do short things rather than a novel?

SHACOCHIS: Writing short stories was probably a factor of a number of things, one of them being that I seriously had no idea what fiction writers were, in the quotidian: what they looked like, how they went about working and living and paying the bills. Writing short stories was, for me, a beginner's attempt at writing fiction, for one thing. And then there's a whole educational system built around the short story. All the writing programs that have evolved in the United States in the last twenty years, starting with the Iowa Writers' Workshop, are essentially based around the short story because it's a manageable form. You can talk about it in a classroom. You can't talk about a student's novel-in-progress in a classroom of ten to twenty students; if they're all working on novels and all at different stages in their novels, it would be unmanageable. The short story is a made-to-order form for the classroom. It's always been there as a customized form for magazines. So it was almost inevitable that I would start by writing stories. And, being so unsure of myself as a fiction writer, I was not about to write a novel until I thought I could do the task at hand, and that seemed to be a short story. I'm trying to write my first novel now, and it's a terrible struggle. I'm glad that

I didn't commit myself to writing one at the beginning, or I suspect I would have defeated myself in the attempt.

CA: Do you think the writers' schools are largely responsible for the renewed commercial acceptance of the short story?

SHACOCHIS: They're directly responsible for it. What's called the short story renaissance is an outgrowth of the writing programs and providing a market cycle for those programs. It's a publishing phenomenon and an educational phenomenon; it's not a writer's phenomenon. The short story has always been around and has always been in relative good health, but, overnight, it seems, publishers decided they had a good, strong market for the short story and indeed they did, with more than two hundred graduate and undergraduate writing programs in the country and thousands of ready-made consumers in the position of being students who hoped to one day produce for that market.

CA: In the island stories in Easy in the Islands, *you were brave enough to tackle the dialect, and it worked. Did that give you any problems in the writing?*

SHACOCHIS: No. I had some mentors in dialect, specifically for the Caribbean dialect—Peter Matthiessen especially. Also, living in the Caribbean helped. The newspapers would always have a column or something written in patois, and the graffiti were written in patois. I had all the models I needed. The hardest part of writing in dialect is having to endure the criticism you get for attempting it: it's too difficult to read, some readers don't want to make the effort to get familiar with the phonetic system; or critics will say quite stupidly that it's condescending to write in a dialect—you're writing about a lower class of people and you're not representing them in their best light. That's a common criticism of dialect from very influential people, and they're so wrong about that. That immediately erases Mark Twain and Charles Dickens and so many other writers trying to establish sociological mobility and cultural breadth in their work.

CA: Without the dialect, that singing quality of the native speech would have been lost in the stories.

SHACOCHIS: Yes. This novel I'm writing is also about the Caribbean and I'm trying to modify the patois a little bit, only because it goes on for so long and when the narrative is extended, the vocabulary that you have to use suddenly increases. In the stories, you could trim that significantly by being very careful what sort of responses you put in dialogue, so you never had to use problematic words and you never had to write a sentence that looked so clumsy because of all the phonetic spelling. It's different with a novel. I've got to streamline the system for my sake and for the reader's sake, but I can't abandon the dialect because that's tantamount to abandoning the culture of the people.

CA: When you're writing a story with a strong autobiographical element, do you ever find it hard to separate the real-life experience enough from yourself to make it good fiction?

SHACOCHIS: No, it's never hard, and that's probably because I have a bad memory. It's so easy to distance myself because I can't remember truly what happened during the course of an event that had an impact on me. I can remember on some level what happened and how I felt, but it doesn't seem real. It always seems more real when I imagine it as if it were all fabricated. I suppose that transference is the source of fiction's credibility and power. And once I start doing that, all of it's accessible in a way that's impossible in pure autobiographical memory.

CA: You were getting stories published while you were at Iowa and came out with several good grants and awards to keep you writing. What were the less obvious benefits from your time there as a student?

SHACOCHIS: The most immediate way it helped was that it convinced me I wasn't making a huge, irrational mistake by having this desire to write. By that time I had been at it long enough without success to think that it was a crazy impulse, that I was deluding myself that I could actually have a life centered around fiction writing. Iowa's a big place. The Workshop has 120 students in it at any given time. When I went to Iowa and immersed myself in that community, for the first time ever I felt that I hadn't made a wrong decision—or that, if I had, I was in good company! That was invaluable, because more than anything else self-doubt is the biggest barrier to getting things done. And acceptance into a community helps reverse the awful sensation of a fall from grace that will not be interrupted. That bleak solitude of not having chosen wisely.

CA: You told Miriam Berkley for Publishers Weekly *that the stories that became* Easy in the Islands *were your master's thesis and ready to be published as a book in 1982, but Crown didn't buy the material until 1984. Did the stories undergo any changes during that time?*

SHACOCHIS: Yes. That was a little too neat an explanation to Miriam. I wrote two more stories after that: the title story and "Redemption Songs." The rest were all published in magazines between '82 and '84, and after they were published in magazines I rewrote them once again, because suddenly the objectivity of print was there and I was able to see what I had only sensed were flaws but had remained invisible both to editors and to myself. When the book was submitted to Crown, there was a final dialogue between myself and Barbara Grossman, my editor there, and the stories were rewritten still once more—not dramatically; only one piece changed in a fundamental way.

Yeah, I'm willingly enslaved to rewriting. Now, when I take a copy of the book somewhere for a public reading and I'm rehearsing a story by reading it to myself beforehand, I'll edit the copy in the book—little obsessive trimmings and alterings. And then when I read it, spontaneously I'll revise it some more. It's crazed. If it wasn't in book form, I'm sure I'd still be tinkering with it. It's an obsessive perfectionism, or whatever the phrase might be, which is based in fear—fear of weaknesses being exposed. It's also a form of procrastination, of indulging in an inconsequential process, and any form of procrastination is something I jump right in on.

CA: You won the 1985 American Book Award for First Fiction for Easy in the Islands, *and it went into a Viking Penguin paperback edition. Those things must have erased some of the self-doubt you've spoken of.*

SHACOCHIS: No. I don't really mean by overemphasis to have the self-doubt become a type of artificial trait or a pretense or an affectation. It might be all of those things in reality, but to me it's something that is constantly gnawing at my willpower. I still, with each thing I do, have a confidence

crisis, a battle to overcome the feeling that I'm really not cut out to be a writer. It never goes away. Each piece I do never feels half as good as what it could be or a third as good as what I read of other people's. There always seems to be a failure of intelligence, a failure of discipline, a failure of motivation. Never, though, a failure of vision—at least from my own perspective. For better or worse, the intentions of my stories are precisely as conceived. Nothing accidental or serendipitous there.

CA: Has the actual process of writing changed in the years you've been at it? You've spoken elsewhere of writing very slowly and finding it hard to sit still.

SHACOCHIS: It's become harder. Mercy me. I write even more slowly, and have even more of a problem sitting still. I wish I could overcome this. It seems I'm going through a phase that's different from the earlier years, when writing was more spontaneous and happy and didn't feel so pressurized. It wasn't under the threat of success.

CA: Many writers say a very successful first book makes the next work very hard because there's the initial triumph to live up to.

SHACOCHIS: Yes. And that pressure manifests itself in each work. When I have to sit down and write five thousand words for *Harper's*, it's five thousand occurrences of insecurity, worrying if that's the best it can be. I've got to rediscover the looseness and the Zen-like lack of control that were there earlier. I'm more than willing to continue taking risks in my writing, but the risks seem less whimsical, less extroverted. It's not that they're more calculated, it's just that I'm more aware that I *am* taking risks. In a way that's sort of a profound loss of innocence in the process of creation.

CA: Your epigraph to Easy in the Islands *is from Joseph Conrad's* Heart of Darkness, *and in an August, 1986,* Esquire *poll you expressed admiration for William Kennedy. What kind of specific inspiration have those two writers provided for your work?*

SHACOCHIS: In literature, Conrad is the father of the modern world, it seems, which is, number one, a global village, and the colonial world as it devolved into a global village with a lot of problems. I like writing about the forces that sweep across the planet. In fiction, they have to embody themselves as characters, and the danger there is in the difficulty of writing beyond archetypical stereotypes. I may get criticism for writing about the exotic, for not paying attention to the home front. The exotic, to some critics and readers, seems a little too glamorous to write about, but the exotic is an entirely relative characteristic to begin with. What's exotic in Kansas is certainly not exotic in Trinidad. Calcutta is not an exotic place to somebody from Bombay. To somebody from Venezuela, Idaho is a remarkably exotic place of the imagination. It's so relative. But what concerns me is that there are enough people who write about the domestic quality of life. That's fine, but there are forces that can suddenly click and the wheel can turn and that domestic life can just be a smear on the landscape; it can be entirely crushed by larger, darker forces moving across the surface of the earth and through mankind. I like to trace the web of those forces of natural and human power in my writing and not ignore them. Americans haven't been consistently good at writing about them, not like, say, the Russians. Americans haven't been very good about writing about how Americans operate in the larger world. Most American writing about that is genre, silly spy intrigues. The people who do write about it—Paul Theroux and Robert Stone and Peter Matthiessen—are considered adventure writers, which is entirely erroneous thinking on the part of the literary establishment. It's very apathetic, and distastefully self-serving. Conrad is an inspiration to overcome the stigma of writing about the so-called exotic, writing about the experience of *the other,* and how contact and conflict with worlds, cultures, people, minds that do not reflect our image or our expectations radically affect our consciousness of our selves. Too many writers today favored by the literary clubhouse are busy portraying anemic insight into the insignificance of experience. What could be more frivolous, more intellectually lazy, more spoiled than this shell-shocked clutch with entropy? These writers should say less, write less, until they have made an effort to develop a system of values. Instead, they pout, and their protests are fatuous, insipid.

William Kennedy has said that realism is fine for what it is, but it's incapable of expressing the full dimension of the human experience. I think that's entirely correct, and I think the realism and the neo-realism and the modernism and the post-modernism in American literature, as baldly lucid as they might be, lack something. There are other dimensions to the quality of human life that aren't expressed so empirically. William Kennedy achieves a fullness of expression in his work. There's a passion and a mythical and indeed mystical depth that come through that I think ring a bell in the psyche of people who read him, unless they're so totally homogenized by contemporary existence that they simply don't have an inner life that goes very deep.

CA: Are you talking about something like the "magical realism" the South American writers are doing so well?

SHACOCHIS: Yes, but "magical realism" is an American term that more appropriately describes a school of painting. The Latins say "lo real maravilloso," which means real *and* marvellous. They fully believe that they're describing reality. I believe it too: the expression of a reality composed of an infinite layering of experience, with only a minority of those layers apparent in everyday modern life. They even try to trick themselves into thinking of something too fantastic, and they always outsmart themselves because, whatever they come up with, as fantastic as it might seem to somebody with a suburban experience, they're writing about the life—the physical, psychological, and spiritual realms—they know and have observed. If somebody has a pig's tail in their book, it's because there are people with pigs' tails in real life. They're trying to communicate their cultural experience, and they're doing it in a way that they think is representational of the multi-layered dimension of human existence. I think it's realistic too. Gabriel Garcia Marquez says that the task of a writer in Latin America or the Caribbean is to convince others of their reality, which they're unwilling to accept. Not the writers, but the people from other cultures, specifically *our* culture, where the only mysteries and the only things fantastic that happen are scientific, technological. Or death, always death, which we treat like an aberration and either sentimentalize or sanitize with cheap philosophy.

CA: Having gone quickly from the student level to the teaching level of writers workshops, how do you feel you're best able to help aspiring writers?

SHACOCHIS: That's a difficult question, and a controversial one. To some extent, the student-teacher relationship is bogus and writing programs are a scam. That doesn't mean they're not of benefit. I think they're of benefit in various ways to almost everybody who participates in them, and they're of benefit to the institutions that support them. But a classroom certainly doesn't make a writer. A classroom is a wonderful place to learn technique. In fact, technique *can* be taught, no sweat at all; it's the easiest thing in the world to teach. The evidence of that is that there are a lot of new writers in this country who are swell with technique, and they've all come out of writing programs. But there's something beyond that, we all know there's something beyond that, that makes a writer, and that simply can't be earned in an institution.

In my own experience as a student, what was valuable to me was to be exposed to a variety of personalities and sensibilities from writers who had had a measure of success. To be able to learn from them as people really was more important than anything instructional that happened in the classroom. Sometimes a writing class can be a huge joke. Not that some teachers don't take them seriously—they do, and most students do. In fact, students take them *too* seriously, because they think it's a guarantee of something, and they can get certified by it. That's entirely untrue. It's a gamble from the word go. You can't go to a writing school as you could a law school or a medical school and come out with something concrete at the end, with the ability to practice law or the ability to practice medicine. You're not certified to practice writing or anything else when you come out of these programs. Except continue a very private struggle against disheartening odds.

CA: Your long story in the January, 1986, issue of Esquire, *"Where Pelham Fell," was completely unlike anything in* Easy in the Islands. *Can you tell me something about how the story happened?*

SHACOCHIS: I can. To people who have only read the stories in *Easy in the Islands,* it's going to look like a wild left turn. But it's not. I've written as many stories that are not about the Caribbean experience as stories that are. They're all different, and I enjoy doing them as much as anything else, if not more. "Where Pelham Fell" grew out of the time when I was living in Charlottesville, Virginia, and wanted to visit my parents or friends outside of Washington, D.C., where I'm from. Route 29 from Charlottesville to the Washington area is dotted with markers commemorating events of American history. The place has seen a lot come and go. There is one marker that I love because of its title, "Where Pelham Fell." I thought, I must have a story called "Where Pelham Fell," because those three words are poetry to me and I love them. So there was that influence, which is more than enough.

Being immersed in the sense of timelessness in the Virginia countryside is a strong motivation to write a story. Another thing is that I always used to go with my brother and a metal detector out in the woods near where we grew up in Virginia. We'd find miniballs and belt buckles and other things that were relics of the Civil War. I'd always had a fascination with that, and I've always kept my eyes to the ground when I've walked around. There are little bits of history on the surface, and they vibrate with a very extraordinary sort of human radiation. I don't know where the notion of the bones in the story came from, but I wanted to write again about black-white relationships. James Alan McPherson was one of my teachers at Iowa, and he told me one time that it was pretty easy for me as a white man to go to the Caribbean and write about black people, but I was chicken to write about blacks in my own home in the United States. I didn't think that was true, but of course I took it seriously and I thought about it and wanted to write something about racial experience in the United States. So there was that too.

CA: You've said in other interviews that there's enough material for a second collection of short stories. Is one definitely scheduled?

SHACOCHIS: No. Again, I guess market strategy is behind that. It probably would look weak in comparison to *Easy in the Islands,* and it's probably a better idea to have the novel come out first. I'm not sure about that stuff, but if there's any way to be smart about it, I'd prefer to be smart.

CA: Do you have goals beyond the novel and the next collection of stories?

SHACOCHIS: I'm not greatly confident about this book I'm working on right now. It might be a good book, but I don't know, which is not an unusual state of mind for me. My confidence sort of surges when I think ahead to a third book and a fourth book, which I have ideas for. My imagination resides more easily in those books—though who knows when they'll be written? But I daydream about them, and then I feel a strength returning, both a desire to write and a need to write.

BIOGRAPHICAL/CRITICAL SOURCES:

BOOKS

Shacochis, Bob, *Easy in the Islands,* Crown, 1985.

PERIODICALS

Los Angeles Times, February 26, 1985.
New York Times Book Review, February 17, 1985.
Publishers Weekly, December 20, 1985.
Time, February 18, 1985.
Times Literary Supplement, March 7, 1986.
Washington Post Book World, March 18, 1985.

—Sketch by Carol Lynn DeKane

—Interview by Jean W. Ross

* * *

SHAHEEN, Jack G(eorge) 1935-

PERSONAL: Born September 21, 1935, in Pittsburgh, Pa.; son of Jack (a foreman) and Nazara (a domestic engineer; maiden name, Jacobs) Shaheen; married Bernice Marie (a research scientist), January 22, 1966; children: Michael, Michele. *Education:* Carnegie Institute of Technology, B.F.A., 1957; Pennsylvania State University, M.A., 1964; University of Missouri, Ph.D., 1969. *Politics:* Independent. *Religion:* Eastern Orthodox.

ADDRESSES: Home—1526 Weber Ln., Edwardsville, Ill. 62026. *Office*—Department of Mass Communications, Southern Illinois University at Edwardsville, P.O. Box 1775, Edwardsville, Ill. 62026. *Agent*—James C.G. Coniff, Megadot, P.O. Box 812, Upper Montclair, N.J. 07043.

CAREER: University of California at Los Angeles, Los Angeles, Calif., special program director, 1965-67; Southern Illinois University, Edwardsville, professor of mass communications, 1969—. American University of Beirut, Beirut,

Lebanon, Fulbright professor, 1974-75; University of Jordan, Amman, Jordan, Fulbright professor, 1981-82. News reporter for KOMU-TV, 1967-68; critic for WSIE-FM Radio, 1969—, and KPLR-TV, 1972-74. Lecturer in communications and Arab stereotypes at universities, academic conferences, and civic organizations, 1973—. Consultant for American Broadcasting Companies (ABC-TV), 1984—, and Institute for International Research, Inc., 1985—. Member of Fulbright Screening Committee, 1985-88. *Military service:* U.S. Army, Intelligence, 1958-60.

MEMBER: International Studies Association, American Federation of Television and Radio Artists, National Academy of Television Arts and Sciences, Association for Professional Broadcasting Education, American-Arab Affairs Council (board member, 1983), Veterans Hospital Radio and T.V. Guild, University Film Association, Popular Culture Association, Fulbright Alumni Association.

AWARDS, HONORS: Named scholar diplomat by U.S. Department of State, 1978, and American Participant Researcher/Teacher by the U.S. Information Agency, 1982 and 1986.

WRITINGS:

(Editor) *Nuclear War Films,* Southern Illinois University Press, 1978.

The TV Arab, Popular Press, 1984.

Author of essays in books and monographs. Television columnist for *Metro East Journal,* 1976-77. Also contributor of more than 150 articles to periodicals, including *Washington Post, Wall Street Journal,* and *Pittsburgh Post Gazette.*

WORK IN PROGRESS: The Hollywood Arab, publication by Syracuse University Press, expected in 1990.

SIDELIGHTS: Jack G. Shaheen told *CA:* "My writings reflect concern for problems such as nuclear war, the environment, and stereotypical portraits of ethnic and minority groups. The works reflect the vision of an academic who seeks out significant themes and examines them with the intent to affect social conditions."

AVOCATIONAL INTERESTS: Traveling in the United States, Europe, and the Middle East; loyalty to Pittsburgh sports teams.

* * *

SHAMES, Laurence 1951-

PERSONAL: Surname is pronounced in one syllable; born January 26, 1951, in Newark, N.J.; son of Irving S. (in sales) and Helen (a homemaker; maiden name, Baron) Shames. *Education:* New York University, B.A., 1972. *Politics:* "Diehard pragmatic liberal."

ADDRESSES: Home and office—New York, N.Y. *Agent*—Sterling Lord Literistic, 1 Madison Ave., New York, N.Y. 10010.

CAREER: Writer, 1972—.

MEMBER: Authors Guild.

AWARDS, HONORS: The Big Time was named to *Business Week*'s list of ten best books for 1986.

WRITINGS:

The Big Time: The Harvard Business School's Most Successful Class—and How It Shaped America, Harper, 1986.

Author of ethics column in *Esquire,* 1982-83. Contributor to magazines and newspapers, including *Saturday Review, Playboy,* and *Vanity Fair.*

WORK IN PROGRESS: A book on contemporary American values, for Times Books.

SIDELIGHTS: Laurence Shames's *The Big Time* was labeled "hard to put down" by Louis Uchitelle in the *New York Times Book Review.* The book details the lives and opinions of the Harvard Business School graduating class of 1949, who first gained national attention in 1974 when *Fortune* magazine reported the amazing success rate of the class's members. Nearly half of its graduates had by then ascended to the top levels of corporate life, and one-fifth of them had achieved millionaire status. Uchitelle praised Shames as "a good storyteller, with a novelist's eye for description, anecdote and vivid metaphor."

Shames told *CA:* "I had never heard of the Harvard Business School's class of 1949 until an editor at Harper & Row suggested I might write a book about the 654 men who comprised it. Her feeling was that everyone liked a good success story, and here were a bunch of them conveniently linked. I saw the project somewhat differently: as an opportunity to explore the attitudes and ambitions of the postwar period, and to trace the effects—both good and bad—of those attitudes in a world grown ever more complicated. Curiously, since the book was superficially about business, people tended to assume it was *pro*-business; this may have been good for sales, but it simply was not the case. Rather, *The Big Time* was about the first generation in American history that had bequeathed *less* opportunity to those that came after.

"The book I'm working on now picks up on this same theme—albeit in a very oblique way. What will take the place, in propping up the national morale and self-esteem, of the sort of automatic economic growth that can no longer be counted on? How will individuals define 'success' when it becomes self-tormenting to define it merely in terms of raises and promotions? Which notion will finally win out in the war between life and lifestyle?"

BIOGRAPHICAL/CRITICAL SOURCES:

PERIODICALS

New York Times Book Review, May 4, 1986.

* * *

SHARP, Martin 1900(?)-1987

OBITUARY NOTICE: Born c. 1900; died December 3, 1987. Editor, public relations manager, and author. Sharp became public relations manager of the British de Havilland aircraft company in 1936, following a period of banking in India and a brief career as assistant editor of *Airplane* magazine. Always an enthusiastic advocate of air transport, Sharp wrote *DH: An Outline of the de Havilland History* in 1960, four years before his retirement from the company.

OBITUARIES AND OTHER SOURCES:

PERIODICALS

Times (London), December 15, 1987.

* * *

SHECHNER, Mark E. 1940-

PERSONAL: Born June 22, 1940, in Newark, N.J.; son of

Herbert and Mary (Picon) Shechner; married Anne Shapiro (a certified public accountant), February 3, 1967; children: Sarah Cecilia. *Education:* University of California, Los Angeles, B.A., 1962, M.A., 1964; University of California, Berkeley, Ph.D., 1970.

ADDRESSES: Office—Department of English, State University of New York at Buffalo, Amherst Campus, Buffalo, N.Y. 14260.

CAREER: State University of New York at Buffalo, assistant professor, 1970-75, associate professor, 1975-79, professor of English, 1979—. Visiting professor at University of Pennsylvania, 1977; Fulbright lecturer at Kobe University, 1988.

AWARDS, HONORS: Fellow of American Council of Learned Societies, 1978-79.

WRITINGS:

Joyce in Nighttown: A Psychoanalytic Inquiry Into Ulysses, University of California Press, 1974.

After the Revolution: Essays in Contemporary Jewish-American Intellectual History, Indiana University Press, 1987.

(Editor) *Preserving the Hunger: An Isaac Rosenfeld Reader,* Wayne State University Press, 1988.

The Conversion of the Jews and Other Essays, Macmillan, in press.

SIDELIGHTS: Mark E. Shechner told *CA:* "At one time I thought of myself as both a Joycean and a psychoanalytic critic. At any rate, those were the identities I came out of graduate school with in 1970. I took up [Irish author James] Joyce because he excited me, and psychoanalysis because it had, or seemed to have, an insurgent edge; it seemed to justify a life of scholarship in an increasingly politicized world, and it gave me privileged insights into the pathological conditions of literature at a time when pathology seemed to be everywhere. Joyce has stayed with me; I never tire of him. But the psychoanalysis has long since been abandoned, not noisily with a convert's fanfare, but quietly, because it no longer seems very interesting to me. Where the study of literature once appealed to me as an adjunct to politics, I now approach it as an antidote to politics. Not that literature is or ought to be non-political, any more than criticism is or ought to be, but the imagination is not a captive of what [English author] E. M. Forster called 'the world of telegrams and anger.' It has its own reasons. I'm now more interested in those reasons.

"I took up a study of contemporary American Jewish writers and intellectuals about fifteen years ago in large measure because I heard voices among them that resonated for me; they seemed like family voices, but they were speaking a strange language. The accents were deeply familiar—I had heard them around the dinner table—but the words were new; they came from a world of ideas that I had no purchase on. Another way to express that is to say that I was in search of a usable past and they turned out to be it. One voice in particular, Isaac Rosenfeld, singled itself out from all the rest, and I sometimes think of him as something of a mix of older brother and patron saint. Anyone who writes, even in a form as marginal as literary criticism, needs a model of how to go about it, and I was fortunate in finding Rosenfeld. He wrote from the heart and the head all at once, and neither disguised the feelings that drove his writing nor subordinated his intelligence to them. The proposition that heart and head are somehow inimical to each other would have bewildered him, and if I've learned anything from him it is how to formulate an emotional language without sounding foolish."

BIOGRAPHICAL/CRITICAL SOURCES:

PERIODICALS

New York Times Book Review, May 10, 1987.

* * *

SHEEAN, Diana 1915(?)-1987 (Diana Forbes-Robertson)

OBITUARY NOTICE: Born c. 1915 in London, England; died of a stroke complicated by pneumonia, December 9, 1987, in London, England. Author. Daughter of the well-known British actors Sir Johnston Forbes-Robertson and Lady Gertrude Forbes-Robertson, Sheean wrote several books under her maiden name, including *The Battle of Waterloo Road* and *War Letters From Britain,* depicting wartime Great Britain, the novel *A Cat and a King,* and *My Aunt Maxine,* a biography of her aunt, American actress Maxine Elliot. In 1935 she married the famous American foreign correspondent, Vincent Sheean, and shortly after, began writing articles for the *New York Herald Tribune* as she traveled in Europe with her husband.

OBITUARIES AND OTHER SOURCES:

PERIODICALS

New York Times, December 16, 1987.

* * *

SHIELDS, David 1956-

PERSONAL: Born July 22, 1956, in Los Angeles, Calif.; son of Milton (a journalist) and Hannah (a journalist; maiden name, Bloom) Shields. *Education:* Brown University, B.A., 1978; University of Iowa, M.F.A. (with honors), 1980.

ADDRESSES: Home—14 Jay St., Canton, N.Y. 13617. *Agent*—**Candida Donadio & Associates, Inc., 231 West 22nd St., New York, N.Y. 10011.**

CAREER: University of Iowa, Iowa City, 1978-80, began as research assistant, became instructor in creative writing and literature; St. Lawrence University, Canton, N.Y., writer in residence, 1985-86, 1987-88. Researcher and writer for former California governor Pat Brown, 1984; visiting lecturer in creative writing at University of California, Los Angeles, spring and summer, 1985.

MEMBER: International P.E.N., Authors Guild, Writers Guild of America—West, Modern Language Association of America, Poets and Writers, Associated Writing Programs, Phi Beta Kappa.

AWARDS, HONORS: James Michener fellowship from Iowa Writers' Workshop, 1980-82; James D. Phelan Award in Literature from San Francisco Foundation, 1981, and Ingram Merrill Foundation Award, 1983, both for "Emile Coue's Unlikely Cure"; a number of grants, including one from National Endowment for the Arts, 1982, Authors League of America, 1983, International P.E.N., 1983, 1986, and 1987, Carnegie Fund, 1984 and 1987, Change, 1985, St. Lawrence University, 1986, and Ludwig Vogelstein Foundation, 1986; MacDowell fellow, 1982; Yaddo fellow, 1982 and 1984; Edna St. Vincent Millay Award from Millay Colony, 1983; Ragdale Foundation fellow, 1983; named winner of fourth P.E.N. Syndicated Science Fiction Project Competition, 1986; William Sloane fellowship in prose from Bread Loaf Writers' Conference, 1986.

WRITINGS:

Heroes (novel), Simon & Schuster, 1984.

Contributor of articles and stories to magazines, including *Iowa Review, Chicago Review, James Joyce Quarterly, Northern Light, Hellcoal,* and *San Francisco Chronicle*.

WORK IN PROGRESS: Dead Languages, a novel; *Perfection,* a novel about "the effect of media-generated norms upon romance."

SIDELIGHTS: In his first novel, *Heroes,* David Shields writes about "two great American preoccupations, Lost Innocence and Sports," recounted James Marcus in the *Philadelphia Inquirer*. Similar themes of spent youth and missed opportunity are also featured in this story that dramatizes the mid-life crisis and ultimate self-realization of a midwestern sportswriter, Al Biederman. A former college basketball star whose career was prematurely ended by an injury sustained on the court, Biederman turned to journalism when he could no longer participate physically in the game. While reporting on basketball for a small town newspaper in Iowa, he discovers a talented college athlete who reminds the middle-aged Biederman of his now diminished athletic prowess. Clinging to a romanticized vision of his past, Biederman sees the young transfer student Belvyn Menkus as the epitome of everything the unsuccessful sportswriter once hoped to become. Ironically, however, Menkus is entangled in some illegal recruiting practices. The admiring Biederman is torn between exposing the wrongdoing—and possibly gaining a more prestigious post at a big city journal—and turning away, thus sacrificing personal attainment for the good of the game. Complicating Biederman's decision-making are several other personal conflicts such as resentment for his wife's success, intolerance for his son's frail health, and an affair with an enamored journalism student.

Heroes garnered favorable reviews from a number of critics and likewise impressed Marcus as a celebration of "the subtler brand of heroism." It "makes a particular virtue of showing how . . . ideals run aground, but nonetheless, survive intact," he added. Diana L. Smith, writing in the *Fort Worth Star-Telegram,* opined that Shields "has an engaging way of incorporating important events . . . with a pleasant mix of hilarity and pathos." Noting that the clarity of the characters and scenes is "excellent," she further assessed that *Heroes* "is a thoroughly enjoyable book." According to Jack Russell's article in the *San Mateo Times,* Shields related that his novel "is about trying to hold onto what we once had, about wanting to get it back, about not wanting ever to give up our good American soul."

Shields told *CA:* "I wrote the first draft of my second novel, *Dead Languages,* while I was a student at the University of Iowa Writers' Workshop. At the same time I was earning my M.F.A. degree, I was a part-time client of the University of Iowa's speech and hearing clinic. I was overwhelmed by the paradox that as a writer I was able to control language but that as a stutterer I was to a certain extent at the mercy of it. Although I have for all intents and purposes overcome my speech problem, I continue to be extraordinarily interested in the psychological origins and philosophic connotations of stuttering. Suffice it to say that my Iowa thesis was a gargantuan, sprawling rough draft of a novel about a boy who confronts his stutter in the context of a family that is committed to the ideal of social justice but addicted to the tension of interpersonal warfare.

"I revised *Dead Languages* and my agent submitted the second draft to more than a dozen publishers who generally admired the verbal energy and sad comedy of the book but were troubled by its claustrophobia and inertia. Over the next four years, I wrote a very different novel titled *Heroes*. I wanted to write a book that wasn't narrowly autobiographical and that was full of character and conflict and action—a solid, traditional novel—and *Heroes* is it. I wrote this book almost exclusively at artists' colonies, where I was impressed by the depth and complexity that a number of visual artists achieved in the collages. An editor had once recommended that I rewrite *Dead Languages* as an autobiographical essay. I paired this suggestion with the collage work I saw being done at the colonies, and I am now reconceiving my first novel as a fragmented family album.

"I hope to create, in the cacophany of competing analyses and definitions and redefinitions, the 'sound' of stuttering. I want to open up the gap between private revery and muddled conversation. As a metaphor, stuttering represents to me nothing less than the beautiful difficulty of human communication."

AVOCATIONAL INTERESTS: Travel (Mexico, Spain).

BIOGRAPHICAL/CRITICAL SOURCES:

PERIODICALS

Fort Worth Star-Telegram, December 16, 1984.
Philadelphia Inquirer, December 8, 1984.
San Mateo Times, August 22, 1984.
Santa Monica Evening Outlook, May 7, 1985.

* * *

SIDEY, Hugh (Swanson) 1927-

PERSONAL: Born September 3, 1927, in Greenfield, Iowa; son of Kenneth H. and Alice Margaret (Swanson) Sidey; married Alice Anne Trowbridge, December 5, 1953; children: Cynthia Anne, Sandra, Bettina, Edwin. *Education:* Iowa State University, B.S., 1950.

ADDRESSES: Home—10825 Stanmore Dr., Potomac, Md. 20854. *Office*—888 16th St. N.W., Washington, D.C. 20006.

CAREER: Journalist. *Adair County Free Press,* Greenfield, Iowa, reporter, 1950; *Nonpareil,* Council Bluffs, Iowa, reporter, 1950-51; *World-Herald,* Omaha, Neb., reporter, 1951-55; *Life,* New York City, reporter, 1955-58; *Time,* New York City, correspondent, 1958—, author of column "The Presidency," 1966—, chief of Washington bureau, 1969-78, Washington contributing editor, 1978—. Has also appeared regularly as a panelist on National Broadcasting Company (NBC-TV) forum "Agronsky and Company." *Military service:* U.S. Army, 1945-46.

WRITINGS:

(With Rodney Fox) *1,000 Ideas for Better News Pictures,* Iowa State College Press, 1956.

John F. Kennedy, President, Atheneum, 1963, new edition, 1964.

A Very Personal Presidency: Lyndon Johnson in the White House, Atheneum, 1968.

(Author of text) *The Memories—JFK, 1961-1963 of Cecil Stoughton, the President's Photographer, and Major General Chester V. Clifton, the President's Military Aide,* Norton, 1973.

(Author of text) *Portrait of a President,* photographs by Fred Ward, Harper, 1975.

(Author of text) *These United States* (Literary Guild Alternate), photographs by Fred J. Maroon, EPM Publications, 1975.

Also contributor to *The Kennedy Circle*.

SIDELIGHTS: During his long career as a journalist, Hugh Sidey has covered seven presidents and written books on three of them—*John F. Kennedy, President; A Very Personal Presidency: Lyndon Johnson in the White House;* and *Portrait of a President,* which chronicles the administration of Gerald R. Ford. Sidey traveled with Johnson to the Vietnam War front; he reported Nixon's China trip; and he accompanied Ford and Carter on their travels around the world. Furthermore, Sidey was granted an exclusive interview for *Time* magazine with President Ronald Reagan just hours before the chief executive's nationally televised August, 1987, press conference on the nine-month-old Iran-*contra* drama that had shaken the nation and scarred his administration. Sidey was also the journalist selected by *People* magazine's editors to compose a profile of Reagan, the first of their "twenty-five most intriguing people of 1987" featured in a special year-end double issue.

Of his three books on these recent White House occupants, *A Very Personal Presidency: Lyndon Johnson in the White House* was the most widely reviewed and highly acclaimed. In the opening notes Sidey describes *A Very Personal Presidency* as a distillation of two million words of "raw material" that he jotted down in ten years—an impressionistic "book of glimpses." The author continues, "None is a total by itself, but it is my hope that when put together in the reader's mind, much like the frames of a motion picture, they will leave a full and fresh impression of Lyndon Johnson's Presidency." Sidey then proceeds to review Johnson's ascension to the presidency; his achievements in the fields of civil rights, health, and education; his concept of the Great Society; his involvement in Vietnam; and his decision not to run again in 1968. The journalist examines both the accomplishments and the failures of the Johnson administration. On the plus side he cites Johnson's grand humanistic and patriotic visions coupled with an ability to get legislation passed. On the minus side he lists Johnson's failure to generate public enthusiasm for his programs and a credibility gap that resulted in public distrust of government. Finally, he recounts incidents and anecdotes that reveal the private side of the man.

Sidey shows how deeply the hard times in the Texas hill country affected Johnson as a youth and how he maintained the conviction that "the world is simply Johnson City in megatons." He posits that Johnson's struggle for wealth and power left him with an "incipient chip on the shoulder" and that his highly successful legislative career shaped—and in some ways misshaped—his presidency. In Sidey's view, Johnson never fully comprehended the difference between legislative and executive power, and his administration suffered for it. His greatest failure, however, Sidey judged, was in the art of communicating. "Language may be the most important tool that a President has for governing this sprawling nation," wrote the author, "and while Johnson was superbly versed in the arcane language of cloakroom and corridor, he never learned to impart his vision for a better America to the people." Moreover, according to Sidey, "there was great truth in the observation of one of [Johnson's] close friends that '90 percent of what he wants is right but 90 percent of the way he does it is wrong.'"

Critics generally agreed with Sidey's analyses of Johnson's strengths and flaws. Larry L. King, writing in *New Republic,* proclaimed that Sidey "did not miss his mark by much." According to King, Sidey "is not blind to presidential shortcomings," adding that the author's "controlled understanding of them, plus his reasoned explanation of *how* LBJ came to be the creature that he [was]—and his willingness to bestow credit when due—leaves the author's credibility intact." Furthermore, King supported Sidey's theory that "despite LBJ's thirty-odd years on the national political scene he remain[ed] very much the small-town boy from Johnson City, his outlooks and decisions irrevocably shaped by his early experiences in a land where brute strength was often necessary to survival and generally was more prized than any virtues save—possibly—cunning."

"Some observations sound hostile," wrote *New York Times Book Review* contributor Richard Strout, but—he hastened to add—"they aren't." Rather, continued the critic, "Sidey's point of view seems to shift: first incredulity, then dismay, then a kind of protective acceptance." Mostly, concluded Strout, Sidey is left baffled by this somehow anachronistic figure, and by the last chapter of his book he "shrugs his shoulders . . . and says simply, 'It is impossible to find your way through the labyrinth of Johnson's mind.'"

Similarly, in an evaluation of *A Very Personal Presidency* for the *New Yorker,* a reviewer called Sidey's book "excellent," lauding its portrayal of "a somewhat asymmetrical personality, given to noble ends and devious means, and flawing wise decisions by coarse speech." The reviewer concluded that although Sidey "does not generalize, his work nonetheless is filled with all sorts of brilliant hints about the qualities that the American Presidency nowadays requires."

BIOGRAPHICAL/CRITICAL SOURCES:

BOOKS

Sidey, Hugh, *A Very Personal Presidency: Lyndon Johnson in the White House,* Atheneum, 1968.

PERIODICALS

Christian Science Monitor, August 3, 1968.
Listener, October 31, 1968.
New Republic, August 3, 1968.
Newsweek, July 15, 1968.
New Yorker, August 10, 1968.
New York Review of Books, October 16, 1975.
New York Times Book Review, July 28, 1968.
Punch, September 25, 1968.
Saturday Review, September 21, 1968.
Time, July 12, 1968.
Times Literary Supplement, September 12, 1968.
Washington Post, August 1, 1968.

—*Sketch by Joanne M. Peters*

* * *

SIEGEL, Seymour 1927-1988

OBITUARY NOTICE: Born September 12, 1927, in Chicago, Ill.; died of a stroke and a circulatory ailment, February 24, 1988, in New York, N.Y. Jewish theologian, educator, and author. Siegel was a leading public figure in the Jewish-American community. As an educator he was associated with the Jewish Theological Seminary in New York City for forty-one years. Appointed Ralph Simon Professor of Theology and Ethics in 1980, he was involved in the social and ethical questions facing the modern Jewish faith and community. As head of

the Committee on Jewish Law and Standards of the Rabbinical Assembly, a position he held for ten years, Siegel played a key role in the decision allowing women to be ordained as Conservative rabbis. He also established close ties with President Ronald Reagan's administration while serving on the President's Commission for the Study of Ethical Problems in Medicine and Biomedical Behavioral Research in 1982 and 1983. He was later appointed executive director of the United States Holocaust Memorial Council; as such he was responsible for organizing the building of a memorial in Washington, D.C., to honor the estimated six million European Jews killed during the Nazi regime of Adolf Hitler. Siegel was a prolific writer of articles and the editor of two books, *Conservative Judaism and Jewish Law* and *God in the Teachings of Conservative Judaism*. His additional writings include *The Jewish Dietary Laws* and *God in Conservative Judaism*.

OBITUARIES AND OTHER SOURCES:

BOOKS

Directory of American Scholars, Volume IV: *Philosophy, Religion, and Law,* 8th edition, Bowker, 1982.
Who's Who in America, 44th edition, Marquis, 1986.

PERIODICALS

Los Angeles Times, February 27, 1988.
New York Times, February 25, 1988.
Washington Post, February 25, 1988.

* * *

SILBER, Evelyn (Ann) 1949-

PERSONAL: Born May 22, 1949, in Welwyn Garden City, England; daughter of Martin H. (an industrialist) and Mavis (Giles) Silber. *Education:* New Hall, Cambridge, M.A., 1972; University of Pennsylvania, M.A., 1973; Clare Hall, Cambridge, Ph.D., 1982.

ADDRESSES: Home—Birmingham, England. *Office*—Birmingham Museum and Art Gallery, Chamberlain Sq., Birmingham B3 3DH, England.

CAREER: Associated Book Publishers, London, England, in marketing production, 1973-75; Birmingham Museum and Art Gallery, Birmingham, England, curator of fine arts, 1979-85, assistant director, 1985—. Lecturer at University of Glasgow, 1978. Member of management council of Ikon Gallery.

MEMBER: Association of Art Historians (honorary secretary).

WRITINGS:

The Sculpture of Epstein: With a Complete Catalogue, Phaidon, 1986.
Jacob Epstein, Leeds City Art Gallery, 1987.

Also author of *Foreign Paintings at Birmingham Museum and Art Gallery: A Summary Catalogue,* 1983, and *Sculpture at Birmingham Museum and Art Gallery: A Summary Catalogue,* 1986. Contributor to art journals.

WORK IN PROGRESS: Research for a book, *Henri Gaudier-Brzeska,* with photographer David Finn, for Thames & Hudson.

SIDELIGHTS: Evelyn Silber told *CA:* "My opportunity to work on the neglected Jewish-American artist, Jacob Epstein, who was one of the most important twentieth-century British artists, came about as a result of his birth centenary, for which I prepared a modest exhibition. This represented a complete change from my former specialty. I was a medievalist, working on the illumination of late medieval manuscripts."

Nearly eighty years ago, Jacob Epstein, a Jewish emigrant from New York, began to produce sculptures whose nudity and style scandalized London. For many years his work was nearly forgotten, but today it is enjoying renewed interest. Silber's book draws attention to the sculptor who, some critics suggest, played an integral role in the development of twentieth-century British sculpture. Because of Epstein's disinterest in recording his works it has been difficult to catalogue his artwork with any degree of accuracy. Peter Fuller wrote in the *Times Literary Supplement:* "Silber is to be commended for the thoroughness and devotion with which she set about her task." The critic added that *The Sculpture of Epstein* is likely to remain the standard work in its field.

BIOGRAPHICAL/CRITICAL SOURCES:

PERIODICALS

Times Literary Supplement, February 6, 1987.

* * *

SILVER, A(aron) David 1941-

PERSONAL: Born March 28, 1941, in Knoxville, Tenn.; son of Leo (an investor) and Sylvia (a community worker; maiden name, Werner) Silver; married Jerilyn Schulman (a psychotherapist), November 22, 1962; children: Claude Amanda, Caleb Borden. *Education:* University of Chicago, B.A., 1962, M.B.A., 1963. *Religion:* Jewish.

ADDRESSES: Home and office—ADS Financial Services, Inc., 524 Camino del Monte Sol, Santa Fe, N.M. 87501.

CAREER: Chase Manhattan Bank, New York City, in credit department, 1964-66; Kuhn, Loeb & Co., New York City, associate in corporate finance department, 1966-70; president of A. David Silver & Co., Inc. (investment banking), 1971-81; general partner of ADS Associates L.P. (venture capital investing), 1982-86; ADS Financial Services, Inc. (merchant bankers), Santa Fe, N.M., president, 1987—. Director of IEC Electronics Corp., Transart Industries, Inc., and Jeffrey Norton Publishers, Inc.; chairman of Temple Beth Shalom Building Fund Committee, 1984-85; chairman of board of trustees of Santa Fe Preparatory School, 1985-87.

MEMBER: Venture Capital Club of New Mexico, University of Chicago Club, Garrison Gold Club, Santa Fe Country Club.

WRITINGS:

Venture Capital, Lane Gate Capital, 1976, Wiley, 1985.
Start-Up Directory, Lane Gate Capital, 1977.
Leveraged Buy-Out Directory, Lane Gate Capital, 1977.
Entrepreneurial Characteristics, Lane Gate Capital, 1977.
Preparing the Business Plan, Lane Gate Capital, 1978.
Corporate Venture Capital Investing, Lane Gate Capital, 1979.
Successful Entrepreneurship, Jeffrey Norton, 1982.
Up Front Financing, Wiley, 1982.
The Entrepreneurial Life, Wiley, 1983.
Who's Who in Venture Capital, Wiley, 1984, 3rd edition, 1986.
Entrepreneurial Megabucks, Wiley, 1986.
The Silver Prescription, Wiley, 1987.

Contributor to periodicals, including *Accounting, America West, Group Practice Journal, High Technology, Los Angeles Business Journal, Nation's Business, New York Times, Success, Venture,* and *Wall Street Journal.*

WORK IN PROGRESS: A First Book of Wealth, for Career Press; *Up Front Money,* for Wiley; *Shifting Winds.*

SIDELIGHTS: A. David Silver informed *CA:* "My personal goal is to see entrepreneurship taught in junior high and high schools. Then young people may learn how to solve society's major problems, rather than having to complain about them or endure them."

* * *

SIMMONS, Mabel Clark 1899-1988

OBITUARY NOTICE: Born September 5, 1899, in Tuscumbia, Mo.; died January 15, 1988. Journalist, free-lance writer, and editor. After majoring in journalism—the only course open to women at that time besides nursing and education—at the University of Missouri, Simmons joined the *Nashville Tennessean* as a reporter in 1922. Following a twenty-seven-year career as a free-lance writer, she joined the New Orleans *Times-Picayune* as literary editor in 1954, where she remained until her retirement in 1987.

OBITUARIES AND OTHER SOURCES:

BOOKS

Who's Who of American Women, 12th edition, Marquis, 1981.

PERIODICALS

Publishers Weekly, March 4, 1988.

* * *

SIMPKIN, Richard E(velyn) 1921-1986

PERSONAL: Born April 25, 1921; died November 3, 1986; married Barbara Grant-Johnson, 1941; children: two sons, one daughter. *Education:* Attended Trinity College, Cambridge; graduate of Army Staff College and Royal Military College of Science.

CAREER: British Army, career officer in Royal Tank Regiment, served in Western Desert and Italy during World War II and became prisoner of war, served in Germany, member of faculty at Staff College and Royal Military College of Science, in charge of equipment branch of Armoured Corps Directorate, 1960-63, commander of First Royal Tank Regiment, 1963-68, appointed director of operational requirements at Ministry of Defence, 1968, retiring as brigadier general in 1971; language consultant and writer, 1971-86.

AWARDS, HONORS: Officer of Order of the British Empire.

WRITINGS:

(Translator) Werner Girbig, *Six Months to Oblivion: The Eclipse of the Luftwaffe Fighter Force,* Allan, 1975.
Broadmanship: A Guide to Safe Boating on the Norfolk Broads, Bayard Books, 1976.
(With Rosemarie Jones) *Business and the Language Barrier,* Business Books, 1976.
The Cruising Yachtsman's Navigator, Barrie & Jenkins, 1977.
Cruising Yachtsman's Troubleshooter, Barrie & Jenkins, 1977.
Seamanship for the Cruising Yachtsman, S. Paul, 1979.
Tank Warfare: An Analysis of Soviet and NATO Tank Philosophy, Brassey's, 1979.
Mechanized Infantry, Brassey's, 1980.
(Editor and translator) Bernard Robin, *Survival at Sea: A Practical Manual of Survival and Advice to the Shipwrecked,* International Marine Publishing, 1981.
Antitank: An Airmechanized Response to Armoured Threats in the Nineties, Brassey's, 1982.
Uniforms of the British Army, Webb & Bower, Volume I: *Cavalry Regiments,* 1982, Volume II: *Infantry Regiments,* 1985.
Human Factors in Mechanized Warfare, Brassey's, 1983.
(Translator) Ferdinand M. Etterlin, *Tanks of the World, 1982-1983: Flottentaschenbuch,* Nautical and Aviation, 1983.
Red Armour: An Examination of the Soviet Mobile Force Concept, Brassey's, 1984.
Race to the Swift: Thoughts on Twenty-first Century Warfare, Brassey's, 1985.
(With John Erickson) *Deep Battle: The Brainchild of Marshall Tukhachevskii,* Pergamon, 1986.

BIOGRAPHICAL/CRITICAL SOURCES:

PERIODICALS

Annals of the American Academy of Political and Social Science, September, 1985.
Times (London), November 4, 1986.*

* * *

SIMS, Patterson 1947-

PERSONAL: Born November 17, 1947, in Philadelphia, Pa.; son of Joseph P., Jr. (a travel agent) and Eleanor (a community organizer; maiden name, Casey) Sims. *Education:* New School for Social Research, B.A., 1972.

ADDRESSES: Seattle Art Museum, Volunteer Park, Seattle, Wash. 98112.

CAREER: O. K. Harris Works of Art, New York City, assistant director, 1969-76; Whitney Museum of American Art, New York City, curator, 1976—. Instructor at New York University, 1975-77. Member of advisory board of Philadelphia's Fabric Workshop and Art Gallery at Robert Lehman College.

MEMBER: Studio in a School Association (member of advisory board).

WRITINGS:

Jan Matulka: A Life in Art, Smithsonian Institution Press, 1979.
(With Emily Rauh Pulitzer) *Ellsworth Kelly: Sculpture,* Whitney Museum of American Art, 1982.
Whitney Museum of American Art: Selected Works From the Permanent Collection, Norton, 1986.

* * *

SITTLER, Joseph 1904-1987

OBITUARY NOTICE: Born September 26, 1904, in Upper Sandusky, Ohio; died of cancer, December 28, 1987, in Chicago, Ill. Theologian, educator, and author. Sittler became emeritus professor of theology at the University of Chicago in 1973, following sixteen years at the university. An internationally famous preacher, and recipient of eleven honorary doctorate degrees for his theological work, Sittler was one of the first religious writers to become involved in ecological issues. His books, *The Ecology of Faith* and *The Care of the Earth,* focused on ecological awareness as a moral duty. His other books include *The Structure of Christian Ethics* and *Gravity and Grace.* Sittler also worked for the World Council of Churches and was active in the international ecumenical movement.

OBITUARIES AND OTHER SOURCES:

BOOKS

Directory of American Scholars, Volume IV: *Philosophy, Religion, and Law,* 6th edition, Bowker, 1974.
Who's Who in America, 40th edition, Marquis, 1978.

PERIODICALS

Chicago Tribune, December 31, 1987.
New York Times, January 4, 1988.

* * *

SMEAD, (Edwin) Howard 1953-

PERSONAL: Born December 4, 1953, in Hagerstown, Md.; son of Edwin Howard, Sr. (a businessman) and Doris (a housewife; maiden name, Evans) Smead. *Education:* University of Maryland, A.B., 1970, M.A., 1972, Ph.D., 1979.

ADDRESSES: Home—219 Manor Circle, Takoma Park, Md. 20912. *Agent*—Wieser & Wieser, 118 East 25th St., New York, N.Y. 10010.

CAREER: Washington Post, Washington, D.C., director of research on night shift, 1972-87; lecturer at University of Maryland at College Park, 1980—.

MEMBER: American Historical Association, Organization of American Historians, Southern Historical Association.

WRITINGS:

Blood Justice: The Lynching of Mack Charles Parker, Oxford University Press, 1986.
The Redneck Waltz (novel), White Mane, 1988.
The Afro-Americans, Chelsea House, 1988.

WORK IN PROGRESS: A satirical novel "about two sisters who move to the District of Columbia in search of fame and fortune"; a horror novel about genetically engineered bacteria; research on the history of violence and race relations in the 1890s.

* * *

SMELLIE, K.
See SMELLIE, Kingsley Bryce (Speakman)

* * *

SMELLIE, K. B.
See SMELLIE, Kingsley Bryce (Speakman)

* * *

SMELLIE, Kingsley Bryce (Speakman) 1897-1987 (K. Smellie, K. B. Smellie)

OBITUARY NOTICE—See index for *CA* sketch: Born November 22, 1897; died November 30, 1987. Educator and author. For most of his career Smellie taught political science at the London School of Economics and Political Science, where he established his reputation as "one of the most intellectually engaging teachers of his generation," according to the London *Times.* His numerous books about politics, written under versions of his name, include *The American Federal System, A Hundred Years of English Government, Reason in Politics, A History of Local Government,* and *Great Britain Since 1688.*

OBITUARIES AND OTHER SOURCES:

BOOKS

Who's Who, 139th edition, St. Martin's, 1987.

PERIODICALS

Times (London), December 2, 1987.

* * *

SMITH, Barbara Clark 1951-

PERSONAL: Born March 30, 1951, in Newark, N.J.; daughter of Harry Clark and Mary (Hughes) Smith; married Daniel Michael Bluestone (a historian), July 28, 1986; children: Hattie. *Education:* University of Pennsylvania, B.A. and M.A., both 1973; Yale University, Ph.D., 1983. *Politics:* "Socialist feminist." *Religion:* Atheist.

ADDRESSES: Office—National Museum of American Art, Smithsonian Institution, Washington, D.C. 20560.

CAREER: Affiliated with National Museum of American History, Washington, D.C.

MEMBER: American Historical Association, Organization of American Historians, American Studies Association, Radical Historians Organization, Phi Beta Kappa.

AWARDS, HONORS: Fellow at John Carter Brown Library, 1986; fellow of American Council of Learned Societies, 1987.

WRITINGS:

After the Revolution: The Smithsonian History of Everyday Life in the Eighteenth Century, Pantheon, 1985.

Member of editorial board of *Radical History Review,* 1980—.

WORK IN PROGRESS: A book on the movement for price controls during the American Revolution.

* * *

SMITH, Darren L. 1958-

PERSONAL: Born December 22, 1958, in Honolulu, Hawaii; son of Jon T. (a computer programmer) and Marilyn (a musician; maiden name, Jaboolian) Smith. *Education:* Oberlin College, B.A., 1980. *Politics:* Democrat. *Religion:* Christian.

ADDRESSES: Home—2100 Northwest Third Ave., Wilton Manors, Fla. 33311. *Office*—Gale Research Co., 1700 East Las Olas Blvd., Fort Lauderdale, Fla. 33301.

CAREER: WSRF/WSHE-Radio, Fort Lauderdale, Fla., disc jockey, 1980-81; Gale Research Co., Fort Lauderdale, assistant editor, 1982-83, associate editor, 1983-85, editor, 1985—. Active in Big Brother/Big Sister program of Broward County.

MEMBER: South Florida Computer Group, Prime User's Group, Young Men's Christian Association.

AWARDS, HONORS: Impromptu Essay Award from Key Club/Kiwanis of State of Florida, 1976, for essay on community service; Armenian Silver Medal from Armenian Students Association, 1976-77, for academic achievement.

WRITINGS:

(Editor with Kay Gill) *International Research Centers Directory,* Gale, 3rd edition, 1985, 4th edition, 1987.
(Editor and contributor) *Gale Directory of Publications,* Gale, 1987.

(Editor) *Directory of International Publications,* Gale, 1988.

WORK IN PROGRESS: North American Parks and Outdoor Recreation Directory.

SIDELIGHTS: Darren L. Smith told *CA:* "I especially enjoy working on international publications because of strong interests in travel, world geography, and politics, and personal experiences gained while living in Lima, Peru, for more than five years. My avocations include archaeology. I have participated in excavations in Mexico and western Florida, and I worked for five months at the Brooklyn Museum in the Department of African, Oceanic, and New World Cultures."

AVOCATIONAL INTERESTS: Travel, scuba diving, all sports (especially racquetball, basketball, and golf), personal computers, collecting chess sets, helping others.

* * *

SMITH, Henry 1905-1988

OBITUARY NOTICE: Born in 1905; died January 29, 1988. Economist, educator, and author. One of the foremost economists of his day, Smith was most noted for his attempts to explain Marxist economic theory within the context of contemporary economic terminology and thought, a topic he dealt with in his 1962 book, *The Economics of Socialism Reconsidered.* After a distinguished academic career at Oxford University's Christ Church College, Smith became a lecturer in business finance at Liverpool University in 1935. Two years later he joined Oxford's Ruskin College as resident economics tutor. Following wartime service at the Ministry of Food, Smith returned to Ruskin College as vice-principal, a position he held until 1970. Author of numerous other books, including *A Prospect of Political Economy,* Smith also served as chairman of a Newfoundland committee of inquiry into the cost of living in 1947, and as a member of Great Britain's Civil Service wage arbitration tribunal between 1948 and 1964.

OBITUARIES AND OTHER SOURCES:

PERIODICALS

Times (London), February 1, 1988.

* * *

SMITH, Ralph Carlisle 1910-

PERSONAL: Born May 24, 1910, in West New York, N.J.; son of Alfred Thomas and Katharine (Haller) Smith; married Harriett V. Petersen (a nurse), May 20, 1954. *Education:* Rensselaer Polytechnic Institute, Ch.E., 1931; George Washington University, J.D., 1939; University of New Mexico, M.A., 1955, Ph.D., 1962. *Religion:* Protestant.

ADDRESSES: Home—838 Arguello Blvd., San Francisco, Calif. 94118.

CAREER: E. I. du Pont de Nemours & Co., Parlin, N.J., chemical engineer, 1931-35; U.S. Patent Office, Washington, D.C., examiner, 1935-37; Colgate/Palmolive Co., Jersey City, N.J., patent consultant, 1938-42; Manhattan Project, Los Alamos, N.M., patent counsel, 1943-47; University of California, Los Alamos National Laboratory, Los Alamos, assistant director, 1947-57; A.C.F. Industries, Washington, D.C., assistant to president of nuclear electronics division, 1957-60; New Mexico Highlands University, Las Vegas, professor of political science, 1961-77, vice-president and academic dean, 1966-70, president of university, 1970-71, president's counsel and graduate dean, 1972-77. Member of University of New Mexico law faculty, 1950-57. Admitted to the Bar of the District of Columbia, 1940, and the Bar of U.S. Supreme Court, 1946; justice of the peace in Los Alamos, 1948-50; county probate judge in Los Alamos, 1950-55; Republican candidate for U.S. Congress, 1956; municipal judge in Las Vegas, 1977. Consultant to Lytle Corporation in Albuquerque, N.M., 1960-61, and Teaching Machines, Inc., in Albuquerque, 1961-63. Chairman of Planning Commission in Las Vegas, 1964-77; member of editorial board of *National Forum,* 1984—. *Military service:* U.S. Army, Corps of Engineers, 1942-47; became lieutenant colonel; received Legion of Merit.

MEMBER: American Institute of Chemists (fellow), American Institute of Chemical Engineers, American Physical Society, American Nuclear Society, American Intellectual Property Law Association, Order of Coif, Sigma Xi, Tau Beta Pi, Phi Kappa Phi, Alpha Tau Omega.

WRITINGS:

(With Samuel Glasstone and others) *The Effects of Atomic Weapons,* U.S. Government Printing Office, 1950.

(With David Hawkins and Edith Truslow) *Project Y: The Los Alamos Story,* Tomash, 1983.

Editor, with Robert R. Davis, of "National Nuclear Energy" series, McGraw, 1951.

SIDELIGHTS: Ralph Carlisle Smith's *Project Y: The Los Alamos Story,* co-authored in 1983 by David Hawkins and Edith Truslow, chronicles the history of the Los Alamos National Laboratory where scientists designed and built the atomic bombs dropped on Hiroshima and Nagasaki, Japan, during World War II. In a critique in the *Los Angeles Times Book Review,* Peter Wyden praised the book, the first draft of which was classified "secret" in 1947, as being "considerably more literate and revealing than most of the genre."

BIOGRAPHICAL/CRITICAL SOURCES:

PERIODICALS

Los Angeles Times Book Review, April 17, 1983.

* * *

SMITH, Roy C(yrus) 1896-

PERSONAL: Born March 6, 1896, in Jones County, Iowa; son of Charles H. (a farmer) and Agnes (a farm wife; maiden name, Walton) Smith; married Marie Cornish, July 18, 1918 (deceased); children: Marshall E. *Education:* Attended public school in Barclay, Kan.

ADDRESSES: Home—501 West Third St., Apt. 310, Davenport, Iowa 52801.

CAREER: Owned grocery store in Elwood, Iowa, 1916-22; American Petroleum Company, Davenport, Iowa, president, 1925-57; farmer in Louisa County, Iowa, 1940-73. Director of Northwest Bank and Trust, 1938-39; member of Iowa Aeronautics Commission, 1959-65. *Military service:* U.S. Army, 1918-19.

MEMBER: American Legion.

WRITINGS:

I Wasn't Like the Cautious Man: The Life of Roy C. Smith, as Told to Robert B. King, Iowa State University Press, 1987.

SIDELIGHTS: Roy C. Smith told *CA:* "I was born in 1896, almost a century ago. During my life I've pursued a great variety of occupations. I've been a farmer, a miner, a horse trainer, a poolhall owner, a railroad section hand, a grocer, a salesman, an airport operator, a banker, and the founder and president of the American Petroleum Co. of Davenport, Iowa. I have had a great many experiences. I've done things and seen things that most people can only dream about. Perhaps because of this my son suggested that I write my experiences down on paper. I figured it would be a good antidote for the imaginative version of my life that some of my neighbors had made up over the years. But a funny thing happened. After my co-author, Robert B. King, prepared the manuscript, one of my relatives read it and said, 'It's a good story, Roy, but no one will ever believe it.' I suppose most people would sooner believe in something that was made up, but I guess there's nothing I can do about that. I'll let my story stand the way it is, and I make no apologies for it."

AVOCATIONAL INTERESTS: Horseback riding, "flying airplanes in younger years."

* * *

SMYTH, Jacqui (Marie) 1960-

PERSONAL: Surname is pronounced like Smith; born October 14, 1960, in Rivers, Manitoba, Canada; daughter of Gordon Kent (a motel owner) and Fay Marie (a restaurant owner; maiden name, Armstrong) Smyth. *Education:* University of Manitoba, B.A., 1981; University of Windsor, M.A., 1987.

ADDRESSES: Home—496 Banning St., Winnipeg, Manitoba, Canada R3G 2E8. *Office*—Department of English, University of Windsor, Windsor, Ontario, Canada N9B 3P4. *Agent*—Gerald Brydon, 201-99 King St., Winnipeg, Manitoba, Canada R3B 1H7.

CAREER: Northern Light, Winnipeg, Manitoba, managing editor and business editor, 1979-82; *CVII,* Winnipeg, managing editor and business editor, 1982-85. Affiliated with department of English at University of Windsor, Windsor, Ontario. Gives readings of poetry and prose.

MEMBER: Manitoba Writers Guild.

AWARDS, HONORS: Writers Choice Award, 1986, for *No Fixed Admission.*

WRITINGS:

No Fixed Admission (novel), Turnstone Press, 1985.

Contributor of poems and prose to magazines, including *Grain, Northern Light, Generation, Waves, Prairie Fire,* and *NeWest Review.*

WORK IN PROGRESS: A collection of short stories.

* * *

SNELLINGS, Rolland
See TOURE, Askia Muhammad Abu Bakr el

* * *

SNOW, Donald M. 1943-

PERSONAL: Born June 22, 1943, in Fort Wayne, Ind.; son of C. A. and Dorothea (an author; maiden name, Johnston) Snow; married Donna Bock (an administrator), May 30, 1969; children: Eric DeVries. *Education:* University of Colorado, Boulder, B.A., 1965, M.A., 1967; Indiana University—Bloomington, Ph.D., 1969.

ADDRESSES: Home—2935 Juniper Lane, Tuscaloosa, Ala. 35405. *Office*—Department of Political Science, University of Alabama, Drawer 1, Tuscaloosa, Ala. 35487.

CAREER: University of Alabama, Tuscaloosa, assistant professor, 1969-77, associate professor, 1977-83, professor of political science, 1983—. Visiting professor at U.S. Air Command and Staff College, 1980; Secretary of the Navy senior research fellow at U.S. Naval War College, 1985-86.

MEMBER: International Studies Association (chairman of Section on Military Studies, 1983-85), Air Force Association, Inter-University Seminar on the Armed Services and Society.

WRITINGS:

The Nuclear Future: Toward a Strategy of Uncertainty, University of Alabama Press, 1983.

(With Gary L. Guertner) *The Last Frontier: An Analysis of the Strategic Defense Initiative,* Lexington Books, 1986.

National Security: Enduring Problems in U.S. Defense Policy, St. Martin's, 1987.

The Necessary Peace: Nuclear Weapons and Superpower Relations, Lexington Books, 1987.

(With Dennis M. Drew) *Making Strategy,* Air University Press, 1987.

(Editor) *Fencers: U.S.-Soviet Relations Face the 1990s,* Lexington Books, 1988.

(With Dennis M. Drew) *The Eagle's Talons: War, Politics, and the American Experience,* Air University Press, 1988.

WORK IN PROGRESS: A manuscript on the evolving impact of the communications revolution on the conduct of international relations and national security affairs.

SIDELIGHTS: Donald M. Snow told *CA:* "A pivotal factor in my development as an academic analyst of military, and especially thermonuclear, policy has been the two years I served on the faculties of professional military education (PME) schools. My interaction with both uniformed and civilian faculty, who bring both theoretical and practical perspectives to issues, has provided both a focus and a practicality difficult to achieve in a purely academic climate. I hope that my work is of value both to academic audiences and policy makers, and the emphasis on practical applications of theoretical ideas that permeates PME has been of great value to me."

* * *

SOBIESKI, Carol 1939-

BRIEF ENTRY: Born March 16, 1939, in Chicago, Ill. American writer for television and film. Sobieski wrote the screenplay for the film "Annie" (1982), a musical adaptation of the popular stage production that had been adapted from the comic-strip about a Depression-era orphan raised by a millionaire. Her other screenwriting credits include "Honeysuckle Rose" (1980), a western featuring acclaimed country singer Willie Nelson as a notorious outlaw, and "The Toy" (1982), in which comedian Richard Pryor appeared as a journalist who agrees to become the human toy of a wealthy man's child. In addition, Sobieski has contributed scripts to films made for television, earning awards from the Writers Guild for "Sunshine" (1973) and its sequel, "Sunshine Christmas" (1977). *Addresses: Home*—P.O. Box 1672, Santa Monica, Calif. 90404. *Agent*—Triad, 10100 Santa Monica Blvd., Los Angeles, Calif.

BIOGRAPHICAL/CRITICAL SOURCES:

PERIODICALS

Los Angeles Times, March 15, 1985.
New Republic, January 31, 1983.
New York Times, May 21, 1982.
Time, December 27, 1982.
Village Voice, June 1, 1982.

* * *

SOSKICE, Janet Martin 1951-

PERSONAL: Born May 16, 1951, in Vancouver, British Columbia, Canada; daughter of Alison Malcolm (in business) and Claire (a nurse; maiden name, Jamieson) Martin; married Oliver Soskice (a painter), July 17, 1982; children: Catherine, Isabelle. *Education:* Cornell University, B.A., 1973; University of Sheffield, M.A., 1975; Oxford University, Ph.D., 1982. *Religion:* Christian.

ADDRESSES: Office—Ripon College, Cuddesdon, Oxfordshire OX9 9EX, England.

CAREER: University of London, Heythrop College, London, England, part-time lecturer in philosophy, 1979-83; Oxford University, Oxford, England, research fellow at Sommerville College, 1980-83, member of theology faculty, 1983—; Ripon College, Cuddesdon, England, lecturer in philosophy, ethics, and doctrine, 1983—.

WRITINGS:

Metaphor and Religious Language, Oxford University Press, 1985.

BIOGRAPHICAL/CRITICAL SOURCES:

PERIODICALS

Times Literary Supplement, November 8, 1985.

* * *

SOUZA FILHO, Henrique de 1945(?)-1988 (Henfil)

OBITUARY NOTICE: Born c. 1945; died of pneumonia and other complications related to acquired immune deficiency syndrome (AIDS), January 4, 1988, in Rio de Janeiro, Brazil. Cartoonist, filmmaker, and author. One of three hemophiliac brothers, all of whom contracted the AIDS virus through transfusions of contaminated blood, Souza Filho was an outspoken critic of the Brazilian government's anti-AIDS policies. Better known in Brazil as "Henfil," a leading political cartoonist, he attempted through his work to lampoon social taboos and the upper classes. Although apparently unsuccessful when syndicated briefly in such American newspapers as the *Chicago Tribune* and the *Detroit News,* Souza Filho's work was said by critics to have played an important role in the downfall of the military regime that ruled Brazil between 1964 and 1985. Souza Filho also made the film "Tanga—It Was in the New York Times," a political comedy about censorship of the press.

OBITUARIES AND OTHER SOURCES:

PERIODICALS

Chicago Tribune, January 7, 1988.
New York Times, January 6, 1988.
Washington Post, January 7, 1988.

SOX, (Harold) David 1936-

PERSONAL: Born April 24, 1936; son of Samuel L. (an Episcopal priest) and Vye (a housewife; maiden name, Coulter) Sox. *Education:* University of North Carolina at Chapel Hill, B.A., 1958; graduate study at Columbia University; Union Theological Seminary, New York, N.Y., M.Div., 1961. *Politics:* Democrat.

ADDRESSES: Home and office—85A Campden Hill Court, London W8 7HW, England. *Agent*—Ralph M. Vicinanza, 342 Park Ave. S., Suite 1205, New York, N.Y. 10016.

CAREER: Assistant at Episcopal church in Upper Montclair, N.J., 1963; chaplain and master of Episcopal school in New York, N.Y., 1964-70; minor canon and chaplain at cathedral in San Francisco, Calif., 1970-73; American School in London, London, England, lecturer, 1974—. Assistant at St. Bride's Church, London, 1985—. *Military service:* U.S. Naval Reserve, 1962-64; became lieutenant.

MEMBER: British Society for the Turin Shroud (general secretary, 1977-80).

WRITINGS:

File on the Shroud, Hodder & Stoughton, 1979.
Image on the Shroud, Allen & Unwin, 1981.
Gospel of Barnabas, Allen & Unwin, 1984.
Relics and Shrines, Allen & Unwin, 1985.
Unmasking the Forger: The Dossena Deception, Unwin Hyman, 1987.

Contributor to magazines, including *Clergy Review.* Literary critic for *Tablet.*

WORK IN PROGRESS: A book on the carbon dating of the Shroud of Turin, publication expected in 1988.

SIDELIGHTS: David Sox told *CA:* "As an American working in London, I find travel extremely important and rewarding. It also gives me the advantage of understanding several cultures and viewpoints. Both as a clergyman and a teacher, I am increasingly worried about American materialism and lack of depth in understanding what is going on in our world today."

BIOGRAPHICAL/CRITICAL SOURCES:

PERIODICALS

Times Literary Supplement, January 3, 1986.

* * *

SOYER, Raphael 1899-1987

OBITUARY NOTICE—See index for *CA* sketch: Born December 25, 1899, in Borisoglebsk, Russia (now U.S.S.R.); immigrated to United States, 1912, naturalized citizen, 1917; died of cancer, November 4 (one source says November 2), 1987, in Manhattan, N.Y. Educator, artist, and author. Soyer, one of three acclaimed artist brothers, earned renown for his realistic paintings of empty city streets, lonely people, dancers, and artists. His work has been exhibited in the United States, France, Italy, and Germany and is represented in permanent collections at the Hirshhorn Museum in Washington, D.C., and in New York City's Metropolitan Museum of Art and Whitney Museum of American Art, among others. During his career Soyer taught art at institutions such as the American Artists School, New School for Social Research, and Art Stu-

dents League and won various awards for art. He also wrote and illustrated books, including *An Artist's Pilgrimage, Homage to Thomas Eakins, Self Revealment,* and his memoirs, titled *Diary of an Artist.*

OBITUARIES AND OTHER SOURCES:

BOOKS

Who's Who in American Art, 17th edition, Bowker, 1986.

PERIODICALS

Chicago Tribune, November 6, 1987.
Los Angeles Times, November 5, 1987.
New York Times, November 5, 1987.
Time, November 16, 1987.
Times (London), November 7, 1987.
Washington Post, November 6, 1987.

* * *

SPARKS, Donald B. 1931-

PERSONAL: Born June 12, 1931, in Pittsburgh, Pa. *Education:* University of Pittsburgh, B.A., 1952; University of Chicago, M.B.A., 1965; Nova University, Ed.D., 1976.

ADDRESSES: Home—14202 Chadbourne, Houston, Tex. 77079. *Office*—Sparks Management Consulting, 10497 Town and Country Way, No. 212, Houston, Tex. 77024.

CAREER: Affiliated with Sparks Management Consulting, Houston, Tex. Member of Houston Committee on Foreign Relations.

MEMBER: Atlantic Council, Army and Navy Club.

WRITINGS:

Administrative Improvement Methods, Gulf Publishing, 1973.
The Dynamics of Effective Negotiation, Gulf Publishing, 1982.

* * *

SPARKS, Will (R.) 1924-1987

OBITUARY NOTICE—See index for *CA* sketch: Born July 15, 1924, in Detroit, Mich.; died of a brain tumor, December 16, 1987, in Brooklyn, N.Y. Administrator, television producer, director, and writer, speech writer, editor, and author. Remembered for the speeches he wrote for U.S. President Lyndon Johnson and Defense Secretary Robert McNamara, Sparks also produced, directed, and wrote more than 150 television films for the NBC-TV series "Wide Wide World." His other writings include articles published in *Life, Look, Saturday Evening Post,* and *Atlantic Monthly* magazines and the books *Who Talked to the President Last?* and *Financial Competition and the Public Interest.* During the later years of his career Sparks served as vice-president for public affairs at Citicorp.

OBITUARIES AND OTHER SOURCES:

PERIODICALS

Los Angeles Times, December 18, 1987.
New York Times, December 18, 1987.
Washington Post, December 18, 1987.

* * *

SPENCER, Benjamin T(ownley) 1904-

PERSONAL: Born April 23, 1904, in Winchester, Ky.; son of Benjamin Townley, Sr. (a teacher) and Elizabeth (a housewife; maiden name, Sellers) Spencer; married Virginia Morrison (a librarian), July 28, 1924; children: Melinda Lee Spencer Fouts. *Education:* Kentucky Wesleyan College, A.B., 1925; graduate study at Johns Hopkins University, 1925-26; University of Cincinnati, Ph.D., 1930. *Politics:* Democrat. *Religion:* Methodist.

CAREER: Kentucky Wesleyan College, Winchester, assistant professor of English, 1926-30; Ohio Wesleyan University, Delaware, assistant professor, 1930-34, associate professor, 1934-37, professor of English, 1937-69, director of library, 1938-40, professor emeritus, 1969—. Smith-Mundt Professor at University of Uppsala and University of Stockholm, 1952-53; visiting professor at Ohio State University, 1952, Wesleyan University, Middletown, Conn., summers, 1958, 1963, 1965, 1967, 1972, Michigan State University, 1970, and Bowling Green State University, 1971; Fulbright professor at University of London and Victoria University of Manchester, both 1959-60.

MEMBER: Modern Language Association of America.

AWARDS, HONORS: Grant from Library of Congress, 1945-46; D.Litt. from Kentucky Wesleyan College, 1949, and Ohio Wesleyan University, 1974; Norman Foerster Award from Modern Language Association of America, 1969, for article "Sherwood Anderson, American Mythopoeist."

WRITINGS:

(Editor) Philip Massinger, *The Bondman,* Princeton University Press, 1932.
(With Daniel Gibson and Mary Cochnower) *Seventeenth Century Studies,* Princeton University Press, 1933.
(Contributor) Merrill Jensen, editor, *Regionalism in America,* University of Wisconsin Press, 1951.
Quest for Nationality: An American Literary Campaign, Syracuse University Press, 1957.
(Author of introduction) C. G. Leland, *Sunshine in Thought,* Scholars' Facsimiles & Reprints, 1959.
(Contributor) Robert Falk, editor, *Literature and Ideas in America,* Ohio University Press, 1975.
Patterns of Nationality, Burt Franklin, 1981.
(Editor) *Memorable Dogs: An Anthology,* Harper, 1985.

Contributor to *English Institute Essays,* Columbia University Press, 1950, and to literature journals.

* * *

SPERBER, Manes 1905-1984

PERSONAL: Born December 12, 1905, in Zablotow, Austria-Hungary (now U.S.S.R.); immigrated to France, 1934, naturalized citizen; died of heart disease, February 5, 1984, in Paris, France; son of David and Yetti (Heger) Sperber; married twice; children: two sons (one from each marriage). *Education:* Studied psychology in Vienna, Austria, during the 1920s.

ADDRESSES: Home—83 rue Notre Dame des Champs, 75006 Paris, France.

CAREER: Teacher and lecturer in Austria and Germany, became professor of psychology at University of Berlin, 1927-33; literary director at Calmann-Levy (publishers), Paris, France, 1936-80; writer. *Military service:* Volunteer with the French Army during World War II.

MEMBER: International P.E.N., Deutsche Akademie fuer Sprache und Dichtung (Darmstadt), Bayerische Akademie fuer

schoene Kuenste (Munich), German Communist Party (1927-37).

AWARDS, HONORS: Remembrance Award from the World Federation of Bergen-Belsen Associations, 1967, for . . . *Than a Tear in the Sea;* Literature Prize from the Bavarian Academy of Fine Arts, 1971; Goethe Prize from the city of Frankfurt am Main, West Germany, 1973; Georg Buechner Prize from the German Academy of Language and Poetry, 1975; Austrian State Prize for European Literature, 1977; Peace Prize from the German Booksellers Association, 1983.

WRITINGS:

Zur Analyse der Tyrannis; Das Unglueck, begabt zu sein: Zwei sozialpsychologische Essays, [Paris], 1938, Europa, 1975.

Et le buisson devint cendre (novel), translation by Sperber and Blanche Gidon, Calmann-Levy, 1949, original German edition published as *Der verbrannte Dornbusch,* 1950, translation by Constantine FitzGibbon published as *The Burned Bramble,* Doubleday, 1951 (published in England as *The Wind and the Flame,* Wingate, 1951) (also see *OMNIBUS VOLUMES*).

Plus profondque l'abime (novel), translation by Sperber and Gidon, Calmann-Levy, 1950, translation by FitzGibbon published as *The Abyss,* Doubleday, 1952 (published in England as *To Dusty Death,* Wingate, 1952), original German edition published as *Tiefer als der Abgrund,* 1961 (also see *OMNIBUS VOLUMES*).

La Baie perdue (Victi victuri vincendi) (novel), translation by Sperber and Gidon, Calmann-Levy, 1952, translation by FitzGibbon published as *Journey Without End,* Doubleday, 1954 (published in England as *The Lost Bay,* Deutsch, 1956), original German edition published as *Die verlorene Bucht,* 1955 (also see *OMNIBUS VOLUMES*).

Le Talon d'Achille: Essais (essays), Calmann-Levy, 1957, translation by FitzGibbon published as *The Achilles Heel,* Deutsch, 1959, Doubleday, 1960.

Zur taeglichen Weltgeschichte (essays and lectures), Kiepenheuer & Witsch, 1967, published as *Essays zur taeglichen Weltgeschichte,* Europa, c. 1981.

Man and His Deeds (essays), translation from the French and German by Joachim Neugroschel, McGraw, 1970.

Alfred Adler; oder, Das Elend der Psychologie, Molden, 1970, translation by Krishna Winston published as *Masks of Loneliness: Alfred Adler in Perspective,* Macmillan, 1974.

Wir und Dostojewskij: Eine Debatte mit Heinrich Boell, Siegfried Lenz, Andre Malraux, Hans Erich Nossack, gefuehrt von Manes Sperber, Hoffmann & Campe, 1972.

Leben in dieser Zeit: Sieben Fragen zur Gewalt, Europa, 1972.

(Author of afterword) Karl Roessing, *Mein Vorurteil gegen diese Zeit: 100 Holzschnitte von Karl Roessing,* Hoffmann & Campe, c. 1974.

Die Wassertraeger Gottes: All das Vergangene . . . (biographies), Europa, 1974 (also see *OMNIBUS VOLUMES*).

Die vergebliche Warnung: All das Vergangene . . . (biographies), Europa, 1975 (also see *OMNIBUS VOLUMES*).

Bis man mir Scherben auf die Augen legt: All das Vergangene . . . (biographies), Europa, c. 1977 (also see *OMNIBUS VOLUMES*).

(With others) *Geist und Ungeist in Wien* (essays and lectures), Institute fuer Wirtschaft und Politik (Vienna), 1978.

Individuum und Gemeinschaft: Versuch einer sozialen Charakterologie, Klett-Cotta, 1978.

Churban; oder, Die unfassbare Gewissheit: Essays, Europa, 1979.

Nur eine Bruecke zwischen Gestern und Morgen, illustrations by Heinrich Susemann, Europa, 1980.

Die Wirklichkeit in der Literatur des 20 Jahrhunderts; Der Freiheitsgedanke in der europaeischen Literatur: Zwei Vortraege (essays and lectures), Nymphenburger, c. 1983.

Ansprachen aus Anlass der Verleihung des Friedenspreises des Deutschen Buchhandels, Buchhaendler-Vereinigung, 1983.

(With Paulo Von Freire and others) *Zwischen Spontaneitaet und Beharrlichkeit,* edited by Ute Crist-Bode, Franz Decker, and Leo Kauffeldt, Extrabuch, 1983.

Wolyna (novel), foreword by Andre Malraux, Europa, 1984.

Ein politisches Leben: Gespraeche mit Leonhard Reinisch (conversations originally recorded for radio, May, 1983), Deutsche Verlags-Anstalt, c. 1984.

Geteilte Einsamkeit: Der Autor und sein Leser, Europa, 1985.

Sein letztes Jahr, edited by Heinz Friedrich, Deutscher Taschenbuch, 1985.

Der schwarze Zaun: Roman (novel), Europa, c. 1986.

Also author of *Alfred Adler: Der Mensch und sein Lehre* (title means "Alfred Adler: The Man and His Teaching"), 1926. Translator of several of his own German writings into French. Contributor to newspapers, including *New York Times Book Review, Encounter,* and *Merkur;* to numerous psychological journals; and to French radio. Editor, until 1933, of the psychological journal *Zeitschrift fuer individualpsychologische Paedagogik und Psychohygiene.*

OMNIBUS VOLUMES

. . . qu'une larme dans l'ocean (novels), translation by Sperber and Gidon, Calmann-Levy, 1952, original German edition published as *Wie eine Traene im Ozean: Romantrilogie* (contains *Der verbrannte Dornbusch, Tiefer als der Abgrund,* and *Die verlorene Bucht*), Kiepenheuer & Witsch, 1961, translation by Constantine FitzGibbon published as *. . . Than a Tear in the Sea* (contains *The Burned Bramble, The Abyss,* and *Journey Without End*), introduction by Andre Malraux, Bergen-Belsen Memorial Press, 1967.

All das Vergangene . . . (biographies; contains *Die Wassertraeger Gottes, Die vergebliche Warnung,* and *Bis man mir Scherben auf die Augen legt*), Europa, c. 1983.

SIDELIGHTS: Manes Sperber was a respected psychologist and author best known for his trilogy of novels, *Wie eine Traene im Ozean,* for which he won the 1967 Remembrance Award honoring literature inspired by the Holocaust. The trilogy, translated by Constantine FitzGibbon and cited variously as *Than a Tear in the Sea, Like a Tear in the Ocean,* and *As a Tear in the Ocean,* documents the rise of communism in Europe during the first half of the twentieth century. The author has also received acclaim for his collections of essays, including *Le Talon d'Achille* (*The Achilles Heel*) and *Man and His Deeds,* and for *Alfred Adler; oder, Das Elend der Psychologie* (*Masks of Loneliness: Alfred Adler in Perspective*), a study of renowned psychiatrist Alfred Adler's psychological theories.

Sperber describes his childhood, one of constant upheaval, in his introduction to *The Achilles Heel*. Born in the small Jewish community of Zablotow in Austria-Hungary (now U.S.S.R.) in 1905, he fled the town several times with his family to escape the battles and epidemics of World War I, finally settling in Vienna, Austria, in 1914. While there he began studying psychology and, still in his teens, became a student and associate of Adler, who originated the theory of individual psychology. Sperber published his first book, a tribute to his instructor titled *Alfred Adler: Der Mensch und sein Lehre* (title

means "Alfred Adler: The Man and His Teaching"), in 1926 and a year later began lecturing on Adler's theories throughout Austria and Germany.

As a young man Sperber was actively involved in politics. In 1927 he joined the German Communist Party and quickly attained a high position in the organization, although the affiliation led to an ideological break with Adler in 1930. A staunch opponent of German National Socialism (Nazism), Sperber was imprisoned for refusing to accept Adolf Hitler's government when the Nazi leader attained dictatorial power in Germany in 1933. After a brief exile in Yugoslavia, Sperber settled in Paris, France, in 1934, later becoming a French citizen. Disillusioned by the devastating effects of Joseph Stalin's oppressive rule in the Soviet Union, the political activist renounced communism in 1937 and declared himself a social democrat. His political disenchantment found creative expression when, three years later, he began writing *Der verbrannte Dornbusch* (*The Burned Bramble*), the first of his three acclaimed novels published collectively in 1961 as *Wie eine Traene im Ozean* (*Than a Tear in the Sea,* 1967). Through the book's three main characters—activists in the communist underground—the author examines his own initial devotion to and eventual rejection of Marxism.

The Burned Bramble, published in the United States in 1951, received critical acclaim as a thorough documentary of pre-World War I communism in Europe. Although several critics, like *Atlantic Monthly*'s Charles J. Rolo, complained that "the profusion of characters [and] the jerky movement from one plot to another" resulted in a confusing, disjointed saga, most also agreed with him that the novel "is an impassioned and profound picture of Communist experience." Renowned author and critic Upton Sinclair, commenting that he "found it a little difficult to keep [the many characters] sorted out," recalled in the *New York Times Book Review:* "I had the same difficulty with a novel [by Leo Tolstoy] called 'War and Peace,' but that did not keep it from being a very great novel." He also compared Sperber's work to three American classics: Sinclair Lewis's *Babbitt,* Theodore Dreiser's *American Tragedy,* and John Steinbeck's *Grapes of Wrath*. "It is both timely and timeless," he declared. "Its author knows what he is writing about, and he knows how to make it real and important to us."

The second novel in the trilogy, *Tiefer als der Abgrund,* was published in the United States as *The Abyss* in 1952. The book focuses on the isolation and despair felt by Doino Faber, one of the central characters in *The Burned Bramble,* as he loses faith in the communist ideology he once espoused and, like the book's author, flees his own country to settle in France. Calling it the weakest novel of the three, critics consider *The Abyss* a necessary element within the trilogy but one that cannot succeed alone. "Its theme of despair [is] less exciting than either disillusionment or hope," which are treated in the other two novels, noted reviewer A. C. Ames in the *Chicago Sunday Tribune*. Critic Philip Driscoll agreed. "The larger theme—of isolation and spiritual desolation—could be genuinely moving," he wrote in the *Commonweal*. "But here we feel little. . . . Faber's position is clearly articulated but it is not dramatized, and the result is an intellectually rewarding but emotionally unsatisfying book." Reviewer William Barrett maintained in the *New York Times Book Review,* however, that "the experiences of Doino Faber are at the very center of European history in this [twentieth] century." And in the *New York Herald Tribune Book Review,* Virgilia Peterson asserted that "as a fiery commentary on [mid-twentieth-century] conflict and as a testament to man's spiritual indestructibility, it can and should receive acclaim."

Die verlorene Bucht, the third book in the trilogy, was published in the United States as *Journey Without End* in 1954. The novel is widely regarded as Sperber's greatest literary accomplishment. Although as complex and vast as *The Burned Bramble* and *The Abyss, Journey Without End* is considered more dramatic and thus more powerful. Set in Yugoslavia during the end of World War II, the novel chronicles the political, economic, and social collapse of Europe. One of the most acclaimed sections of the novel deals with the extermination of Polish Jews in Volhynia. *Journey Without End,* declared Michael Harrington in the *Commonweal,* "is the culmination of an artistic and spiritual progress which was evident in *The Burned Bramble* and *The Abyss*. . . . [It] is a real, perhaps even a lasting, achievement." Distinguished novelist and literary critic Granville Hicks confirmed the importance of the third book in the trilogy. "When [*The Burned Bramble*] appeared in 1951," Hicks explained in the *New York Times Book Review,* "it seemed fair to regard it as another novel about disillusionment with communism, but now [with the publication of *Journey Without End*] it is clear that Sperber's theme is vastly larger than that. He has written about the anguish of Europe between 1931 and 1944, not for the sake of arousing our pity or our indignation but in the hope of making us think."

The author's association with French publishing house Calmann-Levy, where he served as literary director for more than forty years, had led to the publication of his and Blanche Gidon's French translations of his first three novels beginning in 1949, before they appeared in their original German. In 1957 Calmann-Levy also published a collection of six of Sperber's essays, *Le Talon d'Achille,* translated by FitzGibbon as *The Achilles Heel*. The volume includes Sperber's acclaimed "Essay on the Left," which analyzes and supports revolutionary socialism. "Mr. Sperber's essay is essentially not an argument but a cry from the heart," judged a reviewer in the *Times Literary Supplement*. "Indeed, his book runs a whole gamut of cries, for his interests extend to history, psychology and literature as well as politics. In all these fields he has penetrating points to make."

A collection of nine essays appeared in 1970 under the title *Man and His Deeds*. Analyzing prominent individuals and significant events, Sperber studies the influence of extreme social and political conditions on a person's actions. In an essay called "The Assassin," for example, Sperber presents Lee Harvey Oswald, alleged assassin of U.S. President John F. Kennedy in 1963, as "a lonely figure who had lost his humanity and for whom public images alone were real. . . . He committed murder because he lived in a world of political myth," wrote critic George L. Mosse in the *New York Times Book Review*. "Such men for Sperber lose their own substance to an abstract ideological commitment and consequently delude themselves to become tools of their own delusion." Sperber examines a stronger type of person in his essay on *The Mute Prophet,* a novel by Joseph Roth. In "some of the most deeply felt passages in the book," Mosse noted, Sperber admires the novelist's portrayal of Soviet communist leader Leon Trotsky and other men whose "self-control does not break down in extreme situations, and [who] reject the surrogates of all-encompassing ideologies and mass movements."

Sperber's series of recollections about his friend and mentor, the noted psychiatrist Alfred Adler, was published in 1970 as *Alfred Adler; oder, Das Elend der Psychologie*. Krishna Win-

ston's translation of the book was published four years later as *Masks of Loneliness: Alfred Adler in Perspective*. Rather than systematically presenting Adler's theories in textbook format, Sperber offers personal reflections about the psychiatrist's life and compares his theories and methods with those of pioneering psychoanalyst Sigmund Freud. In *Library Journal* Elaine Z. Jennerich praised the author's "new and refreshing look at the pioneer of individual psychology."

In a collection of six informal interviews with publicist and historian Leonhard Reinisch, published in 1984 as *Ein politisches Leben,* Sperber discusses his views on how a person develops his or her political stance and matures through political activity. Sperber himself remained politically active until the end of his life, spurring controversy within the German Writers Union upon his receipt of the 1983 Peace Prize from the German Booksellers Association. Because of his comments supporting an active defense of Europe from Soviet communism, he was asked to return the Peace Prize. Soon after, on February 5, 1984, he died in Paris, France.

BIOGRAPHICAL/CRITICAL SOURCES:

BOOKS

Kreuzer, Franz, *Pan und Apoll: Alfred Adlers Individualpsychologie, erste Uberwindung Sigmund Freuds; Franz Kreuzer im Gespraech mit Alexandra Adler, Manes Sperber, und Walter Toman* (essays, lectures, and conversations), Deuticke, 1984.
Paffenholz, Alfred, *Manes Sperber zur Einfuehrung,* Junius, 1984.

PERIODICALS

Atlantic Monthly, May, 1951.
Chicago Sunday Tribune, June 1, 1952.
Commonweal, July 4, 1952, June 18, 1954.
Library Journal, October 15, 1974.
New York Herald Tribune Book Review, June 1, 1952, June 13, 1954.
New York Times Book Review, March 18, 1951, June 1, 1952, May 23, 1954, November 8, 1970.
Times Literary Supplement, December 25, 1959.
World Literature Today, spring, 1985.*

—Sketch by Christa Brelin

* * *

STANCLIFFE, Michael (Staffurth) 1916-1987

PERSONAL: Born April 8, 1916; died March 26, 1987; son of Harold Emmet Stancliffe (a clergyman); married Barbara Elizabeth Tatlow, 1940; children: two sons, one daughter. *Education:* Received M.A. from Trinity College, Oxford.

CAREER: Curate of St. James, Southbrook, Devizes, 1940-43; priest in charge at Ramsbury, England, 1943-44; curate of Cirencester and priest in charge at Watermoor, 1944-49; chaplain and schoolmaster in Westminster, England, 1949-57; canon of Westminster and rector of local church, 1957-69, dean of Westminster, 1969-86. Preacher at Lincoln's Inn, 1954-57; speaker's chaplain, 1961-69; member of General Synod, 1970-80; chairman of Council for Places of Worship, 1972-75; member of Cathedrals Advisory Commission for England, beginning in 1981; chairman of Francis Holland Schools, London, England, and St. Swithun's School. Fellow of Winchester College, 1973.

WRITINGS:

Symbols and Dances: Sermons, S.P.C.K., 1986.
Jacob's Ladder: Sermons, S.P.C.K., 1987.

BIOGRAPHICAL/CRITICAL SOURCES:

PERIODICALS

Times (London), April 10, 1987.*

* * *

STANN, Francis E. 1912(?)-1987

OBITUARY NOTICE: Born c. 1912; died of emphysema and cancer, November 18, 1987, in Stuart, Fla. Journalist. An award-winning reporter, Stann worked for the *Washington Star* from 1929 to 1973, first as a copy boy and later as a sportswriter and columnist. For his work he won four Washington-area Sportswriter of the Year awards, four Washington-Baltimore Newspaper Guild sports writing awards, and a National Headliners sports writing award. In addition to his work for the *Star,* Stann wrote articles for various magazines.

OBITUARIES AND OTHER SOURCES:

PERIODICALS

Washington Post, November 21, 1987.

* * *

STEARNS, Monroe (Mather) 1913-1987

OBITUARY NOTICE—See index for *CA* sketch: Born September 28, 1913, in New York, N.Y.; died of an apparent respiratory ailment, December 17, 1987. Educator, editor, translator, and author. Stearns taught for fifteen years at institutions including Rutgers University before embarking on a career in publishing, first as an editor for Prentice-Hall and later as managing editor of Bobbs-Merrill. In addition, he was the author of historical books and works for children, among them *Gabriel and His Magic Wand, The Story of New England,* and *Wolfgang Amadeus Mozart,* and he translated *Angelique and the King, The Soldier and the Rose,* and *Wherever They May Be.*

OBITUARIES AND OTHER SOURCES:

BOOKS

The Writers Directory: 1982-1984, Gale, 1981.

PERIODICALS

New York Times, December 31, 1987.

* * *

STEERS, J(ames) A(lfred) 1899-1987

PERSONAL: Born August 8, 1899, in Bedford, England; died March 11, 1987; son of J. A. Steers; married Harriet Wanklyn, 1942; children: one son, one daughter. *Education:* St. Catharine's College, Cambridge, M.A.

CAREER: Senior geography master at secondary school, 1921-22; Cambridge University, Cambridge, England, fellow of St. Catharine's College, 1925, lecturer, 1927-49, professor of geography, 1949-66, professor emeritus, 1966-87, dean and later president of St. Catharine's College. Member of British expedition to the Great Barrier Reef, 1928, expedition leader, 1936; conducted expedition to the Jamaica Cays, 1939. Mem-

ber of Advisory Committee to Improve Sea Defences, beginning in 1954; member of National Parks Commission, 1960-66; chairman of Coastal Conferences, 1966-67; chairman of National Committee of Geography, 1967-72; member of properties committee of National Trust, 1969-76. Visiting professor at University of California, Berkeley, 1959; visiting fellow at Australian National University, 1967; consultant to Conservation Committee of Council of Europe, Ministry of Town and Country Planning, and Scottish Department of Health. *Military service:* 1917-18.

AWARDS, HONORS: Victoria Medal from Royal Geographical Society, 1960; Scottish Geographical Medal, 1969; LL.D. from University of Aberdeen, 1971; Commander of Order of the British Empire, 1973; D.Sc. from University of East Anglia, 1978.

WRITINGS:

An Introduction to the Study of Map Projections, University of London Press, 1927, 15th edition, 1970.
The Unstable Earth: Some Recent Views in Geomorphology, Methuen, 1932, 2nd edition, 1964.
The Coastline of England and Wales, Cambridge University Press, 1946, 2nd edition, 1964.
A Picture Book of the Whole Coast of England and Wales: An Account of Variety in Scenery and Its Causes, Cambridge University Press, 1948, reprinted as *The Coast of England and Wales in Pictures,* 1960.
(With Ian Hepburn) *Flowers of the Coast,* Collins, 1952.
A Guide to Blakeney Point and Scolt Head Island, National Trust, 1952.
The Sea Coast, Collins, 1953, 4th edition, 1969.
The English Coast and the Coast of Wales, Collins, 1966.
Coasts and Beaches, Oliver & Boyd, 1969.
The Coastline of Scotland, Cambridge University Press, 1973.
Coastal Features of England and Wales: Eight Essays, Oleander Press, 1981.

Contributor to scientific journals.

EDITOR

(Also contributor) *Scolt Head Island, the Story of Its Origin: The Plant and Animal Life of the Dunes and Marshes,* W. Heffer & Sons, 1934, revised edition, 1960.
Philip Lake, *Physical Geography,* 2nd edition, Cambridge University Press, 1949, 4th edition, 1958.
Field Studies in the British Isles, Thomas Nelson, 1964.
Blakeney Point and Scolt Head Island, Soman-Wherry Press, 1964.
The Cambridge Region, 1965, British Association for the Advancement of Science, 1965.
(Translator with Cuchlaine A. M. King) Vsevolod Pavlovich Zenkovich, *Processes of Coastal Development,* Oliver & Boyd, 1967.
Applied Coastal Geomorphology, MIT Press, 1971.
Introduction to Coastline Development, MIT Press, 1971.

AVOCATIONAL INTERESTS: Philately, walking, travel.

BIOGRAPHICAL/CRITICAL SOURCES:

PERIODICALS

Economist, August 25, 1973.
Times (London), March 14, 1987.
Times Literary Supplement, March 15, 1974.*

STELL, Geoffrey (Percival) 1944-

PERSONAL: Born November 21, 1944, in Keighley, Yorkshire, England; son of Arthur William (a textile engineer) and Ada (Foster) Stell; married Evelyn Florence Burns, November 6, 1971; children: Catherine Susan, Anthony James. *Education:* University of Leeds, B.A. (with honors), 1966; attended University of Glasgow, 1966-69.

ADDRESSES: Home—Beechmount, Borrowstoun, Bo'ness, West Lothian EH51 9RS, Scotland. *Office*—Royal Commission on the Ancient and Historical Monuments of Scotland, 54 Melville St., Edinburgh EH3 7HF, Scotland.

CAREER: Investigator supervising architectural and industrial surveys for Royal Commission on the Ancient and Historical Monuments of Scotland, Edinburgh, Scotland.

MEMBER: Council for British Archaeology, Scotland (vice-president), Society of Antiquaries of Scotland (fellow; past member of council), Scottish Urban Archaeological Trust Ltd. (member of board of trustees), Scottish Vernacular Buildings Working Group (chairman), Royal Archaeological Institute, Society for Medieval Archaeology, Society for Post-Medieval Archaeology, Vernacular Architecture Group, Society of Antiquaries of London (fellow).

WRITINGS:

(Contributor) Grant G. Simpson, editor, *Scotland's Medieval Burghs: An Archaeological Heritage in Danger,* Society of Antiquaries of Scotland, 1972.
(Editor with Alexander Fenton and D. Bruce Walker) *Building Construction in Scotland: Some Historical and Regional Aspects,* Scottish Vernacular Buildings Working Group, 1976.
(Contributor) J. M. Brown, editor, *Scottish Society in the Fifteenth Century,* Edward Arnold, 1977.
(Contributor) D. H. Caldwell, editor, *Scottish Weapons and Fortifications,* John Donald, 1981.
(Contributor) J. R. Baldwin, editor, *Caithness: A Cultural Crossroads,* Scottish Society for Northern Studies, 1982.
(Editor with Alexander Fenton, and contributor) *Loads and Roads in Scotland and Beyond: Road Transport Over Six Thousand Years,* John Donald, 1984.
(Contributor) K. J. Stringer, editor, *Essays on the Nobility of Medieval Scotland,* John Donald, 1985.
(With Geoffrey D. Hay) *Monuments of Industry,* H.M.S.O., 1986.
Exploring Scotland's Heritage: A Guide to Dumfries and Galloway, H.M.S.O., 1986.
(Contributor) J. R. Baldwin, editor, *Firthlands of Ross and Sutherland,* Scottish Society for Northern Studies, 1986.
(With Mary Harman) *Buildings of St. Kilda,* H.M.S.O., 1988.
(With Michael Lynch and Michael Spearman) *Scottish Medieval Towns,* John Donald, 1988.

Contributor to *Historical Atlas of Scotland c. 400—c. 1600, A Companion to Scottish Culture,* and guide books. Contributor to historical and archaeological journals.

WORK IN PROGRESS: Subeditor and contributor to *Scottish Historical Atlas,* for Conference of Scottish Medievaliers; editing and writing a contribution for *Patterns of Scottish Building,* for Scottish Vernacular Buildings Working Group; with Richard Oram, editing and writing a contribution for *Galloway* volume, for Scottish Society for Northern Studies; writing a contribution for *Scotland and Scandinavia,* for John Donald.

SIDELIGHTS: Geoffrey Stell told *CA:* "Scottish castles and traditional or vernacular buildings are my main interests, usually explored through an integrated approach to building and social history. *Loads and Roads* arose out of a conference that I organized, and my special concern was to demonstrate the importance of land transport in the pre-industrial era. It is time there was a corresponding volume on maritime transport!"

BIOGRAPHICAL/CRITICAL SOURCES:

PERIODICALS

Times Literary Supplement, October 19, 1984.

* * *

STEPHENSON, Andrew M(ichael) 1946-

PERSONAL: Born October 8, 1946, in Maracaibo, Venezuela. *Education:* City University, London, England, B.Sc. (with honors), 1969.

ADDRESSES: Home—High Wycombe, Buckinghamshire, England. *Agent*—Maggie Noach, A. P. Watt Ltd., 26-28 Bedford Row, London WC1R 4HL, England; and Frances Collin, Marie Rodell-Frances Collin Literary Agency, 110 West 40th St., New York, N.Y. 10018.

CAREER: Plessey Telecommunications Research, Taplow, England, design engineer, 1969-76; European representative for Science Fiction Writers of America, 1976-78; writer and science fiction illustrator.

WRITINGS:

(With Christopher Priest) *Inverted World,* New English Library, 1975.
Nightwatch (science fiction novel), Futura, 1977, Dell, 1979.
The Wall of Years (science fiction novel), Futura, 1979, Dell, 1980.

Work represented in anthologies, including *Andromeda 1,* edited by Peter Weston, Futura, 1976, St. Martin's, 1979. Contributor to *Analog.**

* * *

STERBA, Richard F(rancis) 1898-

PERSONAL: Born May 6, 1898, in Vienna, Austria; naturalized U.S. citizen, 1945; son of Yosef (a professor) and Mathilde (a seamstress; maiden name, Fischer) Sterba; married wife, Editha (a psychoanalyst), December 11, 1926; children: Monique Sterba Schneider, Verena Sterba Nichols. *Education:* University of Vienna, M.D., 1923; postdoctoral study at Vienna Psychoanalytic Institute, 1924-27. *Politics:* "No affiliation." *Religion:* "No denomination."

ADDRESSES: Home—861 Whittier, Grosse Pointe, Mich. 48230. *Office*—18228 Mack Ave., Grosse Pointe Farms, Mich. 48236.

CAREER: Wilhelminenspital, Vienna, Austria, intern, 1923-26; University of Vienna, Vienna, resident in psychiatry, 1926-29; Vienna Psychoanalytic Institute, Vienna, training analyst, 1929-38; Chicago Psychoanalytic Institute, Chicago, Ill., training analyst, 1939-46; Wayne State University, Detroit, Mich., clinical professor of psychiatry, 1945-73, professor emeritus, 1973—. Director of Detroit-Cleveland Psychoanalytic Institute, 1946-53.

MEMBER: American Medical Association, American Psychoanalytical Association.

AWARDS, HONORS: Award from Michigan Psychiatric Association.

WRITINGS:

Introduction to the Psychoanalytic Theory of the Libido, Brunner, 1942.
(With wife, Edith Sterba) *Beethoven and His Nephew,* Pantheon, 1954.
Reminiscences of a Viennese Psychoanalyst, Wayne State University Press, 1982.

Contributor of about seventy articles to medical and psychoanalytic journals.

SIDELIGHTS: Richard F. Sterba's *Reminiscences of a Viennese Psychoanalyst* reveals the author's early contacts with the vanguard of psychoanalysis. His acquaintances included the elderly Sigmund Freud, Otto Rank, and Theodor Reik. During the 1920s, Sterba worked closely with the noted Wilhelm Reich to establish an outpatient psychoanalytic clinic for the poor of Vienna. Later the author allied himself with the younger generation of the Vienna Psychoanalytic Society and participated in its often controversial meetings. According to Peter Sedgwick of the *Times Literary Supplement,* "Sterba's notes on these impromptu interventions, on topics crucially important in the comprehension of psychoanalytic concepts, are among the most valuable features of the present memoir." The critic went on to describe the book as "an attractive human document, replete with pen-portraits and a sheaf of photographs."

BIOGRAPHICAL/CRITICAL SOURCES:

PERIODICALS

Times Literary Supplement, November 5, 1982.

* * *

STEVENS, Art 1935-

PERSONAL: Born July 17, 1935, in New York, N.Y.; son of Sol (a clothing executive) and May (a housewife; maiden name, Frank) Stevens; married Eva Sandberg, March 19, 1972. *Education:* City College (now of the City University of New York), B.A., 1957.

ADDRESSES: Home—201 East 21st St., New York, N.Y. 10010. *Office*—Lobsenz-Stevens, Inc., 460 Park Ave. S., New York, N.Y. 10016.

CAREER: English teacher in a New York City junior high school, 1957-58; Prentice-Hall, Inc., Englewood Cliffs, N.J., textbook editor, 1958-60, assistant to public relations director, 1960-61, public relations director, 1961-65; William L. Safire Public Relations, Inc., New York City, account executive, 1966-69, vice-president, 1967-68, president, 1968-69; Lobsenz-Stevens, Inc., New York City, president, 1970—. Instructor at Fairleigh Dickinson University. Member of ethics committee of Public Relations Counselors Academy.

MEMBER: Public Relations Society of America, Publicity Club of New York, Gipsy Trail Club, United Way of Putnam County (board member).

AWARDS, HONORS: Distinguished Service Award from Publicity Club of New York, 1969.

WRITINGS:

The Persuasion Explosion, Acropolis Books, 1985.

Author of humor column for the Sanibel *Island Reporter*. Contributor to business and management journals.

WORK IN PROGRESS: A book of humorous essays; a humor column, for newspaper syndication.

SIDELIGHTS: Art Stevens told *CA:* "Words are power. The accuracy of this aphorism never hit home as profoundly as when my book was published. The ability to turn a phrase, to toss off a tense, or to alter an alliteration is an awesome power.

"I had never written a book before *The Persuasion Explosion*. I had written tons of press releases, feature stories, and article outlines in my capacity as a public relations writer for many clients. But I had never written for *myself*. When I was invited to write *The Persuasion Explosion* by Acropolis Books, a fear swept over me. Would I be able to provide substance out of my own experiences and viewpoints to fill a three hundred-page book? The verdict can best be judged by trivia historians of the twenty-third century.

"A catharsis took place within me, however, that transformed the Dr. Jekyl client writer to the Mr. Hyde of self-expression. The first phase of my metamorphosis began when I forced myself to put my very first words to paper in writing *The Persuasion Explosion*. I was forced to take stock of what I had to say. To my pleasant surprise, not unlike sex, writing got better and better as I went along. Not only did I find that I did indeed have something to contribute, but the manner in which words began to be strung together became eminently joyful. I was addicted. What to write next?

"Several years ago I bought another home in Sanibel, Florida. To keep up with matters that had a bearing on homeowner interests, I subscribed to the weekly *Island Reporter*. Just as Clark Kent tests his ability to turn the awesome power of Superman into actuality as often as necessary, I too wanted to test my newly discovered ability to express my writing skills in real life circumstances. One thing led to another. And lo and behold, I became the weekly humor columnist for the *Island Reporter*. It's been a gas. I'm having a great deal of fun. I no longer have to beat my wife or kick the cat. I now have an outlet for my gripes, frustrations, disappointments, dissatisfaction, and bitterness. It's called humor. And it takes the sting out of life. It pokes fun at it. It enables us to put things in perspective.

"Will I write another book? Maybe it'll be a collection of my humor columns. Maybe it'll be a novel. Maybe it'll be a play. Regardless of what form my next literary contribution to mankind will be, of one thing I'm certain. There's no turning back. It's Mr. Hyde all the way."

AVOCATIONAL INTERESTS: Tennis, pop singing.

BIOGRAPHICAL/CRITICAL SOURCES:

PERIODICALS

Los Angeles Times, December 13, 1985.

* * *

STEVENS, Wallace 1879-1955
(Peter Parasol)

PERSONAL: Born October 2, 1879, in Reading, Pa.; died of cancer, August 2, 1955, in Hartford, Conn.; buried in Cedar Hills Cemetery, Hartford, Conn; son of Garrett Barcalow (a lawyer) and Margaretha Catharine (a schoolteacher; maiden name, Zeller) Stevens; married Elsie Viola Kachel, September 21, 1909; children: Holly Bright. *Education:* Attended Harvard University, 1897-1900; New York Law School, LL.B., 1903.

ADDRESSES: Home—118 Westerly Terrace, Hartford, Conn. 06112.

CAREER: Poet and insurance lawyer. *New York Tribune,* New York City, reporter, 1900-01; law clerk for W. G. Peckham in New York City, 1903-04; admitted to the Bar in New York State, 1904; law partner with Lyman Ward, c. 1904; worked in various law firms in New York City, 1904-08; American Bonding Co. (became Fidelity and Deposit Co.), New York City, lawyer, 1908-13; Equitable Surety Co. (became New England Equitable Insurance Co.), New York City, resident vice-president, 1914-16; Hartford Accident and Indemnity Co., Hartford, Conn., 1916-55, became vice-president, 1934. Lecturer.

MEMBER: National Institute of Arts and Letters.

AWARDS, HONORS: Prize from Players Producing Co., c. 1916, for "Three Travelers Watch a Sunrise"; Levinson Prize from *Poetry,* 1920; poetry prize from *Nation,* 1936; Harriet Monroe Poetry Award, 1946; Bollingen Prize in Poetry, 1950; gold medal from Poetry Society of America, 1951; National Book Award for best poetry, 1951, for *The Auroras of Autumn;* Litt.D., from Bard College, 1951; Litt.D., from Harvard University, 1951; Litt.D., from Mount Holyoke College, 1952; Litt.D., from Columbia University, 1952; National Book Award for best poetry and Pulitzer Prize for poetry, both 1955, both for *The Collected Poems of Wallace Stevens;* L.H.D., from Hartt College of Music, 1955; Litt.D., from Yale University, 1955.

WRITINGS:

Harmonium (poetry; includes "Le Monocle de Mon Oncle," "The Comedian as the Letter C," "The Emperor of Ice Cream," "Thirteen Ways of Looking at a Blackbird," "Peter Quince at the Clavier," "Sunday Morning," "Sea Surface Full of Clouds," and "In the Clear Season of Grapes"), Knopf, 1923, revised edition, 1931.

Ideas of Order (poetry; includes "Farewell to Florida," "The Idea of Order at Key West," "Academic Discourse at Havana," "Like Decorations in a Nigger Cemetery," and "A Postcard From the Volcano"), Alcestis Press, 1935, enlarged edition, Knopf, 1936.

Owl's Clover (poetry), Alcestis Press, 1936, reprinted in *Opus Posthumous* (also see below).

The Man With the Blue Guitar, and Other Poems (poetry; includes "The Man With the Blue Guitar," "A Thought Revolved," and "The Men That Are Falling"), Knopf, 1937.

Parts of a World (poetry; includes "The Poems of Our Climate," "The Well Dressed Man With a Beard," and "Examination of the Hero in a Time of War"), Knopf, 1942.

Notes Toward a Supreme Fiction (poetry), Cummington Press, 1942, reprinted in *Transport to Summer* (also see below).

Esthetique du Mal (poetry), Cummington Press, 1945, reprinted in *Transport to Summer* (also see below).

Transport to Summer (poetry; includes "The Pure Good of Theory," "A Word With Jose Rodriguez-Feo," "Description Without Place," "The House Was Quiet and the World Was Calm," *Notes Toward a Supreme Fiction,* and *Esthetique du Mal;* also see above), Knopf, 1947.

Three Academic Pieces: The Realm of Resemblance, Someone Puts a Pineapple Together, Of Ideal Time and Choice (essays), Cummington Press, 1947, reprinted in *The Necessary Angel: Essays on Reality and the Imagination* (also see below).

A Primitive Like an Orb (poetry), Gotham Book Mart, 1948, reprinted in *The Auroras of Autumn* (also see below).

The Auroras of Autumn (poetry; includes "The Auroras of Autumn," "Large Red Man Reading," "In a Bad Time," "The Ultimate Poem Is Abstract," "Bouquet of Roses in Sunlight," "An Ordinary Evening in New Haven," and *A Primitive Like an Orb;* also see above), Knopf, 1950.

The Relations Between Poetry and Painting (lecture), Museum of Modern Art, 1951.

The Necessary Angel: Essays on Reality and the Imagination (essays; includes "The Noble Rider and the Sound of Words," "The Figure of the Youth as Virile Poet," "Effects of Analogy," "The Realm of Resemblance," "Someone Puts a Pineapple Together," and "Of Ideal Time and Choice" from *Three Academic Pieces;* also see above), Faber, 1960.

Selected Poems, Fortune Press, 1952.

Selected Poems, Faber, 1953.

Raoul Dufy: A Note (nonfiction), Pierre Beres, 1953.

The Collected Poems of Wallace Stevens (includes *The Rock,* previously unpublished section featuring "The Poem That Took the Place of a Mountain," "A Quiet Normal Life," "Final Soliloquy of the Interior Paramour," "The Rock," "The Planet on the Table," and "Not Ideas About the Thing but the Thing Itself"), Knopf, 1954, reprinted, Random House, 1982.

Opus Posthumous (includes *Owl's Clover* and essays "The Irrational Element in Poetry," "The Whole Man: Perspectives, Horizons," "Preface to *Time of Year,*" "John Crowe Ransom: Tennessean," and "Adagia"), edited by Samuel French Morse, Knopf, 1957, reprinted, Random House, 1982.

Poems by Wallace Stevens, edited by Morse, Vintage Books, 1959.

Letters of Wallace Stevens, edited by daughter, Holly Stevens, Knopf, 1966.

The Palm at the End of the Mind: Selected Poems and a Play by Wallace Stevens, edited by Holly Stevens, Knopf, 1971.

Also author of preface to William Carlos Williams's *Collected Poems, 1921-1931,* Objectivist Press, 1934.

Author of plays "Three Travelers Watch a Sunrise," 1916, "Carlos Among the Candles," 1917, and "Bowl, Cat, and Broomstick," c. 1917.

Work represented in numerous anthologies, including *Modern American Poetry, The New Pocket Anthology of American Verse,* and *The Norton Anthology of Modern Poetry.*

Contributor to periodicals, including *Accent, American Letters, Botteghe Oscure, Broom, Contact, Dial, Halcyon, Horizon, Hound and Horn, Kenyon Review, Life and Letters Today, Little Review, Measure, Modern School, Nation, New Republic, Others, Poetry* (some works published under pseudonym Peter Parasol, c. 1914), *Poetry London, Quarterly Review of Literature, Rogue, Secession, Soil, Southern Review, Voices,* and *Wake.*

SIDELIGHTS: Wallace Stevens is one of America's most respected poets. He was a master stylist, employing an extraordinary vocabulary and a rigorous precision in crafting his poems. But he was also a philosopher of aesthetics, vigorously exploring the notion of poetry as the supreme fusion of the creative imagination and objective reality. Because of the extreme technical and thematic complexity of his work, Stevens was sometimes considered a willfully difficult poet. But he was also acknowledged as an eminent abstractionist and a provocative thinker, and that reputation has been sustained throughout the more than thirty years that have passed since his death. In 1975, for instance, noted literary critic Harold Bloom, whose writings on Stevens include the imposing *Wallace Stevens: The Poems of Our Climate,* called him "the best and most representative American poet of our time."

Stevens was born in 1879 in Reading, Pennsylvania. His family belonged to the Dutch Reformed Church, and when Stevens became eligible he enrolled in parochial schools. Stevens's father contributed substantially to the son's early education by providing their home with an extensive library and by encouraging reading. At age twelve Stevens entered public school for boys and began studying classics in Greek and Latin. In high school he became a prominent student, scoring high marks and distinguishing himself as a skillful orator. He also showed early promise as a writer by reporting for the school's newspaper, and after completing his studies in Reading he decided to continue his literary pursuits at Harvard University.

Encouraged by his father, Stevens devoted himself to the literary aspects of Harvard life. By his sophomore year he wrote regularly for the *Harvard Advocate,* and by the end of his third year, as biographer Samuel French Morse noted in *Wallace Stevens: Poetry as Life,* he had received all of the school's honors for writing. In 1899 Stevens joined the editorial board of the *Advocate*'s rival publication, the *Harvard Monthly,* and the following year he assumed the board's presidency and became editor. By that time Stevens had already published poems in both the *Advocate* and the *Monthly,* and as editor he additionally produced stories and literary sketches. Because there was a frequent shortage of manuscript during his tenure as editor, Stevens often published several of his own works in each issue of the *Monthly*. He thus gained further recognition on campus as a prolific and multi-talented writer. Unfortunately, his campus literary endeavors ended in 1900 when a shortage of family funds necessitated his withdrawal from the university.

Leaving Harvard was hardly a setback, though, for Stevens was not working towards a college degree and was not particularly invigorated by the school's literary environment. Once out of Harvard, Stevens decided to work as a journalist, and shortly thereafter he began reporting for the *New York Evening Post*. He published regularly in the newspaper, but he found the work dull and inconsequential. The job proved most worthwhile as a means for Stevens to acquaint himself with New York City. Each day he explored various areas and then recorded his observations in a journal. In the evenings he either attended theatrical and musical productions or remained in his room writing poems or drafting a play.

Stevens soon tired of this life, however, and questioned his father on the possibility of abandoning the newspaper position to entirely devote himself to literature. But his father, while a lover of literature, was also prudent, and he counseled his son to cease writing and commence law studies. Stevens heeded the advice, and in October, 1901, he enrolled at the New York School of Law.

Two years later Stevens graduated, and in 1904 he was admitted to the New York Bar. He then worked briefly in a law

partnership with former Harvard classmate Lyman Ward. After parting from Ward, Stevens worked for various law firms in New York City. In 1908 he accepted a post with the American Bonding Company, an insurance firm, and he stayed with the company when it was purchased by the Fidelity and Deposit Company.

Stevens's early years with the insurance firm brought great personal change. Financially secure, he proposed marriage to Elsie Viola Kachel, who accepted and became his wife in September, 1909. Two years later Stevens's father died, and in 1912 his mother also died.

During this period Stevens apparently wrote no poetry, but he involved himself in New York City's artistic community through his association with several writers, including poets Marianne Moore and William Carlos Williams. Of keen interest to Stevens at this time were the art exhibitions at the many museums and galleries in the city. He developed a fondness for modern painting—eventually becoming a connoisseur and collector—and for Asian art, including painting, pottery, and jewelry. He particularly admired Asian works for their vivid colors and their precision and clarity, qualities that he later imparted to his own art.

By 1913 Stevens was enjoying great success in the field of insurance law. Unlike many aspiring artists, however, he was hardly stifled by steady employment. He soon resumed writing poetry, though in a letter to his wife he confided that writing was "absurd" as well as fulfilling. In 1914 he nonetheless published two poems in the modest periodical *Trend,* and later that year he produced four more verses—portions from an ultimately uncompleted work, "Phases"—for Harriet Monroe's publication *Poetry*. None of these poems were included in Stevens's later volumes, but they are often considered his first mature writings.

After he began publishing his poems Stevens changed jobs again, becoming resident vice-president, in New York City, of the Equitable Surety Company (which, in turn, became the New England Equitable Company). He left that position in 1916 to work for the Hartford Accident and Indemnity Company, where he remained employed for the rest of his life, becoming vice-president in 1934.

This period of job changes was also one of impressive literary achievements for Stevens. In 1915 he produced his first important poems, "Peter Quince at the Clavier" and "Sunday Morning," and in 1916 he published his prize-winning play, "Three Travelers Watch a Sunrise." Another play, "Carlos Among the Candles," followed in 1917, and the comic poem "Le Monocle de Mon Oncle" appeared in 1918. During the next few years Stevens began organizing his poems for publication in a single volume. For inclusion in that prospective volume he also produced several longer poems, including the masterful "Comedian as the Letter C." This poem, together with the early "Sunday Morning" and "Le Monocle de Mon Oncle," proved key to Stevens's volume *Harmonium* when it was published in 1923.

Harmonium bears ample evidence of Stevens's wide-ranging talents: an extraordinary vocabulary, a flair for memorable phrasing, an accomplished sense of imagery, and the ability to both lampoon and philosophize. "Peter Quince at the Clavier," among the earliest poems in *Harmonium,* contains aspects of all these skills. In this poem, a beautiful woman's humiliating encounter with lustful elders becomes a meditation on the nature of beauty (and the beauty of nature). Stevens vividly captures the woman's plight by dramatically contrasting the tranquility of her bath with a jarring interruption by several old folk. Consistent with the narrator's contention that "music is feeling," the woman's plight is emphasized by descriptions of sounds from nature and musical instruments. The poem culminates in a reflection on the permanence of the woman's physical beauty, which, it is declared, exists forever in memory and—through death—in the union of body and nature: "The body dies; the body's beauty lives. / So evenings die, in their green going, / A wave, interminably flowing."

"Peter Quince at the Clavier," with its notion of immortality as a natural cycle, serves as a prelude to the more ambitious "Sunday Morning," in which cyclical nature is proposed as the sole alternative to Christianity in the theologically bankrupt twentieth century. Here Stevens echoes the theme of "Peter Quince at the Clavier" by writing that "death is the mother of beauty," thus confirming that physical beauty is immortal through death and the consequent consummation with nature. Essentially an analysis of one woman's ennui, "Sunday Morning" ends by stripping the New Testament's Jesus Christ of transcendence and consigning him, too, to immortality void of an afterlife but part of "the heavenly fellowship / of men that perish." In this manner "Sunday Morning" shatters the tenets, or illusion, of Christianity—essentially, the spiritual afterlife—and substantiates nature—the joining of corpse to earth—as the only channel to immortality. In her volume *Wallace Stevens: An Introduction to the Poetry,* Susan B. Weston perceived the replacement of Christianity with nature as the essence of the poem, and she called "Sunday Morning" the "revelation of a secular religion."

Less profound, perhaps, but no less impressive are *Harmonium*'s comedic highlights, "Le Monocle de Mon Oncle" and "The Comedian as the Letter C." In "Le Monocle de Mon Oncle" the narrator, a middle-aged poet, delivers an extended, rather flamboyantly embellished, monologue to love in all its embodiments and evocations. He reflects on his own loves and ambitions in such carefree detail that the work seems an amusing alternative to T. S. Eliot's pessimistic poem "The Love Song of J. Alfred Prufrock." Like "Sunday Morning," "Le Monocle de Mon Oncle" celebrates change, and it further suggests that even in fluctuation there is definition—"that fluttering things have so distinct a shade."

In the mock epic "Comedian as the Letter C" Stevens presents a similarly introspective protagonist, Crispin, who is, or has been, a poet, handyman, musician, and rogue. The poem recounts Crispin's adventures from France to the jungle to a lush, Eden-like land where he establishes his own colony and devotes himself to contemplating his purpose in life. During the course of his adventures Crispin evolves from romantic to realist and from poet to parent, the latter two roles being, according to the poem, mutually antagonistic. The poem ends with Crispin dourly viewing his six daughters as poems and questioning the validity of creating anything that must, eventually, become separate from him.

"The Comedian as the Letter C" is a fairly complex work, evincing Stevens's impressive, and occasionally intimidating, vocabulary and his penchant for often obscure humor. Stevens later declared that his own motivations in writing the poem derived from his enthusiasm for "words and sounds." He stated: "I suppose that I ought to confess that by the letter C I meant the sound of the letter C; what was in my mind was to play on that sound throughout the poem. While the sound of that letter has more or less variety . . . , all its shades may

be said to have a comic aspect. Consequently, the letter C is a comedian.''

Although the aforementioned poems are perhaps the most substantial in *Harmonium,* they are hardly the volume's only noteworthy ones. Also among the more than fifty poems that comprise Stevens's first book are ''Thirteen Ways of Looking at a Blackbird,'' an imagistic poem highly reminiscent of the Japanese poetry form haiku, and ''The Emperor of Ice Cream,'' an eloquent exhortation that death is an inevitable aspect of living. These and the other entries in *Harmonium* reveal Stevens as a poet of delicate, but determined, sensibility, one whose perspective is precise without being precious, and whose wit is subtle but not subdued. As Harriet Monroe, founder and first editor of *Poetry,* wrote in reviewing *Harmonium* for her own periodical, ''The delight which one breathes like a perfume from the poetry of Wallace Stevens is the natural effluence of his own clear and untroubled and humorously philosophical delight in the beauty of things as they are.''

Few critics, however, shared Monroe's enthusiasm, or even her familiarity, concerning *Harmonium* following its publication in 1923. The book was ignored in most critical quarters, and was dismissed as a product of mere dilettantism by some of the few reviewers that acknowledged Stevens's art. Although apparently undaunted by the poor reception accorded *Harmonium,* Stevens produced only a few poems during the next several years. Part of this unproductiveness was attributed by Stevens to the birth of his daughter, Holly, in 1924. Like his autobiographical character Crispin, Stevens found that parenting thwarted writing. In a letter to Harriet Monroe he noted that the responsibilities of parenthood were a ''terrible blow to poor literature.''

In 1933, nine years after his daughter's birth, Stevens finally resumed writing steadily. The following year he published his second poetry collection, *Ideas of Order,* and in 1935 he produced an expanded edition of that same work. The poems of *Ideas of Order* are, generally, sparer and gloomier than those of *Harmonium.* Prominent among these bleak works is ''Like Decorations in a Nigger Cemetery,'' comprised of fifty verses on subjects such as aging and dying. Perhaps in reference to these fifty short verses, the racist title refers to the litter that, in Stevens's opinion, accumulated in blacks' cemeteries. He ends this poem by noting the futility of attempts to thwart nature and by commending those individuals who adapt to change: ''Union of the weakest develops strength / Not wisdom. Can all men, together, avenge / One of the leaves that have fallen in autumn? / But the wise avenges by building his city in snow.''

Stevens more clearly explicated his notion of creative imagination in ''The Idea of Order in Key West,'' among the few invigorating poems in *Ideas of Order* and one of the most important works in his entire canon. In this poem Stevens wrote of strolling along the beach with a friend and discovering a girl singing to the ocean. Stevens declares that the girl has created order out of chaos by fashioning a sensible song from her observations of the swirling sea. The concluding stanza extolls the virtues of the singer's endeavor (''The maker's rage to order words of the sea'') and declares that the resulting song is an actual aspect of the singer. In his book *Wallace Stevens: The Making of the Poem,* Frank Doggett called the concluding stanza Stevens's ''hymn to the ardor of the poet to give order to the world by his command of language.''

Following the publication of *Ideas of Order* Stevens began receiving increasing recognition as an important and unique poet. Not all of that recognition, however, was entirely positive. Some critics charged that the obscurity, abstraction, and self-contained, art-for-art's-sake tenor of his work were inappropriate and ineffective during a time of international strife that included widespread economic depression and increasing fascism in Europe. Stevens, comfortably esconced in his half-acre home in Hartford, responded that the world was improving, not degenerating further. He held himself relatively detached from politics and world affairs, although he briefly championed leading Italian fascist Benito Mussolini, and contended that his art actually constituted the most substantial reality. ''Life is not people and scene,'' he argued, ''but thought and feeling. The world is myself. Life is myself.''

Stevens contended that the poet's purpose was to interpret the external world of thought and feeling through the imagination. Like his alter-ego Crispin, Stevens became preoccupied with articulating his perception of the poet's purpose, and he sought to explore that theme in his 1936 book, *Owl's Clover.* But that book—comprised of five explications of various individuals' relations to art—proved verbose and thus uncharacteristically excessive. Immensely displeased, Stevens immediately dismantled the volume and reshaped portions of the work for inclusion in a forthcoming collection.

That volume, *The Man With the Blue Guitar,* succeeded where *Owl's Clover* failed, presenting a varied, eloquently articulated contention of the same theme—the poet, and therefore the imagination, as the explicator of thought and feeling—that had undone him earlier. In the title poem Stevens defends the poet's responsibility to shape and define perceived reality: ''They said, 'You have a blue guitar, / You do not play things as they are.' / The man replied, 'Things as they are / Are changed upon the blue guitar.''' For Stevens, the blue guitar was the power of imagination, and the power of imagination, in turn, was ''the power of the mind over the possibility of things'' and ''the power that enables us to perceive the normal in the abnormal.''

The Man With the Blue Guitar, particularly the thirty-three-part title poem, constituted a breakthrough for Stevens by indicating a new direction: an inexhaustive articulation of the imagination as the supreme perception and of poetry as the supreme fiction. Harold Bloom, in acknowledging Stevens's debacle *Owl's Clover,* described *The Man With the Blue Guitar* as the poet's ''triumph over . . . literary anxieties'' and added that with its completion Stevens renewed his poetic aspirations and vision. ''The poet who had written *The Man With the Blue Guitar* had weathered his long crisis,'' Bloom wrote, ''and at fifty-eight was ready to begin again.''

In subsequent volumes Stevens singlemindedly concentrated on his idea of poetry as the perfect synthesis of reality and the imagination. Consequently, much of his poetry is about poetry. In his next collection, *Parts of a World,* his writing frequently adopts a solipsistic perspective in exemplifying and explicating his definition of poetry. Such poems as ''Prelude to Objects,'' ''Add This to Rhetoric,'' and ''Of Modern Poetry'' all address, to some extent, the self-referential nature of poetry. In ''Of Modern Poetry'' Stevens defined the genre as ''the finding of a satisfaction, and may / Be of a man skating, a woman dancing, a woman / Combing. The poem of the act of the mind.'' In *Wallace Stevens: An Introduction to the Poetry,* Susan B. Weston wrote that in ''Of Modern Poetry,'' as with many poems in *Parts of a World,* ''Stevens cannot say *what* the mind wants to hear; he must be content to write *about* a poetry that would express what the mind wants to hear, and

to render the satisfaction that *might* ensue.'' She added, ''Stevens' is a conditional world indeed.''

Stevens followed *Parts of a World* with *Notes Toward a Supreme Fiction,* which is usually considered his greatest poem on the nature of poetry. This long poem, more an exploration of a definition than it is an actual definition, exemplifies the tenets of supreme fiction even as it articulates them. The poem is comprised of a prologue, three substantial sections, and a coda. The first main section, entitled ''It Must Be Abstract,'' recalls *Harmonium*'s themes by hailing art as the new deity in a theologically deficient age. Abstraction is necessary, Stevens declares, because it fosters the sense of mystery necessary to provoke interest and worship from humanity. The second long portion, ''It Must Change,'' recalls ''Sunday Morning'' in citing change as that which ever renews and sustains life: ''Winter and spring, cold copulars, embrace / And for the particulars of rapture come.'' And in ''It Must Give Pleasure,'' Stevens expresses his conviction that poetry must always be ''a thing final in itself and, therefore, good: / One of the vast repetitions final in themselves and, therefore, good, the going round / And round and round, the merely going round, / Until merely going round is a final good, / The way wine comes at a table in a wood.'' *Notes Toward a Supreme Fiction* concludes with verses describing the poet's pursuit of supreme fiction as ''a war that never ends.'' Stevens, directing these verses to an imaginary warrior, wrote: ''Soldier, there is a war between the mind / And sky, between thought and day and night. It is / For that the poet is always in the sun, / Patches the moon together in his room / to his Virgilian cadences, up down, / Up down. It is a war that never ends.'' This is perhaps Stevens's most impressive description of his own sense of self, and in it he provides his most succinct appraisal of the poet's duty.

Although *Notes Toward a Supreme Fiction* elucidates Stevens's notions of poetry and poet, it was not intended by him to serve as a definitive testament. Rather, he considered the poem as a collection of ideas about the idea of supreme fiction. Writing to Henry Church, to whom the poem is dedicated, Stevens warned that it was not a systematized philosophy but mere notes—''the nucleus of the matter is contained in the title.'' He also reaffirmed his contention that poetry was the supreme fiction, explaining that poetry was supreme because ''the essence of poetry is change and the essence of change is that it gives pleasure.''

Notes Toward a Supreme Fiction was published as a small volume in 1942 and was subsequently included in the 1947 collection, *Transport to Summer*. Also featured in the collection is *Esthetique du Mal,* another long poem first published separately. In this poem Stevens explored the poetic imagination's response to specific provocations: pain and evil. Seconding philosopher Friedrich Nietzsche, Stevens asserted that evil was a necessary aspect of life, and he further declared that it was both inspirational and profitable to the imagination. This notion is most clearly articulated in the poem's eighth section, which begins: ''The death of Satan was a tragedy / For the imagination. A capital / Negation destroyed him in his tenement / And, with him, many blue phenomena.'' In a later stanza, one in which Bloom found the poem's ''central polemic,'' Stevens emphasizes the positive aspect of evil: ''The tragedy, however, may have begun, / Again, in the imagination's new beginning, / In the yes of the realist spoken because he must / Say yes, spoken because under every no / Lay a passion for yes that had never been broken.'' In *Wallace Stevens: The Poems of Our Climate,* Bloom called *Esthetique du Mal* Stevens's ''major humanistic polemic'' of the mid-1940s.

In 1950 Stevens published his last new poetry collection, *The Auroras of Autumn*. The poems in this volume show Stevens further refining and ordering his ideas about the imagination and poetry. Among the most prominent works in this volume is ''An Ordinary Evening in New Haven,'' which constitutes still another set of notes toward a supreme fiction. Here Stevens finds the sublime in the seemingly mundane by recording his contemplations of a given evening. The style here is spare and abstract, resulting in a poem that revels in ambiguity and the elusiveness of definitions: ''It is not the premise that reality / Is solid. It may be a shade that traverses / A dust, a force that traverses a shade.'' In this poem Stevens once again explicates as the supreme synthesis of perception and the imagination and produces a poem about poetry: ''This endlessly elaborating poem / Displays the theory of poetry, / As the life of poetry.'' Other poems in *The Auroras of Autumn* are equally self-reflexive, but they are ultimately less ambitious and less provocative, concerned more with rendering the mundane through abstraction and thus prompting a sense of mystery and, simultaneously, order. As fellow poet Louise Bogan noted in a *New Yorker* review of the collection, only Stevens ''can describe the simplicities of the natural world with more direct skill,'' though she added that his ''is a natural world strangely empty of human beings.''

Stevens followed *The Auroras of Autumn* with a prose volume, *The Necessary Angel,* in which he articulated his poetic notions without resorting to abstraction and obfuscation. In the essay ''The Noble Ride and the Sound of Words'' he addressed the imagination's response to adversity, and in ''The Figure of the Youth as Virile Poet'' he once again championed the imagination as the medium toward a reality transcending mere action and rationalization. Consistent in the volume is Stevens's willingness to render his ideas in a precise, accessible manner. Thus *The Necessary Angel* considerably illuminates his poetry.

By the early 1950s Stevens was regarded as one of America's greatest contemporary poets, an artist whose precise abstractions exerted substantial influence on other writers. Despite this widespread recognition, Stevens kept his position at the Hartford company, perhaps fearing that he would become isolated if he left his lucrative post. In his later years with the firm, Stevens amassed many writing awards, including the Bollingen Prize for Poetry, the National Book Award for *The Auroras of Autumn,* and several honorary doctorates. His greatest accolades, however, came with the 1955 publication of *The Collected Poems of Wallace Stevens,* which earned him the Pulitzer Prize for poetry and another National Book Award. In this volume Stevens gathered nearly all of his previously published verse, save *Owl's Clover,* and added another twenty-five poems under the title ''The Rock.'' Included in this section are some of Stevens's finest and most characteristically abstract poems. Appropriately, the final poem in ''The Rock'' is entitled ''Not Ideas About the Thing But the Thing Itself,'' in which reality and the imagination are depicted as fusing at the instant of perception: ''That scrawny cry—it was / A chorister whose c preceded the choir. / It was part of the colossal sun, / Surrounded by its choral rings, / Still far away. It was like / A new knowledge of reality.''

After publishing his collected verse Stevens succumbed increasingly to cancer and was repeatedly hospitalized. He died in August, 1955.

In the years since his death Stevens's reputation has remained formidable. The obscurity and abstraction of his poetry has proven particularly appealing among students and academicians and has consequently generated extensive criticism. Among the most respected interpreters of Stevens's work are Helen Hennessy Vendler, who has demonstrated particular expertise on the longer poems, and Harold Bloom, whose *Wallace Stevens: The Poems of Our Climate* is probably the most provocative and substantial, if also dense and verbose, of the many volumes attending to Stevens's entire canon. For Bloom, Stevens is "a vital part of the American mythology."

MEDIA ADAPTATIONS: Poems from *Harmonium* were set to music by Vincent Persichetti to form a song cycle; "Thirteen Ways of Looking at a Blackbird" was set to music by John Gruen to form a song cycle and by J. Wisse to form a secular cantata.

AVOCATIONAL INTERESTS: Collecting paintings, walking.

BIOGRAPHICAL/CRITICAL SOURCES:

BOOKS

Alvarez, A., *Stewards of Excellence: Studies in Modern English and American Poets,* Scribner, 1958.

Baird, James, *The Dome and the Rock: Structure in the Poetry of Wallace Stevens,* Johns Hopkins University Press, 1968.

Bates, Milton J., *Wallace Stevens: A Mythology of Self,* University of California Press, 1985.

Beckett, Lucy, *Wallace Stevens,* Cambridge University Press, 1974.

Benamou, Michel, *Wallace Stevens and the Symbolist Imagination,* Princeton University Press, 1972.

Blackmur, R. P., *The Double Agent: Essays in Craft and Elucidation,* Peter Smith, 1962.

Blessing, Richard Allen, *Wallace Stevens' "Whole Harmonium,"* Syracuse University Press, 1970.

Bloom, Harold, *Figures of Capable Imagination,* Seabury, 1976.

Bloom, Harold, *Wallace Stevens: The Poems of Our Climate,* Cornell University Press, 1976.

Bornstein, George, *Transformations of Romanticism in Yeats, Eliot, and Stevens,* University of Chicago Press, 1976.

Boroff, Marie, *Language and the Poet: Verbal Artistry in Frost, Stevens, and Moore,* University of Chicago Press, 1979.

Boroff, Marie, editor, *Wallace Stevens: A Collection of Critical Essays,* Prentice-Hall, 1963.

Brazeau, Peter, *Parts of a World: Wallace Stevens Remembered,* Random House, 1983.

Brown, Ashley, and Robert S. Haller, editors, *The Achievement of Wallace Stevens,* Lippincott, 1962.

Brown, Merle E., *Wallace Stevens: The Poem as Act,* Wayne State University Press, 1970.

Burney, William, *Wallace Stevens,* Twayne, 1968.

Buttel, Robert, *Wallace Stevens: The Making of "Harmonium,"* Princeton University Press, 1967.

Buttel, Robert, and Frank Doggett, editors, *Wallace Stevens: A Celebration,* Princeton University Press, 1980.

Doggett, Frank, *Stevens' Poetry of Thought,* Johns Hopkins University Press, 1966.

Doggett, Frank, *Wallace Stevens: The Making of the Poem,* Johns Hopkins University Press, 1980.

Donaghue, Denis, *Connoisseurs of Chaos: Ideas of Order in Modern American Poetry,* Faber, 1965.

Donaghue, Denis, *The Ordinary Universe: Soundings in Modern Literature,* Faber, 1968.

Ehrenpreis, Irvin, editor, *Wallace Stevens: A Critical Anthology,* Penguin, 1973.

Enck, John J., *Wallace Stevens: Images and Judgments,* Southern Illinois University Press, 1964.

Hines, Thomas J., *The Later Poetry of Wallace Stevens: Phenomenological Parallels With Husserl and Heidegger,* Bucknell University Press, 1976.

Kenner, Hugh, *A Homemade World: The American Modernist Writers,* Knopf, 1975.

Kermode, Frank, *Wallace Stevens,* Oliver & Boyd, 1960.

Kessler, Edward, *Images of Wallace Stevens,* Rutgers University Press, 1972.

LaGuardia, David M., *Advance on Chaos: The Sanctifying Imagination of Wallace Stevens,* University Press of New England, 1983.

Lentricchia, Frank, *The Gaiety of Language: An Essay on the Radical Poetics of W. B. Yeats and Wallace Stevens,* University of California Press, 1968.

Litz, A. Walton, *Introspective Voyager: The Poetic Development of Wallace Stevens,* Oxford University Press, 1972.

McNamara, Peter L., editor, *Critics on Wallace Stevens,* University of Miami Press, 1972.

Morris, Adalaide Kirby, *Wallace Stevens: Imagination and Faith,* Princeton University Press, 1974.

Morse, Samuel French, *Wallace Stevens: Poetry as Life,* Pegasus, 1970.

Nasser, Eugene Paul, *Wallace Stevens: An Anatomy of Figuration,* University of Pennsylvania Press, 1965.

O'Connor, William Van, *The Shaping Spirit: A Study of Wallace Stevens,* Regnery, 1950.

Pack, Robert, *Wallace Stevens: An Approach to His Poetry and Thought,* Rutgers University Press, 1958.

Perlis, Alan, *Wallace Stevens: A World of Transforming Shapes,* Bucknell University Press, 1976.

Richardson, Joan, *Wallace Stevens: The Early Years,* Morrow, 1986.

Riddel, Joseph N., *The Clairvoyant Eye: The Poetry and Poetics of Wallace Stevens,* Louisiana State University Press, 1965.

Sexson, Michael, *The Quest of Self in the Collected Poems of Wallace Stevens,* Edwin Mellen, 1981.

Stern, Herbert J., *Wallace Stevens: Art of Uncertainty,* University of Michigan Press, 1966.

Stevens, Holly, *Souvenirs and Prophecies: The Young Wallace Stevens,* Knopf, 1977.

Sukenick, Ronald, *Wallace Stevens: Musing the Obscure,* New York University Press, 1967.

Tindall, William York, *Wallace Stevens,* University of Minnesota Press, 1961.

Twentieth-Century Literary Criticism, Gale, Volume 3, 1980, Volume 12, 1984.

Vendler, Helen Hennessy, *On Extended Wings: Wallace Stevens' Longer Poems,* Harvard University Press, 1969.

Vendler, Helen Hennessy, *Wallace Stevens,* Harvard University Press,1986.

Wells, Henry W., *Introduction to Wallace Stevens,* Indiana University Press, 1964.

Weston, Susan B., *Wallace Stevens: An Introduction to the Poetry,* Columbia University Press, 1977.

Woodman, Leonora, *Stanza My Stone: Wallace Stevens and the Hermetic Tradition,* Purdue University Press, 1983.

Woodward, Kathleen, *At Last, the Real Distinguished Thing: The Later Poems of Eliot, Pound, Stevens, and Williams,* Ohio State University Press, 1980.

PERIODICALS

American Poetry Review, September-October, 1978.
Arizona Quarterly, autumn, 1955.
Colorado Quarterly, summer, 1960.
Commonweal, September 23, 1955.
Comparative Literature, winter, 1959.
Contemporary Literature, autumn, 1975.
Critical Quarterly, autumn, 1960.
Criticism, winter, 1960, summer, 1965.
Encounter, November, 1979.
English Journal, October, 1959.
Georgia Review, spring, 1976, summer, 1976.
Hudson Review, autumn, 1957.
Journal of Modern Literature, May, 1982.
Kenyon Review, winter, 1957, winter, 1964.
Literary Review, autumn, 1963.
Modern Language Quarterly, September, 1969.
Nation, April 5, 1947.
New England Quarterly, December, 1971.
New Yorker, October 28, 1950.
Poetry, March, 1924, December, 1931, February, 1937, January, 1956.
Sewanee Review, autumn, 1945, spring, 1952, winter, 1957.
Southern Review, July, 1971, July, 1976, October, 1979, January, 1982.
Studies in Romanticism, spring, 1982.
Western Review, autumn, 1955.
Yale Review, spring, 1955, spring, 1967, winter, 1982.*

—Sketch by Les Stone

* * *

STOCK, Guy 1933-

PERSONAL: Born February 18, 1933, in Great Baddow, Essex, England; son of Harry Thomas (a company director) and Dorothy Blanche (a housewife) Stock; married Phyllis Jane Spear (a university lecturer), April 2, 1971; children: Kathleen, Sarah. *Education:* Trinity College, Dublin, M.A., 1955; Birkbeck College, London, B.A., 1964. *Politics:* "Conservative with a small 'c'." *Religion:* Roman Catholic.

ADDRESSES: Home—9 Union Place, Montrose DD10 8QB, Scotland. *Office*—Department of Philosophy, University of Aberdeen, Aberdeen AB9 1FX, Scotland.

CAREER: Patrick, Grainger Ltd. (wholesale provisions merchants), Fordingbridge, England, trainee manager, 1959-60; geography teacher at Roman Catholic school in London, England, 1960-65; University of Aberdeen, Aberdeen, Scotland, lecturer, 1965-73, senior lecturer in philosophy, 1973—. *Military service:* Royal Air Force, flying officer in Education Branch, 1956-59.

MEMBER: Aristotelian Society, Mind Association.

WRITINGS:

(Editor with Anthony Manser) *The Philosophy of F. H. Bradley,* Clarendon Press, 1984.
Bradley, Routledge & Kegan Paul, in press.

Associate editor of *Philosophical Investigations* and *Reid Newsletter.*

WORK IN PROGRESS: Selected Readings in the Philosophy of Bradley, with James Allard, for Oxford University Press.

SIDELIGHTS: Guy Stock told *CA:* "Francis Herbert Bradley, although unfortunately little known outside academic circles, is generally recognized among philosophers as one of the greatest of all English thinkers. He was highly respected by Bertrand Russell and William James even though his idealism and monism stood in stark contrast to their empiricist and pluralistic philosophical systems. T. S. Eliot, who wrote a philosophically excellent but unpresented doctoral thesis on Bradley, said of him that one of the reasons for his indubitable claim to permanence was his 'great gift of style.'

"My interest in Bradley stemmed initially from a prephilosophical interest in the poetry of Eliot and later from an interest in the philosophy of Russell. In the 1920s Russell became the dominant influence in British philosophy but, it seems to me, he did this by force of personality rather than by the cogency of his detailed arguments.

"Scientific realism, of a kind that Russell would in general have approved of, has in the 1970s and 1980s once again become dominant in Anglo-American philosophy. However, again I believe that this dominance cannot be explained by the cogency of contemporary philosophers' arguments. No scientific 'advances' could affect the validity of Bradley's reasoning. And his thought in epistemology, metaphysics, and ethics still offers an alternative which, in my opinion, is nearer the truth than the arid irreligious physicalism and utilitarianism which dominate our contemporary philosophical scene."

AVOCATIONAL INTERESTS: Marathon running.

BIOGRAPHICAL/CRITICAL SOURCES:

PERIODICALS

Times Literary Supplement, November 9, 1984.

* * *

STODDART, Jack Elliott 1916-1988

OBITUARY NOTICE: Born July 24, 1916, in Hamilton, Ontario, Canada; died of a stroke, January 8, 1988, in Naples, Fla. Sales executive and publisher. Stoddart is remembered for making General Publishing one of Canada's most successful publishers. He joined Macmillan Company of Canada in 1936 and served in various capacities, including sales manager, until 1957. He purchased General Publishing that year and, in subsequent years, Musson Book Company; New Press; Simon & Schuster of Canada; Nelson, Foster & Scott; and other publishers. In 1972 Stoddart founded PaperJacks—a paperback book distributor that quickly became successful in both Canada and the United States. He retired as chairman of General Publishing in 1983 but remained chairman of PaperJacks until his death. He was also chairman and president of Stoddart Publishers. Stoddart contributed articles on book publishing to professional journals.

OBITUARIES AND OTHER SOURCES:

BOOKS

The Canadian Who's Who, Volume XXII, University of Toronto Press, 1987.
Who's Who in the East, 19th edition, Marquis, 1983.

PERIODICALS

Publishers Weekly, February 26, 1988.

STOLL, Dennis G(ray) 1912-1987
(Denys Craig)

OBITUARY NOTICE—See index for *CA* sketch: Born May 25, 1912, in London, England; died December 16, 1987. Broadcaster, conductor, composer, and author. Stoll was known both for reconstructing music and dance styles of ancient Egypt for his own compositions in the Egyptian style and for founding the Ancient Egyptian Arts Association. He conducted for organizations such as the Royal Philharmonic Orchestra and the Cairo Symphony, and his musical works include the operas "Akhnaton and Nefertiti" and "Songs of Karnak," "Persian Suite," and the ballet "The Raising of Nefertiti." Among Stoll's prose writings are *Music Festivals of Europe,* the novels *Comedy in Chains* and *The Dove Found No Rest,* and, under the pseudonym Denys Craig, *Man in Ebony.* He also made numerous broadcasts for the British Broadcasting Corporation.

OBITUARIES AND OTHER SOURCES:

BOOKS

International Who's Who in Music and Musicians' Directory, 8th edition, Melrose, 1977.

PERIODICALS

Times (London), December 22, 1987.

* * *

STONE, Howard W. 1942-

PERSONAL: Born March 11, 1942, in Minneapolis, Minn.; son of Walter S. (a postal clerk) and Ruth (a secretary; maiden name, Andren) Stone; married wife, Karen, August 31, 1963; children: Christine M. Po. *Education:* Augsburg College, B.A., 1965; Lutheran Theological Seminary at Philadelphia, M.Div., 1968; School of Theology at Claremont, Ph.D., 1971; postdoctoral study at Arizona State University.

ADDRESSES: Office—Brite Divinity School, Texas Christian University, P.O. Box 32923, Fort Worth, Tex. 76129.

CAREER: Ordained minister of Evangelical Lutheran Church in America, 1971; diplomate of American Association of Pastoral Counselors. Student pastor in Pennsylvania, 1966-68; Lutheran Theological Seminary, Philadelphia, Pa., visiting lecturer in pastoral theology and acting director of field education, 1970-71; Interfaith Counseling Service, Scottsdale, Ariz., executive director, 1971-79; Texas Christian University, Fort Worth, professor of pastoral care and pastoral psychology, 1979—. Visiting scholar at Wescott House, Cambridge University, 1986; lecturer and workshop leader. Vice-president of board of managers of *Journal of Pastoral Care.*

MEMBER: American Association of Marriage and Family Therapists (clinical member), Society for Pastoral Theology.

AWARDS, HONORS: Special Honor Award from Crisis Intervention of Fort Worth, 1984.

WRITINGS:

Suicide and Grief, Fortress, 1972.
(Contributor) *Suicide Prevention in the Seventies,* National Institute of Mental Health, 1973.
Crisis Counseling, Fortress, 1976.
Using Behavioral Methods in Pastoral Counseling, Fortress, 1980.
The Caring Church: A Guide for Lay Pastoral Care, Harper, 1983.
(With James Duke) *The Caring Christian: Schleiermacher's Practical Theology,* Fortress, 1988.
The Word of God and Pastoral Care, Abingdon, 1988.

* * *

STONE, Jerry 1942(?)-1987

OBITUARY NOTICE: Born c. 1942; died after an extended illness, November 24, 1987. Editor. Stone began working for the publishing company Springer-Verlag in New York in 1982 as senior editor. He became executive medical editor four years later. He served previously as senior medical editor at Praeger Publishers and Raven Press and as biological sciences editor at Academic Press.

OBITUARIES AND OTHER SOURCES:

PERIODICALS

Publishers Weekly, December 11, 1987.

* * *

STONE, Natalie
See GOLDENBAUM, Sally

* * *

STOTT, D(enis) H(erbert) 1909-1988

OBITUARY NOTICE—See index for *CA* sketch: Born December 31, 1909, in London, England; died January 22, 1988. Educator and author. In more than forty years as a teacher, Stott earned respect and renown for his work with delinquent children and those with learning disabilities. He did extensive research in the field and published numerous books on the subject, notably *Delinquency and Human Nature, Helping Children With Learning Difficulties, Helping the Maladjusted Child,* and *Delinquency: The Problem and Its Prevention.*

OBITUARIES AND OTHER SOURCES:

PERIODICALS

Times (London), January 26, 1988.

* * *

STRACHEY, James 1889(?)-1967

BRIEF ENTRY: Born c. 1889; died in April, 1967; British psychoanalyst, editor, and translator. Strachey was best known as general editor and principal translator of the twenty-four volume *Standard Edition of the Complete Psychological Works of Sigmund Freud* (Hogarth Press, 1953-74). He was the brother of writer Lytton Strachey and was thus peripherally associated with the Bloomsbury group of British artists that included Virginia Woolf and E. M. Forster. After studying psychoanalysis under Freud and James Glover, Strachey entered the field and began his own practice. With his wife, Alix, who was also a practicing psychoanalyst, Strachey also devoted many years to editing and translating the standard edition of Freud's works. A portion of Strachey's correspondence with his wife was eventually published as *Bloomsbury/Freud: The Letters of James and Alix Strachey, 1924-1925.*

BIOGRAPHICAL/CRITICAL SOURCES:

PERIODICALS

New York Times Book Review, December 29, 1985.
Times (London), May 3, 1967, May 11, 1967.
Times Literary Supplement, March 28, 1986.

* * *

STRAUSS, Walter L(eopold) 1928-1988

OBITUARY NOTICE—See index for *CA* sketch: Born April 23, 1928, in Nuremberg, Germany (now West Germany); immigrated to United States, 1936, naturalized citizen, 1949; died of a heart attack, January 14, 1988, in Manhattan, N.Y. Publisher, editor, and author. Strauss wrote and published numerous books about art masters such as Albrecht Duerer, Hendrick Goltzius, and Rembrandt van Rijn, including several multivolume works considered standard references. In 1973 he founded his own publishing firm, Abaris Books, which produced Strauss's six-volume *Complete Drawings of Albrecht Duerer.* His other writings include *The Human Figure: Albrecht Duerer's Dresden Sketchbook, The Chiaroscuro Woodcuts of the German and Netherlandish Masters of the Sixteenth Century, The Book of Hours of Emperor Maximilian I,* and *The Iconography of Astrology.* Strauss also edited *Tribute to Wolfgang Stechow.*

OBITUARIES AND OTHER SOURCES:

BOOKS

International Authors and Writers Who's Who, 9th edition, [and] *International Who's Who in Poetry,* 6th edition, Melrose, 1982.

PERIODICALS

Publishers Weekly, February 5, 1988.

* * *

STREN, Patti 1949-

PERSONAL: Born August 8, 1949, in Brantford, Ontario, Canada; daughter of Maurie (a manufacturer) and Sadie (a teacher and archivist; maiden name, Goldberg) Stren. *Education:* University of Toronto, B.A., 1971; attended Ontario College of Art, 1972-74; School of Visual Arts, New York City, B.F.A., 1977.

ADDRESSES: Home—365 West End Ave., Apt. 1204, New York, N.Y. 10024. *Office*—c/o Writers' Union of Canada, 24 Ryerson Ave., Toronto, Ontario, Canada M5T 2P3.

CAREER: Author and illustrator of children's books. Worked with children in various settings, including Children's Aid Society in Brantford, Ontario, and Sloan-Kettering Hospital in New York City; taught autistic children in Tel Hashomer Hospital in Tel Aviv, Israel, 1970-71.

MEMBER: Writers' Union of Canada.

AWARDS, HONORS: Canada Council Grant from the Canada Arts Council, 1978, for *There's a Rainbow in My Closet.*

WRITINGS:

JUVENILE; AUTHOR AND ILLUSTRATOR

Hug Me, Harper, 1977.
Bo, the Constrictor That Couldn't, Green Tree, 1978.
Sloan and Philamina; or, How to Make Friends With Your Lunch, Dutton, 1979.
There's a Rainbow in My Closet, Harper, 1979.
I'm Only Afraid of the Dark (at Night!!), Harper, 1982.
Mountain Rose, Dutton, 1982.

OTHER

(Illustrator) Rosemary Allison, *Yaaay Crickets!!!,* privately printed, 1975.
(Illustrator) Mary Kennedy, *Wings,* Scholastic, Inc., 1980.
Hug Me and Other Stories by Patti Stren (recording; includes "Hug Me," "Sloan and Philamina," "I'm Only Afraid of the Dark [at Night!!]," and "Mountain Rose"), Caedmon, 1983.
(Illustrator) Phyllis Green, *Eating Ice Cream With a Werewolf,* Harper, 1983.
(Illustrator) Ronnie Sellers, *My First Day at School,* Caedmon, 1985.
I Was a Fifteen-Year-Old Blimp, Harper, 1985.
(Illustrator) Claudine G. Wirths and Mary Bowman-Kruhm, *I Hate School,* Crowell, 1987.

Also illustrator of the school workbook *Noise Sound Silence,* 1974, and of the "Hug Me" series for Renaissance Greeting Cards. Contributor to magazines, including *Better Homes, Ms.,* and *Self.*

WORK IN PROGRESS: A book for teenagers, tentatively titled *Love Stinks,* for Harper.

SIDELIGHTS: Patti Stren, a best-selling author and illustrator of children's books, is known for the quiet humor in her books and the endearing quality instilled in her pen and ink doodles. Reviewers praise her ability to create picture books that serve equally well as "read-aloud" books for youngsters and "read-alone" books for adults, who can appreciate the witty quips and asides spoken by the cartoon-like characters.

Her first book, *Hug Me,* concerns a porcupine who longs to be hugged, and it has proven as popular among adults as among children. "It's the kind of bright picture book that finds its way into college bookstores and is offered as a love token by yearning swains," proposed a reviewer in *Publishers Weekly.* Presenting a "simple but universal message—our need to love and be loved," wrote Jon C. Stott in the *World of Children's Books,* "Stren's prose is clear and concise. . . . But most importantly, the pen and ink sketches, although simple to the point of plainness, capture Elliot [the porcupine's] inner feelings." Georgess McHargue, reviewing the book for the *New York Times Book Review,* also praised Stren's "wispy line drawings and happy ending" and urged readers to "try the book on the nearest angst-ridden adult."

Stren's second book is about a boa constrictor who would rather hug and kiss other animals than squeeze and swallow them, much to the disgust of his fellow boa constrictors. The idea for *Bo, the Constrictor That Couldn't* "is an excellent one for a picture book," proclaimed Nancy Ward in her critique for *In Review: Canadian Books for Children.* Although she found the introduction "too detailed and too long" to hold the attention of preschoolers, the reviewer affirmed that "the illustrations are large and simple with few details to confuse" the youngsters. In addition, Ward noted that the children to whom she read the book "seemed to enjoy the fact that the hero was a boa constrictor."

"Little humans will undoubtedly chuckle through the pages" of *Sloan and Philamina; or, How to Make Friends With Your*

Lunch, declared a reviewer in *Publishers Weekly.* The book's plot is similar to that of *Bo:* an anteater named Sloan befriends an ant named Philamina instead of eating her. When the anteater colony warns Sloan to devour his new friend "or else," Sloan decides to throw a party for the anteaters and the ants, after which everybody becomes friends. "Blithe and bouncy, the book can gently infuse some positive thoughts on prejudging, and it's fun," asserted Zena Sutherland in the *Bulletin of the Center for Children's Books.* "I even think that the whole story can be seen as an adult tale of love between two people of totally different backgrounds," ventured reviewer Marjorie Kelley. She told readers of *In Review: Canadian Books for Children:* "I can only applaud that philosophy and talent which gives me such delight in reading [*Sloan and Philamina*] aloud and at the same time entertains and entrances the children."

I'm Only Afraid of the Dark (at Night!!) is about an owl, Harold Tribune, who lives at the Arctic Circle and is afraid of the dark. His friend, Gert, tries various amusing tactics to help him get over his fear before winter—with its season-long darkness—sets in. Eventually Harold learns that Gert is afraid of the dark too, and the two friends end up helping each other. Several reviewers criticized the book's setting and illustrations as inaccurate, including Ronald Jobe in *CM,* who stated: "There must be a basic honesty in quality children's books. . . . The facts must be correct: slugs, trees, and bushes in the Arctic?" Leigh Dean, however, writing for the *Children's Book Review Service,* praised the book as "thoroughly satisfying." She added: "The secret of Stren's success [is] her gift to reach the authentic heart and spirit of the child. She does so in a charming, vulnerable, original style."

"In *There's a Rainbow in My Closet,* Patti Stren once again explores the child's need for love and acceptance despite individual differences," determined *Quill and Quire*'s Jacquie Hunt. The story is about shy, insecure Emma, a fourth grader whose grandmother comes to stay with her when Emma's mother goes away on a business trip. The two become close as they discover common interests, such as Emma's love for drawing and painting and Gramma's appreciation of the arts. The book's illustrations are presented as Emma's drawings, through which "Stren lets us experience . . . the excitement and total involvement of the artist during the act of creating," observed Jean Little in *Canadian Children's Literature: A Journal of Criticism and Review.* Although some critics complained that the adult characters in the book are unrealistic, Little pointed out that, "true as this may be, the reader is not concerned about it for this is Emma's story, . . . and Emma is entirely real." Noted Kelley, "The Emmas who read the book will love meeting a character so like themselves. The non-Emmas may get some appreciation of the importance of the particular uniqueness of each of us."

Again celebrating the uniqueness of each individual, Stren's *Mountain Rose* is about an unusual child. Rose, orphaned at the age of six, is ostracized by her peers for being "unusually big—so big 'that she needed her own zip code,'" quoted Arlene Stolzer Sandner in her critique for the *Children's Book Review Service.* Gradually Rose overcomes her insecurity and, as a woman wrestler, learns to feel proud of her size. "The side remarks and hilarious illustrations that fill every page will delight readers as they follow Rose from a disastrous beginning as an outcast in elementary school to the day she becomes Mountain Rose, Champion Wrestler of the World," Sandner wrote. "The story is told in a style that is replete with humour and verve," noted the *Children's Book News,* "[and the] illustrations are skillful and full of wit." A reviewer in *Publishers Weekly* agreed: "Kids will love following the fortunes of Rose. . . . It's the ludicrous setup on each page that will tickle [them]."

Stren wrote her next book, *I Was a Fifteen-Year-Old Blimp,* for pre-adolescents. The story concerns a teenager, Gabby, who becomes bulimic, believing that vomiting after she eats is the only way she can control her weight problem. After becoming aware of her compulsion, Gabby's family and friends help her confront and overcome it. "It will probably surprise few readers," wrote a reviewer in the *Bulletin of the Center for Children's Books,* "that a thinner and happier Gabby rejects the handsome jock on whom she's long had a crush, and turns to the less attractive Mel, who has long been her friend [and] admirer." Mary Ainslie Smith, writing in *Books in Canada,* called the book a "sensitive portrayal of a young person struggling to make sense of her life."

MEDIA ADAPTATIONS: An animated version of *Hug Me* was produced as a "CBS Library Special," November 8, 1981.

BIOGRAPHICAL/CRITICAL SOURCES:

BOOKS

Children's Literature Review, Volume V, Gale, 1983.

PERIODICALS

Books in Canada, December, 1985.
Bulletin of the Center for Children's Books, November, 1979, November, 1985.
Canadian Children's Literature: A Journal of Criticism and Review, number 22, 1981.
Children's Book News, June, 1982.
Children's Book Review Service, May, 1982, September, 1982.
CM, January, 1983.
Flare, February, 1981.
In Review: Canadian Books for Children, autumn, 1978, October, 1979, April, 1980.
New York Times Book Review, October 16, 1977.
Publishers Weekly, August 22, 1977, May 14, 1979, May 7, 1982.
Quill and Quire, February, 1980.
World of Children's Books, spring, 1978.

—*Sketch by Christa Brelin*

* * *

STRICKLER, Susan (Elizabeth) 1952-

PERSONAL: Born January 23, 1952, in Baltimore, Md.; daughter of Richard Stoner (a lawyer) and Joan (O'Connor) Strickler. *Education:* Ecole du Louvre, Certificate, 1972; Mount Holyoke College, B.A., 1973; University of Delaware, M.A., 1977.

ADDRESSES: Office—Worcester Art Museum, 55 Salisbury St., Worcester, Mass. 01609.

CAREER: Toledo Museum of Art, Toledo, Ohio, research associate, 1978-79; Virginia Museum, Richmond, director of special projects, 1979-80; Worcester Art Museum, Worcester, Mass., curator of American art, 1981—, director of curatorial affairs, 1987—.

MEMBER: College Art Association of America, American Association of Museums, Society of Architectural Historians, New England Museums Association.

WRITINGS:

American Paintings, Toledo Museum of Art, 1979.

(Editor) *John Frederick Kensett: An American Master,* Norton, 1985.

American Traditions in Watercolor: The Worcester Art Museum Collection, Abbeville, 1987.

WORK IN PROGRESS: Research on American miniature portraits.

BIOGRAPHICAL/CRITICAL SOURCES:

PERIODICALS

Times Literary Supplement, November 22, 1985.

* * *

STROBEL, Margaret 1946-

PERSONAL: Born February 15, 1946, in Grand Forks, N.D.; daughter of Arthur Fred and Alice (Olson) Strobel; married William J. Barclay, Jr. (an economist), August 30, 1978; children: Jessica. *Education:* Michigan State University, B.A., 1967; University of California, Los Angeles, M.A., 1968, Ph.D., 1975.

ADDRESSES: Home—Oak Park, Ill. *Office*—Women's Studies Program, University of Illinois at Chicago Circle, Box 4348, Chicago, Ill. 60680.

CAREER: Middlebury College, Middlebury, Vt., instructor in history, 1971-72; University of California, Los Angeles, lecturer in history and interim director of Women's Studies Program, 1975-78; San Diego State University, San Diego, Calif., lecturer in women's studies, 1978-79; University of Illinois at Chicago Circle, Chicago, associate professor of women's studies and history, director of Women's Studies Program, 1979—.

MEMBER: American Historical Association, National Women's Studies Association, Coordinating Committee of Women in the Historical Profession.

AWARDS, HONORS: Shared Herskovitz Award from African Studies Association, 1980, for *Muslim Women in Mombasa, 1890-1975.*

WRITINGS:

Muslim Women in Mombasa, 1890-1975, Yale University Press, 1979.

(With Sarah Mirza) *Three Swahili Women: Life Histories From Mombasa, Kenya,* Indiana University Press, 1988.

Contributor to periodicals. Editor of newsletter of Coordinating Committee of Women in the Historical Profession, 1982. Member of editorial board of *Signs: A Journal of Women in Culture and Society.*

WORK IN PROGRESS: A book on European women in the nineteenth and twentieth century British Empire, completion expected in 1989; a study of the Chicago Women's Liberation Union, completion expected in 1990.

SIDELIGHTS: Margaret Strobel told *CA:* "My interest in African women developed from my involvement in the late sixties in the U.S. feminist movement. This added dimensions to my existing studies in African history. My teaching has been in the area of women's studies. My present and future research is concerned with U.S. feminist activities."

BIOGRAPHICAL/CRITICAL SOURCES:

PERIODICALS

Times Literary Supplement, March 7, 1980.

* * *

STROHM, John
See STROHM, John L(ouis)

* * *

STROHM, John L(ouis) 1912-1987
(John Strohm)

OBITUARY NOTICE: Born June 22, 1912, in West Union, Ill.; died of cancer, December 5, 1987, in Woodstock, Ill. Radio commentator, editor, and author. Strohm is best remembered as a founding editor of *National Wildlife* magazine. Before beginning *National Wildlife* in 1962, he served as field editor, assistant editor, and eventually managing editor of *Prairie Farmer,* as well as editor of *Ford Almanac* and associate editor of *Country Gentleman.* Strohm traveled throughout Latin America, China, and the Soviet Union and contributed numerous travel articles to periodicals and publication syndicates. For his writings he received an Overseas Press Club award in 1959, the President's award in 1978, and two Pulitzer Prize nominations. He also worked as a radio broadcaster, conducting the radio program "World Neighbor" for Chicago station WLS during the 1940s. During former U.S. President Dwight D. Eisenhower's administration Strohm served as a speech writer and agricultural advisor. He wrote the books *I Lived With Latin Americans* and *Just Tell the Truth: The Uncensored Story of How the Common People Live Behind the Russian Iron Curtain.* He also edited *The Golden Garden Guide, The Golden Guide to Flowers,* and *The Golden Guide to Lawns, Trees, and Shrubs,* among other publications.

OBITUARIES AND OTHER SOURCES:

BOOKS

Who's Who in America, 41st edition, Marquis, 1980.

PERIODICALS

New York Times, December 10, 1987.

Washington Post, December 11, 1987.

* * *

STRONG, William S. 1951-

PERSONAL: Born March 1, 1951, in Cincinnati, Ohio; son of Robert L. (a lawyer) and Mary J. (a foundation director; maiden name, Sutherland) Strong; married Ann E. Reinke (a publisher), March 31, 1984. *Education:* Harvard University, A.B. (magna cum laude), 1973, J.D., 1977.

ADDRESSES: Office—Kotin, Crabtree & Strong, 61 Chatham St., Boston, Mass. 02109.

CAREER: Herrick & Smith (law firm), Boston, Mass., associate, 1977-82; Kotin, Crabtree & Strong (law firm), Boston, partner, 1982—; Franklin Pierce Law Center, Concord, N.H., adjunct professor of copyright law, 1987—.

MEMBER: American Bar Association, Boston Bar Association.

WRITINGS:

The Copyright Book: A Practical Guide, MIT Press, 1981, 2nd edition, 1984, 3rd edition, in press.

SIDELIGHTS: William S. Strong told *CA* that *The Copyright Book* "is intended for artists, writers, publishers, and lawyers who do not specialize in the field. My primary purpose in writing it was to provide information for the people who are most affected by copyright law, but who have no training in how to protect themselves or are unsure of what they can or cannot do under the law."

* * *

STUEART, Robert D. 1935-

PERSONAL: Born June 1, 1935, in Monticello, Ark.; son of Ira and Lois (Roberts) Stueart; married Marie-Luise Hille; children: Christian F., Sabine. *Education:* Southern State College (now Southern Arkansas University), B.A., 1956; Louisiana State University, M.L.S., 1962; University of Pittsburgh, Ph.D., 1972.

ADDRESSES: Home—43 Avon Rd., Wellesley, Mass. 02181. *Office*—Graduate School of Library and Information Science, Simmons College, 300 The Fenway, Boston, Mass. 02115.

CAREER: University of Colorado, Boulder, librarian, 1962-64; Pennsylvania State University, University Park, associate director of libraries, 1964-68; College of Librarianship Wales, Llanbadarn Fawr, Aberystwyth, Dyfed, visiting lecturer, 1971-72; University of Denver, School of Library and Information Management, Denver, Colo., assistant dean and associate professor, 1972-74; Simmons College, Boston, Mass., dean of Graduate School of Library and Information Science and professor, 1975—.

MEMBER: American Library Association (past chair of publishing committee; past president of Library Education Division), Association for Library and Information Science Education (past president), Beta Phi Mu (past president).

AWARDS, HONORS: Melvil Dewey Award for creative professional achievement and Blackwell Award for *Collection Development* from American Library Association, 1980; distinguished alumnus award from University of Pittsburgh, 1984; outstanding alumnus award from Southern Arkansas University, 1984; First Service Award from Association for Library and Information Science Education, 1987.

WRITINGS:

Area Specialist Bibliographer, Scarecrow, 1973.
Library Management, Libraries Unlimited, 1974, 3rd edition (with Barbara B. Moran), 1987.
Collection Development, JAI Press, 1980.
Academic Librarianship, Neal-Schuman, 1982.
Information Needs of the Eighties, JAI Press, 1982.
Michelle, My Chelle, Winston-Derek, 1987.

Contributor to library journals. Member of editorial board of *Journal of Academic Librarianship, College and Research Libraries*, and *Education for Information*.

WORK IN PROGRESS: Video disc research project.

SIDELIGHTS: Robert D. Stueart told *CA:* "Librarianship, a key profession in our information-rich environment, is constantly evolving and expanding. It is an exciting profession to be in as we approach the twenty-first century."

SUBLETTE, Walter (Edwards) 1940- (S. W. Edwards)

PERSONAL: Born September 6, 1940, in Chicago, Ill.; married wife, Cheryl. *Education:* Attended University of Illinois at Chicago Circle.

ADDRESSES: 5812 North Drake Ave., Chicago, Ill. 60659.

CAREER: Affiliated with *Playboy* in Chicago, Ill., in various positions, including nonfiction projects editor, fiction acquisitions editor, domestic editor. Guest reader at University of Chicago, Long Island University, University of Illinois, and University of Wisconsin—Madison.

MEMBER: Poetry Society of America, Authors Guild, Authors League of America, American Society of Journalists and Authors.

AWARDS, HONORS: Charles McElvy Award for Poetry, 1965.

WRITINGS:

(Under pseudonym S. W. Edwards) *Go Now in Darkness* (novel), Baker, 1964.
The Resurrection on Friday Night (poems), Swallow Press, 1977.

Also author, under pseudonym S. W. Edwards, of play "Natural Murder." Work represented in anthologies, including *Port Chicago Poets*. Contributor to magazines and newspapers, including *New Voices, American Poetry Review, Blackbird*, and *Chicago*. Contributing editor of *Playboy*.*

* * *

SULLIVAN, Earl L. 1942-

PERSONAL: Born August 11, 1942, in Anaconda, Mont.; son of Earl R. (a mail carrier) and Margaret (a housewife; maiden name, Jones) Sullivan; married Jean Wendell (a costume designer), August 10, 1963; children: Mark, Erin, Colin. *Education:* Seattle University, B.A., 1964; Claremont Graduate School, Ph.D., 1970.

ADDRESSES: Home—P.O. Box 2511, Cairo, Egypt. *Office*—Department of Political Science, American University in Cairo, Cairo, Egypt.

CAREER: University of Portland, Portland, Ore., instructor, 1967-68, assistant professor of political science, 1968-73; Cairo American College, Cairo, Egypt, chairman of board of trustees, 1974-79; American University in Cairo, assistant professor, 1973-74, associate professor, 1974-80, professor of political science, 1980—. Visiting scholar at University of California, Los Angeles, 1984-85.

MEMBER: International Studies Association, American Political Science Association, American Society for International Law, Middle East Studies Association.

WRITINGS:

Women in Egyptian Public Life, Syracuse University Press, 1986.

Contributor to *Cairo Papers in Social Science*.

WORK IN PROGRESS: The Conflict Over Palestine, completion expected in 1990.

SIDELIGHTS: G. H. Gardner wrote in *Choice* that Earl L. Sullivan's *Women in Egyptian Public Life* "is a remarkably lucid, uncluttered study of four groups of women who have

made a difference in contemporary Egypt.'' In the preface to his book, Sullivan wrote: ''I thought about doing this study for a long time before beginning the systematic research which led to this volume. Having lived and worked in Egypt since 1973, I was stimulated by a growing awareness of the gap between the Egypt I read about and the Egypt I observed in daily life. The chasm between theory and reality seemed especially serious in the case of women active in Egyptian public life. . . . Conversations with numerous Egyptian women, some of whom are subjects of this book, convinced me that, even as a foreign man, I was in an especially advantageous position to do research on women in the political and economic elite. . . . As the book took shape, it included women in four categories: those who had served in Parliament; the wives of Egypt's presidents; women in the political opposition; [and] women in business.''

Sullivan told *CA:* ''I shall continue to write about women in the Arab world, but my next major research project will be on the conflict over Palestine and Egypt's role in that conflict. What will distinguish this study from the work of others will be the use of game theory and rational choice theory, in addition to more traditional approaches, to explain this important and tendentious issue in a relatively non-ideological and objective manner.''

BIOGRAPHICAL/CRITICAL SOURCES:

PERIODICALS

Choice, September, 1986.
Times Literary Supplement, August 15, 1986.

*　　*　　*

SULLOWAY, Frank J(ones) 1947-

PERSONAL: Born February 2, 1947, in Concord, N.H.; son of Alvah Woodbury (a lawyer and teacher) and Alison (a professor; maiden name, Green) Sulloway. *Education:* Harvard University, B.A., 1969, M.A., 1971, Ph.D., 1978.

ADDRESSES: Office—Department of Psychology, Harvard University, Cambridge, Mass. 02138.

CAREER: Princeton University, Princeton, N.J., research fellow at Institute for Advanced Study, 1977-78; University of California, Berkeley, research fellow at Miller Institute for Basic Research, 1978-79; Massachusetts Institute of Technology, Cambridge, Mass., research fellow, 1980-81; Harvard University, Cambridge, visiting scholar, 1981-82; University of London, London, England, research fellow, 1982-84; Harvard University, visiting scholar, 1984—. Vernon Professor of Biology at Dartmouth College, summer, 1986. Producer of documentary films, including ''Charles Darwin and the Voyage of the Beagle,'' ''The Brazilian Tropical Rain Forest,'' and ''The Galapagos Islands: Darwin's Finches.''

MEMBER: History of Science Society.

AWARDS, HONORS: Pfizer Award from History of Science Society, 1980, for *Freud, Biologist of the Mind: Beyond the Psychoanalytic Legend;* numerous fellowships, including $192,000 MacArthur Prize from MacArthur Foundation, 1984.

WRITINGS:

Freud, Biologist of the Mind: Beyond the Psychoanalytic Legend, Basic Books, 1979.

(Contributor) William R. Woodward and Mitchell G. Ash, editors, *The Problematic Science: Psychology in Nineteenth-Century Thought,* Praeger, 1982.

(Contributor) R. J. Berry, editor, *Evolution in the Galapagos Islands,* Academic Press, 1984.

(Contributor) David Kohn, editor, *The Darwinian Heritage,* Princeton University Press, 1985.

Work anthologized in *Annual Editions: Western Civilization,* Volume 2: *Early Modern Through the Twentieth Century,* edited by William Hughes, Guilford Publishing, 1981.

Contributor to periodicals, including *Studies in the History of Biology, Journal of the History of Biology,* and *Nature.*

WORK IN PROGRESS: Family Constellation and Scientific Revolutions: The Roots of Intellectual Rebellion and *Darwin's Genius: An Intellectual Biography.*

SIDELIGHTS: Frank J. Sulloway is a respected scholar with particular expertise in the history of science. His high standing stems from the importance of his first major publication, *Freud, Biologist of the Mind,* in which he contends that pioneering psychoanalyst Sigmund Freud and his followers deliberately distorted his life and work to fashion a more heroic portrait. In *Freud,* Sulloway's intentions are twofold—to detail Freud's hitherto unacknowledged debt to both science and his peers and to ''elucidate the development and function of the Freud legend.'' But Sulloway's work does not discredit Freud. Rather, it attempts to perceive him free of artifice and distortion.

In *Freud* Sulloway emphasizes that Freud had long denied any relation between psychoanalysis—Freud's creation—and biology. But Sulloway uncovers Freud's ties to seminal evolutionist Charles Darwin, whose concepts of instinctual and irrational behavior were necessary to Freud's own formulations on human motivation. Sulloway also measures Freud's debt to close friend Wilhelm Fliess, an eccentric physician whose sex theories anticipated Freud's notions of latency, sexual preference, and the psyche's unconscious, instinctual component (the id). Sulloway asserts that Freud's followers portrayed Fliess as ''a crank'' scientist and that these followers thus obscured Fliess's important psychobiological contributions to theories now credited solely to Freud.

Among Sulloway's other findings is that Freud once charged sexologist Albert Moll with appropriating Freud's notion of infant sexuality, although Moll presented his own theory years before Freud's appeared and actually converted Freud to this perspective. Similarly, Sulloway notes that when Freud was confronted with evidence linking his ideas to those of philosopher Friedrich Nietzsche, Freud denied having possessed knowledge of Nietzsche's work prior to having published his own findings. Sulloway reveals, however, that Freud had originally studied Nietzsche's work while a student. According to Sulloway, Freud's denial of his own mentors—biologists and philosophers—has somewhat undermined psychoanalysis's stature as a reputable field within the natural sciences and has transformed it into a self-contained school perpetually generated by Freud's subservient followers. Furthermore, Sulloway believes that Freud's efforts to obscure the origins of psychoanalysis have resulted in the misconception that the field is ''pure psychology'' derived from Freud's creative, *original* thinking.

In exploring Freud's reputation as an extraordinarily original thinker, Sulloway reveals that Freud deliberately distorted his past in order to present himself as a solitary, heroic figure grappling with controversial, original ideas despite abuse and

ridicule from the scientific and medical communities. Sulloway disputes Freud's self-portrait, declaring that many scientists and doctors of Freud's time shared his interest and that Freud's willful misrepresentation of his stature distorts the reception accorded psychoanalysis in its early years. Contesting Freud's insistence that his ideas were originally mocked and resisted, Sulloway establishes that Freud's work was actually well received. He cites Freud biographer Ernest Jones's claim that one of Freud's most important writings, *The Interpretation of Dreams,* was either ignored or ridiculed by reviewers. But Sulloway shows that the book actually met with many favorable reviews, and he speculates that Jones, like many others in the psychoanalytic community, proffered a distortion specifically to enhance Freud's reputation as a heroic outsider.

But if Freud, at least in Sulloway's perspective, is hardly the radical and defiant intellect of his legend, he is nonetheless drawn throughout the book as a great figure. Sulloway readily acknowledges Freud's astounding creativity in adapting and synthesizing various concepts—some borrowed from predecessors Moll and Havelock Ellis—into a coherent interpretation and understanding of human behavior and motivation. "What remains today of Freud's insights and influences," Sulloway asserts, "provides ample testimony to his greatness."

Upon publication in 1979, *Freud, Biologist of the Mind* was hailed in many reviews as an extraordinary addition to the literature on Freud and psychoanalysis. Anthony Storr, writing in the *Washington Post Book World,* declared that "Sulloway's book is original and important" for its many revelations about Freud's personality and actual achievements. Storr added that Sulloway's work was also "an important contribution to our understanding of how . . . history can be retrospectively falsified." Similarly, Robert Kirsch wrote in the *Los Angeles Times Book Review* that *Freud* "shows what can be done in the neglected field of intellectual history to recover a sense of the current of ideas and theories." Kirsch described *Freud* as a "closely reasoned" and "fascinating" book, and he commended Sulloway for being both "fair and objective." And *Newsweek* reviewer Jean Strouse called *Freud* "an impressive intellectual biography," adding that "no one before has documented in such painstaking detail how Freud's genius worked to transform his own and others' observations into a thoroughgoing science of mind."

Sulloway has also been active as a scholar of the life and work of evolutionist Charles Darwin and has produced several essays on Darwin's early thought—especially on the *Beagle* voyage's importance in his intellectual development. In this regard Sulloway has shown that, contrary to popular belief, Darwin's conversion to evolutionism did not occur as a sudden realization during the *Beagle* exploration of the Galapagos Islands but developed after his return to England. Sulloway has analyzed the origins of the Galapagos legend and has noted its various functions within the scientific community. As for Darwin's alleged intellectual transformation during the *Beagle* voyage, Sulloway has emphasized the personal changes that accompanied Darwin's growing self-perception as a geological theorist.

Sulloway told *CA* that his most recent research focuses on the psychology and sociology of scientific revolutions. He reported that he has used "multi-variate statistical procedures" to analyze the personal and intellectual backgrounds of more than two thousand participants in sixteen major scientific revolutions since the Copernican era. According to Sulloway, birth order is a "particularly good" indicator of an individual's opinion of revolutionary scientific theory. "Birth order is also closely linked to political and religious persuasions," Sulloway added, "with late borns being more liberal on both measures."

In recognition of his achievement and continued promise as a scholar, Sulloway was awarded a coveted MacArthur Prize from the MacArthur Foundation, a highly respected body which confers fellowships without stipulations of any kind. These cash prizes, sometimes referred to as "genius awards," are given to select individuals to provide them greater flexibility in pursuing the same creative bent that merited recognition. Sulloway's own prize was $192,000 to be received over a five-year period beginning in 1984.

CA INTERVIEW

CA interviewed Frank Sulloway by telephone on July 9, 1986, at Dartmouth College, where he was teaching during the summer.

CA: Both of your parents were teachers, you've told CA. *Did their example encourage you to pursue a scholarly career?*

SULLOWAY: Undoubtedly. I think they were a very important influence. Having parents who teach gives one a role model, and I think it also makes very tangible in one's mind a sense of values and of academic excellence.

CA: Did they concentrate on science or psychology?

SULLOWAY: No, neither of my parents was interested in these fields. My father was initially a lawyer who had an interest in history and literature, and my mother is a professor of English.

CA: Is it true that Freud, Biologist of the Mind *came about almost accidentally? I believe you were originally working on Darwin.*

SULLOWAY: Yes, that's true. I initially turned to Freud as a way of gaining some insights into the problems I encountered in Darwin's life. I was very much interested in the process of scientific creativity, in creativity in general, and in certain legends about Darwin. I thought to myself, if you want to illuminate problems of this sort, you could do worse than to turn to Sigmund Freud, who had a great interest in these issues. So I began reading his work.

CA: What are some of the myths surrounding the life and work of Darwin that you have challenged?

SULLOWAY: At the time I began working on Darwin, in the late 1960s, there was still a consensus that when Darwin had gone on the voyage of the *Beagle* and visited the Galapagos Islands, he had been converted, Eureka-like, to the theory of evolution. We had the image of Darwin, the lone genius, standing on volcanic rock in the Galapagos observing "Darwin's finches" and the giant tortoises and forming a theory of evolution right at that moment. I personally retraced Darwin's voyage around South America; and I knew from having seen firsthand the things he described in his letters that he knew much less about what he was collecting and observing than he did after he returned to England. Only then did many of the world's experts in zoology and botany fill him in on the importance of what he had collected. I also realized Darwin had made a number of crucial errors during the voyage in terms

of what he thought he had collected versus what these specimens turned out to be. He often merged separate species into one, for example, and thus confused biological identities. He could be fooled by things he saw because he was not an expert. And yet it was Darwin, ironically, who subsequently had the scientific vision to recognize his *Beagle* collections in an evolutionary light. This circumstance made me aware how important individual temperament is in revolutionary thinking. It was not the Galapagos Islands, then, that made Darwin; rather it was Darwin who made the Galapagos by daring to think what others would not.

CA: You've written about this in scholarly journals. Will you also do a book on Darwin?

SULLOWAY: I have been working on a biography, which incorporates many of these aspects of the story of his life. I had originally intended to do a biography of Darwin before I ended up doing one of Freud. So, in a way, Freud got me waylaid on the track of scholarly endeavor.

CA: In your work on Freud, you needed the cooperation of many people and institutions. Were you always able to get the help you needed?

SULLOWAY: No, I had some difficulty. I was not able to see the complete letters from Freud to Wilhelm Fliess, which have since been published. That access was denied to me by Freud's daughter Anna. She had given permission to Jeffrey Masson to edit and publish the letters, but she still would not let other scholars see them. One could describe this as an example of misguided favoritism. When the complete letters appeared, it turned out that I had correctly surmised what most of the crucial missing parts were about. Others had looked at the correspondence—Ernest Jones, for example, and Max Schur, who were psychoanalysts in favor with Anna Freud. And one could largely reconstruct from the unpublished passages to which they referred what was actually in the missing parts of the letters. I was very pleased to find that I had not overlooked anything and that I had anticipated a great deal—in fact, probably the bulk of what was missing—and that, indeed, Fliess himself had published lots of things that gave one an intimate image of the collaboration that was going on in his relationship with Freud. So I didn't miss much.

CA: Did you get cooperation in general from other people and institutions?

SULLOWAY: I was allowed to work in Freud's library in London, which was in Anna Freud's house, the house that Freud himself moved to when he emigrated from Vienna. But I think that she was always a little bit suspicious about what I was up to.

CA: Because you weren't a psychoanalyst yourself?

SULLOWAY: Yes. I think she had a reaction that came out of family tradition, which was to distrust biographers or any scholar who was mucking around in old family paper and documents. She seemed to think that people should not be busying themselves with writing biographies of Freud, that if they were interested in Freud, they should be psychoanalysts. All motives were rather suspect if you were working on Freud himself. So she seemed to be a little wary of me.

CA: Then you didn't have an opportunity to interview her extensively about her father?

SULLOWAY: No. The kind of history I was doing was intellectual history, and I did know from talking with her that she knew much less about how Freud developed his ideas than I did. This was old history to her and she was not particularly interested in it. One experience I had with her really sums up our whole relationship. I once made the statement to her that having had access to all the books Freud was reading during his years of crucial discovery had, I felt, advanced my research and understanding of the man by perhaps five years. There was an astonished look on her face. She clearly could not understand that having access to the specific books her father read could tell you much about the creativity of the man. Her puzzlement stemmed from a difference in her view of where her father's creativity must have come from. She saw it as deriving from the context of patients through the analytical process, not from the books he read. But in the context of intellectual history, it was precisely the addition of this literary and conceptual element that made my approach valuable. That was not something she could appreciate, and I could see from the reaction on her face that it really mystified her. I think she said something about it at the time.

CA: How reliable in general have you found the other major biographies of Freud?

SULLOWAY: I would say this about them: that whether they are accurate or inaccurate, those that were written by first- or second-generation analysts like Ernest Jones or Max Schur convey some aspect of psychological reality. The essence of this psychological reality is the Freud legend. So if Ernest Jones says something about Freud that is simply wrong, but Jones believed it, it is sometimes very valuable to know this belief because it conveys the pervasiveness of the Freud legend as it existed in Jones's mind. In this sense, I still feel that the Jones biography is a marvelous book to read. It's the epitome of the Freud legend, and much of the interest of Freud is the legend that surrounds him.

CA: You refer frequently in your book to James Strachey's editorial comments. Were you usually happy with his interpretations?

SULLOWAY: Strachey is a real unsung hero in Freud scholarship. Here is a man who devoted his life to translating and editing the twenty-four volumes of the *Standard Edition* of Freud's works, and many of his editorial essays and sometimes long footnotes are models of careful scholarship. Because they are in the *Standard Edition,* there are often references to them by other Freud scholars—to such-and-such a page and such-and-such a footnote, for example, which may be a Strachey editorial commentary on the relationship of an idea in 1905 to an idea in 1920. But often Strachey's name gets left out of such references by other scholars. He really was a very perceptive editor of Freud's works, a gifted translator, and I benefited greatly from his scholarship. I think there were times when he was swayed too much by the Freud legend, but no one who works with Freud's *Standard Edition* in the English language can do without the assistance of Strachey.

CA: In your biography, I believe, you had no intention of arguing that Freud's ideas were based solely on biology, only that biology was an important source for the theory of psychoanalysis.

SULLOWAY: That's correct. I often was misunderstood on this point. On the one hand, biology was of course very important for Freud. After all, he began his career as a biologist and neurologist, and he continued that career into his mid-forties. On the other hand, biology is something of a bad word in the social sciences. Humanists despise the deterministic, reductionist mode of thinking that is generally associated with this discipline. Freud, of course, was adopted by humanists in the twentieth century as the great hero of poetry and literature; and, when you write a book of the sort I did, it is perhaps inevitable to be typecast as an "overly biological" interpreter of Freud. It was easier for critics to confront a paper dragon than it was to see the more sophisticated argument behind the book, and thus I often got reviewed as representing the notion that psychoanalysis is *only* biology. Psychoanalysis is really a very complicated, sophisticated psychobiology. It is very important to recognize this, and, in fact, this perspective is necessary in order to understand psychoanalysis properly. Moreover, because many of Freud's biological assumptions were erroneous, being based on now-outmoded nineteenth-century theories, understanding these assumptions allows us to see why much of psychoanalysis has turned out to be misguided and wrong.

CA: If so many of the terms that we associate with Freud—infantile sexuality, dream interpretation, and the unconscious, for example—actually preceded Freud, as you've shown in your book, what is truly original in Freud's work?

SULLOWAY: That's a very good question. There are many different forms that originality can take. Freud without question worked with many basic concepts that we now identify with him, such as infantile sexuality and the unconscious and dream interpretation, but that were very widespread in his day. The fact that he is now famous and we have forgotten about all his contemporaries who were working on these same notions has made it appear that Freud was the author of them. When one examines Freud in historical context, then, he seems to be much less original. But Freud took many of these contemporary ideas and gave them a unique Freudian twist. One could say that he transformed many of them. The notion of infantile sexuality as held by, say, Havelock Ellis or Albert Moll in the 1890s is *not* the same notion of infantile sexuality that Freud developed about this time and that became so famous in the twentieth century. The essence of Freud's originality lies in his unique synthesis and transformation of a number of ideas that, in their component parts, appear to be unoriginal.

CA: In an interview for the Italian publication Panorama, *you commented that you were surprised to find that many psychoanalysts liked your book. Has that remained true in the last three or four years?*

SULLOWAY: Yes. This is still one of the overriding surprises for me in terms of the reception of my book, although I think I would now issue a footnote to qualify my *Panorama* remark. When I originally published the book, I thought most analysts would hate it and nonanalytical psychiatrists, psychologists, and lay readers would enjoy it. I was surprised how many analysts actually liked it. They tended, however, to have their training in medicine and the sciences; and what they identified with in the book that I had not anticipated was the notion that Freud really did emerge out of a natural sciences background, and hence that psychoanalysis, no matter how problematic, still has its heart in the natural sciences. On the other hand, many people who were very interested in psychoanalysis but were not analysts themselves were negative about my book, and *they* tended to have a background in the humanities. It surprised me that certain professors of, say, philosophy or English were very put off by my book. I think what bothered them was the notion that I was somehow reducing Freud to the status of a simple-minded biological determinist. The major thesis of the book was much more sophisticated, but that is the way it was often portrayed.

Having said this, I would also say that I have been a little surprised, given the positive reception my book had among many psychoanalysts, that more of a dialogue has not developed in the last six or seven years. It is as if they were appreciative, but that not much could really grow out of it. And I think this represents a problem that is institutional within psychoanalysis, which is that most analysts do not have academic backgrounds. There are not many formal bridges between the world of the analytic community and the universities. I come from a university background, where we are much more used to talking about ideas and fighting for them and having the test of academia, and academic criticism, decide their fate. Analysts, who are mostly trained within analytic institutes, tend to be overprotective of "analytic truth." So, even though there was a great deal of initial interest in my book, there were very few bridges by which that interest could be transformed into a continuing dialogue with analysts. This reflects a more serious problem in psychoanalysis, namely, its rather distant relationship to academic psychology. Thus I merely got a taste of what is a much wider problem for psychoanalysis as a science.

CA: And this dialogue did not take place even overseas? Your book has been translated into other languages.

SULLOWAY: The same problem exists in the various countries where my book has been translated. Just as in the United States, psychoanalysis in Europe is mostly taught in psychoanalytic institutes, and this gives some limits to the intellectual contacts that are generated between analysts and academics. I must say I have had a number of continuing contacts, but they almost always come from psychotherapists and researchers trained in medical or psychiatric traditions rather than in analytic ones.

CA: Do you feel that your biography falls in any way within the province of psychohistory?

SULLOWAY: I would prefer to describe my book as being in the tradition of intellectual history rather than psychohistory. The book is not a typical attempt, in a psychohistorical vein, to reduce Freud's creative life to certain childhood events. Most Freud biography, including the Freud legend itself, ultimately has a "Freudian" psychohistorical core paradigm in which Freud's creativity is derived from his unusual childhood and family constellation. What I was trying to do was to show the limited nature of this paradigm and indeed to restore the forgotten intellectual context and intellectual history surrounding Freud's achievements. In this sense, my book is an antidote to psychohistory rather than an example of it.

CA: How do you feel about psychohistory in general?

SULLOWAY: I tend to be very skeptical of most psychohistory that I read. History is difficult enough to do anyway, and it is even more difficult to establish a *thesis* in history. When one

builds a thesis from a speculative, psychohistorical perspective, one is not only erecting a historical thesis but one is also building on a theory of psychology, usually psychoanalysis, that is itself very problematical. It is like trying to construct a building on quicksand. The foundation is unstable and the building sinks as you build it.

CA: You've received several grants for your research and writing. Have you been doing much teaching in the last ten years or so?

SULLOWAY: I have taught only a limited amount in the last decade. During the time I was a graduate student I was fortunate enough to spend three years in the Society of Fellows at Harvard and, subsequently, to receive the MacArthur Fellowship, which lasts for five years. Recently I have done some teaching, particularly in areas that I am most interested in—the lives of Darwin and Freud and theoretical issues in psychobiology, including sociobiology; and teaching has brought me here this summer to Dartmouth College as the Vernon Professor of Biography.

CA: Would you like to teach more, or would that keep you away from the research too much?

SULLOWAY: As long as I have funds for postdoctoral research, that is my primary aim. But I do intend to have a career in teaching, and I have tried to use my MacArthur Fellowship as a transition into this career.

CA: What writing projects are you involved in now?

SULLOWAY: My research career to date has really gone through three phases. The first was publishing the Freud book, which took me seven years. The second phase, which lasted from the time the book came out until 1984 or 1985, involved publishing a great deal of research that I had done on Darwin prior to getting involved in Freud. This I have done in article form. The third phase is beginning now. It involves a project that I have worked on since the early 1970s, namely, the relationship between birth order and revolutionary temperament, particularly in science but also in other fields. It's a project that involves a large number of biographies and multivariate data analysis. I have collected biographical information on more than two thousand persons and more than a dozen scientific revolutions since the time of Copernicus in the sixteenth century. I have tried to control these samples not only for the major variable I am interested in, which is birth order—that is, whether you are a firstborn or laterborn in the family—but also for other variables that might co-vary with birth order, such as family size, socioeconomic status, religiosity, and nationality. There are more than twenty variables that I am looking at simultaneously with birth order, so my data matrix is two thousand people times twenty variables or about forty thousand data points.

CA: So if I asked a question about your conclusions about the firstborn in the family, that would probably be too simple.

SULLOWAY: There's a simple answer, a less simple answer, and then another even less simple answer. In general one can say that although firstborns tend to be more eminent in all fields of knowledge, they also tend to be more conservative. So there is a sort of paradoxical relationship between birth order and intellectual achievement: firstborns, for example, tend to win more Nobel Prizes in science, but they do not tend to lead scientific revolutions. In fact, they tend to vehemently oppose revolutions in science. Where occasionally there are revolutionary firstborns, the revolution concerned has to be of a circumscribed variety. Einstein was a firstborn, for instance. His work was indeed revolutionary, but the average person in the street certainly did not know what this revolution was all about. On the other hand, the average person did understand the revolutionary significance of what Darwin or Copernicus were proposing. They were laterborns. Their followers also tended to be laterborns, and their opponents tended to be firstborns. Where revolutions have involved deep-seated implications for major issues in politics, religion, or other extra-scientific areas, there are usually major birth-order effects involved. I am doing a book on this, and I will also publish an article summarizing the results.

CA: In the December, 1979, issue of California Monthly *you are quoted as saying, "I work very hard. Long hours. Weekends. I don't take any time off. But I* love *working. It's fun!" Is this still true for you?*

SULLOWAY: This statement makes me sound like a real workaholic! I am still a very hard worker, and I think it's difficult to alter those patterns, but I am no longer such a workaholic. So even though I am still a pretty disciplined worker, my life has diverse things going on.

CA: Where will you go after the summer at Dartmouth?

SULLOWAY: I will be back at Harvard in my capacity as visiting scholar and I will do some teaching on and off, and also work on my book on birth-order and scientific revolutions. I still have another three years to go on my MacArthur fellowships, so for the next three years my career will be primarily research oriented.

BIOGRAPHICAL/CRITICAL SOURCES:

PERIODICALS

California Monthly, December, 1979.
Los Angeles Times Book Review, September 16, 1979.
New Statesman, October 7, 1979.
Newsweek, October 29, 1979.
New York Review of Books, November 8, 1979.
New York Times, October 9, 1979.
New York Times Book Review, February 10, 1980.
Panorama, December 13, 1982.
Partisan Review, summer, 1983.
Psychology Today, December, 1979.
Spectator, November 17, 1979.
Time, July 30, 1979.
Voice Literary Supplement, October, 1981.
Washington Post Book World, September 23, 1979.

—Sketch by Les Stone

—Interview by Walter W. Ross

* * *

SUMIDA, Jon Tetsuro 1949-

PERSONAL: Born July 7, 1949, in Washington, D.C.; son of Theodore T. (an administrator) and Sumi (an administrator; maiden name, Washino) Sumida; married Janet Day (an administrator), August 25, 1975. *Education:* University of California, Santa Cruz, B.A., 1971; University of Chicago, M.A., 1974, Ph.D., 1982. *Politics:* Democrat. *Religion:* Buddhist.

ADDRESSES: Office—Department of History, University of Maryland at College Park, College Park, Md. 20742.

CAREER: Roosevelt University, Chicago, Ill., lecturer in European history, 1980; University of Maryland at College Park, assistant lecturer, 1980-83, assistant professor of European and military history, 1982—.

MEMBER: International Naval Research Organization, Navy Records Society.

AWARDS, HONORS: Archives fellow commoner of Churchill College, Cambridge, 1983; international security studies fellow at Woodrow Wilson Center, 1986.

WRITINGS:

(Editor) *The Pollen Papers: The Privately Circulated Printed Works of Arthur Hungerford Pollen, 1901-1916,* Allen & Unwin, 1984.
In Defense of Naval Supremacy: Finance, Technology, and British Naval Policy, 1889-1914, Allen & Unwin, 1988.
(Editor) *Papers on British Naval Tactics and Gunnery,* Allen & Unwin, 1988.

Contributor to history journals.

BIOGRAPHICAL/CRITICAL SOURCES:

PERIODICALS

Times Literary Supplement, August 31, 1984.

* * *

SUTHERLAND, Roger
See HICKS, Roger W(illiam)

* * *

SWAIN, Marshall (William) 1940-

PERSONAL: Born July 16, 1940, in Kansas City, Mo.; children: two. *Education:* University of Minnesota, B.A., 1963; University of Rochester, Ph.D., 1966.

ADDRESSES: Office—Department of Philosophy, 230 North Oval Mall, Ohio State University, Columbus, Ohio 43210.

CAREER: University of Pennsylvania, Philadelphia, assistant professor of philosophy, 1966-71, research fellow, 1967-69; Ohio State University, Columbus, associate professor, 1971-79, professor of philosophy, 1980—.

MEMBER: American Philosophical Association.

AWARDS, HONORS: Grant from National Science Foundation, 1968-69; fellow of National Endowment for the Humanities, 1974.

WRITINGS:

(Editor and contributor) *Induction, Acceptance, and Rational Belief,* D. Reidel, 1970.
(Editor with George S. Pappas) *Essays on Knowledge and Justification,* Cornell University Press, 1978.
Reasons and Knowledge, Cornell University Press, 1981.

Contributor to philosophy journals.*

* * *

SWEETMAN, Rosita (Anne) 1948-

PERSONAL: Born May 22, 1948, in Dublin, Ireland.

CAREER: Journalist in Dar es Salaam, Tanzania, for *Tanganyika Standard,* and in Dublin, Ireland, for *Irish Press, This Week, Irish Times,* and British Broadcasting Corp.

WRITINGS:

On Our Knees, Pan Books, 1972.
Fathers Come First (novel), M. Joseph, 1974.
On Our Backs: Sexual Attitudes in a Changing Ireland, Pan Books, 1979.

Author of weekly column in *Sunday Independent* (Dublin). Contributor to magazines and newspapers, including London *Observer* and *New Society.*

BIOGRAPHICAL/CRITICAL SOURCES:

PERIODICALS

Times Literary Supplement, October 18, 1974.*

* * *

SYMMES, Robert Edward
See DUNCAN, Robert (Edward)

T

TAKACS, Carol Addison 1926-

PERSONAL: Surname is pronounced "*Tock*-as"; born July 28, 1926, in Columbus, Ohio; daughter of Arthur Colburn (a salesman) and Carol (a sales representative; maiden name, Brooke) Addison; married William Takacs, September 1, 1952 (deceased); children: Catherine Takacs Ake, C. Helen, Edward. *Education:* Kent State University, B.S.Ed. (magna cum laude), 1966, M.A., 1968, Ph.D., 1971. *Politics:* Democrat. *Religion:* Roman Catholic.

ADDRESSES: Home—3633 Sutherland Rd., Shaker Heights, Ohio 44133. *Office*—Department of Educational Psychology, Cleveland State University, Cleveland, Ohio 44115.

CAREER: Manager of a dairy farm in Conneaut, Ohio, 1952-63; Cleveland State University, Cleveland, Ohio, professor of educational psychology, 1970—. Elementary schoolteacher in Conneaut, 1961-63.

WRITINGS:

Enjoy Your Gifted Child, Syracuse University Press, 1986.

Contributor to education journals.

WORK IN PROGRESS: Curriculum for Gifted Education; research on the effects of labeling gifted children and their families.

SIDELIGHTS: Carol Addison Takacs told *CA:* "My book grew out of a desire to allay the anxieties of parents of gifted children and to provide knowledge and recommendations, which should result in more relaxation and enjoyment within the family and contribute to better adjustment for the children."

* * *

TALBERT, Ansel Edward (McLaurine) 1912-1987

OBITUARY NOTICE: Born January 6, 1912, in Washington, D.C.; died October 7, 1987, in Bridgeport, Conn. Radio broadcaster, editor, and author. Throughout his career, Talbert espoused the importance of military aviation. He began writing for the *New York Herald Tribune* in 1936, fulfilling special assignments in Europe, the Soviet Union, the Middle East, Korea, Greenland, the North Pole, and the South Pole, among other locations. From 1950 to 1951 he was chief of the newspaper's Tokyo bureau, and from 1953 until the paper folded in 1966 he served as military and aviation editor. Talbert also served, from 1959 to 1967, as executive editor of publications and vice-president of the Flight Safety Foundation. He later became executive editor of *Air Transport World* magazine and senior editor of *Travel Agent, Travel Agent International,* and *Interline Reporter* magazines. His many awards include the Croix de Chevalier of the Legion of Honor from France, the 1957 James J. Strebig Trophy for outstanding writing on aviation, and the 1959 Gold Medal from the Adventurers Club. During the early 1960s Talbert conducted special radio broadcasts on aerospace and military developments. Author of the well-known syndicated column "Defense and Aviation," Talbert also wrote the books *Famous Airports of the World* and *Newsbreak,* and he co-authored *How I Got That Story* and *The Grand Original: A Biography of Randolph Churchill.*

OBITUARIES AND OTHER SOURCES:

BOOKS

Who's Who in America, 44th edition, Marquis, 1986.

PERIODICALS

New York Times, November 19, 1987.

* * *

TALLY, Ted 1952-

PERSONAL: Born April 9, 1952, in Winston-Salem, N.C.; son of David K. (a school administrator) and Dorothy E. (a teacher; maiden name, Spears) Tally; married Melinda Kahn (an art gallery director), December 11, 1977. *Education:* Yale University, B.A., 1974, M.F.A., 1977.

ADDRESSES: Home—New York, N.Y. *Agent*—Arlene Donovan, International Creative Management, 40 West 57th St., New York, N.Y. 10019.

CAREER: Playwright and screenwriter, 1977—. Playwriting seminar instructor at Yale University, 1977-79; master artist-in-residence at Atlantic Center for the Arts, 1983.

MEMBER: Writer's Guild of America, Dramatists Guild, Playwrights Horizons (member of artistic board).

AWARDS, HONORS: Kazan Award and Theron Rockwell Field Prize, both from Yale University, both 1977, for *Terra Nova;* Columbia Broadcasting System (CBS) Foundation Playwriting

Fellowship from Yale University, 1977; award from Los Angeles newspaper *Drama-Logue,* 1979, for *Terra Nova;* New York State Creative Artists Public Service (CAPS) Grant, 1980; John Gassner Award from the New York Outer Critics Circle, 1981, for *Coming Attractions;* National Endowment for the Arts Grant in Playwriting, 1983-84; Obie Award from the *Village Voice,* 1984, for *Terra Nova;* Guggenheim fellowship, 1985-86; Christopher Award, 1988, for *The Father Clements Story.*

WRITINGS:

PLAYS

Terra Nova (two-act; first produced in New Haven, Conn., at the Yale Repertory Theater, November 18, 1977; produced Off-Broadway at American Place Theater, April 25, 1984), Doubleday, 1981.

Hooters (two-act; first produced Off-Broadway at Playwrights Horizons, April 18, 1978), Dramatists Play Service, 1978.

Coming Attractions (one-act; first produced Off-Broadway at Playwrights Horizons, December 3, 1980), Samuel French, 1982.

Silver Linings (collection of revue sketches; first produced as individual pieces in numerous separate revues), Dramatists Play Service, 1983.

Little Footsteps (two-act; first produced Off-Broadway at Playwrights Horizons, February 13, 1986), Doubleday, 1986.

TELEVISION SCRIPTS

Hooters (adaptation of Tally's play of the same name), Playboy Channel, 1983.

Terra Nova (adaptation with John Bruce of Tally's play of the same name), British Broadcasting Corporation (BBC-TV), 1984.

(Contributor) *The Comedy Zone,* Columbia Broadcasting System (CBS-TV), 1984.

(With Arthur Heineman) *The Father Clements Story,* National Broadcasting Company (NBC-TV), 1987.

Works represented in anthologies, including *Plays From Playwrights Horizons,* 1987.

WORK IN PROGRESS: A film version of *Little Footsteps,* for release by Twentieth Century-Fox; a film version of Glenn Savan's novel *White Palace,* for release by Universal; *Free Spirit,* with A. J. Carothers, for Tri-Star.

SIDELIGHTS: Ted Tally's best-known play, "Terra Nova," made its debut at the Yale Repertory Theater when its author was only twenty-five years old. A Yale drama school student who, according to *People* magazine, "was frankly hurt" that the university "rejected him as an actor," but was "relieved to be accepted for his play-writing credits," Tally featured six of his classmates in his play's premiere performance. As Samuel G. Freedman reported in the *New York Times,* the set was built "out of scrap wood and yards of white muslin from Connecticut's tobacco fields." The audience, however, included New York producers and talent agents, and "Terra Nova" has since been performed Off-Broadway and in countries all over the world, including England, Australia, and Japan. The young playwright's more recent efforts have been in a lighter vein than his darkly dramatic first success, and his comedic credits include "Hooters," "Coming Attractions," "Silver Linings," and "Little Footsteps." Tally has also supplemented his career with scriptwriting for film and television.

"Terra Nova," named for the ship that bears its protagonist to the play's setting, is the story of Antarctic explorer Robert Falcon Scott. Describing himself in Tally's drama as a "footnote to history," Scott is remembered as the Englishman who came in second to Norwegian Roald Amundsen in the race to discover the South Pole. "Terra Nova" depicts Scott's expedition and its tragic end—the slow, torturous death of Scott and his men from exposure and hunger a mere eleven miles from safety—but as Frank Rich pointed out in the *New York Times,* "in a sense, there are three plays here." The historic action is intertwined with the psychological action of Scott's inner thought, and both are tied to the theme of Great Britain's decline as an empire. Though some critics, like Rich, felt that these different aspects did not successfully "converge in a single dramatic entity," others applauded them. J. W. Lambert declared in *Drama* that "structurally the play is ingenious but not obtrusively so."

"Terra Nova" is often performed on a more-or-less completely white set. Speaking of the Off-Broadway production at the American Place Theater, Rich affirmed that "the white stage serves as the terrain of both Antarctica and the hero's mind." Thus Scott's imagined conversations with his wife and with rival Amundsen are presented to the audience. Mrs. Scott appears on stage to re-enact the couple's courtship and to add substance to the conflict in Scott's makeup between duty to country and duty to family. Amundsen's function is to force the hero to question the value of ideals—or, as James Harris put it in *Plays and Players,* to "chide him for being so sentimental as not to take dogs and eat them en route." Tally carefully blends his speculative interpretation of the explorer's psyche with illustrations of the horrible realities of the polar expedition. Many reviewers noted with David Richards the effectiveness of the scene in which Scott's daydreams of a triumphant banquet celebrating the expedition's return dissolve into despair. Richards, critiquing a 1982 performance of "Terra Nova" at the Center Stage in Baltimore, Maryland, for the *Washington Post,* called the drama "an act of poetic conjuration" and described the banquet scene, with Scott and his men "spankingly attired in crisp tuxedoes," thus: "At the height of the festivities, the elegant crystal service is stripped away and the table is instantly transformed into the sled of death. The men are back in a freezing hell." Similarly, Rich praised the "startling images" the play created and cited as an example the scene in which "we see a celebratory group photograph taken at the Pole decompose into a vision of an entire civilization's imminent extinction."

Because "Terra Nova" is "a historical, heroic and narrative work," Freedman labeled it "a play that seems innovative in part by being such a throwback." But, combined with the scenes which take place in Scott's imagination, the more conventional storytelling nature of the play helps make it appeal more broadly. As Freedman explained, a "mix of traditional and modern elements" partially accounts for "the attraction of 'Terra Nova' to so many . . . theaters." Freedman quoted Robert Brustein, artistic director of Yale Repertory Theater when "Terra Nova" made its debut, on his first impressions of the play: "It wasn't going to alienate people who dislike experimental or avant-garde theater. And it wasn't going to alienate those who like experimental or avant-garde theater. It had a wide audience."

Tally's next play, "Hooters," differs greatly from "Terra Nova." A comedy taking its name from a slang term for female breasts, "Hooters" is set in 1972 and concerns two college freshmen vacationing on Cape Cod trying to pick up women. The freshmen, Ricky and Clint, meet two banktellers on holiday, Cheryl and Ronda. Cheryl is attractive and ad-

venturous, Ronda is plain and reticent. Both women are older and more experienced than Ricky and Clint. In the *New York Times,* Richard Eder described the boys' "meeting with Cheryl and Ronda" as having "the quality of two blind men groping at two porcupines." "Hooters" has "a farcical structure and an endless supply of gags about pick-up rituals, about sexual role-playing, [and] about 'hooters' themselves," asserted Rich. He went on to affirm that "Tally, an intelligent writer, is not just interested in locker-room humor; he aspires to make some larger points about men and women in our supposedly liberated age," and praised as the play's best scene one in which Ricky and Clint confront the falseness of their own friendship. Eder applauded Tally's characterization of Cheryl, proclaiming her his "best creation." The reviewer declared: "She is a character with more than one dimension. . . . She loves her body, sex, men; and there is a real warmth and humor contending with her growing conviction that there is something more to life than to be used." John Simon in *New York* concluded the play's best features to be "the generally peppy, often genuinely droll, dialogue, and the consistently smile-producing interaction of the characters."

Tally's "Coming Attractions" also drew superlatives from Simon. Again reviewing for *New York,* he announced that the play contains "that most desiderated and least available commodity in our theater: purposeful satire." "Coming Attractions" spoofs the tendency on the part of American society to make celebrities of notorious criminals. The musical comedy's protagonist, Lonnie Wayne Burke, begins as an incompetent thief holding four hostages. He is taken in hand by a theatrical agent who is down on his luck; with his guidance, Lonnie becomes a headline-grabbing mass-murderer known as "the Halloween Killer." Then, as Rich reports, "like all American celebrities of the first rank, Lonnie is quickly rewarded with book contracts, movie deals, groupies, product tie-ins, nightclub appearances and magazine cover stories." Lonnie also appears on a television talk show in a scene almost universally applauded by critics—other guests include a Palestine Liberation Organization (PLO) terrorist-comedian who needs a translator to tell his jokes—and the host is a parody who "glides about in gold lame, fawning over his murderous guests with obscene abandon," chortled Rich. Simon rhapsodized over "several sequences as exquisitely roguish as anything you have ever delighted in," possibly among them the show's finale, which Rich described as "a singing-and-dancing television special saluting Lonnie's electric-chair execution." Simon concluded that "Coming Attractions" produced "the best kind of laughter there is—the thinking kind."

"Civilized, literate, mind-stretching entertainment" by "an authorial athlete as fit and playful as a fiddle" was the verdict Simon handed down on Tally's 1986 comedy, "Little Footsteps." The play features Ben and Joanie, an upwardly mobile couple in their mid-thirties expecting their first baby. Both have doubts—Joanie is not sure she has chosen the right reasons to become pregnant, and Ben is uncertain that he can be as self-sacrificing as he feels a good parent should be. These doubts explode in marital fighting, and the couple separates. Act II begins with Joanie living with her parents and having the baby's christening party. In Rich's opinion, "Little Footsteps" is "merriest" in this act, which includes a "farcical game of hide-and-seek." Simon avowed that "the scene in which the wised-up Joanie tells a Ben bursting with paternal resolve what infant rearing is really like comes off as sustainedly riotous, verbally and visually, as anything the comic muse has granted a *farceur*."

CA INTERVIEW

CA interviewed Ted Tally by telephone on January 13, 1987, at his home in New York City.

CA: You've called yourself "a real theater rat." You told People *magazine, "I'd push a broom if that was the only thing available." When and how did this love affair begin?*

TALLY: I started out as an actor in junior high school, in ninth grade. My English teacher teased me into trying out for the school play, which was a production of *I Remember Mama.* So there I was, crashing around the stage with a funny Norwegian accent. But I enjoyed it so much that I was really hooked. I just loved the whole camaraderie of the theater and the excitement of it. I had been writing since I was a little kid, writing short stories, poems, and things like that, but the theater seemed so much more festive to me, and less lonesome as a way of being in the arts. So it was a fairly natural transition after acting for a few years to start writing for the theater as well.

CA: When you went to Yale as an undergraduate, had you pretty much decided you wanted to write plays?

TALLY: I had started writing plays in high school. I was in a summer program in the arts in North Carolina called the Governor's School, and we were invited to write plays for the last production of the season. I wrote a play that was produced there and was pretty successful; it was later filmed for television. That encouraged me so much that I wrote another play my senior year in high school. That play was done at a statewide drama festival and also did very well. So by the time I arrived at Yale, I'd had a couple of plays produced, and I felt that there was a real chance that I would want to do that professionally. I chose Yale because it had a drama major, which other schools didn't. It also had a professional, postgraduate drama school.

CA: Did you find the Yale drama school a good place to prepare for your career?

TALLY: In a sense. The chance to work with so many peers in all the different disciplines of theater—designers, directors, actors, and administrators—was very useful, and those contacts have continued through until today. I've found that I learned as much from the other students as I did from the faculty. At that time there was a pretty heavy bent in a lot of the courses for playwrights on literature and on the history of theater, really sort of formal classroom stuff. There were workshop courses, and there were studio courses, but there was probably a bit less emphasis on that than I could have wished. So I found in terms of formal training it was a little bit of a mixed bag. There weren't enough production opportunities for the student playwright, and there were some frustrations for a lot of us. But certainly on balance it turned out to have been a good thing that I went there, because at least I had three years when my only responsibility was to write plays.

CA: You started writing plays at a time when there had been a lot of ferment in the theater; some very experimental things had been done and were still being done to some extent. I wonder if that affected your thinking about the sort of plays you wanted to write?

TALLY: It must have; I think you're influenced by everything that you see or read that's good, whatever style it's in. There was certainly a lot of opportunity to see exciting productions at Yale. They would bring in European directors like Andre Wajda. You'd see these very stunning, eye-opening productions that were not like anything being done anywhere else. I remember a stage version of *The Possessed* that was directed by Wajda. They would do a lot of Brecht and things that were totally alien to me, coming from North Carolina and never having seen much live theater. So that was very exciting. Also, we had a chance to come in contact with a lot of professional writers because of the proximity of the school to New York, more than anything else; and because they had various grants from [television networks] ABC and CBS, they were able to bring in professional playwrights to act as tutors of a sort, maybe to lead a seminar once a week. So you got a chance to meet people like Terrence McNally and David Mamet there and to go over your script with these people. You felt like you were making contact with somebody who was really in the business and not just in an ivory tower. That was an enormous influence. Arthur Kopit, I remember, was very kind to me and very helpful.

CA: I've read about the production of "Terra Nova" at Yale when you were twenty-four. The right people happened to be in the audience, and your career really got moving. How were you attracted to the explorer Robert Scott as the subject of that play?

TALLY: In a sense it began as an academic requirement. I had to write a full-length play in order to get my master's degree, and I was casting about for a subject. I went to a photographic exhibit mounted at one of the residential colleges at Yale. Some of the photographs were made in Antarctica by an undergraduate who was, I think, a biology major; he had gone there on a research expedition and had taken this series of photographs. They were very beautiful, very evocative, especially a series of photographs of Scott's base camp as it looks today. It's been preserved as a sort of museum and it doesn't look much different from the way it looked in 1912. Some half-eaten biscuits were on the shelf; nothing ever deteriorates. They were very haunting photographs. I didn't know much about the historical episode, only that there had been this fateful expedition. I wasn't even sure if it was at the North Pole or the South Pole. The fellow who took the photographs encouraged me to read about it. He said, "There's a great deal of literature on this. You'd find it fascinating." I did, and I began to think of it immediately as a play. I became aware later that it had been made as a movie, but it always struck me as being such an abstract kind of setting, where every place looks pretty much like every other place. There was something that struck me as more dramatic about it, more suited for a stage drama than a movie, and I thought that it would be possible, by setting the play more or less in Scott's mind, to move around from one location to another without basically changing the setting. It just sort of evolved. I was struck by the possibility of doing something that had the kind of scope and feeling of an Elizabethan drama on a bare stage.

CA: You wrote in Yale Drama *about the suspension of disbelief required of audiences for that play.*

TALLY: Yes. It requires so much imaginatively from the audience. You're to imagine it's a freezing temperature, and on this vast and distant continent, and so forth. And the events of the play themselves are so much larger than life, with people going mad and dying in front of your eyes, that I think there's a fine line with producing or performing this play where it's either quite moving or it's a bit silly. I've seen it slip over that line a few times. There are scenes that if they're not done just right look like something out of a Monty Python sketch. And certainly, in a couple of the early productions, in un-air-conditioned theaters and certain other circumstances, it got a little silly at times.

CA: It has been widely produced in other countries. How many now?

TALLY: It's probably had by this point close to a hundred productions of one kind or another, and I would say it's been done in thirteen or fourteen countries.

CA: All your plays seem to be quite different from each other. Have you set out deliberately not to repeat yourself, to try something different each time?

TALLY: I think so. "Terra Nova," I suppose, was a little bit of a fluke. I really set out that time to write a "serious drama," but I think my natural bent is more towards comedy. Comedies are more enjoyable to work on through all the long, frustrating months that you're at the typewriter and at rehearsal. I think creating comedies keeps you going in a more pleasant way. Within that category, I think the subject dictates the style of the play, and I suppose it's writing about very different subjects that's made the plays so different.

CA: Have you directed your own plays?

TALLY: Not since I was an undergraduate.

CA: Is that something you'd like to do, or do you feel it's better not to?

TALLY: I think my time is better spent writing. And I think especially with a new play I need the perspective of an outside observer to help me sense where the revisions should be. I can conceive of directing a revival of one of my plays sometime, but basically, once they're written I become a bit bored with them and want to get on to something new.

CA: Would you comment on your association with Playwrights Horizon and what you feel it's meant to your career?

TALLY: It's been, honestly, an enormous support system for me. I hooked up with Andre Bishop and Playwrights Horizon early on, right after drama school, because my then agent, Helen Merrill, had a close association with that theater, and several playwrights that I had gone to Yale with had worked there, and it became sort of a natural place for me to submit my work. Andre Bishop, who took over the theater from Bob Moss and has run it for the last several years, has become a close friend. It gives me a great sense of security. One of the hardest things for a playwright to latch onto is a place that can be his artistic home. You know the famous Robert Frost quotation "Home is the place where, when you have to go there, / They have to take you in." That's sort of the feeling I have about Playwrights Horizon. There's a sort of moral commitment that Andre makes toward his writers that he will try to produce anything they write in some form. Even if it's only in workshop, he'll find a way to get it on its feet so that they can see it and learn from it. His commitment is an unusual one among producers in that it's much more to a writer's

career—mistakes and all—than to an individual show that might be a hit. That's a very refreshing attitude, and I don't think very many producers have that attitude, though they may pay lip service to it.

CA: It seems to be pretty rare, yes.

TALLY: On top of everything else, it's obviously a hard attitude to maintain financially because you're going to produce a lot of things that are not quite ready to be commercial successes. Andre certainly has had his share of commercial successes, but I don't think that's ever been a criterion in his mind. I just think he's a wonderful man. He has a terrific intelligence and sense of humor. He's very diplomatic; he's good with suggestions about text and staging, but very careful not to advance them too early and not to be too dogmatic about them. I think he makes it possible for playwrights to do their best work by not getting in their way. He assembles the strongest production team that he can around the playwright and then he lets the playwright and the director do their work without interfering. That doesn't sound like a lot, perhaps, but it really is because most artistic directors fancy themselves as stage directors and are not above throwing their weight around to get a script that they want, even if another director might serve it better. Playwrights Horizon is a wonderful sort of place to work.

CA: Do you feel regional theater is doing a good job now?

TALLY: Yes. I've had the opportunity to travel around the country during the past couple of years as one of the judges for a new play contest, and I've been most impressed by the quality of the productions I've seen. Theater people in New York tend to slip too easily into a kind of provincialism of their own, the idea that plays haven't "happened" until they've been done in the Big Apple. I only wish that more regional theater productions could find a showcase in New York; I think you'd find that sort of attitude starting to disappear—which would be a healthy thing for everybody.

CA: For the past several years you've done some writing for television and screen in addition to the plays. In a recent Newsweek *article you were quoted as saying that it's "not just about money or even* mainly *about money. Playwrights want to reach a wider audience. The other thing is that screenwriting is a different kind of storytelling challenge." Have you found that doing screenplays sharpens the playwriting skills?*

TALLY: I may just be deluding myself, but I think it does because I think it makes you more conscious of sheer storytelling. Playwrights love to imagine that they can get away with just the brilliance of their voice, and that just the ping-pong of their dialogue is going to keep an audience enthralled. In the movies there's short patience for that and much more of an attitude of "just tell us a good story" and "tell us what happens next." I think it's a good thing for a playwright to be reminded of that. Movies make you think hard about transitions between scenes, about how not just the scene order but the way in which you get from one scene to the next reinforces the meaning of the story. I think there's also a kind of feeling of freedom that it gives you, a feeling of fresh air, to work in a different form once in a while.

CA: Has the screenwriting forced you to travel much?

TALLY: No. I work at home. I go out to Los Angeles as rarely as I can, usually three or four times a year, to meet about a script or a project before I've been hired for it. But I'm very much of a homebody. I have trouble working anywhere except at home.

CA: Do you feel the increasing number of playwrights working in movies now might enhance the quality of films generally?

TALLY: I think there are an awful lot of good screenwriters out there who don't get the recognition that playwrights get, and I feel it would be presumptuous to say that a bunch of playwrights are going to come in and do the job better than screenwriters. It's a very hard craft. I know playwrights who are not particularly good at screenwriting, and I certainly feel I've got a lot to learn about it myself. I think it works both ways. I hope that playwrights are good for the movie business, and I hope the movie business is not too bad for playwrights in terms of their own work.

CA: Is writing plays still your greatest love?

TALLY: I think so, yes, because of the authority that I'm allowed to have over the work in a theater, because the words can't be changed without my permission, no actor or designer can be hired without my approval, and mainly because of the fact that there's the feeling in the theater, at least if you're lucky enough to have reached a stage where you've had a few productions, that anything you write is going to be done. And of course the greatest frustration in films and television is that often you work very hard on something for a long time and then for whatever vague reason—you may never even know why—your script is not produced. I think a steady diet of that would be awfully bad for you as a writer.

CA: What's in progress now or slated for the near future that you can talk about?

TALLY: I've been working on several things. I wrote a sitcom pilot for ABC, although apparently it's not going to be made. I did a rewrite of a movie for NBC that apparently will be made. I'm working on a movie version of *Little Footsteps* for Twentieth Century-Fox, and I'm supposed to do a movie adaptation of a new novel for Universal. The novel is called *White Palace,* by a writer named Glenn Savan. That's what's going on right now.

BIOGRAPHICAL/CRITICAL SOURCES:

BOOKS

Contemporary Literary Criticism, Volume 42, Gale, 1987.
Tally, Ted, *Coming Attractions,* Samuel French, 1982.
Tally, *Terra Nova,* Samuel French, 1981.

PERIODICALS

Drama, summer, 1979.
Newsweek, December 15, 1986.
New York, December 15, 1980, November 8, 1982, March 17, 1986.
New York Times, May 1, 1978, December 4, 1980, October 21, 1982, April 26, 1984, April 29, 1984, February 28, 1986.
People, October 1, 1979.
Plays and Players, June, 1980.

Washington Post, April 7, 1982.
Yale Drama, summer, 1977.

—*Sketch by Elizabeth Thomas*
—*Interview by Jean W. Ross*

* * *

TAUBER, Edward S(anford) 1908-1988

OBITUARY NOTICE: Born May 10, 1908, in New York, N.Y.; died of complications from a stroke, February 5, 1988, in White Plains, N.Y. Psychiatrist, educator, and author. Tauber was a specialist in psychoanalysis and the neuro-physiology of sleep, and he is remembered for his original research on dreams in animals. From 1936 to 1958 he held positions, including assistant physician and associate in psychiatry, at the Columbia University College for Physicians and Surgeons, and he later served as adjunct professor of psychology at New York and Yeshiva universities. In 1973 he became a resident consultant in the Department of Neurology and Psychiatry at the Montefiore Hospital Medical Center. During World War II Tauber served in the U.S. Army Medical Corps. He wrote, with Maurice R. Green, *Prelogical Experience: An Inquiry Into Dreams and Other Creative Processes* and edited, with Bernard Landis, *In the Name of Life: Essays in Honor of Erich Fromm.* Tauber also contributed to such publications as *Nature* and *Science.*

OBITUARIES AND OTHER SOURCES:

BOOKS

Biographical Directory of the Fellows and Members of the American Psychiatric Association, Bowker, 1977.

PERIODICALS

New York Times, February 6, 1988.

* * *

TAURANAC, John 1939-

PERSONAL: Surname is pronounced "*Tar*-a-nak"; born August 2, 1939, in New York, N.Y.; son of Harold D. (a hotel manager) and Morna Coombs (Roeg) Tauranac; married Jane Apt Bevans (an artist and lawyer), June 17, 1983; children: Margaret Bevans. *Education:* Columbia University, B.A., 1963; New York University, M.A., 1975.

ADDRESSES: Home—900 West End Ave., New York, N.Y. 10025. *Office*—Metropolitan Transportation Authority, 347 Madison Ave., New York, N.Y. *Agent*—Carol Rinzler, Rembar & Curtis, 19 West 44th St., New York, N.Y. 10036.

CAREER: Batten, Barton, Durstine & Osborne (advertising agency), New York City, copywriter; J. Walter Thompson (advertising agency), New York City, copywriter; Associated Councils on the Arts, New York City, director of communications; Metropolitan Transportation Authority, New York City, chief designer of maps and manager of passenger information, 1974—. Member of faculty at New York University.

AWARDS, HONORS: Commendation for Design Excellence from U.S. Department of Transportation and National Endowment for the Arts, 1980, for New York City subway map.

WRITINGS:

Seeing New York, Popular Library, 1976.
Essential New York, Holt, 1979.
Elegant New York, Abbeville, 1985.

Contributor to magazines, including *Travel and Leisure* and *New York.*

SIDELIGHTS: John Tauranac told *CA:* "I give tours of New York City for various groups, including the Municipal Art Society, Classical America, and the mayor's office. I also give illustrated lectures at the New York Historical Society, the Brooklyn Historical Society, and the Schools of Architecture at Columbia and the City University of New York."

BIOGRAPHICAL/CRITICAL SOURCES:

PERIODICALS

AIA Journal, April, 1980.
Journal of the Society of Architectural Historians, February, 1980.
Publishers Weekly, December 13, 1985.

* * *

TAYLOR, Cora (Lorraine) 1936-

PERSONAL: Born January 14, 1936, in Fort Qupappelle, Saskatchewan, Canada; daughter of Harvey and Edith (Kalbfleisch) Traub; married Durward Thomas, 1953 (divorced); married Don Livingston, 1958 (divorced); married Russell Taylor (a physician), November, 1973; children: (first marriage) Granger, Wendy; (second marriage) Clancy, Sean. *Education:* University of Alberta, B.A. and Teaching Certificate, 1973. *Religion:* Anglican.

ADDRESSES: Home—R.R.1, Winterburn, Alberta, Canada T0E 2N0.

CAREER: University of Alberta, University Hospital, Edmonton, medical secretary, 1964-68; Duffield School, Duffield, Alberta, teacher, 1973-75; writer, 1975—.

MEMBER: Canadian Authors Association (Alberta vice-president, 1980-86; national award chairman, 1987).

AWARDS, HONORS: Ross Annett Award from Alberta Writers Guild, Book of the Year Award from Canadian Library Association, and Canada Council award, all 1985, for *Julie;* Arts Award from City of Edmonton, 1987.

WRITINGS:

Julie (young adult novel), Western Producer Prairie Books, 1985.
The Doll (young adult novel), Western Producer Prairie Books, 1987.

Also author of musical plays "Parkland Spirit," 1980, and "Dateline: Stony Plain," 1983. Theater critic for *Allied Arts Bulletin,* 1967. Contributor of articles and stories to magazines, including *Chatelaine, Golden West, Heritage, Magpie,* and *Branching Out.* Editor of *Life Was a Bowl of Chokecherries,* 1980, and *Alberta Poetry Yearbook,* 1980-86.

WORK IN PROGRESS: A story about the Beothuk Indians of Newfoundland; *Screams of the Horses,* nonfiction on horses at war.

BIOGRAPHICAL/CRITICAL SOURCES:

PERIODICALS

CANSCAIP, April, 1987.
Emergency Librarian, March/April, 1987.

TAYLOR, Janelle (Diane Williams) 1944-

PERSONAL: Born June 28, 1944, in Athens, Ga.; daughter of Alton L. Williams (a mechanic) and Frances (a housewife; maiden name, Davis) Edwards; married Michael Howard Taylor (a business manager and accountant), April 8, 1965; children: Angela Michelle, Alisha Melanie. *Education:* Attended Augusta College, 1980-81, and Medical College of Georgia. *Politics:* Republican. *Religion:* Baptist.

ADDRESSES: Home—4366 Deerwood Lane, Evans, Ga. 30809. *Office*—Janelle Taylor Enterprises, Inc., P.O. Box 11646, Augusta, Ga. 30907-8646. *Agent*—Adele Leone Agency, Inc., 26 Nantucket Place, Scarsdale, N.Y. 10583.

CAREER: Worked as orthodontic nurse in Athens, Ga., and Augusta, Ga., 1962-72; Medical College of Georgia, Augusta, medical research assistant, 1977-79; writer, 1979—. Owner of Janelle Taylor Enterprises, Inc., Augusta, Ga. Teaches and lectures on romance literature and creative writing at conferences and schools, including Augusta College, 1982—; critiques manuscript for beginning writers; guest on television and radio programs.

MEMBER: Romance Writers of America, Western Writers of America, Science Fiction Writers of America, Authors Guild, Southeastern Writers, Georgia Romance Writers, Augusta Author's Guild.

AWARDS, HONORS: Honored at Sioux National Celebration in South Dakota, 1983, for first five books of "Ecstasy Saga" series; Maggie Award for Best Historical Romance from Georgia Romance Writers, 1984, for *First Love, Wild Love;* Reviewers Choice Award from *Romantic Times,* 1984, for *Golden Torment;* Indian Series award from *Romantic Times,* 1985, for first five book of "Ecstasy Saga" series; Golden Pen award from *Affaire de Coeur,* 1986, for *Sweet, Savage Heart;* certificate of merit from American University Women, 1986.

WRITINGS:

"ECSTASY SAGA" HISTORICAL ROMANCE SERIES; FOR ZEBRA BOOKS

Savage Ecstasy, 1981.
Defiant Ecstasy, 1982.
Forbidden Ecstasy, 1982.
Brazen Ecstasy, 1983.
Tender Ecstasy, 1983.
Stolen Ecstasy, 1985.
Bittersweet Ecstasy, 1987.
Flames of Ecstasy, in press.

HISTORICAL ROMANCE; FOR ZEBRA BOOKS

Love Me With Fury, 1983.
First Love, Wild Love, 1984.
Golden Torment, 1984.
Savage Conquest, 1985.
Sweet, Savage Heart, 1986.
Destiny's Temptress, 1986.
Fortune's Flames, in press.
Passion's Wild and Free, in press.
Love's Fierce Flames, in press.
Vixen's Rouge, in press.

OTHER

(Contributor) Kathyrn Falk, editor, *How to Write a Romance and Get It Published: With Intimate Advice From the World's Most Popular Romantic Writers,* illustrations by Ignatius Sahula, Crown, 1983.
(Contributor) R. Buhrer, P. Moore, and R. Jones, editors, *Candelight, Romance, and You,* Cookbook Publishers, 1983.
Valley of Fire (contemporary romance), Harlequin, 1984.
(Contributor) Jerry Biederman and Tom Silberkleit, editors, *My First Real Romance: Twenty Bestselling Romance Novelists Reveal the Stories of Their Own First Real Romances,* Stein & Day, 1985.
Moondust and Madness (science fiction romance), Bantam, 1986.
Wild Is My Love (medieval romance), Bantam, 1987.
The Last Viking Queen, Bantam, in press.

Author of short stories and poems; author of newsletter for Janelle Taylor Enterprises, Inc. Contributor of articles and stories to magazines, including *Romantic Times* and *Love Line.*

WORK IN PROGRESS: Another historical romance in "Ecstasy Saga" series for Zebra Books, *Endless Ecstasy,* publication expected in 1990; several historical romances for Zebra Books, including *Passion's Ablaze,* publication expected in 1990; two medieval fantasy romances for Bantam.

SIDELIGHTS: A prolific, best-selling romance novelist, Janelle Taylor is perhaps best known for her historical romance books. Notable among these are the nine titles comprising the author's immensely popular "Ecstasy Saga" series, which features the ongoing love story between a Sioux warrior and a pioneer woman of English ancestry. Set in the northwest territory of the United States during the late 1700's, the fictional romance progresses amid actual events—such as U.S. Army General George Armstrong Custer's defeat at Little Big Horn—and presents what Taylor termed in an article for the *Romantic Times* as "an in-depth look into the life, heart, and mind of the American Indian."

Already interested in native North American history before she began writing the "Ecstasy" novels, the author—considered a meticulous researcher—reported in the *Romantic Times* that she unearthed a number of "inconsistencies and unknown facts" while reading about the topic. "It was amazing to me to learn how many customs were attributed to [American Indians] which were actually begun by the white man," Taylor recalled. Focusing on the Sioux tribes in particular, Taylor wanted to reveal the native North Americans' struggle to survive and protect their lands against non-native settlers and U.S. Army onslaughts. In addition, she decided to portray the native North American as victorious, since—as she pointed out in the *Romantic Times*—"most westerns have the white man as the victor." Taylor further explained to the magazine that native North Americans have been "misunderstood and maligned, and I wanted to reveal their culture and emotions."

Commenting on the historical aspects of her novels, Taylor stated in the *Romantic Times* that she "combined turbulent history with passionate romance," adding, "I tried to intermingle reality with fantasy." Similarly, Taylor incorporated authentic Sioux language into the dialogue of her stories, enhancing what she termed in the *Romantic Times* the "reality, accuracy, and uniqueness" distinguishing her writing. Overall, according to Taylor's synopsis of the "Ecstasy Saga" series, her books provide a balanced account of both the white man's and native North American's motivations while documenting history through a believable love story. In recognition of the realistic depiction of native North Americans and their history and culture presented in her historical romance novels,

Taylor was honored at the Sioux National Celebration in Sisseton, South Dakota, in 1983. Two years later she won the Indian Series award given by the *Romantic Times*.

Giving range to her talents beyond the "Ecstasy Saga" collection, Taylor has written several other historical romances. These include the award-winning national best-seller *First Love, Wild Love*, based on the historic exploits of the Texas Rangers, and another national best-seller, *Savage Conquest*, placed in the post-Civil War American South. She also wrote *Love Me With Fury*, a private adventure set during the War of 1812, and *Golden Torment*, which takes place in the frozen landscape of the Yukon Territory at the time of the gold rush, as well as *Valley of Fire*, a contemporary romance, and *Moondust and Madness*, the first in a series of Taylor's innovative science fiction romances. The "Janelle Taylor Collection" of books, manuscripts, and promotional materials is archived at the University of Georgia Libraries.

Regarding the personal aspects and benefits of her writing, Taylor told *CA:* "I have learned to be more attentive and perceptive in all areas of my life. I have learned patience and persistence, and I have matured both as a person and a woman by developing this previously unused talent. Through the extensive research for my books, I have learned many interesting things about people, places, and history. I have also discovered good qualities in other people—generosity, kindness, warmth, helpfulness, and understanding. Most of all, my work has given me a new sense of self-worth, self-confidence, and a feeling of excitement and accomplishment. It has inspired courage and boldness, given me new outlets and friends, and granted me great pleasure. I learned it is never too late to do anything a person wants badly enough. The only drawback to serious, full-time writing and its other requirements—such as publicity and deadlines—is the weighty demand it places upon your energy and time. But would I give up any of it? Never! Very few things are as exciting, stimulating, and encouraging as the letters and calls I receive from readers and other writers. Writing is a growing experience that I hope to continue for years, and years, and years!

"I doubt I could have become a writer before reaching thirty-four, because I hadn't grown enough emotionally or experienced enough of life. When I did begin it was like a dam breaking, and all my pent-up creativity came pouring out very rapidly and intensely. Now I doubt I can ever stop writing—and you have to love writing to do it because it's a lot of work."

AVOCATIONAL INTERESTS: Collecting models of ships, "sea treasures," souvenir spoons, and book cover art; reading; music; movies (especially old westerns and science fiction films); Indian, American, and English history; sports (football, tennis, fishing, horseback and motorcycle riding, and target practice); chess; exploring the land around her home; working outdoors; travel around the United States.

CA INTERVIEW

CA interviewed Janelle Taylor by telephone on May 29, 1986, at her home in Evans, Georgia.

CA: You've been writing romance novels for six or seven years now?

TAYLOR: Yes, I started in August of 1978.

CA: Do you think writing romances is going to be a permanent career for you?

TAYLOR: Yes. I'm going to do that plus a lot of other kinds of books, too. I just did a science fiction romance for Bantam Books, *Moondust and Madness*, and I'm going to do some medieval fantasy for them. I'd like to go into some other types of things as well, such as contemporary mainstream, and I'd like to write a mystery and a horror novel.

CA: How did you start to write romances?

TAYLOR: I was in medical research, and the doctor I was working with transferred to a medical school in Kentucky. So I wasn't working at the moment. I was watching television one morning, which I don't normally do, and I heard a writer named Kathleen Woodiwiss give a talk. She was talking about people who are constantly fantasizing and making up stories, how they're mentally writing. And she said, "Try putting these down on paper." I had been writing on my own, but had never thought about becoming a professional writer. That statement just struck me, and I started writing. And fortunately I have been successful.

CA: You'd just been writing for yourself before that?

TAYLOR: Yes. I still have things that go back to the eighth grade—short stories and a lot of poetry and anything that would come to my mind. I would just write things down and put them in a drawer. When I decided to be a writer, I started going through the early things I had done and expanded some of them.

CA: Has Kathleen Woodiwiss been one of your favorite novelists?

TAYLOR: Yes, she has. She was one of the first ones to write historical romances. When I first started, historical was the thing that I liked, and it seemed like the best path to go because not too many people would pick up mainstream historical novels. I did want to write about history, and romances were selling.

CA: Have you always had a love for history?

TAYLOR: Yes, I certainly have.

CA: What do you feel romance writers may have in common?

TAYLOR: I think most of them would prefer that their books be taken as books rather than being labeled romance because you can miss so much of the market with that tag. Romance writers seem to be one of the most helpful groups of people; they're constantly helping their competition. I teach at a college here sometimes and go around to high schools giving talks on creative writing. I've only met a couple of romance writers who were not willing to give of their time and talents to help other people get established. That's one big thing I've noticed that romance writers have in common, that sense of wanting to help other people.

CA: Are you often asked to read other writers' works?

TAYLOR: Yes, I am. Normally I do not critique unless it's as part of a class. When I teach at Augusta College here, prospective students are allowed to send in a first chapter and an outline of a book. Then you can generally tell if they've got

talent. But as far as critiquing other things, I really can't do that anymore. A lot of writers do, but I don't because I feel it's dangerous. People are so sue-crazy nowadays that you really have to protect yourself from that. If somebody sends you something like a piece of work you're doing or planning to do, they could say you'd stolen their idea. Also, it's very time-consuming, and I'm heavily contracted for the next several years. My way of helping is to go in and teach the basics of writing and how to prepare a manuscript, a synopsis, a query letter—that type of thing. Most people don't realize what you do when you start writing, that there's a certain way that you have to submit the work. They'll say, "I want to write, so what do I do?" And a lot of times they'll just pick a publisher's name out of a book and send a manuscript in, not realizing that you have to have the right one to send something to. I teach them how to get information and help they need with whatever kind of problem they have. And then I have a tip sheet I print out, because most people will ask the same basic questions.

CA: You've said elsewhere that sometimes people will submit something to you just looking for praise or flattery.

TAYLOR: Yes. Most people think writing is very easy, and they think about instant fame and fortune. It's very rare, you know, that a first book will be a national best-seller. People don't realize that you've got to pay your dues, to put in years of hard work to get your name known so that you can become a big writer. They always just think that there's a lot of money involved. In fact, when I was in New Orleans this past weekend for the American Booksellers Association Convention, I was talking to a girl who said she wanted to write, and I asked her, "What do you want to write?" She said, "I don't know, just anything." So I told her, "Your first problem is that you've got to have a goal in mind. You must want to write history, or write a mystery, or write science fiction. You can't get anywhere just saying you want to write." She said, "Well, I just want to write to make a lot of money so my husband can retire. I'm going to quit my job and start writng." I said, "That's not a good idea if you don't have somebody to support you. It takes a long time, you know, to make money." A lot of people do have the misconception that it's easy.

CA: I read your description of your Dictaphone Dual Display Word Processor in Kathryn Falk's How to Write a Romance and Get It Published. *Are you still as happy as ever with that?*

TAYLOR: Yes, I am. It's not on the market anymore, but I still have mine. In fact, I still have it under contract to be sure it stays in good working order. The writing basics, the mechanics, are so hard, anything you can find to make it easier is worth buying.

CA: When you first started writing professionally, did you write in longhand?

TAYLOR: Yes, my first two books I did in longhand. I had been out of school for about twenty years, so it had been a long time since I had taken typing. When I had to type my first manuscript and then they told me it still was not in the proper form, my career almost ended then and there. It took me about three-and-one-half months to retype. I was what you'd call blissfully ignorant, like some of the students I work with now. I thought you could just sit down and write a book and send it off.

CA: Aren't some of your novels now being translated into foreign languages?

TAYLOR: Yes. I've got one book that's out in 190 countries, I believe the contract says. I've got a Greek copy here, and one from Portugal. We've sold to Italy. And we've got several English editions around the world, of course. The only problem with foreign languages is that the shorter books are easier to sell for translation. The bigger books cost so much to translate that they have to charge a lot more in the foreign editions. My $3.95 paperback books sell for $8.95 overseas. So really, all they buy for translation are the national best-sellers.

CA: With all you're doing, you must have to have a lot of people helping you.

TAYLOR: My husband works for me. He takes care of all the mail, the government papers, and the tax forms. And he sets up the trips with my publishers, sends most of my public relations stuff out, and takes care of our children and the house. It really helps a lot. I couldn't get as much done as I need to do if I didn't have him to help me.

CA: So he really works for you on a full-time basis, then?

TAYLOR: Yes. Right now it's mostly answering letters because we've had especially heavy mail since *Moondust and Madness* came out. When the mail comes in, he spends the rest of the day answering it, almost every afternoon.

CA: Do a lot of people write to you about romance problems of their own?

TAYLOR: Sometimes they do. But mainly people write during hard periods of their life, like after the death of a spouse or the death of a child. I talked to a lady this morning—in fact, I called her—because of the death of a child. People talk about times being so hard now, and that seems to distract them from their present everyday problems. And since the Indian series, I get a great deal of mail from Indians of all tribes telling me how much the series has done for them individually and as a nation. I got an award from the Sioux and the Cherokee for the books because they're told strictly from the Indian point of view. A lot of people write in and say, "I've always been embarrassed to tell anyone I was an Indian until I read your series." And a lot of whites have written to the Indians to get more information on Indian culture and religion and things like that. They've said that it's because of reading my books that they've seen things in a different light and developed this interest. So you really teach people things about history. And people pick up other kinds of things from the books, too. One girl wrote to me and said that she'd always been painfully shy. I'd started off one of my heroines as very shy. After reading the book, this girl realized that there was nothing wrong with being shy and that she could pull out of her shyness by doing certain things.

CA: It's interesting that you mention shyness, because it comes across occasionally, in things you've written about yourself, that you were also shy at one time.

TAYLOR: Very much so.

CA: Do the letters you get help you decide what to write about in future books?

TAYLOR: Yes. In my sixth book in the Indian series, I put a note in the back saying that there would be nine and asking the readers questions such as which book was their favorite and why, who were their favorite characters and why. That gave me some input on what they would like or not like. It was very strange that every one of those letters (and there were probably several thousands that came in) mentioned a minor character, the hero's best friend. I didn't realize that he had so impressed everybody. There were several other characters that a lot of people mentioned, so I'll bring them back, too. That kind of information is good to have if you're continuing a series. Bantam put a note in the back of *Moondust and Madness* asking, "Do you like this new kind of book and would you like to see more?" That was to see what kind of feedback they were getting, because it was mixing the two markets, romance and science fiction. All of the mail on that has said, "Yes, please give us a sequel."

CA: Where did your interest in the Indian culture come from?

TAYLOR: I think it started off with growing up as a tomboy, with two brothers. We played a lot of cowboys and Indians, and that kind of thing. I read a lot of what used to be called boys' books: [Anna Sewell's] *Black Beauty,* Jack London books like *Call of the Wild* and *White Fang*. I did male things; my brothers taught me to fish and track and hunt and shoot. I still go out for target practice all the time.

CA: You like football, don't you?

TAYLOR: Very much so. And I've watched a lot of westerns and read a lot of western novels—like Louis L'Amour's books; I've read him for years. In fact, I saw him this weekend. So my interest in the Indians came from all those things. I noticed that the Sioux Indians seemed to be the last big holdout, and I started reading things about [Chief] Crazy Horse and things by and about [Chief] Sitting Bull. They didn't talk the same way about [General George] Custer as the history books do. Crazy Horse said, "Give me twenty Custers, and I'll wipe out the white nation." I thought, This doesn't sound like what I've been reading in history. The interest in the Sioux was already there when I started to write. With the first two stories, it was as if I'd been plotting them for years because it was very simple and quick to sit down and write them once I decided to do it.

There's an interesting story about the man [Hiram Owen] who does the translating for me. He's a Sioux Indian from South Dakota. After about four books he invited me to come up to the Sioux National Celebration, which is called the Wacipi. They do all of the old dances with the authentic music and costumes and all the religious ceremonies, and they wanted to present me with some gifts. When I met him, I saw he was almost the spitting image of my father, who had been dead for seven years. That's so strange, meeting somebody you've been working with for a long time and finding out that he looks so much like your own father.

CA: Did you tell him?

TAYLOR: No, but my family discussed it that night and later. We all agreed on Hiram's similarities to my father. I think that gave me and Hiram a closer rapport.

CA: Have any of your books found their way to television or the movies?

TAYLOR: No, not yet. There's been some interest from a couple of companies, but with Hollywood it's very slow and hard. They will read your things and get ideas, but I think they like to write their own material because then they don't have to fool with the writer, and they don't have to pay. We're trying to get the books to [actor] Sylvester Stallone; my character seems like the kind he does in his movies, and I would really like to see him play it. We're working with the William Morris Agency in Hollywood on that. We did have an offer from a video company, but the budget was very, very low. It was going to be made as a series and the actors and actresses that they would have used were from lower-grade movies. We objected to that. I wouldn't like my readers to be disappointed if it was not done right. When you see a movie that's from a book you expect to see what you've seen in that book. If it's not well done, or not done closely to the book, readers are really disappointed.

CA: You obviously feel a very strong obligation to your readers.

TAYLOR: I do. When I sign contracts, I think more about terms which are the best for the book than I think about money. I think you owe that to your readers because they're paying their hard-earned money for your books. I don't think you can disappoint them more than one time, or they're not going to buy your work again.

CA: Do a lot of your readers subscribe to your newsletter?

TAYLOR: Yes, they do. We're just printing a new one this week. We're waiting for my next cover to come out. We started the newsletter because so much of the mail that came in would ask basically the same questions: What else have you written? What's it about? When did it come out? What's coming out next? Every time we do a newsletter, we pull about the last ten questions that are asked most frequently by readers. It's so time-consuming to answer mail. Most days, I would say, I get between 150 and 200 letters. It's just impossible to answer those, but you want to. The best way I've found to deal with it is to do a newsletter. It has gone over extremely well. In fact, I'm dropping it back now to twice a year—January and July—because doing it three or four times a year was too time-consuming.

CA: What's your teaching schedule now?

TAYLOR: I teach at Augusta College once a year, though I didn't this year because I was on tour in February, March, and April. And I usually teach at at least four writers' conferences around the country.

CA: Have some of your students written articles and books themselves?

TAYLOR: Yes. In fact, three people out of the class I had last year at Augusta College have [sent] things in to publishers. One publisher has responded to one of the students, and it looks as if she's going to sell her book. With another student, the publisher read three chapters and asked for the rest. We had first, second, and third prizes for work in the class. And what is so strange is that the three people I picked are all going to be published first, from the way it looks. When I picked the first-prize winner, I laughed and said to the class, "You realize that a *man* is going to win." This man's a lawyer, and he does a lot of other things. His time is so short, but he is so talented. His book is a little bit of an intrigue novel. I told

him, "If you don't want to do a romance, these are the other companies you have possibilities of selling this book to. But you're just too good to let this go by." So I have been working with him and with the two girls. You can tell when people have talent, and you really want to encourage it.

CA: You don't have many male students, do you?

TAYLOR: Not too many, but I do have an awful lot of male readers. When I was doing my signing at the American Booksellers Association Convention, I signed probably 50 percent for men. And a lot of the mail I get is from men. Usually a letter from a man saying, "My wife (or my girlfriend) said I should read this." Then they'll ask what else I've done, because they like my style. Because we've been using a romance cover and the books have been in the romance section of the stores, people sometimes don't realize that they're getting about the same thing that they'd get in the mystery and western and other departments. Once they get past the romance image, they realize that they've got a good action-packed book.

CA: How graphic do you think romance novels should be?

TAYLOR: Years ago, everything was what they called virginal romance. Then with the ERA [Equal Rights Amendment] and the sexual revolution, it was as if women were wanting the same thing the man had—books and magazines with different degrees of sensuality. So it got more and more explicit over the years. Now I think it's beginning to swing back the other way. It's like, We've had it, we've seen it, fine. We just wanted to get a look at it. I think now they want more emphasis on the romance and the relationship between the characters rather than the heavy degree of sensuality. I'm glad to see that, because one of the things my publisher usually tells me when I turn a book in is that I don't have enough sensuality. My revisions will usually involve adding more. But it also seems like they're beginning to crack down on some of the covers and titles, and on the content. To me, the story is what's important. You don't want the sensuality to overshadow the story.

CA: Will you go on living in the South?

TAYLOR: Yes, I will. I'm very pleased with it here. We live in the country on twelve acres of land. We've already put in a pool, and now we're putting in a pond. We've had animals before, and we're getting horses again because my girls are riders. I do love Texas and Colorado, but if I ever move, I think it will be to somewhere like St. Simons Island—on the coast of Georgia—because I am also a beach person.

BIOGRAPHICAL/CRITICAL SOURCES:

BOOKS

Kathryn Falk, editor, *How to Write a Romance and Get It Published: With Intimate Advice From the World's Most Popular Romantic Writers,* illustrations by Ignatius Sahula, Crown, 1983.

PERIODICALS

Athens Observer, March 14, 1985.
Augusta Chronicle, April 13, 1981, September 8, 1982, September 21, 1986.
Columbia Sun, October 14, 1986.
Romantic Times, December, 1983.

—*Interview by Walter W. Ross*

TAYLOR, John 1955-

PERSONAL: Born April 20, 1955, in Yokosuka, Japan; son of Jay (an American diplomat) and Elizabeth (Rose) Taylor; married Maureen Sherwood (a journalist), December 19, 1982; children: Jessica. *Education:* University of Chicago, B.A., 1977.

ADDRESSES: Office—*New York,* 755 Second Ave., New York, N.Y. 10017.

CAREER: Newsweek, New York City, editorial assistant, 1980-83; *Business Week,* New York City, staff editor, 1984; *Manhattan, inc.,* New York City, senior writer, 1984-87; *New York,* New York City, contributing editor, 1987—.

WRITINGS:

Storming the Magic Kingdom: Wall Street, the Raiders, and the Battle for Disney, Knopf, 1987.

Contributor to magazines and newspapers, including *Architectural Digest.*

WORK IN PROGRESS: A book about New York City in the 1980s.

SIDELIGHTS: John Taylor's *Storming the Magic Kingdom* details the recent changes Walt Disney Productions went through to become the more varied Walt Disney Company. As David McClintick reported in the *New York Times Book Review,* "Taylor portrays well the diverse cultures and styles of the people and institutions that govern contemporary show business and fight the eternal battle over who should run things." The book recounts how the unsuccessful takeover attempt by famed corporate raider Saul Steinberg weakened the company and allowed the subsequent takeover by Roy E. Disney (nephew of cartoonist and entrepreneur Walt Disney) and his corporate ally Sid Bass. According to Taylor, Roy Disney had reportedly become increasingly disturbed by the drop in Disney stock prices, which he blamed on mismanagement of the company's film studios by his uncle's hand-picked successors. Under the direction of Roy Disney's appointees, the new company has produced films, such as "Down and Out in Beverly Hills" and "Ruthless People," of a type not associated with its previous orientation towards children. These diversification efforts have been largely successful, and Disney stock had risen to record prices by the book's publication.

Taylor "employs the fly-on-the-wall narrative that is now standard for such business tales," described Peter Behr in the *Washington Post Book World,* "recreating the flow of conversations, telephone calls, arguments, conferences and scheming by which the takeover fight progressed." McClintick lauded *Storming the Magic Kingdom* as having "told [its] story quite well overall, capturing the supreme importance of egos and personal relationships in the governance of business, particularly show business." "For those unfamiliar with the combination of ego and economics that drive takeovers," concluded Behr, "the Disney story is a good primer."

Taylor told *CA:* "Growing up abroad and moving every two years or so instilled a sort of restlessness in me that made me very suited for journalism. What interested me in business was the drama and the psychology of the deal. The business side of Hollywood is almost entirely deal-driven, and that is one of the reasons the entertainment industry is so intriguing to write about. The Walt Disney Company made a deal with the corporate raider Saul Steinberg to prevent him from acquiring the company in a hostile takeover and liquidating it. It was

this deal that initially interested me. But as I pursued the story I became more interested in the corporate culture of Disney—the anthropological side of business. Disney is one of the strangest and most fascinating corporations in the country. To research the book, I interviewed virtually all of the participants and combed through the Disney archives.''

BIOGRAPHICAL/CRITICAL SOURCES:

PERIODICALS

Detroit News, May 3, 1987.
Los Angeles Times, June 28, 1987.
New York Times, May 4, 1987.
New York Times Book Review, May 10, 1987.
Washington Post Book World, June 7, 1987.

* * *

TAYLOR, Judy
See HOUGH, Judy Taylor

* * *

TAYLOR, Lord
See TAYLOR, Stephen James Lake

* * *

TAYLOR, Stephen
See TAYLOR, Stephen James Lake

* * *

TAYLOR, Stephen James Lake 1910-1988
(Lord Taylor, Stephen Taylor)

OBITUARY NOTICE: Born December 30, 1910; died February 1, 1988. Member of British Parliament, psychiatrist, sociologist, editor, and author. Taylor began his medical career as a specialist in industrial medicine and mental health. During World War II he served first as a neuro-psychiatric expert in the Royal Navy Reserve and, beginning in 1941, as director of home intelligence for the Ministry of Information. During this time he also conducted the Wartime Social Survey. From 1950 to 1964 Taylor directed the Harlow New Town Development Corporation's industrial health service. He was president and vice-chancellor of the Memorial University of Newfoundland from 1967 to 1973, and afterward he served there as visiting professor of medicine. Taylor was also active in Parliament and helped to form the Labour party's health and education program during the late 1940s. He acted as parliamentary private secretary to the council president during that time and, in 1964, as under secretary of state for the British colonies. In addition to being assistant editor of the publication *Lancet* for a time, Taylor was author and co-author, under various forms of his name, of the books *Good General Practice, The Suburban Neurosis, Battle for Health: A Primer of Social Medicine, National Health Service, Shadows in the Sun,* and *Mental Health and Environment.*

OBITUARIES AND OTHER SOURCES:

PERIODICALS

Times (London), February 3, 1988.

TAYLOR-OLSON, Clara Mae 1899(?)-1988

OBITUARY NOTICE: Born c. 1899; died after a long illness, January 6, 1988, in Pittsburgh, Pa. Educator and author. Taylor-Olson was professor emeritus of nutrition at Columbia University's Teachers College, and she is remembered for her notable work in nutrition education. She co-authored two revisions of a major textbook by Mary Swartz Rose, *Foundations of Nutrition.*

OBITUARIES AND OTHER SOURCES:

PERIODICALS

New York Times, January 15, 1988.

* * *

TEMPLE, Arthur
See NORTHCOTT, (William) Cecil

* * *

TENNANT, Kylie
See RODD, Kathleen Tennant

* * *

TESSLER, Stephanie Gordon 1940-
(Jeffie Ross Gordon, a joint pseudonym)

PERSONAL: Born May 11, 1940, in Los Angeles, Calif.; daughter of Jack (a fireman) and Sylvia (in retail sales; maiden name, Kepniss) Gordon; married Sidney E. Tessler (a certified public accountant and business manager), August 6, 1961; children: Jon Adam, Todd Allyn, Jacklyn Paige. *Education:* Attended Santa Monica College, 1958-59, and University of California, Los Angeles, 1959-60; California State University, Los Angeles, B.A., 1962.

ADDRESSES: Home—Malibu, Calif. *Office*—Malibu Writers Ink., 6925 Grasswood Ave., Malibu, Calif. 90265. *Agent*—Ruth Cohen, Inc., P.O. Box 7626, Menlo Park, Calif. 94025.

CAREER: Elementary schoolteacher in Los Angeles, Calif., 1962-64; real estate agent in Malibu, Calif., 1977—. Co-founder of Malibu Writers Ink. (a critique service for children's book writers), 1980—; teacher of college courses on writing for children, 1980—.

MEMBER: Society of Children's Book Writers, California Writers Club.

AWARDS, HONORS: Named Rebus Writer of the Year by *Highlights for Children,* 1982.

WRITINGS:

YOUNG ADULT NOVELS

Winning Heart, Dutton, 1983.
(With Judith Ross Enderle) *Andrea Whitman: Pediatrics,* Walker & Co., 1983.
(With Enderle) *Monica Ross: Maternity,* Walker & Co., 1983.
Wanted: A Little Love, Berkley Publishing, 1984.
(With Enderle) *Elizabeth Jones: Emergency,* Walker & Co., 1984.
(With Enderle) *Gabriella Ortiz: Hot Line/Crisis Center,* Walker & Co., 1984.
I Double Love You, Berkley Publishing, 1985.
Crazy Crush, Scholastic, Inc., 1985.

WITH ENDERLE, UNDER JOINT PSEUDONYM JEFFIE ROSS GORDON

Jacquelyn (young adult historical novel), Scholastic, Inc., 1985.
Touch of Genius (young adult fantasy novel), Silhouette, 1986.
The Journal of Emily Rose (young adult mystery novel), Silhouette, 1986.
Touch of Magic (young adult fantasy novel), Silhouette, 1987.
Nora (young adult historical novel), Scholastic, Inc., 1987.
Nobody Knows Me (young adult novel), Silhouette, in press.

OTHER

Contributor to magazines, including *Writer's Digest, Highlights for Children,* and *Friend.*

WORK IN PROGRESS: Fiction for the middle grades and young adults; a screenplay for television; research on Egyptology, parapsychology, and England in the time of Elizabeth I.

SIDELIGHTS: Stephanie Gordon Tessler told *CA:* "I began my life in Los Angeles. Fourteen days later, I became a movie extra and remained one for more than thirteen years. As a child, if I wasn't riding around in a covered wagon, I was boarding spaceships or eating lunch with Joan of Arc. Growing up in postwar Los Angeles was hectic and fascinating, filled with wonderful experiences from which I could draw when I finally realized my lifelong dream of becoming an author.

"If I had to choose the most outstanding circumstance of my life, the one that led me down the path to becoming a writer, I would find myself engaged in a mental battle of immense proportions. Was it growing up in the studios where the imagination was all? Or was it the onset of television that brought new dreams right into the living room every day? It could have been that tiny storefront lending library, where the librarian let me check out ten books at a time and keep them as long as I liked. It could have been the influence of my fifth grade teacher, who encouraged my literary flights of fancy.

"As an adult I have traveled through much of America and the world. I have met and been befriended by many fine and truly individual people. I have experienced the joys and tribulations of marriage and motherhood. I have read many great (and not so great) books. I have dreamed dreams, and I have lived life. I have so much to write about. And so, I am a writer."

* * *

TEXON, Meyer 1909-

PERSONAL: Born April 23, 1909, in New York, N.Y.; son of Morris David and Eva (Kaizer) Texon; married Ami Gold, October 26, 1941; children: Stephen J., Sylvia A. Texon Rogers. *Education:* Harvard University, B.A. (cum laude), 1930; New York University, M.D., 1934.

ADDRESSES: Home—365 West End Ave., New York, N.Y. 10024. *Office*—3 East 68th St., New York, N.Y. 10021; and Department of Forensic Medicine, Medical Center, New York University, 520 First Ave., New York, N.Y. 10016.

CAREER: Bellevue Hospital, New York City, N.Y., intern and house physician, 1934-36; City of New York, assistant medical examiner, 1957-61; New York University, New York City, associate professor of forensic medicine, 1974—. Diplomate of American Board of Internal Medicine and Cardiovascular Disease; private practice of cardiology; affiliated with Mount Sinai Hospital and Doctors Hospital.

MEMBER: American College of Physicians, American College of Cardiology, American Heart Association, New York Academy of Medicine, New York County Medical Society (president, 1982-83).

AWARDS, HONORS: Hektoen Medal from American Medical Association, 1958, for *The Hemodynamic Basis of Atherosclerosis.*

WRITINGS:

Heart Disease and Industry, Grune, 1954.
The Hemodynamic Basis of Atherosclerosis, Hemisphere Publishing, 1980.
Can the Cardiac Stand Trial? Hemisphere Publishing, 1987.

Contributor of more than thirty articles to medical journals.

WORK IN PROGRESS: Continuing research on atherosclerosis and coronary heart disease.

SIDELIGHTS: Meyer Texon told *CA:* "All the data from my experience (clinical practice, autopsy specimens, model hydraulic systems, the laws of fluid mechanics, and the experimental production of hemodynamically induced arterial lesions in dogs) support the hemodynamic basis of atherosclerosis. My conclusion is that the effect of the laws of fluid mechanics is the primary causative factor in the development of atherosclerosis."

* * *

THALER, Michael C. 1936-
(Mike Thaler)

ADDRESSES: Home—Box 223 RD1, Stone Ridge, N.Y. 12484.

CAREER: Writer and sculptor. Game designer, teacher, lecturer, songwriter; creator of "Letterman," a feature on the Public Broadcasting Service television series "The Electric Company."

WRITINGS:

JUVENILE; UNDER NAME MIKE THALER

Magic Boy (self-illustrated), Harper, 1961.
The Clown's Smile, Harper, 1962.
The King's Flower, Orion Press, 1963.
Penny Pencil: The Story of a Pencil (self-illustrated), Harper, 1963.
Moonboy, Harper, 1964.
The Prince and the Seven Moons, Macmillan, 1966.
(Editor with William Cole) *The Classic Cartoons,* World Publishing, 1966.
The Rainbow, H. Quist, 1967.
My Little Friend, Lothrop, 1971.
The Smiling Book, Lothrop, 1971.
The Staff, Knopf, 1971.
How Far Will a Rubberband Stretch, Parents Magazine Press, 1974.
What Can a Hippopotamus Be? Parents Magazine Press, 1975.
Funny Bones: Cartoon Monster Riddles, F. Watts, 1976.
Soup With Quackers: Funny Cartoon Riddles, F. Watts, 1976.
There's a Hippopotamus Under My Bed, F. Watts, 1977.
Never Tickle a Turtle: Cartoons, Riddles, and Funny Stories, F. Watts, 1977.
The Chocolate Marshmelephant Sundae, F. Watts, 1978.
Madge's Magic Show, F. Watts, 1978.
What's Up Duck? Cartoons, Riddles, and Jokes, F. Watts, 1978.

The Yellow Brick Toad: Funny Frog Cartoons, Riddles, and Silly Stories, Doubleday, 1978.
My Puppy, Harper, 1980.
The Complete Cootie Book, Avon, 1980.
A Hippopotamus Ate the Teacher, Avon, 1981.
Moonkey, Harper, 1981.
Oinkers Away: Pig Riddles, Cartoons, and Jokes, Archway, 1981.
The Moose Is Loose, Scholastic Inc., 1981.
PAWS: Cat Riddles, Cat Jokes, and Catoons, Archway, 1982.
Owly, Harper, 1982.
Scared Silly: A Monster Riddle and Joke Scare-a-Thon Featuring Bugs Mummy and Count Quackula, Avon, 1982.
The Moon and the Balloon, Hastings House, 1982.
The Pac-Man Riddle and Joke Book, Pocket Books, 1982.
(With William Cole; also illustrator) *Monster Knock Knocks,* Pocket Books, 1982.
Stuffed Feet, Avon, 1983.
It's Me, Hippo! Harper, 1983.
Cream of Creature From the School Cafeteria, Avon, 1985.
Funny Side Up! How to Create Your Own Riddles, Scholastic Inc., 1985.
Montgomery Moose's Favorite Riddles, Scholastic Inc., 1985.
Hippo Lemonade, Harper, 1986.
Upside Down Day, Avon, 1986.
King Kong's Underwear, Avon, 1986.
Mr. Bananahead at Home, Scholastic Inc., 1987.

ILLUSTRATOR

William Cole, *Knock, Knock, the Most Ever,* F. Watts, 1976.
William Cole, *Knock Knocks You've Never Heard Before,* F. Watts, 1977.
William Cole, *Give Up? Cartoon Riddle Rhymes,* F. Watts, 1978.

SIDELIGHTS: Michael C. Thaler told *CA:* "I believe that the most important two things that human beings have—and what *makes* them human—are love and creativity. This belief is the foundation of my books and my life."

* * *

THALER, Mike
See THALER, Michael C.

* * *

THEBERGE, James D.
See THEBERGE, James Daniel

* * *

THEBERGE, James Daniel 1930-1988
(James D. Theberge)

OBITUARY NOTICE—See index for *CA* sketch: Born December 28, 1930 in Rockville Centre (some sources say Oceanside), N.Y.; died after a heart attack, January 20, 1988, in Montego Bay, Jamaica. Economist, educator, civil servant, editor, and author. Theberge spent much of his career in public service, working variously as ambassador to both Nicaragua and Chile, as economic adviser to the U.S. Embassy in Buenos Aires, Argentina, and to the Agency for International Development, and as consultant to the Central Intelligence Agency. He also taught and lectured at institutions in Maryland, Florida, California, England, Brazil, Argentina, Chile, and Germany. Among his writings, published under variations of his name, are *Latin America in the World System, Spain in the Seventies: Economics, Social Structure, Foreign Policy,* and *Reflections of a Diplomat.* Theberge also edited *Economics of Trade and Development, Soviet Seapower in the Caribbean: Political and Strategic Implications,* and, with Alvin Cottrell, *The Western Mediterranean: Its Political, Economic, and Strategic Importance.*

OBITUARIES AND OTHER SOURCES:

BOOKS

Who's Who in America, 44th edition, Marquis, 1986.
The Writers Directory: 1984-1986, St. James Press, 1983.

PERIODICALS

Chicago Tribune, January 24, 1988.
Washington Post, January 23, 1988.

* * *

THOM, Valerie M(acLaren) 1929-

PERSONAL: Surname is pronounced like "Tom"; born January 24, 1929, in Tynemouth, England; daughter of George MacLaren (an army officer) and Agnes (MacEwan) Thom. *Education:* University of Edinburgh, B.Sc., 1949; graduate study at University of Reading.

ADDRESSES: Home—19 Braeside Gardens, Perth PH1 1DB, Scotland.

CAREER: Scottish Colleges of Agriculture, Aberdeen and Perth, Scotland, advisory bacteriologist, 1951-55, 1956-69; assistant warden of Fair Isle Bird Observatory, 1955; Countryside Commission for Scotland, Perth, conservation and education officer, 1969-80; free-lance writer and consultant on "interpretive planning," 1981—. Honorary secretary and director of Fair Isle Bird Observatory Trust.

MEMBER: Royal Society for the Protection of Birds, British Trust for Ornithology, Scottish Wildlife Trust (chairman of Perth branch, 1976-79, 1982-85), Scottish Ornithologists Club (president, 1978-81; honorary president, 1986), Nature Conservancy Council (member of Scottish committee).

WRITINGS:

(With J. H. Davies) *The Macmillan Guide to Britain's Nature Reserves,* Macmillan, 1984.
Birds in Scotland, T. & A. D. Poyser, 1986.
Fair Isle: An Island Saga, John Donald, in press.

Editor of *Scottish Birds,* 1982-87.

SIDELIGHTS: Valerie M. Thom told *CA:* "When World War II broke out I was living in Edinburgh and was evacuated with my school to the Border countryside. My family later moved to a Perthshire glen, where I became involved with the farming activities that led to my studying agriculture at the university. While living in the countryside I also became interested in wildlife in general, but my enthusiasm for birds was not really sparked until 1951, when I visited Fair Isle Bird Observatory for the first time. Subsequently, as a member of the Scottish Ornithologists Club and the Scottish organizer for the monthly wildfowl counts run by the Wildfowl Trust, I made contact with most of the people who were currently active in Scottish ornithology. During the late 1960s I widened my interests and became deeply involved in the work of the Scottish Wildlife Trust (the only Scottish voluntary conservation body concerned with all forms of wildlife).

"My writing activities started in the 1950s, with contributions to weekly 'Nature Notes' and to 'Woman's Hour' on radio. While with the Countryside Commission for Scotland I had the opportunity to work on a wide range of publications, obtaining valuable experience while doing so, and I continued my own writing—mainly small-scale and unpaid efforts!

"*Birds in Scotland* is unique in that it is the only book in print that details the current status and distribution of all species recorded in Scotland; describes changes in status and distribution which have occurred over the last thirty to forty years and relates these, where possible, to habitat changes; and draws together the findings of virtually all the fieldwork, research, and surveys carried out in Scotland—by amateurs as well as professionals—in the last thirty years. It is my hope that *Birds in Scotland* will not only help people to enjoy Scotland's birds but also increase their awareness of man's impact on the Scottish countryside and its wildlife.

"Although there is a growing awareness in Scotland of the need for environmental conservation there are still many conflicts of interest where land use is concerned. Political pressures applied by would-be developers all too often result in permission being granted for land use changes that destroy important semi-natural habitats and are of questionable economic benefit to the nation as a whole. Overlapping or conflicting interests/responsibilities in both the voluntary sector and among government bodies at times make efforts toward conservation less productive, more protracted, and more frustrating than they might otherwise be. Sadly, recent legislation aimed at assisting conservation has, in practice, resulted at times in an increase in conflict rather than a reduction. Scotland—and indeed Britain as a whole—badly needs an overall land use strategy designed to ensure a balance between interests."

AVOCATIONAL INTERESTS: Travel, photography.

BIOGRAPHICAL/CRITICAL SOURCES:

PERIODICALS

Scots Magazine, March, 1987.
Times Literary Supplement, March 13, 1987.

* * *

THOMAS, Phillip Drennon 1938-

PERSONAL: Born August 2, 1938, in Knox City, Tex.; son of J. D. and Mildred Thomas; married wife, Marian (a teacher), April 30, 1960; children: Deborah Thomas Baus, Traci. *Education:* Baylor University, B.A., 1960; University of New Mexico, M.A., 1964, Ph.D., 1965.

ADDRESSES: Home—7104 East 17th St., Wichita, Kan. 67206. *Office*—Fairmount College of Liberal Arts and Sciences, Wichita State University, Wichita, Kan. 67208.

CAREER: Wichita State University, Wichita, Kan., professor of history, 1972—, dean of Fairmount College of Liberal Arts and Sciences, 1984—. Dean of College of Arts and Sciences at University of Alaska, 1981-84; member of editorial board of University of Alaska Press, 1982-83.

MEMBER: Royal Geographical Society (fellow), Kansas Academy of Sciences (chairman of History of Science and Technology Division), Falstaff Literary Society, Phi Alpha Theta, Phi Kappa Phi, Rotary Club.

AWARDS, HONORS: Postdoctoral fellow at Southeastern Institute of Medieval and Renaissance Studies, Duke University, and University of North Carolina at Chapel Hill, 1969; Danforth fellow, 1976—; humanities scholar of Kansas Committee for the Humanities.

WRITINGS:

(Contributor) Daniel Tyler, editor, *Western American History in the Seventies,* Educational Media & Information Systems, 1973.

(Co-author) *These Well-Wooded Shores: The Forest in American History,* University of Nebraska Press, 1985.

(With Thomas R. Cox, Robert S. Maxwell, and Joseph J. Malone) *This Well-Wooded Land: Americans and Their Forests From Colonial Times to the Present,* University of Nebraska Press, 1986.

Contributor to history journals. Book review editor of *Historian.*

WORK IN PROGRESS: Shepherds in Troubled Waters: The Revenue Service in Alaska.

AVOCATIONAL INTERESTS: Alaska, arctic history, aviation, conservation, art, maritime history, American natural history.

* * *

THOMPSON, (Arthur) Denys (Halstead) 1907-1988

OBITUARY NOTICE—See index for *CA* sketch: Born February 15, 1907, in Darlington, Durham, England; died February 28, 1988. Educator, editor, journalist, and author. During an education career spanning more than thirty years, Thompson became an important influence on the teaching of English. His suspicion of the mass media and his conviction that English study could contribute to society's critical ability found expression in his writings, notably *Culture and Environment,* a book he wrote with F. R. Leavis, and his contributions to *The Use of English,* a journal he founded in 1939 as *English in Schools.* Thompson also wrote *The Training of Critical Awareness, Distant Voices,* and *Change and Tradition in Rural England.* Among volumes he edited are *Society in Focus: An Approach to General Studies, Discrimination and Popular Culture,* and assorted anthologies. In addition, Thompson served on the editorial board of the quarterly magazine *Scrutiny.*

OBITUARIES AND OTHER SOURCES:

The Writers Directory: 1982-1984, Gale, 1981.

PERIODICALS

Times (London), March 1, 1988.

* * *

THOMSON, David (Robert Alexander) 1914-1988

OBITUARY NOTICE—See index for *CA* sketch: Born February 17, 1914, in Quetta, India; died in February, 1988. Broadcaster, educator, and author. Thomson, who wrote both fiction and nonfiction, was praised for his evocative use of novelistic technique in his autobiographies, *Woodbrook* and *Nairn in Darkness and Light.* The latter book won the first McVities Award for Scottish Book of the Year in 1987. In 1932 Thomson began his career as a tutor in Ireland, a post he held until 1943 when he became a writer and producer with the British Broadcasting Corporation. He wrote *The People of the Sea: A Journey in Search of the Seal Legend* and *Ronan and Other Stories;* the novels *Daniel* and *Break in the Sun,* the "Danny

Fox" series of children's books; and the nonfiction work *In Camden Town*. With Moyra McGusty he edited *The Irish Journals of Elizabeth Smith, 1840-1850: A Selection.*

OBITUARIES AND OTHER SOURCES:

BOOKS

International Authors and Writers Who's Who, 10th edition, International Biographical Centre, 1986.
The Writers Directory: 1986-1988, St. James Press, 1986.

PERIODICALS

Times (London), March 1, 1988.

* * *

THURMAN, Wallace (Henry) 1902-1934 (Patrick Casey, Ethel Belle Mandrake)

PERSONAL: Born August 16, 1902, in Salt Lake City, Utah; died of tuberculosis, December 22 (one source says December 21), 1934, in New York, N.Y.; buried in Silver Mount Cemetery, New York, N.Y.; son of Oscar and Beulah Thurman; married Louise Thompson (a schoolteacher), August 22, 1928 (separated). *Education:* Attended University of Utah, 1919-20, and University of Southern California, 1922-23.

CAREER: Reporter and editor for *The Looking Glass;* member of the editorial staff of *Messenger,* 1925-26; circulation manager of *World Tomorrow,* 1926; member of editorial staff of McFadden Publications; began as reader, became editor in chief of Macaulay Publishing Co.

WRITINGS:

(With William Jourdan Rapp) "Harlem: A Melodrama of Negro Life in Harlem" (three-act play), first produced on Broadway at Apollo Theater, February 20, 1929.
The Blacker the Berry: A Novel of Negro Life, Macaulay, 1929, AMS Press, 1972.
Infants of the Spring, Macaulay, 1932, reprinted, with afterword by John A. Williams, Southern Illinois University Press, 1979.
(With A. L. Furman) *The Interne,* Macaulay, 1932, University Microfilms, 1973.
"Tomorrow's Children" (screenplay), Bryan Foy Productions, 1934.
"High School Girl" (screenplay), Bryan Foy Productions, 1935.

Also author of unpublished plays, including "Jeremiah, the Magnificent," 1930, "Savage Rhythm," 1931, and "Singing the Blues," 1932; author of column, "Inkling." Founder and editor of *Outlet, Harlem: A Forum of Negro Life,* and *Fire!!* Worked as a ghostwriter, sometimes under the pseudonyms Patrick Casey or Ethel Belle Mandrake, for books and periodicals, including *True Story.*

Works represented in anthologies, including *The Negro Caravan, Anthology of American Negro Literature, The Black Writer of America, Black American Literature: Fiction.* Contributor to periodicals, including *New Republic, Independent, New York Times, Negro World, Opportunity,* and *Dance Magazine.*

SIDELIGHTS: Wallace Thurman settled in New York City at the beginning of the Harlem Renaissance, a period of heightened black literary activity during the mid-1920s. Because of his unconventional lifestyle and penchant for parties and alcohol, he became popular in Harlem social circles, but he was only considered a minor literary figure. His fame lay with his influence on and support of younger and talented writers of the era and with his realistic—although sensationalized—portrayals of the lower classes of black American society. Thurman was lauded as a satirist and often used satire to accuse blacks of prejudice against darker-skinned members of their race. He also rejected the belief that the Harlem Renaissance was a substantial literary movement, claiming that the 1920s produced no outstanding writers and that those who were famous exploited, and allowed themselves to be patronized by, whites. He claimed, as did a number of authors of the decade, that white critics judged black works by lower standards than they judged white efforts. Thurman maintained that black writers were held back from making any great contribution to the canon of Negro literature by their race-consciousness and decadent lifestyles.

Born and raised in the American West, Thurman attended the University of Utah for a year before transferring in 1922 to the University of Southern California in Los Angeles. While in Los Angeles Thurman wrote a column, "Inklings," for a black-oriented newspaper. He then founded a magazine, *Outlet,* hoping to initate on the West Coast a literary renaissance like the one happening in Harlem. *Outlet* lasted only six months, and in 1925 Thurman went east. In New York City he took a job as a reporter and editor at *The Looking Glass,* then became managing editor of the *Messenger,* where his editorial expertise earned him notoriety. He published short works by the poet and author Langston Hughes—not because Thurman thought them good but because they were the best available—and pieces by the writer Zora Neale Hurston. He left in the autumn of 1926 to join the staff of a white-owned periodical, *World Tomorrow.*

In the summer of 1926 Hughes asked Thurman to edit *Fire!!,* a magazine that Hughes and artist and writer Bruce Nugent were planning. Hurston, the author Gwendolyn Bennett, and another artist, Aaron Douglas, were members of the editorial board. The board intended *Fire!!* to "satisfy pagan thirst for beauty unadorned," as was stated in the foreword to the first issue. *Fire!!* would offer a forum for younger black writers who wanted to stand apart from the older, venerated black literati, and it would be strictly literary, with no focus on contemporary social issues. Thurman agreed to edit the magazine and advanced a good deal of the publication money. The first issue featured short stories by Thurman, Hurston, and Bennett, poetry by Hughes, Countee Cullen, and Arna Bontemps, a play by Hurston, illustrations by Douglas, and the first part of a novel by Nugent. But *Fire!!* folded after one issue; it was plagued by financial and distribution problems and received mediocre reviews. It was also ignored by a number of white critics and harshly criticized by some blacks who thought it irreverent.

Two years later Thurman published *Harlem: A Forum of Negro Life,* a more moderate, broader-focused magazine, also devoted to displaying works by younger writers. The new effort, unlike the avant-garde *Fire!!,* would appeal to all age groups and was "to be a general magazine . . . on current events and debates on racial and non racial issues," Thurman wrote to the critic Alain Locke. The first volume contained an essay by Locke, a book review by Thurman, poetry by Alice Dunbar Nelson and Hughes, fiction by Hughes and George Schuyler, a theater review by the editor Theophilus Lewis, and a directory of New York City churches and nightclubs. But *Harlem,* too, failed after its premier issue.

Thurman's first play was entitled "Harlem: A Melodrama of Negro Life in Harlem." It opened on Broadway February 20, 1929, at the Apollo Theater, bringing Thurman immediate success. He collaborated on the drama with William Jourdan Rapp, a white man who later became the editor of *True Story* and would remain Thurman's lifelong friend. "Harlem" centers on the Williams family, who relocate in New York City to escape economic difficulties at the time of the "great migration" of Southerners to the North during the first two decades of the twentieth century. But instead of finding the city a promised land, they encounter many of the problems that often plagued the families of the migration: unemployment and tensions between generations heightened by difficulties in adjusting to city life.

"Harlem" received mixed reviews—ranging from "exciting" to "vulgar"—but was generally considered interesting. It was criticized by blacks who did not care for its focus on the seedier elements of life, like illicit sex, liquor, wild parties thrown to collect rent money, and gambling. R. Dana Skinner stated in a 1929 *Commonweal* review of "Harlem" that he was especially upset by "the particular way in which this melodrama exploits the worst features of the Negro and depends for its effects solely on the explosions of lust and sensuality." Nevertheless, many critics felt it "captured the feel of life" and was "constantly entertaining." "Harlem" played for an impressive ninety-three performances in what was considered a poor theater season and was taken on tour to the West Coast, the Midwest, and Canada.

In 1930 Thurman again collaborated with Rapp on a three-act play, "Jeremiah, the Magnificent," based on black nationalist Marcus Garvey's "back to Africa" movement of the early 1900s. Garvey had called for an exodus of blacks to Africa so that there they could create their own country and attain personal freedoms in a society where they would be in the majority. Although Thurman portrayed Garvey as a vain and unwise man, the playwright thought Garvey did much to promote the black ideal in the hope of fostering Negro unity worldwide. The play remained unpublished and was only performed once, after Thurman had died. Thurman's other unproduced and unpublished plays include "Singing the Blues," written in 1931, and "Savage Rhythm," written the following year.

Thurman's first novel, *The Blacker the Berry,* was published in 1929. Taken from the folk-saying "the blacker the berry, the sweeter the juice," its title was ironic, for the novel was an attack on prejudice within the race. Emma Lou, the protagonist, is a dark-skinned girl from Boise who is looked down upon by her fairer family members and friends. When she attends school at the University of Southern California in Los Angeles she again is scorned, so she travels to Harlem, where she believes that she won't be snubbed because of her dark coloring. But like the Williamses in "Harlem" and Thurman in his own life, Emma Lou is disillusioned with the city. She becomes unhappy with her work, her love affairs, and the pronounced discrimination in the nightclubs, where lighter-skinned females starred in extravagant productions while darker-skinned performers were forced to sing off stage. She uses hair straighteners and skin bleachers, and takes on the appearance and attitudes of the fairer-skinned people who degrade her. She in turn snubs darker men, whom she thinks inferior, and takes up with Alva, a man who is light-skinned but cruel. After viewing Alva in a lovers' embrace with another man, Emma Lou realizes how hypocritical she's become. Critics praised Thurman for devoting a novel to the plight of the dark-skinned black girl, but they faulted him for being too objective: he recounted Emma Lou's tale without handing down any judgment on the world in which she lived. They also criticized Thurman for trying to do too much with *The Blacker the Berry,* accusing him of crafting a choppy, and occasionally incoherent, narrative by touching on too many themes.

Thurman's next novel, *Infants of the Spring,* also is set in 1920s Harlem. The story revolves around Raymond Taylor, a young black author who is trying to write a weighty novel in a decadent, race-oriented atmosphere. Taylor resides in a boardinghouse, nicknamed "Niggeratti Manor," with a number of young blacks who pretend to be aspiring authors. Thurman makes these pretenders the major victims of his satire, suggesting that they have destroyed their creativity by leading such decadent lives. Critics contend that Thurman based his characters on well-known figures of the Harlem Renaissance, including Hughes, Locke, Hurston, Cullen, Nugent, and Douglas.

In *Infants of the Spring* Thurman suggests that all American artists and writers—black and white—are overrated. He vigorously attacks black writers patronized by whites, who praise everything black authors produce, regardless of quality, as novel and ingenious. *Infants* received criticism similar to that of *The Blacker the Berry*. Reviewers objected to Thurman's examining too many issues and not presenting them clearly, and his not making a universal statement about the lifestyles presented. But unlike Thurman's first novel, which was considered too objective, *Infants* was thought to be overly subjective and Thurman overly argumentative. Yet critics praised him for his frank discussion of black society. Assessed Martha Gruening in the *Saturday Review:* "No other Negro writer has so unflinchingly told the truth about color snobbery within the color line, the ins and outs of 'passing' and other vagaries of prejudice. . . . [*Infants of the Spring*'s] quota of truth is just that which Negro writers, under the stress of propaganda and counterpropaganda, have generally and quite understandably omitted from their picture." In addition, critics considered *Infants of the Spring* one of the first books written expressly for black audiences and not white critics.

Thurman's third and final novel, *The Interne,* was a collaboration with Abraham L. Furman, a white man Thurman met while working at Macaulay's Publishing Company. The novel portrays medical life at an urban hospital as seen through the eyes of a young white doctor, Carl Armstrong. In his first three months at the hospital, Armstrong's ideals are shattered, during which time he witnesses staff members' corrupt behavior and comes in contact with bureaucratic red tape. Armstrong himself participates in the vice but soon realizes his own loss of ethics and saves himself by taking up doctoring in the country. Critics could not agree whether Thurman's accounts of medical wrongdoing were based on fact; many claimed that the novel had no semblance of reality while others stressed that incidents were actual, if unusual.

In 1934 Thurman returned to the West Coast to write screenplays. While in California he continued to lead a decadent lifestyle, drank excessively, and wrote two screenplays for Bryan Foy Productions, "Tomorrow's Children," released in 1934, and "High School Girl," released the following year. "Tomorrow's Children" was a production about the Masons, a poor white family supported by the seventeen-year-old daughter. She takes care of her younger brothers and sisters, who are either mentally or physically impaired, her drunken father, and her constantly pregnant mother. Two social workers, sent by a compassionate doctor, declare that if they wish

to receive welfare money, the mother, father, and daughter must be sterilized. "Tomorrow's Children" was based on circumstances rarely explored in Hollywood at that time, and was considered groundbreaking because it used the medical term "vasectomy" to explain the procedure of male sterilization. Because of its revolutionary subject matter, "Tomorrow's Children" was banned in New York when it was released.

In ill health, Thurman returned to New York City in May, 1934, and went on one last drinking binge with his Harlem friends. He collapsed in the middle of the reunion party and was taken, ironically, to City Hospital, on Welfare Island, New York, the institution he condemned in *The Interne*. After spending half a year in the ward for incurables diagnosed with tuberculosis, he died there on December 22, 1934. His funeral services were held in New York City on Christmas Eve.

BIOGRAPHICAL/CRITICAL SOURCES:

BOOKS

Abramson, Doris E., *Negro Playwrights in the American Theatre, 1929-1959,* Columbia University Press, 1969.
Bontemps, Arna, editor, *The Harlem Renaissance Remembered,* Dodd, Mead, 1972.
Dictionary of Literary Biography, Volume 51: *Afro-American Writers from the Harlem Renaissance to 1940,* Gale, 1987.
Twentieth-Century Literary Criticism, Volume 6, Gale, 1982.

PERIODICALS

Black World, November, 1970, February, 1976.
Commonweal, March 6, 1929.
Nation, February 10, 1932.
New Yorker, March 2, 1929.
New York Times, February 21, 1929, March 3, 1929, April 7, 1929, February 28, 1932, June 5, 1932.
Opportunity, April, 1929, October, 1930, January, 1935.
Saturday Review, March 12, 1932, June 22, 1940.
Western American Literature, spring, 1971.*

—Sketch by Carol Lynn DeKane

* * *

TIGAY, Alan M(errill) 1947-

PERSONAL: Born June 23, 1947, in Detroit, Mich.; son of Leonard (a jeweler) and Ethel (a jeweler; maiden name, Cooper) Tigay; married Lois Carlson (a social worker), December 27, 1970; children: Rafael Leonard. *Education:* University of Michigan, B.A., 1969; Columbia University, M.S., 1976. *Religion:* Jewish.

ADDRESSES: Office—Hadassah, 50 West 58th St., New York, N.Y. 10019.

CAREER: Assembly line worker at Ford Motor Company, Detroit, Mich.; probation officer in Chicago, Ill.; United Features Syndicate, New York, N.Y., feature writer, 1976-78; *Near East Report,* Washington, D.C., editor, 1978-80; *Hadassah,* New York City, executive editor, 1980—. Administrator of Harold U. Ribalow Prize for fiction; member of screening committee for National Magazine Awards. President of cooperative apartment complex in New York City, 1983-86.

MEMBER: American Jewish Press Association, American Society of Magazine Editors.

WRITINGS:

(Editor) *Myths and Facts: A Concise Record of the Arab and Israeli Conflict,* 6th edition (Tigay was not associated with earlier editions), Near East Report, 1978.
(Editor) *Myths and Facts 1980: A Concise Record of the Arab and Israeli Conflict,* 7th edition, Near East Report, 1980.
(Editor) *The Jewish Traveler* (guide book), Doubleday, 1987.

Contributor of articles to *People's Almanac* and *Book of Lists.* Also contributor of articles to periodicals, including the Baltimore *Sun,* the *Record, Boston Globe,* the Chicago *Sun Times, Detroit News, Editor & Publisher, Kansas City Star, Milwaukee Journal, National Lampoon, Newark Star-Ledger, New York Times, Washington Star.*

AVOCATIONAL INTERESTS: Collecting newspapers, Gilbert and Sullivan.

* * *

TILLER, Terence (Rogers) 1916-1987

*OBITUARY NOTICE—*See index for *CA* sketch: Born September 19, 1916, in Truro, Cornwall (now Cornwall and Isles of Scilly), England; died December 24, 1987. Broadcaster, educator, editor, translator, playwright, and poet. Tiller, who taught for nearly ten years in England and Egypt and wrote several volumes of metaphysical poetry, was widely known as a radio writer and producer for the British Broadcasting Corporation. From 1946 to 1976 he produced hundreds of popular radio plays and features, including the adaptations and translations "The Wakefield Shepherd's Play" and "The Parlement of Foules" and the original works "The Death of a Friend," "Lilith," and "Final Meeting." Tiller's poetry volumes include the acclaimed collection *Unarm, Eros.* He also edited books such as *New Poems, 1960: A P.E.N. Anthology* and *Chess Treasury of the Air.*

OBITUARIES AND OTHER SOURCES:

BOOKS

Contemporary Poets, 4th edition, St. Martin's, 1985.
The Writers Directory: 1986-1988, St. James Press, 1986.

PERIODICALS

Times (London), January 5, 1988.

* * *

TINER, Ralph W., Jr. 1948-

PERSONAL: Born October 25, 1948, in Stuttgart, West Germany; immigrated to the United States, 1948, naturalized citizen, 1948; son of Ralph W. (a machine operator) and Martha (an executive secretary; maiden name, Wieser) Tiner; married Barbara Dee Jongbloed (an advertising executive), May 24, 1986; children: Andrew. *Education:* University of Connecticut, B.A., 1970, M.S., 1974; Harvard University, M.P.A., 1981; doctoral study at University of Massachusetts at Amherst, 1985—.

*ADDRESSES: Home—*Sherborn, Mass. *Office—*U.S. Fish and Wildlife Service, Newton Corner, Mass. 02158.

CAREER: South Carolina Wildlife and Marine Resources Department, Charleston, marine biologist, 1974-77; U.S. Fish and Wildlife Service, Newton Corner, Mass., regional wetland coordinator, 1977—. *Military service:* U.S. Army National Guard, 1970-76.

MEMBER: Society of Wetland Scientists, American Society of Photogrammetry and Remote Sensing, New England Estuarine Research Society.

WRITINGS:

Wetlands of the United States: Current Status and Recent Trends, U.S. Government Printing Office, 1984.

Wetlands of New Jersey, U.S. Government Printing Office, 1985.

Wetlands of Delaware, U.S. Government Printing Office, 1985.

A Field Guide to Coastal Wetland Plants of the Northeastern United States, University of Massachusetts Press, 1987.

(With Peter Veneman) *Hydric Soils of New England,* University of Massachusetts Cooperative Extension, 1987.

A Field Guide to Nontidal Wetland Identification, U.S. Government Printing Office, 1988.

Wetlands of Rhode Island, U.S. Government Printing Office, 1988.

(With Ken Metzler) *Wetlands of Connecticut,* Connecticut Department of Environmental Protection, 1988.

(With David Burke) *Wetlands of Maryland,* U.S. Government Printing Office, 1988.

(With S. K. Majumdar, F. J. Brenner, and Robert P. Brooks) *Wetlands Ecology, Productivity, and Values: Emphasis on Pennsylvania,* Pennsylvania Academy of Sciences, in press.

SIDELIGHTS: Ralph W. Tiner, Jr., told *CA:* "Through studying biology, especially marine biology, I learned that coastal and other wetlands are important natural resources, not wastelands as many people, unfortunately, still believe. Wetlands are not only homes for a wide variety of fish and wildlife, but they also help improve water quality, reduce flood damage and erosion, and provide a base for an important aquatic food chain that supports our fishing industries. Wetlands are among America's most valuable natural resources. I have been inspired, through my work and writing, to increase public understanding of the values that wetlands offer society."

* * *

TOLSON, M. B.
See TOLSON, Melvin B(eaunorus)

* * *

TOLSON, Melvin B(eaunorus) 1898(?)-1966
(M. B. Tolson)

PERSONAL: Born February 6, 1898 (some sources say 1900), in Moberly, Mo.; died August 29 (one source says 28), 1966; buried in Guthrie, Okla.; son of Alonzo A. (a minister and teacher) and Lera (one source says Leah; maiden name, Hurt) Tolson; married Ruth Southall, January 29, 1922; children: Melvin B., Jr., Arthur, Wiley Wilson, Ruth Marie. *Education:* Attended Fisk University, c. 1918-19; Lincoln University, Lincoln University, Pa., B.A. (with honors), 1923; Columbia University, M.A., 1940.

CAREER: Worked at meat-packing plant; Wiley College, Marshall, Tex., teacher of English and speech, 1924-47, tennis, football, and boxing coach, director of Log Cabin Theatre, organizer of Wiley Forensic Society; Langston University, Langston, Okla., professor of creative literature and director of Dust Bowl Theatre, 1947-65; Tuskegee Institute, Tuskegee Institute, Ala., Avalon Professor of the Humanities, 1965-66. Mayor of Langston, Oklahoma, 1952-58.

AWARDS, HONORS: First place in American Negro Exposition National Poetry Contest, 1939, for "Dark Symphony"; Omega Psi Phi Award for creative writing, 1945; Poet Laureate of Liberia, 1947; Bess Hokin Prize from *Poetry* magazine, 1951, for "E. & O. E."; Knight of the Order of the Star of Africa, 1954; appointed permanent Bread Loaf Fellow in Poetry and Drama, 1954; District of Columbia Citation and Award for Cultural Achievement in Fine Arts, 1965; National Institute and American Academy of Arts and Letters Award in Literature, 1966; honorary doctorates from Lincoln University, 1954 and 1965; fellowships from Rockefeller Foundation and Omega Psi Phi.

WRITINGS:

Rendezvous With America (poetry; includes "Rendezvous With America," "Dark Symphony," "Of Men and Cities," "The Idols of the Tribe," "Ballad of the Rattlesnake," and "Tapestries of Time"), Dodd, 1944.

(And director) "The Fire in the Flint" (play; adapted from Walter White's novel of the same title), first produced in Oklahoma City, Okla., at National Convention of National Association for the Advancement of Colored People, June 28, 1952.

(Under name M. B. Tolson) *Libretto for the Republic of Liberia* (poetry), preface by Allen Tate, Twayne, 1953.

(Under name M. B. Tolson) *Harlem Gallery: Book One, The Curator* (poetry), introduction by Karl Shapiro, Twayne, 1965.

A Gallery of Harlem Portraits (poetry; includes "Harlem," "Hilmar Enick," and "Harold Lincoln"), edited with afterword by Robert M. Farnsworth, University of Missouri Press, 1979.

Caviar and Cabbage (articles), edited with introduction by Farnsworth, University of Missouri Press, 1982.

Author of novel *Beyond the Zaretto;* author of plays, including "Black No More" (adapted from George Schuyler's novel of the same title), 1952, "Black Boy," 1963, "The Moses of Beale Street," and "Southern Front."

Work represented in numerous anthologies, including *Golden Slippers,* fourth edition, edited by Arna Bontemps, Harper, 1941; *The Poetry of the Negro, 1746-1949,* edited by Langston Hughes and Bontemps, Doubleday, 1949; *Black Voices,* edited by Abraham Chapman, New American Library, 1968; *The Writing on the Wall,* edited by Walter Lowenfels, Doubleday, 1969; *Black Poetry,* edited by Dudley Randall, Broadside, 1969; *The Black Experience,* edited by Francis E. Kearns, Viking, 1970; *Black Literature in America,* edited by Houston A. Baker, Jr., McGraw, 1971; *The Black Poets,* edited by Randall, Bantam, 1971; *Afro-American Poetry,* edited by Bernard W. Bell, Allyn & Bacon, 1972; *Black Writers of America,* edited by Richard Barksdale and Keneth Kinnamon, Macmillan, 1972; *The Poetry of Black America,* edited by Arnold Adoff, Harper, 1973; and *Understanding the New Black Poetry,* edited by Stephen Henderson, Morrow, 1973.

Author of weekly column "Caviar and Cabbage" in *Washington Tribune,* 1937-44. Contributor to periodicals, including *American Poet, Arts Quarterly, Atlantic Monthly, Midwest Journal, Modern Monthly, Modern Quarterly, Negro Digest,* and *Pittsburgh Courier.*

SIDELIGHTS: Known for his complex, challenging poetry, Melvin B. Tolson earned little critical attention through most of his life but eventually won a place among America's leading black poets. He was, in the opinion of Allen Tate, author of

the preface to Tolson's *Libretto for the Republic of Liberia,* the first black poet to assimilate "completely the full poetic language of his time and, by implication, the language of the Anglo-American tradition." More, according to Karl Shapiro in his introduction to Tolson's *Harlem Gallery: Book One, The Curator,* Tolson wrote and thought "in Negro," thus adding to the quality of his best work. His sonnets, free verse, and epic poems, which employ both standard English and black idiom, illuminate the lives of black Americans and consider the role of black artists in white society. Noted James R. Payne in *World Literature Today,* Tolson's work is "a rich body of American poetry . . . that will give a great deal of satisfaction to readers."

Publication of Tolson's first collection of poetry, *Rendezvous With America,* came five years after his poem "Dark Symphony" won first place in the American Negro Exposition National Poetry Contest in 1939. "Dark Symphony," included in the collection, "celebrates . . . the historic contribution of black Americans and their struggle to gain recognition for their achievements, ending with a proud and defiant prediction of black accomplishment and cultural realization," asserted Robert M. Farnsworth in *Dictionary of Literary Biography.* Other poems in the volume, written during World War II, address the war's destruction, human aspirations and corruption, and the possibility of achieving "a new democracy of nations," according to Farnsworth. Poet and journalist Frank Marshall Davis, quoted by Farnsworth, characterized Tolson's writing in the volume as mature and masterful but "yet too complex for the masses"; many critics attribute the neglect of much of Tolson's writing to his complexity and erudition.

Appointed poet laureate of Liberia in 1947, Tolson attracted increased attention with his *Libretto for the Republic of Liberia,* an epic poem commemorating the African nation's centennial. Observed poet and critic John Ciardi in *Nation,* Tolson creates "a vision of Africa past, present, and future" with abundant imagery and "prodigious eclecticism." Portraying Liberia as an offshoot of America, newer and smaller with hopes of achieving more, Tolson continues the allusiveness and vision displayed in his earlier work. Ciardi commended the poet's "force of language and . . . rhythm," concluding that Tolson "has established a new dimension for American Negro poetry."

Published in 1965, Tolson's *Harlem Gallery: Book One, The Curator* was the product of years of work and is widely considered a poetic masterpiece. Robert Donald Spector, reviewing the poem for *Saturday Review* the year it appeared, judged that it "marks [Tolson] as one of America's great poets." Originally a sonnet, in the early 1930s it became the book-length *Gallery of Harlem Portraits,* which remained unpublished during Tolson's life; in the 1950s Tolson conceived it as part of a five-book epic about Harlem and black America and revised it as *Harlem Gallery: Book One, The Curator.* A fictional gallery curator "provides the central point of view" in the poem's discussions of black art and life, remarked Farnsworth, "but three major characters, all practicing artists, dramatically amplify the reader's view of the black artist's dilemma and achievement." Stanzas in the style of blues music punctuate the portraits, reinforcing Tolson's points or offering ironic commentary. Payne found such stanzas "very effective, among the most effective elements of the book." Still, while Tolson used black elements such as the blues, focusing on black characters and a black setting, he did not espouse separatism. According to Blyden Jackson's *New Review* critique, "The brotherhood of man and the universality of serious art . . . catalyze [the poem's] perceptions."

Tolson's skillful delineation of character, his ability to turn discussions of aesthetics into social commentary, his breadth of vision, and his deftness with language garnered critical acclaim. Reviewers compared *Harlem Gallery* to works by Walt Whitman, Edgar Lee Masters, Hart Crane, and T. S. Eliot and praised with Spector "the richness and variety of [Tolson's] characters" and the "allusiveness that absorbs classical, Biblical, oriental, and African references." Admitting that *Harlem Gallery* presents the same complexity and involved syntax that rendered Tolson's earlier works somewhat inaccessible, Jackson asserted that "nevertheless [it] is a fine product of the imagination. . . . [Tolson] achieved a memorable presentation of the human comedy and of human values." Responding to other critics' neglect of Tolson's work, Spector declared, "Here is a poet whose language, comprehensiveness, and values demand a critical sensitivity rarely found in any establishment. . . . Whatever his reputation in the present critical climate, Tolson stands firmly as a great American poet."

BIOGRAPHICAL/CRITICAL SOURCES:

BOOKS

Contemporary Literary Criticism, Volume 36, Gale, 1986.
Dictionary of Literary Biography, Volume 48: *American Poets, 1880-1945,* Second Series, Gale, 1986.
Farnsworth, Robert M., *Melvin B. Tolson, 1898-1966: Plain Talk and Poetic Prophecy,* University of Missouri Press, 1984.
Flasch, Joy, *Melvin B. Tolson,* Twayne, 1972.
Gibson, Donald B., editor, *Modern Black Poets: A Collection of Critical Essays,* Prentice-Hall, 1973.
Russell, Mariann, *Melvin B. Tolson's Harlem Gallery,* University of Missouri Press, 1980.
Tolson, M. B., *Harlem Gallery: Book One, The Curator,* introduction by Karl Shapiro, Twayne, 1965.

PERIODICALS

Nation, February 27, 1954.
New Republic, December 4, 1976.
Saturday Review, August 7, 1965.
World Literature Today, winter, 1983.*

—Sketch by Polly A. Vedder

* * *

TOMLIN, E(ric) W(alter) F(rederick) 1913-1988(?)

OBITUARY NOTICE—See index for *CA* sketch: Born January 30, 1913, in London, England; died c. 1988. Educator, civil servant, editor, and author. For thirty years Tomlin served in the British Council Service in Iraq, Turkey, France, and Japan, publishing a number of books based on his observations. His first book was *Turkey: The Modern Miracle,* and he later wrote *Tokyo Essays* and *The Last Country: My Years in Japan.* Tomlin's other major interest was philosophy, which he taught at institutions such as the University of Southern California and University of Nice and wrote about in works such as *The Approach to Metaphysics, Living and Knowing,* and *The Tall Trees of Marshland: Reflections on Life and Time.* He also edited books, notably *T. S. Eliot: A Tribute From Japan* and *Charles Dickens, 1812-1870: A Centennial Volume.*

OBITUARIES AND OTHER SOURCES:

BOOKS

Who's Who, 139th edition, St. Martin's, 1987.

PERIODICALS

Times (London), January 23, 1988.

* * *

TOURE, Askia Muhammad
See TOURE, Askia Muhammad Abu Bakr el

* * *

TOURE, Askia Muhammad Abu Bakr el 1938-
(Askia Muhammad Abu Bakr el-Toure, Rolland Snellings, Askia Muhammad Toure)

PERSONAL: Name originally Rolland Snellings; name changed c. 1970; listed in many sources as Askia Muhammad Toure; born October 13, 1938, in Raleigh, N.C.; son of Clifford R. and Nancy (Bullock) Snellings; married Dona Humphrey in June, 1966 (divorced); married Helen Morton Hobbs (Muslim name, Halima; a writer and editor) in 1970 (divorced); married third wife, Agila; children: (first marriage) Tariq Abdullah bin Toure, (second marriage) Jamil Abdus-Salam bin Toure. *Education:* Attended Art Students League of New York, 1960-62. *Religion:* Muslim.

ADDRESSES: Home—50 West 90th St., New York, N.Y. 10025.

CAREER: Poet, essayist, artist, editor, educator. Lecturer in African history, black studies, and creative writing at colleges and universities, including Yale University, Cornell University, Pennsylvania State University, Columbia University, University of California (Berkeley), San Francisco State College (now University), Central State College, and Queens College. *Military service:* U.S. Air Force, 1956-59.

MEMBER: Rockefeller Foundation (literary fellow), Omega Psi Phi (literary fellow).

AWARDS, HONORS: Modern Poetry Association award, 1952; Columbia University Creative Writing Grant, 1969.

WRITINGS—UNDER NAME ASKIA MUHAMMAD ABU BAKR EL-TOURE, EXCEPT AS NOTED:

(Author of introduction under name Rolland Snellings) *Samory Toure* (illustrated biography), designed by Matthew Meade, illustrated by Tom Feelings, produced by William E. Day, privately printed in New York, 1963.

Earth: For Mrs. Mary Bethune and the African and Afro-American Women, Broadside Press, 1968.

(With Ben Caldwell) *JuJu: Magic Songs for the Black Nation* (collection of poetry and prose), Third World Press, 1970.

Songhai! (collection of poetry and sketches), introduction by John O. Killens, Songhai Press, 1972.

(Contributor, under name Askia Muhammad Abu Bakr el Toure) Joe Goncalves, editor, *Black Art, Black Culture* (collection of articles from *Journal of Black Poetry*), Journal of Black Poetry Press, 1972.

Also author of the record *Black Spirits,* released by Black Forum. Work represented in anthologies, including *Black Fire: An Anthology of Afro-American Writing,* Morrow, 1968; *Black Arts,* Black Arts, 1969, *Black Nationalism in America,* Bobbs-Merrill, 1970; *Natural Process,* Hill & Wang, 1970; *The Poetry of Black America,* Harper, 1973; and *Understanding the New Black Poetry,* Morrow, 1973. Contributor of poetry and articles to periodicals, including *Black Theatre, Black World, Essence, Freedomways, Journal of Black Poetry, Liberation Magazine, Negro Digest, Soulbook,* and *Umbra.*

Staff member of *Umbra* magazine, 1962-63; member of editorial board of *Black America,* 1963-65; co-founder of *Afro World* newspaper, 1965; staff member of *Liberator Magazine,* 1965-66; associate editor of *Black Dialogue;* editor-at-large of *Journal of Black Poetry* (now *Kitabu Cha Jua*).

WORK IN PROGRESS: A volume of poetry, *Sunrise: A New Afrikan Anthem.*

SIDELIGHTS: A historian of African culture and a visionary poet foreseeing a "coming Age of Light" for humanity, Askia Muhammad Abu Bakr el Toure has been a leader of the black aesthetic movement since the early 1960s. The movement, whose influence extends to diverse fields, including poetry, theatre, music, journalism, politics, and religion, seeks to separate the spirit of black people from Western influence and define it in terms of its African origin.

While studying at the Art Students League of New York in the early 1960s, Toure helped compose one of the first books celebrating African heroes and history, *Samory Toure.* Toure collaborated with illustrator Tom Feelings, artist Elombe Brath, and others to produce the illustrated biography of the prominent grandfather of Sekou Toure, who was instrumental in maintaining Guinea's resistance to French domination in the nineteenth century.

After publishing his first book, Toure helped promote numerous journals supporting black awareness, including *Black America,* the black nationalist journal of the Revolutionary Action Movement (RAM), *Liberator Magazine,* and *Black Dialogue.* He eventually became editor-at-large of the *Journal of Black Poetry* (now known as *Kitabu Cha Jua*) after its emergence from *Black Dialogue.* With the newspaper he and author Larry Neal founded in 1965, *Afro World,* Toure helped strengthen the black liberation movement through the documentation of oppression and the analysis of racial injustice in America.

That same year Toure and Neal organized a Harlem Uptown Youth Conference with artists from the Black Arts Repertoir Theatre School, soon after which the Black Arts Theatre opened in Harlem. Black artists, including playwright LeRoi Jones (also known as Amiri Baraka), musicians Sun Ra and Milford Graves, and poets Toure and Neal acted out plays, performed music, and recited poetry in blocked-off streets in New York. "We would serenade the people on the streets of Harlem," Toure recalled, "and it made the authorities nervous as hell. We went all over Harlem and brought to its neglected, colonized masses the messages of Black power, dignity, and beauty."

Just as the nation was changing under the influence of the black arts and black liberation movements, Toure's personal life changed in the course of his activities. After moving with his wife, Dona Humphrey, to San Francisco soon after their marriage in 1966, Toure came under the influence of the Nation of Islam. Converting to the Islamic faith, he changed his name from Rolland Snellings to Askia Muhammad Abu Bakr

el Toure. In his poem "Extension," published in *JuJu: Magic Songs for the Black Nation* in 1970, Toure praises the Islamic faith as "The TRUTH" that can engender "one large community with open doors [and] open minds." Pressures from his religious, social, and political activities, however, contributed to the strain on his marriage, and Toure and his wife divorced after the birth of their son.

After returning to New York, Toure married Helen Morton Hobbs in 1970, who encouraged Toure in his poetry and his newly embraced religion. Called by her Muslim name, Halima, she is probably the inspirational "woman panther-lithe and tawny, a princess come back to haunt me" in Toure's poem "Al Fajr: The Daybreak," published in *Songhai!* in 1972. They, too, divorced, however, after the birth of a son, and Toure moved to Philadelphia in 1974.

Reviewers admired *JuJu* and *Songhai!,* both collections of the visionary poetry and prose Toure composed during the height of his activity with the black aesthetic movement. *JuJu,* which includes three poems and an essay by Toure and a poem by playwright Ben Caldwell, guides the reader through the black person's "quest for national destiny and [his] spiritual identification with the universe," explained Carolyn F. Gerald in *Black World.* In *JuJu*—the title is a West African word meaning "magic"—Toure's epic poetry links the modern black soul to its African heritage through vibrant imagery and long, polyrhythmic lines that imitate classical black music. Inspired by black instrumentalists like John Coltrane and Milford Graves, Toure equates black music with African magic, believing music to be the most authentic expression of the black soul. He explains his belief in an essay he wrote in the *Journal of Black Poetry* in 1968: "When they stripped us of our obvious African culture (robes, drums, language, religion, etc.), the 'abstract' . . . aspect of our culture—our music—was the only thing, in altered form, permitted to remain. . . . As time passed, the Black Musician became *and remains* the major philosopher, priest, myth-maker and cultural hero of the Black Nation."

Praising the intricate form and stirring content of Toure's poetry, Gerald declared that *JuJu* is a collection "well worth buying and reading by all Black people, who stand to gain, in the reading, a greater sense of self."

Reviewer Addison Gayle, Jr., proclaimed in *Black World* that *Songhai!,* like *JuJu,* tells an important "truth: that the strength of Black people lay in a culture outside that of the American, and that [its attainment] is possible only after a return to the values and ethics of our African forefathers." The poetry and prose in *Songhai!,* however, suggests more than simply returning to African origins. In "an imaginative work overflowing with symbols, images, and metaphors of the new African world to come," Gayle pointed out, Toure "envisions the world . . . peopled by strong Black men and women equipped with the grace and endurance to survive." Gayle found that in the "coming Age of Light" of which the poet writes in his "Hymn to the People," Toure predicts "a world, where poet and people feed into each other's creative ethos, where all men are poets, where love and fidelity to the human condition remain sacrosanct."

BIOGRAPHICAL/CRITICAL SOURCES:

BOOK

Dictionary of Literary Biography, Volume 41, *Afro-American Poets Since 1955,* Gale, 1985.

PERIODICALS

Black World, June, 1971, September, 1974.
***Journal of Literary Biography,* Volume 8, 1968.**

—*Sketch by Christa Brelin*

* * *

TREADWELL, Sandy 1946-

PERSONAL: Born March 25, 1946, in London, England; son of John William Ferguson (an army officer and international public relations executive) and Susan (Ord) Treadwell; married Elisabeth Krautter, March 21, 1970; children: Caroline, Zachary. *Education:* University of North Carolina at Chapel Hill, B.A., 1968. *Politics:* Republican. *Religion:* Episcopalian.

ADDRESSES: Home—P.O. Box 371, Westport, N.Y. 12993.

CAREER: Sports Illustrated, New York City, reporter, 1968-71; free-lance journalist, 1971-75, 1979—; *Classic,* New York City, staff writer, 1975-79; Director of Greer Woodycrest Children's Services; trustee of The Day School, New York City; chairman of Essex County Republican Committee. *Military service:* U.S. Army National Guard, 1968-74.

WRITINGS:

The World Marathons, Stewart, Tabori & Chang, 1987.

Contributor to magazines and newspapers, including *New York* and *Sports Illustrated.*

WORK IN PROGRESS: The White House, publication by Stewart, Tabori & Chang expected in 1990; *The Olympic Games: A Centennial Celebration,* completion expected in 1995.

SIDELIGHTS: Sandy Treadwell told *CA:* "I have loved sports all my life. Not being good enough to play at games for a career I did the next best thing—I began writing about sports in college.

"My other great interest is politics. I am looking forward to writing a bit about that subject in the future."

BIOGRAPHICAL/CRITICAL SOURCES:

PERIODICALS

Washington Post Book World, April 20, 1987.

* * *

TROUPE, Quincy (Thomas, Jr.) 1943-

PERSONAL: Born July 23, 1943, in New York, N.Y.; son of Quincy, Sr., and Dorothy (Marshall Smith) Troupe; married Margaret Porter; children: Antoinette, Tymme, Quincy, Porter. *Education:* Grambling College (now Grambling State University), B.A., 1963; Los Angeles City College, A.A., 1967.

ADDRESSES: Home—1925 7th Ave. #7L, New York, N.Y. 10026. *Office*—Department of Performing and Creative Arts, City University of New York, 130 Stuyvesant Place, Staten Island, N.Y. 10301; and School of the Arts, Writing Division, Columbia University, New York, N.Y. 10027. *Agent*—Marie Brown, 412 West 154th St., No. 2, New York, N.Y. 10032.

CAREER: Watts Writers' Movement, Los Angeles, Calif., creative writing teacher, 1966-68; *Shrewd* (magazine), Los Angeles, associate editor, beginning 1968; University of California, Los Angeles, instructor in creative writing and black literature, 1968; Ohio University, Athens, instructor in crea-

tive writing and third world literature, 1969-72; Richmond College, Staten Island, N.Y., instructor in third world literature, beginning in 1972; instructor at institutions including University of California at Berkeley, California State University at Sacramento, and University of Ghana at Legon; College of Staten Island, City University of New York, New York City, associate professor of American and third world literatures and director of poetry center; Columbia University, New York City, member of faculty of Graduate Writing Program, 1985—. Director of Malcolm X Center and the John Coltrane Summer Festivals in Los Angeles, summers of 1969 and 1970. Has given poetry readings at various institutions, including Harvard University, New York University, Howard University, Yale University, Princeton University, Louisiana State University, Dartmouth College, Oberlin College, Ohio State University, University of Michigan, and Michigan State University. Presenter of lecture and readings series "Life Forces: A Festival of Black Roots" at the Church of St. John the Divine in New York City.

MEMBER: Poetry Society of America.

AWARDS, HONORS: International Institute of Education grant for travel in Africa, 1972; National Endowment for the Arts Award in poetry, 1978; grant from New York State Council of the Arts, 1979; American Book Award from the Association of American Publishers, 1980, for *Snake-back Solos;* New York Foundation for the Arts fellowship in poetry, 1987.

WRITINGS:

(Editor) *Watts Poets: A Book of New Poetry and Essays,* House of Respect, 1968.

Embryo Poems, 1967-1971 (includes "South African Bloodstone—For Hugh Masekela," "Chicago—For Howlin Wolf," "Profilin, A Rap/Poem—For Leon Damas," "The Scag Ballet," "Midtown Traffic," "Woke Up Crying the Blues," "The Earthquake of Peru; 1970; In 49 Seconds—For Cesar Vallejo, Great Peruvian Poet," "In the Manner of Rabearivello," "Poem From the Third Eye—For Eugene Redmond," and "Black Star, Black Woman"), Barlenmir, 1972.

(Editor with Rainer Schulte) *Giant Talk: An Anthology of Third World Writings,* Random House, 1975.

(Author of foreword) Arnold Adoff, editor, *Celebrations: A New Anthology of Black American Poetry,* Follet, 1977.

(With David L. Wolper) *The Inside Story of TV's "Roots,"* Warner Books, 1978.

Snake-back Solos: Selected Poems, 1969-1977 (includes "Springtime Ritual," "The Day Duke Raised," "La Marqueta," "For Miles Davis," "Up Sun South of Alaska," "Today's Subway Ride," "New York Streetwalker," "Steel Poles Give Back No Sweat," "Ghanaian Song—Image," and "Memory"), I. Reed Books, 1978.

Skulls Along the River (poetry), I. Reed Books, 1984.

Also founding editor of *Confrontation: A Journal of Third World Literature* and *American Rag;* guest editor of black poetry and black fiction issues of *Mundus Artium* in 1973; senior editor of *River Styx,* 1983—. Work represented in anthologies, including *The New Black Poetry,* 1969; *We Speak as Liberators,* 1970; *New Black Voices,* 1972; *Black Spirits,* 1972; *Poetry of Black America,* 1973; and *A Rock Against the Wind,* 1973. Contributor to periodicals, including *New Directions, Mundus Artium, Iowa Review, Black World, Callaloo, Essence, Antioch Review, Black Creation, Negro American Literature Forum, Umbra, Mediterranean Review, Concerning Poetry, Sumac, Paris Match, Black Review, New York Quarterly,* and *Village Voice.*

WORK IN PROGRESS: An autobiography of Miles Davis, with Miles Davis, for Simon & Schuster; *The Footmans,* a novel; a fourth collection of poems.

SIDELIGHTS: Quincy Troupe is "a poet of great feeling and energy," according to Michael S. Harper, reviewing *Snake-back Solos* in the *New York Times Book Review.* Troupe has also founded and edited magazines such as *Confrontation: A Journal of Third World Literature* and *American Rag,* in addition to having a distinguished academic career. He began teaching creative writing for the Watts Writers' Movement in 1966; his other teaching responsibilities have included courses in black literature and third world literature. Troupe was already an established poet and his scholarly interests had led him to compile *Giant Talk: An Anthology of Third World Writings* with Rainer Schulte when, in 1978, he reached a wider audience with *The Inside Story of TV's "Roots."* The book, which Troupe wrote with David L. Wolper, chronicles the production of the highly successful television miniseries about slavery in America, "Roots," which was based on Alex Haley's book of the same title. Troupe's *Inside Story* has sold over one million copies.

Troupe's first poetic publication came in 1964 when *Paris Match* featured his "What Is a Black Man?" Since then he has contributed poetry to many periodicals in addition to having volumes of his poems published in book form. The first of these, *Embryo Poems,* includes poems which display Troupe's interests in the use of dialect, such as "Profilin, A Rap/Poem—For Leon Damas," and in the area of music, such as "The Scag Ballet." The latter poem depicts the actions of drug addicts as a strange form of dance; another piece likens traffic noises to "black jazz piano." Yet another, "Woke Up Crying the Blues," concerns the assassination of black civil rights leader Martin Luther King, Jr. The sadness the speaker of the poem feels at the loss of "the peaceful man from Atlanta" mingles with the happiness of the news that one of his poems has been accepted for publication, producing a mixture of emotion essential to the singing of a blues song.

Snake-back Solos, Troupe's second volume of poetry, takes its title from a local name—"Snakeback"—for the Mississippi River, recalled from the poet's childhood in St. Louis. Harper cited such poems as "Today's Subway Ride" in praising Troupe's descriptions of "the strange reality of familiar scenes." The subway is painted starkly, its unpleasant atmosphere displayed in "pee smells assaulting nostrils/blood breaking wine stains everywhere." Though Harper faulted the repetition of some of *Snake-back Solos,* including "Up Sun South of Alaska," he lauded "Ghanaian Song—Image" and "Memory" as "striking" and concluded that "the strength and economy" of the poet's "best insights . . . are about people and places he has internalized and often left behind."

Troupe's academic work has also garnered applause from critics. *Giant Talk* was declared "comprehensive" by Jack Slater in the *New York Times Book Review.* The book, which Troupe edited with Rainer Schulte, contains poems, folk talkes, short stories, and novel excerpts by black Americans, native Americans, Hispanic Americans, black Africans, and Central and South Americans. According to Slater, the editors define third world writers as "those who identify with the historically exploited segment of mankind, and who confront the establishment on their behalf"; hence the inclusion of U.S.-born authors along with those native to areas more traditionally identified

with the third world. Slater hailed the editors' decision to group the anthologized pieces by concept rather than by geographical area or genre. By using categories like "Oppression and Protest" and "Ritual and Magic," Troupe and Schulte "have managed to lessen the unwieldiness of *Giant Talk*'s scope. The uninitiated reader can, therefore, savor with as much ease as possible bits and pieces of longer works . . . as well as enjoy complete works by . . . short-story writers and poets."

BIOGRAPHICAL/CRITICAL SOURCES:

BOOKS

Dictionary of Literary Biography, Volume 41: *Afro-American Poets Since 1955,* Gale, 1985.

Troupe, Quincy, *Embryo Poems, 1967-1971,* Barlenmir, 1972.

Troupe, Quincy, and Rainer Schulte, *Giant Talk: An Anthology of Third World Writings,* Random House, 1975.

Troupe, Quincy, *Snake-back Solos: Selected Poems, 1969-1977,* I. Reed Books, 1978.

PERIODICALS

Black Scholar, March/April, 1981.

Freedomways, Volume XX, Number 2, 1980.

New York Times Book Review, November 30, 1975, October 21, 1979.

* * *

TUCK, (John) Anthony 1940-

PERSONAL: Born November 14, 1940, in Surrey, England; son of John Philip (a professor) and Jane Adelaide (a teacher; maiden name, Wall) Tuck; married Amanda Cawley (a teacher), July 17, 1976; children: Robert James, Michael Richard. *Education:* Earned B.A., M.A., and Ph.D. at Jesus College, Cambridge.

ADDRESSES: Home and office—Master's House, Collingwood College, University of Durham, Durham DH1 3LT, England.

CAREER: University of Lancaster, Bailrigg, England, lecturer, 1965-75, senior lecturer in history, 1975-78; University of Durham, Durham, England, master of Collingwood College and honorary lecturer in history, 1978—.

WRITINGS:

Richard II and the English Nobility, St. Martin's, 1973.

Crown and Nobility, 1272-1461: Political Conflict in Late Medieval England, Fontana, 1985.

(Co-editor) *History of Newcastle Royal Grammar School,* Oriel Press, 1986.

Contributor to history journals.

SIDELIGHTS: Anthony Tuck's *Crown and Nobility, 1272-1461* is a political history of medieval England. Critic Nigel Saul praised the book in *Times Literary Supplement,* saying the author "writes in an elegant, racy style which it is a pleasure to read. He is best . . . on the period which he has made very much his own—the reign of Richard II."

BIOGRAPHICAL/CRITICAL SOURCES:

PERIODICALS

Times Literary Supplement, June 6, 1986.

TUDOR-CRAIG, Pamela 1928-
(Pamela Wedgwood)

PERSONAL: Married name, Pamela Wedgwood; born June 26, 1928, in London, England; daughter of Herbert (a musician) and Madeline Wynn (Brours) Reeves; married James Tudor-Craig, 1956 (died, 1969); married John Wedgwood, 1982; children: (first marriage) a daughter. *Education:* Courtauld Institute of Art, London, B.A. (first class honors), 1949, Ph.D., 1952.

ADDRESSES: Home—Home Farm, Leighton Bromswold, near Huntingdon, Cambridgeshire PE18 0FL, England.

CAREER: Society of Antiquaries of London, London, England, secretary to bicentenary exhibition, 1951, cataloguer of possessions, 1953-55; assistant to Nikolaus Pevsner on "Buildings of England" series, 1952-53; cataloguer of pictures for earl of Verulam and earl of Salisbury, 1955-60; assistant to husband, James Tudor-Craig (curator at Ickworth, a national trust house), 1960-69; United States International University at Dropmore, and, later, Ashdown Park, Sussex, England, art historian, 1969-74; British and European Studies Group of London, London, England, art historian, 1974-79; University of London, London, England, teacher in extramural department, 1976-78; Open University, Milton Keynes, Buckinghamshire, England, teacher of art history,1976-77; Institute of Christian Studies, England, teacher of art history: University of Evansville at Harlaxton College, Grantham, England, professor of art history, 1979—.

Lecturer at several institutions in the United States, including the Smithsonian Institution, Boston Museum, Harvard University, Metropolitan Museum in New York City, and University Museum in Philadelphia. Advisory member of numerous committees for the conservation and restoration of historical English cathedrals and churches.

WRITINGS:

One Half of Our Noblest Art: Study of the Sculptures of Wells West Front, Friends of Wells Cathedral, 1986.

(Editor) *Richard III: Catalogue of an Exhibition at the National Portrait Gallery,* National Portrait Gallery, 1986.

(With Richard Foster) *The Secret Life of Paintings* (adapted from television series of same title [also see below]), Boydell, 1986.

(Co-editor with Richard Ollard, and contributor) *For Veronica Wedgewood: These Studies in Seventeenth-Century History* (festschrift), Collins, 1986.

Also co-author of *New Bell's Cathedral Guide to Westminster Abbey,* 1986.

CONTRIBUTOR

Linzee Colchester, editor, *Wells Cathedral: A History,* Open Books, 1982.

Rosemary Horrox, editor, *Richard III in the North,* University of Hull, 1986.

Harlaxton Symposium III: England in the Fifteenth Century, Boydell, in press.

Also contributor to *Anglo-Saxon England,* 1981, *Ivories,* in press, and *Early English Wall Paintings,* edited by David Park, in press. Contributor of articles to periodicals, including *Antiquaries Journal, Archaeological Journal, British Archaeological Journal, Burlington,* and *Country Life.* Contributor to archive volumes on Wells Cathedral, published by Harvey Miller in 1977 and 1978.

RADIO AND TELEVISION SCRIPTS

"Trial of Richard III," telecast by Independent Television, 1984.

(With Richard Foster) "The Secret Life of Paintings" (five-part television series), telecast by British Broadcasting Corporation, 1986.

Author of television scripts "Richard III" and "Round Table at Winchester," and of television series "Light of Experience." Author of two half-hour radio programs about Wells Cathedral and Westminster Abbey.

WORK IN PROGRESS: A monograph on English gothic sculpture, with Paul Williamson, for Harvey Miller; a monograph on medieval Westminster Abbey, with photographs by Malcolm Crowthers, for James & James.

BIOGRAPHICAL/CRITICAL SOURCES:

PERIODICALS

Times Literary Supplement, August 1, 1986.

* * *

TURNER, Stansfield 1923-

PERSONAL: Born December 1, 1923, in Chicago, Ill.; son of Oliver Stansfield (in real estate) and Wilhemina Josephine (Wagner) Turner; married Patricia Busby Whitney, December 23, 1953 (marriage ended, 1984); married Eli Karin Gilbert, March 16, 1985; children: Laurel Turner Echevarria, Geoffrey W. *Education:* Attended Amherst College, 1941-43; United States Naval Academy, B.S., 1946; Oxford University, M.A., 1950; attended Harvard University, 1966. *Religion:* Christian Scientist.

ADDRESSES: Office—1320 Skipwith Rd., McLean, Va. 22101.

CAREER: U.S. Navy, 1946-79; served in Office of the Chief of Naval Operations, 1954-56; commanding officer of U.S.S. *Conquest,* 1956-58, and U.S.S. *Rowan,* 1962-63; served in Office of the Assistant Secretary of Defense for Systems Analysis, 1963-66; became captain, 1966; commanding officer of U.S.S. *Horne,* 1967-68; executive assistant and military aide to secretary of navy, 1968-70; became rear admiral, 1970; commander of carrier task group of Sixth Fleet in the Mediterranean, 1970-71; head of systems analysis division of Office of Chief of Naval Operations, 1971-72; became vice-admiral, 1972; president of Naval War College in Newport, R.I., 1972-74; commander of Second Fleet and North Atlantic Treaty Organization (NATO) Striking Fleet, Atlantic, 1974-75; became admiral, 1975; commander in chief of Allied Forces in Southern Europe (AFSOUTH), 1975-77. Director of intelligence and head of Central Intelligence Agency (CIA) in Washington, D.C., 1977-81; international affairs consultant, television commentator, lecturer, and writer. Member of board of directors of Monsanto Co. and National Life Insurance Co.

AWARDS, HONORS: Military—Legion of Merit Medal and Bronze Star. Civilian—Rhodes Scholarship from Oxford University, 1949-50; National Intelligence Distinguished Service Medal, 1981; National Security Medal, 1981; honorary degrees from several institutions, including Amherst College, 1976, Roger Williams College, 1976, Bryant College, 1976, Salve Regina College, 1977, and Pace University, 1979.

WRITINGS:

Secrecy and Democracy: The CIA in Transition, Houghton, 1985.

Contributor to periodicals, including *U.S. News and World Report* and *New York Times Magazine.*

WORK IN PROGRESS: Terrorism and Democracy, a book on "how we can combat terrorism within the limits of democracy"; a book on the American military.

SIDELIGHTS: Stansfield Turner has enjoyed a long and distinguished career in service to the United States. He spent thirty-one years in the navy, from which he retired in 1979 as a four-star admiral, and he devoted four years to the Central Intelligence Agency (CIA), which he served as director during the presidency of Jimmy Carter. In addition, Turner has worked as a consultant in international affairs, a field in which he evinces considerable expertise, and has sat on the directorial boards of various business organizations, including the Monsanto Company and the National Life Insurance Company. Throughout his career Turner has earned admiration for his thinking and his forthright leadership.

Turner's lengthy tenure in the navy was one of ever increasing distinction. He entered active service after graduating from the Naval Academy and attending Oxford University as a Rhodes Scholar. During the Korean War Turner served at sea, and in 1956 he assumed command of the U.S.S. *Conquest.* In 1962 he held the same post on the U.S.S. *Rowan,* and the next year he began working ashore in both political and military affairs. He returned to sea in 1967 as commanding officer of the U.S.S. *Horne,* a guided-missiles carrier in the Vietnamese theater of war. For that service he was awarded the Bronze Star.

After leaving the *Horne* in 1968, Turner assisted naval secretaries Paul Ignatius and John Chafee on matters ranging from personnel to naval strategy. Turner had been promoted to captain in 1966, and in 1970 he became rear admiral. Two years later he served as president of the navy's war college in Rhode Island, at which time he was promoted once again, this time to vice-admiral. At the academy Turner instituted major academic reforms in the curriculum, but by 1974 he was back at sea as commander of the navy's Second Fleet and NATO's Striking Fleet in the Atlantic Ocean. After serving in these positions Turner was promoted to admiral. That same year—1975—he assumed command of Allied forces in Southern Europe. In 1977 he accepted President Carter's offer of the CIA directorship.

Carter, who had graduated with Turner from the naval academy, accorded his former classmate surprisingly extensive authority over the CIA and even signed an executive order extending Turner's powers to include control of related intelligence groups, including the Federal Bureau of Investigation, the National Security Agency, and State Department Intelligence. In return Turner promised that the CIA, which suffered from low morale and public shame following disclosures of illegal and unethical activities, would adhere to the law and abandon distasteful programs such as drug experimentation.

Turner's main efforts as director of the CIA involved improving the agency's management systems, establishing a satisfactory working relationship with related congressional committees, and integrating the various intelligence organizations more closely. Following initial dissension prompted by Turner's personnel policies, the CIA enjoyed increased public approval. During his tenure Turner avoided major scandal and worked to make the agency more accountable and efficient. He also succeeded in unifying the seemingly disparate factions within the organization and fostered improved relations with the media. And he reaffirmed the CIA's long-standing requirement

that former employees submit for examination any agency-related manuscripts intended for publication. This policy drew media attention when former CIA member Frank Snepp ignored it and published his book *Decent Interval* without agency approval. Snepp was consequently sued by the government and forced to pay $140,000.

Turner eventually fell victim to this policy when he submitted *Secrecy and Democracy* to the agency before the book's 1985 publication. After leaving the CIA in 1981, Turner had considered various writing projects before producing a book that he hoped would elucidate his perspective on the organization. Upon submitting his manuscript, however, Turner was surprised to learn that many passages concerned information deemed classified. He argued that most of the CIA's objections were trivial and that some of the allegedly classified information had already been revealed by equally knowledgeable authorities. Turner also noted that he could ignore the agency's censorship and risk a lawsuit, but he eventually complied with its demands and made more than one hundred deletions.

Despite the alterations, *Secrecy and Democracy* earned commendations from many critical quarters. Writing in the *New York Times Book Review,* Thomas Powers praised Turner's analysis of political ethics regarding espionage and intelligence operations. Powers called *Secrecy and Democracy* "a serious and valuable contribution to a debate that cuts close to the bone of power in a world of sin and danger." Powers also acknowledged Turner's censorship conflict with the CIA and declared that *Secrecy and Democracy* "survived the scissors, and its central arguments are made with a vigorous candor." *New Yorker*'s critic was also impressed with Turner's frank appraisal of both his successes and failures as the agency's director, and *New York Times* reviewer Charles Mohr noted the book's serious nature by stating that it is "wiser than it is entertaining." Mohr called *Secrecy and Democracy* "a valuable primer . . . in the actual art of intelligence."

Turner told *CA* that "it is interesting to reconsider *Secrecy and Democracy* since the Iran-Contra revelations." He added, "The book almost forecasts the problems that American intelligence would re-visit as a result of the Reagan administration's heavy emphasis on covert action, its efforts to overclassify information, and its unwillingness to maintain a good working relationship with the Congress."

Since completing *Secrecy and Democracy,* Turner has remained active as a consultant, television commentator, and lecturer on world affairs. He has also continued writing, and in his next book, *Terrorism and Democracy,* he will analyze American responses to terrorism in the 1980s. Another work, concerning an evaluation of the present American military, is also planned.

AVOCATIONAL INTERESTS: Swimming, tennis, jogging, attending theatrical and musical performances.

CA INTERVIEW

CA interviewed Admiral Stansfield Turner by telephone on June 30, 1986, at his home in McLean, Virginia.

CA: You wrote Secrecy and Democracy *in part "to share the special quality of the period" during which you served as director of Central Intelligence, from 1977 to 1981. When did the idea for the book begin, and how did it grow?*

TURNER: I think I knew from the time I completed the job as director that I wanted to share with the American public the lessons we had learned during that period of transition from almost no accountability of our intelligence organizations to a substantial form of accountability. I felt, however, that I was so close to the issue that it would be inadvisable to start writing immediately. I wanted to gain some perspective, some distance. After I had been out of the government two years, I was working on a different book and not getting very far with it. A friend of mine who was a very close associate, George Thibault, said, "It's time for you to drop that book and do the one on intelligence that you've talked about. You've been out long enough now, and you ought to get it out while the country still needs to understand this." Among other things, the Reagan administration was taking what I thought were rather backward views of how to run intelligence, and I wanted to share with the public what I thought were the more forward-looking views that did include some form of accountability. So, at the end of two years out of office, I started to write this book.

CA: Though the book deals with a complex and sometimes technical subject, it's written in a very clear, accessible style. Was that something you consciously worked hard at?

TURNER: Yes. I wanted to avoid acronyms and discussion of things that only people inside the government would understand. I wanted to reach a broader public, who would hopefully influence the Congress and even the executive branch to continue to keep our intelligence accountable to the American public.

CA: Among your acknowledgments, you gave editor Nan Talese praise for her "patient and sound coaching." In what particular ways was she especially helpful?

TURNER: The first time I produced a book, she looked at it and said, "This won't do. It doesn't have a good theme." So I started all over again—all over in the sense that I tried to work the same material into a different pattern. I sent her another book six months later and she said, "You've got a theme for this one, but it's no good." So we started *again,* and after another four or five months I produced a third book. She was very patient in saying, "You've got a lot of good material here, Turner, but you have not marshalled it together in a way that is both interesting and persuasive."

CA: In an acknowledgments section, you described the delay of the book's completion and publication that resulted from the CIA Publications Review Board's handling of it. How much of the original text would you say was lost through that process?

TURNER: There were something like a hundred deletions, but each of these was small in itself. One major story was lost entirely. It would have been a very good story to have told, and would have been very commendatory of the CIA. They eliminated that—I think with marginal justification; I can't complain totally on it. The other things that they eliminated were about three subjects where they made me talk around the issue rather than address it directly. Nothing is lost to the reader, but it took me endless hours of argumentation to get them to compromise to the point where you can understand it in the book. I had to use euphemisms instead of saying it directly.

CA: You and many other people compared your treatment by the CIA reviewers with that of Frank Snepp, whose book Decent Interval *(1977) was the subject of a government lawsuit. Obviously the two cases are very different, but has your experience in any way caused you to rethink the review requirement and process that you endorsed, and under which Snepp was prosecuted?*

TURNER: Yes. And I'm glad you said "endorsed," because a lot of people claim I founded it, which is not true. My case and Snepp's were entirely opposite. The complaint against Snepp was that he did not submit his book for review. I submitted mine, and they butchered it with deletions that were unnecessary. I think the process of review still is required. The only thing that's changed in my mind is that there's got to be some way of arbitrating these issues. I hope the congressional committees on intelligence will step in and play some role here. The poor citizen like myself is almost at the mercy of the CIA in this regard, and their whole inclination is to keep everything secret that they can. It's very difficult to find a way to appeal. In one instance I threatened to publish what they said I should not publish unless they got an injunction against me. All I wanted was to have a court adjudicate between us. I could have brought a lawsuit on the basis of restraint of my freedom of speech, but that might have taken a couple of years, whereas an injunction is something that moves through the courts very quickly. The CIA refused to get an injunction against me, and left it entirely up to me. I could have published it then, and my lawyer said they couldn't possibly have sued me, since I had warned them. But I didn't want to be the fellow who defied them and published something against their wishes, because I thought it was a poor example for others.

CA: One of the subjects you discussed in Secrecy and Democracy *was the business of thinning the ranks, for which you had received a lot of unfavorable and distorted criticism. Were there any indications that the book succeeded in setting the record straight?*

TURNER: No. Everywhere I go, people still say, "Why did you decimate our human intelligence activities?" As I've explained in the book, I did nothing that was injurious. Nobody was reduced from the overseas component and everybody who left was in the bottom five percent. Now they've reversed a lot of that. There was a story in the *Washington Post* last week that said that the President's Foreign Intelligence Advisory Board, an outside body composed of right-wing, extremely conservative people, said that Mr. Casey's handling of the Howard case—in which Howard was fired from the CIA and then defected to the Soviets—had "devastated our human intelligence capabilities in Moscow," and that there had been "repeated blunders" in Howard's hiring, screening, and dismissal. The accusations that I hurt our human intelligence are largely from the five percent who got fired. And here's the President's Foreign Intelligence Advisory Board officially saying that the *reversal* of my policies on people has resulted in the devastation of one of our major human intelligence activities.

CA: In "Who Killed the CIA?" in Commentary, *Edward Jay Epstein refuted your account of James Angleton's responsibility for the three-year incarceration of Russian defector Yuri Nosenko and said that you had deliberately used Angleton's name as a "tactful metaphor" for the real culprits, whom you prefered "not to confront directly." How would you respond to that criticism?*

TURNER: I think Epstein is both partly incorrect and partly just picking at technicalities. There's no question that Angleton was the man behind the handling of Nosenko. It may well be that the Soviet Branch actually issued the directives. It was Angleton's activity, but it was technically housed in a different branch from his as far as the details for the administration of Nosenko's imprisonment went. I think Epstein was making an effort to be a lawyer and pick a fine technical line. Neither Angleton nor anybody else has disputed the fact that the way Nosenko was handled was managed from Angleton's office.

CA: James Bamford, reviewing your book for Washington Post Book World, *called it "an important book on a dark subject." Thomas Powers, in the* New York Times Book Review, *said that it was "a valuable contribution to a debate that cuts close to the bone of power in a world of sin and danger." Is the book being used in college and university courses as supplemental reading?*

TURNER: Yes. I haven't got a real head count on it, but several professors have told me that they've put it into their curriculum. The paperback just came out a couple of months ago, and since that makes it more affordable, I hope that next fall there will be more college classes in which it will be used. If as you look at the reviews you ask the question "Did the reviewer once play a part in the espionage branch of the CIA?" you can tell whether it's going to be a good review or a bad one.

CA: Yes. It was amazing, for example, that the Los Angeles Times *had asked Frank Snepp to review the book.*

TURNER: It was totally irresponsible of the *Los Angeles Times,* I think, to ask Frank Snepp to write a review. He claims I cost him $150,000. He's hardly likely to be unbiased. The worst review we ever got was in the *Armed Forces Journal.* The interesting thing about it is that the man who wrote it was one of the five percenters I cut, and on the opposite page, the *Journal* had a review of a book that *he* had just written about the KGB. It wasn't the same subject, but our books hit the market at the same time and were in competition for people who wanted to read about spying and intelligence. So he had several reasons to want to blast my book. I have a friend who is on a substantial paper in this country—I can't identify him or his paper—who told me that the "old boys" in the CIA were calling up volunteering to review my book. He fortunately got his newspaper to get a third party involved, somebody who wasn't part of the system, and I got a very favorable review.

CA: You became director of Central Intelligence at a time when the CIA was in low esteem because of the abuses that had been revealed by the Church Committee in 1975, and provisions had been made for the CIA's activities to be overseen by a government committee. How do you think the public's perception of the CIA today compares with then?

TURNER: Between 1976 and 1979, the CIA went up markedly in the public's opinion, partly because we worked at it and partly because the public and even the media began to appreciate that this was an organization that had been beaten over the head more than was healthy for our country. The reputation stayed steady through '79, '80, maybe into '81. But I think it's gone downhill steadily under Reagan. We keep reading certain things in the media: one, that there's an adversarial relationship between the CIA and the Congress; two, that the

CIA is doing illegal or improper things in Nicaragua; three, that the intelligence is being slanted to suit Mr. Reagan and analysts are quitting in complaint of that. Whether these accusations are justified or not—and I'm not saying they are—the impact is a diminution of the reputation of the CIA in our country. There's no question that we mined the harbors of Nicaragua; there's no question that we wrote a manual that condoned assassinations. There's no question that we did liaison with Lebanese intelligence, and that some Lebanese then drove a truck bomb into an apartment building to kill a known terrorist and killed eighty innocent people instead. In all three of those cases, the president of the United States rescinded his orders to the CIA to do those things, thereby acknowledging that we had made a mistake. And I think three mistakes of that sort by one president, in the period of a year and a half, indicate mismanagement.

CA: What do you consider your most important legacies to the CIA?

TURNER: First, instituting and putting into operation the process of accountability through White House and congressional oversight. Second, integrating the CIA into the intelligence community and making the community work better as a group. Third, giving the CIA a new organizational structure that tried to make it operate as one organization rather than three.

CA: In your book, you mentioned the idea you'd had of making available to the business community intelligence that could be useful to business, if that could be done in an equitable way. Did that idea take off?

TURNER: No. We got it started, but it didn't take off. There was such resistance to it that it took me a lot of time and effort just to get it moving. We did get it moving somewhat, but I don't know whether Mr. Casey continued in that direction or not.

CA: There always seems to be a fresh crop of spies being caught, and people love reading about them. Are there any surprises in the pattern now, any new motives for spying?

TURNER: I think we see more cases of people spying today because they think it's a thrilling thing to do. They've read too many John le Carre books. That's frightening because it's more difficult in some ways to predict from just looking at their lives. I think we also have a very dangerous situation whereby there are so many people involved in our technical spying system compared with our human spying system that there's more opportunity for individuals to be suborned by other countries. It takes a lot of people to invent, build, operate, and maintain a satellite. It doesn't take too many people to recruit and operate a single agent. On top of that, people who are responsible for the secrets of blueprints are not as conscientious maybe as people who are responsible for the lives of human beings. So the world of technical spying has opened us to a greater vulnerability to people giving away our secrets. There are more of them, and they don't feel that same sense of intimate responsibility that a handler of a human agent does.

CA: What periodicals do you read to keep abreast of government activities and current events?

TURNER: I read the *New York Times,* the *Christian Science Monitor,* the *Washington Post,* the London *Economist,* and *Business Week.* And I have a clipping service that gives me a sampling of things from all across the American media.

CA: What do you think about television programs that cover government activities and news? Do some of them do a good job?

TURNER: I think "The MacNeil-Lehrer Report" does a good job. The Sunday shows, like "Meet the Press," do a reasonable job. I was recently over in England on a Sunday morning TV show and found it much more informative, much more instructive than any of our Sunday shows. They really encouraged you to speak, and not just take thirty seconds. If you're on "This Week With David Brinkley," you get half an answer out and [panelist] George Will interrupts you. There isn't an effort in American television, in my opinion, to try to get the different views on the table. It's an effort to try to get people to say something embarrassing, something that will make a headline. If you don't get a headline out of a show, it's not a success.

CA: Are you lecturing extensively now?

TURNER: Yes. I'm in the business of lecturing and have several different lectures I give. I talk about this business we've been talking about if people are interested in understanding the intelligence process and the value of accountability. I give lectures on what's happening around the world. But today I'm in demand mainly to give lectures on the question of terrorism and where we're going with that.

CA: Generally speaking, what is your message about terrorism?

TURNER: I think we have to learn to be more patient than we are, and understand that it's going to be the combination of a whole series of small steps against terrorism that will eventually bring it under reasonable control. The idea that one bombing or one other major effort will solve the problem is naive. We do have the problem of how to combat terrorism and still not abandon the democratic principles that we're fighting to preserve.

CA: What was your feeling about the U.S. bombing of Libya in April, 1986?

TURNER: I thought it was done in too much haste, and done with too much enthusiasm for retaliation rather than consideration of whether it would do us any good over the long run. It's the same thing as the [Central American] Contra situation. Nobody thinks the Contras are going to achieve anything, but we still vote to support them. Not many people think we're going to exterminate even Libyan terrorism by the bombing, but we all were very wildly enthusiastic about doing it. It was a catharsis for us, but I don't think in the long run it's going to be a major step toward curing terrorism. I'm not against using military force when appropriate. I just think in this case we had not exhausted other means of reining in Qaddafi before using this one.

CA: You told Beth Duff Sanders for the New York Times Book Review *in the summer of 1985 that you were working on a new book about "improving American military strength and strategy." Is that the book you interrupted to write* Secrecy and Democracy*?*

TURNER: That's it, and I've interrupted it again to write one on terrorism. It will be called *Terrorism and Democracy*. It's

still in the research stages. I'm going to take terrorist incidents against Americans since 1979, when the hostages were captured in Tehran [Iran], and review the way the United States responded as compared with the way other countries have responded in similar circumstances and with other alternatives that might have been considered. I want to try to understand why we did what we did and what options we might have that could be different in the future.

CA: Do you think a Reagan-size defense budget is necessary to improve our strength and strategy?

TURNER: No. I find it difficult from the outside to know what number of dollars are needed. But I'm utterly convinced that we should not be spending as much as we are today, because of the way Reagan is misspending it. We might need this much money if it were well spent, but certainly I don't want to see it spent when it's being misused. The idea that we need an MX missile, for instance, is the most absurd thing that the United States military have proposed for centuries. We're spending where we're strong and we're not spending where we're weak, and that's a crime. The navy is building exactly the wrong kind of navy, not designed with a strategy in mind. We have not got a military strategy in this country today. Mr. Reagan and Mr. Weinberger feel that the military are so good at this that they don't have to oversee what the military do; they can just turn them loose and let them do what they want. Our military system is in the process of being revamped by the Congress. But there's no way that turning money over to the military without supervision is going to get an effective military response. We're tied up with the three military services, each bargaining with the others for what they would like, and nobody is working on an overall strategy.

CA: By all biographical accounts, you have a wide range of interests, including theatre and opera. Do you have time now to enjoy them?

TURNER: Actually more than I did when I was in the government, but I keep extremely busy and don't do as much of that as I would like. My wife and I love to go to the theatre, and that's one of the reasons we like to go to London. When we were there recently, we went to two or three very good shows. We like to go to the Kennedy Center here and make sure we don't miss good things; we just signed up for "Camelot" and Ella Fitzgerald at Wolf Trap this summer. Yes, we like to do those kinds of things. But mainly we like to have people at our house. Last night we had a party for six. It was midnight before we realized it, and here we were solving all the problems of the world—a congressman and his wife, a famous movie actress, another friend, and the two of us. It's very stimulating to get people who are interested in discussion—not pontificating, but reasoning and thinking.

CA: You seem to retain very positive feelings for our country.

TURNER: Yes. We're talking a couple of days before the Fourth of July, and one can't help being particularly patriotic on this one with its emphasis on liberty. I'm so grateful to have had the opportunities that I've had to serve our country, because every one of them has been an exciting challenge, and you just couldn't have these opportunities in many, many other countries of the world. You and I ought to be so grateful. Finally, I have such deep faith that the American system is so much better than that of the Communists that we're going to prevail in this competition, particularly if we don't get carried away with a lot of jingoism and sloganeering. We've got a tremendous advantage over the Soviets because we have an ideology that's sound and they have an ideology that's flawed. We have an ideology that many countries of the world are turning toward today. Almost nobody's turning toward Marxism. We ought to remember that and not bleed ourselves dry building MX missiles and that kind of thing, but build on our strengths, which are our freedom and our ideology and our willingness to communicate.

I have advocated that one of the primary lessons of the Chernobyl [nuclear reactor contamination] incident is that the United States, which surely must have had better information than the LandSat commercial satellites were giving us, should have advised the world what was going on at Chernobyl. We had that capability with our intelligence, unless there was a massive intelligence failure. And why were we sitting back, not letting the world know everything we could that would help calm concerns in Western Europe, for instance? That should have been the beginning of our opening up the world through our intelligence satellites, and releasing as much information from those as we can without jeopardizing our necessary secrecy. That's a challenge that the Soviets could never stand. Openness is anathema to them. We should throw down the gauntlet and say that we're going to tell the whole world what's going on all *around* the world and not let people start wars without warning; not let floods take place without giving every relief we can—which we can do through our satellites; and help people find minerals and water resources and fish and oil through using these marvelous photographic tools to everybody's advantage rather than keeping all this information secret.

BIOGRAPHICAL/CRITICAL SOURCES:

BOOKS

Turner, Stansfield, *Secrecy and Democracy: The CIA in Transition,* Houghton, 1985.

PERIODICALS

Commentary, October, 1985.
Los Angeles Times Book Review, August 11, 1985.
New Republic, March 12, 1977, July 1, 1985.
Newsweek, February 6, 1978.
New York, March 3, 1980.
New Yorker, July 29, 1985.
New York Times, February 8, 1977, May 18, 1983, June 13, 1985.
New York Times Book Review, June 16, 1985.
Time, February 6, 1978.
Washington Post Book World, June 9, 1985.

—Sketch by Les Stone

—Interview by Jean W. Ross

U-V

ULRICH, (John) Homer 1906-1987

OBITUARY NOTICE—See index for *CA* sketch: Born March 27, 1906, in Chicago, Ill.; died after a heart attack, November 28, 1987, in Silver Spring, Md. Musician, educator, journalist, and author. During a career spanning more than forty years, Ulrich made notable contributions to the music program at the University of Maryland and to music literature. He played cello and bassoon with the Chicago Symphony Orchestra from 1929 until 1935, when he accepted his first teaching post. Ulrich became chairman of the music department at the University of Maryland in 1953 and oversaw the department's expansion from five professors, thirty-five students, and one degree program to sixty professors, six hundred students, and nine degree programs before he retired in 1972. His writings in the music field include books such as *Chamber Music, The Education of a Concert-Goer, Famous Women Singers,* and *A Survey of Choral Literature* as well as contributions to encyclopedias and criticism for the *Washington Evening Star*. Beginning in 1972 Ulrich also edited *American Music Teacher*.

OBITUARIES AND OTHER SOURCES:

BOOKS

Directory of American Scholars, Volume I: *History,* 8th edition, Bowker, 1982.

Who's Who in American Music: Classical, 2nd edition, Bowker, 1985.

PERIODICALS

Washington Post, December 1, 1987.

* * *

URBANSKA, Wanda (Marie) 1956-

PERSONAL: Born January 17, 1956, in South Bend, Ind.; daughter of Edmund Stephen (an author and professor) and Marie Mitchell Olesen (an author and professor) Urbanski; married Frank Graham Levering (an orchardist and writer), October 1, 1983. *Education:* Attended Bowdoin College, 1974-75; Harvard University, B.A., 1978. *Religion:* Cultural Christian.

ADDRESSES: Home and office—Route No. 2, Ararat, Va. 24053. *Agent*—Elaine Markson, 44 Greenwich Ave., New York, N.Y. 10011.

CAREER: Free-lance writer for magazines, 1978—; *Paris Review,* New York, N.Y., associate editor, 1978-79; *Los Angeles Herald Examiner,* Los Angeles, Calif., reporter and editor, 1980-83; Levering Orchard, Ararat, Va., vice-president for marketing and sales, 1986—.

WRITINGS:

The Singular Generation: Young Americans in the 1980's, Doubleday, 1986.

Contributor of articles to periodicals, including *Los Angeles Times Book Review, McCall's, Vogue,* and *Glamour.*

WORK IN PROGRESS: A book about simple living in America; a novel based in Washington, D.C., set in the world of journalism.

SIDELIGHTS: Wanda Urbanska told *CA:* "I am a product of writers and have always been surrounded by them. I came to writing as a child, living among books, including my father's impressive list, with titles in Spanish, Polish, and English. My mother's book *Margaret Fuller's 'Woman in the Nineteenth Century'* (Greenwood Press, 1980) is now a classic in its field. My parents were my first inspriation, but now I find material to write about everywhere.

"*The Singular Generation* grew out of a series of articles published in the *Los Angeles Herald* in January 1983 about the second generation of feminism. I wanted to expand those articles into a book, but publishers felt that in 1983 feminism was a non-seller, so they asked me to write about the many influences on the generation. I'm glad they did, as the resulting book was much broader, and included the trend toward being single, the pressure of downward economic mobility, and the changing attitudes toward children and marriage and politics."

BIOGRAPHICAL/CRITICAL SOURCES:

PERIODICALS

New Woman, November, 1986.

* * *

V

See CHEKHOV, Anton (Pavlovich)

VALL, Seymour 1925(?)-1987

OBITUARY NOTICE: Born c. 1925 in Far Rockaway, N.Y.; died of cancer, October 30, 1987, in New York, N.Y. Theatrical fund-raiser and producer, television scriptwriter, and playwright. Vall was co-founder, with Edwin Partikian, of the First Theater Investing Service in 1960. The brokerage firm funded about sixty Broadway and Off-Broadway productions, including "Fiddler on the Roof," "Mame," "Carnival," and "Stop the World . . . I Want to Get Off." Vall produced several shows during the 1960s and 1970s, including "A Funny Thing Happened on the Way to the Forum," and he wrote plays such as "The Really Portable Hamlet Company" and "How to Be a Jewish Mother," the latter based on Dan Greenburg's book of the same title. During the 1950s Vall contributed television scripts to Kraft Theater and plays to the New Dramatists Studio.

OBITUARIES AND OTHER SOURCES:

PERIODICALS

New York Times, November 3, 1987.

* * *

VETTERLING-BRAGGIN, Mary (Katherine) 1947-

PERSONAL: Born June 20, 1947, in Greenfield, Mass.; daughter of Donald Edward and Margaret Mary (Lebert) Vetterling; married Allan Brian Braggin, June 8, 1975; children: Jennifer, Jessica. *Education:* Mount Holyoke College, B.A. (cum laude), 1969; attended Free University of Berlin, 1969-70; Boston University, M.A., 1973, Ph.D., 1976.

ADDRESSES: Home—25 Franklin St., Ramsey, N.J. 07446.

CAREER: Union College, Schenectady, N.Y., instructor in philosophy, 1973-75; E. Leitz, Inc., Rockleigh, N.J., product manager in Microscope Division, 1976-79; general editor of women's studies books for Littlefield, Adams & Co., 1981-83; working for the advancement and rights of emotionally challenged people, 1983—.

MEMBER: American Association of University Professors, American Philosophical Association, Philosophy of Science Association, Society of Women in Philosophy, Society of Business Ethics, Garden State Tennis League, Bergen County Women's Tennis League.

AWARDS, HONORS: Fulbright fellow in West Germany, 1969-70.

WRITINGS:

(With Jane English and Frederick Elliston) *Feminism and Philosophy,* Littlefield, Adams, 1976.
Sexist Language: A Modern Philosophical Analysis, Littlefield, Adams, 1982.
(Contributor) Patrick Grim, editor, *Philosophy of Science and the Occult,* State University of New York Press, 1982.
"Femininity," "Masculinity," and "Androgyny," Littlefield, Adams, 1984.

Contributor to philosophy journals.

* * *

VICKERS, Hugo (Ralph) 1951-

BRIEF ENTRY: Born November 12, 1951, in London, England. British biographer. Following an early career with Burke's Peerage, publishers of biographical reference books on the British aristocracy, Vickers turned to the full-time writing of biographies in 1975 when he began researching the life of Gladys Deacon, a wealthy New England socialite who married the ninth Duke of Marlborough in 1921. The finished work, *Gladys, Duchess of Marlborough* (Weidenfeld & Nicolson, 1979), was the result of four years' extensive research and sixty-five interviews with the former duchess, whom Vickers found, at the age of ninety-four, incarcerated—apparently deranged and disfigured by an accident during cosmetic surgery in her youth—in a mental hospital in Northampton, England.

The publication of *Gladys, Duchess of Marlborough* brought Vickers much critical acclaim as well as a request from Cecil Beaton, English photographer to the Royal Family, to be Beaton's authorized biographer. After five years of painstaking research Vickers published *Cecil Beaton: The Authorized Biography* (Weidenfeld & Nicolson, 1985). He has written several other books, including *We Want The Queen* (Debrett, 1977), an authorized account of Queen Elizabeth's Silver Jubilee Celebrations, and *Debrett's Book of the Royal Wedding* (Debrett, 1981), which includes a biography of Prince Charles. In addition, Vickers has contributed articles to such magazines as *Harper's and Queen, Tatler,* and *Architectural Digest,* and since 1980 has been a regular book reviewer for the London *Times.* In 1977 he served on the London Celebrations Committee for the Queen's Silver Jubilee, and in 1986 was a member of the Queen's Birthday Committee. *Addresses: Home*—62 Lexham Gardens, London W8 5JA, England. *Agent*—Gillon Aitken, 29 Fernshaw Rd., London SW10 0TG, England.

BIOGRAPHICAL/CRITICAL SOURCES:

PERIODICALS

New York Times Book Review, July 7, 1980, June 15, 1986.
Spectator, September 22, 1979.
Times (London), July 25, 1985.

* * *

VIEG, John A.
See VIEG, John Albert

* * *

VIEG, John Albert 1904-1988
(John A. Vieg)

OBITUARY NOTICE—See index for *CA* sketch: Born November 26, 1904, in Fort Dodge, Iowa; died February 12, 1988, in Claremont, Calif. Educator and author. Vieg devoted his career to the study and teaching of political science, working occasionally as administrative and economic analyst for government bureaus. He spent much of his teaching career at Pomona College and received two Fulbright grants to teach at the universities in Oslo, Norway, and Delhi, India. Under variations of his name he wrote several books, including *The Government of Education in Metropolitan Chicago; Progress Versus Utopia: The Use of Plans, Examples, Complaints and Standards in Improving Public Administration;* and, with Henry A. Turner, *The Government and Politics of California.* Vieg also helped write *California Local Finance* and *Elements of Public Administration.*

OBITUARIES AND OTHER SOURCES:

BOOKS

American Men and Women of Science: The Social and Behavioral Sciences, 13th edition, Bowker, 1978.

Who's Who in America, 39th edition, Marquis, 1976.

PERIODICALS

Los Angeles Times, February 18, 1988.

* * *

VILNAY, Zev 1900-1988

OBITUARY NOTICE: Born June 12, 1900, in Haifa, Israel; died January 21, 1988. Geographer, lecturer, and author. Vilnay, a lecturer in the United States, England, and Israel, is remembered for his popular *Israel Guide,* later published as *The Guide to Israel,* which was revised more than twenty times and translated into several languages. He also wrote *Legends of the Land of Israel, Legends of Palestine, Palestine Guide, Israel Encyclopedia, The Holy Land in Old Prints and Maps,* and *Jerusalem: The Capital of Israel.*

OBITUARIES AND OTHER SOURCES:

BOOKS

The Author's and Writer's Who's Who, 6th edition, reprinted, Burke's Peerage, 1971.

Who's Who in World Jewry: A Biographical Dictionary of Outstanding Jews, Olive Books of Israel, 1978.

PERIODICALS

New York Times, January 23, 1988.

* * *

VINTON, Iris 1906(?)-1988

*OBITUARY NOTICE—*See index for *CA* sketch: Born c. 1906 in West Point, Miss.; died of breast cancer, February 6, 1988, in Manhattan, N.Y. Editor and author. Vinton was best known for her novels for young people, including *Flying Ebony,* which was adapted as a motion picture, "The Mooncussers." Her first writings were short plays such as *Just Babies,* published in 1939; *Laffy of the Navy Salvage Divers,* published in 1944, was her first fiction book. Among Vinton's other works are a sequel to *Flying Ebony* titled *The Black Horse Company,* the juvenile biographies *The Story of Robert E. Lee* and *The Story of President Kennedy,* and *The Folkways Omnibus of Children's Games.* She also served as editor of *You and Your Child* magazine during the late 1930s and as associate editor for Breskin Publishing Company in the early 1940s.

OBITUARIES AND OTHER SOURCES:

PERIODICALS

New York Times, February 9, 1988.

* * *

VITEK, John D(ennis) 1942-

PERSONAL: Born August 16, 1942, in St. Paul, Minn.; son of John (a tool and die maker) and Amelia (a housewife; maiden name, Katich) Vitek; married Margaret Elizabeth Kriegl (a student counselor), August 20, 1966; children: Mark V., Alan A. *Education:* Wisconsin State University (now University of Wisconsin)—Stevens Point, B.S., 1964; University of Iowa, M.A., 1970, Ph.D., 1973.

ADDRESSES: Home—Stillwater, Okla. *Office*—Department of Geology, Oklahoma State University, Stillwater, Okla. 74078.

CAREER: Northern Illinois University, DeKalb, cartographer in department of geography, 1965-67; University of Iowa, Iowa City, part-time instructor in geography, 1967-70; State University of New York at Buffalo, assistant professor of geography, 1971-74; University of Michigan, Flint, assistant professor of physical geography, 1974-78, chairman of department, 1976-77; Oklahoma State University, Stillwater, assistant professor, 1978-80, associate professor, 1980-84, professor of geography, 1984-86, professor of geology, 1987—, coordinator of environmental sciences, 1982—, assistant dean of Graduate College, 1982—. Visiting professor at University of Michigan, Ann Arbor, 1977.

MEMBER: Association of American Geographers (chairman of Geomorphology Specialty Groups, 1980-81), American Geophysical Union, American Association for the Advancement of Science, American Geomorphological Field Group, American Quaternary Association, Geological Society of America, Council of Graduate Schools of the United States, British Geomorphological Research Group, Midwestern Association of Graduate Schools, Binghamton Geomorphology Symposium (chairman of steering committee, 1979—), Sigma Xi, Phi Kappa Phi.

WRITINGS:

(Contributor) William M. Marsh, editor, *Environmental Analysis,* McGraw, 1978.

(Editor with Donald R. Coates, and contributor) *Thresholds in Geomorphology,* Allen & Unwin, 1980.

(With Robert E. Norris and Keith D. Harries) *Geography: An Introductory Perspective,* with instructor's manual, C. E. Merrill, 1982.

(With J. F. Rooney, Wilbur Zelinsky, and others) *This Remarkable Continent: An Atlas of United States and Canadian Society and Cultures,* Texas A&M University Press, 1982.

(Contributor) C. J. Johannsen and J. L. Sanders, editors, *Remote Sensing for Resource Management,* Soil Conservation Society of America, 1982.

(Editor with J. R. Giardino and J. F. Schroder, Jr., and contributor) *Rock Glaciers,* Allen & Unwin, 1987.

Contributor of about thirty articles to scholarly journals.

WORK IN PROGRESS: Research on freezing and thawing processes and the ways in which they are changing the face of the earth.

SIDELIGHTS: John D. Vitek told *CA* that he welcomes every opportunity to promote his professional development. In the summer he participates in backpacking trips in order to study sites above the treeline in the Colorado Rocky Mountains. He added: "Through writing I have been able to express my ideas about the processes that are shaping the surface of the earth and human interaction with the earth."

W

WAGNER, Gordon Parsons 1915-1987

OBITUARY NOTICE: Born April 13, 1915, in Redondo Beach, Calif.; died of cancer, December 4, 1987, in Los Angeles, Calif. Aerospace engineer, educator, artist, and poet. Wagner is remembered for his assemblages—abstract collections of wood, metal, and other scraps formed into artistic displays. After working as an aerospace engineer until he reached middle age, Wagner devoted his career to his abstract painting and sculpture. Beginning in 1960 he taught painting, drawing, and sculpture at institutions such as Barnsdall Art Center of Los Angeles and Pitzer College. He received more than seventy awards for his art, and his work is represented in more than five hundred public and private collections and museums. Wagner collected some of his lithographs and poems in a book, *Memories of the Future*.

OBITUARIES AND OTHER SOURCES:

BOOKS

Who's Who in American Art, 17th edition, Bowker, 1986.
Who's Who in the West, 17th edition, Marquis, 1980.

PERIODICALS

Los Angeles Times, December 9, 1987.

* * *

WAKEMAN, John 1928-

PERSONAL: Born September 29, 1928, in London, England; son of Fred (a driver) and Edith (a housemaid; maiden name, Mayo) Wakeman; married Hilary Paulett (an Anglican deacon), March 15, 1957; children: Harry, Matthew, Tully, Theo, Rosie. *Education:* London School of Librarianship, A.L.A., 1949; also attended University of East Anglia. *Politics:* Labour.

ADDRESSES: Home and office—32 Grosvenor Rd., Norwich NR2 2PZ, England.

CAREER: Librarian at public libraries in London, England, 1946-57; Brooklyn Public Library, Brooklyn, N.Y., acting director of public relations department, 1957-59; *Wilson Library Bulletin,* New York, N.Y., editor, 1959-61; free-lance editor and writer, 1962—. *Military service:* Royal Air Force, 1947-49.

WRITINGS:

(Editor) *World Authors: 1950-1970,* H. W. Wilson, 1975.
(Editor) *World Authors: 1970-1975,* H. W. Wilson, 1980.
Hopeless Loves and Happy Endings (poems), Midsummer Press, 1981.
No Room for Doubt (poems), Taxus Press, 1985.
(Editor) *World Film Directors,* H. W. Wilson, 1987.
"The Beach Hut" (television screenplay), first broadcast by Anglia Television, 1987.

Contributor to magazines and newspapers, including *Observer, New Statesman, Holiday, Punch,* and *Poetry*. Co-founder and co-editor of *Rialto*.

WORK IN PROGRESS: Poetry and fiction.

* * *

WALKER, Clive (Phillip) 1954-

PERSONAL: Born February 10, 1954, in Hartlepool, England. *Education:* University of Leeds, LL.B., 1975; Victoria University of Manchester, Ph.D., 1982.

ADDRESSES: Office—Department of Law, University of Leeds, Leeds LS2 9JT, England.

CAREER: University of Manchester, Manchester, England, lecturer in law, 1978-82; University of Leeds, Leeds, England, lecturer in law, 1982—. Solicitor.

WRITINGS:

The Data Protection File, Faculty of Law, University of Leeds, 1985.
The Prevention of Terrorism in British Law, Manchester University Press, 1986.

Contributor of articles and reviews to law journals.

WORK IN PROGRESS: Political Violence and the Law in Ireland, with Gerard Hogan, for Manchester University Press.

* * *

WALLACE, Bill
See WALLACE, William Keith

WALLACE, David J. 1954-

PERSONAL: Born November 13, 1954, in Newport Pagnell, Buckinghamshire, England; immigrated to United States, 1983; son of Sidney John (an engineer) and Lillian (a farm worker; maiden name, Green) Wallace; married Rita Copeland (a professor of English), January 21, 1983. *Education:* Attended Universita Italiana per Stranieri, 1974, 1975; University of York, B.A., 1976; St. Edmund's College, Cambridge, Ph.D., 1983. *Religion:* Roman Catholic.

ADDRESSES: Office—Department of English, University of Texas at Austin, Austin, Tex. 78712.

CAREER: University of Leipzig, Leipzig, East Germany, lecturer in English, 1976-77; English teacher at British School in Arona, Italy, 1977-78; Cambridge University, Cambridge, England, assistant director of studies in English and acting librarian of St. Edmund's College,1981-83; Stanford University, Stanford, Calif., Mellon fellow in English, 1984-85; University of Texas at Austin, assistant professor of English, 1985—.

MEMBER: Modern Language Association of America, New Chaucer Society, American Association of University Professors of Italian, American Association for Italian Studies, Mediaeval Academy of America, Renaissance Society of America.

WRITINGS:

(Contributor) Piero Boitani, editor, *Chaucer and the Italian Trecento,* Cambridge University Press, 1983.
(Contributor) Marion Glasscoe, editor, *The Medieval Mystical Tradition in England,* Boydell & Brewer, 1984.
Chaucer and the Early Writings of Boccaccio, D. S. Brewer, 1985.
(Contributor) Piero Boitani and Jill Mann, editors, *The Cambridge Chaucer Companion,* Cambridge University Press, 1986.
(Contributor) A. J. Minnis and A. B. Scott, editors, *Medieval Literary Theory and Criticism, c. 1100-c.1375: The Commentary Tradition,* Oxford University Press, 1988.
(Contributor) Julian Wasserman, editor, *Essays on the Pearl-Poet,* Syracuse University Press, 1989.

Contributor to *The Chaucer Encyclopedia* and *Medieval France: An Encyclopedia*. Contributor of articles, translations, and reviews to periodicals. Editor of special volume on Dante for *Texas Studies in Literature and Language,* 1990.

WORK IN PROGRESS: "'Whan She Translated Was': A Chaucerian Critique of the Petrarchan Academy," to be included in a volume of essays on new historicism, edited by Lee Patterson, University of California Press, 1988; *Chaucer in Florence and Lombardy,* publication expected in 1992.

AVOCATIONAL INTERESTS: Dance, basketball, foreign languages, "avoiding English food."

* * *

WALLACE, William Keith 1947-
(Bill Wallace)

PERSONAL: Born August 1, 1947, in Chickasha, Okla.; son of Keith and Mabel (a math teacher) Wallace; married Carol Ann Priddle (an elementary school teacher); children: Laurie Beth, Amanda Nicole, Justin Keith. *Education:* University of Science and Arts of Oklahoma, B.S., 1971; Southwestern Oklahoma State University, M.S., 1974; also attended University of Oklahoma. *Politics:* Democrat. *Religion:* "First Christian."

ADDRESSES: Home—Rt. 1, P.O. Box 91, Chickasha, Okla. 73018.

CAREER: Former elementary school teacher; West Elementary School, Chickasha, Okla., principal, since 1977, and physical education teacher. Speaker at schools and universities in various states, including State University of New York and University of South Florida.

AWARDS, HONORS: Bluebonnet Award from Texas Association of School Librarians and Children's Round Table and Sequoyah Children's Book Award from Oklahoma State Department of Education, both 1983, Central Missouri State University Award for Excellence in Children's Literature, 1984, and Nebraska Golden Sowers Award from Nebraska Library Association, 1985, all for *A Dog Called Kitty;* Central Missouri State University Award for Excellence in Children's Literature, 1984, and Pine Tree Book Award, 1985, both for *Trapped in Death Cave*.

WRITINGS:

JUVENILES; UNDER NAME BILL WALLACE

A Dog Called Kitty, Holiday House, 1980.
Trapped in Death Cave, Holiday House, 1984.
Shadow on the Snow, Holiday House, 1985.
Ferret in the Bedroom, Lizards in the Fridge, Holiday House, 1986.
Red Dog, Holiday House, 1987.

Contributor to magazines, including *Western Horseman, Horse Lover's,* and *Hunting Dog*.

WORK IN PROGRESS: Ride the Morning Trail, publication expected in 1988; novels.

SIDELIGHTS: William Keith Wallace told *CA:* "I enjoyed reading good fiction to my fourth grade class. One year we had difficulty finding books to keep their attention. Since I had had some luck with articles and short stories I decided to try my hand with a book for them to listen to. When I found how well they liked the stories, I decided to try them with various publishers. *Shadow on the Snow* was the first book I ever wrote for my students, and it was the third to be published. *Trapped in Death Cave* was the second book I wrote for my class, and it was also the second to become a 'real book.' The third story, *A Dog Called Kitty,* was the first one accepted for publication by Holiday House."

AVOCATIONAL INTERESTS: Hunting, fishing.

* * *

WALLERSTEIN, Judith (Hannah) S(aretsky) 1921-

PERSONAL: Born December 27, 1921, in New York, N.Y.; daughter of Samuel and Augusta (Tucker) Saretsky; married Robert S. Wallerstein, January 26, 1947; children: Michael Jonathan, Nina Beth, Amy Lisa. *Education:* Hunter College (now of the City University of New York), B.A. (cum laude), 1943; Columbia University, M.S.W., 1946; further graduate study at Topeka Institute for Psychoanalysis, 1955-61.

ADDRESSES: Office—Department of Social Welfare, University of California, 2120 Oxford St., Berkeley, Calif. 94720.

CAREER: Community Service Society, New York, N.Y., assistant director of Residential Treatment Center, 1945-47;

Menninger Foundation, Topeka, Kan., senior psychiatric social worker and child therapist, 1949-57; University of Kansas, Lawrence, instructor in social work, 1965-66; University of California, Berkeley, lecturer in social welfare, beginning in 1966. Lecturer at University of Amsterdam, 1967, and Paul Baerwald School of Social Welfare, Jerusalem, Israel, 1970. Member of board of directors of Homewood Terrace Adolescent Treatment Center, San Francisco, Calif., 1971-73; senior consultant to Marin County Community Mental Health Center.

MEMBER: Association for Child Psychoanalysis, American Orthopsychiatric Association, National Association of Social Workers.

AWARDS, HONORS: Koshland Award in Social Welfare, 1975.

WRITINGS:

(With Joan Berlin Kelly) *Surviving the Breakup: How Children and Parents Cope With Divorce,* Basic Books, 1980.

Contributor to magazines.

BIOGRAPHICAL/CRITICAL SOURCES:

PERIODICALS

Elementary School Guidance Counselor, October, 1984.
Spectator, December 13, 1980.*

* * *

WALSH, Maurice 1879-1964

BRIEF ENTRY: Born May 2, 1879, in County Kerry, Ireland; died in 1964. Irish novelist. Walsh served as a customs and excise official for more than thirty years, first in the Highlands of Scotland and later in his native Ireland. It was during his service in Ireland in the 1920s, at the time of the Irish Civil War, that he first began to write at length. Forced to remain indoors at night—the activities of snipers made the streets unsafe after dark—and missing his wife and family who had remained in Scotland, Walsh eased his boredom and loneliness by writing about his memories of the Highlands. The resulting novel, *The Key Above the Door* (W. & R. Chambers, 1926), became a best-seller in Great Britain. Encouraged by this success, Walsh quit his job in 1934 and continued to write out of nostalgia for Scotland and a love of the Irish countryside. His later work included the novels *Blackcock's Feather* (W. & R. Chambers, 1932), *Sons of The Swordmaker* (W. & R. Chambers, 1938), *Thomasheen James, Man-of-No-Work* (W. & R. Chambers, 1941; published simultaneously in the United States as *Thomasheen James*), and *Danger Under the Moon* (W. & R. Chambers, 1956), and a successful short story "The Quiet Man" (Angus & Robertson, 1947), which was later produced as a film, shot in Ireland, starring John Wayne and Maureen O'Hara.

BIOGRAPHICAL/CRITICAL SOURCES:

BOOKS

A Biographical Dictionary of Irish Writers, St. Martin's, 1985.
Fennel, Mary, *Maurice Walsh: "Blackcock's Feather,"* Macmillan, 1973.
Twentieth-Century Authors: A Biographical Dictionary of Modern Literature, H. W. Wilson, 1942.

* * *

WALTON, John K(immons) 1948-

PERSONAL: Born November 18, 1948, in Chesterfield, England; son of Eric (a manager) and Nora (Kimmons) Walton. *Education:* Merton College, Oxford, B.A. (with first class honors), 1970; University of Lancaster, Ph.D., 1974. *Politics:* Socialist.

ADDRESSES: Home—Preston, England. *Office*—Department of History, Furness College, University of Lancaster, Lancaster LA1 4YG, England.

CAREER: Teacher of history and geography at a teacher training college in Bishop's Stortford, England, 1973-74; University of Lancaster, Lancaster, England, lecturer, 1974-86, senior lecturer in history, 1986—. Chairman of Bulk Ward Labour party, 1983-84.

MEMBER: Royal Historical Society (fellow), Economic History Society, Social History Society, Friends of the Earth, Greenpeace.

WRITINGS:

The Blackpool Landlady: A Social History, Manchester University Press, 1978.
(With J. D. Marshall) *The Lake Counties From 1830 to the Mid-Twentieth Century,* Manchester University Press, 1981.
The English Seaside Resort: A Social History, Leicester University Press, 1983.
(Editor with James Walvin) *Leisure in Britain, 1780-1939,* Manchester University Press, 1983.
Lancashire: A Social History, 1558-1939, Manchester University Press, 1987.
The Second Reform Act, Methuen, 1987.
National Trust Guide to Britain, 1750-1914, Philip & Son, in press.

Contributor to academic journals. Review editor of *Urban History Yearbook.*

WORK IN PROGRESS: Research on the cooperative movement and on working class diet in Britain.

SIDELIGHTS: John K. Walton told *CA:* "The formative influences on my development as a historian have been James Campbell and Richard Cobb at Oxford University, J. D. Marshall at the University of Lancaster, and E. P. Thompson through the brilliance of his writings. In my work I seek to understand the lives and relationships of ordinary working people as well as those of the elite. To this end I have tried to analyze first the level of the local and specific and, second, the level of the national, general, and theoretical. Thus, my first work concerns the seaside resort of Blackpool and the landladies who let rooms to its working-class holidaymakers, while my current work attempts to generalize about the whole of British society over a crucially important period. I may address the international dimension later. Meanwhile, I continue to study the local and specific by examining the development of the fast food market in late Victorian England and the growth of the cooperative movement, which sought to provide a collectivist alternative to competitive individualist capitalism.

"My research has led me to adopt a skeptical Marxist framework of analysis and to regard with horror the efforts of British Prime Minister Margaret Thatcher, U.S. President Ronald Reagan, and their supporters to exploit and manipulate the disadvantaged and to accelerate the arms race. One of the key lessons of the past, for me, is the immorality of the 'new right.'"

AVOCATIONAL INTERESTS: Walking, architecture.

WARMINGTON, E(ric) H(erbert) 1898-1987

PERSONAL: Born March 15, 1898; died June 8, 1987; son of John Herbert and Maud (Lockhart) Warmington; married Marian Eveline Robertson, 1922; children: one son, two daughters. *Education:* Peterhouse, Cambridge, B.A. (with first class honors), 1922, M.A., 1925.

CAREER: Assistant schoolmaster, 1922-23; master of classics, 1923-25; University of London, London, England, reader in ancient history, 1925-35, professor of classics, 1935-65, professor emeritus, 1966-87, dean of faculty of arts, 1951-56, acting director of Institute of Education, 1957-58, acting master of Birkbeck College, 1950-51, 1965-66, vice-master, 1954-65, vice-president, beginning in 1966, and fellow. *Military service:* British Army, Garrison Artillery and King's Own Yorkshire Light Infantry, 1917-19.

WRITINGS:

Athens: A Picture of a Great Greek City, Benn, 1928.
The Commerce Between the Roman Empire and India, Cambridge University Press, 1928, 2nd edition, Octagon, 1974.
(With Max Cary) *The Ancient Explorers,* Methuen, 1929, revised edition, Penguin, 1963.
Africa in Ancient and Medieval Times, Cambridge University Press, 1936.
A History of Birkbeck College, University of London, During the Second World War, 1939-1945, Birkbeck College, London, 1954.
(Author of revision) *Petronius,* Heinemann, 1969.

Contributor to *Oxford Classical Dictionary*. Contributor of articles and reviews to periodicals.

EDITOR

(Also translator) *Greek Geography,* Dutton, 1934, reprinted, AMS Press, 1973.
(Also translator) *Remains of Old Latin,* Harvard University Press, Volume I: *Ennius, Caecilius,* 1935, Volume II: *Livius Andronicus, Naevius, Pacuvius, Accius,* 1936, Volume III: *Lucilius: Laws of the Twelve Tables,* 1938, Volume IV: *Archaic Inscriptions,* 1940, revised edition, 1965-82.
(With W. H. Semple) Sidonius, *Poems and Letters,* Volume II, Heinemann, 1965.
(With Philip G. Rouse) *Great Dialogues of Plato,* revised edition, New American Library, 1967.

Editor of "Loeb Classical Library," 1937-74; titles include the five-volume *Greek Anthology,* the nine-volume *Works of Josephus,* the three-volume *Scriptores Historiae Augustae,* Plato's *Statesman and Philebus,* Cicero's *De Inventione,* and *Minor Latin Poets.*

AVOCATIONAL INTERESTS: Gardening, natural history, music.

OBITUARIES:

PERIODICALS

Times (London), June 11, 1987.*

* * *

WARREN, Lansing 1894-1987

OBITUARY NOTICE: Born June 17, 1894, in Waukegan, Ill.; died of a heart ailment, November 14, 1987, in Pasadena, Calif. Journalist. After spending two years in France during World War I as an ambulance driver, Warren served as news editor "and practically the whole editorial staff," according to Warren's *New York Times* obituary, of the *Watsonville Register* in California. He also worked for other California newspapers before joining the Paris bureau of the *New York Times* in 1926. Warren was a correspondent in Switzerland, Italy, and Spain, and he helped break the story of former French Prime Minister Pierre Laval's arrest on December 13, 1940. Warren and his wife, along with several other Americans, were arrested by the Nazis in 1942 and held captive for sixteen months. For his service to France, the French Government awarded him the Croix de Chevalier of the Legion of Honor in 1955.

OBITUARIES AND OTHER SOURCES:

PERIODICALS

New York Times, November 18, 1987.

* * *

WATERFIELD, Gordon 1903-1987

OBITUARY NOTICE—See index for CA sketch: Born May 24, 1903, in Canterbury, Kent, England; died December 17, 1987. Editor, journalist, and author. Waterfield spent more than thirty-five years as a correspondent in Europe, Africa, and Asia and wrote about his adventures and observations in numerous articles and books. He began his journalism career with the *Egyptian Gazette* in 1926 and later wrote extensively for Reuters News Agency and the British Broadcasting Corporation, for which he headed the Eastern and Arabic services at different times. Waterfield was the author of *Lucie Duff Gordon in England, South Africa, and Egypt,* a biography of his great-grandmother, and he also edited a collection of her letters. His other writings include two volumes of memoirs titled *What Happened to France* and *Morning Will Come,* numerous biographies, such as *Layard of Ninevah* and *Professional Diplomat,* and *Egypt.* In 1963 he was named a member of the Order of the British Empire.

OBITUARIES AND OTHER SOURCES:

BOOKS

International Authors and Writers Who's Who, 10th edition, International Biographical Centre, 1986.

PERIODICALS

Times (London), December 18, 1987.

* * *

WEBB, Michael (Dennis Puzey) 1937-

PERSONAL: Born July 12, 1937, in London, England; immigrated to United States, 1969, naturalized citizen, 1973; son of John Puzey (an insurance executive) and Daisy (an artist; maiden name, Pocock) Webb; married B. J. Van Damme (a public relations consultant), 1972 (divorced). *Education:* London School of Economics and Political Science, London, B.Sc. (with honors), 1959.

ADDRESSES: Home—Los Angeles, Calif. *Agent*—Michael Hamilburg, Mitchell Hamilburg Agency, 292 South La Cienega Blvd., Suite 212, Beverly Hills, Calif. 90211.

CAREER: Times, London, England, correspondent, 1959-62; *Country Life,* London, assistant editor, 1962-65; British Film Institute, London, programming manager, 1965-69; American

Film Institute, Washington, D.C., and Los Angeles, Calif., director of national film programming, 1969-80; free-lance writer, producer, and arts consultant, 1980—.

AWARDS, HONORS: Chevalier de l'Ordre des Arts et des Lettres, 1978; Emmy nomination, 1986, for "Hollywood: The Greatest Story Ever Sold."

WRITINGS:

Architecture in Britain Today, Country Life, 1969.
The Magic of Neon, Peregrine Smith, 1983, revised edition, 1987.
Las Vegas Access Guide, Access Press, 1985.
(And co-producer) "The Movie Palaces" (documentary film), released by Smithsonian Institution, 1985.
(And co-producer) "Hollywood: The Greatest Story Ever Sold," first broadcast by KTLA-TV, 1985.
Hollywood: Legend and Reality (Literary Guild selection), Little, Brown, 1986.
Happy Birthday, Hollywood, Motion Picture and Television Fund, 1987.
Los Angeles Access Guide, Access Press, 1987.

Contributor of articles and photographs to magazines, including *America Illustrated, Architectural Digest, Design Quarterly, Historic Preservation, LA Style, Smithsonian, Travel and Leisure,* and *Museum News*. West Coast editor of *Restaurant and Hotel Design;* past contributing editor of *Arts and Architecture*.

WORK IN PROGRESS: A book on the image of the city in films; a book on city squares.

SIDELIGHTS: For the past several years, Michael Webb has worked as a free-lance writer, producer, and arts consultant. He is the guest curator of the critically acclaimed Smithsonian exhibition "Hollywood: Legend and Reality," for which he wrote the companion book. Webb's color photographs have appeared in two of his books and have been published in leading American magazines, including *Time*. A Smithsonian exhibition of his neon photographs has enjoyed wide circulation.

* * *

WEBER, Simon 1910(?)-1987

OBITUARY NOTICE: Born c. 1910; died of a lung ailment (one source says complications from a back injury), December 1, 1987, in New York, N.Y. Journalist. Simon, a Polish emigrant, was editor of the Yiddish-language newspaper *Forward*. He worked for the New York publication for more than forty-five years, beginning as a reporter and retiring in 1986 as top editor. In addition to preserving the Yiddish language and culture, the *Forward* has published the writings of Nobel Prize-winner Isaac Bashevis Singer.

OBITUARIES AND OTHER SOURCES:

PERIODICALS

Los Angeles Times, December 4, 1987.
Washington Post, December 4, 1987.

* * *

WEDGWOOD, Pamela
See TUDOR-CRAIG, Pamela

WEEKES, Mark Kinkead
See KINKEAD-WEEKES, Mark

* * *

WELFARE, Humphrey 1950-

PERSONAL: Born September 25, 1950, in Melbourn, England; son of Kenneth William (a county court registrar) and Patience (a social worker and justice of the peace; maiden name, Ross) Welfare; married Nicola Woods (a teacher), July 15, 1972; children: Rebecca, William, Philippa. *Education:* University of Newcastle upon Tyne, B.A. (with first class honors), 1972, M.Phil., 1974.

ADDRESSES: Home—45 Kenton Rd., Newcastle upon Tyne NE3 4NH, England. *Office*—Royal Commission on the Historical Monuments of England, University of Newcastle upon Tyne, Newcastle upon Tyne NE1 7RU, England.

CAREER: Royal Commission on the Ancient and Historical Monuments of Scotland, Edinburgh, investigator in prehistoric archaeology, 1974-78; Royal Commission on the Historical Monuments of England, archaeological investigator in Salisbury, 1978-83, and Newcastle upon Tyne, 1983—. Director of Cambrook Woods Ltd.

MEMBER: Society of Antiquaries of Scotland (fellow), Institute of Field Archaeologists.

WRITINGS:

(With Richard Muir) *The National Trust Guide to Prehistoric and Roman Britain,* George Philip, 1983.
Wessex, Collins Willow, 1984.
The National Trust Historical Atlas, George Philip, in press.

Contributor to scholarly journals.

WORK IN PROGRESS: "The Prehistoric, Roman, and Medieval Archaeology," to be included in *The Buildings of England: Northumberland,* edited by Elizabeth Williamson, publication by Penguin Books expected in 1990.

SIDELIGHTS: Humphrey Welfare told *CA:* "The intensive weekday involvement in the academic recording of Britain's archaeological heritage provides a contrast to the equally demanding, spare-time task of interpreting that archaeology for a more popular market. Wider public awareness and deeper understanding will pay dividends in a longer-term commitment to conservation. Part of this work is motivated by a desire to raise consciousness from the specific 'visitable' site to the fragile survival of extensive historic landscapes. My own research centers on the native iron-age peoples of northern England and Scotland, and on their reaction to the Roman invasion and occupation. From nine to five, however, specialization has to give way to the work of a 'general practitioner.' The thrill lies not only in the transmission of original knowledge and ideas but also in the recognition of ancient monuments never before recorded. Upland Britain is full of them. Each one has to be fitted into the jigsaw puzzle of our current hypotheses—although more often than not the new piece changes the shape of the puzzle itself. Paradoxically, 'heritage' is a key activity for the future of Britain: tourism is one of the United Kingdom's biggest industries. The future looks good; nevertheless, for me it is the prediction of the past that is easier."

WEST, Anthony (Panther) 1914-1987

OBITUARY NOTICE—See index for *CA* sketch: Born August 4 (one source says August 5), 1914, in Hunstanton, Norfolk, England; died after suffering a stroke, December 27, 1987, in Stonington, Conn. Journalist and author. West, the illegitimate son of writers H. G. Wells and Rebecca West, wrote essays and book reviews for magazines such as *New Yorker* as well as a frank and revealing biography of his father titled *H. G. Wells: Aspects of a Life*. He earned praise for his intelligent, witty, and incisive prose style in both fiction and nonfiction works. In addition, West wrote several novels, including *On a Dark Night, Another Kind, The Trend Is Up,* and the semi-autobiographical *Heritage*. His critical writings include a biography of writer D. H. Lawrence and the essay and review collection *Principles and Persuasions*.

OBITUARIES AND OTHER SOURCES:

BOOKS

Who's Who, 139th edition, St. Martin's, 1987.

PERIODICALS

Newsweek, January 11, 1988.
New York Times, December 28, 1987.
Times (London), December 29, 1987.
Washington Post, December 29, 1987.

* * *

WEST, Thomas R(eed) 1936-

PERSONAL: Born August 4, 1936, in Washington, D.C. *Education:* Princeton University, B.A., 1958; Columbia University, M.A., 1959, Ph.D., 1965.

ADDRESSES: Office—Department of History, Catholic University of America, Washington, D.C. 20064.

CAREER: Michigan State University, East Lansing, assistant professor of American thought and language, 1965-66; Catholic University of America, Washington, D.C., assistant professor, 1966-72, associate professor of American history, 1972—.

MEMBER: American Historical Association.

WRITINGS:

Flesh of Steel: Literature and the Machine in American Culture, Vanderbilt University Press, 1967.
(With David Burner and Robert D. Marcus) *A Giant's Strength: America in the 1960s,* Holt, 1971.
Nature, Community, and Will: A Study in Literary and Social Thought, University of Missouri Press, 1976.
(With Burner) *The Torch Is Passed: The Kennedy Brothers and American Liberalism,* Atheneum, 1984.

BIOGRAPHICAL/CRITICAL SOURCES:

PERIODICALS

American Historical Review, April, 1968.
Los Angeles Times, August 20, 1984.*

* * *

WHEATCROFT, Geoffrey 1945-

PERSONAL: Born December 23, 1945, in London, England; son of Stephen (an economist) and Joyce (a social worker; maiden name, Reed) Wheatcroft. *Education:* New College, Oxford, M.A. (with second class honors), 1968.

ADDRESSES: Office—Sunday Telegraph, 181 Marsh Wall, London E14 9SR, England. *Agent*—Anthony Sheil Associates, 43 Doughty St., London WC1N 2LF, England; Wallace & Sheil Agency Inc., 177 East 70th St., New York, N.Y. 10021.

CAREER: Hamish Hamilton Ltd. (publisher), production assistant and publicity manager, 1968-70; Michael Joseph Ltd. (publisher), editor, 1971-73; Cassell & Co. (publisher), editor, 1974-75; *Spectator* (periodical), assistant editor, 1974-75, literary editor, 1977-81; free-lance journalist, 1981-85; *Evening Standard* (newspaper), editor of "Londoner's Diary," 1985-86; *Daily Telegraph* and *Sunday Telegraph* (newspapers), London, England, columnist, 1986—.

MEMBER: National Union of Journalists, Garrick Club, Beefsteak Club.

WRITINGS:

The Randlords, Weidenfeld & Nicolson, 1985, Atheneum, 1986.

Contributor to periodicals, including *Harper's, New York Times, New Republic, Spectator, Tatler,* and *Field*.

WORK IN PROGRESS: History of the Wagner family of Bayreuth, West Germany, descendants of composer Richard Wagner.

SIDELIGHTS: In *The Randlords,* Geoffrey Wheatcroft discusses the small group of men who became powerful millionaires when the diamond and gold fields of present-day South Africa were discovered in the late nineteenth century. The book's title alludes to Witwatersrand, an area near Johannesburg that became famous for its extensive deposits of gold ore. Much of the volume is devoted to portraits of the individual Randlords, which Bernard A. Weisberger in *Washington Post Book World* praised for their excellence. One unusual tycoon was Barney Bernato, an undistinguished stage performer and son of a London pub owner, who made fortunes in both diamonds and gold only to go insane and commit suicide. Another, J. B. Robinson, was so widely hated that when the British government announced its intention to grant him a title of nobility, he was denounced by noblemen in the House of Lords until he withdrew his name from consideration. Cecil Rhodes, whom *New York Times Book Review* contributor J. A. Livingston called "the central character in the book," was a ferociously ambitious man who believed in the superiority of the British Empire and the white race. He used the influence he acquired as a diamond magnate to build a political career in the British Cape Colony at the southern tip of Africa, where he helped to create a system of legal discrimination against blacks and strove to extend the influence of Great Britain throughout the region. He even tried to draw the British government into war against the neighboring white-dominated republics of Transvaal and the Orange Free State, for which he was censured by a committee of the British House of Commons.

Wheatcroft also explains the economic and technological factors that drove out small miners and brought the Randlords into existence—"complex subjects, which [he] handles with skill," wrote David Welsh in the *Times Literary Supplement*. As the author explains, the vast quantities of diamonds that could be mined favored the rise of a few powerful mine owners who could work together to limit the world's diamond supply and so maintain high prices. South African gold was too deeply buried and of too low a quality to be mined on a small scale,

and so the industry quickly became dominated by the few who could get access to large amounts of money from European investors.

A number of critics were pleased at Wheatcroft's skill in tracing many of the racist practices of contemporary South Africa to the nineteenth-century mining boom. As James North noted in *New Republic,* Wheatcroft "successfully explodes one of the South African government's major rationales" for its system of racial segregation and discrimination—that black and white have never been able to co-exist peacefully in southern Africa. Instead, as North quotes him, "until the middle of the [19th] century black and white had largely ignored each other. What contact there had been was, despite intermittent wars, often amicable and co-operative."

Wheatcroft suggests that race relations permanently worsened when the mining magnates realized that they could maximize their profits through cruelly cheap labor. The black population, who had lived outside the white-controlled mining economy as independent farmers and hunters, were driven into the labor market through a series of racially motivated laws. Black farmers were deprived of the legal title to their land. Men such as Cecil Rhodes supported tax laws that essentially compelled such unemployed blacks to hire themselves to whites in order to earn the money to pay their assessments. Rhodes also sponsored the Master and Servant Bill, giving whites the right to beat their black servants.

Reviewers' reactions to *The Randlords* were generally favorable. Welsh echoed the comments of several critics when he observed that the book has "a freshness and verve that make [it] eminently readable." *The Randlords* "has no pretensions to being scholarly," Welsh added, "but the author has steeped himself in the academic literature and also delved into archival sources." North wished that Wheatcroft had spent a larger proportion of the book discussing the plight of South African blacks, writing that the author "has most of the information, but his treatment is regrettably brief." But John Gross of the *New York Times* thought that although Wheatcroft "refrains from obvious moralizing," he "brings home sharply the human toll exacted by the Randlords' success, and the sorry part they played in shaping South Africa's subsequent history."

Wheatcroft told *CA:* "I am based in London, but I have some experience of traveling in Africa and reporting from there for sundry papers. I have written widely as a journalist on politics and social issues in various countries, as well as on travel, music, sport, food, and wine."

BIOGRAPHICAL/CRITICAL SOURCES:

PERIODICALS

New Republic, May 19, 1986.
New York Review of Books, July 17, 1986.
New York Times, March 4, 1986.
New York Times Book Review, March 30, 1986.
Spectator, August 10, 1985.
Times (London), August 11, 1985.
Times Literary Supplement, October 25, 1985.
Washington Post Book World, June 1, 1986.

* * *

WHEELOCK, Frederic M(elvin) 1902-1987

OBITUARY NOTICE—See index for *CA* sketch: Born September 19, 1902, in Lawrence, Mass.; died of a heart attack, October 29, 1987, in Sharon, Conn. Educator and author. For more than forty years Wheelock taught Latin and classics at institutions such as Haverford College, City College (now of the City University of New York), and University of Toledo, and he wrote several books in his field. *Latin: An Introductory Course Based on Ancient Authors* is his textbook, written with a humanistic emphasis, and his later works include *Latin Literature: A Book of Readings* and *Quintilian as Educator*.

OBITUARIES AND OTHER SOURCES:

BOOKS

Directory of American Scholars, Volume III: *Foreign Languages, Linguistics, and Philology,* 8th edition, Bowker, 1982.

PERIODICALS

New York Times, November 10, 1987.

* * *

WHITAKER, Peter 1952-

PERSONAL: Born June 9, 1952, in Cambridge, England; children: Thomas, Joseph. *Education:* Oxford University, B.A., 1973, D.Phil, 1979; attended University of Berlin, 1974-75; attended University of Hamburg, 1976-78; attended University of London, 1987—.

ADDRESSES: c/o Worcester College, Oxford, Oxford, England.

CAREER: Longdean School and Hemel Hempstead School, Hemel Hempstead, England, teacher of German, French, and general studies, 1978-82; Free-lance translator, 1982—. Union representative, 1986-87.

MEMBER: National Association of Schoolmasters/Union of Women Teachers, British Psychological Society, Association of Educational Psychologists.

WRITINGS:

Brecht's Poetry: A Critical Study, Oxford University Press, 1985.

WORK IN PROGRESS: Poems; translations and research on Heine, Hoelderlin, Brecht, and Biermann.

SIDELIGHTS: Peter Whitaker told *CA:* "I write out of curiosity, out of pain and anger, and always for fun."

BIOGRAPHICAL/CRITICAL SOURCES:

PERIODICALS

Times Literary Supplement, October 3, 1986.

* * *

WHITE, Benton R. 1949-

PERSONAL: Born November 15, 1949, in Houston, Tex.; son of Bowden B. and Nadine (Duffey) White; married Christine Schultz (a college history instructor), June 1, 1985. *Education:* Texas Christian University, B.A., 1972, Ph.D., 1984.

ADDRESSES: Home—320 Quitman, Pittsburg, Tex. 75686. *Office*—Northeast Texas Community College, P.O. Box 1307, Mt. Pleasant, Tex. 75455.

CAREER: Northeast Texas Community College, Mt. Pleasant, instructor in history, 1985—.

MEMBER: Western Writers of America, West Texas Historical Association.

WRITINGS:

The Forgotten Cattle King, Texas A&M University Press, 1986.

WORK IN PROGRESS: Now the Wolf Comes, "a story of the Creek Indians' desperate flight to safety during the American Civil War."

SIDELIGHTS: Benton R. White told *CA:* "I am intrigued with the themes of man in crisis and man against the odds. Life-or-death drama has a way of bringing out the best and worst of human nature. It also makes for a gripping story."

* * *

WHITE, John H(enry) 1945-

PERSONAL: Born March 18, 1945, in Lexington, N.C.; son of Reid Ross and Ruby Mae (Leverette) White; married Emily Lee Miller, May 29, 1966; children: Deborah, Angela, Ruby, John Henry. *Education:* Central Piedmont Community College, A.A.S., 1966. *Religion:* African Methodist Episcopalian.

ADDRESSES: Home—623 East 33rd Pl., Chicago, Ill. 60616. *Office*—Chicago *Sun-Times,* 401 North Wabash Ave., Chicago, Ill. 60611.

CAREER/WRITINGS: Tom Walters Photography, Charlotte, N.C., photographic laboratory technician, 1968-69; *Chicago Daily News,* Chicago, Ill., press photographer, 1969-78; Chicago *Sun-Times,* Chicago, press photographer, 1978—. Volunteer photography teacher at South Side Art Center, Chicago, 1970—; instructor at Columbia College, Chicago, 1978—. Photographer for film "Young, Gifted, and Black," 1971. Member of board of trustees of Bishop William J. Walls Foundation, Yonkers, N.Y. *Military service:* U.S. Marine Corps, photographer, 1966-68.

MEMBER: National Press Photographers Association, Illinois Press Photographers Association, Chicago Press Photographers Association (president, 1977-78; member of board of directors), Chicago Association of Black Journalists.

AWARDS, HONORS: More than two hundred photography awards, including winner of National Press Photography Contest, 1970, World Press Photography Contest, 1971, and National Fire Fighters Contest and National Construction Contest, 1972; photographer of the year awards from Illinois Press Photographers Association, 1971, 1979, and 1982, and Chicago Press Photographers Association, 1972, 1973, 1975, and 1979; Poy Feature Picture Story Award, 1975; Marshall Field Award, 1976; Pulitzer Prize for feature photography, 1982.*

* * *

WHITE, Walter
See WHITE, Walter F(rancis)

* * *

WHITE, Walter F(rancis) 1893-1955
(Walter White)

PERSONAL: Born July 1, 1893, in Atlanta, Ga.; died of a heart attack, March 21, 1955, in New York, N.Y.; son of George (a postal worker) and Madeline (a teacher; maiden name, Harrison) White; married Leah Gladys Powell (a secretary), February 15, 1922 (divorced in 1949); married Poppy Cannon, July 6, 1949; children: (first marriage) Jane, Walter Carl Darrow. *Education:* Atlanta University, B.A., 1916; graduate study at College of the City of New York (now City College of the City University of New York). *Politics:* Democrat. *Religion:* Congregational.

CAREER: Insurance salesman in Atlanta, Ga., 1916-18; National Association for the Advancement of Colored People (NAACP), New York City, assistant secretary, 1918-29, acting secretary, 1929-30, secretary, 1931-55. War correspondent for *New York Post* in European, Mediterranean, Middle East, and Pacific theaters, 1943-45; columnist for newspapers, including *Chicago Defender* and Sunday *Herald Tribune.* Delegate to Second Pan-African Congress, 1921; member of advisory council for the Government of the Virgin Islands, 1934-35; member of governor's committee on the constitutional convention in New York state, 1938; member of executive committee of National Committee for Prevention and Control of Juvenile Delinquency, 1947, and of National Health Assembly, 1948; member of New York mayor's advisory committee on atomic education and committee for commemoration of the golden anniversary of New York, both 1948; member of American Committee on Economic Policy. Consultant to U.S. presidents, including Franklin D. Roosevelt and Harry S. Truman, to United Nations (U.N.) Conference on International Organizations, 1945, and to U.S. delegation to U.N. General Assembly, Paris, France, 1948. Member of board of visitors of New York State Training School for Boys, 1933.

MEMBER: P.E.N. (American Center).

AWARDS, HONORS: Guggenheim fellowship, 1927-28; award for literature from Harmon Foundation, 1929; Spingarn Medal from NAACP, 1937; Sir James Jeans Award from New London Junior College, 1943; Order of Honor and Merit (Haiti), 1950; Star of Ethiopia, 1953; LL.D. from Howard University, 1939, and Atlanta University, 1943.

WRITINGS:

The Fire in the Flint (novel), Knopf, 1924, reprinted, Negro Universities Press, 1969.

(Under name Walter White) *Flight* (novel), Knopf, 1926, reprinted, Negro Universities Press, 1969.

(Under name Walter White) *Rope and Faggot: A Biography of Judge Lynch,* Knopf, 1929, reprinted, Arno Press, 1969.

(Under name Walter White, with Thurgood Marshall) *What Caused the Detroit Riot?* National Association for the Advancement of Colored People, 1943.

(Under name Walter White) *A Rising Wind* (essays), Doubleday, Doran & Co., 1945, reprinted, Negro Universities Press, 1971.

(Under name Walter White) *A Man Called White: The Autobiography of Walter White,* Viking, 1948.

How Far the Promised Land? Viking, 1955.

Contributor to periodicals.

SIDELIGHTS: Walter F. White, who worked for the National Association for the Advancement of Colored People (NAACP) for more than thirty years, was "probably the most stentorian advocate of the Negro's rights" in the United States, commented E. J. Kahn, Jr., in a 1948 *New Yorker* profile. Less than one-quarter Negro by blood, White had light skin, blue eyes, and blond hair but chose to remain in black society, in which he had grown up. He was able to cross the color line at will and frequently posed as a white to gather information in his fight against lynching, segregation, and other discrim-

ination. "The ranking Negro diplomat," according to Kahn, White was "one of the ablest lobbyists in the Capital." His findings and achievements became the basis of several fiction and nonfiction books.

In his first ten years with the NAACP White investigated lynchings in the guise of a white reporter, gathering eyewitness accounts of more than forty incidents of mob violence and putting the information to use in his books. Observed Kahn: White "could gain the confidence of Southern Negroes because he had been conditioned by a boyhood in the colored section of Atlanta [Georgia]. He could hobnob with Southern whites because of his outward resemblance to them and because of a genuine Georgia accent that precluded their suspecting him of being a prying agitator from up North." The evidence he uncovered suggested, as he wrote in *Rope and Faggot: A Biography of Judge Lynch,* that such violence had become "an almost integral part of our national folkways." White traced the origins of lynching to economics—a Southern attempt to put blacks back in their place as industrialization began to make slavery unnecessary—and to intolerance by religious fundamentalists. Writing for the *New York Times Book Review,* Florence Finch Kelly deemed *Rope and Faggot* "a challenge to national self-complacency" and commended its "searching analysis" of the causes of mob violence. In his novel *The Fire in the Flint* White presented another aspect of the subject, showing how the lynching of his brother rouses a complacent black doctor to active opposition of racism. A *New York Times Book Review* critic called it "an inevitable novel [that] deserves serious consideration."

Later in his career, especially after he became secretary of the NAACP, White addressed other concerns in his work and writings, notably discrimination in the armed forces, education, employment, and the arts. His book *A Rising Wind* discusses the conditions of black soldiers abroad during World War II, including their limited participation in active combat. White points out that dangerous combat situations cause race barriers to drop and that black soldiers returning home "will not be content to return to the old way of life in the post-war era," noted *New York Times Book Review* writer John Desmond. White's "reasoned and reserved contribution" to the challenge of improving race relations "deserves to be read," asserted Desmond.

A Man Called White and *How Far the Promised Land?* describe many of the efforts by White and the NAACP to improve conditions for blacks. White spoke personally with congressmen, senators, and presidents, urging them to promote legislation that would uphold and extend black rights, became involved in legal cases addressing discrimination, and lectured extensively to raise public awareness. In his autobiography, *A Man Called White,* he revealed the atrocities against blacks that he witnessed while growing up in black society as well as the progress that has been made. Remarked a *Times Literary Supplement* reviewer, White's autobiography "gains a great deal from being the story of a man who has seen both sides of the fence that separates the two 'races' in America, and who has been able to use his physical characteristics to further his work for the coming of a day when the passions, hatred, crimes and follies associated with 'race' will seem like a morbid memory." Morroe Berger, writing for the *New York Times Book Review,* deemed it "more than personal history" also. "It is part of the history of twentieth century America, a vivid account of the efforts to save democracy by widening its scope and securing its benefits to an increasing number of Americans." Summing up the posthumously published *How Far the Promised Land?,* Gerald W. Johnson wrote in the *New York Times Book Review:* "If there were no other reason this book would command attention as the last word of a man who was cast in the truly heroic mold. But there is another and even better reason—the book is a careful account by a close observer of one of the most remarkable achievements in human history, the rise of the American Negro."

White's accomplishments reflected what Kahn termed his "penchant for taking resolute action," his belief in making a "frontal attack" on discrimination of all kinds. Using lectures, political pressure, and his writings as weapons, he oversaw part of the fight in which "former chattels have climbed almost to the rank of first-class citizens, as far as the law is concerned," wrote Johnson. White's life stands as testimony to what can be achieved "in the tradition of militant democracy, seeking to enforce existing laws which promise equality and to secure further legislation in protection of the civil rights of all," affirmed Berger.

BIOGRAPHICAL/CRITICAL SOURCES:

BOOKS

Cannon, Poppy, *A Gentle Knight: My Husband, Walter White,* Rinehart, 1956.

Twentieth-Century Literary Criticism, Volume 15, Gale, 1985.

Waldron, Edward E., *Walter White and the Harlem Renaissance,* Kennikat Press, 1978.

White, Walter, *Rope and Faggot: A Biography of Judge Lynch,* Knopf, 1929, reprinted, Arno Press, 1969.

White, Walter, *A Man Called White: The Autobiography of Walter White,* Viking, 1948.

PERIODICALS

Commonweal, November 5, 1948.

New Yorker, September 4, 1948, September 11, 1948.

New York Times Book Review, September 14, 1924, April 11, 1926, May 12, 1929, March 4, 1945, September 26, 1948, November 6, 1955.

Times Literary Supplement, December 9, 1926, October 17, 1929, May 27, 1949.*

—*Sketch by Polly A. Vedder*

* * *

WHITEHEAD, William Grant 1943-1987

OBITUARY NOTICE: Born September 19, 1943, in Wilmington, N.C.; died of complications of acquired immune deficiency syndrome (AIDS), October 9, 1987, in Manhattan, N.Y. Publisher and editor. Whitehead, winner of the 1985 Carey-Thomas award for distinguished publishing, was senior editor of Macmillan Publishing Company beginning in 1985. Prior to joining Macmillan he held such positions as editor in chief of Dutton, where he created the popular Obelisk line of paperback reprints, and senior editor at Doubleday & Company.

OBITUARIES AND OTHER SOURCES:

BOOKS

Who's Who in America, 44th edition, Marquis, 1986.

PERIODICALS

New York Times, October 10, 1987.

Publishers Weekly, October 23, 1987.

WICKER, Ireene 1905(?)-1987

OBITUARY NOTICE—See index for *CA* sketch: Name originally Irene Seaton; surname became Hammer following second marriage; born November 24, 1905 (some sources indicate 1900 or 1901), in Quincy, Ill.; died November 17 (one source says November 16), 1987, in West Palm Beach, Fla. Broadcasting personality, scriptwriter, and author of juvenile literature. Wicker gained notoriety as a storyteller on radio and television between 1930 and 1975. Popularly known as the "Lady With a Thousand Voices," she starred in "The Singing Story Lady" show, which became one of radio's most successful programs and eventually prospered on television. Wicker provided all the voices for the show's characters, and she occasionally wrote the stories she performed—several of which later became books or sound recordings for children.

Early in her career Wicker was featured in the radio soap operas "Today's Children" and "Harold Teen"—a favorite with teenagers—and during the 1930s and 1940s she produced a weekly series called "The Ireene Wicker Musical Plays" in which she dramatized operas and folk legends with guest performers, such as Don Ameche, John Houseman, and Agnes Moorehead. The recipient of at least thirty awards, including the prestigious George Foster Peabody Award for lifetime achievement, Wicker also devoted much effort to eliminating violence from broadcasting. In the early 1950s she and well-known stripteaser Gypsy Rose Lee were wrongly accused of being Communist sympathizers, and charges were soon dismissed. Wicker published a number of works for children, including *The Singing Lady's Favorite Stories, Young Master Artists: Boyhoods of Famous Artists, Children's Stories of Famous Composers and Artists,* and *The Legend of the Christmas Rose.*

OBITUARIES AND OTHER SOURCES:

BOOKS

Who's Who in America, 42nd edition, Marquis, 1982.

PERIODICALS

Chicago Tribune, November 20, 1987.
Los Angeles Times, November 19, 1987.
New York Times, November 18, 1987.

* * *

WILBERT, Johannes 1927-

PERSONAL: Born June 23, 1927, in Cologne, Germany; married in 1955; children: two. *Education:* University of Cologne, B.S., 1951, Ph.D., 1955.

ADDRESSES: Home—15300 Whitfield Ave., Pacific Palisades, Calif. 90272. *Office*—Department of Anthropology, University of California, 405 Hilgard Ave., Los Angeles, Calif. 90024.

CAREER: University of Birmingham, Birmingham, England, lecturer in languages, 1951-52; University of California, Los Angeles, began as instructor, became professor of anthropology, 1963—, director of anthropology at LaSalle Foundation for Natural Sciences and director of Latin American Center, 1963-74.

WRITINGS:

(With Miguel Layrisse) *El antigeno del sistema sanguineo Diego,* Fundacion Creole, 1960.

(Editor) *The Evolution of Horticultural Systems in Native South America: Causes and Consequences,* Sociedad de Ciencias Naturales La Salle, 1961.

Indios de la region Orinoco-Ventuari, Fundacion La Salle de Ciencias Naturales, 1963.

Warao Oral Literature, Editorial Sucre, 1964.

Material linguistico Ye, Editorial Sucre, 1964.

(With Layrisse) *Indian Societies of Venezuela: Their Blood Group Types,* Editorial Sucre, 1966.

(Editor) *Textos folkloricos de los indios waraos,* Latin American Center, University of California, Los Angeles, 1969.

(Editor) *Folk Literature of the Warao Indians: Narrative Material and Motif Content,* Latin American Center, University of California, Los Angeles, 1970.

Survivors of El Dorado: Four Indian Cultures of South America, Praeger, 1972.

Yupa Folktales, Latin American Center, University of California, Los Angeles, 1974.

The Thread of Life: Symbolism of Miniature Art From Ecuador, Dumbarton Oaks, 1974.

(Editor) Martin Gusinde, *Folk Literature of the Selknam Indians: Martin Gusinde's Collection of Selknam Narratives,* Latin American Center, University of California, Los Angeles, 1975.

Warao Basketry: Form and Function, Museum of Cultural History, University of California, Los Angeles, 1975.

(Editor) *Enculturation in Latin America: An Anthology,* Latin American Center, University of California, Los Angeles, 1976, new edition, 1979.

(Editor) Gusinde, *Folk Literature of the Yamana Indians: Martin Gusinde's Collection of Yamana Narratives,* University of California Press, 1977.

(Editor) *Folk Literature of the Ge Indians,* Latin American Center, University of California, Los Angeles, Volume I, 1978, Volume II (with Karin Simoneau), 1984.

(Editor with Layrisse) *Demographic and Biological Studies of the Warao Indians,* Latin American Center, University of California, Los Angeles, 1980.

(Editor with Robert A. Hill) Rex Nettleford, *Caribbean Cultural Identity: The Case of Jamaica,* Latin American Center, University of California, Los Angeles, 1980.

Folk Literature of the Toba Indians, Latin American Center, University of California, Los Angeles, 1982.

(Editor with Karin Simoneau) *Folk Literature of the Mataco Indians,* Latin American Center, University of California, Los Angeles, 1982.

(Editor with Simoneau) *Folk Literature of the Bororo Indians,* Latin American Center, University of California, Los Angeles, 1983.

(With Simoneau) *Folk Literature of the Tehuelche Indians,* Latin American Center, University of California, Los Angeles, 1984.

(Editor with Simoneau) *Folk Literature of the Chorote Indians,* Latin American Center, University of California, Los Angeles, 1985.

Also author of *Zur Kenntnis der Yabarana,* 1959. Contributor to anthropology journals. Editor of *Antropologica.**

* * *

WILKIN, Eloise (Burns) 1904-1987

PERSONAL: Born March 30, 1904, in Rochester, N.Y.; died of cardiac arrest following surgery for cancer, October 4, 1987, in Rochester, N.Y.; married; children: Sidney, Jeremy, Deb-

orah Wilkin Springett, Ann Wilkin Murphy. *Education:* Studied art at Mechanics Institute (now Rochester Institute of Technology).

ADDRESSES: Home—504 Surburban Ct., Rochester, N.Y. 14620.

CAREER: Free-lance artist, doll designer, illustrator, and writer. Work exhibited in 1982 at Hartnett Gallery, Rochester, N.Y.

AWARDS, HONORS: New York Herald Tribune Spring Book Festival Award honor, 1940, for *A Good House for a Mouse,* and 1950, for *The Tune Is in the Tree;* lithograph "Lilybet" received Ewald Eisenhardt Memorial Merit Award for excellence in printmaking, 1944; *The Boy With a Drum* and *I Hear: Sounds in a Child's World* were each named children's book of the year by Child Study Association of America.

WRITINGS:

JUVENILE; SELF-ILLUSTRATED

Song of Praise, American Heritage Press, 1970.
The Baby Book, Golden Press, 1973.
Baby's Mother Goose, Golden Press, 1973.
Baby's Christmas, Random House, 1980.
How Big Is Baby? Golden Press, 1980.
Baby Listens, Golden Press, 1981.
Baby Looks, Golden Press, 1981.
Four Baby's First Golden Books, Golden Press, 1981.
The Little Book, Golden Press, 1981.
My Goodnight Book, Golden Press, 1981.
Rock-a-Bye Baby: Nursery Songs and Cradle Games, Random House, 1981.
My Good Morning Book, Golden Press, 1983.
Baby's Bedtime, Grosset, 1985.
Baby's House, Grosset, 1985.
Baby's Playground, Grosset, 1985.
Baby's Toys, Grosset, 1985.
The Eloise Wilkin Treasury: Favorite Nursery Rhymes, Poems, and Stories, edited by Linda C. Falken, Golden Books, 1985.

JUVENILE; ILLUSTRATOR

Esther Burns, *Mrs. Peregrine and the Yak,* Holt, 1938.
E. Burns, *Mrs. Peregrine at the Fair,* Messner, 1939.
Esther Wilkin, *Play With Me,* Golden Press, 1967.
Esther Wilkin, *So Big,* Golden Press, 1968.
Esther Wilkin, selector, *The Golden Treasury of Prayers for Boys and Girls,* Golden Press, 1975.
Esther Wilkin, *To You From Me,* Golden Press, 1977.
Esther Wilkin, *Little Prayers,* Golden Books, 1980.

Also illustrator of a book of poetry by her daughter Deborah Springett, titled *Eloise Wilkin's Book of Poems,* for Golden Press, and of more than sixty other books, including: Irmengarde Eberle, *A Good House for a Mouse,* Messner, 1940; Maud Hart Lovelace, *The Tune Is in the Tree,* Crowell, 1950; Jakob and Wilhelm Grimm, *Hansel and Gretel,* Simon & Schuster, 1954, reissued, Golden Press, 1976; Clement C. Moore, *The Night Before Christmas,* Simon & Schuster, 1955; David L. Harrison, *The Boy With a Drum,* Golden Press, 1971; and Lucille Ogle and Tina Thoburn, *I Hear: Sounds in a Child's World,* American Heritage Press, 1971.

SIDELIGHTS: During a career that spanned more than fifty years, Eloise Wilkin worked on scores of children's books. A prolific, award-winning illustrator, she was well known for her detailed drawings featured cherub-faced childen. A number of her books were joint efforts with her sister, Esther, who provided the text. In addition to her collaborations with numerous other authors, however, Wilkin published several of her own books, including *Baby's Mother Goose, My Goodnight Book,* and *The Eloise Wilkin Treasury: Favorite Nursery Rhymes, Poems, and Stories.* Over the years she worked with various major publishing houses, and by 1944 she was under exclusive contract with Golden Press—a division of Western Publishing Company in New York City. Her forthcoming *Eloise Wilkin's Book of Poems* is a collection combining Wilkin's drawings with verse written by her daughter Deborah Springett.

Aside from her work on children's books, Wilkin designed doll houses and a new-born infant doll that was successfully marketed in the 1960s as "Baby Dear." Despite its simple, functionless design, the soft, stuffed toy proved appealing. In fact, former Soviet Premier Nikita Khrushchev reportedly returned home with several of the dolls purchased during his excursion to a toy store in New York City.

BIOGRAPHICAL/CRITICAL SOURCES:

PERIODICALS

Brighton-Pittsford Post, July 28, 1982.
Daily Herald (Columbia, Tenn.), June 12, 1983.
Upstate New York, January 13, 1980.

OBITUARIES:

PERIODICALS

Democrat and Chronicle (Rochester), October 7, 1987.*

[Place of death provided by Melanie S. Donovan, promotion and publicity representative for Golden Books.]

* * *

WILLEY, F. T.
See WILLEY, Frederick Thomas

* * *

WILLEY, Fred
See WILLEY, Frederick Thomas

* * *

WILLEY, Frederick Thomas 1910-1987
(F. T. Willey, Fred Willey)

OBITUARY NOTICE: Born November 13, 1910; died December 13, 1987. Politician, barrister, fireman, and author. Willey, chairman of the Parliamentary Labour Party from 1979 to 1981, began practicing law in 1936 and was active in British politics throughout his career. From the late 1940s to the early 1950s he acted as a parliamentary secretary. He later served, at different times, as minister of land and natural resources, minister of state for the Ministry of Housing and Local Government, vice-president of the Save the Children Fund, and chairman and member of various parliamentary committees. During World War II he worked in London as an auxiliary fireman, becoming London regional officer of the Fire Brigades Union. Willey contributed articles to legal and political journals and wrote, under various forms of his name, *The Honourable Member, An Enquiry Into Teacher Training, Education Today and Tomorrow,* and *Plan for Shipbuilding.*

OBITUARIES AND OTHER SOURCES:

BOOKS

International Who's Who, 51st edition, Europa, 1987.
Who's Who, 140th edition, St. Martin's, 1988.

PERIODICALS

Times (London), December 16, 1987.

* * *

WILLIAMS, G(erhard) Mennen 1911-1988

OBITUARY NOTICE: Born February 23, 1911, in Detroit, Mich.; died after a stroke, February 2, 1988, in Detroit, Mich. Attorney, judge, politician, educator, and author. Williams, nicknamed "Soapy" as heir to the Mennen soap and toiletry company, served six terms as governor of Michigan from 1949 to 1961. A lawyer with the Social Security Board in 1936, he helped write the legal briefs that upheld the Social Security Act in the U.S. Supreme Court and was on the editorial staff of the *Michigan Law Review*. As governor he was noted for appointing blacks to important posts and fighting employment and housing discrimination. He also presided over road improvements as well as construction of the Mackinac Bridge, then the world's longest suspension bridge. Williams was assistant secretary of state for African affairs from 1960 to 1966, an experience resulting in his 1969 book *Africa for the Africans*. In 1968 he became ambassador to the Philippines, and in 1971 he began a fifteen-year stint as Michigan Supreme Court justice, becoming chief justice in 1983. After his retirement he taught law at the University of Detroit.

OBITUARIES AND OTHER SOURCES:

BOOKS

Current Biography, H. W. Wilson, 1963, March, 1988.
The International Who's Who, 51st edition, Europa, 1987.
McNaughton, Frank, *Mennen Williams of Michigan: Fighter for Progress,* preface by John D. Voelker, Oceana, 1960.
Political Profiles: The Kennedy Years, Facts on File, 1976.

PERIODICALS

Chicago Tribune, February 3, 1988.
Los Angeles Times, February 3, 1988.
New York Times, June 13, 1986, February 3, 1988.
Washington Post, February 3, 1988.

* * *

WILLIAMS, Geraint 1942-

PERSONAL: Born December 13, 1942, in Prestatyn, Flintshire, Wales; son of Albert Thomas (a teacher) and Lyn (a teacher; maiden name, Evans) Williams; married Mary Katharine Meggs, 1970; children: Joshua Tomos, Evan Joseph. *Education:* University of Wales, University College, Swansea, B.A. (with honors), 1963, M.A., 1968.

ADDRESSES: Home—65 Glenalmond Rd., Sheffield S11 7GX, England. *Office*— Department of Politics, University of Sheffield, Sheffield S10 2TN, England.

CAREER: University of Wales, University College, Swansea, lecturer in politics, 1966-68; University of Sheffield, Sheffield, England, lecturer in politics, 1968—. Visiting professor at University of Calgary, 1971-72.

WRITINGS:

(Editor) *J. S. Mill on Politics and Society,* Collins, 1976.
(With R. A. Pearson) *Political Thought and Public Policy in the Nineteenth Century,* Longman, 1984.
(Editor) John C. Rees, *John Stuart Mill's "On Liberty,"* Oxford University Press, 1985.

WORK IN PROGRESS: Continuing research on John Stuart Mill.

SIDELIGHTS: Geraint Williams told *CA:* "My interest in John Stuart Mill developed from an inquiry into the nature of liberty. Research has continued, stimulated by the controversies over the precise nature of Mill's contribution to nineteenth-century political thought. Was he an individualist or a collectivist, a traditional liberal or a new socialist? Many of the common stereotypes of Mill are simply wrong. As an example, he departed from orthodox liberals in rejecting the sanctity of private property. My current research is into his views on the justification of political violence and how this fits in with his belief in the utility of reason. The more Mill is read the less easily is he categorized—this partly accounts for my interest in him."

* * *

WILLIAMS, Raymond (Henry) 1921-1988

OBITUARY NOTICE—See index for *CA* sketch: Born August 31, 1921, in Abergavenny, Monmouthshire (some sources say Llanfihangel Crocorney), Wales; died January 26, 1988, in London, England. Educator, editor, playwright, and author. Known for his interest in the relationship between literature and society, Williams wrote numerous books during his forty-year teaching career. His literary works include *Drama From Ibsen to Eliot, Culture and Society, 1780-1950,* and a critical biography of novelist George Orwell. Among his other writings are the novels *Border Country* and *Second Generation,* the political book *Marxism and Literature,* and the play "A Letter From the Country." Additionally, Williams edited the journal *Politics and Letters* from 1946 to 1947 and the anthology *The Pelican Book of English Prose: From 1780 to the Present Day*. Beginning in 1946 he taught at institutions including Oxford University and Cambridge University's Jesus College.

OBITUARIES AND OTHER SOURCES:

BOOKS

Contemporary Literary Critics, 2nd edition, Gale, 1982.
Contemporary Novelists, 3rd edition, St. Martin's, 1982.
Who's Who, 139th edition, St. Martin's, 1987.

PERIODICALS

New York Times, January 29, 1988.
Times (London), January 27, 1988.

* * *

WILLIAMS, Roger J(ohn) 1893-1988

OBITUARY NOTICE—See index for *CA* sketch: American citizen born abroad; born August 14 (one source says October 14), 1893, in Ootacamund, Madras, India; died of pneumonia, February 20, 1988, in Austin, Tex. Biochemist, educator, and author. A pioneer in vitamin research, Williams discovered the B vitamin pantothenic acid and was an authority on nutrition. His long career as a chemistry teacher at institutions such

as the University of Oregon, Oregon State College, and University of Texas at Austin—where he founded the Clayton Foundation Biochemical Institute—gave him the opportunity to pursue research, and he published many works on his findings. *An Introduction to Organic Chemistry,* Williams's first book, became a popular text for several hundred colleges within one year of its publication. His later writings, which include *What to Do About Vitamins, The Human Frontier, Nutrition and Alcoholism, Biochemical Individuality,* and *Rethinking Education: The Coming Age of Enlightenment,* present Williams's nutritional, humanistic, and educational views in detail. The scientist emphasized the need for a comprehensive science of humankind he labeled "humanics."

OBITUARIES AND OTHER SOURCES:

BOOKS

The International Who's Who, 51st edition, Europa, 1987.

PERIODICALS

Los Angeles Times, February 25, 1988.
New York Times, February 23, 1988.

* * *

WILSON, Callie C(oe) 1917-

PERSONAL: Born April 8, 1917, in Pitkin, La.; daughter of Burrell Columbus (a lumberman) and Ida (Herring) Coe; married Waldo Wilson (an oilman), February 21, 1958 (died June 2, 1979); children: Waldo, Jr. *Education:* Attended Lamar College (now University), 1934-36, and Stanford University, 1936-37.

ADDRESSES: Home and office—2545 Harrison, Beaumont, Tex. 77702.

CAREER: Bookstore manager in Beaumont, Tex.; affiliated with engineering department of Magnolia Petroleum Co.; writer.

WRITINGS:

(With Ellen Walker Rienstra) *A Pride of Kin: A Frank Wardlaw Book,* Texas A&M University Press, 1985.

Contributor of fiction to *Redbook.*

WORK IN PROGRESS: In Her Image, a memoir of the author's mother.

* * *

WILSON, George C. 1927-

PERSONAL: Born July 11, 1927, in New Jersey; son of George Cadman (in sales) and Mary (a physical education teacher; maiden name, Ricalton) Wilson; married Joan Gibbons (a mathematics teacher), March 26, 1955; children: Kathryn Binns, James Ricalton. *Education:* Attended Mercer University, 1945, and Georgia Institute of Technology, 1945-46; Bucknell University, A.B., 1949.

ADDRESSES: Home—4875 Potomac Ave. N.W., Washington, D.C. 20007. *Office—Washington Post,* 1150 15th St. N.W., Washington, D.C. 20071. *Agent*—Raphael Sagalyn, Raphael Sagalyn, Inc., 2813 Bellevue Ter. N.W., Washington, D.C. 20007.

CAREER: Newark Evening News, Newark, N.J., reporter, 1951-55; *Congressional Quarterly,* Washington, D.C., staff writer, 1956-60; *Washington Star,* Washington, D.C., reporter, 1960-61; *Aviation Week and Space Technology,* Washington, D.C., writer, 1961-66; *Washington Post,* Washington, D.C., military correspondent, 1966—. *Military service:* U.S. Navy, Air Corps, 1945-47.

MEMBER: Authors Guild, Tailhook Association.

AWARDS, HONORS: Mark S. Watson Memorial Award, 1971.

WRITINGS:

(With F. Carl Schumacher, Jr.) *Bridge of No Return: The Ordeal of the U.S.S. Pueblo,* Harcourt, 1971.

(With Haynes Johnson) *Army in Anguish,* Simon & Schuster, 1971.

Supercarrier: An Inside Account of Life Aboard the World's Most Powerful Ship, the U.S.S. John F. Kennedy, Macmillan, 1986.

SIDELIGHTS: George C. Wilson told *CA:* "Writing *Supercarrier* involved going to sea for seven months, flying in all its planes, catapulting, and landing at night in an F14 Tomcat fighter. My goal was to 'tell it like it is'—or was."

Wilson happened to be a visitor aboard the four-billion-dollar "supercarrier," the U.S.S. *John F. Kennedy,* in October, 1983, when an Arab truck killed more than two hundred American marines stationed at a U.S. military compound in Beirut, Lebanon. He was still aboard on December 14, when the ship was ordered to carry out a retaliatory air strike which left one American pilot dead and a U.S. bombardier-navigator in enemy hands.

Wilson had boarded the ship for a cruise to the Indian Ocean to interview and observe crewmen at their daily jobs. After the Beirut incident he turned his attention to the details leading to what the journalist considered an expensive and useless air strike. He blamed military bureaucrats whose poor timing and mismanagement may have killed two American fliers. He recorded the findings of his investigation in the book *Supercarrier.*

Clark G. Reynolds of the *Washington Post Book World* described Wilson's book as "high drama, expertly told by a master observer," and "a brilliant social commentary on life at sea in the 1980s." The critic agreed with the author's claim that, despite technological advances, it is still a human being who makes a military decision—one who should be held accountable for his actions.

AVOCATIONAL INTERESTS: The outdoors, fishing.

BIOGRAPHICAL/CRITICAL SOURCES:

PERIODICALS

Washington Post Book World, September 14, 1986.

* * *

WILSON, Robert (Edward) 1951- (R. Edward Gatheridge)

PERSONAL: Born April 30, 1951, in Yonkers, N.Y.; son of Edward Norval and Eleanor (Walzer) Wilson; married Kathryn Williams, June 13, 1981; children: Jessica, Elizabeth. *Education:* Attended William Paterson College, 1969-72, 1974-75. *Politics:* Democrat. *Religion:* Lutheran.

ADDRESSES: Home—2614 Monroe St., Hollywood, Fla. 33020. *Office*—Gale Research Co., 1700 East Las Olas Blvd., Fort Lauderdale, Fla. 33301.

CAREER: New York Yankees, New York, N.Y., professional baseball player, 1972-74; *Press-Chronicle,* Johnson City, Tenn., reporter, 1976-80; *Sunday Post,* Paramus, N.J., reporter, 1981; Gale Research Co., Fort Lauderdale, Fla., editor, 1982—. Free-lance travel writer.

MEMBER: Thomas Wolfe Society.

WRITINGS:

(Editor with Anthony T. Kruzas and Kay Gill) *Government Programs and Projects Directory,* Gale, 1983.
(Editor with Kruzas and Gill) *Encyclopedia of Medical Organizations and Agencies,* 2nd edition, Gale, 1986.
(Editor with Gill) *Consumer Sourcebook,* 5th edition, Gale, 1987.

Contributor of poems to periodicals, including *Essence* (under pseudonym R. Edward Gatheridge). Contributing editor of *Recommend,* 1984—.

WORK IN PROGRESS: A book on Florida folklore and a novel.

SIDELIGHTS: Robert Wilson told *CA* that, as a political journalist, he covered the Tennessee state legislature and U.S. presidential campaigns and conventions.

* * *

WILSON, William P. 1922-

PERSONAL: Born November 6, 1922, in Fayetteville, N.C.; son of Preston P. and Rose V. Wilson; married Elizabeth Taylor; children: Bill, Ben, Karen, Tammy, Bob. *Education:* Duke University, B.S., 1943, M.D., 1947.

ADDRESSES: Home—1209 Virginia Ave., Durham, N.C. 27706. *Office*—Institute of Christian Growth, P.O. Box 2347, Burlington, N.C. 27716-2347.

CAREER: State Hospital, Raleigh, N.C., staff psychiatrist, 1948-49; Duke University, Durham, N.C., instructor, 1949-52, associate in psychiatry, 1952-54, assistant professor, 1955-60, associate professor, 1961-64, professor of psychiatry, 1964—, director of Neurophysiology Research Laboratory, 1949-52, head of Laboratories of Clinical Neurophysiology, 1961-81, head of Division of Biological Psychiatry, 1964-83. Assistant director of psychosurgical section at State Hospital, Butner, N.C., 1949-52; Veterans Administration Hospital, Durham, staff physician, 1955-58, chief of Neurophysiology Laboratories, 1961-76; associate professor and director of psychiatric research at University of Texas Medical Branch at Galveston, 1958-60. Finch Lecturer at Fuller Theological Seminary; lecturer at Western Conservative Baptist Seminary; member of board of directors of CONTACT Teleministry U.S.A.; past president of United Methodist Renewal Services, Inc. *Military service:* U.S. Army, 1943-46.

MEMBER: American Psychiatric Association, American Medical Association, American Epilepsy Society, American Association for the Advancement of Science, American Academy of Neurology, American Electroencephalography Society, Society of Biological Psychiatry, Southern Psychiatric Association, Southern Medical Association, Southern Electroencephalography Society, Medical Society of North Carolina, Durham-Orange County Medical Society, Alpha Omega Alpha.

WRITINGS:

(With Kathryn Slattery) *The Grace to Grow: The Power of Christian Faith in Emotional Healing,* Life Publishers, 1986.

Also editor of *Applications of Electroencephalography in Psychiatry: A Symposium,* published by UMI Research Press.

WORK IN PROGRESS: A book on Christian discipleship; a book on Christian counseling, which will include basic and clinical issues.

SIDELIGHTS: William P. Wilson told *CA:* "One of the major revelations of my life was the fact that people are spiritual beings, and that as such, they can have spiritual disease—although psychiatry calls this existential disease. It is, though, basically spiritual, and I have endeavored through the last twenty years of my career to investigate this more fully and to try to formulate a planned approach to the management of the spiritual problems that people have, whether they are primary or secondary to other psychological problems. This has brought about a major change in my thinking and has resulted in a dramatic change in the way in which I have managed my patients.

"It is my intent in the future to continue to look at the whole concept of spiritual development, as well as spiritual growth, as part of the healing process and to incorporate this into two works on Christian discipleship and Christian counseling."

* * *

WINDSOR, Gerard (Charles) 1944-

PERSONAL: Born December 29, 1944, in Sydney, Australia; son of Harry Matthew (a cardiac surgeon) and Imelda Mary (Burfitt) Windsor; married Louella Ruth Kerr (an antiquarian book dealer), January 27, 1979; children: Harry. *Education:* Australian National University, B.A. (with honors), 1972; University of Sydney, M.A. (with honors), 1974. *Politics:* "Eclectic." *Religion:* Roman Catholic.

ADDRESSES: Home and office—17 Palace St., Petersham, Sydney, New South Wales 2049, Australia. *Agent*—Curtis Brown Australia, Union St., Paddington, New South Wales 2021, Australia.

CAREER: St. Ignatius College, Sydney, Australia, school historian, 1975-76; University of New South Wales, Sydney, tutor in English, 1979-80; Special Broadcasting Service, Sydney, editor in unit responsible for subtitling foreign-language films, 1982-85; writer.

MEMBER: Australian Society of Authors.

AWARDS, HONORS: Australia Council Literature Board, grants, 1978 and 1983, senior fellowship, 1986.

WRITINGS:

The Harlots Enter First (stories), Hale & Iremonger, 1982.
Memories of the Assassination Attempt, and Other Stories, Penguin, 1985.

Contributor of articles, stories, and reviews to magazines and newspapers, including *Australian, Age, Meanjin, Overland, Southerly,* and *Westerly.*

WORK IN PROGRESS: *That Fierce Virgin,* a short, semicomic novel set in Ireland about a woman doctor and an Australian trader.

SIDELIGHTS: Gerard Windsor told *CA* that his writing has been influenced by his continuing interest in Catholicism, Ireland, medicine, sport, and Australian history.

WISHART, David J(ohn) 1946-

PERSONAL: Born August 15, 1946, in Corbridge, England; married in 1971. *Education:* University of Sheffield, B.A., 1967; University of Nebraska, Lincoln, M.A., 1968, Ph.D., 1971.

ADDRESSES: Office—Department of Geography, University of Nebraska, Lincoln, Neb. 68583.

CAREER: University of Arizona, Tucson, assistant professor of geography, 1971-72; Beloit College, Beloit, Wis., assistant professor of geography, 1972-74; University of Nebraska, Lincoln, assistant professor of geography, 1974—.

MEMBER: Survival International, Association of American Geographers.

WRITINGS:

The Fur Trade of the American West, 1807-1840: A Geographical Synthesis, University of Nebraska Press, 1979.

BIOGRAPHICAL/CRITICAL SOURCES:

PERIODICALS

American Historical Review, October, 1980.
Journal of American History, June, 1980.*

* * *

WOHLMUTH, Ed 1935-
(Ed David)

PERSONAL: Surname is pronounced "*Wall*-mith"; born January 18, 1935, in Philadelphia, Pa.; son of Max K. (a travel agent) and Lillian (a teacher and travel agent; maiden name, Farbman) Wohlmuth. *Education:* University of Pennsylvania, B.S., 1956.

ADDRESSES: Home and office—210 Locust St., Philadelphia, Pa. 19106. *Agent*—Nancy Love, 250 East 65th St., New York, N.Y. 10021.

CAREER: Admiral Travel, Inc., Philadelphia, Pa., chief executive officer, 1963-80; Fashion Institute of Philadelphia, Philadelphia, member of business and communications faculty, 1983—. President of Ed Wohlmuth New Rules Seminars (communications seminars for private clients), 1975—. *Military service:* U.S. Army, 1957-59, 1981-82.

WRITINGS:

(Under pseudonym Ed David) *The Intelligent Idiot's Guide to Getting the Most Out of Your Home Video Equipment,* Running Press, 1982.
The Overnight Guide to Public Speaking, Running Press, 1983.
(Contributor) J. R. Brent Ritchie and Charles R. Goeldner, editors, *Travel, Tourism, and Hospitality Research,* Wiley, 1987.

Contributor to magazines, including *Cosmopolitan, Boston, D,* and *St. Louis.* Past contributing editor of *Philadelphia.*

WORK IN PROGRESS: A book on personal and business communications, publication expected in 1988.

SIDELIGHTS: Ed Wohlmuth told *CA:* "I'm frequently told that my writing sounds like me, which I consider high praise. I want to be there in the room with you and talk to you, the reader, as I would a friend. I also know that I must be entertaining to read. I'm just one voice in millions—if I'm not entertaining, who will listen? I learned this lesson from my days working for some great editors at *Philadelphia* magazine—I hope I never forget it!

"Everything I know about public speaking and communications in general comes from hard experience. In 1962, just two weeks after my release from active military service, my father suddenly died and I was forced to operate his business, a thriving company in the package tour field. I had to quickly learn how to communicate with our customers—the major airlines and travel agents throughout North America—or lose a multimillion-dollar enterprise. I made a lot of mistakes. But I also started learning about what works and doesn't work in communications, particularly when you're dealing with large audiences. It started a lifelong fascination with people, why we do what we do, and how ego plays a major role in the way we send and receive information.

"My career as a writer started quite by accident, through a chance meeting with a young publisher who had just inherited his magazine as I had just inherited my travel company. He was looking for someone to write a 'different' type of monthly travel column and I had some ideas. He asked for a sample. It started a long association with *Philadelphia* magazine, first as their monthly travel editor and later as a regular contributor of pieces on home entertainment and electronics.

"My new book follows the pattern established by *The Overnight Guide to Public Speaking*—a fast, punchy, breezy read without (I hope) a single excess or overblown word. This time I'm talking about personal communications, how we deal with each other one-on-one."

* * *

WOLBERG, Lewis Robert 1905-1988

OBITUARY NOTICE—See index for *CA* sketch: Born July 4, 1905, in Odessa, Ukraine, Russia (now U.S.S.R.); died of a heart attack, February 3, 1988, in La Penita, Jalisco, Mexico. Psychiatrist, educator, and author. Wolberg is remembered as the founder of the low-cost Postgraduate Center for Mental Health in New York City and as the author of numerous works on the use of hypnosis in psychoanalysis. Through much of his career he taught psychiatry, first at New York Medical College and later at New York University's medical school. His writings include *The Psychology of Eating, Medical Hypnosis, Psychotherapy and the Behavioral Sciences,* and *The Practice of Psychotherapy: 506 Questions and Answers,* and he contributed to more than twenty-five other scholarly works.

OBITUARIES AND OTHER SOURCES:

PERIODICALS

New York Times, February 12, 1988.

* * *

WOLFE, J(ames) N(athan) 1927-1988

OBITUARY NOTICE: Born September 16, 1927, in Montreal, Quebec, Canada; died January 1, 1988. Educator, governmental consultant, editor, and author. Wolfe, honored as professor emeritus of economics at the University of Edinburgh, began his academic career in 1952 as a lecturer in political economy at the University of Toronto. He later taught economics at the University of California at both Berkeley and Santa Barbara, as well as at Stanford University and the University of Edinburgh, where he remained from 1964 to 1984. During the 1960s and early 1970s he served in England as an

economic consultant to the National Economic Development Office, the Department of Economic Affairs, and the Secretary of State for Scotland. Wolfe edited several books, including *Government and Nationalism in Scotland* and, with C. I. Phillips, *Clinical Practice and Economics*. He was also the co-author of *The Economics of Technical Information Systems, Some Considerations Regarding Forestry Policy in Great Britain,* and *The Church of Scotland: An Economic Survey,* among others.

OBITUARIES AND OTHER SOURCES:

BOOKS

American Men and Women of Science: The Social and Behavioral Sciences, 13th edition, Bowker, 1978.
Who's Who, 140th edition, St. Martin's, 1988.

PERIODICALS

Times (London), January 8, 1988.

* * *

WOLFFE, B. P.
See WOLFFE, Bertram (Percy)

* * *

WOLFFE, Bertram (Percy) 1923(?)-1988
(B. P. Wolffe)

OBITUARY NOTICE: Born c. 1923; died February 23, 1988. Historian, educator, and author. Wolffe is remembered for his 1981 biography *Henry VI,* regarded as a standard work on the fifteenth-century king of England. A specialist in medieval history, Wolffe taught at the University of Nottingham, the University of Edinburgh, and Trinity College, Dublin. In 1959 he became a reader in history at the University of Exeter, where he remained until 1987. He also wrote, under the name B. P. Wolffe, *The Crown Lands, 1461 to 1536: An Aspect of Yorkist and Early Tudor Government* and *The Royal Demesne in English History: The Crown Estate in the Governance of the Realm From the Conquest to 1509*.

OBITUARIES AND OTHER SOURCES:

PERIODICALS

Times (London), February 29, 1988.

* * *

WOOD, Walter Hunt, Sr. 1916(?)-1987

OBITUARY NOTICE: Born c. 1916; died of leukemia, October 29, 1987, in Washington, D.C. Educator and journalist. Wood, a former picture editor for the *Washington Post,* was a co-founder of the journalism department at the University of Maryland. He began his journalistic career with the *Washington Times* in 1936. Three years later he became a police reporter for the *Washington Post,* and in 1940 he was named picture editor. Wood served as a combat correspondent in the South Pacific during World War II, resuming his position at the *Post* after the war. He left the paper in 1952 to become picture editor for the *Washington Evening Star,* where he remained for ten years. During the mid-1960s he served the Baltimore *News-American,* again as picture editor. Wood subsequently edited *American Education* magazine for the U.S. Department of Health, Education, and Welfare (now Department of Health and Human Services), and he later edited *Labor Worklife* magazine for the Labor Department, retiring in 1986. Wood also taught journalism for a time at American and George Washington universities.

OBITUARIES AND OTHER SOURCES:

PERIODICALS

Washington Post, November 1, 1987.

* * *

WOODHEAD, Peter 1944-

PERSONAL: Born November 11, 1944, in Shipley, Yorkshire, England; son of Donald (a headmaster) and Marjorie (a teacher; maiden name, Hutton) Woodhead; married Sylvia Robertshaw (a teacher), August 24, 1970; children: Vanessa, Jonathan. *Education:* University of London, B.A. (with first class honors), 1966; University of Sheffield, M.A., 1969; University of Leicester, M.Phil., 1985.

ADDRESSES: Home—81 Uppingham Rd., Houghton-on-the-Hill, Leicestershire LE7 9HL, England. *Office*—Library, University of Leicester, Leicester, Leicestershire LE1 7RH, England.

CAREER: University of Liverpool, Liverpool, England, assistant librarian, 1969-72; University of Leicester, Leicester, England, head of circulation department, 1973-75, reference librarian in the arts, 1975—. Member of Sconul Advisory Committee on Information Services.

MEMBER: Library Association (associate member).

WRITINGS:

Keyguide to Information Sources in Archaeology, Mansell, 1985.
(With Geoffrey Stansfield) *Keyguide to Information Sources in Museum Studies,* Mansell, in press.

Contributor to library and education journals.

SIDELIGHTS: Peter Woodhead told *CA:* "The aim of the 'Keyguide' series is to provide a guide to the documentation, reference aids, and key organizational sources of information of relatively integrated subject areas—for example, archaeology, cartography, dentistry, museum studies, and so forth. Each keyguide consists of an overview of the subject and its literature, in narrative form, showing how the literature is organized and including references to documentation studies; an annotated bibliography of reference sources; a directory of selected organizations in the field; and an index. Archaeology and museum studies are two of the subjects for which I am responsible as a reference librarian, and I have a personal interest additionally.

"Compiling a keyguide is to some degree rather like putting together a giant jigsaw puzzle. Many of the pieces set down come from my own built-up knowledge, others are adapted from other people's knowledge, others are fitted into the pattern as a result of careful research and checking. Assimilating all the pieces into a unified system is a creative process. The needs of different types of readers—academics, workers in the specialist field, students, librarians and information officers, and so on—must always be borne in mind."

AVOCATIONAL INTERESTS: Fell walking in the English Lake District, long distance walking, tennis, soccer, cricket, planning and maintaining a garden, family life.

WOOSTER, Robert 1956-

PERSONAL: Born August 27, 1956, in Beaumont, Tex.; son of Ralph A. (a professor) and Edna (a legal assistant; maiden name, Jones) Wooster; married Debora Turner, May 14, 1978 (divorced, 1981); married Pat Thomas (a research associate), December 22, 1984. *Education:* Lamar University, B.A., 1977, M.A., 1979; University of Texas at Austin, Ph.D., 1985.

ADDRESSES: Home—6635 South Staples, No. 813, Corpus Christi, Tex. 78413. *Office*—Department of History, Corpus Christi State University, Corpus Christi, Tex. 78412.

CAREER: Research assistant for author James Michener in Austin, Tex., 1982-84; Sam Houston Regional Library, Liberty, Tex., scholar-in-residence, 1985-86; Corpus Christi State University, Corpus Christi, Tex., assistant professor of history, 1986—.

MEMBER: Organization of American Historians, Texas State Historical Association, Western Historical Association.

WRITINGS:

Soldiers, Sutlers, and Settlers: Garrison Life on the Texas Frontier, Texas A&M University Press, 1987.
To Conquer a Lasting Peace: The Military and United States Indian Policy, 1865-1903, Yale University Press, 1988.

Contributor to history journals. Advisory editor of *The Handbook of Texas.*

WORK IN PROGRESS: Fort Davis, Texas, publication expected in 1989; *Nelson A. Miles: A Biography,* publication expected in 1991.

* * *

WORKING, Russell (Craig) 1959-

PERSONAL: Born October 12, 1959, in Long Beach, Calif.; son of Kenneth Calvin (a minister) and Marjorie (a minister and writer; maiden name, Skare) Working. *Education:* Attended Whitworth College, 1979-82. *Religion:* Christian.

ADDRESSES: Home—Grants Pass, Ore. *Office—Grants Pass Daily Courier,* 409 South East Seventh, P.O. Box 1468, Grants Pass, Ore. 97526.

CAREER: Social worker with Haitian refugees in Belle Glade, Fla., 1982-83; *Daily Courier,* Grants Pass, Ore., education reporter, 1985—.

MEMBER: Sons of Hrothgar (chairman, 1980—).

AWARDS, HONORS: Iowa School of Letters Award for short fiction from Iowa Arts Council Writers Workshop and University of Iowa Press, 1986, and H. L. Davis Award from the Oregon Institute for Literary Arts, 1987, both for *Resurrectionists.*

WRITINGS:

Resurrectionists (short story collection), University of Iowa Press, 1987.

Contributor of short story "Halloween, via Dolorosa" to *Paris Review.*

WORK IN PROGRESS: A novel.

* * *

WYMAN, Leland C(lifton) 1897-1988

OBITUARY NOTICE: Born February 20, 1897; died January 13, 1988, in Boston, Mass. Anthropologist, educator, and author. Wyman is remembered for his research on the Navaho Indians, whom he wrote about in such books as *The Red Antway of the Navaho, Blessingway,* and *Sandpaintings of the Navaho Shootingway and the Walcott Collection.* He also wrote *Navaho Indian Ethnoentomology* with Flora L. Bailey and *Navaho Classification of Their Song Ceremonials* with Clyde Kluckhohn, among other works. After teaching physical sciences and, later, Navaho art and culture for forty years at Boston University, Wyman retired as professor emeritus in 1962.

OBITUARIES AND OTHER SOURCES:

BOOKS

Fifth International Directory of Anthropologists, University of Chicago Press, 1975.

PERIODICALS

New York Times, January 22, 1988.

* * *

WYSS, Wallace A(lfred) 1944-

PERSONAL: Born September 19, 1944, in Detroit, Mich.; married Eiko Kikawada. *Education:* Received B.A. from Wayne State University.

CAREER: Copywriter for Campbell-Ewald, 1967-69; copywriter for *Motor Trend,* 1970-73; free-lance automotive writer and photographer.

MEMBER: Sigma Delta Chi.

WRITINGS:

The Wankel Rotary Engine, Petersen Publishing, 1973.
Shelby's Wildlife: The Cobras and Mustangs, Motorbooks International, 1977.
The Super Fords: DeTomasos, Boss Series, and Ford GTs, Zuma Marketing, 1979.
DeTomaso Automobiles, Osprey, 1981.
The New Corvette: A Technical Photoguide to the New Generation, California Autotrend Publications, 1983.

Also author of screenplay "Molsheim Man," 1976.*

Y

YABSLEY, Suzanne 1949-

PERSONAL: Born April 3, 1949, in Oklahoma City, Okla.; daughter of Orval Woodrow (a realtor) and Madge (Gum) Williams; married Gary Yabsley (an attorney), October 6, 1973 (divorced). *Education:* University of Texas at Austin, B.A., 1971; University of Ottawa, B.Ed., 1975. *Politics:* Liberal Democrat.

ADDRESSES: Home—Austin, Tex. *Office*—Farm Credit Banks of Texas, P.O. Box 15919, Austin, Tex. 78761.

CAREER: Texas Rural Legal Aid, Austin, technical writer, 1981; British Columbia Institute of Technology, Burnaby, technical writer, 1981-84; free-lance technical writer in Austin, 1984-86; Farm Credit Banks of Texas, Austin, documentation specialist, 1987—. Member of American Quilt Study Group; founder and member of board of directors of Texas Sesquicentennial Quilt Association; vice-president of Austin Area Quilt Guild, 1980-81; member of Austin Friends of Folk Art.

MEMBER: American International Quilt Association, Society for Technical Communication, Austin Writers League, Austin Association of Women in Computing.

WRITINGS:

Texas Quilts, Texas Women, Texas A&M University Press, 1984.

WORK IN PROGRESS: Articles on Texas lifestyle.

SIDELIGHTS: Suzanne Yabsley told *CA:* ''I grew up quilting. I lived on a cotton farm in the Texas Panhandle with an aunt who always had a quilt 'in the frames', and I learned to love quilts from her and from both of my grandmothers. After I had gone away to the university, I returned home one summer and began working on a quilt with my aunt and her quilting friends. I became fascinated with their talk while they quilted—it was as though the process of quilting set their tongues and imaginations free, thus enabling them to recount and share a wide range of associations and memories. There was some gossiping, of course, but really very little of that sort of thing. Mostly they'd talk about their lives (perhaps a scrap of fabric would trigger a recollection), about their husbands, family, children, history, Texas, politics, religion—every topic imaginable. As they were all elderly, I decided it would be a timely idea to record them and their stories as soon as possible. And so I began the project that became my book, *Texas Quilts, Texas Women*. Eventually I traveled all over the state interviewing quilters, looking at quilts, and making some wonderful friends.

''The book is a history of quilts, quilting, and quiltmakers in Texas, beginning with the quilt's introduction here in the early nineteenth century and ending with a look at the current state of the art. The quilt is placed in a historical context, set against the highlights of Texas's colorful development. I also deal with the issue of *why* women quilt—the artistic, social, and economic needs fulfilled by making quilts. The book includes a discussion of ethnic influences on Texas quilts, a comparison of traditional quilting clubs and modern quilt guilds, and a list of Texas museums that have quilt collections.''

* * *

YOUNG, Brittany
See YOUNG, Sandra

* * *

YOUNG, (Cecil) Edwyn 1913-1988

OBITUARY NOTICE: Born April 29, 1913, in Colombo, Sri Lanka; died March 1, 1988. Anglican priest and author. Young held such unusual positions during his career as chaplain to Raymond's Revue Bar, the Palladium Theater, Collins Music Hall, and other theaters, bars, and stores in London, England, and elsewhere. He was ordained in 1936 and first served as curate to St. Peter's in London Docks. During World War II Young was a priest at St. Francis in North Kensington, and he subsequently served parishes in Broughton, Stepney, and Liverpool as rector and rural dean. In 1947 he became vicar of St. Silas in Pentonville. He was commissary of the Diocese of North Queensland beginning in 1959 and was named canon in 1974. After serving as chaplain of the Queens' Chapel of the Savoy, Young retired in 1984. His autobiography, *No Fun Like Work,* was published in 1970. He also wrote *Young and Grace Full.*

OBITUARIES AND OTHER SOURCES:

BOOKS

Who's Who, 140th edition, St. Martin's, 1988.

PERIODICALS

Times (London), March 3, 1988.

* * *

YOUNG, George Berkeley 1913-1988

OBITUARY NOTICE: Born July 27, 1913, in Madison, Wis.; died January 29, 1988. Business executive, lawyer, educator, and author. Young is remembered for his service to the publishing company Field Enterprises, where he worked from 1954 to 1968. The company's holdings at that time included the Chicago *Sun-Times,* the Chicago *Daily News,* and *World Book Encyclopedia.* Young was named chief operating officer of Field Enterprises in 1965 and a year later was elected chairman of the board. Before joining Field Enterprises Young taught history at Columbia University and Barnard College, and he later lectured in property law at Northwestern University. During World War II he served as a Navy lieutenant in the Office of Strategic Services, which became the Central Intelligence Agency. He earned his law degree in 1948 and soon after joined the Chicago law firm of Isham, Lincoln and Beale, where he became a partner in 1950. After his retirement from Field Enterprises he served on the boards of Chrysler Corporation, First National Bank of Chicago, and other large companies. He was also a director and trustee of many civic and cultural organizations. Young wrote *Politics, Strategy, and American Diplomacy: Studies in Foreign Policy, 1873-1917,* with John A. S. Grenville.

OBITUARIES AND OTHER SOURCES:

BOOKS

The International Year Book and Statesmen's Who's Who, Thomas Skinner Directories, 1985.
Who's Who in America, 44th edition, Marquis, 1986.

PERIODICALS

Chicago Tribune, January 31, 1988.

* * *

YOUNG, Sandra 1952-
(Brittany Young)

PERSONAL: Born May 23, 1952, in Cincinnati, Ohio; daughter of Robert W. (an executive) and Helen F. (a businesswoman) Harrisson; married Frederick M. Young (an industrialist), June 15, 1977; children: Ariel, Ryan. *Education:* Attended Texas Christian University, 1970 and 1972, and University of Wisconsin—Madison, 1974.

ADDRESSES: Home—Racine, Wis. *Agent*—Robin Kaigh, 300 East 54th St., New York, N.Y. 10022.

CAREER: Paralegal assistant in Racine, Wis., 1971-80; writer, 1980—.

MEMBER: Romance Writers of America.

AWARDS, HONORS: Golden Medallion from Romance Writers of America, 1986, for *The Karas Cup.*

WRITINGS:

ROMANCE NOVELS UNDER PSEUDONYM BRITTANY YOUNG

Arranged Marriage, Silhouette, 1982.
A Separate Happiness, Silhouette, 1983.
No Special Consideration, Silhouette, 1983.
The Karas Cup, Silhouette, 1984.
An Honorable Man, Silhouette, 1984.
A Deeper Meaning, Silhouette, 1984.
No Ordinary Man, Silhouette, 1985.
To Catch a Thief, Silhouette, 1985.
Gallagher's Lady, Silhouette, 1986.
All or Nothing, Silhouette, 1986.
Far From Over, Silhouette, 1987.
A Matter of Honor, Silhouette, 1987.
Worth the Risk, Silhouette, in press.
The Kiss of a Stranger, Silhouette, in press.
A Man Called Travers, Silhouette, in press.

WORK IN PROGRESS: The Emperor's Daughter, a historical novel set in Napoleonic France, publication by Pocket Books expected in 1990; *Murder, Texas Style,* a nonfiction book about Texas murder cases.

SIDELIGHTS: Sandra Young told *CA:* "I love history and travel. The majority of my romantic settings are foreign, and I've traveled to nearly all of them. I have a library of nearly five thousand history books, which are now being put to use as I embark on a series of historical novels."

Z

ZACH, Cheryl (Byrd) 1947-
(Jennifer Cole)

PERSONAL: Surname is pronounced "Zack"; born June 9, 1947, in Clarksville, Tenn.; daughter of Smith Henry (a military officer) and Nancy (a sales manager; maiden name, LeGate) Byrd; married Q. J. Wasden, June 2, 1967 (divorced September, 1979); married Charles O. Zach, Jr. (a vice-president of a die casting company), June 20, 1982; children: (first marriage) Quinton John, Michelle Nicole. *Education:* Austin Peay State University, B.A., 1968, M.A., 1977. *Religion:* Episcopalian.

ADDRESSES: Home—Bellflower, Calif. *Agent*—Richard Curtis, 164 East 64th St., New York, N.Y. 10021.

CAREER: High school English teacher in Harrison County, Miss., 1970-71; free-lance journalist, 1976-77; high school English teacher in Dyersburg, Tenn., 1978-82; writer, 1982—.

MEMBER: Romance Writers of America, Society of Children's Book Writers, Phi Kappa Phi.

AWARDS, HONORS: Golden Medallion Awards for best young adult novel from Romance Writers of America, 1984, for *The Frog Princess,* and 1985, for *Waiting for Amanda*.

WRITINGS:

Twice a Fool (romance novel), Harlequin, 1984.
The Frog Princess (young adult romance novel), Silhouette, 1984.
Waiting for Amanda (young adult romance novel), Silhouette, 1985.
Fortune's Child (young adult romance novel), Silhouette, 1985.

UNDER PSEUDONYM JENNIFER COLE

Three's a Crowd (young adult romance novel), Fawcett, 1986.
Star Quality (young adult romance novel), Fawcett, 1987.
Too Many Cooks (young adult romance novel), Fawcett, 1987.
Mollie in Love (young adult romance novel), Fawcett, 1987.

OTHER

Contributor of articles, poems, and stories to magazines and newspapers.

WORK IN PROGRESS: An adult mystery novel.

SIDELIGHTS: Cheryl Zach told *CA:* "Because my father was a career army man, I led a gypsy's life as a child, changing schools ten times in twelve years. I was born in Tennessee and have also lived in Georgia, Mississippi (the Gulf coast), Germany, and Scotland.

"I read early and well, and a deep love for books perhaps made it inevitable that my oldest and greatest ambition would be to create my own. I wrote poems, stories, and plays during childhood and won writing awards in college, but commercial success eluded me. I married, had children, taught school, and continued to write when I could.

"At my first writing conference, at Vanderbilt University in the late seventies, I discovered that writing was not just an art form but also a business. After the first shock, I decided that I wanted my writing to be read, so I began to pay attention to marketing as well as craftsmanship.

"After years of trying to write 'on the side,' while going to school, teaching, and raising my two kids, I remarried, moved to California, and took a year to pursue my lifelong ambition. Thirteen months later, I sold my first novel. My books have been published in six countries outside the United States.

"I came into writing for young people almost by accident, but I do have strong convictions about its importance. I believe young readers deserve the best, and writers for young people have even more responsibility as far as truth and excellence than writers in general."

* * *

ZELDOVICH, Ia(kov) B(orisovich) 1914-1987

OBITUARY NOTICE: First name sometimes transliterated Yakov or Uakov; surname sometimes transliterated Zel'dovich; born March 8, 1914, in Minsk, Russia (now U.S.S.R.); died December 2, 1987. Physicist, educator, and author. Zeldovich's research in astrophysics and related fields was fundamental to the development of the "Black Hole" theory. The physicist, who taught at Moscow University, performed extensive analysis of explosions, and he developed a way of calculating the chain reaction in nuclear fission. He won national and international acclaim for his research, including three Orders of Lenin, four State Prizes of the U.S.S.R., three Hero of Socialist Labor awards, a Lenin Prize, and honorary doc-

torates from the universities of Sussex and Cambridge, among other awards. He co-authored several books in his field, including *Theory of Detonation, Physics of Shock Waves and High-Temperature Hydrodynamic Phenomena, Relativistic Astrophysics, Stars and Relativity,* and *Theory of Shock Waves and Introduction to Gas Dynamics.* Zeldovich supported the "Big Bang" theory of creation, and he collaborated on two books on the subject: *The Theory of Gravity and the Evolution of Stars* and *The Structure and Evolution of the Universe.*

OBITUARIES AND OTHER SOURCES:

BOOKS

The International Who's Who, 51st edition, Europa, 1987.
Who's Who in Socialist Countries, K. G. Saur, 1978.

PERIODICALS

Times (London), December 7, 1987.

* * *

ZIMMERMAN, Dale A. 1928-

PERSONAL: Born June 7, 1928, in Imlay City, Mich.; son of Landis Myron (a dentist) and Leta Pearl (a teacher and dental assistant; maiden name, Marshall) Zimmerman; married Marian Allen (a research assistant and personal secretary), July 29, 1950; children: Allan Dale. *Education:* University of Michigan, B.S., 1950, M.S., 1951, Ph.D., 1956.

ADDRESSES: Home—1011 West Florence St., Silver City, N.M. 88061. *Office*—Department of Biological Science, Western New Mexico University, Silver City, N.M. 88061.

CAREER: Western New Mexico University, Silver City, assistant professor, 1957-60, associate professor, 1960-64, professor of biology, 1965-88, chairman of department of biological science, 1964-81. Visiting curator of birds at University of Michigan's Museum of Zoology, summer, 1958. Conducted ornithological field work in Mexico, South America, Panama, the Galapagos Islands, Africa, India, Nepal, Australia, New Guinea, Borneo, Malaya, and Thailand; leader of foreign ornithological tours for American Automobile Association, Roadrunner Nature Tours, Wings, Inc., Birdquest Ltd., Bruce Safaris, Hanns Ebensten Travel, and Nature Expeditions International. Consultant to Visual Resources for Ornithology.

MEMBER: World Wildlife Society, American Ornithological Union, Wilson Ornithological Society, Cooper Ornithological Society, National Audubon Society, Nature Conservancy, American Birding Association (member of board of directors, 1981-86), East African Natural History Society, East African Wildlife Society.

WRITINGS:

(Editor with Dustin Huntington) *New Mexico Bird Finding Guide,* New Mexico Ornithological Society, 1984.
(With Bruce M. Beehler and Thane K. Pratt; also illustrator) *Birds of New Guinea,* Princeton University Press, 1986.

Contributor of a book chapter to Olin Sewall Pettingill's *The Bird Watcher's America.* Contributor of about seventy-five articles, reviews, and photographs to scientific journals. Editor of regional field notes for *Audubon Field Notes,* 1961-63; member of editorial board of *American Birds.*

WORK IN PROGRESS: Senior author and illustrator of *A Field Guide to the Birds of Kenya,* with Donald A. Turner and David J. Pearson, publication by Princeton University Press and Christopher Helm expected in 1990.

SIDELIGHTS: Dale A. Zimmerman told *CA:* "I have been interested in birds specifically, and the natural world in general, since early childhood. I began serious birdwatching and recordkeeping in 1940, and this has continued to the present. My world life-list numbers almost five thousand species.

"My interest in bird (and other outdoor) photography began in 1946, becoming more sophisticated with time. It has been a serious pursuit for the past two decades. I studied bird painting under George Miksch Sutton for several years in Ann Arbor, Michigan, but did little serious art work until the late 1970s. Painting and drawing now occupy considerable time. Preparing plates for *The Birds of New Guinea* has been particularly time-consuming during the past five years.

"My museum experience with birds began in 1949 and continued through 1955. Between 1949 and 1959 I made four expeditions into Mexico, covering most of that country and collecting selectively for the University of Michigan's Museum of Zoology. Although I have not worked with a major collection on any long-term basis since the late 1950s, I have built up and maintained a small but high quality collection of birds (including virtually all North American species and all but ten or twelve of the world's families) at Western New Mexico University. In 1963, with partial support from the American Museum of Natural History, I undertook preliminary bird population studies in western Kenya and selective collecting elsewhere in Kenya and Uganda. I have made fourteen visits to various parts of Africa since 1961.

"My teaching experience has been varied, as is to be expected in the small college where I have elected to remain, despite opportunities for employment in larger institutions, which would have involved a transfer to urban environments. Over the years I have taught courses in general biology, botany, zoology, genetics, ecology, invertebrate zoology, ornithology, systematic botany, conservation, biogeography, and nature photography. More recent and current teaching has been confined to general biology, systematic botany, and ornithology.

"As I stated in the introduction to my chapter in Pettingill's *The Bird Watcher's America,* birds are a way of life with me. They dominate, in one way or another, most of the things I do. But my training and experience have been broad, and I maintain serious peripheral interests in lepidoptera, certain angiosperms (particularly the Cactaceae), reptiles, mammals, and photography of all of these."

BIOGRAPHICAL/CRITICAL SOURCES:

PERIODICALS

Albuquerque Journal, April 19, 1987.

* * *

ZOHAR, Danah 1944-

ADDRESSES: 29 Warwick Ave., London W.9, England.

CAREER: Free-lance writer.

WRITINGS:

Up My Mother's Flagpole, Stein & Day, 1974.
Israel: The Land and Its People, Macdonald Educational, 1977.
Through the Time Barrier: A Study in Precognition and Modern Physics, Heinemann, 1982, Academy Chicago, 1984.*

ZUCKERMAN, Seth (Abram) 1961-

PERSONAL: Born October 24, 1916, in Northridge, Calif.; son of Frank (an engineer) and Frederica (a chef) Zuckerman. *Education:* Stanford University, A.B. (with distinction), 1983; also attended University of California, Berkeley, 1987. *Religion:* Jewish.

ADDRESSES: *Home*—3788 Army St., San Francisco, Calif. 94110.

CAREER: *Stanford Daily,* Stanford, Calif., news editor, managing editor, and editor in chief, 1978-81; *Stanford Independent,* Stanford, co-founder and editor, 1981-82; writer, 1982—. Intern at *Newsweek,* summers, 1981-83; instructor at Stanford University, 1982-87, and Sierra Community College, 1987—. Member of executive committee of San Francisco mayor's Energy Management Committee; energy consultant.

MEMBER: National Writers Union, Media Alliance, Energy Network.

WRITINGS:

(With Hunter Lovins and Amory Lovins) *Energy Unbound: A Fable for America's Future,* Sierra Books, 1986.

Contributor to magazines and newspapers, including *Nation, Newsweek,* and *Sierra.*

WORK IN PROGRESS: Continuing research on energy and the environment "with particular focus on bioregionalism (place-oriented politics), the effect of energy technologies on the environment, and sustainable forestry practices."

SIDELIGHTS: Seth Zuckerman commented: "My first-grade teacher was convinced I would be a writer. I knew better, though: I would be a scientist. Energy and writing have wound up being my twin fields, and we have both been proven right. I lived in Israel from 1970 to 1978 where I learned to speak fluent Hebrew. I recently returned there at the invitation of the local anti-nuclear group to help dissuade the country from building a nuclear power plant.

"The Lovinses and I wrote *Energy Unbound* because the major previous books on the topic had all been fairly technical. With *Unbound* we hoped to make the issues accessible to the lay reader—the teacher or accountant or carpenter who had been interested in the energy debate but unable to plow through the technical jargon of Amory Lovins's *Soft Energy Paths.* We subtitled the book 'A Fable for America's Future' because it is written entirely in fictional dialogue between Mrs. Eunice Bunnyhut (a Dubuque, Iowa, housewife who is named Secretary of Energy) and her colleagues at the Department of Energy, including Duncan Jefferson Holt, a career bureaucrat who answers Eunice's commonsensical questions about energy and equips her to develop her own energy plan. As the story unfolds, Eunice and the reader gain confidence in the subject and come to formulate their own opinions about it.

"The United States and the world have come a long way toward a sustainable energy path since the first oil shock of 1973. We use energy so much more efficiently that we consume as much energy as we did in 1973, even though gross national product has grown by a third. The impact of many of the improvements we have begun to make—in buildings, automobiles, and industry—will increase over the coming decades. As the energy intensity of our economy declines, and we shift from depletable sources such as coal and oil to renewable sources such as sunlight, wind, and agricultural wastes, the impact of energy use on the environment will decrease.

"I have written lately about battles in which different environmental values conflict with each other—such as the push to use the renewable energy of wind power versus environmentalists' demands for open space. These are tricky issues that challenge ecology activists to figure out what their priorities really are."

* * *

ZWEIG, Ronald W. 1949-

PERSONAL: Born October 17, 1949, in Sydney, Australia; son of Ernst (an engineer) and Anita (a housewife; maiden name, Trief) Zweig; married Hanna Heitner (an information scientist), August 20, 1974; children: Eytan, Alon. *Education:* University of Sydney, B.A. (with honors), 1972; Cambridge University, Ph.D., 1978.

ADDRESSES: *Home*—P.O. Box 1042, Mevasseret Zion 90-805, Israel. *Office*—Department of Jewish History, Tel Aviv University, Tel Aviv, Israel.

CAREER: Hebrew University, Jerusalem, lecturer, 1978-83; Tel Aviv University, Tel Aviv, Israel, senior lecturer in Jewish history, 1983—.

WRITINGS:

Britain and Palestine During the Second World War, Royal Historical Society, 1986.

German Reparations and the Jewish World, Westview, 1987.

Editor of *Studies in Zionism.*

WORK IN PROGRESS: *America and the Jewish Displaced Persons, 1945-1948,* publication expected in 1989.

Contemporary Authors®

Cumulative Index
Volumes 1–124

This Index Includes References to All Entries in the Contemporary Authors Series

Contemporary Authors

Volume 124 brings the total coverage to more than 90,000 writers, both living and deceased, a large portion of whom are missing in similar works. Writers in fiction, general nonfiction, poetry, journalism, drama, motion pictures, television, and other fields are all included in *CA*. Each new volume contains sketches on authors not previously listed in the series. Cumulative index in even-numbered original volumes. All volumes in the series are in print.

Contemporary Authors New Revision Series

Provides completely updated information on authors listed in previously published volumes of *CA*. Sketches from a number of volumes are assessed, and only entries requiring significant change are revised and published in *CA New Revision Series* volumes. Volumes 1-24 are in print. (All volumes published under the former revision system, 1-4 through 41-44 First Revision, will remain in print.)

Contemporary Authors Permanent Series

Consists of updated listings for deceased and inactive authors removed from original volumes 9-36 when these volumes were revised. Two volumes only; both are in print.

Contemporary Authors Autobiography Series

Presents specially commissioned autobiographies by leading writers to complement information in *CA* original and revision volumes. Cumulative index to authors, personal names, titles of works, geographical names, subjects, and schools of writing in each new volume. Volumes 1-6 are in print.

Contemporary Authors Bibliographical Series

Contains primary and secondary bibliographies as well as analytical bibliographical essays by authorities on major modern writers. Cumulative indexes to authors and critics in each new volume. Volumes 1-2 are in print.

And to All Entries in These Gale Series

Authors in the News

Reprints articles from American newspapers and magazines covering writers and other members of the communications media.

Children's Literature Review

Includes excerpts from reviews, criticism, and commentary on works of children's authors and illustrators.

Concise Dictionary of American Literary Biography

Contains illustrated entries on major American authors selected and updated from the *Dictionary of Literary Biography*.

Contemporary Literary Criticism

Presents excerpts from current criticism of the works of today's novelists, poets, playwrights, short story writers, scriptwriters, and other creative writers.

Dictionary of Literary Biography

Encompasses three related series. *Dictionary of Literary Biography* furnishes overviews of authors and their work, placing them in the larger context of literary history. *Dictionary of Literary Biography Documentary Series* illuminates the careers of major figures through a selection of literary documents. *Dictionary of Literary Biography Yearbook* summarizes the past year's literary activity and includes updated and new author entries.

Short Story Criticism

Provides excerpts from criticism of the works of major short story writers of all eras and nationalities.

Something About the Author

Contains heavily illustrated sketches on juvenile and young adult authors and illustrators from all eras.

Something About the Author Autobiography Series

Presents specially commissioned autobiographies by prominent authors and illustrators of books for children.

Twentieth-Century Literary Criticism

Furnishes lengthy excerpts from criticism of the works of novelists, poets, playwrights, short story writers, and other creative writers who died between 1900 and 1960.

Yesterday's Authors of Books for Children

Consists of heavily illustrated sketches on children's authors who died before 1961.

Contemporary Authors

Cumulative Index • Volumes 1-124

Citations to entries in *Contemporary Authors* are identified as follows:

R after number • *Contemporary Authors* First Revision Volumes 1-44
Volume number only • *Contemporary Authors* Original Volumes 45-124
CANR • *Contemporary Authors New Revision Series,* Volumes 1-24
CAP • *Contemporary Authors Permanent Series,* Volumes 1-2
CAAS • *Contemporary Authors Autobiography Series,* Volumes 1-6
CABS • *Contemporary Authors Bibliographical Series,* Volumes 1-2

Citations to entries in other reference works are identified as follows:

AITN • *Authors in the News,* Volumes 1-2
CDALB • *Concise Dictionary of American Literary Biography,* 1941-1968, 1640-1865
CLC • *Contemporary Literary Criticism,* Volumes 1-47
CLR • *Children's Literature Review,* Volumes 1-14
DLB • *Dictionary of Literary Biography,* Volumes 1-67
DLBD • *Dictionary of Literary Biography Documentary Series,* Volumes 1-4
DLBY • *Dictionary of Literary Biography Yearbook,* 1980-1986
SAAS • *Something About the Author Autobiography Series,* Volumes 1-5
SATA • *Something About the Author,* Volumes 1-50
SSC • *Short Story Criticism,* Volume 1
TCLC • *Twentieth-Century Literary Criticism,* Volumes 1-27
YABC • *Yesterday's Authors of Books for Children,* Volumes 1-2

A. A.
See Willis, (George) Anthony Armstrong
A. E.
See Russell, George William
See also DLB 19
See also TCLC 3, 10
A. M.
See Megged, Aharon
Aach, Herb(ert) 1923-1985 Obituary 118
Aaker, David A(llen) 1938- 49-52
Aalben, Patrick
See Jones, Noel
Aallyn, Alysse
See Clark, Melissa
Aalto, (Hugo) Alvar (Henrik) 1898-1976
Obituary 65-68
Aardema, Verna
See Vugteveen, Verna Aardema
See also SATA 4
Aaron, Benjamin 1915- 23-24R
Aaron, Chester 1923- CANR-8
Earlier sketch in CA 21-22R
See also SATA 9
Aaron, Daniel 1912- CANR-7
Earlier sketch in CA 13-14R
Aaron, Hank
See Aaron, Henry Louis
Aaron, Henry Louis 1934- Brief entry 104
Aaron, James Ethridge 1927- 23-24R
Aaron, R. I.
See Aaron, Richard Ithamar
Aaron, Richard Ithamar 1901-1987
Obituary 122
Aaron, Shirley L. 1941- 123
Aaron, Sidney
See Chayefsky, Sidney
Aaron, Stephen 1936-.................... 124
Aaronovitch, Sam 1919- 13-14R
Aarons, Edward S(idney) 1916-1975 93-96
Obituary 57-60
Aarons, Slim 1916- Brief entry 106
Aaronson, Bernard S(eymour) 1924- 29-32R
Aarsleff, Hans 1925- 21-22R
Aaseng, Nate
See Aaseng, Nathan
Aaseng, Nathan 1953- 106
See also SATA 38
Aaseng, Rolf E(dward) 1923- 49-52
Aasheim, Ashley 1942- 115
Abadinsky, Howard 1941- 110
Abagnale, Frank W., Jr. 1948- 112
Abajian, James De Tar 1914- 65-68
Abarbanel, Karin 1950- 65-68
Abarbanel, Sam X. 1914- Brief entry 106
Abasiyanik, Sait Faik 1906-1954
Brief entry 123
Abata, Russell M(ary) 1930- 113
Abate, Frank R(obert) 1951- 118
Abayakoon, Cyrus D. F. 1912- Brief entry .. 115
Abbaanano, Nicola 1901- 33-36R
Abbas, Khwaja Ahmad 1914- 57-60
Abbazia, Patrick 1937- 57-60
Abbe, Elfriede (Martha) 1919- 15-16R
Abbe, George (Bancroft) 1911- CANR-10
Earlier sketch in CA 25-28R
Abbensetts, Michael 1938- 104
Abberley, Aldwyn
See Cowie, Donald
Abbey, Edward 1927- CANR-2
Earlier sketch in CA 45-48
See also CLC 36
Abbey, Lloyd Robert 1943- Brief entry 104
Abbey, Lynn
See Abbey, Marilyn Lorraine
Abbey, Margaret
See York, Margaret Elizabeth
Abbey, Marilyn Lorraine 1948- 119
Abbey, Merrill R. 1905- CANR-3
Earlier sketch in CA 1R
Abbington, John
See Gibson, Walter B(rown)
Abbot, Anthony
See Oursler, (Charles) Fulton
Abbot, Charles G(reeley) 1872-1973 77-80
Obituary 45-48
Abbot, Rick
See Sharkey, John Michael
Abbot, W(illiam) W(right) 1922-
Brief entry 110
Abbot, Willis J(ohn) 1863-1934
Brief entry 119
See also DLB 29
Abbott, Alice
See Borland, Kathryn Kilby
and Speicher, Helen Ross S(mith)
Abbott, Anthony S. 1935- 17-18R
Abbott, Berenice 1898- 106
Abbott, Carl (John) 1944- CANR-11
Earlier sketch in CA 65-68
Abbott, Claude Colleer 1889-1971 ....7-8R
Obituary 89-92
Abbott, Eric Symes 1906-1983 Obituary 110
Abbott, Freeland K(night) 1919-1971 ..... CAP-2
Earlier sketch in CA 25-28
Abbott, George 1887- 93-96
Abbott, H(orace) Porter 1940- 45-48
Abbott, Jack Henry
See Abbott, Rufus Henry
Abbott, Jacob 1803-1879 .... SATA-22
See also DLB 1, 42
Abbott, James H(amilton) 1924- 77-80
Abbott, Jerry (Lynn) 1938- 45-48
Abbott, John J(amison) 1930- 17-18R
Abbott, John Janisen 17-18R
Abbott, Keith 1944- 121
Abbott, L(enwood) B(allard) 1908-1985
Obituary 117
Abbott, Lee K(ittredge) 1947- 124
Abbott, Manager Henry
See Stratemeyer, Edward L.
Abbott, Margaret Evans 1896-1976
Obituary 110
Abbott, Martin 1922-1977 ....33-36R
Abbott, May L(aura) 1916- 9-10R
Abbott, Philip R. 1944- Brief entry 106
Abbott, R(obert) Tucker 1919- CANR-4
Earlier sketch in CA 9-10R
Abbott, Raymond H(erbert) 1942- 57-60
Abbott, Richard H(enry) 1936- 33-36R
Abbott, Robert S. 1868-1940 .... DLB-29
Abbott, Rowland A(ubrey) S(amuel)
1909- 53-56
Abbott, Rufus Henry 1944- 107
Abbott, Sarah
See Zolotow, Charlotte S.
Abbott, Shirley 1934- 113
Abbott, Sidney 1937- 41-44R
Abbott, Walter M(atthew) 1923- 11-12R
Abbotts, John 1947- 73-76
Abboushi, W(asif) F(ahmi) 1931- 29-32R
Abbs, Peter 1942- 93-96
ABC
See Caddick, Arthur
Abcarian, Richard 1929- 33-36R
Abdallah, Omar
See Humbaraci, D(emir) Arslan
Abdel-Malek, Anouar 1924- 29-32R
Abdelsamad, Moustafa H(assan) 1941- 53-56
Abdul, Raoul 1929- 29-32R
See also SATA 12
Abdullah, Achmed 1881-1945 Brief entry ... 115
Abdullahi, Guda 1946- 93-96
Abdul-Rauf, Muhammad 1917- 101
Abe, Kobo 1924- CANR-24
Earlier sketch in CA 65-68
See also CLC 8, 22
Abeel, Erica (Hennefeld) 1937- 113
Brief entry 109
Abel, Alan (Irwin) 1928- CANR-12
Earlier sketch in CA 19-20R
Abel, Bob
See Abel, Robert
Abel, Elie 1920- CANR-8
Earlier sketch in CA 61-64
Abel, Ernest L(awrence) 1943- CANR-14
Earlier sketch in CA 41-44R
Abel, I(orwith) W(ilbur) 1908-1987
Obituary 123
Brief entry 105
Abel, Jeanne 1937- 19-20R
Abel, Lionel 1910- 61-64
Abel, Raymond 1911- SATA-12
Abel, Reuben 1911- 37-40R
Abel, Robert 1913(?)-1987 Obituary 122
Abel, Robert 1931-1981 .... CANR-11
Obituary 105
Earlier sketch in CA 65-68
Abel, Robert H(alsall) 1941- 102
Abel, Theodora M(ead) 1899- 57-60
Abel, Theodore 1896- 23-24R
Abel, Wilhelm 1904- Brief entry 119
Abeles, Elvin 1907- 104
Abell, Arunah S. 1806-1888 .... DLB-43
Abell, George O(gden) 1927-1983 ...... CANR-3
Obituary 111
Earlier sketch in CA 9-10R
Abell, Kathleen 1938- 49-52
See also SATA 9
Abell, Kjeld 1901-1961 Obituary 111
See also CLC 15
Abell, Ron(ald F.) 1932- 119
Abella, Alex 1950- 93-96
Abella, Irving Martin 1940- 49-52
Abels, Harriette S(heffer) 1926- 121
See also SATA 50
Abels, Jules 1913- 61-64
Abel-Smith, Brian 1926- CANR-9
Earlier sketch in CA 21-22R
Abelson, Philip Hauge 1913- Brief entry 107
Abelson, Raziel A(lter) 1921- CANR-6
Earlier sketch in CA 11-12R
Abelson, Robert P(aul) 1928- 41-44R
Abend, Norman A(nchel) 1931- 33-36R
Aber, William M(cKee) 1929- 57-60
Aberbach, Joel D(avid) 1940- CANR-20
Earlier sketch in CA 45-48
Abercrombie, Barbara (Mattes) 1939- 81-84
See also SATA 16
Abercrombie, Lascelles 1881-1938
Brief entry 112
See also DLB 19
Abercrombie, M(innie) L(ouie) J(ohnson)
1909(?)-1984 Obituary 115
Abercrombie, M. L. Johnson
See Abercrombie, M(innie) L(ouie)
J(ohnson)

Abercrombie, Michael 1912-1979
Obituary ... 115
Abercrombie, Nigel J(ames) 1908-1986 ... 101
Obituary ... 118
Abercrombie, Stanley 1935- ... 117
Aberg, Sherrill E. 1924- ... 21-22R
Aberle, David F(riend) 1918- ... 21-22R
Aberle, John Wayne 1919- ... 1R
Aberle, Kathleen Gough 1925- ... CANR-5
Earlier sketch in CA 13-14R
Abernathy, David M(yles) 1933- ... 53-56
Abernathy, (M.) Elton 1913- ... 17-18R
Abernathy, M(abra) Glenn 1921- ... 13-14R
Abernathy, William J(ackson) 1933-1983 .. 93-96
Obituary ... 111
Abernethy, Francis Edward 1925- ... CANR-8
Earlier sketch in CA 21-22R
Abernethy, George Lawrence 1910- ... 2R
Abernethy, Peter L(ink) 1935- ... 69-72
Abernethy, Robert G(ordon) 1927- ... 21-22R
See also SATA 5
Abernethy, Thomas Perkins 1890-1975 ... CAP-1
Obituary ... 111
Earlier sketch in CA 19-20
Abernethy, Virginia 1934- ... 93-96
Abert, Donald B. 1907-1985 Obituary ... 116
Abisch, Roslyn Kroop 1927- ... CANR-10
Earlier sketch in CA 21-22R
See also SATA 9
Abisch, Roz
See Abisch, Roslyn Kroop
Abish, Walter 1931- ... 101
See also CLC 22
Able, James A(ugustus), Jr. 1928- ... 93-96
Ableman, Paul 1927- ... CANR-12
Earlier sketch in CA 61-64
Abler, Ronald F. 1939- ... CANR-4
Earlier sketch in CA 53-56
Abler, Thomas S(truthers) 1941- ... 101
Abley, Mark 1955- ... 120
Abodaher, David J. (Naiph) 1919- ... CANR-10
Earlier sketch in CA 17-18R
See also SATA 17
Abolafia, Yossi ... SATA-46
Abrahall, Clare Hoskyns
See Hoskyns-Abrahall, Clare (Constance Drury)
Abraham, Claude K(urt) 1931- ... 23-24R
Abraham, George 1915- ... 110
Abraham, Gerald Ernest Heal 1904- ... 89-92
Abraham, Henry Julian 1921- ... CANR-18
Earlier sketches in CA 5-6R, CANR-2
Abraham, Katherine 1922- ... 110
Abraham, Katy
See Abraham, Katherine
Abraham, Louis Arnold 1893-1983
Obituary ... 108
Abraham, M(annamplakkal) Francis 1939- ... 110
Abraham, Willard 1916- ... CANR-5
Earlier sketch in CA 13-14R
Abraham, William E. 1934- ... 13-14R
Abraham, William I(srael) 1919- ... 25-28R
Abrahami, Izzy 1930- Brief entry ... 110
Abrahamian, Ervand 1940- ... 110
Abrahams, Doris Caroline
1901(?)-1982(?) Obituary ... 108
Abrahams, Edward 1949- ... 122
Abrahams, Gerald 1907-1980 ... 102
Obituary ... 97-100
Abrahams, Hilary (Ruth) 1938- ... SATA-29
Abrahams, Howard Phineas 1904- ... 57-60
Abrahams, Peter (Henry) 1919- ... 57-60
See also CLC 4
Abrahams, R(aphael) G(arvin) 1934- ... 25-28R
Abrahams, Robert David 1905- ... CAP-2
Earlier sketch in CA 33-36
See also SATA 4
Abrahams, Roger D(avid) 1933- ... CANR-24
Earlier sketches in CA 11-12R, CANR-5
Abrahams, William Miller 1919- ... 61-64
Abrahamsen, Christine Elizabeth 1916- ... 101
Abrahamsen, David 1903- ... 65-68
Abrahamson, Mark J. 1939- ... 101
Abrahamsson, Bengt 1937- ... 97-100
Abrahms, Sally (Ellen) 1953- ... 113
Abram, H(arry) S(hore) 1931-1977 ... 29-32R
Abram, Morris Berthold 1918- ... 108
Abramov, Emil
See Draitser, Emil
Abramov, Fyodor Aleksandrovich
1920-1983 Obituary ... 109
Abramov, S(hene'ur) Zalman 1908-
Brief entry ... 108
Abramovitz, Anita (Zeltner Brooks)
1914- ... 97-100
Abramowitz, Jack 1918- ... CANR-6
Earlier sketch in CA 7-8R
Abramowitz, Shalom Jacob 1835(?)-1917
Brief entry ... 118
Abrams, Alan E(dwin) 1941- ... 89-92
Abrams, Charles 1901-1970 ... CAP-2
Earlier sketch in CA 23-24
Abrams, George J(oseph) 1918-1978 .. CANR-12
Earlier sketch in CA 61-64
Abrams, Harry N(athan) 1904-1979
Obituary ... 93-96
Abrams, Joy 1941- ... 77-80
See also SATA 16
Abrams, Lawrence F. ... 124
See also SATA 47
Abrams, Linsey 1951- ... CANR-18
Earlier sketch in CA 102
Abrams, M(eyer) H(oward) 1912- ... CANR-13
Earlier sketch in CA 57-60
See also DLB 67
See also CLC 24
Abrams, Mark 1906- ... 124
Abrams, Peter D(avid) 1936- ... 33-36R
Abrams, Philip 1933(?)-1981 Obituary ... 105
Abrams, Richard M. 1932- ... 13-14R
Abrams, Sam(uel) 1935- ... 21-22R
Abramsky, Chimen 1916- Brief entry ... 109
Abramson, Doris E. 1925- ... 25-28R
Abramson, Harold Alexander 1889-1980
Obituary ... 102
Abramson, Harold J(ulian) 1934- ... 45-48
Abramson, Jesse P. 1904-1979 Obituary .. 89-92
Abramson, Joan 1932- ... 25-28R
Abramson, Martin 1921- ... 49-52
Abramson, Michael 1944- ... 69-72
Abramson, Paul R(obert) 1937- ... CANR-8
Earlier sketch in CA 61-64
Abrash, Merritt 1930- ... 23-24R
Abrashkin, Raymond 1911-1960 ... 115
See also SATA 50
Abravanel, Elizabeth 1944- ... 112
Abravanel, Elliot D(on) 1942- ... 112
Abrecht, Mary Ellen (Benson) 1945- ... 69-72
Abreu, Maria Isabel 1919- ... 45-48
Abruzzo, Ben(jamine Lawrence)
1930-1985 Obituary ... 115
Absalom, Roger Neil Lewis 1929- ... 111
Abse, Dannie 1923- ... CANR-4
Earlier sketch in CA 53-56
See also CAAS 1
See also DLB 27
See also CLC 7, 29
Abse, David Wilfred 1915- ... 49-52
Abse, Joan 1926- ... 108
Abshire, David M. 1926- ... CANR-8
Earlier sketch in CA 23-24R
Abt, Clark C(laus) 1929- ... CANR-21
Earlier sketch in CA 69-72
Abt, Lawrence Edwin 1915- ... CANR-13
Earlier sketch in CA 33-36R
Abt, Vicki 1942- ... 120
Abu Jaber, Kamel S(aleh) 1932- ... CANR-14
Earlier sketch in CA 21-22R
Abu-Lughod, Ibrahim Ali 1929- ... CANR-10
Earlier sketch in CA 5-6R
Abu-Lughod, Janet L(ouise) 1928- ... CANR-10
Earlier sketch in CA 65-68
Abun-Nasr, Jamil Miri 1932- ... 69-72
Aby, Stephen H. 1949- ... 123
Abzug, Bella (Savitzky) 1920- Brief entry ... 104
Abzug, Martin 1916-1986 Obituary ... 119
Abzug, Robert H(enry) 1945- ... CANR-21
Earlier sketch in CA 104
Academicas Mentor
See Montagu, Ashley
Academic Investor
See Reddaway, W(illiam) Brian
Accola, Louis W(ayne) 1937- ... CANR-12
Earlier sketch in CA 29-32R
Ace, Goodman 1899-1982 ... 61-64
Obituary ... 106
Aceto, Vincent J(ohn) 1932- ... 106
Achard, George
See Torres-Levin, Tereska (Szwarc)
Achard, Marcel
See Ferreol, Marcel Auguste
Achebe, Chinua 1930- ... CANR-6
Earlier sketch in CA 4R
See also SATA 38, 40
See also CLC 1, 3, 5, 7, 11, 26
Achenbaum, W(ilbert) Andrew 1947- ... CANR-15
Earlier sketch in CA 89-92
Acheson, Dean (Gooderham) 1893-1971 .. CAP-2
Obituary ... 33-36R
Earlier sketch in CA 25-28
Acheson, Patricia Castles 1924- ... 3R
Achilles
See Lamb, Charles Bentall
Achinstein, Peter Jacob 1935- ... 111
Achtemeier, Elizabeth (Rice) 1926- ... CANR-8
Earlier sketch in CA 17-18R
Achtemeier, Paul J(ohn) 1927- ... CANR-8
Earlier sketch in CA 17-18R
Achyut
See Birla, Lakshminiwas
Ackart, Robert 1921- ... 109
Acker, Duane Calvin 1931- ... 33-36R
Acker, Helen ... 73-76
Acker, Kathy 1948- ... 122
Brief entry ... 117
See also CLC 45
Acker, Robert Flint 1920- ... 89-92
Acker, William R. B. 1910(?)-1974
Obituary ... 49-52
Ackerley, J(oe) R(andolph) 1896-1967 ... 102
Obituary ... 89-92
Ackerman, Bruce A. 1943- ... CANR-4
Earlier sketch in CA 53-56
Ackerman, Carl W(illiam) 1890-1970 ... 73-76
Obituary ... 29-32R
Ackerman, Diane 1948- ... 57-60
Ackerman, Edward A. 1911-1973
Obituary ... 41-44R
Ackerman, Eugene (Francis)
1888-1974 ... SATA-10
Ackerman, Forrest J(ames) 1916- ... 102
Ackerman, Gerald M(artin) 1928- ... CANR-1
Earlier sketch in CA 45-48
Ackerman, J. Mark 1939- ... 53-56
Ackerman, James S(loss) 1919- ... 9-10R
Ackerman, Nathan W(ard) 1908-1971 ... CAP-2
Earlier sketch in CA 29-32
Ackerman, Robert E(dwin) 1928- ... CANR-20
Earlier sketch in CA 45-48
Ackerman, Robert K. 1933- ... 123
Ackerman, Robert W(illiam) 1910-1980 ... 103
Ackerman, Susan Rose
See Rose-Ackerman, Susan
Ackermann, Paul Kurt 1919- Brief entry ... 104
Ackermann, Robert John 1933-
Brief entry ... 108
Ackerson, Duane (Wright, Jr.) 1942- ... 33-36R
Ackland, Rodney 1908- ... 57-60
Ackley, Charles Walton 1913-1975 ... 41-44R
Ackley, Hugh Gardner 1915- ... 61-64
Ackley, Randall William 1931- ... CANR-6
Earlier sketch in CA 53-56
Ackoff, Russell L(incoln) 1919- ... CANR-15
Earlier sketch in CA 41-44R
Ackroyd, Joyce Irene ... 103
Ackroyd, Peter 1949- Brief entry ... 123
See also CLC 34
Ackroyd, Peter R(unham) 1917- ... 25-28R
Ackworth, Robert Charles 1923- ... 5-6R
Acland, Alice
See Wignall, Anne
Acland, James H. 1917-1976 ... 41-44R
Acomb, Evelyn Martha
See Acomb-Walker, Evelyn
Acomb, Frances (Dorothy) 1907-
Brief entry ... 109
Acomb-Walker, Evelyn 1910- ... 85-88
Acorn, Milton 1923- ... 103
See also DLB 53
See also CLC 15
Acquaviva, Sabino Samele 1927- ... 101
Acquaye, Alfred Allotey 1939- ... 25-28R
Acre, Stephen
See Gruber, Frank
Acred, Arthur 1926- ... 25-28R
Acs, Laszlo (Bela) 1931- ... SATA-32, 42
Acton, Edward J. 1949- ... CANR-2
Earlier sketch in CA 45-48
Acton, Harold Mario Mitchell 1904- ... CANR-3
Earlier sketch in CA 4R
Acton, Jay
See Acton, Edward J.
Acton, Thomas (Alan) 1948- ... 57-60
Acuff, Frederick Gene 1931- Brief entry ... 110
Acuff, Selma Boyd 1924- ... 111
See also SATA 45
Acuna, Rodolfo 1932- Brief entry ... 108
Acuna, Rudy
See Acuna, Rudolfo
Aczel, Tamas 1921- ... 49-52
Ada, Alma Flor 1938- ... 123
See also SATA 43
Adachi, Barbara (Curtis) 1924- ... 49-52
Adair, Cecil
See Everett-Green, Evelyn
Adair, Dennis 1945- ... 107
Adair, Ian 1942- ... CANR-11
Earlier sketch in CA 69-72
Adair, Jack
See Pavey, Don
Adair, James 1709(?)-1783(?) ... DLB-30
Adair, James R. 1923- ... 19-20R
Adair, John G(lenn) 1933- ... 49-52
Adair, Margaret Weeks ?-1971 ... CAP-1
Earlier sketch in CA 13-14
See also SATA 10
Adam, Ben
See Drachman, Julian M(oses)
Adam, Cornel
See Lengyel, Cornel Adam
Adam, Helen 1909- ... CANR-7
Earlier sketch in CA 19-20R
Adam, Heribert 1936- ... 105
Adam, Jan 1920- ... 115
Adam, Michael 1919- ... 53-56
Adam, Ruth (Augusta) 1907- ... 23-24R
Adam, Thomas R(itchie) 1900- ... CAP-1
Earlier sketch in CA 19-20
Adamczewski, Zygmunt 1921- ... 15-16R
Adamec, Ludwig W(arren) 1924- ... CANR-24
Earlier sketches in CA 23-24R, CANR-9
Adamic, Alojzij 1899(?)-1951 Brief entry ... 109
Adamic, Louis
See Adamic, Alojzij
See also DLB 9
Adamov, Arthur 1908-1970 ... CAP-2
Obituary ... 25-28R
Earlier sketch in CA 17-18
See also CLC 4, 25
Adams, A. Don
See Cleveland, Philip Jerome
Adams, A. John 1931- ... 33-36R
Adams, Adrienne 1906- ... CANR-1
Earlier sketch in CA 49-52
See also SATA 8
Adams, Alexander B. 1917(?)-1984
Obituary ... 112
Adams, Alice (Boyd) 1926- ... 81-84
See also DLBY 86
See also CLC 6, 13, 46
Adams, Andy 1859-1935 ... YABC-1
Adams, Andy
See Gibson, Walter B(rown)
Adams, Anne H(utchinson) 1935- ... 41-44R
Adams, Annette
See Rowland, D(onald) S(ydney)
Adams, Ansel (Easton) 1902-1984 ... CANR-10
Obituary ... 112
Earlier sketch in CA 21-22R
See also AITN 1
Adams, Arthur E(ugene) 1917- ... CANR-4
Earlier sketch in CA 7-8R
Adams, Arthur Gray (Jr.) 1935- ... CANR-23
Earlier sketch in CA 107
Adams, Arthur Merrihew 1908- ... 53-56
Adams, Arthur Stanton 1896-1980
Obituary ... 102
Adams, Barbara
See Gardner, Virginia (Marberry)
Adams, Bart
See Bingley, David Ernest
Adams, Betsy
See Pitcher, Gladys
Adams, Brooks 1848-1927 Brief entry ... 123
See also DLB 47
Adams, Bruin
See Ellis, Edward S(ylvester)
Adams, Captain Bruin
See Ellis, Edward S(ylvester)
Adams, Captain J. F. C.
See Ellis, Edward S(ylvester)
Adams, Cedric M. 1902-1961 Obituary ... 89-92
Adams, Charles Francis, Jr. 1835-1915
Brief entry ... 113
See also DLB 47
Adams, Charles J(oseph) 1924- ... CANR-24
Earlier sketches in CA 17-18R, CANR-8
Adams, Charles Lynford 1929- ... 113
Adams, Charlotte 1899- Brief entry ... 107
Adams, Christopher
See Hopkins, Kenneth
Adams, Chuck
See Tubb, E(dwin) C(harles)
Adams, Cindy ... CANR-17
Earlier sketch in CA 23-24R
Adams, Cleve F(ranklin) 1895-1949
Brief entry ... 112
Adams, Clifton 1919- ... CANR-21
Earlier sketch in CA 13-14R
Adams, Clinton 1918- ... 33-36R
Adams, Dale
See Quinn, Elisabeth
Adams, Don(ald Kendrick) 1925- ... 33-36R
Adams, Donald K(napp) 1924-1987
Obituary ... 123
Brief entry ... 111
Adams, Donald R., Jr. 1940- Brief entry ... 113
Adams, Douglas Noel 1952- ... 106
See also DLBY 83
See also CLC 27
Adams, E(lie) M(aynard) 1919- ... 3R
Adams, Edith
See Shine, Deborah
Adams, Elsie B(onita) 1932- ... 69-72
Adams, Eugenia
See Owens, Virginia Stem
Adams, Evangeline (Smith) 1872(?)-1932
Brief entry ... 121
Adams, F(rank) Ramsay 1883-1963 ... 7-8R
Adams, Faith 1960- ... 121
Adams, Florence 1932- ... 49-52
Adams, Francis A(lexandre) 1874-1975
Obituary ... 61-64
Adams, Frank C(lyde) 1916- ... 69-72
Adams, Franklin P(ierce) 1881-1960
Obituary ... 93-96
See also DLB 29
Adams, Frederick C(harles) 1941-
Brief entry ... 105
Adams, George Matthew 1878-1962
Obituary ... 93-96
Adams, George Worthington 1905- ... 41-44R
Adams, Georgia Sachs 1913- ... 37-40R
Adams, Glenda 1939- ... 104
Adams, Graham, Jr. 1928- ... 17-18R
Adams, Harlen M(artin) 1904- ... CAP-1
Earlier sketch in CA 13-14
Adams, Harriet S(tratemeyer)
1894-1982 ... 19-20R
Obituary ... 106
See also SATA 1, 29
See also AITN 2
Adams, Harrison
See Stratemeyer, Edward L.
Adams, Harry Baker 1924- Brief entry ... 106
Adams, Hazard 1926- ... 9-10R
See also SATA 6
Adams, Henry (Brooks) 1838-1918
Brief entry ... 104
See also DLB 12, 47
See also TCLC 4
Adams, Henry H(itch) 1917- ... CANR-13
Earlier sketch in CA 21-22R
Adams, Henry Mason 1907- ... CAP-1
Earlier sketch in CA 17-18
Adams, Henry T.
See Ransom, Jay Ellis
Adams, Herbert Baxter 1850-1901 ... DLB-47
Adams, Herbert Mayow 1893-1985 ... CAP-2
Obituary ... 115
Earlier sketch in CA 25-28
Adams, Howard (Joseph) 1928- ... 89-92
Adams, J(ames) Donald 1891-1968 ... CANR-1
Earlier sketch in CA 2R
Adams, J(ames) Mack 1933- ... 85-88
Adams, James E(dward) 1941- ... 73-76
Adams, James F(rederick) 1927- ... 19-20R
Adams, James Luther 1901- ... 41-44R
Adams, James R(owe) 1934- ... 41-44R
Adams, James Truslow 1878-1949
Brief entry ... 115
See also DLB 17
Adams, Jane (Ellen) 1940- ... 116
Adams, Jay Edward 1929- Brief entry ... 108
Adams, Joey 1911- ... CANR-1
Earlier sketch in CA 49-52
Adams, John 1734-1826 ... DLB-31
Adams, John 1938- ... 111
Adams, John Clarke 1910- ... 3R
Adams, John Coldwell 1927- ... 121
Adams, John Cranford 1903-1986
Obituary ... 121
Adams, John D(avid) 1942- ... 115
Adams, John F(estus) 1930- ... 33-36R
Adams, John M(ilton) 1905-1981 ... 107
Adams, John P. 1923(?)-1983 ... 122
Obituary ... 111

Adams, John Paul
See Kinnaird, Clark
Adams, John Quincy 1767-1848 .... DLB-37
Adams, John R. 1900- 25-28R
Adams, Julian 1919- CANR-11
Earlier sketch in CA 25-28R
Adams, Justin
See Cameron, Lou
Adams, Kenneth Menzies 1922- 103
Adams, Kramer A. 1920- 11-12R
Adams, L(ouis) Jerold 1939- 49-52
Adams, Laura 1943- 53-56
Adams, Laurie 1941- 53-56
See also SATA 33
Adams, Lee (Richard) 1924- Brief entry 111
Adams, Leon D(avid) 1905- 45-48
Adams, Leonie (Fuller) 1899- CAP-1
Earlier sketch in CA 9-10
See also DLB 48
Adams, Les 1934- 97-100
Adams, Lowell
See Joseph, James (Herz)
Adams, Marion 1932- 41-44R
Adams, Mary (Grace Agnes) 1898-1984
Obituary 113
Adams, Maurice 1915(?)-1985 Obituary 116
Adams, Michael (Evelyn) 1920- 33-36R
Adams, Michael C(harles) C(orringham)
1945- 89-92
Adams, Mildred
See Kenyon, Mildred Adams
Adams, Nancy 1943(?)-1987 Obituary 123
Adams, Nathan Miller 1934- 45-48
Adams, Norman (Edward Albert) 1927- 114
Adams, Paul L(ieber) 1924- 61-64
Adams, Percy G(uy) 1914- CANR-4
Earlier sketch in CA 4R
Adams, Perseus 1933- 107
Adams, Philip R. 1908- 85-88
Adams, Phoebe-Lou 1918- Brief entry 121
Adams, Rachel Leona White 1905(?)-1979
Obituary 93-96
Adams, Ramon Frederick 1889-1976
Obituary 65-68
Adams, Ramona Shepherd 1921- 106
Adams, Richard (George) 1920- CANR-3
Earlier sketch in CA 49-52
See also SATA 7
See also CLC 4, 5, 18
See also AITN 1, 2
Adams, Richard E(dward) W(ood) 1931- 106
Adams, Richard N(ewbold) 1924- CANR-12
Earlier sketch in CA 29-32R
Adams, Richard P(errill) 1917-1977 ..... CAP-2
Obituary 69-72
Earlier sketch in CA 33-36
Adams, Robert (Franklin) 1932- 69-72
Adams, Robert H(ickman) 1937- CANR-22
Earlier sketch in CA 105
Adams, Robert Martin 1915- CANR-4
Earlier sketch in CA 5-6R
Adams, Robert McCormick 1926- CANR-12
Earlier sketch in CA 61-64
Adams, Robert P. 1910- 13-14R
Adams, Rolland Leroy 1905(?)-1979
Obituary 89-92
Adams, Russell B(aird), Jr. 1937- 69-72
Adams, Russell L. 1930- 53-56
Adams, Ruth Joyce SATA-14
Adams, Sally Pepper ?-197(?) 41-44R
Adams, Sam 1934- 57-60
Adams, Samuel 1722-1803 .... DLB-31, 43
Adams, Sexton 1936- 25-28R
Adams, (Llewellyn) Sherman 1899-1986
Obituary 120
Adams, Stephen J(on) 1945- 111
Adams, T(homas) W(illiam) 1933- 25-28R
Adams, Terrence Dean 1935- 33-36R
Adams, Theodore Floyd 1898-1980 ...... CAP-1
Obituary 97-100
Earlier sketch in CA 11-12
Adams, Thomas Boylston 1910- 114
Adams, Thomas F. 1927- 15-16R
Adams, Thomas Randolph 1921- 107
Adams, Tricia
See Kite, Pat
Adams, Val 1917(?)-1983 Obituary 109
Adams, Walter 1922- CANR-3
Earlier sketch in CA 2R
Adams, Willi Paul 1940- 105
Adams, William Howard Brief entry 105
Adams, William Taylor 1822-1897 ..... SATA-28
See also DLB 42
Adams, William Yewdale 1927- Brief entry .. 104
Adamski, George 1891-1965 Obituary 112
Adam Smith, Janet (Buchanan) 1905- 113
Adam-Smith, Patricia Jean 1926- 105
Adam-Smith, Patsy
See Adam-Smith, Patricia Jean
Adamson, Alan (Herbert) 1919- 81-84
Adamson, David Grant 1927- 15-16R
Adamson, Donald 1939- 53-56
Adamson, Ed(ward Joseph) 1915(?)-1972
Obituary 37-40R
Adamson, Frank
See Adams, Robert (Franklin)
Adamson, Gareth 1925-1982(?) CANR-11
Obituary 106
Earlier sketch in CA 13-14R
See also SATA 30, 46
Adamson, George Worsley 1913- 107
See also SATA 30
Adamson, Graham
See Groom, Arthur William
Adamson, Hans Christian 1890-1968 ...... 5-6R
Adamson, Joe
See Adamson, Joseph III
Adamson, Joseph III 1945- CANR-21
Earlier sketches in CA 45-48, CANR-1
Adamson, Joy(-Friederike Victoria)
1910-1980 .... CANR-22
Obituary 93-96
Earlier sketch in CA 69-72
See also SATA 11, 22
See also CLC 17
Adamson, Lesley
See Grant-Adamson, Lesley
Adamson, Walter L(uiz) 1946- 107
Adamson, Wendy Writson 1942- 53-56
See also SATA 22
Adamson, William Robert 1927- 23-24R
Adas, Michael 1943- 53-56
Adastra
See Mirepoix, Camille
Adburgham, Alison Haig 1912- CAP-1
Earlier sketch in CA 9-10
Adcock, Almey St. John 1894- 65-68
Adcock, Betty
See Adcock, Elizabeth S(harp)
Adcock, C(yril) John 1904- CAP-1
Earlier sketch in CA 19-20
Adcock, Elizabeth S(harp) 1938- 57-60
Adcock, Fleur 1934- CANR-11
Earlier sketch in CA 25-28R
See also DLB 40
See also CLC 41
Adcock, Frank Ezra 1886-1968 Obituary 106
Addams, Charles (Samuel) 1912- CANR-12
Earlier sketch in CA 61-64
See also CLC 30
Addanki, Sam 1932- 109
Adde, Leo 1927(?)-1975 Obituary 57-60
Addeo, Jovita A. 1939- 103
Addie, Bob 1911(?)-1982 Obituary 105
Addie, Pauline Betz 1919(?)- Brief entry 105
Addington, Arthur Charles 1939- 105
Addington, Larry H(olbrook) 1932- 33-36R
Addison, Gwen
See Harris, Al(fred)
Addison, Herbert 1889-1982 Obituary 108
Addison, Lloyd 1937- 45-48
Addison, William Wilkinson 1905- CANR-5
Earlier sketch in CA 13-14R
Addiss, Stephen 1935- 120
Addleshaw, George William Outram
1907(?)-1982 Obituary 107
Addona, Angelo F. 1925- 25-28R
See also SATA 14
Addy, George M(ilton) 1927- 21-22R
Addy, John 1915- 69-72
Addy, Ted
See Winterbotham, R(ussell) R(obert)
Ade, George 1866-1944 Brief entry 110
See also DLB 11, 25
Ade, Walter Frank Charles 1910- 53-56
Adelberg, Doris
See Orgel, Doris
Adelberg, Roy P. 1928- 17-18R
Adeler, Max
See Clark, Charles Heber
Adelman, Bob 1930- 69-72
Adelman, Clifford 1942- 41-44R
Adelman, Gary 1935- 33-36R
Adelman, Howard 1938- 25-28R
Adelman, Irma Glicman CANR-3
Earlier sketch in CA 5-6R
Adelman, Irving 1926- 21-22R
Adelman, Janet (Ann) 1941- 61-64
Adelman, Morris Albert 1917- Brief entry ... 104
Adelman, Saul J(oseph) 1944- 104
Adelmann, Frederick J(oseph) 1915- 49-52
Adelsberger, Lucie 1895-1971 Obituary .. 33-36R
Adelson, Daniel 1918- 69-72
Adelson, Joseph (Bernard) 1925- 19-20R
Adelson, Leone 1908- 61-64
See also SATA 11
Adelson, Sandra 1934- 105
Adelstein, Michael E. 1922- CANR-15
Earlier sketch in CA 33-36R
Aden, John M(ichael) 1918- 97-100
Adenauer, Konrad 1876-1967 Obituary 112
Adeney, David Howard 1911- 53-56
Ader, Paul (Fassett) 1919- 65-68
Aderman, Ralph M(erl) 1919- 5-6R
Ades, Dawn 1943- 103
Adiseshiah, Malcolm S(athianathan)
1910- 81-84
Adizes, Ichak 1937- 33-36R
Adkins, Arthur W(illiam) H(ope) 1929- 111
Brief entry 104
Adkins, Cecil (Dale) 1932- 115
Adkins, Dorothy C.
See Wood, Dorothy Adkins
Adkins, Jan 1944- 33-36R
See also SATA 8
See also CLR 7
Adkins, Nelson F(rederick) 1897-1976 73-76
Obituary 65-68
Adlard, John 1929- CANR-21
Earlier sketches in CA 57-60, CANR-6
Adlard, (P.) Mark 1932- 65-68
Adleman, Robert H. 1919- 25-28R
Adler, Alfred (F.) 1870-1937 Brief entry ... 119
Adler, B.
See Adler, William
Adler, Betty 1918-1973 .... CAP-1
Earlier sketch in CA 13-14
Adler, Bill
See Adler, William
Adler, C(arole) S(chwerdtfeger) 1932- .. CANR-19
Earlier sketch in CA 89-92
See also SATA 26
See also CLC 35
Adler, Carol 1938- 61-64
Adler, Christopher Edward 1954(?)-1984
Obituary 114
Adler, Cyrus 1863-1940 Brief entry 122
Adler, David A. 1947- CANR-23
Earlier sketches in CA 57-60, CANR-7
See also SATA 14
Adler, Denise Rinker 1908- 102
Adler, Elmer 1884-1962 Obituary 89-92
Adler, France-Michele 1942- 105
Adler, Freda 1934- CANR-11
Earlier sketch in CA 69-72
Adler, H. G. 1910- CANR-10
Earlier sketch in CA 25-28R
Adler, Hans A(rnold) 1921- 49-52
Adler, Helmut E(rnest) 1920- 33-36R
Adler, Irene
See Penzler, Otto
and Storr, Catherine (Cole)
Adler, Irving 1913- CANR-2
Earlier sketch in CA 7-8R
See also SATA 1, 29
Adler, Jack 73-76
Adler, Jacob 1873(?)-1974 Obituary 53-56
Adler, Jacob 1913- 17-18R
Adler, Jacob H(enry) 1919- 15-16R
Adler, John Hans 1912-1980 Obituary ... 97-100
Adler, Kathleen
See Jones, Kathleen Eve
Adler, Larry 1939- 105
See also SATA 36
Adler, Lucile 1922- 105
Adler, Lulla
See Rosenfeld, Lulla
Adler, Manfred 1936- 49-52
Adler, Margot 1946- 107
Adler, Max K(urt) 1905- CANR-3
Earlier sketch in CA 9-10R
Adler, Mortimer J(erome) 1902- CANR-7
Earlier sketch in CA 65-68
Adler, Norman Tenner 1941- CANR-20
Earlier sketch in CA 69-72
Adler, Peggy SATA-22
Adler, Renata 1938- CANR-22
Earlier sketches in CA 49-52, CANR-5
See also CLC 8, 31
Adler, Ruth 1915-1968 .... CANR-4
Obituary 25-28R
Earlier sketch in CA 7-8R
See also SATA 1
Adler, Selig 1909-1984 .... 7-8R
Obituary 114
Adler, Sol 1925- CANR-22
Earlier sketches in CA 19-20R, CANR-7
Adler, Warren 1927- CANR-11
Earlier sketch in CA 69-72
Adler, William 1929- CANR-7
Earlier sketch in CA 11-12R
Adler, William 1951- 124
Adlerblum, Nina H. 1882-1974 Obituary ... 49-52
Adoff, Arnold 1935- CANR-20
Earlier sketch in CA 41-44R
See also SATA 5
See also CLR 7
See also AITN 1
Adolph, E. F.
See Adolph, Edward F(rederick)
Adolph, Edward F(rederick) 1895-1986
Obituary 121
Adomeit, Ruth E(lizabeth) 1910- 111
Adon, Aaron Bar
See Bar-Adon, Aaron
Adony, Raoul
See Launay, Andre (Joseph)
Adorjan, Carol (Madden) 1934- CANR-14
Earlier sketch in CA 41-44R
See also SATA 10
Adorno, Theodor W(iesengrund)
1903-1969 89-92
Obituary 25-28R
Adrian, Arthur A(llen) 1906- CAP-2
Earlier sketch in CA 19-20
Adrian, Charles R. 1922- CANR-3
Earlier sketch in CA 2R
Adrian, Edgar Douglas 1889-1977
Obituary 73-76
Adrian, Mary
See Jorgensen, Mary Venn
Adrian, Rhys Brief entry 106
Adshead, Gladys L(ucy) 1896- 29-32R
See also SATA 3
Advani, Rukun 1955- 119
Ady, Endre 1877-1919 Brief entry 107
See also TCLC 11
Ady, Ronald W(illiam) 1934- 117
Adytum
See Curl, James Stevens
Adzigian, Denise Allard 1952- 97-100
Aebi, Ormond 1916- 89-92
Aeby, Jacquelyn CANR-24
Earlier sketch in CA 29-32R
Aero, Rita 112
Aers, David 1946- CANR-8
Earlier sketch in CA 61-64
Aeschliman, Michael D(avid) 1948- 113
Aesop 620(?)-564(?) B.C. CLR-14
Aesop, Abraham
See Newbery, John
Affabee, Eric
See Stine, R(obert) L(awrence)
Affron, Charles 1935- 21-22R
Afnan, Ruhi Muhsen 1899-1971 .... CAP-2
Earlier sketch in CA 29-32
Africa, Thomas Wilson 1927- 17-18R
Africano, Lillian 1935- CANR-11
Earlier sketch in CA 69-72
Aftel, Mandy 1948- 108
Afterman, Allen 1941- 103
Agan, Patrick 1943- CANR-10
Earlier sketch in CA 65-68
Agan, Raymond J(ohn) 1919- 33-36R
Agan, (Anna) Tessie 1897- CAP-1
Earlier sketch in CA 17-18
Agapida, Fray Antonio
See Irving, Washington
Agar, Brian
See Ballard, (Willis) Todhunter
Agar, Herbert (Sebastian) 1897-1980 65-68
Obituary 102
Agar, Michael H(enry) 1945- CANR-2
Earlier sketch in CA 45-48
Agar, William (Macdonough) 1894-1972
Obituary 37-40R
Agard, H. E.
See Evans, Hilary
Agard, Nadema 1948- SATA-18
Agarossi, Elena 1940- CANR-20
Earlier sketch in CA 97-100
Agarwala, Amar N. 1917- CANR-13
Earlier sketch in CA 23-24R
Agassi, Joseph 1927- CANR-15
Earlier sketch in CA 41-44R
Agassiz, Jean Louis Rodolphe
1807-1873 .... DLB-1
Agay, Denes 1911- 69-72
Agbodeka, Francis 1931- CANR-4
Earlier sketch in CA 53-56
Agee, James (Rufus) 1909-1955
Brief entry 108
See also DLB 2, 26
See also CDALB 1941-1968
See also TCLC 1, 19
See also AITN 1
Agee, Joel 1940- Brief entry 105
Agee, Philip 1935- Brief entry 104
Agee, Warren Kendall 1916- 17-18R
Ager, Cecelia 1902-1981 Obituary 103
Ager, Derek Victor 1923- 107
Ageton, Arthur Ainsley 1900-1971 ...... CANR-1
Obituary 29-32R
Earlier sketch in CA 3R
Aggeler, Geoffrey D(onovan) 1939- 97-100
Aggertt, Otis J. 1916-1973 .... 33-36R
Aghill, Gordon
See Silverberg, Robert
Aginsky, Bernard W(illard) 1905- 85-88
Aginsky, Burt W.
See Aginsky, Bernard W(illard)
Aginsky, Ethel G(oldberg) 1910- 41-44R
Agle, Nan Hayden 1905- CANR-3
Earlier sketch in CA 4R
See also SATA 3
Agnelli, Susanna 1922- 109
Agnew, Edith J(osephine) 1897- CAP-1
Earlier sketch in CA 17-18
See also SATA 11
Agnew, James Barron 1930- 89-92
Agnew, Patience McCormick-Goodhart
1913(?)-1976 Obituary 69-72
Agnew, Peter L(awrence) 1901-1969 ..... CAP-2
Earlier sketch in CA 21-22
Agnew, Spiro T(heodore) 1918-
Brief entry 110
Agniel, Lucien D. 1919- 29-32R
Agnon, S(hmuel) Y(osef Halevi)
1888-1970 .... CAP-2
Obituary 25-28R
Earlier sketch in CA 17-18
See also CLC 4, 8, 14
Agonito, Rosemary (Giambattista) 1937- 122
Brief entry 112
Agor, Weston H(arris) 1939- 49-52
Agostinelli, Maria Enrica 1929- 33-36R
Agranoff, Robert 1936- CANR-14
Earlier sketch in CA 37-40R
Agree, Rose H. 1913- 21-22R
Agress, Hyman 1931- 89-92
Agress, Lynne 1941- 112
Agresto, John 1946- 115
Agronsky, Martin (Zama) 1915- 109
See also AITN 2
Aguero, Kathleen 1949- 73-76
Aguila, Pancho 1945- 105
Aguilar, Luis E. 1926- 23-24R
Aguilar, Rodolfo J(esus) 1936- 53-56
Aguilera, Donna Conant 37-40R
Aguilera, Jaime Roldos
See Roldos Aguilera, Jaime
Aguilera Malta, Demetrio 1909- 124
Aguilera Malta, Demetrio 1909(?)-
Brief entry 111
Aguolu, Christian Chukwunedu 1940- .. CANR-19
Earlier sketch in CA 101
Agus, Irving A(braham) 1910-1984 ...... CAP-2
Obituary 113
Earlier sketch in CA 33-36
Agus, Jacob Bernard 1911-1986 .... CANR-2
Obituary 120
Earlier sketch in CA 7-8R
Aguzzi-Barbagli, Danilo 1924- 49-52
Agwani, Mohammed Shafi 1928- CANR-7
Earlier sketch in CA 17-18R
Aharoni, Yohanan 1919-1976 .... CANR-15
Earlier sketch in CA 25-28R
Ahearn, Barry 1950- 110
Ahearn, Catherine 1949- 114
Ahern, Barnabas M. 1915- CANR-3
Earlier sketch in CA 7-8R
Ahern, Emily M. 1944- 49-52
Ahern, James F(rancis) 1932-1986 ...... 41-44R
Obituary 118
Ahern, John F(rancis) 1936- 61-64
Ahern, Margaret McCrohan 1921- 15-16R
See also SATA 10

Ahern, Thomas Francis 1947- ... CANR-21
Earlier sketches in CA 45-48, CANR-1
Ahern, Tim(othy James) 1952- ... 115
Ahern, Tom
See Ahern, Thomas Francis
Aherne, Brian (de Lacy) 1902-1986
Obituary ... 118
Brief entry ... 117
Aherne, Owen
See Cassill, R(onald) V(erlin)
Ahituv, Niv 1943- ... 117
Ahl, Anna Maria 1926- ... SATA-32
Ahl, Frederick Michael 1941- ... 111
Ahlberg, Allan 1938- ... 114
Brief entry ... 111
See also SATA 35
Ahlberg, Janet 1944- ... 114
Brief entry ... 111
See also SATA 32
Ahlberg, William A. 1922(?)-1985
Obituary ... 116
Ahlborn, Richard Eighme 1933- ... 108
Ahlers, John C(larke) 1927-1983 Obituary .. 110
Ahlert, Richard 1921-1985 Obituary ... 117
Ahlstroem, G(oesta) W(erner) 1918- ... CANR-21
Earlier sketch in CA 45-48
Ahlstrom, G(osta) W(erner)
See Ahlstroem, G(oesta) W(erner)
Ahlstrom, Sydney E(ckman) 1919-1984 ..21-22R
Obituary ... 113
Ahmad, Ishtiaq 1937- ... 53-56
Ahmad, Nafis 1913- ... 17-18R
Ahmad, Suleiman M(uhammad) 1943- ... 110
Ahmann, Mathew H(all) 1931- ... 9-10R
Ahnebrink, Lars 1915- ... 5-6R
Ahnstrom, D(oris) N. 1915- ... 7-8R
Aho, James (Alfred) 1942- ... 107
Ahokas, Jaakko (Alfred) 1923- ... 65-68
Ahrari, Mohammed E. 1945- ... 120
Ahsen, Akhter 1931- ... CANR-10
Earlier sketch in CA 61-64
Ahuja, Savitri 1924- ... 112
Ai 1947- ... 85-88
See also CLC 4, 14
Aichinger, Helga 1937- ... CANR-19
Earlier sketch in CA 25-28R
See also SATA 4
Aichinger, Ilse 1921- ... 85-88
Aichinger, Peter 1933- ... CANR-11
Earlier sketch in CA 61-64
Aickman, Robert (Fordyce) 1914- ... CANR-3
Earlier sketch in CA 7-8R
Aidala, Thomas R(ichard) 1933-
Brief entry ... 112
Aidenoff, Abraham 1913-1976 ... 37-40R
Obituary ... 61-64
Aidoo, (Christina) Ama Ata 1942- ... 101
Aiguillette
See Hargreaves, Reginald (Charles)
Aiken, Clarissa Lorenz 1899- ... CAP-2
Earlier sketch in CA 21-22
See also SATA 12
Aiken, Conrad (Potter) 1889-1973 ... CANR-4
Obituary ... 45-48
Earlier sketch in CA 5-6R
See also SATA 3, 30
See also DLB 9, 45
See also CLC 1, 3, 5, 10
Aiken, George D(avid) 1892-1984
Obituary ... 114
Brief entry ... 111
Aiken, Henry David 1912-1982 ... CANR-1
Obituary ... 106
Earlier sketch in CA 4R
Aiken, Irene (Nixon) ... 93-96
Aiken, Joan (Delano) 1924- ... CANR-23
Earlier sketches in CA 9-10R, CANR-4
See also SATA 2, 30
See also SAAS 1
See also CLC 35
See also CLR 1
Aiken, John (Kempton) 1913- ... 101
Aiken, John R(obert) 1927- ... 33-36R
Aiken, Lewis R(oscoe), Jr. 1931- ... CANR-10
Earlier sketch in CA 25-28R
Aiken, Maurice C. 1909(?)-1983 Obituary ... 109
Aiken, Michael Thomas 1932- ... CANR-9
Earlier sketch in CA 21-22R
Aikin, Charles 1901- ... 7-8R
Aikman, Ann
See McQuade, Ann Aikman
Aikman, David (B. T.) 1944- ... 65-68
Aikman, Lonnelle (Davison) 1901(?)-1986
Obituary ... 121
Aimes, Angelica 1943- ... CANR-14
Earlier sketch in CA 81-84
Ainsbury, Ray
See Paine, Lauran (Bosworth)
and Verrill, A(lphues) Hyatt
Ainsbury, Roy
See Paine, Lauran (Bosworth)
Ainslie, Rosalynde 1932- ... 25-28R
Ainslie, Tom
See Carter, Richard
Ainsworth, Charles H(arold) 1935- ... 49-52
Ainsworth, Dorothy Sears 1894-1976
Obituary ... 69-72
Ainsworth, Ed(ward Maddin)
1902-1968 ... CANR-4
Earlier sketch in CA 5-6R
Ainsworth, G(eoffrey) C(lough) 1905- ... 73-76
Ainsworth, Harriet
See Cadell, (Violet) Elizabeth
Ainsworth, Katherine 1908- ... 29-32R
Ainsworth, Mary D(insmore) Salter
1913- ... CANR-8
Earlier sketch in CA 21-22R
Ainsworth, Norma ... CANR-5
Earlier sketch in CA 15-16R
See also SATA 9
Ainsworth, Patricia
See Bigg, Patricia Nina
Ainsworth, Ray
See Paine, Lauran (Bosworth)
Ainsworth, Roy
See Paine, Lauran (Bosworth)
Ainsworth, Ruth
See Gilbert, Ruth Gallard Ainsworth
See also SATA 7
Ainsworth, Thomas Hargraves, Jr. 1920- ... 123
Ainsworth, William Harrison
1805-1882 ... SATA-24
See also DLB 21
Ainsztein, Reuben 1917-1981 ... 110
Obituary ... 108
Air Chief Marshal Lord Dowding
See Dowding, Hugh Caswell Tremenheere
Aird, Catherine
See McIntosh, Kinn Hamilton
Aird, Eileen M(argaret) 1945- ... 49-52
Airlie, Catherine
See MacLeod, Jean Sutherland
Airola, Paavo (Olavi) 1915- ... 81-84
Aislin
See Mosher, (Christopher) Terry
Aistis, Jonas 1908(?)-1973 Obituary ... 41-44R
Aistrop, Jack 1916- ... CANR-3
Earlier sketch in CA 4R
See also SATA 14
Aitchison, Janet 1962- ... 57-60
Aitken, A(dam) J(ack) 1921- ... CANR-7
Earlier sketch in CA 13-14R
Aitken, Amy 1952- ... 108
See also SATA 40
Aitken, Dorothy 1916- ... CANR-2
Earlier sketch in CA 49-52
See also SATA 10
Aitken, Douglas 1933- ... 115
Aitken, Hugh G(eorge) J(effrey) 1922- ... CANR-3
Earlier sketch in CA 2R
Aitken, Jonathan (William Patrick)
1942- ... 21-22R
Aitken, (John William) Max(well)
1910-1985 Obituary ... 116
Aitken, Thomas, Jr. 1910- ... 2R
Aitken, W(illiam) R(ussell) 1913- ... 41-44R
Aitken, William Maxwell
See Beaverbrook, William Maxwell Aitken
Aitkin, Don(ald Alexander) 1937- ... CANR-15
Earlier sketch in CA 93-96
Aitmatov, Chingiz 1928- ... 103
Ajami, Alfred M(ichel) 1948- Brief entry ... 110
Ajar, Emile
See Kacew, Romain
Ajay, Betty 1918- ... 69-72
Ajayi, J(acob) F(estus) Ade(niyi)
1929- ... CANR-18
Earlier sketch in CA 61-64
Ajegbo, Keith 1946- ... 122
Ajilvsgi, Geyata 1933- ... 124
Akaba, Suekichi 1910- ... SATA-46
Akaha, Tsuneo 1949- ... 120
Akanji, Sangodare
See Beier, Ulli
Akare, Thomas 1950- ... 109
Akashi, Yoji 1928- ... 33-36R
Ake, Claude 1939- ... CANR-10
Earlier sketch in CA 21-22R
Akehurst, M(ichael) B(arton) 1940- ... 25-28R
Akens, David S. 1921- ... CANR-12
Earlier sketch in CA 25-28R
Akenson, Donald Harman 1941- ... CANR-22
Earlier sketches in CA 57-60, CANR-7
Aker, George F(rederick) 1927- ... CANR-15
Earlier sketch in CA 41-44R
Akeret, Robert U(lrich) 1928- ... 45-48
Akers, Alan Burt
See Bulmer, (Henry) Kenneth
Akers, Charles W(esley) 1920- ... 15-16R
Akers, Floyd
See Baum, L(yman) Frank
Akers, Keith 1949- ... 112
Akers, Ronald L(ouis) 1939- ... CANR-1
Earlier sketch in CA 45-48
Akers, Susan Grey 1889-1984 Obituary ... 112
Akhmadulina, Bella Akhatovna 1937- ... 65-68
Akhmatova, Anna 1888-1966 ... CAP-1
Obituary ... 25-28R
Earlier sketch in CA 19-20
See also CLC 11, 25
Akhnaton, Askia
See Eckels, Jon
Akhurst, Bertram A. 1928- ... 45-48
Akin, Wallace E(lmus) 1923- ... 25-28R
Akin, William E(rnest) 1936- ... 116
Akinjogbin, I(saac) A(deagbo) 1930- ... CANR-12
Earlier sketch in CA 21-22R
Akins, Zoe 1886-1958 Brief entry ... 115
See also DLB 26
Akita, George 1926- ... 19-20R
Akmakjian, Hiag 1926- ... 57-60
Akpabot, Samuel Ekpe 1932- ... 101
Akrigg, G(eorge) P(hillip) V(ernon)
1913- ... 25-28R
Aksenov, Vassily
See Aksyonov, Vassily (Pavlovich)
See also CLC 22
Aksyonov, Vassily (Pavlovich) 1932- ... CANR-12
Earlier sketch in CA 53-56
See also CLC 37
Akutagawa Ryunosuke 1892-1927
Brief entry ... 117
See also TCLC 16
Aladjem, Henrietta H. 1917- ... 105
Alailima, Fay C. 1921- ... 33-36R
Alain
See Brustlein, Daniel
Alain-Fournier
See Fournier, Henri Alban
See also DLB 65
See also TCLC 6
Alajalov, Constantin 1900-1987 Obituary ... 123
Al-Amin, Jamil Abdullah 1943- Brief entry .. 112
Alan, Jack
See Green, Alan (Baer)
Alan, Sandy
See Ullman, Allan
Aland, Kurt 1915- ... CANR-12
Earlier sketch in CA 25-28R
Alas (y Urena), Leopoldo (Enrique Garcia)
1852-1901 Brief entry ... 113
Alaya, Flavia (M.) 1935- ... 33-36R
al-Azm, Sadik J. 1934- ... CANR-9
Earlier sketch in CA 21-22R
Alazraki, Jaime 1934- ... CANR-21
Earlier sketch in CA 33-36R
Alba, Nanina 1915-1968 ... DLB-41
Alba, Richard D(enis) 1942- ... 109
Alba, Victor 1916- ... CANR-10
Earlier sketch in CA 23-24R
Alba de Gamez, Cielo Cayetana 1920- ... 93-96
Albanese, Catherine L(ouise) 1940- ... CANR-24
Earlier sketches in CA 65-68, CANR-9
Albaret, Celeste (Gineste) 1891-1984 ... 73-76
Obituary ... 112
Albaugh, Edwin (Doll, Jr.) 1935- ... 89-92
Albaugh, Ralph M. 1909- ... CAP-1
Earlier sketch in CA 13-14
Albaum, Gerald (Sherwin) 1933- ... CANR-14
Earlier sketch in CA 37-40R
Albaum, Melvin 1936- ... 53-56
Albee, Edward (Franklin III) 1928- ... CANR-8
Earlier sketch in CA 7-8R
See also DLB 7
See also CDALB 1941-1968
See also CLC 1, 2, 3, 5, 9, 11, 13, 25
See also AITN 1
Albee, George Sumner 1905-1964 ... 3R
Alber, Mike 1938- ... 25-28R
Albers, Anni 1899- ... CANR-2
Earlier sketch in CA 2R
Albers, Henry H. 1919- ... CANR-6
Earlier sketch in CA 2R
Albers, Josef 1888-1976 ... CANR-3
Obituary ... 65-68
Earlier sketch in CA 4R
Albert, A(braham) Adrian 1905-1972
Obituary ... 37-40R
Albert, Allan (Praigrod) 1945- Brief entry ... 116
Albert, Burton, Jr. 1936- ... CANR-23
Earlier sketches in CA 61-64, CANR-8
See also SATA 22
Albert, Ethel M(ary) 1918- ... 23-24R
Albert, Gail 1942- ... 108
Albert, Harold A. ... 29-32R
Albert, Linda 1939- ... 110
Albert, Louise 1928- ... 69-72
Albert, Marv 1943- ... 101
Albert, Marvin H. ... 73-76
Albert, Mimi (Abriel) 1940- ... 73-76
Albert, Peter J(oseph) 1946- ... 114
Albert, Walter E. 1930- ... 23-24R
Albertazzie, Ralph 1923- ... 101
Alberti, Rafael 1902- ... 85-88
See also CLC 7
Alberti, Robert E(dward) 1938- ... CANR-7
Earlier sketch in CA 61-64
Alberts, David Stephen 1942- ... 29-32R
Alberts, Frances Jacobs 1907- ... 5-6R
See also SATA 14
Alberts, Robert C(arman) 1907- ... 33-36R
Alberts, William W. 1925- ... 21-22R
Albertson, Chris 1931- ... 57-60
Albertson, Dean 1920- ... CANR-3
Earlier sketch in CA 2R
Albertyn, Dorothy
See Black, Dorothy
Albery, Nobuko ... 81-84
Albin, Peter S(teigman) 1934- ... 85-88
Albini, Joseph L(ouis) 1930- ... 61-64
Albinski, Henry Stephen 1931- ... CANR-23
Earlier sketches in CA 23-24R, CANR-8
Albinson, Jack
See Albinson, James P.
Albinson, James P. 1932- ... 57-60
Albion, Lee Smith ... SATA-29
Albion, Robert Greenhalgh 1896-1983 ... CANR-3
Obituary ... 110
Earlier sketch in CA 4R
Albornoz, Claudio Sanchez
See Sanchez Albornoz, Claudio
Albran, Kehlog
See Shacket, Sheldon R(ubin)
Albrand, Martha (a pseudonym)
1914-1981 ... CANR-11
Obituary ... 108
Earlier sketch in CA 13-14R
Albrecht, Lillie (Vanderveer) 1894- ... 7-8R
See also SATA 12
Albrecht, Milton C(harles) 1904- ... CANR-13
Earlier sketch in CA 33-36R
Albrecht, Robert C(harles) 1933- ... 23-24R
Albrecht, Ruth E. 1910- ... 17-18R
Albrecht, William P(rice) 1907- ... 73-76
Albrecht-Carrie, Rene 1904-1978 ... CANR-1
Earlier sketch in CA 3R
Albright, Bets Parker
See Albright, Elizabeth A.
Albright, Bliss (James F.) 1903- ... 33-36R
Albright, Elizabeth A. 1920- ... 108
Albright, Horace M(arden) 1890-1987 ... 124
Obituary ... 122
Albright, John Brannon 1930- ... 65-68
Albright, Joseph (Medill Patterson)
1937- ... 97-100
Albright, Peter 1926- ... 108
Albright, Raymond W(olf) 1901-1965 ... CAP-1
Earlier sketch in CA 9-10
Albright, Roger (Lynch) 1922- ... 106
Albright, Thomas 1935-1984 Obituary ... 112
Albright, William F(oxwell) 1891-1971
Obituary ... 33-36R
Albrow, Martin 1937- ... 33-36R
Albus, James Sacra 1935- ... 124
Alcala-Galiano, Juan Valera y
See Valera y Alcala-Galiano, Juan
Alcalde, E. L.
See Chaij, Fernando
Alcalde, Miguel
See Burgess, M(ichael) R(oy)
Alcantara, Ruben R(eyes) 1940- ... 105
Alcayaga, Lucila Godoy
See Godoy Alcayaga, Lucila
Alchemy, Jack
See Gershator, David
Alchian, Armen A(lbert) 1914- Brief entry ... 110
Alcibiade
See Praz, Mario
Alcock, Gudrun ... SATA-33
Alcock, Vivien 1924- ... 110
See also SATA 38, 45
Alcorn, Alfred 1941- ... 122
Alcorn, John 1935- ... SATA-30, 31
Alcorn, Marvin D. 1902- ... 15-16R
Alcorn, Pat B(arker) 1948- ... 107
Alcorn, Robert Hayden 1909- ... 5-6R
Alcosser, Sandra (B.) 1944- Brief entry ... 124
Alcott, Amos Bronson 1799-1888 ... DLB-1
Alcott, Julia
See Cudlipp, Edythe
Alcott, Louisa May 1832-1888 ... YABC-1
See also DLB 1, 42
See also CLR 1
Alcott, William Andrus 1789-1859 ... DLB-1
Alcyone
See Krishnamurti, Jiddu
Ald, Roy A(llison) ... CANR-24
Earlier sketch in CA 73-76
Alda, Alan 1936- ... 103
Alda, Arlene 1933- ... 114
See also SATA 36, 44
Aldan, Daisy 1923- ... CANR-8
Earlier sketch in CA 13-14R
Aldanov, M. A.
See Aldanov, Mark (Alexandrovich)
Aldanov, Mark (Alexandrovich)
1886(?)-1957 Brief entry ... 118
See also TCLC 23
Aldcroft, Derek H. 1936- ... CANR-12
Earlier sketch in CA 25-28R
Alden, Carella
See Remington, Ella-Carrie
Alden, Dauril 1926- ... 105
Alden, Douglas William 1912- ... 69-72
Alden, Isabella (Macdonald) 1841(?)-1930
Brief entry ... 120
See also YABC 2
See also DLB 42
Alden, Jack
See Barrows, (Ruth) Marjorie
Alden, John D. 1921- ... 17-18R
Alden, John R(ichard) 1908- ... CANR-11
Earlier sketch in CA 61-64
Alden, Michele
See Avallone, Michael (Angelo), Jr.
Alden, Robert L(eslie) 1937- ... 65-68
Alden, Sue
See Francis, Dorothy Brenner
Alder, Francis A(nthony) 1937- ... 61-64
Alder, Henry (Ludwig) 1922- ... 49-52
Alderfer, Clayton P. 1940- ... 37-40R
Alderfer, E. G.
See Alderfer, E. Gordon
Alderfer, E. Gordon 1915- ... 121
Alderfer, Harold F(reed) 1903- ... 11-12R
Alderman, Clifford Lindsey 1902- ... CANR-3
Earlier sketch in CA 3R
See also SATA 3
Alderman, Geoffrey 1944- ... 93-96
Alderman, (Barbara) Joy 1931- ... 61-64
Alderson, Jo(anne) Bartels 1930- ... 65-68
Alderson, (Arthur) Stanley 1927- ... 7-8R
Alderson, Sue Ann 1940- ... SATA-48
Alderson, William T(homas), Jr. 1926- ... 9-10R
Alding, Peter
See Jeffries, Roderic (Graeme)
Aldington, Richard 1892-1962 ... 85-88
See also DLB 20, 36
Aldis, Dorothy (Keeley) 1896-1966 ... 3R
See also SATA 2
See also DLB 22
Aldiss, Brian W(ilson) 1925- ... CANR-5
Earlier sketch in CA 5-6R
See also CAAS 2
See also SATA 34
See also DLB 14
See also CLC 5, 14, 40
Aldon, Adair
See Meigs, Cornelia Lynde
Aldouby, Zwy H(erbert) 1931- ... 33-36R
Aldous, Allan (Charles) 1911- ... SATA-27
Aldous, Anthony Michael 1935- ... 69-72
Aldous, Tony
See Aldous, Anthony Michael
Aldred, Cyril 1914- ... CANR-6
Earlier sketch in CA 57-60

Aldrich, Ann
See Meaker, Marijane
Aldrich, C(larence) Knight 1914- ... 25-28R
Aldrich, Frederic DeLong 1899- ... CAP-1
Earlier sketch in CA 11-12
Aldrich, Jonathan 1936- Brief entry ... 112
Aldrich, Joseph C(offin) 1940- ... 114
Aldrich, Nelson Wilmarth, Jr. 1935-
Brief entry ... 110
Aldrich, Richard (Stoddard) 1902-1986
Obituary ... 119
Aldrich, Ruth I(sabelle) ... 105
Aldrich, Sandra Picklesimer 1945- ... 111
Aldrich, Thomas Bailey 1836-1907
Brief entry ... 111
See also SATA 17
See also DLB 42
Aldridge, A(lfred) Owen 1915- ... 17-18R
Aldridge, Adele 1934- ... 49-52
Aldridge, Alan 1943(?)- ... SATA-33
Aldridge, (Harold Edward) James
1918- ... CANR-13
Earlier sketch in CA 61-64
Aldridge, Jeffrey 1938- ... 25-28R
Aldridge, John W(atson) 1922- ... CANR-3
Earlier sketch in CA 2R
Aldridge, Josephine Haskell ... 73-76
See also SATA 14
Aldridge, Richard Boughton 1930- ... CANR-3
Earlier sketch in CA 9-10R
Aldrin, Edwin E(ugene), Jr. 1930- ... 89-92
Aldwinckle, Russell (Foster) 1911- ... 69-72
Aldyne, Nathan
See McDowell, Michael
Alegria, Fernando 1918- ... CANR-5
Earlier sketch in CA 11-12R
Alegria, Ricardo E. 1921- ... CANR-15
Earlier sketch in CA 25-28R
See also SATA 6
Aleichem, Sholom
See Rabinovitch, Sholem
See also TCLC 1
Aleixandre, Vicente 1898-1984 ... 85-88
Obituary ... 114
See also CLC 9, 36
Alejandro, Carlos Federico Diaz
See Diaz-Alejandro, Carlos Federico
Aleksin, Anatolii Georgievich 1924- ... 109
See also SATA 36
Aleman, Miguel 1903(?)-1983 Obituary ... 110
Alent, Rose Marie Bachem
See Bachem Alent, Rose M(arie Baake)
Alepoudelis, Odysseus
See Elytis, Odysseus
Aleshkovsky, Joseph 1929- Brief entry ... 121
Aleshkovsky, Yuz
See Aleshkovsky, Joseph
See also CLC 44
Alessandra, Anthony J(oseph) 1947- ... 103
Alessandrini, Federico 1906(?)-1983
Obituary ... 109
Alex, Ben (a pseudonym) 1946- ... 114
See also SATA 45
Alex, Marlee (a pseudonym) 1948- ... 114
See also SATA 45
Alexander, Albert 1914- ... 25-28R
Alexander, Alfred 1908-1983 Obituary ... 110
Alexander, Anna B(arbara Cooke) 1913- ... 57-60
See also SATA 1
Alexander, Anne
See Alexander, Anna B(arbara Cooke)
Alexander, Anthony Francis 1920- ... 2R
Alexander, Arthur (Wilson) 1927- ... 7-8R
Alexander, Bevin (Ray) 1928- ... 122
Alexander, Boyd 1913-1980 ... 53-56
Obituary ... 97-100
Alexander, Charles
See Hadfield, (Ellis) Charles (Raymond)
Alexander, Charles C(omer) 1935- ... 15-16R
Alexander, Charles Stevenson 1916- ... CANR-2
Earlier sketch in CA 5-6R
Alexander, Christine 1893-1975 Obituary ... 61-64
Alexander, Christine (Anne) 1949- ... 117
Alexander, Colin James 1920- ... 15-16R
Alexander, Conel Hugh O'Donel
1909-1974 ... 73-76
Alexander, David 1907-1973 ... 1R
Obituary ... 41-44R
Alexander, David M(ichael) 1945- ... 81-84
Alexander, Denis 1945- ... 45-48
Alexander, Edward 1936- ... 15-16R
Alexander, Edward P(orter) 1907- ... 33-36R
Alexander, Edwin P. 1905- ... 29-32R
Alexander, Eric 1910(?)-1982 Obituary ... 106
Alexander, Ernest R(obert) 1933- ... 103
Alexander, Floyce 1938- ... CANR-13
Earlier sketch in CA 33-36R
Alexander, Frances (Laura) 1888- ... 25-28R
See also SATA 4
Alexander, Frank 1943- ... 65-68
Alexander, Franklin Osborne 1897- ... CAP-2
Earlier sketch in CA 25-28
Alexander, Franz (Gabriel) 1891-1964 ... 5-6R
Alexander, George Jonathan 1931- ... 73-76
Alexander, George M(oyer) 1914- ... 7-8R
Alexander, Gil
See Ralston, Gilbert A(lexander)
Alexander, Harold Lee 1934- ... 69-72
Alexander, Henry
See McAllister, Alister
Alexander, Herbert E(phraim) 1927- ... 41-44R
Alexander, Holmes (Moss) 1906-1985 ... 61-64
Obituary ... 118
Alexander, Hubert G(riggs) 1909- ... 23-24R
Alexander, I. J. 1905(?)-1974 Obituary ... 53-56
Alexander, Ian W(elsh) 1911- ... 13-14R
Alexander, J(onathan) J(ames) G(raham)
1935- ... CANR-13
Earlier sketch in CA 21-22R
Alexander, James 1691-1756 ... DLB-24
Alexander, James E(ckert) 1913- ... 73-76
Alexander, Jan
See Banis, Victor J(erome)
Alexander, Janet 1907- ... CANR-4
Earlier sketch in CA 9-10R
Alexander, Jean 1926- ... 49-52
Alexander, Joan
See Wetherell-Pepper, Joan Alexander
Alexander, Jocelyn Anne Arundel 1930- ... CANR-4
Earlier sketch in CA 4R
See also SATA 22
Alexander, John A(leck) 1912- ... 9-10R
Alexander, John Kurt 1941- ... 102
Alexander, John N. 1941- ... 69-72
Alexander, John T(horndike) 1940- ... 33-36R
Alexander, John W(esley) 1918- ... CANR-3
Earlier sketch in CA 5-6R
Alexander, Jon 1940- ... 33-36R
Alexander, Josephine 1909- ... 104
Alexander, (Charles) K(halil) 1923-1980
Obituary ... 103
Alexander, Kate
See Armstrong, Tilly
Alexander, Kathryn
See Caldwell, Kathryn (Smoot)
Alexander, Ken
See Alexander, Kenneth John Wilson
Alexander, Kenneth John Wilson 1922- ... 61-64
Alexander, L(ouis) G(eorge) 1932- ... CANR-19
Earlier sketch in CA 102
Alexander, Lawrence 1939- Brief entry ... 122
Alexander, Leo 1905-1985 Obituary ... 116
Alexander, Lewis M(cElwain) 1921- ... 21-22R
Alexander, Linda 1935- ... 23-24R
See also SATA 2
Alexander, Liza
See Campbell, Louisa D.
Alexander, Lloyd (Chudley) 1924- ... CANR-24
Earlier sketches in CA 1R, CANR-1
See also SATA 3, 49
See also DLB 52
See also CLC 35
See also CLR 1, 5
Alexander, Louis 1917- ... 121
Alexander, Marc 1929- ... CANR-14
Earlier sketch in CA 7-8R
Alexander, Marge
See Edwards, Roselyn
Alexander, Martha 1920- ... 85-88
See also SATA 11
Alexander, Marthann 1907- ... 53-56
Alexander, Martin 1930- ... 49-52
Alexander, Mary Jean McCutcheon ... 11-12R
Alexander, Meena 1951- ... 115
Alexander, Michael (Joseph) 1941- ... CANR-22
Earlier sketch in CA 45-48
Alexander, Michael Van Cleave 1937- ... 102
Alexander, Milton 1917- ... 17-18R
Alexander, Pamela 1948- ... 122
Alexander, Pat(ricia June) 1937- ... 113
Alexander, R(obert) McNeill 1934- ... 124
Alexander, R(obert) P(ercival)
1905(?)-1985 Obituary ... 117
Alexander, Rae Pace
See Alexander, Raymond Pace
Alexander, Ralph (Holland) 1936- ... 115
Alexander, Raymond Pace 1898-1974 ... 97-100
See also SATA 22
Alexander, Ric
See Long, Richard A(lexander)
Alexander, Richard Dale 1929- ... 110
Alexander, Robert
See Gross, Michael (Robert)
Alexander, Robert
See Legat, Michael (Ronald)
Alexander, Robert J. 1918- ... CANR-18
Earlier sketches in CA 1R, CANR-3
Alexander, Robert Lester 1920- ... 108
Alexander, Robert William 1906(?)-1980
Obituary ... 97-100
Alexander, (Eben) Roy 1899(?)-1978 ... 85-88
Obituary ... 81-84
Alexander, Roy 1928- ... 118
Alexander, Shana 1925- ... 61-64
Alexander, Sidney 1912- ... CANR-6
Earlier sketch in CA 11-12R
Alexander, Stanley Walter 1895-1980
Obituary ... 97-100
Alexander, Stella Tucker 1912- ... 105
Alexander, Sue 1933- ... CANR-19
Earlier sketches in CA 53-56, CANR-4
See also SATA 12
Alexander, Taylor Richard 1915- ... 107
Alexander, Theron 1913- ... CANR-3
Earlier sketch in CA 5-6R
Alexander, Thomas G(len) 1935- ... 65-68
Alexander, Thomas W(illiamson), Jr.
1930- ... 9-10R
Alexander, Vincent Arthur 1925-1980
Obituary ... 101
See also SATA 23
Alexander, W(illiam) M(ortimer) 1928- ... 69-72
Alexander, William M(arvin) 1912- ... 33-36R
Alexander, Yonah 1931- ... 61-64
Alexander, Zane
See Alexander, Harold Lee
Alexanderson, Gerald L(ee) 1933- ... 118
Alexandersson, Gunnar V(ilhelm) 1922- ... 17-18R
Alexandre, Philippe 1932- ... 41-44R
Alexandrowicz, Charles Henry
1902-1975 ... CANR-1
Earlier sketch in CA 2R
Alexeev, Wassilij 1906- ... 89-92
Alexeieff, Alexandre A. 1901- ... SATA-14
Alexeyev, Constantin (Sergeivich)
See Stanislavsky, Constantin (Sergeivich)
Alexiou, Margaret 1939- ... 69-72
Alexis, Katina
See Strauch, Katina (Parthemos)
Aley, Albert 1919-1986 Obituary ... 118
Alfandary-Alexander, Mark 1923- ... 7-8R
al-Faruqi, Isma'il Raji 1921- ... CANR-13
Earlier sketch in CA 69-72
Alford, Bernard William Ernest 1937- ... 101
Alford, Norman (William) 1929- ... 37-40R
Alford, Robert R(oss) 1928- ... 41-44R
Alford, Terry (L.) 1945- Brief entry ... 110
Alfred, Richard
See Haverstock, Nathan Alfred
Alfred, William 1922- ... 15-16R
Alfven, Hannes O(lof) G(oesta) 1908- ... 29-32R
Algarin, Miguel 1941- ... CANR-20
Earlier sketch in CA 69-72
Algeo, John (Thomas) 1930- ... CANR-7
Earlier sketch in CA 19-20R
Alger, Horatio, Jr. 1832-1899 ... SATA-16
See also DLB 42
Alger, Leclaire (Gowans) 1898-1969 ... 73-76
See also SATA 15
Alger, Philip Langdon 1894-1979 Obituary ... 109
Algery, Andre
See Coulet du Gard, Rene
Algren, Nelson 1909-1981 ... CANR-20
Obituary ... 103
Earlier sketch in CA 13-14R
See also DLB 9
See also DLBY 81, 82
See also CDALB 1941-1968
See also CLC 4, 10, 33
Alhaique, Claudio 1913- ... 29-32R
Ali, Ahmed 1910- ... CANR-15
Earlier sketch in CA 25-28R
Ali, Chaudhri Mohamad 1905-1980
Obituary ... 105
Ali, Muhammad 1942- Brief entry ... 116
Ali, Salim (A.) 1896-1987 Obituary ... 123
Ali, Tariq 1943- ... CANR-10
Earlier sketch in CA 25-28R
Aliano, Richard Anthony 1946- ... CANR-10
Earlier sketch in CA 65-68
Aliav, Ruth
See Kluger, Ruth
Aliber, Robert Z. 1930- ... CANR-8
Earlier sketch in CA 23-24R
Alibrandi, Tom 1941- ... CANR-12
Earlier sketch in CA 65-68
Alice (Mary Victoria Augusta Pauline),
Princess 1883-1981 Obituary ... 103
Aliesan, Jody 1943- ... CANR-7
Earlier sketch in CA 57-60
Alihan, Milla ... CAP-2
Earlier sketch in CA 29-32
Ali Khan, Shirley 1951- ... 118
Aliki
See Brandenberg, Aliki Liacouras
See also CLR 9
Alilunas, Leo John 1912- ... 17-18R
Alimayo, Chikuyo
See Franklin, Harold L(eroy)
Alinder, Martha Wheelock
See Wheelock, Martha E.
Alinsky, Saul (David) 1909-1972
Obituary ... 37-40R
Alioto, Robert F(ranklyn) 1933- ... 45-48
Alisky, Marvin (Howard) 1923- ... CANR-20
Earlier sketches in CA 13-14R, CANR-5
Alisov, Boris P. 1892-1972 Obituary ... 37-40R
Al-Issa, Ihsan 1931- ... 109
Alitto, Guy S(alvatore) 1942- ... 93-96
Alix, Ernest Kahlar 1939- Brief entry ... 112
Alkema, Chester Jay 1932- ... 53-56
See also SATA 12
Alker, Hayward R(ose), Jr. 1937- ... 17-18R
Alkire, Leland George, (Jr.) 1937- ... 101
Alkire, William Henry 1935- ... 107
Allaback, Steven Lee 1939- ... 97-100
Allaby, (John) Michael 1933- ... CANR-20
Earlier sketches in CA 45-48, CANR-1
Allaire, Joseph L(eo) 1929- ... 41-44R
Allamand, Pascale 1942- ... CANR-12
Earlier sketch in CA 69-72
See also SATA 12
Allan, Alfred K. 1930- ... 17-18R
Allan, D(avid) G(uy) C(harles) 1925- ... CANR-15
Earlier sketch in CA 25-28R
Allan, Elkan 1922- ... 25-28R
Allan, Harry T. 1928- ... 25-28R
Allan, J(ohn) David 1945- ... 41-44R
Allan, John B.
See Westlake, Donald E(dwin)
Allan, Lewis
See Meeropol, Abel
Allan, Mabel Esther 1915- ... CANR-18
Earlier sketches in CA 7-8R, CANR-2
See also SATA 5, 32
Allan, Mea 1909-1982 ... CANR-2
Obituary ... 107
Earlier sketch in CA 7-8R
Allan, Norman B. 1921- Brief entry ... 105
Allan, Robert Alexander 1914-1979
Obituary ... 106
Allan, Robin 1934- ... 107
Allan, Ted 1916- ... 77-80
Allana, Ghulam Ali 1906-1985 Obituary ... 115
Allana, Ghulamali
See Allana, Ghulam Ali
Allanbrook, Wye J(amison) 1943- ... 110
Alland, Alexander, Jr. 1931- ... 21-22R
Alland, Guy 1944- ... 69-72
Allard, Bessie Butler Newsom ?-1987
Obituary ... 122
Allard, Dean C(onrad) 1933- ... CANR-1
Earlier sketch in CA 45-48
Allard, Harry
See Allard, Harry G(rover), Jr.
Allard, Harry G(rover), Jr. 1928- ... 113
See also SATA 42
Allard, Michel (Adrien) 1924-1976
Obituary ... 65-68
Allard, Sven 1896-1975 ... CAP-2
Earlier sketch in CA 29-32
Allard, William Albert 1937- ... 115
Allardt, Erik 1925- ... CANR-13
Earlier sketch in CA 73-76
Allardt, Linda 1926- Brief entry ... 104
Allardyce, Gilbert Daniel 1932- ... 33-36R
Allardyce, Paula
See Torday, Ursula
Allaun, Frank (Julian) 1913- ... 103
Allbeck, Willard Dow 1898- ... 21-22R
Allbeury, Ted
See Allbeury, Theodore Edward le
Bouthillier
Allbeury, Theodore Edward le Bouthillier
1917- ... CANR-5
Earlier sketch in CA 53-56
Allchin, A(rthur) M(acdonald) 1930- ... CANR-17
Earlier sketch in CA 25-28R
Alldridge, James Charles 1910- ... 29-32R
Alldritt, Keith 1935- ... 25-28R
See also DLB 14
Allee, John Gage (Jr.) 1918-1987
Obituary ... 121
Allee, Marjorie Hill 1890-1945 ... SATA-17
Alleger, Daniel E(ugene) 1903- ... 33-36R
Allegro, John Marco 1923-1988 ... CANR-20
Obituary ... 124
Earlier sketches in CA 11-12R, CANR-4
Allen, A(rthur) B(ruce) 1903-1975 ... CAP-2
Earlier sketch in CA 23-24
Allen, A(rvon) Dale, Jr. 1935- ... 21-22R
Allen, Adam
See Epstein, Beryl (M. Williams)
and Epstein, Samuel
Allen, Adam
See Epstein, Beryl (Williams)
and Epstein, Samuel
Allen, Agnes Rogers 1893-1986 Obituary ... 121
Allen, Alex B.
See Heide, Florence Parry
Allen, Allyn
See Eberle, Irmengarde
Allen, Anita
See Schenck, Anita A(llen)
Allen, Arthur A(ugustus) 1885-1964 ... CANR-19
Earlier sketch in CA 2R
Allen, Barbara
See Stuart, (Violet) Vivian (Finlay)
Allen, Betsy
See Cavanna, Betty
Allen, Betty (Jeanne) 1929- ... 113
Allen, Bob 1948- ... 118
Allen, Carl 1961- ... 69-72
Allen, Catherine Blanche 1883- ... 107
Allen, Cecil J(ohn) 1886-1973 ... CAP-2
Earlier sketch in CA 25-28
Allen, Charles Livingstone 1913- ... 111
Allen, Charlotte Vale 1941- ... CANR-12
Earlier sketch in CA 69-72
Allen, Chester
See Holding, Vera Zumwalt
Allen, Chris 1929- ... 29-32R
Allen, Clabon Walter 1904-1987 Obituary ... 124
Allen, Clay
See Paine, Lauran (Bosworth)
Allen, Clifford Edward 1902- ... CAP-1
Earlier sketch in CA 9-10
Allen, Clifton Judson 1901- ... 108
Allen, David 1925- ... 33-36R
Allen, David 1939- ... 115
Allen, David Elliston 1932- ... 25-28R
Allen, David F(ranklyn) 1943- ... 103
Allen, David Grayson 1943- ... 115
Allen, David W. 1922- Brief entry ... 113
Allen, Derek Fortrose 1910-1975 Obituary ... 114
Allen, Dick 1939- ... 33-36R
Allen, Diogenes 1932- ... CANR-10
Earlier sketch in CA 25-28R
Allen, Dizzy
See Allen, H(ubert) R(aymond)
Allen, Don Cameron 1903-1972 ... CANR-4
Earlier sketch in CA 5-6R
Allen, Donald Emerson 1917- ... 45-48
Allen, Donald M(erriam) 1912- ... CANR-10
Earlier sketch in CA 19-20R
Allen, Donald R. 1930- ... 45-48
Allen, Douglas (Malcolm) 1941- ... 113
Allen, Durward L(eon) 1910- ... 41-44R
Allen, Dwight W(illiam) 1931- ... 15-16R
Allen, E. C.
See Ward, Elizabeth Campbell
Allen, Edith Beavers 1920- ... 9-10R
Allen, Edith Marion ... CAP-1
Earlier sketch in CA 15-16
Allen, Edward D(avid) 1923- ... 49-52
Allen, Edward Heron
See Heron-Allen, Edward
Allen, Edward J(oseph) 1907- ... CAP-1
Earlier sketch in CA 17-18
Allen, Edward Switzer 1887-1985
Obituary ... 116
Allen, Elisabeth Offutt 1895- ... 57-60
Allen, (Evelyn) Elizabeth 1918- ... 121
Allen, Elizabeth 1955- ... 122
Allen, Elizabeth
See Thompson, Elizabeth Allen

Allen, Elizabeth Cooper
See Allen, Betty (Jeanne)
Allen, Eric 1916- Brief entry ... 111
Allen, Ethan 1738-1789 ... DLB-31
Allen, Everett S(locum) 1916- Brief entry ... 110
Allen, Francis A(lfred) 1919- ... 15-16R
Allen, Francis R(obbins) 1908- ... 77-80
Allen, Frank 1939- ... 109
Allen, Frederick G(arfield) 1936-1986 ... 57-60
Obituary ... 121
Allen, Frederick S(tetson) 1930-
Brief entry ... 112
Allen, G(eorge) C(yril) 1900-1982 ... CANR-3
Obituary ... 107
Earlier sketch in CA 4R
Allen, G(eorge) Francis 1907- ... CAP-1
Earlier sketch in CA 9-10
Allen, Garland E(dward) 1936- ... 53-56
Allen, Gary
See Allen, Frederick G(arfield)
Allen, Gay Wilson 1903- ... CANR-3
Earlier sketch in CA 7-8R
Allen, Geoffrey Francis 1902- ... CAP-1
Earlier sketch in CA 13-14
Allen, George 1808-1876 ... DLB-59
Allen, George (Herbert) 1922- ... 111
Allen, Gerald 1942- ... CANR-16
Earlier sketch in CA 93-96
Allen, Gertrude E(lizabeth) 1888- ... 61-64
See also SATA 9
Allen, Gilbert (Bruce) 1951- ... 111
Allen, Gina 1918- ... 4R
Allen, Gwenfread Elaine 1904- ... 61-64
Allen, H. Fredericka
See Allen, H(elena) G(ronlund)
Allen, H(elena) G(ronlund) ... 29-32R
Allen, H(ubert) R(aymond) 1919-1987
Obituary ... 122
Allen, Harold B(yron) 1902- ... CANR-10
Earlier sketch in CA 17-18R
Allen, Harold J(oseph) 1925- ... 45-48
Allen, Harry Cranbrook 1917- ... 7-8R
Allen, Hazel
See Hershberger, Hazel Kuhns
Allen, Henry
See Adams, Henry H(itch)
Allen, Henry Wilson 1912- ... 89-92
See also DLBY 85
Allen, Herman R. 1913(?)-1979 Obituary ... 89-92
Allen, (William) Hervey (Jr.) 1889-1949
Brief entry ... 108
See also DLB 9, 45
Allen, Heywood 1935- ... 33-36R
Allen, Howard W. 1931- ... 33-36R
Allen, Ida (Cogswell) Bailey 1885-1973
Obituary ... 110
Allen, Ira R. 1948- ... 65-68
Allen, Irene 1903- ... CAP-1
Earlier sketch in CA 15-16
Allen, Irving L(ewis), Jr. 1931- ... 110
Allen, Ivan, Jr. 1911- ... 109
Allen, Jack 1899- ... SATA-29
Allen, Jack 1914- ... CANR-4
Earlier sketch in CA 9-10R
Allen, James 1739-1808 ... DLB-31
Allen, James
See Ader, Paul (Fassett)
Allen, James B(rown) 1927- ... 105
Allen, James B(eekman) 1931- ... 105
Allen, James Egert 1896-1980 Obituary ... 97-100
Allen, James L(ovic), Jr. 1929- ... CANR-17
Earlier sketch in CA 33-36R
Allen, James S. 1906(?)-1986 Obituary ... 120
Allen, James Smith 1949- ... 111
Allen, Jay Presson 1922- ... 73-76
See also DLB 26
Allen, Jeffrey (Yale) 1948- ... 112
See also SATA 42
Allen, Jeffrey G(rant) 1943- ... 116
Allen, Jerry 1911- ... 11-12R
Allen, Jim
See Allen, James L(ovic), Jr.
Allen, Johannes 1916-1973 ... CANR-14
Earlier sketch in CA 29-32R
Allen, John
See Perry, Ritchie (John Allen)
Allen, John Alexander 1922- ... 25-28R
Allen, John D(aniel) 1898-1972 ... CAP-2
Earlier sketch in CA 33-36
Allen, John Jay 1932- ... CANR-18
Earlier sketch in CA 33-36R
Allen, John Logan 1941- ... 85-88
Allen, John Stuart 1907-1982 Obituary ... 109
Allen, Jon L(ewis) 1931- ... 57-60
Allen, Jordan
See Dumke, Glenn S.
Allen, Judson B(oyce) 1932- ... CANR-17
Earlier sketch in CA 81-84
Allen, K. Eileen 1918- ... 113
Allen, Katharine Martin 1906(?)-1984
Obituary ... 113
Allen, Kenneth (William) 1941- ... 69-72
Allen, Kenneth S. 1913- ... 77-80
Allen, L(ouis) David 1940- Brief entry ... 117
Allen, Lafe Franklin 1914- Brief entry ... 111
Allen, Laura Jean Brief entry ... 110
Allen, Lawrence A. 1926- ... 45-48
Allen, Layman E(dward) 1927- ... 7-8R
Allen, Lee 1915-1969 ... CANR-1
Earlier sketch in CA 2R
Allen, Leonard 1915(?)-1981 Obituary ... 102
Allen, Leroy 1912- ... 65-68
See also SATA 11
Allen, Leslie Christopher 1935- ... CANR-13
Earlier sketch in CA 73-76
Allen, Leslie H. 1887(?)-1973 Obituary ... 49-52
Allen, Linda 1925- ... 102
See also SATA 33
Allen, Loring
See Allen, Robert Loring
Allen, Louis 1922- ... 41-44R
Allen, Louis A. 1917- ... 7-8R
Allen, M(arion) C. 1914- ... 9-10R
Allen, Marcus
See Donicht, Mark Allen
Allen, Marjorie 1931- ... 69-72
See also SATA 22
Allen, Marjory (Gill) 1897- ... CAP-1
Earlier sketch in CA 9-10
Allen, Mark
See Donicht, Mark Allen
Allen, Mary (Charlotte Chocqueel) 1909- ... 109
Allen, Mary
See Cleveland, Mary
Allen, Maury 1932- ... CANR-11
Earlier sketch in CA 17-18R
See also SATA 26
Allen, Merrill J(ames) 1918- ... 69-72
Allen, Merritt Parmelee 1892-1954 ... SATA-22
Allen, Michael (Derek) 1939- ... 77-80
Allen, Michael J(ohn) B(ridgman) 1941- ... 102
Allen, Minerva C(rantz) 1935- ... CANR-6
Earlier sketch in CA 57-60
Allen, Myron Sheppard 1901- ... CAP-1
Earlier sketch in CA 9-10
Allen, Nina (Stroemgren) 1935- ... SATA-22
Allen, Pamela 1934- ... SATA-50
Allen, Pat 1938- ... 118
Allen, Paul 1948- ... 81-84
Allen, Paula Gunn Brief entry ... 112
Allen, Peter Christopher 1905- ... 108
Allen, Phyllis (Greig) ... 65-68
Allen, Phyllis S(loan) 1908- ... 65-68
Allen, Polly Reynolds 1940- ... 110
Allen, R. Earl 1922- ... CANR-6
Earlier sketch in CA 9-10R
Allen, R(onald) R(oyce) 1930- ... 19-20R
Allen, Reginald E. 1931- ... CANR-13
Earlier sketch in CA 33-36R
Allen, Richard (Hugh Sedley) 1903- ... 25-28R
Allen, (Alexander) Richard 1929- ... CANR-11
Earlier sketch in CA 65-68
Allen, Richard C. 1926- ... CANR-17
Earlier sketch in CA 25-28R
Allen, Richard C.
See Taylor, John M(axwell)
Allen, Richard Sanders 1917- ... 21-22R
Allen, Richard V(incent) 1936- ... 21-22R
Allen, Roach Van 1917- ... 11-12R
Allen, Robert 1946- ... 97-100
Allen, Robert
See Garfinkel, Bernard Max
Allen, Robert C(lyde) 1950- ... 117
Allen, Robert Day 1927- ... 107
Allen, Robert F(rances) 1928-1987 ... 33-36R
Obituary ... 123
Allen, Robert J. 1930- ... 15-16R
Allen, Robert L(ee) 1942- ... 101
Allen, Robert Livingston 1916- ... 17-18R
Allen, Robert Loring 1921- ... CANR-6
Earlier sketch in CA 1R
Allen, Robert M. 1909-1979 ... CANR-2
Earlier sketch in CA 1R
Allen, Robert Porter 1905-1963 ... 5-6R
Allen, Robert S(haron) 1900-1981 ... CANR-6
Obituary ... 103
Earlier sketch in CA 57-60
Allen, Robert Thomas 1911- Brief entry ... 110
Allen, Rodney F. 1938- ... 61-64
See also SATA 27
Allen, Roger M(ichael) A(shley) 1942- ... 111
Allen, Ronald B(arclay) 1941- ... 114
Allen, Ronald Royce 1930- ... 113
Allen, Ross R(oundy) 1928- ... 33-36R
Allen, Roy (George Douglas) 1906-1983
Obituary ... 110
Allen, Rupert C(lyde) 1927- ... 65-68
Allen, Ruth
See Peterson, Esther (Allen)
Allen, Ruth Finney 1898-1979 ... 93-96
Obituary ... 85-88
Allen, Sam
See Allen, M(arion) C.
Allen, Samuel 1917- ... 49-52
See also SATA 9
See also DLB 41
Allen, Sarah (Pearson) Sawyer 1920- ... 89-92
Allen, Shirley Seifried 1921- ... 57-60
Allen, Shirley Walter 1883- ... CAP-2
Earlier sketch in CA 25-28
Allen, Stephen (Valentine Patrick William)
1921- ... CANR-18
Earlier sketch in CA 25-28R
Allen, Steve
See Allen, Stephen (Valentine Patrick William)
Allen, Sue P. 1913- ... 25-28R
Allen, Sydney (Earl), Jr. 1929- ... 29-32R
Allen, T. D.
See Allen, Terril Diener
Allen, Terril Diener 1908- ... CANR-2
Earlier sketch in CA 7-8R
See also SATA 35
Allen, Terry D.
See Allen, Terril Diener
Allen, Thomas B(enton) 1929- ... CANR-20
Earlier sketches in CA 15-16R, CANR-5
See also SATA 45
Allen, Tom
See Allen, Thomas B(enton)
Allen, Tony 1945- ... 77-80
Allen, Vernon L(esley) 1933- ... 29-32R
Allen, W(illiam) Sidney 1918- ... 49-52
Allen, Wallace (Wilbur) 1919- ... 118
Allen, Walter Ernest 1911- ... 61-64
See also CAAS 6
Allen, William 1940- ... 65-68
Allen, William A(ustin) 1916- ... CANR-13
Earlier sketch in CA 33-36R
Allen, William R(ichard) 1924- ... 17-18R
Allen, William Sheridan 1932- ... 15-16R
Allen, William Stannard 1913- ... 101
Allen, Woody
See Allen, Heywood
See also DLB 44
See also CLC 16
Allende, Isabel 1942- ... CLC-39
Allendoerfer, Carl B(arnett) 1911-1974 ... CANR-11
Earlier sketches in CA 17-18, CAP-2
Allen of Hurtwood, Lady
See Allen, Marjory (Gill)
Allentuch, Harriet Ray 1933- ... 13-14R
Allentuck, Andrew 1943- ... 111
Allentuck, Marcia Epstein 1928- ... 33-36R
Allerton, Mary
See Govan, Christine Noble
Alley, Brian 1933- ... 111
Alley, Henry Melton 1945- ... 112
Alley, Louis Edward 1914- ... 19-20R
Alley, Norman William 1895-1981
Obituary ... 115
Alley, Rewi 1897-1987 ... CANR-13
Obituary ... 124
Earlier sketch in CA 73-76
Alley, Robert S. 1932- ... 33-36R
Alley, Stephen L(ewis) 1915- Brief entry ... 110
Alleyn, Ellen
See Rossetti, Christina (Georgina)
Allgire, Mildred J. 1910- ... CAP-2
Earlier sketch in CA 25-28
Alliluyeva, Svetlana (Iosifovna Stalina)
1926- ... 57-60
Allin, Clinton Harrop
See Harrop-Allin, Clinton
Allin, Craig Willard 1946- ... 108
Allingham, Margery (Louise)
1904-1966 ... CANR-4
Obituary ... 25-28R
Earlier sketch in CA 5-6R
See also CLC 19
Allingham, Michael 1943- ... 97-100
Allingham, William 1824-1889 ... DLB-35
Allington, Richard L(loyd) 1947- ... 112
See also SATA 35, 39
Allinsmith, Wesley 1923- ... 85-88
Allinson, Beverley (Lynn Rouse) 1936- ... CANR-4
Earlier sketch in CA 49-52
Allinson, Gary D(ean) 1942- ... 77-80
Allis, Frederick Scouller, Jr. 1913- ... 115
Allis, Oswald T(hompson) 1880-1973
Obituary ... 37-40R
Allison, A(ntony) F(rancis) 1916- ... 106
Allison, Alexander Ward 1919- ... 7-8R
Allison, Anne Marie 1931- ... 114
Allison, Anthony C(lifford) 1928- ... 29-32R
Allison, Bob ... SATA-14
Allison, C(hristopher) FitzSimons 1927- ... CANR-4
Earlier sketch in CA 1R
Allison, Clay
See Keevill, Henry J(ohn)
Allison, E. M. A.
See Allison, Eric W(illiam)
and Allison, Mary Ann
Allison, Eric W(illiam) 1947- ... 122
Allison, Graham T(illett), Jr. 1940- ... CANR-2
Earlier sketch in CA 49-52
Allison, Harrison C(larke) 1917- ... 49-52
Allison, Henry E. 1937- Brief entry ... 110
Allison, John Murray 1889- ... 73-76
Allison, Joseph D(avid) 1950- ... 111
Allison, Linda 1948- ... 113
See also SATA 43
Allison, Marian
See Reid, Frances P(ugh)
Allison, Mary Ann 1949- ... 122
Allison, Michael Frederick Lister 1936- ... 57-60
Allison, Mike
See Allison, Michael Frederick Lister
Allison, Penny
See Katz, Carol
Allison, R(ichard) Bruce 1949- ... CANR-19
Earlier sketches in CA 49-52, CANR-3
Allison, Ralph B(rewster) 1931- ... 101
Allison, Rand
See McCormick, Wilfred
Allison, Rosemary 1953- ... 93-96
Allison, Roy (Anthony) 1957- ... 119
Allison, Sam
See Loomis, Noel M(iller)
Allman, James 1943- ... 112
Allman, John 1935- ... 85-88
Allman, T. D. 1944- ... CANR-17
Earlier sketch in CA 93-96
Allmendinger, David F(rederick), Jr.
1938- ... 61-64
See also SATA 35
Allon, Yigal 1918-1980 ... 73-76
Obituary ... 97-100
Allott, Kenneth 1912-1973 Obituary ... 89-92
See also DLB 20
Allott, Miriam 1920- ... 112
Alloway, David N(elson) 1927- ... CANR-10
Earlier sketch in CA 23-24R
Alloway, Lawrence 1926- ... 41-44R
Allport, Gordon (Willard) 1897-1967 ... CANR-3
Obituary ... 25-28R
Earlier sketch in CA 1R
Allport, Susan 1950- ... 124
Allred, Dorald M(ervin) 1923- ... 65-68
Allred, G. Hugh 1932- ... CANR-8
Earlier sketch in CA 61-64
Allred, Gordon T(hatcher) 1930- ... CANR-10
Earlier sketch in CA 17-18R
See also SATA 10
Allred, Ruel A(cord) 1929- ... 106
Allsen, Philip E(dmond) 1932- ... CANR-4
Earlier sketch in CA 53-56
Allsop, Kenneth 1920-1973 ... CANR-6
Earlier sketch in CA 3R
See also SATA 17
Allsopp, (Harold) Bruce 1912- ... CANR-18
Earlier sketches in CA 7-8R, CANR-2
Allston, Washington 1779-1843 ... DLB-1
Allswang, John M(yers) 1937- ... 41-44R
Allum, Nancy (Patricia Eaton) 1920- ... CAP-1
Earlier sketch in CA 9-10
Allvine, Fred C. 1936- ... 61-64
Allvine, Glendon 1893(?)-1977 Obituary ... 73-76
Allward, Maurice (Frank) 1923- ... CANR-19
Earlier sketches in CA 7-8R, CANR-3
Allwood, Martin Samuel 1916- ... 110
Allworth, Edward (Alfred) 1920- ... 101
Allyn, Jennifer
See Jones, Jeannette
Allyn, Paul
See Schosberg, Paul A.
Allyson, Kym
See Kimbro, John M.
Alman, David 1919- ... 9-10R
Al-Marayati, Abid A(min) 1931- ... 33-36R
Almaraz, Felix D(iaz), Jr. 1933- ... 33-36R
Almaz, Michael 1921- ... 81-84
Almedingen, E. M.
See Almedingen, Martha Edith von
See also SATA 3
See also CLC 12
Almedingen, Martha Edith von
1898-1971 ... CANR-1
Earlier sketch in CA 2R
Almon, Bert 1943- ... 110
Almon, Clopper, Jr. 1934- ... 21-22R
Almond, Gabriel Abraham 1911- ... CANR-18
Earlier sketch in CA 101
Almond, Linda Stevens 1881(?)-1987
Obituary ... 121
See also SATA 50
Almond, Paul 1931- ... 73-76
Almond, Richard 1938- ... 53-56
Almonte, Rosa
See Paine, Lauran (Bosworth)
Almquist, Don 1929- ... SATA-11
Almquist, L. Arden 1921- ... 29-32R
Almy, Millie 1915- ... 85-88
Aloian, David 1928- ... 25-28R
Aloma, Rene R(amon) 1947- ... 113
Alonso, Damaso 1898- Brief entry ... 110
See also CLC 14
Alonso, J(uan) M(anuel) 1936- ... 102
Alonso, Maria Teresa Manjon
See Manjon-Alonso, Maria Teresa
Alonso, William 1933- ... CANR-6
Earlier sketch in CA 9-10R
Alotta, Robert I(gnatius) 1937- ... CANR-14
Earlier sketch in CA 65-68
Aloysius, Sister Mary
See Schaldenbrand, Mary
Alpaugh, Craig 1945- ... 117
Alper, Benedict S(olomon) 1905- ... 49-52
Alper, M(ax) Victor 1944- ... 69-72
Alpern, Andrew 1938- ... CANR-11
Earlier sketch in CA 69-72
Alpern, David M(ark) 1942- ... 73-76
Alpern, Gerald D(avid) 1932- ... 53-56
Alperovitz, Gar 1936- ... 49-52
Alpers, Antony 1919- ... CANR-3
Earlier sketch in CA 3R
Alpers, Bernard J. 1900-1981 Obituary ... 105
Alpers, Edward Alter 1941- ... 109
Alpers, Paul (Joel) 1932- ... 85-88
Alpers, Svetlana (Leontief) 1936- ... 115
Alpert, Hollis 1916- ... CANR-23
Earlier sketches in CA 3R, CANR-6
Alpert, Jane (Lauren) 1947- ... 107
Alpert, Mark I(ra) 1942- ... 61-64
Alpert, Paul 1907- ... 41-44R
Alpert, Richard 1931- ... 89-92
Alphonso-Karkala, John B. 1923- ... CANR-14
Earlier sketch in CA 37-40R
Alphonso Karkala, John B.
See Alphonso-Karkala, John B.
Alplaus, N. Y.
See Rubin, Cynthia Elyce
Al-Qazzaz, Ayad (Sayyid Ali) 1941- ... 112
Alred, Gerald J(ames) 1943- ... 105
AlRoy, Gil Carl 1924-1985 ... CANR-17
Obituary ... 116
Earlier sketch in CA 41-44R
Alschuler, Rose Haas 1887-1979 ... CAP-2
Obituary ... 89-92
Earlier sketch in CA 25-28
Alsen, Eberhard 1939- ... 110
Alsop, George 1636-? ... DLB-24
Alsop, Gulielma Fell 1881-1978 Obituary ... 77-80
Alsop, Joseph (Wright) 1910- ... 122
Alsop, Mary O'Hara 1885-1980 ... CANR-4
Obituary ... 102
Earlier sketch in CA 9-10R
See also SATA 2, 24, 34
Alsop, Richard 1761-1815 ... DLB-37
Alsop, Stewart (Johonnot Oliver)
1914-1974 ... 89-92
Obituary ... 49-52
Alsterlund, Betty
See Pilkington, Betty
Alstern, Fred
See Stern, Alfred

Alston, Mary Niven 1918- 33-36R
Alston, Patrick L(ionel) 1926- 25-28R
Alston, Walter Emmons 1911-1984
Obituary 113
Alston, William P(ayne) 1921- CANR-7
Earlier sketch in CA 7-8R
Alswang, Betty 1920(?)-1978 Obituary 77-80
Alt, David 1933- 49-52
Alt, Herschel 1897(?)-1981 Obituary 105
Alt, (Arthur) Tilo 1931- 41-44R
Alta 1942- 57-60
See also CLC 19
Altabe, Joan B. 1935- 53-56
Altbach, Edith Hoshino 1941- 57-60
Altbach, Philip G(eoffrey) 1941- CANR-10
Earlier sketch in CA 25-28R
Altenbernd, (August) Lynn 1918- CANR-1
Earlier sketch in CA 45-48
Alter, J(ohn) Cecil 1879-1964 5-6R
Alter, Jean V(ictor) 1925- 45-48
Alter, Joseph Dinsmore 1923- 111
Alter, Judith (MacBain) 1938- CANR-14
Earlier sketch in CA 81-84
Alter, Judy
See Alter, Judith (MacBain)
Alter, Robert B(ernard) 1935- CANR-1
Earlier sketch in CA 49-52
See also CLC 34
Alter, Robert Edmond 1925-1965 CANR-1
Earlier sketch in CA 3R
See also SATA 9
Alter, Stephen 1956- 109
Alterman, Nathan 1910-1970 Obituary 25-28R
Altfest, Karen Caplan 105
Alth, Max O(ctavious) 1927- CANR-17
Earlier sketch in CA 41-44R
Althauser, Robert P(ierce) 1939- 57-60
Althea
See Braithwaite, Althea
Alther, Lisa 1944- CANR-12
Earlier sketch in CA 65-68
See also CLC 7, 41
Althoff, Phillip 1941- 33-36R
Altholz, Josef L(ewis) 1933- 9-10R
Althouse, Larry
See Althouse, Lawrence Wilson
Althouse, LaVonne 1932- 19-20R
Althouse, Lawrence Wilson 1930- 101
Altick, Richard Daniel 1915- CANR-19
Earlier sketches in CA 3R, CANR-4
Altieri, Charles F(rancis) 1942- 106
Altizer, Thomas J(onathan) J(ackson)
1927- CANR-3
Earlier sketch in CA 1R
Altman, Dennis 1943- CANR-15
Earlier sketch in CA 33-36R
Altman, Edward I(ra) 1941- CANR-22
Earlier sketches in CA 57-60, CANR-7
Altman, Frances 1937- 65-68
Altman, Irwin 1928- 81-84
Altman, Irwin 1930- CANR-21
Earlier sketch in CA 69-72
Altman, Jack 1938- 21-22R
Altman, Larry
See Altman, Irwin
Altman, Nathaniel 1948- CANR-21
Earlier sketches in CA 57-60, CANR-6
Altman, Richard Charles 1932- 41-44R
Altman, Robert 1925- 73-76
See also CLC 16
Altman, Robert A. 1943- 29-32R
Altman, Thomas
See Black, Campbell
Altman, Wilfred 1927- CAP-1
Earlier sketch in CA 9-10
Altmann, Alexander 1906-1987 CANR-8
Obituary 122
Earlier sketch in CA 61-64
Altmann, Berthold 1902(?)-1977
Obituary 69-72
Altoma, Salih J(awad) 1929- 49-52
Altrocchi, Julia Cooley 1893-1972 CAP-1
Earlier sketch in CA 13-14
Altschul, Aaron Mayer 1914- 105
Altschul, b j 1948- 114
Altschul, Selig 1914- 108
Altschuler, Franz 1923- SATA-45
Altsheler, Joseph A(lexander)
1862-1919 YABC-1
Altshuler, Alan Anthony 1936- 108
Altshuler, Edward A. 1919- 19-20R
Aluko, Timothy Mofolorunso 1918- CANR-10
Earlier sketch in CA 65-68
Alurista
See Urista, Alberto H.
Al-Van-Gar
See Radwanski, Pierre A(rthur)
Alvarez, A(lfred) 1929- CANR-3
Earlier sketch in CA 1R
See also DLB 14, 40
See also CLC 5, 13
Alvarez, Alejandro Rodriguez 1903-1965
Obituary 93-96
Alvarez, Eugene 1932- 57-60
Alvarez, John
See del Rey, Lester
Alvarez, Joseph A. 1930- CANR-17
Earlier sketch in CA 33-36R
See also SATA 18
Alvarez, Max Joseph 1960- 112
Alvarez, Walter C(lement) 1884-1978 CANR-10
Earlier sketch in CA 61-64
Alvarez-Altman, Grace (DeJesus) 1926- 33-36R
Alvarez del Vayo, Julio 1891-1975
Obituary 61-64
Alverson, Charles (E.) 1935- CANR-13
Earlier sketch in CA 25-28R
Alverson, Donna 1933- 65-68
Alves, Colin 1930- CANR-2
Earlier sketch in CA 7-8R
Alves, Marcio Moreira 1936- CANR-2
Earlier sketch in CA 45-48
Alves, Michael (Joseph) 1956- 118
Alvey, Edward, Jr. 1902- 53-56
Alvey, R(ichard) Gerald 1935- 121
Alvin, Juliette (Louise) ?-1982 77-80
Obituary 108
Alworth, E. P(aul) 1918- 25-28R
Alwyn, William 1905-1985 Obituary 117
Aly, Bower 1903- CANR-5
Earlier sketch in CA 5-6R
Aly, Lucile Folse 1913- 23-24R
Alyeshmerni, Mansoor 1943- 29-32R
Alyn, Marc (a pseudonym) 1937- 101
Alzado, Lyle (Martin) 1949- Brief entry 110
Alzaga, Florinda 1930- 73-76
Amabile, George 1936- 33-36R
Amacher, Richard Earl 1917- CANR-3
Earlier sketch in CA 3R
Amacher, Ryan C(uster) 1945- 105
Amadi, Elechi (Emmanuel) 1934- CANR-16
Earlier sketch in CA 29-32R
Amado, Jorge 1912- 77-80
See also CLC 13, 40
Amadon, Dean 1912- 61-64
Amalrik, Andrei Alekseyevich 1938-1980
Obituary 102
Amamoo, Joseph Godson 1931- 13-14R
Aman, Mohammed M(ohammed)
1940- CANR-16
Earlier sketches in CA 49-52, CANR-1
Amanda
See Wynne-Tyson, Esme
Amann, Peter H. 1927- 61-64
Amann, Richard 1945- 106
Amann, Ronald 1943- 112
Amann, Victor F(rancis) 1927- 41-44R
Amanuddin, Syed 1934- CANR-17
Earlier sketches in CA 49-52, CANR-1
Amaral, Anthony 1930-1982 CANR-11
Earlier sketch in CA 21-22R
Amare, Rothayne
See Byrne, Stuart J(ames)
Amaron, Douglas 1914-1985 Obituary 117
Amary, Issam B(ahjat) 1942- CANR-8
Earlier sketch in CA 61-64
Amato, Joseph Anthony 1938- CANR-6
Earlier sketch in CA 57-60
Amatora, Sister Mary 9-10R
Amaya, Ismael E(liseo) 1928-1986
Obituary 120
Amaya, Mario (Anthony) 1933-1986 CANR-9
Obituary 119
Earlier sketch in CA 61-64
Amazing Randi, The
See Randi, James
Ambasz, Emilio 1943- 73-76
Amberg, George H. 1901-1971 Obituary 110
Amberg, (Martin) Hans 1913- 77-80
Amberg, Richard H(iller), Jr. 1942- 77-80
Amberg, Richard Hiller 1912-1967
Obituary 114
Ambhanwong, Suthilak 1924- CANR-18
Earlier sketch in CA 73-76
Ambirajan, Srinivasa 1936- CANR-7
Earlier sketch in CA 19-20R
Ambler, C(hristopher) Gifford 1886- SATA-29
Ambler, Effie 1936- 77-80
Ambler, Eric 1909- CANR-7
Earlier sketch in CA 9-10R
See also CLC 4, 6, 9
Ambler, John S(teward) 1932- 49-52
Ambrose, Alice
See Lazerowitz, Alice Ambrose
Ambrose, David (Edwin) 1943- Brief entry 116
Ambrose, Eric (Samuel) 1908- CAP-1
Earlier sketch in CA 11-12
Ambrose, John W(illiam), Jr. 1931- 57-60
Ambrose, Stephen Edward 1936- CANR-3
Earlier sketch in CA 1R
See also SATA 40
Ambrose, W. Haydn 1922- 25-28R
Ambrosi, Hans Georg 1925- 103
Ambrosini, Maria Luisa 33-36R
Ambroz, Oton 1905- 41-44R
Ambrus, Gyozo Laszlo 1935- CANR-11
Earlier sketch in CA 25-28R
See also SATA 41
Ambrus, Victor
See Ambrus, Gyozo Laszlo
See also SAAS 4
Ambrus, Victor G.
See Ambrus, Gyozo Laszlo
See also SATA 1
Amdur, Neil 1939- 106
Amdur, Nikki 1950- 111
Amelio, Ralph J. 1939- 37-40R
Amen, Carol 1934(?)-1987 Obituary 123
Amend, Victor E(arl) 1916- 33-36R
Ament, Pat 1946- 85-88
Amerine, Maynard A(ndrew) 1911- 41-44R
Ameringer, Charles D. 1926- 57-60
Amerman, Lockhart 1911-1969 CAP-2
Earlier sketch in CA 29-32
See also SATA 3
Amery, (Harold) Julian 1919- 61-64
Ames, Charles Edgar 1895-1972 CAP-2
Earlier sketch in CA 25-28
Ames, Delano L. 1906- 107
Ames, Elinor
See Ranzini, Addis Durning
Ames, Evelyn 1908- 57-60
See also SATA 13
Ames, Felicia
See Burden, Jean
Ames, Fisher 1758-1808 DLB-37
Ames, Francis H. 1900- 17-18R
Ames, Gerald 1906- 73-76
See also SATA 11
Ames, Jennifer
See Greig, Maysie
Ames, Jocelyn Green 7-8R
Ames, John 1944- 111
Ames, John Dawes 1904-1987 Obituary 122
Ames, Lee J(udah) 1921- CANR-18
Earlier sketches in CA 4R, CANR-3
See also SATA 3
Ames, Leslie
See Rigoni, Orlando (Joseph)
and Ross, W(illiam) E(dward) D(aniel)
Ames, Lois (Winslow Sisson) 1931- 101
Ames, Louise Bates 1908- CANR-18
Earlier sketches in CA 3R, CANR-3
Ames, Mary Clemmer 1831-1884 DLB-23
Ames, Mildred 1919- CANR-11
Earlier sketch in CA 69-72
See also SATA 22
Ames, Noel
See Barrows, (Ruth) Marjorie
Ames, Norma 1920- CANR-12
Earlier sketch in CA 29-32R
Ames, Rachel 1922- 97-100
Ames, Ruth M(argaret) 1918- 29-32R
Ames, (Polly) Scribner 1908- 69-72
Ames, Van Meter 1898-1985 CAP-1
Obituary 117
Earlier sketch in CA 15-16
Ames, Walter Lansing 1946- 106
Ames, Winslow 1907-? CAP-2
Earlier sketch in CA 25-28
Ames-Lewis, Francis 1943- 108
Amey, Lloyd Ronald 1922- CANR-20
Earlier sketch in CA 45-48
Amfitheatrof, Erik 1931- 89-92
Amft, M(arian) J(anet) 1920-1985
Obituary 117
Ami, Ben
See Eliav, Arie L(ova)
Ami, Shlomo Ben
See Ben-Ami, Shlomo
Amichai, Yehuda 1924- 85-88
See also CLC 9, 22
Amick, Robert Gene 1933- 33-36R
Amidon, Bill (Vincent) 1935-1979 45-48
Obituary 103
Amiel, Barbara 1940- 101
Amiel, Joseph 1937- 101
Amin, Ali 1913(?)-1976 Obituary 65-68
Amin, Samir 1931- CANR-15
Earlier sketch in CA 89-92
Amini, Johari M.
See Kunjufu, Johari M. Amini
See also DLB 41
Amir, Menachem 1930- 45-48
Amis, Breton
See Best, Rayleigh Breton Amis
Amis, Kingsley (William) 1922- CANR-8
Earlier sketch in CA 11-12R
See also DLB 15, 27
See also CLC 1, 2, 3, 5, 8, 13, 40, 44
See also AITN 2
Amis, Martin 1949- CANR-8
Earlier sketch in CA 65-68
See also DLB 14
See also CLC 4, 9, 38
Amishai-Maisels, Ziva
See Maisels, Maxine S.
Amling, Frederick 1926- Brief entry 112
Amlund, Curtis Arthur 1927- 21-22R
Ammar, Abbas 1907(?)-1974 Obituary 53-56
Amme, Carl H., Jr. 1913- 25-28R
Ammer, Christine (Parker) 1931- 106
Ammer, Dean S. 1926- CANR-7
Earlier sketch in CA 19-20R
Ammerman, David L(eon) 1938- 57-60
Ammerman, Gale Richard 1923- 107
Ammerman, Leila T(remaine) 1912- 33-36R
Ammerman, Robert R(ay) 1927- 15-16R
Ammon, Harry 1917- 73-76
Ammons, A(rchie) R(andolph) 1926- CANR-6
Earlier sketch in CA 9-10R
See also DLB 5
See also CLC 2, 3, 5, 8, 9, 25
See also AITN 1
Amo, Tauraatua i
See Adams, Henry (Brooks)
Amoaku, J. K. 1936- 45-48
Amon, Aline 1928- CANR-8
Earlier sketch in CA 61-64
See also SATA 9
Amor, Amos
See Harrell, Irene B(urk)
Amor, Anne Clark 1933- 112
Amore, Roy Clayton 1942- 105
Amory, Anne Reinberg 1931- 17-18R
Amory, Cleveland 1917- 69-72
See also AITN 1
Amory, Mark 1941- 114
Amos, William E. 1926- 17-18R
Amos, Winsom 1921- 49-52
Amosov, N.
See Amosov, N(ikolai) M(ikhailovich)
Amosov, N(ikolai) M(ikhailovich) 1913-
Brief entry 112
Amoss, Berthe 1925- CANR-14
Earlier sketch in CA 21-22R
See also SATA 5
Amplegirth, Antony
See Dent, Anthony Austen
Amprimoz, Alexandre 1948- CANR-15
Earlier sketch in CA 37-40R
Amram, David (Werner III) 1930- 29-32R
Amrine, Michael 1919(?)-1974 73-76
Obituary 49-52
Amsel, Abram 1922- 114
Amstead, B(illy) H(oward) 1921- 23-24R
Amster, Linda 1938- CANR-22
Earlier sketch in CA 45-48
Amsterdam, Morey 1914- Brief entry 111
Amstutz, Arnold E. 1936- 21-22R
Amstutz, Mark R(obert) 1944- 105
Amter, Joseph A. ?-1982 Obituary 109
Amundsen, Kirsten 1932- 37-40R
Amundsen, Roald Engelbregt Gravning
1872-1928 Brief entry 117
Amusin, Joseph 1910-1984 Obituary 113
Amuzegar, Jahangir 1920- CANR-15
Earlier sketch in CA 41-44R
Analyticus
See Wise, James Waterman
Anand, Mulk Raj 1905- 65-68
See also CLC 23
Anand, Valerie 1937- CANR-13
Earlier sketch in CA 73-76
Anania, Michael 1939- 25-28R
Anastaplo, George 1925- 37-40R
Anastas, Lila L. 1940- 122
Anastas, Peter 1937- CANR-1
Earlier sketch in CA 45-48
Anastasi, Anne 1908- CANR-17
Earlier sketches in CA 7-8R, CANR-2
Anastasio, Dina 1941- 107
See also SATA 30, 37
Anastasiou, Clifford (John) 1929- CANR-18
Earlier sketches in CA 49-52, CANR-3
Anastos, Andrea La Sonde (Melrose)
1951- 117
Anatol
See Schnitzler, Arthur
Anatol, A.
See Kuznetsov, Anatoli
Anaya, Rudolfo A(lfonso) 1937- CANR-1
Earlier sketch in CA 45-48
See also CAAS 4
See also CLC 23
Anber, Paul
See Baker, Pauline H(alpern)
Ancel, Marc 1902- CANR-12
Earlier sketch in CA 69-72
Anchell, Melvin 1919- 25-28R
Anchor, Robert 1937- 69-72
Anckarsvard, Karin Inez Maria 1915-1969 9-10R
Obituary 103
See also SATA 6
Ancona, George 1929- CANR-19
Earlier sketches in CA 53-56, CANR-4
See also SATA 12
Andelin, Helen B. 1920- 89-92
Andelman, Eddie 1936- 57-60
Andelman, Samuel L(ouis) 1916-
Brief entry 114
Andelson, Robert V(ernon) 1931- 33-36R
Andereich, Justus
See Steiner, Gerolf
Anders, Edith (Mary) England 1899- CAP-1
Earlier sketch in CA 15-16
Anders, Evelyn 1916- 29-32R
Anders, Jeanne
See Anderson, Joan Wester
Anders, Leslie 1922- 15-16R
Anders, Sarah Frances 1927- 105
Andersch, Alfred 1914-1980 33-36R
Obituary 93-96
Andersch, Elizabeth Genevieve 1913- 7-8R
Andersdatter, Karla M(argaret) 1938- CANR-21
Earlier sketch in CA 104
See also SATA 34
Andersen, Arlow W. 1906- CAP-1
Earlier sketch in CA 11-12
Andersen, Benny (Allan) 1929- 101
Andersen, Christopher P(eter) 1949- CANR-14
Earlier sketch in CA 69-72
Andersen, D(ennis) R(ichard) 1947- 108
Andersen, Doris 1909- CANR-11
Earlier sketch in CA 23-24R
Andersen, Francis Ian 1925- 108
Andersen, Georg 1941- 112
Andersen, Hans Christian 1805-1875 YABC-1
See also CLR 6
Andersen, Jefferson 1955(?)-1979
Obituary 85-88
Andersen, Juel 1923- CANR-22
Earlier sketch in CA 105
Andersen, Kenneth E(ldon) 1933- 37-40R
Andersen, Kurt 1954- CANR-23
Earlier sketch in CA 106
Andersen, Marianne S(inger) 1934- 65-68
Andersen, Marion Lineaweaver
1912(?)-1971 Obituary 29-32R
Andersen, R(udolph) Clifton 1933- 33-36R
Andersen, Richard 1931- CANR-24
Earlier sketches in CA 57-60, CANR-8
Andersen, Richard 1946- 102
Andersen, Ted
See Boyd, Waldo T.
Andersen, Uell Stanley 1917- 3R
Andersen, Wayne V. 1928- 9-10R
Andersen, Wilhelm 1911- 29-32R
Andersen, Yvonne 1932- 29-32R
See also SATA 27
Anderson, A(rthur) J(ames) 1933- 106
Anderson, Alan H., Jr. 1943- 69-72
Anderson, Alan Ross 1925-1973 CAP-2
Obituary 45-48
Earlier sketch in CA 17-18
Anderson, Allan 1915- 97-100

Anderson, Alpha E. 1914-1970 ... CAP-2
Earlier sketch in CA 23-24
Anderson, Ann Kiemel 1945- ... 121
Anderson, Arthur J(ames) O(utram) 1907- ... CANR-15
Earlier sketch in CA 85-88
Anderson, B(asil) W(illiam) 1901-1984
Obituary ... 112
Anderson, Barbara 1948- ... 93-96
Anderson, Barbara Gallatin 1926-
Brief entry ... 111
Anderson, Barry (Franklin) 1935- ... 19-20R
Anderson, Bern 1900-1963 ... 1R
Anderson, Bernard Eric 1936- ... CANR-5
Earlier sketch in CA 53-56
Anderson, Bernhard Word 1916- ... CANR-8
Earlier sketch in CA 57-60
Anderson, Bernice G(oudy) 1894- ... 101
See also SATA 33
Anderson, Bertha Moore 1892- ... 7-8R
Anderson, Beverly
See Nemiro, Beverly Anderson
Anderson, Beverly M.
See Nemiro, Beverly Anderson
Anderson, Bob 1947- ... 69-72
Anderson, Brad(ley Jay) 1924- ... 106
See also SATA 31, 33
Anderson, C(arl) L(eonard) 1901- ... 25-28R
Anderson, Camilla M(ay) 1904- ... 33-36R
Anderson, Carl Dicmann 1912- ... 33-36R
Anderson, Carl L(ennart) 1919- ... 41-44R
Anderson, Carolyn 1941- ... 73-76
Anderson, Catherine Corley 1909- ... 4R
Anderson, Charles Burroughs 1905-1985 ... 65-68
Obituary ... 115
Anderson, Charles C. 1931- ... 29-32R
Anderson, Charles Roberts 1902- ... CANR-3
Earlier sketch in CA 1R
Anderson, Charles W(illiam) 1934- ... 11-12R
Anderson, Charlotte Maria 1923- ... 81-84
Anderson, Chester 1932- Brief entry ... 117
Anderson, Chester G(rant) 1923- ... 25-28R
Anderson, Chuck 1933- ... 49-52
Anderson, Clarence William 1891-1971 ... 73-76
Obituary ... 29-32R
See also SATA 11
Anderson, Clifford
See Gardner, Richard (M.)
Anderson, Colena M(ichael) 1891- ... CANR-11
Earlier sketch in CA 21-22R
Anderson, Cortland 1935-1985 Obituary ... 118
Anderson, Courtney 1906- ... CAP-1
Earlier sketch in CA 19-20
Anderson, Dave
See Anderson, David Poole
See also AITN 2
Anderson, David D(aniel) 1924- ... CANR-5
Earlier sketch in CA 13-14R
Anderson, David L(eonard) 1919- ... 7-8R
Anderson, David Poole 1929- ... 89-92
Anderson, Dillon 1906-1974 ... 3R
Obituary ... 45-48
Anderson, Donald F(rancis) 1938- ... 53-56
Anderson, Donald K(ennedy), Jr. 1922- ... 37-40R
Anderson, Doris (Hilda) 1925- ... 89-92
Anderson, Dwight G(ale) 1938- ... 107
Anderson, E. Ruth 1907- ... 93-96
Anderson, E.W. 1901-1981 Obituary ... 104
Anderson, Earl Robert 1943- ... 111
Anderson, Edgar 1920- ... CANR-13
Earlier sketch in CA 33-36R
Anderson, Einar 1909- ... 15-16R
Anderson, Elbridge Gerry 1907- ... 69-72
Anderson, Elliott 1944- ... 93-96
Anderson, Eloise Adell 1927- ... 53-56
See also SATA 9
Anderson, Emily 1891-1962 ... 124
Anderson, Eric (Douglas) 1949- ... 106
Anderson, Erica 1914- ... 57-60
Anderson, Eugene N(ewton) 1900- ... 29-32R
Anderson, (William) Ferguson 1914- ... 107
Anderson, Frank J(ohn) 1919- ... CANR-4
Earlier sketch in CA 9-10R
Anderson, Fred 1949- ... 117
Anderson, Frederick Irving 1877-1947
Brief entry ... 112
Anderson, Freeman B(urket) 1922- ... 41-44R
Anderson, Gary Clayton 1948- ... 117
Anderson, Gary Lee 1939- Brief entry ... 115
Anderson, George
See Groom, Arthur William
Anderson, George
See Weissman, Jack
Anderson, George B. 1908(?)-1985
Obituary ... 114
Anderson, George Christian 1907-1976 ... CAP-2
Obituary ... 69-72
Earlier sketch in CA 29-32
Anderson, George K(umler) 1901- ... CAP-2
Earlier sketch in CA 23-24
Anderson, George L(aVerne) 1905-1971 ... CANR-9
Earlier sketch in CA 13-14R
Anderson, George Lee 1934- Brief entry ... 111
Anderson, Gerald Dwight 1944- ... 115
Anderson, Gerald H(arry) 1930- ... CANR-7
Earlier sketch in CA 19-20R
Anderson, Godfrey Tryggve 1909- ... 41-44R
Anderson, Grace Fox 1932- ... 121
See also SATA 43
Anderson, H(ugh) Allen (Jr.) 1950- ... 120
Anderson, H(obson) Dewey 1897-1975 ... 65-68
Obituary ... 61-64
Anderson, Harold H(omer) 1897- ... CAP-2
Earlier sketch in CA 21-22
Anderson, Harry V(ernon) 1903-1983
Obituary ... 110
Anderson, Henry P. 1927- ... 33-36R
Anderson, Howard Jeremy 1915(?)-1983
Obituary ... 111
Anderson, Howard Peter 1932- ... 61-64
Anderson, Hugh 1920- ... 9-10R
Anderson, Ian Gibson 1933- ... 85-88
Anderson, Irvine H(enry) 1928- ... CANR-11
Earlier sketch in CA 69-72
Anderson, J(ohn) E(dward) 1903- ... 37-40R
Anderson, J(ohn) K(inloch) 1924- ... CANR-10
Earlier sketch in CA 19-20R
Anderson, J(ohn) Kerby 1951- ... 97-100
Anderson, J. N.
See Anderson, (James) Norman (Dalrymple)
Anderson, J(ohn) R(ichard) L(ane) 1911-1981 ... CANR-18
Obituary ... 104
Earlier sketch in CA 25-28R
See also SATA 15, 27
Anderson, Jack(son Northman) 1922- ... CANR-6
Earlier sketch in CA 57-60
See also AITN 1
Anderson, Jack 1935- ... CANR-24
Earlier sketch in CA 33-36R
Anderson, James C(letus) 1943- ... 111
Anderson, James D(esmond) 1933- ... 49-52
Anderson, James E(lliott) 1933- ... CANR-21
Earlier sketches in CA 9-10R, CANR-6
Anderson, James F(rancis) 1910- ... 41-44R
Anderson, James G(eorge) 1936- ... 25-28R
Anderson, James LaVerne 1940-
Brief entry ... 111
Anderson, James M(axwell) 1933- ... 33-36R
Anderson, (Helen) Jean 1931- ... CANR-14
Earlier sketch in CA 41-44R
Anderson, Jeanne 1934(?)-1979 Obituary ... 85-88
Anderson, Jennifer 1942- ... 57-60
Anderson, Jerry M(aynard) 1933- ... 41-44R
Anderson, Jessica (Margaret) Queale ... CANR-4
Earlier sketch in CA 11-12R
See also CLC 37
Anderson, Joan Wester 1938- ... CANR-24
Earlier sketches in CA 65-68, CANR-9
Anderson, John Bayard 1922- ... 33-36R
Anderson, John F(reeman) 1945- ... 53-56
Anderson, John K.
See Anderson, J(ohn) K(inloch)
Anderson, John L(onzo) 1905- ... 25-28R
Anderson, John M(ueller) 1914- ... 17-18R
Anderson, John Q. 1916-1975 ... CANR-3
Earlier sketch in CA 1R
Anderson, Jon (Victor) 1940- ... CANR-20
Earlier sketch in CA 25-28R
See also CLC 9
Anderson, Joy 1928- ... 25-28R
See also SATA 1
Anderson, Judith H(elena) 1940- ... 123
Anderson, Judith I(cke) 1939- ... 112
Anderson, Ken 1917- ... 25-28R
Anderson, Kenneth Norman 1921- ... CANR-18
Earlier sketch in CA 102
Anderson, Kristin
See Du Breuil, (Elizabeth) L(or)inda
Anderson, LaVere Francis Shoenfelt 1907- ... 101
See also SATA 27
Anderson, Lee 1896-1972 ... 1R
Obituary ... 37-40R
Anderson, Lee Stratton 1925- ... 101
Anderson, Leone Castell 1923- ... SATA-49
Anderson, Lester William 1918-1973 ... 7-8R
Obituary ... 103
Anderson, Lindsay 1923- ... CLC-20
Anderson, Lonzo
See Anderson, John L(onzo)
See also SATA 2
Anderson, Lucia (Lewis) 1922- ... 41-44R
See also SATA 10
Anderson, Luther A(dolph) ... 65-68
Anderson, M(ary) D(esiree) 1902- ... 11-12R
Anderson, Madeleine Paltenghi 1899- ... CAP-1
Earlier sketch in CA 19-20
Anderson, Madelyn Klein ... CANR-11
Earlier sketch in CA 69-72
See also SATA 28
Anderson, Maggie
See Anderson, Margaret
Anderson, Malcolm 1934- ... 33-36R
Anderson, Margaret (Vance) 1917- ... 21-22R
Anderson, Margaret 1948- ... 101
Anderson, Margaret Bartlett 1922- ... 9-10R
Anderson, Margaret C(aroline) 1886-1973 ... 108
Obituary ... 45-48
See also DLB 4
Anderson, Margaret J(ohnson) 1909- ... CANR-3
Earlier sketch in CA 3R
Anderson, Margaret J(ean) 1931- ... CANR-11
Earlier sketch in CA 69-72
See also SATA 27
Anderson, Martin 1936- ... CANR-9
Earlier sketch in CA 15-16R
Anderson, Marvin Walter 1933- ... 41-44R
Anderson, Mary 1939- ... CANR-16
Earlier sketches in CA 49-52, CANR-1
See also SATA 7
Anderson, Matthew Smith 1922- ... 13-14R
Anderson, Maxie (Leroy) 1934-1983
Obituary ... 115
Anderson, Maxwell 1888-1959 Brief entry ... 105
See also DLB 7
See also TCLC 2
Anderson, Mona 1910- ... CANR-6
Earlier sketch in CA 57-60
See also SATA 40
Anderson, (James) Norman (Dalrymple) 1908- ... CANR-4
Earlier sketch in CA 11-12R
Anderson, Norman Dean 1928- ... CANR-15
Earlier sketch in CA 33-36R
See also SATA 22
Anderson, Norman G(ulden) 1913-
Brief entry ... 114
Anderson, O(rvil) Roger 1937- ... 33-36R
Anderson, Odin W(aldemar) 1914- ... 25-28R
Anderson, Olive M(ary) 1915- ... CANR-14
Earlier sketch in CA 81-84
Anderson, Olive Ruth 1926- ... 107
Anderson, P(aul) Howard 1947- ... 61-64
Anderson, Patrick (John MacAllister) 1915-1979 ... 93-96
Obituary ... 85-88
Anderson, Patrick 1936- ... 33-36R
Anderson, Paul E. 1925- ... 33-36R
Anderson, Paul Seward 1913-1975 ... CANR-6
Earlier sketch in CA 4R
Anderson, Paul Y. 1893-1938 ... DLB-29
Anderson, Peggy 1938- ... 93-96
Anderson, Poul (William) 1926- ... CANR-15
Earlier sketches in CA 2R, CANR-2
See also CAAS 2
See also SATA 39
See also DLB 8
See also CLC 15
Anderson, Quentin 1912- ... CANR-3
Earlier sketch in CA 1R
Anderson, R. C. 1883(?)-1976 Obituary ... 69-72
Anderson, R(oy) C(laude) 1931- ... 124
Anderson, Rachel 1943- ... CANR-24
Earlier sketches in CA 21-22R, CANR-9
See also SATA 34
Anderson, Randall C. 1934- ... 41-44R
Anderson, Ray Sherman 1925- ... CANR-10
Earlier sketch in CA 65-68
Anderson, Raymond L(loyd) 1927- ... 106
Anderson, Richard
See Anderson, J(ohn) R(ichard) L(ane)
Anderson, Richard Chase 1934-
Brief entry ... 112
Anderson, Richard Lloyd 1926- ... 37-40R
Anderson, Robert (Woodruff) 1917- ... 21-22R
See also DLB 7
See also CLC 23
See also AITN 1
Anderson, Robert A(ndrew) 1944- ... 109
Anderson, Robert C(harles) 1930- ... 85-88
Anderson, Robert David 1942- ... 73-76
Anderson, Robert H(enry) 1918- ... 49-52
Anderson, Robert Mapes 1929- ... 108
Anderson, Robert Newton 1929- ... 49-52
Anderson, Robert T(homas) 1926- ... 9-10R
Anderson, Robert W(illiam) 1926- ... 19-20R
Anderson, Roberta 1942- ... 115
Brief entry ... 111
Anderson, Rodney Dean 1938- ... 108
Anderson, Ronald Kinloch 1911-1984
Obituary ... 111
Anderson, Roy 1936- ... 15-16R
Anderson, Roy
See Anderson, R(oy) C(laude)
Anderson, Roy Allan 1895- ... CANR-9
Earlier sketch in CA 15-16R
Anderson, Ruth I(rene) 1919- ... CANR-18
Earlier sketch in CA 4R
Anderson, Ruth Nathan 1934- ... 69-72
Anderson, Scarvia (Bateman) 1926- ... CANR-14
Earlier sketch in CA 41-44R
Anderson, Sherwood 1876-1941 ... 121
Brief entry ... 104
See also DLB 4, 9
See also DLBD 1
See also TCLC 1, 10, 24
See also SSC 1
Anderson, Shirley Lord 1934- ... CANR-11
Earlier sketch in CA 65-68
Anderson, Sparky
See Anderson, George Lee
Anderson, Stanford 1934- ... 25-28R
Anderson, Stanley Edwin 1900-1977 ... CANR-3
Earlier sketch in CA 1R
Anderson, Stanley V(ictor) 1928- ... 21-22R
Anderson, Sydney 1927- ... 106
Anderson, T(heodore) W(ilbur, Jr.) 1918- ... 49-52
Anderson, Teresa 1944- ... 85-88
Anderson, Theodore R(obert) 1927- ... 41-44R
Anderson, Thomas 1929- ... 3R
Anderson, Thomas D. 1929- ... 111
Anderson, Tom 1910- ... 69-72
Anderson, Tommy (Nolan) 1918- ... 45-48
Anderson, Totton J(ames) 1909- ... 3R
Anderson, Verily (Bruce) 1915- ... CANR-3
Earlier sketch in CA 7-8R
Anderson, Vernon E(llsworth) 1908- ... CANR-5
Earlier sketch in CA 4R
Anderson, Virgil Antris 1899- ... CANR-16
Earlier sketch in CA 1R
Anderson, Virginia (R. Cronin) 1920- ... 21-22R
Anderson, Vivienne 1916- ... 19-20R
Anderson, W. B.
See Schultz, James Willard
Anderson, Wallace Ludwig 1917- ... 17-18R
Anderson, Walt
See Anderson, Walter Truett
Anderson, Walter 1944- ... 101
Anderson, Walter Truett 1933- ... 105
Anderson, Warren DeWitt 1920- ... 17-18R
Anderson, Wayne 1946- ... 107
Anderson, Wayne Jeremy 1908- ... 49-52
Anderson, Wendell B(ernhard) 1920- ... 105
Anderson, William A(verette) 1937-
Brief entry ... 114
Anderson, William Charles 1920- ... CANR-2
Earlier sketch in CA 7-8R
Anderson, William Davis 1938- ... 33-36R
Anderson, William Eugene 1926-
Brief entry ... 111
Anderson, William G(ary) 1945- ... 115
Anderson, William H(arry) 1905-1972 ... 49-52
Anderson, William Robert 1921- ... 7-8R
Anderson, William Scovil 1927- ... 61-64
Anderson, Wilton T(homas) 1916- ... 17-18R
Anderson Imbert, Enrique 1910- ... CANR-10
Earlier sketch in CA 19-20R
Andersons, Edgars
See Anderson, Edgar
Anders-Richards, Donald 1928- ... 25-28R
Andersson, Ingvar 1899(?)-1974
Obituary ... 53-56
Andersson, Theodore 1903- ... 49-52
Andersson, Theodore M(urdock) 1934- ... 25-28R
Anderton, David A(lbin) 1919- ... CANR-9
Earlier sketch in CA 65-68
Anderton, Joanne (Marie) Gast 1930- ... 61-64
Anderton, Johana Gast
See Anderton, Joanne (Marie) Gast
Andervont, Howard Bancroft 1898-1981
Obituary ... 103
Andonian, Jeanne (Beghian) 1891(?)-1976
Obituary ... 65-68
Andonov-Poljanski, Hristo 1927- ... CANR-9
Earlier sketch in CA 21-22R
Andouard
See Giraudoux, (Hippolyte) Jean
Andrade, Carlos Drummond de
See Drummond de Andrade, Carlos
See also CLC 18
Andrade, E(dward) N(eville) da C(osta) 1887-1971 ... CAP-1
Earlier sketch in CA 11-12
Andrade, Victor (Manuel) 1905- ... 69-72
Andrain, Charles F(ranklin) 1937- ... 69-72
Andre, Evelyn M(arie) 1924- ... CANR-11
Earlier sketch in CA 69-72
See also SATA 27
Andre, (Kenneth) Michael 1946- ... 114
Andre, Rae 1946- ... 116
Andreach, Robert J. 1930- ... 33-36R
Andreano, Ralph L(ouis) 1929- ... CANR-6
Earlier sketch in CA 7-8R
Andreas, Burton G(ould) 1921- ... 81-84
Andreas, Thomas
See Williams, Thomas (Andrew)
Andreasen, Alan R(obert) 1934- ... 65-68
Andreasen, Nancy C(oover) 1938- ... 108
Andreas-Salome, Lou 1861-1937 ... DLB-66
Andreassen, Karl
See Boyd, Waldo T.
Andree, Louise
See Coury, Louise Andree
Andree, R(ichard) V(ernon) 1919- ... CANR-8
Earlier sketch in CA 57-60
Andree, Robert G(erald) 1912-1987 ... 29-32R
Obituary ... 124
Andreissen, David
See Poyer, David
Andreopoulos, Spyros (George) 1929- ... 77-80
Andres, Glenn M(erle) 1941- ... 73-76
Andres, Stefan 1906-1970 Obituary ... 29-32R
Andresen, Jack
See Andresen, John H(enry), Jr.
Andresen, John H(enry), Jr. 1917- ... 57-60
Andresen, Julie
See Tetel, Julie
Andreski, Iris
See Gillespie, I(ris) S(ylvia)
Andreski, Stanislav Leonard 1919- ... 61-64
Andrew, David S. 1943- ... 123
Andrew, J(ames) Dudley 1945- ... CANR-9
Earlier sketch in CA 65-68
Andrew, John (Alfred III) 1943- ... 69-72
Andrew, Malcolm (Ross) 1945- ... 105
Andrew, Prudence (Hastings) 1924- ... CANR-1
Earlier sketch in CA 1R
Andrew, Warren 1910- ... 21-22R
Andrewes, Christopher Howard 1896- ... 17-18R
Andrewes, Patience
See Bradford, Patience Andrewes
Andrews, A. A.
See Paine, Lauran (Bosworth)
Andrews, Allen 1913- ... CANR-1
Earlier sketch in CA 49-52
Andrews, Arthur (Douglas, Jr.) 1923- ... 69-72
Andrews, Barry G(eoffrey) 1943- ... CANR-2
Earlier sketch in CA 49-52
Andrews, Bart 1945- ... CANR-24
Earlier sketches in CA 65-68, CANR-9
Andrews, Benny 1930- ... 106
See also SATA 31
Andrews, Bruce 1948- ... CANR-10
Earlier sketch in CA 49-52
Andrews, Burton (Allen) 1906- ... CAP-2
Earlier sketch in CA 33-36
Andrews, Charles M(cLean) 1863-1943
Brief entry ... 119
See also DLB 17
Andrews, Cicily Fairfield
See West, Rebecca
Andrews, Claire 1940- ... 33-36R
Andrews, Clarence A(delbert) 1912- ... CANR-20
Earlier sketch in CA 33-36R
Andrews, Donald H(atch) 1898-197(?) ... CAP-2
Earlier sketch in CA 23-24
Andrews, Dorothea Harris 1916-1976
Obituary ... 69-72
Andrews, E(ric) M(ontgomery) 1933- ... 93-96
Andrews, Eamonn 1922-1987 ... 120
Obituary ... 124
Andrews, Edgar Harold 1932- ... 105
Andrews, Eleanor Lattimore
See Lattimore, Eleanor Frances

Andrews, Elton V.
See Pohl, Frederik
Andrews, Ernest E(ugene) 1932- 57-60
Andrews, F(rank) Emerson 1902-1978 .. CANR-1
Obituary 81-84
Earlier sketch in CA 4R
See also SATA 22
Andrews, (Earl) Frank 1937- 61-64
Andrews, Frank M(eredith) 1935- CANR-14
Earlier sketch in CA 41-44R
Andrews, George (Clinton) 1926- 21-22R
Andrews, George F(redrick) 1918- 65-68
Andrews, Henry N(athaniel), Jr. 1910- 93-96
Andrews, J. Cutler 1908-1972 Obituary ..37-40R
Andrews, J(ames) S(ydney) 1934- 29-32R
See also SATA 4
Andrews, James David 1924- 53-56
Andrews, James Frederick 1936-1980
Obituary 107
Andrews, James J. C. 1943(?)-1985
Obituary 116
Andrews, James R(obertson) 1936-
Brief entry 117
Andrews, Jan 1942- 122
See also SATA 49
Andrews, John F(rank) 1942- 119
Andrews, John Henry 1939- 107
Andrews, John Malcolm 1936- 117
Andrews, John Williams 1898-1975
Obituary 57-60
Andrews, Julie 1935- 37-40R
See also SATA 7
Andrews, Keith 1930- 33-36R
Andrews, Kenneth R(ichmond) 1916- .. CANR-16
Earlier sketch in CA 1R
Andrews, Kevin 1924- 124
Andrews, Laura
See Coury, Louise Andree
Andrews, Lewis M. 1946- 65-68
Andrews, (William) Linton 1886-1972 .....9-10R
Obituary 120
Andrews, Lucilla Mathew Brief entry 116
Andrews, Lyman 1938- 49-52
Andrews, Margaret E(lizabeth) 33-36R
Andrews, Mark Edwin 1903- CAP-1
Earlier sketch in CA 19-20
Andrews, (Daniel) Marshall 1899(?)-1973
Obituary 45-48
Andrews, Mary Evans 5-6R
Andrews, Michael
See Andrews, Michael Alford
Andrews, Michael Alford 1939- 116
Andrews, Michael F(rank) 1916- 49-52
Andrews, Mike
See Andrews, Michael Alford
Andrews, Paul Revere 1906-1983
Obituary 110
Andrews, Peter 1931- CANR-11
Earlier sketch in CA 17-18R
Andrews, Ralph W(arren) 1897- 9-10R
Andrews, Raymond 1934- CANR-15
Earlier sketch in CA 81-84
Andrews, Robert D.
See Andrews, (Charles) Robert Douglas (Hardy)
Andrews, (Charles) Robert Douglas (Hardy)
1908- CAP-1
Earlier sketch in CA 9-10
Andrews, Roy Chapman 1884-1960 .... SATA-19
Andrews, Stanley 1894- CANR-22
Earlier sketch in CA 45-48
Andrews, V(irginia) C(leo) ?-1986 ..... CANR-21
Obituary 121
Earlier sketch in CA 97-100
See also SATA 50
Andrews, Wayne 1913-1987 .... CANR-3
Obituary 123
Earlier sketch in CA 9-10R
Andrews, William G(eorge) 1930- CANR-7
Earlier sketch in CA 7-8R
Andrews, William R(obert) 1937- 53-56
Andreyev, Leonid (Nikolaevich) 1871-1919
Brief entry 104
See also TCLC 3
Andreyev, Nikolay Efremych 1908-1982
Obituary 106
Andrezel, Pierre
See Blixen, Karen (Christentze Dinesen)
Andrian, Gustave W(illiam) 1918-
Brief entry 114
Andric, Ivo 1892-1975 81-84
Obituary 57-60
See also CLC 8
Andriekus, (Kazimieras) Leonardas
1914- 25-28R
Andrien, Kenneth James 1951- 120
Andriessen, Hendrik (Franciscus)
1892-1981 Obituary 108
Andriola, Alfred J. 1912-1983 Obituary 109
See also SATA 34
Andrist, Ralph K. 1914- CANR-20
Earlier sketches in CA 9-10R, CANR-5
See also SATA 45
Andropov, Yuri (Vladimirovich) 1914-1984
Obituary 111
Andros, Dee G(us) 1924- 69-72
Andros, Phil
See Steward, Samuel M(orris)
Andrus, (Vincent) Dyckman 1942- 102
Andrus, Hyrum L(eslie) 1924- 37-40R
Andrus, Paul 1931- 65-68
Andrus, Vera 1895- CAP-2
Earlier sketch in CA 21-22
Andrzejewski, Jerzy 1909-1983 ....25-28R
Obituary 109
Andrzeyevski, George
See Andrzejewski, Jerzy
Anduze-Dufy, Raphael
See Coulet du Gard, Rene
Anees, Munawar Ahmad 1948- 123
An Elderly Spinster
See Wilson, Margaret (Wilhemina)
Anfousse, Ginette 1944- SATA-48
Angebert, Jean
See Bertrand, Michel
Angebert, Jean-Michel
See Bertrand, Michel
Angebert, Michel
See Bertrand, Michel
Angel, Daniel D. 1939- 33-36R
Angel, Heather 1941- 69-72
Angel, J(ohn) Lawrence 1915-1986 101
Obituary 120
Angel, Marc D(wight) 1945- 101
Angel, Marie 1923- CANR-15
Earlier sketch in CA 29-32R
See also SATA 47
Angelella, Michael 1953- 97-100
Angeles, Jose 1930- 33-36R
Angeles, Peter A. 1931- 33-36R
See also SATA 40
Angeles, Philip 1909- 7-8R
Angeli, Marguerite (Lofft) de
See de Angeli, Marguerite (Lofft)
Angelilli, Frank Joseph
See Angell, Frank Joseph
Angelin, Patricia 119
Angelino, Marie
See Garbutt, Janice (D.) Lovoos
Angelique, Pierre
See Bataille, Georges
Angell, Ernest 1889-1973 Obituary 37-40R
Angell, Frank Joseph 1919- 17-18R
Angell, George 1945- 101
Angell, James Burrill 1829-1916 .... DLB-64
Angell, James W(aterhouse) 1898-1986
Obituary 119
Angell, Judie 1937- 77-80
See also SATA 22
Angell, Madeline 1919- CANR-10
Earlier sketch in CA 65-68
See also SATA 18
Angell, (Ralph) Norman 1872(?)-1967 .... CAP-1
Earlier sketch in CA 13-14
Angell, Richard B(radshaw) 1918- 15-16R
Angell, Robert Cooley 1899- 101
Angell, Roger 1920- CANR-13
Earlier sketch in CA 57-60
See also CLC 26
Angell, Tony 1940- CANR-4
Earlier sketch in CA 53-56
Angelo, Bonnie Brief entry 113
Angelo, Frank 1914- CANR-4
Earlier sketch in CA 53-56
Angelo, Valenti 1897- 73-76
See also SATA 14
Angelocci, Angelo 1926- 23-24R
Angelou, Maya 1928- CANR-19
Earlier sketch in CA 65-68
See also SATA 49
See also DLB 38
See also CLC 12, 35
Anger, Kenneth 1930- 106
Angermann, Gerhard O(tto) 1904- 65-68
Angier, Bradford CANR-7
Earlier sketch in CA 5-6R
See also SATA 12
Angier, Carole 1943- 120
Angier, Roswell P. 1940- 101
Angiolillo, Paul F(rancis) 1917- 105
Anglade, Jean 1915- CANR-20
Earlier sketch in CA 103
Angle, Paul M(cClelland) 1900-1975 ..... CAP-2
Obituary 57-60
Earlier sketch in CA 21-22
See also SATA 20
Anglin, Douglas G(eorge) 1923- CANR-14
Earlier sketch in CA 37-40R
Anglo, Sydney 1934- 89-92
Anglund, Joan Walsh 1926- CANR-15
Earlier sketch in CA 7-8R
See also SATA 2
See also CLR 1
Ango, Fan D.
See Longyear, Barry Brookes
Angoff, Allan 1910- CANR-20
Earlier sketch in CA 45-48
Angoff, Charles 1902-1979 .... CANR-4
Obituary 85-88
Earlier sketch in CA 5-6R
Angremy, Jean-Pierre 1937- 106
Angress, R(uth) K(lueger) 1931- 37-40R
Angress, Werner T(homas) 1920- 13-14R
Angrist, Shirley S(arah) 1933- 25-28R
Angrist, Stanley W(olff) 1933- 25-28R
See also SATA 4
Anguizola, G. A.
See Anguizola, Gustave (A.)
Anguizola, Gustave (A.) 1927- Brief entry ... 116
Angus, Douglas Ross 1909- CANR-3
Earlier sketch in CA 1R
Angus, Fay 1929- CANR-15
Earlier sketch in CA 89-92
Angus, Ian
See Mackay, James (Alexander)
Angus, J(ohn) Colin 1907- 107
Angus, Margaret 1908- 21-22R
Angus, Sylvia 1921-1982 .... CANR-10
Earlier sketch in CA 61-64
Angus, Tom
See Powell, Geoffrey Stewart
Angus-Butterworth, Lionel Milner 1900- . CANR-4
Earlier sketch in CA 53-56
Anhalt, Edward 85-88
See also DLB 26
Anicar, Tom
See Racina, Thom
Anikouchine, William A(lexander) 1929-
Brief entry 117
Anita
See Daniel, Anita
Ankenbrand, Frank, Jr. 1905- CAP-2
Earlier sketch in CA 19-20
Anker, Charlotte 1934- 93-96
Anmar, Frank
See Nolan, William F(rancis)
Anna, Timothy E. 1944- 101
Annan, Noel Gilroy 1916- 61-64
Annand, J(ames) K(ing) 1908- CANR-18
Earlier sketch in CA 101
Annandale, Barbara
See Bowden, Jean
Annas, George J. 1945- 77-80
Anne-Mariel
See Goud, Anne
Annensky, Innokenty Fyodorovich
1856-1909 Brief entry 110
See also TCLC 14
Anness, Milford E(dwin) 1918- 17-18R
Annett, Cora
See Scott, Cora Annett (Pipitone)
Annett, John 1930- 29-32R
Annis, Linda Ferrill 1943- 85-88
Annixter, Jane
See Sturtzel, Jane Levington
Annixter, Paul
See Sturtzel, Howard A(llison)
Anno, Mitsumasa 1926- CANR-4
Earlier sketch in CA 49-52
See also SATA 5, 38
See also CLR 2, 14
Anobile, Richard J(oseph) 1947- CANR-5
Earlier sketch in CA 53-56
Anobile, Ulla (Kakonen) 1945- 111
Anodos
See Coleridge, Mary E(lizabeth)
Anoff, I(sador) S(amuel) 1892- 45-48
Anouilh, Jean (Marie Lucien Pierre)
1910-1987 ....17-18R
Obituary 123
See also CLC 1, 3, 8, 13, 40
Anquillare, John 1942- 105
Ansbacher, Heinz L(udwig) 1904- CAP-1
Earlier sketch in CA 9-10
Ansbacher, Max G. 1935- 89-92
Ansberry, William F. 1926- 33-36R
Anschel, Eugene 1907- 53-56
Anschel, Kurt R. 1936- 41-44R
Anscombe, G(ertrude) E(lizabeth)
M(argaret) 1919- Brief entry 122
Anscombe, Isabelle (Mary) 1954- 108
Ansel, Walter (Charles) 1897-1977 45-48
Obituary 73-76
Ansell, Helen 1940- 25-28R
Ansell, Jack 1925-1976 ....17-18R
Obituary 69-72
Anselm, Felix
See Pollak, Felix
Ansen, Alan 1922- CANR-4
Earlier sketch in CA 1R
Anshen, Melvin (Leon) 1912- 124
Ansley, Gladys Piatt 1906- 5-6R
Anslinger, Harry Jacob 1892-1975 .... CAP-1
Obituary 61-64
Earlier sketch in CA 11-12
Anson, Bill 1907-1983 Obituary 110
Anson, Cyril J(oseph) 1923- 49-52
Anson, Jay 1921-1980 81-84
Obituary 97-100
Anson, John
See Firth, (Frederick) Anson
Anson, Peter Frederick 1889- 9-10R
Anson, Robert Sam 1945- Brief entry 115
Anspach, Donald F. 1942- 69-72
Anstey, Edgar 1917- CANR-3
Earlier sketch in CA 7-8R
Anstey, Edgar
See Slusser, George Edgar
Anstey, F.
See Guthrie, Thomas Anstey
Anstey, Roger T(homas) 1927- 13-14R
Anstey, Vera (Powell) 1889- CAP-1
Earlier sketch in CA 17-18
Anstruther, James
See Maxtone Graham, James Anstruther
An Tai-sung 1931- Brief entry 113
Antell, Gerson 1926- 53-56
Antell, Will D. 1935- 104
See also SATA 31
Anthes, Richard A(llen) 1944- 107
Anthony
See Taber, Anthony Scott
Anthony, Barbara 1932- CANR-21
Earlier sketch in CA 103
See also SATA 29
Anthony, C. L.
See Smith, Dodie
Anthony, Catherine
See Adachi, Barbara (Curtis)
Anthony, David
See Smith, William Dale
Anthony, Diana 1951- 114
Anthony, Edward 1895-1971 73-76
Obituary 33-36R
See also SATA 21
Anthony, Evelyn
See Ward-Thomas, Evelyn Bridget Patricia Stephens
Anthony, Florence
See Ai
Anthony, Geraldine C(ecilia) 1919- CANR-11
Earlier sketch in CA 69-72
Anthony, Gordon
See Stannus, (James) Gordon (Dawson)
Anthony, Inid E. 1925- 104
Anthony, J(oseph) Garner 1899- 61-64
Anthony, James R. 1922- 49-52
Anthony, John
See Beckett, Ronald Brymer
Anthony, John
See Sabini, John Anthony
Anthony, Julie 1948- 106
Anthony, Katharine (Susan) 1877-1965
Obituary 25-28R
Anthony, Michael 1932- CANR-10
Earlier sketch in CA 19-20R
Anthony, Peter
See Shaffer, Anthony (Joshua)
and Shaffer, Peter (Levin)
Anthony, Piers
See Jacob, Piers A(nthony) D(illingham)
See also DLB 8
See also CLC 35
Anthony, Rebecca (Jespersen) 1950- 118
Anthony, Robert N(ewton) 1916- CANR-5
Earlier sketch in CA 15-16R
Anthony, Susan B(rownell) 1916- 89-92
Anthony, William G. 1934- 17-18R
Anthony, William P(hilip) 1943- CANR-13
Earlier sketch in CA 77-80
Anthrop, Donald F. 1935- Brief entry 111
Anticaglia, Elizabeth 1939- CANR-1
Earlier sketch in CA 45-48
See also SATA 12
Antico, John 1924- 29-32R
Antill, James Macquarie 1912- CANR-13
Earlier sketch in CA 33-36R
Antin, David 1932- 73-76
Antin, Mary 1881-1949 Brief entry 118
See also DLBY 84
Antoine, Marc
See Proust, (Valentin-Louis-George-Eugene-) Marcel
Antoine-Dariaux, Genevieve 1914- 57-60
Antolini, Margaret Fishback 1904-1985
Obituary 117
See also SATA 45
Anton, Frank Robert 1920- 41-44R
Anton, Hector R(oque) 1919- 73-76
Anton, John P(eter) 1920- CANR-9
Earlier sketch in CA 21-22R
Anton, Michael J(ames) 1940- 57-60
See also SATA 12
Anton, Rita (Kenter) 1920- 9-10R
Antonacci, Robert J(oseph) 1916- CANR-9
Earlier sketch in CA 7-8R
See also SATA 37, 45
Antoncich, Betty (Kennedy) 1913- 15-16R
Antoni
See Iranek-Osmecki, Kazimierz
Antoniak, Helen Elizabeth 1947- 105
Antonick, Robert J. 1939- 37-40R
Antoninus, Brother
See Everson, William (Oliver)
Antonio, Robert J(ohn) 1945- 120
Antonioni, Michelangelo 1912- 73-76
See also CLC 20
Antoniutti, Ildebrando 1898-1974
Obituary 53-56
Antonovsky, Aaron 1923- CANR-12
Earlier sketch in CA 29-32R
Antony, Jonquil 1916(?)-1980 ....15-16R
Obituary 120
Antoun, Richard T(aft) 1932- 65-68
Antreasian, Garo Z(areh) 1922- 81-84
Antrim, Harry Thomas 1936- 33-36R
Antrim, William H. 1928- 69-72
Antrobus, John 1933- CANR-11
Earlier sketch in CA 57-60
Antschel, Paul 1920-1970 85-88
See also CLC 10, 19
Anttila, Raimo (Aulis) 1935- 33-36R
Anvic, Frank
See Sherman, Jory (Tecumseh)
Anwar, Chairil 1922-1949 Brief entry 121
See also TCLC 22
Anweiler, Oskar 1925- CANR-9
Earlier sketch in CA 65-68
Anyon, G(eorge) Jay 1909- 7-8R
Anzovin, Steven 1954- 124
Aoki, Haruo 1930- 49-52
Aoki, Hisako 1942- 115
See also SATA 45
Aoki, Michiko Y(amaguchi) 107
Apel, Karl-Otto 1922- CANR-22
Earlier sketch in CA 105
Apel, Willi 1893- CANR-2
Earlier sketch in CA 2R
Apelian, Albert Solomon 1893-1986
Obituary 121
Apfel, Necia H(alpern) 1930- CANR-23
Earlier sketch in CA 107
See also SATA 41
Apffel, Edmund R., Jr. 1948- 107
Apgar, Virginia 1909-1974 73-76
Obituary 53-56
Aphrodite, J.
See Livingston, Carole
Apikuni
See Schultz, James Willard
Apilentz
See Apelian, Albert Solomon
Apitz, Bruno 1900-1979 Obituary 85-88
Aplon, Roger 1937- 119
Apolinar, Danny 1934- 61-64

Apollinaire, Guillaume
See Kostrowitzki, Wilhelm Apollinaris de
See also TCLC 3, 8
Aponte, Barbara (Ann) Bockus 1936-
Brief entry ... 111
Apostle, Chris(tos) N(icholas) 1935- ... 21-22R
Apostolon, Billy (Michael) 1930- ... 97-100
Apostolos-Cappadona, Diane 1948- ... 112
App, Austin Joseph 1902-1984 ... 101
Obituary ... 112
Appadorai, A(ngadipuram) 1902- ... 102
Appel, Alfred, Jr. 1934- Brief entry ... 113
Appel, Allan 1946- ... 77-80
Appel, Benjamin 1907-1977 ... CANR-6
Obituary ... 69-72
Earlier sketch in CA 13-14R
See also SATA 21, 39
Appel, Frederic C. 1935(?)-1984 Obituary ... 112
Appel, John J. 1921- ... 33-36R
Appel, Kenneth Ellmaker 1896-1979
Obituary ... 89-92
Appel, Libby E(ve Sundel) 1937- ... 117
Appel, Martin E(liot) 1948- ... CANR-15
Earlier sketch in CA 85-88
See also SATA 45
Appel, Marty
See Appel, Martin E(liot)
Appel, Willa 1946- ... 117
Appel, William 1939- ... 114
Appelbaum, Diana Karter 1953- ... 122
Appelbaum, Judith (Pilpel) 1939- ... CANR-14
Earlier sketch in CA 77-80
Appelbaum, Paul S(tuart) 1951- ... 108
Appelbaum, Stephen A(rthur) 1926- ... 101
Appelfeld, Aharon 1932- Brief entry ... 112
See also CLC 23, 47
Appelman, Hyman (Jedidiah) 1902- ... 5-6R
Appere, Guy 1923- ... 117
Appiah, Peggy 1921- ... 41-44R
See also SATA 15
Appignanesi, Lisa 1946- ... 49-52
Applbaum, Ronald L. 1943- ... CANR-7
Earlier sketch in CA 57-60
Apple, Margot ... SATA-42
Apple, Max (Isaac) 1941- ... CANR-19
Earlier sketch in CA 81-84
See also CLC 9, 33
Apple, Michael W(hitman) 1942- ... 109
Apple, R(aymond) W(alter), Jr. 1934- ... 89-92
Applebaum, Edmond L(ewis) 1924- ... 117
Applebaum, Samuel 1904- ... 65-68
Applebaum, Stan 1922- ... 85-88
See also SATA 45
Applebaum, William 1906-1979(?) ... CANR-6
Earlier sketch in CA 11-12R
Applebee, Arthur N(oble) 1946- ... CANR-14
Earlier sketch in CA 81-84
Appleby, Andrew Bell 1929-1980 ... 108
Appleby, David P. 1925- ... 110
Appleby, John T. 1909(?)-1974 Obituary ... 53-56
Appleby, Jon 1948- ... 33-36R
Appleby, Joyce Oldham 1929- ... CANR-11
Earlier sketch in CA 69-72
Applegarth, Margaret Tyson 1886-1976
Obituary ... 69-72
Applegate, James (Earl) 1923- ... 33-36R
Applegate, Richard 1913(?)-1979
Obituary ... 85-88
Applegath, John 1935- ... 115
Appleman, John Alan 1912-1982 ... CANR-2
Obituary ... 108
Earlier sketch in CA 7-8R
Appleman, M(arjorie) H. 1928- ... 118
Appleman, Margie
See Appleman, M(arjorie) H.
Appleman, Mark J(erome) 1917- ... 29-32R
Appleman, Philip (Dean) 1926- ... CANR-6
Earlier sketch in CA 15-16R
Appleman, Roy Edgar 1904- ... CAP-1
Earlier sketch in CA 9-10
Appleton, Arthur 1913- ... 93-96
Appleton, James Henry 1919- ... CANR-2
Earlier sketch in CA 5-6R
Appleton, Jane (Frances) 1934- ... 102
Appleton, Jay
See Appleton, James Henry
Appleton, Lawrence
See Lovecraft, H(oward) P(hillips)
Appleton, Marion Brymner 1906- ... 105
Appleton, Sarah 1930- ... 37-40R
Appleton, Sheldon Lee 1933- ... 1R
Appleton, Victor ... CAP-2
Earlier sketch in CA 19-20
See also SATA 1
Appleton, Victor II ... 19-20R
See also SATA 1
Appleton, Victor W. II
See Adams, Harriet S(tratemeyer)
Appleton, William S. 1934- ... 101
Appleton, William W(orthen) 1915-
Brief entry ... 113
Applewhite, Cynthia ... 89-92
Applewhite, E(dgar) J(arratt, Jr.) 1919- ... 89-92
Applewhite, Harriet Branson 1940- ... 106
Applewhite, James W(illiam) 1935- ... 85-88
Applewhite, Philip B(oatman) 1938- ... 112
Appley, Lawrence A. 1904- ... 121
Appley, M(ortimer) H(erbert) 1921- ... 15-16R
Appleyard, Donald 1928- ... CANR-4
Earlier sketch in CA 5-6R
Appleyard, Reginald Thomas 1927- ... 17-18R
Applezweig, M. H.
See Appley, M(ortimer) H(erbert)
Apps, Jerold W(illard) 1934- ... CANR-16
Earlier sketches in CA 49-52, CANR-1
Apps, Jerry
See Apps, Jerold W(illard)
apRoberts, Ruth ... 111
Apsler, Alfred 1907- ... CANR-3
Earlier sketch in CA 5-6R
See also SATA 10
Apt, (Jerome) Leon 1929- ... 53-56
Apte, Mahadev L(akshuman) 1931- ... 117
Apted, M(ichael) R. 1919- ... 25-28R
Aptekar, Jane 1935- ... 81-84
Apter, David Ernest 1924- ... CANR-3
Earlier sketch in CA 1R
Apter, Michael J(ohn) 1939- ... 29-32R
Apter, Samson 1910- ... 104
Aptheker, Bettina 1944- ... CANR-6
Earlier sketch in CA 29-32R
Aptheker, Herbert 1915- ... CANR-6
Earlier sketch in CA 5-6R
Aquarius, Qass
See Buskirk, Richard H(obart)
Aquilano, Nicholas Joseph 1930- ... 112
Aquin, Hubert 1929-1977 ... 105
See also DLB 53
See also CLC 15
Aquina, Sister Mary
See Weinrich, A(nna) K(atharina) H(ildegard)
Aquino, Benigno S(imeon), Jr. 1932-1983
Obituary ... 110
Aquino, Ninoy
See Aquino, Benigno S(imeon), Jr.
Arafat, Ibtihaj Said 1934- ... 85-88
Aragbabalu, Omidiji
See Beier, Ulli
Aragon, Louis 1897-1982 ... 69-72
Obituary ... 108
See also CLC 3, 22
Aragones, Sergio 1937- ... 122
See also SATA 39, 48
Araki, James T(omomasa) 1925- ... 15-16R
Arango, Jorge Sanin 1916- ... 61-64
Aranha, Ray 1939- Brief entry ... 112
Aranow, Edward Ross 1909- ... 41-44R
Araoz, Daniel Leon 1930- ... 108
Arapoff, Nancy 1930- ... 29-32R
Arasteh, A(bdol) Reza 1927- ... 105
Arata, Esther S(pring) 1918- ... 89-92
Arata, Luis O(scar) 1950- ... 115
Arbatov, G. A.
See Arbatov, Georgi (Arkadevich)
Arbatov, Georgi (Arkadevich) 1923- ... 116
Arbatov, Yuri Arkadevich
See Arbatov, Georgi (Arkadevich)
Arbeiter, Jean S(onkin) 1937- ... 106
Arberry, A(rthur) J(ohn) 1905-1969 ... CANR-4
Earlier sketch in CA 4R
Arbib, Robert
See Arbib, Robert S(imeon), Jr.
Arbib, Robert S(imeon), Jr. 1915-1987 ... 33-36R
Obituary ... 123
Arbingast, Stanley A(lan) 1910- ... CANR-10
Earlier sketch in CA 17-18R
Arbogast, William F. 1908-1979 Obituary ... 89-92
Arbuckle, Dorothy Fry 1910-1982
Obituary ... 108
See also SATA 33
Arbuckle, Dugald S(inclair) 1912- ... 13-14R
Arbuckle, Robert D(ean) 1940- ... 61-64
Arbuckle, W(endell) S(herwood) 1911-1987 Obituary ... 122
Arbuckle, Wanda Rector 1910- ... 41-44R
Arbuthnot, May Hill 1884-1969 ... 9-10R
See also SATA 2
Arbuzov, Alexei Nikolaevich 1908-1986 ... 69-72
Obituary ... 119
Arca, Julie Anne 1953- ... 111
Arcana, Judith 1943- ... 103
Arce, Hector 1935-1980 ... 97-100
Arceneaux, Thelma Hoffmann Tyler ... AITN-1
Arch, E. L.
See Payes, Rachel C(osgrove)
ar C'Halan, Reun
See Galand, Rene
Archambault, Paul 1937- ... 81-84
Archdeacon, Thomas J(ohn) 1942- ... 65-68
Archer, A. A.
See Joscelyn, Archie L.
Archer, Frank
See O'Connor, Richard
Archer, Fred 1915- ... CANR-7
Earlier sketch in CA 57-60
Archer, Fred C. 1916(?)-1974 Obituary ... 53-56
Archer, Gleason Leonard, Jr. 1916- ... 65-68
Archer, H(orace) Richard 1911-1978 ... CANR-6
Obituary ... 89-92
Earlier sketch in CA 15-16R
Archer, Jane (a pseudonym) ... 113
Archer, Jeffrey (Howard) 1940- ... CANR-22
Earlier sketch in CA 77-80
See also CLC 28
Archer, John H(all) 1914- ... 101
Archer, Jules 1915- ... CANR-6
Earlier sketch in CA 9-10R
See also SATA 4
See also SAAS 5
See also CLC 12
Archer, Lee
See Ellison, Harlan
Archer, Marion Fuller 1917- ... 5-6R
See also SATA 11
Archer, Mildred 1911- ... 104
Archer, Myrtle (Lilly) 1926- ... 102
Archer, Nuala 1955- ... 121
Archer, Peter Kingsley 1926- ... CANR-2
Earlier sketch in CA 7-8R
Archer, Ron
See White, Theodore Edwin
Archer, S. E.
See Soderberg, Percy Measday
Archer, Sellers G. 1908- ... 17-18R
Archer, Stephen H(unt) 1928- ... 19-20R
Archer, Stephen M(urphy) 1934- ... 105
Archer, W(illiam) G(eorge) 1907- ... 57-60
Archer, William 1856-1924 Brief entry ... 108
See also DLB 10
Archerd, Armand ... 115
Brief entry ... 110
Archerd, Army
See Archerd, Armand
Archer Houblon, Doreen (Lindsay) 1899-1977 ... 106
Archibald, (Rupert) Douglas 1919- ... 101
Archibald, Douglas N(elson) 1933-
Brief entry ... 113
Archibald, James Montgomery 1920-1983
Obituary ... 110
Archibald, Joe
See Archibald, Joseph S(topford)
Archibald, John J. 1925- ... 5-6R
Archibald, Joseph S(topford) 1898-1986 ... CANR-5
Obituary ... 118
Earlier sketch in CA 9-10R
See also SATA 3, 47
Archibald, Sandra O(rr) 1945- ... 113
Archibald, William 1924-1970 Obituary ... 29-32R
Arciniegas, German 1900- ... CANR-10
Earlier sketch in CA 61-64
Arcone, Sonya 1925-1978 ... 21-22R
Obituary ... 77-80
Ard, Ben N(eal), Jr. 1922- ... CANR-12
Earlier sketch in CA 33-36R
Ard, William (Thomas) 1922-1962(?) ... 5-6R
Ardagh, John 1928- ... 25-28R
Ardalan, Nader 1939- ... 69-72
Arden, Barbi
See Stoutenburg, Adrien (Pearl)
Arden, Gothard Everett 1905- ... CAP-1
Earlier sketch in CA 11-12
Arden, J. E. M.
See Conquest, (George) Robert (Acworth)
Arden, Jane ... 61-64
Arden, John 1930- ... 15-16R
See also CAAS 4
See also DLB 13
See also CLC 6, 13, 15
Arden, Leon 1932- ... 107
Arden, Noele
See Dambrauskas, Joan Arden
Arden, William
See Lynds, Dennis
Ardener, Edwin (William) 1927-1987 ... 7-8R
Obituary ... 123
Ardies, Tom 1931- ... 33-36R
Ardizzone, Edward (Jeffrey Irving) 1900-1979 ... CANR-8
Obituary ... 89-92
Earlier sketch in CA 5-6R
See also SATA 1, 21, 28
See also CLR 3
Ardizzone, Tony 1949- ... 85-88
Ardley, Neil (Richard) 1937- ... 115
See also SATA 43
Ardmore, Jane Kesner 1915- ... 7-8R
Ardoin, John (Louis) 1935- ... 57-60
Ardrey, Robert 1908-1980 ... 33-36R
Obituary ... 93-96
Arecco, Vera Lustig
See Lustig-Arecco, Vera
Areeda, Phillip E. 1930- ... 23-24R
Arehart-Treichel, Joan 1942- ... CANR-6
Earlier sketch in CA 57-60
See also SATA 22
Arellanes, Audrey Spencer 1920- ... 33-36R
Arem, Joel E(dward) 1943- ... 89-92
Arena, Jay M(orris) 1909- ... 107
Arena, John I. 1929- ... CANR-20
Earlier sketch in CA 45-48
Arenas, Reinaldo 1943- Brief entry ... 124
See also CLC 41
Arendt, Hannah 1906-1975 ... 19-20R
Obituary ... 61-64
Arenella, Roy 1939- ... SATA-14
Arens, Richard 1921-1984 ... 73-76
Obituary ... 112
Arens, William 1940- ... 89-92
Arensberg, Ann 1937- ... 114
See also DLBY 82
Arensberg, Conrad Maynadier 1910- ... 61-64
Arenson, Gloria 1935- ... 118
Arent, Arthur 1904-1972 ... CAP-2
Obituary ... 33-36R
Earlier sketch in CA 23-24
Areskoug, Kaj 1933- ... 29-32R
Aresty, Esther B(radford) ... 9-10R
Areta, Mavis
See Winder, Mavis Areta
Arey, James A. 1936- ... 41-44R
Argan, Giulio Carlo 1909- ... 65-68
Argenti, John 1926- ... 115
Argenti, Philip 1891(?)-1974 Obituary ... 49-52
Argenzio, Victor 1902- ... 53-56
Argersinger, Peter H(ayes) 1944-
Brief entry ... 112
Arghezi, Tudor
See Theodorescu, Ion N.
Argiro, Larry 1909- ... 5-6R
Argo, Ellen
See Johnson, Ellen Argo
Argow, Waldemar 1916- ... 23-24R
Arguedas, Jose Maria 1911-1969 ... 89-92
See also CLC 10, 18
Arguelles, Jose A(nthony) 1939- ... CANR-20
Earlier sketch in CA 45-48
Arguelles, Miriam Tarcov 1943- ... 45-48
Argueta, Manlio 1936- ... CLC-31
Argus
See Osusky, Stefan
Argus
See Phillips-Birt, Douglas Hextall Chedzey
Argyle, Aubrey William 1910- ... CAP-1
Earlier sketch in CA 17-18
Argyle, Michael 1925- ... CANR-9
Earlier sketch in CA 21-22R
Argyris, Chris 1923- ... CANR-20
Earlier sketches in CA 2R, CANR-5
Arian, Alan (Asher) 1938- ... CANR-1
Earlier sketch in CA 49-52
Arian, Edward 1921- ... 33-36R
Arias-Misson, Alain 1936- ... 77-80
Aridas, Chris 1947- ... 112
Ariel
See Moraes, Frank Robert
Aries, Philippe 1914-1984 ... 89-92
Obituary ... 112
Arieti, James Alexander 1948- ... 108
Arieti, Silvano 1914-1981 ... CANR-10
Obituary ... 104
Earlier sketch in CA 21-22R
Arimond, Carroll 1909-1979 Obituary ... 89-92
Aring, Charles D(air) 1904- ... 49-52
Aris, Rutherford 1929- ... 117
Aristides
See Epstein, Joseph
Ariyoshi, Sawako 1931-1984 ... 105
Obituary ... 113
Ariyoshi, Shoichiro 1939(?)-1979
Obituary ... 89-92
Arkell, Anthony John 1898-1980 ... 102
Obituary ... 97-100
Arkhurst, Frederick S(iegfried) 1920- ... 29-32R
Arkhurst, Joyce Cooper 1921- ... 17-18R
Arkin, Alan (Wolf) 1934- ... 112
Brief entry ... 110
See also SATA 32
Arkin, David 1906- ... 21-22R
Arkin, Frieda 1917- ... CANR-11
Earlier sketch in CA 65-68
Arkin, Herbert 1906- ... 7-8R
Arkin, Joseph 1922- ... 7-8R
Arkin, Marcus 1926- ... 53-56
Arkley, Arthur J(ames) 1919- ... 112
Arksey, Laura L(ee) 1936- ... 119
Arkush, Arthur Spencer 1925-1979
Obituary ... 85-88
Arlandson, Leone 1917- ... 29-32R
Arlen, Michael 1895-1956 Brief entry ... 120
See also DLB 36
Arlen, Michael J. 1930- ... CANR-13
Earlier sketch in CA 61-64
Arleo, Joseph 1933- ... 29-32R
Arley, Catherine 1935- ... CANR-2
Earlier sketch in CA 45-48
Arliss, Leslie 1901-1987 Obituary ... 124
Arlott, (Leslie Thomas) John 1914- ... 9-10R
Arlotto, Anthony (Thomas) 1939- ... 33-36R
Arlow, Jacob A. 1912- ... 53-56
Arlt, Roberto 1900-1942 Brief entry ... 123
Armacost, Michael Hayden 1937- ... 101
Armah, Ayi Kwei 1939- ... CANR-21
Earlier sketch in CA 61-64
See also CLC 5, 33
Armand, Louis 1905-1971 ... CAP-2
Obituary ... 33-36R
Earlier sketch in CA 29-32
Armatas, James P. 1931- ... 41-44R
Armatrading, Joan 1950- Brief entry ... 114
See also CLC 17
Armbrister, Trevor 1933- ... 89-92
Armbruster, Carl J. 1929- ... 33-36R
Armbruster, F(ranz) O(wen) 1929- ... 49-52
Armbruster, Francis E(dward) 1923- ... 29-32R
Armbruster, Frank
See Armbruster, Francis E(dward)
Armbruster, Maxim Ethan 1902- ... 1R
Armens, Sven 1921- ... 21-22R
Armentrout, Fred S(herman) 1946- ... 119
Armentrout, William W(infield) 1918- ... 33-36R
Armer, Alberta (Roller) 1904- ... 7-8R
See also SATA 9
Armer, J(ohn) Michael 1937- ... 106
Armer, Laura (Adams) 1874-1963 ... 65-68
See also SATA 13
Armerding, Carl Edwin 1936- ... 104
Armerding, George D. 1899- ... 85-88
Armerding, Hudson Taylor 1918- ... CANR-11
Earlier sketch in CA 23-24R
Armes, Roy (Philip) 1937- ... CANR-13
Earlier sketch in CA 73-76
Armington, John Calvin 1923- ... 53-56
Armistead, Samuel (Gordon) 1927- ... 53-56
Armitage, A(rthur) L(lewellyn) 1916-1984
Obituary ... 112
Armitage, Angus 1902- ... CAP-1
Earlier sketch in CA 13-14
Armitage, David 1943- ... SATA-38
Armitage, E(dward) Liddall 1887- ... CAP-1
Earlier sketch in CA 9-10
Armitage, G(ary) E(dric) 1956- ... 121
Armitage, Merle 1893-1975 Obituary ... 61-64
Armitage, Michael John 1930- ... 117
Armitage, Ronda (Jacqueline) 1943- ... 121
See also SATA 38, 47
Armitage, Shelley S(ue) 1947- ... 121
Armory, Thomas 1691(?)-1788 ... DLB-39
Armour, John
See Paine, Lauran (Bosworth)
Armour, Leslie 1931- ... 110
Armour, Lloyd R. 1922- ... 29-32R
Armour, Richard 1906- ... CANR-4
Earlier sketch in CA 1R
See also SATA 14

Armour, Rollin Stely 1929- 33-36R
Arms, George (Warren) 1912- 5-6R
Arms, Johnson
 See Halliwell, David (William)
Arms, Suzanne 1944- 57-60
Armstrong, (Walter) Alan 1936- 73-76
Armstrong, Ann Seidel 1917- 9-10R
Armstrong, Anne(tte) 1924- 13-14R
Armstrong, Anthony
 See Willis, (George) Anthony Armstrong
Armstrong, Anthony C.
 See Armstrong, Christopher J. R.
Armstrong, (Grace) April (Oursler) 1926- ..89-92
Armstrong, Arthur Hilary 1909- 69-72
Armstrong, Benjamin Leighton 1923- 93-96
Armstrong, Brian G(ary) 1936- 69-72
Armstrong, Charles B. 1923-1985
 Obituary 115
Armstrong, Charlotte 1905-1969 .... CANR-3
 Obituary 25-28R
 Earlier sketch in CA 1R
Armstrong, Christopher J(ohn) R(ichard)
 1935- 69-72
Armstrong, Claude Blakely 1889-1982
 Obituary 108
Armstrong, D(avid) M(alet) 1926- CANR-11
 Earlier sketch in CA 25-28R
Armstrong, (James) David 1945- 107
Armstrong, David M(ichael) 1944- 57-60
Armstrong, Diana 1943- 107
Armstrong, Douglas Albert 1920- 9-10R
Armstrong, Edward Allworthy
 1900-1978 .... CANR-4
 Earlier sketch in CA 7-8R
Armstrong, (Annette) Elizabeth 1917- 25-28R
Armstrong, F. W.
 See Wright, T. M.
Armstrong, Frederick H(enry) 1926- 33-36R
Armstrong, Garner Ted 1929(?)-
 Brief entry 113
Armstrong, George D. 1927- SATA-10
Armstrong, Gerry (Breen) 1929- 15-16R
 See also SATA 10
Armstrong, Gregory T(imon) 1933- 9-10R
Armstrong, Hamilton Fish 1893-1973 93-96
 Obituary 41-44R
Armstrong, Henry H.
 See Arvay, Harry
Armstrong, Herbert W. 1892-1986
 Obituary 118
 Brief entry 116
Armstrong, J(on) Scott 1937- CANR-1
 Earlier sketch in CA 45-48
Armstrong, (A.) James 1924- 29-32R
Armstrong, John A(lexander, Jr.)
 1922- CANR-3
 Earlier sketch in CA 4R
Armstrong, John Borden 1926- 33-36R
Armstrong, John Byron 1917-1976 ....5-6R
 Obituary 65-68
Armstrong, Joseph Gravitt 1943- 101
Armstrong, Judith Mary 1935- 102
Armstrong, Keith F(rancis) W(hitfield)
 1950- 29-32R
Armstrong, Leslie 1940- 124
Armstrong, (Daniel) Louis 1900-1971
 Obituary 29-32R
Armstrong, Louise 117
 Brief entry 111
 See also SATA 33, 43
Armstrong, Marjorie Moore 1912- 89-92
Armstrong, Martin 1882-1974 Obituary ...49-52
Armstrong, O(rland) K(ay) 1893-1987 93-96
 Obituary 122
Armstrong, (Raymond) Paul 1912- 37-40R
Armstrong, Paul B(radford) 1949- 112
Armstrong, Richard 1903- 77-80
 See also SATA 11
Armstrong, Richard G. 1932- 73-76
Armstrong, Robert H(oward) 1936- 108
Armstrong, Robert L(aurence) 1926- 29-32R
Armstrong, Robert Plant 1919-1984 .....41-44R
 Obituary 113
Armstrong, Roger D. 1939- 19-20R
Armstrong, Ruth Gallup 1891- CAP-1
 Earlier sketch in CA 9-10
Armstrong, (Russell) Scott 1945- 108
Armstrong, Terence Ian Fytton
 1912-1970 .... CAP-2
 Obituary 29-32R
 Earlier sketch in CA 17-18
Armstrong, Thomas 1899-1978 ....7-8R
 Obituary 103
Armstrong, Tilly 1927- CANR-23
 Earlier sketch in CA 107
Armstrong, Wallace Edwin 1896-1980
 Obituary 97-100
Armstrong, William A(lexander) 1912- 13-14R
Armstrong, William A(rthur) 1915- 17-18R
Armstrong, William H(oward) 1914- CANR-9
 Earlier sketch in CA 19-20R
 See also SATA 4
 See also CLR 1
 See also AITN 1
Armstrong, William M(artin) 1919- 49-52
Armstrong-Jones, Antony (Charles Robert)
 1930- 118
Armstrong Jones, Tony
 See Armstrong-Jones, Antony (Charles
 Robert)
Armytage, Walter Harry Green 1915- 9-10R
Arnade, Charles W(olfgang) 1927- 33-36R
Arnandez, Richard 1912- CANR-6
 Earlier sketch in CA 15-16R
Arnason, David 1940- 114
Arnason, H(jorvardur) H(arvard)
 1909-1986 .... CANR-13
 Obituary 119
 Earlier sketch in CA 61-64
Arnau, Frank
 See Schmitt, Heinrich
Arnaud, Georges
 See Girard, Henri Georges Charles Achille
Arnaud, Saint Romain
 See Aragon, Louis
Arnaz, Desi
 See Arnaz y de Acha, Desiderio Alberto
 III
Arnaz y de Acha, Desiderio Alberto III
 1917(?)-1986 Obituary 121
 Brief entry 114
Arncliffe, Andrew
 See Walker, Peter N.
Arndt, Elise 1943- 116
Arndt, Ernst H(einrich) D(aniel) 1899- CAP-2
 Earlier sketch in CA 23-24
Arndt, H(einz) W(olfgang) 1915- CANR-10
 Earlier sketch in CA 21-22R
Arndt, Karl John Richard 1903- CANR-23
 Earlier sketches in CA 17-18R, CANR-7
Arndt, Ursula (Martha H.) SATA-39
Arndt, Walter W(erner) 1916- CANR-5
 Earlier sketch in CA 13-14R
Arnebeck, Bob 1947- 108
Arneson, D(on) J(on) 1935- 106
 See also SATA 37
Arnett, Caroline
 See Cole, Lois Dwight
Arnett, Carroll 1927- CANR-11
 Earlier sketch in CA 21-22R
Arnett, Harold E(dward) 1931- CANR-8
 Earlier sketch in CA 21-22R
Arnett, Ross H(arold), Jr. 1919- CANR-17
 Earlier sketches in CA 49-52, CANR-2
Arnette, Robert
 See Silverberg, Robert
Arney, William Ray 1950- 110
Arnez, Nancy Levi 1928- 29-32R
Arnheim, Daniel D(avid) 1930- CANR-5
 Earlier sketch in CA 11-12R
Arnheim, Rudolf 1904- CANR-3
 Earlier sketch in CA 4R
Arno, Enrico 1913-1981 .... SATA-28, 43
Arno, Peter 1904-1968 73-76
 Obituary 25-28R
Arnold, Adlai F(ranklin) 1914- 33-36R
Arnold, Alan 1922- 7-8R
Arnold, Alvin L(incoln) 1929- 93-96
Arnold, Anthony 1928- 111
Arnold, Armin H. 1931- CANR-18
 Earlier sketches in CA 9-10R, CANR-3
Arnold, Arnold (Ferdinand) 1921- CANR-10
 Earlier sketch in CA 19-20R
Arnold, Bob 1952- CANR-21
 Earlier sketch in CA 105
Arnold, Bruce 1936- 93-96
Arnold, Carl
 See Raknes, Ola
Arnold, Caroline 1944- CANR-24
 Earlier sketch in CA 107
 See also SATA 34, 36
Arnold, Carroll C(lyde) 1912- Brief entry 116
Arnold, Charles Harvey 1920- 65-68
Arnold, Charlotte E(lizabeth) Cramer 57-60
Arnold, Corliss Richard 1926- 49-52
Arnold, Denis Midgley 1926-1986 ...... CANR-2
 Obituary 119
 Earlier sketch in CA 7-8R
Arnold, Edmund C(larence) 1913- CANR-3
 Earlier sketch in CA 4R
Arnold, Edwin 1832-1904 .... DLB-35
Arnold, Edwin L(ester Linden)
 1857(?)-1935 Brief entry 109
Arnold, Elliott 1912-1980 .... CANR-24
 Obituary 97-100
 Earlier sketch in CA 19-20R
 See also SATA 5, 22
Arnold, Emily 1939- 109
 See also SATA 50
Arnold, Emmy (von Hollander)
 1884-1980 .... CANR-9
 Earlier sketch in CA 23-24R
Arnold, Eve 1913- 112
Arnold, Francena H(arriet Long) 1888- ... CAP-1
 Earlier sketch in CA 17-18
Arnold, G. L.
 See Lichtheim, George
Arnold, Gary Howard 1942- Brief entry 117
Arnold, Guy 1932- CANR-11
 Earlier sketch in CA 25-28R
Arnold, H(arry) J(ohn) P(hilip) 1932- ... CANR-2
 Earlier sketch in CA 7-8R
Arnold, Heini
 See Arnold, Johann Heinrich
Arnold, Herbert 1935- 37-40R
Arnold, Janet 1932- 93-96
Arnold, Johann Heinrich 1913-1982 122
 Obituary 111
Arnold, John D(avid) 1933- 111
Arnold, Joseph H.
 See Hayes, Joseph
Arnold, June (Davis) 1926- 21-22R
Arnold, L. J.
 See Cameron, Lou
Arnold, Leslie
 See Lazarus, A(rnold) L(eslie)
Arnold, Lloyd R. 1906-1970 .... CAP-2
 Earlier sketch in CA 25-28
Arnold, Lois B(arber) 107
Arnold, Magda B(londiau) 1903- 5-6R
Arnold, Margot
 See Cook, Petronelle Marguerite Mary
Arnold, Marilyn 1935- 122
Arnold, Mary Ann 1918- 65-68
Arnold, Matthew 1822-1888 .... DLB-32, 57
Arnold, Milo Lawrence 1903- 57-60
Arnold, Olga Moore 1900-1981 Obituary ... 102
Arnold, Oren 1900- CANR-2
 Earlier sketch in CA 5-6R
 See also SATA 4
Arnold, Pauline 1894-1974 .... CANR-2
 Earlier sketch in CA 1R
Arnold, Peter 1931- 123
Arnold, Peter 1943- CANR-1
 Earlier sketch in CA 49-52
Arnold, R. Douglas 1950- 101
Arnold, Ray Henry 1895- 5-6R
Arnold, Richard 1912- CANR-3
 Earlier sketch in CA 9-10R
Arnold, Richard E(ugene) 1908- CAP-2
 Earlier sketch in CA 33-36
Arnold, Richard K(lein) 1923- 69-72
Arnold, Robert E(vans) 1932- 49-52
Arnold, Rollo (Davis) 1926- 23-24R
Arnold, Ron 1937- 108
Arnold, Stephen H. 1942- 117
Arnold, Thomas 1795-1842 .... DLB-55
Arnold, Thurman Wesley 1891-1969 ..... CAP-1
 Earlier sketch in CA 15-16
Arnold, William Robert 1933- 29-32R
Arnold, William Van 1941- 110
Arnold-Baker, Charles 1918- 7-8R
Arnold-Forster, Mark 1920-1981 65-68
 Obituary 105
Arnoldy, Julie
 See Bischoff, Julia Bristol
Arnosky, Jim 1946- CANR-12
 Earlier sketch in CA 69-72
 See also SATA 22
Arnothy, Christine 1930- CANR-10
 Earlier sketch in CA 65-68
Arnott, (Margaret) Anne 1916- CANR-13
 Earlier sketch in CA 73-76
Arnott, J(ames) F(ullarton) 1914-1982
 Obituary 108
Arnott, Kathleen 1914- 57-60
 See also SATA 20
Arnott, Peter D(ouglas) 1931- CANR-3
 Earlier sketch in CA 3R
Arnoux, Alexandre (Paul) 1884-1973
 Obituary 37-40R
Arnov, Boris, Jr. 1926- CANR-3
 Earlier sketch in CA 4R
 See also SATA 12
Arnove, Robert Fred 1937- 111
Arnow, Harriette (Louisa) Simpson
 1908-1986 .... CANR-14
 Obituary 118
 Earlier sketch in CA 9-10R
 See also SATA 42, 47
 See also DLB 6
 See also CLC 2, 7, 18
Arnow, L(eslie) Earle 1909- 69-72
Arnstein, Flora Jacobi 1885- 7-8R
Arnstein, Helene S(olomon) 1915- 57-60
 See also SATA 12
Arnstein, Walter L(eonard) 1930- CANR-23
 Earlier sketches in CA 15-16R, CANR-5
Arntson, Herbert E(dward) 1911- 19-20R
 See also SATA 12
Arny, Mary (Travis) 1909- 61-64
Arny, Thomas Travis 1940- 85-88
Aron, Raymond (Claude Ferdinand)
 1905-1983 .... CANR-2
 Obituary 111
 Earlier sketch in CA 49-52
Aron, Robert 1898-1975 93-96
 Obituary 57-60
Aronfreed, Justin 1930- 25-28R
Aronin, Ben 1904-1980 Obituary 102
 See also SATA 25
Aronoff, Myron J(oel) 1940- CANR-24
 Earlier sketch in CA 107
Aronson, Alex 1912- 45-48
Aronson, Alvin 1928- 25-28R
Aronson, Elliot 1932- CANR-12
 Earlier sketch in CA 33-36R
Aronson, Harvey 1929- 85-88
Aronson, J(ay) Richard 1937- 81-84
Aronson, James 1915- 29-32R
Aronson, Joseph 1898- CAP-1
 Earlier sketch in CA 19-20
Aronson, Marvin L. 1925- 41-44R
Aronson, Shlomo 1936- 73-76
Aronson, Theo 1930- CANR-4
 Earlier sketch in CA 11-12R
Aronson, Virginia 1954- 108
Arora, Shirley (Lease) 1930- 4R
 See also SATA 2
Aros, Andrew A(lexandre) 1944- 97-100
Arout, Gabriel 1909-1982 Obituary 106
Arp, Bill
 See Smith, Charles Henry
Arp, Hans
 See Arp, Jean
Arp, Jean 1887-1966 81-84
 Obituary 25-28R
 See also CLC 5
Arpad, Joseph J(ohn) 1937- 49-52
Arpel, Adrien
 See Newman, Adrien Ann
Arps, Louisa Ward 1901-1986 Obituary 118
Arquette, Cliff(ord) 1905-1974 Obituary ...53-56
Arrabal
 See Arrabal, Fernando
 See also CLC 2, 9, 18
Arrabal, Fernando 1932- CANR-15
 Earlier sketch in CA 11-12R
Arre, Helen
 See Ross, Zola Helen
Arre, John
 See Holt, John (Robert)
Arreola, Juan Jose 1918- Brief entry 113
Arrick, Fran CLC-30
Arrighi, Mel 1933-1986 .... CANR-18
 Obituary 120
 Earlier sketches in CA 49-52, CANR-1
Arrington, Leonard James 1917- CANR-9
 Earlier sketch in CA 19-20R
Arrow, Kenneth J(oseph) 1921- CANR-13
 Earlier sketch in CA 15-16R
Arroway, Francis M.
 See Rosmond, Babette
Arrowood, (McKendrick Lee) Clinton
 1939- SATA-19
Arrowsmith, Marvin Lawrence 1913-
 Brief entry 116
Arrowsmith, Pat 1930- 101
Arrowsmith, William Ayres 1924- CANR-4
 Earlier sketch in CA 9-10R
Arroyo, Antonio M. Stevens
 See Stevens-Arroyo, Antonio M.
Arroyo, Stephen J(oseph) 1946- 61-64
Art, Robert (Jeffrey) 1942- 65-68
Artaud, Antonin 1896-1948 Brief entry 104
 See also TCLC 3
Arteaga, Lucio 1924- 49-52
Arteaga, William De
 See De Arteaga, William
Artes, Dorothy Beecher 1919- 57-60
Arther, Richard O. 1928- 17-18R
Arthos, John 1908- 9-10R
Arthur, Alan
 See Edmonds, Arthur Denis
Arthur, Anthony 1937- 119
Arthur, Art(hur) 1911-1985 Obituary 116
Arthur, Burt
 See Shappiro, Herbert (Arthur)
Arthur, Don(ald) R(amsay) 1917-1984 ...29-32R
 Obituary 114
Arthur, Elizabeth 1953- CANR-21
 Earlier sketch in CA 105
Arthur, Eric (Ross) 1898-1982 Obituary 112
Arthur, Frank
 See Ebert, Arthur Frank
Arthur, Gladys
 See Osborne, Dorothy (Gladys) Yeo
Arthur, Herbert
 See Shappiro, Herbert (Arthur)
Arthur, Hugh
 See Christie-Murray, David (Hugh Arthur)
Arthur, Kay L(ee) 1932- 118
Arthur, Lee 122
Arthur, Martin (Forest) 1951- 116
Arthur, Max 1939- 121
Arthur, Percy E. 1910- CAP-1
 Earlier sketch in CA 9-10
Arthur, Robert
 See Feder, Robert Arthur
Arthur, Ruth M(abel) 1905-1979 .... CANR-4
 Obituary 85-88
 Earlier sketch in CA 11-12R
 See also SATA 7, 26
 See also CLC 12
Arthur, Thomas H. 1937- 122
Arthur, Tiffany
 See Pelton, Robert W(ayne)
Arthur, Timothy Shay 1809-1885 ..... DLB-3, 42
Arthur, Tom
 See Arthur, Thomas H.
Arthur, William
 See Neubauer, William Arthur
Arthurs, Peter 1933- 106
Artin, Thomas 1938- Brief entry 116
Artin, Tom
 See Artin, Thomas
Artis, Vicki Kimmel 1945- 53-56
 See also SATA 12
Artmann, H(ans) C(arl) 1921- 101
Artobolevsky, Ivan I. 1905-1977 Obituary ..73-76
Artom, Guido 1906-1982 .... CANR-12
 Earlier sketch in CA 29-32R
Arts, Herwig (W. J.) 1935- 113
Artz, Frederick B(inkerd) 1894-1983 ... CANR-18
 Earlier sketch in CA 1R
Artzybasheff, Boris (Miklailovich)
 1899-1965 .... SATA-14
Aruego, Ariane
 See Dewey, Ariane
Aruego, Jose 37-40R
 See also SATA 6
 See also CLR 5
Arundale, G. S.
 See Arundale, George S(ydney)
Arundale, George S(ydney) 1878-1945
 Brief entry 119
Arundel, Honor (Morfydd) 1919-1973 .... CAP-2
 Obituary 41-44R
 Earlier sketch in CA 21-22
 See also SATA 4, 24
 See also CLC 17
Arundel, Jocelyn
 See Alexander, Jocelyn Anne Arundel
Arundel, Russell M. 1903-1978 Obituary ..77-80
Aruri, Naseer H. 113
Arvay, Harry 1925- CANR-8
 Earlier sketch in CA 57-60
Arvay, Stephen 1937- 114
Arvill, Robert
 See Boote, Robert Edward
Arvin, Kay K(rehbiel) 1922- 65-68
Arvin, (Frederic) Newton (Jr.) 1900-1963
 Obituary 116
Arvio, Raymond Paavo 1930-1986 77-80
 Obituary 120

Ary, Donald E(ugene) 1930- 41-44R
Ary, Sheila M(ary Littleboy) 1929- 13-14R
Arya, Usharbudh 1934- 105
Arzhak, Nikolai
See Daniel, Yuli (Markovich)
Arzoomanian, Raffi
See Arzoomanian, Ralph Sarkis
Arzoomanian, Ralph Sarkis 1937- 118
Arzt, Max 1897-1975 Obituary 61-64
Asals, Frederick (John) 1935- 124
Asamani, Joseph Owusu 1934- 49-52
Asante, Molefi K(ete) 1942- CANR-21
Earlier sketch in CA 33-36R
Asare, Bediako
See Konadu, S(amuel) A(sare)
Asare, Meshack (Yaw) 1945- CANR-11
Earlier sketch in CA 61-64
Asbell, Bernard 1923- CANR-1
Earlier sketch in CA 45-48
Asbjoernsen, Peter Christen
1812-1885 .... SATA-15
Asbury, Herbert 1891-1963 Obituary 116
Ascani, Sparky (Wilson) 1922- 111
Asch, Frank 1946- 41-44R
See also SATA 5
Asch, Nathan 1902-1964 109
See also DLB 4, 28
Asch, Peter 1937- Brief entry 114
Asch, Sholem 1880-1957 Brief entry 105
See also TCLC 3
Ascheim, Skip 1943- 53-56
Ascher, Abraham 1928- 81-84
Ascher, Carol 1941- 105
Ascher, Sheila CANR-23
Earlier sketch in CA 105
Ascher, William (Louis) 1947- 114
Ascherson, Neal 1932- 13-14R
Ascher/Straus
See Ascher, Sheila
and Straus, Dennis
Aschmann, Alberta 1921- CANR-7
Earlier sketch in CA 15-16R
Aschmann, Helen Tann 13-14R
Ascoli, Max 1898-1978 Obituary 77-80
Ash, Anthony Lee 1931- CANR-3
Earlier sketch in CA 49-52
Ash, Bernard 1910- CAP-1
Earlier sketch in CA 19-20
Ash, Brian 1936- Brief entry 114
Ash, Christopher (Edward) 1914- 4R
Ash, David W(ilfred) 1923- 11-12R
Ash, Douglas 1914- CANR-2
Earlier sketch in CA 7-8R
Ash, John 1948- Brief entry 123
See also DLB 40
Ash, Jutta 1942- SATA-38
Ash, Lee (Michael) 1917- 110
Ash, Mary Kay (Wagner) 112
Ash, Maurice Anthony 1917- 101
Ash, Rene Lee 1939- 57-60
Ash, Roberta
See Garner, Roberta
Ash, Sarah Leeds 1904- CAP-1
Earlier sketch in CA 9-10
Ash, Shalom
See Asch, Sholem
Ash, William Franklin 1917- CANR-18
Earlier sketches in CA 7-8R, CANR-2
Ashabranner, Brent (Kenneth) 1921- ... CANR-10
Earlier sketch in CA 7-8R
See also SATA 1
Ashbaugh, Nancy 1929- 73-76
Ashbee, Paul 1918- 93-96
Ashbery, John (Lawrence) 1927- CANR-9
Earlier sketch in CA 7-8R
See also DLB 5
See also DLBY 81
See also CLC 2, 3, 4, 6, 9, 13, 15, 25, 41
Ashbolt, Allan Campbell 1921- 104
Ashbrook, James B(arbour) 1925- CANR-14
Earlier sketch in CA 37-40R
Ashbrook, Joseph 1918-1980 122
Obituary 117
Ashbrook, William (Sinclair) 1922- 29-32R
Ashburne, Jim G. 1912- 4R
Ashby, Cliff 1919- 25-28R
See also CAAS 6
Ashby, Eric 1904- 61-64
Ashby, Gwynneth 1922- 25-28R
See also SATA 44
Ashby, LaVerne 1922- 21-22R
Ashby, (Darrel) LeRoy 1938- 33-36R
Ashby, Lloyd W. 1905- 89-92
Ashby, Neal 1924- 89-92
Ashby, Philip Harrison 1916- 17-18R
Ashcraft, Allan Coleman 1928- 9-10R
Ashcraft, Laura 1945- 107
Ashcraft, Laurie
See Ashcraft, Laura
Ashcraft, Morris 1922- 45-48
Ashcroft, John (David) 1942- 112
Ashdown, Clifford
See Freeman, R(ichard) Austin
Ashdown, Dulcie M(argaret) 1946- 122
Brief entry 112
Ashdown, Paul G(eorge) 1944- 119
Ashe, Arthur (R., Jr.) 1943- CANR-18
Earlier sketch in CA 65-68
Ashe, Douglas
See Bardin, John Franklin
Ashe, Geoffrey (Thomas) 1923- CANR-12
Earlier sketch in CA 7-8R
See also SATA 17
Ashe, Gerald C. 1924(?)-1984 Obituary 112
Ashe, Gordon
See Creasey, John
Ashe, Mary Ann
See Lewis, Mary (Christianna Milne)
Ashe, Penelope
See Greene, Robert W.
and Karman, Mal
and Young, Billie
Asheim, Lester E(ugene) 1914- 19-20R
Ashenfelter, David L. 1948- 108
Ashenfelter, Orley C(lark) 1942- CANR-8
Earlier sketch in CA 61-64
Asher, Don 1926- 73-76
Asher, Harry (Maurice Felix) 1909- CANR-2
Earlier sketch in CA 5-6R
Asher, John A(lexander) 1921- 23-24R
Asher, Maxine 1930- 105
Asher, Miriam
See Mundis, Hester
Asher, Robert 1944- 111
Asher, Robert Eller 1910- 61-64
Asher, Sandra Fenichel 1942- CANR-22
Earlier sketch in CA 105
Asher, Sandy
See Asher, Sandra Fenichel
See also SATA 34, 36
See also DLBY 83
Ashey, Bella
See Breinburg, Petronella
Ashford, Daisy
See Ashford, Margaret Mary
Ashford, Douglas E(lliott) 1928- CANR-16
Earlier sketch in CA 73-76
Ashford, Gerald 1907- 41-44R
Ashford, Janet Isaacs 1949- 113
Ashford, Jeffrey
See Jeffries, Roderic (Graeme)
Ashford, Margaret Mary 1881-1972
Obituary 33-36R
See also SATA 10
Ashford, (H.) Ray 1926- 65-68
Ashford, Theodore Askounes 1908-1987
Obituary 122
Ashley, A.
See Aasheim, Ashley
Ashley, Bernard 1935- 93-96
See also SATA 39, 47
See also CLR 4
Ashley, Elizabeth
See Salmon, Annie Elizabeth
Ashley, (Arthur) Ernest 1906- CAP-1
Earlier sketch in CA 15-16
Ashley, Franklin 1942- CANR-1
Earlier sketch in CA 45-48
Ashley, Graham
See Organ, John
Ashley, Jack 1922- 106
Ashley, Leonard R(aymond) N(elligan)
1928- CANR-24
Earlier sketches in CA 15-16R, CANR-9
Ashley, Maurice (Percy) 1907- 41-44R
Ashley, Michael (Raymond Donald)
1948- CANR-13
Earlier sketch in CA 69-72
Ashley, Nova Trimble 1911- 65-68
Ashley, Paul P(ritchard) 1896-1979 .... CANR-10
Obituary 85-88
Earlier sketch in CA 21-22R
Ashley, Perry J(onathan) 1928- 120
Ashley, Ray
See Abrashkin, Raymond
Ashley, Robert P(aul), Jr. 1915- 17-18R
Ashley, Rosalind Minor 1923- 69-72
Ashley, Sally 1935- 109
Ashley, Steven
See McCaig, Donald
Ashley-Montagu, Montague Francis
See Montagu, (Montague Francis) Ashley
Ashlin, John
See Cutforth, John Ashlin
Ashlock, Patrick (Robert) 1937- 61-64
Ashlock, Robert B. 1930- CANR-12
Earlier sketch in CA 29-32R
Ashman, Howard 1950- Brief entry 122
Ashmead, John, Jr. 1917- 1R
Ashmole, Bernard 1894-1988 106
Obituary 124
Ashmore, Harry S(cott) 1916- 15-16R
Ashmore, Jerome 1901- CAP-2
Earlier sketch in CA 33-36
Ashmore, Lewis
See Raborg, Frederick A(shton), Jr.
Ashmore, Owen 1920- 106
Ashner, Sonie Shapiro 1938- 57-60
Ashryn, Veryl M. 1948- 119
Ashton, Ann
See Kimbro, John M.
Ashton, Dore 1928- CANR-2
Earlier sketch in CA 5-6R
Ashton, (Arthur) Leigh (Bolland)
1897-1983 Obituary 114
Ashton, Robert 1924- CANR-3
Earlier sketch in CA 1R
Ashton, (Margery) Violet 1908- 73-76
Ashton, Warren T.
See Adams, William Taylor
Ashton, Winifred 1888-1965 Obituary 93-96
Ashton-Warner, Sylvia (Constance)
1908-1984 69-72
Obituary 112
See also CLC 19
Ashworth, Kenneth H(ayden) 1932- 41-44R
Ashworth, Mary Wells Knight 1903- 7-8R
Ashworth, Wilfred 1912- 15-16R
Ashworth, William 1920- 7-8R
Asimov, Isaac 1920- CANR-19
Earlier sketches in CA 2R, CANR-2
See also SATA 1, 26
See also DLB 8
See also CLC 1, 3, 9, 19, 26
See also CLR 12
Asimov, Janet
See Jeppson, Janet O(pal)
Asinof, Eliot 1919- CANR-7
Earlier sketch in CA 11-12R
See also SATA 6
Aska, Warabe
See Masuda, Takeshi
Askari, Hussaini Muhammad
See Pereira, Harold Bertram
Askenasy, Hans George 1930- 77-80
Askew, Jack
See Hivnor, Robert
Askew, William C(larence) 1910- 49-52
Askham, Francis
See Greenwood, Julia Eileen Courtney
Askin, A. Bradley 1943- 73-76
Askin, Alma 1911- 57-60
Askin, I(da) Jayne 1940- 109
Askwith, Betty Ellen 1909- CANR-13
Earlier sketch in CA 61-64
Askwith, Herbert 1889-1985 Obituary 117
Brief entry 113
Aslanapa, Oktay 1914- 37-40R
Aslet, Clive (William) 1955- 113
Aspaturian, Vernon V. 1922- 105
Aspel, Michael (Terence) 1933-
Brief entry 117
Aspell, Patrick J(oseph) 1930- 25-28R
Aspin, Les 1938- 108
Aspinall, (Honor) Ruth (Alastair) 1922- .. CANR-2
Earlier sketch in CA 7-8R
Aspinwall, Dorothy B(rown) 1910- 49-52
Aspiz, Harold 1921- 105
Aspler, Tony 1939- 105
Asprey, Robert B. 1923- CANR-6
Earlier sketch in CA 5-6R
Asprin, Robert Lynn 1946- 85-88
Aspy, David N(athanial) 1930- CANR-20
Earlier sketch in CA 45-48
Asquith, Cynthia Mary Evelyn (Charteris)
1887-1960 Obituary 110
Asquith, Glenn Hackney 1904- CANR-16
Earlier sketches in CA 1R, CANR-1
Asquith, Nan
See Pattinson, Nancy Evelyn
Asquith, Stewart 1948- 116
Assael, Henry 1935- 41-44R
Assagioli, Roberto 1893(?)-1974
Obituary 53-56
Asselbroke, Archibald Algernon 1923- 77-80
Asselin, E(dward) Donald 1903-1970 .... CAP-1
Earlier sketch in CA 11-12
Asselineau, Roger (Maurice) 1915- 97-100
Assensoh, A(kwasi) B(retuo) 1946(?)- 120
Assiac
See Fraenkel, Heinrich
Astaire, Fred 1899-1987 Obituary 122
Aster, Sidney 1942- CANR-10
Earlier sketch in CA 65-68
Astier, Pierre A(rthur) G(eorges)
1927- CANR-20
Earlier sketch in CA 45-48
Astill, Kenneth N. 1923- 53-56
Astin, Alexander W(illiam) 1932- CANR-7
Earlier sketch in CA 17-18R
Astin, Helen S(tavridou) 1932- 29-32R
Astiz, Carlos A. 1933- 25-28R
Astley, Joan Bright 1910- 33-36R
Astley, Juliet
See Lofts, Norah (Robinson)
Astley, Thea (Beatrice May) 1925- CANR-11
Earlier sketch in CA 65-68
See also CLC 41
Aston, Athina (Leka) 1934- 117
Aston, James
See White, T(erence) H(anbury)
Aston, Margaret 1932- 73-76
Aston, Michael (Anthony) 1946- 61-64
Aston, Trevor Henry 1925-1985 Obituary ... 118
Astor, (Francis) David (Langhorne) 1912-
Brief entry 113
Astor, Gavin 1918-1984 Obituary 113
Astor, Gerald (Morton) 1926- CANR-24
Earlier sketch in CA 107
Astor, Mary 1906-1987 .... CANR-3
Obituary 123
Earlier sketch in CA 5-6R
Astor, Michael Langhorne 1916-1980 61-64
Obituary 97-100
Astor, Susan 1946- 105
Astrachan, Samuel 1934- 69-72
Astro, Richard 1941- 29-32R
Asturias, Miguel Angel 1899-1974 .... CAP-2
Obituary 49-52
Earlier sketch in CA 25-28
See also CLC 3, 8, 13
Aswad, Betsy (Becker) 1939- 104
Aswell, Mary Louise 1902-1984 Obituary ... 114
Aswin
See Nandakumar, Prema
Atamian, David 1892(?)-1978 Obituary 81-84
Atcheson, Richard 1934- 29-32R
Atchison, Sandra Dallas 1939- CANR-10
Earlier sketch in CA 17-18R
Atchity, Kenneth John 1944- CANR-16
Earlier sketches in CA 49-52, CANR-1
Atchley, Bob
See Atchley, Robert C.
Atchley, Dana W(inslow) 1941- 61-64
Atchley, Robert C. 1939- CANR-1
Earlier sketch in CA 45-48
Atene, Ann
See Atene, (Rita) Anna
Atene, (Rita) Anna 1922- SATA-12
Athanassiadis, Nikos 1904- CANR-17
Earlier sketch in CA 33-36R
Athans, George (Stanley), Jr. 1952- 104
Athas, Daphne 1923- CANR-3
Earlier sketch in CA 4R
Athay, R(obert) E. 1925- 33-36R
Athearn, Robert G(reenleaf) 1914- CANR-3
Earlier sketch in CA 4R
Atheling, William
See Pound, Ezra (Loomis)
Atheling, William, Jr.
See Blish, James (Benjamin)
Atherton, Alexine 1930- 37-40R
Atherton, Gertrude (Franklin Horn)
1857-1948 Brief entry 104
See also DLB 9
See also TCLC 2
Atherton, James C(hristian) 1915- 49-52
Atherton, James S(tephen) 1910- CAP-1
Earlier sketch in CA 15-16
Atherton, Lewis E. 1905- 1R
Atherton, Lucius
See Masters, Edgar Lee
Atherton, Maxine 5-6R
Atherton, Pauline
See Cochrane, Pauline A(therton)
Atherton, Sarah
See Bridgman, Sarah Atherton
Atherton, Wallace N(ewman) 1927- 49-52
Athey, Irene J(owett) 1919- 61-64
Athill, Diana 1917- CANR-2
Earlier sketch in CA 4R
Athlone, Countess of
See Alice (Mary Victoria Augusta Pauline), Princess
Athos
See Walkerley, Rodney Lewis (de Burah)
Athos, Anthony G(eorge) 1934- CANR-19
Earlier sketch in CA 25-28R
Atil, Esin 1938- 113
Atiya, Aziz S. 1898- 7-8R
Atiyah, P(atrick) S(elim) 1931- 37-40R
Atiyeh, George N(icholas) 1923- 57-60
Atkeson, Ray A. 1907- CANR-11
Earlier sketch in CA 69-72
Atkey, Philip 1908-1985 Obituary 118
Brief entry 112
Atkin, Flora B(lumenthal) 1919- CANR-16
Earlier sketch in CA 93-96
Atkin, J. Myron 1927- 45-48
Atkin, Mary Gage 1929- 81-84
Atkin, William Wilson 1912(?)-1976
Obituary 65-68
Atkins, Burton M(ark) 1944- Brief entry 115
Atkins, Chester Burton 1924- Brief entry ... 113
Atkins, Chester G(reenough) 1948- 45-48
Atkins, Chet
See Atkins, Chester Burton
Atkins, G(eorge) Douglas 1943- 114
Atkins, G(eorge) Pope 1934- CANR-17
Earlier sketch in CA 33-36R
Atkins, (Arthur) Harold 1910- 105
Atkins, Harry 1933- 25-28R
Atkins, Hedley (John Barnard) 1905-1983
Obituary 111
Atkins, Jack
See Harris, Mark
Atkins, James G. 1932- 17-18R
Atkins, Jim
See Atkins, James G.
Atkins, John (Alfred) 1916- CANR-19
Earlier sketches in CA 11-12R, CANR-3
Atkins, Josiah 1755(?)-1781 .... DLB-31
Atkins, Kenneth R(obert) 1920- 73-76
Atkins, Meg Elizabeth 102
Atkins, Oliver F. 1916-1977 73-76
Atkins, Ollie
See Atkins, Oliver F.
Atkins, P(eter) W(illiam) 1940- 117
Atkins, Paul Moody 1892-1977 Obituary ...69-72
Atkins, Russell 1926- CANR-1
Earlier sketch in CA 45-48
See also DLB 41
Atkins, Stuart (Pratt) 1914- 25-28R
Atkins, Thomas R(adcliffe) 1939- CANR-8
Earlier sketch in CA 61-64
Atkinson, Allen SATA-46
Atkinson, Anthony Barnes 1944- CANR-11
Earlier sketch in CA 69-72
Atkinson, Basil F(erris) C(ampbell) 1895- ...7-8R
Atkinson, (Justin) Brooks 1894-1984 .. CANR-14
Obituary 111
Earlier sketch in CA 61-64
Atkinson, Carroll (Holloway) 1896- CAP-1
Earlier sketch in CA 15-16
Atkinson, David J(ohn) 1943- 107
Atkinson, Frank 1922- 108
Atkinson, Geoffrey 1955- 118
Atkinson, Hugh C(raig) 1933-1986 49-52
Obituary 120
Atkinson, James 1914- 25-28R
Atkinson, James B(lakely) 1934- 119
Atkinson, Jennifer (Elizabeth) McCabe
1937- Brief entry 116
Atkinson, John W(illiam) 1923- CANR-11
Earlier sketch in CA 23-24R
Atkinson, M. E.
See Frankau, Mary Evelyn Atkinson
Atkinson, Margaret Fleming 73-76
See also SATA 14
Atkinson, Mary
See Hardwick, Mollie
Atkinson, Phillip S. 1921- 25-28R
Atkinson, R(ichard) C(hatham) 1929- 17-18R

Atkinson, Ron 1932- 57-60
Atkinson, Ronald Field 1928- 17-18R
Atkinson, W. W.
 See Atkinson, William Walker
Atkinson, Walter S(ydney) 1891-1978
 Obituary 73-76
Atkinson, William Christopher 1902- 109
Atkinson, William Walker 1862-1932
 Brief entry 120
Atkisson, Arthur A(lbert, Jr.) 1930- 61-64
Atkyns, Glenn C(hadwick) 1921- 49-52
Atlas, Helen Vincent 1931- 101
Atlas, Martin 1914- 5-6R
Atlas, Samuel 1899-1977 Obituary 73-76
Atmore, Anthony 1932- 25-28R
Attaway, Robert J(oseph) 1942- 49-52
Attea, Mary
 See Spahn, Mary Attea
Atteberry, William L(ouis) 1939- 53-56
Attenborough, Bernard George CANR-2
 Earlier sketch in CA 49-52
Attenborough, David Frederick 1926- CANR-6
 Earlier sketch in CA 4R
Attenborough, John 1908- 101
Atterton, Julian (Harold) 1956- 122
Atthill, Robin 1912- 69-72
Atticus
 See Davies, Hunter
 and Fleming, Ian (Lancaster)
 and Pawle, Gerald
Attiyeh, Richard E. 1937- Brief entry 113
Attlee, C. R.
 See Attlee, Clement R(ichard)
Attlee, Clement R(ichard) 1883-1967
 Obituary 112
Attneave, Carolyn L(ewis) 1920- CANR-1
 Earlier sketch in CA 45-48
Attridge, Derek 1945- 105
Attwell, Arthur A(lbert) 1917- 49-52
Attwood, William 1919- 21-22R
Atwater, C(onstance) Elizabeth (Sullivan)
 1923- 15-16R
Atwater, Eastwood 1925- 110
Atwater, Florence (Hasseltine Carroll) SATA-16
Atwater, James David 1928- 101
Atwater, Lynn 1935- 111
Atwater, Montgomery Meigs 1904- 73-76
 See also SATA 15
Atwater, Richard Tupper 1892-1948(?)
 Brief entry 111
 See also SATA 27
Atwood, Ann (Margaret) 1913- 41-44R
 See also SATA 7
Atwood, Drucy
 See Morrison, Eula Atwood
Atwood, Margaret (Eleanor) 1939- CANR-24
 Earlier sketches in CA 49-52, CANR-3
 See also SATA 50
 See also DLB 53
 See also CLC 2, 3, 4, 8, 13, 15, 25, 44
Atwood, Robert B. AITN-2
Atyeo, Don 1950- 93-96
Auberjonois, Fernand 1910- 77-80
Aubert, Alvin (Bernard) 1930- 81-84
 See also DLB 41
Aubert, Rosemary 1946- 113
Aubery, Pierre 1920- 37-40R
Aubey, Robert T(haddeus) 1930- 21-22R
Aubin, Henry (Trocme) 1942- 77-80
Aubin, Penelope 1685-1731(?) DLB-39
Aubrey-Fletcher, Henry Lancelot
 1887-1969 Obituary 111
Aubry, Claude B. 1914-1984 106
 See also SATA 29, 40
Auburn, Mark Stuart 1945- 89-92
Auchincloss, Louis (Stanton) 1917- CANR-6
 Earlier sketch in CA 1R
 See also DLB 2
 See also DLBY 80
 See also CLC 4, 6, 9, 18, 45
Auchmuty, James Johnston 1909-1981 101
 Obituary 109
Auchterlonie, Dorothy
 See Green, Dorothy (Auchterlonie)
Audax
 See Oaksey, John
Audemars, Pierre 1909- CANR-7
 Earlier sketch in CA 19-20R
Auden, Renee
 See West, Uta
Auden, W(ystan) H(ugh) 1907-1973 .... CANR-5
 Obituary 45-48
 Earlier sketch in CA 9-10R
 See also DLB 10, 20
 See also CLC 1, 2, 3, 4, 6, 9, 11, 14,
 43
Audi, Robert (N.) 1941- 123
Audiard, Michel 1920-1985 Obituary 116
Audiberti, Jacques 1900-1965 Obituary .. 25-28R
 See also CLC 38
Auel, Jean M(arie) 1936- CANR-21
 Earlier sketch in CA 103
 See also CLC 31
Auer, J(ohn) Jeffery 1913- CANR-6
 Earlier sketch in CA 11-12R
Auerbach, Aline B.
 See Auerbach, Aline Sophie (Buchman)
Auerbach, Aline Sophie (Buchman)
 1899(?)-1985 Obituary 116
Auerbach, Arnold M. 1912- 17-18R
Auerbach, Erich 1892-1957 Brief entry 118
Auerbach, Erna ?-1975 Obituary 61-64
Auerbach, George 1905(?)-1973 Obituary .. 45-48
Auerbach, Jerold S(tephen) 1936- 21-22R
Auerbach, Jessica (Lynn) 1947- 114
Auerbach, Marjorie (Hoffberg) 9-10R
Auerbach, Nina 1943- CANR-15
 Earlier sketch in CA 85-88
Auerbach, Stevanne 1938- CANR-24
 Earlier sketches in CA 57-60, CANR-8
Auerbach, Stuart C(harles) 1935- 89-92
Auerbach, Sylvia CANR-4
 Earlier sketch in CA 53-56
Aufricht, Hans 1902- 45-48
Augarde, Steve 1950- CANR-21
 Earlier sketch in CA 104
 See also SATA 25
Augarde, Tony 1936- 118
Augarten, Stan 1952- 115
Auge, Bud
 See Auge, Henry J., Jr.
Auge, Henry J., Jr. 1930(?)-1983
 Obituary 109
Augelli, John P(at) 1921- 17-18R
 See also SATA 46
Aughtry, Charles Edward 1925- 7-8R
Augsburger, A(aron) Don(ald) 1925- 21-22R
Augsburger, David W. 1938- CANR-13
 Earlier sketch in CA 33-36R
Augsburger, Myron S. 1929- CANR-6
 Earlier sketch in CA 15-16R
Augspurger, Everett F. 1904(?)-1986
 Obituary 118
Augstein, Rudolf (Karl) 1923- 110
Auguet, Roland (Jacques) 1935- 105
August, Eugene R(obert) 1935- 49-52
August, John
 See De Voto, Bernard (Augustine)
Augustin, Ann Sutherland 1934- 57-60
Augustin, Pius 1934- 19-20R
Augustine, Erich
 See Stoil, Michael Jon
Augustine, Norman R(alph) 1935- 121
Augustson, Ernest
 See Ryden, Ernest Edwin
Augustus, Albert, Jr.
 See Nuetzel, Charles (Alexander)
Aukerman, Dale 1930- 112
Aukerman, Robert C. 1910- 33-36R
Aukofer, Frank A(lexander) 1935- 65-68
Auld, Rhoda L(andsman) 105
Auleta, Michael S. 1909- CAP-2
 Earlier sketch in CA 25-28
Auletta, Ken 1942- CANR-12
 Earlier sketch in CA 69-72
Auletta, Richard P(aul) 1942- 53-56
Auletta, Robert 1940- 119
 Brief entry 115
Aulicino, Armand 1920(?)-1983 Obituary ... 109
Aulick, June L. 1906- 25-28R
Ault, Donald D(uane) 1942- 81-84
Ault, Phil
 See Ault, Phillip H(alliday)
Ault, Phillip H(alliday) 1914- CANR-18
 Earlier sketch in CA 101
 See also SATA 23
Ault, Rosalie Sain 1942- 107
 See also SATA 38
Ault, Roz
 See Ault, Rosalie Sain
Aultman, Donald S. 1930- 19-20R
Aultman, Richard E(ugene) 1933- CANR-9
 Earlier sketch in CA 65-68
Aumann, Francis R(obert) 1901- 41-44R
Aumbry, Alan
 See Bayley, Barrington J(ohn)
Aumont, Jean-Pierre 1913- 29-32R
Aune, Bruce (Arthur) 1933- 73-76
Aung, (Maung) Htin 1909- CANR-3
 Earlier sketch in CA 7-8R
 See also SATA 21
Aunger, Edmund A(lexander) 1949- 112
Auntie Deb
 See Coury, Louise Andree
Auntie Louise
 See Coury, Louise Andree
Aurand, Harold Wilson 1940- 41-44R
Aurand, L(eonard) W(illiam) 1920- 53-56
Aurandt, Paul Harvey 1918- 102
Aurelio, John R. 1937- 111
Aurelius
 See Bourne, Randolph S(illiman)
Aurell, Tage 1895-1976 Obituary 113
Aurner, Robert R(ay) 1898- 7-8R
Aurthur, Robert Alan 1922-1978 81-84
Ausland, John C(ampbell) 1920- 93-96
Auslander, Audrey (May) Wurdemann
 1911-1960 Obituary 116
Auslander, Joseph 1897-1965 Obituary 116
Ausmus, Harry Jack 1937- 115
Austen, Michael (Edward) 1951- 109
Austen, Ralph A. 1937- 25-28R
Auster, Nancy (Eileen) R(oss) 1926- 65-68
Auster, Paul 1947- CANR-23
 Earlier sketch in CA 69-72
 See also CLC 47
Austerlitz, Robert Paul 1923- 111
Austerman, Wayne R. 1948- 122
Austgen, Robert Joseph 1932- 23-24R
Austin, Alfred 1835-1913 .... DLB-35
Austin, Allan Edward 1929- 73-76
Austin, Allen 1922- 33-36R
Austin, Anthony 1919- 33-36R
Austin, (Mildred) Aurelia 53-56
Austin, Barbara Leslie
 See Linton, Barbara Leslie
Austin, Brett
 See Floren, Lee
Austin, Charles M(arshall) 1941- 69-72
Austin, David E(dwards) 1926- 29-32R
Austin, Elizabeth S. 1907- CAP-2
 Earlier sketch in CA 25-28
 See also SATA 5
Austin, Frank
 See Faust, Frederick (Shiller)
Austin, Harry
 See McInerny, Ralph
Austin, Henry Wilfred 1906- 101
Austin, James C(layton) 1923- 13-14R
Austin, James Henry 1925- 81-84
Austin, John 1922- 61-64
Austin, John Langshaw 1911-1960
 Obituary 112
Austin, K(enneth) A(shurst) 1911- 102
Austin, Lettie J(ane) 1925- 65-68
Austin, Lewis 1936- 73-76
Austin, Lloyd James 1915- CAP-1
 Earlier sketch in CA 13-14
Austin, M(ichel) M(ervyn) 1943- CANR-19
 Earlier sketch in CA 85-88
Austin, Margot CAP-1
 Earlier sketch in CA 9-10
 See also SATA 11
Austin, Mary (Hunter) 1868-1934
 Brief entry 109
 See also DLB 9
 See also TCLC 25
Austin, Mary C(arrington) 1915- 7-8R
Austin, Neal F(uller) 1926- 25-28R
Austin, (John) Norman 1937- 89-92
Austin, Oliver L(uther), Jr. 1903- 49-52
 See also SATA 7
Austin, R. G.
 See Gelman, Rita Golden
Austin, (Stewart) Reid 1931- 89-92
Austin, Richard B(uckner), Jr. 1930- 73-76
Austin, Stephen
 See Stevens, Austin N(eil)
Austin, Timothy R(obert) 1952- 117
Austin, Tom
 See Jacobs, Linda C.
Austin, William W(eaver) 1920- 23-24R
Austwick, John
 See Lee, Austin
Ausubel, Herman 1920-1977 .... 1R
 Obituary 69-72
Ausubel, Marynn H. 1913(?)-1980
 Obituary 97-100
Auten, James H(udson) 1938- 41-44R
Auteur, Hillary
 See Gottfried, Theodore Mark
Auth, Tony
 See Auth, William Anthony, Jr.
Auth, William Anthony, Jr. 1942- 111
 Brief entry 108
Autran Dourado, Waldomiro
 See Dourado, Autran
Autrey, C. E. 1904- CANR-2
 Earlier sketch in CA 4R
Autry, Ewart (Arthur) 1900- 15-16R
Autry, (Orvon) Gene 1907- Brief entry 112
Autry, James Arthur 1933- Brief entry 115
Autton, Norman William James 1920- 101
Auty, Phyllis 1910- CANR-2
 Earlier sketch in CA 7-8R
Auty, Robert 1914-1978 Obituary 111
Auvert, Elizabeth CANR-14
 Earlier sketch in CA 37-40R
Auvil, Kenneth W(illiam) 1925- 17-18R
Avakian, Arra S(teve) 1912- 85-88
Avakumovic, Ivan 1926- 41-44R
Avalle-Arce, Juan Bautista 1927- CANR-13
 Earlier sketch in CA 33-36R
Avallone, Michael (Angelo), Jr. 1924- ... CANR-4
 Earlier sketch in CA 7-8R
Avalon, Arthur
 See Woodroffe, John George
Avanzini, John F. 1936- 122
Aveline, Claude 1901- CANR-6
 Earlier sketch in CA 7-8R
Aveni, Anthony F(rancis) 1938- 81-84
Averbach, Albert 1902-1975 .... CAP-2
 Earlier sketch in CA 21-22
Averill, E(dgar) W(aite) 1906-1980 53-56
Averill, Esther 1902- CANR-12
 Earlier sketch in CA 29-32R
 See also SATA 1, 28
Averill, John Hillier 1923-1984 Obituary 111
Averill, Lloyd J(ames) 1923- CANR-10
 Earlier sketch in CA 23-24R
Averitt, Robert T(abor) 1931- 23-24R
Avery, Al
 See Montgomery, Rutherford George
Avery, Burniece 1908- 73-76
Avery, Catherine B(arber) 1909- 57-60
Avery, Edwina Austin 1896-1983 Obituary .. 110
Avery, George C(ostas) 1926- 25-28R
Avery, Gillian (Elise) 1926- CANR-4
 Earlier sketch in CA 9-10R
 See also SATA 7
Avery, Ira 1914- 81-84
Avery, Jeanne 1931- 111
Avery, June
 See Rees, Joan
Avery, Kay 1908- 1R
 See also SATA 5
Avery, Laurence G(reen) 1934- 33-36R
Avery, Lynn
 See Cole, Lois Dwight
Avery, Martin 1955- 113
Avery, Mary Ellen 1927- 118
Avery, Peter 1923- 15-16R
Avery, Richard
 See Cooper, Edmund
Avery, Robert J., Jr. 1911(?)-1983
 Obituary 110
Avery, Robert Sterling 1917- 13-14R
Avery, Valerie 1940- 111
Avey, Albert E(dwin) 1886-1963 .... CAP-1
 Earlier sketch in CA 17-18
Avey, Ruby 1927- CANR-16
 Earlier sketch in CA 89-92
Avi
 See Wortis, Avi
Aviad, Janet 1942- 115
Avice, Claude (Pierre Marie) 1925- CANR-24
 Earlier sketches in CA 61-64, CANR-8
Avila, Lilian Estelle 45-48
Avineri, Shlomo 1933- 25-28R
Avirgan, Anthony Lance 1944- 112
Avirgan, Tony
 See Avirgan, Anthony Lance
Avis, Paul (David Loup) 1947- 120
Avison, Margaret 1918- 17-18R
 See also DLB 53
 See also CLC 2, 4
Avison, N(eville) Howard 1934- 29-32R
Avi-Yonah, M(ichael) 1904-1974 .... CANR-6
 Earlier sketch in CA 7-8R
Avnery, Uri 1923- 105
Avni, Abraham Albert 1921- 33-36R
Avramovic, Dragoslav 1919- CANR-17
 Earlier sketch in CA 41-44R
Avrelin, M.
 See Steinberg, Aaron Zacharovich
Avrett, Robert 1901- 1R
Avrett, Rosalind Case 1933- 110
Avrett, Roz
 See Avrett, Rosalind Case
Avrich, Paul (Henry) 1931- CANR-5
 Earlier sketch in CA 49-52
Avriel, Ehud 1917- 69-72
Avril, Pierre 1930- 29-32R
Avruch, Kevin Andrew 1950- 123
Avrutis, Raymond 1948- 69-72
Awa, Eme Onuoha 1921- 15-16R
Awad, Elias M. 1934- CANR-11
 Earlier sketch in CA 17-18R
Awdry, Wilbert Vere 1911- 103
Awe, Chulho 1927- 33-36R
Awolowo, Obafemi Awo 1909-1987 .... CANR-14
 Obituary 122
 Earlier sketch in CA 65-68
Awoonor, Kofi 1935- CANR-15
 Earlier sketch in CA 29-32R
Axell, Herbert (Ernest) 1915- CANR-14
 Earlier sketch in CA 81-84
Axelrad, Jacob 1899- 61-64
Axelrad, Sidney 1913-1976 122
 Obituary 110
Axelrad, Sylvia Brody 1914- 104
Axelrod, Alan 1952- 110
Axelrod, D(avid) B(ruce) 1943- CANR-1
 Earlier sketch in CA 45-48
Axelrod, George 1922- 65-68
Axelrod, Herbert Richard 1927- 85-88
Axelrod, Joseph 1918- 33-36R
Axelrod, Paul (Douglas) 1949- 110
Axelrod, Robert 1943- 33-36R
Axelrod, Steven Gould 1944- 81-84
Axelson, Eric (Victor) 1913- CANR-9
 Earlier sketch in CA 21-22R
Axford, H. William 1925- 37-40R
Axford, Joseph Mack 1879-1970 .... CAP-2
 Earlier sketch in CA 25-28
Axford, Lavonne B(rady) 1928- 33-36R
Axford, Roger W(illiam) 1920- 33-36R
Axinn, Donald E(verett) 1929- Brief entry ... 115
Axinn, June 1923- 89-92
Axline, W. Andrew 1940- 25-28R
Axtell, James Lewis 1941- 108
Axthelm, Peter M(acrae) 1943- 107
Axton, David
 See Koontz, Dean R(ay)
Axton, W(illiam) F(itch) 1926- 21-22R
Ayal, Igal 1942- 37-40R
Ayala, Francisco 1934- 85-88
Ayala, Mitzi 1941- 110
Ayandele, E(mmanuel) A(yankanmi)
 1936- CANR-13
 Earlier sketch in CA 21-22R
Ayars, Albert L(ee) 1917- 29-32R
Ayars, James S(terling) 1898- CANR-2
 Earlier sketch in CA 5-6R
 See also SATA 4
Ayatey, Siegfried B. Y. 1934- 25-28R
Ayatollah, The
 See Khomeini, Ruhollah (Mussavi)
Ayckbourn, Alan 1939- 21-22R
 See also DLB 13
 See also CLC 5, 8, 18, 33
Aycock, Don M(ilton) 1951- 106
Aydelotte, William Osgood 1910- 57-60
Ayearst, Morley 1899-1983 .... CAP-2
 Obituary 109
 Earlier sketch in CA 29-32
Ayer, A(lfred) J(ules) 1910- CANR-5
 Earlier sketch in CA 7-8R
Ayer, Frederick, Jr. 1917(?)-1974 73-76
 Obituary 45-48
Ayer, Jacqueline 1930- 69-72
 See also SATA 13
Ayer, Margaret ?-1981 .... CANR-13
 Earlier sketch in CA 65-68
 See also SATA 15
Ayers, Bradley Earl 1935- 69-72
Ayers, Donald Murray 1923- 17-18R
Ayers, Edward L(ynn) 1953- 115
Ayers, M(ichael) R(ichard) 1935- 25-28R
Ayers, Robert H(yman) 1918- 45-48
Ayers, Ronald 1948- 61-64
Ayers, Rose
 See Greenwood, Lillian Bethel
Ayerst, David (George Ogilvy) 1904-
 Brief entry 113
Aykroyd, Dan(iel Edward) 1952- 123

Aykroyd, Wallace Ruddell 1899-1979
Obituary ... 110
Aylen, Leo (William) 1935- ... CANR-19
Earlier sketch in CA 102
Aylesworth, Jim 1943- ... CANR-22
Earlier sketch in CA 106
See also SATA 38
Aylesworth, Thomas G(ibbons) 1927- ... CANR-10
Earlier sketch in CA 25-28R
See also SATA 4
See also CLR 6
Ayling, (Harold) Keith (Oliver) 1898-1976 ... 73-76
Obituary ... 69-72
Ayling, Stanley (Edward) 1909- ... CANR-21
Earlier sketch in CA 45-48
Aylmer, Felix
See Jones, Felix Edward Aylmer
Aylmer, G(erald) E(dward) 1926- ... CANR-5
Earlier sketch in CA 13-14R
Aylward, Gladys 1902(?)-1970 Obituary ... 111
Aylward, Marcus
See Alexander, Marc
Aymar, Brandt 1911- ... CANR-16
Earlier sketch in CA 3R
See also SATA 22
Aymar, Gordon C(hristian) 1893- ... 7-8R
Ayme, Marcel (Andre) 1902-1967 ... 89-92
See also CLC 11
Aymes, Sister Maria de la Cruz ... 23-24R
Aynes, Edith A(nnette) 1909- ... 45-48
Aynes, Pat Edith
See Aynes, Edith A(nnette)
Aynesworth, Hugh (G.) 1931- ... 120
Brief entry ... 115
Ayrault, Evelyn West 1922- ... 9-10R
Ayre, Robert (Hugh) 1900- ... 4R
Ayres, Alison
See Carter, Robert A(yres)
Ayres, Carole Briggs
See Briggs, Carole S(uzanne)
Ayres, James Eyvind 1939- ... 103
Ayres, Patricia Miller 1923-1985 Obituary ... 117
See also SATA 46
Ayres, Paul
See Aarons, Edward S(idney)
Ayres, Robert U(nderwood) 1932- ... CANR-16
Earlier sketch in CA 93-96
Ayres, Ruby M(ildred) 1883-1955
Brief entry ... 117
Ayrton, Elisabeth Walshe 1918- ... CANR-21
Earlier sketches in CA 7-8R, CANR-3
Ayrton, Michael 1921-1975 ... CANR-21
Obituary ... 61-64
Earlier sketches in CA 7-8R, CANR-9
See also CLC 7
Aytoun, William Edmonstoune
1813-1865 ... DLB-32
Ayub Khan, Mohammad 1907-1974 ... CAP-2
Earlier sketch in CA 23-24
Ayvazian, L. Fred 1919- ... 69-72
Azaid
See Zaidenberg, Arthur
Azar, Edward E. 1938- ... 49-52
Azarian, Mary 1940- ... 118
Azbel, Mark Ya. 1932- ... 105
Azcarate y Florez, Pablo de 1890-1971
Obituary ... 113
Azevedo, Ross E(ames) ... 105
Aziz, Sartaj 1929- ... 111
Aznavour, Charles
See Aznavourian, Varenagh
Aznavourian, Varenagh 1924- Brief entry ... 112
Azneer, J. Leonard 1921- ... 33-36R
Azorin
See Martinez Ruiz, Jose
See also CLC 11
Azoy, A(nastasio) C. M. 1891- ... CAP-1
Earlier sketch in CA 13-14
Azrael, Judith Anne 1938- ... CANR-10
Earlier sketch in CA 65-68
Azrin, Nathan H(arold) 1930- ... CANR-16
Earlier sketches in CA 45-48, CANR-1
Azuela, Mariano 1873-1952 Brief entry ... 104
See also TCLC 3
Azumi, Atsushi 1907- ... 102
Azumi, Koya 1930- ... 29-32R

B

B., Tania
See Blixen, Karen (Christentze Dinesen)
B. V.
See Thomson, James
Baack, Lawrence James 1943- ... 109
Baade, (Wilhelm Heinrich) W(alter)
1893-1960 Obituary ... 112
Baali, Fuad (G.) 1930- Brief entry ... 117
Baal-Teshuva, Jacob 1929- ... 7-8R
Baar, James A. 1929- ... 102
Baars, Conrad W(alterus) 1919-1981 ... CANR-8
Earlier sketch in CA 57-60
Baars, Donald Lee 1928- ... 121
Baarslag, Karl Herman William 1900-1984
Obituary ... 111
Baastad, Babbis Friis
See Friis-Baastad, Babbis Ellinor
Baatz, Charles A(lbert) 1916- ... 104
Baatz, Olga K. 1921- ... 104
Bab
See Gilbert, W(illiam) S(chwenck)
Baba, Meher 1894-1969 ... 109
Obituary ... 106
Babb, Howard S(elden) 1924-1978 ... 13-14R
Obituary ... 120
Babb, Hugh Webster 1887-197(?) ... CAP-1
Earlier sketch in CA 13-14
Babb, Janice Barbara
See Bentley, Janice Babb
Babb, Lawrence 1902- ... CAP-2
Earlier sketch in CA 33-36
Babb, Lawrence Alan 1941- Brief entry ... 105
Babb, Sanora 1907- ... 15-16R
Babbage, Stuart Barton 1916- ... CANR-8
Earlier sketch in CA 5-6R
Babbidge, Homer D(aniels), Jr.
1925-1984 ... CANR-13
Obituary ... 112
Earlier sketch in CA 61-64
Babbie, Earl (Robert) 1938- ... CANR-23
Earlier sketches in CA 61-64, CANR-8
Babbis, Eleanor
See Friis-Baastad, Babbis Ellinor
Babbitt, Bruce E(dward) 1938- ... 97-100
Babbitt, Irving 1865-1933 ... DLB-63
Babbitt, Natalie 1932- ... CANR-19
Earlier sketches in CA 49-52, CANR-2
See also SATA 6
See also SAAS 5
See also DLB 52
See also CLR 2
Babbitt, Robert
See Bangs, Robert B(abbitt)
Babcock, C(larence) Merton 1908- ... CANR-5
Earlier sketch in CA 5-6R
Babcock, Dennis Arthur 1948- ... 61-64
See also SATA 22
Babcock, Dorothy E(llen) 1931- ... 65-68
Babcock, Frederic 1896- ... 5-6R
Babcock, Frederick Morrison
1897(?)-1983 Obituary ... 110
Babcock, Havilah 1898-1964 ... 122
Obituary ... 110
Babcock, Leland S. 1922- Brief entry ... 106
Babcock, Nicolas
See Lewis, Tom
Babcock, Robert J(oseph) 1928- ... 15-16R
Babe, Thomas 1941- ... 101
Babel, Isaac (Emanuilovich)
See Babel, Isaak (Emmanuilovich)
See also TCLC 13
Babel, Isaak (Emmanuilovich)
1894-1941(?) Brief entry ... 104
See also TCLC 2
Baber, Walter F(rank) 1953- ... 120
Babiiha, Thaddeo K(itasimbwa) 1945- ... 110
Babin, David E. 1925- ... 23-24R
Babin, Maria Teresa 1910- Brief entry ... 107
Babington, Anthony Patrick 1920- ... 61-64
Babits, Mihaly 1883-1941 Brief entry ... 114
See also TCLC 14
Babitz, Eve 1943- ... 81-84
Babitz, Sol 1911- ... 41-44R
Babladelis, Georgia 1931- ... CANR-8
Earlier sketch in CA 23-24R
Babris, Peter J. 1917- ... CANR-10
Earlier sketch in CA 21-22R
Babson, Marian ... 102
Babson, Roger W(ard) 1875-1967
Obituary ... 89-92
Babula, William 1943- ... CANR-21
Earlier sketch in CA 105
Bacall, Lauren 1924- ... 93-96
Bacchelli, Riccardo 1891-1985 ... 29-32R
Obituary ... 117
See also CLC 19
Bacciocco, Edward J(oseph), Jr. 1935- ... 45-48
Bach, Alice (Hendricks) 1942- ... 101
See also SATA 27, 30
Bach, Bert C(oates) 1936- ... 23-24R
Bach, George Leland 1915- ... CANR-3
Earlier sketch in CA 4R
Bach, George Robert 1914- ... 104
Bach, Ira J(ohn) 1906-1985 ... 115
Bach, Kent 1943- ... 85-88
Bach, Marcus (Louis) 1906- Brief entry ... 115
Bach, Orville E(uing), Jr. 1946- ... 115
Bach, P.D.Q.
See Schickele, Peter
Bach, Richard (David) ... CANR-18
Earlier sketch in CA 11-12R
See also SATA 13
See also CLC 14
See also AITN 1
Bach, Wilfrid 1936- ... CANR-10
Earlier sketch in CA 61-64
Bacharach, Alfred L(ouis) 1891-1966 ... CAP-1
Earlier sketch in CA 11-12
Bacharach, Bert(ram Mark) 1898-1983
Obituary ... 110
Bache, Benjamin Franklin 1769-1798 ... DLB-43
Bache, William B. 1922- ... 25-28R
Bachelard, Gaston 1884-1962 ... 97-100
Obituary ... 89-92
Bachem Alent, Rose M(arie Baake) ... 49-52
Bacher, June Masters 1918- ... 108
Bachman, David C(hristian) 1934- ... 124
Bachman, Fred 1949- ... 53-56
See also SATA 12
Bachman, Ingeborg 1926-1973 ... 93-96
Obituary ... 45-48
Bachman, Jerald G(raybill) 1936- ... 41-44R
Bachman, John Walter 1916- ... 5-6R
Bachmann, Gideon 1927- ... 104
Bachmura, Frank T(homas) 1922- ... 45-48
Bachrach, Bernard S. 1939- ... 113
Bachrach, Judy 1948- ... 114
Bacik, James Joseph 1936- ... 105
Back, Joe (W.) 1899-1986 ... CAP-2
Obituary ... 120
Earlier sketch in CA 17-18
Back, Kurt W(olfgang) 1919- ... 13-14R
Backer, Dorothy 1925- ... 85-88
Backer, John H. 1902-1985 ... 33-36R
Obituary ... 116
Backer, Morton 1918- ... 19-20R
Backgammon, Daisy
See Murray, John F(rancis)
Backhouse, Janet 1938- ... 109
Backhouse, Sally 1927- ... 23-24R
Backlund, Ralph T. 1918- ... 73-76
Backman, Carl W(ard) 1923- ... 19-20R
Backman, Jules 1910- ... CANR-3
Earlier sketch in CA 2R
Backman, Melvin (Abraham) 1919- ... 21-22R
Backman, Milton V., Jr. 1927- ... CANR-13
Earlier sketch in CA 33-36R
Backstrom, Charles H(erbert) 1926- ... 13-14R
Backus, Jean L(ouise) 1914-1986 ... 33-36R
Obituary ... 119
Backus, Oswald P(rentiss) III 1921-1972 ... CAP-2
Obituary ... 37-40R
Earlier sketch in CA 33-36
Bacmeister, Rhoda W(arner) 1893- ... CAP-1
Earlier sketch in CA 15-16
See also SATA 11
Bacon, Daisy Sarah 1899(?)-1986
Obituary ... 118
Bacon, Delia 1811-1859 ... DLB-1
Bacon, Edmund N(orwood) 1910- ... 41-44R
Bacon, Edward 1906-1981 ... 29-32R
Obituary ... 102
Bacon, Elizabeth 1914- ... 29-32R
See also SATA 3
Bacon, Elizabeth E(maline) 1904- ... CAP-1
Earlier sketch in CA 19-20
Bacon, Frances Atchinson 1903- ... 4R
Bacon, Joan Chase
See Bowden, Joan Chase
Bacon, John 1940- ... 53-56
Bacon, Josephine Dodge (Daskam)
1876-1961 ... 97-100
See also SATA 48
Bacon, Lenice Ingram 1895- ... 45-48
Bacon, Margaret ... 106
Bacon, Margaret Frances
See Bacon, Peggy
See also SATA 50
Bacon, Margaret Hope 1921- ... 25-28R
See also SATA 6
Bacon, Marion 1901(?)-1975 Obituary ... 57-60
Bacon, Martha Sherman 1917-1981 ... 85-88
Obituary ... 104
See also SATA 18, 27
See also CLR 3
Bacon, Nancy 1940- ... 93-96
Bacon, Peggy 1895-1987 ... CAP-2
Obituary ... 121
Earlier sketch in CA 23-24
See also SATA 2
Bacon, Phillip 1922- ... 41-44R
Bacon, R(onald) L(eonard) 1924- ... 104
See also SATA 26
Bacon, Thomas 1700(?)-1768 ... DLB-31
Bacon, Wallace A(lger) 1914- ... 19-20R
Bacote, Clarence A(lbert) 1906- ... CAP-2
Earlier sketch in CA 33-36
Bacovia, G.
See Vasiliu, Gheorghe
Bacovia, George
See Vasiliu, Gheorghe
See also TCLC 24
Bacque, James 1929- ... 101
Badash, Lawrence 1934- ... CANR-14
Earlier sketch in CA 37-40R
Badawi, M(ohamed) M(ustafa) 1925- ... CANR-1
Earlier sketch in CA 49-52
Badawi, Muhammed Mustafa
See Badawi, M(ohamed) M(ustafa)
Badcock, Christopher Robert 1946- ... 101
Baddeley, Alan D(avid) 1934- ... 69-72
Baddeley, Hermione 1906(?)-1986
Obituary ... 120
Baddeley, V.C. Clinton
See Clinton-Baddeley, V.C.
Bade, Jane (Ruth) 1932- ... 89-92
Bade, Patrick 1951- ... 89-92
Baden-Powell, Dorothy 1920- ... 103
Baden-Powell, Robert (Stephenson Smyth)
1857-1941 Brief entry ... 114
See also SATA 16
Bader, Douglas (Robert Steuart)
1910-1982 ... 101
Obituary ... 107
Bader, Julia 1944- ... 69-72
Bader, Robert S(mith) 1925- ... 120
Badger, John d'Arcy 1917- ... 45-48
Badger, Ralph E(astman) 1890-1978 ... CAP-2
Obituary ... 73-76
Earlier sketch in CA 21-22
Badger, Reid 1942- ... 97-100
Badgley, John 1930- ... 37-40R
Badgley, Robin F(rancis) 1931- ... 101
Badham, Leslie (Stephen Ronald)
1908-1975 Obituary ... 114
Badia, Leonard F(rancis) 1934- ... 113
Badian, Ernst 1925- ... 37-40R
Badillo, Herman 1929- ... 85-88
Badinter, Elisabeth 1944- ... 118
Badough, Rose Marie 1938- ... 117
Badura-Skoda, Eva 1929- ... CANR-14
Earlier sketch in CA 37-40R
Baechler, Jean 1937- ... CANR-13
Earlier sketch in CA 73-76
Baeck, Leo 1873-1956 Brief entry ... 115
Baeder, John 1938- ... 111
Baehr, Consuelo 1938- ... 103
Baehr, Harry William 1907-1987 Obituary ... 123
Baehr, Patricia Goehner 1952- ... 103
Baen, James P. 1943- Brief entry ... 112
Baensch, Willy E(dward) 1893-1972
Obituary ... 37-40R
Baenziger, Hans 1917- ... 49-52
Baer, Adela S(wenson) 1931- ... 101
Baer, Curtis O. 1898- ... 49-52
Baer, Daniel J(oseph) 1929- ... 33-36R
Baer, Donald Merle 1931- ... 81-84
Baer, Earl E. 1928- ... 57-60
Baer, Edith R(uth) 1920- ... CANR-21
Earlier sketch in CA 104
Baer, Eleanora A(gnes) 1907- ... 9-10R
Baer, Gabriel 1919- ... CANR-2
Earlier sketch in CA 7-8R
Baer, George Webster 1935- ... 21-22R
Baer, Hans A. 1944- ... 119
Baer, Jean L. ... CANR-9
Earlier sketch in CA 15-16R
Baer, Jill
See Gilbert, (Agnes) Joan (Sewell)
Baer, John 1886-1970 Obituary ... 29-32R
Baer, Judith A(bbott) 1945- ... 81-84
Baer, Marianne 1932- ... 81-84
Baer, Max Frank 1912- ... 11-12R
Baer, Rosemary 1913- ... 41-44R
Baer, Walter S. III 1937- ... 65-68
Baer, Werner 1931- ... 11-12R
Baerg, Harry J(ohn) 1909- ... CANR-4
Earlier sketch in CA 11-12R
See also SATA 12
Baerwald, Hans H(erman) 1927- ... 33-36R
Baerwald, Sara 1948- ... 61-64
Baetjer, Anna M(edora) 1899-1984
Obituary ... 112
Baetzhold, Howard G(eorge) 1923- ... 29-32R
Baeuml, Franz H(einrich) 1926- ... 49-52
Baez, Joan (Chandos) 1941- ... 21-22R
Bagarag, Shibli
See Lawlor, Patrick Anthony
Bagby, George
See Stein, Aaron Marc
Bagby, Wesley M(arvin) 1922- ... CANR-16
Earlier sketch in CA 4R
Bagdikian, Ben Haig 1920- ... CANR-6
Earlier sketch in CA 11-12R
Bage, Robert 1728-1801 ... DLB-39
Bagehot, Walter 1826-1877 ... DLB-55
Bagg, Graham (William) 1917- ... 57-60
Bagg, Robert Ely 1935- ... CANR-15
Earlier sketch in CA 65-68
Baggaley, Andrew R(obert) 1923- ... 15-16R
Baggett, Nancy 1943- ... 117
Baggley, John (Samuel) 1940- ... 124
Bagin, Don(ald Richard) 1938- ... 77-80
Baginski, Frank 1938- ... 93-96
Bagley, Christopher 1937- ... 119
Bagley, Desmond 1923-1983 ... 19-20R
Obituary ... 109
Bagley, Edward R(osecrans) 1926- ... CANR-5
Earlier sketch in CA 53-56
Bagley, J(ohn) J(oseph) 1908- ... CANR-2
Earlier sketch in CA 7-8R
Bagnel, Joan 1933- ... 49-52
Bagni, Gwen
See Dubov, Gwen Bagni
Bagnold, Enid 1889-1981 ... CANR-5
Obituary ... 103
Earlier sketch in CA 7-8R
See also SATA 1, 25
See also DLB 13
See also CLC 25
Bagramian, Ivan K(ristoforovich)
1897-1982 Obituary ... 107
Bagrjana, Elisaveta
See Belcheva, Elisaveta
Bagryana, Elisaveta
See Belcheva, Elisaveta
Bagster, Hubert
See Trumper, Hubert Bagster
Bagwell, Philip S(idney) 1914- ... CANR-13
Earlier sketch in CA 33-36R
Bagwell, William Francis, Jr. 1923- ... 33-36R
Bahadur, K(rishna) P(rakash) 1924- ... 57-60
Bahat, Dan 1938- ... 77-80
Bahl, Roy W. (Jr.) 1939- ... 23-24R
Bahlke, George W(ilbon) 1934- ... 29-32R
Bahlke, Valerie Worth 1933- ... CANR-15
Earlier sketch in CA 41-44R
Bahlman, Dudley Ward Rhodes 1923- ... 85-88
Bahm, Archie J(ohn) 1907- ... CANR-3
Earlier sketch in CA 11-12R
Bahmueller, Charles F(erdinand) 1942- ... 112
Bahn, Eugene 1906- ... 23-24R
Bahn, Margaret (Elizabeth) Linton
1907-1969 ... CAP-2
Earlier sketch in CA 25-28
Bahr, Edith-Jane 1926- ... 65-68
Bahr, Erhard 1932- ... 33-36R
Bahr, Hermann 1863-1934 Brief entry ... 121
Bahr, Howard M. 1938- ... CANR-12
Earlier sketch in CA 29-32R
Bahr, Jerome 1909- ... 33-36R
Bahr, Robert 1940- ... CANR-9
Earlier sketch in CA 65-68
See also SATA 38
Bahti, Tom ... SATA-31
Baier, Kurt Erich 1917- ... 65-68
Baigell, Matthew 1933- ... 107
Bailes, Kendall E(ugene) 1940- Brief entry ... 112
Bailey, Alfred Goldsworthy 1905- ... 25-28R
Bailey, Alfred M(arshall) 1894-1978 ... 41-44R
Bailey, Alice A(nne La Trobe-Bateman)
1880(?)-1949 Brief entry ... 116
Bailey, Alice Cooper 1890- ... CAP-1
Earlier sketch in CA 15-16
See also SATA 12

Bailey, Anthony 1933- CANR-3
Earlier sketch in CA 3R
Bailey, Barry 1926- 107
Bailey, Bernadine (Freeman) 1901- CANR-7
Earlier sketch in CA 5-6R
See also SATA 14
Bailey, Beryl Loftman 1920(?)-1977
Obituary 69-72
Bailey, Carolyn Sherwin 1875-1961 73-76
See also SATA 14
Bailey, Charles W(aldo) II 1929- CANR-1
Earlier sketch in CA 1R
Bailey, Chris H(arvey) 1946- 65-68
Bailey, Conrad Charles Maitland 1922- 105
Bailey, D. R. Shackleton
See Shackleton Bailey, D(avid) R(oy)
Bailey, David (Royston) 1938- 120
Bailey, David C(harles) 1930- 45-48
Bailey, Derrick Sherwin 1910-1984 CANR-2
Obituary 112
Earlier sketch in CA 5-6R
Bailey, Don 1942- 93-96
Bailey, Dudley 1918- 19-20R
Bailey, Eric 1933- 33-36R
Bailey, F(rancis) Lee 1933- 89-92
Bailey, Frederick George 1924- CANR-9
Earlier sketch in CA 13-14R
Bailey, Frederick Marshman 1882-1967 CAP-1
Earlier sketch in CA 13-14
Bailey, George 1919- CANR-17
Earlier sketch in CA 25-28R
Bailey, Gerald Earl 1929- CANR-10
Earlier sketch in CA 25-28R
Bailey, Gordon Keith 1936- 112
Bailey, H(enry) C(hristopher) 1878-1961
Obituary 108
Bailey, Harold (Walter) 1899- 109
Bailey, Harry A(ugustine), Jr. 1932- 23-24R
Bailey, Helen Miller 1909- 15-16R
Bailey, Herbert S(mith), Jr. 1921-
Brief entry 112
Bailey, Hillary G(oodsell) 1894- 57-60
Bailey, Hugh C(oleman) 1929- 11-12R
Bailey, J(ames) Martin 1929- 49-52
Bailey, J(ames) O(sler) 1903- 17-18R
Bailey, Jackson Holbrook 1925- CANR-21
Earlier sketch in CA 45-48
Bailey, James H(enry) 1919- 106
Bailey, James R(ichard) A(be) 1919- 53-56
Bailey, (Corinne) Jane 1943- 77-80
Bailey, Jane H(orton) 1916- CANR-4
Earlier sketch in CA 53-56
See also SATA 12
Bailey, Joan H(auser) 1922- 21-22R
Bailey, Joe A(llen) 1929- 37-40R
Bailey, John (Robert) 1940- 121
Bailey, John A(medee) 1929- 37-40R
Bailey, Kenneth K(yle) 1923- 23-24R
Bailey, Kenneth P. 1912- CANR-4
Earlier sketch in CA 53-56
Bailey, Lloyd Richard 1936- CANR-15
Earlier sketch in CA 85-88
Bailey, M(innie Elizabeth) Thomas 57-60
Bailey, Maralyn Collins (Harrison) 1941- 53-56
See also SATA 12
Bailey, Matilda
See Radford, Ruby L(orraine)
Bailey, Maurice Charles 1932- 53-56
See also SATA 12
Bailey, Norman A(lishan) 1931- CANR-13
Earlier sketch in CA 21-22R
Bailey, Patrick 1925- 57-60
Bailey, Paul 1937- CANR-16
Earlier sketch in CA 21-22R
See also DLB 14
See also CLC 45
Bailey, Paul Dayton 1906-1987 CANR-6
Obituary 124
Earlier sketch in CA 5-6R
Bailey, Pearl (Mae) 1918- CANR-14
Earlier sketch in CA 61-64
Bailey, Philip James 1816-1902 DLB-32
Bailey, Ralph Edgar 1893- CAP-1
Earlier sketch in CA 17-18
See also SATA 11
Bailey, Raymond H(amby) 1938- CANR-8
Earlier sketch in CA 61-64
Bailey, Richard W(eld) 1939- CANR-10
Earlier sketch in CA 25-28R
Bailey, Robert, Jr. 1945- 49-52
Bailey, Robert W(ilson) 1943- CANR-21
Earlier sketch in CA 69-72
Bailey, Stephen Kemp 1916-1982 CANR-4
Obituary 106
Earlier sketch in CA 1R
Bailey, Sydney D(awson) 1916- CANR-12
Earlier sketch in CA 69-72
Bailey, Thomas A(ndrew) 1902-1983 CANR-18
Obituary 110
Earlier sketch in CA 19-20R
Bailie, Victoria Worley 1894- CAP-1
Earlier sketch in CA 15-16
Bailkey, Nels M(artin) 1911- 33-36R
Baillen, Claude
See Delay-Tubiana, Claude
Baillie, Allan 1943- 118
Baillie, Hugh 1890-1966 Obituary 89-92
See also DLB 29
Baillie, Isobel 1895-1983 Obituary 110
Baillie, Kate 1957- 124
Baillie-Hamilton, George 1894-1986
Obituary 121
Baily, Charles M(ichael) 1944- 117
Baily, Leslie 1906-1976 CAP-2
Earlier sketch in CA 25-28
Baily, Nathan A(riel) 1920- CANR-6
Earlier sketch in CA 9-10R
Baily, Samuel L(ongstreth) 1936- 29-32R
Bailyn, Bernard 1922- CANR-8
Earlier sketch in CA 61-64
See also DLB 17
Bain, A(ndrew) D(avid) 1936- Brief entry 111
Bain, Carl E. 1930- 85-88
Bain, Chester A(rthur) 1912- 29-32R
Bain, Chester Ward 1919- 85-88
Bain, Joe S. 1912- 33-36R
Bain, Kenneth Bruce Findlater 1921-1985 93-96
Obituary 115
Bain, Kenneth Ray 1942- 104
Bain, Robert 1932- 77-80
Bain, Willard S., Jr. 1938- 25-28R
Bainbridge, Beryl 1933- CANR-24
Earlier sketch in CA 21-22R
See also DLB 14
See also CLC 4, 5, 8, 10, 14, 18, 22
Bainbridge, Geoffrey 1923- 7-8R
Bainbridge, John 1913- 13-14R
Bainbridge, William Sims 1940- 120
Baine, Rodney M(ontgomery) 1913- 69-72
Baines, Anthony C(uthbert) 1912- 7-8R
Baines, Frank 1915-1987 Obituary 124
Baines, Jocelyn 1925-1973 106
Obituary 104
Baines, John M. 1935- 41-44R
Baines, John Robert 1946- 123
Bains, Larry
See Sabin, Louis
Bainton, Roland H(erbert) 1894-1984 CANR-5
Obituary 113
Earlier sketch in CA 4R
Bair, Deirdre 1935- 81-84
Bair, Frank E. 1927- 102
Baird, A(lbert) Craig 1883- CAP-1
Earlier sketch in CA 13-14
Baird, Alexander (John) 1925- 11-12R
Baird, Bil
See Baird, William Britton
See also SATA 30
Baird, Duncan H. 1917- 65-68
Baird, Forrest J. 1905- CAP-1
Earlier sketch in CA 19-20
Baird, J(oseph) Arthur 1922- CANR-3
Earlier sketch in CA 5-6R
Baird, J(oseph) L. 1933- 85-88
Baird, Jay Warren 1936- 41-44R
Baird, Jesse Hays 1889- 15-16R
Baird, John D. 1941- 109
Baird, John Edward 1922- 17-18R
Baird, Joseph Armstrong (Jr.) 1922- CANR-12
Earlier sketch in CA 33-36R
Baird, Lorrayne Y. 1927- 112
Baird, Marie-Terese 1918- 57-60
Baird, Martha (Joanna) 1921-1981 CANR-9
Earlier sketch in CA 61-64
Baird, Nancy Disher 1935- CANR-15
Earlier sketch in CA 89-92
Baird, Patrick D(ouglas) 1912-1984
Obituary 112
Baird, Robert D(ahlen) 1933- 53-56
Baird, Ronald J(ames) 1929- 53-56
Baird, Russell N. 1922- 19-20R
Baird, Thomas (P.) 1923- CANR-21
Earlier sketches in CA 53-56, CANR-4
See also SATA 39, 45
Baird, W(illiam) David 1939- 41-44R
Baird, William (Robb) 1924- 15-16R
Baird, William Britton 1904-1987 106
Obituary 122
See also SATA 30
Baird-Smith, Robin 1946- 123
Bairstow, Jeffrey N(oel) 1939- CANR-8
Earlier sketch in CA 61-64
Baity, Elizabeth Chesley 1907- 29-32R
See also SATA 1
Bajema, Carl Jay 1937- CANR-12
Earlier sketch in CA 33-36R
Bakal, Carl 1918- 23-24R
Bakalar, James B. 1943- 97-100
Bakalis, Michael J. 1938- 85-88
Bakan, David 1921- 25-28R
Bakan, Paul 1928- 23-24R
Bakaric, Vladimir 1912-1983 Obituary 114
Bake, William A(lbert) 1938- 110
Bakeless, John (Edwin) 1894-1978 CANR-5
Obituary 118
Earlier sketch in CA 5-6R
See also SATA 9
Bakeless, Katherine Little 1895- 7-8R
See also SATA 9
Bakely, Don(ald Carlisle) 1928- 65-68
Baker, Adelaide N(ichols) 1894-1974 45-48
Baker, Adolph 1917- 53-56
Baker, Al AITN-1
Baker, Alan 1951- CANR-16
Earlier sketch in CA 97-100
See also SATA 22
Baker, (Allen) Albert 1910- 104
Baker, Alfred Thornton 1915(?)-1983
Obituary 110
Baker, Allison
See Crumbaker, Alice
Baker, Alton Wesley 1912- 33-36R
Baker, Asa
See Dresser, Davis
Baker, Augusta 1911- CANR-17
Earlier sketch in CA 1R
See also SATA 3
Baker, Benjamin 1915- 3R
Baker, Betty D(oreen Flook) 1916- CANR-6
Earlier sketch in CA 9-10R
Baker, Betty Lou 1928- CANR-2
Earlier sketch in CA 4R
See also SATA 5
Baker, Bill 1936- 77-80
Baker, Bill
See Baker, C(harles) William
Baker, Bill Russell 1933- 57-60
Baker, Bobby
See Baker, Robert G.
and Baker, Alfred Thornton
Baker, C(harles) William 1919- 57-60
Baker, Carlos (Heard) 1909-1987 CANR-3
Obituary 122
Earlier sketch in CA 5-6R
Baker, Charlotte 1910- 19-20R
See also SATA 2
Baker, Christopher John 1948- Brief entry 117
Baker, D(onald) Philip 1937- 102
Baker, David (Anthony) 1954- 118
Baker, Dennis 1942- 107
Baker, Denys Val 1917-1984 CANR-6
Obituary 113
Earlier sketch in CA 9-10R
Baker, Donald G(ene) 1932- 33-36R
Baker, Donald N(oel) 1936- 23-24R
Baker, Donald W(hitelaw) 1923- CANR-12
Earlier sketch in CA 73-76
Baker, Dorothy 1907-1968 CANR-1
Obituary 25-28R
Earlier sketch in CA 4R
Baker, Eleanor Z(uckerman) 1932- CANR-8
Earlier sketch in CA 57-60
Baker, (Mary) Elizabeth (Gillette) 1923- CANR-3
Earlier sketch in CA 3R
See also SATA 7
Baker, Elizabeth Faulkner 1886(?)-1973 CAP-1
Obituary 41-44R
Earlier sketch in CA 15-16
Baker, Elliott 1922- CANR-2
Earlier sketch in CA 45-48
See also CLC 8
Baker, Elsie 1929- 65-68
Baker, Elsworth F. 1903- CAP-2
Earlier sketch in CA 25-28
Baker, Eric Wilfred 1899-1973 Obituary 45-48
Baker, Eugene H. SATA-50
Baker, F(rederick) Sherman 1902-1976
Obituary 65-68
Baker, Frank 1910- 9-10R
Baker, Frank 1936- CANR-18
Earlier sketches in CA 49-52, CANR-2
Baker, Frank S. 1899(?)-1983 Obituary 109
Baker, Frank S(heaffer) 1910- 17-18R
Baker, Gary G. 1939- 23-24R
Baker, Gayle Cunningham 1950- 105
See also SATA 39
Baker, George 1915-1975 93-96
Obituary 57-60
Baker, George W(alter) 1915- 21-22R
Baker, Gilbert
See Baker, John Gilbert Hindley
Baker, Gladys L(ucille) 1910- 41-44R
Baker, Gordon Pratt 1910- 4R
Baker, Herbert G(eorge) 1920- 41-44R
Baker, Herschel Clay 1914- 61-64
Baker, Houston A., Jr. 1943- CANR-14
Earlier sketch in CA 41-44R
See also DLB 67
Baker, Howard 1905- CAP-2
Earlier sketch in CA 19-20
Baker, Howard H(enry), Jr. 1925- 124
Baker, Howard Henry, Jr. 1925-
Brief entry 113
Baker, Hugh D. R. 1937- CANR-12
Earlier sketch in CA 25-28R
Baker, Ivon 1928- 73-76
Baker, J(ohn) A(lec) 1926- 25-28R
Baker, James C(alvin) 1935- Brief entry 117
Baker, James Lawrence 1941- 53-56
Baker, James R(upert) 1925- 29-32R
Baker, James T. 1940- 85-88
Baker, James Volant 1903- 57-60
Baker, James W. 1924- 77-80
See also SATA 22
Baker, Jane Howard 1950- 110
Baker, Janice E(dla) 1941- 57-60
See also SATA 22
Baker, Jean Hogarth H(arvey) 1933- 41-44R
Baker, Jeannie 1950- 97-100
See also SATA 23
Baker, Jeffrey J(ohn) W(heeler) 1931- CANR-1
Earlier sketch in CA 49-52
See also SATA 5
Baker, Jerry 105
See also AITN 2
Baker, Jim
See Baker, James W.
Baker, John 1901(?)-1971 Obituary 104
Baker, John C(hester) 1909- 106
Baker, John F(leetwood) 1901-1985
Obituary 117
Baker, John F. 1931- 85-88
Baker, John Gilbert Hindley 1910-1986
Obituary 119
Baker, John H(enry) 1936- 33-36R
Baker, John R(andal) 1900-1984 49-52
Obituary 113
Baker, John W(esley) 1920- 61-64
Baker, Joseph E(llis) 1905- 33-36R
Baker, Josephine 1906-1975 Obituary 105
Baker, Keith Michael 1938- 57-60
Baker, Kenneth F(rank) 1908- 49-52
Baker, Laura Nelson 1911- CANR-5
Earlier sketch in CA 5-6R
See also SATA 3
Baker, Lawrence M(anning) 1907- CAP-1
Earlier sketch in CA 13-14
Baker, Leonard S(tanley) 1931-1984 23-24R
Obituary 114
Baker, Letha Elizabeth (Mitts) 1913- 33-36R
Baker, Liva 1930- 29-32R
Baker, Lucinda 1916- 65-68
Baker, Lynn S. 1948- 109
Baker, M(ary) E(llen) Penny 45-48
Baker, Margaret 1890- CANR-6
Earlier sketch in CA 15-16R
See also SATA 4
Baker, Margaret J(oyce) 1918- CANR-22
Earlier sketches in CA 13-14R, CANR-7
See also SATA 12
Baker, Marilyn 1929- Brief entry 111
Baker, Mary Gladys Steel 1892-1974 CAP-1
Earlier sketch in CA 15-16
See also SATA 12
Baker, (Robert) Michael (Graham)
1938- 25-28R
See also SATA 4
Baker, Michael H(enry) C(hadwick)
1937- CANR-23
Earlier sketches in CA 57-60, CANR-8
Baker, Miriam Hawthorn
See Nye, Miriam (Maurine Hawthorn)
Baker
Baker, Nancy C(arolyn Moll) 1944- 81-84
Baker, Nelson B(laisdell) 1905- 17-18R
Baker, Nina (Brown) 1888-1957 SATA-15
Baker, Norma Jean 1926-1962 Obituary 113
Baker, Oleda 1934- 69-72
Baker, Paul R(aymond) 1927- CANR-19
Earlier sketches in CA 11-12R, CANR-4
Baker, Paul T(hornell) 1927- 33-36R
Baker, Pauline H(alpern) 1941- 105
Baker, Pearl Biddlecome 1907- 17-18R
Baker, Peter (Gorton) 1926- CANR-10
Earlier sketch in CA 23-24R
Baker, Philip John Noel
See Noel-Baker, Philip John
Baker, R(onald) J(ames) 1924- 33-36R
Baker, R. R.
See Baker, R(eginald) Robin
Baker, R(eginald) Robin 1944- 110
Baker, Rachel 1904-1978 5-6R
Obituary 103
See also SATA 2, 26
Baker, Ray Stannard 1870-1946
Brief entry 118
Baker, Richard M., Jr. 1924- 15-16R
Baker, Richard St. Barbe 1889-1982 CAP-1
Obituary 110
Earlier sketch in CA 11-12
Baker, Richard Terrill 1913-1981 3R
Obituary 104
Baker, Robert Allen, Jr. 1921- 108
Baker, Robert Andrew 1910- 109
Baker, Robert B(ernard) 1937- CANR-6
Earlier sketch in CA 53-56
Baker, Robert D(onald) 1927- 121
Baker, Robert G. 1928- 85-88
Baker, Robert J(unior) 1920- 116
Baker, Robert K(erry) 1948- 108
Baker, Robin
See Baker, R(eginald) Robin
Baker, Robin Campbell 1941- 17-18R
Baker, (John) Roger 1934- 25-28R
Baker, Rollin H(arold) 1916- 118
Baker, Ronald L(ee) 1937- 105
Baker, Ross K(enneth) 1938- 29-32R
Baker, Russell (Wayne) 1925- CANR-11
Earlier sketch in CA 57-60
See also CLC 31
Baker, Samm Sinclair 1909- CANR-21
Earlier sketches in CA 5-6R, CANR-3
See also SATA 12
Baker, Scott (MacMartin) 1947- 93-96
Baker, Sharon 1938- 117
Baker, Sheridan (Warner, Jr.) 1918- CANR-18
Earlier sketches in CA 7-8R, CANR-2
Baker, Stephen 1921- CANR-19
Earlier sketches in CA 1R, CANR-3
Baker, Susan (Catherine) 1942- 105
See also SATA 29
Baker, T(homas) F(rancis) Timothy
1935- 25-28R
Baker, T(homas) Lindsay 1947- 121
Baker, Thomas George Adames 1920- 108
Baker, Thomas Harrison 1933- 33-36R
Baker, Victor Richard 1945- 109
Baker, Wesley C. 23-24R
Baker, William Avery 1911- CANR-2
Earlier sketch in CA 7-8R
Baker, William D. 1924- 105
Baker, William E(dwin) 1935- 23-24R
Baker, William Howard
See McNeilly, Wilfred Glassford
Baker, William Joseph 1938- CANR-24
Earlier sketch in CA 97-100
Baker, William W(allace) 1921- 73-76
Baker-Carr, Janet 1934- 93-96
Baker White, John 1902- 101
Bakewell, K(enneth) G(raham) B(artlett)
1931- CANR-19
Earlier sketch in CA 102
Bakewell, Paul, Jr. 1889-1972 CAP-1
Earlier sketch in CA 11-12
Bakewell, Peter J(ohn) 1943- 119
Bakhtiar, Laleh Mehree 1938- 69-72
Bakhtin, Mikhail (Mikhailovich) 1895-1975
Obituary 113
Bakish, David (Joseph) 1937- 45-48
Bakjian, Andy 1915- 53-56
Bakke, E(dward) Wight 1903-1971
Obituary 110
Bakke, Mary S(terling) 1904-1987 37-40R
Obituary 121
Bakken, Dick 1941- 106
Bakken, Henry Harrison 1896- CANR-11
Earlier sketch in CA 65-68
Bakker, Cornelius B(ernardus) 1929- 57-60

Bakker, Elna S(undquist) 1921- 69-72
Bakker-Rabdau, Marianne K(atherine)
1935- 73-76
Baklanoff, Eric N. 1925- CANR-13
Earlier sketch in CA 33-36R
Bakr el Toure, Askia Muhammad Abu
See Toure, Askia Muhammad Abu Bakr el
Bakshi, Ralph 1938(?)- Brief entry 112
See also CLC 26
Bakshian, Aram 1944- 102
Bakula, William J(ohn), Jr. 1936- 49-52
Bakwin, Harry 1894-1973 .... CAP-2
Obituary 45-48
Earlier sketch in CA 19-20
Bakwin, Ruth Morris 1898- 19-20R
Balaam
See Lamb, G(eoffrey) F(rederick)
Balaam, David N(orman) 1950- 112
Balaban, John B. 1943- CANR-12
Earlier sketch in CA 65-68
Balabkins, Nicholas (W.) 1926- 11-12R
Balachandran, M(adhavarao) 1938- 102
Balachandran, Sarojini 1934- CANR-18
Earlier sketch in CA 102
Balagura, Saul 1943- 81-84
Balakian, Nona 1919- 85-88
Balakian, Peter 1951- 102
Balanchine, George 1904-1983 111
Obituary 109
Balancy, Pierre Guy Girald 1924-1979
Obituary 89-92
Balandier, Georges (Leon) 1920- CANR-8
Earlier sketch in CA 61-64
Balas, David L(aszlo) 1929- 33-36R
Balaskas, Arthur 1940- 103
Balaskas, Janet (Marion) 1946- 117
Balassa, Bela 1928- CANR-3
Earlier sketch in CA 1R
Balawyder, Aloysius 1924- CANR-15
Earlier sketch in CA 41-44R
Balbontin, Jose Antonio 1893- CAP-1
Earlier sketch in CA 11-12
Balbus
See Huxley, Julian (Sorell)
Balch, Glenn 1902- CANR-3
Earlier sketch in CA 3R
See also SATA 3
Balchen, Bernt 1899-1973 Obituary 45-48
Balchin, John Frederick 1937- 122
Balchin, Nigel (Marlin) 1908-1970 .... CANR-21
Obituary 29-32R
Earlier sketch in CA 97-100
Balchin, W(illiam) G(eorge) V(ictor)
1916- CANR-18
Earlier sketch in CA 101
Balcomb, Raymond E. 1923- 23-24R
Balcon, Michael 1896-1977 77-80
Obituary 73-76
Bald, F(rederick) Clever 1897-1970 .... CAP-1
Earlier sketch in CA 13-14
Bald, R(obert) C(ecil) 1901-1965 .... CANR-6
Earlier sketch in CA 5-6R
Bald, Wambly 1902- DLB-4
Baldanza, Frank 1924- 3R
Baldelli, Giovanni 1914- 45-48
Balderson, Margaret 25-28R
Balderston, Frederick E(mery) 1923-
Brief entry 112
Balderston, John L.
See Balderston, John Lloyd
Balderston, John Lloyd 1889-1954
Brief entry 121
See also DLB 26
Balderston, Katharine Canby 1895-1979
Obituary 93-96
Baldick, Robert 1927-1972 Obituary 89-92
Baldinger, Stanley 1932- 29-32R
Baldinger, Wallace S(pencer) 1905- 3R
Baldree, J(asper) Martin, Jr. 1927- 53-56
Baldridge, Cyrus LeRoy 1889- SATA-29
Baldridge, Mary Humphrey 1937- 114
Baldrige, Letitia (Katherine) CANR-17
Earlier sketch in CA 25-28R
Baldry, Harold (Caparne) 1907- 19-20R
Balducci, Carolyn (Feleppa) 1946- 33-36R
See also SATA 5
Balducci, Ernesto 1922- CANR-12
Earlier sketch in CA 29-32R
Baldwin, Alex
See Butterworth, W(illiam) E(dmund III)
Baldwin, Anne Norris 1938- 29-32R
See also SATA 5
Baldwin, Arthur W. 1904(?)-1976
Obituary 69-72
Baldwin, Bates
See Jennings, John (Edward, Jr.)
Baldwin, Billy
See Baldwin, William, Jr.
Baldwin, Christina 1946- CANR-13
Earlier sketch in CA 77-80
Baldwin, Clara 61-64
See also SATA 11
Baldwin, David A. 1936- 19-20R
Baldwin, Dick
See Raborg, Frederick A(shton), Jr.
Baldwin, Ed(ward A.) 1935- 118
Baldwin, Edward R(obinson) 1935- CANR-21
Earlier sketch in CA 45-48
Baldwin, Faith 1893-1978 .... CANR-4
Obituary 77-80
Earlier sketch in CA 7-8R
See also AITN 1
Baldwin, Gordo
See Baldwin, Gordon C.
Baldwin, Gordon C. 1908- CANR-3
Earlier sketch in CA 4R
See also SATA 12
Baldwin, Hanson W(eightman) 1903- 61-64
Baldwin, James 1841-1925 Brief entry 111
See also SATA 24
Baldwin, James (Arthur) 1924-1987 .... CANR-24
Obituary 124
Earlier sketches in CA 3R, CANR-3
See also CABS 1
See also SATA 9
See also DLB 2, 7, 33
See also CDALB 1941-1968
See also CLC 1, 2, 3, 4, 5, 8, 13, 15,
17, 42
Baldwin, John D. 1930- 101
Baldwin, John W(esley) 1929- 105
Baldwin, Joseph B(urkette) 1918- 111
Baldwin, Joseph Glover 1815-1864 .... DLB-3, 11
Baldwin, Joyce G(ertrude) 1921- CANR-8
Earlier sketch in CA 61-64
Baldwin, Leland D(ewitt) 1897-1981 .... 41-44R
Obituary 103
Baldwin, Margaret
See Weis, Margaret (Edith)
Baldwin, Marshall W(hithed) 1903-1975 61-64
Obituary 57-60
Baldwin, Michael 1930- CANR-3
Earlier sketch in CA 9-10R
Baldwin, Monica 1896(?)-1975 Obituary 104
Baldwin, Ned
See Baldwin, Edward R(obinson)
Baldwin, Raymond Earl 1893-1986
Obituary 121
Baldwin, Rebecca
See Chappell, Helen
Baldwin, Richard S(heridan) 1910- 105
Baldwin, Robert E(dward) 1924- 41-44R
Baldwin, Roger (Nash) 1884-1981
Obituary 105
Baldwin, Roger E(dwin) 1929- 49-52
Baldwin, Stan(ley C.) 1929- CANR-17
Earlier sketches in CA 49-52, CANR-2
See also SATA 28
Baldwin, William, Jr. 1903-1983 Obituary 111
Baldwin, William Lee 1928- CANR-3
Earlier sketch in CA 1R
Bale, Robert Osborne 1912- 1R
Bales, Carol Ann 1940- 45-48
See also SATA 29
Bales, Jack
See Bales, James E(dward)
Bales, James D(avid) 1915- 5-6R
Bales, James E(dward) 1951- 107
Bales, Robert F(reed) 1916- 93-96
Bales, William Alan 1917- 7-8R
Balet, Jan (Bernard) 1913- 85-88
See also SATA 11
Baley, James A. 1918- CANR-5
Earlier sketch in CA 15-16R
Balfort, Neil
See Fanthorpe, R(obert) Lionel
Balfour, A. J.
See Balfour, Arthur James
Balfour, Arthur J.
See Balfour, Arthur James
Balfour, Arthur James 1848-1930
Brief entry 120
Balfour, Conrad George 1928- 53-56
Balfour, Henry H(allowell), Jr. 1940- 117
Balfour, James 1925- 25-28R
Balfour, John
See Moore, James
Balfour, Michael (Leonard) Graham
1908- CANR-6
Earlier sketch in CA 11-12R
Balfour, (John) Patrick Douglas
1904-1976 .... CANR-6
Earlier sketch in CA 9-10R
Balfour-Kinnear, George Purvis Russell
1888- 5-6R
Balian, Lorna 1929- CANR-19
Earlier sketches in CA 53-56, CANR-4
See also SATA 9
Baligh, Helmy H. 1931- 21-22R
Balikci, Asen 1929- 29-32R
Balinky, Alexander 1919- 21-22R
Balint, Michael 1896-1970 .... CAP-1
Earlier sketch in CA 9-10
Balis, Andrea F. 1948- 108
Balizet, Carol 1933- 114
Baljeu, Joost 1925- 97-100
Balk, Alfred (W.) 1930- 25-28R
Balk, H(oward) Wesley 1932- Brief entry 111
Balka, Marie
See Balkany, Marie (Romoka Zelinger) de
Balkany, Marie (Romoka Zelinger) de
1930- 104
Balke, Willem 1933- 107
Balkey, Rita
See Oleyar, Rita Balkey
Balkin, Richard 1938- 77-80
Ball, B. N.
See Ball, Brian N(eville)
Ball, Brian N(eville) 1932- 33-36R
Ball, (Frederick) Clive 1941- Brief entry 114
Ball, David 1937- 65-68
Ball, Desmond (John) 1947- CANR-24
Earlier sketch in CA 106
Ball, Donald W(inston) 1934-1976 122
Obituary 110
Ball, Donna 1951- 108
Ball, Doris Bell (Collier) 1897-1987 .... CANR-18
Obituary 122
Earlier sketches in CA 4R, CANR-2
Ball, Edith L. 1905- 85-88
Ball, (Katherine) Eve(lyn) 1890-1984 122
Obituary 114
Ball, F(rederick) Carlton 1911- 17-18R
Ball, George W(ildman) 1909- 73-76
Ball, Howard 1937- CANR-17
Earlier sketch in CA 33-36R
Ball, Jane Eklund 1921- 33-36R
Ball, John (Dudley, Jr.) 1911- CANR-18
Earlier sketches in CA 7-8R, CANR-3
Ball, John C. 1924- CANR-8
Earlier sketch in CA 7-8R
Ball, John M(iller) 1923- 33-36R
Ball, Joseph H. 1905- CAP-2
Earlier sketch in CA 23-24
Ball, Larry Durwood, Sr. 1940- 123
Ball, M(ary) Margaret 1909- 25-28R
Ball, Marion J(okl) 1940- CANR-15
Earlier sketch in CA 89-92
Ball, Nicole (Janice) 1948- 112
Ball, Robert Edward 1911- 108
Ball, Robert Hamilton 1902- 11-12R
Ball, Robert M(yers) 1914- 97-100
Ball, Sylvia Patricia 1936- 57-60
Ball, Zachary
See Janas, Frankie-Lee
and Masters, Kelly R.
Ballantine, Bill
See Ballantine, William (Oliver)
Ballantine, David 1926- 115
Ballantine, John (Winthrop) 1920- 53-56
Ballantine, John
See da Cruz, Daniel, Jr.
Ballantine, Joseph W. 1890(?)-1973
Obituary 41-44R
Ballantine, Lesley Frost
See Frost, Lesley
Ballantine, Richard 1940- CANR-1
Earlier sketch in CA 45-48
Ballantine, William (Oliver) 1911- 106
Ballantyne, David (Watt) 1924- CANR-10
Earlier sketch in CA 65-68
Ballantyne, Dorothy Joan (Smith) 1922- 7-8R
Ballantyne, R(obert) M(ichael)
1825-1894 .... SATA-24
Ballantyne, Sheila 1936- 101
Ballard, Allen B(utler, Jr.) 1930- 61-64
Ballard, Charles E. 1914(?)-1987 Obituary 123
Ballard, Dean
See Wilkes-Hunter, R(ichard)
Ballard, Edward Goodwin 1910- CANR-13
Earlier sketch in CA 33-36R
Ballard, I. Edward 1909(?)-1985 Obituary 117
Ballard, J(ames) G(raham) 1930- CANR-15
Earlier sketch in CA 7-8R
See also DLB 14
See also CLC 3, 6, 14, 36
See also SSC 1
Ballard, Joan Kadey 1928- 5-6R
Ballard, K. G.
See Roth, Holly
Ballard, Lowell C(lyne) 1904-1986 .... CAP-1
Obituary 120
Earlier sketch in CA 11-12
See also SATA 12, 49
Ballard, (Charles) Martin 1929- 25-28R
See also SATA 1
Ballard, Mignon Franklin 1934- 121
See also SATA 49
Ballard, P. D.
See Ballard, (Willis) Todhunter
Ballard, Robert D(uane) 1942- 112
Ballard, (Willis) Todhunter 1903- 15-16R
Ballard, W. T.
See Ballard, (Willis) Todhunter
Ballard, Willis T.
See Ballard, (Willis) Todhunter
Ballem, John 1925- 81-84
Ballen, Roger 1950- 103
Ballentine, Rudolph 1941- 114
Baller, Warren Robert 1900- 69-72
Ballet, Arthur H(arold) 1924- Brief entry 111
Balliett, Whitney 1926- CANR-13
Earlier sketch in CA 17-18R
Ballin, Caroline 19-20R
Ballingall, James (Gordon Mackie) 1958- 117
Ballinger, Bill S.
See Ballinger, William Sanborn
Ballinger, Harry (Russell) 1892- CAP-2
Earlier sketch in CA 23-24
Ballinger, James Lawrence 1919- 17-18R
Ballinger, Louise Bowen 1909- 15-16R
Ballinger, (Violet) Margaret (Livingstone)
1894-1980 .... CANR-13
Obituary 105
Earlier sketch in CA 61-64
Ballinger, Raymond A. 1907- 7-8R
Ballinger, William A.
See McNeilly, Wilfred Glassford
Ballinger, William Sanborn 1912-1980 .... CANR-1
Obituary 97-100
Earlier sketch in CA 4R
Ballon, Robert J(ean) 1919- CANR-21
Earlier sketch in CA 45-48
Ballonoff, Paul A(lan) 1943- 57-60
Ballou, Arthur W. 1915- 25-28R
Ballou, Ellen B(artlett) 1905- CAP-2
Earlier sketch in CA 29-32
Ballowe, James 1933- CANR-12
Earlier sketch in CA 29-32R
Ballstadt, Carl A. 1931- 124
Balma, Michael J(ames) 1930- 19-20R
Balmain, Pierre (Alexandre) 1914-1982
Obituary 107
Balme, Maurice (George) 1925- 61-64
Balmer, Edwin 1883-1959 Brief entry 114
Balmont, Konstantin (Dmitriyevich)
1867-1943 Brief entry 109
See also TCLC 11
Balmuth, Miriam S. 124
Balogh, Penelope 1916-1975 .... CAP-2
Earlier sketch in CA 25-28
See also SATA 1, 34
Balogh, Thomas 1905-1985 57-60
Obituary 115
Balow, Tom 1931- 45-48
See also SATA 12
Baloyra, Enrique Antonio 1942- 111
Balsdon, (John Percy Vyvian) Dacre
1901-1977 .... CANR-13
Obituary 73-76
Earlier sketch in CA 7-8R
Balsdon, J.P.V.D.
See Balsdon, (John Percy Vyvian) Dacre
Balseiro, Jose Agustin 1900- 81-84
See also AITN 1
Balsiger, David W(ayne) 1945- CANR-11
Earlier sketch in CA 61-64
Balsley, Howard L(loyd) 1913- CANR-4
Earlier sketch in CA 3R
Balsley, Irol Whitmore 1912- 15-16R
Baltake, Joe 1945- 118
Baltazar, Eulalio R. 1925- 19-20R
Baltazzi, Evan Serge 1919- 65-68
Baltensperger, Peter 1938- 115
Balterman, Marcia Ridlon 1942- 25-28R
Baltes, Paul B. 1939- 89-92
Balthasar, Hans Urs von
See von Balthasar, Hans Urs
Balthazar, Earl E(dward) 1918- 53-56
Baltz, Howard B(url) 1930- 29-32R
Baltzell, E(dward) Digby 1915- 33-36R
Baltzer, Hans (Adolf) 1900- SATA-40
Balukas, Jean 1959- Brief entry 111
Balwers, Renato
See La Barre, Weston
Baly, (Alfred) Denis 1913- 19-20R
Baly, Monica Eileen 1914- 102
Balzano, Jeanne (Koppel) 1912- 5-6R
Balzer, Richard J(ay) 1944- 45-48
Balzer, Robert Lawrence 1912- 103
Bambara, Toni Cade 1939- CANR-24
Earlier sketch in CA 29-32R
See also DLB 38
See also CLC 19
Bamber, Linda 1945- 109
Bamberger, Bernard J(acob)
1904-1980 .... CANR-6
Obituary 101
Earlier sketch in CA 13-14R
Bamberger, Carl 1902- CAP-2
Earlier sketch in CA 21-22
Bamberger, Fritz 1902-1984 Obituary 113
Bambrough, (John) Renford 1926- 61-64
Bamdad, A.
See Shamlu, Ahmad
Bamford, James 1946- 123
Bamford, Paul W(alden) 1921- 41-44R
Bamfylde, Walter
See Bevan, Tom
Bamm, Peter
See Emmrich, Curt
Bamman, Henry A. 1918- CANR-7
Earlier sketch in CA 5-6R
See also SATA 12
Ban, (Maria) Eva 1934- 73-76
Ban, Joseph D(aniel) 1926- CANR-23
Earlier sketches in CA 23-24R, CANR-8
Ban, Thomas A. 1929- CANR-10
Earlier sketch in CA 21-22R
Banani, Amin 1926- 33-36R
Banbury, Philip 1914- 102
Bance, Alan F. 1939- 111
Bancroft, Anne 1923- 57-60
Bancroft, Caroline 1900- CAP-2
Earlier sketch in CA 21-22
Bancroft, George 1800-1891 .... DLB-1, 30, 59
Bancroft, Griffing 1907- 29-32R
See also SATA 6
See also AITN 1
Bancroft, Hubert Howe 1832-1918 .... DLB-47
Bancroft, Iris (May Nelson) 1922- CANR-19
Earlier sketch in CA 102
Bancroft, Laura
See Baum, L(yman) Frank
Bancroft, Mary 1903- 118
Bancroft, Peter 1916- 41-44R
Bancroft, Robert
See Kirsch, Robert R.
Bandeira (Filho), Manuel (Carneiro de
Sousa) 1886(?)-1968 Obituary 115
Bandel, Betty 1912- 106
See also SATA 47
Bander, Edward J. 1923- CANR-5
Earlier sketch in CA 15-16R
Bandera, V(ladimir) N(icholas) 1932- 33-36R
Bandi, Hans-Georg 1920- 85-88
Bandinelli, Ranuccio Bianchi 1901(?)-1975
Obituary 53-56
Bandman, Bertram 1930- 21-22R
Bandoff, Hope
See Guthrie, Thomas Anstey
Bandura, Albert 1925- 13-14R
Bandy, (Eugene) Franklin 1914-1987 .... CANR-24
Obituary 122
Earlier sketch in CA 33-36R
Bandy, Leland A. 1935- 77-80
Bandy, Melanie 1932- 114
Bandy, W(illiam) T(homas) 1903- 37-40R
Bandy, Way 1941(?)-1986 123
Obituary 120
Bane, Mary Jo 1942- Brief entry 112
Bane, Michael 1950- 108
Banel, Joseph 1943- 45-48
Baner, Skulda Vanadis 1897-1964 .... CAP-1
Earlier sketch in CA 13-14
See also SATA 10

Banerjee, H(emendra) N(ath) 1929-
Brief entry ... 114
Banerji, Ranan B(ihari) 1928- ... CANR-11
Earlier sketch in CA 29-32R
Banet, Doris Beatrice Robinson 1925- ... 5-6R
Banfield, A(lexander) W(illiam) F(rancis)
1918- ... 61-64
Banfield, Edward C(hristie) 1916- ... 57-60
See also AITN 1
Bang, Betsy 1912- ... 102
See also SATA 37, 48
Bang, Garrett
See Bang, Molly Garrett
Bang, Molly Garrett 1943- ... 102
See also SATA 24
See also CLR 8
Bangert, Ethel E(lizabeth) 1912- ... CANR-1
Earlier sketch in CA 45-48
Bangert, William V(alentine) 1911- ... 45-48
Bangerter, Lowell A(llen) 1941- ... CANR-11
Earlier sketch in CA 69-72
Bangham, Mary Dickerson 1896- ... CAP-2
Earlier sketch in CA 23-24
Banghart, Charles K(enneth) 1910(?)-1980
Obituary ... 97-100
Banghart, Kenneth
See Banghart, Charles K(enneth)
Bangley, Bernard 1935- ... 110
Bangs, Carl (Oliver) 1922- ... CANR-7
Earlier sketch in CA 19-20R
Bangs, Carol Jane 1949- ... 114
Bangs, John Kendrick 1862-1922
Brief entry ... 110
See also DLB 11
Bangs, Lester 1949(?)-1982 Obituary ... 106
Bangs, Richard 1950- ... 122
Bangs, Robert B(abbitt) 1914- ... 37-40R
Banham, (Peter) Reyner 1922- ... 29-32R
Banis, Victor J(erome) 1937- ... 81-84
Banister, Gary L. 1948- ... 57-60
Banister, Manly (Miles) 1914- ... 41-44R
Banister, Margaret 1894(?)-1977
Obituary ... 73-76
Bank, Dena Citron 1912- ... 123
Bank, Mirra 1945- ... 102
Bank, Stephen Paul 1941- ... 110
Bank, Ted
See Bank, Theodore P(aul) II
Bank, Theodore P(aul) II 1923- ... 41-44R
Bank-Jensen, Thea
See Ottesen, Thea Tauber
Bankoff, George Alexis
See Milkomane, George Alexis
Milkomanovich
Bankowsky, Richard James 1928- ... 1R
Banks, Ann 1943- ... 105
Banks, Arthur S. 1926- ... 33-36R
Banks, Carolyn 1941- ... CANR-23
Earlier sketch in CA 105
Banks, Hal N(orman) 1921- ... 102
Banks, Harlan Parker 1913- ... 89-92
Banks, Iain (Menzies) 1954- Brief entry ... 123
See also CLC 34
Banks, J(ohn) Houston 1911- ... 33-36R
Banks, James A(lbert) 1941- ... CANR-13
Earlier sketch in CA 33-36R
Banks, James Houston 1925- ... 89-92
Banks, Jane 1913- ... 65-68
Banks, Jimmy
See Banks, James Houston
Banks, Laura Stockton Voorhees
1908(?)-1980 Obituary ... 101
See also SATA 23
Banks, Lynne Reid
See Reid Banks, Lynne
See also CLC 23
Banks, Oliver 1941- ... 107
Banks, Richard L. 1920- ... 11-12R
Banks, Roger 1929- ... 107
Banks, Ronald F(illmore) 1934- ... 29-32R
Banks, Russell 1940- ... CANR-19
Earlier sketch in CA 65-68
See also CLC 37
Banks, Sara (Jeanne Gordon Harrell)
See Harrell, Sara (Jeanne) Gordon
See also SATA 26
Banks, Taylor
See Banks, Jane
Banks, William L(ove) 1928- ... 112
Bankson, Douglas (Henneck) 1920- ... 45-48
Bankwitz, Philip Charles Farwell 1924- ... 33-36R
Banner, Angela
See Maddison, Angela Mary
Banner, Charla Ann Leibenguth 1942- .. CANR-24
Earlier sketch in CA 106
Banner, Hubert Stewart 1891-1964 ... CAP-1
Earlier sketch in CA 11-12
Banner, James M(orrill), Jr. 1935- ... 49-52
Banner, Lois W(endland) 1939- ... CANR-1
Earlier sketch in CA 49-52
Banner, Melvin Edward 1914- ... 53-56
Banner, William Augustus 1915- ... 45-48
Bannerman, Helen (Brodie Cowan Watson)
1863(?)-1946 Brief entry ... 111
See also SATA 19
Bannerman, Mark
See Lewing, Anthony Charles
Bannerman, Roland
See Hartston, W(illiam) R(oland)
Bannerman, W. Mary 1894-1984 Obituary .. 114
Bannick, Nancy (Meredith) 1926- ... 41-44R
Banning, Evelyn I. 1903- ... 73-76
See also SATA 36
Banning, Lance (Gilbert) 1942- ... 89-92
Banning, Margaret Culkin 1891-1982 ... CANR-4
Obituary ... 105
Earlier sketch in CA 5-6R
Bannister, Don
See Bannister, Donald
Bannister, Donald 1928- ... CANR-9
Earlier sketch in CA 61-64
Bannister, Jo 1951- ... 119
Bannister, Pat
See Davis, Lou Ellen
Bannister, Patricia V. 1923- Brief entry ... 115
Bannister, Robert C(orwin), Jr. 1935- ... 23-24R
Bannister, Sally
See Pratt, James Norwood
Bannock, Graham 1932- ... 33-36R
Bannon, Barbara Anne 1928- ... 101
Bannon, John Francis 1905-1986 ... CANR-4
Obituary ... 119
Earlier sketch in CA 1R
Bannon, Laura ?-1963 ... 3R
See also SATA 6
Bannon, Peter
See Durst, Paul
Banta, Martha 1928- ... 81-84
Banta, R(ichard) E(lwell) 1904- ... CAP-2
Earlier sketch in CA 33-36
Bantel, Linda 1943- ... 113
Banting, Peter M(yles) 1936- ... 112
Bantock, G(eoffrey) H(erman) 1914- ... CANR-11
Earlier sketch in CA 25-28R
Bantock, Gavin (Marcus August) 1939- ... 33-36R
Banton, Coy
See Norwood, Victor G(eorge) C(harles)
Banton, Michael (Parker) 1926- ... CANR-2
Earlier sketch in CA 7-8R
Banville, John 1945- Brief entry ... 117
See also DLB 14
See also CLC 46
Banville, Thomas G(eorge) 1924- ... 81-84
Bany, Mary A. 1913- ... 11-12R
Banz, George 1928- ... 29-32R
Banziger, Hans
See Baenziger, Hans
Bapu
See Khare, Narayan Bhaskar
Barabas, Steven 1904-1983 ... 5-6R
Obituary ... 109
Barach, Alvan L(eroy) 1895-1977
Obituary ... 73-76
Barach, Arnold B(auer) 1913-1987 ... 97-100
Obituary ... 122
Barack, Nathan A. 1913- ... 15-16R
Barackman, Floyd Hays, Jr. 1923- ... 115
Barackman, Paul F(reeman) 1894- ... 1R
Baracks, Barbara 1951- ... 106
Barada, Bill
See Barada, William Richard
Barada, William Richard 1913- ... 45-48
Bar-Adon, Aaron 1923- Brief entry ... 114
Baraheni, Reza 1935- ... 69-72
Barak, Gregg 1948- ... 114
Barak, Michael
See Bar-Zohar, Michael
Baraka, Imamu Amiri
See Jones, (Everett) LeRoi
See also DLB 5, 7, 16, 38
See also CDALB 1941-1968
See also CLC 1, 2, 3, 5, 10, 14, 33
Baral, Robert 1910- ... CAP-1
Earlier sketch in CA 9-10
Baram, Phillip J(ason) 1938- ... 85-88
Baram, Robert 1919- Brief entry ... 112
Baran, Annette 1927- Brief entry ... 114
Baranet, Nancy Neiman 1933- ... 41-44R
Baranov, Alexander A. 1931(?)-1983
Obituary ... 109
Baranson, Jack 1924- ... 119
Barany, George 1922- ... 25-28R
Barasch, Frances K. 1928- ... 37-40R
Barasch, Marc Ian 1949- ... 113
Barasch, Moshe 1920- ... 97-100
Barash, Meyer 1916- ... 1R
Barash, Samuel T(heodore) 1921- ... 107
Barba, Harry 1922- ... CANR-1
Earlier sketch in CA 1R
Barbach, Lonnie (Villoldo) 1946- ... CANR-9
Earlier sketch in CA 61-64
Barbanell, Maurice 1902-1981 Obituary ... 113
Barbara, Dominick A. 1914- ... 37-40R
Barbare, Rholf
See Volkoff, Vladimir
Barbary, James
See Beeching, Jack
Barbash, Jack 1910- ... CANR-16
Earlier sketch in CA 4R
Barbe, Walter Burke 1926- ... 15-16R
See also SATA 45
Barbeau, Arthur E(dward) 1936- ... 49-52
Barbeau, Clayton C(harles) 1930- ... 73-76
Barbeau, Marius 1883-1969 Obituary ... 25-28R
Barbee, David E(dwin) 1936- ... 57-60
Barbee, Phillips
See Sheckley, Robert
Barbellion, W. N. P.
See Cummings, Bruce F(rederick)
See also TCLC 24
Barber, Antonia
See Anthony, Barbara
Barber, Benjamin R. 1939- ... CANR-12
Earlier sketch in CA 29-32R
Barber, Bernard 1918- ... CANR-14
Earlier sketch in CA 65-68
Barber, Charles (Laurence) 1915- ... CANR-22
Earlier sketches in CA 17-18R, CANR-7
Barber, Cyril J(ohn) 1934- ... CANR-9
Earlier sketch in CA 65-68
Barber, D(ulan) F(riar Whilberton)
1940- ... CANR-21
Earlier sketch in CA 61-64
Barber, James David 1930- ... CANR-6
Earlier sketch in CA 15-16R
Barber, James G(eoffrey) 1952- ... 110
Barber, Jesse 1893-1979 Obituary ... 85-88
Barber, John Warner 1798-1885 ... DLB-30
Barber, Joseph 1909-1982 Obituary ... 107
Barber, Lucie W(elles) 1922- ... 108
Barber, Lucy L(ombardi) 1882(?)-1974
Obituary ... 49-52
Barber, Lynda
See Graham-Barber, Lynda
Barber, Lynda Graham
See Graham-Barber, Lynda
Barber, Lynn 1944- ... 97-100
Barber, Noel (John Lysberg) 1909-
Brief entry ... 115
Barber, Philip W. 1903-1981 Obituary ... 103
Barber, Red
See Barber, Walter Lanier
Barber, Richard (William) 1941- ... CANR-13
Earlier sketch in CA 33-36R
See also SATA 35
Barber, Richard J. 1932- ... 29-32R
Barber, Samuel 1910-1981 Obituary ... 103
Barber, Stephen Guy 1921-1980 ... 69-72
Obituary ... 97-100
Barber, T(heodore) X(enophon) 1927- ... 41-44R
Barber, Walter Lanier 1908- Brief entry ... 113
Barber, Willard F(oster) 1909- ... CAP-2
Earlier sketch in CA 21-22
Barber, William Henry 1918- ... 7-8R
Barber, William Joseph 1925- ... CANR-8
Earlier sketch in CA 61-64
Barbera, Henry 1929- ... 105
Barbera, Jack 1945- ... 110
See also CLC 44
Barberis
See Barberis, Franco
Barberis, Franco 1905- ... 25-28R
Barbero, Yves Regis Francois 1943- ... 57-60
Barbet, Pierre
See Avice, Claude (Pierre Marie)
Barbette, Jay
See Spicer, Bart
Barbotin, Edmond 1920- ... 57-60
Barbour, Alan G. 1933- Brief entry ... 117
Barbour, Arthur Joseph 1926- ... 57-60
Barbour, Brian M(ichael) 1943- ... 49-52
Barbour, Douglas (Fleming) 1940- ... CANR-11
Earlier sketch in CA 69-72
Barbour, Frances Martha 1895- ... 17-18R
Barbour, George 1890-1977 Obituary ... 73-76
Barbour, Hugh (Stewart) 1921- ... 23-24R
Barbour, Ian G(raeme) 1923- ... CANR-8
Earlier sketch in CA 21-22R
Barbour, J(ames) Murray 1897-1970 ... CAP-1
Earlier sketch in CA 11-12
Barbour, Kenneth Michael 1921- ... CANR-7
Earlier sketch in CA 7-8R
Barbour, Michael G(eorge) 1942- ... CANR-2
Earlier sketch in CA 49-52
Barbour, Nevill 1895-1972 ... 7-8R
Obituary ... 103
Barbour, Philip L(emont) 1898- ... 11-12R
Barbour, Ralph Henry 1870-1944 ... SATA-16
See also DLB 22
Barbour, Roger W(illiam) 1919- ... 61-64
Barbour, Russell B. 1906- ... CAP-2
Earlier sketch in CA 23-24
Barbour, Ruth P(eeling) 1924- ... 89-92
Barbour, Thomas L.
See Lesure, Thomas B(arbour)
Barbrook, Alec
See Barbrook, Alexander Thomas
Barbrook, Alexander Thomas 1927- ... 45-48
Barbusse, Henri 1873-1935 Brief entry ... 105
See also DLB 65
See also TCLC 5
Barchek, James Robert 1935- ... 41-44R
Barchilon, Jacques 1923- ... CANR-5
Earlier sketch in CA 13-14R
Barchus, Agnes J(osephine) 1893- ... 97-100
Barcia, Jose Rubia
See Rubia Barcia, Jose
Barck, Oscar Theodore, Jr. 1902- ... 21-22R
Barclay, Andrew M(ichael) 1941- ... 113
Barclay, Ann
See Greig, Maysie
Barclay, Barbara 1938- ... 29-32R
Barclay, Bill
See Moorcock, Michael (John)
Barclay, Cyril Nelson 1896- ... 7-8R
Barclay, Glen St. J(ohn) 1930- ... 77-80
Barclay, Harold B. 1924- ... 41-44R
Barclay, Hartley Wade 1903-1978 ... 85-88
Obituary ... 81-84
Barclay, Isabel
See Dobell, I(sabel) M(arian) B(arclay)
Barclay, Oliver R(ainsford) 1919- ... CANR-8
Earlier sketch in CA 57-60
Barclay, Virginia
See McDonnell, Virginia B(leecker)
Barclay, William 1907-1978 ... 77-80
Obituary ... 73-76
Barclay, William Ewert
See Moorcock, Michael (John)
Barcus, James E(dgar) 1938- ... 23-24R
Barcus, Nancy B(idwell) 1937- ... 117
Barcynski, Leon Roger 1949- ... CANR-10
Earlier sketch in CA 93-96
Barcynski, Vivian G(odfrey) 1917- ... CANR-10
Earlier sketch in CA 61-64
Bard, Bernard 1927- ... 25-28R
Bard, Harry 1906-1976 ... 33-36R
Bard, James (Alan) 1925- ... 103
Bard, Morton 1924- ... 97-100
Bard, Patti 1935- ... 21-22R
Bard, Rachel 1921- ... 117
Bardach, John E(ugene) 1915- ... 41-44R
Bardarson, Hjalmar R(oegnvaldur) 1918- .. 57-60
Barden, Leonard (William) 1929- ... CANR-2
Earlier sketch in CA 3R
Bardens, Amey E. 1894(?)-1974
Obituary ... 53-56
Bardens, Dennis (Conrad) 1911- ... 7-8R
Bardi, Pietro Maria 1900- ... CANR-19
Earlier sketch in CA 85-88
Bardin, John Franklin 1916-1981 ... 81-84
Obituary ... 104
Bardis, Panos D(emetrios) 1924- ... CANR-10
Earlier sketch in CA 25-28R
Bard of Avondale
See Jacobs, Howard
Bardolph, Richard 1915- ... 61-64
Bardon, Edward J(ohn) 1933- ... 81-84
Bardon, Jack Irving 1925- ... 101
Bardos, Marie (Dupuis) 1935- ... 13-14R
Bardot, Louis 1896-1975 Obituary ... 61-64
Bardsley, Cuthbert K(illick) N(orman)
1907- ... CAP-2
Earlier sketch in CA 25-28
Bardwell, George E(ldred) 1924- ... 3R
Bardwick, Judith M(arcia) 1933- ... CANR-19
Earlier sketch in CA 103
Bare, Arnold Edwin 1920- ... SATA-16
Bare, Colleen Stanley ... 102
See also SATA 32
Barea, Arturo 1897-1957 Brief entry ... 111
See also TCLC 14
Bareham, Terence 1937- ... 109
Barell, John 1938- ... 111
Barendrecht, Cor W(illiam) 1934- ... 114
Baretski, Charles Allan 1918- ... 77-80
Barfield, (Arthur) Owen 1898- ... CANR-2
Earlier sketch in CA 7-8R
Barfoot, Audrey Ilma 1918-1964 ... 7-8R
Barfoot, Joan 1946- ... 105
See also CLC 18
Barford, Carol 1931- ... 89-92
Barford, Philip (Trevelyan) 1925- ... 93-96
Bargad, Warren 1940- ... 122
Bargar, B(radley) D(uffee) 1924- ... 19-20R
Bargate, Verity 1941(?)-1981 Obituary ... 103
Bargebuhr, Frederick P(erez) 1904- ... CAP-2
Earlier sketch in CA 33-36
Bargellini, Piero 1897-1980(?) Obituary .. 97-100
Barger, Harold 1907- ... CAP-2
Earlier sketch in CA 19-20
Barger, James (David) 1947- ... 57-60
Bar-Hillel, Yehoshua 1915-1975 Obituary ... 115
Baring, Arnulf Martin 1932- ... 41-44R
Baring, Maurice 1874-1945 Brief entry ... 105
See also DLB 34
See also TCLC 8
Baringer, William E(ldon) 1909- ... 1R
Baring-Gould, William Stuart 1913-1967
Obituary ... 25-28R
Barish, Jonas A. 1922- ... 23-24R
Barish, Matthew 1907- ... 57-60
See also SATA 12
Baritz, Loren 1928- ... 15-16R
Barjavel, Rene (Gustave Henri) 1911-
Brief entry ... 107
Bark, Dennis L(aistner) 1942- ... 117
Bark, William (Carroll) 1908- ... CAP-1
Earlier sketch in CA 13-14
Barkalow, Frederick Schenck, Jr. 1914- ... 61-64
Barkan, Elliott Robert 1940- ... 23-24R
Barkan, Leonard 1944- ... 122
Brief entry ... 116
Barkas, J. L. 1948- ... 57-60
Barkas, Janet
See Barkas, J. L.
Barkdoll, Robert S. 1913(?)-1984
Obituary ... 112
Barkee, Asouff
See Strung, Norman
Barker, A(rthur) J(ames) 1918-1981 ... CANR-7
Obituary ... 104
Earlier sketch in CA 15-16R
Barker, A(udrey) L(ilian) 1918- ... CANR-3
Earlier sketch in CA 11-12R
See also DLB 14
Barker, A(nthony) W(ilhelm) 1930- ... 113
Barker, Albert W. 1900- ... CANR-14
Earlier sketch in CA 73-76
See also SATA 8
Barker, Bill
See Barker, William J(ohn)
Barker, Carol (Minturn) 1938- ... 107
See also SATA 31
Barker, Carol M. 1942- ... 45-48
Barker, Charles Albro 1904- ... 93-96
Barker, Charles M., Jr. 1926- ... 15-16R
Barker, Cicely Mary 1895-1973 ... 121
Obituary ... 117
See also SATA 39, 49
Barker, Clive 1952- Brief entry ... 121
Barker, D(erek) R(oland) 1930- ... 7-8R
Barker, Dennis (Malcolm) 1929- ... CANR-14
Earlier sketch in CA 25-28R
Barker, Dudley 1910-1980(?) ... CANR-1
Obituary ... 102
Earlier sketch in CA 2R
Barker, E. M.
See Barker, Elsa (McCormick)
Barker, Elisabeth 1910-1986 Obituary ... 118
Barker, Elliott S(peer) 1886- ... 89-92
Barker, Elsa (McCormick) 1906- ... CAP-2
Earlier sketch in CA 17-18
Barker, Elver A. 1920- ... 25-28R
Barker, Eric 1905-1973 ... 1R
Obituary ... 41-44R

Barker, Ernest 1874-1960 ... 103
Obituary ... 93-96
Barker, Esther T(emperley) 1910- ... CANR-2
Earlier sketch in CA 49-52
Barker, Frank Granville 1923- ... CAP-1
Earlier sketch in CA 11-12
Barker, George Granville 1913- ... CANR-7
Earlier sketch in CA 9-10R
See also DLB 20
See also CLC 8
Barker, Gerard A(rthur) 1930- ... 69-72
Barker, Graham H(arold) 1949- ... 106
Barker, Harley Granville
See Granville-Barker, Harley
See also DLB 10
Barker, Howard 1946- ... 102
See also DLB 13
See also CLC 37
Barker, Jack M. 1924(?)-1985 Obituary ... 117
Barker, James Nelson 1784-1858 ... DLB-37
Barker, Jane 1652-1727(?) ... DLB-39
Barker, Jane Valentine 1930- ... CANR-11
Earlier sketch in CA 65-68
Barker, John W(alton, Jr.) 1933- ... 19-20R
Barker, Joseph 1929- ... 103
Barker, Kenneth S(tacey) 1932- ... 110
Barker, Larry L(ee) 1941- ... CANR-17
Earlier sketch in CA 81-84
Barker, M(uhammad) A(bd-Al-)R(ahman) 1929- ... 116
Barker, Melvern 1907- ... CAP-1
Earlier sketch in CA 9-10
See also SATA 11
Barker, Myrtie Lillian 1910- ... 7-8R
Barker, Nancy Nichols 1925- Brief entry ... 114
Barker, Nicolas (John) 1932- ... 102
Barker, Pat 1943- ... 122
Brief entry ... 117
See also CLC 32
Barker, Philip 1929- ... 114
Barker, Ralph 1917- ... CANR-16
Earlier sketches in CA 2R, CANR-1
Barker, Robert L(ee) 1937- ... 25-28R
Barker, Rodney (Steven) 1942- ... 45-48
Barker, Roger Garlock 1903- ... CANR-11
Earlier sketches in CA 11-12, CAP-1
Barker, Ronald 1921(?)-1976 Obituary ... 65-68
Barker, S. Omar 1894- ... CAP-2
Earlier sketch in CA 17-18
See also SATA 10
Barker, Sally
See McMurry, Sarah L.
Barker, Sebastian 1945- ... 124
Barker, Shirley Frances 1911-1965 ... 5-6R
Barker, T(heodore Cardwell) 1923- ... CANR-5
Earlier sketch in CA 13-14R
Barker, T(erence) S(narr) 1941- ... CANR-21
Earlier sketch in CA 45-48
Barker, Thomas M. 1929- ... 23-24R
Barker, W(illiam) Alan 1923- ... CANR-1
Earlier sketch in CA 3R
Barker, Will 1913-1983 ... 9-10R
Obituary ... 110
See also SATA 8
Barker, William J(ohn) ... 65-68
Barker, William P(ierson) 1927- ... 9-10R
Barker-Benfield, G(raham) J(ohn) 1941-
Brief entry ... 113
Barkhouse, Joyce 1913- ... 93-96
See also SATA 48
Barkin, Carol Brief entry ... 118
See also SATA 42
Barkin, David Peter 1942- ... 37-40R
Barkin, Kenneth D(avid) 1939- ... 41-44R
Barkin, Solomon 1907- ... 9-10R
Barkins, Evelyn (Warner) 1919- ... 29-32R
Barkley, Deanne 1931- Brief entry ... 114
Barkley, James Edward 1941- ... SATA-6
Barkley, T(heodore) M(itchell) 1934- ... 120
Barkley, Vada Lee 1919- ... 57-60
Barkman, Alma 1939- ... 114
Barkman, Paul Friesen 1921- ... 17-18R
Barkow, Al 1932- ... CANR-4
Earlier sketch in CA 53-56
Barks, Carl 1901- ... 115
See also SATA 37
Barks, Coleman (Bryan) 1937- ... CANR-12
Earlier sketch in CA 25-28R
See also DLB 5
Barksdale, E(thelbert) C(ourtland) 1944- ... 57-60
Barksdale, Hiram C(ollier) 1921- ... 11-12R
Barksdale, Richard (Kenneth) 1915- ... 49-52
Barkton, S. Rush
See Brav, Stanley R(osenbaum)
Barkun, Michael 1938- Brief entry ... 114
Barkworth, Peter (Wynn) 1929- ... 107
Barlach, Ernst 1870-1938 ... DLB-56
Barlay, Bennett
See Crossen, Kendell Foster
Barlay, Stephen 1930- ... CANR-12
Earlier sketch in CA 25-28R
Barlett, Donald L(eon) 1936- ... 115
Barley, M. W.
See Barley, Maurice Willmore
Barley, Maurice Willmore 1909- ... 122
Barlin, Anne L(ief) 1916- ... 97-100
Barling, Charles
See Barling, Muriel Vere Mant
Barling, Muriel Vere Mant 1904- ... 7-8R
Barlough, J(effrey) Ernest 1953- ... 49-52
Barlow, Claude W(illis) 1907-1976 ... CAP-2
Earlier sketch in CA 33-36
Barlow, Frank 1911- ... CANR-3
Earlier sketch in CA 9-10R
Barlow, Genevieve 1910- ... 21-22R
Barlow, J(ames) Stanley (Jr.) 1924- ... 41-44R
Barlow, James 1921-1973 ... CAP-1
Obituary ... 41-44R
Earlier sketch in CA 13-14
Barlow, Jane 1857-1917 Brief entry ... 115
Barlow, Joel 1754-1812 ... DLB-37
Barlow, John A(lfred) 1924- ... 21-22R
Barlow, John D(enison) 1934- ... 120
Barlow, Judith E(llen) 1946- ... 107
Barlow, (Emma) Nora 1885- ... CAP-2
Earlier sketch in CA 25-28
Barlow, Robert O.
See Meyer, Heinrich
Barlow, Roger
See Leckie, Robert (Hugh)
Barlow, Samuel L(atham) M(itchell) 1892-1982 Obituary ... 107
Barlow, Sanna Morrison
See Rossi, Sanna Morrison Barlow
Barlow, T(homas) Edward 1931- ... CANR-3
Earlier sketch in CA 45-48
Barlow, Wilfred 1915- ... 101
Barlowe, Raleigh 1914- ... 19-20R
Barltrop, Robert 1922- ... CANR-19
Earlier sketch in CA 73-76
Barman, Alicerose 1919- ... 65-68
Barman, Charles R(oy) 1945- ... 106
Barmann, Lawrence Francis 1932- ... 9-10R
Barmash, Isadore 1921- ... CANR-17
Earlier sketches in CA 45-48, CANR-1
Barna, George 1954- ... 114
Barna, Yon 1927- ... 53-56
Barnabas
See Blandford, Brian E(rnest)
Barnabas
See West, Charles Converse
Barnaby, (Charles) Frank 1927- ... CANR-13
Earlier sketch in CA 33-36R
Barnaby, Ralph S(tanton) 1893- ... 61-64
See also SATA 9
Barnard, (James) Alan 1928- ... 9-10R
Barnard, Charles N(elson III) 1924- ... CANR-1
Earlier sketch in CA 49-52
Barnard, Christiaan (Neethling) 1922- ... CANR-14
Earlier sketch in CA 61-64
Barnard, Ellsworth 1907- ... CANR-11
Earlier sketch in CA 21-22R
Barnard, F(rederick) M(echner) 1921- ... 25-28R
Barnard, Harry 1906-1982 ... CANR-3
Obituary ... 107
Earlier sketch in CA 7-8R
Barnard, Howard Clive 1884-1985 ... 85-88
Obituary ... 117
Barnard, J(ohn) Darrell 1906- ... 7-8R
Barnard, J(ohn) Lawrence 1912-1977 ... 77-80
Obituary ... 73-76
Barnard, John 1681-1770 ... DLB-24
Barnard, (Virail) John 1932- ... 33-36R
Barnard, Mary (Ethel) 1909- ... CAP-2
Earlier sketch in CA 21-22
Barnard, Robert 1936- ... CANR-20
Earlier sketch in CA 77-80
Barnard, William Dean 1942- ... 69-72
Bar-Natan, Moshe
See Louvish, Misha
Barne, Kitty
See Barne, Marion Catherine
Barne, Marion Catherine 1883-1957
Brief entry ... 112
Barner, Bob 1947- ... 93-96
See also SATA 29
Bar Ner, R.
See Brenner, Reeve R(obert)
Barnes, Adrienne Martine
See Martine-Barnes, Adrienne
Barnes, Barry 1943- ... 97-100
Barnes, Chesley Virginia
See Young, Chesley Virginia
Barnes, Clara Ernst 1895- ... 5-6R
Barnes, Clive (Alexander) 1927- ... 77-80
See also AITN 2
Barnes, Djuna 1892-1982 ... CANR-16
Obituary ... 107
Earlier sketch in CA 11-12R
See also DLB 4, 9, 45
See also CLC 3, 4, 8, 11, 29
Barnes, Douglas 1927- ... CANR-19
Earlier sketch in CA 103
Barnes, (Frank) Eric Wollencott 1907-1962 ... SATA-22
Barnes, Gregory Allen 1934- ... CANR-10
Earlier sketch in CA 25-28R
Barnes, Harry Elmer 1889-1968 ... 89-92
Obituary ... 25-28R
Barnes, Hazel E(stella) 1915- ... CANR-3
Earlier sketch in CA 5-6R
Barnes, Henry A. 1906-1968 ... CAP-1
Earlier sketch in CA 15-16
Barnes, Irston Roberts 1904-1988
Obituary ... 124
Barnes, J. 1944- ... 85-88
Barnes, J(ohn) A(rundel) 1918- ... 101
Barnes, Jack 1920- ... 89-92
Barnes, Jack 1940- ... CANR-9
Earlier sketch in CA 61-64
Barnes, James A(nderson) 1898- ... 11-12R
Barnes, James J(ohn) 1931- ... CANR-4
Earlier sketch in CA 11-12R
Barnes, James N(eil) 1944- ... 117
Barnes, Jane
See Casey, Jane Barnes
Barnes, Jim 1933- ... 108
Barnes, Joanna 1934- ... 57-60
Barnes, John 1908- ... CANR-2
Earlier sketch in CA 45-48
Barnes, (Ernest) John (Ward) 1917- ... 108
Barnes, John B(ertram) 1924- ... 33-36R
Barnes, Joseph Fels 1907-1970 Obituary ... 104
Barnes, Julian 1946- ... CANR-19
Earlier sketch in CA 102
See also CLC 42
Barnes, Kenneth Charles 1903- ... 106
Barnes, Leonard (John) 1895- ... CAP-2
Earlier sketch in CA 29-32
Barnes, Malcolm 1909(?)-1984 Obituary ... 114
See also SATA 41
Barnes, Margaret Ayer 1886-1967
Obituary ... 25-28R
See also DLB 9
Barnes, Mary 1923- ... 85-88
Barnes, Melvyn (Peter Keith) 1942- ... 122
Barnes, Patience P(lummer) 1932- ... 108
Barnes, Peter 1931- ... 65-68
See also DLB 13
See also CLC 5
Barnes, Phoebe 1908- ... CAP-2
Earlier sketch in CA 23-24
Barnes, R(ichard) G(ordon) 1932- ... 33-36R
Barnes, Ralph M(osser) 1900-1984 ... CAP-2
Obituary ... 114
Earlier sketch in CA 17-18
Barnes, Robert J(ay) 1925- ... 21-22R
Barnes, Robert M(orson) 1940- ... 45-48
Barnes, Sam(uel) G(ill) 1913- ... 15-16R
Barnes, Samuel H(enry) 1931- ... 23-24R
Barnes, Stephen Emory 1952- ... 105
Barnes, Steven
See Barnes, Stephen Emory
Barnes, Thomas Garden 1930- ... CANR-1
Earlier sketch in CA 1R
Barnes, Timothy David 1942- ... 114
Barnes, Valerie ... 115
Barnes, Viola Florence 1885- ... 3R
Barnes, Walter 1880-1969 Obituary ... 116
Barnes, William 1801-1886 ... DLB-32
Barness, Richard 1917- ... 65-68
Barnet, Richard J. ... 13-14R
Barnet, Sylvan 1926- ... CANR-4
Earlier sketch in CA 4R
Barnetson, William Denholm 1917-1981
Obituary ... 103
Barnett, A. Doak 1921- ... CANR-15
Earlier sketch in CA 5-6R
Barnett, Adam
See Fast, Julius
Barnett, Correlli (Douglas) 1927- ... CANR-15
Earlier sketch in CA 15-16R
Barnett, Franklin 1903- ... 69-72
Barnett, George L(eonard) 1915- ... 29-32R
Barnett, (Nicolas) Guy 1928- ... 19-20R
Barnett, H(omer) G(arner) 1906- ... 45-48
Barnett, Isobel (Morag) 1918-1980
Obituary ... 105
Barnett, James Monroe 1925- ... 114
Barnett, Joe R(ichard) 1933- ... 106
Barnett, L. David
See Laschever, Barnett D.
Barnett, Leo 1925- ... 29-32R
Barnett, Leonard (Palin) 1919- ... CANR-12
Earlier sketches in CA 13-14, CAP-1
Barnett, Lincoln (Kinnear) 1909-1979 ... 102
Obituary ... 89-92
See also SATA 36
Barnett, Malcolm Joel 1941- ... 45-48
Barnett, Marva T(uttle) 1913- ... 57-60
Barnett, Maurice 1917-1980 Obituary ... 97-100
Barnett, Michael 1930- ... 57-60
Barnett, Moneta 1922-1976 ... SATA-33
Barnett, Naomi 1927- ... CANR-7
Earlier sketch in CA 5-6R
See also SATA 40
Barnett, Peter Herbert 1945- ... 124
Barnett, Richard B(aity) 1941- ... 105
Barnett, Richard C(hambers) 1932- ... 33-36R
Barnett, S(amuel) A(nthony) 1915- ... CANR-6
Earlier sketch in CA 13-14R
Barnett, Suzanne Wilson 1940- ... 120
Barnett, Ursula A(nnemarie) 1924- ... 123
Barnett, Vivian E(ndicott) 1944- ... 115
Barnette, Henlee H(ulix) 1911- ... 49-52
Barnette, W(arren) Leslie, Jr. 1910- ... CAP-1
Earlier sketch in CA 11-12
Barnewall, Gordon G(ouverneur) 1924- ... 121
Barney, Harry
See Lottman, Eileen
Barney, Kenneth D. 1921- ... 69-72
Barney, Laura D(reyfus) 1880(?)-1974
Obituary ... 53-56
Barney, LeRoy 1930- ... 33-36R
Barney, Maginel Wright 1881(?)-1966
Obituary ... 111
See also SATA 32, 39
Barney, Natalie (Clifford) 1878(?)-1972
Obituary ... 33-36R
See also DLB 4
Barney, Stephen A(llen) 1942- ... 102
Barney, William L(esko) 1943- ... 41-44R
Barnhart, Clarence L(ewis) 1900- ... 13-14R
See also SATA 48
Barnhart, Joe Edward 1931- ... 41-44R
Barnhill, Myrtle Fait 1896-1986 ... CAP-1
Obituary ... 119
Earlier sketch in CA 15-16
Barnhouse, Donald ... 103
Barnhouse, Donald Grey 1895-1960 ... 123
Obituary ... 113
Barnhouse, Ruth Tiffany 1923- ... CANR-15
Earlier sketch in CA 85-88
Barnie, John 1941- ... 57-60
Barnitt, Nedda Lemmon ... 9-10R
Barnitz, Harry W. 1920-1973 ... CAP-2
Earlier sketch in CA 25-28
Barnoon, Shlomo 1940- ... 41-44R
Barnouw, Adriaan Jacob 1877-1968
Obituary ... 104
See also SATA 27
Barnouw, Erik 1908- ... CANR-12
Earlier sketch in CA 15-16R
Barnouw, Victor 1915- ... 85-88
See also SATA 28, 43
Barn Owl
See Howells, Roscoe
Barnright, Julia
See Bancroft, Iris (May Nelson)
Barns, John W(intour) B(aldwin) 1912-1974 Obituary ... 49-52
Barnsley, Alan Gabriel 1916-1986 ... 13-14R
Obituary ... 121
Barnstone, Aliki 1956- ... 105
Barnstone, Howard 1923-1987 Obituary ... 122
Barnstone, Willis 1927- ... 17-18R
See also SATA 20
Barnum, Jay Hyde 1888(?)-1962 ... SATA-20
Barnum, Richard ... CAP-2
Earlier sketch in CA 19-20
See also SATA 1
Barnum, W(illiam) Paul 1933- ... 29-32R
Barnwell, D. Robinson 1915- ... 19-20R
Barnwell, John (Gibbes, Jr.) 1947- ... 113
Barnwell, William Curtis 1943- ... 103
Baro, Gene 1924-1982 Obituary ... 112
Baroff, George Stanley 1924- ... 101
Baroja (y Nessi), Pio 1872-1956
Brief entry ... 104
See also TCLC 8
Barolini, Antonio 1910-1971 ... CANR-1
Earlier sketch in CA 2R
Barolini, Helen 1925- ... CANR-16
Earlier sketch in CA 73-76
Barolini, Teodolinda 1951- ... 124
Barolsky, Paul 1941- ... 81-84
Baron, (Joseph) Alexander 1917- ... CANR-14
Earlier sketch in CA 7-8R
Baron, David
See Pinter, Harold
Baron, Dennis E(mery) 1944- ... 110
Baron, Elizabeth Frank
See Frank-Baron, Elizabeth
Baron, Frank 1936- ... 119
Baron, Hans 1900- ... 19-20R
Baron, Herman 1941- ... 61-64
Baron, J. W.
See Krauzer, Steven M(ark)
Baron, Mary (Kelley) 1944- ... CANR-2
Earlier sketch in CA 49-52
Baron, Mikan
See Barba, Harry
Baron, Oscar 1908(?)-1976 Obituary ... 65-68
Baron, Othello
See Fanthorpe, R(obert) Lionel
Baron, Robert Alex 1920- ... 41-44R
Baron, Salo W(ittmayer) 1895- ... 69-72
Baron, Samuel H(askell) 1921- ... CANR-3
Earlier sketch in CA 11-12R
Baron, Virginia Olsen 1931- ... 25-28R
See also SATA 28, 46
Baron, (Ora) Wendy 1937- ... 41-44R
Baron Amulree
See Mackenzie, Basil William Sholto
Baron Corvo
See Rolfe, Frederick (William Serafino Austin Lewis Mary)
Barondess, Sue K(aufman) 1926-1977 ... CANR-1
Obituary ... 69-72
Earlier sketch in CA 3R
See also CLC 8
Barone, Michael 1944- ... 93-96
Baron Lloyd of Hampstead
See Lloyd, Dennis
Baron of Remenham
See Thomas, (William) Miles (Webster)
Baroody, Jamil Murad 1905-1979
Obituary ... 85-88
Barooshian, (Dickran) Vahan 1932- ... 85-88
Barr, Alfred H(amilton), Jr. 1902-1981 ... 49-52
Obituary ... 105
Barr, (Chester) Alwyn (Jr.) 1938- ... 33-36R
Barr, Anthony 1921- ... 109
Barr, Betty 1932- ... 97-100
Barr, Beverly ... 61-64
Barr, Densil Neve
See Buttrey, Douglas N(orton)
Barr, Donald 1921- ... 11-12R
See also SATA 20
Barr, Donald Roy 1938- ... 69-72
Barr, Doris W(ilson) 1923- ... 33-36R
Barr, George 1907- ... CANR-1
Earlier sketch in CA 3R
See also SATA 2
Barr, Gladys Hutchison 1904-1976 ... CANR-6
Earlier sketch in CA 1R
Barr, James 1924- ... CANR-20
Earlier sketches in CA 3R, CANR-4
Barr, Jeff 1941- ... 69-72
Barr, Jene
See Cohen, Jene Barr
See also SATA 16, 42
Barr, Jennifer 1945- ... 102
Barr, John J(ay) 1942- ... 61-64
Barr, Margaret Scolari 1901-1987
Obituary ... 124
Barr, Marleen Sandra 1953- ... 120
Barr, O(rlando) Sydney 1919- ... 15-16R
Barr, Pat(ricia Miriam) 1934- ... CANR-12
Earlier sketch in CA 23-24R
Barr, Robert R(ussell) 1931- ... 110
Barr, Stephen 1904- ... CAP-1
Earlier sketch in CA 15-16

Barr, Stringfellow 1897-1982 .... CANR-1
Obituary 106
Earlier sketch in CA 2R
Barr, Tony
See Barr, Anthony
Barr, William G. 1920(?)-1987 Obituary 121
Barraclough, Geoffrey 1908-1984 101
Obituary 114
Barraclough, Solon L(ovett) 1922- 41-44R
Barraga, Natalie Carter 1915- 41-44R
Barral, Mary-Rose 1925- 33-36R
Barranger, M(illy) S(later) 1937- CANR-12
Earlier sketch in CA 29-32R
Barratt, G. R. V.
See Barratt, Glynn (Richard V.)
Barratt, Glynn (Richard V.) 1944-
Brief entry 110
Barratt-Brown, Michael 1918- CANR-17
Earlier sketch in CA 97-100
Barrault, Jean-Louis 1910- 105
Barrax, Gerald William 1933- CANR-10
Earlier sketch in CA 65-68
See also DLB 41
Barre, Michael Lee 1943- 118
Barrell, Geoffrey Richard 1917-1983
Obituary 111
Barrell, Sarah Webb 1946(?)-1979
Obituary 89-92
Barren, Charles (MacKinnon) 1913- CANR-4
Earlier sketch in CA 11-12R
Barreno, Maria Isabel
See Martins, Maria Isabel Barreno de Faria
See also AITN 1
Barrer, Gertrude
See Barrer-Russell, Gertrude
Barrera, Mario 1939- 97-100
Barrer-Russell, Gertrude 1921- SATA-27
Barres, Oliver 1921- 13-14R
Barreto, Afonso Henrique de Lima
See Lima Barreto, Afonso Henrique de
Barrett, Anne Mainwaring (Gillett) 1911- .. CAP-2
Earlier sketch in CA 29-32
Barrett, Bob 1925- 73-76
Barrett, C(harles) Kingsley 1917- CANR-10
Earlier sketch in CA 21-22R
Barrett, C(lifton) Waller 1901- 41-44R
Barrett, Clifford L(eslie) 1894-1971
Obituary 33-36R
Barrett, Dean 1942- 69-72
Barrett, Donald N(eil) 1920- 13-14R
Barrett, Edward L(ouis), Jr. 1917- 25-28R
Barrett, Ethel SATA-44
Barrett, Eugene F(rancis) 1921- 57-60
Barrett, George W(est) 1908- 17-18R
Barrett, George W. 1913(?)-1984
Obituary 114
Barrett, Gerald Van 1936- 37-40R
Barrett, Harold 1925- 81-84
Barrett, Harry B(emister) 1922- 85-88
Barrett, Henry Charles 1923- 53-56
Barrett, Ivan J. 1910- 49-52
Barrett, J(ohn) Edward 1932- 37-40R
Barrett, James H(enry) 1906- 33-36R
Barrett, James Lee 1929- 81-84
Barrett, John Gilchrist 1921- CANR-2
Earlier sketch in CA 5-6R
Barrett, John Henry 1913- 101
Barrett, Judi
See Barrett, Judith
Barrett, Judith 1941- 103
See also SATA 26
Barrett, Laurence I(rwin) 1935- 69-72
Barrett, Leonard E(manuel) 1920- 65-68
Barrett, Linton Lomas 1904- 7-8R
Barrett, Marvin 1920- CANR-11
Earlier sketch in CA 69-72
Barrett, Mary Ellin 1927- 19-20R
Barrett, Max 81-84
Barrett, Maye
See Barrett, Max
Barrett, Michael Dennis 1947- 85-88
Barrett, N. S.
See Barrett, Norman (S.)
Barrett, Nancy Smith 1942- 37-40R
Barrett, Nathan N(oble) 1933- 17-18R
Barrett, Norman (S.) 1935- CANR-24
Earlier sketch in CA 107
Barrett, Patricia 1914-1987 ....5-6R
Obituary 121
Barrett, Paul F(rancis) 1943- 117
Barrett, Raina
See Kelly, Pauline Agnes
Barrett, Ron 1937- SATA-14
Barrett, Rona 1936- 103
See also AITN 1
Barrett, Russel H(unter) 1919- 17-18R
Barrett, Susan (Mary) 1938- Brief entry 109
Barrett, (Roger) Syd 1946- CLC-35
Barrett, Sylvia 1914- 25-28R
Barrett, Ward J. 1927- 29-32R
Barrett, William (Christopher) 1913- ... CANR-11
Earlier sketch in CA 13-14R
See also CLC 27
Barrett, William E(dmund) 1900-1986 .. CANR-22
Obituary 120
Earlier sketch in CA 7-8R
See also SATA 49
Barrett, William R. 1922(?)-1977
Obituary 73-76
Barretto, Larry
See Barretto, Laurence Brevoort
Barretto, Laurence Brevoort 1890-1971
Obituary 33-36R
Barriault, Arthur 1915(?)-1976 Obituary ...65-68
Barricelli, Jean-Pierre 1924- CANR-21
Earlier sketch in CA 105
Barrick, Mac E(ugene) 1933- 33-36R
Barrie, Alexander 1923- CANR-5
Earlier sketch in CA 4R
Barrie, Donald C(onway) 1905- 17-18R
Barrie, J(ames) M(atthew) 1860-1937
Brief entry 104
See also YABC 1
See also DLB 10
See also TCLC 2
Barrie, Jane
See Savage, Mildred (Spitz)
Barrie, Patricia 1946- 122
Barrier, (John) Michael 1940- 109
Barrier, Norman G(erald) 1940- CANR-4
Earlier sketch in CA 53-56
Barriger, John Walker 1899-1976
Obituary 69-72
Barrile, Jackie 1943- 117
Barrington, H. W.
See Brannon, William T.
Barrington, John
See Brownjohn, Alan
Barrington, Maurice
See Brogan, D(enis) W(illiam)
Barrington, Michael
See Moorcock, Michael (John)
Barrington, P. V.
See Barling, Muriel Vere Mant
Barrington, Pamela
See Barling, Muriel Vere Mant
Barrington, Thomas Joseph 1916- 104
Barrio, Raymond 1921- CANR-11
Earlier sketch in CA 25-28R
Barrio-Garay, Jose Luis 1932- 81-84
Barris, Alex 1922- 61-64
Barris, Chuck 1929- Brief entry 109
Barris, George 1925- SATA-47
Barritt, Denis P(hillips) 1914- 21-22R
Barro, Robert Joseph 1944- 97-100
Barrol, Grady
See Bograd, Larry
Barroll, John Leeds III 1928- 101
Barron, Ann Forman 69-72
Barron, Bruce 1960- 123
Barron, Charlie Nelms 1922-1977
Obituary 69-72
Barron, Ed
See Bernhardt, Clyde Edric Barron
Barron, Frank (Xavier) 1922- CANR-8
Earlier sketch in CA 5-6R
Barron, Fred 117
Barron, Gayle 1945- 109
Barron, Gloria Joan 1934- 81-84
Barron, Greg 1952- 110
Barron, Jerome A(ure) 1933- CANR-24
Earlier sketch in CA 45-48
Barron, Milton L. 1918- CANR-18
Earlier sketch in CA 1R
Barron, (Richard) Neil 1934- 102
Barrosse, Thomas 1926- 9-10R
Barrow, Andrew 1945- 97-100
Barrow, Geoffrey W(allis) S(teuart) 1924- CANR-7
Earlier sketch in CA 17-18R
Barrow, Harold M(arion) 1909- 106
Barrow, Henry 1906(?)-1985 Obituary 117
Barrow, John D(avid) 1952- 115
Barrow, Joseph Louis 1914-1981
Obituary 103
Barrow, Keith E. 1954-1983 Obituary 111
Barrow, Kenneth 1945- 119
Barrow, Leo (Lebron) 1925- Brief entry 110
Barrow, Pamela
See Howarth, Pamela
Barrow, R. H. 1894(?)-1984 Obituary 114
Barrow, Rhoda
See Lederer, Rhoda Catharine (Kitto)
Barrow, Robin 1944- CANR-10
Earlier sketch in CA 65-68
Barrow, Terence 1923- 41-44R
Barrow, Thomas C(hurchill) 1929- 23-24R
Barrow, William
See Fuller, Hoyt (William)
Barrows, Anita 1947- 49-52
Barrows, Chester L. 1892(?)-1975
Obituary 104
Barrows, (Ruth) Marjorie 1892(?)-1983 .. CAP-2
Obituary 109
Earlier sketch in CA 21-22
Barrows, R. M.
See Barrows, (Ruth) Marjorie
Barrows, Ruth
See Barrows, (Ruth) Marjorie
Barrows, Susanna Isabel 1944- 108
Barry, Anne 1940- 85-88
Barry, Colman J. 1921- 13-14R
Barry, Herbert III 1930- CANR-14
Earlier sketch in CA 37-40R
Barry, Iris 1895-1969 Obituary 104
Barry, Jack 1939- 69-72
Barry, Jackson G(ranville) 1926- 29-32R
Barry, James Donald 1926- 33-36R
Barry, James P(otvin) 1918- CANR-24
Earlier sketch in CA 37-40R
See also SATA 14
Barry, Jane (Powell) 1925- 7-8R
Barry, Jerome B(enedict) 1894-1975 .... 3R
Obituary 61-64
Barry, Jocelyn
See Bowden, Jean
Barry, John Vincent William 1903-1969 ..... 3R
Obituary 103
Barry, Joseph (Amber) 1917- CANR-14
Earlier sketch in CA 57-60
Barry, June 1925- 15-16R
Barry, Katharina Watjen 1936- 9-10R
See also SATA 4
Barry, Kevin
See Laffan, Kevin (Barry)
Barry, Lucy (Brown) 1934- 19-20R
Barry, Margaret Stuart 1927- 106
Barry, Mary J(ane) 1928- 49-52
Barry, Mike
See Malzberg, Barry N(athaniel)
Barry, Philip 1896-1949 Brief entry 109
See also DLB 7
See also TCLC 11
Barry, Raymond Walker 1894- CAP-1
Earlier sketch in CA 17-18
Barry, Robert (Everett) 1931- CANR-2
Earlier sketch in CA 5-6R
See also SATA 6
Barry, Roger Graham 1935- 102
Barry, Scott 1952- 89-92
See also SATA 32
Barry, Sebastian 1955- 117
Barry, Spranger
See Kauffmann, Stanley
Barry, Stephen P. 1948(?)-1986 123
Obituary 120
Barry, William A(nthony) 1930- 115
Barry, William David 1946- 114
Barsacq, Andre 1909-1973 Obituary 41-44R
Barsacq, Leon 1906-1969 Obituary 113
Barsby, John A. 1935- 121
Barsh, Russel Lawrence 1950- 105
Barsis, Max 1894(?)-1973 Obituary 41-44R
Barsky, Arthur 1900(?)-1982(?) Obituary ... 106
Barson, John 1936- 85-88
Barsotti, C(harles) 1933- 65-68
Barstow, Anne Llewellyn 1929- 111
Barstow, Phyllida 1937- 121
Barstow, Stan(ley) 1928- CANR-1
Earlier sketch in CA 3R
See also DLB 14
Bart, Andre Schwarz
See Schwarz-Bart, Andre
Bart, Benjamin F(ranklin) 1917- 25-28R
Bart, Lionel 1930- 65-68
Bart, Pauline B(ernice) 1930- 53-56
Bart, Peter 1932- CANR-19
Earlier sketch in CA 93-96
Bartek, E(dward) J(ohn) 1921- 37-40R
Bartel, Pauline C(hristine) 1952- 81-84
Bartel, Roland 1919- 17-18R
Bartell, Ernest 1932- 33-36R
Bartels, Robert 1913- 15-16R
Bartels, Robert A. 1923- CANR-16
Earlier sketch in CA 1R
Bartels, Susan Ludvigson
See Ludvigson, Susan
Barten, Harvey H(arold) 1933- 33-36R
Bartenbach, Jean 1918- 115
See also SATA 40
Bartenieff, Irmgard 1900(?)-1981
Obituary 105
Barter, A(lice) K(nar) 1918- 57-60
Barth, Alan 1906-1979 .... CANR-5
Obituary 104
Earlier sketch in CA 2R
Barth, Charles P. 1895- CAP-2
Earlier sketch in CA 25-28
Barth, Christoph F. 1917- 29-32R
Barth, Edna 1914-1980 ....41-44R
Obituary 102
See also SATA 7, 24
Barth, Fredrik 1928- CANR-11
Earlier sketch in CA 65-68
Barth, Gunther 1925- 103
Barth, J(ohn) Robert 1931- 29-32R
Barth, John (Simmons) 1930- CANR-23
Earlier sketches in CA 1R, CANR-5
See also CABS 1
See also DLB 2
See also CLC 1, 2, 3, 5, 7, 9, 10, 14, 27
See also AITN 1, 2
Barth, Karl 1886-1968 Obituary 25-28R
Barth, Lois
See Freihofer, Lois Diane
Barth, Markus Karl 1915- CANR-2
Earlier sketch in CA 7-8R
Barth, Peter S. 1937- 106
Barth, Richard 1943- 81-84
Barth, Roland S(awyer) 1937- CANR-1
Earlier sketch in CA 45-48
Barthel, Diane L(ee) 1949- 115
Barthel, Joan 1932- 114
Brief entry 111
Barthelme, Donald 1931- CANR-20
Earlier sketch in CA 21-22R
See also SATA 7
See also DLB 2
See also DLBY 80
See also CLC 1, 2, 3, 5, 6, 8, 13, 23, 46
Barthelme, Frederick 1943- 122
Brief entry 114
See also DLBY 85
See also CLC 36
Barthelmes, (Albert) Wes(ley, Jr.) 1922-1976 69-72
Obituary 65-68
Barthes, Roland 1915-1980 Obituary 97-100
See also CLC 24
Bartholomay, Julia A. 1923- 45-48
Bartholomew, Barbara 1941- Brief entry 118
See also SATA 42
Bartholomew, Bart
See Bartholomew, Frank H.
Bartholomew, Cecilia 1907- CAP-1
Earlier sketch in CA 13-14
Bartholomew, Ed(ward Ellsworth) 1914- ..25-28R
Bartholomew, Frank H. 1898-1985
Obituary 115
Bartholomew, Jean
See Beatty, Patricia Robbins
Bartholomew, John Eric
See Morecambe, Eric
Bartholomew, Paul C(harles) 1907-1975 .... CANR-10
Earlier sketch in CA 17-18R
Bartier, Pierre 1945- 23-24R
Bartlett, Amy 1949- 124
Bartlett, Basil Hardington 1905-1985
Obituary 115
Bartlett, Bruce R(eeves) 1951- CANR-19
Earlier sketch in CA 89-92
Bartlett, C(hristopher) J(ohn) 1931- 17-18R
Bartlett, Charles (Leffingwell) 1921- 29-32R
Bartlett, David
See Mason, Madeline
Bartlett, Donald L. Brief entry 110
Bartlett, Elizabeth (Winters) CANR-9
Earlier sketch in CA 17-18R
Bartlett, Elsa Jaffe 1935- CANR-15
Earlier sketch in CA 33-36R
Bartlett, Eric George 1920- CANR-19
Earlier sketches in CA 7-8R, CANR-2
Bartlett, F. C.
See Bartlett, Frederic Charles
Bartlett, Frederic Charles 1886-1969
Obituary 115
Bartlett, Gerald (Robert) 1935- 21-22R
Bartlett, Harriett M(oulton) 1897-1987
Obituary 121
Bartlett, Hubert Moyse
See Moyse-Bartlett, Hubert
Bartlett, Irving H(enry) 1923- CANR-9
Earlier sketch in CA 23-24R
Bartlett, Jean Anne 1927- 97-100
Bartlett, John 1820-1905 .... DLB-1
Bartlett, Jonathan 1931- 93-96
Bartlett, Kathleen
See Paine, Lauran (Bosworth)
Bartlett, Kim 1941- 89-92
Bartlett, Lee Anthony 1950- 114
Bartlett, Margaret Farrington 1896- CANR-5
Earlier sketch in CA 5-6R
Bartlett, Marie (Swan) 1918- 21-22R
Bartlett, Merrill L(ewis) 1939- 117
Bartlett, Nancy W(hite) 1913-1972 .... CAP-2
Obituary 41-44R
Earlier sketch in CA 23-24
Bartlett, Paul 1909- CAP-2
Earlier sketch in CA 17-18
Bartlett, Philip A. CAP-2
Earlier sketch in CA 19-20
See also SATA 1
Bartlett, Phyllis 1908(?)-1973 Obituary ...41-44R
Bartlett, Richard A(dams) 1920- CANR-2
Earlier sketch in CA 5-6R
Bartlett, Robert Merrill 1899- CANR-2
Earlier sketch in CA 5-6R
See also SATA 12
Bartlett, Robert V(irgil) 1953- CANR-22
Earlier sketch in CA 104
Bartlett, Ruhl J. 1897- CAP-1
Earlier sketch in CA 11-12
Bartlett, Ruth 19-20R
Bartlett, Vernon 1894-1983 61-64
Obituary 108
Bartley, Diana E(sther) Pelaez-Rivera 1940- 69-72
Bartley, Leigh
See Riker, Leigh
Bartley, Numan V(ache) 1934- CANR-12
Earlier sketch in CA 69-72
Bartley, Robert L(eRoy) 1937- 97-100
Bartley, William Warren III 1934- CANR-15
Earlier sketch in CA 37-40R
Bartocci, Gianni 1925- 23-24R
Bartol, Cyrus Augustus 1813-1900 ...... DLB-1
Bartole, Genevieve 1927- 101
Bartolome de Roxas, Juan
See Rubia Barcia, Jose
Barton, Allen H(oisington) 1924- CANR-10
Earlier sketch in CA 25-28R
Barton, Bruce Walter 1935- 89-92
Barton, Byron 1930- CANR-13
Earlier sketch in CA 57-60
See also SATA 9
Barton, Del 1925-1971 Obituary 103
Barton, Erle
See Fanthorpe, R(obert) Lionel
Barton, Eustace Robert 1854-1943
Brief entry 114
Barton, Fredrick (Preston) 1948- 119
Barton, H. Arnold 1929- 77-80
Barton, Harriett SATA-43
Barton, Humphrey (Douglas Elliott) 1900- CAP-2
Earlier sketch in CA 19-20
Barton, Jim Tom 123
Barton, John (Stuart) 1957- 114
Barton, John Bernard Adie 1928- 81-84
Barton, John H(ays) 1936- 111
Barton, John Mackintosh Tilney 1898- ... CAP-1
Earlier sketch in CA 17-18
Barton, Lee
See Fanthorpe, R(obert) Lionel
Barton, Lew(is Randolph) 1918- 73-76
Barton, M. Xaveria 1910- Brief entry 105
Barton, Margaret D(over) 1902- CAP-1
Earlier sketch in CA 15-16
Barton, Mary Neill 1899- CAP-2
Earlier sketch in CA 19-20
Barton, May Hollis CAP-2
Earlier sketch in CA 19-20
See also SATA 1

Barton, Michael (Lee) 1943- ... 110
Barton, Richard F(leming) 1924- ... 61-64
Barton, Roger A(very) 1903-1976
Obituary ... 65-68
Barton, S. W.
See Whaley, Barton Stewart
Barton, Thomas Frank 1905- ... CANR-1
Earlier sketch in CA 45-48
Barton, V(ernon) Wayne ... 3R
Barton, Walter Elbert 1886-1983 Obituary ... 111
Barton, Wayne 1944- ... 124
Barton, Weldon V. 1938- ... 21-22R
Barton, William (Renald III) 1950- ... CANR-1
Earlier sketch in CA 45-48
Bartos, Otomar J(an) 1927- ... 105
Bartos-Hoeppner, Barbara 1923- ... CANR-10
Earlier sketch in CA 25-28R
See also SATA 5
Bartov, Hanoch 1926- Brief entry ... 117
Bartram, Graham 1946- ... 116
Bartram, John 1699-1777 ... DLB-31
Bartram, William 1739-1823 ... DLB-37
Bartran, Margaret 1913-1976 ... CAP-2
Earlier sketch in CA 29-32
Bartrum, Douglas A(lbert) 1907- ... CANR-6
Earlier sketch in CA 11-12R
Bartsch, Jochen 1906- ... SATA-39
Bartscht, Waltraud 1924- ... 41-44R
Bartusis, Mary Ann 1930- ... 101
Bartz, Albert E(dward) 1933- ... 23-24R
Bartz, Patricia McBride 1921- ... 102
Bartz, Wayne R(onald) 1938- ... 111
Baruch, Dorothy W(alter) 1899-1962 ... SATA-21
Baruch, Ruth-Marion 1922- ... 29-32R
Baruk, Henri Marc 1897- ... 85-88
Barwick, Steven 1921- ... 15-16R
Baryshnikov, Mikhail (Nikolayevich) 1948-
Brief entry ... 113
Barzanti, Sergio 1925- ... 19-20R
Barzilay, Isaac Eisenstein 1915- ... 113
Barzini, Luigi (Giorgio, Jr.)
1908-1984 ... CANR-23
Obituary ... 112
Earlier sketch in CA 13-14R
Bar-Zohar, Michael 1938- ... CANR-12
Earlier sketch in CA 23-24R
Barzun, Jacques (Martin) 1907- ... CANR-22
Earlier sketch in CA 61-64
Bas, Joe 1932- ... 53-56
Bas, Rutger
See Rutgers van der Loeff-Basenau,
An(na) Maria Margaretha
Basa, Eniko Molnar 1939- ... 77-80
Basart, Ann Phillips 1931- ... CANR-1
Earlier sketch in CA 3R
Basche, James 1926- ... 29-32R
Bascio, Patrick 1927- ... 119
Bascom, David 1912- ... 93-96
Bascom, Willard N. 1916- ... CANR-6
Earlier sketch in CA 2R
Bascom, William R(ussel) 1912- ... 19-20R
Basdekis, Demetrios 1930- ... 25-28R
Baseley, Godfrey 1904- ... 102
Basgoz, M(ehmet) Ilhan 1921- ... 113
Bash, Deborah M. Blumenthal 1940- ... 109
Bash, Frank N(ess) 1937- ... 107
Bash, Harry H(arvey) 1926- ... 89-92
Basham, Don W(ilson) 1926- ... 65-68
Basham, Richard Dalton 1945- ... 111
Basham, William Randolph 1933(?)-1986
Obituary ... 118
Bashevis, Isaac
See Singer, Isaac Bashevis
Bashevkin, Sylvia B. 1954- ... 121
Bashira, Damali 1951- ... 57-60
Bashshur, Rashid L. 1933- ... 89-92
Basichis, Gordon (Allen) 1947- ... 85-88
Basil, Douglas C. 1923- ... 41-44R
Basil, Otto 1901-1983 ... 49-52
Obituary ... 113
Basile, Gloria Vitanza 1929- ... CANR-12
Earlier sketch in CA 69-72
Basile, Joseph 1912- ... CANR-11
Earlier sketch in CA 25-28R
Basile, Leon 1955- ... 113
Basile, Robert M(anlius) 1916- ... 53-56
Basilius, Harold A. 1905-1977 ... CANR-2
Earlier sketch in CA 1R
Basinger, Jeanine (Deyling) 1936- ... CANR-18
Earlier sketch in CA 97-100
Basiuk, Victor 1932- ... 93-96
Baskerville, Barnet 1916- ... 4R
Baskerville, Patricia 1951- ... 108
Baskett, John 1930- ... 97-100
Baskette, Floyd K(enneth) 1910- ... 33-36R
Baskin, Barbara H(olland) 1929- ... CANR-22
Earlier sketch in CA 103
Baskin, Esther Tane 1926(?)-1973
Obituary ... 37-40R
Baskin, Leonard 1922- ... 106
See also SATA 27, 30
Baskin, Robert E(dward) 1917-1983
Obituary ... 110
Baskin, Samuel 1921- ... 17-18R
Baskin, Wade 1924-1974 ... CAP-2
Earlier sketch in CA 23-24
Basler, Roy P(rentice) 1906- ... CANR-4
Earlier sketch in CA 5-6R
Basler, Thomas G(ordon) 1940- ... 103
Bason, Fred
See Bason, Frederick (Thomas)
Bason, Frederick (Thomas) 1907-1973 ... 7-8R
Obituary ... 89-92
Bason, Lillian 1913- ... 69-72
See also SATA 20
Bass, Althea 1892- ... CAP-2
Earlier sketch in CA 23-24
Bass, Bernard M(orris) 1925- ... CANR-19
Earlier sketches in CA 1R, CANR-4
Bass, Clarence B(eaty) 1922- ... 5-6R
Bass, Eben E(dward) 1924- ... 107
Bass, Ellen 1947- ... CANR-2
Earlier sketch in CA 49-52
Bass, George F(letcher) 1932- ... 122
Bass, Henry B(enjamin) 1897-1975
Obituary ... 57-60
Bass, Herbert Jacob 1929- ... CANR-1
Earlier sketch in CA 3R
Bass, Howard 1923- ... CANR-2
Earlier sketch in CA 7-8R
Bass, Howard L(arry) 1942- ... 69-72
Bass, Jack 1934- ... CANR-19
Earlier sketch in CA 29-32R
Bass, Jack A(lexander) 1946- ... 97-100
Bass, Kingsley B., Jr.
See Bullins, Ed
Bass, Lawrence W(ade) 1898- ... 49-52
Bass, Madeline Tiger 1934- ... 116
Bass, Milton R. 1923- ... 25-28R
Bass, Robert D(uncan) 1904- ... 61-64
Bass, T. J.
See Bassler, Thomas J(oseph)
See also DLBY 81
Bass, Thomas A. 1951- ... 124
Bass, Virginia W(auchope) 1905- ... 61-64
Bass, William M(arvin III) 1928- ... 41-44R
Bassan, Maurice 1929- ... 25-28R
Bassani, Giorgio 1916- ... 65-68
See also CLC 9
Basse, Eli 1904-1979 Obituary ... 93-96
Basseches, Michael 1950- ... 114
Bassermann, Lujo
See Schreiber, Hermann
Basset, Bernard 1909- ... CANR-6
Earlier sketch in CA 11-12R
Bassett, Edward Eryl 1940- ... 33-36R
Bassett, Flora Marjorie 1890(?)-1980
Obituary ... 97-100
Bassett, George William 1910- ... 102
Bassett, Glenn Arthur 1930- ... 19-20R
Bassett, (Mary) Grace 1927- ... 73-76
Bassett, Jack
See Rowland, D(onald) S(ydney)
Bassett, James E(lias) 1912-1978 ... 61-64
Obituary ... 81-84
Bassett, Jeni 1960(?)- ... SATA-43
Bassett, John Earl, Jr. 1942- ... 123
Bassett, John Keith
See Keating, Lawrence A.
Bassett, John Spencer 1867-1928
Brief entry ... 122
See also DLB 17
Bassett, Marnie
See Bassett, Flora Marjorie
Bassett, Richard 1900- ... CAP-2
Earlier sketch in CA 25-28
Bassett, Ronald 1924- ... 81-84
Bassett, T(homas) D(ay) Seymour
1913- ... CANR-8
Earlier sketch in CA 23-24R
Bassett, William B. K. 1908- ... CAP-1
Earlier sketch in CA 9-10
Bassett, William Travis 1923- ... 11-12R
Bassett, William W. 1932- ... 25-28R
Bassiouni, M. Cherif 1937- ... 29-32R
Bassler, Thomas J(oseph) 1932- ... 115
Basso, Aldo P(eter) 1922- ... 65-68
Basso, (Joseph) Hamilton 1904-1964 ... 89-92
Bassoff, Bruce 1941- ... 69-72
Basten, Fred E(rnest) ... CANR-22
Earlier sketches in CA 57-60, CANR-7
Bastias, Constantine 1901(?)-1972
Obituary ... 37-40R
Bastico, Ettore 1876-1972 Obituary ... 37-40R
Bastin, J(ohn) S(turgus) 1927- ... CANR-11
Earlier sketch in CA 23-24R
Bastlund, Knud 1925- ... 23-24R
Basu, Arindam 1948- ... 61-64
Basu, Asoke (Kumar) 1940- ... 106
Basu, Dipak R. 1951- ... 112
Basu, Kaushik 1952- ... 115
Basu, Romen 1923- ... CANR-13
Earlier sketch in CA 77-80
Bataille, Georges 1897-1962 ... 101
Obituary ... 89-92
See also CLC 29
Bataille, Gretchen M. 1944- ... 102
Batbedat, Jean 1926- ... 37-40R
Batchelder, Alan Bruce 1931- ... 23-24R
Batchelder, Howard T(imothy) 1909- ... CAP-2
Earlier sketch in CA 19-20
Batcheller, John M. 1918- ... 45-48
Batchelor, C(larence) D(aniel) 1888-1977
Obituary ... 73-76
Batchelor, David 1943- ... CANR-18
Earlier sketch in CA 101
Batchelor, Edward, Jr. 1930- ... 110
Batchelor, John 1942- ... 93-96
Batchelor, John (Dennis) 1947- ... 109
Batchelor, John Calvin 1948- ... 105
Batchelor, Joy 1914- ... SATA-29
Batchelor, Julie F(rances) E(lizabeth)
1947- ... 109
Batchelor, Reg
See Paine, Lauran (Bosworth)
Batcher, Elaine Kotler 1944- ... 109
Bate, Lucy 1939- ... 69-72
See also SATA 18
Bate, Norman (Arthur) 1916- ... 4R
See also SATA 5
Bate, Sam 1907- ... 102
Bate, W(alter) Jackson 1918- ... 7-8R
See also DLB 67
Bateman, Barbara Dee 1933- ... 41-44R
Bateman, Robert (Moyes Carruthers)
1922-1973 ... CANR-7
Earlier sketch in CA 7-8R
Bateman, Walter L(ewis) 1916- ... 29-32R
Bates, Alan Lawrence 1923- ... 17-18R
Bates, Arthenia J. 1920- ... 57-60
Bates, Barbara S(nedeker) 1919- ... 17-18R
See also SATA 12
Bates, Betty
See Bates, Elizabeth
See also SATA 19
Bates, Carol Neuls
See Neuls-Bates, Carol
Bates, Caroline (Philbrick) 1932- ... 103
Bates, Charles C(arpenter) 1918- ... 121
Bates, Darrell 1913- ... CAP-1
Earlier sketch in CA 9-10
Bates, David Vincent 1922- ... 110
Bates, Elizabeth 1921- ... CANR-14
Earlier sketch in CA 77-80
Bates, H(erbert) E(rnest) 1905-1974 ... 93-96
Obituary ... 45-48
See also CLC 46
Bates, Helen L. Z.
See Yakobson, Helen B(ates)
Bates, J(ames) Leonard 1919- ... 13-14R
Bates, Jefferson D(avis) 1920- ... CANR-15
Earlier sketch in CA 81-84
Bates, Jerome E. 1917- ... 17-18R
Bates, Kenneth Francis 1904- ... CAP-1
Earlier sketch in CA 13-14
Bates, Lucius Christopher 1901(?)-1980
Obituary ... 101
Bates, Margaret J(ane) 1918- ... 17-18R
Bates, Marston 1906-1974 ... CANR-7
Obituary ... 49-52
Earlier sketch in CA 7-8R
Bates, Paul A(llen) 1920- ... 37-40R
Bates, Peter Watson 1920- ... 102
Bates, Ralph Samuel 1906- ... 3R
Bates, Robert H(inrichs) 1942- ... CANR-11
Earlier sketch in CA 69-72
Bates, Robert L(atimer) 1912- ... 121
Brief entry ... 116
Bates, Ronald (Gordon Nudell) 1924- ... 25-28R
Bates, Scott 1923- ... 49-52
Bates, Stephen 1958- ... 122
Bates, Steven Latimer 1940- ... 114
Bates, Su
See Bates, Susannah (Vacella)
Bates, Susannah (Vacella) 1941- ... 112
Bates, Timothy M(ason) 1946- ... 53-56
Bateson, Charles (Henry) 1903- ... 69-72
Bateson, F(rederick) W(ilse) 1901-1978 . CANR-6
Earlier sketch in CA 5-6R
Bateson, Gregory 1904-1980 ... 41-44R
Obituary ... 101
Batey, Richard (Alexander) 1933- ... 33-36R
Batey, Tom 1946- ... 107
See also SATA 41
Bath, Philip Ernest 1898- ... CAP-1
Earlier sketch in CA 9-10
Batherman, Muriel
See Sheldon, Muriel
Bathke, Edwin A(lbert) 1936- ... 57-60
Bathke, Nancy E(dna) 1938- ... 57-60
Batho, Edith C(lara) 1895- ... CAP-1
Earlier sketch in CA 11-12
Bathurst, Sheila
See Sullivan, Sheila
Batista, Fulgencio
See Batista y Zaldivar, Fulgencio
Batista y Zaldivar, Fulgencio 1901-1973
Obituary ... 111
Batiuk, Thomas M(artin) 1947- ... 69-72
See also SATA 40
Batki, John 1942- ... 45-48
Batman, Richard (Dale) 1932- ... 124
Bator, Robert 1939- ... 115
Batra, Raveendra N(ath) 1943- ... 89-92
Batson, George (Donald) 1918-1977 ... 33-36R
Obituary ... 73-76
Batson, Larry 1930- ... 57-60
See also SATA 35
Battaglia, Anthony 1939- ... 108
Battaglia, Aurelius 1910- ... SATA-33, 50
Battaglia, Elio Lee 1928- ... CANR-1
Earlier sketch in CA 4R
Battalia, O. William 1928- ... 45-48
Battan, Louis J(oseph) 1923- ... 15-16R
Battcock, Gregory 1938-1980 ... CANR-11
Obituary ... 105
Earlier sketch in CA 23-24R
Battelle, Phyllis (Marie) 1922- ... 77-80
Batten, Charles Linwood, Jr. 1942- ... 85-88
Batten, H(arry) Mortimer 1888-1958
Brief entry ... 112
See also SATA 25
Batten, Jack 1932- ... 49-52
Batten, James Knox 1936- ... 102
Batten, James William 1919- ... 33-36R
Batten, Jean (Gardner) 1909-1982 ... 106
Obituary ... 123
Batten, Joyce Mortimer
See Mankowska, Joyce Kells Batten
Batten, Mary 1937- ... 41-44R
See also SATA 5
Batten, (Richard) Peter 1916- ... 97-100
Batten, Thomas Reginald 1904- ... 13-14R
Battenhouse, Roy W(esley) 1912- ... 13-14R
Batterberry, Ariane Ruskin 1935- ... CANR-13
Earlier sketch in CA 69-72
See also SATA 13
Batterberry, Michael Carver 1932- ... 77-80
See also SATA 32
Battersby, James L(yons) 1936- ... 41-44R
Battersby, Martin 1914(?)-1982 Obituary ... 106
Battersby, William J(ohn) 1904-1976 ... CANR-4
Earlier sketch in CA 7-8R
Battestin, Martin C(arey) 1930- ... 15-16R
Battin, B(rinton) W(arner) 1941- ... 112
Battin, Buck
See Battin, B(rinton) W(arner)
Battin, R(osabell) Ray 1925- ... CANR-6
Earlier sketch in CA 11-12R
Battin, Wendy 1953- ... 121
Battis, Emery John 1915- ... 4R
Battiscombe, E(sther) Georgina (Harwood)
1905- ... CANR-14
Earlier sketches in CA 9-10, CAP-1
Battista, Miriam 1912(?)-1980 Obituary ... 103
Battista, O(rlando) A(loysius) 1917- ... CANR-7
Earlier sketch in CA 15-16R
Battisti, Eugenio 1924- ... 37-40R
Battle, Allen Overton 1927- ... 41-44R
Battle, Gerald N(ichols) 1914- ... 57-60
Battle, Jean Allen 1914- ... 25-28R
Battle, Lois 1942- ... 106
Battle, Richard John Vulliamy 1907-1982
Obituary ... 106
Battle, Sol(omon Oden) 1934- ... 25-28R
Battles, (Roxy) Edith 1921- ... 41-44R
See also SATA 7
Battles, Ford Lewis 1915- ... 15-16R
Batto, Bernard Frank 1941- ... 57-60
Batts, Michael S. 1929- ... 41-44R
Batty, C(harles) D(avid) 1932- ... 19-20R
Batty, Joyce D(orothea) 1919- ... 17-18R
Batty, Linda Schmidt 1940- ... 61-64
Battye, Gladys Starkey 1915- Brief entry ... 111
Battye, Louis Neville 1923- ... 7-8R
Baty, Gordon B(ruce) 1938- ... 57-60
Baty, Roger M(endenhall) 1937- ... 77-80
Baty, Wayne 1925- ... CANR-5
Earlier sketch in CA 15-16R
Bauby, Cathrina 1927- ... 49-52
Bauchart
See Camus, Albert
Baudhuin, John S. 1948- ... 112
Baudouy, Michel-Aime 1909- ... CAP-2
Earlier sketch in CA 33-36
See also SATA 7
Bauduc, R.
See Segre, Dan V(ittorio)
Baudy, Nicolas 1904(?)-1971 Obituary ... 33-36R
Bauer, Caroline Feller 1935- ... 77-80
See also SATA 46
Bauer, E. Charles 1916- ... 11-12R
Bauer, Erwin A. 1919- ... CANR-6
Earlier sketch in CA 11-12R
Bauer, Florence Marvyne ... CAP-2
Earlier sketch in CA 17-18
Bauer, Fred 1934- ... CANR-13
Earlier sketch in CA 29-32R
See also SATA 36
Bauer, George C. 1942- ... 73-76
Bauer, George Howard 1933- ... CANR-15
Earlier sketch in CA 29-32R
Bauer, (Jo) Hanna R(uth Goldsmith)
1918- ... 57-60
Bauer, Harry C(harles) 1902-1979 ... CAP-1
Obituary ... 85-88
Earlier sketch in CA 13-14
Bauer, Helen 1900- ... 5-6R
See also SATA 2
Bauer, Josef Martin 1901- ... CANR-5
Earlier sketch in CA 7-8R
Bauer, K(arl) Jack 1926-1987 ... CANR-10
Obituary ... 123
Earlier sketch in CA 25-28R
Bauer, Malcolm Clair 1914- ... 102
Bauer, Maria 1919- ... 117
Bauer, Marion Dane 1938- ... CANR-11
Earlier sketch in CA 69-72
See also SATA 20
Bauer, Nancy 1934- ... 113
Bauer, Peter Thomas 1915- ... 103
Bauer, Raymond A(ugustine)
1916-1977 ... CANR-11
Obituary ... 73-76
Earlier sketch in CA 61-64
Bauer, Robert A(lbert) 1910- ... 69-72
Bauer, Royal D(aniel) M(ichael) 1889- ... 33-36R
Bauer, Walter 1904- ... 101
Bauer, William Waldo 1892-1967 ... CANR-7
Earlier sketch in CA 5-6R
Bauer, Wolfgang L(eander) 1930- ... 15-16R
Bauer, Yehuda 1926- ... CANR-12
Earlier sketch in CA 29-32R
Bauerle, Ruth (Ellen) H(awkins) 1924- ... 112
Bauernfeind, Harry B. 1904- ... CAP-2
Earlier sketch in CA 19-20
Bauerschmidt, Marjorie 1926- ... SATA-15
Baugh, Albert C(roll) 1891-1981 ... 107
Obituary ... 103
Baugh, Daniel A(lbert) 1931- ... 69-72
Baughan, Peter E(dward) 1934- ... 107
Baughman, Dorothy 1940- ... 65-68
Baughman, Ernest W(arren) 1916- ... 33-36R
Baughman, James L(ewis) 1952- ... 118
Baughman, James P(orter) 1936- ... 25-28R
Baughman, John Lee 1913- ... 97-100
Baughman, M(illard) Dale 1919- ... 41-44R
Baughman, Ray Edward 1925- ... CANR-22
Earlier sketches in CA 11-12R, CANR-4
Baughman, Ronald 1940- ... 122
Baughman, Urbanus E., Jr. 1905(?)-1978
Obituary ... 81-84
Baughn, William Hubert 1918- ... CANR-17
Earlier sketch in CA 3R
Baukhage, Hilmar Robert 1889-1976
Obituary ... 65-68
See also AITN 2
Bauland, Peter 1932- ... 25-28R

Baulch, Jerry T. 1913- 77-80
Baulch, Lawrence 1926- 25-28R
Baum, Allyn Z(elton) 1924- 17-18R
See also SATA 20
Baum, Bernard H(elmut) 1926- 37-40R
Baum, Dale 1943- 118
Baum, Daniel (Jay) 1934- CANR-6
Earlier sketch in CA 15-16R
Baum, David William 1940- 53-56
Baum, Gregory 1923- CANR-15
Earlier sketch in CA 25-28R
Baum, L(yman) Frank 1856-1919
Brief entry 108
See also SATA 18
See also DLB 22
See also TCLC 7
Baum, Louis 1948- 124
Baum, Louis F.
See Baum, L(yman) Frank
Baum, Paull F(ranklin) 1886-1964 ....7-8R
Obituary 103
Baum, Rainer C(arl) 1934- 107
Baum, Richard (Dennis) 1940- 57-60
Baum, Richard Fitzgerald 1913- 7-8R
Baum, Robert J(ames) 1941- CANR-17
Earlier sketch in CA 85-88
Baum, Thomas 1940- 65-68
Baum, Vicki 1888-1960 93-96
Baum, Willi 1931- 29-32R
See also SATA 4
Bauman, Clarence 1928- 45-48
Bauman, Edward Walter 1927- 106
Bauman, H(erman) Carl 1913- 9-10R
Baumann, Amy (Brown) Beeching
1922- 21-22R
See also SATA 10
Baumann, Carol Edler 1932- 33-36R
Baumann, Charles Henry 1926- 73-76
Baumann, Charly 1928- 89-92
Baumann, Edward (Weston) 1925- 109
Baumann, Elwood D. Brief entry 111
See also SATA 33
Baumann, Hans 1914- CANR-3
Earlier sketch in CA 7-8R
See also SATA 2
Baumann, Hans Felix S(iegismund)
1893-1985 Obituary 115
Baumann, Kurt 1935- CANR-13
Earlier sketch in CA 77-80
See also SATA 21
Baumann, Walter 1935- 29-32R
Baumbach, Jonathan 1933- CANR-12
Earlier sketch in CA 15-16R
See also CAAS 5
See also DLBY 80
See also CLC 6, 23
Baumback, Clifford M(ason) 1915- CANR-6
Earlier sketch in CA 57-60
Baume, Michael 1930- 25-28R
Baumer, Franklin L(e Van) 1913-
Brief entry 110
Baumer, William H(enry) 1909- CANR-1
Earlier sketch in CA 2R
Baumgaertel, (Max) Walter 1902- 69-72
Baumgard, Herbert Mark 1920- 13-14R
Baumgardt, David 1890-1963 .... CANR-15
Obituary 103
Earlier sketch in CA 4R
Baumgartel, Walter
See Baumgaertel, (Max) Walter
Baumgarten, Sylvia 1933- 112
Baumgartner, Frederic J(oseph) 1945- 110
Baumgartner, John Stanley 1924- 9-10R
Bauml, Franz H.
See Baeuml, Franz H(einrich)
Baumol, William J(ack) 1922- CANR-24
Earlier sketches in CA 13-14R, CANR-7
Baumrin, Bernard H(erbert) 1934- 11-12R
Baumrin, Stefan
See Baumrin, Bernard H(erbert)
Baur, Francis G. 1930- 111
Baur, John E(dward) 1922- 11-12R
Baur, John I(reland) H(owe) 1909-1987
Obituary 122
Baus, Herbert M(ichael) 1914- CANR-11
Earlier sketch in CA 25-28R
Bausani, Alessandro 1921- 45-48
Bausch, Richard (Carl) 1945- 101
Bausch, Robert (Charles) 1945- 109
Bausch, William J. 1929- CANR-11
Earlier sketch in CA 29-32R
Bavarel, Michel (Joseph) 1940- 114
Bavier, Robert Newton (Jr.) 1918- 115
Bavin, Bill 1919- 73-76
Bavinck, J(ohan) H(erman) 1895-1965
Obituary 113
Bawden, Nina
See Kark, Nina Mary (Mabey)
See also DLB 14
See also CLR 2
Bawn, Mary
See Wright, Mary Pamela Godwin
Bax
See Baxter, Gordon F(rancis), Jr.
Bax, Clifford 1886-1962 Obituary 113
See also DLB 10
Bax, Martin C(harles) O(wen) 1933- 65-68
Bax, Roger
See Winterton, Paul
Baxandall, Rosalyn Fraad 1939- 81-84
Baxt, George 1923- 21-22R
Baxter, Angus 1912- 111
Baxter, Anne 1923-1985 114
Obituary 118
Brief entry 111
Baxter, Annette Kar 1926- CANR-4
Earlier sketch in CA 1R
Baxter, Batsell Barrett 1916- 33-36R
Baxter, Charles 1947- 57-60
See also CLC 45
Baxter, Craig 1929- CANR-11
Earlier sketch in CA 25-28R
Baxter, Douglas Clark 1942- 85-88
Baxter, Edna May 1890- CAP-1
Earlier sketch in CA 17-18
Baxter, Eric George 1918- 19-20R
Baxter, Eric P(eter) 1913- 9-10R
Baxter, George Owen
See Faust, Frederick (Shiller)
Baxter, Glen 1944- 109
Baxter, Gordon F(rancis), Jr. 1923- CANR-1
Earlier sketch in CA 45-48
Baxter, Hazel
See Rowland, D(onald) S(ydney)
Baxter, Ian F. G. CANR-11
Earlier sketch in CA 23-24R
Baxter, James Finney III 1893-1975 65-68
Baxter, James K(eir) 1926-1972 77-80
See also CLC 14
Baxter, James P(hinney) III 1893-1975
Obituary 57-60
Baxter, James Sidlow 1903- 73-76
Baxter, John 1939- 29-32R
Baxter, John
See Hunt, E(verette) Howard, Jr.
Baxter, Maurice Glen 1920- 15-16R
Baxter, Michael John 1944- 103
Baxter, Mike
See Baxter, Michael John
Baxter, Patricia E. W. 107
Baxter, Phyllis
See Wallmann, Jeffrey M(iner)
Baxter, Shane V.
See Norwood, Victor G(eorge) C(harles)
Baxter, Stephen B(artow) 1929- 19-20R
Baxter, Valerie
See Meynell, Laurence Walter
Baxter, William F(rancis) 1929- 89-92
Baxter, William T(hreipland) 1906- 107
Bay, Christian 1921- 33-36R
Bay, Howard 1912-1986 81-84
Obituary 121
Bayard, Jean 1923- 114
Baybars, Taner 1936- CANR-4
Earlier sketch in CA 53-56
Bayer, Eleanor
See Perry, Eleanor (Rosenfeld Bayer)
Bayer, Harold
See Gregg, Andrew K.
Bayer, Herbert 1900-1985 Obituary 117
Bayer, Jane E. ?-1985 Obituary 116
See also SATA 44
Bayer, Oliver Weld
See Perry, Eleanor (Rosenfeld Bayer)
Bayer, Ronald 1943- 106
Bayer, Sylvia
See Glassco, John
Bayer, William 1939- 33-36R
Bayer-Berenbaum, Linda 1948- 107
Bayerle, Gustav 1931- 53-56
Bayes, Marjorie 1934- 115
Bayes, Ronald H(omer) 1932- CANR-10
Earlier sketch in CA 25-28R
Bayh, Birch E(vans), Jr. 1928- 41-44R
Bayh, Marvella (Hern) 1933-1979 93-96
Obituary 85-88
Bay Laurel, Alicia
See Laurel, Alicia Bay
Baylen, Joseph O(scar) 1920- CANR-10
Earlier sketch in CA 25-28R
Bayles, Ernest E(dward) 1897- 73-76
Bayles, Michael D(ale) 1941- CANR-18
Earlier sketches in CA 49-52, CANR-1
Bayless, John 1913(?)-1983 Obituary 109
Bayless, Kenneth 1913(?)-1972 Obituary 104
Bayless, Raymond 1920- 85-88
Bayley, Barrington J(ohn) 1937- CANR-14
Earlier sketch in CA 37-40R
Bayley, Charles C(alvert) 1907- 33-36R
Bayley, David H(ume) 1933- 15-16R
Bayley, Edwin Richard 1918- 108
Bayley, John (Oliver) 1925- 85-88
Bayley, Monica Worsley 1919- 111
Bayley, Nicola 1949- 118
See also SATA 41
Bayley, Peter Charles 1921- 101
Bayley, Stephen 1951- 106
Bayley, Viola (Powles) 1911- CANR-5
Earlier sketch in CA 7-8R
Baylis, John 1946- CANR-18
Earlier sketch in CA 101
Bayliss, John Clifford 1919- 13-14R
Bayliss, Timothy
See Baybars, Taner
Baylor, Byrd 1924- 81-84
See also SATA 16
See also CLR 3
Baylor, Robert 1925- 13-14R
Bayly, Joseph T(ate) 1920- 17-18R
Baym, Max I. 1895- 41-44R
Baym, Nina 1936- 112
Bayne, David C(owan) 1918- 41-44R
Bayne, Stephen F(ielding), Jr. 1908-1974
Obituary 45-48
Bayne-Jardine, C(olin) C(harles) 1932- 25-28R
Baynes, Cary F. 1873(?)-1977 Obituary 104
Baynes, Dorothy Colston
See Colston-Baynes, Dorothy
Baynes, John (Christopher Malcolm)
1928- 21-22R
Baynes, Ken 1934- Brief entry 110
Baynes, Pauline (Diana) 1922- 120
See also SATA 19
Baynham, Henry (W. F.) 1933- 29-32R
Bayrd, Edwin 1944- 97-100
Bays, Gwendolyn McKee 13-14R
Bazelon, David T. 1923- 17-18R
Bazelon, Irwin 1922- 102
Bazin, Andre 1918-1958 Brief entry 113
Bazin, Germain (Rene Michel) 1907- CANR-12
Earlier sketch in CA 7-8R
Bazin, Herve
See Herve-Bazin, Jean Pierre Marie
Bazin, Nancy Topping 1934- 41-44R
Bazley, Margaret C. 1938- 106
Bb
See Watkins-Pitchford, Denys James
Beach, Bert Beverly 1928- 57-60
Beach, Charles
See Reid, (Thomas) Mayne
Beach, Charles Amory CAP-2
Earlier sketch in CA 19-20
See also SATA 1
Beach, Dale S. 1923- 15-16R
Beach, David (Williams) 1938- 115
Beach, Earl F(rancis) 1912- 13-14R
Beach, Edward L(atimer) 1918- CANR-6
Earlier sketch in CA 5-6R
See also SATA 12
Beach, Frank Ambrose 1911- 110
Beach, Lynn
See Lance, Kathryn
Beach, Mark B. 1937- 69-72
Beach, Stewart T(aft) 1899-1979 93-96
Obituary 85-88
See also SATA 23
Beach, Sylvia (Woodbridge) 1887-1962 108
See also DLB 4
Beach, Vincent W(oodrow) 1917- 33-36R
Beach, (William) Waldo 1916- 61-64
Beachcomber
See Morton, John (Cameron Andrieu)
Bingham (Michael)
Beachcroft, Nina 1931- CANR-19
Earlier sketch in CA 97-100
See also SATA 18
Beachcroft, T(homas) O(wen) 1902- CAP-1
Earlier sketch in CA 9-10
Beachey, Duane 1948- 112
Beachum, Larry M(ahon) 1948- 113
Beachy, Lucille 1935- 77-80
Beadell, Len 1923- 102
Beadle, Leigh P(atric) 1941- 65-68
Beadle, Muriel (McClure Barnett) 1915- 21-22R
Beadles, William T(homas) 1902- 19-20R
Beagle, Peter S(oyer) 1939- CANR-4
Earlier sketch in CA 11-12R
See also DLBY 80
See also CLC 7
Beaglehole, J(ohn) C(awte) 1901-1971 .... CAP-2
Obituary 33-36R
Earlier sketch in CA 21-22
Beakley, George Carroll, Jr. 1922- CANR-16
Earlier sketches in CA 45-48, CANR-1
Beal, Anthony (Ridley) 1925- 9-10R
Beal, George M(elvin) 1917- CANR-13
Earlier sketch in CA 23-24R
Beal, Graham W(illiam) J(ohn) 1947- 118
Beal, Gwyneth 1943- 69-72
Beal, John Robinson 1906(?)-1985
Obituary 116
Beal, M. F. 1937- 73-76
See also DLBY 81
Beal, Merrill D. 1898- CANR-5
Earlier sketch in CA 2R
Beal, Richard S(mith) 1945-1984 122
Obituary 114
Beale, Betty 73-76
Beale, Calvin L(unsford) 1923- 3R
Beale, Christopher Griffin
See Griffin-Beale, Christopher
Beale, Howard 1898- 109
Beale, Howard K. 1899-1959 .... DLB-17
Beale, Walter H(enry) 1945- Brief entry 118
Bealer, Alex W(inkler III) 1921-1980 .... CANR-2
Obituary 97-100
Earlier sketch in CA 45-48
See also SATA 8, 22
Bealer, George Persson 113
Beales, Derek (Edward Dawson)
1931- CANR-16
Earlier sketch in CA 73-76
Beales, Peter 1936- 122
Bealey, (Frank) William 1922- CANR-2
Earlier sketch in CA 7-8R
Beall, James Lee 1924- CANR-11
Earlier sketch in CA 65-68
Beall, Karen F(riedmann) 1938- 106
Beall, Otho T(hompson), Jr. 1908-1977
Obituary 113
Beals, Alan R(obin) 1928- 37-40R
Beals, Carleton 1893-1979 .... CANR-3
Earlier sketch in CA 4R
See also SATA 12
Beals, Frank Lee 1881-1972 ....7-8R
Obituary 103
See also SATA 26
Beals, Ralph L(eon) 1901- 23-24R
Beam, Alvin Wesley 1912-1982 Obituary 107
Beam, C. Richard 45-48
Beam, George D(ahl) 1934- 69-72
Beam, Philip C(onway) 1910- 97-100
Beaman, Joyce Proctor 1931- 29-32R
Beame, Rona 1934- 45-48
See also SATA 12
Beamer, (George) Charles (Jr.) 1942- 121
See also SATA 43
Beamish, Annie O'Meara de Vic 1883- 15-16R
Beamish, Anthony Hamilton ?-1983
Obituary 109
Beamish, Huldine V. 1904- CAP-1
Earlier sketch in CA 13-14
Beamish, Noel de Vic
See Beamish, Annie O'Meara de Vic
Beamish, Tufton Victor Hamilton
See Chelwood, Tufton Victor Hamilton
Bean, Constance A(ustin) 41-44R
Bean, George E(wart) 1903- 25-28R
Bean, Henry (Schorr) 1945- 109
Bean, Keith F(enwick) 1911- CAP-1
Earlier sketch in CA 11-12
Bean, Lowell John 1931- 41-44R
Bean, Mabel Greene 1898(?)-1977
Obituary 73-76
Bean, Normal
See Burroughs, Edgar Rice
Bean, Orson 1928- 77-80
Bean, Walton (Elbert) 1914- 25-28R
Bean, William B(ennett) 1909- 111
Beaney, Jane
See Udall, Jan Beaney
Bear, Bullen
See Donnelly, Austin Stanislaus
Bear, David 1949- 106
Bear, Greg(ory Dale) 1951- 113
Bear, James A(dam), Jr. 1919- 21-22R
Bear, Joan 1918- 57-60
Bear, John (Boris) 1938- CANR-13
Earlier sketch in CA 73-76
Bear, Roberta Meyer 1942- 21-22R
Bearce, George D(onham) 1922- 11-12R
Bearchell, Charles 1925- 93-96
Beard, Belle Boone 1898-1984 Obituary 114
Beard, Charles A(ustin) 1874-1948
Brief entry 115
See also SATA 18
See also DLB 17
See also TCLC 15
Beard, Dan(iel Carter) 1859-1941 .... SATA-22
Beard, Estle S. 1908-1983 111
Beard, Helen 1931- 113
Beard, James (Andrews) 1903-1985 .... CANR-15
Obituary 114
Earlier sketch in CA 81-84
Beard, James F(ranklin) 1919- 3R
Beard, Marna L(ouise) 1942- 112
Beard, Peter H. 1938- 13-14R
Beard, Robert Eric 1911-1983 Obituary 111
Bearden, James Hudson 1933- 23-24R
Bearden, Romare (Howard) 1914- 102
See also SATA 22
Beardmore, Cedric
See Beardmore, George
Beardmore, George 1908-1979 69-72
See also SATA 20
Beardslee, John W(alter) III 1914- 37-40R
Beardsley, Charles Noel 1914- CANR-2
Earlier sketch in CA 4R
Beardsley, (John) Douglas 1941- 113
Beardsley, Elizabeth Lane 29-32R
Beardsley, John 1952- 109
Beardsley, (Betty) Lou 1925- 118
Beardsley, Monroe C(urtis) 1915-1985 ....17-18R
Obituary 117
Beardsley, Richard K(ing) 1918-1978 .. CANR-11
Obituary 77-80
Earlier sketch in CA 17-18R
Beardsley, Theodore S(terling), Jr.
1930- 33-36R
Beardsworth, Millicent Monica 1915- 103
Beardwood, Roger 1932- 89-92
Beardwood, Valerie Fairfield 5-6R
Beare, Francis W(right) 1902- CANR-16
Earlier sketch in CA 4R
Beare, (M.A.) Nikki 1928- 37-40R
Bearman, Jane (Ruth) 1917- 105
See also SATA 29
Bearne, C(olin) G(erald) 1939- 97-100
Bearss, Edwin C(ole) 1923- CANR-10
Earlier sketch in CA 25-28R
Beaser, Herbert W. 1913(?)-1979
Obituary 85-88
Beasley, Jerry C(arr) 1940- CANR-14
Earlier sketch in CA 37-40R
Beasley, M. Robert 1918- 9-10R
Beasley, Maurine 1936- CANR-20
Earlier sketch in CA 104
Beasley, Rex 1925- 11-12R
Beasley, W(illiam) Conger, Jr. 1940- CANR-4
Earlier sketch in CA 53-56
Beasley, W(illiam) G(erald) 1919- 53-56
Beasley-Murray, George Raymond 1916- ..65-68
Beason, Robert G(ayle) 1927- 114
Beath, Paul Robert 1905- 7-8R
Beaton, Alan A. 1947- 123
Beaton, Anne
See Washington, (Catherine) Marguerite
Beauchamp
Beaton, Cecil (Walter Hardy) 1904-1980 ...81-84
Obituary 93-96
Beaton, George
See Brenan, (Edward Fitz)Gerald
Beaton, (Donald) Leonard 1929-1971 ... CANR-4
Obituary 29-32R
Earlier sketch in CA 7-8R
Beaton, M. C.
See Chesney, Marion
Beaton-Jones, Cynon 1921- 7-8R
Beattie, Ann 1947- 81-84
See also DLBY 82
See also CLC 8, 13, 18, 40
Beattie, Carol 1918- 29-32R
Beattie, Edward J(ames), Jr. 1918- 106
Beattie, Jessie Louise 1896- CANR-17
Earlier sketches in CA 7-8R, CANR-2
Beattie, John (Hugh Marshall) 1915- 37-40R
Beattie, Sally 1941- 122

Beattie, Susan 1938- 123
Beatts, Anne Patricia 1947- 102
Beatty, Elizabeth
See Holloway, Teresa (Bragunier)
Beatty, Hetty Burlingame 1907-1971 .... 4R
Obituary 103
See also SATA 5
Beatty, Jerome, Jr. 1918- CANR-3
Earlier sketch in CA 9-10R
See also SATA 5
Beatty, John (Louis) 1922-1975 .... CANR-4
Obituary 57-60
Earlier sketch in CA 7-8R
See also SATA 6, 25
Beatty, Morgan 1902-1975 Obituary 61-64
Beatty, Patricia Robbins 1922- CANR-3
Earlier sketch in CA 4R
See also SATA 1, 30
See also SAAS 4
Beatty, Rita Gray 1930- 45-48
Beatty, Robert Owen 1924-1976 Obituary ..69-72
Beatty, Warren
See Beaty, Warren
Beatty, William Alfred 1912-19(?) CAP-1
Earlier sketch in CA 13-14
Beatty, William K(ave) 1926- 41-44R
Beaty, Betty CANR-18
Earlier sketch in CA 73-76
Beaty, (Arthur) David 1919- CANR-18
Earlier sketches in CA 4R, CANR-2
Beaty, Janice J(anowski) 1930- 15-16R
Beaty, Jerome 1924- 85-88
Beaty, Shirley MacLean 1934- 103
Beaty, Warren 1937(?)- Brief entry 109
Beaubien, Anne K(athleen) 1947- 123
Beauchamp, Edward R(obert) 1933- 61-64
Beauchamp, Gorman 1938- 121
Beauchamp, Kathleen Mansfield
1888-1923 Brief entry 104
Beauchamp, Kenneth L(loyd) 1939- 29-32R
Beauchamp, Pat
See Washington, (Catherine) Marguerite
Beauchamp
Beauchamp, Tom L. 1939- CANR-13
Earlier sketch in CA 73-76
Beauchemin, Yves 1941- DLB-60
Beauclerk, Helen De Vere 1892-1969
Obituary 114
Beaudoin, Kenneth Lawrence 1913- 29-32R
Beaudouin, John T(yrell) 1920-
Brief entry 114
Beaufitz, William
See Critchley, Julian (Michael Gordon)
Beaufort, John (David) 1912- 104
Beaufre, Andre 1902-1975 65-68
Obituary 57-60
Beaulac, Willard L(eon) 1899- 11-12R
Beaulieu, Victor-Levy 1945- DLB-53
Beauman, E(ric) Bentley 9-10R
Beauman, Katharine (Burgoyne) Bentley
1902- 102
Beaumont, Beverly
See von Block, Sylvia
Beaumont, Charles 1929-1967 ....5-6R
Obituary 103
Beaumont, Charles Allen 1926- 3R
Beaumont, Cyril William 1891-1976 ......13-14R
Obituary 65-68
Beaumont, Francis 1584(?)-1616 .... DLB-58
Beaumont, George Ernest 1888-1974
Obituary 49-52
Beaumont, Keith (Stanley) 1944- 118
Beaumont, Roger A(lban) 1935- 65-68
Beauregard, Erving E. 1920- 111
Beaurline, L(ester) A(lbert) 1927- 21-22R
Beausang, Michael F(rancis), Jr. 1936- 57-60
Beausay, Florence E(dith) 1911- 21-22R
Beausoleil, Beau 1941- CANR-14
Earlier sketch in CA 81-84
Beauvais, Robert 1911- 104
Beauvoir, Simone (Lucie Ernestine Marie
Bertrand) de 1908-1986 ....11-12R
Obituary 118
See also DLBY 86
See also CLC 1, 2, 4, 8, 14, 31, 44
Beaver, Bruce (Victor) 1928- 97-100
Beaver, Frank E(ugene) 1938- 114
Beaver, Harold (Lothar) 1929- 21-22R
Beaver, (Jack) Patrick 1923- 33-36R
Beaver, Paul (Eli) 1953- 115
Beaver, R(obert) Pierce 1906- CANR-7
Earlier sketch in CA 5-6R
Beaver, Stanley H(enry) 1907-1984
Obituary 114
Beaverbrook, William Maxwell Aitken
1879-1964 103
Obituary 89-92
Beazley, John Davidson 1885-1970
Obituary 115
Bebb, Russ(ell H.), Jr. 1930- 49-52
Bebell, Mildred Hoyt 1909- CAP-1
Earlier sketch in CA 15-16
Bebey, Francis 1929- 69-72
Bebler, A(lex) Anton 1937- CANR-2
Earlier sketch in CA 49-52
Becerra, Rosina M. 1939- 122
Becher, Ulrich 1910- 101
Bechervaise, John Mayston 1910- CANR-5
Earlier sketch in CA 15-16R
Bechhoefer, Bernhard G. 1904- 2R
Bechko, Peggy Anne 1950- CANR-2
Earlier sketch in CA 49-52
Becht, J. Edwin 1918- 29-32R
Bechtel, Louise Seaman 1894-1985 ...... CAP-2
Obituary 116
Earlier sketch in CA 29-32
See also SATA 4, 43
Bechtel, Paul M(oyer) 1909- 116
Bechtol, William M(ilton) 1931- 49-52
Beck, Aaron T(emkin) 1921- CANR-11
Earlier sketch in CA 23-24R
Beck, Alan M(arshall) 1942- CANR-21
Earlier sketch in CA 45-48
Beck, Barbara L. 1927- 17-18R
See also SATA 12
Beck, Calvin Thomas 1937- 97-100
Beck, Carl 1930- CANR-1
Earlier sketch in CA 1R
Beck, Clive 1939- 49-52
Beck, Doc
See Beck, Earl Clifton
Beck, Earl Clifton 1891-1977 Obituary 110
Beck, Earl R(ay) 1916- 33-36R
Beck, Emily M(orison) 1915- 114
Beck, Evelyn Torton 1933- CANR-13
Earlier sketch in CA 33-36R
Beck, Harry
See Paine, Lauran (Bosworth)
Beck, Helen L(ouise) 1908- 73-76
Beck, Henry G(abriel) J(ustin) 1914- 11-12R
Beck, Horace P(almer) 1920- 77-80
Beck, Hubert (F.) 1931- CANR-12
Earlier sketch in CA 29-32R
Beck, James (H.) 1930- 85-88
Beck, James Murray 1914- 101
Beck, Joan (Wagner) 1923- Brief entry 118
Beck, John Jacob, Jr. 1941- 53-56
Beck, Julian 1925-1985 102
Obituary 117
Beck, Leslie 1907(?)-1978 Obituary 104
Beck, Lewis White 1913- CANR-2
Earlier sketch in CA 7-8R
Beck, M. Susan 1941- 113
Beck, Marilyn (Mohr) 1928- 65-68
Beck, Pamela 1954- 120
Beck, Paul 1933(?)-1985 Obituary 116
Beck, Phineas
See Chamberlain, Samuel
Beck, Robert Edward 1941- 104
Beck, Robert H(olmes) 1918- 29-32R
Beck, Robert Nelson 1924-1980 .... CANR-4
Earlier sketch in CA 3R
Beck, Thomas D(avis) 1943- 57-60
Beck, Toni 1925- 57-60
Beck, Victor Emanuel 1894-1963 ....5-6R
Beck, Warren 1896-1986 .... CANR-3
Obituary 119
Earlier sketch in CA 1R
Beck, Warren Albert 1918- CANR-6
Earlier sketch in CA 5-6R
Beckel, Graham 1913- 3R
Beckelhymer, (Paul) Hunter 1919- CANR-3
Earlier sketch in CA 2R
Becker, A(dolph) C(arl), Jr. 1920- 65-68
Becker, Abraham S(amuel) 1927- 33-36R
Becker, Albert B. 1903-1972 .... CAP-2
Earlier sketch in CA 29-32
Becker, Arthur P(eter) 1918- 29-32R
Becker, B. Jay 1904-1987 65-68
Obituary 123
Becker, Beril 1901- CAP-1
Earlier sketch in CA 9-10
See also SATA 11
Becker, Bill
See Becker, William
Becker, Bruce 57-60
Becker, Carl 1873-1945 .... DLB-17
Becker, Carol 1947- 124
Becker, Edith C. (Stepien) 1915- 15-16R
Becker, Ernest 1925-1974 97-100
Becker, Florence
See Lennon, Florence Becker
(Tanenbaum)
Becker, Gary S(tanley) 1930- CANR-11
Earlier sketch in CA 61-64
Becker, George J(oseph) 1908- CANR-7
Earlier sketch in CA 5-6R
Becker, Harold K(auffman) 1933- CANR-13
Earlier sketch in CA 29-32R
Becker, Howard Saul 1928- Brief entry 115
Becker, Irving 1945- 122
Becker, Jillian (Ruth) 1932- 77-80
Becker, John (Leonard) 1901- CAP-1
Earlier sketch in CA 11-12
See also SATA 12
Becker, John E(dward) 1930- 49-52
Becker, Joseph M(aria) 1908- CANR-7
Earlier sketch in CA 17-18R
Becker, Joyce 1936- SATA-39
Becker, Jurek 1937- 85-88
See also CLC 7, 19
Becker, Klaus
See Koch, Kurt E(mil)
Becker, Lawrence C(arlyle) 1939- 85-88
Becker, Lucille F(rackman) 1929- CANR-12
Earlier sketch in CA 29-32R
Becker, Manning H. 1922- 13-14R
Becker, Marion Rombauer 1903-1976 ....37-40R
Obituary 69-72
Becker, Marvin Burton 1922- 107
Becker, May Lamberton 1873-1958
Brief entry 112
See also SATA 33
Becker, Murray 1909(?)-1986 Obituary 118
Becker, Olga
See Frank, Rudolf
Becker, Paula Lee 1941- 19-20R
Becker, Peter 1921- 53-56
Becker, Robert O(tto) 1923- 123
Becker, Robin 1951- 110
Becker, Ruby Wirt 1915- 33-36R
Becker, Russell J(ames) 1923- 37-40R
Becker, Samuel L(eo) 1923- CANR-7
Earlier sketch in CA 15-16R
Becker, Seymour 1934- 25-28R
Becker, Stephen (David) 1927- CANR-3
Earlier sketch in CA 7-8R
See also CAAS 1
Becker, Ted
See Becker, Theodore L(ewis)
Becker, Theodore L(ewis) 1932-
Brief entry 116
Becker, Thomas W(illiam) 1933- 7-8R
Becker, Walter 1950- CLC-26
Becker, Wesley C(lemence) 1928- 33-36R
Becker, William 1903(?)-1983 Obituary 110
Beckerman, Bernard 1921-1985 .... CANR-19
Obituary 117
Earlier sketch in CA 4R
Beckerman, Wilfred 1925- CANR-7
Earlier sketch in CA 17-18R
Beckett, Ian F(rederick) W(illiam) 1950- 120
Beckett, J(ames) C(amlin) 1912-
Brief entry 114
Beckett, John A(ngus) 1916- 33-36R
Beckett, Kenneth A(lbert) 1929- CANR-10
Earlier sketch in CA 65-68
Beckett, Lucy 1942- 49-52
Beckett, Ralph L(awrence) 1923- 7-8R
Beckett, Ronald Brymer 1891- 7-8R
Beckett, Samuel (Barclay) 1906- 7-8R
See also DLB 13, 15
See also CLC 1, 2, 3, 4, 6, 9, 10, 11,
14, 18, 29
Beckett, Sheilah 1913- SATA-33
Beckey, Fred W(olfgang) 1923- 109
Beckford, George L(eslie Fitz-Gerald)
1934- 97-100
Beckford, William 1760-1844 .... DLB-39
Beckham, Barry 1944- 29-32R
See also DLB 33
Beckham, Stephen Dow 1941- CANR-12
Earlier sketch in CA 61-64
Beckhart, Benjamin Haggott 1897-1975
Obituary 57-60
Beckingham, Charles Fraser 1914- 61-64
Beckinsale, Monica 1914- 69-72
Beckinsale, Robert Percy 1908- CANR-2
Earlier sketch in CA 7-8R
Becklake, Sue 1943- 120
Beckler, Marion Floyd 1889- CAP-1
Earlier sketch in CA 11-12
Beckles Willson, Robina (Elizabeth)
1930- CANR-20
Earlier sketches in CA 13-14R, CANR-5
Beckman, Aldo Bruce 1934- 73-76
Beckman, Delores 1914- 121
Beckman, Gail McKnight 1938- 53-56
Beckman, Gunnel 1910- CANR-15
Earlier sketch in CA 33-36R
See also SATA 6
See also CLC 26
Beckman, Kaj
See Beckman, Karin
Beckman, Karin 1913- SATA-45
Beckman, Patti
See Boeckman, Patti
Beckman, Per (Frithiof) 1913- SATA-45
Beckman, Robert C(harles) 1934- 120
Beckmann, David M(ilton) 1948- CANR-8
Earlier sketch in CA 61-64
Beckmann, George Michael 1926- 7-8R
Beckmann, Martin J(osef) 1924- 37-40R
Beckmann, Petr 1924- 69-72
Beckner, Weldon (Earnest) 1933- 33-36R
Beckovic, Matiia 1939- 33-36R
Beckson, Karl 1926- CANR-2
Earlier sketch in CA 5-6R
Beckwith, B(rainerd) K(ellogg) 1902- 73-76
Beckwith, Burnham Putnam 1904- 33-36R
Beckwith, Charles E(milio) 1917- 37-40R
Beckwith, John Gordon 1918- 9-10R
Beckwith, Lillian
See Comber, Lillian
Beckwith, Paul 1905-1975 Obituary 113
Beckwith, Yvonne 106
Bedard, Michelle
See MacKenzie, Joan Finnigan
Bedard, Patrick Joseph 1941- 112
Bedau, Hugo Adam 1926- CANR-19
Earlier sketches in CA 11-12R, CANR-4
Beddall, Barbara G(ould) 1919- 33-36R
Beddall-Smith, Charles John 1916- 15-16R
Beddoe, Ellaruth
See Elkins, Ella Ruth
Beddoes, Richard H(erbert) 1926- 37-40R
Bede, Andrew
See Beha, Ernest
Bede, Jean-Albert 1903-1977 Obituary 69-72
Bedeian, Arthur G(eorge) 1946- 110
Bedell, George C(hester) 1928- 41-44R
Bedell, L. Frank 1888- CAP-1
Earlier sketch in CA 15-16
Bedell, Madelon (Jane Berns)
1922(?)-1986 Obituary 119
Bedells, Phyllis 1893-1985 Obituary 116
Bedford, A. N.
See Watson, Jane Werner
Bedford, Ann
See Rees, Joan
Bedford, Annie North
See Watson, Jane Werner
Bedford, Charles Harold 1929- 57-60
Bedford, Donald F.
See Fearing, Kenneth (Flexner)
Bedford, Emmett G(runer) 1922- 45-48
Bedford, Henry F(rederick) 1931- 11-12R
Bedford, Kenneth
See Paine, Lauran (Bosworth)
Bedford, Norton M(oore) 1916- 5-6R
Bedford, Sybille 1911- 11-12R
Bediako, Kwabena Asare
See Kondau, S(amuel) A(sare)
Bedikian, Antriganik A. 1886(?)-1980
Obituary 93-96
Bedinger, Margery 1891- 57-60
Bedinger, Singleton B(erry) 1907- 49-52
Bedini, Silvio A. 1917- CANR-13
Earlier sketch in CA 33-36R
Bednarik, Charles (Philip) 1925- 77-80
Bednarik, Chuck
See Bednarik, Charles (Philip)
Bedoukian, Kerop 1907- 93-96
Bedoyere, Michael De La
See De La Bedoyere, Michael
Bedrij, Orest (John) 1933- CANR-16
Earlier sketch in CA 85-88
Bedsole, Adolph 1914- 15-16R
Bee, Clair (Francis) 1900-1983 .... 4R
Obituary 109
Bee, (John) David (Ashford) 1931- 17-18R
Bee, Helen L. 1939- CANR-16
Earlier sketch in CA 89-92
Bee, Jay
See Brainerd, John W(hiting)
Bee, Robert L(awrence) 1938- 113
Beebe, (Ida) Ann 1919- 41-44R
Beebe, B(urdetta) F(aye)
See Johnson, B(urdetta) F(aye)
See also SATA 1
Beebe, Frank L(yman) 1914- 89-92
Beebe, Frederick S(essions) 1914-1973
Obituary 41-44R
Beebe, H. Keith 1921- 29-32R
Beebe, Lucius 1902-1966 Obituary 25-28R
Beebe, Maurice (Laverne) 1926- CANR-1
Earlier sketch in CA 4R
Beebe, Ralph K(enneth) 1932- 33-36R
Beebe, (Charles) William 1877-1962 73-76
See also SATA 19
Beeby, Betty 1923- SATA-25
Beeby, C(larence) E(dward) 1902- 109
Beech, George T(homas) 1931- 11-12R
Beech, Harold Reginald 1925- 25-28R
Beech, Keyes 1913- 33-36R
Beech, Robert (Paul) 1940- 33-36R
Beech, Webb
See Butterworth, W(illiam) E(dmund III)
Beecham, Justin
See Wintle, Justin (Beecham)
Beecham, Thomas 1879-1961 Obituary 112
Beechcroft, William
See Hallstead, William F(inn III)
Beecher, Catharine Esther 1800-1878 .... DLB-1
Beecher, Henry Ward 1813-1887 ..... DLB-3, 43
Beecher, John 1904-1980 .... CANR-8
Obituary 105
Earlier sketch in CA 5-6R
See also CLC 6
See also AITN 1
Beecher, William (M.) 1933- 65-68
Beechert, Edward D. 1920- 124
Beechhold, Henry F(rank) 1928- 33-36R
Beechick, Ruth 1925- 108
Beeching, Jack 1922- CANR-13
Earlier sketch in CA 21-22R
See also SATA 14
Beechy, Winifred
See Beechy, Winifred Nelson
Beechy, Winifred Nelson 1915- 116
Beecroft, John William Richard 1902-1966 ..5-6R
Beedell, Suzanne (Mollie) 1921- CANR-20
Earlier sketch in CA 69-72
Beeding, Francis
See Palmer, John (Leslie)
and Saunders, Hilary Aidan St. George
Beegle, Charles William 1928- 106
Beegle, Dewey Maurice 1919- 5-6R
Beegle, J(oseph) Allan 1918- 119
Beek, Martin(us) A(drianus) 1909- 13-14R
Beekman, Allan 1913- 33-36R
Beekman, E(ric) M(ontague) 1939- CANR-14
Earlier sketch in CA 33-36R
Beekman, John 1918- 61-64
Beekman, Ross
See Dey, Frederic (Merrill) Van
Rensselaer
Beeks, Graydon 1919- 65-68
Beeler, Nelson F(rederick) 1910- 69-72
See also SATA 13
Beeman, Richard R(oy) 1942- 77-80
Beer, Barrett L(ynn) 1936- 49-52
Beer, Edith Lynn 1930- CANR-11
Earlier sketch in CA 61-64
Beer, Eloise C. S. 1903- 13-14R
Beer, Ethel S(ophia) 1897-1975 .... CAP-2
Obituary 57-60
Earlier sketch in CA 25-28
Beer, Francis Anthony 1939- CANR-10
Earlier sketch in CA 25-28R
Beer, George L. 1872-1920 .... DLB-47
Beer, Jeanette (Mary Ayres) 124
Beer, John B(ernard) 1926- CANR-23
Earlier sketches in CA 5-6R, CANR-7
Beer, Kathleen Costello 1926- 25-28R
Beer, Lawrence W(ard) 1932- 37-40R
Beer, Lisl
See Beer, Eloise C. S.
Beer, Patricia 1924- CANR-13
Earlier sketch in CA 61-64
See also DLB 40
Beer, Ralph (Robert) 1947- 120
Beer, Samuel Hutchison 1911- 61-64
Beer, Vic
See Bird, Vivian
Beer, William Reed 1943- 112

Beerbohm, Henry Maximilian 1872-1956
Brief entry ... 104
See also DLB 34
See also TCLC 1, 24
Beers, Burton F(loyd) 1927- ... CANR-19
Earlier sketch in CA 4R
Beers, Dorothy Sands 1917- ... 49-52
See also SATA 9
Beers, Henry Putney 1907- ... 15-16R
Beers, Lorna 1897- ... 49-52
See also SATA 14
Beers, Paul Benjamin 1931- ... 102
Beers, V(ictor) Gilbert 1928- ... CANR-16
Earlier sketches in CA 49-52, CANR-1
See also SATA 9
Beery, Mary 1907- ... 5-6R
Beesly, Patrick 1913-1986 ... CANR-15
Obituary ... 120
Earlier sketch in CA 85-88
Beeson, Trevor Randall 1926- ... 93-96
Beeton, (Douglas) Ridley 1929- ... 93-96
Beevers, John (Leonard) 1911-1975 ... 61-64
Beezley, P(aul) C. 1895- ... 7-8R
Beezley, William H(oward Taft) 1942- ... 49-52
Befu, Harumi 1930- ... 53-56
Beg, Toran
See McKillop, Norman
Begg, A(lexander) Charles 1912- ... 102
Begg, Howard Bolton 1896- ... 5-6R
Begg, Neil Colquhoun 1915- ... 102
Beggs, David W(hiteford) III 1931-1966 .. CAP-1
Earlier sketch in CA 15-16
Beggs, Donald L(ee) 1941- ... 33-36R
Beggs, Edward Larry 1933- ... 89-92
Begiebing, Robert J(ohn) 1946- ... 122
Begin, Menachem 1913- Brief entry ... 109
Begin, Menahem
See Begin, Menachem
Begleiter, Henri 1935- ... 119
Begley, James 1929- ... 25-28R
Begley, Kathleen A(nne) 1948- ... 77-80
See also SATA 21
Begnal, Michael H(enry) 1939- ... 73-76
Begner, Edith ... CANR-3
Earlier sketch in CA 3R
Beha, Ernest 1908- ... CAP-1
Earlier sketch in CA 13-14
Beha, Sister Helen Marie 1926- ... 21-22R
Behan, Brendan 1923-1964 ... 73-76
See also DLB 13
See also CLC 1, 8, 11, 15
Behan, Leslie
See Gottfried, Theodore Mark
Behara, Devendra Nath 1940- ... 41-44R
Behee, John 1933- ... 112
Behle, William H(arroun) 1909- ... 7-8R
Behler, Ernst 1928- ... 41-44R
Behlmer, George K(inkel) 1948- ... 123
Behlmer, Rudy 1926- ... CANR-8
Earlier sketch in CA 57-60
Behm, Marc 1925- ... 101
Behm, William H(erman), Jr. 1922- ... 15-16R
Behme, Robert Lee 1924- ... 57-60
Behn, Aphra 1640(?)-1689 ... DLB-39
Behn, Harry 1898-1973 ... CANR-5
Obituary ... 53-56
Earlier sketch in CA 7-8R
See also SATA 2, 34
See also DLB 61
Behn, Noel 1928- Brief entry ... 116
Behney, John Bruce 1905- ... 101
Behnke, Charles A(lbert) 1891- ... CAP-2
Earlier sketch in CA 19-20
Behnke, Frances L. ... 33-36R
See also SATA 8
Behnke, John 1945- ... 69-72
Behnke, Leo 1933- ... 111
Behr, Edward 1926- ... CANR-3
Earlier sketch in CA 2R
Behr, Joyce 1929- ... SATA-15
Behr, Marion 1939- ... 105
Behrend, Jeanne 1911- ... 19-20R
Behrens, Earl (Charles) 1892-1985
Obituary ... 116
Behrens, Helen Kindler 1922- ... 61-64
Behrens, Herman D(aniel) 1901- ... 33-36R
Behrens, John C. 1933- ... CANR-14
Earlier sketch in CA 37-40R
Behrens, June York 1925- ... CANR-24
Earlier sketches in CA 17-18R, CANR-8
See also SATA 19
Behrens, Roy R(ichard) 1946- ... 110
Behrman, Carol H(elen) 1925- ... CANR-22
Earlier sketches in CA 61-64, CANR-7
See also SATA 14
Behrman, Cynthia F(ansler) 1931- ... 123
Behrman, Daniel 1923- ... 65-68
Behrman, Jack N(ewton) 1922- ... 29-32R
Behrman, Lucy Creevey
See Creevey, Lucy E.
Behrman, S(amuel) N(athaniel)
1893-1973 ... CAP-1
Obituary ... 45-48
Earlier sketch in CA 15-16
See also DLB 7, 44
See also CLC 40
Behrstock, Barry 1948- ... 106
Beichman, Arnold 1913- ... 49-52
Beichner, Paul E(dward) 1912- ... 33-36R
Beier, Ernst G(unter) 1916- ... 21-22R
Beier, Ulli 1922- ... CANR-4
Earlier sketch in CA 9-10R
Beigel, Allan 1940- ... 101
Beigel, Herbert 1944- ... 97-100
Beigel, Hugo George 1897- ... 37-40R
Beik, Paul H(arold) 1915- ... 15-16R
Beik, William (Humphrey) 1941- ... 123
Beilenson, Edna 1909-1981 ... 85-88
Obituary ... 103
Beilenson, Laurence W. 1899- ... 29-32R
Beiler, Edna 1923- ... CANR-1
Earlier sketch in CA 4R
Beilharz, Edwin A(lanson) 1907-1986 ... 33-36R
Obituary ... 120
Beim, Norman 1923- ... 85-88
Beine, George Holmes 1893- ... 93-96
Beineix, Jean-Jacques 1946- ... 124
Beiner, Ronald 1953- ... 117
Beirne, Brother Killian 1896- ... 21-22R
Beirne, Gerald E(dward) 1936- ... 118
Beirne, Joseph Anthony 1911-1974 ... 45-48
Obituary ... 53-56
Beiser, Arthur 1931- ... 93-96
See also SATA 22
Beiser, Germaine 1931- ... SATA-11
Beisner, Robert L(ee) 1936- ... 25-28R
Beissel, Henry Eric 1929- ... CANR-10
Earlier sketch in CA 65-68
Beisser, Arnold R(ay) 1925- ... 25-28R
Beistle, Shirley
See Climo, Shirley
Beit-Hallahmi, Benjamin 1943- ... 105
Beitler, Ethel Jane (Heinkel) 1906- ... CANR-2
Earlier sketch in CA 5-6R
Beitler, Stanley (Samuel) 1924- ... 5-6R
Beitz, Charles R(ichard) 1949- ... CANR-1
Earlier sketch in CA 49-52
Beitzell, Edwin Warfield 1905(?)-1984
Obituary ... 114
Beitzell, Robert (E.) 1930- Brief entry ... 115
Beitzinger, A(lfons) J(oseph) 1918- ... 45-48
Beizer, Boris 1934- ... 105
Beja, Morris 1935- ... 29-32R
Bejerot, Nils 1921- ... 29-32R
Bekessy, Jean
See Habe, Hans
Bekker, Hugo 1925- ... 41-44R
Bekker-Nielsen, Hans 1933- ... CANR-16
Earlier sketch in CA 25-28R
Belair, Felix, Jr. 1907-1978 Obituary ... 77-80
Belair, Richard L. 1934- ... 15-16R
See also SATA 45
Belaney, Archibald Stansfeld 1888-1938
Brief entry ... 114
See also SATA 24
Belanger, Jerome D(avid) 1938- ... 69-72
Belasco, David 1853-1931 Brief entry ... 104
See also DLB 7
See also TCLC 3
Belcastro, Joseph 1910- ... CAP-2
Earlier sketch in CA 19-20
Belch, Caroline Jean 1916- ... 45-48
Belchem, David
See Belchem, R(onald) F(rederick) K(ing)
Belchem, R(onald) F(rederick) K(ing)
1911-1981 ... 122
Obituary ... 108
Belcher, Jerry 1930-1987 Obituary ... 124
Belcheva, Elisaveta 1893- ... CLC-10
Belden, Gail
See Belden, Louise Conway
Belden, Louise Conway 1910- ... 104
Belden, Wilanne Schneider 1925- ... CANR-23
Earlier sketch in CA 106
Belding, Robert E(dward) 1911- ... 33-36R
Beldone, Phil "Cheech"
See Ellison, Harlan
Belehradek, Jan 1896-1980 Obituary ... 97-100
Beleno
See Azuela, Mariano
Belew, M. Wendell 1922- ... 33-36R
Belfer, Nancy 1930- ... 85-88
Belfield, Eversley (Michael Gallimore)
1918- ... CANR-11
Earlier sketch in CA 25-28R
Belfiglio, Valentine J(ohn) 1934- ... CANR-11
Earlier sketch in CA 49-52
Belford, Lee A(rcher) 1913- ... 19-20R
Belfrage, Cedric 1904- ... CANR-3
Earlier sketch in CA 11-12R
Belfrage, Sally 1936- ... 105
Bel Geddes, Joan
See Geddes, Joan Bel
Belgion, (Harold) Montgomery
1892-1973 ... CAP-1
Earlier sketch in CA 13-14
Belgum, David 1922- ... CANR-6
Earlier sketch in CA 13-14R
Belin, David W. 1928- ... 85-88
Beling, Willard A(dolf) 1919- ... 53-56
Belinkov, Arkady Viktorovich
1922(?)-1970 Obituary ... 29-32R
Belisle, Louis-Alexandre 1902-1985
Obituary ... 117
Belitsky, A(braham) Harvey 1929- ... 33-36R
Belitt, Ben 1911- ... CANR-7
Earlier sketch in CA 13-14R
See also CAAS 4
See also DLB 5
See also CLC 22
Belk, Fred Richard 1937- ... 115
Belkin, Gary S(tuart) 1945- ... 114
Belkin, Samuel 1911-1976 ... CANR-6
Obituary ... 65-68
Earlier sketch in CA 2R
Belkind, Allen 1927- ... 29-32R
Belknap, B. H.
See Ellis, Edward S(ylvester)
Belknap, Boynton
See Ellis, Edward S(ylvester)
Belknap, Boynton, M.D.
See Ellis, Edward S(ylvester)
Belknap, Ivan (Carl) 1916- ... 5-6R
Belknap, Jeremy 1744-1798 ... DLB-30, 37
Belknap, Robert H(arlan) 1917- ... 45-48
Belknap, Robert L(amont) 1929- ... 33-36R
Belknap, S(ally) Yancey 1895- ... CAP-1
Earlier sketch in CA 11-12
Bell, A(rthur) Donald 1920- ... 25-28R
Bell, Adrian (Hanbury) 1901-1980 ... 97-100
Obituary ... 102
Bell, Alan P(aul) 1932- ... CANR-13
Earlier sketch in CA 33-36R
Bell, Anne Olivier 1916- ... 112
Bell, Arthur 1939-1984 ... 85-88
Obituary ... 112
Bell, Barbara Currier 1941- ... 115
Bell, Bernard W(illiam) 1936- Brief entry ... 117
Bell, Betty
See Bell, Lorna Beatrice
Bell, Carol
See Flavell, Carol Willsey Bell
Bell, Carolyn
See Rigoni, Orlando (Joseph)
Bell, Carolyn Shaw 1920- ... 29-32R
Bell, Charles G. 1929- ... 37-40R
Bell, Charles Greenleaf 1916- ... CANR-2
Earlier sketch in CA 4R
Bell, Chip R(ay) 1944- ... 121
Bell, (Arthur) Clive (Howard) 1881-1964 .. 97-100
Obituary ... 89-92
Bell, Colin (John) 1938- ... 29-32R
Bell, Corydon Whitten 1894- ... 7-8R
See also SATA 3
Bell, Daniel 1919- ... CANR-4
Earlier sketch in CA 2R
Bell, David R(obert) 1932- ... 93-96
Bell, David S(heffield) 1945- ... 61-64
Bell, David Victor John 1944- ... CANR-17
Earlier sketches in CA 45-48, CANR-1
Bell, Derrick Albert, Jr. 1930- ... 104
Bell, Earl Hoyt 1903-1963 ... 3R
Bell, Eileen 1907- ... 33-36R
Bell, Elizabeth Rose 1912- ... 106
Bell, Elliot V(allance) 1902-1983 Obituary ... 108
Bell, Emily Mary
See Cason, Mabel Earp
Bell, Gail Winther 1936- ... 41-44R
Bell, Geoffrey (Lakin) 1939- Brief entry ... 114
Bell, Geoffrey Foxall 1896-1984 Obituary ... 111
Bell, Gerald D(ean) 1937- ... 49-52
Bell, Gertrude (Wood) 1911- ... 15-16R
See also SATA 12
Bell, Gina
See Balzano, Jeanne (Koppel)
See also SATA 7
Bell, Gordon Bennett 1934- ... 104
Bell, H(arold) Idris 1879-1967 ... CAP-1
Earlier sketch in CA 13-14
Bell, Harry McAra 1899- ... CAP-1
Earlier sketch in CA 13-14
Bell, Herbert C(lifford Francis) 1881-1966
Obituary ... 113
Bell, Herbert W. 1922- ... 123
Bell, Irene Wood 1944- ... 89-92
Bell, J. Bowyer 1931- ... 19-20R
Bell, Jack L. 1904-1975 ... CANR-6
Obituary ... 61-64
Earlier sketch in CA 1R
Bell, James (Adrian) 1917- ... 73-76
Bell, James B. 1932- ... 101
Bell, James Edward 1941- ... 33-36R
Bell, James K(enton) 1937- ... 25-28R
Bell, James Madison 1826-1902 ... 124
Brief entry ... 122
See also DLB 50
Bell, Janet
See Clymer, Eleanor
Bell, John (Donnelly) 1944- ... 97-100
Bell, John
See Johnson, Victor Hugo
Bell, John C. 1902(?)-1981 Obituary ... 103
Bell, John Elderkin 1913- ... 81-84
Bell, John Patrick 1935- ... 101
Bell, Joseph N. 1921- ... 7-8R
Bell, Josephine
See Ball, Doris Bell (Collier)
Bell, Joyce 1920- ... CANR-8
Earlier sketch in CA 57-60
Bell, Joyce Denebrink 1936- ... 19-20R
Bell, L. Nelson 1894-1973 ... CAP-1
Obituary ... 45-48
Earlier sketch in CA 19-20
Bell, Leland V(irgil) 1934- ... 49-52
Bell, Linda R. 1949- ... 117
Bell, Lorna Beatrice 1902- ... 117
Bell, Louise Price ... CAP-1
Earlier sketch in CA 9-10
Bell, Madison (Smartt) 1957- ... 111
See also CLC 41
Bell, Malcolm (H.) 1931- ... 122
Bell, Margaret E(lizabeth) 1898- ... CANR-1
Earlier sketch in CA 2R
See also SATA 2
Bell, Marvin 1937- ... 23-24R
See also DLB 5
See also CLC 8, 31
Bell, Mary Hayley
See Hayley Bell, Mary
Bell, Michael Davitt 1941- ... CANR-15
Earlier sketch in CA 81-84
Bell, Millicent (L.) ... 114
Bell, Neill 1946- ... 118
See also SATA 50
Bell, Norman (Edward) 1899- ... 61-64
See also SATA 11
Bell, Norman W. 1928- ... CANR-1
Earlier sketch in CA 4R
Bell, Oliver (Sydney) 1913- ... 53-56
Bell, Philip W(ilkes) 1924- ... 29-32R
Bell, Quentin (Claudian Stephen) 1910- ... 57-60
Bell, R(obert) C(harles) 1917- ... CANR-24
Earlier sketches in CA 19-20R, CANR-7
Bell, Raymond Martin 1907- ... 29-32R
See also SATA 13
Bell, Robert (Ivan) 1942- ... 101
Bell, Robert E(ugene) 1914- ... 37-40R
Bell, Robert Roy 1924- ... CANR-1
Earlier sketch in CA 4R
Bell, Robert S(tanley) W(arren) 1871-1921
Brief entry ... 115
See also SATA 27
Bell, Robert Vaughn 1924- ... 110
Bell, Roger 1947- ... 122
Bell, (Caroline) Rose (Buchanan) 1939- ... 29-32R
Bell, Roseann P. 1945- ... 120
Bell, Rudolph M(ark) 1942- ... 45-48
Bell, Sallie Lee ... CANR-1
Earlier sketch in CA 4R
Bell, Sarah Fore 1920- ... 53-56
Bell, Sidney 1929- ... 41-44R
Bell, Stephen (Scott) 1935- ... 65-68
Bell, Thelma Harrington 1896- ... 1R
See also SATA 3
Bell, Thornton
See Fanthorpe, R(obert) Lionel
Bell, Vicars W(alker) 1904- ... CAP-1
Earlier sketch in CA 15-16
Bell, Wendell 1924- ... CANR-4
Earlier sketch in CA 3R
Bell, Whitfield Jenks, Jr. 1914- ... 105
Bell, William J. ... AITN-1
Bell, William Stewart 1921- ... 4R
Bell, Winifred 1914- ... CANR-9
Earlier sketch in CA 19-20R
Bellah, James Warner 1899-1976 ... 7-8R
Obituary ... 69-72
Bellah, Robert N(eelly) 1927- ... 21-22R
Bellairs, George
See Blundell, Harold
Bellairs, John 1938- ... CANR-24
Earlier sketches in CA 23-24R, CANR-8
See also SATA 2
Bellak, Leopold 1916- ... CANR-16
Earlier sketch in CA 85-88
Bellamy, David (James) 1933- Brief entry ... 114
Bellamy, Edward 1850-1898 ... DLB-12
Bellamy, Francis Rufus 1886-1972
Obituary ... 33-36R
Bellamy, Guy 1935- ... CANR-9
Earlier sketch in CA 65-68
Bellamy, Harmon
See Bloom, Herman Irving
Bellamy, James A(ndrew) 1925- ... 49-52
Bellamy, Joe David 1941- ... CANR-15
Earlier sketch in CA 41-44R
Bellamy, Joseph 1719-1790 ... DLB-31
Bellamy, Peter 1914- Brief entry ... 117
Bellamy, Ralph 1904- ... 101
Bellan, Ruben C. 1918- ... 13-14R
Belle, Pamela 1952- ... 115
Beller, Anne Scott ... 77-80
Beller, Elmer Adolph 1894-1980
Obituary ... 97-100
Beller, Jacob 1896- ... CAP-2
Earlier sketch in CA 25-28
Beller, Joel 1926- ... 113
Beller, William Stern 1919- ... 7-8R
Bellerby, (Mary Eireen) Frances Parker
1899-1975 ... 101
Bellhouse, Alan Robert 1914-1980
Obituary ... 108
Belli, Angela 1935- ... 37-40R
Belli, Melvin M(ouron) 1907- ... 104
Bellin, Edward J.
See Kuttner, Henry
Bellingham, Brenda 1931- ... 123
Bellingham, Helen Mary Dorothea
See Beauclerk, Helen De Vere
Bellini delle Stelle, Pier Luigi
1920(?)-1984 Obituary ... 111
Bellis, David James 1944- ... 108
Bellman, Richard (Ernest) 1920-1984 .. CANR-12
Obituary ... 112
Earlier sketch in CA 69-72
Bellman, Samuel Irving 1926- ... CANR-7
Earlier sketch in CA 17-18R
Bellman, Willard F. 1920- ... 113
Bell-Metereau, Rebecca 1949- ... 122
Bello, Francis (Cesare) 1917-1987
Obituary ... 121
Belloc, (Joseph) Hilaire (Pierre)
1870-1953 Brief entry ... 106
See also YABC 1
See also DLB 19
See also TCLC 7, 18
Belloc, Joseph Peter Rene Hilaire
See Belloc, (Joseph) Hilaire (Pierre)
Belloc, Joseph Pierre Hilaire
See Belloc, (Joseph) Hilaire (Pierre)
Belloc, M. A.
See Lowndes, Marie Adelaide (Belloc)
Bellochio, Marco 1939- ... 110
Bellocq, Louise
See Boudat, Marie-Louise
Bellonci, Maria 1902-1986 Obituary ... 120
Bellone, Enrico 1938- ... 106
Bellony, Alice 1925- ... 118
Bellony-Rewald, Alice
See Bellony, Alice
Bellot, Leland J(oseph) 1936- Brief entry ... 115

Bellow, Saul 1915- ... 5-6R
See also CABS 1
See also DLB 2, 28
See also DLBY 82
See also DLBD 3
See also CDALB 1941-1968
See also CLC 1, 2, 3, 6, 8, 10, 13, 15, 25, 33, 34
See also AITN 2
Bellows, Fiona (Ann) 1941- ... 115
Bellows, James G(ilbert) 1922- ... 102
Bellows, Roger Marion 1905- ... 4R
Bellows, Thomas J(ohn) 1935- ... 45-48
Bellush, Bernard 1917- Brief entry ... 120
Bell-Villada, Gene Harold 1941- ... 105
Bellville, Cheryl Walsh 1944- ... 109
See also SATA 49
Bellville, Rod 1944- ... 117
Bell-Zano, Gina
See Balzano, Jeanne (Koppel)
See also SATA 7
Belmont, Eleanor Robson 1879-1979
Obituary ... 97-100
Belmont, Georges 1909- ... 29-32R
Belmont, Herman S. 1920- ... 41-44R
Belmonte, Thomas 1946- ... 93-96
Beloff, Max 1913- ... CANR-18
Earlier sketch in CA 7-8R
Beloff, Michael 1942- ... 21-22R
Beloff, Nora 1919- ... 106
Belok, Michael V(ictor) 1923- ... 33-36R
Beloof, Robert 1923- ... 21-22R
Belote, James H(ine) 1922- ... 33-36R
Belote, Julianne 1929- ... 61-64
Belote, William Milton 1922- ... 49-52
Belotserkovsky, Vladimir Naumovich Bill
See Bill-Belotserkovsky, Vladimir Naumovich
Belous, Russell E. 1925- ... 25-28R
Belozersky, Andrei (Nicolaevich) 1905-1972 Obituary ... 37-40R
Belpre, Pura 1899-1982 ... 73-76
Obituary ... 109
See also SATA 16, 30
Belser, Lee 1925- ... 73-76
Belser, Reimond Karel Maria de 1929- ... CLC-14
Belshaw, Cyril S(hirley) 1921- ... 11-12R
Belshaw, Michael (Horace) 1928- ... 21-22R
Belsky, Dick 1945- ... 122
Belsley, David A(lan) 1939- ... 29-32R
Belth, Joseph M(orton) 1929- ... 112
Belting, Natalia Maree 1915- ... CANR-3
Earlier sketch in CA 1R
See also SATA 6
Belton, John Raynor 1931- ... 69-72
See also SATA 22
Beltran, Alberto 1923- ... SATA-43
Beltran, Miriam 1914- ... 33-36R
Beltran, Pedro (Gerardo) 1897-1979 ... 93-96
Obituary ... 85-88
Belushi, John 1949-1982 Obituary ... 106
Belveal, L(orenzo) Dee 1918- ... 23-24R
Belvedere, Lee
See Grayland, Valerie (Merle Spanner)
Bely, Andrey
See Bugayev, Boris Nikolayevich
See also TCLC 7
Bely, Jeanette L(obach) 1916- ... 33-36R
Belyi, Andrei
See Bugayev, Boris Nikolayevich
Belz, Carl 1937- ... CANR-11
Earlier sketch in CA 29-32R
Belz, Herman (Julius) 1937- ... 65-68
Bemelmans, Ludwig 1898-1962 ... 73-76
See also SATA 15
See also DLB 22
See also CLR 6
Bemis, Samuel Flagg 1891-1973 ... 11-12R
Obituary ... 45-48
See also DLB 17
Bemis, Stephen Edward 1937-1985
Obituary ... 115
Bemister, Henry
See Barrett, Harry B(emister)
Bemmy, Karen (Amy) 1955- ... 123
Bemporad, Jules (Richard) 1937- ... 122
Ben, Ilke
See Harper, Carol Ely
Benagh, Jim 1937- ... CANR-9
Earlier sketch in CA 57-60
Ben-Ami, Shlomo 1943- ... 116
Ben-Amos, Dan 1934- ... CANR-11
Earlier sketch in CA 69-72
Benamou, Michel J(ean) 1929-1978 ... CANR-3
Earlier sketch in CA 5-6R
Benante, Joseph P(hilip) 1936- ... 33-36R
Benarde, Melvin A(lbert) 1923- ... 25-28R
Benardete, Jane Johnson 1930- ... 45-48
Benario, Herbert W. 1929- ... 25-28R
Benarria, Allan
See Goldenthal, Allan Benarria
Benary, Margot
See Benary-Isbert, Margot
Benary-Isbert, Margot 1889-1979 ... CANR-4
Obituary ... 89-92
Earlier sketch in CA 7-8R
See also SATA 2, 21
See also CLC 12
See also CLR 12
Benasutti, Marion 1908- ... 21-22R
See also SATA 6
Benatar, Stephen (Royce) 1937- ... 110
Benavente (y Martinez), Jacinto 1866-1954 Brief entry ... 106
See also TCLC 3
Ben-Avraham, Chofetz Chaim
See Pickering, Stephen
Benbow, Charles (Clarence) 1929- ... 122
Bence, Evelyn ... 110
Bence-Jones, Mark 1930- ... CANR-5
Earlier sketch in CA 13-14R
Bench, Johnny (Lee) 1947- Brief entry ... 113
Benchley, Nathaniel (Goddard) 1915-1981 ... CANR-12
Obituary ... 105
Earlier sketches in CA 4R, CANR-2
See also SATA 3, 25, 28
Benchley, Peter (Bradford) 1940- ... CANR-12
Earlier sketch in CA 17-18R
See also SATA 3
See also CLC 4, 8
See also AITN 2
Benchley, Robert (Charles) 1889-1945
Brief entry ... 105
See also DLB 11
See also TCLC 1
Benda, Harry J(indrich) 1919- ... 11-12R
Benda, Julien 1867-1956 Brief entry ... 120
Bendavid, Avrom 1942- ... 41-44R
Ben-David, Joseph 1920-1986 Obituary ... 118
Bender, Coleman C. 1921- ... 33-36R
Bender, David L(eo) 1936- ... 123
Bender, David R(ay) 1942- ... 102
Bender, Frederic L(awrence) 1943- ... 69-72
Bender, Henry E(dwin), Jr. 1937- ... 33-36R
Bender, James F(rederick) 1905- ... 17-18R
Bender, Jay
See Deindorfer, Robert Greene
Bender, John B(ryant) 1940- ... 65-68
Bender, Louis W. 1927- ... CANR-14
Earlier sketch in CA 33-36R
Bender, Lucy Ellen 1942- ... 25-28R
See also SATA 22
Bender, Marylin 1925- ... CANR-12
Earlier sketch in CA 21-22R
Bender, Norman J(ohn) 1927- ... 118
Bender, Richard 1930- ... 45-48
Bender, Robert M. 1936- ... 33-36R
Bender, Ross Thomas 1929- ... 61-64
Bender, Stephen (Joseph) 1942- ... 61-64
Bender, Thomas 1944- ... CANR-12
Earlier sketch in CA 73-76
Bender, Todd K. 1936- ... CANR-24
Earlier sketches in CA 21-22R, CANR-9
Benderly, Beryl Lieff 1943- ... 108
Bendick, Jeanne 1919- ... CANR-2
Earlier sketch in CA 7-8R
See also SATA 2
See also SAAS 4
See also CLR 5
Bendick, Marc, Jr. 1946- ... 118
Bendick, Robert L(ouis) 1917- ... 61-64
See also SATA 11
Bendiner, Elmer 1916- ... CANR-7
Earlier sketch in CA 57-60
Bendiner, Kenneth Paul 1947- ... 119
Bendiner, Robert 1909- ... 11-12R
Bendit, Gladys Williams 1885- ... CAP-1
Earlier sketches in CA 13-14
Bendit, Laurence John 1898-1974 ... CAP-2
Earlier sketch in CA 25-28
Bendix, Reinhard 1916- ... CANR-4
Earlier sketch in CA 1R
Bendixson, Terence 1934- ... 93-96
Ben-Dov, Meir
See Bernet, Michael M.
Benecke, Gerhard ?-1985 Obituary ... 117
Benedek, Therese 1892-1977 ... 41-44R
Benedetti, Robert L(awrence) 1939- ... 29-32R
Benedetto, Arnold J(oseph) 1916-1966 ... 7-8R
Benedict, Bertram 1892(?)-1978 Obituary ... 77-80
Benedict, Burton 1923- ... 109
Benedict, Dianne 1941- ... 110
Benedict, Dorothy Potter 1889-1979 ... CAP-1
Obituary ... 93-96
Earlier sketch in CA 13-14
See also SATA 11, 23
Benedict, Joseph
See Dollen, Charles Joseph
Benedict, Lois Trimble 1902-1967 ... CAP-2
Earlier sketch in CA 19-20
See also SATA 12
Benedict, Marion 1923- ... 109
Benedict, Michael Les 1945- ... 45-48
Benedict, Rex 1920- ... 19-20R
See also SATA 8
Benedict, Robert P(hilip) 1924-1986 ... 41-44R
Obituary ... 119
Benedict, Stewart H(urd) 1924- ... 13-14R
See also SATA 26
Benedictus, David (Henry) 1938- ... CANR-24
Earlier sketch in CA 73-76
See also DLB 14
Benedikt, Michael 1935- ... CANR-7
Earlier sketch in CA 15-16R
See also DLB 5
See also CLC 4, 14
Benefield, June 1921- ... 45-48
Benell, Florence B(elle) 1912- ... 33-36R
Benell, Julie 1906(?)-1982 Obituary ... 105
Benello, C. George 1926- ... 33-36R
Ben-Ephraim, Gavriel 1946- ... 116
Benes, Jan 1936- ... 29-32R
Benet, Edouard
See Edwards, William B(ennett)
Benet, James 1914- ... CANR-8
Earlier sketch in CA 61-64
Benet, Juan 1927- ... CLC-28
Benet, Laura 1884-1979 ... CANR-6
Obituary ... 85-88
Earlier sketch in CA 9-10R
See also SATA 3, 23
Benet, Mary Kathleen 1943- ... 57-60
Benet, Stephen Vincent 1898-1943
Brief entry ... 104
See also YABC 1
See also DLB 4, 48
See also TCLC 7
Benet, Sula 1906-1982 ... 89-92
Obituary ... 108
See also SATA 21, 33
Benet, William Rose 1886-1950
Brief entry ... 118
See also DLB 45
Benetar, Judith 1941- ... 53-56
Benevolo, Leonardo 1923- ... 89-92
Ben-Ezer, Ehud 1936- ... CANR-24
Earlier sketches in CA 61-64, CANR-8
Benezra, Barbara (Beardsley) 1921- ... 15-16R
See also SATA 10
Benfield, Derek 1926- ... CANR-10
Earlier sketch in CA 23-24R
Benfield, G(raham) J(ohn) Barker
See Barker-Benfield, G(raham) J(ohn)
Benfield, Richard E. 1940- ... 77-80
Benford, Gregory (Albert) 1941- ... CANR-24
Earlier sketches in CA 69-72, CANR-12
See also DLBY 82
Benford, Harry (Bell) 1917- ... 89-92
Benford, Timothy B(artholomew) 1941- ... CANR-11
Earlier sketch in CA 69-72
Benge, Eugene J(ackson) 1896- ... CANR-9
Earlier sketch in CA 57-60
Bengelsdorf, Irving S. 1922- ... 57-60
Bengtson, Vern L. 1941- ... CANR-4
Earlier sketch in CA 49-52
Bengtsson, Arvid 1916- ... 33-36R
Ben-Gurion, David 1886-1973 ... 101
Obituary ... 45-48
Benham, Leslie 1922- ... 9-10R
See also SATA 48
Benham, Lois (Dakin) 1924- ... 9-10R
See also SATA 48
Benham, Mary Lile 1914- ... 102
Ben-Horav, Naphthali
See Kravitz, Nathaniel
Ben-Horin, Meir 1918- ... CANR-14
Earlier sketch in CA 29-32R
Benichou, Paul 1908- ... 57-60
Beniger, James R. 1946- ... 111
Benington, John (Elson) 1921- ... 5-6R
Ben-Israel-Kidron, Hedva ... 33-36R
Benjamin, Alice
See Brooke, Avery (Rogers)
Benjamin, Anna Shaw 1925- ... 41-44R
Benjamin, Annette Francis 1928- ... 19-20R
Benjamin, Bry 1924- ... 19-20R
Benjamin, Burton Richard 1917- ... 101
Benjamin, Claude (Max Edward Pohlman) 1911- ... 9-10R
Benjamin, Curtis G. 1901-1983 ... 122
Obituary ... 111
Benjamin, Edward Bernard 1897- ... 69-72
Benjamin, Gerald 1945- ... 49-52
Benjamin, Harry 1885-1986 ... CAP-1
Obituary ... 120
Earlier sketch in CA 11-12
Benjamin, Herbert S(tanley) 1922- ... 5-6R
Benjamin, Joseph 1921- ... 57-60
Benjamin, Judy-Lynn
See del Rey, Judy-Lynn
Benjamin, Nora
See Kubie, Nora Gottheil Benjamin
Benjamin, Park 1809-1864 ... DLB-3, 59
Benjamin, Philip (Robert) 1922-1966 ... 7-8R
Obituary ... 25-28R
Benjamin, Robert (Irving) 1949- ... 109
Benjamin, Roger W. 1942- ... 37-40R
Benjamin, William E(arl) 1942- ... 25-28R
Benjaminson, Peter 1945- ... CANR-12
Earlier sketch in CA 73-76
Benji, Thomas
See Robinson, Frank M(alcolm)
ben-Jochannan, Yosef 1918- ... CANR-12
Earlier sketch in CA 69-72
Benko, Stephen 1924- ... 11-12R
Benkovitz, Miriam J(eanette) 1911-1986 ... CANR-4
Obituary ... 119
Earlier sketch in CA 11-12R
Benn, Gottfried 1886-1956 Brief entry ... 106
See also DLB 56
See also TCLC 3
Benn, John Andrews 1904-1984 Obituary ... 115
Benn, Matthew
See Siegel, Benjamin
Bennani, B(en) M(ohammed) 1946- ... CANR-13
Earlier sketch in CA 61-64
Benne, Kenneth D(ean) 1908- ... 33-36R
Benner, Judith Ann 1942- ... 122
Benner, Ralph Eugene (Jr.) 1932- ... 33-36R
Bennet, Glin 1927- ... 123
Bennett, A(bram) E(lting Hasbrouck) 1898- ... 65-68
Bennett, Addison C(urtis) 1918- ... CANR-7
Earlier sketch in CA 5-6R
Bennett, Adrian A(rthur) 1941- ... 53-56
Bennett, Alan 1934- ... 103
See also CLC 45
Bennett, Alice
See Ziner, Florence (Feenie)
Bennett, Anna Elizabeth 1914- ... 19-20R
Bennett, Archibald F. 1896- ... CAP-1
Earlier sketch in CA 15-16
Bennett, (Enoch) Arnold 1867-1931
Brief entry ... 106
See also DLB 10, 34
See also TCLC 5, 20
Bennett, Betty T. ... 115
Bennett, Boyce McLean, Jr. 1928- ... 115
Bennett, Bruce (William) 1952- ... 110
Bennett, Bruce L(anyon) 1917- ... 25-28R
Bennett, Charles 1899- ... DLB-44
Bennett, Charles 1901- ... CAP-1
Earlier sketch in CA 15-16
Bennett, Charles 1932- ... 25-28R
Bennett, Charles E(dward) 1910- ... 11-12R
Bennett, Christine
See Neubauer, William Arthur
Bennett, Daniel
See Gilmore, Joseph L(ee)
Bennett, Daphne Nicholson ... 41-44R
Bennett, David H. 1935- ... 25-28R
Bennett, Dennis J. 1917- ... CANR-20
Earlier sketch in CA 49-52
Bennett, Dorothea
See Young, Dorothea Bennett
Bennett, Dwight
See Newton, D(wight) B(ennett)
Bennett, E(thel) M. Granger 1891- ... CAP-1
Earlier sketch in CA 13-14
Bennett, E. N.
See Bennett, Ernest N(athaniel)
Bennett, Edward (Martin) 1924- ... 5-6R
Bennett, Edward M(oore) 1927- ... 33-36R
Bennett, Ernest N(athaniel) 1868-1947
Brief entry ... 119
Bennett, Frances Grant 1899- ... CAP-2
Earlier sketch in CA 25-28
Bennett, Fredna W(illis) 1906- ... CAP-1
Earlier sketch in CA 9-10
Bennett, G. V.
See Bennett, Gareth Vaughan
Bennett, Gareth Vaughan 1929-1987
Obituary ... 124
Bennett, Geoffrey (Martin) 1909-1983 ... 13-14R
Obituary ... 110
Bennett, George 1920- ... 5-6R
Bennett, George Harold 1930- ... 97-100
Bennett, Gertrude Ryder ... 53-56
Bennett, Gordon A(nderson) 1940- ... 29-32R
Bennett, Gordon C. 1935- ... CANR-14
Earlier sketch in CA 33-36R
Bennett, Gwendolyn 1902-1981 ... DLB-51
Bennett, Hal
See Bennett, George Harold
See also DLB 33
See also CLC 5
Bennett, Hall
See Hall, Bennie Caroline (Humble)
Bennett, Harold (Zina) 1936- ... 41-44R
Bennett, Harve
See Fischman, Harve
Bennett, Howard Franklin 1911-1974 ... 4R
Bennett, Isadora 1900-1980 Obituary ... 93-96
Bennett, J(ohn) G(odolphin) 1897-1974
Obituary ... 111
Bennett, Jack Arthur Walter 1911-1981 ... CANR-6
Obituary ... 103
Earlier sketch in CA 9-10R
Bennett, James D(avid) 1926- ... 61-64
Bennett, James Gordon 1795-1872 ... DLB-43
Bennett, James Gordon, Jr. 1841-1918 ... DLB-23
Bennett, James R(ichard) 1932- ... 33-36R
Bennett, James Thomas 1942- ... CANR-23
Earlier sketch in CA 106
Bennett, Jay 1912- ... CANR-11
Earlier sketch in CA 69-72
See also SATA 27, 41
See also SAAS 4
See also CLC 35
Bennett, Jean Francis
See Dorcy, Sister Mary Jean
Bennett, Jeremy
See Bennett, John Jerome Nelson
Bennett, Jill (Crawford) 1934- ... SATA-41
Bennett, Jill 1947- ... 106
Bennett, John 1865-1956 ... YABC-1
See also DLB 42
Bennett, John (Frederic) 1920- ... 29-32R
Bennett, John Jerome Nelson 1939- ... 21-22R
Bennett, John M(ichael) 1942- ... CANR-18
Earlier sketches in CA 49-52, CANR-2
Bennett, John W. 1918- ... 69-72
Bennett, John William 1915- ... CANR-4
Earlier sketch in CA 3R
Bennett, Jonathan (Francis) 1930- ... CANR-1
Earlier sketch in CA 45-48
Bennett, Joseph D. 1922-1972 ... 3R
Obituary ... 33-36R
Bennett, Josephine Waters 1899-1975 ... 3R
Obituary ... 103
Bennett, Judith ?-1979 Obituary ... 85-88
Bennett, Kay Curley 1922- ... 17-18R
Bennett, Lerone, Jr. 1928- ... CANR-2
Earlier sketch in CA 45-48
Bennett, Linda L(eveque) 1946- ... 115
Bennett, Louise (Simone) 1919- ... CLC-28
Bennett, M. J.
See Bennett, Marcia J(oanne)
Bennett, Marcia J(oanne) 1945- ... 114
Bennett, Margaret E(laine) 1893- ... 7-8R
Bennett, Margot 1912-1980 Obituary ... 105
Bennett, Marion T(insley) 1914- ... 11-12R
Bennett, Melba Berry 1901-1968 ... CAP-2
Earlier sketch in CA 19-20
Bennett, Meridan 1927- ... 25-28R
Bennett, Michael 1943-1987 ... 101
Obituary ... 122
Bennett, Mildred R. 1909- ... CAP-2
Earlier sketch in CA 25-28
Bennett, Neville 1937- ... CANR-19
Earlier sketch in CA 102
Bennett, Noel 1939- ... 45-48
Bennett, Norman Robert 1932- ... CANR-18
Earlier sketches in CA 9-10R, CANR-3

Bennett, Patrick (H.) 1931- 122
Bennett, Paul Lewis 1921- CANR-4
Earlier sketch in CA 1R
Bennett, Penelope Agnes 1938- 13-14R
Bennett, Rachel
See Hill, Margaret (Ohler)
Bennett, Rainey 1907- SATA-15
Bennett, Richard 1899- SATA-21
Bennett, Rita (Marie) 1934- CANR-20
Earlier sketch in CA 69-72
Bennett, Robert A(ndrew) 1927- CANR-5
Earlier sketch in CA 13-14R
Bennett, Robert D(onald) 1947- 118
Bennett, Robert L. 1931- 41-44R
Bennett, Robert Russell 1894-1981
Obituary 105
Bennett, Russell H(oradley) 1896- SATA-25
Bennett, Scott (Boyce) 1939- 33-36R
Bennett, Thomas L(eroy) 1942- 85-88
Bennett, Victor 1919- CANR-7
Earlier sketch in CA 7-8R
Bennett, W(illiam) R(obert) 1921- 13-14R
Bennett, William (Ira) 1941- 107
Bennett, William L. 1924- 19-20R
Bennett-Coverley, Louise 1919- 97-100
Bennett-England, Rodney Charles 1936- 61-64
Bennetts, Pamela 1922- 37-40R
Bennie, William A(ndrew) 1921- 69-72
Benning, (Barbara) Lee Edwards 1934- 53-56
Bennion, Barbara Elisabeth 1930- 110
Bennis, Warren G. 1925- CANR-5
Earlier sketch in CA 53-56
Benoff, Mac 1915(?)-1972 Obituary 37-40R
Benoist-Mechin, Jacques 1901-1983 105
Obituary 109
Benoit, Emile 1910-1978 CANR-3
Obituary 77-80
Earlier sketch in CA 7-8R
Benoit, Jacques 1941- DLB-60
Benoit, Leroy James 1913- 33-36R
Benoit, Pierre 1886-1962 Obituary 93-96
Benoit, Pierre Maurice 1906-1987 41-44R
Obituary 122
Benoit, Richard 1899(?)-1969 Obituary 104
Benoliel, Jeanne Quint 1919- 49-52
Bense, Walter F(rederick) 1932- CANR-1
Earlier sketch in CA 45-48
Bensen, Alice R. 1911- 69-72
Bensen, Donald R. 1927- CANR-20
Earlier sketches in CA 9-10R, CANR-5
Bensko, John 1949- 105
Bensman, Joseph 1922- CANR-10
Earlier sketch in CA 23-24R
Bensol, Oscar
See Gilbert, Willie
Benson, A. George 1924- 69-72
Benson, B. A.
See Beyea, Basil
Benson, Ben(jamin) 1915-1959
Brief entry 112
Benson, C(arl) David 1942- 123
Benson, C. Randolph 1923- 29-32R
Benson, Carmen 1921- 57-60
Benson, Charles S(cott) 1922- CANR-8
Earlier sketch in CA 17-18R
Benson, Constantine Walter 1909-1982
Obituary 108
Benson, Daniel
See Cooper, Colin Symons
Benson, Dennis C(arroll) 1936- 37-40R
Benson, E(dward) F(rederic) 1867-1940
Brief entry 114
See also TCLC 27
Benson, Elizabeth P(olk) 1924- 93-96
Benson, Eugene 1928- 89-92
Benson, Frederick R. 1934- 33-36R
Benson, Frederick William 1948- CANR-19
Earlier sketch in CA 101
Benson, Gigi (Dian Daniels) 1941- 108
Benson, Ginny
See Benson, Virginia
Benson, Harry 1929- 108
Benson, Herbert 1935- 85-88
Benson, J(ack) L(eonard) 1920- 105
Benson, Jackson J. 1930- 25-28R
See also CLC 34
Benson, Jeffrey 1937- 120
Benson, Kathleen 1947- 85-88
Benson, Larry D(ean) 1929- 37-40R
Benson, Lyman (David) 1909- 49-52
Benson, Margaret H. Benson 1899- 7-8R
Benson, Mary 1919- CANR-17
Earlier sketches in CA 49-52, CANR-1
Benson, Maxine (Frances) 1939- 65-68
Benson, Rachel
See Jowitt, Deborah
Benson, Raymond 1955- 118
Benson, Richard
See Cooper, Saul
Benson, Robert G(reen) 1930- 29-32R
Benson, Robert S(later) 1942- 33-36R
Benson, Rolf Eric 1951- 102
Benson, Ruth Crego 1937- 41-44R
Benson, Sally 1900-1972 CAP-1
Obituary 37-40R
Earlier sketch in CA 19-20
See also SATA 1, 27, 35
See also CLC 17
Benson, Stella 1892-1933 Brief entry 117
See also DLB 36
See also TCLC 17
Benson, Stephana Vere 1909- 13-14R
Benson, Ted
See Benson, Frederick William
Benson, Thomas Godfrey 1899- CAP-1
Earlier sketch in CA 11-12
Benson, Thomas W(alter) 1937- CANR-19
Earlier sketch in CA 29-32R
Benson, Virginia 1923- 57-60
Benson, Warren S(ten) 1929- 114
Benson, William Howard 1902- 4R
Benstead, Steven 1951- 113
Bensted-Smith, Richard (Brian) 1929- 13-14R
Benstock, Bernard 1930- CANR-7
Earlier sketch in CA 17-18R
Benstock, Shari 1944- 97-100
Bent, Alan Edward 1939- CANR-4
Earlier sketch in CA 49-52
Bent, Charles N. 1935- 23-24R
Bent, Rudyard K(ipling) 1901- CANR-18
Earlier sketch in CA 3R
Benteen, John
See Haas, Ben(jamin) L(eopold)
Bentel, Pearl B(ucklen) 1901- CAP-2
Earlier sketch in CA 21-22
Benthall, Jonathan 1941- 41-44R
Bentham, Frederick 1911- 105
Bentham, Jay
See Bensman, Joseph
Benthic, Arch E.
See Stewart, Harris B(ates), Jr.
Benthul, Herman F(orrest) 1911- 33-36R
Bentley, Beth (Rita) 1928- 101
Bentley, Colin 1936- 118
Bentley, E(dmund) C(lerihew) 1875-1956
Brief entry 108
See also TCLC 12
Bentley, Eric (Russell) 1916- CANR-6
Earlier sketch in CA 7-8R
See also CLC 24
Bentley, G(erald) E(ades), Jr. 1930- CANR-4
Earlier sketch in CA 3R
Bentley, Gerald Eades 1901- 41-44R
Bentley, Howard Beebe 1925- 9-10R
Bentley, Janice Babb 1933- 15-16R
Bentley, Judith (McBride) 1945- CANR-23
Earlier sketch in CA 107
See also SATA 40
Bentley, Margaret 1926- 108
Bentley, Nicolas Clerihew 1907-1978 CANR-11
Obituary 81-84
Earlier sketch in CA 65-68
See also SATA 24
Bentley, Phyllis Eleanor 1894-1977 CANR-3
Earlier sketch in CA 4R
See also SATA 6, 25
Bentley, Richard
See Browning, Alice C(rolley)
Bentley, Roy 1947- SATA-46
Bentley, Sarah 1946- 29-32R
Bentley, Toni 1958- 123
Bentley, Virginia W(illiams) 1908- 57-60
Bentley-Taylor, David 1915- CANR-14
Earlier sketch in CA 77-80
Benton, Dorothy Gilchrist 1919- 57-60
Benton, F(red) Warren 1948- 119
Benton, Helen Hemingway 1902(?)-1974
Obituary 104
Benton, John Frederic 1931-1988 69-72
Obituary 124
Benton, John W. 1933- CANR-12
Earlier sketch in CA 29-32R
Benton, Joseph Nelson, Jr. 1924-1988
Obituary 124
Benton, Josephine Moffett 1905- 7-8R
Benton, Karla
See Rowland, D(onald) S(ydney)
Benton, Kenneth (Carter) 1909- CANR-1
Earlier sketch in CA 49-52
Benton, Lewis R(obert) 1920- 19-20R
Benton, (Joseph) Nelson (Jr.) 1924- 112
Brief entry 110
Benton, Patricia 1907- 5-6R
Benton, Peggie 1906- 49-52
Benton, Richard G(lasscock) 1938- 81-84
Benton, Robert (Douglass) 1932- CANR-2
Earlier sketch in CA 1R
See also DLB 44
Benton, Robert
See Buse, Renee
Benton, Thomas Hart 1889-1975 93-96
Obituary 53-56
Benton, Wilbourn Eugene 1917- 3R
Benton, Will
See Paine, Lauran (Bosworth)
Benton, William 1900-1973 CAP-1
Obituary 41-44R
Earlier sketch in CA 15-16
Bentov, Itzhak 1923(?)-1979 Obituary 85-88
Bentwich, Norman 1883-1971 Obituary 111
Bentz, Thomas 1943- 112
Bentz, William F(rederick) 1940- 53-56
ben Uzair, Salem
See Horne, Richard Henry
Benveniste, Asa 1925- 69-72
Benveniste, Emile 1902-1976 Obituary 115
Benveniste, Guy 1927- CANR-8
Earlier sketch in CA 61-64
Ben-Veniste, Richard 1943- Brief entry 114
Benvenisti, Meron (Shmuel) 1934- CANR-12
Earlier sketch in CA 65-68
Benward, Bruce (Charles) 1921- CANR-9
Earlier sketch in CA 9-10R
Beny, Roloff
See Beny, Wilfred Roy
Beny, Wilfred Roy 1924-1984 23-24R
Obituary 112
Benyo, Richard (Stephen) 1946- CANR-13
Earlier sketch in CA 77-80
Ben-Yosef, Avraham C(haim)
See Matsuba, Moshe
Benz, Ernst (Wilhelm) 1907-1978 CANR-13
Earlier sketch in CA 15-16R
Benz, Frank L(eonard) 1930- 41-44R
Benzie, William 1930- 37-40R
Benziger, Barbara Field 1918- Brief entry 115
Benziger, James 1914- 13-14R
Ben-Zion
See Weinman, Benzion
Benzoni, Juliette (Andree Marguerite)
1920- CANR-18
Earlier sketch in CA 101
Beorse, Bryn 1896- 45-48
Bequaert, Lucia H(umes) 65-68
Beranek, Leo L(eroy) 1914- 7-8R
Beranek, William 1922- 5-6R
Berard, J(ules) Aram 1933- 17-18R
Berardo, Felix M(ario) 1934- CANR-24
Earlier sketches in CA 57-60, CANR-8
Berberova, Nina (Nikolaevna) 1901- CANR-14
Earlier sketch in CA 33-36R
Berbrich, Joan D. 1925- CANR-12
Earlier sketch in CA 29-32R
Berbusse, Edward J(oseph) 1912- 21-22R
Berch, William O.
See Coyne, Joseph E.
Berchen, Ursula 1919- 65-68
Berchen, William 1920- 65-68
Berck, Martin G(ans) 1928- 65-68
Berckman, Evelyn Domenica 1900- CANR-1
Earlier sketch in CA 3R
Bercovici, Rion 1903(?)-1976 Obituary 69-72
Bercovitch, Reuben 1923- 104
Bercovitch, Sacvan 1933- 41-44R
Berczeller, Richard 1902- 11-12R
Berdes, George R. 1931- 29-32R
Berdie, Douglas R(alph) 1946- 53-56
Berdie, Ralph F(reimuth) 1916-1974 CANR-11
Earlier sketch in CA 17-18R
Berding, Andrew H(enry) 1902- 7-8R
Berdyaev, Nicolas
See Berdyaev, Nikolai (Aleksandrovich)
Berdyaev, Nikolai (Aleksandrovich)
1874-1948 Brief entry 120
Bere, Rennie Montague 1907- 65-68
Bereday, George Z(ygmunt) F(ijalkowski)
1920-1983 CANR-4
Obituary 111
Earlier sketch in CA 4R
Bereiter, Carl 1930- Brief entry 113
Berelson, Bernard R(euben) 1912-1979 CANR-3
Obituary 89-92
Earlier sketch in CA 7-8R
Berelson, David 1943- 25-28R
Berelson, Howard 1940- SATA-5
Berenbaum, Linda Bayer
See Bayer-Berenbaum, Linda
Berends, Polly Berrien 1939- 108
See also SATA 38, 50
Berendsohn, Walter A(rthur) 1884- 33-36R
Berendt, Joachim Ernst 1922- CANR-12
Earlier sketch in CA 69-72
Berendzen, Richard (Earl) 1938- 85-88
Berenson, Conrad 1930- 11-12R
Berenstain, Jan(ice) CANR-14
Earlier sketch in CA 25-28R
See also SATA 12
Berenstain, Michael 1951- CANR-14
Earlier sketch in CA 97-100
See also SATA 45
Berenstain, Stan(ley) 1923- CANR-14
Earlier sketch in CA 25-28R
See also SATA 12
Bereny, Gail Rubin 1942- 85-88
Beresford, Anne 1929- 97-100
See also DLB 40
Beresford, Elisabeth 102
See also SATA 25
Beresford, J(ohn) D(avys) 1873-1947
Brief entry 112
Beresford, Maurice Warwick 1920- 13-14R
Beresford-Howe, Constance 1922- 53-56
See also AITN 2
Beresiner, Yasha 1940- CANR-12
Earlier sketch in CA 69-72
Beretta, Lia 1934- 17-18R
Berg, A(ndrew) Scott 1949(?)- 81-84
Berg, Adriane G(ilda) 1948- 119
Berg, Alan (David) 1932- CANR-22
Earlier sketch in CA 45-48
Berg, Barbara J. 124
Berg, Bjoern 1923- SATA-47
Berg, Bjorn
See Berg, Bjoern
See also SATA 47
Berg, Darrel E. 1920- 17-18R
Berg, Dave
See Berg, David
Berg, David 1920- CANR-10
Earlier sketch in CA 21-22R
See also SATA 27
Berg, Fred Anderson 1948- 37-40R
Berg, Frederick S(ven) 1928- 53-56
Berg, Friedrich Kantor
See Kantor-Berg, Friedrich
Berg, Goesta 1903- 69-72
Berg, Irwin August 1913- 13-14R
Berg, Ivar E(lis), Jr. 1929- CANR-13
Earlier sketch in CA 23-24R
Berg, Jean Horton 1913- CANR-4
Earlier sketch in CA 53-56
See also SATA 6
Berg, Joan
See Victor, Joan Berg
Berg, Larry L(ee) 1939- 41-44R
Berg, Lasse 1943- CANR-12
Earlier sketch in CA 73-76
Berg, Leila Rita 1917- 101
Berg, Louis 1901-1972 Obituary 37-40R
Berg, Orley M. 1918- 19-20R
Berg, Paul Conrad 1921- 33-36R
Berg, Richard F(rederick) 1936- 115
Berg, Rick 1951- 93-96
Berg, Ron 1952- SATA-48
Berg, Stephen 1934- CANR-8
Earlier sketch in CA 15-16R
See also DLB 5
Berg, Thomas L(eRoy) 1930- 69-72
Berg, Viola Jacobson 1918- CANR-5
Earlier sketch in CA 53-56
Berg, William 1938- 97-100
Bergamini, David H(owland)
1928-1983 CANR-15
Obituary 110
Earlier sketch in CA 1R
Bergamini, John D. 1925(?)-1982
Obituary 108
Bergaust, Erik 1925-1978 73-76
Obituary 77-80
See also SATA 20
Berge, Carol CANR-7
Earlier sketch in CA 15-16R
Bergel, Egon Ernst 1894-1969 CAP-2
Earlier sketch in CA 21-22
Bergen, Polly 1930- 57-60
Bergendoff, Conrad J(ohn) I(mmanuel)
1895- CANR-13
Earlier sketch in CA 33-36R
Bergengruen, Werner 1892-1964(?)
Obituary 114
See also DLB 56
Berger, Andrew J(ohn) 1915- CANR-14
Earlier sketch in CA 41-44R
Berger, Arthur Asa 1933- CANR-10
Earlier sketch in CA 25-28R
Berger, Bennett Maurice 1926- CANR-4
Earlier sketch in CA 1R
Berger, Bruce 1938- 112
Berger, Carl 1925- 11-12R
Berger, Colonel
See Malraux, (Georges-) Andre
Berger, David 1943- 115
Berger, Elmer 1908- 61-64
Berger, Evelyn Miller 1896- CANR-14
Earlier sketch in CA 37-40R
Berger, Gilda Brief entry 118
See also SATA 42
Berger, H. Jean 1924- 15-16R
Berger, Harry, Jr. 1924- 110
Berger, Hilbert J. 1920- 57-60
Berger, Ivan (Bennett) 1939- CANR-17
Earlier sketch in CA 97-100
Berger, John (Peter) 1926- 81-84
See also DLB 14
See also CLC 2, 19
Berger, John J(oseph) 1945- 69-72
Berger, Josef 1903-1971 7-8R
Obituary 33-36R
See also SATA 36
Berger, Joseph 1924- 41-44R
Berger, Karen 1944- 122
Berger, Klaus 1901- CAP-1
Earlier sketch in CA 13-14
Berger, Marilyn 1935- 101
Berger, Marjorie Sue 1916- 15-16R
Berger, Mark L(ewis) 1942- Brief entry 109
Berger, Melvin H. 1927- CANR-4
Earlier sketch in CA 5-6R
See also SATA 5
See also SAAS 2
See also CLC 12
Berger, Meyer 1898-1959(?) Brief entry 120
See also DLB 29
Berger, Michael (Louis) 1943- CANR-14
Earlier sketch in CA 77-80
Berger, Morroe 1917-1981 CANR-4
Obituary 103
Earlier sketch in CA 1R
Berger, Nan 1914- 113
Berger, Peter Ludwig 1929- CANR-1
Earlier sketch in CA 1R
Berger, Phil 1942- CANR-12
Earlier sketch in CA 61-64
Berger, Rainer 1930- 37-40R
Berger, Raoul 1901- 93-96
Berger, Raymond M(ark) 1950- 109
Berger, Robert W(illiam) 1936- 49-52
Berger, Stuart 1953- 112
Berger, Suzanne E(lizabeth) 1944- 105
Berger, Terry 1933- 37-40R
See also SATA 8
Berger, Thomas (Louis) 1924- CANR-5
Earlier sketch in CA 2R
See also DLB 2
See also DLBY 80
See also CLC 3, 5, 8, 11, 18, 38
Berger, Yves 1934- 85-88
Bergeret, Ida Treat 1889(?)-1978
Obituary 77-80
Bergeron, David M(oore) 1938- CANR-2
Earlier sketch in CA 45-48
Bergeron, Paul H. 1938- 101
Bergeron, Victor (Jules, Jr.) 1902-1984 89-92
Obituary 114
Bergeson, John B(rian) 1935- 69-72
Bergevin, Paul (Emile) 1906- CANR-2
Earlier sketch in CA 7-8R
Bergey, Alyce (Mae) 1934- CANR-7
Earlier sketch in CA 5-6R
See also SATA 45
Berggren, W(illiam) A(lfred) 1931- 123
Berghahn, Volker R(olf) 1938- CANR-20
Earlier sketch in CA 103
Bergier, Jacques 1912-1978 85-88
Obituary 81-84
Bergin, Allen E. 1934- 45-48

Bergin, Kenneth Glenny 1911-1981
Obituary 103
Bergin, Thomas Goddard 1904-1987 .... CANR-3
Obituary 124
Earlier sketch in CA 11-12R
Bergman, Arlene Eisen 1942- 61-64
Bergman, Bernard A(aron) 1894-1980 102
Obituary 97-100
Bergman, Bo 1869-1967 Obituary 25-28R
Bergman, David (L.) 1950- CANR-22
Earlier sketch in CA 106
Bergman, Floyd L(awrence) 1927- CANR-17
Earlier sketches in CA 49-52, CANR-2
Bergman, Hannah E(stermann) 1925- 69-72
Bergman, Hjalmar (Frederik Elgerus)
1883-1931 Brief entry 119
Bergman, (Shmuel) Hugo 1883-1975
Obituary 57-60
Bergman, (Ernst) Ingmar 1918- 81-84
See also CLC 16
Bergman, Ingrid 1915-1982 Obituary 107
Bergman, Jay Asa 1948- 110
Bergman, Jules (Verne) 1929-1987 108
Obituary 121
Bergmann, Ernst W. 1896(?)-1977
Obituary 69-72
Bergmann, Fred L(ouis) 1916- 61-64
Bergmann, Frithjof H. 1930- 101
Bergmann, Peter G(abriel) 1915- 23-24R
Bergonzi, Bernard 1929- CANR-8
Earlier sketch in CA 17-18R
Bergonzo, Jean Louis 1939-19(?) CAP-2
Earlier sketch in CA 25-28
Bergquist, Laura (Cecella) 1918-1982
Obituary 108
Bergreen, Laurence R. 1950- 104
Bergson, Abram 1914- 13-14R
Bergson, Leo
See Stebel, S(idney) L(eo)
Bergstein, Eleanor 1938- CANR-5
Earlier sketch in CA 53-56
See also CLC 4
Bergsten, C. Fred 1941- 111
Bergsten, Staffan 1932- CANR-6
Earlier sketch in CA 57-60
Bergstrom, Louise 1914- 29-32R
Beringause, Arthur F. 1919- 33-36R
Beringer, Richard E. 1933- 81-84
Berk, Fred 1911(?)-1980 Obituary 97-100
Berke, Joel S(ommers) 1936-1981 110
Obituary 105
Berke, Joseph H(erman) 1939- 57-60
Berke, Roberta 1943- 106
Berkebile, Don(ald) H(erbert) 1926- CANR-8
Earlier sketch in CA 61-64
Berkebile, Fred D(onovan) 1900-1978 ......5-6R
Obituary 103
See also SATA 26
Berkeley, Anthony
See Cox, A(nthony) B(erkeley)
Berkeley, David S(helley) 1917- 41-44R
Berkeley, Edmund 1912- Brief entry 112
Berkeley, Ellen Perry 1931- 110
Berkemeyer, William C. 1908- CAP-2
Earlier sketch in CA 25-28
Berkey, Barry Robert 1935- 69-72
See also SATA 24
Berkey, Helen 1898- CAP-2
Earlier sketch in CA 23-24
Berkhofer, Robert Frederick, Jr. 1931- ...15-16R
Berkin, Carol Ruth 1942- CANR-11
Earlier sketch in CA 69-72
Berkley, George E(ugene) 1928-
Brief entry 113
Berkman, Edward O(scar) 1914- CANR-9
Earlier sketch in CA 61-64
Berkman, Harold W(illiam) 1926- CANR-21
Earlier sketches in CA 53-56, CANR-5
Berkman, Richard Lyle 1946- CANR-1
Earlier sketch in CA 45-48
Berkman, Sue 1936- 45-48
Berkman, Ted
See Berkman, Edward O(scar)
Berkoff, Steven 1937- 104
Berkove, Lawrence Ivan 1930- 106
Berkovits, Eliezer 1908- CANR-2
Earlier sketch in CA 4R
Berkovitz, Irving H(erbert) 1924- 57-60
Berkow, Ira 1940- 97-100
Berkowitz, Bernard 1909- AITN-1
Berkowitz, David Sandler 1913- 33-36R
Berkowitz, Freda Pastor 1910- CAP-1
Earlier sketch in CA 9-10
See also SATA 12
Berkowitz, Gerald M(artin) 1942- 110
Berkowitz, Luci 1938- 33-36R
Berkowitz, Marvin 1938- 29-32R
Berkowitz, Morris Ira 1931- 53-56
Berkowitz, Pearl H(enriette) 1921- 23-24R
Berkowitz, Sol 1922- CANR-1
Earlier sketch in CA 45-48
Berkowitz, William R(obby) 1939- 112
Berkson, Bill 1939- CANR-24
Earlier sketches in CA 21-22R, CANR-9
Berkson, William Koller 1944- 102
Berlak, Harold 1932- 33-36R
Berland, Theodore 1929- CANR-18
Earlier sketches in CA 7-8R, CANR-2
Berlanstein, Lenard R(ussell) 1947- 69-72
Berlant, Anthony 1941- Brief entry 112
Berlant, Tony
See Berlant, Anthony
Berle, Adolf A(ugustus), Jr. 1895-1971 ... CAP-2
Obituary 29-32R
Earlier sketch in CA 23-24
Berle, Beatrice Bishop 1902- 114
Berle, Milton 1908- 77-80
See also AITN 1
Berleant, Arnold 1932- 29-32R
Berlin, Ellin (Mackay) 1904- 65-68
Berlin, Ira 1941- 101
Berlin, Irving 1888- 108
Berlin, Irving N. 1917- CANR-13
Earlier sketch in CA 23-24R
Berlin, Isaiah 1909- 85-88
Berlin, Michael J(oseph) 1938- 69-72
Berlin, Normand 1931- 57-60
Berlin, Richard Emmett 1894(?)-1986
Obituary 118
Berlin, Sven 1911- CANR-15
Earlier sketch in CA 85-88
Berlind, Bruce 1926- 33-36R
Berliner, Don 1930- CANR-21
Earlier sketch in CA 105
See also SATA 33
Berliner, Franz 1930- CANR-12
Earlier sketch in CA 29-32R
See also SATA 13
Berliner, Herman A(lbert) 1944- 77-80
Berliner, Joseph S(cholom) 1921- 69-72
Berlitz, Charles (L. Frambach) 1914- CANR-9
Earlier sketch in CA 7-8R
See also SATA 32
Berl-Lee, Maria
See Lee, Maria Berl
Berloni, William 1956- 77-80
Berlye, Milton K. 1915- 49-52
Berlyne, D(aniel) E(llis) 1924- 13-14R
Berman, Arthur I(rwin) 1925- 97-100
Berman, Bennett H(erbert) 1927- 105
Berman, Bruce D(avid) 1944- 41-44R
Berman, Claire 1936- CANR-10
Earlier sketch in CA 25-28R
Berman, Connie 1949- 93-96
Berman, Daniel M(arvin) 1928-1967 .... CANR-1
Earlier sketch in CA 1R
Berman, Ed 1941- 106
Berman, Edgar F(rank) 1915(?)-1987 97-100
Obituary 124
Berman, Eleanor 1934- 85-88
Berman, Emile Zola 1902-1981 Obituary 104
Berman, Harold Joseph 1918- CANR-15
Earlier sketch in CA 89-92
Berman, Larry 1951- 93-96
Berman, Linda 1948- 113
See also SATA 38
Berman, Louise M(arguerite) 1928- 21-22R
Berman, Marshall 1940- 29-32R
Berman, Milton 1924- 1R
Berman, Morton 1924- CANR-2
Earlier sketch in CA 5-6R
Berman, Morton M(ayer) 1899-1986
Obituary 118
Berman, Paul (Lawrence) 1949- 110
Berman, Ronald 1930- 13-14R
Berman, Sanford 1933- 37-40R
Berman, Simeon M(oses) 1935- 49-52
Berman, Susan 1945- CANR-17
Earlier sketch in CA 65-68
Berman, William C(arl) 1932- 41-44R
Bermange, Barry 1933- 57-60
Bermant, Chaim 1929- CANR-6
Earlier sketch in CA 57-60
See also CLC 40
Bermant, Gordon 1936- 120
Bermel, Albert (Cyril) 1927- CANR-11
Earlier sketch in CA 69-72
Bermont, Hubert Ingram 1924- CANR-5
Earlier sketch in CA 9-10R
Bermosk, Loretta Sue 1918- CANR-3
Earlier sketch in CA 11-12R
Bern, Maria Rasputin Soloviev
1900(?)-1977 Obituary 73-76
Berna, Paul 1910- 73-76
See also SATA 15
Bernabei, Alfio 1941- CANR-14
Earlier sketch in CA 77-80
Bernadette
See Watts, (Anna) Bernadette
Bernal, Ignacio 1910- 97-100
Bernal, J(ohn) D(esmond) 1901-1971 97-100
Obituary 33-36R
Bernal, Judith F. 1939- 57-60
Bernal, Martin Gardiner 1937- 104
Bernal y Garcia y Pimentel, Ignacio
1910- CANR-5
Earlier sketch in CA 9-10R
Bernanos, (Paul Louis) Georges
1888-1948 Brief entry 104
See also TCLC 3
Bernard, George 1939- 73-76
Bernard, George I. 1949- SATA-39
Bernard, Guy
See Barber, Stephen Guy
Bernard, H(arvey) Russell 1940- 41-44R
Bernard, Harold W. 1908- CANR-4
Earlier sketch in CA 3R
Bernard, Hugh Y(ancey), Jr. 1919- 23-24R
Bernard, Jack F. 1930- 21-22R
Bernard, Jacqueline (de Sieyes)
1921-1983 ....23-24R
Obituary 117
See also SATA 8, 45
Bernard, Jay
See Sawkins, Raymond H(arold)
Bernard, Jean-Jacques 1888-1972
Obituary 37-40R
Bernard, John 1756-1828 .... DLB-37
Bernard, Kenneth 1930- 41-44R
Bernard, Kenneth A(nderson) 1906- 29-32R
Bernard, Laureat J(oseph) 1922- 25-28R
Bernard, Marley
See Graves, Susan B(ernard)
Bernard, Nelson T(ed), Jr. 1925- 123
Bernard, Oliver 1925- 15-16R
Bernard, Paul Peter 1929- 89-92
Bernard, Richard Marion 1948- 105
Bernard, Robert
See Martin, Robert Bernard
Bernard, Sidney 1918- 29-32R
Bernard, Stefan
See Baumrin, Bernard H(erbert)
Bernard, Thelma Rene 1940- 57-60
Bernard, Will 1915- 93-96
Bernard, William Spencer 1907-1986
Obituary 118
Bernardo, Aldo S(isto) 1920- CANR-4
Earlier sketch in CA 4R
Bernardo, James V. 1913- 17-18R
Bernardo, Stephanie 1947- 112
Bernarn, Terrave
See Burnett, David (Benjamin Foley)
Bernauer, George F. 1941- 29-32R
Bernays, Anne
See Kaplan, Anne Bernays
Bernays, Edward L. 1891- 17-18R
Bernazza, Ann Marie
See Haase, Ann Marie Bernazza
Bernbach, William 1911-1982 Obituary 108
Bernd, Joseph Laurence 1923- 19-20R
Berndt, Ronald Murray 1916- CANR-19
Earlier sketches in CA 5-6R, CANR-3
Berndt, Walter 1900(?)-1979 Obituary 89-92
Berndtson, Arthur 1913- 108
Berne, Eric (Lennard) 1910-1970 .... CANR-4
Obituary 25-28R
Earlier sketch in CA 7-8R
Berne, Leo
See Davies, L(eslie) P(urnell)
Berne, Patricia H(iggins) 1934- 110
Berne, Stanley 1923- CANR-1
Earlier sketch in CA 45-48
Berner, Carl Walter 1902- 49-52
Berner, Jeff 1940- 89-92
Berner, Robert B(arry) 1940- 41-44R
Bernert, Eleanor H.
See Sheldon, Eleanor Bernert
Bernet, Michael M. 1930- 25-28R
Bernhard, Thomas 1931- 85-88
See also CLC 3, 32
Bernhard, Virginia Purington 1937- 112
Bernhardsen, Bris
See Bernhardsen, (Einar) Christian
(Rosenvinge)
Bernhardsen, (Einar) Christian (Rosenvinge)
1923- 29-32R
Bernhardt, Clyde Edric Barron 1905-1986
Obituary 119
Bernhardt, Frances Simonsen 1932- 103
Bernhardt, Karl S. 1901-1967 .... CAP-1
Earlier sketch in CA 13-14
Bernheim, Evelyne 1935- 21-22R
Bernheim, Kayla F. 1946- 108
Bernheim, Marc 1924- 21-22R
Bernheimer, Martin 1936- 69-72
Bernier, Olivier 1941- 105
Berninghausen, David K(nipe) 1916- 111
Berns, Julie 1899(?)-1983 Obituary 111
Berns, Walter (Fred) 1919- CANR-24
Earlier sketch in CA 101
Bernstein, Alvin H(owell) 1939- 89-92
Bernstein, Anne C(arolyn) 1944- 105
Bernstein, Arnold 1920- 29-32R
Bernstein, Barton J(annen) 1936- 37-40R
Bernstein, Basil (Bernard) 1924-
Brief entry 119
Bernstein, Blanche 1912- 110
Bernstein, Burton 1932- CANR-21
Earlier sketches in CA 1R, CANR-4
Bernstein, Carl 1944- 81-84
See also AITN 1
Bernstein, David 1915(?)-1974 Obituary ...53-56
Bernstein, Douglas A. 1942- 45-48
Bernstein, Gail Lee 1939- 115
Bernstein, Gerry 1927- 105
Bernstein, Harry 1909- CANR-1
Earlier sketch in CA 1R
Bernstein, Hillel 1892(?)-1977 Obituary ...69-72
Bernstein, Irving 1916- Brief entry 114
Bernstein, J(erome) S(traus) 1936- 25-28R
Bernstein, Jacob 1946- 104
Bernstein, Jane 1949- 104
Bernstein, Jeremy 1929- 13-14R
Bernstein, Jerry Marx 1908-1969 .... CAP-2
Earlier sketch in CA 25-28
Bernstein, Joanne E(ckstein) 1943- CANR-13
Earlier sketch in CA 77-80
See also SATA 15
Bernstein, John Andrew 1944- 124
Bernstein, Joseph M(ilton) 1908(?)-1975
Obituary 57-60
Bernstein, Leonard 1918- CANR-21
Earlier sketches in CA 2R, CANR-2
Bernstein, Lewis 1915- 33-36R
Bernstein, Margery 1933- 57-60
Bernstein, Marilyn 1929- 21-22R
Bernstein, Marver H(illel) 1919- CANR-2
Earlier sketch in CA 1R
Bernstein, Marvin David 1923- 45-48
Bernstein, Merton C(lay) 1923- 19-20R
Bernstein, Michael Andre 1947- 124
Bernstein, Mordechai 1893-1983 Obituary .. 109
Bernstein, Morey 1919- 23-24R
Bernstein, Norman R. 1927- CANR-13
Earlier sketch in CA 33-36R
Bernstein, Philip S(idney) 1901- 49-52
Bernstein, Richard J(acob) 1932-
Brief entry 113
Bernstein, Richard K. 1934- 105
Bernstein, Seymour 109
Bernstein, Theodore M(enline)
1904-1979 .... CANR-3
Earlier sketch in CA 1R
See also SATA 12, 27
Bernstein, Thomas P(aul) 1937- 113
Bernstein, Walter 1919- 106
Bernzweig, Eli P. 1927- 29-32R
Berofsky, Bernard 1935- 89-92
Berque, Jacques Augustin 1910- 85-88
Berquist, Goodwin F(auntleroy) 1930- 23-24R
Berrellez, Robert 1920(?)-1985 Obituary 116
Berrett, LaMar C(ecil) 1926- 53-56
Berrian, Albert H. 1925- 37-40R
Berriault, Gina 1926- Brief entry 116
Berridge, Celia 1943- 110
Berridge, Elizabeth 1921- CANR-6
Earlier sketch in CA 57-60
Berridge, P(ercy) S(tuart) A(ttwood)
1901- 29-32R
Berrien, Edith Heal
See Heal, Edith
Berrien, F. Kenneth 1909-1971 .... CANR-1
Obituary 29-32R
Earlier sketch in CA 3R
Berrigan, Daniel 1921- CANR-11
Earlier sketch in CA 33-36R
See also CAAS 1
See also DLB 5
See also CLC 4
Berrigan, Edmund Joseph Michael, Jr.
1934-1983 .... CANR-14
Obituary 110
Earlier sketch in CA 61-64
Berrigan, Philip (Francis) 1923- CANR-11
Earlier sketch in CA 15-16R
Berrigan, Ted
See Berrigan, Edmund Joseph Michael,
Jr.
See also DLB 5
See also CLC 37
Berrill, Jacquelyn (Batsel) 1905- 19-20R
See also SATA 12
Berrill, N(orman) J(ohn) 1903- 19-20R
Berrington, Hugh B(ayard) 1928- 49-52
Berrington, John
See Brownjohn, Alan
Berrisford, Judith Mary
See Lewis, Judith Mary
Berry, Adrian M(ichael) 1937- CANR-9
Earlier sketch in CA 57-60
Berry, B. J.
See Berry, Barbara J.
Berry, Barbara J. 1937- 33-36R
See also SATA 7
Berry, Boyd M(cCulloch) 1939- 69-72
Berry, Brewton 1901- CANR-3
Earlier sketch in CA 4R
Berry, Brian J(oe) L(obley) 1934- CANR-5
Earlier sketch in CA 15-16R
Berry, Bryan 1930-1955 Brief entry 112
Berry, Burton Yost 1901- 85-88
Berry, Charles Edward Anderson 1931- 115
Berry, Charles H. 1930- 69-72
Berry, Chuck
See Berry, Charles Edward Anderson
See also CLC 17
Berry, Cicely 1926- 93-96
Berry, D. C. 1942- 45-48
Berry, David (Ronald) 1942- 29-32R
Berry, David (Adams) 1943- 108
Berry, Don (George) 1932- 106
Berry, Edmund G(rindlay) 1915- 3R
Berry, Edward I. 1940- 57-60
Berry, (Julia) Elizabeth 1920- 21-22R
Berry, Erick
See Best, (Evangel) Allena Champlin
Berry, Francis 1915- CANR-5
Earlier sketch in CA 5-6R
Berry, Frederic Aroyce, Jr. 1906-1978
Obituary 77-80
Berry, Geoffrey 1912-1988 Obituary 124
Berry, Helen
See Rowland, D(onald) S(ydney)
Berry, Henry 1926- 85-88
Berry, Herbert 1922- 111
Berry, I. William 1934- 105
Berry, Jack 1918- 37-40R
Berry, James 1932- 23-24R
Berry, James Gomer 1883-1968 Obituary ..89-92
Berry, Jane Cobb 1915(?)-1979 Obituary ...85-88
See also SATA 22
Berry, Jason 1949- 45-48
Berry, Jim 1946- 107
Berry, Jim
See Berry, James
Berry, Jo(ycelyn) 1933- CANR-18
Earlier sketch in CA 102
Berry, John Nichols (III) 1933- Brief entry .. 113
Berry, Jonas
See Ashbery, John (Lawrence)
Berry, Joy Wilt SATA-46
Berry, Katherine F(iske) 1877-19(?) CAP-2
Earlier sketch in CA 17-18
Berry, Lloyd E(ason) 1935- 15-16R
Berry, Lynn 1948- 61-64
Berry, Mary Frances 1938- CANR-14
Earlier sketch in CA 33-36R
Berry, Nicholas O(rlando) 1936- 93-96
Berry, Paul 1919- 102
Berry, R(obert) J(ames) 1934- 121
Berry, Roland (Brian) 1951- 93-96
Berry, Ron(ald Anthony) 1920- 25-28R
Berry, Sister Mary Virginia 1908(?)-1987
Obituary 122
Berry, Stephen Ames 1947- 118
Berry, Thomas 1914- 23-24R
Berry, Thomas Edwin 1930- 102

Berry, Thomas Elliott 1917- 33-36R
Berry, Wallace Taft 1928- CANR-8
Earlier sketch in CA 19-20R
Berry, Wendell (Erdman) 1934- 73-76
See also DLB 5, 6
See also CLC 4, 6, 8, 27, 46
See also AITN 1
Berry, William D(avid) 1926- 73-76
See also SATA 14
Berry, William Turner 1888- CAP-2
Earlier sketch in CA 23-24
Berryman, Charles (Beecher) 1939- 112
Berryman, James Thomas 1902-1971
Obituary 93-96
Berryman, Jim
See Berryman, James Thomas
Berryman, John 1914-1972 .... CAP-1
Obituary 33-36R
Earlier sketch in CA 15-16
See also CABS 2
See also DLB 48
See also CDALB 1941-1968
See also CLC 1, 2, 3, 4, 6, 8, 10, 13, 25
Bersani, Leo 1931- CANR-5
Earlier sketch in CA 53-56
Berscheid, Ellen 1936- 25-28R
Bersianik, Louky 1930- DLB-60
Berson, Harold 1926- 33-36R
See also SATA 4
Berson, Lenora E. 1926- 93-96
Berssenbrugge, Mei-mei 1947- 104
Berst, Charles A(shton) 1932- 41-44R
Berst, Jesse 116
Bertcher, Harvey (Joseph) 1929- 85-88
Bertelson, David (Earl) 1934- 21-22R
Berthelot, Joseph A. 1927- 21-22R
Berthoff, Rowland (Tappan) 1921- 33-36R
Berthoff, Warner (Bement) 1925- CANR-2
Earlier sketch in CA 5-6R
Berthold, Dennis (Alfred) 1942- 117
Berthold, Margot 1922- 73-76
Berthold, Mary Paddock 1909- 53-56
Bertholf, Diana 1946- 115
Berthoud, Jacques (Alexandre) 1935- .. CANR-10
Earlier sketch in CA 19-20R
Berthrong, Donald J(ohn) 1922- 81-84
Berthrong, Evelyn Nagai
See Nagai Berthrong, Evelyn
Bertin, Charles-Francois
See Berlitz, Charles (L. Frambach)
Bertin, Jack
See Bertin, John
Bertin, John 1904-1963 Obituary 116
Bertin, Leonard M. 1918- 15-16R
Bertman, Stephen (Samuel) 1937- 45-48
Bertocci, Peter A(nthony) 1910- 17-18R
Bertolino, James 1942- CANR-17
Earlier sketches in CA 45-48, CANR-1
Bertolucci, Bernardo 1940- 106
See also CLC 16
Berton, Peter (Alexander Menquez) 1922- ..77-80
Berton, Pierre 1920- CANR-2
Earlier sketch in CA 3R
Berton, Ralph 1910- 49-52
Bertonasco, Marc F(rancis) 1934- 89-92
Bertram, Anthony 1897-1978 Obituary 104
Bertram, (George) Colin (Lawder) 1911- ..13-14R
Bertram, James Munro 1910- 65-68
Bertram, Jean De Sales CANR-12
Earlier sketch in CA 45-48
Bertram, Noel
See Fanthorpe, R(obert) Lionel
Bertram-Cox, Jean De Sales
See Bertram, Jean De Sales
Bertrand, Alvin L(ee) 1918- 45-48
Bertrand, Charles
See Carter, David C(harles)
Bertrand, Lewis 1897(?)-1974 Obituary ...53-56
Bertrand, Michel 1944- CANR-13
Earlier sketch in CA 73-76
Berwanger, Eugene H. 21-22R
Berwick, Jean Shepherd 1929- 9-10R
Berwick, Keith (Bennet) 1928- 33-36R
Besag, Frank P. 1935- 119
Besanceney, Paul H. 1924- 45-48
Besant, Annie (Wood) 1847-1933
Brief entry 105
See also TCLC 9
Besas, Peter 1933- 77-80
Beschloss, Michael R(ichard) 1955- 101
Besdine, Matthew 1905(?)-1986 Obituary ... 120
Beshers, James M(onahan) 1931- 4R
Beshoar, Barron B(enedict) 1907- 69-72
Beskow, Bo 1906- CANR-11
Earlier sketch in CA 61-64
Beskow, Elsa (Maartman) 1874-1953 .. SATA-20
Besoyan, Rick 1924(?)-1970 Obituary ...25-28R
Bessborough, Tenth Earl of
See Ponsonby, Frederick Edward Neuflize
Bessell, Peter (Joseph) 1921-1985
Obituary 117
Besser, Gretchen R(ous) 1928- CANR-14
Earlier sketch in CA 41-44R
Besser, Joe 1907-1988 Obituary 124
Besser, Milton 1911-1976 69-72
Obituary 65-68
Bessette, Gerard 1920- CANR-14
Earlier sketch in CA 37-40R
See also DLB 53
Bessie, Alvah 1904-1985 .... CANR-2
Obituary 116
Earlier sketch in CA 5-6R
See also DLB 26
See also CLC 23
Bessie, Constance Ernst 1918(?)-1985
Obituary 115
Bessinger, Jess B(alsor), Jr. 1921- 15-16R
Bessom, Malcolm E(ugene) 1940- 57-60
Bessy, Maurice 1910- CANR-10
Earlier sketch in CA 65-68
Best, Adam
See Carmichael, William Edward
Best, Alan C.G. 1939- 111
Best, (Evangel) Allena Champlin
1892-1974 .... CAP-2
Earlier sketch in CA 25-28
See also SATA 2, 25
Best, Charles H(erbert) 1899-1978 45-48
Obituary 103
Best, Ernest 1917- 114
Best, Ernest E. 1919- 112
Best, G. F. A.
See Best, Geoffrey (Francis Andrew)
Best, Gary A(llen) 1939- 33-36R
Best, Gary Dean 1936- 117
Best, Geoffrey (Francis Andrew) 1928-
Brief entry 114
Best, (Oswald) Herbert 1894- CAP-2
Earlier sketch in CA 25-28
See also SATA 2
Best, Hugh 1920- 115
Best, James J(oseph) 1938- 37-40R
Best, John Wesley 1909- 17-18R
Best, Judith A. 1938- 69-72
Best, Marc
See Lemieux, Marc
Best, Marshall A. 1901(?)-1982 Obituary ... 106
Best, Michael R. 37-40R
Best, Otto F(erdinand) 1929- 69-72
Best, Rayleigh Breton Amis 1905- CAP-1
Earlier sketch in CA 15-16
Best, Robin Hewitson ?-1984 Obituary 113
Best, Thomas W(aring) 1939- 29-32R
Bestall, A(lfred) E(dmeades) 1892-1986
Obituary 119
See also SATA 48
Beste, R(aymond) Vernon 1908- CANR-4
Earlier sketch in CA 4R
Bester, Alfred 1913-1987 .... CANR-12
Obituary 123
Earlier sketch in CA 15-16R
See also DLB 8
Besterman, Theodore (Deocatus Nathaniel)
1904-1976 Obituary 105
Bestic, Alan Kent 1922- 13-14R
Beston, Henry 1888-1968 Obituary 25-28R
Bestor, Arthur (Eugene, Jr.) 1908- CANR-6
Earlier sketch in CA 4R
Bestor, Dorothy K(och) 118
Bestul, Thomas H(oward) 1942- 53-56
Betancourt, Jeanne 1941- 49-52
See also SATA 43
Betancourt, Romulo 1908-1981 104
Betenson, Lula Parker 1884- 61-64
Beth
See Winship, Elizabeth
Beth, Loren Peter 1920- CANR-3
Earlier sketch in CA 4R
Beth, Mary
See Miller, Mary Beth
Bethancourt, T. Ernesto
See Paisley, Tom
See also SATA 11
See also CLR 3
Bethe, H. A.
See Bethe, Hans Albrecht
Bethe, Hans A.
See Bethe, Hans Albrecht
Bethe, Hans Albrecht 1906- Brief entry 115
Bethel, Dell 1929- 29-32R
Bethel, Elizabeth Rauh 1942- 106
Bethel, Paul D(uane) 1919- 25-28R
Bethell, Jean (Frankenberry) 1922- CANR-3
Earlier sketch in CA 9-10R
See also SATA 8
Bethell, Nicholas William 1938- CANR-1
Earlier sketch in CA 45-48
Bethell, Tom 1940- 77-80
Bethers, Ray 1902- CAP-1
Earlier sketch in CA 11-12
See also SATA 6
Bethge, Eberhard 1909- 85-88
Bethlen, T. D.
See Silverberg, Robert
Bethmann, Erich Waldemar 1904- CAP-2
Earlier sketch in CA 23-24
Bethune, J. G.
See Ellis, Edward S(ylvester)
Bethune, J. H.
See Ellis, Edward S(ylvester)
Bethurum, F(rances) Dorothy 1897- CAP-2
Earlier sketch in CA 17-18
Beti, Mongo
See Biyidi, Alexandre
See also CLC 27
Betjeman, John 1906-1984 ....11-12R
Obituary 112
See also DLB 20
See also DLBY 84
See also CLC 2, 6, 10, 34, 43
Betjeman, Penelope Chetwode
See Chetwode, Penelope
Betocchi, Carlo 1899- CANR-4
Earlier sketch in CA 9-10R
Bett, Walter R(eginald) 1903- CAP-1
Earlier sketch in CA 13-14
Bettelheim, Bruno 1903- CANR-23
Earlier sketch in CA 81-84
Bettelheim, Charles 1913- CANR-13
Earlier sketch in CA 73-76
Bettelheim, Frederick A(braham) 1923- 49-52
Betten, Neil B. 1939- 105
Bettenson, Henry (Scowcroft) 1908- 13-14R
Betteridge, Anne
See Potter, Margaret (Newman)
Betteridge, Don
See Newman, Bernard (Charles)
Betteridge, H(arold) T(homas) 1910- 5-6R
Bettersworth, John K(nox) 1909- CANR-2
Earlier sketch in CA 5-6R
Betti, Liliana 1939- 101
Betti, Ugo 1892-1953 Brief entry 104
See also TCLC 5
Bettina
See Ehrlich, Bettina Bauer
Bettis, Joseph Dabney 1936- 33-36R
Bettmann, Otto Ludwig 1903- 17-18R
See also SATA 46
Betts, Charles L(ancaster), Jr. 1908- 101
Betts, Donni 1948- CANR-5
Earlier sketch in CA 53-56
Betts, Doris (Waugh) 1932- CANR-9
Earlier sketch in CA 15-16R
See also DLBY 82
See also CLC 3, 6, 28
Betts, Emmett Albert 1903- 33-36R
Betts, George 1944- CANR-2
Earlier sketch in CA 45-48
Betts, Glynne Robinson 1934- 105
Betts, James
See Haynes, Betsy
Betts, John (Edward) 1939- 106
Betts, Raymond F. 1925- CANR-3
Earlier sketch in CA 3R
Betts, Richard K(evin) 1947- CANR-16
Earlier sketch in CA 85-88
Betts, William W(ilson), Jr. 1926- 33-36R
Betty, L(ewis) Stafford 1942- 118
Betz, Betty 1920- 4R
Betz, Eva Kelly 1897-1968 .... CAP-1
Earlier sketch in CA 11-12
See also SATA 10
Betz, Hans Dieter 1931- CANR-19
Earlier sketches in CA 53-56, CANR-4
Beuf, Ann H(ill) 1939- 85-88
Beum, Robert (Lawrence) 1929- 11-12R
Beurdeley, Michel 1911- 49-52
Beutel, William Charles 1930- 101
Beuttler, Edward Ivan Oakley 73-76
Bevan, Alistair
See Roberts, Keith (John Kingston)
Bevan, Aneurin 1897-1960 Obituary 106
Bevan, Bryan 1913- 13-14R
Bevan, E. Dean 1938- 33-36R
Bevan, Gloria Brief entry 117
Bevan, Jack 1920- 13-14R
Bevan, James (Stuart) 1930- 106
Bevan, Tom 1868-193(?) YABC-2
Bevenot, Maurice 1897-1980 Obituary 105
Beveridge, Albert J. 1862-1927 .... DLB-17
Beveridge, Andrew A(lan) 1945- 93-96
Beveridge, George David, Jr. 1922-1987 102
Obituary 121
Beveridge, Meryle Secrest 1930- 81-84
Beveridge, Oscar Maltman 1913- 11-12R
Beveridge, William (Henry) 1879-1963
Obituary 112
Beveridge, William (Ian Beardmore) 1908- .. 106
Beverley, Mary Frances 1925- 120
Beverley, Robert 1673(?)-1722 ..... DLB-24, 30
BeVier, Michael J(udson) 97-100
Bevilacqua, Alberto 1934- 29-32R
Bevington, David M(artin) 1931- CANR-3
Earlier sketch in CA 3R
Bevington, Helen 1906- 15-16R
Bevis, Em Olivia 1932- CANR-1
Earlier sketch in CA 49-52
Bevis, H(erbert) U(rlin) 1902- CAP-2
Earlier sketch in CA 29-32
Bevis, James
See Cumberland, Marten
Bevlin, Marjorie Elliott 1917- 9-10R
Bewes, Richard 1934- CANR-20
Earlier sketch in CA 102
Bewick, Thomas 1753-1828 .... SATA-16
Bewkes, Eugene Garrett 1895- 7-8R
Bewley, Charles Henry 1888- 5-6R
Bewley, Marius 1918-1973 .... CANR-3
Obituary 41-44R
Earlier sketch in CA 5-6R
Bey, Isabelle
See Bosticco, (Isabel Lucy) Mary
Beye, Charles Rowan 1930- 93-96
Beyea, Basil 1910- 61-64
Beyer, (Richard) Andrew 1943- CANR-11
Earlier sketch in CA 69-72
Beyer, Audrey White 1916- 13-14R
See also SATA 9
Beyer, Edvard (Freydar) 1920- 121
Brief entry 116
Beyer, Evelyn M. 1907- CAP-2
Earlier sketch in CA 25-28
Beyer, Glenn H. 1913-1969 .... CANR-2
Earlier sketch in CA 3R
Beyer, Robert 1913(?)-1978 Obituary 77-80
Beyer, Steven L(arsen) 1943- 123
Beyer, Werner William 1911- 11-12R
Beyerchen, Alan 1945- 81-84
Beyerhaus, Peter (Paul Johannes)
1929- CANR-16
Earlier sketch in CA 93-96
Beyerlin, Walter W(ilhelm) 1929- 124
Beyers, Charlotte K(empner) 1931- 85-88
Beyfus, Drusilla 1927- 107
Beyle, Thad L. 1934- 37-40R
Beynon, Huw 1942- 107
Beynon, John
See Harris, John (Wyndham Parkes Lucas) Beynon
Beytagh, Gonville (Aubie) ffrench
See ffRench-Beytagh, Gonville (Aubie)
Bezencon, Jacqueline (Buxcel) 1924- ... SATA-48
Bezilla, Michael 1950- 111
Bezio, May Rowland ?-1977 Obituary 69-72
Bezruchka, Stephen (Anthony) 1943- 107
Bhagat, G(oberdhan) 1928- 29-32R
Bhagavatula, Murty S. 1921- 29-32R
Bhagwati, Jagdish N. 1934- 19-20R
Bhajan, Yogi
See Yogiji, Harbhajan Singh Khalsa
Bhaktivedanta Swami, A. C.
See Prabhupada, A. C. Bhaktivedanta
Bhana, Surendra 1939- 57-60
Bharati, Agehananda 1923- CANR-4
Earlier sketch in CA 4R
Bhardwaj, Surinder Mohan 1934- 45-48
Bharti, Ma Satya 1942- 102
Bhatia, Hans Raj 1904- 53-56
Bhatia, Jamunadevi 1919- 101
Bhatia, June
See Bhatia, Jamunadevi
Bhatia, Krishan 1926(?)-1974 Obituary 53-56
Bhatnagar, Joti 1935- 41-44R
Bhatt, Jagdish J(eyshanker) 1939- CANR-14
Earlier sketch in CA 77-80
Bhattacharji, Sukumari 1921- 33-36R
Bhattacharya, Bhabani 1906- CANR-9
Earlier sketch in CA 5-6R
Bhave, Vinoba 1895-1982 Obituary 108
Bhutto, Zulfikar Ali 1928-1979 .... CANR-11
Earlier sketch in CA 53-56
Biaggini, Adriana Ivancich 1930(?)-1983
Obituary 109
Biagi, Shirley 1944- CANR-15
Earlier sketch in CA 85-88
Bial, Morrison David 1917- 61-64
Bialik, Chaim Nachman 1873-1934 .....TCLC-25
Bialk, Elisa
See Krautter, Elisa (Bialk)
Bialostocki, Jan 1921- 104
Bialostosky, Don H(oward) 1947- 120
Bianchi, Engene C(arl) 1930- 25-28R
Bianchi, Hombert 1912(?)-1980
Obituary 97-100
Bianchi, Robert S(teven) 1943- 109
Bianco, Lucien Andre 1930- CANR-15
Earlier sketch in CA 85-88
Bianco, Margery (Williams) 1881-1944
Brief entry 109
See also SATA 15
Bianco, Pamela 1906- 85-88
See also SATA 28
Biancolli, Louis Leopold 1907- 65-68
Biasin, Gian-Paolo 1933- 25-28R
Bibb, (David) Porter III 1937- 65-68
Bibby, Cyril 1914- CANR-7
Earlier sketch in CA 13-14R
Bibby, John F(ranklin) 1934- 45-48
Bibby, T(homas) Geoffrey 1917- CANR-4
Earlier sketch in CA 3R
Bibby, Violet 1908- 102
See also SATA 24
Bibee, John 1954- 112
Biberman, Edward 1904-1986 49-52
Obituary 118
Biberman, Herbert 1900-1971 .... CAP-1
Obituary 33-36R
Earlier sketch in CA 15-16
Bibesco, Marthe Lucie 1887-1973 93-96
Obituary 49-52
Bible, Charles 1937- 69-72
See also SATA 13
Bibo, Bobette
See Gugliotta, Bobette
Bicanic, Rudolf 1905-1968 85-88
Bice, Clare 1909-1976 .... SATA-22
Bichler, Joyce 1954- 107
Bichsel, Peter 1935- 81-84
Bick, Edgar Milton 1902-1978 Obituary ...77-80
Bickel, Alexander M(ordecai)
1924-1974 .... CANR-1
Obituary 53-56
Earlier sketch in CA 4R
Bickelhaupt, David L(ynn) 1929- 69-72
Bickerman, Elias J(oseph) 1897-1981 .. CANR-20
Obituary 104
Earlier sketch in CA 25-28R
Bickers, Richard Leslie Townshend
1917- CANR-1
Earlier sketch in CA 45-48
Bickerstaff, Isaac
See Swift, Jonathan
Bickersteth, Geoffrey Langdale 1884-1974
Obituary 49-52
Bickerton, Derek 1926- 61-64
Bicket, Zenas J(ohan) 1932- 37-40R
Bickford, Elwood Dale 1927- 61-64
Bickham, Jack M(iles) 1930- CANR-23
Earlier sketches in CA 7-8R, CANR-8
Bickle, Judith Brundrett ?-19(?) CAP-1
Earlier sketch in CA 13-14
Bickley, R(obert) Bruce, Jr. 1942- CANR-9
Earlier sketch in CA 65-68
Bickman, Martin 1945- 104
Bida, Constantine 1916- CANR-13
Earlier sketch in CA 61-64
Bidart, Frank 19(?)- CLC-33
Bidault, Georges 1899-1983 Obituary 109
Bididdiss, Michael Denis 1942- CANR-4
Earlier sketch in CA 53-56
Biddle, Arthur W(illiam) 1936- 45-48
Biddle, Bruce J(esse) 1928- CANR-7
Earlier sketch in CA 17-18R
Biddle, Francis (Beverley) 1886-1968 ....5-6R
Obituary 103
Biddle, George 1885-1973 Obituary 45-48

INDEX

Biddle, Katherine Garrison Chapin
1890-1977 .... CANR-5
Obituary 73-76
Earlier sketch in CA 5-6R
Biddle, Marcia McKenna 1931- 112
Biddle, Perry H(arvey), Jr. 1932- 57-60
Biddle, Phillips R. 1933- 37-40R
Biddle, Wayne 1948- 106
Biddle, William W(ishart) 1900-19(?) CAP-2
Earlier sketch in CA 17-18
Biderman, Albert D. 1923- CANR-23
Earlier sketches in CA 5-6R, CANR-8
Biderman, Sol 1936- 25-28R
Bidney, David 1908- 11-12R
Bidwell, Dafne (Mary) 1929- 97-100
Bidwell, Marjory Elizabeth Sarah 77-80
Bidwell, Percy W(ells) 1888-19(?) CAP-1
Earlier sketch in CA 9-10
Bieber, Margarete 1879-1978 .... CANR-11
Obituary 77-80
Earlier sketch in CA 19-20R
Biebuyck, Daniel P. 1925- CANR-11
Earlier sketch in CA 25-28R
Biegel, John E(dward) 1925- 49-52
Biegel, Paul 1925- CANR-14
Earlier sketch in CA 77-80
See also SATA 16
Biehler, Robert F(rederick) 1927- 37-40R
Bielby, Cliff 1919-1984 Obituary 111
Bielenberg, Christabel 1909- 29-32R
Bieler, Ludwig 1906-1981 .... 7-8R
Obituary 103
Bielfield, Sidney 1904(?)-1984 Obituary 112
Bielski, Feliks
See Giergielewicz, Mieczyslaw F.
Bielyi, Sergei
See Hollo, Anselm
Biemiller, Carl L(udwig, Jr.) 1912-1979 121
Obituary 106
See also SATA 21, 40
Biemiller, Ruth Cobbett 1914- 37-40R
Bien, David Duckworth 1930- 5-6R
Bien, Joseph Julius 1936- CANR-5
Earlier sketch in CA 53-56
Bien, Peter (Adolph) 1930- 9-10R
Bienek, Horst 1930- 73-76
See also CLC 7, 11
Bienen, Henry Samuel 1939- 81-84
Bienenfeld, Florence L(ucille) 1929- CANR-23
Earlier sketch in CA 106
See also SATA 39
Bienstock, Mike
See Bienstock, Myron Joseph
Bienstock, Myron Joseph 1922- 9-10R
Bienvenu, Bernard J(efferson) 1925- 53-56
Bienvenu, Richard (Thomas) 1936- 61-64
Bier, Jesse 1925- CANR-3
Earlier sketch in CA 7-8R
Bier, William C(hristian) 1911-1980 .... 33-36R
Obituary 97-100
Bierbaum, Margaret 1916- 33-36R
Bierbaum, Otto Julius 1865-1910 .... DLB-66
Bierce, Ambrose (Gwinett) 1842-1914(?)
Brief entry 104
See also DLB 11, 12, 23
See also TCLC 1, 7
Bierhorst, John (William) 1936- CANR-13
Earlier sketch in CA 33-36R
See also SATA 6
Bieri, Arthur Peter 1931- 61-64
Bierley, Paul E(dmund) 1926- CANR-13
Earlier sketch in CA 77-80
Bierman, Arthur K(almer) 1923- 85-88
Bierman, Harold, Jr. 1924- CANR-9
Earlier sketch in CA 19-20R
Bierman, Judah 1917- 114
Bierman, Mildred Thornton 1912- 5-6R
Bierman, Stanley M(elvin) 1935- 106
Biermann, Lillian
See Wehmeyer, Lillian (Mabel) Biermann
Biermann, Wolf 1936- 81-84
Biernatzki, William E(ugene) 1931- CANR-6
Earlier sketch in CA 57-60
Biers, William Richard 1938- CANR-23
Earlier sketch in CA 106
Bierstedt, Robert 1913- CANR-2
Earlier sketch in CA 1R
Biery, William (Richard) 1933- 57-60
Biesanz, Mavis Hiltunen 1919- 33-36R
Biesanz, Richard 1944- 112
Biesterveld, Betty Parsons 1923- CANR-1
Earlier sketch in CA 3R
Bietenholz, Peter G(erard) 1933- 101
Biezanek, Anne C(ampbell) 1927- 17-18R
Bigart, Robert James 1947- 33-36R
Bigelow, Donald N(evius) 1918- 41-44R
Bigelow, Gordon Ellsworth 1919- 110
Bigelow, Karl Worth 1898-1980
Obituary 97-100
Bigelow, Marybelle S(chmidt) 1923- 25-28R
Bigelow, Robert P(ratt) 1927- Brief entry 118
Bigelow, Robert Sydney 1918- 102
Bigg, Patricia Nina 1932- 102
Bigge, Morris L. 1908- 9-10R
Biggers, Earl Derr 1884-1933 Brief entry 108
Biggers, John Thomas 1924- CANR-2
Earlier sketch in CA 3R
Biggle, Lloyd, Jr. 1923- CANR-20
Earlier sketches in CA 13-14R, CANR-5
See also DLB 8
Biggs, Anselm G. 1914- 33-36R
Biggs, Bradley 1920- 124
Biggs, John B(urville) 1934- CANR-6
Earlier sketch in CA 57-60
Biggs, John, Jr. 1895-1979 Obituary 85-88
Biggs, Margaret Key 1933- 114
Biggs, (Marvin) Mouzon, Jr. 1941- 111
Biggs, Peter
See Rimel, Duane (Weldon)
Biggs-Davison, John (Alec) 1918- 13-14R
Bigiaretti, Libero 1906- CANR-12
Earlier sketch in CA 29-32R
Bigler, Vernon 1922- 21-22R
Bignell, Alan 1928- 103
Bigsby, C(hristopher) W(illiam) E(dgar)
1941- CANR-11
Earlier sketch in CA 25-28R
Bihalji-Merin, Oto 1904- CANR-15
Earlier sketch in CA 81-84
Bihler, Penny 1940- 77-80
Bijou, Sidney W(illiam) 1908- CANR-14
Earlier sketch in CA 37-40R
Bikel, Theodore 1924- CANR-1
Earlier sketch in CA 1R
Bikkie, James A(ndrew) 1929- 53-56
Biklen, Douglas Paul 1945- CANR-15
Earlier sketch in CA 85-88
Bilas, Richard A(llen) 1935- 53-56
Bilbo, Queenie ?-1972 Obituary 37-40R
Bilbow, Antony 1932- 25-28R
Bilderback, Dean Loy 1932- 97-100
Bilderback, Diane E(lizabeth) 1951- 110
Bileck, Marvin 1920- SATA-40
Bilek, Arthur J(ohn) 1929- 115
Bilich, Marion Yellin 1949- 114
Bilinsky, Yaroslav 1932- 13-14R
Bilkey, Warren J(oseph) 1920- 29-32R
Bill, Alfred Hoyt 1879-1964 107
See also SATA 44
Bill, J(ohn) Brent 1951- 117
Bill, James A(lban) 1939- Brief entry 114
Bill, Valentine T. 13-14R
Billam, Rosemary 1952- 123
Bill-Belotserkovsky, Vladimir Naumovich
1884-1970 Obituary 104
Biller, Henry B(urt) 1940- 114
Billetdoux, Francois (Paul) 1927- 21-22R
Billett, Roy O(ren) 1891- 13-14R
Billias, George Athan 1919- CANR-6
Earlier sketch in CA 11-12R
Billings, Charlene W(interer) 1941- CANR-24
Earlier sketch in CA 107
See also SATA 41
Billings, Charles E(dward) 1938- 121
Billings, Evelyn L(ivingston) 1918- 112
Billings, Ezra
See Halla, (Robert) Chris(tian)
Billings, Harold (Wayne) 1931- 25-28R
Billings, John Shaw 1898-1975 Obituary 104
Billings, Josh
See Shaw, Henry Wheeler
Billings, Peggy 1928- 25-28R
Billings, Richard N. 1930- 103
Billings, Robert 1949- 113
Billings, Warren M(artin) 1940- 61-64
Billings, William Dwight 1910- 113
Billingsley, Andrew 1926- 57-60
Billingsley, Edward Baxter 1910- CAP-2
Earlier sketch in CA 25-28
Billington, Dora May 1890-1968 .... CAP-1
Earlier sketch in CA 13-14
Billington, Elizabeth T(hain) 101
See also SATA 43, 50
Billington, James H(adley) 1929-
Brief entry 117
Billington, John
See Beaver, (Jack) Patrick
Billington, Joy 1931- 77-80
Billington, Michael 1939- 102
Billington, Monroe Lee 1928- 21-22R
Billington, Rachel 1942- 33-36R
See also CLC 43
See also AITN 2
Billington, Ray Allen 1903-1981 .... CANR-5
Obituary 103
Earlier sketch in CA 1R
Billington, Raymond John 1930- 110
Billmeyer, Fred Wallace, Jr. 1919- 85-88
Billout, Guy (Rene) 1941- 85-88
See also SATA 10
Bills, Robert E(dgar) 1916- 107
Bills, Scott L(aurence) 1948- 112
Billy, Andre 1882-1971 Obituary 29-32R
Bilow, Pat 1941- 106
Bilsland, Bilko
See Bilsland, E(rnest) C(harles)
Bilsland, E(rnest) C(harles) 1931- 69-72
Bimler, Richard William 1940- CANR-14
Earlier sketch in CA 41-44R
Binder, Aaron 1927- 57-60
Binder, David 1931- 65-68
Binder, Eando
See Binder, Otto O(scar)
Binder, Frederick M(elvin) 1931- 29-32R
Binder, Frederick Moore 1920- 41-44R
Binder, Leonard 1927- 61-64
Binder, Otto O(scar) 1911-1974 .... CANR-3
Obituary 53-56
Earlier sketch in CA 4R
Binder, Pearl
See Elwyn-Jones, Pearl Binder
Binding, Rudolf G. 1867-1938 .... DLB-66
Bindman, Arthur J(oseph) 1925- 45-48
Bindoff, Stanley Thomas 1908-1980 73-76
Obituary 102
Bindra, Dalbir 1922-1980 122
Obituary 117
Bing, Elisabeth D. 1914- CANR-11
Earlier sketch in CA 69-72
Bing, Rudolf 1902- 89-92
Bingaman, Ron 1936- 61-64
Binger, Carl A(lfred) L(anning)
1889-1976 73-76
Obituary 65-68
Binger, Norman H(enry) 1914- 33-36R
Binger, Walter 1888(?)-1979 Obituary 85-88
Bingham, (George) Barry, Jr. 1933- 106
Bingham, Caleb 1757-1817 .... DLB-42
Bingham, Caroline 1938- CANR-10
Earlier sketch in CA 57-60
Bingham, Carson
See Cassiday, Bruce (Bingham)
Bingham, Charlotte (Mary Therese)
1942- CANR-11
Earlier sketch in CA 105
Bingham, David A(ndrew) 1926- 53-56
Bingham, Edwin R(alph) 1920- CANR-2
Earlier sketch in CA 5-6R
Bingham, Evangeline M(arguerite) L(adys)
(Elliot) 1899- 65-68
Bingham, Jane Marie 1941- 104
Bingham, John (Michael Ward) 1908- CANR-11
Earlier sketch in CA 21-22R
Bingham, Jonathan Brewster
1914-1986 .... 33-36R
Obituary 119
Bingham, June Rossbach 1919- 4R
Bingham, M(orley) P(aul) 1918- 49-52
Bingham, Madeleine (Mary Ebel)
1912-1988 .... CANR-11
Obituary 124
Earlier sketch in CA 13-14R
Bingham, Melinda 1950- 119
Bingham, Mindy
See Bingham, Melinda
Bingham, Richard D. 1937- 112
Bingham, Robert C(harles) 1927- 21-22R
Bingham, Robert E. 1925- 29-32R
Bingham, Robert Kamerer 1925(?)-1982
Obituary 107
Bingham, Sallie
See Ellsworth, Sallie Bingham
Bingham, Woodbridge 1901-1986
Obituary 119
Bingley, Clive (Hamilton) 1936- 19-20R
Bingley, D. E.
See Bingley, David Ernest
Bingley, David Ernest 1920- CANR-18
Earlier sketches in CA 45-48, CANR-2
Binham, Philip Frank 1924- 107
Binion, Rudolph 1927- CANR-4
Earlier sketch in CA 1R
bin Ishak, Yusof
See Ishak, Yusof bin
Binkley, Anne
See Rand, Ann (Binkley)
Binkley, Luther John 1925- 5-6R
Binkley, Olin T(rivette) 1908- 45-48
Binkley, William Campbell 1889-1970 107
Obituary 104
Binns, Archie (Fred) 1899- 73-76
Binns, J(ames) W(allace) 1940- 53-56
Binswanger, Ludwig 1881-1966 Obituary 107
Binyon, Claude 1905-1978 Obituary 77-80
Binyon, Helen 1904-1982(?) Obituary 114
Binyon, (Robert) Laurence 1869-1943
Brief entry 115
See also DLB 19
Binyon, T(imothy) J(ohn) 1936- 111
See also CLC 34
Binzen, Bill
See Binzen, William
See also SATA 24
Binzen, William 89-92
Biossat, Bruce 1910(?)-1974 Obituary 104
Biot, Francois 1923- 13-14R
Biow, Milton H. 1882(?)-1976 Obituary 65-68
Bioy Casares, Adolfo 1914- CANR-19
Earlier sketch in CA 29-32R
See also CLC 4, 8, 13
Biram, Brenda 1930(?)-1984 Obituary 112
Birch, Alison Wyrley 1922- 85-88
Birch, Anthony H(arold) 1924- CANR-5
Earlier sketch in CA 13-14R
Birch, Bruce C(harles) 1941- CANR-10
Earlier sketch in CA 65-68
Birch, Cyril 1925- 85-88
Birch, Daniel R(ichard) 1937- 101
Birch, David L. 1937- CANR-16
Earlier sketch in CA 25-28R
Birch, Herbert G. 1918-1973 Obituary 41-44R
Birch, L(ouis) C(harles) 1918- 120
Birch, Leo Bedrich 1902- 33-36R
Birch, Lionel ?-1982(?) Obituary 106
Birch, (Evelyn) Nigel (Chetwode)
1906-1981 Obituary 108
Birch, Reginald B(athurst) 1856-1943 .... SATA-19
Birch, William G(arry) 1909- 53-56
Birchall, Ian H(arry) 1939- 97-100
Bircham, Deric Neale 1934- 89-92
Bird, Al
See Mandel, Leon
Bird, Anthony (Cole) 1917- 13-14R
Bird, Brandon
See Evans, George Bird
and Evans, Kay Harris
Bird, C.
See Ellison, Harlan
Bird, Caroline 1915- CANR-11
Earlier sketch in CA 19-20R
Bird, Cordwainer
See Ellison, Harlan
Bird, David 1926(?)-1987 Obituary 121
Bird, Dennis L(eslie) 1930- 116
Bird, Dorothy Maywood 1899- CAP-1
Earlier sketch in CA 17-18
Bird, Florence (Bayard) 1908- 97-100
Bird, George L(loyd) 1900- CANR-2
Earlier sketch in CA 5-6R
Bird, Harrison K. 1910- 85-88
Bird, Isabella L.
See Bishop, Isabella Lucy (Bird)
Bird, James Harold 1923- 102
Bird, Junius Bouton 1907-1982 Obituary 106
Bird, (Cyril) Kenneth 1887-1965 .... CAP-1
Earlier sketch in CA 13-14
Bird, Lewis P(enhall) 1933- CANR-17
Earlier sketch in CA 97-100
Bird, Patricia Amy 1941- CANR-22
Earlier sketches in CA 61-64, CANR-7
Bird, Richard (Miller) 1938- CANR-19
Earlier sketches in CA 11-12R, CANR-4
Bird, Sarah McCabe 1949- 111
Bird, Veronica 1932- 112
Bird, Vivian 1910- 102
Bird, W(illiam) Ernest 1890- CAP-1
Earlier sketch in CA 19-20
Bird, Wendell R(aleigh) 116
Bird, Will R. 1891- 13-14R
Bird, William 1889-1963 Obituary 112
See also DLB 4
Birdsall, Steve 1944- CANR-7
Earlier sketch in CA 53-56
Birdsell, Joseph B(enjamin) 1908- 119
Birdseye, Clarence (Frank) 1886-1956
Brief entry 122
Birdwell, Russell (Juarez) 1903-1977
Obituary 107
Birdwhistell, Ray L. 1918- 45-48
Birenbaum, Arnold 1939- 108
Birenbaum, Halina 1929- 45-48
Birenbaum, Harvey 1936- 109
Birenbaum, William M. 1923- 29-32R
Birimisa, George 1924- 89-92
Birkenhead, Lord
See Smith, Frederick Winston Furneaux
Birkenmayer, Sigmund Stanley 1923- 23-24R
Birket-Smith, Kaj 1893- CAP-1
Earlier sketch in CA 13-14
Birkin, Andrew (Timothy) 1945- 97-100
Birkin, Charles (Lloyd) 1907- 69-72
Birkley, Marilyn 1916- 41-44R
Birkos, Alexander S(ergei) 1936- 25-28R
Birks, Tony 1937- CANR-12
Earlier sketch in CA 69-72
Birksted-Breen, Dana 1946- 102
Birla, Ghanshyamdas 1894-1983 Obituary 110
Birla, Lakshminiwas N. 1909- CAP-1
Earlier sketch in CA 13-14
Birley, Julia (Davies) 1928- 13-14R
Birley, Robert 1903-1982 Obituary 110
Birmelin, Blair T. 1939- 117
Birmingham, David (Bevis) 1938- 19-20R
Birmingham, F(rederic) A(lexander)
1911-1982 .... CANR-11
Obituary 107
Earlier sketch in CA 17-18R
Birmingham, Frances A(therton) 1920- 17-18R
Birmingham, John 1951- 45-48
Birmingham, Lloyd 1924- SATA-12
Birmingham, Maisie 1914- 101
Birmingham, Stephen 1932- CANR-20
Earlier sketches in CA 49-52, CANR-2
See also AITN 1
Birmingham, Walter (Barr) 1913- 17-18R
Birn, Randi (Marie) 1935- 73-76
Birn, Raymond Francis 1935- 102
Birnbach, Martin 1929- 3R
Birnbaum, Eleazar 1929- 37-40R
Birnbaum, Milton 1919- 33-36R
Birnbaum, Norman 1926- CANR-5
Earlier sketch in CA 53-56
Birnbaum, Philip 1904- CANR-1
Earlier sketch in CA 49-52
Birnbaum, Phyllis 1945- 102
Birnberg, Thomas B.
See Brooks, Thomas
Birne, Henry 1921- 17-18R
Birney, Alice L(otvin) 1938- 33-36R
Birney, (Alfred) Earle 1904- CANR-20
Earlier sketches in CA 3R, CANR-5
See also CLC 1, 4, 6, 11
Birnie, Whittlesey 1945- 97-100
Birnkrant, Arthur 1906(?)-1983 Obituary 108
Biro, B(alint) S(tephen) 1921- CANR-11
Earlier sketch in CA 25-28R
Biro, Charlotte Slovak 1904- 57-60
Biro, Val
See Biro, B(alint) S(tephen)
See also SATA 1
Biro, Yvette 111
Birren, Faber 1900- CANR-7
Earlier sketch in CA 13-14R
Birren, James E(mmett) 1918- 17-18R
Birse, A(rthur) H(erbert) 1889- CAP-2
Earlier sketch in CA 23-24
Birstein, Ann 17-18R
Birt, David 1936- CANR-13
Earlier sketch in CA 73-76
Bischof, Ledford Julius 1914- 11-12R
Bischoff, David F(rederick) 1951- 81-84
Bischoff, F(rederick) A(lexander) 1928- 89-92
Bischoff, Julia Bristol 1909-1970 .... CAP-2
Earlier sketch in CA 21-22
See also SATA 12
Bish, Robert L(ee) 1942- 53-56
Bishai, Wilson B. 1923- 33-36R
Bisher, James F(urman) 1918- CANR-2
Earlier sketch in CA 5-6R
Bishin, William R(obert) 1939- 61-64
Bishir, John (William) 1933- 41-44R
Bishop, Bonnie 1943- 103
See also SATA 37
Bishop, Claire (Huchet) 73-76
See also SATA 14
Bishop, Crawford M. 1885- CAP-2
Earlier sketch in CA 17-18

Bishop, Curtis (Kent) 1912-1967 CAP-1
Earlier sketch in CA 11-12
See also SATA 6
Bishop, Donald
See Steward, Samuel M(orris)
Bishop, Donald G. 1907- CANR-3
Earlier sketch in CA 3R
Bishop, Donald H(arold) 1920- 105
Bishop, E. Morchard
See Stonor, Oliver
Bishop, Elizabeth 1911-1979 7-8R
Obituary 89-92
See also CABS 2
See also SATA 24
See also DLB 5
See also CLC 1, 4, 9, 13, 15, 32
Bishop, Eugene C. 1909-1983 Obituary 109
Bishop, Ferman 1922- 23-24R
Bishop, Gavin 1946- 121
Bishop, George (Victor) 1924- CANR-2
Earlier sketch in CA 49-52
Bishop, George W(esley), Jr. 1910- 13-14R
Bishop, Gordon (Bruce) 1938- 118
Bishop, Ian Benjamin 1927- 106
Bishop, Isabella Bird
See Bishop, Isabella Lucy (Bird)
Bishop, Isabella L.
See Bishop, Isabella Lucy (Bird)
Bishop, Isabella Lucy (Bird) 1831-1904
Brief entry 123
Bishop, James 1929- 97-100
Bishop, James Alonzo 1907-1987 19-20R
Obituary 123
Bishop, Jim
See Bishop, James Alonzo
See also AITN 1, 2
Bishop, John 1908- 65-68
Bishop, John 1935- 105
See also CLC 10
Bishop, John L(yman) 1913-1974 CAP-2
Earlier sketch in CA 33-36
Bishop, John Melville 1946- CANR-13
Earlier sketch in CA 77-80
Bishop, John Peale 1892-1944 Brief entry 107
See also DLB 4, 9, 45
Bishop, Joseph W(arren), Jr.
1915-1985 33-36R
Obituary 116
Bishop, Leonard 1922- 15-16R
Bishop, Lloyd (Ormond) 1933- 114
Bishop, Louis Faugeres 1901(?)-1986 122
Obituary 119
Bishop, Maurice 1944-1983 123
Obituary 111
Bishop, Maxine H. 1919- 25-28R
Bishop, Michael 1945- CANR-9
Earlier sketch in CA 61-64
See also AITN 2
Bishop, Morchard
See Stonor, Oliver
Bishop, Morris 1893-1973 CANR-6
Obituary 45-48
Earlier sketch in CA 4R
Bishop, Mrs. J. F.
See Bishop, Isabella Lucy (Bird)
Bishop, Pike
See Obstfeld, Raymond
Bishop, Robert 1938- CANR-15
Earlier sketch in CA 81-84
Bishop, Robert Lee 1931- 15-16R
Bishop, Ron 1922(?)-1988 Obituary 124
Bishop, Susan M. 1921(?)-1970 Obituary 104
Bishop, Tania Kroitor 1906- CAP-2
Earlier sketch in CA 29-32
Bishop, Thomas W(alter) 1929- CANR-18
Earlier sketches in CA 3R, CANR-1
Bishop, Tom
See Bishop, Thomas W(alter)
Bishop, W(illiam) Arthur 1923- 21-22R
Bishop, William W(arner), Jr. 1906- 17-18R
Bishop of Marsland
See Duncan, Ronald
Bishop of Truro
See Leonard, Graham Douglas
Bisignani, Joseph D(aniel) 1947- 112
Biskin, Miriam 1920- 21-22R
Bisque, Anatole
See Bosquet, Alain
Bissell, Claude T(homas) 1916- 101
Bissell, Elaine 81-84
Bissell, Richard (Pike) 1913-1977 CANR-6
Obituary 69-72
Earlier sketch in CA 4R
Bisset, Donald 1910- CANR-13
Earlier sketch in CA 33-36R
See also SATA 7
Bisset, Ronald 1950- 103
bissett, bill 1939- CANR-15
Earlier sketch in CA 69-72
See also DLB 53
See also CLC 18
Bissett, Donald J(ohn) 1930- 97-100
Bisson, Thomas N(oel) 1931- 119
Bissoondoyal, Basdeo 1906- CANR-11
Earlier sketch in CA 25-28R
Bisztray, George 1938- 106
Bita, Lili
See Zaller, Angelika Bita
Bite, Ben
See Schneck, Stephen
Bitker, Marjorie M. 1901- 77-80
Bitsios, Dimitri S. 1915-1984 Obituary 111
Bittel, Lester Robert 1918- CANR-21
Earlier sketches in CA 15-16R, CANR-6
Bitter, Francis 1902-1967 Obituary 113
Bitter, Gary G(len) 1940- CANR-14
Earlier sketch in CA 69-72
See also SATA 22
Bittermann, Henry J(ohn) 1904- 33-36R
Bittinger, Desmond W(right) 1905- 37-40R
Bittinger, Emmert F(oster) 1925- 37-40R
Bittker, Boris I(rving) 1916- Brief entry 109
Bittle, William E(lmer) 1926- 53-56
Bittlinger, Arnold 1928- 49-52
Bittner, Donald F(rancis) 1941- 122
Bittner, Vernon (John) 1932- 69-72
Bittner, William (Robert) 1921- 5-6R
Bitton, Davis 1930- CANR-14
Earlier sketch in CA 33-36R
Biven, W(illiam) Carl 1925- 21-22R
Bivins, John 1940- 85-88
Bixby, Jay Lewis
See Bixby, Jerome Lewis
Bixby, Jerome Lewis 1923- 17-18R
Bixby, Ray Z.
See Tralins, S(andor) Robert
Bixby, William (Courtney) 1920-1986 CANR-6
Obituary 118
Earlier sketch in CA 3R
See also SATA 6, 47
Bixler, Julius Seelye 1894-1985 Obituary 115
Bixler, Norma 1905- 49-52
Bixler, Paul (Howard) 1899- 69-72
Bixler, R(oy) Russell, Jr. 1927- 61-64
Biyidi, Alexandre 1932- 124
Brief entry 114
Bizardel, Yvon 1891- 61-64
Bizzarro, Salvatore 1939- 53-56
Bjarme, Brynjolf
See Ibsen, Henrik (Johan)
Bjerke, Robert Alan 1939- 41-44R
Bjerke, Ward (Ollie) 1920- Brief entry 108
Bjerre, Jens 1921- 11-12R
Bjoerneboe, Jens 1920-1976 69-72
Obituary 65-68
Bjoernson, Bjoernstjerne (Martinius)
1832-1910 Brief entry 104
See also TCLC 7
Bjorklund, Lorence F. 1913-1978 SATA-32, 35
Bjorn, Thyra Ferre 1905-1975 CANR-3
Obituary 57-60
Earlier sketch in CA 5-6R
Bjornard, Reidar B(ernhard) 1917- 33-36R
Bjornson, Bjornstjerne (Martinius)
See Bjoernson, Bjoernstjerne (Martinius)
See also TCLC 7
Bjornson, Richard 1938- 77-80
Bjornson, (Kristjan) Val(dimar) 1906-1987
Obituary 121
Bjornstad, James 1940- 29-32R
Bjorset, Bryniolf
See Beorse, Bryn
Blachford, George 1913- 11-12R
Blachly, Frederick (Frank) 1881(?)-1975
Obituary 57-60
Blachly, Lou 1889- CAP-1
Earlier sketch in CA 13-14
Black, Albert George 1928- 45-48
Black, Algernon David 1900- CANR-2
Earlier sketch in CA 4R
See also SATA 12
Black, Angus 1943- 29-32R
Black, Antony 1936- 121
Black, Betty
See Schwartz, Betty
Black, Bonnie Lee 1945- 107
Black, Brady Forrest 1908- 102
Black, Campbell 1944- 89-92
Black, Charles
See Black, Charles L(und), Jr.
Black, Charles L(und), Jr. 1915- CANR-3
Earlier sketch in CA 1R
Black, Clinton Vane De Brosse 1918- 102
Black, Creed C(arter) 1925- 73-76
Black, Cyril Edwin 1915- CANR-3
Earlier sketch in CA 4R
Black, D. M.
See Black, David (Macleod)
Black, David (Macleod) 1941- 25-28R
See also DLB 40
Black, David
See Way, Robert E(dward)
Black, Dianne (a pseudonym) 1940- 97-100
Black, Dorothy 1899-1985 Obituary 115
Black, Dorothy 1914- 111
Black, Douglas M. 1896(?)-1977 Obituary 104
Black, Duncan 1908- CAP-2
Earlier sketch in CA 19-20
Black, E(dward) L(oring) 1915- 9-10R
Black, Earl 1942- 101
Black, Elizabeth 1908(?)-1987 Obituary 122
Black, Eugene C(harlton) 1927- 11-12R
Black, Eugene R(obert) 1898- CAP-2
Earlier sketch in CA 25-28
Black, Floyd H. 1888-1983 Obituary 111
Black, Gavin
See Wynd, Oswald Morris
Black, Hallie 1943- 108
Black, Harry George 1933- 61-64
Black, Hugh C(leon) 1920- 37-40R
Black, Hugo Lafayette 1886-1971
Obituary 33-36R
Black, Ian Stuart 1915- CANR-6
Earlier sketch in CA 9-10R
Black, Irma Simonton 1906-1972 CANR-6
Obituary 37-40R
Earlier sketch in CA 4R
See also SATA 2, 25
Black, Ishi
See Gibson, Walter B(rown)
Black, Ivan 1904(?)-1979 Obituary 85-88
Black, James A(llen) 1937- 121
Black, James Menzies 1913- CANR-5
Earlier sketch in CA 5-6R
Black, John N(icholson) 1922- CANR-13
Earlier sketch in CA 33-36R
Black, John Wilson 1906- CAP-1
Earlier sketch in CA 17-18
Black, Jonathan
See von Block, Bela W(illiam)
Black, Joseph E. 1921- 11-12R
Black, Kenneth, Jr. 1925- CANR-7
Earlier sketch in CA 15-16R
Black, Kitty
See Black, Dorothy
Black, Lionel
See Barker, Dudley
Black, Maggie
See Black, Margaret K(atherine)
Black, Malcolm Charles Lamont 1928- 85-88
Black, Mansell
See Trevor, Elleston
Black, Margaret K(atherine) 1921- CANR-14
Earlier sketch in CA 29-32R
Black, Martha E(llen) 1901- 33-36R
Black, Mary (Childs) 1922- CANR-13
Earlier sketch in CA 21-22R
Black, Matthew W(ilson) 1895- CAP-2
Earlier sketch in CA 25-28
Black, Max 1909- 61-64
Black, Michael L(awrence) 1940- 121
Black, Millard H. 1912- 25-28R
Black, Misha 1910- CAP-1
Earlier sketch in CA 11-12
Black, Nancy B(reMiller) 1941- Brief entry 107
Black, Percy 1922- 33-36R
Black, Robert 1946- 121
Black, Robert B(ruce) 1920- 109
Black, Robert C(lifford) III 1914- 41-44R
Black, Roe C(oddington) 1926- 89-92
Black, Stanley Warren III 1939- 45-48
Black, Susan Adams 1953- 105
See also SATA 40
Black, Theodore Michael 1919- 109
Black, Veronica
See Peters, Maureen
Black, William Joseph 1934(?)-1977
Obituary 73-76
Black, Winifred 1863-1936 DLB-25
Blackall, Eric Albert 1914- 65-68
Blackamore, Arthur 1679-? DLB-24, 39
Blackbeard, Bill 1926- 97-100
Blackburn, Alexander (Lambert) 1929- 97-100
See also DLBY 85
Blackburn, Barbara
See Leader, (Evelyn) Barbara (Blackburn)
Blackburn, Claire
See Jacobs, Linda C.
Blackburn, George M. III 1950- 123
Blackburn, Graham (John) 1940- CANR-22
Earlier sketch in CA 69-72
Blackburn, John (Fenwick) 1923- CANR-22
Earlier sketches in CA 3R, CANR-2
Blackburn, John(ny) Brewton 1952- SATA-15
Blackburn, Joyce Knight 1920- 17-18R
See also SATA 29
Blackburn, Laurence Henry 1897- 57-60
Blackburn, Michael 1954- 118
Blackburn, Norma Davis 1914- 69-72
Blackburn, Paul 1926-1971 81-84
Obituary 33-36R
See also DLB 16
See also DLBY 81
See also CLC 9, 43
Blackburn, R(obert) M(artin) 1934- 119
Blackburn, Robert T. 1923- 121
Blackburn, Simon 1944- 49-52
Blackburn, Thomas (Eliel Fenwick)
1916-1977 73-76
Obituary 113
See also DLB 27
Blackburn, Thomas C(arl) 1936- CANR-22
Earlier sketch in CA 69-72
Blackburne, Kenneth (William) 1907-1980
Obituary 105
Blackburne, Neville Alfred Edmund 1913- 53-56
Blacker, C(arlos) P(aton) 1895-1975
Obituary 57-60
Blacker, Carmen Elizabeth 1924- 11-12R
Blacker, Irwin R(obert) 1919-1985 CANR-3
Obituary 115
Earlier sketch in CA 3R
Blackett, Patrick (Maynard Stuart)
1897-1974 Obituary 49-52
Blackett, Veronica Heath 1927- 53-56
See also SATA 12
Blackey, Robert 1941- CANR-4
Earlier sketch in CA 53-56
Blackford, Charles Minor III 1898- 69-72
Blackford, Staige D(avis) 1931- 103
Blackhall, David Scott 1910- 7-8R
Blackham, Garth J. 1926- 33-36R
Blackham, H(arold) J(ohn) 1903- 23-24R
Black Hobart
See Sanders, (James) Ed(ward)
Blackie, Bruce L(othian) 1936- 57-60
Blackie, John (Ernest Haldane)
1904-1985 73-76
Obituary 116
Blackie, Pamela 1917- 103
Blacking, John (Anthony Randoll)
1928- CANR-3
Earlier sketch in CA 11-12R
Blackledge, Ethel H(ale) CANR-11
Earlier sketch in CA 23-24R
Blackman, Audrey 1907- 109
Blackman, Sheldon 1935- 33-36R
Blackman, Victor 1922- 103
Blackmer, Donald L. M. 1929- 33-36R
Black-Michaud, Jacob 1938- 61-64
Blackmon, C(harles) Robert 1925- 33-36R
Blackmon, Rosemary Barnsdall
1921(?)-1983 Obituary 111
Blackmore, Charles (David) 1957- 124
Blackmore, Dorothy S. 1914- 41-44R
Blackmore, John T(homas) 1931- CANR-15
Earlier sketch in CA 41-44R
Blackmore, Peter 1909-1984 9-10R
Obituary 114
Blackmore, R(ichard) D(oddridge)
1825-1900 Brief entry 120
See also DLB 18
See also TCLC 27
Blackmore, Robert Long 1919- 113
Blackmur, R(ichard) P(almer) 1904-1965 CAP-1
Obituary 25-28R
Earlier sketch in CA 11-12
See also DLB 63
See also CLC 2, 24
Blackoff, Edward M. 1934- 11-12R
Blackshear, Helen F(riedman) 1911- CANR-10
Earlier sketch in CA 25-28R
Blacksnake, George
See Richardson, Gladwell
Blackstock, Charity
See Torday, Ursula
Blackstock, Lee
See Torday, Ursula
Blackstock, Nelson 1944- 97-100
Blackstock, Paul W(illiam) 1913- 15-16R
Blackstock, Walter 1917- CANR-9
Earlier sketch in CA 5-6R
Blackstone, Bernard 1911-1983 69-72
Obituary 111
Blackstone, Geoffrey Vaughan 1910- CAP-1
Earlier sketch in CA 9-10
Blackstone, Harry
See Blackstone, Harry (Bouton), Jr.
Blackstone, Harry (Bouton), Jr. 1934- 114
Blackstone, Tessa Ann Vosper 1942- CANR-19
Earlier sketch in CA 102
Blackstone, William T(homas) 1931- CANR-11
Earlier sketch in CA 17-18R
Black Tarantula, The
See Acker, Kathy
Blackton, Peter
See Wilson, Lionel
Blackwelder, Bernice Fowler 1902- 3R
Blackwelder, Boyce W. 1913- 19-20R
Blackwelder, Jerry 1950- 122
Blackwell, Basil (Henry) 1889-1984
Obituary 112
Blackwell, Betsy Talbot 1905(?)-1985
Obituary 115
Blackwell, (Samuel) Earl (Jr.) 1913- 81-84
Blackwell, James E(dward) 1926-
Brief entry 114
Blackwell, Leslie 1885- 9-10R
Blackwell, Lois S. 1943- 85-88
Blackwell, (Annie) Louise 1919-1977 37-40R
Blackwell, Marilyn Johns 1948- 116
Blackwell, Muriel F(ontenot) 1929- 108
Blackwell, Richard Joseph 1929- 33-36R
Blackwell, Roger D(ale) 1940- 93-96
Blackwell, William L. 1929- 23-24R
Blackwood, Alan 1932- 110
Blackwood, Algernon (Henry) 1869-1951
Brief entry 105
See also TCLC 5
Blackwood, Andrew W(atterson)
1882-1966 5-6R
Obituary 103
Blackwood, Andrew W(atterson), Jr.
1915- CANR-5
Earlier sketch in CA 1R
Blackwood, Caroline 1931- 85-88
See also DLB 14
See also CLC 6, 9
Blackwood, Cheryl Prewitt 1957- 108
Blackwood, Easley 1903- 115
Blackwood, George D(ouglas) 1919- 13-14R
Blackwood, James R. 1918- 23-24R
Blackwood, Paul Everett 1913- 102
Blade, Alexander
See Hamilton, Edmond
and Silverberg, Robert
Bladel, Roderick L(eRoy) 97-100
Bladen, Ashby 1929- 106
Bladen, V(incent) W(heeler) 1900- 61-64
Blades, Ann 1947- CANR-13
Earlier sketch in CA 77-80
See also SATA 16
Blades, Brian Brewer 1906-1977
Obituary 73-76
Blades, James 1901- 65-68
Bladow, Suzanne Wilson 1937- 61-64
See also SATA 14
Blaffer, Sarah C.
See Hrdy, Sarah Blaffer
Blagden, Cyprian 1906-1962 4R
Blagden, David 1944- 53-56
Blagowidow, George 1923- 77-80
Blaher, Damian J(oseph) 1913- 21-22R
Blaich, Theodore Paul 1902- CAP-1
Earlier sketch in CA 13-14
Blaike, Avona
See MacIntosh, Joan
Blaikie, Robert J. 1923- 33-36R
Blaiklock, Edward Musgrave 1903- CANR-7
Earlier sketch in CA 19-20R
Blaine, James
See Avallone, Michael (Angelo), Jr.
Blaine, John
See Goodwin, Harold Leland
Blaine, Marge
See Blaine, Margery Kay

Blaine, Margery Kay 1937- 61-64
See also SATA 11
Blaine, Thomas R(obert) 1895- 106
Blaine, Tom R.
See Blaine, Thomas R(obert)
Blaine, William L(ee) 1931- 65-68
Blainey, Ann (Warriner) 1935- 25-28R
Blainey, Geoffrey (Norman) 1930- 25-28R
Blair
See Blair-Fish, Wallace Wilfrid
Blair, Anne Denton 1914- 110
See also SATA 46
Blair, Calvin Patton 1924- 15-16R
Blair, Carvel Hall 1924- 49-52
Blair, Charles E. 1920- 25-28R
Blair, Claude 1922- CANR-11
Earlier sketch in CA 7-8R
Blair, Clay Drewry, Jr. 1925- 77-80
See also AITN 2
Blair, Cynthia 1953- 118
Blair, (Robert) Dike 1919- 9-10R
Blair, Don 1933- 65-68
Blair, Dorothy L. 1890- 114
Blair, Dorothy S(ara Greene) 1913-
Brief entry 113
Blair, Edward H. 1938- CANR-7
Earlier sketch in CA 17-18R
Blair, Edward P(ayson) 1910- CANR-11
Earlier sketches in CA 13-14, CAP-1
Blair, Eric Hugh 1903-1950 Brief entry 104
See also SATA 29
Blair, Everetta Love 1907- CAP-2
Earlier sketch in CA 25-28
Blair, Francis Preston 1791-1876 .... DLB-43
Blair, Frank 1915- 93-96
Blair, George S(imms) 1924- 17-18R
Blair, Glenn Myers 1908- 5-6R
Blair, Harry Wallace 1938- 109
Blair, Helen 1910- SATA-29
Blair, J(oseph) Allen 1913- 89-92
Blair, James 1655(?)-1743 .... DLB-24
Blair, Jane N(emec) 1911- 57-60
Blair, Jay 1953- SATA-45
Blair, John Durburrow 1759-1823 .... DLB-37
Blair, John G(eorge) 1934- 15-16R
Blair, John M(alcolm) 1914-1976 73-76
Obituary 69-72
Blair, Kay Reynolds 1942- 33-36R
Blair, Leon Borden 1917- 29-32R
Blair, Lorraine Louise 1899(?)-1984
Obituary 114
Blair, Lucile
See Yeakley, Marjory Hall
Blair, Paxton 1892-1974 Obituary 53-56
Blair, Peter Hunter
See Hunter Blair, Peter
Blair, Philip M(ark) 1928- 41-44R
Blair, Ruth Van Ness 1912- 21-22R
See also SATA 12
Blair, Sam 1932- 53-56
Blair, Shannon
See Kaye, Marilyn
Blair, Thomas (Lucien Vincent) 1926- 106
Blair, Walter 1900- CANR-18
Earlier sketches in CA 5-6R, CANR-3
See also SATA 12
Blair, Wilfrid
See Blair-Fish, Wallace Wilfrid
Blair-Fish, Wallace Wilfrid 1889-1968 .... CAP-2
Earlier sketch in CA 29-32
Blais, Madeleine 1947- 104
Blais, Marie-Claire 1939- 21-22R
See also CAAS 4
See also DLB 53
See also CLC 2, 4, 6, 13, 22
Blaisdell, Anne
See Linington, Elizabeth
Blaisdell, Donald C. 1899- 37-40R
Blaisdell, Foster W(arren) 1927- 69-72
Blaisdell, Harold F. 1914- 65-68
Blaisdell, Paul H(enry) 1908- 61-64
Blaise, Clark 1940- CANR-5
Earlier sketch in CA 53-56
See also CAAS 3
See also DLB 53
See also CLC 29
See also AITN 2
Blake, Alfred
See Janifer, Laurence M(ark)
Blake, Andrew
See Janifer, Laurence M(ark)
Blake, Brian 1918- 109
Blake, Bud
See Blake, Julian Watson
Blake, Christina
See Chandler, Bryn
Blake, David H(aven) 1940- 41-44R
Blake, Eubie
See Blake, James Hubert
Blake, Eugene Carson 1906-1985
Obituary 116
Blake, Fay M(ontaug) 1920- 53-56
Blake, Gary 1944- CANR-15
Earlier sketch in CA 85-88
Blake, Gerald H(enry) 1936- 124
Blake, Harlan Morse 1923- 25-28R
Blake, I(srael) George 1902- 21-22R
Blake, J. W.
See Blake, John William
Blake, James 1922-1979 93-96
Obituary 85-88
Blake, James Hubert 1883-1983 Obituary 109
Blake, Jennifer
See Maxwell, Patricia
Blake, John W.
See Blake, John William
Blake, John William 1911-1987 Obituary 122
Blake, Jonas
See Hardy, C. Colburn
Blake, Judith (Kincade) 1926- 3R
Blake, Julian Watson 1918- 65-68
Blake, Justin
See Bowen, John (Griffith)
Blake, Katherine
See Walter, Dorothy Blake
Blake, Kathleen 1944- 57-60
Blake, Kay
See Walter, Dorothy Blake
Blake, Ken
See Bulmer, (Henry) Kenneth
Blake, L(eslie) J(ames) 1913- CANR-11
Earlier sketch in CA 25-28R
Blake, Minden V(aughan) 1913- 69-72
Blake, Mindy
See Blake, Minden V.
Blake, Monica
See Muir, Marie
Blake, Nelson Manfred 1908- CANR-3
Earlier sketch in CA 1R
Blake, Nicholas
See Day Lewis, C(ecil)
Blake, Norman (Francis) 1934- 93-96
Blake, Patricia 1933- 49-52
Blake, Patrick
See Egleton, Clive (Frederick)
Blake, Paul C. 1916- 25-28R
Blake, Peter (Jost) 1920- CANR-14
Earlier sketch in CA 65-68
Blake, Quentin 1932- CANR-11
Earlier sketch in CA 25-28R
See also SATA 9
Blake, Reed H(arris) 1933- 57-60
Blake, Richard A(loysius) 1939- 93-96
Blake, Robert (Norman William) 1916- CANR-22
Earlier sketch in CA 9-10R
Blake, Robert 1949- SATA-42
Blake, Robert
See Davies, L(eslie) P(urnell)
Blake, Robert R(ogers) 1918- CANR-13
Earlier sketch in CA 23-24R
Blake, Robert W(illiam) 1930- 33-36R
Blake, Sally
See Saunders, Jean
Blake, Sally Mirliss 1925-1986 .... 17-18R
Obituary 118
Blake, Stephanie
See Pearl, Jacques Bain
Blake, Vanessa
See Brown, May
Blake, Walker E.
See Butterworth, W(illiam) E(dmund III)
Blake, Wendon
See Holden, Donald
Blake, William 1757-1827 .... SATA-30
Blake, William J(ames) 1894-1969 .... 5-6R
Obituary 25-28R
Blakeborough, Jack Fairfax
See Fairfax-Blakeborough, John Freeman
Blakeborough, John Freeman Fairfax
See Fairfax-Blakeborough, John Freeman
Blakeley, Phyllis (Ruth) 1922- 61-64
Blakeley, Thomas J(ohn) 1931- CANR-3
Earlier sketch in CA 9-10R
Blakely, R(obert) J(ohn) 1915- 37-40R
Blakemore, Colin (Brian) 1944- 85-88
Blakeney, Jay D.
See Chester, Deborah
Blaker, Alfred A(rthur) 1928- 65-68
Blakeslee, Alton (Lauren) 1913- 105
Blakeslee, Thomas R(obert) 1937- 101
Blakeston, Oswell 1907(?)-1985(?)
Obituary 116
Blakey, George T., Jr. 1939- 120
Blakey, Scott 1936- 85-88
Blakey, Walker Jameson 1940- 69-72
Blakiston, Georgiana 1903- 69-72
Blakiston, Noel 1905-1984 Obituary 115
Blakney, Raymond D. 1897(?)-1970
Obituary 104
Blalock, Hubert Morse, Jr. 1926- CANR-5
Earlier sketch in CA 13-14R
Blalock, Jane B. 1945- Brief entry 112
Blamires, David (Malcolm) 1936- CANR-14
Earlier sketch in CA 65-68
Blamires, Harry 1916- CANR-20
Earlier sketches in CA 9-10R, CANR-5
Blance, Ellen 1931- CANR-7
Earlier sketch in CA 57-60
Blanch, Lesley 1907- 102
Blanch, Robert J. 1938- 21-22R
Blanch, Stuart Yarworth 1918- 106
Blanchard, Allan E(dward) 1929- 69-72
Blanchard, B(irdsall) Everard 1909- 41-44R
Blanchard, Carroll Henry, Jr. 1928- 15-16R
Blanchard, Fessenden Seaver 1888-1963 .... 5-6R
Blanchard, Howard L(awrence) 1909- 7-8R
Blanchard, J. Richard 1912- 89-92
Blanchard, Kendall A(llan) 1942- CANR-11
Earlier sketch in CA 69-72
Blanchard, Kenneth H(artley) 1939- 111
Blanchard, Nina 101
Blanchard, Paula (Barber) 1936- 81-84
Blanchard, Peter 1946- 117
Blanchard, Ralph Harrub 1890-1973 .... CAP-1
Earlier sketch in CA 13-14
Blanchard, William H(enry) 1922- CANR-8
Earlier sketch in CA 23-24R
Blanche, Pierre 1927- 25-28R
Blanchet, Eileen 1924- 57-60
Blanchette, Oliva 1929- 53-56
Blanchot, Maurice 1907- Brief entry 117
Blanck, Gertrude 1914- 85-88
Blanck, Jacob Nathaniel 1906-1974 .... CAP-1
Obituary 53-56
Earlier sketch in CA 11-12
Blanck, Rubin 1914- 25-28R
Blanco, Luis Anado 1903(?)-1975
Obituary 104
Blanco, Richard L(idio) 1926- 57-60
Blanco White, Amber 1887-1981 Obituary 105
Bland, Alexander
See Gosling, Nigel
Bland, E.
See Nesbit, E(dith)
Bland, Fabian
See Nesbit, E(dith)
Bland, Hester Beth 1906- 57-60
Bland, Jeffrey 1946- 106
Bland, Jennifer
See Bowden, Jean
Bland, Larry I(rvin) 1940- 109
Bland, Randall Walton 1942- CANR-5
Earlier sketch in CA 53-56
Blanda, George (Frederick) 1927-
Brief entry 114
Blandenship, Edward Gary 1943- 45-48
Blandford, Brian E(rnest) 1937- 118
Blandford, Percy William 1912- 9-10R
Blanding, Forrest H(arvey) 1917- 111
Blandino, Giovanni 1923- 23-24R
Blane, Gertrude
See Blumenthal, Gertrude
Blane, Howard T(homas) 1926- CANR-10
Earlier sketch in CA 25-28R
Blanford, James T. 1917- 33-36R
Blank, Blanche D(avis) 41-44R
Blank, George (W. III) 1945- 110
Blank, Joseph P. 1919- 93-96
Blank, Leonard 1927- CANR-12
Earlier sketch in CA 33-36R
Blank, Sheldon H(aas) 1896- 4R
Blankenship, A(lbert) B. 1914- CANR-7
Earlier sketch in CA 15-16R
Blankenship, Edward Gary 1943- 45-48
Blankenship, Lela (McDowell) 1886- 7-8R
Blankenship, William D(ouglas) 1934- 33-36R
Blankfort, (Seymour) Michael
1907-1982 .... CANR-2
Obituary 107
Earlier sketch in CA 3R
Blanksten, George I(rving) 1917- CANR-1
Earlier sketch in CA 1R
Blanpied, Pamela Wharton 1937- 102
Blanshard, Brand 1892-1987 .... CANR-16
Obituary 124
Earlier sketch in CA 4R
Blanshard, Paul 1892-1980 Obituary 93-96
Blanton, (Martha) Catherine 1907- 4R
Blantz, Thomas E(dward) 1934- 111
Blanzaco, Andre C. 1934- 29-32R
Blasco Ibanez, Vicente 1867-1928
Brief entry 110
See also TCLC 12
Blase, Melvin G(eorge) 1933- 33-36R
Blaser, Robin (Francis) 1925- CANR-8
Earlier sketch in CA 57-60
Blashford-Snell, John Nicholas 1936- CANR-19
Earlier sketch in CA 102
Blasier, (Stewart) Cole 1925- 23-24R
Blasing, Mutlu Konuk 1944- 89-92
Blasing, Randy 1943- 114
Blass, Birgit A(nnelise) 1940- 29-32R
Blass, Ron(ald J.) 1922-1984 Obituary 114
Blassingame, John W(esley) 1940- 49-52
Blassingame, Wyatt Rainey 1909-1985 .... CANR-3
Obituary 114
Earlier sketch in CA 4R
See also SATA 1, 34, 41
Blatchford, Christie 1951- 73-76
Blathwayt, Jean 1918- 106
Blatt, Burton 1927- CANR-14
Earlier sketch in CA 41-44R
Blatt, Sidney J(ules) 1928- 37-40R
Blatter, Dorothy (Gertrude) 1901- CAP-1
Earlier sketch in CA 11-12
Blatty, William Peter 1928- CANR-9
Earlier sketch in CA 7-8R
See also CLC 2
Blau, Abram 1907-1979 Obituary 85-88
Blau, Eric 1921- 85-88
Blau, Francine D(ee) 1946- 106
Blau, Herbert 1926- 111
Blau, Joseph L(eon) 1909-1986 .... 9-10R
Obituary 121
Blau, Joshua 1919- CANR-7
Earlier sketch in CA 15-16R
Blau, Judith R. 1942- 122
Blau, Milton
See Blau, Eric
Blau, Peter M(ichael) 1918- CANR-1
Earlier sketch in CA 1R
Blau, Sheldon Paul 1935- 57-60
Blau, Tom 1913(?)-1984 Obituary 113
Blau, Yehoshua
See Blau, Joshua
Blau, Zena Smith 1922- CANR-1
Earlier sketch in CA 45-48
Blauer, Ettagale 1940- CANR-24
Earlier sketch in CA 103
See also SATA 49
Blaufarb, Douglas S(amuel) 1918- 85-88
Blaug, Mark 1927- CANR-16
Earlier sketches in CA 3R, CANR-1
Blaukopf, Kurt 1914- Brief entry 114
Blauner, Robert 1929- 17-18R
Blaushild, Babette 1927- 29-32R
Blaustein, Albert Paul 1921- CANR-19
Earlier sketches in CA 3R, CANR-1
Blaustein, Arthur I. 1933- CANR-10
Earlier sketch in CA 25-28R
Blaustein, Elliott H(arold) 1915- 41-44R
Blaustein, Esther 1935- 45-48
Blauw, Johannes 1912- 11-12R
Blaxland, John 1917- 7-8R
Blaxland, W(illiam) Gregory 1918- CANR-3
Earlier sketch in CA 9-10R
Blaylock, James P(aul) 1950- 110
Blayne, Sara
See Howl, Marcia (Yvonne Hurt)
Blayney, Margaret S(tatler) 1926- 53-56
Blayre, Christopher
See Heron-Allen, Edward
Blaze, Wayne 1951- 61-64
Blazek, Douglas 1941- 25-28R
Blazek, Ron(ald David) 1936- 111
Blazer, Dan G(erman) II 1944- 110
Blazer, J.S.
See Scott, Justin
Blazier, Kenneth D(ean) 1933- CANR-11
Earlier sketch in CA 69-72
Bleakley, David (Wylie) 1925- 102
Bleamer, Burton 1906(?)-1986 Obituary 118
Blechman, Barry M. 1943- 97-100
Blechman, Burt 1932- 21-22R
Bledlow, John
See Vale, (Henry) Edmund (Theodoric)
Bledsoe, Albert Taylor 1809-1877 .... DLB-3
Bledsoe, Jerry 1941- 85-88
Bledsoe, Joseph C(ullie) 1918- 33-36R
Bledsoe, Thomas (Alexander) 1914- CANR-9
Earlier sketch in CA 13-14R
Bledsoe, William Ambrose 1906-1981
Obituary 104
Bleeck, Oliver
See Thomas, Ross (Elmore)
Bleeker, Mordecia
See Morgan, Fred Troy
Bleeker, Sonia
See Zim, Sonia Bleeker
See also SATA 2, 26
Blees, Robert A(rthur) 1922- 19-20R
Blegen, Carl (William) 1887-1971
Obituary 33-36R
Blegen, Theodore C. 1891-1969 .... CANR-3
Earlier sketch in CA 5-6R
Blegvad, Erik 1923- 97-100
See also SATA 14
Blegvad, Lenore 1926- CANR-14
Earlier sketch in CA 69-72
See also SATA 14
Blehl, Vincent Ferrer 1921- 11-12R
Bleiberg, Robert Marvin 1924- 103
Bleich, Alan R. 1913- 15-16R
Bleich, Harold 1930(?)-1980 Obituary 93-96
Bleich, J(udah) David 1936- 116
Bleicher, Michael N(athaniel) 1935- 37-40R
Bleier, Robert Patrick 1946- 85-88
Bleier, Rocky
See Bleier, Robert Patrick
Blench, J(ohn) W(heatley) 1926- 15-16R
Blend, Charles D(aniels) 1918- 23-24R
Blenkinsopp, Joseph 1927- 37-40R
Bleser, Carol K. 1935- 107
Blesh, Rudi
See Blesh, Rudolph Pickett
Blesh, Rudolph Pickett 1899-1985 .... 17-18R
Obituary 117
Blessing, Richard Allen 1939- 53-56
Bletter, Robert 1933(?)-1976 Obituary 61-64
Bletter, Rosemarie Haag 1939- 57-60
Blevins, James Lowell 1936- 106
Blevins, Leon W(ilford) 1937- 57-60
Blevins, William L. 1937- 33-36R
Blevins, Winfred (Ernest, Jr.) 1938- CANR-1
Earlier sketch in CA 45-48
Bleything, Dennis H(ugh) 1946- 61-64
Bleznick, Donald W(illiam) 1924- 21-22R
Blicker, Seymour 1940- 77-80
Blicq, Anthony 1926- 33-36R
Bligh, Norman
See Neubauer, William Arthur
Blight, John 1913- CANR-22
Earlier sketch in CA 69-72
Blinder, Alan S(tuart) 1945- 113
Blinder, Elliot 1949- 106
Blinderman, Abraham 1916- 61-64
Blinn, Johna
See Dorsey, Helen
Blinn, Walter Craig 1930- 61-64
Blish, James (Benjamin) 1921-1975 .... CANR-3
Obituary 57-60
Earlier sketch in CA 3R
See also DLB 8
See also CLC 14
Blishen, Bernard Russell 1919- CANR-3
Earlier sketch in CA 4R
Blishen, Edward 1920- CANR-11
Earlier sketch in CA 19-20R
See also SATA 8
Bliss, A(lan) J(oseph) 1921-1985
Obituary 118
Bliss, Carey S(tillman) 1914- 41-44R
Bliss, Corinne Demas 1947- 104
See also SATA 37
Bliss, Dorothy E(lizabeth) 1916-1987 118
Obituary 124
Bliss, Edward, Jr. 1912- 41-44R
Bliss, George William 1918-1978 85-88
Obituary 81-84
Bliss, Lee 1943- 122
Bliss, (John) Michael 1941- 103
Bliss, Reginald
See Wells, H(erbert) G(eorge)
Bliss, Ronald G(ene) 1942- 53-56
See also SATA 12

Blissett, Marlan 1938- 41-44R
Blistein, Elmer M(ilton) 1920- 11-12R
Blitch, Fleming Lee
 See Lee, Fleming
Blitchington, Evelyn G(rant) 1947- 114
Blits, Jan H. 1943- 110
Blitzstein, Marc 1905-1964 Obituary 110
Bliven, Bruce 1889-1977 ..... 37-40R
 Obituary 69-72
Bliven, Bruce, Jr. 1916- CANR-7
 Earlier sketch in CA 19-20R
 See also SATA 2
Bliven, Naomi 1925- 33-36R
Blixen, Karen (Christentze Dinesen)
 1885-1962 ..... CANR-22
 Earlier sketches in CA 25-28, CAP-2
 See also SATA 44
 See also CLC 10
Blizzard, S(amuel) W(ilson, Jr.)
 1914(?)-1976 Obituary 65-68
Bloch, Ariel A(lfred Karl) 1933- 41-44R
Bloch, Barbara 1925- CANR-24
 Earlier sketch in CA 106
Bloch, Bertram 1892-1987 Obituary 122
Bloch, Blanche 1890-1980 Obituary 97-100
Bloch, Chana Florence 1940- 105
Bloch, Dorothy 1912- 93-96
Bloch, E. Maurice 25-28R
Bloch, Ernst 1885-1977 ..... 29-32R
 Obituary 73-76
Bloch, Herbert A(aron David) 1904-1965 ..... 3R
Bloch, Herman D(avid) 1914- 29-32R
Bloch, Lucienne 1909- SATA-10
Bloch, Lucienne S(chupf) 1937- 93-96
Bloch, Marc 1886-1944 Brief entry 118
Bloch, Marie Halun 1910- CANR-19
 Earlier sketches in CA 4R, CANR-4
 See also SATA 6
Bloch, Robert (Albert) 1917- CANR-5
 Earlier sketch in CA 5-6R
 See also SATA 12
 See also DLB 44
 See also CLC 33
Blocher, Henri (Arthur) 1937- CANR-10
 Earlier sketch in CA 65-68
Blochman, Lawrence G(oldtree)
 1900-1975 ..... CAP-2
 Obituary 53-56
 Earlier sketch in CA 19-20
 See also SATA 22
Block, Allan (Forrest) 1923- 49-52
Block, Andrew 1892-1985 Obituary 118
Block, Arthur John 1916(?)-1981
 Obituary 105
Block, Eugene B. 1890- CANR-2
 Earlier sketch in CA 7-8R
Block, Hal 1914(?)-1981 Obituary 104
Block, Herbert (Lawrence) 1909- 111
Block, Irvin 1917- 19-20R
 See also SATA 12
Block, Irving (Leonard) 1930- 118
Block, Jack 1921- 33-36R
Block, Jack 1931- 53-56
Block, Jean Libman 5-6R
Block, Joel D(avid) 1943- CANR-15
 Earlier sketch in CA 89-92
Block, Julian 1934- 106
Block, Lawrence 1938- CANR-6
 Earlier sketch in CA 3R
Block, Libbie 1910(?)-1972 ..... 33-36R
Block, Marvin Avram 1903- 106
Block, Michael 1942- 101
Block, Ned Joel 1942- 117
Block, Paul, Jr. 1911-1987 Obituary 122
Block, Ralph 1889-1974 Obituary 45-48
Block, Rudolph
 See Lessing, Bruno
Block, Seymour Stanton 1918- 89-92
Block, Stanley Byron 1939- 85-88
Block, Thomas H(arris) 1945- CANR-18
 Earlier sketch in CA 101
Block, Walter (Edward) 1941- CANR-22
 Earlier sketches in CA 57-60, CANR-6
Block, Zenas 1916- 107
Blocker, Clyde (Edward) 1918- 33-36R
Blocker, H(arry) Gene 1937- 116
Blockinger, Betty
 See Blocklinger, Peggy O'More
Blocklinger, Peggy O'More 1895- 7-8R
Blocksma, Mary SATA-44
Blodgett, Beverley 1926- 57-60
Blodgett, E(dward) D(ickinson) 1935- 112
Blodgett, Geoffrey Thomas 1931- 17-18R
Blodgett, Harold William 1900- 15-16R
Blodgett, Harriet Eleanor 1919- 33-36R
Blodgett, Richard 1940- CANR-1
 Earlier sketch in CA 49-52
Bloem, Diane Brummel 1935- CANR-16
 Earlier sketch in CA 85-88
Bloesch, Donald G. 1928- 13-14R
Bloesser, Robert 1930- 37-40R
Blofeld, John (Eaton Calthorpe)
 1913-1987 ..... CANR-19
 Obituary 123
 Earlier sketches in CA 53-56, CANR-4
Blok, Alexander (Alexandrovich)
 1880-1921 Brief entry 104
 See also TCLC 5
Blok, Anton 1935- 97-100
Blom, Gaston E(ugene) 1920- 25-28R
Blom, Karl Arne 1946- CANR-11
 Earlier sketch in CA 69-72
Blom, Lynne Anne 1942- 120
Blom-Cooper, Louis Jacques 1926- 7-8R
Blond, Anthony 1928- 106
Blondel, Jean Fernand Pierre 1929- 101
Blondell, (Rose) Joan 1906(?)-1979 115
 Obituary 93-96
Blood, Bob
 See Blood, Robert O(scar), Jr.
Blood, Charles Lewis 1929- 73-76
 See also SATA 28
Blood, Jerome W. 1926- 11-12R
Blood, Marje 41-44R
Blood, Matthew
 See Dresser, Davis
Blood, Robert O(scar), Jr. 1921- CANR-3
 Earlier sketch in CA 4R
Bloodstone, John
 See Byrne, Stuart J(ames)
Bloom, Alan (Herbert Vawser) 1906- CANR-3
 Earlier sketch in CA 9-10R
Bloom, Alexander 1947- 114
Bloom, Claire 1931- 114
Bloom, Daniel Halevi 1949- 120
Bloom, Edward A(lan) 1914- CANR-2
 Earlier sketch in CA 1R
Bloom, Erick Franklin 1944- 57-60
Bloom, Floyd E(lliott) 1936- 120
Bloom, Freddy 1914- 101
 See also SATA 37
Bloom, Gordon F. 1918- 13-14R
Bloom, Harold 1930- 15-16R
 See also DLB 67
 See also CLC 24
Bloom, Harry 1913(?)-1981 Obituary 104
Bloom, Herman Irving 1908- 102
Bloom, John 1921- 7-8R
Bloom, John Porter 1924- 49-52
Bloom, Ken(neth) 1949- 115
Bloom, Lillian D. 1920- CANR-11
 Earlier sketch in CA 17-18R
Bloom, Lloyd SATA-43
Bloom, Lynn (Marie) Z(immerman)
 1934- CANR-21
 Earlier sketches in CA 15-16R, CANR-6
Bloom, Melvyn H(arold) 1938- 45-48
Bloom, Murray Teigh 1916- 19-20R
Bloom, Pauline 41-44R
Bloom, Robert 1930- 17-18R
Bloom, Samuel William 1921- CANR-3
 Earlier sketch in CA 11-12R
Bloom, Ursula 1893-1984 ..... 25-28R
 Obituary 114
Blooman, Percy A. 1906- CAP-1
 Earlier sketch in CA 11-12
Bloomberg, Edward (Michael) 1937- 41-44R
Bloomberg, Marty
 See Bloomberg, Max Arthur
Bloomberg, Max Arthur 1938- 101
Bloomberg, Morton 1936- 53-56
Bloome, Enid P. 1925- 85-88
Bloomfield, Anthony John Westgate 1922- 4R
Bloomfield, Arthur (John) 1931- 65-68
Bloomfield, Arthur Irving 1914- 41-44R
Bloomfield, Aurelius
 See Bourne, Randolph S(illiman)
Bloomfield, B(arry) C(ambray) 1931- CANR-5
 Earlier sketch in CA 11-12R
Bloomfield, Harold H. 1944- CANR-9
 Earlier sketch in CA 57-60
Bloomfield, Lincoln Palmer 1920- CANR-5
 Earlier sketch in CA 1R
Bloomfield, Masse 1923- CANR-8
 Earlier sketch in CA 61-64
Bloomfield, Maxwell H(erron III) 1931- 122
 Brief entry 118
Bloomfield, Morton W(ilfred)
 1913-1987 ..... CANR-2
 Obituary 122
 Earlier sketch in CA 5-6R
Bloomingdale, Teresa 1930- CANR-21
 Earlier sketch in CA 105
Bloomquist, Edward R. 1924- 29-32R
Bloomstein, Morris J. 1928- 25-28R
Blos, Joan W(insor) 1928- CANR-21
 Earlier sketch in CA 101
 See also SATA 27, 33
Blos, Peter 1904- 89-92
Bloss, F(red) Donald 1920- 53-56
Bloss, Meredith 1908-1982 Obituary 107
Blossom, Frederick A. 1878(?)-1974
 Obituary 49-52
Blossom, Thomas 1912- 23-24R
Blotner, Joseph (Leo) 1923- CANR-13
 Earlier sketch in CA 19-20R
 See also AITN 1
Blotnick, Elihu 1939- 106
Blotnick, Srully (D.) 1941(?)- Brief entry 123
Blouet, Brian Walter 1936- CANR-15
 Earlier sketch in CA 93-96
Blough, Glenn O(rlando) 1907- CAP-1
 Earlier sketch in CA 11-12
 See also SATA 1
Blough, Roger M(iles) 1904-1985
 Obituary 117
Blount, Charles (Harold Clavell) 1913- 17-18R
Blount, Margaret 1924- 69-72
Blount, Roy (Alton), Jr. 1941- CANR-10
 Earlier sketch in CA 53-56
 See also CLC 38
Bloustein, Edward J. 1925- 41-44R
Blow, Suzanne (Katherine) 1932- 45-48
Bloy, Leon 1846-1917 Brief entry 121
 See also TCLC 22
Blu, Karen I(sobell) 1941- 121
Blue, Betty (Anne) 1922- CANR-1
 Earlier sketch in CA 45-48
Blue, Frederick Judd 1937- 53-56
Blue, Martha Ward 1942- 104
Blue, Rose 1931- CANR-14
 Earlier sketch in CA 41-44R
 See also SATA 5
Blue, Vida (Rochelle) 1949- Brief entry 112
Blue, Wallace
 See Kraenzel, Margaret (Powell)
Blue, Zachary
 See Stine, R(obert) L(awrence)
Bluebond-Langner, Myra 1948- 81-84
Blue Cloud, Peter (Aroniawenrate) 1933- 117
Bluefarb, Samuel 1919- 37-40R
Bluemle, Andrew (Waltz) 1929- 1R
Blues, Elwood
 See Aykroyd, Dan(iel Edward)
Bluestein, Daniel Thomas 1943- 65-68
Bluestein, Gene 1928- 81-84
Bluestone, Barry A(lan) 1944- 115
Bluestone, George 1928- CANR-1
 Earlier sketch in CA 4R
Bluestone, Max 1926- 15-16R
Bluh, Bonnie 1926- 97-100
Bluhm, Heinz 1907- CAP-1
 Earlier sketch in CA 17-18
Bluhm, William T(heodore) 1923- 15-16R
Blum, Albert A(lexander) 1924- CANR-11
 Earlier sketch in CA 7-8R
Blum, Carol (Kathlyn) O'Brien 1934- CANR-17
 Earlier sketch in CA 101
Blum, D. Steven 1951- 118
Blum, David 1935- 107
Blum, Eleanor 1914- 3R
Blum, Fred 1932- 15-16R
Blum, Harold P. 1929- 103
Blum, Henrik L(eo) 1915- CANR-6
 Earlier sketch in CA 11-12R
Blum, Jerome 1913- CANR-19
 Earlier sketch in CA 1R
Blum, John Morton 1921- CANR-2
 Earlier sketch in CA 7-8R
Blum, Lawrence A. 1943- 124
Blum, Leon 1872-1950 Brief entry 119
Blum, Lucille Hollander 1904- 101
Blum, Mark E. 1937- 121
Blum, Ralph AITN-1
Blum, Richard H(osmer Adams) 1927- 13-14R
Blum, Shirley Neilsen 1932- 33-36R
Blum, Stella 1916-1985 97-100
 Obituary 116
Blum, Virgil C(larence) 1913- 15-16R
Blumberg, Arnold 1925- 33-36R
Blumberg, Dorothy Rose 1904- CAP-2
 Earlier sketch in CA 25-28
Blumberg, Gary 1938- CANR-2
 Earlier sketch in CA 45-48
Blumberg, Harry 1903- 73-76
Blumberg, Leonard U. 1920- 101
Blumberg, Morris B. 1917- 123
Blumberg, Myrna 1932- 23-24R
Blumberg, Nathan(iel) Bernard 1922- 41-44R
Blumberg, Paul (Marvin) 1935- Brief entry 113
Blumberg, Phillip I(rvin) 1919- 101
Blumberg, Rena J(oy) 1934- 109
Blumberg, Rhoda 1917- CANR-9
 Earlier sketch in CA 65-68
 See also SATA 35
Blumberg, Rhoda L(ois Goldstein)
 1926- CANR-6
 Earlier sketch in CA 57-60
Blumberg, Richard E(lliot) 1944- 113
Blumberg, Robert S(tephen) 1945- 57-60
Blume, Friedrich 1893-1975 73-76
Blume, Judy (Sussman) 1938- CANR-13
 Earlier sketch in CA 29-32R
 See also SATA 2, 31
 See also DLB 52
 See also CLC 12, 30
 See also CLR 2
Blumenfeld, Gerry 1906- 23-24R
Blumenfeld, Hans 1892- CAP-2
 Earlier sketch in CA 21-22
Blumenfeld, Harold 1905- 97-100
Blumenfeld, Meyer 1905-1980 Obituary 97-100
Blumenfeld, Samuel L(eon) 1926- 41-44R
Blumenfeld, (F.) Yorick 1932- 25-28R
Blumenson, Martin 1918- CANR-21
 Earlier sketches in CA 4R, CANR-4
Blumenstock, David Irving 1913-1963
 Obituary 116
Blumenthal, Arthur L. 1936- 29-32R
Blumenthal, David Reuben 1938- 112
Blumenthal, Eileen (Flinder) 1948- 120
Blumenthal, Fred(erick G.) 1919(?)-1986
 Obituary 118
Blumenthal, Gerda Renee 1923- 1R
Blumenthal, Gertrude 1907-1971 Obituary 104
 See also SATA 27
Blumenthal, Henry 1911-1987 ..... 29-32R
 Obituary 121
Blumenthal, L. Roy 1908-1975 Obituary 61-64
Blumenthal, Lassor Agoos 1926- 25-28R
Blumenthal, Michael C. 1949- 110
Blumenthal, Monica David 1930-1981 73-76
 Obituary 103
Blumenthal, Norm 97-100
Blumenthal, Shirley 1943- 108
 See also SATA 46
Blumenthal, Sidney 1909- 106
Blumenthal, Susan
 See Tribich, Susan
Blumenthal, Walter Hart 1883- CAP-1
 Earlier sketch in CA 11-12
Blumin, Stuart M(ack) 1940- 65-68
Bluming, Mildred G. 1919- 106
Blumrich, Josef F(ranz) 1913- 93-96
Blumrosen, Alfred W(illiam) 1928- 53-56
Blunck, Hans Friedrich 1888-1961 ..... DLB-66
Blundel, Anne
 See Conley, Enid Mary
Blundell, Harold 1902- 101
Blunden, Edmund (Charles) 1896-1974 ..... CAP-2
 Obituary 45-48
 Earlier sketch in CA 17-18
 See also DLB 20
 See also CLC 2
Blunden, Margaret (Anne) 1939- 23-24R
Blunk, Frank M. 1897(?)-1976 Obituary 69-72
Blunsden, John (Beresford) 1930- 57-60
Blunsdon, Norman (Victor Charles)
 1915-1968 ..... CAP-1
 Earlier sketch in CA 13-14
Blunt, Anthony (Frederick) 1907-1983 113
 Obituary 109
Blunt, Don
 See Booth, Edwin
Blunt, Wilfrid (Jasper Walter)
 1901-1987 ..... CANR-21
 Obituary 121
 Earlier sketches in CA 15-16R, CANR-5
Blunt, Wilfrid Scawen 1840-1922 ..... DLB-19
Bluphocks, Lucien
 See Seldes, Gilbert (Vivian)
Bluth, B(etty) J(ean) 1934- CANR-24
 Earlier sketch in CA 106
Blutig, Eduard
 See Gorey, Edward (St. John)
Bly, Carol(yn) 1930- 108
Bly, Janet (Chester) 1945- 116
 See also SATA 43
Bly, Nellie
 See Cochrane, Elizabeth
Bly, Peter A(nthony) 1944- 116
Bly, Robert 1926- 5-6R
 See also DLB 5
 See also CLC 1, 2, 5, 10, 15, 38
Bly, Robert W(ayne) 1957- 117
 See also SATA 48
Bly, Stephen A(rthur) 1944- 121
 See also SATA 43
Bly, Thomas J. 1918(?)-1979 Obituary 85-88
Blyn, George 1919- CANR-14
 Earlier sketch in CA 37-40R
Blyth, Alan 1929- CANR-1
 Earlier sketch in CA 49-52
Blyth, Chay 1940- Brief entry 110
Blyth, Estelle 1882(?)-1983 Obituary 109
Blyth, Henry 1910-1983 ..... 21-22R
 Obituary 110
Blyth, Jeffrey 1926- 65-68
Blyth, John
 See Hibbs, John
Blyth, Myrna 1939- CANR-10
 Earlier sketch in CA 65-68
Blythe, (William) LeGette 1900- CANR-1
 Earlier sketch in CA 3R
Blythe, Ronald (George) 1922- 7-8R
Blyton, Carey 1932- 49-52
 See also SATA 9
Blyton, Enid (Mary) 1897-1968 77-80
 Obituary 25-28R
 See also SATA 25
Boa, Kenneth 1945- CANR-8
 Earlier sketch in CA 61-64
Boadella, David 1931- 53-56
Boadt, Lawrence 1942- 114
Boak, Arthur Edward Romilly 1888-1962 ..... 5-6R
Boak, (Charles) Denis 1932- 13-14R
Boalch, Donald (Howard) 1914- 11-12R
Boalt, (Hans) Gunnar 1910- CANR-7
 Earlier sketch in CA 57-60
Board, C(hester) Stephen 1942- 57-60
Board, Joseph B(reckinridge), Jr. 1931- 29-32R
Boardman, Arthur 1927- 61-64
Boardman, Charles C. 1932- 29-32R
Boardman, Eunice
 See Meske, Eunice Boardman
Boardman, Fon Wyman, Jr. 1911- CANR-3
 Earlier sketch in CA 4R
 See also SATA 6
Boardman, Francis 1915-1976 Obituary 69-72
Boardman, Gwenn R.
 See Petersen, Gwenn Boardman
 See also SATA 12
Boardman, John 1927- 101
Boardman, Michael Moore 1945- 118
Boardman, Neil S(ervis) 1907- CAP-1
 Earlier sketch in CA 13-14
Boardman, Peter (David) 1950-1982 97-100
 Obituary 108
Boardman, Thomas Leslie 1919-
 Brief entry 111
Boardwell, Robert Lee 1926- 103
Boarino, Gerald L(ouis) 1931- 23-24R
Boarman, Patrick M(adigan) 1922- CANR-9
 Earlier sketch in CA 15-16R
Boas, Claudio Villas
 See Villas Boas, Claudio
Boas, Franz 1858-1942 Brief entry 115
Boas, Guy (Herman Sidney) 1896-1966 ..... CAP-1
 Earlier sketch in CA 11-12
Boas, Jacob 1943- 120
Boas, Louise Schutz 1885- 5-6R
Boas, Marie
 See Hall, Marie Boas
Boas, Maurits Ignatius 1892- CANR-5
 Earlier sketch in CA 3R
Boas, Orlando Villas
 See Villas Boas, Orlando
Boase, Alan Martin 1902-1982 ..... CANR-10
 Obituary 108
 Earlier sketch in CA 7-8R
Boase, Paul H(enshaw) 1915- 37-40R
Boase, Thomas Sherrer Ross 1898-1974 ..... CAP-2
 Earlier sketch in CA 23-24
Boase, Wendy 1944- 106
 See also SATA 28

INDEX

Boateng, E(rnest) A(mano) 1920- CANR-11
Earlier sketch in CA 23-24R
Boateng, Yaw Maurice
See Brunner, Maurice Yaw
Boatman, Don Earl 1913- 4R
Boatner, Mark Mayo III 1921- 21-22R
See also SATA 29
Boatright, Mody Coggin 1896-1970 ..... CANR-3
Obituary 89-92
Earlier sketch in CA 7-8R
Boatwright, Howard (Leake, Jr.) 1918- 53-56
Boatwright, James III 1933- 119
Boaz, Martha (Tearosse) CANR-19
Earlier sketches in CA 9-10R, CANR-3
Boba, Imre 1919- 69-72
Bobb, Bernard E(arl) 1917- 5-6R
Bobbe, Dorothie de Bear 1905-1975 ..... CAP-2
Obituary 57-60
Earlier sketch in CA 25-28
See also SATA 1, 25
Bobbitt, Philip 1948- 108
Bober, Stanley 1932- CANR-11
Earlier sketch in CA 23-24R
Bobette
See Simenon, Georges (Jacques Christian)
Bobinski, George S(ylvan) 1929- 29-32R
Bobker, Lee R(obert) 1925- CANR-9
Earlier sketch in CA 53-56
Bobo, Lawrence (Douglas) 1958- 124
Bobri, Vladimir V. 1898- 105
Bobritsky, Vladimir
See Bobri, Vladimir V.
See also SATA 32, 47
Bobroff, Edith
See Marks, Edith Bobroff
Bobrow, Davis Bernard 1936- CANR-7
Earlier sketch in CA 57-60
Bobrow, Edwin E. 1928- CANR-24
Earlier sketches in CA 23-24R, CANR-8
Bobrowski, Johannes 1917-1965 77-80
Bobst, Elmer H(olmes) 1884-1978 122
Obituary 113
Bocca, Al
See Winter, Bevis (Peter)
Bocca, Geoffrey 1923-1983 Obituary 110
Bochco, Steven 1943- Brief entry 124
See also CLC 35
Bochenski, Innocentius M.
See Bochenski, Joseph M.
Bochenski, Joseph M. 1902- CANR-7
Earlier sketch in CA 5-6R
Bochner, Salomon 1899- 41-44R
Bochroch, Albert R(obert) 1909- 111
Bock, Alan W(illiam) 1943- 41-44R
Bock, Carl H(einz) 1930-19(?) CAP-2
Earlier sketch in CA 19-20
Bock, Fred 1939- CANR-10
Earlier sketch in CA 25-28R
Bock, Frederick 1916- 9-10R
Bock, Hal
See Bock, Harold I.
Bock, Harold I. 1939- 29-32R
See also SATA 10
Bock, Joanne 1940- 57-60
Bock, Paul J(ohn) 1922- 53-56
Bock, Philip K. 1934- CANR-11
Earlier sketch in CA 25-28R
Bock, William Sauts Netamux'we 1939- SATA-14
Bockelman, Wilfred 1920- 37-40R
Bockl, George 1909- 61-64
Bockle, Franz
See Boeckle, Franz
Bockmon, Guy Alan 1926- 7-8R
Bockstoce, John R(oberts) 1944- 121
Bockus, H(erman) William 1915- 53-56
Bocock, Robert (James) 1940- CANR-12
Earlier sketch in CA 69-72
Boczek, Boleslaw Adam 1922- CANR-4
Earlier sketch in CA 3R
Bod, Peter
See Vesenyi, Paul E.
Bodansky, Oscar 1901-1977 Obituary 73-76
Bodard, Lucien (Albert) 1914- Brief entry 116
Bodart, Joni
See Bodart-Talbot, Joni
Bodart-Talbot, Joni 1947- CANR-23
Earlier sketch in CA 106
Boddewyn, J(ean) J. 1929- CANR-17
Earlier sketch in CA 25-28R
Boddie, Charles Emerson 1911- 65-68
Boddington, Craig Thornton 1952- 111
Boddy, David 1940- 119
Boddy, Frederick A(rthur) 1914- 61-64
Boddy, William Charles 1913- 101
Bode, Carl 1911- CANR-20
Earlier sketches in CA 1R, CANR-3
Bode, Elroy 1931- CANR-10
Earlier sketch in CA 25-28R
Bode, Janet 1943- CANR-12
Earlier sketch in CA 69-72
Bode, Roy E. 1948- 77-80
Bodecker, N(iels) M(ogens) 1922-1988 ..... CANR-4
Obituary 124
Earlier sketch in CA 49-52
See also SATA 8
Bodeen, DeWitt 1908- CANR-10
Earlier sketch in CA 25-28R
Bodell, Mary
See Pecsok, Mary Bodell
Boden, Hilda
See Bodenham, Hilda Morris
Boden, Margaret A. 1936- 93-96
Bodenham, Hilda Morris 1901- CANR-6
Earlier sketch in CA 11-12R
See also SATA 13
Bodenheim, Maxwell 1892-1954
Brief entry 110
See also DLB 9, 45
Bodenheimer, Edgar 1908- CANR-20
Earlier sketch in CA 33-36R
Bodet, Jaime Torres
See Torres Bodet, Jaime
Bodett, Thomas Edward 1955- 123
Bodett, Tom
See Bodett, Thomas Edward
Bodey, Hugh (Arthur) 1939- CANR-12
Earlier sketch in CA 61-64
Bodger, Joan
See Mercer, Joan Bodger
Bodian, Nat G. 1921- CANR-20
Earlier sketch in CA 103
Bodie, Idella F(allaw) 1925- 41-44R
See also SATA 12
Bodin, Paul 1909- 65-68
Bodine, Eunice
See Lapp, Eunice Willis Bodine
Bodington, Nancy H(ermione) 1912- 53-56
Bodington, Stephen 1909- 123
Bodker, Cecil 1927- CANR-13
Earlier sketch in CA 73-76
See also SATA 14
See also CLC 21
Bodkin, Cora 1944- 69-72
Bodkin, M(atthias) M'Donnell 1850-1933
Brief entry 114
Bodkin, Maud 1875- CAP-1
Earlier sketch in CA 11-12
Bodkin, Ronald G(eorge) 1936- 33-36R
Bodle, Yvonne Gallegos 1939- 33-36R
Bodmer, Walter Fred 1936- 102
Bodnar, John Edward 1944- 110
Bodo, Murray 1937- CANR-23
Earlier sketches in CA 57-60, CANR-7
Bodo, Peter T. 1949- 85-88
Bodoh, John J(ames) 1931- 45-48
Bodsworth, (Charles) Fred(erick) 1918- CANR-3
Earlier sketch in CA 1R
See also SATA 27
Bodwell, Richard
See Spring, Gerald M(ax)
Boeckle, Franz 1921- 101
Boeckman, Charles 1920- 15-16R
See also SATA 12
Boeckman, Patti 109
Boege, Ulrich Gustav 1940- 97-100
Boegehold, Betty (Doyle) 1913-1985 ..... CANR-12
Obituary 115
Earlier sketch in CA 69-72
See also SATA 42
Boegner, Marc 1881-1970 Obituary 29-32R
Boehlke, Frederick J(ohn), Jr. 1926- 21-22R
Boehlke, Robert R(ichard) 1925- 5-6R
Boehlow, Robert H(enry) 1925- 53-56
Boehm, Christopher 1937- 121
Boehm, Eric H. 1918- 13-14R
Boehm, Herb
See Varley, John (Herbert)
Boehm, Karl 1894-1981 Obituary 105
Boehm, Sydney 1908- DLB-44
Boehm, William D(ryden) 1946- 61-64
Boehme, Lillian R.
See Rodberg, Lillian
Boehning, W. R.
See Bohning, W(olf) R(uediger)
Boehringer, Robert 1885(?)-1974
Obituary 53-56
Boelcke, Willi A(lfred) 1929- Brief entry 107
Boelen, Bernard J(acques) 1916- 41-44R
Boell, Heinrich (Theodor) 1917-1985 ..... CANR-24
Obituary 116
Earlier sketch in CA 21-22R
See also DLBY 85
See also CLC 2, 3, 6, 9, 11, 15, 27, 39
Boeman, John (Sigler) 1923- 108
Boer, Charles 1939- 69-72
See also DLB 5
Boer, Harry R(einier) 1913- CANR-4
Earlier sketch in CA 3R
Boesch, Hans Heinrich 1911-1978
Obituary 116
Boesch, Mark J(oseph) 1917- 21-22R
See also SATA 12
Boesel, David 1938- 41-44R
Boesen, Victor 1908- 37-40R
See also SATA 16
Boesiger, Willi 1904- 102
Boeth, Richard 1933-1982 Obituary 107
Boetie, Dugmore 1920(?)-1966 Obituary 109
Boettcher, Henry J. 1893- CAP-1
Earlier sketch in CA 19-20
Boettcher, Robert B. 1941(?)-1984
Obituary 112
Boettinger, Henry M(aurice) 1924- 73-76
Boeve, Edgar G. 1929- 21-22R
Boewe, Charles (Ernst) 1924- 11-12R
Boff, Vic 1915- 103
Boffey, David Barnes 1945- 110
Bogaduck
See Lindsay, Harold Arthur
Bogan, James 1945- 103
Bogan, Louise 1897-1970 73-76
Obituary 25-28R
See also DLB 45
See also CLC 4, 39, 46
Bogard, Travis (Miller) 1918- 69-72
Bogarde, Dirk
See Van Den Bogarde, Derek Jules Gaspard Ulric Niven
See also DLB 14
See also CLC 19
Bogardus, Emory Stephen 1882-1973
Obituary 116
Bogart, Carlotta 1929- 61-64
Bogart, Leo 1921- CANR-14
Earlier sketch in CA 41-44R
Bogat, Shatan
See Kacew, Romain
Bogatyryov, Konstantin 1924(?)-1976
Obituary 65-68
Bogdanor, Vernon 1943- CANR-14
Earlier sketch in CA 81-84
Bogdanovich, Peter 1939- CANR-21
Earlier sketch in CA 7-8R
Bogen, James Benjamin 1935- 89-92
Bogen, Laurel Ann 1950- 112
Bogen, Nancy R(uth) 1932- 97-100
Boger, Louise Ade 1909- Brief entry 115
Bogert, L(otta) Jean 1888-1970 ..... CAP-1
Earlier sketch in CA 11-12
Boggan, E(lton) Carrington 1943- 101
Boggess, Louise Bradford 1912- CANR-7
Earlier sketch in CA 15-16R
Boggs, Bill
See Boggs, William III
Boggs, James 1919- 77-80
Boggs, Jean Sutherland 1922- 108
Boggs, Marcus 1947- 108
Boggs, Ralph Steele 1901- CAP-1
Earlier sketch in CA 11-12
See also SATA 7
Boggs, W(ilmot) Arthur 1916- 19-20R
Boggs, Wade Hamilton, Jr. 1916- 13-14R
Boggs, William III 1942- 102
Bogin, George 1920- 104
Bogin, Ruth 1920- 122
Bogle, Donald AITN-1
Bogner, Norman 1935- CANR-15
Earlier sketch in CA 7-8R
See also AITN 2
Bogomolny, Robert L(ee) 1938- 121
Bogosian, Eric 1953- CLC-45
Bogoslovsky, Christina Stael 1888(?)-1974 Obituary 49-52
Bograd, Larry 1953- 93-96
See also SATA 33
See also CLC 35
Bogue, Allan G(eorge Britton) 1921- 107
Bogue, Jesse C. 1912(?)-1983 Obituary 111
Bogue, Lucile 1911- CANR-13
Earlier sketch in CA 37-40R
Boguslawski, Dorothy Beers 1911(?)-1978
Obituary 77-80
Bohan, Peter 33-36R
Bohana, Aileen Stein 1951- 103
Bohannan, Paul (James) 1920- 11-12R
Bohdal, Susi 1951- 97-100
See also SATA 22
Bohen, Halcyone H(arger) 1937- 108
Bohen, Sister Marian 1930- 7-8R
Bohi, Charles W(esley) 1940- 89-92
Bohi, M. Janette 1927- 25-28R
Bohlander, Jill 1936- 37-40R
Bohle, Bruce 1918- CANR-9
Earlier sketch in CA 21-22R
Bohle, Edgar (Henry) 1909- 3R
Bohlen, Charles Eustis 1904-1974
Obituary 111
Bohlen, Joe M(erl) 1919- 5-6R
Bohlke, L(andall) Brent 1942-1987 124
Bohlman, (Mary) Edna McCaull 1897- CAP-1
Earlier sketch in CA 9-10
Bohlman, Herbert W(illiam) 1896- CAP-1
Earlier sketch in CA 19-20
Bohn, Frank 1878-1975 Obituary 57-60
Bohn, Joyce Illig 1940(?)-1976 Obituary 69-72
Bohn, Martin J(ohn), Jr. 1938- 116
Bohn, Ralph C. 1930- CANR-11
Earlier sketch in CA 19-20R
Bohner, Charles (Henry) 1927- 118
Bohnet, Michael 1937- 102
Bohning, W(olf) R(uediger) 1942- 111
Bohnstedt, John W(olfgang) 1927- 33-36R
Bohr, Niels (Henrik David) 1885-1962
Obituary 112
Bohr, R(ussell) L(eRoi) 1916- 25-28R
Bohr, Theophilus
See Thistle, Mel(ville William)
Bohrnstedt, George W(illiam) 1938- CANR-20
Earlier sketch in CA 33-36R
Bohrod, Aaron 1907- 23-24R
Boice, James Montgomery 1938- CANR-12
Earlier sketch in CA 29-32R
Boiko, Claire Taylor 1925- 93-96
Boiles, Charles Lafayette (Jr.) 1932- 65-68
Bois, J(oseph) Samuel 1892- 33-36R
Boisgilbert, Edmund
See Donnelly, Ignatius
Boissevain, Jeremy 1928- CANR-21
Earlier sketches in CA 57-60, CANR-6
Boissiere, Robert 1914- 119
Boissoneau, Robert 1937- 105
Boissonneau, Alice 101
Bok, Bart J(an) 1906-1983 49-52
Obituary 110
Bok, Cary W(illiam) 1905-1970
Obituary 29-32R
Bok, Derek Curtis 1930- 106
Bok, Priscilla F(airfield) 1896- 49-52
Bok, Sissela Ann 1934- 112
Bokenkotter, Thomas 1924- CANR-17
Earlier sketch in CA 85-88
Bokser, Ben Zion 1907-1984 ..... CANR-11
Obituary 111
Earlier sketch in CA 65-68
Bokum, Fanny Butcher 1888-1987 ..... 37-40R
Obituary 122
Bokun, Branko 1920- 45-48
Boland, Bridget 1913-1988 101
Obituary 124
Boland, Charles Michael 1917- 11-12R
Boland, Daniel 1891- CAP-1
Earlier sketch in CA 13-14
Boland, Eavan 1944- DLB-40
See also CLC 40
Boland, (Bertram) John 1913-1976 ..... CANR-10
Earlier sketch in CA 9-10R
Boland, Lillian C(anon) 1919- 29-32R
Bolch, Ben W(ilsman) 1938- 57-60
Bolcom, William E(lden) 1938- 93-96
Bold, Alan 1943- 25-28R
Bolding, Amy 1910- 73-76
Boldt, Menno 1930- 120
Bolen, Jean Shinoda 1936- 110
Boles, Donald Edward 1926- CANR-18
Earlier sketch in CA 4R
Boles, Harold W(ilson) 1915- 17-18R
Boles, John B. 1943- CANR-14
Earlier sketch in CA 37-40R
Boles, Paul Darcy 1916-1984 ..... CANR-4
Obituary 112
Earlier sketch in CA 9-10R
See also SATA 9, 38
Bolgan, Anne C(atherine) 1923- 41-44R
Bolgar, (Caius Coriolanus) R(obert) R(alph) 1913-1985 Obituary 117
Bolger, Philip C(unningham) 1927- CANR-6
Earlier sketch in CA 57-60
Bolian, Polly 1925- 33-36R
See also SATA 4
Bolin, Luis (A.) 1894-1969 ..... CAP-2
Earlier sketch in CA 23-24
Boling, Katharine (Singleton) 1933- 57-60
Bolinger, Dwight (L.) 1907- CANR-7
Earlier sketch in CA 15-16R
Bolino, August C(onstantino) 1922- CANR-18
Earlier sketch in CA 4R
Bolitho, Archie A(rdella) 1886- CAP-1
Earlier sketch in CA 9-10
Bolitho, Harold 1939- 103
Bolitho, (Henry) Hector 1897-1974 ..... CAP-1
Obituary 53-56
Earlier sketch in CA 9-10
Bolitho, Ray D.
See Blair, Dorothy S(ara Greene)
Bolkhovitinov, Nikolai Nikolaevich 1930- 97-100
Bolkosky, Sidney M(arvin) 1944- 65-68
Boll, Carl R. 1894- CAP-1
Earlier sketch in CA 17-18
Boll, David 1931- 21-22R
Boll, Ernest
See Boll, Theophilus E(rnest) M(artin)
Boll, Heinrich (Theodor)
See Boell, Heinrich (Theodor)
See also DLBY 85
See also CLC 2, 3, 6, 9, 11, 15, 27
Boll, Theo
See Boll, Theophilus E(rnest) M(artin)
Boll, Theophilus E(rnest) M(artin) 1902- 37-40R
Bolland, O(rlando) Nigel 1943- 110
Bolle, Kees W. 1927- CANR-17
Earlier sketch in CA 25-28R
Bollen, Roger 1942(?)- SATA-29
See also AITN 1
Bollens, John C(onstantinus) 1920-1983 ..... CANR-3
Obituary 111
Earlier sketch in CA 3R
Boller, Paul Franklin, Jr. 1916- CANR-19
Earlier sketches in CA 4R, CANR-3
Bolles, (Edmund) Blair 1911- 9-10R
Bolles, Donald F. 1928-1976 73-76
Obituary 65-68
Bolles, Richard Nelson 1927- CANR-1
Earlier sketch in CA 45-48
Bolles, Robert C(harles) 1928- 21-22R
Bollettieri, Nick J(ames) 1931- 110
Bolliger, Max 1929- 25-28R
See also SATA 7
Bolling, Hal
See Schwalberg, Carol(yn Ernestine Stein)
Bolling, Richard (Walker) 1916- 19-20R
Bolling, Robert 1738-1775 ..... DLB-31
Bolloten, Burnett 1909-1987 93-96
Obituary 123
Bolman, Frederick deWolfe, Jr. 1912-1985 Obituary 117
Bolner, James (Jerome) 1936- 61-64
Bologna, Joseph 77-80
Bolognese, Don
See Bolognese, Donald Alan
Bolognese, Donald Alan 1934- 97-100
See also SATA 24
Bolognese, Elaine Raphael (Chionchio) 1933- 97-100
Bolotowsky, Ilya 1907-1981 Obituary 108
Bolshakoff, Serge 1901- 93-96
Bolster, John 1910-1984 89-92
Obituary 111
Bolsterli, Margaret Jones 1931- 111
Bolt, Bruce A(lan) 1930- CANR-10
Earlier sketch in CA 65-68
Bolt, Carol 1941- 101
See also DLB 60
Bolt, David (Michael) Langstone 1927- CANR-6
Earlier sketch in CA 3R
Bolt, Ernest C(ollier), Jr. 1936- 77-80
Bolt, Lee
See Faust, Frederick (Shiller)
Bolt, Martin 1944- 118
Bolt, Robert (Oxton) 1924- 17-18R
See also DLB 13
See also CLC 14
Bolten, Steven E. 1941- 37-40R
Boltho, Andrea 1939- 69-72

Bolton, Carole 1926- CANR-1
Earlier sketch in CA 49-52
See also SATA 6
Bolton, Evelyn
See Bunting, Anne Evelyn
Bolton, Guy (Reginald) 1884-1979 7-8R
Obituary 89-92
Bolton, Herbert, E. 1870-1953 DLB-17
Bolton, Isabel
See Miller, Mary Britton
Bolton, James 1917(?)-1981 Obituary 103
Bolton, John Robert 1948- 115
Bolton, Kenneth (Ewart) 1914- 9-10R
Bolton, Maisie Sharman 1915- 9-10R
Bolton, Muriel Roy 1909(?)-1983
Obituary 109
Bolton, Theodore 1889(?)-1973 Obituary 45-48
Bolton, W(hitney) F(rench) 1930- 17-18R
Bolton, Whitney 1900-1969 Obituary 25-28R
Bolus, James Michael 1943- 111
Bolus, Jim
See Bolus, James Michael
Boman, Thorleif Gustav 1894- 23-24R
Bomans, Godfried J(an) A(rnold)
1913-1971 CAP-2
Earlier sketch in CA 29-32
Bomar, Cora Paul 1913- 41-44R
Bombardieri, Merle 1949- 107
Bombeck, Erma 1927- CANR-12
Earlier sketch in CA 23-24R
See also AITN 1
Bombelles, Joseph T. 1930- 25-28R
Bomeli, Edwin C(larence) 1920- 21-22R
Bomkauf
See Kaufman, Bob (Garnell)
Bommarito, James W. 1922- 121
Bona, Mercy
See Ziegler, Alan
Bonachea, E(nrique) Rolando 1943- 41-44R
Bonacich, Edna 1940- 45-48
Bonanno, Margaret Wander 1950- 85-88
Bonansea, Bernardino M(aria) 1908- CANR-14
Earlier sketch in CA 41-44R
Bonaparte, Felicia 1937- CANR-11
Earlier sketch in CA 61-64
Bonatti, Walter 1930- CANR-23
Earlier sketch in CA 106
Bonavia, David Michael 1940- 106
Bonavia-Hunt, Noel Aubrey 1882-1965 CAP-1
Earlier sketch in CA 9-10
Bonbright, James C(ummings) 1891-1985 3R
Obituary 117
Bond, Brian 1936- CANR-6
Earlier sketch in CA 57-60
Bond, Charles R(ankin), Jr. 1915- 124
Bond, Christopher Godfrey 1945- 101
Bond, Donald F(rederic) 1898-1987 13-14R
Obituary 121
Bond, Douglas Danford 1911-1976
Obituary 69-72
Bond, E(dward) J(arvis) 1930- 114
Bond, Edward 1934- 25-28R
See also DLB 13
See also CLC 4, 6, 13, 23
Bond, Elaine 1924-1984 Obituary 112
Bond, Evelyn
See Hershman, Morris
Bond, Felicia 1954- SATA-49
Bond, Geoffrey 1924- 29-32R
Bond, Gladys Baker 1912- CANR-2
Earlier sketch in CA 5-6R
See also SATA 14
Bond, Harold 1939- CANR-11
Earlier sketch in CA 65-68
Bond, Horace Mann 1904-1972 CANR-1
Obituary 37-40R
Earlier sketch in CA 1R
Bond, J. Harvey
See Winterbotham, R(ussell) R(obert)
Bond, Jean Carey 106
Bond, Julian 1940- 49-52
Bond, Marshall, Jr. 1908- CAP-2
Earlier sketch in CA 25-28
Bond, Mary Fanning Wickham 1898- 23-24R
Bond, Maurice Francis 1916-1983
Obituary 111
Bond, (Thomas) Michael 1926- CANR-24
Earlier sketches in CA 5-6R, CANR-4
See also SATA 6
See also SAAS 3
See also CLR 1
Bond, Mrs. James
See Bond, Mary Fanning Wickham
Bond, Nancy (Barbara) 1945- CANR-9
Earlier sketch in CA 65-68
See also SATA 22
See also CLR 11
Bond, Nelson S(lade) 1908- CAP-1
Earlier sketch in CA 19-20
Bond, Otto F(erdinand) 1885- 4R
Bond, Ray
See Smith, Richard Rein
Bond, Raymond T. 1893(?)-1981
Obituary 104
Bond, Richmond Pugh 1899- CAP-2
Earlier sketch in CA 33-36
Bond, Ruskin 1934- CANR-14
Earlier sketch in CA 29-32R
See also SATA 14
Bond, Simon 1947- 104
Bond, Ted
See Bond, E(dward) J(arvis)
Bond, William Henry 1915- 124
Bond, William J(oseph) 1941- 108
Bondanella, Peter Eugene 1943- CANR-10
Earlier sketch in CA 65-68
Bonderoff, Jason (Dennis) 1946- 97-100
Bondi, Joseph C. 1936- CANR-11
Earlier sketch in CA 29-32R
Bondurant, Joan V(alerie) 1918- 41-44R
Bone, Edith 1889(?)-1975 Obituary 57-60
Bone, Hugh A(lvin) 1909- CANR-3
Earlier sketch in CA 1R
Bone, Jesse F. 1916- 57-60
Bone, Quentin 1918- 85-88
Bone, Robert (Adamson) 1924- 69-72
Bone, Robert C(larke) 1917- 37-40R
Bonehill, Captain Ralph
See Stratemeyer, Edward L.
Bonelli, Robert Allen 1950- 112
Bonellie, Helen-Janet 1937- 41-44R
Boness, A. James 1928- 37-40R
Bonestell, Chesley 1888-1986 Obituary 119
See also SATA 48
Bonett, Emery
See Coulson, Felicity Carter
Bonett, John
See Coulson, John H(ubert) A(rthur)
Bonetti, Edward 1928- 93-96
Bonewits, Isaac
See Bonewits, P(hilip) E(mmons) I(saac)
Bonewits, P(hilip) E(mmons) I(saac)
1949- 93-96
Boney, Elaine E(mesette) 1921-
Brief entry 110
Boney, F(rancis) N(ash) 1929- CANR-15
Earlier sketch in CA 41-44R
Boney, Mary Lily
See Sheats, Mary Boney
Boney, William Jerry 1930- 23-24R
Bonfante, Larissa CANR-11
Earlier sketch in CA 69-72
Bongar, Emmet W(ald) 1919- 33-36R
Bongartz, Heinz
See Thorwald, Juergen
Bongartz, Roy 1924- 15-16R
Bongie, Laurence L(ouis) 1929- 61-64
Bonham, Barbara Thomas 1926- CANR-7
Earlier sketch in CA 19-20R
See also SATA 7
Bonham, Frank 1914- CANR-4
Earlier sketch in CA 11-12R
See also SATA 1, 49
See also SAAS 3
See also CLC 12
Bonham-Carter, Victor 1913- 9-10R
Bonham Carter, (Helen) Violet (Asquith)
1887-1969 CAP-2
Earlier sketch in CA 17-18
Bonheim, Helmut 1930- CANR-4
Earlier sketch in CA 3R
Bonhoeffer, Dietrich 1906-1945
Brief entry 122
Bonhomme, Denise 1926- 104
Boni, Albert 1892-1981 65-68
Obituary 104
Boni, Margaret Bradford 1893(?)-1974
Obituary 53-56
Bonime, Florence 1907- 49-52
Bonime, Walter 1909- CAP-2
Earlier sketch in CA 17-18
Bonine, Gladys Nichols 1907- CAP-1
Earlier sketch in CA 15-16
Bonington, Christian (John Storey)
1934- CANR-1
Earlier sketch in CA 45-48
Bonini, Charles P(ius) 1933- 13-14R
Bonino, Louise
See Williams, Louise Bonino
Bonjean, Charles M. 1935- 41-44R
Bonk, James 1932- 123
Bonk, Wallace J. 1923- 9-10R
Bonn, Pat
See Bonn, Patricia Carolyn
Bonn, Patricia Carolyn 1948- SATA-43
Bonn, Thomas L. 1939- 109
Bonnamy, Francis
See Walz, Audrey Boyers
Bonnar, Alphonsus 1895-1968 CAP-1
Earlier sketch in CA 9-10
Bonnay, Charles (Louis) 1930-1986
Obituary 119
Bonnefoy, Yves 1923- 85-88
See also CLC 9, 15
Bonnell, Dorothy Haworth 1914- CANR-3
Earlier sketch in CA 4R
Bonnell, F(raser) C(larence) 1908-1983 118
Bonnell, F(lorence Rhodes) W(inn) 1915- 118
Bonnell, John Sutherland 1893- 7-8R
Bonner, Brian 1917- CANR-21
Earlier sketch in CA 104
Bonner, Gerald 1926- CANR-5
Earlier sketch in CA 11-12R
Bonner, James Calvin 1904- CANR-9
Earlier sketch in CA 11-12R
Bonner, Joey 1948- 122
Bonner, John Tyler 1920- 49-52
Bonner, Mary Graham 1890-1974 73-76
Obituary 49-52
See also SATA 19
Bonner, Michael
See Glasscock, Anne Bonner
Bonner, Parker
See Ballard, (Willis) Todhunter
Bonner, Paul Hyde 1893-1968 4R
Obituary 103
Bonner, Raymond T(homas) 1942- 117
Bonner, Terry Nelsen
See Castoro, Laura A(nn)
Bonner, Terry Nelsen
See Krauzer, Steven M(ark)
and Raeschild, Sheila
Bonner, Thomas, Jr. 1942- 110
Bonner, Thomas N(eville) 1923- 11-12R
Bonner, William H(omer) 1924- 53-56
Bonner, William Hallam 1899-1980
Obituary 115
Bonners, Susan SATA-48
Bonnette, Jeanne 1907- 41-44R
Bonnette, Victor
See Roy, Ewell Paul
Bonneville, Douglas A(lan) 1931- 21-22R
Bonney, Bill
See Keevill, Henry J(ohn)
Bonney, H(anning) Orrin 1903-1979 11-12R
Obituary 103
Bonney, Lorraine G(agnon) 1922- CANR-1
Earlier sketch in CA 45-48
Bonney, Merl E(dwin) 1902- CAP-2
Earlier sketch in CA 33-36
Bonney, (Mabel) Therese 1897-1978
Obituary 73-76
Bonnice, Joseph G(regory) 1930- 49-52
Bonnie, Richard J(effrey) 1945- CANR-4
Earlier sketch in CA 53-56
Bonnifield, Paul 1937- 104
Bonnor, William (Bowen) 1920- 11-12R
Bonny, Helen L(indquist) 1921- CANR-19
Earlier sketches in CA 49-52, CANR-2
Bono, Philip 1921- 101
Bonoma, T(homas) V(incent) 1946- CANR-15
Earlier sketch in CA 85-88
Bonomi, Patricia U(pdegraff) 1928- 85-88
Bonsal, Philip Wilson 1903- 85-88
Bonsall, Crosby Barbara (Newell) 1921- 73-76
See also SATA 23
Bontecou, Eleanor 1890(?)-1976
Obituary 65-68
Bontempo, Charles J(oseph) 1931- 61-64
Bontemps, Arna Wendell 1902-1973 CANR-4
Obituary 41-44R
Earlier sketch in CA 1R
See also SATA 2, 24, 44
See also DLB 48, 51
See also CLC 1, 18
See also CLR 6
Bontly, Thomas (John) 1939- 57-60
Bontrager, G(erald) Edwin 1939- 114
Bontrager, John K(enneth) 1923- 65-68
Bonvie, Thomas L. 1940- 114
Bony, Jean (Victor) 1908- 101
Bonzon, Paul-Jacques 1908-1978 93-96
See also SATA 22
Boodman, David M(orris) 1923- 23-24R
Boody, Shirley Bright 1919- 89-92
Boog Watson, Elspeth Janet 1900- CAP-1
Earlier sketch in CA 11-12
Booher, Dianna Daniels 1948- 103
See also SATA 33
Bookbinder, David J(oel) 1951- 101
Bookbinder, Robert 1950- 110
Bookchin, Murray 1921- CANR-1
Earlier sketch in CA 3R
Booker, Anton S.
See Randolph, Vance
Booker, Malcolm (Richard) 1915- 108
Booker, Simeon Saunders 1918- 11-12R
Bookman, Charlotte
See Zolotow, Charlotte S.
Book-Senninger, Claude 1928- 45-48
Bookspan, Martin 1926- 41-44R
Bookstein, Abraham 1940- 53-56
Boom, Alfred B. 1928- CANR-14
Earlier sketch in CA 25-28R
Boom, Corrie ten
See ten Boom, Corrie
Boon, Francis
See Bacon, Edward
Boon, Louis-Paul 1912-1979 CANR-13
Earlier sketch in CA 73-76
Boone, Bruce 1940- 112
Boone, Buford 1909(?)-1983 Obituary 109
Boone, Charles Eugene
See Boone, Pat
Boone, Daniel R. 1927- CANR-12
Earlier sketch in CA 33-36R
Boone, Debby
See Boone, Deborah Ann
Boone, Deborah Ann 1956- 110
Boone, Gene 1962- 113
Boone, Gray Davis 1938- 93-96
Boone, Louis E(ugene) 1941- CANR-15
Earlier sketch in CA 41-44R
Boone, Muriel 1893- 69-72
Boone, Pat 1934- CANR-2
Earlier sketch in CA 4R
See also SATA 7
Boontje
See Boon, Louis-Paul
Boore, W(alter) H(ugh) 1904- CANR-5
Earlier sketch in CA 7-8R
Boorer, Wendy 1931- CANR-6
Earlier sketch in CA 57-60
Boorman, Howard L(yon) 1920- 41-44R
Boorman, John 1933- 121
Brief entry 112
Boorman, Linda (Kay) 1940- 121
See also SATA 46
Boorman, Scott A(rcher) 1949- 29-32R
Boorstein, Edward 1915- 73-76
Boorstin, Daniel J(oseph) 1914- CANR-1
Earlier sketch in CA 3R
See also DLB 17
See also AITN 2
Boorstin, Paul (Terry) 1944- 103
Boos, Frank Holgate 1893-1968 CAP-2
Earlier sketch in CA 33-36
Boot, John C. G. 1936- 19-20R
Boote, Robert Edward 1920- 65-68
Booth, Alan R. 1934- Brief entry 107
Booth, Bradford A(llen) 1909-1968
Obituary 116
Booth, Catherine Bramwell
See Bramwell-Booth, Catherine
Booth, Charles Orrell 1918- 13-14R
Booth, Edwin CANR-7
Earlier sketch in CA 17-18R
Booth, Ernest Sheldon 1915-1984 53-56
See also SATA 43
Booth, Geoffrey
See Tann, Jennifer
Booth, George C(live) 1901- CAP-1
Earlier sketch in CA 11-12
Booth, Graham (Charles) 1935- SATA-37
Booth, Helen Sutton 1890(?)-1985
Obituary 117
Booth, Irwin
See Hoch, Edward D(entinger)
Booth, James 1945- 119
Booth, John A(llan) 1946- 111
Booth, John E(rlanger) 1919- 9-10R
Booth, Ken 1943- 102
Booth, Mark Haworth
See Haworth-Booth, Mark
Booth, Mark Warren 1943- 107
Booth, Martin 1944- 93-96
See also CAAS 2
See also CLC 13
Booth, Nyla 121
Booth, Pat(rick John) 1929- CAP-1
Earlier sketch in CA 9-10
Booth, Paul Henry Gore
See Gore-Booth, Paul Henry
Booth, Philip 1907-1981 106
Booth, Philip 1925- CANR-5
Earlier sketch in CA 5-6R
See also DLBY 82
See also CLC 23
Booth, Rosemary Frances 1928- 53-56
Booth, Stephen 1933- 69-72
Booth, Taylor L(ockwood) 1933- 53-56
Booth, Warren Scripps 1894-1987
Obituary 121
Booth, Wayne C(layson) 1921- CANR-3
Earlier sketch in CA 1R
See also CAAS 5
See also DLB 67
See also CLC 24
Boothby, Robert
See Boothby, Robert John Graham
Boothby, Robert John Graham 1900-1986 117
Obituary 120
Boothroyd, (John) Basil 1910-1988 CANR-13
Obituary 124
Earlier sketch in CA 33-36R
Bootle, Stan Kelly
See Kelly-Bootle, Stan
Booton, (Catherine) Kage 1919- 61-64
Booty, John Everitt 1925- CANR-17
Earlier sketch in CA 85-88
Bopp, Karl Richard 1906-1979 Obituary 107
Bor, Josef 1906-1979 Obituary 115
Bor, Norman 1893(?)-1973 Obituary 104
Boraas, Roger S(tuart) 1926- 33-36R
Borah, Woodrow (Wilson) 1912- CANR-3
Earlier sketch in CA 7-8R
Borch, Ted
See Lund, A. Morten
Borchard, Ruth (Berendsohn) 1910- 15-16R
Borchardt, D(ietrich) H(ans) 1916- CANR-24
Earlier sketches in CA 23-24R, CANR-9
Borchardt, Frank L(ouis) 1938- 33-36R
Borchardt, Rudolf 1877-1945 DLB-66
Borchers, Gladys L. 1891- CAP-1
Earlier sketch in CA 17-18
Borchert, Gerald L(eo) 1932- CANR-14
Earlier sketch in CA 37-40R
Borchert, James 1941- 104
Borchert, Wolfgang 1921-1947 Brief entry 104
See also TCLC 5
Borden, Bob
See Rees, Clair (Francis)
Borden, Charles A. 1912-1968 7-8R
Borden, Henry 1901- 41-44R
Borden, Lee
See Deal, Borden
Borden, Leigh
See Deal, Borden
Borden, M.
See Saxon, Gladys Relyea
Borden, Mary 1886-1968 CAP-1
Obituary 25-28R
Earlier sketch in CA 15-16
Borden, Morton 1925- 11-12R
Borden, Neil Hopper 1895- CANR-6
Earlier sketch in CA 3R
Borden, Norman E(aston), Jr. 1907- 17-18R
Borden, Richard Carman 1900- CAP-1
Earlier sketch in CA 11-12
Borden, William (Vickers) 1938- CANR-10
Earlier sketch in CA 25-28R
Borderieux, Carita 1874-1953 Brief entry 113
Bordes, Francois 1919-1981 Obituary 103
Bordier, Georgette 1924- SATA-16
Bordin, Edward S. 1913- 57-60
Bordin, Ruth B(irgitta) 1917- CANR-11
Earlier sketch in CA 21-22R
Bordley, James III 1900- 69-72
Bordman, Gerald 1931- 107
Bordow, Joan (Wiener) 1944- 85-88
Borea, Phyllis Gilbert 1924- 29-32R
Boreham, Gordon F. 1928- 41-44R
Borek, Ernest 1911-1986 106
Obituary 118
Borel, Jacques 1925- CANR-13
Earlier sketch in CA 33-36R
Borel, Raymond C. 1927- 73-76

Borell, Helene
See Hegeler, Sten
Boreman, Jean 1909- CAP-2
Earlier sketch in CA 21-22
Boren, Henry C(harles) 1921- 17-18R
Boren, James H(arlan) 1925- 41-44R
Borenstein, Audrey F(arrell) 1930- CANR-13
Earlier sketch in CA 77-80
Borenstein, Emily 1923- 104
Borer, Mary (Irene) Cathcart 1906- CANR-4
Earlier sketch in CA 9-10R
Boretz, Allen 1900-1986 Obituary 119
Boretz, Alvin 1919- 124
Brief entry 118
Boretz, Benjamin (Aaron) 1934- 69-72
Borg, Bjoern (Rune) 1956- Brief entry 114
Borg, Bjorn
See Borg, Bjoern (Rune)
Borg, Dorothy 1902- 23-24R
Borg, Walter R(aymond) 1921- CANR-13
Earlier sketch in CA 33-36R
Borgen, Robert 1945- 124
Borges, Jorge Luis 1899-1986 CANR-19
Earlier sketch in CA 21-22R
See also DLBY 86
See also CLC 1, 2, 3, 4, 6, 8, 9, 10, 13, 19, 44
Borgese, Elisabeth Mann 1918- CANR-24
Earlier sketch in CA 73-76
Borghese, Junio Valerio 1906(?)-1974
Obituary 53-56
Borglum, (James) Lincoln (De La Mothe) 1912-1986 122
Obituary 118
Borgmann, Albert 1937- 117
Borgmann, Dmitri A(lfred) 1927-1985 17-18R
Obituary 118
Borgo, Ludovico 1930- 65-68
Borgos, Seth 1952- 119
Borgstrom, Georg A(rne) 1912- 17-18R
Borgzinner, Jon A. 1938-1980 108
Obituary 97-100
Borhek, Mary V(irginia) 1922- 113
Borich, Michael 1949- 105
Boring, Edwin G(arrigues) 1886-1968 CANR-6
Earlier sketch in CA 3R
Boring, M(aynard) Eugene 1935- 107
Boring, Mel 1939- 106
See also SATA 35
Boring, Phyllis Zatlin
See Zatlin, Phyllis
Boris, Edna Z(wick) 1943- 113
Boris, Martin 1930- 89-92
Borja, Corinne 1929- 97-100
See also SATA 22
Borja, Robert 1923- 97-100
See also SATA 22
Bork, Alfred M. 1926- 17-18R
Bork, Robert H(eron) 1927- Brief entry 111
Borkin, Joseph 1911-1979 97-100
Obituary 89-92
Borklund, C(arl) W(ilbur) 1930- 21-22R
Borko, Harold 1922- 15-16R
Borkovec, Thomas D. 1944- 45-48
Borland, Barbara Dodge CAP-1
Earlier sketch in CA 9-10
Borland, Hal
See Borland, Harold Glen
See also SATA 5, 24
Borland, Harold Glen 1900-1978 CANR-6
Obituary 77-80
Earlier sketch in CA 4R
Borland, Kathryn Kilby 1916- CANR-4
Earlier sketch in CA 53-56
See also SATA 16
Borman, Kathryn M. 1941- 117
Bormann, Ernest G(ordon) 1925- 17-18R
Born, Adolf 1930- SATA-49
Born, Ernest Alexander 1898- 102
Born, Max 1882-1970 7-8R
Obituary 25-28R
Borne, Dorothy
See Rice, Dorothy Mary
Borne, Lawrence Roger 1939- 121
Borneman, Ernest 1915- CANR-19
Earlier sketches in CA 9-10R, CANR-3
Borneman, H.
See Gottshall, Franklin Henry
Bornemann, Alfred H. 1908- 13-14R
Bornet, Vaughn Davis 1917- CANR-20
Earlier sketches in CA 3R, CANR-5
Bornheimer, Deane G(ordon) 1935- 89-92
Borning, Bernard C(arl) 1913- CANR-3
Earlier sketch in CA 3R
Bornkamm, Guenther 1905- Brief entry 116
Bornstein, Diane (Dorothy) 1942-1984 CANR-8
Obituary 112
Earlier sketch in CA 57-60
Bornstein, George (Jay) 1941- 29-32R
Bornstein, Morris 1927- CANR-2
Earlier sketch in CA 7-8R
Bornstein, Sam 1913- Brief entry 112
Bornstein-Lercher, Ruth 1927- CANR-8
Earlier sketch in CA 61-64
See also SATA 14
Borntrager, Karl A. 1892- 89-92
Borodacz, William ?-1986 Obituary 118
Borodin, George
See Milkomane, George Alexis Milkomanovich
Boroff, David 1917-1965 CAP-1
Obituary 29-32R
Earlier sketch in CA 11-12
Boroson, Warren 1935- 23-24R
Borovski, Conrad 1930- 37-40R
Borovsky, Natasha 1924- 121
Borowitz, Albert (Ira) 1930- CANR-15
Earlier sketch in CA 85-88
Borowitz, Eugene B(ernard) 1924- CANR-1
Earlier sketch in CA 49-52
Borowski, Tadeusz 1922-1951 Brief entry 106
See also TCLC 9
Borras, Frank Marshall (?)-1980 Obituary 102
Borrello, Alfred 1931- 29-32R
Borrie, John 1915- 103
Borrie, Wilfred David 1913- 109
Borroff, Edith 1925- 65-68
Borroff, Marie 1923- CANR-2
Earlier sketch in CA 7-8R
Borror, Donald J(oyce) 1907- 4R
Borror, Gordon L(amar) 1936- 117
Borrow, George 1803-1881 DLB-21, 55
Borsch, Frederick Houk 1935- CANR-10
Earlier sketch in CA 25-28R
Borski, Lucia Merecka 73-76
See also SATA 18
Borsodi, Ralph 1888-1977 Obituary 73-76
Borson, Roo
See Borson, Ruth Elizabeth
Borson, Ruth Elizabeth 1952- 112
Borst, Raymond R(ichard) 1909- 107
Borsten, Orin 1912- 85-88
Borten, Helen Jacobson 1930- CANR-3
Earlier sketch in CA 5-6R
See also SATA 5
Borth, Christian C. 1895(?)-1976
Obituary 65-68
Bortin, George 114
Bortin, V. G.
See Bortin, George and Bortin, Virginia
Bortin, Virginia 1936- 114
Bortner, Doyle M(cClean) 1915- 33-36R
Bortner, Morton 1925- 33-36R
Bortoli, Georges 1923- 65-68
Borton, Elizabeth
See Trevino, Elizabeth B(orton) de
Borton, John C., Jr. 1938- 29-32R
Borton, Terry
See Borton, John C., Jr.
Bortstein, Larry 1942- 33-36R
See also SATA 16
Bortz, Edward L(eRoy) 1896-1970 CAP-1
Earlier sketch in CA 11-12
Boruch, Robert F(rancis) 1942- 69-72
Borus, Michael E(liot) 1938-1987 37-40R
Obituary 122
Borza, Eugene N(icholas) 1935- 25-28R
Bosanquet, Reggie
See Bosanquet, Reginald
Bosanquet, Reginald 1932-1984 Obituary 113
Bosch, David J(acobus) 1929- 118
Bosch, William Joseph 1928- 29-32R
Bosco, Antoinette (Oppedisano) 1928- 13-14R
Bosco, (Fernand Joseph Marius) Henri 1888-1976 69-72
Obituary 65-68
Bosco, Jack
See Holliday, Joseph
Bosco, Monique 1927- DLB-53
Bose, Buddhadeva 1908- Brief entry 119
Bose, Irene Mott 1899(?)-1974 Obituary 53-56
Bose, N(irmal) K(umar) 1901-1972 CAP-2
Earlier sketch in CA 23-24
Bose, Tarun Chandra 1931- 45-48
Boserup, Ester 1910- 57-60
Boshell, Buris R(aye) 1923- 105
Boshell, Gordon 1908- 77-80
See also SATA 15
Boshinski, Blanche 1922- 21-22R
See also SATA 10
Boskin, Joseph 1929- 25-28R
Boskoff, Alvin 1924- 13-14R
Bosland, Chelcie Clayton 1901- 5-6R
Bosler, Raymond Thomas 1915- 112
Bosley, Harold A(ugustus) 1907-1975 49-52
Obituary 53-56
Bosley, Keith 1937- CANR-6
Earlier sketch in CA 57-60
Boslooper, Thomas 1923- 81-84
Bosmajian, Haig Aram 1928- CANR-7
Earlier sketch in CA 17-18R
Bosmajian, Hamida 1936- 107
Bosquet, Alain 1919- 13-14R
Bosse, Judy 1935- 57-60
Boss, Richard W(oodruff) 1937- 103
Bosschere, Jean de 1878(?)-1953
Brief entry 115
See also TCLC 19
Bosse, Malcolm J(oseph) 1933- 106
See also SATA 35
Bosserman, (Charles) Phillip 1931- 102
Bossert, Steven T(homas) 1948- 104
Bossom, Naomi 1933- 102
See also SATA 35
Bossone, Richard M. 1924- 33-36R
Bosticco, (Isabel Lucy) Mary 102
Bostick, William A(llison) 1913- 89-92
Boston, Charles K.
See Gruber, Frank
Boston, Lucy Maria (Wood) 1892- 73-76
See also SATA 19
See also CLR 3
Boston, Noel 1910-1966 CAP-1
Earlier sketch in CA 15-16
Boston, Robert 1940- 65-68
Bostwick, Burdette Edwards 1908- 106
Boswell
See Gordon, Giles (Alexander Esme)
Boswell, Barbara (S.) 1946- 122
Boswell, Charles (Meigs, Jr.) 1909- 5-6R
Boswell, Jackson Campbell 1934- 61-64
Boswell, Jeanetta 1922- CANR-22
Earlier sketch in CA 106
Boswell, John (Eastburn) 1947- 121
Boswell, Thomas 1947- 118
Bosworth, Allan R(ucker) 1901-1986 4R
Obituary 120
Bosworth, Clifford Edmund 1928- CANR-7
Earlier sketch in CA 13-14R
Bosworth, David 1947- 113
Bosworth, Frank
See Paine, Lauran (Bosworth)
Bosworth, J. Allan 1925- SATA-19
Bosworth, Patricia 1933- 77-80
Bosworth, R(ichard) J(ames) B(oon) 1943- CANR-23
Earlier sketch in CA 106
Botein, Bernard 1900-1974 Obituary 45-48
Botel, Morton 1925- 105
Botham, Noel 1940- 104
Bothmer, Dietrich Felix von
See von Bothmer, Dietrich Felix
Bothwell, Jean ?-1977 CANR-3
Earlier sketch in CA 2R
See also SATA 2
Botjer, George (Francis) 1937- 97-100
Botkin, B(enjamin) A(lbert) 1901-1975 CAP-1
Obituary 57-60
Earlier sketch in CA 15-16
See also SATA 40
Botkin, James W. 1943- 112
Boto, Eza
See Biyidi, Alexandre
Botsch, Robert Emil 1947- 104
Botsford, Keith 1928- 9-10R
Botsford, Ward 1927- 110
Bott, George 1920- 104
Botta, Anne Charlotte (Lynch) 1815-1891 DLB-3
Bottel, Helen 1914- 25-28R
Botterill, Cal(vin Bruce) 1947- 57-60
Bottiglia, William F(ilbert) 1912- 23-24R
Botting, Douglas (Scott) 1934- CANR-16
Earlier sketches in CA 45-48, CANR-1
See also SATA 43
Bottner, Barbara 1943- CANR-23
Earlier sketches in CA 61-64, CANR-8
See also SATA 14
Bottom, Raymond 1927- 33-36R
Bottome, Edgar M. 1937- 33-36R
Bottome, Phyllis
See Forbes-Dennis, Phyllis
Bottomley, Gordon 1874-1948 Brief entry 120
See also DLB 10
Bottomly, Heath 1919- 105
Bottomore, T(homas) B(urton) 1920- CANR-20
Earlier sketches in CA 9-10R, CANR-4
Bottoms, A(nthony) E(dward) 1939- 73-76
Bottoms, David 1949- CANR-22
Earlier sketch in CA 105
See also DLBY 83
Bottoms, Lawrence W(endell) 1908- 89-92
Bottrall, Margaret Florence Saumarez 1909- 104
Bottrall, (Francis James) Ronald 1906- 53-56
See also DLB 20
Botvinnik, Mikhail Moiseyevich 1911- 112
Botwinick, Jack 1923- 41-44R
Bouce, Paul-Gabriel 1936- 73-76
Bouchard, Lois Kalb 1938- 25-28R
Bouchard, Robert H. 1923- 19-20R
Boucher, Alan (Estcourt) 1918- CANR-24
Earlier sketches in CA 5-6R, CANR-9
Boucher, Anthony
See White, William A(nthony) P(arker)
See also DLB 8
Boucher, Frank 1901-1977 122
Obituary 110
Boucher, John G(regory) 1930- 37-40R
Boucher, Jonathan 1738-1804 DLB-31
Boucher, Paul Edward 1893- CAP-1
Earlier sketch in CA 13-14
Boucher, Sandy 1936- 110
Boucher, Wayne I(rving) 1934- 53-56
Boucolon, Maryse 1937- 110
Boudat, Marie-Louise 1909- CAP-1
Earlier sketch in CA 11-12
Boudon, Raymond 1934- 49-52
Boudreau, Eugene H(oward) 1934- 45-48
Boudreaux, Patricia Duncan 1941- 33-36R
Bough, Lee
See Huser, (La)Verne (Carl)
Boughey, Arthur S(tanley) 1913-
Brief entry 113
Boughner, Daniel C(liness) 1909-1974 CAP-2
Obituary 49-52
Earlier sketch in CA 23-24
Boughton, James M(urray) 1940- 41-44R
Boughton, Willis A(rnold) 1885-1977
Obituary 73-76
Bouissac, Paul (Antoine Rene) 1934- 65-68
Boularan, Jacques 1890-1972 Obituary 37-40R
Boulby, Mark 1929- 37-40R
Boulding, Elise (Biorn-Hansen) 1920- CANR-8
Earlier sketch in CA 21-22R
Boulding, Kenneth E(wart) 1910- CANR-7
Earlier sketch in CA 5-6R
Boulet, Susan Seddon 1941- SATA-50
Boulger, James Denis 1931-1979 109
Boulle, Pierre (Francois Marie-Louis) 1912- CANR-24
Earlier sketch in CA 11-12R
See also SATA 22
Boulogne, Jean 1942- 93-96
Boult, Adrian (Cedric) 1889-1983 114
Obituary 109
Boult, S. Kye
See Cochrane, William E.
Boulting, John (Edward) 1913-1985
Obituary 116
Boulting, Sydney Arthur
See Cotes, Peter
Boulton, David 1935- CANR-15
Earlier sketch in CA 25-28R
Boulton, James T(hompson) 1924- 29-32R
Boulton, Jane 1921- 65-68
Boulton, Laura Theresa Craytor 1899(?)-1980 Obituary 110
Boulton, Marjorie 1924- CANR-9
Earlier sketch in CA 65-68
Boulton, Wayne G(ranberry) 1941- 115
Boultwood, Alban 1911- 118
Boulware, Marcus H(anna) 1907- CANR-1
Earlier sketch in CA 45-48
Bouma, Donald H(erbert) 1918- 41-44R
Bouma, Mary La Grand 93-96
Bouman, Pieter M(arinus) 1938- CANR-12
Earlier sketch in CA 29-32R
Bouman, Walter Richard 1929- 29-32R
Boumelha, Penelope Ann 1950- 110
Boumelha, Penny
See Boumelha, Penelope Ann
Boumphrey, Robert Stavely 1916(?)-1987
Obituary 123
Bouraoui, H(edi) A(ndre) 1932- CANR-9
Earlier sketch in CA 65-68
Bourbon, Ken
See Bauer, Erwin A.
Bourdeaux, Michael 1934- CANR-14
Earlier sketch in CA 33-36R
Bourdier, James A(aron) 1929-1987
Obituary 124
Bourdon, David 1934- CANR-13
Earlier sketch in CA 37-40R
See also SATA 46
Bourdon, Sylvia Diane Eve 1949- 85-88
Bouregy, Thomas 1909(?)-1978 Obituary 104
Bouret, Jean 1914- 85-88
Bourget, Paul (Charles Joseph) 1852-1935 Brief entry 107
See also TCLC 12
Bourgholtzer, Frank 1919- 25-28R
Bourguignon, Erika (Eichhorn) 1924- 85-88
Bourjaily, Monte Ferris 1894-1979 97-100
Obituary 85-88
Bourjaily, Vance (Nye) 1922- CANR-2
Earlier sketch in CA 2R
See also CAAS 1
See also DLB 2
See also CLC 8
Bourke, Vernon J(oseph) 1907- CANR-3
Earlier sketch in CA 11-12R
Bourke-White, Margaret 1904-1971 CAP-1
Obituary 29-32R
Earlier sketch in CA 15-16
Bourliaguet, Leonce 1895-1965 102
Bourliere, Francois (Marie Gabriel) 1913-
Brief entry 113
Bourne, Aleck William 1885(?)-1974
Obituary 53-56
Bourne, Charles P. 1931- 11-12R
Bourne, Dorothy D(ulles) 1893-19(?) CAP-2
Earlier sketch in CA 23-24
Bourne, Edward Gaylord 1860-1908 DLB-47
Bourne, Eulalia 97-100
Bourne, Frank Card 1914- 19-20R
Bourne, Geoffrey Howard 1909- 33-36R
Bourne, J(ohn) M. 1949- 124
Bourne, James R. 1897-19(?) CAP-2
Earlier sketch in CA 21-22
Bourne, Joanna Watkins 1949- 112
Bourne, John
See John, Owen
Bourne, Kenneth 1930- CANR-11
Earlier sketch in CA 25-28R
Bourne, L(arry) S(tuart) 1939- CANR-12
Earlier sketch in CA 33-36R
Bourne, Lesley
See Marshall, Evelyn
Bourne, Lyle E(ugene), Jr. 1932- 53-56
Bourne, Miriam Anne 1931- CANR-10
Earlier sketch in CA 21-22R
See also SATA 16
Bourne, Peter
See Jeffries, Graham Montague
Bourne, Peter Geoffrey 1939- CANR-7
Earlier sketch in CA 57-60
Bourne, Randolph S(illiman) 1886-1918
Brief entry 117
See also DLB 63
See also TCLC 16
Bourne, Ruth (May) 1897-1986 33-36R
Obituary 120
Bourneuf, Alice E. 1912-1980 Obituary 102
Bourricaud, Francois 1922- 29-32R
Bouscaren, Anthony Trawick 1920- CANR-5
Earlier sketch in CA 3R
Bouscaren, T(imothy) Lincoln 1884- CAP-1
Earlier sketch in CA 11-12
Bousquet, Marie-Louis Valentin 1887(?)-1975 Obituary 104
Boussard, Jacques Marie 1910- 29-32R
Boustead, John Edmund Hugh 1895-1980
Obituary 97-100
Boutell, Clarence Burley 1908-1981
Obituary 104
Boutell, Clip
See Boutell, Clarence Burley
Boutet de Monvel, (Louis) M(aurice) 1850(?)-1913 SATA-30
Boutilier, Mary A(nn) 1943- 105
Bouton, James Alan 1939- 89-92
Bouton, Jim
See Bouton, James Alan
Bouvard, Marguerite Anne 1937- 37-40R

Bouvier, Emile 1906- 37-40R
Bouvier, Leon F(rancis) 1922- 105
Bova, Ben(jamin William) 1932- CANR-11
Earlier sketch in CA 7-8R
See also SATA 6
See also DLBY 81
See also CLC 45
See also CLR 3
Bovard, Oliver K. 1872-1945 ..... DLB-25
Bovasso, Julie 1930- 25-28R
Bovee, Courtland Lowell 1944- 49-52
Bovee, Ruth
See Paine, Lauran (Bosworth)
Boven, William 1887(?)-1970 Obituary 104
Bovet, Eric D(avid) 1900- 118
Bovey, John (Alden, Jr.) 1913- 107
Bovis, H(enry) Eugene 1928- 29-32R
Bow, Russell 1925- 23-24R
Bowden, Betsy 1948- 107
Bowden, Edwin T(urner), Jr. 1924- CANR-8
Earlier sketch in CA 15-16R
Bowden, Elbert Victor 1924- CANR-15
Earlier sketch in CA 41-44R
Bowden, Gregory Houston 1948- 41-44R
Bowden, Henry Warner 1939- 49-52
Bowden, J(ocelyn) J(ean) 1927- 29-32R
Bowden, Jean 1925- CANR-7
Earlier sketch in CA 53-56
Bowden, Jim
See Spence, William John Duncan
Bowden, Joan Chase 1925- 89-92
See also SATA 38
Bowden, Leonard (Walter) 1933- 17-18R
Bowden, Mary Weatherspoon 1941- 110
Bowden, Roland Heywood 1916- CANR-24
Earlier sketch in CA 106
Bowden, Susan White
See White-Bowden, Susan
Bowder, Diana (Ruth) 1942- 109
Bowditch, James L(owell) 1939- 89-92
Bowdle, Donald N(elson) 1935- 49-52
Bowdler, Roger 1934- 97-100
Bowe, Frank 1947- 104
Bowe, Gabriel P(aul) 1923- 23-24R
Bowe, Kate
See Taylor, Mary Ann
Bowe, (Paul Thomas) Patrick 1945- 106
Bowen, Barbara C(herry) 1937- 37-40R
Bowen, Betty Morgan
See West, Betty
Bowen, Catherine Drinker 1897-1973 .. CANR-15
Obituary 45-48
Earlier sketch in CA 5-6R
See also SATA 7
Bowen, Croswell 1905-1971 Obituary 33-36R
Bowen, David
See Bowen, Joshua David
Bowen, Desmond 1921- 33-36R
Bowen, Earl Kenneth 1918- 5-6R
Bowen, Edmund (John) 1898-1980
Obituary 105
Bowen, Elbert Russell 1918- 13-14R
Bowen, Elizabeth (Dorothea Cole)
1899-1973 ..... CAP-2
Obituary 41-44R
Earlier sketch in CA 17-18
See also DLB 15
See also CLC 1, 3, 6, 11, 15, 22
Bowen, Emrys George 1900-1983
Obituary 111
Bowen, Ezra 1927- 85-88
Bowen, Francis 1811-1890 ..... DLB-1, 59
Bowen, Haskell L. 1929- 41-44R
Bowen, Howard R(othmann) 1908- CANR-8
Earlier sketch in CA 23-24R
Bowen, (Ivor) Ian 1908-1984 105
Obituary 115
Bowen, J(ean) Donald 1922- CANR-8
Earlier sketch in CA 19-20R
Bowen, James Keith 1932- 37-40R
Bowen, John 1916- 103
Bowen, John (Griffith) 1924- CANR-2
Earlier sketch in CA 4R
See also DLB 13
Bowen, Joshua David 1930- 105
See also SATA 22
Bowen, Marjorie
See Campbell, (Gabrielle) Margaret (Vere)
Bowen, Mary
See Hall, Mary Bowen
Bowen, Peter 1939- 57-60
Bowen, Ralph H(enry) 1919- 69-72
Bowen, Richard M. 1928- 23-24R
Bowen, Robert O. 1920- 11-12R
Bowen, Robert Sydney 1900-1977 73-76
Obituary 69-72
See also SATA 21
Bowen, Zack (Rhollie) 1934- 29-32R
Bowen-Judd, Sara (Hutton) 1922-1985 .. CANR-5
Obituary 117
Earlier sketch in CA 9-10R
Bower, Barbara
See Todd, Barbara Euphan
Bower, David A(llan) 1945- 37-40R
Bower, Donald E(dward) 1920- 77-80
Bower, Eli M(ichael) 1917- 89-92
Bower, Fay Louise 1929- 53-56
Bower, Gordon H(oward) 1932- 19-20R
Bower, Joseph L(yon) 1938- 112
Bower, Julia Wells 1903- 41-44R
Bower, Keith
See Beckett, Kenneth A(lbert)
Bower, Louise 1900- CAP-2
Earlier sketch in CA 21-22
Bower, Muriel 1921- 49-52
Bower, Robert T(urrell) 1919- 49-52
Bower, Sharon Anthony 1932- 65-68
Bower, William Clayton 1878- 7-8R
Bowering, George 1935- CANR-10
Earlier sketch in CA 21-22R
See also DLB 53
See also CLC 15, 47
Bowering, Marilyn R(uthe) 1949- 101
See also CLC 32
Bowers, C. A. 1935- 29-32R
Bowers, Claude, G. 1878-1958 ..... DLB-17
Bowers, Edgar 1924- CANR-24
Earlier sketch in CA 7-8R
See also DLB 5
See also CLC 9
Bowers, Faubion 1917- 5-6R
Bowers, Fredson (Thayer) 1905- CANR-2
Earlier sketch in CA 5-6R
Bowers, George K. 1916- CANR-2
Earlier sketch in CA 3R
Bowers, John 1928- 33-36R
Bowers, John Waite 1935- 41-44R
Bowers, Kenneth S. 1937- 97-100
Bowers, Margaretta K(eller) 1908- 5-6R
Bowers, Mary Beacom 1932- 105
Bowers, Neal 1948- 110
Bowers, Q(uentin) David 1938- CANR-16
Earlier sketch in CA 41-44R
Bowers, Ronald (Lee) 1941- 41-44R
Bowers, Warner Fremont 1906- 61-64
Bowers, William 1916-1987 102
Obituary 122
Bowers, William J(oseph) 1935- 97-100
Bowers, William L(avalle) 1930-
Brief entry 114
Bowersock, G(len) W(arren) 1936- 81-84
Bowes, Anne LaBastille
See LaBastille, Anne
Bowett, Derek William 1927- CANR-6
Earlier sketch in CA 9-10R
Bowick, Dorothy Mueller
See Mueller, Dorothy
Bowie, David
See Jones, David Robert
See also CLC 17
Bowie, Janetta (Hamilton) 1907- 102
Bowie, Jim
See Norwood, Victor G(eorge) C(harles)
Bowie, Jim
See Stratemeyer, Edward L.
Bowie, Norman E. 1942- CANR-13
Earlier sketch in CA 33-36R
Bowie, Robert R(ichardson) 1909- CAP-1
Earlier sketch in CA 11-12
Bowie, Sam
See Ballard, (Willis) Todhunter
Bowie, Walter Russell 1882-1969 ..... CANR-3
Earlier sketch in CA 5-6R
Bowker, Francis E. 1917- 41-44R
Bowker, John (Westerdale) 1935- CANR-12
Earlier sketch in CA 25-28R
Bowker, Lee Harrington 1940- 108
Bowker, Margaret 1936- 25-28R
Bowker, R(obin) M(arsland) 1920- 65-68
Bowlby, John 1907- 49-52
Bowle, John (Edward) 1905-1985 ..... CANR-1
Obituary 117
Earlier sketch in CA 4R
Bowler, Jan Brett
See Brett, Jan (Churchill)
Bowler, R(eginald) Arthur 1930- 57-60
Bowles, Chester (Bliss) 1901-1986 69-72
Obituary 119
Bowles, D(elbert) Richard 1910- 33-36R
Bowles, Edmund A(ddison) 1925- 33-36R
Bowles, Ella Shannon 1886-1975
Obituary 57-60
Bowles, Frank H(amilton) 1907-1975 .....15-16R
Obituary 57-60
Bowles, George A., Jr. 1924(?)-1986
Obituary 118
Bowles, Gordon Townsend 1904- CAP-1
Earlier sketch in CA 11-12
Bowles, Jane (Sydney) 1917-1973 ..... CAP-2
Obituary 41-44R
Earlier sketch in CA 19-20
See also CLC 3
Bowles, John 1938- 106
Bowles, Kerwin
See Abeles, Elvin
Bowles, Norma L(ouise) 77-80
Bowles, Paul (Frederick) 1910- CANR-19
Earlier sketches in CA 4R, CANR-1
See also CAAS 1
See also DLB 5, 6
See also CLC 1, 2, 19
Bowles, Samuel III 1826-1878 ..... DLB-43
Bowley, Rex Lyon 1925- 103
Bowling, Ann (Patricia) 1951- 113
Bowling, Jackson M(ichael) 1934- 7-8R
Bowman, Albert Hall 1921- 41-44R
Bowman, Alfred C(onner) 1904-1982 117
Bowman, Bob
See Bowman, Robert T.
Bowman, Bruce 1938- 65-68
Bowman, Clell Edgar 1904- 105
Bowman, David J. 1919- 9-10R
Bowman, Derek 1931- 102
Bowman, Frank Paul 1927- 33-36R
Bowman, Henry A(delbert) 1903- CAP-1
Earlier sketch in CA 13-14
Bowman, Herbert E(ugene) 1917- 65-68
Bowman, James Cloyd 1880-1961 97-100
See also SATA 23
Bowman, Jeanne
See Blocklinger, Peggy O'More
Bowman, John S(tewart) 1931- CANR-19
Earlier sketches in CA 9-10R, CANR-5
See also SATA 16
Bowman, John Wick 1894- CANR-6
Earlier sketch in CA 4R
Bowman, Karl M. 1888-1973 Obituary 41-44R
Bowman, Kathleen (Gill) 1942- 69-72
See also SATA 40
Bowman, Larry G(ene) 1935- Brief entry 115
Bowman, LeRoy 1887-1971 Obituary 33-36R
Bowman, Locke E., Jr. 1927- CANR-2
Earlier sketch in CA 7-8R
Bowman, Marcelle 1914- 25-28R
Bowman, Mary D. 1924- 25-28R
Bowman, Mary Jean 1908- 33-36R
Bowman, Ned A(lan) 1932- 41-44R
Bowman, Paul Hoover 1914- 33-36R
Bowman, Peter 1917(?)-1985 Obituary 114
Bowman, Raymond Albert 1903-1979
Obituary 89-92
Bowman, Robert 1928- 25-28R
Bowman, Robert T. 1910- 73-76
Bowman, Sylvia E(dmonia) 1914- 1R
Bowman, Ward S(imon), Jr. 1911- 49-52
Bowmer, Angus L(ivingston) 1904-1979
Obituary 85-88
Bowne, Ford
See Brown, Forrest
Bowood, Richard
See Daniell, Albert Scott
Bowra, (Cecil) Maurice 1898-1971 ..... CANR-2
Obituary 29-32R
Earlier sketch in CA 4R
Bowring, Richard (John) 1947- 114
Bowser, Eileen 1928- CANR-11
Earlier sketch in CA 69-72
Bowser, Frederick P(ark) 1937- 49-52
Bowser, Joan
See Bowser, Pearl
Bowser, Pearl 1931- CANR-13
Earlier sketch in CA 33-36R
Bowskill, Derek 1928- CANR-13
Earlier sketch in CA 77-80
Bowyer, (Raymond) Chaz 1926- CANR-15
Earlier sketch in CA 93-96
Bowyer, John W(alter) 1921- 37-40R
Bowyer, Mathew J(ustice) 1926- CANR-13
Earlier sketch in CA 37-40R
Box, Edgar
See Vidal, Gore
Box, Sydney 1907-1983 Obituary 109
Boxer, Charles Ralph 1904- 102
Boxerman, David Samuel 1945- 61-64
Boxman
See Chambliss, William J(oseph)
Boy, Angelo V(ictor) 1929- 69-72
Boyajian, Cecile
See Starr, Cecile
Boyarsky, Bill 1936- 25-28R
Boyce, (Joseph) Chris(topher) 1943- 73-76
Boyce, David George 1942- 103
Boyce, George A(rthur) 1898- 53-56
See also SATA 19
Boyce, Gray Cowan 1899- 5-6R
Boyce, Joseph Nelson 1937- 102
Boyce, Richard Fyfe 1896-1985 69-72
Obituary 116
Boyce, Ronald R(eed) 1931- CANR-18
Earlier sketches in CA 11-12R, CANR-3
Boycott, Desmond (Lionel) Morse
See Morse-Boycott, Desmond (Lionel)
Boyd, Alamo
See Bosworth, Allan R(ucker)
Boyd, Andrew (Kirk Henry) 1920- 1R
Boyd, Ann S.
See Schoonmaker, Ann
Boyd, Anne Morris 1884-1974 Obituary 113
Boyd, Beverly M(ary) 1925- 69-72
Boyd, Bob
See Boyd, Robert T(hompson)
Boyd, Carolyn Patricia 1944- 112
Boyd, Carse
See Stacton, David (Derek)
Boyd, Dean (Wallace) 5-6R
Boyd, E(lizabeth) 1904(?)-1974 Obituary ..53-56
Boyd, Edward M. 1927- 120
Boyd, Frank
See Kane, Frank
Boyd, Harper W(hite), Jr. 1917- 15-16R
Boyd, Herb 1938- 110
Boyd, J(ohn) Francis 1910- 7-8R
Boyd, Jack 1932- 49-52
Boyd, James 1888-1944 ..... DLB-9
Boyd, James M(oore) 1919- 33-36R
Boyd, James S(terling) 1917- 49-52
Boyd, John
See Upchurch, Boyd
See also DLB 8
Boyd, John D. 1916- 25-28R
Boyd, Julian P(arks) 1903-1980 65-68
Obituary 97-100
Boyd, Malcolm 1923- CANR-4
Earlier sketch in CA 5-6R
Boyd, Martin a Beckett 1893- CAP-1
Earlier sketch in CA 13-14
Boyd, Maurice 1921- 11-12R
Boyd, Mildred Worthy 1921- 17-18R
Boyd, Myron F(enton) 1909-1978 .....41-44R
Boyd, Nancy
See Millay, Edna St. Vincent
Boyd, Neil
See DeRosa, Peter (Clement)
Boyd, Pauline
See Schock, Pauline
Boyd, R(obert) L(ewis) F(ullarton) 1922- ...57-60
Boyd, Robert H. 1912- 53-56
Boyd, Robert S. 1928- 15-16R
Boyd, Robert T(hompson) 1914- 108
Boyd, Robin 1919- 17-18R
Boyd, Selma
See Acuff, Selma Boyd
Boyd, Shylah 1945- 61-64
Boyd, Sue Abbott 1921- CANR-14
Earlier sketch in CA 65-68
Boyd, Thomas (Alexander) 1898-1935
Brief entry 111
See also DLB 9
Boyd, Waldo T. 1918- CANR-12
Earlier sketch in CA 29-32R
See also SATA 18
Boyd, William 1885- 41-44R
Boyd, William 1952- 120
Brief entry 114
See also CLC 28
Boyd, William C(louser) 1903-1983
Obituary 109
Boyd, William Harland 1912- CANR-11
Earlier sketch in CA 69-72
Boyden, David D(odge) 1910-1986
Obituary 120
Boydston, Jo Ann 1924- 29-32R
Boyer, Brian D. 1939- 45-48
Boyer, Bruce Hatton 1946- 101
Boyer, Carl B(enjamin) 1906-1976
Obituary 65-68
Boyer, Dwight 1912- 65-68
Boyer, Elizabeth (Mary) 1913- 81-84
Boyer, Ernest LeRoy 1928- 110
Boyer, Harold W. 1908- 4R
Boyer, John (William) 1946- 103
Boyer, Mildred (Vinson) 1926- 112
Boyer, Paul Samuel 1935- CANR-18
Earlier sketches in CA 49-52, CANR-1
Boyer, Richard Edwin 1932- 23-24R
Boyer, Richard Lewis 1943- CANR-11
Earlier sketch in CA 69-72
Boyer, Richard O. 1903-1973 Obituary 45-48
Boyer, Robert
See Lake, Kenneth R(obert)
Boyer, Robert E(rnst) 1929- 41-44R
See also SATA 22
Boyer, Ruth Gasink 1913- 114
Boyer, Sophia Ames 1907(?)-1972
Obituary 37-40R
Boyer, William H(arrison) 1924- CANR-22
Earlier sketch in CA 106
Boyer, William W., (Jr.) 1923- 13-14R
Boyers, Margaret Anne 118
Boyers, Peggy
See Boyers, Margaret Anne
Boyers, Robert 1942- CANR-4
Earlier sketch in CA 53-56
Boyesen, Hjalmar Hjorth 1848-1895 ..... DLB-12
Boyington, (Gregory) Pappy 1912-1988
Obituary 124
Boykin, James H(andy) 1914- CANR-2
Earlier sketch in CA 5-6R
Boylan, Boyd
See Whiton, James Nelson
Boylan, Brian Richard 1936- 81-84
Boylan, James (Richard) 1927- CANR-16
Earlier sketches in CA 4R, CANR-1
Boylan, Leona Davis 1910- 61-64
Boylan, Lucile 1906- CAP-1
Earlier sketch in CA 11-12
Boylan, Mary 1913(?)-1984 Obituary 112
Boyle, Andrew 1923- 5-6R
Boyle, Andrew Philip More 1919- 102
Boyle, Ann (Peters) 1916- 29-32R
See also SATA 10
Boyle, Charles 1951- 113
Boyle, Deirdre 1949- 110
Boyle, Edward Charles Gurney 1923-1981
Obituary 108
Boyle, Eleanor Vere (Gordon)
1825-1916 ..... SATA-28
Boyle, Freddie M. 1915(?)-1984 Obituary ... 113
Boyle, Hal
See Boyle, Harold V(incent)
Boyle, Harold V(incent) 1911-1974 101
Obituary 89-92
Boyle, Harry Joseph 1915- CANR-7
Earlier sketch in CA 13-14R
Boyle, J(ohn) A(ndrew) 1916-1979 ..... CANR-9
Obituary 85-88
Earlier sketch in CA 61-64
Boyle, John Hunter 1930- 41-44R
Boyle, John P(hillips) 1931- Brief entry 114
Boyle, (Emily) Joyce 1901- CAP-1
Earlier sketch in CA 13-14
Boyle, Kay 1903- 15-16R
See also CAAS 1
See also DLB 4, 9, 48
See also CLC 1, 5, 19
Boyle, (C.) Kevin 1943- 123
Boyle, Mark
See Kienzle, William X(avier)
Boyle, Mary 1882(?)-1975 Obituary 53-56
Boyle, Patrick CLC-19
Boyle, Robert (Richard) 1915- 15-16R
Boyle, Robert H. 1928- CANR-12
Earlier sketch in CA 19-20R
Boyle, Samuel J. III 1920-1985 Obituary ... 118
Boyle, Sarah Patton 1906- CAP-1
Earlier sketch in CA 15-16
Boyle, Stanley E(ugene) 1927- 41-44R
Boyle, T. Coraghessan 1948- 120
See also DLBY 86
See also CLC 36
Boyle, Ted Eugene 1933- 23-24R
Boyle, Thomas 1939- 118
Boyle, Timm
See Boyle, Timothy R(obert)
Boyle, Timothy R(obert) 1953- 118
Boylen, Margaret Currier 1921-1967 ..... 3R
Obituary 103

Boyles, C(larence) S(cott), Jr. 1905- ... 3R
Boylston, Helen Dore 1895-1984 ... CANR-21
Obituary ... 113
Earlier sketch in CA 73-76
See also SATA 23, 39
Boyne, Walter J(ames) 1929- ... 107
Boynton, Lewis Delano 1909- ... CANR-6
Earlier sketch in CA 5-6R
Boynton, Peter S. 1920(?)-1971 Obituary ... 104
Boynton, Robert W(hitney) 1921-
Brief entry ... 117
Boynton, Sandra 1953- ... SATA-38
Boynton, Searles Roland 1926- ... 77-80
Boyum, Joy Gould 1934- ... 33-36R
Boyum, Keith O(rel) 1945- ... 102
Boz
See Dickens, Charles (John Huffam)
Bozarth-Campbell, Alla (Linda Renee)
1947- ... 105
Boze, Arthur Phillip 1945- ... 57-60
Bozeman, Adda B(ruemmer) 1908- ... CANR-3
Earlier sketch in CA 5-6R
Bozeman, Theodore Dwight 1942- ... 85-88
Braasch, William Frederick 1878- ... CAP-2
Earlier sketch in CA 29-32
Brabazon, James
See Seth-Smith, Leslie James
Brabb, George J(acob) 1925- ... 41-44R
Brabec, Barbara 1937- ... CANR-15
Earlier sketch in CA 93-96
Brabson, George Dana 1900- ... CAP-1
Earlier sketch in CA 19-20
Brace, Edward Roy 1936- ... CANR-19
Earlier sketch in CA 102
Brace, Geoffrey (Arthur) 1930- ... CANR-11
Earlier sketch in CA 69-72
Brace, Gerald Warner 1901-1978 ... 13-14R
Obituary ... 81-84
Brace, Richard Munthe 1915-1977 ... CANR-15
Obituary ... 69-72
Earlier sketch in CA 3R
Brace, Timothy
See Pratt, Theodore
Braceairdle, Cyril 1920- ... 45-48
Bracegirdle, Brian 1933- ... 101
Braceland, Francis J(ames) 1900-1985
Obituary ... 115
Bracewell, Ronald N(ewbold) 1921- ... 57-60
Bracewell-Milnes, (John) Barry 1931- ... CANR-13
Earlier sketch in CA 33-36R
Bracey, Howard E(dwin) 1905- ... 13-14R
Bracey, John H(enry, Jr.) 1941- ... 29-32R
Bracher, Frederick (George) 1905- ... 111
Bracher, Karl Dietrich 1922- ... CANR-17
Earlier sketches in CA 45-48, CANR-1
Bracher, Marjory (Louise) 1906- ... CAP-1
Earlier sketch in CA 15-16
Brack, Harold Arthur 1923- ... 17-18R
Brack, O M, Jr. 1938- ... 41-44R
Brack, Vektris
See Humphrys, Leslie George
Brackbill, Yvonne 1928- ... 23-24R
Bracken, Dorothy K(endall) ... 23-24R
Bracken, Joseph Andrew 1930- ... 37-40R
Bracken, Paul 1948- ... 115
Bracken, Peg 1920- ... CANR-6
Earlier sketch in CA 4R
Brackenbury, Alison 1953- ... DLB-40
Brackenridge, Hugh Henry
1748-1816 ... DLB-11, 37
Brackenridge, R(obert) Douglas 1932- ... 101
Bracker, Jon 1936- ... 17-18R
Brackett, Charles 1892-1969 Obituary ... 113
See also DLB 26
Brackett, Leigh (Douglass) 1915-1978 ... CANR-1
Obituary ... 77-80
Earlier sketch in CA 3R
See also DLB 8, 26
Brackman, Arnold C(harles) 1923-1983 ... CANR-2
Obituary ... 111
Earlier sketch in CA 5-6R
See also AITN 1
Brackney, William (Henry) 1948- ... 123
Bracy, William 1915- ... 61-64
Bradbrook, M(uriel) C(lara) 1909- ... CANR-23
Earlier sketches in CA 13-14R, CANR-7
Bradburn, Norman M. 1933- ... CANR-13
Earlier sketch in CA 37-40R
Bradburne, E(lizabeth) S. 1915- ... 25-28R
Bradbury, Bianca 1908- ... CANR-5
Earlier sketch in CA 13-14R
See also SATA 3
Bradbury, Dorothy E(dith) 1902-1984
Obituary ... 113
Bradbury, Edward P.
See Moorcock, Michael (John)
Bradbury, John M(ason) 1908-1969 ... CAP-1
Earlier sketch in CA 15-16
Bradbury, Katharine L(orraine) 1946- ... 111
Bradbury, Malcolm (Stanley) 1932- ... CANR-1
Earlier sketch in CA 2R
See also DLB 14
See also CLC 32
Bradbury, Parnell 1904- ... 13-14R
Bradbury, Peggy 1930- ... 65-68
Bradbury, Ray (Douglas) 1920- ... CANR-2
Earlier sketch in CA 4R
See also SATA 11
See also DLB 2, 8
See also CLC 1, 3, 10, 15, 42
See also AITN 1, 2
Braddock, Joseph (Edward) 1902-
Brief entry ... 117
Braddock, Richard R(eed) 1920-1974 ... 1R
Obituary ... 103
Braddon, George
See Milkomane, George Alexis
Milkomanovich
Braddon, Mary Elizabeth 1837(?)-1915
Brief entry ... 108
See also DLB 18
Braddon, Russell (Reading) 1921- ... CANR-2
Earlier sketch in CA 4R
Braddy, Haldeen 1908-1980 ... 17-18R
Obituary ... 101
Brade-Birks, S(tanley) Graham 1887- ... CAP-1
Earlier sketch in CA 15-16
Braden, Charles Samuel 1887- ... 5-6R
Braden, Irene A.
See Hoadley, Irene Braden
Braden, Spruille 1894-1978 Obituary ... 115
Braden, Thomas (Wardell) 1918-
Brief entry ... 113
Braden, Tom
See Braden, Thomas
Braden, Waldo W(arder) 1911- ... CANR-5
Earlier sketch in CA 7-8R
Braden, William 1930- ... 23-24R
Bradfield, James McComb 1917- ... 5-6R
Bradfield, Jolly Roger
See Bradfield, Roger
Bradfield, Nancy 1913- ... 29-32R
Bradfield, Richard 1896- ... CAP-2
Earlier sketch in CA 23-24
Bradfield, Roger 1924- ... 19-20R
Bradford, Adam, M.D.
See Wassersug, Joseph D.
Bradford, Alex 1927-1978 Obituary ... 112
Bradford, Andrew 1686-1742 ... DLB-43
Bradford, Ann (Liddell) 1917- Brief entry ... 116
See also SATA 38
Bradford, Barbara Taylor 1933- ... 89-92
Bradford, Benjamin 1925- ... 85-88
Bradford, David F(rantz) 1939- ... 124
Bradford, Dennis E(arle) 1946- ... 118
Bradford, Ernle (Dusgate Selby)
1922-1986 ... 101
Obituary ... 119
Bradford, Gamaliel 1863-1932 ... DLB-17
Bradford, James C(hapin) 1945- ... 111
Bradford, John 1749-1830 ... DLB-43
Bradford, Karleen 1936- ... 112
See also SATA 48
Bradford, Leland P(owers) 1905- ... CANR-9
Earlier sketch in CA 13-14R
Bradford, Leroy 1922- ... 105
Bradford, Lois J(ean) 1936- ... 104
See also SATA 36
Bradford, M(elvin) E(ustace) 1934- ... CANR-13
Earlier sketch in CA 77-80
Bradford, Patience Andrewes 1918- ... 33-36R
Bradford, Peter Amory 1942- ... 61-64
Bradford, Reed H(oward) 1912- ... 49-52
Bradford, Richard (Roark) 1932- ... CANR-2
Earlier sketch in CA 49-52
Bradford, Richard H(eadlee) 1938- ... 89-92
Bradford, Robert W(hitmore) 1918- ... 77-80
Bradford, Roy Hamilton 1920- ... 109
Bradford, Sax(ton) 1907-1966 ... 4R
Bradford, Will
See Paine, Lauran (Bosworth)
Bradford, William 1590-1657 ... DLB-24, 30
Bradford, William C(astle) 1910- ... 9-10R
Bradford, William III 1719-1791 ... DLB-43
Bradlaugh, Charles 1833-1891 ... DLB-57
Bradlee, Benjamin C(rowninshield) 1921- ... 61-64
See also AITN 2
Bradlee, Frederic 1920- ... 21-22R
Bradley, Alfred 1925- ... 105
Bradley, Bert E(dward) 1926- ... 41-44R
Bradley, Bill
See Bradley, William Warren
Bradley, Brigitte L(ooke) 1924- ... 37-40R
Bradley, C. Paul 1918- ... 106
Bradley, Concho
See Paine, Lauran (Bosworth)
Bradley, David (Henry, Jr.) 1950- ... 104
See also DLB 33
See also CLC 23
Bradley, David G. 1916- ... 13-14R
Bradley, Duane
See Sanborn, Duane
Bradley, Ed 1911(?)-1983 Obituary ... 110
Bradley, Ed(ward R.) 1941- ... 113
Brief entry ... 108
Bradley, Erwin S(tanley) 1906- ... CAP-2
Earlier sketch in CA 33-36
Bradley, Harold Whitman 1903- ... 33-36R
Bradley, Hassell 1930- ... 65-68
Bradley, Helen G(enevieve) 1932- ... 112
Bradley, Ian Campbell 1950- ... 103
Bradley, James V(andiver) 1924- ... 37-40R
Bradley, John (Francis Nejez) 1930- ... CANR-10
Earlier sketch in CA 25-28R
Bradley, John Lewis 1917- ... 29-32R
Bradley, Joseph F(rancis) 1917- ... 23-24R
Bradley, Kenneth (Granville) 1904- ... CAP-1
Earlier sketch in CA 13-14
Bradley, Marion Zimmer 1930- ... CANR-7
Earlier sketch in CA 57-60
See also DLB 8
See also CLC 30
Bradley, Marjorie D. 1931- ... 25-28R
Bradley, Matt 1947- ... 105
Bradley, Melanie (Rose) Choukas
See Choukas-Bradley, Melanie (Rose)
Bradley, Michael
See Blumberg, Gary
Bradley, Omar Nelson 1893-1981
Obituary ... 103
Bradley, Preston 1888-1983 Obituary ... 110
Bradley, R. C. 1929- ... CANR-14
Earlier sketch in CA 33-36R
Bradley, Ritamary 1916- ... 49-52
Bradley, Robert A(ustin) 1917- ... 21-22R
Bradley, Sam(uel McKee) 1917- ... 21-22R
Bradley, (Edward) Sculley 1897- ... 89-92
Bradley, Van Allen 1913-1984 ... 37-40R
Obituary ... 114
Bradley, Virginia 1912- ... CANR-8
Earlier sketch in CA 61-64
See also SATA 23
Bradley, William 1934- ... 45-48
Bradley, William Aspenwall 1878-1939
Brief entry ... 107
See also DLB 4
Bradley, William L(ee) 1918- ... 23-24R
Bradley, William Warren 1943- ... 101
Bradlow, Edna Rom ... CAP-1
Earlier sketch in CA 9-10
Bradlow, Frank R(osslyn) 1913- ... CANR-13
Earlier sketches in CA 9-10, CAP-1
Bradner, Enos 1892-1984 ... 57-60
Obituary ... 111
Bradshaw, Brendan 1937- ... 73-76
Bradshaw, George 1909(?)-1973
Obituary ... 45-48
Bradshaw, Gillian (Marucha) 1956- ... 103
Bradshaw, Jon (Wayne) 1937-1986
Obituary ... 121
Bradshaw, Terry (Paxton) 1948- ... 111
Bradshaw, Thornton F(rederick) 1917- ... 108
Bradstreet, Anne 1612(?)-1672 ... DLB-24
See also CDALB 1640-1865
Bradstreet, Vallerie
See Roby, Mary Linn
Bradt, A(cken) Gordon 1896-1983 ... 57-60
Obituary ... 110
Bradway, John S(aeger) 1890- ... CAP-2
Earlier sketch in CA 33-36
Bradwell, James
See Kent, Arthur William Charles
Brady, Alexander 1896-1985 Obituary ... 117
Brady, Charles Andrew 1912- ... 5-6R
Brady, Darlene A(nn) 1951- ... 102
Brady, David W(illiam) 1940- Brief entry ... 114
Brady, Esther Wood 1905-1987 ... 93-96
Obituary ... 123
See also SATA 31
Brady, Frank 1924-1986 ... 15-16R
Obituary ... 120
Brady, Frank 1934- ... CANR-9
Earlier sketch in CA 61-64
Brady, Gene P(aul) 1927- ... 107
Brady, George Stuart 1887-1977
Obituary ... 73-76
Brady, Gerald Peter 1929- ... 5-6R
Brady, Ignatius Charles 1911- ... 113
Brady, Irene 1943- ... CANR-20
Earlier sketch in CA 33-36R
See also SATA 4
Brady, James Winston 1928- ... CANR-21
Earlier sketch in CA 101
Brady, Jane 1934- Brief entry ... 113
Brady, John 1942- ... CANR-10
Earlier sketch in CA 65-68
Brady, John Paul 1928- ... CANR-5
Earlier sketch in CA 13-14R
Brady, Kristin 1949- ... 109
Brady, Leo 1917-1984 ... 69-72
Obituary ... 114
Brady, Lillian 1902- ... 105
See also SATA 28
Brady, Mary Lou 1937- ... 106
Brady, Maureen 1943- ... 112
Brady, Maxine L. 1941- ... 69-72
Brady, Michael 1928- ... 93-96
Brady, Nicholas
See Levinson, Leonard
Brady, Peter
See Daniels, Norman
Brady, Sally Ryder 1939- ... 103
Brady, Terence 1939- ... 106
Braenne, Berit 1918- ... 21-22R
Braestrup, Carl Bjorn 1897-1982 Obituary ... 107
Braestrup, Peter 1929- ... 97-100
Braff, Allan James 1930- ... 108
Braganti, Nancy (Sue) 1941- ... 117
Bragdon, Clifford R(ichardson) 1940- ... 57-60
Bragdon, Elspeth MacDuffie 1897- ... CANR-5
Earlier sketch in CA 5-6R
See also SATA 6
Bragdon, Henry Wilkinson 1906-1980 ... CANR-3
Obituary ... 97-100
Earlier sketch in CA 7-8R
Bragdon, Lillian Jacot ... 73-76
See also SATA 24
Bragg, Arthur N(orris) 1897- ... CAP-1
Earlier sketch in CA 17-18
Bragg, Bill
See Bragg, William Fredrick, Jr.
Bragg, Dobby
See Sykes, Roosevelt
Bragg, Mabel Caroline 1870-1945 ... SATA-24
Bragg, Melvyn 1939- ... CANR-10
Earlier sketch in CA 57-60
See also DLB 14
See also CLC 10
Bragg, Michael 1948- ... SATA-46
Bragg, Richard Geoffrey 1909- ... 121
Bragg, Sir W. H.
See Bragg, William Henry
Bragg, Sir William
See Bragg, William Henry
Bragg, Sir William Henry
See Bragg, William Henry
Bragg, William Fredrick, Jr. 1922- ... 109
Bragg, William Henry 1862-1942
Brief entry ... 123
Bragg, William Lawrence 1890-1971
Obituary ... 115
Braggin, Mary Vetterling
See Vetterling-Braggin, Mary (Katherine)
Braham, Allan (John Witney) 1937- ... 105
Braham, Randolph Lewis 1922- ... CANR-19
Earlier sketches in CA 3R, CANR-5
Brahms, Caryl
See Abrahams, Doris Caroline
Brahs, Stuart J(ohn) 1940- ... 57-60
Brahtz, John F(rederick) Peel 1918- ... 73-76
Braider, Donald 1923-1976 ... CAP-2
Obituary ... 65-68
Earlier sketch in CA 33-36
Braidwood, Robert John 1907- ... 108
Brailsford, Frances
See Wosmek, Frances
Braimah, Joseph Adam 1916- ... 61-64
Braiman, Susan 1943- ... 97-100
Brain, George B(ernard) 1920- ... 41-44R
Brain, J(oy) B(lundell) 1926- ... 118
Brain, James Lewton
See Lewton-Brain, James
Brain, Joseph J. 1920- ... 13-14R
Brain, Robert 1933- ... 73-76
Brainard, Harry Gray 1907- ... 1R
Brainard, Joe 1942- ... CANR-12
Earlier sketch in CA 65-68
Braine, John (Gerard) 1922-1986 ... CANR-1
Obituary ... 120
Earlier sketch in CA 2R
See also DLB 15
See also DLBY 86
See also CLC 1, 3, 41
Brainerd, Barron 1928- ... 33-36R
Brainerd, Charles Jon 1944- ... 103
Brainerd, John W(hiting) 1918- ... 57-60
Braithwaite, Althea 1940- ... CANR-18
Earlier sketch in CA 97-100
See also SATA 23
Braithwaite, (Eustace) E(dward) R(icardo)
1920- ... 106
Braithwaite, Kenneth James
See Barrow, Kenneth
Braithwaite, Max 1911- ... 93-96
Braithwaite, William Stanley (Beaumont)
1878-1962 ... DLB-50, 54
Brake, Mike 1936- ... 93-96
Brakel, Samuel J(ohannes) 1943- ... 33-36R
Brakhage, Stan 1933- ... CANR-15
Earlier sketch in CA 41-44R
Bralver, Eleanor 1913- ... 97-100
Braly, Malcolm 1925-1980 ... CANR-12
Obituary ... 97-100
Earlier sketch in CA 19-20R
Bram, Elizabeth 1948- ... CANR-9
Earlier sketch in CA 65-68
See also SATA 30
Bram, Joseph 1904-1974 Obituary ... 110
Bramall, Eric 1927- ... 9-10R
Braman, Sandra 1951- ... 114
Bramann, Jorn K(arl) 1938- ... 119
Brambell, Wilfrid 1912- ... 113
Bramble, Forbes 1939- ... 89-92
Brameld, Theodore (Burghard Hurt)
1904-1987 ... 17-18R
Obituary ... 123
Bramer, Jennie (Perkins) 1900- ... CAP-1
Earlier sketch in CA 13-14
Bramer, John C(onrad) Jr. 1924- ... 4R
Bramesco, Norton J. 1924- ... 106
Bramlett, John
See Pierce, John Leonard, Jr.
Brammell, P(aris) Roy 1900- ... 65-68
Brammer, Lawrence M(artin) 1922- ... 13-14R
Brammer, William 1930(?)-1978
Obituary ... 77-80
See also CLC 31
Brams, Stanley Howard 1910- ... 11-12R
Brams, Steven J(ohn) 1940- ... CANR-10
Earlier sketch in CA 61-64
Bramsch, Joan 1936- ... 122
Bramson, Leon 1930- ... CANR-4
Earlier sketch in CA 3R
Bramson, Robert M(ark) 1925- ... 108
Bramwell, Charlotte
See Kimbro, John M.
Bramwell, Dana G. 1948- ... 57-60
Bramwell, James Guy 1911- ... 9-10R
Bramwell-Booth, Catherine 1883-1987
Obituary ... 123
Branagan, Thomas 1774-1843 ... DLB-37
Brana-Shute, Gary 1945- ... 111
Branca, Albert A. 1916- ... 15-16R
Brancafort, Benito 1934- ... 37-40R
Brancati, Vitaliano 1907-1954 Brief entry ... 109
See also TCLC 12
Brancato, Gilda 1949- ... 107
Brancato, Robin F(idler) 1936- ... CANR-11
Earlier sketch in CA 69-72
See also SATA 23
See also CLC 35
Branch, Alan E(dward) 1933- ... 105
Branch, Daniel Paulk 1931- ... 17-18R
Branch, Edgar Marquess 1913- ... 13-14R
Branch, Harold F(rancis) 1894-1966 ... 7-8R
Branch, Kip 1947- ... 108
Branch, Mary 1910- ... CANR-10
Earlier sketch in CA 25-28R
Branch, Melville C(ampbell) 1913- ... CANR-14
Earlier sketch in CA 41-44R
Branch, William (Blackwell) 1927- ... CANR-16
Earlier sketch in CA 81-84
Brand, C(larence) E(ugene) 1895- ... CAP-2
Earlier sketch in CA 23-24

Brand, Carl F(remont) 1892- 15-16R
Brand, Charles M(acy) 1932- 23-24R
Brand, Charles Peter 1923- 15-16R
Brand, Christianna
See Lewis, Mary (Christianna Milne)
Brand, Clay
See Norwood, Victor G(eorge) C(harles)
Brand, Eugene L(ouis) 1931- CANR-8
Earlier sketch in CA 61-64
Brand, Garrison
See Brandner, Gary
Brand, Gerd 1921- Brief entry 113
Brand, Irene B. 1929- 124
Brand, Jeanne L(aurel) 1919- 15-16R
Brand, Max
See Faust, Frederick (Shiller)
Brand, Millen 1906-1980 ....21-22R
Obituary 97-100
See also CLC 7
Brand, Myles 1942- 37-40R
Brand, Oscar 1920- CANR-4
Earlier sketch in CA 4R
Brand, Peter
See Larsen, Erling
Brand, Sandra 1918- 85-88
Brand, Stewart 1938- 81-84
See also AITN 1
Brand, Susan
See Roper, Susan Bonthron
Brandabur, Edward 1930- 41-44R
Brande, Ralph T. 1921- 25-28R
Brandeis, Louis Dembitz 1856-1941
Brief entry 118
Brandel, Arthur Meyer 1913(?)-1980
Obituary 102
Brandel, Marc 1919- 108
Brandell, (Erik) Gunnar 1916- CANR-20
Earlier sketch in CA 103
Branden, Barbara CLC-44
Branden, Nathaniel 1930- 33-36R
Branden, Victoria (Fremlin) 101
Brandenberg, Aliki Liacouras 1929- CANR-12
Earlier sketches in CA 4R, CANR-4
See also SATA 2, 35
Brandenberg, Franz 1932- CANR-12
Earlier sketch in CA 29-32R
See also SATA 8, 35
Brandenburg, David J(ohn) 1920-1987
Obituary 123
Brandenburg, Frank R(alph) 1926- 13-14R
Brander, Michael (William) 1924- CANR-7
Earlier sketch in CA 53-56
Brandes, Georg (Morris Cohen)
1842-1927 Brief entry 105
See also TCLC 10
Brandes, Joseph 1928- 5-6R
Brandes, Norman Scott 1923- 57-60
Brandes, Paul D(ickerson) 1920- CANR-2
Earlier sketch in CA 45-48
Brandewyne, (Mary) Rebecca (Wadsworth)
1955- CANR-23
Earlier sketch in CA 107
Brandhorst, Carl T(heodore) 1898- CAP-2
Earlier sketch in CA 25-28
See also SATA 23
Brandi, John 1943- CANR-12
Earlier sketch in CA 73-76
Brandis, Marianne 1938- 117
Brandner, Gary 1933- CANR-17
Earlier sketches in CA 45-48, CANR-1
Brandon, Beatrice
See Krepps, Robert W(ilson)
Brandon, Brumsic, Jr. 1927- 61-64
See also SATA 9
Brandon, Curt
See Bishop, Curtis (Kent)
Brandon, Dick H. 1934-1981 .... CANR-10
Earlier sketch in CA 19-20R
Brandon, Donald (Wayne) 1926- 69-72
Brandon, Dorothy 1899(?)-1977 Obituary ..69-72
Brandon, Frances Sweeney 1916- 9-10R
Brandon, Frank
See Bulmer, (Henry) Kenneth
Brandon, (Oscar) Henry 1916- 49-52
Brandon, James Rodger 1927- CANR-11
Earlier sketch in CA 69-72
Brandon, Jay (Robert) 1953- 119
Brandon, Joe
See Davis, Robert P.
Brandon, John G(ordon) 1879(?)-1941
Brief entry 112
Brandon, Johnny 105
Brandon, Joyce A(lmeta) 1938- 118
Brandon, Robert Joseph 1918- 105
Brandon, Robin
See Brandon, Robert Joseph
Brandon, S(amuel) G(eorge) F(rederick)
1907-1971 102
Brandon, Shelia
See Rayner, Claire (Berenice)
Brandon, William 1914- 77-80
Brandon-Cox, Hugh 1917- 93-96
Brandreth, Gyles 1948- 65-68
See also SATA 28
Brandreth, Henry R(enaud) T(urner)
1914-1984 Obituary 114
Brandstatter, A(rthur) F. 1914- 107
Brandt, Alvin G. 1922- 13-14R
Brandt, Anthony 1936- 69-72
Brandt, Bill 1904(?)-1983 Obituary 111
Brandt, Carol 1904-1984 Obituary 114
Brandt, Catharine 1905- 106
See also SATA 40
Brandt, Floyd S(tanley) 1930- 21-22R
Brandt, Harvey
See Edwards, William B(ennett)
Brandt, Jane Lewis 1915- 97-100
Brandt, Keith
See Sabin, Louis
Brandt, Leslie F. 1919- CANR-23
Earlier sketches in CA 23-24R, CANR-8
Brandt, Lucile (Long Strayer) 1900- CANR-13
Earlier sketch in CA 61-64
Brandt, Nat
See Brandt, Nathan Henry, Jr.
Brandt, Nathan Henry, Jr. 1929- CANR-18
Earlier sketch in CA 102
Brandt, Rex(ford Elson) 1914- CANR-5
Earlier sketch in CA 13-14R
Brandt, Richard B(ooker) 1910-
Brief entry 114
Brandt, Richard M(artin) 1922- 33-36R
Brandt, Roger
See Crawford, William (Elbert)
Brandt, Sue R(eading) 1916- 25-28R
Brandt, Tom
See Dewey, Thomas B.
Brandt, Vincent S. R. 1924- 37-40R
Brandt, William E(dward) 1920- 5-6R
Brandt, Willy 1913- 85-88
Brandt, Yanna Kroyt 1933- 104
Brandts, Robert (Percival) 1930- 69-72
Brandwein, Chaim N(aftali) 1920- 23-24R
Brandys, Marian 1912- 57-60
Branegan, James Augustus III 1950- 124
Branfield, John (Charles) 1931- CANR-14
Earlier sketch in CA 41-44R
See also SATA 11
Branfoot, Gwynneth
See Holder, Gwynneth
Branick, Vincent P(atrick) 1941- 113
Branigan, Keith 1940- 124
Branin, M(anlif) Lelyn 1901- 85-88
Branley, Franklyn M(ansfield) 1915- CANR-14
Earlier sketch in CA 33-36R
See also SATA 4
See also CLC 21
See also CLR 13
Brann, Eva T(oni) H(elene) 1929- 93-96
Brannan, Robert Louis 1927- 21-22R
Brannen, Noah S(amuel) 1924- CANR-11
Earlier sketch in CA 25-28R
Brannen, Ted R. 1924- 17-18R
Branner, Hans Christian 1903-1966 97-100
Obituary 89-92
Branner, R(obert) 1927-1973 .... CANR-3
Obituary 45-48
Earlier sketch in CA 5-6R
Brannigan, Bill
See Brannigan, William
Brannigan, William 1936- 65-68
Brannon, William T. 1906- CAP-1
Earlier sketch in CA 15-16
Branscomb, (Bennett) Harvie 1894- 106
Branscum, Robbie 1937- CANR-8
Earlier sketch in CA 61-64
See also SATA 23
Bransford, Kent Jackson 1953- 97-100
Bransom, (John) Paul 1885-1979 ..... SATA-43
Branson, David 1909- CANR-21
Earlier sketch in CA 41-44R
Branson, Margaret Stimmann 1922- CANR-1
Earlier sketch in CA 49-52
Branston, (Ronald Victor) Brian 1914- 53-56
Brant, Charles S(tanford) 1919- 25-28R
Brant, Irving (Newton) 1885-1976 ....9-10R
Obituary 69-72
Brant, Lewis
See Rowland, D(onald) S(ydney)
Brantley, Cynthia Louise 1943- 109
Branyan, Robert L(ester) 1930- 104
Branzburg, Paul M(arshal) 1941- 73-76
Braque, Georges 1882-1963 Obituary 112
Brasch, Charles (Orwell) 1909-1973 114
Obituary 104
Brasch, Ila Wales 1945- 57-60
Brasch, James D(aniel) 1929- 116
Brasch, Rudolph 1912- CANR-8
Earlier sketch in CA 21-22R
Brasch, Walter Milton 1945- CANR-23
Earlier sketches in CA 57-60, CANR-6
Brasher, Christopher William 1928- 7-8R
Brasher, N(orman) H(enry) 1922- 25-28R
Brasher, Nell 1912- CANR-7
Earlier sketch in CA 61-64
Brasher, Thomas L(owber) 1912- 69-72
Brashers, H(oward) C(harles) 1930- CANR-8
Earlier sketch in CA 7-8R
Brashler, William 1947- CANR-2
Earlier sketch in CA 45-48
Brasier, Virginia 1910- 61-64
Brasier-Creagh, Patrick
See Creagh, Patrick
Brasnett, Bertrand R(ippington)
1893-1988 Obituary 124
Brason, Gill 1942- 112
Brass, Paul Richard 1936- 17-18R
Brassai
See Halasz, Gyula
Brasselle, Keefe 1923(?)-1981 Obituary 104
Brassens, Georges 1921-1981 Obituary 105
Brasseur, Pierre
See Espinasse, Albert
Braswell, George Wilbur, Jr. 1936- 112
Brater, Enoch 1944- 122
Brathwaite, Edward (Kamau) 1930- CANR-11
Earlier sketch in CA 25-28R
See also CLC 11
Brathwaite, Errol (Freeman) 1924- CANR-11
Earlier sketches in CA 57-60, CANR-7
Brathwaite, Sheila R. 1914- 25-28R
Bratt, Elmer Clark 1901-1970 .... 3R
Obituary 103
Bratt, John H(arold) 1909- CANR-9
Earlier sketch in CA 19-20R
Bratter, Herbert Max 1900-1976 Obituary ..65-68
Bratter, Thomas Edward 1939- 120
Brattgarg, Helge (Axel Kristian) 1920- 7-8R
Bratton, Fred Gladstone 1896-19(?) CAP-1
Earlier sketch in CA 11-12
Bratton, Helen 1899- CAP-2
Earlier sketch in CA 23-24
See also SATA 4
Brattstrom, Bayard H(olmes) 1929- 57-60
Braude, Benjamin 1945- 111
Braude, Jacob M(orton) 1896-1970 ..... CANR-5
Earlier sketch in CA 5-6R
Braude, Michael 1909-1986 Obituary 121
Braude, Michael 1936- 17-18R
See also SATA 23
Braude, William Gordon 1907- 33-36R
Braudel, Fernand (Paul) 1902-1985 .... CANR-14
Obituary 117
Earlier sketch in CA 93-96
Braudy, Leo 1941- 37-40R
Braudy, Susan (Orr) 1941- CANR-10
Earlier sketch in CA 65-68
Brauer, Carl M(alcolm) 1946- 85-88
Brauer, George C(harles), Jr. 1925-
Brief entry 113
Brauer, Jerald C(arl) 1921- CANR-13
Earlier sketch in CA 33-36R
Brauer, Kinley J(ules) 1935- 21-22R
Brault, Gerard Joseph 1929- CANR-3
Earlier sketch in CA 7-8R
Brault, Jacques 1933- DLB-53
Braun, Armin C(harles John) 1911-1986
Obituary 120
Braun, Arthur E. 1876-1976 Obituary 69-72
Braun, Edward 1936- Brief entry 115
Braun, Eric 1921- 102
Braun, Henry 1930- 25-28R
Braun, Hugh 1902- 25-28R
Braun, J(oachim) Werner 1914-1972
Obituary 37-40R
Braun, John R(ichard) 1928- 33-36R
Braun, Lev 1913- 41-44R
Braun, Richard Emil 1934- 9-10R
Braun, Sidney D(avid) 1912- CANR-10
Earlier sketch in CA 65-68
Braun, Theodore E. D. 1933- CANR-7
Earlier sketch in CA 15-16R
Braun, Thomas (Felix Rudry Gerhart)
1935- 115
Braunburg, Rudolf 1924- 109
Braund, Hal
See Braund, Harold
Braund, Harold 1913-1988 61-64
Obituary 124
Braunrot, Bruno 1936- 114
Braunstein, Daniel N(orman) 1938- 111
Braunstein, Mark M(athew) 1951- 113
Braunthal, Alfred 1898(?)-1980 Obituary ..93-96
Braunthal, Gerard 1923- 15-16R
Braunthal, Julius 1891-1972 .... CAP-2
Earlier sketch in CA 23-24
Brautigan, Richard (Gary) 1935-1984 53-56
Obituary 113
See also DLB 2, 5
See also DLBY 80, 84
See also CLC 1, 3, 5, 9, 12, 34, 42
Brav, Stanley R(osenbaum) 1908- 25-28R
Braverman, Harry 1920-1976 53-56
Obituary 69-72
Braverman, Kate 1950- 89-92
Bravmann, Rene A. 1939- 85-88
Brawer, Florence B(lum) 1922- 37-40R
Brawley, Ernest 1937- 53-56
Brawley, Paul L(eroy) 1942- 73-76
Brawn, Dympna 1931- 25-28R
Brawne, Michael 1925- 73-76
Braxton, Joanne M. 1950- DLB-41
Bray, Alison
See Rowland, D(onald) S(ydney)
Bray, Allen Farris III 1926- 9-10R
Bray, Douglas W. 1918- 15-16R
Bray, Howard 1929- 105
Bray, J(ohn) J(efferson) 1912- 102
Bray, Thomas 1656-1730 .... DLB-24
Bray, Virginia Elizabeth Nuckolls
1895(?)-1979 Obituary 93-96
Bray, Warwick 1936- CANR-15
Earlier sketch in CA 25-28R
Braybrooke, David 1924- CANR-18
Earlier sketches in CA 11-12R, CANR-3
Braybrooke, Neville (Patrick Bellairs)
1925- 7-8R
Brayce, William
See Rowland, D(onald) S(ydney)
Brayman, Harold 1900-1988 73-76
Obituary 124
Braymer, Marguerite
See Dodd, Marguerite
Braymer, Marjorie Elizabeth 1911- 3R
See also SATA 6
Braynard, Frank O. 1916- CANR-8
Earlier sketch in CA 17-18R
Braza, Jacque
See McKeag, Ernest L(ionel)
Brazeau, Peter (Alden) 1942-1986 111
Obituary 119
Brazell, Karen 1938- 45-48
Brazelton, T(homas) Berry 1918- 97-100
Brazer, Harvey E(lliott) 1922- 111
Brazil, Angela 1869(?)-1947 Brief entry 112
Brazill, William J., Jr. 1935- 53-56
Brazos, Waco
See Jennings, Michael Glenn
Breach, Robert Walter 1927- 15-16R
Breakwell, Glynis M(arie) 1952- 122
Brealey, Richard A. 1936- 53-56
Brean, Herbert (J.) 1907-1973 93-96
Obituary 41-44R
Brearley, Denis 1940- 37-40R
Brears, Peter C(harles) D(avid) 1944- 102
Breasted, Charles 1898(?)-1980 Obituary ..93-96
Breasted, James Henry 1865-1935 ..... DLB-47
Breasted, James Henry, Jr. 1908-1983
Obituary 109
Breathed, Berke 1957- 110
Breathett, George 1925- 13-14R
Breatnac, Seamus
See Walsh, James P(atrick)
Breault, William 1926- CANR-6
Earlier sketch in CA 57-60
Brecher, Charles Martin 1945- CANR-4
Earlier sketch in CA 53-56
Brecher, Edward M(oritz) 1911- CANR-7
Earlier sketch in CA 13-14R
Brecher, Jeremy 1946- CANR-12
Earlier sketch in CA 69-72
Brecher, Michael 1925- CANR-4
Earlier sketch in CA 1R
Brecher, Ruth E(rnestine) 1911-1966 .... CAP-1
Earlier sketch in CA 13-14
Brechner, Irv 1951- 110
Brecht, Arnold 1884-1977 77-80
Obituary 73-76
Brecht, Bertolt 1898-1956 Brief entry 104
See also DLB 56
See also TCLC 1, 6, 13
Brecht, Edith 1895-1975 .... CAP-2
Earlier sketch in CA 25-28
See also SATA 6, 25
Brecht, Eugen Berthold Friedrich
See Brecht, Bertolt
Brecht, George 1924- 106
Breck, Allen duPont 1914- CANR-9
Earlier sketch in CA 13-14R
Breck, Vivian
See Breckenfeld, Vivian Gurney
Breckenfeld, Vivian Gurney 1895- 5-6R
See also SATA 1
Breckenridge, Adam Carlyle 1916- 29-32R
Breckinridge, Mary 1881-1965 Obituary 114
Breckler, Rosemary 1920- 101
Breda, Tjalmar
See DeJong, David C(ornel)
Bredel, Willi 1901-1964 .... DLB-56
Bredemeier, Harry Charles 1920- CANR-8
Earlier sketch in CA 7-8R
Bredemeier, Mary E(lizabeth) 1924- 81-84
Bredes, Don(ald) 1947- 110
Bredow, Miriam
See Wolf, Miriam Bredow
Bredsdorff, Elias Lunn 1912- CAP-1
Earlier sketch in CA 9-10
Bredsdorff, Jan 1942- CANR-13
Earlier sketch in CA 21-22R
Bredvold, Louis I(gnatius) 1888-1977 .... 3R
Obituary 103
Bree, Germaine 1907- CANR-4
Earlier sketch in CA 1R
Breech, (Earl) James 1944- 114
Breed, Paul F. 1916- 33-36R
Breeden, Stanley 1938- 106
Breem, Wallace (Wilfred Swinburne)
1926- Brief entry 113
Breen, Dana
See Birksted-Breen, Dana
Breen, (Joseph) John 1942- 77-80
Breen, Jon L(inn) 1943- 119
Breen, Quirinus 1896-1975 .... CAP-2
Earlier sketch in CA 33-36
Breen, Richard 1935- 110
Breen, Richard L. 1919-1967 Obituary 111
Breen, T(imothy) H(all) 1942- 101
Breen, William J(ames) 1937- 118
Breese, Dave
See Breese, David W(illiam)
Breese, David W(illiam) 1926- 118
Breese, Gerald (William) 1912- 41-44R
Breeskin, Adelyn Dohme 1896-1986 .....33-36R
Obituary 119
Breetveld, Jim Patrick 1925- CANR-2
Earlier sketch in CA 4R
Breeze, Katie 1929- 111
Breffort, Alexandre 1901-1971 Obituary ..29-32R
Breger, Louis 1935- 69-72
Breggin, Peter R(oger) 1936- CANR-15
Earlier sketch in CA 81-84
Bregman, Jacob I(srael Jack) 1923- 41-44R
Bregman, Jay 1940- 109
Brehm, Sharon S(tephens) 1945- 112
Brehm, Shirley A(lice) 1926- 69-72
Breig, Joseph A(nthony) 1905- 5-6R
Breihan, Carl W(illiam) 1916- CANR-1
Earlier sketch in CA 4R
Breillat, Catherine 1950- 33-36R
Breimyer, Harold F(rederick) 1914- 19-20R
Breinburg, Petronella 1927- CANR-4
Earlier sketch in CA 53-56
See also SATA 11
Breines, Paul 1941- 61-64
Breines, Simon 1906- Brief entry 114
Breines, Winifred 1942- 113
Breisach, Ernst Adolf 1923- CANR-18
Earlier sketch in CA 3R
Breisky, William J(ohn) 1928- 53-56
See also SATA 22
Breit, Harvey 1909-1968 .... CANR-6
Obituary 25-28R
Earlier sketch in CA 5-6R
Breit, Marquita E(laine) 1942- 57-60
Breit, William (Leo) 1933- CANR-13
Earlier sketch in CA 33-36R
Breitbart, Vicki 1942- 93-96

Breitenkamp, Edward C(arlton) 1913- CANR-10
Earlier sketch in CA 25-28R
Breitman, George 1916-1986 .... CANR-7
Obituary 119
Earlier sketch in CA 61-64
Breitman, Richard D(avid) 1947- CANR-21
Earlier sketch in CA 105
Breitner, I. Emery 1929- 57-60
Breland, Osmond P(hilip) 1910- 11-12R
Brelis, Dean 1924- 11-12R
Brelis, Nancy (Burns) 1929- 21-22R
Brelsford, W(illiam) V(ernon) 1907- CAP-1
Earlier sketch in CA 13-14
Breman, Paul 1931- 21-22R
Brembeck, Winston Lamont 1912-
Brief entry 115
Bremer, Arthur H(erman) 1950-
Brief entry 113
Bremer, Francis J(ohn) 1947- 93-96
Bremer, Lisa
See Janas, Frankie-Lee
Bremner, Geoffrey 1930- 115
Bremner, John B(urton) 1920-1987
Obituary 123
Bremner, Robert H(amlett) 1917- CANR-9
Earlier sketch in CA 23-24R
Brems, Hans 1915- CANR-10
Earlier sketch in CA 25-28R
Bremser, Bonnie 1939- DLB-16
Bremser, Ray 1934- 17-18R
See also DLB 16
Bremyer, Jayne Dickey 1924- 61-64
Brenan, (Edward Fitz)Gerald 1894-1987 .... CANR-3
Obituary 121
Earlier sketch in CA 4R
Brend, Ruth M(argaret) 1927- 105
Brendel, Otto Johannes 1901-1973 97-100
Brendon, Piers (George Rundle) 1940- 101
Brendtro, Larry K. 1940- 29-32R
Brener, Milton E. 1930- 29-32R
Brengelman, Fred(erick Henry) 1928-
Brief entry 115
Brengelmann, Johannes Clemens 1920- 5-6R
Brennan, Anne 1936- 109
Brennan, Bernard P(atrick) 1918- 5-6R
Brennan, Christopher
See Kininmonth, Christopher
Brennan, Christopher John 1870-1932
Brief entry 117
See also TCLC 17
Brennan, Donald (George) 1926-1980
Obituary 97-100
Brennan, John N(eedham) H(uggard)
1914- CANR-20
Earlier sketches in CA 4R, CANR-4
Brennan, Joseph Gerard 1910- CANR-3
Earlier sketch in CA 3R
Brennan, Joseph K(illorin) 1952- 121
Brennan, Joseph Lomas 1903- CANR-2
Earlier sketch in CA 5-6R
See also SATA 6
Brennan, Joseph Payne 1918- CANR-19
Earlier sketches in CA 4R, CANR-4
Brennan, Lawrence D(avid) 1915- 5-6R
Brennan, Louis A(rthur) 1911-1983 .... 19-20R
Obituary 109
Brennan, Maeve 1917- 81-84
See also CLC 5
Brennan, Matthew J. 1917- 106
Brennan, Maynard J. 1921- 13-14R
Brennan, Michael Joseph, Jr. 1928- 15-16R
Brennan, Neil F(rancis) 1923- 37-40R
Brennan, Niall 1918- 13-14R
Brennan, Nicholas (Stephen) 1948- 106
Brennan, Ray 1908(?)-1972 Obituary 37-40R
Brennan, Richard O(liver) 1916- 89-92
Brennan, Tim
See Conroy, John Wesley
Brennan, Will
See Paine, Lauran (Bosworth)
Brennand, Frank
See Lambert, Eric
Brennecke, John H(enry) 1934- 37-40R
Brenneman, Helen Good 1925- 23-24R
Brenner, Anita 1905-1974 49-52
Obituary 53-56
Brenner, Barbara (Johnes) 1925- CANR-12
Earlier sketch in CA 9-10R
See also SATA 4, 42
Brenner, Elizabeth 1954- 123
Brenner, Erma 1911- 69-72
Brenner, Fred 1920- SATA-34, 36
Brenner, Gerry 1937- 110
Brenner, Isabel
See Schuchman, Joan
Brenner, Lenni 1937- 117
Brenner, Marie 1949- 73-76
Brenner, Rebecca Summer 1945- CANR-10
Earlier sketch in CA 61-64
Brenner, Reeve R(obert) 1936- Brief entry 116
Brenner, Summer
See Brenner, Rebecca Summer
Brenner, Yehojachin Simon 1926- CANR-11
Earlier sketch in CA 21-22R
Brennert, Alan (Michael) 1954- 118
Brenni, Vito J(oseph) 1923- 49-52
Brent, Beryl
See Ince, Martin (Jeffrey)
Brent, Harold Patrick 1943- 33-36R
Brent, Harry
See Brent, Harold Patrick
Brent, Hope 1935(?)-1984 .... SATA-39
Brent, Iris
See Bancroft, Iris (May Nelson)
Brent, Jonathan 1949- 113
Brent, Peter (Ludwig) 1931-1984 .... CANR-13
Obituary 114
Earlier sketch in CA 65-68
Brent, Stuart 73-76
See also SATA 14
Brentano, Bernard von 1901-1964 .... DLB-56
Brentano, Robert 1926- 23-24R
Brent-Dyer, Elinor Mary 1895-1969 101
Brent of Bin Bin
See Franklin, (Stella Maraia Sarah) Miles
Brenton, Howard 1942- 69-72
See also DLB 13
See also CLC 31
Breo, Dennis L. 1942- 124
Brereton, Geoffrey 1906-1979 .... CANR-20
Earlier sketch in CA 25-28R
Bresee, Clyde W. 1916- 122
Bresky, Dushan 53-56
Breslau, Alan Jeffry 1926- 69-72
Breslauer, George W. 1946- CANR-12
Earlier sketch in CA 29-32R
Breslauer, Samuel Daniel 1942- 102
Breslin, Catherine 1936- 93-96
Breslin, Herbert H. 1924- 53-56
Breslin, James 1930- 73-76
Breslin, James E. 1935- 33-36R
Breslin, Jimmy
See Breslin, James
See also CLC 4, 43
See also AITN 1
Breslin, Mark 1952- 121
Breslin, Paul 1946- 111
Breslove, David 1891- 9-10R
Breslow, Lester 1915- 115
Breslow, Lou 1900(?)-1987 Obituary 124
Bressett, Kenneth E(dward) 1928- 93-96
Bressler, Leo A(lbert) 1911- 57-60
Bressler, Marion Ann 1921- 57-60
Bresson, Robert 1907- 110
See also CLC 16
Brestin, Dee 1944- 114
Bretall, Robert Walter 1913-1980 Obituary 110
Bretecher, Claire 1940- Brief entry 113
Bretnor, Reginald 1911- CANR-10
Earlier sketch in CA 65-68
Breton, Albert 1929- 61-64
Breton, Andre 1896-1966 .... CAP-2
Obituary 25-28R
Earlier sketch in CA 19-20
See also DLB 65
See also CLC 2, 9, 15
Bretscher, Paul G(erhardt) 1921- CANR-8
Earlier sketch in CA 17-18R
Brett, Bernard 1925- CANR-17
Earlier sketch in CA 97-100
See also SATA 22
Brett, Bill 1922- 122
Brett, David
See Campbell, Will D(avis)
Brett, Dorothy 1883-1977 Obituary 73-76
Brett, George P(latt), Jr. 1893-1984
Obituary 112
Brett, Grace N(eff) 1900-1975 .... 11-12R
Obituary 120
See also SATA 23
Brett, Hawksley
See Bell, Robert S(tanley) W(arren)
Brett, Jan (Churchill) 1949- 116
See also SATA 42
Brett, John Michael
See Tripp, Miles (Barton)
Brett, Leo
See Fanthorpe, R(obert) Lionel
Brett, Mary Elizabeth 11-12R
Brett, Michael
See Tripp, Miles (Barton)
Brett, Molly
See Brett, Mary Elizabeth
Brett, Peter David 1943- 77-80
Brett, Raymond Laurence 1917- CANR-3
Earlier sketch in CA 1R
Brett, Simon (Anthony Lee) 1945- 69-72
Brettell, Richard (Robson) 1949- 124
Brett-James, (Eliot) Antony 1920-1984 .... CANR-7
Obituary 112
Earlier sketch in CA 7-8R
Bretton, Henry L. 1916- CANR-2
Earlier sketch in CA 5-6R
Brettschneider, Bertram D(onald)
1924-1986 .... 33-36R
Obituary 121
Brett-Smith, Richard 1923- 21-22R
Brett-Young, Jessica (Hankinson)
1883-1970 .... CAP-1
Earlier sketch in CA 9-10
Bretuo, Akwasi
See Assensoh, A(kwasi) B(retuo)
Breuer, Bessie 1893-1975 .... CAP-2
Obituary 61-64
Earlier sketch in CA 17-18
Breuer, Ernest Henry 1902-1972 .... CAP-2
Earlier sketch in CA 19-20
Breuer, Georg 1919- 105
Breuer, Gustav J. 1915-1985 Obituary 114
Breuer, Gustl
See Breuer, Gustav J.
Breuer, Lee 1937- 110
Breuer, Marcel 1902-1981 .... CANR-5
Obituary 104
Earlier sketch in CA 7-8R
Breuer, Miles J(ohn) 1888-1947
Brief entry 112
Breuer, Reinhard 1946- 115
Breuer, William B(entley) 1924- 118
Breugelmans, Rene 1925- 103
Breunig, Jerome Edward 1917- 15-16R
Breunig, LeRoy C(linton) 1915- 61-64
Brew, Douglas James 1949(?)-1985
Obituary 117
Brew, J(ohn) O(tis) 1906- 61-64
Brewer, Annie M. 1925- 107
Brewer, D(erek) S(tanley) 1923- CANR-4
Earlier sketch in CA 1R
Brewer, Edward S(amuel) 1933- CANR-13
Earlier sketch in CA 33-36R
Brewer, (Lucie) Elisabeth 1923- 115
Brewer, Frances Joan 1913-1965 .... CAP-1
Earlier sketch in CA 11-12
Brewer, Fredric (Aldwyn) 1921- 17-18R
Brewer, Garry Dwight 1941- CANR-14
Earlier sketch in CA 33-36R
Brewer, J(ohn) Mason 1896-1975 .... CAP-2
Earlier sketch in CA 25-28
Brewer, Jack A. 1933- 23-24R
Brewer, James H. Fitzgerald 1916- 11-12R
Brewer, Jeutonne P. 1939- CANR-14
Earlier sketch in CA 77-80
Brewer, Kenneth W(ayne) 1941- 110
Brewer, Margaret L. 1929- 29-32R
Brewer, Priscilla J. 1956- 122
Brewer, Sally King 1947- SATA-33
Brewer, Sam Pope 1909(?)-1976
Obituary 65-68
Brewer, Thomas B. 1932- 21-22R
Brewer, William C. 1897(?)-1974
Obituary 53-56
Brewer, Wilmon 1895- 5-6R
Brewi, Janice 1933- 110
Brewington, Marion Vernon 1902-1974 .... CANR-3
Obituary 53-56
Earlier sketch in CA 5-6R
Brewster, Benjamin
See Folsom, Franklin (Brewster)
Brewster, Dorothy 1883-1979 .... CANR-3
Obituary 85-88
Earlier sketch in CA 1R
Brewster, Elizabeth (Winifred) 1922- CANR-10
Earlier sketch in CA 25-28R
See also DLB 60
Brewster, Patience 1952- 121
Brewster, Townsend 1924- 105
Brewton, John E(dmund) 1898- CANR-3
Earlier sketch in CA 5-6R
See also SATA 5
Brewton, Sara Westbrook ?-1976 122
Breyer, N(orman) L(ane) 1942- 49-52
Breyer, Stephen Gerald 1938- 107
Breytenbach, Breyten 1939(?)- Brief entry 113
See also CLC 23, 37
Breza, Tadeusz 1905(?)-1970 Obituary 29-32R
Brezhnev, Leonid I(lyich) 1906-1982
Obituary 108
Brian
See Powell, Brian S(harples)
Brian, Alan B.
See Parulski, George R(ichard), Jr.
Brian, Denis 1923- 25-28R
Briand, Paul L., Jr. 1920- CANR-4
Earlier sketch in CA 2R
Briand, Rena 1935- 29-32R
Briarton, Grendel
See Bretnor, Reginald
Brice, Douglas 1916- 21-22R
Brice, Marshall Moore 1898- 19-20R
Brichant, Colette Dubois 1926- 15-16R
Brick, John 1922-1973 .... CAP-1
Obituary 45-48
Earlier sketch in CA 13-14
See also SATA 10
Brick, Michael 1922-1974 .... CANR-9
Earlier sketch in CA 15-16R
Bricker, Victoria Reifler 1940- 53-56
Brickhill, Paul Chester Jerome 1916- 11-12R
Bricklin, Mark Harris 1939- 111
Brickman, Marshall 1941- 81-84
Brickman, William Wolfgang
1913-1986 .... CANR-17
Obituary 119
Earlier sketches in CA 4R, CANR-1
Brickner, Richard P(ilpel) 1933- CANR-2
Earlier sketch in CA 5-6R
Bricktop
See Smith, Ada Beatrice Queen Victoria
Louisa Virginia
Bricuth, John
See Irwin, John T(homas)
Bridenbaugh, Carl 1903- CANR-4
Earlier sketch in CA 11-12R
Bridge, Ann
See O'Malley, Mary Dolling (Sanders)
Bridge, Don(ald) U(lysses) 1894-1984
Obituary 112
Bridge, Raymond 1943- 69-72
Bridgecross, Peter
See Cardinal, Roger (Thomas)
Bridgeman, Harriet 1942- 85-88
Bridgeman, Richard
See Davies, L(eslie) P(urnell)
Bridgeman, William Barton 1916- 9-10R
Bridger, Adam
See Bingley, David Ernest
Bridger, Gordon (Frederick) 1932- 65-68
Bridgers, Sue Ellen 1942- CANR-11
Earlier sketch in CA 65-68
See also SATA 22
See also SAAS 1
See also DLB 52
See also CLC 26
Bridges, Emily
See Bruggen, Carol (Holmes)
Bridges, Hal 1918- 1R
Bridges, Herb 1929- 110
Bridges, Howard
See Staples, Reginald Thomas
Bridges, James 1936- Brief entry 116
Bridges, Laurie
See Bruck, Lorraine
Bridges, Robert (Seymour) 1844-1930
Brief entry 104
See also DLB 19
See also TCLC 1
Bridges, William (Andrew) 1901- 33-36R
See also SATA 5
Bridges, William (Emery) 1933- CANR-13
Earlier sketch in CA 33-36R
Bridges-Adams, William 1889-1965 .... CAP-1
Earlier sketch in CA 13-14
Bridgman, Elizabeth 1921- 73-76
Bridgman, Sarah Atherton 1889(?)-1975
Obituary 57-60
Bridgwater, (William) Patrick 1931- 7-8R
Bridie, James
See Mavor, Osborne Henry
See also DLB 10
See also TCLC 3
Bridson, Gavin (Douglas Ruthven) 1936- 105
Bridwell, Norman 1928- CANR-20
Earlier sketches in CA 13-14R, CANR-5
See also SATA 4
Briefs, Goetz Antony 1889-1974 .... CAP-2
Obituary 49-52
Earlier sketch in CA 21-22
Briegel, Ann C(arrick) 1915- 33-36R
Brien, Mimi 1929- 111
Brien, Raley
See McCulley, Johnston
Brier, Bob 1943- 102
Brier, Howard M(axwell) 1903-1969 .... CAP-1
Earlier sketch in CA 13-14
See also SATA 8
Brier, Peter A. 1935- 105
Brier, Royce 1894-1975 Obituary 93-96
Brier, Warren Judson 1931- 25-28R
Brierley, David 1936- 107
Brierley, Susan S.
See Isaacs, Susan (Sutherland Fairhurst)
Briffault, Herma 1898-1981 Obituary 104
Briggs, Asa 1921- CANR-7
Earlier sketch in CA 5-6R
Briggs, Austin (Eugene), Jr. 1931- 29-32R
Briggs, B(arry B.) Bruce
See Bruce-Briggs, B(arry B.)
Briggs, Berta N. 1884(?)-1976 Obituary 69-72
Briggs, Carl 1925- 114
Briggs, Carole S(uzanne) 1950- 110
See also SATA 47
Briggs, Charles Frederick 1804-1877 .... DLB-3
Briggs, Charlie 1927- CANR-1
Earlier sketch in CA 49-52
Briggs, Desmond Lawther 1931- 108
Briggs, Dorothy Corkille 1924- 29-32R
Briggs, Ellis O(rmsbee) 1899-1976 73-76
Obituary 65-68
Briggs, F(red) Allen 1916- 33-36R
Briggs, Fred 1932- 73-76
Briggs, G. A. 1891(?)-1978 Obituary 104
Briggs, George M(cSpadden) 1919- 33-36R
Briggs, Jean 1925- 93-96
Briggs, Katharine Mary 1898-1980 .... CANR-12
Obituary 102
Earlier sketch in CA 9-10R
See also SATA 25
Briggs, Kenneth Arthur 1941- 101
Briggs, Kenneth R. 1934- 33-36R
Briggs, L(loyd) Cabot 1909-1975 .... CANR-3
Obituary 57-60
Earlier sketch in CA 5-6R
Briggs, Peter 1921-1975 .... CAP-2
Obituary 57-60
Earlier sketch in CA 25-28
See also SATA 31, 39
Briggs, R(obert) C(ook) 1915- 37-40R
Briggs, Raymond Redvers 1934- 73-76
See also SATA 23
See also CLR 10
Briggs, Shirley Ann 1918- 106
Briggs, Vernon M(ason), Jr. 1937- 73-76
Briggs, Walter Ladd 1919- 69-72
Brigham, Besmilr 1923- CANR-12
Earlier sketch in CA 29-32R
Brigham, John C(arl) 1942- 41-44R
Brighouse, Harold 1882-1958 Brief entry 110
See also DLB 10
Bright, Deborah (Sue Tomberg) 1949- 97-100
Bright, Greg 1951- 93-96
Bright, John 1908- 5-6R
Bright, Pamela Mia 1914- 109
Bright, Richard (Eugene) 1931- 69-72
Bright, Robert 1902- 73-76
See also SATA 24
Bright, Sarah
See Shine, Deborah
Bright, William 1928- 33-36R
Brightbill, Charles K(estner) 1910-1966 .... 2R
Obituary 103
Brightfield, Richard 1927- 118
Brightfield, Rick
See Brightfield, Richard
Brightman, Robert 1920- 105
Brighton, Howard 1925- 57-60
Brighton, Wesley, Jr.
See Lovin, Roger Robert
Brightwell, L(eonard) R(obert) 1889- SATA-29
Brignano, Russell C(arl) 1935- 57-60
Brignetti, Raffaello 1922(?)-1978 Obituary 104
Brigola, Alfredo L(uigi) 1923- 41-44R
Briles, Judith 1946- 106
Briley, John (Richard) 1925- 101
Brilhart, John K. 1929- 23-24R
Brill, Earl H(ubert) 1925- 19-20R
Brill, Leon 1915- 110

Brill, Steven 85-88
Brilliant, Ashleigh 1933- CANR-11
  Earlier sketch in CA 65-68
Brilliant, Eleanor L(uria) 1930- 112
Brilliant, Richard 1929- 33-36R
Briloff, Abraham J(acob) 1917- 61-64
Brim, Orville G(ilbert), Jr. 1923- CANR-2
  Earlier sketch in CA 5-6R
Brimberg, Stanlee 1947- 49-52
  See also SATA 9
Brin, David 1950- CANR-24
  Earlier sketch in CA 102
  See also CLC 34
Brin, Herb(ert Henry) 1915- 49-52
Brin, Ruth Firestone 1921- CANR-8
  Earlier sketch in CA 17-18R
  See also SATA 22
Brinckerhoff, Sidney B(urr) 1933-
  Brief entry 117
Brinckloe, Julie (Lorraine) 1950- 65-68
  See also SATA 13
Brindel, June (Rachuy) 1919- 49-52
  See also SATA 7
Brindle, Reginald Smith
  See Smith Brindle, Reginald
Brindze, Ruth 1903- 73-76
  See also SATA 23
Brinegar, David F(ranklin) 1910- 77-80
Brines, Russell (Dean) 1911- 69-72
Briney, Robert E(dward) 1933- CANR-19
  Earlier sketches in CA 53-56, CANR-4
Bring, Mitchell 1951- 106
Bringhurst, Robert 1946- CANR-21
  Earlier sketches in CA 57-60, CANR-6
Brinitzer, Carl 1907-1974 .... CANR-3
  Obituary 53-56
  Earlier sketch in CA 7-8R
Brink, Andre (Philippus) 1935- 104
  See also CLC 18, 36
Brink, Carol Ryrie 1895-1981 .... CANR-3
  Obituary 104
  Earlier sketch in CA 2R
  See also SATA 1, 27, 31
Brink, T(erry) L(ee) 1949- CANR-15
  Earlier sketch in CA 89-92
Brink, Wellington 1895-1979 Obituary 85-88
Brinker, Paul A. 1919- 25-28R
Brinker, Robert Durie 1901-1983 Obituary .. 111
Brinkerhoff, Dericksen Morgan 1921- 85-88
Brinkley, Alan 1949- 107
Brinkley, Christie 1953- 122
Brinkley, David (McClure) 1920- 97-100
Brinkley, George A. (Jr.) 1931- 17-18R
Brinkley, Joel 1952- 102
Brinkley, Roberta Florence 1892(?)-1967
  Obituary 112
Brinkley, William (Clark) 1917- CANR-11
  Earlier sketch in CA 21-22R
Brinkman, George L(oris) 1942- 53-56
Brinkman, Grover 1903- 73-76
Brinks, Herbert J(ohn) 1935- CANR-12
  Earlier sketch in CA 29-32R
Brinley, Bertrand R(ussell) 1917- 29-32R
Brinner, William M(ichael) 1924- 111
Brinnin, John Malcolm 1916- CANR-1
  Earlier sketch in CA 1R
  See also DLB 48
Brinsmead, H(esba) F(ay) 1922- CANR-10
  Earlier sketch in CA 21-22R
  See also SATA 18
  See also SAAS 5
  See also CLC 21
Brinsmead, Hesba Fay
  See Hungerford, Hesba (Fay) Brinsmead
Brint, Armand Ian 1952- 105
Brinton, (Clarence) Crane 1898-1968 .... 7-8R
  Obituary 25-28R
Brinton, Henry 1901-1977 .... CANR-4
  Earlier sketch in CA 2R
Brinton, Howard Haines 1884-1973 .... CANR-3
  Earlier sketch in CA 7-8R
Brion, Guy
  See Madsen, Axel
Brion, John M. 1922- 23-24R
Brion, Marcel 1895-1984 124
  Obituary 114
Briquebec, John
  See Rowland-Entwistle, (Arthur)
    Theodore (Henry)
Brisbane, Albert 1809-1890 .... DLB-3
Brisbane, Arthur 1864-1936 .... DLB-25
Brisbane, Henry R.
  See Ellis, Edward S(ylvester)
Brisbane, Holly E. 1927- 33-36R
Brisbane, Katharine 1932- CANR-23
  Earlier sketch in CA 107
Brisbane, Robert Hughes 1913- 77-80
Brisco, Patty
  See Matthews, Clayton (Hartley)
  and Matthews, Patricia (Anne)
Briscoe, D(avid) Stuart 1930- CANR-9
  Earlier sketch in CA 17-18R
Briscoe, Jill (Pauline) 1935- CANR-8
  Earlier sketch in CA 61-64
  See also SATA 47
Briscoe, John 1938- 118
Briscoe, Mary Louise 1937- 109
Brisk, Melvin J. 1924-1981 Obituary 104
Briskin, Jacqueline 1927- CANR-13
  Earlier sketch in CA 29-32R
Brisley, Joyce Lankester 1896- 97-100
  See also SATA 22
Brisman, Leslie 1944- 61-64
Brissenden, Paul F(rederick) 1885-1974 .. CAP-2
  Obituary 53-56
  Earlier sketch in CA 17-18
Brissenden, R(obert) F(rancis) 1928- CANR-10
  Earlier sketch in CA 23-24R
Brister, C(ommodore) W(ebster), Jr.
  1926- CANR-7
  Earlier sketch in CA 13-14R
Brister, Richard 1915- 13-14R
Bristol, Goldie M(ae) 1918- 121
Bristol, Julius
  See Abel, Alan (Irwin)
Bristol, Lee Hastings, Jr. 1923-1979 .... CANR-4
  Obituary 89-92
  Earlier sketch in CA 7-8R
Bristow, Allen P. 1929- CANR-8
  Earlier sketch in CA 21-22R
Bristow, Gwen 1903-1980 .... CANR-12
  Obituary 102
  Earlier sketch in CA 19-20R
Bristow, Robert O'Neil 1926- 25-28R
Bristowe, Anthony (Lynn) 1921-19(?) CAP-1
  Earlier sketch in CA 11-12
Britain, Dan
  See Pendleton, Don(ald Eugene)
Britchky, Seymour 1930- 102
Britindian
  See Solomon, Samuel
Britsch, Ralph A(dam) 1912- 101
Britsch, Todd A(dam) 1937- 101
Britt, Albert 1874-1969 .... 5-6R
  Obituary 103
  See also SATA 28
Britt, Dell 1934- 25-28R
  See also SATA 1
Britt, George (William Hughes) 1895-1988
  Obituary 124
Britt, Steuart Henderson 1907-1979 .... CANR-2
  Obituary 85-88
  Earlier sketch in CA 1R
Brittain, Bill
  See Brittain, William
Brittain, Frederick ?-1969 .... CANR-3
  Earlier sketch in CA 7-8R
Brittain, Joan Tucker 1928- 37-40R
Brittain, John A(shleigh) 1923- 73-76
Brittain, Vera (Mary) 1893(?)-1970 .... CAP-1
  Obituary 25-28R
  Earlier sketch in CA 15-16
  See also CLC 23
Brittain, William 1930- CANR-13
  Earlier sketch in CA 77-80
  See also SATA 36
Brittan, Gordon G(oodhue), Jr. 1939- 89-92
Brittan, Samuel 1933- 29-32R
Britten, Milton R(eese) 1924-1985
  Obituary 115
Britten Austin, Paul 1922- CANR-13
  Earlier sketch in CA 23-24R
Britter, Eric V(alentine) B(lakeney)
  1906-1977 Obituary 73-76
Brittin, Norman A(ylsworth) 1906- 19-20R
Brittin, Phil (Henry) 1953- 108
Britton, Bryce 1943- 110
Britton, Christopher (Q.) 1943- Brief entry .. 118
Britton, Dorothea S(prague) 1926- CANR-16
  Earlier sketches in CA 45-48, CANR-1
Britton, Dorothy (Guyver) 1922- 107
Britton, Karl (William) 1909-1983 .... 29-32R
  Obituary 110
Britton, Kate
  See Stegeman, Janet Allais
  See also SATA 49
Britton, Louisa
  See McGuire, Leslie Sarah
Britton, Mattie Lula Cooper 1914- 7-8R
Britton, Peter Ewart 1936- CANR-18
  Earlier sketch in CA 97-100
Brivic, Sheldon Roy 1943- 122
Brkic, Jovan 1927- 41-44R
Bro, Bernard (Gerard Marie) 1925- CANR-17
  Earlier sketch in CA 97-100
Bro, Harmon Hartzell 1919- 25-28R
Bro, Marguerite (Harmon) 1894-1977 77-80
  See also SATA 19, 27
Broad, C(harlie) D(unbar) 1887-1971 101
  Obituary 89-92
Broad, Charles Lewis 1900- 7-8R
Broad, Jay 1930- CANR-19
  Earlier sketch in CA 97-100
Broadbent, Donald E(ric) 1926- 105
Broadbent, Edward 1936- 45-48
Broadbent, W. W. 1919- 69-72
Broaddus, J(ohn) Morgan, Jr. 1929- 21-22R
Broadfoot, Barry 1926- 89-92
Broadhead, Helen Cross 1913- 103
  See also SATA 25
Broadhurst, Allan R. 1932- 5-6R
Broadhurst, Ronald Joseph Callender
  1906- CAP-1
  Earlier sketch in CA 11-12
Broadley, Margaret E(ricson) 1904-1985 .. 97-100
  Obituary 117
Broadribb, Violet 41-44R
Broadus, Catherine 1929- 37-40R
Broadus, Loren, Jr. 1928- 37-40R
Broadus, Robert N(ewton) 1922- 73-76
Broadwell, Martin M. 1927- CANR-13
  Earlier sketch in CA 73-76
Broat, I(sidore) G(erald) 1927- 97-100
Brobeck, Florence 1895-1979 Obituary 85-88
Broby-Johansen, R(udolf) 1900- CANR-12
  Earlier sketch in CA 25-28R
Broce, Thomas Edward 1935- 69-72
Broch, Hermann 1886-1951 Brief entry 117
  See also TCLC 20
Brochmann, Elizabeth 1938- 112
  See also SATA 41
Brochu, Andre 1942- DLB-53
Brock, Alice May 1941- 41-44R
Brock, Arthur Guy Clutton
  See Clutton-Brock, Arthur Guy
Brock, Ben
  See Howells, Roscoe
Brock, Betty 1923- 29-32R
  See also SATA 4
Brock, C(harles) E(dmund)
  1870-1938 .... SATA-32, 42
Brock, D(ewey) Heyward 1941- 53-56
Brock, Delia
  See Ephron, Delia
Brock, Dewey Clifton, Jr. 1930- 7-8R
Brock, Edwin 1927- Brief entry 119
  See also DLB 40
Brock, Emma L(illian) 1886-1974 .... 5-6R
  Obituary 103
  See also SATA 8
Brock, Gavin
  See Lindsay, (John) Maurice
Brock, Gerald Wayne 1948- 57-60
Brock, H(enry) M(atthew) 1875-1960 .. SATA-42
Brock, Horace 1908(?)-1981 Obituary 105
Brock, Horace Rhea 1927- 113
Brock, Lou(is Clark) 1939- Brief entry 113
Brock, Lynn
  See McAllister, Alister
Brock, Mary Duncan Howe 1909(?)-1984
  Obituary 112
Brock, Michael George 1920- 93-96
Brock, P. W.
  See Brock, Patrick Willet
Brock, Patrick Willet 1902- 112
Brock, Peter (de Beauvoir) 1920- CANR-5
  Earlier sketch in CA 11-12R
Brock, Rose
  See Hansen, Joseph
Brock, Russell Claude 1903-1980
  Obituary 105
Brock, Stanley E(dmunde) 1936- 57-60
Brock, Stuart
  See Trimble, Louis P(reston)
Brock, Van(dall) K(line) 1932- CANR-11
  Earlier sketch in CA 61-64
Brock, W(illiam) H(odson) 1936- 23-24R
Brock, William R(anulf) 1916- CANR-20
  Earlier sketches in CA 4R, CANR-4
Brockbank, Reed 1923- 21-22R
Brockelman, Paul T(aylor) 1935- 110
Brockett, Eleanor Hall 1913-1967 .... CAP-1
  Earlier sketch in CA 9-10
  See also SATA 10
Brockett, Oscar Gross 1923- CANR-22
  Earlier sketches in CA 15-16R, CANR-7
Brockley, Fenton
  See Rowland, D(onald) S(ydney)
Brockman, C(hristian) Frank 1902- 5-6R
  See also SATA 26
Brockman, David Drake
  See Drake-Brockman, David
Brockman, Harold 1902-1980 Obituary 101
Brockman, James R(aymond) 1926- 110
Brockman, Norbert 1934- 73-76
Brockriede, Wayne Elmer 1922- CANR-4
  Earlier sketch in CA 4R
Brockway, Allan R(eitz) 1932- 23-24R
Brockway, Edith E. 1914- 17-18R
Brockway, (Archibald) Fenner 1888- CAP-1
  Earlier sketch in CA 11-12
Brockway, George P(ond) 1915- 123
Brockway, Thomas P(armelee) 1898- CAP-2
  Earlier sketch in CA 17-18
Brockway, Wallace 1905-1972 Obituary .. 37-40R
Brod, Max 1884-1968 .... CANR-7
  Obituary 25-28R
  Earlier sketch in CA 7-8R
Brod, Ruth Hagy 1911-1980 Obituary 97-100
Brodatz, Philip 1915- 57-60
Brode, Douglas 1943- 57-60
Brode, Wallace R. 1900(?)-1974
  Obituary 53-56
Broder, David S(alzer) 1929- 97-100
Broder, Patricia Janis 1935- CANR-6
  Earlier sketch in CA 57-60
Broderick, Carlfred B(artholomew)
  1932- CANR-10
  Earlier sketch in CA 25-28R
Broderick, Damien Francis 1944- 111
Broderick, Dorothy M. 1929- 15-16R
  See also SATA 5
Broderick, Francis L(yons) 1922- 101
Broderick, John C(aruthers) 1926- 4R
Broderick, John F. 1909- CAP-2
  Earlier sketch in CA 33-36
Broderick, Richard L(awrence) 1927- CANR-1
  Earlier sketch in CA 45-48
Broderick, Robert C(arlton) 1913- CANR-8
  Earlier sketch in CA 23-24R
Brodeur, Paul (Adrian, Jr.) 1931- 7-8R
Brodeur, Ruth Wallace
  See Wallace-Brodeur, Ruth
Brodhead, John R. 1814-1873 .... DLB-30
Brodhead, Michael John 1935- 105
Brodie, Bernard 1910-1978 .... CANR-10
  Obituary 81-84
  Earlier sketch in CA 17-18R
Brodie, Fawn M(cKay) 1915-1981 .... CANR-10
  Obituary 102
  Earlier sketch in CA 17-18R
Brodie, H(arlowe) Keith H(ammond) 1939- .. 103
Brodie, John (Riley) 1935- Brief entry 115
Brodie, Sally
  See Cavin, Ruth (Brodie)
Brodin, Pierre Eugene 1909- 85-88
Brodine, Karen 1947- 123
Brodine, Virginia Warner 1915- 41-44R
Brodkey, Harold 111
Brodribb, (Arthur) Gerald (Norcott) 1915- .. 113
Brodsky, Archie 1945- CANR-7
  Earlier sketch in CA 61-64
Brodsky, Beverly
  See McDermott, Beverly Brodsky
Brodsky, Iosif Alexandrovich 1940- 41-44R
  See also AITN 1
Brodsky, Joseph
  See Brodsky, Iosif Alexandrovich
  See also CLC 4, 6, 13, 36
Brodsky, Louis Daniel 1941- 111
Brodsky, Michael Mark 1948- CANR-18
  Earlier sketch in CA 102
  See also CLC 19
Brodsky, Stanley L. 1939- 29-32R
Brodsky, Vera
  See Lawrence, Vera Brodsky
Brodwin, Leonora Leet 1929- 53-56
Brody, Baruch A(lter) 1943- CANR-14
  Earlier sketch in CA 33-36R
Brody, David 1930- 33-36R
Brody, Elaine 1923-1987 .... 37-40R
  Obituary 123
Brody, J(acob) J(erome) 1929- 113
Brody, Jane E(llen) 1941- CANR-23
  Earlier sketch in CA 102
Brody, Jules 1928- CANR-9
  Earlier sketch in CA 13-14R
Brody, Marc
  See Wilkes-Hunter, R(ichard)
Brody, Nathan 1935- 111
Brody, Polly 1919- 57-60
Brody, Saul Nathaniel 1938- 53-56
Brody, Sylvia
  See Axelrad, Sylvia Brody
Broe, Mary Lynn 1946- 110
Broe, Ruth Hammond 1912(?)-1983
  Obituary 110
Broeg, Bob
  See Broeg, Robert M.
Broeg, Robert M. 1918- CANR-5
  Earlier sketch in CA 13-14R
Broeger, Achim 1944- 107
  See also SATA 31
Broehl, Wayne G(ottlieb), Jr. 1922- 11-12R
Broek, J(an) O(tto) M(arius) 1904-1974 .. CAP-2
  Earlier sketch in CA 19-20
Broekel, Rainer Lothar 1923- CANR-19
  Earlier sketches in CA 9-10R, CANR-3
  See also SATA 38
Broekel, Ray
  See Broekel, Rainer Lothar
Broeker, Galen 1920- 41-44R
Broekman, Marcel 1922- 57-60
Broer, Lawrence R(ichard) 1938- 69-72
Broer, Marion Ruth 1910- 13-14R
Broesamle, John J(oseph) 1941- 57-60
Brof, Janet 1929- 37-40R
Brog, Molly (Jane) 1950- 113
Brogan, D(enis) W(illiam) 1900-1974 97-100
  Obituary 45-48
Brogan, Elise
  See Urch, Elizabeth
Brogan, Frankie Fonde 1922- 109
Brogan, Gerald E(dward) 1924-1981 .... 29-32R
  Obituary 104
Brogan, James E(dmund) 1941- 41-44R
Brogan, Phil(ip) F(rancis) 1896- 11-12R
Brogan, T(erry) V. F. 1951- 119
Broger, Achim
  See Broeger, Achim
Broglie, Marguerite de 1897-1973
  Obituary 37-40R
Broh, C(harles) Anthony 1945- 61-64
Broh-Kahn, Eleanor 1924- 45-48
Broido, Vera
  See Cohn, Vera
Brokamp, Marilyn 1920- 49-52
  See also SATA 10
Brokaw, Thomas John 1940- 108
Brokaw, Tom
  See Brokaw, Thomas John
Brokensha, David W(arwick) 1923- 25-28R
Brokhin, Yuri 1934- 57-60
Brokhoff, John R(udolph) 1913- CANR-23
  Earlier sketches in CA 61-64, CANR-8
Brolin, Brent C(ruse) 1940- 65-68
Bromage, Mary Cogan 1906- CAP-1
  Earlier sketch in CA 15-16
Bromberg, Walter 1900- 65-68
Bromberger, Merry (Marie Louis)
  1906-1979 Obituary 110
Bromberger, Serge Paul 1912- 29-32R
Brombert, Victor H. 1923- CANR-7
  Earlier sketch in CA 13-14R
Brome, Richard 1590(?)-1652 .... DLB-58
Brome, (Herbert) Vincent CANR-14
  Earlier sketch in CA 77-80
Bromell, Henry 1947- CANR-9
  Earlier sketch in CA 53-56
  See also CLC 5
Bromfield, Louis (Brucker) 1896-1956
  Brief entry 107
  See also DLB 4, 9
  See also TCLC 11
Bromhall, Winifred SATA-26
Bromhead, Peter (Alexander) 1919- 61-64
Bromige, David (Mansfield) 1933- CANR-16
  Earlier sketch in CA 25-28R
Bromiley, Geoffrey W(illiam) 1915- CANR-19
  Earlier sketches in CA 5-6R, CANR-4
Bromke, Adam 1928- 15-16R
Bromley, David G(rover) 1941- 41-44R
Bromley, Dorothy Dunbar 1896-1986
  Obituary 118
Bromley, Dudley 1948- 77-80
Bromley, Gordon 1910- 112
Bromley, John Carter 1937- 33-36R

Bromley, John Selwyn 1913-1985
Obituary ... 116
Brommer, Gerald F(rederick) 1927- ... CANR-21
Earlier sketch in CA 105
See also SATA 28
Bromwich, David (Lee) 1951- Brief entry ... 121
Bronaugh, Robert Brett 1947- ... 106
Brondfield, Jerome 1913- ... 73-76
See also SATA 22
Brondfield, Jerry
See Brondfield, Jerome
Broner, E(sther) M(asserman) 1930- ... CANR-8
Earlier sketch in CA 19-20R
See also DLB 28
See also CLC 19
Bronfeld, Stewart 1929- ... 109
Bronfenbrenner, Martin 1914- ... 13-14R
Bronfenbrenner, Urie 1917- ... CANR-16
Earlier sketch in CA 97-100
Bronin, Andrew 1947- ... 45-48
Bronk, William 1918- ... CANR-23
Earlier sketch in CA 89-92
See also CLC 10
Bronner, Edwin B(laine) 1920- ... CANR-22
Earlier sketches in CA 7-8R, CANR-7
Bronner, Simon J. 1954- ... 121
Bronner, Stephen Eric 1949- ... 113
Bronowski, Jacob 1908-1974 ... CANR-3
Obituary ... 53-56
Earlier sketch in CA 2R
Bronsen, David 1926- ... 37-40R
Bronson, Bertrand Harris 1902-1986 ... 61-64
Obituary ... 118
Bronson, Lita
See Bell, Louise Price
Bronson, Lynn
See Lampman, Evelyn Sibley
Bronson, Oliver
See Rowland, D(onald) S(ydney)
Bronson, Wilfrid Swancourt 1894-1985 ... 73-76
Obituary ... 116
See also SATA 43
Bronson, William (Knox) 1926-1976 ... 41-44R
Obituary ... 65-68
Bronson, Wolfe
See Raborg, Frederick A(shton), Jr.
Bronstein, Arthur J. 1914- ... 9-10R
Bronstein, Leo 1903(?)-1976 Obituary ... 65-68
Bronstein, Lev Davidovich
See Trotsky, Leon
Bronstein, Lynne 1950- ... 77-80
Bronstein, Yetta
See Abel, Jeanne
Bronte, Anne 1820-1849 ... DLB-21
Bronte, Charlotte 1816-1855 ... DLB-21
Bronte, Emily 1818-1848 ... DLB-21, 32
Bronte, Louisa
See Roberts, Janet Louise
Bronwell, Arthur B. 1909- ... 33-36R
Brook, Barry S(helley) 1918- ... CANR-16
Earlier sketch in CA 25-28R
Brook, David 1932- ... 13-14R
Brook, G. L.
See Brook, George Leslie
Brook, George Leslie 1910-1987 ... CANR-5
Obituary ... 123
Earlier sketch in CA 9-10R
Brook, Judith (Penelope) 1926- ... 122
Brook, Judy
See Brook, Judith (Penelope)
Brook, Peter (Stephen Paul) 1925- ... 105
Brook, Victor John Knight 1887-1974 ... 4R
Obituary ... 103
Brooke, A. B.
See Jennings, Leslie Nelson
Brooke, Avery (Rogers) 1923- ... CANR-21
Earlier sketches in CA 57-60, CANR-6
Brooke, Brian 1911- ... 85-88
Brooke, Bryan (Nicholas) 1915- ... CANR-1
Earlier sketch in CA 45-48
Brooke, Carol
See Ramskill, Valerie Patricia Roskams
Brooke, Christopher N(ugent) L(awrence)
1927- ... CANR-18
Earlier sketches in CA 7-8R, CANR-2
Brooke, Dinah 1936- ... CANR-4
Earlier sketch in CA 49-52
Brooke, Eleanor (Golden) 1905(?)-1987
Obituary ... 122
Brooke, Frances 1724-1789 ... DLB-39
Brooke, George Mercer, Jr. 1914- ... 122
Brooke, Harold 1910- Brief entry ... 113
Brooke, Henry 1703(?)-1783 ... DLB-39
Brooke, (Bernard) Jocelyn 1908- ... 5-6R
Brooke, John 1920-1985 Obituary ... 118
Brooke, Joshua
See Miller, Victor (Brooke)
Brooke, L(eonard) Leslie 1862-1940 ... SATA-17
Brooke, Maxey 1913- ... 9-10R
Brooke, Nicholas Stanton 1924- ... 25-28R
Brooke, Rupert (Chawner) 1887-1915
Brief entry ... 104
See also DLB 19
See also TCLC 2, 7
Brooke, (Robert) Tal(iaferro) 1945- ... 93-96
Brooke-Haven, P.
See Wodehouse, P(elham) G(renville)
Brooke-Little, John 1927- ... CANR-10
Earlier sketch in CA 23-24R
Brooker, Clark
See Fowler, Kenneth A(brams)
Brooke-Rose, Christine 1926- ... 13-14R
See also DLB 14
See also CLC 40
Brookes, Edgar Harry 1897- ... CANR-3
Earlier sketch in CA 4R
Brookes, Kenneth John 1909-1984
Obituary ... 111
Brookes, Owen
See Barber, D(ulan) F(riar Whilberton)
Brookes, Pamela 1922- ... 25-28R
Brookes, Reuben Solomon 1914- ... CAP-1
Earlier sketch in CA 9-10
Brookhouse, (John) Christopher 1938- ... 29-32R
Brookhouser, Frank 1912(?)-1975 ... 4R
Obituary ... 61-64
Brookins, Dana 1931- ... 69-72
See also SATA 28
Brookman, Denise Cass 1921- ... 4R
Brookman, Rosina Francesca 1932- ... 61-64
Brookner, Anita 1928- ... 120
Brief entry ... 114
See also CLC 32, 34
Brookover, Wilbur B(one) 1911- ... 33-36R
Brooks, A(lfred) Russell 1906- ... CAP-2
Earlier sketch in CA 33-36
Brooks, Albert
See Einstein, Albert
Brooks, Anita
See Abramovitz, Anita (Zeltner Brooks)
See also SATA 5
Brooks, Anne Tedlock 1905- ... CANR-1
Earlier sketch in CA 4R
Brooks, B. David 1938- ... 113
Brooks, C(larence) Carlyle 1888- ... CAP-1
Earlier sketch in CA 13-14
Brooks, Charles (Gordon) 1920- ... 115
Brooks, Charles B(enton) 1921- ... 3R
Brooks, Charles E(dward) 1921- ... 53-56
Brooks, Charles Timothy 1813-1883 ... DLB-1
Brooks, Charles V. W. 1912- ... 77-80
Brooks, Charlotte K. ... 89-92
See also SATA 24
Brooks, Cleanth 1906- ... 17-18R
See also DLB 63
See also CLC 24
Brooks, D(avid) P. 1915- ... CANR-11
Earlier sketch in CA 25-28R
Brooks, David H(opkinson) 1929- ... 61-64
Brooks, Deems M(arkham) 1934- ... 69-72
Brooks, Douglas
See Brooks-Davies, Douglas
Brooks, Douglas L(ee) 1916- ... 114
Brooks, Emerson M. 1905(?)-1982
Obituary ... 108
Brooks, Gary D(onald) 1942- ... 41-44R
Brooks, George E(dward), Jr. 1933- ... 33-36R
Brooks, Gladys Rice 1886(?)-1984
Obituary ... 111
Brooks, Glenn E(llis), Jr. 1931- ... 2R
Brooks, Gregory 1961- ... 102
Brooks, Gwendolyn 1917- ... CANR-1
Earlier sketch in CA 1R
See also SATA 6
See also DLB 5
See also CDALB 1941-1968
See also CLC 1, 2, 4, 5, 15
See also AITN 1
Brooks, H(arold) Allen 1925- ... CANR-14
Earlier sketch in CA 81-84
Brooks, Harvey 1915- ... 25-28R
Brooks, Hindi Brief entry ... 115
Brooks, Hugh C. 1922- ... 29-32R
Brooks, Hunter O(tis) 1929- ... 77-80
Brooks, James L. 1940- ... 73-76
Brooks, Janice Young 1943- ... CANR-9
Earlier sketch in CA 65-68
Brooks, Jeremy 1926- ... CANR-7
Earlier sketch in CA 5-6R
See also DLB 14
Brooks, Jerome 1931- ... CANR-2
Earlier sketch in CA 49-52
See also SATA 23
Brooks, Jerome E(dmund) 1895(?)-1983
Obituary ... 109
Brooks, John (Nixon) 1920- ... CANR-6
Earlier sketch in CA 15-16R
Brooks, John
See Sugar, Bert Randolph
Brooks, Juanita 1898- Brief entry ... 114
Brooks, Karen 1949- ... 57-60
Brooks, Keith 1923- ... 17-18R
Brooks, (Frank) Leonard 1911- ... 13-14R
Brooks, LeRoy D(avis) II 1943-
Brief entry ... 113
Brooks, Lester 1924- ... CANR-13
Earlier sketch in CA 33-36R
See also SATA 7
Brooks, Louise 1906-1985 Obituary ... 117
Brooks, Lyman Beecher 1910-1984 ... 122
Obituary ... 112
Brooks, Maria (Zagorska) 1933- ... 41-44R
Brooks, Maurice (Graham) 1900- ... SATA-45
Brooks, Mel
See Kaminsky, Melvin
See also DLB 26
See also CLC 12
Brooks, Nelson Herbert 1902-1978
Obituary ... 77-80
Brooks, Noah 1830-1903 ... DLB-42
Brooks, Pat 1931- ... CANR-7
Earlier sketch in CA 57-60
Brooks, Patricia 1926- ... CANR-11
Earlier sketch in CA 25-28R
Brooks, Paul 1909- ... CANR-7
Earlier sketch in CA 15-16R
Brooks, Peter 1938- ... CANR-1
Earlier sketch in CA 45-48
See also CLC 34
Brooks, Peter W(right) 1920- ... 9-10R
Brooks, Philip 1899(?)-1975 Obituary ... 104
Brooks, Polly Schoyer 1912- ... CANR-17
Earlier sketch in CA 4R
See also SATA 12
Brooks, Richard 1912- ... 73-76
See also DLB 44
Brooks, Richard Oliver 1934- ... 112
Brooks, Robert A(ngus) 1920-1976
Obituary ... 65-68
Brooks, Robert Emanuel 1941- ... 57-60
Brooks, Ron(ald George) 1948-
Brief entry ... 111
See also SATA 33
Brooks, Seth Rogers 1901-1987 Obituary ... 123
Brooks, Stewart M. 1923- ... CANR-9
Earlier sketch in CA 17-18R
Brooks, Terry 1944- ... CANR-14
Earlier sketch in CA 77-80
Brooks, Thomas 1941- ... 120
Brooks, Thomas R(eed) 1925- ... 73-76
Brooks, Tim(othy Haley) 1942- ... CANR-19
Earlier sketch in CA 102
Brooks, Van Wyck 1886-1963 ... CANR-6
Earlier sketch in CA 4R
See also DLB 45, 63
See also CLC 29
Brooks, W. Hal 1933- ... 57-60
Brooks, Walter R(ollin) 1886-1958
Brief entry ... 111
See also SATA 17
Brooks, William D(ean) 1929- ... 33-36R
Brooks-Davies, Douglas 1942- ... CANR-12
Earlier sketch in CA 73-76
Brook-Shepherd, (Frederick) Gordon
1918- ... CANR-3
Earlier sketch in CA 9-10R
Brookshier, Frank ... 93-96
Brookter, Marie 1934?- ... AITN-1
Broom, Leonard 1911- ... CANR-5
Earlier sketch in CA 15-16R
Broomall, Robert W(alter) 1946- ... 119
Broome, Charles L(arue) 1925- ... 41-44R
Broome, Harvey 1902-1968 ... 122
Obituary ... 110
Broomell, Myron H(enry) 1906-1970 ... CAP-1
Earlier sketch in CA 9-10
Broomfield, Gerald W(ebb) 1895-1976 ... 7-8R
Obituary ... 103
Broomfield, J(ohn) H(indle) 1935- ... 25-28R
Broomsnodder, B(radley) MacKinley
1940- ... CANR-8
Earlier sketch in CA 15-16R
Brophy, Ann 1931- ... 106
Brophy, Brigid (Antonia) 1929- ... 7-8R
See also CAAS 4
See also DLB 14
See also CLC 6, 11, 29
Brophy, Donald F(rancis) 1934- ... CANR-10
Earlier sketch in CA 23-24R
Brophy, Elizabeth Bergen 1929- ... 61-64
Brophy, James David, Jr. 1926- ... CANR-3
Earlier sketch in CA 4R
Brophy, James J(oseph) 1912- ... 65-68
Brophy, Jere E(dward) 1940- ... CANR-2
Earlier sketch in CA 45-48
Brophy, Jim
See Brophy, James J(oseph)
Brophy, John 1899-1965 ... CAP-1
Earlier sketch in CA 11-12
Brophy, Liam 1910- ... 11-12R
Brophy, Robert J(oseph) 1928- ... CANR-5
Earlier sketch in CA 53-56
Brose, Olive J(ohnson) 1919- ... 41-44R
Brosman, Catharine Savage 1934- ... CANR-21
Earlier sketch in CA 61-64
See also CLC 9
Brosnahan, Leonard Francis 1922- ... 102
Brosnahan, Tom 1945- ... 119
Brosnan, James Patrick 1929- ... CANR-3
Earlier sketch in CA 4R
See also SATA 14
Brosnan, Jim
See Brosnan, James Patrick
Bross, Irwin D(udley) J(ackson) 1921- ... 37-40R
Brossard, Chandler 1922- ... CANR-8
Earlier sketch in CA 61-64
See also CAAS 2
See also DLB 16
Brossard, Nicole 1943- ... 122
See also DLB 53
Brossier, Margaret 1918(?)-1984 Obituary ... 113
Brostowin, Patrick Ronald 1931- ... 15-16R
Brother Antoninus
See Everson, William (Oliver)
Brother Bob
See Buell, Robert Kingery
Brother Choleric
See van Zeller, Claud
Brothers, (M.) Jay 1931- ... 103
Brothers, Joyce (Diane Bauer) 1929- ... CANR-13
Earlier sketch in CA 23-24R
See also AITN 1
Brothers Hildebrandt, The
See Hildebrandt, Tim(othy)
Brotherston, James Gordon 1939- ... CANR-11
Earlier sketch in CA 25-28R
Brotherton, Manfred 1900(?)-1981
Obituary ... 102
Broude, Norma (Freedman) 1941- ... 113
Broudy, Harry S(amuel) 1905- ... CANR-3
Earlier sketch in CA 2R
Broue, Pierre 1926- ... CANR-12
Earlier sketch in CA 69-72
Brough, James 1918- ... 111
Brough, John 1917-1984 Obituary ... 111
Brough, R(obert) Clayton 1950- ... CANR-7
Earlier sketch in CA 57-60
Brougham, John 1810-1880 ... DLB-11
Broughton, Bradford B. 1926- ... 21-22R
Broughton, Diane 1943- ... 81-84
Broughton, Geoffrey 1927- ... 102
Broughton, Jack(sel Markham) 1925- ... 73-76
Broughton, James 1913- ... CANR-2
Earlier sketch in CA 49-52
See also DLB 5
Broughton, Panthea Reid 1940- ... CANR-7
Earlier sketch in CA 57-60
Broughton, Rhoda 1840-1920 ... DLB-18
Broughton, T(homas) Alan 1936- ... CANR-23
Earlier sketches in CA 45-48, CANR-2
See also CLC 19
Brouillette, Jeanne S. ... 4R
Broumas, Olga 1949- ... CANR-20
Earlier sketch in CA 85-88
See also CLC 10
Broun, Emily
See Sterne, Emma Gelders
Broun, Heywood 1888-1939 ... DLB-29
Broun, Heywood Hale 1918- ... CANR-12
Earlier sketch in CA 17-18R
Broun, Heywood Oren 1950(?)-1987
Obituary ... 124
Broun, Hob
See Broun, Heywood Oren
Broussard, Louis 1922- ... 25-28R
Broussard, Vivian L.
See Martinetz, V(ivian) L.
Brouwer, Luitzen Egbertus Jan 1881-1966
Obituary ... 116
Brovka, Petr (Pyatrus Ustinovich)
1905-1980 Obituary ... 105
Brow, Robert 1924- ... CANR-10
Earlier sketch in CA 23-24R
Broward, Donn
See Halleran, Eugene E(dward)
Broward, Robert C. 1926- ... 122
Browder, Earl Russell 1891(?)-1973
Obituary ... 45-48
Browder, Lesley H(ughes), Jr. 1935- ... 45-48
Browder, Olin L(orraine), Jr. 1913- ... 41-44R
Browder, Robert P(aul) 1921- ... 122
Browder, Sue 1946- ... 77-80
Browder, Walter Everett 1939- ... 53-56
Brower, Brock (Hendrickson) 1931- ... 25-28R
Brower, Charles Hendrickson 1901-1984 ... 102
Obituary ... 113
Brower, Charlie
See Brower, Charles Hendrickson
Brower, Daniel R(oberts) 1936- ... 41-44R
Brower, David R(oss) 1912- ... CANR-9
Earlier sketch in CA 61-64
Brower, Kenneth (David) 1944- ... CANR-10
Earlier sketch in CA 25-28R
Brower, Linda A. 1945- ... 33-36R
Brower, Millicent ... CANR-15
Earlier sketch in CA 41-44R
See also SATA 8
Brower, Pauline 1929- ... 77-80
See also SATA 22
Brower, Reuben Arthur 1908-1975 ... CANR-6
Obituary ... 57-60
Earlier sketch in CA 4R
Browin, Frances Williams 1898- ... CAP-1
Earlier sketch in CA 19-20
See also SATA 5
Brown, A(lfred) R(eginald) Radcliffe
See Radcliffe-Brown, A(lfred) R(eginald)
Brown, Alan A. 1929- ... CANR-16
Earlier sketch in CA 25-28R
Brown, Alan R. 1938- ... 105
Brown, Alberta L(ouise) 1894- ... CAP-1
Earlier sketch in CA 11-12
Brown, Alexander (Crosby) 1905- ... CANR-3
Earlier sketch in CA 2R
Brown, Alexis
See Baumann, Amy (Brown) Beeching
Brown, Alice Very
See Very, Alice (N.)
Brown, Allen 1926- ... 15-16R
Brown, Andreas Le 1933- ... 108
Brown, Anne Ensign 1937- ... 101
Brown, Anne S(eddon) K(insolving)
1906-1985 ... 17-18R
Obituary ... 117
Brown, Annice Harris 1897- ... 45-48
Brown, Annora 1899-1987(?) Obituary ... 121
Brown, Anthony Eugene 1937- ... 89-92
Brown, Archibald Haworth 1938- ... CANR-20
Earlier sketch in CA 103
Brown, Arnold 1927- ... 117
Brown, Arthur A(llen) 1900- ... 73-76
Brown, Arthur Wayne 1917- ... CANR-8
Earlier sketch in CA 5-6R
Brown, Ashley 1923- ... CANR-20
Earlier sketches in CA 4R, CANR-3
Brown, B(artley) Frank 1917- ... CANR-4
Earlier sketch in CA 11-12R
Brown, B(essie) Katherine (Taylor)
1917- ... 15-16R
Brown, Barbara B(anker) 1917- ... 69-72
Brown, Barbara W(ood) 1928- ... 105
Brown, Beatrice C.
See Curtis Brown, Beatrice
Brown, Benjamin F. 1930- ... CANR-1
Earlier sketch in CA 45-48
Brown, Bernard E(dward) 1925- ... CANR-21
Earlier sketches in CA 4R, CANR-4
Brown, Bert R(obert) 1936- ... 41-44R
Brown, Beth ... CAP-2
Earlier sketch in CA 21-22
Brown, Betty
See Jones, Elizabeth B(rown)
Brown, Bill
See Brown, William L(ouis)

Brown, Billye Walker
See Cutchen, Billye Walker
Brown, Blanche R. (Levine) 1915- 13-14R
Brown, Bob
See Brown, Robert Carlton
and Brown, Robert Joseph
See also DLB 4, 45
Brown, Bob Burton 1925- 23-24R
Brown, Buck 1936- SATA-45
Brown, Calvin S(mith) 1909- 49-52
Brown, Camille 1917- 9-10R
Brown, Carl F(raser) 1910- 41-44R
Brown, Carol Williams 1941- 111
Brown, Carter
See Yates, A(lan) G(eoffrey)
Brown, Cassie 1919-1986 .... CANR-23
Earlier sketch in CA 45-48
Brown, Cecil 1907-1987 Obituary 123
Brown, Cecil H(ooper) 1944- 109
Brown, Cecil M. 1943- 73-76
See also DLB 33
Brown, Charles
See Cadet, John
Brown, Charles Brockden
1771-1810 .... DLB-37, 59
See also CDALB 1640-1865
Brown, Charles H. 1910- 23-24R
Brown, Charles N(ikki) 1937- 93-96
Brown, Charles T(homas) 1912- 41-44R
Brown, Christopher P(aterson) 1939- .. CANR-10
Earlier sketch in CA 65-68
Brown, Christy 1932-1981 105
Obituary 104
See also DLB 14
Brown, Clarence (Fleetwood, Jr.) 1929-
Brief entry 112
Brown, Clark 1935- 25-28R
Brown, Claude 1937- 73-76
See also CLC 30
Brown, Clifford Waters, Jr. 1942- 77-80
Brown, (John) Clive (Anthony) 1947- 121
Brown, Conrad 1922- SATA-31
Brown, Constantine 1889-1966 .... CAP-1
Earlier sketch in CA 11-12
Brown, Courtney C(onrades) 1904- 77-80
Brown, Croswell 1905(?)-1971 Obituary 104
Brown, Curtis F(ranklin) 1925- 61-64
Brown, Cynthia 1952- 121
Brown, Dale W. 1926- 37-40R
Brown, Daniel G(ilbert) 1924- 45-48
Brown, Daniel Russell
See Curzon, Daniel
Brown, Daphne Faunce
See Faunce-Brown, Daphne (Bridget)
Brown, David 1916- 15-16R
Brown, David (Alan) 1922-1982 Obituary ... 110
Brown, David (Clifford) 1929- 57-60
Brown, David
See Myller, Rolf
Brown, David E(arl) 1938- 113
Brown, David Grant 1936- 15-16R
Brown, David S(pringer) 1915- 29-32R
Brown, Deaver David 1943- 102
Brown, Dee (Alexander) 1908- CANR-11
Earlier sketch in CA 15-16R
See also CAAS 6
See also SATA 5
See also DLBY 80
See also CLC 18, 47
Brown, Delwin (Wray) 1935- Brief entry 117
Brown, Denise Scott 1931- 41-44R
Brown, Dennis A(lbert) 1926-1978 .... CANR-13
Earlier sketch in CA 61-64
Brown, Derek Ernest Denny
See Denny-Brown, Derek Ernest
Brown, Diana 1928- CANR-18
Earlier sketch in CA 101
Brown, Donald Eugene 1909- CAP-1
Earlier sketch in CA 15-16
Brown, Donald Fowler 1909- 41-44R
Brown, Donald Robert 1925- 41-44R
Brown, Doris E. 1910(?)-1975 Obituary ...61-64
Brown, Dorothy
See Oxley, Dorothy (Anne)
Brown, Douglas (Frank Lambert) 1907- ...25-28R
Brown, Douglas
See Gibson, Walter B(rown)
Brown, Drollene P. 1939- 122
Brown, Duane 1937- 33-36R
Brown, E(dward) K(illoran) 1905-1951
Brief entry 107
Brown, E(ugene) Richard 1942- CANR-18
Earlier sketch in CA 97-100
Brown, Edgar S., Jr. 1922- 9-10R
Brown, Edward J(ames) 1909- 25-28R
Brown, Eleanor Frances 1908- 29-32R
See also SATA 3
Brown, Eleanor Gertrude 1887-1968
Obituary 104
Brown, Elizabeth Louise 1924- 53-56
Brown, Elizabeth M(yers) 1915- 107
See also SATA 43
Brown, Emily Clara 1911- 53-56
Brown, Erik 1923- 114
Brown, Ernest Henry Phelps 1906- 108
Brown, Evelyn M. 1911- 21-22R
Brown, F(rancis) Andrew 1915- 41-44R
Brown, F. Keith 1913(?)-1976 Obituary ...69-72
Brown, F(rancis Charles Claypon) Yeats
See Yeats-Brown, F(rancis Charles
Claypon)
Brown, Fern G. 1918- CANR-17
Earlier sketch in CA 97-100
See also SATA 34
Brown, (Robert) Fletch 1923- 116
See also SATA 42
Brown, Forrest 49-52
Brown, (Ernest) Francis 1903- 73-76
Brown, Francis R(obert) 1914- 41-44R
Brown, Frank A(rthur), Jr. 1908- 69-72
Brown, Frank E(dward) 1908- 101
Brown, Frederick 1934- 25-28R
Brown, Frederick G(ramm) 1932- CANR-12
Earlier sketch in CA 29-32R
Brown, Fredric (William) 1906-1972 122
Obituary 33-36R
See also DLB 8
Brown, G(eorge) Neville 1932- 17-18R
Brown, Geoff 1932- 61-64
Brown, George
See Wertmuller, Lina
Brown, George Alfred George
See George-Brown, George Alfred
Brown, George Earl 1883-1964 ....5-6R
See also SATA 11
Brown, George Isaac 1923- 73-76
Brown, George Mackay 1921- CANR-12
Earlier sketch in CA 21-22R
See also CAAS 6
See also SATA 35
See also DLB 14, 27
See also CLC 5
Brown, George Thompson 1921- 111
Brown, Gerald Saxon 1911- 11-12R
Brown, Gerald W(illiam) 1916- 33-36R
Brown, Giles T(yler) 1916- 19-20R
Brown, Ginny
See Brown, Virginia Sharpe
Brown, Gwilym Slater 1928-1974 ....11-12R
Obituary 53-56
Brown, H. Rap
See Al-Amin, Jamil Abdullah
Brown, Harcourt 1900- CANR-20
Earlier sketch in CA 101
Brown, Harold O(gden) J(oseph)
1933- CANR-10
Earlier sketch in CA 25-28R
Brown, Harriett M. 1897- 7-8R
Brown, Harrison Scott 1917-1986 69-72
Obituary 121
Brown, Harry (Peter McNab, Jr.)
1917-1986 69-72
Obituary 120
See also DLB 26
Brown, Harry G(unnison) 1880-1975
Obituary 57-60
Brown, Harry M(atthew) 1921- CANR-10
Earlier sketch in CA 25-28R
Brown, Hazel E(lizabeth) 1893- 57-60
Brown, Helen Gurley 1922- CANR-5
Earlier sketch in CA 7-8R
Brown, Herbert Ross 1902- CAP-1
Earlier sketch in CA 15-16
Brown, Howard Mayer 1930- CANR-3
Earlier sketch in CA 4R
Brown, Hugh Auchincloss 1879-1975
Obituary 61-64
Brown, Huntington 1899- CAP-1
Earlier sketch in CA 19-20
Brown, Ida Mae 1908- CAP-2
Earlier sketch in CA 29-32
Brown, Ina Corinne 5-6R
Brown, Ina Ladd 1905- CAP-1
Earlier sketch in CA 13-14
Brown, Ira Vernon 1922- 5-6R
Brown, Irene Bennett 1932- CANR-12
Earlier sketch in CA 29-32R
See also SATA 3
Brown, Irving
See Adams, William Taylor
Brown, Irwin
See Murray, David Stark
Brown, Ivor (John Carnegie)
1891-1974 .... CANR-12
Obituary 49-52
Earlier sketch in CA 11-12R
See also SATA 5, 26
Brown, J(ames) Douglas 1898-1986
Obituary 118
Brown, J(oseph) P(aul) S(ummers)
1930- 61-64
Brown, James (Wiley) 1909- 77-80
Brown, James (Montgomery) 1921- 4R
Brown, James 1934- CANR-10
Earlier sketch in CA 65-68
Brown, James Alan Calvert 1922-1984
Obituary 114
Brown, James Bush
See Bush-Brown, James
Brown, James Cooke 1921- 29-32R
Brown, James I(saac) 1908- CANR-7
Earlier sketch in CA 17-18R
Brown, James Patrick 1948- 29-32R
Brown, James S(eay), Jr. 1944- 120
Brown, James Wilson 1913- 41-44R
Brown, Jamie 1945- CANR-20
Earlier sketch in CA 101
Brown, Janet 1947- 69-72
Brown, Jay A(llen) 1935- 110
Brown, Jeff
See Brown, Sevellon III
Brown, Jerry Earl 1940- 105
Brown, Jerry Wayne 1936- 25-28R
Brown, Jim (M.) 1940- 69-72
Brown, Jo Giese 1947- 108
Brown, Joan Sayers 1925(?)-1983
Obituary 110
Brown, Joe David 1915-1976 ....13-14R
Obituary 65-68
See also SATA 44
Brown, John 1887- CAP-1
Earlier sketch in CA 13-14
Brown, John 1920- 7-8R
Brown, John (E.) 1934- 25-28R
Brown, John A. 1898- 112
Brown, John Arthur 1914- CANR-11
Earlier sketch in CA 17-18R
Brown, John Buchanan
See Buchanan-Brown, John
Brown, John Gracen 1936- 104
Brown, John J. 1916- 15-16R
Brown, John L(ackey) 1914- 49-52
Brown, John Mason 1900-1969 ....9-10R
Obituary 25-28R
Brown, John Pairman 1923- 33-36R
Brown, John Russell 1923- CANR-11
Earlier sketch in CA 21-22R
Brown, Jonathan (M.) 1939- Brief entry 112
Brown, Joseph E(dward) 1929- CANR-6
Earlier sketch in CA 53-56
Brown, Judith Gwyn 1933- CANR-21
Earlier sketch in CA 93-96
See also SATA 20
Brown, Judith K. 124
Brown, Judith M(argaret) 1944- CANR-15
Earlier sketch in CA 41-44R
Brown, Julia (Prewitt) 1948- 93-96
Brown, Karl 1895(?)-1970 Obituary 104
Brown, Kenneth H. 1936- 13-14R
Brown, Kevin V. 1922- 89-92
Brown, Kitt
See Vandergriff, (Lola) Aola
Brown, L(aurence) B(inet) 1927- 65-68
Brown, L. Carl
See Brown, Leon Carl
Brown, L. J.
See Du Breuil, (Elizabeth) L(or)inda
Brown, Larry
See Brown, Lawrence, Jr.
Brown, Laurene Krasny 1945- 117
Brown, Lawrence, Jr. 1947- Brief entry 114
Brown, Lawrence R. 1904(?)-1986
Obituary 119
Brown, Lee Dolph 1890-1971 Obituary ...29-32R
Brown, Leigh 65-68
Brown, Leland 1914- 1R
Brown, Lennox (John) 1934- 93-96
Brown, Leon Carl 1928- Brief entry 117
Brown, LeRoy Chester 1908- CANR-13
Earlier sketches in CA 11-12, CAP-1
Brown, Les(ter Louis) 1928- CANR-13
Earlier sketch in CA 33-36R
Brown, Leslie H(ilton) 1917-1980 ...... CANR-7
Earlier sketch in CA 9-10R
Brown, Leslie Wilfrid 1912- 17-18R
Brown, Letitia Woods 1915-1976 73-76
Obituary 69-72
Brown, Lloyd Arnold 1907-1966 .... CAP-1
Earlier sketch in CA 11-12
See also SATA 36
Brown, Louis M(orris) 1909- 49-52
Brown, Lyle C(larence) 1926- CANR-15
Earlier sketch in CA 41-44R
Brown, M(ary) L(oretta) T(herese) 15-16R
Brown, Mac Alister 1924- 89-92
Brown, Mahlon A.
See Ellis, Edward S(ylvester)
Brown, Mandy
See Brown, May
Brown, Marc Tolon 1946- 69-72
See also SATA 10
Brown, Marcia 1918- 41-44R
See also SATA 7, 47
See also DLB 61
See also CLR 12
Brown, Marel 1899- 102
Brown, Margaret Wise 1910-1952
Brief entry 108
See also YABC 2
See also DLB 22
See also CLR 10
Brown, Margery (Wheeler) 1920- 25-28R
See also SATA 5
Brown, Marian A. 1911- 73-76
Brown, Marilyn McMeen Miller 1938- ... CANR-6
Earlier sketch in CA 57-60
Brown, Marion Marsh 1908- CANR-3
Earlier sketch in CA 4R
See also SATA 6
Brown, Mark H(erbert) 1900- CAP-2
Earlier sketch in CA 21-22
Brown, Marshall 1945- 111
Brown, Marshall L. 1924- 23-24R
Brown, Marvin L., Jr. 1920- 53-56
Brown, Mary Ellen 1939- 117
Brown, Maurice F(red) 1928-1985 ....41-44R
Obituary 116
Brown, May 1913- 118
Brown, Melissa Mather 1917- 121
Brown, Merle Elliott 1925-1978 108
Brown, Michael 1931- 33-36R
Brown, Michael Barratt
See Barratt-Brown, Michael
Brown, Michael H(arold) 1952- 121
Brown, Michael John 1932- 29-32R
Brown, Milton Perry, Jr. 1928- 9-10R
Brown, Milton W(olf) 1911- Brief entry 113
Brown, Morna Doris 1907- CANR-5
Earlier sketch in CA 5-6R
Brown, Morris Cecil 1943- 37-40R
Brown, Moses
See Barrett, William (Christopher)
Brown, Muriel 1938- 107
Brown, Muriel W(hitbeck) 1892- CAP-2
Earlier sketch in CA 23-24
Brown, Murray 1929- 37-40R
Brown, Myra Berry 1918- CANR-3
Earlier sketch in CA 4R
See also SATA 6
Brown, Nathaniel Hapgood 1929- 101
Brown, Ned 1882(?)-1976 Obituary 65-68
Brown, Neville (George) 1932- 11-12R
Brown, Newell 1917- 97-100
Brown, Norman D(onald) 1935- 53-56
Brown, Norman O(liver) 1913- 21-22R
Brown, Oliver Madox 1855-1874 .... DLB-21
Brown, Palmer 1919- 107
See also SATA 36
Brown, Pamela Beatrice 1924- 13-14R
See also SATA 5
Brown, Parker B(oyd) 1928- 53-56
Brown, Paula 1925- 110
Brown, Peter 1926(?)-1984(?) Obituary 112
Brown, Peter (Robert Lamont) 1935- .. CANR-13
Earlier sketch in CA 23-24R
Brown, Peter Douglas 1925- CANR-16
Earlier sketch in CA 25-28R
Brown, Peter Lancaster
See Lancaster-Brown, Peter
Brown, R(eginald) Allen 1924- CANR-11
Earlier sketch in CA 7-8R
Brown, R(onald) G(ordon) S(clater)
1929- 29-32R
Brown, Rae
See Brown, Forrest
Brown, Ralph Adams 1908- 33-36R
Brown, Raymond Bryan 1923- 19-20R
Brown, Raymond E(dward) 1928- CANR-17
Earlier sketch in CA 97-100
Brown, Raymond George 1924- 109
Brown, Raymond Kay 1936- 102
Brown, Raymond Lamont
See Lamont-Brown, Raymond
Brown, Re Mona 1917- 41-44R
Brown, Rebecca 1956- 124
Brown, Rex V(andesteene) 1933- 53-56
Brown, Richard 1935- 114
Brown, Richard C(arl) 1917- CANR-17
Earlier sketches in CA 7-8R, CANR-2
Brown, Richard D(avid) 1939- 53-56
Brown, Richard E(ugene) 1937- 73-76
Brown, Richard H(olbrook) 1927- 11-12R
Brown, Richard H(arvey) 1940- 109
Brown, Richard Howard 1929- 57-60
Brown, Richard Maxwell 1927- CANR-11
Earlier sketch in CA 19-20R
Brown, Rita Mae 1944- CANR-11
Earlier sketches in CA 45-48, CANR-2
See also CLC 18, 43
Brown, Robert Carlton 1886-1959
Brief entry 107
Brown, Robert Craig 1935- 101
Brown, Robert D. 1924- CANR-20
Earlier sketch in CA 104
Brown, Robert E(ldon) 1907- 7-8R
Brown, Robert Edward 1945- CANR-15
Earlier sketch in CA 65-68
Brown, Robert Fath 1941- 111
Brown, Robert Goodell 1923- 33-36R
Brown, Robert Hanbury 1916- 112
Brown, Robert Joseph 1907- CANR-13
Earlier sketches in CA 9-10, CAP-1
See also SATA 14
Brown, Robert L. 1921- 23-24R
Brown, Robert McAfee 1920- CANR-7
Earlier sketch in CA 13-14R
Brown, Robert T(homas) 1943- 113
Brown, Robin 1937- 97-100
Brown, Roderick (Langmere) Haig-
See Haig-Brown, Roderick (Langmere)
Brown, Roger Glenn 1941- 77-80
Brown, Roger H(amilton) 1931- 11-12R
Brown, Roger William 1925- 15-16R
Brown, Ronald 1900- 81-84
Brown, Rosalie
See Moore, Rosalie (Gertrude)
See also SATA 9
Brown, Rosel George 1926-1967 Obituary .. 102
Brown, Rosellen 1939- CANR-14
Earlier sketch in CA 77-80
See also CLC 32
Brown, Rosemary (Eleanor) 1938-
Brief entry 115
Brown, Roswell
See Webb, Jean Francis
Brown, Roy (Frederick) 1921-1982 65-68
Obituary 117
See also SATA 39
Brown, Sanborn C(onner) 1913-1981 .. CANR-11
Obituary 106
Earlier sketch in CA 17-18R
Brown, Sanford J(ay) 1946- 118
Brown, Sevellon III 1913-1983 Obituary 110
Brown, Seyom 1933- CANR-17
Earlier sketch in CA 65-68
Brown, Sheldon S. 1933- 122
Brown, Sheldon S. 1937- CANR-7
Earlier sketch in CA 53-56
Brown, Sidney DeVere 1925- 33-36R
Brown, Stanley (Branson) 1914- 49-52
Brown, Stanley C(oleman) 1928- 77-80
Brown, Stanley H(arold) 1927- 45-48
Brown, Stephen W. 1940- CANR-13
Earlier sketch in CA 33-36R
Brown, Sterling Allen 1901- 85-88
See also DLB 48, 51, 63
See also CLC 1, 23
Brown, Steven R(andall) 1939- 49-52
Brown, Stuart C(ampbell) 1938- 29-32R
Brown, Stuart Gerry 1912- 23-24R
Brown, Susan Jenkins 1896- 85-88
Brown, T. E. 1830-1897 .... DLB-35
Brown, T(illman) Merritt 1913- 41-44R
Brown, Terence 1944- CANR-19
Earlier sketch in CA 102
Brown, Theo W(atts) 1934- CANR-8
Earlier sketch in CA 61-64
Brown, Theodore L(awrence) 1928- 33-36R

INDEX

Brown, Theodore M(orey) 1925- ... 33-36R
Brown, Thomas H. 1930- ... 57-60
Brown, Tina 1953- ... 118
Brief entry ... 116
Brown, Tony
See Brown, W. Anthony
Brown, Truesdell S(parhawk) 1906- ... 15-16R
Brown, Turner, Jr.
See Hample, Stuart
Brown, Velma Darbo 1921- ... 97-100
Brown, Vinson 1912- ... CANR-1
Earlier sketch in CA 4R
See also SATA 19
Brown, Virginia (Suggs) 1924- ... 69-72
Brown, Virginia Pounds 1916- ... 114
Brown, Virginia Sharpe 1916- ... 13-14R
Brown, W. Anthony 1933- Brief entry ... 110
Brown, W(illiam) Norman 1892-1975 ... 61-64
Obituary ... 57-60
Brown, Wallace 1933- ... 17-18R
Brown, Walter Lee 1924- ... 33-36R
Brown, Walter R(eed) 1929- ... CANR-2
Earlier sketch in CA 45-48
See also SATA 19
Brown, Warner
See Boroson, Warren
Brown, Warren (William) 1894-1978 ... 85-88
Obituary ... 81-84
Brown, Warren A. 1917(?)-1985 Obituary ... 117
Brown, Wayne 1944- ... 101
Brown, Weldon A(mzy) 1911- ... 65-68
Brown, Wenzell 1912- ... CANR-5
Earlier sketch in CA 1R
Brown, Wilfred (Banks Duncan) 1908-1985 ... 9-10R
Obituary ... 116
Brown, Wilfred A(rthur) Gavin
See Gavin-Brown, Wilfred A(rthur)
Brown, Will
See Ainsworth, William Harrison
Brown, Will C.
See Boyles, C. S(cott), Jr.
Brown, William Campbell 1928- ... 57-60
Brown, William E(nglish) 1907-1975 ... CAP-2
Earlier sketch in CA 29-32
Brown, William F(rank) 1920- ... 33-36R
Brown, William F(erdinand) 1928- ... 33-36R
Brown, William Hill 1765-1793 ... DLB-37
Brown, William J. ... 97-100
Brown, William James 1889- ... 7-8R
Brown, William L(ouis) 1910-1964 ... 4R
See also SATA 5
Brown, William Wells 1813-1884 ... DLB-3, 50
Brown, Zenith Jones 1898-1983 ... 11-12R
Obituary ... 110
Brown-Azarowicz, Marjory F. 1922- ... 33-36R
Brownback, Paul 1940- ... 113
Browne, Anthony (Edward Tudor) 1946- ... 97-100
See also SATA 44, 45
Browne, Barum
See Saunders, Hilary Aidan St. George
Browne, Charles Farrar 1834-1867 ... DLB-11
Browne, Colette (Victoria) 1950- ... 121
Browne, Courtney 1915- ... 21-22R
Browne, Dik
See Browne, Richard
See also SATA 38
See also AITN 1
Browne, E(lliott) Martin 1900-1980 ... CAP-2
Obituary ... 97-100
Earlier sketch in CA 25-28
Browne, G(erald) P(eter) 1930- ... 23-24R
Browne, Gary Lawson 1939- ... 101
Browne, George Stephenson 1890-1970 ... CAP-2
Earlier sketch in CA 29-32
Browne, Hablot Knight 1815-1882 ... SATA-21
Browne, Harry 1933- ... CANR-3
Earlier sketch in CA 49-52
Browne, Harry
See Browne, Henry
Browne, Henry 1918- ... 102
Browne, Howard 1908- ... 73-76
Browne, (Clyde) Jackson 1948(?)- ... 120
See also CLC 21
Browne, Joseph William 1914- ... 105
Browne, Joy 1944- ... 97-100
Browne, Malcolm W(ilde) 1931- ... 17-18R
Browne, Matthew
See Rands, William Brighty
Browne, Michael Dennis 1940- ... CANR-15
Earlier sketch in CA 29-32R
See also DLB 40
Browne, Ray B(roadus) 1922- ... CANR-11
Earlier sketch in CA 19-20R
Browne, Raymond 1897- ... 73-76
Browne, Richard 1917- ... SATA-38
Browne, Robert
See Karlins, Marvin
Browne, Robert S(pan) 1924- ... CANR-14
Earlier sketch in CA 37-40R
Browne, Roland A. 1910- ... 65-68
Browne, Sam
See Smith, Ronald Gregor
Browne, Theodore R. 1911(?)-1979
Obituary ... 81-84
Browne, Walter A(nderson) 1895- ... 37-40R
Browne, William P(aul) 1945- ... 109
Browne, Wynyard (Barry) 1911-1964
Obituary ... 113
See also DLB 13
Brownell, Blaine Allison 1942- ... 65-68
Brownell, John Arnold 1924- ... 21-22R
Browning, Alice C(rolley) 1907-1985
Obituary ... 117
Browning, Christopher R(obert) 1944- ... 112
Browning, Columban
See Browning, William
Browning, David (George) 1938- ... 37-40R
Browning, Dixie Burrus 1930- ... 110
Browning, Don S(pencer) 1934- ... CANR-2
Earlier sketch in CA 49-52
Browning, (Grayson) Douglas 1929- ... 15-16R
Browning, Elizabeth 1924- ... 57-60
Browning, Elizabeth Barrett 1806-1861 ... DLB-32
Browning, Frank 1946- ... 107
Browning, Gordon 1938- ... 37-40R
Browning, Iben 1918- Brief entry ... 113
Browning, John S.
See Williams, Robert Moore
Browning, L. J.
See Du Breuil, (Elizabeth) L(or)inda
Browning, Mary 1887- ... CAP-1
Earlier sketch in CA 11-12
Browning, Norma Lee 1914- ... CANR-8
Earlier sketch in CA 61-64
Browning, Peter 1928- ... 104
Browning, Preston M(ercer), Jr. 1929- ... 57-60
Browning, Reed 1938- ... 57-60
Browning, Robert 1812-1889 ... YABC-1
See also DLB 32
Browning, Robert 1914- ... CANR-13
Earlier sketch in CA 33-36R
Browning, Robert L(ynn) 1924- ... CANR-16
Earlier sketch in CA 85-88
Browning, Rufus P(utnam) 1934- ... 124
Browning, (Zerilda) Sinclair 1946- ... 112
Browning, Tod 1882-1962 Obituary ... 117
See also CLC 16
Browning, Wilfrid (Robert Francis) 1918- ... 7-8R
Browning, William 1921- ... 113
Brownjohn, Alan 1931- ... 25-28R
See also SATA 6
See also DLB 40
Brownlee, O(swald) H(arvey) 1917- ... 65-68
Brownlee, W(illiam) H(ugh) 1917- ... 9-10R
Brownlee, W(ilson) Elliot, Jr. 1941- ... 69-72
Brownlee, Walter 1930- ... 57-60
Brownlie, Ian 1932- ... CANR-2
Earlier sketch in CA 5-6R
Brownlow, Cecil Alexander III 1926-1988
Obituary ... 124
Brownlow, Kevin 1938- ... CANR-12
Earlier sketch in CA 25-28R
Brownmiller, Susan 1935- ... 103
Brownrigg, Walter Grant 1940- ... 110
Brownson, Orestes Augustus 1803-1876 ... DLB-1, 59
Brownson, William C(larence), Jr. 1928- ... 69-72
Brownstein, Karen (Osney) 1944- ... 124
Brownstein, Michael 1943- ... 33-36R
Brownstein, Oscar Lee 1928- ... 113
Brownstein, Rachel M. 1937- ... 122
Brownstein, Ronald J. 1958- ... 106
Brownstein, Samuel C. 1909- ... 7-8R
Brownstone, David M. 1928- ... CANR-21
Earlier sketch in CA 104
Broxholme, John Franklin 1930- ... CANR-12
Earlier sketch in CA 65-68
Broxon, Mildred Downey 1944- ... 107
Broy, Anthony 1916- ... 102
Broyard, Anatole 1920- ... 105
Broyles, J(ohn) Allen 1934- ... 11-12R
Broyles, William Dodson, Jr. 1944- ... 73-76
Brozek, Josef (Maria) 1913- ... 45-48
Brozen, Yale 1917- ... 109
Bru, Hedin
See Jacobsen, Hans Jacob
Brubach, Holly 1953- ... 110
Brubacher, John Seiler 1898- ... CANR-1
Earlier sketch in CA 2R
Brubaker, Dale L(ee) 1937- ... CANR-4
Earlier sketch in CA 53-56
Brubaker, Earl R(oy) 1932- ... 107
Brubaker, Sterling 1924- ... 21-22R
Bruccoli, Matthew J(oseph) 1931- ... CANR-7
Earlier sketch in CA 11-12R
See also CLC 34
Bruce, Ben F., Jr. 1920- ... 13-14R
Bruce, Curt 1946- ... 97-100
Bruce, David (Kirkpatrick Este) 1898-1977
Obituary ... 105
Bruce, Debra 1951- ... 118
Bruce, Dickson D., Jr. 1946- ... 53-56
Bruce, Donald (James) 1930- ... 17-18R
Bruce, Dorita Fairlie 1885-1970 Obituary ... 107
See also SATA 27
Bruce, F(rederick) F(yvie) 1910- ... CANR-19
Earlier sketches in CA 2R, CANR-3
Bruce, George 1909- ... 65-68
Bruce, Harold (R., Jr.) 1934(?)-1987
Obituary ... 122
Bruce, Harry J. 1931- ... 23-24R
Bruce, Janet
See Campbell, Janet Bruce
Bruce, Jeannette M. 1922- ... 5-6R
Bruce, Lennart 1919- ... CANR-13
Earlier sketch in CA 33-36R
Bruce, Lenny
See Schneider, Leonard Alfred
See also CLC 21
Bruce, Leo
See Croft-Cooke, Rupert
Bruce, Mary 1927- ... 25-28R
See also SATA 1
Bruce, Monica
See Melaro, Constance L(oraine)
Bruce, Philip Alexander 1856-1933 ... DLB-47
Bruce, R(aymon) R(ene) 1934- ... 89-92
Bruce, Robert 1927- ... CAP-1
Earlier sketch in CA 9-10
Bruce, Robert V(ance) 1923- ... 53-56
Bruce, Shelley
See Merklinghaus, Michele
Bruce, Sylvia (Valerie) 1936- ... 33-36R
Bruce, Violet R(ose) ... 29-32R
Bruce-Briggs, B(arry B.) ... 112
Bruce Lockhart, Robin 1920- ... 25-28R
Bruce-Novoa
See Bruce-Novoa, John David
Bruce-Novoa, John David 1944-
Brief entry ... 117
Bruce-Novoa, Juan
See Bruce-Novoa, John David
Bruch, Hilde ... 53-56
See also AITN 1
Bruchac, Joseph III 1942- ... CANR-13
Earlier sketch in CA 33-36R
See also SATA 42
Bruchey, Stuart (Weems) 1917- ... 33-36R
Bruck, Lilly 1918- ... 109
Bruck, Lorraine 1921- ... SATA-46
Brucker, Clara (Hantel) 1892(?)-1980
Obituary ... 97-100
Brucker, Gene (Adam) 1924- Brief entry ... 114
Brucker, Herbert 1898-1977 ... CANR-4
Obituary ... 69-72
Earlier sketch in CA 5-6R
Brucker, Roger W(arren) 1929- ... CANR-11
Earlier sketch in CA 65-68
Bruckman, Clyde 1894-1955 ... DLB-26
Bruder, Judith ... 97-100
Bruegel, Johann Wolfgang 1905-1986 ... 77-80
Obituary ... 121
Bruegel, John Wolfgang
See Bruegel, Johann Wolfgang
Brueggemann, Walter (A.) 1933-
Brief entry ... 117
Bruegmann, Robert 1948- ... 101
Bruehl, Anton 1900-1982 Obituary ... 110
Bruemmer, Fred 1929- ... 102
See also SATA 47
Bruening, William H(arry) 1943- ... 57-60
Bruess, Clint E. 1941- ... 33-36R
Bruff, Nancy
See Gardner, Nancy Bruff
Bruffee, Kenneth A. 1934- ... 37-40R
Bruggen, Carol (Holmes) 1932- ... 117
Brugger, Bill
See Brugger, William
Brugger, Robert J. 1943- ... CANR-16
Earlier sketch in CA 85-88
Brugger, William 1941- ... CANR-12
Earlier sketch in CA 73-76
Bruggink, Donald J. 1929- ... CANR-7
Earlier sketch in CA 13-14R
Bruhn, Eric (Belton Evers) 1928-1986
Obituary ... 118
Bruhn, John Glyndon 1934- ... 89-92
Bruin, John
See Brutus, Dennis
Bruins, Elton J(ohn) 1927- ... 53-56
Bruland, Esther (Byle) 1956- ... 116
Bruller, Jean (Marcel) 1902- ... CANR-12
Earlier sketch in CA 65-68
Brulls, Christian
See Simenon, Georges (Jacques Christian)
Brumback, Carl V. 1917(?)-1987 Obituary ... 123
Brumbaugh, Robert Sherrick 1918- ... CANR-3
Earlier sketch in CA 5-6R
Brumbaugh, Thomas B(rendle) 1921- ... 49-52
Brumble, H(erbert) David III 1943- ... 107
Brumgardt, John R(aymond) 1946- ... 97-100
Brumm, Ursula 1919- ... 29-32R
Brummel, Mark Joseph 1933- ... 103
Brummet, R. Lee 1921- ... 23-24R
Brummitt, Wyatt B. 1897- ... 11-12R
Brun, Ellen 1933- ... 103
Brun, Henri 1939- ... 53-56
Bruna, Dick 1927- ... 112
See also SATA 30, 43
See also CLR 7
Brundage, Burr Cartwright 1912- ... 41-44R
Brundage, Dorothy J(une) 1930- ... 104
Brundage, James A(rthur) 1929- ... CANR-7
Earlier sketch in CA 5-6R
Brundage, John Herbert 1926- ... 101
Brundage, Percival F(lack) 1892-1979 ... 101
Obituary ... 89-92
Brune, Lester H(ugo) 1926- ... CANR-13
Earlier sketch in CA 33-36R
Bruneau, Jean
See Sylvestre, (Joseph Jean) Guy
Bruneau, Thomas C. 1939- ... 53-56
Bruner, Edward M. 1924- ... 121
Bruner, Herbert B. 1894(?)-1974
Obituary ... 53-56
Bruner, Jerome S(eymour) 1915- ... CANR-1
Earlier sketch in CA 45-48
Bruner, Margaret E. (Baggerly) 1886-197(?) ... CAP-1
Earlier sketch in CA 17-18
Bruner, Richard W(allace) 1926- ... 49-52
Bruner, Wally 1931- ... 49-52
Brunet, Michel 1917-1985 ... CANR-18
Obituary ... 117
Earlier sketch in CA 102
Brunetti, Cledo 1910-1971 ... CAP-2
Earlier sketch in CA 29-32
Brunetti, Mendor Thomas 1894-1979
Obituary ... 89-92
Brunhoff, Jean de 1899-1937 Brief entry ... 118
See also SATA 24
See also CLR 4
Brunhoff, Laurent de 1925- ... 73-76
See also SATA 24
See also CLR 4
Brunhouse, Robert Levere 1908- ... CANR-2
Earlier sketch in CA 49-52
Bruni, (Toni) Roxanna 1952- ... 114
Bruning, Nancy P(auline) 1948- ... CANR-23
Earlier sketch in CA 106
Brunn, Harry O(tis), Jr. 1919- ... 2R
Brunner, Edmund de S(chweinitz) 1889-1973 ... CAP-1
Obituary ... 45-48
Earlier sketch in CA 15-16
Brunner, Elizabeth 1920-1983 Obituary ... 111
Brunner, James A(lbertus) 1923- ... 37-40R
Brunner, John (Kilian Houston) 1934- ... CANR-2
Earlier sketch in CA 1R
See also CLC 8, 10
Brunner, Maurice Yaw 1950- ... 103
Brunner, Theodore F(riederich) 1934- ... 33-36R
Brunnings, Florence E(mery) 1916- ... 112
Bruno, Frank
See St. Bruno, Albert Francis
Bruno, Frank J(oe) 1930- ... 107
Bruno, Harold R., Jr. 1928- ... 77-80
Bruno, James Edward 1940- ... 41-44R
Bruno, Michael 1921- ... 33-36R
Bruno, Vincent J. 1926- ... 65-68
Bruns, Frederick R., Jr. 1913(?)-1979
Obituary ... 85-88
Bruns, George 1914(?)-1983 Obituary ... 109
Bruns, J(ames) Edgar 1923- ... CANR-2
Earlier sketch in CA 5-6R
Bruns, William A(lan) 1942- ... 113
Bruns, William J(ohn), Jr. 1935- ... 37-40R
Brunskill, Ronald (William) 1929- ... 85-88
Brunstein, Karl (Avrum) 1933- ... 97-100
Brunt, P(eter) A(stbury) 1917- ... 101
Bruntjen, Scott 1943- ... 111
Brunton, David W(alter) 1929- ... 41-44R
Brunton, Paul 1898-1981 Obituary ... 115
Bruntz, George G. 1901- ... 7-8R
Brunvand, Jan Harold 1933- ... 108
Brus, Wlodzimierz 1921- ... 73-76
Brush, Craig B(alcombe) 1930- ... 21-22R
Brush, Douglas P(eirce) 1930- ... CANR-7
Earlier sketch in CA 57-60
Brush, John E(dwin) 1919- ... 33-36R
Brush, Judith M(arie) 1938- ... CANR-7
Earlier sketch in CA 57-60
Brush, Stephen G(eorge) ... 73-76
Brushwood, John S(tubbs) 1920- ... CANR-9
Earlier sketch in CA 21-22R
Brusiloff, Phyllis 1935- ... 57-60
Bruss, Elizabeth W(issman) 1944-1981 ... 108
Brussel, Jacob 1900(?)-1979 Obituary ... 104
Brussel, James Arnold 1905- ... CANR-3
Earlier sketch in CA 4R
Brust, Harold
See Cheyney, (Reginald Evelyn) Peter (Southouse)
Brust, Steven K. (Zoltan) 1955- ... 115
Brustein, Robert S(anford) 1927- ... CANR-7
Earlier sketch in CA 11-12R
Bruster, Bill(y) G(lenn) 1940- ... 111
Brustlein, Daniel 1904- ... SATA-40
Brustlein, Janice Tworkov ... 9-10R
See also SATA 40
Bruteau, Beatrice 1930- ... 57-60
Bruton, Eric (Moore) 1915- ... CANR-23
Earlier sketches in CA 13-14R, CANR-5
Bruton, Henry J(ackson) 1921- ... 23-24R
Bruton, J(ack) G(ordon) 1914- ... 11-12R
Brutten, Gene J. 1928- ... 37-40R
Brutten, Milton 1922- ... 45-48
Brutus
See Spooner, John D.
Brutus, Dennis 1924- ... CANR-2
Earlier sketch in CA 49-52
See also CLC 43
Bruun, Bertel 1937- ... 45-48
Bruun, (Arthur) Geoffrey 1898- ... 1R
Bruun, Ruth Dowling 1937- ... 108
Bruyn, Kathleen 1903- ... CAP-2
Earlier sketch in CA 33-36
Bruzelius, Caroline 1949- ... 121
Bry, Adelaide 1920- ... 33-36R
Bry, Gerhard 1911- ... 41-44R
Bryan, Ashley F. 1923- ... 107
See also SATA 31
Bryan, C(ourtlandt) D(ixon) B(arnes) 1936- ... CANR-13
Earlier sketch in CA 73-76
See also CLC 29
Bryan, Carter R(oyston) 1911- ... 33-36R
Bryan, Christopher 1935- ... CANR-20
Earlier sketch in CA 104
Bryan, Dorothy M. 1896(?)-1984 Obituary ... 114
See also SATA 39
Bryan, G(eorge) McLeod 1920- ... 4R
Bryan, George B(arton) 1939- ... 117
Bryan, J(oseph) III 1904- ... CANR-11
Earlier sketch in CA 61-64
Bryan, J(ack) Y(eaman) 1907- ... 73-76
Bryan, John E. 1931- ... CANR-4
Earlier sketch in CA 53-56
Bryan, Julien (Hequembourg) 1899-1974
Obituary ... 53-56
Bryan, M(erwyn) Leonard 1937- ... 103
Bryan, Marian K(nighton) 1900(?)-1974
Obituary ... 53-56
Bryan, Martin 1908- ... 2R
Bryan, Mavis
See O'Brien, Marian P(lowman)
Bryan, Mina R(uese) 1908-1985 Obituary ... 115
Bryan, Sharon 1943- ... 115
Bryan, (William) Wright 1905- ... 77-80
Bryans, Robert Harbinson 1928- ... CANR-11
Earlier sketch in CA 7-8R
Bryans, Robin
See Bryans, Robert Harbinson
Bryant, Anita
See Green, Anita Jane

Bryant, Arthur (Wynne Morgan)
1899-1985 ... 105
Obituary ... 114
Bryant, Bear
See Bryant, Paul W(illiam)
Bryant, Bernice (Morgan) 1908- ... CAP-1
Earlier sketch in CA 9-10
See also SATA 11
Bryant, Beth Elaine 1936- ... 15-16R
Bryant, Cyril E(ric, Jr.) 1917- ... 61-64
Bryant, Donald C(ross) 1905- ... 13-14R
Bryant, Dorothy 1930- ... CANR-19
Earlier sketches in CA 53-56, CANR-4
Bryant, Edward (Albert) 1928- ... CANR-11
Earlier sketch in CA 11-12R
Bryant, Edward (Winslow, Jr.) 1945- ... CANR-1
Earlier sketch in CA 45-48
Bryant, Gay 1945- ... CANR-13
Earlier sketch in CA 73-76
Bryant, Henry A(llen), Jr. 1943- ... CANR-4
Earlier sketch in CA 53-56
Bryant, J(oseph) A(llen), Jr. 1919- ... 5-6R
Bryant, James C(ecil), Jr. 1931- ... 49-52
Bryant, Jerry H(olt) 1928- ... 33-36R
Bryant, Katherine Cliffton 1912- ... 13-14R
Bryant, Keith L(ynn), Jr. 1937- ... 49-52
Bryant, Margaret M. 1900- ... CANR-4
Earlier sketch in CA 4R
Bryant, Paul W(illiam) 1913-1983 ... 111
Obituary ... 108
Bryant, Ralph C(lement) 1938- ... 117
Bryant, Robert H(arry) 1925- ... 23-24R
Bryant, Shasta M(onroe) 1924- ... 41-44R
Bryant, T(homas) Alton 1926- ... CANR-10
Earlier sketch in CA 25-28R
Bryant, Traphes L(emon) 1914- ... 77-80
Bryant, Verda E. 1910- ... CAP-2
Earlier sketch in CA 21-22
Bryant, William Cullen
1794-1878 ... DLB-3, 43, 59
See also CDALB 1640-1865
Bryant, Willis Rooks 1892-1965 ... 7-8R
Obituary ... 103
Bryce, Gladysann 1934- ... 116
Bryce, James 1934- ... 112
Bryce, Murray D(avidson) 1917- ... 13-14R
Brychta, Alex 1956- ... CANR-20
Earlier sketch in CA 103
See also SATA 21
Bryde, John F(rancis) 1920- ... 33-36R
Bryden, Bill
See Bryden, William Campbell Rough
Bryden, John Marshall 1941- ... CANR-1
Earlier sketch in CA 49-52
Bryden, John R(ennie) 1913- ... 33-36R
Bryden, William Campbell Rough 1942- ... 105
Bryer, Jackson R(obert) 1937- ... CANR-18
Earlier sketches in CA 9-10R, CANR-3
Bryer, (Alastair) Robin (Mornington)
1944- ... 111
Bryers, Paul 1945- ... 73-76
Bryfonski, Dedria (Anne) 1947- ... 101
Bryher
See Ellerman, Annie Winifred
Bryks, Rachmil 1912-1974 ... 97-100
Brymer, Jack 1915- ... 110
Brynildsen, Ken(neth) 1944- ... 110
Brynner, Yul
See Khan, Taidje
Bryson, Bernarda 1905- ... 49-52
See also SATA 9
Bryson, Conrey 1905- ... 93-96
Bryson, Phillip J(ames) 1939- ... 69-72
Bryson, Reid Allen 1920- ... 101
Bryson, W(illiam) Hamilton 1941- ... 114
Bryusov, Valery Yakovlevich 1873-1924
Brief entry ... 107
See also TCLC 10
Brzezinski, Zbigniew K(azimierz) 1928- ... CANR-5
Earlier sketch in CA 3R
Buba, Joy Flinsch 1904- ... SATA-44
Bubar, Margaret Weber 1920(?)-1978
Obituary ... 77-80
Bubb, Mel
See Whitcomb, Ian
Bube, Richard H. 1927- ... CANR-8
Earlier sketch in CA 23-24R
Bubeck, Mark I(rving) 1928- ... 61-64
Buber, Martin 1878-1965 Obituary ... 25-28R
Bubner, Rudiger
See Bubner, Ruediger
Bubner, Ruediger 1941- ... 121
Buccellati, Giorgio 1937- ... 41-44R
Bucchieri, Theresa F. 1908- ... 73-76
Bucco, Martin 1929- ... CANR-14
Earlier sketch in CA 29-32R
Buchan, Alastair (Francis) 1918-1976 ... 73-76
Obituary ... 65-68
Buchan, Bryan 1945- ... 107
See also SATA 36
Buchan, David
See Womack, David A(lfred)
Buchan, James 1916- Brief entry ... 119
Buchan, John 1875-1940 Brief entry ... 108
See also YABC 2
See also DLB 34
Buchan, Kate
See Erskine, Barbara
Buchan, Norman Findlay 1922- ... 109
Buchan, Perdita 1940- ... 21-22R
Buchan, Stuart 1942-1987 ... 57-60
Obituary ... 123
Buchan, Thomas Buchanan 1931- ... CANR-16
Earlier sketch in CA 25-28R
Buchan, Tom
See Buchan, Thomas Buchanan
Buchanan, A(lbert) Russell 1906- ... 13-14R
Buchanan, Annette 1933- ... 118
Buchanan, Betty (Joan) 1923- ... 101
Buchanan, Chuck
See Rowland, D(onald) S(ydney)
Buchanan, Colin O(gilvie) 1934- ... 25-28R
Buchanan, Cynthia 1942- ... CANR-1
Earlier sketch in CA 45-48
Buchanan, Cynthia D(ee) 1937- ... 7-8R
Buchanan, Daniel C(rump) 1892- ... 19-20R
Buchanan, (Eric) David 1933- ... 57-60
Buchanan, David A(lan) 1949- ... 118
Buchanan, Donald W(illiam) 1908-19(?) ... CAP-1
Earlier sketch in CA 11-12
Buchanan, George (Henry Perrott)
1904- ... CANR-3
Earlier sketch in CA 11-12R
Buchanan, George Wesley 1921- ... CANR-14
Earlier sketch in CA 37-40R
Buchanan, James J(unkin) 1925- ... 33-36R
Buchanan, James McGill 1919- ... CANR-22
Earlier sketches in CA 5-6R, CANR-3
Buchanan, Keith 1919- ... CANR-10
Earlier sketch in CA 23-24R
Buchanan, Laura
See King, Florence
Buchanan, Marie ... CANR-10
Earlier sketch in CA 65-68
Buchanan, Patrick
See Corley, Edwin (Raymond)
Buchanan, Pegasus 1920- ... 11-12R
Buchanan, R(obert) A(ngus) 1930- ... CANR-7
Earlier sketch in CA 17-18R
Buchanan, Robert 1841-1901 ... DLB-18, 35
Buchanan, Thomas G(ittings) 1919- ... 2R
Buchanan, Wiley T(homas), Jr.
1914-1986 Obituary ... 118
Buchanan, William
See Buck, William Ray
Buchanan, William J(esse) 1926- ... 73-76
Buchanan-Brown, John 1929- ... 102
Buchard, Robert 1931- ... 33-36R
Buchdahl, Gerd 1914- ... 57-60
Bucheister, Patt 1942- ... 122
Buchele, William Martin 1895- ... 57-60
Buchen, Irving H. 1930- ... 25-28R
Bucher, Bradley 1932- ... 37-40R
Bucher, Charles A(ugustus) 1912- ... CANR-3
Earlier sketch in CA 11-12R
Bucher, Francois 1927- ... CANR-3
Earlier sketch in CA 5-6R
Bucher, Glenn R(ichard) 1940- ... 57-60
Bucher, Magnus 1927- ... 41-44R
Buchheim, Lothar-Guenther 1918- ... 85-88
See also CLC 6
Buchheimer, Naomi Barnett
See Barnett, Naomi
Buchheit, Lee C(harles) 1950- ... 81-84
Buchler, Justus 1914- ... 5-6R
Buchman, Dian Dincin ... CANR-8
Earlier sketch in CA 61-64
Buchman, Frank N(athan) D(aniel)
1878-1961 Obituary ... 112
Buchman, Herman 1920- ... 41-44R
Buchman, Marion ... 121
Buchman, Randall L(oren) 1929- ... CANR-1
Earlier sketch in CA 45-48
Buchman, Sidney 1902-1975 ... 93-96
Obituary ... 61-64
See also DLB 26
Buchwald, Art(hur) 1925- ... CANR-21
Earlier sketch in CA 5-6R
See also SATA 10
See also CLC 33
See also AITN 1
Buchwald, Emilie 1935- ... CANR-2
Earlier sketch in CA 49-52
See also SATA 7
Buck, Ashley ?-1980 Obituary ... 97-100
Buck, Charles (Henry, Jr.) 1915- ... 33-36R
Buck, Doris P(itkin) 1898(?)-1980
Obituary ... 102
Buck, Edith V(irginia) 1919- ... 117
Buck, Frederick Silas ... 7-8R
Buck, George C(rawford) 1918- ... 69-72
Buck, Harry M(erwyn, Jr.) 1921- ... CANR-13
Earlier sketch in CA 33-36R
Buck, James H. 1924- ... 104
Buck, Joan Juliet 1948- ... 108
Buck, John Lossing 1890-1975 ... CANR-2
Obituary ... 61-64
Earlier sketch in CA 45-48
Buck, John N(elson) 1906- ... CAP-2
Earlier sketch in CA 29-32
Buck, Lewis 1925- ... 73-76
See also SATA 18
Buck, Margaret Waring 1910- ... 5-6R
See also SATA 3
Buck, Marion A(shby) 1909- ... CAP-1
Earlier sketch in CA 13-14
Buck, Paul H(erman) 1899-1978
Obituary ... 81-84
Buck, Pearl S(ydenstricker) 1892-1973 ... CANR-1
Obituary ... 41-44R
Earlier sketch in CA 2R
See also SATA 1, 25
See also DLB 9
See also CLC 7, 11, 18
See also AITN 1
Buck, Peggy S(ullivan) 1930- ... 65-68
Buck, Philip W(allenstein) 1900- ... 65-68
Buck, Robert N. 1914- ... 103
Buck, Stratton 1906- ... CAP-2
Earlier sketch in CA 17-18
Buck, Vernon E(llis) 1934- ... 37-40R
Buck, William Ray 1930- ... 4R
Buckeridge, Anthony (Malcolm) 1912- ... CANR-2
Earlier sketch in CA 49-52
See also SATA 6
Buckeye, Donald A(ndrew) 1930- ... 49-52
Buckholdt, David R. 1942- ... 101
Buckholtz, Eileen (Garber) 1949- ... 117
See also SATA 47
Buckhout, Robert 1935- ... 45-48
Buckingham, Burdette H. 1907(?)-1977
Obituary ... 73-76
Buckingham, Clyde E(dwin) 1907- ... CAP-1
Earlier sketch in CA 15-16
Buckingham, James (William) 1932- ... 29-32R
Buckingham, Jamie
See Buckingham, James (William)
Buckingham, Robert W(illiam) III ... 113
Buckingham, Walter S(amuel), Jr.
1924-1967 ... 1R
Obituary ... 103
Buckingham, Willis J(ohn) 1938- ... 29-32R
Buckland, Michael K(eeble) 1941- ... 97-100
Buckland, Raymond 1934- ... 73-76
Buckle, (Christopher) Richard (Sandford)
1916- ... 97-100
Buckler, Ernest 1908-1984 ... CAP-1
Obituary ... 114
Earlier sketch in CA 11-12
See also SATA 47
See also CLC 13
Buckler, John 1945- ... 121
Buckler, William Earl 1924- ... CANR-20
Earlier sketches in CA 1R, CANR-5
Buckley, Anthony D. 1945- ... 120
Buckley, Doris Heather
See Buckley Neville, Heather
Buckley, Fergus Reid 1930- ... 21-22R
Buckley, Fiona
See Anand, Valerie
Buckley, Francis J(oseph) 1928- ... CANR-13
Earlier sketch in CA 33-36R
Buckley, Helen E(lizabeth) 1918- ... CANR-3
Earlier sketch in CA 5-6R
See also SATA 2
Buckley, James Lane 1923- ... 61-64
Buckley, Jerome Hamilton 1917- ... CANR-3
Earlier sketch in CA 2R
Buckley, Julian Gerard 1905- ... 41-44R
Buckley, Mary L(orraine) ... 53-56
Buckley, Michael F. 1880(?)-1977
Obituary ... 69-72
Buckley, Michael J(oseph) 1931- ... 73-76
Buckley, Peter 1938- ... 112
Buckley, Priscilla 1921- ... 81-84
Buckley, Roger N(orman) 1937- ... 97-100
Buckley, Shawn 1943- ... 93-96
Buckley, Suzanne Shelton 1946- ... 108
Buckley, Thomas H(ugh) 1932- ... 29-32R
Buckley, Vincent (Thomas) 1925- ... 101
Buckley, Walter (Frederick) 1921- ... 121
Buckley, William F(rank), Jr. 1925- ... CANR-24
Earlier sketches in CA 4R, CANR-1
See also DLBY 80
See also CLC 7, 18, 37
See also AITN 1
Buckley Neville, Heather 1910- ... 103
Bucklin, Louis P(ierre) 1928- ... 97-100
Buckman, Peter 1941- ... CANR-11
Earlier sketch in CA 65-68
Buckmaster, Henrietta
See Stephens, Henrietta Henkle
See also SATA 6
Buckminster, Joseph Stevens
1784-1812 ... DLB-37
Bucknall, Barbara J(ane) 1933- ... CANR-14
Earlier sketch in CA 33-36R
Buckner, Robert (Henry) 1906- ... 3R
See also DLB 26
Buckner, Sally Beaver 1931- ... 61-64
Buckstead, Richard C(hris) 1929- ... 49-52
Buckvar, Felice (Spitz) 1938- ... 107
Buczkowski, Leopold 1905- ... 41-44R
Buday, George
See Buday, Gyorgy
Buday, Gyorgy 1907- ... 107
Budberg, Moura 1892(?)-1974 Obituary ... 53-56
Budbill, David 1940- ... 73-76
Budd, Edward C(arhart) 1920- ... 23-24R
Budd, Elaine 1925- ... 101
Budd, Kenneth George 1904-1972 ... CAP-1
Earlier sketch in CA 13-14
Budd, Lillian (Peterson) 1897- ... CANR-4
Earlier sketch in CA 2R
See also SATA 7
Budd, Louis J(ohn) 1921- ... CANR-3
Earlier sketch in CA 4R
Budd, Mavis ... CANR-19
Earlier sketch in CA 102
Budd, Richard W. 1934- ... 23-24R
Budd, Thomas ?-1698 ... DLB-24
Budd, William C(laude) 1923- ... 49-52
Buddee, Paul Edgar 1913- ... 103
Budden, Laura M(adeline) 1894- ... 7-8R
Bude, John
See Elmore, Ernest Carpenter
Budenz, Louis F(rancis) 1891-1972
Obituary ... 89-92
Budge, Ian 1936- ... CANR-12
Earlier sketch in CA 29-32R
Budgen, Frank Spencer Curtis 1882-1971
Obituary ... 29-32R
Budick, Sanford 1942- ... 33-36R
Budimir, (Simo) Velimir 1926- ... 65-68
Budinger, Peyton Bailey 1939- ... 114
Budoff, Penny Wise 1939- ... 110
Budrys, Algirdas Jonas 1931- ... CANR-20
Earlier sketches in CA 2R, CANR-4
See also DLB 8
Budrys, Algis
See Budrys, Algirdas Jonas
Budurowycz, Bohdan B(asil) 1921- ... CANR-3
Earlier sketch in CA 5-6R
Budzik, Janet K. Sims 1942- ... 37-40R
Buechner, (Carl) Frederick 1926- ... CANR-11
Earlier sketch in CA 13-14R
See also DLBY 80
See also CLC 2, 4, 6, 9
Buechner, John C(harles) 1934- ... 23-24R
Buechner, Thomas S(charman) 1926- ... 49-52
Buehler, Curt F(erdinand) 1905-1985 ... 1R
Obituary ... 117
Buehlmann, Walbert 1916- ... 115
Buehnau, Ludwig
See Schreiber, Hermann
Buehner, Andrew J(ohn) 1905- ... 17-18R
Buehr, Walter Franklin 1897-1971 ... CANR-3
Obituary ... 33-36R
Earlier sketch in CA 5-6R
See also SATA 3
Buehrig, Edward H(enry) 1910- ... 37-40R
Buehrig, Gordon M. 1904- ... 101
Buel, Richard (Van Wyck), Jr. 1933- ... CANR-13
Earlier sketch in CA 73-76
Bueler, Lois E(aton) 1940- ... 57-60
Bueler, William Merwin 1934- ... 37-40R
Buell, Frederick H(enderson) 1942- ... 33-36R
Buell, John (Edward) 1927- ... 2R
See also DLB 53
See also CLC 10
Buell, Jon A. 1939- ... 102
Buell, Lawrence 1939- ... 49-52
Buell, Robert Kingery 1908-1971 ... CAP-2
Earlier sketch in CA 25-28
Buell, Victor P(aul) 1914- ... CANR-8
Earlier sketch in CA 21-22R
Buelow, George J. 1929- ... 21-22R
Buendia, Manuel
See Giron, Manuel Buendia Tellez
Buenker, John D(avid) 1937- ... CANR-16
Earlier sketches in CA 45-48, CANR-1
Bueno, Jose de la Torre 1905(?)-1980
Obituary ... 93-96
Bueno de Mesquita, Bruce James 1946- ... 108
Buergenthal, Thomas 1934- ... 37-40R
Buerkle, Jack Vincent 1923- ... 41-44R
Buero Vallejo, Antonio 1916- ... CANR-24
Earlier sketch in CA 106
See also CLC 15, 46
Bueschel, Richard M. 1926- ... CANR-11
Earlier sketch in CA 25-28R
Buetow, Harold A(ndrew) 1919- ... 53-56
Buettner-Janusch, John 1924- ... 49-52
Bufalari, Giuseppe 1927- ... CANR-16
Earlier sketch in CA 25-28R
Buferd, Norma Bradley 1937- ... 69-72
Buff, Conrad 1886-1975 ... SATA-19
Buff, Mary Marsh 1890-1970 Obituary ... 116
See also SATA 19
Buffa, Dudley W. 1940- ... 121
Buffalo Chuck
See Barth, Charles P.
Buffaloe, Neal D(ollison) 1924- ... 53-56
Buffington, Albert F(ranklin) 1905- ... 33-36R
Buffington, Robert (Ray) 1933- ... 21-22R
Bufkin, Ernest Claude, Jr. 1929- ... 101
Buford, Thomas O(liver) 1932- ... 29-32R
Bugayev, Boris Nikolayevich 1880-1934
Brief entry ... 104
Bugbee, Emma 1888(?)-1981 Obituary ... 105
See also SATA 29
Bugbee, Ruth Carson 1903- ... CANR-1
Earlier sketch in CA 1R
Bugental, James F(rederick) T(homas)
1915- ... CANR-10
Earlier sketch in CA 23-24R
Bugg, James L(uckin), Jr. 1920- ... 7-8R
Bugg, Ralph 1922- ... 73-76
Buggie, Frederick D(enman) 1929- ... 97-100
Buglass, Leslie J. 1917- ... 13-14R
Bugliarello, George 1927- ... 41-44R
Bugliosi, Vincent (T.) 1934- ... CANR-13
Earlier sketch in CA 73-76
Buhite, Russell D(evere) 1938- ... 101
Buhle, Mari Jo 1943- ... 108
Buhler, Charlotte B(ertha) 1893-197(?) ... CAP-2
Earlier sketch in CA 17-18
Buhler, Curt F(erdinand)
See Buehler, Curt F(erdinand)
Buhlmann, Walbert
See Buehlmann, Walbert
Buisseret, David 1934- ... 124
Buist, Charlotte
See Patterson, Charlotte (Buist)
Buist, Vincent 1919(?)-1979 Obituary ... 89-92
Buitenhuis, Peter (Martinus) 1925- ... 25-28R
Buitrago, Ann Mari 1929- ... 105
Bukalski, Peter J(ulian) 1941- ... CANR-15
Earlier sketch in CA 41-44R
Buker, George E(dward) 1923- ... 53-56
Bukharin, Nikolai (Ivanovich) 1888-1938
Brief entry ... 120
Bukowski, Charles 1920- ... 17-18R
See also DLB 5
See also CLC 2, 5, 9, 41
Buktenica, Norman A(ugust) 1930- ... 33-36R
Bulatkin, Eleanor Webster 1913- ... 33-36R
Bulatovic, Miodrag 1930- ... CANR-21
Earlier sketch in CA 5-6R
Buley, R(oscoe) Carlyle 1893-1968 ... CAP-2
Obituary ... 25-28R
Earlier sketch in CA 21-22
Bulfinch, Thomas 1796-1867 ... SATA-35
Bulgakov, Mikhail (Afanas'evich)
1891-1940 Brief entry ... 105
See also TCLC 2, 16

Bulger, William T(homas) 1927- 69-72
Bulgya, Alexander Alexandrovich
1901-1956 Brief entry 117
Bulka, Reuven P(inchas) 1944- 113
Bulkeley, Christy C. AITN-2
Bulkley, Dwight H(atfield) 1919- 105
Bull, Angela (Mary) 1936- CANR-24
Earlier sketches in CA 21-22R, CANR-9
See also SATA 45
Bull, Geoffrey Taylor 1921- CANR-3
Earlier sketch in CA 9-10R
Bull, George (Anthony) 1929- 115
Bull, Guyon B(oys) G(arrett) 1912- CANR-5
Earlier sketch in CA 7-8R
Bull, Hedley Norman 1932-1985 .... 5-6R
Obituary 116
Bull, John 1914- 69-72
Bull, Norman John 1916- CANR-16
Earlier sketch in CA 93-96
See also SATA 41
Bull, Odd 1907- 81-84
Bull, Peter (Cecil) 1912-1984 .... CANR-11
Obituary 112
Earlier sketch in CA 25-28R
See also SATA 39
Bull, Robert J(ehu) 1920- 97-100
Bull, Storm 1913- 11-12R
Bull, William E(merson) 1909-1972 .... CAP-1
Earlier sketch in CA 15-16
Bulla, Clyde Robert 1914- CANR-18
Earlier sketches in CA 7-8R, CANR-3
See also SATA 2, 41
Bullard, E(dgar) John III 1942- 33-36R
Bullard, Fred Mason 1901- 25-28R
Bullard, Helen 1902- CANR-7
Earlier sketch in CA 17-18R
Bullard, Oral 1922- CANR-23
Earlier sketches in CA 61-64, CANR-8
Bullard, Pamela 1948- 106
Bullard, Roger A(ubrey) 1937- 33-36R
Bulle, Florence (Elizabeth) 1925- CANR-15
Earlier sketch in CA 93-96
Bulleid, H(enry) A(nthony) V(aughan)
1912- CANR-13
Earlier sketches in CA 9-10, CAP-1
Bullen, Dana R(ipley) 1931- 73-76
Bullen, Keith Edward 1906-1976 Obituary ... 106
Bullen, Robert 1926(?)-1976 Obituary 69-72
Buller, Herman 1923- 61-64
Bulliet, Richard W(illiams) 1940- CANR-7
Earlier sketch in CA 57-60
Bullingham, Rodney
See Sladen, Norman St. Barbe
Bullins, Ed 1935- CANR-24
Earlier sketch in CA 49-52
See also DLB 7, 38
See also CLC 1, 5, 7
Bullis, Harry Amos 1890-1963 .... CAP-2
Earlier sketch in CA 17-18
Bullis, Jerald 1944- CANR-1
Earlier sketch in CA 49-52
Bullitt, John M(arshall) 1921-1985
Obituary 117
Bullitt, Orville H(orwitz) 1894-1979 .... 33-36R
Obituary 89-92
Bullitt, Stimson 1919- 112
Bullitt, William C(hristian) 1891-1967
Obituary 89-92
Bullock, Alan Louis Charles 1914- 1R
Bullock, Alice 1904- 89-92
Bullock, Barbara
See Bullock-Wilson, Barbara
Bullock, C(larence) Hassell 1939- 89-92
Bullock, Charles S(pencer) III 1942- ... CANR-13
Earlier sketch in CA 33-36R
Bullock, Frederick W(illiam) B(agshawe)
1903-19(?) CANR-4
Earlier sketch in CA 7-8R
Bullock, Henry 1907(?)-1973 Obituary ... 41-44R
Bullock, Michael 1918- CANR-7
Earlier sketch in CA 19-20R
Bullock, Paul 1924-1986 .... CANR-11
Obituary 118
Earlier sketch in CA 29-32R
Bullock-Wilson, Barbara 1945- 65-68
Bullough, Bonnie 1927- CANR-11
Earlier sketch in CA 69-72
Bullough, D(onald) A(uberon) 1928- 107
Bullough, Geoffrey 1901-1982 .... CANR-5
Obituary 106
Earlier sketch in CA 4R
Bullough, Vern (LeRoy) 1928- CANR-11
Earlier sketches in CA 9-10R, CANR-4
Bullough, William A(lfred) 1933- 101
Bulman, Joan (Carroll Boone) 1904- 103
Bulman, Oliver (Meredith Boone)
1902-1974 Obituary 49-52
Bulmer, (Henry) Kenneth 1921- CANR-9
Earlier sketch in CA 15-16R
Bulmer, Martin 1943- 113
Bulmer-Thomas, Ivor 1905- CAP-1
Earlier sketch in CA 11-12
Buloff, Joseph 1899(?)-1985 Obituary 115
Bulpin, T(homas) V(ictor) 1918- CANR-4
Earlier sketch in CA 11-12R
Bultmann, Rudolf Karl 1884-1976 .... 7-8R
Obituary 65-68
Bulwer-Lytton, Edward 1803-1873 .... DLB-21
Bumagin, Victoria E. 1923- 89-92
Bump, Jerome 1943- 109
Bumppo, Nathaniel John Balthazar
1940- 97-100
Bumppo, Natty
See Bumppo, Nathaniel John Balthazar
Bumpus, Jerry 1937- CANR-10
Earlier sketch in CA 65-68
See also DLBY 81
Bumstead, Kathleen Mary 1918- 121
Bumsted, J(ohn) M(ichael) 1938- 41-44R
Bunce, Alan 1939- 77-80
Bunce, Frank David 1907- CAP-1
Earlier sketch in CA 11-12
Bunce, Linda Susan (Staines) 1956- 107
Bunch, Clarence 53-56
Bunch, David R. 29-32R
Bunche, Ralph Johnson 1904-1971
Obituary 33-36R
Bundy, Clarence E(verett) 1906- 85-88
Bundy, William P(utnam) 1917- 104
Bunge, Mario A(ugusto) 1919- 9-10R
Bunge, Nancy L(iddell) 1942- 124
Bunge, Robert Pierce 1930- 124
Bunge, Walter R(ichard) 1911- 25-28R
Bung Karno
See Sukarno, (Ahmed)
Buni, Andrew 1931- 21-22R
Bunim, Irving M. 1901(?)-1980 Obituary ... 103
Bunin, Catherine 1967- 93-96
See also SATA 30
Bunin, Ivan Alexeyevich 1870-1953
Brief entry 104
See also TCLC 6
Bunin, Sherry 1925- 93-96
See also SATA 30
Buning, Sietze
See Wiersma, Stanley M(arvin)
Bunke, H(arvey) Charles 1922- 11-12R
Bunker, Edward 1933- 41-44R
Bunker, Gerald Edward 1938- 37-40R
Bunker, Linda K. 1947- 111
Bunn, John T(homas) 1924- 37-40R
Bunn, John W. 1898- CAP-2
Earlier sketch in CA 23-24
Bunn, Ronald F(reeze) 1929- 21-22R
Bunn, Scott (Middelton) 1943- 111
Bunn, Thomas 1944- 69-72
Bunnell, Peter C(urtis) 1937- CANR-12
Earlier sketch in CA 33-36R
Bunnell, William S(tanley) 1925- CAP-1
Earlier sketch in CA 11-12
Bunt, Lucas N(icolaas) H(endrik) 1905- ... 69-72
Bunting, A. E.
See Bunting, Anne Evelyn
Bunting, Anne Evelyn 1928- CANR-19
Earlier sketches in CA 53-56, CANR-5
See also SATA 18
Bunting, Bainbridge 1913-1981 .... CANR-8
Earlier sketch in CA 61-64
Bunting, Basil 1900-1985 .... CANR-7
Obituary 115
Earlier sketch in CA 53-56
See also DLB 20
See also CLC 10, 39, 47
Bunting, Eve
See Bunting, Anne Evelyn
Bunting, Glenn (Davison) 1957- SATA-22
Bunting, Josiah 1939- 45-48
Bunuan, Josefina S(antiago) 1935- 33-36R
Bunuel, Luis 1900-1983 101
Obituary 110
See also CLC 16
Bunyan, John 1628-1688 .... DLB-39
Bunzel, John H(arvey) 1924- 17-18R
Buol, S(tanley) W(alter) 1934- 49-52
Burack, Abraham Saul 1908-1978 .... CANR-4
Obituary 77-80
Earlier sketch in CA 11-12R
Burack, Elmer H(oward) 1927- CANR-16
Earlier sketch in CA 37-40R
Burack, Sylvia K. 1916- CANR-9
Earlier sketch in CA 21-22R
See also SATA 35
Burak, Linda (Gallina) 116
Buranelli, Vincent 1919- CANR-20
Earlier sketches in CA 11-12R, CANR-5
Burbank, Addison (Buswell)
1895-1961 .... SATA-37
Burbank, Garin 1940- 69-72
Burbank, Natt B(ryant) 1903- CAP-2
Earlier sketch in CA 25-28
Burbank, Nelson L(incoln) 1898- CAP-1
Earlier sketch in CA 11-12
Burbank, Rex James 1925- CANR-18
Earlier sketch in CA 1R
Burbidge, Peter George 1919-1985
Obituary 116
Burbridge, Branse 1921- 97-100
Burby, Raymond J(oseph) III 1942- ... CANR-11
Earlier sketch in CA 69-72
Burby, William E(dward) 1893- CAP-1
Earlier sketch in CA 11-12
Burch, Claire R. 1925- 101
Burch, Francis F(loyd) 1932- 29-32R
Burch, George Bosworth 1902-1973 122
Obituary 109
Burch, Jennings Michael 1941- 118
Burch, Mark H(etzel) 1953- 122
Burch, Mary Lou 1914- 104
Burch, Monte G. 1943- 103
Burch, Pat 1944- 57-60
Burch, Philip H. 1930- 106
Burch, Preston M. 1884-1978 Obituary ... 77-80
Burch, Robert J(oseph) 1925- CANR-17
Earlier sketches in CA 5-6R, CANR-2
See also SATA 1
See also DLB 52
Burcham, Nancy A(nn) 1942- 89-92
Burchard, John Ely 1898-1975 .... CANR-6
Obituary 61-64
Earlier sketch in CA 3R
Burchard, Max N(orman) 1925- 23-24R
Burchard, Peter Duncan 1921- CANR-18
Earlier sketches in CA 5-6R, CANR-3
See also SATA 5
Burchard, Rachael C(aroline) 1921- 33-36R
Burchard, S. H.
See Burchard, Sue
Burchard, Sue 1937- CANR-19
Earlier sketches in CA 53-56, CANR-4
See also SATA 22
Burchardt, Bill
See Burchardt, William Robert
Burchardt, Nellie 1921- 21-22R
See also SATA 7
Burchardt, William Robert 1917- CANR-16
Earlier sketch in CA 89-92
Burchell, Mary
See Cook, Ida
Burchell, R(obert) A(rthur) 1941- 106
Burchett, Randall E. ?-1971 .... 3R
Obituary 103
Burchett, Wilfred (Graham) 1911-1983 .. CANR-2
Obituary 110
Earlier sketch in CA 49-52
Burchfield, Joe D(onald) 1937- 85-88
Burchfield, Robert William 1923- CANR-14
Earlier sketch in CA 41-44R
Burchwood, Katharine T(yler) 57-60
Burck, Jacob 1907-1982 Obituary 106
Burckel, Nicholas C(lare) 1943- CANR-19
Earlier sketch in CA 103
Burckhardt, C(arl) J(akob) 1891-1974 93-96
Obituary 49-52
Burd, Laurence Hull 1915-1983 Obituary ... 109
Burd, Van Akin 1914- 41-44R
Burda, R(obert) W(arren) 1932- 73-76
Burden, Jean 1914- CANR-3
Earlier sketch in CA 9-10R
Burden, William Douglas 1898-1978
Obituary 81-84
Burder, John 1940- 110
Burdett, Winston 1913- 29-32R
Burdette, Franklin L. 1911-1975 65-68
Obituary 61-64
Burdge, Rabel J(ames) 1937- 69-72
Burdick, Donald W(alter) 1917- 53-56
Burdick, Eric 1934- 29-32R
Burdick, Eugene (Leonard) 1918-1965 .... 5-6R
Obituary 25-28R
See also SATA 22
Burdick, Loraine 1929- 57-60
Burdon, R(andal) M(athews) 1896- CAP-1
Earlier sketch in CA 13-14
Bureau, William H(obbs) 1913- 102
Buren, Martha Margareta Elisabet 1910- .. CAP-1
Earlier sketch in CA 13-14
Burfield, Eva
See Ebbett, (Frances) Eva
Burford, E(phraim) J(ohn) 1905- 124
Burford, Eleanor
See Hibbert, Eleanor Burford
Burford, Lolah 41-44R
Burford, Roger L(ewis) 1930- 41-44R
Burford, William (Skelly) 1927- CANR-7
Earlier sketch in CA 7-8R
Burg, Dale R(onda) 1942- CANR-23
Earlier sketch in CA 106
Burg, David
See Dolberg, Alexander
Burg, David F(rederick) 1936- 116
Burge, Doris 1909- 120
Burge, Ethel 1916- 65-68
Burgeon, G. A. L.
See Barfield, (Arthur) Owen
Burger, Albert E. 1941- 37-40R
Burger, Alfred 1905- 122
Burger, Angela Sutherland (Brown) 1936- .. 81-84
Burger, Carl 1888-1967 .... CAP-2
Earlier sketch in CA 19-20
See also SATA 9
Burger, Chester 1921- 11-12R
Burger, Edward J(ames), Jr. 1933- 110
Burger, George V(anderkarr) 1927- 57-60
Burger, Henry G. 1923- CANR-15
Earlier sketch in CA 41-44R
Burger, Jack
See Burger, John R(obert)
Burger, John
See Marquard, Leo(pold)
Burger, John R(obert) 1942- 81-84
Burger, Nash K(err) 1908- CAP-2
Earlier sketch in CA 23-24
Burger, Robert E(ugene) 1931- 85-88
Burger, Robert S. 1913- 29-32R
Burger, Ronna Cheryl 1947- 117
Burger, Ruth P(azen) 1917- 17-18R
Burger, Sarah Greene 1935- 69-72
Burgess, Ann Marie
See Gerson, Noel Bertram
Burgess, Anthony
See Wilson, John (Anthony) Burgess
See also DLB 14
See also CLC 1, 2, 4, 5, 8, 10, 13, 15,
22, 40
See also AITN 1
Burgess, C(hester) F(rancis) 1922- 21-22R
Burgess, Charles (Orville) 1932- 33-36R
Burgess, Christopher Victor 1921- 9-10R
Burgess, Em
See Burgess, Mary Wyche
Burgess, Eric (Alexander) 1912- 101
Burgess, Eric 1920- CANR-18
Earlier sketches in CA 5-6R, CANR-3
Burgess, (Frank) Gelett 1866-1951
Brief entry 113
See also SATA 30, 32
See also DLB 11
Burgess, Helen S(teers) 1906-1987
Obituary 123
Burgess, Jackson (Visscher) 1927- 11-12R
Burgess, Jane K. 1928- CANR-13
Earlier sketch in CA 73-76R
Burgess, John H(enry) 1923- 33-36R
Burgess, John Lawie 1912-1987 Obituary .. 121
Burgess, John W. 1844-1931 .... DLB-47
Burgess, Linda Cannon 1911- 73-76
Burgess, Lorraine Marshall 1913- 106
Burgess, M(argaret) Elaine 15-16R
Burgess, M(ichael) R(oy) 1948- CANR-6
Earlier sketch in CA 57-60
Burgess, Mary Wyche 1916- 61-64
See also SATA 18
Burgess, Michael
See Gerson, Noel Bertram
Burgess, Norman 1923- 25-28R
Burgess, Philip M(ark) 1939- CANR-16
Earlier sketch in CA 25-28R
Burgess, Robert F(orrest) 1927- CANR-11
Earlier sketch in CA 25-28R
See also SATA 4
Burgess, Robert H(errmann) 1913- CANR-5
Earlier sketch in CA 9-10R
Burgess, Robert L. 1938- 29-32R
Burgess, Thornton Waldo 1874-1965 73-76
See also SATA 17
See also DLB 22
Burgess, Trevor
See Trevor, Elleston
Burgess, W(arren) Randolph 1889-1978 .. CAP-2
Obituary 81-84
Earlier sketch in CA 29-32
Burgess-Kohn, Jane
See Burgess, Jane K.
Burgett, Donald R(obert) 1925- 21-22R
Burggraaff, Winfield J. 1940- Brief entry ... 114
Burghard, August 1901- CANR-7
Earlier sketch in CA 19-20R
See also AITN 2
Burghardt, Andrew Frank 1924- 5-6R
Burghardt, Walter J(ohn) 1914- CANR-19
Earlier sketches in CA 2R, CANR-4
Burgin, C(harles) David 1939- 73-76
Burgin, (Weston) Richard 1947- 25-28R
Burgos, Joseph A(gner), Jr. 1945- 106
Burgoyne, Elizabeth
See Pickles, M(abel) Elizabeth
Burgwyn, Diana 1937- 108
Burgwyn, Mebane Holoman 1914- 49-52
See also SATA 7
Burhoe, Ralph Wendell 1911- 17-18R
Buri, Fritz 1907- CANR-8
Earlier sketch in CA 19-20R
Burian, Jarka M(arsano) 1927- 33-36R
Burian, Richard M(artin) 1941- 121
Burich, Nancy J(ane) 1943- 29-32R
Burick, Si(mon) 1909-1986 85-88
Obituary 121
Burk, Bill E(ugene) 1932- 65-68
Burk, Bruce 1917- 61-64
Burk, John Daly 1772(?)-1808 .... DLB-37
Burke, Alan Dennis 1949- 106
Burke, Anna Mae Walsh 1938- 111
Burke, Avid J. 1906- 23-24R
Burke, C(letus) J(oseph) 1917-1973 45-48
Burke, Carl F(rancis) 1917- 25-28R
Burke, Carol 1950- CANR-14
Earlier sketch in CA 65-68
Burke, Colin Bradley 1936- 113
Burke, David 1927- CANR-23
Earlier sketch in CA 105
See also SATA 46
Burke, Desmond William Lardner
See Lardner-Burke, Desmond William
Burke, Edmund M. 1928- 11-12R
Burke, Fielding
See Dargan, Olive (Tilford)
Burke, Fred G(eorge) 1926- 13-14R
Burke, Gerald 1914- CANR-1
Earlier sketch in CA 45-48
Burke, J(ohn) Bruce 1933- 37-40R
Burke, J(ackson) F(rederick Augustine)
1915- CANR-12
Earlier sketch in CA 65-68
Burke, James 1936- 102
Burke, James Lee 1936- CANR-22
Earlier sketches in CA 15-16R, CANR-7
Burke, James Wakefield 1916- CANR-1
Earlier sketch in CA 45-48
Burke, John (Frederick) 1922- CANR-9
Earlier sketch in CA 7-8R
Burke, John
See O'Connor, Richard
Burke, John Emmett 1908- 37-40R
Burke, John Garrett 1917- 77-80
Burke, John J(oseph), Jr. 1942- 114
Burke, Jonathan
See Burke, John (Frederick)
Burke, Joseph (Terence Anthony) 1913- ... 103
Burke, Kenneth (Duva) 1897- 5-6R
See also DLB 45, 63
See also CLC 2, 24
Burke, Leda
See Garnett, David
Burke, Maggie
See Snyder, Marilyn
Burke, (Omar) Michael 1927- 73-76
Burke, Owen
See Burke, John (Frederick)
Burke, (Ulick) Peter 1937- CANR-16
Earlier sketch in CA 25-28R
Burke, Ralph
See Silverberg, Robert
Burke, Richard C(ullen) 1932- 53-56
Burke, Robert E(ugene) 1921- 21-22R
Burke, Russell 1946- 33-36R
Burke, S(amuel) M(artin) 1906- 49-52

Burke, Shifty
See Benton, Peggie
Burke, Stanley 1923- 101
Burke, T(homas) Patrick 1934- 121
Burke, Ted 1934(?)-1978 Obituary 77-80
Burke, Thomas 1886-1945 Brief entry 113
Burke, Tom 73-76
Burke, Vee
See Burke, Velma Whitgrove
Burke, Velma Whitgrove 1921- CANR-4
Earlier sketch in CA 53-56
Burke, Vincent John 1919-1973 122
Obituary 111
Burke, Virginia M. 1916- 45-48
Burke, W. Warner 1935- CANR-14
Earlier sketch in CA 37-40R
Burkert, Nancy Ekholm 1933- SATA-24
Burkert, Walter 1931- 103
Burket, Harriet 1908- 37-40R
Burkett, David (Young III) 1934- CANR-9
Earlier sketch in CA 65-68
Burkett, Eva M(ae) 1903- 33-36R
Burkett, Jack 1914- 101
Burkett, Molly 1932- CANR-9
Earlier sketch in CA 53-56
Burkey, Richard M(ichael) 1930- 93-96
Burkhalter, Barton R. 1938- CANR-11
Earlier sketch in CA 25-28R
Burkhardt, Richard Wellington 1918- 2R
Burkhart, Charles 1924- 15-16R
Burkhart, James A(ustin) 1914-1979 9-10R
Burkhart, John E(rnest) 1927- 116
Burkhart, Kathryn Watterson 1942- 45-48
Burkhart, Kitsi
See Burkhart, Kathryn Watterson
Burkhart, Robert E(dward) 1937- 29-32R
Burkhead, Jesse 1916- CANR-3
Earlier sketch in CA 4R
Burkholder, J(ames) Peter 1954- 119
Burkholder, John Richard 1928- 115
Burkholz, Herbert 1932- CANR-11
Earlier sketch in CA 25-28R
Burkill, T(om) A(lec) 1912- 33-36R
Burkitt, Denis (Parsons) 1911- 112
Burkle, Howard R(ussell) 1925-
Brief entry 107
Burkman, Katherine H. 1934- 29-32R
Burkowsky, Mitchell R(oy) 1931- 29-32R
Burks, Ardath Walter 1915- 107
Burks, Arthur W(alter) 1915- 49-52
Burks, David D. 1924- 33-36R
Burks, Edward C. 1921(?)-1983 Obituary 111
Burks, Gordon E(ngledow) 1904- 4R
Burks, Ned
See Burks, Edward C.
Burl, (Harry) Aubrey (Woodruff) 1926- 97-100
Burland, Brian (Berkeley) 1931- CANR-23
Earlier sketches in CA 15-16R, CANR-7
See also SATA 34
Burland, C. A.
See Burland, Cottie (Arthur)
Burland, Cottie (Arthur) 1905- CANR-5
Earlier sketch in CA 5-6R
See also SATA 5
Burleigh, Anne Husted 1941- 29-32R
Burleigh, David Robert 1907- 4R
Burleigh, John H. S. 1894-1985 Obituary 116
Burley, George (Joseph) 1939- Brief entry 107
Burley, W(illiam) J(ohn) 1914- CANR-13
Earlier sketch in CA 33-36R
Burling, Robbins 1926- 17-18R
Burlingame, (William) Roger 1889-1967 5-6R
See also SATA 2
Burlingame, Virginia (Struble) 1900- CAP-2
Earlier sketch in CA 23-24
Burlingham, Dorothy (Tiffany) 1891-1979 109
Obituary 93-96
Burma, John H(armon) 1913- CANR-5
Earlier sketch in CA 1R
Burman, Alice Caddy 1896(?)-1977 SATA-24
Burman, Ben Lucien 1896-1984 CANR-8
Obituary 114
Earlier sketch in CA 5-6R
See also SATA 6, 40
Burman, Jose Lionel 1917- 109
Burmeister, Edwin 1939- 29-32R
Burmeister, Eva (Elizabeth) 1899- CAP-1
Earlier sketch in CA 13-14
Burmeister, Jon 1933- 29-32R
Burmeister, Lou E(lla) 1928- 45-48
Burn, A(ndrew) R(obert) 1902- CANR-17
Earlier sketches in CA 4R, CANR-1
Burn, Barbara 1940- CANR-17
Earlier sketch in CA 85-88
Burn, Doris 1923- 29-32R
See also SATA 1
Burn, Duncan (Lyall) 1902-1988 Obituary 124
Burn, Gordon 1948- 123
Burn, J(oshua) Harold 1892-1982 CAP-1
Obituary 108
Earlier sketch in CA 11-12
Burn, Mary (Wynn) 1910- 122
Burnaby, John 1891-1978 CAP-1
Obituary 104
Earlier sketch in CA 13-14
Burnam, Tom 1913- 61-64
Burne, Glen
See Green, Alan (Baer)
Burne, Glenn S. 1921- 21-22R
Burne, Kevin G. 1925- 15-16R
Burner, David (B.) 1937- CANR-10
Earlier sketch in CA 25-28R
Burness, Tad
See Burness, Wallace B(inny)
Burness, Wallace B(inny) 1933- CANR-21
Earlier sketch in CA 69-72
Burnet, George Bain 1894- CAP-2
Earlier sketch in CA 23-24
Burnet, (Frank) Macfarlane 1899-1985 73-76
Obituary 117
Burnet, Mary E(dith) 1911- 53-56
Burnett, Alfred David 1937- CANR-19
Earlier sketch in CA 102
Burnett, Anne Pippin 1925- 113
Burnett, Avis 1937- 41-44R
Burnett, Ben G(eorge) 1924-1975 CANR-3
Earlier sketch in CA 4R
Burnett, Calvin 1921- 33-36R
Burnett, Collins W. 1914- CANR-3
Earlier sketch in CA 11-12R
Burnett, Constance Buel 1893-1975 5-6R
See also SATA 36
Burnett, David (Benjamin Foley)
1931-1971 11-12R
Obituary 33-36R
Burnett, David (Alan) 1946- 121
Burnett, Dorothy Kirk 1924- 7-8R
Burnett, Frances (Eliza) Hodgson
1849-1924 Brief entry 108
See also YABC 2
See also DLB 42
Burnett, Hallie Southgate (Zeisel) CANR-6
Earlier sketch in CA 13-14R
Burnett, Janet 1915- 49-52
Burnett, Joe Ray 1928- 17-18R
Burnett, John 1925- 57-60
Burnett, June 1936- 113
Burnett, Laurence 1907- 49-52
Burnett, Leo 1891-1971 Obituary 116
Burnett, Leon R. 1925(?)-1983 Obituary 109
Burnett, W(illiam) R(iley) 1899-1982 CANR-22
Obituary 106
Earlier sketch in CA 7-8R
See also DLB 9
Burnett, Whit(ney Ewing) 1899-1973 CAP-2
Obituary 41-44R
Earlier sketch in CA 13-14
Burnette, O(llen) Lawrence, Jr. 1927- 33-36R
Burney, Anton
See Hopkins, Kenneth
Burney, Elizabeth (Mary) 1934- 23-24R
Burney, Eugenia 1913- 29-32R
Burney, Fanny 1752-1840 DLB-39
Burnford, Sheila (Philip Cochrane Every)
1918-1984 CANR-1
Obituary 112
Earlier sketch in CA 2R
See also SATA 3, 38
See also CLR 2
Burnham, Alan 1913-1984 15-16R
Obituary 112
Burnham, David (Bright) 1933- 122
Burnham, Dorothy E(dith) 1921- 65-68
Burnham, (Linden) Forbes (Sampson)
1923-1985 Obituary 117
Burnham, J. W.
See Burnham, Jack (Wesley)
Burnham, Jack (Wesley) 1931- 115
Burnham, James 1905-1987 Obituary 123
Burnham, John
See Beckwith, Burnham Putnam
Burnham, John C(hynoweth) 1929- 33-36R
Burnham, Richard 1940- 118
Burnham, Robert Ward, Jr. 1913- 19-20R
Burnham, Sophy 1936- 41-44R
See also AITN 1
Burnham, Walter Dean 1930- 101
Burnim, Kalman A(aron) 1928- 2R
Burningham, John Mackintosh 1936- 73-76
See also SATA 16
See also CLR 9
Burnley, (John) David 1941- 117
Burnley, Judith CANR-16
Earlier sketch in CA 97-100
Burns, Aidan 1943- 121
Burns, Alan 1929- CANR-5
Earlier sketch in CA 11-12R
See also DLB 14
Burns, Alan Cuthbert 1887-1980 Obituary 102
Burns, Alma 1919- 81-84
Burns, Arthur F(rank) 1904-1987 15-16R
Obituary 122
Burns, Betty 1909- CAP-2
Earlier sketch in CA 19-20
Burns, Bobby
See Burns, Vincent Godfrey
Burns, Carol 1934- 29-32R
Burns, Chester R(ay) 1937- 103
Burns, David D. 1942- 114
Burns, E(dward) Bradford 1932- 17-18R
Burns, Edward McNall 1897-1972 1R
Obituary 103
Burns, Eedson Louis Millard
1897-1985 CANR-5
Obituary 117
Earlier sketch in CA 7-8R
Burns, Eveline M(abel Richardson)
1900-1985 Obituary 117
Burns, Geoff 1954- 115
Burns, George 1896- 112
Burns, Gerald P(hillip) 1918- 17-18R
Burns, Helen M(arie) 1922- 110
Burns, Hobert Warren 1925- 4R
Burns, James MacGregor 1918- CANR-19
Earlier sketch in CA 7-8R
Burns, James W(illiam) 1937- 33-36R
Burns, Jean (Ellen) 1934- 103
Burns, Jim 1936- 101
Burns, Joan Simpson 1927- 65-68
Burns, John Horne 1916-1953 Brief entry 115
See also DLBY 85
Burns, John McLauren 1932- Brief entry 109
Burns, John V. 1907- CAP-2
Earlier sketch in CA 33-36
Burns, Marilyn SATA-33
Burns, Michael 1947- 121
Burns, Norman T(homas) 1930- 69-72
Burns, Olive Ann 1924- 120
Burns, Paul C. CANR-4
Earlier sketch in CA 3R
See also SATA 5
Burns, Ralph J. 1901- CAP-2
Earlier sketch in CA 25-28
Burns, Ray
See Burns, Raymond (Howard)
Burns, Raymond (Howard) 1924- SATA-9
Burns, Rex (Sehler) 1935- CANR-13
Earlier sketch in CA 77-80
Burns, Richard Dean 1929- CANR-8
Earlier sketch in CA 19-20R
Burns, Richard W(ebster) 1920- 69-72
Burns, Robert Edward 1919- 111
Burns, Robert Grant 1938- CANR-16
Earlier sketch in CA 25-28R
Burns, Robert I(gnatius) 1921- CANR-7
Earlier sketch in CA 19-20R
Burns, Robert M(ilton) C(lark), Jr. 1940- 102
Burns, Ruby V(ermillion) 1901- 106
Burns, Scott
See Burns, Robert M(ilton) C(lark), Jr.
Burns, Sheila
See Bloom, Ursula
Burns, Tex
See L'Amour, Louis (Dearborn)
Burns, Thomas (Jr.) 1928- CANR-14
Earlier sketch in CA 41-44R
Burns, Thomas Stephen 1927- 49-52
Burns, Tom 1913- CANR-22
Earlier sketches in CA 5-6R, CANR-5
Burns, Vincent Godfrey 1893-1979 41-44R
Obituary 85-88
See also AITN 2
Burns, Wayne 1918- CANR-1
Earlier sketch in CA 2R
Burns, William A. 1909- CANR-11
Earlier sketches in CA 13-14, CAP-1
See also SATA 5
Burns, Zed H(ouston) 1903- 33-36R
Burnshaw, Stanley 1906- 9-10R
See also DLB 48
See also CLC 3, 13, 44
Burnside, Wesley M(ason) 1918- 65-68
Buros, Oscar Krisen 1905-1978 Obituary 77-80
Burow, Daniel R(obert) 1931- CANR-11
Earlier sketch in CA 29-32R
Burr, Alfred Gray 1919- 25-28R
Burr, Anne 1937- 25-28R
See also CLC 6
Burr, Charles 1922(?)-1976 Obituary 69-72
Burr, Gray 1919- 69-72
Burr, John R(oy) 1933- 45-48
Burr, Keith 1946- 115
Burr, Lonnie 1943- 103
See also SATA 47
Burr, Samuel Engle, Jr. 1897-1987
Obituary 124
Burr, Wesley R(ay) 1936- 37-40R
Burrell, Berkeley G(raham) 1919-1979 33-36R
Obituary 89-92
Burrell, David B(akewell) 1933- 33-36R
Burrell, Evelyn Patterson 1920- CANR-7
Earlier sketch in CA 53-56
Burrell, Roy E(ric) C(harles) 1923- 33-36R
Burridge, Kenelm (Oswald Lancelot)
1922- 93-96
Burrin, Frank K. 1920- 25-28R
Burrington, David E. 1931- 73-76
Burris, B. C(ullen) 1924- 21-22R
Burris-Meyer, Harold 1902- 41-44R
Burros, Marian (Fox) 89-92
Burroughs, Ben(jamin F.) 1918-1980 65-68
Obituary 122
Burroughs, Edgar Rice 1875-1950
Brief entry 104
See also SATA 41
See also DLB 8
See also TCLC 2
Burroughs, Jean Mitchell 1908- 65-68
See also SATA 28
Burroughs, John 1837-1921 Brief entry 109
See also DLB 64
Burroughs, Margaret Taylor (Goss)
1917- 23-24R
See also DLB 41
Burroughs, Polly 1925- 25-28R
See also SATA 2
Burroughs, Raleigh (Simpson) 1901- 106
Burroughs, William (Seward), Jr.
1947-1981 73-76
Obituary 112
See also DLB 16
Burroughs, William S(eward) 1914- CANR-20
Earlier sketch in CA 9-10R
See also DLB 2, 8, 16
See also DLBY 81
See also CLC 1, 2, 5, 15, 22, 42
See also AITN 2
Burrow, James Gordon 1922- CANR-2
Earlier sketch in CA 5-6R
Burrow, John A(nthony) 1932- 97-100
Burrow, John W(yon) 1935- CANR-12
Earlier sketch in CA 21-22R
Burroway, Janet (Gay) 1936- CANR-12
Earlier sketch in CA 21-22R
See also CAAS 6
See also SATA 23
See also DLB 6
Burrowes, Michael Anthony Bernard 1937- 103
Burrowes, Mike
See Burrowes, Michael Anthony Bernard
Burrows, Abe
See Burrows, Abram Solman
Burrows, Abram Solman 1910-1985 110
Obituary 116
Burrows, David J(ames) 1936- 41-44R
Burrows, E(dwin) G(ladding) 1917- CANR-14
Earlier sketch in CA 77-80
Burrows, Fredrika Alexander 1908- CANR-6
Earlier sketch in CA 57-60
Burrows, James C. 1944- 29-32R
Burrows, John 1945- 101
Burrows, Miles 1936- 21-22R
Burrows, Millar 1889-1980 81-84
Obituary 97-100
Burrows, William E. 1937- 65-68
Burrows, William R(ichard) 1942- 117
Burrup, Percy E. 1910- 4R
Bursk, Christopher 1943- CANR-24
Earlier sketch in CA 85-88
Bursk, Edward C(ollins) 1907- CANR-5
Earlier sketch in CA 4R
Burstall, Aubrey F(rederic) 1902-1984
Obituary 113
Burstein, Alvin G(eorge) 1931- 85-88
Burstein, John 1949- CANR-21
Earlier sketch in CA 69-72
See also SATA 40
Burstein, Patricia (Ann) 1945- 108
Burstein, Paul 1946- 123
Burstiner, Irving 1919- 104
Burston, W. H. 1915-1981 Obituary 103
Burstyn, Harold L(ewis) 1930- CANR-5
Earlier sketch in CA 11-12R
Burt, Al(vin Victor, Jr.) 1927- 25-28R
Burt, Alfred LeRoy 1888- CAP-1
Earlier sketch in CA 9-10
Burt, Cyril (Lodowic) 1883-1971 CAP-1
Obituary 33-36R
Earlier sketch in CA 13-14
Burt, Donald X(avier) 1929- 116
Burt, Frances R(iemer) 1917- 69-72
Burt, Jesse Clifton 1921-1976 CANR-4
Earlier sketch in CA 9-10R
See also SATA 20, 46
Burt, John J. 1934- CANR-11
Earlier sketch in CA 29-32R
Burt, Larry W(ayne) 1950- 122
Burt, Leonard James 1892-1983 Obituary 114
Burt, Mala S(chuster) 1943- 112
Burt, Nathaniel 1913- 19-20R
Burt, Olive Woolley 1894- CANR-5
Earlier sketch in CA 7-8R
See also SATA 4
Burt, Robert Amsterdam 1939- 102
Burt, Roger B(ivens) 1939- 113
Burt, Samuel M(athew) 1915- 23-24R
Burt, Simon 1947- 123
Burt, William Henry 1903- 106
Burtchaell, James Tunstead 1934- CANR-11
Earlier sketch in CA 25-28R
Burtis, C(harles) Edward 1907- 41-44R
Burtle, James (L.) 1919- Brief entry 113
Burtness, Paul Sidney 1923- 19-20R
Burton, Anthony 1933- 61-64
Burton, Anthony 1934- 97-100
Burton, Arthur 1914-1982 CANR-10
Earlier sketch in CA 21-22R
Burton, Carl D. 1913- 4R
Burton, David H(enry) 1925- CANR-3
Earlier sketch in CA 49-52
Burton, Dolores Marie 1932- 25-28R
Burton, Dwight L(owell) 1922- 61-64
Burton, Edward J. 1917- 23-24R
Burton, (Alice) Elizabeth 1908- CANR-15
Earlier sketch in CA 65-68
Burton, Gabrielle 1939- 45-48
Burton, Genevieve 1912- 33-36R
Burton, H(arry) M(cGuire Philip)
1898(?)-1979 Obituary 93-96
Burton, Hal
See Burton, Harold Bernard
Burton, Harold Bernard 1908- 97-100
Burton, Hester (Wood-Hill) 1913- CANR-10
Earlier sketch in CA 9-10R
See also SATA 7
See also CLR 1
Burton, Ian 1935- 19-20R
Burton, Ivor Flower 1923- 109
Burton, Jane 105
Burton, Joe Wright 1907-1976 107
Burton, John A(ndrew) 1944- CANR-14
Earlier sketch in CA 65-68
Burton, John Wear 1915- 103
Burton, Katherine (Kurz) 1890-1969 77-80
Burton, Leslie
See McGuire, Leslie Sarah
Burton, Lindy 1937- 25-28R
Burton, Lloyd E. 1922- 53-56
Burton, Marilee Robin 1950- 121
See also SATA 46
Burton, Martin A. 1911-1984 Obituary 114
Burton, Mary E(lizabeth) 1900- 106
Burton, Maurice 1898- CANR-9
Earlier sketch in CA 65-68
See also SATA 23
Burton, Nelson, Jr. 1942- 57-60
Burton, Philip 1904- 25-28R
Burton, Richard 1925-1984 Obituary 113
Burton, Richard F. 1821-1890 DLB-55
Burton, Robert (Wellesley) 1941- CANR-17
Earlier sketches in CA 45-48, CANR-1
See also SATA 22
Burton, Robert E(dward) 1927- CANR-13
Earlier sketch in CA 61-64
Burton, Robert H(enderson) 1934- 37-40R

Burton, Roger V(ernon) 1928- ... 45-48
Burton, S(amuel) H(olroyd) 1919- ... 102
Burton, Thomas
See Longstreet, Stephen
Burton, Thomas G(lenn) 1935- ... 105
Burton, Virginia Lee 1909-1968 ... CAP-1
Obituary ... 25-28R
Earlier sketch in CA 13-14
See also SATA 2
See also DLB 22
See also CLR 11
Burton, William H(enry) 1890-1964 ... CANR-1
Earlier sketch in CA 3R
See also SATA 11
Burton, William L(ester) 1928- ... 21-22R
Burton-Bradley, Burton Gyrth 1914- ... 77-80
Burtschi, Mary 1911- ... CANR-19
Earlier sketches in CA 11-12R, CANR-5
Burtt, E(dwin) A. 1892- ... 7-8R
Burtt, Everett Johnson, Jr. 1914- ... 11-12R
Burtt, George 1914- ... CANR-11
Earlier sketch in CA 61-64
Burtt, Harold E(rnest) 1890- ... CAP-2
Earlier sketch in CA 17-18
Burwash, Peter 1945- ... 119
Bury, Frank
See Harris, Herbert
Bury, J(ohn) P(atrick) T(uer) 1908- ... 19-20R
Buryn, Ed(ward Casimir) 1934- ... 85-88
Busbee, Shirlee (Elaine) 1941- ... 77-80
Busby, Edith (A. Lake) ?-1964 Obituary ... 109
See also SATA 29
Busby, F. M. 1921- ... CANR-24
Earlier sketches in CA 65-68, CANR-9
Busby, John 1928- ... 116
Busby, Jonathan
See Allen, Eric
Busby, Mabel Janice
See Stanford, Sally
Busby, Roger (Charles) 1941- ... 105
Buscaglia, Felice Leonardo 1924- ... 112
Brief entry ... 110
Buscaglia, Leo F.
See Buscaglia, Felice Leonardo
Busch, Briton Cooper 1936- ... CANR-8
Earlier sketch in CA 23-24R
Busch, Francis X(avier) 1879-1975 ... CAP-1
Obituary ... 61-64
Earlier sketch in CA 13-14
Busch, Frederick 1941- ... 33-36R
See also CAAS 1
See also DLB 6
See also CLC 7, 10, 18, 47
Busch, Hans (Peter) 1914- ... 109
Busch, Julia 1940- ... 57-60
Busch, Niven 1903- ... CANR-7
Earlier sketch in CA 13-14R
See also DLB 44
Busch, Noel F(airchild) 1906-1985 ... 49-52
Obituary ... 117
Busch, Phyllis S. 1909- ... 107
See also SATA 30
Busch, Ronald 1928-1987 Obituary ... 123
Buschkuehl, Matthias 1953- ... 121
Buschkuhl, Matthias
See Buschkuehl, Matthias
Buse, R. F.
See Buse, Renee
Buse, Renee 1914(?)-1979 Obituary ... 85-88
Buse, Rueben C. 1932- ... 109
Busey, James L. 1916- ... 5-6R
Bush, Alan (Dudley) 1900- ... 110
Bush, Barbara Holstein 1935- ... CANR-12
Earlier sketch in CA 69-72
Bush, Barry (Michael) 1938- ... 110
Bush, Charlie Christmas 1888(?)-1973 ... 107
Obituary ... 104
Bush, Christopher
See Bush, Charlie Christmas
Bush, Clifford L(ewis) 1915- ... 33-36R
Bush, Donald J(ohn) ... 114
Bush, (John Nash) Douglas 1896-1983 ... 37-40R
Obituary ... 109
Bush, Eric Wheler 1899-1985 ... 65-68
Obituary ... 117
Bush, George Edward, Jr. 1938- ... 109
Bush, George P(ollock) 1892- ... 19-20R
Bush, George S(idney) 1925- ... 110
Bush, Grace A(bhau) 1936- ... 104
Bush, Jim 1926- ... 57-60
Bush, John W(illiam) 1917-1976 ... CAP-2
Earlier sketch in CA 33-36
Bush, L(uther) Russ(ell III) 1944- ... 121
Bush, Larry
See Bush, Lawrence Dana
Bush, Lawrence Dana 1951- ... 109
Bush, Lewis William 1907- ... 81-84
Bush, Martin H(arry) 1930- ... CANR-12
Earlier sketch in CA 29-32R
Bush, Patricia (Jahns) 1932- ... CANR-24
Earlier sketch in CA 105
Bush, Richard C(larence) 1923-
Brief entry ... 114
Bush, Robert (Burton) 1917- ... 116
Bush, Robert (Ray) 1920-1972
Obituary ... 33-36R
Bush, Ronald ... CLC-34
Bush, Sargent, Jr. 1937- ... 65-68
Bush, Ted J. 1922- ... 19-20R
Bush, Vannevar 1890-1974 ... 97-100
Obituary ... 53-56
Bush, William (Shirley, Jr.) 1929- ... CANR-14
Earlier sketch in CA 37-40R
Busha, Charles Henry 1931- ... CANR-5
Earlier sketch in CA 53-56
Bush-Brown, James 1892-1985 ... 7-8R
Obituary ... 118
Bush-Brown, Louise 1896(?)-1973
Obituary ... 49-52
Bushell, Don(ald Gair), Jr. 1934-
Brief entry ... 113
Bushell, Raymond 1910- ... CANR-20
Earlier sketches in CA 15-16R, CANR-5
Bushey, Jerry 1941- ... 108
Bushinsky, Jay (Joseph Mason) 1932- ... 77-80
Bushman, Claudia L(auper) 1934- ... CANR-22
Earlier sketch in CA 106
Bushman, Richard L(yman) 1931- ... CANR-22
Earlier sketch in CA 21-22R
Bushmiller, Ernest Paul 1905-1982 ... 29-32R
Obituary ... 107
See also AITN 1
Bushmiller, Ernie
See Bushmiller, Ernest Paul
See also SATA 31
Bushnell, David S(herman) 1927- ... 41-44R
Bushrui, S(uheil) B(adi) 1929- ... 17-18R
Bushyager, Linda E(yster) 1947- ... 93-96
Busia, Kofi Abrefa 1913- ... 69-72
Buske, Morris Roger 1912- ... 13-14R
Buskin, Martin 1930-1976 Obituary ... 65-68
Buskirk, Richard H(obart) 1927- ... CANR-1
Earlier sketch in CA 1R
Busoni, Rafaello 1900-1962 Obituary ... 117
See also SATA 16
Buss, Arnold H. 1924- ... CANR-4
Earlier sketch in CA 1R
Buss, Claude Albert 1903- ... 109
Buss, Leo W. 1953- ... 121
Buss, Martin J(ohn) 1930- ... 33-36R
Bussard, Paul 1904-1983 Obituary ... 109
Bussche, Henri O(mer) A(ntoine) Van den
1920-1965 ... CANR-5
Earlier sketch in CA 7-8R
Busse, Thomas V(alentine) 1941-1986 ... 77-80
Obituary ... 119
Bussey, Ellen M(arion) 1926- ... CANR-2
Earlier sketch in CA 49-52
Bussieres, Simone 1918- ... 53-56
Bustad, Leo Kenneth 1920- ... 106
Bustamante, A(gustin) Jorge 1938- ... 33-36R
Bustanoby, Andre S(teven) 1930- ... 101
Bustard, Robert 1938- ... 65-68
Busteed, Marilyn 1937- ... 61-64
Bustos, F(rancisco)
See Borges, Jorge Luis
Bustos Domecq, H(onorio)
See Bioy Casares, Adolfo
and Borges, Jorge Luis
Buswell, J(ames) Oliver, Jr. 1895- ... 5-6R
Butcher, Fanny
See Bokum, Fanny Butcher
Butcher, Geoffrey (Arthur John) 1936- ... 111
Butcher, Grace 1934- ... 25-28R
Butcher, H(arold) J(ohn) 1920- ... 23-24R
Butcher, Harry Cecil 1901-1985 Obituary ... 115
Butcher, James Neal 1933- ... CANR-14
Earlier sketch in CA 33-36R
Butcher, (Anne) Judith 1927- ... 57-60
Butcher, (Charles) Philip 1918- ... CANR-4
Earlier sketch in CA 4R
Butcher, Russell Devereux 1938- ... CANR-8
Earlier sketch in CA 61-64
Butcher, Thomas Kennedy 1914- ... CAP-1
Earlier sketch in CA 11-12
Butchvarov, Panayot K. 1933- ... 33-36R
Butck, Zulie
See Jones, Thomas W(arren)
Butera, Mary C. 1925- ... 21-22R
Buteux, Paul E. 1939- ... 121
Buth, Lenore 1932- ... 89-92
Buthelezi, Gatsha 1928- ... 102
Butland, Gilbert J(ames) 1910- ... 21-22R
Butler, Albert 1923- ... CANR-5
Earlier sketch in CA 15-16R
Butler, Annie L(ouise) 1920- ... 33-36R
Butler, Arthur D. 1923- ... 4R
Butler, B. C.
See Butler, Basil Christopher
Butler, Basil Christopher 1902-1986 ... CANR-2
Obituary ... 120
Earlier sketch in CA 1R
Butler, Beverly Kathleen 1932- ... CANR-4
Earlier sketch in CA 2R
See also SATA 7
Butler, Bill
See Butler, Ernest Alton
and Butler, William Huxford
Butler, Bishop B. C.
See Butler, Basil Christopher
Butler, Charles Henry 1894-19(?) ... CAP-2
Earlier sketch in CA 23-24
Butler, Christina Violet 1884-1982
Obituary ... 106
Butler, Christopher
See Butler, Basil Christopher
Butler, Colin Gasking 1913- ... 109
Butler, David Edgeworth 1924- ... CANR-13
Earlier sketch in CA 7-8R
Butler, David Francis 1928- ... 41-44R
Butler, David Jonathon 1946- ... 69-72
Butler, E(dward) H(arry) 1913- ... 13-14R
Butler, Edgar W(ilbur) 1929- ... 77-80
Butler, Erica Bracher 1905- ... CAP-2
Earlier sketch in CA 17-18
Butler, Ernest Alton 1926- ... 33-36R
Butler, Francelia McWilliams 1913- ... CANR-3
Earlier sketch in CA 11-12R
Butler, G(eorge) Paul 1900- ... CAP-2
Earlier sketch in CA 17-18
Butler, George D. 1893- ... 19-20R
Butler, George Tyssen 1943- ... 103
Butler, Grace Kipp Pratt
See Pratt-Butler, Grace Kipp
Butler, (Frederick) Guy 1918- ... CANR-18
Earlier sketch in CA 101
Butler, Gwendoline Williams 1922- ... CANR-6
Earlier sketch in CA 11-12R
Butler, Hal 1913- ... 57-60
Butler, Iris 1905- ... 21-22R
Butler, Ivan
See Beuttler, Edward Ivan Oakley
Butler, J. Donald 1908- ... 1R
Butler, Jack 1944- ... 114
Butler, James 1904- ... CAP-1
Earlier sketch in CA 11-12
Butler, James H(armon) 1908- ... 41-44R
Butler, James R(amsay) M(ontagu)
1889-1975 ... CAP-1
Earlier sketch in CA 13-14
Butler, Jean Campbell (MacLaurin)
1918- ... 11-12R
Butler, Jean Rouverol 1916- ... 97-100
Butler, Jeffrey (Ernest) 1922- ... 65-68
Butler, Jerry P. 1944- ... 65-68
Butler, Joan
See Alexander, Robert William
Butler, John Alfred Valentine
1899-1977 ... CANR-5
Obituary ... 106
Earlier sketch in CA 5-6R
Butler, Joseph Thomas 1932- ... 15-16R
Butler, Joyce 1933- ... CANR-9
Earlier sketch in CA 65-68
Butler, Juan 1942-1981 ... DLB-53
Butler, Lionel Harry 1923-1981 ... 110
Obituary ... 105
Butler, Lucius (Albert, Jr.) 1928- ... 69-72
Butler, Margaret Gwendoline ... 104
Butler, Marilyn (Speers) 1937- ... 102
Butler, Mildred Allen 1897- ... CAP-2
Earlier sketch in CA 29-32
Butler, Natalie Sturges 1908- ... 53-56
Butler, Nathan
See Sohl, Jerry
Butler, Octavia E(stelle) 1947- ... CANR-24
Earlier sketches in CA 73-76, CANR-12
See also DLB 33
See also CLC 38
Butler, Pat(rick) (Trevor) 1929- ... 7-8R
Butler, Rab
See Butler, Richard Austen
Butler, Richard 1925- ... CANR-8
Earlier sketch in CA 57-60
Butler, Richard
See Allbeury, Theodore Edward le
Bouthillier
Butler, Richard Austen 1902-1982
Obituary ... 106
Butler, Rick 1946- ... 97-100
Butler, Robert Albert 1934- ... CANR-11
Earlier sketch in CA 61-64
Butler, Robert Lee 1918- ... 57-60
Butler, Robert N(eil) 1927- ... 41-44R
Butler, Robert Olen (Jr.) 1945- ... 112
Butler, Rohan D'Olier 1917- ... 109
Butler, Ron(ald William) 1934- ... 69-72
Butler, Samuel 1835-1902 Brief entry ... 104
See also DLB 18, 57
See also TCLC 1
Butler, Sandra (Ada) 1938- ... 105
Butler, Stanley 1914- ... 57-60
Butler, Stefan Congrat
See Congrat-Butler, Stefan
Butler, Stuart Thomas 1926- ... 107
Butler, Suzanne
See Perreard, Suzanne Louise Butler
Butler, Ted
See Schweitzer, Darrell
Butler, Walter C.
See Faust, Frederick (Shiller)
Butler, Walter E(rnest) 1898- ... CANR-5
Earlier sketch in CA 7-8R
Butler, William 1929- ... 107
Butler, William E(lliott II) 1939- ... CANR-11
Earlier sketch in CA 25-28R
Butler, William F(rank) 1917-1972
Obituary ... 113
Butler, William Huxford 1934- ... 57-60
Butlin, Martin (Richard Fletcher)
1929- ... CANR-19
Earlier sketches in CA 7-8R, CANR-2
Butor, Michel (Marie Francois) 1926- ... 9-10R
See also CLC 1, 3, 8, 11, 15
Butow, Robert J. C. 1924- ... 13-14R
Butrym, Zofia Teresa 1927- ... 103
Butscher, Edward 1943- ... 97-100
Butt, (Howard) Edward, Jr. 1927- ... 57-60
Butt, (Dorcas) Susan 1938- ... 89-92
Buttaci, Sal(vatore) St. John 1941- ... CANR-9
Earlier sketch in CA 65-68
Buttel, Robert (William) 1923- ... 102
Buttenwieser, Paul (Arthur) 1938- ... 104
Butter, Peter (Herbert) 1921- ... 7-8R
Butterfield, Fox 1939- ... 119
Butterfield, Herbert 1900- ... 2R
Butterfield, Lyman H(enry) 1909-1982
Obituary ... 106
Butterfield, Roger (Place) 1907-1981 ... CAP-1
Obituary ... 103
Earlier sketch in CA 9-10
Butterfield, Stephen T(homas) 1942- ... 57-60
Butterick, George F. 1942- ... CANR-11
Earlier sketch in CA 69-72
Butters, Dorothy Gilman 1923- ... CANR-2
Earlier sketch in CA 4R
See also SATA 5
Butterworth, Douglas Stanley 1930- ... 108
Butterworth, Emma Macalik 1928- ... 105
See also SATA 43
Butterworth, F(rank) Edward (Jr.) 1917- ... 29-32R
Butterworth, Hezekiah 1839-1905 ... DLB-42
Butterworth, Lionel Milner Angus
See Angus-Butterworth, Lionel Milner
Butterworth, Michael 1924-1986 ... CANR-10
Obituary ... 121
Earlier sketch in CA 25-28R
Butterworth, Oliver 1915- ... 4R
See also SATA 1
Butterworth, W(illiam) E(dmund III)
1929- ... CANR-18
Earlier sketches in CA 2R, CANR-2
See also SATA 5
Butti, Ken(neth Michael) 1950- ... 104
Buttigeig, Anton 1912-1983 Obituary ... 109
Buttimer, Anne 1938- ... 37-40R
Buttinger, Joseph 1906- ... 21-22R
Buttinger, Muriel Gardiner 1901-1985 ... 77-80
Obituary ... 115
Buttitta, Anthony 1907- ... 81-84
Buttitta, Tony
See Buttitta, Anthony
Buttlar, Lois J(acqueline) 1934- ... 112
Buttle, Myra
See Purcell, Victor
Button, Daniel E(van) 1917- ... 89-92
Button, Dick 1929- ... 11-12R
Button, James W(ickham) 1942- ... 81-84
Button, Kenneth John 1948- ... CANR-20
Earlier sketch in CA 103
Button, (Henry) Warren 1922- ... 97-100
Buttress, Frederick Arthur 1908- ... 33-36R
Buttrey, Douglas N(orton) ... CANR-18
Earlier sketch in CA 101
Buttrick, George Arthur 1892-1980 ... 61-64
Obituary ... 93-96
Butts, David P. 1932- ... 11-12R
Butts, Jane Roberts 1929-1984 ... CANR-15
Earlier sketch in CA 41-44R
Butts, Porter (Freeman) 1903- ... 41-44R
Butts, R. Freeman 1910- ... 15-16R
Butwell, Richard 1929- ... CANR-1
Earlier sketch in CA 45-48
Butzer, Karl W(ilhelm) 1934- ... CANR-8
Earlier sketch in CA 23-24R
Buultjens, (Edward) Ralph 1936- ... CANR-4
Earlier sketch in CA 53-56
Buxbaum, Edith 1902- ... CAP-2
Earlier sketch in CA 25-28
Buxbaum, Martin 1912- ... 17-18R
Buxbaum, Melvin H. 1934- ... 53-56
Buxbaum, Robert C(ourtney) 1930- ... 97-100
Buxton, Anne (Arundel) Brief entry ... 115
Buxton, Anthony 1892(?)-1970 Obituary ... 104
Buxton, (Evelyn June) Bonnie 1940- ... 69-72
Buxton, Charles R(oberts) 1913- ... 65-68
Buxton, Claude E(lmo) 1912- Brief entry ... 114
Buxton, David Roden 1910- ... 104
Buxton, Edward F(ulton) 1917- ... 41-44R
Buxton, Harold J(ocelyn) 1880-1976
Obituary ... 104
Buxton, (Edward) John (Mawby) 1912- ... CANR-5
Earlier sketch in CA 9-10R
Buxton, Thomas H(amilton) 1940- ... 57-60
Buys, Donna 1944- ... 102
Buzan, Barry 1946- ... 119
Buzo, Alexander (John) 1944- ... CANR-17
Earlier sketch in CA 97-100
Buzzard, John Huxley 1912-1984 Obituary ... 112
Buzzati, Dino 1906-1972 Obituary ... 33-36R
See also CLC 36
Buzzell, Robert (Dow) 1933- ... 104
Buzzle, Buck
See Rubin, Charles J.
Buzzotta, V. R(alph) 1931- ... 37-40R
Byars, Betsy (Cromer) 1928- ... CANR-18
Earlier sketch in CA 33-36R
See also SATA 4, 46
See also SAAS 1
See also DLB 52
See also CLC 35
See also CLR 1
Byatt, A(ntonia) S(usan Drabble)
1936- ... CANR-13
Earlier sketch in CA 13-14R
See also DLB 14
See also CLC 19
Bychowski, Gustav 1895-1972 Obituary ... 33-36R
Byck, Robert 1933- ... 109
Bye, Beryl (Joyce Rayment) 1926- ... CANR-11
Earlier sketch in CA 61-64
Bye, Ranulph (deBayeux) 1916- ... 53-56
Bye, Raymond T(aylor) 1892- ... 7-8R
Byerly, Henry Clement 1935- ... 53-56
Byerly, Kenneth R(hodes) 1908- ... 2R
Byers, David (Milner) 1941- ... 53-56
Byers, Edward A(dams) 1939- ... 119
Byers, Edward E. 1921- ... CANR-3
Earlier sketch in CA 4R
Byers, (Amy) Irene 1906- ... CANR-3
Earlier sketch in CA 11-12R
Byers, R(ichard) McCulloch 1913- ... 69-72
Byfield, Barbara Ninde 1930- ... CANR-4
Earlier sketch in CA 4R
See also SATA 8
Byham, William C(larence) 1936- ... CANR-17
Earlier sketch in CA 25-28R
Bykau, Vasilii Uladzimiravich
See Bykov, Vasily Vladimirovich
Bykov, Vasily Vladimirovich 1924- ... 102
Byles, Mather 1707-1788 ... DLB-24
Bylinsky, Gene (Michael) 1930- ... 77-80
Bynagle, Hans E(dward) 1946- ... 120
Byng, Douglas 1893-1987 Obituary ... 123
Bynner, Witter 1881-1968 ... CANR-4
Obituary ... 25-28R
Earlier sketch in CA 3R
See also DLB 54

Bynum, David E(liab) 1936- CANR-20
Earlier sketch in CA 37-40R
Bynum, Terrell Ward 1941- CANR-18
Earlier sketch in CA 101
Byock, Jesse L(ewis) 1945- 110
Byrd, Bobby
See Byrd, Robert James
Byrd, C. L.
See Rosenkrantz, Linda
Byrd, Cecil Kash 1913- 19-20R
Byrd, Eldon A(rthur) 1939- 45-48
Byrd, Elizabeth 1912- CANR-5
Earlier sketch in CA 5-6R
See also SATA 34
Byrd, Emmett
See Hinden, Michael C(harles)
Byrd, John Crowe
See Hinden, Michael C(harles)
Byrd, Martha 1930- 29-32R
Byrd, Richard E(dward) 1931- CANR-7
Earlier sketch in CA 57-60
Byrd, Robert (John) 1942- SATA-33
Byrd, Robert James 1942- 65-68
Byrd, William II 1674-1744 .... DLB-24
Byrne, Charles Raymond 1916-1983
Obituary 111
Byrne, David 1953(?)- CLC-26
Byrne, Donald E(dward), Jr. 1942- 73-76
Byrne, Donn (Erwin) 1931- CANR-20
Earlier sketches in CA 11-12R, CANR-5
Byrne, Edmund F(rancis) 1933- 29-32R
Byrne, Edward M. 1935- 29-32R
Byrne, Frank L(oyola) 1928- 23-24R
Byrne, Gary C. 1942- 49-52
Byrne, Herbert Winston 1917- 4R
Byrne, James E. 1945- 81-84
Byrne, John 1940- 104
Byrne, John Keyes 1926- 102
See also CLC 19
Byrne, Muriel St. Clare 1895-1983 .... CAP-1
Obituary 111
Earlier sketch in CA 17-18
Byrne, Peter 1925- 65-68
Byrne, Ralph
See Burns, Ralph J.
Byrne, Richard Hill 1915- 21-22R
Byrne, Robert (Eugene) 1928- Brief entry ... 110
Byrne, Robert 1930- CANR-13
Earlier sketch in CA 73-76
Byrne, Stuart J(ames) 1913- 102
Byrnes, Edward T(homas) 1929- 53-56
Byrnes, Eugene F. 1890(?)-1974
Obituary 49-52
Byrnes, Garrett D(avis) 1904(?)-1985
Obituary 118
Byrnes, James Francis 1879-1972
Obituary 112
Byrnes, Joseph Francis 1939- 114
Byrnes, Robert F. 1917- CANR-10
Earlier sketch in CA 25-28R
Byrnes, Thomas Edmund 1911- 15-16R
Byrom, James
See Bramwell, James Guy
Byrom, (Robert) Michael 1925- 7-8R
Byron, Carl R(oscoe) 1948- 97-100
Byron, Christopher M. 1944- 77-80
Byron, Gilbert 1903- 17-18R
Byron, John
See Armstrong, John Byron
Byron, William J(ames) 1927- 81-84
Bytwerk, Randall Lee 1950- 109
Bywater, William G(len), Jr. 1940- 61-64

C

C.3.3.
See Wilde, Oscar (Fingal O'Flahertie Wills)
C. E. M.
See Mastrangelo, Charles E.
Caballero, Ann Mallory 1928- 19-20R
Cabanis, Jose 1922- Brief entry 111
Cabaniss, J(ames) Allen 1911- 1R
See also SATA 5
Cabarga, Leslie 1954- CANR-13
Earlier sketch in CA 77-80
Cabassa, Victoria 1912- 49-52
Cabbell, Edward J. 1946- 121
Cabbell, Paul 1942- 53-56
Cabeen, David Clark 1886-19(?) CAP-1
Earlier sketch in CA 13-14
Cabell, James Branch 1879-1958
Brief entry 105
See also DLB 9
See also TCLC 6
Cabibi, John F(rank) J(oseph) 1912- 53-56
Cable, George Washington 1844-1925
Brief entry 104
See also DLB 12
See also TCLC 4
Cable, James (Eric) 1920- CANR-15
Earlier sketch in CA 85-88
Cable, John L(aurence) 1934- CANR-21
Earlier sketch in CA 69-72
Cable, Mary 1920- CANR-11
Earlier sketch in CA 25-28R
See also SATA 9
Cable, Thomas Monroe 1942- Brief entry ... 106
Cabot, Blake 1905(?)-1974 Obituary 53-56
Cabot, John Moors 1901-1981 Obituary 103
Cabot, Robert (Moors) 1924- 29-32R
Cabot, Thomas Dudley 1897- 93-96
Cabot, Tracy 1941- 81-84
Cabral, Alberto
See White, Richard Alan
Cabral, Amilcar 1921-1973 Obituary 111
Cabral, O. M.
See Cabral, Olga
Cabral, Olga 1909- CANR-10
Earlier sketch in CA 25-28R
See also SATA 46
Cabrera, James C. 1935- 109
See also CLC 5, 25, 45
Cabrera Infante, G(uillermo) 1929- 85-88
Caccia-Dominioni, Paolo 1896- 21-22R
Cacciatore, Vera (Signorelli) 1911- CANR-5
Earlier sketch in CA 7-8R
Cachia, Pierre J. E. 1921- CANR-11
Earlier sketch in CA 25-28R
Cacoyannis, Michael 1922- 101
Cadbury, Henry J(oel) 1883-1974 .... CAP-1
Obituary 53-56
Earlier sketch in CA 15-16
Cadbury, Paul Strangman 1895-1984
Obituary 114
Cadden, Joseph E. 1911(?)-1980
Obituary 101
Caddick, Arthur 1911-1987 Obituary 122
Caddy, Alice
See Burman, Alice Caddy
Cade, Alexander
See Methold, Kenneth (Walter)
Cade, Toni
See Bambara, Toni Cade
Cadell, (Violet) Elizabeth 1903- CANR-11
Earlier sketch in CA 57-60
Cadenhead, Ivie E(dward), Jr. 1923- 41-44R
Cadet, John 1935- 77-80
Cadieux, Charles L. 1919- 57-60
Cadieux, (Joseph Arthur) Lorenzo
1903-1976 49-52
Obituary 103
Cadieux, (Joseph David Romeo) Marcel
1915-1981 Obituary 108
Cadle, Dean 1920- 25-28R
Cadmus
See Buchan, John
Cadogan, Alexander (George Montagu)
1884-1968 Obituary 106
Cadogan, Mary (Rose) 1928- 106
Cadwallader, Clyde T(homas) 5-6R
Cadwallader, Sharon 1936- CANR-17
Earlier sketches in CA 49-52, CANR-1
See also SATA 7
Cady, Arthur 1920-1983 Obituary 109
Cady, Edwin Harrison 1917- CANR-4
Earlier sketch in CA 2R
Cady, Ernest (Albert) 1899-1985 Obituary .. 117
Cady, (Walter) Harrison 1877(?)-1970
Obituary 116
See also SATA 19
Cady, Jack A(ndrew) 1932- CANR-9
Earlier sketch in CA 65-68
Cady, John Frank 1901- CANR-4
Earlier sketch in CA 1R
Cady, Steve (Noel) 1927- 45-48
Caedmon, Father
See Wahl, Thomas (Peter)
Caefer, Raymond J(ohn) 1926- 17-18R
Caemmerer, Richard R(udolph) 1904- ... CANR-5
Earlier sketch in CA 1R
Caen, Herb (Eugene) 1916- CANR-1
Earlier sketch in CA 1R
See also AITN 1
Caesar, (Eu)Gene (Lee) 1927- CANR-1
Earlier sketch in CA 3R
Cafferty, Bernard 1934- 41-44R
Cafferty, Pastora San Juan 1940- 114
Caffey, David L(uther) 1947- 45-48
Caffrey, John G(ordon) 1922- 17-18R
Caffrey, Kate CANR-1
Earlier sketch in CA 49-52
Cagan, Phillip D(avid) 1927- 17-18R
Cage, John (Milton, Jr.) 1912- CANR-9
Earlier sketch in CA 13-14R
See also CLC 41
Caggiano, Philip 1949- 114
Cagle, Malcolm W(infield) 1918- 108
See also SATA 32
Cagle, William R(ea) 1933- 65-68
Cagney, James (Francis, Jr.)
1899(?)-1986 Obituary 118
Brief entry 115
Cagney, Peter
See Winter, Bevis (Peter)
Cahalan, (John) Don(ald) 1912- 102
Cahalane, Victor H(arrison) 1901- CAP-2
Earlier sketch in CA 23-24
Cahan, Abraham 1860-1951 Brief entry 108
See also DLB 9, 25, 28
Cahen, Alfred B. 1932- 17-18R
Cahill, Audrey Fawcett 1929- 23-24R
Cahill, Daniel J(oseph) 1929- 69-72
Cahill, Fred V(irgil), Jr. 1916-1984
Obituary 112
Cahill, Gilbert A. 1912- Brief entry 107
Cahill, James F(rancis) 1926- CANR-6
Earlier sketch in CA 1R
Cahill, Jane (Miller) 1901- CAP-2
Earlier sketch in CA 23-24
Cahill, Kevin Michael 1936- CANR-18
Earlier sketch in CA 102
Cahill, Robert S. 1933- 15-16R
Cahill, Susan Neunzig 1940- 37-40R
Cahill, Thomas (Quinn) 1940- 49-52
Cahill, Tom
See Cahill, Thomas (Quinn)
Cahn, Edgar S. 1935- 29-32R
Cahn, Rhoda 1922- 81-84
See also SATA 37
Cahn, Robert 1917- 108
Cahn, Sammy 1913- 85-88
Cahn, Steven M. 1942- CANR-13
Earlier sketch in CA 21-22R
Cahn, William 1912-1976 ....23-24R
Obituary 69-72
See also SATA 37
Cahn, Zvi 1896- CAP-2
Earlier sketch in CA 23-24
Cahnman, Werner J(acob) 1902- 49-52
Caiden, Gerald E(lliot) 1936- CANR-14
Earlier sketch in CA 29-32R
Caidin, Martin 1927- CANR-2
Earlier sketch in CA 2R
See also AITN 2
Caiger-Smith, Alan 1930- 13-14R
Caillois, Roger 1913-1978 .... CANR-13
Obituary 85-88
Earlier sketch in CA 25-28R
Caillou, Alan
See Lyle-Smythe, Alan
Cain, Arthur H(omer) 1913- CANR-4
Earlier sketch in CA 4R
See also SATA 3
Cain, Bob
See Cain, Robert Owen
Cain, Bruce E. 1948- 122
Cain, George 1943- DLB-33
Cain, Glen G. 1933- 21-22R
Cain, Guillermo
See Cabrera Infante, G(uillermo)
Cain, Jackson
See Gleason, Robert
Cain, James M(allahan) 1892-1977 ...... CANR-8
Obituary 73-76
Earlier sketch in CA 17-18R
See also CLC 3, 11, 28
See also AITN 1
Cain, Mary (Dawson) 1904-1984 Obituary .. 112
Cain, Maureen 1938- 73-76
Cain, Michael Peter 1941- 93-96
Cain, Robert Owen 1934- 65-68
Cain, T. G. S. 1944- 124
Cain, Thomas H(enry) 1931- 93-96
Caine, (Thomas Henry) Hall 1853(?)-1931
Brief entry 122
Caine, Jeffrey (Andrew) 1944- 85-88
Caine, Lynn 1924(?)-1987 Obituary 124
Caine, Mark
See Raphael, Frederic (Michael)
Caine, Mitchell
See Sparkia, Roy (Bernard)
Caine, Stanley P(aul) 1940- 41-44R
Caine, Sydney 1902- CAP-2
Earlier sketch in CA 25-28
Caines, Jeannette (Franklin) SATA-43
Caird, George Bradford 1917-1984 61-64
Obituary 112
Caird, Janet 1913- CANR-2
Earlier sketch in CA 49-52
Cairncross, Alec
See Cairncross, Alexander Kirkland
Cairncross, Alexander Kirkland 1911- ... CANR-8
Earlier sketch in CA 61-64
Cairncross, Frances (Anne) 1944- 57-60
Cairney, John 1930- 105
Cairns, David 1904- CANR-11
Earlier sketch in CA 61-64
Cairns, (Thomas) Dorian 1901-1972
Obituary 37-40R
Cairns, Earle E(dwin) 1910- CANR-18
Earlier sketch in CA 1R
Cairns, Grace Edith 1907- CANR-18
Earlier sketch in CA 1R
Cairns, Huntington 1904-1985 .... CANR-5
Obituary 114
Earlier sketch in CA 53-56
Cairns, J(ames) F(ord) 1914- 105
Cairns, John C(ampbell) 1924- CANR-5
Earlier sketch in CA 13-14R
Cairns, Thomas W(illiam) 1931- 23-24R
Cairns, Trevor 1922- 33-36R
See also SATA 14
Cairns-Smith, A(lexander) G(raham) 1931- .. 123
Cairo, Jon
See Romano, Deane Louis
Caitlin, Elise 1953- 111
Cake, Patrick
See Welch, Timothy L.
Calabrese, Alphonse F. X. 1923- 69-72
Calabrese, Anthony 1938- 89-92
Calabresi, Guido 1932- CANR-20
Earlier sketch in CA 41-44R
Calaferte, Louis 1928- CANR-17
Earlier sketches in CA 45-48, CANR-1
Calais, Jean
See Rodefer, Stephen
Calamandrei, Mauro 1925- 69-72
Calamari, John D(aniel) 1921- 37-40R
Calasibetta, Charlotte M(ankey) 1917- 103
Calde, Mark A(ugustine) 1945- 69-72
Caldecott, Moyra 1927- CANR-13
Earlier sketch in CA 77-80
See also SATA 22
Caldecott, Randolph (J.) 1846-1886 ... SATA-17
See also CLR 14
Calder, Alexander 1898-1976 Obituary 111
Calder, Angus 1942- 29-32R
Calder, C(larence) R(oy), Jr. 1928- 81-84
Calder, Daniel Gillmore 1939- 103
Calder, Jason
See Dunmore, John
Calder, Jenni 1941- CANR-1
Earlier sketch in CA 45-48
Calder, Kent E(yring) 1948- 107
Calder, Lyn
See Calmenson, Stephanie
Calder, Nigel (David Ritchie) 1931- CANR-11
Earlier sketch in CA 21-22R
Calder, Ritchie
See Ritchie-Calder, Peter Ritchie
Calder, Robert
See Mundis, Jerrold
Calder, Robert Lorin 1941- 65-68
Calder-Marshall, Arthur 1908- 61-64
Calderon, Jose Vasconcelos
See Vasconcelos (Calderon), Jose
Calderone, Mary S(teichen) 1904- 104
See also AITN 1
Calderwood, Ivan E. 1899- 57-60
Calderwood, James D(ixon) 1917- CANR-3
Earlier sketch in CA 5-6R
Calderwood, James L(ee) 1930- 21-22R
Caldicott, Helen 1938- Brief entry 114
Caldicott, Helen (Mary) 1938- 124
Caldwell, Ben 1937- Brief entry 117
See also DLB 38
Caldwell, Ben(jamin) 1937- 124
Caldwell, Bettye (McDonald) 1924- 104
Caldwell, C(harles) Edson 1906-1974 .... CAP-2
Earlier sketch in CA 29-32
Caldwell, Dan (Edward) 1948- 112
Caldwell, Edward S(abiston) 1928- 65-68
Caldwell, Erskine (Preston) 1903-1987 .. CANR-2
Obituary 121
Earlier sketch in CA 2R
See also CAAS 1
See also DLB 9
See also CLC 1, 8, 14
See also AITN 1
Caldwell, Gaylon L(oray) 1920- 33-36R
Caldwell, Harry B(oynton) 1935- 37-40R
Caldwell, Helen F. 1904- 77-80
Caldwell, Inga Gilson 1897- 61-64
Caldwell, Irene Catherine (Smith)
1908-1979 ....9-10R
Obituary 103
Caldwell, James
See Lowry, Robert (James Collas)
Caldwell, John 1928- CANR-12
Earlier sketch in CA 73-76
Caldwell, John C(ope) 1913- CANR-13
Earlier sketch in CA 23-24R
See also SATA 7
Caldwell, Joseph H(erman) 1934- 23-24R
Caldwell, Kathryn (Smoot) 1942- 69-72
Caldwell, Louis O(liver) 1935- 69-72
Caldwell, Lynton (Keith) 1913- CANR-12
Earlier sketch in CA 29-32R
Caldwell, (James Alexander) Malcolm
1931-1978 .... CANR-17
Earlier sketch in CA 25-28R
Caldwell, Marge 1914- 97-100
Caldwell, Nat(han Green) 1912-1985
Obituary 115
Caldwell, Oliver Johnson 1904- 37-40R
Caldwell, Robert G(ranville) 1882-1976
Obituary 65-68
Caldwell, Robert Graham 1904- 19-20R
Caldwell, (Janet Miriam) Taylor (Holland)
1900-1985 .... CANR-5
Obituary 116
Earlier sketch in CA 5-6R
See also CLC 2, 28, 39
Caldwell, William A(nthony) 1906-1986
Obituary 119
Calef, Wesley (Carr) 1914- 13-14R
Caley, Rod
See Rowland, Donald S(ydney)
Calhoon, Richard P(ercival) 1909- 57-60
Calhoon, Robert M(cCluer) 1935- CANR-4
Earlier sketch in CA 53-56
Calhoun, Calfrey C. 1928- 37-40R
Calhoun, Chad
See Goulart, Ron(ald Joseph)
Calhoun, Conyus 1946- 111
Calhoun, Daniel F(airchild) 1929- 65-68
Calhoun, Don Gilmore 1914- 85-88
Calhoun, Donald W(allace) 1917- 104
Calhoun, Eric
See Turner, Robert H(arry)
Calhoun, James Frank 1941- 109
Calhoun, John Caldwell 1782-1850 ...... DLB-3
Calhoun, Mary
See Wilkins, Mary Huiskamp
See also SATA 2
Calhoun, Richard James 1926- 33-36R
Calhoun, Robert L(owery) 1896-1983
Obituary 110
Calhoun, Thomas 1940- 89-92
Calia, Vincent F(rank) 1926- 53-56
Calian, Carnegie Samuel 1933- 25-28R
Caliban
See Reid, J(ohn) C(owie)
Califano, Joseph A(nthony), Jr. 1931- ... CANR-2
Earlier sketch in CA 45-48
Calin, William (Compaine) 1936- CANR-11
Earlier sketch in CA 21-22R
Calisch, Edith Lindeman 1898-1984
Obituary 114
Calisher, Hortense 1911- CANR-22
Earlier sketches in CA 4R, CANR-1
See also DLB 2
See also CLC 2, 4, 8, 38
Calistro, Paddy
See Calistro McAuley, Patricia Ann
Calistro McAuley, Patricia Ann 1948- 118
Calitri, Charles J(oseph) 1916- 5-6R
Calitri, Princine 33-36R
Calkin, Homer Leonard 1912- 41-44R
Calkin, Ruth Harms 1918- 102
Calkins, Fay
See Alailima, Fay C.
Calkins, Franklin
See Stratemeyer, Edward L.
Calkins, Rodello 1920- Brief entry 105

INDEX

Call, Alice E(lizabeth) LaPlant 1914- ... 13-14R
Call, Hughie Florence 1890- ... 7-8R
See also SATA 1
Calladine, Andrew G(arfield) 1941- ... 102
Calladine, Carole E(lizabeth) 1942- ... 102
Callaghan, Barry 1937- ... 101
Callaghan, Catherine A. 1931- ... 33-36R
Callaghan, Mary Rose 1944- ... 118
Callaghan, Morley Edward 1903- ... 9-10R
See also CLC 3, 14, 41
Callaghan, Thomas 1924- ... 114
Callahan, Charles C(lifford) 1910- ... CAP-2
Earlier sketch in CA 17-18
Callahan, Claire Wallis 1890- ... 7-8R
Callahan, Daniel 1930- ... 21-22R
Callahan, Dorothy M(onahan) 1934- ... 114
See also SATA 35, 39
Callahan, John
See Gallun, Raymond Z(inke)
Callahan, John F(rancis) 1912- ... 33-36R
Callahan, Nelson J. 1927- ... 33-36R
Callahan, North 1908- ... CANR-2
Earlier sketch in CA 1R
Callahan, Philip Serna 1923- ... 102
See also SATA 25
Callahan, Raymond (Aloysius) 1938- ... 69-72
Callahan, Sidney Cornelia 1933- ... 17-18R
Callahan, Sterling G. 1916- ... 21-22R
Callahan, Steven (Patrick) 1952- ... 120
Callan, Edward T. 1917- ... 17-18R
Callan, Jamie 1954- ... 109
Callan, John P(atrick) 1939- ... 111
Callan, Richard J(erome) 1932- ... 53-56
Callard, Maurice (Frederick Thomas) 1912- ... CANR-3
Earlier sketch in CA 1R
Callard, Thomas Henry 1912- ... 9-10R
Callas, Theo
See McCarthy, Shaun (Lloyd)
Callaway, Bernice (Anne) 1923- ... 121
See also SATA 48
Callaway, Joseph A(tlee) 1920- ... 65-68
Callaway, Kathy 1943- ... 107
See also SATA 36
Callcott, George H(ardy) 1929- ... 29-32R
Callcott, Margaret Law 1929- ... 61-64
Callcott, Wilfrid H(ardy) 1895-1969
Obituary ... 112
Calle, Francisco Rosillo
See Rosillo-Calle, Francisco
Callen, Larry
See Callen, Lawrence Willard, Jr.
Callen, Lawrence Willard, Jr. 1927- ... CANR-12
Earlier sketch in CA 73-76
See also SATA 19
Callen, William B. 1930- ... 23-24R
Callenbach, Ernest 1929- ... CANR-21
Earlier sketches in CA 57-60, CANR-6
Callender, Charles 1928- ... 41-44R
Callender, Julian
See Lee, Austin
Callender, Wesley P(ayne), Jr. 1923- ... 17-18R
Calleo, David P(atrick) 1934- ... CANR-10
Earlier sketch in CA 17-18R
Callihan, E(lmer) L(ee) 1903- ... CAP-2
Earlier sketch in CA 25-28
Callinan, Bernard James 1913- ... 110
Callis, Helmut G(unther) 1906- ... CANR-5
Earlier sketch in CA 53-56
Callis, Robert 1920- ... 37-40R
Callison, Brian 1934- ... 29-32R
Callister, Frank 1916- ... 13-14R
Callmann, Rudolf 1892-1976 ... 69-72
Obituary ... 65-68
Callow, Alexander B., Jr. 1925- ... 21-22R
Callow, James T(homas) 1928- ... 41-44R
Callow, Philip Kenneth 1924- ... CANR-21
Earlier sketches in CA 13-14R, CANR-6
Calloway, Cab(ell III) 1907- Brief entry ... 113
Calloway, Doris Howes 1923- ... 21-22R
Callum, Myles 1934- ... 9-10R
Callwood, June 1924- ... CANR-24
Earlier sketch in CA 101
Calman, Alvin R(ose) 1895-1983 Obituary ... 110
Calmann, John 1935-1980 ... 21-22R
Obituary ... 97-100
Calmann-Levy, Robert 1899-1982
Obituary ... 108
Calmenson, Stephanie 1952- ... CANR-24
Earlier sketch in CA 107
See also SATA 37
Calmer, Edgar 1907-1986 ... CANR-20
Obituary ... 118
Earlier sketch in CA 69-72
See also DLB 4
Calmer, Ned
See Calmer, Edgar
Calmus, Lawrence 1943- ... 111
Calnan, T(homas) D(aniel) 1915- ... 29-32R
Calne, Roy Yorke 1930- ... 61-64
Calonne, David Stephen 1953- ... 114
Caltagirone, Carmen L(illian) 1950- ... 114
Calter, Paul (William) 1934- ... CANR-14
Earlier sketch in CA 41-44R
Calverley, C. S. 1831-1884 ... DLB-35
Calvert, Elinor H.
See Lasell, Elinor H.
Calvert, George Henry 1803-1889 ... DLB-1, 64
Calvert, John
See Leaf, (Wilbur) Munro
Calvert, Laura D. 1922- ... 37-40R
Calvert, Mary 1941- ... 93-96
Calvert, Monte A(lan) 1938- ... 21-22R
Calvert, Patricia 1931- ... CANR-21
Earlier sketch in CA 105
See also SATA 45
Calvert, Peter (Anthony Richard) 1936- ... CANR-11
Earlier sketch in CA 25-28R
Calvert, Robert, Jr. 1922- ... 25-28R
Calvez, Jean-Yves 1927- ... 57-60
Calvin, Henry
See Hanley, Clifford
Calvin, Ross 1890(?)-1970 Obituary ... 104
Calvin, William H(oward) 1939- ... 123
Calvino, Italo 1923-1985 ... CANR-23
Obituary ... 116
Earlier sketch in CA 85-88
See also CLC 5, 8, 11, 22, 33, 39
Calvocoressi, Peter (John Ambrose) 1912- ... 65-68
Cam, Helen Maud 1885-1968 ... CAP-1
Earlier sketch in CA 13-14
Camara, Helder Pessoa 1909- ... 61-64
Camber, Andrew
See Bingley, David Ernest
Cambon, Glauco (Gianlorenzo) 1921- ... CANR-7
Earlier sketch in CA 19-20R
Camden, Archie 1888-1979 ... 114
Camejo, Peter Miguel 1939- Brief entry ... 105
Camerini, Mario 1895-1981 Obituary ... 103
Cameron, A(rchibald) J(ames) 1920- ... 73-76
Cameron, Alan (Douglas Edward) 1938- ... CANR-8
Earlier sketch in CA 61-64
Cameron, Allan Gillies 1930- ... 102
Cameron, Allan W(illiams) 1938- ... 33-36R
Cameron, Angus de Mille 1913- ... 102
Cameron, Angus Fraser 1941-1983 ... 122
Obituary ... 109
Cameron, Ann 1943- ... 101
See also SATA 27
Cameron, Betsy 1949- ... 101
Cameron, (Jack) Bruce 1913-1979 ... 2R
Cameron, Constance Carpenter 1937- ... 49-52
Cameron, D. A.
See Cameron, Donald (Allan)
Cameron, D. Y.
See Cook, Dorothy Mary
Cameron, David R(obertson) 1941- ... 73-76
Cameron, Donald (Allan) 1937- ... CANR-8
Earlier sketch in CA 23-24R
Cameron, Donald
See Bryans, Robert Harbinson
Cameron, Edna M. 1905- ... CAP-1
Earlier sketch in CA 9-10
See also SATA 3
Cameron, Eleanor (Frances) 1912- ... CANR-22
Earlier sketches in CA 4R, CANR-2
See also SATA 1, 25
See also DLB 52
See also CLR 1
Cameron, Eleanor Cranston ... 118
Cameron, Eleanor Elford 1910- ... 77-80
Cameron, Elizabeth
See Nowell, Elizabeth Cameron
Cameron, Elizabeth Jane 1910-1976 ... CANR-1
Obituary ... 69-72
Earlier sketch in CA 3R
See also SATA 30, 32
Cameron, Elspeth 1943- ... 113
Cameron, Frank T. 1909- ... CAP-1
Earlier sketch in CA 19-20
Cameron, George Glenn 1905-1979
Obituary ... 89-92
Cameron, Harold W. 1905- ... 81-84
Cameron, Hope
See Morritt, Hope
Cameron, Ian
See Payne, Donald Gordon
Cameron, J(ames) M(unro) 1910- ... CANR-2
Earlier sketch in CA 7-8R
Cameron, (Mark) James (Walter) 1911-1985 ... 23-24R
Obituary ... 114
Cameron, James R(eese) 1929- ... 33-36R
Cameron, John 1914- ... 29-32R
Cameron, Julie
See Cameron, Lou
Cameron, Kate
See Du Breuil, (Elizabeth) L(or)inda
Cameron, Kenneth 1922- ... 103
Cameron, Kenneth Neill 1908- ... CANR-3
Earlier sketch in CA 11-12R
Cameron, Kenneth Walter 1908- ... CANR-24
Earlier sketches in CA 21-22R, CANR-8
Cameron, Kim S(terling) 1946- ... 109
Cameron, Lorna
See Fraser, Anthea
Cameron, Lou 1924- ... CANR-21
Earlier sketches in CA 3R, CANR-4
Cameron, M(alcolm) G(ordon) Graham
See Graham-Cameron, M(alcolm) G(ordon)
Cameron, M. Graham
See Graham-Cameron, M(alcolm) G(ordon)
Cameron, Mary Owen 1915- ... 15-16R
Cameron, Meribeth E(lliott) 1905- ... 1R
Cameron, Mike Graham
See Graham-Cameron, M(alcolm) G(ordon)
Cameron, Neil 1920-1985 Obituary ... 115
Cameron, Peter 1959- ... CLC-44
Cameron, Polly 1928- ... 17-18R
See also SATA 2
Cameron, Roderick (William) 1913-1985
Obituary ... 117
Brief entry ... 113
Cameron, Rondo (Emmett) 1925- ... CANR-5
Earlier sketch in CA 1R
Cameron, Sharon 1947- ... 123
Cameron, Silver Donald
See Cameron, Donald (Allan)
Cameron, William Bruce 1920- ... 37-40R
Cameron, William J(ames) 1926-
Brief entry ... 116
Cameron Watt, Donald 1928- ... CANR-14
Earlier sketch in CA 77-80
Camilleri, Joseph A. 1944- ... 117
Caminada, Jerome (Charles) 1911-1985
Obituary ... 117
Camm, John 1718-1778 ... DLB-31
Cammack, Floyd M(cKee) 1933- ... CANR-6
Earlier sketch in CA 11-12R
Cammann, Schuyler (van Rensselaer) 1912- ... 9-10R
Cammarata, Jerry F(rank) 1947- ... 81-84
Cammer, Leonard 1913- ... 65-68
Camner, James 1950- ... 108
Camoin, Francois Andre 1939- ... 61-64
Camp, Candace P(auline) 1949- ... 102
Camp, Charles L. 1893-1975 Obituary ... 61-64
See also SATA 31
Camp, Dalton Kingsley 1920- ... 61-64
Camp, Fred V(alterma) 1911- ... 49-52
Camp, James 1923- ... 33-36R
Camp, John (Michael Francis) 1915- ... 93-96
Camp, Roderic (Ai) 1945- ... CANR-18
Earlier sketch in CA 102
Camp, T(homas) Edward 1929- ... 13-14R
Camp, Walter (Chauncey) 1859-1925 ... YABC-1
Camp, Wesley D(ouglass) 1915- ... 19-20R
Camp, William (Newton Alexander) 1926- ... 61-64
Campa, Arthur L(eon) 1905- ... 73-76
Campaigne, Jameson Gilbert 1914-1985 ... 2R
Obituary ... 114
Campana, Dino 1885-1932 Brief entry ... 117
See also TCLC 20
Campanella, Francis B. 1936- ... 53-56
Campanile, Archille 1900(?)-1977
Obituary ... 69-72
Campanile, Pasquale Festa
See Festa Campanile, Pasquale
Campbell, A. C.
See Campbell, Andrew C.
Campbell, Alan K. 1923- ... CANR-3
Earlier sketch in CA 5-6R
Campbell, Alexander 1912-1977 ... 61-64
Obituary ... 69-72
Campbell, Alistair 1907-1974 ... CAP-1
Earlier sketch in CA 17-18
Campbell, Alla (Linda Renee) Bozarth
See Bozarth-Campbell, Alla (Linda Renee)
Campbell, (Elizabeth) Andrea 1963- ... SATA-50
Campbell, Andrew C. 1923- Brief entry ... 114
Campbell, (Albert) Angus 1910-1980
Obituary ... 105
Campbell, Angus
See Chetwynd-Hayes, R(onald Henry Glynn)
Campbell, Ann R. 1925- ... 21-22R
See also SATA 11
Campbell, Archibald Bruce 1881- ... CAP-1
Earlier sketch in CA 15-16
Campbell, Arnold Everitt 1906-1980
Obituary ... 108
Campbell, Arthur A(ndrews) 1924- ... 1R
Campbell, Ballard Crooker, Jr. 1940- ... 104
Campbell, Beatrice Murphy
See Murphy, Beatrice M.
Campbell, Bernard G(rant) 1930- ... 23-24R
Campbell, Blanche 1902- ... 5-6R
Campbell, Bruce
See Epstein, Samuel
Campbell, Camilla 1905- ... CAP-2
Earlier sketch in CA 25-28
See also SATA 26
Campbell, Carlos Cardozo 1937- ... 102
Campbell, Charles Arthur 1897-1974
Obituary ... 49-52
Campbell, Charles S(outter) 1911- ... 69-72
Campbell, Clive
See MacRae, Donald G.
Campbell, Colin Dearborn 1917- ... 33-36R
Campbell, Cy(ril Calvin) 1925- ... 97-100
Campbell, D(onald)
See Gilford, C(harles) B(ernard)
Campbell, D(onald) Ross 1939- ... 117
Campbell, Dan H(ampton) 1907-1974
Obituary ... 112
Campbell, David (Watt Ian) 1915-1979 ... 97-100
Campbell, David A(itken) 1927- ... CANR-11
Earlier sketch in CA 25-28R
Campbell, David (John) Graham
See Graham-Campbell, David (John)
Campbell, David P. 1934- ... 23-24R
Campbell, Dennis M(arion) 1945- ... 73-76
Campbell, Don(ald Guy) 1922- ... 19-20R
Campbell, Donald 1940- ... 69-72
Campbell, Duane E(ugene) 1941- ... 116
Campbell, E(lwood) G(ordon) 1923- ... 107
Campbell, E. Simms 1906-1971 Obituary ... 93-96
Campbell, Edward D(unscomb) C(hristian), Jr. 1946- ... 106
Campbell, Edward F(ay), Jr. 1932- ... 15-16R
Campbell, Elizabeth McClure 1891- ... 37-40R
Campbell, Enid (Mona) 1932- ... 109
Campbell, Ernest Q(ueener) 1926- ... 37-40R
Campbell, Eugene Edward 1915- ... 23-24R
Campbell, Ewing 1940- ... CANR-13
Earlier sketch in CA 73-76
Campbell, F(enton) Gregory, Jr. 1939- ... 69-72
Campbell, Francis Stuart
See Kuehnelt-Leddihn, Erik (Maria) Ritter von
Campbell, G(aylon) S(anford) 1940- ... 107
Campbell, George F(rederick) 1915- ... CANR-14
Earlier sketch in CA 65-68
Campbell, Graeme 1931- ... 77-80
Campbell, Hannah ... 11-12R
Campbell, Herbert James 1925- ... 97-100
Campbell, Hope 1925- ... CANR-10
Earlier sketch in CA 61-64
See also SATA 20
Campbell, Howard E(rnest) 1925- ... CANR-7
Earlier sketch in CA 57-60
Campbell, Ian 1899-1978 ... 53-56
Obituary ... 103
Campbell, Ian 1942- ... CANR-9
Earlier sketch in CA 65-68
Campbell, J(ames) Arthur 1916- ... 53-56
Campbell, Jack K(enagy) 1927- ... 23-24R
Campbell, James 1920- ... 57-60
Campbell, James E(dward) 1945- ... 107
Campbell, James Edwin 1867-1896 ... DLB-50
Campbell, James Howard 1928- ... 113
Campbell, James Marshall 1895-1977 ... 73-76
Obituary ... 69-72
Campbell, Jane 1934- ... 41-44R
Campbell, Jane
See Edwards, Jane Campbell
Campbell, Janet Bruce 1955- ... 121
Campbell, (Mary) Jean 1943- ... 115
Campbell, Jeff(erson) H(olland) 1931- ... 41-44R
Campbell, Jeffrey
See Black, Campbell
Campbell, Jeremy 1931- ... 109
Campbell, Jim
See Campbell, James Howard
Campbell, Joan 1929- ... 109
Campbell, Joanna
See Bly, Carol(yn)
Campbell, John 1653-1728 ... DLB-43
Campbell, John 1947- ... 114
Campbell, John Coert 1911- ... CANR-3
Earlier sketch in CA 4R
Campbell, John Creighton 1941- ... 111
Campbell, John Franklin 1940(?)-1971
Obituary ... 33-36R
Campbell, John Lorne 1906- ... 29-32R
Campbell, John R(oy) 1933- ... 53-56
Campbell, John W(ood) 1910-1971 ... CAP-2
Obituary ... 29-32R
Earlier sketch in CA 21-22
See also DLB 8
See also CLC 32
Campbell, Joseph 1904-1987 ... CANR-3
Obituary ... 124
Earlier sketch in CA 4R
Campbell, Judith
See Pares, Marion (Stapylton)
Campbell, Karen
See Beaty, Betty
Campbell, Karlyn Kohrs 1937- ... CANR-18
Earlier sketches in CA 53-56, CANR-4
Campbell, Keith 1938- ... 106
Campbell, Keith Oliver 1920- ... 110
Campbell, Ken 1941- ... 77-80
Campbell, Kenneth 1901(?)-1979
Obituary ... 85-88
Campbell, Lawrence James 1931- ... 106
Campbell, Litta Belle 1886-1980 ... CANR-5
Earlier sketch in CA 5-6R
Campbell, Louisa D. 1958- ... 121
Campbell, Luke
See Madison, Thomas A.
Campbell, Malcolm J(ames) 1930- ... CANR-21
Earlier sketches in CA 57-60, CANR-6
Campbell, Margaret ... 69-72
Campbell, (Gabrielle) Margaret (Vere) 1886-1952 Brief entry ... 116
Campbell, Margaret 1916- ... 106
Campbell, Maria 1940- ... 102
Campbell, Marjorie Wilkins ... 97-100
Campbell, Michael Mussen 1924-1984 ... 102
Obituary ... 113
Campbell, Oscar James, Jr. 1879-1970
Obituary ... 29-32R
Campbell, Patricia J(ean) 1930- ... 103
See also SATA 45
Campbell, Patricia Piatt 1901- ... 25-28R
Campbell, Patrick Gordon 1913-1980
Obituary ... 102
Campbell, Patty
See Campbell, Patricia J(ean)
Campbell, Paul N. 1923- ... 21-22R
Campbell, Penelope 1935- ... 33-36R
Campbell, Peter (Walter) 1926- ... CANR-11
Earlier sketches in CA 13-14, CAP-1
Campbell, Peter Anthony 1935- ... 21-22R
Campbell, R. T.
See Todd, Ruthven
Campbell, R. W.
See Campbell, Rosemae Wells
Campbell, R(obert) Wright 1927- ... CANR-24
Earlier sketches in CA 57-60, CANR-6, 21
Campbell, (John) Ramsey 1946- ... CANR-7
Earlier sketch in CA 57-60
See also CLC 42
Campbell, Randolph B(luford) 1940- ... 41-44R
Campbell, Rex R. 1931- ... 41-44R
Campbell, Rita Ricardo
See Ricardo-Campbell, Rita
Campbell, Robert 1922-1977 ... CANR-8
Obituary ... 73-76
Earlier sketch in CA 53-56
Campbell, Robert
See Campbell, R(obert) Wright
Campbell, Robert B(lair) 1923- ... 69-72
Campbell, Robert C(harles) 1924- ... 49-52
Campbell, Robert Dale 1914- ... 11-12R
Campbell, Robert Wellington 1926- ... CANR-3
Earlier sketch in CA 1R
Campbell, Rod 1945- ... SATA-44

Campbell, Rosemae Wells 1909- 13-14R
See also SATA 1
Campbell, (Ignatius) Roy (Dunnachie) 1901-1957 Brief entry 104
See also DLB 20
See also TCLC 5
Campbell, Sheldon 1919- 41-44R
Campbell, Sid 1944- 118
Campbell, Stanley W(allace) 1926- 49-52
Campbell, Stephen K(ent) 1935- 49-52
Campbell, Thomas F. 1924- 21-22R
Campbell, Thomas M(oody) 1936- 49-52
Campbell, Wilfred
See Campbell, William
See also TCLC 9
Campbell, Will D(avis) 1924- CANR-22
Earlier sketches in CA 7-8R, CANR-7
Campbell, William 1858(?)-1918 Brief entry 106
Campbell, William Edward March 1893-1954 Brief entry 108
Campbell-Johnson, Alan 1913- 65-68
Campbell-Purdie, Wendy 1925- 21-22R
Campen, Richard N(ewman) 1912- 69-72
Camper, Shirley
See Soman, Shirley
Campion, Joan 1940- 124
Campion, Nardi Reeder 1917- CANR-6
Earlier sketch in CA 4R
See also SATA 22
Campion, Rosamond
See Rosmond, Babette
Campion, Sidney R(onald) 1891- CAP-1
Earlier sketch in CA 9-10
Campion, Thomas 1567-1620 DLB-58
Camplin, Jamie (Robert) 1947- 97-100
Campling, Christopher R(ussell) 1925- 113
Campling, Elizabeth 1948- 123
Campolo, Anthony, Jr. 1935- CANR-11
Earlier sketch in CA 69-72
Camps, Francis Edward 1905-1972 37-40R
Campton, David 1924- CANR-20
Earlier sketches in CA 7-8R, CANR-5
Camus, Albert 1913-1960 89-92
See also CLC 1, 2, 4, 9, 11, 14, 32
Camus, Raoul Francois 1930- 65-68
Camus, (Jean) Renaud (Gabriel) 1946- 108
Camuti, Louis J(oseph) 1893-1981 101
Obituary 103
Canada, Lena 1942- 93-96
Canaday, John E(dwin) 1907-1985 CANR-7
Obituary 116
Earlier sketch in CA 13-14R
Canan, James William 1929- 61-64
Canary
See Conn, Canary Denise
Canary, Robert H(ughes) 1939- CANR-11
Earlier sketch in CA 29-32R
Canavan, Francis 1917- 118
Canaway, W(illiam) H(amilton) 1925- 93-96
Canby, Courtlandt 1914- 118
Canby, Henry Seidel 1878-1961 Obituary 89-92
Canby, Vincent 1924- 81-84
See also CLC 13
Cancale
See Desnos, Robert
Cancellare, Frank 1910-1985 Obituary 116
Cancian, Francesca M(icaela) 1937- 57-60
Cancian, Francis Alexander 1934- CANR-7
Earlier sketch in CA 53-56
Cancian, Frank
See Cancian, Francis Alexander
Candelaria, Frederick (Henry) 1929- 17-18R
Candelaria, Nash 1928- CANR-11
Earlier sketch in CA 69-72
Candell, Victor 1903-1977 SATA-24
Candida
See Hoffman, Lisa
Candilis, Wray O. 1927- CANR-10
Earlier sketch in CA 25-28R
Candland, Douglas Keith 1934- CANR-2
Earlier sketch in CA 5-6R
Candler, Julie 1919- 65-68
Candlin, Enid Saunders 1909- CANR-1
Earlier sketch in CA 45-48
Candy, Edward
See Neville, B(arbara) Alison (Boodson)
Cane, Melville (Henry) 1879-1980 CANR-8
Obituary 97-100
Earlier sketches in CA 4R, CANR-6
Canellopoulos, Panayiotis 1902-1986
Obituary 120
Canemaker, John 1943- 81-84
Caner, Mary Paul 1893- CAP-2
Earlier sketch in CA 21-22
Canetti, Elias 1905- CANR-23
Earlier sketch in CA 21-22R
See also CLC 3, 14, 25
Caney, Steven 1941- 104
Canfield, Cass 1897-1986 41-44R
Obituary 118
Canfield, (Fayette) Curtis 1903-1986
Obituary 120
Canfield, D(elos) Lincoln 1903- 25-28R
Canfield, Dorothy
See Fisher, Dorothy (Frances) Canfield
Canfield, Gae Whitney 1931- 113
Canfield, James D(avid) 1937- 117
Canfield, James K(eith) 1925- 25-28R
Canfield, James Lewis 1942- 121
Canfield, Jane White 1897-1984 109
Obituary 112
See also SATA 32, 38
Canfield, John A(lan) 1941- 37-40R
Canfield, Kenneth French 1909- CAP-1
Earlier sketch in CA 15-16
Canfield, Leon Hardy 1886- 3R
Canfield, Muriel 1935- 115
Cang, Joel 1899-1974 CAP-2
Earlier sketch in CA 29-32
Cangemi, Sister Marie Lucita 1920- 21-22R
Canham, Erwin D(ain) 1904-1982 CAP-1
Obituary 105
Earlier sketch in CA 13-14
Canham, Kingsley 1945- 57-60
Caniff, Milton (Arthur) 1907- 85-88
See also AITN 1
Cann, Marjorie Mitchell 1924- 89-92
Cannam, Peggie 1925- 13-14R
Cannan, Denis 1919- CANR-7
Earlier sketch in CA 57-60
Cannan, Gilbert E. 1884-1955 Brief entry 111
See also DLB 10
Cannan, Joanna
See Pullein-Thompson, Joanna Maxwell
Cannell, Kathleen Biggar (Eaton) 1891-1974 106
See also DLB 4
Cannell, Skipwith 1887-1957 DLB-45
Canning, Jeff(rey Michael) 1947- 73-76
Canning, John 1920- 89-92
Canning, Ray R(ussell) 1920- 41-44R
Canning, Victor 1911-1986 CANR-6
Obituary 118
Earlier sketch in CA 13-14R
Cannon, Alexander 1896-1963(?) Obituary 111
Cannon, Beth 1951- 69-72
Cannon, Bill
See Cannon, William S.
Cannon, Cornelia (James) 1876-1969
Obituary 109
See also SATA 28
Cannon, Garland (Hampton) 1924- CANR-13
Earlier sketch in CA 33-36R
Cannon, Grant Groesbeck 1911-1969
Obituary 117
Cannon, Harold C(harles) 1930- 45-48
Cannon, Helen 1921- 101
Cannon, James Monroe III 1918- 2R
Cannon, James P. 1890(?)-1974
Obituary 53-56
Cannon, Jimmy 1909-1973 Obituary 104
Cannon, John (Ashton) 1918- 49-52
Cannon, John
See Newton, Michael
Cannon, Le Grand, Jr. 1899-1979
Obituary 93-96
Cannon, Lou(is S.) 1933- 29-32R
Cannon, Mark W(ilcox) 1928- 15-16R
Cannon, Poppy
See White, Poppy Cannon
Cannon, Ravenna
See Mayhar, Ardath
Cannon, William Ragsdale 1916- CANR-18
Earlier sketches in CA 1R, CANR-4
Cannon, William S. 1918- 29-32R
Canny, Nicholas P(atrick) 1944- 69-72
Cano-Ballesta, Juan 1932- CANR-1
Earlier sketch in CA 49-52
Canon, Lance Kirkpatrick 1939- 45-48
Canovan, Margaret 1939- 81-84
Cansdale, George (Soper) 1909- 9-10R
Cant, Gilbert 1909-1982 Obituary 107
Cant, Reginald (Edward) 1914-1987
Obituary 122
Cantacuzene, Julia 1876-1975 Obituary 61-64
Cantacuzino, Sherban 1928- 118
Cantelon, John E(dward) 1924- 11-12R
Cantelon, Philip L(ouis) 1940- 124
Canterbery, E(stes) Ray 1935- 41-44R
Cantin, Eileen 1931- 53-56
Cantin, Eugene Thorpe 1944- 45-48
Cantinat, Jean 1902- 29-32R
Cantor, Arthur 1920- 29-32R
Cantor, Eli 1913- CANR-14
Earlier sketch in CA 77-80
Cantor, Gilbert M. 1929(?)-1987 Obituary 122
Cantor, Leonard M(artin) 1927- 69-72
Cantor, Louis 1934- 29-32R
Cantor, Milton 1925- Brief entry 112
Cantor, Muriel G. 1923- CANR-12
Earlier sketch in CA 33-36R
Cantor, Norman F(rank) 1929- 102
Cantor, Paul A(rthur) 1945- 89-92
Cantor, Paul David 1916-1979 Obituary 89-92
Cantori, Louis J. 1934- 29-32R
Cantrell, J(ohn) A(nthony) 1952- 123
Cantril, Albert H(adley) 1940- 111
Cantu, Robert Clark 1938- 108
Cantwell, Aston
See Platt, Charles
Cantwell, Dennis P(atrick) 1940- 57-60
Cantwell, Lois 1951- 121
Cantwell, Robert Emmett 1908-1978 CANR-4
Obituary 81-84
Earlier sketch in CA 5-6R
See also DLB 9
Cantzlaar, George La Fond 1906-1967 CAP-1
Earlier sketch in CA 15-16
Canuck, Abe
See Bingley, David Ernest
Canusi, Jose
See Barker, S. Omar
Canutt, Enos Edward 1895(?)-1986
Obituary 119
Brief entry 114
Canutt, Yakima
See Canutt, Enos Edward
Canzoneri, Robert (Wilburn) 1925- 19-20R
Capaldi, Nicholas 1939- 21-22R
Cape, Judith
See Page, P(atricia) K(athleen)
Cape, Peter (Irwin) 1929- 108
Cape, William H(enry) 1920- 11-12R
Capeci, Dominic Joseph, Jr. 1940- 77-80
Capek, Karel 1890-1938 Brief entry 104
See also TCLC 6
Capek, Milic 1909- CANR-4
Earlier sketch in CA 4R
Capel, Roger
See Sheppard, Lancelot C(apel)
Capelle, Russell B(eckett) 1917- 7-8R
Capen, Joseph 1658-1725 DLB-24
Capers, Gerald Mortimer, Jr. 1909- 5-6R
Capitan, William H(arry) 1933- 29-32R
Capitanchik, Maurice 1929(?)-1985
Obituary 118
Capitman, William G(ardiner) 1921-1975 122
Obituary 111
Capizzi, Michael 1941- 41-44R
Caplan, Arthur L(eonard) 1950- CANR-22
Earlier sketch in CA 106
Caplan, David 1947- 105
Caplan, Edwin H(arvey) 41-44R
Caplan, Frank 110
Caplan, Gerald 1917- CANR-18
Earlier sketch in CA 25-28R
Caplan, Harry 1896- CAP-2
Earlier sketch in CA 23-24
Caplan, Lionel 33-36R
Caplan, Ralph 1925- 15-16R
Caplan, Ronald Mervyn 1937- 107
Caplan, Theresa 110
Caplan, Thomas (Mark) 1946- 107
Caples, John 1900- 23-24R
Caplin, Alfred Gerald 1909-1979 57-60
Obituary 89-92
See also SATA 21
Caplovitz, David 1928- 41-44R
Caplow, Theodore 1920- CANR-20
Earlier sketches in CA 4R, CANR-4
Capon, Edmund (George) 1940- 107
Capon, (Harry) Paul 1912-1969 5-6R
Obituary 103
Capon, Peter
See Oakley, Eric Gilbert
Capon, Robert Farrar 1925- Brief entry 106
Caponigri, A(loysius) Robert 1915- 37-40R
Caporale, Rocco 1927- 37-40R
Capote, Truman 1924-1984 CANR-18
Obituary 113
Earlier sketch in CA 7-8R
See also DLB 2
See also DLBY 80, 84
See also CDALB 1941-1968
See also CLC 1, 3, 8, 13, 19, 34, 38
Capouya, Emile 122
Brief entry 118
Capp, Al
See Caplin, Alfred Gerald
Capp, Glenn Richard 1910- CANR-3
Earlier sketch in CA 1R
Capp, Richard 1935- 81-84
Cappadona, Diane Apostolos
See Apostolos-Cappadona, Diane
Cappel, Constance 1936- CANR-10
Earlier sketch in CA 21-22R
See also SATA 22
Cappelluti, Frank Joseph 1935-1972 37-40R
Capper, Douglas Parode 1898(?)-1979 9-10R
Obituary 103
Cappo, Joseph 1936- 77-80
Cappon, Daniel 1921- 19-20R
Cappon, Lester J(esse) 1900-1981 106
Obituary 104
Capps, Benjamin (Franklin) 1922- CANR-7
Earlier sketch in CA 7-8R
See also SATA 9
Capps, Carroll M. 1917(?)-1971 Obituary 112
Capps, Clifford Lucille Sheats 1902-1976 37-40R
Capps, Donald E(ric) 1939- CANR-12
Earlier sketch in CA 29-32R
Capps, Jack Lee 1926- 23-24R
Capps, Walter H(olden) 1934- CANR-12
Earlier sketch in CA 29-32R
Cappy Dick
See Cleveland, George
Capra, Frank 1897- 61-64
See also CLC 16
Capra, Fritjof 1939- 107
Capretta, Patrick J(ohn) 1929- 21-22R
Caprio, Betsy
See Caprio, Elizabeth Blair
Caprio, Elizabeth Blair 1933- 110
Caprio, Frank S(amuel) 1906- 101
Capron, Alexander Morgan 1944- 115
Capron, Jean F. 1924- 21-22R
Capron, Louis (Bishop) 1891- CAP-1
Earlier sketch in CA 9-10
Capron, Walter Clark 1904-1979 CAP-1
Obituary 89-92
Earlier sketch in CA 17-18
Capron, William M(osher) 1920- 29-32R
Capstick, Peter Hathaway 1940- 102
Captain Kangaroo
See Keeshan, Robert J.
Captain Wheeler
See Ellis, Edward S(ylvester)
Captain X
See Power-Waters, Brian
Caputi, Anthony (Francis) 1924- CANR-3
Earlier sketch in CA 1R
Caputo, David A(rmand) 1943- 65-68
Caputo, Philip 1941- 73-76
See also CLC 32
Caputo, Robert 1949- 101
Caradon, Lord
See Foot, Hugh Mackintosh
Caraley, Demetrios 1932- 103
Caraman, Philip 1911- CANR-21
Earlier sketches in CA 11-12R, CANR-6
Caramello, Charles 1948- 112
Carano, Paul 1919- 19-20R
Caras, Roger A(ndrew) 1928- CANR-5
Earlier sketch in CA 4R
See also SATA 12
Caras, Tracy 1953- 113
Carawan, Candie
See Carawan, Carolanne M.
Carawan, Carolanne M. 1939- 19-20R
Carawan, Guy H., Jr. 1927- 19-20R
Carballido, Emilio 1925- 33-36R
Carbaugh, Robert J(ohn) 1946- 65-68
Carbery, Thomas F. 29-32R
Carbine, Patricia (Theresa) 1931- 107
Carbonell, Reyes 1917- 9-10R
Carbonnier, Jeanne 1894-1974 CAP-2
Earlier sketch in CA 33-36
See also SATA 3, 34
Carbury, A.B.
See Carr, Albert H. Z(olotkoff)
Carcopino, Jerome 1881(?)-1970
Obituary 104
Card, Orson Scott 1951- 102
See also CLC 44, 47
Cardarelli, Joseph 1944- 77-80
Carden, Karen W(ilson) 1946- CANR-1
Earlier sketch in CA 49-52
Carden, Maren Lockwood 53-56
Carden, Patricia J. 1935- 41-44R
Cardenal, Ernesto 1925- CANR-2
Earlier sketch in CA 49-52
See also CLC 31
Cardenas, Daniel N(egrete) 1917- 45-48
Cardenas, Gilbert 1947- 97-100
Cardew, Cornelius 1936-1981 Obituary 108
Cardew, Michael (Ambrose) 1901-1983 49-52
Obituary 109
Cardiff, Gray Emerson 1949- 89-92
Cardinal, Ora 1913- 111
Cardinal, Roger (Thomas) 1940- CANR-18
Earlier sketches in CA 45-48, CANR-1
Cardinal, Sister Mary Ora
See Cardinal, Ora
Cardona, George 1936- 119
Cardona-Hine, Alvaro 1926- CANR-5
Earlier sketch in CA 9-10R
Cardone, Samuel S(teve) 1938- 19-20R
Cardozo, Arlene Rossen 1938- CANR-19
Earlier sketch in CA 102
Cardozo, Benjamin N(athan) 1870-1938
Brief entry 117
Cardozo, Michael H. 1910- 33-36R
Cardozo, Nancy 103
Cardozo, Peter 1916- 61-64
Cardui, Van
See Wayman, Tony Russell
Cardui, Vanessa
See Wayman, Tony Russell
Cardus, Neville 1889-1975 CANR-11
Obituary 57-60
Earlier sketch in CA 61-64
Cardwell, D(onald) S(tephen) L(owell) 1919- 101
Cardwell, Guy A(dams) 1905- 15-16R
Care, Felicity
See Coury, Louise Andree
Care, Norman S. 1937- 25-28R
Careless, J(ames) M(aurice) S(tockford) 1919- 102
Carens, James Francis 1927- CANR-12
Earlier sketch in CA 61-64
Cares, Paul B. 1911- 11-12R
Caress, James M. 1947- 122
Caress, Jay
See Caress, James M.
Carette, Louis 1913- 85-88
Carew, Dorothy 1910(?)-1973 Obituary 41-44R
Carew, Dudley Charles 1903-1981
Obituary 103
Carew, Jan (Rynveld) 1925- 77-80
See also SATA 40
Carew, Jocelyn
See Aeby, Jacquelyn
Carew, John Mohun 1921-1980 CANR-7
Earlier sketch in CA 13-14R
Carew, Rod(ney Cline) 1945- 104
Carew, Tim
See Carew, John Mohun
Carewe, S. C.
See Du Breuil, (Elizabeth) L(or)inda
Carey, Anne
See Nevill, Barry St-John
Carey, Bonnie 1941- SATA-18
Carey, Diane 1954- 122
Carey, Eileen
See O'Casey, Eileen (Reynolds)
Carey, Ernestine Gilbreth 1908- 5-6R
See also SATA 2
See also CLC 17
Carey, Gary 1938- CANR-15
Earlier sketch in CA 57-60
Carey, James Charles 1915- 15-16R
Carey, Jane Perry (Clark) 1898-1981 73-76
Obituary 105
Carey, John 1934- CANR-6
Earlier sketch in CA 57-60
Carey, John A(ndrew) 1949- 109
Carey, Kenneth Moir 1908-1979 Obituary 108
Carey, M. V.
See Carey, Mary (Virginia)
Carey, Mary (Virginia) 1925- CANR-17
Earlier sketch in CA 81-84
See also SATA 39, 44
Carey, Mathew 1760-1839 DLB-37

Carey, Michael (Sausmarez) 1913-1985
Obituary ... 118
Carey, Michael
See Burton, Edward J.
Carey, Michael L(awrence) 1948- ... 65-68
Carey, Mother Marme Aimee 1931- ... 15-16R
Carey, Omer L. 1929- ... CANR-23
Earlier sketches in CA 23-24R, CANR-8
Carey, Peter 1943- Brief entry ... 123
See also CLC 40
Carey, Richard John 1925- ... 53-56
Carey, Robert George 1926- Brief entry ... 108
Carey-Jones, N(orman) S(tewart) 1911- ... 21-22R
Carfagne, Cyril
See Jennings, Leslie Nelson
Carfagno, Vincent R. 1935- ... 41-44R
Carfax, Catherine
See Fairburn, Eleanor
Cargas, Harry J(ames) 1932- ... CANR-21
Earlier sketches in CA 15-16R, CANR-6
Cargill, Jennifer S(ue) 1944- ... 109
Cargill, Oscar 1898-1972 ... CANR-15
Obituary ... 33-36R
Earlier sketch in CA 2R
Cargill, Robert L. 1929- ... 25-28R
Cargo, David N(iels) 1932- ... 57-60
Cargo, Robert T. 1933- ... 85-88
Cargoe, Richard
See Payne, (Pierre Stephen) Robert
Carhart, Arthur Hawthorne 1892- ... CAP-1
Earlier sketch in CA 9-10
Caridi, Ronald J. 1941- ... 25-28R
Carigiet, Alois 1902-1985 ... 73-76
Obituary ... 119
See also SATA 24, 47
Carin, Arthur A. 1928- ... 29-32R
Carini, Edward 1923- ... 61-64
See also SATA 9
Carkeet, David 1946- ... 102
Carl, Beverly May 1932- ... CANR-4
Earlier sketch in CA 53-56
Carl, Lillian Stewart 1949- ... 118
Carle, Eric 1929- ... CANR-10
Earlier sketch in CA 25-28R
See also SATA 4
See also CLR 10
Carlell, Lodowick 1602-1675 ... DLB-58
Carlen, Claudia 1906- ... 106
Carleton, Barbee Oliver 1917- ... 23-24R
Carleton, Captain L. C.
See Ellis, Edward S(ylvester)
Carleton, Captain Latham C.
See Ellis, Edward S(ylvester)
Carleton, Latham C.
See Ellis, Edward S(ylvester)
Carleton, Mark T. 1935- ... CANR-12
Earlier sketch in CA 33-36R
Carleton, R(eginal) Milton 1899-1986 ... 69-72
Obituary ... 120
Carleton, Will(iam McKendree) 1845-1912
Brief entry ... 115
Carleton, William G(raves) 1903- ... CAP-2
Earlier sketch in CA 25-28
Carley, V(an Ness) Royal 1906-1976 ... CAP-2
Earlier sketch in CA 29-32
See also SATA 20
Carli, Angelo 1937- ... 49-52
Carlile, Clark S(tites) 1912- ... 41-44R
Carlile, Henry 1934- ... 33-36R
Carlin, Gabriel S. 1921- ... 4R
Carlin, Thomas W(illard) 1918- ... 25-28R
Carline, Richard (Cotton) 1896-1980
Obituary ... 105
Carling, Francis 1945- ... 25-28R
Carlino, Lewis John 1932- ... 77-80
Carlinsky, Dan 1944- ... CANR-23
Earlier sketches in CA 21-22R, CANR-8
Carlisle, Carol Jones 1919- ... 29-32R
Carlisle, Clark
See Holding, James (Clark Carlisle, Jr.)
Carlisle, D. M.
See Cook, Dorothy Mary
Carlisle, Douglas H(ilton) 1921- ... 45-48
Carlisle, E(rvin) Fred 1935- ... 53-56
Carlisle, Fred 1915- ... 73-76
Carlisle, Henry (Coffin) 1926- ... CANR-15
Earlier sketch in CA 13-14R
See also CLC 33
Carlisle, Howard M(yron) 1928- ... 69-72
Carlisle, Lilian (Matarose) Baker 1912- ... 53-56
Carlisle, Olga Andreyev 1930- ... CANR-7
Earlier sketch in CA 13-14R
See also SATA 35
Carlisle, Regis 1955- ... CANR-17
Earlier sketch in CA 77-80
Carlisle, Rodney P. 1936- ... 45-48
Carlisle, Thomas (Fiske) 1944- ... 53-56
Carlisle, Thomas John 1913- ... CANR-18
Earlier sketch in CA 101
Carlock, John R(obert) 1921- ... 33-36R
Carlon, Patricia Bernardette ... 13-14R
Carlquist, Sherwin 1930- ... 13-14R
Carls, (John) Norman 1907- ... CAP-2
Earlier sketch in CA 17-18
Carlsen, G(eorge) Robert 1917- ... CANR-24
Earlier sketches in CA 19-20R, CANR-8
See also SATA 30
Carlsen, James C(aldwell) 1927- ... 25-28R
Carlsen, Ruth C(hristoffer) 1918- ... CANR-24
Earlier sketches in CA 19-20R, CANR-8
See also SATA 2
Carlson, Andrew R(aymond) 1934- ... 29-32R
Carlson, Arthur E(ugene) 1923- ... 37-40R
Carlson, Avis D(ungan) 1896-1987 ... 73-76
Obituary ... 121
Carlson, Bernice Wells 1910- ... CANR-2
Earlier sketch in CA 5-6R
See also SATA 8
Carlson, Betty 1919- ... CANR-2
Earlier sketch in CA 3R
Carlson, C. C.
See Carlson, Carole C.
Carlson, Carl Walter 1907- ... 49-52
Carlson, Carole C. 1925- ... 113
Carlson, Dale Bick 1935- ... CANR-3
Earlier sketch in CA 11-12R
See also SATA 1
Carlson, Daniel (Bick) 1960- ... 105
See also SATA 27
Carlson, Edgar M(agnus) 1908- ... 105
Carlson, Ellsworth C. 1917- Brief entry ... 105
Carlson, Elof Axel 1931- ... 45-48
Carlson, Eric W(alter) 1910- ... 25-28R
Carlson, Esther Elisabeth 1920- ... 5-6R
Carlson, Harry Gilbert 1930- ... 109
Carlson, John A(llyn) 1933- ... 29-32R
Carlson, Judith Lee 1952- ... 104
Carlson, Leland H(enry) 1908- ... 19-20R
Carlson, Lewis H(erbert) 1934- ... 41-44R
Carlson, Loraine 1923- ... CANR-14
Earlier sketch in CA 37-40R
Carlson, Marvin 1935- ... CANR-8
Earlier sketch in CA 23-24R
Carlson, Nancy L(ee) 1953- ... 110
See also SATA 45
Carlson, Natalie Savage 1906- ... CANR-3
Earlier sketch in CA 4R
See also SATA 2
See also SAAS 4
Carlson, P. M.
See Carlson, Patricia M(cElroy)
Carlson, Patricia M(cElroy) 1940- ... 114
Carlson, Paul Robins 1928- ... 101
Carlson, Raymond 1906-1983 Obituary ... 109
Carlson, Reynold Edgar 1901- ... CANR-4
Earlier sketch in CA 4R
Carlson, Richard 1912(?)-1977 Obituary ... 73-76
Carlson, Richard Stocks 1942- ... 57-60
Carlson, Rick J. 1940- ... 65-68
Carlson, Robert E(ugene) 1922- ... 41-44R
Carlson, Ron 1947- ... 105
Carlson, Ronald L. 1934- ... CANR-13
Earlier sketch in CA 33-36R
Carlson, Roy L(incoln) 1930- ... 41-44R
Carlson, Ruth (Elizabeth) Kearney 1911- ... 29-32R
Carlson, Theodore L(eonard) 1905- ... 45-48
Carlson, Vada F. 1897- ... CANR-10
Earlier sketch in CA 23-24R
See also SATA 16
Carlson, William H(ugh) 1898- ... CAP-2
Earlier sketch in CA 23-24
Carlson, William S(amuel) 1905- ... 4R
Carlston, Kenneth S. 1904- ... 5-6R
Carlstrom, Nancy White 1948- ... 121
See also SATA 48
Carlton, Alva
See Delk, Robert Carlton
Carlton, Charles 1941- ... 53-56
Carlton, Charles Merritt 1928- ... 45-48
Carlton, David 1938- ... 103
Carlton, Henry F(isk) 1893(?)-1973
Obituary ... 41-44R
Carlton, Lessie 1903- ... 49-52
Carlton, Robert G(oodrich) 1927- ... 19-20R
Carlton, Roger
See Rowland, D(onald) S(ydney)
Carlton, Wendy 1949- ... 101
Carlut, Charles E. 1911- Brief entry ... 107
Carlyle, Jane Welsh 1801-1866 ... DLB-55
Carlyle, Thomas 1795-1881 ... DLB-55
Carm, Mac
See Armstrong, Keith F(rancis) W(hitfield)
Carmack, Robert M. 1934- ... 45-48
Carman, Barry (Francis) 1922- ... 118
Carman, (William) Bliss 1861-1929
Brief entry ... 104
See also TCLC 7
Carman, Dulce
See Drummond, Edith Marie Dulce Carman
Carman, J(ustice) Neale 1897-1972 ... CAP-1
Earlier sketch in CA 9-10
Carman, Robert A(rchibald) 1931- ... CANR-7
Earlier sketch in CA 57-60
Carman, William Y(oung) 1909- ... 13-14R
Carmel, Catherine 1939- ... 69-72
Carmel, Hesi 1937- ... 103
Carmell, Aryeh 1917- ... 118
Carmen, Arlene 1936- ... 69-72
Carmen, Sister (M.) Joann 1941- ... 21-22R
Carmen Sylva
See Elisabeth (Ottilie Luise), Queen (Pauline)
Carmer, Carl (Lamson) 1893-1976 ... CANR-4
Obituary ... 69-72
Earlier sketch in CA 7-8R
See also SATA 30, 37
Carmer, Elizabeth Black 1904- ... SATA-24
Carmi, T.
See Charny, Carmi
Carmichael, Ann
See MacAlpine, Margaret H(esketh Murray)
Carmichael, Calum M. 1938- ... 53-56
Carmichael, Carrie
See Carmichael, Harriet
See also SATA 40
Carmichael, D(ouglas) R(oy) 1941- ... 33-36R
Carmichael, Fred 1924- ... CANR-10
Earlier sketch in CA 19-20R
Carmichael, Harriet ... 115
Carmichael, Harry
See Ognall, Leopold Horace
Carmichael, Hoagland Howard 1899-1981
Obituary ... 108
Carmichael, Hoagy
See Carmichael, Hoagland Howard
Carmichael, Joel 1915- ... CANR-2
Earlier sketch in CA 1R
Carmichael, John P(eerless) 1902-1986
Obituary ... 119
Carmichael, Leonard 1898-1973 ... 41-44R
Obituary ... 45-48
Carmichael, Oliver C(romwell) 1891-1966 ... CAP-1
Earlier sketch in CA 9-10
Carmichael, Peter A(rchibald) 1897- ... CAP-2
Earlier sketch in CA 17-18
Carmichael, Stokely 1941- ... 57-60
Carmichael, Thomas N(ichols) 1919-1972 ... CAP-2
Earlier sketch in CA 29-32
Carmichael, William Edward 1922- ... 37-40R
Carmilly, Moshe 1908- ... 41-44R
Carmines, Al(vin Allison, Jr.) 1936- ... 103
Carmody, Denise Lardner 1935- ... 93-96
Carmody, Jay 1900(?)-1973 Obituary ... 41-44R
Carmoy, Guy de 1907- ... 89-92
Carnac, Carol
See Rivett, Edith Caroline
Carnac, Levin
See Griffith-Jones, George Chetwynd
Carnahan, Walter H(ervey) 1891- ... CAP-1
Earlier sketch in CA 9-10
Carnall, Geoffrey 1927- ... 15-16R
Carnap, Rudolf P. 1891-1970 ... CAP-1
Obituary ... 29-32R
Earlier sketch in CA 9-10
Carnarvon, The Earl of
See Herbert, Henry George Alfred Marius Victor Francis
Carnegie, Dorothy Vanderpool ... AITN-1
Carnegie, Raymond Alexander 1920- ... CANR-11
Earlier sketch in CA 23-24R
Carnegie, Sacha
See Carnegie, Raymond Alexander
Carnegy, Patrick 1940- ... 81-84
Carneiro, Maurina Pereira
See Pereira Carneiro, Maurina
Carnell, Corbin Scott 1929- ... CANR-10
Earlier sketch in CA 65-68
Carnell, E. J.
See Carnell, (Edward) John
Carnell, Edward John 1919-1967 ... CAP-1
Earlier sketch in CA 13-14
Carnell, (Edward) John 1912-1972 ... 25-28R
Obituary ... 104
Carner, Mosco 1904-1985 ... CANR-12
Obituary ... 116
Earlier sketches in CA 11-12, CAP-1
Carnes, Conrad D(ew) 1936- ... 85-88
Carnes, Mark C(hristopher) 1950- ... 112
Carnes, Paul N(athaniel) 1921-1979
Obituary ... 85-88
Carnes, Ralph L(ee) 1931- ... 33-36R
Carnes, Valerie Folts-Bohanan 1945- ... 33-36R
Carnevali, Doris L(orrain) ... CANR-21
Earlier sketch in CA 69-72
Carney, Daniel 1944- ... 119
Carney, Dora Sanders 1903-1986
Obituary ... 120
Carney, James (Patrick) 1914- ... 21-22R
Carney, John J(oseph), Jr. 1932- ... 69-72
Carney, John Otis 1922- ... CANR-3
Earlier sketch in CA 1R
Carney, Matthew 1922- ... 108
Carney, Richard Edward 1929- ... 37-40R
Carney, T(homas) F(rancis) 1931- ... CANR-17
Earlier sketches in CA 49-52, CANR-1
Carney, W(illiam) Alderman 1922- ... 25-28R
Carnicelli, D(omenick) D. 1931- ... 61-64
Carnochan, W(alter) B(liss) 1930- ... 33-36R
Carnot, Joseph B(arry) 1941- ... 45-48
Carnoy, Martin 1938- ... CANR-10
Earlier sketch in CA 65-68
Caro, Francis G(eorge) 1936- ... CANR-11
Earlier sketch in CA 69-72
Caro, Robert A. ... 101
Caroe, Olaf Kirkpatrick 1892-1981 ... 113
Carol, Bill J.
See Knott, William C(ecil, Jr.)
Carol, Jacqueline
See Cooper, Jacqueline
Caroli, Betty Boyd 1938- ... 118
Caroll, Nonie 1926- ... 103
Caron, Roger 1938- ... 89-92
Carona, Philip B(en) 1925- ... CANR-4
Earlier sketch in CA 4R
Caronia, Guiseppe 1884(?)-1977
Obituary ... 69-72
Caroselli, Remus F(rancis) 1916- ... 97-100
See also SATA 36
Carossa, Hans 1878-1956 ... DLB-66
Carosso, Vincent Phillip 1922- ... CANR-3
Earlier sketch in CA 9-10R
Carothers, J. Edward 1907- ... 41-44R
Carothers, Robert Lee 1942- ... 45-48
Carousso, Georges 1909- ... 89-92
Carozzi, Albert V(ictor) 1925- ... 53-56
Carp, Frances Merchant 1918- ... 23-24R
Carpelan, Bo (Gustaf Bertelsson) 1926- ... CANR-2
Earlier sketch in CA 49-52
See also SATA 8
Carpenter
See Arnold, June (Davis)
Carpenter, (John) Allan 1917- ... CANR-3
Earlier sketch in CA 9-10R
See also SATA 3
Carpenter, Andrew 1943- ... 93-96
Carpenter, Cal
See Carpenter, Clarence A(lfred)
Carpenter, Charles A. (Jr.) 1929- ... 33-36R
Carpenter, Charles H(ope), Jr. 1916- ... 111
Carpenter, Clarence A(lfred) 1921- ... 116
Carpenter, Clarence Ray 1905-1975
Obituary ... 57-60
Carpenter, David A(llen) 1949- ... 111
Carpenter, David C. 1941- ... 121
Carpenter, Don(ald Richard) 1931- ... CANR-1
Earlier sketch in CA 45-48
See also CLC 41
Carpenter, Duffy
See Hurley, John J(erome)
Carpenter, Elizabeth Sutherland 1920- ... 41-44R
Carpenter, Frances 1890-1972 ... CANR-4
Obituary ... 37-40R
Earlier sketch in CA 5-6R
See also SATA 3, 27
Carpenter, Francis Ross 1925- ... 101
Carpenter, Fred
See Hand, (Andrus) Jackson
Carpenter, Frederic Ives (Jr.) 1903- ... 5-6R
Carpenter, Humphrey (William Bouverie) 1946- ... CANR-13
Earlier sketch in CA 89-92
Carpenter, J(ohn) D(avid) 1948- ... 115
Carpenter, James A. 1928- ... 37-40R
Carpenter, John A(lcott) 1921-1978 ... 11-12R
Obituary ... 77-80
Carpenter, John Jo
See Reese, John (Henry)
Carpenter, John R. 1936- ... CANR-9
Earlier sketch in CA 65-68
Carpenter, Joyce Frances ... 33-36R
Carpenter, Kenneth J(ohn) 1923- ... 124
Carpenter, Liz
See Carpenter, Elizabeth Sutherland
Carpenter, Margaret Haley ?-1985 ... 5-6R
Obituary ... 116
Carpenter, Marjorie 1896- ... 45-48
Carpenter, Michael (Anthony) 1940- ... 119
Carpenter, Mimi Gregoire 1947- ... 111
Carpenter, Nan Cooke 1912- ... 25-28R
Carpenter, Patricia (Healy Evans) 1920- ... 29-32R
See also SATA 11
Carpenter, Peter 1922- ... 15-16R
Carpenter, Rhys 1889-1980 ... 57-60
Obituary ... 93-96
Carpenter, Richard C(oles) 1916- ... 15-16R
Carpenter, William 1940- ... 106
Carpenter, Willow
See Browning, (Zerilda) Sinclair
Carpentier (y Valmont), Alejo 1904-1980 ... CANR-11
Obituary ... 97-100
Earlier sketch in CA 65-68
See also CLC 8, 11, 38
Carper, Jean Elinor 1932- ... CANR-7
Earlier sketch in CA 17-18R
Carper, L. Dean 1931- ... 49-52
Carpozi, George, Jr. 1920- ... CANR-11
Earlier sketch in CA 13-14R
Carr, A.H.Z.
See Carr, Albert H. Z(olotkoff)
Carr, Albert H. Z(olotkoff) 1902-1971 ... CANR-1
Obituary ... 33-36R
Earlier sketch in CA 4R
Carr, Archie (Fairly, Jr.) 1909-1987 ... 15-16R
Obituary ... 122
Carr, Arthur C(harles) 1918- ... 37-40R
Carr, Arthur Japheth 1914- ... 57-60
Carr, Bruce (A.) 1938- ... 114
Carr, C(harles) T(elford) 1905-1976
Obituary ... 65-68
Carr, Catharine
See Wade, Rosalind Herschel
Carr, David William 1911- ... 37-40R
Carr, Donald Eaton 1903- ... 15-16R
Carr, Dorothy Stevenson Laird 1912- ... 9-10R
Carr, Edward Hallet 1892-1982 ... CANR-14
Obituary ... 108
Earlier sketch in CA 61-64
Carr, Edwin George 1937- ... 61-64
Carr, Gerald F(rancis) 1930- ... 118
Carr, Glyn
See Styles, (Frank) Showell
Carr, Gwen B. 1924- ... 41-44R
Carr, Harriett Helen 1899- ... CAP-1
Earlier sketch in CA 9-10
See also SATA 3
Carr, Herbert R(eginald) C(ulling) 1896-1986 Obituary ... 119
Carr, Ian (Henry Randell) 1933- ... 110
Carr, J(ames) L(loyd) 1912- ... 102
Carr, Janet Baker
See Baker-Carr, Janet
Carr, Jay Phillip 1936- ... 89-92
Carr, Jess(e Crowe, Jr.) 1930- ... CANR-12
Earlier sketch in CA 29-32R
Carr, (Bettye) Jo (Crisler) 1926- ... 21-22R
Carr, John C(harles) 1929- ... 53-56
Carr, John Dickson 1906-1977 ... CANR-3
Obituary ... 69-72
Earlier sketch in CA 49-52
See also CLC 3
Carr, John Laurence 1916- ... 49-52
Carr, Josephine 1952- ... 111
Carr, Lois Green 1922- ... 61-64
Carr, Margaret 1935- ... 105
Carr, Mary Jane 1899-1988 ... CAP-1
Obituary ... 124
Earlier sketch in CA 9-10
See also SATA 2
Carr, Michael Harold 1935- ... 109
Carr, Pat M(oore) 1932- ... CANR-14
Earlier sketch in CA 65-68

Carr, Philippa
See Hibbert, Eleanor Burford
Carr, Raymond 1919- ... CANR-8
Earlier sketch in CA 19-20R
Carr, Robert K(enneth) 1908-1979 ... 93-96
Obituary ... 85-88
Carr, Roberta
See Roberts, Irene
Carr, Robyn 1951- ... 115
Carr, Roland T. 1908(?)-1983 ... 122
Obituary ... 111
Carr, Stephen L(amoni) ... 57-60
Carr, Terry (Gene) 1937- ... 81-84
Carr, Virginia Mason
See Vaughan, Virginia M(ason)
Carr, Virginia Spencer 1929- ... 61-64
See also CLC 34
Carr, Warren Tyree 1917- ... 7-8R
Carr, William 1921- ... 73-76
Carr, William G(eorge) 1901- ... 53-56
Carr, William H(enry) A(lexander)
1924- ... CANR-7
Earlier sketch in CA 15-16R
Carraco, Carol Crowe
See Crowe-Carraco, Carol
Carranco, Lynwood 1921- ... CANR-21
Earlier sketches in CA 57-60, CANR-6
Carras, Mary C(alliope) ... 85-88
Carrasco, David ... 112
Carrel, Alexis 1873-1944 Brief entry ... 120
Carrel, Mark
See Paine, Lauran (Bosworth)
Carrell, Norman (Gerald) 1905- ... CAP-2
Earlier sketch in CA 25-28
Carrera Andrade, Jorge 1903-1978
Obituary ... 85-88
Carrick, A. B.
See Lindsay, Harold Arthur
Carrick, Carol 1935- ... CANR-17
Earlier sketches in CA 45-48, CANR-1
See also SATA 7
Carrick, Donald 1929- ... CANR-20
Earlier sketches in CA 53-56, CANR-5
See also SATA 7
Carrick, Edward
See Craig, Edward Anthony
Carrick, John
See Crosbie, (Hugh) Provan
Carrick, Malcolm 1945- ... CANR-14
Earlier sketch in CA 77-80
See also SATA 28
Carrier, Constance 1908- ... 33-36R
Carrier, Esther Jane 1925- ... 19-20R
Carrier, Jean-Guy 1945- ... 101
Carrier, Lark 1947- ... SATA-50
Carrier, Roch 1937- ... DLB-53
See also CLC 13
Carrier, Warren (Pendleton) 1918- ... CANR-18
Earlier sketches in CA 9-10R, CANR-3
Carrigan, Andrew G(ardner) 1935- ... CANR-1
Earlier sketch in CA 45-48
Carrigan, D(avid) Owen 1933- ... 25-28R
Carrigan, Richard A(lfred), Jr. 1932- ... 112
Carrighar, Sally ... 93-96
See also SATA 24
Carriker, Robert C(harles) 1940- ... 69-72
Carrillo, Lawrence W(ilbert) 1920- ... 15-16R
Carringer, Robert L. 1941- ... CANR-17
Earlier sketch in CA 97-100
Carrington, Charles Edmund 1897- ... 7-8R
Carrington, Frank G(amble, Jr.) 1936- ... 57-60
Carrington, George C(abell), Jr. 1928- ... 122
Brief entry ... 118
Carrington, Grant 1938- ... 104
Carrington, Leonora 1917- ... 124
Brief entry ... 114
Carrington, Molly
See Matthews, C(onstance) M(ary)
Carrington, Paul D(eWitt) 1931- ... 29-32R
Carrington, Richard (Temple Murray)
1921- ... 9-10R
Carrington, William Langley 1900-1970 ... CAP-1
Earlier sketch in CA 13-14
Carris, Joan Davenport 1938- ... 106
See also SATA 42, 44
Carrison, Daniel J. 1917- ... 37-40R
Carrithers, David W. 1943- ... 110
Carrithers, Gale H(emphill), Jr. 1932- ... 41-44R
Carrithers, Wallace M(axwell) 1911- ... 25-28R
Carrol, Shana
See Newcomb, Kerry
and Schaefer, Frank
Carroll, Anne Kristin
See Gales, Barbara J.
Carroll, Archie B(enjamin III) 1943- ... 109
Carroll, B(illy) D(an) 1940- ... 53-56
Carroll, Berenice A(nita) 1932- ... 41-44R
Carroll, C(armal) Edward 1923- ... 29-32R
Carroll, Carroll 1902- ... 101
Carroll, Charles Francis 1936- ... 53-56
Carroll, Curt
See Bishop, Curtis (Kent)
Carroll, Daniel B(ernard) 1928-1977 ... 41-44R
Carroll, Dennis 1940- ... 114
Carroll, Donald K(ingery) 1909- ... CAP-2
Earlier sketch in CA 17-18
Carroll, Elizabeth
See James, Elizabeth
Carroll, Faye 1937- ... 23-24R
Carroll, Gladys Hasty 1904- ... CANR-5
Earlier sketch in CA 3R
See also DLB 9
Carroll, Herbert A(llen) 1897- ... CAP-1
Earlier sketch in CA 11-12
Carroll, Jackson W(alker) 1932- ... CANR-16
Earlier sketch in CA 85-88
Carroll, James P. 1943(?)- ... 81-84
See also CLC 38
Carroll, Jeffrey 1950- ... 85-88
Carroll, Jim 1951- ... 45-48
See also CLC 35
Carroll, John 1735-1815 ... DLB-37
Carroll, John 1944- ... CANR-7
Earlier sketch in CA 57-60
Carroll, John B(issell) 1916- ... CANR-3
Earlier sketch in CA 1R
Carroll, John J(oseph) 1924- ... 15-16R
Carroll, John M(elvin) 1928- ... 37-40R
Carroll, John Millar 1925- ... CANR-23
Earlier sketches in CA 5-6R, CANR-8
Carroll, Jonathan 1949- ... CANR-21
Earlier sketch in CA 105
Carroll, Joseph T(homas) 1935- ... 102
Carroll, Joy 1924- ... 102
Carroll, Kenneth Lane 1924- ... 37-40R
Carroll, L(awrence) Patrick 1936- ... 111
Carroll, (Archer) Latrobe 1894- ... CANR-3
Earlier sketch in CA 4R
See also SATA 7
Carroll, Laura
See Parr, Lucy
Carroll, Lewis
See Dodgson, Charles Lutwidge
See also DLB 18
See also CLR 2
Carroll, Loren 1904-1978 ... 85-88
Obituary ... 81-84
Carroll, Martin
See Carr, Margaret
Carroll, Paul 1927- ... 25-28R
See also DLB 16
Carroll, Paul Vincent 1900-1968 ... 9-10R
Obituary ... 25-28R
See also DLB 10
See also CLC 10
Carroll, Peter N(eil) 1943- ... 102
Carroll, Phil 1895-1971 ... CAP-1
Earlier sketch in CA 13-14
Carroll, Raymond ... SATA-47
Carroll, Robert
See Alpert, Hollis
Carroll, Robert P(eter) 1941- ... 105
Carroll, Rosalynn
See Katz, Carol
Carroll, Ruth (Robinson) 1899- ... CANR-1
Earlier sketch in CA 4R
Carroll, St. Thomas Marion
See Carroll, Tom M.
Carroll, Sheila Baker 1918(?)-1984
Obituary ... 113
Carroll, Sister Mary Gerald 1913- ... 23-24R
Carroll, Stephen J(ohn), Jr. 1930- ... 41-44R
Carroll, Ted
See Carroll, Thomas Theodore, Jr.
Carroll, Theodus 1928- ... 69-72
Carroll, Thomas J. 1909-1971 ... 2R
Obituary ... 103
Carroll, Thomas Theodore, Jr. 1925- ... 11-12R
Carroll, Tom M. 1950- ... 53-56
Carroll, Vern 1933- ... 57-60
Carroll, Vinnette (Justine) ... 123
Carroll, Vinnette (Justine) 1922-
Brief entry ... 114
Carron, Malcolm 1917- Brief entry ... 105
Carrott, Richard G. 1924- ... 85-88
Carrouges, Michel
See Couturier, Louis (Joseph)
Carrow, Milton M(ichael) 1912- ... CANR-16
Earlier sketch in CA 25-28R
Carr-Saunders, Alexander (Morris)
1886-1966 ... CANR-20
Obituary ... 103
Earlier sketch in CA 3R
Carruth, Estelle 1910- ... 9-10R
Carruth, Gorton Veeder 1925- ... CANR-6
Earlier sketch in CA 57-60
Carruth, Hayden 1921- ... CANR-4
Earlier sketch in CA 9-10R
See also SATA 47
See also DLB 5
See also CLC 4, 7, 10, 18
Carruthers, Ben F(rederick) 1911- ... 114
Carruthers, Malcolm Euan 1938- ... 102
Carry, (Benjamin) Peter 1942- ... 105
Carryaway, Nick
See Murray, John F(rancis)
Carryl, Charles E. 1841-1920 ... DLB-42
Carsac, Francis
See Bordes, Francois
Carsberg, Bryan Victor 1939- ... CANR-12
Earlier sketch in CA 29-32R
Carse, James P(earce) 1932- ... 23-24R
Carse, Robert 1902-1971 ... CANR-1
Obituary ... 29-32R
Earlier sketch in CA 4R
See also SATA 5
Carskadon, Thomas R. 1901(?)-1983(?)
Obituary ... 108
Carson, Ada Lou 1932- ... 110
Carson, Alan 1951- ... 115
Carson, Captain James
See Stratemeyer, Edward L.
Carson, Ciaran 1948- Brief entry ... 112
Carson, Clayborne 1944- ... 105
Carson, F(ranklin) John 1920- ... 11-12R
Carson, Gerald (Hewes) 1899- ... CANR-16
Earlier sketches in CA 4R, CANR-1
Carson, Hampton L(awrence) 1914- ... 5-6R
Carson, Herbert L(ee) 1929- ... 29-32R
Carson, J(ohn) Franklin 1920- ... 15-16R
See also SATA 1
Carson, Jane Dennison ?-1984 Obituary ... 114
Carson, Kit
See Carson, Xanthus
Carson, Mary 1934- ... 41-44R
Carson, Rachel Louise 1907-1964 ... 77-80
See also SATA 23
Carson, Ray F(ritziof) 1939- ... 61-64
Carson, Robert 1909-1983 ... 21-22R
Obituary ... 108
Carson, Robert B. 1934- ... CANR-6
Earlier sketch in CA 57-60
Carson, Robert C(harles) 1930- ... 29-32R
Carson, Ronald A(lan) 1940- ... 119
Carson, Rosalind
See Chittenden, Margaret
Carson, Ruth
See Bugbee, Ruth Carson
Carson, S. M.
See Gorsline, (Sally) Marie
Carson, William Glasgow Bruce 1891- ... 5-6R
Carson, Xanthus 1910- ... 57-60
Carstairs, George Morrison 1916- ... 69-72
Carstairs, Kathleen
See Pendower, Jacques
Carsten, Francis Ludwig 1911- ... 13-14R
Carstens, Grace Pearce ... 2R
Carstensen, Roger Norwood 1920- ... CANR-2
Earlier sketch in CA 5-6R
Carswell, Catherine 1879-1946 ... DLB-36
Carswell, Evelyn M(edicus) 1919- ... 57-60
Carswell, John (Patrick) 1918- ... CANR-21
Earlier sketch in CA 9-10R
Carswell, Leslie
See Stephens, Rosemary
Carte, Gene E(dward) 1938- ... 61-64
Carter, Alan 1936- ... 33-36R
Carter, Albert Howard 1913-1970 ... CAP-2
Earlier sketch in CA 25-28
Carter, Alfred Edward 1914- ... 33-36R
Carter, Amon Giles, Jr. 1919-1982
Obituary ... 111
Carter, Angela 1940- ... CANR-12
Earlier sketch in CA 53-56
See also DLB 14
See also CLC 5, 41
Carter, Ann
See Brooks, Anne Tedlock
Carter, Anne
See Brooks, Anne Tedlock
Carter, Anne Pitts 1925- Brief entry ... 106
Carter, Ashley
See Whittington, Harry (Benjamin)
Carter, Barbara (Ellen) 1925- ... CANR-10
Earlier sketch in CA 53-56
Carter, Boyd (George) 1908-1980 ... CANR-7
Earlier sketch in CA 13-14R
Carter, Bruce
See Hough, Richard (Alexander)
Carter, Burnham 1901(?)-1979 Obituary ... 89-92
Carter, Byron L. 1924- ... 23-24R
Carter, C(edric) O(swald) 1917-1984
Obituary ... 112
Carter, Carolle J(ean) 1934- ... 81-84
Carter, Charles Frederick 1919- ... CANR-20
Earlier sketches in CA 1R, CANR-4
Carter, Charles H(oward) 1927- ... 11-12R
Carter, Charles W(ebb) 1905- ... 21-22R
Carter, Dan T. 1940- ... 65-68
Carter, David C(harles) 1946- ... 45-48
Carter, Don E(arl) 1917- ... 73-76
Carter, Dorothy Sharp 1921- ... 49-52
See also SATA 8
Carter, E. Lawrence 1910- ... 25-28R
Carter, Edward Julian 1902-1982 ... 5-6R
Obituary ... 107
Carter, Elliott Cook 1908- ... 89-92
Carter, Ernestine Marie ?-1983 Obituary ... 110
Carter, Everett 1919- ... 13-14R
Carter, Forrest 1927(?)-1979 ... 107
See also SATA 32
Carter, Frances Monet 1923- ... 37-40R
Carter, Frances Tunnell ... 37-40R
Carter, George F(rancis) 1912- ... CANR-4
Earlier sketch in CA 7-8R
Carter, Gwendolen M(argaret) 1906- ... CANR-19
Earlier sketches in CA 1R, CANR-4
Carter, Harold 1925- ... 33-36R
Carter, Harry Graham 1901-1982 Obituary ... 106
Carter, Harvey L(ewis) 1904- ... 23-24R
Carter, Helene 1887-1960 ... SATA-15
Carter, Henry
See Leslie, Frank
Carter, Henry Hare 1905- ... 41-44R
Carter, (William) Hodding 1907-1972 ... CAP-1
Obituary ... 33-36R
Earlier sketch in CA 13-14
See also SATA 2, 27
Carter, Hugh 1895- ... 37-40R
Carter, Hurricane
See Carter, Rubin
Carter, J(ohn) Anthony 1943- ... 61-64
Carter, James E(dward) 1935- ... CANR-22
Earlier sketches in CA 57-60, CANR-7
Carter, James Earl, Jr. 1924- ... 69-72
Carter, James Puckette 1933- ... 33-36R
Carter, James Richard 1940- ... 33-36R
Carter, Jane (Borsch) Robbins
See Robbins-Carter, Jane (Borsch)
Carter, Janet 1938- ... 104
Carter, Jimmy
See Carter, James Earl, Jr.
Carter, John (Waynflete) 1905-1975 ... 7-8R
Obituary ... 57-60
Carter, John Franklin 1897-1967
Obituary ... 25-28R
Carter, John Mack 1928- ... 103
Carter, John Stewart 1912-1965 ... CAP-1
Earlier sketch in CA 11-12
Carter, John T(homas) 1921- ... 33-36R
Carter, Joseph 1912-1984 ... 49-52
Obituary ... 112
Carter, K(ay) Codell 1939- ... 110
Carter, Katharine J(ones) 1905- ... 5-6R
See also SATA 2
Carter, Landon 1710-1778 ... DLB-31
Carter, Lief Hastings 1940- ... CANR-6
Earlier sketch in CA 57-60
Carter, (Bessie) Lillian (Gordy) 1898-1983 ... 118
Obituary ... 111
Brief entry ... 105
Carter, Lin 1930- ... 41-44R
See also DLBY 81
Carter, Lonnie 1942- ... CANR-9
Earlier sketch in CA 65-68
Carter, Luther J(ordan) 1927- ... 57-60
Carter, M(argaret) L(ouise) 1948- ... 33-36R
Carter, Margaret (Mary) 1923- ... 107
Carter, Martin (Wylde) 1927- ... 102
Carter, Mary ... CANR-5
Earlier sketch in CA 9-10R
Carter, Mary Ellen 1923- ... 25-28R
Carter, Mary Kennedy ... 65-68
Carter, Neil 1913- ... 17-18R
Carter, Nevada
See Paine, Lauran (Bosworth)
Carter, Nicholas
See Dey, Frederic (Merrill) Van
Rensselaer
Carter, Nick
See Avallone, Michael (Angelo), Jr.
and Ballard, (Willis) Todhunter
and Crider, (Allen) Bill(y)
and Dey, Frederic (Merrill) Van
Rensselaer
and Granbeck, Marilyn
and Hayes, Ralph E(ugene)
and Lynds, Dennis
and Randisi, Robert J(oseph)
and Rasof, Henry
and Smith, Martin Cruz
and Swain, Dwight V(reeland)
and Wallmann, Jeffrey M(iner)
Carter, Paul A(llen) 1926- ... CANR-13
Earlier sketch in CA 33-36R
Carter, Paul J(efferson), Jr. 1912-1975 ... CAP-2
Earlier sketch in CA 21-22
Carter, Peter 1929- ... 69-72
Carter, Phyllis Ann
See Eberle, Irmengarde
Carter, Ralph
See Neubauer, William Arthur
Carter, Randolph 1914- ... 101
Carter, Richard 1918- ... CANR-8
Earlier sketch in CA 61-64
Carter, Richard D(uane) 1929- ... 111
Carter, Robert A(yres) 1923- ... 33-36R
Carter, Robert M(ack) 1925- ... 33-36R
Carter, Roger 1939- ... 119
Carter, (Eleanor) Rosalynn (Smith) 1927- ... 113
Carter, Rubin 1937- Brief entry ... 113
Carter, Samuel III 1904- ... 57-60
See also SATA 37
Carter, Victor A(lbert) 1902- ... CAP-1
Earlier sketch in CA 9-10
Carter, William 1934- ... 33-36R
Carter, William Ambrose 1899- ... CAP-1
Earlier sketch in CA 17-18
Carter, William Beverly, Jr. 1921-1982
Obituary ... 110
Carter, William E. 1926-1983 ... 19-20R
Obituary ... 110
See also SATA 1, 35
Carter, William Lee 1925- ... 1R
Carter, Worrall Reed 1885(?)-1975
Obituary ... 57-60
Carterette, Edward C(alvin) 1921- ... 41-44R
Carter-Harrison, Paul
See Harrison, Paul Carter
Carter-Ruck, Peter F(rederick) 1914- ... 97-100
Cartey, Wilfred (George Onslow) 1931- ... 73-76
Carthy, Mother Mary Peter 1911- ... 13-14R
Cartland, Barbara (Hamilton) 1901- ... CANR-6
Earlier sketch in CA 11-12R
Cartledge, Paul 1947- ... 124
Cartledge, Samuel Antoine 1903- ... 3R
Cartlidge, Barbara 1922- ... 121
Cartlidge, Michelle 1950- ... 93-96
See also SATA 37, 49
Cartnal, Alan 1950- ... 105
Cartner, William Carruthers 1910- ... 73-76
See also SATA 11
Carto, Willis A(llison) 1926- ... 114
Cartter, Allan Murray 1922-1976 ... CANR-8
Earlier sketch in CA 5-6R
Cartwright, Desmond S(pencer) 1924- ... 89-92
Cartwright, Gary 1934- ... 89-92
Cartwright, James McGregor
See Jennings, Leslie Nelson
Cartwright, Joseph H. 1939- ... 73-76
Cartwright, N.
See Scofield, Norma Margaret Cartwright
Cartwright, Rosalind Dymond 1922- ... 81-84
Cartwright, Sally 1923- ... CANR-2
Earlier sketch in CA 49-52
See also SATA 9
Cartwright, Vanessa
See Preston, Harry
Cartwright, William H(olman) 1915- ... 9-10R
Carty, James William, Jr. 1925- ... 53-56
Caruba, Alan 1937- ... 65-68
Caruso, Enrico 1873-1921 Brief entry ... 115
Caruso, John Anthony 1907- ... 33-36R
Carus-Wilson, Eleanora M(ary) 1897- ... 7-8R
Caruth, Donald L(ewis) 1935- ... 29-32R
Caruthers, Osgood 1915-1985 Obituary ... 117

Caruthers, William Alexander 1802-1846 .. DLB-3
Carvajal, Ricardo
See Meneses, Enrique
Carvalho-Neto, Paulo de 1923- CANR-4
Earlier sketch in CA 53-56
Carvell, Fred J. 1934- 29-32R
Carver, Dave
See Bingley, David Ernest
Carver, Frank G(ould) 1928- 49-52
Carver, Fred D(onald) 1936- 29-32R
Carver, Jeffrey A(llan) 1949- CANR-18
Earlier sketch in CA 101
Carver, John
See Gardner, Richard (M.)
Carver, Jonathan 1710-1780 .... DLB-31
Carver, (Richard) Michael (Power)
1915- CANR-14
Earlier sketch in CA 69-72
Carver, Norman F., Jr. 1928- 41-44R
Carver, Raymond 1938- CANR-17
Earlier sketch in CA 33-36R
See also DLBY 84
See also CLC 22, 36
Carver, Saxon Rowe 1905- CAP-1
Earlier sketch in CA 13-14
Carvic, Heron ?-1980 53-56
Obituary 103
Carwell, L'Ann
See McKissack, Patricia (L'Ann) C(arwell)
Cary
See Cary, Louis F(avreau)
Cary, Barbara Knapp 1912(?)-1975
Obituary 61-64
See also SATA 31
Cary, Bob 1921- 105
Cary, Diana Serra
See Cary, Peggy-Jean Montgomery
Cary, Harold Whiting 1903- CAP-1
Earlier sketch in CA 9-10
Cary, James Donald 1919- 5-6R
Cary, John H. 1926- 11-12R
Cary, (Arthur) Joyce (Lune) 1888-1957
Brief entry 104
See also DLB 15
See also TCLC 1
Cary, Jud
See Tubb, E(dwin) C(harles)
Cary, Lee J(ames) 1925- 29-32R
Cary, Louis F(avreau) 1915- SATA-9
Cary, Lucian 1886-1971 ....33-36R
Cary, Otis 1921- 61-64
Cary, Peggy-Jean Montgomery 1918- 57-60
Cary, Richard 1909- 23-24R
Cary, William L(ucius) 1910-1983
Obituary 109
Cary, Zenja Saft 1932(?)-1983 Obituary 110
Caryl, Jean
See Kaplan, Jean Caryl Korn
Caryl, Warren 1920- 23-24R
Casada, James A(llen) 1942- 109
Casado, Pablo Gil 1931- 49-52
Casady, Cort (Boon) 1947- CANR-22
Earlier sketch in CA 105
Casady, Donald Rex 1926- 15-16R
Casalandra, Estelle
See Estelle, Sister Mary
Casale, Joan T(herese) 1935- 61-64
Casale, Ottavio M(ark) 1934- 104
Casals, Pablo
See Casals, Pau Carlos Salvador Defillo
de
Casals, Pau Carlos Salvador Defillo de
1876-1973 93-96
Obituary 45-48
Casas, Penelope 1943- 114
Casberg, Melvin Augustus 1909- 104
Cascio, Chuck 1946- 93-96
Casdorph, Herman Richard 1928- 101
Casdorph, Paul D(ouglas) 1932- 106
Case, Brian (David) 1937- 25-28R
Case, David 1937- 107
Case, Elinor Rutt 1914- 4R
Case, Fred E. 1918- CANR-4
Earlier sketch in CA 5-6R
Case, Geoffrey 77-80
Case, Jack Gaylord 1918(?)-1970
Obituary 104
Case, John 1944- 114
Case, Josephine Young 1907- CAP-2
Earlier sketch in CA 25-28
Case, Justin
See Gleadow, Rupert Seeley
Case, L. L.
See Lewin, Leonard C(ase)
Case, Leland D(avidson) 1900- 17-18R
Case, Lynn M(arshall) 1903- 15-16R
Case, Marshal T(aylor) 1941- 57-60
See also SATA 9
Case, Maurice 1910-1968 .... CAP-2
Earlier sketch in CA 19-20
Case, Michael
See Howard, Robert West
Case, Patricia J(une) 1952- 110
Case, Victoria 1897- 7-8R
Case, Walter 1909(?)-1983 Obituary 110
Casebier, Allan (Frank) 1934- 65-68
Casebier, Marjorie
See McCoy, Marjorie Casebier
Casebier, Virginia (Eleanor) 1918- 41-44R
Caseley, Judith 1951- 121
Caseleyr, Cam(ille Auguste Marie) 1909- .. CAP-1
Earlier sketch in CA 9-10
Casely-Hayford, J(oseph) E(phraim)
1866-1930 Brief entry 123
See also TCLC 24
Casement, Richard 1942-1982 Obituary 108
Casemore, Robert 1915- 73-76

Casewit, Curtis W(erner) 1922- CANR-21
Earlier sketches in CA 13-14R, CANR-6
See also SATA 4
Casey, Beatrice Vivian 1898(?)-1986
Obituary 120
Casey, Bill Harris 1930- 1R
Casey, Brigid 1950- 49-52
See also SATA 9
Casey, Daniel J(oseph) 1937- CANR-22
Earlier sketches in CA 57-60, CANR-6
Casey, Douglas R(obert) 1946- Brief entry .. 118
Casey, Edward Scott 1939- 102
Casey, Genevieve M(ary) 1916- 116
Casey, Gladys
See Grier, Barbara G(ene Damon)
Casey, Jack
See Casey, John
Casey, Jane Barnes 1942- 104
Casey, John (Dudley) 1939- CANR-23
Earlier sketch in CA 69-72
Casey, John 1950- 120
Casey, Juanita 1925- 49-52
See also DLB 14
Casey, Kevin 1940- 25-28R
Casey, Lawrence B. 1905-1977 73-76
Obituary 69-72
Casey, Mart
See Casey, Michael T.
Casey, Michael 1947- 65-68
See also DLB 5
See also CLC 2
Casey, Michael T. 1922- 21-22R
Casey, Patrick
See Thurman, Wallace (Henry)
Casey, Richard Gardiner 1890-1976 61-64
Obituary 65-68
Casey, Robert J(oseph) 1890-1962
Obituary 89-92
Casey, Rosemary 1904-1976 Obituary 65-68
Casey, Rosemary Alice (Christmann)
1922- 5-6R
Casey, Thomas Francis 1923- 15-16R
Casey, W. Wilson 1954- 107
Casey, Warren 1935- 101
See also CLC 12
Casey, William J(oseph) 1913-1987
Obituary 122
Casey, William Van Etten 1914- 57-60
Casgrain, Therese F. 1896(?)-1981 110
Obituary 108
Cash, Anthony 1933- 102
Cash, Arthur H(ill) 1922- Brief entry 110
Cash, Grace (Savannah) 1915- 23-24R
Cash, Grady
See Cash, Grace (Savannah)
Cash, J(ames) Allan 1901- CANR-4
Earlier sketch in CA 7-8R
Cash, John R.
See Cash, Johnny
Cash, Johnny 1932- Brief entry 110
Cash, Joseph H(arper) 1927- 41-44R
Cash, Kevin (Richard) 1926-1985 77-80
Obituary 115
Cash, Philip 1931- 106
Cash, Sebastian
See Smithells, Roger (William)
Cashen, Richard A(nthony) 1938- 112
Cashin, Edward J(oseph, Jr.) 1927- CANR-9
Earlier sketch in CA 21-22R
Cashin, Edward L(awrence)
See Cashin, Edward J(oseph, Jr.)
Cashin, James A. 1911-1982 .... CANR-10
Earlier sketch in CA 17-18R
Cashman, John
See Davis, Timothy Francis Tothill
Cashman, Paul Harrison 1924- 15-16R
Cashman, Sean Dennis 1943- 107
Cashmore, E. Ellis 1949- 116
Cashmore, Ernest
See Cashmore, E. Ellis
Caskey, John L. 1908- 15-16R
Casler, Lawrence (Ray) 1932- 49-52
Casmier, Adam A(nthony) 1934- 33-36R
Casmir, Fred L. 1928- 37-40R
Casner, A(ndrew) James 1907- CANR-4
Earlier sketch in CA 7-8R
Caso, Adolph 1934- CANR-7
Earlier sketch in CA 57-60
Casolaro, Daniel 1949- 114
Cason, Mabel Earp 1892-1965 .... CAP-1
Earlier sketch in CA 13-14
See also SATA 10
Casona, Alejandro
See Alvarez, Alejandro Rodriguez
Casotti, Fred 1923- 93-96
Caspari, Ernest W(olfgang) 1909- 41-44R
Caspary, Vera 1899-1987 .... CANR-9
Obituary 122
Earlier sketch in CA 13-14R
Casper, Barry M(ichael) 1939- 69-72
Casper, Bill, Jr.
See Casper, William Earl, Jr.
Casper, Billy
See Casper, William Earl, Jr.
Casper, Henry W. 1909- 37-40R
Casper, Jonathan D(avid) 1942- 53-56
Casper, Joseph Andrew 1941- 65-68
Casper, Leonard Ralph 1923- 2R
Casper, Linda Ty
See Ty-Casper, Linda
Casper, William Earl, Jr. 1931- 121
Casque, Sammy
See Davis, Sydney Charles Houghton
Casriel, H(arold) Daniel 1924-1983 ......15-16R
Obituary 110
Cass, Carl Bartholomew 1901- CAP-1
Earlier sketch in CA 9-10

Cass, James (Michael) 1915- 101
Cass, Joan E(velyn) CANR-20
Earlier sketches in CA 4R, CANR-5
See also SATA 1
Cass, Ronald A(ndrew) 1949- 106
Cass, Zoe
See Low, Lois Dorothea
Cassady, Carolyn 1923- DLB-16
Cassady, Neal 1926-1968 .... DLB-16
Cassady, Ralph, Jr. 1900-1978 .... CANR-4
Obituary 77-80
Earlier sketch in CA 2R
Cassandra
See Connor, William (Neil)
Cassara, Ernest 1925- 41-44R
Cassata, Mary B. 1930- 121
Cassavetes, John 1929- 85-88
See also CLC 20
Cassedy, James H(iggins) 1919- 4R
Cassedy, Sylvia 1930- CANR-22
Earlier sketch in CA 105
See also SATA 27
Cassel, Don 1942- 110
Cassel, Lili
See Wronker, Lili Cassel
Cassel, Mana-Zucca 1891-1981 Obituary ... 103
Cassel, Russell N. 1911- 37-40R
Cassel, Virginia Cunningham 105
Cassell, Anthony K. 1941- 120
Cassell, Frank A(llan) 1941- 33-36R
Cassell, Frank Hyde 1916- 37-40R
Cassell, Richard A(llan) 1921- 23-24R
Cassell, Sylvia 1924- 5-6R
Cassells, Cyrus (Curtis III) 1957- 112
Cassells, John
See Duncan, W(illiam) Murdoch
Casselman, Karen Leigh 1942- 107
Cassels, Alan 1929- CANR-13
Earlier sketch in CA 33-36R
Cassels, Louis 1922-1974 .... CANR-4
Obituary 45-48
Earlier sketch in CA 9-10R
Casserley, H(enry) C(yril) 1903- CANR-9
Earlier sketch in CA 65-68
Casserley, Julian Victor Langmead 1909- ..9-10R
Casserly, John J(oseph) 1927- 120
Cassiday, Bruce (Bingham) 1920- CANR-19
Earlier sketches in CA 1R, CANR-4
Cassidy, Claude
See Paine, Lauran (Bosworth)
Cassidy, Daniel J(ames) 1956- 119
Cassidy, Frederic Gomes 1907- 4R
Cassidy, George
See Vance, William E.
Cassidy, Harold G(omes) 1906- 25-28R
Cassidy, John 1928- 114
Cassidy, John A(lbert) 1908- 33-36R
Cassidy, John R(ufus) 1922- 89-92
Cassidy, Jude (Anne) 1955- 121
Cassidy, Michael 1936- 97-100
Cassidy, Richard J(oseph) 1942- 114
Cassidy, Vincent H. 1923- 21-22R
Cassidy, William L(awrence Robert) 103
Cassilis, Robert
See Edwardes, Michael (F. H.)
Cassill, Kay 89-92
Cassill, R(onald) V(erlin) 1919- CANR-7
Earlier sketch in CA 9-10R
See also CAAS 1
See also DLB 6
See also CLC 4, 23
Cassils, Peter
See Keele, Kenneth D(avid)
Cassin, Rene Samuel 1887-1976
Obituary 65-68
Cassinelli, C(harles) W(illiam, Jr.) 1925- 3R
Cassity, (Allen) Turner 1929- CANR-11
Earlier sketch in CA 17-18R
See also CLC 6, 42
Casso, Evans J(oseph) 1914- 57-60
Cassola, Albert M(aria) 1915- CAP-1
Earlier sketch in CA 9-10
Cassola, Carlo 1917-1987 101
Obituary 121
Casson, Hugh Maxwell 1910- CANR-20
Earlier sketch in CA 103
Casson, Lionel 1914- CANR-3
Earlier sketch in CA 9-10R
Casstevens, Thomas W(illiam) 1937- 19-20R
Cast, David (Jesse Dale) 1942- 109
Castagna, Edwin 1909-1983 .... CAP-2
Obituary 111
Earlier sketch in CA 17-18
Castagnola, Lawrence A. 1933- CANR-12
Earlier sketch in CA 29-32R
Castaneda, Carlos 1931- 25-28R
See also CLC 12
Castaneda, Hector-Neri 1924- CANR-19
Earlier sketches in CA 7-8R, CANR-3
Castaneda, James A(gustin) 1933- 41-44R
Castel, Albert 1928- CANR-5
Earlier sketch in CA 1R
Castel, J(ean) G(abriel) 1928- CANR-9
Earlier sketch in CA 21-22R
Castellan, N(orman) John, Jr. 1939- 37-40R
Castellaneta, Carlo 1930- CANR-11
Earlier sketch in CA 13-14R
Castellano, Giuseppe 1893-1977 Obituary ..73-76
Castellanos, Jane Mollie Robinson
1913- 11-12R
See also SATA 9
Castellanos, Rosario 1915-1974 Obituary ..53-56
Castellon, Federico 1914-1971 .... SATA-48
Castells, Manuel 1942- 115
Castells, Matilde O(livella) 1929- 69-72
Castelnuovo-Tedesco, P(ietro) 1925- 21-22R

Castetter, William Benjamin 1914- CANR-4
Earlier sketch in CA 4R
Castillo, Edmund L. 1924- 29-32R
See also SATA 1
Castillo, Richard Griswold del
See Griswold del Castillo, Richard
Castillo Puche, Jose Luis 1919-
Brief entry 110
Castle, Anthony (Percy) 1938- 113
Castle, Charles 1939- 33-36R
Castle, Coralie 1924- 57-60
Castle, Damon
See Smith, Richard Rein
Castle, Edgar Bradshaw 1897-1973
Obituary 104
Castle, Emery N(eal) 1923- 4R
Castle, Frances
See Leader, (Evelyn) Barbara (Blackburn)
Castle, Kate 123
Castle, Keith 1927(?)-1985 Obituary 118
Castle, Lee
See Ogan, George F.
and Ogan, Margaret E. (Nettles)
Castle, Marian (Johnson) CAP-2
Earlier sketch in CA 17-18
Castle, Mort 1946- CANR-14
Earlier sketch in CA 81-84
Castle, Paul
See Howard, Vernon (Linwood)
Castle, Robert
See Hamilton, Edmond
Castle, Robert W., Jr. 1929- 25-28R
Castle, Sue G(aronzik) 1942- 105
Castle, Terry (Jacqueline) 1953- 112
Castle, Tony
See Castle, Anthony (Percy)
Castle, William 1914-1977 77-80
Obituary 69-72
Castleman, Harry 1953- 109
Castleman, Michael 1950- 108
Castleman, (Esther) Riva 1930-
Brief entry 117
Castlemon, Harry
See Fosdick, Charles Austin
Castles, Francis G(eoffrey) 1943- CANR-17
Earlier sketch in CA 25-28R
Castles, Lance 1937- 25-28R
Castleton, Virginia 1925- 49-52
Castor, Grahame (Douglas) 1932- CANR-7
Earlier sketch in CA 15-16R
Castor, Henry 1909- 17-18R
Castoro, Laura A(nn) 1948- 124
Castro, Americo 1885-1972 ....37-40R
Castro, Antonio 1946- 53-56
Castro, Fidel 1927- Brief entry 110
Castro, Jan Garden 1945- 120
Castro, Tony
See Castro, Antonio
Castro-Klaren, Sara 1942- 61-64
Castronovo, David 1945- 114
Castro Ruz, Fidel
See Castro, Fidel
Casty, Alan Howard 1929- CANR-4
Earlier sketch in CA 3R
Caswall, Edward 1814-1878 .... DLB-32
Caswell, Helen (Rayburn) 1923- 33-36R
See also SATA 12
Caswell, Margaret (Betsy) R(oss)
1903(?)-1982 Obituary 107
Catala, Rafael 1942- CANR-13
Earlier sketch in CA 73-76
Catalano, Donald B(ernard) 1920- 57-60
Catalano, Joseph S(tellario) 1928- 102
Cataldo, Michael F. 1947- 122
Catanese, Anthony James (Jr.) 1942- .. CANR-14
Earlier sketch in CA 29-32R
Catania, A(nthony) Charles 1936- 37-40R
Catanzariti, John 1942- 124
Cate, Benjamin W(ilson) 1931- 73-76
Cate, Curtis 1924- CANR-9
Earlier sketch in CA 53-56
Cate, Curtis Wolsey 1884-1976 Obituary ..61-64
Cate, Dick
See Cate, Richard Edward Nelson
Cate, Richard Edward Nelson 1932- 73-76
See also SATA 28
Cate, Robert L(ouis) 1932- 111
Cate, William Burke 1924- 13-14R
Cateora, Philip Rene 1932- 7-8R
Cater, (Silas) Douglass 1923- CANR-1
Earlier sketch in CA 4R
Cates, Ray A., Jr. 1940- 29-32R
Cates, Tory
See Bird, Sarah McCabe
Cathcart, Helen CANR-2
Earlier sketch in CA 7-8R
Cathcart, Robert S(tephen) 1923- 101
Cather, Willa (Sibert) 1873-1947
Brief entry 104
See also SATA 30
See also DLB 9, 54
See also DLBD 1
See also TCLC 1, 11
Catherall, Arthur 1906- 7-8R
See also SATA 3
Cathers, David M. 1941- 111
Cathers, Ken 1951- 112
Catherwood, (Henry) Frederick (Ross)
1925- 106
Cathey, Cornelius Oliver 1908- 3R
Cathon, Laura E(lizabeth) 1908- 5-6R
See also SATA 27
Catledge, Turner 1901-1983 57-60
Obituary 109
See also AITN 1

Catlin, George E(dward) G(ordon)
1896-1979 ....13-14R
Obituary 85-88
Catlin, Warren Benjamin 1881-1968 .... 4R
Obituary 103
Catlin, Wynelle 1930- 65-68
See also SATA 13
Catling, Darrel (Charles) 1909- 7-8R
Catling, Patrick Skene 1925- Brief entry 115
Catlow, Joanna
See Lowry, Joan (Catlow)
Cato
See Howard, Peter D(unsmore)
Cato, Nancy (Fotheringham) 1917- CAP-1
Earlier sketch in CA 49-52
Catoir, John T. 1931- CANR-11
Earlier sketch in CA 25-28R
Caton, Charles E(dwin) 1928- 9-10R
Caton, Hiram P. 1936- CANR-4
Earlier sketch in CA 53-56
Caton-Thompson, Gertrude 1888-1985 122
Obituary 116
Catron, Louis E. 1932- 45-48
Cattan, Henry 1906- 29-32R
Cattaui, Georges 1896-1974 .... CAP-2
Earlier sketch in CA 25-28
Cattell, Everett L(ewis) 1905- 4R
Cattell, Psyche 1893- 41-44R
Cattell, Raymond Bernard 1905- CANR-2
Earlier sketch in CA 7-8R
Catto, Max(well Jeffrey) 1909- 105
Catton, (Charles) Bruce 1899-1978 ..... CANR-7
Obituary 81-84
Earlier sketch in CA 5-6R
See also SATA 2, 24
See also DLB 17
See also CLC 35
See also AITN 1
Catton, William Bruce 1926- CANR-1
Earlier sketch in CA 4R
Catton, William R(obert), Jr. 1926- 109
Catudal, Honore M(arc, Jr.) 1944- CANR-12
Earlier sketch in CA 69-72
Catz, Max
See Glaser, Milton
Caudell, Marian 1930- 121
Caudill, Harry M(onroe) 1922- CANR-14
Earlier sketch in CA 33-36R
Caudill, Rebecca 1899-1985 .... CANR-2
Obituary 117
Earlier sketch in CA 5-6R
See also SATA 1, 44
Caudill, William W(ayne) 1914-1983
Obituary 110
Caudwell, Christopher
See Sprigg, C(hristopher) St. John
Cauffield, Margaret E(ileen) 1932- 122
Caughey, John L(yon) 1941- 115
Caughey, John Walton 1902- Brief entry ... 106
Caulder, Colline 1945- 113
Cauldwell, Frank
See King, Francis H(enry)
Cauley, John R(owan) 1908-1976
Obituary 65-68
Cauley, Lorinda Bryan 1951- 101
See also SATA 43, 46
Cauley, Terry
See Cauley, Troy Jesse
Cauley, Troy Jesse 1902- CANR-1
Earlier sketch in CA 4R
Caulfield, Malachy Francis 1915- CANR-14
Earlier sketch in CA 77-80
Caulfield, Max
See Caulfield, Malachy Francis
Caulfield, Peggy F. 1926-1987 ....7-8R
Obituary 123
Caulfield, Sean 1925- 108
Cauliflower, Sebastian
See Seldes, Gilbert (Vivian)
Cauman, Samuel 1910-1971 .... CAP-2
Earlier sketch in CA 23-24
See also SATA 48
Caunitz, William 1935- CLC-34
Causley, Charles (Stanley) 1917- CANR-5
Earlier sketch in CA 9-10R
See also SATA 3
See also DLB 27
See also CLC 7
Caute, David 1936- CANR-1
Earlier sketch in CA 3R
See also CAAS 4
See also DLB 14
See also CLC 29
Cautela, Joseph R(ichard) 1927- 106
Cauthen, Baker James 1909-1985
Obituary 115
Cauthen, Irby Bruce, Jr. 1919- 111
Cauthen, W(ilfred) Kenneth 1930- CANR-7
Earlier sketch in CA 7-8R
Cauvin, Jean-Pierre (Bernard) 1936- 116
Cauwels, Janice M(arie) 1949- 110
Cava, Esther Laden 1916- 37-40R
Cavafy, C(onstantine) P(eter)
See Kavafis, Konstantinos Petrou
See also TCLC 2, 7
Cavaiani, Mabel 1919- CANR-21
Earlier sketches in CA 57-60, CANR-6
Cavalcanti, Alberto (de Almeida)
1897-1982 Obituary 107
Cavalier, Julian 1931- CANR-2
Earlier sketch in CA 49-52
Cavaliero, Glen 1927- CANR-13
Earlier sketch in CA 73-76
Cavallari, Alberto 1927- CANR-10
Earlier sketch in CA 23-24R
Cavallaro, Ann (Abelson) 1918- 5-6R
Cavallo, Diana 1931- CANR-2
Earlier sketch in CA 1R
See also SATA 7
Cavallo, Evelyn
See Spark, Muriel (Sarah)
Cavallo, Robert M. 1932- CANR-10
Earlier sketch in CA 65-68
Cavan, Romilly 1914(?)-1975 Obituary 61-64
Cavan, Sherri 1938- 19-20R
Cavanagh, Gerald F(rancis) 1931- 41-44R
Cavanagh, Helen (Carol) 1939- 104
See also SATA 37, 48
Cavanagh, John B. 1908-1983 Obituary 110
Cavanagh, John Richard 1904- CAP-2
Earlier sketch in CA 19-20
Cavanagh, Richard E(dward) 1946- 121
Cavanah, Frances 1899-1982 ....15-16R
See also SATA 1, 31
Cavanaugh, Arthur 1926- 17-18R
Cavani, Liliana 1936- 110
Cavanna, Betty 1909- CANR-6
Earlier sketch in CA 9-10R
See also SATA 1, 30
See also SAAS 4
See also CLC 12
Cavanna, Elizabeth Allen
See Cavanna, Betty
Cave, Alfred A. 1935- 37-40R
Cave, Hugh Barnett 1910- CANR-2
Earlier sketch in CA 7-8R
Cave, Roderick (George James Munro)
1935- CANR-2
Earlier sketch in CA 7-8R
Cave, Thomas
See Steward, Samuel M(orris)
Cavell, Stanley (Louis) 1926- CANR-11
Earlier sketch in CA 61-64
Cavelti, Peter C(hristian) 1948- 116
Cavendish, J(ean) M(avis) 1932- 118
Cavendish, Richard 1930- CANR-20
Earlier sketches in CA 9-10R, CANR-5
Caveney, Philip (Richard) 1951- CANR-19
Earlier sketch in CA 102
Caverhill, Nicholas
See Kirk-Greene, Anthony (Hamilton
Millard)
Caverhill, William Melville 1910-1983
Obituary 111
Cavers, David F(arquhar) 1902- 19-20R
Cavert, Samuel McCrea 1888-1976 ......37-40R
Cavert, Walter Dudley 1891- 1R
Caves, Richard E(arl) 1931- CANR-19
Earlier sketches in CA 4R, CANR-4
Cavett, Dick
See Cavett, Richard A.
Cavett, Richard A. 1936- 108
Cavin, Ruth (Brodie) 1918- CANR-8
Earlier sketch in CA 61-64
See also SATA 38
Cavitch, David 1933- 29-32R
Cavnes, Max P(arvin) 1922- 11-12R
Cavrell, Jean 1927- 107
Cawein, Madison 1865-1914 .... DLB-54
Cawelti, John G(eorge) 1929- 23-24R
Cawley, Linda 1949- 113
Cawley, Robert Ralston 1893-1973 ...... CAP-2
Obituary 41-44R
Earlier sketch in CA 21-22
Cawley, Winifred 1915- 69-72
See also SATA 13
Cawood, John W. 1931- 33-36R
Caws, Ian 1945- 118
Caws, Mary Ann 1933- CANR-10
Earlier sketch in CA 25-28R
Caws, Peter (James) 1931- CANR-8
Earlier sketch in CA 17-18R
Cawthorne, Graham 1906(?)-1980
Obituary 97-100
Caxton, Pisistratus
See Lytton, Edward G(eorge) E(arle)
and L(ytton) Bulwer-Lytton, Baron
Cayce, Edgar E(vans) 1918- 23-24R
Cayce, Hugh Lynn 1907-1982 ....25-28R
Obituary 107
Cayley, Michael (Forde) 1950- 53-56
Cayrol, Jean 1911- 89-92
See also CLC 11
Cayton, Horace R(oscoe) 1903-1970 ..... CAP-1
Obituary 29-32R
Earlier sketch in CA 13-14
Cazalet-Keir, Thelma 25-28R
Cazamian, Louis Francois 1877-1965
Obituary 93-96
Cazden, Elizabeth 1950- 65-68
Cazden, Norman 1914- 37-40R
Cazden, Robert E. 1930- 33-36R
Cazeau, Charles J(ay) 1931- 104
Cazeaux, Isabelle 1926- 53-56
Cazel, Fred A(ugustus), Jr. 1921- 11-12R
Cazelles, Brigitte Jacqueline 1944- 102
Cazemajou, Jean 1924- 73-76
Cazet, Denys 1938- 108
See also SATA 41
Cazzola, Gus 1934- 108
Cebula, Richard J(ohn) 1944- 111
Cebulash, Mel 1937- CANR-12
Earlier sketch in CA 29-32R
See also SATA 10
Cecchetti, Giovanni 1922- Brief entry 107
Cecelski, Elizabeth 1953- 119
Cech, John O(tto) 1944- 120
Cecil, (Edward Christian) David (Gascoyne)
1902-1986 .... CANR-13
Obituary 118
Earlier sketch in CA 61-64
Cecil, Henry
See Leon, Henry Cecil
Cecil, Hugh Mortimer
See Roberts, William
Cecil, Lamar (John Ryan, Jr.) 1932- 21-22R
Cecil, Lord David
See Cecil, (Edward Christian) David
(Gascoyne)
Cecil, R. H.
See Hewitt, Cecil Rolph
Cecil, Robert 1913- 53-56
Ceder, Georgiana Dorcas 2R
See also SATA 10
Cefkin, J. Leo 1916- 25-28R
Cegielka, Francis A(nthony) 1908- 37-40R
Ceitho, Dewi
See Jones, Evan David
Cela, Camilo Jose 1916- CANR-21
Earlier sketch in CA 21-22R
See also CLC 4, 13
Celaeno
See Harper, George W(illiam)
Celan, Paul
See Antschel, Paul
Celeste, Sister Marie 49-52
Celestino, Martha Laing 1951- 107
See also SATA 39
Celine, Louis-Ferdinand
See Destouches, Louis Ferdinand
See also CLC 1, 3, 4, 7, 9, 15, 47
Cell, Edward (Charles) 1928- 21-22R
Cell, John W(hitson) 1935- 41-44R
Cellario, Alberto R. 1910(?)-1984
Obituary 112
Celler, Emanuel 1888-1981 Obituary 108
Celnik, Max 1933- 17-18R
Celoria, Francis (S. C.) 1926- 102
Cemach, Harry P(aul) 1917- 57-60
Cenci, Louis 1918- 17-18R
Cendrars, Blaise
See Sauser-Hall, Frederic
Censer, Jane T(urner) 1951- 123
Cente, H. F.
See Rocklin, Ross Louis
Center, Allen Harry 1912- CANR-4
Earlier sketch in CA 5-6R
Cento
See Cobbing, Bob
Centore, F. F. 1938- 25-28R
Ceram, C. W.
See Marek, Kurt W(illi)
Ceravolo, Joseph 1934- 102
Cerf, Bennett (Alfred) 1898-1971 .... CAP-2
Obituary 29-32R
Earlier sketch in CA 19-20
See also SATA 7
Cerf, Christopher (Bennett) 1941- 25-28R
See also SATA 2
Cerf, Jay H(enry) 1923-1974 .... CAP-2
Obituary 53-56
Earlier sketch in CA 19-20
Cerling, Charles (Edward), Jr. 1943- 111
Cermak, Laird S(cott) 1942- CANR-4
Earlier sketch in CA 53-56
Cermak, Martin
See Duchacek, Ivo D(uka)
Cerminara, Gina 17-18R
Cerney, James Vincent 1914- 23-24R
Cernuda (y Bidon), Luis 1902-1963
Obituary 89-92
Cerra, Frances 1946- 97-100
Cerri, Lawrence J. 1923- CANR-17
Earlier sketch in CA 89-92
Cerruti, James Smith 1918- 103
Certner, Simon 1909(?)-1979 Obituary 89-92
Cerutti, Maria Antonietta 1932- 25-28R
Cerutti, Toni
See Cerutti, Maria Antonietta
Cerutty, Percy Wells 1895-1975 .... CAP-2
Obituary 61-64
Earlier sketch in CA 25-28
Cervantes, Alfonso J(uan) 1920-1983
Obituary 110
Cervantes, Lucius F. 1914- 15-16R
Cerveri, Doris 1914- 101
Cervon, Jacqueline
See Moussard, Jacqueline
Cerwinske, Laura 1948- 111
Cerych, Ladislav 1925- CANR-7
Earlier sketch in CA 15-16R
Cesaire, Aime (Fernand) 1913- CANR-24
Earlier sketch in CA 65-68
See also CLC 19, 32
Cesara, Manda
See Poewe, Karla
Cetin, Frank Stanley 1921- 4R
See also SATA 2
Cetron, Marvin Jerome 1930- 107
Cetta, Lewis T(homas) 1933- 53-56
Cevasco, George A(nthony) 1924- CANR-2
Earlier sketch in CA 5-6R
Chabe, Alexander M(ichael) 1923- 53-56
Chaber, M. E.
See Crossen, Kendell Foster
Chabod, Federico 1901-1960 Obituary 116
Chabrol, Claude 1930- 110
See also CLC 16
Chace, James (Clarke) 1931- CANR-1
Earlier sketch in CA 3R
Chace, William M(urdough) 1938- 69-72
Chacholiades, Miltiades 1937- CANR-1
Earlier sketch in CA 45-48
Chacko, David 1942- 49-52
Chacko, George K(uttickal) 1930- CANR-13
Earlier sketch in CA 73-76
Chaconas, D(oris) J. 1938- 21-22R
Chadbourne, Richard M(cClain) 1922- 23-24R
Chadeayne, Lee 1933- 53-56
Chadourne, Marc 1896(?)-1975 Obituary ..53-56
Chadwick, Bruce A(lbert) 1940- 97-100
Chadwick, Henry 1920- CANR-9
Earlier sketch in CA 21-22R
Chadwick, James 1891-1974 Obituary 49-52
Chadwick, Janet (Bachand) 1933- 97-100
Chadwick, (Gerald William St.) John
1915- 25-28R
Chadwick, John 1920- 4R
Chadwick, Lee 1909- 69-72
Chadwick, Lester CAP-2
Earlier sketch in CA 19-20
See also SATA 1
Chadwick, Margaret Lee (Gill) 1893-1984
Obituary 112
Chadwick, Nora Kershaw 1891-1972 ..... CAP-1
Earlier sketch in CA 15-16
Chadwick, (William) Owen 1916- CANR-19
Earlier sketches in CA 4R, CANR-1
Chadwick, Ronald P(aul) 1935- 116
Chadwin, Mark Lincoln 1939- CANR-17
Earlier sketch in CA 25-28R
Chaet, Bernard 1924- 69-72
Chafe, Wallace L. 1927- 29-32R
Chafe, William H(enry) 1942- CANR-12
Earlier sketch in CA 49-52
Chafetz, Henry 1916-1978 .... CANR-3
Obituary 73-76
Earlier sketch in CA 1R
Chafetz, Janet Saltzman 1942- 69-72
Chafetz, Morris E(dward) 1924- CANR-5
Earlier sketch in CA 13-14R
Chaffee, Allen CAP-1
Earlier sketch in CA 9-10
See also SATA 3
Chaffee, John 1946- 85-88
Chaffee, Steven Henry 1935- 106
Chaffin, Lillie D(orton) 1925- CANR-13
Earlier sketch in CA 33-36R
See also SATA 4
Chaffin, Yule M. 1914- 23-24R
Chafin, Andrew 1937- 53-56
Chagall, David 1930- CANR-3
Earlier sketch in CA 9-10R
Chagall, Marc 1887-1985 122
Obituary 114
Chagla, M(ohamedali) C(urrim) 1900-1981
Obituary 108
Chai, Chen kang 1916- 21-22R
Chai, Ch'u 1906- 9-10R
Chai, Hon-chan 1931- 23-24R
Chai, Winberg 1932- CANR-9
Earlier sketch in CA 5-6R
Chaij, Fernando 1909- CANR-8
Earlier sketch in CA 21-22R
Chaikin, Miriam 1928- CANR-14
Earlier sketch in CA 81-84
See also SATA 24
Chais, Pamela (Herbert) 1930- 73-76
Chaisson, Eric (Joseph) 1946- 108
Chajkowsky, William E(ugene) 1938- 116
Chakerian, Charles (Garabed) 1904- 45-48
Chakour, Charles M. 1929- 33-36R
Chakravarty, Amiya (Chandra) 1901- CANR-1
Earlier sketch in CA 1R
Chakravarty, Birendra Narayan
1904-1980(?) 102
Chalfant, Edward Allan 1921- 111
Chalfont, Alun
See Jones, (Alun) Arthur Gwynne
Chalhoub, Michael 1932- 89-92
Chalidze, Valery Nikolaevich 1938- 103
Chalk, John Allen 1937- 57-60
Chalk, Ocania 1927- CANR-1
Earlier sketch in CA 45-48
Chalker, Jack L(aurence) 1944- 73-76
Chall, Jeanne S(ternlicht) 1921- CANR-10
Earlier sketch in CA 25-28R
Challand, Helen J(ean) 1921- 121
Brief entry 118
Challans, Mary 1905-1983 81-84
Obituary 111
See also SATA 23, 36
Challice, Kenneth
See Hutchin, Kenneth Charles
Challinor, John 1894- 73-76
Challis, George
See Faust, Frederick (Shiller)
Challoner, H. K.
See Mills, J(anet) M(elanie) A(ilsa)
Challoner, Robert
See Butterworth, Michael
Chalmers, David Mark 1927- 25-28R
Chalmers, Eric Brownlie 1929- 102
Chalmers, Floyd S(herman) 1898- CAP-2
Earlier sketch in CA 25-28
Chalmers, George 1742-1825 .... DLB-30
Chalmers, Harvey II 1890-1971
Obituary 33-36R
Chalmers, John W. 1910- 93-96
Chalmers, Malcolm 1956- 120
Chalmers, Mary (Eileen) 1927- 5-6R
See also SATA 6
Chalon, Jean 1935- CANR-16
Earlier sketch in CA 97-100
Chalon, Jon
See Chaloner, John Seymour
Chaloner, John Seymour 1924- 93-96
Chaloner, W. H.
See Chaloner, William Henry
Chaloner, William Henry 1914-1987
Obituary 122
Chamberlain, Anne 1917- 77-80
Chamberlain, Betty 1908-1983 ....33-36R
Obituary 109
Chamberlain, Elinor 1901- CAP-1
Earlier sketch in CA 15-16

Chamberlain, Houston Stewart
1855-1927(?) Brief entry 120
Chamberlain, John (Rensselaer) 1903- 57-60
Chamberlain, Jonathan Mack 1928- 101
Chamberlain, Joseph Miles 1923- 107
Chamberlain, Margaret 1954- SATA-46
Chamberlain, Mary (Christina) 1947- 115
Chamberlain, Muriel Evelyn 1932- CANR-16
Earlier sketch in CA 93-96
Chamberlain, Narcisse 1924- 15-16R
Chamberlain, Neil Wolverton 1915- CANR-6
Earlier sketch in CA 13-14R
Chamberlain, (Arthur) Neville 1869-1940
Brief entry 113
Chamberlain, Robert Lyall 1923- 15-16R
Chamberlain, Samuel 1895-1975 .... CAP-2
Obituary 53-56
Earlier sketch in CA 23-24
Chamberlain, Samuel S. 1851-1916 .... DLB-25
Chamberlain, Wilson
See Crandall, Norma
Chamberlain, Wilt(on Norman) 1936- 103
Chamberland, Paul 1939- DLB-60
Chamberlin, E(ric) R(ussell) 1926- CANR-19
Earlier sketch in CA 97-100
Chamberlin, Enid C. S. 1900(?)-1982(?)
Obituary 106
Chamberlin, J. E(ward) 1943- 85-88
Chamberlin, J(ohn) Gordon 1914- CANR-4
Earlier sketch in CA 3R
Chamberlin, Judi 1944- 81-84
Chamberlin, Leslie J(oseph) 1926- 53-56
Chamberlin, M. Hope 1920-1974 45-48
Obituary 49-52
Chamberlin, Mary 1914- 45-48
Chamberlin, Waldo 1905- 65-68
Chamberlin, William Henry 1897-1969 .....5-6R
See also DLB 29
Chambers, Aidan 1934- CANR-12
Earlier sketch in CA 25-28R
See also SATA 1
See also CLC 35
Chambers, Anthony H(ood) 1943- 108
Chambers, Bradford 1922-1984 Obituary ... 113
See also SATA 39
Chambers, Charles Haddon 1860-1921
Brief entry 110
See also DLB 10
Chambers, Clarke A(lexander) 1921- 41-44R
Chambers, Dewey W. 1929- CANR-12
Earlier sketch in CA 29-32R
Chambers, Edward J(ames) 1925- 17-18R
Chambers, Frances 1940- 111
Chambers, Frank P(entland) 1900- CAP-1
Earlier sketch in CA 9-10
Chambers, Howard V.
See Lowenkopf, Shelly A(lan)
Chambers, James 1948- Brief entry 124
Chambers, Jane 1937-1983 85-88
Obituary 109
Chambers, Jessie
See Lawrence, D(avid) H(erbert Richards)
Chambers, John W. 1933- 124
See also SATA 46
Chambers, Jonathan David 1898-1970 .. CANR-3
Earlier sketch in CA 4R
Chambers, Lenoir 1891-1970 111
Obituary 104
Chambers, M(erritt) M(adison) 1899- ... CANR-5
Earlier sketch in CA 9-10R
Chambers, Margaret Ada Eastwood
1911- 9-10R
See also SATA 2
Chambers, Mortimer Hardin, Jr. 1927- .. CANR-6
Earlier sketch in CA 11-12R
Chambers, Peggy
See Chambers, Margaret Ada Eastwood
Chambers, Peter
See Phillips, D(ennis) J(ohn Andrew)
Chambers, R(aymond) J(ohn) 1917- 17-18R
Chambers, Robin Bernard 1942- 103
Chambers, W(illiam) Walker 1913- 29-32R
Chambers, (David) Whittaker 1901-1961
Obituary 89-92
Chambers, William E. 1943- 73-76
Chambers, William Nisbet 1916- CANR-8
Earlier sketch in CA 7-8R
Chambers, William Trout 1896- CAP-1
Earlier sketch in CA 13-14
Chambers-Schiller, Lee Virginia 1948- 120
Chambertin, Ilya
See von Block, Bela W(illiam)
and von Block, Sylvia
Chambliss, Bill
See Chambliss, William J(oseph)
Chambliss, William C. 1908(?)-1975
Obituary 57-60
Chambliss, William J(ones) 1923- 15-16R
Chambliss, William J(oseph) 1933- CANR-14
Earlier sketch in CA 77-80
Chamelin, Neil Charles 1942- 69-72
Chametzky, Jules 1928- 33-36R
Chamlee, Ruth Miller 1893(?)-1983
Obituary 110
Champagne, Marian 1915- 7-8R
Champe, Flavia Waters 1902- 115
Champernowne, David (Gawen) 1912- 104
Champigny, Robert J(ean) 1922- 33-36R
Champion, Dick
See Champion, Richard Gordon
Champion, John C(arr) 1923- CANR-8
Earlier sketch in CA 17-18R
Champion, John E(lmer) 1922- 13-14R
Champion, Larry S(tephen) 1932- CANR-9
Earlier sketch in CA 23-24R
Champion, R(ichard) A(nnells) 1925- 29-32R
Champion, Richard Gordon 1931- 77-80
Champkin, Peter 1918- 7-8R
Champlin, Charles (Davenport) 1926- 69-72
Champlin, James R(aymond) 1928- 21-22R
Champlin, John Michael 1937- 110
Champlin, Joseph M(asson) 1930- CANR-20
Earlier sketches in CA 49-52, CANR-1
Champlin, Tim
See Champlin, John Michael
Champney, Freeman 1911- 25-28R
Chamson, Andre J(ules) L(ouis)
1900-1983 .... CANR-2
Obituary 111
Earlier sketch in CA 7-8R
Ch'An, Chu
See Blofeld, John (Eaton Calthorpe)
Ch'an, Chu
See Blofeld, John (Eaton Calthorpe)
Chan, Loren Briggs 1943- CANR-8
Earlier sketch in CA 57-60
Chanaidh, Fear
See Campbell, John Lorne
Chanakya
See Panikkar, K(avalam) Madhava
Chanan, Ben
See Yaffe, Richard
Chanan, Gabriel 1942- CANR-7
Earlier sketch in CA 57-60
Chanan, Michael 1946- 106
Chance, John Newton 1911-1983 102
Obituary 110
Chance, Jonathan
See Chance, John Newton
Chance, Michael R(obin) A(lexander)
1915- 85-88
Chance, Roger (James Ferguson)
1893-1987 Obituary 122
Chance, Stephen
See Turner, Philip
Chancellor, John 1900-1971 .... CAP-2
Earlier sketch in CA 23-24
Chancellor, John (William) 1927- 109
See also AITN 1
Chancellor, Paul 1900-1975 Obituary 57-60
Chand, Meira (Angela) 1942- 106
Chand, Munshi Prem
See Srivastava, Dhanpat Rai
Chand, Prem
See Srivastava, Dhanpat Rai
Chanda, Asok Kumar 1902- 19-20R
Chandler, A(rthur) Bertram 1912-1984 . CANR-13
Earlier sketch in CA 21-22R
Chandler, Alfred D(upont), Jr. 1918- CANR-4
Earlier sketch in CA 9-10R
Chandler, Alice 1931- 53-56
Chandler, Allison 1906- CAP-1
Earlier sketch in CA 9-10
Chandler, B. J. 1921- 2R
Chandler, Billy Jaynes 1932- 122
Chandler, Bryn 1945- 118
Chandler, Caroline A(ugusta)
1906-1979 ....17-18R
Obituary 93-96
See also SATA 22, 24
Chandler, David (Geoffrey) 1934- CANR-11
Earlier sketch in CA 25-28R
Chandler, David Leon CANR-16
Earlier sketches in CA 49-52, CANR-1
Chandler, David Porter 1933- 45-48
See also SATA 28
Chandler, E(dwin) Russell, Jr. 1932- 77-80
Chandler, Edna Walker 1908-1982 ...... CANR-4
Obituary 108
Earlier sketch in CA 4R
See also SATA 11, 31
Chandler, Frank
See Harknett, Terry
Chandler, George 1915- CANR-5
Earlier sketch in CA 9-10R
Chandler, Harry 1864-1944 .... DLB-29
Chandler, Howard 1915(?)-1981 Obituary ... 104
Chandler, Jennifer (Westwood) 1940- ... CANR-9
Earlier sketch in CA 65-68
Chandler, Linda S(mith) 1929- CANR-23
Earlier sketch in CA 106
See also SATA 39
Chandler, Margaret Kueffner 1922- 17-18R
Chandler, Norman 1899-1973 Obituary 89-92
Chandler, Otis 1927- 111
Chandler, Raymond 1888-1959
Brief entry 104
See also TCLC 1, 7
Chandler, Richard Eugene 1916- 5-6R
Chandler, Robert 1953- 112
See also SATA 40
Chandler, Robert Wilbur 1921- 102
Chandler, Ruth Forbes 1894-1978 .... 4R
Obituary 103
See also SATA 2, 26
Chandler, S(tanley) Bernard 1921- 21-22R
Chandler, T(ony) J(ohn) 1928- 107
Chandler, Tertius 1915- CANR-19
Earlier sketch in CA 102
Chandola, Anoop C. 1937- CANR-14
Earlier sketch in CA 37-40R
Chandonnet, Ann F. 1943- CANR-23
Earlier sketches in CA 61-64, CANR-8
Chandor, (Peter John) Anthony 1932- 29-32R
Chandos, Fay
See Swatridge, Irene Maude (Mossop)
Chandos, John
See McConnell, John Lithgow Chandos
Chandra, Pramod 1930- 77-80
Chandrasekhar, Sripati 1918- 89-92
Chaneles, Sol 1926- 41-44R
Chaney, Jill 1932- CANR-11
Earlier sketch in CA 25-28R
Chaney, Norman 1935- 110
Chaney, Otto Preston, Jr. 1931- 33-36R
Chaney, William A(lbert) 1922- 33-36R
Chang, Chen-chi 1920- Brief entry 115
Chang, Ch'eng-chi
See Chang, Chen-chi
Chang, Chung-yuan 1900- 117
Chang, Constance D(an) 1917- 61-64
Chang, Dae H(ong) 1928- CANR-6
Earlier sketch in CA 57-60
Chang, Garma C. C.
See Chang, Chen-chi
Chang, Hsin-hai 1900- 7-8R
Chang, Isabelle C(hin) 1924- 21-22R
Chang, Jen-chi 1903- CAP-1
Earlier sketch in CA 11-12
Chang, Kia-Ngau 1889- 5-6R
Chang, Kwang-chih 1931- CANR-15
Earlier sketch in CA 41-44R
Chang, Lee
See Levinson, Leonard
Chang, Parris (Hsu-Cheng) 1936- CANR-6
Earlier sketch in CA 57-60
Chang, Raymond 1939- 121
Chang, Richard T(aiwon) 1933- 61-64
Chang-Rodriguez, Eugenio 1926- CANR-21
Earlier sketches in CA 9-10R, CANR-6
Chanin, Abraham (Solomon) 1921- 89-92
Chankin, Donald O(liver) 1934- 57-60
Channel, A. R.
See Catherall, Arthur
Channels, Vera G(race) 1915- 69-72
Channing, Edward (Perkins) 1856-1931
Brief entry 122
See also DLB 17
Channing, Edward Tyrrell 1790-1856 .. DLB-1, 59
Channing, Steven A. 1940- CANR-13
Earlier sketch in CA 33-36R
Channing, William Ellery 1780-1842 .. DLB-1, 59
Channing, William Ellery II 1817-1901 .... DLB-1
Channing, William Henry 1810-1884 .. DLB-1, 59
Channon, Henry 1897-1958 Brief entry 121
Chanover, E(dmond) Pierre 1932- 29-32R
Chanover, Hyman 1920- CANR-2
Earlier sketch in CA 49-52
Chansky, Norman M(orton) 1929- 21-22R
Chant, Barry (Mostyn) 1938- CANR-11
Earlier sketch in CA 65-68
Chant, Donald (Alfred) 1928- CANR-18
Earlier sketch in CA 101
Chant, Joy
See Rutter, Eileen Joyce
Chant, Ken(neth David) 1933- 89-92
Chantiles, Vilma Liacouras 1925- CANR-6
Earlier sketch in CA 57-60
Chantler, David T(homas) 1925- 93-96
Chao, Buwei Yang 1889-1981 61-64
Obituary 120
Chao, Evelina 1949- 120
Chao, Kang 1929- 33-36R
Chao, Paul 1919- 114
Chao, Yuen Ren 1892-1982 .... CAP-2
Obituary 106
Earlier sketch in CA 21-22
Chapel, Paul 1926- 25-28R
Chapelle, Howard I(rving) 1901-1975 .... CAP-2
Obituary 57-60
Earlier sketch in CA 25-28
Chapian, Marie 1938- CANR-22
Earlier sketch in CA 106
See also SATA 29
Chapin, Alene Olsen Dalton 1915(?)-1986
Obituary 119
See also SATA 47
Chapin, Dwight Allan 1938- 41-44R
Chapin, F(rancis) Stuart, Jr. 1916- CANR-2
Earlier sketch in CA 7-8R
Chapin, Harry (Forster) 1942-1981 105
Obituary 104
Chapin, Henry 1893-1983 93-96
Obituary 110
Chapin, June Roediger 1931- CANR-13
Earlier sketch in CA 37-40R
Chapin, Katherine Garrison
See Biddle, Katherine Garrison Chapin
Chapin, Kim 1942- CANR-9
Earlier sketch in CA 53-56
Chapin, Louis Le Bourgeois, Jr.
1918-1981 103
Chapin, Ned 1927- 15-16R
Chapin, Schuyler G(arrison) 1923- 77-80
Chapin, Victor 1919(?)-1983 Obituary 109
Chapin, William 1918- 37-40R
Chaplin, Bill
See Chaplin, W. W.
Chaplin, Charles Spencer 1889-1977 81-84
Obituary 73-76
See also CLC 16
Chaplin, Charlie
See Chaplin, Charles Spencer
See also DLB 44
Chaplin, George 1914- 69-72
See also AITN 2
Chaplin, James P(atrick) 1919- CANR-1
Earlier sketch in CA 1R
Chaplin, L(inda) Tarin 1941- 116
Chaplin, Sid(ney) 1916-1986 .... CANR-16
Obituary 118
Earlier sketches in CA 9-10, CAP-1
Chaplin, W. W. 1895(?)-1978 Obituary ...81-84
Chapman, A(rthur) H(arry) 1924- CANR-19
Earlier sketch in CA 25-28R
Chapman, Abraham 1915- 45-48
Chapman, Allen
See Stratemeyer, Edward L.
Chapman, Alvah H., Jr. 1921- AITN-2
Chapman, Brian 1923- 9-10R
Chapman, Carleton B(urke) 1915- 69-72
Chapman, Charles F(rederic) 1881-1976
Obituary 65-68
Chapman, Christine 1933- CANR-12
Earlier sketch in CA 73-76
Chapman, Clark Russell 1945- 110
Chapman, Colin 1937- 29-32R
Chapman, (William) Donald 1923- 109
Chapman, Dorothy Hilton 1934- 57-60
Chapman, Edmund H(aupt) 1906- CAP-1
Earlier sketch in CA 15-16
Chapman, (Constance) Elizabeth (Mann)
1919- CAP-1
Earlier sketch in CA 9-10
See also SATA 10
Chapman, Elwood N. 1916- 37-40R
Chapman, Frances
See Chapman, Frank M(onroe)
Chapman, Frank
See Chapman, Frank M(onroe)
Chapman, Frank M(onroe) 1930- 113
Chapman, G(eorge) W(arren) Vernon
1925- 29-32R
Chapman, Gaynor 1935- SATA-32
Chapman, George 1559(?)-1634 .... DLB-62
Chapman, Graham 1941- 116
See also CLC 21
Chapman, Guy (Patterson) 1889-1972 101
Obituary 89-92
Chapman, Hester W(olferstan)
1899-1976 .... CANR-9
Obituary 65-68
Earlier sketch in CA 9-10R
Chapman, J. Dudley 1928- CANR-8
Earlier sketch in CA 23-24R
Chapman, James (Keith) 1919- CANR-15
Earlier sketch in CA 41-44R
Chapman, Jean 97-100
See also SATA 34
Chapman, Jennifer 1950- 118
Chapman, John 1900-1972 Obituary 33-36R
Chapman, John Jay 1862-1933
Brief entry 104
See also TCLC 7
Chapman, John L(eslie) 1920- 2R
Chapman, John Roy 1927- CANR-15
Earlier sketch in CA 77-80
Chapman, John Stanton Higham
1891-1972 Obituary 107
See also SATA 27
Chapman, Joseph Irvine 1912- 61-64
Chapman, June R(amey) 1918- 7-8R
Chapman, Karen C. 1942- 65-68
Chapman, Kenneth F(rancis) 1910- CAP-1
Earlier sketch in CA 15-16
Chapman, Kenneth G. 1927- 15-16R
Chapman, Laura 1935- 105
Chapman, Loren J(ames) 1927- 53-56
Chapman, M(ary) Winslow 1903- 93-96
Chapman, Marie M(anire) 1917- CANR-11
Earlier sketch in CA 61-64
Chapman, Maristan
See Chapman, John Stanton Higham
Chapman, Nancy W(hisnant) Collins
See Collins-Chapman, Nancy W(hisnant)
Chapman, Phil 1944- 121
Chapman, Raymond 1924- CANR-2
Earlier sketch in CA 7-8R
Chapman, Richard Arnold 1937-
Brief entry 105
Chapman, Rick M. 1943- 49-52
Chapman, Robert (DeWitt) 1937- 107
Chapman, Robert L(undquist) 1920- 122
Chapman, Roger E(ddington) 1916- 23-24R
Chapman, Ronald (George) 1917- 7-8R
Chapman, Ruth 1912(?)-1979 Obituary 104
Chapman, Samuel Greeley 1929- CANR-9
Earlier sketch in CA 19-20R
Chapman, Stanley D(avid) 1935- CANR-9
Earlier sketch in CA 21-22R
Chapman, Stepan 41-44R
Chapman, Steven
See Chapman, Stepan
Chapman, Sydney 1888-1970 106
Chapman, Vera 1898- 81-84
See also SATA 33
Chapman, Victoria L(ynn) 1944- 57-60
Chapman, Walker
See Silverberg, Robert
Chapman-Mortimer, William Charles
1907- 13-14R
Chapnick, Howard 1922- 65-68
Chappel, Bernice M(arie) 1910- CANR-16
Earlier sketch in CA 89-92
Chappell, Clovis G(illham) 1882-1972 65-68
Chappell, Fred 1936- CANR-8
Earlier sketch in CA 7-8R
See also CAAS 4
See also DLB 6
See also CLC 40
Chappell, Gordon (Stelling) 1939- 57-60
Chappell, Helen 1947- 104
Chappell, Jeannette
See Kalt, Jeannette Chappell
Chappell, Mollie 102
Chappell, Vere Claiborne 1930- 7-8R
Chappell, Warren 1904- CANR-8
Earlier sketch in CA 19-20R
See also SATA 6
Chappell, William (Evelyn) 1908- 106
Chapple, Eliot D(ismore) 1909- 41-44R
Chapple, (Clement) Gerald 1937- 111
Chapple, J(ohn) A(lfred) V(ictor) 1928- ...21-22R
Chapple, Richard L(ynn) 1944- 112
Chapple, Steve 1949- 77-80
Chaput, Donald (Charles) 1933- 122
Brief entry 117

Char, K. T. Narasimha
See Narasimha Char, K. T.
Char, Rene(-Emile) 1907-1988 ....15-16R
Obituary 124
See also CLC 9, 11, 14
Char, Tin-Yuke 1905- 57-60
Char, Wai Jane Chun 1912- 118
Char, Yum
See Barrett, Dean
Charanis, Peter 1908-1985 ....37-40R
Obituary 115
Charbonneau, Louis (Henry) 1924- 85-88
Charby, Jay
See Ellison, Harlan
Charchat, Isaac 1904(?)-1985 Obituary 116
Chard, (Maire) Brigid 1934- 105
Chard, Judy 1916- CANR-14
Earlier sketch in CA 77-80
Chard, Leslie F. II 1934- 33-36R
Chardiet, Bernice (Kroll) 1927(?)- 103
See also SATA 27
Chardin, Pierre Teilhard de
See Teilhard de Chardin, (Marie Joseph) Pierre
Chargaff, Erwin 1905- CANR-18
Earlier sketch in CA 101
Charhadi, Driss ben Hamed 13-14R
Chari, V. Krishna 1924- 19-20R
Charland, William (Alfred), Jr. 1937- 97-100
Charles, Amy M(arie) 1922- 116
Charles, C(arol) M(organ) 1931- CANR-1
Earlier sketch in CA 49-52
Charles, David
See Mondey, David (Charles)
Charles, Don C(laude) 1918- 11-12R
Charles, Donald
See Meighan, Donald Charles
Charles, Franklin
See Adams, Cleve F(ranklin)
Charles, Gerda CANR-1
Earlier sketch in CA 1R
See also DLB 14
Charles, Gordon H(ull) 1920- 104
Charles, Henry
See Harris, Marion Rose (Young)
Charles, Louis
See Stratemeyer, Edward L.
Charles, Mark
See Bickers, Richard Leslie Townshend
Charles, Nathanael
See Franklin, Benjamin V
Charles, Nicholas
See Kuskin, Karla (Seidman)
Charles, Ray
See Robinson, Ray Charles
Charles, Robert
See Smith, Robert Charles
Charles, Sascha 1896(?)-1972 Obituary ..37-40R
Charles, Searle F(ranklin) 1923- 11-12R
Charles, Theresa
See Swatridge, Charles (John)
and Swatridge, Irene Maude (Mossop)
Charles, Will
See Willeford, Charles (Ray III)
Charles-Roux, Edmonde 1920- 85-88
Charles the Clown
See Kraus, Charles E.
Charleston, Robert E.
See Robinson, Charles M. III
Charleston, Robert Jesse 1916- 102
Charlesworth, Arthur Riggs 1911- 53-56
Charlesworth, James Clyde 1900-1974 ....9-10R
Obituary 45-48
Charlesworth, John Kaye 1889- CAP-1
Earlier sketch in CA 9-10
Charlesworth, Maxwell John 1925- CANR-18
Earlier sketches in CA 4R, CANR-2
Charlier, Patricia (Mary) Simonet 1923- ...37-40R
Charlier, Roger H(enri) 1921- CANR-13
Earlier sketch in CA 37-40R
Charlip, Remy 1929- 33-36R
See also SATA 4
See also CLR 8
Charlot, Jean 1898-1979 .... CANR-4
Earlier sketch in CA 7-8R
See also SATA 8, 31
Charlot, John (Pierre) 1941- 120
Charlot, Martin (Day) 1944- 114
Charlotte, Susan 1954- 109
Charlson, David
See Holmes, David Charles
Charlton, Donald Geoffrey 1925- CANR-17
Earlier sketches in CA 4R, CANR-1
Charlton, Evan 1912-1983 Obituary 110
Charlton, Jack
See Charlton, John
Charlton, James (Mervyn) 1939- 81-84
Charlton, John 1935- 109
Charlton, John
See Woodhouse, Martin (Charlton)
Charlton, Linda
See Murray, Linda Charlton
Charlton, Michael (Alan) 1923- SATA-34
Charlwood, D(onald) E(rnest) 1915- CANR-9
Earlier sketch in CA 23-24R
Charlwood, Don
See Charlwood, D(onald) E(rnest)
Charmatz, Bill 1925- 29-32R
See also SATA 7
Charnance, L. P.
See Hannaway, Patricia H(inman)
Charnas, Suzy McKee 1939- CANR-18
Earlier sketch in CA 93-96
Charney, Ann 102
Charney, David H. 1923- CANR-15
Earlier sketch in CA 81-84
Charney, George 1905(?)-1975 Obituary ...61-64
Charney, Hanna K(urz) 1931- 49-52
Charney, Maurice (Myron) 1929- CANR-18
Earlier sketches in CA 9-10R, CANR-3
Charnin, Martin (Jay) 1934- 103
Charnley, John 1911-1982 Obituary 107
Charnley, Mitchell V(aughn) 1898- 69-72
Charnock, Joan 1903- CAP-2
Earlier sketch in CA 33-36
Charny, Carmi 1925- CANR-7
Earlier sketch in CA 15-16R
Charny, Israel W(olf) 1931- 57-60
Charosh, Mannis 1906- 29-32R
See also SATA 5
Charques, Dorothy (Taylor) 1899-1976 73-76
Obituary 65-68
Charriere, Henri 1906-1973 101
Charron, Shirley 1935- 69-72
Charry, Elias 1906- 69-72
Charter, S(teve) P. R. 1915(?)-1984
Obituary 114
Charteris, Hugo (Francis Guy) 1922-1970 ... 105
Obituary 89-92
Charteris, James Donald 1948- 117
Charteris, Leslie 1907- CANR-10
Earlier sketch in CA 7-8R
Charters, Alexander N(athaniel) 1916- 120
Charters, Ann (Danberg) 1936- CANR-9
Earlier sketch in CA 17-18R
Charters, Samuel (Barclay) 1929- CANR-9
Earlier sketch in CA 9-10R
Chartham, Robert
See Seth, Ronald (Sydney)
Chartier, Emilio
See Estenssoro, Hugo
Chartkoff, Joseph L(ouis) 1942- 119
Chartkoff, Kerry K(ona) 1943- 119
Charvat, Frank John 1918- 1R
Charvet, John 1938- CANR-15
Earlier sketch in CA 85-88
Chary, Frederick B(arry) 1939- 49-52
Charyn, Jerome 1937- CANR-7
Earlier sketch in CA 7-8R
See also CAAS 1
See also DLBY 83
See also CLC 5, 8, 18
Chasan, Daniel Jack 1943- 29-32R
Chase, A(lice) Elizabeth 1906- CAP-1
Earlier sketch in CA 11-12
Chase, Adam
See Fairman, Paul W.
and Marlowe, Stephen
and Thomson, James C(utting)
Chase, Alan (Louis) 1929- 2R
Chase, Alice
See McHargue, Georgess
Chase, Alston Hurd 1906- 5-6R
Chase, Borden
See Fowler, Frank
See also DLB 26
Chase, Chris AITN-1
Chase, Cleveland B(ruce) 1904(?)-1975
Obituary 53-56
Chase, Clinton I(rvin) 1927- 106
Chase, Cora G(ingrich) 1898- CANR-7
Earlier sketch in CA 61-64
Chase, Donald 1943- 53-56
Chase, Elaine R(aco) 1949- 114
Chase, Emily
See Sachs, Judith
and White, Carol
Chase, Gilbert 1906- 17-18R
Chase, Glen
See Levinson, Leonard
Chase, Harold W(illiam) 1922- CANR-4
Earlier sketch in CA 11-12R
Chase, Ilka 1905-1978 .... CANR-9
Obituary 77-80
Earlier sketch in CA 61-64
Chase, James Hadley
See Raymond, Rene (Brabazon)
Chase, James S(taton) 1932- 85-88
Chase, Judith Wragg 1907- 41-44R
Chase, Larry
See Chase, Lawrence
Chase, Lawrence 1943- 97-100
Chase, Loriene Eck 102
Chase, Loring D. 1916- 25-28R
Chase, Lyndon
See Chard, Judy
Chase, Mary (Coyle) 1907-1981 77-80
Obituary 105
See also SATA 17, 29
Chase, Mary Ellen 1887-1973 .... CAP-1
Obituary 41-44R
Earlier sketch in CA 15-16
See also SATA 10
See also CLC 2
Chase, Mildred Portney 1921- 106
Chase, Naomi Feigelson 1932- 104
Chase, Otta Louise 1909- 49-52
Chase, Philander D(ean) 1943- 124
Chase, Richard 1904- 61-64
Chase, Samuel B(rown), Jr. 1932- 5-6R
Chase, Stuart 1888-1985 65-68
Obituary 117
Chase, Sylvia (Belle) 1938- 115
Brief entry 110
Chase, Virginia Lowell
See Perkins, Virginia Chase
Chase, W. Linwood 1897(?)-1983
Obituary 110
Chase-Riboud, Barbara (Dewayne Tosi)
1939- 113
See also DLB 33
Chasin, Barbara 1940- 69-72
Chasins, Abram 1903-1987 .... CANR-14
Obituary 122
Earlier sketch in CA 37-40R
Chasman, Herbert 1938- 121
Chastain, Madye Lee 1908- 5-6R
See also SATA 4
Chasteen, Edgar R(ay) 1935- 33-36R
Chastenet de Castaing, Jacques
1893-1978 Obituary 77-80
Chaston, Gloria Duncan 1929- 69-72
Chatalbash, Ron 1959- 111
Chatelain, Nicolas 1913-1976 Obituary 65-68
Chatelet, Albert 1928- CANR-6
Earlier sketch in CA 13-14R
Chater, Elizabeth (Eileen) 1910- 111
Chatfield, (Earl) Charles (Jr.) 1934- 37-40R
Chatfield, Hale 1936- CANR-13
Earlier sketch in CA 33-36R
Chatfield, Michael 1934- CANR-10
Earlier sketch in CA 25-28R
Chatham, Doug(las) M. 1938- CANR-8
Earlier sketch in CA 61-64
Chatham, James R(ay) 1931- 33-36R
Chatham, Josiah G(eorge) 1914- 49-52
Chatham, Larry
See Bingley, David Ernest
Chatham, Russell 1939- 69-72
Chatman, Seymour B(enjamin) 1928- 37-40R
Chatov, Robert 1927- 105
Chatt, Orville K(eith) 1924- 53-56
Chatterje, Sarat Chandra 1876-1936(?)
Brief entry 109
Chatterjee, Margaret (Gantzer) 1925- ... CANR-20
Earlier sketches in CA 7-8R, CANR-3
Chatterji, Saratchandra
See Chatterje, Sarat Chandra
See also TCLC 13
Chatterji, Suniti Kumar 1890- 81-84
Chatterton, Wayne 1921- 37-40R
Chatwin, (Charles) Bruce 1940- 85-88
See also CLC 28
Chaudhuri, Haridas 1913- CANR-4
Earlier sketch in CA 7-8R
Chaudhuri, Sukanta 1950- 57-60
Chauffard, Rene-Jacques 1920(?)-1972
Obituary 37-40R
Chauncy, Charles 1705-1787 .... DLB-24
Chauncy, Nan(cen Beryl Masterman)
1900-1970 .... CANR-4
Earlier sketch in CA 3R
See also SATA 6
See also CLR 6
Chaundler, Christine 1887-1972 .... CAP-2
Earlier sketch in CA 29-32
See also SATA 1, 25
Chauvin, Remy 1913- 108
Chavasse, Michael Louis Maude
1923-1983 Obituary 110
Chavchavadze, Paul 1899-1971 .... CAP-2
Obituary 29-32R
Earlier sketch in CA 25-28
Chavel, Charles Ber 1906- CANR-4
Earlier sketch in CA 49-52
Chaves, Jonathan 1943- CANR-9
Earlier sketch in CA 65-68
Chavez, Angelico 1910- 93-96
Chavez, John R(ichard) 1949- 118
Chavez, Patricia 1934- 103
Chaviaras, Strates 1935- 105
Chayefsky, Paddy
See Chayefsky, Sidney
See also DLB 7, 44
See also DLBY 81
See also CLC 23
Chayefsky, Sidney 1923-1981 .... CANR-18
Obituary 104
Earlier sketch in CA 11-12R
Chayes, Abram 1922- CANR-14
Earlier sketch in CA 65-68
Chaytor, Lee
See Chater, Elizabeth (Eileen)
Chazanof, William 1915- 33-36R
Chaze, (Lewis) Elliott 1915- 113
Cheape, Charles Windsor 1945- 105
Cheatham, K(aryn) Follis 1943- 81-84
Cheavens, (Sam) Frank 1905- 33-36R
Cheavens, Martha Louise (Schuck)
1898-1975 Obituary 57-60
Check, Otto Premier
See Berman, Ed
Check, William A. 1943- 118
Checkland, S(ydney) G(eorge)
1916-1986 ....17-18R
Obituary 118
Chedid, Andree 1920- CLC-47
Cheech
See Marin, Richard Anthony
Cheek, Frances Edith 1923- 41-44R
Cheeks, James E. 1930- 124
Cheesman, Paul R. 1921- CANR-1
Earlier sketch in CA 49-52
Cheetham, Erika 1939- 109
Cheetham, Hal
See Cheetham, J(ames) H(arold)
Cheetham, J(ames) H(arold) 1921- 108
Cheetham, Nicholas (John Alexander)
1910- CANR-15
Earlier sketch in CA 81-84
Cheever, Ezekiel 1615-1708 .... DLB-24
Cheever, George Barrell 1807-1890 ..... DLB-59
Cheever, John 1912-1982 .... CANR-5
Obituary 106
Earlier sketch in CA 7-8R
See also CABS 1
See also DLB 2
See also DLBY 80, 82
See also CDALB 1941-1968
See also CLC 3, 7, 8, 11, 15, 25
See also SSC 1
Cheever, Susan 1943- 103
See also DLBY 82
See also CLC 18
Cheffins, Ronald I. 1930- 45-48
Cheifetz, Dan 1926- 69-72
Cheifetz, Philip M(orris) 1944- 53-56
Chein, Isidor 1912- Brief entry 105
Chejne, Anwar G(eorge) 1923-1983 .... CANR-18
Earlier sketch in CA 25-28R
Chekenian, Aram Haigaz 1900-1986
Obituary 119
Chekenian, Jane
See Gerard, Jane
Chekhonte, Antosha
See Chekhov, Anton (Pavlovich)
Chekhov, Anton (Pavlovich) 1860-1904 124
Brief entry 104
See also TCLC 3, 10
Chekhova, Olga 1897-1980 Obituary 97-100
Chekki, Dan(esh) A(yyappa) 1935- CANR-23
Earlier sketches in CA 61-64, CANR-7
Cheldelin, Larry V(ernon) 1945- 116
Chelf, Carl P. 1937- 37-40R
Chelius, James R(obert) 1943- 115
Chellis, Marcia 1940- 121
Chelminski, Rudolph 1934- 93-96
Chelton, John
See Durst, Paul
Chelwood, Tufton Victor Hamilton 1917- ...65-68
Chen, Anthony 1929- CANR-14
Earlier sketch in CA 37-40R
See also SATA 6
Chen, Ching-chih 1937- CANR-22
Earlier sketch in CA 106
Ch'En, Chi-yun 1933- 108
Chen, Chung-Hwan 1906- 45-48
Chen, Edwin (Hung-teh) 1934- Brief entry .. 116
Chen, Jack 1908- CANR-15
Earlier sketch in CA 41-44R
Chen, Janey 1922- 73-76
Ch'en, Jerome 1921- CANR-9
Earlier sketch in CA 15-16R
Chen, Joseph Tao 1925- 37-40R
Chen, Kan 1928- 49-52
Chen, Kenneth K(uan-) S(heng) 1907- 19-20R
Chen, King C(hing) 1926- CANR-4
Earlier sketch in CA 53-56
Chen, Kuan I. 1926- 41-44R
Chen, Lincoln C(hih-ho) 1942- 49-52
Chen, Nai-Ruenn 1927- CANR-9
Earlier sketch in CA 23-24R
Chen, Philip S(tanley) 1903-1978 ...... CANR-5
Earlier sketch in CA 9-10R
Chen, Samuel Shih-Tsai 1915- 41-44R
Chen, Theodore Hsi-En 1902- CANR-17
Earlier sketches in CA 2R, CANR-1
Chen, Tony
See Chen, Anthony
Chen, Vincent 1917- 37-40R
Chen, Yuan-tsung 1932- 106
Chenault, Lawrence R(oyce) 1897- CAP-2
Earlier sketch in CA 17-18
Chenault, Nell
See Smith, Linell Nash
Chenery, Hollis Burnley 1918- 111
Chenery, Janet (Dai) 1923- 103
See also SATA 25
Chenery, William Ludlow 1884-1974 97-100
Obituary 53-56
Chenevix Trench, Charles Pocklington
1914- 9-10R
Cheney, Anne 1944- 61-64
Cheney, Brainard (Bartwell) 1900- CAP-2
Earlier sketch in CA 25-28
Cheney, C. R.
See Cheney, Christopher Robert
Cheney, Christopher Robert 1906-1987
Obituary 123
Cheney, Cora 1916- CANR-4
Earlier sketch in CA 3R
See also SATA 3
Cheney, Ednah Dow (Littlehale)
1824-1904 .... DLB-1
Cheney, Frances Neel 1906- 33-36R
Cheney, Glenn Alan 1951- 109
Cheney, Jean E. 1921- 118
Cheney, Lois A. 1931- 29-32R
Cheney, Lynne 1941- 89-92
Cheney, Margaret 1921- 101
Cheney, Richard B(ruce) 1941- 113
Cheney, Robert S(impson) 1922- 118
Cheney, Roberta Carkeek 1912- 73-76
Cheney, Ruth G(ordon) 1908- 113
Cheney, Sheldon Warren 1886-1980
Obituary 102
Cheney, Ted
See Cheney, Theodore Albert
Cheney, Theodore A. Rees
See Cheney, Theodore Albert
Cheney, Theodore Albert 1928- CANR-23
Earlier sketches in CA 61-64, CANR-8
See also SATA 11
Cheney, Thomas E. 1901- 41-44R
Cheney-Coker, Syl 1945- 101
Cheng, Chu-yuan 1927- CANR-20
Earlier sketches in CA 15-16R, CANR-5
Cheng, F.T.
See Cheng, Tien-hsi

INDEX

Cheng, Hang-Sheng 1927- 69-72
Cheng, Hou-Tien 1944- 69-72
Cheng, J(ames) Chester 1926- 9-10R
Cheng, James K(uo) C(hiang) 1936- 25-28R
Cheng, Judith 1955- SATA-36
Cheng, Ronald Ye-lin 1933- 41-44R
Cheng, Tien-hsi 1884-1970 Obituary 104
Cheng, Yi
See Cheng, James K(uo) C(hiang)
Cheng, Ying-wan 41-44R
Chen Hwei
See Stevenson, William
Chen Jo-hsi
See Tuann, Lucy H(siu-mei Chen)
Chennault, Anna (Chan) 1925- 61-64
Chennells, Roy D. 1912(?)-1981 Obituary .. 105
Chenneviere, Daniel
See Rudhyar, Dane
Chenoweth, Vida S. 1928- CANR-11
Earlier sketch in CA 25-28R
Cheraskin, Emanuel 1916- 53-56
Cherim, Stanley M(arshall) 1929- 53-56
Cherington, Paul Whiton 1918-1974 .... CANR-6
Obituary 53-56
Earlier sketch in CA 4R
Chermayeff, Ivan 1932- 97-100
See also SATA 47
Chermayeff, Serge 1900- 21-22R
Chernaik, Judith 1934- CANR-11
Earlier sketch in CA 61-64
Chernenko, Konstantin Ustinovich
1911-1985 Obituary 115
Cherner, Anne 1954- 109
Chernev, Irving 1900-1981 Obituary 105
Cherniavsky, Michael 1923(?)-1973
Obituary 41-44R
Chernik, Barbara E(ileen) 1938- 117
Chernin, Kim 1940- 107
Cherniss, Harold
See Cherniss, Harold Fredrik
Cherniss, Harold Fredrik 1904-1987 93-96
Obituary 123
Cherniss, Michael D(avid) 1940- 37-40R
Cherniss, Norman A(rnold) 1926-1984 122
Obituary 114
Chernoff, Dorothy A.
See Ernst, (Lyman) John
Chernoff, Goldie Taub 1909- 33-36R
See also SATA 10
Chernoff, John Miller 1947- 105
Chernofsky, Jacob L. 1928- 73-76
Chernow, Burt 1933- 110
Chernow, Carol 1934- 57-60
Chernow, Fred B. 1932- 57-60
Chernowitz, Maurice E. 1909-1977
Obituary 73-76
Cherns, Albert
See Cherns, Albert B(ernard)
Cherns, Albert B(ernard) 1921-1987
Obituary 122
Cherrington, Ernest H(urst), Jr. 1909- 33-36R
Cherrington, John 1909- 116
Cherrington, Leon G. 1926- 33-36R
Cherry, C. Conrad 1937- CANR-11
Earlier sketch in CA 23-24R
Cherry, Caroline L(ockett) 1942- 57-60
Cherry, Carolyn Janice 1942- CANR-10
Earlier sketch in CA 65-68
Cherry, Charles L(ester) 1942- 57-60
Cherry, (Edward) Colin 1914-1979 .... CANR-12
Obituary 93-96
Earlier sketch in CA 69-72
Cherry, George Loy 1905- 5-6R
Cherry, Kelly CANR-3
Earlier sketch in CA 49-52
See also DLBY 83
See also AITN 1
Cherry, Lynne 1952- SATA-34
Cherry, Sheldon H(arold) 1934- 49-52
Cherryh, C. J.
See Cherry, Carolyn Janice
See also DLBY 80
See also CLC 35
Cherryholmes, Anne
See Price, Olive
Chervin, Ronda 1937- CANR-21
Earlier sketches in CA 57-60, CANR-6
Cherwinski, Joseph 1915- CANR-5
Earlier sketch in CA 15-16R
Chesbro, George C(lark) 1940- 77-80
Chesebro, James William 1944- 108
Chesen, Eli S. 1944- 37-40R
Chesham, Henry
See Bingley, David Ernest
Chesham, Sallie 29-32R
Chesher, Kim 1955- CANR-19
Earlier sketch in CA 102
Chesher, Richard (Harvey) 1940- 106
Cheshire, David 1944- 97-100
Cheshire, Geoffrey Leonard 1917- CAP-1
Earlier sketch in CA 13-14
Cheshire, Herbert 1925(?)-1985 Obituary ... 118
Cheshire, Maxine 1930- 108
Cheskin, Louis 1909-1981 .... CANR-5
Obituary 105
Earlier sketch in CA 5-6R
Chesler, Bernice 1932- CANR-16
Earlier sketch in CA 25-28R
Chesler, Phyllis 1940- CANR-4
Earlier sketch in CA 49-52
Cheslock, Louis 1898- CAP-1
Earlier sketch in CA 11-12
Chesney, Inga L. 1928- 45-48
Chesney, Kellow (Robert) 1914- 29-32R
Chesney, Marion 1936- 115
Brief entry 111
Chesney, Weatherby
See Hyne, C(harles) J(ohn) Cutcliffe
(Wright)
Chesnoff, Richard Z(eltner) 1937- CANR-10
Earlier sketch in CA 25-28R
Chesnut, J(ames) Stanley 1926- 23-24R
Chesnutt, Charles Waddell 1858-1932
Brief entry 106
See also DLB 12, 50
See also TCLC 5
Chesnutt, David R(ogers) 1940- 122
Chess, Stella 1914- 85-88
Chess, Victoria 1939- 107
See also SATA 33
Chessare, Michele SATA-42
Chesser, Eustace 1902-1973 .... CANR-4
Obituary 45-48
Earlier sketch in CA 9-10R
Chessex, Jacques 1934- 65-68
Chessman, Caryl (Whittier) 1921-1960 73-76
Chessman, G(eorge) Wallace 1919- 15-16R
Chessman, Ruth (Green) 1910- CAP-2
Earlier sketch in CA 17-18
Chester, Alfred 1929(?)-1971 Obituary ... 33-36R
Chester, Allan Griffith 1900-1976 Obituary .. 111
Chester, Deborah 1957- CANR-18
Earlier sketch in CA 102
Chester, Edward W(illiam) 1935- CANR-13
Earlier sketch in CA 23-24R
Chester, Laura 1949- CANR-9
Earlier sketch in CA 65-68
Chester, Michael (Arthur) 1928- CANR-1
Earlier sketch in CA 3R
Chester, (Daniel) Norman 1907-1986 109
Obituary 120
Chester, Peter
See Phillips, D(ennis) J(ohn Andrew)
Chesterman, Charles W(esley) 1913- 107
Chesterman, Clement (Clapton)
1894-1983 Obituary 110
Chesterson, Denise
See Robins, Denise (Naomi)
Chesterton, A(rthur) K(enneth) 1899- CAP-1
Earlier sketch in CA 11-12
Chesterton, G(ilbert) K(eith) 1874-1936
Brief entry 104
See also SATA 27
See also DLB 10, 19, 34
See also TCLC 1, 6
See also SSC 1
Chestor, Rui
See Courtier, S(idney) H(obson)
Chetham-Strode, Warren 1896- CAP-1
Earlier sketch in CA 13-14
Chethimattam, John B(ritto) 1922- 25-28R
Chetin, Helen 1922- CANR-12
Earlier sketch in CA 29-32R
See also SATA 6
Chetwin, Grace 123
See also SATA 50
Chetwode, Penelope 1910-1986 102
Obituary 119
Chetwynd, Berry
See Rayner, Claire (Berenice)
Chetwynd, Tom 1938- 45-48
Chetwynd-Hayes, R(onald Henry Glynn)
1919- CANR-12
Earlier sketch in CA 61-64
Chetwynd-Talbot, Edward Hugh Frederick
1909- 116
Cheung, Steven N(g-) S(heong) 1935- ... 25-28R
Cheuse, Alan 1940- 49-52
Chevalier, Christa 1937- CANR-24
Earlier sketch in CA 107
See also SATA 35
Chevalier, Elizabeth (Pickett) 1896-1984
Obituary 111
Chevalier, Haakon (Maurice) 1901-1985 ... 61-64
Obituary 116
Chevalier, Louis 1911- 85-88
Chevalier, Maurice 1888-1972 Obituary ... 33-36R
Chevalier, Paul Eugene George 1925- 106
Chevallier, Gabriel 1895-1969 Obituary 113
Chevallier, Raymond 1929- 103
Chevigny, Bell Gale 1936- 57-60
Chevigny, Paul G. 1935- 97-100
Cheville, Roy A(rthur) 1897- 97-100
Chew, Allen F. 1924- 33-36R
Chew, Peter 1924- 57-60
Chew, Ruth 1920- CANR-14
Earlier sketch in CA 41-44R
See also SATA 7
Cheyette, Irving 1904- CANR-22
Earlier sketch in CA 69-72
Cheyney, Arnold B. 1926- CANR-23
Earlier sketches in CA 23-24R, CANR-8
Cheyney, Edward P. 1861-1947 .... DLB-47
Cheyney, (Reginald Evelyn) Peter
(Southouse) 1896-1951 Brief entry 113
Chi, Madeleine 1930- CANR-11
Earlier sketch in CA 69-72
Chi, Richard Hu See-Yee 1918- 37-40R
Chi, Wen-shun 1910- 13-14R
Chiang Kai-shek 1886(?)-1975 Obituary 112
Chiang Pin-chin 1904-1986 Obituary 118
Chiang Yee 1903-1977 .... CANR-15
Obituary 73-76
Earlier sketch in CA 65-68
Chiara, Piero 1913-1986 .... CANR-8
Obituary 121
Earlier sketch in CA 53-56
Chiarenza, Carl 1935- 109
Chiari, Joseph 1911- CANR-4
Earlier sketch in CA 7-8R
Chiaromonte, Nicola ?-1972 Obituary 104
Chiba, Atsuko 1941(?)-1987 Obituary 123
Chibnall, Marjorie (McCallum) 1915- 29-32R
Chicago, Judy 1939- CANR-21
Earlier sketch in CA 85-88
Chichester, Francis (Charles) 1901-1972 .. CAP-1
Obituary 37-40R
Earlier sketch in CA 13-14
Chichester, Jane
See Longrigg, Jane Chichester
Chick, Edson M(arland) 1924- 23-24R
Chickering, Arthur W. 1927- 29-32R
Chickering, Roger (Philip) 1942- 73-76
Chickos, James Speros 1941- 49-52
Chicorel, Marietta 85-88
Chidsey, Donald Barr 1902-1981 .... CANR-2
Obituary 103
Earlier sketch in CA 5-6R
See also SATA 3, 27
Chidzero, Bernard Thomas Gibson 1927- 3R
Chief Standing Bear
See Standing Bear, Luther
Chieger, Bob 1945- 114
Chielens, Edward E(rnest) 1943- 53-56
Ch'ien, Ts'un-hsun
See Tsien, Tsuen-hsuin
Ch'ien Chung-shu 1910- CLC-22
Chiesa, Francesco 1871(?)-1973 Obituary .. 104
Chignon, Niles
See Lingeman, Richard R(oberts)
Chigounis, Evans 1931- 45-48
Chilcote, Ronald H. 1935- CANR-24
Earlier sketches in CA 21-22R, CANR-8
Chilcott, John H(enry) 1924- 41-44R
Child, Alan
See Langner, Lawrence
Child, Francis James 1825-1896 .... DLB-1, 64
Child, Heather 1912- 11-12R
Child, Irvin L(ong) 1915- 41-44R
Child, John 1922- 93-96
Child, Julia 1912- CANR-19
Earlier sketch in CA 41-44R
Child, Kenneth 1916-1983 Obituary 111
Child, Lydia Maria 1802-1880 .... DLB-1
Child, Philip 1898-1978 .... CAP-1
Earlier sketch in CA 13-14
See also SATA 47
See also CLC 19
Child, Roderick 1949- 25-28R
Childers, (Robert) Erskine 1870-1922
Brief entry 113
Childers, Thomas (Allen) 1940- 37-40R
Childress, Alice 1920- CANR-3
Earlier sketch in CA 45-48
See also SATA 7, 48
See also DLB 7, 38
See also CLC 12, 15
See also CLR 14
Childress, James Franklin 1940- CANR-11
Earlier sketch in CA 65-68
Childress, William 1933- 41-44R
Childs, Barney 1926- 23-24R
Childs, Brevard S(prings) 1923-
Brief entry 117
Childs, C. Sand
See Childs, Maryanna
Childs, David (Haslam) 1933- CANR-14
Earlier sketch in CA 37-40R
Childs, George W. 1829-1894 .... DLB-23
Childs, H(alla) Fay (Cochrane)
1890-1971 .... CAP-1
Earlier sketch in CA 15-16
See also SATA 1, 25
Childs, Harwood Lawrence 1898-1972 ... CAP-2
Obituary 37-40R
Earlier sketch in CA 25-28
Childs, J(ames) Rives 1893-1987
Obituary 123
Childs, James Bennett 1896-1977
Obituary 73-76
Childs, Marilyn Grace Carlson 1923- 9-10R
Childs, Marquis W(illiam) 1903- CANR-12
Earlier sketch in CA 61-64
Childs, Maryanna 1910- 9-10R
Childs, Timothy 1941- 97-100
Childs, W(illiam) H(arold) J(oseph)
1905(?)-1983 Obituary 109
Chiles, Robert E(ugene) 1923- 17-18R
Chiles, Webb 1941- 108
Chill, Dan S(amuel) 1945- 69-72
Chilman, Catherine (Earles) S(treet) 1914- .. 121
Chilson, Richard William 1943- CANR-6
Earlier sketch in CA 57-60
Chilson, Robert 1945- 69-72
Chilton, Irma 1930- CANR-19
Earlier sketch in CA 103
Chilton, John (James) 1932- CANR-8
Earlier sketch in CA 61-64
Chilton, Lance 1944- 123
Chilton, Shirley R(ay) 1923- 77-80
Chilver, Guy (Edward Farquhar)
1910-1982 109
Obituary 107
Chilver, Peter 1933- CANR-17
Earlier sketch in CA 25-28R
Chimaera
See Farjeon, Eleanor
Chin, Chuan
See Chi, Richard Hu See-Yee
Chin, Frank (Chew, Jr.) 1940- 33-36R
Chin, Richard (M.) 1946- 121
Chin, Robert 1918- 61-64
Chinard, Gilbert 1882(?)-1972 Obituary 104
Chinas, Beverly N(ewbold) 1924- 89-92
Chinery, Michael 1938- CANR-20
Earlier sketch in CA 103
See also SATA 26
Ching, James C(hristopher) 1926- 37-40R
Ching, Julia (Chia-yi) 1934- 101
Chinitz, Benjamin 1924- 9-10R
Chinmoy, Sri 1931- CANR-2
Earlier sketch in CA 49-52
Chinn, Laurene Chambers 1902-1978 .... 2R
Obituary 103
Chinn, Robert (Edward) 1928- 69-72
Chinn, William G. 1919- 33-36R
Chinoy, Ely 1921-1975 .... CANR-1
Obituary 57-60
Earlier sketch in CA 3R
Chinoy, Helen Krich 1922- 17-18R
Chinweizu 1943- 103
Chipasula, Frank (Mkalawile) 1949- 121
Chipman, Bruce L(ewis) 1946- 37-40R
Chipman, Donald E(ugene) 1928- 29-32R
Chipman, John S(omerset) 1926- 104
Chipp, D(onald) L(eslie) 1925- 108
Chipp, Herschel B(rowning) 1913- 25-28R
Chipperfield, Joseph Eugene
1912-1980(?) CANR-6
Earlier sketch in CA 9-10R
See also SATA 2
Chirenje, J. Mutero 1935- 65-68
Chirovsky, Nicholas L. 1919- CANR-4
Earlier sketch in CA 53-56
Chisholm, A(rthur) M(urray) 1872-1960
Obituary 114
Chisholm, A(lan) R(owland) 1888- 7-8R
Chisholm, Anne 109
Chisholm, Hugh J., Jr. 1913-1972
Obituary 37-40R
Chisholm, K. Lomneth 1919- 61-64
Chisholm, Mary K(athleen) 1924- 37-40R
Chisholm, Matt
See Watts, Peter Christopher
Chisholm, Michael (Donald Inglis)
1931- 37-40R
Chisholm, R(obert) F(erguson) 1904- CAP-2
Earlier sketch in CA 29-32
Chisholm, Roderick Milton 1916- 102
Chisholm, Roger K. 1937- 33-36R
Chisholm, Sam(uel) Whitten 1919- 5-6R
Chisholm, Shirley (Anita St. Hill) 1924- ... 29-32R
Chisholm, William S(herman), Jr. 1931- ... 49-52
Chishti, Hakim M.
See Thomson, Robert
Chislett, (Margaret) Anne 1943- CLC-34
Chisolm, Lawrence W(ashington) 1929- .. 11-12R
Chissell, Joan Olive 61-64
Chitham, Edward (Harry Gordon)
1932- CANR-19
Earlier sketch in CA 103
Chitnis, Anand C. 1942- 123
Chitrabhanu, Gurudev Shree 1922- 89-92
Chittenden, Elizabeth F. 1903- 61-64
See also SATA 9
Chittenden, Hiram Martin 1858-1917 .... DLB-47
Chittenden, Margaret 1935- CANR-19
Earlier sketches in CA 53-56, CANR-4
See also SATA 28
Chittick, Donald Ernest 1932- 115
Chittick, William O(liver) 1937- 41-44R
Chittum, Ida 1918- CANR-14
Earlier sketch in CA 37-40R
See also SATA 7
Chitty, Arthur Benjamin 1914- CANR-20
Earlier sketches in CA 53-56, CANR-4
Chitty, Letitia 1897-1982 Obituary 108
Chitty, Susan Elspeth 1929- CAP-1
Earlier sketch in CA 9-10
Chitty, Thomas Willes 1926- 7-8R
See also CLC 11
Chitwood, B(illy) J(ames) 1931- 97-100
Chitwood, Marie Downs 1918- 9-10R
Chitwood, Oliver Perry 1874-1971 .... CAP-1
Earlier sketch in CA 13-14
Chiu, Hong-Yee 1932- 53-56
Chiu, Hungdah 1936- CANR-14
Earlier sketch in CA 37-40R
Chivers, Thomas Holley 1809-1858 .... DLB-3
Chi-wei
See Shu, Austin Chi-wei
Chlamyda, Jehudil
See Peshkov, Alexei Maximovich
Chloros, A(lexander) G(eorge) 1926-1982
Obituary 108
Chloros, Aleck George
See Chloros, A(lexander) G(eorge)
Chmaj, Betty E. 1930- 97-100
Chmielarz, Sharon 1940- 121
Chmielewski, Edward 1928- 13-14R
Ch'o, Chou
See Shu-Jen, Chou
Cho, Yong Hyo 1934- Brief entry 105
Cho, Yong Sam 1925- 5-6R
Choate, Ernest A(lfred) 1900- 49-52
Choate, Gwen Peterson 1922- 3R
Choate, J(ulian) E(rnest, Jr.) 1916- 33-36R
Choate, Judith (Newkirk) 1940- 105
See also SATA 30
Choate, R. G.
See Choate, Gwen Peterson
Chobanian, Aram V(an) 1929- 108
Chochlik
See Radwanski, Pierre A(rthur)
Chodes, John 1939- CANR-9
Earlier sketch in CA 61-64
Chodorov, Edward 1904- 102
Chodorov, Jerome 1911- CANR-15
Earlier sketch in CA 65-68
Chodorov, Stephan 1934- 17-18R
Chodorow, Nancy (Julia) 1944- 105
Chogyam Trungpa 1939-1987 .... CANR-12
Obituary 122
Earlier sketch in CA 25-28R
Choi Sunu 1916-1984 Obituary 115
Choldin, Marianna Tax 1942- 109

Choleric, Brother
See van Zeller, Claud
Chomette, Rene Lucien 1898-1981
Obituary 103
See also CLC 20
Chommie, John C(ampbell) 1914-1974 ... CAP-2
Earlier sketch in CA 29-32
Chomsky, A(vram) Noam 1928- 17-18R
Chomsky, William 1896-1977 77-80
Obituary 73-76
Chong
See Chong, Thomas
Chong, Kyona-Jo
See Chung, Kyuna Cho
Chong, Peng-Khuan 25-28R
Chong, Thomas 1938- Brief entry 112
Chong, Tommy
See Chong, Thomas
Choper, Jesse H(erbert) 1935- CANR-5
Earlier sketch in CA 15-16R
Chopin, Kate
See Chopin, Katherine
See also DLB 12
See also TCLC 5, 14
Chopin, Katherine 1851-1904 122
Brief entry 104
Chorafas, Dimitris N. 1926- CANR-20
Earlier sketches in CA 7-8R, CANR-4
Chorao, (Ann Mc)Kay (Sproat) 1936- .. CANR-19
Earlier sketches in CA 49-52, CANR-1
See also SATA 8
Chorell, Walentin 1912-1984(?) Obituary ... 111
Chorley, Katharine Campbell (Hopkinson)
1897-1986 Obituary 120
Chorley, R. J.
See Chorley, Richard John
Chorley, Richard J(ohn) 1927- 121
Chorley, Richard J.
See Chorley, Richard John
Chorley, Richard John 1927- Brief entry 116
Chorny, Merron 1922- 41-44R
Choron, Jacques 1904-1972 .... CAP-1
Obituary 33-36R
Earlier sketch in CA 9-10
Chorpenning, Charlotte (Lee Barrows)
1872-1955 Brief entry 114
See also SATA 37
Chothia, Jean 1944- 105
Chotzinoff, Samuel 1889-1964 Obituary ... 93-96
Chou, Ya-luu 1924- 41-44R
Choucri, Nazli 1943- CANR-14
Earlier sketch in CA 81-84
Choudhury, G(olam) W(ahed) 1926- ... CANR-17
Earlier sketch in CA 25-28R
Chou En-lai 1898-1976 Obituary 112
Choukas, Michael (Eugene) 1901- CAP-2
Earlier sketch in CA 17-18
Choukas-Bradley, Melanie (Rose) 1952- 124
Chouraqui, Andre (Nathanael) 1917- ... CANR-10
Earlier sketch in CA 65-68
Chow, Gregory C. 1929- 13-14R
Chow, Yung-Teh 1916- 37-40R
Chowder, Ken 1950- 102
Chowdhary, Savitri Devi (Dumra) 1907- .. CAP-1
Earlier sketch in CA 11-12
Chowning, Larry S(hepherd) 1949- 111
Choy, Bong-youn 1914- 69-72
Chrimes, Stanley Bertram 1907-1984 ......7-8R
Obituary 113
Chrislock, Carl H(endrick) 1917- 45-48
Chrisman, Arthur Bowie 1889-1953 ..... YABC-1
Chrisman, Harry E. 1906- 4R
Chrisman, Katherine (G.) 1940(?)-1987
Obituary 122
Christ, Carl F(inley) 1923- 21-22R
Christ, Carol T(ecla) 1944- 93-96
Christ, Henry I(rvine) 1915- CANR-2
Earlier sketch in CA 7-8R
Christ, John M(ichael) 1934- 106
Christ, Karl 1923- 120
Christ, Ronald 1936- CANR-10
Earlier sketch in CA 25-28R
Christaller, Walter 1893-1969 Obituary 115
Christelow, Eileen 1943- 111
See also SATA 35, 38
Christen, Robert J. 1928-1981 Obituary 108
Brief entry 107
Christensen, Ann 1946- 108
Christensen, Anna
See Mayer, Deborah Anne
Christensen, Clyde M. 1905- 53-56
Christensen, David E(mun) 1921- 15-16R
Christensen, Edward L. 1913- 25-28R
Christensen, Eleanor Ingalls 1913- 53-56
Christensen, Erwin O(ttomar) 1890- CAP-1
Earlier sketch in CA 13-14
Christensen, Francis 1902-19(?) CAP-2
Earlier sketch in CA 23-24
Christensen, Gardell Dano 1907- 9-10R
See also SATA 1
Christensen, Harold T(aylor) 1909- 45-48
Christensen, J(ack) A(rden) 1927- 53-56
Christensen, James L(ee) 1922- 97-100
Christensen, Jerome 1948- 110
Christensen, Jo Ippolito
See Christensen, Yolanda Maria Ippolito
Christensen, Otto H(enry) 1898- 33-36R
Christensen, Paul 1943- CANR-15
Earlier sketch in CA 77-80
Christensen, Sandra 1944- 110
Christensen, Yolanda Maria Ippolito
1943- CANR-7
Earlier sketch in CA 57-60
Christenson, Cornelia V(os) 1903- CAP-2
Earlier sketch in CA 33-36
Christenson, Evelyn (Carol) 1922- 117
Christenson, Larry 1928- CANR-8
Earlier sketch in CA 57-60
Christenson, Nordis 1929- 108
Christenson, Reo M. 1918- 37-40R
Christesen, Barbara 1940- 107
See also SATA 40
Christesen, Clement Byrne 1911- 102
Christgau, Alice Erickson 1902- CAP-2
Earlier sketch in CA 17-18
See also SATA 13
Christgau, John (Frederick) 1934- 103
Christgau, Robert (Thomas) 1942- 65-68
Christian, A. B.
See Yabes, Leopoldo Y(abes)
Christian, Barbara T. 1943- 110
Christian, C(urtis) W(allace) 1927- 21-22R
Christian, Carol (Cathay) 1923- 53-56
Christian, Frederick
See Gehman, Richard (Boyd)
Christian, Garth Hood 1921-1967 .... CAP-1
Earlier sketch in CA 9-10
Christian, George (Eastland) 1927- 65-68
Christian, Glynn 1942- 115
Christian, Henry A(rthur) 1931- CANR-14
Earlier sketch in CA 33-36R
Christian, James L(ee) 1927- 57-60
Christian, Jill
See Dilcock, Noreen
Christian, John
See Dixon, Roger
Christian, Louise
See Grill, Nannette L.
Christian, Marcus Bruce 1900- 73-76
Christian, Mary Blount 1933- CANR-17
Earlier sketches in CA 45-48, CANR-1
See also SATA 9
Christian, Peter
See Steinbrunner, (Peter) Chris(tian)
Christian, Portia 1908- 103
Christian, Rebecca 1952- 107
Christian, Reginald Frank 1924- CANR-3
Earlier sketch in CA 5-6R
Christian, Roy Cloberry 1914- 93-96
Christian, Shirley (Ann) 1938- Brief entry ... 119
Christian, William A(rmistead), Jr. 1944- ... 107
Christiani, Dounia Bunis 1913- 15-16R
Christians, Clifford Glenn 1939- 104
Christiansen, Arthur 1904-1963 .... 2R
Christiansen, Eugene Martin 1944- 121
Christiansen, Harley Duane 1930- CANR-4
Earlier sketch in CA 53-56
Christiansen, Keith 1947- 112
Christiansen, Michael Robin 1927-1984
Obituary 113
Christiansen, Richard (Dean) 1931- 121
Christianson, Elin B(allantyne) 1936- 111
Christianson, Gale E. 1942- 81-84
Christianson, John Robert 1934- 23-24R
Christie
See Ichikawa, Kon
Christie, Agatha (Mary Clarissa)
1890-1976 .... CANR-10
Obituary 61-64
Earlier sketch in CA 19-20R
See also SATA 36
See also DLB 13
See also CLC 1, 6, 8, 12, 39
See also AITN 1, 2
Christie, George C(ustis) 1934- 37-40R
Christie, Hugh
See Christie-Murray, David (Hugh Arthur)
Christie, Ian R(alph) 1919- CANR-20
Earlier sketches in CA 7-8R, CANR-2
Christie, Jean 1912- 101
Christie, John Aldrich 1920- 65-68
Christie, Keith
See Haynes, Alfred H(enry)
Christie, Lindsay H. 1906(?)-1976
Obituary 61-64
Christie, Milton 1921- 17-18R
Christie, (Ann) Philippa CANR-4
Earlier sketch in CA 7-8R
Christie, Trevor L. 1905-1969 .... CAP-2
Earlier sketch in CA 21-22
Christie-Murray, David (Hugh Arthur)
1913- CANR-4
Earlier sketch in CA 53-56
Christine, Charles T(hornton) 1936- 33-36R
Christine, Dorothy Weaver 1934- 33-36R
Christ-Janer, Albert W. 1910-1973 ..... CANR-4
Obituary 45-48
Earlier sketch in CA 1R
Christman, Don(ald) R. 1919- 17-18R
Christman, Elizabeth 1914- 89-92
Christman, Henry 1906-1980 Obituary 103
Christman, Henry Max 1932- 65-68
Christman, Luther (Parmalee) 1915- 124
Christman, R(aymond) J(ohn) 1919- 89-92
Christmas, Joyce 1939- 123
Christodoulou, Anastasios 1932- 120
Christoff, Peter K. 1911- 121
Christol, Carl Quimby 1914- CANR-4
Earlier sketch in CA 5-6R
Christoph, James B(ernard) 1928- CANR-4
Earlier sketch in CA 5-6R
Christopher, Beth
See Steinke, Ann (Elizabeth)
Christopher, Georgia B. 1932- 111
Christopher, Joe R(andell) 1935- CANR-4
Earlier sketch in CA 53-56
Christopher, John
See Youd, Samuel
See also CLR 2
Christopher, John B. 1914- 13-14R
Christopher, Kenneth
See Brophy, Donald F(rancis)
Christopher, Louise
See Hale, Arlene
Christopher, Matt(hew F.) 1917- CANR-5
Earlier sketch in CA 2R
See also SATA 2, 47
Christopher, Maurine (Brooks) 65-68
Christopher, Milbourne 1914(?)-1984 105
Obituary 113
See also SATA 46
Christopher, Nicholas 1951- 108
Christopher, Robert Collins 1924- 102
Christophersen, Paul (Hans) 1911- 57-60
Christowe, Stoyan 1898- 65-68
Christy, Betty 1924- 57-60
Christy, George 11-12R
Christy, Howard Chandler 1873-1952 .. SATA-21
Christy, Joe
See Christy, Joseph M.
Christy, Joseph M. 1919- CANR-14
Earlier sketch in CA 29-32R
Christy, Marian 1932- 65-68
Christy, Teresa E(lizabeth) 1927- 73-76
Chroman, Eleanor 1937- 45-48
Chroman, Nathan 1929- 77-80
Chronic, Halka (Pattison) 1923- 118
Chroust, Anton-Hermann 1907- CAP-1
Earlier sketch in CA 9-10
Chruden, Herbert J(efferson) 1918- 5-6R
Chu, Arthur (T. S.) 1916- 81-84
Chu, Daniel 1933- 15-16R
See also SATA 11
Chu, Godwin C(hien) 1927- 114
Chu, Grace (Goodyear) 1916- 81-84
Chu, Grace Zia 1899- CANR-4
Earlier sketch in CA 5-6R
Chu, Kong 1926- 49-52
Chu, Louis H. 1915- 15-16R
Chu, Samuel C. 1929- 69-72
Ch'u, Tung-tsu 1910- CANR-2
Earlier sketch in CA 1R
Chu, Valentin (Yuan-ling) 1919- 9-10R
Chu, W. R.
See Chu, Arthur (T. S.)
Chubb, Elmer
See Masters, Edgar Lee
Chubb, Judith (Ann) 1947- 113
Chubb, Thomas Caldecot 1899-1972 .... CANR-6
Obituary 33-36R
Earlier sketch in CA 2R
Chubin, Barry 1943- 124
Chudacoff, Howard P(eter) 1943- 45-48
Chudley, Ron(ald Alexander) 1937- 110
Chuikov, Vasili Ivanovich 1900-1982
Obituary 106
Chukovskaya, Lydia (Korneeva) 1907-
Brief entry 117
Chukovsky, Kornei (Ivanovich)
1882-1969 .... CANR-4
Obituary 25-28R
Earlier sketch in CA 7-8R
See also SATA 5, 34
Chulak, Armando ?-1975 Obituary 109
Chuman, Frank Fujio 1917- 69-72
Chun, Jinsie K(yung) S(hien) 1902- 49-52
Chun, Richard 1935- 65-68
Chung, Connie
See Chung, Constance Yu-Hwa
Chung, Constance Yu-Hwa 1946-
Brief entry 119
Chung, Edward K(oo-Young) 1931- 107
Chung, Hyung C(han) 1931- 57-60
Chung, Joseph Sang-hoon 1929- 49-52
Chung, Kyung Cho 1921- 33-36R
Chung-yu, Chu
See Hsu, Benedict (Pei-Hsiung)
Chunn, Jay Carrington II 1938- 116
Chupack, Henry 1915- 49-52
Church, Albert M(arion) 1940- 111
Church, Benjamin 1734-1778 .... DLB-31
Church, Jeffrey
See Kirk, Richard (Edmund)
Church, Joseph 1918- 1R
Church, Margaret 1920- 15-16R
Church, Peter
See Nuttall, Jeff
Church, Ralph (Bruce) 1927- 37-40R
Church, Richard 1893-1972 .... CANR-3
Obituary 33-36R
Earlier sketch in CA 4R
See also SATA 3
Church, Robert L(eValley) 1938- 61-64
Church, Ronald James Harrison
See Harrison Church, Ronald James
Church, Roy A. 1935- 124
Church, Ruth Ellen (Lovrien) CANR-7
Earlier sketch in CA 5-6R
Church, Suzanne
See Bates, Susannah (Vacella)
Church, William Farr 1912- Brief entry 105
Churchill, Allen 1911-1988 97-100
Obituary 124
Churchill, Bill
See Churchill, Gail Winston
Churchill, Caryl 1938- CANR-22
Earlier sketch in CA 102
See also DLB 13
See also CLC 31
Churchill, Creighton 1912-1984 69-72
Obituary 114
Churchill, David 1935- 106
Churchill, E(lmer) Richard 1937- CANR-11
Earlier sketch in CA 17-18R
See also SATA 11
Churchill, Edward Delos 1895-1972
Obituary 37-40R
Churchill, Elizabeth
See Hough, Richard (Alexander)
Churchill, Gail Winston 1903(?)-1984
Obituary 112
Churchill, Guy E. 1926- 29-32R
Churchill, Joyce
See Harrison, M(ichael) John
Churchill, Linda R. 1938- CANR-11
Earlier sketch in CA 21-22R
Churchill, R(eginald) C(harles) 1916- 9-10R
Churchill, Randolph (Frederick Edward
Spencer) 1911-1968 Obituary 89-92
Churchill, Reba 1932(?)-1985 Obituary 116
Churchill, Rhona Adelaide 1913- 7-8R
Churchill, Samuel 1911- 17-18R
Churchill, Sarah (Millicent Hermione)
1914-1982 Obituary 107
Churchill, Winston (Leonard Spencer)
1874-1965 97-100
Churchland, Patricia Smith 1943- 123
Churchman, C(harles) West 1913- CANR-9
Earlier sketch in CA 23-24R
Churchman, Michael 1929- 37-40R
Chute, B(eatrice) J(oy) 1913-1987 .... 4R
Obituary 123
See also SATA 2
Chute, Carolyn 1947- 123
See also CLC 39
Chute, Marchette (Gaylord) 1909- CANR-5
Earlier sketch in CA 4R
See also SATA 1
Chute, Robert M. 1926- 109
Chute, Rupert
See Cleveland, Philip Jerome
Chute, William J(oseph) 1914- 11-12R
Chwalek, Henryka C. 1918- 17-18R
Chwast, Jacqueline 1932- CANR-5
Earlier sketch in CA 49-52
See also SATA 6
Chwast, Seymour 1931- SATA-18
Chyet, Stanley F. 1931- 33-36R
Cialente, Fausta
See Terni-Cialente, Fausta
Cianciolo, Patricia Jean 1929- CANR-13
Earlier sketch in CA 37-40R
Ciaramitaro, Andrew James 1955- 110
Ciaramitaro, Barbara 1946- 107
Ciarcia, Steve 1947- 110
Ciardi, John (Anthony) 1916-1986 ...... CANR-5
Obituary 118
Earlier sketch in CA 7-8R
See also CAAS 2
See also SATA 1, 46
See also DLB 5
See also DLBY 86
See also CLC 10, 40, 44
Ciccorella, Aubra Dair 65-68
Cicellis, Kay 1926- CANR-3
Earlier sketch in CA 3R
Cicognani, Amleto Giovanni Cardinal
1883-1973 Obituary 45-48
Cicourel, Aaron V. 1928- 53-56
Cid Perez, Jose (Diego) 1906- CANR-4
Earlier sketch in CA 53-56
Ciechanowski, Jan 1888(?)-1973
Obituary 41-44R
Cienciala, Anna M(aria) 1929- 89-92
Cieplak, Tadeusz N(owak) 1918- CANR-11
Earlier sketch in CA 69-72
Cigler, Allan J(ames) 1943- 111
Cikovsky, Nicolai, Jr. 1933- 113
Cilffriw, Gwynfor
See Griffith, Thomas Gwynfor
Cimbollek, Robert (Carl) 1937- 57-60
Ciment, Michel 1938- 97-100
Cimino, Michael 1943- 105
See also CLC 16
Cinberg, Bernard L. 1905-1979 Obituary ..85-88
Cinel, Dino 1941- 111
Cioffari, Vincenzo 1905- 17-18R
Cioffi, Lou(is James) 1926- 120
Brief entry 109
Cioran, E(mil) M. 1911- 25-28R
Cipes, Robert M. 1930- 23-24R
Ciplijauskaite, Birute 1929- CANR-14
Earlier sketch in CA 37-40R
Cipolla, Carlo M(anlio) 1922- CANR-18
Earlier sketches in CA 7-8R, CANR-2
Cipolla, Joan Bagnel
See Bagnel, Joan
Cipriano, Anthony (John) 1941- 102
Circus, Anthony
See Hoch, Edward D(entinger)
Circus, Jim
See Rosevear, John
Cire
See Hayden, Eric W(illiam)
Ciria, Alberto 1934- 73-76
Cirino, Linda D(avis) 1941- 65-68
Cirino, Robert 1937- 61-64
Cismaru, Alfred 1933- 61-64
Ciszek, Walter 1904- CAP-1
Earlier sketch in CA 13-14
Citati, Pietro 1930- CANR-4
Earlier sketch in CA 53-56
Citino, David 1947- 104
Citrine, Walter McLennan 1887-1983
Obituary 109
Cittafino, Ricardo
See Bickers, Richard Leslie Townshend
Ciuba, Edward J(oseph) 1935- 61-64
Civille, John R(aphael) 1940- CANR-11
Earlier sketch in CA 69-72
Cizmar, Paula 1949- 122
Claassen, Harold 1905- CAP-2
Earlier sketch in CA 19-20
Clabaugh, Gary K(enneth) 1940- 69-72
Clabby, John 1911- 104

Clack, Robert Wood 1886-1964 ... 122
Obituary ... 110
Claerbaut, David 1946- ... CANR-1
Earlier sketch in CA 45-48
Claffey, William J. 1925- ... 23-24R
Claflin, Edward 1949- ... 97-100
Clagett, John (Henry) 1916- ... CANR-6
Earlier sketch in CA 7-8R
Clagett, Marshall 1916- ... CANR-5
Earlier sketch in CA 1R
Claghorn, Charles Eugene 1911- ... 57-60
Clague, Ewan 1896-1987 ... 29-32R
Obituary ... 122
Clague, Maryhelen 1930- ... 81-84
Claiborne, Craig 1920- ... CANR-5
Earlier sketch in CA 2R
Claiborne, Robert (Watson, Jr.) 1919- . CANR-12
Earlier sketch in CA 29-32R
Clain-Stefanelli, Vladimir 1914-1982 ... 111
Obituary ... 108
Clair, Andree ... 29-32R
See also SATA 19
Clair, Bernard (Eddy) 1951- ... 102
Clair, Rene
See Chomette, Rene Lucien
See also CLC 20
Claire, Keith
See Andrews, Claire
Claire, Keith
See Andrews, Keith
Claire, William Francis 1935- ... CANR-7
Earlier sketch in CA 57-60
Clairmont, Elva 1937- ... 117
Clammer, David 1943- ... 69-72
Clampett, Bob 1914(?)-1984 Obituary ... 112
See also SATA 38
See also AITN 1
Clampett, Robert
See Clampett, Bob
See also SATA 44
Clampitt, Amy ... 110
See also CLC 32
Clancy, Francis Michael 1903-1986
Obituary ... 121
Clancy, John Gregory 1922- ... 13-14R
Clancy, Joseph P(atrick) 1928- ... CANR-18
Earlier sketch in CA 101
Clancy, King
See Clancy, Francis Michael
Clancy, Laurence James 1942- ... 108
Clancy, Laurie
See Clancy, Laurence James
Clancy, Thomas H(anley) 1923- ... CANR-7
Earlier sketch in CA 15-16R
Clancy, Tom 1947- ... CLC-45
Clancy, William 1922-1982 Obituary ... 106
Clanton, (Orval) Gene 1934- ... 41-44R
Clanton, Gordon 1942- ... 57-60
Clapham, Arthur Roy 1904- ... 109
Clapham, John 1908- ... CANR-10
Earlier sketch in CA 25-28R
Clapp, James Gordon 1909-1970 ... CAP-1
Earlier sketch in CA 9-10
Clapp, Margaret (Antoinette) 1910-1974
Obituary ... 49-52
Clapp, Patricia 1912- ... CANR-10
Earlier sketch in CA 25-28R
See also SATA 4
See also SAAS 4
Clapp, Verner W(arren) 1901-1972
Obituary ... 37-40R
Clapper, Raymond 1892-1944 ... DLB-29
Clapperton, Richard 1934- ... 25-28R
Clar, C(harles) Raymond 1903- ... 37-40R
Clardy, Andrea Fleck 1943- ... CANR-17
Earlier sketch in CA 97-100
Clardy, J(esse) V. 1929- ... 33-36R
Clare, Elizabeth
See Cook, Dorothy Mary
Clare, Ellen
See Sinclair, Olga
Clare, Francis D.
See Aschmann, Alberta
Clare, George P. 1920- ... 111
Clare, Helen
See Hunter Blair, Pauline (Clarke)
Clare, John 1793-1864 ... DLB-55
Clare, Josephine 1933- ... 73-76
Clare, Margaret
See Maison, Margaret (Mary Bowles)
Clarens, Carlos (Figueredo y)
1936(?)-1987 ... 21-22R
Obituary ... 121
Clareson, Thomas D(ean) 1926- ... CANR-18
Earlier sketches in CA 2R, CANR-2
Clarfield, Gerard Howard 1936- ... 103
Claridge, Gordon S. 1932- ... 21-22R
Clarie, Thomas C(ashin) 1943- ... 93-96
Clarin
See Alas (y Urena), Leopoldo (Enrique
Garcia)
Clarizio, Harvey F(rank) 1934- ... 33-36R
Clark, Admont Gulick 1919- ... 53-56
Clark, Al C.
See Goines, Donald
Clark, Alan 1928- ... 13-14R
Clark, Alfred Alexander Gordon 1900-1958
Brief entry ... 112
Clark, Alice S(andell) 1922- ... 41-44R
Clark, Andrew Hill 1911-1975 ... CAP-2
Earlier sketch in CA 25-28
Clark, Ann L(ivezey) 1913- ... CANR-7
Earlier sketch in CA 19-20R
Clark, Ann Nolan 1896- ... CANR-2
Earlier sketch in CA 5-6R
See also SATA 4
See also DLB 52

Clark, Anne 1909- ... 29-32R
Clark, Anne
See Amor, Anne Clark
Clark (of Herriotshall), Arthur Melville
1895- ... 9-10R
Clark, Badger
See Paine, Lauran (Bosworth)
Clark, Ben T. 1928- ... 53-56
Clark, Bill
See Clark, William A(rthur)
Clark, Billy C(urtis) 1928- ... CANR-22
Earlier sketch in CA 2R
Clark, (Robert) Brian 1932- ... 41-44R
See also CLC 29
Clark, Bruce B(udge) 1918- ... 69-72
Clark, Burton R(obert) 1921- ... 110
Clark, C. E. Frazer, Jr. 1925- ... 33-36R
Clark, C. H. Douglas 1890- ... CAP-2
Earlier sketch in CA 23-24
Clark, C(harles) M(anning) H(ope)
1915- ... 97-100
Clark, Carol (Lois) 1948- ... 57-60
Clark, Catherine Anthony (Smith) 1892- .. CAP-1
Earlier sketch in CA 11-12
Clark, Champ 1923- ... 108
See also SATA 47
Clark, Charles E(dwin) 1929- ... 29-32R
Clark, Charles Heber 1841-1915
Brief entry ... 111
See also DLB 11
Clark, Charles Tallifero 1917- ... 15-16R
Clark, China (Debra) 1950- ... 45-48
Clark, Christopher (Anthony) Stuart
See Stuart-Clark, Christopher (Anthony)
Clark, Clifford E(dward), Jr. 1941- ... 81-84
Clark, Colin (Grant) 1905- ... CANR-8
Earlier sketch in CA 61-64
Clark, D.M.J.
See Clark, Douglas
Clark, David
See Hardcastle, Michael
Clark, David Allen
See Ernst, (Lyman) John
Clark, David Gillis 1933- ... 53-56
Clark, David Ridgley 1920- ... CANR-9
Earlier sketch in CA 17-18R
Clark, Dennis E. 1916- ... 29-32R
Clark, Dennis J. 1927- ... CANR-1
Earlier sketch in CA 1R
Clark, Diana Cooper
See Cooper-Clark, Diana
Clark, Dick
See Clark, Richard Wagstaff
Clark, Don(ald Rowlee) 1925- ... 57-60
Clark, Don(ald Henry) 1930- ... 29-32R
Clark, Donald E. 1933- ... CANR-8
Earlier sketch in CA 23-24R
Clark, Dora Mae 1893- ... 41-44R
Clark, Dorothy Park 1899- ... 5-6R
Clark, Douglas 1919- ... 114
Clark, E. Ritchie 1912- ... 122
Clark, Edward W(illiam) 1943- ... 123
Clark, Eleanor 1913- ... 11-12R
See also DLB 6
See also CLC 5, 19
Clark, Electa 1910- ... 69-72
Clark, Eliot (Candee) 1883-1980
Obituary ... 97-100
Clark, Ella E(lizabeth) 1896- ... 105
Clark, Ellery Harding, Jr. 1909- ... CANR-10
Earlier sketch in CA 65-68
Clark, Elmer Talmage 1886-1966 ... 7-8R
Clark, Eric 1911- ... CANR-9
Earlier sketch in CA 13-14R
Clark, Eric 1937- ... 102
Clark, Eugenie 1922- ... 49-52
Clark, Evans 1888-1970 Obituary ... 104
Clark, F(rederick) Stephen 1908-1977 .. CANR-14
Earlier sketch in CA 21-22R
Clark, Francis 1919- ... 19-20R
Clark, Frank J(ames) 1922- ... CANR-17
Earlier sketch in CA 13-14R
See also SATA 18
Clark, Fred George 1890-1972 Obituary .. 37-40R
Clark, Gail 1944- ... CANR-16
Earlier sketch in CA 97-100
Clark, Garel
See Garelick, May
Clark, Garth (Reginald) 1947- ... 115
Clark, George Norman 1890-1979 ... 65-68
Obituary ... 85-88
Clark, George Sidney Roberts Kitson
See Kitson Clark, George Sidney Roberts
Clark, Gerald 1918- ... 13-14R
Clark, Gordon H(addon) 1902-1985 ... CANR-17
Earlier sketches in CA 3R, CANR-1
Clark, (John) Grahame (Douglas)
1907- ... CANR-10
Earlier sketch in CA 65-68
Clark, Gregory 1892-1977 Obituary ... 89-92
Clark, Harry 1917- ... 61-64
Clark, Harry Hayden 1901-1971 ... CAP-2
Earlier sketch in CA 29-32
Clark, Henry B(alsley) II 1930- ... CANR-8
Earlier sketch in CA 5-6R
Clark, Howard
See Haskin, Dorothy C(lark)
Clark, J(onathan) C(harles) D(ouglas)
1951- ... 121
Clark, J(ohn) H(oward) 1929- ... 106
Clark, J(eff) R(ay) 1947- ... CANR-22
Earlier sketch in CA 106
Clark, J. R.
See Clark, John R(ussell)
Clark, James Anthony 1907- ... 65-68
Clark, James C. 1947- ... 122
Clark, James M(ilford) 1930- ... 21-22R

Clark, James V(aughan) 1927- ... 13-14R
Clark, Jean C(ashman) 1920- ... 93-96
Clark, Jere Walton 1922- ... 23-24R
Clark, Jerome L. 1928- ... 37-40R
Clark, Jerry E(ugene) 1942- ... 73-76
Clark, Joan 1934- ... 93-96
Clark, John Desmond 1916- ... 61-64
Clark, John Drury 1907- ... 37-40R
Clark, John G(arretson) 1932- ... 19-20R
Clark, John Maurice 1884-1963 ... 5-6R
Clark, John Pepper 1935- ... CANR-16
Earlier sketch in CA 65-68
See also CLC 38
Clark, John R(ussell) 1927- ... 120
Clark, John R(ichard) 1930- ... 37-40R
Clark, John R(alph) K(ukeakalani) 1946- ... 101
Clark, John W(illiams) 1907- ... 13-14R
Clark, Joseph D(eadrick) 1893- ... CAP-2
Earlier sketch in CA 33-36
Clark, Joseph James 1893-1971 ... CAP-2
Obituary ... 29-32R
Earlier sketch in CA 19-20
Clark, Joseph L(ynn) 1881- ... CAP-2
Earlier sketch in CA 17-18
Clark, Katerina 1941- ... 110
Clark, Katharine (Jarman) 1911(?)-1986
Obituary ... 118
Clark, Keith 1939- ... 124
Clark, Kenneth (Mackenzie) 1903-1983 ... 93-96
Obituary ... 109
Clark, Kenneth B(ancroft) 1914- ... 33-36R
Clark, L. D. 1922- ... CANR-1
Earlier sketch in CA 2R
Clark, Laurence (Walter) 1914- ... 13-14R
Clark, LaVerne Harrell 1929- ... CANR-11
Earlier sketch in CA 15-16R
Clark, Leonard 1905-1981 ... CANR-7
Obituary ... 105
Earlier sketch in CA 13-14R
See also SATA 29, 30
Clark, Leonard H(ill) 1915- ... CANR-4
Earlier sketch in CA 53-56
Clark, Leroy D. ... CANR-11
Earlier sketch in CA 61-64
Clark, Lewis Gaylord 1808-1873 ... DLB-3, 64
Clark, Lindley H(oag), Jr. 1920- ... 65-68
Clark, Lydia Benson
See Meaker, Eloise
Clark, Mabel Margaret (Cowie) 1903-1975 .. 101
Clark, Malcolm (Hamilton), Jr. 1917- ... 106
Clark, (Charles) Manning (Hope) 1915- ... 9-10R
Clark, Marden J. 1916- ... 61-64
Clark, Margaret Goff 1913- ... CANR-20
Earlier sketches in CA 3R, CANR-5
See also SATA 8
Clark, Marguerite Sheridan 1892(?)-1982
Obituary ... 107
Clark, Maria Louisa Guidish 1926- ... 5-6R
Clark, Marion L. 1943-1977 ... 77-80
Obituary ... 73-76
Clark, Marjorie A. 1911- ... 33-36R
Clark, Mark (Wayne) 1896-1984 Obituary ... 112
Clark, (Bennett) Marsh 1928-1985 ... 122
Obituary ... 117
Clark, Mary T. ... 37-40R
Clark, Mary Higgins 1931- ... CANR-16
Earlier sketch in CA 81-84
See also SATA 46
Clark, Mary Jane 1915- ... 57-60
Clark, Mary Lou
See Clark, Maria Louisa Guidish
Clark, Mary Margaret 1929- ... 113
Clark, Mary T(wibill) ... 102
Clark, Mavis Thorpe 1912- ... CANR-8
Earlier sketch in CA 57-60
See also SATA 8
See also SAAS 5
See also CLC 12
Clark, Melissa 1949- ... CANR-22
Earlier sketch in CA 104
Clark, Merle
See Gessner, Lynne
Clark, Michael D(orsey) 1937- ... 111
Clark, Miles (Morton) 1920- ... 23-24R
Clark, Naomi 1932- ... 77-80
Clark, Neal 1950- ... 113
Clark, Neil M(cCullough) 1890- ... 7-8R
Clark, Norman H(arold) 1925- ... 69-72
Clark, Parlin
See Trigg, Harry Davis
Clark, Patricia Finrow 1929- ... 17-18R
See also SATA 11
Clark, (William) Ramsey 1927- ... 29-32R
Clark, Randall 1957- ... 120
Clark, Richard Charles 1935- Brief entry ... 114
Clark, Richard Wagstaff 1929- Brief entry ... 113
Clark, Robert Alfred 1908- ... 101
Clark, Robert E(ugene) 1912- ... 41-44R
Clark, Robert E(dward) D(avid) 1906- .. CANR-21
Earlier sketch in CA 7-8R
Clark, Robert L(loyd), Jr. 1945- ... 103
Clark, Rolf 1937- ... 114
Clark, Romane Lewis 1925- ... 17-18R
Clark, Ronald Harry 1904- ... 110
Clark, Ronald William 1916-1987 ... 25-28R
Obituary ... 122
See also SATA 2
Clark, Ruth C(ampbell) 1920- ... 69-72
Clark, Samuel 1945- ... 89-92
Clark, Samuel Delbert 1910- ... CANR-11
Earlier sketches in CA 13-14, CAP-1
Clark, Septima Poinsette 1898-1987 ... 7-8R
Obituary ... 124
Clark, Stephen R(ichard) L(yster)
1945- ... CANR-13
Earlier sketch in CA 77-80
Clark, Sue C(assidy) 1935- ... 41-44R

Clark, Sydney A(ylmer) 1890-1975 ... CANR-4
Obituary ... 57-60
Earlier sketch in CA 7-8R
Clark, Terry N(ichols) 1940- ... 25-28R
Clark, Thomas D(ionysious) 1903- ... CANR-4
Earlier sketch in CA 5-6R
Clark, Thomas Willard 1941- ... 81-84
Clark, Tom
See Clark, Thomas Willard
Clark, Truman R(oss) 1935- ... 61-64
Clark, Van D(eusen) 1909- ... CAP-1
Earlier sketch in CA 13-14
See also SATA 2
Clark, Virginia
See Gray, Patricia (Clark)
Clark, Walter Houston 1902- ... 37-40R
Clark, Walter Van Tilburg 1909-1971 ... 9-10R
Obituary ... 33-36R
See also SATA 8
See also DLB 9
See also CLC 28
Clark, Wesley James 1950- ... 112
Clark, William (Donaldson) 1916-1985 ... 29-32R
Obituary ... 116
Clark, William A(rthur) 1931- ... 33-36R
Clark, William Bedford 1947- ... 109
Clark, William Smith II 1900-1969 ... CAP-2
Earlier sketch in CA 25-28
Clarke, Anna 1919- ... CANR-18
Earlier sketch in CA 102
Clarke, Arthur C(harles) 1917- ... CANR-2
Earlier sketch in CA 4R
See also SATA 13
See also CLC 1, 4, 13, 18, 35
Clarke, Arthur G(ladstone) 1887- ... CAP-2
Earlier sketch in CA 17-18
Clarke, Austin 1896-1974 ... CAP-2
Obituary ... 49-52
Earlier sketch in CA 29-32
See also DLB 10, 20
See also CLC 6, 9
Clarke, Austin C(hesterfield) 1934- ... CANR-14
Earlier sketch in CA 25-28R
See also DLB 53
See also CLC 8
Clarke, Basil F(ulford) L(owther)
1908-1978 ... CANR-4
Obituary ... 89-92
Earlier sketch in CA 7-8R
Clarke, Boden
See Burgess, M(ichael) R(oy)
Clarke, Brenda (Margaret Lilian) 1926- . CANR-24
Earlier sketches in CA 65-68, CANR-9
Clarke, Captain Jafar
See Nesmith, Robert I.
Clarke, Charles (Richard Astley) 1944- ... 118
Clarke, Charles Galloway 1899-1983
Obituary ... 110
Clarke, Clorinda 1917- ... 25-28R
See also SATA 7
Clarke, D(avid) Waldo 1907- ... 9-10R
Clarke, David E(gerton) 1920- ... 17-18R
Clarke, David Leonard 1937-1976
Obituary ... 111
Clarke, Derrick Harry 1919- ... 103
Clarke, Dorothy Clotelle
See Shadi, Dorothy Clotelle Clarke
Clarke, Dudley (Wrangel) 1899-1974 ... CAP-1
Earlier sketch in CA 15-16
Clarke, Duncan L(ynn) 1941- ... CANR-16
Earlier sketch in CA 97-100
Clarke, Dwight Lancelot 1885-1971 ... 1R
Obituary ... 103
Clarke, Ernest George 1927- ... 102
Clarke, Garry E(vans) 1943- ... 77-80
Clarke, George Timothy ... CANR-1
Earlier sketch in CA 4R
Clarke, George Wallace
See Wallace-Clarke, George
Clarke, Gillian 1937- ... 106
See also DLB 40
Clarke, H. Harrison 1902- ... CANR-5
Earlier sketch in CA 3R
Clarke, Hans Thacher 1887-1972
Obituary ... 37-40R
Clarke, Harry Eugene, Jr. 1921- ... 5-6R
Clarke, Henry Charles 1899- ... 102
Clarke, Hockley
See Clarke, Henry Charles
Clarke, Howard William 1929- ... 37-40R
Clarke, Hugh Vincent 1919- ... CANR-19
Earlier sketch in CA 102
Clarke, I. F.
See Clarke, Ignatius (Ian) Frederick
Clarke, Ian
See Clarke, Ignatius (Ian) Frederick
Clarke, Ignatius (Ian) Frederick 1918- ... 116
Clarke, J(ohn) F(rederick) Gates 1905- ... CAP-1
Earlier sketch in CA 13-14
Clarke, Jack Alden 1924- ... 29-32R
Clarke, James F(ranklin) 1906- ... 69-72
Clarke, James Freeman 1810-1888 ... DLB-1, 59
Clarke, James Hall
See Rowland-Entwistle, (Arthur)
Theodore (Henry)
Clarke, James W(eston) 1937- ... 110
Clarke, Joan (Lorraine) 1920- ... 104
Clarke, Joan B. 1921- ... SATA-27, 42
Clarke, Joan Dorn 1924- ... 11-12R
Clarke, John (Campbell) 1913-19(?) ... CAP-1
Earlier sketch in CA 15-16
Clarke, John
See Laklan, Carli
and Sontup, Dan(iel)
Clarke, John Henrik 1915- ... CANR-24
Earlier sketch in CA 53-56
See also AITN 1

Clarke, John Joseph 1879- CANR-5
Earlier sketch in CA 7-8R
Clarke, Kenneth W(endell) 1917- 17-18R
Clarke, Lea
See Rowland-Entwistle, (Arthur) Theodore (Henry)
Clarke, Lige 1942- 41-44R
Clarke, Martin Lowther 1909- CANR-2
Earlier sketch in CA 7-8R
Clarke, Mary 1923- 104
Clarke, Mary Stetson 1911- CANR-8
Earlier sketch in CA 21-22R
See also SATA 5
Clarke, Mary Washington 1913- CANR-11
Earlier sketch in CA 25-28R
Clarke, Mary Whatley 1899- CANR-2
Earlier sketch in CA 7-8R
Clarke, Michael
See Newlon, (Frank) Clarke
Clarke, Nicholas Goodrick
See Goodrick-Clarke, Nicholas
Clarke, P(eter) F(rederick) 1942- 73-76
Clarke, Pauline
See Hunter Blair, Pauline (Clarke)
Clarke, Peter 1936- 104
Clarke, Rebecca Sophia 1833-1906
Brief entry 119
See also DLB 42
Clarke, Richard (William Barnes)
1910-1975 Obituary 115
Clarke, Richard
See Paine, Lauran (Bosworth)
Clarke, Robert
See Paine, Lauran (Bosworth)
and Platt, Charles
Clarke, Robin Harwood 1937- CANR-9
Earlier sketch in CA 15-16R
Clarke, Ron 1937- 107
Clarke, Ronald Francis 1933- 21-22R
Clarke, Shirley 1925- CLC-16
Clarke, Simon 1946- 122
Clarke, Stephan P(aul) 1945- 69-72
Clarke, Thomas E(mmet) 1918- 53-56
Clarke, Thomas Ernest Bennett 1907- .. CANR-19
Earlier sketch in CA 103
Clarke, Thurston 1946- CANR-13
Earlier sketch in CA 77-80
Clarke, Tom E(ugene) 1915- 5-6R
Clarke, William Dixon 1927- 5-6R
Clarke, William Kendall 1911(?)-1981
Obituary 104
Clarke, William M(alpas) 1922- CANR-15
Earlier sketch in CA 41-44R
Clarke, William Thomas 1932- 57-60
Clarke-Stewart, K(athleen) Alison 1932- 113
Clark-Kennedy, Archibald Edmund
1893-1985 Obituary 117
Clarkson, Adrienne 1939- 49-52
Clarkson, E(dith) Margaret 1915- CANR-20
Earlier sketches in CA 4R, CANR-5
See also SATA 37
Clarkson, Ewan 1929- CANR-17
Earlier sketch in CA 25-28R
See also SATA 9
Clarkson, Geoffrey P. E. 1934- CANR-2
Earlier sketch in CA 5-6R
Clarkson, Helen
See McCloy, Helen (Worrell Clarkson)
Clarkson, J. F.
See Tubb, E(dwin) C(harles)
Clarkson, Jan Nagel 1943- 93-96
Clarkson, Jesse Dunsmore 1897-1973 .....5-6R
Obituary 45-48
Clarkson, L(eslie) A(lbert) 1933- 73-76
Clarkson, Orman
See Richardson, Gladwell
Clarkson, Paul S(tephen) 1905- 29-32R
Clarkson, Stephen 1937- 41-44R
Clarkson, Tom 1913- 103
Clary, Jack 1932- 57-60
Clasen, Claus-Peter 1931- 41-44R
Clash, The
See Headon, (Nicky) Topper
and Jones, Mick
and Simonon, Paul
and Strummer, Joe
See also CLC 30
Clasper, Paul D(udley) 1923- 4R
Claspy, Everett M. 1907(?)-1973
Obituary 41-44R
Claster, Daniel S(tuart) 1932- 23-24R
Clatworthy, Nancy M(oore) K. 1924- 124
Claude, Richard (P.) 1934- 29-32R
Claudel, Alice Moser CANR-2
Earlier sketch in CA 49-52
Claudel, Paul (Louis Charles Marie)
1868-1955 Brief entry 104
See also TCLC 2, 10
Claudia, Sister Mary 1906- CAP-1
Earlier sketch in CA 9-10
Claudia, Susan
See Johnston, William
Claus, Hugo (Maurice Julius) 1929-
Brief entry 116
Claus, Marshall R. 1936-1970 .... CAP-2
Earlier sketch in CA 29-32
Clausen, Aage R. 1932- 49-52
Clausen, Andy 1943- Brief entry 117
See also DLB 16
Clausen, Connie 1923- 1R
Clausen, Dennis M(onroe) 1943- 106
Clausen, W. V.
See Clausen, Wendell (Vernon)
Clausen, Wendell (Vernon) 1923- 121
Clauser, Suzanne (P.) 1929- 37-40R
Clavel, Bernard (Charles Henri) 1923- ... CANR-2
Earlier sketch in CA 45-48
Clavel, Maurice 1920-1979 Obituary 85-88
Clavell, James (duMaresq) 1925- 25-28R
See also CLC 6, 25
Claverie, Jean 1946- SATA-38
Clawson, Marion 1905- CANR-10
Earlier sketch in CA 65-68
Clawson, Robert W(ayne) 1939- 108
Clay, Bertha M.
See Dey, Frederic (Merrill) Van Rensselaer
Clay, Cassius M.
See Clay, Cassius Marcellus
Clay, Cassius Marcellus 1810-1903
Brief entry 120
See also DLB 43
Clay, Cassius Marcellus
See Ali, Muhammad
Clay, Charles Travis 1885-1978 Obituary ..77-80
Clay, Comer 1910- 45-48
Clay, Diskin 1938- 115
Clay, Duncan
See Diehl, W(illiam) W(ells)
Clay, Floyd M(artin) 1927- 45-48
Clay, Grady E. 1916- 93-96
Clay, James 1924- 17-18R
Clay, Jim
See Clay, James
Clay, Lucius D(uBignon) 1897-1978 81-84
Obituary 77-80
Clay, Marie M(ildred) 1926- CANR-22
Earlier sketches in CA 61-64, CANR-8
Clay, Patrice 1947- 106
See also SATA 47
Clay, Roberta 1900- CAP-2
Earlier sketch in CA 29-32
Claybaugh, Amos L(incoln) 1917- 69-72
Claydon, Leslie Francis 1923- 53-56
Clayes, Stanley A(rnold) 1922- 29-32R
Claypool, Jane
See Miner, Jane Claypool
Clayre, Alasdair 1935-1984 102
Obituary 111
Clayton, Aileen Bowen 1918-1981 113
Clayton, Barbara
See Pluff, Barbara Littlefield
Clayton, Bruce 1939- 69-72
Clayton, C. Guy 1936- 122
Clayton, Charles C(urtis) 1902- 73-76
Clayton, Donald D(elbert) 1935- 65-68
Clayton, (Francis) Howard 1918- CANR-12
Earlier sketch in CA 29-32R
Clayton, Howard 1929- 65-68
Clayton, James E(dwin) 1929- 11-12R
Clayton, James L. 1931- CANR-12
Earlier sketch in CA 29-32R
Clayton, Jo 1939- 81-84
Clayton, John 1892-1979 ....33-36R
Obituary 89-92
Clayton, John
See Beevers, John (Leonard)
Clayton, John J(acob) 1935- CANR-11
Earlier sketch in CA 25-28R
Clayton, Keith (M.) 1928- CANR-11
Earlier sketch in CA 23-24R
Clayton, Paul C(lark) 1932- 61-64
Clayton, Richard Henry Michael 1907- ... CANR-4
Earlier sketch in CA 5-6R
Clayton, Susan
See Bailey, Alfred Goldsworthy
Clayton, Sylvia 103
Clayton, Thomas (Swoverland) 1932- 41-44R
Clayton, Thompson B(owker) 1904- 57-60
Claytor, Gertrude Boatwright
1890(?)-1973 Obituary 45-48
Cleage, Albert B., Jr. 1911- 65-68
Cleall, Charles 1927- 7-8R
Clear, Todd R. 1949- 117
Cleare, John 1936- 65-68
Clearman, Brian (Patrick Joseph) 1941- 115
Cleary, Beverly (Atlee Bunn) 1916- CANR-19
Earlier sketches in CA 1R, CANR-2
See also SATA 2, 43
See also DLB 52
See also CLR 2, 8
Cleary, David Powers 1915- 106
Cleary, Florence Damon 1896- 81-84
Cleary, James W(illiam) 1927- 19-20R
Cleary, Johanna L. 1961- 122
Cleary, Jon 1917- CANR-3
Earlier sketch in CA 4R
Cleary, Robert E(dward) 1932- 41-44R
Cleator, P(hilip) E(llaby) 1908- 102
Cleaver, Anastasia N. CANR-18
Earlier sketch in CA 97-100
Cleaver, Bill 1920-1981 73-76
See also SATA 22, 27
See also DLB 52
See also CLR 6
Cleaver, Carole 1934- 49-52
See also SATA 6
Cleaver, Dale G. 1928- 17-18R
Cleaver, (Leroy) Eldridge 1935- CANR-16
Earlier sketch in CA 21-22R
See also CLC 30
Cleaver, Elizabeth (Mrazik) 1939-1985 97-100
Obituary 117
See also SATA 23, 43
See also CLR 13
Cleaver, Hylton Reginald 1891-1961 73-76
See also SATA 49
Cleaver, Nancy
See Mathews, Evelyn Craw
Cleaver, Vera 1919- 73-76
See also SATA 22
See also DLB 52
See also CLR 6
Cleaver, William J(oseph) 1920-1981
Obituary 104
Cleaves, Emery N(udd) 1902- 33-36R
Cleaves, Freeman 1904- 4R
Cleaves, Peter S(hurtleff) 1943- 69-72
Clebsch, William Anthony 1923-1984 ....15-16R
Obituary 113
Clecak, Peter (E.) 1938- 41-44R
Cleckley, Hervey Milton 1903-1984 122
Obituary 111
Cleese, John (Marwood) 1939- 116
Brief entry 112
See also CLC 21
Cleeve, Brian (Talbot) 1921- CANR-16
Earlier sketches in CA 49-52, CANR-1
Clegg, Alec
See Clegg, Alexander Bradshaw
Clegg, Alexander Bradshaw 1909- 85-88
Clegg, Charles (Myron, Jr.) 1916- CANR-17
Earlier sketch in CA 25-28R
Clegg, Jerry S(tephen) 1933- 77-80
Clegg, John 1909- 118
Clegg, Reed K. 1907- CAP-1
Earlier sketch in CA 13-14
Clegg, Stewart (Roger) 1947- CANR-11
Earlier sketch in CA 69-72
Cleghorn, Reese 1930- 25-28R
Cleishbotham, Jebediah
See Scott, Sir Walter
Cleland, Charles C(arr) 1924- CANR-14
Earlier sketch in CA 41-44R
Cleland, Charles E(dward) 1936- 111
Cleland, David I. 1926- CANR-10
Earlier sketch in CA 25-28R
Cleland, Hugh
See Clarke, John (Campbell)
Cleland, John 1710-1789 .... DLB-39
Cleland, Mabel
See Widdemer, Mabel Cleland
Cleland, (Joseph) Max(well) 1942-
Brief entry 113
Cleland, Morton
See Rennie, James Alan
Cleland, W(illiam) Wendell 1888-1972
Obituary 37-40R
Clelland, Catherine
See Townsend, Doris McFerran
Clelland, Richard C(ook) 1921- 19-20R
Clem, Alan L(eland) 1929- CANR-3
Earlier sketch in CA 11-12R
Clemeau, Carol
See Esler, Carol Clemeau
Clemen, Wolfgang Hermann 1909- CANR-2
Earlier sketch in CA 2R
Clemence, Richard V(ernon) 1910- 1R
Clemenceau, Georges (Eugene Benjamin)
1841-1929 Brief entry 114
Clemenko, Harold B. 1905-1984 Obituary ... 113
Clemens, Alphonse H. 1905-1977
Obituary 73-76
Clemens, Bryan T. 1934- 97-100
Clemens, Cyril AITN-2
Clemens, Diane S(haver) 1936- 29-32R
Clemens, Rodgers
See Lovin, Roger Robert
Clemens, Samuel Langhorne 1835-1910
Brief entry 104
See also YABC 2
See also DLB 11, 12, 23, 64
Clemens, Virginia Phelps 1941- CANR-15
Earlier sketch in CA 85-88
See also SATA 35
Clemens, Walter C., Jr. 1933- CANR-7
Earlier sketch in CA 17-18R
Clement, A(lfred) J(ohn) 1915- 25-28R
Clement, Charles Baxter 1940- 105
Clement, Evelyn Geer 1926- 53-56
Clement, George H. 1909- 29-32R
Clement, Hal
See Stubbs, Harry C(lement)
See also DLB 8
Clement, Herbert F(lint) 1927- 81-84
Clement, Jane Tyson 1917- 25-28R
Clement, Roland C(harles) 1912- 49-52
Clement, Wallace 1949- 111
Clements, A(rthur) L(eo) 1932- 29-32R
Clements, Barbara Evans 1945- 89-92
Clements, Bruce 1931- CANR-5
Earlier sketch in CA 53-56
See also SATA 27
Clements, Colleen D(ianne) 1936- 110
Clements, E(llen) Catherine (Scott)
1920- 15-16R
Clements, E(ileen) H(elen) 1905- CAP-1
Earlier sketch in CA 9-10
Clements, Frank A. 1942- 93-96
Clements, Harold M., Sr. 1907- 69-72
Clements, John 1916- CANR-11
Earlier sketch in CA 69-72
Clements, Julia 1906- CAP-1
Earlier sketch in CA 13-14
Clements, Kendrick Alling 1939- 110
Clements, Marcelle 1948- 121
Clements, Robert John 1912- CANR-5
Earlier sketch in CA 4R
Clements, Robert W(illiam) 1939- 110
Clements, Ronald Ernest 1929- 15-16R
Clements, Tad S. 1922- 25-28R
Clements, Traverse 1900(?)-1977
Obituary 69-72
Clements, William 1933(?)-1983 Obituary .. 110
Clements, William M(orris) 1943- 106
Clemhout, Simone 1934- 73-76
Cleminshaw, Clarence Higbee 1902-1985
Obituary 116
Brief entry 106
Clemmons, Francois 1945- 41-44R
Clemmons, Robert S(tarr) 1910- CAP-2
Earlier sketch in CA 21-22
Clemmons, William (Preston) 1932- 57-60
Clemo, Jack
See Clemo, Reginald John
See also DLB 27
Clemo, Reginald John 1916- CANR-6
Earlier sketch in CA 13-14R
Clemo, Richard F(rederick) 1920-1976
Obituary 65-68
Clemoes, Peter Alan Martin 1920- 102
Clemons, Elizabeth
See Nowell, Elizabeth Cameron
Clemons, Harry 1879-19(?) CAP-1
Earlier sketch in CA 13-14
Clemons, Lulamae 1917- 73-76
Clemons, Walter, Jr. 1929- CANR-6
Earlier sketch in CA 4R
Clendenen, Clarence Clemens 1899- 3R
Clendenin, John C(ameron) 1903- 19-20R
Clendenin, William R(itchie) 1917-1979 ...13-14R
Obituary 120
Clendenning, John 1934- 123
Clendenning, Sheila T. 1939- 25-28R
Cleobury, Frank Harold 1892- CAP-1
Earlier sketch in CA 13-14
Clephane, Irene (Amy) 13-14R
Clepper, Henry (Edward) 1901-1987 .... CANR-1
Obituary 122
Earlier sketch in CA 45-48
Clepper, Irene E(lizabeth) 53-56
Clerc, Charles 1926- CANR-14
Earlier sketch in CA 37-40R
Clerici, Gianni 1930- 65-68
Clerihew, E.
See Bentley, E(dmund) C(lerihew)
Clerk, N. W.
See Lewis, C(live) S(taples)
Clery, (Reginald) Val(entine) 1924- CANR-3
Earlier sketch in CA 49-52
Cleugh, Mary F(rances) 1913- CANR-4
Earlier sketch in CA 3R
Cleve, Janita
See Rowland, D(onald) S(ydney)
Cleve, John
See Offutt, Andrew J(efferson V)
Cleveland, Bob
See Cleveland, George
Cleveland, Carles 1952- 85-88
Cleveland, Clifford S.
See Goldsmith, David H(irsh)
Cleveland, George 1903(?)-1985 Obituary .. 116
See also SATA 43
Cleveland, (James) Harlan 1918- CANR-4
Earlier sketch in CA 2R
Cleveland, Harold van B(uren) 1916- ... CANR-13
Earlier sketch in CA 23-24R
Cleveland, John
See McElfresh, (Elizabeth) Adeline
Cleveland, Leslie 1921- 102
Cleveland, Mary 1917- 104
Cleveland, Philip Jerome 1903- 11-12R
Cleveland, Ray L(eRoy) 1929- 21-22R
Cleveland, Sidney E(arl) 1919- 9-10R
Cleven, Cathrine
See Cleven, Kathryn Seward
Cleven, Kathryn Seward 4R
See also SATA 2
Clevenger, Ernest Allen, Jr. 1929- CANR-8
Earlier sketch in CA 57-60
Clevenger, Theodore, Jr. 1929- 41-44R
Clever, (Warren) Glenn 1918- 57-60
Cleverdon, (Thomas) Douglas (James)
1903-1987 ....29-32R
Obituary 123
Cleverley Ford, D(ouglas) W(illiam)
1914- CANR-11
Earlier sketch in CA 25-28R
Cleves, Bernard
See Moore, Bernard
Clevin, Joergen 1920- 29-32R
See also SATA 7
Clevin, Jorgen
See Clevin, Joergen
Clew, Jeffrey Robert 1928- CANR-21
Earlier sketches in CA 57-60, CANR-6
Clew, William J(oseph) 1904- 77-80
Clewes, Dorothy (Mary) 1907- CANR-3
Earlier sketch in CA 5-6R
See also SATA 1
Clews, Roy 1937- 65-68
Click, J(ohn) W(illiam) 1936- 57-60
Cliff, Jimmy
See Chambers, James
See also CLC 21
Cliff, Michelle 1946- 116
Clifford, Derek Plint 1915- CANR-4
Earlier sketch in CA 7-8R
Clifford, Eth
See Rosenberg, Ethel (Clifford)
Clifford, Francis
See Thompson, A(rthur) L(eonard) B(ell)
Clifford, George 1934(?)-1985 Obituary 118
Clifford, Geraldine Joncich 1931- 25-28R
Clifford, H(enry) Dalton 1911- 9-10R
Clifford, Harold B(urton) 1893- CAP-1
Earlier sketch in CA 11-12
See also SATA 10
Clifford, James L(owry) 1901-1978 ..... CANR-6
Obituary 77-80
Earlier sketch in CA 3R
Clifford, John
See Bayliss, John Clifford
Clifford, John E(dward) 1935- 37-40R
Clifford, John Garry 1942- 53-56
Clifford, John McLean 1904-1979 85-88
Clifford, John W(illiam) 1918- 19-20R

INDEX

Clifford, Laurie B(erry) 1948- ... 112
Clifford, Margaret Cort 1929- ... CANR-23
Earlier sketch in CA 25-28R
See also SATA 1
Clifford, Martin 1910- ... CANR-11
Earlier sketch in CA 25-28R
Clifford, Martin
See Hamilton, Charles Harold St. John
Clifford, Mary Louise Beneway 1926- ... CANR-3
Earlier sketch in CA 5-6R
See also SATA 23
Clifford, Nicholas R(owland) 1930- ... 21-22R
Clifford, Peggy
See Clifford, Margaret Cort
Clifford, Richard J(ohn) 1934- ... 112
Clifford, Sarah 1916-1976 ... CANR-11
Earlier sketch in CA 25-28R
Clifford, Theodore
See von Block, Sylvia
Cliffton, Katherine Potter
See Bryant, Katherine Cliffton
Clift, Virgil Alfred 1912- ... 9-10R
Clift, Wallace Bruce 1926- ... 110
Clifton, Bernice Marie 1901(?)-1985 ... 7-8R
Obituary ... 116
Clifton, Bud
See Stacton, David (Derek)
Clifton, Fred J. 1935(?)-1984 Obituary ... 114
Clifton, Harry
See Hamilton, Charles Harold St. John
Clifton, Jack (Whitney) 1912- ... 106
Clifton, James A(lfonso) 1927- ... CANR-10
Earlier sketch in CA 25-28R
Clifton, James M(alcolm) 1930- ... 112
Clifton, Lewis
See Linedecker, Clifford L.
Clifton, (Thelma) Lucille 1936- ... CANR-24
Earlier sketches in CA 49-52, CANR-2
See also SATA 20
See also DLB 5, 41
See also CLC 19
See also CLR 5
Clifton, Marguerite Ann 1925- ... 15-16R
Clifton, Mark (Irvin) 1906-1963 Obituary ... 117
Clignet, Remi Pierre 1931- ... 104
Climo, Shirley 1928- ... CANR-24
Earlier sketch in CA 107
See also SATA 35, 39
Clinard, Dorothy Long 1909- ... 5-6R
Clinard, Helen Hall 1931- ... 124
Clinard, Marshall B(arron) 1911- ... CANR-4
Earlier sketch in CA 7-8R
Clinard, Turner N(orman) 1917- ... 37-40R
Clinch, Nicholas (Bayard) 1930- ... 111
Clinchy, Everett R(oss) 1896-1986
Obituary ... 118
Cline, Bev
See Fink Cline, Beverly
Cline, Beverly
See Fink Cline, Beverly
Cline, Beverly Fink
See Fink Cline, Beverly
Cline, C(harles) Terry, Jr. 1935- ... CANR-8
Earlier sketch in CA 61-64
Cline, Catherine Ann 1927- ... 19-20R
Cline, Charles (William) 1937- ... CANR-7
Earlier sketch in CA 61-64
Cline, Denzel C(ecil) 1903- ... CAP-2
Earlier sketch in CA 21-22
Cline, Edward 1946- ... 101
Cline, G(loria) Griffen 1929- ... 7-8R
Cline, Joan
See Hamilton, Joan Lesley
Cline, Linda 1941- ... 65-68
Cline, Ray Steiner 1918- Brief entry ... 106
Cline, Rodney 1903- ... 61-64
Cline, Victor (Bailey) 1925- ... 65-68
Clinebell, Howard J., Jr. 1922- ... CANR-13
Earlier sketch in CA 33-36R
Clinton, (Lloyd) D(eWitt) 1946- ... 116
Clinton, Dirk
See Silverberg, Robert
Clinton, F. G.
See Campbell, R(obert) Wright
Clinton, Iris A. (Corbin) 1901- ... CAP-1
Earlier sketch in CA 11-12
Clinton, Jeff
See Bickham, Jack M(iles)
Clinton, Jon
See Prince, J(ack) H(arvey)
Clinton, Richard Lee 1938- ... CANR-23
Earlier sketches in CA 61-64, CANR-8
Clinton, Rupert
See Bulmer, (Henry) Kenneth
Clinton-Baddeley, V.C. 1911(?)-1970
Obituary ... 104
Clipman, William 1954- ... 106
Clipper, Lawrence Jon 1930- ... 49-52
Clish, (Lee) Marian 1946- ... SATA-43
Clissmann, Anne
See Clune, Anne
Clissold, (John) Stephen (Hallet)
1913-1982 ... 110
Obituary ... 107
Clistier, Adeline
See Denny, Alma
Clithero, Myrtle E(ly) 1906- ... CAP-2
Earlier sketch in CA 25-28
Clithero, Sally
See Clithero, Myrtle E(ly)
Clive, Clifford
See Hamilton, Charles Harold St. John
Clive, Geoffrey 1927-1976 ... 33-36R
Clive, John 1933- ... 103
Clive, John Leonard 1924- ... 85-88
Clive, Mary 1907- ... 21-22R
Clive, William
See Bassett, Ronald
Clodfelter, (William) Frank(lin) 1911- ... 103
Clodfelter, Micheal 1946- ... 69-72
Cloeren, Hermann J(osef) 1934- ... 41-44R
Cloete, Stuart 1897-1976 ... CANR-3
Obituary ... 65-68
Earlier sketch in CA 1R
Clogan, Paul M(aurice) 1934- ... 33-36R
Clogg, Clifford C(ollier) 1949- ... 112
Cloke, Richard 1916- ... CANR-11
Earlier sketch in CA 69-72
Clokey, Richard Montgomery 1936-
Brief entry ... 107
Clones, N(icholas) J. ... 97-100
Clopton, Beverly Virginia B(eck) ... 106
Clor, Harry M(ortimer) 1929- ... 53-56
Clore, Gerald L(ewis, Jr.) 1939- ... 37-40R
Close, A. Kathryn 1908(?)-1973
Obituary ... 41-44R
Close, Henry T(hompson) 1928- ... 4R
Close, Reginald Arthur 1909- ... 17-18R
Close, Upton
See Hall, Josef Washington
Closen, Michael L. 1949- ... 121
Closs, August 1898- ... CANR-2
Earlier sketch in CA 5-6R
Closs, Elizabeth
See Traugott, Elizabeth Closs
Clotfelter, Beryl E(dward) 1926- ... 53-56
Clotfelter, Cecil F. 1929- ... 53-56
Clotfelter, Mary (Eunice) L(ong) ... 103
Clothier, Peter (Dean) 1936- ... 65-68
Cloud, (Joseph) Fred (Jr.) 1925- ... 15-16R
Cloud, Patricia
See Strother, Pat Wallace
Cloud, Preston (Ercelle) 1912- ... 93-96
Cloud, Yvonne
See Kapp, Yvonne (Mayer)
Cloudsley-Thompson, J(ohn) L(eonard)
1921- ... CANR-23
Earlier sketches in CA 19-20R, CANR-8
See also SATA 19
Clough, Arthur Hugh 1819-1861 ... DLB-32
Clough, B(renda) W(ang) 1955- ... 116
Clough, Francis F(rederick) 1912- ... CAP-1
Earlier sketch in CA 9-10
Clough, Neil 1950- ... 112
Clough, Ralph Nelson 1916- Brief entry ... 105
Clough, Rosa Trillo 1906- ... 13-14R
Clough, Shepard B(ancroft) 1901- ... CANR-4
Earlier sketch in CA 1R
Clough, William 1911(?)-1976 Obituary ... 69-72
Clough, William A. 1899- ... CAP-2
Earlier sketch in CA 21-22
Clough, Wilson O(ber) 1894- ... 17-18R
Clouse, Robert Gordon 1931- ... CANR-12
Earlier sketch in CA 29-32R
Clouser, John William 1932- ... 61-64
Clout, Hugh Donald 1944- ... CANR-15
Earlier sketch in CA 41-44R
Cloutier, Cecile
See Cloutier-Wojciechowska, Cecile
See also DLB 60
Cloutier, David 1951- ... CANR-7
Earlier sketch in CA 57-60
Cloutier-Wojciechowska, Cecile 1930- ... CANR-12
Earlier sketch in CA 65-68
Clover, Frank Metlar III 1940- ... 101
Clow, Martha de Mey 1932- ... 29-32R
Cloward, Richard Andrew 1926- ... 41-44R
Clower, Robert W(ayne) 1926- ... 89-92
Clowney, Edmund P(rosper) 1917- ... CANR-8
Earlier sketch in CA 5-6R
Clowse, Converse Dilworth 1929-
Brief entry ... 108
Clubb, Louise George 1930- ... 69-72
Clubb, O(liver) Edmund 1901- ... 37-40R
Clubb, Oliver E., Jr. 1929- ... 5-6R
Clubbe, John 1938- ... CANR-11
Earlier sketch in CA 25-28R
Cluff, Charles E. 1937- ... 65-68
Clugston, Richard 1938- ... 41-44R
Clum, John M(acKenzie) 1941- ... 69-72
Clun, Arthur
See Polsby, Nelson W(oolf)
Clune, Anne 1945- ... 103
Clune, Francis Patrick 1893-1971 ... CAP-2
Obituary ... 29-32R
Earlier sketch in CA 23-24
Clune, Frank
See Clune, Francis Patrick
Clune, Henry W. 1890- ... CANR-5
Earlier sketch in CA 2R
Clunies Ross, Anthony (Ian) 1932- ... 53-56
Clurman, Harold 1901-1980 ... CANR-2
Obituary ... 101
Earlier sketch in CA 4R
Cluster, Dick 1947- ... 97-100
Clute, Morrel J. 1912- ... 13-14R
Clute, Robert E(ugene) 1924- ... 41-44R
Clutha, Janet Paterson Frame 1924- ... CANR-2
Earlier sketch in CA 4R
Clutterbuck, David Ashley 1947- ... 113
Clutterbuck, Richard 1917- ... CANR-9
Earlier sketch in CA 23-24R
Clutton-Brock, Arthur Guy 1906- ... 110
Cluver, Eustace Henry 1894- ... CAP-1
Earlier sketch in CA 9-10
Cluysenaar, Anne (Alice Andree Jackson)
1936- ... 102
Clyde, Leslie
See Kipps, Harriet C(lyde)
Clyde, Norman Asa 1885-1972 ... 41-44R
Clyde Cool
See Frazier, Walt(er)
Clymer, Eleanor 1906- ... CANR-9
Earlier sketch in CA 61-64
See also SATA 9
Clymer, (Joseph) Floyd 1895-1970
Obituary ... 104
Clymer, Kenton James 1943- Brief entry ... 109
Clymer, Reuben Swinburne 1878- ... CAP-1
Earlier sketch in CA 11-12
Clynder, Monica
See Muir, Marie
Clyne, James F. 1898(?)-1977 Obituary ... 69-72
Clyne, Patricia (Edwards) ... 101
See also SATA 31
Clyne, Terence
See Blatty, William Peter
Clytus, John 1929- ... 29-32R
Cnudde, Charles F. 1938- ... 29-32R
Coad, F(rederick) Roy 1925- ... 103
Coad, Oral Sumner 1887- ... 45-48
Coade, Jessie 1911- ... 120
Coakley, Lakme 1912- ... 69-72
Coakley, Mary Lewis ... CAP-1
Earlier sketch in CA 15-16
Coale, Samuel Chase 1943- ... CANR-11
Earlier sketch in CA 65-68
Coalson, Glo 1946- ... 103
See also SATA 26
Coan, Eugene V(ictor) 1943- ... 110
Coan, Otis W(elton) 1895- ... CAP-2
Earlier sketch in CA 33-36
Coan, Richard Welton 1928- ... CANR-12
Earlier sketch in CA 69-72
Coates, Austin 1922- ... 102
Coates, Belle 1896- ... 5-6R
See also SATA 2
Coates, Charles R(obert) 1915- ... 106
Coates, Donald R(obert) 1922- ... CANR-2
Earlier sketch in CA 49-52
Coates, Doreen (Frances) 1912- ... 107
Coates, Gary J(oseph) 1947- ... 110
Coates, Geoffrey Edward 1917- ... 37-40R
Coates, J(ohn) F(rancis) 1922- ... 123
Coates, Ken 1930- ... 123
Coates, Robert M(yron) 1897-1973 ... 5-6R
Obituary ... 41-44R
See also DLB 4, 9
Coates, Ruth Allison 1915- ... 57-60
See also SATA 11
Coates, William Ames 1916-1973 ... 37-40R
Coates, Willson H(avelock) 1899-1976 ... 37-40R
Obituary ... 69-72
Coats, Alice M(argaret) 1905- ... 53-56
See also SATA 11
Coats, George W. 1936- ... 23-24R
Coats, Peter 1910- ... CANR-1
Earlier sketch in CA 49-52
Coatsworth, Elizabeth (Jane)
1893-1986 ... CANR-4
Obituary ... 120
Earlier sketch in CA 7-8R
See also SATA 2, 49
See also DLB 22
See also CLR 2
Cobb, Alice 1909- ... 7-8R
Cobb, Carl W(esley) 1926- ... 21-22R
Cobb, Charles E., Jr. 1943- ... DLB-41
Cobb, David 1934- ... 112
Cobb, Faye Davis 1932- ... 9-10R
Cobb, Frank I. 1869-1923 ... DLB-25
Cobb, Geoffrey Belton 1892(?)-1971
Obituary ... 104
Cobb, Irvin S. 1876-1944 ... DLB-11, 25
Cobb, James Charles 1947- ... 112
Cobb, Jane
See Berry, Jane Cobb
Cobb, John B(oswell), Jr. 1925- ... CANR-2
Earlier sketch in CA 3R
Cobb, Jonathan 1946- ... 93-96
Cobb, Nathan 1943- ... 105
Cobb, R. C.
See Cobb, Richard (Charles)
Cobb, Richard (Charles) 1917- Brief entry ... 116
Cobb, Robert A. 1941- ... 69-72
Cobb, Roger W(illiam) 1941- ... 104
Cobb, Vicki 1938- ... CANR-14
Earlier sketch in CA 33-36R
See also SATA 8
See also CLR 2
Cobban, Alfred 1901-1968 Obituary ... 111
Cobbett
See Ludovici, Anthony M(ario)
Cobbett, Richard
See Pluckrose, Henry (Arthur)
Cobbett, William 1762-1835 ... DLB-43
Cobbing, Bob 1920- ... 101
Cobbledick, James R. 1935- ... 97-100
Cobbs, John L(ewis) 1917- Brief entry ... 115
Cobbs, Price M(ashaw) 1928- ... 23-24R
Coben, Lawrence A(llan) 1926- ... 111
Coben, Stanley 1929- ... 122
Cober, Alan E(dwin) 1935- ... SATA-7
Cobham, Sir Alan
See Hamilton, Charles Harold St. John
Coble, John (Lawrence) 1924- ... 9-10R
Cobleigh, Ira U(nderwood) 1903- ... 81-84
Coblentz, Stanton A(rthur) 1896- ... CANR-21
Earlier sketch in CA 5-6R
Cobley, John 1914- ... 13-14R
Cobrin, Harry Aaron 1902- ... CAP-2
Earlier sketch in CA 29-32
Coburn, Andrew 1932- ... CANR-4
Earlier sketch in CA 53-56
Coburn, Broughton 1951- ... 111
Coburn, D(onald) L(ee) 1938- ... 89-92
See also CLC 10
Coburn, John Bowen 1914- ... CANR-2
Earlier sketch in CA 4R
Coburn, Karen Levin 1941- ... 65-68
Coburn, Kathleen 1905- ... 93-96
Coburn, Louis 1915- ... 104
Coburn, Thomas B(owen) 1944- ... 110
Coburn, Walt 1889- ... CAP-1
Earlier sketch in CA 9-10
Cocagnac, Augustin Maurice(-Jean)
1924- ... CANR-17
Earlier sketch in CA 25-28R
See also SATA 7
Coccioli, Carlo 1920- ... CANR-9
Earlier sketch in CA 13-14R
Cochard, Thomas S(ylvester) 1893- ... 57-60
Cochet, Gabriel 1888-1973 Obituary ... 45-48
Cochran, Bert 1917-1984 ... 45-48
Obituary ... 113
Cochran, Bobbye A. 1949- ... SATA-11
Cochran, Charles L(eo) 1940- ... 57-60
Cochran, Clarke E(dward) 1945- ... 107
Cochran, Elizabeth
See Cochrane, Elizabeth
Cochran, Hamilton 1898-1977 ... CANR-6
Obituary ... 73-76
Earlier sketch in CA 3R
Cochran, Jacqueline 1910(?)-1980
Obituary ... 101
Cochran, Jeff
See Durst, Paul
Cochran, John A(rthur) 1921- ... 122
Cochran, John R(obert) 1937- ... 41-44R
Cochran, Leslie H(ershel) 1939- ... CANR-2
Earlier sketch in CA 49-52
Cochran, Rice E.
See Monroe, Keith
Cochran, Thomas C(hilds) 1902- ... CANR-8
Earlier sketch in CA 61-64
See also DLB 17
Cochrane, Arthur C(aspersz) 1909- ... CANR-4
Earlier sketch in CA 7-8R
Cochrane, Elizabeth 1867-1922 Brief entry ... 118
See also DLB 25
Cochrane, Eric W. 1928-1985 ... 49-52
Obituary ... 118
Cochrane, Glynn 1940- ... 53-56
Cochrane, Hugh (Ferrier) 1923- ... 103
Cochrane, James D(avid) 1938- ... 29-32R
Cochrane, James L. 1941- ... CANR-13
Earlier sketch in CA 33-36R
Cochrane, Jennifer (Ann Frances) 1936- ... 102
Cochrane, Louise Morley 1918- ... 11-12R
Cochrane, Pauline A(therton) 1929- ... 110
Cochrane, Willard W(esley) 1914- ... CANR-11
Earlier sketch in CA 23-24R
Cochrane, William E. 1926- ... 97-100
Cochrane de Alencar, Gertrude E. L.
1906- ... 7-8R
Cochran-Smith, Marilyn 1951- ... 115
Coch-y-Bonddhu
See Arnold, Richard
Cockburn, Alexander 1941- Brief entry ... 123
Cockburn, (Francis) Claud 1904-1981 ... 102
Obituary ... 105
Cockburn, Thomas Aiden 1912- ... 9-10R
Cockcroft, George Powers 1932- ... 116
Cockcroft, James D(onald) 1935- ... CANR-10
Earlier sketch in CA 25-28R
Cockcroft, John (Douglas) 1897-1967 ... CAP-2
Earlier sketch in CA 21-22
Cockerell, H(ugh) A(nthony) L(ewis)
1909- ... CAP-1
Earlier sketch in CA 13-14
Cockerell, Sydney M(orris) 1906-1987
Obituary ... 124
Cockerill, John A. 1845-1896 ... DLB-23
Cockett, Mary ... CANR-19
Earlier sketches in CA 9-10R, CANR-4
See also SATA 3
Cockfield, Jamie (Hartwell) 1945- ... 115
Cocking, Clive 1938- ... 105
Cocking, J(ohn) M(artin) 1914- ... 53-56
Cockrell, Amanda
See Crowe, Amanda Cockrell
Cockrell, Marian (Brown) 1909- ... CAP-2
Earlier sketch in CA 17-18
Cocks, Geoffrey (Campbell) 1948- ... 121
Cockshut, A(nthony) O(liver) J(ohn)
1927- ... CANR-10
Earlier sketch in CA 19-20R
Coco, James (Emil) 1930(?)-1987
Obituary ... 121
Cocozzella, Peter 1937- ... 37-40R
Cocozzoli, Gary R(ichard) 1951- ... 119
Cocteau, Jean (Maurice Eugene Clement)
1889-1963 ... CAP-2
Earlier sketch in CA 25-28
See also DLB 65
See also CLC 1, 8, 15, 16, 43
Codding, George A(rthur), Jr. 1923- ... CANR-13
Earlier sketch in CA 33-36R
Code, Grant Hyde 1896-1974 ... 49-52
Codel, Martin 1903(?)-1973 Obituary ... 41-44R
Codel, Michael R(ichard) 1939- ... 73-76
Coder, S(amuel) Maxwell 1902- ... CANR-14
Earlier sketch in CA 37-40R
Codere, Helen (Frances) 1917- ... 69-72
Codevilla, (Maria) Angelo 1943- ... 61-64
Codrescu, Andrei 1946- ... CANR-13
Earlier sketch in CA 33-36R
See also CLC 46
Codrington, Kenneth de Burgh 1899-1986
Obituary ... 118
Cody, Al
See Joscelyn, Archie L.
Cody, C. S.
See Waller, Leslie
Cody, D(ouglas) Thane R(omney) 1932- ... 57-60
Cody, Fred 1916- ... 107

Cody, James P.
See Rohrbach, Peter Thomas
Cody, John 1925- 101
Cody, John J. 1930- 29-32R
Cody, Martin L(eonard) 1941- 53-56
Cody, Walt
See Norwood, Victor G(eorge) C(harles)
Coe, Charles Norton 1915- 4R
Coe, Christine Sadler
See Sadler, Christine
Coe, Douglas
See Epstein, Beryl (M. Williams)
and Epstein, Samuel
Coe, Fred(erick) 1914-1979 Obituary 85-88
Coe, Lloyd 1899(?)-1976 Obituary 69-72
See also SATA 30
Coe, Malcolm (James) 1930- 123
Coe, Max
See Bourne, Randolph S(illiman)
Coe, Michael Douglas 1929- CANR-19
Earlier sketches in CA 4R, CANR-4
Coe, Michelle E(ileen) 1917- 106
Coe, Peter 1929-1987 Obituary 122
Coe, Ralph T(racy) 1929- CANR-1
Earlier sketch in CA 2R
Coe, Richard L(ivingston) 1916- 65-68
Coe, Richard N(elson) 1923- CANR-12
Earlier sketch in CA 25-28R
Coe, Rodney Michael 1933- 41-44R
Coe, Tucker
See Westlake, Donald E(dwin)
Coe, William C(harles) 1930- 37-40R
Coel, Margaret 1937- 106
Coelho, George Victor 1918- CANR-1
Earlier sketch in CA 45-48
Coen, Rena Neumann 1925- 15-16R
See also SATA 20
Coens, Sister Mary Xavier 1918- 21-22R
Coerr, Eleanor (Beatrice) 1922- CANR-11
Earlier sketch in CA 25-28R
See also SATA 1
Coetzee, J(ohn) M. 1940- 77-80
See also CLC 23, 33
Cofer, Charles N(orval) 1916- 37-40R
Cofer, Judith Ortiz 1952- 115
Coffee, Lenore J. 1897(?)-1984 Obituary 113
See also DLB 44
Coffey, Alan R. 1931- 33-36R
Coffey, Brian
See Koontz, Dean R(ay)
Coffey, (Helen) Dairine 1933- 21-22R
Coffey, J(oseph) I(rving) 1916- 41-44R
Coffey, John W(ill), Jr. 1925- 45-48
Coffey, Marilyn 1937- CANR-2
Earlier sketch in CA 45-48
Coffey, Robert E(dward) 1931- 65-68
Coffey, Thomas Patrick 1928- 120
Coffin, Arthur B. 1929- 29-32R
Coffin, Berton 1910- CANR-5
Earlier sketch in CA 11-12R
Coffin, David R(obbins) 1918- 5-6R
Coffin, Dean 1911- 33-36R
Coffin, Frank M(orey) 1919- 11-12R
Coffin, Geoffrey
See Mason, F(rancis) van Wyck
Coffin, George S(turgis) 1903- 7-8R
Coffin, Harold 1905(?)-1981 Obituary 104
Coffin, Harold Glen 1926- 115
Coffin, Joseph (John) 1899- 57-60
Coffin, Lewis A(ugustus) III 1932- 61-64
Coffin, Lyn 1943- 110
Coffin, Patricia 1912-1974 CAP-2
Obituary 49-52
Earlier sketch in CA 33-36
Coffin, Robert P(eter) Tristram 1892-1955
Brief entry 123
See also DLB 45
Coffin, Tristram 1912- 23-24R
Coffin, Tristram Potter 1922- CANR-2
Earlier sketch in CA 5-6R
Coffin, William Sloane, Jr. 1924- 103
Coffinet, Julien 1907- 61-64
Coffman, Barbara Frances 1907- CAP-1
Earlier sketch in CA 15-16
Coffman, Charles DeWitt 1909- 102
Coffman, Edward M. 1929- 33-36R
Coffman, Paul B(rown) 1900- CAP-2
Earlier sketch in CA 21-22
Coffman, Ramon Peyton 1896- CAP-2
Earlier sketch in CA 17-18
See also SATA 4
Coffman, Virginia (Edith) 1914- CANR-2
Earlier sketch in CA 49-52
Cofyn, Cornelius
See Saunders, Hilary Aidan St. George
Cogane, Gerald
See Fonarow, Jerry
Coger, Leslie Irene 1912- 21-22R
Coggan, (Frederick) Donald 1909- 17-18R
Coggan, Philip A(nnett) 1917- 117
Coggins, Jack (Banham) 1914- CANR-2
Earlier sketch in CA 7-8R
See also SATA 2
Coggins, Ross 1927- 15-16R
Coghill, Nevill (Henry Kendall Aylmer)
1899-1980 CANR-11
Obituary 102
Earlier sketch in CA 13-14R
Coghlan, Brian (Laurence Dillon) 1926- 17-18R
Coghlan, Margaret M. 1920- 106
Cogley, John 1916-1976 CANR-2
Obituary 65-68
Earlier sketch in CA 45-48
Cogswell, Coralie (Norris) 1930- 15-16R
Cogswell, Fred(erick William) 1917- CANR-18
Earlier sketches in CA 7-8R, CANR-3
See also DLB 60
Cogswell, James A(rthur) 1922- 33-36R
Cogswell, Mason Fitch 1761-1830 DLB-37
Cogswell, Theodore R. 1918- CANR-4
Earlier sketch in CA 4R
Cohan, Avery B(erlow) 1914-1977 61-64
Obituary 69-72
Cohan, Tony 1939- 108
Cohane, John Philip 1911- 101
Cohane, Tim(othy) 1912- 9-10R
Cohart, Mary 1911- 57-60
Cohen, Aaron (Samuel) 1935- 110
Cohen, Aharon 1910- 69-72
Cohen, Albert 1895(?)-1981 Obituary 105
Cohen, Albert J. 1903(?)-1984 Obituary 114
Cohen, Albert Kircidel 1918- 13-14R
Cohen, Allan Y. 1939- 33-36R
Cohen, Amnon 1936- 85-88
Cohen, Anne Billings 1937- 57-60
Cohen, Anthea 1913- CANR-18
Earlier sketch in CA 97-100
Cohen, Arthur A(llen) 1928-1986 CANR-17
Obituary 120
Earlier sketches in CA 4R, CANR-1
See also DLB 28
See also CLC 7, 31
Cohen, Arthur M. 1927- 33-36R
Cohen, B(enjamin) Bernard 1922- 11-12R
Cohen, Barbara 1932- CANR-19
Earlier sketches in CA 53-56, CANR-4
See also SATA 10
Cohen, Benjamin J(erry) 1937- CANR-18
Earlier sketch in CA 101
Cohen, Benjamin Victor 1894-1983 CAP-1
Obituary 110
Earlier sketch in CA 11-12
Cohen, Bernard 1937- 103
Cohen, Bernard Lande 1902- 29-32R
Cohen, Bernard P. 1930- 45-48
Cohen, Bruce J. 1938- 89-92
Cohen, Carl 1931- CANR-5
Earlier sketch in CA 3R
Cohen, Charles 1943- 111
Cohen, Daniel (E.) 1936- CANR-20
Earlier sketches in CA 45-48, CANR-1
See also SATA 8
See also SAAS 4
Cohen, David 1952- 108
Cohen, David Steven 1943- 53-56
Cohen, Donna 1947- 122
Cohen, Dorothy H. 1915- Brief entry 105
Cohen, Edgar H. 1913- 29-32R
Cohen, Edmund D(avid) 1943- 57-60
Cohen, Edward H. 1941- Brief entry 115
Cohen, Edward M(artin) 1936- 23-24R
Cohen, Elaine (Marsha Perlman) 1938- 110
Cohen, Elie Aron 1909- 53-56
Cohen, Eliot A(sher) 1956- 113
Cohen, Florence Chanock 1927- 5-6R
Cohen, Gary B(ennett) 1948- 107
Cohen, Gary G. 1934- CANR-7
Earlier sketch in CA 57-60
Cohen, George Michael 1931- 81-84
Cohen, Harry 1936- 106
Cohen, (Henry) Hennig 1919- CANR-5
Earlier sketch in CA 3R
Cohen, Henry 1933- 33-36R
Cohen, Howard Martin 1926- Brief entry 107
Cohen, I. Bernard 1914- 69-72
Cohen, Ira Sheldon 1924- CANR-10
Earlier sketch in CA 5-6R
Cohen, Jacob 1918- 123
Cohen, Jean Louise 1946- 111
Cohen, Jene Barr 1900-1985 CANR-3
Obituary 115
Earlier sketch in CA 5-6R
Cohen, Jerome Alan 1930- CANR-13
Earlier sketch in CA 49-52
Cohen, Jerome B(ernard) 1915-1986 9-10R
Obituary 121
Cohen, Joan Lebold 1932- CANR-13
Earlier sketch in CA 25-28R
See also SATA 4
Cohen, John 1911- CANR-6
Earlier sketch in CA 13-14R
Cohen, John Michael 1903- CANR-4
Earlier sketch in CA 7-8R
Cohen, Joseph 1926- CANR-10
Earlier sketch in CA 65-68
Cohen, Jozef 1921- 29-32R
Cohen, Judith Beth 1943- 118
Cohen, Kalman J(oseph) 1931- 15-16R
Cohen, Kathleen Rogers 1933- 53-56
Cohen, Keith 1945- 101
Cohen, Lawrence Jonathan 1923- 65-68
Cohen, Leonard (Norman) 1934- CANR-14
Earlier sketch in CA 21-22R
See also DLB 53
See also CLC 3, 38
Cohen, Margie K(anter) 1912- 109
Cohen, (Stephen) Marshall 1929- CANR-23
Earlier sketches in CA 45-48, CANR-2
Cohen, Martin A(aron) 1928- Brief entry 113
Cohen, Marvin 1931- CANR-17
Earlier sketch in CA 25-28R
Cohen, Matt 1942- 61-64
See also DLB 53
See also CLC 19
Cohen, Michael P. 1944- 121
Cohen, Mike
See Cohen, Morris
Cohen, Miriam 1926- 106
See also SATA 29
Cohen, Morris 1912- 17-18R
Cohen, Morris L(eo) 1927- 49-52
Cohen, Mortimer J. 1894-1972 Obituary 104
Cohen, Morton N(orton) 1921- CANR-5
Earlier sketch in CA 2R
Cohen, Myron 1903(?)-1986 Obituary 118
Cohen, Nancy Wainer 1947- 111
Cohen, Naomi W(iener) 1927- Brief entry 114
Cohen, Norm(an) 1936- 109
Cohen, Octavus Roy 1891-1959
Brief entry 112
Cohen, Paul Andrew 1934- 115
Cohen, Paul S. 1945- 123
Cohen, Peter Zachary 1931- CANR-12
Earlier sketch in CA 33-36R
See also SATA 4
Cohen, Richard Murry 1938- CANR-19
Earlier sketch in CA 103
Cohen, Robert 1938- CANR-12
Earlier sketch in CA 29-32R
Cohen, Robert Carl 1930- 57-60
See also SATA 8
Cohen, Roberta G. 1937- 49-52
Cohen, Ronald 1930- CANR-13
Earlier sketch in CA 33-36R
Cohen, Ronald Dennis 1940- 105
Cohen, Ronald Jay 1949- 97-100
Cohen, Rosalyn
See Higgins, Rosalyn (Cohen)
Cohen, S. Alan 1933- 29-32R
Cohen, S. Ralph 1917-1983 Obituary 110
Cohen, Sanford 1920- 1R
Cohen, Sara Kay Sherman 1943- 102
Cohen, Sarah Blacher 1936- 81-84
Cohen, Scott 1946- 116
Cohen, Selma Jeanne 1920- 25-28R
Cohen, Seymour Jay 1922- 25-28R
Cohen, Sharleen Cooper CANR-19
Earlier sketch in CA 97-100
Cohen, Sheldon S. 1931- 25-28R
Cohen, Sherry Suib 1934- 102
Cohen, Sidney 1910-1987 15-16R
Obituary 122
Cohen, Stanley 1928- CANR-15
Earlier sketch in CA 29-32R
Cohen, Stephen 1941- 118
Cohen, Stephen D(avid) 1942- 111
Cohen, Stephen F(rand) 1938- 49-52
Cohen, Stephen S. 1941- 33-36R
Cohen, Stephen Z(olman) 1931- 121
Cohen, Steve (Michael) 1951- 114
Cohen, Stewart 1940- 65-68
Cohen, Susan 1938- CANR-20
Earlier sketches in CA 53-56, CANR-5
Cohen, Warren I. 1934- CANR-9
Earlier sketch in CA 21-22R
Cohen, Wilbur J(oseph) 1913-1987 CANR-17
Obituary 122
Earlier sketch in CA 25-28R
Cohen, William A(lan) 1937- CANR-19
Earlier sketch in CA 103
Cohen, William B(enjamin) 1941- 37-40R
Cohen, William Howard 1927- 17-18R
Cohen, William S(ebastian) 1940- 108
Cohen, Yehudi A(ryeh) 1928- 113
Cohen-Stratyner, Barbara Naomi 1951- 113
Cohler, Bertram J(oseph) 1938- 109
Cohler, David Keith 1940- 104
Cohn, Adrian A. 1922- 25-28R
Cohn, Alan M(artin) 1926- 110
Cohn, Angelo 1914- CANR-4
Earlier sketch in CA 5-6R
See also SATA 19
Cohn, Arthur 1910- 110
Cohn, Dorrit 1924- 93-96
Cohn, Elchanan 1941- 73-76
Cohn, Haim H(erman) 1911- 45-48
Cohn, Helen Desfosses
See Desfosses, Helen
Cohn, Jan Kadetsky 1933- 102
Cohn, Jules 1930- 33-36R
Cohn, Keith E(van) 1935- 107
Cohn, Lester
See Cole, Lester
Cohn, Marguerite A. 1898(?)-1984
Obituary 113
Cohn, Marvin L(ester) 1924- 105
Cohn, Nik 1946- 102
Cohn, Norman 1915- 57-60
Cohn, Robert Greer 1921- 9-10R
Cohn, Roy M(arcus) 1927-1986 108
Obituary 119
Cohn, Rubin (Goodman) 1911-1986 57-60
Obituary 119
Cohn, Ruby 1922- 93-96
Cohn, Stanley H(arold) 1922- 29-32R
Cohn, Theodore 1923- 89-92
Cohn, Vera 1907- 97-100
Cohn, Victor (Edward) 1919- 65-68
Cohon, Barry
See Cohon, Baruch J(oseph)
Cohon, Baruch J(oseph) 1926- 29-32R
Cohon, Beryl David 1898- CANR-6
Earlier sketch in CA 1R
Coigney, Virginia 1917- 103
Coit, John Hamilton 1947(?)-1986
Obituary 118
Coit, Lew Garrison 1897(?)-1985 Obituary 116
Coit, Margaret Louise 1919- CANR-5
Earlier sketch in CA 1R
See also SATA 2
Cojeen, Robert H. 1920- 37-40R
Coke, Tom S(tephen) 1943- 115
Coke, Van Deren 1921- CANR-22
Earlier sketches in CA 15-16R, CANR-7
Coker, C(harles) F(rederick) W(illiams)
1932-1983 Obituary 110
Coker, Elizabeth Boatwright 1909- 45-48
Coker, Gylbert 1944- 93-96
Coker, Jerry 1932- CANR-6
Earlier sketch in CA 11-12R
Coker, Syl Cheney
See Cheney-Coker, Syl
Colacci, Mario 1910- 5-6R
Coladarci, Arthur Paul 1917- 5-6R
Colaiaco, James A(lfred) 1945- 115
Colander, Pat(ricia) 1952- 110
Colaneri, John Nunzio 1930- 103
Colaw, Emerson S. 1921- 13-14R
Colbach, Edward M(ichael) 1939- 69-72
Colbeck, Maurice 1925- CANR-5
Earlier sketch in CA 15-16R
Colberg, Marshall R(udolph) 1913- CANR-1
Earlier sketch in CA 1R
Colbert, Anthony 1934- 89-92
See also SATA 15
Colbert, Douglas A(lbert) 1933- 57-60
Colbert, Edwin Harris 1905- CANR-8
Earlier sketch in CA 61-64
Colbert, Evelyn S(peyer) 1918- 102
Colbert, James 1951- 122
Colbert, Roman 1921- 53-56
Colbourn, H(arold) Trevor 1927- 33-36R
Colburn, C(lyde) William 1939- 37-40R
Colburn, David Richard 1942- 110
Colburn, George A(bbott) 1938- 41-44R
Colby, Averil 1900-1983(?) Obituary 108
Colby, Benjamin N(ick) 1931- 61-64
Colby, C(arroll) B(urleigh) 1904-1977 CANR-6
Earlier sketch in CA 4R
See also SATA 3, 35
Colby, Douglas (Steven) 1954- 116
Colby, Elbridge 1891-1982 CAP-1
Obituary 108
Earlier sketch in CA 15-16
Colby, Jean Poindexter 1909- CANR-5
Earlier sketch in CA 4R
See also SATA 23
Colby, Joan 1939- CANR-13
Earlier sketch in CA 77-80
Colby, Robert A(lan) 1920- 53-56
Colby, Roy (Edward) 1910- 25-28R
Colby, Vineta (Blumoff) 1922- 11-12R
Colby, William Egan 1920- 81-84
Colchie, Elizabeth Schneider
See Schneider, Elizabeth (Susan)
Colden, Cadwallader 1688-1776 DLB-24, 30
Coldham, James D(esmond Bowden)
1924-1987 113
Obituary 121
Coldrey, Jennifer (M.) 1940- 121
Coldsmith, Don(ald Charles) 1926- CANR-21
Earlier sketch in CA 105
Coldwell, David F(rederick) C(larke)
1923- 17-18R
Coldwell, Joan 1936- 106
Coldwell, M(ichael) J. 1888-1974
Obituary 53-56
Cole, Adrian 1949- 121
Cole, Andrew Thomas, Jr. 1933- 102
Cole, Ann 1937- 65-68
Cole, Ann Kilborn
See Callahan, Claire Wallis
Cole, Annette
See Steiner, Barbara A(nnette)
Cole, Arthur C(harles) 1886-1976
Obituary 65-68
Cole, Barry 1936- CANR-16
Earlier sketch in CA 25-28R
See also DLB 14
Cole, Bill
See Cole, William Shadrack
Cole, Bruce 1938- CANR-15
Earlier sketch in CA 65-68
Cole, Burt 1930- 73-76
Cole, C(harles) Robert 1939- 65-68
Cole, Cannon
See Cook, Arlene Ethel
Cole, Charles C(hester), Jr. 1922- 118
Cole, Charles L(eland) 1927- 69-72
Cole, Charles Woolsey 1906-1978 CANR-22
Obituary 77-80
Earlier sketch in CA 69-72
Cole, Clifford A. 1915- 13-14R
Cole, Cozy
See Cole, William R.
Cole, Dandridge MacFarlan 1921- 13-14R
Cole, David Chamberlain 1928- Brief entry 106
Cole, Davis
See Elting, Mary
Cole, Donald Barnard 1922- 5-6R
Cole, Doris 1938- 89-92
Cole, Douglas 1934- CANR-2
Earlier sketch in CA 5-6R
Cole, E(ugene) R(oger) 1930- CANR-19
Earlier sketches in CA 53-56, CANR-4
Cole, Eddie-Lou 1909- 65-68
Cole, Edward B(ender) 1923- 107
Cole, Edward C(yrus) 1904- 15-16R
Cole, Frank R(aymond) 1892- 69-72
Cole, G(eorge) D(ouglas) H(oward)
1889-1959 Brief entry 108
Cole, George F(raser) 1935- 65-68
Cole, (Roger) Henri 1956- 121
Cole, Howard C(handler) 1934- 49-52
Cole, Hubert (Archibald Noel) 1908- CANR-5
Earlier sketch in CA 7-8R
Cole, J(ohn) A(lfred) 1905- CAP-1
Earlier sketch in CA 15-16
Cole, J. P.
See Cole, John P(eter)
Cole, Jack
See Stewart, John (William)
Cole, Jackson
See Germano, Peter B.
and Schisgall, Oscar
Cole, Janet
See Hunter, Kim

Cole, Jennifer
See Zach, Cheryl (Byrd)
Cole, Joan 1957- 113
Cole, Joanna 1944- 115
See also SATA 37, 49
See also CLR 5
Cole, John N(elson) 1923- 93-96
Cole, John P(eter) 1928- CANR-19
Earlier sketches in CA 5-6R, CANR-3
Cole, John Y(oung), Jr. 1940- CANR-19
Earlier sketch in CA 103
Cole, Jonathan R(ichard) 1942- 53-56
Cole, Juan R(icardo) I(rfan) 1952- 121
Cole, K. C. 1946- 105
Cole, (Edmund) Keith 1919- CANR-19
Earlier sketch in CA 102
Cole, Larry 1936- 45-48
Cole, Leonard A(aron) 1933- 81-84
Cole, Leonard Leslie 1909-1980 103
Cole, Lester 1904(?)-1985 Obituary 117
Cole, Lewis 1946- 109
Cole, Lois Dwight 1903-1979 .... CANR-4
Obituary 104
Earlier sketch in CA 2R
See also SATA 10, 26
Cole, Luella (Winifred) 1893-19(?) CAP-1
Earlier sketch in CA 19-20
Cole, Margaret Alice CANR-6
Earlier sketch in CA 11-12R
Cole, Margaret Isabel 1893-1980 .... CANR-4
Obituary 97-100
Earlier sketch in CA 5-6R
Cole, Martha 1916(?)-1986 Obituary 118
Cole, Mary
See Hanna, Mary T.
Cole, Michael 1938- 97-100
Cole, Michelle 1940- 29-32R
Cole, Monica M(ary) 1922- 4R
Cole, Richard Cargill 1926- 124
Cole, Robert E(van) 1937- 69-72
Cole, Robert H. 1918- 33-36R
Cole, Roger L. 1933- 25-28R
Cole, Sandi Gelles
See Gelles-Cole, Sandi
Cole, Sheila R(otenberg) 1939- CANR-4
Earlier sketch in CA 53-56
See also SATA 24
Cole, Sonia (Mary) 1918-1982 93-96
Obituary 106
Cole, Stephen 1941- 29-32R
Cole, Stephen
See Webbe, Gale D(udley)
Cole, Sylvan, Jr. 1918- 69-72
Cole, (Andrew) Thomas (Jr.) 1933- 33-36R
Cole, W(illiam) Owen 1931- 118
Cole, Wayne S. 1922- 23-24R
Cole, Wendell 1914- 23-24R
Cole, William (Rossa) 1919- CANR-7
Earlier sketch in CA 9-10R
See also SATA 9
Cole, William Earle 1904- 17-18R
Cole, William Graham 1917- 19-20R
Cole, William R. 1909-1981 Obituary 108
Cole, William Shadrack 1937- 101
Colean, Miles Lanier 1898- CAP-2
Earlier sketch in CA 21-22
Coleburt, J(ames) Russell 1920- 13-14R
Colecchia, Francesca Maria 89-92
Colegate, Isabel 1931- CANR-22
Earlier sketches in CA 17-18R, CANR-8
See also DLB 14
See also CLC 36
Colegrove, Kenneth 1886-1975 .... CANR-4
Obituary 53-56
Earlier sketch in CA 5-6R
Coleman, A(llan) D(ouglass) 1943- CANR-15
Earlier sketch in CA 73-76
Coleman, Almand R(ouse) 1905- CAP-2
Earlier sketch in CA 29-32
Coleman, Arthur 1924- 81-84
Coleman, Bernard D(avid) 1919- 25-28R
Coleman, Bob
See Coleman, Robert David
Coleman, Bruce P(umphrey) 1931- 37-40R
Coleman, Buck
See Richardson, Gladwell
Coleman, Clayton W(ebster) 1901- 29-32R
Coleman, D(onald) C(uthbert) 1920- 13-14R
Coleman, Dorothy Gabe 1935- 93-96
Coleman, Elliott 1906-1980 .... 19-20R
Obituary 97-100
Coleman, Emily Holmes 1899-1974 105
See also DLB 4
Coleman, Evelyn Scherabon
See Firchow, Evelyn Scherabon
Coleman, Felicia Slatkin 1916(?)-1981
Obituary 102
Coleman, Francis Xavier Jerome 1939- 108
Coleman, J(ohn) Winston, Jr. 1898- 49-52
Coleman, James A(ndrew) 1921- 5-6R
Coleman, James C(ovington) 1914- CANR-1
Earlier sketch in CA 2R
Coleman, James S(amuel) 1926- 13-14R
Coleman, James Smoot 1919- 3R
Coleman, John R(oyston) 1921- CANR-1
Earlier sketch in CA 4R
See also AITN 1
Coleman, Kenneth 1916- CANR-8
Earlier sketch in CA 23-24R
Coleman, Lee
See Lapidus, Elaine
Coleman, Lonnie 1920-1982 77-80
Obituary 107
Coleman, Lucile 73-76
Coleman, Marion (Reeves) Moore
1900- CANR-11
Earlier sketch in CA 17-18R
Coleman, Michael C(hristopher) 1946- 119
Coleman, Patricia R(egister) 1936- 109
Coleman, Peter J(arrett) 1926- 7-8R
Coleman, Raymond James 1923- 49-52
Coleman, Richard J(ames) 1941- 41-44R
Coleman, Richard M(ark) 1951- 121
Coleman, Richard Patrick 1927- 33-36R
Coleman, Robert David 1951- 121
Coleman, Robert E(merson) 1928- CANR-7
Earlier sketch in CA 15-16R
Coleman, Robert William Alfred 1916- 11-12R
Coleman, Roy V. 1885-1971 Obituary 104
Coleman, Terry 1931- CANR-10
Earlier sketch in CA 15-16R
Coleman, Thomas R. 1942- 57-60
Coleman, Vernon 1946- 81-84
Coleman, Wanda 1946- 119
Coleman, William L(eRoy) 1938- CANR-21
Earlier sketch in CA 69-72
See also SATA 34, 49
Coleman, William V(incent) 1932- CANR-9
Earlier sketch in CA 57-60
Coleman-Norton, P(aul) R(obinson)
1898-1971 Obituary 29-32R
Colen, B. D. 1946- CANR-23
Earlier sketch in CA 65-68
Colenbrander, Joanna 1908- 121
Coleridge, John
See Binder, Otto O(scar)
Coleridge, M. E.
See Coleridge, Mary E(lizabeth)
Coleridge, Mary E(lizabeth) 1861-1907
Brief entry 116
See also DLB 19
Coles, Alan 1927- 124
Coles, Cyril Henry 1899-1965 .... CAP-1
Earlier sketch in CA 9-10
Coles, Don 1928- 115
See also CLC 46
Coles, Flournoy (Arthur), Jr. 1915- 57-60
Coles, Harry L(ewis) 1920- 9-10R
Coles, John M(orton) 1930- CANR-12
Earlier sketch in CA 29-32R
Coles, Kaines Adlard 1901-1985 .... CAP-1
Obituary 117
Earlier sketch in CA 13-14
Coles, Manning
See Coles, Cyril Henry
Coles, Robert (Martin) 1929- CANR-3
Earlier sketch in CA 45-48
See also SATA 23
Coles, Robert R(eed) 1908(?)-1985
Obituary 116
Coles, S(ydney) F(rederick) Arthur 1896- 7-8R
Coles, Susan Vaughan Ebershoff
See Ebershoff-Coles, Susan Vaughan
Coles, William Allan 1930- 33-36R
Coles, William E., Jr. 1932- CANR-10
Earlier sketch in CA 61-64
Coletta, Paolo Enrico 1916- CANR-14
Earlier sketch in CA 41-44R
Colette, (Sidonie-Gabrielle) 1873-1954
Brief entry 104
See also DLB 65
See also TCLC 1, 5, 16
Colette, Jacques 1929- 89-92
Colford, Paul D(ennis) 1953- 110
Colford, William E(dward) 1908-1971 .... 7-8R
Obituary 33-36R
Colgin, Russell W(eymount) 1925- 121
Colgrave, Bertram 1888-1968 .... CAP-2
Earlier sketch in CA 25-28
Colie, Rosalie L(ittell) 1924-1972 Obituary 106
Colimore, Vincent J(erome) 1914- 37-40R
Colin, Ann
See Ure, Jean
Colin, Jean
See Bell, Joyce
Colina, Tessa Patterson 1915- CANR-7
Earlier sketch in CA 19-20R
Colinvaux, Paul (Alfred) 1930- CANR-14
Earlier sketch in CA 41-44R
Colish, Marcia L. 1937- CANR-10
Earlier sketch in CA 25-28R
Coll, Regina A(udrey) 1929- 112
Collard, Edgar Andrew 1911- 102
Collas, J. P. 1911-1984 Obituary 114
Colledge, Malcolm A(ndrew) R(ichard)
1939- CANR-10
Earlier sketch in CA 25-28R
Collen, Neil
See Lee, Lincoln
Coller, Richard Walter 1925- 119
Collett, Rosemary K(ing) 1931- 69-72
Colletta, Nat J(oseph) 1944- 104
Colley, Ann C(heetham) 1940- 112
Colley, Iain 1940- 97-100
Collias, Joe G. 1928- CANR-14
Earlier sketch in CA 41-44R
Collie, Michael (John) 1929- CANR-18
Earlier sketches in CA 49-52, CANR-3
Collier, (John) Basil 1908- CANR-2
Earlier sketch in CA 7-8R
Collier, Boyd D(ean) 1938- 57-60
Collier, Calhoun C(rofford) 1916- 25-28R
Collier, Christopher 1930- CANR-13
Earlier sketch in CA 33-36R
See also SATA 16
See also CLC 30
Collier, David 1942- 69-72
Collier, David S(wanson) 1923-1983 .... 21-22R
Obituary 111
Collier, Douglas
See Fellowes-Gordon, Ian (Douglas)
Collier, Ethel 1903- 65-68
See also SATA 22
Collier, Eugenia W(illiams) 1928- 49-52
Collier, Gaydell M(aier) 1935- 93-96
Collier, Gaylan Jane 1924- 37-40R
Collier, (Alan) Graham 1923- 19-20R
Collier, (James) Graham 1937- 105
Collier, Herbert L(eon) 1933- 103
Collier, James L(incoln) 1928- CANR-4
Earlier sketch in CA 9-10R
See also SATA 8
See also CLC 30
Collier, Jane
See Hampson, Zena
Collier, John 1901-1980 .... CANR-10
Obituary 97-100
Earlier sketch in CA 65-68
Collier, Johnnie Lucille
See Collier, Lucille Ann
Collier, Joy
See Millar, (Minna Henrietta) Joy
Collier, Kenneth Gerald 1910- CANR-18
Earlier sketch in CA 85-88
Collier, Leo(nard) D(awson) 1908- 7-8R
Collier, Louise Wilbourn 1925- 109
Collier, Lucille Ann 1919(?)- Brief entry 109
Collier, Lucy Ann
See Collier, Lucille Ann
Collier, Margaret
See Taylor, Margaret Stewart
Collier, Peter 1939- 65-68
Collier, Phyllis K(ay) 1939- 110
Collier, Richard 1924- CANR-5
Earlier sketch in CA 4R
Collier, Simon 1938- 23-24R
Collier, Zena
See Hampson, Zena
See also SATA 23
Colligan, Francis J(ames) 1908-19(?) CAP-2
Earlier sketch in CA 19-20
Collignon, Jean Henri 1918- 3R
Collignon, Joseph 1930- 89-92
Collin, Marion (Cripps) 1928- CANR-5
Earlier sketch in CA 9-10R
Collin, Richard H(arvey) 1932- 122
Collin, Richard Oliver 1940- 105
Collings, Ellsworth 1887- 73-76
Collings, I. J(illie) 115
Collings, Michael R(obert) 1947- 111
Collingwood, Charles (Cummings)
1917-1985 .... 29-32R
Obituary 117
Collingwood, R(obin) G(eorge)
1889(?)-1943 Brief entry 117
Collins, Alice H(esslein) 1907- 65-68
Collins, Arnold Quint 1935- 73-76
Collins, Barbara J(ane) 1929- CANR-6
Earlier sketch in CA 57-60
Collins, Barry 1941- 102
Collins, Barry E(merson) 1937- CANR-7
Earlier sketch in CA 13-14R
Collins, Beulah Stowe 1923-1983 122
Obituary 110
Collins, Carvel 1912- CANR-8
Earlier sketch in CA 17-18R
Collins, Charles C. 1919- 25-28R
Collins, Charles William 1880-1964
Obituary 89-92
Collins, Christopher 1936- 49-52
Collins, Cindy
See Smith, Richard Rein
Collins, Clark
See Reynolds, Dallas McCord
Collins, Colette
See Knaack, Twila
Collins, D.
See Bulleid, H(enry) A(nthony) V(aughan)
Collins, David A(lmon) 1931- 23-24R
Collins, David R(aymond) 1940- CANR-11
Earlier sketch in CA 29-32R
See also SATA 7
Collins, Desmond 1940- CANR-14
Earlier sketch in CA 73-76
Collins, Donald E(dward) 1934- 122
Collins, Douglas 1912-1972 Obituary 33-36R
Collins, F(rederick) Herbert 1890- CAP-1
Earlier sketch in CA 11-12
Collins, Fletcher, Jr. 1906- 53-56
Collins, Freda
See Collins, Frederica Joan Hale
Collins, Frederica Joan Hale 1904- CAP-1
Earlier sketch in CA 13-14
Collins, Gary (Ross) 1934- CANR-22
Earlier sketches in CA 57-60, CANR-7
Collins, George R(oseborough) 1917- CANR-1
Earlier sketch in CA 4R
Collins, Harold R(eeves) 1915- 25-28R
Collins, Henry 1917- 17-18R
Collins, Henry B(ascom), Jr. 1899-1987
Obituary 123
Collins, Herbert Ridgeway 1932- 118
Collins, Hunt
See Hunter, Evan
Collins, Jackie CANR-22
Earlier sketch in CA 102
Collins, James Daniel 1917- CANR-5
Earlier sketch in CA 2R
Collins, Jean E(lizabeth) 1948- 110
Collins, Joan 1933- 116
Collins, Jodie 1941- 121
Collins, John H. 1893- 4R
Collins, John J(oseph) 1946- 112
Collins, John Lawrence, Jr. 1929- CANR-19
Earlier sketch in CA 65-68
Collins, John M(artin) 1921- 49-52
Collins, Joseph B. 1898(?)-1975
Obituary 53-56
Collins, Joseph T. 1939- 120
Collins, Judith Graham 1942- 115
Collins, Judy (Marjorie) 1939- 103
Collins, June Irene 1935- 37-40R
Collins, Kathleen 1931- 119
Collins, L(ewis) John 1905-1982 .... CAP-1
Obituary 108
Earlier sketch in CA 13-14
Collins, Larry
See Collins, John Lawrence, Jr.
Collins, Linda 1931- CLC-44
Collins, Lorraine (Hill) 1931- 57-60
Collins, Mabel
See Cook, Mabel Collins
Collins, Margaret (Brandon James) 1909- 89-92
Collins, Marie (Margaret) 1935- 53-56
Collins, Marjorie A(nn) 1930- CANR-11
Earlier sketch in CA 65-68
Collins, Marva (Deloise Nettles) 1936- 111
Collins, Max (Allan), Jr. 1948- 103
Collins, Meghan 1926- 101
Collins, Michael 1930- CANR-5
Earlier sketch in CA 53-56
Collins, Michael
See Lynds, Dennis
Collins, Mortimer 1827-1876 .... DLB-21, 35
Collins, Myron D(ean) 1901- CAP-1
Earlier sketch in CA 15-16
Collins, Myrtle T(elleen) 1915- 101
Collins, Nancy W.
See Collins-Chapman, Nancy W(hisnant)
Collins, Norman Richard 1907-1982 105
Obituary 107
Collins, Orvis F(loyd) 1918- 69-72
Collins, Pat(ricia) Lowery 1932- CANR-24
Earlier sketch in CA 107
See also SATA 31
Collins, Peter (Sheridan) 1942- 77-80
Collins, Philip (Arthur William) 1923- CANR-22
Earlier sketches in CA 7-8R, CANR-8
Collins, R(obert) G(eorge) 1926- 112
Collins, Raymond F(rancis) 1935- 112
Collins, Robert 1924- CANR-15
Earlier sketch in CA 89-92
Collins, Robert E(mmet) 1927- 69-72
Collins, Robert M. 1943- 110
Collins, Robert O(akley) 1933- CANR-22
Earlier sketches in CA 3R, CANR-4
Collins, Rowland Lee 1934-1985 .... 9-10R
Obituary 116
Collins, Ruth Philpott 1890-1975 .... CANR-4
Obituary 53-56
Earlier sketch in CA 2R
See also SATA 30
Collins, Thomas Hightower 1910- 102
Collins, Trish 1927- 106
Collins, Wilkie 1824-1889 .... DLB-18
Collins, Will
See Corley, Edwin (Raymond)
Collins, William Alexander Roy 1900-1976
Obituary 69-72
Collins, William Bernard 1913- 7-8R
Collins-Chapman, Nancy W(hisnant) 1933- 112
Collinson, Laurence (Henry) 1925- 103
Collinson, Roger (Alfred) 1936- 110
Collis, John Stewart 1900-1984 61-64
Obituary 112
Collis, Kevin F(rancis) 1930- 107
Collis, Louise 1925- 21-22R
Collis, Maurice 1889-1973 .... CANR-4
Obituary 89-92
Earlier sketch in CA 5-6R
Collis, William Robert Fitzgerald 1900- CAP-1
Earlier sketch in CA 9-10
Collison, David (John) 1937- 105
Collison, Koder M(acklin) 1910- 53-56
Collison, Robert Lewis Wright 1914- CANR-2
Earlier sketch in CA 5-6R
Colliss, Gertrude Florence Mary (Jones)
1908- 7-8R
Collodi, Carlo
See Lorenzini, Carlo
See also CLR 5
Collom, Jack 1931- 77-80
Colloms, Brenda 1919- CANR-7
Earlier sketch in CA 61-64
See also SATA 40
Collyer, Mary 1716(?)-1763(?) DLB-39
Collyns, Robin 1940- 69-72
Colm, Gerhard 1897-1968 .... 5-6R
Obituary 103
Colman, Arthur D. 1937- 33-36R
Colman, Benjamin 1673-1747 .... DLB-24
Colman, E(rnest) A(drian) M(ackenzie)
1930- 57-60
Colman, George
See Glassco, John
Colman, Hila CANR-7
Earlier sketch in CA 15-16R
See also SATA 1
Colman, John E. 1923- 23-24R
Colman, Juliet Benita 1944- 61-64
Colman, Libby Lee 1940- 33-36R
Colman, Morris 1899(?)-1981 .... SATA-25
Colmer, John (Anthony) 1921- CANR-15
Earlier sketch in CA 85-88
Colmer, Michael (J.) 1942- CANR-21
Earlier sketch in CA 69-72
Colodny, Robert G. 1915- CANR-14
Earlier sketch in CA 37-40R
Colombo, Dale
See Monroe, Keith
Colombo, Furio 1931- 111
Colombo, John Robert 1936- CANR-11
Earlier sketch in CA 25-28R
See also SATA 50
See also DLB 53
Colonel Sanders
See Sanders, Harland

Colonius, Lillian 1911- ... 23-24R
See also SATA 3
Colony, Horatio 1900-1977 ... 37-40R
Colorado, Antonio J.
See Colorado Capella, Antonio Julio
Colorado Capella, Antonio Julio 1903- ... 19-20R
See also SATA 23
Colquhoun, Archibald 1912-1964
Obituary ... 89-92
Colquhoun, Frank 1909- ... 106
Colquhoun, Ithell 1906- ... 13-14R
Colquhoun, Keith 1927- ... 102
Colquitt, Betsy Feagan 1926- ... 53-56
Colson, Charles W(endell) 1931- ... 102
Colson, Elizabeth 1917- ... 53-56
Colson, Frederick
See Geis, Richard E(rwin)
Colson, Greta (Scotchmur) 1913- ... CAP-1
Earlier sketch in CA 9-10
Colson, Howard P(aul) 1910- ... 29-32R
Colson, Laramie
See Richardson, Gladwell
Colston, Lowell G(wen) 1919-1985 ... 53-56
Obituary ... 118
Colston-Baynes, Dorothy 1881(?)-1973
Obituary ... 104
Colt, Clem
See Nye, Nelson C(oral)
Colt, John W. 1900(?)-1983 Obituary ... 111
Colt, Martin
See Epstein, Beryl (M. Williams)
and Epstein, Samuel
Colt, Winchester Remington
See Hubbard, L(afayette) Ron(ald)
Colt, Zandra
See Stevenson, Florence
Coltart, James M(ilne) 1903-1986
Obituary ... 120
Colter, Cyrus 1910- ... CANR-10
Earlier sketch in CA 65-68
See also DLB 33
Colter, Shayne
See Norwood, Victor G(eorge) C(harles)
Coltharp, Lurline H(ughes) 1913- ... 17-18R
Coltman, Ernest Vivian
See Dudley, Ernest
Coltman, Will
See Bingley, David Ernest
Colton, C(larence) E(ugene) 1914- ... CANR-2
Earlier sketch in CA 5-6R
Colton, Harold S(ellers) 1881-1970 ... CANR-3
Earlier sketch in CA 3R
Colton, Helen 1918- ... 57-60
Colton, James
See Hansen, Joseph
Colton, James B(yers) II 1908- ... 37-40R
Colton, Joel 1918- ... CANR-2
Earlier sketch in CA 4R
Colton, Timothy J. 1947- ... 124
Coltrane, James
See Wohl, James P(aul)
Colum, Padraic 1881-1972 ... 73-76
Obituary ... 33-36R
See also SATA 15
See also CLC 28
Columella
See Moore, Clement Clarke
Colver, A(nthony) Wayne 1923- ... 93-96
Colver, Alice Mary (Ross) 1892- ... 69-72
Colver, Anne 1908- ... CANR-2
Earlier sketch in CA 45-48
See also SATA 7
Colvert, James B(rumley) 1921- ... 116
Colvett, Latayne
See Scott, Latayne Colvett
Colville, Derek Kent 1923- Brief entry ... 105
Colville, John Rupert 1915-1987 ... CANR-10
Obituary ... 124
Earlier sketch in CA 61-64
Colvin, Brenda 1897-1981 Obituary ... 108
Colvin, Clare 1943- ... 123
Colvin, Elaine Wright 1942- ... 106
Colvin, Howard Montagu 1919- ... 61-64
Colvin, Ian G(oodhope) 1912-1975 ... CAP-2
Obituary ... 57-60
Earlier sketch in CA 19-20
Colvin, James
See Moorcock, Michael (John)
Colvin, Ralph W(hitmore) 1920-1981 ... 107
Obituary ... 104
Colwell, C(harles) Carter 1932- ... 41-44R
Colwell, Eileen (Hilda) 1904- ... CANR-12
Earlier sketch in CA 29-32R
See also SATA 2
Colwell, Ernest Cadman 1901-1974 ... CANR-4
Obituary ... 53-56
Earlier sketch in CA 5-6R
Colwell, Richard J(ames) 1930- ... 69-72
Colwell, Robert 1931- ... 33-36R
Colwin, Laurie 1944- ... CANR-20
Earlier sketch in CA 89-92
See also DLBY 80
See also CLC 5, 13, 23
Colyer, Penrose 1940- ... CANR-20
Earlier sketches in CA 65-68, CANR-14
Coman, Dale Rex 1906- ... 81-84
Coman, Edwin Truman, Jr. 1903- ... 11-12R
Comaromi, John P(hillip) 1937- ... 111
Comay, Joan ... 103
Comber, Lillian 1916- ... CANR-3
Earlier sketch in CA 9-10R
Combs, A(rthur) W(right) 1912- ... CANR-10
Earlier sketch in CA 17-18R
Combs, Ann 1935- ... 117
Combs, David 1934- ... 108
Combs, Eugene 1934- ... 118
Combs, James E(verett) 1941- ... CANR-19
Earlier sketch in CA 101
Combs, Jerald A(rthur) 1937- ... 110
Combs, Richard Earl 1934- ... 33-36R
Combs, Robert
See Murray, John
Combs, (Elisha) Tram(mell, Jr.) 1924- ... 13-14R
Comden, Betty 1919- ... CANR-2
Earlier sketch in CA 49-52
See also DLB 44
Comeau, Arthur M. 1938- ... 61-64
Comer, James P(ierpont) 1934- ... 61-64
Comey, Dennis J. 1896-1987 Obituary ... 123
Comey, James Hugh 1947- ... 65-68
Comfort, Alex(ander) 1920- ... CANR-1
Earlier sketch in CA 4R
See also CLC 7
Comfort, Howard 1904- ... 37-40R
Comfort, Iris Tracy ... CANR-6
Earlier sketch in CA 13-14R
Comfort, Jane Levington
See Sturtzel, Jane Levington
Comfort, Mildred Houghton 1886- ... 9-10R
See also SATA 3
Comfort, Montgomery
See Campbell, (John) Ramsey
Comfort, Richard A(llen) 1933- ... 21-22R
Comidas, Chinas
See Genser, Cynthia
Comini, Alessandra 1934- ... 93-96
Comins, Ethel M(ae) ... CANR-8
Earlier sketch in CA 61-64
See also SATA 11
Comins, Jeremy 1933- ... CANR-14
Earlier sketch in CA 65-68
See also SATA 28
Comitas, Lambros 1927- Brief entry ... 113
Comito, Terry Allen 1935- ... 109
Commager, Henry Steele 1902- ... 21-22R
See also SATA 23
See also DLB 17
Commager, (Henry) Steele (Jr.)
1932-1984 Obituary ... 112
Commins, William Dollard, Sr. 1899-1983
Obituary ... 109
Commire, Anne ... CANR-21
Earlier sketch in CA 69-72
Committe, Thomas C. 1922- ... 65-68
Commoner, Barry 1917- ... 65-68
Como, (Michael) William 1925- ... 69-72
Comparetti, Alice 1907- ... 37-40R
Compere, Mickie
See Davidson, Margaret
Complo, Sister Jannita Marie 1935- ... 57-60
Comprone, Joseph J(ohn) 1943- ... CANR-5
Earlier sketch in CA 53-56
Compton, Ann
See Prebble, Marjorie Mary Curtis
Compton, Arthur Holly 1892-1962
Obituary ... 116
Compton, D(avid) G(uy) 1930- ... CANR-17
Earlier sketch in CA 25-28R
Compton, Guy
See Compton, D(avid) G(uy)
Compton, Henry (Pasfield) 1909- ... 9-10R
Compton, James V(incent) 1928- ... 29-32R
Compton, Piers 1903- ... 122
Compton-Burnett, I(vy) 1892-1969 ... CANR-4
Obituary ... 25-28R
Earlier sketch in CA 4R
See also DLB 36
See also CLC 1, 3, 10, 15, 34
Compton-Hall, (Patrick) Richard 1929- . CANR-24
Earlier sketch in CA 107
Comrey, Andrew Laurence 1923-
Brief entry ... 106
Comroe, Julius H(iram), Jr. 1911-1984 ... 122
Obituary ... 113
Comstock, Anthony 1844-1915 Brief entry ... 110
See also TCLC 13
Comstock, Christine 1942- ... CANR-20
Earlier sketch in CA 104
Comstock, George Adolphe 1932- ... 124
Comstock, Helen 1893-1970 ... CANR-4
Obituary ... 89-92
Earlier sketch in CA 5-6R
Comstock, Henry B. 1908- ... CAP-2
Earlier sketch in CA 33-36
Comstock, Mary Bryce 1934- ... 105
Comstock, W(illiam) Richard 1928- ... 73-76
Comte, The Great
See Hawkesworth, Eric
Comus
See Ballantyne, R(obert) M(ichael)
Comyns, Barbara
See Comyns-Carr, Barbara Irene Veronica
Comyns-Carr, Barbara Irene Veronica
1912- ... 7-8R
Conacher, D(esmond) J(ohn) 1918- ... 25-28R
Conacher, J(ames) B(lennerhasset)
1916- ... 25-28R
Conan Doyle, Adrian Malcolm 1910-1970 ... 7-8R
Obituary ... 29-32R
Conan Doyle, Arthur
See Doyle, Arthur Conan
Conant, Eaton H. 1930- ... 53-56
Conant, Howard (Somers) 1921- ... CANR-8
Earlier sketch in CA 17-18R
Conant, James Bryant 1893-1978 ... 15-16R
Obituary ... 77-80
Conant, Kenneth John 1894- ... 2R
Conant, Ralph W(endell) 1926- ... CANR-14
Earlier sketch in CA 29-32R
Conant, Roger 1909- Brief entry ... 107
Conard, Alfred Fletcher 1911- ... 15-16R
Conard, Joseph W. 1911- ... 13-14R
Conarroe, Joel (Osborne) 1934- ... 29-32R
Conarroe, Richard R(iley) 1928- ... 69-72
Conaway, James (Alley) 1941- ... 33-36R
Conconi, Charles N. 1938- ... 77-80
Conde, Jesse C(lay) 1912- ... 57-60
Conde, Maryse
See Boucolon, Maryse
Condee, Ralph Waterbury 1916- ... 17-18R
Condit, Carl Wilbur 1914- ... CANR-4
Earlier sketch in CA 3R
Condit, Martha Olson 1913- ... 73-76
See also SATA 28
Condliffe, John B(ell) 1891-1981 ... CAP-1
Obituary ... 106
Earlier sketch in CA 15-16
Condon, David Rensing 1924- ... 114
Condon, E(dward) U(hler) 1902-1974
Obituary ... 112
Condon, Eddie 1905-1973 Obituary ... 45-48
Condon, George Edward 1916- ... CANR-1
Earlier sketch in CA 45-48
Condon, Jack
See Condon, John C(arl), Jr.
Condon, John C(arl), Jr. 1938- ... CANR-10
Earlier sketch in CA 23-24R
Condon, Richard (Thomas) 1915- ... CANR-23
Earlier sketches in CA 1R, CANR-2
See also CAAS 1
See also CLC 4, 6, 8, 10, 45
Condon, Robert 1921(?)-1972 Obituary ... 37-40R
Condor, Gladyn
See Davison, Gladys Patton
Condray, Bruno
See Humphrys, Leslie George
Condry, William Moreton 1918- ... 103
Cone, Carl B. 1916- ... 11-12R
Cone, Edward Toner 1917- ... 110
Cone, Fairfax Mastick 1903-1977 ... 73-76
Obituary ... 69-72
Cone, Ferne Geller 1921- ... 107
See also SATA 39
Cone, James H. 1938- ... 33-36R
Cone, John F(rederick) 1926- ... 17-18R
Cone, Molly Lamken 1918- ... CANR-16
Earlier sketches in CA 4R, CANR-1
See also SATA 1, 28
Cone, William F. 1919- ... 57-60
Conerly, Perian Collier 1926- ... 5-6R
Coney, Michael G(reatrex) 1932- ... 97-100
Confer, Vincent 1913- ... 21-22R
Conford, Ellen 1942- ... CANR-13
Earlier sketch in CA 33-36R
See also SATA 6
See also CLR 10
Confucius
See Lund, Philip R(eginald)
Congdon, Constance S. 1944- ... 123
Congdon, Herbert Wheaton 1876-1965 ... 5-6R
Congdon, Kirby 1924- ... CANR-7
Earlier sketch in CA 15-16R
Congdon, William Grosvenor 1912- ... CANR-24
Earlier sketches in CA 17-18R, CANR-7
Conger, (Seymour) Beach III 1912-1969
Obituary ... 115
Conger, John (Janeway) 1921- ... CANR-6
Earlier sketch in CA 13-14R
Conger, Lesley
See Suttles, Shirley (Smith)
Congrat-Butler, Stefan 1914(?)-1979 ... 103
Obituary ... 89-92
Congreve, Willard J(ohn) 1921- ... 57-60
Congreve, William 1670-1729 ... DLB-39
Conil, Jean 1917- ... CANR-13
Earlier sketch in CA 13-14R
Conine, (Odie) Ernest 1925- ... 69-72
Coniston, Ed
See Bingley, David Ernest
Conkin, Paul K(eith) 1929- ... 33-36R
Conkle, E(llsworth) P(routy) 1899- ... 65-68
Conklin, Barbara P. 1927- ... 109
Conklin, Gladys Plemon 1903- ... CANR-4
Earlier sketch in CA 2R
See also SATA 2
Conklin, Groff 1904-1968 ... CANR-3
Earlier sketch in CA 1R
Conklin, Harold C(olyer) 1926- ... 118
Conklin, John E(van) 1943- ... CANR-14
Earlier sketch in CA 37-40R
Conklin, Mike 1944- ... 120
Conklin, Paul ... 115
Brief entry ... 111
See also SATA 33, 43
Conkling, Hilda 1910- ... SATA-23
Conlay, Iris 1910- ... CAP-1
Earlier sketch in CA 11-12
Conley, Ellen Alexander 1938- ... CANR-20
Earlier sketch in CA 103
Conley, Enid Mary 1917- ... CANR-10
Earlier sketch in CA 65-68
Conley, John (Allan) 1912- ... 61-64
Conley, Phillip Mallory 1887- ... 69-72
Conley, Robert J(ackson) 1940- ... CANR-15
Earlier sketch in CA 41-44R
Conley, Verena Andermatt 1943- ... 117
Conlin, David A. 1897- ... 17-18R
Conlin, Joseph R. 1940- ... 49-52
Conlon, Denis J. 1932- ... 37-40R
Conlon, Kathleen (Annie) 1943-
Brief entry ... 114
Conly, Robert Leslie 1918(?)-1973 ... 73-76
Obituary ... 41-44R
See also SATA 23
Conn, Canary Denise 1949- ... 57-60
Conn, Charles Paul 1945- ... CANR-6
Earlier sketch in CA 57-60
Conn, Charles William 1920- ... CANR-10
Earlier sketch in CA 23-24R
Conn, Frances G. 1925- ... 33-36R
Conn, Jan E(velyn) 1952- ... 110
Conn, Martha Orr 1935- ... 93-96
Conn, Peter J. 1942- ... 33-36R
Conn, Stetson 1908- ... CAP-1
Earlier sketch in CA 9-10
Conn, Stewart 1936- Brief entry ... 117
Conn, Walter E(ugene) 1940- ... 110
Connable, Alfred 1931- ... 81-84
Connally, Eugenia (Maye) Horstman 1931- .. 103
Connell, Brian (Reginald) 1916- ... CANR-4
Earlier sketch in CA 4R
Connell, Evan S(helby), Jr. 1924- ... CANR-2
Earlier sketch in CA 4R
See also CAAS 2
See also DLB 2
See also DLBY 81
See also CLC 4, 6, 45
Connell, Francis J. 1888- ... CAP-1
Earlier sketch in CA 13-14
Connell, Jon 1952- ... 97-100
Connell, K(enneth) H(ugh) 1917-1973 ... CAP-2
Earlier sketch in CA 25-28
Connell, Kirk
See Chapman, John Stanton Higham
Connell, Maureen 1931- ... 104
Connell, William Fraser 1916- ... 104
Connellan, Leo 1928- ... 81-84
Connelly, Douglas 1949- ... 121
Connelly, Marc(us Cook) 1890-1980 ... 85-88
Obituary ... 102
See also SATA 25
See also DLB 7
See also DLBY 80
See also CLC 7
Connelly, Owen (Sergeson, Jr.) 1924- ... 19-20R
Connelly, Philip M(arshal) 1904(?)-1981
Obituary ... 104
Connelly, Thomas L(awrence) 1938- ... CANR-11
Earlier sketch in CA 19-20R
Connely, Willard 1888-1967 ... CAP-2
Earlier sketch in CA 17-18
Conner, Berenice Gillete 1908- ... 65-68
Conner, Floyd D(avis) 1951- ... 119
Conner, Patrick (Roy Mountifort) 1947- ... 106
Conner, Patrick Reardon 1907- ... 7-8R
Conner, Paul Willard 1937-1984 ... 17-18R
Obituary ... 114
Conner, Rearden
See Conner, Patrick Reardon
Conner, Valerie Jean 1945- ... 114
Conners, Bernard F. 1926- ... 41-44R
Conners, Kenneth Wray 1909- ... 29-32R
Connery, Donald S(tuart) 1926-
Brief entry ... 114
Connery, George Edward 1907(?)-1985
Obituary ... 116
Connery, John (R.) 1913-1987 Obituary ... 124
Connery, Robert H(owe) 1907- ... 41-44R
Connett, Eugene Virginius III 1891-1969 .. CAP-1
Earlier sketch in CA 13-14
Connette, Earle 1910- ... CAP-1
Earlier sketch in CA 15-16
Connick, C(harles) Milo 1917- ... 3R
Conniff, Frank 1914-1971 Obituary ... 93-96
Conniff, James C(lifford) G(regory) ... 23-24R
Conniff, Michael L(ee) 1942- ... 118
Conniff, Richard 1951- ... 124
Connolly, Cyril (Vernon) 1903-1974 ... CAP-2
Obituary ... 53-56
Earlier sketch in CA 21-22
Connolly, Francis X(avier) 1909-1965 ... CAP-1
Earlier sketch in CA 13-14
Connolly, Jerome P(atrick) 1931- ... SATA-8
Connolly, Paul
See Wicker, Thomas Grey
Connolly, Peter 1935- ... 103
See also SATA 47
Connolly, Ray 1940- ... 101
Connolly, Robert D(uggan, Jr.) 1917- ... 69-72
Connolly, Thomas Edmund 1918- ... CANR-4
Earlier sketch in CA 3R
Connolly, Vivian 1925- ... CANR-1
Earlier sketch in CA 49-52
Connor, J. Robert 1927- ... 123
Connor, Jim 1935- ... 107
Connor, John Anthony 1930- ... 15-16R
Connor, Joyce Mary 1929- ... CANR-10
Earlier sketch in CA 65-68
Connor, Kevin
See O'Rourke, Frank
Connor, Lawrence S(tanton) 1925- ... 89-92
Connor, Patricia 1943- ... 25-28R
Connor, Ralph
See Gordon, Charles William
Connor, Seymour V(aughan) 1923- ... 53-56
Connor, Susanna Pflaum
See Pflaum, Susanna Whitney
Connor, Tony
See Connor, John Anthony
See also DLB 40
Connor, W(alter) Robert 1934- ... 41-44R
Connor, Walter Downing 1942- ... 106
Connor, William (Neil) 1909(?)-1967
Obituary ... 25-28R
Connors, Bruton
See Rohen, Edward
Connors, Dorsey ... 45-48
Connors, John Stanley 1925-1984
Obituary ... 112
Connors, Joseph 1945- ... 106
Conolly, L(eonard) W(illiam) 1941- ... 106
Conolly, Violet 1901(?)-1988(?) Obituary ... 124
Conor, Glen
See Cooney, Michael
Conot, Robert E. 1929- ... CANR-2
Earlier sketch in CA 45-48
Conover, C(harles) Eugene 1903- ... 7-8R

Conover, Carole 1941- 89-92
Conover, Chris 1950- SATA-31
Conover, David (Beals) 1919-1983 115
Conover, Hobart H. 1914- 15-16R
Conover, Jessica Arline Wilcox
 See Jones, Candy
Conquest, Edwin Parker, Jr. 1931- 29-32R
Conquest, Ned
 See Conquest, Edwin Parker, Jr.
Conquest, Owen
 See Hamilton, Charles Harold St. John
Conquest, (George) Robert (Acworth) 1917- CANR-9
 Earlier sketch in CA 15-16R
 See also DLB 27
Conrad, Alfred Borys 1899(?)-1979
 Obituary 104
Conrad, Andree 1945- 29-32R
Conrad, Barnaby (Jr.) 1922- CANR-6
 Earlier sketch in CA 9-10R
Conrad, Brenda
 See Brown, Zenith Jones
Conrad, David Eugene 1928- 17-18R
Conrad, Earl 1912-1986 .... CANR-10
 Obituary 118
 Earlier sketch in CA 1R
Conrad, Edna (G.) 1893- CAP-2
 Earlier sketch in CA 33-36
Conrad, Hal
 See Conrad, Harold
Conrad, Harold 1911- 112
Conrad, Jack (Randolph) 1923- 11-12R
Conrad, John W(ilfred) 1935- CANR-4
 Earlier sketch in CA 53-56
Conrad, Jon(athan) J(ames) 1920- 114
Conrad, Joseph 1857-1924 Brief entry 104
 See also SATA 27
 See also DLB 10, 34
 See also TCLC 1, 6, 13, 25
Conrad, Kenneth
 See Lottich, Kenneth V(erne)
Conrad, L. K.
 See Conrad, Andree
Conrad, Pam 1947- 121
Conrad, Pam(ela) 1947- SATA-49
Conrad, Paul (Francis) 1924- 113
Conrad, Robert 1928- 41-44R
Conrad, Robert Arnold
 See Hart, Moss
Conrad, Susan P(hinney) 1941-
 Brief entry 113
Conrad, Sybil 1921- 23-24R
Conrad, Tod
 See Wilkes-Hunter, R(ichard)
Conrad, Will C. 1882- CAP-1
 Earlier sketch in CA 13-14
Conradis, Heinz 1907- CAP-1
 Earlier sketch in CA 13-14
Conrads, Ulrich 1923- 9-10R
Conran, Anthony 1931- CANR-14
 Earlier sketch in CA 65-68
Conran, Shirley (Ida) 1932- CANR-22
 Earlier sketch in CA 103
Conran, Terence Orby 1931- 85-88
Conron, (Alfred) Brandon 1919- 17-18R
Conrow, Robert 1942- 57-60
Conroy, Barbara 1934- 111
Conroy, Charles W. 1922- 15-16R
Conroy, Frank 1936- 77-80
Conroy, (Francis) Hilary 1919- 115
Conroy, Jack
 See Conroy, John Wesley
 See also SATA 19
 See also DLBY 81
Conroy, John Wesley 1899- CANR-3
 Earlier sketch in CA 7-8R
Conroy, Mary 1941- 110
Conroy, Michael R(alph) 1945- CANR-9
 Earlier sketch in CA 53-56
Conroy, Pat 1945- CANR-24
 Earlier sketch in CA 85-88
 See also DLB 6
 See also CLC 30
 See also AITN 1
Conroy, Patricia 1941- 93-96
Conroy, Peter V(incent), Jr. 1944- 53-56
Conroy, Robert
 See Goldston, Robert (Conroy)
Considine, Bob
 See Considine, Robert (Bernard)
 See also AITN 2
Considine, Douglas M(axwell) 1915- CANR-11
 Earlier sketch in CA 69-72
Considine, John J(oseph) 1897- 3R
Considine, Robert (Bernard) 1906-1975 93-96
 Obituary 61-64
Consilvio, Thomas 1947- 57-60
Consolo, Dominick P(eter) 1923- 33-36R
Constable, John W. 1922- 81-84
Constable, Trevor James 1925- 89-92
Constable, W(illiam) G(eorge) 1887-1976 ....5-6R
 Obituary 65-68
Constant, Alberta Wilson 1908-1981 .... CANR-4
 Obituary 109
 Earlier sketch in CA 4R
 See also SATA 22, 28
Constantelos, Demetrios J. 1927- CANR-24
 Earlier sketches in CA 21-22R, CANR-8
Constantin, James A. 1922- 13-14R
Constantin, Robert W(ilfrid) 1937- 25-28R
Constantine, David 1944- DLB-40
Constantine, Greg(ory John) 1938- 117
Constantine, K. C. (a pseudonym) 1935(?)- Brief entry 114
Constantine, Larry L(eRoy) 1943- CANR-14
 Earlier sketch in CA 81-84
Constantine, Mildred 1914- 112
 Brief entry 105
Constantine, Stephen 1947- 120
Constantino, Renato 1919- 118
Conton, William (Farquhar) 1925- 4R
Contoski, Victor 1936- CANR-17
 Earlier sketch in CA 25-28R
Contosta, David R(ichard) 1945- 104
Contreras, Heles 1933- CANR-14
 Earlier sketch in CA 37-40R
Converse, John Marquis 1909-1980
 Obituary 102
Converse, Paul D(ulaney) 1889-1968 .... CAP-2
 Earlier sketch in CA 17-18
Converse, Philip E. 1928- CANR-6
 Earlier sketch in CA 13-14R
Convict Writer, The
 See Torok, Lou
Conway, Alan (Arthur) 1920- CANR-2
 Earlier sketch in CA 1R
Conway, Arlington B.
 See Burns, Eedson Louis Millard
Conway, David 1939- 106
Conway, Denise
 See Prebble, Marjorie Mary Curtis
Conway, Freda 1911- 25-28R
Conway, Gordon
 See Hamilton, Charles Harold St. John
Conway, J(ohn) D(onald) 1905-1967 .... CANR-2
 Earlier sketch in CA 2R
Conway, Jim 1932- 116
Conway, Joan Ditzel 1933- 97-100
Conway, John Seymour 1929- 25-28R
Conway, (Mary) Margaret 1935- 37-40R
Conway, Moncure Daniel 1832-1907 .... DLB-1
Conway, Peter
 See Milkomane, George Alexis Milkomanovich
Conway, Sally 1934- 116
Conway, Theresa (Ann) 1951- CANR-19
 Earlier sketch in CA 103
Conway, Thomas D(aniel) 1934- 21-22R
Conway, Thomas Daniel 1933- 112
Conway, Tim
 See Conway, Thomas Daniel
Conway, Tom
 See Yates, A(lan) G(eoffrey)
Conway, Troy
 See Avallone, Michael (Angelo), Jr.
Conway, Ward
 See Westmoreland, Reg(inald Conway)
Conway, William J. 1904-1983 Obituary 110
Conybeare, Charles Augustus
 See Eliot, T(homas) S(tearns)
Conyers, James E(rnest) 1932- 41-44R
Conyngham, William Joseph 1924- 53-56
Conyus
 See Calhoun, Conyus
Conze, Edward J. D. 1904- 13-14R
Conzelman, James Gleason 1898-1970
 Obituary 104
Conzelman, Jimmy
 See Conzelman, James Gleason
Coogan, Daniel 1915- 21-22R
Coogan, John W(illiam) 1947- 107
Coogan, Joseph Patrick 1925- CANR-4
 Earlier sketch in CA 3R
Coogan, Michael David 1942- Brief entry 112
Cook, Adrian 1940- 49-52
Cook, Alan Hugh 1922- 106
Cook, Albert Spaulding 1925- CANR-16
 Earlier sketches in CA 1R, CANR-1
Cook, Alice H(anson) 1903- 115
Cook, Alice Rice 1899-1973 Obituary 41-44R
Cook, Ann Jennalie 1934- 105
Cook, Arlene Ethel 1936- 65-68
Cook, Bernadine 1924- SATA-11
Cook, Beverly Blair 1926- 37-40R
Cook, Blanche Wiesen 1941- CANR-4
 Earlier sketch in CA 53-56
Cook, Bruce 1932- 33-36R
Cook, Chris(topher) 1945- CANR-23
 Earlier sketches in CA 57-60, CANR-6
Cook, Daniel 1914- 33-36R
Cook, Daniel J(oseph) 1938- 53-56
Cook, David (John) 1929- 107
Cook, David 1940- CANR-22
 Earlier sketch in CA 103
Cook, David A. 1945- 107
Cook, David C(harles) III 1912- 57-60
Cook, David T. 1946- 65-68
Cook, Don(ald Paul) 1920- CANR-14
 Earlier sketch in CA 15-16R
Cook, Don Lewis 1928- 69-72
Cook, Dorothy Mary 1907- CANR-20
 Earlier sketch in CA 103
Cook, Ebenezer 1667(?)-1732(?) DLB-24
Cook, Edward M(arks), Jr. 1944- 123
 Brief entry 118
Cook, Eugene 1917(?)-1986 Obituary 120
Cook, F(rederick) P. 1937- 93-96
Cook, Fred J(ames) 1911- CANR-23
 Earlier sketches in CA 9-10R, CANR-3
 See also SATA 2
Cook, Geoffrey 1946- 77-80
Cook, George Allan 1916- 23-24R
Cook, George S. 1920- 49-52
Cook, Gervis Frere
 See Frere-Cook, Gervis
Cook, Gladys Emerson 5-6R
Cook, Gladys Moon 1907- 33-36R
Cook, Glen (Charles) 1944- 122
Cook, Glenn J. 1913- 25-28R
Cook, Gregory M(orton) 1942- 117
Cook, Harold Reed 1902- 15-16R
Cook, Hugh C(hristopher) B(ult) 1910- 57-60
Cook, Ida ?-1987(?) Obituary 121
Cook, (Harold) J. 1952- 120
Cook, J(ames) Gordon 1916- 11-12R
Cook, Jack
 See Cook, John Augustine
Cook, (Harold) James 1926- 73-76
Cook, James Graham 1925-1966 .... 2R
 Obituary 103
Cook, James W(yatt) 1932- 69-72
Cook, Jeffrey 1934- 97-100
Cook, Joan Marble 1920- 57-60
Cook, John Augustine 1940- 45-48
Cook, John Lennox 1923- 106
Cook, Joseph Jay 1924- CANR-2
 Earlier sketch in CA 3R
 See also SATA 8
Cook, Lennox
 See Cook, John Lennox
Cook, Louise (Celia) 1942-1984 Obituary 112
Cook, Luther T(ownsend) 1901- 89-92
Cook, Lyn
 See Waddell, Evelyn Margaret
Cook, Mabel Collins 1851-1927(?)
 Brief entry 121
Cook, Margaret G(erry) 1903- 5-6R
Cook, Marjorie 1920- 81-84
Cook, Mark 1942- CANR-14
 Earlier sketch in CA 37-40R
Cook, Mary Jane 1929- 93-96
Cook, Melva Janice 1919- CANR-9
 Earlier sketch in CA 23-24R
Cook, Melvin A(lonzo) 1911- CANR-2
 Earlier sketch in CA 49-52
Cook, (Will) Mercer 1903-1987 77-80
 Obituary 124
Cook, Michael 1931- 123
Cook, Michael 1933- 93-96
 See also DLB 53
Cook, Michael Lewis 1929- 112
Cook, Myra B. 1933- 23-24R
Cook, Nilla Cram 1908-1982 Obituary 108
Cook, Olive 1916- CANR-19
 Earlier sketches in CA 7-8R, CANR-3
Cook, Olive Rambo 1892- 13-14R
Cook, P(auline) Lesley 1922- 15-16R
Cook, Paul H(arlin) 1950- 106
Cook, Peter D(onald) 1939- 112
Cook, Petronelle Marguerite Mary 1925- CANR-15
 Earlier sketch in CA 81-84
Cook, Ramona Graham 5-6R
Cook, Ramsay 1931- 102
Cook, Raymond Allen 1919- 45-48
Cook, Reginald L. 1903- 65-68
Cook, Richard I(rving) 1927- 23-24R
Cook, Robert Andrew 1912- 117
Cook, Robert I. 1920- 33-36R
Cook, Robert William Arthur 1931- 25-28R
Cook, Robin 1940- 111
 Brief entry 108
 See also CLC 14
Cook, Robin
 See Cook, Robert William Arthur
Cook, Roderick 1932- 9-10R
Cook, Roy
 See Silverberg, Robert
Cook, Stanley 1922- 93-96
Cook, Stephani 1944- CANR-23
 Earlier sketch in CA 106
Cook, Stephen 1949- 118
Cook, Stuart W(ellford) 1913- CANR-1
 Earlier sketch in CA 4R
Cook, Sylvia (Carol) 1938- 49-52
Cook, Terry 1942- CANR-12
 Earlier sketch in CA 73-76
Cook, Thomas H. 1947- 111
Cook, Thomas Ira 1907-1976 Obituary 111
Cook, W(illiam) Robert 1928- 115
Cook, Warren L. 1925- 37-40R
Cook, (George) Whitfield 1909- 107
Cook, William H(arleston) 1931- 104
Cook, William J(esse), Jr. 1938- 29-32R
Cook, William Wallace 1867-1933
 Brief entry 116
Cooke, (Alfred) Alistair 1908- CANR-9
 Earlier sketch in CA 57-60
 See also AITN 1
Cooke, Ann
 See Cole, Joanna
Cooke, Arthur
 See Lowndes, Robert A(ugustine) W(ard)
Cooke, Barbara
 See Alexander, Anna B(arbara Cooke)
Cooke, Barclay 1912-1981 97-100
 Obituary 105
Cooke, Bernard J. 1922- CANR-9
 Earlier sketch in CA 15-16R
Cooke, Charles Harris 1904(?)-1977
 Obituary 73-76
Cooke, David Coxe 1917- CANR-2
 Earlier sketch in CA 2R
 See also SATA 2
Cooke, Deryck (Victor) 1919-1976
 Obituary 115
Cooke, Donald Ewin 1916-1985 .... CANR-4
 Obituary 117
 Earlier sketch in CA 4R
 See also SATA 2, 45
Cooke, Edward F(rancis) 1923- 41-44R
Cooke, Gerald 1925- 13-14R
Cooke, Gilbert William 1899- CAP-1
 Earlier sketch in CA 11-12
Cooke, Greville (Vaughan Turner) 1894- 13-14R
Cooke, Hereward Lester 1916-1973 .... CANR-1
 Obituary 45-48
 Earlier sketch in CA 3R
Cooke, Hope 1940- 108
Cooke, Jacob E(rnest) 1924- 2R
Cooke, James Francis 1875-1960
 Obituary 115
Cooke, John Byrne 1940- 119
Cooke, John D(aniel) 1892-1972 Obituary .. 106
Cooke, John Esten 1830-1886 .... DLB-3
Cooke, John Estes
 See Baum, L(yman) Frank
Cooke, John Fletcher
 See Fletcher-Cooke, John
Cooke, Joseph R(obinson) 1926- 65-68
Cooke, M. E.
 See Creasey, John
Cooke, Margaret
 See Creasey, John
Cooke, Michael, F.R.C.S.
 See Cook, Michael Lewis
Cooke, Michael G(eorge) 1934- 110
Cooke, Philip Pendleton 1816-1850 ... DLB-3, 59
Cooke, Robert (Gordon) 1930-1987 101
 Obituary 121
Cooke, Robert William 1935- 123
Cooke, Rose Terry 1827-1892 .... DLB-12
Cooke, Terence James 1921-1983
 Obituary 110
Cooke, Thomas D(arlington) 1933- 115
Cooke, William 1942- CANR-14
 Earlier sketch in CA 33-36R
Cookridge, E. H.
 See Spiro, Edward
Cookson, Catherine (McMullen) 1906- ... CANR-9
 Earlier sketch in CA 15-16R
 See also SATA 9
Cookson, Frank Barton 1912-1977
 Obituary 69-72
Cookson, Peter W. 1913- 49-52
Cookson, Peter W., Jr. 1942- 121
Cookson, William 1939- 49-52
Cool, Joyce 1938- 111
Cool, Ola C. 1890(?)-1977 Obituary 69-72
Coolbrith, Ina 1841-1928 .... DLB-54
Coole, W. W.
 See Kulski, Wladyslaw W(szebor)
Cooley, John Kent 1927- 15-16R
Cooley, Lee Morrison 1919- CANR-3
 Earlier sketch in CA 9-10R
Cooley, Leland Frederick 1909- CANR-4
 Earlier sketch in CA 5-6R
Cooley, Margaret L. 1906(?)-1985
 Obituary 117
Cooley, Peter (John) 1940- CANR-21
 Earlier sketch in CA 69-72
Cooley, Richard A(llen) 1925- 21-22R
Coolidge, Archibald C(ary), Jr. 1928- 37-40R
Coolidge, Clark 1939- 33-36R
Coolidge, Harold Jefferson 1904-1985
 Obituary 115
Coolidge, Olivia E(nsor) 1908- CANR-2
 Earlier sketch in CA 5-6R
 See also SATA 1, 26
Coolidge, Susan
 See Woolsey, Sarah Chauncy
Cooling, Benjamin Franklin 1938- 53-56
Coolwater, John
 See Conniff, James C(lifford) G(regory)
Coomaraswamy, A. K.
 See Coomaraswamy, Ananda K(entish)
Coomaraswamy, Ananda K(entish) 1877-1947 Brief entry 115
Coombes, B. L. 1894(?)-1974 Obituary 53-56
Coombs, Charles Anthony 1918-1981 109
 Obituary 105
Coombs, Charles I(ra) 1914- CANR-19
 Earlier sketches in CA 5-6R, CANR-4
 See also SATA 3, 43
Coombs, Chick
 See Coombs, Charles I(ra)
Coombs, Douglas (Stafford) 1924- 13-14R
Coombs, H. Samm 1928- 93-96
Coombs, Herbert Cole 1906- 93-96
Coombs, Murdo
 See Davis, Frederick C(lyde)
Coombs, Orde M. 1939(?)-1984 73-76
 Obituary 113
Coombs, Patricia 1926- CANR-1
 Earlier sketch in CA 4R
 See also SATA 3
Coombs, (Robert) Peter 1913- 116
Coombs, Philip H(all) 1915- CANR-23
 Earlier sketches in CA 17-18R, CANR-8
Coombs, Robert H(olman) 1934- 41-44R
Coon, Carleton Stevens 1904-1981 .... CANR-2
 Obituary 104
 Earlier sketch in CA 5-6R
Coon, Gene L(ee) 1924-1973 .... CANR-15
 Obituary 103
 Earlier sketch in CA 2R
Coon, Martha Sutherland 1884- CAP-2
 Earlier sketch in CA 25-28
Coon, Nelson 1895- 69-72
Coon, Stephen 1948- 57-60
Cooney, Barbara 1917- CANR-3
 Earlier sketch in CA 5-6R
 See also SATA 6
Cooney, Caroline B. 1947- 97-100
 See also SATA 41, 48
Cooney, David M(artin) 1930- 17-18R
Cooney, Eugene J(erome) 1931- 45-48
Cooney, John 1942- 115
Cooney, Michael 1921- 25-28R
Cooney, Nancy Evans 1932- 105
 See also SATA 42
Cooney, Seamus (Anthony) 1933- 53-56
Cooney, Timothy J. 1929- 107
Coons, Frederica Bertha (Safley) 1910- ...17-18R
Coons, William R(ichard) 1934- 41-44R
Coontz, Otto 1946- 105
 See also SATA 33

Coop, Howard 1928- ... 25-28R
Coope, Rosalys 1921- ... 45-48
Cooper, Alfred Morton 1890- ... CAP-1
Earlier sketch in CA 11-12
Cooper, Alice 1948- ... 106
Cooper, Allan 1954- ... 118
Cooper, Allan D. 1952- ... 121
Cooper, Arnold Cook 1933- ... 19-20R
Cooper, B(rian) Lee 1942- ... 117
Cooper, Barbara (Ann) 1929- ... 9-10R
Cooper, Bernarr 1912- ... 41-44R
Cooper, Bev 1936- ... 119
Cooper, Brian (Newman) 1919- ... CANR-22
Earlier sketch in CA 4R
Cooper, Bruce M(ichael) 1925- ... CANR-9
Earlier sketch in CA 15-16R
Cooper, Bryan (Robert Wright) 1932- ... 25-28R
Cooper, C(hristopher) D(onald) H(untington) 1942- ... 29-32R
Cooper, Carl
See Cooper, Kenneth C(arlton)
Cooper, Charles M(uhlenberg) 1909- ... 41-44R
Cooper, Charles W(illiam) 1904- ... CAP-2
Earlier sketch in CA 21-22
Cooper, Chester L. 1917- ... 29-32R
Cooper, Christopher (John) 1941- ... 107
Cooper, (Brenda) Clare 1935- ... 118
Cooper, Colin Symons 1926- ... 102
Cooper, Darien B(rown) 1934- ... 116
Cooper, Darien B(irla) 1937- ... CANR-16
Earlier sketches in CA 49-52, CANR-1
Cooper, David (Graham) 1931-1986 ... 97-100
Obituary ... 119
Cooper, David E. 1942- ... 49-52
Cooper, Derek Macdonald 1925- ... 102
Cooper, Diana (Olivia Winifred Maud Manners) 1892(?)-1986 Obituary ... 119
Cooper, Dominic (Xavier) 1944- ... 65-68
Cooper, Douglas 1911-1984 Obituary ... 112
Cooper, Edmund 1926- ... 33-36R
Cooper, Elizabeth Ann 1927- ... 3R
Cooper, Elizabeth Keyser ... CANR-1
Earlier sketch in CA 4R
See also SATA 47
Cooper, Emmanuel 1938- ... CANR-3
Earlier sketch in CA 49-52
Cooper, Esther
See Kellner, Esther
Cooper, (C.) Everett
See Burgess, M(ichael) R(oy)
Cooper, Frank E(dward) 1910-1968 ... CAP-2
Earlier sketch in CA 21-22
Cooper, Giles (Stannus) 1918-1966
Obituary ... 113
See also DLB 13
Cooper, Gladys 1888-1971 Obituary ... 33-36R
Cooper, Gordon 1932- ... 61-64
See also SATA 23
Cooper, Grace Rogers 1924- ... 41-44R
Cooper, Hannah
See Spence, William John Duncan
Cooper, Harold E(ugene) 1928- ... 45-48
Cooper, Harold H. 1911(?)-1976
Obituary ... 69-72
Cooper, Harold R. 1911(?)-1978
Obituary ... 77-80
Cooper, Henry S(potswood) F(enimore), Jr. 1933- ... CANR-13
Earlier sketch in CA 69-72
Cooper, Henry St. John
See Creasey, John
Cooper, I(rving) S(pencer) 1922-1985 ... 69-72
Obituary ... 117
Cooper, Jacqueline 1924- ... 107
Cooper, James A.
See Stratemeyer, Edward L.
Cooper, James Fenimore 1789-1851 ... SATA-19
See also DLB 3
See also CDALB 1640-1865
Cooper, James L(ouis) 1934- ... 53-56
Cooper, James M. 1939- ... 45-48
Cooper, Jamie Lee ... 9-10R
Cooper, Jane (Marvel) 1924- ... CANR-17
Earlier sketch in CA 25-28R
Cooper, Jeff 1920- ... 41-44R
Cooper, Jefferson
See Fox, G(ardner) F(rancis)
Cooper, Jeremy (Francis Peter) 1946- ... 93-96
Cooper, Jilly 1937- ... 105
Cooper, John 1934-1984 Obituary ... 113
Cooper, John C(harles) 1933- ... CANR-9
Earlier sketch in CA 23-24R
Cooper, John Cobb 1887- ... 5-6R
Cooper, John Dean
See Cooper, Jeff
Cooper, John E(llsworth) 1922- ... 25-28R
Cooper, John Irwin 1905- ... 41-44R
Cooper, John L. 1936- ... CANR-13
Earlier sketch in CA 21-22R
Cooper, John M(iller) 1912- ... 21-22R
Cooper, John Milton, Jr. 1940-
Brief entry ... 105
Cooper, John O(wen) 1938- ... 89-92
Cooper, John R. ... CAP-2
Earlier sketch in CA 19-20
See also SATA 1
Cooper, Joseph Bonar 1912- ... 19-20R
Cooper, Joseph D(avid) 1917-1975 ... CANR-4
Obituary ... 57-60
Earlier sketch in CA 5-6R
Cooper, Kay 1941- ... CANR-16
Earlier sketches in CA 45-48, CANR-1
See also SATA 11
Cooper, Kenneth C(arlton) 1948- ... 110
Cooper, Kenneth Schaaf 1918- ... 9-10R
Cooper, Kent 1880-1965 Obituary ... 89-92
See also DLB 29
Cooper, Lee Pelham 1926- ... CANR-4
Earlier sketch in CA 5-6R
See also SATA 5
Cooper, Leslie M(uir) 1930- ... 41-44R
Cooper, Lester (Irving) 1919-1985 ... 108
Obituary ... 116
See also SATA 32, 43
Cooper, Lettice (Ulpha) 1897- ... CANR-5
Earlier sketch in CA 9-10R
See also SATA 35
Cooper, Louise 1952- ... 107
Cooper, Louise Field 1905- ... CANR-4
Earlier sketch in CA 4R
Cooper, Lynna
See Fox, G(ardner) F(rancis)
Cooper, Mae (Klein) ... 17-18R
Cooper, Mario 1905- ... 23-24R
Cooper, Martin Du Pre 1910-1986 ... 103
Obituary ... 118
Cooper, Matthew (Heald) 1952- ... 85-88
Cooper, Mattie Lula
See Britton, Mattie Lula Cooper
Cooper, Michael (John) 1930- ... 15-16R
Cooper, Michele F(reda) 1941- ... 85-88
Cooper, Morley
See Cooper, Alfred Morton
Cooper, Neil (Louis) 1930- ... 119
Cooper, Parley J(oseph) 1937- ... CANR-10
Earlier sketch in CA 65-68
Cooper, Patricia J(ean) 1936- ... 97-100
Cooper, Paul 1926- ... 49-52
Cooper, Paul F(enimore) 1900(?)-1970
Obituary ... 104
Cooper, Paulette 1944- ... 37-40R
Cooper, Peter Lee 1949- ... 111
Cooper, Philip (Jr.) 1926- ... 33-36R
Cooper, Phyllis 1939- ... 53-56
Cooper, Richard N(ewell) 1934- ... CANR-10
Earlier sketch in CA 25-28R
Cooper, Robert G(ravlin) 1943- ... 110
Cooper, Robert St. John 1905(?)-1984
Obituary ... 111
Cooper, Sandi E. 1936- ... 49-52
Cooper, Saul 1934- ... 3R
Cooper, Signe Skott 1921- ... CANR-4
Earlier sketch in CA 53-56
Cooper, Sister Mary Ursula 1925- ... 5-6R
Cooper, Sophie
See Amory, Mark
Cooper, Susan 1935- ... CANR-15
Earlier sketch in CA 29-32R
See also SATA 4
See also CLR 4
Cooper, Sylvia 1903- ... CAP-2
Earlier sketch in CA 17-18
Cooper, Wayne 1938- ... 93-96
Cooper, Wendy (Lowe) 1919- ... CANR-6
Earlier sketch in CA 13-14R
Cooper, Wilhelmina (Behmenburg) 1939(?)-1980 Obituary ... 97-100
Cooper, Will 1929- ... 69-72
Cooper, William
See Hoff, Harry S(ummerfield)
Cooper, William F(razier) 1932- ... 69-72
Cooper, William Hurlbert 1924- ... 49-52
Cooper, William J(ames), Jr. 1940- ... 69-72
Cooper, William W(ager) 1914- ... 15-16R
Cooper, Wyatt (Emory) 1927-1978 ... 73-76
Obituary ... 77-80
See also AITN 2
Cooper-Clark, Diana 1945- ... 109
Cooper-Klein, Nina
See Cooper, Mae (Klein)
Cooperman, Hasye 1909- ... 37-40R
Cooperman, Stanley 1929-1976 ... CAP-2
Earlier sketch in CA 33-36
Coopersmith, Harry 1903- ... CAP-2
Earlier sketch in CA 21-22
Coopersmith, Jerome 1925- ... 73-76
Coopersmith, Stanley 1926- ... 21-22R
Cooter, Roger James 1948- ... 123
Cootner, Paul H(arold) 1930- ... 11-12R
Coover, James B(urrell) 1925- ... CANR-23
Earlier sketches in CA 57-60, CANR-6
Coover, Robert (Lowell) 1932- ... CANR-3
Earlier sketch in CA 45-48
See also DLB 2
See also DLBY 81
See also CLC 3, 7, 15, 32, 46
Coox, Alvin D(avid) 1924- ... 29-32R
Copani, Peter 1942- ... 89-92
Cope, David 1941- ... 33-36R
Cope, Edward A(llen) 1948- ... 121
Cope, Jack
See Cope, Robert Knox
Cope, Jackson I(rving) 1925- ... 103
Cope, Myron 1929- ... 57-60
Cope, Oliver 1902- Brief entry ... 109
Cope, Robert Knox 1913- ... 9-10R
Cope, (Vincent) Zachary 1881-1974 ... CAP-1
Earlier sketch in CA 9-10
Copel, Sidney L(eroy) 1930- ... 23-24R
Copelan, Rachel 1934- ... 114
Copeland, Ann
See Furtwangler, Virginia W(alsh)
Copeland, Bill
See Copeland, Paul William
Copeland, Bonnie Chapman 1919- ... 101
Copeland, Carolyn Faunce 1930- ... 65-68
Copeland, E(dwin) Luther 1916- ... CANR-3
Earlier sketch in CA 11-12R
Copeland, Helen 1920- ... 25-28R
See also SATA 4
Copeland, James Isaac 1910- ... 106
Copeland, Lennie 1946- ... 120
Copeland, Melvin T. 1884-1975 ... CAP-2
Obituary ... 57-60
Earlier sketch in CA 21-22
Copeland, Miles 1916- ... 29-32R
Copeland, Morris A(lbert) 1895- ... CAP-1
Earlier sketch in CA 17-18
Copeland, Paul W. ... 105
See also SATA 23
Copeland, Paul William 1917- ... 25-28R
Copeland, Ray (M.) 1926-1984 Obituary ... 112
Copeland, Ross H. 1930- ... 25-28R
Copeland, Stewart (Armstrong) 1952- ... CLC-26
Copeland, Thomas Wellsted 1907-1979 ... 5-6R
Copeman, George H(enry) 1922- ... CANR-8
Earlier sketch in CA 7-8R
Copenhaver, Charles L(eonard) 1915-1982
Obituary ... 107
Coper, Rudolf 1904- ... CAP-1
Earlier sketch in CA 13-14
Copetas, A. Craig 1951- ... 121
Copi, Irving M(armer) 1917- ... CANR-5
Earlier sketch in CA 1R
Coplan, Kate M(ildred) 1901- ... 7-8R
Copland, Aaron 1900- ... 7-8R
Coplans, John (Rivers) 1920- Brief entry ... 112
Copleston, Frederick Charles (John Paul) 1907- ... CANR-7
Earlier sketch in CA 13-14R
Copley, Gerald L. C.
See Cole, Lester
Copley (Diana) Heather Pickering 1918- ... SATA-45
Coplin, William D(avid) 1939- ... CANR-12
Earlier sketch in CA 23-24R
Copman, Louis 1934- ... 57-60
Copp, Andrew James (III) 1916- ... 25-28R
Copp, E. Anthony 1945- ... 102
Copp, Jim
See Copp, Andrew James (III)
Coppa, Frank John 1937- ... CANR-13
Earlier sketch in CA 33-36R
Coppard, A(lfred) E(dgar) 1878-1957
Brief entry ... 114
See also YABC 1
See also TCLC 5
Coppard, Audrey 1931- ... 29-32R
Coppe, Abiezer
See Taylor, John (Alfred)
Coppee, Francois 1842-1908 ... TCLC-25
Coppel, Alec 1909(?)-1972 Obituary ... 33-36R
Coppel, Alfred 1921- ... CANR-10
Earlier sketch in CA 19-20R
See also DLBY 83
Copper, (Robert) Arnold (de Vignier) 1934- ... 97-100
Copper, John Franklin 1940- ... CANR-11
Earlier sketch in CA 69-72
Copper, Marcia S(nyder) 1934- ... 53-56
Copperman, Paul 1947- ... 101
Copperud, Roy H. 1915- ... 11-12R
Coppock, John (Oates) 1914- ... 13-14R
Coppock, John Terence 1921- ... 102
Coppock, Joseph D(avid) 1909- ... 49-52
Coppola, Francis Ford 1939- ... 77-80
See also DLB 44
See also CLC 16
Coppola, Raymond T(homas) 1947- ... 102
Coram, Christopher
See Walker, Peter N.
Corballis, Michael C(harles) 1936- ... 115
Corbally, John Edward, Jr. 1924- ... 5-6R
Corbett, Chan
See Schachner, Nat(han)
Corbett, Christopher 1951- ... 123
Corbett, Edward P(atrick) J(oseph) 1919- ... CANR-9
Earlier sketch in CA 17-18R
Corbett, Elizabeth (Frances) 1887-1981 ... CANR-2
Obituary ... 102
Earlier sketch in CA 5-6R
Corbett, Grahame ... 116
See also SATA 36, 43
Corbett, J(ack) Elliott 1920- ... 29-32R
Corbett, James A(rthur) 1908- ... 65-68
Corbett, Janice M. 1935- ... 37-40R
Corbett, (John) Patrick 1916- ... 17-18R
Corbett, Pearson H(arris) 1900- ... CAP-1
Earlier sketch in CA 9-10
Corbett, Richmond McLain 1902- ... CAP-1
Earlier sketch in CA 15-16
Corbett, Ruth 1912- ... 29-32R
Corbett, Scott 1913- ... CANR-23
Earlier sketches in CA 3R, CANR-1
See also SATA 2, 42
See also SAAS 2
See also CLR 1
Corbett, Thomas H(enry) 1938- ... 77-80
Corbett, W(illiam) J(esse) 1938- ... SATA-44, 50
Corbin, Arnold 1911- ... 9-10R
Corbin, Charles B. 1940- ... CANR-14
Earlier sketch in CA 29-32R
Corbin, Claire 1913- ... 41-44R
Corbin, Donald A(lvin) 1920- ... 33-36R
Corbin, H(ayman) Dan 1912- ... 41-44R
Corbin, Iris
See Clinton, Iris A. (Corbin)
Corbin, John B(oyd) 1935- ... CANR-22
Earlier sketch in CA 105
Corbin, Richard 1911- ... CANR-3
Earlier sketch in CA 7-8R
Corbin, Sabra Lee
See Malvern, Gladys
Corbin, William
See McGraw, William Corbin
Corbishley, Thomas 1903-1976 ... CANR-7
Obituary ... 65-68
Earlier sketch in CA 13-14R
Corbitt, Helen Lucy 1906-1978 ... CANR-4
Obituary ... 89-92
Earlier sketch in CA 7-8R
Corby, Dan
See Catherall, Arthur
Corcoran, Barbara 1911- ... CANR-11
Earlier sketch in CA 23-24R
See also CAAS 2
See also SATA 3
See also DLB 52
See also CLC 17
Corcoran, Gertrude B(eatty) 1922- ... 29-32R
Corcoran, Jean (Kennedy) 1926- ... 3R
Corcos, Lucille 1908-1973 ... 21-22R
See also SATA 10
Cord, Barry
See Germano, Peter B.
Cord, Robert L. 1935- ... 33-36R
Cord, Steven Benson 1928- ... 21-22R
Cord, William O. 1921- ... 37-40R
Cordasco, Francesco 1920- ... CANR-21
Earlier sketches in CA 13-14R, CANR-6
Cordelier, Maurice
See Giraudoux, (Hippolyte) Jean
Cordell, Alexander
See Graber, Alexander
Cordell, Richard Albert 1896- ... 1R
Corden, W(arner) M(ax) 1927- ... 33-36R
Corder, Brice W(ood) 1936- ... 53-56
Corder, Eric
See Mundis, Jerrold
Corder, George Edward 1904- ... 110
Corder, Jim(my Wayne) 1929- ... 17-18R
Cordier, Andrew W(ellington) 1901-1975
Obituary ... 106
Cordier, Gilbert
See Scherer, Jean-Marie Maurice
Cordier, Ralph Waldo 1902- ... 37-40R
Cordingley, Patrick 1944- ... 114
Cordingly, David 1938- ... 93-96
Cordis, Lonny
See Donson, Cyril
Cords, Nicholas J. 1929- ... 105
Cordtz, Dan 1927- ... 73-76
Cordwell, Miriam 1908-1986 ... 89-92
Obituary ... 120
Corea, Gena
See Corea, Genoveffa
Corea, Genoveffa 1946- ... 81-84
Corelli, Marie
See Mackay, Mary
See also DLB 34
Coren, Alan 1938- ... 69-72
See also SATA 32
Corey, Dorothy ... CANR-11
Earlier sketch in CA 69-72
See also SATA 23
Corey, Gerald F(rancis) 1937- ... 114
Corey, Paul (Frederick) 1903- ... CANR-2
Earlier sketch in CA 5-6R
Corey, Stephen 1948- ... 124
Corfe, Thomas Howell 1928- ... 103
See also SATA 27
Corfe, Tom
See Corfe, Thomas Howell
Corfield, Conrad Laurence 1893-1980
Obituary ... 105
Corfman, Eunice (Luccock) 1928-1980
Obituary ... 97-100
Corina, Maurice 1936- ... 57-60
Cork, Patrick
See Cockburn, (Francis) Claud
Cork, Richard (Graham) 1947- ... CANR-24
Earlier sketch in CA 107
Corke, Helen 1882- ... CAP-1
Earlier sketch in CA 9-10
Corke, Hilary 1921- ... 97-100
Corkey, R(obert) 1881-1966 ... CAP-1
Earlier sketch in CA 15-16
Corkran, David Hudson, Jr. 1902- ... 5-6R
Corkran, Herbert, Jr. 1924- ... 29-32R
Corle, Edwin 1906-1956 ... DLBY-85
Corless, Roger (Jonathan) 1938- ... 108
Corlett, William 1938- ... 103
See also SATA 39, 46
Corlew, Robert Ewing 1922- ... 110
Corley, (Thomas) Anthony (Buchanan) 1923- ... 2R
Corley, Edwin (Raymond) 1931-1981 ... CANR-12
Obituary ... 105
Earlier sketch in CA 25-28R
Corley, Ernest
See Bulmer, (Henry) Kenneth
Corley, Nora T(eresa) ... 118
Corley, Ray
See Corley, Edwin (Raymond)
Corley, Robert N(eil) 1930- ... CANR-19
Earlier sketches in CA 11-12R, CANR-3
Corliss, Charlotte N(uzum) 1932- ... 53-56
Corliss, William R(oger) 1926- ... CANR-16
Earlier sketches in CA 45-48, CANR-1
Cormack, Alexander James Ross 1942- ... 65-68
Cormack, James Maxwell Ross 1909-1975 ... CAP-1
Earlier sketch in CA 9-10
Cormack, M(argaret) Grant 1913- ... 3R
See also SATA 11
Cormack, Margaret Lawson 1912- ... 3R
Cormack, Maribelle B. 1902-1984 ... SATA-39
Cormack, Sandy
See Cormack, Alexander James Ross
Corman, Avery 1935- ... 85-88
Corman, Cid
See Corman, Sidney
See also CAAS 2
See also DLB 5
See also CLC 9

Corman, Sidney 1924- 85-88
Cormier, Bruno M. 1919- Brief entry 114
Cormier, Frank 1927- 23-24R
Cormier, Ramona 1923- 49-52
Cormier, Raymond J(oseph) 1938- CANR-19
Earlier sketches in CA 53-56, CANR-4
Cormier, Robert (Edmund) 1925- CANR-23
Earlier sketches in CA 3R, CANR-5
See also SATA 10, 45
See also DLB 52
See also CLC 12, 30
See also CLR 12
Cormillot, Albert E. J. 1938- 69-72
Corn, Alfred 1943- 104
See also DLBY 80
See also CLC 33
Corn, Ira George, Jr. 1921-1982 85-88
Obituary 106
Cornea, Carol
See Koch, Kurt E(mil)
Cornebise, Alfred E(mile) 1929- 115
Cornehls, James V(ernon) 1936- 93-96
Cornelisen, Ann 1926- CANR-17
Earlier sketch in CA 25-28R
corneliszavandenheuvel
See van den Heuvel, Cornelisz A.
Cornelius, Carol 1942- 115
See also SATA 40
Cornelius, Temple H. 1891-1964 .... CAP-1
Earlier sketch in CA 11-12
Cornelius, Wanda Pyle 1936- 105
Cornell, Douglas B. 1906(?)-1982
Obituary 106
Cornell, Felix M. 1896(?)-1970 Obituary 104
Cornell, Francis Griffith 1906-1979
Obituary 89-92
Cornell, George W. 1920- 9-10R
Cornell, J.
See Cornell, Jeffrey
Cornell, James (Clayton, Jr.) 1938- CANR-11
Earlier sketch in CA 69-72
See also SATA 27
Cornell, Jean Gay 1920- CANR-1
Earlier sketch in CA 45-48
See also SATA 23
Cornell, Jeffrey 1945- SATA-11
Cornell, Katherine 1898(?)-1974 Obituary .. 49-52
Cornell, Tim 1946- 115
Corner, E. J. H.
See Corner, Edred John Henry
Corner, Edred John Henry 1906-
Brief entry 116
Corner, George W(ashington) 1889-1981 ... 102
Obituary 104
Corner, Philip 1933- 23-24R
Cornett, Joe D(elayne) 1935- 53-56
Corney, Estelle 1911- 115
Cornfeld, Gaalyah 1902- CANR-12
Earlier sketch in CA 73-76
Cornford, A(ndrew) J(ohn) 1942- 112
Cornforth, Maurice 1909-1980 .... CANR-4
Obituary 102
Earlier sketch in CA 5-6R
Corngold, Stanley Alan 1934- CANR-14
Earlier sketch in CA 37-40R
Cornillon, John Raymond Koppleman
1941- 17-18R
Cornish, Dudley T(aylor) 1915- 19-20R
Cornish, Edward (Seymour) 1927- 108
Cornish, John (Buckley) 1914- 25-28R
Cornish, Sam(uel James) 1935- CANR-24
Earlier sketch in CA 41-44R
See also SATA 23
See also DLB 41
Cornish, W(illiam) R(odolph) 1937- 29-32R
Cornman, James W(elton) 1929-1978 .. CANR-11
Earlier sketch in CA 69-72
Cornock, (John) Stroud 1938- 25-28R
Cornuelle, Richard C. 1927- 17-18R
Cornwall, E(spie) Judson 1924- CANR-6
Earlier sketch in CA 57-60
Cornwall, I(an) W(olfran) 1909- 11-12R
Cornwall, J. Spencer 1888(?)-1983
Obituary 109
Cornwall, James (Handyside) Marshall
See Marshall-Cornwall, James
(Handyside)
Cornwall, Jim
See Rikhoff, James C.
Cornwall, John 1928- 115
Cornwall, Martin
See Cavendish, Richard
Cornwall, Nellie
See Sloggett, Nellie
Cornwell, Bernard 1944- 104
Cornwell, David (John Moore) 1931- ... CANR-13
Earlier sketch in CA 7-8R
See also CLC 9, 15
Cornwell, Elmer E(ckert), Jr. 1924-
Brief entry 118
Cornwell, Smith
See Smith, David (Jeddie)
Coronel, Jorge Icaza
See Icaza Coronel, Jorge
Corporal Trim
See Bolger, Philip C(unningham)
Corradi, Gemma 1939- 23-24R
Corradi, Juan E. 1943- 113
Corrall, Alice Enid 1916- 7-8R
Corre, Alan D. 1931- 37-40R
Correa
See Galbraith, Jean
Correa, Gustavo 1914- 49-52
Correia-Afonso, John 1924- CANR-13
Earlier sketch in CA 33-36R
Corren, Grace
See Hoskins, Robert
Correu, Larry M. 1931- 114
Correy, Lee
See Stine, G(eorge) Harry
Corrie, Elva
See Clairmont, Elva
Corrigan, (Helen) Adeline 1909- 69-72
See also SATA 23
Corrigan, Barbara 1922- 57-60
See also SATA 8
Corrigan, Francis Joseph 1919- 7-8R
Corrigan, John D(avitt) 1900- 41-44R
Corrigan, John Thomas 1936- CANR-10
Earlier sketch in CA 65-68
Corrigan, Ralph L(awrence), Jr. 1937- ... 33-36R
Corrigan, Robert A(nthony) 1935- 9-10R
Corrigan, Robert W(illoughby) 1927- CANR-6
Earlier sketch in CA 7-8R
Corrin, Sara 1918- 120
See also SATA 48
Corrin, Stephen 121
See also SATA 48
Corrington, John William 1932- CANR-8
Earlier sketch in CA 13-14R
See also DLB 6
Corriveau, Monique (Chouinard)
1927-1976 .... CANR-12
Obituary 122
Earlier sketch in CA 61-64
Corrothers, James D. 1869-1917 .... DLB-50
Corry, Emmett 1934- 111
Corry, J(ames) A(lexander) 1899-1985
Obituary 120
Corsa, Helen Storm 1915- 19-20R
Corsaro, Francesco Andrea 1924- 85-88
Corsaro, Frank
See Corsaro, Francesco Andrea
Corsaro, Maria C(ecelia) 1949- 107
Corsel, Ralph 1920- 25-28R
Corsi, Jerome R(obert) 1946- 89-92
Corsini, Raymond J. 1914- CANR-21
Earlier sketches in CA 4R, CANR-3
Corso, (Nunzio) Gregory 1930- 7-8R
See also DLB 5,16
See also CLC 1, 11
Corson, Fred Pierce 1896-1985 .... CAP-2
Obituary 115
Earlier sketch in CA 23-24
Corson, Hazel W. 1906- CANR-2
Earlier sketch in CA 2R
Corson, John J(ay) 1905- CANR-5
Earlier sketch in CA 1R
Corson, Richard 41-44R
Corson-Finnerty, Adam Daniel 1944- ... CANR-14
Earlier sketch in CA 81-84
Corstanje, Auspicius van
See van Corstanje, Charles
Corstanje, Charles van
See van Corstanje, Charles
Cort, David 1904-1983 .... 9-10R
Obituary 111
Cort, M. C.
See Clifford, Margaret Cort
Cort, Margaret
See Clifford, Margaret Cort
Cortada, James W(illiam) 1946-
Brief entry 114
Cortazar, Julio 1914-1984 .... CANR-12
Earlier sketch in CA 21-22R
See also CLC 2, 3, 5, 10, 13, 15, 33, 34
Cortazzi, (Henry Arthur) Hugh 1924- 115
Cortazzo, Carman 1936- 109
Corteen, Wes
See Norwood, Victor G(eorge) C(harles)
Cortes, Carlos E(liseo) 1934- CANR-8
Earlier sketch in CA 61-64
Cortes, Juan B(autista) 1925- 37-40R
Cortese, A(nthony) James 1917- 65-68
Cortesi, Lawrence
See Cerri, Lawrence J.
Cortez, Jayne 1936- CANR-13
Earlier sketch in CA 73-76
See also DLB 41
Cortez-Villon, Juan
See Herzinger, Kim A(llen)
Cortinez, Carlos 1934- 123
Cortner, Richard C(arroll) 1935- 104
Cortright, Barbara 1927- 112
Cortright, David 1946- 57-60
Corty, Floyd L(ouis) 1916- 13-14R
Corwen, Leonard 1921- CANR-15
Earlier sketch in CA 93-96
Corwin, Adele Beatrice Lewis 1922- 123
Corwin, Cecil
See Kornbluth, C(yril) M.
Corwin, Edward S(amuel) 1878-1963 122
Obituary 113
Corwin, Judith H(offman) 1946- 113
See also SATA 10
Corwin, Norman 1910- CANR-24
Earlier sketches in CA 4R, CANR-1
See also AITN 2
Corwin, Ronald G(ary) 1932- CANR-23
Earlier sketches in CA 19-20R, CANR-8
Cory, Caroline
See Freeman, Kathleen
Cory, Corrine
See Cory, Irene E.
Cory, Daniel 1904-1972 Obituary 37-40R
Cory, David 1872-1966 Obituary 25-28R
Cory, Desmond
See McCarthy, Shaun (Lloyd)
Cory, Howard L.
See Jardine, Jack
Cory, Irene E. 1910- 49-52
Cory, Jean-Jacques 1947- 57-60
Cory, Ray
See Marshall, Mel(vin D.)
Cory, William Johnson 1823-1892 .... DLB-35
Corya, I. E.
See Cory, Irene E.
Cosby, Bill
See Cosby, William Henry, Jr.
Cosby, William Henry, Jr. 1937- 81-84
Cosby, Yvonne Shepard 1886(?)-1980
Obituary 97-100
Cose, Ellis Jonathan 1951- 119
Cosell, Howard 1920- 108
Cosentino, Andrew J(oseph) 1931- 120
Cosentino, Donald J(ohn) 1941- 108
Coser, Lewis A. 1913- CANR-4
Earlier sketch in CA 3R
Coser, Rose Laub 1916- 15-16R
Cosgrave, John O'Hara II 1908-1968 .... CANR-1
Earlier sketch in CA 4R
See also SATA 21
Cosgrave, Patrick 1941- 33-36R
Cosgrove, Carol Ann 1943- 29-32R
Cosgrove, Margaret (Leota) 1926- CANR-6
Earlier sketch in CA 9-10R
See also SATA 47
Cosgrove, Mark P. 1947- 85-88
Cosgrove, Maynard G(iles) 1895- 57-60
Cosgrove, Rachel
See Payes, Rachel C(osgrove)
Cosgrove, Richard A(lfred) 1941- 104
Cosgrove, Stephen E(dward) 1945- CANR-22
Earlier sketch in CA 69-72
See also SATA 40
See also AITN 1
Cosh, (Ethel Eleanor) Mary 7-8R
Cosic, Dobrica 1921- Brief entry 122
See also CLC 14
Coskey, Evelyn 1932- 41-44R
See also SATA 7
Coslow, Sam 1905-1982 77-80
Obituary 106
Cosman, Carol 104
Cosman, Madeleine Pelner 1937-
Brief entry 105
Cosneck, Bernard Joseph 1912- 49-52
Cosner, Shaaron 1940- 116
See also SATA 43
Coss, Thurman L. 1926- 13-14R
Cossart, Theophilus
See Glass, Montague (Marsden)
Cosseboom, Kathy Groehn
See El-Messidi, Kathy Groehn
Cossi, Olga 1921- 81-84
Cosslett, Tess 1947- 115
Cossman, E(li) Joseph 1918- 19-20R
Cost, March
See Morrison, Margaret Mackie
Costa, Albert Bernard 1929- 13-14R
Costa, Gustavo 1930- 37-40R
Costa, Horacio (L.) de la 1916-1977
Obituary 112
Costa, Richard Hauer 1921- 21-22R
Costabel, Eva Deutsch 1924- SATA-45
Costain, Thomas B(ertram) 1885-1965 .... 5-6R
Obituary 25-28R
See also DLB 9
See also CLC 30
Costantin, M(ary) M(cCaffrey) 1935- 45-48
Costantini, Humberto 1924(?)-1987
Obituary 122
Costas, Orlando E(nrique) 1942-1987 101
Obituary 124
Costas, Procope 1900(?)-1974 Obituary ... 53-56
Costello, Anne 1937- 102
Costello, Chris 1947- 107
Costello, David F(rancis) 1904- 33-36R
See also SATA 23
Costello, Donald P(aul) 1931- 19-20R
Costello, Elvis 1955- CLC-21
Costello, Grace Seymour 1883-1983
Obituary 110
Costello, John E(dward) 1943- 85-88
Costello, Joseph P(atrick) 1924- 115
Costello, Michael
See Detzer, Karl
Costello, Peter 1946- 93-96
Costello, William Aloysious 1904-1969 .... 4R
Obituary 103
Costelloe, M(artin) Joseph 1914- 41-44R
Coster, Robert
See Barltrop, Robert
Costigan, Daniel M. 1929- CANR-14
Earlier sketch in CA 33-36R
Costigan, Giovanni 1905- CAP-1
Earlier sketch in CA 15-16
Costigan, James 1928- 73-76
Costikyan, Edward N. 1924- 19-20R
Costinescu, Tristan
See Gross, Terence
Costis, Harry George 1928- 45-48
Costley, Bill
See Costley, William K(irkwood), Jr.
Costley, William K(irkwood), Jr. 1942- ... 81-84
Costonis, John J(oseph) 1937- CANR-4
Earlier sketch in CA 49-52
Cote, Richard G(eorge) 1934- 69-72
Cotes, Peter 1912- CANR-4
Earlier sketch in CA 7-8R
Cothem, Fayly H(ardcastle) 1926- 4R
Cothen, Joe H(erbert) 1926- 113
Cothran, J(oseph) Guy 1897- CAP-2
Earlier sketch in CA 29-32
Cothran, Jean 1910- 93-96
Cotich, Felicia 1926- 115
Cotler, Gordon 1923- 2R
Cotler, Sherwin B(arry) 1941- 65-68
Cotlow, Lewis N(athaniel) 1898-1987 65-68
Obituary 122
Cotner, Robert Crawford 1906- 37-40R
Cotner, Thomas E. 1916- 37-40R
Cott, Hugh B(amford) 1900-1987
Obituary 122
Cott, Jonathan 1942- 53-56
See also SATA 23
Cott, Nancy F. 1945- 81-84
Cottam, Clarence 1899-1974 97-100
See also SATA 25
Cottam, Keith M. 1941- 81-84
Cottam, Walter P(ace) 1894- CAP-1
Earlier sketch in CA 15-16
Cotten, Nell(ie) Wyllie 1908- 4R
Cotter, Charles H(enry) 1919- 13-14R
Cotter, Cornelius Philip 1924- CANR-1
Earlier sketch in CA 3R
Cotter, Edward F(rancis) 1917- CANR-6
Earlier sketch in CA 7-8R
Cotter, James Finn 1929- 33-36R
Cotter, Janet M(errill) 1914- 61-64
Cotter, Joseph S., Sr.
See Cotter, Joseph Seamon, Sr.
Cotter, Joseph Seamon, Jr. 1895-1919 .. DLB-50
Cotter, Joseph Seamon, Sr. 1861-1949 124
See also DLB 50
Cotter, Richard V(ern) 1930- CANR-14
Earlier sketch in CA 41-44R
Cotterell, Geoffrey 1919- 7-8R
Cotterell, (Francis) Peter 1930- CANR-1
Earlier sketch in CA 49-52
Cotterill, Rodney M(ichael) J(ohn) 1933- 118
Cottle, Charles
See Anderson, Robert C(harles)
Cottle, Thomas J. 1937- CANR-17
Earlier sketch in CA 33-36R
Cottle, William C(ullen) 1913- 41-44R
Cottler, Joseph 1899- CAP-2
Earlier sketch in CA 25-28
See also SATA 22
Cotton, (Thomas) Henry 1907-1987
Obituary 124
Cotton, John 1584-1652 .... DLB-24
Cotton, John 1925- CANR-11
Earlier sketch in CA 65-68
Cotton, John W(healdon) 1925- 33-36R
Cotton, Norris 1900- 103
Cottrell, Alan (Howard) 1919- CANR-10
Earlier sketch in CA 65-68
Cottrell, Alan P. 1935-1984 120
Cottrell, Alvin J. 1925(?)-1984 Obituary 112
Cottrell, (William) Fred(erick) 1903- 3R
Cottrell, Jack (Warren) 1938- CANR-23
Earlier sketch in CA 107
Cottrell, Leonard 1913-1974 .... CANR-4
Earlier sketch in CA 5-6R
See also SATA 24
Cottrell, Leonard S(later), Jr. 1899-1985 ... 107
Obituary 115
Cottrell, Robert D(uane) 1930- 53-56
Couch, Arthur Thomas Quiller
See Quiller-Couch, Arthur Thomas
Couch, Helen F(ox) 1907- CAP-2
Earlier sketch in CA 17-18
Couch, Osma Palmer
See Tod, Osma Gallinger
Coudenhove-Kalergi, Richard N(icolas)
1894-1972 Obituary 37-40R
Coudert, Allison P(ierce) 1941- 110
Coudert, Jo 1923- 17-18R
Couffer, Jack 1924- CANR-1
Earlier sketch in CA 3R
Couger, J(ames) Daniel 1929- CANR-8
Earlier sketch in CA 53-56
Coughlan, John W. 1927- 21-22R
Coughlan, Margaret N(ourse) 1925- 107
Coughlan, (John) Robert 1914- 65-68
Coughlan, William C(arlisle), Jr. 1946- 115
Coughlin, Bernard J. 1922- 15-16R
Coughlin, Charles E(dward) 1891-1979
Obituary 97-100
Coughlin, George G(ordon) 1900- 107
Coughlin, Joseph Welter 1919- 4R
Coughlin, Violet L(ouise) 73-76
Coughran, Larry C. 1925- 21-22R
Coughtry, Jay 1945- 111
Couldery, Fred(erick) A(lan) J(ames)
1928- 11-12R
Coulet du Gard, Rene 1919- CANR-4
Earlier sketch in CA 53-56
Coulette, Henri Anthony 1927- CANR-14
Earlier sketch in CA 65-68
Coulling, Sidney Baxter 1924- 102
Couloumbis, Theodore A. 1935- CANR-7
Earlier sketch in CA 17-18R
Coulson, C(harles) A(lfred) 1910-1974 .. CANR-4
Earlier sketch in CA 7-8R
Coulson, Felicity Carter 1906- 11-12R
Coulson, John H(ubert) A(rthur) 1906- ... 11-12R
Coulson, Juanita (Ruth) 1933- CANR-9
Earlier sketch in CA 25-28R
Coulson, N. J.
See Coulson, Noel J(ames)
Coulson, Noel J(ames) 1928-1986 124
Coulson, Noel James 1928-1986 Obituary .. 120
Coulson, Robert 1924- 49-52
Coulson, Robert S(tratton) 1928- CANR-24
Earlier sketches in CA 23-24R, CANR-9
Coulson, William D(onald) E(dward)
1942- 89-92
Coulter, E(llis) Merton 1890-1981 .... CANR-3
Obituary 104
Earlier sketch in CA 11-12R
Coulter, Edwin M(artin) 1937- 104
Coulter, John (William) 1888- CANR-3
Earlier sketch in CA 7-8R
Coulter, N(orman) Arthur, Jr. 1920- 65-68
Coulter, Stephen 1914- Brief entry 109

Coulton, James
See Hansen, Joseph
Council, Norman Briggs 1936- 102
Cound, John J(ames) 1928- 37-40R
Counsell, John William 1905-1987 57-60
Obituary 121
Counselman, Mary Elizabeth 1911- 106
Count, Earl W(endel) 1899- 37-40R
Counter, Kenneth (Norman Samuel) 1930- 25-28R
Countess of Romanones
See Quintanilla, Maria Aline Griffith y Dexter, Condesa de
Countryman, The
See Whitlock, Ralph
Countryman, Vern 1917- 15-16R
Counts, Charles Richard 1934- 49-52
Counts, George S(ylvester) 1889-1974 5-6R
Obituary 53-56
Couper, Heather 1949- 124
Couper, J(ohn) M(ill) 1914- 45-48
Couperus, Louis (Marie Anne) 1863-1923
Brief entry 115
See also TCLC 15
Coupey, Philippe 1937- 104
Coupling, J. J.
See Pierce, John Robinson
Courage, James Francis 1903-1963 77-80
Courant, Richard 1888-1972 Obituary 33-36R
Courlander, Harold 1908- CANR-18
Earlier sketches in CA 11-12R, CANR-3
See also SATA 6
Cournos, John 1881-1966 CAP-2
Earlier sketch in CA 13-14
See also DLB 54
Couroucli, Jennifer 1922- 29-32R
Course, Alfred George 1895- 9-10R
Course, Edwin 1922- 77-80
Coursen, Herbert R(andolph), Jr. 1932- CANR-19
Earlier sketches in CA 53-56, CANR-4
Court, Harold
See Swycaffer, Jefferson P(utnam)
Court, Margaret Smith 1942- Brief entry 106
Court, Sharon
See Rowland, D(onald) S(ydney)
Court, W(illiam) H(enry) B(assano) 1905(?)-1971 Obituary 104
Court, Wesli 1940- CANR-11
Earlier sketch in CA 69-72
Court, Wesli
See Turco, Lewis (Putnam)
Courtenay, Ashley (Reginald) 1888-1986
Obituary 121
Courtenay, William J(ames) 1935- 11-12R
Courter, Gay 1944- CANR-7
Earlier sketch in CA 57-60
Courthion, Pierre (Barthelemy) 1902- CANR-14
Earlier sketch in CA 81-84
Courtice, Katie 1942- 121
Courtier, S(idney) H(obson) 1904-197(?) CAP-2
Earlier sketch in CA 25-28
Courtine, Robert 1910- CANR-14
Earlier sketch in CA 81-84
Courtis, Stuart Appleton 1874-1969
Obituary 105
See also SATA 29
Courtland, Roberta
See Dern, Erolie Pearl Gaddis
Courtneidge, Cicely 1893-1980 Obituary 105
Courtney, Dayle
See Goldsmith, Howard
Courtney, Gwendoline CAP-1
Earlier sketch in CA 9-10
Courtney, John
See Judd, Frederick Charles
Courtney, Nicholas (Piers) 1944- 113
Courtney, Ragan 1941- 97-100
Courtney, (John) Richard 1927- CANR-23
Earlier sketch in CA 105
Courtney, Robert
See Ellison, Harlan
and Robinson, Frank M(alcolm)
Courtney, William J(ohn) 1921- 102
Courtney, Winifred F(isk) 1918- 109
Courtwright, David T(odd) 1952- 110
Courville, Donovan A(mos) 1901- 45-48
Coury, Louise Andree 1895(?)-1983
Obituary 109
See also SATA 34
Couse, Harold C. 1925- 17-18R
Cousens, Frances Reissman 1913-1985
Obituary 115
Couser, G(riffith) Thomas 1946- 89-92
Cousins, Albert Newton 1919- 41-44R
Cousins, Geoffrey (Esmond) 1900- 25-28R
Cousins, Margaret 1905- CANR-1
Earlier sketch in CA 4R
See also SATA 2
Cousins, Norman 1915- CANR-13
Earlier sketch in CA 17-18R
Cousins, Peter Edward 1928- 104
Cousse, Raymond 1942- 101
Cousteau, Jacques-Yves 1910- CANR-15
Earlier sketch in CA 65-68
See also SATA 38
See also CLC 30
Cousteau, Philippe Pierre 1940-1979 33-36R
Obituary 89-92
Coustillas, Pierre 1930- 73-76
Coutard, Wanda Lundy Hale 1902(?)-1982
Obituary 106
Coutinho, Joaquim 1886(?)-1978
Obituary 77-80
Couto, Richard A. 1941- CANR-15
Earlier sketch in CA 89-92
Coutts, Frederick Lee 1899- 109
Couture, Andrea 1943- 85-88
Couturier, Louis (Joseph) 1910- 101
Couzyn, Jeni 1942- 85-88
Covarrubias, Barbara Faith 1932- 113
Covatta, Anthony Gallo 1944- 53-56
Covell, Alan C(arter) 1952- 118
Covell, Jon Carter 1910- CANR-17
Earlier sketch in CA 97-100
Coven, Brenda 110
Coveney, James 1920- 41-44R
Coventry, Francis 1725-1754 DLB-39
Coventry, John 1915- 93-96
Cover, Arthur Byron 1950- 107
Cover, Robert M. 1943-1986 57-60
Obituary 119
Coverdale, John F(oy) 1940- 73-76
Coverley, Louise Bennett
See Bennett-Coverley, Louise
Covert, James Thayne 1932- 37-40R
Covert, Paul 1941- CANR-20
Earlier sketch in CA 103
Covey, Cyclone 1922- 21-22R
Covey, Stephen R. 1932- CANR-12
Earlier sketch in CA 33-36R
Covici, Pascal, Jr. 1930- 2R
Coville, Bruce 1950- CANR-22
Earlier sketch in CA 97-100
See also SATA 32
Coville, Walter J(oseph) 1914- CANR-5
Earlier sketch in CA 7-8R
Covin, Theron Michael 1947- 57-60
Covina, Gina 1952- 101
Covington, James W. 1917- 33-36R
Covington, Martin Vaden 1936- 37-40R
Covino, Frank 1931- 57-60
Covino, Joseph, Jr. 1954- 113
Covvey, H(arry) Dominic J(oseph) 1944- 110
Cowan, Alan
See Gilchrist, Alan W.
Cowan, Charles Donald 1923- 102
Cowan, Edward James 1944- 103
Cowan, G(ordon) 1933- 25-28R
Cowan, G(eorge) H(amilton) 1917- 17-18R
Cowan, Geoffrey 1942- 97-100
Cowan, George McKillop 1916- 102
Cowan, Gregory M(ac) 1935-1979 CANR-9
Earlier sketch in CA 65-68
Cowan, Henry J(acob) 1919- CANR-19
Earlier sketches in CA 53-56, CANR-4
Cowan, Ian Borthwick 1932- CANR-24
Earlier sketches in CA 61-64, CANR-8
Cowan, J(oseph) L(loyd) 1929- 25-28R
Cowan, James C(ostello) 1927- 29-32R
Cowan, Janice 1941- 97-100
Cowan, Louise (Shillingburg) 1916- 3R
Cowan, Lyn 1942- 116
Cowan, Michael H(eath) 1937- 23-24R
Cowan, Peter (Walkinshaw) 1914- CANR-9
Earlier sketch in CA 21-22R
Cowan, Richard O(lsen) 1934- 53-56
Cowan, Robert Granniss 1895- CAP-1
Earlier sketch in CA 11-12
Cowan, Ruth Schwartz 1941- 115
Cowan, Stuart DuBois 1917- 104
Cowan, Walter G(reaves) 1912- 120
Cowan, Wood (Messick) 1896-1977 69-72
Coward, Noel (Pierce) 1899-1973 CAP-2
Obituary 41-44R
Earlier sketch in CA 17-18
See also DLB 10
See also CLC 1, 9, 29
See also AITN 1
Cowart, David (Guyland) 1947- 104
Cowasjee, Saros 1931- CANR-20
Earlier sketches in CA 11-12R, CANR-5
Cowden, Dudley J(ohnstone) 1899- 41-44R
Cowden, Jeanne 1918- 85-88
Cowden, Joanna Dunlap 1933- 53-56
Cowdrey, A(lbert) E(dward) 1933- 17-18R
Cowdrey, (Michael) Colin 1932- 105
Cowell, (John) Adrian 1934- 103
Cowell, Cyril 1888- CAP-2
Earlier sketch in CA 21-22
Cowell, Frank Richard 1897- CANR-8
Earlier sketch in CA 53-56
Cowell, Henry Dixon 1897-1965 Obituary 116
Cowen, David L(aurence) 1909- 15-16R
Cowen, Emory L(eland) 1926- 69-72
Cowen, Eve
See Werner, Herma
Cowen, Frances
See Munthe, Frances
Cowen, Ida 1898- 45-48
Cowen, Robert Churchill 1927- 13-14R
Cowen, Ron(ald) 1944- 85-88
Cowen, Roy C(hadwell) 1930- CANR-12
Earlier sketch in CA 33-36R
Cowen, Zelman 1919- CANR-1
Earlier sketch in CA 1R
Cowgill, Donald O(len) 1911- 37-40R
Cowherd, Raymond Gibson 1909- 124
Cowie, Alexander 1896- 33-36R
Cowie, Donald 1911- 116
Cowie, Evelyn E(lizabeth) 1924- CANR-9
Earlier sketch in CA 13-14R
Cowie, Hamilton Russell 1931- 102
Cowie, Leonard W(allace) 1919- CANR-9
Earlier sketch in CA 13-14R
See also SATA 4
Cowie, Mervyn (Hugh) 1909- CAP-1
Earlier sketch in CA 9-10
Cowie, Peter 1939- CANR-18
Earlier sketches in CA 49-52, CANR-1
Cowle, Jerome Milton 1917- 93-96
Cowle, Jerry
See Cowle, Jerome Milton
Cowler, Rosemary (Elizabeth) 1925- 25-28R
Cowles, Fleur CANR-24
Earlier sketches in CA 11-12R, CANR-4
See also AITN 1
Cowles, Frank, Jr. 1918- 57-60
Cowles, Gardner 1861-1946 DLB-29
Cowles, Gardner A., Jr. 1903-1985
Obituary 116
Cowles, Ginny 1924- 57-60
Cowles, John, Sr. 1898-1983 Obituary 109
Cowles, Kathleen
See Krull, Kathleen
Cowles, Lois Thornburg 1909-1980
Obituary 101
Cowles, Mike
See Cowles, Gardner A., Jr.
Cowles, Raymond B(ridgeman) 1896-1975
Obituary 61-64
Cowles, S(amuel) Macon, Jr. 1916- 23-24R
Cowles, Virginia (Spencer) 1912-1983 CANR-12
Obituary 110
Earlier sketch in CA 65-68
Cowley, Joseph (Gilbert) 1923- 106
Cowley, (Cassia) Joy 1936- CANR-11
Earlier sketch in CA 25-28R
See also SATA 4
Cowley, Malcolm 1898- CANR-3
Earlier sketch in CA 5-6R
See also DLB 4, 48
See also DLBY 81
See also CLC 39
Cowlin, Dorothy
See Whalley, Dorothy
Cowling, Elizabeth 1910- Brief entry 110
Cowling, Ellis 1905- CAP-1
Earlier sketch in CA 15-16
Cowling, Maurice John 1926- CANR-3
Earlier sketch in CA 7-8R
Cowlishaw, Ranson 1894- 7-8R
Cowper, Richard
See Middleton-Murry, John (Jr.)
Cox, A(nthony) B(erkeley) 1893-1970 97-100
Cox, Albert W(esley) 1921- 53-56
Cox, Allan 1937- 93-96
Cox, Alva Irwin, Jr. 1925- 19-20R
Cox, Archibald 1912- 73-76
Cox, (Christopher) Barry 1931- 103
Cox, Bertha Mae (Hill) 1901- 19-20R
Cox, Bill 1910- 9-10R
Cox, C. Benjamin 1925- 97-100
Cox, Carol 1946- 117
Cox, Charles B(rian) 1928- 25-28R
Cox, Claire 1919- CANR-2
Earlier sketch in CA 5-6R
Cox, Constance 1915- CANR-24
Earlier sketches in CA 21-22R, CANR-9
Cox, David (Dundas) 1933- 119
Cox, Donald William 1921- CANR-4
Earlier sketch in CA 4R
See also SATA 23
Cox, Edith Muriel 102
Cox, Edward Finch 1946- 29-32R
Cox, Edward Franklin 1925- 33-36R
Cox, Edward Locksley 1943- 121
Cox, Edwin B(urk) 1930- 37-40R
Cox, Erle (Harold) 1873-1950 Brief entry 112
Cox, Eugene L. 1931- 21-22R
Cox, Frank D. 1933- 29-32R
Cox, Fred(erick) M(oreland) 1928- CANR-1
Earlier sketch in CA 45-48
Cox, Gary D(uane) 1947- 113
Cox, Geoffrey Sandford 1910- 103
Cox, George W(yatt) 1935- 115
Cox, Harvey (Gallagher, Jr.) 1929- 77-80
See also AITN 1
Cox, (William) Harvey 1939- 45-48
Cox, Hebe 1909- CAP-1
Earlier sketch in CA 13-14
Cox, Hugh Brandon
See Brandon-Cox, Hugh
Cox, Hugh S(towell) 1874-1969 CAP-2
Earlier sketch in CA 21-22
Cox, J(ohn) Gray 1952- 123
Cox, J. Halley 1910-1974 Obituary 112
Cox, Jack
See Cox, John Roberts
Cox, James Anthony 1926- 104
Cox, James M(elville) 1925- 13-14R
Cox, James Middleton, Jr. 1903-1974
Obituary 89-92
Cox, James W(illiam) 1923- 33-36R
Cox, Jeri
See Kimes, Beverly Rae
Cox, Joan (Irene) 1942- 101
Cox, John H(enry) 1907-1975 Obituary 115
Cox, John Roberts 1915-1981 CANR-14
Earlier sketch in CA 29-32R
See also SATA 9
Cox, John Stuart 1931- 117
Cox, Joseph A. 1896(?)-1980 Obituary 97-100
Cox, Joseph Mason Andrew 1930- CANR-2
Earlier sketch in CA 49-52
Cox, Joseph W(illiam) 1937- 81-84
Cox, Keith (Kohn) 1931- CANR-12
Earlier sketch in CA 69-72
Cox, Kevin R. 1939- 37-40R
Cox, LaWanda Fenlason 1909- 9-10R
Cox, Lee Sheridan 1916- 25-28R
Cox, Marie-Therese Henriette 1925- 105
Cox, Marion Monroe 1898-1983 Obituary 110
Cox, Martha Heasley 1919- 15-16R
Cox, Mary Elizabeth
See Headapohl, Betty R.
Cox, Maxwell E. 1922- 25-28R
Cox, Miriam Stewart 11-12R
Cox, Molly
See Cox, Marie-Therese Henriette
Cox, Oliver Cromwell 1901-1974 3R
Obituary 103
Cox, P(atrick) Brian 45-48
Cox, Palmer 1840-1924 Brief entry 111
See also SATA 24
See also DLB 42
Cox, R(obert) David 1937- CANR-13
Earlier sketch in CA 29-32R
Cox, R(alph) Merritt 1939- 33-36R
Cox, Rachel Dunaway 1904- 33-36R
Cox, Reavis 1900- CAP-1
Earlier sketch in CA 15-16
Cox, Richard 1931- CANR-11
Earlier sketch in CA 21-22R
Cox, Richard Howard 1925- CANR-8
Earlier sketch in CA 13-14R
Cox, Thomas R(ichard) 1933- 53-56
Cox, Victoria
See Garretson, Victoria Diane
Cox, Wallace (Maynard) 1924-1973 97-100
Obituary 41-44R
Cox, Wally
See Cox, Wallace (Maynard)
See also SATA 25
Cox, Warren E(arle) 1895-1977 CAP-2
Obituary 69-72
Earlier sketch in CA 33-36
Cox, William (Robert) 1901- CANR-24
Earlier sketches in CA 11-12R, CANR-6
See also SATA 31, 46
Cox, William E(dwin), Jr. 1930- 106
Cox, William Trevor 1928- CANR-4
Earlier sketch in CA 11-12R
See also CLC 9, 14
Coxe, Antony D(acres) Hippisley
See Hippisley Coxe, Antony D(acres)
Coxe, George Harmon 1901- 57-60
Coxe, Louis (Osborne) 1918- 13-14R
See also DLB 5
Coxe, Tench 1755-1824 DLB-37
Cox-George, Noah Arthur William 1915- CANR-6
Earlier sketch in CA 13-14R
Coxhead, Elizabeth 1909(?)-1979
Obituary 89-92
Cox-Johnson, Ann
See Saunders, Ann Loreille
Coy, Harold 1902- CANR-4
Earlier sketch in CA 7-8R
See also SATA 3
Coyle, David Cushman 1887-1969 CANR-15
Obituary 103
Earlier sketch in CA 1R
Coyle, L(eslie) Patrick 1934- 110
Coyle, Lee
See Coyle, Leo (Perry)
Coyle, Leo (Perry) 1925- 41-44R
Coyle, William 1917- CANR-2
Earlier sketch in CA 4R
Coyne, John (P.) 1940- CANR-12
Earlier sketch in CA 93-96
Coyne, John R(ichard), Jr. 1935- 37-40R
Coyne, Joseph E. 1918- 13-14R
Coysh, A(rthur) W(ilfred) 1905- CANR-13
Earlier sketch in CA 73-76
Coysh, Victor 1906- CANR-8
Earlier sketch in CA 61-64
Coze, Paul 1903(?)-1974 Obituary 53-56
Cozzens, James Gould 1903-1978 CANR-19
Obituary 81-84
Earlier sketch in CA 11-12R
See also DLB 9
See also DLBY 84
See also DLBD 2
See also CDALB 1941-1968
See also CLC 1, 4, 11
Crabb, Alfred Leland 1884- CAP-1
Earlier sketch in CA 13-14
Crabb, Cecil V., Jr. 1924- 13-14R
Crabb, E(dmund) W(illiam) 1912- CAP-1
Earlier sketch in CA 11-12
Crabb, Lawrence J(ames), Jr. 1944- CANR-14
Earlier sketch in CA 65-68
Crabb, Richard 1914- 23-24R
Crabbe, Buster
See Crabbe, Clarence Linden
Crabbe, Clarence Linden 1908-1983 CANR-11
Obituary 109
Earlier sketch in CA 69-72
Crabtree, Arthur B(amford) 1910- CAP-2
Earlier sketch in CA 17-18
Crabtree, Judith 1928- 118
Crabtree, T(homas) T(avron) 1924- 23-24R
Crackel, Theodore J(oseph) 1938- 33-36R
Crackers, Fritz
See Frank, Philip Norman
Cracknell, Basil Edward 1925- 103
Cracraft, James (Edward) 1939- 53-56
Cracroft, Richard Holton 1936- 53-56
Craddock, Charles Egbert
See Murfree, Mary Noailles
Craddock, Patricia (Bland) 1938- CANR-4
Earlier sketch in CA 53-56
Craddock, William J(ames) 1946- 85-88
Cradock, Thomas 1718-1770 DLB-31
Craft, Maurice 1932- CANR-11
Earlier sketch in CA 65-68
Craft, Michael 1928- 25-28R
Craft, Robert 1923- CANR-7
Earlier sketch in CA 11-12R
Craft, Ruth Brief entry 110
See also SATA 31
Crafts, Glenn Alty 1918- 11-12R
Crafts, Kathy 1952- 109
Crafts, Roger Conant 1911- 106
Cragg, D. J.
See Cragg, Dan

Cragg, Dan 1939- ... 115
Cragg, Gerald R(obertson) 1906- ... 61-64
Cragg, (Albert) Kenneth 1913- ... CANR-22
Earlier sketches in CA 17-18R, CANR-7
Craghan, John Francis 1936- ... 53-56
Crago, Hugh 1946- ... 116
Crago, Maureen 1939- ... 116
Crago, T(homas) Howard 1907- ... CAP-1
Earlier sketch in CA 15-16
Crahan, Margaret E(llen) 1939- ... 114
Craib, Ian 1945- ... 69-72
Craig, A. A.
See Anderson, Poul (William)
Craig, Albert M(orton) 1927- ... 37-40R
Craig, Alec
See Craig, Alexander George
Craig, Alexander George 1897- ... CAP-1
Earlier sketch in CA 9-10
Craig, Alisa
See MacLeod, Charlotte (Matilda Hughes)
Craig, Archibald Campbell 1888-1985
Obituary ... 117
Craig, Barbara M(ary St. George) 1914- ... 37-40R
Craig, Bill 1930- ... 33-36R
Craig, Charlotte M(arie) 1929- ... 73-76
Craig, Christine (Angela) 1943- ... 120
Craig, Daniel H. 1811-1895 ... DLB-43
Craig, David 1932- ... CANR-14
Earlier sketch in CA 41-44R
Craig, David
See Tucker, James
Craig, Denys
See Stoll, Dennis G(ray)
Craig, Don(ald) Laurence 1946- ... 73-76
Craig, E(velyn) Quita 1917- ... 103
Craig, Edward Anthony 1905- ... 15-16R
Craig, Edward (Henry) Gordon 1872-1966
Obituary ... 25-28R
Craig, Eleanor 1929- ... 93-96
Craig, Elizabeth (Josephine)
1883-1980 ... CANR-11
Obituary ... 101
Earlier sketch in CA 11-12R
Craig, Georgia
See Dern, Erolie Pearl Gaddis
Craig, Gerald M(arquis) 1916- ... 9-10R
Craig, Gordon A(lexander) 1913- ... CANR-17
Earlier sketch in CA 25-28R
Craig, H(enry) A(rmitage) L(lewellyn)
1921-1978 ... 85-88
Obituary ... 81-84
Craig, Hazel Thompson 1904- ... 2R
Craig, Helen 1934- ... 117
See also SATA 46, 49
Craig, James 1930- ... 73-76
Craig, Jasmine
See Cresswell, Jasmine (Rosemary)
Craig, Jean T. 1936- ... 7-8R
Craig, John David 1903- ... CAP-2
Earlier sketch in CA 17-18
Craig, John Eland
See Chipperfield, Joseph Eugene
Craig, John Ernest 1921- ... 101
See also SATA 23
Craig, John H(erbert) 1885- ... CAP-1
Earlier sketch in CA 9-10
Craig, Jonathan
See Smith, Frank E.
Craig, Larry
See Coughran, Larry C.
Craig, Lee
See Sands, Leo G(eorge)
Craig, M. Jean ... 73-76
See also SATA 17
Craig, Margaret (Maze) 1911-1964 ... 3R
See also SATA 9
Craig, Mary (Francis) 1923- ... CANR-4
Earlier sketch in CA 3R
See also SATA 6
Craig, (Elizabeth) May 1889(?)-1975 ... 101
Obituary ... 89-92
Craig, Nancy
See Maslin, Alice
Craig, Pamela Tudor
See Tudor-Craig, Pamela
Craig, Peggy
See Kreig, Margaret B. (Baltzell)
Craig, Philip R. 1933- ... 25-28R
Craig, Raymond C. 1928- ... 124
Craig, Richard B(lythe) 1935- ... 53-56
Craig, Robert B(ruce) 1944- ... 49-52
Craig, Robert C(harles) 1921- ... 17-18R
Craig, Robert D(ean) 1934- ... CANR-14
Earlier sketch in CA 81-84
Craig, Vera
See Rowland, D(onald) S(ydney)
Craig, Webster
See Russell, Eric Frank
Craig, William Lane 1949- ... 116
Craige, Betty Jean 1946- ... 117
Craighead, Frank C(ooper), Jr. 1916- ... 97-100
Craighead, W(ade) Edward 1942-
Brief entry ... 118
Craigie, E(dward) Horne 1894- ... CAP-2
Earlier sketch in CA 25-28
Craik, Arthur
See Craig, Alexander George
Craik, Dinah Maria (Mulock)
1826-1887 ... SATA-34
See also DLB 35
Craik, Kenneth H(enry) 1936- ... CANR-1
Earlier sketch in CA 45-48
Craik, Thomas Wallace 1927- ... 106
Craik, W(endy) A(nn) 1934- ... 25-28R
Craille, Wesley
See Rowland, D(onald) S(ydney)

Crain, Jeff
See Meneses, Enrique
Crain, John 1926(?)-1979 Obituary ... 89-92
Crain, Robert L(ee) 1934- ... CANR-13
Earlier sketch in CA 21-22R
Crain, Sharie 1942- ... 77-80
Craine, Eugene R(ichard) 1917-1977 ... 33-36R
Craker, Lyle E(ugene) 1941- ... 116
Cram, Mildred 1889- ... 49-52
Cramer, Clarence H(enley) 1905-1982 ... CANR-9
Earlier sketch in CA 13-14R
Cramer, George H. 1913- ... 23-24R
Cramer, Harold 1927- ... 29-32R
Cramer, J(an) S(olomon) 1928- ... 29-32R
Cramer, James 1915- ... 23-24R
Cramer, John Francis 1899-1967 ... CAP-1
Earlier sketch in CA 17-18
Cramer, Kathryn 1943- ... 25-28R
Cramer, Richard L(ouis) 1947- ... 102
Cramer, Richard S(eldon) 1928- ... 29-32R
Cramer, Stanley H. 1933- ... 29-32R
Cramp, Rosemary (Jean) 1929- ... 121
Crampton, C(harles) Gregory 1911- ... 21-22R
Crampton, Georgia Ronan 1925- ... 57-60
Crampton, Helen
See Chesney, Marion
Crampton, Roger C. 1929- ... 33-36R
Cranbrook, James L.
See Edwards, William B(ennett)
Cranch, Christopher Pearse
1813-1892 ... DLB-1, 42
Crandall, James E(dward) 1930- ... 41-44R
Crandall, Joy
See Martin, Joy
Crandall, Norma 1907- ... 69-72
Crandall, Robert Warren 1940- ... 124
Crandell, Anne (Elizabeth) Shaver
See Shaver-Crandell, Anne Elizabeth
Crandell, Richard F. 1901-1974 Obituary ... 53-56
Crane, Alex
See Wilkes-Hunter, R(ichard)
Crane, Barbara (Joyce) 1934- ... 107
See also SATA 31
Crane, Bill
See Crane, William B.
Crane, Caroline 1930- ... CANR-19
Earlier sketches in CA 11-12R, CANR-3
See also SATA 11
Crane, Catherine C(owle) 1940- ... 101
Crane, Diana 1933- ... 89-92
Crane, Donald P(aul) 1933- ... 61-64
Crane, (Lauren) Edgar 1917- ... 17-18R
Crane, Edna Temple
See Eicher, (Ethel) Elizabeth
Crane, Elaine Forman 1939- ... 122
Crane, Frank H. 1912- ... 89-92
Crane, (Harold) Hart 1899-1932
Brief entry ... 104
See also DLB 4, 48
See also TCLC 2, 5
Crane, Hewitt D(avid) 1927- ... 116
Crane, James G(ordon) 1927- ... 15-16R
Crane, Jim
See Crane, James G(ordon)
Crane, Joan St. C(lair) 1927- ... 73-76
Crane, Julia G(orham) 1925- ... 41-44R
Crane, M. A.
See Wartski, Maureen (Ann Crane)
Crane, Milton 1917-1985 Obituary ... 117
Crane, Morley Benjamin 1890-1983
Obituary ... 110
Crane, Philip Miller 1930- ... 11-12R
Crane, R(onald) S(almon) 1886-1967 ... 85-88
See also DLB 63
See also CLC 27
Crane, Richard (Arthur) 1944- ... 77-80
Crane, Robert
See Robertson, Frank C(hester)
and Sellers, Con(nie Leslie, Jr.)
Crane, Robert Dickson 1929- ... 81-84
Crane, Royston Campbell 1901-1977
Obituary ... 89-92
See also SATA 22
Crane, Stephen (Townley) 1871-1900
Brief entry ... 109
See also YABC 2
See also DLB 12, 54
See also TCLC 11, 17
Crane, Sylvia E(ngel) 1918- ... 33-36R
Crane, Theodore Rawson 1929- ... 97-100
Crane, Verner W(inslow) 1889-1974
Obituary ... 113
Crane, Walter 1845-1915 ... SATA-18
Crane, Wilder (Willard) 1928- ... 45-48
Crane, William B. 1904-1981 ... 107
Crane, William D(wight) 1892- ... 5-6R
See also SATA 1
Crane, William Earl 1899- ... 103
Cranfield, Charles E(rnest) B(urland)
1915- ... CANR-18
Earlier sketches in CA 7-8R, CANR-2
Cranfield, Geoffrey Alan 1920- ... 7-8R
Cranford, Clarence William 1906- ... 2R
Cranford, Robert J(oshua) 1908- ... CAP-2
Earlier sketch in CA 17-18
Cranin, A(braham) Norman 1927- ... 73-76
Cranko, John 1927-1973 Obituary ... 45-48
Crankshaw, Edward 1909-1984 ... CANR-23
Obituary ... 114
Earlier sketch in CA 25-28R
Cranny, Titus 1921- ... 25-28R
Cranor, Phoebe 1923- ... 112
Cranston, Edward
See Fairchild, William
Cranston, Maurice (William) 1920- ... CANR-3
Earlier sketch in CA 5-6R
Cranston, Mechthild ... 53-56

Cranton, Elmer M(itchell) 1932- ... 118
Cranwell, John Philips 1904- ... 61-64
Crapanzano, Vincent 1939- ... CANR-5
Earlier sketch in CA 53-56
Crapol, Edward P(aul) 1936- ... 45-48
Crapps, Robert W. 1925- ... 53-56
Crapsey, Adelaide 1878-1914 ... DLB-54
Crary, Catherine S. 1909- ... CAP-1
Earlier sketch in CA 15-16
Crary, Elizabeth (Ann) 1942- ... SATA-43
Crary, Margaret (Coleman) 1906- ... 7-8R
See also SATA 9
Crary, Ryland W(esley) 1913-1984
Obituary ... 113
Crase, Douglas 1944- ... 106
Crassweller, Robert D. 1915- ... 21-22R
Craster, John Montagu 1901-1975
Obituary ... 108
Crathern, Alice Tarbell 1894-1973
Obituary ... 110
Craton, Michael (John) 1931- ... 41-44R
Cratty, Bryant J. 1929- ... CANR-11
Earlier sketch in CA 25-28R
Craven, Avery (Odelle) 1885(?)-1980
Obituary ... 113
See also DLB 17
Craven, George M(ilton) 1929- ... 61-64
Craven, Margaret 1901-1980 ... 103
See also CLC 17
Craven, Roy C., Jr. 1924- ... 69-72
Craven, Thomas 1889-1969 ... 97-100
See also SATA 22
Craven, Wesley Frank (Jr.) 1905-1981 ... 61-64
Obituary ... 103
Cravens, Gwyneth ... 85-88
Cravens, Hamilton 1938- ... 103
Craveri, Marcello 1914- ... 21-22R
Crawells, Carl
See Herm, Gerhard
Crawford, Alan 1953- ... 101
Crawford, Ann Fears 1932- ... CANR-9
Earlier sketch in CA 21-22R
Crawford, Bill
See Crawford, William Hulfish
Crawford, C(harles) Merle 1924- ... 45-48
Crawford, Char 1935- ... 57-60
Crawford, Charles 1752-1815(?) ... DLB-31
Crawford, Charles F. ?-1983 Obituary ... 109
Crawford, Charles O(len) 1934- ... 37-40R
Crawford, Charles P. 1945- ... CANR-24
Earlier sketch in CA 45-48
See also SATA 28
Crawford, Charles W(ann) 1931- ... CANR-8
Earlier sketch in CA 61-64
Crawford, Cheryl 1902-1986 Obituary ... 120
Brief entry ... 112
Crawford, Christina 1939- ... 85-88
Crawford, Clan, Jr. 1927- ... 57-60
Crawford, David L. 1890(?)-1974
Obituary ... 45-48
Crawford, Deborah 1922- ... 49-52
See also SATA 6
Crawford, Donald W(esley) 1938- ... 45-48
Crawford, F(rancis) Marion 1854-1909
Brief entry ... 107
See also TCLC 10
Crawford, Fred D. 1947- ... 117
Crawford, Fred Roberts 1924- ... CANR-2
Earlier sketch in CA 45-48
Crawford, Iain (Padruig) 1922- ... CANR-23
Earlier sketch in CA 3R
Crawford, James M. 1925- ... 89-92
Crawford, Jean 1907(?)-1976 Obituary ... 104
Crawford, Jerry L(eroy) 1934- ... 106
Crawford, Joan
See Le Sueur, Lucille
Crawford, Joanna 1941- ... 11-12R
Crawford, John E(dmund) 1904-1971 ... CAP-2
Earlier sketch in CA 17-18
See also SATA 3
Crawford, John R. 1915(?)-1976
Obituary ... 65-68
Crawford, John Richard 1932- ... 106
Crawford, John S(herman) 1928- ... 106
Crawford, John W(illiam) 1914- ... 3R
Crawford, John W(illiam) 1936- ... CANR-4
Earlier sketch in CA 53-56
Crawford, Joyce 1931- ... 25-28R
Crawford, Kenneth G(ale) 1902-1983 ... 81-84
Obituary ... 108
Crawford, Linda 1938- ... CANR-23
Earlier sketch in CA 65-68
Crawford, Marion (Kirk) 1910(?)-1988
Obituary ... 124
Crawford, Matsu W(offord) 1902- ... CAP-2
Earlier sketch in CA 17-18
Crawford, Max 1938- ... 77-80
Crawford, Mel 1925- ... SATA-33, 44
Crawford, Oliver 1917- ... 85-88
Crawford, Patricia ... 103
Crawford, Phyllis 1899- ... SATA-3
Crawford, Richard (Arthur) 1935- ... CANR-9
Earlier sketch in CA 57-60
Crawford, Robert
See Rae, Hugh C(rauford)
Crawford, Robert Platt 1893- ... CAP-2
Earlier sketch in CA 17-18
Crawford, Stanley (Gottlieb) 1937- ... 69-72
Crawford, T(erence Gordon) S(harman)
1945- ... 29-32R
Crawford, Tad 1946- Brief entry ... 114
Crawford, Thelmar Wyche 1905- ... 4R
Crawford, Theresa 1956- ... 110
Crawford, Vaughn Emerson 1917(?)-1981
Obituary ... 104
Crawford, Walter B(yron) 1919- ... 116

Crawford, William (Elbert) 1929- ... CANR-4
Earlier sketch in CA 3R
Crawford, William H. 1907(?)-1973
Obituary ... 104
Crawford, William Hulfish 1913-1982
Obituary ... 105
Crawford, William P(atrick) 1922- ... 106
Crawley, Aidan Merivale 1908- ... 61-64
Crawley, C(harles) W(illiam) 1899- ... 109
Crawley, Gerard M(arcus) 1938- ... 106
Crawley, Thomas Edward 1920- ... 111
Cray, Ed(ward) 1933- ... CANR-16
Earlier sketch in CA 81-84
Crayder, Dorothy ... 33-36R
See also SATA 7
Crayder, Teresa
See Colman, Hila
Crayon, Geoffrey
See Irving, Washington
Crayon, Porte
See Strother, David Hunter
Craz, Albert G. 1926- ... CANR-8
Earlier sketch in CA 17-18R
See also SATA 24
Creager, Alfred L(eon) 1910- ... 19-20R
Creagh, Patrick 1930- ... CANR-18
Earlier sketch in CA 25-28R
Creagh-Osborne, Richard 1928- ... CANR-7
Earlier sketch in CA 11-12R
Creamer, J. Shane 1929- Brief entry ... 116
Creamer, Robert W. 1922- ... 21-22R
Crean, John Edward, Jr. 1939- ... 41-44R
Crean, Patrick (G.) 1949- ... 123
Creasey, John 1908-1973 ... CANR-8
Obituary ... 41-44R
Earlier sketch in CA 5-6R
See also CLC 11
Creasy, Robert K(enwood) 1934- ... 118
Creasy, Rosalind R. ... 110
Crechales, Anthony George 1926- ... 29-32R
Crechales, Tony
See Crechales, Anthony George
Crecine, John Patrick 1939- ... CANR-7
Earlier sketch in CA 57-60
Crecy, Jeanne
See Williams, Jeanne
Credland, Peter (Francis) 1946- ... 69-72
Credle, Ellis 1902- ... CANR-9
Earlier sketch in CA 15-16R
See also SATA 1
Credo
See Creasey, John
Creed, David
See Guthrie, James Shields
Creekmore, Betsey B(eeler) 1915- ... 69-72
Creekmore, Mildred C. 1905(?)-1987
Obituary ... 123
Creel, George 1876-1953 Brief entry ... 115
See also DLB 25
Creel, Herrlee G(lessner) 1905- ... 85-88
Creel, Stephen Melville 1938- ... 69-72
Creeley, Robert (White) 1926- ... CANR-23
Earlier sketch in CA 4R
See also DLB 5, 16
See also CLC 1, 2, 4, 8, 11, 15, 36
Creelman, James 1859-1915 ... DLB-23
Creelman, Marjorie B(roer) 1908- ... CAP-2
Earlier sketch in CA 21-22
Creer, Thomas L(aselle) 1934- ... CANR-22
Earlier sketch in CA 69-72
Creese, Bethea ... CANR-5
Earlier sketch in CA 9-10R
Creeth, Edmund Homer 1928- ... 102
Creevey, Lucy E. 1940- ... 29-32R
Cregan, David (Appleton Quartus)
1931- ... CANR-1
Earlier sketch in CA 45-48
See also DLB 13
Creger, Ralph (Clinton) 1914- ... 15-16R
Cregier, Don M(esick) 1930- ... 69-72
Crehan, Stewart 1942- ... 118
Crehan, Thomas 1919- ... CANR-2
Earlier sketch in CA 7-8R
Creigh, Dorothy (Weyer) 1921- ... 105
Creighton, Don
See Drury, Maxine Cole
Creighton, Donald Grant 1902-1979 ... 101
Obituary ... 93-96
Creighton, (Mary) Helen 1899- ... 41-44R
Creighton, Helen (Evelyn) 1914- ... 33-36R
Creighton, Joanne V(anish) 1942- ... 69-72
Creighton, Luella Bruce 1901- ... CAP-1
Earlier sketch in CA 17-18
Creighton, Thomas 1915(?)-1987
Obituary ... 123
Creighton, Thomas H(awk) 1904-1984 ... CANR-6
Obituary ... 114
Earlier sketch in CA 7-8R
Crellin, John 1916- ... 69-72
Cremeans, Charles D(avis) 1915- ... 7-8R
Cremer, Jan 1940- ... 15-16R
Cremer, Robert Roger 1947- ... 61-64
Cremer, Robert Wyndham Ketton
See Ketton-Cremer, Robert Wyndham
Cremin, Lawrence A(rthur) 1925- ... 33-36R
Crena de Iongh, Mary (Dows Herter Norton)
1894(?)-1985 Obituary ... 116
Crena de Iongh, Daniel 1888-1970 ... CAP-2
Obituary ... 29-32R
Earlier sketch in CA 25-28
Crennen, Robert Earl 1929-1984 Obituary ... 112
Crenner, James 1938- ... 13-14R
Crenshaw, James L. 1934- ... CANR-14
Earlier sketch in CA 37-40R
Crenshaw, Mary Ann ... CANR-8
Earlier sketch in CA 57-60
Crepeau, Richard C(harles) 1941- ... 105

Cressey, Donald R(ay) 1919-1987 ... CANR-6
Obituary ... 123
Earlier sketch in CA 13-14R
Cressey, William W. 1939- ... 33-36R
Cresson, Bruce Collins 1930- ... 45-48
Cresswell, Helen 1934- ... CANR-8
Earlier sketch in CA 17-18R
See also SATA 1, 48
Cresswell, Jasmine (Rosemary) 1941- ... 110
Creston, Dormer
See Colston-Baynes, Dorothy
Creswell, K(eppel) A(rchibald) C(ameron) 1879- ... CAP-1
Earlier sketch in CA 9-10
Cretan, Gladys (Yessayan) 1921- ... 29-32R
See also SATA 2
Cretcher, Dorothy 1934- ... 112
Cretzmeyer, F(rancis) X(avier), Jr. 1913- ... 15-16R
Crevecoeur, Michel Guillaume Jean de 1735-1813 ... DLB-37
Crew, Francis Albert Eley 1888-1973 ... CAP-2
Earlier sketch in CA 17-18
Crew, Helen (Cecilia) Coale 1866-1941
Brief entry ... 121
See also YABC 2
Crew, Louie 1936- ... 81-84
Crewe, Jonathan V(ere) 1941- ... 116
Crews, Clyde F. 1944- ... 116
Crews, Donald ... 108
See also SATA 30, 32
See also CLR 7
Crews, Frederick C(ampbell) 1933- ... CANR-1
Earlier sketch in CA 3R
Crews, Harry (Eugene) 1935- ... CANR-20
Earlier sketch in CA 25-28R
See also DLB 6
See also CLC 6, 23
See also AITN 1
Crews, Judson (Campbell) 1917- ... CANR-24
Earlier sketches in CA 15-16R, CANR-7
Crews, William J. 1931- ... 25-28R
Cribb, Larry 1934- ... 109
Cribbet, John E(dward) 1918- ... 19-20R
Cribbin, James J(oseph) 1915- ... 121
Crichton, James Dunlop 1907- ... CANR-5
Earlier sketch in CA 15-16R
Crichton, Jennifer 1957- ... 123
Crichton, John 1916- ... 19-20R
Crichton, Kyle Samuel 1896-1960
Obituary ... 89-92
Crichton, (John) Michael 1942- ... CANR-13
Earlier sketch in CA 25-28R
See also SATA 9
See also DLBY 81
See also CLC 2, 6
See also AITN 2
Crichton, Robert 1925- ... 17-18R
See also AITN 1
Crick, Bernard (Rowland) 1929- ... CANR-5
Earlier sketch in CA 1R
Crick, Donald Herbert 1916- ... 102
Crick, Francis (Harry Compton) 1916- ... 121
Brief entry ... 113
Crick, Michael (Lawrence) 1958- ... 118
Criden, Joseph 1916- ... 77-80
Criden, Yosef
See Criden, Joseph
Crider, (Allen) Bill(y) 1941- ... 112
Cridland, Nancy C. 1932- ... 111
Crighton, John C(lark) 1903- ... 33-36R
Crighton, Richard E. 1921- ... 109
Crile, Barney
See Crile, George, Jr.
Crile, George, Jr. 1907- ... 89-92
Crim, Keith R(enn) 1924- ... 29-32R
Crim, Mort 1935- ... 41-44R
Crimmins, James Custis 1935- ... CANR-11
Earlier sketch in CA 5-6R
Crinkley, Richmond 1940- ... 29-32R
Cripe, Helen 1932- ... CANR-8
Earlier sketch in CA 61-64
Cripps, (Matthew) Anthony (Leonard) 1913- ... 13-14R
Cripps, L(ouise) L(ilian) 1914- ... 97-100
Cripps, Thomas (Robert) 1932- ... 97-100
Crisler, Fritz
See Crisler, Herbert Orin
Crisler, Herbert Orin 1899-1982 Obituary ... 107
Crisler, Lois (Brown) ?-1971 Obituary ... 104
Crisp, Anthony Thomas 1937- ... 101
Crisp, C(olin) G(odfrey) 1936- ... 37-40R
Crisp, Frank R(obson) 1915- ... 9-10R
Crisp, Norman James 1923- ... 93-96
Crisp, Quentin 1908- ... 116
Brief entry ... 109
Crisp, Robert (James) ... 1R
Crisp, Tony
See Crisp, Anthony Thomas
Crispin, A(nn) C(arol) 1950- ... 113
Crispin, Edmund
See Montgomery, (Robert) Bruce
See also CLC 22
Crispin, John 1936- ... 53-56
Crispin, Ruth Helen Katz 1940- ... 93-96
Crispo, John 1933- ... 37-40R
Crissey, Elwell 1899- ... CAP-2
Earlier sketch in CA 23-24
Crist, Judith (Klein) 1922- ... CANR-17
Earlier sketch in CA 81-84
See also AITN 1
Crist, Lyle M(artin) 1924- ... 53-56
Crist, Raymond E. 1904- ... 73-76
Crist, Steven G(ordon) 1956- ... 101
Cristabel
See Abrahamsen, Christine Elizabeth
Cristina, Frank
See Laughlin, Tom
Cristina, Teresa
See Laughlin, Tom
Cristofer, Michael 1945(?)- Brief entry ... 110
See also DLB 7
See also CLC 28
Cristol, Vivian ... 19-20R
Cristy, Ann
See Mittermeyer, Helen (Hayton Monteith)
Cristy, R. J.
See De Cristoforo, R. J.
Criswell, Cloyd M. 1908- ... CAP-1
Earlier sketch in CA 17-18
Criswell, W(allie) A(mos) 1909- ... 19-20R
Critchfield, Howard J(ohn) 1920- ... 53-56
Critchfield, Richard (Patrick) 1931- ... CANR-16
Earlier sketch in CA 41-44R
Critchley, Edmund M(ichael) R(hys) 1931- ... 21-22R
Critchley, Julian (Michael Gordon) 1930- ... 85-88
Critchley, Lynne
See Radford, Richard F(rancis), Jr.
Critchley, T(homas) A(lan) 1919- ... 29-32R
Crites, Ronald W(ayne) 1945- ... CANR-18
Earlier sketch in CA 102
Crites, Stephen D(ecatur) 1931- ... 41-44R
Critic
See Martin, (Basil) Kingsley
Criticus
See Harcourt, Melville and Roe, F(rederic) Gordon
Crittenden, Mabel (Buss) 1917- ... 103
Crnjanski, Milos 1893- ... CAP-1
Earlier sketch in CA 9-10
Crobaugh, Emma ... AITN-2
Croce, Arlene 1934- ... 104
Croce, Benedetto 1866-1952 Brief entry ... 120
Crocetti, Guido M. 1920-1979 ... 85-88
Crocker, Helen Bartter 1929- ... 69-72
Crocker, Lester G(ilbert) 1912- ... CANR-5
Earlier sketch in CA 5-6R
Crocker, Lionel (George) 1897- ... CAP-2
Earlier sketch in CA 25-28
Crocker, Mary Wallace 1941- ... 93-96
Crocker, Thomas Dunstan 1936-
Brief entry ... 108
Crocker, Walter Russell 1902- ... 17-18R
Crockett, Albert Stevens 1873-1969
Obituary ... 89-92
Crockett, Christina
See Gray, Linda Crockett
Crockett, David 1786-1836 ... DLB-3, 11
Crockett, G(eorge) Ronald 1906- ... CAP-1
Earlier sketch in CA 11-12
Crockett, H(arold) Dale 1933- ... 111
Crockett, James Underwood 1915-1979 ... CANR-13
Obituary ... 89-92
Earlier sketch in CA 33-36R
Crockett, S(amuel) R(utherford) 1860-1914 Brief entry ... 116
Crocombe, Ronald G(ordon) 1929- ... 15-16R
Crofford, Emily (Ardell) 1927- ... 107
Crofford, Lena H(enrichson) 1908- ... CAP-1
Earlier sketch in CA 9-10
Croft, Julian (Charles Basset) 1941- ... 124
Croft, Michael (John) 1922-1986 Obituary ... 121
Croft, Peter John 1929-1984 ... 122
Obituary ... 114
Croft, Sutton
See Lunn, Arnold
Croft-Cooke, Rupert 1903-1979 ... CANR-4
Obituary ... 89-92
Earlier sketch in CA 9-10R
Croft-Murray, Edward 1907-1980 Obituary ... 102
Crofton, Denis Hayes 1908- ... 109
Crofts, Freeman Wills 1879-1957
Brief entry ... 115
Crofts, John E(rnest) V(ictor) 1887-1972 ... CAP-2
Earlier sketch in CA 25-28
Crofut, William E. III 1934- ... 25-28R
See also SATA 23
Crohn, Burrill B(ernard) 1884-1983
Obituary ... 110
Croise, Jacques
See Schakovskoy, Zinaida
Croizier, Ralph 1935- ... 61-64
Croll, Carolyn 1945- ... 123
Croly, Jane Cunningham 1829(?)-1901
Brief entry ... 118
See also DLB 23
Croman, Dorothy Young
See Rosenberg, Dorothy
Cromie, Alice Hamilton 1914- ... CANR-3
Earlier sketch in CA 11-12R
See also SATA 24
Cromie, Robert (Allen) 1909- ... CANR-16
Earlier sketches in CA 2R, CANR-1
Cromie, William J(oseph) 1930- ... 13-14R
See also SATA 4
Crommelynck, Fernand 1885-1970
Obituary ... 89-92
Crompton, Anne Eliot 1930- ... CANR-13
Earlier sketch in CA 33-36R
See also SATA 23
Crompton, John
See Lamburn, John Battersby Crompton
Crompton, Louis (William) 1925- ... 33-36R
Crompton, Margaret (Norah Mair) 1901- ... CAP-1
Earlier sketch in CA 13-14
Crompton, Richmal
See Lamburn, Richmal Crompton
Cromwell, Chester R. 1925- ... 89-92
Cromwell, Elsie
See Lee, Elsie
Cromwell, Harvey 1907- ... 17-18R
Cromwell, John 1887-1979 Obituary ... 89-92
Cromwell, John 1914(?)-1979 Obituary ... 89-92
Cromwell, Link
See Kaye, Lenny
Cromwell, Richard Sidney 1925- ... 53-56
Cronbach, Abraham 1882-1965 ... 3R
See also SATA 11
Crone, Alla 1923- ... 113
Crone, G(erald) R(oe) 1899-1982 ... 121
Crone, (Hans-) Rainer 1942- ... CANR-14
Earlier sketch in CA 33-36R
Crone, Ruth 1919- ... 9-10R
See also SATA 4
Croner, Helga 1914- ... 107
Croner, John A(lton) 1916- ... 121
Cronin, A(rchibald) J(oseph) 1896-1981 ... CANR-5
Obituary ... 102
Earlier sketch in CA 1R
See also SATA 25, 47
See also CLC 32
Cronin, George 1933- ... 101
Cronin, James E(mmet) 1908- ... CANR-24
Earlier sketch in CA 45-48
Cronin, John F(rancis) 1908- ... 37-40R
Cronin, Joseph M(arr) 1935- ... 49-52
Cronin, Sylvia 1929- ... 89-92
Cronin, Thomas E(dward) 1940- ... CANR-20
Earlier sketch in CA 85-88
Cronin, Vincent (Archibald Patrick) 1924- ... CANR-5
Earlier sketch in CA 9-10R
Cronkhite, Bernice Brown 1893-1983
Obituary ... 110
Cronkite, Walter (Leland, Jr.) 1916- ... 69-72
See also AITN 1, 2
Cronley, Jay 1943- ... 81-84
Cronne, H(enry) A(lfred) 1904- ... 65-68
Cronon, E(dmund) David 1924- ... CANR-1
Earlier sketch in CA 3R
Cronon, William (John) 1954- ... 111
Cronus, Diodorus
See Taylor, Richard
Cronyn, Hume 1911- ... 123
Crook, Bette (Jean) 1921- ... 73-76
Crook, Beverly Courtney ... 115
See also SATA 35, 38
Crook, Compton Newby 1908- ... 121
Crook, David 1910- ... 97-100
Crook, Howard (Hawthorne) 1937- ... 107
Crook, Isabel 1915- ... 97-100
Crook, J(ohn) A(nthony) 1921- ... 23-24R
Crook, J(oseph) Mordaunt 1937- ... 41-44R
Crook, Margaret Brackenbury 1886- ... CAP-1
Earlier sketch in CA 15-16
Crook, Roger H(awley) 1921- ... CANR-4
Earlier sketch in CA 2R
Crook, W. Melvin 1912(?)-1984 Obituary ... 112
Crook, William 1933- ... 102
Crookall, Robert 1890- ... 33-36R
Crookenden, Napier 1915- ... CANR-11
Earlier sketch in CA 69-72
Crooks, James B(enedict) 1933- ... 25-28R
Cropp, Ben(jamin) 1936- ... 33-36R
Cropper, Margaret 1886-1980 Obituary ... 102
Crosbie, John S(haver) 1920- ... CANR-12
Earlier sketch in CA 73-76
Crosbie, (Hugh) Provan 1912- ... 9-10R
Crosbie, Sylvia Kowitt 1938- ... 73-76
Crosby, Alexander L. 1906-1980 ... 29-32R
Obituary ... 93-96
See also SATA 2, 23
Crosby, Alfred W., Jr. 1931- ... 19-20R
Crosby, Bing
See Crosby, Harry Lillis
Crosby, (Mary Jacob) Caresse 1892-1970
Obituary ... 25-28R
See also DLB 4, 48
Crosby, Donald A(llen) 1932- ... 53-56
Crosby, Donald F(rancis) 1933- ... 77-80
Crosby, Faye J. 1947- ... 114
Crosby, Harry 1898-1929 Brief entry ... 107
See also DLB 4, 48
Crosby, Harry H(erbert) 1919- ... CANR-5
Earlier sketch in CA 15-16R
Crosby, Harry Lillis 1904-1977 Obituary ... 73-76
Crosby, Henry Grew
See Crosby, Harry
Crosby, Henry Sturgis
See Crosby, Harry
Crosby, James O('Hea) 1924- ... 89-92
Crosby, Jeremiah
See Crosby, Michael (Hugh)
Crosby, John (Campbell) 1912- ... CANR-4
Earlier sketch in CA 1R
Crosby, John F. 1931- ... CANR-7
Earlier sketch in CA 17-18R
Crosby, Michael (Hugh) 1940- ... CANR-11
Earlier sketch in CA 19-20R
Crosby, Muriel (Estelle) 1908- ... 19-20R
Crosby, Philip B(ayard) 1926- ... 73-76
Crosby, Ruth 1897- ... 49-52
Crosby, Sumner McK(night) 1909-1982 ... 13-14R
Obituary ... 108
Crosher, G. R. ... 69-72
See also SATA 14
Crosland, Andrew T(ate) 1944- ... 53-56
Crosland, (Charles) Anthony (Raven) 1918-1977 ... 73-76
Obituary ... 69-72
Crosland, Margaret 1920- ... CANR-21
Earlier sketches in CA 49-52, CANR-1
Cross, Aleene Ann 1922- ... 29-32R
Cross, Amanda
See Heilbrun, Carolyn G(old)
Cross, Anthony (Glenn) 1936- ... CANR-17
Earlier sketch in CA 37-40R
Cross, (Alan) Beverley 1931- ... 102
Cross, Claire 1932- ... 23-24R
Cross, Colin (John) 1928-1985 ... CANR-7
Obituary ... 118
Earlier sketch in CA 9-10R
Cross, Donna Woolfolk 1947- ... 97-100
Cross, Frank Moore, Jr. 1921- ... 65-68
Cross, Gary Scott 1946- ... 115
Cross, Gilbert B. ... CANR-23
Earlier sketch in CA 105
Cross, Gillian (Clare) 1945- ... 111
See also SATA 38
Cross, Helen Reeder
See Broadhead, Helen Cross
Cross, Herbert James 1934- ... 45-48
Cross, Ira Brown 1880-1977 Obituary ... 106
Cross, James
See Parry, Hugh J(ones)
Cross, Jennifer 1932- ... 29-32R
Cross, John Keir 1914-1967 ... 73-76
Cross, John R(ay) 1939- ... 120
Cross, K(enneth) G(ustav) W(alter) 1927-1967 ... CAP-1
Earlier sketch in CA 15-16
Cross, K(athryn) Patricia 1926- ... CANR-13
Earlier sketch in CA 33-36R
Cross, Leslie (Frank) 1909-1977 ... 65-68
Obituary ... 89-92
Cross, M. Claire
See Cross, Claire
Cross, Milton (John) 1897-1975 Obituary ... 53-56
Cross, Nigel 1942- ... 116
Cross, Ralph D(onald) 1931- ... CANR-17
Earlier sketch in CA 93-96
Cross, Richard 1950(?)-1983 Obituary ... 110
Cross, Richard K(eith) 1940- ... CANR-12
Earlier sketch in CA 33-36R
Cross, Robert Brandt 1914- ... 37-40R
Cross, Robert Dougherty 1924- ... 3R
Cross, Robert Singlehurst 1925- ... 7-8R
Cross, (Alfred) Rupert (Neal) 1912-1980
Obituary ... 102
Cross, (Alfred) Rupert (Neale) 1912-1980 ... 105
Cross, Samuel S(tephen) 1919- ... 45-48
Cross, Sister Mary Francilda 1902(?)-1984 Obituary ... 114
Cross, Stewart
See Drago, Harry Sinclair
Cross, T. T.
See da Cruz, Daniel, Jr.
Cross, Theodore L(amont) 1924- ... 45-48
Cross, Thomas B. 1949- ... 123
Cross, Victor
See Coffman, Virginia (Edith)
Cross, Wilbur Lucius III 1918- ... CANR-2
Earlier sketch in CA 4R
See also SATA 2
Crossan, Darryl
See Smith, Richard Rein
Crosscountry
See Campbell, Thomas F.
Crossen, Ken
See Crossen, Kendell Foster
Crossen, Kendell Foster 1910- ... CANR-4
Earlier sketch in CA 4R
Crosser, Paul K. 1902-1976 ... CANR-3
Earlier sketch in CA 3R
Crossette, George 1910-1984 Obituary ... 114
Crossley, Archibald M(addock) 1896-1985
Obituary ... 116
Crossley-Holland, Kevin 1941- ... 41-44R
See also SATA 5
See also DLB 40
Crossman, Richard (Howard Stafford) 1907-1974 ... 61-64
Obituary ... 49-52
Croteau, John T(ougas) 1910- ... 9-10R
Crothers, George D. 1909- ... CAP-1
Earlier sketch in CA 15-16
Crothers, J(essie) Frances 1913- ... 33-36R
Crothers, Jessie F.
See Crothers, J(essie) Frances
Crothers, Rachel 1878(?)-1958 Brief entry ... 113
See also DLB 7
See also TCLC 19
Crotty, William J(oseph) 1936- ... CANR-13
Earlier sketch in CA 21-22R
Crouch, Harold (Arthur) 1940- ... CANR-15
Earlier sketch in CA 89-92
Crouch, Marcus 1913- ... CANR-23
Earlier sketches in CA 9-10R, CANR-5
See also SATA 4
Crouch, Steve 1915-1983 ... CANR-9
Obituary ... 109
Earlier sketch in CA 53-56
Crouch, Thomas W(illiam) 1932- ... 73-76
Crouch, Tom D. 1944- ... 106
Crouch, W(illiam) George (Alfred) 1903-1970 ... 5-6R
Obituary ... 89-92
Crouch, Winston Winford 1907-
Brief entry ... 106
Croudace, Glynn 1917- ... 29-32R
Crouse, Russell M. 1893-1966 ... 77-80
Obituary ... 25-28R
Crouse, Timothy 1947- ... 77-80
Crouse, William H(arry) 1907- ... CANR-6
Earlier sketch in CA 7-8R
Crout, George C(lement) 1917- ... CANR-11
Earlier sketch in CA 29-32R
See also SATA 11
Crout, Robert Rhodes 1946- ... 116
Crouzet, Francois Marie-Joseph 1922- ... CANR-19
Earlier sketches in CA 9-10R, CANR-3

Croves, Hal
See Traven, B.
Crovitz, Herbert F(loyd) 1932- ... 29-32R
Crow, Alice (von Bauer) 1894-1966 ... CAP-1
Earlier sketch in CA 15-16
Crow, C(harles) P(atrick) 1938- ... 102
Crow, Charles L(loyd) 1940- ... 112
Crow, Donna Fletcher 1941- ... 108
See also SATA 40
Crow, Duncan 1920- ... 85-88
Crow, Elizabeth Smith 1946- ... 103
Crow, Francis Luther
See Luther, Frank
Crow, Jeffrey J(ay) 1947- ... CANR-19
Earlier sketch in CA 85-88
Crow, John A(rmstrong) 1906- ... 13-14R
Crow, Lester D(onald) 1897-1983 ... CAP-1
Obituary ... 110
Earlier sketch in CA 15-16
Crow, Mark (Alan) 1948- ... 57-60
Crow, Martin M(ichael) 1901- ... CAP-2
Earlier sketch in CA 19-20
Crow, William Bernard 1895-1976 ... CAP-1
Obituary ... 65-68
Earlier sketch in CA 13-14
Crowbate, Ophelia Mae
See Smith, C. U.
Crowcroft, Andrew 1923- ... 23-24R
Crowcroft, Jane
See Crowcroft, Peter
Crowcroft, Peter 1923- ... 101
Crowder, Christopher M. D. 1922- ... 103
Crowder, Michael 1934- ... CANR-1
Earlier sketch in CA 2R
Crowder, Richard (Henry) 1909- ... CAP-1
Earlier sketch in CA 17-18
Crowe, Amanda Cockrell 1948- ... 101
Crowe, Bettina Lum 1911- ... 9-10R
See also SATA 6
Crowe, C. B.
See Gibson, Walter B(rown)
Crowe, Cecily (Teague) Brief entry ... 115
Crowe, Charles 1928- ... 17-18R
Crowe, Charles Monroe 1902-1978 ... 3R
Obituary ... 103
Crowe, E. Odell 1925(?)-1983 Obituary ... 110
Crowe, F. J.
See Johnston, Jill
Crowe, Frederick Ernest 1915- ... 111
Crowe, Gregory D(ennis) 1963- ... 116
Crowe, John
See Lynds, Dennis
Crowe, Kenneth C(harles) 1934- ... 103
Crowe, Philip Kingsland 1908-1976 ... 65-68
Obituary ... 69-72
Crowe, Robert L(ee) 1937- ... 69-72
Crowe, Sylvia 1901- ... CAP-1
Earlier sketch in CA 9-10
Crowe-Carraco, Carol 1943- ... 93-96
Crowell, George H. 1931- ... 25-28R
Crowell, Grace Noll 1877-1969 ... 107
See also SATA 34
Crowell, Joan 1921- ... 57-60
Crowell, Muriel Beyea 1916- ... 57-60
Crowell, Norton B. 1914- ... 11-12R
Crowell, Pers 1910- ... 29-32R
See also SATA 2
Crowell, Robert Leland 1909- ... 109
Crowfield, Christopher
See Stowe, Harriet (Elizabeth) Beecher
Crowl, Philip A(xtell) 1914- ... 110
Crowley, Aleister
See Crowley, Edward Alexander
See also TCLC 7
Crowley, Arthur McBlair 1945- ... 107
See also SATA 38
Crowley, Daniel J(ohn) 1921- ... CANR-9
Earlier sketch in CA 21-22R
Crowley, Edward Alexander 1875-1947
Brief entry ... 104
Crowley, Ellen T(eresa) 1943- ... CANR-17
Earlier sketch in CA 97-100
Crowley, Frances G(eyer) 1921- ... 105
Crowley, George (David) 1913-1987
Obituary ... 123
Crowley, J(oseph) Donald 1932- ... 122
Crowley, James B. 1929- ... 23-24R
Crowley, John 1942- ... 61-64
See also DLBY 82
Crowley, John Edward 1943- ... 53-56
Crowley, John W(illiam) 1945- ... 69-72
Crowley, Mart 1935- ... 73-76
See also DLB 7
Crowley, Mary C. 1915- ... 97-100
Crowley, Raymond 1895-1982 Obituary ... 106
Crown, David A. 1928- ... CANR-10
Earlier sketch in CA 25-28R
Crown, Paul 1928- ... 19-20R
Crownfield, Gertrude 1867-1945 ... YABC-1
Crowson, P(aul) S(piller) 1913- ... 53-56
Crowther, Betty 1939- ... 61-64
Crowther, (Francis) Bosley 1905-1981 ... 65-68
Obituary ... 103
Crowther, Duane S(wofford) 1934- ... CANR-17
Earlier sketch in CA 25-28R
Crowther, Geoffrey 1907-1972 Obituary ... 33-36R
Crowther, James Gerald 1899- ... 73-76
See also SATA 14
Crowther, Jean D(ecker) 1937- ... 120
Crowther, Wilma 1918- ... 7-8R
Crowther-Hunt, Norman Crowther
1920-1987 Obituary ... 121
Croxford, Leslie 1944- ... 81-84
Croxton, Anthony H(ugh) 1902- ... 61-64
Croxton, Frederick E(mory) 1899- ... CAP-2
Earlier sketch in CA 23-24

Croy, Homer 1883-1965 ... 110
Obituary ... 89-92
See also DLB 4
Crozet, Charlotte 1926- ... 25-28R
Crozetti, R(uth G.) Warner
See Warner-Crozetti, R(uth G.)
Crozier, Brian (Rossiter) 1918- ... CANR-3
Earlier sketch in CA 11-12R
Crozier, Lorna 1948- ... 113
Crud
See Crumb, R(obert)
Cruden, Robert 1910- ... 33-36R
Cruger, Melvin J. 1925(?)-1983 Obituary ... 111
Cruickshank, Allan D(udley) 1907-1974
Obituary ... 53-56
Cruickshank, Charles (Greig) 1914- ... CANR-9
Earlier sketch in CA 23-24R
Cruickshank, Helen Gere 1907- ... CAP-1
Earlier sketch in CA 13-14
Cruickshank, John 1924- ... CANR-20
Earlier sketches in CA 3R, CANR-4
Cruickshank, Marjorie 1920-1983 ... 122
Obituary ... 111
Cruickshank, William M(ellon) 1915- ... 89-92
Cruikshank, George 1792-1878 ... SATA-22
Crumarums
See Crumb, R(obert)
Crumb, R(obert) 1943- ... 106
See also CLC 17
Crumbaker, Alice 1911- ... 81-84
Crumbaugh, James C(harles) 1912- ... 37-40R
Crumbley, D. Larry 1941- ... CANR-12
Earlier sketch in CA 29-32R
Crumbum
See Crumb, R(obert)
Crumley, James 1939- ... CANR-21
Earlier sketch in CA 69-72
See also DLBY 84
Crumm, Lloyd C(arlton), Jr. 1927- ... CANR-10
Earlier sketch in CA 65-68
Crummey, Robert O(wen) 1936- ... CANR-17
Earlier sketch in CA 25-28R
Crump, Barry (John) 1935- ... CANR-8
Earlier sketch in CA 13-14R
Crump, Fred H., Jr. 1931- ... CANR-19
Earlier sketches in CA 11-12R, CANR-3
See also SATA 11
Crump, Galbraith Miller 1929- ... 57-60
Crump, Geoffrey (Herbert) 1891- ... CAP-1
Earlier sketch in CA 13-14
Crump, J(ames) Irving 1887-1979 ... 73-76
Obituary ... 89-92
See also SATA 21
Crump, Kenneth G(ordon), Jr. 1931- ... 23-24R
Crump, Spencer (M., Jr.) 1933- ... CANR-9
Earlier sketch in CA 23-24R
Crump, (Stephen) Thomas 1929- ... 49-52
Crumpacker, Laurie 1941- ... 118
Crumpet, Peter
See Buckley, Fergus Reid
Crumpler, Frank H(unter) 1935- ... 77-80
Crumpler, Gus H(unt) 1911- ... 69-72
Crumrine, N(orman) Ross II 1934- ... CANR-8
Earlier sketch in CA 15-16R
Crumski
See Crumb, R(obert)
Crum the Bum
See Crumb, R(obert)
Crunden, Reginald
See Cleaver, Hylton Reginald
Crunden, Robert M. 1940- ... CANR-15
Earlier sketch in CA 29-32R
Crunk
See Crumb, R(obert)
Cruse, Harold ... 77-80
Cruso, Thalassa 1909- ... 65-68
Crussi, F(rank) Gonzalez
See Gonzalez-Crussi, F(rank)
Crustt
See Crumb, R(obert)
Crutcher, Anne Neilson 1919-1983
Obituary ... 111
Crutcher, Chris(topher C.) 1946- ... 113
Cruz, Joan Carroll 1931- ... 73-76
Cruz, Ray(mond) 1933- ... SATA-6
Cruz, Victor Hernandez 1949- ... CANR-14
Earlier sketch in CA 65-68
See also DLB 41
Cryer, Gretchen 1935- Brief entry ... 114
See also CLC 21
Cryer, Gretchen (Kiger) 1935- ... 123
Crying Wind
See Stafford, Linda (Crying Wind)
Crystal, David 1941- ... CANR-23
Earlier sketches in CA 17-18R, CANR-7
Crystal, John C(urry) 1920- ... 102
Csath, Geza 1887-1919 Brief entry ... 111
See also TCLC 13
Csicsery-Ronay, Istvan 1917- ... 21-22R
Csikos-Nagy, Bela 1915- ... 73-76
Ctvrtek, Vaclav 1911-1976 Obituary ... 107
See also SATA 27
Cua, Antonio S. 1932- ... CANR-7
Earlier sketch in CA 17-18R
Cuban, Larry 1934- ... CANR-12
Earlier sketch in CA 29-32R
Cubas, Braz
See Dawes, Robyn M(ason)
Cuber, John F(rank) 1911- ... 9-10R
Cubeta, Paul Marsden 1925- ... 7-8R
Cuciti, Peggy L. 1949- ... 123
Cudahy, Brian J(ames) 1936- ... 41-44R
Cuddihy, John Murray 1922- ... 85-88
Cuddon, John Anthony 1928- ... CANR-19
Earlier sketches in CA 7-8R, CANR-3
Cuddy, Don 1925- ... 69-72
Cudjoe, Selwyn Reginald 1943- ... 118

Cudlip, David 1933- ... CLC-34
Cudlipp, Edythe 1929- ... CANR-12
Earlier sketch in CA 33-36R
Cudlipp, Hugh 1913- Brief entry ... 116
Cuelho, Art 1943- ... 61-64
Cuevas, Clara 1933- ... 57-60
Cuff, Barry
See Koste, Robert Francis
Cuff, Robert Dennis 1941- Brief entry ... 109
Cuffari, Richard 1925-1978 ... SATA-6, 25
Cuisenaire, Emile-Georges 1891(?)-1976
Obituary ... 61-64
Cuisenier, Jean 1927- ... CANR-20
Earlier sketch in CA 73-76
Culbert, David H(olbrook) 1943- ... 112
Culbert, Samuel Alan 1938- ... 69-72
Culbert, T(homas) Patrick 1930-
Brief entry ... 107
Culbertson, Don S(tuart) 1927- ... 11-12R
Culbertson, Hugh M. ... 77-80
Culbertson, J(ohn) M(athew) 1921- ... 11-12R
Culbertson, James T(homas) 1911- ... 118
Culbertson, Judi 1941- ... 85-88
Culbertson, Manie 1927- ... 49-52
Culbertson, Paul T(homas) 1905- ... 37-40R
Culex
See Stanier, Maida Euphemia Kerr
Culhane, Claire 1918- ... 118
Culhane, Shamus 1908- ... 121
Culican, William 1929(?)-1984 Obituary ... 113
Culkin, Ann Marie 1918- ... 9-10R
Cull, John G(uinn, Jr.) 1934- ... 41-44R
Cullen, Charles T(homas) 1940- ... 53-56
Cullen, Countee 1903-1946 ... 124
Brief entry ... 108
See also SATA 18
See also DLB 4, 48, 51
See also TCLC 4
Cullen, George Francis 1901-1980
Obituary ... 102
Cullen, Joseph P(atrick) 1920- ... 49-52
Cullen, Lee Stowell 1922- ... 103
Cullen, Maurice R(aymond), Jr. 1927- ... 73-76
Cullen, Patrick (Colborn) 1940- ... 29-32R
Cullen, Peta
See Pyle, Hilary
Culler, A(rthur) Dwight 1917- ... 17-18R
Culler, Annette Lorena
See Penney, Annette Culler
Culler, Jonathan 1944- ... 104
See also DLB 67
Culleton, Beatrice 1949- ... 120
Culley, Thomas R(obert) 1931- ... 33-36R
Culliford, Pierre 1928- ... 124
See also SATA 40
Culliford, Stanley George 1920- ... 65-68
Culligan, Joe
See Culligan, Matthew J(oseph)
Culligan, Matthew J(oseph) 1918- ... CANR-20
Earlier sketch in CA 81-84
Cullinan, Bernice Ellinger 1926- ... 104
Cullinan, Elizabeth 1933- ... CANR-11
Earlier sketch in CA 25-28R
Cullinan, Gerald 1916- ... 23-24R
Cullinane, Leo Patrick 1907(?)-1978
Obituary ... 77-80
Culliney, John L. 1942- ... 65-68
Cullingford, Cecil H(oward) D(unstan)
1904- ... CANR-7
Earlier sketch in CA 7-8R
Cullingford, Guy
See Taylor, Constance Lindsay
Cullingworth, J(ohn) Barry 1929- ... CANR-1
Earlier sketch in CA 4R
Cullman, Marguerite Wagner 1908- ... 1R
Cullman, W(illiam) Arthur 1914- ... 113
Cullman, W. Arthur 1914- Brief entry ... 111
Cullmann, Oscar 1902- ... 106
Cullop, Charles P. 1927- ... 25-28R
Cully, Iris V(irginia Arnold) 1914- ... CANR-17
Earlier sketches in CA 3R, CANR-1
Cully, Kendig Brubaker 1913- ... CANR-17
Earlier sketches in CA 2R, CANR-1
Culotta, Nino
See O'Grady, John (Patrick)
Culp, Delos Poe 1911- ... 17-18R
Culp, John H(ewett, Jr.) 1907- ... 29-32R
Culp, Louanna McNary 1901-1965 ... CAP-1
Earlier sketch in CA 15-16
See also SATA 2
Culp, Paula 1941- ... 57-60
Culpepper, R(ichard) Alan 1946- ... 115
Culpepper, Robert H(arrell) 1924- ... 77-80
Culross, Michael (Gerard) 1942- ... 33-36R
Culshaw, John (Royds) 1924-1980 ... CANR-11
Obituary ... 97-100
Earlier sketch in CA 23-24R
Culver, Dwight W(endell) 1921- ... 9-10R
Culver, Elsie Thomas 1898- ... CAP-2
Earlier sketch in CA 21-22
Culver, Kathryn
See Dresser, Davis
Culver, Kenneth Leon 1903- ... 103
Culver, Robert Duncan 1916- ... 120
Culver, Roger B(ruce) 1940- ... 104
Cum, R.
See Crumb, R(obert)
Cumberland, Charles C(urtis)
1914-1970 ... CANR-2
Earlier sketch in CA 4R
Cumberland, John Hammett 1924-
Brief entry ... 106
Cumberland, Kenneth Brailey 1913- ... 53-56
Cumberland, Marten 1892-1972 ... CAP-1
Earlier sketch in CA 11-12
Cumberland, William Henry 1929- ... 19-20R

Cumberlege, Marcus (Crossley) 1938- ... CANR-17
Earlier sketch in CA 97-100
Cumberlege, Vera 1908- ... 81-84
Cumbler, John T(aylor) 1946- ... 89-92
Cumes, J(ames) W(illiam) C(rawford)
1922- ... 73-76
Cuming, Geoffrey John 1917- ... CANR-18
Earlier sketches in CA 7-8R, CANR-3
Cuming, Pamela 1944- ... 107
Cumings, Bruce Glenn 1943- ... 107
Cumming, Patricia (Arens) 1932- ... CANR-11
Earlier sketch in CA 61-64
Cumming, Primrose Amy 1915- ... 33-36R
See also SATA 24
Cumming, Robert 1945- ... 106
Cumming, Robert Denoon 1916-
Brief entry ... 107
Cumming, William P(atterson) 1900- ... 33-36R
Cummings, Ann
See Rudolph, Lee (Norman)
Cummings, Arthur J. 1920(?)-1979
Obituary ... 89-92
Cummings, Betty Sue 1918- ... CANR-14
Earlier sketch in CA 73-76
See also SATA 15
Cummings, Bruce F(rederick) 1889-1919
Brief entry ... 123
Cummings, Charles 1940- ... 107
Cummings, D(onald) W(ayne) 1935- ... 101
Cummings, E(dward) E(stlin) 1894-1962 ... 73-76
See also DLB 4, 48
See also CLC 1, 3, 8, 12, 15
Cummings, Florence
See Bonime, Florence
Cummings, Jack
See Cummings, John W(illiam), Jr.
Cummings, Jean 1930- ... 33-36R
Cummings, John W(illiam), Jr. 1940- ... 117
Cummings, Larry L(ee) 1937- ... 53-56
Cummings, Milton C(urtis), Jr. 1933- ... 13-14R
Cummings, Monette 1914- ... 116
Cummings, Parke 1902-1987 ... CAP-1
Obituary ... 123
Earlier sketch in CA 13-14
See also SATA 2
Cummings, Pat 1950- ... 122
See also SATA 42
Cummings, Paul 1933- ... CANR-8
Earlier sketch in CA 21-22R
Cummings, Ray(mond King) 1887-1957
Brief entry ... 113
See also DLB 8
Cummings, Richard (Marshall) 1938- ... 113
Cummings, Richard
See Gardner, Richard (M.)
Cummings, Richard LeRoy 1933- ... 45-48
Cummings, Scott ... 112
Cummings, Thomas G(erald) 1944- ... CANR-16
Earlier sketch in CA 97-100
Cummings, Violet M(ay) 1905- ... 57-60
Cummings, W(alter) T(hies) 1933- ... 3R
Cummins, D. Duane 1935- ... CANR-14
Earlier sketch in CA 37-40R
Cummins, Geraldine Dorothy 1890-1969 ... CAP-1
Earlier sketch in CA 9-10
Cummins, James 1948- ... 122
Cummins, Maria Susanna 1827-1866 ... YABC-1
See also DLB 42
Cummins, Paul F. 1937- ... 33-36R
Cummins, Walter (Merrill) 1936- ... CANR-15
Earlier sketch in CA 41-44R
Cundiff, Edward William 1919- ... CANR-4
Earlier sketch in CA 4R
Cundiff, Margaret Joan 1932- ... 112
Cundy, Henry Martyn 1913- ... 7-8R
Cuneo, Gilbert Anthony 1913-1978
Obituary ... 77-80
Cuneo, John R(obert) 1911- ... 53-56
Cuney, William Waring 1906-1976 ... DLB-51
Cunha, Euclides (Rodrigues Pimenta) da
1866-1909 Brief entry ... 123
See also TCLC 24
Cunha, George Martin 1911- ... 25-28R
Cuninggim, Merrimon 1911- ... 41-44R
Cunliffe, Barrington Windsor 1939- ... CANR-24
Earlier sketches in CA 53-56, CANR-9
Cunliffe, Barry
See Cunliffe, Barrington Windsor
Cunliffe, Elaine ... 33-36R
Cunliffe, John Arthur 1933- ... CANR-11
Earlier sketch in CA 61-64
See also SATA 11
Cunliffe, Marcus (Falkner) 1922- ... CANR-10
Earlier sketch in CA 21-22R
See also SATA 37
Cunliffe, William Gordon 1929- ... 25-28R
Cunningham, Aline ... CANR-9
Earlier sketch in CA 57-60
Cunningham, Barry 1940- ... 73-76
Cunningham, Bob
See May, Julian
Cunningham, Captain Frank
See Glick, Carl (Cannon)
Cunningham, Cathy
See Cunningham, Chet
Cunningham, Chet 1928- ... CANR-19
Earlier sketches in CA 49-52, CANR-4
See also SATA 23
Cunningham, Dale S(peers) 1932- ... CANR-8
Earlier sketch in CA 15-16R
See also SATA 11
Cunningham, Donald H(ayward) 1935- ... CANR-20
Earlier sketch in CA 103
Cunningham, E. V.
See Fast, Howard (Melvin)
Cunningham, Floyd F(ranklin) 1899- ... CAP-1
Earlier sketch in CA 15-16

Cunningham, H(orace) H(erndon)
1913-1969 .... CAP-1
Earlier sketch in CA 11-12
Cunningham, Imogen 1883-1976
Obituary 65-68
Cunningham, J(ames) V(incent)
1911-1985 .... CANR-1
Obituary 115
Earlier sketch in CA 1R
See also DLB 5
See also CLC 3, 31
Cunningham, James F. 1901- CAP-2
Earlier sketch in CA 19-20
Cunningham, John D(onovan) 1933- 111
Cunningham, Joseph F. X. 1925- 69-72
Cunningham, Joseph Sandy 1928- 61-64
Cunningham, Julia (Woolfolk) 1916- ... CANR-19
Earlier sketches in CA 9-10R, CANR-4
See also SATA 1, 26
See also SAAS 2
See also CLC 12
Cunningham, Laura 1947- CANR-23
Earlier sketch in CA 85-88
Cunningham, Lawrence 1935- CANR-15
Earlier sketch in CA 85-88
Cunningham, Lyda Sue Martin 1938- 19-20R
Cunningham, Mary (Elizabeth) 1951- 114
Cunningham, Michael 1952- CLC-34
Cunningham, Michael A(lan) 1945- 41-44R
Cunningham, Noble E., Jr. 1926- 81-84
Cunningham, Paul James, Jr. 1917- 73-76
Cunningham, R(onnie) Walter 1932- 103
Cunningham, Richard 1939- 101
Cunningham, Robert Louis 1926- 41-44R
Cunningham, Robert M(aris), Jr. 1909- . CANR-1
Earlier sketch in CA 49-52
Cunningham, Robert Stanley 1907- 53-56
Cunningham, Rosemary 1916- 9-10R
Cunningham, Virginia
See Holmgren, Virginia C(unningham)
Cunningham, W(infield) Scott
1899(?)-1986 Obituary 118
Cunninghame Graham, R(obert) B(ontine)
1852-1936 Brief entry 119
See also TCLC 19
Cunnington, Phillis 1887-1974 Obituary ...53-56
Cunz, Dieter 1910-1969 .... CAP-2
Earlier sketch in CA 19-20
Cuomo, George (Michael) 1929- CANR-7
Earlier sketch in CA 7-8R
See also DLBY 80
Cuomo, Mario Matthew 1932- 103
Cupitt, Don 1934- CANR-14
Earlier sketch in CA 41-44R
Cuppleditch, David 1946- 116
Cuppy, Will(iam Jacob) 1884-1949
Brief entry 108
See also DLB 11
Cure, Karen 1949- CANR-9
Earlier sketch in CA 65-68
Curiae, Amicus
See Fuller, Edmund (Maybank)
Curie, Eve 1904- CAP-1
Earlier sketch in CA 9-10
See also SATA 1
Curie, Marie (Sklodowska) 1867-1934
Brief entry 118
Curl, David H. 1932- 93-96
Curl, Donald Walter 1935- 33-36R
Curl, James Stevens 1937- CANR-14
Earlier sketch in CA 37-40R
Curle, Adam
See Curle, Charles T. W.
Curle, Charles T. W. 1916- 33-36R
Curler, (Mary) Bernice 1915- 85-88
Curley, Arthur 1938- CANR-9
Earlier sketch in CA 21-22R
Curley, Charles 1949- 57-60
Curley, Daniel 1918- CANR-18
Earlier sketches in CA 11-12R, CANR-3
See also SATA 23
Curley, Dorothy Nyren
See Nyren, Dorothy Elizabeth
Curley, Michael J. 1900-1972 Obituary ...37-40R
Curley, Walter J(oseph) P(atrick) 1922- 53-56
Curling, Audrey 61-64
Curling, Bill
See Curling, Bryan William Richard
Curling, Bryan William Richard 1911- 102
Curnow, (Thomas) Allen (Monro) 1911- ...69-72
Curnow, Frank
See Atkinson, Frank
Curnow, Ray(mond) 1928- 117
Curran, Bob
See Curran, Robert
Curran, Charles A(rthur) 1913- 33-36R
Curran, Charles E. 1934- CANR-14
Earlier sketch in CA 23-24R
Curran, Charles John 1921-1980 Obituary .. 105
Curran, Dolores 1932- CANR-6
Earlier sketch in CA 57-60
Curran, Donald J. 1926- 45-48
Curran, Francis X. 1914- 17-18R
Curran, Jan Goldberg 1937- 101
Curran, Joseph M(aroney) 1932- 103
Curran, Mona (Elisa) 7-8R
Curran, Peter Malcolm 1922- 103
Curran, Phil(ip) R(ead) 1911- 73-76
Curran, Robert 1923- 89-92
Curran, Samuel (Crowe) 1912- 109
Curran, Stuart (Alan) 1940- 29-32R
Curran, Susan 1952- 113
Curran, Thomas J(oseph) 1929- 45-48
Curran, Ward S(chenk) 1935- 41-44R
Curran, William John 1925- 108
Curren, Polly 1917- CANR-4
Earlier sketch in CA 4R
Current, Richard N(elson) 1912- CANR-5
Earlier sketch in CA 2R
Current-Garcia, Eugene 1908- 19-20R
Currer-Briggs, Noel 1919- CANR-13
Earlier sketch in CA 73-76
Currey, Cecil B(arr) 1932- 25-28R
Currey, R(onald) F(airbridge) 1894-1983 .. CAP-1
Obituary 109
Earlier sketch in CA 9-10
Currey, R(alph) N(ixon) 1907- 93-96
Currey, Richard 1949- 117
Currie, Ann (Brooke Peterson)
1922(?)-1980 Obituary 102
Currie, Barton Wood 1878-1962 Obituary ... 116
Currie, David
See Allen, Sydney (Earl), Jr.
Currie, David P. 1936- Brief entry 106
Currie, Donald Glenne 1926-1984
Obituary 111
Currie, Ellen 19(?)- CLC-44
Currie, Lauchlin (Bernard) 1902- CANR-15
Earlier sketch in CA 73-76
Currie, Mary Montgomerie Lamb Singleton
See Fane, Violet
Currie, Robert 1937- 112
Currier, Alvin C. 1932- 23-24R
Currier, Frederick P(lumer) 1923- 85-88
Currier, Richard L(eon) 1940- 57-60
Curro, Evelyn Malone 1907- 7-8R
Curry, Andrew 1931- 57-60
Curry, Avon
See Bowden, Jean
Curry, David 1942- 69-72
Curry, Dean C(onrad) 1952- 118
Curry, Estell H. 1907- CAP-2
Earlier sketch in CA 23-24
Curry, F. Hayden 1940- 108
Curry, George E(dward) 1947- 69-72
Curry, Gladys J.
See Washington, Gladys J(oseph)
Curry, Jane L(ouise) 1932- CANR-24
Earlier sketches in CA 17-18R, CANR-7
See also SATA 1
Curry, Jennifer 1934- 77-80
Curry, Kenneth 1910- CANR-8
Earlier sketch in CA 17-18R
Curry, Leonard Preston 1929- 29-32R
Curry, Lerond (Loving) 1938- 33-36R
Curry, Martha Mulroy 1926- 61-64
Curry, Paul (J.) 1917-1986 49-52
Obituary 118
Curry, Peggy Simson 1911-1987 ...... CANR-12
Obituary 121
Earlier sketch in CA 33-36R
See also SATA 8, 50
Curry, Richard Orr 1931- 15-16R
Curry, Thomas A. 1901(?)-1976 Obituary ..69-72
Curry, Windell
See Sujata, Anagarika
Curry-Lindahl, Kai 1917- CANR-19
Earlier sketches in CA 49-52, CANR-2
Curtayne, Alice 1898- 53-56
Curteis, Ian Bayley 1935- 103
Curti, Merle Eugene 1897- CANR-4
Earlier sketch in CA 5-6R
See also DLB 17
Curtin, James R(udd) 1922- 19-20R
Curtin, Mary Ellen 1922- 57-60
Curtin, Patricia (W.) Romero 1935- CANR-14
Earlier sketch in CA 37-40R
Curtin, Philip
See Lowndes, Marie Adelaide (Belloc)
Curtin, Phillip D. 1922- CANR-7
Earlier sketch in CA 13-14R
Curtin, William M(artin) 1927- 53-56
Curtis, Alan R(obert) 1936- 105
Curtis, Anthony 1926- CANR-18
Earlier sketch in CA 101
Curtis, (Hubert) Arnold 1917- CANR-12
Earlier sketch in CA 29-32R
Curtis, Bruce (Richard) 1944- SATA-30
Curtis, Carol Edwards 1943- 77-80
Curtis, Charles J(ohn) 1921- 21-22R
Curtis, Charles Ralph 1899- 7-8R
Curtis, Charlotte (Murray) 1928-1987 .....9-10R
Obituary 122
See also AITN 2
Curtis, David Paul 1942- CANR-13
Earlier sketch in CA 23-24R
Curtis, Donald 1915- CANR-20
Earlier sketch in CA 103
Curtis, Edith Roelker 1893-1977 .... 1R
Obituary 103
Curtis, George William 1824-1892 .... DLB-1, 43
Curtis, Gerald 1904-1983 Obituary 109
Curtis, Howard J(ames) 1906-1972
Obituary 37-40R
Curtis, J(osiah) Montgomery 1905-1982
Obituary 108
Curtis, Jack 1922- 103
Curtis, Jackie
See Holder, John, Jr.
Curtis, James (Richard) 1953- 108
Curtis, James C. 1938- Brief entry 105
Curtis, James Malcolm 1940- 119
Curtis, Jared Ralph 1936- 101
Curtis, John
See Prebble, John Edward Curtis
Curtis, Lewis Perry 1900-1976 .... CAP-2
Obituary 65-68
Earlier sketch in CA 23-24
Curtis, Lindsay R(aine) 1916- 41-44R
Curtis, Lynn A(lan) 1943- 61-64
Curtis, Margaret James 1897- 3R
Curtis, Marjorie
See Prebble, Marjorie Mary Curtis
Curtis, Mark H(ubert) 1920- 5-6R
Curtis, Michael Raymond 1923- CANR-22
Earlier sketch in CA 103
Curtis, Norman 1914- 45-48
Curtis, Patricia 1924- CANR-18
Earlier sketch in CA 69-72
See also SATA 23
Curtis, Paul
See Czura, R(oman) P(eter)
Curtis, Peter
See Lofts, Norah (Robinson)
Curtis, Philip (Delacourt) 1920- 109
Curtis, Price
See Ellison, Harlan
Curtis, Richard (Alan) 1937- 106
See also SATA 29
Curtis, Richard Hale
See Levinson, Leonard
and Rothweiler, Paul Roger
Curtis, Richard Kenneth 1924- 4R
Curtis, Rosemary Ann (Stevens) 1935- 9-10R
Curtis, Sharon 1951- Brief entry 116
Curtis, Thomas (Dale) 1952- Brief entry 116
Curtis, Thomas Bradford 1911- 61-64
Curtis, Tom
See Pendower, Jacques
Curtis, Tony 1925- 73-76
Curtis, Tony 1946- CANR-22
Earlier sketch in CA 106
Curtis, Wade
See Pournelle, Jerry (Eugene)
Curtis, Will
See Nunn, William Curtis
Curtis, William J(oseph) R. 1948- 110
Curtis Brown, Beatrice 1901-1974 .... CAP-2
Earlier sketch in CA 25-28
Curtiss, John S(helton) 1899- CAP-2
Earlier sketch in CA 19-20
Curtiss, Mina (Stein Kirstein) 1896-1985
Obituary 118
Curtiss, Ursula Reilly 1923-1984 .... CANR-5
Obituary 114
Earlier sketch in CA 4R
Curtler, Hugh Mercer 1937- CANR-15
Earlier sketch in CA 89-92
Curto, Josephine J. 1927- 19-20R
Curwin, Richard L(eonard) 1944- 77-80
Curzon, Clare
See Buchanan, Marie
Curzon, Daniel 73-76
Curzon, Lucia
See Stevenson, Florence
Curzon, Sam
See Krasney, Samuel A.
Curzon, Virginia
See Hawton, Hector
Cusac, Marian H(ollingsworth) 1932- 33-36R
Cusack, (Ellen) Dymphna 1902-198(?) . CANR-11
Earlier sketch in CA 9-10R
Cusack, Lawrence X(avier) 1919- 5-6R
Cusack, Michael J(oseph) 1928- 69-72
Cush, Carol Gregor
See Gregor, Carol
Cushing, Barry E(dwin) 1945- CANR-4
Earlier sketch in CA 53-56
Cushing, Jane 1922- 29-32R
Cushing, Mary W(atkins) 189(?)-1974
Obituary 53-56
Cushing, Richard Cardinal
See Cushing, Richard James
Cushing, Richard James 1895-1970
Obituary 112
Cushion, John P(atrick) 1915- 93-96
Cushman, Clarissa Fairchild 1889-1980
Obituary 93-96
Cushman, Dan 1909- CANR-18
Earlier sketches in CA 5-6R, CANR-3
Cushman, Doug 1953- 117
Cushman, Jerome 2R
See also SATA 2
Cushman, Joseph David, Jr. 1925- 111
Cushman, Keith (Maxwell) 1942- 124
Cushman, Robert F(airchild) 1918- 77-80
Cushman, Stephen B. 1956- 123
Cusick, Philip A. 1937- 69-72
Cuskelly, Eugene James 1924- 7-8R
Cuskey, (Raymond) Walter 1934- 41-44R
Cuss, (Theodore Patrick) Camerer
1909(?)-1970 Obituary 104
Cussler, Clive (Eric) 1931- CANR-21
Earlier sketches in CA 45-48, CANR-1
Custer, Chester Eugene 1920- 41-44R
Custer, Clint
See Paine, Lauran (Bosworth)
Cutchen, Billye Walker 1930- CANR-13
Earlier sketch in CA 77-80
See also SATA 15
Cutcliffe, Stephen H(osmer) 1947- 116
Cutforth, John Ashlin 1911- 9-10R
Cutforth, Rene 1909(?)-1984 123
Obituary 112
Cuthbert, Diana Daphne Holman-Hunt
1913- 4R
Cuthbert, Eleonora Isabel (McKenzie)
1902- CAP-1
Earlier sketch in CA 11-12
Cuthbert, Mary
See Hellwig, Monika Konrad
Cuthbertson, Gilbert Morris 1937- 57-60
Cuthbertson, Tom 1945- CANR-1
Earlier sketch in CA 45-48
Cutler, Bruce 1930- CANR-18
Earlier sketches in CA 4R, CANR-2
Cutler, Carl C(uster) 1878-1966 .... 4R
Obituary 103
Cutler, Carol 1926- CANR-19
Earlier sketch in CA 103
Cutler, Charles L(ocke, Jr.) 1930- 65-68
Cutler, Daniel S(olomon) 1951- 120
Cutler, Donald R. 1930- 23-24R
Cutler, (May) Ebbitt 1923- CANR-4
Earlier sketch in CA 49-52
See also SATA 9
Cutler, Irving H. 1923- CANR-9
Earlier sketch in CA 23-24R
Cutler, Ivor 1923- CANR-9
Earlier sketch in CA 7-8R
See also SATA 24
Cutler, Katherine Noble 1905- CANR-4
Earlier sketch in CA 5-6R
Cutler, Roland 1938- 102
Cutler, Samuel
See Folsom, Franklin (Brewster)
Cutler, William Worcester III 1941- 103
Cutler, Winnifred B(erg) 1944- 117
Cutlip, Scott M. 1915- 5-6R
Cutrer, Thomas W(illiam) 1947- 123
Cutright, Paul Russell 1897- 65-68
Cutright, Phillips 1930- 5-6R
Cutshall, Alden 1911- CANR-3
Earlier sketch in CA 9-10R
Cutsumbis, Michael N(icholas) 1935- 45-48
Cutt, W(illiam) Towrie 1898-1981 81-84
Obituary 115
See also SATA 16
Cutten, M. J.
See Cutten, Mervyn (James)
Cutten, Mervyn (James) 1916- 120
Cutter, Donald C(olgett) 1922- CANR-13
Earlier sketch in CA 33-36R
Cutter, Fred 1924- 57-60
Cutter, Robert Arthur 1930- CANR-8
Earlier sketch in CA 57-60
Cutter, Tom
See Randisi, Robert J(oseph)
Cutter, Tom
See Wallmann, Jeffrey M(iner)
Cutting, Edith E(lsie) 1918- 106
Cuttino, G(eorge) P(eddy) 1914- 23-24R
Cuttle, Evelyn Roeding 57-60
Cuttler, Charles D(avid) 1913- 29-32R
Cutts, John P. 1927-1986 45-48
Obituary 121
Cutts, Richard 1923- 33-36R
Cutul, Ann-Marie 1945- 103
Cuyler, Louise E. 1908- 23-24R
Cuyler, Margery S(tuyvesant) 1948- 117
See also SATA 39
Cuyler, Stephen
See Bates, Barbara S(nedeker)
Cuyler, Susanna (Stevens) 1946- 61-64
Cykler, Edmund A(lbert) 1903- 11-12R
Cylwicki, Albert 1932- 116
Cynan
See Evans-Jones, Albert
Cynthia
See King, Florence
Cyr, Don(ald Joseph) 1935- 103
Cyr, John Edwin 1915- 103
Czaczkes, Shmuel Yosef
See Agnon, S(hmuel) Y(osef Halevi)
Czaja, Michael 1911- 57-60
Czaplinski, Suzanne 1943- 61-64
Czerniawski, Adam 1934- CANR-14
Earlier sketch in CA 37-40R
Czerny, Peter G(erd) 1941- 65-68
Czestochowski, Joseph S(tephen) 1950- 113
Czobor, Agnes 1920- 37-40R
Czura, R(oman) P(eter) 1913- 89-92

D

D. P.
See Wells, H(erbert) G(eorge)
Daane, Calvin J(ohn) 1925- 41-44R
Daane, James 1914- 23-24R
Dabberdt, Walter F. 1942- CANR-23
Earlier sketch in CA 107
Dabbs, Jack Autrey 1914- 17-18R
Dabbs, James McBride 1896-1970 ...... CAP-1
Earlier sketch in CA 15-16
Dabcovich, Lydia 124
See also SATA 47
Dabit, Eugene 1898-1936 .... DLB-65
Dabkin, Edwin Franden 1898(?)-1976
Obituary 65-68
Dabney, Dick 1933-1981 69-72
Obituary 105
Dabney, Joseph Earl 1929- 49-52
Dabney, Ross H. 1934- 23-24R
Dabney, Virginius 1901- CANR-1
Earlier sketch in CA 45-48
Dabney, William M(inor) 1919- 9-10R
Daborne, Robert 1580(?)-1628 .... DLB-58
D'Abreu, Gerald Joseph 1916-19(?) CAP-2
Earlier sketch in CA 19-20
Dabringhaus, Erhard 1917- 115
Dabrowska, Maria (Szumska) 1889-1965 ... 106
See also CLC 15
Dabydeen, Cyril 1945- Brief entry 122
Dabydeen, David 1955- CLC-34
DaCal, Ernesto Guerra 1911- CANR-19
Earlier sketches in CA 5-6R, CANR-4
Dace, Letitia (Skinner) 1941- 106
Dace, Tish
See Dace, Letitia (Skinner)
Dace, (Edwin) Wallace 1920- 61-64
Dacey, Norman F(ranklyn) 1908- CANR-2
Earlier sketch in CA 7-8R
Dacey, Philip 1939- CANR-14
Earlier sketch in CA 37-40R
Dachman, Ken 1958- 110

Dachs, David 1922-1980 ... CANR-11
Earlier sketch in CA 69-72
Dack, Gail Monroe 1901-1976 Obituary ... 111
da Cruz, Daniel, Jr. 1921- ... CANR-19
Earlier sketches in CA 7-8R, CANR-3
Dacy, Douglas Calvin 1927- Brief entry ... 104
Dadie, Bernard B(inlin) 1916- ... CANR-17
Earlier sketch in CA 25-28R
Daedalus
See Bramesco, Norton J.
Daehlin, Reidar A. 1910- ... CAP-1
Earlier sketch in CA 17-18
Daem, Thelma (Mary) Bannerman 1914- ... 5-6R
Daemer, Will
See Miller, (H.) Bill(y)
and Wade, Robert (Allison)
Daemmrich, Horst S. 1930- ... CANR-1
Earlier sketch in CA 45-48
Daenzer, Bernard John 1916- ... 53-56
Dagan, Avigdor 1912- ... CANR-13
Earlier sketch in CA 33-36R
Dagenais, James J(oseph) 1928- ... 41-44R
Dager, Edward Z(icca) 1921- ... 61-64
Dagerman, Stig (Halvard) 1923-1954
Brief entry ... 117
See also TCLC 17
Dagg, Anne Innis 1933- ... CANR-11
Earlier sketch in CA 69-72
Daglish, Eric Fitch 1892-1966 ... 102
D'Agostino, Angelo 1926- ... 19-20R
D'Agostino, Dennis John 1957- ... 106
D'Agostino, Giovanna P. 1914- ... 57-60
D'Agostino, Joseph David 1929- ... 69-72
Dagover, Lil 1897-1980 Obituary ... 105
Daheim, Mary 1937- ... 110
Dahinden, Justus 1925- ... 81-84
Dahl, Arlene 1928- Brief entry ... 105
Dahl, Borghild (Margarethe) 1890-1984 . CANR-2
Obituary ... 112
Earlier sketch in CA 3R
See also SATA 7, 37
Dahl, Curtis 1920- ... CANR-2
Earlier sketch in CA 4R
Dahl, Georg 1905- ... 85-88
Dahl, Gordon J. 1932- ... 49-52
Dahl, Linda 1949- ... 122
Dahl, Murdoch Edgcumbe 1914- ... CAP-1
Earlier sketch in CA 9-10
Dahl, Nils A(lstrup) 1911- ... 65-68
Dahl, Roald 1916- ... CANR-6
Earlier sketch in CA 1R
See also SATA 1, 26
See also CLC 1, 6, 18
See also CLR 1, 7
Dahl, Robert Alan 1915- ... 65-68
Dahlberg, Arthur O. ... 124
Dahlberg, Edward 1900-1977 ... 9-10R
Obituary ... 69-72
See also DLB 48
See also CLC 1, 7, 14
Dahlberg, Edwin T(heodore) 1892-1986 .. CAP-2
Obituary ... 120
Earlier sketch in CA 17-18
Dahlberg, Jane S. 1923- ... 23-24R
Dahlinger, John Cote 1923-1984 Obituary .. 114
Dahlstedt, Marden 1921- ... CANR-1
Earlier sketch in CA 45-48
See also SATA 8
Dahlstrand, Frederick Charles 1945- ... 111
Dahlstrom, Earl C(arl) 1914- ... 17-18R
Dahm, Charles W(illiam) 1937- ... 107
Dahms, Alan M(artin) 1937- ... 49-52
Dahmus, Joseph Henry 1909- ... 21-22R
Dahood, Mitchell (Joseph) 1922-1982 .. CANR-20
Obituary ... 106
Earlier sketch in CA 25-28R
Dahrendorf, Ralf 1929- ... CANR-3
Earlier sketch in CA 3R
Daiches, David 1912- ... CANR-7
Earlier sketch in CA 5-6R
Daigh, Ralph (Foster) 1907-1986 Obituary .. 121
Daigon, Arthur 1928- ... 33-36R
Daiken, Leslie Herbert 1912- ... 4R
Dailey, Charles A(lvin) 1923- ... 89-92
Dailey, Janet (Ann) 1944- ... CANR-17
Earlier sketch in CA 89-92
Daily, Jay E(lwood) 1923- ... 33-36R
Daims, Diva 1925- ... 113
Dain, Martin J. 1924- ... 15-16R
See also SATA 35
Dain, Norman 1925- ... 11-12R
Dain, Phyllis 1929- ... 69-72
Dainton, (William) Courtney 1920- ... 9-10R
Daiute, Robert James 1926- ... 13-14R
Dakers, Elaine Kidner 1905-1978 ... 85-88
Dakin, Arthur Hazard 1905- Brief entry ... 106
Dakin, D(avid) Martin 1908- ... 73-76
Dakin, Edwin Franden 1898-1976
Obituary ... 104
Dakin, (David) Julian 1939-1971 ... CAP-2
Earlier sketch in CA 25-28
Dalal, Nergis 1920- Brief entry ... 116
Daland, Robert T(heodore) 1919- ... 21-22R
Dalbor, John B(ronislaw) 1929- ... 17-18R
Dalcourt, Gerard J. 1927- ... 33-36R
Dale, (Mary) Alzina Stone 1931- ... 114
Dale, Antony 1912- ... 107
Dale, Arbie Myron, Jr. 1924- ... 122
Dale, Celia (Marjorie) ... CANR-3
Earlier sketch in CA 7-8R
Dale, Colin
See Lawrence, T(homas) E(dward)
See also TCLC 18
Dale, D(ion) M(urray) C(rosbie) 1930- ... 23-24R
Dale, Doris Cruger 1927- ... 116
Dale, Edgar 1900-1985 Obituary ... 117
Dale, Edward Everett 1879-1972 ... CANR-4
Earlier sketch in CA 5-6R
Dale, Edwin L., Jr. 1923- ... 69-72
Dale, Ernest 1917- ... 13-14R
Dale, George E.
See Asimov, Isaac
Dale, Jack
See Holliday, Joseph
Dale, James 1886-1985 ... CAP-2
Obituary ... 116
Earlier sketch in CA 33-36
Dale, John B. 1905- ... 13-14R
Dale, Kathleen 1895-1984 Obituary ... 112
Dale, Laura A(bbott) 1919-1983 Obituary ... 113
Dale, Magdalene L(arsen) 1904- ... 15-16R
Dale, Margaret J(essy) Miller 1911- ... CANR-19
Earlier sketches in CA 7-8R, CANR-3
See also SATA 39
Dale, Norman
See Denny, Norman (George)
Dale, Paul W(orthen) 1923- ... 25-28R
Dale, Peter (John) 1938- ... CANR-16
Earlier sketches in CA 45-48, CANR-1
See also DLB 40
Dale, Reginald R. 1907- ... 21-22R
Dale, Richard 1932- ... 33-36R
Dale, Richard
See Lansdale, Joe R(ichard)
Dale, Robert D(ennis) 1940- ... 113
Dale, Roman
See Czura, R(oman) P(eter)
d'Alelio, Ellen F. 1938- ... 17-18R
Dales, Douglas S. 1907(?)-1985 Obituary .. 114
Dales, Richard C(lark) 1926- ... CANR-24
Earlier sketch in CA 45-48
Daleski, H(illel) M(atthew) 1926- ... 33-36R
D'Alessandro, Robert (Philip) 1942- ... 61-64
Dalet, Roger (Charles) 1927- ... 107
Daley, Adeline 1922(?)-1984 Obituary ... 112
Daley, Arthur (John) 1904-1974 ... CAP-2
Obituary ... 45-48
Earlier sketch in CA 23-24
Daley, Bill
See Appleman, John Alan
Daley, Eliot A. 1936- ... 97-100
Daley, Joseph A(ndrew) 1927- ... 53-56
Daley, Robert 1930- ... CANR-24
Earlier sketches in CA 2R, CANR-2
Dalfiume, Richard Myron 1936- ... 25-28R
D'Alfonso, John 1918- ... 29-32R
Dalgleish, Oakley Hedley 1910-1963
Obituary ... 115
Dalgliesh, Alice 1893-1979 ... 73-76
Obituary ... 89-92
See also SATA 17, 21
Dalglish, Edward R(ussell) 1913- ... 37-40R
Dali, Salvador (Domenech Felipe Jacinto)
1904- ... 104
Dall, Caroline Wells (Healey) 1822-1912 .. DLB-1
D'Allard, Hunter
See Ballard, (Willis) Todhunter
Dallas, Athena Gianakas
See Dallas-Damis, Athena G(ianakas)
Dallas, E. S. 1828-1879 ... DLB-55
Dallas, John
See Duncan, W(illiam) Murdoch
Dallas, Philip 1921- ... 61-64
Dallas, Ruth 1919- ... CANR-10
Earlier sketch in CA 65-68
Dallas, Sandra
See Atchison, Sandra Dallas
Dallas-Damis, Athena G(ianakas) 1925- ... 81-84
Dallek, Robert 1934- ... CANR-17
Earlier sketch in CA 25-28R
D'Allenger, Hugh
See Kershaw, John (Hugh D'Allenger)
Dallimore, Arnold A(rthur) 1911- ... 112
Dallin, Alexander 1924- ... CANR-19
Earlier sketches in CA 1R, CANR-5
Dallin, Leon 1918- ... CANR-1
Earlier sketch in CA 1R
Dallmann, Martha (Elsie) 1904- ... 4R
Dallmayr, Fred R(einhard) 1928- ... CANR-1
Earlier sketch in CA 49-52
Dally, Ann Mullins 1926- ... CANR-21
Earlier sketches in CA 7-8R, CANR-3
Dalmas, John
See Jones, John R(obert)
D'Alonzo, C(onstance) Anthony
1912-1972 Obituary ... 37-40R
Dalpadado, J(ames) Kingsley (Evold)
1922- ... 112
Dalphin, John R(obert) 1942- ... 118
Dal Poggetto, Newton Francis 1922- ... 61-64
d'Alpuget, Blanche 1944- ... 114
Dalrymple, Byron W(illiam) 1910- ... CANR-6
Earlier sketch in CA 57-60
Dalrymple, Douglas J(esse) 1934- ... 73-76
Dalrymple, Gertrude Bradley 1901(?)-1984
Obituary ... 113
Dalrymple, Ian (Murray) 1903- ... 115
Dalrymple, Jean 1910- ... CANR-5
Earlier sketch in CA 5-6R
Dalrymple, Willard 1921- ... 23-24R
Dalsass, Diana 1947- ... 106
Dalton, Alene
See Chapin, Alene Olsen Dalton
Dalton, Anne 1948- ... SATA-40
Dalton, Claire
See Burns, Alma
Dalton, Clive
See Clark, F(rederick) Stephen
Dalton, (John) David 1944- ... 97-100
Dalton, Dennis (Gilmore) 1938- ... 115
Dalton, Dorothy 1915- ... 21-22R
Dalton, Elizabeth 1936- ... 85-88
Dalton, Gene W(ray) 1928- ... 25-28R
Dalton, George 1926- Brief entry ... 106
D'Alton, Louis (Lynch) 1900-1951
Brief entry ... 110
See also DLB 10
Dalton, Priscilla
See Avallone, Michael (Angelo), Jr.
Dalton, Richard 1930- ... 57-60
Dalton, Stephen 1937- ... 85-88
Dalven, Rae 1904- ... 33-36R
Daly, Anne 1896- ... CAP-2
Earlier sketch in CA 29-32
Daly, Cahal Brendan 1917- ... 104
Daly, Carroll John 1889-1958 Brief entry ... 112
Daly, Donald F(remont) ... 69-72
Daly, Edith Iglauer ... CANR-14
Earlier sketch in CA 77-80
Daly, Elizabeth 1878-1967 ... CAP-2
Obituary ... 25-28R
Earlier sketch in CA 23-24
Daly, Emily Joseph 1913- ... 9-10R
Daly, Faye Kennedy 1936- ... 97-100
Daly, Herman E. 1938- ... 89-92
Daly, Jim
See Stratemeyer, Edward L.
Daly, John Jay 1888(?)-1976 Obituary ... 69-72
Daly, Kathleen N(orah) Brief entry ... 115
See also SATA 37
Daly, (Arthur) Leo 1920- ... 105
Daly, Lowrie John 1914- ... 15-16R
Daly, Mary 1928- ... 25-28R
Daly, Mary Tinley 1904(?)-1979 ... 85-88
Daly, Maureen
See McGivern, Maureen Daly
See also SATA 2
See also SAAS 1
See also CLC 17
Daly, Nicholas 1946- ... 111
See also SATA 37
Daly, Niki
See Daly, Nicholas
Daly, Robert 1943- ... 104
Daly, Robert Welter 1916-1975 ... 9-10R
Obituary ... 103
Daly, Saralyn R(uth) 1924- ... 57-60
Daly, Sister Mary Virginia 1925- ... 17-18R
Daly, T(homas) A(ugustine) 1871-1948
Brief entry ... 111
See also DLB 11
Dalzel, Peter
See Dalzel Job, P(atrick)
Dalzel Job, P(atrick) 1913- ... 13-14R
Dalzell, Robert (Fenton), Jr. 1937- ... 81-84
Dam, Hari N(arayan) 1921- ... 57-60
Dam, Kenneth W. 1932- ... CANR-12
Earlier sketch in CA 69-72
Damachi, (Godwin) Ukandi 1942- ... CANR-2
Earlier sketch in CA 45-48
Damas, Leon 1912-1978 Obituary ... 73-76
D'Amato, Alex 1919- ... CANR-18
Earlier sketch in CA 81-84
See also SATA 20
D'Amato, Anthony A. 1937- ... 29-32R
D'Amato, Barbara 1938- ... 69-72
D'Amato, Janet (Potter) 1925- ... CANR-18
Earlier sketches in CA 49-52, CANR-1
See also SATA 9
Damaz, Paul F. 1917- ... 7-8R
d'Amboise, Christopher 1960- ... 115
Dambrauskas, Joan Arden 1933- ... 104
D'Ambrosio, Charles A. 1932- ... 23-24R
D'Ambrosio, Richard A(nthony) 1927- ... 102
D'Ambrosio, Vinnie-Marie 1928- ... 45-48
Dame, Lawrence 1898- ... CAP-1
Earlier sketch in CA 11-12
D'Amelio, Dan 1927- ... 33-36R
Dameron, J(ohn) Lasley 1925- ... 53-56
Damerst, William A. 1923- ... 19-20R
Damiani, Bruno Mario 1942- ... 57-60
D'Amico, John Francis 1947(?)-1987
Obituary ... 124
Damis, John 1940- ... 118
Damm, John S. 1926- ... 37-40R
Damon, Gene
See Grier, Barbara G(ene Damon)
Damon, S(amuel) Foster 1893-1971 ... 101
See also DLB 45
Damon, Virgil Green 1895-1972 ... CAP-1
Obituary ... 37-40R
Earlier sketch in CA 9-10
Damor, Hakji
See Lesser, R(oger) H(arold)
D'Amore, Arcangelo R. T. 1920-1986
Obituary ... 118
Damore, Leo 1929- ... 81-84
Damrosch, Helen
See Tee-Van, Helen Damrosch
Damrosch, Leopold, Jr. 1941- ... 45-48
Damsker, Matt(hew Harry) 1951- ... 108
Damtoft, Walter A(tkinson) 1922- ... 57-60
Dana, Amber
See Paine, Lauran (Bosworth)
Dana, Barbara 1940- ... CANR-8
Earlier sketch in CA 19-20R
See also SATA 22
Dana, Charles Anderson 1819-1897 ... DLB-3, 23
Dana, E. H.
See Hamel Dobkin, Kathleen
Dana, Richard
See Paine, Lauran (Bosworth)
Dana, Richard H(enry) 1927- ... CANR-15
Earlier sketch in CA 85-88
Dana, Richard Henry, Jr. 1815-1882 ... SATA-26
See also DLB 1
Dana, Robert (Patrick) 1929- ... 33-36R
Dana, Rose
See Ross, W(illiam) E(dward) D(aniel)
Danachair, Caoimhin O
See Danaher, Kevin
Danagher, Edward F. 1919- ... 11-12R
Danaher, Kevin 1913- ... 33-36R
See also SATA 22
Danan, Alexis 1889(?)-1979 Obituary ... 89-92
Danby, Hope (Smedley) 1899- ... CAP-1
Earlier sketch in CA 13-14
Danby, John B(lench) 1905-1983
Obituary ... 109
Danby, Mary
See Calvert, Mary
Danby, Miles William 1925- ... 13-14R
Dance, E(dward) H(erbert) 1894- ... 37-40R
Dance, F(rancis) E(sburn) X(avier)
1929- ... CANR-16
Earlier sketches in CA 4R, CANR-1
Dance, Frank E. X.
See Dance, F(rancis) E(sburn) X(avier)
Dance, Jim 1924(?)-1983 Obituary ... 110
Dance, S(tanley) Peter 1932- ... CANR-13
Earlier sketch in CA 69-72
Dance, Stanley (Frank) 1910- ... CANR-8
Earlier sketch in CA 17-18R
Danco, Katharine L(eck) 1929- ... 112
Danco, Katy
See Danco, Katharine L(eck)
Danco, Leon A(ntoine) 1923- ... 112
Dancocks, Daniel G. 1950- ... 120
D'Ancona, Mirella Levi 1919- ... CANR-6
Earlier sketch in CA 53-56
Dancy, John Christopher 1920- ... 107
Dandrea, Don(ald E.) 1936- ... 120
D'Andrea, Kate
See Steiner, Barbara A(nnette)
D'Andrea, Paul 1939- ... 120
Dandridge, Raymond Garfield
1882-1930 ... DLB-51
Dandy, James Edgar 1903-1976 Obituary ... 104
Dane, Carl
See Adams, F(rank) Ramsay
Dane, Clemence
See Ashton, Winifred
See also DLB 10
Dane, Les(lie A.) 1925- ... 89-92
Dane, Mark
See Avallone, Michael (Angelo), Jr.
Dane, Mary
See Morland, Nigel
Dane, Nathan II 1916-1980 ... 108
Obituary ... 97-100
Dane, Zel
See Timms, E(dward) V(ivian)
Daneff, Stephen Constantine 1931- ... 106
Daneke, Gregory A(llen) 1950- ... 112
Danelski, David J. 1930- ... 15-16R
Danenberg, Leigh 1893-1976 Obituary ... 69-72
Danford, Howard G(orby) 1904- ... CAP-1
Earlier sketch in CA 11-12
Danforth, Art(hur Louis) 1913(?)-1987
Obituary ... 122
Danforth, John 1660-1730 ... DLB-24
Danforth, Loring M(andell) 1949- ... 111
Danforth, Samuel I 1626-1674 ... DLB-24
Danforth, Samuel II 1666-1727 ... DLB-24
Dangaard, Colin (Edward) 1942- ... 85-88
D'angelo, Edward 1932- ... 37-40R
D'Angelo, Frank J(oseph) 1928- ... 120
D'Angelo, Lou
See D'Angelo, Luciano
D'Angelo, Luciano 1932- ... 33-36R
Dangerfield, Balfour
See McCloskey, (John) Robert
Dangerfield, Clint
See Norwood, Victor G(eorge) C(harles)
Dangerfield, George (Bubb) 1904-1986 ... 9-10R
Obituary ... 121
Dangerfield, Harlan
See Padgett, Ron
Dangerfield, Rodney 1922(?)- ... 102
Danhof, Clarence H(enry) 1911- ... 37-40R
Dani, Ahmad Hasan 1920- ... 13-14R
Daniel, Anita 1893(?)-1978 Obituary ... 77-80
See also SATA 23, 24
Daniel, Anne
See Steiner, Barbara A(nnette)
Daniel, Charles 1933- ... 114
Daniel, Cletus E(dward) 1943- ... 107
Daniel, (Elbert) Clifton, Jr. 1912-
Brief entry ... 113
Daniel, Colin
See Windsor, Patricia (Frances)
Daniel, Daniel 1890(?)-1981 Obituary ... 104
Daniel, Elna Worrell
See Stone, Elna
Daniel, Emmett Randolph 1935- ... 102
Daniel, Errol Valentine ... 111
Daniel, George Bernard, Jr. 1927- ... 15-16R
Daniel, Glenda 1943- ... 111
Daniel, Glyn (Edmund) 1914-1986 ... CANR-13
Obituary ... 121
Earlier sketch in CA 57-60
Daniel, Hawthorne 1890- ... 5-6R
See also SATA 8
Daniel, James 1916- ... 69-72
Daniel, Jerry C(layton) 1937- ... 33-36R
Daniel, John M. 1825-1865 ... DLB-43
Daniel, Julie Goldsmith 1949- ... CANR-14
Earlier sketch in CA 77-80
Daniel, Lorne (MacLeod Lyons) 1953- ... 118
Daniel, Norman (Alexander) 1919- ... CANR-6
Earlier sketch in CA 57-60
Daniel, Pete 1938- ... CANR-14
Earlier sketch in CA 37-40R
Daniel, Price, Jr. 1941-1981 Obituary ... 103
Daniel, Ralph T(homas) 1921- ... 53-56
Daniel, Robert L(eslie) 1923- ... 33-36R

Daniel, Robert W(oodham) 1915- 25-28R
Daniel, Samuel 1562(?)-1619 .... DLB-62
Daniel, Stephen H(artley) 1950- 119
Daniel, Urcel 1908(?)-1984 Obituary 113
Daniel, Walter C(larence) 1922- 110
Daniel, Yuli (Markovich) 1925- 116
Daniele, Joseph William 1927- 89-92
Daniell, Albert Scott 1906-1965 .... CANR-3
Earlier sketch in CA 5-6R
Daniell, David Scott
See Daniell, Albert Scott
Daniell, Jere Rogers 1932- CANR-11
Earlier sketch in CA 29-32R
Daniell, Rosemary 1935- 118
Danielle, Maria 1945- 114
Danielli, James Frederic 1911-1984
Obituary 113
Daniells, Lorna M(cLean) 1918- CANR-18
Earlier sketch in CA 89-92
Daniells, Roy 1902- 57-60
Danielou, Alain 1907- CANR-14
Earlier sketch in CA 73-76
Danielou, Jean 1905-1974 .... CAP-2
Obituary 49-52
Earlier sketch in CA 23-24
Daniel-Rops, Henri
See Petiot, Henri Jules Charles
Daniels, Anna Kleegman 1893-1970
Obituary 29-32R
Daniels, Arlene Kaplan 1930- CANR-12
Earlier sketch in CA 29-32R
Daniels, Brett
See Adler, Renata
Daniels, Bruce C(olin) 1943- 122
Daniels, David 1933- 53-56
Daniels, Derick January 1926- Brief entry 112
Daniels, Dewey
See McKimmey, James
Daniels, Dorothy 1915- CANR-15
Earlier sketch in CA 89-92
Daniels, Draper 1913-1983 53-56
Obituary 109
Daniels, Elizabeth Adams 1920- 37-40R
Daniels, Farrington 1889-1972 ....5-6R
Obituary 37-40R
Daniels, Frank Arthur 1904-1986 Obituary .. 121
Daniels, Frank James 1900(?)-1983
Obituary 110
Daniels, George H. 1935- CANR-10
Earlier sketch in CA 25-28R
Daniels, George M(orris) 1927- 29-32R
Daniels, Guy 1919- 21-22R
See also SATA 7, 11
Daniels, Harold R(obert) 1919- 17-18R
Daniels, James R(aymond) 1956- 121
Daniels, Jim
See Daniels, James R(aymond)
Daniels, John Clifford 1915- 13-14R
Daniels, John S.
See Overholser, Wayne D.
Daniels, Jonathan 1902-1981 49-52
Obituary 105
Daniels, Josephus 1862-1948 Brief entry ... 122
See also DLB 29
Daniels, Kate 1953- 124
Daniels, Les(lie Noel III) 1943- CANR-24
Earlier sketches in CA 65-68, CANR-9
Daniels, Mary 1937- 93-96
Daniels, Max
See Gellis, Roberta L(eah Jacobs)
Daniels, Norman CANR-15
Earlier sketch in CA 89-92
Daniels, Norman 1942- CANR-22
Earlier sketch in CA 106
Daniels, Pamela 1937- 101
Daniels, R(obertson) Balfour 1900- 49-52
Daniels, Randy (Allan) 1949- 81-84
Daniels, Robert V(incent) 1926- CANR-2
Earlier sketch in CA 1R
Daniels, Roger 1927- CANR-23
Earlier sketches in CA 7-8R, CANR-8
Daniels, Sally 1931- 3R
Daniels, Shouri
See Ramanujan, Molly
Daniels, Steven Lloyd 1945-1973 ....33-36R
Daniels, Velma Seawell 1931- 108
Danielson, Elena S(chafer) 1947- 116
Danielson, J. D.
See James, M. R.
Danielson, Michael N(ils) 1934- 33-36R
Danielson, Wayne Allen 1929- 77-80
Danielsson, Bengt (Emmerik) 1921- ... CANR-23
Earlier sketch in CA 107
Daniere, Andre L(ucien) 1926- 11-12R
Daniloff, Nicholas 1934- 85-88
Danilov, Victor J(oseph) 1924- CANR-21
Earlier sketches in CA 13-14R, CANR-6
Daninos, Pierre 1913- CANR-15
Earlier sketch in CA 77-80
Danish, Barbara 1948- 57-60
Dank, Gloria Rand 1955- 114
See also SATA 46
Dank, Leonard D(ewey) 1929- SATA-44
Dank, Milton 1920- CANR-11
Earlier sketch in CA 69-72
See also SATA 31
Danker, Frederick William 1920- CANR-5
Earlier sketch in CA 15-16R
Danker, W(illiam) John 1914- 15-16R
Dankleff, Richard E(lden) 1925- 114
Danky, James Philip 1947- CANR-12
Earlier sketch in CA 69-72
Danly, Robert Lyons 1947- 108
Dann, Colin (Michael) 1943- 108
Dann, Jack 1945- CANR-2
Earlier sketch in CA 49-52
Dann, Max 1955- 118
Dann, Uriel 1922- 25-28R
Dannay, Frederic 1905-1982 .... CANR-1
Obituary 107
Earlier sketch in CA 1R
See also CLC 11
Dannelley, Paul (Edward, Jr.) 1919- 122
Dannemiller, Lawrence 1925- 1R
Dannenfeldt, Karl H(enry) 1916- 25-28R
Danner, Margaret (Essie) 1915- 29-32R
See also DLB 41
Dannett, Sylvia G. L. 1909- CANR-4
Earlier sketch in CA 2R
D'Annunzio, Gabriele 1863-1938
Brief entry 104
See also TCLC 6
Danoff, I. Michael 1940- 97-100
Danowski, T(haddeus) S(tanley)
1914-1987 ....11-12R
Obituary 123
Danska, Herbert 1928- 29-32R
Danson, Lawrence Neil 1942- 85-88
d'Antibes, Germain
See Simenon, Georges (Jacques
Christian)
Danto, Arthur C(oleman) 1924- 17-18R
Danto, Bruce L. 1927- CANR-7
Earlier sketch in CA 53-56
Danton, J(oseph) Periam 1908- 11-12R
Danton, Rebecca
See Roberts, Janet Louise
Dantzic, Cynthia Maris 1933- 101
Dantzig, George Bernard 1914- Brief entry .. 106
Danvers, Jack
See Caseleyr, Cam(ille Auguste Marie)
Danzig, Allan (Peter) 1931- 45-48
Danzig, Allison 1898-1987 ....37-40R
Obituary 121
Danzig, Fred P(aul) 1925- 65-68
Danziger, Edmund J(efferson), Jr. 1938- ... 102
Danziger, Kurt 1926- 41-44R
Danziger, Marlies K(allmann) 1926- CANR-16
Earlier sketch in CA 25-28R
Danziger, Paula 1944- 115
Brief entry 112
See also SATA 30, 36
See also CLC 21
Danziger, Sheldon H. 1948- 119
Daoud, Hazim S. 1930-1976 122
Dapper, Gloria 1922- 19-20R
Dapping, William Osborne 1880-1969
Obituary 115
D'Aprix, Roger M. 1932- 33-36R
Darack, Arthur J. 1918- 115
Darbelnet, Jean (Louis) 1904- CANR-10
Earlier sketch in CA 25-28R
Darby, Catherine
See Peters, Maureen
Darby, Gene Kegley 1921- CANR-2
Earlier sketch in CA 5-6R
Darby, Henry Clifford 1909- 7-8R
Darby, J. N.
See Govan, Christine Noble
Darby, John 1940- 105
Darby, Michael 1944- 116
Darby, Patricia (Paulsen) 73-76
See also SATA 14
Darby, Ray(mond) 1912- 17-18R
See also SATA 7
d'Arch Smith, Timothy 1936- 15-16R
Darcy, Clare 102
D'Arcy, G(eorge) Minot 1930- 9-10R
D'Arcy, Jean (Marie) 1913-1983 Obituary 109
Darcy, Jean
See Lepley, Jean Elizabeth
D'Arcy, Margaretta 1934- 104
D'Arcy, Martin C(yril) 1888-1976 .... CANR-3
Obituary 69-72
Earlier sketch in CA 7-8R
D'Arcy, Pamela
See Roby, Mary Linn
D'Arcy, Paul F(rancis) 1921- 19-20R
d'Arcy, Willard
See Cox, William (Robert)
Darden, Lloyd (Nestor) 1931- Brief entry ... 113
Darden, Norma Jean 114
Dardess, William R(aymond) 1936- 77-80
Dardess, John W(olfe) 1937- 45-48
Dardig, Jill C(arolyn) 1948- 69-72
Dardis, Tom 1926- CANR-9
Earlier sketch in CA 65-68
Dare, Evelyn
See Everett-Green, Evelyn
Dareff, Hal 1920- 65-68
Darga, Bert 1931- 110
Dargan, Olive (Tilford) 1869-1968
Obituary 111
Dargo, George 1935- 115
d'Argyre, Gilles
See Klein, Gerard
Dariaux, Genevieve Antoine
See Antoine-Dariaux, Genevieve
Darien, Peter
See Bassett, William B. K.
Daringer, Helen Fern 1892- CAP-2
Earlier sketch in CA 17-18
See also SATA 1
Dario, Ruben
See Sarmiento, Felix Ruben Garcia
See also TCLC 4
Darion, Joe
See Darion, Joseph
Darion, Joseph 1917- Brief entry 113
Dark, Alvin Ralph 1922- 105
Dark, Harris Edward 1922- 57-60
Dark, Johnny
See Norwood, Victor G(eorge) C(harles)
Dark, Philip J(ohn) C(rosskey) 1918- ... CANR-18
Earlier sketches in CA 49-52, CANR-2
Darke, Marjorie 1929- CANR-15
Earlier sketch in CA 81-84
See also SATA 16
Darley, F(elix) O(ctavius) C(arr)
1822-1888 .... SATA-35
Darley, John M(cConnon) 1938- 93-96
Darling, Arthur Burr 1892-1971 ....5-6R
Obituary 33-36R
Darling, David J. SATA-44
Darling, Edward 1907-1974 .... CANR-3
Obituary 53-56
Earlier sketch in CA 49-52
Darling, Frank Clayton 1925- 19-20R
Darling, Frank Fraser
See Fraser Darling, Frank
Darling, Jay Norwood 1876-1962
Obituary 93-96
Darling, John R(othburn) 1937- 93-96
Darling, Kathy
See Darling, Mary Kathleen
Darling, Lois MacIntyre 1917- CANR-3
Earlier sketch in CA 5-6R
See also SATA 3
Darling, Louis, Jr. 1916-1970 .... CANR-3
Obituary 89-92
Earlier sketch in CA 7-8R
See also SATA 3, 23
Darling, Mary Kathleen 1943- CANR-4
Earlier sketch in CA 53-56
See also SATA 9
Darling, Richard L(ewis) 1925- 23-24R
Darlington, Alice B(enning) 1906-1973 ... CAP-2
Obituary 41-44R
Earlier sketch in CA 25-28
Darlington, C(yril) D(ean) 1903-1981 ... CANR-10
Obituary 108
Earlier sketch in CA 9-10R
Darlington, Charles F. 1904-1986 .... CAP-2
Obituary 119
Earlier sketch in CA 25-28
Darlington, Joy 1947- 89-92
Darlington, William Aubrey (Cecil) 1890- .. CAP-1
Earlier sketch in CA 15-16
Darlow, Michael (George) 1934- 104
Darlton, Clark
See Ernsting, Walter
Darmstadter, Joel 1928- 121
Darnay, Arsen (Julius) 1936- 111
Darnton, John Townsend 1941-
Brief entry 119
Darnton, Robert (Choate) 1939- 116
Brief entry 113
Darr, Ann 1920- CANR-7
Earlier sketch in CA 57-60
Darracott, Joseph C(orbould) 1934- 106
Darrah, William C(ulp) 1909- 57-60
Darroch, Maurice A. 1903-19(?) CAP-2
Earlier sketch in CA 19-20
Darroch, Sandra Jobson 1942- 89-92
Darrow, Ralph C(arroll) 1918- 61-64
Darrow, Richard W(illiam) 1915-1976 ....21-22R
Obituary 120
Darrow, Whitney (Jr.) 1909- CANR-14
Earlier sketch in CA 61-64
See also SATA 13
Dart, John 1936- 65-68
Dart, Raymond A(rthur) 1893- CAP-1
Earlier sketch in CA 13-14
Darton, G(erald) C(hristopher)
1913(?)-1987 Obituary 122
Darvas, Nicolas 1920- 61-64
Darveaux, Terry A(lan) 1943- 65-68
Darvill, Fred T(homas), Jr. 1927- CANR-6
Earlier sketch in CA 57-60
Darwall, Stephen L(eicester) 1946- 113
Darwin, Charles 1809-1882 .... DLB-57
Darwin, Len
See Darwin, Leonard
Darwin, Leonard 1916- SATA-24
Darwin, M. B.
See McDavid, Raven I(oor), Jr.
Dary, David A. 1934- CANR-13
Earlier sketch in CA 29-32R
Daryush, Elizabeth 1887-1977 .... CANR-3
Earlier sketch in CA 49-52
See also DLB 20
See also CLC 6, 19
Das, Deb Kumar 1935- 102
Das, Durga 1900-1974 .... CAP-2
Obituary 49-52
Earlier sketch in CA 29-32
Das, Gurcharan 1943- 33-36R
Das, Jagannath Prasad 1931- CANR-6
Earlier sketch in CA 57-60
Das, Kamala 1934- 101
Das, Manmath Nath 1926- CANR-8
Earlier sketch in CA 15-16R
Dasent, Sir George Webbe 1817-1896 .. SATA-29
Das Gupta, Jyotirindra 1933- 53-56
Dash, Joan 1925- 49-52
Dash, Samuel 1925- Brief entry 105
Dash, Tony 1945- 33-36R
Dashiell, Alfred Sheppard 1901-1970
Obituary 89-92
Dashti, Ali 1894- 85-88
Dashwood, Robert Julian 1899- CAP-1
Earlier sketch in CA 13-14
da Silva, Howard 1909-1986 Obituary 118
DaSilva, Leon
See Wallmann, Jeffrey M(iner)
DaSilva, Zenia Sacks 1925- 121
Daskam, Josephine Dodge
See Bacon, Josephine Dodge (Daskam)
Dasmann, Raymond (Fredric) 1919- CANR-2
Earlier sketch in CA 7-8R
Dass, Ram
See Alpert, Richard
Dassault, Marcel (Bloch) 1892-1986
Obituary 119
Brief entry 115
Dassonville, Michel A(uguste) 1927- 73-76
Dater, Henry M. 1909(?)-1974 Obituary ...49-52
Datesh, John Nicholas 1950- 97-100
Dathorne, O(scar) R(onald) 1934- 57-60
Daube, David 1909- CANR-1
Earlier sketch in CA 4R
Daubeny, Peter (Lauderdale) 1921-1975 ...61-64
Dauber, Kenneth Marc 1945- 114
Daudet, Leon 1867-1942 Brief entry 121
Dauenhauer, Richard L(eonard) 1942- .. CANR-11
Earlier sketch in CA 61-64
Dauer, Dorothea W. 1917- 37-40R
Dauer, Manning J(ulian) 1909- 89-92
Dauer, Rosamond 1934- CANR-10
Earlier sketch in CA 65-68
See also SATA 23
Dauer, Victor Paul 1909- 19-20R
Daugert, Stanley M(atthew) 1918- 19-20R
Daughdrill, James H(arold), Jr. 1934- 41-44R
Daughen, Joseph R(obert) 1935- 33-36R
Daugherty, Charles Michael 1914- 73-76
See also SATA 16
Daugherty, James (Henry) 1889-1974 73-76
Obituary 49-52
See also SATA 13
Daugherty, Richard D(eo) 1922- 108
See also SATA 35
Daugherty, Sarah Bowyer 1949- 106
Daugherty, Sonia Medwedeff ?-1971
Obituary 104
See also SATA 27
Daughtrey, Anne Scott 1920- 19-20R
d'Aulaire, Edgar Parin 1898-1986 49-52
Obituary 119
See also SATA 5, 47
See also DLB 22
d'Aulaire, Ingri (Mortenson) 1904-1980 ...49-52
Obituary 102
See also SATA 5, 24
See also DLB 22
Daumal, Rene 1908-1944 Brief entry 114
See also TCLC 14
Dauster, Frank (Nicholas) 1925- 53-56
Dauten, Carl Anton 1913-1976 .... CANR-3
Earlier sketch in CA 5-6R
Dauw, Dean C(harles) 1933- CANR-6
Earlier sketch in CA 53-56
D'Avanzo, Mario Louis 1931- 41-44R
Davar, Ashok 69-72
Dave, Shyam
See Gantzer, Hugh
Daveluy, Paule Cloutier 1919- 9-10R
See also SATA 11
Davenant, William 1606-1668 .... DLB-58
Davenport, Elaine 1946- 102
Davenport, Francine
See Tate, Velma
Davenport, Francis Garvin 1905-1975
Obituary 111
Davenport, Gene L(ooney) 1935- 33-36R
Davenport, Guy (Mattison, Jr.) 1927- .. CANR-23
Earlier sketch in CA 33-36R
See also CLC 6, 14, 38
Davenport, Gwen 1910- 11-12R
Davenport, John 1905-1987 Obituary 122
Davenport, Marcia 1903- 9-10R
Davenport, Robert DLB-58
Davenport, Spencer
See Stratemeyer, Edward L.
Davenport, T(homas) R(odney) H(ope)
1926- 77-80
Davenport, Walter 1889-1971 Obituary 104
Davenport, William H. 1908- CANR-4
Earlier sketch in CA 4R
Daventry, Leonard John 1915- 19-20R
Daves, Delmer Lawrence 1904(?)-1977
Obituary 73-76
See also DLB 26
Daves, Francis Marion 1903- 45-48
Daves, Jessica 1898(?)-1974 Obituary 53-56
Daves, Michael 1938- 9-10R
See also SATA 40
Davey, Cyril J(ames) 1911- CANR-18
Earlier sketches in CA 7-8R, CANR-2
Davey, Frank 1907(?)-1983 Obituary 109
Davey, Frank
See Davey, Frankland Wilmot
See also DLB 53
Davey, Frankland Wilmot 1940- CANR-13
Earlier sketch in CA 65-68
Davey, Gilbert (Walter) 1913- CANR-12
Earlier sketches in CA 9-10, CAP-1
Davey, Harold W(illiam) 1915-1986 120
Davey, Jocelyn
See Raphael, Chaim
Davey, John
See Richey, David
Daviau, Donald G(eorge) 1927- CANR-14
Earlier sketch in CA 81-84
David, A. R.
See David, A(nn) Rosalie
David, A(nn) Rosalie 1946- 114
David, Alfred 1929- 85-88
David, Anne 1924-1987 .... CANR-12
Obituary 122
Earlier sketch in CA 29-32R
David, Carl 1949- 108
David, Ed
See Wohlmuth, Ed
David, Emily
See Alman, David
David, Gerald 1941- 114

David, Heather M(acKinnon) 1937- ... 37-40R
David, Henry 1907-1984 Obituary ... 111
David, Henry P. 1923- ... CANR-6
Earlier sketch in CA 15-16R
David, Irene 1921- ... 110
David, Jack 1946- ... 110
David, Jay
See Adler, William
David, Jonathan
See Ames, Lee J(udah)
David, Joseph Ben
See Ben-David, Joseph
David, Lester 1914- ... CANR-14
Earlier sketch in CA 37-40R
David, Marjorie 1950- ... 112
David, Martin H(eidenhain) 1935- ... 37-40R
David, Michael Robert 1932- ... 53-56
David, Nicholas
See Morgan, Thomas Bruce
David, Paul A(llan) 1935- ... 97-100
David, Paul T(heodore) 1906- ... CANR-2
Earlier sketch in CA 5-6R
David, Rosalie
See David, A(nn) Rosalie
David, Saul 1921- ... 124
Brief entry ... 114
David, Stephen M(ark) 1934-1985 ... 33-36R
Obituary ... 115
David, William
See Sandman, Peter M(ark)
David-Neel, Alexandra 1868-1969
Obituary ... 25-28R
Davidow, Mike 1913- ... 57-60
Davidow-Goodman, Ann
See Goodman, Ann (Davidow)
Davids, Anthony 1923- ... 41-44R
Davids, Bob
See Davids, L(eonard) Robert
Davids, L(eonard) Robert 1926- ... 115
Davids, Lewis Edmund 1917- ... 37-40R
Davids, Richard Carlyle 1913- ... 97-100
Davidson, Abraham A. 1935- ... 53-56
Davidson, Alan Eaton 1924- ... 103
Davidson, Alastair 1939- ... 29-32R
Davidson, Alice Joyce 1932- ... 115
See also SATA 45
Davidson, Angus (Henry Gordon)
1898-1980 ... 25-28R
Obituary ... 97-100
Davidson, Arnold E(dward) 1936- ... 111
Davidson, Avram 1923- ... 101
See also DLB 8
Davidson, Basil 1914- ... CANR-17
Earlier sketches in CA 1R, CANR-1
See also SATA 13
Davidson, Bill
See Davidson, William
Davidson, Bill R.
See Davidson, William R.
Davidson, Caroline 1953- ... 122
Davidson, Cathy Notari 1949- ... CANR-23
Earlier sketch in CA 106
Davidson, Chalmers Gaston 1907- ... 29-32R
Davidson, Chandler 1936- ... 45-48
Davidson, Clarissa Start
See Lippert, Clarissa Start
Davidson, Clifford 1932- ... 45-48
Davidson, David 1908-1985 ... 49-52
Obituary ... 117
Davidson, Diane 1924- ... 29-32R
Davidson, Donald (Grady) 1893-1968 ... CANR-4
Obituary ... 25-28R
Earlier sketch in CA 7-8R
See also DLB 45
See also CLC 2, 13, 19
Davidson, Donald 1917- ... CANR-2
Earlier sketch in CA 45-48
Davidson, E(phraim) E(dward) 1923- ... 33-36R
Davidson, Ellen Prescott ... 49-52
Davidson, Eugene (Arthur) 1902- ... CANR-3
Earlier sketch in CA 3R
Davidson, Eva Rucker 1894(?)-1974
Obituary ... 53-56
Davidson, F(rank) G(eoffrey) 1920- ... 29-32R
Davidson, Frank P(aul) 1918- ... 116
Davidson, Glen W(illiam) 1936- ... CANR-9
Earlier sketch in CA 61-64
Davidson, Gustav 1895-1971 Obituary ... 29-32R
Davidson, H(ilda) R(oderick) Ellis
1914- ... CANR-11
Earlier sketch in CA 17-18R
Davidson, Harold G(ordon) 1912- ... 65-68
Davidson, Henry A(lexander) 1905-1973
Obituary ... 45-48
Davidson, Herbert A(lan) 1932- ... 19-20R
Davidson, Hugh
See Hamilton, Edmond
Davidson, Hugh M(acCullough) 1918- ... 102
Davidson, Irwin Delmore 1906-1981
Obituary ... 105
Davidson, James Dale 1947- ... 107
Davidson, James West 1946- ... CANR-15
Earlier sketch in CA 85-88
Davidson, Jeffrey P(hilip) 1951- ... 122
Davidson, Jessica 1915- ... CANR-14
Earlier sketch in CA 41-44R
See also SATA 5
Davidson, John 1857-1909 Brief entry ... 118
See also DLB 19
See also TCLC 24
Davidson, John
See Reid, Charles (Stuart)
Davidson, John Wells 1903-1986
Obituary ... 120
Davidson, Judith 1953- ... 116
See also SATA 40
Davidson, Julian M. 1931- ... 102
Davidson, Lionel 1922- ... CANR-1
Earlier sketch in CA 4R
See also DLB 14
Davidson, Margaret 1936- ... CANR-17
Earlier sketch in CA 25-28R
See also SATA 5
Davidson, Marion
See Garis, Howard Roger
Davidson, Marshall B(owman) 1907- ... 33-36R
Davidson, Mary R. 1885-1973 ... 5-6R
See also SATA 9
Davidson, Mary S. 1940- ... 107
Davidson, Max D. 1899(?)-1977
Obituary ... 73-76
Davidson, Michael 1944- ... 106
Davidson, Michael
See Rorvik, David M(ichael)
Davidson, Michael Childers 1897- ... 29-32R
Davidson, Mickie
See Davidson, Margaret
Davidson, Mildred 1935- ... 93-96
Davidson, Morris 1898-1979 ... 85-88
Davidson, Muriel 1924(?)-1983 Obituary ... 110
Davidson, Norman 1933- ... 119
Davidson, Paul 1930- ... CANR-6
Earlier sketch in CA 13-14R
Davidson, Philip (Grant) 1902- ... 73-76
Davidson, R.
See Davidson, Raymond
Davidson, Raymond 1926- ... SATA-32
Davidson, Robert F(ranklin) 1902- ... 49-52
Davidson, Roger H(arry) 1936- ... CANR-24
Earlier sketches in CA 21-22R, CANR-9
Davidson, Rosalie 1921- ... 69-72
See also SATA 23
Davidson, Sandra Calder 1935- ... 41-44R
Davidson, Sara 1943- ... 81-84
See also CLC 9
Davidson, Sol M. 1924- ... 17-18R
Davidson, William 1918- ... 93-96
Davidson, William R. 1929(?)-1987
Obituary ... 122
Davidson, William Robert 1919- ... 19-20R
Davidson-Houston, J(ames) Vivian
1901-1965 ... 7-8R
Davie, Donald (Alfred) 1922- ... CANR-1
Earlier sketch in CA 3R
See also CAAS 3
See also DLB 27
See also CLC 5, 8, 10, 31
Davie, Elspeth Brief entry ... 120
Davie, Ian 1924- ... 102
Davie, Maurice R(ea) 1893-1964 ... 7-8R
Davie, Michael 1924- ... 57-60
Davie, Peter (Edward Sidney) 1936- ... 114
Davied, Camille
See Rose, Camille Davied
Davie-Martin, Hugh
See McCutcheon, Hugh Davie-Martin
Davies, A(lfred) Mervyn 1899-1976 ... 17-18R
Obituary ... 69-72
Davies, Ada Hilton 1893- ... CAP-2
Earlier sketch in CA 17-18
Davies, Alan T(rewartha) 1933- ... 33-36R
Davies, Alfred T(homas) 1930- ... 15-16R
Davies, Andrew (Wynford) 1936- ... 105
See also SATA 27
Davies, Bettilu D(onna) 1942- ... CANR-18
Earlier sketch in CA 101
See also SATA 33
Davies, Christie
See Davies, John Christopher Hughes
Davies, Colin
See Elliot, Ian
Davies, (George) Colliss (Boardman)
1912- ... CAP-1
Earlier sketch in CA 11-12
Davies, D(avid) Jacob 1916-1974 ... 7-8R
Obituary ... 103
Davies, Daniel R. 1911- ... 37-40R
Davies, David Margerison 1923- ... 7-8R
Davies, David Michael 1929- Brief entry ... 109
Davies, David W(illiam) 1908- ... CANR-3
Earlier sketch in CA 9-10R
Davies, Duncan (Sheppey) 1921-1987 ... 124
Obituary ... 122
Davies, Ebenezer Thomas 1903- ... CAP-1
Earlier sketch in CA 13-14
Davies, Eileen Winifred 1910- ... CAP-1
Earlier sketch in CA 13-14
Davies, Evelyn 1924- ... CANR-8
Earlier sketch in CA 61-64
Davies, Evelyn A(dele) 1915- ... 61-64
Davies, Harriet Vaughn 1879(?)-1978
Obituary ... 77-80
Davies, Horton (Marlais) 1916- ... CANR-7
Earlier sketch in CA 5-6R
Davies, Hugh Sykes 1909-1984(?)
Obituary ... 113
Davies, Hunter 1936- ... CANR-12
Earlier sketch in CA 57-60
See also SATA 45
Davies, (David) Ioan 1936- ... 21-22R
Davies, Ivor K(evin) 1930- ... 53-56
Davies, J. Clarence III 1937- ... 29-32R
Davies, J. Kenneth 1925- ... 57-60
Davies, James Chowning 1918- ... 45-48
Davies, Joan 1934- ... 124
See also SATA 47, 50
Davies, John Christopher Hughes 1941- ... 93-96
Davies, John Evan Weston 1914- ... 113
Brief entry ... 111
Davies, John Gordon 1919- ... 69-72
Davies, John K(enyon) 1937- ... 120
Davies, John Paton, Jr. 1908- ... 11-12R
Davies, L(eslie) P(urnell) 1914- ... CANR-9
Earlier sketch in CA 21-22R
Davies, Laurence 1926- ... 57-60
Davies, Mansel Morris 1913- ... 9-10R
Davies, Margaret C(onstance Brown)
1923- ... 9-10R
Davies, Margaret Lloyd 1935- ... 106
Davies, Marion
See Douras, Marion Cecilia
Davies, Martin Brett 1936- ... 102
Davies, Merton E(dward) 1917- ... 85-88
Davies, Morton Rees 1939- ... 37-40R
Davies, (Claude) Nigel (Byam) 1920- ... CANR-19
Earlier sketch in CA 102
Earlier sketch in CA 9-10R
Davies, Norman 1939- ... 41-44R
Davies, Oliver 1905- ... CAP-2
Earlier sketch in CA 25-28
Davies, P.C.W.
See Davies, Paul (Charles William)
Davies, Paul (Charles William) 1946- ... 106
Davies, (William Thomas) Pennar 1911- ... 13-14R
Davies, Peter 1937- ... 53-56
Davies, Piers (Anthony David) 1941- ... 103
Davies, R(onald) E. G. 1921- ... 17-18R
Davies, R(eginald) T(horne) 1923- ... 9-10R
Davies, R(obert) W(illiam) 1925- ... CANR-13
Earlier sketch in CA 33-36R
Davies, Ray(mond Douglas) 1944-
Brief entry ... 116
See also CLC 21
Davies, Rhys 1903-1978 ... CANR-4
Obituary ... 81-84
Earlier sketch in CA 9-10R
See also CLC 23
Davies, Richard Llewelyn
See Llewelyn-Davies, Richard
Davies, Richard O. 1937- ... 19-20R
Davies, (William) Robertson 1913- ... CANR-17
Earlier sketch in CA 33-36R
See also CLC 2, 7, 13, 25, 42
Davies, Rod 1941- ... 61-64
Davies, Rosemary Reeves 1925- ... 49-52
Davies, Rupert Eric 1909- ... CANR-18
Earlier sketches in CA 5-6R, CANR-3
Davies, Ruth A(nn) 1915- ... 29-32R
Davies, Samuel 1723-1761 ... DLB-31
Davies, Stan Gebler 1943- ... 65-68
Davies, Stanley Powell 1892-1985
Obituary ... 115
Davies, Stevan L(awrence) 1948- ... 107
Davies, Sumiko 1942- ... SATA-46
Davies, T(refor) Rendall 1913- ... CAP-1
Earlier sketch in CA 9-10
Davies, Thomas 1941- ... 115
Davies, Thomas M(ockett), Jr. 1940- ... CANR-6
Earlier sketch in CA 57-60
Davies, Tom
See Davies, Thomas
Davies, W(illiam) H(enry) 1871-1940
Brief entry ... 104
See also DLB 19
See also TCLC 5
Davies, Walter C.
See Kornbluth, C(yril) M.
Davies, William David 1911- ... CANR-1
Earlier sketch in CA 1R
Davies, Wyndham (Roy) 1926- ... 25-28R
Davin, D(aniel) M(arcus) 1913- ... CANR-3
Earlier sketch in CA 9-10R
Davinson, Donald E(dward) 1932- ... CANR-3
Earlier sketch in CA 7-8R
Daviot, Gordon
See Mackintosh, Elizabeth
See also DLB 10
Davis, Adelle 1904-1974 ... 37-40R
Obituary ... 49-52
Davis, Allen F(reeman) 1931- ... CANR-10
Earlier sketch in CA 23-24R
Davis, Allen III 1929- ... 108
Davis, Allison 1902-1983 Obituary ... 111
Brief entry ... 106
Davis, Andrew Jackson 1826-1910
Brief entry ... 120
Davis, Angela (Yvonne) 1944- ... CANR-10
Earlier sketch in CA 57-60
Davis, Ann E(lizabeth) 1932- ... 69-72
Davis, Archie K. 1911- ... 124
Davis, Arthur G. 1915- ... 15-16R
Davis, Arthur Hoey 1868-1935 Brief entry ... 121
Davis, Arthur Kennard 1910- ... CAP-1
Earlier sketch in CA 13-14
Davis, Arthur Kyle, Jr. 1897-19(?) ... CAP-2
Earlier sketch in CA 17-18
Davis, Arthur P(aul) 1904- ... 61-64
Davis, Audrey
See Paine, Lauran (Bosworth)
Davis, Barbara 1955- ... 108
Davis, Barbara Kerr 1946- ... 104
Davis, Ben Reeves 1927- ... 77-80
Davis, (Mary) Bernice
See Curler, (Mary) Bernice
Davis, Berrie 1922- ... 101
Davis, Bertram H(ylton) 1918- ... CANR-1
Earlier sketch in CA 4R
Davis, Bette
See Davis, Ruth Elizabeth
Davis, Bette J. 1923- ... 93-96
See also SATA 15
Davis, Bill C. 1951- ... 110
Davis, Burke 1913- ... CANR-4
Earlier sketch in CA 1R
See also SATA 4
Davis, Calvin DeArmond 1927- ... 5-6R
Davis, Charles 1923- ... CANR-21
Earlier sketch in CA 5-6R
Davis, Charles A. 1795-1867 ... DLB-11
Davis, Charles T(ill) 1929- ... 37-40R
Davis, Christopher 1928- ... CANR-3
Earlier sketch in CA 9-10R
See also SATA 6
Davis, Cliff
See Smith, Richard Rein
Davis, Clive E(dward) 1914- ... 17-18R
Davis, Clyde Brion 1894-1962 ... 5-6R
See also DLB 9
Davis, Creath 1939- ... CANR-21
Earlier sketches in CA 57-60, CANR-6
Davis, Curtis Carroll 1916- ... CANR-6
Earlier sketch in CA 9-10R
Davis, Curtis Wheeler 1928-1986 Obituary ... 119
Davis, D(elbert) Dwight 1908-1965
Obituary ... 111
See also SATA 33
Davis, D(onald) Evan 1923-1979 ... 19-20R
Obituary ... 122
Davis, Daniel S(heldon) 1936- ... 45-48
See also SATA 12
Davis, Daphne ... 65-68
Davis, David Brion 1927- ... CANR-9
Earlier sketch in CA 19-20R
Davis, David C(harles) L. 1928- ... 33-36R
Davis, David Howard 1941- ... 53-56
Davis, Deane C(handler) 1900- ... 108
Davis, Dick 1945- ... DLB-40
Davis, Don
See Dresser, Davis
Davis, Donald Gordon, Jr. 1939- ... CANR-6
Earlier sketch in CA 53-56
Davis, Dorothy Salisbury 1916- ... CANR-14
Earlier sketch in CA 37-40R
Davis, Douglas (Matthew) 1933- ... 111
Davis, Douglas F(redell) 1935- ... 105
Davis, E. Adams
See Davis, Edwin Adams
Davis, Earl C(linton) 1938- ... 111
Davis, Earle (Rosco) 1905- ... 65-68
Davis, Edwin Adams 1904- ... CAP-2
Earlier sketch in CA 25-28
Davis, Eleanor Harmon 1909- ... 106
Davis, Elise Miller 1915- ... 69-72
Davis, Elizabeth
See Davis, Lou Ellen
Davis, Elizabeth G. 1910(?)-1974
Obituary ... 53-56
Davis, Elwood Craig 1896- ... CANR-3
Earlier sketch in CA 1R
Davis, F(loyd) James 1920- ... CANR-4
Earlier sketch in CA 3R
Davis, Fitzroy K. 1912-1980 ... 49-52
Obituary ... 102
Davis, Flora 1934- ... CANR-10
Earlier sketch in CA 65-68
Davis, Forest K(endall) 1918- ... 41-44R
Davis, Francis 1946- ... 123
Davis, Frank G(reene) 1915- ... 85-88
Davis, Frank Marshall 1905-1987 Obituary ... 123
See also DLB 51
Davis, Franklin M(ilton), Jr. 1918-1981 ... CANR-4
Earlier sketch in CA 3R
Davis, Fred 1925- ... 13-14R
Davis, Frederick Barton 1909-1975 ... CANR-17
Obituary ... 116
Earlier sketch in CA 3R
Davis, Frederick C(lyde) 1902-1977
Obituary ... 115
Davis, Garold N(eil) 1932- ... 41-44R
Davis, Gary A(lan) 1938- ... 106
Davis, Genevieve 1928- ... 65-68
Davis, Genny Wright 1948- ... 105
Davis, George 1939- ... CANR-9
Earlier sketch in CA 65-68
Davis, George L(ittleton), Sr. 1921- ... 57-60
Davis, Gerry 1930- Brief entry ... 117
Davis, Gibbs 1953- ... 111
See also SATA 41, 46
Davis, Gil
See Gilmore, Don
Davis, Gilbert 1899-1983 Obituary ... 109
Davis, Gordon
See Hunt, E(verette) Howard, Jr.
and Levinson, Leonard
Davis, Gordon B(itter) 1930- ... CANR-4
Earlier sketch in CA 53-56
Davis, Grania 1943- ... CANR-16
Earlier sketch in CA 85-88
See also SATA 50
Davis, Grant Miller 1937- ... CANR-11
Earlier sketch in CA 29-32R
Davis, Gwen 1936- ... CANR-2
Earlier sketch in CA 3R
See also AITN 1
Davis, H(enry) Grady 1890- ... CAP-2
Earlier sketch in CA 21-22
Davis, Harley
See Green, Kay
Davis, Harold Eugene 1902- ... CANR-1
Earlier sketch in CA 3R
Davis, Harold Lenoir 1896-1960 Obituary ... 89-92
See also DLB 9
Davis, Harold S(eaton) 1919- ... 57-60
Davis, Harriet Eager 1892(?)-1974
Obituary ... 49-52
Davis, Harry Rex 1921- ... 3R
Davis, Henry P. 1894(?)-1970 Obituary ... 104
Davis, Herbert (John) 1893-1967 ... CANR-1
Earlier sketch in CA 3R
Davis, Hope Hale ... 25-28R
Davis, Hope Harding 1915(?)-1976
Obituary ... 69-72
Davis, Horace B(ancroft) 1898- ... 23-24R
Davis, Horance G(ibbs), Jr. 1924- ... 65-68
Davis, Howard V(aughn) 1915- ... 25-28R
Davis, Hubert J(ackson) 1904- ... 107
See also SATA 31

Davis, I(rene) M(ary) 1926- 61-64
Davis, J(ohn) Cary 1905- 41-44R
Davis, J. Morton 1929- 124
Davis, J(ames) William 1908- 102
Davis, Jack Leonard 1917- 106
Davis, James Allan 1929- CANR-1
Earlier sketch in CA 1R
Davis, James C(urran) 1895-1981
Obituary 108
Davis, James C(ushman) 1931-
Brief entry 117
Davis, James H. 1932- 89-92
Davis, James Kotsilibas
See Kotsilibas-Davis, James
Davis, James Richard 1936- 65-68
Davis, James Robert 1945- CANR-16
Earlier sketch in CA 85-88
See also SATA 32
Davis, James W(arren, Jr.) 1935- 29-32R
Davis, Jan Haddle 1950- 93-96
Davis, Jean Reynolds 1927- 61-64
Davis, Jean Walton 1909- 3R
Davis, Jed H(orace, Jr.) 1921- 17-18R
Davis, Jerome 1891-1979 .... CANR-3
Obituary 89-92
Earlier sketch in CA 5-6R
Davis, Jim
See Davis, James Robert
and Smith, Richard Rein
Davis, Jinnie Y(eh) 1945- 107
Davis, Joe 1901-1978 Obituary 112
Davis, Joe Lee 1906-1974 ....5-6R
Obituary 103
Davis, Johanna 1937-1974 ....41-44R
Obituary 53-56
Davis, John 1774-1854 .... DLB-37
Davis, John D(avid) 1937- 29-32R
Davis, John H(erbert) 1904- 29-32R
Davis, John H. 1929- CANR-18
Earlier sketch in CA 25-28R
Davis, John J(ames) 1936- 33-36R
Davis, John King 1884-1967 .... CAP-1
Earlier sketch in CA 9-10
Davis, Joseph C(ole) 1908- 97-100
Davis, Joseph S(tancliffe) 1885-1975 101
Obituary 57-60
Davis, Judith 1925- 106
Davis, Julia 1900- CANR-1
Earlier sketch in CA 4R
See also SATA 6
Davis, Julian 1902(?)-1974 Obituary 53-56
Davis, K(eith) 1918- CANR-20
Earlier sketches in CA 4R, CANR-5
Davis, Karen Padgett 1942- 112
Davis, Keith F. 1952- 123
Davis, Ken(neth Pickett) 1906- 49-52
Davis, Kenneth Culp 1908- Brief entry 115
Davis, Kenneth R(exton) 1921- 19-20R
Davis, Kenneth S. 1912- 15-16R
Davis, Kingsley 1908- CANR-8
Earlier sketch in CA 15-16R
Davis, L(awrence) J(ames) 1940- CANR-11
Earlier sketch in CA 25-28R
Davis, Lance E(dwin) 1928- 53-56
Davis, Lanny J(esse) 1945- 57-60
Davis, Lawrence B(ennion) 1939- 45-48
Davis, Lennard J. 1949- 116
Davis, Lenwood G. 1939- 25-28R
Davis, Lew A(rter) 1930- 21-22R
Davis, Lloyd (Moore) 1931- 69-72
Davis, Lou Ellen 1936- 81-84
Davis, Louis E(lkin) 1918- 53-56
Davis, Louise Littleton 1921- 103
See also SATA 25
Davis, Loyal Edward 1896-1982 Obituary 107
Davis, Luther 1921- 105
Davis, M(orris) Edward 1899- 7-8R
Davis, Maggie (Hill) CANR-9
Earlier sketch in CA 15-16R
Davis, Maralee G.
See Gibson, Maralee G.
Davis, Marc 1934- 29-32R
Davis, Margaret Banfield 1903- CAP-1
Earlier sketch in CA 11-12
Davis, Margaret Thomson 1926- 102
See also DLB 14
Davis, Marguerite 1889- SATA-34
Davis, Marilyn K(ornreich) 1928- 5-6R
Davis, Martha 1942- CANR-4
Earlier sketch in CA 49-52
Davis, Mary L(ee) 1935- CANR-4
Earlier sketch in CA 49-52
See also SATA 9
Davis, Mary Octavia 1901- CAP-2
Earlier sketch in CA 25-28
See also SATA 6
Davis, Maxine
See McHugh, Maxine Davis
Davis, Melodie M(iller) 1951- 113
Davis, Melton S(amillow) 1910- 41-44R
Davis, (John) Michael 1940- 33-36R
Davis, Michael Justin 1925- 102
Davis, Mildred 77-80
Davis, Mildred Ann (Campbell) 1916- 5-6R
Davis, Millard C. 1930- 69-72
Davis, Monte 1949- 103
Davis, Morris 1933- CANR-11
Earlier sketch in CA 61-64
Davis, Morton D(avid) 1930- 65-68
Davis, Moshe 1916- CANR-20
Earlier sketches in CA 9-10R, CANR-4
Davis, Murray S(tuart) 1940- 53-56
Davis, Myrna (Mushkin) 1936- 69-72
Davis, Natalie Zemon 1928- 53-56
Davis, Neil 1934(?)-1985 Obituary 117
Davis, Neil
See Davis, T(homas) Neil
Davis, Nolan 1942- 49-52
Davis, Norah Deakin 1941- 111
Davis, Norman 1913- Brief entry 106
Davis, Norman Maurice 1936- 69-72
Davis, Nuel Pharr 1915- 29-32R
Davis, Olivia 1922- 81-84
Davis, Ossie 1917- 112
See also DLB 7, 38
Davis, Patrick (David Channer) 1925- 93-96
Davis, Paxton 1925- CANR-3
Earlier sketch in CA 9-10R
See also SATA 16
Davis, Peter (Frank) 1937- 107
Davis, Philip E(dward) 1927- 49-52
Davis, Philip J. 1923- 124
Davis, Polly Ann 1931- 102
Davis, R. G. 1933- 57-60
Davis, R(alph) H(enry) C(arless) 1918- CANR-6
Earlier sketch in CA 7-8R
Davis, Ralph C(urrier) 1894- 33-36R
Davis, Rebecca (Blaine) Harding
1831-1910 Brief entry 104
See also TCLC 6
Davis, Rex D. 1924- 11-12R
Davis, Richard CANR-7
Earlier sketch in CA 53-56
Davis, Richard Beale 1907- CANR-2
Earlier sketch in CA 5-6R
Davis, Richard Harding 1864-1916
Brief entry 114
See also DLB 12, 23
See also TCLC 24
Davis, Richard W. 1935- 33-36R
Davis, Robert 1881-1949 .... YABC-1
Davis, Robert Con 1948- CANR-23
Earlier sketch in CA 104
Davis, Robert Murray 1934- CANR-12
Earlier sketch in CA 33-36R
Davis, Robert P. 1929- CANR-3
Earlier sketch in CA 7-8R
Davis, Robert Ralph, Jr. 1941- 37-40R
Davis, Rocky 1927- 61-64
Davis, Ronald L(eroy) 1936- 37-40R
Davis, Rosemary 7-8R
Davis, Rosemary L.
See Davis, Rosemary
Davis, Roy Eugene 1931- CANR-6
Earlier sketch in CA 11-12R
Davis, Rupert (Charles) Hart
See Hart-Davis, Rupert (Charles)
Davis, Russell Gerard 1922- 7-8R
See also SATA 3
Davis, Ruth Elizabeth 1908- CANR-21
Earlier sketch in CA 61-64
Davis, Sammy, Jr. 1925- 108
Davis, Samuel 1930- 29-32R
Davis, Samuel Cole 1764-1809 .... DLB-37
Davis, Sandra T. W. 1937- 124
Davis, Stanley Nelson 1924- 108
Davis, Steven Andrew 1947- 112
Davis, Stratford
See Bolton, Maisie Sharman
Davis, Suzanne
See Sugar, Bert Randolph
Davis, Sydney Charles Houghton 1887- 7-8R
Davis, Sylvan 1927(?)-1984 Obituary 112
Davis, T. N.
See Davis, T(homas) Neil
Davis, T(homas) Neil 1932- 123
Davis, Terence 1924- 21-22R
Davis, Thomas J(oseph) 1946- CANR-4
Earlier sketch in CA 53-56
Davis, Timothy Francis Tothill 1941- 81-84
Davis, Tom Edward 1929- 85-88
Davis, Verne Theodore 1889-1973 .... 4R
See also SATA 6
Davis, (Benton) Vincent (Jr.) 1930- CANR-23
Earlier sketches in CA 19-20R, CANR-7
Davis, W(illiam) Jackson 1942- 107
Davis, W(arren) Jefferson 1885-1973 .... CAP-2
Earlier sketch in CA 29-32
Davis, W(illiam) N(ewell), Jr. 1915- 81-84
Davis, Walter A(lbert III) 1942- 114
Davis, Walter Richardson 1928- 102
Davis, Wayne H(arry) 1930- 33-36R
Davis, Wiley H. 1913- 25-28R
Davis, William 1933- CANR-10
Earlier sketch in CA 65-68
Davis, William C(harles) 1946- CANR-23
Earlier sketches in CA 61-64, CANR-8
Davis, William H(atcher) 1939- 33-36R
Davis, William S(terling) 1943- 111
Davis, William Virgil 1940- CANR-23
Earlier sketch in CA 106
Davis, Winston (Bradley) 1939- 104
Davis-Friedmann, Deborah 1945- 118
Davis-Gardner, Angela 1942- 110
Davis-Goff, Annabel 1942- 85-88
Davison, Edward 1898-1970 Obituary 29-32R
Davison, Frank Dalby 1893-1970 Obituary 116
See also CLC 15
Davison, Geoffrey 1927- 110
Davison, Gladys Patton 1905- CAP-1
Earlier sketch in CA 15-16
Davison, Jane 1932(?)-1981 Obituary 104
Davison, Jean 1937- CANR-10
Earlier sketch in CA 65-68
Davison, Kenneth E(dwin) 1924- 11-12R
Davison, Lawrence H.
See Lawrence, D(avid) H(erbert Richards)
Davison, Ned J. 1926- 45-48
Davison, Peter 1928- CANR-3
Earlier sketch in CA 9-10R
See also CAAS 4
See also DLB 5
See also CLC 28
Davison, Roderic H(ollett) 1916- 37-40R
Davison, Verne E(lbert) 1904- 69-72
Davisson, Charles Nelson 1917- 25-28R
Davisson, William I. 1929- CANR-11
Earlier sketch in CA 19-20R
Davis-Weyer, Caecilia 1929- 41-44R
Davitt, Thomas E(dward) 1904-1980 ....25-28R
Obituary 117
Davitz, Joel R(obert) 1926- Brief entry 114
Davy, Francis X(avier) 1916- 29-32R
Davy, George Mark Oswald 1898-1983
Obituary 110
Davy, John Charles 1927-1984 Obituary 114
Davys, Mary 1674-1732 .... DLB-39
Dawdy, Doris Ostrander 53-56
Dawe, (Donald) Bruce 1930- CANR-11
Earlier sketch in CA 69-72
Dawe, Donald G. 1926- 33-36R
Dawe, Frederick
See Gettings, Fred
Dawe, (Chartres) Gerald 1952- 114
Dawe, Roger David 1934- CANR-3
Earlier sketch in CA 11-12R
Dawes, Dorothy
See Cooper, Parley J(oseph)
Dawes, Frank 1933- 69-72
Dawes, Nathaniel Thomas, Jr. 1937- 49-52
Dawes, Neville 1926- 13-14R
Dawes, Robyn M(ason) 1936- 37-40R
Dawidowicz, Lucy S. 1915- CANR-18
Earlier sketch in CA 25-28R
Dawis, Rene V(illaneuva) 1928- 45-48
Dawisha, Adeed Isam 1944- CANR-18
Earlier sketch in CA 102
Dawisha, Karen (Lea) 1949- 120
Dawkins, Cecil 1927- 7-8R
Dawkins, Richard 1941- 69-72
Dawley, David 1941- 45-48
Dawley, Powel Mills 1907- 57-60
Dawlish, Peter
See Kerr, James Lennox
Dawn, C(larence) Ernest 1918- 61-64
Dawood, N(essim) J(oseph) 1927- 49-52
Dawson, Alan David 1942- 77-80
Dawson, Carl 1938- CANR-1
Earlier sketch in CA 45-48
Dawson, Christopher (Henry)
1889-1970 .... CANR-6
Obituary 29-32R
Earlier sketch in CA 3R
Dawson, Elizabeth
See Geach, Christine
Dawson, Elmer A. CAP-2
Earlier sketch in CA 19-20
See also SATA 1
Dawson, Fielding 1930- 85-88
See also CLC 6
Dawson, Frank G(ates, Jr.) 1925- 69-72
Dawson, George G(lenn) 1925- 37-40R
Dawson, Giles E(dwin) 1903- CAP-2
Earlier sketch in CA 19-20
Dawson, Grace S(trickler) 1891- 17-18R
Dawson, Howard A. 1895(?)-1979
Obituary 89-92
Dawson, Jan 1939(?)-1980 Obituary 101
Dawson, Jennifer CANR-10
Earlier sketch in CA 57-60
Dawson, Jerry F. 1933- 33-36R
Dawson, Joseph G(reen) III 1945- 110
Dawson, Mary 1919- 21-22R
See also SATA 11
Dawson, Mildred A(gnes) 1897- CANR-12
Earlier sketch in CA 17-18R
Dawson, Minnie E. 1906-1978 85-88
Dawson, Peter
See Faust, Frederick (Shiller)
Dawson, (John) Philip 1928- 21-22R
Dawson, Richard E(vans) 1939- 73-76
Dawson, Robert (Merril) 1941- 21-22R
Dawson, Robert L(ewis) 1943- 105
Dawson, William 1704-1752 .... DLB-31
Dawson-Scott, C(atharine) A(my)
1865-1934 Brief entry 113
Day, A(rthur) Grove 1904- CANR-23
Earlier sketches in CA 21-22R, CANR-8
Day, Alan Charles Lynn 1924- 1R
Day, Alan J(ohn) 1942- 105
Day, Albert Edward 1884-1973 .... CAP-2
Obituary 45-48
Earlier sketch in CA 23-24
Day, Albert M. 1897-1979 93-96
Obituary 85-88
Day, Alice Taylor 1928- 19-20R
Day, Benjamin Henry 1810-1889 .... DLB-43
Day, Beth (Feagles) 1924- CANR-18
Earlier sketches in CA 9-10R, CANR-3
See also SATA 33
Day, Bradford M(arshall) 1916- 104
Day, Clarence (Shepard, Jr.) 1874-1935
Brief entry 108
See also DLB 11
See also TCLC 25
Day, Clarence Burton 1889-1987 Obituary 121
Day, David 1944- 93-96
Day, Donald
See Harding, Donald Edward
Day, Dorothy 1897-1980 65-68
Obituary 102
See also DLB 29
Day, Douglas (Turner III) 1932- CANR-8
Earlier sketch in CA 9-10R
Day, Gardiner Mumford 1900-1981
Obituary 104
Day, George 1950- 117
Day, George Harold 1900- CAP-1
Earlier sketch in CA 13-14
Day, Gwynn McLendon 1908- CAP-1
Earlier sketch in CA 11-12
Day, Houston
See Day, Sam Houston
Day, J(ames) Edward 1914- 17-18R
Day, J(ohn) Laurence 1934- 65-68
Day, James F(rancis) 1917- 33-36R
Day, James Wentworth 1899-1983(?) CANR-10
Obituary 108
Earlier sketch in CA 13-14R
Day, John 1574(?)-1640(?) DLB-62
Day, John A(rthur) 1913- 17-18R
Day, John Patrick 1919- 7-8R
Day, John R(obert) 1917- CANR-9
Earlier sketch in CA 7-8R
Day, Kenneth 1912- 11-12R
Day, LeRoy Judson 1917- 23-24R
Day, Lincoln H(ubert) 1928- 19-20R
Day, Lucille 1947- 110
Day, M(ichael) H(erbert) 1927- 102
Day, Martin Steele 1917- CANR-7
Earlier sketch in CA 5-6R
Day, Maurice 1892- SATA-30
Day, Max
See Cassiday, Bruce (Bingham)
Day, Melvin Norman 1923- 109
Day, Michael
See Dempewolff, Richard F(rederic)
Day, Nancy Raines 1951- 111
Day, (Truman) Owen 1890- 69-72
Day, Paul Woodford 1916- 25-28R
Day, Peter (Morton) 1914- 1R
Day, Price 1907-1978 85-88
Obituary 81-84
Day, R(oss) H(enry) 1927- 29-32R
Day, Ralph L(ewis) 1926- CANR-7
Earlier sketch in CA 7-8R
Day, Richard B(ruce) 1942- 49-52
Day, Richard E. 1929- 33-36R
Day, Richard Hollis 1933- 114
Day, Robert Adams 1924- 53-56
Day, Sam Houston 1896-1984 Obituary 113
Day, Stacey B(iswas) 1927- 33-36R
Day, Thomas 1748-1789 .... YABC-1
See also DLB 39
Dayan, Moshe 1915-1981 .... CANR-22
Obituary 105
Earlier sketch in CA 23-24R
Dayan, Yael 1939- 89-92
See also AITN 1
Dayananda, James Yesupriya 1934- 81-84
Day Lewis, C(ecil) 1904-1972 .... CAP-1
Obituary 33-36R
Earlier sketch in CA 15-16
See also DLB 15, 20
See also CLC 1, 6, 10
Daynes, Byron W(ilford) 1937- 110
Daysh, G(eorge) H(enry) J(ohn)
1901-1987 Obituary 122
Dayton, Donald W(ilber) 1942- CANR-24
Earlier sketch in CA 69-72
Dayton, Edward R(isedorph) 1924- CANR-16
Earlier sketch in CA 85-88
Dayton, Eldorous L. 1906-1987 Obituary 122
Dayton, Irene 1922- CANR-6
Earlier sketch in CA 57-60
Dazai, Osamu
See Tsushima, Shuji
See also TCLC 11
d'Azevedo, Warren L. 1920- 93-96
Dazey, Agnes J(ohnston) CAP-2
Earlier sketch in CA 23-24
See also SATA 2
Dazey, Frank M. CAP-2
Earlier sketch in CA 23-24
See also SATA 2
Deacon, Eileen
See Geipel, Eileen
Deacon, George Edward Raven 1906-1984
Obituary 114
Deacon, Joseph John 1920- 69-72
Deacon, Richard 1922-1984 Obituary 113
Deacon, Richard
See McCormick, (George) Donald (King)
Deacon, Ruth E. 1923- 102
Deacon, William Arthur 1890-1964
Obituary 89-92
Deagon, Ann (Fleming) 1930- 57-60
Deak, Edward Joseph, Jr. 1943- 53-56
Deak, Francis 1899-1972 Obituary 33-36R
Deak, Istvan 1926- CANR-11
Earlier sketch in CA 25-28R
Deakin, Frederick William 1913- CANR-5
Earlier sketch in CA 7-8R
Deakin, James 1929- CANR-24
Earlier sketches in CA 21-22R, CANR-8
Deakin, Motley F. 1920- 120
Deakin, Rose 1937- 109
Deakins, Roger Lee 1933- 61-64
Deal, Babs H(odges) 1929- CANR-1
Earlier sketch in CA 1R
Deal, Borden 1922-1985 .... CANR-2
Obituary 114
Earlier sketch in CA 4R
See also DLB 6
Deal, William S(anford) 1910- CANR-3
Earlier sketch in CA 7-8R
Deale, Kenneth Edwin Lee 1907-19(?) CANR-4
Earlier sketch in CA 7-8R
Dealey, E(dward) M(usgrove) 1892-1969 .... CAP-2
Earlier sketch in CA 23-24
Dealey, Ted
See Dealey, E(dward) M(usgrove)
deAlmeida, Hermione (Beatrice) 1950- 118
Dean, Abner 1910-1982 Obituary 107
Dean, Amber 1902-1985 .... CANR-2
Obituary 116
Earlier sketch in CA 5-6R

Dean, Anabel 1915- ... CANR-14
Earlier sketch in CA 37-40R
See also SATA 12
Dean, Barbara 1946- ... 113
Dean, Basil 1888- ... 69-72
Dean, Beryl 1911- ... 9-10R
Dean, Burton V(ictor) 1924- ... CANR-20
Earlier sketches in CA 45-48, CANR-1
Dean, Christopher G(eorge) 1940- ... 111
Dean, Dorothy 1932(?)-1987 Obituary ... 121
Dean, Dwight G(antz) 1918- ... 17-18R
Dean, E. Douglas 1916- ... 97-100
Dean, Edith M(ae) 1915- ... 111
Dean, Edwin R(obinson) 1933- ... 17-18R
Dean, Frances Mary 1905(?)-1983
Obituary ... 110
Dean, Herbert Morris 1938- ... 105
Dean, Howard E(dward) 1916- ... 41-44R
Dean, Ida
See Grae, Ida
Dean, Jeffrey S. 1939- ... 37-40R
Dean, (Alfreda) Joan 1925- ... 101
Dean, Joan FitzPatrick 1949- ... 118
Dean, Joel 1906- ... 33-36R
Dean, John
See Bumppo, Nathaniel John Balthazar
Dean, John A(urie) 1921- ... 53-56
Dean, John Wesley III 1938- ... 105
Dean, Karen Strickler 1923- ... 109
See also SATA 49
Dean, Leonard Fellows 1909- Brief entry ... 105
Dean, Luella Jo 1908(?)-1977 Obituary ... 69-72
Dean, Malcolm 1948- ... 105
Dean, Morton 1935- ... 69-72
Dean, Nancy 1930- ... 65-68
Dean, Nell Marr 1910- ... 21-22R
Dean, Roger 1944- Brief entry ... 114
Dean, Roy 1925- ... CANR-6
Earlier sketch in CA 57-60
Dean, Stanley (Rochelle) 1908- ... 73-76
Dean, Vera Micheles 1903-1972
Obituary ... 37-40R
Dean, Warren 1932- ... 29-32R
Dean, William D(enard) 1937- ... 37-40R
Dean, William F(rishe) 1899-1981
Obituary ... 105
Dean, Winton Basil 1916- ... CANR-10
Earlier sketch in CA 65-68
Dean, Yetive H(ornor) 1909- ... CAP-1
Earlier sketch in CA 9-10
de Andrade, Carlos Drummond
See Drummond de Andrade, Carlos
DeAndrea, William L(ouis) 1952- ... CANR-20
Earlier sketch in CA 81-84
Deane, Dee Shirley 1928- ... 81-84
Deane, Elisabeth
See Beilenson, Edna
Deane, Herbert Andrew 1921- ... 1R
Deane, James G(arner) 1923- ... 89-92
Deane, Lorna
See Wilkinson, Lorna Hilda Kathleen
Deane, Nancy H(ilts) 1939- ... 29-32R
Deane, Norman
See Creasey, John
Deane, Seamus (Francis) 1940- ... 118
Deane, Shirley Joan 1920- ... CANR-2
Earlier sketch in CA 3R
de Angeli, Marguerite (Lofft)
1889-1987 ... CANR-3
Obituary ... 122
Earlier sketch in CA 5-6R
See also SATA 1, 27
See also DLB 22
See also CLR 1
See also AITN 2
DeAngelis, William 1943- ... 113
de Antonio, Emile 1922- ... 117
Brief entry ... 113
de Aragon, Ray John 1946- ... 115
Dearden, Harold 1882(?)-1962 Obituary ... 116
Dearden, James A(rthur) 1924-1976 ... 33-36R
Dearden, James S(hackley) 1931- ... CANR-12
Earlier sketch in CA 25-28R
Dearden, John 1919- ... 33-36R
Deardorff, Robert 1912- ... 61-64
Deardorff, Tom 1940- ... 89-92
Dearing, James (William) 1959- ... 114
Dearing, Vinton Adams 1920- ... 110
Dearlove, John 1944- ... 97-100
DeArmand, Frances Ullmann
1904(?)-1984 ... 7-8R
Obituary ... 112
See also SATA 10, 38
de Armas, Frederick A(lfred) 1945- ... 37-40R
de Armas, Jose R(afael) 1924- ... 113
DeArment, Robert K(endall) 1925- ... 93-96
Dearmer, Geoffrey 1893- ... CAP-2
Earlier sketch in CA 23-24
Dearmin, Jeannie Tarascou 1924- ... 7-8R
Dearstyne, Howard (Best) 1903-1979 ... 121
Obituary ... 85-88
De Arteaga, William 1943- ... 111
Deary, Terry 1946- ... 110
See also SATA 41
Deason, Hilary J(ohn) 1903- ... 73-76
d'Easum, Cedric (Godfrey) 1907- ... CANR-12
Earlier sketch in CA 73-76
d'Easum, Dick
See d'Easum, Cedric (Godfrey)
Deasy, C(ornelius) M(ichael) 1918- ... 93-96
Deasy, Mary (Margaret) 1914- ... 5-6R
Deaton, Charles W. 1942- ... 93-96
Deaton, John (Graydon) 1939- ... CANR-11
Earlier sketch in CA 61-64
Deats, Paul (Kindred), Jr. 1918- ... 13-14R
Deats, Randy 1954- ... 93-96
Deats, Richard L(ouis) 1932- ... 23-24R
Deaux, George 1931- ... 7-8R
Deaux, Kay 1941- ... 114
DeBakey, Michael E(llis) 1908- ... 73-76
de Banke, Cecile 1889-1965 ... CAP-1
Earlier sketch in CA 13-14
See also SATA 11
de Bary, Brett
See Nee, Brett de Bary
deBary, William Theodore ... 57-60
DeBeaubien, Philip Francis 1913-1979
Obituary ... 85-88
de Beausobre, Iulia
See Namier, Julia
de Beauvoir, Simone (Lucie Ernestine Marie Bertrand)
See Beauvoir, Simone (Lucie Ernestine Marie Bertrand) de
de Bedts, Ralph F(ortes) 1914- ... 11-12R
De Beer, E(smond) S(amuel) 1895- ... CAP-1
Earlier sketch in CA 13-14
de Beer, Gavin R(ylands) 1899-1972 ... CAP-1
Earlier sketch in CA 15-16
DeBenedetti, Charles Louis 1943-1987 ... 102
Obituary ... 121
DeBerard, Ella 1900- ... 73-76
Deberdt-Malaquais, Elisabeth 1937- ... 57-60
de Betancourt, Cressy
See Dobkin De Rios, Marlene
DeBetz, Barbara Holstein ... 123
de Beus, Jacobus Gysbertus 1909- ... 102
Debevec Henning, Sylvie Marie 1948- ... 109
Debicki, Andrew P(eter) 1934- ... 37-40R
Debicki, Roman 1896- ... 3R
de Blank, Joost 1908-1968 ... CAP-1
Earlier sketch in CA 13-14
De Blasis, Celeste (N.) 1946- ... CANR-4
Earlier sketch in CA 53-56
de Blij, Harm J(an) 1935- ... CANR-23
Earlier sketches in CA 15-16R, CANR-8
Debo, Angie 1890-1988 ... 69-72
Obituary ... 124
DeBoer, John C(harles) 1923- ... 29-32R
DeBoer, John James 1903-1969 ... CANR-3
Earlier sketch in CA 3R
de Bois, Helma
See de Bois, Wilhelmina J. E.
de Bois, Wilhelmina J. E. 1923- ... 19-20R
de Boissiere, Ralph (Anthony) 1907- ... 106
DeBold, Richard C. 1927- ... 23-24R
DeBolt, Margaret Wayt 1930- ... 115
De Bona, Maurice, Jr. 1926- ... 65-68
de Bono, Edward 1933- ... CANR-10
Earlier sketch in CA 23-24R
De Bonville, Bob 1926- ... 69-72
De Borchgrave, Arnaud 1926- ... 73-76
De Borhegyi, Suzanne Sims 1926- ... 5-6R
de Born, Edith ... 25-28R
De Bow, James Dunwoody Brownson
1820-1867 ... DLB-3
DeBoy, James J(oseph), Jr. 1942- ... 113
Debray, (Jules) Regis 1942- ... 21-22R
Debreczeny, Paul 1932- ... CANR-12
Earlier sketch in CA 33-36R
De Breffny, Brian 1931- ... 77-80
Debrett, Hal
See Dresser, Davis
Debreu, Gerard 1921- ... CANR-23
Earlier sketch in CA 37-40R
de Brissac, Malcolm
See Dickinson, Peter
de Broglie, L.
See de Broglie, Louis (Victor Pierre Raymond)
de Broglie, Louis (Victor Pierre Raymond)
1892-1987 Obituary ... 122
de Brunhoff, Jean
See Brunhoff, Jean de
De Brunhoff, Laurent
See Brunhoff, Laurent de
de Bruyn, Monica (Jean) G(rembowicz)
1952- ... 65-68
See also SATA 13
Debus, Allen G(eorge) 1926- ... CANR-14
Earlier sketch in CA 37-40R
Debussy, (Achille) Claude 1862-1918
Brief entry ... 118
Decalo, Samuel 1937- ... 121
de Camp, Catherine Crook 1907- ... CANR-20
Earlier sketches in CA 21-22R, CANR-9
See also SATA 12
DeCamp, Graydon 1934- ... 97-100
de Camp, L(yon) Sprague 1907- ... CANR-20
Earlier sketches in CA 2R, CANR-1, 9
See also SATA 9
See also DLB 8
de Campi, John Webb 1939- ... 69-72
De Campos, L.
See Dahl, Linda
De Canio, Stephen J(ohn) 1942- ... 57-60
De Capite, Raymond Anthony 1924- ... 2R
Decarie, Therese Gouin 1923- ... 41-44R
DeCarl, Lennard 1940- ... 81-84
de Castro, Fernando J(ose) 1937- ... 53-56
De Castro, Josue 1908-1973 ... 33-36R
De Caux, Len
See De Caux, Leonard Howard
De Caux, Leonard Howard 1899- ... 29-32R
Decaux, Lucile
See Bibesco, Marthe Lucie
DeCecco, John Paul 1925- ... 19-20R
de Cervera, Alejo 1919- ... 23-24R
de Chair, Somerset (Struben) 1911- ... CANR-1
Earlier sketch in CA 45-48
DeChancie, John 1946- ... 118
Dechant, Emerald V(ictor) 1926- ... 11-12R
DeChant, John A(loysius) 1917-1974 ... CAP-2
Obituary ... 53-56
Earlier sketch in CA 23-24
de Chardin, Pierre Teilhard
See Teilhard de Chardin, (Marie Joseph) Pierre
deCharms, Richard Iv 1927- ... 41-44R
de Chasca, Edmund V(illela) 1903-
Brief entry ... 117
de Chatellerault, Victor
See Beaudoin, Kenneth Lawrence
Dechert, Charles R(ichard) 1927- ... CANR-10
Earlier sketch in CA 21-22R
de Chirico, Giorgio 1888-1978 ... 89-92
Obituary ... 81-84
De Christoforo, Ron(ald) 1951- ... 81-84
Deci, Edward L(ewis) 1942- ... 53-56
Decker, Beatrice 1919- ... 61-64
Decker, Donald M(ilton) 1923- ... 37-40R
Decker, Duane 1910-1964 ... 7-8R
See also SATA 5
Decker, Hannah S(hulman) 1937- ... 85-88
Decker, Leslie E(dward) 1930- ... 11-12R
Decker, Robert Owen 1927- ... 65-68
Decker, William 1926- Brief entry ... 115
Deckers, Jeanine 1933(?)-1985 Obituary ... 115
Deckert, Alice Mae ... 15-16R
DeClements, Barthe 1920- ... CANR-22
Earlier sketch in CA 105
See also SATA 35
De Cock, Liliane 1939- ... CANR-2
Earlier sketch in CA 45-48
Decolta, Ramon
See Whitfield, Raoul
DeConde, Alexander 1920- ... CANR-6
Earlier sketch in CA 5-6R
de Costa, (George) Rene 1939- ... 102
deCoste, Fredrik 1910- ... CAP-2
Earlier sketch in CA 21-22
DeCoster, Cyrus C(ole) 1914- ... 49-52
deCourcy Hinds, Michael 1947- ... 114
DeCoursey, Virginia 1924- ... 114
deCoy, Robert H(arold), Jr. 1920- ... 25-28R
de Crespigny, (Richard) Rafe (Champion)
1936- ... 57-60
De Cristoforo, R(omeo) J(ohn) 1917- ... CANR-3
Earlier sketch in CA 11-12R
DeCrow, Karen 1937- ... 33-36R
Decter, Midge (Rosenthal) 1927- ... CANR-2
Earlier sketch in CA 45-48
Dedek, John F. 1929- ... 33-36R
Dederick, Robert 1919- Brief entry ... 116
de Dienes, Andre 1913- ... 41-44R
Dedijer, Vladimir 1914- ... CANR-4
Earlier sketch in CA 2R
Dedina, Michel 1933- ... 33-36R
Dedini, Eldon 1921- ... 65-68
Dedmon, Emmett 1918-1983 ... CANR-5
Obituary ... 110
Earlier sketch in CA 11-12R
Dee, Henry
See Torbett, Harvey Douglas Louis
Dee, Ruby
See Wallace, Ruby Ann
Deedy, John 1923- ... 33-36R
See also SATA 24
Deegan, Paul Joseph 1937- ... 102
See also SATA 38, 48
Deeken, Alfons 1932- ... 77-80
Deeley, Roger 1944- ... 53-56
Deelman, Christian Felling 1937-1964 ... CAP-1
Earlier sketch in CA 11-12
Deemer, Bill 1945- ... 17-18R
Deemer, Charles (Robert, Jr.) 1939- ... 73-76
Deen, Edith Alderman 1905- ... CANR-2
Earlier sketch in CA 7-8R
Deener, David R(ussell) 1920- ... 19-20R
Deeping, (George) Warwick 1877-1950
Brief entry ... 114
Deeps, Frederick
See Speed, F(rederick) Maurice
Deer, Irving 1924- ... 17-18R
Deer, Sandra 1940- ... CLC-45
Deese, James (Earle) 1921- ... CANR-5
Earlier sketch in CA 4R
Deeter, Allen C. 1931- ... 45-48
de Extramuros, Quixote
See Espino, Federico (Licsi, Jr.)
DeFalco, Joseph Michael 1931- ... 15-16R
DeFanti, Charles 1942- ... 89-92
DeFelice, Louise P(aula) 1945- ... 61-64
De Felitta, Frank (Paul) 1921- ... 61-64
Deferrari, Roy J(oseph) 1890-1969 ... CAP-1
Earlier sketch in CA 13-14
DeFerrari, Sister Teresa Mary 1930- ... 9-10R
Deffner, Donald L(ouis) 1924- ... CANR-11
Earlier sketch in CA 17-18R
de Filippo, Eduardo 1900-1984 Obituary ... 114
de Fletin, P.
See Fielden, T(homas) P(erceval)
Defoe, Daniel 1660(?)-1731 ... SATA-22
See also DLB 39
de Fontaine, Felix Gregory 1834-1896 ... DLB-43
deFontaine, Wade Hampton 1893-1969 ... 5-6R
Obituary ... 103
De Forbes
See Forbes, DeLoris (Florine) Stanton
Deford, Frank 1938- ... 33-36R
deFord, Miriam Allen 1888-1975 ... CANR-4
Earlier sketch in CA 3R
deFord, Sara (Whitcraft) 1916- ... 25-28R
DeForest, Charlotte B. 1879-1971 ... CAP-2
Earlier sketch in CA 25-28
De Forest, John William 1826-1906
Brief entry ... 119
See also DLB 12
De Forest, Lee 1873-1961 Obituary ... 112
de Forrest, Julie
See DeWitt, Edith Openshaw
de Fossard, R(onald) A(lfred) 1929- ... 41-44R
de Fox, Lucia Ungaro
See Lockert, Lucia (Alicia Ungaro Fox)
deFrance, Anthony
See DiFranco, Anthony (Mario)
DeFrancis, John 1911- Brief entry ... 106
DeFrees, Madeline 1919- ... CANR-4
Earlier sketch in CA 11-12R
deFreres, Sebastian J(ean) 1936- ... 121
de Funiak, William Q(uinby) 1901- ... 33-36R
de Gamez, Cielo Cayetana Alba
See Alba de Gamez, Cielo Cayetana
de Gamez, Tana
See Alba de Gamez, Cielo Cayetana
Degani, Meir H(ershtenkorn) 1909- ... 102
DeGarmo, Kenneth Scott 1943- ... 81-84
de Gaulle, Charles (Andre Joseph Marie)
1890-1970 Obituary ... 111
de Gaury, Gerald 1897-1984 ... 15-16R
Obituary ... 112
Degen, Bruce ... SATA-47
Degen, Bruce 1945- ... 124
Degenhardt, Henry W(illiam) 1910- ... CANR-23
Earlier sketch in CA 106
De Gennaro, Angelo Anthony 1919- ... 15-16R
Degenshein, George A. 1918(?)-1979
Obituary ... 93-96
De George, Richard T(homas) 1933- ... CANR-17
Earlier sketches in CA 7-8R, CANR-2
DeGering, Etta Fowler 1898- ... CAP-1
Earlier sketch in CA 9-10
See also SATA 7
Degh, Linda 1920- ... 85-88
Deghy, Guy (Stephen) 1912- ... CAP-1
Earlier sketch in CA 9-10
DeGidio, Sandra 1943- ... 112
Degler, Carl N(eumann) 1921- ... CANR-3
Earlier sketch in CA 7-8R
Degler, Stanley E. 1929- ... 25-28R
Degnan, James Philip 1933- ... 41-44R
de Gourmont, Remy
See Gourmont, Remy de
De Graeff, Allen
See Blaustein, Albert Paul
de Graff, Robert F(air) 1895-1981
Obituary ... 105
See also DLBY 81
de Graffe, Richard
See St. Clair, Leonard
DeGraft, Joseph Coleman 1932- ... 73-76
de Graft-Johnson, John Coleman 1919- ... 21-22R
de Gramont, Sanche
See Morgan, Ted
DeGrave, Philip
See DeAndrea, William L(ouis)
de Grazia, Alfred 1919- ... CANR-5
Earlier sketch in CA 15-16R
De Grazia, Ettore 1909-1982 ... CANR-13
Earlier sketch in CA 61-64
De Grazia, Sebastian 1917- ... 65-68
De Grazia, Ted
See De Grazia, Ettore
See also SATA 39
DeGre, Muriel (Harris) 1914-1971 ... CAP-1
Earlier sketch in CA 17-18
de Greene, Kenyon B(renton) ... CANR-14
Earlier sketch in CA 37-40R
De Gregori, Thomas R(oger) 1935- ... CANR-12
Earlier sketch in CA 29-32R
DeGregorio, William A(lfred) 1946- ... 117
DeGregory, Jerry L(ouis) 1945- ... 119
de Groat, Diane 1947- ... 107
See also SATA 31
DeGrood, David H. 1937- ... 33-36R
DeGroot, Alfred Thomas 1903- ... CANR-5
Earlier sketch in CA 5-6R
de Groot, Roy Andries 1910-1983
Obituary ... 110
deGros, J. H.
See Villiard, Paul
de Grummond, Lena Young ... CANR-1
Earlier sketch in CA 4R
See also SATA 6
de Grunwald, Constantine ... 9-10R
de Guadaloupe, Brother Jose
See Mojica, Jose
Deguine, Jean-Claude 1943- ... 81-84
de Guingand, Francis Wilfred 1900-1979
Obituary ... 89-92
de Gunzburg, Nicholas
See Gunzburg, Nicholas de
deGuzman, Daniel 1911- ... 93-96
De Haan, Margaret
See Freed, Margaret De Haan
De Haan, Richard W. 1923- ... 23-24R
De Haas, Elsa 1901- ... 45-48
de Hamel, Christopher 1950- ... 120
de Hamel, Joan Littledale 1924- ... 103
de Hart, Allen 1926- ... 119
de Hartmann, Olga 1883(?)-1979
Obituary ... 89-92
de Hartog, Jan 1914- ... CANR-1
Earlier sketch in CA 2R
See also CLC 19
Dehn, Olive 1914- ... 117
Dehn, Paul (Edward) 1912-1976 ... 89-92
Dehoney, W(illiam) Wayne 1918- ... 19-20R
de Hostos, E. M.
See Hostos (y Bonilla), Eugenio Maria de
de Hostos, Eugenio M.
See Hostos (y Bonilla), Eugenio Maria de
Dehqani-Tafti, H. B. 1920- ... 106
Dehr, Dorothy 1915- ... 29-32R
Dei-Anang, Michael 1909- ... 53-56
Deibler, William E. 1932- ... 89-92

Deighton, Lee (Cecil) 1906-1987 Obituary 122
Deighton, Lee C(ecil) 1906-1987 124
Deighton, Len
See Deighton, Leonard Cyril
See also CLC 4, 7, 22, 46
Deighton, Leonard Cyril 1929- CANR-19
Earlier sketch in CA 11-12R
Deikman, Arthur J(oseph) 1929- 65-68
Deindorfer, Robert Greene 1922-1983 .... CANR-3
Obituary 109
Earlier sketch in CA 11-12R
Deindorfer, Scott 1967- 81-84
Deinzer, Harvey T. 1908- 17-18R
de Iongh, Mary (Dows Herter Norton) Crena
See Crena de Iongh, Mary (Dows Herter Norton)
Deiss, Joseph Jay 1915- CANR-14
Earlier sketch in CA 33-36R
See also SATA 12
Deitz, Susan 1934- 110
De Jaegher, Raymond-Joseph 1905-1980 .... CAP-2
Obituary 93-96
Earlier sketch in CA 21-22
De Jong, Arthur J(ay) 1934- 69-72
DeJong, David C(ornel) 1905-1967 .... 5-6R
See also SATA 10
deJong, Dola 5-6R
See also SATA 7
De Jong, Gerald Francis 1921- 61-64
de Jong, Gerrit, Jr. 1892- 37-40R
De Jong, Gordon F(rederick) 1935- 25-28R
DeJong, Meindert 1906- 15-16R
See also SATA 2
See also DLB 52
See also CLR 1
De Jong, Peter 1945- 69-72
de Jonge, Alex 1938- CANR-5
Earlier sketch in CA 53-56
De Jonge, Marinus 1925- 123
de Jongh, James 1942- 85-88
de Journlet, Marie
See Little, Paul H(ugo)
de Jouvenel, Bertrand
See de Jouvenel des Ursins, Edouard Bertrand
de Jouvenel des Ursins, Edouard Bertrand 1903-1987 Obituary 121
De Jovine, F(elix) Anthony 1927-1976 .... CAP-2
Earlier sketch in CA 29-32
Deju, Raul A(ntonio) 1946- 53-56
DeKalb, Lorimer
See Knorr, Marian L(ockwood)
de Kay, James T(ertius) 1930- CANR-10
Earlier sketch in CA 25-28R
de Kay, Ormonde, Jr. 1923- 49-52
See also SATA 7
de Kerpely, Theresa 1898- 119
deKieffer, Donald (Eulette) 1945- 112
de Kiewiet, Cornelis W(illem) 1902-1986 Obituary 118
de Kiewiet, Cornelius W(illiam)
See de Kiewiet, Cornelis W(illem)
de Kiewit, Cornelis W(illem)
See de Kiewiet, Cornelis W(illem)
de Kiriline, Louise
See Lawrence, Louise de Kiriline
Dekker, Carl
See Laffin, John (Alfred Charles) and Lynds, Dennis
Dekker, George 1934- 104
Dekker, Thomas 1572(?)-1632 .... DLB-62
Dekle, Bernard 1905- 17-18R
Dekmejian, Richard Hrair 1933- 37-40R
Deknatel, F(rederick) B(rockway) 1905-1973 Obituary 45-48
Dekobra, Maurice
See Tessier, (Ernst) M(aurice)
De Koenigswerther, Edwin Raymond 1930- 49-52
DeKok, David (Paul) 1953- 124
DeKosky, Robert K. 1945- 93-96
DeKoster, Lester Ronald 1915- 13-14R
De Koven, Bernard 1941- 85-88
De Koven, Bernie
See De Koven, Bernard
Dekovic, Gene 1922- 108
deKruif, Paul (Henry) 1890-1971 .... 9-10R
Obituary 29-32R
See also SATA 5, 50
de Kun, Nicolas 1923- 17-18R
De La Bedoyere, Michael 1900-1973 Obituary 104
Delacato, Carl H(enry) 1923- 41-44R
Delacorte, Peter 1943- 105
de la Costa, Horacio (L.)
See Costa, Horacio (L.) de la
Delacour, Jean
See Delacour, Jean Theodore
Delacour, Jean Theodore 1890-1985 Obituary 117
Delacre, Lulu 1957- SATA-36
DeLacy, Margaret (Eisenstein) 1951- 122
DeLaet, Sigfried J(an) 1914- CANR-18
Earlier sketches in CA 7-8R, CANR-3
Delafield, E. M.
See Dashwood, Edmee Elizabeth Monica de la Pasture
See also DLB 34
de la Garza, Rodolfo O(ropea) 1942- 77-80
De Lage, Ida 1918- CANR-14
Earlier sketch in CA 41-44R
See also SATA 11
de La Glannege, Roger-Maxe
See Legman, G(ershon)
De La Grange, Henry Louis 1924- 69-72
de la Guardia, Ernesto, Jr. 1904-1983 Obituary 109
de Laguna, Frederica (Annis) 1906- 37-40R
de Laguna, Grace Mead A(ndrus) 1878-1978 .... CAP-1
Obituary 77-80
Earlier sketch in CA 11-12
Delahanty, Randolph
See Delehanty, Randolph
Delahay, E(ileen) A(vril) 1915-1982 .... 25-28R
Obituary 117
De La Iglesia, Maria Elena 1936- 29-32R
de la Mare, Albinia Catherine 1932- 33-36R
de la Mare, Richard (Herbert Ingpen) 1901-1986 Obituary 118
de la Mare, Walter (John) 1873-1956
Brief entry 110
See also SATA 16
See also DLB 19
See also TCLC 4
DeLamarter, Jeanne
See Bonnette, Jeanne
DeLamotte, Roy Carroll 1917- CANR-15
Earlier sketch in CA 41-44R
DeLancey, Mark W(akeman) 1939- 93-96
Deland, Margaret(ta Wade Campbell) 1857-1945 Brief entry 122
Delaney, Bud
See Delaney, Francis, Jr.
Delaney, C(ornelius) F. 1938- CANR-16
Earlier sketch in CA 25-28R
Delaney, Daniel J(oseph) 1938- 41-44R
Delaney, Denis
See Green, Peter (Morris)
Delaney, Edmund T. 1914- 15-16R
Delaney, Francis, Jr. 1931- 57-60
Delaney, Franey
See O'Hara, John (Henry)
Delaney, Harry 1932- 25-28R
See also SATA 3
Delaney, Jack J(ames) 1921- 21-22R
Delaney, John Joseph 1910-1985 .... CANR-5
Obituary 115
Earlier sketch in CA 1R
DeLaney, Joseph Lawrence 1917- 102
Delaney, Lolo M(ae) 1937- 57-60
Delaney, Marshall
See Fulford, Robert
Delaney, Mary Murray 1913- 53-56
Delaney, Ned
See Delaney, Thomas Nicholas III
See also SATA 28
Delaney, Norman Conrad 1932- 37-40R
Delaney, Robert Finley 1925- CANR-6
Earlier sketch in CA 1R
Delaney, Shelagh 1939- 19-20R
See also DLB 13
See also CLC 29
Delaney, Steve 1938- 121
Brief entry 110
Delaney, Thomas Nicholas III 1951- CANR-10
Earlier sketch in CA 65-68
Delaney, William A(nthony) 1926- 106
de Lange, Nicholas (Robert Michael) 1944- CANR-15
Earlier sketch in CA 89-92
Delano, Anthony 1930- 102
Delano, Hugh 1933- 65-68
See also SATA 20
Delano, Isaac O. 1904- 25-28R
Delano, Kenneth J(oseph) 1934- 57-60
de Lantagne, Cecile
See Cloutier-Wojciechowska, Cecile
Delany, George (Battle) 1946- 114
Delany, Kevin F(rancis) X(avier) 1927- 73-76
Delany, Martin Robinson 1812-1885 .... DLB-50
Delany, Paul 1937- CANR-19
Earlier sketch in CA 29-32R
Delany, Samuel R(ay), Jr. 1942- 81-84
See also DLB 8, 33
See also CLC 8, 14, 38
Delany, Sheila 1940- 112
de la Pena, Augustin (Mateo) 1942- 115
Delaplane, Stanton Hill 1907- 25-28R
Delaporte, Ernest P(ierre) 1924- 97-100
Delaporte, Theophile
See Green, Julien (Hartridge)
de la Portilla, Marta (Rosa) 1927- 61-64
De Lapp, Ardyce Lucile 1903- 97-100
DeLapp, George Leslie 1895- 102
De La Ramee, (Marie) Louise 1839-1908 .... SATA-20
de la Renta, Francoise de Langiade 1921(?)-1983 Obituary 110
De La Roche, Mazo 1885-1961 85-88
See also CLC 14
Delasanta, Rodney 1932- 33-36R
de las Cuevas, Raymon
See Harrington, Mark Raymond
de la Torre, Jose 1943- 112
De La Torre, Lillian
See McCue, Lillian Bueno
de la Torre, Victor Raul Haya
See Haya de la Torre, Victor Raul
DeLatte, Carolyn E(lizabeth) 1943- 112
Delattre, Pierre 1930- 105
Delatush, Edith G. 1921- 124
de Laubenfels, David J(ohn) 1925- 53-56
de Launay, Jacques F(orment) 1924- CANR-3
Earlier sketch in CA 11-12R
Delaune, (Jewel) Lynn (de Grummond) CANR-21
Earlier sketch in CA 4R
See also SATA 7
DeLaura, David J(oseph) 1930- 23-24R
DeLaurentis, Louise Budde 1920- 7-8R
See also SATA 12
de la Warr, George Walter 1904-1969 .... CAP-1
Earlier sketch in CA 15-16
Delay, Claude
See Delay-Tubiana, Claude
Delay-Tubiana, Claude 1934- CANR-4
Earlier sketch in CA 53-56
Delbanco, Nicholas (Franklin) 1942- 19-20R
See also CAAS 2
See also DLB 6
See also CLC 6, 13
del Barco, Lucy Salamanca 19-20R
Del Boca, Angelo 1925- 25-28R
Delbridge, Rosemary 1949(?)-1981 Obituary 105
del Castillo, Michel 1933- 109
See also CLC 38
del Castillo, Richard Griswold
See Griswold del Castillo, Richard
Delcroix, Carlo 1896-1977 Obituary 73-76
Delderfield, Eric R(aymond) 1909- CANR-4
Earlier sketch in CA 53-56
See also SATA 14
Delderfield, Ronald Frederick 1912-1972 73-76
Obituary 37-40R
See also SATA 20
Delear, Frank J. 1914- CANR-9
Earlier sketch in CA 21-22R
Deledda, Grazia (Cosima) 1875(?)-1936
Brief entry 123
See also TCLC 23
DeLeeuw, Adele Louise 1899- CANR-1
Earlier sketch in CA 4R
See also SATA 1, 30
DeLeeuw, Cateau 1903-1975 .... CANR-3
Earlier sketch in CA 4R
de Leeuw, Hendrik 1891-1977 Obituary 73-76
Delehanty, Randolph 1944- 106
de Leiris, Alain 1922- 73-76
DeLeon, David (Henry) 1947- Brief entry 114
de Lerma, Dominique-Rene 1928- CANR-1
Earlier sketch in CA 45-48
Delessert, Etienne 1941- CANR-13
Earlier sketch in CA 21-22R
See also SATA 27, 46
DeLey, Herbert (Clemone, Jr.) 1936- 21-22R
Delfano, M. M.
See Flammonde, Paris
Delfgaauw, Bernard(us Maria Ignatius) 1912- 23-24R
Delgado, Alan (George) 1909- CANR-5
Earlier sketch in CA 11-12R
Delgado, Jose Manuel R(odriguez) 1915- 29-32R
Delgado, Ramon (Louis) 1937- CANR-15
Earlier sketch in CA 85-88
D'Elia, Donald John 1933- 57-60
D'Elia, Maria
See Goudiss, Maria Agnes D'Elia
Delibes, Miguel
See Delibes Setien, Miguel
See also CLC 8, 18
Delibes Setien, Miguel 1920- CANR-1
Earlier sketch in CA 45-48
Deligiorgis, Stavros (George) 1933- 61-64
DeLillo, Don 1936- CANR-21
Earlier sketch in CA 81-84
See also DLB 6
See also CLC 8, 10, 13, 27, 39
de Lima, Agnes 1887(?)-1974 Obituary 53-56
De Lima, Clara Rosa 1922- CANR-6
Earlier sketch in CA 57-60
de Lima, Sigrid 1921- 25-28R
Delinsky, Barbara (Ruth Greenberg) 1945- 111
Delisle, Francoise 1886(?)-1974 Obituary 53-56
De Lisser, Herbert George 1878-1944
Brief entry 109
See also TCLC 12
Delius, Anthony (Ronald St. Martin) 1916- CANR-12
Earlier sketch in CA 17-18R
Delk, Robert Carlton 1920- 45-48
Dell, Belinda
See Bowden, Jean
Dell, Christopher 1927- 65-68
Dell, E(dward) T(homas), Jr. 1923- 15-16R
Dell, Edmund 1921- 103
Dell, Floyd 1887-1969 Obituary 89-92
See also DLB 9
Dell, Jeffrey 1899-1985(?) Obituary 116
Dell, Roberta E(lizabeth) 1946- 81-84
Dell, Sidney 1918- CANR-17
Earlier sketches in CA 5-6R, CANR-2
Della Femina, Jerry 1936- Brief entry 111
Della-Piana, Gabriel M. 1926- 73-76
delle Stelle, Pier Luigi Bellini
See Bellini delle Stelle, Pier Luigi
Dellin, Lubomir A. D. 1920- 45-48
Dellinger, David (T.) 1915- 65-68
Delloff, Irving Arthur 1920- 15-16R
Delman, David 1924- Brief entry 115
Delmar, Ken 1941- 121
Del Mar, Marcia 1950- 105
Delmar, Roy
See Wexler, Jerome (LeRoy)
Delmar, Vina (Croter) 1905- 65-68
Delmer, Denis Sefton 1904- 5-6R
Delmonico, Andrea
See Morrison, Eula Atwood
De Loach, Allen (Wayne) 1939- CANR-16
Earlier sketch in CA 85-88
DeLoach, Charles F. 1927- 37-40R
DeLoach, Clarence, Jr. 1936- 57-60
Delon, Floyd G(urney) 1929- CANR-21
Earlier sketch in CA 69-72
de Lone, Richard H. 1940- 101
DeLone, Ruth
See Rankin, Ruth (DeLone) I(rvine)
DeLong, Lea Rosson 1947- 119
DeLong, Thomas A(nderton) 1935- 106
de Longchamps, Joanne (Cutten) 1923- CANR-3
Earlier sketch in CA 11-12R
De Lora, Joann S.
See Sandlin, Joann S(chepers) De Lora
DeLorean, John Z(achary) 1925- 122
DeLorenzo, Lorisa Mernette 1951- 117
DeLorenzo, Robert John 1947- 117
Deloria, Vine (Victor), Jr. 1933- CANR-20
Earlier sketches in CA 53-56, CANR-5
See also SATA 21
See also CLC 21
Delorme, Andre
See Julien, Charles-Andre
Delorme, Michele
See Cranston, Mechthild
Delort, Robert 1932- 102
de los Reyes, Gabriel 45-48
de los Rios, Francisco Giner
See Giner de los Rios, Francisco
Deloughery, Grace L. 1933- 33-36R
de Loune, Henry
See Popham, Peter (Nicholas Home)
Delp, Michael W(illiam) 1948- 77-80
Delpar, Helen 1936- 53-56
Delphos, Omar
See Ald, Roy A(llison)
del Rey, Judy-Lynn 1943-1986 124
Obituary 118
del Rey, Lester 1915- CANR-17
Earlier sketch in CA 65-68
See also SATA 22
See also DLB 8
Delta
See Dennett, Herbert Victor
Delton, Jina 1961- 106
Delton, Judy 1931- CANR-8
Earlier sketch in CA 57-60
See also SATA 14
Delton, Julie 1959- 108
DeLuca, A(ngelo) Michael 1912-1976 .... 21-22R
Obituary 120
De Luca, Charles J. 1927- 73-76
De Lucca, John 1920- 41-44R
Delulio, John 1938- SATA-15
Delumeau, Jean 1923- 97-100
De Luna, Frederick Adolph 1928- 65-68
Delupis, Ingrid 1939- 103
Del Vecchio, John M(ichael) 1947- 110
See also CLC 29
Delving, Michael
See Williams, Jay
DeLynn, Jane 1946- 77-80
DeLyser, Femmy 1935- 110
Delzell, Charles F(loyd) 1920- CANR-2
Earlier sketch in CA 2R
Demac, Donna A. 1952- 121
de Madariaga, Isabel 1919- 107
Demaine, Don
See Drinkall, Gordon (Don)
de Man, Paul 1919(?)-1983 Obituary 111
See also DLB 67
de Mandiargues, Andre Pieyre
See Pieyre de Mandiargues, Andre
De Manio, Jack 1914- 61-64
Demant, Vigo Auguste 1893-1983 Obituary 109
de Mar, Esmeralda
See Mellen, Ida M(ay)
Demaray, Donald E(ugene) 1926- CANR-16
Earlier sketches in CA 3R, CANR-1
De Marco, Angelus A. 1916- 11-12R
De Marco, Arlene AITN-1
DeMarco, Donald 1937- CANR-24
Earlier sketches in CA 61-64, CANR-7
de Mare, Eric S. 1910- CANR-6
Earlier sketch in CA 9-10R
deMare, George 1912- 23-24R
Demarest, Bruce A(lvin) 1935- 118
Demarest, Chris(topher) L(ynn) 1951- 109
See also SATA 44, 45
Demarest, Doug
See Barker, Will
Demarest, Michael 1924(?)-1984 Obituary 112
Demarest, Phyllis Gordon 1911-1969 Obituary 104
Demarest, Rosemary Regina 1914- 116
Demarest, Victoria Booth(-Clibborn) 1890-1982 124
Obituary 112
Demaret, James Newton 1910-1983 Obituary 111
Demaret, Jimmy
See Demaret, James Newton
Demaret, Pierre 1943- CANR-12
Earlier sketch in CA 61-64
De Maria, Robert 1928- CANR-5
Earlier sketch in CA 1R
De Marinis, Rick 1934- CANR-9
Earlier sketch in CA 57-60
Demaris, Ovid
See Desmarais, Ovid E.
DeMartini, Rodney J(ames) 1947- 113
De Martino, Manfred F(rank) 1924-
Brief entry 117
Demas, Vida 1927- 49-52
See also SATA 9
deMatteo, Donna 1941- 25-28R
de Mauny, Erik 1920- CANR-13
Earlier sketch in CA 33-36R
deMause, Lloyd 1931- 65-68
Dembo, L(awrence) S(anford) 1929- CANR-2
Earlier sketch in CA 1R
Dembry, R. Emmet
See Murfree, Mary Noailles

Demby, William 1922- 81-84
See also DLB 33
de Medici, Marino 1933- 89-92
De Mejo, Oscar 1911- 111
See also SATA 40
Dement, William Charles 1928- Brief entry 105
De Mente, Boye 1928- CANR-8
Earlier sketch in CA 23-24R
de Menton, Francisco
See Chin, Frank (Chew, Jr.)
Demeny, Janos 1915- 118
Demers, James 1942- 97-100
de Mesne, Eugene (Frederick Peter
Cheshire) 41-44R
de Mesquita, Bruce James Bueno
See Bueno de Mesquita, Bruce James
de Messieres, Nicole 1930- 107
See also SATA 39
Demetillo, Ricaredo 1920- 102
Demetrakopoulos, Stephanie Anne 1937- 111
Demetrius, James Kleon 1924- CANR-13
Earlier sketch in CA 21-22R
Demetz, Peter 1922- CANR-14
Earlier sketch in CA 65-68
Demi
See Hitz, Demi
De Michael, Don(ald Anthony) 1928-1982
Obituary 106
Demijohn, Thom
See Disch, Thomas M(ichael)
and Sladek, John
de Milan, Sister Jean
See Jean, Gabrielle (Lucille)
D'Emilio, A. Edward 1919(?)-1987
Obituary 122
de Mille, Agnes
See Prude, Agnes George
DeMille, Alexandria
See Du Breuil, (Elizabeth) L(or)inda
De Mille, Cecil B(lount) 1881-1959
Brief entry 115
DeMille, Nelson 1943- CANR-6
Earlier sketch in CA 57-60
De Mille, Nelson
See Levinson, Leonard
de Mille, Richard 1922- CANR-13
Earlier sketch in CA 23-24R
Deming, Barbara 1917-1984 CANR-15
Earlier sketch in CA 85-88
Deming, Kirk
See Drago, Harry Sinclair
Deming, Louise Macpherson 1916-1976
Obituary 61-64
Deming, Richard 1915- CANR-3
Earlier sketch in CA 11-12R
See also SATA 24
Deming, Robert H. 1937- 21-22R
DeMirjian, Arto, Jr. 1931- 57-60
De Molen, Richard Lee 1938- 45-48
Demone, Harold W(ellington), Jr.
1924- CANR-9
Earlier sketch in CA 5-6R
De Monfried, Henri 1879(?)-1974
Obituary 53-56
Demong, Phyllis 1920- 106
de Montalvo, Luis Galvez
See Avalle-Arce, Juan Bautista
DeMonte, Claudia 1947- 114
de Montebello, Guy-Philippe Lannes
1936- 45-48
de Montfort, Guy
See Johnson, Donald Mcl(ntosh)
de Montherlant, Henry (Milon)
See Montherlant, Henry (Milon) de
DeMontreville Polak, Doris 1904(?)-1974
Obituary 49-52
De Mordaunt, Walter J(ulius) 1925- 33-36R
Demorest, Jean-Jacques 1920- 5-6R
Demorest, Stephen 1949- CANR-20
Earlier sketch in CA 101
De Morny, Peter
See Wynne-Tyson, Esme
Demos, Paul 1888-1983 Obituary 109
Demotes, Michael
See Burgess, M(ichael) R(oy)
DeMott, Benjamin 1924- 5-6R
De Mott, Donald W(arren) 1928- 61-64
de Mourgues, Odette (Marie Helene Louise)
1914- 7-8R
Dempewolff, Richard F(rederic) 1914- CANR-1
Earlier sketch in CA 4R
Dempsey, David Knapp 1914- CANR-2
Earlier sketch in CA 7-8R
Dempsey, Hugh Aylmer 1929- CANR-11
Earlier sketch in CA 69-72
Dempsey, Jack
See Dempsey, William Harrison
Dempsey, Lotta 101
Dempsey, Paul K(enneth) 1935- CANR-19
Earlier sketch in CA 25-28R
Dempsey, Richard A(llen) 1932- 61-64
Dempsey, William Harrison 1895-1983 89-92
Obituary 109
Dempster, Barry 1952- 113
Dempster, Chris 1943- 106
Dempster, Derek David 1924- 15-16R
Dempster, Stuart 1936- 104
Demske, James Michael 1922- 29-32R
Demura, Fumio 1940- CANR-12
Earlier sketch in CA 61-64
Demuth, Norman (Frank) 1898-1968 CAP-1
Earlier sketch in CA 13-14
Demuth, Patricia Brennan 1948- 118
Den, Petr
See Radimsky, Ladislaw
Denali, Peter
See Holm, Don(ald Raymond)
de Natale, Francine
See Malzberg, Barry N(athaniel)
Denbeaux, Fred J. 1914- 7-8R
Denbie, Roger
See Green, Alan (Baer)
Denbigh, Kenneth George 1911- 106
Den Boer, James (Drew) 1937- CANR-10
Earlier sketch in CA 23-24R
Denby, Edwin (Orr) 1903-1983 Obituary 110
Dendel, Esther (Sietmann Warner) 1910- 102
Dender, Jay
See Deindorfer, Robert Greene
Dendle, Brian J(ohn) 1936- 116
Dendy, Marshall C(oleman) 1902- CAP-2
Earlier sketch in CA 17-18
DeNeef, Arthur Leigh 1942- 102
Deneen, James R. 1928- 45-48
Denenberg, Herbert S(idney) 1929- 37-40R
de Neufville, Richard 1939- 53-56
Denevan, William M(axfield) 1931- 41-44R
de Nevers, Noel (Howard) 1932- 37-40R
DeNevi, Donald P. 1937- 37-40R
Denfeld, Duane (Henry) 1939- 41-44R
Deng, William 1929- 13-14R
Dengler, Dieter 1938- 102
Dengler, Marianna (Herron) 1935- 102
Dengler, Sandy 1939- 112
See also SATA 40
Denham, Alice 1933- 23-24R
Denham, Avery Strakosch ?-1970
Obituary 104
Denham, Bertie 1927- 93-96
Denham, H(enry) M(angles) 1897- 61-64
Denham, John 1615-1669 DLB-58
Denham, Mary Orr 1918- CANR-2
Earlier sketch in CA 4R
Denham, Reginald 1894-1983 CAP-1
Obituary 109
Earlier sketch in CA 15-16
Denham, Robert D(ayton) 1938- 53-56
Denham, Sully
See Budd, Mavis
Denhardt, Robert Moorman 1912- 101
den Hollander, A(rie) Nicolaas Jan
1906-1976 CAP-2
Earlier sketch in CA 29-32
Denholm, Therese Mary Zita White 1933- 9-10R
Denholtz, Elaine (Grudin) CANR-13
Earlier sketch in CA 73-76
Dening, Greg 1931- 107
Denis, Armand 1896(?)-1971 Obituary 104
Denis, Charlotte
See Plimmer, Charlotte
and Plimmer, Denis
Denis, Julio
See Cortazar, Julio
Denis, Manuel Maldonado
See Maldonado-Denis, Manuel
Denis, Michaela Holdsworth 13-14R
Denis, Paul 1909- 21-22R
Denisoff, R. Serge 1939- 33-36R
Denison, Barbara 1926- 13-14R
Denison, Corrie
See Partridge, Eric (Honeywood)
Denison, Edward F(ulton) 1915- 23-24R
Denison, (John) Michael (Terence
Wellesley) 1915- 109
Denison, Norman 1925- 65-68
Denker, Henry 1912- 33-36R
See also AITN 1
Denkler, Horst 1935- CANR-19
Earlier sketches in CA 53-56, CANR-4
Denkstein, Vladimir 1906- 103
Denlinger, A(nna) Martha 1931- 113
Denman, D(onald) R(obert) 1911- CANR-8
Earlier sketch in CA 61-64
Denmark, Florence L. 1932- 85-88
Dennehy, Raymond L(eo) 1934- 109
Dennes, William Ray 1898- 73-76
Dennett, Daniel C. 1942- 97-100
Dennett, Herbert Victor 1893- CANR-5
Earlier sketch in CA 7-8R
Denney, Diana 1910- 104
See also SATA 25
Denney, Myron Keith 1930- 102
Denney, Reuel (Nicholas) 1913- CANR-2
Earlier sketch in CA 4R
Dennie, Joseph 1768-1812 DLB-37, 43, 59
Denning, A. T.
See Denning, Alfred Thompson
Denning, Alfred Thompson 1899-
Brief entry 115
Denning, Basil W. 1928- 33-36R
Denning, Melita
See Barcynski, Vivian G(odfrey)
Denning, Patricia
See Willis, Corinne Denneny
Dennis, Arthur
See Edmonds, Arthur Denis
Dennis, Benjamin G. 1929- 45-48
Dennis, Carl 1939- 77-80
Dennis, Charles 1946- CANR-17
Earlier sketch in CA 65-68
Dennis, Deborah Ellis 1950- 116
Dennis, Everette E. 1942- 41-44R
Dennis, Henry C(harles) 1918- 41-44R
Dennis, James M(unn) 1932- 102
Dennis, John V(alue) 1916- 107
Dennis, Landt 1937- 65-68
Dennis, Lane T(imothy) 1943- 93-96
Dennis, Lawrence 1893-1977 Obituary 73-76
Dennis, Morgan 1891?-1960 SATA-18
Dennis, Nigel (Forbes) 1912- 25-28R
See also DLB 13, 15
See also CLC 8
Dennis, Patrick
See Tanner, Edward Everett III
Dennis, Peggy 1909- 77-80
Dennis, Peter (John) 1945- 41-44R
Dennis, Ralph AITN-1
Dennis, Richard (John) 1949- 118
Dennis, Robert C. 1920-1983 101
Obituary 110
Dennis, Rutledge M(elvin) 1939- 115
Dennis, Suzanne Easton 1922- 25-28R
Dennis, Wayne 1905-1976 17-18R
Obituary 69-72
Dennis, Wesley 1903-1966 SATA-18
Dennis-Jones, H(arold) 1915- CANR-8
Earlier sketch in CA 57-60
Dennison, A(lfred) Dudley, Jr. 1914- CANR-9
Earlier sketch in CA 57-60
Dennison, George (Harris) 1925-1987 101
Obituary 123
See also CAAS 6
Dennison, George M(arshel) 1935- 53-56
Dennison, Milo
See Cantwell, Lois
Dennison, Peter (John) 1942- 124
Dennison, Sam 1926- 109
Dennison, Shane 1933- 73-76
Denniston, Denise 1946- 69-72
Denniston, Elinore 1900-1978 Obituary 81-84
See also SATA 24
Denniston, Lyle (William) 1931- 65-68
Denny, Alma 1912- 89-92
Denny, Brian
See Doughty, Bradford
Denny, Carol
See Brandt, Carol
Denny, John Howard 1920- CAP-1
Earlier sketch in CA 9-10
Denny, Ludwell 1894-1970 Obituary 29-32R
Denny, M(aurice) Ray 1918- CANR-14
Earlier sketch in CA 41-44R
Denny, Norman (George) 1901-1982 107
See also SATA 43
Denny-Brown, Derek Ernest 1901-1981
Obituary 103
Dennys, Joyce (a pseudonym) 1895- 121
Dennys, Rodney Onslow 1911- 85-88
Denoeu, Francois 1898-1975 53-56
Denomme, Robert T. 1930- 25-28R
Denoon, Donald (John Noble) 1940- CANR-14
Earlier sketch in CA 73-76
DeNovo, John A(ugust) 1916- 11-12R
Densen-Gerber, Judianne 1934- 37-40R
Denslow, W(illiam) W(allace)
1856-1915 SATA-16
Denson, John Lee 1903-1982 Obituary 108
Dent, Alan (Holmes) 1905-1978 CANR-5
Earlier sketch in CA 9-10R
Dent, Anthony Austen 1915- CANR-15
Earlier sketch in CA 25-28R
Dent, Colin 1921- 13-14R
Dent, Harold (Collett) 1894- CANR-5
Earlier sketch in CA 7-8R
Dent, Harry (Shuler) 1930- 81-84
Dent, Lester 1904(?)-1959 Brief entry 112
Dent, Robert William 1917- 105
Dent, Thomas C(ovington) 1932-
Brief entry 122
Dent, Tom
See Dent, Thomas C(ovington)
See also DLB 38
Dentan, Robert C(laude) 1907- CANR-2
Earlier sketch in CA 1R
Dentinger, Jane 1951- 123
Dentinger, Stephen
See Hoch, Edward D(entinger)
Dentler, Robert A(rnold) 1928- CANR-17
Earlier sketches in CA 3R, CANR-1
Denton, Charles F(rederick) 1942- 37-40R
Denton, D. Keith 1948- 112
Denton, Daniel 1626(?)-1703 DLB-24
Denton, H(arry) M. 1882- CAP-1
Earlier sketch in CA 11-12
Denton, J(effrey) H(oward) 1939- CANR-15
Earlier sketch in CA 41-44R
Denton, Jeremiah A(ndrew), Jr. 1924- 69-72
Denton, Wallace 1928- 3R
d'Entreves, Alexander (Passerin)
1902-1985 Obituary 118
Dentry, Robert
See White, Osmar Egmont Dorkin
Denues, Celia 1915- 41-44R
Den Uyl, Douglas J(ohn) 1950- 117
Denver, Boone
See Rennie, James Alan
Denver, Drake C.
See Nye, Nelson C(oral)
Denver, Rod
See Edson, J(ohn) T(homas)
Denver, Walt
See Sherman, Jory (Tecumseh)
Denvir, Bernard 1917- 115
Denys, Teresa (a pseudonym) 1947- 105
Denzel, Justin F(rancis) 1917- CANR-4
Earlier sketch in CA 53-56
See also SATA 38, 46
Denzer, Ann Wiseman
See Wiseman, Ann (Sayre)
Denzer, Peter W(orthington) 1921- 7-8R
Denzin, Norman K(ent) 1941- CANR-12
Earlier sketch in CA 29-32R
de Obaldia, Rene
See Obaldia, Rene de
de Oca, Marco Antonio Montes
See Montes de Oca, Marco Antonio
de Oliveira, Paulo C(arlos) 1953- 114
Deon, Michel 1919- CANR-16
Earlier sketch in CA 37-40R
De Palma, Brian (Russell) 1940- 109
See also CLC 20
de Paola, Thomas Anthony 1934- CANR-2
Earlier sketch in CA 49-52
See also SATA 11
de Paola, Tomie
See de Paola, Thomas Anthony
See also DLB 61
See also CLR 4
de Paor, Risteard
See Power, Richard
Depas, Spencer 1925- 69-72
DePaul, Edith
See Delatush, Edith G.
DePauw, Linda Grant 1940- CANR-9
Earlier sketch in CA 21-22R
See also SATA 24
Depel, Jim 1936- 73-76
de Pereda, Prudencio 1912- CANR-4
Earlier sketch in CA 1R
Depestre, Rene 1926- Brief entry 113
Depew, Arthur M(c Kinley) 1896-1976 41-44R
Depew, Wally
See Depew, Walter Westerfield
Depew, Walter Westerfield 1924- 5-6R
De Pietro, Albert 1913- 69-72
de Polman, Willem
See Nichols, Dale (William)
De Polnay, Peter 1906-1984 73-76
Obituary 114
DePorte, Anton W. 1928- 124
DePorte, Michael V(ital) 1939- 49-52
Depp, Roberta J. 1947- 101
de Pre, Jean-Anne
See Avallone, Michael (Angelo), Jr.
DePree, Gladis (Lenore) 1933- 101
DePree, Gordon 1930- 101
Depta, Victor M(arshall) 1939- 49-52
De Puy, Norman R(obert) 1929- 97-100
Dequasie, Andrew 1929- 114
D'Erasmo, Martha 1939- 81-84
Derber, Milton 1915- Brief entry 106
Derby, George Horatio 1823-1861 DLB-11
Derby, Pat 1942- 69-72
de Regniers, Beatrice Schenk (Freedman)
1914- CANR-6
Earlier sketch in CA 13-14R
See also SATA 2
Dereksen, David
See Stacton, David (Derek)
Deren, Eleanora 1908(?)-1961 Obituary 111
Deren, Maya
See Deren, Eleanora
See also CLC 16
Derenberg, Walter J(ulius) 1903-1975
Obituary 61-64
De Reneville, Mary Margaret Motley
Sheridan 1912- 5-6R
de Reyna, Rudy 1914- CANR-10
Earlier sketch in CA 57-60
Derfler, (Arnold) Leslie 1933- CANR-9
Earlier sketch in CA 7-8R
deRham, Edith 1933- 15-16R
Derham, (Arthur) Morgan 1915- 13-14R
Der Hovanessian, Diana 124
Deric, Arthur J. 1926- 23-24R
Dering, Joan (Rosalind Cordelia) 1917- 9-10R
De Risi, William J(oseph) 1938- 53-56
de Rivera, Joseph H(osmer) 1932- 41-44R
Derleth, August (William) 1909-1971 CANR-4
Obituary 29-32R
Earlier sketch in CA 1R
See also SATA 5
See also DLB 9
See also CLC 31
Derman, Lou 1914(?)-1976 Obituary 65-68
Derman, Sarah Audrey 1915- CANR-17
Earlier sketch in CA 4R
See also SATA 11
Dermid, Jack 1923- 49-52
Dermout, Maria
See Dermout-Ingermann, Helena Antonia
Maria Elisabeth
Dermout-Ingermann, Helena Antonia Maria
Elisabeth 1888-1962 Obituary 114
Dern, Erolie Pearl Gaddis 1895-1966 CANR-6
Obituary 25-28R
Earlier sketch in CA 2R
Dern, Karl L(udwig) 1894- 57-60
Dern, Peggy
See Dern, Erolie Pearl Gaddis
Dernburg, Thomas F(rederick) 1930- CANR-2
Earlier sketch in CA 1R
Der Nersessian, Sirarpie 1896- 102
de Robeck, Nesta 1886- CAP-2
Earlier sketch in CA 25-28
De Rochemont, Richard (Guertis)
1903-1982 Obituary 108
de Rocher, Gregory (David) 1943- 114
DeRoin, Nancy 1934- 65-68
de Romaszkan, Gregor 1894- 15-16R
de Roo, Anne Louise 1931- 103
See also SATA 25
de Roos, Robert (William) 1912- 11-12R
de Ropp, Robert S(ylvester) 1913- 19-20R
Deror, Yehezkel
See Dror, Yehezkel
DeRosa, Peter (Clement) 1932- CANR-9
Earlier sketch in CA 21-22R
DeRosier, Arthur H(enry), Jr. 1931- 29-32R
De Rosis, Helen A. 1918- 122
Brief entry 107
De Rossi, Claude J(oseph) 1942- 53-56
Derossi, Flavia 1926- 112
de Rothschild, Pauline (Fairfax-Potter)
1908(?)-1976 Obituary 65-68
de Rougemont, Denis 1906-1985
Obituary 118

De Roussan, Jacques 1929- Brief entry 110
See also SATA 31
de Roussan, Jacques 1929- 123
Derr, Richard L(uther) 1930- 53-56
Derr, Thomas Sieger 1931- 53-56
Derrett, J(ohn) Duncan M(artin) 1922- . CANR-21
Earlier sketches in CA 15-16R, CANR-6
Derrick, Graham
See Raby, Derek Graham
Derrick, Lionel
See Cunningham, Chet
Derrick, Paul 1916- CAP-1
Earlier sketch in CA 9-10
Derricotte, Toi 1941- 113
Derrida, Jacques 1930- Brief entry 124
See also CLC 24
Derriman, James Parkyns 1922- 106
Derry, John W(esley) 1933- CANR-3
Earlier sketch in CA 5-6R
Derry, (Thomas) Ramsay 1939- 110
Derry, Thomas Kingston 1905- CANR-4
Earlier sketch in CA 1R
Derry Down Derry
See Lear, Edward
Dershowitz, Alan M. 1938- CANR-11
Earlier sketch in CA 25-28R
Dersonnes, Jacques
See Simenon, Georges (Jacques Christian)
Dertouzos, Michael L. 1936- 23-24R
Derum, James Patrick 1893- CAP-1
Earlier sketch in CA 13-14
De Ruth, Jan 1922- 33-36R
Dervin, Brenda 1938- 29-32R
Dervin, Daniel A(rthur) 1935- 57-60
Derwent, Lavinia 69-72
See also SATA 14
Derwin, Jordan 1931- 13-14R
Dery, Tibor 1894-1977 Obituary 73-76
Desai, Anita 1937- 81-84
See also CLC 19, 37
Desai, P(rasannavadan) B(hagwanji) 1924- 29-32R
Desai, Ram 1926- 7-8R
Desai, Rashmi H(arilal) 1928- 15-16R
Desai, Rupin W(alter) 1934- 45-48
de Ste. Croix, G(eoffrey) E(rnest) M(aurice) 1910- 73-76
de Saint-Gall, Auguste Amedee
See Strich, Christian
de St. Jorre, John 1936- 102
de Saint-Luc, Jean
See Glassco, John
de Saint Phalle, Therese 1930- CANR-21
Earlier sketch in CA 29-32R
de Saint Phalle, Thibaut 1918- 108
DeSalvo, Joseph S(alvatore) 1938- 45-48
DeSalvo, Louise A(nita) 1942- CANR-23
Earlier sketch in CA 102
Desan, Wilfrid 1908- 61-64
Desani, G(ovindas) V(ishnoodas) 1909- 45-48
de Santillana, Giorgio Diaz 1902- CAP-1
Earlier sketch in CA 13-14
DeSantis, Mary Allen (Carpe) 1930- 9-10R
De Santis, Vincent P. 1916- CANR-4
Earlier sketch in CA 11-12R
De Santo, Charles P(asquale) 1923- 116
De Satge, John (Cosmo) 1928-1984 124
Obituary 113
Desatnick, Robert L(awrence) 1931- 41-44R
de Sausmarez, (Lionel) Maurice 1915-1969 .... CAP-1
Earlier sketch in CA 11-12
de Saussure, Eric 1925- 105
Desbarats, Peter 1933- CANR-10
Earlier sketch in CA 17-18R
See also SATA 39
Desbiens, Jean-Paul 1927- DLB-53
Desborough, Vincent Robin d'Arba 1914-1978 Obituary 111
Descargues, Pierre 1925- CANR-14
Earlier sketch in CA 37-40R
Deschampsneufs, Henry Pierre Bernard 1911- CANR-6
Earlier sketch in CA 7-8R
de Schanschieff, Juliet Dymoke 1919- 106
Descharnes, Robert (Pierre) 1926- 69-72
Deschenaux, Jacques 1945- 61-64
Deschin, Celia Spalter 1903- 104
Deschin, Jacob 1900(?)-1983 Obituary 110
Deschler, Lewis 1905-1976 Obituary 65-68
Deschner, Donald (Anthony) 1933- 21-22R
Deschner, (Hans) Guenther 1941- 41-44R
Deschner, (Hans) Gunther
See Deschner, (Hans) Guenther
Deschner, John 1923- 81-84
de Schweinitz, Karl 1887-1975 61-64
de Selincourt, Aubrey 1894-1962 73-76
See also SATA 14
de Sena, Jorge 1919-1978 Obituary 77-80
De Seversky, Alexander P(rocofieff) 1894-1974 Obituary 53-56
DeSeyn, Donna E. 1933- 21-22R
Desfosses, Helen 1945- 41-44R
Des Gagniers, Jean 1929- CANR-9
Earlier sketch in CA 65-68
DeShazo, Edith K(ind) 1920- 61-64
DeShazo, Elmer Anthony 1924- 37-40R
Deshen, Shlomo 1935- 57-60
Deshler, G(eorge) Byron 1903- 53-56
DeSiano, Francis P(atrick) 1945- 112
De Sica, Vittorio 1901(?)-1974 Obituary 117
See also CLC 20
Desiderato, Otello 1926- 37-40R
De Simone, Daniel V. 1930- 25-28R
Desmarais, Barbara G.
See Taylor, Barbara G.
Des Marais, Louise M(ercier) 1923- 110
Desmarais, Ovid E. 1919- CANR-23
Earlier sketches in CA 4R, CANR-4
Desmond, Adrian J(ohn) 1947- CANR-8
Earlier sketch in CA 61-64
Desmond, Alice Curtis 1897- CANR-2
Earlier sketch in CA 4R
See also SATA 8
Desmond, (Clarice) J(oanne) Patrick (Scholes) 1910- 11-12R
Desmond, John 1909(?)-1977 Obituary 73-76
Desmond, John F(rancis) 1939- 112
Desmond, Ray 1925- 120
Desmond, Robert W(illiam) 1900- CANR-12
Earlier sketch in CA 73-76
Desmond, Shaw 1877-1960 Obituary 89-92
Desmonde, William H(erbert) 1921- 1R
Desnos, Robert 1900-1945 Brief entry 121
See also TCLC 22
De Sola, John
See Morland, Nigel
De Sola, Ralph 1908- 53-56
Despalatovic, Elinor Murray 1933- 105
Despert, J(uliette) Louise 1892- 69-72
Desplaines, Baroness Julie
See Jennings, Leslie Nelson
Despland, Michel 1936- 49-52
Despres, Leo A(rthur) 1932- 25-28R
Des Pres, Terrence 1939-1987 73-76
Obituary 124
Dessau, Joanna 1921- CANR-24
Earlier sketch in CA 106
Dessauer, John H(ans) 1905- 104
Dessauer, John P(aul) 1924- 53-56
Dessel, Norman F(rank) 1932- 61-64
Dessen, Alan C(harles) 1935- 69-72
Dessent, Michael H(arold) 1942- 110
Dessi, Giuseppe 1909- 65-68
d'Estaing, Valery Giscard
See Giscard d'Estaing, Valery
De Steuch, Harriet Henry 1897(?)-1974 Obituary 49-52
Destler, Chester McArthur 1904-1984 .. CANR-16
Obituary 114
Earlier sketch in CA 5-6R
Destler, I. M. 1939- CANR-15
Earlier sketch in CA 89-92
Destouches, Louis Ferdinand 1894-1961 ... 85-88
See also CLC 9, 15
Destry, Vince
See Norwood, Victor G(eorge) C(harles)
De Sua, William Joseph 1930- 15-16R
de Swaan, Abram 1942- CANR-13
Earlier sketch in CA 69-72
de Sylva, Donald Perrin 1928- 53-56
de Tabley, Lord 1835-1895 .... DLB-35
De Tarr, Francis 1926- 17-18R
Deter, Dean (Allen) 1945- 53-56
de Teran, Lisa St. Aubin
See St. Aubin de Teran, Lisa
Deterline, William A(lexander) 1927- CANR-8
Earlier sketch in CA 7-8R
de Terra, Helmut 1900-1981 Obituary 104
de Terra, Rhoda Hoff 1901- 2R
Detherage, May 1908- CAP-2
Earlier sketch in CA 23-24
Dethier, Vincent Gaston 1915- CANR-9
Earlier sketch in CA 65-68
Dethlefsen, Merle 1934- 119
Dethloff, Henry C(lay) 1934- 23-24R
De Thomasis, Louis 1940- 123
Detine, Padre
See Olsen, Ib Spang
de Tirtoff, Romain 1892- 69-72
Detjen, Ervin W(infred) 1909- CAP-2
Earlier sketch in CA 19-20
Detjen, Mary (Elizabeth) Ford 1904- CAP-1
Earlier sketch in CA 13-14
de Todany, James
See Beaudoin, Kenneth Lawrence
de Toledano, Ralph
See Toledano, Ralph de
de Tolignac, Gaston
See Griffith, D(avid Lewelyn) W(ark)
De Tolnay, Charles Erich 1899- 73-76
de Tonquedec, Jospeh
See Tonquedec, Joseph de
de Trevino, Elizabeth B.
See Trevino, Elizabeth B(orton) de
Detro, Gene 1935- CANR-12
Earlier sketch in CA 61-64
Detter, Ingrid
See Delupis, Ingrid
Detweiler, Robert 1932- 33-36R
Detwiler, Donald S(caife) 1933- 37-40R
Detz, Joan (Marie) 1951- 118
Detz, Phyllis 1911- CAP-2
Earlier sketch in CA 33-36
Detzer, David William 1937- 93-96
Detzer, Karl 1891- CAP-1
Earlier sketch in CA 9-10
Detzler, Jack J. 1922- 33-36R
Detzler, Wayne Alan 1936- 105
Deuchar, Margaret 1952- 113
Deuel, Thorne 1890-1984 Obituary 112
Deutrich, Mabel E. 1915- 5-6R
Deutsch, Alfred H(enry) 1914- 116
Deutsch, Arnold R. 1919- 101
Deutsch, Babette 1895-1982 .... CANR-4
Obituary 108
Earlier sketch in CA 4R
See also SATA 1, 33
See also DLB 45
See also CLC 18
Deutsch, Bernard Francis 1925- 15-16R
Deutsch, Eberhard Paul 1897-1980
Obituary 93-96
Deutsch, Eliot (Sandler) 1931- CANR-10
Earlier sketch in CA 65-68
Deutsch, Harold C(harles) 1904- 21-22R
Deutsch, Helen 1906- 112
Brief entry 108
Deutsch, Helene (Rosenbach) 1884-1982
Obituary 106
Deutsch, Herbert A(rnold) 1932- 89-92
Deutsch, Hermann Bacher 1889-1970
Obituary 93-96
Deutsch, John James 1911-1976 Obituary .. 111
Deutsch, Karl W(olfgang) 1912- 41-44R
Deutsch, Marilyn Weisberg 1950- 102
Deutsch, Morton 1920- 1R
Deutsch, Ronald M(artin) 1928- CANR-4
Earlier sketch in CA 3R
Deutscher, Irwin 1923- 25-28R
Deutscher, Isaac 1907-1967 .... CANR-4
Obituary 25-28R
Earlier sketch in CA 5-6R
Deutscher, Max 1916(?)-1979 Obituary ... 93-96
Deutscher, Thomas (Brian) 1949- 124
Deutschkron, Inge 1922- 29-32R
Deutschman, Alan (Barry) 1965- 116
Devadutt, Vinjamuri E(verett) 1908- CAP-2
Earlier sketch in CA 23-24
De Vaere, Ulric Josef 1932- 3R
Devahuti, D. 1929- 45-48
Devajee, Ved
See Gool, Reshard
Deval, Gord 1930- 124
Deval, Jacques
See Boularan, Jacques
De Valera, Eamon 1882-1975 Obituary 89-92
De Valera, Sinead 1879(?)-1975 Obituary .. 53-56
See also SATA 30
de Valois, Ninette 1898- Brief entry 115
Devaney, John 1926- CANR-23
Earlier sketches in CA 19-20R, CANR-7
See also SATA 12
Devaraja, N(and) K(ishore) 1917- 104
Devas, Nicolette (Macnamara) 1911-1987(?) 13-14R
Obituary 122
DeVault, M(arion) Vere 1922- CANR-20
Earlier sketches in CA 1R, CANR-4
De Vaux, Roland 1903-1971 Obituary 33-36R
De Veaux, Alexis 1948- 65-68
See also DLB 38
D'Evelyn, Katherine E(dith) 1899- 17-18R
Dever, Joseph 1919-1970 .... CAP-2
Obituary 29-32R
Earlier sketch in CA 19-20
Dever, William Gwinn 1933- Brief entry 109
Deveraux, Jude
See White, Jude Gilliam
de Vere, Aubrey 1814-1902 .... DLB-35
de Vere, Jane
See Watson, Julia
Deverell, William H(erbert) 1937- 115
Devereux, Frederick L(eonard), Jr. 1914- CANR-1
Earlier sketch in CA 49-52
See also SATA 9
Devereux, George 1908- 69-72
Devereux, Hilary 1919- 13-14R
Devereux, Robert (Essex) 1922- 5-6R
Deverson, Harry 1909(?)-1972 Obituary 104
De Vet, Charles V(incent) 1911- 102
Devi, Indra 1899- CAP-1
Earlier sketch in CA 13-14
Devi, Nila
See Woody, Regina Jones
Devi, Ragini 1894(?)-1982 Obituary 110
Deview, Lucille 1920- 73-76
De Vilbiss, Philip
See Mebane, John (Harrison)
Deville, Rene
See Kacew, Romain
de Villiers, Gerard 1929- 61-64
de Vilmorin, Louise Leveque
See Vilmorin, Louise Leveque de
de Vinck, Antoine 1924- 53-56
de Vinck, Catherine 1922- CANR-6
Earlier sketch in CA 57-60
de Vinck, (Baron) Jose M. G. A. 1912- ... 19-20R
Devine, D(avid) M(cDonald) 1920- CANR-1
Earlier sketch in CA 4R
Devine, Dominic
See Devine, D(avid) M(cDonald)
Devine, Donald J. 1937- 81-84
Devine, (Mary) Elizabeth 1938- 116
Devine, George 1941- CANR-1
Earlier sketch in CA 45-48
Devine, Janice 1909(?)-1973 Obituary ... 41-44R
Devine, (Joseph) Lawrence 1935- 73-76
Devine, Thomas G. 1928- 17-18R
DeVinney, Richard 1936- 45-48
Devins, Joseph H(erbert), Jr. 1930- 21-22R
DeVitis, Angelo A(nthony) 1925- 107
De Vito, Joseph Anthony 1938- 37-40R
Devkota, Laxmiprasad 1909-1959
Brief entry 123
See also TCLC 23
Devletoglou, Nicos E. 1936- 41-44R
Devlin, Bernadette (Josephine) 1947- 105
Devlin, Diana (Mary) 1941- 114
Devlin, Gerard M(ichael) 1933- 105
Devlin, Harry 1918- CANR-8
Earlier sketch in CA 65-68
See also SATA 11
Devlin, John C. 1911(?)-1984 Obituary 113
Devlin, John J(oseph), Jr. 1920- 37-40R
Devlin, L. Patrick 1939- 61-64
Devlin, Otis 1916- 117
Devlin, Patrick (Arthur) 1905- 69-72
Devlin, (Dorothy) Wende 1918- CANR-8
Earlier sketch in CA 61-64
See also SATA 11
DeVoe, Shirley Spaulding 1899- 77-80
Devol, Kenneth S(towe) 1929- 49-52
Devon, D. G.
See Demorest, Stephen and Gross, Michael (Robert)
Devon, John Anthony
See Payne, (Pierre Stephen) Robert
Devor, John W(esley) 1901- CAP-1
Earlier sketch in CA 11-12
Devore, Irven 1934- 23-24R
DeVorkin, David H(yam) 1944- 108
De Vorsey, Louis, Jr. 1929- 21-22R
DeVos, George A(lphonse) 1922- CANR-11
Earlier sketch in CA 21-22R
De Vos, Karen Helder 1939- 102
de Vosjoli, Philippe L. Thyraud 1920- 29-32R
De Voto, Bernard (Augustine) 1897-1955
Brief entry 113
See also DLB 9
de Vries, Anne 1904-1964 Obituary 116
De Vries, Carrow 1906- 53-56
deVries, Egbert 1901- 61-64
de Vries, Herbert A. 1917- CANR-13
Earlier sketch in CA 33-36R
de Vries, Jan 1943- 69-72
de Vries, Leonard
See Vries, Leonard de
de Vries, Manfred F. R. Kets
See Kets de Vries, Manfred F. R.
De Vries, Peter 1910- 17-18R
See also DLB 6
See also DLBY 82
See also CLC 1, 2, 3, 7, 10, 28, 46
de Vries, Rachel (Guido) 1947- 123
De Vries, Simon J(ohn) 1921- 57-60
De Vries, Walter (Dale) 1929- 69-72
Dew, Charles B(urgess) 1937- 21-22R
Dew, Donald 1928- 106
Dew, Edward MacMillan 1935- 81-84
Dew, Joan King 1932- 104
Dew, Robb Forman 1946- 104
de Waal, Frans 1948- 110
De Waal, Ronald Burt 1932- CANR-14
Earlier sketch in CA 37-40R
de Waal, Victor (Alexander) 1929- 29-32R
de Waal Malefijt, Annemarie 1914-1982 ... 61-64
Obituary 109
De Waard, E(lliott) John 1935- CANR-2
Earlier sketch in CA 49-52
See also SATA 7
Dewald, Paul A. 1920- 19-20R
Dewar, Deborah 1946(?)-1986 Obituary 118
Dewar, Diana III 1928(?)-1984 Obituary 112
Dewar, Margaret E(lizabeth) 1948- 114
Dewar, Mary (Williamson) 1921- 15-16R
Dewart, Leslie 1922- 9-10R
de Water, Frederic F(ranklyn) Van
See Van de Water, Frederic F(ranklyn)
Dewdney, Christopher 1951- DLB-60
Dewdney, John Christopher 1928- 103
Dewdney, Selwyn (Hanington) 1909- 69-72
DeWeerd, Harvey A. 1902- 73-76
DeWeese, Gene
See DeWeese, Thomas Eugene
DeWeese, Jean
See DeWeese, Thomas Eugene
DeWeese, Thomas Eugene 1934- CANR-24
Earlier sketches in CA 65-68, CANR-9
See also SATA 45, 46
De Wet, Don Finch 1919- CANR-1
Earlier sketch in CA 1R
de Wet, Hugh Oloff 1912(?)-1976(?)
Obituary 104
Dewey, Ariane 1937- CANR-3
Earlier sketch in CA 49-52
See also SATA 7
Dewey, Bradley R. 1934- 29-32R
Dewey, Donald O(dell) 1930- 37-40R
Dewey, Edward R(ussell) 1895-1978 .... 41-44R
Dewey, Frank L. 1906- 122
Dewey, Godfrey 1887-1977 .... CAP-2
Obituary 73-76
Earlier sketch in CA 29-32
Dewey, Irene Sargent 1896- CAP-2
Earlier sketch in CA 17-18
Dewey, Jennifer (Owings) SATA-48
Dewey, John 1859-1952 Brief entry 114
Dewey, Kenneth Francis 1940- 112
See also SATA 39
Dewey, Melvil 1851-1931 Brief entry 118
Dewey, Melville Louis Kossuth
See Dewey, Melvil
Dewey, Robert D(yckman) 1923- 9-10R
Dewey, Robert E(ugene) 1923- 13-14R
Dewey, Thomas B(lanchard) 1915- CANR-1
Earlier sketch in CA 3R
Dewhirst, Ian 1936- 102
Dewhurst, Eileen (Mary) 1929- 109
Dewhurst, J(ames) Frederic 1895-1967 ... CAP-2
Earlier sketch in CA 17-18
Dewhurst, Keith 1931- CANR-18
Earlier sketch in CA 61-64
Dewhurst, Kenneth 1919- CANR-2
Earlier sketch in CA 7-8R
deWit, Dorothy (May Knowles) 1916-1980 .. 113
Obituary 109
See also SATA 28, 39
DeWitt, Addison
See Newman, Kim (James)
DeWitt, Edith Openshaw 1920- 111
DeWitt, James
See Lewis, Mildred D.
DeWitt, John 1910(?)-1984 Obituary 113

Dewlen, Al 1921- ... CANR-2
Earlier sketch in CA 2R
de Wohl, Louis 1903-1961 Obituary ... 111
De Wolf, L. Harold 1905- ... CANR-2
Earlier sketch in CA 2R
DeWolf, Rose (Doris) 1934- ... CANR-11
Earlier sketch in CA 29-32R
de Wolfe, Ivor
See Hastings, Hubert de Cronin
de Wolfe, Ivy
See Hastings, Hubert de Cronin
Dewsbury, Donald A(llen) 1939- ... CANR-15
Earlier sketch in CA 89-92
Dexter, Al
See Poindexter, Clarence Albert
Dexter, Beverly L(iebherr) 1943- ... 114
Dexter, Byron (Vinson) 1900-1973
Obituary ... 113
Dexter, (Norman) Colin 1930- ... CANR-10
Earlier sketch in CA 65-68
Dexter, John
See Zachary, Hugh
Dexter, Lewis Anthony 1915- ... CANR-4
Earlier sketch in CA 11-12R
Dexter, Martin
See Faust, Frederick (Shiller)
Dexter, (Ellen) Pat(ricia) Egan ... 81-84
Dexter, Pete 1943- ... CLC-34
Dexter, Susan (Elizabeth) 1955- ... 108
Dey, Frederic (Merrill) Van Rensselaer
1865-1922 Brief entry ... 113
Dey, Joseph C(harles), Jr. 1907- ... CAP-1
Earlier sketch in CA 11-12
Dey, Marmaduke
See Dey, Frederic (Merrill) Van
Rensselaer
Deyermond, Alan D(avid) 1932- ... CANR-6
Earlier sketch in CA 13-14R
Deyneka, Anita 1943- ... CANR-11
Earlier sketch in CA 61-64
See also SATA 24
Deyneka, Peter (N., Sr.) 1898-1987
Obituary ... 123
de Young, M. H. 1849-1925 ... DLB-25
DeYoung, Mary 1949- ... 112
Deyrup, Astrith Johnson 1923- ... 65-68
See also SATA 24
Deza, Ernest C. 1923- ... 53-56
Dhalla, Nariman K. 1925- ... 25-28R
Dharmi, Santana 1914- ... CANR-20
Earlier sketch in CA 101
d'Harnoncourt, Anne (Julie) 1943- ... 120
Dhavamony, Mariasusai 1925- ... 33-36R
Dhiegh, Khigh (Alx) ... 93-96
Dhokalia, (Ramaa) Prasad 1925- ... 41-44R
Dhrymes, Phoebus J(ames) 1932- ... CANR-12
Earlier sketch in CA 29-32R
Diack, Hunter 1908-1974 ... CAP-2
Earlier sketch in CA 21-22
Dial, Joan 1937- ... CANR-24
Earlier sketch in CA 81-84
Diallo, Nafissatou (Niang) 1941-? ... 116
Diamant, Lincoln 1923- ... 33-36R
Diamond, Ann
See McLean, Anne (Julia)
Diamond, Arthur Sigismund 1897- ... CAP-1
Earlier sketch in CA 9-10
Diamond, Cora A(nn) 1937- ... 121
Diamond, Donna 1950- ... 115
See also SATA 30, 35
Diamond, Edwin 1925- ... CANR-9
Earlier sketch in CA 15-16R
Diamond, Graham 1945- ... 85-88
Diamond, Harold J(ames) 1934- ... 110
Diamond, I(sidore) A. L. 1920- ... 81-84
See also DLB 26
Diamond, Jacqueline
See Hyman, Jackie Diamond
Diamond, Jay 1934- ... CANR-14
Earlier sketch in CA 65-68
Diamond, John 1907- ... 109
Diamond, John 1934- ... 85-88
Diamond, Malcolm L(uria) 1924- ... 25-28R
Diamond, Marc 1944- ... 119
Diamond, Martin 1919-1977 ... 77-80
Obituary ... 73-76
Diamond, Milton 1934- ... 89-92
Diamond, Neil 1941- ... 108
See also CLC 30
Diamond, Norma Joyce 1933- Brief entry ... 108
Diamond, Petra
See Sachs, Judith
Diamond, Rebecca
See Sachs, Judith
Diamond, Robert Mach 1930- ... CANR-7
Earlier sketch in CA 9-10R
Diamond, Sander A. 1942- ... 49-52
Diamond, Selma 1920-1985 Obituary ... 116
Diamond, Sigmund 1920- ... 3R
Diamond, Solomon 1906- ... 102
Diamond, Stanley 1922- ... 102
Diamond, Stephen A(rthur) 1946- ... 89-92
Diamond, William 1917- ... 65-68
Diamonstein, Barbaralee D. ... CANR-15
Earlier sketch in CA 85-88
Diara, Agadem Lumumba 1947- ... 65-68
Diara, Schavi M(ali) 1948- ... CANR-11
Earlier sketch in CA 61-64
Dias, Earl Joseph 1916- ... 23-24R
See also SATA 41
Diaz, Janet W(inecoff) 1935- ... 53-56
Diaz-Alejandro, Carlos Federico 1937-1985
Obituary ... 116
Diaz-Guerrero, Rogelio 1918- ... 101
Diaz Plaja, Guillermo 1909-1984 Obituary ... 113
di Bassetto, Corno
See Shaw, George Bernard
DiBattista, Maria 1947- ... 113
Dibb, Paul 1939- ... CANR-1
Earlier sketch in CA 45-48
Dibba, Ebou 1943- ... 124
Dibble, J(ames) Birney 1925- ... 17-18R
Dibble, Nancy Ann 1942- ... 103
Dibble, Vadna Davis 1902(?)-1983
Obituary ... 110
Dibdin, Michael 1947- ... 77-80
Dibelius, Otto (Friedrich Karl) 1880-1967
Obituary ... 114
Dibell, Ansen
See Dibble, Nancy Ann
Di Bella, Anna 1933- Brief entry ... 110
Dible, Donald M(eredith) 1936- ... 110
Dibner, Andrew Sherman 1926-
Brief entry ... 110
Dibner, Bern 1897- ... 107
Dibner, Martin 1911- ... CANR-4
Earlier sketch in CA 2R
DiBona, Joseph E. 1927- Brief entry ... 109
Di Cavalcanti, Emiliano 1898(?)-1976
Obituary ... 69-72
Dice, Lee R. 1889(?)-1976 Obituary ... 69-72
Di Certo, J(oseph) J(ohn) 1933- ... CANR-13
Earlier sketch in CA 23-24R
Di Cesare, Mario A(nthony) 1928- ... CANR-3
Earlier sketch in CA 5-6R
Dichter, Ernest 1907- ... 19-20R
Dichter, Harry 1900(?)-1978(?) Obituary ... 104
Di Cicco, Pier Giorgio 1949- ... CANR-17
Earlier sketch in CA 97-100
See also DLB 60
Dick, Bernard F(rancis) 1935- ... CANR-9
Earlier sketch in CA 21-22R
Dick, Daniel T. 1946- ... 61-64
Dick, Everett 1898- ... 25-28R
Dick, Ignace 1926- ... CANR-12
Earlier sketch in CA 25-28R
Dick, Kay 1915- ... CANR-15
Earlier sketch in CA 15-16R
Dick, Philip K(indred) 1928-1982 ... CANR-16
Obituary ... 106
Earlier sketches in CA 49-52, CANR-2
See also DLB 8
See also CLC 10, 30
Dick, R. A.
See Leslie, Josephine Aimee Campbell
Dick, Robert C. 1938- ... 37-40R
Dick, Susan 1940- ... 120
Dick, Trella Lamson 1889-1974 ... 7-8R
See also SATA 9
Dick, Trevor J.O. 1934- Brief entry ... 106
Dick, William M(ilner) 1933- ... 41-44R
Dickason, David Howard 1907-1974 ... CAP-2
Earlier sketch in CA 33-36
Dicke, Robert H(enry) 1916- ... 53-56
Dicken, E(ric) W(illiam) Trueman 1919- ... 9-10R
Dickens, A(rthus) G(eoffrey) 1910- ... 53-56
Dickens, Charles (John Huffam)
1812-1870 ... SATA-15
See also DLB 21, 55
Dickens, Floyd, Jr. 1940- ... 111
Dickens, Frank
See Huline-Dickens, Frank William
Dickens, Jacqueline B(ass) 1941- ... 112
Dickens, Milton 1908- ... 2R
Dickens, Monica (Enid) 1915- ... CANR-2
Earlier sketch in CA 7-8R
See also SATA 4
Dickens, Norman
See Eisenberg, Lawrence B(enjamin)
Dickens, Peter (Gerald Charles)
1917-1987 ... 124
Obituary ... 122
Dickens, Roy S(elman), Jr. 1938- ... CANR-9
Earlier sketch in CA 65-68
Dickenson, Fred 1909-1986 Obituary ... 119
Dickenson, James R. 1931- ... 65-68
Dicker, Eva Barash 1936- ... 107
Dicker, Ralph Leslie 1914- ... 65-68
Dickerman, Edmund H. 1935- Brief entry ... 110
Dickerson, F(rederick) Reed 1909- ... 17-18R
Dickerson, Grace Leslie 1911- ... 5-6R
Dickerson, John 1939- ... 57-60
Dickerson, Martha Ufford 1922- ... 81-84
Dickerson, Nancy H(anschman) 1930- ... 69-72
Dickerson, Oliver M(orton) 1875-1966
Obituary ... 106
Dickerson, Robert B(radford), Jr. 1955- ... 106
Dickerson, Roy Ernest 1886-1965 ... 7-8R
Obituary ... 103
See also SATA 26
Dickerson, William E(ugene) 1897-1971 ... CAP-2
Earlier sketch in CA 21-22
Dickey, Charley 1920- ... 69-72
Dickey, Franklin M(iller) 1921- ... 23-24R
Dickey, Glenn (Ernest, Jr.) 1936- ... CANR-4
Earlier sketch in CA 53-56
Dickey, James (Lafayette) 1923- ... CANR-10
Earlier sketch in CA 11-12R
See also CABS 2
See also DLB 5
See also DLBY 82
See also CLC 1, 2, 4, 7, 10, 15, 47
See also AITN 1, 2
Dickey, Lee
See Bremyer, Jayne Dickey
Dickey, R(obert) P(reston) 1936- ... 29-32R
Dickey, William 1928- ... CANR-24
Earlier sketch in CA 9-10R
See also DLB 5
See also CLC 3, 28
Dickie, Edgar P(rimrose) 1897- ... CAP-1
Earlier sketch in CA 11-12
Dickie, George (Thomas) 1926- ... 33-36R
Dickie, James 1934- ... 97-100
Dickie, John 1923- ... 13-14R
Dickie, Margaret (McKenzie) 1935- ... 123
Dickie-Clark, H(amish) F(indlay) 1922- ... 21-22R
Dickins, A. S. M.
See Dickins, Anthony (Stewart Mackay)
Dickins, Anthony (Stewart Mackay)
1914-1987 Obituary ... 124
Dickinson, A(lan) E(dgar) F(rederic)
1899- ... 73-76
Dickinson, A(rthur) T(aylor), Jr. 1925- ... 7-8R
Dickinson, Donald C. 1927- ... 23-24R
Dickinson, Edward C(live) 1938- ... 61-64
Dickinson, Eleanor 1931- ... 65-68
Dickinson, Emily (Elizabeth)
1830-1886 ... SATA-29
See also DLB 1
Dickinson, H(arry) T(homas) 1939- ... 33-36R
Dickinson, John 1732-1808 ... DLB-31
Dickinson, John K(ellogg) 1918- ... 25-28R
Dickinson, Jonathan 1688-1747 ... DLB-24
Dickinson, Leon T. 1912- ... 13-14R
Dickinson, Lois Stice 1898(?)-1970
Obituary ... 104
Dickinson, Margaret
See Muggeson, Margaret Elizabeth
Dickinson, Mary 1949- ... 110
See also SATA 41, 48
Dickinson, Patric Thomas 1914- ... CANR-3
Earlier sketch in CA 9-10R
See also DLB 27
Dickinson, Peter 1927- ... 41-44R
See also SATA 5
See also CLC 12, 35
Dickinson, Peter A(llen) 1926- ... 102
Dickinson, Richard D(onald) N(ye, Jr.)
1929- Brief entry ... 109
Dickinson, Robert Eric 1905- ... CANR-3
Earlier sketch in CA 5-6R
Dickinson, Ruth F(rankenstein) 1933- ... 37-40R
Dickinson, (William) Stirling 1909- ... CAP-2
Earlier sketch in CA 33-36
Dickinson, Susan 1931- ... 57-60
See also SATA 8
Dickinson, Thorold (Barron) 1903-1984 ... 45-48
Obituary ... 112
Dickinson, W(illiam) Croft 1897-1963 ... CANR-6
Earlier sketch in CA 3R
See also SATA 13
Dickinson, William Boyd 1908-1978 ... 85-88
Obituary ... 81-84
Dick-Lauder, George (Andrew) 1917- ... 102
Dickler, Gerald 1912- ... 11-12R
Dickmeyer, Lowell A. 1939- ... 109
Dicks, Henry V(ictor) 1900- ... 102
Dicks, Russell Leslie 1906-1965 ... CAP-1
Earlier sketch in CA 15-16
Dickson, Carr
See Carr, John Dickson
Dickson, Carter
See Carr, John Dickson
Dickson, Charles W., Jr. 1926- ... 25-28R
Dickson, Franklyn 1941- ... 53-56
Dickson, George E(dmond) 1918- ... 49-52
Dickson, Gordon R(upert) 1923- ... CANR-6
Earlier sketch in CA 9-10R
See also DLB 8
Dickson, Helen
See Reynolds, Helen Mary Greenwood
Campbell
Dickson, K. A.
See Dickson, Kwesi A(botsia)
Dickson, Kwesi A(botsia) 1929-
Brief entry ... 109
Dickson, (Horatio Henry) Lovat
1902-1987 ... 13-14R
Obituary ... 121
Dickson, Margaret (Smith) 1947- ... 114
Dickson, Mora (Hope-Robertson) 1918- ... CANR-5
Earlier sketch in CA 15-16R
Dickson, Naida 1916- ... 37-40R
See also SATA 8
Dickson, Paul 1939- ... 33-36R
Dickson, Peter George Muir 1929- ... 13-14R
Dickson, Robert J(ames) 1919- ... 21-22R
Dickson, Stanley 1927- ... 53-56
Dickstein, Morris 1940- ... 85-88
Di Cyan, Erwin 1918- ... 37-40R
Didato, Salvatore V. 1926- ... 122
Brief entry ... 107
Didinger, Ray 1946- ... 93-96
Didion, Joan 1934- ... CANR-14
Earlier sketch in CA 5-6R
See also DLB 2
See also DLBY 81, 86
See also CLC 1, 3, 8, 14, 32
See also AITN 1
di Donato, Georgia 1932- ... 103
di Donato, Pietro 1911- ... 101
See also DLB 9
Didsbury, Howard F(rancis), Jr. 1924- ... 111
Didsbury, Peter 1946- ... 112
Diebold, Janet
See Sylvester, Janet Hart
Diebold, Janet Oline
See Sylvester, Janet Hart
Diebold, John (Theurer) 1926- ... 53-56
Diebold, William, Jr. 1918- ... CANR-6
Earlier sketch in CA 13-14R
Dieckmann, Ed(ward Adolph), Jr.
1920- ... CANR-21
Earlier sketch in CA 102
Dieckmann, Liselotte 1902- ... 97-100
Diederich, Bernard 1926- ... 77-80
Diefendorf, Barbara B(oonstoppel) 1946- ... 124
Diefendorf, Jeffry M(indlin) 1945- ... 104
Diefenthaler, Jon 1943- ... 124
Diego, Gerardo
See Diego Cendoya, Gerardo
Diego Cendoya, Gerardo 1896-1987
Obituary ... 123
Diehl, (Robert) Digby 1940- ... CANR-7
Earlier sketch in CA 53-56
Diehl, James M(ichael) 1938- ... 85-88
Diehl, Katharine Smith 1906- ... CAP-1
Earlier sketch in CA 11-12
Diehl, Kemper 1918- ... 118
Diehl, Lorraine B(uscaglia) 1940- ... 119
Diehl, W(illiam) W(ells) 1916- ... 19-20R
Diehl, William (Francis, Jr.) 1924- ... CANR-13
Earlier sketch in CA 101
Diehm, Floyd L(ee) 1925- Brief entry ... 110
Diekhoff, John S(iemon) 1905-1976 ... CAP-2
Obituary ... 69-72
Earlier sketch in CA 29-32
Diekman, John R(aymond) 1946- ... 110
Diekmann, Godfrey 1908- ... CANR-2
Earlier sketch in CA 4R
Diel, Paul 1893- ... 103
Diener, Royce 1918- Brief entry ... 110
Dienes, C(harles) Thomas 1940- ... CANR-11
Earlier sketch in CA 69-72
Dienstag, Eleanor 1938- ... 65-68
Dienstein, William 1909- ... CAP-1
Earlier sketch in CA 17-18
Dierenfield, Richard B(ruce) 1922- ... 19-20R
Dierickx, C(harles) W(allace) 1921- ... 61-64
Dierks, Jack Cameron 1930- ... 29-32R
Diers, Carol Jean 1933- ... 33-36R
Diesing, Paul R. 1922- ... CANR-2
Earlier sketch in CA 1R
Dieska, L. Joseph 1913- ... 37-40R
Dieskau, Dietrich Fischer
See Fischer-Dieskau, Dietrich
Dieter, William 1929- ... 114
Dietl, (Kirsten) Ulla 1940- ... 33-36R
Dietrich, John E(rb) 1913- ... 17-18R
Dietrich, Noah 1889-1982 ... 45-48
Obituary ... 106
Dietrich, R(ichard) F(arr) 1936- ... 23-24R
Dietrich, Richard V(incent) 1924- ... CANR-19
Earlier sketches in CA 53-56, CANR-4
Dietrich, Robert
See Hunt E(verette) Howard, Jr.
Dietrich, Wilson G. 1916- ... 25-28R
Dietz, Betty Warner
See Dietz, Elisabeth H.
Dietz, David H(enry) 1897-1984 ... CANR-2
Obituary ... 114
Earlier sketch in CA 1R
See also SATA 10, 41
Dietz, Elisabeth H. 1908- ... 29-32R
Dietz, Howard 1896-1983 ... 53-56
Obituary ... 110
Dietz, Lew 1907- ... CANR-3
Earlier sketch in CA 5-6R
See also SATA 11
Dietz, Marjorie (Priscilla) J(ohnson)
1918- ... CANR-14
Earlier sketch in CA 65-68
Dietz, Norman D. 1930- ... CANR-10
Earlier sketch in CA 23-24R
Dietz, Peter O(wen) 1935- ... 33-36R
Dietze, Charles Edgar 1919- ... 69-72
Dietze, Gottfried 1922- ... 23-24R
Dietzel, Paul F(ranklin) 1924- ... 21-22R
Diez Del Corral, Luis 1911- ... 13-14R
Diez de Medina, Raul 1909(?)-1985
Obituary ... 117
DiFranco, Anthony (Mario) 1945- ... 118
See also SATA 42
Di Franco, Fiorenza 1932- ... CANR-17
Earlier sketches in CA 45-48, CANR-1
DiGaetani, John Louis 1943- ... 114
Digennaro, Joseph 1939- ... 53-56
Digges, Jeremiah
See Berger, Josef
Digges, Sister Mary Laurentia 1910- ... CAP-2
Earlier sketch in CA 21-22
Diggins, John P(atrick) 1935- ... 37-40R
Diggle, James 1944- ... CANR-13
Earlier sketch in CA 61-64
Diggory, James C(lark) 1920- ... CANR-9
Earlier sketch in CA 23-24R
Diggory, Terence (Elliott) 1951- ... 112
Diggs, Bernard James 1916- Brief entry ... 106
Diggs, Elizabeth 1939- ... 109
Diggs, Ellen Irene ... 114
Diggs, Irene
See Diggs, Ellen Irene
DiGiacomo, James J(oseph) 1924- ... 112
Di Girolamo, Vittorio 1928- ... 45-48
D'Ignazio, Fred(erick) 1949- ... 110
See also SATA 35, 39
Di Grazia, Thomas ?-1983 ... SATA-32
di Guisa, Giano
See Praz, Mario
Dihoff, Gretchen 1942- ... 41-44R
Dijkstra, Bram (Abraham Jan) 1938- ... 37-40R
Dike, Kenneth Onwuka 1917-1983
Obituary ... 111
Dikshit, R(amesh) D(utta) 1939- ... CANR-10
Earlier sketch in CA 65-68
Dikty, Julian May
See May, Julian
Dil, Zakhmi
See Hilton, Richard
DiLauro, Stephen 1950- ... 112
Dilcock, Noreen 1907- ... 103
Di Lella, Alexander A. 1929- ... 23-24R
DiLello, Richard 1945- ... 41-44R
Di Leo, Joseph H. 1902- ... 33-36R
Diles, Dave 1931- ... CANR-8
Earlier sketch in CA 57-60

Dilke, Annabel (Mary) 1942- CAP-1
Earlier sketch in CA 11-12
Dilke, Caroline (Sophia) 1940- 102
Dilke, O(swald) A(shton) W(entworth)
1915- 69-72
Dilks, David (Neville) 1938- CANR-8
Earlier sketch in CA 61-64
Dill, Alonzo T(homas, Jr.) 1914- 37-40R
Dill, Clarence C(leveland) 1884-1978
Obituary 115
Dill, (George) Marshall, Jr. 1916- 4R
Dillard, Annie 1945- CANR-3
Earlier sketch in CA 49-52
See also SATA 10
See also DLBY 80
See also CLC 9
Dillard, Dudley 1913- 25-28R
Dillard, Emil L(ee) 1921- 57-60
Dillard, Heath (Portmann) 1933- 119
Dillard, J(oey) L(ee) 1924- CANR-14
Earlier sketch in CA 41-44R
Dillard, Polly Hargis 1916- CANR-5
Earlier sketch in CA 11-12R
See also SATA 24
Dillard, R(ichard) H(enry) W(ilde)
1937- CANR-10
Earlier sketch in CA 21-22R
See also DLB 5
See also CLC 5
Dille, John M. 1921(?)-1971 Obituary . . .33-36R
Dille, Robert Crabtree 1924(?)-1983
Obituary 109
Dillehay, Ronald C(lifford) 1935- 23-24R
Dillenbeck, Marsden V. CAP-2
Earlier sketch in CA 25-28
Dillenberger, Jane 1916- CANR-23
Earlier sketches in CA 17-18R, CANR-7
Dillenberger, John 1918- CANR-17
Earlier sketches in CA 4R, CANR-2
Diller, Edward 1925- 85-88
Diller, Phyllis (Ada) 1917- CANR-22
Earlier sketch in CA 81-84
Dilles, James 1923- 1R
Dilley, Clyde H(obson) 1939- 113
Dilley, Frank B(rown) 1931- 15-16R
Dilliard, Irving (Lee) 1904- 21-22R
Dilligan, Robert J(ames) 1940- Brief entry . . 108
Dilling, Judith
See Rhoades, Judith G(rubman)
Dilling, Yvonne 1955- 118
Dillingham, Beth 1927- 53-56
Dillingham, William B(yron) 1930- 15-16R
Dillistone, Frederick W(illiam) 1903- CANR-5
Earlier sketch in CA 4R
Dillman, Audrey 1922(?)-1984 Obituary 113
Dillman, David D. 1900(?)-1983 Obituary . . . 110
Dillon, Barbara 1927- 110
See also SATA 39, 44
Dillon, Bert 1937- 77-80
Dillon, Conley Hall 1906-1987 . . . . CANR-17
Obituary 123
Earlier sketch in CA 1R
Dillon, David 1941- .69-72
Dillon, Diane 1933- SATA-15
Dillon, Eilis 1920- CANR-4
Earlier sketch in CA 9-10R
See also CAAS 3
See also SATA 2
See also CLC 17
Dillon, George 1906-1968 Obituary 89-92
Dillon, George Lewis 1944- 102
Dillon, J(ames) T(homas) 1940- 33-36R
Dillon, John M(yles) 1939- 77-80
Dillon, Lawrence S(amuel) 1910- 45-48
Dillon, Leo 1933- SATA-15
Dillon, Martin 1949- 61-64
Dillon, Merton L. 1924- 13-14R
Dillon, Millicent (Gerson) 1925- CANR-12
Earlier sketch in CA 65-68
Dillon, Richard H(ugh) 1924- CANR-8
Earlier sketch in CA 19-20R
Dillon, Wallace Neil 1922- 3R
Dillon, Wilton S(terling) 1923- 37-40R
Dillow, Harry C. 1922- 123
Dilorenzo, Ronald Eugene 1931-
Brief entry 110
Dilson, Jesse 1914- 25-28R
See also SATA 24
Diltz, Bert Case 1894- CANR-9
Earlier sketch in CA 65-68
Dimancescu, Dan 1943- 113
di Marco, Gino
See Weiss, Irving J.
Di Marco, Luis Eugenio 1937- CANR-2
Earlier sketch in CA 45-48
Dimberg, Ronald G(ilbert) 1938- 61-64
Dimbleby, Jonathan 1944- 119
Brief entry 108
Di Meglio, Clara 1933- 97-100
DiMeglio, John E(dward) 1934- 77-80
DiMento, Joseph F(rank) 1947- 69-72
di Michele, Mary 1949- CANR-17
Earlier sketch in CA 97-100
Dimick, John M. 1898(?)-1983 Obituary . . . 111
Dimick, Kenneth M. 1937- 29-32R
Dimmette, Celia (Puhr) 1896- CAP-2
Earlier sketch in CA 29-32
Dimmitt, Richard Bertrand 1925- 17-18R
Dimock, Edward Cameron, Jr. 1929- 102
Dimock, Gladys Ogden 1908- 7-8R
Dimock, Hedley G(ardiner) 1928- 5-6R
Dimock, Marshall E(dward) 1903- CANR-2
Earlier sketch in CA 1R
DiMona, Joseph 104
Dimond, E(dmunds) Grey 1918- 85-88
Dimond, Mary Clark .93-96
Dimond, Stanley E(llwood) 1905- 15-16R
Dimond, Stuart J. 1938- 33-36R
Dimondstein, Geraldine 1926- 33-36R
Dimont, Madelon 1938- 41-44R
Dimont, Max I. 1912- 19-20R
Dimont, Penelope
See Mortimer, Penelope (Ruth)
Dimrecken, B. Grayer
See de Mille, Richard
Dimson, Wendy
See Baron, (Ora) Wendy
Din, Gilbert C. 1932- 118
Dinan, Carolyn SATA-47
Dineley, David Lawrence 1927- 101
Diner, Hasia R(ena) 1946- CANR-9
Earlier sketch in CA 61-64
Diner, Steven J(ay) 1944- 110
Dinerman, Beatrice 1933- 13-14R
Dinerman, Helen Schneider 1921(?)-1974
Obituary 53-56
Dinerstein, Herbert S(amuel) 1919-
Brief entry 108
Dines, (Harry) Glen 1925- 9-10R
See also SATA 7
Dines, Michael 1916- 103
Dinesen, Isak
See Blixen, Karen (Christentze Dinesen)
See also CLC 10, 29
Ding, J. N.
See Darling, Jay Norwood
Dinges, John (Charles) 1941- 101
Dingle, Graeme 1945- 123
Dingle, Herbert 1890-1978 . . . . .13-14R
Obituary 122
Ding Ling
See Chiang Pin-chin
Dingman, Roger 1938- 93-96
Dings, John (Garetson) 1939- 41-44R
Dingwall, E(ric) J(ohn) 1890-1986 89-92
Obituary 120
Dingwall, W(illiam) Orr 1934- CANR-13
Earlier sketch in CA 21-22R
Dinhofer, A(lfred) 1929- 25-28R
Dinitz, Simon 1926- CANR-14
Earlier sketch in CA 37-40R
Dinkin, Robert J. 1940- Brief entry 107
Dinkmeyer, Don C. 1924- CANR-15
Earlier sketch in CA 41-44R
Dinman, Bertram David 1925- Brief entry . . . 109
Dinnan, James A. 1929- 69-72
Dinneen, Betty 1929- CANR-8
Earlier sketch in CA 57-60
Dinnerstein, Harvey 1928- 112
See also SATA 42
Dinnerstein, Leonard 1934- CANR-24
Earlier sketches in CA 23-24R, CANR-9
Dino
See Dinhofer, A(lfred)
Dinsdale, Tim(othy Kay) 1924-1987 . . . . . CANR-2
Obituary 124
Earlier sketch in CA 3R
See also SATA 11
Dinsky, Lazar 1891(?)-1976 Obituary 69-72
Dinsmore, Herman H. 1900(?)-1980
Obituary 97-100
Dintenfass, Mark 1941- CANR-11
Earlier sketch in CA 25-28R
See also DLBY 84
Dintiman, George B(lough) 1936- CANR-20
Earlier sketches in CA 53-56, CANR-5
Dinwiddie, Elza Teresa 110
Diole, Philippe V. 1908- 53-56
Diomede, John K.
See Effinger, George Alec
Dion, Gerard 1912- 41-44R
Dion, Sister Anita 1918- CANR-2
Earlier sketch in CA 7-8R
Dione, Robert L(ester) 1922- 57-60
Dionisopoulos, P(anagiotes) Allan
1921- 29-32R
Diop, Cheikh Anta 1923-1986 Obituary 118
Brief entry 110
Dior, Christian 1905-1957 Brief entry 115
DiOrio, Al(bert John) 1950- CANR-9
Earlier sketch in CA 57-60
Diotima
See Wynne-Tyson, Esme
DiPalma, Ray(mond) 1943- CANR-24
Earlier sketch in CA 29-32R
DiPasquale, Dominic 1932- 57-60
DiPego, Gerald F(rancis) 1941- 85-88
DiPerna, Paula 1949- 112
DiPersio, Michael S(alvatore) 1934- 110
Di Peso, Charles C(orradino) 1920- 57-60
Di Pietro, Robert Joseph 1932- CANR-7
Earlier sketch in CA 17-18R
Diplomaticus
See Guerra y Sanchez, Ramiro
Dipper, Alan 1922- 49-52
Dipple, Brian William 1943- 108
Dipple, Elizabeth 1937- 33-36R
di Prima, Diane 1934- CANR-13
Earlier sketch in CA 17-18R
See also DLB 5, 16
Dirac, P.A.M.
See Dirac, Paul A(drien) M(aurice)
Dirac, Paul A(drien) M(aurice) 1902-1984
Obituary 113
Dire, Eloise (Evangeline) Hodge 1907- 118
DiRenzo, Gordon J(ames) 1934- CANR-4
Earlier sketch in CA 53-56
Diringer, David 1900-1975 . . . . CANR-6
Obituary 57-60
Earlier sketch in CA 4R
Dirk
See Gringhuis, Richard H.
Dirk, R.
See Dietrich, Richard V(incent)
Dirks, Raymond L(ouis) 1934- 106
Dirks, Rudolph 1877-1968 Obituary 106
See also SATA 31
Dirksen, Alvin Joseph 1915- 110
Dirksen, Charles J(oseph) 1912- 5-6R
Dirksen, Louella Carver 1899-1979 103
Obituary 89-92
Dirlik, Arif 1940- 97-100
di Roccaferrera Ferrero, Giuseppe M.
1912- CANR-7
Earlier sketch in CA 15-16R
Dirrim, Allen Wendell 1929- 23-24R
Dirscherl, Denis 1934- 21-22R
Dirvin, Joseph I. 1917- CANR-2
Earlier sketch in CA 7-8R
Di Scala, Spencer M(ichael) 1941- 102
Disch, Thomas M(ichael) 1940- CANR-17
Earlier sketch in CA 23-24R
See also CAAS 4
See also DLB 8
See also CLC 7, 36
Dischell, Judy
See Lalli, Judy
Disher, Maurice Willson 1893-1969 . . . . . . CAP-1
Earlier sketch in CA 9-10
Dishman, Pat(ricia L.) 1939- 19-20R
d'Isly, Georges
See Simenon, Georges (Jacques
Christian)
Disney, Doris Miles 1907-1976 . . . . CANR-3
Obituary 65-68
Earlier sketch in CA 5-6R
Disney, Walt(er Elias) 1901-1966 Obituary . . 107
See also SATA 27, 28
See also DLB 22
Dison, Norma 1928- .53-56
Dispenza, Joseph Ernest 1942- 81-84
Disraeli, Benjamin 1804-1881 . . . . DLB-21, 55
Disraeli, Robert 1903- CAP-1
Earlier sketch in CA 11-12
Disston, Harry 1899- 41-44R
Distel, Peter
See Koch, Kurt E(mil)
Distler, Paul Francis 1911- 7-8R
Ditchburn, R(obert) W(illiam) 1903-1987 . . 69-72
Obituary 122
Ditcum, Steve
See Crumb, R(obert)
Dito Und Idem
See Elisabeth (Ottilie Luise), Queen
(Pauline)
Ditsky, John (Michael) 1938- CANR-9
Earlier sketch in CA 65-68
Dittes, James E(dward) 1926- 61-64
Dittmer, Lowell 1941- 89-92
Ditton, James
See Clark, Douglas
Dittrich, John E(dward) 1931- 112
Ditzel, Paul C(alvin) 1926- 41-44R
Ditzen, Lowell Russell 1913-1987 . . . . . . .17-18R
Obituary 122
Ditzen, Rudolf 1893-1947 Brief entry 123
Ditzion, Sidney 1908-1975 . . . . .41-44R
Obituary 57-60
Divale, William T(ulio) 1942- 33-36R
Di Valentin, Maria Messuri 1911- CANR-5
Earlier sketch in CA 5-6R
See also SATA 7
Diverres, Armel Hugh 1914- 9-10R
Divine, Arthur Durham 1904-1987 103
Obituary 122
Divine, David
See Divine, Arthur Durham
Divine, Floy (Sherman) 1881-1986 113
Obituary 118
Divine, Robert A(lexander) 1929- CANR-20
Earlier sketches in CA 5-6R, CANR-3
Divine, Thomas F(rancis) 1900- 37-40R
DiVitto, Barbara A(nn) 1947- 118
Divoky, Diane 1939- 33-36R
Dix, Albert V. 1901(?)-1983 Obituary 109
Dix, Dorothea Lynde 1802-1887 . . . . DLB-1
Dix, Dorothy
See Gilmer, Elizabeth Meriwether
Dix, Robert H. 1930- 23-24R
Dix, William (Shepherd) 1910-1978
Obituary 77-80
Dixon, Bernard 1938- CANR-10
Earlier sketch in CA 65-68
Dixon, Christa Klingbeil 1935- 102
Dixon, Colin J. 1933- 105
Dixon, Dougal 1947- 107
See also SATA 45
Dixon, Franklin W. .19-20R
See also SATA 1
Dixon, Franklin W.
See Adams, Harriet S(tratemeyer)
and McFarlane, Leslie
Dixon, George
See Willis, Ted
Dixon, Graham (Peter) 1956- 121
Dixon, H(arry) Vernor 1908- CAP-1
Earlier sketch in CA 9-10
Dixon, Janice T(horne) 1932- 107
Dixon, Jeane 1918- CANR-21
Earlier sketch in CA 65-68
Dixon, Jeanne 1936- 105
See also SATA 31
Dixon, John W(esley), Jr. 1919- CANR-3
Earlier sketch in CA 11-12R
Dixon, Joseph L(awrence) 1896- 61-64
Dixon, Kenneth L. 1915(?)-1986 Obituary . . 119
Dixon, Marjorie (Mack) 1887- CAP-2
Earlier sketch in CA 23-24
Dixon, Paige
See Corcoran, Barbara
Dixon, Penelope A(nn) 1948- 113
Dixon, Peter L(ee) 1931- CANR-2
Earlier sketch in CA 45-48
See also SATA 6
Dixon, Pierson (John) 1904-1965 . . . . CAP-1
Earlier sketch in CA 15-16
Dixon, Richard Watson 1833-1900
Brief entry 122
See also DLB 19
Dixon, Robert G(alloway) 1920-1980
Obituary 97-100
Dixon, Roger 1930- .53-56
Dixon, Roger Edmund 1935-1983
Obituary 109
Dixon, Rosie
See Wood, Christopher (Hovelle)
Dixon, Ruth
See Barrows, (Ruth) Marjorie
Dixon, S(ydney) L(awrence) 1930- 69-72
Dixon, Stephen 1936- CANR-17
Earlier sketch in CA 89-92
Dixon, Wheeler Winston 1950- 121
Dizard, Wilson P(aul) 1922- 17-18R
Dizenzo, Charles (John) 1938- 25-28R
Dizney, Henry (Franklin) 1926- 33-36R
Djassi, Abel
See Cabral, Amilcar
Djeddah, Eli 1911- .37-40R
Djerassi, Carl 1923- Brief entry 111
Djonovich, Dusan J. 1920- 69-72
Dluhosch, Eric 1927- 25-28R
Dluznowsky, Moshe 1906-1977 Obituary . . 73-76
Dmytryshyn, Basil 1925- CANR-11
Earlier sketch in CA 21-22R
Doak, (Dearle) Donn(ell) 1930- 65-68
Doak, Wade Thomas 1940- CANR-6
Earlier sketch in CA 57-60
Doan, Daniel 1914- 103
Doan, Eleanor Lloyd CANR-1
Earlier sketch in CA 4R
Doane, Donald P(aul) 1911- 77-80
Doane, Gilbert H(arry) 1897- CAP-1
Earlier sketch in CA 11-12
Doane, Marion S.
See Woodward, Grace Steele
Doane, Pelagie 1906-1966 . . . . CANR-6
Earlier sketch in CA 4R
See also SATA 7
Dobb, Maurice (Herbert) 1900-1976 . . . . CANR-4
Obituary 69-72
Earlier sketch in CA 9-10R
Dobbie, Elliott Van Kirk 1907-1970
Obituary 111
Dobbin, John E. 1914-1979 . . . . .9-10R
Obituary 103
Dobbin, Muriel 1935- 118
Dobbins, Austin C(harles) 1919- 57-60
Dobbins, Charles G(ordon) 1908- CAP-1
Earlier sketch in CA 15-16
Dobbins, Dorothy Wyeth 1929- 69-72
Dobbins, Gaines Stanley 1886-1978 . . . . . CANR-2
Earlier sketch in CA 3R
Dobbins, Marybelle King 1900- 41-44R
Dobbs, Betty Jo Teeter 1930- 69-72
Dobbs, Farrell 1907-1983 . . . . CANR-14
Obituary 111
Earlier sketch in CA 49-52
Dobbs, Greg 1946- 65-68
Dobbs, Kildare (Robert Eric) 1923- CANR-19
Earlier sketch in CA 102
Dobbyn, John F(rancis) 1937- 53-56
Dobelis, M(iervaldis) C(hristian) 1929- 116
Dobell, Byron (Maxwell) 1927- Brief entry . . 112
Dobell, I(sabel) M(arian) B(arclay) 1909- . . CAP-1
Earlier sketch in CA 17-18
See also SATA 11
Dobell, Sydney 1824-1874 . . . . DLB-32
Dober, Richard P. 11-12R
Dobie, Ann B(rewster) 1935- 106
Dobie, Bertha McKee 1890(?)-1974
Obituary 53-56
Dobie, Edith 1894-1975 . . . . CAP-2
Obituary 57-60
Earlier sketch in CA 23-24
Dobie, J(ames) Frank 1888-1964 . . . . CANR-6
Earlier sketch in CA 1R
See also SATA 43
Dobin, Abraham 1907- 53-56
Dobinson, Charles Henry 1903-1980
Obituary 102
Dobkin, Alexander 1908-1975 Obituary 57-60
See also SATA 30
Dobkin, Bruce H. 1947- 122
Dobkin, Kathleen Hamel
See Hamel Dobkin, Kathleen
Dobkin, Kathy
See Hamel Dobkin, Kathleen
Dobkin, Kaye
See Hamel Dobkin, Kathleen
Dobkin, Marjorie Housepian 1923- CANR-13
Earlier sketch in CA 33-36R
Dobkin De Rios, Marlene 1939- CANR-12
Earlier sketch in CA 61-64
Dobkins, J(ames) Dwight 1943- 49-52
Dobler, Bruce 1939- CANR-7
Earlier sketch in CA 53-56
Dobler, Lavinia G. 1910- CANR-2
Earlier sketch in CA 4R
See also SATA 6
Doblin, Alfred
See Doeblin, Alfred
See also TCLC 13
Dobner, Maeva Park 1918- 29-32R
Dobney, Frederick J(ohn) 1943- 53-56
Dobraczynski, Jan 1910- CAP-1
Earlier sketch in CA 11-12

Dobree, Bonamy 1891-1974 ... CANR-4
Obituary ... 53-56
Earlier sketch in CA 5-6R
Dobriansky, Lev E. 1918- ... CANR-2
Earlier sketch in CA 1R
Dobrin, Arnold 1928- ... CANR-11
Earlier sketch in CA 25-28R
See also SATA 4
Dobrin, Arthur 1943- ... CANR-8
Earlier sketch in CA 61-64
Dobrin, Ronald L. 1938- ... 120
Dobriner, William M(ann) 1922- ... 65-68
Dobrovolsky, Sergei P(avlovich) 1908- ... CAP-2
Earlier sketch in CA 33-36
Dobrow, Larry 1925- ... 123
Dobrowolski, Tomasz B. 1914(?)-1976
Obituary ... 65-68
Dobschiner, Johanna-Ruth 1925- ... 97-100
Dobson, Austin 1840-1921 ... DLB-35
Dobson, (Richard) Barrie 1931- ... 33-36R
Dobson, Christopher (Joseph Edward)
1927- ... 97-100
Dobson, Dennis 1919(?)-1979(?)
Obituary ... 104
Dobson, E. Philip 1910- ... CAP-1
Earlier sketch in CA 13-14
Dobson, Elinore (Lucille) 1934- ... 114
Dobson, Eric John 1913-1984 ... CANR-5
Obituary ... 112
Earlier sketch in CA 15-16R
Dobson, Eugene 1936- Brief entry ... 113
Dobson, James (Clayton, Jr.) 1936- ... 29-32R
Dobson, Jessie ?-1984 Obituary ... 113
Dobson, John M(cCullough) 1940- ... 37-40R
Dobson, Julia 1941- ... 106
See also SATA 48
Dobson, Julia M(argaret) 1937- ... 73-76
Dobson, Margaret J(une) 1931- ... 53-56
Dobson, Rosemary 1920- ... 77-80
Dobson, Terry 1937- ... 81-84
Dobson, Theodore E(lliott) 1946- ... 109
Dobson, William A(rthur) C(harles) H(arvey)
1913- ... 15-16R
Doby, John T(homas) 1920- Brief entry ... 114
Doby, Tibor 1914- ... 5-6R
Dobyns, Henry F(armer) 1925- ... CANR-15
Earlier sketch in CA 37-40R
Dobyns, Lloyd (Allen, Jr.) 1936- ... 119
Brief entry ... 110
Dobyns, Stephen 1941- ... CANR-18
Earlier sketches in CA 45-48, CANR-2
See also CLC 37
Dobzhansky, Theodosius 1900-1975 ... CAP-1
Obituary ... 61-64
Earlier sketch in CA 13-14
Doc Abraham
See Abraham, George
Docherty, James L.
See Raymond, Rene (Brabazon)
Docherty, Thomas 1955- ... 120
Dockeray, J(ames) C(arlton) 1907-1984 ... 45-48
Obituary ... 114
Dockery, Wallene T. 1941- ... CANR-22
Earlier sketch in CA 105
See also SATA 27
Dockrell, William Bryan 1929- ... CANR-14
Earlier sketch in CA 37-40R
Dockstader, Frederick J. 1919- ... 13-14R
Doc Lochard
See Lochard, Metz T(ullus) P(aul)
Doctorow, E(dgar) L(aurence) 1931- ... CANR-2
Earlier sketch in CA 45-48
See also DLB 2, 28
See also DLBY 80
See also CLC 6, 11, 15, 18, 37, 44
See also AITN 2
Doctors, Samuel I(saac) 1936- ... CANR-5
Earlier sketch in CA 53-56
Doctor X
See Nourse, Alan E(dward)
Doczi, George Frederic 1909- ... 113
Dodd, A(rthur) E(dward) 1913- ... 9-10R
Dodd, Anne W(escott) 1940- ... 93-96
Dodd, Arthur Herbert 1893(?)-1975
Obituary ... 57-60
Dodd, Bella V.
See Dodd, Maria Assunta Isabella Visono
Dodd, Charles (Harold) 1884-1973
Obituary ... 45-48
Dodd, Donald B(radford) 1940- ... CANR-6
Earlier sketch in CA 57-60
Dodd, Ed(ward) Benton 1902- ... 73-76
See also SATA 4
Dodd, Edward
See Dodd, Edward Howard, Jr.
Dodd, Edward Howard, Jr. 1905- ... 49-52
Dodd, James Harvey 1892-1969 ... 1R
Obituary ... 103
Dodd, Lynley (Stuart) 1941- ... 107
See also SATA 35
Dodd, Marguerite 1911- ... 7-8R
Dodd, Maria Assunta Isabella Visono
1904-1969 Obituary ... 111
Dodd, Philip W. 1904(?)-1983 Obituary ... 110
Dodd, Stuart C(arter) 1900-1975 ... 41-44R
Dodd, Susan M. 1946- ... 116
Dodd, Thomas J. 1907-1971 Obituary ... 29-32R
Dodd, Wayne (Donald) 1930- ... 33-36R
Dodd, William E. 1869-1940 ... DLB-17
Dodderidge, Esme 1916- ... 97-100
Dodds, E(ric) R(obertson) 1893-1979 ... 101
Dodds, Edward Charles 1899-1973
Obituary ... 115
Dodds, Gordon Barlow 1932- ... 5-6R
Dodds, John W(endell) 1902- ... 5-6R
Dodds, Robert Clyde 1918- ... 7-8R
Dodds, Robert H(ungerford) 1914-1976 ... CAP-2
Earlier sketch in CA 29-32
Dodds, Tracy 1952- ... 85-88
Dodek, Miriam (Joyce) Selker 1909-1986
Obituary ... 118
Doder, Dusko 1937- ... 102
Doderer, Heimito von
See von Doderer, Heimito
Dodge, Bayard 1888-1972 Obituary ... 111
Dodge, Bertha S(anford) 1902- ... CANR-2
Earlier sketch in CA 5-6R
See also SATA 8
Dodge, Calvert R(enaul) 1931- ... 61-64
Dodge, Daniel
See Du Breuil, (Elizabeth) L(or)inda
Dodge, David (Francis) 1910- ... 65-68
Dodge, David L(aurence) 1931-
Brief entry ... 112
Dodge, Dick 1918(?)-1974 Obituary ... 49-52
Dodge, Dorothy R(ae) 1927- ... 45-48
Dodge, Ernest Stanley 1913-1980 ... CANR-2
Obituary ... 97-100
Earlier sketch in CA 1R
Dodge, Fremont
See Grimes, Lee
Dodge, Gil
See Hano, Arnold
Dodge, H(arry) Robert 1929- ... 29-32R
Dodge, Langdon
See Wolfson, Victor
Dodge, Lowell 1940- ... 33-36R
Dodge, Marshall 1935- ... 89-92
Dodge, Mary (Elizabeth) Mapes
1831(?)-1905 Brief entry ... 109
See also SATA 21
See also DLB 42
Dodge, Nicholas A. 1933- ... 65-68
Dodge, Norton T(ownshend) 1927- ... CANR-16
Earlier sketch in CA 25-28R
Dodge, Peter 1926- ... 37-40R
Dodge, Richard Holmes 1926- ... CANR-8
Earlier sketch in CA 13-14R
Dodge, Steve
See Becker, Stephen (David)
Dodge, Wendell P(hillips) 1883-1976
Obituary ... 65-68
Dodgson, Charles Lutwidge 1832-1898 ... YABC-2
See also CLR 2
Dodson, Daniel B. 1918- ... CANR-3
Earlier sketch in CA 11-12R
Dodson, Fitzhugh (James) 1923- ... CANR-24
Earlier sketch in CA 29-32R
Dodson, James L. 1910- ... 53-56
Dodson, Kenneth MacKenzie 1907- ... 3R
See also SATA 11
Dodson, Leonidas 1900-1977 Obituary ... 111
Dodson, Oscar H(enry) 1905- ... 7-8R
Dodson, Owen (Vincent) 1914-1983 ... CANR-24
Obituary ... 110
Earlier sketch in CA 65-68
Dodson, Richard S(licer), Jr. 1896- ... CAP-1
Earlier sketch in CA 11-12
Dodson, Susan 1941- ... 97-100
See also SATA 40, 50
Dodson, Tom 1914- ... 29-32R
Dodwell, Peter C(arpenter) 1930- ... 29-32R
Doebler, Charles H. 1925- ... 23-24R
Doebler, John (Willard) 1932- ... 89-92
Doeblin, Alfred 1878-1957 Brief entry ... 110
See also DLB 66
See also TCLC 13
Doehring, Donald G(ene) 1927- ... 29-32R
Doell, Charles E(dward) 1894- ... CAP-1
Earlier sketch in CA 15-16
Doely, Sarah Bentley
See Bentley, Sarah
Doenecke, Justus Drew 1938- ... CANR-20
Earlier sketch in CA 104
Doenim, Susan
See Effinger, George Alec
Doenitz, Karl 1891-1980 Obituary ... 103
Doerffler, Alfred 1884- ... 2R
Doering, Jeanne
See Zornes, Jeanne Doering
Doeringer, Peter B(rantley) 1941- ... CANR-12
Earlier sketch in CA 61-64
Doerksen, Nan 1934- ... 123
See also SATA 50
Doerkson, Margaret 1921- ... 105
Doermann, Humphrey 1930- ... 25-28R
Doernberg, Myrna 1939- ... 120
Doerr, Arthur H(arry) 1924- ... 41-44R
Doerr, Harriet 1910- ... 122
Brief entry ... 117
See also CLC 34
Doerschuk, Anna Beatrice 1880(?)-1974
Obituary ... 49-52
Doeser, Linda (Ann) 1950- ... 81-84
Doesticks, Q. K. Philander, P. B.
See Thomson, Mortimer
Doezema, Linda Pegman 1948- ... 102
Dogan, Mattei 1920- ... CANR-12
Earlier sketch in CA 25-28R
Dogg, Professor R. L.
See Berman, Ed
Doggett, Frank 1906- ... CANR-12
Earlier sketches in CA 21-22, CAP-2
Doggett, Rachel H. 1943- ... 124
Dogyear, Drew
See Gorey, Edward (St. John)
Dohan, Mary Helen 1914- ... 85-88
Dohen, Dorothy M. 1923-1984 Obituary ... 111
Doherty, Barbara 1931- ... 116
Doherty, Catherine de Hueck 1900- ... CANR-12
Earlier sketch in CA 65-68
Doherty, Charles Hugh 1913- ... 9-10R
See also SATA 6
Doherty, Dennis J. 1932- ... 102
Doherty, Eddie
See Doherty, Edward J(oseph)
Doherty, Edward J(oseph) 1890-1975 ... 65-68
Obituary ... 57-60
Doherty, Herbert J(oseph), Jr. 1926- ... 3R
Doherty, Ivy Duffy
See Doherty, Ivy R. Duffy
Doherty, Ivy R. Duffy 1922- ... CANR-5
Earlier sketch in CA 11-12R
Doherty, Robert W. 1935- ... 21-22R
Doherty, William 1911(?)-1984 Obituary ... 113
Doherty, William Thomas, Jr. 1923- ... 53-56
Dohme, Alvin R(obert) L(ouis) 1910- ... 110
Dohrenwend, Barbara Snell
1927-1982 ... CANR-11
Earlier sketch in CA 25-28R
Doig, Desmond 1921-1983 ... 69-72
Obituary ... 111
Doig, Ivan 1939- ... CANR-24
Earlier sketch in CA 81-84
Doig, Jameson W. 1933- ... CANR-15
Earlier sketch in CA 37-40R
Doimi di Delupis, Ingrid
See Delupis, Ingrid
Dolan, Anthony R(ossi) 1948- ... 73-76
Dolan, Edward F(rancis), Jr. 1924- ... 33-36R
See also SATA 31, 45
Dolan, Edwin G(eorge) 1943- ... 123
Dolan, Jay P(atrick) 1936- ... 81-84
Dolan, John Patrick 1923-1982(?) ... CANR-2
Obituary ... 106
Earlier sketch in CA 5-6R
Dolan, John Richard 1893- ... 9-10R
Dolan, Josephine A(loyse) 1913- ... 49-52
Dolan, Paul 1910- ... 9-10R
Dolan, Winthrop W(iggin) 1909- ... 57-60
Dolbeare, Kenneth M(arsh) 1930-
Brief entry ... 113
Dolberg, Alexander 1933- ... 33-36R
Dolbier, Maurice (Wyman) 1912- ... 65-68
Dolby, James L(ouis) 1926- ... 45-48
Dolce, Philip C(harles) 1941- ... 57-60
Dolch, Edward William 1889-1961 ... SATA-50
Dolch, Marguerite Pierce 1891-1978 ... SATA-50
Dolci, Danilo (Bruno Pietro) 1924-
Brief entry ... 116
Dolden, A(lfred) Stuart 1893- ... 105
Dole, Gertrude E(velyn) 1915- ... 41-44R
Dole, Jeremy H(askell) 1932- ... 17-18R
Dolezel, Lubomir 1922- ... 45-48
Dolgoff, Ralph L. 1932- ... 33-36R
Dolgoff, Sam 1902- ... 102
Dolgun, Alexander (Michael) 1926-1986 ... 104
Obituary ... 120
Doliber, Earl L(awrence) 1947- ... 49-52
Dolim, Mary N(uzum) 1925- ... 19-20R
Dolin, Anton
See Healey-Kay, (Sydney Francis) Patrick (Chippendall)
Dolin, Edwin 1928- ... 45-48
Doliner, Roy 1932- ... CANR-16
Earlier sketches in CA 1R, CANR-1
Dolinger, Jane ... AITN-2
Dolinsky, Meyer 1923- ... 57-60
Dolinsky, Mike
See Dolinsky, Meyer
Dolit, Alan 1934- ... 61-64
Doll, (William) Richard (Shaboe) 1912- ... 108
Doll, Ronald C. 1913- ... CANR-8
Earlier sketch in CA 13-14R
Doll, Susan Marie 1954- ... 118
Dollar, Jimmy
See Shaginyan, Marietta Sergeyevna
Dollar, Truman E. 1937- ... 97-100
Dollard, John 1900(?)-1980 Obituary ... 102
Dollar Investor
See D'Ambrosio, Charles A.
Dollen, Charles Joseph 1926- ... CANR-21
Earlier sketches in CA 7-8R, CANR-6
Dolley, Michael 1925-1983 ... 123
Obituary ... 109
Dolliver, Barbara Babcock 1927- ... 7-8R
Dolloff, Eugene Dinsmore 1890-1972 ... 1R
Obituary ... 103
Dolmatch, Theodore B(ieley) 1924- ... 41-44R
Dolmetsch, Carl R(ichard, Jr.) 1924- ... 21-22R
Dolmetsch, Christopher L(ee) 1950- ... 111
Dolphin, Robert, Jr. 1935- ... 29-32R
Dols, Michael W(alters) 1942- ... 69-72
Dolson, Frank(lin Robert) 1933- ... 112
Dolson, Hildegarde
See Lockridge, Hildegarde (Dolson)
See also SATA 5
Doman, Glenn J(oseph) 1919- ... 61-64
Doman, June
See Beveridge, Meryle Secrest
Domanska, Janina ... CANR-11
Earlier sketch in CA 17-18R
See also SATA 6
See also AITN 1
Domaradzki, Theodore F(elix) 1910- ... CANR-1
Earlier sketch in CA 45-48
Domb, Cyril 1920- ... 109
Dombrowski, James A. 1897-1983
Obituary ... 109
Domecq, H(onorio) Bustos
See Bioy-Casares, Adolfo
and Borges, Jorge Luis
Domencich, Thomas A. ... 29-32R
Domergue, Maurice 1907- ... 25-28R
Dom Helder
See Camara, Helder Pessoa
Domhoff, G(eorge) William 1936- ... 45-48
Dominguez, Jorge Ignacio 1945- ... 102
Dominguez, Richard H(enry) 1941- ... 102
Domini, Jon
See LaRusso, Dominic A(nthony)
Domini, Rey
See Lorde, Audre (Geraldine)
Dominian, Jack 1929- ... 104
Dominic, R. B.
See Hennissart, Martha
and Latsis, Mary J(ane)
Dominic, Sister Mary
See Gallagher, Sister Mary Dominic
Dominick, Raymond Hunter III 1945- ... 110
Dominique
See Proust, (Valentin-Louis-George-Eugene-) Marcel
Domino, John
See Averill, Esther
Dominowski, Roger L. 1939- ... CANR-1
Earlier sketch in CA 45-48
Dominy, Eric (Norman) 1918- ... 11-12R
Domjan, Joseph (Spiri) 1907- ... CANR-24
Earlier sketches in CA 9-10R, CANR-3
See also SATA 25
Domke, Helmut Georg 1914-1974 ... CAP-1
Earlier sketch in CA 13-14
Domke, Martin 1892- ... CAP-1
Earlier sketch in CA 15-16
Dommen, Arthur J(ohn) 1934- ... 11-12R
Dommermuth, William P. 1925- ... 17-18R
Dommeyer, Frederick Charles 1909- ... 37-40R
Domville, Eric 1929- ... 41-44R
Don, A
See Stephen, Leslie
Donabedian, Avedis 1919- ... CANR-12
Earlier sketch in CA 73-76
Donagan, Alan (Harry) 1925- ... 5-6R
Donagan, Barbara (Galley) 1927- ... 17-18R
Donaghy, Henry J. 1930- ... 53-56
Donaghy, William A. 1910(?)-1975
Obituary ... 53-56
Donahoe, Bernard (Frances) 1932- ... 17-18R
Donahue, Don 1942- ... 69-72
Donahue, Francis J. 1917- ... 19-20R
Donahue, George T. 1911- ... 19-20R
Donahue, Jack 1917- ... CANR-17
Earlier sketch in CA 97-100
Donahue, June (Geserick) 1918(?)-1984
Obituary ... 111
Donahue, Kenneth 1915- ... 102
Donahue, Phil(lip John) 1935- ... 107
Donahue, Roy L(uther) 1908- ... CANR-15
Earlier sketch in CA 89-92
Donahue, Thomas John 1943- ... 112
Donald, Aida DiPace 1930- ... 21-22R
Donald, Anabel 1944- ... 122
Donald, Bruce H(arry) 1935- ... 111
Donald, David Herbert 1920- ... CANR-4
Earlier sketch in CA 11-12R
See also DLB 17
Donald, Larry W(atson) 1945- ... 93-96
Donald, Maxwell 1897-1978 Obituary ... 89-92
Donald, R. V.
See Floren, Lee
Donald, Vivian
See Mackinnon, Charles Roy
Donalds, Gordon
See Shirreffs, Gordon D(onald)
Donaldson, Betty 1923- ... 103
Donaldson, Bryna Stevens 1924- ... 116
Donaldson, E(thelbert) Talbot
1910-1987 ... CANR-2
Obituary ... 122
Earlier sketch in CA 49-52
Donaldson, Elvin F. 1903-1972 ... 1R
Obituary ... 103
Donaldson, Frances (Annesley) 1907- ... CANR-12
Earlier sketch in CA 61-64
Donaldson, Frances (Gertrude) F(laacke)
1892(?)-1987 Obituary ... 122
Donaldson, Gordon 1913- ... CANR-22
Earlier sketches in CA 13-14R, CANR-5
Donaldson, (Charles) Ian (Edward)
1935- ... CANR-12
Earlier sketch in CA 69-72
Donaldson, John W. 1893(?)-1979
Obituary ... 85-88
Donaldson, Kenneth 1908- ... 73-76
Donaldson, Malcolm 1884-1973 ... CAP-1
Earlier sketch in CA 9-10
Donaldson, Margaret 1926- ... CANR-20
Earlier sketch in CA 103
Donaldson, Norman 1922- ... 33-36R
Donaldson, Robert Herschel 1943- ... CANR-15
Earlier sketch in CA 85-88
Donaldson, Sam(uel Andrew) 1934- ... 111
Brief entry ... 109
Donaldson, Scott 1928- ... CANR-11
Earlier sketch in CA 25-28R
Donaldson, Stephen R. 1947- ... CANR-13
Earlier sketch in CA 89-92
See also CLC 46
Donaldson, (Charles) William 1935- ... 77-80
Donart, Arthur C(harles) 1936- ... 37-40R
Donat, Anton
See Donart, Arthur C(harles)
Donat, John (Annesley) 1933- ... 15-16R
Donato, Anthony 1909- ... CAP-1
Earlier sketch in CA 15-16
Donavan, John
See Morland, Nigel
Donawerth, Jane (Lynn) 1947- ... 118
Donceel, Joseph F. 1906- ... CANR-1
Earlier sketch in CA 4R
Donchess, Barbara (Briggs) 1922- ... 57-60
Dondis, Donis A(snin) 1924- ... 85-88
Donelson, Irene W(itmer) 1913- ... 19-20R
Donelson, Kenneth L(avern) 1927- ... 69-72

Donelson, Kenneth W(ilber) 1910- 19-20R
Donem, Sue
See Ross, Stanley Ralph
Doner, Mary Frances 1893- 15-16R
Doney, Willis (Frederick, Jr.) 1925- 21-22R
Donfried, Karl Paul 1940- 108
Donheiser, Alan D. 1936- 37-40R
Donicht, Mark Allen 1946- 93-96
Doniger, Lester (Laurence) 1909-1971
Obituary 104
Donin, Hayim Halevy 1928- 77-80
Donington, Robert 1907- 33-36R
Donis, Miles 1937-1979 ....29-32R
Obituary 93-96
Donkin, Nance (Clare) 1915- CANR-20
Earlier sketch in CA 103
Donleavy, J(ames) P(atrick) 1926- CANR-24
Earlier sketch in CA 9-10R
See also DLB 6
See also CLC 1, 4, 6, 10, 45
See also AITN 2
Donley, Carol C(ram) 1937- 122
Donley, Marshall O(wen), Jr. 1932- CANR-14
Earlier sketch in CA 65-68
Donna, Natalie 1934-1979 .... CANR-6
Earlier sketch in CA 11-12R
See also SATA 9
Donnachie, Ian Lowe 1944- 105
Donnan, Marcia Jeanne 1932- 104
Donne, Maxim
See Duke, Madelaine (Elizabeth)
Donnell, David 1939(?)- CLC-34
Donnell, John C(orwin) 1919- 41-44R
Donnell, John D(ouglas) 1920- CANR-5
Earlier sketch in CA 53-56
Donnellan, Michael T(homas) 1931- 37-40R
Donnelley, Dixon 1915-1982 Obituary 105
Donnell-Kotrozo, Carol 1947- 113
Donnelly, Alton S(tewart) 1920- 23-24R
Donnelly, Austin Stanislaus 1923- 112
Donnelly, Desmond L(ouis) 1920- 15-16R
Donnelly, Doris (Krimper) 1940- 123
Donnelly, Dorothy (Boillotat) 1903- CANR-3
Earlier sketch in CA 5-6R
Donnelly, Ignatius 1831-1901 Brief entry ... 110
See also DLB 12
Donnelly, James A. III 1929(?)-1984
Obituary 112
Donnelly, James H(oward), Jr. 1941- 29-32R
Donnelly, James S(tephen), Jr. 1943- 102
Donnelly, John 1941- 93-96
Donnelly, John Patrick 1934- 81-84
Donnelly, Joseph P(eter) 1905-1982 81-84
Obituary 108
Donnelly, Sister Gertrude Joseph 1920- ..15-16R
Donner, Fred McGraw 1945- 106
Donner, Joern 1933- CANR-9
Earlier sketch in CA 13-14R
Donner, Stanley T(emple) 1910- 61-64
Donnison, David Vernon 1926- 106
Donnison, F(rank) S(iegfried) V(ernon)
1898- 3R
Donnison, Jean 1925- 77-80
Donnithorne, Audrey 1922- 17-18R
Donno, Elizabeth Story 1921- CANR-5
Earlier sketch in CA 1R
Donoghue, Denis 1928- CANR-16
Earlier sketch in CA 17-18R
Donoghue, Mildred R(ansdorf) CANR-10
Earlier sketch in CA 25-28R
Donoghue, Quentin 1937- 122
Donoghue, William E(lliott) 1941- 116
Donohoe, Thomas 1917- 53-56
Donohoe, Tom 1957- 123
Donohue, James F(itzgerald) 1934- 73-76
Donohue, John J. 1926- 122
Donohue, John K. 1909- CAP-1
Earlier sketch in CA 11-12
Donohue, John W(aldron) 1917- CANR-3
Earlier sketch in CA 5-6R
Donohue, Joseph (Walter, Jr.) 1935- 69-72
Donohue, Mark 1937-1975 57-60
Obituary 89-92
Donohue, Martin
See Gibson, Walter B(rown)
Donoso, Jose 1924- 81-84
See also CLC 4, 8, 11, 32
Donoughue, Bernard 1934- 17-18R
Donovan, Bonita R. 1947- 73-76
Donovan, Bonnie
See Donovan, Bonita R.
Donovan, Edward J(oseph) 1904- 5-6R
Donovan, Frank (Robert) 1906-1975 .... CANR-6
Obituary 61-64
Earlier sketch in CA 4R
See also SATA 30
Donovan, Hedley (Williams) 1914- 115
Brief entry 110
Donovan, James A., Jr. 1917- 23-24R
Donovan, James Britt 1916-1970 ....9-10R
Obituary 89-92
Donovan, John 1919- CANR-2
Earlier sketch in CA 2R
Donovan, John 1928- 97-100
See also SATA 29
See also CLC 35
See also CLR 3
Donovan, John C(hauncey) 1920-1984 ...37-40R
Obituary 114
Donovan, Josephine (Campbell) 1941- . CANR-24
Earlier sketch in CA 106
Donovan, Robert Alan 1921- 19-20R
Donovan, Robert J(ohn) 1912- CANR-18
Earlier sketches in CA 1R, CANR-2
Donovan, Timothy Paul 1927- 53-56
Donovan, William
See Berkebile, Fred D(onovan)
Donow, Herbert S(tanton) 1936- 112
Don Roberto
See Cunninghame Graham, R(obert)
B(ontine)
Donskoi, Mark Semyonovich 1901-1981
Obituary 103
Donson, Cyril 1919- CANR-11
Earlier sketch in CA 23-24R
Don-Yehiya, Eliezer 1938- 111
Donze, Mary Terese 1911- 108
Doob, Anthony N(ewcomb) 1943- 33-36R
Doob, Leonard W(illiam) 1909- CANR-2
Earlier sketch in CA 5-6R
See also SATA 8
Doob, Penelope Billings Reed 1943- 53-56
Doody, Francis Stephen 1917- 15-16R
Doody, Margaret (Anne) 1939- CANR-11
Earlier sketch in CA 69-72
Doog, K. Caj
See Good, I(rving) John
Doohan, Leonard 1941- 118
Dooley, Arch R(ichard) 1925- 13-14R
Dooley, D(avid) J(oseph) 1921- CANR-16
Earlier sketch in CA 25-28R
Dooley, Ebon
See Ebon
Dooley, Howard J(ohn) 1944- 53-56
Dooley, John 1929(?)-1985 Obituary 119
Dooley, Patrick K(iaran) 1942- 53-56
Dooley, Peter C(hamberlain) 1937- 49-52
Dooley, Roger B(urke) 1920- CANR-22
Earlier sketch in CA 4R
Dooley, Thomas A(nthony) 1927-1961
Obituary 93-96
Dooley, William G(ermain) 1905(?)-1975
Obituary 57-60
Doolin, Dennis James 1933- 15-16R
Doolittle, Hilda 1886-1961 97-100
See also DLB 4, 45
See also CLC 14
Doolittle, Jerome (Hill) 1933- 53-56
Doone, Jice
See Marshall, James Vance
Dooren, Ingrid van
See van Dooren, Ingrid
Doorly, Ruth K. 1919- 25-28R
Doornkamp, John Charles 1938- CANR-7
Earlier sketch in CA 57-60
Dopuch, Nicholas 1929- 61-64
Dor, Ana
See Ceder, Georgiana Dorcas
Doran, Adelaide L(eMert) 1908- 116
Doran, Charles F(rancis) 1943- 73-76
Doran, Madeleine 1905- 121
Dorant, Gene
See Lent, D(ora) Geneva
Doray, Maya 1922- 45-48
Dorcy, Sister Mary Jean 1914- 9-10R
Dordick, Herbert S(halom) 1925- 116
Dore, Anita Wilkes 1914- 29-32R
Dore, Claire (Morin) 1934- 9-10R
Dore, (Louis Christophe Paul) Gustave
1832-1883 .... SATA-19
Dore, Ronald Philip 1925- CANR-15
Earlier sketch in CA 89-92
Doreian, Patrick 1942- 45-48
Doremus, Robert 1913- SATA-30
Doremus, Thomas Edmund 1922-1962 ...... 2R
Doreski, William 1946- CANR-17
Earlier sketches in CA 45-48, CANR-1
Dorey, T(homas) A(lan) 1921- 17-18R
Dorff, Richard C. 1933- 110
Dorff, Elliot N. 1943- 124
Dorfman, Ariel 1942- Brief entry 124
Dorfman, Dan 1932- 116
Brief entry 110
Dorfman, Eugene 1917- 29-32R
Dorfman, Gerald Allen 1939- 118
Dorfman, John 1947- CANR-12
Earlier sketch in CA 69-72
Dorfman, Joseph 1904- 45-48
Dorfman, Nancy S(chelling) 1922- 53-56
Dorfman, Nat N. 1895-1977 Obituary 73-76
Dorfman, Robert 1916- 17-18R
Dorge, Jeanne Emilie Marie
See Marie-Andre du Sacre-Coeur, Sister
Dorgeles, Roland 1886-1973 .... DLB-65
Doria, Charles 1938- 73-76
Dorian, Edith M(cEwen) 1900- CAP-1
Earlier sketch in CA 9-10
See also SATA 5
Dorian, Frederick 1902- CAP-1
Earlier sketch in CA 11-12
Dorian, Harry
See Hamilton, Charles Harold St. John
Dorian, Marguerite 19-20R
See also SATA 7
Dorian, Nancy C(urrier) 1936- 104
Dorin, Patrick C(arberry) 1939- CANR-15
Earlier sketch in CA 93-96
Doris, John Lawrence 1923- 102
Doris, Lillian 1899- 5-6R
Dorland, Henry
See Ash, Brian
Dorland, Michael 1948- 102
Dorliae, Peter Gondro 1935- 29-32R
Dorliae, Saint
See Dorliae, Peter Gondro
Dorman, Luke
See Bingley, David Ernest
Dorman, Michael 1932- CANR-5
Earlier sketch in CA 15-16R
See also SATA 7
Dorman, N. B. 1927- 106
See also SATA 39
Dorman, Sonya 1924- 73-76
Dormandy, Clara 1905- CAP-1
Earlier sketch in CA 9-10
d'Ormesson, Jean (Bruno Waldemar
Francois-de-Paule Lefevre) 1925-
Brief entry 111
Dormon, James H(unter), Jr. 1936- 23-24R
Dorn, Edward (Merton) 1929- 93-96
See also DLB 5
See also CLC 10, 18
Dorn, Frank 1901-1981 .... CANR-24
Obituary 104
Earlier sketch in CA 29-32R
Dorn, Jacob H(enry) 1939- 21-22R
Dorn, Phyllis Moore 1910(?)-1978
Obituary 77-80
Dorn, Sylvia O'Neill 1918- 69-72
Dorn, William S. 1928- 65-68
Dornan, James E., Jr. 1938(?)-1979
Obituary 85-88
Dornberg, John Robert 1931- CANR-1
Earlier sketch in CA 3R
Dornbusch, C(harles) E(mil) 1907- CAP-1
Earlier sketch in CA 9-10
Dorner, Peter Paul 1925- CANR-14
Earlier sketch in CA 37-40R
Doro, Edward 1910- 23-24R
Doro, Marion Elizabeth 1928- 89-92
Doroch, Efim Yakovlevitch 1908(?)-1972
Obituary 37-40R
Doronzo, Emmanuel 1903- 23-24R
Doroshkin, Milton 1914- 33-36R
Dorothy, R. D.
See Charques, Dorothy (Taylor)
Dorpalen, Andreas 1911-1982 ....19-20R
Obituary 109
Dorr, Donal 1935- 118
Dorr, Rheta (Louise) Childe 1866-1948
Brief entry 116
See also DLB 25
Dorries, William (Lyle) 1923- 37-40R
Dorris, Michael Anthony 1945- CANR-19
Earlier sketch in CA 102
Dorris, R(obert) T. 1913- 29-32R
Dors, Diana
See Fluck, Diana
Dorsan, Luc
See Simenon, Georges (Jacques
Christian)
Dorsange, Jean
See Simenon, Georges (Jacques
Christian)
Dorsen, Norman 1930- 37-40R
Dorset, Gerald (Harris) 1920- 112
Dorset, Phyllis (Flanders) 1924- 25-28R
Dorset, Ruth
See Ross, W(illiam) E(dward) D(aniel)
Dorsett, Danielle
See Daniels, Dorothy
Dorsett, Lyle W(esley) 1938- CANR-9
Earlier sketch in CA 23-24R
Dorsey, David Frederick, Jr. 1934- 115
Dorsey, Hebe 1925-1987 Obituary 124
Dorsey, Helen 1928- 110
Dorsey, John M(orris) 1900- CANR-4
Earlier sketch in CA 5-6R
Dorsey, John R(ussell) 1938- 118
Dorsey, John Thornton, Jr. 1924- 111
Dorson, Richard M(ercer) 1916-1981 106
Obituary 105
See also SATA 30
Dorsonville, Max 1943- 65-68
Dorst, Jean (Pierre) 1924- CANR-19
Earlier sketches in CA 5-6R, CANR-3
Dorst, Tankred 1925- 41-44R
Dorwart, J(effrey) M(ichael) 1944- 97-100
Dorwart, Reinhold August 1911- 65-68
Dorworth, Alice Grey 1907- 5-6R
Dosa, Marta Leszlei 45-48
Doskocilova, Hana 1936- CANR-23
Earlier sketches in CA 61-64, CANR-8
Doskow, Minna 1937- 118
Dos Passos, John (Roderigo)
1896-1970 .... CANR-3
Obituary 29-32R
Earlier sketch in CA 2R
See also DLB 4, 9
See also DLBD 1
See also CLC 1, 4, 8, 11, 15, 25, 34
Doss, Helen (Grigsby) 1918- CANR-6
Earlier sketch in CA 9-10R
See also SATA 20
Doss, Margot Patterson CANR-12
Earlier sketch in CA 29-32R
See also SATA 6
Doss, Richard W(eller) 1933- Brief entry ... 112
Dossage, Jean
See Simenon, Georges (Jacques
Christian)
dos Santos, Joyce Audy Brief entry 118
See also SATA 42
Dossick, Philip 1941- 81-84
Doster, Williem C(lark) 1921- 13-14R
Dothard, Robert Loos 1909(?)-1979
Obituary 85-88
Dotsenko, Paul 1894- 117
Dotson, Floyd 1917- 25-28R
Dotson, John L(ouis), Jr. 1937- 105
Dotson, Lillian O. 1921- 25-28R
Dotson, Robert Charles 1946- Brief entry ... 119
Dott, R(obert) H(enry), Jr. 1929- 53-56
Dottig
See Grider, Dorothy
Dotts, M. Franklin 1929- 57-60
Dotts, Maryann J. 1933- CANR-12
Earlier sketch in CA 33-36R
See also SATA 35
Doty, Brant Lee 1921- 19-20R
Doty, C(harles) Stewart 1928- 65-68
Doty, Carolyn 1941- CANR-23
Earlier sketch in CA 105
Doty, Gladys 1908- 53-56
Doty, Gresdna Ann 1931- 41-44R
Doty, James Edward 1922- 37-40R
Doty, Jean Slaughter 1929- CANR-2
Earlier sketch in CA 45-48
See also SATA 28
Doty, Richard (George) 1942- 109
Doty, Robert McIntyre 1933- 102
Doty, Roy 1922- CANR-8
Earlier sketch in CA 53-56
See also SATA 28
Doty, William G(uy) 1939- CANR-20
Earlier sketches in CA 53-56, CANR-5
Doty, William Lodewick 1919-1979 ...... CANR-1
Earlier sketch in CA 4R
Doubiago, Sharon 1946- 112
Doubleday, Neal Frank 1905-1976 ....41-44R
Doubrovsky, Serge 1928- Brief entry 110
Doubtfire, Dianne (Abrams) 1918- CANR-17
Earlier sketches in CA 4R, CANR-1
See also SATA 29
Doucet, Clive 1946- 118
Doucette, Leonard E(ugene) 1936- 33-36R
Douds, Charles Tucker 1898-1982
Obituary 106
Dougall, Herbert E(dward) 1902- CAP-1
Earlier sketch in CA 19-20
Dougan, Michael B(ruce) 1944- 69-72
Dougherty, Betty 1922- 61-64
Dougherty, Charles 1922- SATA-18
Dougherty, Ching-yi (Hsu) 1915- 5-6R
Dougherty, David Mitchell 1903- 113
Dougherty, James (Patrick) 1937- 106
Dougherty, James E(dward) 1923-
Brief entry 111
Dougherty, Joanna Foster
See Foster, Joanna
Dougherty, John J(oseph) 1907-1986
Obituary 118
Dougherty, Jude P(atrick) 1930- 45-48
Dougherty, Richard 1921-1986 .... CANR-2
Obituary 121
Earlier sketch in CA 1R
Dougherty, Richard M. 1935- 33-36R
Doughtie, Edward (Orth) 1935- 45-48
Doughty, Bradford 1921- 65-68
Doughty, Charles M(ontagu) 1843-1926
Brief entry 115
See also DLB 19, 57
See also TCLC 27
Doughty, Nina Beckett 1911- 53-56
Doughty, Oswald 1889- CAP-1
Earlier sketch in CA 9-10
Doughty, Paul L(arrabee) 1930- 85-88
Doughty, Robin W. 1941- 122
Douglas, Albert
See Armstrong, Douglas Albert
Douglas, Althea (Cleveland McCoy) 1926- ... 124
Douglas, Ann C.
See Welch, Ann Courtenay (Edmonds)
Douglas, Carole Nelson 1944- 107
Douglas, Charles H(erbert) 1926-
Brief entry 109
Douglas, Christopher
See Neill, Christopher Harry Douglas
Douglas, David C(harles) 1898-1982 73-76
Obituary 107
Douglas, Ellen
See Haxton, Josephine Ayres
Douglas, Ellen
See Williamson, Ellen Douglas
Douglas, Emily (Taft) 1899- 107
Douglas, George H(alsey) 1934- CANR-14
Earlier sketch in CA 81-84
Douglas, Glenn
See Duckett, Alfred
Douglas, Gregory A.
See Cantor, Eli
Douglas, Helen Bee
See Bee, Helen L.
Douglas, Helen Gahagan 1900-1980
Obituary 101
Douglas, J(ames) D(ixon) 1922- CANR-21
Earlier sketches in CA 13-14R, CANR-6
Douglas, James McM.
See Butterworth, W(illiam) E(dmund III)
Douglas, Jeff
See Offutt, Andrew J(efferson V)
Douglas, John (Frederick James) 1929- 116
Douglas, Kate
See Douglas, Kathleen
Douglas, Kathleen 1949- 117
Douglas, Kathryn
See Ewing, Kathryn
Douglas, Keith 1920-1944 .... DLB-27
Douglas, Leonard M(arvin) 1910-? CAP-2
Earlier sketch in CA 23-24
Douglas, Lloyd C.
See Douglas, Lloyd Cassel
Douglas, Lloyd Cassel 1877-1951
Brief entry 120
Douglas, Louis H(artwell) 1907- 21-22R
Douglas, Mack R. 1922- 21-22R
Douglas, Marjory Stoneman 1890- CANR-2
Earlier sketch in CA 1R
See also SATA 10
See also AITN 2
Douglas, Mary (Tew) 1921- 97-100
Douglas, Michael
See Crichton, (John) Michael
Douglas, Mike 1925- 89-92
Douglas, (George) Norman 1868-1952
Brief entry 119
See also DLB 34

Douglas, Paul Howard 1892-1976 69-72
Douglas, R. M.
See Mason, Douglas R(ankine)
Douglas, Robert
See Andrews, (Charles) Robert Douglas (Hardy)
Douglas, Roy (Ian) 1924- CANR-13
Earlier sketch in CA 73-76
Douglas, Scott
See Smith, William Scott
Douglas, Shane
See Wilkes-Hunter, R(ichard)
Douglas, Thorne
See Haas, Ben(jamin) L(eopold)
Douglas, William A(llison) 1934- 45-48
Douglas, William O(rville) 1898-1980 .. CANR-21
Obituary 93-96
Earlier sketch in CA 9-10R
Douglas-Hamilton, James 1942- CANR-13
Earlier sketch in CA 33-36R
Douglas-Home, Alec
See Home, Alexander Frederick
Douglas-Home, Charles (Cospatrick)
1937-1985 Obituary 117
Douglas-Home, Henry 1907-1980 103
Obituary 101
Douglas-Home, Robin 1932-1968 .... CAP-2
Earlier sketch in CA 25-28
Douglas Home, William
See Home, William Douglas
Douglass, Amanda Hart
See Wallmann, Jeffrey M(iner)
Douglass, Barbara 1930- 114
See also SATA 40
Douglass, Billie
See Delinsky, Barbara (Ruth Greenberg)
Douglass, Donald McNutt 1899-1975 .... 3R
Obituary 103
Douglass, Elisha Peairs 1915- 81-84
Douglass, Frederick 1817(?)-1895 ..... SATA-29
See also DLB 1, 43, 50
See also CDALB 1640-1865
Douglass, Harl R(oy) 1892- 5-6R
Douglass, Herbert Edgar 1927- CANR-13
Earlier sketch in CA 73-76
Douglass, James W. 1937- CANR-10
Earlier sketch in CA 25-28R
Douglass, Malcolm P(aul) 1923- CANR-13
Earlier sketch in CA 73-76
Douglass, Marcia Kent
See Doty, Gladys
Douglass, Paul F(ranklin) 1904- CANR-3
Earlier sketch in CA 5-6R
Douglass, Robert W. 1934- 57-60
Douglass, William 1691(?)-1752 .... DLB-24
Douglass, William A(nthony) 1939- 69-72
Douglas-Scott-Montagu, Edward
See Montagu of Beaulieu, Edward John Barrington
Doulis, Thomas 1931- CANR-11
Earlier sketch in CA 5-6R
Doulos, Jay
See Joyce, Jon L(oyd)
Doumato, Lamia 1947- 103
Dourado, Autran 1926- 25-28R
See also CLC 23
Douras, Marion Cecilia 1897-1961
Obituary 111
Douty, Esther M(orris) 1909-1978 ...... CANR-3
Obituary 85-88
Earlier sketch in CA 5-6R
See also SATA 8, 23
Douty, Norman F(ranklin) 1899- 49-52
Douvan, Elizabeth (Ann Malcolm) 1926- 106
Dove, Rita 1952- 109
Doveglion
See Villa, Jose Garcia
Dover, C(larence) J(oseph) 1919- 13-14R
Dover, K(enneth) J(ames) 1920- CANR-12
Earlier sketch in CA 25-28R
Dover Wilson, John 1881-1969
Obituary 25-28R
Dovey, Ken 1947- 120
Dovlatov, Sergei 1941- 115
Dow, Blanche H(innan) 1893-1973
Obituary 41-44R
Dow, Emily R. 1904- CAP-1
Earlier sketch in CA 11-12
See also SATA 10
Dow, George Francis 1868-1936
Brief entry 122
Dow, J(ose) Kamal 1936- 29-32R
Dow, Marguerite R(uth) 1926- 116
Dow, Neal 1906- 19-20R
Dow, Sterling 1903- CAP-2
Earlier sketch in CA 21-22
Dowd, Douglas F(itzgerald) 1919- 7-8R
Dowd, Laurence P(hillips) 1914- 17-18R
Dowd, Maxine
See Jensen, Maxine Dowd
Dowd, Merle E(dward) 1918- 85-88
Dowdell, Dorothy (Florence) Karns
1910- CANR-20
Earlier sketches in CA 11-12R, CANR-5
See also SATA 12
Dowden, Anne Ophelia 1907- CANR-18
Earlier sketches in CA 11-12R, CANR-3
See also SATA 7
Dowden, Edward 1843-1913 .... DLB-35
Dowden, George 1932- CANR-22
Earlier sketches in CA 53-56, CANR-4
Dowdey, Clifford (Shirley, Jr.) 1904- 11-12R
Dowdey, Landon Gerald 1923- 89-92
See also SATA 11
Dowding, Hugh Caswell Tremenheere
1882-1970 Obituary 112
Dowdy, Andrew 1936- 49-52
Dowdy, Homer E(arl) 1922- 7-8R
Dowdy, Mrs. Regera
See Gorey, Edward (St. John)
Dowell, Coleman 1925-1985 .... CANR-10
Obituary 117
Earlier sketch in CA 25-28R
Dowell, Jack (Larder) 1908- 57-60
Dowell, Richard W(alker) 1931- 116
Dower, Penn
See Pendower, Jacques
Dowie, James Iverne 1911- 41-44R
Dowie, Mark 1939- 85-88
Dowler, James Ross 1925- 29-32R
Dowley, D. M.
See Marrison, L(eslie) W(illiam)
Dowley, Timothy Edward 1946- CANR-18
Earlier sketch in CA 101
Dowling, Allan D. 1903-1983 Obituary 117
Dowling, Allen 1900- 29-32R
Dowling, Basil (Cairns) 1910- 97-100
Dowling, David (Hurst) 1950- 118
Dowling, Eddie 1894-1976 Obituary 65-68
Dowling, Harry Filmore 1904- 102
Dowling, Joseph A(lbert) 1926- 37-40R
Dowling, Maria 1955- 123
Dowling, Thomas, Jr. 1921- 85-88
Dowling, Tom
See Dowling, Thomas, Jr.
Down, Goldie (Malvern) 1918- CANR-11
Earlier sketch in CA 25-28R
Down, Michael (Graham) 1951- 118
Downard, William L. 1940- 49-52
Downer, Alan S(eymour) 1912-1970 ..... CAP-1
Obituary 33-36R
Earlier sketch in CA 11-12
Downer, Marion 1892(?)-1971 Obituary ..33-36R
See also SATA 25
Downes, Bryan Trevor 1939- 33-36R
Downes, David A(nthony) 1927- 33-36R
Downes, Edward (Olin Davenport) 1911- 105
Downes, Kerry 1930- 119
Downes, Mollie Patricia Panter
See Panter-Downes, Mollie Patricia
Downes, Quentin
See Harrison, Michael
Downes, Randolph C(handler) 1901-1975 ..49-52
Obituary 61-64
Downey, Bill
See Downey, William L(eslie)
Downey, Fairfax D(avis) 1893- CANR-1
Earlier sketch in CA 2R
See also SATA 3
Downey, Glanville 1908- CANR-1
Earlier sketch in CA 1R
Downey, Harris 13-14R
Downey, James 1939- 101
Downey, Lawrence William (Lorne)
1921- 17-18R
Downey, Murray William 1910- CANR-1
Earlier sketch in CA 4R
Downey, William L(eslie) 1922- 110
Downie, Freda (Christina) 1929- 106
Downie, Jill 1938- 108
Downie, John 1931- 108
Downie, Leonard, Jr. 1942- CANR-1
Earlier sketch in CA 49-52
Downie, Mary Alice Dawe 1934- CANR-10
Earlier sketch in CA 25-28R
See also SATA 13
Downie, N(orville) M(organ) 1910- 17-18R
Downing, A(rthur) B(enjamin) 1915- 29-32R
Downing, Chris(tine) 1931- 57-60
Downing, Douglas 1957- 114
Downing, J., Major
See Davis, Charles A.
Downing, John (Allen) 1922- CANR-20
Earlier sketches in CA 53-56, CANR-5
Downing, Lester N. 1914- CANR-10
Earlier sketch in CA 25-28R
Downing, Major Jack
See Smith, Seba
Downing, Paul B(utler) 1938- 104
Downing, Warwick 1931- 53-56
Downs, Anthony 1930- 49-52
Downs, Brian W(esterdale) 1893-1984
Obituary 112
Downs, Cal W. 1936- 103
Downs, Donald (Alexander) 1948- 119
Downs, Hugh (Malcolm) 1921- CANR-2
Earlier sketch in CA 45-48
Downs, Hunton (Leache) 1918- 4R
Downs, Jacques M. 1926- 37-40R
Downs, James Francis 1926- 81-84
Downs, Lenthiel H(owell) 1915- 25-28R
Downs, Norton 1918-1985 .... 1R
Obituary 114
Downs, Robert Bingham 1903- CANR-17
Earlier sketches in CA 1R, CANR-2
Downs, Robert C. S. 1937- CANR-1
Earlier sketch in CA 45-48
Downs, William Randall, Jr. 1914-1978 ...81-84
Obituary 77-80
Dowse, Robert E. 1933- 21-22R
Dowse, (Dale) Sara 1938- 119
Dowsey-Magog, Paul 1950- 105
Dowson, Ernest Christopher 1867-1900
Brief entry 105
See also DLB 19
See also TCLC 4
Dowst, Somerby Rohrer 1926- 33-36R
Dowty, Alan K. 1940- 122
Doxey, Roy W(atkins) 1908- 41-44R
Doxey, William S(anford, Jr.) 1935- CANR-9
Earlier sketch in CA 65-68
Doxiadis, Constantinos Apostolos
1913-1975 ....41-44R
Obituary 57-60
Doyle, A. Conan
See Doyle, Arthur Conan
Doyle, Adrian M. C.
See Conan Doyle, Adrian Malcolm
Doyle, Arthur Conan 1859-1930 122
Brief entry 104
See also SATA 24
See also DLB 18
See also TCLC 7
Doyle, Brian 1930- 53-56
Doyle, Charles (Desmond) 1928- CANR-11
Earlier sketch in CA 25-28R
Doyle, Charlotte Lackner 1937- 81-84
Doyle, Conan
See Doyle, Arthur Conan
Doyle, David
See Carter, David C(harles)
Doyle, Denis P. 1940- 109
Doyle, Don H(arrison) 1946- CANR-14
Earlier sketch in CA 81-84
Doyle, Donovan
See Boegehold, Betty (Doyle)
Doyle, Edward (Gerard) 1949- 118
Doyle, Edward Park 1907-1985 Obituary ... 115
Doyle, Esther M. 1910- 45-48
Doyle, Frank D. 1909(?)-1983 Obituary 109
Doyle, Gerald A. 1898(?)-1986 Obituary 119
Doyle, Harold Edmund
See Stearns, Harold Edmund
Doyle, James (Stephen) 1935- 73-76
Doyle, Jerry
See Doyle, Gerald A.
Doyle, John Robert, Jr. 1910- 25-28R
Doyle, Kirby 1932- DLB-16
Doyle, Mary Ellen 1932- 114
Doyle, Michael W. 1948- 120
Doyle, Mike
See Doyle, Charles (Desmond)
Doyle, Paul A. 1925- CANR-22
Earlier sketches in CA 15-16R, CANR-7
Doyle, Richard 1824-1883 .... SATA-21
Doyle, Richard 1948- 85-88
Doyle, Richard Edward 1929- 113
Doyle, Richard J(ames) 1923- 65-68
Doyle, Robert V(aughn) 1916- CANR-9
Earlier sketch in CA 65-68
Doyle, Sir A. Conan
See Doyle, Arthur Conan
Doyle, Sir Arthur Conan
See Doyle, Arthur Conan
Doyno, Victor A(nthony) 1937- 37-40R
Dozer, Donald Marquand 1905- CANR-1
Earlier sketch in CA 2R
Dozier, Craig Lanier 1920- 41-44R
Dozier, Edward P. 1916-1971 Obituary ...29-32R
Dozier, Robert R. 1932- 120
Dozier, Zoe
See Browning, Dixie Burrus
Dozois, Gardner R(aymond) 1947- 108
Dr. A
See Asimov, Isaac
and Silverstein, Alvin
Dr. Alphabet
See Morice, Dave
Dr. Hip
See Schoenfeld, Eugene
Dr. Hippocrates
See Schoenfeld, Eugene
Dr. NO
See Many, Seth E(dward)
Dr. Seuss
See Geisel, Theodor Seuss
See also CLR 9
Dr. Spektor
See Glut, Donald F(rank)
Drabble, Margaret 1939- CANR-18
Earlier sketch in CA 15-16R
See also SATA 48
See also DLB 14
See also CLC 2, 3, 5, 8, 10, 22
Drabble, Phil 1914- 102
Drabek, Jan 1935- 93-96
Drabek, Thomas E(dward) 1940- CANR-16
Earlier sketches in CA 45-48, CANR-1
Drache, Sharon 1943- 118
Drachkovitch, Milorad M. 1921- 19-20R
Drachler, Jacob 1909- 61-64
Drachler, Rose 1911- CANR-4
Earlier sketch in CA 53-56
Drachman, Edward Ralph 1940- 29-32R
Drachman, Julian M(oses) 1894- 61-64
Drachman, Theodore S(olomon) 1904- 81-84
Drackett, Phil(ip Arthur) 1922- CANR-3
Earlier sketch in CA 9-10R
Draco, F.
See Davis, Julia
Drage, Charles H(ardinge) 1897- CANR-2
Earlier sketch in CA 7-8R
Drager, Marvin 1920- 81-84
Dragnich, Alex N. 1912- CANR-15
Earlier sketch in CA 89-92
Drago, Edmund Leon 1942- 109
Drago, Harry Sinclair 1888-1979 113
Obituary 89-92
Drago, Sinclair
See Drago, Harry Sinclair
Dragon, Caroline
See Du Breuil, (Elizabeth) L(or)inda
Dragonette, Jessica (?)-1980 Obituary ...97-100
Dragonwagon, Crescent 1952- CANR-12
Earlier sketch in CA 65-68
See also SATA 11, 41
Drahos, Mary 1927- 116
Draitser, Emil 1937- CANR-18
Earlier sketch in CA 89-92
Drakakis, John 1944- 120
Drake, Albert (Dee) 1935- CANR-13
Earlier sketch in CA 33-36R
Drake, Alice Hutchins 1889(?)-1975
Obituary 61-64
Drake, Asa (a pseudonym) 113
Drake, Barbara (Ann) 1939- CANR-13
Earlier sketch in CA 33-36R
Drake, Bonnie
See Delinsky, Barbara (Ruth Greenberg)
Drake, Charles D(ominic) 1924- 116
Drake, David (Allen) 1945- CANR-17
Earlier sketch in CA 93-96
Drake, Donald C(harles) 1935- 85-88
Drake, Elizabeth 1948- 109
Drake, Francis Vivian 1894-1971 Obituary .. 104
Drake, Frank
See Hamilton, Charles Harold St. John
Drake, Frank D(onald) 1930- 19-20R
Drake, Frederick Charles 1937- 119
Drake, George Randolph 1938- CANR-11
Earlier sketch in CA 69-72
Drake, Harold Allen 1942- 97-100
Drake, Joan H(oward) CANR-24
Earlier sketch in CA 13-14R
Drake, Kimbal
See Gallagher, Rachel
Drake, Lisl
See Beer, Eloise C. S.
Drake, Michael 1935- CANR-16
Earlier sketch in CA 25-28R
Drake, Paul Winter 1944- 106
Drake, Richard Bryant 1925- 37-40R
Drake, Robert (Young, Jr.) 1930- 19-20R
Drake, (John Gibbs) St. Clair (Jr.) 1911- ..65-68
Drake, (Bryant) Stillman 1910- CANR-18
Earlier sketch in CA 41-44R
Drake, W. Anders
See Eshbach, Lloyd Arthur
Drake, W(inbourne) Magruder 1914- 41-44R
Drake, W(alter) Raymond 1913- CANR-5
Earlier sketch in CA 53-56
Drake, William D(onovan) 1922- 21-22R
Drake, William Daniel 1941- 69-72
Drake, William E(arle) 1903- CAP-1
Earlier sketch in CA 17-18
Drake-Brockman, David 1933- 114
Drakeford, John W. 1914- CANR-5
Earlier sketch in CA 4R
Dralle, Elizabeth (Mary) 1910- 4R
Drane, James F. 1930- CANR-7
Earlier sketch in CA 15-16R
Drane, John (William) 1946- CANR-15
Earlier sketch in CA 93-96
Drange, Theodore M. 1934- 37-40R
Dransfield, Michael (John Pender)
1948-1977 ....37-40R
Draper, Alfred 1924- CANR-13
Earlier sketch in CA 33-36R
Draper, Cena C(hristopher) 1907- CANR-10
Earlier sketch in CA 17-18R
Draper, Edgar 1926- 15-16R
Draper, (Ellinor) Elizabeth (Nancy)
1915- 17-18R
Draper, Hal 1914- CANR-24
Earlier sketches in CA 17-18R, CANR-7
Draper, Hastings
See Jeffries, Roderic (Graeme)
Draper, James T(homas), Jr. 1935- 89-92
Draper, Jo 1949- 119
Draper, John W. 1811-1882 .... DLB-30
Draper, John William 1893-1976 ...... CANR-16
Obituary 69-72
Earlier sketches in CA 9-10, CAP-1
Draper, Lyman C. 1815-1891 .... DLB-30
Draper, Norman R(ichard) 1931- 53-56
Draper, Ronald Philip 1928- 69-72
Draper, Theodore 1912- 13-14R
Draper, Thomas 1928- 108
Drapier, M. B.
See Swift, Jonathan
Drapkin, Herbert 1916- 33-36R
Drapkin, Israel 1906- 57-60
Draskovich, Slobodan M. 1910-1982 93-96
Obituary 108
Drath, Viola Herms 1926- CANR-14
Earlier sketch in CA 65-68
Drawbell, James Wedgwood 1899- 65-68
Drawson, Blair 1943- 85-88
See also SATA 17
Dray, William H(erbert) 1921- CANR-13
Earlier sketch in CA 33-36R
Drayer, Adam Matthew 1913- 9-10R
Drayham, William
See Nathan, George Jean
See also TCLC 18
Drayne, George
See McCulley, Johnston
Drazan, Joseph Gerald 1943- 110
Dreadstone, Carl
See Campbell, (John) Ramsey
Drebinger, John 1891(?)-1979 Obituary ...89-92
Drefus, Jean-Paul Etienne 1909-1985
Obituary 117
Dreger, Georgia 1918- 115
Dreger, Ralph Mason 1913- 73-76
Dreher, Carl 1896-1976 73-76
Dreher, Diane Elizabeth 1946- 119
Dreher, Melanie (Creagan) 1943- 114
Dreifort, John E. 1943- 45-48
Dreifus, Claudia 1944- CANR-1
Earlier sketch in CA 45-48
Dreifuss, Kurt 1897- CANR-16
Earlier sketches in CA 1R, CANR-1
Dreikurs, Rudolf 1897-1972 .... CANR-6
Obituary 33-36R
Earlier sketch in CA 3R

Dreiser, Theodore (Herman Albert)
1871-1945 Brief entry ... 106
See also DLB 9, 12
See also DLBD 1
See also TCLC 10, 18
Dreiser, Vera ... 69-72
Dreiss-Tarasovic, Marcia M(argaret)
1943- ... 65-68
Dreitzel, Hans Peter 1935- ... 41-44R
Drekmeier, Charles 1927- ... 4R
Drennen, D(onald) A(rthur) 1925- ... CANR-17
Earlier sketches in CA 4R, CANR-2
Dresang, Eliza (Carolyn Timberlake)
1941- ... 69-72
See also SATA 19
Dresbach, Glen Ward 1889-1968 ... 7-8R
Drescher, Joan E(lizabeth) 1939- ... 106
See also SATA 30
Drescher, John M(ummau) 1928- ... CANR-16
Earlier sketches in CA 49-52, CANR-1
Drescher, Sandra 1957- ... CANR-16
Earlier sketch in CA 85-88
Drescher, Seymour 1934- ... CANR-4
Earlier sketch in CA 11-12R
Drescher-Lehman, Sandra
See Drescher, Sandra
Dresner, Hal 1937- ... 15-16R
Dresner, Samuel H(ayim) 1923- ... CANR-9
Earlier sketch in CA 5-6R
Dressel, Paul L(eroy) 1910- ... CANR-3
Earlier sketch in CA 11-12R
Dresser, Davis 1904-1977 ... 77-80
Obituary ... 69-72
Dresser, Helen
See McCloy, Helen (Worrell Clarkson)
Dressman, Dennis L(ee) 1945- ... 106
Dressman, Denny
See Dressman, Dennis L(ee)
Dressman, John 1947- ... 122
Dretske, Frederick I(rwin) 1932- ... CANR-10
Earlier sketch in CA 25-28R
Dreux, William B(ehan) 1911- ... 89-92
Dreves, Veronica R. 1927-1986 Obituary ... 121
See also SATA 50
Drew, Bernard 1926(?)-1984 Obituary ... 111
Drew, Donald J. 1920- ... 57-60
Drew, Elizabeth 1887-1965 ... 5-6R
Drew, Elizabeth 1935- ... 104
Drew, Fraser Bragg Robert 1913- ... 13-14R
Drew, George A(lexander) 1894-1973
Obituary ... 113
Drew, Katherine Fischer 1923- ... 9-10R
Drew, Kenneth
See Cockburn, (Francis) Claud
Drew, Mary Anne
See Cassiday, Bruce (Bingham)
Drew, Morgan
See Price, Robert
Drew, Patricia (Mary) 1938- ... 77-80
See also SATA 15
Drew, Philip 1943- ... 107
Drew-Bear, Robert 1901- ... CAP-2
Earlier sketch in CA 33-36
Drewery, Mary 1918- ... 25-28R
See also SATA 6
Drewry, Guy Carleton 1901- ... 5-6R
Drewry, Henry N. 1924- ... 97-100
Drewry, John E(ldridge) 1902-1983
Obituary ... 109
Drexel, Jay B.
See Bixby, Jerome Lewis
Drexler, Arthur 1925-1987 ... 97-100
Obituary ... 121
Drexler, J. F.
See Paine, Lauran (Bosworth)
Drexler, K(im) Eric 1955- ... 121
Drexler, Rosalyn 1926- ... 81-84
See also CLC 2, 6
Dreyer, Carl Theodor 1889-1968 Obituary ... 116
See also CLC 16
Dreyer, Edward C. 1937- ... 21-22R
Dreyer, Frederick 1932- ... 111
Dreyer, Peter (Richard) 1939- ... 81-84
Dreyfack, Raymond ... CANR-24
Earlier sketches in CA 65-68, CANR-9
Dreyfus, Edward A(lbert) 1937- ... 37-40R
Dreyfus, Fred
See Rosenblatt, Fred
Dreyfus, Hubert L(ederer) 1929- ... 33-36R
Dreyfus, Kay 1942- ... 124
Dreyfuss, Henry 1904-1972 ... 45-48
Obituary ... 37-40R
Dreyfuss, Joel 1945- ... 97-100
Dreyfuss, Larry 1928- ... 65-68
Dreyfuss, Randolph (Lowell) 1956- ... 97-100
Drial, J. E.
See Laird, Jean E(louise)
Dribben, Judith Strick 1923- ... 37-40R
Driberg, Thomas Edward Neil 1905-1976 ... 65-68
Obituary ... 104
Driberg, Tom
See Driberg, Thomas Edward Neil
Drieu la Rochelle, Pierre(-Eugene)
1893-1945 Brief entry ... 117
See also TCLC 21
Driftwood, Penelope
See De Lima, Clara Rosa
Drimmer, Frederick 1916- ... CANR-23
Earlier sketches in CA 61-64, CANR-7
Drinan, Adam
See Macleod, Joseph (Todd Gordon)
Drinan, Robert F(rederick) 1920- ... CANR-3
Earlier sketch in CA 11-12R
Dring, Nathaniel
See McBroom, R. Curtis
Drinkall, Gordon (Don) 1927- ... 9-10R
Drinkle, Ruth Wolfley 1903- ... 93-96
Drinkrow, John
See Hardwick, (John) Michael (Drinkrow)
Drinkwater, Francis Harold 1886- ... CANR-1
Earlier sketch in CA 3R
Drinkwater, John 1882-1937 Brief entry ... 109
See also DLB 10, 19
Drinkwater, Terry 1936- ... 69-72
Drinnon, Richard 1925- ... CANR-6
Earlier sketch in CA 13-14R
Driscoll, Gertrude 1898(?)-1975 Obituary ... 61-64
Driscoll, Peter (John) 1942- ... CANR-2
Earlier sketch in CA 49-52
Driscoll, R(obert) E(ugene) 1949- ... 85-88
Driskell, David Clyde 1931- ... 102
Driver, C(harles) J(onathan) 1939- ... 29-32R
Driver, Christopher (Prout) 1932- ... 57-60
Driver, Cynthia C.
See Lovin, Roger Robert
Driver, Edwin D(ouglas) 1925- ... 114
Driver, Godfrey Rolles 1892-1975 ... CAP-2
Obituary ... 57-60
Earlier sketch in CA 21-22
Driver, Harold Edson 1907- ... CANR-6
Earlier sketch in CA 2R
Driver, Tom F(aw) 1925- ... CANR-1
Earlier sketch in CA 1R
Driving Hawk, Virginia
See Sneve, Virginia Driving Hawk
Droege, Thomas Arthur 1931- ... 113
Droescher, Vitus B(ernward) 1925- ... 33-36R
Drogheda, Earl of
See Moore, Charles Garrett Ponsonby
Droit, Michel (Arnould Arthur) 1923- ... CANR-11
Earlier sketch in CA 7-8R
Droppers, Carl Hyink 1918- ... 7-8R
Drop Shot
See Cable, George Washington
Dror, Yehezkel 1928- ... CANR-13
Earlier sketch in CA 21-22R
Drossaart Lulofs, H(endrik) J(oan)
1906- ... 15-16R
Drotar, David Lee 1952- ... 112
Drotning, Phillip T(homas) 1920- ... CANR-10
Earlier sketch in CA 25-28R
Drought, James (William) 1931-1983 ... CANR-20
Obituary ... 110
Earlier sketch in CA 7-8R
Drouin, Francis M. 1901- ... 37-40R
Drouin, Marie-Josee 1949- ... 116
Drowatzky, John N(elson) 1936- ... 89-92
Drower, E(thel) S(tefana May)
1879-1972 ... CAP-1
Earlier sketch in CA 11-12
Drown, Harold J(ames) 1904- ... 49-52
Drown, Merle 1943- ... 109
Drowne, Tatiana B(alkoff) 1913- ... 19-20R
Droz, Eugenie 1893(?)-1976 Obituary ... 104
Droze, Wilmon H(enry) 1924- ... CANR-10
Earlier sketch in CA 17-18R
Drubert, John H. 1925- ... 45-48
Druce, Christopher
See Pulling, Christopher Robert Druce
Drucker, H(enry) M(atthew) 1942- ... 106
Drucker, Malka 1945- ... CANR-14
Earlier sketch in CA 81-84
See also SATA 29, 39
Drucker, Mark L(ewis) 1947- ... 107
Drucker, Peter F(erdinand) 1909- ... 61-64
Drukker, J.
See Presser, (Gerrit) Jacob
Druks, Herbert 1937- ... CANR-9
Earlier sketch in CA 21-22R
Drum, Bob
See Drum, Robert F.
Drum, Robert F. 1918- ... 5-6R
Drumheller, Sidney J(ohn) 1923- ... 53-56
Drummond, Alison 1903- ... 112
Drummond, Donald F(rasier) 1914- ... CANR-4
Earlier sketch in CA 3R
Drummond, Dorothy W(eitz) 1928- ... 41-44R
Drummond, Edith Marie Dulce Carman
1883-1970 ... CAP-1
Earlier sketch in CA 9-10
Drummond, Ellen Lane 1897- ... 3R
Drummond, Harold D. 1916- ... CANR-12
Earlier sketch in CA 33-36R
Drummond, Ian (Macdonald) 1933- ... 37-40R
Drummond, J.
See Chance, John Newton
Drummond, Jack 1923(?)-1978 Obituary ... 81-84
Drummond, John 1900-1982 Obituary ... 106
Drummond, John Dodds 1944- ... 102
Drummond, June 1923- ... CANR-7
Earlier sketch in CA 13-14R
Drummond, Kenneth H(erbert) 1922- ... 19-20R
Drummond, Maldwin Andrew Cyril
1932- ... CANR-14
Earlier sketch in CA 73-76
Drummond, Richard H(enry) 1916- ... 41-44R
Drummond, (James) Roscoe 1902-1983 ... 104
Obituary ... 110
Drummond, V(iolet) H(ilda) 1911- ... 13-14R
See also SATA 6
Drummond, Walter
See Silverberg, Robert
Drummond, William Henry 1854-1907 ... TCLC-25
Drummond, William Joe 1944- ... 77-80
Drummond de Andrade, Carlos 1902-1987
Obituary ... 123
See also CLC 18
Druon, Maurice (Samuel Roger Charles)
1918- ... CANR-12
Earlier sketch in CA 13-14R
Drury, Alan 1949- ... 106
Drury, Allen (Stuart) 1918- ... CANR-18
Earlier sketch in CA 57-60
See also CLC 37
Drury, Clare Marie
See Hoskyns-Abrahall, Clare (Constance
Drury)
Drury, Clifford Merrill 1897- ... CANR-3
Earlier sketch in CA 9-10R
Drury, George H(erbert) 1940- ... 121
Drury, James Westbrook 1919- ... 7-8R
Drury, John 1898-1972 ... 5-6R
Obituary ... 33-36R
Drury, Margaret Josephine 1937- ... 53-56
Drury, Maxine Cole 1914- ... 5-6R
Drury, Michael ... 49-52
Drury, Roger W(olcott) 1914- ... 65-68
See also SATA 15
Drury, S(hadia) B(asilious) 1950- ... 116
Drury, Treesa Way 1937- ... 53-56
Drutman, Irving 1910-1978 ... 85-88
Obituary ... 81-84
Druxman, Michael Barnett 1941- ... CANR-16
Earlier sketches in CA 49-52, CANR-1
Drvota, Mojmir 1923- ... 57-60
Dryansky, G. Y. ... 49-52
Dryden, Cecil P(earl) 1887- ... 25-28R
Dryden, Edgar A. 1937- ... 89-92
Dryden, John
See Rowland, D(onald) S(ydney)
Dryden, Ken(neth Wayne) 1947- ... 105
Dryden, Lennox
See Steen, Marguerite
Drysdale, Frank R(eiff) 1943- ... 89-92
Drysdale, George Russell 1912-1981
Obituary ... 108
Drysdale, Vera Louise 1923- ... 115
Drzazga, John 1907- ... CAP-1
Earlier sketch in CA 11-12
Drzemczewski, Andrew (Zbigniew) 1951- ... 116
D'Souza, Dinesh 1961- ... 118
Dua, R(am) P(arkash) 1930- ... 25-28R
Duan, Le
See Le Duan
Duane, Diane (Elizabeth) 1952- ... SATA-46
Duane, Jim
See Hurley, Vic
Duane, William 1760-1835 ... DLB-43
Duarte, Joseph S(imon) 1913- ... 57-60
Dubal, David 1944- ... 118
Duball, Michael
See Ald, Roy A(llison)
Dubanevich, Arlene 1950- ... 116
Dubay, Robert W. 1943- ... 65-68
DuBay, Sandra 1954- ... CANR-23
Earlier sketch in CA 107
Dubay, Thomas Edward 1921- ... CANR-6
Earlier sketch in CA 1R
DuBay, William H. 1934- ... 17-18R
Dube, Marcel 1930- Brief entry ... 117
See also DLB 53
Dube, Pierre Herbert 1943- ... CANR-10
Earlier sketch in CA 65-68
Duberman, Lucile 1926- ... 69-72
Duberman, Martin 1930- ... CANR-2
Earlier sketch in CA 1R
See also CLC 8
Duberstein, Helen 1926- ... CANR-1
Earlier sketch in CA 45-48
Dubh, Cathal O
See Duff, Charles (St. Lawrence)
Dubie, Norman (Evans) 1945- ... CANR-12
Earlier sketch in CA 69-72
See also CLC 36
Dubin, Robert 1916- ... CANR-1
Earlier sketch in CA 45-48
Dubin, Samuel Sanford 1914- ... 37-40R
Dubinsky, David 1892-1982 Obituary ... 107
Dubitsky, Cora Marie 1933- ... 124
Dubkin, Lois Knudson 1911- ... 7-8R
du Blane, Daphne
See Groom, Arthur William
Dublin, Jack 1915- ... 23-24R
Dublin, Thomas Louis 1946- ... 101
Dubnick, Mel(vin Jay) 1946- ... 112
Dubnick, Randa Kay 1948- ... 112
Dubofsky, Melvyn 1934- ... CANR-16
Earlier sketches in CA 49-52, CANR-1
Dubois, Charles
See Counselman, Mary Elizabeth
Du Bois, David G(raham) 1925- ... 65-68
Dubois, Elfrieda T(heresia Pichler) 1916- ... 9-10R
DuBois, Ellen Carol 1947- Brief entry ... 113
DuBois, Josiah Ellis, Jr. 1912-1983
Obituary ... 114
Dubois, M.
See Kent, Arthur William Charles
DuBois, Paul M(artin) 1945- ... 102
DuBois, Paul Z(inkhan) 1936- ... 111
DuBois, Rochelle (Lynn) Holt 1946- ... CANR-7
Earlier sketch in CA 57-60
DuBois, Rosemary
See Durrant, Rita D(elores)
Du Bois, Shirley Graham 1907-1977 ... 77-80
Obituary ... 69-72
See also SATA 24
Du Bois, W(illiam) E(dward) B(urghardt)
1868-1963 ... 85-88
See also SATA 42
See also DLB 47, 50
See also CLC 1, 2, 13
du Bois, William (Sherman) Pene
1916- ... CANR-17
Earlier sketch in CA 5-6R
See also SATA 4
See also DLB 61
See also CLR 1
Dubos, Rene (Jules) 1901-1982 ... 5-6R
Obituary ... 106
DuBose, Fred 1945- ... 118
DuBose, LaRocque (Russ) 1926- ... 23-24R
See also SATA 2
DuBose, Louise Jones 1901- ... CAP-1
Earlier sketch in CA 13-14
Dubout, C(harles) A(lbert) 1905-1976
Obituary ... 65-68
Dubov, Gwen Bagni ... 97-100
Dubov, Paul ?-1979 ... 97-100
Obituary ... 89-92
DuBow, Fredric L(ee) 1944- ... 25-28R
Du Breuil, (Elizabeth) L(or)inda 1924-1980 ... 104
DuBrin, Andrew J(ohn) 1935- ... CANR-15
Earlier sketch in CA 41-44R
Du Broff, Nedra 1931- ... 110
Du Broff, Sidney 1929- ... CANR-9
Earlier sketch in CA 21-22R
Dubrovin, Vivian 1931- ... CANR-9
Earlier sketch in CA 57-60
DuBruck, Alfred J(oseph) 1922- ... 37-40R
DuBruck, Edelgard (Conradt) 1925- ... 19-20R
Dubs, Homer H(asenpflug) 1892-1969 ... CAP-1
Earlier sketch in CA 15-16
Dubus, Andre 1936- ... CANR-17
Earlier sketch in CA 21-22R
See also CLC 13, 36
Dubus, Elizabeth Nell 1933- ... 110
Duby, Georges (Michel Claude) 1919- ... CANR-22
Earlier sketch in CA 104
Duca Minimo
See D'Annunzio, Gabriele
Du Cane, Peter 1901-1984 Obituary ... 114
du Cann, Charles Garfield Lott
1889(?)-1983 Obituary ... 109
Ducas, Dorothy 1905- ... 5-6R
Ducas, Dorothy
See Herzog, Dorothy Ducas
Ducasse, C(urt) J(ohn) 1881-1969 ... CANR-6
Earlier sketch in CA 4R
Duce, Robert 1908- ... 7-8R
Duchacek, Ivo D(uka) 1913-1988 ... CANR-1
Obituary ... 124
Earlier sketch in CA 3R
Du Chaillu, Paul (Belloni) 1835(?)-1903
Brief entry ... 112
See also SATA 26
Duchamp, (Henri-Robert) Marcel
1887-1968 ... 116
Obituary ... 110
Ducharme, Rejean 1941- ... DLB-60
Duche, Jean 1915- ... CANR-9
Earlier sketch in CA 9-10R
Duchene, Louis-Francois 1927- ... 105
Duchesne, Antoinette
See Paine, Lauran (Bosworth)
Duchesne, Jacques
See Saint-Denis, Michel Jacques
Duchesne, Janet 1930- Brief entry ... 111
See also SATA 32
Duchess of Windsor
See Windsor, (Bessie) Wallis Warfield
(Spencer) Simpson
Duckat, Walter Benjamin 1911- ... 29-32R
Ducker, Bruce 1938- ... 65-68
Duckert, Mary 1929- ... 53-56
Duckett, Alfred A. 1917(?)-1984 ... 45-48
Obituary ... 114
Duckett, Eleanor Shipley 1880(?)-1976
Obituary ... 69-72
Duckham, A(lec) N(arraway) 1903- ... 73-76
Duckham, Baron Frederick 1933- ... 103
Duckworth, Alistair M(cKay) 1936- ... 41-44R
Duckworth, F(rancis) R(obinson)
G(ladstone) 1881-1964 Obituary ... 113
Duckworth, George E(ckel) 1903-1972 ... CANR-1
Obituary ... 33-36R
Earlier sketch in CA 4R
Duckworth, Leslie Blakey 1904- ... 105
Ducornet, Erica 1943- ... CANR-14
Earlier sketch in CA 37-40R
See also SATA 7
Ducornet, Rikki
See Ducornet, Erica
Duda, Margaret B(arbalich) 1941- ... 65-68
Dudden, Arthur P(ower) 1921- ... CANR-3
Earlier sketch in CA 5-6R
Dudek, Louis 1918- ... CANR-1
Earlier sketch in CA 45-48
See also CLC 11, 19
Dudley, B(illy) J(oseph) 1931- ... 25-28R
Dudley, Barbara Hudson 1921- ... 65-68
Dudley, Carl Safford 1932- ... 116
Dudley, Donald Reynolds 1910-1972 ... CANR-4
Earlier sketch in CA 7-8R
Dudley, Edward 1926- ... 45-48
Dudley, Ernest 1908- ... 13-14R
Dudley, Geoffrey A(rthur) 1917- ... CANR-6
Earlier sketch in CA 15-16R
Dudley, Guilford A(llerton) 1921-1972 ... 41-44R
Dudley, Guilford, Jr. 1907- ... CAP-2
Earlier sketch in CA 19-20
Dudley, Helen
See Hope Simpson, Jacynth
Dudley, Jay
See Chapman, J. Dudley
Dudley, Lavinia P(ratt) 1891(?)-1984
Obituary ... 113
Dudley, Louise 1884- ... 73-76
Dudley, Martha Ward 1909(?)-1985
Obituary ... 117
See also SATA 45
Dudley, Nancy
See Cole, Lois Dwight
Dudley, Robert
See Baldwin, James
Dudley, Ruth H(ubbell) 1905- ... 61-64
See also SATA 11
Dudley Edwards, Ruth 1944- ... 107

Dudley-Smith, Timothy 1926- ... 103
Dudman, Richard (Beebe) 1918- ... 45-48
Due, Linnea A. 1948- ... 105
Dueker, Christopher W(ayne) 1939- ... 57-60
Dueker, Joyce S(utherlin) 1942- ... 57-60
Dueland, Joy V(ivian) ... 106
See also SATA 27
Duell, Charles Halliwell 1905-1970
Obituary ... 104
Duerr, Edwin 1904- ... 73-76
Duerrenmatt, Friedrich 1921- ... 17-18R
See also CLC 1, 4, 8, 11, 15, 43
Dufault, Peter Kane 1923- ... 33-36R
Duff, Annis (James) 1904(?)-1986
Obituary ... 120
See also SATA 49
Duff, Charles (St. Lawrence)
1894-1966 ... CANR-2
Earlier sketch in CA 4R
Duff, David (Skene) 1912- Brief entry ... 118
Duff, Ernest A(rthur) 1929- ... 25-28R
Duff, Gerald 1938- ... 45-48
Duff, John B. 1931- ... CANR-1
Earlier sketch in CA 45-48
Duff, Maggie
See Duff, Margaret K.
Duff, Margaret K. ... CANR-14
Earlier sketch in CA 37-40R
See also SATA 37
Duff, Raymond S(tanley) 1923- ... 23-24R
Duffee, David E(ugene) 1946- ... 104
Duffey, Bernard I. 1917- ... 114
Duffey, Margery 1926- ... 73-76
Duffield, Anne (Tate) 1893- ... CAP-1
Earlier sketch in CA 15-16
Duffin, Henry Charles 1884- ... CAP-1
Earlier sketch in CA 9-10
Duffus, R(obert) L(uther) 1888-1972 ... 101
Obituary ... 37-40R
Duffy, Ben
See Duffy, Bernard C.
Duffy, Bernard C. 1902-1972 Obituary ... 37-40R
Duffy, Carol Ann 1955- ... 119
Duffy, Charles 1940- ... 104
Duffy, Clinton T(ruman) 1898-1982
Obituary ... 108
Duffy, Dennis 1938- ... 113
Duffy, Edmund 1899-1962 Obituary ... 93-96
Duffy, Elizabeth 1904-19(?) ... CAP-2
Earlier sketch in CA 19-20
Duffy, Francis R(amon) 1915- ... 49-52
Duffy, Helene (Krainovich) 1926- ... 19-20R
Duffy, John 1915- ... CANR-8
Earlier sketch in CA 19-20R
Duffy, John J(oseph) 1934- ... 57-60
Duffy, Maureen 1933- ... 25-28R
See also DLB 14
See also CLC 37
Duffy, Regis Anthony 1934- ... 110
Dufrechou, Carole
See Monroe, Carole
Dufty, William 1916- ... 65-68
Dugan, Alan 1923- ... 81-84
See also DLB 5
See also CLC 2, 6
Dugan, George 1909-1982 Obituary ... 107
Dugan, J(ohn) Raymond 1935- ... 121
Dugan, Jack
See Butterworth, W(illiam) E(dmund III)
Dugan, James (Thomas) 1912-1967 ... CANR-4
Earlier sketch in CA 5-6R
Dugan, Michael (Gray) 1947- ... CANR-14
Earlier sketch in CA 77-80
See also SATA 15
Dugard, C. J(ohn) R. 1936- ... 85-88
du Gard, Roger Martin
See Martin du Gard, Roger
Dugdale, Robert
See Hardy, Henry
Duggan, Alfred Leo 1903-1964 ... 73-76
See also SATA 25
Duggan, George Henry 1912- ... 17-18R
Duggan, Joseph J(ohn) 1938- ... 29-32R
Duggan, Mary M. 1921- ... 25-28R
Duggan, Maurice (Noel) 1922-1974 ... CANR-17
Obituary ... 53-56
Earlier sketch in CA 73-76
See also SATA 30, 40
Duggan, William 1952- ... 122
Duggan, William Redman 1915- ... 69-72
Duggans, Pat
See Connolly, Robert D(uggan, Jr.)
Dugger, Ronnie 1930- ... CANR-12
Earlier sketch in CA 21-22R
Duggins, James (Harry), Jr. 1933- ... 37-40R
Dughi, Nancy ... 3R
Dugmore, Clifford W(illiam) 1909- ... 13-14R
Duguid, Charles 1884- ... 109
Duguid, John Bright 1895-1980 Obituary ... 102
Duguid, Robert
See Pring-Mill, Robert D(uguid) F(orrest)
Duhamel, Georges 1884-1966 ... 81-84
Obituary ... 25-28R
See also DLB 65
See also CLC 8
Duhamel, Marcel 1900(?)-1977 Obituary ... 104
Duhamel, P(ierre) Albert 1920- ... 5-6R
du Hault, Jean
See Grindel, Eugene
Duhl, Leonard J. 1926- ... 13-14R
Duignan, Peter 1926- ... CANR-11
Earlier sketch in CA 13-14R
Duiker, William J(ohn) 1932- ... CANR-16
Earlier sketch in CA 85-88
Duis, Perry R. 1943- ... 124
Dujardin, Edouard (Emile Louis)
1861-1949 Brief entry ... 109
See also TCLC 13
du Jardin, Rosamond Neal 1902-1963 ... 3R
Obituary ... 103
See also SATA 2
Duka, Ivo
See Duchacek, Ivo D(uka)
Duke, Alvah (Carter) 1908- ... 45-48
Duke, Benjamin 1931- ... 49-52
Duke, Charles (Richard) 1940- ... CANR-11
Earlier sketch in CA 69-72
Duke, David C. 1940- ... 112
Duke, Donald Norman 1929- ... CANR-7
Earlier sketch in CA 19-20R
Duke, Forrest R(eagan) 1918- ... 77-80
Duke, James T(aylor) 1933- ... 65-68
Duke, John
See Chalmers, Floyd S(herman)
Duke, Judith S(ilverman) 1934- ... 118
Duke, Madelaine (Elizabeth) 1925- ... CANR-9
Earlier sketch in CA 57-60
Duke, Maurice 1934- ... 112
Duke, Michael Geoffrey Hare
See Hare Duke, Michael Geoffrey
Duke, Richard DeLaBarre 1930- ... 57-60
Duke, Robin (Antony Hare) 1916-1984
Obituary ... 115
Duke, Vernon 1903-1969 ... CAP-2
Earlier sketch in CA 29-32
Duke, Will
See Gault, William Campbell
Duke-Elder, Stewart 1896-1978 Obituary ... 77-80
Dukelsky, Vladimir
See Duke, Vernon
Duke Of Beaufort
See Somerset, Henry Hugh Arthur
FitzRoy
Duker, Abraham G(ordon) 1907- ... 53-56
Duker, Sam 1905-1978 ... 15-16R
Obituary ... 77-80
Dukert, Joseph M(ichael) 1929- ... CANR-3
Earlier sketch in CA 5-6R
Dukes, Ashley 1885-1959 Brief entry ... 110
See also DLB 10
Dukes, Paul 1889-1967 Obituary ... 112
Dukes, Paul 1934- ... CANR-9
Earlier sketch in CA 23-24R
Dukes, Philip
See Bickers, Richard Leslie Townshend
Dukes, Tyrone 1946(?)-1983 Obituary ... 110
Dukore, Bernard F. 1931- ... CANR-12
Earlier sketch in CA 25-28R
Dukore, Margaret Mitchell 1950- ... CANR-23
Earlier sketch in CA 106
Dulac, Edmund 1882-1953 ... SATA-19
Dulack, Thomas 1935- ... 25-28R
Dulany, Don E., Jr. 1928- ... 69-72
Dulany, Harris 1940- ... 33-36R
Dulieu, Jean
See van Oort, Jan
Dull, Jonathan R(omer) 1942- ... 69-72
Dulles, Allen W(elsh) 1893-1969 ... CAP-2
Earlier sketch in CA 23-24
Dulles, Avery (Robert) 1918- ... CANR-21
Earlier sketches in CA 9-10R, CANR-3
Dulles, Eleanor Lansing 1895- ... 9-10R
Dulles, Foster Rhea 1900-1970 ... CAP-1
Obituary ... 29-32R
Earlier sketch in CA 13-14
Dulles, John Foster 1888-1959 Brief entry ... 115
Dulles, John W(atson) F(oster) 1913- ... CANR-1
Earlier sketch in CA 4R
Duloup, Victor
See Volkoff, Vladimir
Dulsey, Bernard M. 1914- ... 11-12R
Dumarchais, Pierre 1882-1970 Obituary ... 29-32R
Dumarchey, Pierre
See Dumarchais, Pierre
Dumas, Alexandre 1802-1870 ... SATA-18
Dumas, Andre 1918- ... CANR-13
Earlier sketch in CA 73-76
Dumas, Claire
See Van Weddingen, Marthe
Dumas, Claudine
See Malzberg, Barry N(athaniel)
du Mas, Frank (Maurice) 1918- ... 106
Dumas, Frederic 1913- ... 69-72
Dumas, Gerald J. 1930- ... 25-28R
Dumas, Henry L. 1934-1968 ... 85-88
See also DLB 41
See also CLC 6
Dumas, Jacqueline 1946- ... 123
Dumas, Philippe 1940- ... 107
du Maurier, Daphne 1907- ... CANR-6
Earlier sketch in CA 5-6R
See also SATA 27
See also CLC 6, 11
Dumbleton, William A(lbert) 1927- ... 37-40R
Dumery, Henry 1920- ... 101
Dumezil, Georges (Edmond Raoul)
1898-1986 Obituary ... 120
Dumitriu, Petru 1924- Brief entry ... 116
Dumke, Edward J. 1946- ... 124
Dumke, Glenn S. 1917- ... 112
Dummett, Michael Anthony Eardley 1925- ... 102
Dumond, Dwight Lowell 1895-1976 ... 69-72
Obituary ... 65-68
Dumont, Jean-Paul 1940- ... CANR-12
Earlier sketch in CA 73-76
Dumoulin, Heinrich 1905- ... CANR-4
Earlier sketch in CA 5-6R
Dumpleton, John Le F(evre) 1924- ... 13-14R
Dumpty, Humpty S.
See Denenberg, Herbert S(idney)
Dun, Angus 1892-1971 Obituary ... 33-36R
Dun, Mao
See Yen-Ping, Shen
Dunas, Joseph C. 1900- ... 19-20R
Dunathan, Arni T(homas) 1936- ... 53-56
Dunaway, David King 1948- ... 107
Dunaway, John M(arson) 1945- ... 89-92
Dunayevskaya, Raya 1910-1987 Obituary ... 122
Dunbabin, J(ohn) P(aul) D(elacour)
1938- ... 69-72
Dunbabin, Jean 1939- ... 119
Dunbar, Alice
See Nelson, Alice Ruth Moore Dunbar
Dunbar, Alice Moore
See Nelson, Alice Ruth Moore Dunbar
Dunbar, Charles Stuart 1900- ... 107
Dunbar, David
See Baxter, Craig
Dunbar, Dorothy 1923- ... 11-12R
Dunbar, Edward
See Smith, David MacLeod
Dunbar, Ernest 1927- ... 25-28R
Dunbar, Janet 1901- ... CANR-6
Earlier sketch in CA 9-10R
Dunbar, John Greenwell 1930- ... 23-24R
Dunbar, Maxwell John 1914- ... 103
Dunbar, Paul Laurence 1872-1906 ... 124
Brief entry ... 104
See also SATA 34
See also DLB 50, 54
See also TCLC 2, 12
Dunbar, Robert E(verett) 1926- ... CANR-15
Earlier sketch in CA 85-88
See also SATA 32
Dunbar, Robert George 1907- ... 114
Dunbar, Tony 1949- ... 33-36R
Dunbar, Willis F(rederick) 1902-1970 ... CANR-4
Earlier sketch in CA 5-6R
Dunbar-Nelson, Alice
See Nelson, Alice Ruth Moore Dunbar
Dunbar-Nelson, Alice Moore
See Nelson, Alice Ruth Moore Dunbar
Dunbaugh, Frank Montgomery 1895- ... 45-48
Duncan, A(nthony) D(ouglas) 1930- ... 33-36R
Duncan, Alastair 1942- ... 117
Duncan, Alex
See Duke, Madelaine (Elizabeth)
Duncan, Alistair (Charteris) 1927- ... 61-64
Duncan, Archibald A(lexander) M(cBeth)
1926- ... 81-84
Duncan, Ardinelle Bean 1913- ... 4R
Duncan, (Reid) Bingham 1911- ... 85-88
Duncan, Bowie 1941- ... 33-36R
Duncan, C(yril) J(ohn) 1916- ... 25-28R
Duncan, Carl P(orter) 1921- Brief entry ... 115
Duncan, Charles T(homas) 1914- ... 19-20R
Duncan, Chester 1913- ... 93-96
Duncan, Clyde H. 1903- ... 19-20R
Duncan, David 1913- ... 7-8R
Duncan, David Douglas 1916- Brief entry ... 112
See also AITN 1
Duncan, Delbert J(ames) 1895- ... 41-44R
Duncan, Denis (Macdonald) 1920- ... CANR-23
Earlier sketch in CA 107
Duncan, Dora Angela
See Duncan, Isadora
Duncan, Dougal 1921- ... 102
Duncan, Elmer H(ubert) 1933- ... 69-72
Duncan, Florence Belle 1917(?)-1980
Obituary ... 97-100
Duncan, Frances (Mary) 1942- ... CANR-17
Earlier sketch in CA 97-100
See also SATA 48
Duncan, George
See Davison, Geoffrey
Duncan, Gregory
See McClintock, Marshall
Duncan, Hugh Dalziel 1909-1970 ... CAP-2
Earlier sketch in CA 23-24
Duncan, Irma 1897-1977 ... 49-52
Obituary ... 73-76
Duncan, Isadora 1878(?)-1927 Brief entry ... 118
Duncan, Jane
See Cameron, Elizabeth Jane
Duncan, Joseph E(llis) 1921- ... 5-6R
Duncan, Julia Coley
See Sather, Julia Coley Duncan
Duncan, Julia K. ... CAP-2
Earlier sketch in CA 19-20
See also SATA 1
Duncan, Kenneth S(andilands) 1912- ... 9-10R
Duncan, Kunigunde 1886- ... 7-8R
Duncan, Lois 1934- ... CANR-23
Earlier sketches in CA 3R, CANR-2
See also SATA 1, 36
See also SAAS 2
See also CLC 26
Duncan, Marion Moncure 1913-1978
Obituary ... 77-80
Duncan, Norman 1871-1916 Brief entry ... 117
See also YABC 1
Duncan, Otis Dudley 1921- ... CANR-22
Earlier sketches in CA 13-14R, CANR-6
Duncan, Pam 1938- ... 37-40R
Duncan, Pope A(lexander) 1920- ... 15-16R
Duncan, Robert (Edward) 1919-1988 ... 11-12R
See also DLB 5, 16
See also CLC 1, 2, 4, 7, 15, 41
Duncan, Robert (Edward) 1919-1988
Obituary ... 124
Duncan, Robert F. 1890(?)-1974
Obituary ... 53-56
Duncan, Robert L(ipscomb) 1927- ... 106
See also CAAS 2
Duncan, Ronald 1914-1982 ... CANR-4
Obituary ... 107
Earlier sketch in CA 7-8R
See also DLB 13
Duncan, T. Bentley 1929- ... 77-80
Duncan, Thomas (William) 1905- ... CANR-1
Earlier sketch in CA 2R
Duncan, W(illiam) Murdoch 1909-1976 ... CANR-6
Earlier sketch in CA 15-16R
Duncan, W. R.
See Duncan, Robert L(ipscomb)
Duncan, W. Raymond 1936- ... 41-44R
Duncan, Wilbur H(oward) 1910- ... 116
Duncan, William (Robert) 1944- ... 115
Duncanson, Michael E(dward) 1948- ... 57-60
Duncombe, David C(ameron) 1928- ... 29-32R
Duncombe, Frances (Riker) 1900- ... 25-28R
See also SATA 25
Dundee, Robert
See Kirsch, Robert R.
Dundes, Alan 1934- ... CANR-9
Earlier sketch in CA 23-24R
Dundy, Elaine 1937- ... 97-100
Dunford, Judith 1933- ... 107
Dungan, David L(aird) 1936- ... 123
Dunham, Arthur 1893- ... 33-36R
Dunham, Barrows 1905- ... 7-8R
Dunham, Bob
See Dunham, Robert
Dunham, Donald Carl 1908- ... CANR-17
Earlier sketch in CA 4R
Dunham, H(enry) Warren 1906-1985 ... CANR-8
Obituary ... 118
Earlier sketch in CA 13-14R
Dunham, John L. 1939- ... 29-32R
Dunham, Katherine 1910- ... CANR-17
Earlier sketch in CA 65-68
Dunham, Lowell 1910- ... 37-40R
Dunham, (Bertha) Mabel 1881-1957
Brief entry ... 114
Dunham, Montrew Goetz 1919- ... 19-20R
Dunham, Robert 1931- ... 69-72
Dunham, William Huse, Jr. 1901- ... 49-52
Dunhill, Alfred H(enry) 1896(?)-1971
Obituary ... 104
Dunhill, Mary 1907(?)-1988 Obituary ... 124
Dunkel, Harold Baker 1912- ... 5-6R
Dunkel, Richard H(adley) 1933- ... 73-76
Dunkell, Samuel (V.) 1919- Brief entry ... 115
Dunkelman, Ben(jamin) 1913- Brief entry ... 111
Dunkerley, Elsie Jeanette ?-1960 Obituary ... 116
Dunkerley, Roderic 1884- ... CAP-1
Earlier sketch in CA 13-14
Dunkin, Paul S(haner) 1905-1975 ... CAP-2
Earlier sketch in CA 33-36
Dunkle, William F(rederick), Jr. 1911- ... 53-56
Dunkley, Christopher 1944- ... 121
Dunkling, Leslie Alan 1935- ... CANR-14
Earlier sketch in CA 81-84
Dunkman, William E(dward) 1903- ... CAP-2
Earlier sketch in CA 25-28
Dunlap, Aurie N(ichols) 1907-1977 ... 37-40R
Dunlap, G(eorge) D(ale) 1923- ... 49-52
Dunlap, Jan ... 65-68
Dunlap, Jane
See Davis, Adelle
Dunlap, John 1747-1812 ... DLB-43
Dunlap, Joseph R(iggs) 1913- ... 85-88
Dunlap, Leslie W(hittaker) 1911- ... 37-40R
Dunlap, Lon
See McCormick, Wilfred
Dunlap, Orrin E(lmer), Jr. 1896-1970 ... CAP-1
Earlier sketch in CA 11-12
Dunlap, William 1766-1839 ... DLB-30, 37, 59
Dunlay, Thomas W. 1944- ... 112
Dunleavy, Gareth W(inthrop) 1923- ... 33-36R
Dunleavy, Janet Egleson 1928- ... CANR-21
Earlier sketches in CA 57-60, CANR-6
Dunleavy, Patrick 1952- ... 123
Dunlop, Agnes M.R. ?-1982 ... CANR-9
Earlier sketch in CA 15-16R
Dunlop, Derrick Melville 1902-1980
Obituary ... 101
Dunlop, Douglas Morton 1909-1987
Obituary ... 123
Dunlop, Eileen (Rhona) 1938- ... CANR-14
Earlier sketch in CA 73-76
See also SATA 24
Dunlop, Ian G(eoffrey) D(avid) 1925- ... CANR-24
Earlier sketches in CA 9-10R, CANR-5
Dunlop, John B. 1942- ... 57-60
Dunlop, John Thomas 1914- ... CANR-5
Earlier sketch in CA 13-14R
Dunlop, Richard (B.) 1921- ... CANR-7
Earlier sketch in CA 17-18R
Dunlop, Robert 1953- ... 116
Dunmore, John 1923- ... CANR-23
Earlier sketch in CA 106
Dunmore, Spencer (Sambrook) 1928- ... CANR-13
Earlier sketch in CA 33-36R
Dunn, Alan (Cantwell) 1900-1974 ... CAP-2
Obituary ... 49-52
Earlier sketch in CA 33-36
Dunn, Carola 1946- ... 118
Dunn, Catherine M(ary) 1930- ... 37-40R
Dunn, Charles W(illiam) 1915- ... 49-52
Dunn, Delmer D(elano) 1941- ... 25-28R
Dunn, Donald H(arley) 1929- ... 33-36R
Dunn, Douglas (Eaglesham) 1942- ... CANR-2
Earlier sketch in CA 45-48
See also DLB 40
See also CLC 6, 40
Dunn, Edgar S(treeter), Jr. 1921- ... 9-10R
Dunn, Edward D. 1883(?)-1978 Obituary ... 77-80
Dunn, Esther Cloudman 1891-1977
Obituary ... 73-76
Dunn, Ethel (Deikman) 1932- ... 23-24R
Dunn, Frederick Sherwood 1893-1962
Obituary ... 113
Dunn, Halbert Louis 1896-1975 Obituary ... 61-64
Dunn, (Henry) Hampton 1916- ... 57-60

Dunn, Harold 1929- 9-10R
Dunn, Harris
See Doerffler, Alfred
Dunn, Harvey T(homas) 1884-1952 .... SATA-34
Dunn, Hugh Patrick 1916- 122
Dunn, James
See Wilkes-Hunter, R(ichard)
Dunn, James D(ouglas Grant) 1939- 73-76
Dunn, James Taylor 1912- CANR-20
Earlier sketches in CA 7-8R, CANR-4
Dunn, Jean 1921- 109
Dunn, Jerry G. 1916- CANR-11
Earlier sketch in CA 23-24R
Dunn, John (Montfort) 1940- CANR-11
Earlier sketch in CA 69-72
Dunn, Joseph (Willcox, Jr.) 1937- 122
Dunn, Judith F.
See Bernal, Judith F.
Dunn, Judy
See Spangenberg, Judith Dunn
Dunn, Katherine (Karen) 1945- 33-36R
Dunn, Kaye
See Dunham, Katherine
Dunn, Lloyd W. 1906- 57-60
Dunn, Marion Herndon 1920- 29-32R
Dunn, Mary Lois 1930- CANR-12
Earlier sketch in CA 61-64
See also SATA 6
Dunn, Mary Maples 1931- 114
Dunn, Nell
See Sandford, Nell Mary
Dunn, Patience (Louise Ralli) 1922- 7-8R
Dunn, Peter N(orman) 1926- 122
Dunn, Richard S(lator) 1928- Brief entry ... 112
Dunn, Ronald (Louis) 1936- Brief entry 120
Dunn, S. P.
See Dunn, Stephen P(orter)
Dunn, Samuel Watson 1918- CANR-5
Earlier sketch in CA 1R
Dunn, Si 1944- 77-80
Dunn, Stephen 1939- CANR-12
Earlier sketch in CA 33-36R
See also CLC 36
Dunn, Stephen P(orter) 1928- 124
Dunn, Stuart 1900- 57-60
Dunn, Thomas G(eorge) 1950- 119
Dunn, Thomas Tinsley 1901- 107
Dunn, Waldo H(ilary) 1882-1969 .... CAP-2
Earlier sketch in CA 21-22
Dunn, Walter Scott, Jr. 1928- 101
Dunn, William J. 1906- 33-36R
Dunn, William L(awrence, Jr.) 1924- 37-40R
Dunn, William Robert 1916- 113
Dunnahoo, Terry 1927- CANR-14
Earlier sketch in CA 41-44R
See also SATA 7
Dunnam, Maxie D(enton) 1934- 73-76
Dunnan, Nancy 1941- 112
Dunne, Colin 1937- 123
Dunne, Dominick 1925- 121
Dunne, Finley Peter 1867-1936 Brief entry .. 108
See also DLB 11, 23
Dunne, George H(arold) 1905- CANR-5
Earlier sketch in CA 3R
Dunne, Gerald T. 1919- CANR-1
Earlier sketch in CA 45-48
Dunne, John Gregory 1932- CANR-14
Earlier sketch in CA 25-28R
See also DLBY 80
See also CLC 28
Dunne, John S(cribner) 1929- 15-16R
Dunne, (Christopher) Lee 1934- 120
Dunne, Mary Collins 1914- CANR-14
Earlier sketch in CA 41-44R
See also SATA 11
Dunne, Mary Jo
See Dunne, Mary Collins
Dunne, Philip 1908- CANR-11
Earlier sketches in CA 9-10, CAP-1
See also DLB 26
Dunne, Robert Williams 1895-1977
Obituary 69-72
Dunnell, Robert C(hester) 1942- 89-92
Dunner, Joseph 1908-1978 .... CANR-14
Earlier sketch in CA 21-22R
Dunnett, Alastair M(acTavish) 1908- 65-68
Dunnett, Dorothy 1923- CANR-3
Earlier sketch in CA 4R
Dunnett, Margaret (Rosalind) 1909-1977 ... 108
See also SATA 42
Dunnigan, Alice Allison 1906-1983
Obituary 109
Dunning, Brad 1957- 102
Dunning, Bruce 1940- 77-80
Dunning, Chester S(idney) L(arson) 1949- .. 116
Dunning, Edward
See Gilbert, R(obert) A(ndrew)
Dunning, Eric (Geoffrey) 1936- 116
Dunning, John 1942- CANR-16
Earlier sketch in CA 93-96
Dunning, John H(arry) 1927- CANR-21
Earlier sketch in CA 104
Dunning, Lawrence 1931- 77-80
Dunning, Ralph Cheever 1878-1930
Brief entry 107
See also DLB 4
Dunning, Robert William 1938- CANR-20
Earlier sketches in CA 53-56, CANR-5
Dunning, (Arthur) Stephen (Jr.) 1924- . CANR-12
Earlier sketch in CA 25-28R
Dunning, William A. 1857-1922 .... DLB-17
Dunnington, Hazel Brain 1912- 21-22R
du Nouey, Pierre (-Andre-Leon) Lecomte
See Lecomte du Nouey, Pierre
(-Andre-Leon)
Dunoyer, Maurice
See Domergue, Maurice
Dunoyer De Segonzac, Andre 1884-1974
Obituary 53-56
Dunphy, Jack 1914- 25-28R
Dunrea, Olivier 1953- SATA-46
Dunrea, Olivier Jean-Paul Dominique
1953- 124
Dunsany, Edward John Moreton Drax
Plunkett 1878-1957 Brief entry 104
See also DLB 10
Dunsheath, Joyce (Houchen) 1902- 7-8R
Dunsheath, Percy 1886- 107
Dunsmore, Roger 1938- 110
Dunson, Josh 1941- 25-28R
Dunstan, Andrew
See Chandler, A(rthur) Bertram
Dunstan, Don(ald Allan) 1926- 110
Dunstan, Reginald (Ernest) 1914- 21-22R
Dunster, Mark 1927- 85-88
Dunsterville, G(alfrid) C. K. 1905- CAP-1
Earlier sketch in CA 9-10
Dunston, Arthur John 1922- 109
Dunton, (Arnold) Davidson 1912-1987
Obituary 121
Dunton, Samuel Cady 1910(?)-1975
Obituary 61-64
Dupee, F(rederick) W(ilcox) 1904-1979 ... CAP-1
Obituary 85-88
Earlier sketch in CA 13-14
du Perry, Jean
See Simenon, Georges (Jacques
Christian)
Dupin, August Dupont
See Taylor, John (Alfred)
Dupin, Jacques 1927- Brief entry 119
Duplessis, Yves
See Duplessis, Yvonne
Duplessis, Yvonne 1912- CANR-3
Earlier sketch in CA 9-10R
Dupont, Paul
See Frewin, Leslie Ronald
Dupre, Catherine CANR-16
Earlier sketch in CA 25-28R
Dupre, J(osef) Stefan 1936- 102
Dupre, Louis CANR-18
Earlier sketches in CA 9-10R, CANR-3
Dupree, A(nderson) Hunter 1921- 11-12R
Dupree, Louis 1925- 41-44R
Dupres, Henri
See Fawcett, F(rank) Dubrez
Duprey, Richard A(llen) 1929- CANR-6
Earlier sketch in CA 7-8R
Dupuis, Adrian M(aurice) 1919- 11-12R
Dupuy, R(ichard) Ernest 1887-1975 .... CANR-6
Obituary 57-60
Earlier sketch in CA 4R
Dupuy, T(revor) N(evitt) 1916- CANR-18
Earlier sketches in CA 4R, CANR-2
See also SATA 4
Durac, Jack
See Rachman, Stanley Jack
Durack, Mary 1913- CANR-17
Earlier sketch in CA 97-100
Duram, James C(arl) 1939- CANR-4
Earlier sketch in CA 53-56
Duran, Gloria Diana Bradley 1924- 107
Duran, Manuel E. 1925- CANR-11
Earlier sketch in CA 25-28R
Duran, Richard (Paul) 1943- 114
Durand, G. Forbes
See Burgess, M(ichael) R(oy)
Durand, John Dana 1913-1981 .... CANR-9
Earlier sketch in CA 61-64
Durand, Loup 1933- 124
Durand, Loyal, Jr. 1902-1970 .... CAP-2
Earlier sketch in CA 21-22
Durand, Lucile
See Bersianik, Louky
Durand, Robert 1944- 57-60
Durandeaux, Jacques 1926- 25-28R
Durang, Christopher (Ferdinand) 1949- 105
See also CLC 27, 38
Durant, Ariel K(aufman) 1898-1981 ..... CANR-4
Obituary 105
Earlier sketch in CA 11-12R
Durant, David N(orton) 1925- 77-80
Durant, Frederick C(lark) III 1916- 113
Durant, Henry 1902-1982 Obituary 107
Durant, John 1902- CANR-5
Earlier sketch in CA 9-10R
See also SATA 27
Durant, Stuart 1932- 104
Durant, Will(iam James) 1885-1981 .... CANR-4
Obituary 105
Earlier sketch in CA 11-12R
Durante, James Francis 1893-1980
Obituary 93-96
Durante, Jimmy
See Durante, James Francis
Duranty, Walter 1884-1957 .... DLB-29
Duras, Marguerite 1914- 25-28R
See also CLC 3, 6, 11, 20, 34, 40
Duratschek, (Mary) Claudia 1894- 37-40R
Duratschek, Sister Mary Claudia
See Duratschek, (Mary) Claudia
Durbahn, Walter E. 1895(?)-1981
Obituary 102
Durban, (Rosa) Pam 1947- 123
Durban, Pam 1947- CLC-39
Durband, Alan 1927- CANR-20
Earlier sketches in CA 7-8R, CANR-2
Durbin, Brice 1899(?)-1983 Obituary 111
Durbin, Mary Lou 1927- 21-22R
Durbin, Richard Louis 1928- CANR-7
Earlier sketch in CA 53-56
Durbridge, Francis (Henry) 1912- CANR-24
Earlier sketches in CA 77-80, CANR-6
Durcan, Paul 1944- CLC-43
Durden, Robert Franklin 1925- 9-10R
Durey, Michael (John) 1947- 107
Durfee, David A(rthur) 1929- 29-32R
Durgnat, Raymond (Eric) 1932- 19-20R
Durham, Frank (Edington) 1935- 114
Durham, John 1925- 107
Durham, John
See Paine, Lauran (Bosworth)
Durham, John I 1933- CANR-13
Earlier sketch in CA 29-32R
Durham, Mae
See Roger, Mae Durham
Durham, Marilyn 1930- 49-52
Durham, Philip 1912-1977 .... CANR-7
Earlier sketch in CA 11-12R
Durka, Gloria 1939- CANR-14
Earlier sketch in CA 65-68
Durkee, Mary C. 1921- 13-14R
Durkin, Barbara W(ernecke) 1944- 123
Durkin, Henry P(aul) 1940- 53-56
Durkin, Joseph Thomas 1903- CAP-1
Earlier sketch in CA 11-12
Durland, Frances Caldwell 1892- 113
Durland, William R(eginald) 1931- CANR-7
Earlier sketch in CA 57-60
Durnbaugh, Donald F. 1927- CANR-8
Earlier sketch in CA 21-22R
Durnin, Richard G(erry) 1920- 110
Durning, Addis
See Ranzini, Addis Durning
Duroche, Leonard L(eRoy) 1933- 37-40R
DuRocher, Richard J(ames) 1955- 118
Duroselle, Jean-Baptiste (Marie Lucien
Charles) 1917- CANR-18
Earlier sketches in CA 9-10R, CANR-3
Durr, Fred
See Durr, Frederick R(oland) E(ugene)
Durr, Frederick R(oland) E(ugene)
1921-1978 ....37-40R
Durr, William Kirtley 1924- 15-16R
Durrani, Mahmood Khan 1914- CAP-1
Earlier sketch in CA 13-14
Durrant, Digby 1926- CANR-13
Earlier sketch in CA 21-22R
Durrant, Rita D(elores) 1932- 108
Durrant, Theo
See Offord, Lenore Glen
Durrell, Donald D(e Witt) 1903- CANR-8
Earlier sketch in CA 17-18R
Durrell, Gerald (Malcolm) 1925- CANR-4
Earlier sketch in CA 7-8R
See also SATA 8
Durrell, Jacqueline Sonia Rasen 1929- ...23-24R
Durrell, Jacquie
See Durrell, Jacqueline Sonia Rasen
Durrell, Lawrence (George) 1912- 9-10R
See also DLB 15, 27
See also CLC 1, 4, 6, 8, 13, 27, 41
Durrell, Zoe C(ompton) 1910- 89-92
Durrenberger, Robert Warren 1918- ... CANR-10
Earlier sketch in CA 23-24R
Durrenmatt, Friedrich
See Duerrenmatt, Friedrich
Durslag, Melvin 1921- 101
Durst, Paul 1921- 23-24R
d'Urstelle, Pierre
See Dorst, Jean (Pierre)
Durville, Hector 1849-1923 Brief entry 117
Dury, George H(arry) 1916- 113
Durzak, Manfred 1938- CANR-1
Earlier sketch in CA 49-52
du Sautoy, Peter (Francis De Courcy)
1921- 5-6R
Dusay, Katherine M(ulholland) 1943- 118
Duscha, Julius (Carl) 1924- 73-76
Dusenberry, William Howard 1908- CAP-1
Earlier sketch in CA 19-20
Dusenbury, Winifred L.
See Frazer, Winifred L(oesch)
Dushkin, Alexander M(ordecai) 1890-1976
Obituary 65-68
Dushnitzky-Shner, Sara 1913- 29-32R
Duska, Ronald 1937- 97-100
Duskin, Ruthie
See Feldman, Ruth Duskin
Dusky, Lorraine 1942- 85-88
Du Soe, Robert C. 1892-1958 .... YABC-2
Dussel, Enrique D. 1934- 89-92
Dussere, Carol
See Dussere, Carolyn T(homas)
Dussere, Carolyn T(homas) 1942- 103
Dussinger, John A(ndrew) 1935- 113
Duster, Alfreda Barnett 1904-1983
Obituary 109
Duster, Troy 1936- 29-32R
Dustin, Charles
See Giesy, J(ohn) U(lrich)
Duthie, Charles S. 1911- CAP-2
Earlier sketch in CA 29-32
Dutile, Fernand N(eville) 1940- 107
Dutourd, Jean Hubert 1920- 65-68
Dutt, R(ajani) Palme 1896-1974 .... CAP-1
Obituary 53-56
Earlier sketch in CA 11-12
Dutta, Reginald 1914- 61-64
Dutta, Rex
See Dutta, Reginald
Dutton, Bertha P(auline) 1903- 122
Brief entry 117
Dutton, Frederick G(ary) 1923- Brief entry .. 111
Dutton, Geoffrey (Piers Henry) 1922- .. CANR-17
Earlier sketches in CA 45-48, CANR-1
Dutton, H(arold) I. ?-1984 Obituary 116
Dutton, Joan Parry 1908- 11-12R
Dutton, John M(ason) 1926- 41-44R
Dutton, Mary 1922- 33-36R
Dutton, Paul 1943- 112
Dutton, Ralph (Stawell) 1898-1985 ......13-14R
Obituary 116
Dutton, Richard Edward 1929- Brief entry .. 106
Dutz
See Davis, Mary Octavia
Duun, Olav 1876-1939 Brief entry 121
Duus, Masayo 1938- 89-92
Duus, Peter 1933- 25-28R
DuVal, F(rancis) Alan 1916- 33-36R
Duval, Jean-Jacques 1930- 69-72
DuVal, John 1940- 120
Duval, Katherine
See James, Elizabeth
Duval, Margaret
See Robinson, Patricia Colbert
Duvall, Evelyn Millis 1906- CANR-1
Earlier sketch in CA 4R
See also SATA 9
Duvall, Richard M. 1934- 45-48
Duvall, Robert (Selden) 1931- Brief entry ... 116
Duvall, W(illiam) Clyde (Jr.) 1917- 19-20R
DuVaul, Virginia C.
See Coffman, Virginia (Edith)
Duveen, Geoffrey 1883-1975 Obituary 61-64
Duveneck, Josephine Whitney 1891-1978 ... 114
Duverger, Maurice 1917- 65-68
Duvoisin, Roger Antoine 1904-1980 ... CANR-11
Obituary 101
Earlier sketch in CA 13-14R
See also SATA 2, 23, 30
See also DLB 61
DuWors, Richard E(dward) 1914- 45-48
Duy, Pham 1927- 61-64
Duyckinck, Evert Augustus
1816-1878 .... DLB-3, 64
Duyckinck, George Long 1823-1863 ..... DLB-3
Dvoretzky, Edward 1930- CANR-14
Earlier sketch in CA 37-40R
Dvorkin, David 1943- 118
Dvornik, Francis 1893-1975 .... CANR-6
Obituary 61-64
Earlier sketch in CA 3R
Dwaraki, Leela 1942- 106
Dweck, Susan 1943- 33-36R
Dwiggins, Don 1913- CANR-23
Earlier sketches in CA 17-18R, CANR-8
See also SATA 4
Dwight, Allan
See Cole, Lois Dwight
Dwight, John Sullivan 1813-1893 .... DLB-1
Dwight, Olivia
See Hazzard, Mary
Dwight, Timothy 1752-1817 .... DLB-37
Dworkin, Andrea 1946- CANR-16
Earlier sketch in CA 77-80
See also CLC 43
Dworkin, Gerald 1937- 53-56
Dworkin, James B(arnet) 1948- 112
Dworkin, R. M.
See Dworkin, Ronald M(yles)
Dworkin, Rita 1928- 23-24R
Dworkin, Ronald
See Dworkin, Ronald M(yles)
Dworkin, Ronald M(yles) 1931-
Brief entry 123
Dwoskin, Charles 1922(?)-1980 Obituary ... 102
Dwoskin, Stephen 1939- 89-92
Dwyer, John 1930- 113
Dwyer, Judith A(nne) 1948- 117
Dwyer, K. R.
See Koontz, Dean R(ay)
Dwyer, T. Ryle 1944- 105
Dwyer, Thomas A. 1923- 115
Dwyer, Vincent Michael 1912-1987
Obituary 123
Dwyer-Joyce, Alice 1913- CANR-4
Earlier sketch in CA 53-56
Dyal, James A. 1928- CANR-10
Earlier sketch in CA 7-8R
Dyal, William M., Jr. 1928- 21-22R
Dyall, Valentine 1908-1985 Obituary 117
Dybek, Stuart 1942- 97-100
Dyck, Anni 1931- 25-28R
Dyck, Cornelius J(ohn) 1921- 89-92
Dyck, Harvey L(eonard) 1934- 69-72
Dyck, J. William 1918- 57-60
Dyck, Martin 1927- 41-44R
Dyckman, John William 1922-1987 ..... CANR-2
Obituary 123
Earlier sketch in CA 3R
Dyckman, Thomas Richard 1932- CANR-13
Earlier sketch in CA 33-36R
Dye, Anne G.
See Phillips, Anne G(arvey)
Dye, Charles
See MacLean, Katherine
Dye, David L. 1925- 23-24R
Dye, Dwight L(atimer) 1931- 118
Dye, Frank Charles 1930- 103
Dye, H(ershel) Allan 1931- 93-96
Dye, Harold E(ldon) 1907- CANR-24
Earlier sketch in CA 29-32R
Dye, James W(ayne) 1934- 23-24R
Dye, Margaret 1932- 81-84
Dye, Thomas R(oy) 1935- CANR-12
Earlier sketch in CA 33-36R
Dyen, Isidore 1913- 53-56
Dyer, Beverly 1921- 61-64
Dyer, Braven 1900(?)-1983 Obituary 110
Dyer, Brian
See Petrocelli, Orlando R(alph)
and Rothery, Brian
Dyer, C. Raymond
See Dyer, Charles (Raymond)
Dyer, Charles (Raymond) 1928- 21-22R
See also DLB 13

INDEX

Dyer, Elinor Mary Brent
See Brent-Dyer, Elinor Mary
Dyer, Esther R(uth) 1950- ... 102
Dyer, Frederick C. 1918- ... 19-20R
Dyer, George Bell 1903-1978 ... 85-88
Obituary ... 81-84
Dyer, George E(dward) 1928-1974 ... 37-40R
Dyer, George J(ohn) 1927- ... 15-16R
Dyer, James (Frederick) 1934- ... 102
See also SATA 37
Dyer, John M. 1920- ... 13-14R
Dyer, John Percy 1902-1975 ... 3R
Obituary ... 103
Dyer, Judith Clements 1947- ... 112
Dyer, K(enneth) F(rank) 1939- ... 114
Dyer, Lucinda 1947- ... 105
Dyer, Raymond
See Dyer, Charles (Raymond)
Dyer, T(homas) A(llan) 1947- ... 101
Dyer, Thomas G(eorge) 1943- ... 107
Dyer, Wayne W(alter) 1940- ... 69-72
Dyer, William G(ibb) 1925- ... CANR-14
Earlier sketch in CA 41-44R
Dygard, Thomas J. 1931- ... CANR-15
Earlier sketch in CA 85-88
See also SATA 24
Dygat, Stanislaw 1914-1978 Obituary ... 111
Dygert, James H(erbert) 1934- ... CANR-10
Earlier sketch in CA 65-68
Dyk, Walter 1899-1972 Obituary ... 37-40R
Dyke, John 1935- ... CANR-12
Earlier sketch in CA 25-28R
See also SATA 35
Dykema, Karl W(ashburn) 1906-1970 ... CAP-2
Earlier sketch in CA 25-28
Dykeman, Richard M(ills) 1943- ... 93-96
Dykeman, Wilma ... CANR-1
Earlier sketch in CA 2R
Dykes, Archie R(eece) 1931- ... CANR-7
Earlier sketch in CA 17-18R
Dykes, Jack
See Owen, Jack
Dykes, Jeff(erson) C(henowth) 1900- ... CANR-17
Earlier sketches in CA 5-6R, CANR-2
Dykhuizen, George 1899- ... 49-52
Dykstra, Craig Richard 1947- ... 112
Dykstra, Gerald 1922- ... 45-48
Dykstra, Robert R. 1930- ... 25-28R
Dylan, Bob 1941- ... 41-44R
See also DLB 16
See also CLC 3, 4, 6, 12
Dymally, Mervyn M(alcolm) 1926- ... 41-44R
Dyment, Clifford (Henry) 1914-1971 ... CAP-1
Obituary ... 33-36R
Earlier sketch in CA 9-10
Dymoke, Juliet
See de Schanschieff, Juliet Dymoke
Dymond, Dorothy 1891-1985 Obituary ... 117
Dymond, Rosalind
See Cartwright, Rosalind Dymond
Dymsza, William A(lexander) 1920- ... CANR-2
Earlier sketch in CA 49-52
Dynes, Russell R(owe) 1923- ... CANR-23
Earlier sketches in CA 11-12R, CANR-6
Dyott, George (Miller) 1883-1972
Obituary ... 37-40R
Dyrness, William A(rthur) 1943- ... CANR-13
Earlier sketch in CA 33-36R
Dyroff, Jan Michael 1942- ... 61-64
Dyson, A(nthony) E(dward) 1928- ... 57-60
Dyson, Anne Jane 1912- ... 21-22R
Dyson, Freeman J(ohn) 1923- ... CANR-17
Earlier sketch in CA 89-92
Dyson, Geoffrey Harry George 1914-1981
Obituary ... 114
Dyson, Lowell Keith 1929- ... 107
Dyson, R(obert) W(illiam) 1949- ... 123
Dywasuk, Colette Taube 1941- ... 45-48
Dziech, Billie Wright 1941- ... 113
Dziewanowski, M(arian) Kamil 1913- ... 29-32R
Dzwonkoski, Peter 1940- ... 123

E

E. V. B.
See Boyle, Eleanor Vere (Gordon)
Eadie, Donald 1919- ... 33-36R
Eadie, John W(illiam) 1935- ... 104
Eagan, Andrea Boroff 1943- ... 73-76
Eagan, Barbara Tiritilli 1935(?)-1986
Obituary ... 118
Eagar, Frances (Elisabeth Stuart)
1940-1978 ... 61-64
Obituary ... 120
See also SATA 11
Eager, Edward McMaken 1911-1964 ... 73-76
See also SATA 17
See also DLB 22
Eager, Mary Ann 1905(?)-1984 Obituary ... 111
Eager, Molly
See Eager, Mary Ann
Eagle, Chester (Arthur) 1933- ... 57-60
Eagle, Dorothy 1912- ... CANR-9
Earlier sketch in CA 23-24R
Eagle, Joanna 1934- ... 25-28R
Eagle, Mike 1942- ... SATA-11
Eagle, Robert H(arold) 1921-1969 ... CAP-2
Earlier sketch in CA 21-22
Eagles, Douglas Alan 1943- ... 110
Eaglesfield, Francis
See Guirdham, Arthur
Eagleson, John 1941- ... 53-56
Eagleton, Terence (Francis) 1943- ... CANR-23
Earlier sketches in CA 57-60, CANR-7
Eagleton, Terry
See Eagleton, Terence (Francis)
Eagleton, Thomas Francis 1929-
Brief entry ... 105
Eagly, Robert V(ictor) 1933- ... 49-52
Eaker, Ira
See Eaker, Ira C(larence)
Eaker, Ira C(larence) 1896-1987 Obituary ... 123
Eakin, Frank Edwin, Jr. 1936- ... 53-56
Eakin, Mary K(atherine) 1917- ... CANR-1
Earlier sketch in CA 4R
Eakin, Mary Mulford 1914- Brief entry ... 106
Eakin, Paul John 1938- ... 120
Eakin, Richard M(arshall) 1910- ... 61-64
Eakin, Sue 1918- ... 69-72
Eakins, David W(alter) 1923- ... 49-52
Eakins, Pamela 1953- ... 117
Eales, John R(ay) 1910- ... 11-12R
Ealy, Lawrence O(rr) 1915- ... 33-36R
Eames, Alexandra 1942- ... 105
Eames, Andrew (John) 1958- ... 124
Eames, David 1934- ... 77-80
Eames, Edwin 1930- ... CANR-14
Earlier sketch in CA 41-44R
Eames, Hugh 1917- ... 45-48
Eames, John Douglas 1915- ... 69-72
Eames, S(amuel) Morris 1916- ... 57-60
Ear, The
See McLellan, Diana
Eardley, George C(harles) 1926- ... 57-60
Earhart, H(arry) Byron 1935- ... CANR-14
Earlier sketch in CA 37-40R
Earl, David M(agarey) 1911- ... 13-14R
Earl, Donald (Charles) 1931- ... 57-60
Earl, Johnrae 1919(?)-1978 Obituary ... 77-80
Earl, Lawrence 1915- ... 9-10R
Earl, Paul Hunter 1945- ... CANR-2
Earlier sketch in CA 49-52
Earle, (Mary) Alice Morse 1853(?)-1911
Brief entry ... 117
Earle, Jean
See Burge, Doris
Earle, Marilee
See Zdenek, Marilee
Earle, Olive L(ydia) 1888- ... 23-24R
See also SATA 7
Earle, Peter G. 1923- ... 17-18R
Earle, Ralph 1907- ... CANR-4
Earlier sketch in CA 1R
Earle, William
See Johns, William Earle
Earle, William Alexander 1919- ... 85-88
Earley, Martha
See Westwater, Sister Agnes Martha
Earley, Tom 1911- ... CAP-2
Earlier sketch in CA 33-36
Earll, Tony
See Buckland, Raymond
Earl Mountbatten of Burma
See Mountbatten, Louis (Francis Albert Victor Nicholas)
Earl of Arran
See Gore, Arthur Kattendyke S(trange) D(avid) A(rchibald)
Earl of Carnarvon
See Herbert, Henry George Alfred Marius Victor Francis
Earl of Longford
See Pakenham, Edward Arthur Henry
Earlson, Ian Malcolm
See Dorn, William S.
Early, James 1923- ... 45-48
Early, Richard E(lliott) 1908- ... 102
Early, Robert 1940- ... 49-52
Earnest, Ernest (Penney) 1901- ... 33-36R
Earney, Fillmore C(hristy) F(idelis) 1931- ... 57-60
Earnshaw, Anthony 1924- ... 53-56
Earnshaw, Brian 1929- ... CANR-11
Earlier sketch in CA 25-28R
See also SATA 17
Earp, Virgil
See Keevill, Henry J(ohn)
Eason, Ruth P. 1898(?)-1978 Obituary ... 81-84
Easson, James 1895-1979 ... 7-8R
Obituary ... 103
Easson, Roger R(alph) 1945- ... 112
Easson, William M(cAlpine) 1931- ... 65-68
East, Ben 1898- ... 33-36R
East, Bob 1920(?)-1985 Obituary ... 115
East, Charles 1924- ... 17-18R
East, John Marlborough 1936- ... 21-22R
East, John Porter 1931-1986 ... 17-18R
Obituary ... 119
East, Michael
See West, Morris L(anglo)
East, P. D. 1921-1971 ... 2R
Obituary ... 103
East, W(illiam) Gordon 1902- ... 69-72
Eastaugh, Kenneth 1929- ... 106
Eastaway, Edward
See Thomas, (Philip) Edward
Easterlin, Richard A(inley) 1926- ... 109
Easterman, Alexander Levvey 1890-1983
Obituary ... 110
Eastham, Thomas 1923- ... 77-80
Easthope, Gary 1945- ... 69-72
Eastin, Roy B(randon) 1917- ... 41-44R
Eastlake, William (Derry) 1917- ... CANR-5
Earlier sketch in CA 5-6R
See also CAAS 1
See also DLB 6
See also CLC 8
Eastland, Terry 1950- ... 97-100
Eastlick, John Taylor 1912- ... 106
Eastman, Addison J. 1918- ... 85-88
Eastman, Ann Heidbreder 1933- ... CANR-14
Earlier sketch in CA 37-40R
Eastman, Arthur M(orse) 1918- ... 23-24R
Eastman, Carol ... 116
See also DLB 44
Eastman, Charles ... 116
Eastman, Charles A(lexander)
1858-1939 ... YABC-1
Eastman, Edward Roe 1885- ... CAP-1
Earlier sketch in CA 13-14
Eastman, Frances Whittier 1915- ... 3R
Eastman, G. Don
See Oosterman, Gordon
Eastman, Harry Claude MacColl 1923-
Brief entry ... 105
Eastman, Joel Webb 1939- ... 15-16R
Eastman, John 1935- ... 117
Eastman, Lloyd E. 1929- Brief entry ... 112
Eastman, Max (Forrester) 1883-1969 ... 11-12R
Obituary ... 25-28R
Eastman, May (Forrester) 1883- ... 11-12R
Eastman, P(hilip) D(ey) 1909-1986 ... 107
Obituary ... 118
See also SATA 33, 46
Eastman, Richard M(orse) 1916- ... 17-18R
Eastman, Robert E. 1913- ... 93-96
Eastman, Roger (Herbert) 1931- ... 53-56
Easton, Allan 1916- ... CANR-20
Earlier sketches in CA 49-52, CANR-2
Easton, Carol 1933- ... 65-68
Easton, David 1917- ... 33-36R
Easton, Edward
See Malerich, Edward P.
Easton, Loyd D(avid) 1915- ... 21-22R
Easton, Robert (Olney) 1915- ... CANR-7
Earlier sketch in CA 15-16R
Easton, Stewart Copinger 1907- ... CANR-18
Earlier sketches in CA 1R, CANR-2
Easton, Thomas A(twood) 1944- ... 114
Eastwick, Ivy (Ethel) O(live) ... CANR-2
Earlier sketch in CA 5-6R
See also SATA 3
Eastwood, C(harles) Cyril 1916- ... 7-8R
Eastwood, Cyril
See Eastwood, C(harles) Cyril
Eatock, Marjorie 1927- ... 89-92
Eaton, Anne T(haxter) 1881-1971
Obituary ... 111
See also SATA 32
Eaton, Charles Edward 1916- ... CANR-20
Earlier sketches in CA 5-6R, CANR-2
Eaton, Clement 1898-1980 ... CANR-4
Obituary ... 118
Earlier sketch in CA 1R
Eaton, Evelyn (Sybil Mary) 1902- ... 53-56
Eaton, Faith (Sybil) 1927- ... 103
Eaton, George L.
See Verral, Charles Spain
Eaton, J(ohn) H(erbert) 1927- ... CANR-19
Earlier sketches in CA 3R, CANR-4
Eaton, Janet
See Givens, Janet E(aton)
Eaton, Jeanette 1886-1968 ... 73-76
See also SATA 24
Eaton, John
See Bodington, Stephen
Eaton, Joseph W. 1919- ... CANR-4
Earlier sketch in CA 4R
Eaton, Leonard K. 1922- ... 21-22R
Eaton, Marcia M(uelder) 1938- ... 113
Eaton, Theodore H(ildreth), Jr. 1907- ... 53-56
Eaton, Tom 1940- ... CANR-15
Earlier sketch in CA 41-44R
See also SATA 22
Eaton, Trevor 1934- ... 23-24R
Eaton, William Edward 1943- ... 69-72
Eauclaire, Sally 1950- ... 118
Eaves, James Clifton 1912- ... 13-14R
Eaves, Morris (Emery) 1944- ... 120
Eaves, T(homas) C(ary) Duncan 1918- ... 77-80
Eavey, Charles B(enton) 1889- ... 5-6R
Eavey, Louise Bone 1900- ... 5-6R
Eayrs, James George 1926- Brief entry ... 106
Eban, Abba (Solomon) 1915- ... 57-60
Eban, Aubrey
See Eban, Abba (Solomon)
Ebb, Fred 1935- ... CANR-24
Earlier sketch in CA 69-72
Ebbesen, Ebbe B(ruce) 1944- ... CANR-2
Earlier sketch in CA 49-52
Ebbett, (Frances) Eva 1925- ... 103
Ebbett, Eve
See Ebbett, (Frances) Eva
Ebejer, Francis 1925- ... CANR-16
Earlier sketch in CA 29-32R
Ebel, Alex 1927- ... SATA-11
Ebel, Henry 1938- ... 53-56
Ebel, Robert L(ouis) 1910- ... 89-92
Ebel, Suzanne
See Goodwin, Suzanne
Ebeling, Gerhard 1912- ... CANR-5
Earlier sketch in CA 9-10R
Ebeling, Walter 1907- ... 119
Ebenstein, Ronnie Sue 1946- ... 103
Ebenstein, William 1910-1976 ... CANR-6
Obituary ... 65-68
Earlier sketch in CA 2R
Eber, Dorothy (Margaret) Harley 1930- ... 41-44R
See also SATA 27
Eber, Irene 1929- ... 102
Eberhard, Wolfram 1909- ... CANR-2
Earlier sketch in CA 49-52
Eberhardt, Newman Charles 1912- ... 1R
Eberhardt, Peter
See Adams, Robert (Franklin)
Eberhart, Dikkon 1946- ... 93-96
Eberhart, George M(artin) 1950- ... 105
Eberhart, Mignon G(ood) 1899- ... 73-76
See also AITN 2
Eberhart, (Wilfred) Perry 1924- ... 19-20R
Eberhart, Richard 1904- ... CANR-2
Earlier sketch in CA 1R
See also DLB 48
See also CDALB 1941-1968
See also CLC 3, 11, 19
Eberle, Irmengarde 1898-1979 ... CANR-2
Obituary ... 85-88
Earlier sketch in CA 4R
See also SATA 2, 23
Eberle, Paul 1928- ... 101
Eberman, (Gilbert) Willis 1917- ... 9-10R
Ebershoff-Coles, Susan Vaughan 1941- ... 102
Ebersohn, Wessel (Schalk) 1940- ... 97-100
Ebersole, A(lva) V(ernon), Jr. 1919- ... CANR-14
Earlier sketch in CA 37-40R
Eberstadt, Charles F. 1914(?)-1974
Obituary ... 53-56
Eberstadt, Fernanda 1960- ... CLC-39
Eberstadt, Lindley E. 1910(?)-1985
Obituary ... 115
Ebert, Alan 1935- ... CANR-16
Earlier sketch in CA 85-88
Ebert, Arthur Frank 1902-1984 ... 7-8R
Obituary ... 114
Ebert, John E(dward) 1922- ... 106
Ebert, Katherine 1921- ... 107
Ebert, Roger (Joseph) 1942- ... CANR-22
Earlier sketch in CA 69-72
Eberwein, Jane Donahue 1943- ... 111
Eberwein, Robert Thomas 1940- ... 111
Eblana, Sister 1907- ... CAP-1
Earlier sketch in CA 11-12
Eble, Kenneth Eugene 1923- ... CANR-19
Earlier sketches in CA 1R, CANR-4
Eblen, Jack Ericson 1936- ... 33-36R
Eblis, J. Philip
See Phillips, James W.
Ebon 1942- ... DLB-41
Ebon, Martin 1917- ... CANR-10
Earlier sketch in CA 23-24R
Ebsen, Buddy
See Ebsen, Christian
Ebsen, Christian 1908- ... 103
Ebsworth, (George Arthur) Raymond
1911- ... 4R
Eby, Cecil D(eGrotte) 1927- ... CANR-4
Earlier sketch in CA 1R
Eby, Richard E(ngle) 1912- ... 112
Eccles, David (McAdam) 1904- ... 53-56
Eccles, Frank 1923- ... 103
Eccles, Henry E. 1898- ... CAP-1
Earlier sketch in CA 15-16
Eccles, John Carew 1903- ... CANR-9
Earlier sketch in CA 65-68
Eccles, W(illiam) J(ohn) 1917- ... 9-10R
Eccles Williams, Ferelith 1920- ... CANR-21
Earlier sketch in CA 105
Eccli, Sandra Fulton 1936- ... 102
Echegaray (y Eizaguirre), Jose (Maria Waldo) 1832-1916 Brief entry ... 104
See also TCLC 4
Echeruo, Michael J(oseph) C(hukwudalu)
1937- ... CANR-8
Earlier sketch in CA 57-60
Echevarria, Roberto Gonzalez
See Gonzalez-Echevarria, Roberto
Echeverria, Durand 1913- ... 9-10R
Echewa, T(homas) Obinkaram 1940- ... 73-76
Echlin, Edward P. 1930- ... 23-24R
Echo
See Proust, (Valentin-Louis-George-Eugene-) Marcel
Echols, Barbara E(llen) 1934- ... 106
Echols, John M(inor) 1913-1982 ... CANR-2
Obituary ... 107
Earlier sketch in CA 5-6R
Echols, Margit 1944- ... 97-100
Eck, Diana L. 1945- ... 107
Eckardt, A(rthur) Roy 1918- ... CANR-14
Earlier sketch in CA 37-40R
Eckardt, Alice L(yons) 1923- ... CANR-14
Earlier sketch in CA 37-40R
Eckaus, Richard S(amuel) 1926- ... 45-48
Eckblad, Edith Berven 1923- ... 17-18R
See also SATA 23
Eckbo, Garrett 1910- ... 25-28R
Ecke, Betty Tseng Yu-ho 1924- ... CANR-6
Earlier sketch in CA 7-8R
Ecke, Wolfgang 1927-1983 Obituary ... 111
See also SATA 37
Eckel, Malcolm W(illiam) 1912- ... 61-64
Eckel, Paul E(dward) 1908-1986 Obituary ... 119
Eckelberry, Grace Kathryn 1902- ... CAP-2
Earlier sketch in CA 33-36
Eckels, Jon ... CANR-3
Earlier sketch in CA 49-52
Ecker, Beverly A. 1938- ... 116
Ecker, H(erman) Paul 1922-1976 ... CAP-2
Earlier sketch in CA 29-32
Ecker-Racz, L. Laszlo 1906- ... 49-52
Eckerson, Olive Taylor 1901- ... 2R
Eckert, Allan W. 1931- ... CANR-14
Earlier sketch in CA 13-14R
See also SATA 27, 29
See also CLC 17
Eckert, Edward K(yle) 1943- ... 77-80
Eckert, Horst 1931- ... 37-40R
See also SATA 8
Eckert, Ruth E(lizabeth) 1905- ... 13-14R
Eckes, Alfred Edward, Jr. 1942- ... CANR-9
Earlier sketch in CA 61-64
Eckhardt, Bob
See Eckhardt, Robert Christian
Eckhardt, Robert Christian 1913- ... 85-88
Eckhardt, Tibor 1888-1972 Obituary ... 37-40R

Eckholm, Erik P(eter) 1949- CANR-6
Earlier sketch in CA 57-60
Eckley, Grace 1932- 45-48
Eckley, Mary M. 102
Eckley, Wilton Earl, Jr. 1929- 49-52
Eckman, Frederick (Willis) 1924- 33-36R
Eckman, Lester S(amuel) 1937- CANR-2
Earlier sketch in CA 49-52
Eckmar, F. R.
See De Hartog, Jan
Eckstein, Alexander 1915-1976 .... CANR-6
Obituary 69-72
Earlier sketch in CA 1R
Eckstein, Gustav 1890-1981 57-60
Obituary 104
Eckstein, Harry 1924- CANR-1
Earlier sketch in CA 3R
Eckstein, Jerome 1928- 114
Eckstein, Otto 1927-1984 .... CANR-14
Obituary 112
Earlier sketch in CA 15-16R
Eclov, Shirley
See Pfoutz, Shirley Eclov
Eco, Umberto 1932- CANR-12
Earlier sketch in CA 77-80
See also CLC 28
Economou, George 1934- 25-28R
Ecroyd, Donald H(owarth) 1923- CANR-4
Earlier sketch in CA 3R
Edari, Ronald S(amuel) 1943- 65-68
Edberg, Rolf 1912- CANR-11
Earlier sketch in CA 69-72
Eddings, David 1931- 110
Eddins, Dwight L. 1939- 33-36R
Eddison, E(ric) R(ucker) 1882-1945
Brief entry 109
See also TCLC 15
Eddison, John 1916- CANR-23
Earlier sketches in CA 61-64, CANR-8
Eddison, Roger (Tatham) 1916- CAP-1
Earlier sketch in CA 11-12
Eddleman, H(enry) Leo 1911- CANR-9
Earlier sketch in CA 13-14R
Eddy, C.M., Jr.
See Eddy, Clifford Martin, Jr.
Eddy, Clifford Martin, Jr. 1896-1967
Obituary 113
Eddy, Edward D(anforth, Jr.) 1921- 73-76
Eddy, Elizabeth M. 1926- 21-22R
Eddy, John J(ude) 1933- 73-76
Eddy, John P(aul) 1932- CANR-9
Earlier sketch in CA 61-64
Eddy, John Percy 1881-1975 Obituary 61-64
Eddy, Mary (Morse) Baker 1821-1910
Brief entry 113
Eddy, Paul 1944- CANR-15
Earlier sketch in CA 73-76
Eddy, Roger (Whittlesey) 1920- 17-18R
Eddy, Samuel K(ennedy) 1926- CANR-17
Earlier sketch in CA 3R
Ede, Janina 1937- SATA-33
Ede, Lisa S. 1947- 123
Edel, Abraham 1908- 3R
Edel, (Joseph) Leon 1907- CANR-22
Earlier sketches in CA 3R, CANR-1
See also CLC 29, 34
Edel, Matthew (David) 1941- 29-32R
Edelberg, Cynthia Dubin 1940- 89-92
Edelen, Georges 1924- 93-96
Edell, Celeste 3R
See also SATA 12
Edelman, Alice Fisher 1940- 112
Edelman, Elaine 113
See also SATA 50
Edelman, Gerald Maurice 1929- 112
Edelman, John W(alter) 1893-1971
Obituary 113
Edelman, Lily (Judith) 1915-1981 61-64
Obituary 102
See also SATA 22
Edelman, Marian Wright 1939- 124
Edelman, Maurice 1911-1975 65-68
Obituary 61-64
Edelman, Murray 1919- 33-36R
Edelman, Nathan 1911-1971 Obituary 113
Edelman, Paul S. 1926- 9-10R
Edelsberg, Herman 1909-1986 Obituary 120
Edelson, Edward 1932- CANR-13
Earlier sketch in CA 19-20R
Edelson, Julie 1949- 122
Edelson, Marshall 1928- Brief entry 111
Edelstein, Arthur CANR-9
Earlier sketch in CA 65-68
Edelstein, David S(imeon) 1913- 61-64
Edelstein, J. M. 1924- 53-56
Edelstein, Morton A. 1925- 69-72
Edelstein, Scott 1954- 122
Edelstein, Stuart J. 1941- 122
Eden, Alvin N(oam) 1926- CANR-9
Earlier sketch in CA 61-64
Eden, (Robert) Anthony 1897-1977 77-80
Obituary 69-72
Eden, Dorothy (Enid) 1912-1982 81-84
Obituary 106
Eden, Laura
See Harrison, Claire E.
Eden, Robert 1942- 113
Edens, Cooper 1945- SATA-49
Edens, (Bishop) David 1926- 108
See also SATA 39
Eder, George Jackson 1900- 85-88
Eder, Richard (Gray) 1932- Brief entry 123
Edes, Benjamin 1732-1803 .... DLB-43
Edey, Maitland A(rmstrong) 1910- CANR-6
Earlier sketch in CA 57-60
See also SATA 25
Edgar, David 1948- CANR-12
Earlier sketch in CA 57-60
See also DLB 13
See also CLC 42
Edgar, Donald 1916- 121
Edgar, Frank Terrell Rhoades 1932- 69-72
Edgar, Josephine
See Mussi, Mary
Edgar, Ken 1925- 49-52
Edgar, Neal Lowndes 1927-1983 69-72
Obituary 110
Edge, David O(wen) 1932- 73-76
Edge, Findley B(artow) 1916- 5-6R
Edgerton, Clyde (C.) 1944- Brief entry 118
See also CLC 39
Edgerton, Franklin 1885-1963 Obituary 110
Edgerton, Gary Richard 1952- 111
Edgerton, Harold Eugene 1903- CANR-5
Earlier sketch in CA 53-56
Edgerton, Joseph S. 1900(?)-1983
Obituary 109
Edgerton, Lucile Selk 1896-1987 Obituary .. 122
Edgerton, Robert B(reckenridge) 1931- 53-56
Edgerton, William B(enbow) 1914- 29-32R
Edgeworth, Maria 1767-1849 .... SATA-21
Edgington, Eugene S(inclair) 1924- 25-28R
Edgley, Charles K(enneth) 1943- 57-60
Edgley, Roy 1925- 29-32R
Edgren, Harry D(aniel) 1899- CAP-2
Earlier sketch in CA 33-36
Edgy, Wardore
See Gorey, Edward (St. John)
Edholm, O(tto) G(ustav) 1909-1985
Obituary 115
Edie, James M. 1927- 11-12R
Ediger, Peter J. 1926- 33-36R
Edinborough, Arnold 1922- 73-76
Edinger, Edward F(erdinand) 1922- 69-72
Edington, Andrew 1914- 73-76
Edison, Judith
See Paul, Judith Edison
Edison, Michael (G.) 1937- Brief entry 110
Edkins, Anthony 1927- 97-100
Edkins, Diana M(aria) 1947- 41-44R
Edler, Peter 1934- 107
Edlin, Herbert Leeson 1913-1976 .... CANR-9
Obituary 69-72
Earlier sketch in CA 61-64
Edlin, Rosabelle Alpern 1914- 11-12R
Edman, David 1930- 37-40R
Edman, Marion (Louise) 1901- CAP-1
Earlier sketch in CA 17-18
Edman, Victor Raymond 1900-1967 .... CANR-6
Earlier sketch in CA 3R
Edmands, Allan 1942- 117
Edmands, Dodie 1947- 116
Edmiston, (Helen) Jean (Mary) 1913- 13-14R
Edmiston, Susan 1940- 65-68
Edmond, Jay
See Jones, Jack
Edmond, Mary 1916- 121
Edmonds, Alan
See Edmonds, Arthur Denis
Edmonds, Ann C.
See Welch, Ann Courtenay (Edmonds)
Edmonds, Arthur Denis 1932- 73-76
Edmonds, C(ecil) J(ohn) 1889- CAP-1
Earlier sketch in CA 13-14
Edmonds, Charles
See Carrington, Charles Edmund
Edmonds, Helen G(rey) 1911- 65-68
Edmonds, I(vy) G(ordon) 1917- CANR-13
Earlier sketch in CA 33-36R
See also SATA 8
Edmonds, Jae
See Edmonds, James A.
Edmonds, James A. 1947- 118
Edmonds, Margaret Hammett 101
Edmonds, Margot
See Edmonds, Margaret Hammett
Edmonds, Paul
See Kuttner, Henry
Edmonds, R(obert) H(umphrey) G(ordon)
1920- 69-72
Edmonds, (Sheppard) Randolph
1900-1983 .... DLB-51
Edmonds, Robert 1913- 112
Edmonds, Robin
See Edmonds, R(obert) H(umphrey)
G(ordon)
Edmonds, Ronald R. 1935-1983 Obituary .. 110
Edmonds, Vernon H. 1927- 37-40R
Edmonds, Walter D(umaux) 1903- CANR-2
Earlier sketch in CA 7-8R
See also SATA 1, 27
See also SAAS 4
See also DLB 9
See also CLC 35
Edmondson, Clifton Earl 1937- 102
Edmondson, G. C. 1922- CANR-11
Earlier sketch in CA 57-60
Edmondson, Garry C.
See Edmondson, G. C.
Edmondson, Wallace
See Ellison, Harlan
Edmonson, Harold A(rthur) 1937- 41-44R
Edmonson, Munro Sterling 1924- 33-36R
Edmund, Sean
See Pringle, Laurence P.
Edmunds, H(enry) Tudor 1897- 106
Edmunds, Malcolm 1938- 73-76
Edmunds, (Thomas) Murrell 1898- CANR-4
Earlier sketch in CA 4R
Edmunds, Simeon 1917- 17-18R
Edmunds, Stahrl W(illiam) 1917- 69-72
Edom, Clifton C. 1907- 105
Edric, Robert
See Armitage, G(ary) E(dric)
Edrich, William J(ohn) 1916-1986
Obituary 120
Edsall, Florence S(mall) 1898(?)-1986
Obituary 119
Edsall, Marian (Stickney) 1920- 49-52
See also SATA 8
Edschmid, Kasimir
See Schmid, Eduard
See also DLB 56
Edson, Harold
See Hall, Asa Zadel
Edson, J(ohn) T(homas) 1928- CANR-12
Earlier sketch in CA 29-32R
Edson, Peter 1896-1977 Obituary 73-76
Edson, Russell 33-36R
See also CLC 13
Eduardi, Guillermo
See Edwards, William B(ennett)
Edwa
See Edwards, Bill
Edwardes, Allen
See Kinsley, D(aniel) A(llan)
Edwardes, Michael (F. H.) 1923- CANR-10
Earlier sketch in CA 57-60
Edwards, A. W. F. 1935- 73-76
Edwards, Al
See Nourse, Alan E(dward)
Edwards, Alexander
See Fleischer, Leonore
Edwards, Allen J(ack) 1926- 33-36R
Edwards, Allen L. 1914- CANR-10
Earlier sketch in CA 25-28R
Edwards, Anne 1927- CANR-13
Earlier sketch in CA 61-64
See also SATA 35
Edwards, Anne-Marie 1932- CANR-16
Earlier sketch in CA 85-88
Edwards, Anthony David 1936- 15-16R
Edwards, Audrey 1947- 81-84
See also SATA 31
Edwards, Bertram
See Edwards, Herbert Charles
Edwards, Betty 1926- 105
Edwards, Bill 1929(?)-1987 Obituary 121
Edwards, Blake 1922- 81-84
Edwards, Bob
See Edwards, Robert Alan
Edwards, Bronwen Elizabeth
See Rose, Wendy
Edwards, Carl N(ormand) 1943- 57-60
Edwards, Cecile Pepin 1916- 5-6R
See also SATA 25
Edwards, Charles Edward 1930- 17-18R
Edwards, Charles Mundy, Jr. 1903-1985 .. 45-48
Obituary 117
Edwards, Charlotte 29-32R
Edwards, Christine 1902- CAP-1
Earlier sketch in CA 19-20
Edwards, Clifford D(uane) 1934- 61-64
Edwards, Corwin D. 1901-1979 .... CANR-10
Obituary 85-88
Earlier sketch in CA 19-20R
Edwards, David C(harles) 1937- 41-44R
Edwards, David L(awrence) 1929- CANR-12
Earlier sketch in CA 7-8R
Edwards, David Vandeusen 1941-
Brief entry 105
Edwards, Donald (Isaac) 1904- 65-68
Edwards, Donald Earl
See Harding, Donald Edward
Edwards, Dorothy 1903(?)-1934
Brief entry 122
Edwards, Dorothy 1914-1982 .... CANR-12
Obituary 107
Earlier sketch in CA 25-28R
See also SATA 4, 31
Edwards, Douglas 1917- 118
Brief entry 110
Edwards, Edgar O(wen) 1919- CANR-6
Earlier sketch in CA 2R
Edwards, Eli
See McKay, Claude
Edwards, Eli
See McKay, Festus Claudius
Edwards, Elizabeth
See Inderlied, Mary Elizabeth
Edwards, Elwyn Hartley 1927- CANR-8
Earlier sketch in CA 61-64
Edwards, F. E.
See Nolan, William F(rancis)
Edwards, Francis
See Brandon, Johnny
Edwards, Frank Allyn 1908-1967 .... CANR-1
Earlier sketch in CA 4R
Edwards, G(erald) B(asil) 1899-1976
Obituary 110
See also CLC 25
Edwards, Gawain
See Pendray, George Edward
Edwards, George 1914- 53-56
Edwards, George Charles III 1947- CANR-24
Earlier sketch in CA 107
Edwards, Gerald (Kenneth Savery) Hamilton
See Hamilton-Edwards, Gerald (Kenneth
Savery)
Edwards, Gillian (Mary) 1918- 25-28R
Edwards, Gunvor 107
See also SATA 32
Edwards, Gus 1939- 108
See also CLC 43
Edwards, Harry (Jr.) 1942- 111
Brief entry 109
Edwards, Harry
See Edwards, Henry James
Edwards, Harvey 1929- 25-28R
See also SATA 5
Edwards, Hazel (Eileen) 1945- 124
Edwards, Henry James 1893-1976 ...... 13-14R
Obituary 122
Edwards, Herbert Charles 1912- 9-10R
See also SATA 12
Edwards, Hilton 1903- 65-68
Edwards, I(orwerth) E(iddon) S(tephen)
1909- CANR-7
Earlier sketch in CA 13-14R
Edwards, James Don(ald) 1926- CANR-4
Earlier sketch in CA 9-10R
Edwards, Jane Campbell 1932- 15-16R
See also SATA 10
Edwards, Jaroldeen 1932- 102
Edwards, Jerome E(arl) 1937- 37-40R
Edwards, John 1943- 118
Edwards, John Milton
See Cook, William Wallace
Edwards, Jonathan 1703-1758 .... DLB-24
Edwards, Jonathan, Jr. 1745-1801 ..... DLB-37
Edwards, Josephine Cunnington 1904- ... 15-16R
Edwards, Julia Spalding 1920- 37-40R
Edwards, Julie
See Andrews, Julie
Edwards, Julie
See Stratemeyer, Edward L.
Edwards, June
See Bhatia, Jamunadevi
Edwards, Junius 1929- DLB-33
Edwards, K(enneth) Morgan 1912- 5-6R
Edwards, Kate F(lournoy) 1877-1980 107
Edwards, Lee 1932- CANR-10
Earlier sketch in CA 25-28R
Edwards, Lee R. 1942- 124
Edwards, Linda Strauss 1948- SATA-42, 49
Edwards, Lyford Paterson 1882-1984
Obituary 113
Edwards, Lynne 1943- 73-76
Edwards, Margaret (Alexander) 1902- CAP-2
Earlier sketch in CA 29-32
Edwards, Marie Babare 57-60
Edwards, Mark U(lin), Jr. 1946- CANR-10
Earlier sketch in CA 65-68
Edwards, Marvin L(ouis) 1915- 13-14R
Edwards, Max
See Benjamin, Claude (Max Edward
Pohlman)
Edwards, Michael 1932- 85-88
Edwards, Michael 1938- CANR-22
Earlier sketch in CA 106
Edwards, Monica le Doux Newton 1912- ... 9-10R
See also SATA 12
Edwards, Nicky 1958- 122
Edwards, Norman
See White, Theodore Edwin
and Carr, Terry (Gene)
Edwards, O(tis) C(arl), Jr. 1928- 53-56
Edwards, Oliver
See Haley, William (John)
Edwards, Olwen
See Gater, Dilys
Edwards, Owen Dudley 1938- CANR-7
Earlier sketch in CA 57-60
Edwards, P(rior) Max(imilian) H(emsley)
1914- 37-40R
Edwards, Page L., Jr. 1941- CANR-1
Earlier sketch in CA 45-48
Edwards, Paul 1923- 85-88
Edwards, Paul 1940- 123
Edwards, Paul Geoffrey 1926- 57-60
Edwards, Paul M(adison) 1933- 41-44R
Edwards, Peter (William) 1934- 109
Edwards, Philip 1923- CANR-12
Earlier sketch in CA 25-28R
Edwards, Phoebe
See Bloch, Barbara
Edwards, Phyllis Irene 1916-1984
Obituary 114
Edwards, R. M.
See Edwards, Roselyn
Edwards, (H. C.) Ralph 1894- CAP-1
Earlier sketch in CA 15-16
Edwards, Rem B(lanchard, Jr.) 1934- 37-40R
Edwards, Richard 1524-1566 .... DLB-62
Edwards, Richard Alan 1934- 69-72
Edwards, Richard C. 1944- CANR-2
Earlier sketch in CA 45-48
Edwards, Robert Alan 1947- 121
Edwards, Ron(ald George) 1930- 105
Edwards, Roselyn 1929- 25-28R
Edwards, Ruth Dudley
See Dudley Edwards, Ruth
Edwards, S. W.
See Sublette, Walter (Edwards)
Edwards, S. W.
See Sublette, Walter Edwards
Edwards, Sally (Cary) 1929- 25-28R
See also SATA 7
Edwards, Samuel
See Gerson, Noel Bertram
Edwards, Stephen
See Palestrant, Simon S.
Edwards, T(homas) Bentley 1906- CAP-2
Earlier sketch in CA 23-24
Edwards, Thomas R(obert) Jr. 1928- 5-6R
Edwards, Tilden Hampton, Jr. 1935- ... CANR-18
Earlier sketch in CA 102
Edwards, Verne E(rvie), Jr. 1924- 33-36R
Edwards, Ward 1927- 21-22R
Edwards, William 1896- CAP-1
Earlier sketch in CA 13-14
Edwards, William B(ennett) 1927- 5-6R
Edward VIII 1894-1972 Obituary 33-36R
Edwin, Brother B.
See Arnandez, Richard

Eekelaar, John M(ichael) 1942- ... 116
Eekman, Thomas 1923- ... 81-84
Eells, George 1922- ... CANR-14
  Earlier sketch in CA 21-22R
Eells, Robert J(ames) 1944- ... 102
Efemey, Raymond (Frederick) 1928- ... 21-22R
Effinger, George Alec 1947- ... CANR-23
  Earlier sketch in CA 37-40R
  See also DLB 8
Efird, James M(ichael) 1932- ... CANR-14
  Earlier sketch in CA 37-40R
Efron, Alexander 1897- ... CAP-2
  Earlier sketch in CA 29-32
Efron, Arthur 1931- ... CANR-21
  Earlier sketch in CA 69-72
Efron, Benjamin 1908- ... CANR-5
  Earlier sketch in CA 5-6R
Efron, Edith Carol 1922- ... 102
Efron, Marina Ivanovna Tsvetaeva
  See Tsvetaeva (Efron), Marina Ivanovna
Efron, Marshall 1938(?)- Brief entry ... 112
Efros, Israel (Isaac) 1891-1981 ... 21-22R
  Obituary ... 102
Efros, Susan Elyse 1947- ... 104
Efrot
  See Efros, Israel (Isaac)
Egami, Tomi 1899- ... 61-64
Egan, Beresford Patrick 1905-1984
  Obituary ... 111
Egan, David R(onald) 1943- ... 102
Egan, E(dward) W(elstead) 1922- ... CANR-9
  Earlier sketch in CA 23-24R
  See also SATA 35
Egan, Ferol 1923- ... 29-32R
Egan, Fred(erick Julian) 1905(?)-1986
  Obituary ... 118
Egan, Gerard 1930- ... CANR-12
  Earlier sketch in CA 29-32R
Egan, Harvey Daniel 1937- ... 113
Egan, John P. 1934- ... 110
Egan, Lesley
  See Linington, Elizabeth
Egan, Melinda A(nne) 1950- ... 102
Egan, Michael 1941- ... 45-48
Egan, Philip S(idney) 1920- ... 4R
Egan, Robert 1945- ... 77-80
Egbert, Donald Drew 1902-1973 ... CAP-2
  Obituary ... 37-40R
  Earlier sketch in CA 23-24
Egbert, Virginia Wylie
  See Kilborne, Virginia Wylie
Egbuna, Obi B(enue Joseph) 1938- ... 102
Egejuru, Phanuel Akubueze ... 106
Egelhof, Joseph (Baird) 1919(?)-1980
  Obituary ... 97-100
Egermeier, Elsie E(milie) 1890- ... 5-6R
Egerton, Frank N(icholas) III 1936- ... 110
Egerton, George W(illiam) 1942- ... 85-88
Egerton, John (Walden) 1935- ... 85-88
Egerton, Lucy
  See Malleson, Lucy Beatrice
Egg, Maria 1910- ... 29-32R
Egg-Benes, Maria
  See Egg, Maria
Eggeling, Hans Friedrich 1878-1977 ... 4R
  Obituary ... 73-76
Eggenberger, David 1918- ... 11-12R
  See also SATA 6
Eggenschwiler, David 1936- ... 37-40R
Egger, M(aurice) David 1936- ... 57-60
Egger, Rowland (Andrews) 1908-1979 .. CANR-4
  Earlier sketch in CA 5-6R
Eggers, J(ohn) Philip 1940- ... 33-36R
Eggers, William T. 1912- ... 29-32R
Eggert, Gerald G(ordon) 1926- ... 21-22R
Eggert, James Edward 1943- ... CANR-23
  Earlier sketch in CA 107
Eggert, Jim
  See Eggert, James Edward
Eggleston, Edward 1837-1902 Brief entry ... 111
  See also SATA 27
  See also DLB 12
Eggleston, Wilfrid 1901-1986 ... CANR-8
  Obituary ... 119
  Earlier sketch in CA 23-24R
Egielski, Richard 1952- ... SATA-11, 49
Egler, Frank E(dwin) 1911- ... 29-32R
Egleson, Janet F.
  See Dunleavy, Janet Egleson
Egleton, Clive (Frederick) 1927- ... CANR-22
  Earlier sketch in CA 103
Egoff, Sheila A. 1918- Brief entry ... 116
Egremont, Max 1948- ... 93-96
Eguchi, Shinichi 1914-1979 Obituary ... 85-88
Egypt, Ophelia Settle 1903-1984 ... 81-84
  Obituary ... 112
  See also SATA 16, 38
Ehle, John (Marsden, Jr.) 1925- ... 9-10R
  See also CLC 27
Ehlers, Henry James 1907- ... 15-16R
Ehlert, Lois (Jane) 1934- ... SATA-35
Ehmann, James 1948- ... 109
Ehninger, Douglas W(agner)
  1913-1979 ... CANR-4
  Earlier sketch in CA 5-6R
Ehre, Edward 1905- ... 11-12R
Ehre, Milton 1933- ... 53-56
Ehrenberg, Miriam ... 124
Ehrenberg, Otto 1926- ... 124
Ehrenberg, Victor (Leopold) 1891-1976 .. CANR-4
  Obituary ... 65-68
  Earlier sketch in CA 7-8R
Ehrenbourg, Ilya (Grigoryevich)
  See Ehrenburg, Ilya (Grigoryevich)
Ehrenburg, Ilya (Grigoryevich) 1891-1967 ... 102
  Obituary ... 25-28R
  See also CLC 18, 34
Ehrenburg, Ilyo (Grigoryevich)
  See Ehrenburg, Ilya (Grigoryevich)
Ehrenfeld, David W(illiam) 1938- ... 81-84
Ehrenhalt, Alan 1947- ... 112
Ehrenpreis, Anne Henry 1927- ... 53-56
Ehrenpreis, Irvin 1920-1985 ... 121
  Obituary ... 116
  Brief entry ... 110
Ehrenreich, Barbara 1941- ... CANR-16
  Earlier sketch in CA 73-76
Ehrenreich, Herman 1900(?)-1970
  Obituary ... 104
Ehrensvaerd, Goesta (Carl Henrik)
  1910- ... CANR-2
  Earlier sketch in CA 49-52
Ehrenwald, Jan 1900- ... CANR-2
  Earlier sketch in CA 49-52
Ehrenzweig, Albert A(rmin) 1906-1974 ... CAP-2
  Earlier sketch in CA 29-32
Ehresmann, Donald L(ouis) 1937- ... 69-72
Ehresmann, Julia M. 1939- ... 33-36R
Ehret, Christopher 1941- ... 37-40R
Ehrhardt, Reinhold 1900- ... 29-32R
Ehrhart, W(illiam) D(aniel) 1948- ... CANR-7
  Earlier sketch in CA 61-64
Ehricke, Krafft A(rnold) 1917-1984
  Obituary ... 114
Ehrlich, Amy 1942- ... CANR-14
  Earlier sketch in CA 37-40R
  See also SATA 25
Ehrlich, Anne (Fitzhugh) Howland
  1933- ... CANR-8
  Earlier sketch in CA 61-64
Ehrlich, Arnold 1923- ... 33-36R
Ehrlich, Bettina Bauer 1903- ... CAP-1
  Earlier sketch in CA 13-14
  See also SATA 1
Ehrlich, Cyril 1925- ... 103
Ehrlich, Eugene H. 1922- ... CANR-5
  Earlier sketch in CA 3R
Ehrlich, Everett M. 1950- ... 112
Ehrlich, Howard J. 1932- ... 19-20R
Ehrlich, Isaac 1938- ... 118
Ehrlich, Jack
  See Ehrlich, John Gunther
Ehrlich, Jacob Wilburn 1900-1971
  Obituary ... 33-36R
Ehrlich, Jake
  See Ehrlich, Jacob Wilburn
Ehrlich, John Gunther 1930- ... CANR-4
  Earlier sketch in CA 3R
Ehrlich, Leonard Harry 1924- ... 102
Ehrlich, Max 1909-1983 ... CANR-1
  Obituary ... 115
  Earlier sketch in CA 3R
Ehrlich, Nathaniel J(oseph) 1940- ... 53-56
Ehrlich, Otto Hild 1892-1979 Obituary ... 85-88
Ehrlich, Paul R(alph) 1932- ... CANR-8
  Earlier sketch in CA 65-68
Ehrlich, Robert S. 1935- ... 23-24R
Ehrlich, Thomas 1934- ... 113
Ehrlich, Walter 1921- ... 53-56
Ehrlichman, John Daniel 1925- ... 65-68
Ehrman, John (Patrick William) 1920- ... CANR-4
  Earlier sketch in CA 5-6R
Ehrman, Lee 1935- ... 69-72
Ehrmann, Herbert B(rutus) 1891-1970 ... CAP-2
  Earlier sketch in CA 25-28
Ehrsam, Theodore George 1909- ... 45-48
Eibl-Eibesfeldt, Irenaeus 1928- ... CANR-3
  Earlier sketch in CA 9-10R
Eibling, Harold Henry 1905-197(?) ... 37-40R
Eiby, George 1918- ... 53-56
Eich, Guenter 1907-1972 ... 111
  Obituary ... 93-96
  See also CLC 15
Eich, Gunter
  See Eich, Guenter
Eichelbaum, Stanley 1926- ... 73-76
Eichelberger, Clark M(ell) 1896-1980
  Obituary ... 93-96
Eichelberger, Clayton L. 1925- ... 41-44R
Eichelberger, Rosa Kohler 1896- ... 102
Eichenberg, Fritz 1901- ... CANR-6
  Earlier sketch in CA 57-60
  See also SATA 9, 50
Eichenlaub, John Ellis 1922- ... CANR-4
  Earlier sketch in CA 1R
Eicher, David J(ohn) 1961- ... 113
Eicher, (Ethel) Elizabeth ... 17-18R
Eicher, Joanne B(ubolz) 1930- ... 49-52
Eichhorn, David Max 1906- ... CAP-1
  Earlier sketch in CA 11-12
Eichhorn, Werner 1899- ... 29-32R
Eichler, Margrit 1942- ... 107
  See also SATA 35
Eichman, Mark 1949- ... 109
Eichner, Alfred S. 1937-1988 ... CANR-5
  Obituary ... 124
  Earlier sketch in CA 15-16R
Eichner, Hans 1921- ... CANR-19
  Earlier sketches in CA 5-6R, CANR-4
Eichner, James A. 1927- ... 15-16R
  See also SATA 4
Eichner, Maura 1915- ... CANR-14
  Earlier sketch in CA 37-40R
Eichorn, Dorothy H(ansen) 1924- ... 49-52
Eickhoff, Andrew R(obert) 1924- ... 21-22R
Eicoff, Alvin Maurey 1921- ... 112
Eid, Leif 1908(?)-1976 Obituary ... 65-68
Eidelberg, Ludwig 1898-1970 ... CAP-1
  Obituary ... 29-32R
  Earlier sketch in CA 19-20
Eidelberg, Paul 1928- ... 23-24R
Eidenberg, Eugene 1939- ... 81-84
Eidesheim, Julie 1884-1972 Obituary ... 104
Eidsmoe, John 1945- ... 114
Eidsvik, Charles Vernon 1943- ... 101
Eidt, Robert C. 1923- ... 33-36R
Eiduson, Bernice Tabackman 1921- ... 1R
Eifert, Virginia (Louise) S(nider)
  1911-1966 ... CANR-15
  Earlier sketch in CA 1R
  See also SATA 2
Eigen, Manfred 1927- ... 108
Eigen, Michael 1936- ... 115
Eigner, Edwin M(oss) 1931- ... 21-22R
Eigner, Larry
  See Eigner, Laurence (Joel)
  See also DLB 5
  See also CLC 9
Eigner, Laurence (Joel) 1927- ... CANR-6
  Earlier sketch in CA 9-10R
Eiland, Howard 1948- ... 111
Eiland, Murray L(ee) 1936- ... 85-88
Eilon, Samuel 1923- ... CANR-4
  Earlier sketch in CA 7-8R
Eimer, D(ean) Robert 1927- ... 13-14R
Eimerl, Sarel (Henry) 1925- ... 21-22R
Einbond, Bernard Lionel 1937- ... 37-40R
Einhorn, Virginia Hilu
  See Hilu, Virginia
Einsel, Mary E. 1929- ... 29-32R
Einsel, Naiad ... SATA-10
Einsel, Walter 1926- ... SATA-10
Einstein, Albert 1879-1955 Brief entry ... 121
Einstein, Albert 1947- ... 113
  Brief entry ... 109
Einstein, Charles 1926- ... 65-68
Einstein, Elizabeth (Ann) 1939- ... 109
Einstein, Stanley 1934- ... CANR-4
  Earlier sketch in CA 53-56
Einstoss, Ron 1930(?)-1977 Obituary ... 69-72
Einzig, Paul 1897-1973 ... CANR-5
  Obituary ... 89-92
  Earlier sketch in CA 11-12R
Einzig, Susan 1922- ... SATA-43
Eirelin, Glenn
  See Evans, Glen
Eisdorfer, Carl 1930- ... 41-44R
Eisele, Albert A(lois) 1936- ... 41-44R
Eisele, Robert H. 1948- ... 108
Eiseley, Loren Corey 1907-1977 ... CANR-6
  Obituary ... 73-76
  Earlier sketch in CA 3R
  See also CLC 7
Eiseman, Alberta 1925- ... 77-80
  See also SATA 15
Eiseman, Alvord L. 1916- ... 112
Eisen, Carol G.
  See Rinzler, Carol Eisen
Eisen, Jack 1925- ... 73-76
Eisenach, Eldon J(ohn) 1938- ... 106
Eisenberg, Azriel (Louis) 1903- ... CANR-10
  Earlier sketch in CA 49-52
  See also SATA 12
Eisenberg, Benjamin 1916-1984 Obituary ... 112
Eisenberg, Daniel Bruce 1946- ... CANR-6
  Earlier sketch in CA 57-60
Eisenberg, Dennis (Harold) 1929- ... 25-28R
Eisenberg, Gerson G. 1909- ... 81-84
Eisenberg, Hershey H. 1927- ... 104
Eisenberg, Howard 1946- ... 101
Eisenberg, Larry 1919- ... 33-36R
Eisenberg, Lawrence B(enjamin) ... 77-80
Eisenberg, Lee 1946- ... CANR-9
  Earlier sketch in CA 61-64
Eisenberg, Lisa 1949- ... 110
  See also SATA 50
Eisenberg, Maurice 1902-1972 Obituary .. 37-40R
Eisenberg, Phyllis Rose 1924- ... 111
  See also SATA 41
Eisenberg, Ralph 1930-1973 ... CANR-3
  Obituary ... 45-48
  Earlier sketch in CA 5-6R
Eisenberg, Ronald L(ee) 1945- ... CANR-13
  Earlier sketch in CA 73-76
Eisenberger, Kenneth 1948- ... 81-84
Eisenbud, Jule 1908- ... 49-52
Eisendrath, Craig R. 1936- ... 49-52
Eisenhower, Dwight D(avid)
  1890-1969 ... CANR-24
  Earlier sketch in CA 65-68
Eisenhower, John S(heldon) D(oud)
  1922- ... CANR-14
  Earlier sketch in CA 33-36R
Eisenhower, Julie Nixon 1948- ... 114
Eisenhower, Milton S(tover) 1899-1985 ... 73-76
  Obituary ... 116
Eisenman, Peter D(avid) 1932- ... 108
Eisenmenger, Robert Waltz 1926- ... 37-40R
Eisenschiml, Otto 1880-1963 ... 3R
Eisenson, Jon 1907- ... 19-20R
Eisenstadt, A(braham) S(eldin) 1920- ... CANR-4
  Earlier sketch in CA 11-12R
Eisenstadt, Shmuel N(oah) 1923- ... 25-28R
Eisenstaedt, Alfred 1898- ... 108
Eisenstat, Jane Sperry 1920- ... 4R
Eisenstein, Elizabeth L(ewisohn) 1923- ... 89-92
Eisenstein, Ira 1906- ... 21-22R
Eisenstein, James 1940- Brief entry ... 111
Eisenstein, Phyllis 1946- ... CANR-16
  Earlier sketch in CA 85-88
Eisenstein, Sam(uel Abraham) 1932- ... CANR-16
  Earlier sketch in CA 61-64
Eisenstein, Sergei (Mikhailovich)
  1898-1948 Brief entry ... 114
Eiserer, Leonard Arnold 1948- ... 73-76
Eisinger, Chester E(manuel) 1915- ... 23-24R
Eisinger, Peter K(endall) 1942- ... 69-72
Eisler, Colin (Tobias) 1931- ... 85-88
Eisler, Frieda Goldman
  See Goldman-Eisler, Frieda
Eisler, Georg 1928- Brief entry ... 106
Eisler, George B. 1892(?)-1983 Obituary ... 111
Eisler, Hanns 1898-1962 Obituary ... 116
Eisler, Lawrence 1920- ... 122
Eisler, Paul (Erich) 1922- ... 61-64
Eisler, Riane Tennenhaus 1931- ... 73-76
Eisman, Hy 1927- ... 65-68
Eisman, Mark 1948- ... 108
Eismann, Bernard N(orman) 1933- ... 4R
Eisner, Betty Grover 1915- ... 29-32R
Eisner, Elliot W(ayne) 1933- ... 123
  Brief entry ... 118
Eisner, Gisela (Spanglet) 1925- ... CAP-1
  Earlier sketch in CA 9-10
Eisner, Kurt 1867-1919 ... DLB-66
Eisner, Lotte (Henriette) 1896-1983 ... CANR-14
  Obituary ... 111
  Earlier sketch in CA 45-48
Eisner, Robert 1922- ... 107
Eisner, Sigmund 1920- ... 124
Eisner, Simon
  See Kornbluth, C(yril) M.
Eisner, Victor 1921- ... 53-56
Eisner, Vivienne
  See Margolis, Vivienne
Eisner, Will(iam Erwin) 1917- ... 108
  See also SATA 31
Eiss, Harry Edwin 1950- ... 124
Eissenstat, Bernard W. 1927- ... 45-48
Eister, Allan W(ardell) 1915-1979 ... CANR-2
  Earlier sketch in CA 45-48
Eiteman, David (Kurt) 1930- ... 45-48
Eiteman, Wilford J(ohn) 1902- ... CANR-4
  Earlier sketch in CA 1R
Eitinger, Leo S(hua) 1912- ... CANR-16
  Earlier sketch in CA 89-92
Eitington, Julius E. 1918- ... 120
Eitner, Lorenz E.A. 1919- ... CANR-5
  Earlier sketch in CA 1R
Eitzen, Allan 1928- ... SATA-9
Eitzen, D(avid) Stanley 1934- ... CANR-19
  Earlier sketches in CA 53-56, CANR-4
Eitzen, Ruth (Carper) 1924- ... 41-44R
  See also SATA 9
Ekblaw, Sidney E(verette) 1903- ... 37-40R
Ekdahl, Janis (Kay) 1946- Brief entry ... 112
Ekeblad, Frederick A(lfred) 1917- ... 5-6R
Ekeh, Peter P(almer) 1937- ... 102
Ekeloef, (Bengt) Gunnar 1907-1968 ... 123
  Obituary ... 25-28R
  See also CLC 27
Ekelof, (Bengt) Gunnar
  See Ekeloef, (Bengt) Gunnar
  See also CLC 27
Ekins, Paul (Whitfield) 1950- ... 123
Ekirch, A(rthur) Roger 1950- ... 109
Ekirch, Arthur A., Jr. 1915- ... CANR-2
  Earlier sketch in CA 7-8R
Ekker, Charles 1930- ... 37-40R
Eklund, Gordon (Stewart) 1945- ... CANR-24
  Earlier sketch in CA 33-36R
  See also DLBY 83
Eklund, Jane Mary
  See Ball, Jane Eklund
Ekman, Paul 1934- ... CANR-14
  Earlier sketch in CA 37-40R
Ekman, Rosalind 1933- ... 33-36R
Ekola, Giles C(hester) 1927- ... 17-18R
Ekstein, Rudolf 1912- ... CANR-4
  Earlier sketch in CA 5-6R
Eksteins, Modris 1943- ... 77-80
Ekvall, Robert B(rainerd) 1898- ... CANR-5
  Earlier sketch in CA 1R
Ekwall, Eldon E(dward) 1933- ... CANR-12
  Earlier sketch in CA 29-32R
Ekwensi, C. O. D.
  See Ekwensi, Cyprian (Odiatu Duaka)
Ekwensi, Cyprian (Odiatu Duaka)
  1921- ... CANR-18
  Earlier sketch in CA 29-32R
  See also CLC 4
Ela, Jonathan P(ell) 1945- ... 81-84
Elaine
  See Leverson, Ada
  See also TCLC 18
Elam, Richard M(ace, Jr.) 1920- ... 61-64
  See also SATA 9
El-Aref, Aref ?-1973 Obituary ... 41-44R
Elashoff, Janet Dixon 1942- ... 61-64
Elath, Eliahu 1903- ... 13-14R
El-Ayouty, Yassin 1928- ... CANR-14
  Earlier sketch in CA 29-32R
Elazar, Daniel J(udah) 1934- ... CANR-13
  Earlier sketch in CA 21-22R
El-Baz, Farouk 1938- ... CANR-10
  Earlier sketch in CA 25-28R
Elbert, Edmund J(oseph) 1923- ... 37-40R
Elbert, George A. 1911- ... 61-64
Elbert, Samuel H(oyt) 1907- ... CANR-5
  Earlier sketch in CA 1R
Elbert, Virginie Fowler 1912- ... CANR-8
  Earlier sketch in CA 61-64
Elbin, Paul Nowell 1905- ... 69-72
Elbing, Alvar O(liver), Jr. 1928- ... 21-22R
Elbing, Carol J(eppson) 1930- ... 21-22R
Elbogen, Paul 1894- ... 5-6R
Elborn, Geoffrey 1950- ... 109
Elbow, Peter (Henry) 1935- ... CANR-12
  Earlier sketch in CA 65-68
Elbrecht, Paul G. 1921- ... 17-18R
El Bundukhari
  See Dent, Anthony Austen
Elcock, Howard J(ames) 1942- ... CANR-12
  Earlier sketch in CA 29-32R
El Crummo
  See Crumb, R(obert)
Eldefonso, Edward 1933- ... CANR-14
  Earlier sketch in CA 23-24R

Elder, Betty Doak 1938- 112
Elder, Ellen Rozanne 1940- 111
Elder, Gary 1939- 73-76
Elder, Glen(nard) H(oll), Jr. 1934- CANR-3
Earlier sketch in CA 49-52
Elder, John William 1933- 111
Elder, Karl 1948- 77-80
Elder, Leon
See Young, Noel
Elder, Lonne III 1931- 81-84
See also DLB 7, 38, 44
Elder, Mark 1935- CANR-2
Earlier sketch in CA 49-52
Elder, Michael (Aiken) 1931- 33-36R
Elder, Robert E(llsworth) 1915- 1R
Elder, Shirley (A.) 1931- Brief entry 118
Eldersveld, Samuel James 1917- 111
Eldjarn, Kristjan (Thorarinsson)
1916-1982 Obituary 110
Eldred, Vince 1924- 69-72
Eldredge, H(anford) Wentworth 1909- 41-44R
Eldredge, Laurence H(oward) 1902- CAP-2
Earlier sketch in CA 25-28
Eldridge, Colin Clifford 1942- 107
Eldridge, Frank R. 1889(?)-1976
Obituary 69-72
Eldridge, J(ohn) E. T. 1936- CANR-11
Earlier sketch in CA 25-28R
Eldridge, Marian (Favel Clair) 1936- 118
Eldridge, Paul 1888- 9-10R
Eldridge, Retha Hazel (Giles) 1910- CAP-1
Earlier sketch in CA 13-14
Eleanor, Sister Joseph 25-28R
Elegant, Robert S(ampson) 1928- CANR-1
Earlier sketch in CA 4R
Elek, Paul 1906(?)-1976 Obituary 69-72
el-Erian, Abdullah Ali 1920-1981 Obituary 108
Elethea, Abba
See Thompson, James W.
Elevitch, M(orton) D. 1925- CANR-2
Earlier sketch in CA 49-52
Eley, Lynn W. 1925- CANR-16
Earlier sketch in CA 25-28R
Elfenbein, Julien 1897-1983 CANR-5
Obituary 109
Earlier sketch in CA 2R
Elfman, Blossom 1925- CANR-17
Earlier sketches in CA 45-48, CANR-2
See also SATA 8
Elford, Homer J. R. 1912- CANR-9
Earlier sketch in CA 23-24R
Elgar, Edward (William) 1857-1934
Brief entry 116
Elgar, Frank 1899- 102
Elgin, Kathleen 1923- 25-28R
See also SATA 39
Elgin, Mary
See Stewart, Dorothy Mary
Elgin, (Patricia Anne) Suzette Haden
1936- CANR-8
Earlier sketch in CA 61-64
el Hajjam, Mohammed ben Chaib
1940- CANR-17
Earlier sketch in CA 97-100
Elia
See Lamb, Charles
Eliach, Yaffa 1935- 110
Eliade, Mircea 1907-1986 65-68
Obituary 119
See also CLC 19
Elias, Albert J. 1920- 81-84
Elias, C(laude) E(dward), Jr. 1924- 13-14R
Elias, Christopher 1925- 33-36R
Elias, Eileen
See Davies, Eileen Winifred
Elias, Horace J(ay) 1910- CANR-16
Earlier sketch in CA 89-92
Elias, John L(awrence) 1933- 69-72
Elias, Robert H(enry) 1914- 61-64
Elias, Taslim Olawale 1914- CANR-21
Earlier sketches in CA 13-14R, CANR-6
Elias, Thomas S. 1942- 114
Eliason, Joyce 1934- 77-80
Eliav, Arie L(ova) 1921- CANR-11
Earlier sketch in CA 69-72
Elicker, Charles W. 1951-1978 Obituary 115
Elieff, Deanne D(esmond) 1926- 113
Elinson, Jack 1917- CANR-20
Earlier sketches in CA 45-48, CANR-2
Elioseff, Lee Andrew 1933- 17-18R
Eliot, Alexander 1919- CANR-1
Earlier sketch in CA 49-52
Eliot, Anne
See Cole, Lois Dwight
Eliot, Dan
See Silverberg, Robert
Eliot, George 1819-1880 DLB-21, 35, 55
Eliot, George Fielding 1894-1971
Obituary 29-32R
Eliot, John 1604-1690 DLB-24
Eliot, Sonny 1926- 81-84
Eliot, T(homas) S(tearns) 1888-1965 7-8R
Obituary 25-28R
See also DLB 7, 10, 45, 63
See also CLC 1, 2, 3, 6, 9, 10, 13, 15,
24, 34, 41
Eliot, Thomas H(opkinson) 1907- 89-92
Eliot Hurst, M(ichael) E(liot) 1938- 57-60
Eliovson, Sima (Benveniste) 1919- CANR-20
Earlier sketches in CA 13-14R, CANR-5
Elis, Islwyn Ffowc 1924- 93-96
Elisabeth (Ottilie Luise), Queen (Pauline)
1843-1916 Brief entry 123
Eliscu, Frank 1912- 57-60
Elisofon, Eliot 1911-1973 Obituary 41-44R
See also SATA 21
Elison, George 1937- 53-56
Elizabeth Marie, Sister 1914- 11-12R
Elkholy, Abdo A. 1925- 23-24R
Elkin, Benjamin 1911- CANR-4
Earlier sketch in CA 4R
See also SATA 3
Elkin, Frederick 1918- 41-44R
Elkin, H. V.
See Hinkle, Vernon
Elkin, Judith Laikin 1928- CANR-19
Earlier sketches in CA 53-56, CANR-4
Elkin, Stanley L(awrence) 1930- CANR-8
Earlier sketch in CA 11-12R
See also DLB 2, 28
See also DLBY 80
See also CLC 4, 6, 9, 14, 27
Elkin, Stephen L(loyd) 1941- 93-96
Elkind, David 1931- CANR-1
Earlier sketch in CA 45-48
Elkins, Dov Peretz 1937- CANR-12
Earlier sketch in CA 29-32R
See also SATA 5
Elkins, Ella Ruth 1929- 25-28R
Elkins, Stanley Maurice 1925- 102
Elkins, T(homas) H(enry) 1926-
Brief entry 111
Elkins, William R. 1926- 33-36R
Elkon, Juliette
See Elkon-Hamelecourt, Juliette
Elkon-Hamelecourt, Juliette 1912- 57-60
Elkouri, Frank 1921- 69-72
Elkus, Jonathan Britton 1931- 111
Ellacott, S(amuel) E(rnest) 1911- CANR-3
Earlier sketch in CA 7-8R
See also SATA 19
Elledge, Jim 1950- CANR-19
Earlier sketch in CA 102
Elledge, Scott CLC-34
Elledge, W(aymon) Paul 1938- 25-28R
Ellen, Barbara 1938- 7-8R
Ellenberger, Henri F(rederic) 1905- CAP-2
Earlier sketch in CA 29-32
Ellenbogen, Eileen 1917- 104
Ellender, Raphael 1906-1972 Obituary 37-40R
Ellens, J(ay) Harold 1932- CANR-7
Earlier sketch in CA 57-60
Ellenson, Gene 1921- 57-60
Eller, John 1935- 105
Eller, Ronald D 1948- 110
Eller, Scott
See Holinger, William (Jaques)
Eller, Vernard (Marion) 1927- CANR-24
Earlier sketches in CA 23-24R, CANR-9
Eller, William 1921- 77-80
Ellerbeck, Rosemary (Anne L'Estrange) CANR-24
Earlier sketch in CA 106
Ellerbee, Linda 1944- 115
Brief entry 110
Ellerman, Annie Winifred 1894-1983 104
Obituary 108
Ellery, John Blaise 1920- 9-10R
Ellet, Elizabeth F. 1818(?)-1877 DLB-30
Ellett, Marcella H. 1931- 23-24R
Ellfeldt, Lois 1910- 33-36R
Ellicott, V. L.
See Ellicott, Valcoulon MeMoyne
Ellicott, Valcoulon MeMoyne 1893-1983
Obituary 109
Ellin, E(lizabeth) M(uriel) 1905- CAP-2
Earlier sketch in CA 29-32
Ellin, Stanley (Bernard) 1916-1986 CANR-4
Obituary 119
Earlier sketch in CA 3R
Elling, Karl A(lwin) 1935- 25-28R
Elling, Ray H. 1929- 33-36R
Ellingsworth, Huber W. 1928- CANR-10
Earlier sketch in CA 21-22R
Ellington, Duke
See Ellington, Edward Kennedy
Ellington, Edward Kennedy 1899-1974 97-100
Obituary 49-52
Ellington, James W(esley) 1927- 37-40R
Ellington, Mercer (Kennedy) 1919-
Brief entry 113
Ellington, Richard 1915(?)-1980 Obituary 102
Ellinwood, Leonard Webster 1905- 4R
Elliot, Asa
See Blinder, Elliot
Elliot, Daniel
See Feldman, Leonard
Elliot, Edith M(arie Farmer) 1912- 23-24R
Elliot, Elisabeth (Howard) 1926- CANR-6
Earlier sketch in CA 7-8R
Elliot, Geraldine
See Bingham, Evangeline M(arguerite)
L(adys) (Elliot)
Elliot, Ian 1925- 69-72
Elliot, Jeffrey M. 1947- CANR-24
Earlier sketch in CA 106
Elliott, Alan C(urtis) 1952- CANR-18
Earlier sketch in CA 102
Elliott, Allan
See Elliott, K(enneth) A(llan) C(aldwell)
Elliott, Aubrey (George) 1917- 93-96
Elliott, Bob 1923- Brief entry 109
Elliott, Brian (Robinson) 1910- 25-28R
Elliott, Bruce (Walter Gardner Lively Stacy)
1915(?)-1973 Obituary 41-44R
Elliott, C(larence) Orville 1913- 33-36R
Elliott, Chip
See Elliott, E(scalus) E(mmert) III
Elliott, David W. 1939- 45-48
Elliott, Don
See Silverberg, Robert
Elliott, Donald 1928- 69-72
Elliott, Douglas B(yron) 1947- 113
Elliott, E(scalus) E(mmert) III 1945- 29-32R
Elliott, Emory 1942- CANR-23
Earlier sketch in CA 69-72
Elliott, Errol T(homas) 1894- 69-72
Elliott, George P(aul) 1918-1980 CANR-2
Obituary 97-100
Earlier sketch in CA 1R
See also CLC 2
Elliott, Harley 1940- CANR-4
Earlier sketch in CA 49-52
Elliott, Hugh (Francis Ivo) 1913-
Brief entry 112
Elliott, James Francis 1914-1981 Obituary 110
Elliott, Jan Walter 1939- 37-40R
Elliott, Janice 1931- CANR-8
Earlier sketch in CA 15-16R
See also DLB 14
See also CLC 47
Elliott, John 1938- 25-28R
Elliott, John E(d) 1931- CANR-5
Earlier sketch in CA 3R
Elliott, John H(uxtable) 1930- CANR-3
Earlier sketch in CA 7-8R
Elliott, John H(all) 1935- Brief entry 113
Elliott, John R., Jr. 1937- 25-28R
Elliott, Jumbo
See Elliott, James Francis
Elliott, K(enneth) A(llan) C(aldwell)
1903-1986 108
Obituary 119
Elliott, Kit 1936- 29-32R
Elliott, Lawrence 1924- CANR-21
Earlier sketches in CA 7-8R, CANR-3
Elliott, Leonard M. 1902- CAP-1
Earlier sketch in CA 13-14
Elliott, Lesley 1905- CANR-14
Earlier sketch in CA 77-80
Elliott, Malissa Childs 1929(?)-1979 101
Obituary 85-88
Elliott, Mark Rowe 1947- CANR-24
Earlier sketch in CA 107
Elliott, Neil 1939- 25-28R
Elliott, Osborn 1924- CANR-12
Earlier sketch in CA 69-72
Elliott, P(hilip) R(oss) C(ourtney)
1943(?)-1983 Obituary 110
Elliott, Ralph H. 1925- CANR-2
Earlier sketch in CA 3R
Elliott, Raymond Pruitt 1904- 17-18R
Elliott, Richard V. 1934- 33-36R
Elliott, Robert
See Garfinkel, Bernard Max
Elliott, Robert B.
See Elliott, Bob
Elliott, Robert C(arl) 1914-1981 CANR-21
Earlier sketch in CA 1R
Elliott, Roberta 97-100
Elliott, Russell Richard 1912- 69-72
Elliott, Sarah M(cCarn) 1930- 41-44R
See also SATA 14
Elliott, Sheldon D(ouglass) 1906-1972
Obituary 33-36R
Elliott, Spencer H(ayward) 1883-1967 CAP-1
Earlier sketch in CA 11-12
Elliott, Sumner Locke 1917- CANR-21
Earlier sketches in CA 7-8R, CANR-2
See also CLC 38
Elliott, Susan (Anthony) 1947- 104
Elliott, Thomas Joseph 1941- 49-52
Elliott, Ward E(dward) Y(andell) 1937- 85-88
Elliott, William Douglas 1938- CANR-9
Earlier sketch in CA 65-68
Elliott, William III 1788-1863 DLB-3
Elliott, William M(arion), Jr. 1903- CAP-1
Earlier sketch in CA 9-10
Elliott, William Yandell 1896-1979
Obituary 85-88
Ellis, A. E. CLC-7
Ellis, Albert 1913- CANR-17
Earlier sketches in CA 2R, CANR-2
Ellis, Alec (Charles Owen) 1932- CANR-1
Earlier sketch in CA 45-48
Ellis, Alice Thomas
See Haycraft, Anna
See also CLC 40
Ellis, (Mary) Amabel (Nassau Strachey)
Williams
See Williams-Ellis, (Mary) Amabel
(Nassau Strachey)
Ellis, Amanda M. 1898-1969 CAP-2
Earlier sketch in CA 23-24
Ellis, Anyon
See Rowland-Entwistle, (Arthur)
Theodore (Henry)
Ellis, Audrey CANR-10
Earlier sketch in CA 65-68
Ellis, B(yron) Robert 1940- 53-56
Ellis, Bret Easton 1964- 123
Brief entry 118
See also CLC 39
Ellis, Brooks (Fleming) 1897-1976
Obituary 65-68
Ellis, C(uthbert) Hamilton 1909- 13-14R
Ellis, Carl F., Jr. 1946- 121
Ellis, Carolyn Sue 1950- 122
Ellis, Charles D(aniel) 1937- Brief entry 115
Ellis, Charles Drummond 1895-1980
Obituary 105
Ellis, Charles Howard 1895- CAP-1
Earlier sketch in CA 13-14
Ellis, Clyde T(aylor) 1908- CAP-2
Earlier sketch in CA 23-24
Ellis, David Maldwyn 1914- 9-10R
Ellis, Dock (Phillip, Jr.) 1945- Brief entry 111
Ellis, E. S.
See Ellis, Edward S(ylvester)
Ellis, Edward Robb 1911- 25-28R
Ellis, Edward S(ylvester) 1840-1916
Brief entry 122
See also YABC 1
See also DLB 42
Ellis, Ella Thorp 1928- CANR-2
Earlier sketch in CA 49-52
See also SATA 7
Ellis, Elma I(srael) 1918- 33-36R
Ellis, Florence Hawley 1906- 61-64
Ellis, (J.) Frank(lyn) 1904(?)-1976
Obituary 65-68
Ellis, Frank Hale 1916- 73-76
Ellis, Frank K. 1933- 25-28R
Ellis, Harry Bearse 1921- CANR-2
Earlier sketch in CA 1R
See also SATA 9
Ellis, (Henry) Havelock 1859-1939
Brief entry 109
See also TCLC 14
Ellis, Helen E. (Oickle) 1926- 120
Ellis, Henry C(arlton) 1927- CANR-17
Earlier sketch in CA 97-100
Ellis, Herbert
See Wilson, Lionel
Ellis, Hilda Roderick
See Davidson, H(ilda) R(oderick) Ellis
Ellis, Howard S(ylvester) 1898- 49-52
Ellis, Howard W(oodrow) 1914- CANR-17
Earlier sketch in CA 4R
Ellis, Humphry F(rancis) 1907- 7-8R
Ellis, J(ames) H(ervey) S(tewart) 1893- CAP-2
Earlier sketch in CA 23-24
Ellis, J(ohn) R(ichard) 1938- 85-88
Ellis, Jack C(lare) 1922- 89-92
Ellis, Jack D. 1941- 121
Ellis, James 1935- 37-40R
Ellis, Jody 1925- 57-60
Ellis, John M(artin) 1936- CANR-3
Earlier sketch in CA 49-52
Ellis, John Marion 1917- 49-52
Ellis, John O(liver) 1917- 85-88
Ellis, John Tracy 1905- CANR-5
Earlier sketch in CA 3R
Ellis, Joseph J(ohn) 1943- 53-56
Ellis, Joyce K. (Eileen) 1950- 116
Ellis, Julie 1933- Brief entry 111
Ellis, Kathy
See Bentley, Margaret
Ellis, Keith Stanley 1927- 102
Ellis, L(ewis) Ethan 1898-1977 CANR-4
Earlier sketch in CA 5-6R
Ellis, Landon
See Ellison, Harlan
Ellis, Leigh 1959- 105
Ellis, Leo R(oy) 1909- 11-12R
Ellis, M(adeleine) B(lanche) 1915- 69-72
Ellis, M(arion) LeRoy 1928- 37-40R
Ellis, Marc H. 1952- CANR-24
Earlier sketch in CA 107
Ellis, Mark Karl 1945- 103
Ellis, Mary Jackson 1916- CANR-17
Earlier sketch in CA 4R
Ellis, Mary Leith 1921- 23-24R
Ellis, Mel(vin Richard) 1912-1984 13-14R
Obituary 113
See also SATA 7, 39
Ellis, Norman R. 1924- 13-14R
Ellis, Olivia
See Wintle, Anne
Ellis, Peter Berresford 1943- CANR-21
Earlier sketch in CA 81-84
Ellis, Peter F(rancis) 1921- 115
Ellis, Ray C. 1898- CAP-2
Earlier sketch in CA 21-22
Ellis, Richard 1938- 104
Ellis, Richard E(manuel) 1937- 61-64
Ellis, Richard N(athaniel) 1939- 33-36R
Ellis, Richard White Bernard 1902- CAP-1
Earlier sketch in CA 15-16
Ellis, Ron(ald Walter) 1941- 77-80
Ellis, (Christopher) Royston (George)
1941- 7-8R
Ellis, Sarah 1952- 123
Ellis, Scott
See Schorr, Mark
Ellis, Ulrich Ruegg 1904-1981 Obituary 108
Ellis, Wesley
See Wallmann, Jeffrey M(iner)
Ellis, William 1918- 49-52
Ellis, William Donohue 1918- 49-52
Ellison, Alfred 1916- 1R
Ellison, Craig W(illiam) 1944- CANR-6
Earlier sketch in CA 57-60
Ellison, Fred P(ittman) 1922- Brief entry 113
Ellison, George R. 1907(?)-1983 Obituary 110
Ellison, Gerald Alexander 1910- CAP-1
Earlier sketch in CA 13-14
Ellison, Glenn 1911- 89-92
Ellison, Glenn "Tiger"
See Ellison, Glenn
Ellison, H(enry) L(eopold) 1903- CANR-6
Earlier sketch in CA 7-8R
Ellison, Harlan 1934- CANR-5
Earlier sketch in CA 5-6R
See also DLB 8
See also CLC 1, 13, 42
Ellison, Henry 1931-1965 7-8R
Ellison, Herbert J(ay) 1929- 15-16R
Ellison, James E. 1927- 15-16R
Ellison, James Whitfield 1929- CANR-1
Earlier sketch in CA 3R
Ellison, Jerome 1907-1981 29-32R
Obituary 104
Ellison, John Malcus 1889-1979 4R
Ellison, Katherine (White) 1941- 101

Ellison, Lucile Watkins 1907(?)-1979 ... 109
Obituary ... 93-96
See also SATA 22, 50
Ellison, Max 1914-1985 ... 57-60
Obituary ... 116
See also AITN 1
Ellison, Ralph (Waldo) 1914- ... CANR-24
Earlier sketch in CA 11-12R
See also DLB 2
See also CDALB 1941-1968
See also CLC 1, 3, 11
Ellison, Randall Erskine 1904-1984
Obituary ... 113
Ellison, Reuben Young 1907- ... 15-16R
Ellison, Virginia H(owell) 1910- ... 33-36R
See also SATA 4
Ellison, William McLaren 1919(?)-1978
Obituary ... 81-84
Elliston, Frederick Allen 1944- ... 105
Elliston, Thomas R(alph) 1919-1977
Obituary ... 73-76
Elliston, Valerie Mae (Watkinson) 1929- ... 9-10R
Ellithorpe, Harold (Earle) 1925- ... 77-80
Ellman, Michael 1942- ... 45-48
Ellmann, Richard (David) 1918-1987 ... CANR-2
Obituary ... 122
Earlier sketch in CA 1R
Ellsberg, Daniel 1931- ... 69-72
Ellsberg, Edward 1891- ... 7-8R
See also SATA 7
Ellsworth, L(ida) E(lizabeth) 1948- ... 118
Ellsworth, P(aul) T(heodore) 1897- ... 17-18R
Ellsworth, Ralph Eugene 1907- ... CANR-2
Earlier sketch in CA 3R
Ellsworth, S(amuel) George 1916- ... 45-48
Ellsworth, Sallie Bingham 1937- ... CANR-18
Earlier sketch in CA 1R
Ellsworth, Scott 1954- ... 109
Ellul, Jacques 1912- ... 81-84
Ellvinger, Barbara Anne Price
See Price, Barbara Anne Ellvinger
Ellwood, Edith E(lizabeth)
See Muesing-Ellwood, Edith E(lizabeth)
Ellwood, Gracia-Fay 1938- ... 29-32R
Ellwood, Robert S(cott), Jr. 1933- ... CANR-14
Earlier sketch in CA 41-44R
El Mallakh, Ragaei (William) 1925- ... 112
Elman, Richard 1934- ... 19-20R
See also CAAS 3
See also CLC 19
Elman, Robert 1930- ... CANR-3
Earlier sketch in CA 45-48
Elmandjra, Mahdi 1933- ... 89-92
Elmblad, Mary (B.) 1927- ... 108
El-Meligi, A(bdel) Moneim 1923- ... 19-20R
Elmen, Paul H. 1913- ... 89-92
Elmendorf, Mary Lindsay 1917- ... 57-60
Elmer, Carlos Hall 1920- ... 102
Elmer, Gary W. 1941- ... 122
Elmer, Irene (Elizabeth) 1937- ... 4R
El-Messidi, Kathy Groehn 1946- ... 57-60
Elmhirst, Leonard Knight 1893-1974
Obituary ... 115
Elmore, Ernest Carpenter 1901-1957
Brief entry ... 114
Elmore, (Carolyn) Patricia 1933- ... 114
See also SATA 35, 38
Elms, Alan C(linton) 1938- ... 69-72
Elmslie, Kenward 1929- ... CANR-9
Earlier sketch in CA 21-22R
Elmslie, William Alexander Leslie
1885-1965 ... CAP-1
Earlier sketch in CA 13-14
Elmstrom, George P. 1925- ... 5-6R
El Muhajir 1944- ... 49-52
Elon, Amos 1926- Brief entry ... 121
Elovitz, Mark H(arvey) 1938- ... 69-72
Elphick, Richard Hall 1943- ... 112
Elphinstone, Francis
See Powell-Smith, Vincent (Walter Francis)
Elphinstone, Murgatroyd
See Kahler, Hugh (Torbert) MacNair
Elrick, George S(eefurth) 1921- ... 112
Elron
See Hubbard, L(afayette) Ron(ald)
el Ropo, Smokestack
See Perry, Charles
El Saadawi, Nawal 1931- ... 118
El Saffar, Ruth (Ann) 1941- ... 69-72
Elsasser, Albert B(ertrand) 1918- ... CANR-22
Earlier sketch in CA 69-72
Elsasser, Glen Robert 1935- ... 65-68
Elsberry, Terence 1943- ... 45-48
Elsbree, Langdon 1929- ... 33-36R
Else, Gerald Frank 1908-1982 ... 61-64
Obituary ... 107
Elsea, Janet G(ayle) 1942- ... 119
Elsen, Albert E(dward) 1927- ... CANR-11
Earlier sketch in CA 7-8R
El-Shabazz, El Hajj Malik
See Little, Malcolm
Elshtain, Jean Bethke 1941- ... 106
Elsmere, Jane Shaffer 1932- ... 37-40R
Elsner, Gisela 1937- ... 9-10R
Elsner, Henry, Jr. 1930- ... 21-22R
Elsom, John Edward 1934- ... 65-68
Elson, Edward L(ee) R(oy) 1906- ... CANR-3
Earlier sketch in CA 5-6R
Elson, Lawrence M(cClellan) 1935- ... 53-56
Elson, R. N.
See Nelson, R. Faraday
Elson, Robert T(ruscott) 1906-1987 ... 77-80
Obituary ... 121
Elson, Ruth Miller 1917- ... 15-16R
Elspeth
See Bragdon, Elspeth MacDuffie
Elstar, Dow
See Gallun, Raymond Z(inke)
Elstob, Peter 1915- ... CANR-1
Earlier sketch in CA 3R
Elston, Allan Vaughan 1887-1976 ... CANR-3
Earlier sketch in CA 3R
Elston, Gene 1922- ... 33-36R
Elston, Robert 1934-1987 Obituary ... 124
Elston, Wilbur E(vans) 1913- Brief entry ... 112
Elstun, Esther N(ies) 1935- ... 117
Elsy, (Winifred) Mary ... 93-96
Elting, John R(obert) 1911- ... 112
Elting, Mary 1906- ... CANR-19
Earlier sketches in CA 9-10R, CANR-4
See also SATA 2
Elton, Edwin J(oel) 1939- ... 53-56
Elton, Geoffrey R(udolph) 1921- ... CANR-3
Earlier sketch in CA 11-12R
Elton, John
See Marsh, John
Elton, W(illiam) R. 1921- Brief entry ... 111
el-Toure, Askia Muhammad Abu Bakr
See Toure, Askia Muhammad Abu Bakr el
Eltringham, S(tewart) K(eith) 1929- ... 110
Eluard, Paul
See Grindel, Eugene
See also TCLC 7
El Uqsor
See Borgmann, Dmitri A(lfred)
Elvin, Drake
See Beha, Ernest
Elvin, Harold 1909-1985 ... CANR-4
Obituary ... 115
Earlier sketch in CA 7-8R
Elvin, (Herbert) Lionel 1905- ... CAP-1
Earlier sketch in CA 13-14
Elvin, Mark 1938- ... 73-76
Elward, James (Joseph) 1928- ... CANR-12
Earlier sketch in CA 29-32R
Elwart, Joan Potter 1927- ... 25-28R
See also SATA 2
Elwell, Fayette Herbert 1885- ... 7-8R
Elwell, Jerry MacElroy 1922- ... 57-60
Elwell, Stillman J. 1894-1977 Obituary ... 110
Elwell, Walter A(lexander) 1937- ... 119
Elwell-Sutton, L(aurence) P(aul)
1912-1984 ... 5-6R
Obituary ... 114
Elwin, Malcolm 1903-1973 Obituary ... 89-92
Elwin, William
See Ebenstein, William
Elwood, Catharyn 1903(?)-1975 Obituary ... 61-64
Elwood, Douglas J(ames) 1924- ... 116
Elwood, Muriel 1902- ... CAP-1
Earlier sketch in CA 9-10
Elwood, Roger 1943- ... CANR-10
Earlier sketch in CA 57-60
Elwyn-Jones, Pearl Binder 1904- ... 107
Ely, David 1927- ... 53-56
Ely, Donald P(aul) 1930- ... 29-32R
Ely, James W(allace), Jr. 1938- ... 73-76
Ely, John Hart 1938- ... 103
Ely, Paul (Henri) 1897-1975 Obituary ... 53-56
Ely, Virginia (Shackelford) 1899- ... CANR-24
Earlier sketch in CA 4R
Elytis, Odysseus 1911- ... 102
See also CLC 15
Elzinga, Kenneth G(erald) 1941- ... CANR-13
Earlier sketches in CA 49-52, CANR-1
Emans, Robert 1934- ... 53-56
Emanuel, James A. 1921- ... CANR-12
Earlier sketch in CA 29-32R
See also DLB 41
Ember, Carol R(uchlis) 1943- ... 77-80
Emberley, Barbara A(nne) 1932- ... CANR-5
Earlier sketch in CA 5-6R
See also SATA 8
See also CLR 5
Emberley, Ed(ward Randolph) 1931- ... CANR-5
Earlier sketch in CA 5-6R
See also SATA 8
See also CLR 5
Emberley, Michael 1960- ... 104
See also SATA 34
Embey, Philip
See Philipp, Elliot Elias
Emblen, D(onald) L(ewis) 1918- ... 33-36R
Embling, John 1952- ... 111
Emboden, William A., Jr. 1935- ... CANR-14
Earlier sketch in CA 41-44R
Embree, Ainslie Thomas 1921- ... CANR-2
Earlier sketch in CA 4R
Embry, Margaret Jacob 1919-1975 ... CANR-3
Earlier sketch in CA 1R
See also SATA 5
Emecheta, (Florence Onye) Buchi 1944- ... 81-84
See also CLC 14
Emeneau, Murray Barnson 1904- ... CANR-5
Earlier sketch in CA 1R
Emenegger, Bob
See Emenegger, Robert
Emenegger, Robert 1933- ... 102
Emenhiser, JeDon A(llen) 1933- ... 37-40R
Emerick, Kenneth F(red) 1925- ... 53-56
Emerson, Alice B. ... CAP-2
Earlier sketch in CA 19-20
See also SATA 1
Emerson, Caroline D. 1891-1973 ... CAP-1
Obituary ... 45-48
Earlier sketch in CA 17-18
Emerson, Caryl (Geppert) 1944- ... 123
Emerson, Connie 1930- ... 109
Emerson, (Alan) David 1900- ... CANR-2
Earlier sketch in CA 7-8R
Emerson, Donald (Conger) 1913- ... 21-22R
Emerson, Earl W. 1948- ... 123
Emerson, Everett Harvey 1925- ... CANR-22
Earlier sketches in CA 15-16R, CANR-5
Emerson, Frank C(reighton) 1936- ... 53-56
Emerson, H(enry) O(liver) 1893- ... CAP-2
Earlier sketch in CA 23-24
Emerson, James G(ordon), Jr. 1926- ... 19-20R
Emerson, Laura S(alome) 1907- ... CAP-1
Earlier sketch in CA 15-16
Emerson, Mary Lee
See Kennedy, Mary
Emerson, O. B. 1922- ... CANR-16
Earlier sketch in CA 25-28R
Emerson, Ralph Waldo 1803-1882 ... DLB-1, 59
See also CDALB 1640-1865
Emerson, Ronald
See Scotland, James
Emerson, Ru 1944- ... 121
Emerson, Rupert 1899-1979 ... CANR-2
Obituary ... 85-88
Earlier sketch in CA 1R
Emerson, Thomas I(rwin) 1907- ... 21-22R
Emerson, William 1769-1811 ... DLB-37
Emerson, William K(eith) 1925- ... 41-44R
See also SATA 25
Emery, Alan E(glin) H(eathcote) 1928- ... 69-72
Emery, Allan C(omstock), Jr. 1919- ... 104
Emery, Anne (McGuigan) 1907- ... CANR-2
Earlier sketch in CA 3R
See also SATA 1, 33
Emery, David A(mos) 1920- ... 29-32R
Emery, Edwin 1914- ... CANR-11
Earlier sketch in CA 69-72
Emery, Fred 1933- ... 65-68
Emery, Gary 1942- ... 110
Emery, Kenneth Orris 1914- ... 107
Emery, Michael 1940- ... 73-76
Emery, Pierre-Yves 1929- ... 101
Emery, Robert F(irestone) 1927- ... 37-40R
Emery, Walter Byron 1907-1973 ... CANR-22
Earlier sketch in CA 1R
Emett, Rowland 1906- ... 102
Emig, Janet Ann ... 73-76
Emma, Ronald David 1920- ... 25-28R
Emmanuel, Philip D. 1909- ... CAP-1
Earlier sketch in CA 15-16
Emmanuel, Pierre
See Mathieu, Noel Jean
Emme, Eugene M(orlock) 1919-1985 ... CANR-8
Obituary ... 116
Earlier sketch in CA 15-16R
Emmel, Thomas C. 1941- Brief entry ... 111
Emmens, Carol Ann 1944- ... 106
See also SATA 39
Emmerich, Andre 1924- ... 9-10R
Emmerick, R(onald) E(ric) 1937- ... CANR-11
Earlier sketch in CA 25-28R
Emmerson, Donald K(enneth) 1940- ... CANR-14
Earlier sketch in CA 65-68
Emmerson, Henry Russell 1899- ... 7-8R
Emmerson, John K(enneth)
1908-1984 ... CANR-14
Obituary ... 112
Earlier sketch in CA 57-60
Emmerson, Richard Kenneth 1948- ... 106
Emmet, Dorothy Mary 1904- ... 9-10R
Emmet, E(ric) R(evell) 1909- ... 107
Emmett, Bruce 1949- ... 57-60
Emmitt, Robert (P.) 1925- ... 29-32R
Emmons, Charles F(rank) 1942- ... 110
Emmons, Della (Florence) Gould
1890-1983 Obituary ... 111
See also SATA 39
Emmons, Michael 1938- ... 107
Emmrich, Curt 1897-1975 ... CAP-2
Earlier sketch in CA 29-32
Emmrich, Kurt
See Emmrich, Curt
Emorey, N.
See Ellison, Jerome
Emory, Alan (Steuer) 1922- ... CANR-12
Earlier sketch in CA 69-72
Empey, Arthur Guy 1883-1963 Obituary ... 107
Empey, LaMar T. 1923- ... 29-32R
Employee X
See Fautsko, Timothy F(rank)
Empringham, Antoinette F(leur) 1939- ... 124
Empringham, Toni
See Empringham, Antoinette F(leur)
Empson, William 1906-1984 ... 17-18R
Obituary ... 112
See also DLB 20
See also CLC 3, 8, 19, 33, 34
Emrich, Duncan (Black Macdonald)
1908-197(?) ... CANR-9
Earlier sketch in CA 61-64
See also SATA 11
Emshwiller, Carol ... 53-56
Emsley, Clare
See Plummer, Clare (Emsley)
Emsley, Michael Gordon 1930- ... 97-100
Emslie, M. L.
See Simpson, Myrtle L(illias)
Emswiler, Sharon Neufer 1944- ... 119
Emy, Hugh (Vincent) 1944- ... 77-80
Encausse, Gerard (Anaclet Vincent)
1865-1916 Brief entry ... 113
Encel, Sol
See Encel, Solomon
Encel, Solomon 1925- ... 115
Enchi, Fumiko (Ueda) 1905-1986 Obituary ... 121
See also CLC 31
Endacott, G(eorge) B(eer) 1901- ... 7-8R
Endacott, M(arie) Violet 1915- ... 11-12R
Ende, Jean 1947- ... 53-56
Ende, Michael 1930(?)- ... 124
Brief entry ... 118
See also SATA 42
See also CLC 31
See also CLR 14
Ende, Richard Chaffey von
See von Ende, Richard Chaffey
Enderle, Judith (Ann) Ross 1941- ... CANR-22
Earlier sketch in CA 106
See also SATA 38
Enders, Richard
See Fenster, Robert
Endfield, Mercedes
See von Block, Bela W(illiam)
Endicott, Stephen Lyon 1928- ... 107
Endler, Norman S(olomon) 1931- ... CANR-9
Earlier sketch in CA 23-24R
Endo, Mitsuko 1942- ... 65-68
Endo, Shusaku 1923- ... CANR-21
Earlier sketch in CA 29-32R
See also CLC 7, 14, 19
Endore, (Samuel) Guy 1900-1970 ... CANR-6
Obituary ... 25-28R
Earlier sketch in CA 2R
Endres, Clifford 1941- ... 108
Endy, Melvin B(ecker), Jr. 1938- ... 81-84
Enelow, Allen J(ay) 1922- ... CANR-7
Earlier sketch in CA 19-20R
Enfield, Carrie
See Smith, Susan Vernon
Engberg, Edward 1928- ... 21-22R
Engberg, Holger L(aessoe) 1930- ... 37-40R
Engberg, (Johanna) Susan 1940- ... 117
Engdahl, Sylvia Louise 1933- ... CANR-14
Earlier sketch in CA 29-32R
See also SATA 4
See also SAAS 5
See also CLR 2
Engebrecht, P(atricia) A(nn) 1935- ... 57-60
Engel, Alan S(tuart) 1932- ... 37-40R
Engel, Bernard F. 1921- ... 13-14R
Engel, Herbert M. 1918- ... 120
Engel, Howard 1931- ... 112
Engel, J. Ronald 1936- ... 124
Engel, James F. 1934- ... CANR-13
Earlier sketch in CA 23-24R
Engel, (Aaron) Lehman 1910-1982 ... 41-44R
Obituary ... 107
Engel, Louis (Henry, Jr.) 1909-1982 ... 21-22R
Obituary ... 108
Engel, Lyle Kenyon 1915-1986 ... 85-88
Obituary ... 120
Engel, Madeline H(elena) 1941- ... 85-88
Engel, Marian 1933-1985 ... CANR-12
Earlier sketch in CA 25-28R
See also DLB 53
See also CLC 36
Engel, Mary June Montgomery
1920(?)-1985 Obituary ... 117
Engel, Monroe 1921- ... 7-8R
Engel, Pauline Newton 1918- ... 17-18R
Engel, Peter H. 1935- ... CANR-15
Earlier sketch in CA 81-84
Engel, S(rul) Morris (von) 1931- ... CANR-14
Earlier sketch in CA 37-40R
Engel, Salo 1908-1972 ... CAP-2
Earlier sketch in CA 33-36
Engel, Samuel G. 1904-1984 Obituary ... 112
Engelberg, Edward 1929- ... 37-40R
Engelhardt, Frederick
See Hubbard, L(afayette) Ron(ald)
Engelhart, Margaret S. 1924- ... 122
Engelking, L. L. 1903(?)-1980 Obituary ... 102
Engelman, Rose C. 1919(?)-1979
Obituary ... 89-92
Engelmann, Hugo O(tto) 1917- ... 41-44R
Engelmann, Larry 1941- ... 101
Engelmann, Ruth 1919- ... 106
Engelmann, Siegfried E. 1931- ... CANR-13
Earlier sketch in CA 23-24R
Engelmayer, Sheldon David 1945- ... 114
Engels, Donald (W.) 1946- ... 102
Engels, John David 1931- ... CANR-6
Earlier sketch in CA 15-16R
Engels, Norbert (Anthony) 1903- ... CAP-2
Earlier sketch in CA 17-18
Engeman, Thomas S(ledge) 1944- ... 109
Engen, Rodney K(ent) 1948- ... CANR-15
Earlier sketch in CA 65-68
Enger, Norman L. 1937- ... CANR-10
Earlier sketch in CA 25-28R
Engerman, Stanley L(ewis) 1936- ... 53-56
Enggass, Robert 1921- ... CANR-9
Earlier sketch in CA 13-14R
Engh, M(ary) J(ane) 1933- ... 69-72
Engh, Rohn 1938- ... 69-72
Engholm, Eva 1909- ... 93-96
Engl, Lieselotte 1918- ... 49-52
Engl, Theodor 1925- ... 49-52
England, Anthony Bertram 1939- ... 85-88
England, Barry 1932- ... 25-28R
England, E. M.
See Anders, Edith (Mary) England
England, E Squires
See Ball, Sylvia Patricia
England, George Allan 1877-1936
Brief entry ... 112
England, George W(illiam) 1927- ... 104
England, John C(arol) 1930- ... 116
England, Martha Winburn 1909- ... CAP-1
Earlier sketch in CA 11-12
England, Maurice Derrick 1908-1980 ... 104
England, Rodney Charles Bennett
See Bennett-England, Rodney Charles
England, Wilbur Birch 1903- ... 4R

Engle, Eloise
See Paananen, Eloise (Katherine)
See also SATA 9
Engle, Jeff(rey) 1947- 103
Engle, John D(avid), Jr. 1922- CANR-7
Earlier sketch in CA 57-60
Engle, Louise Boardman Proctor
1897(?)-1987 Obituary 121
Engle, Parke F. 1900(?)-1984 Obituary 111
Engle, Paul (Hamilton) 1908- CANR-5
Earlier sketch in CA 1R
See also DLB 48
Engle, T(helburn) L(aRoy) 1901- 13-14R
Englebert, Victor 1933- 57-60
See also SATA 8
Englefield, Ronald 1891-1975 Obituary 105
Englekirk, John E(ugene) 1905-1983
Obituary 112
Engleman, Finis E(wing) 1895- 11-12R
Engler, Larry 1949- 53-56
Engler, Richard E(mil), Jr. 1925- 37-40R
Engler, Robert 1922- CANR-2
Earlier sketch in CA 3R
Englert, Clement Cyril 1910- CANR-5
Earlier sketch in CA 1R
English, Adrian J(oseph) 1939- 118
English, Arnold
See Hershman, Morris
English, Barbara (Anne) 1933- CANR-13
Earlier sketch in CA 33-36R
English, Charles
See Nuetzel, Charles (Alexander)
English, David 1931- 69-72
English, Deirdre (Elena) 1948- 85-88
English, E(ugene) Schuyler 1899-1981 107
Obituary 103
English, Earl (Franklin) 1905- 37-40R
English, Edward (H.) 19(?)-1973
Obituary 41-44R
English, Fenwick Walter 1939- CANR-1
Earlier sketch in CA 45-48
English, Isobel 1925- 53-56
English, James W(ilson) 1915- 21-22R
See also SATA 37
English, (Emma) Jean M(artin) 1937- 29-32R
English, John W(esley) 1940- 69-72
English, Maurice 1909-1983 .... CANR-12
Obituary 111
Earlier sketch in CA 9-10R
English, O(liver) Spurgeon 1901- CAP-2
Earlier sketch in CA 33-36
English, Ronald (Frederick) 1913- CAP-1
Earlier sketch in CA 9-10
English, Thomas H(opkins) 1895- CANR-2
Earlier sketch in CA 5-6R
English, Thomas Saunders 1928-
Brief entry 105
Englizian, H. Crosby 1923- 23-24R
Engquist, Richard 1933- 29-32R
Engren, Edith
See McCaig, Robert Jesse
Engs, Robert Francis 1943- 101
Engstrand, Iris (H.) Wilson 1935- 107
Engstrom, Ted W.
See Engstrom, Theodore W(ilhelm)
Engstrom, Theodore W(ilhelm) 1916- CANR-9
Earlier sketch in CA 65-68
Engstrom, W(infred) A(ndrew) 1925- 57-60
Enis, Ben M(elvin) 1942- CANR-22
Earlier sketches in CA 57-60, CANR-7
Enke, Stephen 1916-1974 65-68
Obituary 53-56
Enloe, Cynthia H(olden) 1938- CANR-17
Earlier sketch in CA 37-40R
Enlow, David R(oland) 1916- CANR-10
Earlier sketch in CA 7-8R
Ennes, James Marquis, Jr. 1933- 102
Ennis, Bruce J. 1940- Brief entry 110
Ennis, Robert H(ugh) 1927- CANR-10
Earlier sketch in CA 25-28R
Eno, Susan 101
Enoch, Kurt 1895-1982 Obituary 106
Enockson, Paul G(eorge) 1938- 110
Enomiya-Lassalle, Hugo M(akibi) 1898- 23-24R
Enquist, Per Olov 1934- Brief entry 109
Enrick, Norbert Lloyd 1920- CANR-6
Earlier sketch in CA 15-16R
Enright, D(ennis) J(oseph) 1920- CANR-1
Earlier sketch in CA 4R
See also SATA 25
See also DLB 27
See also CLC 4, 8, 31
Enright, Elizabeth 1909-1968 61-64
Obituary 25-28R
See also SATA 9
See also DLB 22
See also CLR 4
Enright, Maureen Patricia Ford
1908(?)-1983 Obituary 111
Enroth, Clyde A(dolph) 1926- 37-40R
Enscoe, Gerald (Eugene) 1926- CANR-10
Earlier sketch in CA 5-6R
Ense, Wolfgang
See Frank, Rudolf
Ensign, Thomas 1940- 101
Ensign, Tod
See Ensign, Thomas
Ensley, Evangeline 1907- 122
Brief entry 114
Ensley, Francis Gerald 1907- CAP-1
Earlier sketch in CA 15-16
Enslin, Morton S(cott) 1897- 19-20R
Enslin, Theodore (Vernon) 1925- CANR-19
Earlier sketches in CA 53-56, CANR-4
See also CAAS 3
Ensminger, Marion Eugene 1908- CANR-16
Earlier sketches in CA 49-52, CANR-1
Ensor, Allison (Rash) 1935- 25-28R
Ensor, (Alick Charles) David(son)
1906-1987 Obituary 121
Enstrom, Robert (William) 1946- 104
Enteman, Willard F(inley) 1936- 33-36R
Entenza, John Dymock 1905-1984
Obituary 112
Enterline, James Robert 1932- 41-44R
Enthoven, Alain C(harles) 1930- 49-52
Entine, Alan D(avid) 1936- 23-24R
Entwisle, Doris R(oberts) 1924- 5-6R
Entwistle, Florence Vivienne 1889(?)-1982
Obituary 105
Entwistle, Harold 1923- 29-32R
Entwistle, Noel (James) 1936- CANR-16
Earlier sketch in CA 93-96
Entwistle, (Arthur) Theodore (Henry)
Rowland
See Rowland-Entwistle, (Arthur)
Theodore (Henry)
Enyeart, James L(yle) 1943- 113
Enys, Sarah L.
See Sloggett, Nellie
Enz, Jacob J(ohn) 1919- 41-44R
Enzensberger, Hans Magnus 1929- 119
Brief entry 116
See also CLC 43
Enzler, Clarence J. 1910(?)-1976
Obituary 69-72
Epafrodito
See Wagner, C(harles) Peter
Epand, Len 1950- 85-88
Epernay, Mark
See Galbraith, John Kenneth
Ephraim, Gavriel Ben
See Ben-Ephraim, Gavriel
Ephron, Delia 1944- CANR-12
Earlier sketch in CA 97-100
See also SATA 50
Ephron, Henry 1911- 73-76
Ephron, Nora 1941- CANR-12
Earlier sketch in CA 65-68
See also CLC 17, 31
See also AITN 2
Ephron, Phoebe (Wolkind) 1916-1971
Obituary 33-36R
Epler, Percy H. 1872-1975 Obituary 57-60
Epp, Eldon Jay 1930- CANR-7
Earlier sketch in CA 19-20R
Epp, Frank H(enry) 1929- 29-32R
Epp, Margaret A(gnes) 1913- CANR-3
Earlier sketch in CA 11-12R
See also SATA 20
Eppard, Philip B(lair) 1945- 112
Eppenbach, Sarah 1947- 114
Eppenstein, Louise (Kohn) 1892-1987
Obituary 123
Epperly, Elizabeth Rollins 1951- 106
Epperson, Gordon 1921- 25-28R
Eppie
See Naismith, Helen
Eppinga, Jacob D. 1917- 33-36R
Eppinger, Josh 1940- 89-92
Eppink, Norman R(oland) 1906- 53-56
Epple, Anne Orth 1927- 33-36R
See also SATA 20
Epps, Bernard 1936- DLB-53
Epps, Edgar G(ustavas) 1929- 49-52
Epps, Garrett 1950- 69-72
Epps, Preston H(erschel) 1888- 37-40R
Epps, Robert L(ee) 1932- 17-18R
Epsilon
See Betjeman, John
Epstein, Ann Wharton
See Wharton, Annabel Jane
Epstein, Anne Merrick 1931- 69-72
See also SATA 20
Epstein, Barbara 1928- Brief entry 110
Epstein, Benjamin Robert 1912-1983 45-48
Obituary 109
Epstein, Beryl (M. Williams) 1910- CANR-18
Earlier sketches in CA 7-8R, CANR-2
See also SATA 1, 31
Epstein, Charlotte 1921- CANR-8
Earlier sketch in CA 61-64
Epstein, Cy(ril Robert) 1942- Brief entry 108
Epstein, Cynthia Fuchs 1933- CANR-14
Earlier sketch in CA 29-32R
Epstein, Daniel Mark 1948- CANR-2
Earlier sketch in CA 49-52
See also CLC 7
Epstein, David G(eorge) 1943- 69-72
Epstein, Dena J. 1916- 41-44R
Epstein, Edmund L(loyd) 1931- 118
Epstein, Edward Jay 1935- CANR-13
Earlier sketch in CA 19-20R
Epstein, Edwin M(ichael) 1937- 25-28R
Epstein, Ellen Robinson 1947- 115
Epstein, Erwin H(oward) 1939- 29-32R
Epstein, Eugene 1944- 69-72
Epstein, Fritz T(heodor) 1898-1979 .... CANR-22
Earlier sketch in CA 69-72
Epstein, Helen 1947- 89-92
Epstein, Howard M(ichael) 1927- 23-24R
Epstein, Jacob 1880-1959 Brief entry 120
Epstein, Jacob 1956- 114
See also CLC 19
Epstein, Jason 1928- 57-60
Epstein, Joseph 1937- 119
Brief entry 112
See also CLC 39
Epstein, Judith Sue 1947- 69-72
Epstein, Julius 1901-1975 Obituary 57-60
Epstein, Julius J. 1909- 124
Brief entry 113
See also DLB 26
Epstein, June CANR-13
Earlier sketch in CA 73-76
Epstein, Lee 1958- 119
Epstein, Leon D. 1919- 13-14R
Epstein, Leslie 1938- CANR-23
Earlier sketch in CA 73-76
See also CLC 27
Epstein, Melech (Michael) 1889(?)-1979
Obituary 89-92
Epstein, Morris 1921-1973 .... CAP-1
Obituary 45-48
Earlier sketch in CA 15-16
Epstein, Perle S(herry) 1938- CANR-9
Earlier sketch in CA 65-68
See also SATA 27
Epstein, Philip G. 1909-1952 Brief entry 117
See also DLB 26
Epstein, Samuel 1909- CANR-18
Earlier sketches in CA 9-10R, CANR-4
See also SATA 1, 31
Epstein, Samuel S(tanley) 1926- 115
Epstein, Seymour 1917- CANR-5
Earlier sketch in CA 3R
Epstein, William 1912- CANR-11
Earlier sketch in CA 69-72
Epstein, William H(enry) 1944- 61-64
Epton, Nina C(onsuelo) CANR-11
Earlier sketch in CA 5-6R
Equiano, Olaudah 1745(?)-1797 .... DLB-37, 50
Eramus, M. Nott
See Stuber, Stanley I(rving)
Erasmus, Charles J(ohn) 1921- 1R
Erasmus, M. Nott
See Stuber, Stanley I(rving)
Erazmus, Edward T. 1920- Brief entry 106
Erb, Alta Mae 1891- CAP-1
Earlier sketch in CA 9-10
Erb, Paul 1894- 9-10R
Erb, Peter C. 1943- 113
Erbsen, Claude E. 1938- 89-92
Ercoli, Ercole
See Togliatti, Palmiro
Erdahl, Carol Syvertsen 1932- 108
Erdahl, Lowell O. 1931- 109
Erdman, David V(orse) 1911- CANR-17
Earlier sketches in CA 1R, CANR-1
Erdman, Howard Loyd 1935- 23-24R
Erdman, Loula Grace ?-1976 .... CANR-10
Earlier sketch in CA 7-8R
See also SATA 1
Erdman, Nikolai R. 1902(?)-1970
Obituary 29-32R
Erdman, Paul E(mil) 1932- CANR-13
Earlier sketch in CA 61-64
See also CLC 25
See also AITN 1
Erdoes, Richard 1912- 77-80
See also SATA 28, 33
Erdos, Paul L(ouis) 1914- 29-32R
Erdrich, Louise 1954- 114
See also CLC 39
Erdt, Terrence 1942- 106
Erenberg, Arthur 1909(?)-1980 Obituary 114
Erenburg, Ilya (Grigoryevich)
See Ehrenburg, Ilya (Grigoryevich)
Erens, Patricia 1938- 93-96
Erhard, Ludwig 1897-1977 Obituary 112
Erhard, Thomas A. 1923- CANR-13
Earlier sketch in CA 33-36R
Erhard, Walter 1920- SATA-30
Eric, Kenneth
See Henley, Arthur
Erichsen, Heino R(ichard) 1924- 110
Erichsen-Nelson, Jean 1934- 109
Ericksen, Ephraim Gordon 1917- 7-8R
Ericksen, Gerald L(awrence) 1931- 29-32R
Ericksen, Kenneth J(errold) 1939- 37-40R
Ericksen, Stanford Clark 1911- Brief entry 108
Erickson, Arthur (Charles) 1924- 89-92
Erickson, Arvel Benjamin 1905-1974 .... CAP-2
Earlier sketch in CA 21-22
Erickson, Bonnie H(eather) 1944- 112
Erickson, Carolly 1943- CANR-11
Earlier sketch in CA 69-72
Erickson, Don 1932- 110
Erickson, Donald A(rthur) 1925- 29-32R
Erickson, E(rnst) Walfred 1911- CANR-5
Earlier sketch in CA 7-8R
Erickson, Edsel L(ee) 1928- 53-56
Erickson, Erling Arthur 1934- 33-36R
Erickson, John 1929- 101
Erickson, Keith V. 1943- 29-32R
Erickson, M(elvin) E(ddy) 1918-19(?) 11-12R
Erickson, Marilyn T. 1936- 73-76
Erickson, Marion J. 1913- 17-18R
Erickson, Millard J. 1932- 93-96
Erickson, Milton H(yland) 1901-1980 106
Obituary 97-100
Erickson, Phoebe CANR-3
Earlier sketch in CA 1R
Erickson, Robert 1917- Brief entry 109
Erickson, Russell E(verett) 1932- 93-96
See also SATA 27
Erickson, Sabra Rollins 1912- CANR-5
Earlier sketch in CA 5-6R
See also SATA 35
Erickson, Stephen A(nthony) 1940- 85-88
Erickson, W(alter) Bruce 1938- 49-52
Ericson, Edward E(inar) 1939- 69-72
Ericson, Joe Ellis 1925- 41-44R
Ericson, Julia
See Leisy, James (Franklin)
Ericson, Walter
See Fast, Howard Melvin
Ericsson, Emily (Alice) 1904-1976
Obituary 65-68
Ericsson, Mary Kentra 1910- CANR-20
Earlier sketches in CA 4R, CANR-5
Ericsson, Ronald James 1935- 110
Erikson, Erik H(omburger) 1902- 25-28R
Erikson, Kai T(heodor) 1931- Brief entry 107
Erikson, Mel 1937- SATA-31
Erikson, Roy L. 1939(?)-1985 Obituary 116
Erikson, Stanley 1906- 37-40R
Eriksson, Buntel
See Bergman, (Ernst) Ingmar
Eriksson, Edward 1941- 77-80
Eriksson, Marguerite A. 1911- 13-14R
Eringer, Robert 1954- 114
Erisman, Fred (Raymond) 1937- 110
Erlander, Tage Fritiof 1901-1985 Obituary 116
Erlanger, Baba
See Trahey, Jane
Erlanger, Ellen (Louise) 1950- CANR-15
Earlier sketch in CA 85-88
Erlanger, Philippe 1903- CANR-20
Earlier sketches in CA 7-8R, CANR-5
Erlich, Alexander 1912-1985 Obituary 114
Erlich, Lillian (Feldman) 1910- CANR-5
Earlier sketch in CA 4R
See also SATA 10
Erlich, Victor 1914- CANR-3
Earlier sketch in CA 11-12R
Ermarth, Elizabeth 1939- 117
Ermine, Will
See Drago, Harry Sinclair
Ermolaev, Herman Sergei 1924- 107
Ernest, Victor (Hugo) 1911- CAP-2
Earlier sketch in CA 33-36
Ernest, William
See Berkebile, Fred D(onovan)
Ernharth, Ronald Louis 1936- 45-48
Erno, Richard B. 1923- 15-16R
Ernst, Barbara 1945- 65-68
Ernst, Carl Henry 1938- 45-48
Ernst, Clara
See Barnes, Clara Ernst
Ernst, Earle 1911- 5-6R
Ernst, Eldon G(ilbert) 1939- 85-88
Ernst, Jimmy 1920-1984 Obituary 112
Ernst, (Lyman) John 1940- 45-48
See also SATA 39
Ernst, Joseph Albert 1931- Brief entry 109
Ernst, Kathryn (Fitzgerald) 1942- CANR-12
Earlier sketch in CA 61-64
See also SATA 25
Ernst, Lisa Campbell 1957- 114
See also SATA 44
Ernst, Margaret Samuels 1894- CAP-1
Earlier sketch in CA 13-14
Ernst, Margot Klebe 1939- 23-24R
Ernst, Max 1891-1976 Obituary 65-68
Ernst, Morris L(eopold) 1888-1976 .... CANR-7
Obituary 65-68
Earlier sketch in CA 7-8R
Ernst, Paul 1866-1933 .... DLB-66
Ernst, Robert 1915- 23-24R
Ernst, Sheila 1941- 109
Ernsting, Walter 1920- 37-40R
Erny, Pierre Jean Paul 1933- CANR-13
Earlier sketch in CA 73-76
Eron, Carol (Lehman) 1945- 112
Eron, Leonard D(avid) 1920- Brief entry 110
Errington, Frederick (Karl) 1940- 104
Erskine, Barbara 1944- 123
Erskine, Chester 1904(?)-1986 Obituary 121
Erskine, Jim 1956- 107
Erskine, John 1879-1951 Brief entry 112
See also DLB 9
Erskine, Laurie York 1894(?)-1976
Obituary 69-72
Erskine, Margaret
See Williams, (Margaret) Wetherby
Erskine, Noel Leo 116
Erskine, Rosalind
See Longrigg, Roger (Erskine)
Erskine, Thomas L(eonard) 1939- 65-68
Erskine, Wilson Fiske 1911-1972(?) 4R
Erskine-Lindop, Audrey (Beatrice Noel)
1920-1986 69-72
Obituary 121
Erte
See De Tirtoff, Romain
Ertel, (Richard) James 1922-1985 .... 9-10R
Obituary 117
Ertz, Susan 1894-1985 .... 5-6R
Obituary 116
Ervin, Janet Halliday 1923- 29-32R
See also SATA 4
Ervin, Sam(uel) J(ames), Jr. 1896-1985 119
Obituary 115
Brief entry 113
Ervin, Susan
See Ervin-Tripp, Susan Moore
Ervin, Theodore Robert 1928- 15-16R
Ervine, St. John Greer 1883-1971
Obituary 29-32R
See also DLB 10
Ervin-Tripp, Susan Moore 1927- 53-56
Erwin, Annabel
See Barron, Ann Forman
Erwin, Edward (James) 1937- 29-32R
Erwin, John D(raper) 1883-1983 Obituary 109
Erwin, John Seymour 1911- 105
Erwin, Will
See Eisner, Will(iam Erwin)
Esau, Helmut 1941- 57-60
Escandon, Ralph 1928- CANR-14
Earlier sketch in CA 37-40R
Escarpenter, Claudio 1922-1977 .... 17-18R
Obituary 120
Escarraz, Donald Ray 1932- 21-22R
Eschelbach, Claire John 1929- 1R

Escher, Franklin (Jr.) 1915- ... 11-12R
Escherich, Elsa Falk 1888- ... 5-6R
Eschholz, Paul A(nderson) 1942- ... CANR-14
Earlier sketch in CA 37-40R
Eschmeyer, R(einhart) E(rnst) 1898- ... 105
Eschmeyer, William N(eil) 1939- ... 112
Escott, Colin 1949- ... 107
Escott, Jonathan 1922- ... CANR-20
Earlier sketch in CA 65-68
Escott, Paul David 1947- ... 93-96
Escriva, Josemaria
See Escriva de Balaguer, Josemaria
Escriva de Balaguer, Josemaria
1902-1975 Obituary ... 57-60
Eseki, Bruno
See Mphahlele, Ezekiel
Esenin, Sergei (Alexandrovich) 1895-1925
Brief entry ... 104
See also TCLC 4
Esfandiary, F. M. ... CANR-8
Earlier sketch in CA 17-18R
Eshbach, Lloyd Arthur 1910- ... 118
Eshelman, Byron E(lias) 1915- ... 3R
Esherick, Joseph W(harton) 1942- ... 65-68
Eshleman, Clayton 1935- ... 33-36R
See also CAAS 6
See also DLB 5
See also CLC 7
Eshleman, Edwin D(uing) 1920-1985
Obituary ... 114
Eshleman, J. Ross 1936- ... 101
Eshmeyer, R. E.
See Eschmeyer, R(einhart) E(rnst)
See also SATA 29
Eskelin, Neil J(oyner) 1938- ... 33-36R
Eskelund, Karl 1918-1972 ... CAP-2
Earlier sketch in CA 23-24
Eskenazi, Gerald 1936- ... CANR-7
Earlier sketch in CA 61-64
Eskey, Kenneth 1930- ... 77-80
Eskin, Frada 1936- ... 37-40R
Eskow, John 1949- ... 105
Eskow, Seymour 1924- ... 11-12R
Esler, Anthony (James) 1934- ... CANR-8
Earlier sketch in CA 23-24R
Esler, Carol Clemeau 1935- ... 108
Esler, William K. 1930- ... CANR-5
Earlier sketch in CA 53-56
Esman, Aaron H(irsh) 1924- ... CANR-11
Earlier sketch in CA 61-64
Esman, Milton J. 1918- ... 81-84
Esmein, Jean 1923- ... 49-52
Esmond, Harriet
See Burke, John (Frederick)
Esohg, Lama
See Ghose, Amal
Eson, Morris E. 1921- ... 15-16R
Espeland, Pamela (Lee) 1951- ... 107
See also SATA 38
Espenshade, Edward B(owman), Jr. 1910- ... 4R
Esper, Erwin A(llen) 1895-19(?) ... CAP-1
Earlier sketch in CA 15-16
Espey, John (Jenkins) 1913- ... CANR-4
Earlier sketch in CA 7-8R
Espinasse, Albert 1905-1972 Obituary ... 37-40R
'Espinasse, Margaret 1903(?)-1980
Obituary ... 114
Espino, Federico (Licsi, Jr.) 1939- ... 93-96
Espinosa, Jose E(dmundo) 1900-1967 ... CAP-2
Earlier sketch in CA 25-28
Espinosa, Rudy
See Espinoza, Rudolph Louis
Espinoza, Rudolph Louis 1933- ... 73-76
Esposito, John C(abrino) 1940- ... 33-36R
Esposito, John L(ouis) 1940- ... 116
Esposito, Joseph L(ouis) 1941- ... 114
Esposito, Phil(ip Anthony) 1942-
Brief entry ... 108
Espriu, Salvador 1913-1985 Obituary ... 115
See also CLC 9
Espy, Richard 1952- ... 105
Espy, Willard R(ichardson) 1910- ... CANR-2
Earlier sketch in CA 49-52
See also SATA 38
Esquenazi-Mayo, Roberto 1920- ... 45-48
Essame, Hubert 1896-1976 ... 49-52
Obituary ... 65-68
Esse, James
See Stephens, James
Esser, Robin 1933- ... 29-32R
Esses, Michael (Isaiah) 1923- Brief entry ... 110
Essex, Harry J. ... 33-36R
Essex, Mary
See Bloom, Ursula
Essex, Rosamund (Sibyl) 1900-1985 ... 107
Obituary ... 116
Essick, Robert N(ewman) 1942- ... CANR-19
Earlier sketches in CA 53-56, CANR-5
Esslin, Martin (Julius) 1918- ... 85-88
Esslinger, Dean R(obert) 1942- ... 61-64
Esslinger, Pat M.
See Carr, Pat M(oore)
Essoe, Gabe (Attila) 1944- ... 25-28R
Essop, Ahmed 1931- ... 123
Essrig, Harry 1912- ... 108
Estabrook, Robert Harley 1918- ... 69-72
Estabrooks, George H. 1896(?)-1973
Obituary ... 45-48
Estang, Luc 1911- ... 61-64
Estarellas, Juan 1918- ... CANR-2
Earlier sketch in CA 45-48
Estaver, Marguerite M. 1893- ... 97-100
Estelle, Sister Mary 1907- ... CAP-1
Earlier sketch in CA 11-12
Estenssoro, Hugo 1946- ... 69-72
Estep, Irene Compton ... 3R
See also SATA 5
Estep, W(illiam) R(oscoe), Jr. 1920- ... CANR-9
Earlier sketch in CA 13-14R
Esterbrook, Tom
See Hubbard, L(afayette) Ron(ald)
Estergreen, M. Morgan
See Estergreen, Marian Morgan
Estergreen, Marian Morgan 1910- ... 17-18R
Esterly, Glenn 1942- ... 33-36R
Estermann, Carlos ?-1976 Obituary ... 105
Esterow, Milton 1928- ... 19-20R
Estes, Bill 1941- ... 107
Estes, Eleanor 1906- ... CANR-20
Earlier sketches in CA 2R, CANR-5
See also SATA 7
See also DLB 22
See also CLR 2
Estes, J(oseph) Worth 1934- ... 104
Estes, John E(dward) 1939- ... 57-60
Estes, Rice 1907- ... CAP-1
Earlier sketch in CA 11-12
Estes, Richard J. 1942- ... 118
Estes, Steve(n Douglas) 1952- ... 97-100
Estes, Winston M. 1917- ... 29-32R
Estess, Ted L(ynn) 1942- ... 114
Estey, George F. 1924- ... 33-36R
Esthus, Raymond Arthur 1925- ... 15-16R
Estleman, Loren D. 1952- ... 85-88
Estner, Lois J(ane) 1947- ... 114
Estock, Anne (Martin) 1923- ... 4R
Estoril, Jean
See Allan, Mabel Esther
Estrada, Doris (Perkins) 1923- ... 19-20R
Estrada, Jacquelyn (Ann) 1946- ... 29-32R
Estrin, Herman A. 1915- ... CANR-7
Earlier sketch in CA 17-18R
Estroff, Sue E. 1950- ... 105
Esty, John Cushing, Jr. 1928- Brief entry ... 106
Eszterhas, Joe
See Eszterhas, Joseph A.
Eszterhas, Joseph A. Brief entry ... 124
Etchebaster, Pierre 1894-1980 ... 102
Obituary ... 97-100
Etchemendy, Nancy 1952- ... 106
See also SATA 38
Etcheson, Craig Carlyle 1955- ... 117
Etcheson, Warren W(ade) 1920- ... 41-44R
Etchison, Birdie L(ee) 1937- ... 106
See also SATA 38
Etchison, Dennis (William) 1943- ... 118
Brief entry ... 115
Eterovich, Adam S(lav) 1930- ... 49-52
Eterovich, Francis Hyacinth 1913- ... 37-40R
Ethell, Jeffrey L(ance) 1947- ... CANR-18
Earlier sketch in CA 101
Etheridge, Eugene Wesley 1925- ... 7-8R
Etherington, Charles Leslie 1903- ... 7-8R
Etherton, Michael (James) 1939- ... 121
Ethridge, James M(erritt) 1921- ... 114
Ethridge, Mark Foster 1896-1981 Obituary ... 103
Ethridge, Mark Foster, Jr. 1924-1985
Obituary ... 115
Ethridge, Willie Snow 1900-1983(?) ... 17-18R
Obituary ... 108
See also AITN 1
Etienne
See King-Hall, (William) Stephen (Richard)
Etkin, Anne (Dunwody Little) 1923- ... 73-76
Etmekjian, James 1915- ... CANR-3
Earlier sketch in CA 5-6R
Eton, Robert
See Meynell, Laurence Walter
Etra, Jonathan 1952- ... 102
Ets, Marie Hall 1893- ... CANR-4
Earlier sketch in CA 3R
See also SATA 2
See also DLB 22
Ets-Hokin, Judith Diane 1938- ... 61-64
Etteldorf, Raymond P. 1911- ... 9-10R
Etter, Dave 1928- ... CANR-24
Earlier sketches in CA 19-20R, CANR-8
Etter, Les(ter Frederick) 1904- ... 25-28R
Etter, Patricia A. 1932- ... 120
Ettin, Andrew V(ogel) 1943- ... 124
Ettinger, Elzbieta 1925- ... 29-32R
Ettinger, Richard Prentice 1893-1971
Obituary ... 29-32R
Ettinger, Robert C(hester) W(ilson)
1918- ... 15-16R
Ettinghausen, Maurice Leon 1883-1974
Obituary ... 116
Ettinghausen, Richard 1906-1979 ... CANR-9
Obituary ... 85-88
Earlier sketch in CA 65-68
Ettleson, Abraham 1897- ... CAP-2
Earlier sketch in CA 23-24
Ettlinger, Gerard H(erman) 1935- ... 61-64
Ettlinger, L(eopold) D(avid) 1913-
Brief entry ... 111
Etulain, Richard W(ayne) 1938- ... CANR-16
Earlier sketches in CA 45-48, CANR-1
Etzioni, Amitai (Werner) 1929- ... CANR-22
Earlier sketches in CA 2R, CANR-5
Etzioni, Minerva M(orales) 1938(?)-1985
Obituary ... 118
Etzkorn, K(laus) Peter 1932- ... 49-52
Etzkowitz, Henry 1940- ... 25-28R
Etzold, Thomas H(erman) 1945- ... CANR-14
Earlier sketch in CA 81-84
Eubank, (Weaver) Keith (Jr.) 1920- ... CANR-2
Earlier sketch in CA 7-8R
Eubank, Nancy 1934- ... 41-44R
Eubanks, Ralph T(ravis) 1920- ... 17-18R
Eucken, Rudolf (Christof) 1846-1926
Brief entry ... 119
Eulau, Heinz 1915- Brief entry ... 107
Eulenspiegel, Alexander
See Shea, Robert (Joseph)
Eulert, Don(ald Dean) 1935- ... CANR-18
Earlier sketches in CA 49-52, CANR-2
Euller, John E(lmer) 1926- ... 9-10R
Eulo, Ken 1939- Brief entry ... 109
Eunson, (John) Dale 1904- ... 41-44R
See also SATA 5
Eunson, Robert C(harles) 1912-1975 ... 13-14R
Obituary ... 61-64
Euphan
See Todd, Barbara Euphan
Euphemides, Aristos
See von Koerber, Hans Nordewin
Eurich, Alvin C(hristian) 1902-1987 ... 17-18R
Obituary ... 123
Eurich, Nell 1919- ... CANR-12
Earlier sketch in CA 73-76
European
See Mosley, Oswald (Ernald)
Eusden, John (Dykstra) 1922- ... 45-48
Eustace, Cecil John 1903- ... 49-52
Eustace, May (Corcoran) 1904- ... 7-8R
Eustace, Robert
See Barton, Eustace Robert
Eustis, Alvin Allen, Jr. 1917- ... 102
Eustis, Laurette
See Murdock, Laurette P.
Eustis, O. B.
See Eustis, Orville B.
Eustis, Orville B. 1913-1986 ... 124
Euwe, Machgielis 1901-1981 Obituary ... 105
Euwe, Max
See Euwe, Machgielis
Evain, Elaine 1931- ... 57-60
Evan, Carol
See Goldsmith, Carol Evan
Evan, Evin
See Faust, Frederick (Shiller)
Evan, William (Martin) 1922- ... CANR-2
Earlier sketch in CA 3R
Evang, Karl 1902- ... 65-68
Evanier, David Brief entry ... 108
Evanoff, Vlad 1916- ... CANR-6
Earlier sketch in CA 5-6R
Evans, A(lfred) Alexander 1905- ... CAP-1
Earlier sketch in CA 9-10
Evans, Abbie Huston 1881- ... 57-60
Evans, Alan
See Stoker, Alan
Evans, Albert 1917- ... 85-88
Evans, Alice Frazer 1939- ... 112
Evans, Arthur Bruce 1948- ... 61-64
Evans, Barbara Lloyd
See Lloyd Evans, Barbara
Evans, Benjamin Ifor 1899-1982 Obituary ... 107
Evans, Bennett
See Berger, Ivan (Bennett)
Evans, Bergen (Baldwin) 1904-1978 ... CANR-4
Obituary ... 77-80
Earlier sketch in CA 5-6R
Evans, C(harles) Stephen 1948- ... CANR-13
Earlier sketch in CA 33-36R
Evans, (Jean) Cherry (Drummond) 1928- ... CAP-1
Earlier sketch in CA 9-10
Evans, Christopher (Riche) 1931-1979 ... 102
Evans, Clifford 1916(?)-1983 Obituary ... 110
Evans, Constance May 1890- ... 11-12R
Evans, D(avid) Ellis 1930- ... CANR-16
Earlier sketch in CA 25-28R
Evans, Dale
See Rogers, Dale Evans
Evans, David Allan 1940- ... 49-52
Evans, David Beecher 1928- Brief entry ... 105
Evans, David Huhn, Jr. 1944- ... 110
Evans, David R(ussell) 1937- ... CANR-17
Earlier sketch in CA 33-36R
Evans, David R(ichard) 1940- ... 116
Evans, David S(tanley) 1916- ... 41-44R
Evans, Debra 1953- ... 122
Evans, Don 1938- ... 111
Evans, Donald 1884-1921 Brief entry ... 123
See also DLB 54
Evans, Donald (Dwight) 1927- ... 41-44R
Evans, Donald P(aul) 1930- ... CANR-7
Earlier sketch in CA 57-60
Evans, Dorinda 1944- ... 121
Evans, E(myr) Estyn 1905- ... CANR-5
Earlier sketch in CA 5-6R
Evans, E(dward) Everett 1893-1958
Brief entry ... 113
Evans, Edward G(ordon), Jr. 1916- ... 45-48
Evans, Eli N. 1936- ... 45-48
See also AITN 1
Evans, Elizabeth 1932- ... 53-56
Evans, Ellen
See Du Breuil, (Elizabeth) L(or)inda
Evans, Emerald
See Du Breuil, (Elizabeth) L(or)inda
Evans, Eric J(ohn) 1945- ... 108
Evans, Eva (Knox) 1905- ... 73-76
See also SATA 27
Evans, Evan
See Faust, Frederick (Shiller)
Evans, F.M.G.
See Higham, Florence May Grier
Evans, (Francis) Fallon 1925- ... 1R
Evans, Fanny-Maude 1914- ... 117
Evans, Frances Monet Carter
See Carter, Frances Monet
Evans, Frank Bernard 1927- ... 114
Evans, G(ayle) Edward 1937- ... 33-36R
Evans, G(eraint) N(antglyn) D(avies)
1935-1971 ... CAP-2
Earlier sketch in CA 33-36
Evans, Gareth Lloyd
See Lloyd Evans, Gareth
Evans, Geoffrey (Charles) 1901-1987 ... 19-20R
Obituary ... 121
Evans, George Bird 1906- ... CANR-2
Earlier sketch in CA 2R
Evans, George Ewart 1909-1988(?) ... 61-64
Obituary ... 124
Evans, George Henry 1805-1856 ... DLB-43
Evans, George W(illiam) II 1920- ... 21-22R
Evans, Glen 1921- ... 85-88
Evans, Gordon H(eyd) 1930- ... 15-16R
Evans, Gwynfor 1912- ... 61-64
Evans, Harold 1911-1983 Obituary ... 109
Evans, Harold Matthew 1928- ... 41-44R
Evans, Harris
See Evans, George Bird
and Evans, Kay Harris
Evans, Herndon J. 1895-1976 ... 69-72
Evans, Hilary 1929- ... CANR-20
Earlier sketches in CA 3R, CANR-5
Evans, Howard Ensign 1919- ... CANR-6
Earlier sketch in CA 7-8R
Evans, Hubert Reginald 1892-1986 ... 103
Obituary ... 119
See also SATA 48
Evans, Humphrey (Marshall, Jr.) 1914- ... 29-32R
Evans, I(drisyn) O(liver) 1894-1977 ... CANR-15
Earlier sketch in CA 13-14R
Evans, Idella M(arie Crowe) 1924- ... 29-32R
Evans, Ilona 1918(?)-1980 Obituary ... 102
Evans, J(ames) A(llan) S(tewart) 1931- ... 37-40R
Evans, J. Martin 1935- ... 85-88
Evans, J(ack) N(aunton) 1920- ... 25-28R
Evans, J(ohn) Robert 1942- ... CANR-7
Earlier sketch in CA 57-60
Evans, Jacob A. 1920- ... 25-28R
Evans, James Allen 1926(?)-1983
Obituary ... 110
Evans, Jay 1925- ... 61-64
Evans, Jean 1939- ... 102
Evans, Jessica
See Lottman, Eileen
Evans, Joan 1893-1977 ... 15-16R
Obituary ... 73-76
Evans, John
See Browne, Howard
Evans, John Lewis 1930- ... 85-88
Evans, John W(alker) 1904- ... 33-36R
Evans, John X(avier) 1933- ... 37-40R
Evans, Jonathan
See Freemantle, Brian Harry
Evans, Joseph S., Jr. 1909(?)-1978 ... 85-88
Obituary ... 81-84
Evans, Joseph W(illiam) 1921- ... 23-24R
Evans, Julia (Rendel) 1913- ... 15-16R
Evans, K(athleen) M(arianne) 1911- ... 9-10R
Evans, Katherine (Floyd) 1901-1964 ... 5-6R
See also SATA 5
Evans, Kay Harris 1906- ... CANR-2
Earlier sketch in CA 2R
Evans, (Cyril) Kenneth 1917- ... 53-56
Evans, Kenneth R. 1938- Brief entry ... 110
Evans, Laurence 1923- ... 37-40R
Evans, Lawrence Watt 1954- ... 102
Evans, Lloyd (Lloyd Thomas) 1927- ... 69-72
Evans, Louis Hadley, Sr. 1897-1981 ... 116
Evans, Luther Harris 1902-1981 ... CANR-9
Obituary ... 106
Earlier sketch in CA 17-18R
Evans, M(edford) Stanton 1934- ... 65-68
Evans, Mari ... CANR-2
Earlier sketch in CA 49-52
See also SATA 10
See also DLB 41
Evans, Mark ... 65-68
See also SATA 19
Evans, Marvin R(ussell) 1915- ... 49-52
Evans, Mary 1946- ... 122
Evans, Mary Ann
See Eliot, George
Evans, Max 1925- ... CANR-1
Earlier sketch in CA 4R
Evans, Medford (Bryon) 1907- ... 25-28R
Evans, Mel 1912(?)-1984 Obituary ... 112
Evans, Melbourne G(riffith) 1912- ... CAP-2
Earlier sketch in CA 33-36
Evans, Morgan
See Davies, L(eslie) P(urnell)
Evans, N(orman) Dean 1925- ... CANR-13
Earlier sketch in CA 21-22R
Evans, Nancy 1950- ... 77-80
Evans, Nathaniel 1742-1767 ... DLB-31
Evans, Oliver 1915- ... 19-20R
Evans, Patricia Healy
See Carpenter, Patricia (Healy Evans)
Evans, Paul Richer 1925- Brief entry ... 106
Evans, Philip 1944- Brief entry ... 110
Evans, Rand B(oyd) 1942- Brief entry ... 107
Evans, Richard 1939- ... 106
Evans, Richard Evan 1898-1983 Obituary ... 109
Evans, Richard I(sadore) 1922-
Brief entry ... 108
Evans, Richard L(ouis) 1906-1971 ... 11-12R
Obituary ... 103
Evans, Robert Allen 1937- ... 112
Evans, Robert F(ranklin) 1930-1974 ... CAP-2
Earlier sketch in CA 23-24
Evans, Robert Henry 1937- ... 23-24R
Evans, Robert, Jr. 1932- ... 19-20R
Evans, Robert L(eonard) 1917- ... 49-52
Evans, Robert Owen 1919- ... 13-14R
Evans, Robert P. 1918- ... 13-14R
Evans, Rodney E(arl) 1939- ... 49-52
Evans, Rowland, Jr. 1921- ... CANR-15
Earlier sketch in CA 23-24R
Evans, Rupert N. 1921- ... 37-40R
Evans, Sara 1943- ... 93-96
Evans, Sebastian 1830-1909 ... DLB-35

Evans, Shirlee 1931- 61-64
Evans, Stanley G(eorge) 1912-1965 ...... CAP-1
Earlier sketch in CA 9-10
Evans, Stuart 1934- 124
Brief entry 118
Evans, Susan H(ope) 1951- 115
Evans, Tabor
See Cameron, Lou
and Knott, William C(ecil, Jr.)
Evans, Thomas W(illiam) 1930- 45-48
Evans, Travers Moncure 1938- 57-60
Evans, Virginia Moran 1909- CANR-5
Earlier sketch in CA 7-8R
Evans, W(illiam) Glyn 1918- 89-92
Evans, W(illiam) McKee 1923- 23-24R
Evans, Walker 1903-1975 Obituary 89-92
Evans, (William Edis) Webster 1908- 41-44R
Evans, Wilbur 1913- 97-100
Evans, William 1895- 81-84
Evans, William David 1912-1985 Obituary .. 117
Evans, William Howard 1924- 23-24R
Evans, William R. 1938- 105
Evans Davies, Gloria 1932- 7-8R
Evansen, Virginia Besaw 1921- 13-14R
Evans-Jones, Albert 1895- 7-8R
Evans-Pritchard, Edward Evan 1902-1973 ..65-68
Evarts, Esther
See Benson, Sally
Evarts, Hal G(eorge) 1887-1934
Brief entry 121
Evarts, Hal G. (Jr.) 1915- CANR-2
Earlier sketch in CA 49-52
See also SATA 6
Eve, Barbara
See Reiss, Barbara Eve
Eveland, Bill
See Eveland, Wilbur Crane
Eveland, Wilbur Crane 1918- 101
Eveling, (Harry) Stanley 1925- 61-64
Evely, Louis 1910- 85-88
Evelyn, Anthony
See Ward-Thomas, Evelyn Bridget
Patricia Stephens
Evelyn, (John) Michael 1916- CANR-22
Earlier sketches in CA 5-6R, CANR-6
Evenhuis, Gertie 1932- 107
Evered, James F(letcher) 1928- 107
Everest, Allan S(eymour) 1913- CANR-11
Earlier sketch in CA 29-32R
Everett, Alexander Hill 1790-1847 ...... DLB-59
Everett, Arthur (W., Jr.) 1914- 103
Everett, Donald E(dward) 1920- 9-10R
Everett, Edward 1794-1865 .... DLB-1, 59
Everett, Gail
See Hale, Arlene
Everett, Glenn D. 1921- 69-72
Everett, Peter 1931- 69-72
Everett, Peter W(illiam) 1924- 15-16R
Everett, T(homas) H(enry) 1903(?)-1986
Obituary 120
Everett, Walter 1936- 93-96
Everett-Green, Evelyn 1856-1932
Brief entry 114
Evergood, Philip 1901-1973 Obituary 41-44R
Everhart, James W(illiam), Jr. 1924- 89-92
Everhart, Jim
See Everhart, James W(illiam), Jr.
Everitt, Alan (Milner) 1926- CANR-11
Earlier sketch in CA 21-22R
Everitt, Arva Graham Johnson
1916(?)-1982 Obituary 107
Everitt, Bridget Mary 1924- 45-48
Everitt, C(harles) W(illiam) F(rancis)
1934- 65-68
Everitt, David Samuel 1952- 110
Everman, Welch D(uane) 1946- 57-60
Evernden, Margery 1916- 5-6R
See also SATA 5
Evers, (James) Charles 1923(?)-
Brief entry 111
Evers, Christopher 1940- 122
Eversley, D(avid) E(dward) C(harles)
1921- CANR-1
Earlier sketch in CA 4R
Eversole, Finley T. 1933- 9-10R
Everson, Dale Millar 1928- 17-18R
Everson, David H. 1941- 124
Everson, Ida Gertrude 1898- 37-40R
Everson, R(onald) G(ilmour) 1903- 19-20R
See also CLC 27
Everson, William (Oliver) 1912- CANR-20
Earlier sketch in CA 9-10R
See also DLB 5, 16
See also CLC 1, 5, 14
Everson, William Keith 1929- CANR-2
Earlier sketch in CA 4R
Everton, Macduff 1947- 104
Evertts, Eldonna L(ouise) 1917- 21-22R
Everwine, Peter Paul 1930- 73-76
Every, George 1909- CANR-6
Earlier sketch in CA 13-14R
Eves, Douglas 1922- 119
Evetts, Julia 1944- 69-72
Evins, Joseph Landon 1910- 61-64
Evitts, William J(oseph) 1942- 121
Brief entry 112
EVOE
See Knox, Edmund George Valpy
Evoy, John J(oseph) 1911- 5-6R
Evslin, Bernard 1922- CANR-9
Earlier sketch in CA 23-24R
See also SATA 28, 45
Evslin, Dorothy 1923- 57-60
Evtushenko, Evgenii Aleksandrovich
See Yevtushenko, Yevgeny
(Alexandrovich)
Ewald, Wendy Taylor 1951- 120
Ewald, William Bragg, Jr. 1925- 107
Ewart, Andrew 1911- 17-18R
Ewart, Charles
See Lyte, Charles
Ewart, Gavin (Buchanan) 1916- CANR-17
Earlier sketch in CA 89-92
See also DLB 40
See also CLC 13, 46
Ewbank, Henry L(ee), Jr. 1924- 73-76
Ewbank, Walter F(rederick) 1918- CANR-17
Earlier sketch in CA 25-28R
Ewell, Barbara C(laire) 1947- 114
Ewell, Judith 1943- 107
Ewen, David 1907-1985 .... CANR-2
Obituary 118
Earlier sketch in CA 3R
See also SATA 4, 47
Ewen, Elizabeth 1943- 124
Ewen, Frederic 1899- 73-76
Ewen, Robert B. 1940- CANR-15
Earlier sketch in CA 37-40R
Ewen, Stuart 1945- CANR-12
Earlier sketch in CA 69-72
Ewens, James 1939- 116
Ewers, Hanns Heinz 1871-1943
Brief entry 109
See also TCLC 12
Ewers, John C(anfield) 1909- CANR-22
Earlier sketches in CA 19-20R, CANR-7
Ewert, David 1922- 105
Ewing, Alfred Cyril 1899-1973 .... CANR-4
Earlier sketch in CA 5-6R
Ewing, David Walkley 1923- CANR-5
Earlier sketch in CA 1R
Ewing, Donald M. 1895(?)-1978
Obituary 81-84
Ewing, Elizabeth 1904- 41-44R
Ewing, Frederick R.
See Sturgeon, Theodore Hamilton
Ewing, George W(ilmeth) 1923- 45-48
Ewing, John Alexander 1923- Brief entry ... 105
Ewing, John Melvin 1925- 53-56
Ewing, John S(inclair) 1916- 13-14R
Ewing, Juliana (Horatia Gatty)
1841-1885 .... SATA-16
See also DLB 21
Ewing, Kathryn 1921- CANR-7
Earlier sketch in CA 61-64
See also SATA 20
Ewing, Sherman 1901-1975 Obituary 57-60
Ewton, Ralph W(aldo), Jr. 1938- 81-84
Ewy, Donna 1934- CANR-14
Earlier sketch in CA 33-36R
Ewy, Rodger 1931- CANR-14
Earlier sketch in CA 33-36R
Exall, Barry
See Nugent, John Peer
Excellent, Matilda
See Farson, Daniel (Negley)
Exell, Frank Kingsley 1902- 5-6R
Exley, Frederick (Earl) 1929- 81-84
See also DLBY 81
See also CLC 6, 11
See also AITN 2
Exley, Jo Ella Powell 1940- 122
Exman, Eugene 1900-1975 .... CAP-1
Obituary 61-64
Earlier sketch in CA 17-18
Ex - R. S. M.
See Lindsay, Harold Arthur
Exton, Clive (Jack Montague) 1930- 61-64
Exton, William, Jr. 1907- 45-48
Eyck, Frank 1921- CANR-11
Earlier sketch in CA 25-28R
Eye, Glen G(ordon) 1904- CANR-2
Earlier sketch in CA 49-52
Eyen, Jerome
See Eyen, Tom
Eyen, Tom 1941- CANR-22
Earlier sketch in CA 25-28R
Eyerly, Jeannette Hyde 1908- CANR-19
Earlier sketches in CA 4R, CANR-4
See also SATA 4
Eyestone, Robert 1942- 41-44R
Eykman, Christoph 1937- 41-44R
Eyles, Wilfred Charles 1891- CAP-2
Earlier sketch in CA 17-18
Eyre, Annette
See Worboys, Anne(tte Isobel) Eyre
Eyre, Dorothy
See McGuire, Leslie Sarah
Eyre, Katherine Wigmore 1901-1970
Obituary 104
See also SATA 26
Eyre, Richard M(elvin) 1944- CANR-13
Earlier sketch in CA 61-64
Eyre, Ronald 1929- 104
Eyre, S(amuel) R(obert) 1922- 23-24R
Eysenck, Hans J(urgen) 1916- CANR-4
Earlier sketch in CA 9-10R
Eysman, Harvey (Allen) 1939- 104
Eyster, C(harles) William 1917- 29-32R
Eyvindson, Peter (Knowles) 1946- 124
Ezekiel, Mordecai J(oseph) B(rill)
1899-1974 65-68
Obituary 53-56
Ezekiel, Nissim 1924- 61-64
Ezekiel, Raphael S. 1931- 53-56
Ezekiel, Tish O'Dowd 1943- CLC-34
Ezell, Harry E(ugene) 1918-1974 .... 3R
Obituary 103
Ezell, John Samuel 1917- 1R
Ezell, Macel D. 1934- 77-80
Ezera, Kalu 1925- 15-16R
Ezergailis, Andrew 1930- 89-92
Ezorsky, Gertrude 89-92
Ezzell, Marilyn 1937- 109
See also SATA 38, 42

F

F.P.A.
See Adams, Franklin P(ierce)
Faas, Larry A(ndrew) 1936- 29-32R
Fabbri, Diego 1911-1980 Obituary 105
Fabbri, Nancy Rash 1940- 103
Fabe, Maxene 1943- 77-80
See also SATA 15
Faber, Adele 1928- 77-80
Faber, Charles F(ranklin) 1926- CANR-12
Earlier sketch in CA 29-32R
Faber, Doris (Greenberg) 1924- CANR-8
Earlier sketch in CA 17-18R
See also SATA 3
Faber, Frederick William 1814-1863 ..... DLB-32
Faber, Harold 1919- CANR-8
Earlier sketch in CA 15-16R
See also SATA 5
Faber, John Henry 1918- 15-16R
Faber, Nancy W(eingarten) 1909-1976 .....5-6R
Obituary 65-68
Faber, Richard Stanley 1924- 61-64
Faber-Kaiser, Andreas 1944- 73-76
Fabian, Donald L(eroy) 1919- 23-24R
Fabian, Josephine C(unningham)
1903-1984 .... CAP-1
Obituary 114
Earlier sketch in CA 9-10
Fabian, Robert (Honey) 1901-1978 81-84
Obituary 77-80
Fabian, Ruth
See Quigley, Aileen
Fabinyi, Andrew 1908-1978 Obituary 108
Fabio, Sarah Webster 1928-1979 ...... CANR-22
Earlier sketch in CA 69-72
Fabisch, Judith Patricia 1938- CANR-19
Earlier sketch in CA 103
Fabos, Julius Gy(ula) 1932- 97-100
Fabre, Genevieve E. 1936- 109
Fabre, Jean Henri (Casimir)
1823-1915 .... SATA-22
Fabre, Michel J(acques) 1933- CANR-16
Earlier sketches in CA 45-48, CANR-1
Fabrega, Horacio, Jr. 1934- 73-76
Fabri, Ralph 1894-1975 .... CAP-2
Obituary 57-60
Earlier sketch in CA 19-20
Fabricand, Burton Paul 1923- 93-96
Fabricant, Carole 1944- 113
Fabricius, Johan (Johannes) 1899- CANR-5
Earlier sketch in CA 53-56
Fabrizio, Ray 1930- 33-36R
Fabrizius, Peter
See Fabry, Joseph B(enedikt)
and Knight, Max
Fabry, Joseph B(enedikt) 1909- 25-28R
Fabrycky, Wolter Joseph 1932- 21-22R
Fabun, Don 1920- 45-48
Fackenheim, Emil L(udwig) 1916- 23-24R
Facklam, Margery (Metz) 1927- CANR-21
Earlier sketches in CA 7-8R, CANR-6
See also SATA 20
Fackler, Eli
See Fackler, Elizabeth
Fackler, Elizabeth 1947- 118
Fackre, Gabriel Joseph 1926- CANR-7
Earlier sketch in CA 17-18R
Facos, James F(rancis) 1924- 41-44R
Factor, Regis A(nthony) 1937- 118
Fader, Daniel 1930- 33-36R
Fader, Shirley Sloan 1931- CANR-14
Earlier sketch in CA 77-80
Faderman, Lillian 1940- CANR-16
Earlier sketch in CA 33-36R
Fadeyev, A.
See Bulgya, Alexander Alexandrovich
Fadeyev, Alexander
See Bulgya, Alexander Alexandrovich
Fadiman, Clifton (Paul) 1904- CANR-9
Earlier sketch in CA 61-64
See also SATA 11
Fadiman, Edwin, Jr. 1925- 29-32R
Fadiman, James 1939- 33-36R
Fadiman, Jeffrey A(ndrew) 1936- 116
Fadner, Frank (Leslie) 1910-1987 ....11-12R
Obituary 123
Faegre, Torvald 1941- 89-92
Faelten, Sharon 1950- CANR-23
Earlier sketch in CA 106
Faessler, Shirley 1921(?)- 106
Fagan, Brian Murray 1936- CANR-14
Earlier sketch in CA 41-44R
Fagan, Edward R(ichard) 1924- CANR-20
Earlier sketches in CA 9-10R, CANR-5
Fage, John Donnelly 1921- CANR-7
Earlier sketch in CA 7-8R
Fagen, Donald 1948- CLC-26
Fagen, Richard R. 1933- CANR-22
Earlier sketches in CA 17-18R, CANR-7
Fagen, Stanley Alan 1936- 102
Fager, Charles E(ugene) 1942- 21-22R
Fagerstrom, Stan 1923- 57-60
Fagg, Elizabeth
See Olds, Elizabeth Fagg
Fagg, John (Edwin) 1916- 81-84
Fagg, William Buller 1914- 102
Fagles, Robert 1933- Brief entry 104
Fagley, Richard M(artin) 1910- 2R
Fagon, Alfred 1937-1986 Obituary 120
Fagothey, Austin 1901- CAP-1
Earlier sketch in CA 11-12
Fague, William Robert 1927- 109
Fagundo, Ana Maria 1938- 37-40R
Fagunwa, D(aniel) O(lorunfemi)
1910(?)-1963 Obituary 116
Fagyas, Maria 33-36R
Faherty, William B(arnaby) 1914- CANR-5
Earlier sketch in CA 7-8R
Fahey, Frank M(ichael) 1917- 101
Fahey, James C(harles) 1903-1974
Obituary 53-56
Fahlstrom, Oyvind (Axel Christian)
1928-1976 Obituary 69-72
Fahnestock, Beatrice Beck 1899(?)-1980
Obituary 97-100
Fahs, Ivan J. 1932- 45-48
Fahs, Sophia Blanche Lyon 1876-1978
Obituary 77-80
Fahy, Christopher 1937- CANR-11
Earlier sketch in CA 69-72
Fain, Haskell 1926- 33-36R
Fain, Tyrus Gerard 1933- 104
Fainlight, Ruth (Esther) 1931- CANR-8
Earlier sketch in CA 19-20R
Fainsod, Merle 1907-1972 .... CAP-1
Obituary 33-36R
Earlier sketch in CA 15-16
Fainstein, Norman Ira 1944- 102
Fainstein, Susan S. 1938- 93-96
Fainzilberg, Ilya Arnoldovich 1897-1937
Brief entry 120
Fair, A. A.
See Gardner, Erle Stanley
Fair, Charles M. 1916- CANR-10
Earlier sketch in CA 15-16R
Fair, Harold L(loyd) 1924- 89-92
Fair, James 1898(?)-1984 Obituary 112
Fair, James R(utherford), Jr. 1920- 29-32R
Fair, Marvin L(uke) 1897(?)-1983
Obituary 110
Fair, Ray C(larence) 1942- 29-32R
Fair, Ronald L. 1932- 69-72
See also DLB 33
See also CLC 18
Fair, Sylvia 1933- 69-72
See also SATA 13
Fairbairn, Ann
See Tait, Dorothy
Fairbairn, Douglas 1926- 33-36R
Fairbairn, Garry L. 1947- 77-80
Fairbairn, Helen
See Southard, Helen Fairbairn
Fairbairn, Ian J(ohn) 1933- 53-56
Fairbairns, Zoe (Ann) 1948- CANR-21
Earlier sketch in CA 103
See also CLC 32
Fairbank, Alfred John 1895-1982 .... CANR-6
Obituary 106
Earlier sketch in CA 7-8R
Fairbank, John K(ing) 1907- CANR-3
Earlier sketch in CA 1R
Fairbanks, Carol 1935- 69-72
Fairbanks, Henry G(eorge) 1914-
Brief entry 112
Fairbrother, Nan 1913-1971 .... CANR-3
Obituary 33-36R
Earlier sketch in CA 7-8R
Fairburn, Eleanor 1928- CANR-8
Earlier sketch in CA 61-64
Fairchild, Hoxie Neale 1894-1973 ....7-8R
Obituary 45-48
Fairchild, John B(urr) 1927- Brief entry 117
Fairchild, Louis W. 1901-1981 Obituary 105
Fairchild, William 73-76
Fairclough, Chris 1951- 112
Faire, Zabrina
See Stevenson, Florence
Fairfax, Ann
See Chesney, Marion
Fairfax, Beatrice
See Manning, Marie
and McCarroll, Marion C(lyde)
Fairfax, Felix
See Gibson, Walter B(rown)
Fairfax, John 1930- 97-100
Fairfax, John 1937- 49-52
Fairfax, Warwick (Oswald) 1901-1987
Obituary 121
Fairfax-Blakeborough, Jack
See Fairfax-Blakeborough, John Freeman
Fairfax-Blakeborough, John Freeman
1883-1978(?) 102
Fairfax-Lucy, Brian (Fulke
Cameron-Ramsay) 1898-1974 .... CAP-2
Earlier sketch in CA 29-32
See also SATA 6, 26
Fairfield, Darrell
See Larkin, Rochelle
Fairfield, John
See Livingstone, Harrison Edward
Fairfield, Leslie P(arke) 1941- Brief entry ... 107
Fairfield, Richard 1937- 41-44R
Fairfield, Roy P(hillip) 1918- 33-36R
Fairhall, David Keir 1934- 103
Fairholme, Elizabeth 1910- 97-100
Fairless, Caroline S. 1947- 105
Fairley, Barker 1887-1986 .... 1R
Obituary 121
Fairley, Irene R. 1940- 73-76
Fairley, James Stewart 1940- 102
Fairley, M(ichael) C(harles) 1937- CANR-14
Earlier sketch in CA 37-40R
Fairley, Peter 1930- CANR-24
Earlier sketch in CA 29-32R
Fairlie, Gerard 1899-1983 Obituary 109
See also SATA 34
Fairlie, Henry (Jones) 1924- 104
Fairman, Charles 1897- 45-48

Fairman, Herbert Walter 1907-1982 ... 111
Obituary ... 108
Fairman, Honora C. 1927(?)-1978
Obituary ... 81-84
Fairman, Joan A(lexandra) 1935- ... 33-36R
See also SATA 10
Fairman, Paul W. 1916-1977 Obituary ... 114
Fairn, (Richard) Duncan 1906-1986
Obituary ... 119
Fairweather, Eugene Rathbone 1920-
Brief entry ... 108
Fairweather, George W. 1921- ... 15-16R
Fairweather, Janet (Anne) 1945- ... 124
Fairweather, Sally (Hallberg) 1917- ... 112
Fairweather, Virginia 1922- ... 29-32R
Faison, S(amson) Lane, Jr. 1907- ... 89-92
Faissler, Margareta 1902- ... 7-8R
Fait, Hollis F. 1918- ... CANR-5
Earlier sketch in CA 1R
Faith, Barbara
See Covarrubias, Barbara Faith
Faith, William Robert
See Fague, William Robert
Faithfull, Gail 1936- ... 57-60
See also SATA 8
Faiz, Faiz Ahmad 1912(?)-1984 Obituary ... 115
Fakhry, Majid 1923- ... 29-32R
Fakinos, Aris 1935- ... 81-84
Falassi, Alessandro 1945- ... 105
Falb, Lewis W(illiam) 1935- ... 102
Falck, (Adrian) Colin 1934- ... 65-68
Falco, Gian
See Papini, Giovanni
Falco, Maria J(osephine) 1932- ... CANR-12
Earlier sketch in CA 61-64
Falcoff, Mark 1941- ... 65-68
Falcon
See Nestle, John Francis
Falcon, Richard
See Shapiro, Samuel
Falcon, Walter Phillip 1936- Brief entry ... 109
Falcon, William D(yche) 1932- ... 17-18R
Falcon-Barker, Ted 1923- ... 25-28R
Falconer, A. F.
See Falconer, Alexander Frederick
Falconer, Alexander Frederick 1908-1987
Obituary ... 122
Falconer, Alun ?-1973 Obituary ... 104
Falconer, James
See Kirkup, James
Falconer, Kenneth
See Kornbluth, C(yril) M.
Falconer, Lee N.
See May, Julian
Falero, Frank, Jr. 1937- ... 37-40R
Fales, Dean Abner, Jr. 1925- Brief entry ... 110
Fales, Edward (Daniel, Jr.) 1906- ... 97-100
Falk, Charles J(ohn) 1899-1971 ... CAP-2
Earlier sketch in CA 23-24
Falk, Doris Virginia 1919- Brief entry ... 111
Falk, Elsa
See Escherich, Elsa Falk
Falk, Eugene H(annes) 1913- ... 116
Falk, Gerhard 1931- ... 117
Falk, Harvey 1932- Brief entry ... 112
Falk, I(sidore) S(ydney) 1899-1984
Obituary ... 114
Falk, Irving A. 1921- ... 23-24R
Falk, Kathryn 1940- ... CANR-20
Earlier sketch in CA 97-100
Falk, Lee Harrison 1915- ... 97-100
Falk, Leslie A. 1915- ... 11-12R
Falk, Louis A. 1896(?)-1979 Obituary ... 85-88
Falk, Marvin W. 1943- ... 122
Falk, Minna Regina 1900-1983 Obituary ... 109
Falk, Pamela S. 1953- ... 122
Falk, Quentin 1948- ... 122
Falk, Richard A(nderson) 1930- ... CANR-12
Earlier sketch in CA 5-6R
Falk, Robert 1914- ... 89-92
Falk, Roger (Salis) 1910- ... 65-68
Falk, S(tephen) J(ohn) 1942- ... 124
Falk, Signi Lenea 1906- ... 7-8R
Falk, Stanley L(awrence) 1927- ... CANR-2
Earlier sketch in CA 3R
Falk, Susan Meyers 1942- ... 117
Falk, Toby
See Falk, S(tephen) J(ohn)
Falk, Ursula Adler ... 114
Falk, Ze'ev W(ilhelm) 1923- ... CANR-15
Earlier sketch in CA 21-22R
Falkender, Baroness Marcia
See Williams, Marcia
Falkirk, Richard
See Lambert, Derek
Falkland, Samuel
See Heijermans, Herman
Falkner, Leonard 1900- ... 23-24R
See also SATA 12
Falkner, Murry (Charles) 1899- ... CAP-2
Earlier sketch in CA 23-24
Falk-Roenne, Arne 1920- ... CANR-14
Earlier sketch in CA 23-24R
Falkus, Hugh Edward Lance 1917- ... 111
Fall, Bernard B. 1926-1967 ... CANR-6
Obituary ... 25-28R
Earlier sketch in CA 4R
Fall, Frieda Kay 1913- ... 41-44R
Fall, Thomas
See Snow, Donald Clifford
Fallaci, Oriana 1930- ... CANR-15
Earlier sketch in CA 77-80
See also CLC 11
Fallada, Hans
See Ditzen, Rudolf
See also DLB 56
Fallaw, Wesner 1907- ... 4R
Faller, Kevin 1920- ... CANR-4
Earlier sketch in CA 53-56
Fallere, Felicia
See Knist, F(rances) Emma
Fallers, Lloyd A(shton, Jr.) 1925-1974 ... CANR-4
Obituary ... 49-52
Earlier sketch in CA 9-10R
Falley, Margaret Dickson 1898-1983
Obituary ... 110
Fallon, Carlos 1909- ... 41-44R
Fallon, Eileen Brydon 1954- ... 118
Fallon, Frederic (Michael) 1944-1970 ... 41-44R
Fallon, George
See Bingley, David Ernest
Fallon, Jack
See Fallon, John W(illiam)
Fallon, John W(illiam) 1924- ... 77-80
Fallon, Martin
See Patterson, Henry
Fallon, Padraic 1905-1974 ... 103
Obituary ... 89-92
Fallon, Peter 1951- Brief entry ... 106
Fallon, Robert T(homas) 1927- ... 121
Fallows, James M(ackenzie) 1949- ... CANR-2
Earlier sketch in CA 45-48
Falls, C(harles) B(uckles) 1874-1960
Obituary ... 116
See also SATA 27, 38
Falls, Cyril Bentham 1888- ... CAP-1
Earlier sketch in CA 13-14
Falls, Joe 1928- ... 77-80
Fallwell, Marshall Leigh, Jr. 1943- ... 69-72
Falorp, Nelson P.
See Jones, Stephen (Phillip)
Falstein, Louis 1909- ... 97-100
See also SATA 37
Faludy, George 1913- ... 21-22R
See also CLC 42
Faludy, Gyoergy
See Faludy, George
Falvey, Jack 1938- ... 122
Falwell, Jerry 1933- ... 102
Fama, Eugene F. 1939- Brief entry ... 113
Famiglietti, Eugene Paul 1931(?)-1980
Obituary ... 97-100
Famularo, Joseph John 1922- ... CANR-4
Earlier sketch in CA 1R
Fan, Kuang Huan 1932- ... 23-24R
Fanburg, Walter H. 1936- Brief entry ... 114
Fancher, Betsy 1928- ... DLBY-83
Fancher, Ewilda 1928- ... 61-64
Fancher, Raymond E(lwood), Jr. 1940- ... 69-72
Fanchon, Lisa
See Floren, Lee
Fancutt, Walter 1911- ... CANR-12
Earlier sketches in CA 9-10, CAP-1
Fandel, John 1925- ... CANR-23
Earlier sketch in CA 69-72
Fane, Bron
See Fanthorpe, R(obert) Lionel
Fane, Julian Charles 1927- ... CANR-6
Earlier sketch in CA 13-14R
Fane, Violet 1843-1905 ... DLB-35
Fang, Chaoying 1908(?)-1985 Obituary ... 116
Fang, Irving E. 1929- ... 49-52
Fang, Josephine (Maria) Riss 1922- ... 69-72
Fanger, Donald (Lee) 1929- ... 15-16R
Fann, K(uang) T(ih) 1937- ... 61-64
Fann, William E(dwin) 1930- ... CANR-2
Earlier sketch in CA 49-52
Fannin, Allen 1939- ... 69-72
Fanning, Buckner 1926- ... 69-72
Fanning, Charles (Frederick, Jr.) 1942- ... 81-84
Fanning, Leonard M(ulliken) 1888-1967 ... 7-8R
See also SATA 5
Fanning, Louis A(lbert) 1927- ... 69-72
Fanning, Michael 1942- ... 89-92
Fanning, Odom 1920- ... 53-56
Fanning, Robbie 1947- ... CANR-14
Earlier sketch in CA 77-80
Fanon, Frantz 1925-1961 ... 116
Obituary ... 89-92
Fanshawe, David 1942- ... 97-100
Fant, Joseph Lewis III 1928- ... 13-14R
Fant, Louis J(udson), Jr. 1931- ... 37-40R
Fanta, J. Julius 1907- ... 33-36R
Fante, John (Thomas) 1911-1983 ... CANR-23
Obituary ... 109
Earlier sketch in CA 69-72
See also DLBY 83
Fantel, Hans 1922- ... 49-52
Fanthorpe, Patricia Alice 1938- ... CANR-14
Earlier sketch in CA 89-92
Fanthorpe, R(obert) Lionel 1935- ... CANR-14
Earlier sketch in CA 73-76
Fantini, Mario D. ... 77-80
Farabee, Barbara 1944- ... 57-60
Faraday, Ann 1935- ... 77-80
Faragher, John Mack 1945- Brief entry ... 111
Farago, Ladislas 1906-1980 ... CANR-10
Obituary ... 102
Earlier sketch in CA 65-68
Farah, Caesar Elie 1929- ... 41-44R
Farah, Madelain 1934- ... 73-76
Farah, Nuruddin 1945- ... 106
Faralla, Dana 1909- ... 49-52
See also SATA 9
Faralla, Dorothy W.
See Faralla, Dana
Faramelli, Norman Joseph 1932-
Brief entry ... 109
Farau, Alfred 1904-1972 Obituary ... 37-40R
Farb, Peter 1929-1980 ... CANR-12
Obituary ... 97-100
Earlier sketch in CA 15-16R
See also SATA 12, 22
Farber, Bernard 1922- ... 23-24R
Farber, Donald C. ... CANR-13
Earlier sketch in CA 29-32R
Farber, Edward (Rolke) 1914-1982
Obituary ... 110
Farber, Joseph C. 1903- ... 33-36R
Farber, Leslie Hillel 1912-1981 ... 110
Obituary ... 103
Farber, Marvin 1901- ... 49-52
Farber, Norma 1909-1984 ... 102
Obituary ... 112
See also SATA 25, 38
See also DLB 61
Farber, Paul Lawrence 1944- ... 112
Farber, Seymour M(organ) 1912- ... 57-60
Farber, Stephen E. 1943- ... CANR-19
Earlier sketch in CA 103
Farber, Susan L. 1945- ... 106
Farber, Thomas (David) 1944- ... 103
Farberman, Harvey A(lan) 1939- ... 45-48
Farberow, Norman L(ouis) 1918- ... CANR-7
Earlier sketch in CA 19-20R
Farca, Marie C. 1935- ... 37-40R
Farel, Conrad
See Bardens, Dennis (Conrad)
Farely, Alison
See Poland, Dorothy (Elizabeth Hayward)
Farer, Tom J. 1935- ... CANR-8
Earlier sketch in CA 17-18R
Farewell, Nina
See Cooper, Mae (Klein)
Fargis, Paul (McKenna) 1939- ... CANR-13
Earlier sketch in CA 21-22R
Fargo, Doone
See Norwood, Victor G(eorge) C(harles)
Fargo, Joe
See Rikhoff, James C.
Fargue, Leon-Paul 1876(?)-1947
Brief entry ... 109
See also TCLC 11
Farhi, Moris 1935- ... CANR-13
Earlier sketch in CA 77-80
Faria, A(nthony) J(ohn) 1944- ... CANR-19
Earlier sketch in CA 102
Faricy, Robert L(eo) 1926- ... CANR-15
Earlier sketch in CA 37-40R
Faridi, S. N.
See Faridi, Shah Nasiruddin Mohammad
Faridi, Shah Nasiruddin Mohammad
1929- ... 29-32R
Faries, Clyde J. 1928- ... 37-40R
Faries, David A(llan) 1938- ... 112
Farigoule, Louis
See Romains, Jules
Farina, John 1950- ... 114
Farina, Richard 1936(?)-1966 ... 81-84
Obituary ... 25-28R
See also CLC 9
Faris, (Earl) Barry 1889-1966 Obituary ... 114
Faris, Robert E. L(ee) 1907- ... 17-18R
Faris, Wendy B(ush) 1945- ... 115
Farish, Donald J(ames) 1942- ... 106
Farish, Margaret Kennedy 1918- ... 7-8R
Farjeon, (Eve) Annabel 1919- ... 53-56
See also SATA 11
Farjeon, Eleanor 1881-1965 ... CAP-1
Earlier sketch in CA 11-12
See also SATA 2
Farkas, Emil 1946- ... 69-72
Farkas, Philip 1914- ... 49-52
Farley, Carol 1936- ... CANR-10
Earlier sketch in CA 21-22R
See also SATA 4
Farley, (William) Edward 1929- ... 61-64
Farley, Eugene J. 1916- ... CANR-12
Earlier sketch in CA 33-36R
Farley, James A(loysius) 1888-1976
Obituary ... 65-68
Farley, Jean 1928- ... 23-24R
Farley, Miriam Southwell 1907(?)-1975
Obituary ... 57-60
Farley, Rawle 1922- ... 45-48
Farley, Walter 1920- ... CANR-8
Earlier sketch in CA 19-20R
See also SATA 2, 43
See also DLB 22
See also CLC 17
Farley-Hills, David 1931- ... 73-76
Farlie, Barbara L(eitzow) 1936- ... 65-68
Farlow, John King
See King-Farlow, John
Farmacevten
See Holm, Sven (Aage)
Farmar, Hugh William 1908-1987
Obituary ... 123
Farmer, Albert J(ohn) 1894-1976 ... 23-24R
Obituary ... 120
Farmer, Bernard James 1902- ... 7-8R
Farmer, Bertram Hughes 1916- ... 104
Farmer, Charles J(oseph) 1943- ... CANR-10
Earlier sketch in CA 57-60
Farmer, Don 1938- ... 65-68
Farmer, Gary R(ay) 1923- ... 57-60
Farmer, Gene 1919-1972 Obituary ... 37-40R
Farmer, Herbert Henry 1892-1981(?)
Obituary ... 102
Farmer, Kathleen 1946- ... CANR-10
Earlier sketch in CA 65-68
Farmer, Laurence 1895(?)-1976 Obituary ... 65-68
Farmer, Martha L(ouise) 1912- ... 23-24R
Farmer, Norman K(ittrell, Jr.) 1934- ... 123
Farmer, Penelope (Jane) 1939- ... CANR-9
Earlier sketch in CA 15-16R
See also SATA 39, 40
See also CLR 8
Farmer, Peter 1950- ... SATA-38
Farmer, Philip Jose 1918- ... CANR-4
Earlier sketch in CA 3R
See also DLB 8
See also CLC 1, 19
Farmer, R. L.
See Lamont, Rosette C(lementine)
Farmer, Richard Neil 1928- ... CANR-8
Earlier sketch in CA 17-18R
Farmer, Robert Allen 1938- ... 23-24R
Farmer, William R(euben) 1921- ... 123
Brief entry ... 109
Farmer Jones
See Jones, Bryan L.
Farmiloe, Dorothy Alicia 1920- ... CANR-8
Earlier sketch in CA 61-64
Farnash, Hugh
See Luff, S(tanley) G(eorge) A(nthony)
Farndale, W(illiam) A(rthur) J(ames)
1916- ... CANR-11
Earlier sketch in CA 25-28R
Farner, Donald S(ankey) 1915- ... 53-56
Farnham, Burt
See Clifford, Harold B(urton)
Farnham, Emily 1912- ... 69-72
Farnham, Marynia F. 1900(?)-1979
Obituary ... 85-88
Farnham, Thomas J(avery) 1938- ... CANR-4
Earlier sketch in CA 53-56
Farnie, D(ouglas) A(ntony) 1926- ... CANR-12
Earlier sketch in CA 73-76
Farnsworth, Clyde A. 1908(?)-1984
Obituary ... 112
Farnsworth, Dana (Lyda) 1905-1986 ... 61-64
Obituary ... 119
Farnsworth, E(dward) Allan 1928- ... 15-16R
Farnsworth, James
See Pohle, Robert W(arren), Jr.
Farnsworth, Jerry 1895- ... CAP-1
Earlier sketch in CA 15-16
Farnsworth, Lee W(infield) 1932- ... 33-36R
Farnsworth, Paul Randolph 1899- ... CAP-2
Earlier sketch in CA 29-32
Farnsworth, Robert M. 1929- ... 53-56
Farnum, K. T.
See Rips, Ervine M(ilton)
Farnworth, Warren 1935- ... 93-96
Farny, Michael H(olt) 1934- ... 65-68
Faron, Louis C. 1923- ... 11-12R
Farquhar, Aardvark Z. 1929- ... 113
Farquhar, Francis P(eloubet) 1887-1975 ... CAP-1
Obituary ... 57-60
Earlier sketch in CA 19-20
Farquhar, Margaret C(utting) 1905- ... 69-72
See also SATA 13
Farquharson, Alexander 1944- ... SATA-46
Farquharson, Charlie
See Harron, Don(ald)
Farquharson, Martha
See Finley, Martha
Farr, Bill
See Farr, William T.
Farr, David M. L. 1922- ... 37-40R
Farr, Diana (Pullein-Thompson) ... CANR-20
Earlier sketches in CA 15-16R, CANR-7
Farr, Dorothy M(ary) 1905- ... 77-80
Farr, Douglas
See Gilford, C(harles) B(ernard)
Farr, Finis (King) 1904-1982 ... CANR-1
Obituary ... 105
Earlier sketch in CA 3R
See also SATA 10
Farr, John
See Webb, Jack (Randolph)
Farr, Judith 1937- ... CANR-12
Earlier sketch in CA 29-32R
Farr, Kenneth R(aymond) 1942- ... 73-76
Farr, Michael 1924- ... 29-32R
Farr, Roger C. ... 33-36R
Farr, Sidney Saylor 1932- ... 114
Farr, Walter Greene, Jr. 1925- Brief entry ... 106
Farr, William T. 1934-1987 Obituary ... 121
Farra, Madame E.
See Fawcett, F(rank) Dubrez
Farrant, Leda 1927- ... 21-22R
Farrar, John C(hipman) 1896-1974 ... 65-68
Obituary ... 53-56
Farrar, Lancelot Leighton, Jr. 1932- ... CANR-4
Earlier sketch in CA 53-56
Farrar, Larston Dawn 1915-1970 ... 2R
Obituary ... 29-32R
Farrar, Margaret Petherbridge 1897-1984
Obituary ... 113
Farrar, Richard B(artlett), Jr. 1939- ... 65-68
Farrar, Ronald T(ruman) 1935- ... 33-36R
Farrar, Rowena Rutherford 1903- ... 108
Farrar, Susan Clement 1917- ... 101
See also SATA 33
Farrar-Hockley, Anthony Heritage 1924- ... 69-72
Farrell, Alan 1920- ... 15-16R
Farrell, Anne A. 1916- ... 25-28R
Farrell, Barry 1935(?)-1984 Obituary ... 114
Farrell, Ben
See Cebulash, Mel
Farrell, Bryan (Henry) 1923- ... CANR-2
Earlier sketch in CA 49-52
Farrell, C(larence) Frederick, Jr. 1934- ... 122
Farrell, Catharine
See O'Connor, Sister Mary Catharine
Farrell, Cliff 1899- ... 65-68
Farrell, David
See Smith, Frederick E(screet)
Farrell, Desmond
See Organ, John
Farrell, Edith R(odgers) 1933- ... 122
Farrell, Edmund J(ames) 1927- ... 120
Farrell, Francis (Thomas) 1912-1983
Obituary ... 109

Farrell, Frank
See Farrell, Francis (Thomas)
Farrell, J(ames) G(ordon) 1935-1979 73-76
Obituary 89-92
See also DLB 14
See also CLC 6
Farrell, James T(homas) 1904-1979 ..... CANR-9
Obituary 89-92
Earlier sketch in CA 5-6R
See also DLB 4, 9
See also DLBD 2
See also CLC 1, 4, 8, 11
Farrell, John J(oseph) 1934- Brief entry 110
Farrell, John Philip 1939- 102
Farrell, Kathleen (Amy) 1912- 7-8R
Farrell, Kirby 1942- 33-36R
Farrell, M. J.
See Keane, Mary Nesta (Skrine)
Farrell, Matthew Charles 1921- 49-52
Farrell, Melvin L(loyd) 1930- CANR-5
Earlier sketch in CA 13-14R
Farrell, Michael 1944- CANR-23
Earlier sketch in CA 69-72
Farrell, Patricia
See Zelver, Patricia (Farrell)
Farrell, Robert T(homas) 1938- 93-96
Farrell, Susan Caust 1944- 112
Farrell, William E. 1936(?)-1985 Obituary 115
Farrelly, M(ark) John 1927- 15-16R
Farren, David
See McFerran, Douglass David
Farren, Richard J.
See Betjeman, John
Farrer, Claire R(afferty) 1936- CANR-10
Earlier sketch in CA 65-68
Farrer, (Bryan) David 1906-1983 ..... 25-28R
Obituary 109
Farrer, Katharine Dorothy (Newton) 1911- 7-8R
Farrer, Keith Thomas Henry 1916- 110
Farrimond, John 1913- 102
Farrington, Benjamin 1891-1974 65-68
Obituary 53-56
See also SATA 20
Farrington, (Mary) Elizabeth Pruett
1898-1984 Obituary 113
Farrington, S(elwyn) Kip, Jr. 1904-1983 73-76
Obituary 109
See also SATA 20
Farris, John 101
Farris, Martin T(heodore) 1925- CANR-11
Earlier sketch in CA 21-22R
Farris, Paul L(eonard) 1919- 11-12R
Farrison, William Edward 1902- 29-32R
Farriss, N(ancy) M(arguerite) 1938- 25-28R
Farrow, J.
See Fonarow, Jerry
Farrow, James S.
See Tubb, E(dwin) C(harles)
Farson, Daniel (Negley) 1927- CANR-16
Earlier sketch in CA 93-96
Farson, (James Scott) Negley 1890-1960
Obituary 93-96
Farstad, Arthur L(eonard) 1935- 109
Farthing, Alison 1936- 117
See also SATA 36, 45
Farwell, Byron E. 1921- CANR-9
Earlier sketch in CA 15-16R
Farwell, George Michell 1911-1976 ..... 21-22R
Obituary 69-72
Farwell, Loring C(hapman) 1915-
Brief entry 111
Farzan, Massud 1936- 53-56
Fasana, Paul James 1933- CANR-14
Earlier sketch in CA 37-40R
Fasel, George W(illiam) 1938- 23-24R
Fasold, Ralph W(illiam August) 1940- 29-32R
Fass, Paula S. 1947- Brief entry 112
Fassbinder, Rainer Werner 1946-1982 93-96
Obituary 106
See also CLC 20
Fassett, James 1904-1986 49-52
Obituary 121
Fassler, Joan (Grace) 1931- 61-64
See also SATA 11
Fast, Barbara 1924- 104
Fast, Howard (Melvin) 1914- CANR-1
Earlier sketch in CA 2R
See also SATA 7
See also DLB 9
See also CLC 23
Fast, Jonathan David 1948- 77-80
Fast, Julius 1919- CANR-11
Earlier sketch in CA 25-28R
Fastlife
See Grogan, Emmett
Fatchen, Max 1920- CANR-11
Earlier sketch in CA 25-28R
See also SATA 20
Fate, Terry 1949- 116
Fatemi, Nasrollah S(aifpour) 1910- 77-80
Father Xavier
See Hurwood, Bernhardt J.
Fatigati, (Frances) Evelyn 1948- 77-80
See also SATA 24
Fatio, Louise 1904- 37-40R
See also SATA 6
Fatjo, Thomas Joseph, Jr. 1940- 107
Fatouros, A(rghyrios) A. 1932- 15-16R
Fatout, Paul 1897- 23-24R
Fatt, Amelia 1943- 118
Faucher, Real 1940- 101
Faucher, W. Thomas 1945- 57-60
Faulhaber, Charles Bailey 1941- 53-56
Faulhaber, Martha 1926- 33-36R
See also SATA 7
Faulk, John Henry 1913- 102
Faulk, Odie B. 1933- CANR-14
Earlier sketch in CA 25-28R
Faulkner, Alex 1905(?)-1983 Obituary 109
Faulkner, Anne Irvin 1906- CANR-2
Earlier sketch in CA 4R
See also SATA 23
Faulkner, Charles H. 1937- 25-28R
Faulkner, Edwin J. 1900(?)-1987 Obituary 121
Faulkner, Elsie 1905- 65-68
Faulkner, Frank
See Ellis, Edward S(ylvester)
Faulkner, Harold Underwood 1890-1968 ..... 1R
Obituary 103
Faulkner, John 1901-1963 ..... CANR-1
Earlier sketch in CA 2R
Faulkner, Joseph E. 1928- 45-48
Faulkner, Nancy
See Faulkner, Anne Irvin
Faulkner, Peter 1933- CANR-20
Earlier sketches in CA 7-8R, CANR-3
Faulkner, Ray (Nelson) 1906- 5-6R
Faulkner, Trader 1930- 102
Faulkner, Virginia (Louise) 1913-1980 ..... CANR-11
Earlier sketch in CA 65-68
Faulkner, (Herbert Winthrop) Waldron
1898-1979 93-96
Obituary 85-88
Faulkner, William (Cuthbert) 1897-1962 81-84
See also DLB 9, 11, 44
See also DLBY 86
See also DLBD 2
See also CLC 1, 3, 6, 8, 9, 11, 14, 18, 28
See also SSC 1
Faulknor, Cliff(ord Vernon) 1913- CANR-8
Earlier sketch in CA 19-20R
Faulks, Neville 1908-1985 Obituary 118
Faunce, Roland Cleo 1905- 1R
Faunce, William A(lden) 1928- 25-28R
Faunce-Brown, Daphne (Bridget) 1938- 115
Faupel, John F(rancis) 1906- 7-8R
Faure, Lucie 1908-1977 Obituary 73-76
Faure, William C(aldwell), Jr. 1949- 109
Faurot, Albert 1914- 77-80
Faurot, Jean H(iatt) 1911- 29-32R
Faurot, Jeannette 1943- 106
Faurot, Ruth Marie 1916- 85-88
Fauset, Arthur Huff 25-28R
Fauset, Jessie Redmon 1884(?)-1961 109
See also DLB 51
See also CLC 19
Fausold, Martin L. 1921- 23-24R
Fausset, Hugh I'Anson 1895-1965
Obituary 93-96
Faust, Clarence H(enry) 1901-1975
Obituary 57-60
Faust, Drew Gilpin 1947- 110
Faust, Frederick (Shiller) 1892-1944(?)
Brief entry 108
Faust, Irvin 1924- 33-36R
See also DLB 2, 28
See also DLBY 80
See also CLC 8
Faust, Naomi F(lowe) 61-64
Fausti, Remo P(hilip) 1917- 41-44R
Fauth, Robert T. 1916- 1R
Fautsko, Timothy F(rank) 1945- 85-88
Faux, Marian 1945- CANR-14
Earlier sketch in CA 81-84
Fava, Sylvia Fleis 1927- 115
Faverty, Frederic Everett 1902-1981 45-48
Obituary 104
Faville, David Ernest 1899-1970 ..... 1R
Obituary 103
Favret, Andrew G. 1925- 19-20R
Favretti, Rudy J(ohn) 1932- CANR-4
Earlier sketch in CA 53-56
Fawcett, Brian 1906- 102
Fawcett, Chris 1950- 107
Fawcett, Clara Hallard 1887- CAP-1
Earlier sketch in CA 15-16
Fawcett, Claude W(eldon) 1911- 49-52
Fawcett, F(rank) Dubrez 1891-1968 ..... CAP-1
Earlier sketch in CA 9-10
Fawcett, J(ames) E(dmund) S(anford)
1913- 97-100
Fawcett, Ken(neth Richard) 1944- 104
Fawcett, Marion
See Sanderson, Sabina W(arren)
Fawcett, Robin P(owell) 1937- 119
Fawcett, Roger Knowlton 1909-1979
Obituary 89-92
Fawkes, Guy
See Benchley, Robert (Charles)
Fawkes, Richard (Brian) 1944- CANR-20
Earlier sketch in CA 103
Fax, Elton Clay 1909- CANR-15
Earlier sketch in CA 13-14R
See also SATA 25
Faxon, Alicia Craig 1931- 69-72
Faxon, Arba D. 1895(?)-1975 Obituary 61-64
Faxon, Lavinia
See Russ, Lavinia
Fay, Allen 1934- 123
Brief entry 118
Fay, Erica
See Stopes, Marie (Charlotte) Carmichael
Fay, Frederic L(eighton) 1890- CAP-2
Earlier sketch in CA 21-22
Fay, Gerard (Francis Arthur) 1913-1968 ..... CAP-1
Earlier sketch in CA 15-16
Fay, Gordon S(haw) 1912- 53-56
Fay, John 1921- 57-60
Fay, Leo (Charles) 1920- 15-16R
Fay, Mary Helen
See Fagyas, Maria
Fay, Peter Ward 1924- 57-60
Fay, S(amuel) P(rescott), Jr. 1926- 89-92
Fay, Stanley
See Stanley, Fay Grissom (Shulman)
Fay, Stephen 1938- 25-28R
Fay, Thomas A(rthur) 1927- 102
Faye, Jean Pierre 1925- 102
Fayer, Mischa Harry 1902-1977 ..... CANR-6
Earlier sketch in CA 1R
Fayerweather, John 1922- CANR-1
Earlier sketch in CA 3R
Fazakas, Ray 1932- 101
Fazakerley, George Raymond 1921- 13-14R
Fazal, M(uhammad) A(bul) 1939- 29-32R
Fazzano, Joseph E. 1929- 7-8R
Feagans, Lynne 1945- 117
Feagans, Raymond (John) 1953- 57-60
Feagin, Joe R(ichard) 1938- CANR-13
Earlier sketch in CA 37-40R
Feagles, Anita M(acRae) 1927- CANR-4
Earlier sketch in CA 4R
See also SATA 9
Feagles, Elizabeth
See Day, Beth (Feagles)
Feague, Mildred H. 1915- 29-32R
See also SATA 14
Feal-Deibe, Carlos 1935- 37-40R
Fear, David E. 1941- 53-56
Fear Chanaidh
See Campbell, John Lorne
Fearing, Kenneth (Flexner) 1902-1961 93-96
See also DLB 9
Fearon, George Edward 1901- CAP-1
Earlier sketch in CA 9-10
Fearon, John D(aniel) 1920- 37-40R
Fearon, Peter (Shaun) 1942- 29-32R
Fears, Gerald 81-84
Feather, John 1947- 122
Feather, Leonard G(eoffrey) 1914- 61-64
Feather, Norman 1904-1978 Obituary 111
Feather, Norman T(homas) 1930- 73-76
Featherstone, D.
See Warren, David
Featherstone, Helen 1944- 102
Featherstone, Joseph (Luke) 1940- 33-36R
Featherstonehaugh, Francis
See MacGregor, Alasdair Alpin (Douglas)
Feaver, George (Arthur) 1937- 29-32R
Feaver, J(ohn) Clayton 1911- CAP-2
Earlier sketch in CA 25-28
Feaver, William Andrew 1942- 103
Fecamps, Elise
See Creasey, John
Fecher, Charles A(dam) 1917- 81-84
Fecher, Constance
See Heaven, Constance
Fechter, Alyce Shinn 1909- CAP-1
Earlier sketch in CA 15-16
Feck, Luke 1935- 69-72
Fedde, Norman A(ndreas) 1914- 7-8R
Fedden, Henry (Romilly) 1908- 9-10R
Fedden, Robin
See Fedden, Henry (Romilly)
Fedder, Edwin H(ersh) 1929- 37-40R
Fedder, Norman J(oseph) 1934- CANR-9
Earlier sketch in CA 21-22R
Fedder, Ruth 1907- CANR-2
Earlier sketch in CA 5-6R
Feder, Bernard 1924- CANR-15
Earlier sketch in CA 33-36R
Feder, Ernest 1913- 37-40R
Feder, Jane 1940- 93-96
Feder, Jose 1917- 105
Feder, Karah (Tal) 1920- 17-18R
Feder, Lillian 41-44R
Feder, Paula (Kurzband) 1935- 105
See also SATA 26
Feder, Robert Arthur 1909-1969 Obituary 110
See also SATA 35
Federbusch, Simon
See Federbush, Simon
Federbush, Arnold 1935- 104
Federbush, Simon 1892(?)-1969 Obituary 115
Federico, Ronald Charles 1941- 89-92
Federman, Raymond 1928- CANR-10
Earlier sketch in CA 17-18R
See also DLBY 80
See also CLC 6, 47
Federoff, Alexander 1927(?)-1979
Obituary 89-92
Federspiel, J(uerg) F. 1931- CLC-42
Fedin, Konstantin A(lexandrovich)
1892-1977 81-84
Obituary 73-76
Fedler, Fred 1940- 97-100
Fedoroff, Alexander 1927-1979 ..... CANR-5
Earlier sketch in CA 3R
Fedorov, Yevgeny Konstantinovich
1910-1981 Obituary 106
Feduccia, (John) Alan 1943- 124
Fedyshyn, Oleh S(ylvester) 1928- 49-52
Fee, Gordon D(onald) 1934- 117
Feegel, John R(ichard) 1932- CANR-9
Earlier sketch in CA 57-60
Feeley, Kathleen 1929- 33-36R
Feeley, Malcolm McCollum 1942-
Brief entry 105
Feeley, Pat(ricia Falk) 1941- 81-84
Feelings, Muriel (Grey) 1938- 93-96
See also SATA 16
See also CLR 5
Feelings, Thomas 1933- 49-52
See also SATA 8
Feelings, Tom
See Feelings, Thomas
See also CLR 5
Feely, Terence John 1928- 106
Feenberg, Eugene 1906-1977 Obituary 73-76
Feeney, Leonard 1897-1978 81-84
Obituary 77-80
Feeney, Stephanie S(inger) 1939- 118
Feenstra, Henry John 1936- 37-40R
Feerick, John D(avid) 1936- 69-72
Fegan, Camilla 1939- 21-22R
Fegan, Patrick W. 1947- 111
Fegely, Thomas D(avid) 1941- 97-100
Fehl, Philipp P(inhas) 1920- 33-36R
Fehr, Howard Franklin 1901-1982
Obituary 106
Fehren, Henry 1920- CANR-9
Earlier sketch in CA 21-22R
Fehrenbach, T(heodore) R(eed, Jr.)
1925- CANR-1
Earlier sketch in CA 1R
See also SATA 33
Fehrenbacher, Don E. 1920- CANR-2
Earlier sketch in CA 1R
Fehrman, Carl (Abraham Daniel) 1915-
Brief entry 113
Feibes, Walter 1928- 53-56
Feibleman, James K(ern) 1904- CANR-22
Earlier sketches in CA 5-6R, CANR-7
See also AITN 2
Feibleman, Peter S(teinam) 1930- 110
Brief entry 108
Feider, Paul 1951- 114
Feied, Frederick (James) 1925- 13-14R
Feierman, Steven 1940- 53-56
Feifel, Herman 1915- 101
Feiffer, Jules 1929- 19-20R
See also SATA 8
See also DLB 7, 44
See also CLC 2, 8
Feig, Barbara Krane 1937- 104
See also SATA 34
Feig, Douglas 1946- 114
Feigelson, Naomi
See Chase, Naomi Feigelson
Feigenbaum, Lawrence H. 1918- 25-28R
Feigert, Frank B(rook) 1937- CANR-19
Earlier sketches in CA 53-56, CANR-4
Feigl, Herbert 1902- CAP-1
Earlier sketch in CA 13-14
Feigon, Lee (Nathan) 1945- 117
Fei-Kan, Li
See Li Fei-kan
Feikema, Feike
See Manfred, Frederick (Feikema)
Feil, Hila 1942- 37-40R
See also SATA 12
Feild, Reshad 1934- 69-72
Feilding, Charles (Rudolph) 1902- CAP-2
Earlier sketch in CA 25-28
Feilen, John
See May, Julian
Feiler, Seymour 1919- 41-44R
Fein, Albert 1930- 115
Fein, Helen 1934- 110
Fein, Irving A(shley) 1911- 69-72
Fein, John M(orton) 1922- 120
Fein, Judith 1941- 107
Fein, Leah Gold 49-52
Fein, Leonard J. 1934- 13-14R
Fein, Rashi 1926- 122
Fein, Richard J(acob) 1929- 45-48
Feinberg, Abraham L. 1899-1986 ..... 11-12R
Obituary 120
Feinberg, Barbara Jane 1938- CANR-22
Earlier sketch in CA 106
Feinberg, Barry (Vincent) 1938- 29-32R
Feinberg, Bea 1920- 81-84
Feinberg, Gerald 1933- CANR-12
Earlier sketch in CA 25-28R
Feinberg, Gloria (Granditer) 1923-
Brief entry 109
Feinberg, Hilda 49-52
Feinberg, Joel 1926- CANR-22
Earlier sketch in CA 17-18R
Feinberg, Lawrence B(ernard) 1940- 73-76
Feinberg, Leonard 1914- CANR-2
Earlier sketch in CA 5-6R
Feinberg, Mortimer R(obert) 1922- 102
Feinberg, Renee 1940- 112
Feinberg, Walter 1937- 57-60
Feinbloom, Deborah Heller 1940- 65-68
Feingold, Ben(jamin) F(ranklin)
1900-1982 97-100
Obituary 106
Feingold, Eugene (Neil) 1931- CANR-22
Earlier sketch in CA 17-18R
Feingold, Henry L(eo) 1931- 29-32R
Feingold, Jessica 1910- CAP-2
Earlier sketch in CA 25-28
Feingold, Michael 1945- 89-92
Feingold, S. Norman 1914- CANR-13
Earlier sketch in CA 13-14R
Feininger, Andreas (Bernhard Lyonel)
1906- CANR-20
Earlier sketch in CA 85-88
Feinman, Jeffrey 1943- CANR-10
Earlier sketch in CA 65-68
Feinsilver, Alexander 1910- 15-16R
Feinsilver, Lillian Mermin 1917- 29-32R
Feinsinger, Nathan Paul 1902-1983
Obituary 111
Feinstein, Alan (Shawn) 1931- 25-28R
Feinstein, Elaine 1930- 69-72
See also CAAS 1
See also DLB 14, 40
See also CLC 36
Feinstein, George W(illiamson) 1913- 73-76
Feinstein, Lloyd L(eonard) 1941- 113
Feinstein, Moshe 1895-1986 Obituary 118
Feinstein, Otto 1930- 104

Feinstein, Sherman C. 1923- ... CANR-7
Earlier sketch in CA 57-60
Feintuch, Burt H. 1949- ... 124
Feirstein, Bruce 1953- ... 108
Feirstein, Frederick 1940- ... CANR-1
Earlier sketch in CA 45-48
Feis, Herbert 1893-1972 ... CAP-1
Obituary ... 33-36R
Earlier sketch in CA 9-10
Feis, Ruth (Stanley-Brown) 1892- ... CAP-2
Earlier sketch in CA 19-20
Feise, Ernst 1884-1966 ... CAP-2
Earlier sketch in CA 17-18
Feist, Aubrey (Noel Lydston) 1903- ... 41-44R
Feit, E(wald) Edward 1924- ... CANR-10
Earlier sketch in CA 7-8R
Feitel, Donald G. 1925(?)-1976 Obituary ... 65-68
Feith, Herbert 1930- ... 4R
Feiwel, George R(ichard) 1929- ... CANR-23
Earlier sketches in CA 17-18R, CANR-8
Feiwel, Raphael Joseph 1907-1985
Obituary ... 117
Fejes, Claire 1920- ... CANR-13
Earlier sketch in CA 21-22R
Fejes, Endre 1923- ... 25-28R
Fejto, Francois (Philippe) 1909- ... 29-32R
Fekrat, M. Ali 1937- ... 45-48
Felber, Stanley B. 1932- ... 77-80
Feld, Bernard T(aub) 1919- ... 104
Feld, Michael 1938- ... 33-36R
Feld, Rose Caroline 1895-1981 Obituary ... 105
Feld, Ross 1947- ... CANR-16
Earlier sketch in CA 33-36R
Feld, Werner (Joachim) 1910- ... CANR-24
Earlier sketches in CA 21-22R, CANR-8
Feldbaum, Eleanor G. 1935- ... 117
Feldberg, Michael 1943- ... 113
Feldenkrais, Moshe (Pinchas) 1904- ... 73-76
Felder, Paul
See Wellen, Edward (Paul)
Felder, Raoul Lionel 1934- ... 33-36R
Felderman, Eric 1944- ... 69-72
Feldkamp, Fred 1915(?)-1981 Obituary ... 105
Feldkamp, Phyllis ... 102
Feldman, Abraham J(ehiel) 1893-1977 ... 81-84
Obituary ... 73-76
Feldman, Alan 1945- ... CANR-13
Earlier sketch in CA 73-76
Feldman, Anne (Rodgers) 1939- ... 73-76
See also SATA 19
Feldman, Annette Gerber 1913- ... 69-72
Feldman, Burton 1926- ... 33-36R
Feldman, Edmund Burke 1924- ... 33-36R
Feldman, Edwin B(arry) 1925- ... CANR-2
Earlier sketch in CA 7-8R
Feldman, Ellen (Bette) 1941- ... CANR-18
Earlier sketch in CA 97-100
Feldman, George J(ay) 1904- ... CAP-1
Earlier sketch in CA 13-14
Feldman, Gerald D(onald) 1937- ... CANR-9
Earlier sketch in CA 21-22R
Feldman, Herbert (H. S.) 1910- ... 29-32R
Feldman, Irving (Mordecai) 1928- ... CANR-1
Earlier sketch in CA 1R
See also CLC 7
Feldman, Kenneth A. 1937- ... 29-32R
Feldman, Leon A(ryeh) 1921- ... CANR-16
Earlier sketch in CA 97-100
Feldman, Leonard 1927- ... 69-72
Feldman, Leslie ... AITN-1
Feldman, Louis H(arry) 1926- ... 53-56
Feldman, M(aurice) P(hilip) 1933- ... 41-44R
Feldman, Marty 1934(?)-1982 ... 110
Obituary ... 108
Feldman, Robert A.
See Feldman, Robert Alan
Feldman, Robert Alan 1953- ... 123
Feldman, Ruth 1911- ... 106
Feldman, Ruth Duskin 1934- ... 119
Feldman, Samuel Nathan 1931- ... 25-28R
Feldman, Sandor S. 1891(?)-1973
Obituary ... 41-44R
Feldman, Saul D(aniel) 1943- ... 41-44R
Feldman, Sidney 1902(?)-1986 Obituary ... 121
Feldman, Silvia (Dash) 1928- ... 97-100
Feldman, Sol(omon) E. 1933- ... 25-28R
Feldman, Sophie 1930-1978 Obituary ... 108
Feldmann, Susan Judith 1928-1969
Obituary ... 104
Feldmeir, Daryle M(atthew) 1923-1987 ... 73-76
Obituary ... 122
Feldon, Leah 1944- ... 97-100
Feldstein, Martin S(tuart) 1939- ... 73-76
Feldstein, Paul J(oseph) 1933- ... 89-92
Feldstein, Stuart A(lan) 1948- ... 113
Feldt, Allan Gunnar 1932- ... 41-44R
Feldzamen, A(lvin) N(orman) 1931- ... 25-28R
Felheim, Marvin 1914- ... 1R
Felice, Cynthia 1942- ... 107
Felix
See Vincent, Felix
Felix, David 1921- ... 45-48
Felkenes, George T(heodore) 1930- ... CANR-8
Earlier sketch in CA 57-60
Felker, Clay S(chuette) 1925- ... 73-76
Felker, Evelyn H. 1933- ... 57-60
Felker, Jere L. 1934- ... 23-24R
Felknor, Bruce L(ester) 1921- ... 21-22R
Fell, Barry
See Fell, H(oward) Barraclough
Fell, Derek (John) 1939- ... 108
Fell, H(oward) Barraclough 1917- ... 33-36R
Fell, James E(dward), Jr. 1944- ... 107
Fell, John L(ouis) 1927- ... 53-56
Fell, Joseph P(hineas) III 1931- ... CANR-6
Earlier sketch in CA 15-16R
Fellini, Federico 1920- ... 65-68
See also CLC 16
Fellman, Gordon 1934- ... 53-56
Fellman, Michael (Dinion) 1943- ... 45-48
Fellmeth, Robert C(harles) 1945- ... CANR-2
Earlier sketch in CA 49-52
Fellner, William John 1905-1983 ... CANR-2
Obituary ... 110
Earlier sketch in CA 1R
Fellowes, Anne
See Mantle, Winifred (Langford)
Fellowes-Gordon, Ian (Douglas) 1921- ... CANR-10
Earlier sketch in CA 7-8R
Fellows, Brian John 1936- ... 25-28R
Fellows, Donald Keith 1920- ... 41-44R
Fellows, Hugh P. 1915- ... 37-40R
Fellows, Jay 1940- ... CANR-11
Earlier sketch in CA 61-64
Fellows, Lawrence (Perry) 1924- ... 49-52
Fellows, Malcolm Stuart 1924- ... 11-12R
Fellows, Muriel H. ... 53-56
See also SATA 10
Fellows, Otis (Edward) 1908- ... CANR-1
Earlier sketch in CA 4R
Fellows, Richard A(stley) 1947- ... 121
Felmly, Lloyd McPherson 1894-1984
Obituary ... 112
Fels, Rendigs 1917- ... 37-40R
Felsen, Henry Gregor 1916- ... CANR-1
Earlier sketch in CA 4R
See also SATA 1
See also SAAS 2
See also CLC 17
Felsenstein, Walter 1901-1975 Obituary ... 111
Felsenthal, Carol 1949- ... 108
Felsher, Howard D. 1927- ... 19-20R
Felstein, Ivor 1933- ... 41-44R
Felstiner, L. John, Jr. 1936- ... 45-48
Felt, Jeremy P(ollard) 1930- ... 23-24R
Felt, Margaret Elley 1917- ... 9-10R
Felter, Emma K. (Schroeder) 1896- ... CAP-1
Earlier sketch in CA 15-16
Felton, Bruce 1946- ... 65-68
Felton, Cornelius Conway 1807-1862 ... DLB-1
Felton, Harold William 1902- ... CANR-1
Earlier sketch in CA 3R
See also SATA 1
Felton, John Richard 1917- ... 89-92
Felton, Ronald Oliver 1909- ... CANR-3
Earlier sketch in CA 11-12R
See also SATA 3
Felton, Sandra 1935- ... 120
Felts, Shirley 1934- ... SATA-33
Feltskog, E(lmer) N. 1935- ... 37-40R
Felver, Charles S(tanley) 1916- ... 33-36R
Femiano, Samuel D. 1932- ... 21-22R
Femina, Jerry Della
See Della Femina, Jerry
Fen, Elisaveta
See Jackson, Lydia
Fenady, Andrew J. 1928- ... CANR-13
Earlier sketch in CA 77-80
Fenander, Elliot W(atkins) 1938- ... 21-22R
Fenberg, Matilda 1888(?)-1977 Obituary ... 73-76
Fenby, Eric (William) 1906- ... 25-28R
Fendell, Bob 1925- ... 57-60
Fendelman, Helaine Woll 1942- ... 69-72
Fenderson, Lewis H., Jr. 1907-1983 ... 106
Obituary ... 111
See also SATA 37, 47
Fenelon, Fania 1918-1983 ... 77-80
Obituary ... 111
Fenelon, Kevin G(erard) 1898-1983 ... 73-76
Obituary ... 109
Feng, Chin
See Liu, Sydney (Chieh)
Fenger, Henning Johannes Hauch 1921- ... 73-76
Fenical, Marlin Edward 1907-1983
Obituary ... 110
Fenichel, Carol Hansen 1935- ... 119
Fenichell, Stephen 1956- ... 108
Fenick, Barbara 1951- ... 118
Fenik, Bernard Carl 1934- ... 122
Fenin, George N(icolaievich) 1916- ... 9-10R
Fenlon, Dick 1930- ... 89-92
Fenlon, Paul Edward 1921- ... 15-16R
Fenn, Charles (Henry) 1907- ... 9-10R
Fenn, Dan H(untington), Jr. 1923- ... CANR-1
Earlier sketch in CA 3R
Fenn, Elizabeth A. 1959- ... 115
Fenn, Henry Courtenay 1894-1978
Obituary ... 81-84
Fennario, David 1947- ... DLB-60
Fennell, Francis L(e Roy), Jr. 1942- ... 116
Fennell, John L(ister) I(llingworth)
1918- ... CANR-19
Earlier sketches in CA 3R, CANR-1
Fennell, William Oscar 1916- ... 101
Fennelly, Catherine 1918- ... 37-40R
Fennelly, John F(auntleroy) 1899-1974
Obituary ... 53-56
Fennelly, Tony 1945- ... 119
Fennema, Owen Richard 1929- ... CANR-3
Earlier sketch in CA 49-52
Fenner, Carol Elizabeth 1929- ... CANR-3
Earlier sketch in CA 7-8R
See also SATA 7
Fenner, H(arry) Wolcott 1911-1972 ... CAP-2
Obituary ... 37-40R
Earlier sketch in CA 33-36
Fenner, James 1923- ... 37-40R
Fenner, James R.
See Tubb, E(dwin) C(harles)
Fenner, Kay Toy ... CAP-1
Earlier sketch in CA 9-10
Fenner, Mildred Sandison 1910- ... 33-36R
Fenner, Phyllis R(eid) 1899-1982 ... CANR-2
Obituary ... 106
Earlier sketch in CA 5-6R
See also SATA 1, 29
Fenner, Theodore (Lincoln) 1919- ... 37-40R
Fennimore, Keith John 1917- ... 57-60
Fenno, John 1751-1798 ... DLB-43
Fenno, R(ichard) Francis, Jr. 1926- ... 7-8R
Fensch, Edwin A. 1903- ... CAP-1
Earlier sketch in CA 15-16
Fensch, Thomas 1943- ... CANR-11
Earlier sketch in CA 25-28R
Fenster, Robert 1946- ... 113
Fenster, Valmai (Ruth) Kirkham
1939-1984 ... 110
Obituary ... 114
Fensterheim, Herbert 1921- ... 112
Fenstermaker, J(oseph) Van 1933- ... 29-32R
Fenten, Barbara D(oris) 1935- ... CANR-5
Earlier sketch in CA 53-56
See also SATA 26
Fenten, D(onald) X. 1932- ... CANR-5
Earlier sketch in CA 33-36R
See also SATA 4
Fenton, Carroll Lane 1900-1969 ... CANR-6
Obituary ... 29-32R
Earlier sketch in CA 1R
See also SATA 5
Fenton, Clyde 1901-1982 Obituary ... 106
Fenton, Edward 1917- ... CANR-13
Earlier sketch in CA 9-10R
See also SATA 7
Fenton, Frank 1903-1971 Obituary ... 33-36R
Fenton, Freda
See Rowland, D(onald) S(ydney)
Fenton, James Martin 1949- ... 102
See also DLB 40
See also CLC 32
Fenton, John C(harles) 1921- ... CAP-1
Earlier sketch in CA 9-10
Fenton, John H(arold) 1921- ... 37-40R
Fenton, John Y(oung) 1933- ... 53-56
Fenton, Joseph Clifford 1906- ... 7-8R
Fenton, Mildred Adams 1899- ... 77-80
See also SATA 21
Fenton, Shane
See Stardust, Alvin
Fenton, Sophia Harvati 1914- ... 33-36R
Fenton, Thomas Patrick 1943- ... 89-92
Fenton, Thomas Trail 1930- ... 102
Fenton, William N(elson) 1908- ... 93-96
Fentress, John Simmons 1925(?)-1981
Obituary ... 104
Fenvessy, Stanley J(ohn) 1918- ... 106
Fenwick, Charles G(hequiere) 1880-1973
Obituary ... 41-44R
Fenwick, Kay
See Bean, Keith F(enwick)
Fenwick, (Ian Graham) Keith 1941- ... 102
Fenwick, Millicent Hammond 1910- ... 112
Fenwick, Patti
See Grider, Dorothy
Fenwick, Sheridan 1942- ... 69-72
Fenwick-Owen, Roderic (Franklin Rawnsley)
1921- Brief entry ... 111
Fenyvesi, Charles 1937- ... 102
Feola, Jose (Maria) 1926- ... 69-72
Feravolo, Rocco Vincent 1922- ... CANR-1
Earlier sketch in CA 1R
See also SATA 10
Ferazani, Larry 1938- ... 61-64
Ferber, Andrew 1935- ... 53-56
Ferber, Edna 1887-1968 ... 7-8R
Obituary ... 25-28R
See also SATA 7
See also DLB 9, 28
See also CLC 18
See also AITN 1
Ferber, Ellen 1939- ... 102
Ferber, Robert 1922- ... 37-40R
Ferdinand, Theodore N(ichols) 1929- ... 23-24R
Ferdinand, Vallery III
See Salaam, Kalamu ya
Ferdon, Edwin N(elson), Jr. 1913- ... 21-22R
Ferejohn, John A(rthur) 1944- ... 53-56
Ferencz, Benjamin B(erell) 1920- ... CANR-19
Earlier sketch in CA 97-100
Fergus, Patricia M(arguerita) 1918- ... 53-56
Ferguson, Alfred R(iggs) 1915-1974 ... CANR-6
Obituary ... 49-52
Earlier sketch in CA 1R
Ferguson, Annabelle Evelyn 1923- ... 102
Ferguson, Arthur B(owles) 1913- ... 5-6R
Ferguson, Bob
See Ferguson, Robert Bruce
Ferguson, C(harles) E(lmo) 1928- ... 19-20R
Ferguson, Cecil 1931- ... SATA-45
Ferguson, Charles Albert 1921- ... 69-72
Ferguson, Charles Austin 1937- ... 121
Ferguson, Charles W. 1901-1987 ... 15-16R
Obituary ... 124
Ferguson, Chris(topher Wilson) 1944- ... 57-60
Ferguson, Clarence Clyde, Jr.
1924-1983 ... CANR-6
Obituary ... 111
Earlier sketch in CA 7-8R
Ferguson, David L. 1930- ... 73-76
Ferguson, Donald N(ivison) 1882-1985 ... 5-6R
Obituary ... 116
Ferguson, E(lmer) James 1917- ... 61-64
Ferguson, Everett 1933- ... 33-36R
Ferguson, Franklin C(ole) 1934- ... 69-72
Ferguson, Harry 1903-1980 Obituary ... 97-100
Ferguson, Helen
See Kavan, Anna
Ferguson, Howard 1908- ... CAP-1
Earlier sketch in CA 11-12
Ferguson, J(ohn) Halcro 1920-1968 ... 1R
Obituary ... 103
Ferguson, James M(ilton) 1936- ... 23-24R
Ferguson, John 1921- ... CANR-8
Earlier sketch in CA 5-6R
Ferguson, John Henry 1907- ... 13-14R
Ferguson, M(ilton) Carr 1931- ... 49-52
Ferguson, Margaret W(illiams) 1948- ... 112
Ferguson, Marilyn 1938- ... 114
Brief entry ... 110
Ferguson, Mary Anne 1918- ... 77-80
Ferguson, Oliver W(atkins) 1924- ... 5-6R
Ferguson, Pamela 1943- ... 101
Ferguson, Peter R(oderick) I(nnes)
1933- ... CANR-3
Earlier sketch in CA 7-8R
Ferguson, Robert Bruce 1927- ... 69-72
See also SATA 13
Ferguson, Robert D(ouglas) 1921- ... 19-20R
Ferguson, Robert W(illiam) 1940- ... CANR-12
Earlier sketch in CA 61-64
Ferguson, Rowena 1904- ... 85-88
Ferguson, Samuel 1810-1886 ... DLB-32
Ferguson, Suzanne 1939- ... 57-60
Ferguson, Ted 1936- ... 65-68
Ferguson, Tom 1943- ... 107
Ferguson, Trevor 1947- ... 116
Ferguson, Walter (W.) 1930- ... 107
See also SATA 34
Ferguson, William (Rotch) 1943- ... 49-52
Ferguson, William M(cDonald) 1917- ... 117
Ferguson, William Scott 1875-1954 ... DLB-47
Fergusson, Adam 1932- Brief entry ... 112
Fergusson, Bernard Edward 1911-1980 ... CANR-7
Obituary ... 102
Earlier sketch in CA 9-10R
Fergusson, Erna 1888-1964 ... CAP-1
Earlier sketch in CA 13-14
See also SATA 5
Fergusson, Francis (De Liesseline)
1904-1986 ... CANR-3
Obituary ... 121
Earlier sketch in CA 11-12R
Fergusson, Harvey 1890-1971 Obituary ... 33-36R
Fergusson, James 1904-1973 Obituary ... 104
Fergusson, Rosalind (Joyce) 1953- ... 117
Fergusson Hannay, Doris 1902(?)-1982 ... CANR-6
Obituary ... 107
Earlier sketch in CA 9-10R
Fericano, Paul F(rancis) 1951- ... CANR-12
Earlier sketch in CA 69-72
Ferkiss, Victor C(hristopher) 1925- ... 21-22R
Ferland, Carol 1936- ... 102
Ferlinghetti, Lawrence (Monsanto)
1919(?)- ... CANR-3
Earlier sketch in CA 7-8R
See also DLB 5, 16
See also CDALB 1941-1968
See also CLC 2, 6, 10, 27
Ferlita, Ernest (Charles) 1927- ... CANR-11
Earlier sketch in CA 29-32R
Ferm, Betty 1926- ... 23-24R
Ferm, Deane William 1927- ... CANR-13
Earlier sketch in CA 33-36R
Ferm, Max A(rnold) 1929- ... 116
Ferm, Robert Livingston 1931- ... 13-14R
Ferm, Vergilius (Ture Anselm)
1896-1974 ... 9-10R
Obituary ... 49-52
Ferman, Edward L(ewis) 1937- ... 106
Ferman, Joseph W(olfe) 1906-1975
Obituary ... 104
Fermi, Enrico 1901-1954 Brief entry ... 115
Fermi, Laura 1907-1977 ... CANR-6
Earlier sketch in CA 2R
See also SATA 6, 28
Fermor, Patrick Leigh 1915- ... 81-84
Fern, Alan M(axwell) 1930- ... CANR-12
Earlier sketch in CA 33-36R
Fern, Eugene A. 1919-1987 ... CANR-16
Obituary ... 123
Earlier sketch in CA 4R
See also SATA 10
Fern, Fanny
See Parton, Sara Payson Willis
Fernald, John (Bailey) 1905-1985 ... CAP-2
Obituary ... 115
Earlier sketch in CA 23-24
Fernandez, Benedict J. (III) 1936- ... 85-88
Fernandez, Gladys Craven 1939- ... 106
Fernandez, Happy Craven
See Fernandez, Gladys Craven
Fernandez, James William 1930- ... CANR-23
Earlier sketch in CA 107
Fernandez, John P(eter) 1941- ... CANR-10
Earlier sketch in CA 65-68
Fernandez, Jose S(alvador) 1893-1967
Obituary ... 113
Fernandez, Joseph A. 1921- ... 37-40R
Fernandez, Julio A. 1936- ... 33-36R
Fernandez de la Reguera, Ricardo
1914- ... CANR-3
Earlier sketch in CA 7-8R
Fernandez-Marina, R(amon) 1909- ... 41-44R
Fernando, Ajith 1948- ... 122
Fernando, Lloyd 1926- ... 77-80
Fernea, Elizabeth Warnock 1927- ... CANR-12
Earlier sketch in CA 15-16R
Fernea, Robert Alan 1932- ... 33-36R
Fernett, Gene 1924- ... 49-52
Fernie, Eric (Campbell) 1939- ... 119
Ferns, H(enry) S(tanley) 1913- ... CANR-19
Earlier sketches in CA 5-6R, CANR-4
Fernsworth, Lawrence 1893(?)-1977(?)
Obituary ... 89-92
Ferracuti, Franco 1927- ... CANR-11
Earlier sketch in CA 25-28R

Ferrante, Don
See Gerbi, Antonello
Ferrante, Joan M(arguerite Aida) 1936- 85-88
Ferrar, Harold 1935- Brief entry 116
Ferrarini, Elizabeth M. 1948- 124
Ferraro, Gary P(aul) 1940- 89-92
Ferrars, E. X.
See Brown, Morna Doris
Ferrars, Elizabeth
See Brown, Morna Doris
Ferrater-Mora, Jose 1912- 3R
Ferre, Frederick 1933- 13-14R
Ferre, Gustave A. 1918- 4R
Ferre, Nels F(redrik) S(olomon)
1908-1971 .... CAP-2
Earlier sketch in CA 29-32
Ferreira de Castro, Jose Maria 1898-1974 ... 102
Obituary 49-52
Ferrell, Mallory Hope 1935- CANR-13
Earlier sketch in CA 33-36R
Ferrell, Robert H(ugh) 1921- CANR-22
Earlier sketches in CA 5-6R, CANR-6
Ferrell, Robert W(illingham) 1913- 15-16R
Ferreol, Marcel Auguste 1899-1974 97-100
Obituary 53-56
Ferrer, Aldo 1927- CANR-11
Earlier sketch in CA 25-28R
Ferrer, Gabriel (Francisco Victor) Miro
See Miro (Ferrer), Gabriel (Francisco Victor)
Ferrer, Sister Vincent
See Doherty, Barbara
Ferres, John H(oward) 1932- 41-44R
Ferridge, Philippa 1933- CANR-18
Earlier sketch in CA 102
Ferrier, Janet Mackay 1919- 9-10R
Ferrier, Lucy
See Penzler, Otto
Ferril, Thomas Hornsby 1896- 65-68
Ferrini, Vincent 1913- DLB-48
Ferris, Helen Josephine 1890-1969 77-80
See also SATA 21
Ferris, James Cody CAP-2
Earlier sketch in CA 19-20
See also SATA 1
Ferris, James Cody
See McFarlane, Leslie
Ferris, Jean 1939- 116
See also SATA 50
Ferris, Norman (Bernard) 1931- 81-84
Ferris, Paul (Frederick) 1929- CANR-22
Earlier sketches in CA 7-8R, CANR-3
Ferris, Theodore P(arker) 1908-1972
Obituary 37-40R
Ferris, Timothy 1944- CANR-11
Earlier sketch in CA 69-72
Ferris, Tom
See Walker, Peter N.
Ferriss, Abbott Lamoyne 1915- 29-32R
Ferritor, Daniel Edward 1939- 49-52
Ferro, Marc 1924- 77-80
Ferro, Robert Michael 1941- 29-32R
Ferron, Jacques 1921-1985 Brief entry 117
See also DLB 60
Ferron, Madeleine 1922- DLB-53
Ferruolo, Stephen C(arl) 1949- 120
Ferry, Anne Davidson 1930- 19-20R
Ferry, Charles 1927- CANR-16
Earlier sketch in CA 97-100
See also SATA 43
Ferry, David (Russell) 1924- 13-14R
Ferry, W(illiam) Hawkins 1914(?)-1988 61-64
Obituary 124
Fersh, Seymour H. 1926- CANR-14
Earlier sketch in CA 37-40R
Ferster, C(harles) B(ohris) 1922-1981 97-100
Obituary 102
Ferster, Dorothy C(oben) 1922- 111
Ferster, Marilyn B(ender)
See Gilbert, Marilyn B(ender)
Ferullo, Dan 1948- 106
Feshbach, Norma Deitch 1926- CANR-8
Earlier sketch in CA 61-64
Feshbach, Seymour 1925- CANR-8
Earlier sketch in CA 37-40R
Fesler, James W(illiam) 1911- 23-24R
Fesperman, John (Thomas, Jr.) 1925- .. CANR-2
Earlier sketch in CA 5-6R
Fess, Philip E. 1931- 33-36R
Fessel, Murray 1927- 21-22R
Fessenden, Katherine 1896(?)-1974
Obituary 53-56
Fessenden, Seth A(rthur) 1903-1976 ... CANR-10
Earlier sketch in CA 17-18R
Fessenko, Tatiana (Sviatenko) 1915- 13-14R
Fessler, Loren W. 1923- 9-10R
Fest, Joachim C. 1926- 49-52
Fest, Thorrel B(rooks) 1910- CAP-1
Earlier sketch in CA 15-16
Festa Campanile, Pasquale 1927-1986
Obituary 118
Festa-McCormick, Diana 117
Festinger, Leon 1919- 3R
Fetherling, Dale 1941- 77-80
Fetler, Andrew 1925- 15-16R
Fetridge, William Harrison 1906- 73-76
Fetros, John G. 1932- 57-60
Fetscher, Iring 1922- CANR-12
Earlier sketch in CA 69-72
Fettamen, Ann
See Hoffman, Anita
Fetter, Elizabeth Head 1904-1973 ....7-8R
Obituary 41-44R
Fetter, Frank Whitson 1899- 106
Fetter, Richard (Leland) 1943- CANR-15
Earlier sketch in CA 89-92
Fetterley, Judith 1938- Brief entry 113
Fetterman, Elsie 1927- 97-100
Fetterman, John (Davis) 1920-1975 93-96
Obituary 61-64
Fettig, Art(hur John) 1929- CANR-13
Earlier sketch in CA 73-76
Fetz, Ingrid 1915- SATA-30
Fetzer, John F(rancis) 1931- 61-64
Feucht, Oscar E(mil) 1895- 103
Feuchtwanger, E(dgar) J(oseph)
1924- CANR-11
Earlier sketch in CA 69-72
Feuchtwanger, Lion 1884-1958 Brief entry .. 104
See also DLB 66
See also TCLC 3
Feuer, Avrohom Chaim 1946- 113
Feuer, Kathryn Beliveau 1926- 102
Feuer, Lewis S(amuel) 1912- CANR-3
Earlier sketch in CA 7-8R
Feuerlicht, Ignace CAP-2
Earlier sketch in CA 33-36
Feuerlicht, Roberta Strauss 1931- 19-20R
Feuerstein, Georg 1947- 123
Feuerstein, Phyllis A. 1930- 105
Feuerwerger, Marvin C(harles) 1950- 104
Feuerwerker, Albert 1927- CANR-8
Earlier sketch in CA 23-24R
Feulner, Edwin J(ohn), Jr. 1941- 115
Feulner, Patricia N(ancy) 1946- 105
Feur, D. C.
See Stahl, Fred Alan
Fey, Harold E(dward) 1898- 19-20R
Feydeau, Georges (Leon Jules Marie)
1862-1921 Brief entry 113
See also TCLC 22
Feydy, Anne Lindbergh
See Sapieyevski, Anne Lindbergh
See also SATA 32
Feynman, R. P.
See Feynman, Richard Phillips
Feynman, Richard P.
See Feynman, Richard Phillips
Feynman, Richard Phillips 1918-
Brief entry 119
Fezler, William 1945- 122
ffolliott, Rosemary 1934- 97-100
ffrench-Beytagh, Gonville (Aubie) 1912- 103
ffrench Blake, Neil (St. John) 1940- 69-72
ffrench Blake, Robert L(ifford) V(alentine)
1913- 61-64
Fiacc, Padraic
See O'Connor, Patrick Joseph
Fialkowski, Barbara 1946- 77-80
Fiammenghi, Gioia 1929- SATA-9
Fiandt, Mary K. 1914- 89-92
Fiarotta, Noel
See Ficarotta, Noel
See also SATA 15
Fiarotta, Phyllis
See Ficarotta, Phyllis
See also SATA 15
Fiber, Alan 102
Ficarotta, Noel 1944- CANR-11
Earlier sketch in CA 69-72
Ficarotta, Phyllis 1942- CANR-11
Earlier sketch in CA 69-72
Fichtelius, Karl-Erik 1924- 53-56
Fichter, Andrew J(ohn) 1945- 117
Fichter, George S. 1922- CANR-23
Earlier sketches in CA 17-18R, CANR-7
See also SATA 7
Fichter, Joseph 1908- CANR-19
Earlier sketches in CA 1R, CANR-4
Ficke, Arthur Davison 1883-1945 .... DLB-54
Ficken, Frederick A(rthur) 1910-1978
Obituary 81-84
Ficker, Victor B. 1937- CANR-13
Earlier sketch in CA 33-36R
Fickert, Kurt J(on) 1920- CANR-14
Earlier sketch in CA 37-40R
Fickett, Harold L., Jr. 1918- 15-16R
Fickett, Lewis P., Jr. 1926- 21-22R
Fickle, James Edward 1939- 106
Fickling, G. G.
See Fickling, Skip Forrest
Fickling, Skip Forrest 1925- 7-8R
Fidelio
See Hunt, Edgar H(ubert)
Fidler, Kathleen (Annie) 1899-1980 .... CANR-20
Obituary 117
Earlier sketch in CA 25-28R
See also SATA 3, 45
Fidrych, Mark 1954- Brief entry 112
Fie, Jacquelyn Joyce 1937- 57-60
Fiedler, Fred E(dward) 1922- 23-24R
Fiedler, Jean(nette Feldman) CANR-11
Earlier sketch in CA 29-32R
See also SATA 4
Fiedler, Leslie A(aron) 1917- CANR-7
Earlier sketch in CA 11-12R
See also DLB 28, 67
See also CLC 4, 13, 24
Fiedler, Lois (Wagner) 1928- 17-18R
Fieg, Victor P. 1924- 106
Field, Adelaide (Anderson) 1916- 106
Field, Andrew 1938- 97-100
See also CLC 44
Field, Arthur J(ordan) 1927-1975 ....33-36R
Field, Barbara 1935- 110
Field, Carol 1940- 113
Field, Charles
See Rowland, D(onald) S(ydney)
Field, Daniel 1938- 65-68
Field, David D(udley) 1918- 73-76
Field, Dawn Stewart 1940- 57-60
Field, Dick 1912- 57-60
Field, Edward 1924- CANR-10
Earlier sketch in CA 13-14R
See also SATA 8
Field, Eleanor S. 1932- 122
Field, Elinor Whitney 1889-1980 Obituary ... 109
See also SATA 28
Field, Ernest R. 1925- 7-8R
Field, Eugene 1850-1895 .... SATA-16
See also DLB 23, 42
Field, Frances Fox 1913(?)-1977
Obituary 69-72
Field, Frank 1936- 21-22R
Field, Frank Chester
See Robertson, Frank C(hester)
Field, Frank McCoy 1887-1978 45-48
Obituary 103
Field, G(eorge) W(allis) 1914- 37-40R
Field, Gans T.
See Wellman, Manly Wade
Field, George B(rooks) 1929- 101
Field, Gordon Lawrence 1939- 17-18R
Field, Harry
See Field, Henry
Field, Hartry H(amlin) 1946- 124
Field, Hazel E(lizabeth) 1891-19(?) CAP-1
Earlier sketch in CA 19-20
Field, Henry 1902-1986 69-72
Obituary 118
Field, Irving M(edcraft) 1934- 25-28R
Field, James A(lfred), Jr. 1916- 25-28R
Field, Joanna
See Milner, Marion (Blackett)
Field, John (Leslie) 1910- 33-36R
Field, John P(aul) 1936- 37-40R
Field, Joyce W(olf) 1932- 29-32R
Field, Leslie A. 1926- 29-32R
Field, Mark G(eorge) 1923- 37-40R
Field, Michael 1915-1971 Obituary 29-32R
Field, Minna (Kagan) 25-28R
Field, Nathan 1587-1620(?) DLB-58
Field, Penelope
See Giberson, Dorothy (Dodds)
Field, Peter
See Hobson, Laura Z(ametkin)
Field, Phyllis Frances 1946- 107
Field, Rachel (Lyman) 1894-1942
Brief entry 109
See also SATA 15
See also DLB 9, 22
Field, Stanley 1911- CANR-9
Earlier sketch in CA 21-22R
Field, Thomas P(arry) 1914- 9-10R
Field, Walter S(herman) 1899- 49-52
Fielden, Charlotte 93-96
Fielden, T(homas) P(erceval) 1882- 7-8R
Fielder, Mildred (Craig) 1913- CANR-10
Earlier sketch in CA 15-16R
Fielding, A. W.
See Wallace, Alexander Fielding
Fielding, Daphne Winifred Louise 1904- ...9-10R
Fielding, G(ordon) J. 1934- 97-100
Fielding, Gabriel
See Barnsley, Alan Gabriel
Fielding, Henry 1707-1754 .... DLB-39
Fielding, Joy 1945- CANR-2
Earlier sketch in CA 49-52
Fielding, Nancy (Parker) 1913-1983
Obituary 111
Brief entry 108
Fielding, Raymond E. 1931- CANR-8
Earlier sketch in CA 17-18R
Fielding, Sarah 1710-1768 .... DLB-39
Fielding, Temple (Hornaday)
1913-1983 .... CANR-14
Obituary 109
Earlier sketch in CA 21-22R
Fielding, Waldo L. 1921- 45-48
Fielding, William J(ohn) 1886- 15-16R
Fielding, Xan
See Wallace, Alexander Fielding
Fields, Alan
See Duprey, Richard A(llen)
Fields, Arthur C. 1926(?)-1974 Obituary ...49-52
Fields, Beverly 1917- 49-52
Fields, Dorothy 1905-1974 93-96
Obituary 49-52
Fields, Gracie 1898-1979 Obituary 112
Fields, Howard K(enneth) 1938- 81-84
Fields, James Thomas 1817-1881 .... DLB-1
Fields, Jeff AITN-2
Fields, Joseph 1895-1966 Obituary 25-28R
Fields, Julia 1938- 73-76
See also DLB 41
Fields, Kenneth (Wayne) 1939- Brief entry .. 110
Fields, Nora 49-52
Fields, Rick 1942- CANR-9
Earlier sketch in CA 65-68
Fields, Rona M(arcia) 1934- 69-72
Fields, Totie
See Feldman, Sophie
Fields, Victor A(lexander) 1901- 5-6R
Fields, W. C. 1880-1946 .... DLB-44
Fields, Wilbert J. 1917- 15-16R
Fields, Wilmer Clemont 1922- Brief entry ... 106
Fieler, Frank B(ernard) 1933- 41-44R
Fiene, Donald M(ark) 1930- 69-72
Fiene, Ernest 1894-1965 .... CAP-1
Earlier sketch in CA 13-14
Fiennes, Ranulph (Twisleton-Wykeham)
1944- CANR-20
Earlier sketches in CA 45-48, CANR-3
Fiennes, Richard
See Twisleton-Wykeham-Fiennes, Richard Nathaniel
Fiering, Norman Sanford 1935- 105
Fierro, Robert Daniel 1945- 109
Fierstein, Harvey (Forbes) 1954-
Brief entry 123
See also CLC 33
Fieser, Louis F(rederick) 1899-1977
Obituary 73-76
Fieser, Max E(ugene) 1930- 13-14R
Fiester, Mark (Lafayette) 1907- 65-68
Fieve, Ronald R(obert) 1930- Brief entry ... 107
Fife, Austin E(dwin) 1909- 53-56
Fife, Dale (Odile Hollerbach) 1901- CANR-19
Earlier sketch in CA 85-88
See also SATA 18
Fife, Robert Oldham 1918- 37-40R
Fifer, Ken 1947- 104
Fifield, William 1916-1987 .... CANR-9
Obituary 124
Earlier sketch in CA 15-16R
Fifo, Ray
See Glazar, Bob
Fifoot, Cecil Herbert Stuart 1899-1975
Obituary 107
Figes, Eva 1932- CANR-4
Earlier sketch in CA 53-56
See also DLB 14
See also CLC 31
Figgins, Ross 1936- CANR-11
Earlier sketch in CA 69-72
Figh, Margaret Gillis 1896- CAP-2
Earlier sketch in CA 29-32
Fighter Pilot, A
See Johnston, H(ugh) A(nthony) S(tephen)
Figler, Howard Elliot 1939- Brief entry 109
Figler, Stephen K(enneth) 1942- 117
Figueroa, John J(oseph Maria) 1920-
Brief entry 108
Figueroa, John L(ewis) 1936- 65-68
Figueroa, Loida
See Figueroa-Mercado, Loida
Figueroa, Pablo 1938- 61-64
See also SATA 9
Figueroa-Chapel, Ramon 1935- 45-48
Figueroa-Mercado, Loida 1917- CANR-9
Earlier sketch in CA 57-60
Figurito, Joseph 1922- 29-32R
Fijan, Carol 1918- 53-56
See also SATA 12
Fikso, Eunice Cleland 1927- 7-8R
Filas, Francis L(ad) 1915-1985 .... CANR-2
Obituary 115
Earlier sketch in CA 5-6R
Filby, P(ercy) William 1911- CANR-3
Earlier sketch in CA 9-10R
Filene, Peter G. 1940- 21-22R
Filep, Robert Thomas 1931- CANR-19
Earlier sketches in CA 45-48, CANR-1
Filicchia, Ralph 1935- 103
Filip, Raymond 1950- 113
Filipovitch, Anthony J(oseph) 1947- 102
Filippo, Eduardo de
See de Filippo, Eduardo
Fill, Joseph Herbert 1924- Brief entry 112
Filler, Louis 1912- CANR-2
Earlier sketch in CA 1R
Fillmer, Henry Thompson 1932- 23-24R
Fillmore, Lowell 1882- CAP-1
Earlier sketch in CA 9-10
Fillmore, Parker H(oysted) 1878-1944 ... YABC-1
Fillmore, Roscoe Alfred 1887- 7-8R
Filmer, Henry
See Childs, J(ames) Rives
Filosa, Gary Fairmont Randolph de Marco II
1931- 65-68
Filson, Floyd V(ivian) 1896- 61-64
Filson, John 1753(?)-1788 .... DLB-37
Filstrup, Chris
See Filstrup, E(dward) Christian
Filstrup, E(dward) Christian 1942- 113
See also SATA 43
Filstrup, Jane (Merrill) 1946- 110
Filstrup, Janie
See Filstrup, Jane (Merrill)
Finan, John J(oseph) 1925- 117
Finberg, H(erbert) P(atrick) R(eginald)
1900-1974 .... CAP-1
Obituary 53-56
Earlier sketch in CA 15-16
Finch, Christopher 1939- Brief entry 112
Finch, Donald George 1937- 53-56
Finch, Henry LeRoy 1918- 41-44R
Finch, Matthew
See Fink, Merton
Finch, Robert (Duer Claydon) 1900- ... CANR-24
Earlier sketches in CA 57-60, CANR-9
See also CLC 18
Finch(-Rayner), Sheila 1935- 121
Fincham, A(nthony) A(rthur) 1943- 117
Fincher, Cameron Lane 1926- 41-44R
Fincher, Ernest B(arksdale) 1910-1985 .. CANR-9
Obituary 115
Earlier sketch in CA 53-56
Finck, Furman J(oseph) 1900- CAP-2
Earlier sketch in CA 33-36
Fincke, Gary (William) 1945- 57-60
Finckenauer, James O(liver) 1939- 108
Finder, Joseph 1958- 113
Finder, Martin
See Salzmann, Siegmund
Findlater, Richard
See Bain, Kenneth Bruce Findlater
Findlay, Bruce Allyn 1895-1972 .... CAP-1
Earlier sketch in CA 13-14
Findlay, Campbell K(irkman) 1909- 7-8R
Findlay, David K. 1901- CAP-1
Earlier sketch in CA 13-14
Findlay, James Arthur 1883-1964
Obituary 111

INDEX

Findlay, James F(ranklin), Jr. 1930- 49-52
Findlay, John N(iemeyer) 1903-1987 .... CANR-5
Obituary 123
Earlier sketch in CA 7-8R
Findlay, Robert R. 1932- 45-48
Findley, Carter Vaughn 1941- 102
Findley, Paul 1921- 29-32R
Findley, Timothy 1930- CANR-12
Earlier sketch in CA 25-28R
See also DLB 53
See also CLC 27
Findling, John Ellis 1941- 102
Fine, Anne 1947- 105
See also SATA 29
Fine, Benjamin 1905-1975 .... CANR-4
Obituary 57-60
Earlier sketch in CA 5-6R
Fine, Carla 1946- 112
Fine, Elsa Honig 1930- 49-52
Fine, Estelle
See Jelinek, Estelle C.
Fine, Gary Alan 1950- 111
Fine, I(sadore) V. 1918- 19-20R
Fine, John (Van Antwerp), Jr. 1939- 117
Fine, Judylaine 1948- 117
Fine, Nathan 1893(?)-1979 Obituary 89-92
Fine, Ralph Adam 1941- 29-32R
Fine, Reuben 1914- CANR-12
Earlier sketch in CA 17-18R
Fine, S(eymour) Morton 1930- 104
Fine, Seymour H(oward) 1925- 111
Fine, Sidney 1920- CANR-1
Earlier sketch in CA 1R
Fine, Warren 1943- 21-22R
Fine, William Michael 1924- 15-16R
Fineberg, Robert Gene 1940- 107
Finegan, Jack 1908- CANR-1
Earlier sketch in CA 1R
Finegan, T(homas) Aldrich 1929-
Brief entry 108
Fineman, Irving 1893- 5-6R
Finer, Leslie 1921- 15-16R
Finer, Samuel Edward 1915- 41-44R
Finestone, Harold 1920- Brief entry 110
Finestone, Harry 1920- 45-48
Fingarette, Herbert 1921- 77-80
Finger, Charles J(oseph) 1869(?)-1941
Brief entry 119
See also SATA 42
Finger, Seymour Maxwell 1915- 104
Finger, William R(atliff) 1947- 111
Fingerhut, Eugene R. 1932- 111
Fingesten, Peter 1916-1987 .... 15-16R
Obituary 123
Finifter, Ada W(eintraub) 1938- CANR-21
Earlier sketch in CA 104
Fink, Arthur Emil 1903- 1R
Fink, Augusta 1916- CANR-13
Earlier sketch in CA 33-36R
Fink, Edith 1918- 61-64
Fink, Eli E. 1908(?)-1979 Obituary 85-88
Fink, Gary M. 1936- 53-56
Fink, Joanne 1954- 123
Fink, Joseph 1915- 57-60
Fink, Lawrence Alfred 1930- 97-100
Fink, Merton 1921- 9-10R
Fink, Paul Jay 1933- 53-56
Fink, Stevanne Auerbach
See Auerbach, Stevanne
Fink, William B(ertrand) 1916- 41-44R
See also SATA 22
Fink, Z(era) S(ilver) 1902- CAP-1
Earlier sketch in CA 9-10
Fink Cline, Beverly 1951- 113
Finke, Blythe Foote 1922- 65-68
See also SATA 26
Finke, Jack A. 1918(?)-1979 Obituary 89-92
Finkel, Donald 1929- CANR-9
Earlier sketch in CA 23-24R
Finkel, George (Irvine) 1909-1975 .... CAP-2
Earlier sketch in CA 17-18
See also SATA 8
Finkel, Lawrence S. 1925- 13-14R
Finkel, LeRoy 1939- 105
Finkelhor, David 1947- 118
Finkelhor, Dorothy Cimberg 1902- 110
Finkell, Max
See Catto, Max(well Jeffrey)
Finkelman, Paul 1949- CANR-22
Earlier sketch in CA 105
Finkelstein, Bonnie B(lumenthal) 1946- 85-88
Finkelstein, Jacob Joel 1922-1974
Obituary 53-56
Finkelstein, Leonid Vladimirovitch 1924- 23-24R
Finkelstein, Louis 1895- 13-14R
Finkelstein, Marina S. 1921(?)-1972
Obituary 33-36R
Finkelstein, Milton 1920- 89-92
Finkelstein, Miriam 1928- 108
Finkelstein, Sidney 1910(?)-1974
Obituary 45-48
Finkle, Jason L(eonard) 1926- 23-24R
Finklehoffe, Fred F. 1910-1977 Obituary 73-76
Finkler, Kaja 1935- 114
Finlator, John Haywood 1911- 102
Finlay, Campbell K(irkman) 1909- 7-8R
Finlay, David J(ames) 1934- CANR-16
Earlier sketch in CA 25-28R
Finlay, Fiona
See Stuart, (Violet) Vivian (Finlay)
Finlay, Ian Hamilton 1925- 81-84
See also DLB 40
Finlay, Matthew Henderson 1916- 13-14R
Finlay, William
See Mackay, James (Alexander)
Finlay, Winifred Lindsay Crawford
(McKissack) 1910- 9-10R
See also SATA 23
Finlayson, Ann 1925- 29-32R
See also SATA 8
Finlayson, Roderick (David) 1904- 81-84
Finler, Joel W(aldo) 1938- 77-80
Finletter, Thomas K(night) 1893-1980
Obituary 101
Finley, Gerald Eric 1931- 105
Finley, Glenna
See Witte, Glenna Finley
Finley, Harold M(arshall) 1916- 17-18R
Finley, James 1943- 97-100
Finley, Joseph E(dwin) 1919- 69-72
Finley, Lewis M(erren) 1929- 61-64
Finley, M(oses) I. 1912-1986 .... CANR-10
Obituary 119
Earlier sketch in CA 5-6R
Finley, Martha 1828-1909 Brief entry 118
See also SATA 43
See also DLB 42
Finman, Ted 1931- Brief entry 110
Finn, David 1921- 73-76
Finn, Doug(las Arthur) 1946- 118
Finn, Edward E(rnest) 1908- 115
Finn, Geraldine 1947- 118
Finn, James 1924- Brief entry 108
Finn, Jonathan 1884(?)-1971 Obituary 29-32R
Finn, R. Welldon
See Finn, Reginald Patrick Arthur
Welldon
Finn, Ralph L(eslie) 1912- CANR-9
Earlier sketch in CA 7-8R
Finn, Reginald Patrick Arthur Welldon
1900-1971 .... CANR-10
Earlier sketch in CA 13-14R
Finn, Rex Welldon
See Finn, Reginald Patrick Arthur
Welldon
Finnegan, Robert
See Ryan, Paul William
Finnegan, Ruth H(ilary) 1933- CANR-12
Earlier sketch in CA 25-28R
Finneran, Richard J(ohn) 1943- CANR-12
Earlier sketch in CA 29-32R
Finnerty, Adam Daniel
See Corson-Finnerty, Adam Daniel
Finnerty, Daniel John
See Corson-Finnerty, Adam Daniel
Finney, Ben R(udolph) 1933- CANR-1
Earlier sketch in CA 45-48
Finney, Charles G(randison) 1905-1984 .... CAP-2
Obituary 112
Earlier sketch in CA 29-32
Finney, Gertrude Elva (Bridgeman) 1892- . CAP-1
Earlier sketch in CA 15-16
Finney, Gretchen Ludke 1901- 9-10R
Finney, Humphrey S. 1902- 97-100
Finney, Jack
See Finney, Walter Braden
See also DLB 8
Finney, Mark
See Muir, Kenneth (Arthur)
Finney, Nathaniel Solon 1903-1982
Obituary 108
Finney, Patricia 1958- 97-100
Finney, Paul B(urnham) 1929- 73-76
Finney, Shan 1944- 111
Finney, Theodore M(itchell) 1902- 61-64
Finney, Walter Braden 1911- Brief entry 110
Finnigan, Joan
See MacKenzie, Joan Finnigan
Finnin, (Olive) Mary 106
Finocchiaro, Mary (Bonomo) 1913- 29-32R
Fins, Alice 1944- 110
Fiore, Edith 1930- 85-88
Fiore, Michael V. 1934- 45-48
Fiore, Peter Amadeus 1927- 33-36R
Fiore, Robert Louis 1935- 73-76
Fiore, Silvestro 1921- 19-20R
Fiorenza, Elisabeth Schuessler 1938- 106
Fiorenza, Francis S(chuessler) 1941- 115
Fiori, Pamela A. 1944- 89-92
Fiorina, Morris Paul, Jr. 1946- 85-88
Fiorino, A(ngelo) John 1926- 29-32R
Fiorio, Franco Emilio 1912-1975 Obituary 61-64
Firbank, Louis 1942- Brief entry 117
Firbank, (Arthur Annesley) Ronald
1886-1926 Brief entry 104
See also DLB 36
See also TCLC 1
Firchow, Evelyn Scherabon 1932- CANR-11
Earlier sketch in CA 23-24R
Firchow, Peter (Edgerly) 1937- 37-40R
Firebrace, Aylmer (Newton George) 1886- 7-8R
Fires, Alicia
See Oglesby, Joseph
Fireside, Harvey 1929- 29-32R
Firestone, Harvey S(amuel), Jr.
1898-1973 Obituary 41-44R
Firestone, O(tto) J(ohn) 1913- 41-44R
Firestone, Tom
See Newcomb, Duane G(raham)
Firey, Walter Irving (Jr.) 1916- 1R
Firkins, Peter (Charles) 1926- 107
Firmage, George J(ames) 1928- 9-10R
Firmat, Gustavo (Francisco) Perez
See Perez-Firmat, Gustavo (Francisco)
Firmin, Charlotte 1954- CANR-23
Earlier sketch in CA 106
See also SATA 29
Firmin, Giles 1615-1697 .... DLB-24
Firmin, Peter 1928- CANR-17
Earlier sketch in CA 81-84
See also SATA 15
Firsoff, V(aldemar) Axel 1910- 93-96
First, Ruth 1925-1982 .... CANR-10
Obituary 107
Earlier sketch in CA 53-56
Firth, (Frederick) Anson 1902- 117
Firth, Grace (Ushler) 1922- 73-76
Firth, J. R.
See Firth, John Rupert
Firth, John Rupert 1890-1960 Obituary 116
Firth, Raymond (William) 1901- 65-68
Firth, Robert E. 1921- 77-80
Firth, Tony 1937(?)-1980 Obituary 97-100
Fisch, Edith L. 1923- 77-80
Fisch, Gerald G(rant) 1922- 15-16R
Fisch, Harold 1923- 37-40R
Fisch, Martin L. 1924- 109
Fisch, Max H(arold) 1900- 33-36R
Fisch, Richard 1926- Brief entry 106
Fischbach, Julius 1894- CANR-2
Earlier sketch in CA 7-8R
See also SATA 10
Fischel, Walter J(oseph) 1902-1973 .... CAP-2
Obituary 41-44R
Earlier sketch in CA 23-24
Fischer, Alfred (George) 1920- 73-76
Fischer, Ann 1919-1971 .... CAP-2
Earlier sketch in CA 25-28
Fischer, Arlene 1934- 111
Fischer, Bobby
See Fischer, Robert James
Fischer, Bruno 1908- 77-80
Fischer, Carl H(ahn) 1903- 17-18R
Fischer, Claude S(erge) 1948- 107
Fischer, David Hackett 1935- 17-18R
Fischer, Dietrich 1941- 117
Fischer, Donald E(dward) 1935- 41-44R
Fischer, Edward (Adam) 1914- CANR-16
Earlier sketches in CA 1R, CANR-1
Fischer, Ernst 1899-1972 Obituary 37-40R
Fischer, Fritz 1908- CANR-9
Earlier sketch in CA 65-68
Fischer, George 1923- CANR-9
Earlier sketch in CA 53-56
Fischer, George 1932- 25-28R
Fischer, Gerald C(harles) 1928- CANR-9
Earlier sketch in CA 23-24R
Fischer, J(ohn) L(yle) 1923- 19-20R
Fischer, Joel 1939- CANR-19
Earlier sketches in CA 53-56, CANR-4
Fischer, John 1910-1978 .... CANR-4
Obituary 81-84
Earlier sketch in CA 9-10R
Fischer, John Martin 1952- 124
Fischer, LeRoy H(enry) 1917- CANR-8
Earlier sketch in CA 17-18R
Fischer, Louis 1896-1970 .... CAP-1
Obituary 25-28R
Earlier sketch in CA 11-12
Fischer, Michael R(obert) 1949- 118
Fischer, Robert H. 1918- 37-40R
Fischer, Robert James 1943- 103
Fischer, Roger Adrian 1939- Brief entry 109
Fischer, Vera Kistiakowsky
See Kistiakowsky, Vera
Fischer, Victor 1924- Brief entry 110
Fischer, William F(rank) 1934- Brief entry 111
Fischer, Wolfgang Georg 1933- 33-36R
Fischer-Dieskau, Dietrich 1925- 97-100
Fischer-Galati, Stephen A(lexander) 1924-
Brief entry 117
Fischer-Nagel, Andreas 1951- 123
Fischer-Nagel, Heiderose 1956- 123
Fischetti, John 1916-1980 Obituary 102
Fischl, Viktor
See Dagan, Avigdor
Fischler, Stan(ley I.) Brief entry 116
See also SATA 36
Fischman, Harve 1930- Brief entry 113
Fischman, Leonard L(ipman) 1919- CANR-10
Earlier sketch in CA 15-16R
Fischtrom, Harvey 1933-1974 .... CAP-2
Obituary 53-56
Earlier sketch in CA 25-28
Fish, Byron 1908- 45-48
Fish, Julian
See Campbell, Blanche
Fish, Kenneth L(loyd) 1926- 29-32R
Fish, Margery (Townshend) 1892-1969 .. CANR-4
Earlier sketch in CA 7-8R
Fish, Peter Graham 1937- 69-72
Fish, Robert L. 1912-1981 .... CANR-13
Obituary 103
Earlier sketch in CA 13-14R
Fish, Roy J(ason) 1930- 123
Fish, Roy Jason 1930- Brief entry 118
Fish, Stanley Eugene 1938- Brief entry 112
See also DLB 67
Fishback, Margaret
See Antolini, Margaret Fishback
Fishbane, Michael A(lton) 1943- 113
Fishbein, Harold Dennis 1938- Brief entry .. 105
Fishbein, Meyer H(arry) 1916- 41-44R
Fishbein, Morris 1889-1976 .... CANR-4
Obituary 69-72
Earlier sketch in CA 7-8R
Fishburn, Hummel 1901- CAP-1
Earlier sketch in CA 19-20
Fishburn, Janet Forsythe 1937- 108
Fishburn, Peter C(lingerman) 1936- 45-48
Fishel, Elizabeth 1950- 103
Fishel, Leslie H(enry), Jr. 1921- 23-24R
Fishel, Wesley R(obert) 1919-1977 73-76
Obituary 69-72
Fisher, A(rnold) Garth 1933- 104
Fisher, A(rthur) Stanley T(heodore) 1906- .. 93-96
Fisher, Aileen (Lucia) 1906- CANR-17
Earlier sketches in CA 5-6R, CANR-2
See also SATA 1, 25
Fisher, Alan 1929- 121
Fisher, Alan W(ashburn) 1939- 53-56
Fisher, Alden L(owell) 1928-1970 .... CAP-2
Earlier sketch in CA 25-28
Fisher, Allan C(arroll), Jr. 1919- 112
Fisher, Allan G(eorge) B(arnard)
1895-1976 .... 33-36R
Fisher, Allen J. 1907(?)-1980 Obituary 102
Fisher, Ameel J(oseph) 1909- 104
Fisher, Arthur 1931- 110
Fisher, Barbara 1940- 104
See also SATA 34, 44
Fisher, Bart (Steven) 1943- 45-48
Fisher, Benjamin Franklin IV 1940- 112
Fisher, Bob
See Fisher, Robert Percival
Fisher, Bruce 1931- 118
Fisher, C(harles) William 1916- CANR-6
Earlier sketch in CA 7-8R
Fisher, Charles Alfred 1916-1982(?)
Obituary 105
Fisher, Clavin C(argill) 1912- 65-68
See also SATA 24
Fisher, Clay
See Allen, Henry Wilson
Fisher, David E(limelech) 1932- CANR-22
Earlier sketches in CA 53-56, CANR-4
Fisher, Dominic (Mayne Maitland) 1953- 124
Fisher, Don 1933(?)-1983 Obituary 111
Fisher, Dorothy (Frances) Canfield
1879-1958 Brief entry 114
See also YABC 1
See also DLB 9
Fisher, Douglas 1934- 102
Fisher, Douglas 1954- 118
Fisher, Douglas Mason 1919- 89-92
Fisher, Edward 1902- 2R
Fisher, Elizabeth 1941- 117
Fisher, Ernest Arthur 1887- 13-14R
Fisher, Esther Oshiver 1910- 85-88
Fisher, Eugene J(oseph) 1943- CANR-22
Earlier sketch in CA 105
Fisher, Florence (Anna) 1928- Brief entry 112
Fisher, Franklin M(arvin) 1934- 17-18R
Fisher, Fred L(ewis) 1911- CANR-5
Earlier sketch in CA 4R
Fisher, (Donald) Gary 1938- 103
Fisher, Gene H. 1922- 41-44R
Fisher, Gene L(ouis) 1947- 81-84
Fisher, George W. 1910(?)-1987 Obituary .. 124
Fisher, Glen H(arry) 1922- Brief entry 111
Fisher, Glenn W(illiam) 1924- 53-56
Fisher, Gordon N(eil) 1928-1985 Obituary .. 117
Fisher, Harold H. 1890-1975 Obituary 61-64
Fisher, Harvey Irvin 1916- 69-72
Fisher, Helen E(lizabeth) 1945- 108
Fisher, Humphrey J(ohn) 1933- 33-36R
Fisher, J(ohn) R(obert) 1943- CANR-1
Earlier sketch in CA 45-48
Fisher, J(oseph) Thomas 1936- 33-36R
Fisher, James (Maxwell McConnell)
1912-1970 Obituary 89-92
Fisher, James R(aymond), Jr. 1937- 81-84
Fisher, Joe 1947- 103
Fisher, Johanna 1922- 93-96
Fisher, John (Oswald Hamilton) 1909- 81-84
See also SATA 15
Fisher, John C(harles) 1927- 41-44R
Fisher, John H(urt) 1919- CANR-11
Earlier sketch in CA 21-22R
Fisher, Kenneth L(awrence) 1950- 118
Fisher, Kim N. 1948- 121
Fisher, Laine
See Howard, James A(rch)
Fisher, Laura Harrison 1934- 15-16R
See also SATA 5
Fisher, Lawrence V. 1923- 19-20R
Fisher, Lee 1908- 33-36R
Fisher, Leonard Everett 1924- CANR-2
Earlier sketch in CA 3R
See also SATA 4, 34
See also SAAS 1
See also DLB 61
Fisher, Lillian Estelle 1891- CAP-1
Earlier sketch in CA 15-16
Fisher, Lois H(amilton) 1936- 113
Fisher, Lois I. 1948- 113
See also SATA 35, 38
Fisher, Lois Jeannette 1909- 7-8R
Fisher, Louis 1934- 37-40R
Fisher, M(ary) F(rances) K(ennedy) 1908- .. 77-80
Fisher, Malcolm R(obertson) 1923-
Brief entry 110
Fisher, Margaret B(arrow) 1918- 17-18R
Fisher, Margery (Turner) 1913- 73-76
See also SATA 20
Fisher, Margot
See Paine, Lauran (Bosworth)
Fisher, Marvin 1927- 21-22R
Fisher, Mary L. 1928- 33-36R
Fisher, Michael John 1933- CANR-3
Earlier sketch in CA 2R
Fisher, Miles Mark 1899-1970 .... CAP-1
Earlier sketch in CA 15-16
Fisher, Miriam Louise (Scharfe) 1939- 15-16R
Fisher, Morris 1922- 21-22R
Fisher, Neal F(loyd) 1936- 106
Fisher, Nigel 1913- 102
Fisher, Norman George 1910-1972
Obituary 107
Fisher, Peter Jack 1930- 69-72
Fisher, Philip 1941- 113
Fisher, Philip A(rthur) 1907- 61-64
Fisher, R. A.
See Fisher, Ronald A(ylmer)
Fisher, Ralph Talcott, Jr. 1920- 41-44R
Fisher, Rhoda Lee 1924- 65-68

Fisher, Richard 1936- 19-20R
Fisher, Richard B(ernard) 1919- 77-80
Fisher, Robert (Tempest) 1943- 109
See also SATA 47
Fisher, Robert C(harles) 1930- 53-56
Fisher, Robert J(ay) 1924- 61-64
Fisher, Robert Percival 1935- 93-96
Fisher, Roger (Dummer) 1922- 37-40R
Fisher, Ronald A(ylmer) 1890-1962
Obituary 112
Fisher, Roy 1930- CANR-16
Earlier sketch in CA 81-84
See also DLB 40
See also CLC 25
Fisher, Rudolph 1897-1934 124
Brief entry 107
See also DLB 51
See also TCLC 11
Fisher, Seymour 1922- CANR-12
Earlier sketch in CA 33-36R
Fisher, Shelton 1911-1985 Obituary 115
Fisher, Sidney Thomson 1908- 124
Fisher, Sterling Wesley 1899(?)-1978 85-88
Obituary 81-84
Fisher, Susan M(ichal) 1937- 119
Fisher, Sydney G.
See Fisher, Sydney George
Fisher, Sydney George 1856-1927
Brief entry 122
See also DLB 47
Fisher, Vardis (Alvero) 1895-1968 ....5-6R
Obituary 25-28R
See also DLB 9
See also CLC 7
Fisher, Wade
See Norwood, Victor G(eorge) C(harles)
Fisher, Wallace E. 1918- CANR-10
Earlier sketch in CA 23-24R
Fisher, Walter R. 1931- 15-16R
Fisher, Welthy Honsinger 1879-1980 .... CANR-2
Obituary 102
Earlier sketch in CA 4R
Fisher, Wesley Andrew 1944- 104
Fisher, William Bayne 1916-1984 65-68
Obituary 113
Fishler, Mary Shiverick 1920- 7-8R
Fishman, Betty G(oldstein) 1918- 7-8R
Fishman, Burton J(ohn) 1942- 45-48
Fishman, Charles 1942- CANR-7
Earlier sketch in CA 57-60
Fishman, George Samuel 1937- 25-28R
Fishman, Jack 1920- CANR-7
Earlier sketch in CA 9-10R
Fishman, Joshua A(aron) 1926- CANR-15
Earlier sketch in CA 41-44R
Fishman, Ken 1950- 105
Fishman, Leo 1914-1975 ....19-20R
Obituary 120
Fishman, Lew 1939- CANR-11
Earlier sketch in CA 61-64
Fishman, Robert (Lawrence) 1946- 112
Fishman, Sterling 1932- 45-48
Fishof, David 1956- 115
Fishwick, Marshall William 1923- CANR-6
Earlier sketch in CA 7-8R
Fisk, E(rnest) K(elvin) 1917- 19-20R
Fisk, McKee 1900- CAP-2
Earlier sketch in CA 21-22
Fisk, Nicholas 1923- CANR-11
Earlier sketch in CA 65-68
See also SATA 25
Fisk, Samuel 1907- 57-60
Fiske, Edward B. 1937- CANR-16
Earlier sketch in CA 85-88
Fiske, John 1608-1677 .... DLB-24
Fiske, John 1842-1901 .... DLB-47, 64
Fiske, Marjorie CANR-1
Earlier sketch in CA 45-48
Fiske, Roger E(lwyn) 1910- 13-14R
Fiske, Sharon
See Hill, Pamela
Fiske, Tarleton
See Bloch, Robert (Albert)
Fisketjon, Gary 1954- Brief entry 123
Fiskin, A(bram) M. I. 1916-1975 .... CAP-2
Earlier sketch in CA 23-24
Fison, Joseph Edward 1906-1972
Obituary 114
Fiss, Owen M(itchell) 1938- 112
Fiszel, Henryk 1910- 29-32R
Fiszman, Joseph R. 1921- 41-44R
Fitch, Alger Morton, Jr. 1919- 53-56
Fitch, Bob
See Fitch, Robert Beck
Fitch, Clarke
See Sinclair, Upton (Beall)
Fitch, (William) Clyde 1865-1909
Brief entry 110
See also DLB 7
Fitch, Donald S(heldon) 1949- 106
Fitch, Edwin M(edbery) 1902- CAP-2
Earlier sketch in CA 25-28
Fitch, George Ashmore 1883-1979
Obituary 85-88
Fitch, Geraldine T(ownsend) 1892(?)-1976
Obituary 69-72
Fitch, James Marston 1909- 89-92
Fitch, John IV
See Cormier, Robert (Edmund)
Fitch, Kenneth (Leonard) 1929- 49-52
Fitch, Lyle C(raig) 1913- 15-16R
Fitch, Raymond E(dward) 1930- 110
Fitch, Robert Beck 1938- 21-22R
Fitch, Stanley K. 1920- 29-32R
Fitch, Thomas 1700(?)-1774 .... DLB-31
Fitch, William Clyde 1865-1909 .... DLB-7
Fitch, Willis Stetson 1896(?)-1978
Obituary 81-84
Fite, Gilbert C(ourtland) 1918- 33-36R
Fite, James David 1933- 107
Fite, Mack
See Schneck, Stephen
Fitler, Mary Biddle 1878(?)-1966
Obituary 25-28R
Fitschen, Dale 1937- 77-80
See also SATA 20
Fitt, Mary
See Freeman, Kathleen
Fitter, Richard Sidney Richmond
1913- CANR-11
Earlier sketch in CA 65-68
Fitting, Greer A. 1943- 81-84
Fitting, James E. 1939- 45-48
Fitting, Melvin (Chris) 1942- CANR-11
Earlier sketch in CA 29-32R
Fitton, James 1899-1982 Obituary 106
Fitts, Dudley 1903-1968 93-96
Obituary 25-28R
Fitts, Henry (King) 1914- 113
Fitts, William Howard 1918- 21-22R
Fitz, Jean DeWitt 1912- 29-32R
Fitzalan, Roger
See Trevor, Elleston
Fitzell, John 1922- 13-14R
Fitzgerald, Arlene J. CANR-8
Earlier sketch in CA 23-24R
Fitzgerald, Barbara
See Value, Barbara Ann
Fitzgerald, Barry Charles 1939- 37-40R
FitzGerald, Brian Seymour Vesey
See Vesey-FitzGerald, Brian Seymour
FitzGerald, C(harles) P(atrick) 1902- CANR-11
Earlier sketch in CA 19-20R
Fitzgerald, Captain Hugh
See Baum, L(yman) Frank
Fitz-Gerald, Carolyn 1932- 41-44R
FitzGerald, Cathleen 1932-1987 ....33-36R
Obituary 121
See also SATA 50
Fitzgerald, E(dmund) V(alpy) K(nox)
1947- 73-76
FitzGerald, Edward 1809-1883 .... DLB-32
Fitzgerald, Edward 1898(?)-1982 Obituary .. 108
Fitzgerald, Edward Earl 1919- 73-76
See also SATA 20
Fitzgerald, Ellen
See Stevenson, Florence
Fitzgerald, Ernest A. 1925- CANR-12
Earlier sketch in CA 29-32R
Fitzgerald, F(rancis) A(nthony) 1940- ... SATA-15
Fitzgerald, F(rancis) Scott (Key)
1896-1940 123
Brief entry 110
See also DLB 4, 9
See also DLBY 81
See also DLBD 1
See also TCLC 1, 6, 14
See also AITN 1
FitzGerald, Frances 1940- 41-44R
FitzGerald, Garret 1926- 109
Fitzgerald, George R. 1932- CANR-17
Earlier sketch in CA 97-100
Fitzgerald, Gerald (Pierce) 1930- 37-40R
Fitzgerald, Gerald E(dward) 1920- 25-28R
Fitz Gerald, Gregory 1923- CANR-1
Earlier sketch in CA 49-52
Fitzgerald, Hal
See Johnson, Joseph E(arl)
Fitzgerald, Harold Alvin 1896-1984
Obituary 114
Fitzgerald, Hiram E(arl) 1940- CANR-16
Earlier sketch in CA 77-80
Fitzgerald, Jack
See Shea, John Gerald
Fitzgerald, James A(ugustine) 1892- CANR-1
Earlier sketch in CA 1R
Fitzgerald, James V. 1889(?)-1976
Obituary 69-72
Fitzgerald, John
See Fazzano, Joseph E.
Fitzgerald, John Dennis 1907- 93-96
See also SATA 20
See also CLR 1
Fitzgerald, John Joseph 1928- 37-40R
Fitzgerald, Judith 1952- 113
Fitzgerald, Julia
See Watson, Julia
FitzGerald, Kathleen Whalen 1938- 109
FitzGerald, Laurine Elisabeth 1930- 37-40R
Fitzgerald, Lawrence P(ennybaker)
1906-1976 .... CANR-2
Earlier sketch in CA 3R
Fitzgerald, Maury 1906(?)-1986 Obituary ... 121
Fitzgerald, Merni Ingrassia 1955- 124
Fitzgerald, Michael G(arrett) 1950- 77-80
Fitzgerald, Nancy 1951- 85-88
Fitzgerald, Patrick (John) 1928- 9-10R
Fitzgerald, Penelope 1916- 85-88
See also DLB 14
See also CLC 19
Fitzgerald, Randall 1950- 118
Fitzgerald, Richard (Ambrose) 1938- 45-48
Fitzgerald, Robert (Stuart) 1910-1985 .... CANR-1
Obituary 114
Earlier sketch in CA 2R
See also DLBY 80
See also CLC 39
FitzGerald, Robert D(avid) 1902- 19-20R
See also CLC 19
FitzGerald, Stephen (Arthur) 1938- 97-100
Fitzgerald, Tamsin 1950- 97-100
Fitzgerald, Thomas 1819-1891 .... DLB-23
Fitzgerald, Zelda (Sayre) 1900-1948
Brief entry 117
See also DLBY 84
FitzGibbon, (Robert Louis) Constantine
(Lee-Dillon) 1919-1983 .... CANR-2
Obituary 109
Earlier sketch in CA 4R
Fitzgibbon, Russell H(umke)
1902-1979 .... CANR-14
Earlier sketch in CA 65-68
FitzGibbon, Theodora (Joanne Eileen
Winifred) Rosling 1916- CANR-3
Earlier sketch in CA 7-8R
Fitzgibbons, James P. 1912(?)-1983
Obituary 110
Fitzhardinge, Joan Margaret 1912- CANR-23
Earlier sketches in CA 15-16R, CANR-6
See also SATA 2
Fitzhenry, Robert Irvine 1918- 110
Fitzhugh, Louise 1928-1974 .... CAP-2
Obituary 53-56
Earlier sketch in CA 29-32
See also SATA 1, 24, 45
See also DLB 52
See also CLR 1
Fitzhugh, Robert Tyson 1906-1981
Obituary 104
Fitzhugh, William 1651(?)-1701 .... DLB-24
Fitzlyon, (Cecily) April (Mead) 1920- 7-8R
Fitzlyon, Kyril 1910- 93-96
Fitzmaurice, George 1877-1963 Obituary ..93-96
Fitzmyer, Joseph A(ugustine) 1920- CANR-5
Earlier sketch in CA 9-10R
Fitzpatrick, Daniel Robert 1891-1969
Obituary 89-92
Fitzpatrick, James K(evin) 1942- 65-68
Fitzpatrick, Joseph P(atrick) 1913- 17-18R
Fitzpatrick, Kathryn 1934- 113
FitzPatrick, Paul Joseph 1894-1984
Obituary 111
Fitzpatrick, Tom 1927- Brief entry 111
FitzRalph, Matthew
See McInerny, Ralph
Fitz-Randolph, Jane (Currens) 1915- 103
Fitzroy, Rosamond
See Briggs, Desmond Lawther
Fitzsimmons, Cleo 1900- 1R
Fitzsimmons, Thomas 1926- CANR-15
Earlier sketch in CA 33-36R
Fitz-Simon, Christopher 1934- 113
Fitzsimons, Louise 1932- 61-64
Fitzsimons, M(athew) A(nthony) 1912- ...13-14R
Fitzsimons, Neal 1928- 33-36R
FitzSimons, Raymund CANR-15
Earlier sketch in CA 33-36R
FitzSimons, Ruth M(arie Mangan) 53-56
Fitzwilliam, Michael
See Lyons, J. B.
Fivelson, Scott 1954- 117
Fix, Paul
See Morrison, Paul Fix
Fix, William R. 1941- CANR-15
Earlier sketch in CA 85-88
Fixler, Michael 1927- 15-16R
Fixx, James F(uller) 1932-1984 .... CANR-13
Earlier sketch in CA 73-76
Fixx, Jim
See Fixx, James F(uller)
Fizer, John 1925- 53-56
Fjelde, Rolf (Gerhard) 1926- 17-18R
Flach, Frederic F(rancis) 1927- 81-84
Flachmann, Michael 1942- 117
Flack, Audrey 1931- 106
Flack, Dora D(utson) 1919- CANR-21
Earlier sketches in CA 57-60, CANR-6
Flack, Elmer Ellsworth 1894- 17-18R
Flack, Marjorie 1897-1958 Brief entry 112
See also YABC 2
Flack, Naomi John White CANR-1
Earlier sketch in CA 1R
See also SATA 35, 40
Flacks, Niki 1943- 110
Flacks, Richard 1938- 49-52
Fladeland, Betty 1919- 45-48
Flader, Susan L. 1941- 81-84
Flagg, Fannie 1941- 111
Flagg, Kenneth
See Ayvazian, L. Fred
Flagstad, Kirsten 1895-1962 Obituary 112
Flaherty, Daniel Leo 1929- 89-92
Flaherty, David H(arris) 1940- 25-28R
Flaherty, Doug(las Ernest) 1939- 33-36R
Flaherty, Gloria 1938- 85-88
Flaherty, Joe 1936(?)-1983 Obituary 111
Flaherty, Robert J(oseph) 1884-1951
Brief entry 115
Flaherty, Robert Joseph 1933- 73-76
Flaherty, Vincent X. 1908(?)-1977
Obituary 73-76
Flaiano, Ennio 1910-1972 Obituary 37-40R
Flake, Chad J(ohn) 1929- 29-32R
Flamholtz, Eric 1943- 57-60
Flamm, Dudley 1931- 25-28R
Flamm, Gerald R(obert) 1916- 77-80
Flamm, Jerry
See Flamm, Gerald R(obert)
Flammarion, (Nicolas) Camille 1842-1925
Brief entry 120
Flammarion, Henri (Claude) 1910-1985
Obituary 117
Flammer, Philip M(eynard) 1928- 45-48
Flammonde, Paris 19-20R
Flanagan, Dorothy Belle
See Hughes, Dorothy B(elle)
Flanagan, John C(lemans) 1906- CANR-1
Earlier sketch in CA 4R
Flanagan, John T(heodore) 1906- 19-20R
Flanagan, Joseph David Stanislaus
1903- 13-14R
Flanagan, Neal M. 1920-1985 ....19-20R
Obituary 117
Flanagan, Robert (James) 1941- 33-36R
Flanagan, Thomas (James Bonner) 1923- ... 108
See also DLBY 80
See also CLC 25
Flanagan, William G(eorge) 1940- CANR-15
Earlier sketch in CA 93-96
Flanagan, William G(eorge) 1942- 119
Flanagan, William I. 1916(?)-1986
Obituary 118
Flanders, Helen Hartness 1890-1972 .... CAP-1
Obituary 33-36R
Earlier sketch in CA 15-16
Flanders, Henry Jackson, Jr. 1921- 33-36R
Flanders, James P(rescott) 1942- 69-72
Flanders, Jane (Hess) 1940- 110
Flanders, Michael (Henry) 1922-1975 ... CANR-4
Obituary 57-60
Earlier sketch in CA 7-8R
Flanders, Ned A. 1918- 37-40R
Flanders, Ralph Edward 1880-1970 .... CAP-1
Earlier sketch in CA 11-12
Flanders, Rebecca
See Ball, Donna
Flanders, Robert Bruce 1930- 19-20R
Flanery, E(dward) B(oyd) 1932- 61-64
Flanigan, Lloyd A(llen) 1933- 33-36R
Flanner, Hildegarde
See Monhoff, June Hildegarde Flanner
See also DLB 48
Flanner, Janet 1892-1978 .... CANR-13
Obituary 81-84
Earlier sketch in CA 65-68
See also DLB 4
Flannery, Edward H(ugh) 1912- 15-16R
Flannery, Harry W. 1900-1975 .... CAP-1
Obituary 57-60
Earlier sketch in CA 9-10
Flannery, James W(illiam) 1936-
Brief entry 110
Flannery, Peter 1951- 104
Flannery, Sean
See Hagberg, David J(ames)
Flasch, Joy 1932- 37-40R
Flaster, Donald J(ohn) 1932- 115
Flath, Arnold W(illiam), J. 1929- 65-68
Flato, Charles 1908(?)-1984 Obituary 111
Flattau, Edward 1937- 65-68
Flavell, Carol Willsey Bell 1939- 73-76
Flavell, John H(urley) 1928- CANR-11
Earlier sketch in CA 19-20R
Flavin, Martin 1883-1967 ....5-6R
Obituary 25-28R
See also DLB 9
Flavius, Brother
See Ellison, James E.
Flaxman, Traudl 1942- 25-28R
Flayderman, Phillip C(harles) 1930-1969 .. CAP-2
Earlier sketch in CA 23-24
Fleck, Betty
See Paine, Lauran (Bosworth)
Fleck, Henrietta 1903- 77-80
Fleck, Richard Francis 1937- CANR-18
Earlier sketch in CA 102
Flecker, (Herman) James Elroy 1884-1915
Brief entry 109
See also DLB 10, 19
Fleece, Jeffrey (Atkinson) 1920- 17-18R
Fleege, Urban H(erman) 1908- CANR-1
Earlier sketch in CA 45-48
Fleer, Jack D(avid) 1937- 25-28R
Fleeson, Doris 1901-1970 Obituary 93-96
See also DLB 29
Fleetwood, Frances 1902- CANR-17
Earlier sketches in CA 45-48, CANR-1
Fleetwood, Frank
See Fleetwood, Frances
Fleetwood, Hugh (Nigel) 1944- Brief entry .. 112
Fleetwood-Hesketh, (Charles) Peter
(Fleetwood) 1905-1985 Obituary 115
Flegg, (Henry) Graham 1924- 114
Fleischbein, Sister M. Catherine Frederic
1902- 5-6R
Fleischer, Leonore Brief entry 109
See also SATA 47
Fleischer, Manfred P(aul) 1928- 29-32R
Fleischer, Max 1889-1972 Obituary 109
See also SATA 30
Fleischer, Nathaniel S. 1888(?)-1972
Obituary 37-40R
Fleischhauer-Hardt, Helga 1936- 102
See also SATA 30
Fleischman, Harry 1914- CANR-3
Earlier sketch in CA 5-6R
Fleischman, Paul 1952- 113
See also SATA 32, 39
Fleischman, (Albert) Sid(ney) 1920- CANR-5
Earlier sketch in CA 3R
See also SATA 8
See also CLR 1
Fleischmann, Glen H(arvey) 1909- 33-36R
Fleischmann, Harriet 1904- CAP-2
Earlier sketch in CA 21-22
Fleischmann, Raoul H(erbert) 1885-1969
Obituary 115
Fleischmann, Wolfgang Bernard 1928- 116
Fleisher, Belton Mendel 1935- 69-72
Fleisher, Frederic 1933- 21-22R
Fleisher, Martin 1925- 45-48
Fleisher, Michael (Lawrence) 1942- 25-28R
Fleisher, Robbin 1951-1977 .... SATA-49
Fleisher, Wilfried 1897(?)-1976 Obituary ..65-68
Fleishman, Avrom (Hirsch) 1933- 21-22R

Fleishman, Edwin A(lan) 1927- ... CANR-11
Earlier sketch in CA 21-22R
Fleishman, Seymour 1918- Brief entry ... 111
See also SATA 32
Fleisser, Marieluise
See Haindl, Marieluise
See also DLB 56
Flemer, William III 1922- ... 61-64
Fleming, Alice Mulcahey 1928- ... CANR-2
Earlier sketch in CA 4R
See also SATA 9
Fleming, Amalia 1912-1986 Obituary ... 118
Fleming, Berry 1899- ... CANR-18
Earlier sketches in CA 1R, CANR-2
Fleming, C(harlotte) M(ary) 1894- ... 7-8R
Fleming, D(enna) F(rank) 1893- ... CANR-1
Earlier sketch in CA 1R
Fleming, David A(rnold) 1939- ... 93-96
Fleming, Donald M(ethuen) 1905-1986
Obituary ... 121
Fleming, Elizabeth P. 1888-1985 Obituary ... 119
See also SATA 48
Fleming, George J(oseph) 1917- ... 37-40R
Fleming, Gerald 1921- ... 53-56
Fleming, Guy
See Masur, Harold Q.
Fleming, H(orace) K(ingston) 1901- ... 33-36R
Fleming, Harold (Lee) 1927- ... 17-18R
Fleming, Harold M(anchester)
1900-19(?) ... CAP-2
Earlier sketch in CA 21-22
Fleming, Ian (Lancaster) 1908-1964 ... 7-8R
See also SATA 9
See also CLC 3, 30
Fleming, Irene 1923(?)-1979 Obituary ... 89-92
Fleming, Jennifer Baker 1943- ... 77-80
Fleming, Joan Margaret 1908-1980 ... 81-84
Obituary ... 102
Fleming, June 1935- ... 110
Fleming, Lady Amalia
See Fleming, Amalia
Fleming, Laurence (William Howie) 1929- ... 107
Fleming, Macklin 1911- ... 77-80
Fleming, Miles 1919- ... 29-32R
Fleming, Oliver
See MacDonald, Philip
Fleming, (Robert) Peter 1907-1971
Obituary ... 33-36R
Fleming, Ray(mond) 1945- ... 115
Fleming, Robert H(enry) 1912-1984
Obituary ... 114
Fleming, Ronald Lee 1941- ... 108
Fleming, Sandford 1888- ... CAP-1
Earlier sketch in CA 9-10
Fleming, Susan 1932- ... CANR-14
Earlier sketch in CA 81-84
See also SATA 32
Fleming, Theodore B(owman), Jr. 1917- ... 45-48
Fleming, Thomas (James) 1927- ... CANR-10
Earlier sketch in CA 7-8R
See also SATA 8
See also CLC 37
Fleming, William (Coleman) 1909- ... 17-18R
Flemming, Nicholas Coit 1936- ... 97-100
Flemmons, Jerry 1936- ... 124
Flender, Harold 1924- ... 49-52
Flesch, Janos Laszlo 1933(?)-1983
Obituary ... 111
Flesch, Rudolf (Franz) 1911-1986 ... CANR-3
Obituary ... 120
Earlier sketch in CA 9-10R
Flesch, Y.
See Flesch, Yolande (Catarina)
Flesch, Yolande (Catarina) 1950- ... 122
Flescher, Irwin 1926- ... 37-40R
Flescher, Joachim 1906(?)-1976
Obituary ... 65-68
Fletcher, Adele (Whitely) 1898- ... CAP-1
Earlier sketch in CA 17-18
Fletcher, Alan Mark 1928- ... 73-76
Fletcher, Angus (John Stewart) 1930- ... 104
Fletcher, Anthony John 1941- ... 73-76
Fletcher, Arnold Charles 1917- ... 17-18R
Fletcher, Banister F.
See Fletcher, Banister Flight
Fletcher, Banister Flight 1866-1953
Brief entry ... 123
Fletcher, Barbara (Helen) 1935- ... 110
Fletcher, Basil Alais 1900-1983 ... 65-68
Obituary ... 109
Fletcher, Charlie May Hogue 1897- ... 9-10R
See also SATA 3
Fletcher, Colin 1922- ... CANR-11
Earlier sketch in CA 13-14R
See also SATA 28
See also AITN 1
Fletcher, David
See Barber, D(ulan) F(riar Whilberton)
Fletcher, Dirk
See Cunningham, Chet
Fletcher, Geoffrey Scowcroft 1923- ... 103
Fletcher, George U.
See Pratt, (Murray) Fletcher
Fletcher, Grace Nies 1895- ... 7-8R
Fletcher, H(arry) L(utf) V(erne)
1902-197(?) ... CANR-4
Earlier sketch in CA 11-12R
Fletcher, Harold Roy 1907-1978 Obituary ... 111
Fletcher, Harris Francis 1892-1979 ... 1R
Obituary ... 103
Fletcher, Harvey 1884-1981 Obituary ... 108
Fletcher, Helen Jill 1911- ... 9-10R
See also SATA 13
Fletcher, Henry Lancelot Aubrey
See Aubrey-Fletcher, Henry Lancelot
Fletcher, Ian 1920- Brief entry ... 124
Fletcher, (Minna) Inglis ... 7-8R
See also AITN 1
Fletcher, J(oseph) S(mith) 1863-1935
Brief entry ... 109
Fletcher, Jesse C. 1931- ... CANR-4
Earlier sketch in CA 11-12R
Fletcher, John 1579-1625 ... DLB-58
Fletcher, John (Walter James) 1937- ... CANR-15
Earlier sketch in CA 81-84
Fletcher, John C(aldwell) 1931- ... 124
Fletcher, John Gould 1886-1950
Brief entry ... 107
See also DLB 4, 45
Fletcher, Joseph (Francis III) 1905- ... CANR-11
Earlier sketch in CA 21-22R
Fletcher, Leon 1921- ... 49-52
Fletcher, Lucille
See Wallop, Lucille Fletcher
Fletcher, Marilyn P(endleton) 1940- ... 106
Fletcher, Marjorie 1941- Brief entry ... 113
Fletcher, Mary ... AITN-1
Fletcher, (William) Miles (III) 1946- ... 114
Fletcher, Richard E. 1917(?)-1983
Obituary ... 109
See also SATA 34
Fletcher, Rick
See Fletcher, Richard E.
Fletcher, Robert H. 1885(?)-1972
Obituary ... 37-40R
Fletcher, Roger A(nthony) 1942- ... 121
Fletcher, Ronald 1921- ... CANR-13
Earlier sketch in CA 33-36R
Fletcher, Sir Banister
See Fletcher, Banister Flight
Fletcher, William C(atherwood) 1932- ... 23-24R
Fletcher, William W(higham) 1918- ... CANR-15
Earlier sketch in CA 81-84
Fletcher, Winston 1937- ... 118
Fletcher-Cooke, John 1911- ... 102
Fleur, Anne 1901- ... SATA-31
Fleur, Paul
See Pohl, Frederik
Fleure, H. J.
See Fleure, Herbert John
Fleure, Herbert John 1877-1969 Obituary ... 115
Fleuridas, Ellie Rae
See Sherman, Eleanor Rae
Fleury, Delphine
See Amatora, Sister Mary
Flew, Antony G(arrard) N(ewton)
1923- ... CANR-18
Earlier sketches in CA 5-6R, CANR-3
Flexner, Eleanor 1908- ... 45-48
Flexner, James Thomas 1908- ... CANR-2
Earlier sketch in CA 4R
See also SATA 9
Flexner, Stuart Berg 1928- ... CANR-11
Earlier sketch in CA 15-16R
Flick, Carlos Thomas 1927- ... 89-92
Fliegel, Frederick C(hristian) 1925- ... 49-52
Flieger, Wilhelm 1931- ... 25-28R
Flier, Michael S(tephen) 1941- ... CANR-14
Earlier sketch in CA 37-40R
Fliess, Peter J(oachim) 1915- ... 21-22R
Flinders, Neil J. 1934- ... 21-22R
Flink, James J(ohn) 1932- Brief entry ... 112
Flink, Salomon J. 1906-1983 ... CANR-17
Earlier sketch in CA 2R
Flinn, M(ichael) W(alter) 1917-1983 ... CANR-13
Obituary ... 110
Earlier sketch in CA 19-20R
Flint, Betty M. 1920- ... 23-24R
Flint, Cort R(ay) 1915- ... 49-52
Flint, E. de P.
See Fielden, T(homas) P(erceval)
Flint, F(rank) S(tuart) 1885-1960 Obituary ... 113
See also DLB 19
Flint, Homer Eon 1892-1924 Brief entry ... 114
Flint, John E(dgar) 1930- ... 37-40R
Flint, Lucy 1954- ... 115
Flippo, Chet 1943- ... 89-92
Flippo, Edwin B(ly) 1925- ... CANR-13
Earlier sketch in CA 33-36R
Flitner, David P(erkins), Jr. 1949- ... CANR-1
Earlier sketch in CA 45-48
See also SATA 7
Floan, Howard R(ussell) 1918- ... 19-20R
Floethe, Louise Lee 1913- ... CANR-2
Earlier sketch in CA 1R
See also SATA 4
Floethe, Richard 1901- ... 33-36R
See also SATA 4
Floherty, John Joseph 1882-1964 ... SATA-25
Flood, Charles Bracelen 1929- ... 41-44R
Flood, Curt(is Charles) 1938- Brief entry ... 115
Flood, E(dward) Thadeus 1932- ... 49-52
Flood, John M(ichael) 1947- ... 115
Flood, Kenneth Urban 1925- ... 11-12R
Flood, Robert G. 1935- ... CANR-22
Earlier sketch in CA 106
Flook, Maria 1952- ... 110
Flora, Fletcher 1914-1969 ... CANR-3
Earlier sketch in CA 1R
Flora, James (Royer) 1914- ... CANR-3
Earlier sketch in CA 5-6R
See also SATA 1, 30
Flora, Joseph M(artin) 1934- ... CANR-21
Earlier sketches in CA 15-16R, CANR-5
Flora, Paul 1922- Brief entry ... 113
Floren, Lee 1910- ... CANR-18
Earlier sketches in CA 5-6R, CANR-3
Florence, Philip Sargant 1890-1982
Obituary ... 106
Florence, Ronald 1942- ... CANR-15
Earlier sketch in CA 33-36R
Florentin, Eddy 1923- ... 49-52
Flores, Angel 1900- ... CANR-19
Earlier sketch in CA 103
Flores, Dan Louie 1948- ... 121
Flores, Ivan 1923- ... CANR-22
Earlier sketches in CA 19-20R, CANR-7
Flores, Janis 1946- ... CANR-10
Earlier sketch in CA 65-68
Flores, John 1943- ... 77-80
Florescu, Radu R. 1925- ... 41-44R
Florez, Pablo de Azcarate y
See Azcarate y Florez, Pablo de
Florian, Douglas 1950- ... 123
See also SATA 19
Florian, Tibor 1908- ... 73-76
Florin, Lambert F. 1905- ... CANR-7
Earlier sketch in CA 17-18R
Florinsky, Michael T(imothy)
1894-1981 ... CANR-15
Obituary ... 105
Earlier sketch in CA 1R
Floriot, Rene 1902-1975 Obituary ... 61-64
Florit, Eugenio 1903- ... 104
Florman, Samuel C(harles) 1925- ... 102
Florovsky, Georges (Vasilievich)
1893-1979 Obituary ... 111
Flory, Charles D(avid) 1902- ... 41-44R
Flory, Harry R. 1899-1976 Obituary ... 69-72
Flory, Jane Trescott 1917- ... CANR-3
Earlier sketch in CA 9-10R
See also SATA 22
Flory, Julia McCune 1882-1971 ... CAP-2
Obituary ... 29-32R
Earlier sketch in CA 21-22
Flory, Paul J(ohn) 1910-1985 Obituary ... 117
Floud, Roderick 1942- ... CANR-1
Earlier sketch in CA 45-48
Flower, Dean S. 1938- ... 21-22R
Flower, Desmond (John Newman) 1907- ... 9-10R
Flower, Elizabeth Farquhar 1914- ... 103
Flower, Harry A(lfred) 1901- ... CAP-1
Earlier sketch in CA 11-12
Flower, (Harry) John 1936- ... 37-40R
Flower, Margaret Cameron Coss ... 61-64
Flower, (Walter) Newman 1879-1964
Obituary ... 109
Flower, Raymond (Charles) 1921- ... 108
Flowerdew, Phyllis ... 103
See also SATA 33
Flowers, Ann Moore 1923- ... 9-10R
Flowers, Betty S(ue) 1947- ... 65-68
Flowers, Charles 1942- ... 29-32R
Flowers, Charles E(ly, Jr.) 1920- ... 93-96
Flowers, John V(ictor) 1938- ... 106
Flowers, Paul Abbott 1905-1984 Obituary ... 112
Floyd, Barry Neil 1925- ... 33-36R
Floyd, Gareth 1940- ... SATA-31
Floyd, Harriet 1925- ... 69-72
Floyd, Lois Gray 1910(?)-1978 ... 85-88
Obituary ... 81-84
Floyd, Samuel A(lexander), Jr. 1937- ... 115
Floyd, Troy S(mith) 1920- ... 37-40R
Floyd, W(illiam) E(dward) G(regory)
1939- ... 33-36R
Floyd, William Anderson 1928- ... 29-32R
Fluchere, Henri (Auguste) 1898-1987
Obituary ... 123
Fluchere, Henri 1914- ... 77-80
See also SATA 40
Fluck, Diana 1931-1984 Obituary ... 113
Fluck, Reginald Alan Paul 1928- ... 9-10R
Flume, Violet S(igoloff) ... 116
Flumiani, Carlo M(aria) 1911- ... CANR-9
Earlier sketch in CA 15-16R
Fluno, Robert Y(ounger) 1916- ... 33-36R
Flusser, Martin 1947- ... 73-76
Flute, Molly
See Lottman, Eileen
Fly, Claude L(ee) 1905- ... 97-100
Flyat, Sten G(unnar) 1911- ... 11-12R
Flying Officer X
See Bates, H(erbert) E(rnest)
Flynn, Barbara 1928- ... SATA-9
Flynn, Bernice (Lydia Carlson) 1922- ... 114
Flynn, Carol Houlihan 1945- ... 112
Flynn, Charles F(rederick) 1949- ... 57-60
Flynn, David H(oughton) 1953- ... 115
Flynn, Don
See Flynn, Donald R(obert)
Flynn, Donald R(obert) 1928- ... CANR-12
Earlier sketch in CA 29-32R
Flynn, Elizabeth Gurley 1890-1964
Obituary ... 111
Flynn, Fahey 1916-1983 Obituary ... 110
Flynn, George L. 1931- ... CANR-24
Earlier sketches in CA 65-68, CANR-9
Flynn, George Q(uitman) 1937- ... 25-28R
Flynn, Gerard (Cox) 1924- ... 41-44R
Flynn, Jackson
See Bensen, Donald R.
and Shirreffs, Gordon D(onald)
Flynn, James Joseph 1911- ... 23-24R
Flynn, James R. 1934- ... 21-22R
Flynn, John Joseph 1936- ... 19-20R
Flynn, John Thomas 1882-1964 Obituary ... 89-92
Flynn, Leslie Bruce 1918- ... CANR-17
Earlier sketches in CA 1R, CANR-2
Flynn, Paul P(atrick) 1942- ... 37-40R
Flynn, Robert (Lopez) 1932- ... 29-32R
Flynt, Candace 1947- ... 102
Flynt, Larry ... AITN-2
Flynt, Wayne 1940- ... CANR-13
Earlier sketch in CA 37-40R
Flythe, Starkey S(harp), Jr. 1935- ... 69-72
Fo, Dario 1926- Brief entry ... 116
See also CLC 32
Foat Tugay, Emine 1897- ... CAP-1
Earlier sketch in CA 13-14
Foda, Aun
See Foxe, Arthur N(orman)
Fodaski-Black, Martha 1929- ... 73-76
Fodor, Eugene 1905- ... CANR-14
Earlier sketch in CA 21-22R
Fodor, M. W. 1890(?)-1977 Obituary ... 69-72
Fodor, Nandor 1895-1964 Obituary ... 112
Fodor, R(onald) V(ictor) 1944- ... CANR-15
Earlier sketch in CA 65-68
See also SATA 25
Foell, Earl W(illiam) 1929- ... 69-72
Foerster, Eberhard
See Weisenborn, Guenther
Foerster, Leona M(itchell) 1930- ... 89-92
Foerster, Lotte B(rand) 1910-1986 ... 77-80
Obituary ... 119
Foerster, Norman 1887- ... 7-8R
Foff, Arthur R(aymond) 1925-1973 ... CAP-2
Earlier sketch in CA 33-36
Fogarty, Jonathan Titulescu, Esq.
See Farrell, James T(homas)
Fogarty, Michael P(atrick) 1916- ... CANR-9
Earlier sketch in CA 21-22R
Fogarty, Robert S(tephen) 1938- ... CANR-9
Earlier sketch in CA 65-68
Fogel, Daniel
See Kahn-Fogel, Daniel (Mark)
Fogel, Daniel (Mark) Kahn
See Kahn-Fogel, Daniel (Mark)
Fogel, Ephim G(regory) 1920- ... 120
Fogel, Robert W(illiam) 1926- ... CANR-13
Earlier sketch in CA 77-80
Fogel, Ruby ... 19-20R
Fogelquist, Donald Frederick 1906- ... 69-72
Fogelson, Robert M(ichael) 1937- ... 81-84
Fogg, Sam R. 1917(?)-1987 Obituary ... 123
Fogle, Bruce 1944- ... 106
Fogle, French R(owe) 1912- ... 37-40R
Fogle, Richard Harter 1911- ... CANR-5
Earlier sketch in CA 7-8R
Foglio, Frank 1921- ... 57-60
Foiles, Keith Andrew 1926-1983 Obituary ... 109
Foin, Theodore C(hin) 1940- ... 93-96
Foisie, Jack 1919- ... 104
Fokkema, D(ouwe) W(essel) 1931- ... CANR-23
Earlier sketches in CA 19-20R, CANR-7
Fol, Alexander 1933- Brief entry ... 111
Foladare, Joseph 1909- ... 102
Folb, Edith A(rlene) 1938- ... 102
Folch-Ribas, Jacques 1928- ... 69-72
Folds, Thomas M. ... 93-96
Folejewski, Zbigniew 1910- ... CANR-7
Earlier sketch in CA 17-18R
Foley, Allen Richard 1898-1978 ... 45-48
Obituary ... 77-80
Foley, (Anna) Bernice Williams 1902- ... CANR-12
Earlier sketch in CA 29-32R
See also SATA 28
Foley, Charles 1908- ... CAP-1
Earlier sketch in CA 15-16
Foley, Daniel J(oseph) 1913- ... CANR-5
Earlier sketch in CA 7-8R
Foley, Doug 1942- ... 57-60
Foley, Duncan K(arl) 1942- ... 93-96
Foley, Gerald (Patrick) 1936- ... CANR-11
Earlier sketch in CA 69-72
Foley, Helen
See Fowler, Helen Rosa Huxley
Foley, (Cedric) John 1917-1974 ... CANR-4
Obituary ... 53-56
Earlier sketch in CA 9-10R
Foley, John Miles 1947- ... 111
Foley, June 1944- ... 109
See also SATA 44
Foley, Leonard 1913- ... 89-92
Foley, (Mary) Louise Munro 1933- ... 37-40R
See also SATA 40
Foley, Martha 1897(?)-1977 ... 117
Obituary ... 73-76
Foley, Mary Mix 1918- ... 102
Foley, Michael F(rancis) 1940-1984
Obituary ... 113
Foley, Paul 1914-1983 Obituary ... 111
Foley, Rae
See Denniston, Elinore
Foley, Richard N. 1910(?)-1980 Obituary ... 102
Foley, Scott
See Dareff, Hal
Foley, Vincent D. 1933- ... 57-60
Foley, William E. 1938- ... 33-36R
Foley, Winifred 1914- ... 102
Folk, Jerry ... 114
Folkard, Charles James 1878-1963
Obituary ... 109
See also SATA 28
Folke, Will
See Bloch, Robert (Albert)
Folkenflik, Robert 1939- Brief entry ... 111
Folkers, George Fulton 1929- ... 49-52
Folkerts, George W(illiam) 1938- ... 53-56
Folkman, Jerome (Daniel) 1907- ... CAP-2
Earlier sketch in CA 29-32
Folland, H(arold) F(reeze) 1906- ... 49-52
Follen, Eliza Lee (Cabot) 1787-1860 ... DLB-1
Follett, Helen Thomas 1884(?)-1970
Obituary ... 107
See also SATA 27
Follett, James 1939- Brief entry ... 112
Follett, Ken(neth Martin) 1949- ... CANR-13
Earlier sketch in CA 81-84
See also DLBY 81
See also CLC 18
Follett, Robert J(ohn) R(ichard) 1928- ... CANR-23
Earlier sketches in CA 21-22R, CANR-8
Folley, Terence T. 1931- ... 21-22R
Folley, Vern L(eRoy) 1936- ... 49-52

Folliard, Edward T(homas) 1899-1976
  Obituary ... 69-72
Follis, Anne Bowen 1947- ... 106
Follmann, J(oseph) F., Jr. 1908- ... CANR-7
  Earlier sketch in CA 19-20R
Folmar, J. Kent
  See Folmar, John Kent
Folmar, John Kent 1932- ... 116
Folmsbee, Stanley J(ohn) 1899-1974 ... CAP-2
  Earlier sketch in CA 29-32
Folsom, Anne (Ferril) 1922- Brief entry ... 114
Folsom, Burton W(hitmore), Jr. 1947- ... 118
Folsom, Franklin (Brewster) 1907- ... CANR-2
  Earlier sketch in CA 3R
  See also SATA 5
Folsom, Jack
  See Folsom, John B(entley)
Folsom, John B(entley) 1931- ... 45-48
Folsom, Kenneth E(verett) 1921- ... 21-22R
Folsom, Marion Bayard 1893- ... CAP-2
  Earlier sketch in CA 17-18
Folsom, Marvin Hugh 1929- ... 57-60
Folsom, Michael (Brewster) 1938- ... 112
  See also SATA 40
Folsom, Robert S(lade) 1915- ... 77-80
Folta, Jeannette R. 1934- ... 25-28R
Foltin, Lore Barbara 1913-19(?) ... CAP-2
  Earlier sketch in CA 25-28
Foltz, William J(ay) 1936- ... 11-12R
Fomon, Samuel J(oseph) 1923- ... 53-56
Fonarow, Jerry 1935- ... CANR-4
  Earlier sketch in CA 53-56
Fonda, Henry (Jaynes) 1905-1982
  Obituary ... 107
Fonda, Peter 1939(?)- Brief entry ... 112
Fon Eisen, Anthony T. 1917- ... 15-16R
Foner, Eric 1943- ... CANR-12
  Earlier sketch in CA 29-32R
Foner, Jack D(onald) 1910- ... 77-80
Foner, Nancy 1945- ... 53-56
Foner, Philip (Sheldon) 1910- ... CANR-3
  Earlier sketch in CA 11-12R
Fong, Wen Chih 1930- ... 103
Fong-Torres, Ben 1945- ... 93-96
Fonseca, Aloysius Joseph 1915- ... CANR-9
  Earlier sketch in CA 15-16R
Fonseca, John R. 1925- ... CANR-8
  Earlier sketch in CA 19-20R
Fonstad, Karen Wynn 1945- ... 104
Fontaine, Andre 1910- ... 65-68
Fontaine, Andre (Lucien Georges)
  1921- ... CANR-12
  Earlier sketch in CA 25-28R
Fontaine, Joan 1917- ... 81-84
Fontana, Bernard L(ee) 1931- ... CANR-7
  Earlier sketch in CA 19-20R
Fontana, Biancamaria 1952- ... 124
Fontana, Thomas M. 1951- Brief entry ... 113
Fontana, Vincent James 1923- ... 15-16R
Fontanet, Joseph 1921-1980 Obituary ... 105
Fontcreuse, Marquis de
  See Jaeger, Cyril Karel Stuart
Fontenay, Charles L(ouis) 1917- ... 25-28R
Fontenelle, Don H(arris) 1946- ... 106
Fontenot, Chester J. 1950- ... 112
Fontenot, Mary Alice 1910- ... CANR-14
  Earlier sketch in CA 37-40R
  See also SATA 34
Fontenrose, Joseph 1903- ... 7-8R
Fonteyn, Margot
  See Fonteyn de Arias, Margot
Fonteyn de Arias, Margot 1919- ... 117
  Brief entry ... 110
Fonzi, Bruno 1913(?)-1976 Obituary ... 65-68
Foon, Dennis 1951- ... 111
Fooner, Michael ... 81-84
  See also SATA 22
Foord, Archibald Smith 1914-1969 ... CAP-1
  Earlier sketch in CA 11-12
Foot, Hugh Mackintosh 1907- ... 11-12R
Foot, M(ichael) R(ichard) D(aniell)
  1919- ... CANR-3
  Earlier sketch in CA 7-8R
Foot, Michael 1913- ... 108
Foot, Paul Mackintosh 1937- ... 17-18R
Foot, Philippa Ruth 1920- ... 101
Foote, A(von) Edward 1937- ... CANR-13
  Earlier sketch in CA 73-76
Foote, Arthur 1911- ... 114
Foote, Darby Mozelle 1942- ... 61-64
Foote, Dorothy Norris (McBride) 1908- ... CAP-2
  Earlier sketch in CA 21-22
Foote, Geoffrey 1950- ... 123
Foote, Horton 1916- ... 73-76
  See also DLB 26
Foote, Shelby 1916- ... CANR-3
  Earlier sketch in CA 5-6R
  See also DLB 2, 17
Foote, Timothy (Gilson) 1926- ... 93-96
Foote, Victoria 1954- ... 118
Foote, Wilder 1905-1975 Obituary ... 57-60
Foote-Smith, Elizabeth 1913- ... 69-72
Footman, David (John) 1895-1983 ... 97-100
  Obituary ... 111
Footner, (William) Hulbert 1879-1944
  Brief entry ... 114
Foran, Donald J. 1943- ... 33-36R
Forberg, Ati
  See Forberg, Beate Gropius
  See also SATA 22
Forberg, Beate Gropius 1925- ... 105
Forbes, Bryan 1926- ... 69-72
  See also SATA 37
Forbes, Cabot L.
  See Hoyt, Edwin P(almer), Jr.
Forbes, Calvin 1945- ... 49-52
  See also DLB 41
Forbes, Clarence A(llen) 1901- ... 77-80
Forbes, Colin
  See Sawkins, Raymond H(arold)
Forbes, Daniel
  See Kenyon, Michael
Forbes, DeLoris (Florine) Stanton
  1923- ... CANR-5
  Earlier sketch in CA 11-12R
Forbes, Donald (Galen) 1918-1987
  Obituary ... 122
Forbes, Elliot 1917- ... 9-10R
Forbes, Eric Gray 1933-1984 ... CANR-10
  Obituary ... 114
  Earlier sketch in CA 65-68
Forbes, Esther 1891-1967 ... CAP-1
  Obituary ... 25-28R
  Earlier sketch in CA 13-14
  See also SATA 2
  See also DLB 22
  See also CLC 12
Forbes, Graham B. ... CAP-2
  Earlier sketch in CA 19-20
  See also SATA 1
Forbes, Henry W(illiam) 1918- ... 4R
Forbes, J(ohn) V(an) G(elder) 1916- ... 9-10R
Forbes, Jack D. 1934- ... CANR-4
  Earlier sketch in CA 1R
Forbes, Joanne R. (Triebel) 1930- ... 37-40R
Forbes, John Douglas 1910- ... 53-56
Forbes, Kathryn
  See McLean, Kathryn (Anderson)
Forbes, Malcolm S(tevenson) 1919- ... 69-72
Forbes, Murray (M.) 1906-1987 Obituary ... 121
Forbes, (Christopher) Patrick 1925- ... 25-28R
Forbes, Rosita
  See McGrath, Joan Rosita (Torr)
Forbes, Stanton
  See Forbes, DeLoris (Florine) Stanton
Forbes, Thomas Rogers 1911- ... 41-44R
Forbes-Boyd, Eric 1897- ... 15-16R
Forbes-Dennis, Phyllis 1884-1963
  Obituary ... 93-96
Forbes-Robertson, Diana
  See Sheean, Diana
Forbis, Judith 1934- ... 101
Forbis, William H. 1918- ... CANR-15
  Earlier sketch in CA 37-40R
Forbus, Ina B(ell) ... 4R
Force, Peter 1790-1868 ... DLB-30
Force, Roland W(ynfield) 1924- ... 41-44R
Force, William M. 1916- ... 21-22R
Forcey, Charles B(udd) 1925- ... CANR-1
  Earlier sketch in CA 1R
Forche, Carolyn (Louise) 1950- ... 117
  Brief entry ... 109
  See also DLB 5
  See also CLC 25
Forchheimer, Paul 1913- ... 53-56
Forcione, Alban Keith 1938- ... CANR-13
  Earlier sketch in CA 33-36R
Ford, A(lec) G(eorge) 1926- ... 5-6R
Ford, Adam 1940- ... 111
Ford, Agnes Gibbs 1902- ... CAP-2
  Earlier sketch in CA 21-22
Ford, Albert Lee
  See Stratemeyer, Edward L.
Ford, Alice 1906- ... CAP-1
  Earlier sketch in CA 19-20
Ford, Amasa B. 1922- ... 21-22R
Ford, Arthur A. 1897-1971 Obituary ... 112
Ford, Arthur L(ewis) 1937- ... 57-60
Ford, Barbara Brief entry ... 112
  See also SATA 34
Ford, Betty
  See Ford, Elizabeth Anne Bloomer
Ford, Boris 1917- ... 112
Ford, Brian J(ohn) 1939- ... CANR-15
  Earlier sketch in CA 41-44R
  See also SATA 49
Ford, Cathy Diane 1952- ... 105
Ford, Charles Henri 1913- ... CANR-13
  Earlier sketch in CA 25-28R
  See also DLB 4, 48
Ford, Colin John 1934- ... 85-88
Ford, Collier
  See Ford, James L(awrence) C(ollier)
Ford, Corey 1902-1969 Obituary ... 25-28R
  See also DLB 11
Ford, D(ouglas) W(illiam) Cleverley
  1914- ... CANR-24
  Earlier sketches in CA 61-64, CANR-9
Ford, Daniel (Francis) 1931- ... CANR-11
  Earlier sketch in CA 17-18R
Ford, David
  See Harknett, Terry
Ford, Donald (Frank William) 1924- ... 7-8R
Ford, Donald H(erbert) 1926- ... 41-44R
Ford, Edmund Brisco 1901-1988 ... 85-88
  Obituary ... 124
Ford, Edsel 1928-1970 ... CAP-1
  Obituary ... 29-32R
  Earlier sketch in CA 15-16
Ford, Edward (Charles) 1928- ... 89-92
Ford, Eileen (Otte) 1922- ... 120
Ford, Elaine 1938- ... CANR-19
  Earlier sketch in CA 102
Ford, Elbur
  See Hibbert, Eleanor Burford
Ford, Elizabeth
  See Bidwell, Marjory Elizabeth Sarah
Ford, Elizabeth Anne Bloomer 1918- ... CANR-23
  Earlier sketch in CA 105
Ford, Florence
  See Novelli, Florence
Ford, Ford Madox 1873-1939 Brief entry ... 104
  See also DLB 34
  See also TCLC 1, 15
Ford, Frank B(ernard) 1932- ... 85-88
Ford, Franklin L(ewis) 1920- ... 19-20R
Ford, Fred
  See Doerffler, Alfred
Ford, George (Jr.) ... 107
  See also SATA 31
Ford, George Barry 1885-1978 Obituary ... 81-84
Ford, George D. 1880(?)-1974 Obituary ... 53-56
Ford, George H(arry) 1914- ... CANR-2
  Earlier sketch in CA 3R
Ford, George L(onnie) 1914- ... 7-8R
Ford, Gerald R(udolph, Jr.) 1913- ... 114
  Brief entry ... 110
Ford, Gordon B(uell), Jr. 1937- ... CANR-13
  Earlier sketch in CA 21-22R
Ford, Guy B(arrett) 1922- ... 5-6R
Ford, Harvey Seabury 1905(?)-1978
  Obituary ... 73-76
Ford, Henry 1863-1947 Brief entry ... 115
Ford, Henry II 1917-1987 Obituary ... 123
  Brief entry ... 111
Ford, Herbert Paul 1927- ... 19-20R
Ford, Hilary
  See Youd, Samuel
Ford, Hildegarde
  See Morrison, Velma Ford
Ford, Hugh D. 1925- Brief entry ... 114
Ford, J. Massingberd
  See Ford, Josephine Massyngbaerde
Ford, James Allan 1920- ... CAP-1
  Earlier sketch in CA 9-10
Ford, James L(awrence) C(ollier) 1907- ... 29-32R
Ford, Jesse Hill (Jr.) 1928- ... CANR-1
  Earlier sketch in CA 2R
  See also DLB 6
Ford, John 1586-? ... DLB-58
Ford, John 1895-1973 Obituary ... 45-48
  See also CLC 16
Ford, Josephine Massyngbaerde ... 41-44R
Ford, Kathleen 1932- ... 25-28R
Ford, Kirk
  See Spence, William John Duncan
Ford, Lee 1936- ... 25-28R
Ford, Leighton F. S. 1931- ... 19-20R
Ford, LeRoy 1922- ... 11-12R
Ford, Leslie
  See Brown, Zenith Jones
Ford, Lewis
  See Patten, Lewis B(yford)
Ford, Marcia
  See Radford, Ruby L(orraine)
Ford, Marcus Peter 1950- ... 108
Ford, Margaret Patricia 1925- ... 9-10R
Ford, Mary Forker 1905- ... 11-12R
Ford, Murray J(ohn) S(tanley) 1923- ... 93-96
Ford, Nancy K(effer) 1906-1961 Obituary ... 109
  See also SATA 29
Ford, Nick Aaron 1904-1982 ... CANR-11
  Earlier sketch in CA 25-28R
Ford, Norman D(ennis) 1921- ... CANR-10
  Earlier sketch in CA 23-24R
Ford, Norrey
  See Dilcock, Noreen
Ford, Patrick 1914- ... 23-24R
Ford, Paul F(rancis X.) 1947- ... CANR-22
  Earlier sketch in CA 105
Ford, Percy 1894-1983 Obituary ... 110
Ford, Philip J(ohn) 1949- ... 115
Ford, Phyllis M(arjorie) 1928- ... CANR-13
  Earlier sketch in CA 33-36R
Ford, R(obert) A(rthur) D(ouglass)
  1915- ... CANR-19
  Earlier sketch in CA 97-100
Ford, R(ichard) Clyde 1870-1951
  Brief entry ... 121
Ford, Richard 1944- ... CANR-11
  Earlier sketch in CA 69-72
  See also CLC 46
Ford, Richard Brice 1935- ... 37-40R
Ford, Robert E. 1913-1975 ... CAP-2
  Earlier sketch in CA 29-32
Ford, Robert N(icholas) 1909- ... 33-36R
Ford, Stephen 1949- ... 77-80
Ford, Thomas R(obert) 1923- ... 49-52
Ford, Thomas W(ellborn) 1924- ... 21-22R
Ford, W(illiam) Clay(ton, Jr.) 1946- ... 93-96
Ford, W(illiam) Herschel 1900- ... CANR-5
  Earlier sketch in CA 9-10R
Ford, Webster
  See Masters, Edgar Lee
Ford, Whitey
  See Ford, Edward (Charles)
Ford, Worthington C. 1858-1941 ... DLB-47
Forde, Gerhard O(laf) 1927- ... 89-92
Forde-Johnston, James (Leo) 1927- ... CANR-3
  Earlier sketch in CA 9-10R
Fordham, Frieda 1903-1988 Obituary ... 124
Fordham, Peta 1905- ... 106
Fordin, Hugh 1935- ... 57-60
Fordyce, Rachel (Poole) 1942- ... 121
  Brief entry ... 118
Fore, William Frank 1928- ... 7-8R
Forell, George W(olfgang) 1919- ... CANR-16
  Earlier sketches in CA 1R, CANR-1
Foreman, Carl 1914-1984 ... 41-44R
  Obituary ... 113
  See also DLB 26
Foreman, Clark H(owell) 1902-1977
  Obituary ... 69-72
Foreman, Gene 1934- ... 77-80
Foreman, Harry 1915- ... 33-36R
Foreman, Kenneth Joseph 1891- ... CAP-2
  Earlier sketch in CA 33-36
Foreman, L(eonard) L(ondon) 1901- ... CANR-5
  Earlier sketch in CA 5-6R
Foreman, Lawton Durant 1913- ... 9-10R
Foreman, Michael 1938- ... CANR-10
  Earlier sketch in CA 23-24R
  See also SATA 2
Foreman, Richard 1937- ... 65-68
Foreman, Russell 1921- ... 77-80
Forer, Lois G(oldstein) 1914- ... 29-32R
Forer, Lucille K(remith) ... 37-40R
Forer, Mort 1922- ... 97-100
Fores, John 1914- ... 25-28R
Forest, Antonia ... 103
  See also SATA 29
Forest, Ilse 1896- ... CAP-2
  Earlier sketch in CA 19-20
Forest, Lee
  See Woods, Clee
Forester, Bruce (Michael) 1939- ... 107
Forester, C(ecil) S(cott) 1899-1966 ... 73-76
  Obituary ... 25-28R
  See also SATA 13
  See also CLC 35
Forester, Frank
  See Herbert, Henry William
Foreyt, John P(aul) 1943- ... 118
Forez
  See Mauriac, Francois (Charles)
Forgie, George B(arnard) 1941- ... 89-92
Forgus, Ronald (Henry) 1928- ... 41-44R
Forio, Robert
  See Weiss, Irving J.
Forisha, Barbara L.
  See Forisha-Kovach, Barbara L(usk)
Forisha-Kovach, Barbara L(usk) 1941- ... 107
Forkosch, Morris D(avid) 1908- ... 41-44R
Form, William H. 1917- ... 65-68
Forma, Warren 1923- ... 45-48
Forman, Brenda 1936- ... CANR-6
  Earlier sketch in CA 9-10R
  See also SATA 4
Forman, Celia Adler 1890(?)-1979
  Obituary ... 85-88
Forman, Charles William 1916- ... 13-14R
Forman, Harrison 1904-1978 ... 5-6R
  Obituary ... 77-80
Forman, Henry James 1879-1966 ... 7-8R
Forman, James Douglas 1932- ... CANR-19
  Earlier sketches in CA 9-10R, CANR-4
  See also SATA 8
Forman, Joan ... 102
Forman, Jonathan 1887-1974 ... CAP-2
  Earlier sketch in CA 23-24
Forman, Leona S. 1940- ... 25-28R
Forman, Marc A(llan) 1935- ... 57-60
Forman, Max Leon 1909- ... 112
Forman, Milos 1932- ... 109
Forman, Robert E(dgar) 1924- ... 11-12R
Forman, Shepard (Lewis) 1938-
  Brief entry ... 112
Forman, (James Adam) Sholto 1915- ... 25-28R
Formby, William A(rthur) 1943- ... 109
Formento, Dan 1954- ... 112
Formhals, Robert W(illard) Y(ates)
  S(arguszko) 1919- ... 53-56
Formisano, Ronald P. 1939- Brief entry ... 115
Formwalt, Lee W(illiam) 1949- ... 119
Fornari, Franco 1921- ... CANR-12
  Earlier sketch in CA 29-32R
Fornari, Harry D(avid) 1919- ... 69-72
Fornell, Earl Wesley 1915-1969 ... 1R
  Obituary ... 103
Fornes, Maria Irene 1930- ... 25-28R
  See also DLB 7
  See also CLC 39
Forno, Lawrence J(oseph) 1943- ... 37-40R
Forrest, Alfred Clinton 1916-1978 ... 49-52
  Obituary ... 103
Forrest, Caleb
  See Telfer, Dariel (Doris)
Forrest, David
  See Forrest-Webb, Robert
Forrest, Derek W(illiam) 1926- ... 77-80
Forrest, Earle Robert 1883-1969 ... 3R
  Obituary ... 103
Forrest, Felix C.
  See Linebarger, Paul M(yron) A(nthony)
Forrest, Gary Gran 1943- ... 113
Forrest, James Taylor 1921- ... 115
Forrest, John Galbraith 1898-1982
  Obituary ... 107
Forrest, Julian
  See Wagenknecht, Edward (Charles)
Forrest, Julie de
  See DeWitt, Edith Openshaw
Forrest, Leon 1937- ... 89-92
  See also DLB 33
  See also CLC 4
Forrest, Norman
  See Morland, Nigel
Forrest, Richard (Stockton) 1932- ... CANR-9
  Earlier sketch in CA 57-60
Forrest, Sybil
  See Markun, Patricia Maloney
Forrest, W(illiam) G(eorge) 1925- ... 25-28R
Forrest, Wilbur S. 1887-1977 Obituary ... 69-72
Forrestal, Dan J(oseph), Jr. 1912- ... 77-80
Forrester, Frank H. 1919(?)-1986
  Obituary ... 119
Forrester, Helen
  See Bhatia, Jamunadevi
  See also SATA 48
Forrester, Jay W(right) 1918- ... CANR-1
  Earlier sketch in CA 45-48
Forrester, Larry 1924- ... 25-28R
Forrester, Leland S. 1905(?)-1978
  Obituary ... 81-84
Forrester, Marian
  See Schachtel, Roger (Bernard)

Forrester, Mary
See Humphries, Mary
Forrester, (William) Ray 1911- ... 23-24R
Forrester, Rex Desmond 1928- ... 103
Forrester, Victoria 1940- ... 108
See also SATA 35, 40
Forrest-Webb, Robert 1929- ... CANR-4
Earlier sketch in CA 49-52
Forsberg, (Charles) Gerald 1912- ... 102
Forsberg, Malcolm I. 1908- ... 21-22R
Forsberg, Roberta Jean 1914- Brief entry ... 105
Forsee, (Frances) Aylesa ... CANR-1
Earlier sketch in CA 4R
See also SATA 1
Forshay-Lunsford, Cin 1965- ... 119
Forssmann, Werner Theodor Otto
1904-1979 Obituary ... 111
Forster, Arnold 1912- ... 15-16R
Forster, E(dward) M(organ) 1879-1970 ... CAP-1
Obituary ... 25-28R
Earlier sketch in CA 13-14
See also DLB 34
See also CLC 1, 2, 3, 4, 9, 10, 13, 15, 22, 45
Forster, Kent 1916- ... 23-24R
Forster, Mark Arnold
See Arnold-Forster, Mark
Forster, Merlin H(enry) 1928- ... 41-44R
Forster, Peter 1926(?)-1982 Obituary ... 107
Forster, Robert 1926- ... 41-44R
Forstman, H(enry) Jackson 1929- ... 15-16R
Forsyth (Outram), Anne 1933- ... CANR-12
Earlier sketch in CA 29-32R
Forsyth, Bill 1948- ... 122
Forsyth, David J(ames) C(ameron)
1940- ... 41-44R
Forsyth, David P(ond) 1930- ... 9-10R
Forsyth, Frederick 1938- ... 85-88
See also CLC 2, 5, 36
Forsyth, George H(oward), Jr. 1901- ... 37-40R
Forsyth, Ilene (Haering) 1928- ... 37-40R
Forsyth, James (Law) 1913- ... 73-76
Forsyth, Richard S(andes) 1948- ... 116
Forsythe, Elizabeth 1927- ... 93-96
Forsythe, Irene
See Hanson, Irene (Forsythe)
Forsythe, Robert
See Crichton, Kyle Samuel
Forsythe, Sidney A. 1920- ... 41-44R
Fort, John 1942- ... 77-80
Fort, Paul 1872-1960 Obituary ... 114
Fort, Williams Edwards, Jr. 1905- ... 37-40R
Fortas, Abe 1910-1982 Obituary ... 106
Forte, Allen 1926- ... 41-44R
Forte, Dan 1935- ... 65-68
Forte, David F. 1941- ... 53-56
Fortebraccia, Donato
See Forte, Dan
Forten, Charlotte
See Grimke, Charlotte L(ottie) Forten
Forten, Charlotte L.
See Grimke, Charlotte L(ottie) Forten
See also DLB 50
See also TCLC 16
Fortes, Meyer 1906-1983 Obituary ... 109
Fortescue, William (Archer Irvine) 1945- ... 122
Fortman, Edmund J. 1901- ... CANR-11
Earlier sketch in CA 21-22R
Fortnum, Peggy
See Nuttall-Smith, Margaret Emily Noel
See also SATA 26
Fortune, T(imothy) Thomas 1856-1928
Brief entry ... 112
See also DLB 23
Forty, Adrian 1948- ... 123
Forty, George 1927- ... CANR-15
Earlier sketch in CA 89-92
Forward, Luke
See Patrick, Johnstone G(illespie)
Forward, Robert L(ull) 1932- ... CANR-20
Earlier sketch in CA 103
Forzano, Giovacchino 1884-1970 Obituary ... 104
Fosburgh, Hugh (Whitney) 1916-1976
Obituary ... 69-72
Fosburgh, Lacey 1942- ... CANR-22
Earlier sketch in CA 85-88
Fosburgh, Liza 1930- ... 112
Fosburgh, Pieter Whitney 1914(?)-1978
Obituary ... 77-80
Foscue, Edwin Jay 1899-1972 ... 4R
Obituary ... 103
Fosdick, Charles Austin 1842-1915
Brief entry ... 119
See also DLB 42
Fosdick, Harry Emerson 1878-1969
Obituary ... 25-28R
Fosdick, Raymond B(laine) 1883-1972
Obituary ... 37-40R
Foshay, Toby (Avard) 1950- ... 119
Foshee, John (Hugh) 1931- ... 69-72
Foskett, D(ouglas) J(ohn) 1918- ... CANR-5
Earlier sketch in CA 1R
Foskett, Daphne 1911- ... 102
Foskett, Reginald 1909-1973 ... CAP-2
Earlier sketch in CA 21-22
Foss, Christopher F(rank) 1946- ... 93-96
Foss, Dennis C(arleton) 1947- ... 104
Foss, Phillip Oliver ... 15-16R
Foss, William O(tto) 1918- ... 19-20R
Fosse, Alfred
See Jelly, George Oliver
Fosse, Bob
See Fosse, Robert Louis
See also CLC 20
Fosse, Robert Louis 1927-1987 Obituary ... 123
Brief entry ... 110
Fossey, Dian 1932-1985 ... 113
Obituary ... 118
Fossum, Robert H. 1923- ... 25-28R
Foster, Alan Dean 1946- ... CANR-22
Earlier sketches in CA 53-56, CANR-5
Foster, Brad W. 1955- ... SATA-34
Foster, Brian 1920- Brief entry ... 112
Foster, Carno A(ugustus) 1916- ... 41-44R
Foster, Catharine Osgood 1907- ... 65-68
Foster, Cedric 1900-1975 Obituary ... 89-92
Foster, Charles Howell 1913- ... 19-20R
Foster, Charles Irving 1898-197? ... 1R
Foster, Charles R(obert) 1927- ... 110
Foster, Charles William 1939- ... 57-60
Foster, Daniel W(illet) 1930- ... 108
Foster, David 1908- ... 97-100
Foster, David Manning 1944- ... CANR-18
Earlier sketch in CA 97-100
Foster, David William (Anthony) 1940- ... CANR-22
Earlier sketches in CA 21-22R, CANR-8
Foster, Don(ald) 1948- ... 33-36R
Foster, Donald (LeRoy) 1928- ... 53-56
Foster, Doris Van Liew 1899- ... 102
See also SATA 10
Foster, Dorothy 1936- ... 93-96
Foster, E(lizabeth) C(onnell) 1902- ... 53-56
See also SATA 9
Foster, Earl M(asters) 1940- ... 57-60
Foster, Edward Halsey 1942- ... CANR-18
Earlier sketches in CA 49-52, CANR-2
Foster, Elizabeth 1902- ... 85-88
See also SATA 12
Foster, Elizabeth 1905-1963 ... 4R
See also SATA 10
Foster, Elizabeth Read 1912- ... 106
Foster, F. Blanche 1919- ... 61-64
See also SATA 11
Foster, (Reginald) Francis 1896-1975 ... 109
Obituary ... 107
Foster, Frederick
See Godwin, John (Frederick)
Foster, G(eorge) Allen 1907-1969 ... 9-10R
See also SATA 26
Foster, Genevieve Stump 1893-1979 ... CANR-4
Obituary ... 89-92
Earlier sketch in CA 5-6R
See also SATA 2, 23
See also DLB 61
See also CLR 7
Foster, Genevieve W(akeman) 1902- ... 69-72
Foster, George
See Haswell, Chetwynd John Drake
Foster, George M(cClelland, Jr.) 1913-
Brief entry ... 113
Foster, H. Lincoln 1906- ... CAP-1
Earlier sketch in CA 19-20
Foster, Hal
See Foster, Harold (Rudolf)
See also AITN 2
Foster, Hannah Webster 1758-1840 ... DLB-37
Foster, Harold (Rudolf) 1892-1982
Obituary ... 107
See also SATA 31
Foster, Harold D(ouglas) 1943- ... 111
Foster, Henry Hubbard, Jr. 1911- ... CANR-2
Earlier sketch in CA 1R
Foster, Herbert L(awrence) 1928- ... 57-60
Foster, Herbert W. 1920(?)-1979
Obituary ... 89-92
Foster, Idris Llywelyn 1911-1984 Obituary ... 113
Foster, Iris
See Posner, Richard
Foster, Jack Donald 1930- ... 29-32R
Foster, James C(aldwell) 1943- ... CANR-7
Earlier sketch in CA 57-60
Foster, Jeanne Robert (Ollivier)
1884-1970 Obituary ... 104
Foster, Joanna 1928- ... CANR-8
Earlier sketch in CA 5-6R
Foster, John 1648-1681 ... DLB-24
Foster, John 1915- ... 7-8R
Foster, John (Thomas) 1925- ... 33-36R
See also SATA 8
Foster, John Burt, Jr. 1945- ... 106
Foster, John L(awrence) 1930- ... 53-56
Foster, Joseph O'Kane 1898- ... 49-52
Foster, Julian F(rancis) S(herwood)
1926- ... 29-32R
Foster, K(enneth) Neill 1935- ... CANR-4
Earlier sketch in CA 53-56
Foster, Laura Louise (James) 1918- ... 17-18R
See also SATA 6
Foster, Lee 1923(?)-1977 Obituary ... 69-72
Foster, Lee Edwin 1943- ... 33-36R
Foster, Lynn 1952- ... 113
Foster, M(ichael) A(nthony) 1939- ... CANR-9
Earlier sketch in CA 57-60
Foster, Malcolm (Burton) 1931- ... 109
Foster, Margaret Lesser 1899(?)-1979
Obituary ... 89-92
See also SATA 21
Foster, Margery S(omers) 1914- ... 5-6R
Foster, Marguerite H. 1909- ... CAP-2
Earlier sketch in CA 21-22
Foster, Marian Curtis 1909-1978 ... 73-76
Obituary ... 85-88
See also SATA 23
Foster, Marion
See Shea, Shirley
Foster, Mark Stewart 1939- ... 106
Foster, Martha S(tanding) ... 5-6R
Foster, Michael 1904-1956 Brief entry ... 110
See also DLB 9
Foster, Michael S(immler) 1942- ... 117
Foster, Nancy Haston ... 122
Foster, O'Kane
See Foster, Joseph O'Kane
Foster, Paul 1931- ... CANR-9
Earlier sketch in CA 21-22R
Foster, Peter 1947- ... 108
Foster, Philip (John) 1927- ... 69-72
Foster, Richard
See Crossen, Kendell Foster
Foster, Richard J(ames) 1942- ... CANR-15
Earlier sketch in CA 85-88
Foster, Robert A(lfred) 1949- ... 81-84
Foster, Ruel Elton 1916- ... 33-36R
Foster, Shirley 1943- ... 122
Foster, Timothy R(ichard) V(ernon) 1938- ... 112
Foster, Virginia Ramos ... 29-32R
Foster, Walter Roland 1925- Brief entry ... 116
Foster-Harris, William 1903(?)-1978
Obituary ... 104
Fothergill, (Arthur) Brian 1921- ... 19-20R
Fothergill, Philip G(ilbert) 1908- ... 7-8R
Fotheringham, Nick 1943- ... 121
Fottler, Myron David 1941- ... CANR-14
Earlier sketch in CA 37-40R
Foucault, Michel 1926-1984 ... 105
Obituary ... 113
See also CLC 31, 34
Fougasse
See Bird, (Cyril) Kenneth
Fought, John G(uy) 1938- Brief entry ... 113
Fouhy, Ed(ward Michael) 1934- ... 69-72
Foulds, Elfrida Vipont 1902- ... CANR-4
Earlier sketch in CA 53-56
Foulke, Adrienne 1915- ... 65-68
Foulke, Robert (Dana) 1930- ... 45-48
Foulke, Roy Anderson 1896- ... CANR-1
Earlier sketch in CA 4R
Foulkes, A(lbert) Peter 1936- ... 37-40R
Foulkes, (William) David 1935- Brief entry ... 107
Foulkes, Fred K. 1941- ... CANR-12
Earlier sketch in CA 33-36R
Fountain, Charles (Francis) 1950- ... 118
Fountain, Leatrice 1924- ... 23-24R
Fouraker, Lawrence Edward 1923- ... 1R
Four Corners, George
See Viereck, George Sylvester
Fourest, Henri-Pierre 1911- Brief entry ... 109
Fourest, Michel
See Wynne-Tyson, (Timothy) Jon (Lyden)
Fournet, Jean-Claude 1932- ... 124
Fournier, Frank
See Chapman, Frank M(onroe)
Fournier, Henri Alban 1886-1914
Brief entry ... 104
Fournier, Pierre 1916- ... CANR-16
Earlier sketch in CA 89-92
See also CLC 11
Fourth, Clifton
See Morse, H(enry) Clifton Iv
Fourth Brother, The
See Aung, (Maung) Htin
Foust, Paul J(ohn) 1920- ... 49-52
Fouste, E(thel) Bonita Rutledge 1926- ... 15-16R
Fout, John C(alvin) 1937- ... 57-60
Fowke, Edith (Margaret) 1913- ... 37-40R
See also SATA 14
Fowkes, Robert Allen 1913- Brief entry ... 106
Fowle, Eleanor Cranston
See Cameron, Eleanor Cranston
Fowler, Alastair (David Shaw) 1930- ... 15-16R
Fowler, Austin 1928- ... 23-24R
Fowler, Carolyn ... 117
Fowler, Charles B(runer) 1931- ... CANR-24
Earlier sketches in CA 57-60, CANR-8
Fowler, David Covington 1921- ... 1R
Fowler, David Henry 1924- Brief entry ... 112
Fowler, Don D. 1936- ... CANR-15
Earlier sketch in CA 33-36R
Fowler, Doreen (Angela) 1948- ... 119
Fowler, Douglas 1940- ... 57-60
Fowler, Elaine W(ootten) 1914- ... 93-96
Fowler, Elizabeth Millspaugh 1921- ... 102
Fowler, Eugene Devlan 1890-1960 ... 97-100
Obituary ... 89-92
Fowler, Frank 1900-1971 Obituary ... 113
Fowler, Gene 1931- ... CANR-20
Earlier sketches in CA 53-56, CANR-5
Fowler, Gene
See Fowler, Eugene Devlan
Fowler, George P(almer) 1909- ... 41-44R
Fowler, Guy 1893(?)-1966 Obituary ... 25-28R
Fowler, Harry (Jr.) 1934- ... CANR-1
Earlier sketch in CA 45-48
Fowler, Heather T.
See Remoff, Heather T(rexler)
Fowler, Helen Rosa Huxley 1917- ... CAP-1
Earlier sketch in CA 9-10
Fowler, James W(iley) III 1940- ... 104
Fowler, Jim
See Fowler, James W(iley) III
Fowler, John M(ajor) 1926- ... 103
Fowler, Kenneth A(brams) 1900-1987 ... 7-8R
Obituary ... 122
Fowler, Marian (Elizabeth) 1929- ... 114
Fowler, Mark 1949- ... 65-68
Fowler, Mary Elizabeth 1911- ... CAP-2
Earlier sketch in CA 29-32
Fowler, Mary Jane
See Wheeler, Mary Jane
Fowler, (Edward) Michael (Coulson) 1929- ... 109
Fowler, Raymond Dalton, Jr. 1930-
Brief entry ... 110
Fowler, Raymond E(veleth) 1933- ... 85-88
Fowler, Richard A(lan) 1948- ... 113
Fowler, Robert H(oward) 1926- ... 73-76
Fowler, Roger 1938- ... 65-68
Fowler, Sandra (Lynn) 1937- ... 106
Fowler, Virginie
See Elbert, Virginie Fowler
Fowler, Wilfred 1907- ... CAP-1
Earlier sketch in CA 13-14
Fowler, Will 1922- ... 5-6R
Fowler, William Morgan, Jr. 1944- ... CANR-1
Earlier sketch in CA 45-48
Fowler, Wilton B(onham) 1936- ... 53-56
Fowles, Jib 1940- ... 69-72
Fowles, John 1926- ... 7-8R
See also SATA 22
See also DLB 14
See also CLC 1, 2, 3, 4, 6, 9, 10, 15, 33
Fowlie, Wallace 1908- ... CANR-5
Earlier sketch in CA 5-6R
Fox, Adam 1883-1977 ... CANR-10
Earlier sketches in CA 13-14, CAP-1
Fox, Aileen 1907- ... CANR-5
Earlier sketch in CA 7-8R
Fox, Alan John ... 15-16R
Fox, Alistair 1948- ... 116
Fox, Allan M(ark) 1948- ... 41-44R
Fox, Annette Baker 1912- Brief entry ... 109
Fox, Anthony
See Fullerton, Alexander (Fergus)
Fox, Bill
See Fox, William
Fox, Brian
See Ballard, (Willis) Todhunter
Fox, C(arol) Lynn 1948- ... 110
Fox, Charles Elliot 1878- ... CAP-1
Earlier sketch in CA 9-10
Fox, Charles Philip 1913- ... CANR-1
Earlier sketch in CA 1R
See also SATA 12
Fox, Col. Victor J.
See Winston, R(obert) A(lexander)
Fox, Connie
See Fox, Hugh (Bernard, Jr.)
Fox, Daniel Michael 1938- ... 112
Fox, David J(oseph) 1927- ... 15-16R
Fox, Dorothea Warren 1914- ... 61-64
Fox, Douglas A(llan) 1927- ... CANR-17
Earlier sketch in CA 41-44R
Fox, Douglas McMurray 1940- ... CANR-15
Earlier sketch in CA 33-36R
Fox, E(dward) Inman 1933- ... 17-18R
Fox, Edward J(ackson) 1913- ... 2R
Fox, Edward L. 1938- Brief entry ... 110
Fox, Edward Whiting 1911- Brief entry ... 106
Fox, Eleanor
See St. John, Wylly Folk
Fox, Fontaine Talbot, Jr. 1884-1964
Obituary ... 89-92
See also SATA 23
Fox, Frances Margaret
See Field, Frances Fox
Fox, Frank W(ayne) 1940- ... 109
Fox, Fred 1903(?)-1981 Obituary ... 104
See also SATA 27
Fox, Frederic Ewing 1917-1981 ... 4R
Obituary ... 103
Fox, Freeman
See Hamilton, Charles Harold St. John
Fox, G(ardner) F(rancis) 1911- ... CANR-5
Earlier sketch in CA 5-6R
Fox, G(eoffrey) P. 1938- ... CANR-11
Earlier sketch in CA 23-24R
Fox, Gail 1942- ... CANR-19
Earlier sketch in CA 103
Fox, George (Richard) 1934- ... 37-40R
Fox, Gilbert T(heodore) 1915- ... 69-72
Fox, Gill
See Fox, Gilbert T(heodore)
Fox, Grace (Estelle) 1899-1984 ... 37-40R
Obituary ... 111
Fox, Grace
See Anderson, Grace Fox
Fox, Grace Imogene 1907- ... 2R
Fox, H(enry) B(enjamin) 1910- ... 57-60
Fox, Helen Morgenthau 1885(?)-1974
Obituary ... 45-48
Fox, Hugh (Bernard, Jr.) 1932- ... CANR-11
Earlier sketch in CA 25-28R
Fox, Jack C(urtis) 1925-1987 ... 21-22R
Obituary ... 122
Fox, Jack Vernon 1918-1982 Obituary ... 106
Fox, James (Lyttleton) 1945- ... 120
Fox, James M. ... 102
Fox, John 1906-1984 Obituary ... 114
Fox, John
See Todd, John (Murray)
Fox, John H(oward) 1925- ... CANR-8
Earlier sketch in CA 5-6R
Fox, John (William), Jr. 1862(?)-1919
Brief entry ... 108
See also DLB 9
Fox, Joseph M(ichael) 1934- ... 106
Fox, Karl A(ugust) 1917- ... CANR-7
Earlier sketch in CA 17-18R
Fox, Larry ... 106
See also SATA 30
Fox, Levi 1914- ... CANR-14
Earlier sketch in CA 77-80
Fox, Logan J(ordan) 1922- ... 53-56
Fox, Lorraine 1922-1976 ... SATA-11, 27
Fox, Lucia
See Lockert, Lucia (Alicia Ungaro Fox)
Fox, Marcia R(ose) 1942- ... 105
Fox, Mary Virginia 1919- ... CANR-12
Earlier sketch in CA 29-32R
See also SATA 39, 44
Fox, Matthew (Timothy) 1940- Brief entry ... 109
Fox, Michael A(llen) 1940- ... CANR-19
Earlier sketch in CA 103
Fox, Michael W(ilson) 1937- ... CANR-14
Earlier sketch in CA 73-76
See also SATA 15

Fox, Milton S. 1904-1971 Obituary 33-36R
Fox, Nancy L. 1917- 122
Fox, Norman A(rnold) 1911-1960
Obituary 114
Fox, Owen
See Farmer, Bernard James
Fox, Paula 1923- CANR-20
Earlier sketch in CA 73-76
See also SATA 17
See also DLB 52
See also CLC 2, 8
See also CLR 1
Fox, Ralph H(artzler) 1913-1973 Obituary . . 49-52
Fox, Ray Errol 1941- 85-88
Fox, Renee C(laire) 1928- 49-52
Fox, Richard G(abriel) 1939- 41-44R
Fox, Richard Wightman 1945- 93-96
Fox, Robert 1943- 77-80
Fox, Robert Barlow 1930- 15-16R
Fox, Robert J. 1927- CANR-17
Earlier sketches in CA 45-48, CANR-1
See also SATA 33
Fox, Ruth 1895- 73-76
Fox, Samuel 1905- CAP-2
Earlier sketch in CA 21-22
Fox, Samuel J. 1919- 53-56
Fox, Sharon E(lizabeth) 1938- 45-48
Fox, Siv Cedering 1939- 41-44R
Fox, Sonny 1925- 41-44R
Fox, Stephen
See Furthmann, Julius Grinnell
Fox, Stephen R. 1945- CANR-12
Earlier sketch in CA 29-32R
Fox, Ted
See Fox, Gilbert T(heodore)
Fox, Ted
See Fox, Theodore J.
Fox, Terry Curtis 1948- 117
Fox, Theodore J. 1954- 123
Fox, Uffa 1898-1972 Obituary 37-40R
Fox, V. Helen
See Couch, Helen F(ox)
Fox, Vernon (Brittain) 1916- 37-40R
Fox, Willard 1919- 21-22R
Fox, William 1919(?)-1985 Obituary 116
Fox, William Lloyd 1921- 17-18R
Fox, William McNair 1924- 5-6R
Fox, William Price (Jr.) 1926- CANR-11
Earlier sketch in CA 17-18R
See also DLB 2
See also DLBY 81
See also CLC 22
Fox, William Thornton Rickert 1912-
Brief entry 108
Fox, William W(ellington) 1909- 4R
Foxall, Raymond (Jehoiada Campbell)
1916- CANR-5
Earlier sketch in CA 9-10R
Foxe, Arthur N(orman) 1902-1982 ...... CANR-4
Obituary 108
Earlier sketch in CA 9-10R
Foxell, Nigel 1931- 97-100
Fox-Genovese, Elizabeth 1941- CANR-10
Earlier sketch in CA 65-68
Foxley, William M(cLachlan) 1926-1978 . . . 77-80
Foxley-Norris, Christopher Neil 1917- 109
Fox-Lockert, Lucia
See Lockert, Lucia (Alicia Ungaro Fox)
Foxman, Sherri 1950- 112
Fox-Martin, Milton 1914(?)-1977
Obituary 69-72
Foxon, A(ndrew David) 1956- 121
Foxon, David Fairweather 1923- 102
Fox-Sheinwold, Patricia 102
Foxworth, Thomas G(ordon) 1937- 114
Foxx, Jack
See Pronzini, Bill
Foxx, Redd 1922- 89-92
Foxx, Richard M(ichael) 1944- CANR-17
Earlier sketches in CA 45-48, CANR-1
Foxx, Rosalind
See Haydon, June
and Simpson, Judith H(olroyd)
Foxx, Teralene S. 1939- 122
Foy, George 1952- 116
Foy, Kenneth R(ussell) 1922- 25-28R
Foy, Nancy 1934- CANR-2
Earlier sketch in CA 45-48
Fozdar, Jamshed K(hodadad) 1926- 49-52
Fracchia, Charles A(nthony) 1937- 89-92
Frackenpohl, Arthur R(oland) 1924- 19-20R
Frackman, Nathaline 1903(?)-1977
Obituary 69-72
Fraddle, Farragut
See Mearns, David Chambers
Fradin, Dennis Brindell 1945- 69-72
See also SATA 29
Fradkin, Elvira (Thekla) Kush
1890(?)-1972 Obituary 37-40R
Fradkin, Philip L(awrence) 1935- 107
Fraelich, Richard O(ddly) 1924- 7-8R
Fraenkel, Gerd 1919-1970 .... CAP-1
Earlier sketch in CA 11-12
Fraenkel, Gottfried S(amuel) 1901-1984
Obituary 114
Fraenkel, Heinrich 1897- 15-16R
Fraenkel, Jack R(unnels) 1932- 29-32R
Fraenkel, Michael 1896-1957 Brief entry 107
See also DLB 4
Fraenkel, Osmond K. 1888-1983 .... CAP-2
Obituary 109
Earlier sketch in CA 23-24
Frager, Robert 1940- 81-84
Frahm, Anne B. Schwerdt 1927- 9-10R
Fraiberg, Louis Benjamin 1913- 3R
Fraiberg, Selma 1918-1981 97-100
Obituary 105
Fraine, Harold G(eorge) 1900- 4R
Frair, Wayne Franklin 1926- 113
Fraistat, Neil (Richard) 1952- 122
Fraistat, Rose Ann C. 1952- 123
Frake, Warner
See Musciano, Walter A.
Frakes, George Edward 1932- 29-32R
Fraley, Oscar (B.) 1914- Brief entry 109
Fram, Eugene Harry 1929- 17-18R
Frame, Donald M(urdoch) 1911- 17-18R
Frame, Janet
See Clutha, Janet Paterson Frame
See also CLC 2, 3, 6, 22
Frame, Paul 1913- Brief entry 111
See also SATA 33
Framo, James L(awrence) 1922- CANR-15
Earlier sketch in CA 41-44R
Frampton, Hollis 1936-1984 Obituary 112
Frampton, Kenneth Brian 1930- 105
Frampton, Merle E(lbert) 1903- CAP-2
Earlier sketch in CA 25-28
Frampton, Peter (Kenneth) 1950-
Brief entry 117
Franc, Helen M. 1908- 103
Franca, Celia 1921- 89-92
Franca, Jose-Augusto 1922- CANR-19
Earlier sketch in CA 102
France, Anatole
See Thibault, Jacques Anatole Francois
See also TCLC 9
France, Anna Kay 1940- 103
France, Beulah Sanford 1891-1971
Obituary 33-36R
France, Claire
See Dore, Claire (Morin)
France, Evangeline
See France-Hayhurst, Evangeline
(Chaworth-Musters)
France, Harold L(eroy) 1930- 49-52
France, Malcolm 1928- 23-24R
France, Pierre Mendes
See Mendes-France, Pierre
France, Richard 1938- 93-96
See also DLB 7
France-Hayhurst, Evangeline
(Chaworth-Musters) 1904- CAP-1
Earlier sketch in CA 9-10
Francesca, Rosina
See Brookman, Rosina Francesca
Franchere, Ruth 73-76
See also SATA 18
Franchi, Eda
See Vickers, Antoinette L.
Francis, Anne
See Bird, Florence (Bayard)
and Wintle, Anne
Francis, Arlene 1912- 89-92
Francis, Arthur
See Gershwin, Ira
Francis, Basil (Hoskins) 1906- CAP-1
Earlier sketch in CA 13-14
Francis, C.D.E.
See Howarth, Patrick (John Fielding)
Francis, Cat
See Francis, Emile (Percy)
Francis, Charles
See Holme, Bryan
Francis, Clare 1946- CANR-15
Earlier sketch in CA 77-80
Francis, Convers 1795-1863 .... DLB-1
Francis, Daniel 1947- 111
Francis, Daniel
See Cranny, Titus
Francis, (Alan) David 1900- 21-22R
Francis, David Noel 1904- 7-8R
Francis, Dee
See Haas, Dorothy F.
Francis, Dennis S. 1943(?)-1980 Obituary . . 102
Francis, Devon (Earl) 1901-1986 61-64
Obituary 118
Francis, Dick 1920- CANR-9
Earlier sketch in CA 7-8R
See also CLC 2, 22, 42
Francis, Dorothy Brenner 1926- CANR-24
Earlier sketches in CA 21-22R, CANR-9
See also SATA 10
Francis, Emile (Percy) 1926- Brief entry 112
Francis, Frank Chalton 1901- 65-68
Francis, Gloria A(ileen) 1930- Brief entry ... 113
Francis, H(erbert) E(dward, Jr.) 1924- . CANR-10
Earlier sketch in CA 25-28R
Francis, Helen Dannefer 1915- 15-16R
Francis, John M(ichael) 1939- 118
Francis, Marilyn 1920- CANR-3
Earlier sketch in CA 5-6R
Francis, Michael J(ackson) 1938- 89-92
Francis, Michel
See Cattaui, Georges
Francis, Mother Mary
See Aschmann, Alberta
Francis, Nelle (Trew) 1914- 37-40R
Francis, Pamela (Mary) 1926- 29-32R
See also SATA 11
Francis, Philip
See Lockyer, Roger
Francis, Philip S(heridan) 1918- 17-18R
Francis, R. Mabel 1880-19(?) CAP-2
Earlier sketch in CA 25-28
Francis, Richard (H.) 1945- CANR-24
Earlier sketch in CA 102
Francis, Robert (Churchill) 1901-1987 ... CANR-1
Obituary 123
Earlier sketch in CA 1R
See also CLC 15
Francis, Roy G. 1919- 1R
Francis, Wayne L(ouis) 1935- 41-44R
Francisco, Charles 1930- 109
Francisco, Clyde Taylor 1916- Brief entry ... 106
Francis-Williams, Lord
See Williams, Edward Francis
Franck, Frederick 1909- CANR-5
Earlier sketch in CA 3R
Franck, Harry Alverson 1881-1962
Obituary 110
Franck, Irene M(ary) 1941- CANR-21
Earlier sketch in CA 104
Franck, Phyllis 1928- 53-56
Franck, Sebastian
See Jacoby, Henry
Franck, Thomas M. 1931- 33-36R
Francke, Donald Eugene 1910-1978
Obituary 81-84
Francke, Linda Bird 1939- CANR-15
Earlier sketch in CA 85-88
Franco, Jean 1914-1971 .... CAP-2
Earlier sketch in CA 25-28
Franco, Jean 1924- CANR-9
Earlier sketch in CA 23-24R
Franco, Johan (Henri Gustave) 1908- 97-100
Franco, Marjorie 114
See also SATA 38
Francoeur, Anna K(otlarchyk) 1940- 53-56
Francoeur, Robert T(homas) 1931- CANR-14
Earlier sketch in CA 37-40R
Francois, Andre 1915- 93-96
See also SATA 25
Francois, Pierre 1932- 19-20R
Francois, William E. 1924- CANR-5
Earlier sketch in CA 15-16R
Francoise
See Seignobosc, Francoise
Francois-Poncet, Andre 1887-1978
Obituary 73-76
Franda, Marcus F. 1937- CANR-9
Earlier sketch in CA 23-24R
Frandsen, Arden N. 1902- 3R
Frandsen, Julius 1907-1976 Obituary 69-72
Franey, Pierre 1921- CANR-15
Earlier sketch in CA 89-92
Frank, Adolph F(rederick) 1918- 106
Frank, Andre Gunder 1929- 21-22R
Frank, Anne 1929-1945(?) Brief entry 113
See also SATA 42
See also TCLC 17
Frank, Benis M. 1925- 37-40R
Frank, Benjamin 1902-1984 Obituary 113
Frank, Bernhard 1931- 105
Frank, Charles E(dward) 1911- 21-22R
Frank, Charles Paul 1935- Brief entry 112
Frank, Charles Raphael (Jr.) 1937- 37-40R
Frank, Daniel B. 1956- 117
Frank, Elizabeth 1945- Brief entry 121
See also CLC 39
Frank, Florence Kiper 1885(?)-1976
Obituary 65-68
Frank, Gerold 1907- Brief entry 109
Frank, Goldalie 1908- CAP-1
Earlier sketch in CA 17-18
Frank, H(ans) Eric 1921- 49-52
Frank, Harry Thomas 1933-1980 53-56
Obituary 103
Frank, Helene
See Vautier, Ghislaine
Frank, Helmut J(ack) 1922- CANR-7
Earlier sketch in CA 19-20R
Frank, Irving 1910- CAP-2
Earlier sketch in CA 21-22
Frank, Isaiah 1917- CANR-1
Earlier sketch in CA 2R
Frank, Jacqueline ?-1982 Obituary 114
Frank, Janet
See Dunleavy, Janet Egleson
Frank, Jeffrey 1942- 21-22R
Frank, Jerome (New) 1889-1957
Brief entry 121
Frank, Jerome D(avid) 1909- CANR-3
Earlier sketch in CA 7-8R
Frank, John G. 1896(?)-1978 Obituary 81-84
Frank, Joseph 1916- CANR-1
Earlier sketch in CA 1R
Frank, Joseph (Nathaniel) 1918- 77-80
Frank, Josette 1893- CAP-1
Earlier sketch in CA 19-20
See also SATA 10
Frank, Katherine 124
Frank, Lawrence K(elso) 1890-1968 .... 3R
Obituary 103
Frank, Lee
See Griffin, Arthur J.
Frank, Leonhard 1882-1961 Obituary 116
See also DLB 56
Frank, Mary 1933- SATA-34
Frank, Melvin 1913- DLB-26
Frank, Morton 1912- 102
Frank, Murray 1908-1977 ....37-40R
Obituary 73-76
Frank, Nathalie D. 1918- 11-12R
Frank, Pat (Harry Hart) 1907-1964 ....5-6R
Frank, Peter (Solomon) 1950- CANR-15
Earlier sketch in CA 81-84
Frank, Philip Norman 1943- 113
Frank, Philipp (G.) 1884-1966 Obituary . . 25-28R
Frank, R., Jr.
See Ross, Frank (Xavier), Jr.
Frank, Reuven 1920- 81-84
Frank, Robert G(regg), Jr. 1943-
Brief entry 113
Frank, Robert J(oseph) 1939- 65-68
Frank, Robert Worth, Jr. 1914- 13-14R
Frank, Roberta 1941- 115
Frank, Ronald E(dward) 1933- CANR-18
Earlier sketches in CA 7-8R, CANR-3
Frank, Rudolf 1886-1979 121
Frank, Sheldon 1943- 77-80
Frank, Stanley B. 1908-1979 ....7-8R
Obituary 85-88
Frank, T. C.
See Laughlin, Tom
Frank, Thaisa 1943- 117
Frank, Waldo (David) 1889-1967 93-96
Obituary 25-28R
See also DLB 9, 63
Frank, William G.
See Frank, Rudolf
Frank, William L(uke) 1929- 106
Frankau, Mary Evelyn Atkinson 1899- CAP-1
Earlier sketch in CA 9-10
See also SATA 4
Frankau, Pamela 1908-1967 Obituary 25-28R
Frank-Baron, Elizabeth 1911(?)-1982
Obituary 108
Franke, C(arl) W(ilfred) 1928- 23-24R
Franke, Christopher 1941- 77-80
Franke, David 1938- 49-52
Franke, Herbert W. 1927- Brief entry 110
Franke, Holly L(ambro) 1943- 49-52
Frankel, A(rthur) Steven 1942- 53-56
Frankel, Bernice 61-64
See also SATA 9
Frankel, Charles 1917-1979 .... CANR-4
Obituary 89-92
Earlier sketch in CA 5-6R
Frankel, Edward 1910- 85-88
See also SATA 44
Frankel, Eliot 1922- 77-80
Frankel, Flo 1923- 105
Frankel, Hans H(ermann) 1916- 61-64
Frankel, Haskel 1926- 89-92
Frankel, Hermann F. 1899(?)-1977
Obituary 69-72
Frankel, J(oseph) 1913- CANR-3
Earlier sketch in CA 7-8R
Frankel, Julie 1947- 113
See also SATA 34, 40
Frankel, Max 1930- 65-68
Frankel, Otto (Herzberg) 1900- 108
Frankel, Sandor 1943- 33-36R
Frankel, Tobia (Brown) 1935(?)-1987
Obituary 122
Frankel, William 1917- 106
Frankel, Zygmunt 1929- 41-44R
Franken, Rose 1895(?)- DLBY-84
Frankena, William K(laas) 1908- CANR-10
Earlier sketch in CA 19-20R
Frankenberg, Celestine Gilligan 9-10R
Frankenberg, Lloyd 1907-1975 .... CANR-6
Obituary 57-60
Earlier sketch in CA 2R
Frankenberg, Robert 1911- SATA-22
Frankenstein, Alfred Victor 1906-1981 ... CANR-2
Obituary 104
Earlier sketch in CA 3R
Frankenstein, Carl 1905- 9-10R
Frankenthal, Kate 1889-1976 Obituary 65-68
Frankfort, Ellen 1936-1987 ....29-32R
Obituary 122
Frankforter, A(lbertus) Daniel (III) 1939- ...81-84
Frankfurt, Harry Gordon 1929- 41-44R
Frankfurter, Felix 1882-1965 Brief entry 124
Frankl, Viktor E(mil) 1905- 65-68
Frankland, Mark 1934- 69-72
Frankland, (Anthony) Noble 1922- CANR-14
Earlier sketch in CA 65-68
Franklin, A.
See Arnold, Adlai F(ranklin)
Franklin, Ada C(rogman) ?-1983 Obituary ... 111
Franklin, Adele 1887(?)-1977 Obituary 69-72
Franklin, Alexander (John) 1921- 13-14R
Franklin, Alfred White 1905- CANR-7
Earlier sketch in CA 57-60
Franklin, Ben(jamin) A. 1927- 89-92
Franklin, Benjamin 1706-1790 ...... DLB-24, 43
See also CDALB 1640-1865
Franklin, Benjamin
See Hasek, Jaroslav (Matej Frantisek)
Franklin, Benjamin V 1939- 115
Franklin, Billy J(oe) 1940- 33-36R
Franklin, Bob 1949- 124
Franklin, Burt 1903-1972 .... CAP-1
Earlier sketch in CA 15-16
Franklin, Charles
See Usher, Frank (Hugh)
Franklin, Colin 1923- 77-80
Franklin, Denson Nauls 1914- 1R
Franklin, Edward Herbert 1930- 15-16R
Franklin, Elizabeth
See Campbell, Hannah
Franklin, Eugene
See Bandy, (Eugene) Franklin
Franklin, George E. 1890-1971 .... CAP-1
Earlier sketch in CA 19-20
Franklin, H. Bruce 1934- CANR-9
Earlier sketch in CA 5-6R
Franklin, Harold 1926- 29-32R
See also SATA 13
Franklin, Harold L(eroy) 1934- 57-60
Franklin, Harry 1906- CANR-12
Earlier sketches in CA 13-14, CAP-1
Franklin, J(ennie) E(lizabeth) 1937- 61-64
Franklin, James 1697-1735 .... DLB-43
Franklin, Jay
See Carter, John Franklin
Franklin, Jerome L(ee) 1943- 102
Franklin, Jimmie Lewis 1939- Brief entry ... 106
Franklin, Joe 1926- Brief entry 108
Franklin, John Hope 1915- CANR-3
Earlier sketch in CA 5-6R
Franklin, Jon Daniel 1942- 104
Franklin, Kay 1933- 118
Franklin, Keith
See Foy, Kenneth R(ussell)

Franklin, Linda Campbell 1941- 105
Franklin, Marc A. 1932- 29-32R
Franklin, Marshall 1929- 53-56
Franklin, Max
See Deming, Richard
Franklin, (Stella Maraia Sarah) Miles
1879-1954 Brief entry 104
See also TCLC 7
Franklin, Nat
See Bauer, Erwin A.
Franklin, Olga 1912-1985 102
Obituary 115
Franklin, R(alph) W(illiam) 1937- CANR-9
Earlier sketch in CA 23-24R
Franklin, Richard 1918- 21-22R
Franklin, S(amuel) Harvey 1928- 105
Franklin, Sidney 1903-1976 Obituary 65-68
Franklin, Steve
See Stevens, Franklin
Franklin, Ursula 1929- 112
Franklyn, Charles Aubrey Hamilton
1896- 11-12R
Franklyn, Julian 1899-1970 Obituary 112
Franklyn, Robert Alan 1918- 89-92
Franko, Lawrence G. 1942- 37-40R
Frankowski, Leo 1943- 120
Franks, C(harles) E(dward) S(elwyn)
1936- 77-80
Franks, Claudia Stillman 1947- 117
Franks, Cyril Maurice 1923- 15-16R
Franks, Ed
See Brandon, Johnny
Franks, Kenny Arthur 1945- 123
Franks, Lucinda 1946- 53-56
Franks, Maurice R(udolph) 1942- 112
Franks, Robert S(leightholme) 1871-1963 ...7-8R
Fransella, Fay CANR-13
Earlier sketch in CA 25-28R
Frantz, Charles 1925- CANR-3
Earlier sketch in CA 5-6R
Frantz, Harry Warner 1891-1982 Obituary .. 106
Frantz, Joe B. 1917- CANR-1
Earlier sketch in CA 1R
Frantz, Ralph Jules 1902-1979 77-80
Obituary 89-92
See also DLB 4
Frantzen, Allen J. 1947- 121
Franz, Barbara E(van) 1946- 110
Franz, Carl 1944- 107
Franz, William S(trasser) 1945- 110
Franzblau, Abraham N(orman)
1901-1982 ....29-32R
Obituary 108
Franzblau, Rose N(adler) 1905-1979 .....29-32R
Obituary 89-92
Franzen, Gosta Knut 1906- 41-44R
Franzen, Lavern G(erhardt) 1926- CANR-7
Earlier sketch in CA 61-64
Franzen, Nils-Olof 1916- 29-32R
See also SATA 10
Franzero, Carlo Maria 1892-1986 .... CANR-5
Obituary 120
Earlier sketch in CA 2R
Franzero, Charles Marie
See Franzero, Carlo Maria
Franzius, Enno 1901- 25-28R
Franzmann, Martin H. 1907-1976 ...... CANR-3
Earlier sketch in CA 1R
Franzwa, Gregory M. 1926- CANR-9
Earlier sketch in CA 23-24R
Frary, Michael 1918- 77-80
Frasca, John (Anthony) 1916-1979 ..... CANR-3
Obituary 93-96
Earlier sketch in CA 49-52
Frascatoro, Gerald
See Hornback, Bert G(erald)
Frascino, Edward 1938- 114
Brief entry 111
See also SAAS 33, 48
Frascona, Joseph Lohengrin 1910- 17-18R
Frasconi, Antonio 1919- CANR-1
Earlier sketch in CA 1R
See also SATA 6
Frase, Larry E. 1945- 41-44R
Frase, Robert W(illiam) 1912- 33-36R
Fraser, Alex
See Brinton, Henry
Fraser, Allan 1900- 57-60
Fraser, Amy Stewart 1892- CANR-9
Earlier sketch in CA 49-52
Fraser, Anthea CANR-10
Earlier sketch in CA 65-68
Fraser, Antonia (Pakenham) 1932- 85-88
See also SATA 32
See also CLC 32
Fraser, Arthur Ronald 1888-1974
Obituary 53-56
Fraser, Arvonne S. 1925- 33-36R
Fraser, B. Kay 1941- 69-72
Fraser, Betty
See Fraser, Elizabeth Marr
Fraser, Blair 1909-1968 .... CAP-2
Earlier sketch in CA 23-24
Fraser, Bruce (Donald) 1910- 109
Fraser, Colin 1935- 21-22R
Fraser, Conon 1930- CAP-1
Earlier sketch in CA 9-10
Fraser, D(onald) M(urray) 1946-1985 117
Fraser, (William) Dean 1916- 45-48
Fraser, Diane Lynch
See Lynch-Fraser, Diane
Fraser, Dorothy May 1903(?)-1980
Obituary 102
Fraser, Douglas 1910- 102
Fraser, Douglas Ferrar 1929- CANR-4
Earlier sketch in CA 4R
Fraser, Edith Emily Rose Oram 1903- CAP-1
Earlier sketch in CA 11-12
Fraser, Elise Parker 1903- 3R
Fraser, Elizabeth Marr 1928- SATA-31
Fraser, Eric (George) 1902-1983 ...... SATA-38
Fraser, Flora 1958- 124
Fraser, G(eorge) S(utherland) 1915-1980 ..85-88
Obituary 105
See also DLB 27
Fraser, George MacDonald 1925- CANR-2
Earlier sketch in CA 45-48
See also CLC 7
Fraser, Gordon Holmes 1898- CAP-1
Earlier sketch in CA 15-16
Fraser, Hamish 1913-1986 Obituary 120
Fraser, (William Jocelyn) Ian 1897-1974
Obituary 53-56
Fraser, J(ulius) T(homas) 1923- CANR-8
Earlier sketch in CA 61-64
Fraser, James
See White, Alan
Fraser, Jane
See Pilcher, Rosamunde
Fraser, Janet Hobhouse
See Hobhouse, Janet
Fraser, John 1931- 29-32R
Fraser, Kathleen 1937- 106
Fraser, Maxwell
See Fraser, Dorothy May
Fraser, Morris 1941- 102
Fraser, Neil McCormick 1902- 7-8R
Fraser, Peter (Malcolm) 1928-1987 107
Obituary 121
Fraser, Peter (Shaw) 1932- 33-36R
Fraser, Raymond 1941- Brief entry 107
Fraser, Ronald
See Fraser, Arthur Ronald
Fraser, Ronald
See Tiltman, Ronald Frank
Fraser, Russell A(lfred) 1927- 37-40R
Fraser, Stewart Erskine 1929- CANR-10
Earlier sketch in CA 15-16R
Fraser, Stuart
See Wood, James (Alexander Fraser)
Fraser, Sylvia 1935- CANR-16
Earlier sketches in CA 45-48, CANR-1
Fraser, W(aller) B(rown) 1905- CAP-2
Earlier sketch in CA 25-28
Fraser, W(illiam) Hamish 1941- 103
Fraser, W(illiam) Lionel 18(?)-1965 ...... CAP-1
Earlier sketch in CA 9-10
Fraser Darling, Frank 1903-1979 61-64
Obituary 89-92
Fraser Harrison, Brian 1918- CAP-1
Earlier sketch in CA 9-10
Fraser Roberts, J(ohn) A(lexander)
See Roberts, J(ohn) A(lexander) Fraser
Frasier, James E(dwin) 1923- 17-18R
Frassanito, William A(llen) 1946- CANR-9
Earlier sketch in CA 57-60
Frasure, David W(illiam) 1942- 113
Fratcher, William F(ranklin) 1913- CANR-3
Earlier sketch in CA 5-6R
Frater Perdurabo
See Crowley, Edward Alexander
Fraticelli, Marco 1945- 118
Fratti, Mario 1927- 77-80
Frautschi, R(ichard) L(ane) 1926- 19-20R
Frawley, Ernest D(avid) 1920-1984
Obituary 114
Frawley, William John 1953- 114
Fraydas, Stan 1918- 57-60
Frayling, Christopher 1946- 110
Frayn, Michael 1933- 5-6R
See also DLB 13, 14
See also CLC 3, 7, 31, 47
Frazee, Charles A(aron) 1929- 37-40R
Frazee, Steve 1909- CANR-5
Earlier sketch in CA 7-8R
Frazer, Andrew
See Marlowe, Stephen
Frazer, Fred
See Avallone, Michael (Angelo), Jr.
Frazer, J(ames) G(eorge) 1854-1941
Brief entry 118
Frazer, Mark Petrovich
See Maclean, Donald Duart
Frazer, Robert Caine
See Creasey, John
Frazer, Robert W(alter) 1911- 17-18R
Frazer, Sir James George
See Frazer, J(ames) G(eorge)
Frazer, William J(ohnson), Jr. 1924- 17-18R
Frazer, Winifred Dusenbury
See Frazer, Winifred L(oesch)
Frazer, Winifred L(oesch) 25-28R
Frazer-Hurst, Douglas 1883- CAP-1
Earlier sketch in CA 9-10
Frazetta, Frank 1928- 104
Frazier, Allie M. 1932- Brief entry 110
Frazier, Anitra 1937- 113
Frazier, Arthur
See Bulmer, (Henry) Kenneth
Frazier, Claude A(lbee) 1920- 29-32R
Frazier, Cliff(ord) 1934- Brief entry 109
Frazier, Edward Franklin 1894-1962
Obituary 108
Frazier, George 1911-1974 .... CAP-2
Obituary 49-52
Earlier sketch in CA 25-28
Frazier, Ian 1951- CLC-46
Frazier, Kendrick (Crosby) 1942- CANR-17
Earlier sketch in CA 101
Frazier, Neta Lohnes CANR-1
Earlier sketch in CA 2R
See also SATA 7
Frazier, Sarah
See Wirt, Winola Wells
Frazier, Shervert Hughes 1921- 85-88
Frazier, Thomas R(ichard) 1931- 33-36R
Frazier, Walt(er) 1945- 103
Frears, J(ohn) R(ussell) 1936- 107
Freas, Frank Kelly 1922- CANR-21
Earlier sketch in CA 102
Freburger, William J. 1940- 115
Frech, Frances 1923- 97-100
Freddi, Cris 1955- 106
Frede, Richard 1934- 69-72
Fredeman, William E(van) 1928- 33-36R
Fredenburgh, Franz A(lvah) 1906- 33-36R
Frederic, Harold 1856-1898 .... DLB-12, 23
Frederic, Mike
See Cox, William (Robert)
Frederic, Sister M. Catherine
See Fleischbein, M. Catherine Frederic
Frederick, Carl Louis 1942- 65-68
Frederick, Dick
See Dempewolff, Richard F(rederic)
Frederick, John
See Faust, Frederick (Shiller)
Frederick, John H(utchinson) 1896- 1R
Frederick, John Towner 1893-1975
Obituary 111
Frederick, Lee
See Nussbaum, Al(bert F.)
Frederick, Oswald
See Snelling, O(swald) F(rederick)
Frederick, Pauline 1908- 102
Frederick, Robert Allen 1928- CANR-3
Earlier sketch in CA 45-48
Fredericks, Carlton 1910-1987 .... CANR-7
Obituary 123
Earlier sketch in CA 53-56
See also AITN 1
Fredericks, Frank
See Franck, Frederick
Fredericks, Frohm
See Kerner, Fred
Fredericks, Pierce Griffin 1920-1985 .....13-14R
Obituary 117
Fredericks, Vic
See Majeski, William
Frederika (Louise), Queen 1917-1981
Obituary 108
Frederiksen, Alan Ryle 1935- 113
Frederiksen, Martin W. 1930-1980
Obituary 101
Frederikson, Edna 1904- 49-52
Fredge, Frederique 1906- CAP-2
Earlier sketch in CA 21-22
Fredman, Alice G(reen) 1924- 102
Fredman, Henry John 1927- 29-32R
Fredman, John
See Fredman, Henry John
Fredman, Ruth Gruber 1934- 106
Fredricks, Edgar J(ohn) 1942- 25-28R
Fredrickson, George M(arsh) 1934- CANR-24
Earlier sketches in CA 19-20R, CANR-8
Fredrickson, Olive A(lta) 1901- 49-52
Fredriksson, Don 1926- 110
Fredriksson, Kristine 1940- 122
Free
See Hoffman, Abbie
Free, Ann Cottrell 9-10R
Free, James S(tillman) 1908- 77-80
Free, Lloyd A. 1908- 15-16R
Free, William Joseph 1933- 11-12R
Free, William Norris 1933- 25-28R
Freeborn, Brian (James) 1939- 65-68
Freeborn, Richard H. 1926- CANR-1
Earlier sketch in CA 3R
Freed, Alvyn M. 1913- CANR-8
Earlier sketch in CA 61-64
See also SATA 22
Freed, Arthur 1894-1973 Obituary 41-44R
Freed, Barry
See Hoffman, Abbie
Freed, Donald 1932- 85-88
Freed, Louis Franklin 1903- 7-8R
Freed, Lynn 1945- 108
Freed, Margaret De Haan 1917- 73-76
Freed, Ray 1939- 117
Freedberg, S(ydney) J(oseph) 1914- ... CANR-17
Earlier sketches in CA 1R, CANR-1
Freedeman, Charles E(ldon) 1926- 102
Freedgood, Lillian (Fischel) 1911- 15-16R
Freedgood, Morton 1912- Brief entry 108
See also AITN 1
Freedland, Michael 1934- CANR-11
Earlier sketch in CA 65-68
Freedland, Nat(haniel) 1936- 65-68
Freedley, George (Reynolds)
1904-1967 .... CANR-4
Earlier sketch in CA 5-6R
Freedman, Alfred M(ordecai) 1917- CANR-4
Earlier sketch in CA 49-52
Freedman, Arthur M(erton) 1916- 41-44R
Freedman, Benedict 1919- 69-72
See also SATA 27
Freedman, Daniel X. 1921- 41-44R
Freedman, David M(ichael) 1949- 112
Freedman, David Noel 1922- CANR-1
Earlier sketch in CA 4R
Freedman, Hy 1914- 85-88
Freedman, Leonard 1924- CANR-1
Earlier sketch in CA 1R
Freedman, M(orris) David 1938- CANR-16
Earlier sketch in CA 41-44R
Freedman, Marcia K(ohl) 1922- CANR-10
Earlier sketch in CA 25-28R
Freedman, Maurice 1920-1975 .... CAP-2
Obituary 61-64
Earlier sketch in CA 25-28
Freedman, Mervin B. 1920- 29-32R
Freedman, Monroe H(enry) 1928-
Brief entry 107
Freedman, Morris 1920- CANR-3
Earlier sketch in CA 7-8R
Freedman, Nancy 1920- CANR-19
Earlier sketches in CA 45-48, CANR-1
See also SATA 27
Freedman, Paul H(arris) 1949- 122
Freedman, Ralph (William Bernard) 1920-
Brief entry 117
Freedman, Richard 1932- 77-80
Freedman, Robert Owen 1941- CANR-13
Earlier sketch in CA 33-36R
Freedman, Ronald 1917- CANR-6
Earlier sketch in CA 11-12R
Freedman, Russell (Bruce) 1929- CANR-23
Earlier sketches in CA 19-20R, CANR-7
See also SATA 16
Freedman, Samuel Sumner 1927- 112
Freedman, Warren 1921- 17-18R
Freehill, Maurice F(rancis) 1915- 7-8R
Freehling, Alison Goodyear 1941- 112
Freehof, Solomon B(ennett) 1892- 93-96
Freeland, Jay
See McLeod, John Freeland
Freeland, John Maxwell 1920- 13-14R
Freeland, Richard M. 1941- 81-84
Freeland, Stephen L. 1911(?)-1977
Obituary 69-72
Freeley, Austin J. 1922- 5-6R
Freeling, Nicolas 1927- CANR-17
Earlier sketches in CA 49-52, CANR-1
See also CLC 38
Freely, Maureen 1952- 97-100
Freeman, A. Myrick III 1936- 85-88
Freeman, Anne Frances 1936- 4R
Freeman, Arthur 1938- CANR-1
Earlier sketch in CA 2R
Freeman, Barbara C(onstance) 1906- 73-76
See also SATA 28
Freeman, Bill
See Freeman, William Bradford
Freeman, Bjorn
See Pratney, William Alfred
Freeman, C(lifford) Wade 1906- 7-8R
Freeman, Charles K. 1900-1980
Obituary 97-100
Freeman, Cynthia
See Feinberg, Bea
Freeman, Darlene 1934- 29-32R
Freeman, Dave
See Freeman, David
Freeman, David 1922- 102
Freeman, David 1945- Brief entry 108
Freeman, David Hugh 1924- CANR-17
Earlier sketch in CA 1R
Freeman, Don 1908-1978 77-80
See also SATA 17
Freeman, Donald Cary 1938- 53-56
Freeman, Donald McKinley 1931- CANR-15
Earlier sketch in CA 37-40R
Freeman, Douglas Southall 1886-1953
Brief entry 109
See also DLB 17
See also TCLC 11
Freeman, Eugene 1906- 41-44R
Freeman, G(raydon) L(a Verne) 1904- .. CANR-13
Earlier sketch in CA 13-14R
Freeman, Gary 1945- 93-96
Freeman, Gillian 1929- CANR-3
Earlier sketch in CA 7-8R
Freeman, Harrop A(rthur) 1907- 15-16R
Freeman, Harry 1906-1978 77-80
Freeman, Howard E(dgar) 1929- CANR-23
Earlier sketches in CA 5-6R, CANR-6
Freeman, Ira Henry 1906- CAP-1
Earlier sketch in CA 15-16
Freeman, Ira Maximilian 1905- 73-76
See also SATA 21
Freeman, James Dillet 1912- 19-20R
Freeman, James Montague 1936- 102
Freeman, Jean Kenny 1929- 115
Freeman, Jean Todd 1929- 25-28R
Freeman, Jo 1945- CANR-8
Earlier sketch in CA 61-64
Freeman, John Crosby 1941- 15-16R
Freeman, Joseph 1897-1965 Obituary 89-92
Freeman, Kathleen 1897-1959 Brief entry ... 112
Freeman, Larry
See Freeman, G(raydon) L(a Verne)
Freeman, Lea David 1887(?)-1976
Obituary 69-72
Freeman, Legh Richmond 1842-1915 ... DLB-23
Freeman, Leslie J(ane) 1944- 106
Freeman, Linton C(larke) 1927- 69-72
Freeman, Lucy (Greenbaum) 1916- CANR-3
Earlier sketch in CA 5-6R
See also SATA 24
Freeman, Mae (Blacker) 1907- 73-76
See also SATA 25
Freeman, Margaret B. 1899-1980 109
Obituary 97-100
Freeman, Margaret C(ooper) 1913- 57-60
Freeman, Margaret N(adgwick) 1915- 11-12R
Freeman, Mary Eleanor Wilkins 1852-1930
Brief entry 106
See also DLB 12
See also TCLC 9
See also SSC 1
Freeman, Max Herbert 1907- Brief entry 109
Freeman, Morton S(igmund) 1912- 118
Freeman, Paul 1929(?)-1980 Obituary 101
Freeman, Peter J.
See Calvert, Patricia

Freeman, R(ichard) Austin 1862-1943
Brief entry ... 113
See also TCLC 21
Freeman, R(ichard) B(roke) 1915-1986
Obituary ... 120
Freeman, Richard B(arry) 1944- ... CANR-15
Earlier sketch in CA 85-88
Freeman, Richard Borden 1908- ... CANR-17
Earlier sketch in CA 1R
Freeman, Roger A(dolf) 1904- ... 25-28R
Freeman, Roger A(nthony Wilson)
1928- ... CANR-10
Earlier sketch in CA 65-68
Freeman, Roger L(ouis) 1928- ... CANR-12
Earlier sketch in CA 69-72
Freeman, Ruth B(enson) 1906- ... 41-44R
Freeman, Ruth (Lazear) S(underlin)
1907- ... CANR-13
Earlier sketches in CA 15-16, CAP-1
Freeman, Susan Tax 1938- ... 85-88
Freeman, Thomas 1919- ... 93-96
Freeman, Thomas Walter 1908- ... 7-8R
Freeman, Tony ... SATA-44
Freeman, Walter (Jackson, Jr.)
1895-1972 ... CAP-1
Obituary ... 33-36R
Earlier sketch in CA 17-18
Freeman, Warren S(amuel) 1911- ... 5-6R
Freeman, William Bradford 1938- ... SATA-48
Freeman-Grenville, Greville Stewart Parker
1918- ... CANR-3
Earlier sketch in CA 7-8R
Freeman-Ishill, Rose 1895- ... CAP-1
Earlier sketch in CA 9-10
Freemantle, Brian Harry 1936- ... CANR-16
Earlier sketch in CA 65-68
Freemon, Frank R(eed) 1938- ... 45-58
Freer, Coburn 1939- Brief entry ... 105
Freer, Harold Wiley 1906- ... CAP-2
Earlier sketch in CA 21-22
Freese, Arthur S. 1917- ... 77-80
Freestrom, Hubert J. 1928- ... 37-40R
Freeth, Zahra 1925- ... 121
Fregault, Guy 1918-1977 ... 101
Frege, (Friedrich Ludwig) Gottlob
1848-1925 Brief entry ... 120
Fregly, Bert 1922- ... CANR-8
Earlier sketch in CA 57-60
Fregosi, Claudia (Anne Marie) 1946- ... 69-72
See also SATA 24
Frei, Eduardo
See Frei Montalva, Eduardo Frei
Frei, Hans W(ilhelm) 1922- Brief entry ... 111
Freiberg, Stanley K(enneth) 1923- ... 112
Freid, Jacob L. 1913- ... CANR-17
Earlier sketch in CA 3R
Freidel, Frank (Burt, Jr.) 1916- ... CANR-5
Earlier sketch in CA 3R
Freidenreich, Harriet Pass 1947- ... 114
Freides, Thelma K(atz) 1930- ... 49-52
Freidin, Seymour K(enneth) 1917- ... CANR-2
Earlier sketch in CA 4R
Freidson, Eliot 1923- ... CANR-8
Earlier sketch in CA 5-6R
Freihofer, Lois Diane 1933- ... 15-16R
Freilich, Joan S(herman) 1941- ... 57-60
Freilich, Morris 1928- ... 37-40R
Frei Montalva, Eduardo 1911-1982
Obituary ... 110
Freire, Paulo 1921- Brief entry ... 116
Freire-Maia, Newton 1918- ... 29-32R
Freitas, Margarete Elisabeth 1927- ... 45-48
Freivalds, John 1944- ... 69-72
Freixedo, Salvador 1923- ... 29-32R
Fremantle, Anne 1910- ... 15-16R
Fremgen, James Morgan 1933- ... 19-20R
Fremlin, Celia
See Goller, Celia (Fremlin)
Fremont, W. B.
See Bowers, Warner Fremont
Fremont-Smith, Eliot 1929- ... 105
French, Alfred 1916- ... 102
French, Allen 1870-1946 Brief entry ... 122
See also YABC 1
French, Ashley
See Robins, Denise (Naomi)
French, Bevan M(eredith) 1937- ... 97-100
French, Brandon 1944- ... 89-92
French, Calvin L(eonard) 1934- ... 53-56
French, Charles E(zra) 1923- ... CANR-1
Earlier sketch in CA 45-48
French, David 1939- ... 101
See also DLB 53
French, Doris
See Shackleton, Doris (Cavell)
French, Dorothy Kayser 1926- ... CANR-3
Earlier sketch in CA 9-10R
See also SATA 5
French, Edward L(ivingstone) 1916-1969 . CAP-2
Earlier sketch in CA 21-22
French, Fiona 1944- ... 29-32R
See also SATA 6
French, Herbert E(liot) 1912- ... 45-48
French, Kathryn
See Mosesson, Gloria R(ubin)
French, Marilyn 1929- ... CANR-3
Earlier sketch in CA 69-72
See also CLC 10, 18
French, Michael 1944- ... 89-92
See also SATA 38, 49
French, Paul
See Asimov, Isaac
French, Peter 1918- ... 4R
French, Peter A(ndrew) 1942- ... CANR-17
Earlier sketches in CA 45-48, CANR-1
French, Philip (Neville) 1933- ... 103
French, R(obert) B(utler) D(igby)
1904-1981 ... CAP-2
Obituary ... 104
Earlier sketch in CA 25-28
French, R(oger) K(enneth) 1938- ... 118
French, Richard (De Land) 1947- ... CANR-11
Earlier sketch in CA 69-72
French, Ruth M. 1921(?)-1987 Obituary ... 122
French, Scott Robert 1948- ... 57-60
French, Simon 1957- ... CANR-22
Earlier sketch in CA 105
French, Warren G(raham) 1922- ... CANR-16
Earlier sketches in CA 1R, CANR-1
French, Wendell L(owell) 1923- ... 116
French, Will 1890(?)-1979 Obituary ... 89-92
French, William (Harold) 1926- ... 69-72
French, William Marshall 1907- ... CAP-1
Earlier sketch in CA 15-16
Frend, A.
See Cleveland, Philip Jerome
Frend, W(illiam) H(ugh) C(lifford)
1916- ... CANR-9
Earlier sketch in CA 21-22R
Freneau, Philip 1752-1832 ... DLB-37, 43
Frenkel, Jacob A(haron) 1943- ... 89-92
Frenkel, Richard E(ugene) 1924- ... 21-22R
Frentzen, Jeffrey 1956- ... 109
Frenz, Horst 1912- ... 29-32R
Frenzel, Louis (Earl), Jr. 1938- ... 112
Frere, A. S.
See Frere-Reeves, Alexander Stuart
Frere, Emile (George) 1917-1974 ... 41-44R
Frere, James Arnold 1920- ... 7-8R
Frere, Paul 1917- ... CANR-14
Earlier sketch in CA 7-8R
Frere, Sheppard (Sunderland) 1916- ... 21-22R
Frere-Cook, Gervis 1928- Brief entry ... 111
Frere-Reeves, Alexander Stuart 1892-1984
Obituary ... 114
Frerichs, A(lbert) C(hristian) 1910- ... CAP-2
Earlier sketch in CA 25-28
Freschet, Berniece (Louise Speck)
1927- ... CANR-11
Earlier sketch in CA 19-20R
Frese, Dolores Warwick 1936- ... CANR-9
Earlier sketch in CA 5-6R
Fretheim, Terence E(rling) 1936- ... CANR-11
Earlier sketch in CA 25-28R
Fretter, T. W.
See Andre, (Kenneth) Michael
Fretter, William Bache 1916- ... 113
Fretwell, Stephen DeWitt 1942- ... 53-56
Freuchen, (Lorence) Peter (Elfred)
1886-1957 Brief entry ... 114
Freud, Anna 1895-1982 ... 112
Obituary ... 108
Freud, Clement (Raphael) 1924- ... 102
Freud, Sigmund 1856-1939 Brief entry ... 115
Freudberg, Frank 1953- ... 118
Freudenberger, Herman 1922- ... 13-14R
Freudenheim, Leslie Ann Mandelson
1941- ... 69-72
Freudenheim, Yehoshua (Oskar)
1894-1975 ... CAP-2
Earlier sketch in CA 21-22
Freudenthal, Hans 1905- ... CANR-11
Earlier sketch in CA 25-28R
Freund, E(rnest) Hans 1905- ... 1R
Freund, Edith 1931- ... 118
Freund, Gerald 1930- ... CANR-1
Earlier sketch in CA 4R
Freund, Gisele 1912- ... 49-52
Freund, John E(rnst) 1921- ... 13-14R
Freund, Otto Kahn
See Kahn-Freund, Otto
Freund, Paul A(braham) 1908- ... 1R
Freund, Philip (Herbert) 1909- ... CANR-12
Earlier sketch in CA 13-14R
Freund, Rudolf 1915-1969 ... SATA-28
Freundlich, August L. 1924- ... 49-52
Frevert, Peter 1938- ... 81-84
Frew, David R(ichard) 1943- ... 77-80
Frewer, Glyn (M.) 1931- ... CANR-10
Earlier sketch in CA 15-16R
See also SATA 11
Frewin, Leslie Ronald 1917- ... CANR-11
Earlier sketch in CA 7-8R
Frey, Andrew 1905(?)-1983 Obituary ... 109
Frey, Erich A. 1931- ... 45-48
Frey, Frederick Ward 1929- ... 53-56
Frey, Henry A. 1923- ... 33-36R
Frey, John Andrew 1929- ... 89-92
Frey, Leonard H(amilton) 1927- ... 29-32R
Frey, Marlys 1931- ... CANR-10
Earlier sketch in CA 25-28R
Frey, Richard L. 1905- ... 89-92
Freyer, Frederic
See Ballinger, William Sanborn
Freyre, Gilberto (de Mello) 1900-
Brief entry ... 116
Freytag, Joseph
See Cooper, Parley J(oseph)
Freytag, Josephine
See Cooper, Parley J(oseph)
Friar, Kimon 1911- ... 85-88
Friar Tuck
See Tucker, Irwin St. John
Fribourg, Marjorie G. 1920- ... CANR-4
Earlier sketch in CA 3R
Frick, C. H.
See Irwin, Constance Frick
Frick, Constance
See Irwin, Constance Frick
Frick, Ford Christopher 1894-1978
Obituary ... 89-92
Frick, George F(rederick) 1925- ... 13-14R
Fricke, Cedric V. 1928- ... 15-16R
Friday, Nancy 1937- ... 77-80
Friday, Peter
See Harris, Herbert
Frideres, James S(tephen) 1943- ... 113
Fridy, (William) Wallace 1910- ... CANR-17
Earlier sketch in CA 1R
Friebert, Stuart (Alyn) 1931- ... 65-68
Fried, Barbara 1924- ... 45-48
Fried, Charles 1935- ... CANR-12
Earlier sketch in CA 29-32R
Fried, Eleanor L.
See Furman, Eleanor L.
Fried, Emanuel 1913- ... 73-76
Fried, Erich 1921- Brief entry ... 114
Fried, Eunice ... 124
Fried, Frederick 1908- ... 77-80
Fried, John J(ames) 1940- ... CANR-12
Earlier sketch in CA 33-36R
Fried, Jonathan L(ester) 1955- ... 113
Fried, Joseph P. 1939- ... 37-40R
Fried, Lawrence 1926-1983 Obituary ... 110
Fried, Marc (Allen) 1922- ... 77-80
Fried, Marc B(ernard) 1944- ... 77-80
Fried, Mary McKenzie Hill 1914- ... 93-96
Fried, Morton H(erbert) 1923-1986 ... 21-22R
Obituary ... 121
Fried, Peter A(lexander) 1943- ... 108
Fried, Richard M(ayer) 1941- ... 73-76
Fried, William 1945- ... 57-60
Friedan, Betty (Naomi) 1921- ... CANR-18
Earlier sketch in CA 65-68
Friedberg, Ardy 1935- ... 108
Friedberg, Gertrude (Tonkonogy) ... 21-22R
Friedberg, Joan Brest 1927- ... 124
Friedberg, Maurice 1929- ... CANR-5
Earlier sketch in CA 1R
Friede, Eleanor Kask 1920- ... 101
Friedelbaum, Stanley H(erman) 1927- ... 37-40R
Friedell, Aaron 1890(?)-1985 Obituary ... 116
Frieden, Bernard J. 1930- ... CANR-10
Earlier sketch in CA 15-16R
Frieden, Ken(neth) 1955- ... 118
Friedenberg, Edgar Zodiag 1921- ... 65-68
Friedenberg, Walter Drew 1928- ... 89-92
Friedenreich, Harriet Pass
See Freidenreich, Harriet Pass
Friedenthal, Richard 1896-1979 ... 103
Obituary ... 89-92
Frieder, Emma 1891- ... CAP-2
Earlier sketch in CA 33-36
Friederich, Werner P(aul) 1905- ... 15-16R
Friederichsen, Kathleen (Hockman)
1910- ... 19-20R
Friedgut, Theodore H. 1931- ... 89-92
Friedheim, Robert L(yle) 1934- ... CANR-12
Earlier sketch in CA 21-22R
Friedkin, William 1939- ... 107
Friedl, Ernestine 1920- ... 37-40R
Friedl, John 1945- ... CANR-4
Earlier sketch in CA 53-56
Friedlaender, Saul 1932- Brief entry ... 117
Friedlaender, Walter (Ferdinand)
1873-1966 Obituary ... 115
Friedland, Ronald Lloyd 1937-1975 ... CAP-2
Obituary ... 57-60
Earlier sketch in CA 33-36
Friedland, Ronnie 1945- ... 106
Friedland, Seymour 1928- ... CANR-17
Earlier sketch in CA 25-28R
Friedland, William H. 1923- ... 13-14R
Friedlander, Albert H(oschander) 1927- .. CANR-9
Earlier sketch in CA 23-24R
Friedlander, Howard 1941- ... 105
Friedlander, Joanne K(ohn) 1930- ... 61-64
See also SATA 9
Friedlander, Saul
See Friedlaender, Saul
Friedlander, Stanley Lawrence 1938- ... 17-18R
Friedlander, Walter A(ndreas) 1891- ... 37-40R
Friedman, Alan
See Horowitz, Shel Alan
Friedman, Alan Warren 1939- ... 25-28R
Friedman, Albert B(arron) 1920- ... CANR-17
Earlier sketch in CA 1R
Friedman, Alice R. 1900- ... 41-44R
Friedman, Arnold D'Arcy 1900-1981
Obituary ... 109
Friedman, Arnold P(hineas) 1909- ... CANR-1
Earlier sketch in CA 45-48
Friedman, Avner 1932- ... 53-56
Friedman, B(ernard) H(arper) 1926- ... CANR-3
Earlier sketch in CA 2R
See also CLC 7
Friedman, Bernard 1896-1983 Obituary ... 110
Friedman, Bruce Jay 1930- ... 11-12R
See also DLB 2, 28
See also CLC 3, 5
Friedman, Charles 1902-1984 Obituary ... 113
Friedman, David 1945- ... 89-92
Friedman, Edward Ludwig 1903- ... 3R
Friedman, Elizabeth 1893(?)-1980
Obituary ... 102
Friedman, Estelle (Ehrenwald) 1920- ... 5-6R
See also SATA 7
Friedman, Frieda 1905- ... SATA-43
Friedman, Hal
See Friedman, Harold
Friedman, Harold 1942- ... 89-92
Friedman, Herbert 1916- Brief entry ... 112
Friedman, Ina R(osen) 1926- ... 53-56
See also SATA 41, 49
Friedman, Irving S(igmund) 1915- ... CANR-3
Earlier sketch in CA 45-48
Friedman, Isaiah 1921- ... 53-56
Friedman, Jerrold David
See Gerrold, David
Friedman, John S(aul) 1942- ... 118
Friedman, Josephine Troth 1928- ... 77-80
Friedman, Josh Alan 1956- ... 122
Friedman, Joy Troth
See Friedman, Josephine Troth
Friedman, Judi 1935- ... 65-68
See also AITN 2
Friedman, Julian R. 1920(?)-1983
Obituary ... 111
Friedman, Kathi V(allone) 1943- ... 114
Friedman, Ken(neth Scott) ... 65-68
Friedman, Kenneth 1939- ... 25-28R
Friedman, Lawrence J. 1940- ... 53-56
Friedman, Lawrence Meir 1930- ... CANR-5
Earlier sketch in CA 15-16R
Friedman, Lenemaja 1924- ... 61-64
Friedman, Leon 1933- ... 81-84
Friedman, Lester David 1945- ... 108
Friedman, Marcia 1925- ... 57-60
Friedman, Marvin 1930- ... SATA-33, 42
Friedman, Maurice S(tanley) 1921- ... 15-16R
Friedman, Melvin J(ack) 1928- ... 21-22R
Friedman, Meyer 1910- Brief entry ... 113
Friedman, Michael H(enry) 1945- ... 101
Friedman, Michael J(an) 1955- ... 119
Friedman, Michaele Thompson 1944- ... 111
Friedman, Mickey
See Friedman, Michaele Thompson
Friedman, Milton 1912- ... CANR-22
Earlier sketches in CA 1R, CANR-1
Friedman, Murray 1926- ... 57-60
Friedman, Myles I(van) 1924- ... CANR-6
Earlier sketch in CA 57-60
Friedman, Nancy 1950- ... 107
Friedman, Norman 1925- ... CANR-1
Earlier sketch in CA 1R
Friedman, Paul 1899-1972 Obituary ... 37-40R
Friedman, Paul 1937- ... 122
Friedman, Paul Belais 1953- ... 110
Friedman, Ralph 1916- ... 69-72
Friedman, Rochelle (Rame) 1942- ... 112
Friedman, Rose D(irector) ... CANR-22
Earlier sketch in CA 101
Friedman, (Eve) Rosemary (Tibber)
1929- ... CANR-21
Earlier sketches in CA 7-8R, CANR-3
Friedman, Roslyn Berger 1924- ... 19-20R
Friedman, Roy 1934- ... 25-28R
Friedman, Sanford 1928- ... 73-76
Friedman, Sara Ann 1935- ... 77-80
Friedman, Saul S. 1937- ... 57-60
Friedman, Stuart 1913- ... 2R
Friedman, Susan Stanford 1943- ... 109
Friedman, Thomas L(oren) 1953- ... 109
Friedman, Warner G(eorge) 1934- ... 97-100
Friedman, Winifred 1923(?)-1975
Obituary ... 61-64
Friedmann, Arnold 1925- ... 41-44R
Friedmann, Deborah Davis
See Davis-Friedmann, Deborah
Friedmann, Georges 1902(?)-1977
Obituary ... 104
Friedmann, Herbert 1900-1987 ... 106
Obituary ... 122
Friedmann, John 1926- ... CANR-15
Earlier sketch in CA 85-88
Friedmann, Thomas 1947- ... 118
Friedmann, Wolfgang (Gaston)
1907-1972 ... CANR-6
Earlier sketch in CA 3R
Friedmann, Yohanan 1936- ... 33-36R
Friedrich, Anton
See Strich, Christian
Friedrich, Carl Joachim 1901-1984 ... 69-72
Obituary ... 113
Friedrich, Dick
See Friedrich, Richard
Friedrich, Gustav W(illiam) 1941-
Brief entry ... 111
Friedrich, Otto (Alva) 1929- ... CANR-3
Earlier sketch in CA 5-6R
See also SATA 33
Friedrich, Paul 1927- ... CANR-12
Earlier sketch in CA 29-32R
Friedrich, Priscilla 1927- ... 113
See also SATA 39
Friedrich, Richard 1936- ... 103
Friedrichs, Christopher R(ichard) 1947- ... 89-92
Friedrichs, Robert W(inslow) 1923- ... 49-52
Friedson, Anthony M(artin) 1924- ... 108
Friel, Brian 1929- ... 21-22R
See also DLB 13
See also CLC 5, 42
Frielink, A(braham) Barend 1917- ... 21-22R
Friend, Joseph H(arold) 1909-1972 ... CAP-2
Earlier sketch in CA 25-28
Friend, Krebs 1895(?)-1967(?) ... DLB-4
Friend, Robert 1913- ... CANR-7
Earlier sketch in CA 13-14R
Friendlich, Dick
See Friendlich, Richard J.
Friendlich, Richard J. 1909- ... CAP-1
Earlier sketch in CA 15-16
See also SATA 11
Friendly, Alfred 1911-1983 ... 101
Obituary ... 111
Friendly, Fred W. 1915- ... CANR-14
Earlier sketch in CA 23-24R
Friendly, Henry Jacob 1903-1986 ... 103
Obituary ... 118
Friermood, Elisabeth Hamilton 1903- ... CANR-1
Earlier sketch in CA 1R
See also SATA 5
Fries, Albert Charles 1908- ... CANR-4
Earlier sketch in CA 1R
Fries, Fritz Rudolf 1935- ... CANR-11
Earlier sketch in CA 25-28R
Fries, James Franklin 1938- ... 89-92

Fries, Robert Francis 1911- 106
Friesen, Garry 1947- 114
Friesen, Gerald 1943- 120
Friesen, Patrick 1945- 113
Friess, Horace L(eland) 1900-1975 65-68
Obituary 61-64
Friggens, Arthur (Henry) 1920- 103
Friis, Babbis
See Friis-Baastad, Babbis Ellinor
Friis, Erik J(ohan) 1913- 69-72
Friis, Harald T(rap) 1893-1976 Obituary 65-68
Friis-Baastad, Babbis Ellinor 1921-1970 19-20R
See also SATA 7
See also CLC 12
Frijling-Schreuder, E(lisabeth) C. M. 1908- 61-64
Frillmann, Paul W. 1911-1972 CAP-2
Obituary 37-40R
Earlier sketch in CA 25-28
Frimbo, E. M.
See Whitaker, Rogers E(rnest) M(alcolm)
Friml, Rudolf 1879-1972 Obituary 37-40R
Frimmer, Steven 1928- 33-36R
See also SATA 31
Frimoth, Lenore B(eck) 1927- 5-6R
Frings, Ketti 1915-1981 101
Obituary 103
Frings, Manfred S. 1925- CANR-8
Earlier sketch in CA 17-18R
Frink, Maurice 1895-1972 CAP-2
Earlier sketch in CA 25-28
Frinta, Mojmir S(vatopluk) 1922- 25-28R
Fripp, Patricia 1945- 93-96
Frisbie, Louise K(elley) 1913- 61-64
Frisbie, Margery (Rowbottom) 1923- 5-6R
Frisbie, Richard P(atrick) 1926- CANR-17
Earlier sketches in CA 5-6R, CANR-2
Frisby, Terence (Peter Michael) 1932- 65-68
Frisch, Karl (Ritter) von 1886-1982 85-88
Obituary 115
Frisch, Max (Rudolf) 1911- 85-88
See also CLC 3, 9, 14, 18, 32, 44
Frisch, Morton J. 1923- 33-36R
Frisch, O(tto) R(obert) 1904- 11-12R
Frisch, Paul Z. 1926(?)-1977 Obituary 73-76
Frisch, Ragnar Anton Kittil 1895-1973
Obituary 115
Frischauer, Willi 1906- CANR-7
Earlier sketch in CA 7-8R
Frischer, Bernard D(avid) 1949- 113
Frischwasser-Ra'Anan, H. F.
See Ra'Anan, Uri
Friskey, Margaret (Richards) 1901- CANR-2
Earlier sketch in CA 5-6R
See also SATA 5
Frison, George C(arr) 1924- 93-96
Fritchman, Stephen Hole 1902-
Brief entry 105
Frith, H(arold) J(ames) 1921- 102
Frith, Nigel (Andrew Silver) 1941- 69-72
Fritsch, Albert Joseph 1933- 102
Fritsch, Bruno 1926- CANR-11
Earlier sketch in CA 69-72
Fritsch, Charles Theodore 1912- 112
Fritschler, A. Lee 1937- 33-36R
Fritz
See Whitehall, Harold
Fritz, Henry E(ugene) 1927- 19-20R
Fritz, Jean (Guttery) 1915- CANR-16
Earlier sketches in CA 4R, CANR-5
See also SATA 1, 29
See also SAAS 2
See also DLB 52
See also CLR 2, 14
Fritz, Leah 1931- 93-96
Fritze, Julius Arnold 1918- 103
Fritzsch, Harald 1943- 113
Frobish, Nestle J(ohn) 1930- 101
Froboess, Harry (August) 1899- CAP-2
Earlier sketch in CA 17-18
Froehlich, Gustav 1902-1987 Obituary 124
Froehlich, Margaret W(alden) 1930- 115
Froelich, Robert E. 1929- CANR-3
Earlier sketch in CA 45-48
Frohlich, Gustav
See Froehlich, Gustav
Frohlich, Norman 1941- 77-80
Frohman, Charles E(ugene) 1901-1976 CAP-2
Earlier sketch in CA 29-32
Frohock, W(ilbur) M(errill) 1908-1984 73-76
Obituary 113
Froissard, Lily Powell 45-48
Froissart, Jean 1338(?)-1410(?) SATA-28
Froman, Elizabeth Hull 1920-1975 CAP-1
Obituary 53-56
Earlier sketch in CA 15-16
See also SATA 10
Froman, Lewis A(crelius), Jr. 1935- 5-6R
Froman, Robert (Winslow) 1917- CANR-1
Earlier sketch in CA 4R
See also SATA 8
Frome, David
See Brown, Zenith Jones
Frome, Michael 1920- CANR-16
Earlier sketches in CA 4R, CANR-1
Fromer, Margot J(oan) 1939- 110
Fromkin, David 1932- 109
Fromkin, Howard L(arry) 1939- 121
Brief entry 118
Fromkin, Victoria A(lexandria) 1923- 89-92
Fromm, Erich 1900-1980 73-76
Obituary 97-100
Fromm, Erika 1910- 9-10R
Fromm, Gary 1933- CANR-7
Earlier sketch in CA 17-18R
Fromm, Gloria G(likin) 1931- Brief entry 112
Fromm, Harold 1933- 23-24R
Fromm, Herbert 1905- CANR-1
Earlier sketch in CA 49-52
Fromm, Lilo 1928- 81-84
See also SATA 29
Fromme, Babbette Brandt 1925- 106
Frommer, Harvey 1937- 103
See also SATA 41
Frommer, Myrna 1941- 111
Froncek, Thomas (Walter) 1942- 81-84
Frondizi, Risieri 1910- 41-44R
Frontier, Tex
See Miller, J(ames) P.
Frooks, Dorothy 1899- 57-60
Froomkin, Joseph 1927- CANR-13
Earlier sketch in CA 23-24R
Frosch, Thomas Richard 1943- 69-72
Froscher, Wingate 1918- 1R
Frost, A(rthur) B(urdett) 1851-1928 SATA-19
Frost, Carol 1948- CANR-11
Earlier sketch in CA 69-72
Frost, David (Paradine) 1939- 69-72
Frost, Erica
See Supraner, Robyn
Frost, Ernest 1918- 9-10R
Frost, Everett L(loyd) 1942- 65-68
Frost, Frank (Jasper) 1929- 89-92
Frost, Frederick
See Faust, Frederick (Shiller)
Frost, Gavin 1930- CANR-1
Earlier sketch in CA 45-48
Frost, Gerhard Emanuel 1909- CAP-1
Earlier sketch in CA 9-10
Frost, Gregory 1951- 118
Frost, Helen 1898- CAP-1
Earlier sketch in CA 13-14
Frost, James A(rthur) 1918- 37-40R
Frost, Jason
See Obstfeld, Raymond
Frost, Joe L. 1933- 25-28R
Frost, Joni
See Paine, Lauran (Bosworth)
Frost, Lawrence A(ugust) 1907- CANR-11
Earlier sketch in CA 69-72
Frost, Lesley 1899-1983 21-22R
Obituary 110
See also SATA 14, 34
Frost, Leslie Miscampbell 1895-1973
Obituary 41-44R
Frost, M(ax) Gilbert 1908- CAP-1
Earlier sketch in CA 13-14
Frost, Marjorie 1914- 25-28R
Frost, Paul
See Castle, Anthony (Percy)
Frost, Peter Kip 1936- 33-36R
Frost, Richard 1929- 33-36R
Frost, Richard H(indman) 1930- 25-28R
Frost, Richard T. 1926-1972 CAP-1
Obituary 37-40R
Earlier sketch in CA 15-16
Frost, Robert (Lee) 1874-1963 89-92
See also SATA 14
See also DLB 54
See also CLC 1, 3, 4, 9, 10, 13, 15, 26, 34, 44
Frost, Robert Carlton 1926- 53-56
Frost, S. E., Jr. 1899- CAP-2
Earlier sketch in CA 19-20
Frost, Stanley Brice 1913- 61-64
Frost, William 1917- 41-44R
Frostic, Gwen 1906- 19-20R
Frostick, Michael 1917- 9-10R
Frothingham, Octavius Brooks 1822-1895 DLB-1
Froude, James Anthony 1818-1894 DLB-18, 57
Frow, John 1948- 120
Froy, Herald
See Deghy, Guy (Stephen) and Waterhouse, Keith Spencer
Frucht, Phyllis 1936- 57-60
Fruchtenbaum, Arnold G(enekovich) 1943- CANR-11
Earlier sketch in CA 61-64
Fruchter, Benjamin 1914- 1R
Fruchter, Norman D. 81-84
Frude, Neil 1946- 114
Fruehling, Rosemary T(herese) 1933- CANR-13
Earlier sketch in CA 33-36R
Frugoni, Cesare 1881-1978 Obituary 73-76
Fruhan, William E(dward), Jr. 1943- 41-44R
Frum, Barbara 1937- 101
Fruman, Norman 1923- 37-40R
Frumkes, Lewis Burke 1939- 114
Frumkin, Gene 1928- CANR-4
Earlier sketch in CA 9-10R
Frumkin, Robert M. 1928- CANR-9
Earlier sketch in CA 23-24R
Fruton, Joseph S(tewart) 1912- 49-52
Fruzzetti, Lina M(aria) 1942- 113
Fry, Alan 1931- CANR-1
Earlier sketch in CA 45-48
Fry, Barbara 1932- 25-28R
Fry, C(harles) George 1936- CANR-14
Earlier sketch in CA 37-40R
Fry, Christine 1943- 107
Fry, Christopher 1907- CANR-9
Earlier sketch in CA 17-18R
See also DLB 13
See also CLC 2, 10, 14
Fry, David
See Roper, William L(eon)
Fry, Dennis Butler 1907-1983 109
Obituary 110
Fry, Donald K(lein, Jr.) 1937- 25-28R
Fry, E(dwin) Maxwell 1899-1987 65-68
Obituary 123
Fry, Earl H(oward) 1947- 102
Fry, Edward Bernard 1925- CANR-5
Earlier sketch in CA 9-10R
See also SATA 35
Fry, Hilary G. 1922- 19-20R
Fry, Howard T(yrrell) 1919- 37-40R
Fry, John 1930- 93-96
Fry, Maggie Culver 1900- AITN-1
Fry, Maxwell
See Fry, E(dwin) Maxwell
Fry, Michael G(raham) 1934- CANR-23
Earlier sketch in CA 69-72
Fry, P(atricia) Eileen 1947- 104
Fry, Plantagenet Somerset
See Somerset Fry, (Peter George Robin) Plantagenet
Fry, Roger (Eliot) 1866-1934 Brief entry 115
Fry, Ronald W(illiam) 1949- 57-60
Fry, Rosalie Kingsmill 1911- 9-10R
See also SATA 3
Fry, Thomas Frederick 1919- 118
Fry, Tom
See Fry, Thomas Frederick
Fry, William F(inley, Jr.) 1924- 5-6R
Fryatt, Norma R. 57-60
Fryburger, Vernon R(ay), Jr. 1918- 4R
Fryd, Norbert 1913-1976 Obituary 65-68
Frydman, Szajko 1911- 25-28R
Frye, (Charles) Alton 1936- 21-22R
Frye, Ellen 1940- 49-52
Frye, John 1910- 49-52
Frye, Keith 1935- 53-56
Frye, (Herman) Northrop 1912- CANR-8
Earlier sketch in CA 5-6R
See also DLB 67
See also CLC 24
Frye, Richard N(elson) 1920- CANR-3
Earlier sketch in CA 5-6R
Frye, Roland Mushat 1921- 9-10R
Frye, William R(uggles) 1918- 73-76
Fryer, Donald S.
See Sidney-Fryer, Donald
Fryer, Holly C(laire) 1908- CAP-1
Earlier sketch in CA 19-20
Fryer, Jonathan 1950- 85-88
Fryer, Judith 1939- 69-72
Fryer, Mary Beacock 1929- 97-100
Fryer, William T. 1900(?)-1980 Obituary 93-96
Frykenberg, Robert Eric 1930- 25-28R
Fryklund, Verne C(harles) 1896- 13-14R
Frykman, John H(arvey) 1932- 33-36R
Frym, Gloria 1947- 105
Frymier, Jack R(immel) 1925- 19-20R
Fryscak, Milan 1932- 53-56
Fuchida, Mitsuo 1902(?)-1976 Obituary 65-68
Fuchs, Daniel 1909- 81-84
See also CAAS 5
See also DLB 9, 26, 28
See also CLC 8, 22
Fuchs, Daniel 1934- CANR-14
Earlier sketch in CA 37-40R
See also CLC 34
Fuchs, Elinor 1933- 105
Fuchs, Erich 1916- 29-32R
See also SATA 6
Fuchs, Estelle 57-60
Fuchs, Guenter Bruno 1928-1977
Obituary 114
Fuchs, Jacob 1939- 23-24R
Fuchs, Jerome H(erbert) 1922- 69-72
Fuchs, Josef 1912- 21-22R
Fuchs, Lawrence H. 1927- CANR-5
Earlier sketch in CA 3R
Fuchs, Lucy 1935- CANR-12
Earlier sketch in CA 73-76
Fuchs, Roland J(ohn) 1933- CANR-14
Earlier sketch in CA 81-84
Fuchs, Victor R(obert) 1924- CANR-18
Earlier sketches in CA 1R, CANR-2
Fuchs, Vivian (Ernest) 1908- CANR-21
Earlier sketch in CA 104
Fuchshuber, Annegert 1940- 112
See also SATA 43
Fucilla, Joseph G(uerin) 1897- 89-92
Fucini, Joseph J(ames) 1951- 120
Fucini, Suzy 1951- 120
Fudge, William Kingston 1904-1985
Obituary 116
Fuegi, John 1936- 37-40R
Fueloep-Miller, Rene 1891-1963 Obituary 110
Fuentes, Carlos 1928- CANR-10
Earlier sketch in CA 69-72
See also CLC 3, 8, 10, 13, 22, 41
See also AITN 2
Fuentes, Martha Ayers 1923- 73-76
Fuentes, Roberto 1934- 57-60
Fuentes Mohr, Alberto 1928(?)-1979
Obituary 85-88
Fuerer-Haimendorf, Christoph von 1909- CANR-13
Earlier sketch in CA 15-16R
Fuermann, George Melvin 1918- 103
Fufuka, Karama
See Morgan, Sharon A(ntonia)
Fugard, Athol 1932- 85-88
See also CLC 5, 9, 14, 25, 40
Fugate, Bryan I(rven) 1943- 120
Fugate, Francis L(yle) 1915- 25-28R
Fugate, Joe K. 1931- 23-24R
Fugate, Roberta B(auslin) 1917- 111
Fugate, Terence (McCuddy) 1930- 5-6R
Fuhrman, Eva D(raper) 1929- 110
Fuhrman, Ellsworth R(aymond) 1946- 112
Fuhrman, Lee 1903(?)-1977 Obituary 73-76
Fuhrmann, Joseph T(heodore) 1940- 73-76
Fuhro, Wilbur J. 1914- 11-12R
Fujikawa, Gyo 1908- 113
See also SATA 30, 39
Fujita, Tamao 1905- 37-40R
See also SATA 7
Fujiwara, Michiko 1946- 77-80
See also SATA 15
Fujiwara, Yoichi 1909- CANR-22
Earlier sketch in CA 105
Fuka, Vladimir 1926-1977 Obituary 104
See also SATA 27
Fukei, Gladys Arlene (Harper) 1920- 15-16R
Fuks, Ladislav 1923- 118
Fukuda, Haruko 1946- 109
Fukuda, Tsutomu 1905- 103
Fukui, Haruhiro 1935- 29-32R
Fukutake, Tadashi 1917- CANR-5
Earlier sketch in CA 13-14R
Fukuyama, Yoshio 1921- 41-44R
Fulbright, J(ames) William 1905- 9-10R
Fulbrook, Mary (Jean Alexandra) 1951- 121
Fulco, William J(ames) 1936- 49-52
Fuld, James J. 1916- 23-24R
Fuld, Leonard M. 1953- 120
Fulda, Carl H. 1909-1975 CAP-2
Earlier sketch in CA 33-36
Fuldauer, Ivan 1927- 69-72
Fuldheim, Dorothy (Snell) 1893- 49-52
Fulford, Robert 1932- 89-92
Fulford, Roger (Thomas Baldwin) 1902-1983 65-68
Obituary 109
Fulks, Bryan 1897- 97-100
Full, Harold 1919- 17-18R
Fuller, Alfred C(arl) 1885-1973 Obituary 45-48
Fuller, Beverley 1927- 69-72
Fuller, Blair 1927- 9-10R
Fuller, Catherine Leuthold 1916- 29-32R
See also SATA 9
Fuller, Charles (H., Jr.) 1939- 112
Brief entry 108
See also DLB 38
See also CLC 25
Fuller, Curtis G. 1912- Brief entry 120
Fuller, Daniel P(ayton) 1925- Brief entry 112
Fuller, David O(tis) 1903- 53-56
Fuller, Dorothy Mason 1898- 101
Fuller, Edgar 1904-1973 Obituary 45-48
Fuller, Edmund (Maybank) 1914- 77-80
See also SATA 21
Fuller, Edward C. 1907- 53-56
Fuller, Elizabeth 1946- 113
Fuller, Harold 1940- 65-68
Fuller, Helen 1914(?)-1972 Obituary 37-40R
Fuller, Henry Blake 1857-1929 Brief entry 108
See also DLB 12
Fuller, Hoyt (William) 1927-1981 53-56
Obituary 103
Fuller, Iola
See McCoy, Iola Fuller
Fuller, Jean (Violet) Overton 1915- CANR-19
Earlier sketches in CA 7-8R, CANR-4
Fuller, John (Harold) CAP-1
Earlier sketch in CA 9-10
Fuller, John (Leopold) 1937- CANR-9
Earlier sketch in CA 21-22R
See also DLB 40
Fuller, John Frederick Charles 1878-1966 CAP-1
Earlier sketch in CA 15-16
Fuller, John G(rant, Jr.) 1913- CANR-2
Earlier sketch in CA 1R
Fuller, Lois Hamilton 1915- 4R
See also SATA 11
Fuller, Lon (Luvois) 1902-1978 CAP-2
Obituary 77-80
Earlier sketch in CA 33-36
Fuller, Margaret
See Ossoli, Sarah Margaret (Fuller marchesa d')
Fuller, Miriam Morris 1933- 37-40R
Fuller, Paul E(ugene) 1932- 73-76
Fuller, Peter (Michael) 1947- 97-100
Fuller, R(ichard) Buckminster (Jr.) 1895-1983 CANR-12
Obituary 109
Earlier sketch in CA 11-12R
Fuller, Reginald H(orace) 1915- CANR-18
Earlier sketches in CA 5-6R, CANR-3
Fuller, Robert C(harles) 1952- 116
Fuller, Roger
See Tracy, Don(ald Fiske)
Fuller, Roy (Broadbent) 1912- 7-8R
See also DLB 15, 20
See also CLC 4, 28
Fuller, Sam
See Fuller, Samuel (Michael)
Fuller, Samuel (Michael) 1911(?)-
Brief entry 112
Fuller, Samuel 1912- DLB-26
Fuller, Sarah Margaret 1810-1850 DLB-1, 59
See also CDALB 1640-1865
Fuller, Wayne E(dison) 1919- 15-16R
Fuller, William A(lbert) 1924- 41-44R
Fullerton, Alexander (Fergus) 1924- CANR-23
Earlier sketches in CA 19-20R, CANR-7
Fullerton, Gail Jackson 1927- 37-40R
Fullerton, Gail Putney
See Fullerton, Gail Jackson
Fullinwider, Robert King 1942- 108
Fullinwider, S. P(endleton) 1933-
Brief entry 109
Fullmer, Daniel W(arren) 1922- CANR-13
Earlier sketch in CA 33-36R
Fullmer, June Z(immerman) 1920- 25-28R
Fulmer, Robert M(arion) 1939- CANR-10
Earlier sketch in CA 57-60
Fulop-Miller, Rene
See Fueloep-Miller, Rene
Fulton, A(lbert) R(ondthaler) 1902- 1R
Fulton, Alice 1952- 116

Fulton, Gere (Burke) 1939- 53-56
Fulton, Len 1934- 57-60
See also DLBY 86
Fulton, Norman 1927- 37-40R
Fulton, Paul C(edric) 1901-1985 .... CAP-1
Obituary 118
Earlier sketch in CA 15-16
Fulton, Robert Lester 1926- Brief entry 105
Fulton, Robin 1937- CANR-16
Earlier sketch in CA 33-36R
See also DLB 40
Fults, John Lee 1932- 53-56
See also SATA 33
Fultz, Walter J. 1924(?)-1971 Obituary 104
Fulweiler, Howard Wells 1932- 77-80
Fumento, Rocco 1923- 2R
Funabashi, Seiichi 1904(?)-1976
Obituary 65-68
Funai, Mamoru (Rolland) 1932- SATA-46
Fundaburk, Emma Lila 1922- 41-44R
Funderburk, Guy B(ernard) 1902- 45-48
Funderburk, Thomas R(ay) 1928- 19-20R
Fung, Gong
See Goon, Fook Mun
Fung, Raymond (Wai Man) 1940- 123
Funigiello, Philip J. 1939- 65-68
Funk, Arthur Layton 1914- 23-24R
Funk, Charles Earle, Jr. 1913- 122
Funk, Peter V(an) K(euren) 1921- CANR-13
Earlier sketch in CA 21-22R
Funk, Rainer 1943- 109
Funk, Robert W(alter) 1926- 33-36R
Funk, Thompson 1911- CANR-2
Earlier sketch in CA 49-52
See also SATA 7
Funk, Tom
See Funk, Thompson
Funk, Wilfred (John) 1883-1965 Obituary 89-92
Funke, Lewis 1912- 49-52
See also SATA 11
Funston, Richard Y(ork) 1943- 123
Brief entry 118
Funt, Julian 1907(?)-1980 Obituary 97-100
Funt, Marilyn 1937- 102
Fuoss, Robert Martin 1912-1980
Obituary 93-96
Furbank, P(hilip) N(icholas) 1920- CANR-18
Earlier sketch in CA 21-22R
Furbee, Leonard J. 1896(?)-1975
Obituary 61-64
Furchgott, Terry 1948- 105
See also SATA 29
Furcolo, Foster 1917- 117
Furer, Howard B(ernard) 1934- 33-36R
Furer-Haimendorf, Christoph von
See Fuerer-Haimendorf, Christoph von
Furey, Michael
See Ward, Arthur Henry Sarsfield
Furfey, Paul Hanly 1896- CAP-2
Earlier sketch in CA 23-24
Furgurson, Ernest B(aker, Jr.) 1929- 73-76
Furgurson, Pat
See Furgurson, Ernest B(aker, Jr.)
Furley, David John 1922- 108
Furlong, Monica (Mavis) 1930- Brief entry 117
Furlonge, Geoffrey (Warren) 1903-1984
Obituary 114
Furman, Bess 1894-1969 Obituary 115
Furman, Eleanor L. 1913- CANR-12
Earlier sketch in CA 29-32R
Furman, Laura 1945- 104
See also DLBY 86
Furman, Roger 1924(?)-1983 Obituary 111
Furnas, J(oseph) C(hamberlain) 1905- 77-80
Furneaux, Robin
See Smith, Frederick William Robin
Furneaux, Rupert 1908- CANR-1
Earlier sketch in CA 4R
Furness, Edna L(ue) 1906- 37-40R
Furness, Horace Howard 1833-1912 .... DLB-64
Furness, William Henry 1802-1896 .... DLB-1
Furnier, Vincent Damon
See Cooper, Alice
Furnish, Dorothy Jean 1921- 106
Furnish, Victor Paul 1931- CANR-10
Earlier sketch in CA 23-24R
Furniss, Edgar S(tephenson) 1890-1972
Obituary 37-40R
Furniss, Norman Francis 1922- 1R
Furniss, Tim 1948- 109
See also SATA 49
Furniss, W(arren) Todd 1921- 57-60
Furphy, Joseph 1843-1912 .... TCLC-25
Furrer, Juerg 1939- 69-72
Furry, Elda 1890-1966 113
Obituary 89-92
Furse, John 1932- 109
Furst, Alan 1941- CANR-12
Earlier sketch in CA 69-72
Furst, Lilian Renee 1931- CANR-18
Earlier sketch in CA 102
Furtado, Celso 1920- CANR-9
Earlier sketch in CA 17-18R
Furth, Alex
See Sasuly, Richard
Furth, George 1932- 73-76
Furth, Hans G. 1920- 45-48
Furthman, Jules
See Furthmann, Julius Grinnell
See also DLB 26
Furthmann, Julius Grinnell 1888-1966
Obituary 113
Furtwangler, Albert (J.) 1942- 118
Furtwangler, Virginia W(alsh) 1932- 118
Furukawa, Toshi 1924- CANR-2
Earlier sketch in CA 45-48
See also SATA 24
Fusco, Margie 1949- 85-88
Fusero, Clemente 1913-1975 81-84
Fusfeld, Daniel R(oland) 1922- 45-48
Fuson, Benjamin Willis 1911- 37-40R
Fuson, Robert H(enderson) 1927- 89-92
Fuss, Peter 1932- CANR-9
Earlier sketch in CA 23-24R
Fussell, Betty
See Fussell, Betty Harper
Fussell, Betty Harper 1927- 121
Fussell, Edwin 1922- 53-56
Fussell, G(eorge) E(dwin) 1889- CANR-3
Earlier sketch in CA 7-8R
Fussell, Paul 1924- CANR-21
Earlier sketches in CA 19-20R, CANR-8
Fussner, F(rank) Smith 1920- CANR-5
Earlier sketch in CA 1R
Futrell, Allan W. 1952- 123
Futrell, Gene Allen 1928- 107
Futrelle, Jacques 1875-1912 Brief entry 113
See also TCLC 19
Futuyma, Douglas Joel 1942- 108
Fyffe, Don(ald Lewis) 1925- 25-28R
Fyleman, Rose (Amy) 1877-1957
Brief entry 111
See also SATA 21
Fyler, John (Morgan) 1943- 89-92
Fyodorov, Yevgeny Konstantinovich
See Fedorov, Yevgeny Konstantinovich
Fysh, Wilmot Hudson 1895- 17-18R
Fyson, J(enny) G(race) 1904- CAP-2
Earlier sketch in CA 21-22
See also SATA 42
Fyvel, T. R.
See Feiwel, Raphael Joseph
Fyvel, Tosco Raphael
See Feiwel, Raphael Joseph

G

G. B.
See Boas, Guy (Herman Sidney)
Gaa, Charles J(ohn) 1911- 19-20R
Gaan, Margaret 1914- 81-84
Gaard, David 1945- 25-28R
Gaathon, A(ryeh) L(udwig) 1898- 49-52
Gabbard, Lucina P(aquet) 1922- 110
Gabbett, Harry 1910(?)-1985 Obituary 116
Gabel, (W.) Creighton 1931- Brief entry 106
Gabel, Joseph 1912- 101
Gabel, Margaret 1938- 33-36R
Gabel, Medard 1946- CANR-11
Earlier sketch in CA 65-68
Gabin, Sanford B(yron) 1936- 114
Gable, Tom 1944- 93-96
Gablehouse, Charles 1928- 21-22R
Gablik, Suzi 1934- 33-36R
Gabo, Naum 1890-1977 .... CAP-2
Obituary 73-76
Earlier sketch in CA 33-36
Gabor, Dennis 1900-1979 .... 17-18R
Obituary 120
Gabor, Georgia M. 1930- 108
Gabor, Mark 1939- 81-84
Gaboury, Antonio 1919- CANR-2
Earlier sketch in CA 45-48
Gabre-Medhin, Tsegaye (Kawessa) 1936- 101
Gabre-Tsadick, Marta 1932- 115
Gabriel, A(strik) L. 1907- CANR-6
Earlier sketch in CA 7-8R
Gabriel, H(enry) 1922- 77-80
Gabriel, Joyce 1949- 97-100
Gabriel, Jueri (Evald) 1940- 93-96
Gabriel, Mabel McAfee 1884(?)-1976
Obituary 65-68
Gabriel, Philip L(ouis) 1918- 93-96
Gabriel, Ralph Henry 1890-1987 .... 13-14R
Obituary 122
Gabriel, Richard Alan 1942- Brief entry 104
Gabriel, Roman 1940- Brief entry 107
Gabriel-Robinet, Louis 1909-1975
Obituary 61-64
Gabrielson, Frank 1911(?)-1980 Obituary 93-96
Gabrielson, Ira N(oel) 1889-1977 .... CAP-1
Obituary 73-76
Earlier sketch in CA 9-10
Gabrielson, James B. 1917- 29-32R
Gabrys, Ingrid Schubert
See Schubert-Gabrys, Ingrid
Gach, Gary 1947- 77-80
Gach, Michael Reed 1952- 110
Gackenbach, Dick 1927- 115
See also SATA 30, 48
Gadamer, Hans-Georg 1900- 85-88
Gadd, David 1912- 57-60
Gadd, Maxine 1940- 116
Gadda, Carlo Emilio 1893-1973 89-92
See also CLC 11
Gaddes, Peter
See Sheldon, Peter
Gaddis, J. Wilson 1910(?)-1975 Obituary 57-60
Gaddis, John Lewis 1941- 45-48
Gaddis, Peggy
See Dern, Erolie Pearl Gaddis
Gaddis, Thomas E(ugene) 1908-1984 .... CANR-16
Obituary 114
Earlier sketch in CA 29-32R
Gaddis, Vincent H. 1913- 15-16R
See also SATA 35
Gaddis, William 1922- CANR-21
Earlier sketch in CA 19-20R
See also DLB 2
See also CLC 1, 3, 6, 8, 10, 19, 43
Gaddy, C(urtis) Welton 1941- 61-64
Gadler, Steve J. 1905- 97-100
See also SATA 36
Gadney, Reg 1941- CANR-18
Earlier sketches in CA 49-52, CANR-3
Gado, Frank 1936- 49-52
Gadpaille, Warren J(oseph) 1924- 61-64
Gaebelein, Frank Ely 1899- CANR-2
Earlier sketch in CA 13-14R
Gaeddert, Lou Ann (Bigge) 1931- CANR-13
Earlier sketch in CA 73-76
See also SATA 20
Gaedeke, Ralph M(ortimer) 1941- CANR-24
Earlier sketches in CA 65-68, CANR-9
Gaeng, Paul A. 1924- 37-40R
Gaer, Joseph 1897-1969 .... 9-10R
Obituary 122
Gaer, Yossef
See Gaer, Joseph
Gaess, Roger 1943- 104
Gaff, Jerry G(ene) 1936- 85-88
Gaffney, Edward McGlynn, Jr. 1941- 114
Gaffney, James 1931- CANR-6
Earlier sketch in CA 57-60
Gaffney, (Merrill) Mason 1923- CANR-3
Earlier sketch in CA 49-52
Gag, Flavia 1907-1979 .... 7-8R
Obituary 104
See also SATA 24
Gag, Wanda (Hazel) 1893-1946
Brief entry 113
See also YABC 1
See also DLB 22
See also CLR 4
Gagan, Bernard 1915-1984 Obituary 112
Gagarin, Michael 1942- 89-92
Gagarin, Yuri (Alekseevich) 1934-1968
Obituary 112
Gage, Diane 1954- 116
Gage, Edwin 1943- 85-88
Gage, Joy P. 1930- 114
Gage, Nathaniel Lees 1917- 69-72
Gage, Nicholas
See Ngagoyeanes, Nicholas
Gage, William 1915-1973 .... CAP-2
Earlier sketch in CA 25-28
Gage, William W(hitney) 1925- 15-16R
Gage, Wilson
See Steele, Mary Q(uintard Govan)
Gager, John Goodrich, Jr. 1937-
Brief entry 104
Gager, Nancy Land 1932(?)-1980
Obituary 93-96
Gagliano, Frank 1931- CANR-1
Earlier sketch in CA 45-48
Gagliardo, John G(arver) 1933- 23-24R
Gagliardo, Ruth Garver 1895(?)-1980
Obituary 104
See also SATA 22
Gagne, Cole 1954- 112
Gagne, Robert M(ills) 1916- 121
Brief entry 116
Gagnier, Ed 1936- 65-68
Gagnon, Jean-Louis 1913- 23-24R
Gagnon, John H(enry) 1931- 33-36R
Gagnon, Madeleine 1938- DLB-60
Gagnon, Paul Adelard 1925- Brief entry 104
Gahagan, Helen
See Douglas, Helen Gahagan
Gahagan, Jayne D. 1929(?)-1983
Obituary 110
Gaherty, Sherry 1951- 57-60
Gail, Marzieh CANR-11
Earlier sketch in CA 69-72
Gailey, Harry A(lfred) 1926- CANR-16
Earlier sketches in CA 45-48, CANR-1
Gailey, James H(erbert), Jr. 1916- 7-8R
Gailmor, William S. 1910(?)-1970
Obituary 104
Gaine, Hugh 1726-1807 .... DLB-43
Gainer, Bernard 1944- Brief entry 109
Gaines, Bill
See Gaines, William Maxwell
Gaines, Charles (Latham, Jr.) 1942- 119
Gaines, Diana 1912- 1R
Gaines, Ernest J(ames) 1933- CANR-24
Earlier sketches in CA 11-12R, CANR-6
See also DLB 2, 33
See also DLBY 80
See also CLC 3, 11, 18
See also AITN 1
Gaines, Jack
See Gaines, Jacob
Gaines, Jacob 1918- 101
Gaines, Pierce Welch 1905- 15-16R
Gaines, Richard L. 1925- 49-52
Gaines, William Maxwell 1922- Brief entry 108
Gainham, Sarah
See Ames, Rachel
Gains, Larry 1900-1983 Obituary 110
Gainsbrugh, Glen M. 1949- 25-28R
Gainsbrugh, Martin R(euben) 1907-1977
Obituary 69-72
Gainsburg, Joseph (Charles) 1894- 7-8R
Gainza Paz, Alberto 1899-1977 77-80
Obituary 73-76
Gaite, Francis
See Coles, Cyril Henry
Gaither, Gant 1917- 11-12R
Gaither, Norman 1937- 112
Gaitskell, Charles D(udley) 1908- 29-32R
Gaitskell, H.T.N.
See Gaitskell, Hugh (Todd Naylor)
Gaitskell, Hugh (Todd Naylor) 1906-1963
Obituary 112
Gajdusek, Robert Elemer 1925- 102
Gajdusek, Robin
See Gajdusek, Robert Elemer
Gal, Allon 1934- CANR-1
Earlier sketch in CA 45-48
Gal, Hans 1890- 5-6R
Gal, Istvan 1912-1982 Obituary 107
Gal, Laszlo 1933- SATA-32
Galai, Shmuel 1933- 107
Galambos, Louis (Paul) 1931- 81-84
Galamian, Ivan (Alexandrovitch)
1903-1981 Obituary 108
Galand, Rene 1923- CANR-24
Earlier sketch in CA 45-48
Galanoy, Terry 1927- CANR-4
Earlier sketch in CA 45-48
Galanskov, Yuri 1939(?)-1972 Obituary 37-40R
Galantay, Ervin Yvan 1930- 101
Galante, Pierre 1909- 15-16R
Galanter, Eugene 1924- 1R
Galanter, Marc 1931- 122
Galarza, Ernesto 1905-1984 Obituary 113
Galassi, Jonathan (White) 1949- 101
Galati, Stephen A(lexander) Fischer
See Fischer-Galati, Stephen A(lexander)
Galatopoulos, Stelios 1932- Brief entry 110
Galay, Ted 1941- 122
Galbraith, Clare K(earney) 1919- 33-36R
Galbraith, Georgie Starbuck 1909-1980 .... CAP-1
Obituary 97-100
Earlier sketch in CA 9-10
Galbraith, Jean 1906- 37-40R
Galbraith, John Kenneth 1908- 21-22R
Galbraith, John S. 1916- CANR-6
Earlier sketch in CA 5-6R
Galbraith, Madelyn 1897-1976 .... CAP-2
Earlier sketch in CA 33-36
Galbraith, Vivian Hunter 1889-1976 73-76
Obituary 69-72
Galbreath, Robert (Carroll) 1938- 41-44R
Galdone, Paul 1907(?)-1986 .... CANR-13
Obituary 121
Earlier sketch in CA 73-76
See also SATA 17, 49
Gale, Barry 1935- 110
Gale, Bill
See Gale, William
Gale, Elliot N(yman) 1938- Brief entry 110
Gale, Herbert M(orrison) 1907- CAP-1
Earlier sketch in CA 15-16
Gale, John
See Gaze, Richard
Gale, Linda A(nn) 1939- 112
Gale, Patrick (Evelyn Hugh Sadler) 1962- 124
Gale, Raymond F(loyd) 1918- 25-28R
Gale, Richard M. 1932- 25-28R
Gale, Richard Nelson 1896-1982 Obituary 107
Gale, Robert L(ee) 1919- CANR-18
Earlier sketches in CA 11-12R, CANR-3
Gale, Vi 33-36R
Gale, William 1925- 97-100
Gale, William C.
See Giles, Carl H(oward)
Gale, William Daniel 1906- 107
Gale, Zona 1874-1938 Brief entry 105
See also DLB 9
See also TCLC 7
Galeano, Eduardo (Hughes) 1940- CANR-13
Earlier sketch in CA 29-32R
Galella, Ron 1931- CANR-14
Earlier sketch in CA 53-56
See also AITN 1
Galenson, Walter 1914- CANR-11
Earlier sketch in CA 25-28R
Gales, Barbara J. 1940- CANR-14
Earlier sketch in CA 81-84
Galewitz, Herb 1928- CANR-14
Earlier sketch in CA 41-44R
Galfo, Armand J. 1924- 17-18R
Galiano, Juan Valera y Alcala
See Valera y Alcala-Galiano, Juan
Galich, Alexander 1918(?)-1977 Obituary 73-76
Galilea, Segundo 1928- 105
Galinsky, Ellen 1942- CANR-9
Earlier sketch in CA 65-68
See also SATA 23
Galinsky, G(otthard) Karl 1942- 33-36R
Gall, Auguste Amedee de Saint
See Strich, Christian
Gall, Elizabeth Cornelia 1898- 37-40R
Gall, Meredith D(amien) 1942- CANR-21
Earlier sketches in CA 53-56, CANR-6
Gall, Morris 1907- 45-48
Gall, Sally M(oore) 1941- 110
Gallager, Gale
See Oursler, Will(iam Charles)
Gallagher, Buell Gordon 1904- 65-68
Gallagher, Charles A(ugustus) 1927- CANR-9
Earlier sketch in CA 61-64
Gallagher, David P. 1944- 45-48
Gallagher, Dorothy 1935- 65-68
Gallagher, Edward J. 1892(?)-1978
Obituary 81-84
Gallagher, Idella J(ane Smith) 1917-
Brief entry 108
Gallagher, J(ames) Roswell 1903- 57-60
Gallagher, James J(ohn) 1926- 114
Gallagher, John F(redrick) 1936- 19-20R
Gallagher, (John) Joseph 1929- 122
Gallagher, Kent G(rey) 1933- 33-36R
Gallagher, Louis J(oseph) 1885-1972
Obituary 37-40R
Gallagher, (Joseph) Mark 1953- 123
Gallagher, Marsha V. 1943- 117
Gallagher, Mary 1947- 97-100
Gallagher, Matthew P(hilip) 1919- 5-6R
Gallagher, Maureen 1938- 118
Gallagher, Neil 1941- 114
Gallagher, Patricia CANR-11
Earlier sketch in CA 65-68

Gallagher, Patrick (Francis) 1930- 45-48
Gallagher, Rachel 89-92
Gallagher, Richard (Farrington) 1926- ... CANR-6
Earlier sketch in CA 3R
Gallagher, Richard
See Levinson, Leonard
Gallagher, Robert E(mmett) 1922- 13-14R
Gallagher, Sister Mary Dominic 1917- 19-20R
Gallagher, Tess 1943- 106
See also CLC 18
Gallagher, Thomas (Michael) CANR-5
Earlier sketch in CA 1R
Gallagher, Vera 1917- 115
Gallagher, William M. 1923-1975
Obituary 89-92
Gallaher, Art, Jr. 1925- CANR-3
Earlier sketch in CA 2R
Gallaher, John G(erard) 1928- Brief entry ... 112
Gallahue, David L(ee) 1943- CANR-13
Earlier sketch in CA 77-80
Gallahue, John (Jeremiah) 1930-
Brief entry 110
Gallant, Christine C. 1940- Brief entry 106
Gallant, Mavis 1922- 69-72
See also DLB 53
See also CLC 7, 18, 38
Gallant, Roy A(rthur) 1924- CANR-4
Earlier sketch in CA 7-8R
See also SATA 4
See also CLC 17
Gallant, T(homas) Grady 1920- 5-6R
Gallati, Mary Ernestine 7-8R
Gallati, Robert R. J. 1913- CANR-1
Earlier sketch in CA 3R
Galle, F(rederick) C(harles) 1919- 61-64
Galle, William 1938- 93-96
Gallegly, J(oseph) S(tephen) 1898- 5-6R
Gallen, John (J.) 1932- Brief entry 113
Galler, David 1929- 25-28R
Galler, Meyer 1914- 89-92
Gallerite, The
See Bason, Frederick (Thomas)
Gallery, Dan
See Gallery, Daniel V.
Gallery, Daniel V. 1901-1977 ....15-16R
Obituary 69-72
Gallico, Paul (William) 1897-1976 ..... CANR-23
Obituary 69-72
Earlier sketch in CA 7-8R
See also SATA 13
See also DLB 9
See also CLC 2
See also AITN 1
Gallie, Duncan (Ian Dunbar) 1946- 123
Gallie, Menna (Patricia Humphreys)
1920- CANR-1
Earlier sketch in CA 2R
Gallie, W(alter) B(ryce) 1912- 85-88
Gallimard, Gaston 1881-1975 Obituary 61-64
Gallimore, Ronald 1938- 65-68
Gallin, Sister Mary Alice 1921- 13-14R
Gallinger, Osma Couch
See Tod, Osma Gallinger
Gallison, Kate
See Gallison, Kathleen
Gallison, Kathleen 1939- 120
Gallistel, C(harles) R(ansom) 1941- 119
Gallix, Francois 1939- 109
Gallman, Waldemar J(ohn) 1899-1980 ... CAP-1
Obituary 101
Earlier sketch in CA 11-12
Gallner, Sheldon M(ark) 1949- 53-56
Gallo, Max 1932- 85-88
Gallo, Rose Adrienne 1938- Brief entry 107
Gallois, Claire 1938- CANR-18
Earlier sketch in CA 85-88
Gallon, Arthur J(ames) 1915- 57-60
Gallop, David 1928- 65-68
Gallop, Jane 1952- 107
Galloping Gourmet
See Kerr, Graham
Galloway, A(llan) D(ouglas) 1920- 25-28R
Galloway, David D(arryl) 1937- CANR-16
Earlier sketch in CA 21-22R
Galloway, George Barnes 1898-1967 .... 1R
Obituary 103
Galloway, John C. 1915-1970 .... CAP-2
Earlier sketch in CA 25-28
Galloway, Jonathan F(uller) 1939- 77-80
Galloway, Joseph L(ee) 1941- CANR-12
Earlier sketch in CA 73-76
Galloway, Margaret C(ecilia) 1915- 13-14R
Galloway, Patricia Kay 1945- 112
Galloway, Priscilla 1930- 112
Gallu, Samuel 85-88
See also AITN 2
Gallucci, Robert L(ovis) 1946- 61-64
Gallun, Raymond Z(inke) 1911- CANR-9
Earlier sketch in CA 65-68
Gallup, Dick 1941- 33-36R
Gallup, Donald (Clifford) 1913- CANR-11
Earlier sketch in CA 25-28R
Gallup, George (Horace) 1901-1984 ... CANR-13
Earlier sketch in CA 15-16R
Gallwey, W. Timothy 1938- CANR-4
Earlier sketch in CA 53-56
Gallwitz, Klaus 1930- Brief entry 109
Galouye, Daniel Francis 1920- 9-10R
Galper, Harvey 1937- 119
Galston, Arthur William 1920- 102
Galsworthy, John 1867-1933 Brief entry 104
See also DLB 10, 34
See also TCLC 1
Galt, Alfreda Sill 114
Galt, Serena
See Donald, Anabel
Galt, Thomas Franklin, Jr. 1908- 7-8R
See also SATA 5
Galt, Tom
See Galt, Thomas Franklin, Jr.
Galton, Francis 1822-1911 Brief entry 121
Galton, Lawrence 1913- CANR-6
Earlier sketch in CA 57-60
Galub, Jack 1915- 85-88
Galus, Henry S(tanley) 1923- 7-8R
Galvez de Montalvo, Luis
See Avalle-Arce, Juan Bautista
Galvin, Brendan 1938- CANR-24
Earlier sketches in CA 45-48, CANR-1
See also DLB 5
Galvin, James 1951- 108
See also CLC 38
Galvin, John R(ogers) 1929- CANR-13
Earlier sketch in CA 23-24R
Galvin, Patrick Joseph 1927- CANR-18
Earlier sketch in CA 102
Galvin, Thomas J(ohn) 1932- CANR-10
Earlier sketch in CA 15-16R
Galway, James 1939- Brief entry 105
Gam, Rita (Elenore) 1927- 45-48
Gambaccini, Peter 1950- 105
Gambill, Edward Lee 1936- 112
Gambino, Thomas D(ominic) 1942- 101
Gamble, Andrew (Michael) 1947- CANR-12
Earlier sketch in CA 69-72
Gamble, Frederick (John) 1904- CAP-1
Earlier sketch in CA 9-10
Gamble, Mary
See Murry, Mary Middleton
Gamble, Michael (Wesley) 1943- 110
Gamble, Sidney David 1890-1968 .... CAP-1
Earlier sketch in CA 11-12
Gamble, Teri (Susan) Kwal 1947- 110
Gambrell, Herbert (Pickens) 1898- 1R
Gambrill, Eileen 1934- CANR-15
Earlier sketch in CA 89-92
Gambs, John S(ake) 1899- 15-16R
Gamer, Robert E(manuel) 1938- 65-68
Gamerman, Martha 1941- 77-80
See also SATA 15
Gamm, David B(ernard) 1948- 69-72
Gammage, Allen Z. 1917- CANR-11
Earlier sketch in CA 5-6R
Gammage, Bill
See Gammage, William Leonard
Gammage, William Leonard 1942- CANR-10
Earlier sketch in CA 57-60
Gammell, Susanna Valentine Mitchell
1897(?)-1979 Obituary 85-88
Gammie, John G(lenn) 1929- 121
Gammon, Roland I. 1920-1981 49-52
Obituary 103
Gammon, Samuel Rhea (III) 1924-
Brief entry 112
Gammond, Peter 1925- CANR-14
Earlier sketch in CA 81-84
Gamoran, Mamie (Goldsmith) 1900- CANR-3
Earlier sketch in CA 5-6R
Gamow, George 1904-1968 102
Obituary 93-96
Gamson, William A. 1934- CANR-13
Earlier sketch in CA 33-36R
Gamst, Frederick C(harles) 1936- CANR-11
Earlier sketch in CA 29-32R
Gance, Abel 1889-1981 Obituary 108
Ganci, Dave 1937- 115
Gandalac, Lennard
See Berne, Eric (Lennard)
Gandee, Lee R(auss) 1917- 33-36R
Gandevia, Bryan Harle 1925- CANR-22
Earlier sketch in CA 106
Gandhi, Indira (Priyadarshini Nehru)
1917-1984 Obituary 113
Gandhi, M. K.
See Gandhi, Mohandas Karamchand
Gandhi, Mahatma
See Gandhi, Mohandas Karamchand
Gandhi, Mohandas Karamchand
1869-1948 Brief entry 121
Gandley, Kenneth Royce 1920- CANR-12
Earlier sketch in CA 69-72
Gandolfo, Joe M. 1936- 105
Gandossy, Robert P. 1951- 120
Gangel, Kenneth O(tto) 1935- CANR-17
Earlier sketch in CA 25-28R
Gangemi, Kenneth 1937- 29-32R
Gangewere, Robert J(ay) 1936- 89-92
Ganley, Albert Charles 1918- 13-14R
Ganley, Gladys Dickens 1929- 113
Ganley, Oswald Harold 1929- 112
Gann, Ernest Kellogg 1910- CANR-1
Earlier sketch in CA 4R
See also CLC 23
See also AITN 1
Gann, L(ewis) H(enry) 1924- CANR-3
Earlier sketch in CA 7-8R
Gannett, Frank E(rnest) 1876-1957
Brief entry 117
See also DLB 29
Gannett, Lewis Stiles 1891-1966
Obituary 89-92
Gannett, Ruth Chrisman (Arens)
1896-1979 .... SATA-33
Gannett, Ruth Stiles 1923- 21-22R
See also SATA 3
Gannon, Robert Haines 1931- CANR-4
Earlier sketch in CA 11-12R
See also SATA 8
Gannon, Robert I(gnatius) 1893-1978 .... CAP-1
Obituary 77-80
Earlier sketch in CA 15-16
Gannon, Thomas M(ichael) 1936- 109
Gans, Bruce Michael 1951- 81-84
Gans, Eric L. 1941- 33-36R
Gans, Herbert J. 1927- CANR-6
Earlier sketch in CA 1R
Gans, Roma 1894- 77-80
See also SATA 45
Gansberg, Judith M. 1947- 85-88
Ganshof, Francois-Louis 1895- CAP-2
Earlier sketch in CA 19-20
Gans-Ruedin, E(rwin) 1915- 65-68
Ganss, George Edward 1905- 49-52
Gant, Chuck
See Galub, Jack
Gant, Jonathan
See Adams, Clifton
Gant, Matthew
See Hano, Arnold
Gant, Phyllis 1922- 57-60
Gant, Richard
See Freemantle, Brian Harry
Gantner, Neilma 1922- 104
Gantos, Jack
See Gantos, John (Bryan), Jr.
Gantos, John (Bryan), Jr. 1951- CANR-15
Earlier sketch in CA 65-68
See also SATA 20
Gantry, Susan Nadler 1947- 61-64
Gantt, Fred, Jr. 1922-197(?) CANR-3
Earlier sketch in CA 11-12R
Gantt, William Andrew Horsley 1893-1980 .. 102
Obituary 97-100
Gantz, Charlotte Orr 1909- 49-52
Gantzer, Hugh 1931- 61-64
Ganz, Arthur (Frederick) 1928- 49-52
Ganz, David L(awrence) 1951- 105
Ganz, Margaret 1927- 45-48
Ganz, Yaffa 1938- 115
Ganzalass, Martin Richard 1941- 33-36R
Ganzel, Dewey Alvin, Jr. 1927- 25-28R
Gapanov, Boris 1934(?)-1972 Obituary ...37-40R
Gar, The
See Garfinkel, Charles H.
Gara, Larry 1922- 53-56
Garab, Arra M. 1930- 81-84
Garard, Ira D(ufresne) 1888- 73-76
Garavaglia, Louis A(ubrey) 1940- 119
Garb, Solomon 1920- CANR-9
Earlier sketch in CA 15-16R
Garbarino, Joseph W. 1919- 53-56
Garbarino, Merwyn S(tephens) 77-80
Garber, Emil 1901(?)-1985 Obituary 115
Garber, Eugene K. 1932- CANR-6
Earlier sketch in CA 57-60
Garber, Frederick 1929- 53-56
Garber, Lawrence (Arnold) 1937- 122
Garber, Lee O(rville) 1900- 37-40R
Garbett, Colin (Campbell) 1881- CAP-1
Earlier sketch in CA 9-10
Garbini, Giovanni 1931- CANR-9
Earlier sketch in CA 21-22R
Garbo, Norman 1919- CANR-9
Earlier sketch in CA 17-18R
Garbutt, Bernard 1900- Brief entry 110
See also SATA 31
Garbutt, Janice (D.) Lovoos 124
Garceau, Oliver 1911- CAP-2
Earlier sketch in CA 29-32
Garchik, Morton (Lloyd) 1929- 119
Garcia, Ann O'Neal 1939- 108
Garcia, C(elso-) R(amon) 1921- 118
Garcia, F(laviano) Chris 1940- CANR-4
Earlier sketch in CA 53-56
Garcia, George Haddad
See Haddad-Garcia, George
Garcia, Mario R(amon) 1947- 77-80
Garcia Castaneda, Salvador 1932- 61-64
Garcia Lorca, Federico 1898-1936
Brief entry 104
See also TCLC 1, 7
Garcia Marquez, Gabriel (Jose) 1928- .. CANR-10
Earlier sketch in CA 33-36R
See also CLC 2, 3, 8, 10, 15, 27, 47
Gard, Janice
See Latham, Jean Lee
Gard, Joyce
See Reeves, Joyce
Gard, Richard A(bbott) 1914- CANR-1
Earlier sketch in CA 1R
Gard, Robert Edward 1910- 85-88
See also SATA 18
Gard, Roger Martin du
See Martin du Gard, Roger
Gard, (Sanford) Wayne 1899-1986 .... 2R
Obituary 120
See also SATA 49
Gardam, Jane 1928- CANR-18
Earlier sketches in CA 49-52, CANR-2
See also SATA 28, 39
See also DLB 14
See also CLC 43
See also CLR 12
Garden, Alexander 1685(?)-1756 .... DLB-31
Garden, Bruce
See Mackay, James (Alexander)
Garden, Edward J(ames) C(larke) 1930- ..25-28R
Garden, Graeme 1943- 107
Garden, John
See Fletcher, H(arry) L(utf) V(erne)
Garden, Nancy 1938- CANR-13
Earlier sketch in CA 33-36R
See also SATA 12
Garden, Robert Hal 1937- 69-72
Gardiner, C(linton) Harvey 1913- CANR-16
Earlier sketches in CA 1R, CANR-1
Gardiner, Charles Wrey 1901-1981
Obituary 103
Gardiner, Dorothy 1894-1979 Obituary 93-96
Gardiner, Glenn Lion 1896-1962 .... 3R
Gardiner, Judy 1922- CANR-9
Earlier sketch in CA 21-22R
Gardiner, Mary Summerfield 1896-1982
Obituary 106
Gardiner, Muriel
See Buttinger, Muriel Gardiner
Gardiner, Patrick (Lancaster) 1922- CANR-5
Earlier sketch in CA 1R
Gardiner, Robert K. A. 1914- 21-22R
Gardiner, Robert W(orthington) 1932- 53-56
Gardiner, Stephen 1925- 97-100
Gardinier, David E(lmer) 1932- 112
Gardiol, Rita M(azzetti) 81-84
Gardner, Alan (Harold) 1925- 21-22R
Gardner, Angela Davis
See Davis-Gardner, Angela
Gardner, Anne
See Shultz, Gladys Denny
Gardner, Beau SATA-50
Gardner, (Robert) Brian 1931- 13-14R
Gardner, Carl 1931- 107
Gardner, D(avid) Bruce 1924- 49-52
Gardner, David P(ierpont) 1933- 21-22R
Gardner, Dic
See Gardner, Richard (M.)
Gardner, Dorothy E. M. 1900-1972 ...... CAP-2
Earlier sketch in CA 23-24
Gardner, E(dward) Clinton 1920- 15-16R
Gardner, Eldon J(ohn) 1909- 41-44R
Gardner, Erle Stanley 1889-1970 ...... CANR-13
Obituary 25-28R
Earlier sketch in CA 7-8R
Gardner, Frank Matthias 1908-1980
Obituary 109
Gardner, G(erald) B(rosseau) 1884-1964
Obituary 112
Gardner, Gerald 1929- CANR-5
Earlier sketch in CA 2R
Gardner, Helen (Louise) 1908- 97-100
Gardner, Herb CLC-44
Gardner, Howard 1943- CANR-9
Earlier sketch in CA 65-68
Gardner, Hugh 1910-1986 Obituary 120
See also SATA 49
Gardner, Hy 1908- 101
Gardner, Isabella (Stewart) 1915-1981 ...97-100
Obituary 104
Gardner, Jack Irving 1934- 102
Gardner, Jani 1943- 25-28R
Gardner, Jeanne LeMonnier 1925- 19-20R
See also SATA 5
Gardner, Jeffrey
See Fox, G(ardner) F(rancis)
Gardner, John Champlin, Jr. 1933-1982 ...65-68
Obituary 107
See also SATA 31, 40
See also DLB 2
See also DLBY 82
See also CLC 2, 3, 5, 7, 8, 10, 18, 28, 34
See also AITN 1
Gardner, John E(dward) 1917- 17-18R
Gardner, John Edmund 1926- CANR-15
Earlier sketch in CA 103
See also CLC 30
Gardner, John W(illiam) 1912- CANR-4
Earlier sketch in CA 1R
Gardner, Joseph L. 1933- 29-32R
Gardner, Lawrence
See Brannon, William T.
Gardner, Leonard 1934- Brief entry 111
Gardner, Lewis 1943- 65-68
Gardner, Lloyd C(alvin) 1934- CANR-3
Earlier sketch in CA 11-12R
Gardner, (Alice) Lucille 1913- 69-72
Gardner, Marilyn 101
Gardner, Martin 1914- 73-76
See also SATA 16
Gardner, Mary 1936- 124
Gardner, Mary A(delaide) 1920- 21-22R
Gardner, Nancy Bruff 1915- 15-16R
Gardner, Noel
See Kuttner, Henry
Gardner, Paul 69-72
Gardner, R(ufus) H(allette III) 1918- 33-36R
Gardner, Ralph D(avid) 1923- CANR-6
Earlier sketch in CA 15-16R
Gardner, Richard (M.) 1931- CANR-10
Earlier sketch in CA 21-22R
See also SATA 24
Gardner, Richard A. 1931- 33-36R
See also SATA 13
Gardner, Richard Kent 1928- 69-72
Gardner, Richard N(ewton) 1927- 89-92
Gardner, Riley W(etherell) 1921- 13-14R
Gardner, Robert 1911- 61-64
Gardner, Robert 1929- SATA-43
Gardner, Sheldon 1934- 104
See also SATA 33
Gardner, Virginia (Marberry) 1904- 112
Gardner, Wanda Kirby 1914- 73-76
Gardner, Wayland Downing 1928- 73-76
Gardner, William Earl 1928- CANR-18
Earlier sketches in CA 7-8R, CANR-3
Gardner, William Henry 1902-1969 ...... CAP-1
Earlier sketch in CA 15-16
Gardner, Wynelle B. 1918- 65-68
Gardner-Smith, Percival 1888-1985 ...... CAP-2
Obituary 116
Earlier sketch in CA 17-18
Gardons, S. S.
See Snodgrass, W(illiam) D(e Witt)
Garduk, Harry David 1910(?)-1985
Obituary 116
Gare, Fran
See Mandell, Fran Gare
Gareau, Etienne 1915- 45-48

Gareau, Frederick H(enry) 1923- ... 5-6R
Gareffa, Peter M(ichael) 1952- ... 118
Garelick, May 1910- ... 73-76
See also SATA 19
Garetz, Mark 1953- ... 112
Garfield, Brian (Wynne) 1939- ... CANR-6
Earlier sketch in CA 2R
Garfield, Eugene 1925- ... 114
Garfield, Evelyn Picon 1940- ... CANR-9
Earlier sketch in CA 57-60
Garfield, James B. 1881-1984 Obituary ... 112
See also SATA 6, 38
Garfield, Leon 1921- ... 17-18R
See also SATA 1, 32
See also CLC 12
Garfield, Patricia L(ee) 1934- ... 85-88
Garfield, Sol L(ouis) 1918- ... CANR-12
Earlier sketch in CA 29-32R
Garfield, Sydney 1916(?)-1988 Obituary ... 124
Garfinkel, Alan 1941- ... CANR-21
Earlier sketch in CA 105
Garfinkel, Bernard Max 1929- ... CANR-17
Earlier sketch in CA 25-28R
Garfinkel, Charles H. 1939- ... 112
Garfinkel, Charlie
See Garfinkel, Charles H.
Garfinkel, Herbert 1920- ... 1R
Garfinkel, Perry 1948- ... 121
Garfinkle, Adam M. 1951- ... 112
Garfinkle, Louis (Alan) 1928- Brief entry ... 112
Garfitt, Roger 1944- ... CANR-13
Earlier sketch in CA 33-36R
Garforth, Francis William 1917- ... 9-10R
Garfunkel, Louis X. 1897(?)-1972
Obituary ... 37-40R
Gargan, Edward T(homas) 1922-
Brief entry ... 111
Gargan, William (Michael) 1950- ... 111
Gargan, William Dennis 1905-1979
Obituary ... 106
Garibaldi, Gerald 1951- ... 108
Gariepy, Henry 1930- ... CANR-2
Earlier sketch in CA 49-52
Garioch, Robert Sutherland 1909-1981 ... 103
Garis, Howard Roger 1873-1962 ... 73-76
See also SATA 13
See also DLB 22
Garis, Robert (Erwin) 1925- ... 19-20R
Garitano, Rita 1939- ... 118
Garlan, Patricia Wallace 1926- ... 120
Garland, Bennett
See Garfield, Brian (Wynne)
Garland, Charles T(albot) 1910(?)-1976
Obituary ... 69-72
Garland, George
See Roark, Garland
Garland, (Hannibal) Hamlin 1860-1940
Brief entry ... 104
See also DLB 12
See also TCLC 3
Garland, Madge 1900- ... 25-28R
Garland, Mary 1922- ... 89-92
Garland, Phyl(lis T.) 1935- ... 69-72
Garland, Robert (Sandford John) 1947- ... 120
Garlick, Peter C(yril) 1923- ... 41-44R
Garlick, Raymond 1926- ... CANR-4
Earlier sketch in CA 53-56
Garlington, Phil 1943- ... 81-84
Garlington, Warren K(ing) 1923- ... 11-12R
Garlinski, Jozef 1914- ... 108
Garment, Grace R. 1927(?)-1976
Obituary ... 104
Garmey, Jane 1942- ... 114
Garmon, William S. 1926- ... 21-22R
Garms, Walter I(rving, Jr.) 1925- ... 120
Garn, Edwin Jacob 1932- ... 107
Garn, Jake
See Garn, Edwin Jacob
Garneau, Michel 1939- ... DLB-53
Garneau, (Hector de) Saint-Denys
1912-1943 Brief entry ... 111
See also TCLC 13
Garner, Alan 1934- ... CANR-15
Earlier sketch in CA 73-76
See also SATA 18
See also CLC 17
Garner, Claud Wilton 1891- ... 11-12R
Garner, Dwight L. 1913- ... 25-28R
Garner, Graham
See Rowland, D(onald) S(ydney)
Garner, H(essle) F(ilmore) 1926- ... 73-76
Garner, Harry Hyman 1910- ... 17-18R
Garner, Helen 1942- Brief entry ... 124
Garner, Hugh 1913-1979 ... 69-72
See also CLC 13
Garner, Joseph John Saville 1908-1983
Obituary ... 111
Garner, (Samuel) Paul 1910- ... 37-40R
Garner, Roberta 1943- ... 85-88
Garner, Rolf
See Berry, Bryan
Garner, (Lafayette) Ross 1914- ... 33-36R
Garner, Wendell R(ichard) 1921- ... CANR-11
Earlier sketch in CA 5-6R
Garner, William 1920- ... CANR-12
Earlier sketch in CA 29-32R
Garner, William R(obin) 1936- ... 21-22R
Garnet, Eldon 1946- ... CANR-9
Earlier sketch in CA 61-64
Garnett, A(rthur) Campbell 1894-1970 ... CANR-2
Earlier sketch in CA 1R
Garnett, Bill
See Garnett, William John
Garnett, Christopher Browne 1906-1975
Obituary ... 61-64
Garnett, David 1892-1981 ... CANR-17
Obituary ... 103
Earlier sketch in CA 5-6R
See also DLB 34
See also CLC 3
Garnett, Eve C. R. ... CANR-2
Earlier sketch in CA 4R
See also SATA 3
Garnett, Richard (Duncan Carey) 1923- ... 7-8R
Garnett, Roger
See Morland, Nigel
Garnett, Tay 1894(?)-1977 Obituary ... 73-76
Garnett, William John 1941- ... 102
Garnham, Nicholas 1937- ... 33-36R
Garofalo, Reebee
See Garofalo, Robert L.
Garofalo, Robert L. 1944- ... 77-80
Garoogian, Andrew 1928- Brief entry ... 113
Garoogian, Rhoda 1933- ... CANR-19
Earlier sketch in CA 102
Garos, Stephanie
See Katz, Steve
Garoyan, Leon 1925- ... CANR-5
Earlier sketch in CA 4R
Garrad, Larch S(ylvia) 1936- ... 61-64
Garrard, Gene
See Garrard, Jeanne Sue
Garrard, J(ohn) G(ordon) 1934-
Brief entry ... 114
Garrard, Jeanne Sue ... 81-84
Garrard, L(ancelot) A(ustin) 1904- ... CAP-1
Earlier sketch in CA 9-10
Garraty, John A. 1920- ... CANR-2
Earlier sketch in CA 1R
See also SATA 23
See also DLB 17
Garreau, Joel 1948- ... 101
Garret, Maxwell R. 1917- ... 106
See also SATA 39
Garretson, Lucy Reed 1936- ... 97-100
Garretson, Robert L. 1920- ... 19-20R
Garretson, Victoria Diane 1945- ... 108
See also SATA 44
Garrett, Albert Charles 1915-1983
Obituary ... 109
Garrett, Alfred B. 1906- ... 5-6R
Garrett, Charles 1925-1977 Obituary ... 73-76
Garrett, Clarke 1935- ... 73-76
Garrett, Eileen J(eanette) 1893-1970 ... CAP-2
Earlier sketch in CA 25-28
Garrett, Franklin M(iller) 1906- ... 57-60
Garrett, Garet 1878-1954 Brief entry ... 122
Garrett, George (Palmer) 1929- ... CANR-1
Earlier sketch in CA 2R
See also CAAS 5
See also DLB 2, 5
See also DLBY 83
See also CLC 3, 11
Garrett, Gerald R. 1940- ... CANR-12
Earlier sketch in CA 73-76
Garrett, Gerard 1928- ... 73-76
Garrett, Helen 1895- ... SATA-21
Garrett, Howard 1931- ... 61-64
Garrett, James Leo, Jr. 1925- ... CANR-13
Earlier sketch in CA 33-36R
Garrett, (Ruth) Jane 1914- ... 105
Garrett, Jennifer 1960- ... 122
Garrett, John (Allen) 1920- ... CANR-16
Earlier sketch in CA 33-36R
Garrett, Leonard J(oseph) 1926- ... 17-18R
Garrett, Leslie 1931- ... 19-20R
Garrett, Lillian ... 29-32R
Garrett, Peter K. 1940- ... 25-28R
Garrett, Richard 1920- ... CANR-16
Earlier sketch in CA 81-84
Garrett, Romeo Benjamin 1910- ... 37-40R
Garrett, Stephen A(rmour) 1939- ... 111
Garrett, Thomas M(ichael) 1924- ... CANR-5
Earlier sketch in CA 4R
Garrett, Thomas S(amuel) 1913-1980 ... CANR-3
Earlier sketch in CA 3R
Garrett, Tom
See Garrett, Thomas S(amuel)
Garrett, Truman
See Judd, Margaret Haddican
Garrett, Wendell D(ouglas) 1929- ... 9-10R
Garrett, William 1890-1967 ... CAP-1
Earlier sketch in CA 11-12
Garrigan, Owen (Walter) 1928- ... 23-24R
Garrigue, Jean 1914-1972 ... CANR-20
Obituary ... 37-40R
Earlier sketch in CA 7-8R
See also CLC 2, 8
Garrigue, Sheila 1931- ... 69-72
See also SATA 21
Garrison, Barbara 1931- ... SATA-19
Garrison, Christian (Bascom) 1942- ... 65-68
Garrison, Frederick
See Sinclair, Upton (Beall)
Garrison, James (Dale) 1943- ... 61-64
Garrison, Jim (C.) 1921- Brief entry ... 111
Garrison, Joan
See Neubauer, William Arthur
Garrison, Karl C(laudius) 1900- ... 37-40R
Garrison, Omar V. 1913- ... 33-36R
Garrison, Paul 1918- ... 122
Garrison, Phil
See Brandner, Gary
Garrison, R. Benjamin 1926- ... CANR-5
Earlier sketch in CA 13-14R
Garrison, Webb B(lack) 1919- ... CANR-18
Earlier sketches in CA 1R, CANR-2
See also SATA 25
Garrison, William Lloyd 1805-1879 ... DLB-1, 43
See also CDALB 1640-1865
Garrison, Winfred Ernest 1874-1969 ... CANR-6
Earlier sketch in CA 1R
Garrity
See Gerrity, David James
Garrity, Dave
See Gerrity, David James
Garrity, Devin Adair 1905-1981 ... 107
Obituary ... 103
Garrity, Joan Terry 1940- ... 69-72
See also AITN 1
Garrity, Richard (George) 1903- ... 77-80
Garrity, Terry
See Garrity, Joan Terry
Garrod, Rene J(eannette) 1954- ... 120
Garrow, David J(effries) 1953- ... 93-96
Garroway, Dave
See Garroway, David Cunningham
Garroway, David Cunningham 1913-1982
Obituary ... 107
Garry, Charles R. 1909- ... 73-76
Garside, Charles, Jr. 1927-1987 Obituary ... 122
Garside, Roger R(amsay) 1938- ... 107
Garskof, Michele Hoffnung
See Hoffnung, Michele
Garson, Barbara ... 33-36R
Garson, Clee
See Fairman, Paul W.
Garson, G(eorge) David 1943- ... CANR-4
Earlier sketch in CA 53-56
Garson, Helen Sylvia 1925- ... 107
Garson, Noel George 1931- ... 29-32R
Garson, Paul 1946- ... 49-52
Garst, Doris Shannon 1894- ... 4R
See also SATA 1
Garst, John Fredric 1932- ... 45-48
Garst, Robert E(dward) 1900-1980 ... 108
Obituary ... 97-100
Garst, Shannon
See Garst, Doris Shannon
Garstang, Jack
See Garstang, James Gordon
Garstang, James Gordon 1927- ... 13-14R
Garstein, Oskar Bernhard 1924- ... 13-14R
Gart, Murray Joseph 1924- ... 103
Garten, Hugh F(rederick) 1904-1975 ... CANR-3
Earlier sketch in CA 7-8R
Gartenberg, Egon 1911- ... 57-60
Gartenberg, Leo 1906- ... 11-12R
Garth, Will
See Hamilton, Edmond
and Kuttner, Henry
Garthoff, Raymond L(eonard) 1929- ... 7-8R
Garthwaite, Malaby
See Dent, Anthony Austen
Garthwaite, Marion H(ook) 1893- ... 5-6R
See also SATA 7
Gartland, Robert Aldrich 1927- ... 19-20R
Gartman, Louise 1920- ... 17-18R
Gartner, Alan 1935- ... CANR-15
Earlier sketch in CA 33-36R
Gartner, Carol B(licker) 1935- ... 114
Gartner, Chloe (Maria) 1916- ... CANR-20
Earlier sketches in CA 2R, CANR-5
Gartner, Lloyd P. 1927- ... CANR-2
Earlier sketch in CA 1R
Gartner, Michael G(ay) 1938- ... 77-80
Garton, Charles 1926- ... CANR-21
Earlier sketch in CA 45-48
Garton, Janet 1944- ... 114
Garton, Jean Staker 1929- ... 114
Garton, Malinda D(ean) (?)-1976 ... 1R
Obituary ... 103
See also SATA 26
Garton, Nancy Wells 1908- ... 7-8R
Garton, Nina R. 1905- ... CAP-2
Earlier sketch in CA 21-22
Garve, Andrew
See Winterton, Paul
Garver, Richard B(ennett) 1934- ... 33-36R
Garvey, Amy Jacques 1896(?)-1973
Obituary ... 45-48
Garvey, Edward B. 1914- ... 41-44R
Garvey, Gerald (Thomas) 1935-
Brief entry ... 112
Garvey, John 1944- ... CANR-14
Earlier sketch in CA 65-68
Garvey, Marcus (Moziah, Jr.) 1887-1940 ... 124
Brief entry ... 120
Garvey, Mona 1934- ... 29-32R
Garvey, Robert 1908-1983 ... 107
Obituary ... 109
Garvey, Terence Willcocks 1915- ... 103
Garvie, A(lexander) F(emister) 1934- ... 73-76
Garvin, Charles D. 1929- ... CANR-6
Earlier sketch in CA 57-60
Garvin, (Hilda) Katharine 1904- ... 7-8R
Garvin, Lawrence 1945- ... 53-56
Garvin, Paul L(ucian) 1919- ... CANR-5
Earlier sketch in CA 15-16R
Garvin, Philip 1947- ... 73-76
Garvin, Richard M. 1934- ... 49-52
Garvin, Thomas Christopher 1943- ... 113
Garvin, Tom
See Garvin, Thomas Christopher
Garvin, William 1922- ... 25-28R
Garwood, Darrell (Nelson) 1909- ... 29-32R
Gary, Romain
See Kacew, Romain
See also CLC 25
Garza, Roberto J(esus) 1934- ... 104
Garzilli, Enrico 1937- ... 41-44R
Gascar, Pierre
See Fournier, Pierre
See also CLC 11
Gascoigne, Bamber 1935- ... CANR-10
Earlier sketch in CA 25-28R
Gascoigne, Marguerite
See Lazarus, Marguerite
Gascon, The
See Miller, F(rederick) W(alter)
G(ascoyne)
Gascoyne, David (Emery) 1916- ... CANR-10
Earlier sketch in CA 65-68
See also DLB 20
See also CLC 45
Gash, Jonathan
See Grant, John
Gash, Norman 1912- ... CANR-1
Earlier sketch in CA 3R
Gaskell, Elizabeth Cleghorn 1810-1865 ... DLB-21
Gaskell, Jane 1941- ... CANR-11
Earlier sketch in CA 7-8R
Gaskell, (John) Philip (Wellesley) 1926- ... CANR-3
Earlier sketch in CA 7-8R
Gaskell, Thomas F. 1916- ... 17-18R
Gaskill, Harold V. 1905-1975 Obituary ... 57-60
Gaskin, Catherine 1929- ... CANR-10
Earlier sketch in CA 65-68
Gaskin, David Edward 1939- ... 69-72
Gasnick, Roy M(ichael) 1933- ... 117
Gasparini, Graziano 1926- ... 41-44R
Gasparotti, Elizabeth Seifert 1897-1983 ... CANR-2
Obituary ... 110
Earlier sketch in CA 3R
Gasper, Louis 1911- ... 13-14R
Gasperini, Jim 1952- ... 122
See also SATA 49
Gasque, W(oodrow) Ward 1939- ... CANR-15
Earlier sketch in CA 65-68
Gass, William H(oward) 1924- ... 19-20R
See also DLB 2
See also CLC 1, 2, 8, 11, 15, 39
Gassan, Arnold 1930- ... 73-76
Gassert, Robert G(eorge) 1921- ... 17-18R
Gasset, Jose Ortega y
See Ortega y Gasset, Jose
Gassier, Pierre 1915- ... 49-52
Gassner, John Waldhorn 1903-1967 ... CANR-3
Obituary ... 25-28R
Earlier sketch in CA 2R
Gassner, Julius S(tephen) 1915- ... 37-40R
Gast, Kelly P.
See Edmondson, G. C.
Gaster, T(heodor) Herzl 1906- ... 73-76
Gastil, Raymond D(uncan) 1931- ... 29-32R
Gastmann, Albert (Lodewijk) 1921- ... 97-100
Gaston, Edwin W(illmer), Jr. 1925- ... CANR-2
Earlier sketch in CA 1R
Gaston, Georg M(eri-) A(kri) 1938- ... 109
Gaston, Jerry (Collins) 1940- ... CANR-1
Earlier sketch in CA 45-48
Gaston, Wilber
See Gibson, Walter B(rown)
Gat, Dimitri V(sevolod) 1936- ... 29-32R
Gatch, Milton McC(ormick, Jr.) 1932- ... 29-32R
Gatell, Frank Otto 1931- ... 9-10R
Gatenby, Greg 1950- ... 97-100
Gatenby, Rosemary 1918- ... CANR-9
Earlier sketch in CA 21-22R
Gater, Dilys 1944- ... 112
See also SATA 41
Gater, Hubert 1913(?)-1980 Obituary ... 101
Gates, Arthur Irving 1890-1972
Obituary ... 37-40R
Gates, David Murray 1921- ... 81-84
Gates, Doris 1901-1987 ... CANR-1
Obituary ... 124
Earlier sketch in CA 4R
See also SATA 1, 34
See also SAAS 1
See also DLB 22
Gates, Frieda 1933- ... 93-96
See also SATA 26
Gates, Henry Louis, Jr. 1950- ... 109
See also DLB 67
Gates, J(eannette) M(cPherson) 1924- ... CANR-7
Earlier sketch in CA 57-60
Gates, Jean Key 1911- ... 33-36R
Gates, John A(lexander) 1898- ... 5-6R
Gates, John D. 1939- ... 89-92
Gates, John Floyd 1915- ... 1R
Gates, Lillian Francis 1901- ... CAP-2
Earlier sketch in CA 25-28
Gates, Natalie ... 23-24R
Gates, Norman T(immins) 1914- ... 77-80
Gates, Paul W(allace) 1901- ... CANR-2
Earlier sketch in CA 1R
Gates, Robbins L(adew) 1922- ... 15-16R
Gates, William Byram 1917-1975
Obituary ... 61-64
Gatewood, Willard B., Jr. 1931- ... 17-18R
Gathercole, Adrienne Lois
See Kaeppler, Adrienne Lois
Gatheridge, R. Edward
See Wilson, Robert (Edward)
Gathorne-Hardy, Jonathan G. 1933- ... 104
See also SATA 26
Gatley, Jimmy 1931(?)-1985 Obituary ... 115
Gatley, Richard Harry 1936- ... 101
Gatlin, Douglas S. 1928- ... 21-22R
Gatlin, Lila L(ee) 1928- ... 101
Gatner, Elliott S(herman) M(ozian)
1914- ... CANR-3
Earlier sketch in CA 11-12R
Gato, J. A.
See Keller, John E(sten)
Gattey, Charles Neilson 1921- ... CANR-20
Earlier sketches in CA 13-14R, CANR-5
Gatti, Arthur Gerard 1942- ... 65-68
Gatti, Daniel Jon 1946- ... 45-48
Gatti, Enzo
See Gatti, Vincenzo
Gatti, Richard DeY 1947- ... 45-48
Gatti, Vincenzo 1942- ... CANR-8
Earlier sketch in CA 61-64

Gattmann, Eric 1925- ... 49-52
Gatty, Juliana Horatia
See Ewing, Juliana (Horatia Gatty)
Gatty, Margaret Scott 1809-1873 ... SATA-27
Gatty, Ronald 1929- ... 85-88
Gatzke, Hans W(ilhelm) 1915-1987 ... CANR-5
Obituary ... 123
Earlier sketch in CA 1R
Gauch, Patricia Lee 1934- ... CANR-9
Earlier sketch in CA 57-60
See also SATA 26
Gauchat, Dorothy 1921- ... 97-100
Gaudet, Frederick J(oseph) 1902-1977 ... 7-8R
Obituary ... 73-76
Gaudiose, Dorothy M(arie) 1920- ... 89-92
Gauer, Harold 1914- ... 15-16R
Gaugh, Harry F. ... 116
Gauld, Charles A(nderson) 1911- ... 15-16R
Gaulden, Ray 1914- ... CANR-8
Earlier sketch in CA 17-18R
Gauldie, Enid 1928- ... CANR-14
Earlier sketch in CA 77-80
Gauldie, (William) Sinclair 1918- ... 33-36R
Gaulle, Charles (Andre Joseph Marie) de
See de Gaulle, Charles (Andre Joseph Marie)
Gault, Clare 1925- ... 97-100
See also SATA 36
Gault, Frank 1926-1982 ... CANR-11
Earlier sketch in CA 69-72
See also SATA 30, 36
Gault, Mark
See Cournos, John
Gault, William Campbell 1910- ... CANR-16
Earlier sketches in CA 49-52, CANR-1
See also SATA 8
Gaumnitz, Jack E(rwin) 1935- ... 120
Gaumnitz, Walter Herbert 1891-1979
Obituary ... 89-92
Gaunt, Leonard 1921- ... CANR-3
Earlier sketch in CA 7-8R
Gaunt, Michael
See Robertshaw, (James) Denis
Gaunt, Peter
See Eshbach, Lloyd Arthur
Gaunt, William 1900-1980 ... CANR-6
Obituary ... 97-100
Earlier sketch in CA 9-10R
Gauquelin, Michel (Roland) 1928- ... 57-60
Gaur, Albertine 1932- ... 121
Gaus, Gerald F. 1952- ... 112
Gaustad, Edwin Scott 1923- ... CANR-1
Earlier sketch in CA 4R
Gaver, Becky
See Gaver, Rebecca
Gaver, Jack 1906-1974 ... 97-100
Obituary ... 53-56
Gaver, Jessyca (Russell) 1915- ... CANR-9
Earlier sketch in CA 53-56
Gaver, Mary Virginia 1906- ... 1R
Gaver, Rebecca 1952- ... SATA-20
Gavett, J(oseph) William 1921- ... 25-28R
Gavett, Thomas W(illiam) 1932- ... 15-16R
Gavin
See Frost, Gavin
Gavin, Amanda
See Gibson-Jarvie, Clodagh
Gavin, Bill
See Gavin, William S.
Gavin, Catherine ... CANR-1
Earlier sketch in CA 4R
Gavin, Eileen A. 1931- ... 45-48
Gavin, James M(aurice) 1907- ... CAP-1
Earlier sketch in CA 15-16
Gavin, Jamila 1941- ... 110
Gavin, Thomas 1941- ... 85-88
Gavin, Thomas F. 1910- ... 108
Gavin, William
See Houston, Douglas (Norman)
Gavin, William S. 1907(?)-1985 Obituary ... 114
Gavin-Brown, Wilfred A(rthur) 1904- ... CAP-1
Earlier sketch in CA 9-10
Gavron, Daniel 1935- ... CANR-12
Earlier sketch in CA 29-32R
Gavronsky, Serge 1932- ... CANR-9
Earlier sketch in CA 65-68
Gavshon, Arthur L(eslie) 1916- ... 7-8R
Gaw, Walter A. 1904- ... 1R
Gawain, Shakti 1948- ... 93-96
Gawaine, John
See Hamilton-Hill, Donald
Gawron, Jean Mark 1953- ... 103
Gawsworth, John
See Armstrong, Terence Ian Fytton and Bates, H(erbert) E(rnest)
Gawthrop, Louis C. 1930- ... 81-84
Gaxotte, Pierre 1895-1982 ... 111
Obituary ... 108
Gay, A. Nolder
See Koelsch, William Alvin
Gay, Amelia
See Hogarth, Grace (Weston Allen)
Gay, Carlo T(eofilo) E(berhard) 1913- ... 49-52
Gay, Ebenezer 1696-1787 ... DLB-24
Gay, Francis
See Gee, H(erbert) L(eslie)
Gay, John E(dward) 1942- ... 81-84
Gay, Kathlyn 1930- ... CANR-8
Earlier sketch in CA 21-22R
See also SATA 9
Gay, Peter (Jack) 1923- ... CANR-18
Earlier sketch in CA 13-14R
Gay, Volney P(atrick) 1948- ... 117
Gay, Zhenya 1906-1978 ... 73-76
See also SATA 19
Gaya-Nuno, Juan Antonio 1913-1975 ... 81-84
Gayarre, Charles E. A. 1805-1895 ... DLB-30
Gay-Crosier, Raymond 1937- ... CANR-15
Earlier sketch in CA 41-44R
Gaydos, Michael J. 1940- ... 53-56
Gaye, Carol
See Shann, Renee
Gaye, Marvin (Penze) 1939-1984 Obituary ... 112
See also CLC 26
Gay-Kelly, Doreen 1952- ... 61-64
Gayle, Addison, Jr. 1932- ... CANR-13
Earlier sketch in CA 25-28R
Gayle, Emma
See Fairburn, Eleanor
Gayle, Marilyn
See Hoff, Marilyn
Gayle, Stephen H. 1948(?)-1982 Obituary ... 107
Gayles, Anne Richardson 1923- ... 53-56
Gaylin, Willard (M.) 1925- ... CANR-13
Earlier sketch in CA 23-24R
Gaylord, Billy
See Gaylord, William (Gilbert)
Gaylord, Edward King 1873-1974
Obituary ... 89-92
Gaylord, Sherwood Boyd 1914-
Brief entry ... 105
Gaylord, William (Gilbert) 1945-1985 ... 69-72
Obituary ... 118
Gayn, Mark J. 1909-1981 Obituary ... 105
Gayre, G(eorge) R(obert) 1907- ... CANR-4
Earlier sketch in CA 7-8R
Gayre of Gayre, R.
See Gayre, G(eorge) R(obert)
Gayre of Gayre and Nigg, Robert
See Gayre, G(eorge) R(obert)
Gazaway, Rena 1910- ... CAP-2
Earlier sketch in CA 29-32
Gazda, George M(ichael) 1931- ... CANR-13
Earlier sketch in CA 61-64
Gazdanov, Gaito 1903-1971 Obituary ... 104
Gazdanov, Georgii
See Gazdanov, Gaito
Gaze, Richard 1917- ... 4R
Gazell, James A(lbert) 1942- ... 49-52
Gazi, Stephen 1914-1978 ... 45-48
Obituary ... 103
Gazis, Denos C(onstantinos) 1930- ... 57-60
Gazley, John G(erow) 1895- ... 61-64
Gazzaniga, Michael S(aunders) 1939- ... 121
Gdanski, Marek
See Thee, Marek
Geach, Christine 1930- ... CANR-10
Earlier sketch in CA 25-28R
Geach, Patricia Sullivan 1916- ... 29-32R
Geach, Peter Thomas 1916- ... 103
Gealt, Adelheid (Medicus) 1946- ... 114
Geanakoplos, Deno John 1916- ... CANR-2
Earlier sketch in CA 1R
Geaney, Dennis J(oseph) 1914- ... CANR-20
Earlier sketches in CA 7-8R, CANR-5
Gear, C. William 1935- ... 53-56
Gear, Sheila 1942- ... 114
Geare, Michael 1919- ... 117
Geare, Mildred Mahler 1888(?)-1977
Obituary ... 73-76
Gearey, John 1926- ... CANR-23
Earlier sketch in CA 45-48
Gearhart, Sally Miller 1931- ... 57-60
Gearheart, B(ill) R. 1928- ... CANR-9
Earlier sketch in CA 23-24R
Gearing, Catherine 1916- ... 103
Gearing, Fred(erick) O(smond) 1922- ... 29-32R
Gearing-Thomas, G.
See Norwood, Victor G(eorge) C(harles)
Geary, Douglas 1931- ... 13-14R
Geary, Frederick Charles 1886(?)-1975(?)
Obituary ... 104
Geary, Herbert Valentine (Rupert) 1894-1965 ... CAP-1
Earlier sketch in CA 9-10
Geary, Patrick J(oseph) 1948- ... 104
Geary, Roger 1950- ... 123
Geasland, Jack
See Geasland, John Buchanan, Jr.
Geasland, John Buchanan, Jr. 1944- ... 81-84
Gebhard, Anna Laura Munro 1914- ... 7-8R
Gebhard, Bruno (Frederic) 1901- ... 73-76
Gebhard, Paul H(enry) 1917- ... 5-6R
Gebhart, Benjamin 1923- ... 53-56
Gebler, Carlo (Ernest) 1954- Brief entry ... 119
See also CLC 39
Gebler, Ernest 1915- ... CANR-3
Earlier sketch in CA 7-8R
Geck, Francis J(oseph) 1900- ... 73-76
Geckle, George L. 1939- ... 77-80
Gecys, Casimir C. 1904- ... CAP-2
Earlier sketch in CA 19-20
Gedda, George 1941- ... 77-80
Geddes, Charles L(ynn) 1928- ... CANR-2
Earlier sketch in CA 49-52
Geddes, Gary 1940- ... DLB-60
Geddes, Joan Bel 1916- ... 57-60
Geddes, Virgil 1897- ... DLB-4
Geddie, John 1937- ... 69-72
Gedo, John E. 1927- ... 121
Gedo, Mary M(athews) 1925- ... 104
Geduld, Harry M(aurice) 1931- ... CANR-20
Earlier sketches in CA 11-12R, CANR-5
Gedye, George Eric Rowe 1890-1970
Obituary ... 93-96
Gee, H(erbert) L(eslie) 1901-1977 ... 11-12R
Obituary ... 103
See also SATA 26
Gee, Maurice (Gough) 1931- ... 97-100
See also SATA 46
See also CLC 29
Geemis, Joseph (Stephen) 1935- ... 69-72
Geen, Russell Glenn 1932- ... CANR-22
Earlier sketch in CA 104
Geer, Charles 1922- ... 108
See also SATA 32, 42
Geer, Stephen (DuBois) 1930- ... 69-72
Geer, William D. 1906(?)-1976 Obituary ... 104
Geertz, Clifford 1926- ... 33-36R
Geertz, Hildred 1927- ... 77-80
Geeslin, Campbell 1925- ... 102
Geffen, Maxwell Myles 1896-1980
Obituary ... 102
Geffen, Roger 1919- ... 17-18R
Gefvert, Constance J(oanna) 1941- ... 53-56
Gega, Peter C(hristopher) 1924- ... 73-76
Geggus, David Patrick 1949- ... 114
Geherin, David J(ohn) 1943- ... CANR-17
Earlier sketch in CA 101
Gehlbach, Frederick Renner 1935- ... 106
Gehlen, Reinhard 1902-1979 Obituary ... 89-92
Gehman, Betsy Holland 1932- ... 19-20R
Gehman, Christian 1948- ... 119
Gehman, Henry Snyder 1888- ... 13-14R
Gehman, Richard (Boyd) 1921-1972 ... CANR-16
Obituary ... 33-36R
Earlier sketch in CA 3R
Gehr, Mary ... SATA-32
Gehrels, Franz 1922- ... 101
Gehri, Alfred 1896(?)-1972 Obituary ... 33-36R
Gehris, Paul 1934- ... 45-48
Geier, Arnold 1926- ... 4R
Geier, Woodrow A. 1914- ... 21-22R
Geigel Polanco, Vicente 1904-1979
Obituary ... 85-88
Geiger, Don(ald) Jesse 1923- ... 7-8R
Geiger, H(omer) Kent 1922- ... CANR-5
Earlier sketch in CA 1R
Geiger, Louis G. 1913- ... 13-14R
Geiger, Ray(mond Aloysius) 1910- ... 118
See also AITN 1
Geiger, Theodore 1915- Brief entry ... 114
Geipel, Eileen 1932- ... 107
See also SATA 30
Geipel, John 1937- ... CANR-13
Earlier sketch in CA 73-76
Geiringer, Irene (Steckel) 1899-1983
Obituary ... 111
Geiringer, Karl 1899- ... 13-14R
Geis, Darlene Stern ... CANR-5
Earlier sketch in CA 1R
See also SATA 7
Geis, Florence L(indauer) 1933- ... CANR-8
Earlier sketch in CA 57-60
Geis, Gilbert 1925- ... CANR-6
Earlier sketch in CA 11-12R
Geis, Richard E(rwin) 1927- ... 101
Geisel, Helen 1898-1967 Obituary ... 107
See also SATA 26
Geisel, Theodor Seuss 1904- ... CANR-13
Earlier sketch in CA 15-16R
See also SATA 1, 28
See also DLB 61
See also CLR 1
Geiser, Robert L(ee) 1931- ... 97-100
Geisert, Arthur 1941- ... 120
Geisinger, David L. 1938- ... 110
Geisler, Norman L(eo) 1932- ... CANR-10
Earlier sketch in CA 25-28R
Geismar, L(udwig) L(eo) 1921- ... CANR-11
Earlier sketch in CA 25-28R
Geismar, Maxwell (David) 1909-1979 ... 4R
Obituary ... 104
Geissman, Erwin William 1920-1980
Obituary ... 101
Geist, Harold 1916- ... CANR-22
Earlier sketches in CA 17-18R, CANR-7
Geist, Kenneth L(ee) 1936- ... 81-84
Geist, Robert John 1912- ... 41-44R
Geist, Roland C. 1896- ... 89-92
Geist, Sidney 1914- Brief entry ... 112
Geist, Valerius 1938- ... CANR-8
Earlier sketch in CA 61-64
Geitgey, Doris A. 1920- ... 53-56
Geiwitz, P(eter) James 1938- ... CANR-11
Earlier sketch in CA 29-32R
Gelatt, Roland 1920-1986 ... 13-14R
Obituary ... 121
Gelb, Arthur 1924- ... CANR-21
Earlier sketch in CA 3R
Gelb, Barbara (Stone) 1926- ... CANR-21
Earlier sketch in CA 3R
Gelb, Ignace J(ay) 1907-1985 ... 11-12R
Obituary ... 118
Gelb, Joyce 1940- ... 61-64
Gelb, Leslie H(oward) 1937- ... CANR-19
Earlier sketch in CA 103
Gelb, Norman 1929- ... 108
Gelbart, Larry (Simon) 1923- ... 73-76
See also CLC 21
Gelber, Harry G. 1926- ... 25-28R
Gelber, Jack 1932- ... CANR-2
Earlier sketch in CA 4R
See also DLB 7
See also CLC 1, 6, 14
Gelber, Lionel (Morris) 1907- ... 15-16R
Gelber, Steven M(ichael) 1943- ... 53-56
Geld, Ellen Bromfield 1932- ... 37-40R
Geldard, Frank A(rthur) 1904-1984 ... 41-44R
Obituary ... 114
Geldart, William 1936- ... SATA-15
Gelderman, Carol Wettlaufer 1935- ... 105
Gelernt, Jules 1928- ... 23-24R
Gelfand, Elissa D(eborah) 1949- ... 114
Gelfand, Lawrence Emerson 1926- ... CANR-3
Earlier sketch in CA 7-8R
Gelfand, Morris Arthur 1908- ... 49-52
Gelfman, Dick 1947- ... 122
Gelfman, Judith S(chlein) 1937- ... 65-68
Gelfond, Rhoda 1946- ... CANR-12
Earlier sketch in CA 49-52
Gelinas, Paul J. 1911- ... 41-44R
See also SATA 10
Gell, Frank
See Kowet, Don
Gell, Paul (Frederick William) 1928- ... 116
Gellatly, Peter 1923- Brief entry ... 111
Geller, Allen 1941- ... 25-28R
Geller, Bruce 1930-1978 Obituary ... 77-80
Geller, Evelyn
See Gottesfeld, Evelyn
Geller, Uri 1946- ... 69-72
Gellerman, Saul W(illiam) 1929- ... CANR-8
Earlier sketch in CA 5-6R
Gellert, Judith 1925- ... 33-36R
Gellert, Lew
See Wellen, Edward (Paul)
Gelles, Richard J. 1946- ... CANR-22
Earlier sketches in CA 61-64, CANR-8
Gelles, Sandi
See Gelles-Cole, Sandi
Gelles-Cole, Sandi 1949- ... 121
Gelley, Alexander 1933- Brief entry ... 108
Gellhorn, Ernst 1893-1973 ... CAP-2
Earlier sketch in CA 21-22
Gellhorn, Martha Ellis 1908- ... 77-80
See also DLBY 82
See also CLC 14
Gellhorn, Walter 1906- ... 13-14R
Gellinek, Christian 1930- ... CANR-9
Earlier sketch in CA 23-24R
Gellinek, Janis Little
See Solomon, Janis Little
Gellis, Roberta L(eah Jacobs) 1927- ... CANR-22
Earlier sketches in CA 7-8R, CANR-3
Gellman, Estelle Sheila 1941- ... 53-56
Gellman, Irwin F(rederick) 1942- ... CANR-1
Earlier sketch in CA 45-48
Gellner, Ernest (Andre) 1925- ... CANR-22
Earlier sketches in CA 7-8R, CANR-4
Gellner, John 1907- ... 29-32R
Gellrich, Jesse M. 1942- ... 118
Gelman, David Graham 1926- ... 103
Gelman, Mitch(ell Barry) 1962- ... 124
Gelman, Rita Golden 1937- ... CANR-16
Earlier sketch in CA 81-84
Gelman, Steve 1934- ... CANR-16
Earlier sketch in CA 25-28R
See also SATA 3
Gelman, Woodrow 1915(?)-1978 Obituary ... 104
Gelman, Woody
See Gelman, Woodrow
Gelmis, Joseph S(tephan) 1935- ... 45-48
Gelperin, L.
See Halpern, Leivick
Gelpi, Albert 1931- ... 33-36R
Gelpi, Barbara Charlesworth 1933- ... 112
Gelpi, Donald L. 1934- ... CANR-7
Earlier sketch in CA 17-18R
Geltman, Max 1906(?)-1984 Obituary ... 112
Gelula, Abner Joseph 1906-1985 Obituary ... 116
Gelven, (Charles) Michael 1937- ... 29-32R
Gelzer, Matthias 1886-1974 ... CAP-2
Earlier sketch in CA 25-28
Gemme, Francis Robert 1934- ... 23-24R
Gemme, Leila Boyle 1942- ... 81-84
Gemmell, Alan Robertson 1913- ... 114
Gemmett, Robert J(ames) 1936- ... 33-36R
Gemmill, Jane Brown 1898- ... 1R
Gemmill, Paul F. 1890(?)-1976 Obituary ... 69-72
Gemming, Elizabeth 1932- ... CANR-16
Earlier sketch in CA 65-68
See also SATA 11
Gems, (Iris) Pam(ela) 1925- ... 107
See also DLB 13
Genauer, Emily 1911- ... 106
Gendel, Evelyn W. 1916(?)-1977 Obituary ... 104
See also SATA 27
Gendell, Murray 1924- ... CANR-5
Earlier sketch in CA 9-10R
Gendlin, Eugene T. 1926- ... 3R
Gendron, George M. 1949- ... 93-96
Gendzier, Irene Lefel 1936- ... 23-24R
Gendzier, Stephen J(ules) 1930- ... 33-36R
General, Lloyd 1924(?)-1986 Obituary ... 119
Genet
See Flanner, Janet
Genet, Jean 1910-1986 ... CANR-18
Earlier sketch in CA 13-14R
See also DLBY 86
See also CLC 1, 2, 5, 10, 14, 44, 46
Genevoix, Maurice Charles Louis 1890-1980 Obituary ... 102
See also DLB 65
Geng, Veronica 1941- ... 124
Brief entry ... 119
Genn, Calder
See Gillie, Christopher
Gennaro, Joseph F(rancis), Jr. 1924- ... 101
Genne, Elizabeth Steel 1911- Brief entry ... 108
Genne, William H. 1910- ... 17-18R
Genovese, Eugene D(ominick) 1930- ... CANR-10
Earlier sketch in CA 69-72
See also DLB 17
Genoves Tarazaga, Santiago 1923-
Brief entry ... 107
Gensemer, Robert Eugene 1936-
Brief entry ... 110
Genser, Cynthia 1950- ... 69-72
Gensler, Kinereth 1922- ... 116
Genszler, G(eorge) William II 1915- ... CANR-9
Earlier sketch in CA 65-68
Gent, Peter 1942- ... 89-92
See also DLBY 82
See also CLC 29
See also AITN 1
Genthe, Charles V(incent) 1937- ... 29-32R
Gentil, Richard 1917- ... 102

Gentile, Gennaro L. 1946- ... 115
Gentile, Giovanni 1875-1944 Brief entry ... 119
Gentle, Mary 1956- ... 106
See also SATA 48
Gentleman, David (William) 1930- ... CANR-15
Earlier sketch in CA 25-28R
See also SATA 7
Gentles, Frederick (Ray) 1912- ... 29-32R
Gentry, Byron B. 1913- ... 15-16R
Gentry, Curt 1931- ... CANR-5
Earlier sketch in CA 11-12R
Gentry, Dwight L. 1919- ... 1R
Gentry, Marshall Bruce 1953- ... 121
Gentry, Peter
See Newcomb, Kerry
and Schaefer, Frank
Gentz, William Howard 1918- ... 107
Gentzler, J(ennings) Mason 1930- ... 93-96
Geoff
See Dyson, Geoffrey Harry George
Geoffrey, Theodate
See Wayman, Dorothy G.
Geoghegan, Sister Barbara 1902- ... CAP-1
Earlier sketch in CA 11-12
Geoghegan, Thomas Dolan 1917(?)-1987
Obituary ... 121
Georgakas, Dan 1938- ... CANR-22
Earlier sketches in CA 45-48, CANR-1
George, Alexander Lawrence 1920- ... 15-16R
George, Alfred Raymond 1912- ... 108
George, Charles H(illes) 1922- ... 11-12R
George, Chief Dan 1899-1981 ... 110
Obituary ... 108
George, Claude Swanson, Jr. 1920- ... 15-16R
George, Collins Crusor 1909- ... 77-80
George, Dan
See George, Chief Dan
George, David
See Vogenitz, David George
George, E(dgar) Madison 1907-1975 ... 4R
Obituary ... 103
George, Emery E(dward) 1933- ... CANR-16
Earlier sketch in CA 41-44R
George, Eugene
See Chevalier, Paul Eugene George
George, Henry 1839-1897 ... DLB-23
George, Jay
See Strachan, J(ohn) George
George, Jean Craighead 1919- ... 7-8R
See also SATA 2
See also DLB 52
See also CLC 35
See also CLR 1
George, John E(dwin) 1936- ... 53-56
George, John L(othar) 1916- ... 7-8R
See also SATA 2
George, Jonathan
See Burke, John (Frederick)
and Theiner, George
George, M(ary) Dorothy ... CAP-1
Earlier sketch in CA 15-16
George, Malcom F(arris) 1930- ... 57-60
George, Marion
See Benjamin, Claude (Max Edward
Pohlman)
George, Mary Carolyn Hollers Jutson
1930- ... CANR-12
Earlier sketch in CA 73-76
George, Mary Yanaga 1940- ... 29-32R
George, N(orvil) L(ester) 1902- ... CAP-2
Earlier sketch in CA 29-32
George, Nelson 1957- ... 119
George, Peter 1924-1966 Obituary ... 25-28R
George, Richard R(obert) 1943- ... 104
George, Robert Esmonde Gordon
1890-1969 ... CAP-1
Earlier sketch in CA 11-12
George, Rolf 1930- ... 110
George, Roy E(dwin) 1923- ... CANR-14
Earlier sketch in CA 37-40R
George, S(idney) C(harles) 1898- ... 53-56
See also SATA 11
George, Sally 1945- ... 105
George, Sara 1947- ... 65-68
George, Stefan (Anton) 1868-1933
Brief entry ... 104
See also TCLC 2, 14
George, Susan Akers 1934- ... 77-80
George, W(illiam) Lloyd 1900(?)-1975
Obituary ... 53-56
See also SATA 30
George, W(illiam) R(ichard) P(hilip)
1912- ... 69-72
George, Wilfred R(aymond) 1928- ... 111
George, Wilma
See Crowther, Wilma
George-Brown, George Alfred 1914-1985
Obituary ... 116
Brief entry ... 110
Georges, Georges Martin
See Simenon, Georges (Jacques
Christian)
Georges, Robert A(ugustus) 1933- ... 111
Georgescu-Roegen, Nicholas 1906- ... CANR-9
Earlier sketch in CA 23-24R
Georges-Michel, Michel 1883-1985
Obituary ... 116
Georgi, Charlotte ... CANR-17
Earlier sketches in CA 2R, CANR-2
Georgiana, Sister
See Terstegge, Mabel Alice
Georgiou, Constantine 1927- ... 15-16R
See also SATA 7
Georgiou, Steven Demetre 1948- ... 101
Georgopoulos, Basil S(pyros) 1926- ... 73-76
Gephart, William J(ay) 1928- ... 69-72
Geraci, Philip C. 1929- ... 77-80
Gerald, J(ames) Edward 1906- ... 5-6R
Gerald, John Bart 1940- ... CANR-22
Earlier sketches in CA 7-8R, CANR-7
Gerald, Ziggy
See Zeigerman, Gerald
Gerard, Albert S(tanislas) 1920- ... CANR-13
Earlier sketch in CA 29-32R
Gerard, Andrew
See Gatti, Arthur Gerard
Gerard, Charles (Franklin) 1914- ... 29-32R
Gerard, Dave 1909- ... 53-56
Gerard, David 1923- ... 77-80
Gerard, Elaine
See Ryder, Eileen
Gerard, Gaston
See Ostergaard, G(eoffrey) N(ielsen)
Gerard, H(arold) B(enjamin) 1923-
Brief entry ... 110
Gerard, Jane 1930- ... 2R
Gerard, Jean Ignace Isidore
1803-1847 ... SATA-45
Gerard, Jules B(ernard) 1929- ... 110
Gerard, Karen (Nina) 1932- ... 120
Gerard, Louise 1878(?)-1970 Obituary ... 104
Gerard, Ralph W(aldo) 1900-1974
Obituary ... 49-52
Gerard-Libois, Jules C. 1923- ... 33-36R
Geras, Adele (Daphne) 1944- ... CANR-19
Earlier sketch in CA 97-100
See also SATA 23
Geras, Norman (Myron) 1943- ... CANR-19
Earlier sketch in CA 102
Gerasimov, Gennadi (Ivanovitch) 1930- ... 69-72
Gerasimov, Innokentii Petrovich
1905-1985 Obituary ... 115
Gerasimov, Mikhail Mikhaylovich
1907-1970 Obituary ... 107
Gerassi, John 1931- ... CANR-8
Earlier sketch in CA 7-8R
Geraud, (Charles Joseph) Andre
1882-1974 ... 69-72
Obituary ... 53-56
Gerber, Albert B(enjamin) 1913- ... 17-18R
Gerber, Barbara (Lin) 1942- ... 117
Gerber, Bobbie
See Gerber, Barbara (Lin)
Gerber, Dan 1940- ... 33-36R
Gerber, David A(llison) 1944- ... 77-80
Gerber, Douglas E(arl) 1933- ... CANR-15
Earlier sketch in CA 29-32R
Gerber, Ellen W. 1936- Brief entry ... 107
Gerber, Helmut E. 1920-1981 ... CANR-10
Earlier sketch in CA 23-24R
Gerber, Israel J(oshua) 1918- ... 77-80
Gerber, John 1907(?)-1981 Obituary ... 103
Gerber, John C(hristian) 1908- ... 102
Gerber, Merrill Joan 1938- ... CANR-10
Earlier sketch in CA 15-16R
Gerber, Philip Leslie 1923- Brief entry ... 108
Gerber, Rudolph Joseph 1938- ... 105
Gerber, Sanford E(dwin) 1933- ... CANR-1
Earlier sketch in CA 49-52
Gerber, William 1908- ... 37-40R
Gerbers, Teresa 1933- ... 53-56
Gerbi, Antonello 1904-1976 ... 77-80
Gerbner, George 1919- ... CANR-1
Earlier sketch in CA 45-48
Gerboth, Walter W(illiam) 1925-1984 ... 15-16R
Obituary ... 112
Gerden, Friedrich Carl
See Greve, Felix Paul (Berthold Friedrich)
Gerdes, Florence Marie 1919- ... 25-28R
Gerdts, William H. 1929- ... CANR-10
Earlier sketch in CA 15-16R
Gergely, Tibor 1900-1978 ... 107
Obituary ... 106
See also SATA 20
Gergen, Kenneth J(ay) 1934- ... 33-36R
Gerhard, Happy 1920- ... 57-60
Gerhardi, William Alexander
See Gerhardie, William Alexander
Gerhardie, William Alexander
1895-1977 ... CANR-18
Obituary ... 73-76
Earlier sketch in CA 25-28R
See also DLB 36
See also CLC 5
Gerhardt, Lydia A(nn) 1934- ... CANR-10
Earlier sketch in CA 61-64
Gerhart, Gail M. 1943- ... 85-88
Gerhart, Genevra 1930- ... 57-60
Gerig, Reginald R(oth) 1919- ... 57-60
Gerin, Winifred 1901(?)-1981 ... CANR-20
Obituary ... 104
Earlier sketch in CA 25-28R
Geringer, Laura 1948- ... 107
See also SATA 29
Gerlach, Barbara A(nn) 1946- ... 114
Gerlach, Don R(alph) 1932- ... 9-10R
Gerlach, John 1941- ... 101
Gerlach, Larry R(euben) 1941- Brief entry ... 109
Gerlach, Luther P(aul) 1930- ... 41-44R
Gerlach, Russel L(ee) 1939- ... 89-92
Gerlach, Vernon S(amuel) 1922- ... 61-64
Gerler, William R(obert) 1917- ... 65-68
See also SATA 47
Germain, Edward B. 1937- ... 89-92
Germain, Walter 1889-1962 Obituary ... 112
German, Donald R(obert) 1931-1986 ... CANR-22
Obituary ... 119
Earlier sketches in CA 57-60, CANR-7
German, Gene Arlin 1933- ... 45-48
German, Joan W(olfe) 1933- ... CANR-22
Earlier sketches in CA 57-60, CANR-7
German, Tony 1924- ... 97-100
Germane, Gayton E. 1920- ... CANR-18
Earlier sketches in CA 1R, CANR-2
Germani, Gino 1911-1979 ... CANR-7
Earlier sketch in CA 53-56
Germanicus
See Dunner, Joseph
Germann, A(lbert) C(arl) 1921- ... 1R
Germann, Richard Wolf 1930- ... 104
Germano, Peter B. 1913- Brief entry ... 116
Germany, (Vera) Jo(sephine) ... CANR-9
Earlier sketch in CA 65-68
Germar, Herb
See Germar, William H(erbert)
Germar, William H(erbert) 1911- ... 23-24R
Germeshausen, Anna Louise 1906-1968
Obituary ... 108
Germino, Dante (Lee) 1931- ... 53-56
Germond, Jack W. 1928- ... 112
Brief entry ... 108
Gernert, Eleanor Towles 1928- ... 37-40R
Gernes, Sonia 1942- ... 107
Gernsback, Hugo 1884-1967 Obituary ... 93-96
See also DLB 8
Gernsheim, Helmut 1913- ... CANR-22
Earlier sketches in CA 7-8R, CANR-5
Gernstein, Mordicai Brief entry ... 117
See also SATA 36
Geroely, Kalman
See Gabel, Joseph
Gerold, Karl 1906-1973 Obituary ... 41-44R
Gerold, William 1932- ... 17-18R
Geroly, Kalman
See Gabel, Joseph
Gerosa, Guido 1933- ... 73-76
Gerould, Daniel C. 1928- ... 29-32R
Gerow, Edwin 1931- ... 53-56
Gerow, Josh(ua R.) 1941- ... 103
Gerrard, Jean 1933- ... 115
Gerrard, Roy 1935- ... 110
See also SATA 45, 47
Gerrietts, John 1912- ... 77-80
Gerring, Ray H. 1926- ... 13-14R
Gerrish, B(rian) A(lbert) 1931- ... CANR-4
Earlier sketch in CA 5-6R
Gerrity, David James 1923- ... CANR-4
Earlier sketch in CA 2R
Gerrold, David 1944- ... 93-96
See also DLB 8
Gerschenkron, Alexander (Pavlovich)
1904-1978 ... CANR-1
Earlier sketch in CA 45-48
Gersh, Harry 1912- ... CANR-1
Earlier sketch in CA 4R
Gershator, David 1937- ... 115
Gershator, Phillis 1942- ... 102
Gershen, Martin 1924-1985 ... 33-36R
Obituary ... 114
Gershenson, Daniel E(noch) 1935- ... 5-6R
Gershman, Herbert S. 1926-1971 ... CAP-2
Obituary ... 33-36R
Earlier sketch in CA 25-28
Gershon, Karen
See Tripp, Karen
Gershoy, Leo 1897-1975 ... CAP-1
Obituary ... 57-60
Earlier sketch in CA 13-14
Gershwin, Ira 1896-1983 Obituary ... 110
Brief entry ... 108
Gerson, Corinne 1927- ... 93-96
See also SATA 37
Gerson, Louis Leib 1921- ... 19-20R
Gerson, Noel Bertram 1914- ... 81-84
See also SATA 22
Gerson, Walter (Max) 1935- ... 41-44R
Gerson, Wolfgang 1916- ... 33-36R
Gersoni, Diane 1947- ... 53-56
Gersoni-Stavn, Diane
See Gersoni, Diane
Gerstad, John (Leif) 1924-1981 ... 103
Obituary ... 105
Gerstein, Arnold A. 1940- ... 124
Gerstein, Linda (Groves) 1938- Brief entry ... 110
Gerstein, Mordicai 1935- ... SATA-47
Gerstenberger, Donna Lorine 1929- ... CANR-4
Earlier sketch in CA 7-8R
Gerster, Georg (Anton) 1928- ... 37-40R
Gerster, Patrick G(eorge) 1942- ... 57-60
Gerstine, Jack
See Gerstine, John
Gerstine, John 1915- ... 7-8R
Gerstl, Joel E. 1932- ... 21-22R
Gerstle, Kurt H(erman) 1923- ... 53-56
Gerstner, Edna Suckau 1914- ... 2R
Gerstner, John H(enry) 1914- ... CANR-2
Earlier sketch in CA 1R
Gert, Bernard 1934- ... 29-32R
Gerteiny, Alfred G(eorges) 1930- ... 21-22R
Gerteis, Louis S(axton) 1942- ... 45-48
Gerth, Donald Rogers 1928- ... 45-48
Gerth, Hans Heinrich 1908-1978
Obituary ... 81-84
Gertler, Menard M. 1919- ... 11-12R
Gertler, T. ... 121
Brief entry ... 116
See also CLC 34
Gertman, Samuel 1915- ... 1R
Gertz, Elmer 1906- ... CANR-11
Earlier sketch in CA 15-16R
Gertz, Theodore G(erson) 1936- ... 115
Gertzog, Irwin N(orman) 1933- ... 29-32R
Gerulaitis, Leonardas Vytautas 1928- ... 77-80
Gervais, C(harles) H(enry) 1946- ... 97-100
Gervais, Marty
See Gervais, C(harles) H(enry)
Gervasi, Frank H(enry) 1908- ... CAP-1
Earlier sketch in CA 15-16
Gerwig, Anna Mary (Gerwig) 1907- ... CAP-2
Earlier sketch in CA 17-18
Gerwin, Donald 1937- ... 25-28R
Gerzon, Mark ... 81-84
Gesch, Dorothy K(atherine) 1923- ... 29-32R
Gesch, Roy G(eorge) 1920- ... 23-24R
Geschickter, Charles F(reeborn)
1901-1987 Obituary ... 123
Geschwender, James A(rthur) 1933- ... 41-44R
Gesell, Arnold Lucius 1880-1961 Obituary ... 116
Geserick, June
See Donahue, June (Geserick)
Gesner, Carol 1922- ... 29-32R
Gesner, Clark 1938- ... 109
See also SATA 40
Gesner, Elsie Miller 1919- ... 17-18R
Gessert, Kate Rogers 1948- ... 113
Gessner, Lynne 1919- ... CANR-10
Earlier sketch in CA 25-28R
See also SATA 16
Geston, Mark S(ymington) 1946- ... 102
See also DLB 8
Gethers, Peter 1953- ... 103
Gething, Thomas W(ilson) 1939- ... 41-44R
Getlein, Dorothy Woolen 1921- ... 9-10R
Getlein, Frank 1921- ... CANR-6
Earlier sketch in CA 9-10R
Gettel, Ronald 1931- ... 112
Gettens, Rutherford John 1900(?)-1974
Obituary ... 49-52
Gettings, Eunice J. 1901(?)-1978
Obituary ... 81-84
Gettings, Fred 1937- ... 123
Gettleman, Marvin E. 1933- ... 37-40R
Gettleman, Susan
See Braiman, Susan
Getty, Gerald W(inkler) 1913- ... 57-60
Getty, Hilda F. 1938- ... 61-64
Getty, J(ean) Paul 1892-1976 ... 69-72
Obituary ... 65-68
Getty, Mary Ann 1943- ... 114
Getz, Gene A(rnold) 1932- ... CANR-12
Earlier sketch in CA 29-32R
Getz, Malcolm 1945- ... CANR-18
Earlier sketch in CA 101
Getz, Oscar 1897-1983 Obituary ... 110
Getzels, Jacob Warren 1912- ... 45-48
Getzoff, Carole 1943- ... 61-64
Geubtner, Virginia Reidel
See Reidel-Geubtner, Virginia
Gevirtz, Don L(ee) 1928- ... 121
Gevirtz, Eliezer 1950- ... 121
See also SATA 49
Gevirtz, Stanley 1929- Brief entry ... 109
Gewe, Raddory
See Gorey, Edward (St. John)
Gewecke, Clifford George, Jr. 1932- ... 23-24R
Gewehr, Wolf M(ax) 1939- ... CANR-1
Earlier sketch in CA 45-48
Gewirth, Alan 1912- Brief entry ... 107
Gewirtz, Jacob L(eon) 1924- ... 45-48
Gewirtz, Leonard Benjamin 1918- ... 1R
Geyer, Alan (Francis) 1931- ... 9-10R
Geyer, Georgie Anne 1935- ... CANR-17
Earlier sketch in CA 29-32R
Geyl, Pieter (Catharinus Arie) 1887-1966 ... 103
Obituary ... 89-92
Geyman, John P. 1931- ... CANR-14
Earlier sketch in CA 37-40R
Gezi, Kal
See Gezi, Kalil I(smail)
Gezi, Kalil I(smail) 1930- ... CANR-17
Earlier sketch in CA 25-28R
Ghadimi, Hossein 1922- ... 61-64
Ghai, Dharam P. 1936- ... CANR-15
Earlier sketch in CA 21-22R
Gheddo, Piero 1929- ... CANR-15
Earlier sketch in CA 73-76
Ghelardi, Robert (Anthony) 1939- ... 69-72
Ghelderode, Michel de 1898-1962 ... 85-88
See also CLC 6, 11
Gheorghiu, (Constantin) Virgil 1916- ... 33-36R
Gherity, James Arthur 1929- ... 17-18R
Ghigna, Charles 1946- ... 77-80
Ghine, Wunnakyawhtin U Ohn
See Maurice, David (John Kerr)
Ghiotto, Renato 1923- ... 49-52
Ghiradella, Robert 1934- ... 114
Ghiselin, Brewster 1903- ... CANR-13
Earlier sketch in CA 13-14R
See also CLC 23
Ghiselin, Michael T(enant) 1939- ... 49-52
Ghiselli, Edwin E(rnest) 1907- ... 37-40R
Ghnassia, Maurice (Jean-Henri) 1920- ... 49-52
Ghose, Amal 1929- ... 106
Ghose, Sri Chinmoy Kumar
See Chinmoy, Sri
Ghose, Sudhin(dra) N(ath) 1899- ... 7-8R
Ghose, Zulfikar 1935- ... 65-68
See also CLC 42
Ghosh, Amitav 1956- ... CLC-44
Ghosh, Arun Kumar 1930- ... CANR-10
Earlier sketch in CA 23-24R
Ghosh, Dipali 1945- ... 124
Ghosh, Jyotis Chandra 1904(?)-1975
Obituary ... 57-60
Ghosh, Tapan 1928- ... 53-56
Ghougassian, Joseph P(eter) 1944- ... 49-52
Ghurye, G(ovind) S(adashiv) 1893- ... CANR-3
Earlier sketch in CA 5-6R
Giacosa, Giuseppe 1847-1906 Brief entry ... 104
See also TCLC 7
Giacumakis, George, Jr. 1937- ... 41-44R
Giallombardo, Rose (Mary) 1925- ... 61-64
Giamatti, A(ngelo) Bartlett 1938- ... 97-100
Giamatti, Valentine 1911-1982 Obituary ... 106
Gianakaris, C(onstantine) J(ohn) 1934- ... 25-28R
Giannaris, George (B.) 1936- ... CANR-22
Earlier sketches in CA 45-48, CANR-2

Giannestras, Nicholas James 1909-1978
Obituary ... 105
Giannetti, Louis D. 1937- ... 33-36R
Giannone, Richard 1934- ... 21-22R
Giannoni, Carlo Borromeo 1939- ... 41-44R
Giap Vo Nguyen
See Vo Nguyen Giap
Giardina, Anthony 1950- ... 118
Giardina, Denise 1951- ... 119
Giauque, William Francis 1895-1982
Obituary ... 106
Gibaldi, Joseph 1942- ... CANR-15
Earlier sketch in CA 89-92
Gibans, Nina Freedlander 1932- ... 116
Gibb, Hamilton (Alexander Rosskeen)
1895-1971 ... CANR-6
Obituary ... 33-36R
Earlier sketch in CA 4R
Gibb, Jack (Rex) 1914- ... 17-18R
Gibb, Lee
See Deghy, Guy (Stephen)
and Waterhouse, Keith (Spencer)
Gibbard, Graham S(tewart) 1942- ... 53-56
Gibbens, T(revor) C(harles) N(oel)
1912-1983 Obituary ... 111
Gibberd, Frederick 1908-1984 Obituary ... 111
Gibbon, Lewis Grassic
See Mitchell, James Leslie
See also TCLC 4
Gibbon, (William) Monk 1896-1987 ... 69-72
Obituary ... 124
Gibbon, Vivian 1917- ... 103
Gibbons, Barbara (Halloran) 1934- ... CANR-10
Earlier sketch in CA 61-64
Gibbons, Bob
See Gibbons, Robert
Gibbons, Brian 1938- ... CANR-11
Earlier sketch in CA 25-28R
Gibbons, Don C(ary) 1926- Brief entry ... 110
Gibbons, Euell (Theophilus) 1911-1975 ... CAP-2
Obituary ... 61-64
Earlier sketch in CA 23-24
See also AITN 1
Gibbons, Faye 1938- ... 109
Gibbons, Felton L(ewis) 1929- ... 124
Gibbons, (Raphael) Floyd (Phillips)
1887-1939 Brief entry ... 113
See also DLB 25
Gibbons, Gail 1944- ... CANR-12
Earlier sketch in CA 69-72
See also SATA 23
See also CLR 8
Gibbons, Helen Bay 1921- ... 17-18R
Gibbons, J. Whitfield 1939- ... 114
Gibbons, John William 1907-1983
Obituary ... 109
Gibbons, Maurice 1931- ... 89-92
Gibbons, Reginald 1947- ... CANR-18
Earlier sketch in CA 97-100
Gibbons, Robert 1949- ... 116
Gibbons, Stella 1902- ... 13-14R
Gibbons, Whit
See Gibbons, J. Whitfield
Gibbs, A(twood) James 1922- ... 19-20R
Gibbs, A(nthony) M(atthews) 1933- ... 33-36R
Gibbs, Alonzo (Lawrence) 1915- ... CANR-5
Earlier sketch in CA 5-6R
See also SATA 5
Gibbs, Anthony 1902-1975 ... CAP-2
Earlier sketch in CA 29-32
Gibbs, Barbara 1912- ... 25-28R
Gibbs, C. Earl 1935- ... 69-72
Gibbs, Esther 1904- ... 57-60
Gibbs, George 1870-1942 Brief entry ... 120
Gibbs, Henry
See Rumbold-Gibbs, Henry St. John Clair
Gibbs, Jack P(orter) 1927- ... 122
Brief entry ... 118
Gibbs, James A.
See Gibbs, James Atwood
Gibbs, James Atwood 1922- ... CANR-11
Earlier sketch in CA 69-72
Gibbs, Jim
See Gibbs, James Atwood
Gibbs, Joanifer 1947- ... 57-60
Gibbs, John G(amble) 1930- ... 41-44R
Gibbs, Mark 1920- ... 7-8R
Gibbs, Mary Ann
See Bidwell, Marjory Elizabeth Sarah
Gibbs, (Cecilia) May 1877-1969 Obituary ... 104
See also SATA 27
Gibbs, Paul T(homas) 1897- ... 11-12R
Gibbs, Peter Bawtree 1903- ... 2R
Gibbs, Philip (Hamilton) 1877-1962
Obituary ... 89-92
Gibbs, Rafe
See Gibbs, Raphael Sanford
Gibbs, Raphael Sanford 1912- ... 7-8R
Gibbs, Tony
See Gibbs, Wolcott, Jr.
Gibbs, William E. 1936-19(?) ... CAP-2
Earlier sketch in CA 21-22
Gibbs, Wolcott, Jr. 1935- ... 85-88
See also SATA 40
Gibbs-Smith, Charles Harvard
1909-1981 ... CANR-4
Obituary ... 108
Earlier sketch in CA 11-12R
Gibbs-Wilson, Kathryn (Beatrice)
1930- ... CANR-10
Earlier sketch in CA 65-68
Gibby, Robert Gwyn 1916- ... 13-14R
Giberson, Dorothy (Dodds) ... CANR-2
Earlier sketch in CA 3R
Gibian, George 1924- ... CANR-19
Earlier sketches in CA 1R, CANR-5
Giblin, Charles Homer 1928- ... 41-44R
Giblin, James Cross 1933- ... CANR-24
Earlier sketch in CA 106
See also SATA 33
Gibney, Frank (Bray) 1924- ... CANR-11
Earlier sketch in CA 69-72
Gibney, Harriet
See Harvey, Harriet
Giboire, Clive (John) 1945- ... 118
Gibran, Jean 1933- ... 69-72
Gibran, Kahlil 1883-1931 Brief entry ... 104
See also TCLC 1, 9
Gibson, Alexander Dunnett 1901-1978
Obituary ... 77-80
Gibson, Arrell Morgan 1921- ... 41-44R
Gibson, Charles (Edmund) 1916- ... 7-8R
Gibson, Charles 1920- ... 21-22R
Gibson, Charline 1937- ... 69-72
Gibson, D. Parke 1930-1979 ... 93-96
Obituary ... 85-88
Gibson, Derlyne 1936- ... 23-24R
Gibson, Donald B. 1933- ... 25-28R
Gibson, E(rnest) Dana 1906- ... 29-32R
Gibson, E(dward) Lawrence 1935- ... 93-96
Gibson, Elizabeth 1949- ... 118
Gibson, Elsie (Edith) 1907- ... 61-64
Gibson, Eva 1939- ... 114
Gibson, Evan K(eith) 1909- ... 105
Gibson, Frank K. 1924- ... 37-40R
Gibson, George H(orner) 1932-
Brief entry ... 114
Gibson, Gerald Don 1938- ... 104
Gibson, Gertrude Hevener 1906- ... 5-6R
Gibson, Gifford Guy 1943- ... 77-80
Gibson, Graeme 1934- ... DLB-53
Gibson, H(amilton) B(ertie) 1914- ... 102
Gibson, Harry Clark
See Hubler, Richard Gibson
Gibson, James (Charles) 1919- ... 117
Gibson, James C.
See Gibson, James (Charles)
Gibson, James J(erome) 1904- ... 85-88
Gibson, James L(awrence) 1935- ... CANR-8
Earlier sketch in CA 5-6R
Gibson, James W(illiam) 1932- ... 41-44R
Gibson, Janice T(horne) 1934- ... 41-44R
Gibson, John 1907- ... 33-36R
Gibson, John M(endinghall) 1899-19(?) ... 2R
Gibson, Josephine
See Hine, Al(fred Blakelee)
and Hine, Sesyle Joslin
Gibson, Karon Rose (White) 1946- ... 105
Gibson, Maralee G. 1924- ... 17-18R
Gibson, Margaret 1944- ... 77-80
Gibson, Margaret 1948- ... 103
Gibson, Miles 1947- ... CANR-18
Earlier sketch in CA 102
Gibson, Morgan 1929- ... CANR-14
Earlier sketch in CA 25-28R
Gibson, (William) Morris(on) 1916- ... 117
Gibson, Nevin H(erman) 1915- ... 49-52
Gibson, Raymond E(ugene) 1924- ... 23-24R
Gibson, Reginald Walter 1901- ... CAP-1
Earlier sketch in CA 13-14
Gibson, Richard (Thomas) 1931- ... 41-44R
Gibson, Robert (Donald Davidson) 1927- ... 65-68
Gibson, Robert L(eone) 1927- ... 121
Gibson, Robert William, Jr. 1923- ... 107
Gibson, Ronald George 1909- ... 109
Gibson, Rosemary
See Newell, Rosemary
Gibson, Shirley 1927- ... 103
Gibson, (William) Walker 1919- ... CANR-1
Earlier sketch in CA 1R
Gibson, Walter B(rown) 1897-1985 ... 110
Obituary ... 118
Brief entry ... 108
Gibson, Walter Samuel 1932- ... 102
Gibson, Wilfrid Wilson 1878-1962
Obituary ... 113
See also DLB 19
Gibson, William ... CLC-39
Gibson, William 1914- ... CANR-9
Earlier sketch in CA 9-10R
See also DLB 7
See also CLC 23
Gibson, William Carleton 1913- ... 19-20R
Gibson, William E(dward) 1944- ... 33-36R
Gibson, William M(erriam) 1912- ... 121
Gibson-Jarvie, Clodagh 1923- ... 105
Gichon, Mordechai 1922- ... 89-92
Gicovate, Bernard 1922- ... 37-40R
Gidal, Nachum
See Gidal, Tim N(achum)
Gidal, Peter 1946- ... 103
Gidal, Sonia (Epstein) 1922- ... CANR-14
Earlier sketch in CA 7-8R
See also SATA 2
Gidal, Tim N(achum) 1909- ... CANR-20
Earlier sketches in CA 5-6R, CANR-14
See also SATA 2
Gidalewitsch, Nachum
See Gidal, Tim N(achum)
Giddings, James Louis 1909-1964 ... CAP-1
Earlier sketch in CA 11-12
Giddings, John Calvin 1930- ... 109
Giddings, Robert (Lindsay) 1935- ... CANR-9
Earlier sketch in CA 23-24R
Giddins, Gary 1948- ... CANR-13
Earlier sketch in CA 77-80
Giddy, Ian H. 1948- ... 114
Gide, Andre (Paul Guillaume) 1869-1951 ... 124
Brief entry ... 104
See also DLB 65
See also TCLC 5, 12
Gideonse, Harry David 1901-1985
Obituary ... 115
Gidley, Charles
See Wheeler, (Charles) Gidley
Gidley, (Gustavus) M(ick) 1941- ... 102
Gidlow, Elsa 1898-1986 ... 77-80
Obituary ... 119
Gidney, James B. 1914- ... 45-48
Giedion, Sigfried 1888(?)-1968 Obituary ... 116
Giegling, John A(llan) 1935- ... 29-32R
See also SATA 17
Giele, Janet Z(ollinger) 1934- ... 114
Gielgud, Gwen Bagni
See Dubov, Gwen Bagni
Gielgud, (Arthur) John 1904- Brief entry ... 111
Gielgud, Val (Henry) 1900- ... CANR-5
Earlier sketch in CA 9-10R
Giere, Ronald N(elson) 1938- ... CANR-4
Earlier sketch in CA 49-52
Giergielewicz, Mieczyslaw F. 1901-1983 ... CAP-2
Obituary ... 113
Earlier sketch in CA 25-28
Gierow, Karl Ragnar (Knut) 1904-1982
Obituary ... 108
Giersch, Julius
See Arnade, Charles W(olfgang)
Giertz, Bo H(arald) 1905- ... CANR-9
Earlier sketch in CA 23-24R
Gies, Frances 1915- ... CANR-9
Earlier sketch in CA 25-28R
Gies, Joseph (Cornelius) 1916- ... CANR-9
Earlier sketch in CA 7-8R
Gies, Thomas G(eorge) 1921- ... 33-36R
Giesbrecht, Martin Gerhard 1933- ... CANR-4
Earlier sketch in CA 53-56
Giesey, Ralph E(dwin) 1923- ... 25-28R
Giessler, Phillip Bruce 1938- ... CANR-8
Earlier sketch in CA 61-64
Giesy, J(ohn) U(lrich) 1877-1947
Brief entry ... 112
Giff, Patricia Reilly 1935- ... CANR-18
Earlier sketch in CA 101
See also SATA 33
Giffen, Daniel H. 1938- ... 107
Giffin, Frederick Charles 1938- ... 41-44R
Giffin, James Manning 1935- ... 105
Giffin, Sidney F. 1907-1977 Obituary ... 73-76
Gifford, Barry (Colby) 1946- ... CANR-9
Earlier sketch in CA 65-68
See also CLC 34
Gifford, Denis 1927- ... CANR-18
Earlier sketch in CA 101
Gifford, Don (Creighton) 1919- ... 53-56
Gifford, Edward S(tewart), Jr. 1907- ... CAP-2
Earlier sketch in CA 19-20
Gifford, Francis Newton
See Gifford, Frank
Gifford, Frank 1930- Brief entry ... 109
Gifford, Griselda 1931- ... CANR-24
Earlier sketch in CA 107
See also SATA 42
Gifford, (Charles) Henry 1913- ... 17-18R
Gifford, James Fergus, Jr. 1940- ... 57-60
Gifford, Prosser 1929- ... CANR-18
Earlier sketch in CA 101
Gifford, Terry 1946- ... CANR-24
Earlier sketch in CA 106
Gifford, Thomas (Eugene) 1937- ... 77-80
Gifford-Jones, W.
See Walker, Kenneth Francis
Giggal, Kenneth 1927- ... CANR-20
Earlier sketch in CA 104
Giglio, Ernest D(avid) 1931- ... 33-36R
Giguere, Diane 1937- ... 25-28R
See also DLB 53
Giguere, Roland 1929- ... DLB-60
Gih, Andrew 1901- ... 23-24R
Gil, David G(eorg) 1924- ... CANR-12
Earlier sketch in CA 29-32R
Gil, Federico Guillermo 1915- ... CANR-2
Earlier sketch in CA 1R
Gilb, Corinne Lathrop 1925- ... 17-18R
Gilbar, Steven 1941- ... 106
Gilbert, Alan Graham 1944- ... 112
Gilbert, Allan H. 1888- ... 9-10R
Gilbert, Amy M(argaret) 1895- ... 49-52
Gilbert, Ann
See Taylor, Ann
Gilbert, Anna
See Lazarus, Marguerite
Gilbert, Anne 1927- ... CANR-7
Earlier sketch in CA 57-60
Gilbert, Anthony
See Malleson, Lucy Beatrice
Gilbert, Arlene E(lsie) 1934- ... 49-52
Gilbert, Arthur 1926-1976 ... CANR-9
Earlier sketch in CA 19-20R
Gilbert, Ben W(illiam) 1918- ... 45-48
Gilbert, Benjamin Franklin 1918- ... CANR-22
Earlier sketches in CA 17-18R, CANR-7
Gilbert, Bentley B(rinkerhoff) 1924- ... 25-28R
Gilbert, Bill 1931- ... 105
Gilbert, Celia 1932- ... 115
Gilbert, Charles 1913- ... 41-44R
Gilbert, Christine B(ell) 1909- ... 103
Gilbert, Christopher 1949- ... 120
Gilbert, Creighton (Eddy) 1924- ... CANR-15
Earlier sketch in CA 33-36R
Gilbert, David T(hompson) 1953- ... 106
Gilbert, Doris Wilcox ... 17-18R
Gilbert, Doug 1938-1979 Obituary ... 104
Gilbert, Douglas 1942- ... 53-56
Gilbert, Douglas L. 1925- ... 15-16R
Gilbert, Edmund W(illiam) 1900-1973 ... 65-68
Gilbert, Edwin 1907-1976 ... 77-80
Obituary ... 69-72
Gilbert, Felix 1905- Brief entry ... 106
Gilbert, George 1922- ... 69-72
Gilbert, Glenn Gordon 1936- ... CANR-13
Earlier sketch in CA 33-36R
Gilbert, Gordon Allan 1942- ... 103
Gilbert, Gorman 1943- ... 114
Gilbert, Gustave M. 1911-1977 Obituary ... 69-72
Gilbert, Harriett 1948- ... CANR-9
Earlier sketch in CA 57-60
See also SATA 30
Gilbert, Harry 1946- ... 106
Gilbert, Herman Cromwell 1923- ... CANR-12
Earlier sketch in CA 29-32R
Gilbert, Jack 1925- ... 123
Gilbert, Jack (Glenn) 1925(?)- Brief entry ... 116
Gilbert, Jack G(lenn) 1934- ... 25-28R
Gilbert, James 1935- ... 29-32R
Gilbert, Jarvey 1917- ... 33-36R
Gilbert, (Agnes) Joan (Sewell) 1931- ... 21-22R
See also SATA 10
Gilbert, John (Raphael) 1926- ... 107
See also SATA 36
Gilbert, Julie Goldsmith
See Daniel, Julie Goldsmith
Gilbert, Manu
See West, Joyce (Tarlton)
Gilbert, Marilyn B(ender) 1926- ... CANR-1
Earlier sketch in CA 4R
Gilbert, Martin 1936- ... 11-12R
Gilbert, Michael Francis 1912- ... CANR-1
Earlier sketch in CA 1R
Gilbert, Milton 1909(?)-1979 Obituary ... 93-96
Gilbert, Miriam
See Presberg, Miriam Goldstein
Gilbert, Nan
See Gilbertson, Mildred Geiger
Gilbert, Neil 1940- ... 77-80
Gilbert, R(obert) A(ndrew) 1942- ... 124
Gilbert, Robert E(mile) 1939- ... 53-56
Gilbert, Rod(rigue Gabriel) 1941-
Brief entry ... 109
Gilbert, Russell Wieder 1905-1985 ... 45-48
Obituary ... 115
Gilbert, Ruth Gallard Ainsworth 1908- ... CANR-4
Earlier sketch in CA 9-10R
Gilbert, S(tuart) R(eid) 1948- ... 101
Gilbert, Sandra M(ortola) 1936- ... CANR-14
Earlier sketch in CA 41-44R
Gilbert, Sara (Dulaney) 1943- ... CANR-6
Earlier sketch in CA 57-60
See also SATA 11
Gilbert, Stephen 1912- ... 25-28R
Gilbert, W(illiam) S(chwenck) 1836-1911
Brief entry ... 104
See also SATA 36
See also TCLC 3
Gilbert, Willie 1916- ... 45-48
Gilbert, (Lerman) Zack 1925- ... 65-68
Gilberts, Helen 1909- ... 29-32R
Gilbertson, Merrill Thomas 1911- ... 11-12R
Gilbertson, Mildred Geiger 1908- ... CANR-2
Earlier sketch in CA 5-6R
See also SATA 2
Gilbo, Patrick F(rancis) 1937- ... 107
Gilboa, Amir 1917-1984 Obituary ... 114
Gilboa, Yehoshua A. 1918- ... 29-32R
Gilborn, Alice 1936- ... 69-72
Gilbreath, Alice 1921- ... CANR-10
Earlier sketch in CA 25-28R
See also SATA 12
Gilbreath, (Larry) Kent 1945- ... 45-48
Gilbreth, Frank B., Jr. 1911- ... 9-10R
See also SATA 2
See also CLC 17
Gilbreth, Lillian Moller 1878-1972
Obituary ... 33-36R
Gilcher, Edwin L. 1909- ... 29-32R
Gilchrist, Agnes A(ddison) 1907-1976
Obituary ... 65-68
Gilchrist, Alan W. 1913- ... 21-22R
Gilchrist, Andrew (Graham) 1910- ... 109
Gilchrist, Ellen 1935- ... 116
Brief entry ... 113
See also CLC 34
Gilchrist, J(ohn Thomas) 1927- ... 25-28R
Gilday, Robert M. 1925(?)-1980 Obituary ... 101
Gilden, Bert 1915(?)-1971 ... CAP-1
Obituary ... 29-32R
Earlier sketch in CA 11-12
Gilden, K.B.
See Gilden, Bert
and Gilden, Katya
Gilden, Katya ... 11-12R
Gilder, Eric 1911- ... CANR-15
Earlier sketch in CA 89-92
Gilder, George F. 1939- ... CANR-9
Earlier sketch in CA 17-18R
See also AITN 1
Gilder, Richard Watson 1844-1909 ... DLB-64
Gilder, Rosamond de Kay 1891-1986 ... 1R
Obituary ... 120
Gildersleeve, Thomas R(obert) 1927- ... 29-32R
Gildner, Gary 1938- ... CANR-12
Earlier sketch in CA 33-36R
Gildner, Judith 1943- ... 89-92
Gildrie, Richard P(eter) 1945- ... 73-76
Gildzen, Alex 1943- ... 41-44R
Gilead, Zerubavel 1912- ... 123
Giles, C(harles) W(ilfred) Scott
See Scott-Giles, C(harles) W(ilfred)
Giles, Carl H(oward) 1935- ... 29-32R
Giles, Elizabeth
See Holt, John (Robert)
Giles, Frederick John 1928- ... 93-96
Giles, Geoffrey J(ohn) 1947- ... 122
Giles, Gordon A.
See Binder, Otto O(scar)
Giles, Henry 1809-1882 ... DLB-64
Giles, James R(ichard) 1937- ... 73-76

Giles, Janice Holt 1909-1979 .... CANR-3
Earlier sketch in CA 1R
Giles, John 1921- 104
Giles, Kris
See Nielsen, Helen Berniece
Giles, Mary E(lizabeth) 1934- 108
Giles, Molly 1942- CLC-39
Giles, Raymond
See Holt, John (Robert)
Giles, Robert H(artmann) 1933-
Brief entry 122
Gilfillan, Edward S(mith), Jr. 1906- 57-60
Gilfond, Henry CANR-24
Earlier sketches in CA 23-24R, CANR-9
See also SATA 2
Gilford, C(harles) B(ernard) 1920- 17-18R
Gilford, Madeline Lee 1923- 85-88
Gilge, Jeanette 1924- 61-64
See also SATA 22
Gilgen, Albert R(udolph) 1930- 37-40R
Gilgoff, Alice 1946- 85-88
Gilgun, John F(rancis) 1935- 117
Gilhooley, Jack
See Gilhooley, John
Gilhooley, John 1940- 85-88
Gilhooley, Leonard 1921- 37-40R
Gilien, Sasha 1925(?)-1971 Obituary 33-36R
Giliomee, Hermann (Buhr) 1938- 102
Gilison, Jerome Martin 1935- 103
Gilkes, A(ntony) N(ewcombe) 1900- 5-6R
Gilkey, Langdon (Brown) 1919- CANR-7
Earlier sketch in CA 19-20R
Gilkyson, Bernice Kenyon 1898(?)-1982
Obituary 106
Gill, Alan
See Gillepsie, Alfred
Gill, Bartholomew
See McGarrity, Mark
Gill, Bob 1931- 4R
Gill, Brendan 1914- 73-76
Gill, (Ronald) Crispin 1916- CANR-12
Earlier sketch in CA 21-22R
Gill, David (Lawrence William) 1934- CANR-12
Earlier sketch in CA 29-32R
Gill, Derek (Lewis Theodore) 1919- CANR-19
Earlier sketches in CA 49-52, CANR-4
See also SATA 9
Gill, Dominic 1941- 106
Gill, (Arthur) Eric (Rowton Peter Joseph)
1882-1940 Brief entry 120
Gill, Evan Robertson 1892- 11-12R
Gill, Frederick (Cyril) 1898- 7-8R
Gill, I(nayat) K(hera) 1924- 61-64
Gill, Jerry H. 1933- CANR-12
Earlier sketch in CA 33-36R
Gill, John Edward 1938- 106
Gill, Joseph 1901- CANR-3
Earlier sketch in CA 9-10R
Gill, Kay 1944- 111
Gill, Margery Jean 1925- SATA-22
Gill, Merton M(ax) 1914- 122
Gill, Patrick
See Creasey, John
Gill, Peter 1939- CANR-22
Earlier sketch in CA 103
Gill, Richard 1922- 41-44R
Gill, Richard T(homas) 1927- CANR-13
Earlier sketch in CA 23-24R
Gill, Traviss 1891- CAP-1
Earlier sketch in CA 13-14
Gillan, Garth J. 1939- 102
Gillan, Patricia Wagstaff 1936- 102
Gillchrest, Muriel Noyes 1905- 25-28R
Gillelan, G(eorge) Howard 1917- CANR-6
Earlier sketch in CA 2R
Gillen, Lucy
See Stratton, Rebecca
Gillen, Mollie 1908- 41-44R
Gillen, Robert L(eonard) 1946- 114
Gillenson, Lewis William 1918- 7-8R
Giller, Robert M(aynard) 1942- 124
Gilles, Albert S(imeon), Sr. 1888- 57-60
Gilles, Anthony E(ugene) 1945- 114
Gilles, Daniel 1917- 103
Gillese, John Patrick 1920- 13-14R
Gillespie, A(braham) Lincoln, Jr.
1895-1950 Brief entry 115
See also DLB 4
Gillespie, Alfred 1924- 77-80
Gillespie, Dizzy
See Gillespie, John Birks
Gillespie, Gerald 1933- CANR-10
Earlier sketch in CA 25-28R
Gillespie, I(ris) S(ylvia) 1923- 65-68
Gillespie, James E(rnest), Jr. 1940- 53-56
Gillespie, Janet Wicks 1913- 7-8R
Gillespie, John Birks 1917- 104
Gillespie, John E. 1921- 17-18R
Gillespie, John T(homas) 1928- CANR-13
Earlier sketch in CA 73-76
Gillespie, Kingsley 1895-1984 Obituary 112
Gillespie, Link
See Gillespie, A(braham) Lincoln, Jr.
Gillespie, Marcia Ann AITN-2
Gillespie, Neal C(ephas) 1933- 33-36R
Gillespie, Robert B(ryne) 1917- 110
Gillespie, Robert W. 1922(?)-1983
Obituary 110
Gillespie, Susan
See Turton-Jones, Edith Constance
(Bradshaw)
Gillet, Lev 1892(?)-1980 Obituary 97-100
Gillett, Charlie 1942- 33-36R
Gillett, Eric (Walkey) 1893-1978 .... CANR-3
Earlier sketch in CA 7-8R
Gillett, J(ohn) D(avid) 1913- 49-52
Gillett, Margaret 1930- CANR-17
Earlier sketches in CA 1R, CANR-2
Gillett, Mary (Bledsoe) CAP-2
Earlier sketch in CA 25-28
See also SATA 7
Gillette, Arnold S(impson) 1904- CANR-2
Earlier sketch in CA 1R
Gillette, Henry Sampson 1915- 7-8R
See also SATA 14
Gillette, J(ay) Michael 1939- 113
Gillette, Michael
See Gillette, J(ay) Michael
Gillette, Paul 1938- 53-56
Gillette, Virginia M(ary) 1920- 57-60
Gillette, William 1933- 108
Gillham, Bill
See Gillham, W(illiam) E(dwin) C(harles)
Gillham, D. G. 1921- 21-22R
Gillham, W(illiam) E(dwin) C(harles) 1936- .. 113
See also SATA 42
Gilliam, Dorothy B(utler) 1936- 97-100
Gilliam, Florence DLB-4
Gilliam, Stan 1946- SATA-35, 39
Gilliam, Terry (Vance) 1940- 113
Brief entry 108
See also CLC 21
Gillian, Jerry
See Gilliam, Terry (Vance)
Gillian, Kay
See Smith, Kay Nolte
Gilliatt, Penelope (Ann Douglass) 1932- .. 15-16R
See also DLB 14
See also CLC 2, 10, 13
See also AITN 2
Gillie, Christopher 1914- 102
Gillie, Oliver (John) 1937- CANR-12
Earlier sketch in CA 65-68
Gillies, John 1925- CANR-12
Earlier sketch in CA 73-76
Gillies, Mary Davis 1900- CAP-2
Earlier sketch in CA 25-28
Gilligan, Edmund 1898-1973 Obituary 45-48
Gilligan, Sonja Carl 1936- 57-60
Gilliland, Alexis A(rnaldus) 1931- 108
Gilliland, Charles
See Muller, Charles G(eorge Geoffrey)
Gilliland, Charles Edward, Jr. 1916-1975
Obituary 110
Gilliland, (Cleburne) Hap 1918- CANR-5
Earlier sketch in CA 53-56
Gillin, Caroline J(ulia) 1932- 45-48
Gillin, Donald George 1930- 33-36R
Gillin, John P(hilip) 1907-1973 .... 41-44R
Obituary 45-48
Gillingham, John (Bennett) 1940- CANR-18
Earlier sketch in CA 97-100
Gillings, Richard John 1902- 77-80
Gillion, Kenneth Lowell (Oliver) 1929- 93-96
Gillis, Daniel 1935- 106
Gillis, Everett A(lden) 1914- CANR-15
Earlier sketch in CA 41-44R
Gillis, John R. 1939- 33-36R
Gillis, Patricia Ingle 1932- Brief entry 108
Gillis, Phyllis 1945- 116
Gillispie, Charles C(oulston) 1918- 13-14R
Gillman, Olga Marjorie 1894- 7-8R
Gillman, Richard 1929- 17-18R
Gillmer, Thomas C(harles) 1911- CANR-6
Earlier sketch in CA 57-60
Gillmer, Tom
See Gillmer, Thomas C(harles)
Gillmor, C(harles) Stewart 1938- 45-48
Gillmor, Daniel S. 1917(?)-1975 Obituary .. 61-64
Gillmor, Donald M(iles) 1926- 41-44R
Gillmor, Frances 1903- CAP-2
Earlier sketch in CA 17-18
Gillmore, David 1934- 23-24R
Gillmore, Margalo 1897-1986 Obituary 119
Gillon, Adam 1921- CANR-8
Earlier sketch in CA 7-8R
Gillon, Diana (Pleasance Case) 1915- 15-16R
Gillon, Meir Selig 1907- 15-16R
Gillott, Jacky 1939-1980 102
See also DLB 14
Gillquist, Peter E. 1938- CANR-12
Earlier sketch in CA 29-32R
Gilluly, James 1896-1980 Obituary 102
Gillum, Helen L(ouise) 1909- 69-72
Gilman, C(harles) Malcolm B(rookfield)
1898-1981 107
Gilman, Caroline (Howard) 1794-1888 .... DLB-3
Gilman, Charlotte (Anna) Perkins (Stetson)
1860-1935 Brief entry 106
See also TCLC 9
Gilman, Dorothy
See Butters, Dorothy Gilman
Gilman, Esther 1925- SATA-15
Gilman, George G.
See Harknett, Terry
Gilman, J. D.
See Fishman, Jack
and Orgill, Douglas
Gilman, James
See Gilmore, Joseph L(ee)
Gilman, Richard 1925- CANR-5
Earlier sketch in CA 53-56
Gilman, Robert Cham
See Coppel, Alfred
Gilman, Sander L(awrence) 1944- CANR-5
Earlier sketch in CA 53-56
Gilman, Stephen 1917- 107
Gilman, William 1909-1978 .... 3R
Gilman, William H(enry) 1911-1976 .... 17-18R
Obituary 65-68
Gilmer, Ann
See Ross, W(illiam) E(dward) D(aniel)
Gilmer, B(everley) von Haller 1909- CANR-5
Earlier sketch in CA 5-6R
Gilmer, Elizabeth Meriwether
1861(?)-1951 Brief entry 114
See also DLB 29
Gilmer, Francis Walker 1790-1826 .... DLB-37
Gilmer, (Frank) Walker 1935- 33-36R
Gilmer, Wesley, Jr. 1928- 115
Gilmore, Alec 1928- 93-96
Gilmore, Al-Tony 1946- CANR-7
Earlier sketch in CA 57-60
Gilmore, Cecile
See MacMillan, Cecile
Gilmore, Charles L(ee) 33-36R
Gilmore, Christopher Cook 1940- CANR-17
Earlier sketch in CA 101
Gilmore, Daniel F(rancis) 1922- 65-68
Gilmore, Don 1930- 29-32R
Gilmore, Eddy (Lanier King) 1907- 7-8R
Gilmore, Edith Spacil 1920- 4R
Gilmore, Gene 1920- 33-36R
Gilmore, Grant 1910-1982 Obituary 111
Gilmore, Harold L(awrence) 1931- 53-56
Gilmore, Haydn 1928- 85-88
Gilmore, Iris 1900- 97-100
See also SATA 22
Gilmore, J. Herbert, Jr. 1925- 33-36R
Gilmore, Jene Carlton 1933- 33-36R
Gilmore, John 1935- 25-28R
Gilmore, Joseph L(ee) 1929- 81-84
Gilmore, Maeve ?-1983 102
Obituary 110
Gilmore, Mary (Jean Cameron) 1865-1962 .. 114
See also SATA 49
Gilmore, Richard 1943- 107
Gilmore, Thomas B(arry, Jr.) 1932- 73-76
Gilmore, William J(ames) 1945- 120
Gilmour, David 1944- CLC-35
Gilmour, Garth (Hamilton) 1925- CAP-1
Earlier sketch in CA 9-10
Gilmour, H. B. 1939- 81-84
Gilmour, Robert S(cott) 1940- 69-72
Gilmour, Robin 1943- 124
Gilner, Elias 1888(?)-1976 Obituary 65-68
Gilot, Francoise 1921- 108
Gilpatrick, Eleanor G(ottesfocht) 1930- .. CANR-9
Earlier sketch in CA 23-24R
Gilpin, Alan 1924- CANR-11
Earlier sketch in CA 25-28R
Gilpin, Alec Richard 1920- 45-48
Gilpin, John 1930-1983 Obituary 114
Gilpin, Laura 1891-1979 Obituary 111
Gilpin, Robert G., Jr. 1930- 5-6R
Gilroy, Frank D(aniel) 1925- 81-84
See also DLB 7
See also CLC 2
Gilroy, Harry 1908(?)-1981 Obituary 104
Gilroy, Thomas Laurence 1951- 103
Gilroy, Tom
See Gilroy, Thomas Laurence
Gilson, Barbara
See Gilson, Charles James Louis
Gilson, Charles James Louis 1878-1943 . YABC-2
Gilson, Etienne Henry 1884-1978 102
Obituary 81-84
Gilson, Goodwin Woodrow 1918- 17-18R
Gilson, Jamie 1933- 111
See also SATA 34, 37
Gilson, Thomas Q(uinleven) 1916- 7-8R
Gilstrap, Robert L(awrence) 1933- 9-10R
Gilzean, Elizabeth Houghton Blanchet
1913- 9-10R
Gimbel, John 1922- CANR-2
Earlier sketch in CA 2R
Gimbutas, Marija (Alseika) 1921- 13-14R
Gimmestad, Victor E(dward) 1912-1982 ... 57-60
Obituary 109
Gimpel, Herbert J. 1915- 17-18R
Gimpel, Jean 1918- 69-72
Gimson, Alfred Charles 1917-1985 .... 7-8R
Obituary 116
Ginandes, Shepard 1928- 41-44R
Ginder, Richard 1914- 65-68
Gindin, James 1926- CANR-2
Earlier sketch in CA 5-6R
Giner de los Rios, Francisco 1839-1915
Brief entry 105
Gingell, Benjamin Broughton 1924- 104
Ginger, Ann Fagan 1925- CANR-19
Earlier sketches in CA 53-56, CANR-4
Ginger, Helen 1916- 19-20R
Ginger, John 1933- 25-28R
Gingerich, Martin E(llsworth) 1933- 118
Gingerich, Melvin 1902-1975 .... CAP-2
Earlier sketch in CA 25-28
Gingerich, Owen (Jay) 1930- CANR-22
Earlier sketches in CA 53-56, CANR-5
Ginglend, David R. 1913- 17-18R
Gingold, Hermione (Ferdinanda)
1897-1987 .... 7-8R
Obituary 122
Gingrich, Arnold 1903-1976 .... 13-14R
Obituary 69-72
Gingrich, F(elix) Wilbur 1901- CAP-2
Earlier sketch in CA 17-18
Giniger, Carol Virginia Wilkins
1929(?)-1985 Obituary 117
Giniger, Kenneth Seeman 1919- CANR-3
Earlier sketch in CA 7-8R
Ginn, Robert Jay, Jr. 1946- 107
Ginnings, Harriett W.
See Harriett
Ginns, Patsy (Lee) M(oore) 1937- 69-72
Ginns, Ronald 1896- CAP-1
Earlier sketch in CA 11-12
Ginori Lisci, Leonardo 1908-1987
Obituary 122
Ginott, Haim G. 1922-1973 Obituary 45-48
Ginsberg, Allen 1926- CANR-2
Earlier sketch in CA 2R
See also DLB 5, 16
See also CDALB 1941-1968
See also CLC 1, 2, 3, 4, 6, 13, 36
See also AITN 1
Ginsberg, Benjamin 1947- 121
Ginsberg, Joanne
See Summerfield, Joanne
Ginsberg, Leon H(erman) 1936- 105
Ginsberg, Louis 1895-1976 .... 15-16R
Obituary 65-68
Ginsberg, Morris 1889-1970 Obituary 116
Ginsberg, Robert 1937- 25-28R
Ginsburg, Herbert (Paul) 1939- CANR-12
Earlier sketch in CA 73-76
Ginsburg, Mirra CANR-11
Earlier sketch in CA 19-20R
See also SATA 6
Ginsburg, Ruth Bader 1933- 53-56
Ginsburg, Seymour 1927- CANR-13
Earlier sketch in CA 21-22R
Ginsburgh, Robert N(eville) 1923- 15-16R
Ginsburgs, George 1932- CANR-4
Earlier sketch in CA 53-56
Ginsbury, Norman 1902- 7-8R
Ginter, Maria 1922- 105
Ginther, John R(obert) 1922- Brief entry ... 107
Gintis, Herbert 1940- 57-60
Ginzberg, Eli 1911- CANR-8
Earlier sketch in CA 5-6R
Ginzberg, Yevgeniya 1906(?)-1977
Obituary 69-72
Ginzburg, Natalia 1916- 85-88
See also CLC 5, 11
Ginzburg, Ralph 1929- 21-22R
Giono, Jean 1895-1970 .... CANR-2
Obituary 29-32R
Earlier sketch in CA 45-48
See also CLC 4, 11
Giordan, Alma Roberts 1917- 57-60
Giordan, Marion ?-1983 Obituary 110
Giordanetti, Elmo 1925-1984 Obituary 113
Giorno, John 1936- 33-36R
Gioseffi, Daniela 1941- CANR-3
Earlier sketch in CA 45-48
Giovacchini, Peter L(ouis) 1922- 101
Giovannetti, Alberto 1913- 9-10R
Giovanni, Nikki 1943- CANR-18
Earlier sketch in CA 29-32R
See also CAAS 6
See also SATA 24
See also DLB 5, 41
See also CLC 2, 4, 19
See also CLR 6
See also AITN 1
Giovannitti, Len 1920- 15-16R
Giovanopoulos, Paul (Arthur) 1939- SATA-7
Giovene, Andrea 1904- 85-88
See also CLC 7
Gipe, George 1933-1986 77-80
Obituary 120
Gippius, Zinaida (Nikolayevna) 1869-1945
Brief entry 106
Gipson, Fred(erick Benjamin)
1908-1973 .... CANR-3
Obituary 45-48
Earlier sketch in CA 3R
See also SATA 2, 24
Gipson, John (Durwood) 1932- 61-64
Gipson, Lawrence Henry 1880-1971 .... CANR-3
Obituary 33-36R
Earlier sketch in CA 7-8R
See also DLB 17
Giragosian, Newman H. 1922- 93-96
Girard, Hazel Batten 1901- 112
Girard, Henri Georges Charles Achille
1917-1987 Obituary 121
Girard, James P(reston) 1944- 69-72
Girard, Joe 1928- CANR-9
Earlier sketch in CA 77-80
Girard, Linda (Walvoord) 1942- 114
See also SATA 41
Girard, Marvin Eugene 1924- 112
Girard, Mustang Marve
See Girard, Marvin Eugene
Girard, Rene N(oel) 1923- CANR-4
Earlier sketch in CA 9-10R
Girard, Robert C(olby) 1932- 101
Girardi, Joe
See Girard, Joe
Girardot, Norman J(ohn) 1943- 110
Giraud, Marcel 1900- 77-80
Giraudoux, (Hippolyte) Jean 1882-1944
Brief entry 104
See also DLB 65
See also TCLC 2, 7
Girdlestone, Cuthbert Morton
1895-1975 .... CANR-3
Obituary 65-68
Earlier sketch in CA 7-8R
Girion, Barbara 1937- CANR-15
Earlier sketch in CA 85-88
See also SATA 26
Girling, John L(awrence) S(cott) 1926- 106
Girling, Richard 1945- 108
Girod, Gerald R(alph) 1939- 53-56
Girod, Gordon H. 1920- 1R
Girodias, Maurice 1919- Brief entry 112
Girodo, Michel 1945- 81-84
Giron, Manuel Buendia Tellez
1926(?)-1984 Obituary 112
Gironella, Jose Maria 1917- 101
See also CLC 11

Giroud, Francoise 1916- ... CANR-17
Earlier sketch in CA 81-84
See also AITN 1
Giroux, E. X.
See Shannon, Doris
Giroux, Henry A(rmand) 1943- ... 112
Giroux, Joan 1922- ... 93-96
Giroux, Robert 1914- ... 107
Girson, Rochelle ... 23-24R
Girtin, Thomas 1913- ... 9-10R
Girtin, Tom
See Girtin, Thomas
Girvan, Helen (Masterman) 1891- ... 73-76
Girvetz, Harry K(enneth) 1910-1974
Obituary ... 111
Girzaitis, Loretta 1920- ... CANR-2
Earlier sketch in CA 49-52
Giscard, Valery
See Giscard d'Estaing, Valery
Giscard d'Estaing, Valery 1926-
Brief entry ... 111
Gish, Arthur G. 1939- ... 29-32R
Gishford, Anthony (Joseph) 1908-1975
Obituary ... 53-56
Gisolfi, Anthony M. 1909- ... CAP-2
Earlier sketch in CA 17-18
Gisselquist, David 1947- ... 112
Gissen, Max 1909(?)-1984 Obituary ... 114
Gissing, George (Robert) 1857-1903
Brief entry ... 105
See also DLB 18
See also TCLC 3, 24
Gist, Noel P(itts) 1899- ... CANR-1
Earlier sketch in CA 2R
Gist, Ronald R. 1932- ... 23-24R
Gitchoff, G(eorge) Thomas 1938- ... 53-56
Gitchoff, Tom
See Gitchoff, G(eorge) Thomas
Gitelman, Zvi Y(echiel) 1940- Brief entry ... 112
Gitin, David (Daniel) 1941- ... CANR-2
Earlier sketch in CA 49-52
Gitin, Maria (Brians) 1946- ... CANR-8
Earlier sketch in CA 61-64
Gitisetan, Dariush ... 118
Gitisetan, Darrin Dariush
See Gitisetan, Dariush
Gitlin, Murray 1903- ... 4R
Gitlin, Todd 1943- ... 29-32R
Gitlow, A(braham) Leo 1918- ... 1R
Gitlow, Benjamin 1891-1965 Obituary ... 89-92
Gittell, Marilyn 1931- ... CANR-9
Earlier sketch in CA 21-22R
Gittelsohn, Roland B(ertram) 1910- ... CANR-2
Earlier sketch in CA 5-6R
Gittelson, Celia ... 105
Gitter, A. George 1926- ... 102
Gittinger, J(ames) Price ... 41-44R
Gittings, Jo (Grenville) Manton 1919- ... CANR-3
Earlier sketch in CA 5-6R
See also SATA 3
Gittings, John 1938- ... CANR-9
Earlier sketch in CA 21-22R
Gittings, Robert (William Victor) 1911- ... 25-28R
See also SATA 6
Gittins, Diana 1946- ... 113
Gittleman, Edwin 1929- ... 21-22R
Gittleman, Sol 1934- ... 65-68
Gittler, Joseph B(ertram) 1912- ... 37-40R
Giudici, Ann Couper 1929- ... 73-76
Giuliani, George A. 1938- ... 120
Giunti, Renato 1905-1983 Obituary ... 109
Giurlani, Aldo
See Palazzeschi, Aldo
Giuseppi, John (Anthony) 1900- ... CAP-2
Earlier sketch in CA 23-24
Giuttari, Theodore Richard 1931- ... 29-32R
Givens, David B(radley) 1944- ... 119
Givens, Janet E(aton) 1932- ... 111
Givens, John 1943- ... 77-80
Givner, Abraham 1944- ... 89-92
Givner, Joan Mary 1936- ... 108
Gizycka, Eleanor M.
See Patterson, Eleanor Medill
Gizzi, Michael 1949- ... 117
Glaab, Charles N(elson) 1927- ... CANR-8
Earlier sketch in CA 5-6R
Glad, Betty 1929- ... 21-22R
Glad, Donald 1915- ... 15-16R
Glad, Paul W(ilbur) 1926- ... 73-76
Gladden, E(dgar) Norman 1897- ... 21-22R
Gladden, Vivianne Cervantes 1927- ... 102
Glade, William P(atton), Jr. 1929- ... 41-44R
Gladilin, Anatoly (Tikhonovich) 1935- ... CANR-18
Earlier sketch in CA 101
Gladish, David F(rancis) 1928- ... 41-44R
Gladkov, Fyodor (Vasilyevich)
1883-1958 ... TCLC-27
Gladney Glasserow, Marion 1925- ... 118
Gladstone, Arthur M. 1921- ... 97-100
Gladstone, Eve
See Werner, Herma
Gladstone, Gary 1935- ... 29-32R
See also SATA 12
Gladstone, Josephine 1938- ... 21-22R
Gladstone, M(yron) J. 1923- ... 53-56
See also SATA 37
Gladstone, Maggie
See Gladstone, Arthur M.
Gladstone, Meredith 1939- ... 69-72
Gladstone, William Ewart 1809-1898 ... DLB-57
Gladwin, William Zachary
See Zollinger, Gulielma
Gladych, B. Michael 1910- ... 5-6R
Glaettli, Walter E(ric) 1920- ... 21-22R
Glahe, Fred R(ufus) 1934- ... CANR-14
Earlier sketch in CA 37-40R
Glaister, John 1892-1971 Obituary ... 104
Glamis, Walter
See Schachner, Nat(han)
Glanville, Brian (Lester) 1931- ... CANR-3
Earlier sketch in CA 7-8R
See also SATA 42
See also DLB 15
See also CLC 6
Glanville, Maxwell 1918- ... 85-88
Glanville, Ranulph 1946- ... 114
Glanz, Edward C(oleman) 1924- ... 1R
Glanz, Rudolf 1892-1978 ... CANR-3
Earlier sketch in CA 49-52
Glanzman, Louis S. 1922- ... SATA-36
Glapthorne, Henry 1610-1643(?) ... DLB-58
Glaser, Daniel 1918- ... 61-64
Glaser, Dianne E(lizabeth) 1937- ... 77-80
See also SATA 31, 50
Glaser, E(ric) M(ichael) 1913- ... 23-24R
Glaser, Edward 1918-1972 Obituary ... 37-40R
Glaser, Eleanor Dorothy
See Zonik, Eleanor Dorothy
Glaser, Elton 1945- ... 111
Glaser, Eva Schocken 1918-1982 Obituary ... 105
Glaser, Isabel Joshlin 1929- ... 77-80
Glaser, Kurt 1914- ... CANR-5
Earlier sketch in CA 1R
Glaser, Lynn 1943- ... 21-22R
Glaser, Milton 1929- ... CANR-11
Earlier sketch in CA 17-18R
See also SATA 11
Glaser, Robert 1921- ... CANR-7
Earlier sketch in CA 17-18R
Glaser, Rollin Oliver 1932- ... CANR-10
Earlier sketch in CA 25-28R
Glaser, William A(rnold) 1925- ... CANR-21
Earlier sketches in CA 1R, CANR-6
Glasgow, Douglas G. ... 108
Glasgow, Ellen (Anderson Gholson)
1873(?)-1945 Brief entry ... 104
See also DLB 9, 12
See also TCLC 2, 7
Glasgow, Eric 1924- ... 69-72
Glasgow, Gordon H(enry) H(arper)
1926- ... 29-32R
Glasgow, Jack
See Larson, Doran
Glasgow, Mary Cecilia 1905-1983
Obituary ... 111
Glasheen, Adaline 1920- ... 101
Glasheen, Patrick 1897- ... CAP-1
Earlier sketch in CA 13-14
Glaskin, G(erald) M(arcus) 1923- ... CANR-5
Earlier sketch in CA 53-56
Glaskowsky, Nicholas A(lexander), Jr.
1928- ... CANR-3
Earlier sketch in CA 5-6R
Glaspell, Susan (Keating) 1882(?)-1948
Brief entry ... 110
See also YABC 2
See also DLB 7, 9
Glasrud, Bruce (Alden) 1940- ... 41-44R
Glass, Albert J(ulius) 1908-1983 Obituary ... 109
Glass, Andrew ... SATA-46
Glass, Andrew J(ames) 1935- ... 65-68
Glass, Bill 1935- ... CANR-13
Earlier sketch in CA 73-76
Glass, David Victor 1911-1978 ... 85-88
Obituary ... 81-84
Glass, Ian Cameron 1926- ... 77-80
Glass, Joanna (McClelland) 1936- ... 81-84
Glass, John F(ranklin) 1936- ... 53-56
Glass, Justine C.
See Corrall, Alice Enid
Glass, Malcolm (Sanford) 1936- ... CANR-20
Earlier sketch in CA 104
Glass, Montague (Marsden) 1877-1934
Brief entry ... 117
See also DLB 11
Glass, Sandra
See Shea, Robert (Joseph)
Glass, Stanley T(homas) 1932- ... 21-22R
Glassberg, B(ertrand) Y(ounker)
1902-19(?) ... CAP-1
Earlier sketch in CA 15-16
Glassburner, Bruce 1920- ... 33-36R
Glassco, John 1909-1981 ... CANR-15
Obituary ... 102
Earlier sketch in CA 15-16R
See also CLC 9
Glasscock, Amnesia
See Steinbeck, John (Ernst)
Glasscock, Anne Bonner 1924- ... 3R
Glasse, Robert Marshall 1929- ... 29-32R
Glasser, Allen 1918- ... 9-10R
Glasser, Paul H(arold) 1929- ... CANR-15
Earlier sketch in CA 29-32R
Glasser, Ronald J. 1940(?)- ... CLC-37
Glasser, Selma ... 110
Glasser, Stephen A(ndrew) 1943- ... 53-56
Glasser, William 1925- ... 73-76
Glasserow, Mario N.
See Gladney Glasserow, Marion
Glasserow, Marion Gladney
See Gladney Glasserow, Marion
Glassford, Wilfred
See McNeilly, Wilfred Glassford
Glassgold, Peter 1939- ... 103
Glassie, Henry H(aywood) 1914-1987
Obituary ... 124
Glassman, Bernard Tetsugen 1939- ... 112
Glassman, Jon David 1944- ... 69-72
Glassman, Michael 1899- ... 15-16R
Glassman, Peter Joel 1945- ... 113
Glassman, Ronald M. 1937- Brief entry ... 111
Glassner, Lester 1939- ... 107
Glassner, Martin Ira 1932- ... CANR-15
Earlier sketch in CA 41-44R
Glasson, Thomas Francis 1906- ... CAP-1
Earlier sketch in CA 9-10
Glassop, (Jack) Lawson 1913-1966 ... CAP-1
Earlier sketch in CA 9-10
Glasstone, Victor 1924- ... CANR-10
Earlier sketch in CA 65-68
Glatstein, Jacob 1896-1971 Obituary ... 33-36R
Glatthorn, Allan A. 1924- ... 15-16R
Glatzer, Hal 1946- ... 57-60
Glatzer, Nahum Norbert 1903- ... CANR-7
Earlier sketch in CA 13-14R
Glauber, Uta (Heil) 1936- ... 29-32R
See also SATA 17
Glaus, Marlene 1933- ... 23-24R
Glauser, Friedrich 1896-1938 ... DLB-56
Glavin, John P(atrick) 1933- ... 57-60
Glazar, Bob 1954- ... 115
Glaze, Andrew (Louis III) 1920- ... CANR-24
Earlier sketches in CA 17-18R, CANR-8
Glaze, Eleanor 1930- ... 49-52
Glaze, Thomas E(dward) 1914- ... 2R
Glazebrook, G(eorge) P(arkin) de
T(wenebrokes) 1899- ... 102
Glazebrook, Philip 1937- ... 29-32R
Glazener, Mary U(nderwood) 1921- ... 19-20R
Glazer, Daphne (Fae) 1938- ... 119
Glazer, Nathan 1923- ... 5-6R
Glazer, Nona Y.
See Glazer-Malbin, Nona
Glazer, Sidney 1905-1983 ... 1R
Obituary ... 111
Glazer, Tom 1914- ... CANR-8
Earlier sketch in CA 61-64
See also SATA 9
Glazer-Malbin, Nona 1932- ... 33-36R
Glazier, Kenneth MacLean 1912- ... 11-12R
Glazier, Lyle (Edward) 1911- ... 37-40R
Glazier, Stephen 1947- ... 108
Glazner, Joseph Mark 1945- ... 104
Gleadow, Rupert Seeley 1909-1974 ... 9-10R
Obituary ... 103
Gleasner, Diana (Cottle) 1936- ... CANR-15
Earlier sketch in CA 65-68
See also SATA 29
Gleason, Abbott 1938- ... CANR-21
Earlier sketch in CA 104
Gleason, Eugene Franklin 1914- ... 4R
Gleason, Gene
See Gleason, Eugene Franklin
Gleason, Harold 1892- ... CAP-1
Earlier sketch in CA 9-10
Gleason, John (Marquis) 1942- ... 107
Gleason, John J(ames), Jr. 1934- ... 120
Gleason, Judith 1929- ... CANR-9
Earlier sketch in CA 61-64
See also SATA 24
Gleason, Ralph J(oseph) 1917-1975 ... 65-68
Obituary ... 61-64
Gleason, Robert 1945- ... 118
Gleason, Robert J(ames) 1906- ... 73-76
Gleason, Robert Walter 1917- ... CANR-4
Earlier sketch in CA 1R
Gleason, S(arel) Everett 1905-1974
Obituary ... 53-56
Gleaves, Robert M(ilnor) 1938- ... 53-56
Gleaves, Suzanne 1904- ... 11-12R
Gleckner, Robert Francis 1925- ... CANR-17
Earlier sketches in CA 3R, CANR-2
Gledhill, Alan 1895-1983 ... CAP-1
Obituary ... 110
Earlier sketch in CA 9-10
Gleeson, Ruth (Ryall) 1925- ... 9-10R
Gleiman, Lubomir 1923- ... 41-44R
Gleisser, Marcus D(avid) 1923- ... 19-20R
Gleitman, Lila R. 1929- ... 114
Glen, Duncan (Munro) 1933- ... CANR-12
Earlier sketch in CA 21-22R
Glen, Eugene
See Fawcett, F(rank) Dubrez
Glen, Frank Grenfell 1933- ... 106
Glen, J(ohn) Stanley 1907-1986 ... CAP-1
Obituary ... 118
Earlier sketch in CA 9-10
Glen, Robert S. 1925- ... 29-32R
Glenday, Alice 1920- ... 57-60
Glendenning, Donn
See Paine, Lauran (Bosworth)
Glendenning, Raymond Carl 1907-1974
Obituary ... 114
Glendinning, Richard 1917- ... 21-22R
See also SATA 24
Glendinning, Sally
See Glendinning, Sara W(ilson)
Glendinning, Sara W(ilson) 1913- ... CANR-2
Earlier sketch in CA 49-52
See also SATA 24
Glendinning, Victoria 1937- Brief entry ... 120
Glendon, Mary Ann 1938- ... 41-44R
Glenn, Armon 1912- ... 107
Glenn, Christine Genevieve 1947- ... 115
Glenn, Edmund S(tanislas) 1915- ... 113
Glenn, Frank 1901-1982 Obituary ... 106
Glenn, Harold T(heodore) 1910- ... CANR-5
Earlier sketch in CA 7-8R
Glenn, Jacob B. 1905-1974 ... CANR-4
Obituary ... 49-52
Earlier sketch in CA 9-10R
Glenn, James
See Paine, Lauran (Bosworth)
Glenn, Jerry (Hesmer, Jr.) 1938- ... 45-48
Glenn, Lois (Ruth) 1941- ... 61-64
Glenn, Mel 1943- ... 123
See also SATA 45
Glenn, Morton B(ernard) 1922- ... 61-64
Glenn, Norval Dwight 1933- ... 17-18R
Glennon, James 1900- ... 25-28R
Glennon, Maurade 1926- ... 25-28R
Glenny, Lyman A. 1918- ... CANR-7
Earlier sketch in CA 19-20R
Glenny, Michael Valentine 1927- ... 102
Gles, Margaret Breitmaier 1940- ... 57-60
See also SATA 22
Gleser, Goldine C(ohnberg) 1915- ... 17-18R
Gless, Darryl James 1945- ... 102
Glessing, Robert J(ohn) 1930- ... 29-32R
Gliauda, Jurgis 1906- ... CANR-3
Earlier sketch in CA 5-6R
Glick, Carl (Cannon) 1890-1971 ... 7-8R
Obituary ... 103
See also SATA 14
Glick, Edward Bernard 1929- ... CANR-8
Earlier sketch in CA 23-24R
Glick, G(arland) Wayne 1921- ... 25-28R
Glick, Paul C(harles) 1910- ... 5-6R
Glick, Paula Brown
See Brown, Paula
Glick, Ruth (Burtnick) 1942- ... CANR-16
Earlier sketch in CA 89-92
Glick, Thomas F(rederick) 1939- ... CANR-15
Earlier sketch in CA 29-32R
Glick, Virginia Kirkus 1893-1980 ... CAP-2
Obituary ... 101
Earlier sketch in CA 21-22
See also SATA 23
Glick, Wendell 1916- ... 111
Glickman, Albert S(eymour) 1923- ... 53-56
Glickman, Arthur P. 1940- ... 61-64
Glickman, Beatrice Marden 1919- ... 102
Glickman, S(teven) Craig 1947- ... 116
Glickman, Susan 1953- ... 116
Glicksberg, Charles Irving 1900- ... CANR-2
Earlier sketch in CA 1R
Glicksman, Abraham M(orton) 1911- ... 5-6R
Glidden, Frederick D(illey) 1908-1975 ... CAP-2
Obituary ... 61-64
Earlier sketch in CA 21-22
Glidden, Horace Knight 1901- ... CAP-1
Earlier sketch in CA 15-16
Glidewell, John Calvin 1919- ... CANR-23
Earlier sketches in CA 15-16R, CANR-7
Glieberman, Herbert A(llen) 1930- ... 112
Gliewe, Unada (Grace) 1927- ... CANR-12
Earlier sketch in CA 29-32R
See also SATA 3
Glikes, Erwin 1937- ... 15-16R
Glimcher, Arnold B. 1938- ... 81-84
Glines, Carroll V(ane), Jr. 1920- ... CANR-2
Earlier sketch in CA 2R
See also SATA 19
Gliozzo, Charles 1932- ... 45-48
Glissant, Edouard 1928- ... CLC-10
Glisson, Jerry (Lee) 1923- ... 113
Gloag, John (Edwards) 1896-1981 ... CANR-10
Obituary ... 104
Earlier sketch in CA 65-68
Gloag, Julian 1930- ... CANR-10
Earlier sketch in CA 65-68
See also CLC 40
See also AITN 1
Glob, Peter Vilhelm 1911-1985 ... 97-100
Obituary ... 117
Globe, Leah Ain 1900- ... 107
See also SATA 41
Glock, Charles Y(oung) 1919- ... CANR-5
Earlier sketch in CA 53-56
Glock, Marvin D(avid) 1912- ... 23-24R
Glogau, Art(hur H.) 1922- ... 53-56
Glogau, Lillian Flatow Fleischer 1925- ... 85-88
Glogowski, Maryruth F(rancine) P(helps)
1950- ... 120
Glorfeld, Louis E(arl) 1916- ... 53-56
Glos, Raymond E(ugene) 1903- ... 23-24R
Glovach, Linda 1947- ... CANR-14
Earlier sketch in CA 37-40R
See also SATA 7
Glover, Albert Gould 1942- ... 89-92
Glover, Bob
See Glover, Robert H.
Glover, Denis (James Matthews)
1912-1980 ... 77-80
Obituary ... 101
See also SATA 7
Glover, Donald E(llsworth) 1933- ... 116
Glover, Harry 1912- ... 77-80
Glover, Janice 1919- ... 17-18R
Glover, John D(esmond) 1915- ... CANR-2
Earlier sketch in CA 5-6R
Glover, Judith 1943- ... CANR-22
Earlier sketch in CA 106
Glover, Leland E(llis) 1917- ... 9-10R
Glover, Michael 1922- ... CANR-23
Earlier sketches in CA 19-20R, CANR-8
Glover, Robert H. 1946- ... 116
Glover, (David) Tony "Harp Dog"
1939- ... 15-16R
Glowacki, Janusz 1938- ... 116
Glubb, John Bagot 1897-1986 ... CANR-5
Obituary ... 118
Earlier sketch in CA 9-10R
Glubb Pasha
See Glubb, John Bagot
Glubok, Shirley (Astor) 1933- ... CANR-4
Earlier sketch in CA 5-6R
See also SATA 6
See also CLR 1
Gluck, Felix 1923-1981 Obituary ... 103
See also SATA 25
Gluck, Herb 1925- ... CANR-2
Earlier sketch in CA 45-48
Gluck, Jay 1927- ... CANR-12
Earlier sketch in CA 21-22R
Gluck, Louise 1943- ... 33-36R
See also DLB 5
See also CLC 7, 22, 44

Gluck, Robert 1947- ... 113
Gluckin, Doreen Sandra 1949- ... 108
Gluckman, Max 1911-1975 ... 9-10R
Obituary ... 57-60
Glucksberg, Harold 1939- ... 105
Glueck, Eleanor T(ouroff) 1898-1972 ... CANR-9
Obituary ... 37-40R
Earlier sketches in CA 17-18, CAP-2
Glueck, Louise
See Gluck, Louise
See also DLB 5
See also CLC 7, 22
Glueck, Nelson 1900-1971 ... CAP-2
Earlier sketch in CA 17-18
Glueck, Sheldon 1896-1980 ... CANR-9
Obituary ... 97-100
Earlier sketch in CA 5-6R
Glueck, William Frank 1934- ... 33-36R
Glueckauf, Eugen 1906-1981 Obituary ... 108
Gluss, Brian 1930- ... 104
Glustrom, Simon W. 1924- ... 21-22R
Glut, Donald F(rank) 1944- ... CANR-13
Earlier sketch in CA 33-36R
Gluyas, Constance 1920- Brief entry ... 115
Gluzman, Brian
See Gluss, Brian
Glyn, Anthony 1922- ... 53-56
Glyn, Caroline 1947- ... CANR-5
Earlier sketch in CA 11-12R
Glyn, Richard Hamilton 1907-1980 ... 105
Obituary ... 102
Glynn, James A. 1941- ... 57-60
Glynn, Jeanne Davis 1932- ... 29-32R
Glynn, Prudence (Loveday) 1935-1986
Obituary ... 120
Glynn, Thomas P(eter) 1935- ... 93-96
Glynne-Jones, M(arjorie) L(ilian) 1936-
Brief entry ... 111
Glynne-Jones, William 1907- ... 7-8R
See also SATA 11
Gmelch, George 1944- ... 103
Gmelch, Sharon Bohn 1947- ... 103
Gmelch, Walter H(oward) 1947- ... 112
Gnaegy, Charles 1938- ... 89-92
Gnagey, Thomas D(avid) 1938- ... 49-52
Gnagy, Jon
See Gnagy, Michael Jacques
Gnagy, Michael Jacques 1907(?)-1981
Obituary ... 103
Gnarowski, Michael 1934- ... 41-44R
Gniffke, Rudolf
See Hartmann, Rudolf A.
Gnosticus
See Weschcke, Carl L(ouis)
Gnuse, Robert K(arl) 1947- ... 121
Go, Puan Seng 1904- ... CAP-2
Earlier sketch in CA 29-32
Goacher, Denis 1925- ... 104
Goaman, Muriel
See Cox, Edith Muriel
Gobar, Ash 1930- ... 41-44R
Gobbato, Imero 1923- ... SATA-39
Gobbi, Tito 1915-1984 Obituary ... 112
Brief entry ... 105
Goble, Dorothy ... 93-96
See also SATA 26
Goble, Frank G. 1917- ... 112
Goble, (Lloyd) Neil 1933- ... 29-32R
Goble, Paul 1933- ... CANR-16
Earlier sketch in CA 93-96
See also SATA 25
Goble, Warwick (?)-1943 ... SATA-46
Gocek, Matilda A(rkenbout) 1923- ... CANR-1
Earlier sketch in CA 49-52
Gockel, Herman W. 1906- ... CANR-1
Earlier sketch in CA 1R
Godard, Jean-Luc 1930- ... 93-96
See also CLC 20
Godbold, E(dward) Stanly, Jr. 1942- ... 37-40R
Godbout, Jacques 1933- ... DLB-53
Goddard, Alfred
See Harper, Carol Ely
Goddard, Burton L(eslie) 1910- ... 23-24R
Goddard, Donald 1934- ... CANR-11
Earlier sketch in CA 17-18R
Goddard, Gladys Benjamin 1881(?)-1976
Obituary ... 61-64
Goddard, J(ack) R. 1930- ... 29-32R
Goddard, Kenneth (William) 1946- ... 110
Goddard, Morrill 1865-1937 ... DLB-25
Goddard, Robert Hutchings 1882-1945
Brief entry ... 118
Goddard, William 1740-1817 ... DLB-43
Godden, Geoffrey 1929- ... 102
Godden, Jon 1906-1984 ... 77-80
Obituary ... 112
Godden, Rumer 1907- ... CANR-4
Earlier sketch in CA 7-8R
See also SATA 3, 36
Gode, Alexander
See Gode von Aesch, Alexander
(Gottfried Friedrich)
Godechot, Jacques Leon 1907- ... CANR-9
Earlier sketch in CA 65-68
Godefroy, Vincent 1912- ... 69-72
Godel, Kurt
See Goedel, Kurt
Gode von Aesch, Alexander (Gottfried
Friedrich) 1906-1970 ... CAP-1
Earlier sketch in CA 9-10
See also SATA 14
Godey, John
See Freedgood, Morton
Godfrey, Cuthbert John ... 7-8R
Godfrey, (William) Dave 1938- ... CANR-11
Earlier sketch in CA 69-72
See also DLB 60
Godfrey, Eleanor S(mith) 1914- ... 69-72
Godfrey, Ellen 1942- ... 113
Godfrey, Frederick M. 1901-1974 ... CAP-1
Earlier sketch in CA 13-14
Godfrey, Henry F. 1906-1975 ... CAP-2
Earlier sketch in CA 25-28
Godfrey, Jane
See Bowden, Joan Chase
Godfrey, Laurie R(ohde) 1945- ... 113
Godfrey, Lionel (Robert Holcombe) 1932- ... 81-84
Godfrey, Michael A. 1940- ... CANR-14
Earlier sketch in CA 81-84
Godfrey, Peter 1917- ... 124
Godfrey, Thomas 1736-1763 ... DLB-31
Godfrey, Vincent H. 1895(?)-1975
Obituary ... 57-60
Godfrey, William
See Youd, Samuel
Godin, Gabriel 1929- ... 73-76
Godine, David R(ichard) 1944- ... 101
Godley, John
See Kilbracken, John (Raymond Godley)
Godly, J. P.
See Plawin, Paul
Godman, Arthur 1916- ... CANR-24
Earlier sketch in CA 106
Godolphin, Francis R(ichard) B(orrow)
1903-1974 ... 65-68
Obituary ... 53-56
Godown, Marian Bailey ... 103
Godoy Alcayaga, Lucila 1889-1957
Brief entry ... 104
Godsey, John Drew 1922- ... 13-14R
Godshalk, William Leigh 1937- ... 41-44R
Godson, John 1937- ... 77-80
Godson, Joseph 1913-1986 Obituary ... 120
Godson, Roy (S.) 1942- Brief entry ... 111
Godwin, Anthony Richard James Wylie
1920(?)-1976 Obituary ... 104
Godwin, Gail 1937- ... CANR-15
Earlier sketch in CA 29-32R
See also DLB 6
See also CLC 5, 8, 22, 31
Godwin, Gaylord 1906(?)-1979 Obituary ... 85-88
Godwin, George (Stanley) 1889- ... 5-6R
Godwin, Harry 1901-1985 ... 109
Obituary ... 117
Godwin, John (Frederick) 1922- ... CANR-19
Earlier sketch in CA 102
Godwin, John 1929- ... CANR-16
Earlier sketches in CA 4R, CANR-1
Godwin, Joscelyn 1945- ... CANR-12
Earlier sketch in CA 69-72
Godwin, Parke 1816-1904 Brief entry ... 119
See also DLB 3, 64
Godwin, Tony
See Godwin, Anthony Richard James
Wylie
Godwin, William 1756-1836 ... DLB-39
Goebbels, Josef
See Goebbels, (Paul) Joseph
Goebbels, (Paul) Joseph 1897-1945
Brief entry ... 115
Goebbels, Joseph Paul
See Goebbels, (Paul) Joseph
Goebel, Dorothy (Burne) 1898-1976 ... 69-72
Obituary ... 65-68
Goebel, Julius, Jr. 1893(?)-1973
Obituary ... 45-48
Goedecke, W(alter) Robert 1928- ... 29-32R
Goedel, Kurt 1906-1978 Obituary ... 108
Goedertier, Joseph M. 1907- ... CAP-2
Earlier sketch in CA 25-28
Goedicke, Hans 1926- ... CANR-19
Earlier sketches in CA 45-48, CANR-1
Goedicke, Patricia (McKenna) 1931- ... CANR-11
Earlier sketch in CA 25-28R
Goedicke, Victor (Alfred) 1912- ... 17-18R
Goel, M(adan) Lal 1936- ... 53-56
Goeller, Carl 1930- ... 23-24R
Goelz, Paul Cornelius 1914- ... 109
Goen, Clarence C(urtis), Jr. 1924- ... 2R
Goen, Rayburne Wyndham, Jr. 1942- ... 107
Goen, Tex, Jr.
See Goen, Rayburne Wyndham, Jr.
Goeney, William M(orton) 1914- ... 5-6R
Goerdt, Arthur L(inus) 1912- ... 41-44R
Goergen, Donald 1943- ... 61-64
Goering, Helga
See Wallmann, Jeffrey M(iner)
Goerling, Lars 1931-1966 ... CAP-2
Obituary ... 25-28R
Earlier sketch in CA 21-22
Goerner, E(dward) A(lfred) 1929- ... 49-52
Goertz, Donald C(harles) 1939- ... 53-56
Goertzel, Ted George 1942- ... 69-72
Goetchius, Eugene Van Ness 1921- ... 118
Goethals, George W. 1920- ... 13-14R
Goetsch-Trevelyan, Katherine
See Trevelyan, Katherine
Goettel, Elinor 1930- ... 29-32R
See also SATA 12
Goetz, Billy E. 1904- ... CAP-1
Earlier sketch in CA 13-14
Goetz, Delia 1898- ... 73-76
See also SATA 22
Goetz, Ignacio L. 1933- ... 37-40R
Goetz, Joseph (William) 1933- ... 118
Goetz, Lee Garrett 1932- ... 25-28R
Goetze, Albrecht E. R. 1897-1971
Obituary ... 33-36R
Goetzmann, William H. 1930- ... 23-24R
Goetz-Stankiewicz, Marketa ... 122
Goff, Charles Ray 1889-1984 Obituary ... 114
Goff, Frederick Richmond 1916-1982 ... CANR-7
Obituary ... 108
Earlier sketch in CA 17-18R
Goff, Martyn 1923- ... CANR-2
Earlier sketch in CA 7-8R
Goffart, Walter (Andre) 1934- ... CANR-16
Earlier sketch in CA 37-40R
Goffe, Thomas 1592(?)-1629 ... DLB-58
Goffen, Rona 1944- ... 121
Goffin, Raymond C. 1890(?)-1976
Obituary ... 65-68
Goffman, Erving 1922-1982 ... CANR-9
Obituary ... 108
Earlier sketch in CA 23-24R
Goffstein, M(arilyn) B(rooke) 1940- ... CANR-9
Earlier sketch in CA 21-22R
See also SATA 8
See also DLB 61
See also CLR 3
Gofman, John W(illiam) 1918- ... 65-68
Goforth, Ellen
See Francis, Dorothy Brenner
Gogarty, Oliver St. John 1878-1957
Brief entry ... 109
See also DLB 15, 19
See also TCLC 15
Goggin, Terrence P(atrick) 1941- ... 103
Gogisgi
See Arnett, Carroll
Goh, Cheng-Teik 1943- ... 41-44R
Gohdes, Clarence Louis Frank 1901- ... 13-14R
Gohman, Fred Joseph 1918- ... 7-8R
Goines, Donald 1937-1974 Obituary ... 114
See also DLB 33
See also AITN 1
Goines, Donald 1937(?)-1974 ... 124
Goins, Ellen H(aynes) 1927- ... 33-36R
Goist, Park Dixon 1936- ... 37-40R
Goitein, S(helomo) D(ov) 1900-1985 ... CANR-8
Obituary ... 115
Earlier sketch in CA 61-64
Goitein, Solomon Dob Fritz
See Goitein, S(helomo) D(ov)
Gokak, Vinayak Krishna 1909- ... 69-72
Gokhale, Balkrishna Govind 1919- ... CANR-4
Earlier sketch in CA 1R
Gokhale, Namita 1956- ... 123
Golan, Aviezer 1922- ... 104
Golan, Matti 1936- ... 101
Golann, Cecil Paige 1921- ... 33-36R
See also SATA 11
Golann, Stuart E(ugene) 1936- ... 57-60
Golant, William 1937- ... 65-68
Golay, Frank H(indman) 1915- ... CANR-1
Earlier sketch in CA 2R
Golbin, Andree 1923- ... SATA-15
Golburgh, Stephen J. 1935- ... 21-22R
Gold, Aaron 1937-1983 ... 101
Obituary ... 109
Gold, Alan R(obert) 1948- ... 45-48
Gold, Artie 1947- ... 114
Gold, Barbara K(irk) 1945- ... 110
Gold, Don 1931- ... CANR-9
Earlier sketch in CA 61-64
Gold, Doris B. 1919- ... CANR-9
Earlier sketch in CA 23-24R
Gold, Douglas 1894- ... CAP-1
Earlier sketch in CA 11-12
Gold, Herbert 1924- ... CANR-17
Earlier sketch in CA 11-12R
See also DLB 2
See also DLBY 81
See also CLC 4, 7, 14, 42
Gold, Ivan 1932- ... CANR-3
Earlier sketch in CA 5-6R
Gold, Joseph 1933- ... 21-22R
Gold, Lee 1919(?)-1985 Obituary ... 116
Gold, Martin 1931- ... 29-32R
Gold, Michael
See Granich, Irving
See also DLB 9, 28
Gold, Milton J. 1917- ... 17-18R
Gold, Phyllis
See Goldberg, Phyllis
See also SATA 21
Gold, Robert S(tanley) 1924- ... 53-56
Gold, Seymour M(urray) 1933- ... CANR-21
Earlier sketch in CA 41-44R
Gold, Sharlya ... CANR-8
Earlier sketch in CA 61-64
See also SATA 9
Gold, Victor Roland 1924- ... 53-56
Gold, William E(mil) 1912- ... 69-72
Goldbarth, Albert 1948- ... CANR-6
Earlier sketch in CA 53-56
See also CLC 5, 38
Goldbeck, David M. 1942- ... 49-52
Goldbeck, Frederick E(rnest) 1902- ... 102
Goldbeck, Nikki 1947- ... 49-52
Goldbeck, Willis 1899(?)-1979 Obituary ... 89-92
Goldberg, Alvin Arnold 1931- ... 41-44R
Goldberg, Anatol 1910-1982 Obituary ... 117
See also CLC 34
Goldberg, Arnold I(rving) 1929- ... CANR-19
Earlier sketch in CA 103
Goldberg, Arthur J(oseph) 1908- ... 65-68
Goldberg, Barney 1918- ... 23-24R
Goldberg, Benjamin 1915- ... 120
Goldberg, Carl 1938- ... CANR-18
Earlier sketches in CA 49-52, CANR-3
Goldberg, Dick 1947- ... 97-100
See also DLB 7
Goldberg, Dorothy K(urgans)
1909(?)-1988 ... 103
Obituary ... 124
Goldberg, E(lliott) Marshall 1930- ... CANR-11
Earlier sketch in CA 69-72
Goldberg, Edward M(orris) 1931- ... 53-56
Goldberg, Fats
See Goldberg, Larry
Goldberg, George 1935- ... 69-72
Goldberg, Gerald Jay 1929- ... 49-52
Goldberg, Harvey E(llis) 1939- ... 45-48
Goldberg, Herb 1937- ... CANR-9
Earlier sketch in CA 61-64
Goldberg, Herbert S. 1926- ... 5-6R
See also SATA 25
Goldberg, Herman Raphael 1915- ... CANR-5
Earlier sketch in CA 11-12R
Goldberg, Hillel 1946- ... 116
Goldberg, Hyman 1908(?)-1970 Obituary ... 104
Goldberg, Jacob 1948- ... 120
Goldberg, Jan
See Curran, Jan Goldberg
Goldberg, Joan Rachel 1955- ... 110
Goldberg, Jonathan 1943- ... 122
Goldberg, Joseph P(hilip) 1918- ... 37-40R
Goldberg, Kenneth P(hilip) 1945- ... 116
Goldberg, Larry 1934- ... 113
Goldberg, Leah 1911-1970 Obituary ... 25-28R
Goldberg, Louis 1908- ... 13-14R
Goldberg, Louis
See Grant, Louis T(heodore)
Goldberg, Lucianne Cummings 1935- ... 85-88
Goldberg, M(ilton) A(llan) 1919-1970 ... CAP-2
Earlier sketch in CA 25-28
Goldberg, M(elvyn) Hirsh 1942- ... 73-76
Goldberg, Marie Waife
See Waife-Goldberg, Marie
Goldberg, Maxwell Henry 1907- ... CANR-24
Earlier sketch in CA 103
Goldberg, Miriam Levin 1914- ... 41-44R
Goldberg, Moses H(aym) 1940- ... CANR-15
Earlier sketch in CA 93-96
Goldberg, Nathan 1903(?)-1979 Obituary ... 85-88
Goldberg, Norman L(ewis) 1906- ... 81-84
Goldberg, P(ercy) Selvin 1917- ... 7-8R
Goldberg, Philip 1944- ... CANR-15
Earlier sketch in CA 85-88
Goldberg, Phyllis 1941- ... 57-60
Goldberg, Ray A(llan) 1926- ... 49-52
Goldberg, Reuben L(ucius) 1883-1970 ... CANR-9
Earlier sketch in CA 5-6R
Goldberg, Robert Alan 1949- ... 105
Goldberg, RoseLee 1947- ... 120
Goldberg, Rube
See Goldberg, Reuben L(ucius)
Goldberg, Samuel Louis 1926- ... 112
Goldberg, Sidney 1931- ... 77-80
Goldberg, Stan J. 1939- ... 49-52
See also SATA 26
Goldberg, Steven 1941- ... 53-56
Goldberger, Arthur Stanley 1930- ... 9-10R
Goldberger, Judith M. 1948- ... 112
Goldberger, Nancy Rule 1937- ... 124
Goldberger, Paul (Jesse) 1950-
Brief entry ... 122
Golde, Peggy 1930- ... 37-40R
Golde, Roger A(lan) 1934- ... 69-72
Goldemberg, Isaac 1945- ... CANR-11
Earlier sketch in CA 69-72
Goldemberg, Rose Leiman ... CANR-2
Earlier sketch in CA 49-52
Golden, Arthur 1924- ... 33-36R
Golden, Harry (Lewis) 1902-1981 ... CANR-2
Obituary ... 104
Earlier sketch in CA 2R
Golden, James L. 1919- Brief entry ... 109
Golden, Jeffrey S. 1950- ... 33-36R
Golden, L(ouis) L(awrence) L(ionel)
1909(?)-1983 ... 23-24R
Obituary ... 111
Golden, Leon 1930- ... 19-20R
Golden, Marita 1950- ... 111
Golden, Morris 1926- ... 3R
Golden, Robert Edward 1945- ... 65-68
Golden, Ruth I(sbell) 1910- ... CAP-2
Earlier sketch in CA 17-18
Golden, Samuel A(dler) 1909- Brief entry ... 110
Golden, Sean V(alentine) 1948- ... 107
Golden, Sherry (Lazar) 1945- ... 123
Goldenbaum, Sally 1941- ... 124
Goldenberg, Edie N. 1945- ... 69-72
Goldenberg, Herbert 1926- ... 41-44R
Goldenberg, I(sidore) Ira 1936- ... 110
Goldenberg, Robert 1942- ... 109
Golden Silver
See Storm, Hyemeyohsts
Goldensohn, Barry 1937- ... 77-80
Goldenson, Daniel R. 1944- ... 25-28R
Goldenson, Robert M(yar) 1908- ... 29-32R
Goldenthal, Allan Benarria 1920- ... 19-20R
Goldfader, Edward H. 1930- ... 29-32R
Goldfarb, Clare R(osett) 1934- ... 113
Goldfarb, Nathan 1913- ... 15-16R
Goldfarb, Ronald L. 1933- ... CANR-9
Earlier sketch in CA 23-24R
Goldfarb, Russell M. 1934- ... 37-40R
Goldfarb, Sally F(ay) 1957- ... 104
Goldfeder, Cheryl
See Pahz, (Anne) Cheryl Suzanne
Goldfeder, James
See Pahz, James Alon
Goldfeder, Jim
See Pahz, James Alon
Goldfein, Donna 1933- ... 116
Goldfrank, David M. ... 118
Goldfrank, Esther S(chiff) 1896- ... 61-64
Goldfrank, Helen Colodny 1912- ... CANR-3
Earlier sketch in CA 2R
See also SATA 6
Goldfried, Marvin R(obert) 1936- ... 37-40R
Goldgar, Bertrand A(lvin) 1927- ... 65-68
Goldhaber, Gerald Martin 1944- ... CANR-9
Earlier sketch in CA 57-60
Goldhamer, Herbert 1907-1977 ... CANR-2
Earlier sketch in CA 45-48

Goldhurst, Richard 1927- ... 57-60
Goldhurst, William 1929- ... 5-6R
Goldie, Frederick 1914-1980 Obituary ... 105
Goldie, Terrence William 1950- ... 113
Goldie, Terry
 See Goldie, Terrence William
Goldin, Augusta 1906- ... CANR-7
 Earlier sketch in CA 19-20R
 See also SATA 13
Goldin, Grace 1916- ... 115
Goldin, Judah 1914- ... 33-36R
Goldin, Kathleen Mckinney 1943-
 Brief entry ... 118
Goldin, Milton 1927- ... 61-64
Goldin, Stephen 1947- ... 77-80
Golding, Lawrence A(rthur) 1926- ... 61-64
Golding, Louis 1907- ... CAP-1
 Earlier sketch in CA 9-10
Golding, Martin Philip 1930- ... 101
Golding, Morton J(ay) 1925- ... 21-22R
Golding, Peter 1947- ... 103
Golding, William (Gerald) 1911- ... CANR-13
 Earlier sketch in CA 7-8R
 See also DLB 15
 See also CLC 1, 2, 3, 8, 10, 17, 27
Goldknopf, David 1918- ... 53-56
Goldman, A(ndrew) E. O. 1947- ... 57-60
Goldman, Alan H(arris) 1945- ... 93-96
Goldman, Albert 1927- ... CANR-9
 Earlier sketch in CA 19-20R
Goldman, Alex J. 1917- ... 49-52
Goldman, Alvin I(ra) 1938- ... 77-80
Goldman, Alvin L. 1938- ... CANR-1
 Earlier sketch in CA 45-48
Goldman, Arnold (Melvyn) 1936- ... 17-18R
Goldman, Bernard 1922- ... 53-56
Goldman, Bo 1932- ... 112
 Brief entry ... 109
Goldman, Bruce (Eliot) 1942- ... 61-64
Goldman, Carl A(lexander) 1942- ... 101
Goldman, Charles R(emington) 1930- ... 53-56
Goldman, Dave 1927- ... 107
Goldman, Emma 1869-1940 Brief entry ... 110
 See also TCLC 13
Goldman, Eric (Frederick) 1915- ... 7-8R
Goldman, Frederick 1921- ... 81-84
Goldman, George D(avid) 1923- ... 107
Goldman, Howard H(irsch) 1949- ... 112
Goldman, Irving 1911- ... 29-32R
Goldman, Jacquelin (Roberta) 1934- ... 69-72
Goldman, James A. 1927- ... CANR-1
 Earlier sketch in CA 45-48
Goldman, Lee A. 1946- ... 25-28R
Goldman, Leo 1920- ... 85-88
Goldman, Lorraine 1940- ... 111
Goldman, Marcus Selden 1894- ... 41-44R
Goldman, Marshall I(rwin) 1930- ... 9-10R
Goldman, Martin (Raymond Rubin)
 1920- ... 69-72
Goldman, Martin 1950(?)-1984 Obituary ... 113
Goldman, Merle 1931- ... 33-36R
Goldman, Michael (Paul) 1936- ... CANR-8
 Earlier sketch in CA 17-18R
Goldman, Norma Wynick 1922- ... 110
Goldman, Peter (Louis) 1933- ... CANR-24
 Earlier sketches in CA 21-22R, CANR-8
Goldman, Phyllis W. 1927- ... 29-32R
Goldman, Ralph M(orris) 1920- ... 89-92
Goldman, Richard Franko 1910-1980 ... CANR-5
 Obituary ... 93-96
 Earlier sketch in CA 11-12R
Goldman, Ronald ... 23-24R
Goldman, Sheldon 1939- ... 23-24R
Goldman, Sherli E(vens) 1930- ... 25-28R
Goldman, Shifra M(eyerowitz) 1926- ... 106
Goldman, Susan 1939- ... 65-68
Goldman, William W. 1931- ... 9-10R
 See also DLB 44
 See also CLC 1
Goldman-Eisler, Frieda 1909(?)-1982
 Obituary ... 105
Goldmann, Lucien 1913-1970 ... CAP-2
 Earlier sketch in CA 25-28
 See also CLC 24
Goldmann, Nahum 1895-1982 Obituary ... 107
Goldmark, Peter C(arl) 1906-1977 ... 77-80
 Obituary ... 73-76
Goldner, Bernard (Burton) 1919- ... 5-6R
Goldner, Jack 1900- ... CAP-2
 Earlier sketch in CA 25-28
Goldner, Nancy 1943- ... 57-60
Goldner, Orville (Charles) 1906- ... 53-56
Goldovsky, Boris 1908- ... CANR-16
 Earlier sketch in CA 81-84
Goldring, Douglas 1887-1960 Obituary ... 93-96
Goldring, Patrick (Thomas Zachary)
 1921- ... 29-32R
Goldsberry, Steven 1949- ... CLC-34
Goldsborough, June 1923- ... SATA-19
Goldscheider, Calvin 1941- ... 122
 Brief entry ... 108
Goldscheider, Ludwig 1896- ... 7-8R
Goldschmidt, Clara Malraux
 See Malraux, Clara (Goldschmidt)
Goldschmidt, Walter Rochs 1913- ... 9-10R
Goldschmidt, Yaagov 1927- ... 29-32R
Goldsen, Rose Kohn 1918- ... 1R
Goldsmith
 See Miller, Lynne (Ellen)
Goldsmith, Arnold L(ouis) 1928- ... 41-44R
Goldsmith, Arthur (A., Jr.) 1926- ... CANR-5
 Earlier sketch in CA 15-16R
Goldsmith, Barbara 1931- ... CANR-5
 Earlier sketch in CA 53-56
Goldsmith, Carol Evan 1930- ... 29-32R
Goldsmith, David H(irsh) 1933- ... 117
Goldsmith, Donald 1943- ... 77-80
Goldsmith, Edward ... 104
Goldsmith, Emanuel S(idney) 1935-
 Brief entry ... 109
Goldsmith, Howard 1943- ... CANR-21
 Earlier sketch in CA 101
 See also SATA 24
Goldsmith, Ilse Sondra (Weinberg)
 1933- ... 37-40R
Goldsmith, Jack 1931- ... 57-60
Goldsmith, Joel S. 1892(?)-1964 Obituary ... 109
Goldsmith, John Herman Thorburn
 1903-1987 Obituary ... 122
Goldsmith, Oliver 1728-1774 ... SATA-26
 See also DLB 39
Goldsmith, Peter
 See Priestley, J(ohn) B(oynton)
Goldsmith, Raymond W(illiam) 1904- ... 115
Goldsmith, Robert Hillis 1911- ... 49-52
Goldsmith, Sharon S(weeney) 1948- ... 57-60
Goldsmith, Walter (Kenneth) 1938- ... 120
Goldson, Rae L(illian) Segalowitz 1893- ... 7-8R
Goldstein, Abraham 1903(?)-1982
 Obituary ... 106
Goldstein, Abraham S(amuel) 1925- ... 33-36R
Goldstein, Alvin H., Sr. 1902-1972
 Obituary ... 33-36R
Goldstein, Arthur D(avid) 1937- ... 73-76
Goldstein, Bernard R. 1938- ... 57-60
Goldstein, David 1933- ... CANR-11
 Earlier sketch in CA 19-20R
Goldstein, Donald M(aurice) 1932- ... 108
Goldstein, E. Ernest 1918- ... 11-12R
Goldstein, Edward 1923- ... 11-12R
Goldstein, Ernest A. 1933- ... 110
Goldstein, Gersham 1938- Brief entry ... 108
Goldstein, Howard 1922- ... 93-96
Goldstein, Irwin L. 1937- ... 41-44R
Goldstein, Israel 1896-1986 ... 53-56
 Obituary ... 119
Goldstein, Jack 1930- ... 73-76
Goldstein, Jeffrey H(askell) 1942- ... CANR-14
 Earlier sketch in CA 81-84
Goldstein, Jerome 1931- ... 101
Goldstein, Joan 1932- ... 114
Goldstein, Jonathan A(mos) 1929- ... 25-28R
Goldstein, Joseph 1923- ... 19-20R
Goldstein, Kenneth M(ichael) 1940- ... 33-36R
Goldstein, Kenneth S. 1927- Brief entry ... 107
Goldstein, Laurence 1937(?)-1972
 Obituary ... 33-36R
Goldstein, Laurence 1943- ... 93-96
Goldstein, Leo S. 1924- ... 15-16R
Goldstein, Leon J. 1927- ... 69-72
Goldstein, Lisa 1953- ... 108
Goldstein, Malcolm 1925- ... 49-52
Goldstein, Marc 1948- ... 109
Goldstein, Martin E(ugene) 1939- ... 41-44R
Goldstein, Melvyn C. 1938- ... 121
Goldstein, Michael J(oseph) 1930- ... 103
Goldstein, Milton 1915- ... CANR-24
 Earlier sketch in CA 45-48
Goldstein, Nathan 1927- ... CANR-16
 Earlier sketches in CA 45-48, CANR-1
 See also SATA 47
Goldstein, Philip 1910- ... 53-56
 See also SATA 23
Goldstein, Rhoda L.
 See Blumberg, Rhoda L(ois Goldstein)
Goldstein, Richard 1944- ... 25-28R
Goldstein, Roberta Butterfield 1917- ... 11-12R
Goldstein, Ruth M(artha) 1913- ... 113
Goldstein, Ruth Tessler 1924- ... 69-72
Goldstein, Sidney 1927- ... CANR-9
 Earlier sketch in CA 23-24R
Goldstein, Stanley 1922- ... 103
Goldstein, Stephen R(obert) 1938- ... CANR-13
 Earlier sketch in CA 61-64
Goldstein, Stewart 1941- ... 65-68
Goldstein, Thomas Eugene 1913-
 Brief entry ... 108
Goldstein, William Isaac 1932- ... 15-16R
Goldstein-Jackson, Kevin 1946- ... 106
Goldstine, Herman Heine 1913- ... 110
Goldston, Robert (Conroy) 1927- ... CANR-13
 Earlier sketch in CA 17-18R
 See also SATA 6
Goldstone, Aline L(ewis) 1878(?)-1976
 Obituary ... 65-68
Goldstone, Harmon H(endricks) 1911- ... 77-80
Goldstone, Herbert 1921- ... 77-80
Goldstone, Lawrence A.
 See Treat, Lawrence
Goldstone, Richard H. 1921- ... 33-36R
Goldsworthy, David 1938- ... 33-36R
Goldsworthy, Graeme 1934- ... 114
Goldsworthy, Peter 1951- ... 118
Goldthorpe, J(ohn) E(rnest) 1921- ... 49-52
Goldthwaite, Eaton K. 1907- ... 25-28R
Goldthwaite, Richard A. 1933- Brief entry ... 108
Goldwater, Barry (Morris) 1909- ... 41-44R
Goldwater, Eleanor Lowenstein
 1909(?)-1980 Obituary ... 102
Goldwater, John ... AITN-1
Goldwater, Robert 1907-1973 Obituary ... 41-44R
Goldwater, Walter Delmar 1907-1985
 Obituary ... 116
Goldwin, Robert Allen 1922- ... 102
Goldwyn, Robert M(alcolm) 1930- ... 122
Gole, Victor Leslie 1903- ... CANR-23
 Earlier sketch in CA 107
Goleman, Daniel 1946- ... 111
Golembiewski, Robert T(homas)
 1932- ... CANR-21
 Earlier sketches in CA 5-6R, CANR-6
Golenbock, Peter 1946- ... CANR-8
 Earlier sketch in CA 57-60
Golenpaul, Ann 1907(?)-1986 Obituary ... 119
Golf, Loyal E.
 See Golv, Loyal E(ugene)
Golffing, Francis (Charles) 1910- ... CANR-5
 Earlier sketch in CA 5-6R
Goliard, Roy
 See Shipley, Joseph T(wadell)
Golightly, Bonnie H(elen) 1919- ... 2R
Goll, Reinhold W(eimar) 1897- ... 7-8R
 See also SATA 26
Gollan, Robin 1917- ... 13-14R
Gollancz, Victor 1893-1967 Obituary ... 116
Golledge, Reginald G(eorge) 1937- ... 41-44R
Goller, Celia (Fremlin) 1914- ... CANR-5
 Earlier sketch in CA 13-14R
Golley, Frank Benjamin 1930- Brief entry ... 106
Gollin, Gillian Lindt
 See Lindt, Gillian
Gollings, Franklin O. A. 1919- ... 23-24R
Gollmar, Robert H. 1903(?)-1987
 Obituary ... 123
Gollwitzer, Heinz 1917- ... 25-28R
Gologor, Ethan 1940- ... 101
Golomb, Claire 1928- ... 103
Golomb, Louis 1943- ... CANR-16
 Earlier sketch in CA 85-88
Golombek, Harry 1911- ... 103
Golon, Serge(anne) 1903-1972
 Obituary ... 37-40R
Golovine, Michael N(icholas) 1903-1965 ... 5-6R
Golson, G. Barry 1944- ... 69-72
Golv, Loyal E(ugene) 1926- ... CANR-1
 Earlier sketch in CA 4R
Golz, R(einhardt) Lud 1936- ... CANR-5
 Earlier sketch in CA 13-14R
Gom, Leona 1946- ... 116
Gombault, Charles Henri 1907-1983
 Obituary ... 110
Gomberg, Adeline Wishengrad 1915- ... 19-20R
Gomberg, William 1911-1985 ... 17-18R
 Obituary ... 118
Gombossy, Zoltan
 See Gabel, Joseph
Gombrich, E(rnst) H(ans Josef) 1909- ... CANR-5
 Earlier sketch in CA 53-56
Gombrowicz, Witold 1904-1969 ... CAP-2
 Obituary ... 25-28R
 Earlier sketch in CA 19-20
 See also CLC 4, 7, 11
Gomery, Douglas 1945- ... 110
Gomez, David F(ederico) 1940- ... 49-52
Gomez, Joseph A(nthony) 1942- ... 104
Gomez, Rudolph 1930- ... 53-56
Gomez de la Serna, Ramon 1888-1963
 Obituary ... 116
 See also CLC 9
Gomez-Gil, Alfredo 1936- ... 41-44R
 See also AITN 1
Gomori, George 1934- ... CANR-9
 Earlier sketch in CA 23-24R
Gompertz, Rolf 1927- ... CANR-11
 Earlier sketch in CA 69-72
Gongora, Maria Eugenia 1948- ... 104
Gonick, Jean 1950- ... 121
Gontarski, S(tanley) E. 1942- ... 114
Gonzales, John
 See Terrall, Robert
Gonzales, Manuel G(arcia) 1943- ... 111
Gonzales, Pancho
 See Gonzales, Richard Alonzo
Gonzales, Richard Alonzo 1928-
 Brief entry ... 105
Gonzales, Sylvia Alicia 1943- ... 77-80
Gonzalez, Alfonso 1927- ... 41-44R
Gonzalez, Angel 1925- ... CANR-15
 Earlier sketch in CA 85-88
Gonzalez, Arturo 1928- ... 77-80
Gonzalez, Catherine Gunsalus
 See Gunsalus Gonzalez, Catherine
Gonzalez, Edward 1933- Brief entry ... 109
Gonzalez, Gloria 1940- ... CANR-24
 Earlier sketch in CA 65-68
 See also SATA 23
Gonzalez, Jaime Jose 1925- ... 103
Gonzalez, Justo L(uis) 1937- ... CANR-16
 Earlier sketch in CA 29-32R
Gonzalez, N(estor) V(icente) M(adali)
 1915- ... CANR-2
 Earlier sketch in CA 4R
Gonzalez, Nancie L(oudon) 1929- ... 103
Gonzalez, Richard F(lorentz) 1927- ... 114
Gonzalez, Sergio A(ntonio) Torres
 See Torres Gonzalez, Sergio A(ntonio)
Gonzalez-Aller, Faustino 1922- ... 81-84
Gonzalez-Crussi, F(rank) 1936- Brief entry ... 121
Gonzalez-Echevarria, Roberto 1943- ... 106
Gonzalez-Gerth, Miguel 1926- ... 69-72
Gonzalez Lopez, Emilio 1903- ... CANR-2
 Earlier sketch in CA 49-52
Gonzalez-Mena, Janet 1937- ... 111
Gonzalez-Paz, Elsie E. 1913- ... 45-48
Gonzalez-Wippler, Migene 1936- ... 109
Gooby, Peter Taylor
 See Taylor-Gooby, Peter
Gooch, Bob
 See Gooch, Robert M(iletus)
Gooch, Brison D(owling) 1925- ... 13-14R
Gooch, Bryan Niel Shirley 1937- ... 93-96
Gooch, George Peabody 1873-1968 ... 7-8R
Gooch, Robert M(iletus) 1919- ... CANR-13
 Earlier sketch in CA 77-80
Gooch, Stan(ley Alfred) 1932- ... CANR-14
 Earlier sketch in CA 77-80
Gooch, Steve 1945- ... CANR-20
 Earlier sketch in CA 101
Good, Carter V(ictor) 1897- ... 7-8R
Good, Edwin M(arshall) 1928- ... CANR-11
 Earlier sketch in CA 17-18R
Good, H(arry) G(ehman) 1880-1971 ... 2R
 Obituary ... 103
Good, I(rving) John 1916- ... CANR-3
 Earlier sketch in CA 5-6R
Good, Lawrence R. 1924- ... 15-16R
Good, Paul 1929- ... 85-88
Good, Robert Crocker 1924- ... 73-76
Good, Thomas L(indall) 1943- ... CANR-22
 Earlier sketches in CA 57-60, CANR-8
Goodacre, Elizabeth Jane 1929- ... 102
Goodall, Daphne Machin
 See Machin Goodall, Daphne (Edith)
Goodall, Jane 1934- ... CANR-2
 Earlier sketch in CA 45-48
Goodall, John Strickland 1908- ... 33-36R
 See also SATA 4
Goodall, Leonard E. 1937- ... 85-88
Goodall, Marcus C(ampbell) 1914- ... 33-36R
Goodall, Melanie
 See Drachman, Julian M(oses)
Goodall, Norman 1896-1985 Obituary ... 115
Goodall, Vanne Morris
 See Morris-Goodall, Vanne
Goodavage, Joseph F. 1925- ... 25-28R
Goodbody, Slim
 See Burstein, John
Goodchild, Peter 1939- ... 106
Goode, Barry 1938- ... 118
Goode, Diane 1949- ... SATA-15
Goode, Erich 1938- ... CANR-16
 Earlier sketches in CA 49-52, CANR-1
Goode, Gerald 1899(?)-1983 Obituary ... 111
Goode, James 1924- ... 123
Goode, James M. 1939- ... 93-96
Goode, John 1927- ... 103
Goode, Kenneth G. 1932- ... 49-52
Goode, Richard (Benjamin) 1916- ... 17-18R
Goode, Ruth 1905- ... 77-80
Goode, Stephen H(ogue) 1924- ... CANR-2
 Earlier sketch in CA 45-48
Goode, Stephen Ray 1943- ... CANR-18
 Earlier sketch in CA 57-60
 See also SATA 40
Goode, William Josiah 1917- ... 102
Goodell, Charles E(llsworth) 1926-1987 ... 81-84
 Obituary ... 121
Goodell, Donald (James) 1938- ... 45-48
Goodell, John S. 1939- ... 73-76
Goodell, Rae 1944- ... 77-80
Goodenough, Erwin R(amsdell)
 1893-1965 ... 7-8R
Goodenough, Evelyn
 See Pitcher, Evelyn G(oodenough)
Goodenough, Ward Hunt 1919- ... CANR-2
 Earlier sketch in CA 4R
Goodenow, Earle 1913- ... SATA-40
Gooders, John 1937- ... CANR-6
 Earlier sketch in CA 57-60
Goodfellow, Peter 1935- ... 115
Goodfield, (Gwyneth) June 1927- ... 9-10R
Goodfriend, Arthur 1907- ... 5-6R
Goodgold, Edwin 1944- ... CANR-23
 Earlier sketch in CA 21-22R
Goodhart, Arthur Lehman 1891-1978 ... 85-88
 Obituary ... 81-84
Goodhart, Robert S(tanley) 1909- ... 89-92
Goodheart, Barbara 1934- ... 33-36R
Goodheart, Eugene 1931- ... CANR-18
 Earlier sketches in CA 5-6R, CANR-3
Goodin, Gayle 1938- ... 33-36R
Goodin, Robert Edward 1950- ... CANR-22
 Earlier sketch in CA 105
Gooding, Cynthia 1924- ... 33-36R
Gooding, John (Ervine) 1940- ... 21-22R
Gooding, Judson 1926- ... 73-76
Gooding, Kathleen (Tinney) ... 116
Goodis, David 1917-1967 ... 1R
Goodkin, Sanford R(onald) 1929- ... 104
Goodkind, Henry M. 1904(?)-1970
 Obituary ... 104
Goodlad, John I. 1920- ... CANR-19
 Earlier sketches in CA 7-8R, CANR-3
Goodman, A(lvin) Harold 1924- ... 103
Goodman, A(dolph) W(inkler) 1915- ... 57-60
Goodman, Ann (Davidow) 1932- ... 107
Goodman, Arnold Abraham 1913- ... 109
Goodman, Benjamin David 1909(?)-1986
 Obituary ... 119
Goodman, Benny
 See Goodman, Benjamin David
Goodman, Celia (Mary) 1916- ... 123
Goodman, Charles S(chaffner) 1916- ... 33-36R
Goodman, David (Allen) 1941- ... 119
Goodman, David Michael 1936- ... 19-20R
Goodman, David S. 1917- ... 29-32R
Goodman, Deborah Lerme 1956- ... 121
 See also SATA 49, 50
Goodman, Edward J(ulius) 1916- ... 111
Goodman, Elaine 1930- ... 37-40R
 See also SATA 9
Goodman, Elizabeth B. 1912- ... 25-28R
Goodman, Ellen (Holtz) 1941- ... 104
Goodman, Elliot R(aymond) 1923- ... 1R
Goodman, Emily Jane 1940- ... 65-68
Goodman, Eugene B(enedict) 1922- ... 113
Goodman, Felicitas D(aniels) 1914- ... CANR-23
 Earlier sketches in CA 53-56, CANR-4
Goodman, George J(erome) W(aldo)
 1930- ... 21-22R
Goodman, Grant K(ohn) 1924- ... CANR-15
 Earlier sketch in CA 41-44R
Goodman, Harriet Wilinsky ... 111
Goodman, Herman 1894-1971 Obituary ... 105
Goodman, James M(arion) 1929- ... 117
Goodman, Jay S. 1940- ... 37-40R
Goodman, Joan Elizabeth 1950- ... SATA-50

Goodman, Jonathan 1931- CANR-13
Earlier sketch in CA 33-36R
Goodman, Joseph Irving 1908- 102
Goodman, Kenneth S. 1927- 25-28R
Goodman, Lenn Evan 1944- 53-56
Goodman, Leonard H(enry) 1941- 103
Goodman, Linda 1925- 89-92
Goodman, Louis Wolf 1942- 25-28R
Goodman, Michael B(arry) 1949- 107
Goodman, Mitchell 1923- CANR-4
Earlier sketch in CA 4R
Goodman, (Henry) Nelson 1906- 45-48
Goodman, Norman 1934- CANR-17
Earlier sketches in CA 49-52, CANR-1
Goodman, Paul 1911-1972 CAP-2
Obituary 37-40R
Earlier sketch in CA 19-20
See also CLC 1, 2, 4, 7
Goodman, Percival 1904- 2R
Goodman, Philip 1911- 33-36R
Goodman, Randolph 1908- CANR-2
Earlier sketch in CA 7-8R
Goodman, Rebecca Gruver 1931- 77-80
Goodman, Richard Merle 1932- CANR-18
Earlier sketch in CA 102
Goodman, Roger B. 1919- CANR-9
Earlier sketch in CA 23-24R
Goodman, Ronald A. 1938- 73-76
Goodman, Rubin Robert 1913-1978
Obituary 81-84
Goodman, Saul 1919- 103
Goodman, Seymour S. 1931- CANR-22
Earlier sketch in CA 45-48
Goodman, Sonya
See Arcone, Sonya
Goodman, Stanley J(oshua) 1910- 110
Goodman, Steve 1948-1984 Obituary 113
Goodman, Walter 1927- CANR-7
Earlier sketch in CA 9-10R
See also SATA 9
Goodnough, David L. 1930- 93-96
Goodnow, Henry F(rank) 1917- 15-16R
Goodnow, Jacqueline (Jarrett) 1924- CANR-5
Earlier sketch in CA 15-16R
Goodovitch, I(srael) M(eir) 1934- 25-28R
Goodpaster, Andrew J(ackson) 1915- 109
Goodpaster, Kenneth E(dwin) 1944- CANR-17
Earlier sketch in CA 97-100
Goodreau, William Joseph, Jr. 1931- 4R
Goodrich, David L(loyd) 1930- 85-88
Goodrich, Donna Clark 1938- 117
Goodrich, Foster E(dward) 1908-1972
Obituary 37-40R
Goodrich, Frances 1890(?)-1984 Obituary 111
See also DLB 26
Goodrich, Frances C. 1933- 23-24R
Goodrich, L(uther) Carrington
1894-1986 CANR-2
Obituary 120
Earlier sketch in CA 7-8R
Goodrich, Leland Matthew 1899- 81-84
Goodrich, Lloyd 1897-1987 69-72
Obituary 122
Goodrich, Norma Lorre 1917- 53-56
Goodrich, Robert E(dward), Jr. 1909- 33-36R
Goodrich, Samuel Griswold 1793-1860 SATA-23
See also DLB 1, 42
Goodrich, William Lloyd 1910(?)-1975
Obituary 61-64
Goodrick, Edward W(illiam) 1913- 111
Goodrick-Clarke, Nicholas 1953- 123
Goodrum, Charles A(lvin) 1923- CANR-12
Earlier sketch in CA 25-28R
Goodsall, Robert Harold 1891-19(?) CANR-4
Earlier sketch in CA 7-8R
Goodsell, Charles T(rue) 1932- CANR-8
Earlier sketch in CA 61-64
Goodsell, Fred Field 1880-1976 3R
Obituary 69-72
Goodson, Felix E(mmett) 1922- 49-52
Goodspeed, Donald J(ames) 1919- 5-6R
Goodspeed, Edgar Johnson 1871-1962
Obituary 93-96
Goodspeed, Peter 1944- 110
Goodstein, David B. 1932(?)-1985
Obituary 116
Goodstein, Leonard D(avid) 1927- CANR-13
Earlier sketch in CA 33-36R
Goodstein, R(euben) L(ouis) 1912-1985 53-56
Obituary 116
Goodwin, Albert 1906- 5-6R
Goodwin, Bennie Eugene II 1933- 112
Goodwin, Craufurd D(avid) W(ycliffe)
1934- CANR-14
Earlier sketch in CA 37-40R
Goodwin, Dave 1926- 113
Goodwin, Derek 1920- 93-96
Goodwin, Donald W(illiam) 1931- 65-68
Goodwin, Doris (Helen) Kearns 1943- CANR-23
Earlier sketch in CA 103
Goodwin, Eugene D.
See Kaye, Marvin (Nathan)
Goodwin, Geoffrey (Lawrence) 1916- 106
Goodwin, Hal
See Goodwin, Harold Leland
Goodwin, Harold 1919- 57-60
Goodwin, Harold Leland 1914- CANR-2
Earlier sketch in CA 4R
See also SATA 13
Goodwin, John Lonnen 1921- 108
Goodwin, John R(obert) 1929- 77-80
Goodwin, Leonard 1929- 41-44R
Goodwin, Mark
See Matthews, Stanley G(oodwin)
Goodwin, (Trevor) Noel 1927- 124
Goodwin, R(ichard) M(urphey) 1913- CANR-12
Earlier sketch in CA 29-32R
Goodwin, Richard N(aradhof) 1931-
Brief entry 111
Goodwin, Robert L. 1928(?)-1983
Obituary 109
Goodwin, Stephen 1943- CANR-8
Earlier sketch in CA 57-60
See also DLBY 82
Goodwin, Suzanne CANR-14
Earlier sketch in CA 77-80
Goodwyn, Floyd L(owell) 1940- 113
Goodwyn, Lawrence 1928- 23-24R
Goody, Joan Edelman 1935- 17-18R
Goodyear, Frank H., Jr. 1944- 122
Goodyear, John H(enry) III 1941- 111
Gookin, Daniel 1612-1687 DLB-24
Gool, Reshard 1931- 97-100
Goolagong, Evonne 1951- 89-92
Goold-Adams, Richard 1916- 13-14R
Goon, Fook Mun 1917(?)-1984 Obituary 113
Gooneratne, (Malini) Yasmine 1935- CANR-18
Earlier sketch in CA 29-32R
Goor, Nancy (Ruth Miller) 1944- 113
See also SATA 34, 39
Goor, Ron(ald Stephen) 1940- 113
See also SATA 34, 39
Goossen, Agnes
See Epp, Margaret A(gnes)
Goossen, Irvy W. 37-40R
Goot, Mary Vander
See Vander Goot, Mary
Gopal, Sarvepalli 1923- 104
Gopalakrishnan, Chennat 1936- 112
Gopen, George D(avid) 1945- 113
Goralski, Robert 1928- 105
Goran, Lester 1928- 45-48
Goran, Morris 1918- CANR-2
Earlier sketch in CA 3R
Gorbanevskaya, Natalya 1936- 111
Gorbatov, Alexander V. 1891(?)-1973
Obituary 45-48
Gorden, Raymond L(owell) 1919- 53-56
Gordenker, Leon 1923- 23-24R
Gordett, Marea (Beth) 1949- 117
Gordh, George (Rudolph) 1912- 13-14R
Gordimer, Nadine 1923- CANR-3
Earlier sketch in CA 5-6R
See also CLC 3, 5, 7, 10, 18, 33
Gordin, Richard Davis 1928- 53-56
Gordis, Robert 1908- CANR-9
Earlier sketch in CA 13-14R
Gordon, Ad
See Hano, Arnold
Gordon, Alan F. 1947- 102
Gordon, Albert I(saac) 1903-1968 CAP-1
Earlier sketch in CA 11-12
Gordon, Alex
See Cotler, Gordon
Gordon, Alison (Ruth) 1943- 121
Gordon, Alvin J. 1912- 33-36R
Gordon, Ambrose, Jr. 1920-1987 33-36R
Obituary 122
Gordon, Andrew (Mark) 1945- 115
Gordon, Angela
See Paine, Lauran (Bosworth)
Gordon, Anne Wolrige
See Wolrige Gordon, Anne
Gordon, Antoinette K. 1892(?)-1975
Obituary 57-60
Gordon, Archibald Victor Dudley
1913-1984 Obituary 114
Gordon, Archie
See Gordon, Archibald Victor Dudley
Gordon, Arthur 1912- 5-6R
Gordon, Barbara 1935- CANR-17
Earlier sketch in CA 89-92
Gordon, Barry (Lewis John) 1934- 102
Gordon, Bernard K. 1932- 85-88
Gordon, Bernard Ludwig 1931- 29-32R
See also SATA 27
Gordon, Bertram M(artin) 1943- 101
Gordon, Beverly 1948- 93-96
Gordon, Burton L(e Roy) 1920- 114
Gordon, Caroline 1895-1981 CAP-1
Obituary 103
Earlier sketch in CA 11-12
See also DLB 4, 9
See also DLBY 81
See also CLC 6, 13, 29
Gordon, Charles William 1860-1937
Brief entry 109
Gordon, Colonel H. R.
See Ellis, Edward S(ylvester)
Gordon, Cyrus H(erzl) 1908- CANR-5
Earlier sketch in CA 4R
Gordon, Dane R. 1925- 33-36R
Gordon, David Cole 1922- 25-28R
Gordon, David J. 1929- Brief entry 105
Gordon, Diana
See Andrews, Lucilla Mathew
Gordon, Diana R(ussell) 1938- 49-52
Gordon, Donald
See Payne, Donald Gordon
Gordon, Donald Craigie 1911- 19-20R
Gordon, Donald E(dward) 1931-1984
Obituary 112
Gordon, Donald Ramsay 1929- CANR-14
Earlier sketch in CA 37-40R
Gordon, Doreen
See Chard, Judy
Gordon, Dorothy 1893-1970 73-76
See also SATA 20
Gordon, Edmund Wyatt 1921- 37-40R
Gordon, Edwin 1927- CANR-10
Earlier sketch in CA 17-18R
Gordon, Ernest 1916- CANR-2
Earlier sketch in CA 1R
Gordon, (Alexander) Esme 1910- 108
Gordon, Esther S(aranga) 1935- CANR-7
Earlier sketch in CA 53-56
See also SATA 10
Gordon, Ethel Edison 1915- 53-56
Gordon, Felice 1939- 97-100
Gordon, Frederick CAP-2
Earlier sketch in CA 19-20
See also SATA 1
Gordon, Fritz
See Jarvis, Fred(erick) G(ordon, Jr.)
Gordon, Gary
See Edmonds, I(vy) G(ordon)
Gordon, George
See Hasford, (Jerry) Gustav
Gordon, George Byron 1911- 33-36R
Gordon, George J(acob) 1943- 111
Gordon, George N(ewton) 1926- CANR-5
Earlier sketch in CA 1R
Gordon, Gerald 1909- CAP-1
Earlier sketch in CA 13-14
Gordon, Giles (Alexander Esme) 1940- 41-44R
See also DLB 14
Gordon, Gordon 1912- CANR-7
Earlier sketch in CA 5-6R
Gordon, Guanetta Stewart 37-40R
Gordon, Hal
See Goodwin, Harold Leland
Gordon, Harold J(ackson), Jr. 1919- 33-36R
Gordon, Harry
See Gordon, Henry Alfred
Gordon, (Charles) Harry (Clinton) Pirie
See Pirie-Gordon, (Charles) Harry
(Clinton)
Gordon, Henry Alfred 1925- CANR-5
Earlier sketch in CA 53-56
Gordon, I(an) R(obert) F(raser) 1939- 69-72
Gordon, Ian
See Fellowes-Gordon, Ian (Douglas)
Gordon, Ian A(listair) 1908- CANR-11
Earlier sketch in CA 25-28R
Gordon, Ida L. 1907- CAP-2
Earlier sketch in CA 33-36
Gordon, Ira J(ay) 1923- 69-72
Gordon, (Gilbert) James 1918- 61-64
Gordon, Jane
See Lee, Elsie
Gordon, Jeffie Ross
See Enderle, Judith (Ann) Ross
Gordon, Jeffie Ross
See Tessler, Stephanie Gordon
Gordon, Joanne J(oy) 1956- 108
Gordon, John (Rutherford) 1890-1974
Obituary 104
Gordon, John (William) 1925- CANR-11
Earlier sketch in CA 103
Gordon, John
See Gesner, Clark
Gordon, John Fraser 1916- CANR-22
Earlier sketch in CA 105
Gordon, John Steele 1944- 57-60
Gordon, Kermit 1916-1976 Obituary 65-68
Gordon, Kurtz
See Kurtz, C(larence) Gordon
Gordon, Leland J(ames) 1897- 41-44R
Gordon, Leonard 1935- 53-56
Gordon, Leonard A. 1938- 37-40R
Gordon, Leonard H. D. 1928- 29-32R
Gordon, Lesley
See Elliott, Lesley
Gordon, Lew
See Baldwin, Gordon C.
Gordon, Lillian L. 1925-1977 29-32R
Gordon, Lincoln 1913- 117
Gordon, (Irene) Linda 1940- CANR-10
Earlier sketch in CA 65-68
Gordon, Lois G. 1938- CANR-13
Earlier sketch in CA 33-36R
Gordon, Lou 1917(?)-1977 Obituary 69-72
Gordon, Margaret (Anna) 1939- SATA-9
Gordon, Margaret T(aber) 1939- 81-84
Gordon, Mark 1942- 118
Gordon, Mary (Catherine) 1949- 102
See also DLB 6
See also DLBY 81
See also CLC 13, 22
Gordon, Mary Ebbitt
See Winters, Catherine (Mary)
Gordon, Michael 1940- 41-44R
Gordon, Michael (David) 1952- 123
Gordon, Mildred 1912-1979 CANR-7
Obituary 85-88
Earlier sketch in CA 5-6R
See also SATA 24
Gordon, Mitchell 1925- 7-8R
Gordon, Myron J(ules) 1920- CANR-6
Earlier sketch in CA 5-6R
Gordon, Nancy
See Heinl, Nancy G(ordon)
Gordon, Noah 1926- 17-18R
Gordon, Oliver
See Emerson, H(enry) O(liver)
Gordon, Patricia 1909- 21-22R
Gordon, Percival Hector 1884-1975 41-44R
Gordon, Peter
See Wilkes-Hunter, R(ichard)
Gordon, R(ichard) L(aurence) 1920-
Brief entry 114
Gordon, Ray
See Wainwright, Gordon Ray
Gordon, Rex
See Hough, S(tanley) B(ennett)
Gordon, Richard
See Ostlere, Gordon (Stanley)
Gordon, Richard A(lewis) 1934- 29-32R
Gordon, Robert A(aron) 1908-1978 CANR-4
Obituary 77-80
Earlier sketch in CA 5-6R
Gordon, Robert C(oningsby) 1921- 5-6R
Gordon, Robert J. 1947- 121
Gordon, Ruth 1896-1985 81-84
Obituary 117
Gordon, Samuel 1907(?)-1984 Obituary 114
Gordon, Sanford D(aniel) 1924- 33-36R
Gordon, Selma
See Lanes, Selma Gordon
Gordon, Shirley 1921- 97-100
See also SATA 41, 48
Gordon, Sol 1923- CANR-4
Earlier sketch in CA 53-56
See also SATA 11
See also CLC 26
Gordon, Steve 1938(?)-1982 Obituary 108
Gordon, Stewart
See Shirreffs, Gordon D(onald)
Gordon, Strathearn 1902-1983 Obituary 109
Gordon, Suzanne 1945- CANR-4
Earlier sketch in CA 49-52
Gordon, Sydney 1914- 29-32R
Gordon, Theodore J. 1930- 17-18R
Gordon, Thomas 1918- 29-32R
Gordon, Tom
See Thomas, Gordon
Gordon, Walter Kelly 1930- 33-36R
Gordon, Walter L(ockhart) 1906-1987 97-100
Obituary 122
Gordon, Wendell (Chaffee) 1916- 19-20R
Gordone, Charles 1925- 93-96
See also DLB 7
See also CLC 1, 4
Gordons, The
See Gordon, Gordon
and Gordon, Mildred
Gordon Walker, Patrick (Chrestien)
1907- 29-32R
Gordon-Watson, Mary 1948- 112
Gordy, Berry, Sr. 1888-1978 102
Gore, Albert (Arnold) 1907- Brief entry 112
Gore, Arthur Kattendyke S(trange) D(avid)
A(rchibald) 1910-1983 Obituary 109
Gore, John Francis 1885-1983 Obituary 110
Gore, Robert Hayes 1886-1972 Obituary 89-92
Gore, William Jay 1924- 11-12R
Goreau, Angeline 1951- 102
Gore-Booth, Paul Henry 1909-1984
Obituary 113
Gorecki, Jan 1926- 57-60
Gorelick, Bryna Siegel
See Siegel-Gorelick, Bryna
Gorelick, Molly C. 1920- 23-24R
See also SATA 9
Gorelik, Mordecai 1899- CAP-2
Earlier sketch in CA 23-24
Goren, Arthur A(ryeh) 1926- Brief entry 111
Goren, Charles H(enry) 1901- 69-72
Goren, Judith 1933- 61-64
Gorenko, Anna Andreevna
See Akhmatova, Anna
Gorenstein, Paul 1934- 114
Gorenstein, Shirley 1928- 73-76
Gorer, Geoffrey (Edgar) 1905-1985 69-72
Obituary 116
Gores, Joe
See Gores, Joseph N(icholas)
Gores, Joseph N(icholas) 1931- CANR-10
Earlier sketch in CA 25-28R
Gorey, Edward (St. John) 1925- CANR-9
Earlier sketch in CA 7-8R
See also SATA 27, 29
See also DLB 61
Gorey, Hays 57-60
Gorham, Charles Orson 1911-1975 CANR-6
Obituary 61-64
Earlier sketch in CA 1R
See also SATA 36
Gorham, J(eanne) U(rich) 1920- 53-56
Gorham, Maurice Anthony Coneys 1902- 9-10R
Gorham, Michael
See Folsom, Franklin (Brewster)
Gorkin, Jess 1913-1985 Obituary 115
Gorky, Maxim
See Peshkov, Alexei Maximovich
See also TCLC 8
Gorling, Lars
See Goerling, Lars
Gorman, Beth
See Paine, Lauran (Bosworth)
Gorman, Burton W(illiam) 1907- 29-32R
Gorman, George H. 1916-1982 Obituary 106
Gorman, Ginny
See Zachary, Hugh
Gorman, John Andrew 1938- 41-44R
Gorman, Katherine ?-1972 CAP-2
Earlier sketch in CA 29-32
Gorman, Ralph 1897-1972 Obituary 37-40R
Gorman, T. Walter 1916(?)-1972
Obituary 37-40R
Gorman, Thomas David 1919-1986 123
Obituary 120
Gorman, Tom
See Gorman, Thomas David
Gormley, Beatrice 1942- 113
See also SATA 35, 39
Gormley, Gerard (Joseph) 1931- CANR-14
Earlier sketch in CA 81-84
Gormley, Mike 1945- 69-72
Gorn, Janice L(eonora) 1915- 53-56
Gorn, Mordechai Martin 1890-1986
Obituary 119
Gorney, Roderic 1924- 73-76
Gorney, Sondra 1918- 45-48
Gornick, Vivian 1935- 101
Goro, Fritz 1901-1986 Obituary 121
Gorodetsky, Gabriel 1945- 69-72

INDEX

Gorog, Judith (Allen) 1938- 114
See also SATA 39
Gorrell, Robert Mark 1914- CANR-5
Earlier sketch in CA 3R
Gorsline, Douglas (Warner) 1913-1985 .. CANR-9
Obituary 116
Earlier sketch in CA 61-64
See also SATA 11, 43
Gorsline, (Sally) Marie 1928- 106
See also SATA 28
Gorsline, S. M.
See Gorsline, (Sally) Marie
Gorst, Elliot Marcet 1885-1973 Obituary 104
Gortner, Ross A(iken), Jr. 1912- 5-6R
Gortner, Willis Alway 1913- 108
Gorton, Richard A. 1932- CANR-7
Earlier sketch in CA 57-60
Goryan, Sirak
See Saroyan, William
Goscilo, Helena 1945- 118
Goscinny, Rene 1926-1977 117
Obituary 113
See also SATA 39, 47
Gosden, Freeman F(isher) 1899-1982
Obituary 108
Gosden, Peter Henry John Heather 1927- .. 93-96
Gosdin, Rex 1938(?)-1983 Obituary 109
Gose, Elliott B(ickley), Jr. 1926- 33-36R
Goshay, Robert C. 1931- 15-16R
Goshen, Charles E(rnest) 1916- CANR-13
Earlier sketch in CA 21-22R
Goshgarian, Gary 1942- 112
Goshorn, Elizabeth 1953- 61-64
Goslin, David A. 1936- 9-10R
Gosling, J(ustin) C(yril) B(ertrand) 1930- .. 77-80
Gosling, John Neville 1905- 7-8R
Gosling, Nigel 1909-1982 Obituary 106
Gosling, Paula 1939- 111
Gosling, William Flower 1901- 7-8R
Goslovich, Marianne
See Brown, Morris Cecil
Gosnell, Betty
See Gosnell, Elizabeth Duke Tucker
Gosnell, Elizabeth Duke Tucker 1921- 29-32R
Gosnell, Harold F(oote) 1896- 41-44R
Goss, Clay 1946- 57-60
Gosse, Edmund (William) 1849-1928
Brief entry 117
See also DLB 57
Gosselin, Chris(topher C.) 1929- 110
Gossett, Philip 1941- CANR-15
Earlier sketch in CA 89-92
Gossett, Thomas F. 1916- 13-14R
Gossman, Lionel 1929- CANR-7
Earlier sketch in CA 17-18R
Gostelow, Mary 1943- CANR-8
Earlier sketch in CA 61-64
Goswami, Maggie 1937- 117
Gotesky, Rubin 1906- 45-48
Gotfurt, Frederick 1902(?)-1973 Obituary ... 104
Gotlieb, Phyllis Fay (Bloom) 1926- CANR-7
Earlier sketch in CA 15-16R
See also CLC 18
Gotlieb, Sondra 1936- Brief entry 111
Gotoff, Harold C(harles) 1936- Brief entry .. 112
Gots, Ronald E(ric) 1943- 65-68
Gotshalk, D(ilman) W(alter) 1901-1973 .. CANR-6
Earlier sketch in CA 1R
Gott, K(enneth) D(avidson) 1923- 81-84
Gott, Richard (Willoughby) 1938- 81-84
Gottehrer, Barry H. 1935- 13-14R
Gotterer, Malcolm H(arold) 1924- 37-40R
Gottesfeld, Evelyn 1948- 104
Gottesfeld, Mary L. 1926(?)-1984
Obituary 113
Gottesman, Irving I(sadore) 1930- 37-40R
Gottesman, Ronald 1933- CANR-13
Earlier sketch in CA 33-36R
Gottesman, S. D.
See Kornbluth, C(yril) M.
and Lowndes, Robert A(ugustine) W(ard)
and Pohl, Frederik
Gottfried, Alex 1919- 1R
Gottfried, Manfred 1900-1985 Obituary 117
Gottfried, Martin 1933- CANR-14
Earlier sketch in CA 23-24R
Gottfried, Robert Steven 1949- 111
Gottfried, Theodore Mark 1928- CANR-18
Earlier sketch in CA 33-36R
Gottlieb, Adolph 1903-1974 Obituary 49-52
Gottlieb, Beatrice M. 1889(?)-1979
Obituary 89-92
Gottlieb, Bernhardt Stanley 1898- 2R
Gottlieb, Carla 1912- 119
Gottlieb, Darcy 1922- 77-80
Gottlieb, Elaine 61-64
Gottlieb, Gerald 1923- 5-6R
See also SATA 7
Gottlieb, Lois Davidson 1926- 17-28R
Gottlieb, Moshe R(aphael) 1931- 113
Gottlieb, Naomi R(uth) 1925- 57-60
Gottlieb, Paul 1936- 93-96
Gottlieb, Robin (Grossman) 1928- CANR-2
Earlier sketch in CA 4R
Gottlieb, (Anne Ruth) Vera 1945- 117
Gottlieb, William P(aul) 1917- 101
See also SATA 24
Gottman, John M(ordechai) 1942- CANR-12
Earlier sketch in CA 69-72
Gottschalk, Elin Toona
See Toona, Elin(-Kai)
Gottschalk, Louis (Reichenthal)
1899-1975 .... CANR-9
Obituary 57-60
Earlier sketch in CA 15-16R
Gottschalk, Louis A(ugust) 1916- CANR-19
Earlier sketches in CA 53-56, CANR-5
Gottschalk, Paul A. 1939- 61-64
Gottschalk, Shimon S. 1929- 89-92
Gottschalk, Stephen 1940- 77-80
Gottsegen, Abby J. 1956- 105
Gottsegen, Gloria Behar 1930- 77-80
Gottshall, Franklin Henry 1902- CANR-2
Earlier sketch in CA 7-8R
Gottwald, Norman Karol 1926- 108
Gotwals, Vernon (Detwiler, Jr.) 1924- 5-6R
Gotz, Ignacio L.
See Goetz, Ignacio L.
Gotzsche, Anne-Lise 1939- 97-100
Goud, Anne 1917- 61-64
Goudeket, Maurice 1889-1977 Obituary ...69-72
Goudey, Alice E. 1898- 73-76
See also SATA 20
Goudge, Elizabeth (de Beauchamp)
1900-1984 .... CANR-5
Obituary 112
Earlier sketch in CA 7-8R
See also SATA 2, 38
Goudie, Andrew Shaw 1945- CANR-17
Earlier sketches in CA 49-52, CANR-1
Goudinoff, Peter Alexis 1941- 112
Goudiss, Maria Agnes D'Elia 1941- 114
Goudsmit, Samuel A(braham) 1902-1978
Obituary 81-84
Gouge, Orson
See Larner, Jeremy
Gough, Barry Morton 1938- CANR-11
Earlier sketch in CA 61-64
Gough, Catherine
See Mulgan, Catherine
See also SATA 24
Gough, John W(iedhofft) 1900- 15-16R
Gough, Kathleen
See Aberle, Kathleen Gough
Gough, Philip 1908- SATA-45
Gough, Vera 25-28R
Gougov, Nikola Delchev 1914- 45-48
Goulart, Frances Sheridan 1938- CANR-7
Earlier sketch in CA 57-60
Goulart, Ron(ald Joseph) 1933- CANR-7
Earlier sketch in CA 25-28R
See also SATA 6
Gould, Alan
See Canning, Victor
Gould, Alfred Ernest 1909- 7-8R
Gould, Beatrice Blackmar 1898- CAP-2
Earlier sketch in CA 25-28
Gould, Bruce Grant 1942- CANR-22
Earlier sketch in CA 45-48
Gould, Carol C. 1946- 103
Gould, Cecil (Hilton Monk) 1918- CANR-9
Earlier sketch in CA 21-22R
Gould, Chester 1900-1985 77-80
Obituary 116
See also SATA 43, 49
Gould, Douglas Parsons 1919- 2R
Gould, Ed(win Orrin) 1936- CANR-16
Earlier sketch in CA 93-96
Gould, Felix CAP-1
Earlier sketch in CA 11-12
Gould, James A(dams) 1922- 33-36R
Gould, James Warren 1924- CANR-2
Earlier sketch in CA 5-6R
Gould, Jay R(eid) 1906- CANR-24
Earlier sketch in CA 45-48
Gould, Jean R(osalind) 1919- CANR-21
Earlier sketches in CA 5-6R, CANR-3
See also SATA 11
Gould, Joan 1927- 107
Gould, John (Thomas) 1908- 65-68
Gould, John A(llen) 1944- 57-60
Gould, Joseph E(dmund) 1912- 11-12R
Gould, Josiah B(ancroft) 1928- 45-48
Gould, Joy
See Boyum, Joy Gould
Gould, Leroy C. 1937- 93-96
Gould, Leslie 1902-1977 Obituary 73-76
Gould, Lettie
See Paxson, Ethel
Gould, Lewis L(udlow) 1939- 41-44R
Gould, Lilian CANR-2
Earlier sketch in CA 49-52
See also SATA 6
Gould, Lois 1938(?)- 77-80
See also CLC 4, 10
Gould, Marilyn 1928- SATA-15
Gould, Mary Earle 1885- 7-8R
Gould, Maurice M. 1909- CANR-5
Earlier sketch in CA 7-8R
Gould, Milton Samuel 1909- 93-96
Gould, P(eter) Robin 1932- 3R
Gould, Philip 1925- 124
Gould, Randall 1898(?)-1979 Obituary 89-92
Gould, Richard A(llan) 1939- CANR-7
Earlier sketch in CA 53-56
Gould, Roger L(ouis) 1935- Brief entry 110
Gould, Ronald 1904- 102
Gould, Shirley (Goldman) 81-84
Gould, Stephen Jay 1941- CANR-10
Earlier sketch in CA 77-80
Gould, Wallace 1882-1940 .... DLB-54
Gould, Warwick 1947- 110
Gould, Wesley Larson 1917- CANR-2
Earlier sketch in CA 2R
Gould, William B(enjamin) 1936-
Brief entry 118
Goulden, Joseph C. (Jr.) 1934- CANR-8
Earlier sketch in CA 17-18R
Goulden, Mark 1896(?)-1980 Obituary 101
Goulder, Grace
See Izant, Grace Goulder
Goulding, Brian 1933- 103
Goulding, Dorothy Jane 1923- 65-68
Goulding, Peter Geoffrey 1920- 106
Goulding, Ray(mond Walter) 1922- 85-88
Gouldner, Alvin W(ard) 1920-1980 .... CANR-17
Obituary 102
Earlier sketch in CA 13-14R
Gouled, Vivian G(loria) 1911- 41-44R
Goulet, Denis A. 1931- CANR-15
Earlier sketch in CA 41-44R
Goulet, John 1942- 85-88
Goulet, Robert (Joseph) 1924- 3R
Goulet, Rosalina Morales 1930- 119
Goulett, Harlan M(ador) 1927-1969 ...... CAP-2
Earlier sketch in CA 21-22
Goulianos, Joan Rodman 1939- 49-52
Gouliashki, (Stoianov) Andrei 1914- ... CANR-19
Earlier sketch in CA 101
Goullart, Peter 1902- CAP-1
Earlier sketch in CA 13-14
Goulson, Carlyn Floyd 1922- 113
Goulson, Cary F.
See Goulson, Carlyn Floyd
Gourdie, Thomas 1913- CANR-1
Earlier sketch in CA 4R
Gourevitch, Doris-Jeanne 19-20R
Gourevitch, Peter A(lexis) 1943- 112
Gourhan, Andre (Georges Leandre) Leroi
See Leroi-Gourhan, Andre (Georges
Leandre)
Gouri, Haim 1923- 103
Gourlay, Elizabeth 1917- 112
Gourley, G(erald) Douglas 1911- 2R
Gourley, Jay 1947- 73-76
Gourlie, Norah Dundas CAP-1
Earlier sketch in CA 9-10
Gourmont, Remy de 1858-1915
Brief entry 109
See also TCLC 17
Gourse, Leslie 1939- 4R
Gouzenko, Igor 1919-1982 Obituary 107
Govan, Christine Noble 1898- CANR-2
Earlier sketch in CA 4R
See also SATA 9
Govan, Thomas P(ayne) 1907-1979 ..... CANR-2
Earlier sketch in CA 45-48
Gove, Philip Babcock 1902-1972 .... CAP-1
Obituary 37-40R
Earlier sketch in CA 13-14
Gove, Samuel K(imball) 1923- 33-36R
Gove, Walter R(oberts) 1938- 118
Goveia, Elsa V(esta) 1925- 21-22R
Govenar, Alan B(ruce) 1952- 109
Gover, (John) Robert 1929- 11-12R
Govern, Elaine 1939- 53-56
See also SATA 26
Govier, Katherine 1948- CANR-18
Earlier sketch in CA 101
Govinda, Anagarika Brahmacari 1898- .. CANR-14
Earlier sketch in CA 23-24R
Govinda, Lama Anagarika Brahmacari
See Govinda, Anagarika Brahmacari
Govoni, Albert P(eter) 1914-1982 53-56
Obituary 108
Govoni, Laura E. 1914- 33-36R
Govorchin, Gerald Gilbert 1912- 13-14R
Gow, Donald 1920- 41-44R
Gow, Ronald 1897- CANR-13
Earlier sketches in CA 25-28, CAP-2
Gowan, Donald E(lmer) 1929- 69-72
Gowan, John Curtis 1912-1986 .... CANR-5
Obituary 121
Earlier sketch in CA 13-14R
Gowans, Alan 1923- CANR-18
Earlier sketches in CA 1R, CANR-2
Gowar, Antonia
See Dunford, Judith
and Margolis, Susanna
Gowen, (Samuel) Emmett 1902- CAP-1
Earlier sketch in CA 11-12
Gowen, James A(nthony) 1928- 17-18R
Gower, Herschel 1919- 5-6R
Gowers, Ernest (Arthur) 1880-1966
Obituary 89-92
Gowin, D(ixie) Bob 1925- 108
Gowing, Lawrence (Burnett) 1918- 11-12R
Gowing, Margaret (Margaret Mary) 1921- .. 81-84
Gowing, Peter Gordon 1930- 53-56
Gowland, Mariano E(zequiel) 1933- 7-8R
Goy, Richard J(ohn) 1947- 118
Goyder, George Armin 1908- 105
Goyen, (Charles) William 1915-1983 .. CANR-6
Obituary 110
Earlier sketch in CA 7-8R
See also DLB 2
See also DLBY 83
See also CLC 5, 8, 14, 40
See also AITN 2
Goyeneche, Gabriel
See Avalle-Arce, Juan Bautista
Goyer, Robert S(tanton) 1923- CANR-16
Earlier sketch in CA 41-44R
Goytisolo, Juan 1931- 85-88
See also CLC 5, 10, 23
Gozzi, Raymond D(ante) 1920- 116
Graaf, Peter
See Youd, Samuel
Grabar, Andre 1896- 111
Grabar, Oleg 1929- 124
Grabbe, Paul 1902- 93-96
Graber, Alexander 1914- CANR-1
Earlier sketch in CA 2R
See also SATA 7
Graber, Doris A. 1923- CANR-13
Earlier sketch in CA 33-36R
Graber, Gerry S(amuel) 1928- 81-84
Graber, Richard (Fredrick) 1927- 85-88
See also SATA 26
Grabianski, Janusz 1928-1976 .... CANR-2
Earlier sketch in CA 45-48
See also SATA 30, 39
Grabill, Joseph L. 1931- 29-32R
Grabner-Haider, Anton 1940- 73-76
Grabo, Norman Stanley 1930- 1R
Graboff, Abner 1919- 107
See also SATA 35
Grabois, Aryeh 1930- 105
Grabosky, Peter Nils 1945- 85-88
Grabow, Stephen (Harris) 1943- 121
Grabowski, Z(bigniew) Anthony 1903- 7-8R
Graburn, Nelson H(ayes) H(enry) 1936- . CANR-1
Earlier sketch in CA 45-48
Gracchus, Sidney J(oseph) 1930- 97-100
Grace, F(rances Jane) 111
See also SATA 45
Grace, Gerald R(upert) 1936- CANR-22
Earlier sketch in CA 45-48
Grace, Helen K(ennedy) 1935- 53-56
Grace, Joan C(arroll) 1921- 61-64
Grace, John Patrick 1942- 112
Grace, Joseph
See Hornby, John (Wilkinson)
Grace, Sherrill E(lizabeth) 1944- 110
Grace, William J(oseph), Jr. 1948- 111
Grace, William Joseph 1910- CAP-1
Earlier sketch in CA 13-14
Gracey, Harry L(ewis) 1933- 41-44R
Gracia, Jorge J(esus) E(miliano) 1942- 109
Gracie, Archibald 1859-1912 Brief entry 122
Gracq, Julien
See Poirier, Louis
See also CLC 11
Gracy, David B(ergen) II 1941- CANR-16
Earlier sketch in CA 25-28R
Gracza, Margaret Young 1928- 15-16R
Grad, Bonnie L(ee) 1949- 117
Grad, Eli 1928- 115
Grad, Frank P. 1924- 33-36R
Grade, Arnold (Edward) 1928- 29-32R
Grade, Chaim 1910-1982 93-96
Obituary 107
See also CLC 10
Gradidge, Roderick 1929- 117
Gradon, Pamela O(live) E(lizabeth)
1915- 97-100
Grady, Don(ald Wyndham) 1929- 115
Grady, Henry W. 1850-1889 .... DLB-23
Grady, James (Thomas) 1949- CANR-22
Earlier sketch in CA 104
Grady, Ronan Calistus, Jr. 1921- 49-52
Grady, Tex
See Webb, Jack (Randolph)
Grae, Ida 1918- 97-100
Graeber, Charlotte Towner SATA-44
Graebner, Alan 1938- 61-64
Graebner, Norman A. 1915- CANR-24
Earlier sketches in CA 15-16R, CANR-7
Graebner, Walter 1909- CAP-1
Earlier sketch in CA 15-16
Graebner, William Sievers 1943- 104
Graedon, Joe (David) 1945- 77-80
Graef, Hilda C(harlotte) 1907- 7-8R
Graeff, Grace M. 1918- 23-24R
Graeme, Bruce
See Jeffries, Graham Montague
Graeme, David
See Jeffries, Graham Montague
Graeme, Roderic
See Jeffries, Roderic (Graeme)
Graeme, Sheila 1944- 25-28R
Graf, Le Roy Philip 1915- 41-44R
Graf, Oskar Maria 1894-1967 Obituary 115
See also DLB 56
Graf, Rudolf F. 1926- 11-12R
Grafe, Felix
See Greve, Felix Paul (Berthold Friedrich)
Graff, George 1886-1973 Obituary 41-44R
Graff, Gerald (Edward) 1937- 29-32R
Graff, Henry F(ranklin) 1921- CANR-17
Earlier sketches in CA 1R, CANR-1
Graff, Polly Anne Colver
See Colver, Anne
Graff, S. Stewart 1908- 49-52
See also SATA 9
Grafton, Ann
See Owens, Thelma
Grafton, Carl 1942- 53-56
Grafton, Sue 1940- 108
Graglia, Lino A(nthony) 1930- 69-72
Graham, A(lexander) John 1930- CANR-8
Earlier sketch in CA 15-16R
Graham, A(lexander) S(teel) 1917- 104
Graham, Ada 1931- CANR-4
Earlier sketch in CA 29-32R
See also SATA 11
Graham, Aelred 1907-1984 .... CANR-5
Obituary 114
Earlier sketch in CA 7-8R
Graham, Alice Walworth 1905- CANR-5
Earlier sketch in CA 2R
Graham, Alistair (Dundas) 1938- 49-52
Graham, Andrew Guillemard 1913-1981
Obituary 103
Graham, Angus (Charles) 1919- 17-18R
Graham, Billy
See Graham, William Franklin
Graham, Brenda Knight 1942- 103
See also SATA 32
Graham, Carlotta
See Wallmann, Jeffrey M(iner)
Graham, Caroline 1931- 119
Graham, Charles S.
See Tubb, E(dwin) C(harles)
Graham, Charlotte
See Bowden, Joan Chase

Graham, Clarence H. 1906-1971
 Obituary 33-36R
Graham, David (Duane) 1927- 69-72
Graham, Desmond 1940- 73-76
Graham, Don B. 1940- CANR-18
 Earlier sketch in CA 102
Graham, Donald W(ilkinson) 1903- CAP-2
 Earlier sketch in CA 29-32
Graham, Eleanor 1896-1984 73-76
 Obituary 112
 See also SATA 18, 38
Graham, Elizabeth
 See Edmonds, Arthur Denis
Graham, Frank, Jr. 1925- CANR-4
 Earlier sketch in CA 11-12R
 See also SATA 11
Graham, Fred P(atterson) 1931- 37-40R
Graham, Gene S(wann) 1924- 41-44R
Graham, George J(ackson), Jr. 1938- 45-48
Graham, Gerald (Sandford) 1903- 102
Graham, Grace 1910- CAP-1
 Earlier sketch in CA 13-14
Graham, Harry Edward 1940- 29-32R
Graham, Henry 1930- 103
Graham, Howard Jay 1905- CAP-2
 Earlier sketch in CA 33-36
Graham, Hugh
 See Barrows, (Ruth) Marjorie
Graham, Hugh Davis 1936- CANR-13
 Earlier sketch in CA 23-24R
Graham, Ian (James Alastair) 1923- CANR-2
 Earlier sketch in CA 45-48
Graham, Ilse 1914- CANR-8
 Earlier sketch in CA 57-60
Graham, J. W. 1925- 93-96
Graham, J(ames) Walter 1906- 4R
Graham, James
 See Patterson, Henry
Graham, John 1926- 33-36R
 See also SATA 11
Graham, John
 See Phillips, David Graham
Graham, John Alexander 1941- 25-28R
Graham, John Remington 1940- 33-36R
Graham, John Thomas 1928- 53-56
Graham, Jorie 1951- 111
Graham, Jory 1925-1983 .... CANR-13
 Obituary 109
 Earlier sketch in CA 29-32R
Graham, Joseph M. 1911(?)-1971
 Obituary 104
Graham, Katharine (Meyer) 1917- 105
 See also AITN 1
Graham, (George) Kenneth 1936- 77-80
Graham, Kennon
 See Harrison, David L(ee)
Graham, Larry
 See Graham, Lawrence (Otis)
Graham, Lawrence (Otis) 1962- 116
Graham, Lawrence S(herman) 1936- 45-48
Graham, Lee E. 1913(?)-1977 Obituary 73-76
Graham, Lloyd M. 1889- 97-100
Graham, Loren R. 1933- CANR-13
 Earlier sketch in CA 21-22R
Graham, Lorenz (Bell) 1902- 9-10R
 See also SATA 2
 See also SAAS 5
 See also CLR 10
Graham, Malcolm 1923- 53-56
Graham, Margaret Althea 1924- 11-12R
Graham, Margaret Bloy 1920- 77-80
 See also SATA 11
Graham, Matthew
 See Arnold, Peter
Graham, Michael 1898-1972 Obituary 104
Graham, Michael Angelo 1921-1985
 Obituary 117
Graham, Milton D(uke) 1916- 45-48
Graham, Neile 1958- 113
Graham, (Roger) Neill 1941- 109
Graham, Neill
 See Duncan, W(illiam) Murdoch
Graham, Otis L., Jr. 1935- CANR-11
 Earlier sketch in CA 21-22R
Graham, Patricia Albjerg 1935- 25-28R
Graham, Peter W(illiam) 1951- 121
Graham, Philip Leslie 1915-1963
 Obituary 89-92
Graham, R(obert) B(ontine) Cunninghame
 See Cunninghame Graham, R(obert) B(ontine)
Graham, Rachel (Metcalf) 1895- CAP-1
 Earlier sketch in CA 15-16
Graham, Ramona
 See Cook, Ramona Graham
Graham, Richard 1934- CANR-15
 Earlier sketch in CA 29-32R
Graham, Robert
 See Haldeman, Joe (William)
Graham, Robert G. 1925- CANR-12
 Earlier sketch in CA 25-28R
Graham, Robin Lee 1949- 49-52
 See also SATA 7
Graham, Ruth
 See Evans, Jean
Graham, Sean 1920- 21-22R
Graham, Sheilah 1908(?)- 108
 See also AITN 1
Graham, Shirley
 See Du Bois, Shirley Graham
Graham, Stephen 1884-1975 Obituary 93-96
Graham, (Maude Fitzgerald) Susan 1912- 19-20R
Graham, Thomas F(rancis) 1923- 23-24R
Graham, Tom
 See Lewis, (Harry) Sinclair
Graham, Vanessa
 See Fraser, Anthea
Graham, Victor E(rnest) 1920- 93-96
Graham, Virginia
 See Guttenberg, Virginia
Graham, W(illiam) Fred 1930- 33-36R
Graham, W(illiam) S(ydney) 1918-1986 73-76
 Obituary 118
 See also DLB 20
 See also CLC 29
Graham, William Franklin 1918- CANR-20
 Earlier sketch in CA 9-10R
Graham, Winston (Mawdsley) 1910- CANR-22
 Earlier sketches in CA 49-52, CANR-2
 See also CLC 23
Graham-Barber, Lynda 1944- 113
 See also SATA 42
Graham-Cameron, M.
 See Graham-Cameron, M(alcolm) G(ordon)
Graham-Cameron, M(alcolm) G(ordon) 1931- 123
 See also SATA 45
Graham-Cameron, Mike
 See Graham-Cameron, M(alcolm) G(ordon)
Graham-Campbell, David (John) 1912- 113
Grahame, Kenneth 1859-1932 Brief entry 108
 See also YABC 1
 See also DLB 34
 See also CLR 5
Graham Scott, Peter 1923- 108
Graham-White, Anthony 1940- 61-64
Graham-Yooll, Andrew M(ichael) 1944- 108
Grahn, Judith L. 1940- 122
 Brief entry 116
Grahn, Judy
 See Grahn, Judith L.
Grainger, A(nthony) J(ohn) 1929- 33-36R
Grainger, J(ohn) H(erbert) 1917- 77-80
Grainger, Margaret 1936- 116
Gralapp, Leland Wilson 1921- 15-16R
Gram, Harold A(lbert) 1927- 25-28R
Gram, Moltke (Stefanus) 1938- CANR-13
 Earlier sketch in CA 69-72
Gramatky, Hardie 1907-1979 .... CANR-3
 Obituary 85-88
 Earlier sketch in CA 2R
 See also SATA 1, 23, 30
 See also DLB 22
 See also AITN 1
Grambs, Jean D(resden) 1919- CANR-7
 Earlier sketch in CA 17-18R
Gramet, Charles 3R
Gramick, Jeannine 1942- 113
Grammaticus
 See Blaiklock, Edward Musgrave
Grampp, William D(yer) 1914- 33-36R
Grams, Armin 1924- 45-48
Granados, Paul
 See Kent, Arthur William Charles
Granat, Robert 1925- CANR-2
 Earlier sketch in CA 2R
Granatstein, J(ack) L(awrence) 1939- CANR-10
 Earlier sketch in CA 25-28R
Granbeck, Marilyn 1927- 77-80
Granberg, W(ilbur) J(ohn) 1906- 5-6R
Granberry, Edwin 1897- CAP-2
 Earlier sketch in CA 21-22
Granby, Milton
 See Wallmann, Jeffrey M(iner)
Grand, Samuel 1912- 107
 See also SATA 42
Granda, Chabuca
 See Larco, Isabel Granda
Grande, Luke M. 1922- CANR-2
 Earlier sketch in CA 7-8R
Grande Vitesse
 See Walkerley, Rodney Lewis (de Burah)
Grandfield, Raymond J(oseph) 1931- 53-56
Grandower, Elissa
 See Waugh, Hillary Baldwin
Grandville, J. J.
 See Gerard, Jean Ignace Isidore
Grandville, Jean Ignace Isidore Gerard
 See Gerard, Jean Ignace Isidore
Grandy, Richard (Edward) 1942- 77-80
Grange, Chris
 See Gnaegy, Charles
Grange, Cyril 1900- CAP-1
 Earlier sketch in CA 15-16
Grange, Peter
 See Nicole, Christopher Robin
Granger, Bruce Ingham 1920- 1R
Granger, Byrd Howell 1912- 107
Granger, Clive W(illiam) J(ohn) 1934- CANR-8
 Earlier sketch in CA 11-12R
Granger, Darius John
 See Marlowe, Stephen
Granger, Margaret Jane 1925(?)-1977
 Obituary 104
 See also SATA 27
Granger, Peggy
 See Granger, Margaret Jane
Granich, Irving 1894-1967 97-100
 Obituary 45-48
Granick, David 1926- 2R
Granick, Harry 1898- 85-88
Granik, (S.) Theodore 1906-1970
 Obituary 89-92
Granit, Arthur 1917- 120
Granite, Harvey R. 1927- CANR-15
 Earlier sketch in CA 33-36R
Granite, Tony
 See Politella, Dario
Grannis, Chandler B(rinkerhoff) 1912-
 Brief entry 111
Granovetter, Mark S. 1943- 85-88
Granovsky, Anatoli 1922-1974 Obituary 53-56
Granowsky, Alvin 1936- 21-22R
Gransden, Antonia 1928- 77-80
Granstaff, Bill 1925- SATA-10
Grant, Alan
 See Kennington, (Gilbert) Alan
Grant, Alexander T(homas) K(ingdom) 1906- 53-56
Grant, Ambrose
 See Raymond, Rene (Brabazon)
Grant, Anthony
 See Pares, Marion (Stapylton)
Grant, Barbara M(oll) 1932- 53-56
Grant, Ben
 See Granbeck, Marilyn
Grant, Brian W. 1939- CANR-7
 Earlier sketch in CA 57-60
Grant, Bruce 1893-1977 .... CANR-6
 Obituary 69-72
 Earlier sketch in CA 1R
 See also SATA 5, 25
Grant, Bruce Alexander 1925- 107
Grant, C.B.S.
 See Haga, Enoch J.
Grant, Charles L. 1942- 85-88
Grant, Cynthia D. 1950- CANR-20
 Earlier sketch in CA 104
 See also SATA 33
Grant, David
 See Thomas, Craig (David)
Grant, Don
 See Glut, Donald F(rank)
Grant, Donald J. 1939-1984 Obituary 113
Grant, Dorothy 1927- 114
Grant, Dorothy Fremont 1900- CAP-2
 Earlier sketch in CA 23-24
Grant, Elliott Mansfield 1895-1969 .... CANR-5
 Earlier sketch in CA 7-8R
Grant, Ellsworth Strong 1917- 57-60
Grant, Eva 1907- 49-52
 See also SATA 7
Grant, Evva H. 1913-1977 Obituary 104
 See also SATA 27
Grant, Frederick C(lifton) 1891-1974 .... 1R
 Obituary 49-52
Grant, Gerald 1938- 81-84
Grant, Gordon 1875-1962 102
 See also SATA 25
Grant, Gwen(doline Ellen) 1940- CANR-22
 Earlier sketch in CA 106
 See also SATA 47
Grant, H. Roger 1943- 89-92
Grant, Harry J(ohnston) 1881-1963
 Obituary 114
 See also DLB 29
Grant, Hilda Kay 1910- 4R
Grant, Isabel F(rances) 1887-1983
 Obituary 110
Grant, J(ohn) B(arnard) 1940- CANR-6
 Earlier sketch in CA 57-60
Grant, Jack
 See Grant, J(ohn) B(arnard)
Grant, James Edward 1905-1966 Obituary 113
 See also DLB 26
Grant, James G. 1926(?)-1979 Obituary 89-92
Grant, James Russell 1924- CANR-17
 Earlier sketch in CA 101
Grant, Jane (Cole) 1895-1972 .... CAP-2
 Obituary 33-36R
 Earlier sketch in CA 25-28
Grant, Jane
 See Leader, (Evelyn) Barbara (Blackburn)
Grant, Joan
 See Kelsey, Joan Marshall
Grant, Joanne B(enzel) 1940- 106
Grant, John 1933- 77-80
Grant, John E(rnest) 1925- 41-44R
Grant, John J. 1932- 53-56
Grant, John Webster 1919- CANR-6
 Earlier sketch in CA 7-8R
Grant, Judith 1929- 21-22R
Grant, Kay 23-24R
Grant, Kerry S. 1945- 121
Grant, Landon
 See Gribble, Leonard (Reginald)
Grant, (Alice) Leigh 1947- SATA-10
Grant, Louis T(heodore) 1943- 53-56
Grant, Madeleine Parker 1895- 73-76
Grant, Mary A(melia) 1890- CAP-2
 Earlier sketch in CA 25-28
Grant, Mary Kathryn 1941- 81-84
Grant, Matthew G.
 See May, Julian
Grant, Maxwell
 See Gibson, Walter B(rown) and Lynds, Dennis
Grant, Michael 1914- CANR-4
 Earlier sketch in CA 4R
Grant, Myrna (Lois) 1934- CANR-4
 Earlier sketch in CA 53-56
 See also SATA 21
Grant, Neil 1938- CANR-15
 Earlier sketch in CA 33-36R
 See also SATA 14
Grant, Nigel (Duncan Cameron) 1932- CANR-7
 Earlier sketch in CA 17-18R
Grant, Ozro F. 1908- CAP-2
 Earlier sketch in CA 21-22
Grant, Richard B(abson) 1925- CANR-4
 Earlier sketch in CA 3R
Grant, Robert B(ruce) 1933- 45-48
Grant, Robert M(cQueen) 1917- 65-68
Grant, Roderick 1941- Brief entry 112
Grant, Ulysses S. III 1881-1968 Obituary 111
Grant, Verne E(dwin) 1917- 53-56
Grant, Vernon W(esley) 1904- 17-18R
Grant, W(illiam) Leonard 1914- 19-20R
Grant, Wilson Wayne 1941- 97-100
Grant, Wyn(ford) 1947- 114
Grant, Zalin (Belton) 1941- 73-76
Grant-Adamson, Lesley 1942- 121
Grantham, Alexander (William George Herder) 1899- CAP-2
 Earlier sketch in CA 19-20
Grantham, Dewey Wesley 1921- CANR-1
 Earlier sketch in CA 1R
Grantland, Keith
 See Beaumont, Charles
Granton, Ester Fannie 1914(?)-1980
 Obituary 101
Grant Wallace, Lewis
 See Wallace, Lewis Grant
Granville, Joseph E(nsign) 1923- 65-68
Granville, W. Wilfred 1905- CAP-1
 Earlier sketch in CA 9-10
Granville-Barker, Harley 1877-1946
 Brief entry 104
 See also TCLC 2
Grape, Oliver
 See Wood, Christopher (Hovelle)
Grapho
 See Oakley, Eric Gilbert
Grass, Guenter (Wilhelm) 1927- CANR-20
 Earlier sketch in CA 13-14R
 See also CLC 1, 2, 4, 6, 11, 15, 22, 32
Grassi, Joseph A(ugustus) 1922- CANR-19
 Earlier sketch in CA 103
Grasso, Domenico 1917- 73-76
Grasty, Charles H. 1863-1924 .... DLB-25
Grathwohl, Larry D(avid) 1947- 65-68
Grattan, C(linton) Hartley 1902-1980 .... CANR-1
 Obituary 101
 Earlier sketch in CA 4R
Grattan, Virginia L(ee) 1932- 115
Grattan-Guinness, I. 1941- 73-76
Gratton, Thomas
 See Hulme, T(homas) E(rnest)
Gratus, Jack 1935- 93-96
Grau, Joseph A(ugust) 1921- 65-68
Grau, Shirley Ann 1929- CANR-22
 Earlier sketch in CA 89-92
 See also DLB 2
 See also CLC 4, 9
Graubard, Mark A. 1904- CANR-5
 Earlier sketch in CA 1R
Graubard, Paul S. 1932- 103
Graubard, Stephen R(ichards) 1924-
 Brief entry 113
Graubart, David 1907(?)-1984 Obituary 112
Grauer, Ben(jamin Franklin) 1908-1977
 Obituary 69-72
Grauer, Neil A(lbert) 1947- 122
Grauman, Lawrence, Jr. 1935- 33-36R
Graupe, Daniel 1934- 41-44R
Graupera, Carlos M(anuel) 1915- 41-44R
Grava, Sigurd 1934- 77-80
Gravagnuolo, Benedetto 1949- 112
Grave, S(elwyn) A(lfred) 1916- 5-6R
Gravel, Fern
 See Hall, James Norman
Gravel, Mike 1930- 41-44R
Gravely, William B(ernard) 1939- 49-52
Graver, Jane (Ann) 1931- 117
Graver, Lawrence 1931- 25-28R
Graver, Suzanne 1936- 117
Graversen, Pat 1935- 109
Graves, Allen W(illis) 1915- 17-18R
Graves, Barbara Farris 1938- 41-44R
Graves, Charles Parlin 1911-1972 .... CANR-4
 Obituary 37-40R
 Earlier sketch in CA 5-6R
 See also SATA 4
Graves, Edgar B(aldwin) 1898-1983
 Obituary 109
Graves, Eleanor MacKenzie 1926- 102
Graves, John (Alexander III) 1920- CANR-9
 Earlier sketch in CA 13-14R
 See also DLBY 83
Graves, Leon B(erneil) 1946- 29-32R
Graves, Nora Calhoun 1914- 73-76
Graves, Phillip E(arl) 1945- 115
Graves, Richard 1715-1804 .... DLB-39
Graves, Richard L(atshaw) 1928- 57-60
Graves, Richard L(ayton) 1931- 53-56
Graves, Richard Perceval 1945- CANR-9
 Earlier sketch in CA 65-68
 See also CLC 44
Graves, Robert (von Ranke) 1895-1985 .... CANR-5
 Obituary 117
 Earlier sketch in CA 5-6R
 See also SATA 45
 See also DLB 20
 See also DLBY 85
 See also CLC 1, 2, 6, 11, 39, 44, 45
Graves, Susan B(ernard) 1933- 41-44R
Graves, Tricia
 See Graversen, Pat
Graves, W(illiam) Brooke 1899- CAP-1
 Earlier sketch in CA 9-10
Graves, Wallace 1922- 33-36R
Graveson, R(onald) H(arry) 1911- 122
Grawbarger, Josephine (Clara) 1908- 121
Grawoig, Sheila
 See Raeschild, Sheila
Gray, Alasdair 1934- CLC-41
Gray, Alexander 1882-1968 .... 7-8R
Gray, Alfred O(rren) 1914- CANR-7
 Earlier sketch in CA 19-20R
Gray, Amlin 1946- CLC-29
Gray, Angela
 See Daniels, Dorothy
Gray, Anne 1931- CANR-9
 Earlier sketch in CA 65-68

Gray, Asa 1810-1888 ... DLB-1
Gray, Barry 1916- ... 61-64
Gray, Basil 1904- ... CAP-1
Earlier sketch in CA 9-10
Gray, Betsy
See Poole, Gray Johnson
Gray, Bettyanne 1934- ... 81-84
Gray, Bradford H(itch) 1942- ... 57-60
Gray, Captain Bill
See Gray, William Bittle
Gray, Charles A(ugustus) 1938- ... 19-20R
Gray, Clifford F. 1930- ... 25-28R
Gray, Darrell 1945- ... 65-68
Gray, David 1838-1861 ... DLB-32
Gray, David 1927-1983 Obituary ... 110
Gray, Dorothea Helen Forbes ?-1983
Obituary ... 110
Gray, Dorothy (Kamer) 1936- ... 69-72
Gray, Dorothy Kate 1918- ... 102
Gray, Douglas 1930- ... 117
Gray, Dulcie ... CANR-24
Earlier sketches in CA 7-8R, CANR-3
Gray, Dwight E(lder) 1903- ... CAP-2
Earlier sketch in CA 23-24
Gray, Eden 1907- ... 93-96
Gray, Edna Redmond 1905(?)-1983
Obituary ... 110
Gray, Edwyn 1927- ... 41-44R
Gray, Elizabeth Janet
See Vining, Elizabeth Gray
Gray, Ellington
See Jacob, Naomi Ellington
Gray, Ernest
See Gray, Ernest Alfred
Gray, Ernest A.
See Gray, Ernest Alfred
Gray, Ernest Alfred 1908- ... 118
Gray, Farnum 1940- ... 49-52
Gray, Floyd (Francis) 1926- ... CANR-10
Earlier sketch in CA 25-28R
Gray, Francine du Plessix 1930- ... CANR-11
Earlier sketch in CA 61-64
See also CAAS 2
See also CLC 22
Gray, Genevieve S(tuck) 1920- ... 33-36R
See also SATA 4
Gray, George Hugh 1922- ... CANR-7
Earlier sketch in CA 17-18R
Gray, Gibson 1922- ... 33-36R
Gray, Giles Wilkeson 1889- ... 7-8R
Gray, Gordon 1909-1982 Obituary ... 109
Gray, H(enry) Peter 1924- Brief entry ... 111
Gray, Harold (Lincoln) 1894-1968 ... 107
See also SATA 32, 33
Gray, Harold James 1907- ... 107
Gray, Harriet
See Robins, Denise (Naomi)
Gray, J(esse) Glenn 1913-1977 ... 37-40R
Obituary ... 73-76
Gray, J(ames) M(artin) 1930- ... 53-56
Gray, J(ohn) Richard 1929- ... CANR-5
Earlier sketch in CA 3R
Gray, J(ohn) Stanley 1894- ... CAP-2
Earlier sketch in CA 17-18
Gray, Jack 1927- ... 103
Gray, James 1899- ... 13-14R
Gray, James H(enry) 1906- ... 97-100
Gray, James R(obert) 1921- ... 33-36R
Gray, Jane
See Evans, Constance May
Gray, Jeffrey A(lan) 1934- ... 104
Gray, Jenny
See Gray, Genevieve S(tuck)
Gray, John (Henry) 1866-1934 Brief entry ... 119
See also TCLC 19
Gray, John 1913- ... 11-12R
Gray, John E(dmund) 1922- ... 65-68
Gray, John Milner 1889-1970 Obituary ... 29-32R
Gray, John Morgan 1907- ... 103
Gray, John Rodger 1913-1984 Obituary ... 113
Gray, John S(tephens) 1910- ... 73-76
Gray, John W(ylie) 1935- ... 19-20R
Gray, Juanita R(uth) 1918- ... 61-64
Gray, Lee Learner 1924- ... 73-76
Gray, Linda Crockett 1943- ... 109
Gray, Margaret K. 1949- ... 123
Gray, Marian
See Pierce, Edith Gray
Gray, Marianne 1947- ... 110
Gray, Martin 1926- ... CANR-14
Earlier sketch in CA 77-80
See also AITN 1
Gray, Mayo Loiseau 1938- ... 104
Gray, Michael H(aslam) 1946- ... 103
Gray, Nicholas Stuart 1922-1981 ... CANR-11
Obituary ... 103
Earlier sketch in CA 21-22R
See also SATA 4, 27
Gray, Nicolete (Mary) 1911- ... 103
Gray, Nigel 1941- ... 85-88
See also SATA 33
Gray, (Lucy) Noel (Clervaux) 1898-1983 ... 65-68
See also SATA 47
Gray, Oscar S(halom) 1926- ... 29-32R
Gray, Parke H. 1936(?)-1987 Obituary ... 121
Gray, Patricia (Clark) ... 29-32R
See also SATA 7
Gray, Patsey
See Gray, Patricia (Clark)
Gray, Peter 1908- ... 41-44R
Gray, Philip
See Perlman, Jess
Gray, Ralph D(ale) 1933- ... CANR-24
Earlier sketches in CA 21-22R, CANR-8
Gray, Richard
See Gray, J(ohn) Richard
Gray, Richard B(utler) 1922- ... CANR-2
Earlier sketch in CA 1R
Gray, Richard G(eorge) 1932-1984
Obituary ... 114
Gray, Robert F(red) 1912- ... 19-20R
Gray, Robert Keith 1923- ... 4R
Gray, Robert Mack 1922- ... 13-14R
Gray, Ronald (Douglas) 1919- ... CANR-22
Earlier sketches in CA 17-18R, CANR-7
Gray, Ronald Francis 1918- ... 7-8R
Gray, Russell
See Fischer, Bruno
Gray, Simon 1936- ... 23-24R
See also CAAS 3
See also DLB 13
See also CLC 9, 14, 36
See also AITN 1
Gray, Stephen E. 1925- ... 73-76
Gray, Tony
See Gray, George Hugh
Gray, Vanessa
See Aeby, Jacquelyn
Gray, Wellington Burbank 1919-1977 ... 1R
Obituary ... 103
Gray, William Bittle 1891-1974 ... CANR-11
Earlier sketch in CA 13-14R
Gray, William R(alph) 1946- ... 97-100
Gray, Wood 1905(?)-1977 Obituary ... 69-72
Graybar, Lloyd J(oseph) 1938- ... 57-60
Graybeal, David M(cConnell) 1921- ... 17-18R
Graybill, Florence Curtis 1898- ... 97-100
Graybill, Ron(ald D.) 1944- ... 33-36R
Grayeff, Felix 1906- ... 77-80
Grayland, Eugene C(harles)
1916-1976 ... CANR-11
Earlier sketches in CA 9-10, CAP-1
Grayland, V. Merle
See Grayland, Valerie (Merle Spanner)
Grayland, Valerie (Merle Spanner) ... CANR-11
Earlier sketch in CA 9-10R
See also SATA 7
Graymont, Barbara ... 81-84
Graysmith, Robert 1942- ... 117
Grayson, A(lbert) K(irk) 1935- ... 41-44R
Grayson, Alice Barr
See Grossman, Jean Schick
Grayson, Benson Lee 1932- ... 93-96
Grayson, C(harles) Jackson, Jr. 1923- ... 106
Grayson, Cary Travers, Jr. 1919- ... CANR-10
Earlier sketch in CA 17-18R
Grayson, Cecil 1920- ... 13-14R
Grayson, Charles 1905-1973 Obituary ... 41-44R
Grayson, David
See Baker, Ray Stannard
Grayson, Henry (Wesley) 1910- ... 41-44R
Grayson, Janet 1934- ... 53-56
Grayson, L(inda) M(ary) 1947- ... 89-92
Grayson, Marion F. 1906-1976 ... CANR-4
Obituary ... 69-72
Earlier sketch in CA 5-6R
Grayson, Melvin J(ay) 1924- ... 45-48
Grayson, Richard (A.) 1951- ... CANR-14
Earlier sketch in CA 85-88
See also CLC 38
Grayson, Robert A. 1927- ... 33-36R
Grayson, Ruth (King) 1926- ... 73-76
Grayson, William John 1788-1863 ... DLB-3, 64
Graystone, Lynn
See Brennan, Joseph Lomas
Grayzel, Solomon 1896-1980 ... CANR-4
Earlier sketch in CA 4R
Grazhdanin, Misha
See Burgess, M(ichael) R(oy)
Graziano, Anthony M(ichael) 1932- ... 93-96
Grealey, Thomas Louis 1916- ... 81-84
Grealis, Walt(er) 1929- ... 77-80
Grealy, Desmond 1923(?)-1979 Obituary ... 85-88
Grean, Stanley 1920- ... 29-32R
Great Merlini, The
See Rawson, Clayton
Greatorex, Wilfred 1921- ... 103
Greaves, H(arold) R(ichard) G(oring)
1907- ... 5-6R
Greaves, (Brian) John 1898- ... 103
Greaves, Margaret 1914- ... CANR-18
Earlier sketch in CA 25-28R
See also SATA 7
Greaves, Percy L(aurie), Jr. 1906- ... 49-52
Greaves, Richard L(ee) 1938- ... CANR-16
Earlier sketch in CA 33-36R
Grebanier, Bernard (David N.)
1903-1977 ... CANR-10
Earlier sketch in CA 23-24R
Grebe, Maria Ester 1928- ... 25-28R
Greben, Stanley E(dward) 1927- ... 120
Greber, Judith 1939- ... 116
Grebstein, Lawrence C(harles) 1937- ... 29-32R
Grebstein, Sheldon Norman 1928- ... CANR-5
Earlier sketch in CA 1R
Greco, Jose 1918- ... 85-88
Greco, Margaret
See Fry, Barbara
Gree, Alain 1936- ... 89-92
See also SATA 28
Greeley, Andrew M(oran) 1928- ... CANR-7
Earlier sketch in CA 7-8R
See also CLC 28
Greeley, Dana McLean 1908-1986
Obituary ... 119
Greeley, Horace 1811-1872 ... DLB-3, 43
Greeley, Valerie 1953- ... 118
Green, A(dwin) Wigfall 1900-1971(?) ... CAP-1
Earlier sketch in CA 9-10
Green, Abel 1900-1973 Obituary ... 41-44R
Green, Adam
See Weisgard, Leonard Joseph
Green, Adolph 1915- Brief entry ... 110
See also DLB 44
Green, Alan (Baer) 1906-1975 ... 53-56
Obituary ... 57-60
Green, Alan Singer 1907- ... 85-88
Green, Andrew (Malcolm) 1927- ... CANR-12
Earlier sketch in CA 73-76
Green, Anita Jane 1940- ... 85-88
Green, Anna Katharine 1846-1935
Brief entry ... 112
Green, Anne (Mitchell) 1947- ... 120
Green, Anne M. 1922- ... 1R
Green, Arnold W(ilfred) 1914- ... 5-6R
Green, Arthur S(amuel) 1927- ... 5-6R
Green, Ben K. 1911(?)-1974 Obituary ... 115
See also AITN 1
Green, Benny
See Green, Bernard
Green, Bernard 1927- ... 25-28R
Green, Betty Radley 1926-1978 Obituary ... 111
Green, Bryan S(tuart) W(estmacott)
1901- ... CAP-1
Earlier sketch in CA 13-14
Green, Celia (Elizabeth) 1935- ... 65-68
Green, Constance McLaughlin 1897-1975 ... 9-10R
Obituary ... 61-64
Green, D.
See Casewit, Curtis W(erner)
Green, Daniel W(illiam) E(dward) 1958- ... 121
Green, David 1942- ... 77-80
Green, David Bronte 1910- ... 13-14R
Green, David M(arvin) 1932- ... 41-44R
Green, Deborah 1948- ... 104
Green, Dennis Howard 1922- ... 110
Green, Donald E(dward) 1936- ... CANR-1
Earlier sketch in CA 45-48
Green, Donald Ross 1924- ... 37-40R
Green, Dorothy (Auchterlonie) 1915- ... 112
Green, Duff 1791-1875 ... DLB-43
Green, Edith Pinero 1929- ... CANR-15
Earlier sketch in CA 77-80
Green, Edward 1920- ... 15-16R
Green, Edwin 1948- ... 116
Green, Elizabeth A(dine) H(erkimer)
1906- ... 23-24R
Green, Elmer Ellsworth 1917- ... 103
Green, Ernestene L(everne) 1939- ... 57-60
Green, Evelyn Everett
See Everett-Green, Evelyn
Green, F(rederick) C(harles) 1891-1964
Obituary ... 89-92
Green, Fitzhugh 1917- ... 77-80
Green, Fletcher Melvin 1895-1978 ... CANR-6
Earlier sketch in CA 1R
Green, Frederick Pratt 1903- ... 102
Green, Galen 1949- ... 57-60
Green, George D(avid) 1938- Brief entry ... 114
Green, George MacEwan 1931- ... 81-84
Green, George S(herman) 1930- ... 97-100
Green, Georgia M. 1944- ... 93-96
Green, Gerald 1922- ... CANR-8
Earlier sketch in CA 15-16R
See also DLB 28
Green, Gil(bert) 1906- ... 73-76
Green, H(enry) Gordon 1912- ... 110
Green, Hannah ... 73-76
See also CLC 3
Green, Hannah
See Greenberg, Joanne (Goldenberg)
Green, Harold P(aul) 1922- ... 13-14R
Green, Harvey 1946- ... 115
Green, Henry
See Yorke, Henry Vincent
See also DLB 15
See also CLC 2, 13
Green, Hollis Lynn 1933- ... 103
Green, J(ames) C. R. 1949- ... 104
Green, James L(eroy) 1919- ... 17-18R
Green, Jane 1937- ... 61-64
See also SATA 9
Green, Jane Nugent 1918- ... 61-64
Green, Janet 1939- ... 112
Green, Jeffrey P(hillip) 1944- ... 111
Green, Jim 1941- ... 114
Green, Joann 1938- ... 115
Green, John Alden 1925- ... CANR-3
Earlier sketch in CA 7-8R
Green, John L(afayette), Jr. 1929- ... CANR-22
Earlier sketch in CA 45-48
Green, Jonas 1712-1767 ... DLB-31
Green, Jonathan (William) 1939- ... CANR-9
Earlier sketch in CA 61-64
Green, Joseph 1706-1780 ... DLB-31
Green, Joseph 1931- ... 29-32R
Green, Joseph F(ranklin), Jr. 1924- ... 15-16R
Green, Judith
See Galbraith, Jean
and Rodriguez, Judith Green
Green, Julien (Hartridge) 1900- ... 21-22R
See also DLB 4
See also CLC 3, 11
Green, Kay 1927- ... 117
Green, Landis K(night) 1940- ... 57-60
Green, Lawrence W(inter) 1940- ... CANR-12
Earlier sketch in CA 69-72
Green, Leslie Claude 1920- ... 13-14R
Green, Lewis W(allace) 1932- ... 119
Green, Louis 1929- ... 45-48
Green, Marc Edward 1943- ... 117
Green, Margaret (Murphy) 1926- ... CANR-1
Earlier sketch in CA 2R
Green, Mark J(oseph) 1945- ... 41-44R
Green, Martin (Burgess) 1927- ... CANR-9
Earlier sketch in CA 17-18R
Green, Martyn 1899-1975 Obituary ... 57-60
Green, Mary McBurney 1896- ... CAP-2
Earlier sketch in CA 29-32
Green, Mary Moore 1906- ... CAP-1
Earlier sketch in CA 13-14
See also SATA 11
Green, Maureen Patricia 1933- ... 101
Green, (James) Maurice (Spurgeon)
1906-1987 Obituary ... 123
Green, Maurice B(erkeley) 1920- ... 77-80
Green, Maurice R(ichard) 1922- ... 15-16R
Green, Maury 1916- ... 29-32R
Green, Michael Frederick 1927- ... CANR-19
Earlier sketch in CA 102
Green, Milton D(ouglas) 1903- ... 41-44R
Green, Morton 1937- ... 57-60
See also SATA 8
Green, Norma B(erger) 1925- ... 41-44R
See also SATA 11
Green, O. O.
See Durgnat, Raymond (Eric)
Green, Otis H(oward) 1898- ... 9-10R
Green, Paul (Eliot) 1894-1981 ... CANR-3
Obituary ... 103
Earlier sketch in CA 5-6R
See also DLB 7, 9
See also DLBY 81
See also CLC 25
See also AITN 1
Green, Paul E(dgar) 1927- ... CANR-11
Earlier sketch in CA 69-72
Green, Peter (Morris) 1924- ... CANR-4
Earlier sketch in CA 5-6R
Green, Peter
See Bulmer, (Henry) Kenneth
Green, Phyllis 1932- ... CANR-17
Earlier sketches in CA 45-48, CANR-1
See also SATA 20
Green, Rayna (Diane) 1942- ... 114
Green, Reginald Herbold 1935- ... CANR-17
Earlier sketch in CA 25-28R
Green, Richard ... AITN-1
Green, Richard 1936- Brief entry ... 111
Green, Robert
See Smith, Richard Rein
Green, Robert D(avid) 1942- ... 77-80
Green, Robert L(ee) 1933- ... CANR-15
Earlier sketch in CA 65-68
Green, Roger C(urtis) 1932- ... CANR-24
Earlier sketch in CA 45-48
Green, Roger James 1944- ... 123
Green, Roger (Gilbert) Lancelyn
1918-1987 ... CANR-2
Obituary ... 123
Earlier sketch in CA 4R
See also SATA 2
Green, Roland (James) 1944- ... 77-80
Green, Ronald Michael 1942- ... 85-88
Green, Rosalie B(eth) 1917- ... 4R
Green, Rose Basile 1914- ... CANR-15
Earlier sketch in CA 41-44R
Green, Samuel 1921(?)-1983 Obituary ... 111
Green, Samuel 1948- ... 77-80
Green, Sharon 1942- ... 120
Green, Sheila Ellen 1934- ... CANR-17
Earlier sketches in CA 4R, CANR-2
See also SATA 8
Green, Smith Wendell 1917(?)-1987
Obituary ... 124
Green, Stanley 1923- ... CANR-17
Earlier sketches in CA 4R, CANR-1
Green, Susan 1941- ... 81-84
Green, Thomas F. 1927- ... 57-60
Green, Thomas J(ohn) 1946- ... 113
Green, Timothy (Seton) 1936- ... CANR-22
Earlier sketches in CA 49-52, CANR-5
Green, Vivian Hubert Howard 1915- ... 9-10R
Green, William 1926- ... 53-56
Green, William A., Jr. 1935- ... 85-88
Green, William Baillie 1927- ... 118
Green, William M(ark) 1929- ... 45-48
Greenacre, Phyllis 1894- ... 5-6R
Greenall, Jack 1905-1983 Obituary ... 110
Greenawalt, R(obert) Kent 1936- ... 33-36R
Greenaway, Catherine 1846-1901
Brief entry ... 113
Greenaway, George W(illiam) 1903- ... 118
Greenaway, Gladys 1901- ... 93-96
Greenaway, Kate
See Greenaway, Catherine
See also YABC 2
See also CLR 6
Greenbank, Anthony Hunt 1933- ... CANR-19
Earlier sketches in CA 49-52, CANR-4
See also SATA 39
Greenbaum, Fred 1930- ... 37-40R
Greenbaum, Leonard 1930- ... 21-22R
Greenbaum, Sidney 1929- ... CANR-15
Earlier sketch in CA 33-36R
Greenberg, Alvin (David) 1932- ... 33-36R
Greenberg, Arthur
See Granit, Arthur
Greenberg, Barbara L(evenson) 1932- ... 53-56
Greenberg, Bernard 1922- ... 69-72
Greenberg, Bernard L(ouis) 1917- ... 41-44R
Greenberg, Bradley S(ander) 1934- ... 104
Greenberg, Carl 1908-1984 Obituary ... 114
Greenberg, Clement 1909- ... CANR-2
Earlier sketch in CA 1R
Greenberg, Daniel A. 1934- ... 5-6R
Greenberg, Daniel S. 1931- ... 29-32R
Greenberg, Dolores 1934- ... 112
Greenberg, Douglas 1947- ... 117
Greenberg, Edward (Seymour) 1942- ... 53-56
Greenberg, Eliezer 1897(?)-1977
Obituary ... 69-72
Greenberg, Eric Rolfe 1945- ... 114
Greenberg, Harvey R. 1935- ... 33-36R
See also SATA 5
Greenberg, Herbert 1935- ... 25-28R

Greenberg, Ira A(rthur) 1924- ... CANR-2
Earlier sketch in CA 49-52
Greenberg, Ivan 1908-1973 ... 85-88
Greenberg, Jae W. 1894(?)-1974
Obituary ... 104
Greenberg, James B(rian) 1945- ... 105
Greenberg, Jan W(eingarten) 1943- ... 118
Greenberg, Joanne (Goldenberg)
1932- ... CANR-14
Earlier sketch in CA 7-8R
See also SATA 25
See also CLC 7, 30
Greenberg, Joseph Harold 1915- ... 102
Greenberg, Judith Anne
See Azrael, Judith Anne
Greenberg, Kenneth R(ay) 1930- ... 57-60
Greenberg, Kenneth S. 1947- ... 124
Greenberg, Louis M. 1933- Brief entry ... 112
Greenberg, Martin Harry 1941- ... 49-52
Greenberg, Milton 1927- ... 25-28R
Greenberg, Morrie
See Greenberg, Morris S.
Greenberg, Morris S. 1924- ... 33-36R
Greenberg, Moshe 1928- ... 15-16R
Greenberg, Paul 1937- ... 69-72
Greenberg, Pearl 1927- ... 93-96
Greenberg, Polly 1932- ... 85-88
See also SATA 43
Greenberg, Robert Arthur 1930- ... CANR-4
Earlier sketch in CA 1R
Greenberg, Selig 1904- ... 49-52
Greenberg, Selma 1930- ... 29-32R
Greenberg, Sidney 1917- ... CANR-3
Earlier sketch in CA 9-10R
Greenberg, Simon 1901- ... CANR-14
Earlier sketch in CA 77-80
Greenberg, Stan 1931- ... 119
Greenberg, Stanley Bernard 1945- ... 53-56
Greenberg, Uri Zvi 1898-1981 Obituary ... 103
Greenberger, Allen J(ay) 1937- ... 41-44R
Greenberger, Howard 1924- ... 45-48
Greenberger, Martin 1931- ... CANR-8
Earlier sketch in CA 61-64
Greenbie, Barrie B(arstow) 1920- ... 107
Greenbie, Marjorie Barstow 1889(?)-1976
Obituary ... 61-64
Greenblat, Cathy S(tein) 1940- Brief entry ... 118
Greenblatt, Augusta 1912- ... CANR-6
Earlier sketch in CA 57-60
Greenblatt, Edwin 1920- ... 49-52
Greenblatt, M(anuel) H(arry) 1922-1972 ... CAP-2
Earlier sketch in CA 17-18
Greenblatt, Robert Benjamin 1906-1987 ... CAP-1
Obituary ... 123
Earlier sketch in CA 11-12
Greenblatt, Stephen J(ay) 1943- ... 49-52
Greenblum, Joseph 1925- ... 23-24R
Greenburg, Dan 1936- ... CANR-9
Earlier sketch in CA 13-14R
Greenburger, Francis 1949- ... 85-88
Greenburger, Ingrid Elisabeth 1913- ... 104
Greene, A(lvin) C(arl) 1923- ... CANR-14
Earlier sketch in CA 37-40R
Greene, Adam
See Scott, Peter Dale
Greene, Anthony Hamilton Millard Kirk
See Kirk-Greene, Anthony (Hamilton Millard)
Greene, Asa 1789-1838 ... DLB-11
Greene, Bert 1923- ... CANR-6
Earlier sketch in CA 57-60
Greene, Bette 1934- ... CANR-4
Earlier sketch in CA 53-56
See also SATA 8
See also CLC 30
See also CLR 2
Greene, Bob
See Greene, Robert Bernard, Jr.
Greene, Carla 1916- ... CANR-1
Earlier sketch in CA 4R
See also SATA 1
Greene, Carol ... SATA-44
Greene, Charles Jerome 1910-1983
Obituary ... 110
Greene, Constance C(larke) 1924- ... CANR-8
Earlier sketch in CA 61-64
See also SATA 11
Greene, David B(eckwith) 1939- ... 117
Greene, David H. 1913- ... 23-24R
Greene, David L(ouis) 1944- Brief entry ... 114
Greene, David M(ason) 1920- ... 118
Greene, Donald J(ohnson) 1916- ... CANR-2
Earlier sketch in CA 1R
Greene, Ellin 1927- ... 77-80
See also SATA 23
Greene, Felix 1909-1985 ... CANR-6
Obituary ... 116
Earlier sketch in CA 3R
Greene, Fred
See Cadet, John
Greene, Gael ... CANR-10
Earlier sketch in CA 13-14R
See also CLC 8
Greene, Graham 1904- ... 15-16R
See also SATA 20
See also DLB 13, 15
See also DLBY 85
See also CLC 1, 3, 6, 9, 14, 18, 27, 37
See also AITN 2
Greene, Harris 1921- ... 15-16R
Greene, Harry A. 1889- ... CAP-2
Earlier sketch in CA 17-18
Greene, Harry J(oseph) 1906- ... 57-60
Greene, Herbert 1898- ... CAP-1
Earlier sketch in CA 9-10
Greene, Howard R. 1937- ... 61-64
Greene, Hugh (Carleton) 1910-1987 ... 102
Obituary ... 121
Greene, Jack P(hillip) 1931- ... CANR-18
Earlier sketches in CA 11-12R, CANR-3
Greene, James H. 1915- ... 17-18R
Greene, Janet (Churchill) 1917- ... 5-6R
Greene, Janice Presser
See Presser, Janice
Greene, Jay E(lihu) 1914- ... CANR-5
Earlier sketch in CA 5-6R
Greene, Jerry
See Greene, Charles Jerome
Greene, John C(olton) 1917- ... 89-92
Greene, John William, Jr. 1946- ... 89-92
Greene, Johnny
See Greene, John William, Jr.
Greene, Jonathan Edward 1943- ... CANR-12
Earlier sketch in CA 33-36R
Greene, Laura 1935- ... CANR-23
Earlier sketch in CA 107
See also SATA 38
Greene, Lawrence J. 1943- ... 113
Greene, Lee S(eifert) 1905- ... CANR-5
Earlier sketch in CA 13-14R
Greene, Leonard M(ichael) 1918- ... 109
Greene, Lorenzo Johnston 1899-1988
Obituary ... 124
Greene, Mabel
See Bean, Mabel Greene
Greene, Mark R. 1923- ... CANR-5
Earlier sketch in CA 2R
Greene, Maxine 1917- ... CANR-13
Earlier sketch in CA 23-24R
Greene, Mott T(uthill) 1945- ... 110
Greene, Naomi 1942- ... 45-48
Greene, Nathanael 1935- ... 25-28R
Greene, Owen (John) 1954- ... 124
Greene, Pamela
See Forman, Joan
Greene, Philip L(eon) 1924- Brief entry ... 113
Greene, Reynolds W(illiam), Jr. 1924- ... CANR-2
Earlier sketch in CA 5-6R
Greene, Richard C. 1941- ... 111
Greene, Richard Leighton 1904-1983 ... CANR-2
Obituary ... 111
Earlier sketch in CA 5-6R
Greene, Robert 1558-1592 ... DLB-62
Greene, Robert
See Deindorfer, Robert Greene
Greene, Robert Bernard, Jr. 1947- ... 107
Greene, Robert W. 1929- ... 104
Greene, Robert W(illiam) 1933-
Brief entry ... 111
Greene, Ruth Altman 1896- ... 73-76
Greene, Shirley E(dward) 1911- ... 3R
Greene, Stephanie 1953- ... 61-64
Greene, Stephen 1914-1979 Obituary ... 89-92
Greene, Thomas M(cLernon) 1926- ... 9-10R
Greene, Victor R(obert) 1933- ... 25-28R
Greene, Vivian ... AITN-2
Greene, Wade 1933- ... SATA-11
Greene, Walter E. 1929- ... 25-28R
Greene, Wilda 1911- ... CANR-9
Earlier sketch in CA 23-24R
Greene, William C. 1933- ... 15-16R
Greene, Yvonne
See Flesch, Yolande (Catarina)
Greenebaum, Louise G(uggenheim)
1919- ... 69-72
Greener, Leslie 1900-1974 ... CAP-2
Earlier sketch in CA 21-22
Greener, Michael (John) 1931- ... 25-28R
Greenewalt, Crawford Hallock 1902- ... CANR-2
Earlier sketch in CA 2R
Greenfeder, Paul 1925(?)-1983 Obituary ... 109
Greenfeld, Howard ... CANR-19
Earlier sketch in CA 81-84
See also SATA 19
Greenfeld, Josh 1927(?)- Brief entry ... 116
Greenfield, Darby
See Ward, Philip
Greenfield, Edward 1928- Brief entry ... 110
Greenfield, Eloise 1929- ... CANR-19
Earlier sketches in CA 49-52, CANR-1
See also SATA 19
See also CLR 4
Greenfield, Gerald Michael 1943- ... 114
Greenfield, Harry I. 1922- Brief entry ... 109
Greenfield, Howard 1937(?)-1986
Obituary ... 118
Greenfield, Irving A. 1928- ... 33-36R
Greenfield, James Lloyd 1924- ... 73-76
Greenfield, Jeff 1943- ... CANR-24
Earlier sketch in CA 37-40R
Greenfield, Jerome 1923- ... 7-8R
Greenfield, Jerry
See Greenfield, Jerome
Greenfield, Jonas Carl 1926- Brief entry ... 110
Greenfield, Meg 1930- Brief entry ... 123
Greenfield, Norman S(amuel) 1923- ... 41-44R
Greenfield, Patricia Marks 1940- ... CANR-24
Earlier sketches in CA 21-22R, CANR-9
Greenfield, Sidney M(artin) 1932- ... 21-22R
Greenfield, Stanley B(rian) 1922- ... 11-12R
Greenfield, Thelma N. 1922- ... 25-28R
Greengold, Jane
See Stevens, Jane Greengold
Greengrass, Mark 1949- ... 118
Greengroin, Artie
See Brown, Harry (Peter McNab, Jr.)
Greenhalgh, P(eter) A(ndrew) L(ivsey)
1945- ... CANR-1
Earlier sketch in CA 49-52
Greenhaus, Thelma Nurenberg
1903-1984 ... 69-72
Obituary ... 113
See also SATA 45
Greenhaw, H(arold) Wayne 1940- ... CANR-24
Earlier sketches in CA 23-24R, CANR-9
Greenhill, Basil (Jack) 1920- ... CANR-17
Earlier sketches in CA 7-8R, CANR-2
Greenhood, (Clarence) David 1895-1983 ... 2R
Obituary ... 109
Greenhouse, Linda 1947- ... 77-80
Greenhow, Robert 1800-1854 ... DLB-30
Greenhut, Melvin L. 1921- ... 15-16R
Greening, Hamilton
See Hamilton, Charles Harold St. John
Greenland, Colin 1954- ... 117
Greenlaw, Jean-Pierre 1910- ... 69-72
Greenlaw, Paul S(tephen) 1930- ... CANR-5
Earlier sketch in CA 2R
Greenleaf, Barbara Kaye 1942- ... 29-32R
See also SATA 6
Greenleaf, Peter 1910- ... 85-88
See also SATA 33
Greenleaf, Richard Edward 1930- ... 25-28R
Greenleaf, Stephen (Howell) 1942- ... 102
Greenleaf, William 1917- ... 9-10R
Greenlee, Douglas 1935-1979 ... 45-48
Obituary ... 103
Greenlee, J(acob) Harold 1918- ... 19-20R
Greenlee, James W(allace) 1933- ... CANR-11
Earlier sketch in CA 69-72
Greenlee, Sam 1930- ... 69-72
Greenlick, Merwyn R(onald) 1935- ... 41-44R
Greenman, Robert 1939- ... 115
Greenman, Russell Lester 1904-1983
Obituary ... 111
Greenough, Horatio 1805-1852 ... DLB-1
Greenough, William Croan 1914- ... 15-16R
Greenslade, S(tanley) L(awrence)
1905-1977 Obituary ... 111
Greenson, Ralph R(omeo) 1911-
Brief entry ... 114
Greenspan, Bud 1927- ... 103
Greenspan, Cappy Petrash
See Greenspan, Constance Anne Petrash
Greenspan, Charlotte L. 1921- ... 33-36R
Greenspan, Constance Anne Petrash
1932(?)-1983 Obituary ... 110
Greenspan, Elaine 1929- ... 110
Greenspan, Emily 1953- ... 124
Greenspan, Sophie 1906- ... 97-100
Greenspoon, Leonard J(ay) 1945- ... 111
Greenspun, H(erman) M(ilton) 1909- ... CAP-2
Earlier sketch in CA 21-22
See also AITN 2
Greenspun, Hank
See Greenspun, H(erman) M(ilton)
Greenspun, Roger (Austin) 1929- ... 102
Greenstein, Fred I(rwin) 1930- ... CANR-4
Earlier sketch in CA 49-52
Greenstock, David Lionel 1912- ... 9-10R
Greenstone, J. David 1937- ... 25-28R
Greenup, Ruth (Robinson) 1912(?)-1984
Obituary ... 113
Greenwald, Harold 1910- ... CANR-4
Earlier sketch in CA 1R
Greenwald, Jerry 1923- ... 57-60
Greenwald, Sheila
See Green, Sheila Ellen
Green-Wanstall, Kenneth 1918- ... 15-16R
Greenway, Hugh D(avids) S(cott) 1935- ... 73-76
Greenway, John 1919- ... 11-12R
Greenway, Roger S(elles) 1934- ... CANR-4
Earlier sketch in CA 53-56
Greenwell, Dora 1821-1882 ... DLB-35
Greenwood, David Charles 1927-1984 ... 61-64
Obituary ... 112
Greenwood, Duncan 1919- ... 21-22R
Greenwood, Edward Alister 1930- ... CANR-12
Earlier sketch in CA 29-32R
Greenwood, Frank 1924- ... CANR-10
Earlier sketch in CA 25-28R
Greenwood, Gordon 1913- ... CANR-9
Earlier sketch in CA 21-22R
Greenwood, Gordon E(dward) 1935- ... 37-40R
Greenwood, Grace
See Lippincott, Sara Jane Clarke
Greenwood, Julia Eileen Courtney 1910- ... CAP-1
Earlier sketch in CA 13-14
Greenwood, Kathryn Moore 1922- ... 93-96
Greenwood, Lillian Bethel 1932- ... 104
Greenwood, Marianne (Hederstrom)
1926- ... CANR-6
Earlier sketch in CA 11-12R
Greenwood, Ned H. 1932- Brief entry ... 110
Greenwood, Ted
See Greenwood, Edward Alister
Greenwood, Theresa 1936- ... 29-32R
Greenwood, Val D(avid) 1937- ... 73-76
Greenwood, Walter 1903-1974 ... 93-96
Obituary ... 53-56
See also DLB 10
Greer, Ann Lennarson 1944- ... 53-56
Greer, Art(hur Ellis, Jr.) 1929- ... 81-84
Greer, Ben 1948- ... 102
See also DLB 6
Greer, Carlotta C(herryholmes)
1879-1965 ... CAP-1
Earlier sketch in CA 15-16
Greer, Francesca
See Janas, Frankie-Lee
Greer, Georgeanna H(errmann) 1922- ... CANR-6
Earlier sketch in CA 57-60
Greer, Germaine 1939- ... 81-84
See also AITN 1
Greer, Herb 1929- ... CANR-8
Earlier sketch in CA 7-8R
Greer, Louise 1899- ... CAP-1
Earlier sketch in CA 15-16
Greer, Philip 1930-1985 Obituary ... 116
Greer, Rebecca Ellen 1935- ... 103
Greer, Richard
See Silverberg, Robert
Greer, Rita 1942- ... 97-100
Greer, Scott (Allen) 1922- ... 45-48
Greer, Thomas H(oag) 1914- ... 23-24R
Greeson, Janet 1952- ... 121
Greet, Brian Aubrey 1922- ... 105
Greet, Kenneth (Gerald) 1918- ... CANR-6
Earlier sketch in CA 7-8R
Greet, T(homas) Y(oung) 1923- ... 15-16R
Greet, William Cabell 1901-1972
Obituary ... 37-40R
Greever, William S(t. Clair) 1916- ... 5-6R
Greeves, Frederic 1903-1985 Obituary ... 115
Greevy, David U(pton) 1953- ... 112
Greg, W. R. 1809-1881 ... DLB-55
Greger, Debora 1949- ... 112
Gregersen, Edgar (Alstrup) 1937- ... 120
Gregg, Andrew K. 1929- ... CANR-15
Earlier sketch in CA 29-32R
Gregg, Charles T(hornton) 1927- ... CANR-14
Earlier sketch in CA 81-84
Gregg, Davis W(einert) 1918- ... 17-18R
Gregg, Hubert 1916- ... 102
Gregg, James E(rwin) 1927- ... 23-24R
Gregg, James R. 1914- ... 23-24R
Gregg, Jess 1926- ... 61-64
Gregg, John E(dwin) 1925- ... 45-48
Gregg, Larry
See Leighton, Lauren G(ray)
Gregg, Linda (Alouise) 1942- ... 113
Gregg, Martin
See McNeilly, Wilfred Glassford
Gregg, Pauline ... 7-8R
Gregg, Richard A(lexander) 1927- ... 15-16R
Gregg, Robert J(ohn) 1912- Brief entry ... 110
Gregg, Walter H(arold) 1919- ... 73-76
See also SATA 20
Gregg, William H. 1904(?)-1983 Obituary ... 109
Gregor, A(nthony) James 1929- ... 57-60
Gregor, Arthur 1923- ... CANR-11
Earlier sketch in CA 25-28R
See also SATA 36
See also CLC 9
Gregor, Carol 1943- ... 117
Gregor, Howard F(rank) 1920- ... CANR-2
Earlier sketch in CA 7-8R
Gregor, Lee
See Pohl, Frederik
Gregor, Rex H. 1922- ... 15-16R
Gregori, Leon 1919- ... SATA-15
Gregorian, Joyce Ballou 1946- ... CANR-24
Earlier sketch in CA 107
See also SATA 30
Gregorian, Vartan 1935- ... 29-32R
Gregorich, Barbara 1943- ... 117
Gregorios, Paulos Mar 1922- ... CANR-11
Earlier sketch in CA 25-28R
Gregorowski, Christopher 1940- ... CANR-15
Earlier sketch in CA 89-92
See also SATA 30
Gregory, Bettina 1946- ... 69-72
Gregory, Chuck
See Gnaegy, Charles
Gregory, Diana (Jean) 1933- ... 97-100
See also SATA 42, 49
Gregory, Dick 1932- ... CANR-7
Earlier sketch in CA 45-48
Gregory, Elizabeth
See Gilford, C(harles) B(ernard)
Gregory, Freida 1938- ... 69-72
Gregory, H(ollingsworth) F(ranklin) 1906- ... 69-72
Gregory, Harry
See Gottfried, Theodore Mark
Gregory, Hilton
See Ferguson, Charles W.
Gregory, Horace (Victor) 1898-1982 ... CANR-22
Obituary ... 106
Earlier sketches in CA 7-8R, CANR-3
See also DLB 48
Gregory, Isabella Augusta (Persse)
1852-1932 Brief entry ... 104
See also DLB 10
See also TCLC 1
Gregory, J. Dennis
See Williams, John A(lfred)
Gregory, James 1912- ... 77-80
Gregory, Jean
See Ure, Jean
Gregory, K(enneth) J(ohn) 1938- ... 107
Gregory, Kenneth (Malcolm) 1921- ... 73-76
Gregory, Lisa
See Camp, Candace P(auline)
Gregory, Lydia
See Carey, Diane
Gregory, Mark
See Burch, Monte G.
Gregory, Paul Roderick 1941- ... 53-56
Gregory, Peter 1924- ... 41-44R
Gregory, R(ichard) L(angton) 1923- ... 57-60
Gregory, Richard Claxton
See Gregory, Dick
Gregory, Robert G(ranville) 1924- ... 41-44R
Gregory, Robert Lloyd 1892- ... 29-32R
Gregory, Ross 1933- ... 29-32R
Gregory, Roy 1935- ... 37-40R
Gregory, Ruth W(ilhelmine) 1910- ... 77-80
Gregory, Sean
See Hossent, Harry
Gregory, Sinda 1947- ... 115
Gregory, Stephan
See Pendleton, Don(ald Eugene)
Gregory, Stephen
See Penzler, Otto
Gregory, Susan 1945- ... 108
Gregory, Thomas B(ernard) 1940- ... 45-48
Gregory, Timothy E(dmund) 1943- ... 111

Gregory, Vahan 1927- 69-72
Gregory, Violet L(efler) 1907- CANR-8
Earlier sketch in CA 57-60
Gregory, William King 1876-1970
Obituary 29-32R
Gregory, Yvonne 1919(?)-1979 Obituary 89-92
Gregson, Paul
See Oakley, Eric Gilbert
Gregston, Gene 1925- 81-84
Greider, William (F.) 117
Greif, E(dwin) Charles 1915- 1R
Greif, Martin 1938- CANR-10
Earlier sketch in CA 65-68
Greiff, Barrie S(anford) 1935- Brief entry 114
Greig, Cicely ?-1983 Obituary 116
Greig, Maysie 1902-1971 102
Obituary 104
Greiner, Donald J(ames) 1940- CANR-16
Earlier sketches in CA 45-48, CANR-1
Greinke, (Lawrence) Eric 1948- 41-44R
Greisman, Joan Ruth 1937- 103
See also SATA 31
Grele, Ronald J(ohn) 1934- 73-76
Gremillion, Joseph 1919- 102
Gremmels, Marion Louise Chapman 1924- 111
Grenander, M(ary) E(lizabeth) 1918- CANR-4
Earlier sketch in CA 53-56
Grendahl, J(ay) Spencer 1943- 29-32R
Grendler, Paul F(rederick) 1936- 41-44R
Grendon, Edward
See LeShan, Lawrence L(ee)
Grendon, Stephen
See Derleth, August (William)
Grene, Marjorie (Glicksman) 1910- CANR-8
Earlier sketch in CA 13-14R
Grenelle, Lisa
See Munroe, Elizabeth L(ee)
Grenfell, Joyce (Irene) 1910-1979 CANR-20
Obituary 89-92
Earlier sketch in CA 81-84
Grenier, Judson A(chille) 1930- 89-92
Grenier, Mildred 1917- CANR-12
Earlier sketch in CA 29-32R
Grennan, Margaret R(ose) 41-44R
Grenville, Bryan P(eter) 1955- 117
Grenville, J(ohn) A(shley) S(oames)
1928- CANR-5
Earlier sketch in CA 11-12R
Grenville, Kate 1950- 118
Grenville, Pelham
See Wodehouse, P(elham) G(renville)
Grenyer, Norman 1913-1983 Obituary 110
Gresham, Anthony
See Russell, Roy
Gresham, Claude Hamilton, Jr. 1922- CANR-8
Earlier sketch in CA 7-8R
Gresham, Elizabeth (Fenner) 1904- 81-84
Gresham, Grits
See Gresham, Claude Hamilton, Jr.
Gresham, Perry E(pler) 1907- 45-48
Gresser, Seymour 1926- 29-32R
Gresser, Sy
See Gresser, Seymour
Gressley, Gene M(aurice) 1931- CANR-10
Earlier sketch in CA 17-18R
Greteman, James 1933- 112
Greteman, Jim
See Greteman, James
Gretz, Susanna 1937- 29-32R
See also SATA 7
Gretzer, John SATA-18
Gretzky, Walter 1938- 120
Greulach, Victor A(ugust) 1906- 49-52
Greve, Elsa
See Greve, Felix Paul (Berthold Friedrich)
Greve, Felix Paul (Berthold Friedrich)
1879-1948 Brief entry 104
Greville, Fulke 1554-1628 DLB-62
Grew, James Hooper 1906- 103
Grew, Raymond 1930- 13-14R
Grewdead, Roy
See Gorey, Edward (St. John)
Grewer, Eira M(ary) 1931- 21-22R
Grex, Leo
See Gribble, Leonard (Reginald)
Grey, Abby (Bartlett) Weed 1903(?)-1983
Obituary 110
Grey, Anthony 1938- 29-32R
Grey, Beryl (Elizabeth) 1927- 109
Grey, Brenda
See Mackinlay, Leila Antoinette Sterling
Grey, Carenna Jane
See Kalpakian, Laura Anne
Grey, Carol
See Lowndes, Robert A(ugustine) W(ard)
Grey, Charles
See Tubb, E(dwin) C(harles)
Grey, David Lennox 1935- 93-96
Grey, Dorothy 1913- 120
Grey, Elizabeth
See Hogg, Elizabeth (Tootill)
Grey, Georgina
See Roby, Mary Linn
Grey, Ian 1918- CANR-2
Earlier sketch in CA 7-8R
Grey, Jerry 1926- CANR-20
Earlier sketches in CA 53-56, CANR-5
See also SATA 11
Grey, Lindsey
See Peel, Colin D(udley)
Grey, Marian Powys 1883(?)-1972
Obituary 104
Grey, Robert Waters 1943- 49-52
Grey, Robin
See Gresham, Elizabeth (Fenner)
Grey, Vivian (Hoffman) 17-18R
Grey, Zane 1872(?)-1939 Brief entry 104
See also DLB 9
See also TCLC 6
Grey Owl
See Belaney, Archibald Stansfeld
Greyser, Stephen A. 1935- 33-36R
Gri
See Denney, Diana
Gribbin, John 1946- 113
Gribbin, Lenore S. 1922- 33-36R
Gribbin, William James 1943- CANR-17
Earlier sketches in CA 45-48, CANR-1
Gribble, Charles E(dward) 1936- 41-44R
Gribble, Harry Wagstaff (Graham)
1891(?)-1981 Obituary 102
Gribble, James 1938- 29-32R
Gribble, Jennifer 1937- 116
Gribble, Leonard (Reginald) 1908- CANR-7
Earlier sketch in CA 53-56
Gribbons, Warren D(avid) 1921- 29-32R
Grice, Frederick 1910- CANR-3
Earlier sketch in CA 11-12R
See also SATA 6
Grice, Grimes
See Kamp, Irene Kittle
Grice, Julia (Haughey) 1940- CANR-16
Earlier sketch in CA 77-80
Gridban, Volsted
See Tubb, E(dwin) C(harles)
Grider, Dorothy 1915- SATA-31
Gridley, Marion E(leanor) 1906-1974 45-48
Obituary 103
See also SATA 26, 35
Gridley, Roy E. 1935- Brief entry 109
Gridzewski, Mieczylawski 1895(?)-1970
Obituary 104
Grieb, Kenneth J. 1939- CANR-12
Earlier sketch in CA 29-32R
Grieb, Lyndal 1940- 61-64
Grieder, Josephine 1939- 53-56
Grieder, Terence 1931- 114
Grieder, Theodore 1926- 45-48
Grieder, Walter 1924- 41-44R
See also SATA 9
Grieg, Michael 1922- 19-20R
Grieg, (Johan) Nordahl (Brun) 1902-1943
Brief entry 107
See also TCLC 10
Grier, B. R. 1913- 25-28R
Grier, Barbara G(ene Damon) 1933- 107
Grier, Edward F(rancis) 1917- 121
Grier, Eldon 1917- 113
Grier, Frances Belle Powner
1886(?)-1980(?) Obituary 104
Grier, Roosevelt 1932- 113
Grier, Rosey
See Grier, Roosevelt
Grierson, Edward 1914- CANR-4
Earlier sketch in CA 3R
Grierson, Francis Durham 1888-1972
Obituary 104
Grierson, Herbert John Clifford 1886-1960
Obituary 93-96
Grierson, John 1898-1972 Obituary 116
Grierson, John 1909-1977 CAP-2
Obituary 69-72
Earlier sketch in CA 19-20
Grierson, (Monica) Linden 1914- CAP-1
Earlier sketch in CA 9-10
Gries, Tom 1923(?)-1977 Obituary 69-72
Griese, Arnold A(lfred) 1921- CANR-1
Earlier sketch in CA 49-52
See also SATA 9
Grieson, Ronald Edward 1943- CANR-1
Earlier sketch in CA 49-52
Griesse, Carolyn 1941- 107
Griessman, Benjamin Eugene 1934- 41-44R
Griest, Guinevere L(indley) 1924- 65-68
Grieve, Andrew W. 1925- 11-12R
Grieve, C(hristopher) M(urray) 1892-1978 7-8R
Obituary 85-88
See also CLC 11, 19
Grieves, Forest L(eslie) 1938- 53-56
Grifalconi, Ann 1929- CANR-9
Earlier sketch in CA 7-8R
See also SATA 2
Griff
See Fawcett, F(rank) Dubrez
and McKeag, Ernest L(ionel)
Griffen, Edmund
See Du Breuil, (Elizabeth) L(or)inda
Griffen, (James) Jeff(erds) 1923- 15-16R
Griffin, A(rthur) H(arold) 1911- CANR-9
Earlier sketch in CA 21-22R
Griffin, Al 1919- 33-36R
Griffin, Anne J.
See Griffin, Arthur J.
Griffin, Arthur J. 1921- CANR-1
Earlier sketch in CA 49-52
Griffin, Barbara C(ook) 1945- 53-56
Griffin, Bryan F(rederick) 120
Brief entry 113
Griffin, C. F.
See Fikso, Eunice Cleland
Griffin, C. S.
See Griffin, Clifford S(tephen)
Griffin, C(harles) W(illiam) 1925- 53-56
Griffin, Charles C(arroll) 1902-1976
Obituary 65-68
Griffin, Charles Henry 1922- 19-20R
Griffin, Clifford S(tephen) 1929-
Brief entry 111
Griffin, (George) Dan(iel) 1937-1984
Obituary 112
Griffin, David Ray 1939- 77-80
Griffin, Donald (Redfield) 1915- CANR-15
Earlier sketch in CA 37-40R
Griffin, Dustin H(adley) 1943- 120
Griffin, Edward M(ichael) 1937- 89-92
Griffin, Emilie Russell Dietrich 1936- CANR-21
Earlier sketch in CA 103
Griffin, Ernest G(eorge) 1916- 25-28R
Griffin, Gerald G(ehrig) 1933- CANR-9
Earlier sketch in CA 57-60
Griffin, Gillett Good 1928- SATA-26
Griffin, Glen C. 1934- CANR-17
Earlier sketch in CA 29-32R
Griffin, (Arthur) Gwyn 1922(?)-1967
Obituary 89-92
Griffin, Jacqueline P. 1927- 33-36R
Griffin, James A. 1934- 29-32R
Griffin, John Howard 1920-1980 CANR-2
Obituary 101
Earlier sketch in CA 2R
See also AITN 1
Griffin, John Q(uealy) 1948- 77-80
Griffin, Judith Berry 108
See also SATA 34
Griffin, Keith B(roadwell) 1938- CANR-7
Earlier sketch in CA 57-60
Griffin, (Samuel) Marvin 1907-1982
Obituary 108
Griffin, Mary 1916- 61-64
Griffin, Mary Claire 1924- 19-20R
Griffin, Peter CLC-39
Griffin, Robert 1936- 53-56
Griffin, Russell M(organ) 1943- 114
Griffin, Stuart 1917- 7-8R
Griffin, Susan 1943- CANR-3
Earlier sketch in CA 49-52
Griffin, W. E. B.
See Butterworth, W(illiam) E(dmund III)
Griffin, Walter 1937- 73-76
Griffin, (Henry) William 1935- 93-96
Griffin, William D(enis) 1936- 122
Griffin, William Lloyd 1938- 21-22R
Griffin-Beale, Christopher 1947- 118
Griffiss, James E(dward) 1928-
Brief entry 118
Griffith, A. Kinney 1897- CANR-17
Earlier sketch in CA 2R
Griffith, A(rthur) Leonard 1920- CANR-5
Earlier sketch in CA 9-10R
Griffith, Albert J(oseph, Jr.) 1932- 37-40R
Griffith, Benjamin Woodward, Jr.
1922- CANR-20
Earlier sketches in CA 1R, CANR-5
Griffith, Corinne 1898(?)-1979 Obituary 89-92
Griffith, D(avid Lewelyn) W(ark)
1875-1948 Brief entry 119
Griffith, Elizabeth 1727(?)-1793 DLB-39
Griffith, Ernest S(tacey) 1896- 13-14R
Griffith, Francis 1906- 106
Griffith, G(uy) T(hompson) 1908-1985
Obituary 117
Griffith, George
See Griffith-Jones, George Chetwynd
Griffith, Helen V(irginia) 1934- CANR-22
Earlier sketch in CA 105
See also SATA 39
Griffith, Jeannette
See Eyerly, Jeannette Hyde
Griffith, Jerry 1932- 53-56
Griffith, Kathryn 1923- 73-76
Griffith, Kenneth 1921- CANR-21
Earlier sketch in CA 69-72
Griffith, Lawrence
See Griffith, D(avid Lewelyn) W(ark)
Griffith, Leon Odell 1921- CANR-2
Earlier sketch in CA 3R
Griffith, Lucille B(lanche) 1905- 17-18R
Griffith, Patricia Browning 1935- CANR-13
Earlier sketch in CA 77-80
Griffith, Paul 1921-1983 23-24R
Obituary 109
Griffith, Richard (Edward) 1912-1969 CANR-6
Earlier sketch in CA 1R
Griffith, Robert 1940- 45-48
Griffith, Samuel Blair II 1906-1983
Obituary 109
Griffith, Thomas 1915- 23-24R
Griffith, Thomas Gwynfor 1926- 103
Griffith, William E(dgar) 1920- 61-64
Griffith, Winthrop 1931- 11-12R
Griffith-Jones, George Chetwynd
1857-1906 Brief entry 112
Griffiths, A(lan) Bede 1906- CANR-7
Earlier sketch in CA 13-14R
Griffiths, Brian 1941- 120
Griffiths, Bryn(lyn) David 1933- 101
Griffiths, Daniel E(dward) 1917- 25-28R
Griffiths, G(ordon) D(ouglas) 1910-1973 CAP-2
Earlier sketch in CA 21-22
See also SATA 20
Griffiths, G. D.
See Griffiths, (Edith) Grace (Chalmers)
Griffiths, (Edith) Grace (Chalmers)
1921- CANR-22
Earlier sketch in CA 106
Griffiths, Helen 1939- CANR-7
Earlier sketch in CA 19-20R
See also SATA 5
See also SAAS 5
Griffiths, John C(harles) 1934- 108
Griffiths, John Gwyn 1911- 106
Griffiths, Kitty Anna 105
Griffiths, Louise (Benckenstein) 1907- 3R
Griffiths, (Thomas) Mel(vin) 1910- 85-88
Griffiths, Michael C(ompton) 1928- CANR-14
Earlier sketch in CA 37-40R
Griffiths, Naomi 1934- 101
Griffiths, Paul (Anthony) 1947- 107
Griffiths, Percival Joseph 1899- 103
Griffiths, Ralph A(lan) 1937- CANR-22
Earlier sketch in CA 105
Griffiths, Richard M(athias) 1935- CANR-8
Earlier sketch in CA 17-18R
Griffiths, Robert David 1952- 118
Griffiths, Robert L. III
See Pauker, John
Griffiths, Sally 1934- 25-28R
Griffiths, Trevor 1935- 97-100
See also DLB 13
See also CLC 13
Griffiths, Vincent Llewellyn 1902(?)-1984
Obituary 113
Grigg, Charles M(eade) 1918- 13-14R
Grigg, John (Edward Poynder) 1924- 104
Griggs, Charles Irwin 1902- 1R
Griggs, Earl Leslie 1899- 73-76
Griggs, Gary B(ruce) 1943- 118
Griggs, Lee 1928- 69-72
Griggs, Sutton Elbert 1872-1930(?)
Brief entry 123
See also DLB 50
Griggs, Tamar 1941- 77-80
Grigoli, Valorie 1955- 122
Grigsby, Gordon 1927- CANR-19
Earlier sketch in CA 97-100
Grigson, Geoffrey (Edward Harvey)
1905-1985 CANR-20
Obituary 118
Earlier sketch in CA 25-28R
See also DLB 27
See also CLC 7, 39
Grigson, Jane 1928- CANR-20
Earlier sketches in CA 49-52, CANR-1
Grill, Johnpeter Horst 1943- 112
Grill, Nannette L. 1935- 65-68
Grilli, Peter M. 1942- 120
Grilliot, Harold J(ohn) 1937- 107
Grillo, John 1942- Brief entry 117
Grillo, Ralph David 1940- 49-52
Grillo, Virgil 1938- 53-56
Grim, John A(llen) 1946- 117
Grim, Patrick 1950- 115
Grim, Ronald E(ugene) 1946- 118
Grimal, Pierre Antoine 1912- CANR-7
Earlier sketch in CA 13-14R
Grimaldi, J(ohn) V. 1916- CANR-19
Earlier sketches in CA 5-6R, CANR-3
Grimault, Berthe 1940- 13-14R
Grimble, Ian 1921- CANR-18
Earlier sketches in CA 7-8R, CANR-2
Grimble, Reverend Charles James
See Eliot, T(homas) S(tearns)
Grime, Harol (Riley) 1896-1984 Obituary 114
Grimes, Alan P. 1919- CANR-1
Earlier sketch in CA 1R
Grimes, (Lewis) Howard 1915- 25-28R
Grimes, Johnnie Marie 103
Grimes, Joseph E(vans) 1928- 37-40R
Grimes, Lee 1920- 61-64
Grimes, Martha 117
Brief entry 113
Grimes, Nikki 1950- 77-80
Grimes, Orville F(rank), Jr. 1943- 106
Grimes, Paul 1924- 77-80
Grimes, Ronald L. 1943- CANR-17
Earlier sketches in CA 45-48, CANR-1
Grimes, W(illiam) H(enry) 1892-1972
Obituary 33-36R
Grimke, Angelina (Emily) Weld 1880-1958 124
Grimke, Angelina Weld 1880-1958 DLB-50, 54
Grimke, Charlotte L(ottie) Forten
1837(?)-1914 124
Brief entry 117
Grimley, Mildred H(ess) 1919- 5-6R
Grimm, Charles John 1898(?)-1983
Obituary 111
Grimm, Charlie
See Grimm, Charles John
Grimm, Cherry Barbara 1930- 101
See also SATA 43
Grimm, Hans 1875-1959 DLB-66
Grimm, Harold J(ohn) 1901- 13-14R
Grimm, Jacob Ludwig Karl 1785-1863 SATA-22
Grimm, Reinhold 1931- CANR-23
Earlier sketches in CA 61-64, CANR-8
Grimm, Wilhelm Karl 1786-1859 SATA-22
Grimm, William C(arey) 1907- 49-52
See also SATA 14
Grimond, Joseph 1913- 108
Grimsditch, Herbert Borthwick 1898-1971
Obituary 104
Grimshaw, Allen Day 1929- CANR-9
Earlier sketch in CA 65-68
Grimshaw, James A(lbert), Jr. 1940- 109
Grimshaw, Mark
See McKeag, Ernest L(ionel)
Grimshaw, Nigel (Gilroy) 1925- CANR-17
Earlier sketch in CA 101
See also SATA 23
Grimsley, Gordon
See Groom, Arthur William
Grimsley, Linda 1940- 81-84
Grimsley, Ronald 1915- CANR-3
Earlier sketch in CA 7-8R
Grimsley, Will (Henry) 1914- 33-36R
Grimstead, Hettie 1903- Brief entry 115
Grimsted, David Allen 1935- 25-28R
Grimsted, Patricia Kennedy 1935- 77-80
Grindal, Bruce T. 1940- 41-44R
Grindal, Gracia (Marie) 1943- 116
Grindea, Miron 1909- CANR-5
Earlier sketch in CA 7-8R
Grindel, Carl W(illiam) 1905- 85-88
Grindel, Eugene 1895-1952 Brief entry 104
Grindel, John Anthony 1937- 65-68
Grindell, Robert M(aclean) 1933- 15-16R

Grinder, Michael 1942- ... 61-64
Grindle, Carleton
See Page, Gerald W(ilburn)
Grindley, John (Thomas Ellam) 1926- ... 25-28R
Grindley, (Jane) Sally 1953- ... 121
Grindrod, Muriel (Kathleen) 1902- ... 7-8R
Gringhuis, Dirk
See Gringhuis, Richard H.
Gringhuis, Richard H. 1918-1974 ... CANR-5
Earlier sketch in CA 2R
See also SATA 6, 25
Grinnell, David
See Wollheim, Donald A(llen)
Grinnell, George Bird 1849-1938 ... SATA-16
Grinnell, Isabel Hoopes 1899(?)-1988
Obituary ... 124
Grinsell, Leslie Valentine 1907- ... CANR-3
Earlier sketch in CA 9-10R
Grinspoon, Lester 1928- ... 81-84
Grinstead, David 1939- ... 105
Grinstein, Alexander 1918- ... CANR-5
Earlier sketch in CA 15-16R
Gripari, Pierre 1925- ... 29-32R
Gripe, Maria (Kristina) 1923- ... CANR-17
Earlier sketch in CA 29-32R
See also SATA 2
See also CLR 5
Grise, Jeannette
See Thomas, Jeannette Grise
Grisewood, Harman (Joseph Gerard)
1906- ... CAP-2
Earlier sketch in CA 29-32
Grisez, Germain G. 1929- ... CANR-21
Earlier sketches in CA 15-16R, CANR-6
Grisham, Noel 1916- ... CANR-10
Earlier sketch in CA 25-28R
Grispino, Joseph Aloysius 1922- ... 17-18R
Grissim, John 1941- ... 113
Griswold, Charles L., Jr. 1951- ... 123
Griswold, Erwin N(athaniel) 1904- ... CAP-1
Earlier sketch in CA 15-16
Griswold, Lawrence T. 1904(?)-1984
Obituary ... 113
Griswold, Rufus Wilmot 1815-1857 ... DLB-3, 59
Griswold, Wesley S(outhmayd) 1909- ... 3R
Griswold del Castillo, Richard 1942- ... 101
Gritsch, Eric W. 1931- ... CANR-10
Earlier sketch in CA 23-24R
Grivas, Theodore 1922- ... 9-10R
Grizzard, Lewis 1946- Brief entry ... 123
Grob, Alan 1932- Brief entry ... 113
Grob, Gerald N. 1931- ... CANR-20
Earlier sketches in CA 1R, CANR-5
Grobman, Alex 1946- ... 116
Groch, Judith (Goldstein) 1929- ... 9-10R
See also SATA 25
Grode, Redway
See Gorey, Edward (St. John)
Grodnick, Susan 1951- ... 122
Groemping, Franz A(lbert) 1909(?)-1987
Obituary ... 123
Groenbjerg, Kirsten A(ndersen) 1946- ... CANR-15
Earlier sketch in CA 85-88
Groene, Bertram Hawthorne 1923- ... 45-48
Groene, Janet 1936- ... 37-40R
Groenhoff, Edwin L. 1924- ... 57-60
Groennings, Sven O. 1934- ... 45-48
Groenoset, Dagfinn 1920- ... 93-96
Groeschel, Benedict J(oseph) 1933- ... 115
Grof, Stanislav 1931- ... 73-76
Groff, Patrick J(ohn) 1924- ... 41-44R
Groff, Warren F(rederick) 1924- ... 53-56
Grogan, Emmett 1942-1978 ... 41-44R
Groh, Ed(win Charles) 1910- ... 49-52
Groh, George W. 1922-1984 ... 85-88
Obituary ... 114
Grohman, Joann Sills 1928- ... 107
Grohskopf, Bernice ... CANR-3
Earlier sketch in CA 5-6R
See also SATA 7
Groia, Phil(ip) 1941- ... 53-56
Grol, Lini R(icharda) 1913- ... CANR-8
Earlier sketch in CA 61-64
See also SATA 9
Grollman, Earl A. 1925- ... 23-24R
See also SATA 22
Grollman, Sharon Hya 1954- ... CANR-15
Earlier sketch in CA 81-84
Grollmes, Eugene E. 1931- ... 29-32R
Gromacki, Robert Glenn 1933- ... CANR-19
Earlier sketches in CA 53-56, CANR-4
Gromada, Thaddeus V(ladimir) 1929- ... 45-48
Groman, George L. 1928- ... 23-24R
Grombach, John V(alentin) 1901- ... 103
Gronbeck, Bruce E(lliott) 1941-
Brief entry ... 118
Gronbjerg, Kirsten A(ndersen)
See Groenbjerg, Kirsten A(ndersen)
Grondona, L(eo) St. Clare 1890-1982 ... 103
Obituary ... 108
Groneman, Chris Harold 1906- ... CANR-1
Earlier sketch in CA 4R
Gronert, Bernard G(eorge) 1920-1985
Obituary ... 116
Gronewold, Sue Ellen
See Gronewold, Susan Ellen
Gronewold, Susan Ellen 1947- ... 115
Groninger, William C. 1928(?)-1983
Obituary ... 111
Gronowicz, Antoni 1913-1985 ... 25-28R
Obituary ... 117
Groocock, J(ohn) M(ichael) 1929- ... 57-60
Groom, Arthur William 1898-1964 ... CANR-1
Earlier sketch in CA 4R
See also SATA 10
Groom, Bernard 1892- ... CAP-2
Earlier sketch in CA 21-22
Groom, Nigel 1924- ... 117
Groom, Winston 1943- ... 85-88
Groome, Thomas H(enry) 1945- ... 110
Gropius, Walter 1883-1969 Obituary ... 25-28R
Gropman, Donald S(heldon) 1936- ... 101
Gropp, Louis (Oliver) 1935- ... 120
Gropper, William 1897-1977 ... 102
Obituary ... 89-92
Grosbard, Ulu 1929- ... 25-28R
Grose, B(url) Donald 1943- ... CANR-22
Earlier sketch in CA 45-48
Grose, Christopher (Waldo) 1939-
Brief entry ... 114
Grose, Peter (Bolton) 1934- Brief entry ... 119
Groseclose, Elgin E. 1899-1983 ... CAP-2
Obituary ... 109
Earlier sketch in CA 21-22
Groseclose, Kel(vin) 1940- ... 113
Grosman, Brian A(llen) 1935- ... 73-76
Grosman, Ladislav 1921- ... 102
Grosman, Tatyana 1904-1982 Obituary ... 107
Grosofsky, Leslie
See Gross, Leslie
Gross, Alan 1947- ... CANR-24
Earlier sketch in CA 89-92
See also SATA 43
Gross, Anthony 1905-1984 Obituary ... 114
Gross, Beatrice 1935- ... 77-80
Gross, Ben Samuel 1891-1979 ... 97-100
Obituary ... 89-92
Gross, Bertram M(yron) 1912- ... CANR-9
Earlier sketch in CA 15-16R
Gross, Beverly 1938- ... 29-32R
Gross, Carl H. 1911- ... 15-16R
Gross, Daniel R(ussell) 1942- ... 53-56
Gross, David C(harles) 1923- ... 102
Gross, Ernest A(rnold) 1906- ... 7-8R
Gross, Feliks 1906- ... CANR-12
Earlier sketch in CA 29-32R
Gross, Franz B(runo) 1919- ... 29-32R
Gross, Gerald 1932- ... 11-12R
Gross, Hanns 1928- ... 41-44R
Gross, Harvey S(eymour) 1922- ... CANR-8
Earlier sketch in CA 15-16R
Gross, Helen Shimota 1931- ... 11-12R
Gross, Irma H(annah) 1892- ... CAP-1
Earlier sketch in CA 15-16
Gross, James A. 1933- ... 57-60
Gross, Joel 1951- ... CANR-14
Earlier sketch in CA 29-32R
Gross, Johannes Heinrich 1916- ... 29-32R
Gross, John 1935- ... 29-32R
Gross, John J. 1912-1970 ... CAP-2
Earlier sketch in CA 25-28
Gross, John Owen 1894-1971 ... CAP-2
Earlier sketch in CA 17-18
Gross, Kenneth 1954- ... 118
Gross, Kenneth G. 1939- ... 25-28R
Gross, Leonard 1928- ... 118
Brief entry ... 112
Gross, Leslie 1927- ... 7-8R
Gross, Llewellyn (Zwicker) 1914- ... 25-28R
Gross, Martin (Arnold) 1934- ... CANR-11
Earlier sketch in CA 15-16R
Gross, Martin L(ouis) 1925- ... CANR-7
Earlier sketch in CA 9-10R
Gross, Mary Anne 1943- ... 49-52
Gross, Michael 1891(?)-1979 Obituary ... 97-100
Gross, Michael (Robert) 1952- ... CANR-20
Earlier sketch in CA 93-96
Gross, Milt 1895-1953 ... DLB-11
Gross, Milton ... AITN-1
Gross, Milton 1912(?)-1973 Obituary ... 41-44R
Gross, Neal 1920-1981 Obituary ... 108
Gross, Phyllis P(ennebaker) 1915- ... 93-96
Gross, Richard Edmund 1920- ... CANR-1
Earlier sketch in CA 2R
Gross, Ronald 1935- ... CANR-5
Earlier sketch in CA 7-8R
Gross, Ruth Belov 1929- ... SATA-33
Gross, S(amuel Harry) 1933- ... 45-48
Gross, Sarah Chokla 1906-1976 ... 61-64
Obituary ... 65-68
See also SATA 9, 26
Gross, Seymour L. 1926- ... CANR-3
Earlier sketch in CA 1R
Gross, Sheldon H(arvey) 1921- ... 81-84
Gross, Shelley 1938- ... 21-22R
Gross, Shelly
See Gross, Sheldon H(arvey)
Gross, Stuart D. 1914- ... 57-60
Gross, Suzanne 1933- ... 19-20R
Gross, Terence 1947- ... 101
Gross, Theodore L(awrence) 1930- ... CANR-14
Earlier sketch in CA 41-44R
Gross, Walter 1923- ... 21-22R
Gross, William Joseph 1894- ... CAP-1
Earlier sketch in CA 11-12
Grossack, Irvin Millman 1927- ... 97-100
Grossack, Martin Myer 1928- ... CANR-6
Earlier sketch in CA 11-12R
Grossbach, Robert 1941- ... CANR-13
Earlier sketch in CA 33-36R
Grossberger, Lewis 1940(?)- Brief entry ... 121
Grossen, Neal E. 1943- ... 93-96
Grosser, Alfred 1925- ... CANR-20
Earlier sketches in CA 45-48, CANR-2
Grosser, Arthur E(dward) 1934- ... 116
Grosser, Morton 1931- ... CANR-17
Earlier sketch in CA 97-100
Grosshans, Henry 1921- ... 29-32R
Grossholtz, Jean 1929- ... 15-16R
Grossinger, Richard (Selig) 1944- ... CANR-19
Earlier sketch in CA 103
Grossinger, Tania 1937- ... CANR-4
Earlier sketch in CA 53-56
Grosskurth, Phyllis 1924- ... CANR-9
Earlier sketch in CA 15-16R
Grossman, Alfred 1927- ... 7-8R
Grossman, Allen (R.) 1932- ... CANR-16
Earlier sketches in CA 4R, CANR-1
Grossman, Edith Marian 1936- ... 108
Grossman, Ellie ... 110
Grossman, Frances Kaplan 1939- ... 57-60
Grossman, Gary H(oward) 1948- ... 69-72
Grossman, Herbert 1934- ... 17-18R
Grossman, Jean Schick 1894-1972
Obituary ... 37-40R
Grossman, Joan (Adess) 1940- ... 120
Grossman, Joan Delaney 1928- ... 111
Grossman, Julian 1931- ... 53-56
Grossman, Kurt R. 1897-1972 Obituary ... 33-36R
Grossman, Lawrence 1945- ... 65-68
Grossman, Lee 1931- ... 69-72
Grossman, Manuel Lester 1939-
Brief entry ... 106
Grossman, Martin (Allen) 1943- ... CANR-13
Earlier sketch in CA 77-80
Grossman, Martin A. 1951- ... 102
Grossman, Mary Louise 1930- ... 77-80
Grossman, Morton Charles 1919- ... CANR-2
Earlier sketch in CA 4R
Grossman, Nancy 1940- ... SATA-29
Grossman, Richard L(ee) 1921- ... 97-100
Grossman, Robert 1940- ... SATA-11
Grossman, Ronald P(hilip) 1934- ... 21-22R
Grossman, Samuel 1897- ... 53-56
Grossman, Sebastian P. 1934- ... 23-24R
Grossman, Shelly 1928(?)-1975 Obituary ... 57-60
Grossman, Vasily (Semenovich)
1905-1964 Brief entry ... 124
See also CLC 41
Grossman, William L(eonard) 1906-1980 ... CAP-2
Obituary ... 97-100
Earlier sketch in CA 23-24
Grossmann, Reinhardt S. 1931- ... CANR-20
Earlier sketch in CA 33-36R
Grossu, Sergiu 1920- ... CANR-8
Earlier sketch in CA 57-60
Grossvogel, David I. 1925- ... CANR-4
Earlier sketch in CA 1R
Grosswirth, Marvin 1931-1984 ... 33-36R
Obituary ... 112
Grosvenor, Donna K(erkam) 1938- ... 109
Grosvenor, Gilbert (Hovey) 1875-1966
Obituary ... 93-96
Grosvenor, Kali Diana 1960- ... 69-72
Grosvenor, Melville Bell 1901-1982 ... 69-72
Obituary ... 106
Grosvenor, Verta Mae 1938- ... 69-72
Groten, Dallas 1951- ... 115
Groth, Alexander J(acob) 1932- ... CANR-14
Earlier sketch in CA 41-44R
Groth, Jeanette L(ue) 1947- ... 111
Groth, John 1908- ... 101
See also SATA 21
Grotjahn, Martin 1904- ... CANR-15
Earlier sketch in CA 41-44R
Grotowski, Jerzy 1933- Brief entry ... 105
Grounds, Roger (Ransford Paterson)
1938- ... 97-100
Grounds, Vernon C(arl) 1914- ... 122
Groundwater, William 1906(?)-1982
Obituary ... 106
Groupe, Darryl R.
See Bunch, David R.
Groussard, Serge 1921- ... 108
Grout, Donald Jay 1902-1987 ... 102
Obituary ... 121
Grout, Jack 1910- ... 69-72
Grout, Ruth E(llen) 1901- ... CAP-2
Earlier sketch in CA 17-18
Grove, Fred(erick) 1913- ... CANR-17
Earlier sketches in CA 3R, CANR-2
Grove, Frederick Philip
See Greve, Felix Paul (Berthold Friedrich)
See also TCLC 4
Grove, Jack William 1920- ... 7-8R
Grove, Lee E(dmonds) ?-1971 Obituary ... 104
Grove, Pearce S(eymour) 1930- ... 73-76
Grove, Will O.
See Brister, Richard
Grovelands, Sarah
See Schneider, Myra
Grover, David H(ubert) 1925- ... 15-16R
Grover, David S(teele) 1939- ... 89-92
Grover, John W(agner) 1927- ... 77-80
Grover, Linda 1934- ... 29-32R
Grover, Philip 1929- ... 104
Groves, Colin Peter 1942- ... 61-64
Groves, Don(ald) George ... 106
Groves, Francis Richard 1889- ... CAP-1
Earlier sketch in CA 13-14
Groves, Georgina
See Symons, (Dorothy) Geraldine
Groves, H(arry) E(dward) 1921- ... 5-6R
Groves, Harold M(artin) 1897- ... 5-6R
Groves, Naomi Jackson 1910- ... 117
Groves, Paul 1930- ... CANR-17
Earlier sketch in CA 93-96
Groves, Reg(inald) 1908- ... 13-14R
Groves, Ruth Clouse 1902- ... CAP-2
Earlier sketch in CA 17-18
Grow, Lawrence 1939- ... CANR-10
Earlier sketch in CA 73-76
Grozny, I. L.
See Berger, Ivan (Bennett)
Grub, Phillip D. 1932- ... CANR-14
Earlier sketch in CA 25-28R
Grubar, Francis S(tanley) 1924- ... 33-36R
Grubb
See Crumb, R(obert)
Grubb, Davis Alexander 1919-1980 ... CANR-4
Obituary ... 101
Earlier sketch in CA 2R
See also DLB 6
Grubb, Frederick (Crichton-Stuart) 1930- ... 101
Grubb, Kenneth George 1900-1980 ... CAP-1
Obituary ... 97-100
Earlier sketch in CA 9-10
Grubb, Norman (Percy) 1895- ... CANR-13
Earlier sketches in CA 15-16, CAP-1
Grubb, W. Norton 1948- ... 110
Grubbs, David H(arold) 1929- ... 117
Grubbs, Donald H. 1936- ... 81-84
Grubbs, Frank Leslie, Jr. 1931- ... 29-32R
Grubbs, Robert L(owell) 1919- ... CANR-2
Earlier sketch in CA 2R
Grube, Georges M(aximilien) A(ntoine)
1899- ... CAP-1
Earlier sketch in CA 13-14
Grubel, Herbert G(unter) 1934- ... CANR-5
Earlier sketch in CA 9-10R
Gruber, Frank 1904-1969 ... CAP-1
Obituary ... 25-28R
Earlier sketch in CA 13-14
Gruber, Frederick C(harles) 1903- ... 49-52
Gruber, Gary R. 1940- ... CANR-24
Earlier sketches in CA 53-56, CANR-9
Gruber, Helmut 1928- ... 103
Gruber, Howard E(rnest) 1922- ... 119
Brief entry ... 113
Gruber, Ira D(empsey) 1934- Brief entry ... 110
Gruber, Jacob W(illiam) 1921- ... 1R
Gruber, Joseph John, Jr. 1930- ... CANR-6
Earlier sketch in CA 7-8R
Gruber, Katherine 1952- ... 123
Gruber, Martin Jay 1937- ... CANR-8
Earlier sketch in CA 53-56
Gruber, Ruth ... CANR-12
Earlier sketch in CA 25-28R
Gruber, Terry (deRoy) 1953- ... 97-100
Gruberg, Martin 1935- ... 33-36R
Grubian, Motel 1909(?)-1972 Obituary ... 104
Grudin, Louis 1898- ... 1R
Gruelle, John (Barton) 1880-1938
Brief entry ... 115
See also SATA 32, 35
Gruelle, Johnny
See Gruelle, John (Barton)
See also DLB 22
Gruelle, Worth ... AITN-2
Gruen, Erich S(tephen) 1935- Brief entry ... 111
Gruen, John 1926- ... CANR-8
Earlier sketch in CA 17-18R
Gruen, Victor (David) 1903-1980 ... CANR-10
Obituary ... 97-100
Earlier sketch in CA 15-16R
Gruenbaum, Adolf 1923- ... CANR-20
Earlier sketches in CA 9-10R, CANR-5
Gruenbaum, Ludwig
See Gaathon, A(ryeh) L(udwig)
Gruenberg, Benj(amin) C(harles)
1875-1965 ... CAP-1
Earlier sketch in CA 13-14
Gruenberg, Sidonie Matsner 1881-1974 ... CAP-1
Obituary ... 49-52
Earlier sketch in CA 15-16
See also SATA 2, 27
Gruenberger, Fred J(oseph) 1918- ... 118
Grueneberg, Hans 1907-1982 Obituary ... 108
Gruenhagen, Robert W. 1932- ... 29-32R
Gruening, Ernest (Henry) 1887-1974 ... 49-52
Gruenstein, Peter 1947- ... 77-80
Gruenther, Alfred M(aximilian) 1899-1983
Obituary ... 109
Gruffydd, Peter 1935- ... 104
Gruhn, Carrie Myers 1907- ... CAP-1
Earlier sketch in CA 11-12
Gruits, Patricia Beall 1923- ... 105
Gruliow, Leo 1913- ... 5-6R
Grumbach, Doris (Isaac) 1918- ... CANR-9
Earlier sketch in CA 5-6R
See also CAAS 2
See also CLC 13, 22
Grumbling Gourmet, The
See Chapman, Frank M(onroe)
Grumelli, Antonio 1928- ... 37-40R
Grumet, Robert Steven 1949- ... 102
Grumich, Charles A. 1905(?)-1981
Obituary ... 104
Grumley, Michael 1941- ... 29-32R
Grumme, Marguerite (Evelyn) ... 5-6R
Grummer, Arnold E(dward) 1923- ... 106
See also SATA 49
Grun, Bernard 1901-1972 Obituary ... 37-40R
Grunbaum, Adolf
See Gruenbaum, Adolf
Grund, Josef Carl 1920- ... 73-76
Grundberg, Andy
See Grundberg, John Andrew
Grundberg, John Andrew 1947- ... 103
Grundlehner, Philip 1945- ... 115
Grundstein, Nathan D(avid) 1913- ... CANR-15
Earlier sketch in CA 37-40R
Grundt, Leonard 1936- ... 57-60
Grundy, J(ohn) B(rownsdon) C(lowes)
1902-1987 Obituary ... 123
Grundy, J(ohn) Owen 1911-1985 Obituary ... 114
Grundy, Joan 1920- ... 109
Grundy, Kenneth W(illiam) 1936- ... CANR-12
Earlier sketch in CA 73-76
Grundy, Lester H. 1914(?)-1985 Obituary ... 116
Gruneau, Richard S(teven) 1948- ... 110
Gruneberg, Hans
See Grueneberg, Hans
Grunfeld, Frederic V(olker) 1929-1987 ... CANR-18
Obituary ... 124
Earlier sketch in CA 73-76

Grunge
See Crumb, R(obert)
Grunlan, Stephen Arthur 1942- ... CANR-18
Earlier sketch in CA 101
Grunwald, Constantine de
See de Grunwald, Constantine
Grunwald, Henry Anatole 1922- ... 107
Grunwald, Joseph 1920- ... 115
Grunwald, Lisa 1959- ... 120
See also CLC 44
Grunwald, Stefan 1933- ... 29-32R
Grupp, Stanley E(ugene) 1927- ... 53-56
Grusa, Jiri 1938- ... 117
Grusd, Edward Elihu 1904- ... CAP-2
Earlier sketch in CA 19-20
Gruskin, Alan D(aniel) 1904-1970 ... CAP-1
Obituary ... 29-32R
Earlier sketch in CA 11-12
Gruson, Edward S. 1929- ... 45-48
Gruss, Edmond C(harles) 1933- ... 53-56
Grutz, Mariellen Procopio 1946- ... 93-96
Grutzmacher, Harold M(artin), Jr.
1930- ... 29-32R
Gruver, Rebecca
See Goodman, Rebecca Gruver
Gruver, William R. II 1929- ... 45-48
Grylls, David (Stanway) 1947- ... 85-88
Grylls, Rosalie Glynn ... 65-68
Grynberg, Henryk 1936- ... 29-32R
Gryst, Edward (George) 1911- ... 2R
Grzimek, Bernhard (Klemens Maria H. P.)
1909-1987 Obituary ... 121
Guadaloupe, Brother Jose de
See Mojica, Jose
Guado, Sergio
See Gerosa, Guido
Guandagnolo, Joseph F(rancis) 1912- ... 5-6R
Guandolo, John 1919- ... 21-22R
Guaragna, Salvatore 1893-1981 Obituary ... 105
Guard, Dave
See Guard, David
Guard, David 1934- ... 77-80
Guardia, Ernesto de la, Jr.
See de la Guardia, Ernesto, Jr.
Guardo, Carol Joan 1939- ... 103
Guare, John 1938- ... CANR-21
Earlier sketch in CA 73-76
See also DLB 7
See also CLC 8, 14, 29
Guarendi, Raymond N(icholas) 1952- ... 120
Guareschi, Giovanni 1908-1968 ... 105
Obituary ... 25-28R
Guarino, M(artin) Vincent 1939- ... 41-44R
Guback, Thomas H(enry) 1937- ... 25-28R
Gubar, Susan (David) 1944- ... 108
Gubern, Santiago (Garriga-Nogues)
1933- ... CANR-2
Earlier sketch in CA 45-48
Gubert, Betty Kaplan 1934- ... 112
Gubrium, Jaber F(andy) 1943- ... CANR-4
Earlier sketch in CA 53-56
Gubser, Nicholas J. 1938- ... 19-20R
Guccione, Robert, Jr. ... AITN-2
Guches, Richard (Clement) 1938- ... 115
Guck, Dorothy 1913- ... 49-52
See also SATA 27
Gudde, Erwin G(ustav) 1889-1969 ... CANR-4
Earlier sketch in CA 5-6R
Gudenian, Haig (Krikor) 1918-1985(?)
Obituary ... 115
Guder, Eileen (Likens) 1919- ... 17-18R
Gudiol, Jose
See Gudiol i Ricart, Josep
Gudiol i Ricart, Josep 1904- ... 81-84
Gudiol Ricart, Jose M.
See Gudiol i Ricart, Josep
Gudiol Ricart, Josep
See Gudiol i Ricart, Josep
Gudjonsson, Halldor Kiljan 1902- ... 103
Gudschinsky, Sarah C(aroline)
1919-1975 ... CAP-2
Earlier sketch in CA 33-36
Guede, Norina (Maria Esterina) Lami
1913- ... 9-10R
Guehenne, Jean
See Guehenno, Jean Marcel Jules Marie
Guehenno, Jean Marcel Jules Marie
1890-1978 Obituary ... 104
Guelich, Robert A(llison) 1939- ... CANR-17
Earlier sketches in CA 45-48, CANR-2
Guemple, Lee 1930- ... 41-44R
Guenette, Robert (Homer) 1935- ... 25-28R
Guenter, Erich
See Eich, Guenter
Guenther, Charles (John) 1920- ... 29-32R
Guenther, Herbert V. 1917- ... 73-76
Guenther, John (Lewis) ... CANR-9
Earlier sketch in CA 5-6R
Guenther, (Robert) Wallace 1929- ... 65-68
Guerard, Albert Joseph 1914- ... CANR-2
Earlier sketch in CA 3R
See also CAAS 2
Guerin, Wilfred L(ouis) 1929- ... 17-18R
Guerlac, Henry (Edward) 1910-1985
Obituary ... 116
Guerlac, Rita 1916- ... 116
Guerney, Bernard G(uilbert), Jr. 1930- ... 93-96
Guerney, Bernard Guilbert 1894-1979
Obituary ... 85-88
Guernsey, Bruce H(ubbard) 1944- ... 108
Guernsey, James Lee 1923- ... 37-40R
Guernsey, Otis L(ove), Jr. 1918- ... 89-92
Guerny, Gene
See Gurney, Gene
Guerra, Emilio Louis 1909-1980
Obituary ... 97-100
Guerrant, Edward Owings 1911- ... 23-24R
Guerra y Sanchez, Ramiro 1880-1970
Obituary ... 104
Guerrero, Rogelio Diaz
See Diaz-Guerrero, Rogelio
Guerrette, Richard H(ector) 1930- ... 49-52
Guerrier, Dennis 1923- ... 29-32R
Guers-Villate, Yvonne 1924- ... 41-44R
Guess, Edward Preston 1925- ... 73-76
Guest, A(nthony) G(ordon) 1930- ... CANR-1
Earlier sketch in CA 2R
Guest, Barbara 1920- ... CANR-11
Earlier sketch in CA 25-28R
See also DLB 5
See also CLC 34
Guest, Edgar A(lbert) 1881-1959
Brief entry ... 112
Guest, Harry
See Guest, Henry Bayly
Guest, Henry Bayly 1932- ... CANR-9
Earlier sketch in CA 65-68
Guest, Ivor (Forbes) 1920- ... CANR-20
Earlier sketches in CA 7-8R, CANR-2
Guest, Judith (Ann) 1936- ... CANR-15
Earlier sketch in CA 77-80
See also CLC 8, 30
Guett, Dieter 1924- ... 65-68
Gueulette, David G(eorge) 1941- ... 111
Guevara, Che
See Guevara, (Serna) Ernesto
Guevara, (Serna) Ernesto 1928-1967
Obituary ... 111
Guffey, George R(obert) 1932- Brief entry ... 118
Guffin, Gilbert L. 1906- ... 17-18R
Gugas, Chris 1921- ... 97-100
Gugelyk, M(yron) Ted 1938- ... 120
Guggenheim, Edward Armand 1901-1970
Obituary ... 104
Guggenheim, Harry Frank 1890-1971
Obituary ... 89-92
Guggenheim, Marguerite 1898-1979
Obituary ... 105
Guggenheim, Peggy
See Guggenheim, Marguerite
Guggenheimer, Richard 1906-1977 ... 41-44R
Obituary ... 69-72
Guggenmos, Josef 1922- ... 81-84
Guggisberg, C(harles) A(lbert) W(alter)
1913- ... 81-84
Gugliotta, Bobette 1918- ... CANR-14
Earlier sketch in CA 41-44R
See also SATA 7
Guhin, Michael A(lan) 1940- ... 41-44R
Guice, John D(avid) W(ynne) 1931- ... 41-44R
Guicharnaud, June 1922- ... 93-96
Guido, (Cecily) Margaret 1912- ... 65-68
Guild, Lurelle Van Arsdale 1898- ... CAP-2
Earlier sketch in CA 29-32
Guild, Nicholas M. 1944- ... 93-96
See also CLC 33
Guild, Thelma S(croggs) 1911- ... 118
Guild, Vera Palmer 1906- Brief entry ... 106
Guilds, John C(aldwell, Jr.) 1924- ... 77-80
Guiles, Fred Lawrence 1920- ... CANR-12
Earlier sketch in CA 25-28R
Guilford, J(oy) Paul 1897- ... CANR-4
Earlier sketch in CA 1R
Guilford, Joan S. 1928- ... 29-32R
Guillaume, Alfred 1888-19(?) ... CAP-1
Earlier sketch in CA 15-16
Guillaume, Jeanette G. Flierl 1899- ... 2R
See also SATA 8
Guille, Frances V(ernor) 1908-1975 ... 45-48
Obituary ... 61-64
Guillemin, Henri 1903- ... 81-84
Guillemin, Jacques
See Sartre, Jean-Paul
Guillen, Jorge 1893-1984 ... 89-92
Obituary ... 112
See also CLC 11
Guillen (y Batista), Nicolas (Cristobal)
1902- Brief entry ... 116
Guillet, Edwin C(larence) 1898-1975 ... 107
Guillet, Jacques 1910- ... 102
Guillevic, (Eugene) 1907- ... 93-96
See also CLC 33
Guillois
See Desnos, Robert
Guillot, Rene 1900-1969 ... 49-52
See also SATA 7
Guilloux, Louis 1899-1980 Obituary ... 104
Guilmartin, John Francis, Jr. 1940- ... 53-56
Guimary, Donald L(ee) 1932- ... 73-76
Guimond, James K. 1936- ... 25-28R
Guin, Wyman (Woods) 1915- ... 102
Guinagh, Kevin (Joseph) 1897- ... 17-18R
Guinan, Michael D(amon) 1939- ... 117
Guinee, Kathleen K. 1902(?)-1982
Obituary ... 109
Guiney, Louise Imogen 1861-1920 ... DLB-54
Guiney, Mortimer 1930- ... 53-56
Guinn, Paul (Spencer, Jr.) 1928- ... 15-16R
Guinness, Bryan (Walter) 1905- ... 102
Guinness, (Ian) Os(wald) 1941- ... 65-68
Guinther, John 1927- ... CANR-11
Earlier sketch in CA 69-72
Guion, Robert M(organ) 1924- ... CANR-7
Earlier sketch in CA 17-18R
Guirdham, Arthur 1905- ... 103
Guisewite, Cathy (Lee) 1950- ... 113
Brief entry ... 111
Guisinger, Stephen Edward 1941- ... 103
Guitar, Mary Anne 1922- Brief entry ... 113
Guiterman, Arthur 1871-1943 Brief entry ... 120
See also DLB 11
Guither, Harold D. 1927- ... 29-32R
Gula, Richard M(ichael) 1947- ... 109
Gula, Robert J(ohn) 1941- ... 97-100
Gulick, Bill
See Gulick, Grover C.
Gulick, Edward Vose 1915- ... 113
Gulick, Grover C. 1916- ... CANR-17
Earlier sketch in CA 33-36R
Gulick, Robert Lee, Jr. 1912-1987
Obituary ... 122
Gulik, Robert H(ans) van
See van Gulik, Robert H(ans)
Gulker, Virgil G. 1947- ... 65-68
Gullace, Gino 1925- ... CANR-17
Earlier sketch in CA 69-72
Gullans, Charles (Bennett) 1929- ... CANR-18
Earlier sketches in CA 4R, CANR-4
Gullason, Thomas A(rthur) 1924- ... CANR-8
Earlier sketch in CA 23-24R
Gulley, Halbert E(dison) 1919- ... CANR-6
Earlier sketch in CA 5-6R
Gulley, Norman 1920- ... 33-36R
Gullick, Charles Francis William Rowley
1907- ... 7-8R
Gullick, Etta 1916- ... 89-92
Gullick, John M(ichael) 1916- ... 15-16R
Gulliford, Andrew 1953- ... 120
Gulliford, Ronald 1920- ... 13-14R
Gulliver, Harold S. 1935- ... 97-100
Gulliver, Lemuel
See Hastings, Macdonald
Gulston, Charles 1913-1981 ... 122
Gummere, Richard M(ott), Jr. 1912- ... 45-48
Gump, Richard (Benjamin) 1906- ... CAP-1
Earlier sketch in CA 9-10
Gump, Sally
See Stanford, Sally
Gumpertz, Robert 1925- ... 69-72
Gunders, Henry 1924- ... 29-32R
Gundersheimer, Karen ... SATA-44
Gundersheimer, Werner L. 1937- ... 53-56
Gunderson, Doris V. ... 29-32R
Gunderson, Frank L(ester) 1902-1983
Obituary ... 110
Gunderson, Keith (Robert) 1935- ... 33-36R
Gunderson, Robert Gray 1915- ... 1R
Gundrey, Elizabeth 1924- ... CANR-6
Earlier sketch in CA 13-14R
See also SATA 23
Gundry, Robert H(orton) 1932- ... 29-32R
Gundry, Stanley Norman 1937- ... 114
Gundy, Elizabeth ... 112
Gundy, H(enry) Pearson) 1905- ... 45-48
Guney, Yilmaz 1937(?)-1984 Obituary ... 113
Gunji, Masakatsu 1913- ... 29-32R
Gunn, Bill
See Gunn, William Harrison
See also DLB 38
See also CLC 5
Gunn, Christopher Eaton 1944- ... 117
Gunn, Diana Maureen 1926- ... CANR-18
Earlier sketch in CA 97-100
Gunn, Drewey Wayne 1939- ... 57-60
Gunn, Elizabeth
See Gunn, Diana Maureen
Gunn, Giles B(uckingham) 1938- ... 57-60
Gunn, Helen Montgomery 1900(?)-1987
Obituary ... 122
Gunn, J(ohn) A(lexander) W(ilson)
1937- ... CANR-20
Earlier sketch in CA 25-28R
Gunn, James E(dwin) 1923- ... CANR-22
Earlier sketches in CA 11-12R, CANR-5
See also CAAS 2
See also SATA 35
See also DLB 8
Gunn, John (Charles) 1937- ... 49-52
Gunn, Mrs. Aneas 1870-1961 Obituary ... 115
Gunn, Neil M(iller) 1891-1973 Obituary ... 37-40R
See also DLB 15
Gunn, Peter (Nicholson) 1914- ... CANR-18
Earlier sketches in CA 25-28R, CANR-10
Gunn, Sister Agnes Marie 1928- ... 17-18R
Gunn, Thom(son William) 1929- ... CANR-9
Earlier sketch in CA 17-18R
See also DLB 27
See also CLC 3, 6, 18, 32
Gunn, William Harrison 1934- ... CANR-12
Earlier sketch in CA 13-14R
See also AITN 1
Gunnars, Kristjana 1948- ... 113
See also DLB 60
Gunnarsson, Gunnar 1889-1975 Obituary ... 61-64
Gunnell, Bryn 1933- ... 103
Gunnell, John G. 1933- ... 25-28R
Gunneweg, Antonius H. J. 1922- ... CANR-16
Earlier sketch in CA 89-92
Gunning, Monica Olwen 1930- ... 65-68
Gunning, Robert 1908-1980 ... CAP-2
Obituary ... 97-100
Earlier sketch in CA 25-28
Gunsalus Gonzalez, Catherine 1934-
Brief entry ... 107
Gunston, Bill
See Gunston, William Tudor
Gunston, William Tudor 1927- ... CANR-19
Earlier sketches in CA 49-52, CANR-3
See also SATA 9
Gunstone, A(ntony) J. H. 1937(?)-1984
Obituary ... 112
Gunter, (J.) Bradley (Hunt) 1940- ... 29-32R
Gunter, Pete A(ddison) Y(ancey)
1936- ... CANR-15
Earlier sketch in CA 33-36R
Gunterman, Bertha Lisette 1886(?)-1975
Obituary ... 104
See also SATA 27
Gunther, A(lbert) E(verard) 1903- ... 29-32R
Gunther, Bernard 1929- ... CANR-2
Earlier sketch in CA 45-48
Gunther, Gerald 1927- ... CANR-13
Earlier sketch in CA 33-36R
Gunther, John 1901-1970 ... 11-12R
Obituary ... 25-28R
See also SATA 2
Gunther, Max 1927- ... 15-16R
Gunther, Peter F. 1920- ... 11-12R
Gunther, Richard (Paul) 1946- ... 103
Gunton, Sharon R(ose) 1952- ... 102
Guntrip, Harry
See Guntrip, Henry James Samuel
Guntrip, Henry James Samuel
1901-1975 ... CANR-5
Earlier sketch in CA 7-8R
Gunzburg, Nicholas de 1904-1981
Obituary ... 103
Guppy, Nicholas (Gareth Lechmere)
1925- ... CANR-6
Earlier sketch in CA 7-8R
Gupta, Brijen K(ishore) 1929- ... CANR-16
Earlier sketches in CA 45-48, CANR-1
Gupta, Marie (Jacqueline) 1946- ... 57-60
Gupta, Pranati Sen
See Sen Gupta, Pranati
Gupta, Ram Chandra 1927- ... CANR-13
Earlier sketch in CA 23-24R
Gupta, S(ushil) (Kumar) 1927- ... 57-60
Gupta, Shiv K(umar) 1930- ... 57-60
Gupta, Sulekh Chandra 1928- ... 15-16R
Guptara, Prabhu S(iddhartha) 1949- ... 81-84
Guptill, Nathanael M(ann) 1917- ... 45-48
Gura, Philip F(rancis) 1950- ... 111
Gurdus, Luba Krugman 1914- ... 120
Gurik, Robert 1932- ... DLB-60
Gurin, Joel 1953- ... 108
Gurko, Leo 1914- ... CANR-5
Earlier sketch in CA 5-6R
See also SATA 9
Gurko, Miriam ... 4R
See also SATA 9
Gurman, Alan S(tephen) 1945- ... CANR-5
Earlier sketch in CA 53-56
Gurnee, Jeanne 1926- ... 93-96
Gurnee, Russell H(ampton) 1922- ... 107
Gurney, A(lbert) R(amsdell), Jr. 1930- ... 77-80
See also CLC 32
Gurney, Gene 1924- ... CANR-9
Earlier sketch in CA 7-8R
Gurney, George 1939- ... 119
Gurney, J. Eric ... CANR-2
Earlier sketch in CA 4R
Gurney, Nancy Jack 1915(?)-1973
Obituary ... 45-48
Gurney, Peter
See Gurney, A(lbert) R(amsdell), Jr.
Gurr, Andrew (John) 1936- ... 33-36R
Gurr, Ted Robert 1936- ... CANR-16
Earlier sketch in CA 41-44R
Gurrey, Percival 1890-1980 Obituary ... 97-100
Gurtov, Melvin 1941- Brief entry ... 112
Gurwitsch, Aron 1901-1973 ... CAP-1
Obituary ... 41-44R
Earlier sketch in CA 15-16
Gusfield, Joseph R. 1923- ... 53-56
Gusikoff, Lynne
See Hawes, Lynne Gusikoff Salop
Guss, Donald L(eroy) 1929- ... 17-18R
Guss, Leonard M. 1926- ... 21-22R
Gussman, Boris (William) 1914- ... 5-6R
Gussow, Alan 1931- Brief entry ... 111
Gussow, Joan Dye 1928- ... 29-32R
Gussow, Mel 1933- ... 107
Gustaf, King of Sweden 1882-1973
Obituary ... 45-48
Gustafson, Alrik 1903-1970 ... 4R
Obituary ... 103
Gustafson, Anita 1942- ... 112
See also SATA 45
Gustafson, Donald F. 1934- ... 11-12R
Gustafson, James M(oody) 1925- ... 25-28R
Gustafson, Paula Catherine 1941- ... 106
Gustafson, Ralph (Barker) 1909- ... CANR-8
Earlier sketch in CA 23-24R
See also CLC 36
Gustafson, Richard C(larence) 1933-1977
Obituary ... 111
Gustafson, Richard F(olke) 1934- ... 19-20R
Gustafson, Sarah R.
See Riedman, Sarah R(egal)
Gustafson, Scott 1956- ... SATA-34
Gustafson, W(illiam) Eric 1933- ... 57-60
Gustafsson, Lars 1936- ... 85-88
Gustaitis, Rasa 1934- ... 25-28R
Gustavson, Carl G(ustav) 1915- ... 19-20R
Gustin, Lawrence Robert 1937- ... 57-60
Gustkey, Earl 1940- ... 57-60
Gut, Gom
See Simenon, Georges (Jacques
Christian)
Gutch, John 1905-1988 Obituary ... 124
Gutcheon, Beth R(ichardson) 1945- ... CANR-2
Earlier sketch in CA 49-52
Gutek, Gerald L(ee) 1935- ... CANR-17
Earlier sketch in CA 81-84
Gutenberg, Arthur W(illiam) 1920- ... 37-40R
Guterman, Norbert 1900-1984 Obituary ... 113
Guterman, Simeon L(eonard) 1907- ... 41-44R
Guterman, Stanley S(anford) 1934- ... 29-32R
Gutheim, Frederick 1908- ... CANR-9
Earlier sketch in CA 23-24R
Guthke, Karl S(iegfried) 1933- ... CANR-15
Earlier sketch in CA 41-44R
Guthman, Edwin 1919- ... 33-36R
Guthman, William H(arold) 1924- ... 57-60
Guthmann, Harry G. 1896- ... 3R

Guthrie, A(lfred) B(ertram), Jr. 1901- .. CANR-24
Earlier sketch in CA 57-60
See also DLB 6
See also CLC 23
Guthrie, Anne 1890-1979 ... 5-6R
See also SATA 28
Guthrie, Arlo (Davy) 1947- ... 113
Guthrie, David
See Allen, H(ubert) R(aymond)
Guthrie, Donald 1916- ... CANR-23
Earlier sketches in CA 13-14R, CANR-7
Guthrie, Harvey Henry, Jr. 1924- ... 13-14R
Guthrie, Hugh
See Freeman, John Crosby
Guthrie, Hunter 1901-1974 ... 65-68
Obituary ... 53-56
Guthrie, Isobel
See Grieve, C(hristopher) M(urray)
Guthrie, James Shields 1931- ... CANR-15
Earlier sketch in CA 33-36R
Guthrie, James W. 1936- ... 41-44R
Guthrie, John 1908- ... 106
Guthrie, John A(lexander) 1907- ... 1R
Guthrie, Judith Bretherton 1905(?)-1972
Obituary ... 37-40R
Guthrie, Marjorie (Greenblatt Mazia)
1917-1983 Obituary ... 117
Guthrie, Ramon 1896-1973 ... 5-6R
Obituary ... 45-48
See also DLB 4
Guthrie, Robert V(al) 1930- ... 53-56
Guthrie, Russell Dale 1936- Brief entry ... 106
Guthrie, T.
See Guthrie, (William) Tyrone
Guthrie, Thomas Anstey 1856-1934
Brief entry ... 113
Guthrie, (William) Tyrone 1900-1971 ... 123
Obituary ... 29-32R
Guthrie, William Keith Chambers
1906-1981 ... CANR-11
Obituary ... 103
Earlier sketch in CA 65-68
Guthrie, Woodrow Wilson 1912-1967 ... 113
Obituary ... 93-96
Guthrie, Woody
See Guthrie, Woodrow Wilson
See also CLC 35
Gutierrez, Donald 1932- ... 109
Gutierrez-Vega, Zenaida 1924- ... CANR-19
Earlier sketch in CA 41-44R
Gutin, Bernard 1934- ... 112
Gutkin, Harry 1915- ... 101
Gutkind, Erwin A(nton) 1886-1968 ... CANR-8
Earlier sketch in CA 7-8R
Gutkind, Lee 1943- ... CANR-20
Earlier sketches in CA 53-56, CANR-5
Gutkind, Peter C(laus) W(olfgang) 1925- ... 116
Gutman, Bill ... SATA-43
Gutman, Herbert G(eorge) 1928-1985 ... 65-68
Obituary ... 116
Gutman, Judith Mara 1928- ... 21-22R
Gutman, Kellie O. 1952- ... 124
Gutman, Naham 1899(?)-1981 Obituary ... 102
See also SATA 25
Gutman, Richard J(ay) S(tephen) 1949- ... 101
Gutman, Robert 1926- ... 45-48
Gutman, Robert W. 1925- ... 25-28R
Gutman, Walter
See Gutman, Walter Knowlton
Gutman, Walter Knowlton 1903-1986
Obituary ... 119
Gutmann, James 1897- ... CAP-2
Earlier sketch in CA 21-22
Gutmann, Joseph 1923- ... CANR-17
Earlier sketches in CA 49-52, CANR-1
Gutmann, Myron P. 1949- Brief entry ... 105
Gutnik, Martin J(erome) 1942- ... CANR-3
Earlier sketch in CA 49-52
Gutsche, Thelma 1915- ... 23-24R
Gutstein, Morris A(aron) 1905-1987
Obituary ... 122
Gutt, Dieter
See Guett, Dieter
Guttenberg, Barnett ... 89-92
Guttenberg, Virginia 1914- ... 81-84
Guttentag, Marcia 1932-1977 ... CANR-8
Earlier sketch in CA 57-60
Gutteridge, Anne C(hristine) 1943- ... 108
Gutteridge, Bernard 1916-1985 Obituary ... 117
Gutteridge, Don(ald George) 1937- ... CANR-9
Earlier sketch in CA 65-68
Gutteridge, Lindsay 1923- ... 49-52
Gutteridge, Richard (Joseph Cooke) 1911- .. 122
Gutteridge, William F(rank) 1919- ... 15-16R
Gutterson, Herbert (Lindsley, Jr.) 1915- ... 9-10R
Gutting, Gary (Michael) 1942- ... 103
Guttmacher, Alan F(rank) 1898-1974 ... CANR-6
Obituary ... 49-52
Earlier sketch in CA 4R
Guttmacher, Manfred S(chanfarber)
1898-1966 ... CAP-1
Earlier sketch in CA 11-12
Guttmann, Alexander ... 29-32R
Guttmann, Allen 1932- ... CANR-16
Earlier sketches in CA 4R, CANR-1
Guttridge, Leonard F(rancis) 1918- ... 85-88
Guttsman, Wilhelm Leo 1920- ... 11-12R
Gutwirth, Samuel William 1903-1983
Obituary ... 111
Gutzke, Manford G(eorge) 1896- ... 17-18R
Guy, Anne W(elsh) ... 5-6R
Guy, David 1948- ... 105
Guy, Harold A. 1904- ... 17-18R
Guy, Ray 1939- ... DLB-60
Guy, Rosa (Cuthbert) 1928- ... CANR-14
Earlier sketch in CA 17-18R
See also SATA 14
See also DLB 33
See also CLC 26
See also CLR 13
Guyer, Paul 1948- ... CANR-24
Earlier sketch in CA 105
Guymer, (Wilhelmina) Mary 1909- ... SATA-50
Guyot, James F(ranklin) 1932- ... 53-56
Guyton, Arthur C(lifton) 1919- ... CANR-7
Earlier sketch in CA 19-20R
Guzie, Tad W(alter) 1934- ... CANR-5
Earlier sketch in CA 15-16R
Guzman, Ralph C. 1924-1985 Obituary ... 117
Guzzo, Sandra E(lizabeth) 1941- ... 120
Guzzwell, John 1930- ... 13-14R
Gwaltney, Francis Irby 1921- ... CANR-2
Earlier sketch in CA 4R
Gwaltney, John Langston 1928- ... 77-80
Gwendolyn
See Bennett, (Enoch) Arnold
Gwilliam, Kenneth M(ason) 1937- ... 17-18R
Gwin, Lucy 1943- ... 109
Gwinup, Thomas 1932- ... 73-76
Gwirtzman, Milton S. 1933- ... 29-32R
Gwyn, Julian 1937- ... 57-60
Gwyn, Richard J. 1934- ... CANR-17
Earlier sketch in CA 25-28R
Gwyn, W(illiam) B(rent) 1927- ... CANR-5
Earlier sketch in CA 15-16R
Gwynn, Denis (Rolleston) 1893- ... CAP-1
Earlier sketch in CA 13-14
Gwynn, Mary 1952- ... 111
Gwynn, Robin D(avid) 1942- ... 121
Gwynne, Erskine 1898-1948 Brief entry ... 107
See also DLB 4
Gwynne, Fred(erick Hubbard) 1926- ... 113
See also SATA 27, 41
Gwynne, Oscar A.
See Ellis, Edward S(ylvester)
Gwynne, Oswald A.
See Ellis, Edward S(ylvester)
Gwynne, Peter 1941- ... 89-92
Gwynne-Jones, Allan 1892-1982 Obituary .. 107
Gwynne-Thomas, E(ric) H(ubert) 1917- ... 120
Gyftopoulos, Elias Panayiotis 1927- ... 104
Gyldenvand, Lily M. 1917- ... CANR-6
Earlier sketch in CA 15-16R
Gyllenhammar, Pehr G(ustaf) 1935- ... CANR-13
Earlier sketch in CA 73-76
Gyoergyi, Albert (von Nagyrapolt) Szent
See Szent-Gyoergyi, Albert (von Nagyrapolt)
Gyorgy, Andrew 1917- ... 122
Gyorgyey, Clara 1936- ... 77-80
Gyorgyi, Albert (von Nagyrapolt) Szent
See Szent-Gyoergyi, Albert (von Nagyrapolt)
Gysbers, Norman C(harles) 1932- ... 61-64
Gysin, Brion 1916-1986 ... 117
Obituary ... 120
Brief entry ... 113
See also DLB 16
Gzowski, Peter 1934- ... 106

H

H. D.
See Doolittle, Hilda
See also CLC 3, 8, 14, 31, 34
H. F. E.
See Everett-Green, Evelyn
H. M. S.
See Kirk-Greene, Anthony (Hamilton Millard)
H. M. W.
See Wang, Hui-Ming
Haaby, Lawrence O. 1915- ... 33-36R
Haac, Oscar A(lfred) 1918- ... 33-36R
Haack, Susan 1945- ... 61-64
Haaf, Beverly T(erhune) 1936- ... 97-100
Haaften, Julia Van
See Van Haaften, Julia
Haag, Jessie Helen 1917- ... CANR-5
Earlier sketch in CA 15-16R
Haaker, Ann M. ... 25-28R
Haakonssen, Knud 1947- ... 124
Haan, Aubrey Edwin 1908- ... 1R
Haar, Charles M(onroe) 1920- ... 33-36R
Haar, Francis 1908- ... 53-56
Haar, Franklin B. 1906- ... CAP-1
Earlier sketch in CA 11-12
Haar, James 1929- ... 21-22R
Haarer, Alec Ernest 1894-1970 ... CANR-4
Earlier sketch in CA 7-8R
Haarhoff, Theodore Johannes 1892-1971 . CAP-1
Earlier sketch in CA 13-14
Haas, Albert E. 1917- ... 23-24R
Haas, Ben(jamin) L(eopold) 1926-1977 .. CANR-8
Obituary ... 73-76
Earlier sketch in CA 9-10R
Haas, Carolyn Buhai 1926- ... CANR-9
Earlier sketch in CA 65-68
See also SATA 43
Haas, Charlie 1952- ... 73-76
Haas, Dorothy F. ... CANR-20
Earlier sketches in CA 7-8R, CANR-3
See also SATA 43, 46
See also SAAS 43
Haas, Ernst 1921-1986 Obituary ... 120
Haas, Ernst B(ernard) 1924- ... 81-84
Haas, Gerda (Schild) 1922- ... 110
Haas, Harold I(rwin) 1925- ... 29-32R
Haas, Irene 1929- ... 97-100
See also SATA 17
Haas, Irvin 1916- ... 41-44R
Haas, J(ohn) Eugene 1926- ... 41-44R
Haas, James E(dward) 1943- ... CANR-7
Earlier sketch in CA 61-64
See also SATA 40
Haas, Jessie 1959- ... 114
Haas, Kenneth B(rooks), Sr. 1898- ... CANR-6
Earlier sketch in CA 57-60
Haas, Kurt ... 53-56
Haas, LaVerne 1942- ... 49-52
Haas, Lynne 1939- ... 65-68
Haas, Marilyn L(oomis) 1931- ... 117
Haas, Mary Odin 1910- ... CAP-1
Earlier sketch in CA 13-14
Haas, Mary R(osamond) 1910- ... 11-12R
Haas, Merle S. 1896(?)-1985 Obituary ... 114
See also SATA 41
Haas, Michael 1938- ... 53-56
Haas, Raymond Michael 1935- ... 37-40R
Haas, Robert Bartlett 1916- Brief entry ... 108
Haas, Robert Lewis 1936- ... 101
Haase, Ann Marie Bernazza 1942- ... 33-36R
Haase, John 1923- ... CANR-14
Earlier sketch in CA 7-8R
Haavikko, Paavo Juhani 1931- ... 106
See also CLC 18, 34
Habbema, Koos
See Heijermans, Herman
Habe, Hans 1911-1977 ... CANR-2
Obituary ... 73-76
Earlier sketch in CA 45-48
Habel, Norman C. 1932- ... 17-18R
Habenstreit, Barbara 1937- ... 29-32R
See also SATA 5
Haber, Audrey 1940- ... CANR-13
Earlier sketch in CA 33-36R
Haber, Carole R. 1951- ... 124
Haber, Eitan 1940- ... 104
Haber, Heinz 1913- ... 73-76
Haber, Jack 1939-1984 ... 69-72
Obituary ... 114
Haber, Joyce 1932- ... 65-68
Haber, Louis 1910- ... 29-32R
See also SATA 12
Haber, Ralph Norman 1932- ... 33-36R
Haber, Samuel 1928- ... 9-10R
Haber, Tom Burns 1900- ... CAP-2
Earlier sketch in CA 17-18
Haber, William 1899- ... CAP-2
Earlier sketch in CA 21-22
Haberer, Joseph 1929- ... 65-68
Haberler, Gottfried 1900- ... 103
Haberly, David T(ristram) 1942- ... 106
Haberly, Loyd 1896-1981 ... 105
Obituary ... 103
Haberman, Daniel 1933- ... 110
Haberman, Donald (Charles) 1933- ... 21-22R
Haberman, Martin 1932- ... 57-60
Haberman, Shelby J(oel) 1947- ... 103
Habermann, Helen M(argaret) 1927- ... 53-56
Habermas, Juergen 1929- ... 109
Habermas, Jurgen
See Habermas, Juergen
Haberstroh, Chadwick John 1927- ... 41-44R
Habgood, John Stapylton 1927- ... CANR-22
Earlier sketches in CA 15-16R, CANR-5
Habig, Marion A(lphonse) 1901-1984 .. CANR-20
Obituary ... 114
Earlier sketches in CA 7-8R, CANR-5
Hablutzel, Philip 1935- ... 37-40R
Habsburg-Lothringen, Geza Louis Eusebius Gebhard Ralphael Albert Maria von
See von Habsburg-Lothringen, Geza Louis Eusebius Gebhard Ralphael Albert Maria
Hach, Clarence Woodrow 1917- ... 13-14R
Hachey, Thomas E(ugene) 1938- ... 37-40R
Hachten, Harva ... 108
Hachten, William Andrews 1924- ... 107
Hacikyan, A(gop) J. 1931- ... 33-36R
Hack, Walter G. 1925- ... 29-32R
Hackady, Hal Brief entry ... 105
Hacker, Andrew 1929- ... CANR-1
Earlier sketch in CA 1R
Hacker, Carlotta 1931- ... 118
Hacker, Frederick J. 1914- Brief entry ... 104
Hacker, Leonard
See Hackett, Buddy
Hacker, Louis M(orton) 1899-1987 ... 17-18R
Obituary ... 122
Hacker, Marilyn 1942- ... 77-80
See also CLC 5, 9, 23
Hacker, Mary Louise 1908- ... CAP-2
Earlier sketch in CA 17-18
Hacker, Rose (Goldbloom) 1906- ... 13-14R
Hacker, Shyrle 1910- ... 101
Hackes, Peter Sidney 1924- ... 102
Hackett, Albert 1900- ... DLB-26
Hackett, Blanche Ann 1924- ... 73-76
Hackett, Buddy 1924- Brief entry ... 108
Hackett, Cecil Arthur 1908- ... 13-14R
Hackett, Charles J(oseph) 1915- ... 73-76
Hackett, Donald F. 1918- ... 29-32R
Hackett, Francis 1883-1962 ... 108
Obituary ... 89-92
Hackett, Herbert L(ewis) 1917-1964 ... 2R
Hackett, Jan Michele 1952- ... 105
Hackett, John W. 1924- ... 17-18R
Hackett, John Winthrop 1910- ... 89-92
Hackett, Laura Lyman 1916- ... 17-18R
Hackett, Lee
See Arkley, Arthur J(ames)
Hackett, Marie G. 1923- ... 37-40R
Hackett, Pat ... 105
Hackett, Paul 1920- ... 29-32R
Hackett, Peter 1940- Brief entry ... 108
Hackett, Philip 1941- ... 77-80
Hackett, Roger F(leming) 1922- ... 77-80
Hackett, William H. Y., Jr. 1921(?)-1986
Obituary ... 118
Hackford, Robert 1921(?)-1983 Obituary ... 111
Hackforth-Jones, (Frank) Gilbert 1900- ... 15-16R
Hacking, Ian 1936- ... 69-72
Hackleman, Michael A(lan) 1946- ... 106
Hackler, James C(ourtland) 1930- ... 112
Hackman, J(ohn) Richard 1940- ... CANR-1
Earlier sketch in CA 49-52
Hackman, Martha L. 1912- ... 29-32R
Hackney, Alan 1924- ... 7-8R
Hackney, Sheldon 1933- ... 41-44R
Hackney, Vivian 1914- ... 23-24R
Hadas, Moses 1900-1966 ... CANR-6
Obituary ... 25-28R
Earlier sketch in CA 1R
Hadas, Pamela White 1946- ... CANR-16
Earlier sketch in CA 93-96
Hadas, Rachel 1948- ... 111
Hadawi, Sami 1904- ... CANR-13
Earlier sketch in CA 23-24R
Haddad, George M. 1910- ... 17-18R
Haddad, Robert M(itchell) 1930- ... 69-72
Haddad, William Frederick 1928-
Brief entry ... 108
Haddad, Yvonne Y(azbeck) 1935- ... 108
Haddad-Garcia, George 1954- ... 107
Haddan, Eugene E. 1918- Brief entry ... 108
Hadden, Jeffrey K(eith) 1936- ... 106
Hadden, Maude Miner 1880-1967 ... CAP-2
Earlier sketch in CA 17-18
Haddix, Cecille
See Haddix-Kontos, Cecille P.
Haddix-Kontos, Cecille P. 1937- ... 69-72
Haddo, Oliver
See Puechner, Ray
Haddock, Sally 1954- ... 121
Haddon, Christopher
See Palmer, John (Leslie)
Haddox, John H(erbert) 1929- ... 45-48
Hader, Berta (Hoerner) 1890(?)-1976 ... 73-76
Obituary ... 65-68
See also SATA 16
Hader, Elmer Stanley 1889-1973 ... 73-76
See also SATA 16
Hadfield, Alice M(ary) 1908- ... 108
Hadfield, (Ellis) Charles (Raymond)
1909- ... CANR-7
Earlier sketch in CA 13-14R
Hadfield, E. C. R.
See Hadfield, (Ellis) Charles (Raymond)
Hadfield, Miles H(eywood) 1903-1982 ... CAP-1
Obituary ... 106
Earlier sketch in CA 15-16
Hadfield, Vic(tor Edward) 1940-
Brief entry ... 106
Hadham, John
See Parkes, James William
Hadik, Laszlo 1932(?)-1973 Obituary ... 45-48
Hadingham, Evan 1951- ... 102
Hadley, Arthur T. 1924- ... 89-92
Hadley, Charles D(avid), Jr. 1942- ... 110
Hadley, Eleanor M(artha) 1916- ... 29-32R
Hadley, Franklin
See Winterbotham, R(ussell) R(obert)
Hadley, Hamilton 1896- ... CAP-1
Earlier sketch in CA 9-10
Hadley, Jay 1947- ... 114
Hadley, Lee 1934- ... CANR-19
Earlier sketch in CA 101
See also SATA 38, 47
Hadley, Leila 1925- ... CANR-14
Earlier sketch in CA 41-44R
Hadley, Michael L(lewellyn) 1936- ... 118
Hadley, Morris 1894-1979 Obituary ... 85-88
Hadley Chase, James
See Raymond, Rene (Brabazon)
Hadlich, Roger L(ee) 1930- Brief entry ... 108
Hadlow, Leonard Harold 1908- ... CAP-1
Earlier sketch in CA 13-14
Hadrill, Andrew (Frederic) Wallace
See Wallace-Hadrill, Andrew (Frederic)
Hadrill, John Michael Wallace
See Wallace-Hadrill, John Michael
Hadwiger, Don F. 1930- ... 21-22R
Haeberle, Erwin J(akob) 1936- ... 29-32R
Haebich, Kathryn A. 1899- ... 7-8R
Haedrich, Marcel (pseudonym) 1913- ... 85-88
Haefele, John W(illiam) 1913- ... 3R
Haefner, Richard 1929- ... 108
Haegerstrand, (Stig) Torsten (Erik) 1916-
Brief entry ... 116
Haegg, Tomas 1938- ... 111
Haegglund, Bengt 1920- ... CANR-10
Earlier sketch in CA 25-28R
Haekkerup, Per 1915-1979 Obituary ... 85-88
Haenicke, Diether H. 1935- ... 33-36R
Haentzschel, Adolph T(heodore)
1881-1971 ... 2R
Obituary ... 103
Haering, Bernhard 1912- ... CANR-9
Earlier sketch in CA 7-8R
Haertling, Peter 1933- ... CANR-22
Earlier sketch in CA 101
Haessly, Jacqueline 1937- ... 120
Hafemeister, David W(alter) 1934- ... 124
Hafen, Ann Woodbury 1893-1970
Obituary ... 111
Hafen, Brent Q(ue) 1940- ... 112
Hafen, LeRoy R(euben) 1893- ... 65-68
Hafer, W(illiam) Keith ... 108
Haffenden, Philip Spencer 1926- ... 61-64
Haffner, J. Lilliwhite
See Speed, F(rederick) Maurice

Hafley, James 1928- 17-18R
Hafner, Lawrence E. 1924- CANR-10
Earlier sketch in CA 25-28R
Hafner, Marylin 1925- SATA-7
Haga, Enoch J. 1931- 25-28R
Hagan, Arthur Peter 1912- 107
Hagan, Charles B(anner) 1905- 37-40R
Hagan, Chet 1922- 107
Hagan, John T(homas) 1926- 25-28R
Hagan, Kenneth J(ames) 1936- 41-44R
Hagan, Patricia
See Howell, Patricia Hagan
Hagan, William T(homas) 1918- CANR-8
Earlier sketch in CA 5-6R
Hagar, George
See Maria Del Rey, Sister
Hagarty, Britt 1949- 110
Hagberg, David J(ames) 1942- 106
Hagbrink, Bodil 1936- 104
Hage, Jerald 1932- 37-40R
Hagedorn, Hermann 1882-1964 Obituary 116
Hagedorn, Robert (Bruce) 1925- 49-52
Hagee, John C(harles) 1940- CANR-3
Earlier sketch in CA 45-48
Hagelman, Charles W(illiam), Jr. 1920- 21-22R
Hagelstange, Rudolf 1912- 81-84
Hageman, Howard G(arberich) 1921- CANR-5
Earlier sketch in CA 3R
Hagen, Clifford (Warren, Jr.) 1943- 29-32R
Hagen, Elizabeth Pauline 1915- 13-14R
Hagen, Everett E(inar) 1906- CANR-1
Earlier sketch in CA 2R
Hagen, John Milton 1902- 57-60
Hagen, John William 1940- 61-64
Hagen, Lorinda
See Du Breuil, (Elizabeth) L(or)inda
Hagen, Richard L(ionel) 1935- 93-96
Hagen, Uta 1919- 77-80
Hager, Alice Rogers 1894-1969 5-6R
Obituary 103
See also SATA 26
Hager, Henry B. 1926- 19-20R
Hager, Jean 1932- 101
Hager, Robert M. 1938- 65-68
Hagerman, Paul Stirling 1949- 106
Hagerstrand, (Stig) Torsten (Erik)
See Haegerstrand, (Stig) Torsten (Erik)
Hagerty, James C(ampbell) 1909-1981
Obituary 103
Hagerty, Nancy K. 1935- 33-36R
Hagerty, Sheward 1930-1983 Obituary 109
Hagg, G. Eric 1908(?)-1979 Obituary 85-88
Hagg, Tomas
See Haegg, Tomas
Haggai, Thomas Stephens 1931- 93-96
Haggard, H(enry) Rider 1856-1925
Brief entry 108
See also SATA 16
See also TCLC 11
Haggard, Howard W. 1902- 121
Haggard, Merle 1937- Brief entry 112
Haggard, Paul
See Longstreet, Stephen
Haggard, Raymond (Gordon Rider) 1921-
Brief entry 109
Haggard, Virginia 1915- 122
Haggard, William
See Clayton, Richard Henry Michael
Haggerson, Nelson L. 1927- 41-44R
Haggerty, Brian A(rthur) 1943- 113
Haggerty, James J(oseph) 1920- 41-44R
See also SATA 5
Haggerty, P(atrick) E(ugene) 1914-1980
Obituary 105
Haggett, Peter 1933- 73-76
Haggie, Paul 1949- 124
Haggin, B(ernard) H. 1900-1987 CANR-18
Obituary 122
Earlier sketch in CA 102
Hagiwara, Michio Peter 1932- CANR-13
Earlier sketch in CA 73-76
Hagler, Erwin Harrison 1947- 120
Hagler, Skeeter
See Hagler, Erwin Harrison
Haglund, Elaine J(ean) 1937- 109
Hagman, Bette 1922- 53-56
Hagman, Donald Gerald 1932-1982
Obituary 114
Hagner, Donald Alfred 1936- 110
Hagon, Priscilla
See Allan, Mabel Esther
Hagopian, John V. 1923- 41-44R
Hagopian, Mark N. 1940- 49-52
Hagstrom, Jerry 1947- 111
Hagstrom, Julie 1950- 111
Hagstrom, Warren Olaf 1930- 21-22R
Hagstrum, Jean (Howard) 1913- 17-18R
Hague, Douglas Chalmers 1926- CANR-20
Earlier sketch in CA 69-72
Hague, Harlan 1932- 116
Hague, (Susan) Kathleen 1949- SATA-45, 49
Hague, Michael R. 1948- 123
Brief entry 111
See also SATA 32, 48
Hague, William Edward, Jr. 1919- 85-88
Hagy, Ruth Geri
See Brod, Ruth Hagy
Hahn, Emily 1905- CANR-1
Earlier sketch in CA 3R
See also SATA 3
Hahn, Fred 1906- 45-48
Hahn, Gloria 1926-1987 Obituary 123
Hahn, H. George 1942- 107
Hahn, Hannelore CANR-3
Earlier sketch in CA 7-8R
See also SATA 8
Hahn, Harlan 1939- 33-36R
Hahn, James (Sage) 1947- CANR-17
Earlier sketches in CA 49-52, CANR-2
See also SATA 9
Hahn, (Mona) Lynn 1949- CANR-17
Earlier sketches in CA 49-52, CANR-2
See also SATA 9
Hahn, Mary Downing 1937- 122
See also SATA 44, 50
Hahn, Otto 1879-1968 Obituary 112
Hahn, Paul H. 1932- 117
Hahn, Robert H. 1920- 123
Hahn, Robert O(scar) 1916- 69-72
Hahn, Roger 1932- 33-36R
Hahn, Steven 1951- 123
Hahner, June E(dith) 1940- CANR-11
Earlier sketch in CA 25-28R
Hahon, James
See Swift, Patrick
Haiblum, Isidore 1935- CANR-19
Earlier sketches in CA 53-56, CANR-4
Haidu, Peter 1931- 37-40R
Haig, Alexander M(eigs), Jr. 1924-
Brief entry 124
Haig, (Irvine Reid) Stirling 1936- 33-36R
Haigaz, Aram
See Chekenian, Aram Haigaz
Haig-Brown, Roderick (Langmere)
1908-1976 CANR-4
Obituary 69-72
Earlier sketch in CA 7-8R
See also SATA 12
See also CLC 21
Haigerty, Leo James 1924- 1R
Haight, Amanda 1939- 77-80
Haight, Anne Lyon 1895-1977 CAP-2
Obituary 73-76
Earlier sketch in CA 33-36
See also SATA 30
Haight, Gordon S(herman) 1901-1985 CAP-2
Obituary 118
Earlier sketch in CA 25-28
Haight, John McVickar, Jr. 1917- 29-32R
Haight, M. R. 1938- 124
Haight, Mabel V. Jackson
See Jackson-Haight, Mabel V.
Hail, Marshall 1905- 7-8R
Haile, H(arry) G(erald) 1931- 65-68
Hailey, Arthur 1920- CANR-2
Earlier sketch in CA 3R
See also DLBY 82
See also CLC 5
See also AITN 2
Hailey, Elizabeth Forsythe 1938- CANR-15
Earlier sketch in CA 93-96
See also CAAS 1
See also CLC 40
Hailey, Johanna
See Howl, Marcia (Yvonne Hurt)
Hailey, Johanna
See Jarvis, Sharon
Hailey, Oliver 1932- CANR-15
Earlier sketch in CA 41-44R
Hailey, Sheila 1927- 85-88
Hailperin, Herman 1899-1973 7-8R
Obituary 103
Hailstones, Thomas J(ohn) 1919- 41-44R
Hailwood, Mike
See Hailwood, Stanley Michael Bailey
Hailwood, Stanley Michael Bailey
1940-1981 Obituary 108
Haiman, Franklyn S(aul) 1921- 37-40R
Haimann, Theo 1911- CANR-2
Earlier sketch in CA 5-6R
Haime, Agnes Irvine Constance (Adams)
1884- CAP-1
Earlier sketch in CA 9-10
Haimes, Norma 53-56
Haimowitz, Morris (Loeb) 1918- 37-40R
Haimowitz, Natalie Reader 1923- 53-56
Haimson, Leopold H. 1917- Brief entry 109
Hainaux, Rene 1918- 73-76
Haindl, Marieluise 1901-1974 Obituary 49-52
Haine, Edgar A. 1908- 97-100
Haines, Charles 1928- 41-44R
Haines, Charles G(rove) 1906-1976
Obituary 65-68
Haines, Edward Burdette 1910-1984
Obituary 112
Haines, Francis 1899- 5-6R
Haines, Francis D., Jr. 1923- 53-56
Haines, Gail Kay 1943- CANR-14
Earlier sketch in CA 37-40R
See also SATA 11
Haines, George H(enry), Jr. 1937- 33-36R
Haines, Harry B. 1949(?)-1984 Obituary 112
Haines, John (Meade) 1924- CANR-13
Earlier sketch in CA 19-20R
See also DLB 5
Haines, John
See Richardson, Gladwell
Haines, Max 1931- CANR-15
Earlier sketch in CA 85-88
Haines, Pamela Mary 1929- CANR-24
Earlier sketch in CA 106
Haines, Perry Franklin 1889- 5-6R
Haines, Walter W(ells) 1918- 1R
Haines, William Wister 1908- CAP-1
Earlier sketch in CA 9-10
Haining, Peter 1940- CANR-1
Earlier sketch in CA 45-48
See also SATA 14
Hainworth, Henry Charles 1914- 109
Hair, Donald S(herman) 1937- 69-72
Hair, P(aul) E(dward) H(edley) 1926- 25-28R
Hair, William Ivy 1930- 29-32R
Haire, Wilson John 1932- 101
Haislip, Harvey (Shadle) 1889-1978 2R
Obituary 103
Haislip, John 1925- 33-36R
Haislip, Martha Pratt 1889(?)-1984
Obituary 112
Haithcox, John Patrick 1933- 29-32R
Haj, Fareed 1935- 29-32R
Hake, Thomas Gordon 1809-1895 DLB-32
Hakeda, Yoshito S. 1924(?)-1983
Obituary 110
Hakes, Joseph Edward 1916- 11-12R
Hakim, Seymour 1933- 65-68
Hakutani, Yoshinobu 1935- 101
Halaby, Najeeb E(lias) 1915- Brief entry 107
Halacy, D(aniel) S(tephen), Jr. 1919- CANR-9
Earlier sketch in CA 7-8R
See also SATA 36
Halal, William E. 1933- 123
Halam, Ann
See Jones, Gwyneth A.
Halas, Celia (Mary) 1922- 103
Halas, George Stanley 1895-1983
Obituary 111
Halas, John 1912- 108
Halasz, Gyula 1899-1984 Obituary 113
Halasz, Nicholas 1895-1985 19-20R
Obituary 116
Halbach, Edward C(hristian), Jr. 1931- 93-96
Halberg, Arvo Kusta
See Hall, Gus
Halberstadt, John 1941- 49-52
Halberstadt, William Harold 1930- 4R
Halberstam, David 1934- CANR-10
Earlier sketch in CA 69-72
Halberstam, Michael J(oseph)
1932-1980 CANR-10
Obituary 102
Earlier sketch in CA 65-68
Halbert, Frederic (Leslie) 1945- 122
Brief entry 118
Halbert, Sandra (Edith) 1943- 123
Halbrook, Stephen P. 121
Halcomb, Ruth 1936- 97-100
Halcrow, Harold Graham 1911- 19-20R
Haldane, A(rchibald) R(ichard) B(urdon)
1900-1982 120
Obituary 108
Haldane, J(ohn) B(urdon) S(anderson)
1892-1964 101
Haldane, R(obert) A(ylmer) 1907- 69-72
Haldane, Roger John 1945- SATA-13
Haldane-Stevenson, James Patrick
1910- CANR-14
Earlier sketch in CA 45-48
Haldeman, Charles (Heuss) 1931- 7-8R
Haldeman, H(arry) R(obbins) 1926- 81-84
Haldeman, Jack C(arroll II) 1941-
Brief entry 119
Haldeman, Joe (William) 1943- CANR-6
Earlier sketch in CA 53-56
See also DLB 8
Haldeman, Linda (Wilson) 1935- 85-88
Hale, Agnes Burke 1890-1981 Obituary 103
Hale, Allean Lemmon 1914- 33-36R
Hale, Arlene 1924-1982 CANR-1
Earlier sketch in CA 1R
See also SATA 49
Hale, Charles A(dams) 1930- 25-28R
Hale, Clarence B(enjamin) 1905- 69-72
Hale, David G(eorge) 1938- 45-48
Hale, Dennis 1944- 25-28R
Hale, Edward Everett 1822-1909
Brief entry 119
See also SATA 16
See also DLB 1, 42
Hale, Francesca
See Halpern, Frances J(oy)
Hale, Francis Joseph 1922- 53-56
Hale, Frank (Wilbur), Jr. 1927- 65-68
Hale, Helen
See Mulcahy, Lucille Burnett
Hale, Irina 1932- 105
See also SATA 26
Hale, J. Russell 1918- 101
Hale, Janet Campbell 1947- 49-52
Hale, John (Barry) 1926- 102
Hale, John Rigby 1923- CANR-19
Earlier sketch in CA 102
Hale, Judson (Drake) 1933- 69-72
Hale, Julian A(nthony) S(tuart) 1940- 41-44R
Hale, Kathleen 1898- 73-76
See also SATA 17
Hale, Leo Thomas
See Ebon
Hale, Leon 1921- CANR-10
Earlier sketch in CA 19-20R
Hale, (Charles) Leslie 1902-1985 CAP-1
Obituary 116
Earlier sketch in CA 15-16
Hale, Linda (Howe) 1929- 5-6R
See also SATA 6
Hale, Lionel Ramsay 1909-1977 Obituary 107
Hale, Lucretia P.
See Hale, Lucretia Peabody
Hale, Lucretia Peabody 1820-1900
Brief entry 122
See also SATA 26
See also DLB 42
Hale, Margaret
See Higonnet, Margaret Randolph
Hale, Michael
See Bullock, Michael
Hale, Nancy 1908- 5-6R
See also SATA 31
See also DLBY 80
Hale, Nathan Cabot 1925- 53-56
Hale, Oron James 1902- 13-14R
Hale, Patricia Whitaker 1922- 53-56
Hale, Philip
See Eastwood, C(harles) Cyril
Hale, Richard W(alden) 1909-1976
Obituary 65-68
Hale, Robert Beverly 1901-1985 Obituary 117
Hale, Robert William 1937- 114
Hale, Sarah Josepha (Buell)
1788-1879 DLB-1, 42
Hale, Wanda
See Coutard, Wanda Lundy Hale
Hale, William Harlan 1910-1974 93-96
Obituary 49-52
Hales, Ann
See Hales-Tooke, Ann (Mary Margaret)
Hales, E(dward) E(lton) Y(oung) 1908- 85-88
Hales, Edward John 1927- 106
Hales, Loyde (Wesley) 1933- 89-92
Hales, Norman
See Young, Vernon
Hales-Tooke, Ann (Mary Margaret) 1926- 123
Brief entry 116
Halevi, Z'ev ben Shimon
See Kenton, Warren
Haley, Alex (Palmer) 1921- 77-80
See also DLB 38
See also CLC 8, 12
Haley, Andrew G(allagher) 1904- CAP-1
Earlier sketch in CA 15-16
Haley, Bruce Everts 1933- Brief entry 108
Haley, Earl. J. 1898(?)-1987 Obituary 122
Haley, Gail E(inhart) 1939- CANR-14
Earlier sketch in CA 21-22R
See also SATA 28, 43
Haley, James L(ewis) 1951- 77-80
Haley, Jay 1923- CANR-9
Earlier sketch in CA 23-24R
Haley, Joseph E. 1915- 15-16R
Haley, K(enneth) H(arold) D(obson)
1920- 25-28R
Haley, Margaret Angela 1861-1939
Brief entry 112
Haley, Michael 1952- 109
Haley, Neale 41-44R
Haley, (Harry) Russell 1934- 118
Haley, William (John) 1901-1987 Obituary 123
Half, Robert 1918- 107
Haliburton, Thomas Chandler
1796-1865 DLB-11
Halifax, Joan (Squire) 1942- 85-88
Halio, Jay L(eon) 1928- CANR-10
Earlier sketch in CA 25-28R
Halivni, David
See Weiss, David
Halivni, David Weiss
See Weiss, David
Halkett, John G(eorge) 1933- 57-60
Halkin, Shimon 1899- 53-56
Halkin, Simon
See Halkin, Shimon
Hall, Adam
See Trevor, Elleston
Hall, Adele 1910- 4R
See also SATA 7
Hall, Adrian 1927- CANR-22
Earlier sketch in CA 106
Hall, Al(fred) Rupert 1920- 9-10R
Hall, Alice Clay 1900- 73-76
Hall, Andrew 1935- 21-22R
Hall, Angus 1932- CANR-13
Earlier sketch in CA 21-22R
Hall, Ann
See Duckert, Mary
Hall, Anna Gertrude 1882-1967 CAP-1
Earlier sketch in CA 11-12
See also SATA 8
Hall, Anthony Stewart 1945- 102
Hall, Ariel Perry 1906- 69-72
Hall, Arlene Stevens 1923- 19-20R
Hall, Asa Zadel 1875-1965 CANR-4
Earlier sketch in CA 3R
Hall, Austin 1882(?)-1933 Brief entry 114
Hall, Aylmer
See Hall, Norah E. L.
Hall, B(axter) C(larence) 1936- CANR-9
Earlier sketch in CA 57-60
Hall, B. K. 1932- 106
Hall, Bennie Caroline (Humble) 4R
Hall, Borden
See Yates, Raymond F(rancis)
Hall, Brian P(atrick) 1935- CANR-9
Earlier sketch in CA 61-64
See also SATA 31
Hall, C(onstance) Margaret 1937- CANR-12
Earlier sketch in CA 73-76
Hall, Calvin (Springer) 1909- 13-14R
Hall, Cameron
See del Rey, Lester
Hall, Cameron P(arker) 1898- 49-52
Hall, Carolyn Vosburg 1927- 61-64
Hall, Caryl
See Hansen, Caryl (Hall)
Hall, Challis A(lva), Jr. 1917-1968 1R
Obituary 103
Hall, Charles A(rthur) M(ann) 1924-
Brief entry 107
Hall, Clarence W(ilbur) 1902-1985
Obituary 114
Hall, Claudia
See Floren, Lee
Hall, Clifton L. 1898- CAP-1
Earlier sketch in CA 11-12
Hall, D(onald) J(ohn) 1903- 13-14R
Hall, Daniel George Edward 1891-1979 103
Hall, David D(risko) 1936- Brief entry 108
Hall, Don 1929- 110
Hall, Don Alan 1938- 108

Hall, Donald (Andrew, Jr.) 1928- CANR-2
Earlier sketch in CA 7-8R
See also SATA 23
See also DLB 5
See also CLC 1, 13, 37
Hall, Donald Ray 1933- 33-36R
Hall, Dorothy Judd 122
Hall, Douglas 1931- SATA-43
Hall, Douglas John 1928- CANR-14
Earlier sketch in CA 69-72
Hall, Douglas Kent 1938- 33-36R
Hall, Edward Twitchell (Jr.) 1914- 65-68
Hall, Elizabeth 1929- CANR-14
Earlier sketch in CA 65-68
Hall, Elizabeth Cornelia 1898- 37-40R
Hall, Elvajean 1910- CANR-8
Earlier sketch in CA 15-16R
See also SATA 6
Hall, Eric J(ohn) 1933- 97-100
Hall, Evan
See Halleran, Eugene E(dward)
Hall, F. H. 1926- 77-80
Hall, Fernau 102
Hall, Frederic Sauser
See Sauser-Hall, Frederic
Hall, Gene E(rwin) 1941- 93-96
Hall, Geoffrey Fowler 1888-1970 .... CAP-1
Earlier sketch in CA 13-14
Hall, George 1941- CANR-15
Earlier sketch in CA 85-88
Hall, George F(ridolph) 1908- CANR-22
Earlier sketch in CA 45-48
Hall, George R. 1930- 123
Hall, Georgette Brockman 1915- 57-60
Hall, Geraldine M(arion) 1935- 33-36R
Hall, Gimone 1940- CANR-15
Earlier sketch in CA 29-32R
Hall, Gladys 1891(?)-1977 Obituary 73-76
Hall, Gordon Langley
See Simmons, Dawn Langley
Hall, Gus 1910- Brief entry 108
Hall, Gwendolyn Midlo 1929- 41-44R
Hall, H(essel) Duncan 1891-1976 .... CAP-2
Obituary 65-68
Earlier sketch in CA 29-32
Hall, Halbert Weldon 1941- 53-56
Hall, Haywood 1898- 77-80
Hall, Helen 1892- 104
Hall, Henry M(arion) 1877- 5-6R
Hall, J(ohn) C(live) 1920- 101
Hall, J(ames) Curtis 1926- 53-56
Hall, J. De P.
See McKelway, St. Clair
Hall, J. Tillman 1916- CANR-6
Earlier sketch in CA 4R
Hall, Jacquelyn (Dowd) 1943- 97-100
Hall, James 1918- 102
Hall, James (Herrick, Jr.) 1933- 53-56
Hall, James
See Kuttner, Henry
Hall, James Andrew 1935- 118
Hall, James B(yron) 1918- CANR-1
Earlier sketch in CA 3R
Hall, James Baker 1935- 116
Hall, James Norman 1887-1951
Brief entry 123
See also SATA 21
See also TCLC 23
Hall, James W(illiam) 1937- CANR-22
Earlier sketch in CA 45-48
Hall, Jay C.
See Hall, John C.
Hall, Jean R(ogers) 1941- 105
Hall, Jerome 1901- CAP-1
Earlier sketch in CA 11-12
Hall, Jesse
See Boesen, Victor
Hall, John 1937- 93-96
Hall, John C. 1915- 57-60
Hall, John F. 1919- CANR-17
Earlier sketch in CA 1R
Hall, John O. P. 1911- 11-12R
Hall, John Whitney 1916- 25-28R
Hall, Josef Washington 1894-1960
Obituary 89-92
Hall, Joseph (Sargent) 1906- 41-44R
Hall, Julie (Ann) 1943- Brief entry 110
Hall, Kathleen M(ary) 1924- CANR-3
Earlier sketch in CA 7-8R
Hall, Katy
See McMullan, Kate (Hall)
Hall, Katy
See McMullan, Kate Hall
Hall, Kendall
See Heath, Harry E(ugene), Jr.
Hall, Kenneth F(ranklin) 1926- 19-20R
Hall, Kermit L(ance) 1944- 101
Hall, Laurence James 1940- 97-100
Hall, Lawrence Sargent 1915- 4R
Hall, (Frederick) Leonard 1899- 65-68
Hall, Linda B(iesele) 1939- CANR-23
Earlier sketch in CA 106
Hall, Livingston 1903- CAP-2
Earlier sketch in CA 21-22
Hall, Louis Brewer 1920- 110
Hall, Luella J(emima) 1890-1973 45-48
Obituary 103
Hall, Lynn 1937- CANR-9
Earlier sketch in CA 23-24R
See also SATA 2, 47
See also SAAS 4
Hall, Malcolm 1945- CANR-4
Earlier sketch in CA 49-52
See also SATA 7
Hall, Manly Palmer 1901- 93-96
Hall, Marie Boas 1919- 11-12R
Hall, Marjory
See Yeakley, Marjory Hall
Hall, Mark W. 1943- 33-36R
Hall, Martin Hardwick 1925- 33-36R
Hall, Mary Ann 1942- 116
Hall, Mary Bowen 1932- 23-24R
Hall, MaryAnne 1934- 29-32R
Hall, Michael Garibaldi 1926- 15-16R
Hall, Monty 1924- Brief entry 108
Hall, N(orman) John 1933- CANR-12
Earlier sketch in CA 61-64
Hall, Nancy Lee 1923- 57-60
Hall, Natalie Watson 1923- 7-8R
Hall, Noel (Frederick) 1902-1983 Obituary .. 109
Hall, Norah E. L. 1914- 97-100
Hall, O. M.
See Hall, Oakley (Maxwell)
Hall, Oakley (Maxwell) 1920- CANR-3
Earlier sketch in CA 9-10R
Hall, Patrick 1932- 21-22R
Hall, Penelope C(oker) 1933- 19-20R
Hall, Peter (Geoffrey) 1932- CANR-24
Earlier sketches in CA 17-18R, CANR-8
Hall, Phil 1953- 102
Hall, R(obert) Cargill 1937- CANR-1
Earlier sketch in CA 49-52
Hall, (Marguerite) Radclyffe 1886(?)-1943
Brief entry 110
See also TCLC 12
Hall, Richard (Seymour) 1925- CANR-9
Earlier sketch in CA 17-18R
Hall, (Patrick) Richard Compton
See Compton-Hall, (Patrick) Richard
Hall, Richard H(ammond) 1934- CANR-13
Earlier sketch in CA 77-80
Hall, Robert A(nderson), Jr. 1911- CANR-5
Earlier sketch in CA 13-14R
Hall, Robert Benjamin 1918- 57-60
Hall, Robert Burnett, Jr. 1923- Brief entry .. 109
Hall, Robert E(lliott) 1924- CANR-13
Earlier sketch in CA 19-20R
Hall, Robert E(rnest) 1943- 114
Hall, Robert Lee 1941- 73-76
Hall, Robert T(om) 1938- Brief entry 110
Hall, Rodney 1935- 109
Hall, Roger (Wolcott) 1919- 29-32R
Hall, Roger 1945- 112
Hall, Rosalys Haskell 1914- 11-12R
See also SATA 7
Hall, Ross H(ume) 1926- 61-64
Hall, Rubylea (Ray) 1910- CAP-2
Earlier sketch in CA 17-18
Hall, Ruth 1933(?)-1981 Obituary 104
Hall, Steven (Leonard) 1960- 93-96
Hall, Susan 1940- 57-60
Hall, T(homas) William 1921- 118
Hall, Ted Byron 1902- CAP-2
Earlier sketch in CA 33-36
Hall, Thor 1927- 37-40R
Hall, Tom T. 1936- 102
Hall, Tony
See Hall, Anthony Stewart
Hall, Tord (Erik Martin) 1910- 29-32R
Hall, Trevor H(enry) 1910- CANR-16
Earlier sketch in CA 29-32R
Hall, Van Beck 1934- 45-48
Hall, Vernon, Jr. 1913- CANR-3
Earlier sketch in CA 7-8R
Hall, Wade H. 1934- CANR-6
Earlier sketch in CA 7-8R
Hall, Walter (Earl, Jr.) 1940- CANR-13
Earlier sketch in CA 21-22R
Hall, Wayne E(dward) 1947- 105
Hall, William N(orman) 1915-1974
Obituary 53-56
Hall, Willis 1929- 101
Hall, Wilson (Dudley) 1922- 69-72
Halla, (Robert) Chris(tian) 1949- CANR-18
Earlier sketch in CA 77-80
Hallahan, William H(enry) Brief entry 109
Hallahmi, Benjamin Beit
See Beit-Hallahmi, Benjamin
Hallam, Arthur Henry 1811-1833 .... DLB-32
Hallam, (Samuel Benoni) Atlantis 1915- 5-6R
Hallam, Elizabeth M. 1950- 123
Hallam, H(erbert) E(noch) 1923- 23-24R
Hallam, J(ohn) Harvey 1917- 13-14R
Hallas, Richard
See Knight, Eric (Mowbray)
Hallberg, Charles William 1899- CAP-1
Earlier sketch in CA 17-18
Hallberg, Edmond C. 1931- Brief entry 111
Hallberg, Peter 1916- CANR-4
Earlier sketch in CA 53-56
Hall-Clarke, James
See Rowland-Entwistle, (Arthur)
Theodore (Henry)
Halle, Jean-Claude 1939- CANR-17
Earlier sketch in CA 93-96
Halle, Katherine Murphy 41-44R
Halle, Kay
See Halle, Katherine Murphy
Halle, Louis J(oseph) 1910- CANR-2
Earlier sketch in CA 4R
Halleck, Fitz-Greene 1790-1867 .... DLB-3
Halleck, Seymour L(eon) 1929- CANR-13
Earlier sketch in CA 21-22R
Haller, Archibald O(rben), Jr. 1926- 45-48
Haller, Bill
See Bechko, Peggy Anne
Haller, Dorcas Woodbury 1946- 117
See also SATA 46
Haller, Ellis M(etcalf) 1915-1981 Obituary .. 103
Haller, John Samuel, Jr. 1940- 61-64
Haller, Mark H(ughlin) 1928- CANR-5
Earlier sketch in CA 11-12R
Haller, Mike 1945- 110
Haller, Robert S(pencer) 1933- CANR-2
Earlier sketch in CA 2R
Haller, Robin Meredith 1944- 65-68
Haller, William 1885-1974 Obituary 49-52
Halleran, Eugene E(dward) 1905- 4R
Hallet, Jean-Pierre 1927- 19-20R
Hallett, Ellen Kathleen 1899- CAP-1
Earlier sketch in CA 15-16
Hallett, Garth L(ie) 1927- CANR-13
Earlier sketch in CA 69-72
Hallett, George H(ervey), Jr. 1895-1985
Obituary 116
Hallett, Graham 1929- CANR-16
Earlier sketch in CA 25-28R
Hallett, Judith Peller 1944- 124
Hallett, Kathryn J(osephine) 1937- 57-60
Hallett, Robin 1926- 103
Halley, Anne 1928- 121
Halley, Laurence
See O'Keeffe, Laurence
Hallgarten, George W(olfgang) F(elix)
1901-1975 65-68
Obituary 57-60
Hallgarten, Peter A(lexander) 1931- 97-100
Hallgarten, Siegfried Fritz 1902- CANR-18
Earlier sketches in CA 7-8R, CANR-3
Hallgren, Chris 1947- 115
Halliburton, David (Garland) 1933-
Brief entry 116
Halliburton, Richard 1900-1939
Brief entry 114
Halliburton, Rudia, Jr. 1929- 81-84
Halliburton, Warren J. 1924- CANR-24
Earlier sketch in CA 33-36R
See also SATA 19
Halliday, Brett
See Dresser, Davis
and Terrall, Robert
Halliday, David 1948- 113
Halliday, Dorothy
See Dunnett, Dorothy
Halliday, E(rnest) M(ilton) 1913- 3R
Halliday, Ena
See Baumgarten, Sylvia
Halliday, F(rank) E(rnest) 1903-1982 .... CANR-2
Obituary 106
Earlier sketch in CA 2R
Halliday, Fred 1937- 53-56
Halliday, James
See Symington, David
Halliday, Jerry 1949- 69-72
Halliday, Jon 1939- 97-100
Halliday, M(ichael) A(lexander) K(irkwood)
1925- Brief entry 112
Halliday, Michael
See Creasey, John
Halliday, Richard 1905-1973 Obituary 41-44R
Halliday, Tim (Richard) 1945- 112
Halliday, William R(oss) 1926- 49-52
Hallie, Philip P. 1922- CANR-9
Earlier sketch in CA 15-16R
Hallier, Amedee 1913- 73-76
Halligan, Nicholas 1917- CANR-5
Earlier sketch in CA 13-14R
Hallin, Emily Watson CANR-10
Earlier sketch in CA 25-28R
See also SATA 6
Hallinan, Hazel Hunkins 1891(?)-1982
Obituary 106
Hallinan, Nancy 1921- CANR-3
Earlier sketch in CA 9-10R
Hallinan, P(atrick) K(enneth) 1944- CANR-11
Earlier sketch in CA 69-72
See also SATA 37, 39
Hallinan, Vincent 1896- 4R
Hallion, Richard P(aul, Jr.) 1948- 41-44R
Halliwell, David (William) 1936- CANR-11
Earlier sketch in CA 65-68
Halliwell, Leslie 1929- CANR-16
Earlier sketches in CA 49-52, CANR-1
Hall-Jones, Frederick George 1891-1982
Obituary 108
Hallman, Frank Curtis 1943(?)-1975
Obituary 104
Hallman, G(eorge) Victor III 1930- 101
Hallman, Howard W(esley) 1928- 116
Hallman, Ralph J(efferson) 1911- 13-14R
Hallman, Ruth 1929- CANR-15
Earlier sketch in CA 85-88
See also SATA 28, 43
Hallo, William W. 1928- CANR-15
Earlier sketch in CA 37-40R
Hallock, G. B. F.
See Hallock, Gerard B(enjamin) F(leet)
Hallock, Gerard B(enjamin) F(leet)
1856-1953 Brief entry 122
Hallock, Robert Lay 1898(?)-1986
Obituary 120
Halloran, Richard (Colby) 1930- 29-32R
Halloway, Vance 1916- 53-56
Hallowell, A(lfred) Irving 1892-1974 ....7-8R
Obituary 53-56
Hallowell, Christopher L. 1945- 93-96
Hallowell, John H(amilton) 1913- CANR-5
Earlier sketch in CA 15-16R
Hallpike, C. R. 1938- 41-44R
Hall-Quest, (Edna) Olga W(ilbourne)
1899-1986 ....7-8R
Obituary 118
See also SATA 11, 47
Halls, Geraldine (Mary) 1919- 103
Halls, W(ilfred) D(ouglas) 1918- CANR-5
Earlier sketch in CA 3R
Hallstead, William F(inn III) 1924- CANR-21
Earlier sketches in CA 5-6R, CANR-6
See also SATA 11
Hallstein, Walter 1901-1982 Obituary 106
Hallstroem, Per (August Leonard)
1866-1960 Obituary 116
Hallstrom, Per (August Leonard)
See Hallstroem, Per (August Leonard)
Hallus, Tak
See Robinett, Stephen (Allen)
Hallward, Michael 1889- 49-52
See also SATA 12
Halm, George N(ikolaus) 1901- 23-24R
Halman, Talat Sait 1931- CANR-4
Earlier sketch in CA 53-56
Halmos, Paul 1911-1977 .... CANR-8
Earlier sketch in CA 17-18R
Halper
See Halpern, Leivick
Halper, Albert 1904-1984 .... CANR-3
Obituary 111
Earlier sketch in CA 7-8R
See also DLB 9
Halper, Nathan 1908(?)-1983 Obituary 110
Halper, Thomas 1942- 41-44R
Halperin, David M(artin) 1952- 117
Halperin, Don A(kiba) 1925- 57-60
Halperin, Edwin G. 1935(?)-1987
Obituary 123
Halperin, Irving 1922- 29-32R
Halperin, John 1941- CANR-6
Earlier sketch in CA 53-56
Halperin, Mark (Warren) 1940- CANR-9
Earlier sketch in CA 65-68
Halperin, Maurice 1906- 73-76
Halperin, Morton H. 1938- CANR-3
Earlier sketch in CA 11-12R
Halperin, S(amuel) William 1905-1979 ...97-100
Obituary 85-88
Halperin, Samuel 1930- CANR-1
Earlier sketch in CA 1R
Halpern, A(braham) M(eyer) 1914- 19-20R
Halpern, Barbara Kerewsky
See Kerewsky-Halpern, Barbara
Halpern, Barbara Strachey 1912- 106
Halpern, Ben(jamin) 1912- Brief entry 115
Halpern, Daniel 1945- 33-36R
See also CLC 14
Halpern, Frances J(oy) 114
Halpern, Howard Marvin 1929- 93-96
Halpern, Joel M. 1929- CANR-3
Earlier sketch in CA 7-8R
Halpern, L.
See Halpern, Leivick
Halpern, Leivick 1888-1962 Obituary 114
Halpern, Manfred 1924- 11-12R
Halpern, Martin 1929- CANR-7
Earlier sketch in CA 5-6R
Halpern, Oscar Saul 1912- 97-100
Halpern, Paul G. 1937- 45-48
Halpern, Paul J(oseph) 1942- CANR-7
Earlier sketch in CA 57-60
Halpern, Stephen Mark 1940- 57-60
Halpert, Inge D. 1926- 23-24R
Halpert, Stephen 1941- 37-40R
Halpin, Andrew W(illiams) 1911- 19-20R
Halprin, Anna Schuman 1920- 85-88
Halprin, Lawrence 1916- 41-44R
Hals, Ronald M. 1926- 33-36R
Halsall, Elizabeth 1916- 33-36R
Halsall, Eric 1920- 107
Halsband, Robert 1914- CANR-8
Earlier sketch in CA 19-20R
Halsell, Grace (Eleanor) 1923- CANR-13
Earlier sketch in CA 23-24R
See also SATA 13
See also AITN 1
Halsey, A(lbert) H(enry) 1923- CANR-7
Earlier sketch in CA 17-18R
Halsey, Elizabeth 1890- CAP-2
Earlier sketch in CA 17-18
Halsey, Elizabeth Tower 1903(?)-1976
Obituary 65-68
Halsey, George Dawson 1889-1970 .... 4R
Obituary 103
Halsey, Margaret (Frances) 1910- 81-84
Halsey, Martha T. 1932- CANR-14
Earlier sketch in CA 37-40R
Halsey, William D(arrach) 1918-
Brief entry 117
Halsman, Philippe 1906-1979 .... CANR-10
Obituary 89-92
Earlier sketch in CA 23-24R
Halstead, Murat 1829-1908 .... DLB-23
Halstead, William Perdue 1906-1982
Obituary 109
Halsted, Anna Roosevelt 1906-1975
Obituary 61-64
See also SATA 30
Halstock, Max
See Caulfield, Malachy Francis
Halter, Carl 1915- 17-18R
Halter, Jon C(harles) 1941- CANR-13
Earlier sketch in CA 61-64
See also SATA 22
Halton, David 1940- 73-76
Halton, Eugene Rochberg
See Rochberg-Halton, Eugene
Haltrecht, Montague 1932- 29-32R
Halverson, Alton C. O. 1922- 61-64
Halverson, Richard C. 1916- CANR-3
Earlier sketch in CA 1R
Halverson, Richard P(aul) 1941- 109
Halverson, William H(agen) 1930- 37-40R
Halvorson, Arndt L(eroy) 1915- CANR-3
Earlier sketch in CA 7-8R
Halward, Leslie G. 1904(?)-1976
Obituary 65-68
Ham, Wayne 1938- CANR-11
Earlier sketch in CA 21-22R
Hamachek, Don E. 1933- 17-18R

Hamada, Hirosuke 1893- ... 45-48
Hamady, Walter ... AITN-1
Hamalainen, Pekka Kalevi 1938- ... 97-100
Hamalian, Leo 1920- ... CANR-2
Earlier sketch in CA 5-6R
See also SATA 41
Hamberg, Daniel 1924- ... 1R
Hamberger, Conrad P. 1900- ... 15-16R
Hamberger, John 1934- ... 69-72
See also SATA 14
Hambletonian
See Fairfax-Blakeborough, John Freeman
Hamblett, Theora 1895(?)-1977 Obituary ... 69-72
Hamblin, C(harles) L(eonard) 1922- ... 25-28R
Hamblin, Dora Jane 1920- ... 37-40R
See also SATA 36
Hamblin, Douglas H. 1923- ... 115
Hamblin, Robert L(ee) 1927- ... 97-100
Hamblin, W. K. 1928- ... 53-56
Hamburg, Carl H(einz) 1915- ... 37-40R
Hamburg, David A(llen) 1925- Brief entry ... 109
Hamburg, Morris 1922- Brief entry ... 114
Hamburger, Ernest 1891(?)-1980
Obituary ... 97-100
Hamburger, Estelle 1898(?)-1983
Obituary ... 110
Hamburger, Kaete 1896- ... CANR-14
Earlier sketch in CA 29-32R
Hamburger, Max 1897-1970 ... CAP-2
Earlier sketch in CA 17-18
Hamburger, Michael (Peter Leopold)
1924- ... CANR-2
Earlier sketch in CA 7-8R
See also CAAS 4
See also DLB 27
See also CLC 5, 14
Hamburger, Michael J(ay) 1938- ... CANR-3
Earlier sketch in CA 45-48
Hamburger, Philip 1914- ... 5-6R
Hamburger, Robert (A., Jr.) 1943- ... CANR-8
Earlier sketch in CA 61-64
Hamburgh, Max 1922- ... 61-64
Hamby, Alonzo L. 1940- ... CANR-15
Earlier sketch in CA 37-40R
Hamel, Peter Michael 1947- ... 97-100
Hamel Dobkin, Kathleen 1945- ... 110
Hamelin, Louis-Edmond 1923- ... 110
Hamell, Patrick Joseph 1910- ... CAP-1
Earlier sketch in CA 15-16
Hamelman, Paul W(illiam) 1930-1976 ... 41-44R
Hamer, David Allan 1938- ... 45-48
Hamer, Frank 1929- ... 105
Hamer, Mick 1946- ... 109
Hamer, Philip (May) 1891-1971 Obituary ... 104
Hamermesh, Daniel S(elim) 1943-
Brief entry ... 110
Hamermesh, Morton 1915- ... 5-6R
Hamerow, Theodore S(tephen) 1920- ... 49-52
Hamerstrom, Frances 1907- ... 69-72
See also SATA 24
Hames, (Alice) Inez 1892- ... 29-32R
Hamey, J(ohn) A(nthony) 1956- ... 109
Hamey, L(eonard) A(rnold) 1918- ... 109
Hamil, Sharon Hide 1939- ... 122
Hamil, Thomas Arthur 1928- ... 73-76
See also SATA 14
Hamill, Denis 1951- ... 110
Hamill, Ethel
See Webb, Jean Francis
Hamill, Pete 1935- ... CANR-18
Earlier sketch in CA 25-28R
See also CLC 10
Hamill, Robert H(offman) 1912-1975 ... CAP-2
Earlier sketch in CA 33-36
Hamilton, Adam
See Granbeck, Marilyn
Hamilton, (John) Alan 1943- ... 115
Hamilton, Alex John 1939- ... 103
Hamilton, Alexander 1712-1756 ... DLB-31
Hamilton, Alexander 1755(?)-1804 ... DLB-37
Hamilton, Alfred Starr 1914- ... 53-56
Hamilton, Alice
See Cromie, Alice Hamilton
Hamilton, B(ertram) L(awson) St. John
1914- ... 15-16R
Hamilton, Beth Alleman 1927- ... 110
Hamilton, (Arthur Douglas) Bruce
1900-1974 Obituary ... 109
Hamilton, Buzz
See Hemming, Roy
Hamilton, Carl 1914- ... 53-56
Hamilton, Carlos D. 1908- ... 69-72
Hamilton, Charles 1913- ... CANR-20
Earlier sketches in CA 7-8R, CANR-3
Hamilton, Charles D(aniel) 1940-
Brief entry ... 112
Hamilton, Charles F(ranklin) 1915- ... 89-92
Hamilton, Charles Granville
1905-1984 ... CANR-15
Earlier sketch in CA 41-44R
Hamilton, Charles Harold St. John
1875-1961 ... 73-76
See also SATA 13
Hamilton, Charles Vernon 1929- ... 77-80
Hamilton, Charles W(alter) 1890- ... 7-8R
Hamilton, Cicely (Mary) 1872-1952
Brief entry ... 113
See also DLB 10
Hamilton, Clare
See Lawless, Bettyclare Hamilton
Hamilton, Clive
See Lewis, C(live) S(taples)
Hamilton, Dave
See Troyer, Byron L(eRoy)
Hamilton, David (Boyce, Jr.) 1918- ... 29-32R
Hamilton, David (Peter) 1935- ... 119
Hamilton, (Charles) Denis 1918- ... 109
Hamilton, Donald (Bengtsson) 1916- ... CANR-18
Earlier sketches in CA 4R, CANR-2
Hamilton, Dorothy (Drumm) 1906-1983 ... 33-36R
Obituary ... 110
See also SATA 12, 35
Hamilton, Earl J(efferson) 1899- ... CAP-1
Earlier sketch in CA 9-10
Hamilton, Edith 1867-1963 ... 77-80
See also SATA 20
Hamilton, Edmond 1904-1977 ... CANR-3
Earlier sketch in CA 2R
See also DLB 8
See also CLC 1
Hamilton, Edward G. 1897- ... CAP-1
Earlier sketch in CA 11-12
Hamilton, Eleanor Poorman 1909- ... CANR-2
Earlier sketch in CA 1R
Hamilton, (Muriel) Elizabeth (Mollie)
1906- ... CAP-1
Earlier sketch in CA 9-10
See also SATA 23
Hamilton, Elizabeth 1928- ... 97-100
Hamilton, Ernest
See Merril, Judith
Hamilton, Eugene (Jacob) Lee
See Lee-Hamilton, Eugene (Jacob)
Hamilton, Floyd (Garland) 1908(?)-1984
Obituary ... 113
Hamilton, Franklin
See Silverberg, Robert
Hamilton, Franklin Willard 1923- ... 33-36R
Hamilton, Gail
See Corcoran, Barbara
Hamilton, Gene 1943- ... 120
Hamilton, George Baillie
See Baillie-Hamilton, George
Hamilton, George Rostrevor 1888-1967
Obituary ... 93-96
Hamilton, Henry W. 1898- ... 33-36R
Hamilton, Hervey
See Robins, Denise (Naomi)
Hamilton, Holman 1910-1980 ... CANR-10
Obituary ... 97-100
Earlier sketch in CA 13-14R
Hamilton, Horace E(rnst) 1911- ... 21-22R
Hamilton, Howard Devon 1920- ... 13-14R
Hamilton, (Robert) Ian 1938- ... 106
See also DLB 40
Hamilton, J(ames) A(lan) B(ousfield)
1899-1971 Obituary ... 116
Hamilton, J(ames) Wallace 1900-1968 ... CAP-1
Earlier sketch in CA 13-14
Hamilton, Jack
See Brannon, William T.
Hamilton, James Robertson 1921- ... 103
Hamilton, Janet 1951- ... 114
Hamilton, Jean Tyree 1909- ... 33-36R
Hamilton, Joan Lesley 1942- ... 102
Hamilton, John
See Hayden, Sterling
Hamilton, John Maxwell 1947- ... 121
Hamilton, Julia
See Watson, Julia
Hamilton, Katie 1945- ... 118
Hamilton, Kay
See DeLeeuw, Cateau
Hamilton, Kenneth (Morrison) 1917- ... 17-18R
Hamilton, Marshall Lee 1937- ... 37-40R
Hamilton, Mary (E.) 1927- ... 123
Hamilton, Michael (Pollock) 1927- ... 29-32R
Hamilton, Milton W(heaton) 1901- ... CAP-1
Earlier sketch in CA 15-16
Hamilton, Mollie
See Kaye, M(ary) M(argaret)
Hamilton, Morse 1943- ... 108
See also SATA 35
Hamilton, Nancy 1908-1985 Obituary ... 115
Hamilton, Neill Q. 1925- ... 61-64
Hamilton, (Charles) Nigel 1944- ... 101
Hamilton, (Anthony Walter) Patrick
1904-1962 Obituary ... 113
See also DLB 10
Hamilton, Patrick Macfarlan 1892-1977
Obituary ... 108
Hamilton, Paul
See Dennis-Jones, H(arold)
Hamilton, Peter (Edward) 1947- ... 73-76
Hamilton, Raphael N(oteware) 1892- ... CAP-2
Earlier sketch in CA 29-32
Hamilton, Richard 1922- Brief entry ... 116
Hamilton, Richard F(rederick) 1930- ... 108
Hamilton, Robert W.
See Stratemeyer, Edward L.
Hamilton, Ronald 1909- ... 15-16R
Hamilton, Russell G(eorge) 1934- ... 61-64
Hamilton, Seena M. 1926- ... 17-18R
Hamilton, Virginia 1936- ... CANR-20
Earlier sketch in CA 25-28R
See also SATA 4
See also DLB 33, 52
See also CLC 26
See also CLR 1, 11
Hamilton, W(illiam) B(askerville)
1908-1972 ... CAP-1
Obituary ... 37-40R
Earlier sketch in CA 17-18
Hamilton, W(illis) D(avid) 1936- ... 105
Hamilton, Wade
See Floren, Lee
Hamilton, Wallace 1919-1983 ... CANR-15
Obituary ... 110
Earlier sketch in CA 85-88
Hamilton, Walter 1908-1988 ... 109
Obituary ... 124
Hamilton, William 1939- ... CANR-15
Earlier sketch in CA 69-72
Hamilton, William B(aillie) 1930- ... 102
Hamilton, William, Jr. 1924- ... 53-56
Hamilton-Edwards, Gerald (Kenneth Savery)
1906- ... CANR-14
Earlier sketch in CA 21-22R
Hamilton-Hill, Donald 1915-1985 Obituary ... 117
Hamizrachi, Yoram 1942- ... 107
Hamlet, Ova
See Lupoff, Richard A(llen)
Hamley, Dennis 1935- ... CANR-11
Earlier sketch in CA 57-60
See also SATA 39
Hamlin, Charles Hughes 1907- ... 69-72
Hamlin, Gladys E(va) ... 37-40R
Hamlin, Griffith Askew 1919- ... 37-40R
Hamlin, Marjorie (Day) 1921- ... 105
Hamlin, Wilfrid G(ardiner) 1918- ... 93-96
Hamm, Charles Edward 1925- ... 103
Hamm, Cleve 1927(?)-1984 Obituary ... 112
Hamm, Edward Frederick, Jr. 1908-1985
Obituary ... 115
Hamm, Glenn B(ruce) 1936- ... 53-56
Hamm, Jack 1916- ... CANR-9
Earlier sketch in CA 7-8R
Hamm, Marie Roberson 1917- ... 65-68
Hamm, Michael Franklin 1943- ... 89-92
Hamm, Robert M(acGowan) 1950- ... 116
Hamm, Russell Leroy 1926- ... CANR-2
Earlier sketch in CA 7-8R
Hammack, David C(onrad) 1941- ... 115
Hammack, James W., Jr. 1937- ... 81-84
Hamman, Henry (Longley) 1946- ... 119
Hamman, Ray T(racy) 1945- ... 69-72
Hammar, Russell A(lfred) 1920- ... 104
Hammarskjoeld, Dag (Hjalmar Agne Carl)
1905-1961 ... 77-80
Hammarskjold, Dag
See Hammarskjoeld, Dag (Hjalmar Ange Carl)
Hammel, Eric M(axwell) 1946- ... 107
Hammel, Faye 1929- ... CANR-5
Earlier sketch in CA 3R
Hammen, Carl Schlee 1923- ... 53-56
Hammen, Oscar J(ohn) 1907- ... CAP-2
Earlier sketch in CA 25-28
Hammer, Carl, Jr. 1910- ... 53-56
Hammer, David Harry 1893(?)-1978
Obituary ... 81-84
Hammer, Emanuel F(rederick) 1926- ... 29-32R
Hammer, Jacob
See Oppenheimer, Joel (Lester)
Hammer, Jeanne-Ruth 1912- ... 9-10R
Hammer, Jefferson J(oseph) 1933- ... 41-44R
Hammer, Kenneth M. 1918- ... 85-88
Hammer, Richard 1928- ... CANR-11
Earlier sketch in CA 25-28R
See also SATA 6
Hammer, Signe ... 102
Hammerman, Donald R. 1925- ... 15-16R
Hammerman, Gay M(orenus) 1926- ... 33-36R
See also SATA 9
Hammerstein, Oscar (Greeley Glendenning)
II 1895-1960 ... 101
Hammes, John A(nthony) 1924- ... 13-14R
Hammes, Tobi Gillian Sanders
1948(?)-1987 Obituary ... 122
Hammett, (Samuel) Dashiell 1894-1961 ... 81-84
See also CLC 3, 5, 10, 19, 47
See also AITN 1
Hammil, Joel 1909- ... 114
Hamming, Richard W. 1915- ... 57-60
Hammon, Jupiter 1711-? ... DLB-31, 50
Hammond, Albert L(anphier) 1892-1970 ... 4R
Obituary ... 103
Hammond, Antony Derek 1938- ... 114
Hammond, Brean S(imon) 1951- ... 119
Hammond, Charles Montgomery, Jr.
1922- ... 106
Hammond, Dorothy 1924- ... 69-72
Hammond, Edwin Hughes 1919- ... 13-14R
Hammond, Gerald (Arthur Douglas) 1926- ... 107
Hammond, Guyton B(owers) 1930- ... 17-18R
Hammond, J(ames) D(illard) 1933- ... CANR-22
Earlier sketch in CA 45-48
Hammond, Jane
See Poland, Dorothy (Elizabeth Hayward)
Hammond, John (Henry, Jr.) 1910-1987 ... 106
Obituary ... 123
Hammond, John ?-1663 ... DLB-24
Hammond, Keith
See Kuttner, Henry
Hammond, Laurence ... 104
Hammond, Lawrence 1925- ... 81-84
Hammond, Mac (Sawyer) 1926- ... 19-20R
Hammond, Mason 1903- ... 65-68
Hammond, N(icholas) G(eoffrey)
L(empriere) 1907- ... CANR-21
Earlier sketches in CA 13-14R, CANR-5
Hammond, Norman 1944- ... CANR-19
Earlier sketches in CA 49-52, CANR-3
Hammond, Paul 1947- ... 57-60
Hammond, Paul Y(oung) 1929- ... CANR-2
Earlier sketch in CA 4R
Hammond, Peter B(oyd) 1928- ... 69-72
Hammond, Philip C. 1924- ... 5-6R
Hammond, Phillip E(verett) 1931- ... CANR-7
Earlier sketch in CA 19-20R
Hammond, Ralph
See Hammond Innes, Ralph
Hammond, Richard J(ames) 1911-1982 ... 61-64
Obituary ... 122
Hammond, Ross W(illiam) 1918- ... 33-36R
Hammond, Thomas T(aylor) 1920- ... 9-10R
Hammond, W(illiam) Rogers 1920- ... 45-48
Hammond, Winifred G(raham) 1899- ... 107
See also SATA 29
Hammond Innes, Ralph 1913- ... CANR-4
Earlier sketch in CA 5-6R
Hammonds, Michael (Galen) 1942- ... 45-48
Hammontree, Marie (Gertrude) 1913- ... 5-6R
See also SATA 13
Hamner, Earl (Henry), Jr. 1923- ... 73-76
See also DLB 6
See also CLC 12
See also AITN 2
Hamner, Robert Daniel 1941- ... 106
Hamod, (Hamode) Sam(uel) 1936- ... CANR-22
Earlier sketch in CA 45-48
Hamori, Laszlo Dezso 1911- ... 9-10R
Hamovitch, Mitzi Berger 1924- ... 112
Hamp, Eric P(ratt) 1920- ... 17-18R
Hampden, John 1898- ... 109
Hampden-Turner, Charles M. 1934- ... 33-36R
Hampl, Patricia 1946- ... CANR-21
Earlier sketch in CA 104
Hample, Stuart 1926- ... 108
Hampsch, George H(arold) 1927- ... 15-16R
Hampshire, Joyce Gregorian
See Gregorian, Joyce Ballou
Hampshire, Stuart (Newton) 1914-
Brief entry ... 116
Hampshire, Susan 1942- Brief entry ... 112
Hampson, Anne ... 117
Brief entry ... 111
Hampson, (Richard) Denman 1929- ... SATA-15
Hampson, Frank 1918(?)-1985 Obituary ... 117
See also SATA 46
Hampson, Norman 1922- ... 25-28R
Hampson, Zena 1926- ... CANR-19
Earlier sketches in CA 4R, CANR-3
Hampton, Christopher 1929- ... CANR-4
Earlier sketch in CA 53-56
Hampton, Christopher (James) 1946- ... 25-28R
See also DLB 13
See also CLC 4
Hampton, David
See Fairclough, Chris
Hampton, David R(ichard) 1933- ... 81-84
Hampton, H(arold) Duane 1932- ... 33-36R
Hampton, Kathleen 1923- ... 4R
Hampton, Mark
See Norwood, Victor G(eorge) C(harles)
Hampton, Robert E. 1924- ... 33-36R
Hampton, William (Albert) 1929- ... CANR-13
Earlier sketch in CA 33-36R
Hamre, Leif 1914- ... CANR-4
Earlier sketch in CA 5-6R
See also SATA 5
Hamrick, Samuel J., Jr. 1929- ... 120
Brief entry ... 115
Hams, Thomas M., Jr. 1928- ... 11-12R
Hamsa, Bobbie 1944- ... 106
See also SATA 38
Hamscher, Albert N(elson) 1946- ... 73-76
Hamsher, J. Herbert 1938- ... 57-60
Hamshere, Cyril (Eric) 1912- ... 41-44R
Hamson, C. J.
See Hamson, Charles John
Hamson, Charles John 1905-1987
Obituary ... 124
Hamsun, Knut
See Pedersen, Knut
See also TCLC 2, 14
Hamsund, Knut Pedersen
See Pedersen, Knut
Han, Seung Soo 1936- ... CANR-2
Earlier sketch in CA 45-48
Han, Sungjoo 1940- ... 53-56
Han, Suyin 1917- ... 19-20R
Hanagan, Eva (Helen) 1923- ... 101
Hanagan, Michael Patrick 1947- ... 109
Hanaghan, Jonathan 1887-1967 ... 65-68
Hanami, Tadashi (Akamatsu) 1930- ... 89-92
Hanan, Patrick Dewes 1927- ... 106
Hanau, Laia 1916- ... 89-92
Hanawalt, Barbara A(nn) 1941- ... 101
Hanbury, Victor
See Losey, Joseph (Walton)
Hanbury-Tenison, Marika 1938-1982 ... 104
Obituary ... 108
Hanbury-Tenison, (Airling) Robin 1936- ... 57-60
Hance, Kenneth G(ordon) 1903- ... 85-88
Hance, William A(dams) 1916- ... 11-12R
Hanchett, William 1922- ... 33-36R
Hancock, Alice Van Fossen 1890- ... 2R
Hancock, Carla ... 89-92
Hancock, Carol Helen Brooks
See Hancock, Morgan
Hancock, Edward L(eslie) 1930- ... CANR-1
Earlier sketch in CA 45-48
Hancock, Geoffrey 1946- ... CANR-19
Earlier sketch in CA 101
Hancock, Harold B(ell) 1913- ... 53-56
Hancock, Joy Bright 1898-1986 Obituary ... 120
Hancock, Keith
See Hancock, W(illiam) K(eith)
Hancock, Leslie 1941- ... 23-24R
Hancock, Lyn 1938- ... 77-80
Hancock, M. Donald 1939- ... 33-36R
Hancock, Malcolm 1936- ... 25-28R
Hancock, Mary A. 1923- ... 37-40R
See also SATA 31
Hancock, Maxine 1942- ... CANR-8
Earlier sketch in CA 61-64
Hancock, Morgan 1941- ... 103
Hancock, Niel Anderson 1941- ... CANR-21
Earlier sketch in CA 97-100
Hancock, Ralph Lowell 1903- ... CAP-1
Earlier sketch in CA 9-10
Hancock, Roger Nelson 1929- ... 97-100
Hancock, Sheila 1942- ... 49-52
Hancock, Sibyl 1940- ... CANR-16
Earlier sketches in CA 49-52, CANR-1
See also SATA 9
Hancock, Taylor 1920- ... 97-100

Hancock, W(illiam) K(eith) 1898- CANR-5
Earlier sketch in CA 7-8R
Hand, G(eoffrey) J(oseph Philip Macaulay)
1931- 25-28R
Hand, J(oan) C(arole) 1943- 57-60
Hand, (Andrus) Jackson 1913- CANR-10
Earlier sketch in CA 61-64
Hand, John
See Pierson, John H(erman) G(roesbeck)
Hand, Thomas A(lypius) 1915- 13-14R
Hand, Wayland D(ebs) 1907-1986 .... 41-44R
Obituary 120
Handel, Gerald 1924- CANR-11
Earlier sketch in CA 23-24R
Handelman, Howard 1943- 57-60
Handelman, John R(obert) 1948- 77-80
Handelsman, Judith Florence 1948- 61-64
Handforth, Thomas (Schofield) 1897-1948
Brief entry 120
See also SATA 42
Handke, Peter 1942- 77-80
See also CLC 5, 8, 10, 15, 38
Handl, Irene 1902(?)-1987 103
Obituary 124
Handler, Jerome S(idney) 1933- 53-56
Handler, Joel F. 1932- Brief entry 113
Handler, Julian Harris 1922- 21-22R
Handler, Meyer Srednick 1905-1978
Obituary 77-80
Handler, Milton 1903- 61-64
Handler, Philip 1917-1981 .... 33-36R
Obituary 105
Handley, Graham Roderick 1926- CANR-24
Earlier sketch in CA 105
Handley-Taylor, Geoffrey 1920- CANR-7
Earlier sketch in CA 7-8R
Handlin, Mary (Flug) 1913-1976 .... CAP-2
Obituary 65-68
Earlier sketch in CA 33-36
Handlin, Oscar 1915- CANR-23
Earlier sketches in CA 3R, CANR-5
See also DLB 17
Handman, Herbert Ira 1932- 89-92
Handover, P(hyllis) M(argaret)
1923(?)-1974 .... 9-10R
Obituary 53-56
Handscombe, Richard 1935- 37-40R
Handville, Robert (Tompkins) 1924- ... SATA-45
Handy, Edward Smith Craighill
1893(?)-1980 Obituary 102
Handy, Robert T(heodore) 1918- CANR-2
Earlier sketch in CA 7-8R
Handy, Rollo 1927- 11-12R
Handy, Toni 1930- 97-100
Handy, W(illiam) C(hristopher) 1873-1958
Brief entry 121
Handy, William J. 1918- 45-48
Hane, Mikiso 1922- CANR-15
Earlier sketch in CA 81-84
Hane, Roger 1940-1974 .... SATA-20
Hanenkrat, Frank (Thomas) 1939- 93-96
Haner, F(rederick) T(heodore) 1929- 53-56
Hanes, Bailey C(ass) 1915- 77-80
Hanes, Elizabeth Sill 2R
Hanes, Frank Borden 1920- 1R
Hanes, Mary (a pseudonym) 1940(?)-
Brief entry 117
Haney, David P. 1938- CANR-21
Earlier sketches in CA 57-60, CANR-6
Haney, Eleanor H(umes) 1931- Brief entry .. 114
Haney, John B. 1931- 29-32R
Haney, Lynn 1941- CANR-1
Earlier sketch in CA 49-52
See also SATA 23
Haney, Thomas K. 1936- 15-16R
Haney, Thomas R. 45-48
Haney, William V. 1925- 17-18R
Hanff, Helene CANR-3
Earlier sketch in CA 7-8R
See also SATA 11
Hanfmann, George M(axim) A(nossov)
1911-1986 Obituary 118
Brief entry 117
Hanford, Lloyd D(avid) 1901-1979 ..... CANR-11
Earlier sketch in CA 15-16R
Hanford, S. A. 1898-1978 Obituary 81-84
Hang, T(ing-)Y(ung) 1908(?)-1987
Obituary 122
Hangen, (Putnam) Welles 1930- 9-10R
Hanifi, M(ohammed) Jamil 1935- 61-64
Haning, Bob
See Haning, James R(obert)
Haning, James R(obert) 1928- CANR-2
Earlier sketch in CA 45-48
Hanke, Howard August 1911- 1R
Hanke, Lewis (Ulysses) 1905- 65-68
Hankey, Cyril Patrick 1886-1973 .... 4R
Obituary 103
Hankey, Rosalie A.
See Wax, Rosalie (Amelia) H.
Hankey, Roy 1932- 108
Hankin, (Edward Charles) St. John (Emile
Clavering) 1869-1909 Brief entry 110
See also DLB 10
Hankins, Clabe
See McDonald, Erwin L(awrence)
Hankins, Frank Hamilton 1877-1970
Obituary 104
Hankins, John Erskine 1905- 49-52
Hankins, Norman E(lijah) 1935- CANR-11
Earlier sketch in CA 61-64
Hankins, Thomas Leroy 1933- 108
Hankinson, Cyril (Francis James) 1895- .. CAP-1
Earlier sketch in CA 9-10
Hankla, Cathryn 1958- 116
Hanks, Lucien M(ason) 1910- 37-40R
Hanks, Stedman Shumway 1889-1979
Obituary 85-88
Hanle, Dorothea Zack 1917- 13-14R
Hanley, Boniface Francis 1924- 9-10R
Hanley, Clifford 1922- CANR-23
Earlier sketches in CA 9-10R, CANR-3
See also DLB 14
Hanley, Elizabeth
See Du Breuil, (Elizabeth) L(or)inda
Hanley, Evelyn A(lice) 1916-1980 .... 41-44R
Obituary 97-100
Hanley, Gerald (Anthony) 1916- CANR-6
Earlier sketch in CA 3R
Hanley, Hope Anthony 1926- CANR-5
Earlier sketch in CA 11-12R
Hanley, James 1901-1985 73-76
Obituary 117
See also CLC 3, 5, 8, 13
Hanley, Katharine Rose 1932- 37-40R
Hanley, Michael F. IV 1941- 65-68
Hanley, Mike
See Hanley, Michael F. IV
Hanley, Theodore Dean 1917- 7-8R
Hanley, Thomas O'Brien 1918- CANR-1
Earlier sketch in CA 1R
Hanley, William 1931- 41-44R
Hanlon, Emily 1945- 77-80
See also SATA 15
Hanlon, John J(oseph) 1912- 57-60
Hanmer, Davina
See Courtney, Nicholas (Piers)
Hann, C. M. 1953- 121
Hann, Jacquie 1951- CANR-13
Earlier sketch in CA 73-76
See also SATA 19
Hanna, Alfred Jackson 1893-1978 ...... CANR-2
Earlier sketch in CA 45-48
Hanna, David 1917- CANR-6
Earlier sketch in CA 57-60
Hanna, Frank A(llan) 1907-1978 Obituary ... 111
Hanna, J. Marshall 1907- CANR-24
Earlier sketch in CA 1R
Hanna, John Paul 1932- CANR-1
Earlier sketch in CA 45-48
Hanna, Lavone Agnes 1896- 13-14R
Hanna, Mary Carr 1905- 45-48
Hanna, Mary T. 1935- 97-100
Hanna, Paul R(obert) 1902- 45-48
See also SATA 9
Hanna, Thomas 1928- CANR-1
Earlier sketch in CA 1R
Hanna, William John 1931- CANR-8
Earlier sketch in CA 61-64
Hannaford, John 1918- 45-48
Hannah, (Juliel) Barbara 1891- 97-100
Hannah, Barry 1942- 110
Brief entry 108
See also DLB 6
See also CLC 23, 38
Hannak, Johann Jacques 1892- CAP-1
Earlier sketch in CA 9-10
Hannam, Charles 1925- CANR-11
Earlier sketch in CA 61-64
See also SATA 50
Hannan, Joseph F(rancis) 1923- CANR-3
Earlier sketch in CA 9-10R
Hannas, Linda 1913- 113
Hannau, Hans W(alter) 1904- CANR-10
Earlier sketch in CA 23-24R
Hannavy, John Michael 1946- CANR-11
Earlier sketch in CA 69-72
Hannaway, Patricia H(inman) 1929- 61-64
Hannaway, Patti
See Hannaway, Patricia H(inman)
Hannay, Allen 1946- 109
Hannay, Doris Fergusson
See Fergusson Hannay, Doris
Hannay, James 1827-1873 .... DLB-21
Hannay, Margaret Patterson 1944- CANR-21
Earlier sketch in CA 104
Hanneman, Audre (Louise) 1926- 23-24R
Hanney, Peter 1930-1976 Obituary 105
Hannibal
See Alexander, Stanley Walter
Hannibal, Edward 1936- 29-32R
Hannifin, Jerry (Bernard) 1917- 77-80
Hanning, Hugh 1925- 25-28R
Hanning, Robert William 1938- 93-96
Hannula, Reino 1918- 105
Hannum, Alberta Pierson 1906-1985 65-68
Obituary 115
Hano, Arnold 1922- CANR-5
Earlier sketch in CA 9-10R
See also SATA 12
Hanrahan, Barbara 1939- Brief entry 121
Hanrahan, John D(avid) 1938- CANR-15
Earlier sketch in CA 77-80
Hanrieder, Wolfram F. 1931- CANR-23
Earlier sketches in CA 23-24R, CANR-8
Hansberry, Lorraine (Vivian) 1930-1965 109
Obituary 25-28R
See also DLB 7, 38
See also CDALB 1941-1968
See also CLC 17
Hansel, C(harles) E(dward) M(ark) 1917-
Brief entry 115
Hansel, Robert R(aymond) 1936-
Brief entry 110
Hansell, Antonina
See Looker, Antonina (Hansell)
Hansen, Al(fred Earl) 1927- 19-20R
Hansen, Alvin H(arvey) 1887-1975 ...... CAP-1
Obituary 57-60
Earlier sketch in CA 15-16
Hansen, Bertrand Lyle 1922- 9-10R
Hansen, Carl (Francis) 1906-1983 ...... CANR-2
Obituary 110
Earlier sketch in CA 5-6R
Hansen, Carol
See Fenichel, Carol Hansen
Hansen, Caryl (Hall) 1929- 108
See also SATA 39
Hansen, Cecil
See Huffaker, Clair
Hansen, Cecil Dan
See Huffaker, Clair
Hansen, Chadwick (Clarke) 1926- 29-32R
Hansen, Donald A(ndrew) 1933- 73-76
Hansen, Donald Charles 1935- 33-36R
Hansen, Emmanuel 1937- 104
Hansen, Flemming 1938- 93-96
Hansen, Forest Warnyr 1931- 45-48
Hansen, Gary B(arker) 1935- CANR-21
Earlier sketches in CA 11-12R, CANR-3
Hansen, Harry 1884-1977 73-76
Obituary 69-72
Hansen, Joseph 1923- CANR-16
Earlier sketch in CA 29-32R
See also CLC 38
Hansen, Joyce 1942- 105
See also SATA 39, 46
Hansen, Kenneth H(arvey) 1917- 13-14R
Hansen, Klaus J(uergen) 1931- 21-22R
Hansen, Mary Lewis (Patterson) 1933- ... 17-18R
Hansen, Niles M(aurice) 1937- CANR-13
Earlier sketch in CA 25-28R
Hansen, Norman J. 1918- 29-32R
Hansen, Richard H(erbert) 1929- 4R
Hansen, Rodney Thor 1940- 53-56
Hansen, Roger D(ennis) 1935- 105
Hansen, Ron 1947- CANR-17
Earlier sketch in CA 89-92
Hansen, Rosanna 1947- 105
Hansen, Terrence Leslie 1920-1974 ...... 37-40R
Hansen, W(illiam) Lee 1928- 29-32R
Hansen, William F(reeman) 1941- 49-52
Hanser, Richard (Frederick) 1909-1981 .. CANR-8
Earlier sketch in CA 5-6R
See also SATA 13
Hanshew, Thomas W. 1857-1914
Brief entry 113
Hansi
See Hirschmann, Maria Anne
Hanson, A(lbert) H(enry) 1913-1971 .... CANR-4
Obituary 89-92
Earlier sketch in CA 7-8R
Hanson, Agnes O(lin) 1905- 107
Hanson, Anne Coffin 1921- 23-24R
Hanson, Anthony Tyrrell 1916- CANR-24
Earlier sketches in CA 23-24R, CANR-9
Hanson, Dirk 1950- 111
Hanson, E(ugene) Kenneth 1930- 13-14R
Hanson, Earl D(orchester) 1927- CANR-12
Earlier sketch in CA 73-76
Hanson, Earl Parker 1899-1978 .... 41-44R
Hanson, F(ridolf) Allan 1939- 41-44R
Hanson, Harvey 1941- 65-68
Hanson, Howard (Harold) 1896-1981
Obituary 103
Hanson, Howard Gordon 1931- 23-24R
Hanson, Irene (Forsythe) 1898- 49-52
Hanson, Isabel 1929- 106
Hanson, James Arthur 1940- 49-52
Hanson, Jim 1953- 97-100
Hanson, Joan 1938- CANR-15
Earlier sketch in CA 33-36R
See also SATA 8
Hanson, Joseph E. 1894(?)-1971
Obituary 104
See also SATA 27
Hanson, June Andrea 1941- 97-100
Hanson, Kenneth O(stlin) 1922- CANR-7
Earlier sketch in CA 53-56
See also CLC 13
Hanson, Kristine 1958- 123
Hanson, Michael James 1942- 61-64
Hanson, Norwood Russell 1924-1967 ... CANR-8
Earlier sketch in CA 7-8R
Hanson, Paul D(avid) 1939- 61-64
Hanson, Pauline 45-48
Hanson, Peggy 1934- CANR-12
Earlier sketch in CA 29-32R
Hanson, Philip 1936- 103
Hanson, R(ichard) P(atrick) C(rosland)
1916- CANR-9
Earlier sketch in CA 23-24R
Hanson, Richard S(imon) 1931- 37-40R
Hanson, Robert Carl 1926- 37-40R
Hanson, Robert P(aul) 1918- 11-12R
Hanson, Ruth Katie 1900- 7-8R
Hanson, Simon
See Hanson, Richard S(imon)
Hanson, William S(tewart) 1950- 123
Hansten, Philip D. 1943- 33-36R
Hanushek, Eric Alan 1943- 41-44R
Hanzlicek, C(harles) G(eorge) 1942- ... CANR-12
Earlier sketch in CA 73-76
Hao, Qian
See Qian Hao
Hao, Yen-ping 1934- 53-56
Hapgood, Charles Hutchins 1904- 19-20R
Hapgood, David 1926- 15-16R
Hapgood, Fred 1942- 93-96
Hapgood, Ruth K(nott) 1920- 49-52
Happe, Peter 1932- 45-48
Happel, Robert A. 1916- 2R
Happel, Stephen 1944- 114
Happold, F(rederick) C(rossfield) 1893- 101
Haq, Mahbub ul 1934- 15-16R
Harald, Eric
See Boesen, Victor
Haraldsson, Erlendur 1931- 101
Harap, Henry 1893-1981 Obituary 104
Harap, Louis 1904- 57-60
Harari, Ehud 1935- 65-68
Harary, Keith 1953- 120
Harary, Stuart Blue
See Harary, Keith
Harasymiw, Bohdan 1936- 124
Haraway, Donna Jeanne 1944- 73-76
Harbach, Otto (Abels) 1873-1963
Obituary 112
Harbage, Alfred (Bennett) 1901-1976 ... CANR-5
Obituary 65-68
Earlier sketch in CA 5-6R
Harbaugh, John W(arvelle) 1926- 49-52
Harbaugh, William Henry 1920- 1R
Harberger, Arnold C. 1924- CANR-6
Earlier sketch in CA 15-16R
Harbert, Earl N(orman) 1934- CANR-13
Earlier sketch in CA 33-36R
Harbert, Mary Ann 1945- 61-64
Harbeson, Georgiana Brown 1894(?)-1980
Obituary 101
Harbeson, Gladys Evans 21-22R
Harbeson, John Willis 1938- 57-60
Harbin, Calvin E(dward) 1916- 23-24R
Harbin, Robert
See Williams, Ned
Harbinson, Robert
See Bryans, Robert Harbinson
Harbinson, W(illiam) A(llen) 1941- CANR-9
Earlier sketch in CA 61-64
Harbison, Frederick Harris 1912-1976
Obituary 65-68
Harbison, Peter 1939- 65-68
Harbison, Robert 1940- 102
Harbottle, Michael (Neale) 1917- 29-32R
Harbron, John D(avison) 1924- 11-12R
Harburg, E(dgar) Y(ipsel) 1896-1981 85-88
Obituary 103
Harburg, Yip
See Harburg, E(dgar) Y(ipsel)
Harbury, Colin (Desmond) 1922- 102
Harcave, Sidney S(amuel) 1916- 19-20R
Harcleroad, Fred F(arley) 1918- CANR-23
Earlier sketches in CA 19-20R, CANR-8
Harcourt, Ellen Knowles 1890(?)-1984
Obituary 111
See also SATA 36
Harcourt, G(eoffrey) C(olin) 1931- CANR-16
Earlier sketch in CA 25-28R
Harcourt, Melville 1909- 7-8R
Harcourt, Palma CANR-14
Earlier sketch in CA 77-80
Harcourt, Peter 1931- 81-84
Hard, Edward W(ilhelm), Jr. 1939- 85-88
Hard, Frederick 1897- CAP-2
Earlier sketch in CA 25-28
Hard, Margaret (Steel) 1888(?)-1974
Obituary 49-52
Hard, T. W.
See Hard, Edward W(ilhelm), Jr.
Hard, Walter (Rice) 1882-1966 Obituary 116
Hardach, Gerd 1941- 105
Hardaway, Francine 1941- 81-84
Hardcastle, Michael 1933- CANR-12
Earlier sketch in CA 25-28R
See also SATA 38, 47
Harden, Donald B(enjamin) 1901- 5-6R
Harden, Edgar F(rederick) 1932- 123
Harden, Oleta Elizabeth (McWhorter)
1935- 37-40R
Harden, (John) William 1903- 93-96
Harder, Eleanor (Loraine) 1925- 37-40R
Harder, Geraldine Gross 1926- 53-56
Harder, Raymond Wymbs, Jr. 1920- 85-88
Hardesty, Nancy A(nn) 1941- CANR-23
Earlier sketches in CA 57-60, CANR-8
Hardesty, Von 1939- 112
Hardgrave, Robert L(ewis), Jr. 1939- .. CANR-11
Earlier sketch in CA 25-28R
Hardie, Frank 1911- 33-36R
Hardiman, James W. 1919- 33-36R
Hardin, Charles M(eyer) 1908- 49-52
Hardin, Clement
See Newton, D(wight) B(ennett)
Hardin, Garrett James 1915- CANR-9
Earlier sketch in CA 17-18R
Hardin, J. D.
See Riefe, Alan
and Sheldon, Walter J.
Hardin, James N(eal) 1939- 114
Hardin, Paul III 1931- 25-28R
Hardin, Peter
See Vaczek, Louis
Hardin, Richard F(rancis) 1937- 45-48
Hardin, Robert 1934- 77-80
Hardin, Tim 1941(?)-1981 Obituary 102
Hardin, Tom
See Bauer, Erwin A.
Hardin, Wes
See Keevill, Henry J(ohn)
Harding, A(nthony) F(ilmer) 1946- 77-80
Harding, Barbara 1926- 41-44R
Harding, Bertita (Leonarz de) 1902- 5-6R
Harding, Carl B.
See Barker, Elver A.
Harding, D(ouglas) E(dison) 1909-
Brief entry 116
Harding, D(enys Clement) W(yatt)
1906- CANR-16
Earlier sketches in CA 15-16, CAP-1
Harding, D(ennis) W(illiam) 1940- 41-44R
Harding, Davis P. 1915(?)-1970 Obituary ... 104
Harding, Donald Edward 1916- CANR-4
Earlier sketch in CA 53-56
Harding, Harold F(riend) 1903- 37-40R
Harding, Harry (Jr.) 1946- 109

Harding, Jack 1914- ... 29-32R
Harding, James 1929- ... CANR-14
Earlier sketch in CA 33-36R
Harding, John 1948- ... 97-100
Harding, Kenneth
See Little, Paul H(ugo)
Harding, Lee 1937- ... 106
See also SATA 31, 32
Harding, Maria
See Goudiss, Maria Agnes D'Elia
Harding, Matt
See Floren, Lee
Harding, Matthew Whitman
See Floren, Lee
Harding, Peter
See Burgess, M(ichael) R(oy)
Harding, Sandra G. 1935- ... 120
Harding, T(imothy) D. 1948- ... 85-88
Harding, Thomas G(rayson) 1937- ... 21-22R
Harding, Virginia Hamlet 1909- ... 45-48
Harding, Walter Roy 1917- ... CANR-17
Earlier sketches in CA 1R, CANR-1
Harding, Wes
See Keevill, Henry J(ohn)
Harding, William Harry 1945- ... 93-96
Hardinge, Helen (Mary Cecil) 1901- ... CAP-2
Earlier sketch in CA 29-32
Hardingham, John (Frederick Watson) 1916- ... CAP-1
Earlier sketch in CA 11-12
Hardison, O(sborne) B(ennett, Jr.) 1928- ... CANR-6
Earlier sketch in CA 5-6R
Hardman, John (David) 1944- ... 45-48
Hardman, Keith (Jordan) 1931- ... 116
Hardman, Richards Lynden 1924- ... 15-16R
Hardon, John A(nthony) 1914- ... CANR-2
Earlier sketch in CA 2R
Hardoy, Jorge Enrique 1926- ... 33-36R
Hardt, Helga Fleischhauer
See Fleischhauer-Hardt, Helga
Hardt, J(ohn) Pearce 1922- ... CANR-3
Earlier sketch in CA 5-6R
Hardwick, Adam
See Connor, John Anthony
Hardwick, Clyde T(homas) 1915- ... 5-6R
Hardwick, Elizabeth 1916- ... CANR-3
Earlier sketch in CA 7-8R
See also DLB 6
See also CLC 13
Hardwick, Homer
See Rogers, Paul (Patrick)
Hardwick, (John) Michael (Drinkrow) 1924- ... CANR-2
Earlier sketch in CA 49-52
Hardwick, Mollie ... CANR-2
Earlier sketch in CA 49-52
Hardwick, Richard Holmes, Jr. 1923- ... CANR-9
Earlier sketch in CA 7-8R
See also SATA 12
Hardwick, Sylvia
See Doherty, Ivy R. Duffy
Hardy, Adam
See Bulmer, (Henry) Kenneth
Hardy, Alan 1932- ... 73-76
Hardy, Alexander G(eorge) 1920-1973
Obituary ... 45-48
Hardy, Alice Dale ... CAP-2
Earlier sketch in CA 19-20
See also SATA 1
Hardy, Alister C(lavering) 1896-1985 ... 85-88
Obituary ... 116
Hardy, Barbara (Gladys) ... 85-88
Hardy, C. Colburn 1910- ... CANR-21
Earlier sketches in CA 53-56, CANR-6
Hardy, David A(ndrews) 1936- ... CANR-8
Earlier sketch in CA 61-64
See also SATA 9
Hardy, Dennis 1941- ... 124
Hardy, Douglas
See Andrews, (Charles) Robert Douglas (Hardy)
Hardy, Edward R(ochie) 1908- ... CAP-1
Earlier sketch in CA 15-16
Hardy, Eric ... 61-64
Hardy, Evelyn 1902- ... 23-24R
Hardy, Henry 1949- ... 113
Hardy, J(ohn) P(hillips) 1933- ... 25-28R
Hardy, Jason
See Oxley, William
Hardy, John Edward 1922- ... 13-14R
Hardy, Jon 1958- ... 123
Hardy, Jonathan G. Gathorne
See Gathorne-Hardy, Jonathan G.
Hardy, Laura
See Holland, Sheila
Hardy, Leroy C(lyde) 1927- ... 29-32R
Hardy, Melissa Arnold 1952- ... 102
Hardy, Michael (James Langley) 1933- ... 25-28R
Hardy, Peter 1931- ... 65-68
Hardy, Richard E(arl) 1938- ... 37-40R
Hardy, Richard P(eter) 1940- ... 117
Hardy, Ronald Harold 1919- ... 7-8R
Hardy, Stuart
See Schisgall, Oscar
Hardy, Thomas 1840-1928 ... 123
Brief entry ... 104
See also DLB 18, 19
See also TCLC 4, 10, 18
Hardy, Tom 1943- ... 116
Hardy, W(illiam) G(eorge) 1895-1979 ... CANR-5
Earlier sketch in CA 7-8R
Hardy, Willene S(chaefer) 1937- ... 112
Hardy, William M(arion) 1922- ... CANR-2
Earlier sketch in CA 2R
Hardyck, Curtis D(ale) 1929- ... 29-32R
Hare, A(lexander) Paul 1923- ... CANR-2
Earlier sketch in CA 2R
Hare, Bill
See Hare, William Moorman
Hare, Cyril
See Clark, Alfred Alexander Gordon
Hare, David 1947- ... 97-100
See also DLB 13
See also CLC 29
Hare, Douglas Robert Adams 1929- ... 45-48
Hare, Eric B. 1894- ... CAP-1
Earlier sketch in CA 15-16
Hare, F(rederick) Kenneth 1919- ... CANR-14
Earlier sketch in CA 37-40R
Hare, John 1935- ... 21-22R
Hare, Nathan 1934- ... CANR-24
Earlier sketch in CA 41-44R
Hare, Norma Q(uarles) 1924- ... 101
See also SATA 41, 46
Hare, Peter H. 1935- ... 33-36R
Hare, R(ichard) M(ervyn) 1919- ... CANR-2
Earlier sketch in CA 7-8R
Hare, Richard (Gilbert) 1907-1966 ... CAP-1
Earlier sketch in CA 13-14
Hare, Ronald 1899- ... 77-80
Hare, Thomas Blenman
See Hare, Thomas William
Hare, Thomas William 1952- ... 122
Hare, Van Court, Jr. 1929- ... 25-28R
Hare, William 1944- ... 111
Hare, William Moorman 1934- ... 101
Hare Duke, Michael Geoffrey 1925- ... 111
Harel, Isser 1912- ... CANR-10
Earlier sketch in CA 65-68
Hareven, Shulamith 1931- Brief entry ... 117
Hareven, Tamara K. 1937- ... CANR-13
Earlier sketch in CA 25-28R
Harford, David K(ennedy) 1947- ... 49-52
Harford, Henry
See Hudson, W(illiam) H(enry)
Harger, Rolla N(eil) 1890-1983 Obituary ... 114
Harger, William Henderson 1936- ... 57-60
Hargrave, John Gordon 1894-1982
Obituary ... 110
Hargrave, Leonie
See Disch, Thomas M(ichael)
Hargrave, O. T. 1936- ... 33-36R
Hargrave, Rowena 1906- ... 33-36R
Hargraves, Thomas
See Ainsworth, Thomas Hargraves, Jr.
Hargreaves, Harry 1922- ... 7-8R
Hargreaves, John D(esmond) 1924- ... 9-10R
Hargreaves, Mary W(ilma) M(assey) 1914- ... CANR-14
Earlier sketch in CA 37-40R
Hargreaves, Reginald (Charles) 1888- ... CAP-1
Earlier sketch in CA 9-10
Hargreaves-Mawdsley, W(illiam) Norman 1921-1980 ... CANR-7
Earlier sketch in CA 9-10R
Hargroder, Charles M(erlin) 1926- ... 73-76
Hargrove, Barbara Watts 1924- ... 33-36R
Hargrove, Erwin C. 1930- Brief entry ... 111
Hargrove, James 1947- ... 120
See also SATA 50
Hargrove, Jim
See Hargrove, James
Hargrove, Katharine T. ... 33-36R
Hargrove, Marion 1919- ... DLB-11
Hargrove, Merwin Matthew 1910- ... 11-12R
Hargrove, Nancy Duvall 1941- ... 97-100
Hargrove, Richard J(ohn), Jr. 1941- ... 116
Harik, Iliya F. 1934- ... CANR-16
Earlier sketch in CA 25-28R
Haring, Bernard
See Haering, Bernhard
Haring, Firth 1937- ... 25-28R
Haring, Jo 1934- ... 116
Haring, Joseph E(merick) 1931- ... 33-36R
Haring, Norris G. 1923- ... CANR-2
Earlier sketch in CA 2R
Haring, Philip S(myth) 1915- ... 37-40R
Harington, Donald 1935- ... CANR-7
Earlier sketch in CA 15-16R
Harjo, Joy 1951- ... 114
Hark, Mildred
See McQueen, Mildred Hark
Harkabi, Yehoshafat 1921- ... 73-76
Harkavy, Robert E(dward) 1936- ... 111
Harkaway, Hal
See Stratemeyer, Edward L.
Harker, Kenneth 1927- ... 97-100
Harker, Ronald 1909- ... 77-80
Harkey, Ira B(rown), Jr. 1918- ... 57-60
Harkey, William G. 1914- ... 25-28R
Harkins, Arthur M(artin) 1936- ... 97-100
Harkins, Paul W(illiam) 1911- ... 116
Harkins, Philip 1912- ... 29-32R
See also SATA 6
Harkins, William E(dward) 1921- ... 33-36R
Harkness, Bruce 1923- ... 13-14R
Harkness, D(avid) W(illiam) 1937- ... CANR-15
Earlier sketch in CA 29-32R
Harkness, David J(ames) 1913- ... CANR-3
Earlier sketch in CA 9-10R
Harkness, Edward 1947- ... 77-80
Harkness, Georgia (Elma) 1891-1974 ... CANR-6
Obituary ... 53-56
Earlier sketch in CA 1R
Harkness, Gladys Estelle Suiter 1908(?)-1973 Obituary ... 41-44R
Harkness, Jack
See Harkness, John Leigh
Harkness, John Leigh 1918- ... 120
Harkness, Marjory Gane 1880-19(?) ... CAP-2
Earlier sketch in CA 23-24
Harknett, Terry 1936- ... CANR-21
Earlier sketches in CA 57-60, CANR-6
Harlan
See Shaw, William Harlan
Harlan, Elizabeth 1945- ... 111
See also SATA 35, 41
Harlan, Glen
See Cebulash, Mel
Harlan, John Marshall 1899-1971
Obituary ... 33-36R
Harlan, Louis R(udolph) 1922- ... 23-24R
See also CLC 34
Harlan, William K(eith) 1938- ... 45-48
Harle, Elizabeth
See Roberts, Irene
Harlequin
See Reed, A(lexander) W(yclif)
Harley, John
See Marsh, John
Harling, Thomas
See Eastham, Thomas
Harlow, Enid 1939- ... 102
Harlow, Francis H(arvey) 1928- ... 57-60
Harlow, Harry F(rederick) 1905- ... 97-100
Harlow, Joan Hiatt 1932- ... 89-92
Harlow, LeRoy F(rancis) 1913- ... 85-88
Harlow, Lewis A(ugustus) 1901- ... CAP-1
Earlier sketch in CA 13-14
Harlow, Neal 1908- ... 109
Harlow, Robert 1923- ... DLB-60
Harlow, Samuel Ralph 1885-1972 ... 2R
Harlow, Samuel Ralph 1885-1972 ... 37-40R
Harlow, W(illiam) M(orehouse) 1900-1986 ... 13-14R
Obituary ... 119
Harman, Alec
See Harman, Richard Alexander
Harman, Claire
See Schmidt, Claire Harman
Harman, David 1944- ... 105
Harman, Fred 1902(?)-1982 Obituary ... 106
See also SATA 30
Harman, Gilbert H(elms) 1938- ... 73-76
Harman, Harry E. III 1917- ... 116
Harman, Hugh 1903-1982 Obituary ... 108
See also SATA 33
Harman, Jane
See Harknett, Terry
Harman, Jeanne Perkins 1919- ... CANR-11
Earlier sketch in CA 69-72
Harman, Mark 1951- ... 118
Harman, Nicholas 1933- ... 101
Harman, P(eter) M(ichael) 1943- ... 110
Harman, R. Alec
See Harman, Richard Alexander
Harman, Richard Alexander 1917- ... CANR-5
Earlier sketch in CA 11-12R
Harman, Willis W(alter) 1918- ... 7-8R
Harmel, Robert 1950- ... 110
Harmelink, Barbara (Mary) ... 61-64
See also SATA 9
Harmer, Mabel 1894- ... 11-12R
See also SATA 45
Harmer, Ruth Mulvey 1919- ... 9-10R
Harmin, Merrill 1928- ... 89-92
Harmon, A(llen) J(ackson) 1926- ... 21-22R
Harmon, Frederick G(ardner) 1932- ... 119
Harmon, Gary L. 1935- ... 37-40R
Harmon, Glynn 1933- ... 45-48
Harmon, H. H.
See Williams, Robert Moore
Harmon, James Judson 1933- ... 23-24R
Harmon, Jim
See Harmon, James Judson
Harmon, Lily 1912- ... 105
Harmon, Lyn S. 1930- ... 21-22R
Harmon, Margaret 1906- ... 69-72
See also SATA 20
Harmon, Maurice 1930- ... CANR-9
Earlier sketch in CA 23-24R
Harmon, Nolan B(ailey) 1892- ... 89-92
Harmon, (Norman) Paul 1942- ... 122
Harmon, Robert Bartlett 1932- ... CANR-23
Earlier sketches in CA 17-18R, CANR-8
Harmon, Susanna M(arie) 1940- ... 57-60
Harmon, William (Ruth) 1938- ... CANR-14
Earlier sketch in CA 33-36R
See also CLC 38
Harms, Ernest 1895-1974 ... CAP-1
Obituary ... 49-52
Earlier sketch in CA 13-14
Harms, John 1900- ... 17-18R
Harms, Leroy Stanley 1928- ... CANR-8
Earlier sketch in CA 53-56
Harms, Robert T(homas) 1932- ... 37-40R
Harms, Valerie 1940- ... CANR-2
Earlier sketch in CA 49-52
Harmsel, Henrietta Ten
See Ten Harmsel, Henrietta
Harmsen, Dorothy B. Bahneman ... 103
Harmsen, Frieda 1931- ... 107
Harmston, Olivia
See Weber, Nancy
Harmsworth, Esmond Cecil 1898-1978
Obituary ... 89-92
Harnack, Curtis (Arthur) 1927- ... CANR-22
Earlier sketches in CA 4R, CANR-2
Harnack, R(obert) Victor 1927- ... 15-16R
Harnan, Terry 1920- ... 45-48
See also SATA 12
Harnden, Ruth Peabody ... 73-76
Harned, David Baily 1932- Brief entry ... 112
Harner, James L(owell) 1946- ... 110
Harner, Michael J(ames) 1929- Brief entry ... 114
Harness, Charles L(eonard) 1915-
Brief entry ... 113
See also DLB 8
Harnett, Bertram 1923- ... 119
Harnett, Cynthia (Mary) 1893-1981 ... CAP-1
Obituary ... 111
Earlier sketch in CA 9-10
See also SATA 5, 32
Harnetty, Peter 1927- ... 37-40R
Harnik, Bernard 1910- ... 93-96
Harnsberger, Caroline Thomas 1902- ... 61-64
Harnwell, Gaylord Probasco 1903-1982
Obituary ... 106
Haro, Robert P(eter) 1936- ... 33-36R
Harodoy, Jorge Enrique 1926- ... 33-36R
Harold, Fred(erick) G(ordon) 1937- ... 118
Haroldson, William
See King, Harold
Haroutunian, Joseph 1904-1968 Obituary ... 111
Harper, Anita 1943- ... 114
See also SATA 41
Harper, Bill
See Harper, William A(rthur)
Harper, Carol Ely ... 61-64
Harper, Daniel
See Brossard, Chandler
Harper, David
See Corley, Edwin (Raymond)
Harper, Douglas A(lbert) 1948- ... 117
Harper, Elaine
See Hallin, Emily Watson
Harper, Floyd H(enry) 1899-1978
Obituary ... 77-80
Harper, Frances Ellen Watkins 1825-1911
Brief entry ... 111
See also DLB 50
See also TCLC 14
Harper, George Mills 1914- Brief entry ... 114
Harper, George W(illiam) 1927- ... 113
Harper, Harold W. ... 89-92
Harper, Harry H(alsted), Jr. 1910-1983
Obituary ... 110
Harper, Howard 1904- ... 19-20R
Harper, Howard M(orrall), Jr. 1930- ... CANR-22
Earlier sketch in CA 21-22R
Harper, J(ohn) Russell 1914-1983 ... CANR-13
Earlier sketch in CA 33-36R
Harper, James E(dwin) 1927- ... 41-44R
Harper, Joan (Marie) 1932- ... 101
Harper, John C(arsten) 1924- ... 103
Harper, John Dickson 1910- ... 103
Harper, Karen 1945- ... 114
Harper, Kate
See Harper, Katherine E(rna)
Harper, Katherine E(rna) 1946- ... 103
Harper, M(ichael) J(ohn) K(ennedy) 1935- ... 116
Harper, Marvin Henry 1901- ... 49-52
Harper, Mary Wood
See Dixon, Jeanne
Harper, Michael 1931- ... CANR-15
Earlier sketch in CA 65-68
Harper, Michael S(teven) 1938- ... CANR-24
Earlier sketch in CA 33-36R
See also DLB 41
See also CLC 7, 22
Harper, Paula (Hays) 1938- ... 105
Harper, Robert A(lexander) 1924- ... 17-18R
Harper, Robert J(ohnston) C(raig) 1927- ... 13-14R
Harper, Stephen (Dennis) 1924- ... 97-100
Harper, Tom 1923(?)-1983 Obituary ... 110
Harper, Wilhelmina 1884-1973 ... CAP-1
Earlier sketch in CA 17-18
See also SATA 4, 26
Harper, William A(rthur) 1944- ... 77-80
Harpham, Geoffrey Galt 1946- ... 111
Harpole, Charles H(enry) 1943- ... 111
Harpole, Patricia Chayne 1933- ... 37-40R
Harpur, Patrick 1950- ... 114
Harr, Wilber C. 1908-1971 ... 1R
Obituary ... 103
Harragan, Betty Lehan 1921- ... CANR-17
Earlier sketch in CA 77-80
Harrah, Barbara K. 1938- ... 107
Harrah, David 1926- ... 7-8R
Harrah, David Fletcher 1949- ... 65-68
Harrah, Michael 1940- ... 115
See also SATA 41
Harral, Stewart 1906-1964 ... 5-6R
Harrar, E(llwood) S(cott) 1905- ... CAP-1
Earlier sketch in CA 11-12
Harrar, J(acob) George 1906-1982
Obituary ... 110
Harre, John 1931- ... 23-24R
Harre, (Horace) Rom(ano) 1927- ... CANR-21
Earlier sketches in CA 5-6R, CANR-2
Harrell, Allen W(aylan) 1922- ... 29-32R
Harrell, Costen J(ordan) 1885- ... 7-8R
Harrell, David Edwin, Jr. 1930- ... CANR-15
Earlier sketch in CA 37-40R
Harrell, Irene B(urk) 1927- ... CANR-9
Earlier sketch in CA 23-24R
Harrell, John G(rinnell) 1922- ... CANR-18
Earlier sketches in CA 11-12R, CANR-3
Harrell, Sara (Jeanne) Gordon 1940- ... 105
Harrell, (Clyde) Stevan 1947- ... 106
Harrell, Thomas Willard 1911- ... 1R
Harrelson, Walter (Joseph) 1919- ... 11-12R
Harrer, Heinrich 1912- ... CANR-7
Earlier sketch in CA 17-18R
Harrier, Richard C(harles) 1923- ... 122
Brief entry ... 117
Harries, Joan 1922- ... 107
See also SATA 39
Harries, Karsten 1937- ... 25-28R
Harries, Richard (Douglas) 1936- ... 116
Harriett 1905- ... 77-80
Harriford, Daphne
See Harris, Marion Rose (Young)
Harrigan, Anthony (Hart) 1925- ... 21-22R

Harrigan, Kathryn Rudie 1951- 109
Harrigan, Stephen 1948- 122
Harriman, Ann 1932- 111
Harriman, Averell
See Harriman, W(illiam) Averell
Harriman, Edward 1922- 114
Harriman, Margaret 1928- 21-22R
Harriman, Richard L(evet) 1944- 33-36R
Harriman, Sarah 1942- 57-60
Harriman, W(illiam) Averell 1891-1986
Obituary 119
Brief entry 111
Harrington, Alan 1919- 73-76
Harrington, Charles (Christopher)
1942- CANR-9
Earlier sketch in CA 65-68
Harrington, Curtis 1928- 103
Harrington, Denis J(ames) 1932- 69-72
Harrington, Donald Szantho 1914- 21-22R
Harrington, Elbert W(ellington) 1901- 37-40R
Harrington, Evelyn Davis 1911- CANR-4
Earlier sketch in CA 7-8R
Harrington, Geri CANR-21
Earlier sketches in CA 57-60, CANR-6
Harrington, Harold David 1903-1981 ... CANR-11
Earlier sketch in CA 25-28R
Harrington, Jack 1918- 57-60
Harrington, Jeremy 1932- 41-44R
Harrington, Joseph Daniel 1923- 89-92
Harrington, K.
See Bean, Keith F(enwick)
Harrington, Lyn
See Harrington, Evelyn Davis
See also SATA 5
Harrington, Mark Raymond 1882-1971 ... CAP-2
Earlier sketch in CA 17-18
Harrington, Michael 1928- CANR-19
Earlier sketch in CA 19-20R
Harrington, Norman W. 1922(?)-1987
Obituary 123
Harrington, (Peter) Ty(rus) 1951- 102
Harrington, William 1931- CANR-19
Earlier sketches in CA 11-12R, CANR-4
Harriott, Edwin Thomas 1933- 117
Harriott, Ted
See Harriott, Edwin Thomas
Harris, Alan 1928- 7-8R
Harris, Albert J(osiah) 1908- CANR-5
Earlier sketch in CA 2R
Harris, Alex(ander Eisemann) 1949- 124
Harris, Alf(red) 1928- 53-56
Harris, Alice Kessler 1941- CANR-14
Earlier sketch in CA 37-40R
Harris, Andrea
See Connolly, Vivian
and Walker, Irma Ruth (Roden)
Harris, Andrew
See Poole, Frederick King
Harris, Aurand 1915- CANR-16
Earlier sketch in CA 93-96
See also SATA 37
Harris, Barbara J. 1942- 115
Harris, Barbara S(eger) 1927- 49-52
Harris, Ben(jamin) Charles 1907-1978 57-60
Obituary 89-92
Harris, Ben(jamin) M(axwell) 1923- CANR-2
Earlier sketch in CA 5-6R
Harris, Benjamin (?)-1720(?) DLB-42, 43
Harris, Bernice K(elly) 1892-1973 ....5-6R
Obituary 45-48
Harris, Bertha 1937- 29-32R
Harris, Beulah ?-1970 Obituary 104
Harris, Bill 1933- 109
Harris, Brian
See King, Harold
Harris, Brownie 1949- 107
Harris, Carl V(ernon) 1937- 97-100
Harris, Charlaine 1951- 105
Harris, Charles 1923- 102
Harris, Charles B(urt) 1940- 53-56
Harris, Charles H(ouston) III 1937- 15-16R
Harris, Chauncy D(ennison) 1914- 29-32R
Harris, Chester W(illiam) 1910- CAP-1
Earlier sketch in CA 11-12
Harris, Christie (Lucy) Irwin 1907- CANR-6
Earlier sketch in CA 7-8R
See also SATA 6
See also CLC 12
Harris, Clyde E., Jr. 23-24R
Harris, Colver
See Colver, Anne
Harris, Curtis C(lark), Jr. 1930- 53-56
Harris, Cyril 1891- CAP-1
Earlier sketch in CA 11-12
Harris, Dale B(enner) 1914- 15-16R
Harris, Daniel A(rthur) 1942- 89-92
Harris, David (Victor) 1946- 69-72
Harris, David W. 1948- Brief entry 107
Harris, Del(mer William) 1937- CANR-8
Earlier sketch in CA 61-64
Harris, Dorothy Joan 1931- CANR-1
Earlier sketch in CA 45-48
See also SATA 13
Harris, Douglas H(ershel, Jr.) 1930- 25-28R
Harris, Edward Arnold 1910-1976
Obituary 65-68
Harris, Elliot 1932- 25-28R
Harris, Ernest E(dward) 1914- 33-36R
Harris, Errol E(ustace) 1908- CANR-18
Earlier sketches in CA 49-52, CANR-2
Harris, F(rank) Brayton 1932- 21-22R
Harris, Frank 1856(?)-1931 Brief entry 109
See also TCLC 24
Harris, Fred (Roy) 1930- 77-80
Harris, Frederick John 1943- 57-60
Harris, Gene Gray 1929- 17-18R
Harris, George Washington
1814-1869 .... DLB-3, 11
Harris, Geraldine (Rachel) 1951- 116
Harris, Gertrude (Margaret) 1916- 57-60
Harris, H(arold) A(rthur) 1902- 49-52
Harris, Helen(a Barbara Mary) 1927- 61-64
Harris, Herbert 1911- 102
Harris, Herbert 1914(?)-1974 Obituary 49-52
Harris, Hyde
See Harris, Timothy Hyde
Harris, Ian (Anthony) 1937- 107
Harris, Irving David 1914- 13-14R
Harris, James E(dward) 1928- Brief entry ... 110
Harris, Jana 1947- 105
Harris, Jane Allen 1918- 4R
Harris, Jane Gary 111
Harris, Janet 1932-1979 ....33-36R
Obituary 93-96
See also SATA 4, 23
Harris, Janice Hubbard 1943- 118
Harris, Jay S(tephen) 1938- 85-88
Harris, Jed
See Horowitz, Jacob
Harris, Jessica L.
See Milstead, Jessica L(ee)
Harris, Joel Chandler 1848-1908
Brief entry 104
See also YABC 1
See also DLB 11, 23, 42
See also TCLC 2
Harris, John (Roy) 1915- CANR-2
Earlier sketch in CA 5-6R
Harris, John 1916- 93-96
Harris, John (Wyndham Parkes Lucas)
Beynon 1903-1969 102
Obituary 89-92
See also CLC 19
Harris, John S(harp) 1917- 29-32R
Harris, John S(terling) 1929- 65-68
Harris, Jonathan 1921- 121
Harris, Joseph E(arl) 1929- 122
Brief entry 117
Harris, Joseph Pratt 1896-1985 .... 3R
Obituary 115
Harris, Julian (Earle) 1896- 2R
Harris, Julie 1925- 103
Harris, Karen H(arriman) 1934- CANR-22
Earlier sketch in CA 103
Harris, Kathleen
See Humphries, Adelaide M.
Harris, Kathryn Gibbs
See Gibbs-Wilson, Kathryn (Beatrice)
Harris, Kenn 1947- 116
Harris, Kenneth 1904-1983 Obituary 109
Harris, Larry M.
See Janifer, Laurence M(ark)
Harris, Lavinia
See Johnston, Norma
Harris, Leon A., Jr. 1926- CANR-3
Earlier sketch in CA 9-10R
See also SATA 4
Harris, Leonard 1929- CANR-9
Earlier sketch in CA 65-68
Harris, Lloyd J(ohn) 1947- 61-64
Harris, Lorle K(empe) 1912- 97-100
See also SATA 22
Harris, Louis 1921- 13-14R
Harris, Louise 1903- CANR-7
Earlier sketch in CA 19-20R
Harris, M(iddleton) A. 1908-1977
Obituary 111
Harris, MacDonald
See Heiney, Donald (William)
Harris, Madalene 1925- 105
Harris, Marcia Lee 1951- 109
Harris, Marie 1943- CANR-20
Earlier sketch in CA 104
Harris, Marilyn
See Springer, Marilyn Harris
Harris, Marion Rose (Young) 1925- CANR-12
Earlier sketches in CA 9-10, CAP-1
Harris, Marjorie Silliman 1890- CAP-1
Earlier sketch in CA 13-14
Harris, Mark 1922- CANR-2
Earlier sketch in CA 7-8R
See also CAAS 3
See also DLB 2
See also DLBY 80
See also CLC 19
Harris, Mark C(harles) 1955- 113
Harris, Mark Jonathan 1941- CANR-21
Earlier sketch in CA 104
See also SATA 32
Harris, Marshall (Dees) 1903- CANR-1
Earlier sketch in CA 4R
Harris, Marvin 1927- 124
Brief entry 110
Harris, Mary B(ierman) 1943- 53-56
Harris, Mary Imogene 49-52
Harris, Mary K. 1905-1966 .... CAP-1
Earlier sketch in CA 15-16
Harris, Mary Law 1892(?)-1980 Obituary ... 102
Harris, Maynard L(awrence) 1902-1974
Obituary 116
Harris, Michael H(ope) 1941- 57-60
Harris, Michael R(ichard) 1936- 29-32R
Harris, Miles F(itzgerald) 1913- CANR-6
Earlier sketch in CA 7-8R
Harris, P(eter) B(ernard) 1929- 104
Harris, Patricia 57-60
Harris, Philip R(obert) 1926- CANR-8
Earlier sketch in CA 17-18R
Harris, R(ansom) Baine 1927- 73-76
Harris, R(obert) J(ohn) C(ecil)
1922-1980 .... CANR-15
Earlier sketch in CA 65-68
Harris, R(obert) Laird 1911- CANR-1
Earlier sketch in CA 4R
Harris, Radie 65-68
Harris, Rex 1904-1985 Obituary 118
Harris, Richard (S.) 1928(?)-1987
Obituary 123
Harris, Richard 1934- 107
Harris, Richard Colebrook 1936- 97-100
Harris, Richard H. 1942- 103
Harris, Richard J(ohn) 1948- 115
Harris, Richard N(elson) 1942- 77-80
Harris, Ricky 1922- 103
Harris, Robert (Jennings) 1907- 5-6R
Harris, Robert Dalton 1921- 93-96
Harris, Robert Harry 1941- 108
Harris, Robert Samuel 1904-1983
Obituary 111
Harris, Robert T(aylor) 1912- 7-8R
Harris, Robin
See Shine, Deborah
Harris, Robin S(utton) 1919- 21-22R
Harris, Roger
See Wilson, R(oger) H(arris) L(ebus)
Harris, Ronald W(alter) 1916- 7-8R
Harris, Rosemary (Jeanne) CANR-13
Earlier sketch in CA 33-36R
See also SATA 4
Harris, Roy J. 1903(?)-1980 Obituary 93-96
Harris, S(eymour) E(dwin) 1897-1974 65-68
Obituary 53-56
Harris, Sara Lee
See Stadelman, S(ara) L(ee)
Harris, Sheldon H(oward) 1928- 37-40R
Harris, Sherwood 1932- 97-100
See also SATA 25
Harris, Stephen E. 1943- Brief entry 111
Harris, Stephen L(eRoy) 1937- 29-32R
Harris, Steven Michael 1957- 121
Harris, (William) Stewart 1922- 104
Harris, Styron 1936- 112
Harris, Sydney J(ustin) 1917-1986 .... CANR-11
Obituary 120
Earlier sketch in CA 61-64
Harris, T George 1924- 69-72
Harris, Thistle Y.
See Stead, Thistle Yolette
Harris, Thomas 1940(?)- 113
Harris, Thomas A(nthony) 1913(?)- 93-96
Harris, Thomas Cunningham 1908-1985
Obituary 114
Harris, Thomas J. 1892(?)-1983 Obituary .. 109
Harris, Thomas O(rville) 1935- 73-76
Harris, Timothy Hyde 1946- 101
Harris, (Jonathan) Toby 1953- 118
Harris, Tom
See Harris, Thomas Cunningham
Harris, Trudier 1948- 115
Harris, Walter A. 1929- 29-32R
Harris, Warren G(ene) 1936- 77-80
Harris, Wendell V. 1932- 111
Harris, William Bliss 1901(?)-1981
Obituary 104
Harris, William C. 1933- 23-24R
Harris, William Foster
See Foster-Harris, William
Harris, William Hamilton 1944- 111
Harris, William J(oseph) 1942- CANR-19
Earlier sketches in CA 53-56, CANR-5
Harris, (Theodore) Wilson 1921- CANR-11
Earlier sketch in CA 65-68
See also CLC 25
Harrison, Allan E(ugene) 1925- CANR-6
Earlier sketch in CA 57-60
Harrison, Barbara 1941- CANR-12
Earlier sketch in CA 29-32R
Harrison, Barbara Grizzuti 1934- CANR-15
Earlier sketch in CA 77-80
Harrison, Bennett 1942- 53-56
Harrison, Bernard 1933- 93-96
Harrison, Beverly Wildung 1932- 111
Harrison, Bill
See Harrison, William C.
Harrison, Billy R. 1937- 121
Harrison, Brian Fraser
See Fraser Harrison, Brian
Harrison, C. William 1913- 107
See also SATA 35
Harrison, Carey 1944- 61-64
Harrison, Chip 1952- 29-32R
Harrison, Claire E. 1946- 111
Harrison, Cynthia Ellen 1946- 57-60
Harrison, David L(akin) 1926- 117
Harrison, David L(ee) 1937- 93-96
See also SATA 26
Harrison, Deloris 1938- 61-64
See also SATA 9
Harrison, Don(ald Dean) 1941- 112
Harrison, Edward Hardy 1926- 116
Harrison, Eric George William Warde
1893-1987 Obituary 124
Harrison, Everett F(alconer) 1902- CAP-1
Earlier sketch in CA 11-12
Harrison, Francis Llewelyn 1905-1987
Obituary 124
Harrison, Frank Llewelyn
See Harrison, Francis Llewelyn
Harrison, Frank R(ussell) III 1935- 53-56
Harrison, Fred 1917- 29-32R
Harrison, Frederic 1831-1923 .... DLB-57
Harrison, G(eorge) B(agshawe) 1894- ... CANR-3
Earlier sketch in CA 1R
Harrison, George Russell 1898- CAP-2
Earlier sketch in CA 19-20
Harrison, Hank 1940- 41-44R
Harrison, Harry (Max) 1925- CANR-21
Earlier sketches in CA 4R, CANR-5
See also SATA 4
See also DLB 8
See also CLC 42
Harrison, Helen Amy 1943- 114
Harrison, Helen P(atricia) 1935- 102
Harrison, Howard 1930- 7-8R
Harrison, J(ohn) F(letcher) C(lews)
1921- CANR-10
Earlier sketch in CA 25-28R
Harrison, J(ames) P. 77-80
Harrison, James (Thomas) 1937- CANR-8
Earlier sketch in CA 15-16R
Harrison, Jay S(molens) 1927-1974
Obituary 53-56
Harrison, Jim
See Harrison, James (Thomas)
See also DLBY 82
See also CLC 6, 14, 33
Harrison, Joan (Mary) 1909- 104
Harrison, John A(rmstrong) 1915-
Brief entry 111
Harrison, John Baugham 1907- 1R
Harrison, John M(arshall) 1914- 25-28R
Harrison, John R(aymond) 1933- 101
See also AITN 2
Harrison, K(enneth) C(ecil) 1915- CANR-3
Earlier sketch in CA 9-10R
Harrison, Keith Edward 1932- 73-76
Harrison, Louise C(ollbran) 1908- CAP-1
Earlier sketch in CA 11-12
Harrison, Lowell H(ayes) 1922- 37-40R
Harrison, M(ichael) John 1945- 53-56
Harrison, Marcus 1924- 102
Harrison, Martin 1930- 49-52
Harrison, Mary
See Fabbri, Nancy Rash
Harrison, Max 69-72
Harrison, Michael 1907- 97-100
Harrison, Michelle Jessica 1942- 109
Harrison, Molly 1909- 108
See also SATA 41
Harrison, Nicolas 1937(?)-1984 Obituary ... 114
Harrison, Paul Carter 1936- Brief entry 117
See also DLB 38
Harrison, Paul M. 1923- 53-56
Harrison, Randall P(aul) 1929- CANR-11
Earlier sketch in CA 69-72
Harrison, Raymond H. 1911- 17-18R
Harrison, Richard A(rnold) 1945- 107
Harrison, Richard John 1920- 109
Harrison, Robert (Ligon) 1932- 25-28R
Harrison, Roland Kenneth 1920- 49-52
Harrison, Rosina 1899- 102
Harrison, (Thomas) Ross 1943- CANR-9
Earlier sketch in CA 61-64
Harrison, Royden John 1927- 17-18R
Harrison, S(ydney) Gerald 1924- 13-14R
Harrison, Sarah 1946- 102
Harrison, Saul I. 1925- CANR-10
Earlier sketch in CA 21-22R
Harrison, Selig S(eidenman) 1927- 85-88
Harrison, Stanley R. 1927- 41-44R
Harrison, Ted
See Harrison, Edward Hardy
Harrison, Tony 1937- 65-68
See also DLB 40
See also CLC 43
Harrison, Wallace (Kirkman) 1895-1981
Obituary 108
Harrison, Whit
See Whittington, Harry (Benjamin)
Harrison, Wilfrid 1909- CAP-1
Earlier sketch in CA 11-12
Harrison, William 1933- CANR-9
Earlier sketch in CA 19-20R
Harrison, William C. 1919- 25-28R
Harrison Church, Ronald James 1915- ...15-16R
Harriss, C(lement) Lowell 1912- CANR-2
Earlier sketch in CA 1R
Harriss, Joseph 1936- 57-60
Harriss, R(obert) P(reston) 1902- 73-76
Harriss, Will(ard Irvin) 1922- 111
See also CLC 34
Harrisse, Henry 1829-1910 .... DLB-47
Harrity, Richard 1907-1973 Obituary 41-44R
Harrod, Leonard Montague 1905- 15-16R
Harrod, Roy Forbes 1900-1978 ....9-10R
Obituary 103
Harrold, William E(ugene) 1936- 41-44R
Harron, Don(ald) 1924- 104
Harrop-Allin, Clinton 1936- 107
Harroun, Catherine 1907- 109
Harrow, Benjamin 1888-1970 Obituary 104
Harrowe, Fiona
See Hurd, Florence
Harrower, Elizabeth 1928- 101
Harrower, Molly 1906- 5-6R
Harry, M.
See Lewis, Sasha Gregory
Harsany, Peter 1913- 111
Harsch, Ernest 1951- 69-72
Harsch, Hilya
See Jelly, George Oliver
Harsch, Joseph C(lose) 1905- 102
Harsent, David 1942- 93-96
See also DLB 40
Harsh, George 1908(?)-1980 Obituary 93-96
Harsh, Wayne C. 1924- CANR-15
Earlier sketch in CA 29-32R
Harshaw, Ruth H(etzel) 1890-1968
Obituary 107
See also SATA 27
Harshbarger, David Dwight 1938- 53-56
Harson, Sley
See Ellison, Harlan

Harss, Luis 1936- ... 17-18R
Harstad, Peter Tjernagel 1935- ... 37-40R
Harston, Ruth 1944- ... 41-44R
Hart, A(rthur) Tindal 1908- ... 9-10R
Hart, Albert Bushnell 1854-1943
Brief entry ... 116
See also DLB 17
Hart, Albert Gailord 1909- ... CAP-2
Earlier sketch in CA 23-24
Hart, Alexandra 1939- ... CANR-6
Earlier sketch in CA 57-60
Hart, Allan H(untley) 1935- ... 106
Hart, Archibald D(aniel) 1932- ... CANR-15
Earlier sketch in CA 93-96
Hart, Barry
See Bloom, Herman Irving
Hart, Basil Henry Liddell
See Liddell Hart, Basil Henry
Hart, Benjamin 1958- Brief entry ... 118
Hart, Bruce 1938- ... 107
See also SATA 39
Hart, Carol 1944- ... 65-68
Hart, Carole 1943- ... 107
See also SATA 39
Hart, Carolyn G(impel) 1936- ... 15-16R
Hart, David K(irkwood) 1933- ... 123
Brief entry ... 117
Hart, Donald J(ohn) 1917- ... 11-12R
Hart, Douglas C. 1950- ... 101
Hart, Edward J(ack) 1941- ... 53-56
Hart, Edward L. 1916- ... CANR-14
Earlier sketch in CA 37-40R
Hart, Ellis
See Ellison, Harlan
Hart, Ernest H(untley) 1910- ... 102
Hart, Frances (Newbold) Noyes
1890-1943 Brief entry ... 112
Hart, Francis
See Paine, Lauran (Bosworth)
Hart, Francis Dudley 1909- ... 108
Hart, Gary (Warren) 1936- Brief entry ... 114
Hart, Gary (Warren) 1936(?)- ... 124
Hart, Gavin 1939- ... 106
Hart, George L. III 1942- ... 93-96
Hart, H(erbert) L(ionel) A(dolphus)
1907- ... CANR-2
Earlier sketch in CA 4R
Hart, Henry C(owles) 1916- ... 1R
Hart, Henry Hersch 1886-1968 ... CAP-1
Earlier sketch in CA 9-10
Hart, Herbert Michael 1928- ... 11-12R
Hart, Hornell (Norris) 1888-1967 Obituary ... 111
Hart, James D(avid) 1911- ... CANR-1
Earlier sketch in CA 1R
Hart, Jane (Meyers) 1922- ... 107
Hart, Jeffrey Allen 1947- ... 109
Hart, Jim Allee 1914- ... 13-14R
Hart, John 1942- ... 109
Hart, John 1948- ... CANR-11
Earlier sketch in CA 65-68
Hart, John E(dward) 1917- ... 33-36R
Hart, John Fraser 1924- ... 37-40R
Hart, John Lewis 1931- ... CANR-4
Earlier sketch in CA 49-52
Hart, Johnny
See Hart, John Lewis
See also AITN 1
Hart, Joseph 1945- ... 85-88
Hart, Judith 1924- ... 109
Hart, Kate
See Kramer, Roberta
Hart, Kitty 1926- ... 117
Hart, Larry 1920- ... 33-36R
Hart, Lois B(orland) 1941- ... 117
Hart, Marie 1932- ... 41-44R
Hart, Marilyn M(cGuire) 1926- ... 45-48
Hart, Milton R. 1896(?)-1983 Obituary ... 109
Hart, Moss 1904-1961 ... 109
Obituary ... 89-92
See also DLB 7
Hart, Oliver 1723-1795 ... DLB-31
Hart, Patricia Susan 1950- ... 118
Hart, Patrick 1925- ... 53-56
Hart, Ray L(ee) 1929- ... 29-32R
Hart, Richard (Harry) 1908- ... CAP-1
Earlier sketch in CA 9-10
Hart, Robert A(llan) 1929- Brief entry ... 117
Hart, Roderick P(atrick) 1945- ... 106
Hart, Sandra Lynn Housby 1948- ... 108
Hart, Stan 1929- ... 118
Hart, Stephanie 1949- ... 97-100
Hart, Sue
See Hart, Susanne
Hart, Susanne 1927- ... CANR-20
Earlier sketch in CA 102
Hart, V(orhis) Donn 1918- ... 15-16R
Hart, Walter 1906(?)-1973 Obituary ... 45-48
Hart, Winston Scott 1903(?)-1979
Obituary ... 89-92
Hartcup, Adeline 1918- ... 116
Hartcup, Guy 1919- ... 29-32R
Hart-Davis, Duff 1936- ... 29-32R
Hart-Davis, Phyllida
See Barstow, Phyllida
Hart-Davis, Rupert (Charles) 1907-
Brief entry ... 115
Harte, (Francis) Bret(t) 1836(?)-1902
Brief entry ... 104
See also SATA 26
See also DLB 12, 64
See also TCLC 1, 25
Harte, Marjorie
See McEvoy, Marjorie Harte
Harte, Samantha
See Hart, Sandra Lynn Houseby
Harte, Thomas Joseph 1914-1974
Obituary ... 53-56
Hartel, Klaus Dieter
See Vandenberg, Philipp
Hartendorp, A(bram) V(an) H(eyningen)
1893- ... CAP-1
Earlier sketch in CA 15-16
Harter, Eugene C(laudius) 1926- ... 119
Harter, Helen (O'Connor) 1905- ... 7-8R
Harter, Hugh A(nthony) 1922- ... 110
Harter, Kenneth W. 1912(?)-1984
Obituary ... 112
Harter, Lafayette George, Jr. 1918- ... 9-10R
Hartford, Claire 1913- ... 29-32R
Hartford, Ellis F(ord) 1905- ... CAP-1
Earlier sketch in CA 13-14
Hartford, (George) Huntington II 1911- ... 17-18R
Hartford, Margaret E(lizabeth) 1917- ... 41-44R
Hartford, Via
See Donson, Cyril
Harth, Erica ... 116
Harth, Erich 1919- ... 107
Harth, (John) Phillip 1926- Brief entry ... 116
Harth, Robert 1940- ... 33-36R
Harthan, John Plant 1916- ... 102
Harthoorn, A(ntonie) M(arinus) 1923- ... 53-56
Hartich, Alice 1888- ... CAP-2
Earlier sketch in CA 17-18
Harting, Emilie Clothier 1942- ... 73-76
Hartje, Robert G(eorge) 1922- ... 25-28R
Hartjen, Clayton A(lfred) 1943- ... 69-72
Hartke, Vance 1919- ... 25-28R
Hartland, Michael 1941- ... 110
Hartlaub, Felix 1913(?)-1945 ... DLB-56
Hartlaub, G(ustav) F(riedrich) 1884-1963
Obituary ... 112
Hartley, Dorothy 1893-1985 ... 105
Obituary ... 118
Hartley, Ellen (Raphael) 1915-1980 ... CANR-4
Earlier sketch in CA 7-8R
See also SATA 23
Hartley, Fred Allan III 1953- ... 106
See also SATA 41
Hartley, John I(rvin) 1921- ... 7-8R
Hartley, Keith 1940- ... 115
Hartley, L(eslie) P(oles) 1895-1972 ... 45-48
Obituary ... 37-40R
See also DLB 15
See also CLC 2, 22
Hartley, Livingston 1900- ... 61-64
Hartley, Lodwick (Charles) 1906-1979 ... CANR-1
Earlier sketch in CA 1R
Hartley, Margaret L(ohlker) 1909-1983 ... 97-100
Obituary ... 110
Hartley, Marie 1905- ... 11-12R
Hartley, Marsden 1877-1943 Brief entry ... 123
See also DLB 54
Hartley, Peter (Roy) 1933- ... 103
Hartley, Rachel M. 1895- ... 7-8R
Hartley, Robert F(rank) 1927- ... CANR-11
Earlier sketch in CA 69-72
Hartley, Shirley Foster 1928- ... CANR-13
Earlier sketch in CA 73-76
Hartley, William B(rown) 1913-1980 ... CANR-4
Earlier sketch in CA 7-8R
See also SATA 23
Hartling, Peter
See Haertling, Peter
Hartman, Berl
See Hartman, Berl Mendelson
Hartman, Berl Mendelson 1938- ... 122
Hartman, (Howard) Carl 1917- ... 122
Hartman, Carl 1928- ... 104
Hartman, Charles O(ssian) 1949- ... 108
Hartman, Chester W(arren) 1936- ... 57-60
Hartman, David N. 1921- ... 15-16R
Hartman, Evert 1937- ... 113
See also SATA 35, 38
Hartman, Geoffrey H. 1929- Brief entry ... 117
See also DLB 67
See also CLC 27
Hartman, George E(dward) 1926- ... 41-44R
Hartman, Hermene D(emaris) 1948- ... 122
Hartman, Jan 1938- ... 65-68
Hartman, Jane E(vangeline) 1928- ... CANR-22
Earlier sketch in CA 105
See also SATA 47
Hartman, John J(acob) 1942- ... 49-52
Hartman, Louis F(rancis) 1901-1970 ... CAP-2
Earlier sketch in CA 23-24
See also SATA 22
Hartman, Mary S(usan) 1941- ... 81-84
Hartman, Nancy Carol 1942- ... 53-56
Hartman, Olov 1906-1982 ... CANR-14
Earlier sketch in CA 29-32R
Hartman, Patience
See Zawadsky, Patience
Hartman, Rachel (Frieda) 1920-1972 ... 7-8R
Obituary ... 33-36R
Hartman, Rhondda Evans 1934- ... 61-64
Hartman, Robert K(intz) 1940- ... 41-44R
Hartman, Robert S. 1910-1973 ... CAP-2
Obituary ... 45-48
Earlier sketch in CA 17-18
Hartman, Roger
See Mehta, Rustam Jehangir
Hartman, Shirley 1929- ... 57-60
Hartman, William E(llis) 1919- ... 69-72
Hartman, William T(aylor) 1942- ... 117
Hartmann, Edward George 1912- ... 41-44R
Hartmann, Ernest 1934- ... 21-22R
Hartmann, Franz 1838-1912 Brief entry ... 115
Hartmann, Frederick Howard 1922- ... CANR-16
Earlier sketches in CA 2R, CANR-1
Hartmann, Heinz 1894-1970 Obituary ... 104
Hartmann, Helmut Henry 1931- ... 105
Hartmann, Klaus 1925- ... 21-22R
Hartmann, Michael 1944- ... 97-100
Hartmann, Rudolf A. 1937- Brief entry ... 111
Hartmann, Sadakichi 1867-1944 ... DLB-54
Hartmann, Susan M(arie) 1940- ... 41-44R
Hartmann, William K(enneth) 1939- ... 69-72
Hartnack, Justus 1912- ... 41-44R
Hartnett, D(avid) W(illiam) 1952- ... 122
Hartnett, Ken(neth Owen) 1934- ... 118
Hartnoll, Phyllis 1906- ... 81-84
Hartocollis, Peter 1922- ... CANR-1
Earlier sketch in CA 45-48
Hartog, Diana 1942- ... 123
Hartog, Joseph 1933- ... 102
Hartshorn, Ruth M. 1928- ... SATA-11
Hartshorne, Charles 1897- ... CANR-4
Earlier sketch in CA 9-10R
Hartshorne, Richard 1899- ... 7-8R
Hartshorne, Thomas L(lewellyn) 1935- ... 37-40R
Hart-Smith, William 1911- ... CANR-11
Earlier sketch in CA 23-24R
Hartsoe, Colleen Ivey 1925- ... 109
Hartston, W(illiam) R(oland) 1947- ... 116
Hartsuch, Paul Jackson 1902- ... 57-60
Hartt, Julian 1916(?)-1984 Obituary ... 113
Hartung, Albert Edward 1923- ... 103
Hartup, Willard W(ert) 1927- ... 25-28R
Hartwell, Dickson Jay 1906-1981 ... CAP-1
Obituary ... 103
Earlier sketch in CA 11-12
Hartwell, Nancy
See Callahan, Claire Wallis
Hartwell, Ronald Max 1921- ... 25-28R
Hartwick, Sylvia
See Doherty, Ivy R. Duffy
Hartwig, Marie (Dorothy) 1906- ... 1R
Hartwig, Richard E(ric) 1942- ... 118
Hartz, Fred R. 1933- ... 122
Hartz, Jim ... AITN-2
Hartz, Louis 1919-1986 Obituary ... 118
Hartzler, Daniel David 1941- ... 61-64
Haruf, Kent 19(?)- ... CLC-34
Harvard, Andrew Carson 1949- ... 69-72
Harvard, Charles
See Gibbs-Smith, Charles Harvard
Harvard, Stephen 1948- ... 57-60
Harvester, Simon
See Rumbold-Gibbs, Henry St. John Clair
Harvey, Anne 1933- ... 121
Harvey, Anthony Peter 1940- ... 106
Harvey, Barbara (Fitzgerald) 1928- ... 116
Harvey, C(harles) J(ohn) D(errick)
1922- ... 11-12R
Harvey, David 1935- ... 123
Harvey, David (W.) 1935- Brief entry ... 117
Harvey, David Dow 1931- ... 65-68
Harvey, Donald J(oseph) 1922- ... 41-44R
Harvey, Earle Sherburn 1906- ... 109
Harvey, Edith 1908(?)-1972 Obituary ... 104
See also SATA 27
Harvey, Edward Burns 1939- ... 41-44R
Harvey, Frank 1912-1981 Obituary ... 105
Harvey, Frank (Laird) 1913- ... 7-8R
Harvey, Gina P(aula) 1922- ... 45-48
Harvey, Harriet 1924- ... 109
Harvey, Ian Douglas 1914-1987 ... CAP-1
Obituary ... 121
Earlier sketch in CA 9-10
Harvey, James C(ardwell) 1925- ... 45-48
Harvey, James O. 1926- ... 17-18R
Harvey, Joan M(argaret) 1918- ... 102
Harvey, John F(rederick) 1921- ... CANR-23
Earlier sketches in CA 15-16R, CANR-8
Harvey, John Hooper 1911- ... CANR-21
Earlier sketches in CA 7-8R, CANR-6
Harvey, John Robert 1942- ... 93-96
Harvey, Jonathan 1939- ... 61-64
Harvey, Karen (E.) G(iddens) 1944- ... 117
Harvey, Kenneth 1919(?)-1979 Obituary ... 89-92
Harvey, Lashley Grey 1900- ... 37-40R
Harvey, Maria Luisa Alvarez 1938- ... 53-56
Harvey, Marian 1927- ... 89-92
Harvey, Michael G. 1944- ... 110
Harvey, Mose Lofley 1910-1985 Obituary ... 115
Harvey, Nancy Lenz 1935- ... 65-68
Harvey, Nigel 1916- ... CANR-13
Earlier sketch in CA 73-76
Harvey, O. J. 1927- ... 37-40R
Harvey, P(aul) D(ean) A(dshead) 1930- ... 112
Harvey, Paul
See Aurandt, Paul Harvey
Harvey, Rachel
See Bloom, Ursula
Harvey, Richard B(lake) 1930- ... 49-52
Harvey, Robert 1884- ... 7-8R
Harvey, Ruth C(harlotte) 1918-1980 ... 1R
Obituary ... 102
Harvey, Van A(ustin) 1926- ... 33-36R
Harvey, Virginia I(sham) 1917- ... 57-60
Harvey, William Burnett 1922- ... 41-44R
Harvey Wood, (Elizabeth) Harriet 1934- ... 123
Harvie-Watt, George Steven 1903- ... 109
Harward, Donald W. 1939- ... 93-96
Harward, Timothy Blake 1932- ... 25-28R
Harwell, Ann (Manning) J. 1936- ... 57-60
Harwell, Ernie
See Harwell, William Earnest
Harwell, Richard Barksdale 1915- ... CANR-17
Earlier sketches in CA 4R, CANR-2
Harwell, William Earnest 1918- Brief entry ... 116
Harwick, B. L.
See Keller, Beverly (Lou)
Harwin, Brian
See Henderson, LeGrand
Harwit, Martin Otto 1931- ... 105
Harwood, Alan 1935- ... 113
Harwood, Alice (Mary) ... 7-8R
Harwood, (Henry) David 1938- ... 104
Harwood, Edwin 1939- ... 29-32R
Harwood, Gina
See Battiscombe, E(sther) Georgina
(Harwood)
Harwood, Gwen(doline Nessie) 1920- ... 97-100
Harwood, Jonathan 1943- ... 103
Harwood, Lee 1939- ... CANR-9
Earlier sketch in CA 21-22R
See also DLB 40
Harwood, Pearl Augusta (Bragdon)
1903- ... 13-14R
See also SATA 9
Harwood, Raymond C(harles) 1906-1987
Obituary ... 122
Harwood, Ronald 1934- ... CANR-4
Earlier sketch in CA 4R
See also DLB 13
See also CLC 32
Harzfeld, Lois 1932- ... 107
Hasan, Saiyid Zafar 1930- ... 73-76
Hasbrouck, Kenneth E. 1916- ... 49-52
Hasegawa, Nyozekan 1875-1969 Obituary ... 111
Hasegawa, Tsuyoshi 1941- ... 109
Hasek, Jaroslav (Matej Frantisek)
1883-1923 Brief entry ... 104
See also TCLC 4
Hasel, Gerhard F(ranz) 1935- ... CANR-15
Earlier sketch in CA 41-44R
Haselden, Kyle (Emerson) 1913-1968 ... 5-6R
Haseler, Stephen Michael Alan 1942- ... 85-88
Haseley, Dennis ... SATA-44
Hasenclever, Herbert Frederick 1924-1978
Obituary ... 81-84
Hasford, (Jerry) Gustav 1947- ... 85-88
Hashmi, Aurangzeb Alamgir 1951- ... CANR-16
Earlier sketch in CA 77-80
Haskell, Arnold L(ionel) 1903-1981(?) ... CANR-7
Obituary ... 102
Earlier sketch in CA 5-6R
See also SATA 6
Haskell, Douglas 1899-1979 Obituary ... 89-92
Haskell, Edward Froehlich 1906-
Brief entry ... 105
Haskell, Francis (James Herbert) 1928- ... CANR-6
Earlier sketch in CA 11-12R
Haskell, John Duncan, Jr. 1941- ... 107
Haskell, Martin R(oy) 1912- ... 41-44R
Haskett, Edythe Rance 1915- ... 23-24R
Haskin, Dorothy C(lark) 1905- ... 5-6R
Haskin, Gretchen 1936- ... 103
Haskins, Barbara
See Stone, Barbara Haskins
Haskins, Charles Homer 1870-1937 ... DLB-47
Haskins, George Lee 1915- ... CANR-1
Earlier sketch in CA 1R
Haskins, Ilma 1919- ... 45-48
Haskins, James S. 1941- ... 33-36R
See also SATA 9
See also CLR 3
Haskins, Jim
See Haskins, James S.
See also SAAS 4
Haskins, Sam(uel Joseph) 1926- ... 103
Haslam, Gerald W. 1937- ... CANR-11
Earlier sketch in CA 29-32R
Hasler, Eveline 1937- ... 106
Hasler, Joan 1931- ... 29-32R
See also SATA 28
Haslerud, George M(artin) 1906- ... 45-48
Hasley, Louis (Leonard) 1906- ... 37-40R
Hasley, Lucile (Charlotte Hardman)
1909- ... CAP-1
Earlier sketch in CA 11-12
Hasling, John 1928- ... 33-36R
Haslip, Joan 1912- ... 107
Hasluck, Paul (Meernaa Caedwalla) 1905- ... 109
Haspel, Eleanor C. 1944- ... 69-72
Hass, C(harles) Glen 1915- ... 17-18R
Hass, Eric 1905(?)-1980 Obituary ... 102
Hass, Hans 1919- ... 108
Hass, Michael 1938- ... 37-40R
Hass, Robert 1941- ... 111
See also CLC 18, 39
Hassall, Christopher (Vernon) 1912-1963
Obituary ... 89-92
Hassall, Joan 1906- ... SATA-43
Hassall, Mark (William Cory) 1940- ... CANR-13
Earlier sketch in CA 73-76
Hassall, William Owen 1912- ... 15-16R
Hassan, Ihab Habib 1925- ... CANR-19
Earlier sketches in CA 7-8R, CANR-3
Hassan, William Ephraim, Jr. 1923- ... 33-36R
Hasse, John Edward 1948- ... 119
Hassel, David John 1923- ... 113
Hassel, Odd 1897-1981 Obituary ... 108
Hassel, Sven 1917- ... 93-96
Hassenger, Robert (Leo) 1937- ... 21-22R
Hassing, Per 1916- ... 37-40R
Hassler, Donald M. (II) 1937- ... CANR-14
Earlier sketch in CA 41-44R
Hassler, Jon (Francis) 1933- ... CANR-21
Earlier sketch in CA 73-76
See also SATA 19
Hassler, Warren W., Jr. 1926- ... 9-10R
Hassler, William T(homas) 1954- ... 104
Hassrick, Peter H(eyl) 1941- ... CANR-16
Earlier sketches in CA 49-52, CANR-1
Hast, Adele 1931- ... 119
Hastings, Adrian 1929- ... CANR-23
Earlier sketches in CA 19-20R, CANR-7
Hastings, Alan
See Williamson, Geoffrey
Hastings, Arthur Claude 1935- ... 37-40R
Hastings, Beverly
See Barkin, Carol
and James, Elizabeth
Hastings, Cecily Mary Eleanor 1924- ... 7-8R

Hastings, Graham
See Jeffries, Roderic (Graeme)
Hastings, Harrington
See Marsh, John
Hastings, Hubert de Cronin 1902-1986 109
Obituary 121
Hastings, Hudson
See Kuttner, Henry
Hastings, Ian 1912- 45-48
Hastings, Macdonald 1909- CANR-9
Earlier sketch in CA 53-56
Hastings, March
See Levinson, Leonard
Hastings, Margaret 1910- 41-44R
Hastings, (Macdonald) Max 1945- 81-84
Hastings, Michael (Gerald) 1938- 97-100
Hastings, Paul G(uiler) 1914- CANR-24
Earlier sketch in CA 2R
Hastings, Philip Kay 1922- 102
Hastings, Phyllis (Dora Hodge) CANR-8
Earlier sketch in CA 9-10R
Hastings, Robert J. 1924- 122
Hastings, Robert Paul 1933- 73-76
Hastings, Selina CLC-44
Hastings, William T(homson) 1881- 7-8R
Haston, Dougal 1940-1977 Obituary 105
Hastorf, Albert H(erman) 1920- 97-100
Hasty, Ronald W. 1941- CANR-4
Earlier sketch in CA 53-56
Haswell, Chetwynd John Drake 1919- 41-44R
Haswell, Harold Alanson, Jr. 1912- 45-48
Haswell, Jock
See Haswell, Chetwynd John Drake
Haszard, Patricia Moyes 1923- CANR-13
Earlier sketch in CA 19-20R
Hatch, Alden 1898-1975 65-68
Obituary 57-60
Hatch, (Alden) Denison 1935- 33-36R
Hatch, Elvin (James) 1937- 45-48
Hatch, Eric S(towe) 1902(?)-1973
Obituary 41-44R
Hatch, James V(ernon) 1928- 41-44R
Hatch, John (Charles) 1917- 11-12R
Hatch, Mary Cottam 1912-1970 Obituary 109
See also SATA 28
Hatch, Nathan O(rr) 1946- Brief entry 109
Hatch, Preble D(elloss) K(ellogg) 1898- CAP-2
Earlier sketch in CA 23-24
Hatch, Raymond N(orris) 1911- 21-22R
Hatch, Richard A(llen) 1940- CANR-9
Earlier sketch in CA 21-22R
Hatch, Robert McConnell 1910- 93-96
Hatch, William H(enry) P(aine) 1875-1972
Obituary 37-40R
Hatcher, George W. 1906(?)-1983
Obituary 110
Hatcher, Harlan (Henthorne) 1898- CAP-2
Earlier sketch in CA 19-20
Hatcher, John 1942- 33-36R
Hatcher, John S(outhall) 1940- 97-100
Hatcher, Nat(han) B(razzell) 1897- 4R
Hatcher, Robert Anthony 1937- 93-96
Hatcher, William S(pottswood) 1935- 123
Hatem, Mohamed Abdel-Kader
See Hatim, Muhammad 'Abd al-Qadir
Hatfield, Antoinette Kuzmanich 1929- 85-88
Hatfield, Dorothy B(lackmon) 1921- 53-56
Hatfield, Elaine (Catherine) 1937- CANR-17
Earlier sketches in CA 25-28R, CANR-10
Hatfield, Henry Caraway 1912- 65-68
Hatfield, Mark O(dom) 1922- 77-80
Hatfield, Michael (Vernon) 1935- 119
Hathaway, Baxter L. 1909- CANR-5
Earlier sketch in CA 3R
Hathaway, Bo 1942- 106
Hathaway, Dale E(rnest) 1925- 9-10R
Hathaway, Jan
See Neubauer, William Arthur
Hathaway, Lulu (Bailey) 1903- 13-14R
Hathaway, Mavis
See Avery, Ira
Hathaway, Nancy 1946- 108
Hathaway, Sibyl Collings 1884-1974 ..... 4R
Obituary 103
Hathaway, Starke R(osecrans) 1903-1984 ..... 5-6R
Obituary 113
Hathaway, William 1944- 73-76
Hathcock, Louise 4R
Hathorn, Richmond Y(ancey) 1917- CANR-1
Earlier sketch in CA 2R
Hatim, Muhammad 'Abd al-Qadir 1918- 89-92
Hatlen, Burton (Norval) 1936- 109
Hatley, George B(erton) 1924- 106
Hatlo, Jimmy 1898-1963 Obituary 93-96
See also SATA 23
Hatmon, Paul W. 1921- 106
Hatt, Harold E(rnest) 1932- 21-22R
Hatta, Mohammed 1902-1980 Obituary 97-100
Hattaway, Herman (Morell) 1938- 65-68
Hattaway, Michael 1941- 116
Hatteras, Owen
See Nathan, George Jean
See also TCLC 18
Hatteras, Owen III
See McDavid, Raven I(oor), Jr.
Hatterer, Lawrence J(ohn) 1925-
Brief entry 118
Hattersley, Ralph (Marshall, Jr.) 1921- 103
Hattersley, Roy (Sydney George) 1932- 103
Hattersley-Smith, Geoffrey (Francis) 1923- 118
Hattery, Lowell H(arold) 1916- 19-20R
Hatton, Ragnhild Marie 1913- CANR-12
Earlier sketch in CA 25-28R
Hatton, Robert Wayland 1934- 37-40R
Hatton, Thomas J(enison) 1935- 114
Hattwick, Richard E(arl) 1938- 73-76
Hatvary, George Egon 53-56
Hatzenbuehler, Ronald L(ee) 1945- 117
Hatzfeld, Helmut A(nthony) 1892-1979 97-100
Obituary 85-88
Hauberg, Clifford A(lvin) 1906- 37-40R
Hauck, Allan 1925- 3R
Hauck, Paul A(nthony) 1924- CANR-14
Earlier sketch in CA 41-44R
Hauck, Richard Boyd 1936- 53-56
Hauerwas, Stanley Martin 1940- 57-60
Haug, C(harles) James 1946- 116
Haugaard, Erik Christian 1923- CANR-3
Earlier sketch in CA 7-8R
See also SATA 4
See also CLR 11
Haugaard, William Paul 1929- 25-28R
Hauge, Sharon K(aye) 1943- 116
Haugen, Edmund Bennett 1913- 19-20R
Haugen, Einar (Ingvald) 1906- CANR-9
Earlier sketch in CA 21-22R
Haugh, Richard (Stanley) 1942- CANR-9
Earlier sketch in CA 57-60
Haugh, Robert F(ulton) 1910- 61-64
Haughey, John C. 1930- 77-80
Haughey, Thomas Brace 1943- 113
Haught, James A(lbert, Jr.) 1932-
Brief entry 122
Haught, John F(rancis) 1942- 85-88
Haughton, Claire Shaver 1901- 85-88
Haughton, Rosemary (Luling) 1927- 7-8R
Haughton, Sidney Henry 1888-1982
Obituary 107
Haughton-James, Jean Rosemary
1924-1981 Obituary 105
Haugland, Vern(on Arnold) 1908-1984 93-96
Obituary 113
Hauk, Maung
See Hobbs, Cecil (Carlton)
Haule, James M(ark) 1945- 109
Hauman, Doris 1898- SATA-32
Hauman, George 1890-1961 ..... SATA-32
Haun, Paul 1906-1969 ..... CAP-2
Earlier sketch in CA 17-18
Hau'Ofa, Epeli 1939- 124
Haupt, Christopher (Charles Herbert)
Lehmann
See Lehmann-Haupt, Christopher
(Charles Herbert)
Haupt, Zygmunt 1907(?)-1975 Obituary 61-64
Hauptly, Denis J(ames) 1945- 118
Hauptman, Terry 1947- 111
Hauptmann, Carl 1858-1921 ..... DLB-66
Hauptmann, Gerhart (Johann Robert)
1862-1946 Brief entry 104
See also DLB 66
See also TCLC 4
Haury, Emil W(alter) 1904- 65-68
Hausdorff, Don 1927- 45-48
Hauser, Bengamin Gayelord 1895-1984
Obituary 114
Brief entry 111
Hauser, Carl Maria 1895-1985 Obituary 117
Hauser, Charles McCorkle 1929- 69-72
Hauser, Gayelord
See Hauser, Bengamin Gayelord
Hauser, Hillary 1944- CANR-11
Earlier sketch in CA 69-72
Hauser, Margaret L(ouise) 1909- CAP-1
Earlier sketch in CA 11-12
See also SATA 10
Hauser, Marianne 1910- CANR-13
Earlier sketches in CA 11-12, CAP-1
See also DLBY 83
Hauser, Phillip M(orris) 1909- 17-18R
Hauser, Robert Mason 1942- 109
Hauser, Thomas 1946- 85-88
Hauser, William B(arry) 1939- 69-72
Hausknecht, Murray 1925- 37-40R
Hausknecht, Richard 1929- 121
Hausman, Gerald 1945- CANR-17
Earlier sketches in CA 45-48, CANR-2
See also SATA 13
Hausman, Gerry
See Hausman, Gerald
Hausman, Patricia 1953- 107
Hausman, Warren H. 1939- 17-18R
Hausmann, Bernard A(ndrew) 1899- CAP-2
Earlier sketch in CA 23-24
Hausmann, Manfred 1898-1986 Obituary 120
Hausmann, Winifred 1922- CANR-11
Earlier sketch in CA 21-22R
Hausrath, Alfred Hartmann 1901- 41-44R
Haussig, Hans Wilhelm 1916- 29-32R
Hauther, Brenda 1951- 113
Hautzig, Deborah 1956- 89-92
See also SATA 31
Hautzig, Esther Rudomin 1930- CANR-20
Earlier sketches in CA 2R, CANR-5
See also SATA 4
Havard, William C(lyde), Jr. 1923- CANR-5
Earlier sketch in CA 2R
Havel, J(ean) E(ugene Martial) 1928- 41-44R
Havel, Vaclav 1936- 104
See also CLC 25
Havelock, Christine Mitchell 1924- 85-88
Havelock, Eric A. 1903- CAP-1
Earlier sketch in CA 15-16
Havelock, Ronald G(eoffrey) 1935- 85-88
Haveman, Robert H. 1936- 19-20R
Havemann, Ernest (Carl) 1912- 4R
Havemann, Joel 1943- 85-88
Havemann, Robert (Hans Gunther)
1910-1982 Obituary 110
Havemeyer, Loomis 1886-1971
Obituary 33-36R
Haven, Richard 1924- 25-28R
Havens, Daniel F(rederick) 1931- 69-72
Havens, George R(emington)
1890-1977 ..... CANR-4
Obituary 73-76
Earlier sketch in CA 7-8R
Havens, Gordon 1903-1983 Obituary 111
Havens, Leston Laycock 1924- 119
Havens, Murray Clark 1932- 41-44R
Havens, Shirley E(lise) 1925- 89-92
Havens, Thomas R. H. 1939- CANR-15
Earlier sketch in CA 41-44R
Haver, Ronald D. 1939- 109
Haverkamp-Begemann, Egbert 1923- CANR-11
Earlier sketch in CA 19-20R
Haverstick, John (Mitchell) 1919- 25-28R
Haverstock, Mary Sayre 1932- 81-84
Haverstock, Nathan Alfred 1931- 53-56
Haviaras, Stratis
See Chaviaras, Strates
See also CLC 33
Havighurst, Alfred F(reeman) 1904- 33-36R
Havighurst, Marion Boyd (?)-1974 ..... CAP-1
Obituary 49-52
Earlier sketch in CA 13-14
Havighurst, Robert J(ames) 1900- 23-24R
Havighurst, Walter (Edwin) 1901- CANR-1
Earlier sketch in CA 3R
See also SATA 1
Haviland, Virginia 1911-1988 ..... CANR-12
Obituary 124
Earlier sketch in CA 17-18R
See also SATA 6
Havill, Steven 1945- 108
Havis, Allan 1951- 108
Havlice, Patricia Pate 1943- CANR-12
Earlier sketch in CA 29-32R
Havlik, John F(ranklin) 1917-1984 ..... CANR-24
Earlier sketch in CA 45-48
Havoc, June 1916- 107
Havran, Martin J. 1929- CANR-1
Earlier sketch in CA 2R
Havrevold, Finn 1905- 109
Havrilesky, Thomas M(ichael) 1939- CANR-19
Earlier sketches in CA 53-56, CANR-4
Haw, Richard Claude 1913- CAP-1
Earlier sketch in CA 9-10
Hawes, Evelyn (Johnson) 15-16R
See also AITN 1
Hawes, Frances Cooper (Richmond)
1897- CAP-1
Earlier sketch in CA 9-10
Hawes, Gene R(obert) 1922- CANR-18
Earlier sketches in CA 7-8R, CANR-3
Hawes, Grace M. 1926- 69-72
Hawes, Hampton 1929(?)-1977 Obituary 69-72
Hawes, John T. 1906(?)-1983 Obituary 109
Hawes, Joseph M(ilton) 1938- 53-56
Hawes, Judy 1913- 33-36R
See also SATA 4
Hawes, Louis 1931- 114
Hawes, Lynne Gusikoff Salop 1931- CANR-22
Earlier sketch in CA 106
Hawes, William (Kenneth) 1931- 77-80
Hawgood, John Arkas 1905-1971
Obituary 104
Hawk, Alex
See Garfield, Brian (Wynne)
Hawk, Grace E. 1905-1983 Obituary 110
Hawk, Philip B(ovier) 1874-1966 Obituary 116
Hawke, David Freeman 1923- CANR-18
Earlier sketch in CA 102
Hawke, Gary Richard 1942- 102
Hawke, Nancy
See Nugent, Nancy
Hawke, Simon
See Yermakov, Nicholas
Hawken, William R. 1917- CANR-5
Earlier sketch in CA 9-10R
Hawker, Robert Stephen 1803-1875 ..... DLB-32
Hawkes, (Charles Francis) Christopher
1905- Brief entry 105
Hawkes, Glenn R(ogers) 1919- 17-18R
Hawkes, (Jessie) Jacquetta (Hopkins)
1910- CANR-15
Earlier sketch in CA 69-72
Hawkes, John (Clendennin Burne, Jr.)
1925- CANR-2
Earlier sketch in CA 4R
See also DLB 2, 7
See also DLBY 80
See also CLC 1, 2, 3, 4, 7, 9, 14, 15,
27
Hawkes, Robert E(rnest) 1930- 113
Hawkes, Terence 1932- 17-18R
Hawkesworth, (Elizabeth) Celia 1942- 121
Hawkesworth, Eric 1921- 29-32R
See also SATA 13
Hawkins, A. Desmond
See Hawkins, (Alec) Desmond
Hawkins, Arthur 1903- CANR-8
Earlier sketch in CA 21-22R
See also SATA 19
Hawkins, Brett W(illiam) 1937- CANR-11
Earlier sketch in CA 21-22R
Hawkins, (Alec) Desmond 1908- CANR-9
Earlier sketch in CA 65-68
Hawkins, Edward H. 1934- 85-88
Hawkins, Frances P(ockman) 1913- 105
Hawkins, Gary J(ames) 1937- 115
Hawkins, Gerald S(tanley) 1928- 19-20R
Hawkins, Gordon 1919- 41-44R
Hawkins, Harriett B(loker) 1934-
Brief entry 112
Hawkins, Hugh (Dodge) 1929- 1R
Hawkins, Jack
See Hawkins, John Edward
Hawkins, Jim 1944- 73-76
Hawkins, John C(harles) 1948- 106
Hawkins, John Edward 1910-1973 120
Obituary 111
Hawkins, John Noel 1944- CANR-8
Earlier sketch in CA 61-64
Hawkins, John P. 1946- 120
Hawkins, Odie 1937- 57-60
Hawkins, Peter S(tephen) 1945- 110
Hawkins, (Helena Ann) Quail 1905- 17-18R
See also SATA 6
Hawkins, Robert 1923- CANR-14
Earlier sketch in CA 21-22R
Hawkins, Robert O(usley), Jr. 1938- 117
Hawkins, Walter Everette 1883 ?- DLB-50
Hawkins, William (Waller) 1912- 4R
Hawkinson, John (Samuel) 1912- 23-24R
See also SATA 4
Hawkinson, Lucy (Ozone) 1924-1971 103
See also SATA 21
Hawks, Howard (Winchester) 1896-1977
Obituary 73-76
Hawksworth, Henry D. 1933- 73-76
Hawley, Amos H(enry) 1910- 37-40R
Hawley, Beatrice
See Jagel, Beatrice Hawley
Hawley, Cameron 1905-1969 ..... 1R
Obituary 25-28R
Hawley, Donald Frederick 1921- 108
Hawley, Donald Thomas 1923- CANR-11
Earlier sketch in CA 65-68
Hawley, Ellis W. 1929- CANR-7
Earlier sketch in CA 19-20R
Hawley, Florence M.
See Ellis, Florence Hawley
Hawley, Gessner G. 1906(?)-1983
Obituary 110
Hawley, Henrietta Ripperger 1890(?)-1974
Obituary 49-52
Hawley, Isabel (Allen) L(ockwood)
1935- CANR-7
Earlier sketch in CA 57-60
Hawley, Jane Stouder 1936- 23-24R
Hawley, John Stratton 1941- 110
Hawley, Mabel C. CAP-2
Earlier sketch in CA 19-20
See also SATA 1
Hawley, Richard A. 1945- 123
Hawley, Robert C(oit) 1933- CANR-22
Earlier sketches in CA 57-60, CANR-7
Hawley, Willis D(avid) 1938- 114
Haworth, Lawrence 1926- 5-6R
Haworth, Mary
See Young, Mary Elizabeth Reardon
Haworth-Booth, Mark 1944- 124
Haworth-Booth, Michael 1896- 7-8R
Haws, Duncan 1921- 97-100
Hawthorn, Jeremy 1942- 97-100
Hawthorne, Captain R. M.
See Ellis, Edward S(ylvester)
Hawthorne, (Ivy Ellen) Jennie Crawley
1916- CAP-1
Earlier sketch in CA 9-10
Hawthorne, Julian 1846-1934 ..... TCLC-25
Hawthorne, Nathaniel 1804-1864 ..... YABC-2
See also DLB 1
See also CDALB 1640-1865
Hawton, Hector 1901- 15-16R
Haxton, Josephine Ayres 1921- 115
Hay, David M(cKechnie) 1935- 53-56
Hay, Dennis 1952- 105
Hay, Denys 1915- 13-14R
Hay, Eloise K(napp) 1926- 11-12R
Hay, Jacob 1920- 25-28R
Hay, James G(ordon) 1936- CANR-4
Earlier sketch in CA 53-56
Hay, John (Milton) 1838-1905 Brief entry 108
See also DLB 12, 47
Hay, John 1915- CANR-9
Earlier sketch in CA 65-68
See also SATA 13
Hay, Leon Edwards 25-28R
Hay, Peter 1935- 21-22R
Hay, Robert D(ean) 1921- CANR-8
Earlier sketch in CA 61-64
Hay, Sara Henderson 1906-1987 ..... CAP-1
Obituary 123
Earlier sketch in CA 15-16
Hay, Stephen N(orthup) 1925- 7-8R
Hay, Thomas Robson 1888-1974
Obituary 49-52
Hay, Timothy
See Brown, Margaret Wise
Haya de la Torre, Victor Raul 1895-1979
Obituary 89-92
Hayakawa, S(amuel) I(chiye) 1906- CANR-20
Earlier sketch in CA 15-16R
Hayami, Yujiro 1932- 77-80
Hayano, David M(amoru) 1942- 115
Hayaseca y Eizaguirre, Jorge
See Echegaray (y Eizaguirre), Jose (Maria
Waldo)
Hayashi, Tetsumaro 1929- CANR-14
Earlier sketch in CA 37-40R
Hayashi Fumiko 1904-1951 ..... TCLC-27
Haycock, Ken(neth) Roy 1948- 104
Haycock, Ronald G. 1942- 123
Haycraft, Anna 122
Haycraft, Howard 1905- 23-24R
See also SATA 6
Haycraft, Molly Costain 1911- 15-16R
See also SATA 6
Hayden, Albert A(rthur) 1923- 33-36R
Hayden, C. Gervin
See Wicker, Randolfe Hayden
Hayden, Carl T(rumbull) 1877-1972
Obituary 33-36R
Hayden, Dolores 1945- CANR-9
Earlier sketch in CA 65-68

Hayden, Donald E(ugene) 1915- ... CANR-10
Earlier sketch in CA 25-28R
Hayden, Eric W(illiam) 1919- ... CANR-2
Earlier sketch in CA 5-6R
Hayden, Gwendolen Lampshire 1904- .. SATA-35
Hayden, Howard K. 1930- ... 19-20R
Hayden, Jay
See Paine, Lauran (Bosworth)
Hayden, Jay G. 1884-1971 Obituary ... 89-92
Hayden, John O(lin) 1932- ... CANR-10
Earlier sketch in CA 25-28R
Hayden, Julia Elizabeth 1939(?)-1981
Obituary ... 104
Hayden, Julie
See Hayden, Julia Elizabeth
Hayden, Martin S(choll) 1912- ... 69-72
Hayden, (Holden) Mike 1920-1984 ... 120
Hayden, Naura 1942- ... CANR-12
Earlier sketch in CA 73-76
Hayden, Robert C(arter), Jr. 1937- ... CANR-24
Earlier sketch in CA 69-72
See also SATA 28, 47
Hayden, Robert E(arl) 1913-1980 ... CANR-24
Obituary ... 97-100
Earlier sketch in CA 69-72
See also CABS 2
See also SATA 19, 26
See also DLB 5
See also CDALB 1941-1968
See also CLC 5, 9, 14, 37
Hayden, Sterling 1916-1986 ... 111
Obituary ... 119
Hayden, Stirling
See Hayden, Sterling
Hayden, Thomas E(mmet) 1939- ... 107
Hayden, Tom
See Hayden, Thomas E(mmet)
Hayden, Torey L(ynn) 1951- ... 103
Haydn, Hiram 1907-1973 ... CAP-1
Obituary ... 45-48
Earlier sketch in CA 9-10
Haydn, Richard 1905-1985 Obituary ... 115
Haydon, A(lbert) Eustace 1880-1975
Obituary ... 61-64
Haydon, Glen 1896-1966 ... CAP-1
Earlier sketch in CA 9-10
Haydon, June 1932- ... 109
Haydon, Roger (Malcolm) 1950- ... 118
Hayek, F(riedrich) A(ugust von) 1899- .. CANR-20
Earlier sketch in CA 93-96
Hayes, Alden C(ary) 1916- ... 57-60
Hayes, Alfred 1911-1985 ... 106
Obituary ... 117
Hayes, Ann L(ouise) 1924- ... 25-28R
Hayes, Anna Hansen 1886- ... 3R
Hayes, Bartlett (Harding, Jr.) 1904-1988 .. 77-80
Obituary ... 124
Hayes, Billy ... 97-100
Hayes, Carlton J(oseph) H(untley)
1882-1964 ... CANR-3
Earlier sketch in CA 1R
See also SATA 11
Hayes, Dorsha ... 77-80
Hayes, Douglas A(nderson) 1918- ... CANR-18
Earlier sketch in CA 2R
Hayes, E(ugene) Nelson 1920- ... 29-32R
Hayes, Edward C. 1937- ... 45-48
Hayes, Edward L(ee) 1931- ... 29-32R
Hayes, Elvin 1945- Brief entry ... 111
Hayes, Francis Clement 1904- ... CAP-2
Earlier sketch in CA 21-22
Hayes, Geoffrey 1947- ... CANR-9
Earlier sketch in CA 65-68
See also SATA 26
Hayes, Grace Person 1919- ... 33-36R
Hayes, Harold T(homas) P(ace) 1926- .. CANR-22
Earlier sketch in CA 69-72
Hayes, James T(homas) 1923- ... 29-32R
Hayes, John F. 1904- ... CAP-1
Earlier sketch in CA 13-14
See also SATA 11
Hayes, John H(aralson) 1934- ... CANR-21
Earlier sketch in CA 69-72
Hayes, John Michael 1919- ... 108
See also DLB 26
Hayes, John P(hillip) 1949- ... CANR-15
Earlier sketch in CA 93-96
Hayes, John R(ichard) 1929- ... 108
Hayes, John S. 1910-1981 Obituary ... 108
Hayes, Joseph 1918- ... CANR-7
Earlier sketch in CA 17-18R
Hayes, Louis D. 1940- ... 29-32R
Hayes, Margaret 1925- ... 21-22R
Hayes, Mary Anne 1956- ... 105
Hayes, Mary-Rose 1939- ... 102
Hayes, Nelson (Taylor) 1903-1971 ... 4R
Obituary ... 33-36R
Hayes, Paul J(ames) 1922- ... 57-60
Hayes, Paul Martin 1942- ... 77-80
Hayes, Penny (a pseudonym) 1940- ... 121
Hayes, Ralph E(ugene) 1927- ... CANR-15
Earlier sketch in CA 21-22R
Hayes, Robert M(ayo) 1926- ... 11-12R
Hayes, Samuel P(erkins) 1910- ... CANR-3
Earlier sketch in CA 5-6R
Hayes, Sheila 1937- ... CANR-22
Earlier sketch in CA 106
See also SATA 50
Hayes, Steven C(harles) 1948- ... 112
Hayes, W. Woodrow
See Hayes, Wayne Woodrow
Hayes, Wayland J(ackson) 1893-1972 ... CAP-1
Earlier sketch in CA 13-14
Hayes, Wayne Woodrow 1913-1987
Obituary ... 121
Hayes, Will ... 5-6R
See also SATA 7
Hayes, William D(imitt) 1913- ... 7-8R
See also SATA 8
Hayes, Wilson
See Gibbs-Wilson, Kathryn (Beatrice)
Hayes, Woody
See Hayes, Wayne Woodrow
Hayes, Zachary (Jerome) 1932- ... 115
Hayford, Fred Kwesi 1937- ... 45-48
Hayford, Harrison (Mosher) 1916- ... 118
Hayford, J(oseph) E(phraim) Casely
See Casely-Hayford, J(oseph) E(phraim)
Hayford, Taria
See Haydon, June
Hayley Bell, Mary ... 25-28R
Hayman
See Peel, H(azel) M(ary)
Hayman, Carol Bessent 1927- ... 53-56
Hayman, David 1927- ... CANR-7
Earlier sketch in CA 17-18R
Hayman, John L(uther), Jr. 1929- ... 25-28R
Hayman, LeRoy 1916- ... 85-88
Hayman, Max 1908- ... 19-20R
Hayman, Ronald 1932- ... CANR-18
Earlier sketch in CA 25-28R
See also CLC 44
Haymes, Robert C. 1931- ... 33-36R
Hayn, Annette 1922- ... 65-68
Haynal, Andre (Emeric) 1930- ... 120
Hayne, Paul Hamilton 1830-1886 ... DLB-3, 64
Haynes, Alfred H(enry) 1910- ... 7-8R
Haynes, Anne
See Madlee, Dorothy (Haynes)
Haynes, Betsy 1937- ... CANR-8
Earlier sketch in CA 57-60
See also SATA 37, 48
Haynes, Brian 1939- ... 111
Haynes, Glynn W(alker) 1936- ... 65-68
Haynes, James 1932- ... 110
Haynes, Lincoln 1924- ... 116
Haynes, Linda
See Swinford, Betty (June Wells)
Haynes, Maria S(chnee) 1912- ... 25-28R
Haynes, Mary 1938- ... 111
Haynes, Pat
See McKeag, Ernest L(ionel)
Haynes, Renee (Oriana) 1906- ... 49-52
Haynes, Richard F(rederick) 1935- ... 49-52
Haynes, Robert Talmadge, Jr. 1926- ... 4R
Haynes, Robert Vaughn 1929- ... 41-44R
Haynes, Sybille 1926- ... 57-60
Haynes, William Warren 1921- ... CANR-8
Earlier sketch in CA 5-6R
Haynie, Hugh 1927- ... 121
Haynie, Sandra (B.) 1943- Brief entry ... 121
Hays, (Lawrence) Brooks 1898-1981 ... CAP-1
Obituary ... 105
Earlier sketch in CA 11-12
Hays, David G(lenn) 1928- ... CANR-14
Earlier sketch in CA 21-22R
Hays, Elinor Rice ... 1R
Hays, H(offman) R(eynolds) 1904-1980 ... 81-84
Obituary ... 105
See also SATA 26
Hays, Helen Ireland 1903- ... 61-64
Hays, Paul R. 1903-1980 ... CAP-2
Obituary ... 93-96
Earlier sketch in CA 19-20
Hays, Peter L. 1938- ... 33-36R
Hays, R. Vernon 1902- ... 89-92
Hays, Richard D. 1942- ... 37-40R
Hays, Robert Glenn 1935- ... 53-56
Hays, Samuel Pfrimmer 1921- ... 103
Hays, Terence E(ugene) 1942- ... 69-72
Hays, Wilma Pitchford 1909- ... CANR-5
Earlier sketch in CA 1R
See also SATA 1, 28
See also SAAS 3
Haystead, Wes
See Haystead, Wesley
Haystead, Wesley 1942- ... CANR-22
Earlier sketches in CA 57-60, CANR-6
Hayter, Alethea 1911- ... 29-32R
Hayter, Earl W(iley) 1901- ... 41-44R
Hayter, William Goodenough 1906- ... CANR-9
Earlier sketch in CA 21-22R
Haythornthwaite, Philip John 1951- ... CANR-19
Earlier sketch in CA 103
Hayton, Richard Neil 1916- ... 57-60
Hayward, Brooke 1937- ... 81-84
Hayward, Charles H(arold) 1898- ... CANR-7
Earlier sketch in CA 9-10R
Hayward, Jack 1931- ... CANR-21
Earlier sketches in CA 57-60, CANR-6
Hayward, John F(orrest) 1916-1983 ... 11-12R
Obituary ... 109
Hayward, John F(rank) 1918- ... 5-6R
Hayward, Linda 1943- ... 112
See also SATA 39
Hayward, Max 1925(?)-1979 ... 93-96
Obituary ... 85-88
Hayward, Richard 1893- ... CAP-1
Earlier sketch in CA 9-10
Hayward, Richard
See Kendrick, Baynard H(ardwick)
Haywood, Carolyn 1898- ... CANR-20
Earlier sketches in CA 7-8R, CANR-5
See also SATA 1, 29
Haywood, Charles 1904- ... CANR-22
Earlier sketch in CA 3R
Haywood, Dixie 1933- ... 105
Haywood, Eliza 1693(?)-1756 ... DLB-39
Haywood, H(erbert) Carl(ton) 1931- ... CANR-3
Earlier sketch in CA 49-52
Haywood, Harry
See Hall, Haywood
Haywood, John Alfred 1913- ... 19-20R
Haywood, Richard Mansfield 1905-1977 .. CAP-2
Obituary ... 69-72
Earlier sketch in CA 33-36
Haywood, Richard Mowbray 1933- ... 25-28R
Hazam, Louis J. 1911-1983 Obituary ... 110
Hazan, Marcella (Maddalena) 1924-
Brief entry ... 116
Hazan, Victor 1928- ... 114
Hazard, David 1955- ... 116
Hazard, Harry W(illiams) 1918- ... 122
Hazard, Jack
See Booth, Edwin
Hazard, John N(ewbold) 1909- ... 1R
Hazard, Leland 1893- ... 17-18R
Hazard, Patrick D. 1927- ... 13-14R
Hazel, Paul 1944- ... 114
Hazelrigg, Meredith K(ent) 1942- ... 33-36R
Hazelton, Alexander
See Armstrong, William A(lexander)
Hazelton, Roger 1909- ... CANR-16
Earlier sketches in CA 4R, CANR-1
Hazen, Allen T(racy) 1904- ... CAP-1
Earlier sketch in CA 13-14
Hazen, Barbara Shook 1930- ... CANR-22
Earlier sketch in CA 105
See also SATA 27
Hazen, Helen 1943- ... 116
Hazen, Robert M(iller) 1948- ... 112
Hazlehurst, Cameron 1941- ... 103
Hazlett, Bill
See Hazlett, William Scott
Hazlett, William Scott 1931-1983 Obituary .. 110
Hazlitt, Henry 1894- ... CANR-3
Earlier sketch in CA 5-6R
Hazlitt, Joseph
See Strage, Mark
Hazo, Robert G. 1931- ... 23-24R
Hazo, Samuel (John) 1928- ... CANR-8
Earlier sketch in CA 7-8R
Hazzard, Lowell B(restel) 1898-1978
Obituary ... 77-80
Hazzard, Mary 1928- ... 105
Hazzard, Shirley 1931- ... CANR-4
Earlier sketch in CA 9-10R
See also DLBY 82
See also CLC 18
Heacox, Cecil E. 1903- ... 101
Head, Alice Maud 1886-1981 Obituary ... 116
Head, Ann
See Morse, Anne Christensen
Head, Bessie 1937-1986 ... 29-32R
Obituary ... 119
See also CLC 25
Head, Constance 1939- ... 37-40R
Head, Edith 1898(?)-1981 Obituary ... 105
Head, Gay
See Hauser, Margaret L(ouise)
Head, Gwen 1940- ... 89-92
Head, K(enneth) Maynard 1938- ... 110
Head, (Joanne) Lee 1931-1983 ... 65-68
Obituary ... 110
Head, Matthew
See Canaday, John E(dwin)
Head, Richard G(lenn) 1938- ... 53-56
Head, Robert V. 1929- ... CANR-15
Earlier sketch in CA 41-44R
Head, Sydney W(arren) 1913- ... CANR-9
Earlier sketch in CA 65-68
Head, Timothy E. 1934- ... 15-16R
Headapohl, B. R.
See Headapohl, Betty R.
Headapohl, Betty R. 1940- ... 122
Headings, Mildred J. 1908- ... 37-40R
Headington, Bonnie Jay 1940- ... 114
Headington, Christopher John Magenis
1930- Brief entry ... 106
Headley, Elizabeth
See Cavanna, Betty
Headley, Joel T. 1813-1897 ... DLB-30
Headon, (Nicky) Topper 1956(?)- ... CLC-30
Headstrom, (Birger) Richard 1902- ... CANR-13
Earlier sketches in CA 4R, CANR-2
See also SATA 8
Heady, Earl O(rel) 1916- ... CANR-8
Earlier sketch in CA 19-20R
Heady, Eleanor B(utler) 1917- ... 41-44R
See also SATA 8
Heady, Harold F(ranklin) 1916- ... 53-56
Heagney, Anne 1901- ... 7-8R
Heal, Edith 1903- ... CANR-2
Earlier sketch in CA 4R
See also SATA 7
Heal, Jeanne (Bennett) 1917- ... CAP-1
Earlier sketch in CA 9-10
Heald, Charles Brehmer 1882-1974
Obituary ... 49-52
Heald, Edward Thornton 1885- ... 17-18R
Heald, Morrell 1922- Brief entry ... 111
Heald, Timothy (Villiers) 1944- ... CANR-2
Earlier sketch in CA 49-52
Healey, B. J.
See Healey, Ben (James)
Healey, Ben (James) 1908- ... CANR-17
Earlier sketch in CA 77-80
Healey, Brooks
See Albert, Burton, Jr.
Healey, Denis Winston 1917- ... 110
Healey, F(rancis) G(eorge) 1903- ... CAP-2
Earlier sketch in CA 21-22
Healey, James 1936- ... 53-56
Healey, James Stewart 1931- ... 57-60
Healey, Joseph G(raham) 1938- ... 116
Healey, Larry 1927- ... 101
See also SATA 42, 44
Healey, Robert (Mathieu) 1921- ... 61-64
Healey-Kay, (Sydney Francis) Patrick
(Chippendall) 1904-1983 Obituary ... 111
Healy, David F(rank) 1926- ... 19-20R
Healy, Dermot 1947- ... 114
Healy, Fleming 1911- ... 7-8R
Healy, George Robert 1923- ... 19-20R
Healy, George W(illiam), Jr. 1905- ... 69-72
Healy, John D(elaware) 1921- ... 93-96
Healy, Kent T(enney) 1902-1985 Obituary .. 114
Healy, Patrick III 1910- Brief entry ... 110
Healy, Paul F(rancis) 1915-1984 ... 17-18R
Obituary ... 114
Healy, Richard J. 1916- ... 25-28R
Healy, Sean D(esmond) 1927- ... CANR-11
Earlier sketch in CA 25-28R
Healy, Sister Kathleen ... 61-64
Healy, Timothy S. 1923- ... 41-44R
Heaney, John J. 1925- ... CANR-5
Earlier sketch in CA 9-10R
Heaney, Seamus (Justin) 1939- ... 85-88
See also DLB 40
See also CLC 5, 7, 14, 25, 37
Heap, Desmond 1907- ... CANR-15
Earlier sketches in CA 9-10, CAP-1
Heaps, Willard A(llison) 1908- ... 85-88
See also SATA 26
Heard, (George) Alexander 1917- ... 17-18R
Heard, (Henry Fitz) Gerald 1889-1971 ... CAP-2
Obituary ... 29-32R
Earlier sketch in CA 21-22
Heard, H. F.
See Heard, (Henry Fitz) Gerald
Heard, J(oseph) Norman 1922- ... 11-12R
Heard, Nathan C(liff) 1936- ... 53-56
See also DLB 33
Hearder, Harry 1924- ... 5-6R
Hearn, Charles R(alph) 1937- ... 77-80
Hearn, Janice W. 1938- ... 65-68
Hearn, John 1920- ... 97-100
Hearn, (Patricio) Lafcadio (Tessima Carlos)
1850-1904 Brief entry ... 105
See also DLB 12
See also TCLC 9
Hearn, M(illard) F(illmore, Jr.) 1938- ... 115
Hearn, Sneed
See Gregg, Andrew K.
Hearnden, Arthur (George) 1931- ... 65-68
Hearne, Betsy Gould 1942- ... 114
See also SATA 38
Hearne, John (Edgar Caulwell) 1926-
Brief entry ... 116
Hearnshaw, Leslie Spencer 1907- ... 89-92
Hearon, Shelby 1931- ... CANR-18
Earlier sketch in CA 25-28R
See also AITN 2
Hearsey, John E(dward) N(icholl)
1928- ... CANR-8
Earlier sketch in CA 7-8R
Hearst, David Whitmire 1915-1986
Obituary ... 119
Hearst, George Randolph 1904-1972
Obituary ... 89-92
Hearst, James 1900-1983 ... CANR-15
Earlier sketch in CA 85-88
Hearst, William Randolph 1863-1951
Brief entry ... 118
See also DLB 25
Heartman, Harold
See Mebane, John (Harrison)
Heasman, Kathleen Joan 1913- ... CAP-1
Earlier sketch in CA 9-10
Heater, Derek (Benjamin) 1931- ... CANR-6
Earlier sketch in CA 57-60
Heath, Catherine 1924- ... 93-96
See also DLB 14
Heath, Charles C(hastain) 1921- ... 69-72
Heath, Charles D(ickinson) 1941- ... 121
See also SATA 46
Heath, Douglas H(amilton) 1925- ... 17-18R
Heath, Dwight B(raley) 1930- ... CANR-7
Earlier sketch in CA 17-18R
Heath, Edward Richard George 1916- ... 33-36R
Heath, G. Louis 1944- ... 37-40R
Heath, Harry E(ugene), Jr. 1919- ... 85-88
Heath, (Ernest) James 1920- ... 17-18R
Heath, Jim F(rank) 1931- ... 29-32R
Heath, Mary Ellen 1928- ... 115
Heath, Monica
See Fitzgerald, Arlene J.
Heath, (Charles) Monro 1899-1966 ... CAP-1
Earlier sketch in CA 9-10
Heath, Peter (Lauchlan) 1922- ... 41-44R
Heath, Robert W. 1931- ... 13-14R
Heath, Roy 1917- ... 11-12R
Heath, Roy A(ubrey) K(elvin) 1926- ... 106
Heath, Royton E(dward) 1907- ... 9-10R
Heath, Sandra
See Wilson, Sandra
Heath, Terrence (George) 1936- ... 97-100
Heath, Veronica
See Blackett, Veronica Heath
Heath, William (Webster) 1929- ... 2R
Heathcott, Mary
See Keegan, Mary Heathcott
Heath-Stubbs, John (Francis Alexander)
1918- ... 13-14R
See also DLB 27
Heat-Moon, William Least
See Trogdon, William (Lewis)
See also CLC 29
Heaton, Charles Huddleston 1928- ... CANR-20
Earlier sketch in CA 2R
Heaton, Eric William 1920- ... 61-64
Heaton, Herbert 1890-1973 ... 7-8R
Obituary ... 41-44R
Heaton, Peter 1919- ... 104
Heaton, Rose Henniker 1884-1975
Obituary ... 61-64
Heaton-Ward, William Alan 1919- ... 102

Heatter, Gabriel 1890-1972 Obituary 89-92
Heaven, Constance 1911- CANR-18
Earlier sketches in CA 49-52, CANR-2
See also SATA 7
Hebard, Edna L(aura Henriksen) 1913- 9-10R
Hebb, D(onald) O(lding) 1904-1985 ...... CANR-2
Obituary 118
Earlier sketch in CA 2R
Hebblethwaite, Brian Leslie 1939- 109
Hebblethwaite, Peter 1930- 69-72
Hebden, Mark
See Harris, John
Hebert, Anne 1916- 85-88
See also CLC 4, 13, 29
Hebert, Ernest 1941- 102
Hebert, F(elix) Edward 1901-1979 110
Obituary 106
Hebert, (Arthur) Gabriel 1886-1963 ...... 3R
Hebert, Jacques 1923- CANR-11
Earlier sketch in CA 25-28R
See also DLB 53
Hebert, Tom 1938- 69-72
Hebson, Ann (Hellebusch) 1925- 19-20R
Hechinger, Fred M(ichael) 1920- 77-80
Hechler, Ken 1914- 109
Hecht, Anthony (Evan) 1923- CANR-6
Earlier sketch in CA 11-12R
See also DLB 5
See also CLC 8, 13, 19
Hecht, Ben 1894-1964 85-88
See also DLB 7, 9, 25, 26, 28
See also CLC 8
Hecht, George J(oseph) 1895-1980
Obituary 97-100
See also SATA 22
Hecht, Henri Joseph 1922- 29-32R
See also SATA 9
Hecht, James L(ee) 1926- 33-36R
Hecht, Joseph C. 1924- 29-32R
Hecht, Marie B(ergenfeld) 1918- 21-22R
Hecht, Robert A(nthony) 1929- 114
Hecht, Roger 1926- 17-18R
Hecht, Warren Jay 1946- 103
Hechter, Michael 1943- 69-72
Hechtkopf, Henryk 1910- SATA-17
Hechtlinger, Adelaide 1914- 29-32R
Heck, Bessie Holland 1911- 7-8R
See also SATA 26
Heck, Frank H(opkins) 1904- 69-72
Heck, Harold J(oseph) 1906- 41-44R
Heck, Peter M. 1937- 53-56
Heck, Suzanne Wright 1939- 53-56
Heckart, Barbara Hooper 1937- 118
Heckart, Beverly Anne 1938- 103
Heckel, Robert V. 1925- 11-12R
Heckelmann, Charles N(ewman) 1913- 49-52
Hecker, Isaac Thomas 1819-1888 ...... DLB-1
Heckert, J(osiah) Brooks 1893- 7-8R
Heckler, Jonellen (Beth) 1943- 109
Heckman, Hazel 1904- 21-22R
Heckman, William O(scar) 1921- 21-22R
Heckmann, Wolf 1929- 114
Heckscher, August 1913- 3R
Hedayat, Sadeq 1903-1951 Brief entry 120
See also TCLC 21
Hedberg, Nancy 1944- 122
Hedde, Wilhelmina G(enevava) 1895- 7-8R
Hedden, Walter Page 1898(?)-1976
Obituary 65-68
Hedden, Worth Tuttle 1896-1985 ...... CAP-2
Obituary 117
Earlier sketch in CA 21-22
Hedderwick, Mairi 1939- SATA-30
Hederman, Thomas M(artin), Jr.
1911-1985 Obituary 114
Hedge, Frederic Henry 1805-1890 ...... DLB-1, 59
Hedge, Leslie (Joseph) 1922- 11-12R
Hedgeman, Anna Arnold 1899- CAP-1
Earlier sketch in CA 15-16
Hedges, Bob A(tkinson) 1919- 45-48
Hedges, David (Paget) 1930- 45-48
Hedges, Elaine R(yan) 1927- CANR-7
Earlier sketch in CA 57-60
Hedges, Inez (Kathleen) 1947- 116
Hedges, Joseph
See Harknett, Terry
Hedges, Sid(ney) G(eorge) 1897-1974 ...... CANR-4
Earlier sketch in CA 11-12R
See also SATA 28
Hedges, Trimble R(aymond) 1906- CAP-2
Earlier sketch in CA 21-22
Hedges, Ursula M. 1940- 29-32R
Hedges, William L(eonard) 1923- 37-40R
Hedin, Mary 103
Hedley, George (Percy) 1899- CAP-2
Earlier sketch in CA 19-20
Hedley, (Gladys) Olwen 1912- CANR-9
Earlier sketch in CA 61-64
Hedlund, Ronald D(avid) 1941- 33-36R
Hedren, Paul L(eslie) 1949- 114
Hedrick, Addie M. 1903- CAP-2
Earlier sketch in CA 25-28
Hedrick, Basil C(alvin) 1932- CANR-21
Earlier sketch in CA 33-36R
Hedrick, Floyd D(udley) 1927- 33-36R
Hedrick, Joan Doran 1944- 107
Hedrick, Travis K. 1904(?)-1977
Obituary 69-72
Heeney, Brian 1933- 89-92
Heer, David MacAlpine 1930- 15-16R
Heer, John E(dward), Jr. 1921-19(?)
Obituary 113
Heer, Nancy Whittier 33-36R
Heeresma, Heere 1932- 25-28R
Heeresma Inc.
See Heeresma, Heere
Heermance, J. Noel 1939- 25-28R
Heerwagen, Paul K. 1895- 29-32R
Heezen, Bruce C(harles) 1924-1977 49-52
Obituary 69-72
Heffer, Eric S(amuel) 1922- 123
Heffern, Richard 1950- 61-64
Heffernan, James A(nthony) W(alsh)
1939- 25-28R
Heffernan, Michael 1942- CANR-18
Earlier sketch in CA 77-80
Heffernan, Patrick
See O'Heffernan, Patrick
Heffernan, Paul 1905(?)-1983 Obituary 110
Heffernan, Thomas (Patrick Carroll)
1939- 81-84
Heffernan, Thomas Farel 1933- 107
Heffernan, William A. 1937- 25-28R
Heffley, Wayne 1927- 11-12R
Heffner, Richard D(ouglas) 1925- 69-72
Heffron, Dorris 1944- 49-52
Hefley, James C(arl) 1930- CANR-7
Earlier sketch in CA 13-14R
Heflin, Donald
See Wallmann, Jeffrey M(iner)
Hefner, Hugh (Marston) 1926- Brief entry 110
See also AITN 1
Hefner, Paul
See Tabori, Paul
Hefner, Robert W(illiam) 1952- 119
Hefter, Richard 1942- CANR-23
Earlier sketch in CA 107
See also SATA 31
Hegarty, Edward J. 1891- CANR-5
Earlier sketch in CA 2R
Hegarty, Ellen 1918- 37-40R
Hegarty, Reginald Beaton 1906-1973 ...... CAP-1
Obituary 41-44R
Earlier sketch in CA 15-16
See also SATA 10
Hegarty, Sister M(ary) Loyola
See Hegarty, Ellen
Hegarty, Walter 1922- 65-68
Hegel, Richard 1927- CANR-6
Earlier sketch in CA 57-60
Hegel, Robert Earl 1943- 108
Hegeler, Sten 1923- 107
Hegeman, Elizabeth Blair 1942- 61-64
Heger, Theodore Ernest 1907- 33-36R
Hegesippus
See Schonfield, Hugh J(oseph)
Heggoy, Alf Andrew 1938- CANR-14
Earlier sketch in CA 37-40R
Hegi, Ursula 1946- 104
Heginbotham, Stanley J. 1938-
Brief entry 106
Heglar, Mary Schnall 1934- 49-52
Hegner, William 1928- 93-96
Hegre, Theodore A. 1908-1984 Obituary 115
Hegstad, Roland R(ex) 1926- 57-60
Heiber, Helmut 1924- 49-52
Heiby, Walter A(lbert) 1918- 21-22R
Heichberger, Robert Lee 1930- 53-56
Heichelheim, Fritz M(oritz) 1901-1968
Obituary 116
Heicher, Merlo K. W. 1882-1967 ...... CAP-1
Earlier sketch in CA 13-14
Heidbreder, Margaret Ann
See Eastman, Ann Heidbreder
Heide, Florence Parry 1919- CANR-19
Earlier sketch in CA 93-96
See also SATA 32
Heide, Robert 1939- CANR-20
Earlier sketch in CA 103
Heidegger, Martin 1889-1976 81-84
Obituary 65-68
See also CLC 24
Heideman, Eugene P. 1929- 69-72
Heiden, Carol A. 1939- 57-60
Heiden, Konrad 1901-1966 Obituary 116
Heidenreich, Charles A(lbert) 1917- 25-28R
Heidenstam, (Carl Gustaf) Verner von
1859-1940 Brief entry 104
See also TCLC 5
Heiderstadt, Dorothy 1907- CANR-1
Earlier sketch in CA 4R
See also SATA 6
Heidi, Gloria 69-72
Heidingsfield, Myron S. 1914-1969 ...... 4R
Obituary 103
Heidish, Marcy Moran 1947- 101
See also DLBY 82
Heiferman, Ronald Ian 1941- 61-64
Heifetz, Harold 1919- CANR-10
Earlier sketch in CA 25-28R
Heifetz, Milton D. 1921- 57-60
Heifner, Jack 1946- 105
See also CLC 11
Heiges, P. Myers 1887-1968 ...... CAP-1
Earlier sketch in CA 15-16
Heijermans, Herman 1864-1924
Brief entry 123
See also TCLC 24
Heijke, John 1927- 21-22R
Heikal, Muhammed Hassanein 1923-
Brief entry 112
Heil, John 112
Heil, Ruth 1947- 112
Heilbron, J(ohn) L(ewis) 1934- CANR-19
Earlier sketches in CA 53-56, CANR-4
Heilbroner, Joan Knapp 1922- 2R
Heilbroner, Robert L(ouis) 1919- CANR-21
Earlier sketches in CA 1R, CANR-4
Heilbronner, Walter L(eo) 1924- 25-28R
Heilbrun, Carolyn G(old) 1926- CANR-1
Earlier sketch in CA 45-48
See also CLC 25
Heilbrun, Lois Hussey 1922(?)-1987
Obituary 123
Heilbrunn, Otto 1906-1969 ...... CAP-1
Earlier sketch in CA 15-16
Heilig, Matthias R. 1881-? CAP-2
Earlier sketch in CA 23-24
Heiliger, Edward Martin 1909- 13-14R
Heilman, Arthur (William) 1914- CANR-5
Earlier sketch in CA 5-6R
Heilman, Grant 1919- 53-56
Heilman, Joan Rattner CANR-21
Earlier sketches in CA 57-60, CANR-6
See also SATA 50
Heilman, Robert Bechtold 1906- CANR-9
Earlier sketch in CA 15-16R
Heilman, Samuel C(hiel) 1946- 69-72
Heilner, Van Campen 1899-1970
Obituary 29-32R
Heim, Alice (Winifred) 1913- CANR-14
Earlier sketch in CA 33-36R
Heim, Bruno Bernard 1911- 89-92
Heim, Kathleen M(cEntee) 1948- 111
Heim, Ralph Daniel 1895- 73-76
Heiman, Ernest J(ean) 1930- CANR-4
Earlier sketch in CA 53-56
Heiman, Grover G(eorge, Jr.) 1920- CANR-6
Earlier sketch in CA 5-6R
Heiman, Judith 1935- 3R
Heiman, Marcel 1909-1976 Obituary 65-68
Heimann, Susan 1940- 33-36R
Heimarck, Theodore 1906- 7-8R
Heimbeck, Raeburne S(eeley) 1930- 29-32R
Heimberg, Marilyn Markham
See Ross, Marilyn (Ann) Heimberg
Heimdahl, Ralph 1909- 69-72
Heimer, Mel(vin Lytton) 1915-1971 ...... CANR-4
Obituary 29-32R
Earlier sketch in CA 2R
Heimert, Alan (Edward) 1928- 7-8R
Heimler, Eugene 1922- CANR-8
Earlier sketch in CA 13-14R
Heimlich, Henry Jay 1920- 102
Heimsath, Charles H. 1928- 19-20R
Hein, Eleanor C(harlotte) 1933- 61-64
Hein, John 1921- CANR-16
Earlier sketches in CA 45-48, CANR-1
Hein, Leonard William 1916- 53-56
Hein, Lucille Eleanor 1915- CANR-2
Earlier sketch in CA 7-8R
See also SATA 20
Hein, Norvin 1914- 61-64
Hein, Piet 1905- CANR-4
Earlier sketch in CA 49-52
Hein, Rolland Neal 1932- 112
Heinberg, Paul (Julius) 1924- CANR-23
Earlier sketch in CA 45-48
Heindel, Richard Heathcote 1912-1979
Obituary 89-92
Heine, Carl 1936- 57-60
Heine, Lala Koehn
See Koehn-Heine, Lala
Heine, Ralph W(illiam) 1914- 41-44R
Heine, William C(olbourne) 1919- 97-100
Heineman, Benjamin Walter, Jr. 1944- 105
Heinemann, George Alfred 1918- SATA-31
Heinemann, Katherine 1918- 77-80
Heinemann, Larry C(urtiss) 1944- 110
Heinemann, Ronald L(ynton) 1939- 112
Heinen, Hubert (Plummer) 1937- 41-44R
Heiney, Donald (William) 1921- CANR-3
Earlier sketch in CA 3R
See also CLC 9
Heinke, Clarence H. 1912- 53-56
Heinl, Nancy G(ordon) 1916- 81-84
Heinl, Robert Debs, Jr. 1916-1979 ...... CANR-4
Obituary 85-88
Earlier sketch in CA 7-8R
Heinlein, Robert A(nson) 1907- CANR-20
Earlier sketches in CA 2R, CANR-1
See also SATA 9
See also DLB 8
See also CLC 1, 3, 8, 14, 26
Heinrich, Bernd 1940- 109
Heinrich, Willi 1920- CANR-15
Earlier sketch in CA 93-96
Heinrichs, Waldo H(untley), Jr. 1925- 122
Heins, A(rthur) James 1931- 7-8R
Heins, Ethel L(eah) 1918- 102
Heins, Marjorie 1946- 69-72
Heins, Paul 1909- 69-72
See also SATA 13
Heinsohn, A(ugereau) G(ray), Jr. 1896- CAP-1
Earlier sketch in CA 11-12
Heinsohn, Thomas William 1934-
Brief entry 118
Heinsohn, Tommy
See Heinsohn, Thomas William
Heintz, Ann Christine 1930- CANR-8
Earlier sketch in CA 61-64
Heintz, Bonnie L(ee) 1924- 69-72
Heintz, John 1936- 45-48
Heintze, Carl 1922- 57-60
See also SATA 26
Heintzelman, Donald S(haffer) 1938- CANR-16
Earlier sketch in CA 93-96
Heinz, G.
See Gerard-Libois, Jules C.
Heinz, W(ilfred) C(harles) 1915- CANR-4
Earlier sketch in CA 5-6R
See also SATA 26
Heinz, William Frederick 1899-1976 ...... CANR-12
Earlier sketch in CA 61-64
Heinze, Robert H(arold) 1920-1984
Obituary 113
Heinzelman, Kurt 1947- 101
Heinzen, Mildred
See Masters, Mildred
Heinzerling, Larry E(dward) 1945- 73-76
Heinzerling, Lynn Louis 1906-1983
Obituary 111
Heinzman(n), George (Melville) 1916- 2R
Heirich, Max 1931- 29-32R
Heise, David R(euben) 1937- 89-92
Heise, Edward Tyler 1912- 1R
Heise, Kenan 1933- 57-60
Heisenberg, Werner 1901-1976 Obituary 65-68
Heiser, Charles B(ixler), Jr. 1920- 45-48
Heiser, Victor George 1893-1972
Obituary 33-36R
Heiserman, Arthur Ray 1929-1975 ...... CANR-15
Obituary 103
Earlier sketch in CA 1R
Heiserman, David L(ee) 1940- CANR-8
Earlier sketch in CA 61-64
Heisey, Alan Milliken 1928- 57-60
Heiskell, John Netherland 1872-1972
Obituary 89-92
Heisler, Martin O. 1938- CANR-23
Earlier sketch in CA 45-48
Heiss, Jerold (Sheldon) 1930- Brief entry 111
Heissenbuettel, Helmut 1921- 81-84
Heisserer, Andrew Jackson 1935- 111
Heitler, Walter (Heinrich) 1904-1981 ...... CANR-8
Earlier sketch in CA 13-14R
Heitman, Sidney 1924- 11-12R
Heitner, Robert R. 1920- 5-6R
Heitzmann, William Ray 1948- CANR-17
Earlier sketch in CA 97-100
Heizer, Robert Fleming 1915-1979 102
Hekker, Terry 1932- 97-100
Hekman, Susan J(ean) 1949- 114
Helbig, Althea K. 1928- CANR-17
Earlier sketch in CA 97-100
Helbing, Terry 1951- 89-92
Helbling, Robert E(ugene) 1923- 49-52
Helck, C. Peter 1893- CANR-1
Earlier sketch in CA 3R
Held, David 1951- 110
Held, Jack Preston 1926- 33-36R
Held, Jacqueline 1936- CANR-14
Earlier sketch in CA 73-76
Held, Joseph 1930- 45-48
Held, Julius Samuel 1905- 103
Held, Peter
See Vance, John Holbrook
Held, R(over) Burnell 1921- 33-36R
Held, Ray E(ldred) 1918- 45-48
Held, Richard 1922- 41-44R
Held, Virginia (Potter) 1929- CANR-16
Earlier sketches in CA 1R, CANR-1
Helder, Dom
See Camara, Helder Pessoa
Heldman, Dan C(hristopher) 1943- 110
Heldman, Gladys M(edalie) 1922-
Brief entry 111
Heleniak, Kathryn Moore 110
Helfen, Otto J. Maenchen
See Maenchen, Otto John
Helfert, Erich A(nton) 1931- 9-10R
Helfgott, Daniel (Andrew) 1952- CANR-22
Earlier sketch in CA 106
Helfgott, Roy B. 1925- 81-84
Helfman, Elizabeth S(eaver) 1911- CANR-5
Earlier sketch in CA 5-6R
See also SATA 3
Helfman, Harry 1910- 25-28R
See also SATA 3
Helforth, John
See Doolittle, Hilda
Helfritz, Hans 1902- 41-44R
Helgerson, Richard 1940- 116
Helgesen, Sally 1948- 115
Helion, Jean 1904-1987 Obituary 124
Helitzer, Florence (Saperstein) 1928- 19-20R
Hellberg, Hans-Eric 1927- CANR-18
Earlier sketch in CA 101
See also SATA 38
Hellegers, Andre E. 1926-1979 Obituary 85-88
Hellen, J(ohn) A(nthony) 1935- 61-64
Hellenhofferu, Vojtech Kapristian z
See Hasek, Jaroslav (Matej Frantisek)
Heller
See Iranek-Osmecki, Kazimierz
Heller, Abraham M. 1898-1975 Obituary 57-60
Heller, Bernard 1896-1976 Obituary 65-68
Heller, Celia S(topnicka) 37-40R
Heller, David (A.) 1922-1968 ...... CAP-1
Earlier sketch in CA 9-10
Heller, David 1957- 124
Heller, Deane Fons 1924- 9-10R
Heller, Erich 1911- CANR-8
Earlier sketch in CA 13-14R
Heller, Francis H(oward) 1917- 1R
Heller, H(einz) Robert 1940- CANR-22
Earlier sketch in CA 69-72
Heller, Herbert L. 1908- 21-22R
Heller, Jean 1942- 73-76
Heller, John 1896(?)-1987 Obituary 124
Heller, John H(erbert) 1921- 114
Heller, Joseph 1923- CANR-8
Earlier sketch in CA 7-8R
See also CABS 1
See also DLB 2, 28
See also DLBY 80
See also CLC 1, 3, 5, 8, 11, 36
See also AITN 1
Heller, Keith 1949- 119
Heller, Linda 1944- 108
See also SATA 40, 46
Heller, Mark (Francis) 1914- CANR-10
Earlier sketch in CA 61-64
Heller, Michael 1937- 45-48
Heller, Mike
See Hano, Arnold

Heller, Peter 1920- ... CANR-14
Earlier sketch in CA 41-44R
Heller, Rachelle S(ara) 1943- ... 111
Heller, Reinhold (August Friedrich) 1940- ... 77-80
Heller, Robert 1899(?)-1973 Obituary ... 41-44R
Heller, Robert W(illiam) 1933- ... 25-28R
Heller, Shelly
See Heller, Rachelle S(ara)
Heller, Sipa 1897(?)-1980 Obituary ... 97-100
Heller, Trudy (Marie) 1944- ... 115
Heller, Walter W(olfgang) 1915-1987 ... 21-22R
Obituary ... 122
Heller, Wilson Battin 1893-1983 Obituary ... 110
Hellerman, Herbert 1927- ... 53-56
Hellerstein, David (Joel) 1953- ... 120
Hellerstein, Jerome R. 1907- ... CAP-1
Earlier sketch in CA 13-14
Hellerstein, Kathryn (Ann) 1952- ... 114
Hellie, Ann 1925- ... CANR-15
Earlier sketch in CA 77-80
Hellie, Richard 1937- ... CANR-14
Earlier sketch in CA 33-36R
Hellinga, Wytze (Gs) 1908-1985 Obituary ... 116
Hellinger, Douglas A(lan) 1948- ... CANR-21
Earlier sketch in CA 69-72
Hellinger, Stephen H(enry) 1948- ... CANR-21
Earlier sketch in CA 69-72
Hellison, Donald R(aymond) 1938- ... 53-56
Hellman, Anna 1902(?)-1972 Obituary ... 33-36R
Hellman, Arthur D(avid) 1942- ... 69-72
Hellman, C(larisse) Doris 1910-1973
Obituary ... 41-44R
Hellman, Geoffrey T(heodore) 1907-1977 ... 69-72
Obituary ... 73-76
Hellman, Hal
See Hellman, Harold
Hellman, Harold 1927- ... CANR-10
Earlier sketch in CA 25-28R
See also SATA 4
Hellman, Hugo E. 1908- ... CAP-2
Earlier sketch in CA 19-20
Hellman, Judith Adler 1945- ... 113
Hellman, Lillian (Florence) 1905-1984 ... 13-14R
Obituary ... 112
See also DLB 7
See also DLBY 84
See also CLC 2, 4, 8, 14, 18, 34, 44
See also AITN 1, 2
Hellman, Peter 1943- ... 107
Hellman, Robert 1919-1984 ... 17-18R
Obituary ... 113
Hellmann, Donald C(harles) 1933- ... 45-48
Hellmann, Ellen 1908- ... 106
Hellmann, John 1948- ... CANR-24
Earlier sketch in CA 105
Hellmuth, Jerome 1911- ... 15-16R
Hellmuth, William Frederick, Jr. 1920- ... CANR-4
Earlier sketch in CA 2R
Hellstrom, Ward 1930- ... 33-36R
Hellwig, Monika Konrad 1929- ... 37-40R
Helly, Dorothy O. 1931- ... 122
Hellyer, A(rthur) G(eorge) L(ee) 1902- ... CANR-19
Earlier sketches in CA 9-10R, CANR-4
Hellyer, Arthur
See Hellyer, A(rthur) G(eorge) L(ee)
Hellyer, Clement David 1914- ... 118
Hellyer, David Tirrell 1913- ... 17-18R
Hellyer, Jill 1925- ... 118
Hellyer, Paul (Theodore) 1923- ... CANR-14
Earlier sketch in CA 69-72
Helm, Bertrand P. 1929- ... 37-40R
Helm, Ernest Eugene 1928- ... CANR-2
Earlier sketch in CA 1R
Helm, Everett 1913- ... 49-52
Helm, P(eter) J(ames) 1916- ... CANR-3
Earlier sketch in CA 9-10R
Helm, Robert Meredith 1917- ... 17-18R
Helm, Thomas (William) 1919- ... 7-8R
Helmer, John 1946- ... 41-44R
Helmer, William F. 1926- ... 33-36R
Helmer, William J(oseph) 1936- ... 73-76
Helmericks, Bud
See Helmericks, Harmon R.
Helmericks, Constance (Chittenden)
1918-1987 ... 9-10R
Obituary ... 122
Helmericks, Harmon R. 1917- ... 29-32R
Helmering, Doris Wild 1942- ... 65-68
Helmers, George Dow 1906- ... 61-64
Helmholz, R(ichard) H(enry) 1940- ... 61-64
Helmi, Jack
See Sands, Leo G(eorge)
Helming, Ann 1924-19(?) ... CANR-2
Earlier sketch in CA 4R
Helmker, Judith Anne 1940- ... 33-36R
Helmlinger, (Benita) Trudy 1943- ... 69-72
Helmore, G(eoffrey) A(nthony) 1922- ... 29-32R
Helm-Pirgo, Marian 1897- ... 77-80
Helmreich, Ernst Christian 1902- ... 1R
Helmreich, Jonathan Ernst 1936-
Brief entry ... 105
Helmreich, Paul C(hristian) 1933- ... 53-56
Helmreich, Robert Louis 1937- ... 65-68
Helmreich, William B. 1945- ... 105
Helms, Jesse (Alexander, Jr.) 1921-
Brief entry ... 124
Helms, Randel 1942- ... 49-52
Helms, Roland Thomas, Jr. 1940- ... 102
Helms, Tom
See Helms, Roland Thomas, Jr.
Helmstadter, Gerald C. 1925- ... 15-16R
Heloise
See Reese, Heloise (Bowles)
Helper, Rose ... 77-80
Helpern, Milton 1902-1977 ... 73-76
Obituary ... 69-72
Helprin, Mark 1947- ... 81-84
See also DLBY 85
See also CLC 7, 10, 22, 32
Helps, Racey 1913-1971 ... CAP-2
Obituary ... 29-32R
Earlier sketch in CA 23-24
See also SATA 2, 25
Helson, Harry 1898- ... CAP-1
Earlier sketch in CA 11-12
Helterman, Jeffrey A. 1942- ... 103
Helton, David (Kirby) 1940- ... 25-28R
Helton, Tinsley 1915- ... 1R
Helvick, James
See Cockburn, (Francis) Claud
Helweg, Hans H. 1917- ... SATA-33, 50
Helwig, David (Gordon) 1938- ... 33-36R
See also DLB 60
Helyar, Jane Penelope Josephine
1933- ... CANR-10
Earlier sketch in CA 21-22R
Hembree, Charles R. 1938- ... 33-36R
Hemdahl, Reuel Gustaf 1903-1977 ... 37-40R
Hemenway, Robert 1921- ... 33-36R
Hemenway, Ruby 1884(?)-1987 Obituary ... 123
Hemery, Eric 1914- ... 111
Hemesath, Caroline 1899- ... 61-64
Hemingway, Ernest 1899-1961 ... 77-80
See also DLB 4, 9
See also DLBY 81
See also DLBD 1
See also CLC 1, 3, 6, 8, 10, 13, 19, 30, 34, 39, 41, 44
See also SSC 1
Hemingway, Gregory H. 1931(?)-
Brief entry ... 112
Hemingway, Leicester C. 1915-1982
Obituary ... 107
Hemingway, Mary Welsh 1908-1986 ... 73-76
Obituary ... 121
Hemingway, Patricia Drake 1926-1978 ... 69-72
Obituary ... 73-76
Hemingway, Taylor
See Rywell, Martin
Heminway, John (H., Jr.) 1944- ... 25-28R
Hemleben, Sylvester John 1902- ... CAP-2
Earlier sketch in CA 25-28
Hemley, Cecil Herbert 1914-1966 ... CANR-1
Obituary ... 25-28R
Earlier sketch in CA 3R
Hemley, Elaine Gottlieb
See Gottlieb, Elaine
Hemlow, Joyce 1906- ... 7-8R
Hemming, John (Henry) 1935- ... CANR-12
Earlier sketch in CA 29-32R
Hemming, Roy 1928- ... 61-64
See also SATA 11
Hemmings, F(rederic) W(illiam) J(ohn)
1920- ... 97-100
Hemmings, Susan 1941- ... 118
Hempel, Amy 1951- Brief entry ... 118
See also CLC 39
Hempel, Carl G.
See Hempel, Carl Gustav
Hempel, Carl Gustav 1905- Brief entry ... 116
Hemphill, A. Marcus 1930(?)-1986
Obituary ... 120
Hemphill, Betty
See Hemphill, Elizabeth Anne
Hemphill, Charles F., Jr. 1917- ... 101
Hemphill, Christopher (Glenn) 1950-1987
Obituary ... 122
Hemphill, Elizabeth Anne 1920- ... 115
Hemphill, George 1922- ... 15-16R
Hemphill, Herbert Waide, Jr. 1929- ... 116
Hemphill, John K(nox) 1919- ... 53-56
Hemphill, Martha Locke 1904-1973 ... 37-40R
See also SATA 37
Hemphill, Paul 1936- ... CANR-12
Earlier sketch in CA 49-52
See also AITN 2
Hemphill, W(illiam) Edwin 1912- ... 21-22R
Hempstone, Smith 1929- ... CANR-1
Earlier sketch in CA 3R
Hemschemeyer, Judith 1935- ... 49-52
Henaghan, Jim 1919- ... 102
Henahan, Donal 1921- Brief entry ... 111
Henault, Marie (Josephine) 1921- ... 33-36R
Henbest, Nigel 1951- ... 124
Henchman, Daniel 1689-1761 ... DLB-24
Hencken, Hugh O'Neill 1902-1981
Obituary ... 104
Hendee, John C(lare) 1938- ... 93-96
Hendel, Charles William 1890-1982 ... CANR-13
Obituary ... 108
Earlier sketches in CA 15-16, CAP-1
Hendel, Samuel 1909-1984 ... CANR-1
Obituary ... 113
Earlier sketch in CA 4R
Hendelson, William H. 1904-1975
Obituary ... 104
Henderley, Brooks ... CAP-2
Earlier sketch in CA 19-20
See also SATA 1
Henderlite, Rachel 1905- ... 2R
Hendershot, Ralph 1896(?)-1979
Obituary ... 89-92
Henderson, Alexander (John) 1910- ... CAP-1
Earlier sketch in CA 15-16
Henderson, Algo D(onmyer) 1897- ... CANR-1
Earlier sketch in CA 1R
Henderson, Alice Corbin 1881-1949 ... DLB-54
Henderson, Archibald 1877-1963
Obituary ... 93-96
Henderson, Archibald 1916- ... 53-56
Henderson, Bert C. 1904- ... CAP-1
Earlier sketch in CA 9-10
Henderson, Bill 1941- ... 33-36R
Henderson, Brian 1941- ... 112
Henderson, C(rispin) A(listair) P(oland)
1955- ... 119
Henderson, C(harles) William 1925- ... 65-68
Henderson, Charles, Jr. 1923- ... 45-48
Henderson, Charles P(ackard), Jr.
1941- ... 41-44R
Henderson, Dan Fenno 1921- ... 19-20R
Henderson, David 1942- ... CANR-10
Earlier sketch in CA 25-28R
See also DLB 41
Henderson, Dion (Winslow) 1921-1984 ... CANR-5
Obituary ... 114
Earlier sketch in CA 9-10R
Henderson, Donald
See Laughlin, Tom
Henderson, Dwight F. 1937- ... 41-44R
Henderson, Edwin Bancroft 1883-1977
Obituary ... 116
Henderson, Eva Pendleton 1890- ... 115
Henderson, G(eorge) P(atrick) 1915- ... 29-32R
Henderson, G(eorge) P(oland) 1920- ... 37-40R
Henderson, George 1931- ... 25-28R
Henderson, George L(eslie) 1925- ... 69-72
Henderson, George Wylie 1904- ... DLB-51
Henderson, Harold G(ould) 1889-1974
Obituary ... 53-56
Henderson, Harold H(ale) 1928- ... 114
Henderson, Harry B(rinton), Jr. 1914-
Brief entry ... 109
Henderson, Ian 1910-1969 ... CAP-2
Earlier sketch in CA 17-18
Henderson, Isabel 1933- ... 25-28R
Henderson, James 1934- ... CANR-13
Earlier sketch in CA 33-36R
Henderson, James Youngblood 1944- ... 110
Henderson, Jean Carolyn Glidden 1916- ... 102
Henderson, Jennifer 1929- ... 107
Henderson, John 1906(?)-1982 Obituary ... 108
Henderson, John 1915- ... 7-8R
Henderson, John S(teele) 1919- ... 5-6R
Henderson, John W(illiam) 1910- ... 25-28R
Henderson, K(enneth) D(avid) D(ruitt)
1903- ... CAP-1
Earlier sketch in CA 15-16
Henderson, Kathy 1949- ... 123
Henderson, (Alan) Keith 1883-1982 ... 107
Obituary ... 106
Henderson, Keith M. 1934- ... 23-24R
Henderson, Laurance G. 1924(?)-1977
Obituary ... 73-76
Henderson, Laurence 1928- ... 53-56
Henderson, Lawrence W. 1921- ... 103
Henderson, LeGrand 1901-1965 ... 5-6R
See also SATA 9
Henderson, Linda Dalrymple 1948- ... 124
Henderson, Lois T(hompson) 1918- ... 81-84
Henderson, Mary
See Mavor, Osborne Henry
Henderson, Mary C. 1928- ... 77-80
Henderson, Michael (Douglas) 1932- ... 110
Henderson, Nancy 1943- ... 41-44R
Henderson, Nancy Wallace 1916- ... 97-100
See also SATA 22
Henderson, Paul (III) 1939- Brief entry ... 122
Henderson, Peter 1904-1983 ... 108
Obituary ... 111
Henderson, Philip (Prichard)
1906-1977 ... CANR-14
Obituary ... 104
Earlier sketches in CA 9-10, CAP-1
Henderson, Randall 1888- ... CAP-1
Earlier sketch in CA 13-14
Henderson, Richard 1924- ... CANR-20
Earlier sketches in CA 13-14R, CANR-5
Henderson, Richard B(eveir) 1921- ... 77-80
Henderson, Richard I(van) 1926- ... CANR-11
Earlier sketch in CA 69-72
Henderson, Robert 1906- ... 106
Henderson, Robert M. 1926- ... 33-36R
Henderson, Robert W(augh) 1920- ... 4R
Henderson, Robert William 1888-1985
Obituary ... 117
Henderson, S(hirley) P(rudence) A(nn)
1929- ... 37-40R
Henderson, Stephen E. 1925- ... 29-32R
Henderson, Sylvia
See Ashton-Warner, Sylvia (Constance)
Henderson, Thomas W(alter) 1949- ... 73-76
Henderson, Vivian (Wilson) 1923-1976 ... 65-68
Obituary ... 61-64
Henderson, W(illiam) O(tto) 1904- ... CANR-4
Earlier sketch in CA 2R
Henderson, William III 1922- ... 17-18R
Henderson, William L(eroy) 1927- ... 33-36R
Henderson, Zenna (Chlarson) 1917- ... CANR-1
Earlier sketch in CA 2R
See also SATA 5
See also DLB 8
Henderson-Howat, Gerald
See Howat, Gerald Malcolm David
Hendin, David (Bruce) 1945- ... 41-44R
Hendin, Herbert (Martin) 1926-
Brief entry ... 117
Hendin, Josephine 1946- ... 102
Hendley, Coit (Taylor), Jr. 1920-1985
Obituary ... 116
Hendon, William S(cott) 1933- ... 45-48
Hendra, Tony 1945- ... 102
Hendren, Ron 1945- ... 77-80
Hendrich, Paula Griffith 1928- ... CANR-1
Earlier sketch in CA 4R
Hendrick, George 1929- ... CANR-23
Earlier sketches in CA 13-14R, CANR-8
Hendrick, Irving G(uilford) 1936- ... 81-84
Hendrick, Ives 1898-1972 ... CAP-1
Obituary ... 33-36R
Earlier sketch in CA 11-12
Hendrick, T(homas) W(illiam) 1909- ... 108
Hendricks, Faye N(eidhold) 1913- ... 69-72
Hendricks, Frances Wade Kellam 1900- ... 37-40R
Hendricks, Gay 1945- ... 73-76
Hendricks, George D. 1913- ... 5-6R
Hendricks, J(ames) Edwin 1935- ... CANR-15
Earlier sketch in CA 41-44R
Hendricks, Robert J(oseph) 1944- ... 45-48
Hendricks, Walter 1892-1979 Obituary ... 103
Hendricks, William Lawrence 1929- ... CANR-17
Earlier sketches in CA 49-52, CANR-2
Hendrickson, Donald E(ugene) 1941- ... 93-96
Hendrickson, James E. 1932- ... 21-22R
Hendrickson, Paul 1944- ... 108
Hendrickson, Robert 1933- ... CANR-1
Earlier sketch in CA 49-52
Hendrickson, Robert A(ugustus)
1923- ... CANR-12
Earlier sketch in CA 29-32R
Hendrickson, Walter Brookfield, Jr.
1936- ... CANR-1
Earlier sketch in CA 3R
See also SATA 9
Hendrie, Don(ald Franz), Jr. 1942- ... CANR-18
Earlier sketches in CA 49-52, CANR-3
Hendriks, A(rthur) L(emiere) 1922- ... 97-100
Hendriksen, Eldon Sende 1917- ... 15-16R
Hendry, Allan 1950- ... 106
Hendry, J(ames) F(indlay) 1912- ... 29-32R
Hendry, Thomas 1929- ... 69-72
Hendry, Tom
See Hendry, Thomas
Hendy, Philip (Anstiss) 1900-1980
Obituary ... 102
Henegan, Lucius Herbert, Jr.
1902(?)-1979 Obituary ... 85-88
Heneman, Herbert Gerhard, Jr. 1916- ... CANR-1
Earlier sketch in CA 1R
Henfil
See Souza Filho, Henrique de
Henfrey, Colin (Vere Fleetwood) 1941- ... 15-16R
Henfrey, Norman 1929- ... 25-28R
Henig, Gerald S(heldon) 1942- ... 57-60
Henig, Martin (Edward) 1942- ... 114
Henig, Robin Marantz 1953- ... 108
Henig, Ruth B(eatrice) 1943- ... 49-52
Henig, Suzanne 1936- ... CANR-2
Earlier sketch in CA 45-48
Henige, David 1938- ... 103
Heninger, S(imeon) K(ahn), Jr. 1922- ... CANR-1
Earlier sketch in CA 1R
Henisch, Heinz K. 1922- ... 73-76
Henissart, Paul 1923- ... 29-32R
Henke, Dan (Ferdinand) 1924- ... 53-56
Henke, Emerson O(verbeck) 1916- ... CANR-12
Earlier sketch in CA 17-18R
Henkel, Barbara Osborn 1921- ... 11-12R
Henkel, Stephen C. 1933- ... 37-40R
Henkels, Robert M(acAllister), Jr. 1936- ... 57-60
Henkes, Kevin 1960- ... 114
See also SATA 43
Henkes, Robert 1922- ... CANR-13
Earlier sketch in CA 33-36R
Henkin, Harmon 1940(?)-1980 Obituary ... 101
Henkin, Louis 1917- ... CANR-13
Earlier sketch in CA 33-36R
Henle, Faye ?-1972 Obituary ... 37-40R
Henle, Fritz 1909- ... 73-76
Henle, James 1891(?)-1973 Obituary ... 37-40R
Henle, Jane 1913- ... 77-80
Henle, Mary 1913- ... 33-36R
Henle, Robert John 1909- ... 110
Henle, Theda O. 1918- ... 33-36R
Henley, Arthur 1921- ... 21-22R
Henley, Beth
See Henley, Elizabeth Becker
See also DLBY 86
See also CLC 23
Henley, Elizabeth Becker 1952- ... 107
Henley, Gail 1952- ... CANR-21
Earlier sketch in CA 89-92
Henley, Karyn 1952- ... 102
Henley, Nancy Eloise Main 1934-
Brief entry ... 106
Henley, Norman 1915- ... 17-18R
Henley, Virginia 1935- ... 109
Henley, W(illiam) Ballentine 1905- ... 61-64
Henley, Wallace (Boynton) 1941- ... CANR-14
Earlier sketch in CA 65-68
Henley, William Ernest 1849-1903
Brief entry ... 105
See also DLB 19
See also TCLC 8
Henn, Harry George 1919- ... 45-48
Henn, Thomas Rice 1901-1974 ... CANR-4
Earlier sketch in CA 7-8R
Hennacy, Ammon 1893-1970 Obituary ... 104
Henne, Frances E. 1906-1985 Obituary ... 118
Hennedy, Hugh L(ouis) 1929- ... 41-44R
Henneman, John Bell, Jr. 1935- ... 45-48
Hennesey, James J. 1926- ... 33-36R
Hennessey, Caroline
See von Block, Bela W(illiam)
and von Block, Sylvia
Hennessey, R(oger) A(nthony) S(ean)
1937- ... 29-32R
Hennessy, Bernard C. 1924- ... 15-16R
Hennessy, David James George 1932- ... CANR-22
Earlier sketch in CA 106
Hennessy, James Pope
See Pope-Hennessy, James
Hennessy, Jossleyn (Michael Stephen
Philip) 1903- ... 9-10R
Hennessy, Mary L. 1927- ... 23-24R

Hennessy, Max
See Harris, John
Hennessy, Peter 1947- ... 123
Hennessy, Thomas C(hristopher) 1916- ... 115
Hennig, Margaret (Marie) 1940- ... 81-84
Henning, Charles N(athaniel) 1915- ... 1R
Henning, Daniel H(oward) 1931- ... CANR-2
Earlier sketch in CA 45-48
Henning, Edward B. 1922- ... 19-20R
Henning, Standish 1932- Brief entry ... 107
Henning, Sylvie Marie Debevec
See Debevec Henning, Sylvie Marie
Henninger, G. Ross 1898-1984 Obituary ... 112
Hennings, Dorothy Grant 1935- ... CANR-4
Earlier sketch in CA 53-56
Hennings, Josephine Silva 1899(?)-1985
Obituary ... 117
Hennissart, Martha ... 85-88
Henrey, Madeleine 1906- ... CANR-6
Earlier sketch in CA 13-14R
Henrey, Mrs. Robert
See Henrey, Madeleine
Henrey, Robert
See Henrey, Madeleine
Henri, Adrian (Maurice) 1932- ... CANR-15
Earlier sketch in CA 25-28R
Henri, Florette 1908-1985 ... 73-76
Obituary ... 117
Henri, G.
See Clement, George H.
Henrichsen, Walt(er Arlie), Jr. 1934- ... 89-92
Henricks, Kaw
See Wolfe, Charles Keith
Henries, A. Doris Banks 1913(?)-1981
Obituary ... 103
Henriksen, Thomas H(ollinger) 1939- ... 112
Henriod, Lorraine 1925- ... 45-48
See also SATA 26
Henriques, Veronica 1931- ... 102
Henry, Avril (Kay) 1935- ... 123
Henry, Bessie Walker 1921- ... 9-10R
Henry, Bill
See Henry, William Mellors
Henry, Buck 1930- ... 77-80
See also DLB 26
Henry, Carl F(erdinand) H(oward)
1913- ... CANR-21
Earlier sketches in CA 13-14R, CANR-6
Henry, (William) Claud 1914- ... 45-48
Henry, Daniel
See Kahnweiler, Daniel-Henry
Henry, David Dodds 1905- ... 106
Henry, David Lee
See Hill, R. Lance
Henry, Eric P(utnam) 1943- ... 108
Henry, Fran Worden 1948- ... 111
Henry, Frances 1931- ... 77-80
Henry, Francoise 1902-1982 Obituary ... 106
Henry, Harold Wilkinson 1926- ... 37-40R
Henry, Harriet
See De Steuch, Harriet Henry
Henry, James P(aget) 1914- ... 104
Henry, James S(helburne) 1950- ... 49-52
Henry, Janet Cope 1925(?)-1986 Obituary ... 118
Henry, Jeanne Heffernan 1940- ... 105
Henry, Joanne Landers 1927- ... 17-18R
See also SATA 6
Henry, Joseph B. 1901- ... CAP-2
Earlier sketch in CA 17-18
Henry, Jules 1904-1969 Obituary ... 109
Henry, Kenneth 1920- ... 57-60
Henry, Laurin L(uther) 1921- ... 2R
Henry, Marguerite ... CANR-9
Earlier sketch in CA 19-20R
See also SATA 11
See also DLB 22
See also CLR 4
Henry, Marion
See del Rey, Lester
Henry, O.
See Porter, William Sydney
See also TCLC 1, 19
Henry, Oliver
See Porter, William Sydney
Henry, Peter 1926- ... 109
Henry, Robert Selph 1889-1970 ... CANR-17
Obituary ... 103
Earlier sketch in CA 1R
See also DLB 17
Henry, Shirley 1925(?)-1972 Obituary ... 33-36R
Henry, Sondra 1930- ... 119
Henry, T. E.
See Rowland-Entwistle, (Arthur)
Theodore (Henry)
Henry, Vera 1909(?)-1987 ... CAP-2
Obituary ... 123
Earlier sketch in CA 21-22
Henry, W. P. 1929- ... 19-20R
Henry, Will
See Allen, Henry Wilson
Henry, William A(lfred) III 1950-
Brief entry ... 116
Henry, William Earl 1917- Brief entry ... 108
Henry, William Mellors 1890-1970
Obituary ... 89-92
Henschel, Elizabeth Georgie ... 107
Henschke, Alfred
See Klabund
Hensey, Frederick G(erald) 1931- ... 89-92
Hensey, Fritz
See Hensey, Frederick G(erald)
Henshall, A(udrey) S(hore) 1927- ... 11-12R
Henshaw, James Ene 1924- ... 101
Henshaw, Richard 1945- ... 101
Henshaw, Tom 1924- ... 103
Henshel, Richard L(ee) 1939- ... 57-60
Hensley, Charles S(tanley) 1919- ... 41-44R
Hensley, Jeff (Lane) 1947- ... 117
Hensley, Joe L. 1926- ... CANR-14
Earlier sketch in CA 33-36R
Hensley, (Malcolm) Stewart 1914(?)-1976
Obituary ... 65-68
Henslin, James M(arvin) 1937- ... CANR-15
Earlier sketch in CA 41-44R
Henson, Clyde E(ugene) 1914- ... 5-6R
Henson, James Maury 1936- ... 124
Brief entry ... 106
See also SATA 43
Henson, Jim
See Henson, James Maury
Henson, Margaret Swett 1924- ... 122
Henstra, Friso 1928- ... SATA-8
Henthorn, William E(llsworth) 1928- ... 41-44R
Hentoff, Nat(han Irving) 1925- ... CANR-5
Earlier sketch in CA 2R
See also CAAS 6
See also SATA 27, 42
See also CLC 26
See also CLR 1
Henty, G(eorge) A(lfred) 1832-1902
Brief entry ... 112
See also DLB 18
Hentz, Caroline Lee (Whiting) 1800-1856 ... DLB-3
Henwood, James N. J. 1932- ... 29-32R
Henze, Donald F(rank) 1928- ... 23-24R
Hepburn, Andrew H. 1899(?)-1975
Obituary ... 57-60
Hepburn, James Gordon 1922- ... 85-88
Hepburn, Ronald W(illiam) 1927- ... 13-14R
Hepner, Harry W(alker) 1893-1984 ... 29-32R
Obituary ... 114
Hepner, James O(rville) 1933- ... 57-60
Heppenheimer, T(homas) A(dolph)
1947- ... CANR-16
Earlier sketch in CA 93-96
Heppenstall, Margit Strom 1913- ... 23-24R
Heppenstall, (John) Rayner 1911-1981 ... 4R
Obituary ... 103
See also CLC 10
Hepple, Alex 1904(?)-1983 Obituary ... 111
Hepple, Bob (Alexander) 1934- ... CANR-12
Earlier sketch in CA 29-32R
Hepple, Peter 1927- ... 81-84
Heppner, Sam(uel) 1913-1983 ... 25-28R
Obituary ... 109
Hepworth, James B. 1910- ... 1R
Hepworth, James Michael 1938- ... CANR-13
Earlier sketch in CA 73-76
Hepworth, Mike
See Hepworth, James Michael
Hepworth, (Charles) Philip 1912- ... 17-18R
Her
See Deal, Borden
Herail, Rene James 1939- ... 118
Herald, Earl Stannard 1914-1973 Obituary ... 112
Herald, George William 1911- ... 73-76
Herald, Kathleen
See Peyton, Kathleen Wendy
Heraud, Brian J(eremy) 1934- ... 73-76
Heravi, Mehdi 1940- ... 29-32R
Herber, Bernard P. 1929- ... 21-22R
Herber, Harold L. 1929- ... 108
Herber, Lewis
See Bookchin, Murray
Herberg, Will 1909-1977 ... 73-76
Obituary ... 69-72
Herberger, Charles F. 1920- ... 41-44R
Herbers, John N. 1923- ... 33-36R
Herbert, A(lan) P(atrick) 1890-1971 ... 97-100
Obituary ... 33-36R
See also DLB 10
Herbert, Anthony B(ernard) 1930- ... 77-80
Herbert, Arthur
See Shappiro, Herbert (Arthur)
Herbert, Cecil
See Hamilton, Charles Harold St. John
Herbert, Cynthia Ridgeway 1943- ... 118
Herbert, David T(homas) 1935- ... CANR-18
Earlier sketches in CA 49-52, CANR-2
Herbert, Don 1917- ... 29-32R
See also SATA 2
Herbert, Eugenia W(arren) 1929- ... 93-96
Herbert, Frank (Patrick) 1920-1986 ... CANR-5
Obituary ... 118
Earlier sketch in CA 53-56
See also SATA 9, 37, 47
See also DLB 8
See also CLC 12, 23, 35, 44
Herbert, Gilbert 1924- ... CANR-23
Earlier sketch in CA 107
Herbert, Henry George Alfred Marius Victor
Francis 1898-1987 Obituary ... 123
Herbert, Henry William 1807-1858 ... DLB-3
Herbert, Ian 1939- ... 111
Herbert, (Edward) Ivor (Montgomery)
1925- ... CANR-19
Earlier sketches in CA 53-56, CANR-4
Herbert, James 1943- ... 81-84
Herbert, Jean (Daniel Fernand)
1897-1980 ... CANR-9
Earlier sketch in CA 17-18R
Herbert, John (David) 1924- ... CANR-13
Earlier sketch in CA 23-24R
Herbert, John
See Brundage, John Herbert
See also DLB 53
Herbert, Kevin (Barry John) 1921- ... 17-18R
Herbert, Marie 1941- ... 69-72
Herbert, Martin 1933- ... 103
Herbert, Miranda C(arleton) 1950- ... 97-100
Herbert, Robert L(ouis) 1929- ... CANR-5
Earlier sketch in CA 11-12R
Herbert, Theodore T(erence) 1942- ... CANR-15
Earlier sketch in CA 65-68
Herbert, Thomas Walter, Jr. 1938- ... 104
Herbert, Victor 1927- ... 112
Herbert, Wally
See Herbert, Walter William
Herbert, Walter William 1934- ... CANR-15
Earlier sketch in CA 69-72
See also SATA 23
Herbert, (Alfred Francis) Xavier
1901-1984 ... 69-72
Obituary ... 114
Herbert, Zbigniew 1924- ... 89-92
See also CLC 9, 43
Herbertson, Gary J. 1938- ... 25-28R
Herblock
See Block, Herbert (Lawrence)
Herbrand, Jan(ice M.) 1931- ... 49-52
Herbruck, Christine Comstock
See Comstock, Christine
Herbst, Anthony F(rancis) 1941- ... 114
Herbst, Josephine (Frey) 1897-1969 ... 7-8R
Obituary ... 25-28R
See also DLB 9
See also CLC 34
Herbst, Jurgen (F. H.) 1928- ... 37-40R
Herbst, Robert L(eroy) 1935- ... 61-64
Hercules, Frank (E. M.) ... CANR-2
Earlier sketch in CA 2R
See also DLB 33
Herd, Dale 1940- ... 61-64
Herdan, Gustav 1897- ... 2R
Herdeck, Donald E. 1924- ... 53-56
Herdt, Gilbert H(enry) 1949- ... 105
Herdt, Sheryll (Enette) Patterson 1941- ... 57-60
Hereford, John
See Fletcher, H(arry) L(utf) V(erne)
Heren, Louis (P.) 1919- ... CANR-12
Earlier sketch in CA 25-28R
Herfindahl, Orris C(lemens) 1918-1972 ... 41-44R
Obituary ... 37-40R
Herge
See Remi, Georges
See also CLR 6
Hergenhahn, B(aldwin) R(oss) 1934- ... 123
Brief entry ... 118
Hergesheimer, Joseph 1880-1954
Brief entry ... 109
See also DLB 9
See also TCLC 11
Herget, Paul 1908(?)-1981 Obituary ... 105
Herian, V.
See Gregorian, Vartan
Heriat, Philippe
See Payelle, Raymond-Gerard
Herington, C. J(ohn) 1924- ... CANR-15
Earlier sketch in CA 29-32R
Heriot, Angus 1927- ... 7-8R
Heriteau, Jacqueline 1925- ... CANR-16
Earlier sketches in CA 45-48, CANR-1
Herity, Michael 1929- ... 49-52
Herken, Gregg (Franklin) 1947- ... CANR-20
Earlier sketch in CA 104
Herkimer, L(awrence) R(ussell) 1925(?)- ... 110
See also SATA 42
Herlihy, David 1930- ... 41-44R
Herlihy, James Leo 1927- ... CANR-2
Earlier sketch in CA 1R
See also CLC 6
Herlin, Hans 1925- ... 77-80
Herling, John 1907- Brief entry ... 112
Herm, Gerhard 1931- ... CANR-22
Earlier sketch in CA 104
Hermalyn, Gary 1952- ... 123
Herman, A(rthur) L(udwig) 1930- ... 65-68
Herman, Ben 1927- ... 104
Herman, Charlotte 1937- ... CANR-15
Earlier sketch in CA 41-44R
See also SATA 20
Herman, Donald L. 1928- ... CANR-4
Earlier sketch in CA 53-56
Herman, Esther 1935- ... 102
Herman, George E(dward) 1920- ... 69-72
Herman, George R(ichard) 1925- ... 5-6R
Herman, Jan (Jacob) 1942- ... 45-48
Herman, John R(ufus) 1928- ... 119
Herman, Judith 1943- ... 49-52
Herman, Justin B. 1907(?)-1983 Obituary ... 111
Herman, Kenneth Neil 1954- ... 77-80
Herman, Louis Jay 1925- ... 53-56
Herman, Marguerite Shalett 1914-1977 ... 41-44R
Herman, Masako ... 103
Herman, Melvin (Jerome) 1922-
Brief entry ... 111
Herman, Melvin 1922(?)-1983 Obituary ... 109
Herman, Simon N(athan) 1912- ... 29-32R
Herman, Sondra R(enee) 1932- ... 25-28R
Herman, Stanley M. 1928- ... 25-28R
Herman, Vic(tor J.) 1919- ... 107
Herman, Victor 1916(?)-1985 Obituary ... 115
Herman, Walter
See Wager, Walter H(erman)
Hermand, Jost 1930- ... CANR-14
Earlier sketch in CA 41-44R
Hermann, Donald H(arold) J(ames)
1943- ... CANR-17
Earlier sketches in CA 45-48, CANR-2
Hermann, Edward J(ulius) 1919- ... 17-18R
Hermann, John 1917- ... 49-52
Hermann, Philip J. 1916- ... 117
Hermann, (Theodore) Placid 1909-19(?) ... CAP-1
Earlier sketch in CA 15-16
Hermanns, Peter
See Brannon, William T.
Hermanns, William 1895- ... CANR-15
Earlier sketch in CA 37-40R
Hermans, Willem Frederik 1921- ... CAP-1
Earlier sketch in CA 9-10
Hermansen, Gustav 1909- ... 117
Hermansen, John 1918- ... 45-48
Hermanson, Dennis (Everett) 1947- ... SATA-10
Hermeren, Goeran A. 1938- ... CANR-15
Earlier sketch in CA 89-92
Hermes
See Flammarion, (Nicolas) Camille
Hermes, Patricia 1936- ... CANR-22
Earlier sketch in CA 104
See also SATA 31
Hern, (George) Anthony 1916- ... 23-24R
Hern, Nicholas 1944- ... 115
Hernadi, Paul 1936- ... CANR-15
Earlier sketch in CA 41-44R
Hernandez, Al 1909- ... CAP-2
Earlier sketch in CA 21-22
Hernandez, Amado V. 1903-1970
Obituary ... 112
Hernandez, Frances 1926- ... 37-40R
Hernandez, Juana Amelia ... 45-48
Hernandez, Luis F. 1923- ... 61-64
Hernandez, Pedro F(elix) 1925- ... 45-48
Herndl, George C. 1927- ... 33-36R
Herndon, Booton 1915- ... CANR-4
Earlier sketch in CA 9-10R
Herndon, James 1926- ... 89-92
Herndon, Venable 1927- ... 109
Herner, Charles H. 1930- ... 29-32R
Hernes, Helga Maria 1938- ... CANR-20
Earlier sketch in CA 103
Hernon, Peter 1944- ... CANR-8
Earlier sketch in CA 61-64
Hernton, Calvin C(oolidge) 1934- ... CANR-3
Earlier sketch in CA 11-12R
See also DLB 38
Hero, Alfred O(livier), Jr. 1924- ... 21-22R
Herold, Brenda 1948- ... 33-36R
Herold, J(ean) Christopher 1919-1964 ... CAP-1
Earlier sketch in CA 9-10
Heron, Alasdair I(ain) C(ampbell) 1942- ... 115
Heron, David Winston 1920- ... 112
Heron, Laurence Tunstall 1902- ... 49-52
Heron, Patrick 1920- ... 109
Heron-Allen, Edward 1861-1943
Brief entry ... 113
Herpel, George L(loyd) 1921- ... CANR-15
Earlier sketch in CA 41-44R
Herr, Dan(iel J.) 1917- ... 2R
Herr, Edwin L. 1933- ... 37-40R
Herr, Ethel 1936- ... 112
Herr, Michael 1940(?)- ... 89-92
Herr, Richard 1922- ... 4R
Herrero, Stephen M(atthew) 1939- ... 118
Herreshoff, David 1921- ... 21-22R
Herreshoff, L. Francis 1890-1972 ... CAP-1
Obituary ... 37-40R
Earlier sketch in CA 13-14
Herrick, Bruce Hale 1936- ... CANR-7
Earlier sketch in CA 19-20R
Herrick, Joy Field 1930- ... 101
Herrick, Marvin Theodore 1899-1966 ... CANR-1
Earlier sketch in CA 1R
Herrick, Neal Q(uentin) 1927- ... 49-52
Herrick, Robert (Welch) 1868-1938
Brief entry ... 119
See also DLB 9,12
Herrick, Robert L(ee) 1930- ... 61-64
Herrick, Tracy Grant 1933- ... 112
Herrick, Walter R(ussell), Jr. 1918- ... 23-24R
Herrick, William 1915- ... CANR-9
Earlier sketch in CA 23-24R
See also DLBY 83
Herridge, Robert 1914(?)-1981 Obituary ... 104
Herring, George C., Jr. 1936- ... CANR-14
Earlier sketch in CA 41-44R
Herring, Hubert Clinton 1889-1967
Obituary ... 105
Herring, Jack W(illiam) 1925- ... 115
Herring, Ralph A(lderman) 1901-19(?) ... CAP-2
Earlier sketch in CA 21-22
Herring, Reuben 1922- ... CANR-7
Earlier sketch in CA 19-20R
Herring, Robert H(erschel) 1938- ... CANR-21
Earlier sketch in CA 105
Herrington, James L(awrence) 1928- ... 73-76
Herrington, Pat
See Herrington, Patricia (Murphy)
Herrington, Patricia (Murphy) 1927- ... 114
Herrington, Stuart A. 1941- ... 109
Herriot, James
See Wight, James Alfred
See also CLC 12
Herriot, Peter 1939- ... 29-32R
Herriott, Robert E. 1929- ... CANR-7
Earlier sketch in CA 17-18R
Herrmann, Dorothy 1941- ... 107
See also CLC 44
Herrmann, Frank 1927- ... CANR-10
Earlier sketch in CA 21-22R
Herrmann, John 1900-1959 Brief entry ... 107
See also DLB 4
Herrmann, Klaus J(acob) 1929- ... 37-40R
Herrmann, Luke John 1932- ... 103
Herrmann, Nina 1943- ... 77-80
Herrmann, R(obert) L(awrence) 1928- ... 109
Herrmann, Richard K. 1952- ... 124
Herrmann, Robert O(mer) 1932- ... 41-44R
Herrmann, Taffy
See Herrmann, Dorothy
Herrmanns, Ralph 1933- ... CANR-18
Earlier sketches in CA 9-10R, CANR-3
See also SATA 11
Herrnstadt, Richard L. 1926- ... 33-36R
Herrnstein, Barbara
See Smith, Barbara Herrnstein
Herrnstein, Richard J(ulius) 1930-
Brief entry ... 107
Herron, Don 1952- ... 111

Herron, Edward A(lbert) 1912- ... 5-6R
See also SATA 4
Herron, Ima Honaker 1899- ... CAP-2
Earlier sketch in CA 25-28
Herron, Lowell William 1916- ... 2R
Herron, Orley R., Jr. 1933- ... CANR-12
Earlier sketch in CA 25-28R
Herron, Shaun 1912- ... 29-32R
Herron, William George 1933- ... 37-40R
Herschberger, Ruth (Margaret) 1917- ... 33-36R
Herschensohn, Bruce 1932- ... 69-72
Herscher, Uri David 1941- ... 107
Hersey, George Leonard 1927- ... 41-44R
Hersey, Jean 1902- ... CANR-3
Earlier sketch in CA 11-12R
Hersey, John (Richard) 1914- ... 17-18R
See also SATA 25
See also DLB 6
See also CLC 1, 2, 7, 9, 40
Hersey, William Dearborn 1910- ... CAP-1
Earlier sketch in CA 11-12
Hersh, Burton 1933- ... 73-76
Hersh, Jacques 1935- ... 103
Hersh, Seymour M. 1937- ... CANR-15
Earlier sketch in CA 73-76
See also AITN 1
Hershan, Stella K. 1915- ... 33-36R
Hershatter, Richard Lawrence 1923- ... 81-84
Hershberg, David 1935- ... 45-48
Hershberger, Hazel Kuhns ... 5-6R
Hershenson, David Bert 1933- ... 41-44R
Hershenson, Maurice (Eugene) 1933- ... 41-44R
Hersher, Leonard 1925- ... 41-44R
Hershey, Burnet 1896-1971 ... CAP-2
Obituary ... 33-36R
Earlier sketch in CA 25-28
Hershey, Daniel 1931- ... CANR-16
Earlier sketch in CA 89-92
Hershey, Ed
See Hershey, Edward (Norman)
Hershey, Edward (Norman) 1944-
Brief entry ... 118
Hershey, Gerald L. 1931- ... 53-56
Hershey, Lenore ... 104
Hershey, Nathan 1930- ... 117
Hershey, Robert Delp 1909- ... 69-72
Hershfield, Harry 1885-1974 Obituary ... 53-56
Hershhorn, Bernard S(eymour) 1928- ... 119
Hershkowitz, Leo 1924- ... 25-28R
Hershman, Morris 1926- ... CANR-5
Earlier sketch in CA 53-56
Hershon, Robert 1936- ... CANR-13
Earlier sketch in CA 33-36R
Herskovits, Frances Shapiro 1897-1972
Obituary ... 33-36R
Herskowitz, Herbert Bennett 1925- ... 17-18R
Herskowitz, Mickey ... 81-84
Herst, Herman, Jr. 1909- ... CANR-2
Earlier sketch in CA 4R
Herstein, Sheila R. 1942- ... 119
Herter, Christian A(rchibald) 1895-1966
Obituary ... 116
Hertling, G(unter) H. 1930- ... 41-44R
Hertling, James E. 1935- ... 93-96
Hertsens, Marcel 1918- ... 9-10R
Hertweck, Alma Louise 1937- ... 122
Hertz, Aleksander 1895-1983 Obituary ... 109
Hertz, Grete Janus 1915- ... 101
See also SATA 23
Hertz, Jackoline G. 1920- ... 69-72
Hertz, Jacky
See Hertz, Jackoline G.
Hertz, Karl H(erbert) 1917- ... 73-76
Hertz, Peter Donald 1933- ... 37-40R
Hertz, Richard C(ornell) 1916- ... 21-22R
Hertz, Solange (Strong) 1920- ... 7-8R
Hertzberg, Arthur 1921- ... 19-20R
Hertzberg, Hazel W(hitman) 1918- ... 73-76
Hertzberg, Sidney 1910-1984 Obituary ... 114
Hertzler, Daniel 1925- ... 115
Hertzler, Joyce O(ramel) 1895-1975 ... 1R
Obituary ... 103
Hertzler, Lois Shank 1927- ... 57-60
Hertzman, Lewis 1927- ... 11-12R
Herum, John (Maurice) 1931- ... 61-64
Herve, Jean-Luc
See Humbaraci, D(emir) Arslan
Herve-Bazin, Jean Pierre Marie 1911- ... 81-84
Hervent, Maurice
See Grindel, Eugene
Hervey, Evelyn
See Keating, H(enry) R(eymond) F(itzwalter)
Hervey, Jane
See McGaw, Naomi Blanche Thoburn
Hervey, Michael 1920- ... 11-12R
Herwig, Holger H(einrich) 1941- ... CANR-7
Earlier sketch in CA 61-64
Herz, Irene 1948- ... 93-96
Herz, Jerome Spencer ... 45-48
Herz, Jerry
See Herz, Jerome Spencer
Herz, John H(ermann) 1908- ... 41-44R
Herz, Martin F(lorian) 1917-1983 ... CANR-9
Obituary ... 111
Earlier sketch in CA 23-24R
Herz, Peggy 1936- ... 37-40R
Herz, Stephanie M(argarette) 1900- ... 101
Herzberg, Donald Gabriel 1925-1980
Obituary ... 101
Herzberg, Joseph Gabriel 1907-1976
Obituary ... 65-68
Herzberger, Maximillian Jacob 1899-1982
Obituary ... 106
Herzel, Catherine (Williams) 1908- ... 5-6R
Herzfeld, Thomas J. 1945- ... 107
Herzinger, Kim A(llen) 1946- ... 114
Herzka, Heinz (Stefan) 1935- ... 37-40R
Herzog, Arthur (III) 1927- ... CANR-9
Earlier sketch in CA 19-20R
Herzog, Chaim 1918- ... 103
Herzog, Dorothy Ducas 1905(?)-1987
Obituary ... 123
Herzog, E.
See Maurois, Andre
Herzog, Frederick 1925- ... 116
Herzog, Gerard 1920- ... 104
Herzog, John P(hillip) 1931- ... 29-32R
Herzog, Kristin (K. H.) 1929- ... 114
Herzog, Stephen J(oel) 1938- ... 33-36R
Herzog, Werner 1942- ... 89-92
See also CLC 16
Herzstein, Robert Edwin 1940- ... CANR-7
Earlier sketch in CA 57-60
Hesburgh, Theodore M(artin) 1917- ... 13-14R
Heschel, Abraham Joshua 1907-1972 ... CANR-4
Obituary ... 37-40R
Earlier sketch in CA 7-8R
Heseltine, George Coulehan 1895-1980
Obituary ... 97-100
Heseltine, Nigel 1916- ... 9-10R
Heskes, Irene 1928- ... 93-96
Hesketh, (Charles) Peter (Fleetwood) Fleetwood
See Fleetwood-Hesketh, (Charles) Peter (Fleetwood)
Hesketh, Phoebe Rayner 1909- ... CANR-14
Earlier sketches in CA 9-10, CAP-1
Heskett, J(ames) L(ee) 1933- ... CANR-8
Earlier sketch in CA 13-14R
Hesky, Olga ?-1974 ... CAP-2
Obituary ... 53-56
Earlier sketch in CA 25-28
Hesla, David H(eimarck) 1929- ... 33-36R
Heslep, Robert D(urham) 1930- ... 37-40R
Heslin, Jo-Ann 1946- ... CANR-16
Earlier sketch in CA 93-96
Heslin, Richard 1936- ... 37-40R
Heslop, J. Malan 1923- ... 37-40R
Hespro, Herbert
See Robinson, Herbert Spencer
Hess, Albert G(unter) 1909- ... CAP-1
Earlier sketch in CA 19-20
Hess, Alexander 1898(?)-1981 Obituary ... 105
Hess, Bartlett L(eonard) 1910- ... CANR-21
Earlier sketch in CA 61-64
Hess, Beth B(owman) ... CANR-24
Earlier sketches in CA 65-68, CANR-9
Hess, Earl J(ohn) 1955- ... 118
Hess, Eckhard H(einrich) 1916-1986 ... 57-60
Obituary ... 118
Hess, Gary R(ay) 1937- ... 21-22R
Hess, Hannah S(pier) 1934- ... 45-48
Hess, Hans 1908-1975 Obituary ... 53-56
Hess, J(ohn) Daniel 1937- ... 116
Hess, John L(oft) 1917- ... 102
Hess, John M(ilton) 1929- ... 23-24R
Hess, Karen 1918- ... 105
Hess, Karl 1923- ... 81-84
Hess, Lilo 1916- ... CANR-12
Earlier sketch in CA 33-36R
See also SATA 4
Hess, Margaret Johnston 1915- ... CANR-21
Earlier sketches in CA 57-60, CANR-6
Hess, Robert D(aniel) 1920- ... CANR-13
Earlier sketch in CA 23-24R
Hess, Robert L. 1932- ... 29-32R
Hess, (Walther Richard) Rudolf 1894-1987 Obituary ... 123
Hess, Stephen 1933- ... CANR-10
Earlier sketch in CA 19-20R
Hess, Thomas B(aer) 1920-1978 ... 81-84
Obituary ... 77-80
Hess, William N. 1925- ... 29-32R
Hesse, Hermann 1877-1962 ... CAP-2
Earlier sketch in CA 17-18
See also SATA 50
See also DLB 66
See also CLC 1, 2, 3, 6, 11, 17, 25
Hesse, Mary (Brenda) 1924- ... CANR-12
Earlier sketch in CA 19-20R
Hesselgesser, Debra 1939- ... 69-72
Hesselgrave, David J(ohn) 1924- ... 81-84
Hesseltine, William Best 1902-1963 ... 4R
Hessert, Paul 1925- ... 33-36R
Hessing, Dennis
See Dennis-Jones, H(arold)
Hession, Charles H(enry) 1911- ... 33-36R
Hession, Roy 1908- ... 81-84
Hessler, Gene 1928- ... 73-76
Hesslink, George K. 1940-1980 ... 21-22R
Obituary ... 120
Hest, Amy 1950- ... 115
Hester, Hubert Inman 1895- ... CANR-5
Earlier sketch in CA 5-6R
Hester, Hugh Bryan 1895-1983 Obituary ... 111
Hester, James J. 1931- ... 37-40R
Hester, Kathleen B. 1905- ... CAP-2
Earlier sketch in CA 19-20
Hester, Marcus B. 1937- ... 33-36R
Hester, Randolph Thompson, Jr. 1944- ... 113
Hester, Thomas R(oy) 1946- ... 113
Hesterman, Vicki 1951- ... 112
Heston, Alan (Wiley) 1934- ... 97-100
Heston, Charlton 1924- ... 110
Brief entry ... 108
Heston, Edward 1908(?)-1973 Obituary ... 45-48
Heston, Leonard L(ancaster) 1930- ... 101
Heth, Meir 1932- ... 23-24R
Hetherington, (Hector) Alastair 1919- ... 109
Hetherington, Eileen Mavis (Plenderleith) 1926- ... 115
Hetherington, Hugh W(illiam) 1903- ... 5-6R
Hetherington, John (Aikman) 1907-1974 ... 93-96
Obituary ... 53-56
Hethmon, Robert H(enry) 1925- ... 15-16R
Hettinger, Herman Strecker 1902-1972
Obituary ... 37-40R
Hettlinger, Richard F(rederick) 1920- ... CANR-7
Earlier sketch in CA 19-20R
Hetzell, Margaret Carol 1917-1978 ... 85-88
Obituary ... 81-84
Hetzler, Florence M(ary) 1926- ... 107
Hetzler, Stanley Arthur 1919- ... 37-40R
Hetzron, Robert 1937- ... 33-36R
Heuer, John (Michael) 1941- ... CANR-14
Earlier sketch in CA 69-72
Heuer, Kenneth John 1927- ... 110
See also SATA 44
Heuman, William 1912-1971 ... CANR-7
Earlier sketch in CA 7-8R
See also SATA 21
Heumann, Milton 1947- ... 110
Heuscher, Julius E(rnst) 1918- ... 11-12R
Heuss, John 1908-1966 ... CAP-1
Earlier sketch in CA 9-10
Heussler, Robert 1924- ... CANR-8
Earlier sketch in CA 5-6R
Heussner, Ralph C(lyde), Jr. 1949- ... 119
Heuterman, Thomas H(enry) 1934- ... 101
Heuvelmans, Bernard (Joseph Pierre) 1916- ... 97-100
Heuvelmans, Martin 1903- ... 49-52
Heuyer, Georges 1884-1977 Obituary ... 73-76
Hevener, John W(atts) 1933- ... 103
Heward, Edmund (Rawlings) 1912- ... 93-96
Heward, William L(ee) 1949- ... CANR-4
Earlier sketch in CA 53-56
Hewat, Alexander 1743(?)-1824 ... DLB-30
Hewens, Frank Edgar 1912- ... 45-48
Hewer, Humphrey Robert 1903-1974
Obituary ... 105
Hewes, Agnes Danforth 1874-1963
Obituary ... 113
See also SATA 35
Hewes, Cady
See De Voto, Bernard (Augustine)
Hewes, Dorothy W. 1922- ... 37-40R
Hewes, Hayden 1943- ... 85-88
Hewes, Henry 1917- ... 13-14R
Hewes, Jeremy Joan 1944- ... 77-80
Hewes, Laurence (Ilsley) 1902- ... 105
Hewes, Leslie 1906- ... 41-44R
Hewett, Anita 1918- ... 21-22R
See also SATA 13
Hewett, Dorothy Coade 1923- ... 97-100
Hewett, John H(arris) 1952- ... 115
Hewett, William S. 1924- ... 21-22R
Hewins, Geoffrey Shaw 1889- ... CAP-1
Earlier sketch in CA 9-10
Hewins, Ralph Anthony 1909-1984(?) ... CAP-1
Obituary ... 112
Earlier sketch in CA 9-10
Hewison, Robert 1943- ... 81-84
Hewitson, John Nelson 1917- ... 29-32R
Hewitt, Arthur Wentworth 1883- ... 69-72
Hewitt, Bernard (Wolcott) 1906- ... 13-14R
Hewitt, Cecil Rolph 1901- ... CANR-18
Earlier sketch in CA 102
Hewitt, David (Sword) 1942- ... 118
Hewitt, Don (S.) 1922- Brief entry ... 119
Hewitt, Emily Clark 1944- ... CANR-2
Earlier sketch in CA 45-48
Hewitt, Foster (William) 1903(?)-1985
Obituary ... 115
Hewitt, Garnet (William) 1939- ... 110
Hewitt, Geof (George F.) 1943- ... 33-36R
Hewitt, H(erbert) J(ames) 1890- ... 13-14R
Hewitt, James 1928- ... CANR-21
Earlier sketches in CA 57-60, CANR-6
Hewitt, Jean D(aphne) 1925- ... 77-80
Hewitt, John (Harold) 1907-1987 ... CANR-16
Obituary ... 123
Earlier sketch in CA 97-100
See also DLB 27
Hewitt, John P(aul) 1941- ... 53-56
Hewitt, Philip Nigel 1945- ... 81-84
Hewitt, Robert L. 1917(?)-1983 Obituary ... 111
Hewitt, Sue Whitsett 1919(?)-1984
Obituary ... 111
Hewitt, William Henry 1936- ... 17-18R
Hewlett, Dorothy (?)-1979 Obituary ... 85-88
Hewlett, Frank West 1909(?)-1983
Obituary ... 110
Hewlett, Maurice (Henry) 1861-1923
Brief entry ... 121
See also DLB 34
Hewlett, Richard Greening 1923- ... 9-10R
Hewlett, Roger S. 1911(?)-1977 Obituary ... 73-76
Hewlett, Sylvia Ann 1946- ... 123
Brief entry ... 118
Hewlett, Virginia B. 1912(?)-1979
Obituary ... 85-88
Hewson, John 1930- ... 37-40R
Hexner, Ervin Paul 1893-1968 ... 7-8R
Obituary ... 103
Hext, Harrington
See Phillpotts, Eden
Hextall, David
See Phillips-Birt, Douglas Hextall Chedzey
Hexter, J(ack) H. 1910- ... 13-14R
Hey, John D(enis) 1944- ... 106
Hey, Nigel S(tewart) 1936- ... 33-36R
See also SATA 20
Heyd, David 1945- ... 118
Heydenburg, Harry E. 1891(?)-1979
Obituary ... 89-92
Heydenreich, Ludwig Heinrich 1903-
Brief entry ... 105
Heydon, Peter Richard 1913-1971 ... CAP-1
Earlier sketch in CA 19-20
Heyduck-Huth, Hilde 1929- ... 57-60
See also SATA 8
Heyel, Carl 1908- ... CANR-22
Earlier sketches in CA 19-20R, CANR-7
Heyen, William 1940- ... 33-36R
See also DLB 5
See also CLC 13, 18
Heyer, Georgette 1902-1974 ... 93-96
Obituary ... 49-52
Heyerdahl, Thor 1914- ... CANR-22
Earlier sketches in CA 7-8R, CANR-5
See also SATA 2
See also CLC 26
Heyler, David B., Sr. 1905(?)-1983
Obituary ... 110
Heyliger, William 1884-1955 ... YABC-1
Heym, Georg (Theodor Franz Arthur) 1887-1912 Brief entry ... 106
See also TCLC 9
Heym, Stefan 1913- ... CANR-4
Earlier sketch in CA 9-10R
See also CLC 41
Heyman, Abigail 1942- ... 57-60
Heyman, Ken(neth Louis) 1930- ... 112
See also SATA 34
Heyman, Neil Michael 1937- ... 113
Heymann, Frederick Gotthold 1900-1983
Obituary ... 111
Heymanns, Betty 1932- ... 85-88
Heymanson, Randal 1903-1984 Obituary ... 113
Heyn, Ernest V(ictor) 1904- Brief entry ... 111
Heyne, Paul 1931- ... 89-92
Heynen, Jim 1940- ... 77-80
Heyns, Barbara 1943- ... 85-88
Heyrman, Christine Leigh 1950- ... 115
Heyse, Paul (Johann Ludwig von) 1830-1914 Brief entry ... 104
See also TCLC 8
Heyst, Axel
See Grabowski, Z(bigniew) Anthony
Heyward, Carter 1945- ... 65-68
Heyward, Dorothy (Hartzell Kuhns) 1890-1961 Obituary ... 112
See also DLB 7
Heyward, (Edwin) DuBose 1885-1940
Brief entry ... 108
See also SATA 21
See also DLB 7, 9, 45
Heywood, Christopher 1928- ... 41-44R
Heywood, Hugh Christopher Lempriere 1896-1987 Obituary ... 122
Heywood, Karen 1946- ... SATA-48
Heywood, Lorimer D. 1899(?)-1977
Obituary ... 73-76
Heywood, Philip 1938- ... 69-72
Heywood, Rosalind 1895- ... 89-92
Heywood, Terence ... CAP-1
Earlier sketch in CA 9-10
Heywood, Thomas 1573(?)-1641 ... DLB-62
Heyworth, Peter (Lawrence Frederick) 1921- ... 65-68
Heyworth-Dunne, James ?-1974 Obituary ... 53-56
Hezel, Francis X(avier) 1939- ... 118
Hiaasen, Carl 1953- ... CANR-22
Earlier sketch in CA 105
Hian
See Higginson, William J(ohn)
Hiat, Elchik
See Katz, Menke
Hibbard, George Richard 1915- ... 85-88
Hibbard, Howard 1928-1984 ... CANR-9
Obituary ... 114
Earlier sketch in CA 53-56
Hibben, Frank Cummings 1910- ... CANR-2
Earlier sketch in CA 1R
Hibberd, Andrew Stuart 1893-1983(?)
Obituary ... 111
Hibberd, Jack 1940- ... 103
Hibbert, Christopher 1924- ... CANR-2
Earlier sketch in CA 4R
See also SATA 4
Hibbert, Eleanor Burford 1906- ... CANR-9
Earlier sketch in CA 17-18R
See also SATA 2
See also CLC 7
Hibbett, Howard (Scott) 1920- ... 106
Hibbs, Ben 1901-1975 ... 65-68
Obituary ... 104
Hibbs, Douglas A(lbert), Jr. 1944- ... CANR-3
Earlier sketch in CA 49-52
Hibbs, John 1925- ... CANR-19
Earlier sketch in CA 103
Hibbs, Paul 1906- ... CAP-1
Earlier sketch in CA 15-16
Hibdon, James E(dward) 1924- ... 25-28R
Hick, John (Harwood) 1922- ... CANR-22
Earlier sketches in CA 9-10R, CANR-6
Hickel, Walter J(oseph) 1919- ... 41-44R
Hicken, Victor 1921- ... 21-22R
Hickerson, J(ohn) Mel(ancthon) 1897- ... 25-28R
Hickey, Edward Shelby 1928(?)-1978 ... 85-88
Obituary ... 81-84
Hickey, Joseph J(ames) 1907- ... 41-44R
Hickey, Michael 1929- ... 102
Hickey, Neil 1931- ... 1R
Hickey, Raymond 1936- ... 114
Hickey, William
See Driberg, Thomas Edward Neil
Hickford, Jessie 1911- ... 53-56
Hickin, Norman E(rnest) 1910- ... CANR-15
Earlier sketch in CA 85-88
Hickinbotham, Tom 1903-1983 Obituary ... 111
Hickler, Holly 1923- ... 117
Hickling, C(harles) F(rederick) 1902-1977
Obituary ... 117

Hickman, Bert G(eorge), Jr. 1924- 108
Hickman, C(harles) Addison 1916- 103
Hickman, Charles 1905-1983 Obituary 109
Hickman, (Gertrud) Hannah 1928- 123
Hickman, Hoyt L(eon) 1927- 121
Hickman, Janet 1940- CANR-10
Earlier sketch in CA 65-68
See also SATA 12
Hickman, Martha Whitmore 1925- CANR-10
Earlier sketch in CA 25-28R
See also SATA 26
Hickman, Martin B(erkeley) 1925- 65-68
Hickman, Peggy 1906- 73-76
Hickok, Dorothy Jane 1912- 73-76
Hickok, Lorena A. 1892(?)-1968 73-76
See also SATA 20
Hickok, Robert (Blair) 1927- 61-64
Hickok, Will
See Harrison, C. William
Hicks, Charles B(alch) 1916- 7-8R
Hicks, Clifford B. 1920- CANR-24
Earlier sketches in CA 5-6R, CANR-9
See also SATA 50
Hicks, Darryl E(dwin) 1948- 120
Hicks, David E. 1931- CANR-7
Earlier sketch in CA 11-12R
Hicks, Donald A(lbert) 1947- 111
Hicks, Eleanor B.
See Coerr, Eleanor (Beatrice)
Hicks, George L(eon) 1935- 65-68
Hicks, Granville 1901-1982 .... CANR-13
Obituary 107
Earlier sketch in CA 9-10R
Hicks, Harvey
See Stratemeyer, Edward L.
Hicks, J. L.
See Hicks, Jim(my Lyn)
Hicks, Jack 1942- 97-100
Hicks, James L. 1915(?)-1986 Obituary 118
Hicks, Jim(my Lyn) 1937- 107
Hicks, John (Richard) 1904- CANR-13
Earlier sketch in CA 65-68
Hicks, John (Kenneth) 1918- 25-28R
Hicks, John D(onald) 1890-1972 .... CANR-2
Earlier sketch in CA 4R
Hicks, John Edward 1890(?)-1971
Obituary 104
Hicks, John H(arland) 1919- 45-48
Hicks, John V(ictor) 1907- 110
Hicks, Raymond L. 1926- 61-64
Hicks, Robert E(lden) 1920- Brief entry 109
Hicks, Roger W(illiam) 1950- 124
Hicks, Ronald G(raydon) 1934- 73-76
Hicks, Tyler Gregory 1921- 103
Hicks, Ursula Kathleen (Webb) 1896-1985 .. 103
Obituary 117
Hicks, Warren B(raukman) 1921- 33-36R
Hicks, Wilson 1897-1970 Obituary 29-32R
Hicky, Daniel Whitehead 1902- AITN-1
Hidden, (Frederick) Norman 1913- 77-80
Hidore, John J. 1932- CANR-21
Earlier sketches in CA 57-60, CANR-6
Hidy, Muriel E(mmie) 1906- 97-100
Hidy, Ralph W(illard) 1905- 7-8R
Hieatt, A(llen) Kent 1921- 21-22R
Hieatt, Constance B(artlett) 1928- CANR-23
Earlier sketches in CA 5-6R, CANR-8
See also SATA 4
Hiebel, Friedrich 1903- CANR-11
Earlier sketch in CA 65-68
Hiebert, Clarence 1927- 61-64
Hiebert, D(avid) Edmond 1910- 19-20R
Hiebert, Paul (Gerhardt) 1892- CANR-17
Earlier sketches in CA 23-24, CAP-2
Hiebert, Ray Eldon 1932- CANR-7
Earlier sketch in CA 17-18R
See also SATA 13
Hiernaux, Jean 1921- 57-60
Hieronymus, Clara (Booth) 1913- 73-76
Hiers, John Turner 1945- 102
Hiers, Richard H(yde) 1932- 53-56
Hiesberger, Jean Marie 1941- 41-44R
Hiesinger, Kathryn B(loom) 1943- 119
Hiestand, Dale L(eroy) 1925- 41-44R
Hifler, Joyce (Sequichie) 1925- 21-22R
Higashiuchi, Yoshio 1915(?)-1987
Obituary 122
Higbe, (Walter) Kirby 1915-1985 Obituary .. 116
Higbee, Edward (Counselman) 1910- 15-16R
Higbee, Kenneth Leo 1941- 101
Higby, Mary Jane 25-28R
Higdon, David Leon 1939- 77-80
Higdon, Hal 1931- CANR-3
Earlier sketch in CA 11-12R
See also SATA 4
Higenbottam, Frank 1910-1982 Obituary 117
Higenbottam, Frank 1910- 25-28R
Higgie, Lincoln William 1938- 7-8R
Higginbotham, A(loysius) Leon, Jr. 1928- .. 110
Higginbotham, (Prieur) Jay 1937- CANR-17
Earlier sketch in CA 93-96
Higginbotham, John E. 1933- 29-32R
Higginbotham, R(obert) Don 1931- 17-18R
Higginbotham, Sanford Wilson 1913-
Brief entry 105
Higginbotham, Virginia 1935- 115
Brief entry 110
Higginbottom, J(effrey) Winslow
1945- SATA-29
Higgins, A(lbert) C(orbin) 1930- 37-40R
Higgins, A(ngus) J(ohn) B(rockhurst)
1911- 13-14R
Higgins, Aidan 1927- 11-12R
See also DLB 14
Higgins, Alice 1924(?)-1974 Obituary 53-56
Higgins, Chester (Archer, Jr.) 1946- 73-76
Higgins, Colin 1941- 33-36R
See also DLB 26
Higgins, Dick
See Higgins, Richard C(arter)
Higgins, Don 1928- CANR-14
Earlier sketch in CA 25-28R
Higgins, George V(incent) 1939- CANR-17
Earlier sketch in CA 77-80
See also CAAS 5
See also DLB 2
See also DLBY 81
See also CLC 4, 7, 10, 18
Higgins, Ink
See Weiss, Morris S(amuel)
Higgins, Jack
See Patterson, Henry
Higgins, James E(dward) 1926- 73-76
Higgins, Jean C. 1932- 29-32R
Higgins, John A(loysius) 1931- CANR-13
Earlier sketch in CA 77-80
Higgins, John J(oseph) 1935- 45-48
Higgins, Judith Holden 1930- 102
Higgins, Lionel G(eorge) 1891-1985 123
Higgins, Marguerite 1920-1966 .... 5-6R
Obituary 25-28R
Higgins, Paul C. 1950- 106
Higgins, Paul Lambourne 1916- CANR-17
Earlier sketches in CA 3R, CANR-2
Higgins, Reynold Alleyne 1916- 25-28R
Higgins, Richard C(arter) 1938- CANR-8
Earlier sketch in CA 13-14R
Higgins, Ronald 1929- 81-84
Higgins, Rosalyn (Cohen) 1937- CANR-3
Earlier sketch in CA 11-12R
Higgins, Thomas J(oseph) 1899- CANR-5
Earlier sketch in CA 1R
Higgins, Trumbull 1919- 19-20R
Higgins, W(illiam) Robert 1938- 37-40R
Higginson, Fred H(all) 1921- 1R
Higginson, Margaret V(alliant) 1923- 105
Higginson, Thomas Wentworth
1823-1911 .... DLB-1, 64
Higginson, William J(ohn) 1938- 123
Higgs, David (Clive) 1939- 61-64
Higgs, E(ric) S(idney) 1908-1976 .... 11-12R
Obituary 69-72
Higgs, Gerald B. 1921- 106
Higgs, Gertrude Monro
See Monro-Higgs, Gertrude
Higgs, Robert J(ackson) 1932- 115
High, Dallas M. 1931- 21-22R
High, Monique Raphel 1949- CANR-21
Earlier sketch in CA 102
High, Philip E(mpson) 1914- 97-100
High, Stanley (Hoflund) 1895-1961
Obituary 89-92
Higham, Charles 1931- CANR-17
Earlier sketch in CA 33-36R
Higham, David 1895-1978 .... CANR-2
Earlier sketch in CA 4R
Higham, David (Michael) 1949- SATA-50
Higham, Florence May Grier 1896-1980
Obituary 97-100
Higham, John 1920- CANR-6
Earlier sketch in CA 1R
Higham, Robin (David Stewart) 1925- ... CANR-1
Earlier sketch in CA 2R
Higham, Roger 1935- 33-36R
Higham, T. F.
See Higham, Thomas Farrant
Higham, Thomas Farrant 1890-1975
Obituary 116
Highberger, Ruth 1917- 65-68
Highet, Gilbert (Arthur) 1906-1978 ..... CANR-6
Obituary 73-76
Earlier sketch in CA 1R
Highet, Helen
See MacInnes, Helen (Clark)
Highland, Dora
See Avallone, Michael (Angelo), Jr.
Highland, Monica
See Kendall, Lisa See
Highsmith, (Mary) Patricia 1921- CANR-20
Earlier sketches in CA 3R, CANR-1
See also CLC 2, 4, 14, 42
Highsmith, Richard M(organ), Jr. 1920- .. 37-40R
Hightower, Florence Cole 1916-1981 .... 4R
Obituary 103
See also SATA 4, 27
Hightower, John M(urmann) 1909-1987
Obituary 121
Hightower, Paul
See Collins, Thomas Hightower
Highwater, Jamake (Mamake) 1942- ... CANR-10
Earlier sketch in CA 65-68
See also SATA 30, 32
See also DLB 52
See also DLBY 85
See also CLC 12
Higley, John (Clark) 1938- Brief entry 116
Higman, B(arry) W(illiam) 1943- 81-84
Higman, Francis M(ontgomery) 1935- .. CANR-12
Earlier sketch in CA 25-28R
Hignett, Sean 1934- 49-52
Hignonnet, Margaret Randolph 1941- 61-64
Hignonnet, Patrice Louis-Rene 1938- 65-68
Higson, James D(oran) 1925- 49-52
Hijuelos, Oscar 1951- 123
Hikmet, Nazim 1902-1963 Obituary 93-96
See also CLC 40
Hilary, Christopher 1927(?)-1979
Obituary 89-92
Hilberg, Raul 1926- 33-36R
Hilberry, Conrad (Arthur) 1928- CANR-10
Earlier sketch in CA 25-28R
Hilborn, Ann 1942- 109
Hilborn, Harry (Warren) 1900- CAP-2
Earlier sketch in CA 33-36
Hildebidle, John 1946- 114
Hildebrand, George H(erbert) 1913- CANR-8
Earlier sketch in CA 17-18R
Hildebrand, Grant 1934- 57-60
Hildebrand, Joel H(enry) 1881-1983 ..... CAP-1
Obituary 109
Earlier sketch in CA 11-12
Hildebrand, Verna 1924- CANR-13
Earlier sketch in CA 33-36R
Hildebrandt, Franz 1909-1985 118
Hildebrandt, Greg 1939- 104
See also SATA 33
Hildebrandt, Tim(othy) 1939- 122
Brief entry 111
See also SATA 33
Hildebrandts, The
See Hildebrandt, Tim(othy)
Hilder, Rowland 1905- SATA-36
Hilderbrand, Robert Clinton 1947- 105
Hildesheimer, Wolfgang 1916- 101
Hildick, E. W.
See Hildick, (Edmund) Wallace
Hildick, (Edmund) Wallace 1925- 25-28R
See also SATA 2
Hildreth, Gertrude Howell 1898-1984
Obituary 112
Hildreth, Margaret Holbrook 1927- 89-92
Hildreth, Richard 1807-1865 ..... DLB-1, 30, 59
Hildum, Donald C(layton) 1930- 23-24R
Hildyard, Nicholas 1955- 122
Hilfer, Anthony Channell 1936- 73-76
Hilfiker, David 1945- 123
Hilgard, Ernest R(opiequet) 1904- 113
Hilgartner, Stephen 1956- 111
Hilger, Sister Mary Inez 1891-1977 73-76
Hilken, Glen A. 1936- 61-64
Hill, Ab
See Hill, Abram (Barrington)
Hill, Abram (Barrington) 1910(?)-1986
Obituary 120
Hill, Adrian Keith Graham 1895-1977 77-80
Hill, Alexis
See Glick, Ruth (Burtnick)
Hill, Alfred T(uxbury) 1908- 21-22R
Hill, Archibald A(nderson) 1902- 49-52
Hill, Barrington Julian Warren 1915- 7-8R
Hill, Bennett D(avid) 1934- 111
Hill, Bob
See Hill, Robert C(ecil)
Hill, Brian (Merrikin) 1896- CAP-1
Earlier sketch in CA 9-10
Hill, Carol (Dechellis) 1942- 77-80
Hill, (John Edward) Christopher 1912- . CANR-22
Earlier sketches in CA 9-10R, CANR-4
Hill, Claude 1911- 23-24R
Hill, Clifford S. 1927- CANR-7
Earlier sketch in CA 13-14R
Hill, Daniel G., Jr. 1896(?)-1979
Obituary 89-92
Hill, Dave
See Hill, David Charles
Hill, David Charles 1936- CANR-11
Earlier sketch in CA 19-20R
Hill, Deborah 1936- 108
Hill, Dee
See Zucker, Dolores Mae Bolton
Hill, Denise 1919- CANR-23
Earlier sketch in CA 106
Hill, (Richard) Desmond 1920-1984 .... 7-8R
Obituary 114
Hill, Devra Z.
See Zucker, Dolores Mae Bolton
Hill, Dilys M(ary) 1935- 61-64
Hill, Donald (Routledge) 1922- 122
Hill, Donald Hamilton
See Hamilton-Hill, Donald
Hill, Donna (Marie) CANR-7
Earlier sketch in CA 15-16R
See also SATA 24
Hill, Douglas (Arthur) 1935- CANR-4
Earlier sketch in CA 53-56
See also SATA 39
Hill, Draper
See Hill, L(eroy) Draper, Jr.
Hill, Earle 1941- 33-36R
Hill, Eileen
See Stack, Nicolete Meredith
Hill, Elizabeth Starr 1925- 17-18R
See also SATA 24
Hill, Ellen Wise 1942- 77-80
Hill, Eric 1927- CLR-13
Hill, Ernest 1915- 53-56
Hill, Errol Gaston 1921- 45-48
Hill, Evan 1919- CANR-5
Earlier sketch in CA 11-12R
Hill, Fiona
See Pall, Ellen Jane
Hill, (Charles) Fowler 1901(?)-1973
Obituary 37-40R
Hill, (James William) Francis 1899-1980
Obituary 108
Hill, Frank Ernest 1888-1969 73-76
Hill, Gene 1928- 97-100
Hill, Geoffrey (William) 1932- CANR-21
Earlier sketch in CA 81-84
See also DLB 40
See also CLC 5, 8, 18, 45
Hill, George E(dward) 1907- CAP-1
Earlier sketch in CA 17-18
Hill, George Roy 1921- 122
Brief entry 110
See also CLC 26
Hill, Gladwin 1914- 25-28R
Hill, Grace Brooks CAP-2
Earlier sketch in CA 19-20
See also SATA 1
Hill, Grace Livingston 1865-1947 .... YABC-2
Hill, (Norman) Graham 1929-1975
Obituary 108
Hill, H. D. N.
See Disston, Harry
Hill, Hamlin (Lewis) 1931- CANR-18
Earlier sketches in CA 11-12R, CANR-3
Hill, Harold E(verett) 1905- CANR-11
Earlier sketch in CA 69-72
Hill, Helen
See Miller, Helen Hill
Hill, Helen M(orey) 1915- 57-60
See also SATA 27
Hill, Henry Bertram 1907- 1R
Hill, Herbert 1924- 65-68
Hill, Hyacinthe
See Anderson, Virginia (R. Cronin)
Hill, I(saac) William 1908- 65-68
Hill, J(ohn) C(ampbell) 1888- 37-40R
Hill, James
See Jameson, (Margaret) Storm
Hill, James N(ewlin) 1934- 33-36R
Hill, Jim Dan 1897- CAP-1
Earlier sketch in CA 11-12
Hill, John Hugh 1905- CANR-5
Earlier sketch in CA 2R
Hill, John L. 1960- 124
Hill, John P(aul) 1936- 29-32R
Hill, John S(tanley) 1929- 37-40R
Hill, John Wiley 1890-1977 Obituary 69-72
Hill, Kathleen Louise 1917- CANR-3
Earlier sketch in CA 9-10R
See also SATA 4
Hill, Kay
See Hill, Kathleen Louise
Hill, Ken(neth) 1937- 108
Hill, King
See Robertson, Frank C(hester)
Hill, Knox C(alvin) 1910- CAP-1
Earlier sketch in CA 19-20
Hill, L(eslie) A(lexander) 1918- 23-24R
Hill, L(eroy) Draper, Jr. 1935- CANR-12
Earlier sketch in CA 17-18R
Hill, Larry D(ean) 1935- 73-76
Hill, Lawson (Traphagen) 1927- 118
Hill, Lee H(alsey) 1899-1974 .... 37-40R
Obituary 45-48
Hill, Leslie Pinckney 1880-1960 .... DLB-51
Hill, Lew
See Skene-Melvin, (Lewis) David (St.
Columb)
Hill, Lorna 1902- CANR-14
Earlier sketches in CA 9-10, CAP-1
See also SATA 12
Hill, Lowell Dean 1930- 114
Hill, M(elba) Anne 1953- 123
Hill, Margaret (Ohler) 1915- CANR-16
Earlier sketches in CA 4R, CANR-1
See also SATA 36
Hill, Marnesba D. 1913- 101
Hill, Marvin S(idney) 1928- 61-64
Hill, Mary A. 1939- 102
Hill, Mary Raymond 1923- CANR-6
Earlier sketch in CA 57-60
Hill, Mary V. 1941- 102
Hill, Meg
See Hill, Margaret (Ohler)
Hill, Mike 1944- 122
Hill, Monica
See Watson, Jane Werner
Hill, Nancy Klenk 1936- 108
Hill, Napoleon 1883(?)-1970 Obituary 104
Hill, Nellie
See Hill, Ellen Wise
Hill, Norman Llewellyn 1895- 7-8R
Hill, Pamela 1920- CANR-16
Earlier sketches in CA 49-52, CANR-1
Hill, Pati 69-72
Hill, Peter Proal 1926- 33-36R
Hill, Philip G(eorge) 1934- 33-36R
Hill, Polly
See Humphreys, Mary Eglantyne Hill
Hill, R(ufus) Carter 1945- 110
Hill, R. Lance 1943- CANR-11
Earlier sketch in CA 65-68
Hill, Ralph Nading 1917-1987 .... CANR-1
Obituary 124
Earlier sketch in CA 4R
Hill, Rebecca 1944- 111
Hill, Reginald (Charles) 1936- 73-76
Hill, Reuben (Lorenzo, Jr.) 1912-1985
Obituary 117
Hill, Richard 1901- CANR-1
Earlier sketch in CA 1R
Hill, Richard (Fontaine) 1941- 33-36R
Hill, Richard E. 1920- 33-36R
Hill, Richard Johnson 1925- CANR-4
Earlier sketch in CA 9-10R
Hill, Robert C(ecil) 1929- 118
Hill, Robert W(hite) 1919-1982 .... 9-10R
Obituary 107
See also SATA 12, 31
Hill, Rosalind M(ary) T(heodosia) 1908- .. CAP-1
Earlier sketch in CA 11-12
Hill, Roscoe E(arl) 1936- 37-40R
Hill, Rowland
See Wallace-Clarke, George
Hill, Roy Gerald 1926- 111
Hill, Ruth A.
See Viguers, Ruth Hill
Hill, Ruth Beebe 1913- 89-92
Hill, Ruth Livingston
See Munce, Ruth Hill
Hill, Samuel E(rvin) 1913- 17-18R

Hill, Samuel S(mythe), Jr. 1927- ... CANR-5
Earlier sketch in CA 11-12R
Hill, Selima 1945- ... 117
Hill, "Sir" John 1714(?)-1775 ... DLB-39
Hill, Stephen 1946- ... 111
Hill, Susan 1942- ... 33-36R
See also DLB 14
See also CLC 4
Hill, Thomas English 1909- ... 13-14R
Hill, W. M.
See Dodd, Edward Howard, Jr.
Hill, W(illiam) Speed 1935- ... 41-44R
Hill, Walter 1942- Brief entry ... 109
See also DLB 44
Hill, Weldon
See Scott, William R(alph)
Hill, West T(hompson), Jr. 1915- ... 37-40R
Hill, Wilhelmina 1902- ... 57-60
Hill, William Joseph 1924- ... 37-40R
Hill, Winfred F(arrington) 1929- ... 29-32R
Hillaby, John (D.) 1917- Brief entry ... 109
Hillam, Ray C. 1928- Brief entry ... 107
Hillard, James M(ilton) 1920- ... 73-76
Hillary, Edmund (Percival) 1919- ... 112
Hillary, Peter 1954- ... 123
Hillas, Julian
See Dashwood, Robert Julian
Hillbruner, Anthony 1914- ... 41-44R
Hillcourt, William 1900- ... 93-96
See also SATA 27
Hillegas, Mark R(obert) 1926- ... 33-36R
Hillel, Yehoshua Bar
See Bar-Hillel, Yehoshua
Hillenbrand, Barry R. 1941- ... 73-76
Hillenbrand, Martin Joseph 1915- ... 108
Hiller, Catherine 1946- ... 106
Hiller, Doris
See Nussbaum, Al(bert) F.
Hiller, Flora
See Hurd, Florence
Hiller, Ilo (Ann) 1938- ... 121
Hiller, Lejaren A(rthur), Jr. 1924- ... 1R
Hillerbrand, Hans J(oachim) 1931-
Brief entry ... 111
Hillerich, Robert L(ee) 1927- ... 112
Hillerman, Anne 1949- ... 118
Hillerman, Tony 1925- ... CANR-21
Earlier sketch in CA 29-32R
See also SATA 6
Hillers, Delbert R(oy) 1932- ... 77-80
Hillers, H(erman) W(illiam) 1925- ... 73-76
Hillert, Margaret 1920- ... CANR-17
Earlier sketches in CA 49-52, CANR-1
See also SATA 8
See also AITN 1
Hillery, George A(nthony), Jr. 1927- ... 25-28R
Hilles, Frederick W(hiley) 1900-1975 ... 5-6R
Obituary ... 61-64
Hillgarth, J(ocelyn) N(igel) 1929- ... 37-40R
Hillgruber, Andreas 1925- ... 106
Hilliard, Jan
See Grant, Kay
Hilliard, Noel (Harvey) 1929- ... CANR-7
Earlier sketch in CA 11-12R
See also CLC 15
Hilliard, Robert L. 1925- ... 107
Hilliard, Sam B(owers) 1930- ... 61-64
Hillier, Bevis 1940- ... 29-32R
Hillier, Jack R(onald) 1912- ... CANR-3
Earlier sketch in CA 7-8R
Hillier, James Martin 1941- ... 113
Hillier, Jim
See Hillier, James Martin
Hillier, Tristram (Paul) 1905-1983
Obituary ... 114
Hilliker, Grant 1921- ... 33-36R
Hilling, David 1935- ... CANR-12
Earlier sketch in CA 29-32R
Hillinger, Brad 1952- ... 73-76
Hillis, Charles Richard 1913- ... 13-14R
Hillis, Dave 1945- ... 57-60
Hillis, Dick
See Hillis, Charles Richard
Hillix, W(illiam) A(llen) 1927- ... 89-92
Hillman, Arthur 1909-1985 Obituary ... 115
Hillman, Barry L(eslie) 1942- ... 102
Hillman, Howard 1934- ... CANR-20
Earlier sketch in CA 41-44R
Hillman, James 1926- ... 89-92
Hillman, Martin
See Hill, Douglas (Arthur)
Hillman, Priscilla 1940- ... 108
See also SATA 39, 48
Hillman, Ruth Estelyn 1925- ... 53-56
Hillocks, George, Jr. 1934- ... 53-56
Hill-Reid, William Scott 1890- ... 7-8R
Hills, C(harles) A(lbert) R(eis) 1955- ... CANR-23
Earlier sketch in CA 106
See also SATA 39
Hills, Christopher B. 1926- ... 114
Hills, Denis (Cecil) 1913- ... CANR-10
Earlier sketch in CA 65-68
Hills, George 1918- ... 25-28R
Hills, L(awrence) Rust 1924- ... 25-28R
Hills, Lee 1906- ... 101
See also AITN 2
Hills, P. J.
See Hills, Philip J(ames)
Hills, Patricia Gorton Schulze 1936- ... 103
Hills, Philip J(ames) 1933- Brief entry ... 117
Hills, Stuart Lee 1932- ... 33-36R
Hills, Theo(dore) L(ewis) 1925- ... 7-8R
Hills, Tina ... AITN-2
Hillson, Maurie 1925- ... 17-18R
Hillstrom, Tom 1943- ... 102
Hillus, Wilhelm
See Hillers, H(erman) W(illiam)

Hillway, Tyrus 1912- ... CANR-4
Earlier sketch in CA 2R
Hillyard, Brian P. 1949- ... 111
Hillyer, Robert (Silliman) 1895-1961
Obituary ... 89-92
See also DLB 54
Hilscher, Herb(ert H.) 1902-1987
Obituary ... 122
Hilsdale, (Eric) Paul 1922- ... 11-12R
Hilsenrath, Edgar 1926- ... 49-52
Hilsman, Roger 1919- ... 5-6R
Hilt, Douglas Richard 1932- ... 65-68
Hiltebeital, Alf 1942- ... 103
Hiltner, Seward 1909-1984 ... CANR-1
Obituary ... 114
Earlier sketch in CA 3R
Hilton, Alec
See Chesser, Eustace
and Fullerton, Alexander
Hilton, Alice Mary 1924- ... 29-32R
Hilton, Bruce 1930- ... CANR-8
Earlier sketch in CA 7-8R
Hilton, Conrad N(icholson) 1887-1979
Obituary ... 81-84
Hilton, Della (Marion) 1934- ... 69-72
Hilton, Earl (Raymond) 1914- ... 23-24R
Hilton, George W(oodman) 1925- ... CANR-4
Earlier sketch in CA 1R
Hilton, Howard H(oyt, Jr.) 1926- ... 105
Hilton, Irene Pothus ... 3R
See also SATA 7
Hilton, James 1900-1954 Brief entry ... 108
See also SATA 34
See also DLB 34
See also TCLC 21
Hilton, John Buxton 1921- ... CANR-5
Earlier sketch in CA 53-56
Hilton, Lewis B. 1920- ... CANR-8
Earlier sketch in CA 57-60
Hilton, (Howard) Nelson 1950- ... 110
Hilton, Peter 1913- ... 69-72
Hilton, R(odney) H(oward) Brief entry ... 112
Hilton, Ralph 1907- ... 29-32R
See also SATA 8
Hilton, Richard 1894- ... CAP-1
Earlier sketch in CA 9-10
Hilton, Rodney
See Hilton, R(odney) H(oward)
Hilton, Ronald 1911- ... 29-32R
Hilton, Suzanne 1922- ... CANR-12
Earlier sketch in CA 29-32R
See also SATA 4
Hilton, Thomas Leonard 1924- ... 13-14R
Hilton Smith, Robert D(ennis) ?-1974
Obituary ... 53-56
Hilts, Philip J(ames) 1947- ... 110
Hilu, Virginia 1929(?)-1976 Obituary ... 104
Hilvert, John (Peter Paul) 1945- ... 124
Him
See Deal, Borden
Him, George 1900-1982 Obituary ... 106
See also SATA 30
Himber, Jacob 1907- ... 105
Himelick, (James) Raymond 1910- ... 33-36R
Himelstein, Morgan Y(ale) 1926- ... 5-6R
Himes, Chester (Bomar) 1909-1984 ... CANR-22
Obituary ... 114
Earlier sketch in CA 25-28R
See also DLB 2
See also CLC 2, 4, 7, 18
Himes, Joseph S(andy) 1908- ... 25-28R
Himler, Ann 1946- ... 53-56
See also SATA 8
Himler, Ronald (Norbert) 1937- ... CANR-5
Earlier sketch in CA 53-56
See also SATA 6
Himmelfarb, Gertrude 1922- ... 49-52
Himmelfarb, Milton 1918- ... 101
Himmelheber, Diana Martin 1938- ... 19-20R
Himmelman, John (Carl) 1959- ... 114
See also SATA 47
Himmelstein, Jerome L(ionel) 1948- ... 113
Himstreet, William Charles 1923- ... CANR-16
Earlier sketches in CA 1R, CANR-1
Hinchcliff, Peter Bingham 1929- ... 102
Hinchliffe, Arnold P. 1930- ... CANR-14
Earlier sketch in CA 77-80
Hinckle, Warren James III 1938- ... 89-92
Hinckley, Barbara 1937- ... 57-60
Hinckley, Helen
See Jones, Helen Hinckley
Hinckley, Ted C(harles) 1925- ... 57-60
Hind, Dolores (Ellen) 1931- ... SATA-49
Hind, Robert James 1931- ... 45-48
Hinde, Richard Standish Elphinstone
1912- ... CAP-1
Earlier sketch in CA 9-10
Hinde, Robert Aubrey 1923- ... 109
Hinde, Thomas
See Chitty, Thomas Willes
See also CLC 6, 11
Hinde, Wendy 1919- ... 103
Hindemith, Paul 1895-1963 Obituary ... 112
Hinden, Michael C(harles) 1941- ... 109
Hinderer, Walter (Hermann) 1934- ... CANR-1
Earlier sketch in CA 45-48
Hindin, Nathan
See Bloch, Robert (Albert)
Hindle, Brooke 1918- ... CANR-23
Earlier sketches in CA 15-16R, CANR-7
Hindle, Lee J(ohn) 1965- ... 117
Hindle, W(ilfred) H(ope) 1903-1967 ... CAP-2
Earlier sketch in CA 23-24
Hindley, Geoffrey 1935- ... 109
Hindman, Jane F(erguson) 1905- ... CANR-10
Earlier sketch in CA 25-28R
Hindman, Jo(sephine Long) 1910- ... 97-100

Hinds, Dudley S. 1926- ... 115
Hinds, E. M.
See Hinds, (Evelyn) Margery
Hinds, (Evelyn) Margery ... 9-10R
Hinds, Michael deCourcy
See deCourcy Hinds, Michael
Hindus, Maurice (Gerschon) 1891-1969
Obituary ... 25-28R
Hindus, Michael S(tephen) 1946- ... 105
Hindus, Milton Henry 1916- ... CANR-7
Earlier sketch in CA 19-20R
Hine, Al(fred Blakelee) 1915- ... CANR-2
Earlier sketch in CA 1R
Hine, (William) Daryl 1936- ... CANR-20
Earlier sketches in CA 2R, CANR-1
See also DLB 60
See also CLC 15
Hine, Frederick R. 1925- ... 37-40R
Hine, James R. 1909- ... CANR-17
Earlier sketches in CA 45-48, CANR-2
Hine, Robert Van Norden, Jr. 1921- ... CANR-1
Earlier sketch in CA 1R
Hine, Sesyle Joslin 1929- ... 15-16R
Hine, Thomas 1947- ... 123
Hine, Virginia H(aglin) 1920- ... 97-100
Hiner, Louis C(hase) 1919- ... 73-76
Hines, Anna G(rossnickle) 1946- ... 114
See also SATA 45
Hines, Barry (Melvin) 1939- ... 102
Hines, Bede F(rancis) 1918- ... 45-48
Hines, Earl Kenneth 1905-1983 Obituary ... 109
Hines, Fatha
See Hines, Earl Kenneth
Hines, Neal O(ldfield) 1908- ... CANR-2
Earlier sketch in CA 7-8R
Hines, Paul (David) 1934- ... 29-32R
Hines, Robert Stephan 1926- ... CANR-3
Earlier sketch in CA 9-10R
Hines, Thomas S(pight) 1936- ... CANR-5
Earlier sketch in CA 53-56
Hines, William H. 1909(?)-1976 Obituary ... 65-68
Hinger, Charlotte 1940- ... 123
Hingley, Ronald F(rancis) 1920- ... 7-8R
Hingorani, R(up) C. 1925- ... 29-32R
Hinkel, John V.
See Hinkel, John Vincent
Hinkel, John Vincent 1906-1986 Obituary ... 121
Hinkemeyer, Michael T(homas) 1940- ... CANR-11
Earlier sketch in CA 69-72
Hinkle, Douglas P(addock) 1923- ... 69-72
Hinkle, Gerald H(ahn) 1931- ... 89-92
Hinkle, Olin Ethmer 1902- ... 3R
Hinkle, Vernon 1935- ... 109
Hinkson, James 1943- ... 69-72
Hinkson, Katharine Tynan
See Tynan, Katharine
Hinkson, Pamela 1900(?)-1982 Obituary ... 107
Hinman, Charlton (Joseph Kadio)
1911-1977 ... CANR-3
Obituary ... 89-92
Earlier sketch in CA 5-6R
Hinman, George W., Jr. 1891-1977
Obituary ... 73-76
Hinman, Robert B(enedict) 1920- ... 5-6R
Hinnebusch, Paul (Gerard) 1917- ... 114
Hinnebusch, William A(quinas) 1908- ... 37-40R
Hinnells, John R(ussell) 1941- ... 49-52
Hinrichsen, Max (Henry) 1901-1965 ... CAP-1
Earlier sketch in CA 13-14
Hinshaw, Cecil E(ugene) 1911- ... 15-16R
Hinshaw, H(orton) Corwin 1902- ... 104
Hinshaw, Randall (Weston) 1915- ... CANR-15
Earlier sketch in CA 41-44R
Hinshaw, Robert E(ugene) 1933- ... 57-60
Hinshaw, Seth B(ennett) 1908- ... 112
Hinshelwood, Cyril (Norman) 1897-1967
Obituary ... 116
Hinsley, F(rancis) H(arry) 1918- ... 17-18R
Hinson, E(dward) Glenn 1931- ... CANR-8
Earlier sketch in CA 21-22R
Hinson, (Grady) Maurice 1930- ... CANR-17
Earlier sketches in CA 45-48, CANR-2
Hinterhoff, Eugene 1895- ... CAP-1
Earlier sketch in CA 9-10
Hintikka, (Kaarlo) Jaakko (Juhani)
1929- ... CANR-2
Earlier sketch in CA 2R
Hinton, Ann Pearlman 1941- ... 108
Hinton, Bernard L. 1937- ... 33-36R
Hinton, Harold C(lendenin) 1924- ... 19-20R
Hinton, John 1926- ... 49-52
Hinton, Nigel 1941- ... 85-88
Hinton, Richard W.
See Angoff, Charles
Hinton, S(usan) E(loise) 1950- ... 81-84
See also SATA 19
See also CLC 30
See also CLR 3
Hinton, Sam 1917- ... 73-76
See also SATA 43
Hinton, Ted C. 1904(?)-1977 Obituary ... 73-76
Hinton, William H. 1919- ... CANR-18
Earlier sketch in CA 25-28R
Hintz, (Loren) Martin 1945- ... CANR-12
Earlier sketch in CA 65-68
See also SATA 39, 47
Hintze, Guenther 1906- ... CAP-2
Earlier sketch in CA 21-22
Hintze, Naomi A. 1909- ... CANR-1
Earlier sketch in CA 45-48
Hinxman, Margaret 1924- ... 124
Hinz, Evelyn J. 1938- ... CANR-10
Earlier sketch in CA 65-68
Hipp, George
See Abrams, George J(oseph)

Hippisley Coxe, Antony D(acres)
1912-1988 ... 103
Obituary ... 124
Hippius, Zinaida
See Gippius, Zinaida (Nikolayevna)
See also TCLC 9
Hipple, Theodore W(allace) 1935- ... CANR-10
Earlier sketch in CA 65-68
Hipple, Walter J(ohn), Jr. 1921- ... 41-44R
Hippler, Arthur E(dwin) 1935- ... 57-60
Hipps, Juanita Redmond 1913(?)-1979
Obituary ... 85-88
Hipskind, Judith 1945- ... 97-100
Hipskind, Verne K(enneth) 1925-1975 ... CAP-2
Earlier sketch in CA 21-22
Hirano, Marsha
See Hirano-Nakanishi, Marsha J(oyce)
Hirano-Nakanishi, Marsha J(oyce) 1949- ... 119
Hiraoka, Kimitake 1925-1970 ... 97-100
Obituary ... 29-32R
Hiro, Dilip ... CANR-14
Earlier sketch in CA 77-80
Hirsch, Abby 1946- ... 45-48
Hirsch, Barbara B. 1938- ... 73-76
Hirsch, Charles S. 1942- ... 105
Hirsch, David H. 1930- ... 97-100
Hirsch, E(ric) Donald, Jr. 1928- ... 25-28R
See also DLB 67
Hirsch, Edward 1950- ... CANR-20
Earlier sketch in CA 104
See also CLC 31
Hirsch, Ernest A(lbert) 1924-1977 ... CANR-11
Earlier sketch in CA 25-28R
Hirsch, Foster (Lance) 1943- ... CANR-17
Earlier sketches in CA 45-48, CANR-2
Hirsch, Fred 1931-1978 ... 25-28R
Obituary ... 77-80
Hirsch, Herbert 1941- ... CANR-15
Earlier sketch in CA 41-44R
Hirsch, Karen 1941- ... 105
Hirsch, Lester M. 1925- ... 17-18R
Hirsch, Linda 1949- ... 105
Hirsch, Marianne 1949- ... 113
Hirsch, Mark David 1910- ... 89-92
Hirsch, Miriam F. 1927- ... 106
Hirsch, Monroe J(erome) 1917- ... 41-44R
Hirsch, Morris Isaac 1915- ... 103
Hirsch, Phil 1926- ... 102
See also SATA 35
Hirsch, S. Carl 1913- ... CANR-2
Earlier sketch in CA 7-8R
See also SATA 2
Hirsch, Seev 1931- ... 33-36R
Hirsch, Steven R(ichard) 1937- ... 113
Hirsch, Thomas L. 1931- ... 49-52
Hirsch, Walter 1919- ... 15-16R
Hirsch, Werner Z. 1920- ... CANR-7
Earlier sketch in CA 19-20R
Hirsch, William Randolph
See Kitman, Marvin
and Lingeman, Richard R(oberts)
Hirschberg, Cornelius 1901- ... CAP-2
Earlier sketch in CA 17-18
Hirschfeld, Albert 1903- ... CANR-2
Earlier sketch in CA 1R
Hirschfeld, Burt 1923- Brief entry ... 111
Hirschfeld, Charles 1913- Brief entry ... 105
Hirschfeld, Herman 1905- ... CAP-1
Earlier sketch in CA 15-16
Hirschfield, Robert S(idney) 1928- ... 45-48
Hirschhorn, Clive 1940- ... CANR-9
Earlier sketch in CA 57-60
Hirschhorn, Howard H(arvey) 1931- ... CANR-16
Earlier sketch in CA 93-96
Hirschhorn, Richard Clark 1933- ... 69-72
Hirschi, Ron 1948- ... 120
Hirschi, Travis 1935- ... CANR-13
Earlier sketch in CA 77-80
Hirschman, Albert O. 1915- ... CANR-16
Earlier sketches in CA 1R, CANR-1
Hirschman, Jack 1933- ... CANR-22
Earlier sketch in CA 105
Hirschmann, Linda (Ann) 1941- ... 106
See also SATA 40
Hirschmann, Maria Anne ... 85-88
Hirschmeier, Johannes 1921- ... CANR-5
Earlier sketch in CA 13-14R
Hirsh, James E(ric) 1946- ... 109
Hirsh, Marilyn 1944- ... CANR-16
Earlier sketches in CA 49-52, CANR-1
See also SATA 7
Hirshberg, Al(bert Simon) 1909-1973 ... CANR-4
Obituary ... 41-44R
Earlier sketch in CA 4R
See also SATA 38
Hirshfield, Daniel S. 1942- ... 29-32R
Hirshson, Stanley Philip 1928- ... 2R
Hirst, David W(ayne) 1920- ... 37-40R
Hirst, Paul H(eywood) 1927- ... 65-68
Hirst, Paul Quentin 1946- ... 104
Hirst, Rodney Julian 1920- ... 11-12R
Hirst, Stephen M(ichael) 1939- ... 53-56
Hirst, Wilma E(llis) 1914- ... 15-16R
Hirt, Michael L(eonard) 1934- ... 9-10R
Hisamatsu, (Hoseki) Shin'ichi 1889- ... 81-84
Hiscock, Bruce 1940- ... 122
Hiscock, Eric 1899- ... 109
Hiscock, Eric C(harles) 1908-1986 ... 107
Obituary ... 120
Hiscocks, C(harles) Richard 1907- ... 53-56
Hiser, Iona Seibert ... CANR-2
Earlier sketch in CA 3R
See also SATA 4
Hiskett, Mervyn 1920- ... 61-64
Hislop, Codman 1906- ... CAP-2
Earlier sketch in CA 33-36
Hisrich, Robert D(ale) 1944- ... 112

Hiss, Alger 1904- ... 33-36R
Hiss, Tony 1941- ... 77-80
Hissey, Jane (Elizabeth) 1952- ... 124
Hitchcock, Alfred (Joseph) 1899-1980
  Obituary ... 97-100
  See also SATA 24, 27
  See also CLC 16
Hitchcock, Alma Reville 1899-1982
  Obituary ... 107
Hitchcock, George 1914- ... CANR-13
  Earlier sketch in CA 33-36R
Hitchcock, H(ugh) Wiley 1923- ... CANR-17
  Earlier sketches in CA 45-48, CANR-1
Hitchcock, Henry-Russell 1903-1987
  Obituary ... 122
Hitchcock, James 1938- ... 33-36R
Hitchcock, Raymond (John) 1922- ... 85-88
Hitchcock, Susan Tyler 1950- ... CANR-18
  Earlier sketch in CA 102
Hitchens, Dolores 1908(?)-1973 Obituary ... 45-48
Hitchin, Martin Mewburn 1917- ... 13-14R
Hitching, (John) Francis 1933- ... 103
Hitchman, James H. 1932- ... 37-40R
Hitchman, Janet 1916-1980 ... 23-24R
  Obituary ... 97-100
Hite, James (Cleveland) 1941- ... 53-56
Hite, Molly 1947- ... 124
Hite, Shere D. 1942- ... 81-84
Hitiris, Theodore 1938- ... 41-44R
Hitler, Adolf 1889-1945 Brief entry ... 117
Hitrec, Joseph George 1912-1972 ... CAP-2
  Earlier sketch in CA 17-18
Hitsman, J(ohn) Mackay 1917-1970 ... CAP-1
  Earlier sketch in CA 17-18
Hitt, Russell T(rovillo) 1905- ... 4R
Hitt, William D(ee) 1929- ... 49-52
Hitte, Kathryn 1919- ... 21-22R
  See also SATA 16
Hitti, Philip K(huri) 1886-1978 ... CANR-6
  Obituary ... 81-84
  Earlier sketch in CA 2R
Hitz, Demi 1942- ... CANR-8
  Earlier sketch in CA 61-64
  See also SATA 11
Hitz-Holman, Betsy
  See Holman, Betsy Hitz
Hively, Pete (Chester) 1934- ... 69-72
Hivnor, Robert 1916- ... 65-68
Hix, Charles (Arthur) 1942- ... CANR-21
  Earlier sketch in CA 102
Hixon, Don L(ee) 1942- ... 73-76
Hixson, Joseph R(andolph) 1927- ... 65-68
Hixson, Richard F. 1932- ... 23-24R
Hixson, William B(utler), Jr. 1940- ... 37-40R
Hjelte, George 1893-1979 ... CANR-23
  Earlier sketch in CA 29-32R
Hjortsberg, William (Reinhold) 1941- ... 33-36R
Hlasko, Marek 1933(?)-1969 Obituary ... 25-28R
Hlybinny, Vladimir
  See Seduro, Vladimir
Hnizdovsky, Jacques 1915- ... SATA-32
Ho, Alfred K(uo-liang) 1919- ... 25-28R
Ho, Minfong 1951- ... 77-80
  See also SATA 15
Ho, Ping-ti 1917- ... CANR-11
  Earlier sketch in CA 5-6R
Hoa, Nguyen-Dinh
  See Nguyen-dinh-Hoa
Hoadley, Irene Braden 1938- ... 29-32R
Hoadley, Walter E(vans) 1916- ... 102
Hoag, Edwin 1926- ... 15-16R
Hoagland, Edward 1932- ... CANR-2
  Earlier sketch in CA 3R
  See also DLB 6
  See also CLC 28
Hoagland, Everett (III) 1942- ... 33-36R
  See also DLB 41
Hoagland, Jimmie Lee 1940- ... 101
Hoagland, John 1947(?)-1984 Obituary ... 112
Hoagland, Kathleen M(ary) Dooher
  1909(?)-1984 ... 7-8R
  Obituary ... 112
Hoagland, Mahlon B(ush) 1921- ... 85-88
Hoang Van Chi 1915- ... CANR-7
  Earlier sketch in CA 13-14R
Hoare, Merval Hannah 1914- ... 103
Hoare, Robert J(ohn) 1921-1975 ... CANR-6
  Earlier sketch in CA 11-12R
  See also SATA 38
Hoare, Wilber W., Jr. 1921-1976
  Obituary ... 65-68
Hoban, Lillian 1925- ... CANR-23
  Earlier sketch in CA 69-72
  See also SATA 22
Hoban, Russell (Conwell) 1925- ... CANR-23
  Earlier sketch in CA 7-8R
  See also SATA 1, 40
  See also DLB 52
  See also CLC 7, 25
  See also CLR 3
Hoban, Tana ... CANR-23
  Earlier sketch in CA 93-96
  See also SATA 22
  See also CLR 13
Hobart, Alice Nourse 1882-1967 ... 7-8R
  Obituary ... 25-28R
Hobart, Alice Tisdale
  See Hobart, Alice Nourse
Hobart, Billie 1935- ... 49-52
Hobart, Lois (Elaine) ... 5-6R
  See also SATA 7
Hobbing, Enno 1920- ... 89-92
Hobbs, Anne
  See Purdy, Anne S.
Hobbs, Cecil (Carlton) 1907- ... 23-24R
Hobbs, Charles R(ene) 1931- ... 15-16R
Hobbs, (Carl) Fredric 1931- ... 81-84
Hobbs, Herschel Harold 1907- ... CANR-2
  Earlier sketch in CA 7-8R
Hobbs, J. Kline 1928- ... 108
Hobbs, John Leslie 1916-1964 ... 7-8R
Hobbs, Michael 1934- ... 111
Hobbs, Perry
  See Blackmur, R(ichard) P(almer)
Hobbs, Peter V(ictor) 1936- ... 53-56
Hobbs, Richard (Wright) 1931- ... 123
  Brief entry ... 118
Hobbs, Robert C(arleton) 1946- ... CANR-24
  Earlier sketch in CA 106
Hobbs, William (Beresford) 1939- ... 21-22R
Hobbs, Williston C. 1925(?)-1978
  Obituary ... 81-84
Hobby, Bertram Maurice 1905-1983
  Obituary ... 110
Hobby, Gladys L(ounsbury) 1910- ... 119
Hobby, Oveta Culp 1905- ... 81-84
Hobby, William P. 1932- ... 85-88
Hobday, Victor C(arr) 1914- ... 97-100
Hobel, Phil
  See Fanthorpe, R(obert) Lionel
Hoben, John B. 1908- ... 37-40R
Hoberecht, Earnest 1918- ... 23-24R
Hoberman, Gerald 1943- ... 111
Hoberman, Mary Ann 1930- ... 41-44R
  See also SATA 5
Hobfoll, Stevan E(arl) 1951- ... 123
Hobgood, Burnet M. 1922- ... 101
Hobhouse, Christina 1941- ... 25-28R
Hobhouse, Hermione 1934- ... CANR-15
  Earlier sketch in CA 41-44R
Hobhouse, Janet 1948- ... 57-60
Hobkirk, Michael D(algliesh) 1924- ... 119
Hobley, Leonard Frank 1903- ... CANR-5
  Earlier sketch in CA 13-14R
Hobsbaum, Philip (Dennis) 1932- ... CANR-3
  Earlier sketch in CA 9-10R
  See also DLB 40
Hobsbawm, Eric J(ohn Ernest) 1917- ... CANR-3
  Earlier sketch in CA 5-6R
Hobson, Anthony (Robert Alwyn) 1921- ... 33-36R
Hobson, Burton (Harold) 1933- ... CANR-2
  Earlier sketch in CA 7-8R
  See also SATA 28
Hobson, Edmund (Schofield) 1931- ... 45-48
Hobson, Fred Colby, Jr. 1943- ... CANR-5
  Earlier sketch in CA 53-56
Hobson, Geary 1941- ... 122
Hobson, Hank
  See Hobson, Harry
Hobson, Harold 1904- ... 81-84
Hobson, Harry 1908- ... CAP-1
  Earlier sketch in CA 9-10
Hobson, Julius W(ilson) 1922(?)-1977 ... 102
Hobson, Laura Z(ametkin) 1900-1986 ... 19-20R
  Obituary ... 118
  See also DLB 28
  See also CLC 7, 25
Hobson, Mary 1926- ... 106
Hobson, Polly
  See Evans, Julia (Rendel)
Hobson, William 1911- ... 103
Hobzek, Mildred J(ane) 1919- ... 101
Hoch, Edward D(entinger) 1930- ... CANR-11
  Earlier sketch in CA 29-32R
Hoch, Paul L(awrence) 1942- ... 65-68
Hochbaum, H(ans) Albert 1911- ... 103
Hochfield, George 1926- ... 2R
Hochhuth, Rolf 1931- ... 7-8R
  See also CLC 4, 11, 18
Ho Chi Minh 1890(?)-1969 Obituary ... 112
Hochman, Harold M(arvin) 1936- ... 108
Hochman, Sandra 1936- ... 7-8R
  See also DLB 5
  See also CLC 3, 8
Hochman, Shel 1944- ... 69-72
Hochman, Shirley D(ean) 1917- ... 61-64
Hochman, Stanley Richard 1928- ... 103
Hochschild, Adam 1942- Brief entry ... 121
Hochschild, Arlie Russell 1940- ... 57-60
  See also SATA 11
Hochschild, Harold K. 1892-1981
  Obituary ... 103
Hochstein, Rolaine ... CANR-23
  Earlier sketch in CA 45-48
Hochstetter, Leo D. 1911(?)-1987
  Obituary ... 122
Hochwaelder, Fritz 1911-1986 ... 29-32R
  Obituary ... 120
  See also CLC 36
Hochwald, Werner 1910- ... 19-20R
Hochwalder, Fritz
  See Hochwaelder, Fritz
  See also CLC 36
Hockaby, Stephen
  See Mitchell, Gladys (Maude Winifred)
Hockenberry, Hope
  See Newell, Hope Hockenberry
Hocker, Karla
  See Hoecker, Karla
Hockett, Charles F(rancis) 1916- ... 19-20R
Hocking, Anthony 1938- ... 102
Hocking, Brian 1914-1974 ... CAP-2
  Earlier sketch in CA 17-18
Hocking, Mary (Eunice) 1921- ... CANR-18
  Earlier sketch in CA 101
  See also CLC 13
Hocking, William Ernest 1873-1966 ... CAP-1
  Earlier sketch in CA 13-14
Hockley, G(raham) C(harles) 1931- ... 29-32R
Hockney, David 1937- Brief entry ... 116
Hocks, Richard A(llen) 1936- ... 81-84
Hodder-Williams, Christopher 1926- ... CANR-1
  Earlier sketch in CA 2R
Hode, W(illiam) Stanley 1903- ... 17-18R
Hodeir, Andre 1921- ... CANR-15
  Earlier sketch in CA 85-88
Hodes, Aubrey 1927- ... 33-36R
Hodes, Scott 1937- ... 49-52
Hodgart, Matthew (John Caldwell)
  1916- ... CANR-9
  Earlier sketch in CA 7-8R
Hodge, Alan 1915-1979 Obituary ... 89-92
Hodge, David W(ayne) 1935- ... 61-64
Hodge, Francis (Richard) 1915- ... CANR-12
  Earlier sketch in CA 33-36R
Hodge, Gene (Meany) 1898- ... 45-48
Hodge, James L(ee) 1935- ... 41-44R
Hodge, Jane Aiken 1917- ... CANR-3
  Earlier sketch in CA 7-8R
Hodge, Marshall Bryant 1925-19(?) ... CAP-2
  Earlier sketch in CA 23-24
Hodge, P(aul) W(illiam) 1934- ... CANR-14
  Earlier sketch in CA 33-36R
  See also SATA 12
Hodge, William H(oward) 1932- ... CANR-15
  Earlier sketch in CA 65-68
Hodgell, P(atricia) C(hristine) 1951- ... 109
  See also SATA 42
Hodges, C(yril) Walter 1909- ... CANR-5
  Earlier sketch in CA 15-16R
  See also SATA 2
Hodges, Carl G. 1902-1964 ... 7-8R
  See also SATA 10
Hodges, Donald Clark 1923- ... CANR-24
  Earlier sketches in CA 53-56, CANR-6
Hodges, Doris M(arjorie) 1915- ... CANR-11
  Earlier sketch in CA 25-28R
Hodges, Elizabeth Jamison ... 11-12R
  See also SATA 1
Hodges, Gil(bert Ray) 1924-1972
  Obituary ... 109
Hodges, Graham R(ushing) 1915- ... 5-6R
Hodges, Harold Mellor 1922- ... 19-20R
Hodges, Henry (Woolmington MacKenzie)
  1920- ... 37-40R
Hodges, Henry G. 1888- ... 7-8R
Hodges, Herbert Arthur 1905-1976 ... 73-76
  Obituary ... 69-72
Hodges, John C(unyus) 1892-1967 ... 5-6R
  Obituary ... 103
Hodges, Louis W. 1933- ... 81-84
Hodges, Luther (Hartwell) 1898-1974
  Obituary ... 53-56
Hodges, Margaret Moore 1911- ... CANR-2
  Earlier sketch in CA 1R
  See also SATA 1, 33
Hodges, Richard E(dwin) 1928- ... CANR-15
  Earlier sketch in CA 41-44R
Hodges, Turner
  See Morehead, Albert H(odges)
Hodges, Zane Clark 1932- ... CANR-15
  Earlier sketch in CA 41-44R
Hodgetts, A(lfred) Birnie 1911- ... 101
Hodgetts, Blake Christopher 1967- ... 114
  See also SATA 43
Hodgetts, J(ohn) E(dwin) 1917- ... 13-14R
Hodgetts, Richard M(ichael) 1942- ... CANR-23
  Earlier sketches in CA 57-60, CANR-8
Hodgins, Bruce W(illard) 1931- ... 37-40R
Hodgins, Eric 1899-1971 ... 104
  Obituary ... 29-32R
Hodgins, Jack 1938- ... 93-96
  See also DLB 60
  See also CLC 23
Hodgkin, Robert Allason 1916- ... 102
Hodgkin, Robin A.
  See Hodgkin, Robert Allason
Hodgkin, Thomas Lionel 1910-1982
  Obituary ... 115
Hodgkinson, Christopher 1928- ... 115
Hodgkinson, Edith 1959- ... 117
Hodgkinson, Liz 1943- ... 124
Hodgkinson, Marie Elisabeth
  1921(?)-1983 Obituary ... 110
Hodgkiss, A(lan) G(eoffrey) 1921- ... 124
Hodgman, Helen 1945- Brief entry ... 117
  See also DLB 14
Hodgson, D(avid) H(argraves) 1939- ... 25-28R
Hodgson, David
  See Lewis, David
Hodgson, Derek 1929- ... 118
Hodgson, Godfrey (Michael Talbot)
  1934- ... 25-28R
Hodgson, Leonard 1889-1969 ... CAP-1
  Earlier sketch in CA 9-10
Hodgson, Margaret
  See Ballinger, (Violet) Margaret
  (Livingstone)
Hodgson, Marshall G. S. 1922-1968 ... CAP-2
  Earlier sketch in CA 21-22
Hodgson, Martha (Keeling) 1906- ... 57-60
Hodgson, Norma
  See Russell, Norma Hull Lewis
Hodgson, Pat 1928- ... CANR-7
  Earlier sketch in CA 57-60
Hodgson, Peter Crafts 1934- ... CANR-15
  Earlier sketch in CA 29-32R
Hodgson, Peter E(dward) 1928- ... 11-12R
Hodgson, Phyllis 1909- ... CAP-1
  Earlier sketch in CA 13-14
Hodgson, Ralph 1871-1962 ... 102
  See also DLB 19
Hodgson, Richard Sargeant 1924- ... CANR-7
  Earlier sketch in CA 15-16R
Hodgson, Robert D(avid) 1923- ... 7-8R
Hodgson, William Hope 1877(?)-1918
  Brief entry ... 111
  See also TCLC 13
Hodin, J(osef) P(aul) 1905- ... 41-44R
Hodnett, Edward 1901-1984 ... CANR-5
  Obituary ... 114
  Earlier sketch in CA 13-14R
Hodsdon, Nicholas E(dward) 1941- ... 49-52
Hodsdon, Nick
  See Hodsdon, Nicholas E(dward)
Hodson, Henry V(incent) 1906- ... CANR-3
  Earlier sketch in CA 7-8R
Hoebel, Edward Adamson 1906- ... CANR-1
  Earlier sketch in CA 4R
Hoecker, Karla 1901- ... CANR-2
  Earlier sketch in CA 49-52
Hoehling, A(dolph) A. 1915- ... CANR-1
  Earlier sketch in CA 1R
Hoehling, Mary 1914- ... 93-96
Hoehn, Richard A(lbert) 1936- ... 116
Hoehner, Harold W. 1935- ... 37-40R
Hoekema, Anthony A(ndrew) 1913- ... 11-12R
Hoeksema, Gertrude 1921- ... 106
Hoel, Robert F(loyd) 1942- ... 53-56
Hoelterhoff, Manuela (Vali) 1949- ... 120
  Brief entry ... 114
Hoelzel, Alfred 1934- ... 41-44R
Hoenig, J(ulius) 1916- ... 29-32R
Hoenig, Sidney B(enjamin) 1907-1979 ... CANR-2
  Earlier sketch in CA 45-48
Hoeniger, F(rederick) David 1921- ... 41-44R
Hoenigswald, Henry M(ax) 1915- ... 13-14R
Hoequist, Charles Ernest, Jr. 1954- ... 108
Hoest, Bill
  See Hoest, William P.
Hoest, William P. 1926- ... CANR-23
  Earlier sketch in CA 69-72
Hoetink, H(armannus) 1931- ... 23-24R
Hoeveler, Diane Long 1949- ... 102
Hoexter, Corinne K. 1927- ... 49-52
  See also SATA 6
Hoey, Joanne Nobes 1936- ... 106
Hofer, Philip 1898-1984 Obituary ... 114
Hoff, Carol 1900- ... CAP-2
  Earlier sketch in CA 21-22
  See also SATA 11
Hoff, Ebbe Curtis 1906- ... 57-60
Hoff, Harry S(ummerfield) 1910- ... CANR-20
  Earlier sketches in CA 4R, CANR-2
Hoff, Marilyn 1942- ... CANR-7
  Earlier sketch in CA 17-18R
Hoff, Syd(ney) 1912- ... CANR-4
  Earlier sketch in CA 5-6R
  See also SATA 9
  See also SAAS 4
Hoffa, James R(iddle) 1913-1975(?)
  Obituary ... 109
Hoffecker, Carol E(leanor) 1938- ... 85-88
Hoffecker, (John) Savin 1908- ... 5-6R
Hoffeld, Donald R(aymond) 1933- ... 29-32R
Hoffeld, Laura 1946(?)-1982 Obituary ... 106
Hoffenberg, Jack 1906-1977 ... 81-84
Hoffenberg, Mason 1922(?)-1986
  Obituary ... 119
Hoffenstein, Samuel Goodman 1890-1947
  Brief entry ... 111
  See also DLB 11
Hoffer, Charles R(ussell) 1929- ... CANR-22
  Earlier sketches in CA 15-16R, CANR-7
Hoffer, Eric 1902-1983 ... CANR-18
  Obituary ... 109
  Earlier sketch in CA 15-16R
Hoffer, Thomas William 1938- ... 118
Hoffer, William 1943- ... 65-68
Hofferbert, Richard I(ra) 1937- ... 29-32R
Hoffine, Lyla 1897- ... 2R
Hoffman, Abbie 1936- ... CANR-8
  Earlier sketch in CA 21-22R
Hoffman, Abraham 1938- ... 106
Hoffman, Adeline M(ildred)
  1908-1979 ... CANR-23
  Earlier sketch in CA 29-32R
Hoffman, Alice 1952- ... 77-80
Hoffman, Anita 1942- ... 69-72
Hoffman, Arthur S. 1926- ... CANR-10
  Earlier sketch in CA 25-28R
Hoffman, Arthur W(olf) 1921- ... 5-6R
Hoffman, Bengt R(uno) 1913- ... 69-72
Hoffman, Bernard G(ilbert) 1925- ... 41-44R
Hoffman, Betty Hannah 1918- ... 9-10R
Hoffman, Calvin 1908(?)-1986 Obituary ... 118
Hoffman, Charles Fenno 1806-1884 ... DLB-3
Hoffman, Daniel (Gerard) 1923- ... CANR-4
  Earlier sketch in CA 3R
  See also DLB 5
  See also CLC 6, 13, 23
Hoffman, David Herbert 1932(?)-1985
  Obituary ... 115
Hoffman, Dominic M. 1913- ... 116
Hoffman, Donald S(tone) 1936- ... 57-60
Hoffman, Edward ... 106
Hoffman, Edwin D. ... 101
  See also SATA 49
Hoffman, Elizabeth P(arkinson) 1921- ... 77-80
Hoffman, Frederick J(ohn) 1909-1967 ... CANR-6
  Earlier sketch in CA 4R
Hoffman, Gail 1896- ... 5-6R
Hoffman, George W(alter) 1914- ... 13-14R
Hoffman, Harry G. 1911(?)-1977
  Obituary ... 69-72
Hoffman, Helmut 1912- ... CANR-17
  Earlier sketch in CA 3R
Hoffman, Herbert H(einz) 1928- ... 117
Hoffman, Hester R(osalyn) 1895- ... CAP-1
  Earlier sketch in CA 9-10
Hoffman, Jo Ann S. 1942- ... 81-84
Hoffman, Joseph G(ilbert) 1909-1974 ... 65-68
  Obituary ... 53-56
Hoffman, Joy 1954- ... 108
Hoffman, Julius Jennings 1895-1983
  Obituary ... 110

INDEX

Hoffman, L. Richard 1930- 13-14R
Hoffman, Lee 1932- CANR-18
Earlier sketch in CA 25-28R
Hoffman, Lisa 1919- 29-32R
Hoffman, Lois Wladis 1929- 13-14R
Hoffman, Marshall 1942- 106
Hoffman, Michael Allen 1944- 106
Hoffman, Michael J(erome) 1939- 29-32R
Hoffman, Nancy Jo 1942- 107
Hoffman, Paul 1934-1984 ....CANR-1
Obituary 112
Earlier sketch in CA 45-48
Hoffman, Philip T(homas) 1947- 119
Hoffman, Phyllis M(iriam) 1944- CANR-12
Earlier sketch in CA 29-32R
See also SATA 4
Hoffman, Richard L(ester) 1937-1981 .. CANR-23
Earlier sketch in CA 29-32R
Hoffman, Robert C. 1899(?)-1985
Obituary 116
Hoffman, Robert L. 1937- 37-40R
Hoffman, Ronald 1941- Brief entry 112
Hoffman, Rosekrans 1926- CANR-15
Earlier sketch in CA 89-92
See also SATA 15
Hoffman, Ross John Swartz 1902- 65-68
Hoffman, Stanley 1944- 77-80
See also CLC 5
Hoffman, Willa M(athews) 1914- 61-64
Hoffman, William 1925- CANR-9
Earlier sketch in CA 21-22R
Hoffman, William M(oses) 1939- CANR-11
Earlier sketch in CA 57-60
See also CLC 40
Hoffmann, Ann (Marie) 1930- 37-40R
Hoffmann, Banesh 1906-1986 ....CANR-3
Obituary 119
Earlier sketch in CA 7-8R
Hoffmann, Charles 1921- 106
Hoffmann, Charles G. 1921- 15-16R
Hoffmann, Donald 1933- 25-28R
Hoffmann, E(rnst) T(heodor) A(madeus)
1776-1822 ....SATA-27
Hoffmann, Eleanor 1895- CAP-1
Earlier sketch in CA 15-16
Hoffmann, Erik P(eter) 1939- CANR-13
Earlier sketch in CA 33-36R
Hoffmann, Felix 1911-1975 ....CAP-2
Obituary 57-60
Earlier sketch in CA 29-32
See also SATA 9
Hoffmann, Frank W(illiam) 1949- 106
Hoffmann, Hilde 1927- 25-28R
Hoffmann, Leon-Francois 1932- 49-52
Hoffmann, Malcolm A(rthur) 1912- 65-68
Hoffmann, Margaret Jones 1910- CANR-2
Earlier sketch in CA 5-6R
See also SATA 48
Hoffmann, Peggy
See Hoffmann, Margaret Jones
Hoffmann, Peter (Conrad Werner)
1930- CANR-14
Earlier sketch in CA 81-84
Hoffmann, Peter R. 1935- 108
Hoffmann, Stanley 1928- CANR-5
Earlier sketch in CA 15-16R
Hoffmann, Stanley (H.) 1928- CANR-14
Earlier sketch in CA 81-84
Hoffmann, Yoel 1937- 97-100
Hoffmeister, Adolf 1903-1973 Obituary ...41-44R
Hoffmeister, Donald F(rederick) 1916- 53-56
Hoffnung, Michele 1944- 81-84
Hofheinz, Roy Mark, Jr. 1935- 110
Hofinger, Johannes 1905- CAP-1
Earlier sketch in CA 19-20
Hofling, Charles K(reimer) 1920- 41-44R
Hofman, Anton
See Hollo, Anselm
Hofmann, Adele Dellenbaugh 1926- 97-100
Hofmann, Hans 1923- CANR-4
Earlier sketch in CA 3R
Hofmann, Melita C(ecelia) ?-1976 ....5-6R
Obituary 69-72
Hofmann, Michael 1957- DLB-40
Hofmann, Paul Leopold 1912- 107
Hofmann, William J(ohn) 1931- 114
Hofmannsthal, Hugo von 1874-1929
Brief entry 106
See also TCLC 11
Hofsinde, Robert 1902-1973 73-76
Obituary 45-48
See also SATA 21
Hofsommer, Don(ovan) L(owell)
1938- CANR-24
Earlier sketches in CA 65-68, CANR-9
Hofstadter, Albert 1910- 33-36R
Hofstadter, Douglas R(ichard) 1945- 105
Hofstadter, Richard 1916-1970 ....CANR-4
Obituary 29-32R
Earlier sketch in CA 4R
See also DLB 17
Hofstede, Geert H.
See Hofstede, Gerard H(endrik)
Hofstede, Gerard H(endrik) 1928- CANR-15
Earlier sketch in CA 41-44R
Hofstetter, Richard R(yan) 1956- 117
Hofvendahl, Russ(ell Lloyd) 1921- 116
Hogan, Bernice Harris 1929- CANR-7
Earlier sketch in CA 15-16R
See also SATA 12
Hogan, Dennis P. 1950- 110
Hogan, Desmond 1950- 102
See also DLB 14
Hogan, Inez 1895- CANR-1
Earlier sketch in CA 4R
See also SATA 2
Hogan, James P(atrick) 1941- CANR-15
Earlier sketch in CA 81-84
Hogan, John Charles 1919- 17-18R
Hogan, John D. 1927- 45-48
Hogan, Judy 1937- CANR-16
Earlier sketch in CA 77-80
Hogan, Lawrence D(aniel) 1944- 124
Hogan, Linda 1947- 120
Hogan, Michael 1943- CANR-14
Earlier sketch in CA 77-80
Hogan, Paul 1927- 61-64
Hogan, (Robert) Ray 1908- CANR-4
Earlier sketch in CA 9-10R
Hogan, Robert (Goode) 1930- CANR-19
Earlier sketches in CA 4R, CANR-1
Hogan, Robert F(rancis) 1927- 41-44R
Hogan, Thom(as Eugene, Jr.) 1952- 103
Hogan, Ursula 1899- 5-6R
Hogan, Willard N(ewton) 1909- CAP-2
Earlier sketch in CA 21-22
Hogan, William Francis 1930- 25-28R
Hogan, William T. 1919- 97-100
Hogarth, Burne 1911- 93-96
Hogarth, Charles
See Bowen, (Ivor) Ian
and Creasey, John
Hogarth, Douglas
See Phillips-Birt, Douglas Hextall Chedzey
Hogarth, Emmett
See Polonsky, Abraham (Lincoln)
Hogarth, Grace (Weston Allen) 1905- 89-92
Hogarth, John
See Finnin, (Olive) Mary
Hogarth, Jr.
See Kent, Rockwell
Hogarth, Paul 1917- 49-52
See also SATA 41
Hogben, Lancelot T. 1895-1975 73-76
Obituary 61-64
Hogbin, H(erbert) Ian 1904- 9-10R
Hogbotel, Sebastian
See Gott, K(enneth) D(avidson)
Hoge, Cecil C(unningham), Sr. 1913- 116
Hoge, Dean Richard 1937- 53-56
Hoge, James O(tey) 1944- 89-92
Hoge, Phyllis
See Thompson, Phyllis Hoge
Hoge, Warren McClamroch 1941- 102
Hogendorn, Jan S(tafford) 1937- CANR-14
Earlier sketch in CA 37-40R
Hogg, Beth
See Hogg, Elizabeth (Tootill)
Hogg, Clayton L(eRoy) 1924- 104
Hogg, Elizabeth (Tootill) 1917- CANR-10
Earlier sketch in CA 7-8R
Hogg, Garry 1902-1976 ....CANR-10
Earlier sketch in CA 23-24R
See also SATA 2
Hogg, Helen (Battles) Sawyer 1905- 69-72
Hogg, Ian V(ernon) 1926- CANR-12
Earlier sketch in CA 29-32R
Hogg, Oliver Frederick Gillilan 1887-1979 ..93-96
Obituary 85-88
Hogg, Quintin McGarel 1907- CANR-14
Earlier sketches in CA 11-12, CAP-1
Hogg, Robert (Lawrence) 1942- 53-56
Hogg, W(illiam) Richey 1921- 2R
Hoggart, Richard 1918- 9-10R
Hogins, James Burl 1936- 53-56
Hogner, Dorothy Childs 33-36R
See also SATA 4
Hogner, Nils 1893-1970 77-80
See also SATA 25
Hogrefe, Pearl CAP-1
Earlier sketch in CA 15-16
Hogrogian, Nonny 1932- CANR-2
Earlier sketch in CA 45-48
See also SATA 7
See also SAAS 1
See also CLR 2
Hogue, Arthur R(eed) 1906-1986 ....37-40R
Obituary 118
Hogue, C(harles) B(illy) 1928- 69-72
Hogue, Charles Leonard 1935- 105
Hogue, Richard 1946- 49-52
Hoguet, Susan Ramsay 1945- 119
Hogwood, Christopher (Jarvis Haley)
1941- Brief entry 120
Hoh, Diane 1937- 120
See also SATA 48
Hohenberg, Dorothy Lannuier
1905(?)-1977 Obituary 73-76
Hohenberg, John 1906- CANR-6
Earlier sketch in CA 13-14R
Hohenberg, Paul M(arcel) 1933- 25-28R
Hohendahl, Peter Uwe 1936- CANR-17
Earlier sketches in CA 45-48, CANR-2
Hohenstein, C(harles) Louis 1930- 116
Hohenstein, Henry J(ohn) 1931- 53-56
Hohenzollern, Friedrich Wilhelm (Victor
Albert) 1859-1941 Brief entry 120
Hohimer, Frank 1928- 57-60
Hohl, Ludwig 1904-1980 ....DLB-56
Hohler, Robert T(illman) 1951- 123
Hohlfelder, Robert Lane 1938- 45-48
Hohn, Hazel (Stamper) 7-8R
Hohnen, David 1925- 21-22R
Hohoff, Tay
See Torrey, Therese von Hohoff
Hoig, Stan(ley Warlick) 1924- CANR-1
Earlier sketch in CA 1R
Hoijer, Harry 1904-1976 73-76
Obituary 65-68
Hoisington, Harland 1896(?)-1973
Obituary 45-48
Hoke, Helen L. 1903- 73-76
See also SATA 15
Hoke, John (Lindsay) 1925- 41-44R
See also SATA 7
Holabird, Katharine 1948- 121
Holaday, Allan Gibson 1916- 37-40R
Holan, Vladimir 1905-1980 Obituary 114
Holbeach, Henry
See Rands, William Brighty
Holbeche, Philippa Jack 1919- CAP-1
Earlier sketch in CA 9-10
Holberg, Ruth L(angland) 1889- 5-6R
See also SATA 1
Holbik, Karel 1920- 37-40R
Holbo, Paul Sothe 1929- 25-28R
Holborn, Hajo 1902-1969 ....CAP-2
Earlier sketch in CA 25-28
Holborn, Louise W. 1898-19(?) CAP-2
Earlier sketch in CA 25-28
Holborn, Mark 1949- 104
Holbrook, Bill 1921- 61-64
Holbrook, David (Kenneth) 1923- CANR-3
Earlier sketch in CA 7-8R
See also DLB 14, 40
Holbrook, Jennifer Kearns 1931- 102
Holbrook, Peter
See Glick, Carl (Cannon)
Holbrook, Sabra
See Erickson, Sabra Rollins
Holbrook, Stewart Hall 1893-1964 ....CAP-1
Earlier sketch in CA 9-10
See also SATA 2
Holburn, James 1900-1988 Obituary 124
Holck, Manfred, Jr. 1930- 19-20R
Holcomb, Adele M(ansfield) 1930- 113
Holcomb, Donald F(rank) 1925- 97-100
Holcomb, George L. 1911- 45-48
Holcomb, Jerry (Leona) 1927- 25-28R
Holcombe, Arthur N(orman) 1884-1977 .. CAP-2
Obituary 73-76
Earlier sketch in CA 29-32
Holcombe, Randall G(regory) 1950- 111
Holcroft, Thomas 1745-1809 ....DLB-39
Holden, Anthony (Ivan) 1947- 101
Holden, Anton 1934- 108
Holden, Curry
See Holden, William Curry
Holden, David (Shipley) 1924-1977 ......41-44R
Holden, Donald 1931- CANR-18
Earlier sketches in CA 45-48, CANR-2
Holden, Edith 1871-1920 Brief entry 113
Holden, Elizabeth Rhoda 1943- CANR-16
Earlier sketch in CA 97-100
Holden, Genevieve
See Pou, Genevieve Long
Holden, George S(cott) 1926- 106
Holden, Inez 1906-1974 Obituary 53-56
Holden, Jonathan 1941- CANR-16
Earlier sketches in CA 45-48, CANR-1
Holden, Matthew
See Parkinson, Roger
Holden, Matthew, Jr. 1931- 57-60
Holden, Molly 1927-1981 ....25-28R
See also DLB 40
Holden, Paul E. 1894(?)-1976 Obituary ...65-68
Holden, Raymond (Peckham)
1894-1972 ....CANR-4
Obituary 37-40R
Earlier sketch in CA 7-8R
Holden, Ursula 1921- CANR-22
Earlier sketch in CA 101
See also CLC 18
Holden, Vincent F. 1911-1972 Obituary ..37-40R
Holden, W. C.
See Holden, William Curry
Holden, W(illis) Sprague 1909-1973 .... 1R
Obituary 45-48
Holden, William Curry 1898(?)-
Brief entry 117
Holder, Glenn 1906- 41-44R
Holder, Gwynneth 1943- 119
Holder, John, Jr. 1947-1985 103
Obituary 116
Holder, Ray 1913- 102
Holder, William G. 1937- CANR-10
Earlier sketch in CA 25-28R
Holdgate, Martin Wyatt 1931- 109
Holdheim, William Wolfgang 1926- CANR-2
Earlier sketch in CA 1R
Holding, Charles H. 1897- CAP-1
Earlier sketch in CA 11-12
Holding, Elizabeth Sanxay 1889-1955
Brief entry 111
Holding, James (Clark Carlisle, Jr.)
1907- 25-28R
See also SATA 3
Holding, Vera Zumwalt 1894-1984
Obituary 114
Holditch, W(illiam) Kenneth 1933- 119
Holdren, Bob R. 1922- 37-40R
Holdren, John P(aul) 1944- 33-36R
Holdstock, Robert (P.) CLC-39
Holdsworth, Christopher (John) 1931- 124
Holdsworth, Irene CAP-1
Earlier sketch in CA 9-10
Holdsworth, Mary (Zvegintzov) 1908- CAP-1
Earlier sketch in CA 15-16
Hole, Christina 1896-1985 Obituary 118
Hole, Tahu Ronald Charles Pearce
1908-1985 Obituary 118
Holenstein, Elmar 1937- CANR-11
Earlier sketch in CA 65-68
Holford, Ingrid 1920- 102
Holford, William Graham 1907-1975
Obituary 108
Holiday, F(rederick) W(illiam) 1921- 25-28R
Holiday, Homer
See DeBeaubien, Philip Francis
Holinger, William (Jacques) 1944- 123
Holisher, Desider 1901-1972 ....CAP-2
Obituary 37-40R
Earlier sketch in CA 19-20
See also SATA 6
Holl, Adelaide Hinkle 1910- CANR-2
Earlier sketch in CA 4R
See also SATA 8
Holl, Adolf 1930- 101
Holl, Jack M. 1937- 57-60
Holl, Kristi D(iane) 1951- 114
Holladay, Sylvia A(gnes) 1936- 57-60
Holladay, William L(ee) 1926- 53-56
Holland, Ada Morehead 1911- 122
Holland, Alma Boice 29-32R
Holland, Barbara A(dams) 1925- 57-60
Holland, Brud
See Holland, Jerome H(eartwell)
Holland, Cecelia (Anastasia) 1943- CANR-9
Earlier sketch in CA 17-18R
Holland, Cecil Fletcher 1907-1978
Obituary 77-80
Holland, Deborah K(atherine) 1947- 57-60
Holland, DeWitte T(almage) 1923- 45-48
Holland, Elizabeth (Anne) 1928- 124
Holland, Francis Ross, Jr. 1927- 33-36R
Holland, Glen A. 1920- 37-40R
Holland, Harrison M(elsher) 1921- 117
Holland, Hilda 1901(?)-1975 Obituary 57-60
Holland, Isabelle 1920- CANR-10
Earlier sketch in CA 21-22R
See also SATA 8
See also CLC 21
Holland, Jack 1947- 105
Holland, Jack H. 1922- 81-84
Holland, James C(larence) 1935- 112
Holland, James Gordon 1927- 1R
Holland, James R. 1944- 37-40R
Holland, Janice 1913-1962 73-76
See also SATA 18
Holland, Jerome H(eartwell) 1916-1985
Obituary 114
Holland, John L(ewis) 1919- CANR-17
Earlier sketch in CA 25-28R
See also SATA 20
Holland, Joyce (Flint) 1921- 5-6R
Holland, Joyce
See Morice, Dave
Holland, Katrin
See Albrand, Martha
Holland, Kel
See Whittington, Harry (Benjamin)
Holland, Kenneth 1948- 118
Holland, Kenneth J(ohn) 1918- 33-36R
Holland, Laurence B(edwell) 1920-1980 ..19-20R
Obituary 102
Holland, Louise Adams 1893- 89-92
Holland, Lynwood M. 1905- 41-44R
Holland, Lys
See Gater, Dilys
Holland, Marcus
See Caldwell, (Janet Miriam) Taylor
(Holland)
Holland, Marion 1908- 61-64
See also SATA 6
Holland, Norman N(orwood) 1927- 17-18R
See also DLB 67
Holland, Patricia G. 1940- 115
Holland, Philip Welsby 1917- 109
Holland, Robert 1940- 33-36R
Holland, Sheila 1937- CANR-15
Earlier sketch in CA 85-88
Holland, Thomas E(dward) 1934- 53-56
Holland, Tim 1931- 57-60
Holland, Vyvyan (Beresford) 1886-1967 ..97-100
Obituary 25-28R
Holland, William E. 1940- 124
Hollander, A(rie) Nicolaas Jan den
See den Hollander, A(rie) Nicolaas Jan
Hollander, Hans 1899-1986 103
Obituary 120
Hollander, Herbert S. 1904(?)-1976
Obituary 69-72
Hollander, John 1929- CANR-1
Earlier sketch in CA 4R
See also SATA 13
See also DLB 5
See also CLC 2, 5, 8, 14
Hollander, Lee M(ilton) 1880- 1R
Hollander, Paul 1932- CANR-13
Earlier sketch in CA 37-40R
Hollander, Paul
See Silverberg, Robert
Hollander, Phyllis 1928- CANR-18
Earlier sketch in CA 97-100
See also SATA 39
Hollander, Richard Isaac 1912-1985
Obituary 117
Hollander, Robert 1933- CANR-5
Earlier sketch in CA 13-14R
Hollander, Sophie Smith 1911- 15-16R
Hollander, Stanley C(harles) 1919- 37-40R
Hollander, Zander 1923- CANR-18
Earlier sketch in CA 65-68
Hollands, Roy (Derrick) 1924- 114
Hollaway, Otto 1903- 69-72
Hollberg, John
See Hall, Gus
Holldobler, Turid 1939- SATA-26
Holleb, Arthur Irving 1921- 103
Hollender, Edward A. 1899- 105
Hollenweger, Walter J(acob) 1927- CANR-19
Earlier sketches in CA 53-56, CANR-4
Holler, Frederick L. 1921- 97-100
Holler, Ronald F. 1938- 53-56
Holleran, Andrew 1943(?)- CLC-38
Holles, Everett R. 1904(?)-1978 Obituary ..77-80

Holles, Robert Owen 1926- CANR-18
Earlier sketches in CA 7-8R, CANR-3
Holley, Bobbie Lee 1927- 33-36R
Holley, Edward Gailon 1927- CANR-6
Earlier sketch in CA 7-8R
Holley, Frederick S. 1924- 109
Holley, I(rving) B(rinton), Jr. 1919- CANR-14
Earlier sketch in CA 37-40R
Holley, Marietta 1836(?)-1926 Brief entry ... 118
See also DLB 11
Holli, Melvin G(eorge) 1933- CANR-11
Earlier sketch in CA 25-28R
Hollick, Ann L(orraine) 1941- 57-60
Holliday, Barbara Gregg 1917- 73-76
Holliday, James
See Gray, Simon
Holliday, Joe
See Holliday, Joseph
Holliday, Joseph 1910- CAP-2
Earlier sketch in CA 29-32
See also SATA 11
Hollindale, Peter 1936- 103
Holling, Holling C(lancy) 1900-1973
Obituary 106
See also SATA 15, 26
Hollingdale, R(eginald) J(ohn) 1930- 102
Hollinghurst, Alan 1954- 114
Hollings, Michael 1921- 81-84
Hollingshead, August deBelmont
1907-1980 ....13-14R
Obituary 120
Hollingshead, (Ronald) Kyle 1941- CANR-11
Earlier sketch in CA 23-24R
Hollingsworth, Alvin C(arl) 1930- SATA-39
Hollingsworth, Dorothy Frances 1916- 85-88
Hollingsworth, Harold M(arvin) 1932- 53-56
Hollingsworth, J(oseph) Rogers 1932- . CANR-22
Earlier sketches in CA 13-14R, CANR-7
Hollingsworth, Kent 1929- 81-84
Hollingsworth, Lyman B(urgess) 1919- 45-48
Hollingsworth, Margaret 1942- 123
See also DLB 60
Hollingsworth, Mary H(ead) 1910- 69-72
Hollingsworth, Paul M. 1932- 29-32R
Hollingworth, Clare 1911- 121
Hollinrake, Roger (Barker) 1929- 115
Hollis, (Maurice) Christopher 1902-1977 ...73-76
Obituary 69-72
Hollis, Daniel W(alker) 1922- 5-6R
Hollis, Daniel W(ebster) III 1942- 118
Hollis, Florence 1907-1987 Obituary 123
Hollis, Harry Newcombe, Jr. 1938- 57-60
Hollis, Helen Rice 1908- 61-64
Hollis, James R(ussell) 1940- 41-44R
Hollis, Jim
See Summers, Hollis (Spurgeon, Jr.)
Hollis, Joseph W(illiam) 1922- 25-28R
Hollis, Lucile U(ssery) 1921- 25-28R
Hollis, Marcia 1937- 114
Hollister, Bernard C(laiborne) 1938- CANR-3
Earlier sketch in CA 49-52
Hollister, C(harles) Warren 1930- CANR-1
Earlier sketch in CA 4R
Hollister, Charles A(mmon) 1918- 17-18R
Hollister, George E(rwin) 1905- CAP-2
Earlier sketch in CA 17-18
Hollister, Herbert A(llen) 1933- 104
Hollister, Leo E. 1920- CANR-14
Earlier sketch in CA 23-24R
Hollister, William G(ray) 1915- 122
Hollmann, Clide John 1896-1966 ....7-8R
Hollo, Anselm 1934- CANR-9
Earlier sketch in CA 21-22R
See also DLB 40
Hollom, Philip Arthur Dominic 1912- 15-16R
Hollon, W. Eugene 1913- CANR-2
Earlier sketch in CA 1R
See also AITN 1
Hollow, John Walter 1939- 111
Holloway, Brenda W(ilmar) 1908- CAP-1
Earlier sketch in CA 9-10
Holloway, David 1924- 107
Holloway, (Rufus) Emory 1885-1977 49-52
Obituary 73-76
Holloway, (Percival) Geoffrey 1918- 49-52
Holloway, George (Edward Talbot)
1921- 25-28R
Holloway, Harry (Albert) 1925- 11-12R
Holloway, James Y(oung) 1927- 53-56
Holloway, John 1920- CANR-3
Earlier sketch in CA 7-8R
See also DLB 27
Holloway, Joseph E(dward) 1948- 111
Holloway, Marcella M(arie) 1913- 89-92
Holloway, Mark 1917- 21-22R
Holloway, Maurice 1920- 11-12R
Holloway, Robert J. 1921- 15-16R
Holloway, Stanley 1890-1982 Obituary 106
Holloway, Teresa (Bragunier) 1906- 19-20R
See also SATA 26
Holloway, Thomas H(alsey) 1944- 106
Holloway, W(illiam) V(ernon) 1903- CANR-2
Earlier sketch in CA 1R
Hollowell, John 1945- 102
Hollowood, Albert Bernard 1910-1981 .....9-10R
Obituary 103
Holly, J(ohn) Fred 1915- CANR-6
Earlier sketch in CA 5-6R
Holly, Joan C(arol) 1932- CANR-1
Earlier sketch in CA 4R
Holly, Joan Hunter
See Holly, Joan C(arol)
Holly, Michael Ann 1944- 121
Hollyday, Frederic B(lackmar) M(umford)
1928- 45-48
Holm, (Else) Anne (Lise) 1922- 19-20R
See also SATA 1
Holm, Bill
See Holm, Oscar William
Holm, Don(ald Raymond) 1918- 33-36R
Holm, John Cecil 1904-1981 Obituary 116
Holm, Marilyn D. (Franzen) 1944- 19-20R
Holm, Oscar William 1925- Brief entry 117
Holm, Sven (Aage) 1902- CAP-1
Earlier sketch in CA 11-12
Holman, Betsy Hitz 1951- 119
Holman, Bob
See Holman, Robert
Holman, C(larence) Hugh 1914-1981 ... CANR-21
Earlier sketch in CA 5-6R
Holman, Dennis (Idris) 1915- 9-10R
Holman, Felice 1919- CANR-18
Earlier sketches in CA 7-8R, CANR-3
See also SATA 7
Holman, Harriet R. 1912- 37-40R
Holman, L(loyd) Bruce 1939- 61-64
Holman, Mary A(lida) 1933- 93-96
Holman, Portia Grenfell 1903-1983
Obituary 109
Holman, Robert 1936- 116
Holman, William R(oger) 1926- 49-52
Holmans, Alan Edward 1934- 3R
Holme, Bryan 1913- 103
See also SATA 26
Holme, (Edith) Constance 1880(?)-1955
Brief entry 118
See also DLB 34
Holme, K. E.
See Hill, (John Edward) Christopher
Holme, Thea 1903- 41-44R
Holmelund, Paul 1890- 7-8R
Holmer, Paul L(eroy) 1916- 37-40R
Holmes, Ann 1936(?)-1985 Obituary 114
Holmes, Arthur 1890-1965 Obituary 116
Holmes, Arthur F. 1924- 33-36R
Holmes, Barbara Ware 1945- 120
Holmes, Burnham 1942- 97-100
Holmes, C. Raymond 1929- 57-60
Holmes, Charles M(ason) 1923- 29-32R
Holmes, Charles S(hiveley) 1916-1976 ...41-44R
Obituary 61-64
Holmes, Charles Warfield 1931-1984
Obituary 112
Holmes, Colin 1938- CANR-11
Earlier sketch in CA 25-28R
Holmes, David Charles 1919- 9-10R
Holmes, David M(orton) 1929- 33-36R
Holmes, Douglas 1933- 41-44R
Holmes, Edward M(orris) 1910- CANR-14
Earlier sketch in CA 37-40R
Holmes, Efner Tudor 1949- 65-68
Holmes, Eric M(ills) 1943- 121
Holmes, Frank Wakefield 1924- 109
Holmes, Frederic L(awrence) 1932- 93-96
Holmes, Geoffrey (Shorter) 1928- 25-28R
Holmes, Grant
See Fox, James M.
Holmes, H. H.
See White, William A(nthony) P(arker)
Holmes, Jack D(avid) L(azarus) 1930- .. CANR-24
Earlier sketch in CA 41-44R
Holmes, Jay
See Holmes, Joseph Everett
Holmes, Jeffrey 1934- 120
Holmes, John (Albert) 1904-1962
Obituary 115
Holmes, John 1913- 104
Holmes, John
See Souster, (Holmes) Raymond
Holmes, John Clellon 1926- CANR-4
Earlier sketch in CA 9-10R
See also DLB 16
Holmes, John Haynes 1879-1964
Obituary 89-92
Holmes, John L. 1925- 115
Holmes, John W(endell) 1910- Brief entry .. 109
Holmes, Jon 1948- 114
Holmes, Joseph Everett 1922- CANR-1
Earlier sketch in CA 3R
Holmes, Joseph R. 1928(?)-1983
Obituary 109
Holmes, Kenneth L(loyd) 1915- 37-40R
Holmes, Kim R(ene) 1952- 111
Holmes, Lowell D(on) 1925- 33-36R
Holmes, Marjorie (Rose) 1910- CANR-23
Earlier sketches in CA 3R, CANR-5
See also SATA 43
See also AITN 1
Holmes, Martin (Rivington) 1905- CANR-1
Earlier sketch in CA 49-52
Holmes, (John) Michael (Aleister) 1931- ..25-28R
Holmes, Michael Stephan 1942- 77-80
Holmes, Nancy 1921- 69-72
Holmes, Olive 1911- 115
Holmes, Oliver Wendell 1809-1894 .... SATA-34
See also DLB 1
See also CDALB 1640-1865
Holmes, Oliver Wendell, Jr. 1841-1935
Brief entry 114
Holmes, Parker Manfred 1895- CAP-1
Earlier sketch in CA 13-14
Holmes, Paul Allen 1901-1985 .... CAP-2
Obituary 114
Earlier sketch in CA 19-20
Holmes, Paul Carter 1926- CANR-11
Earlier sketch in CA 23-24R
Holmes, Peggy 1898- 121
Holmes, Raymond
See Souster, (Holmes) Raymond
Holmes, (Edward) Richard 1946- 106
Holmes, Rick
See Hardwick, Richard Holmes, Jr.
Holmes, Robert A(lexander) 1943- 57-60
Holmes, Robert L(awrence) 1935- 41-44R
Holmes, Robert Merrill 1925- 89-92
Holmes, Tiffany 1944- 97-100
Holmes, Tommy 1903-1975 Obituary 57-60
Holmes, Urban T(igner) 1900-1972 ...... CAP-2
Earlier sketch in CA 21-22
Holmes, W(ilfred) J(ay) 1900- 29-32R
Holmes, William Kersley 1882- CAP-1
Earlier sketch in CA 9-10
Holmgren, Helen Jean 1930- 97-100
See also SATA 45
Holmgren, Norah 1939- 102
Holmgren, Sister George Ellen
See Holmgren, Helen Jean
Holmgren, Virginia C(unningham) 1909- 107
See also SATA 26
Holmquist, Anders 1933- 29-32R
Holmquist, Eve 1921- 53-56
See also SATA 11
Holmstrand, Marie Juline (Gunderson)
1908- 5-6R
Holmstrom, (John) Edwin 1898- CAP-1
Earlier sketch in CA 11-12
Holmstrom, Lynda Lytle 1939- 33-36R
Holmvik, Oyvind 1914- 19-20R
Holod, Renata O. 1942- 119
Holoien, Martin O. 1928- 112
Holquist, (James) Michael 1935- CANR-17
Earlier sketches in CA 45-48, CANR-2
Holroyd, Michael (de Courcy Fraser)
1935- CANR-18
Earlier sketches in CA 53-56, CANR-4
Holroyd, Sam
See Burton, S(amuel) H(olroyd)
Holroyd, Stuart 1933- 93-96
Holsaert, Eunice ?-1974 Obituary 53-56
Holsinger, Jane Lumley 17-18R
Holske, Katherine ?-1973 Obituary 104
Holsopple, Barbara 1943- 73-76
Holst, Hermann E. von 1841-1904 .... DLB-47
Holst, Imogen (Clare) 1907-1984 Obituary .. 112
Holst, Johan J(oergen) 1937- CANR-11
Earlier sketch in CA 25-28R
Holst, Lawrence E(berhardt) 1929- 61-64
Holsti, Kalevi J(acque) 1935- 23-24R
Holsti, Ole R(udolf) 1933- CANR-11
Earlier sketch in CA 25-28R
Holt, Andrew
See Anhalt, Edward
Holt, Edgar Crawshaw 1900-1975 ...... CANR-6
Obituary 61-64
Earlier sketch in CA 3R
Holt, Elizabeth B(asye) G(ilmore)
1906(?)-1987 124
Holt, Gavin
See Rodda, Charles
Holt, Helen
See Paine, Lauran (Bosworth)
Holt, (Laurence) James 1939- 25-28R
Holt, John 1721-1784 .... DLB-43
Holt, John (Caldwell) 1923-1985 69-72
Obituary 117
Holt, John (Robert) 1926- CANR-11
Earlier sketch in CA 25-28R
Holt, John Agee 1920- 1R
Holt, Kaare 1917- Brief entry 111
Holt, Kare
See Holt, Kaare
Holt, L. Emmett, Jr. 1895-1974 Obituary ..53-56
Holt, Lee E(lbert) 1912- 13-14R
Holt, Margaret 1937- 17-18R
See also SATA 4
Holt, Margaret Van Vechten (Saunders)
1899-1963 Obituary 111
See also SATA 32
Holt, Michael (Paul) 1929- CANR-5
Earlier sketch in CA 53-56
See also SATA 13
Holt, Michael F(itzgibbon) 1940- 81-84
Holt, Pat Mayo 1920- 111
Holt, Rackham
See Holt, Margaret Van Vechten
(Saunders)
Holt, Robert R(utherford) 1917- CANR-15
Earlier sketch in CA 41-44R
Holt, Robert T. 1928- 37-40R
Holt, Rochelle L.
See DuBois, Rochelle (Lynn) Holt
See also SATA 41
Holt, Stephen
See Thompson, Harlan (Howard)
Holt, Stephen
See Thompson, Harlan H(oward)
Holt, Tex
See Joscelyn, Archie L.
Holt, Thelma Jewett 1913- 29-32R
Holt, Thomas J(ung) 1928- 102
Holt, Victoria
See Hibbert, Eleanor Burford
Holt, Will 1929- 105
Holt, William 1897-1977 .... CAP-1
Obituary 69-72
Earlier sketch in CA 17-18
Holtan, Orley I. 1933- 33-36R
Holtby, Robert Tinsley 1921- 108
Holter, Don W. 1905- 37-40R
Holthusen, Hans Egon 1913- 45-48
Holtje, Herbert F(ranklin) 1931- CANR-8
Earlier sketch in CA 61-64
Holton, Felicia Antonelli 1921- 69-72
Holton, Gerald (James) 1922- 15-16R
Holton, Leonard
See Wibberley, Leonard (Patrick
O'Connor)
Holton, (William) Milne 1931- 41-44R
Holton, Richard H(enry) 1926- Brief entry .. 107
Holtrop, William Frans 1908- 57-60
Holtz, Avraham 1934- 29-32R
Holtz, Barry W(illiam) 1947- 109
Holtz, Herman R(alph) 1919- 105
Holtze, Sally Holmes 1952- 123
Holtzman, Abraham 1921- CANR-2
Earlier sketch in CA 3R
Holtzman, Harry 1912-1987 Obituary 123
Holtzman, Jerome 1926- CANR-4
Earlier sketch in CA 53-56
Holtzman, Paul D(ouglas) 1918- 33-36R
Holtzman, Wayne H(arold) 1923- CANR-15
Earlier sketch in CA 37-40R
Holtzman, Will 1951- 102
Holub, Miroslav 1923- CANR-10
Earlier sketch in CA 21-22R
See also CLC 4
Holub, Robert C(harles) 1949- 114
Holum, Dianne 1951- 123
Holway, John 1929- 57-60
Holyer, Erna Maria 1925- CANR-12
Earlier sketch in CA 29-32R
See also SATA 22
Holyer, Ernie
See Holyer, Erna Maria
Holz, Loretta (Marie) 1943- CANR-10
Earlier sketch in CA 65-68
See also SATA 17
Holz, Robert K(enneth) 1930- 53-56
Holzapfel, Rudolf Patrick 1938- CAP-1
Earlier sketch in CA 11-12
Holzberger, William George 1932- 53-56
Holzer, Hans 1920- CANR-22
Earlier sketches in CA 13-14R, CANR-7
Holzer, Harold 1949- 116
Holzman, Franklyn Dunn 1918- 61-64
Holzman, Philip Seidman 1922- 37-40R
Holzman, Red
See Holzman, William
Holzman, Robert S(tuart) 1907- CANR-2
Earlier sketch in CA 1R
Holzman, William 1920- 101
Holzner, Burkart 1931- 93-96
Hom, Ken 1949- 109
Homan, Robert Anthony 1929- 7-8R
Homans, Abigail Adams 1879-1974
Obituary 104
Homans, George Caspar 1910- 107
Homans, Peter 1930- CANR-11
Earlier sketch in CA 23-24R
Homberger, Eric (Ross) 1942- CANR-23
Earlier sketch in CA 106
Homburger, Erik
See Erikson, Erik H(omburger)
Home, Alexander Frederick 1903- 102
Home, Charles (Cospatrick) Douglas
See Douglas-Home, Charles (Cospatrick)
Home, Henry Douglas
See Douglas-Home, Henry
Home, Michael
See Bush, Charlie Christmas
Home, William Douglas 1912- 102
See also DLB 13
Homer, Frederic D(onald) 1939- 65-68
Homer, Sidney 1902-1983 Obituary 110
Homer, Williams Innes 1929- 15-16R
Homes, Geoffrey
See Mainwaring, Daniel
Homewood, Charles H. 1914(?)-1984
Obituary 112
Homewood, Harry
See Homewood, Charles H.
Homola, Priscilla 1947- 116
Homola, Samuel 1929- 97-100
Homosap
See Nuttall, Jeff
Homrighausen, Elmer George 1900- 45-48
Homsher, Lola Mae 1913- 2R
Homze, Alma C. 1932- 29-32R
See also SATA 17
Homze, Edward L. 1930- 33-36R
Honan, Park 1928- CANR-14
Earlier sketch in CA 77-80
Honan, William H(olmes) 1930- 123
Honce, Charles E. 1895-1975 Obituary 61-64
Honderich, Ted 1933- CANR-14
Earlier sketch in CA 33-36R
Hone, Joseph 1937- CANR-14
Earlier sketch in CA 65-68
Hone, Ralph E(merson) 1913- CANR-9
Earlier sketch in CA 23-24R
Honey, Martha S(pencer) 1945- 112
Honey, P(atrick) J(ames) 1922- 13-14R
Honey, William (Houghton) 1910- 33-36R
Honeycombe, Gordon 1936- CANR-15
Earlier sketch in CA 77-80
Honeycutt, Benjamin L(awrence) 1938- 57-60
Honeycutt, Roy L(ee), Jr. 1926- 41-44R
Honeyman, Brenda
See Clarke, Brenda (Margaret Lilian)
Hong, Edna H. 1913- CANR-9
Earlier sketch in CA 21-22R
Hong, Howard V(incent) 1912- CANR-9
Earlier sketch in CA 21-22R
Hong, Jane Fay 1954- 93-96
Hong, Yong Ki 1929(?)-1979 Obituary 85-88
Honhart, Frederick L(ewis III) 1943- 112
Honig, Donald 1931- CANR-24
Earlier sketches in CA 19-20R, CANR-9
See also SATA 18
Honig, Edwin 1919- CANR-4
Earlier sketch in CA 7-8R
See also DLB 5
See also CLC 33
Honig, Louis 1911-1977 77-80
Obituary 73-76
Honigfeld, Gilbert
See Howard, Gilbert

Honigmann, E(rnst) A(nselm) J(oachim) 1927- ... CANR-9
Earlier sketch in CA 21-22R
Honigmann, John J(oseph) 1914-1977 .. CANR-2
Earlier sketch in CA 1R
Honnalgere, Gopal 1944- ... 73-76
Honness, Elizabeth H. 1904- ... 25-28R
See also SATA 2
Honnold, John Otis, Jr. 1915- ... CANR-8
Earlier sketch in CA 15-16R
Honore, Antony Maurice 1921- ... CANR-1
Earlier sketch in CA 3R
Honour, Hugh 1927- ... 103
Honourable Member for X
See de Chair, Somerset (Struben)
Honri, Peter 1929- ... 103
Hoobler, Dorothy ... CANR-11
Earlier sketch in CA 69-72
See also SATA 28
Hoobler, Thomas ... CANR-11
Earlier sketch in CA 69-72
See also SATA 28
Hood, Buck 1907(?)-1983 Obituary ... 110
Hood, David Crockett 1937- ... 37-40R
Hood, Donald W(ilbur) 1918- ... 37-40R
Hood, Dora (Ridout) 1885- ... CAP-2
Earlier sketch in CA 17-18
Hood, F(rancis) C(ampbell) 1895-1971 ... CAP-1
Earlier sketch in CA 13-14
Hood, Flora M(ae) 1898- ... 5-6R
Hood, Graham 1936- ... 77-80
Hood, Hugh (John Blagdon) 1928- ... CANR-1
Earlier sketch in CA 49-52
See also DLB 53
See also CLC 15, 28
Hood, Joseph F. 1925- ... 33-36R
See also SATA 4
Hood, Margaret Page 1892- ... 3R
Hood, Robert E. 1926- ... 23-24R
See also SATA 21
Hood, Sarah
See Killough, (Karen) Lee
Hood, (Martin) Sinclair (Frankland) 1917- ... CANR-9
Earlier sketch in CA 21-22R
Hood, William (Joseph) 1920- ... 109
Hoofnagle, Keith Lundy 1941- ... 15-16R
Hoogasian-Villa, Susie 1921-1978 ... 17-18R
Obituary ... 114
Hoogenboom, Ari (Arthur) 1927- ... 45-48
Hoogenboom, Olive 1927- ... 23-24R
Hoogestraat, Wayne E. ... 7-8R
Hook, Andrew 1932- ... 53-56
Hook, Diana ffarington 1918- ... 61-64
Hook, Donald D(wight) 1928- ... CANR-4
Earlier sketch in CA 53-56
Hook, Frances 1912- ... 105
See also SATA 27
Hook, Frank S(cott) 1922- ... 23-24R
Hook, J(ulius) N(icholas) 1913- ... CANR-17
Earlier sketches in CA 5-6R, CANR-2
Hook, Judith 1941(?)-1984 Obituary ... 113
Hook, Martha 1936- ... 105
See also SATA 27
Hook, Sidney 1902- ... CANR-7
Earlier sketch in CA 11-12R
Hooke, Nina Warner 1907- ... 73-76
Hooker, C(lifford) A(lan) 1942- ... CANR-19
Earlier sketches in CA 49-52, CANR-4
Hooker, Craig Michael 1951- ... 57-60
Hooker, Frances
See Horovitz, Frances Margaret
Hooker, James Ralph 1929- ... 21-22R
Hooker, (Peter) Jeremy 1941- ... CANR-22
Earlier sketch in CA 77-80
See also DLB 40
See also CLC 43
Hooker, Richard
See Hornberger, H. Richard
Hooker, Richard J(ames) 1912- ... 122
Hooker, Ruth 1920- ... 69-72
See also SATA 21
Hooker, Stanley (George) 1907-1984
Obituary ... 112
Hooker, Thomas 1586-1647 ... DLB-24
Hookham, Hilda Henriette (Kuttner) 1915- ... 9-10R
Hooks, G(aylor) Eugene 1927- ... 4R
Hooks, Gene
See Hooks, G(aylor) Eugene
Hooks, William H(arris) 1921- ... CANR-19
Earlier sketch in CA 81-84
See also SATA 16
Hoole, Daryl Van Dam 1934- ... 23-24R
Hoole, W(illiam) Stanley 1903- ... CANR-7
Earlier sketch in CA 17-18R
Hooper, Byrd
See St. Clair, Byrd Hooper
Hooper, David (Vincent) 1915- ... 85-88
Hooper, Douglas 1927- ... CANR-18
Earlier sketch in CA 25-28R
Hooper, Finley (Allison) 1922- ... 123
Hooper, Hedley Colwill 1919- ... 124
Hooper, John W(illiam) 1926- ... 29-32R
Hooper, Johnson Jones 1815-1862 ... DLB-3,11
Hooper, Kay 1957- ... 122
Hooper, Meredith (Jean) 1939- ... CANR-22
Earlier sketch in CA 106
See also SATA 28
Hooper, Paul F(ranklin) 1938- ... CANR-18
Earlier sketch in CA 101
Hooper, Peter
See Hooper, Hedley Colwill
Hooper, Walter (McGehee) 1931- ... CANR-22
Earlier sketches in CA 17-18R, CANR-7
Hooper, William Loyd 1931- ... CANR-19
Earlier sketches in CA 5-6R, CANR-3
Hoopes, Clement R. 1906-1979 ... 73-76
Obituary ... 89-92
Hoopes, David S. 1928- ... 118
Hoopes, Donelson F(arquhar) 1932- ... 33-36R
Hoopes, James 1944- ... CANR-10
Earlier sketch in CA 65-68
Hoopes, Lyn Littlefield 1953- ... 120
See also SATA 44, 49
Hoopes, Ned E(dward) 1932- ... 17-18R
See also SATA 21
Hoopes, Robert (Griffith) 1920- ... CANR-1
Earlier sketch in CA 2R
Hoopes, Roy 1922- ... CANR-15
Earlier sketch in CA 21-22R
See also SATA 11
Hoopes, Townsend Walter 1922- ... 97-100
Hoople, Cheryl G. Brief entry ... 111
See also SATA 32
Hoops, Richard A(llen) 1933- ... 41-44R
Hoor, Elvie (Marie Mortensen) Ten
See Ten Hoor, Elvie (Marie Mortensen)
Hoornik, Ed(uard Jozef Antonie Marie) 1910-1970 Obituary ... 104
Hoos, Ida Russakoff 1912- ... 19-20R
Hooson, David J. M. 1926- ... 19-20R
Hooten, William J(arvis) 1900- ... 61-64
Hooton, Charles
See Rowe, Vivian C(laud)
Hoover, Calvin Bryce 1897-1974 ... CAP-1
Obituary ... 49-52
Earlier sketch in CA 13-14
Hoover, Dorothy Estheryne 1918- ... 49-52
Hoover, Dwight W(esley) 1926- ... 33-36R
Hoover, Edgar M. 1907- ... 13-14R
Hoover, F(rancis) Louis 1913- ... 41-44R
Hoover, H(elen) M(ary) 1935- ... CANR-22
Earlier sketch in CA 105
See also SATA 33, 44
Hoover, Hardy 1902- ... 29-32R
Hoover, Helen (Drusilla Blackburn) 1910-1984 ... 21-22R
Obituary ... 113
See also SATA 12, 39
Hoover, Herbert (Clark) 1874-1964 ... 108
Obituary ... 89-92
Hoover, Herbert Theodore 1930- ... 106
Hoover, J(ohn) Edgar 1895-1972 ... CANR-2
Obituary ... 33-36R
Earlier sketch in CA 3R
Hoover, John P. 1910- ... 53-56
Hoover, Kenneth H(arding) 1920- ... CANR-7
Earlier sketch in CA 57-60
Hoover, Marjorie L(awson) 1910- ... 41-44R
Hoover, Mary B(idgood) 1917- ... 93-96
Hoover, Thomas 1941- ... 102
Hopcraft, Arthur 1932- ... CANR-14
Earlier sketch in CA 25-28R
Hope, A(lec) D(erwent) 1907- ... 21-22R
See also CLC 3
Hope, A(shley) Guy 1914- ... 25-28R
Hope, Amanda
See Lewis, Judith Mary
Hope, Andrew
See Hern, (George) Anthony
Hope, Bob 1903- ... 101
Hope, Brian
See Creasey, John
Hope, C(harles) E(velyn) G(raham) 1900-1971 ... CAP-1
Earlier sketch in CA 15-16
Hope, Christopher (David Tully) 1944- ... 106
Hope, David
See Fraser, Douglas
Hope, Felix
See Williamson, Claude C(harles) H.
Hope, Jack 1940- ... 81-84
Hope, Jane 1938- ... 110
Hope, Karol ... 93-96
Hope, Laura Lee ... 19-20R
See also SATA 1
Hope, Laura Lee
See Adams, Harriet S(tratemeyer)
Hope, Margaret
See Knight, Alanna
Hope, Marjorie (Cecelia) 1923- ... 29-32R
Hope, Norman Victor 1908-1983 Obituary ... 110
Hope, Quentin M(anning) 1923- ... 13-14R
Hope, Ronald (Sidney) 1921- ... CANR-3
Earlier sketch in CA 9-10R
Hope, Welborn 1903- ... 29-32R
Hope-Jones, Arthur 1911-1984 Obituary ... 112
Hopes, David Brendan 1953- ... 109
Hope Simpson, Jacynth 1930- ... CANR-7
Earlier sketch in CA 13-14R
See also SATA 12
Hope-Wallace, Philip (Adrian) 1911-1979
Obituary ... 93-96
Hopewell, S(ydney) 1924- ... 25-28R
Hopf, Alice
See Hopf, Alice (Martha) L(ightner)
Hopf, Alice (Martha) L(ightner) 1904-1988 ... CANR-9
Obituary ... 124
Earlier sketch in CA 19-20R
See also SATA 5
Hopke, William E. 1918- ... 21-22R
Hopkin, Alannah 1949- ... 109
Hopkins, A. T.
See Turngren, Annette
Hopkins, Antony 1921- ... CANR-17
Earlier sketch in CA 101
Hopkins, Bill 1928- ... 11-12R
Hopkins, C(harles) Howard 1905- ... 123
Hopkins, Clark 1895-1976 Obituary ... 109
See also SATA 34
Hopkins, David 1948- ... 122
Hopkins, Donald R(oswell) 1941- ... 123
Hopkins, Fred W(right), Jr. 1935- ... 69-72
Hopkins, George E(mil) 1937- ... 33-36R
Hopkins, Gerard Manley 1844-1889 .. DLB-35, 57
Hopkins, Harry 1913- ... 29-32R
Hopkins, J(ohn) F(eely) 1922- ... 102
Hopkins, J. L. 1938- ... 77-80
Hopkins, Jack W(alker) 1930- ... 25-28R
Hopkins, James Franklin 1909- ... 1R
Hopkins, Jasper (Stephen, Jr.) 1936- .. CANR-14
Earlier sketch in CA 37-40R
Hopkins, Jerry 1935- ... CANR-18
Earlier sketch in CA 25-28R
Hopkins, John (Richard) 1931- ... 85-88
See also CLC 4
Hopkins, Joseph G(erard) E(dward) 1909- ... CANR-5
Earlier sketch in CA 1R
See also SATA 11
Hopkins, Joseph Martin 1919- ... 49-52
Hopkins, Kenneth 1914- ... CANR-17
Earlier sketches in CA 3R, CANR-1
Hopkins, Lee (Wallace) ... 57-60
Hopkins, Lee Bennett 1938- ... 25-28R
See also SATA 3
See also SAAS 4
Hopkins, Lemuel 1750-1801 ... DLB-37
Hopkins, Lightnin'
See Hopkins, Sam
Hopkins, Lyman
See Folsom, Franklin (Brewster)
Hopkins, Marjorie 1911- ... 21-22R
See also SATA 9
Hopkins, Mark W(yatt) 1931- ... 29-32R
Hopkins, Milton 1906-1983 Obituary ... 109
Hopkins, Nicholas S(nowden) 1939- ... 77-80
Hopkins, Pauline Elizabeth 1859-1930 ... DLB-50
Hopkins, Prynce (C.) 1885-1970 ... CAP-2
Earlier sketch in CA 21-22
Hopkins, Pryns
See Hopkins, Prynce (C.)
Hopkins, Raymond F(rederick) 1939- ... 49-52
Hopkins, Robert A. 1923- ... 89-92
Hopkins, Robert S(ydney) ... 115
Hopkins, Sam 1912-1982 Obituary ... 106
Hopkins, Samuel 1721-1803 ... DLB-31
Hopkins, Terence K(ilbourne) 1928- ... 11-12R
Hopkins, Thomas H(ollis) 1945- ... 116
Hopkins, Thomas J(ohns) 1930- ... 37-40R
Hopkins, Viola
See Winner, Viola Hopkins
Hopkins, Vivian C. 1909- ... CAP-2
Earlier sketch in CA 33-36
Hopkinson, Diana 1912- ... 29-32R
Hopkinson, Francis 1737-1791 ... DLB-31
Hopkinson, Henry Thomas 1905- ... 19-20R
Hopkirk, Peter 1930- ... 107
Hopley, George
See Hopley-Woolrich, Cornell George
Hopley-Woolrich, Cornell George 1903-1968 ... CAP-1
Earlier sketch in CA 13-14
Hoppe, Art(hur Watterson) 1925- ... CANR-3
Earlier sketch in CA 7-8R
Hoppe, Eleanor Sellers 1933- ... 73-76
Hoppe, Emil Otho 1878- ... 11-12R
Hoppe, Joanne 1932- ... 81-84
See also SATA 42
Hoppe, Ronald A. 1931- ... 45-48
Hoppen, K(arl) Theodore 1941- ... 119
Hoppenstedt, Elbert M. 1917- ... 3R
Hopper, Columbus B(urwell) 1931- ... 33-36R
Hopper, David H. 1927- ... 23-24R
Hopper, Dennis 1936- ... 114
Hopper, Hedda
See Furry, Elda
Hopper, John 1934- ... 17-18R
Hopper, Nancy J. 1937- ... 115
See also SATA 35, 38
Hopper, R(obert) J(ohn) 1910-1987 ... 123
Hopper, Robert 1945- ... CANR-9
Earlier sketch in CA 65-68
Hopper, Vincent Foster 1906-1976 ... CANR-6
Obituary ... 61-64
Earlier sketch in CA 1R
Hoppin, Richard H(allowell) 1913- ... 41-44R
Hoppock, Robert 1901- ... 1R
Hopson, Dan, Jr. 1930- ... 23-24R
Hopson, Janet L(ouise) 1950- ... 89-92
Hopwood, Robert R. 1910- ... CAP-1
Earlier sketch in CA 13-14
Hora, F. Bayard 1909(?)-1984 Obituary ... 112
Horak, M. Stephan 1920- ... 11-12R
Horan, Francis Harding 1900-1978
Obituary ... 81-84
Horan, James David 1914-1981 ... CANR-9
Obituary ... 105
Earlier sketch in CA 13-14R
Horan, (Harold) Joseph Taaffe 1898(?)-1985 Obituary ... 117
Horan, William D. 1933- ... 25-28R
Horatio
See Proust, (Valentin-Louis-George-Eugene-) Marcel
Horatio, Algernon ... 89-92
Horatio, Jane
See Cudlipp, Edythe
Horbach, Michael 1924-1986 ... 29-32R
Obituary ... 120
Horchler, Richard (Thomas) 1925- ... 5-6R
Horchow, (Samuel) Roger 1928- ... 106
Horder, Mervyn 1910- ... 104
Hordern, William (Edward) 1920- ... 13-14R
Hordon, Harris E(ugene) 1942- ... 53-56
Horecky, Paul Louis 1913- ... CANR-2
Earlier sketch in CA 7-8R
Horelick, Arnold L(awrence) 1928- ... CANR-8
Earlier sketch in CA 17-18R
Horgan, Denis E. 1941- ... 101
Horgan, Edward R. 1934- ... 109
Horgan, John J(oseph) 1910- ... 61-64
Horgan, John Joseph 1881-1967 Obituary .. 116
Horgan, Paul 1903- ... CANR-9
Earlier sketch in CA 13-14R
See also SATA 13
See also DLBY 85
See also CLC 9
Hori, Ichiro 1910-1974 ... CAP-2
Earlier sketch in CA 25-28
Horie, Shigeo 1903- ... CAP-1
Earlier sketch in CA 13-14
Horikoshi, Jiro 1904(?)-1982 Obituary ... 110
Horka-Follick, Lorayne Ann 1940- ... 29-32R
Horkheimer, Max 1895-1973 Obituary ... 41-44R
Horman, Richard E. 1945- ... 29-32R
Horn, D(avid) B(ayne) 1901-1969 ... CANR-6
Earlier sketch in CA 4R
Horn, Daniel 1934- ... 21-22R
Horn, Edward Newman 1903(?)-1976
Obituary ... 65-68
Horn, Francis H(enry) 1908- ... 53-56
Horn, George F(rancis) 1917- ... CANR-8
Earlier sketch in CA 7-8R
Horn, Henry Eyster 1913- ... 23-24R
Horn, Jeanne P. 1925- ... 5-6R
Horn, John L(eonard) 1928- ... CANR-14
Earlier sketch in CA 37-40R
Horn, Linda L(ouise) 1947- ... 101
Horn, Maurice 1931- ... CANR-22
Earlier sketch in CA 89-92
Horn, Pamela (Lucy Ray) 1936- ... 69-72
Horn, Peter (Rudolf Gisela) 1934- ... 103
Horn, Peter
See Kuttner, Henry
Horn, Pierre L(aurence) 1942- ... 119
Horn, Richard 1954- ... 105
Horn, Robert M. 1933- ... 29-32R
Horn, Siegfried H(erbert) 1908- ... 37-40R
Horn, Stefan F. 1900- ... CAP-1
Earlier sketch in CA 15-16
Horn, (John) Stephen 1931- ... 15-16R
Horn, Stephen (McCaffrey Moore) 1931- ... 45-48
Horn, Thomas D. 1918- ... 13-14R
Horn, Vivi 1878(?)-1971 Obituary ... 104
Horn, Walter (William) 1908- ... 23-24R
Hornback, Bert G(erald) 1935- ... CANR-22
Earlier sketch in CA 29-32R
Hornbaker, Alice 1927- ... 77-80
Hornbein, Thomas Frederic 1930- ... 53-56
Hornberger, H. Richard ... 105
Hornberger, Theodore 1906-1975 ... CANR-3
Earlier sketch in CA 5-6R
Hornblow, Arthur, Jr. 1893-1976 ... 89-92
Obituary ... 65-68
See also SATA 15
Hornblow, Leonora (Schinasi) 1920- ... 73-76
See also SATA 18
Hornblower, Harry C.
See Shriver, Harry C(lair)
Hornbruch, Frederick William, Jr. 1913- ... 109
Hornby, John (Wilkinson) 1913- ... 9-10R
Hornby, Leslie 1949- ... 103
Hornby, Richard 1938- ... 89-92
Hornby, William H(arry) 1923- ... 106
Horne, A(lexander) D(ouglas) 1932- ... 109
Horne, Alistair (Allan) 1925- ... CANR-9
Earlier sketch in CA 5-6R
Horne, Bernard Shea 1905-1970 Obituary .. 104
Horne, Chevis Ferber 1914- ... CANR-16
Earlier sketch in CA 97-100
Horne, Cynthia Miriam 1939- ... 7-8R
Horne, Donald (Richmond) 1921- ... CANR-20
Earlier sketch in CA 103
Horne, Frank (Smith) 1899-1974
Obituary ... 53-56
See also DLB 51
Horne, Geoffrey 1916- ... 9-10R
Horne, Howard
See Payne, (Pierre Stephen) Robert
Horne, Hugh Robert 1915- ... 7-8R
Horne, Kenneth 1900-1975 Obituary ... 115
Horne, Lewis 1932- ... 110
Horne, Peter 1947- ... 69-72
Horne, R(alph) A(lbert) 1929- ... 106
Horne, Richard Henry 1803-1884 ... SATA-29
See also DLB 32
Horne, Roman L(emuel) 1901-1987
Obituary ... 121
Horne, Shirley (Faith) 1919- ... 49-52
Horner, Althea (Jane) 1926- ... 81-84
See also SATA 36
Horner, Dave 1934- ... 17-18R
See also SATA 12
Horner, David Stuart 1900(?)-1983(?)
Obituary ... 111
Horner, George F(rederick) 1899-1974 ... CAP-2
Earlier sketch in CA 33-36
Horner, J. C.
See Horner, John Curwen
Horner, John Curwen 1922- ... 103
Horner, Joyce Mary 1903-1980 Obituary ... 112
Horner, Kenric Lancaster 1902-1973
Obituary ... 111
Horner, Lance
See Horner, Kenric Lancaster
Horner, Thomas Marland 1927- ... 37-40R
Horner, Tom (Julian) 1913- ... 121
Horner, Winifred Bryan 1922- ... 118
Horney, Karen (Clementine Theodore Danielsen) 1885-1952 Brief entry ... 114
Horngren, Charles T(homas) 1926- ... 57-60
Hornig, Doug 1943- ... 117

Hornik, Edith Lynn
See Beer, Edith Lynn
Hornman, Wim 1920- Brief entry 106
Hornos, Axel 1907- CAP-2
Earlier sketch in CA 29-32
See also SATA 20
Hornsby, Albert Sidney 1898(?)-1978
Obituary 104
Hornsby, Alton, Jr. 1940- 37-40R
Hornsby, Ken 1934- 105
Hornsby, Roger A. 1926- 21-22R
Hornstein, Harvey A. 1938- 53-56
Hornstein, Lillian Herlands 1909- 45-48
Hornstein, Reuben Aaron 1912- 106
Hornung, Clarence Pearson 1899- CANR-9
Earlier sketch in CA 17-18R
Hornung, E(rnest) W(illiam) 1866-1921
Brief entry 108
Hornung, Erik 1933- 117
Hornung, Maximilian 1942- 107
Horobin, Ian M. 1899-1976 Obituary 69-72
Horovitz, Frances Margaret 1938-1983
Obituary 111
Horovitz, Israel 1939- 33-36R
See also DLB 7
Horovitz, Michael 1935- 81-84
Horowitz, Al
See Horowitz, I(srael) A.
Horowitz, David 1903- 69-72
Horowitz, David (Joel) 1939- 15-16R
Horowitz, David A. 1941- 89-92
Horowitz, David Charles 1937- 89-92
Horowitz, Edward 1904- CANR-4
Earlier sketch in CA 3R
Horowitz, Esther 1920- 49-52
Horowitz, Gene 1930- 77-80
Horowitz, I(srael) A. 1907-1973
Obituary 41-44R
Horowitz, Ira 1934- 41-44R
Horowitz, Irving Louis 1929- 41-44R
Horowitz, Jacob 1900-1979 Obituary 89-92
Horowitz, Joseph 1948- 109
Horowitz, Laura (Godofsky) 1943-1983
Obituary 110
Horowitz, Leonard M(artin) 1937- 37-40R
Horowitz, Lois 1940- 119
Horowitz, Mardi J(on) 1934- 33-36R
Horowitz, Michael M. 1933- CANR-15
Earlier sketch in CA 41-44R
Horowitz, Morris A(aron) 1919- CANR-9
Earlier sketch in CA 65-68
Horowitz, Robert S. 1924- 9-10R
Horowitz, Shel Alan 1956- 120
Horrell, C. William 1918- CANR-13
Earlier sketch in CA 61-64
Horrock, Berta Crone 1896(?)-1983
Obituary 110
Horrock, Nicholas (Morton) 1936- 49-52
Horrocks, Brian (Gwynne) 1895-1985
Obituary 114
Horrocks, Edna M. 1908- CAP-2
Earlier sketch in CA 17-18
Horrocks, John E(dwin) 1913- 7-8R
Horsbrugh, Ian 1941- 111
Horsburgh, David Michael 1923-1984
Obituary 114
Horsburgh, H(oward) J(ohn) N(eate)
1918- 25-28R
Horsefield, J(ohn) Keith 1901- 7-8R
Horsely, Ramsbottom
See Berne, Eric (Lennard)
Horseman, Elaine Hall 1925- 15-16R
Horsley, David
See Bingley, David Ernest
Horsley, James (Allen) 1938- 45-48
Horsman, Reginald 1931- CANR-17
Earlier sketches in CA 4R, CANR-2
Horst, Irvin B(uckwalter) 1915- 41-44R
Horst, Samuel (Levi) 1919- 21-22R
Horstman, Allen (Henry) 1943- 122
Horton, Arthur MacNeill, Jr. 1947- 114
Horton, Felix Lee
See Floren, Lee
Horton, Frank E. 1939- 29-32R
Horton, George Moses 1797(?)-1883(?) . DLB-50
Horton, James O(liver) 1943- 114
Horton, John (William) 1905- CANR-18
Earlier sketches in CA 9-10R, CANR-3
Horton, Louise 1916- CANR-2
Earlier sketch in CA 49-52
Horton, Lowell 1936- 53-56
Horton, Patricia Campbell 1943- 89-92
Horton, Paul Burleigh 1916- CANR-20
Earlier sketch in CA 1R
Horton, Paul Chester 1942- 106
Horton, Rod W(illiam) 1910- 49-52
Horton, Russell M. 1946- 97-100
Horton, Stanley M(onroe) 1916- CANR-6
Earlier sketch in CA 57-60
Horton, Susan R. 1941- 109
Horvat, Branko 1928- 53-56
Horvath, Betty 1927- 19-20R
See also SATA 4
Horvath, Janos 1921- 41-44R
Horvath, Joan 1944- 81-84
Horvath, Odon von
See Horvath, Oedoen von
Horvath, Oedoen von 1901-1938
Brief entry 118
Horvath, Violet M. 1924- 29-32R
Horwich, Frances R(appaport) 1908- CAP-1
Earlier sketch in CA 15-16
See also SATA 11
Horwitz, Elinor Lander CANR-13
Earlier sketch in CA 77-80
See also SATA 33, 45
Horwitz, Julius 1920-1986 .... CANR-12
Obituary 119
Earlier sketch in CA 9-10R
See also CLC 14
Horwitz, Richard P(aul) 1949- 122
Horwitz, Simi L(ouise) 1949- 103
Horwitz, Sylvia L(aibman) 1911- 61-64
Horwood, Harold (Andrew) 1923- CANR-9
Earlier sketch in CA 21-22R
See also DLB 60
Hoselitz, Bert(hold) F(rank) 1913- CANR-1
Earlier sketch in CA 1R
Hosford, Bowen I. 1916- CANR-24
Earlier sketch in CA 107
Hosford, Dorothy (Grant) 1900-1952 ... SATA-22
Hosford, Jessie 1892- 41-44R
See also SATA 5
Hosford, Philip L(ewis) 1926- 57-60
Hosford, Ray E. 1933- 85-88
Hosie, Stanley W(illiam) 1922- 25-28R
Hosier, Helen Kooiman 1928- CANR-8
Earlier sketch in CA 61-64
Hosier, Peter
See Clark, Douglas
Hosken, Fran(ziska) P(orges) 1919- CANR-6
Earlier sketch in CA 57-60
Hoskin, Cyril Henry 1911(?)-1981
Obituary 102
Hosking, Eric (John) 1909- CANR-17
Earlier sketch in CA 101
Hosking, Geoffrey A(lan) 1942- CANR-19
Earlier sketch in CA 85-88
Hoskins, Katharine Bail 1924- 65-68
Hoskins, Katherine (de Montalant) 1909- . CAP-2
Earlier sketch in CA 25-28
Hoskins, Robert 1933- 29-32R
Hoskins, William George 1908- 13-14R
Hoskyns-Abrahall, Clare (Constance
Drury) 29-32R
See also SATA 13
Hosley, Richard 1921- CANR-8
Earlier sketch in CA 7-8R
Hosmer, Charles B(ridgham), Jr. 1932- ..15-16R
Hosmon, Robert Stahr 1943- 45-48
Hosokawa, Bill
See Hosokawa, William K.
Hosokawa, William K. 1915- CANR-11
Earlier sketch in CA 29-32R
Hospers, John, Jr. 1918- CANR-2
Earlier sketch in CA 1R
Hospital, Janette Turner 1942- 108
See also CLC 42
Hoss, Marvin Allen 1929- 29-32R
Hoss, Norman 1923(?)-1983 Obituary 111
Hossent, Harry 1916- CAP-1
Earlier sketch in CA 9-10
Hostetler, Marian 1932- CANR-24
Earlier sketches in CA 65-68, CANR-9
Hostetter, B(enjamin) Charles 1916- CANR-1
Earlier sketch in CA 4R
Hostler, Charles W(arren) 1919- 23-24R
Hostos, E. M. de
See Hostos (y Bonilla), Eugenio Maria de
Hostos, Eugenio M. de
See Hostos (y Bonilla), Eugenio Maria de
Hostos, Eugenio Maria
See Hostos (y Bonilla), Eugenio Maria de
Hostos (y Bonilla), Eugenio Maria de
1839-1903 Brief entry 123
See also TCLC 24
Hostovsky, Egon 1908-1973 Obituary 89-92
Hostrop, Richard Winfred 1925- 25-28R
Hotaling, Edward 1937- 77-80
Hotchkiss, Bill 1936- 104
Hotchkiss, Jeanette 1901- 23-24R
Hotchkiss, Ralf D. 1947- 33-36R
Hotchner, A(aron) E(dward) 1920- 69-72
Hotchner, Tracy 1950- 102
Hothem, Lar(ry Lee) 1938- 106
Hothersall, David 1940- 111
Hotson, John H(argrove) 1930- 25-28R
Hotspur
See Curling, Bryan William Richard
Hottois, James W. 1943- 77-80
Hotz, Robert B(ergmann) 1914- 101
Hou, Chi-ming 1924- 23-24R
Hou, Fu-Wu
See Houn, Franklin W.
Houblon, Doreen (Lindsay) Archer
See Archer Houblon, Doreen (Lindsay)
Houchin, Thomas D(ouglas) 1925- 77-80
Houck, Carter 1924- CANR-14
Earlier sketch in CA 77-80
See also SATA 22
Houck, John W(illiam) 1931- CANR-11
Earlier sketch in CA 29-32R
Houdini
See Lovecraft, H(oward) P(hillips)
Houdini, Merlin X.
See Borgmann, Dmitri A(lfred)
Houedard, Pierre-Sylvester 1924- 103
Houfe, Simon (Richard) 1942- CANR-19
Earlier sketch in CA 103
Hougan, Carolyn 19(?)- CLC-34
Hougan, James Richard 1942- 77-80
Hougan, Jim
See Hougan, James Richard
Hough, (Helen) Charlotte 1924- CANR-5
Earlier sketch in CA 9-10R
See also SATA 9
Hough, Denny C. 1925(?)-1983 Obituary ... 111
Hough, Emerson 1857-1923 Brief entry 120
See also DLB 9
Hough, George A(nthony) III 1920- 121
Brief entry 117
Hough, Graham (Goulder) 1908- 69-72
Hough, Henry Beetle 1896-1985 .... CANR-2
Obituary 116
Earlier sketch in CA 1R
Hough, Henry W(ade) 1906-197(?) 25-28R
Obituary 122
Hough, Hugh 1924-1986 73-76
Obituary 119
Hough, Jerry F(incher) 1935- Brief entry ... 114
Hough, John T., Jr. 1946- 33-36R
Hough, Joseph C(arl), Jr. 1933- 23-24R
Hough, Judy Taylor 1932- 124
Hough, Lindy Downer 1944- CANR-8
Earlier sketch in CA 61-64
Hough, Louis 1914- 37-40R
Hough, Richard (Alexander) 1922- CANR-18
Earlier sketches in CA 5-6R, CANR-3
See also SATA 17
Hough, S(tanley) B(ennett) 1917- CANR-3
Earlier sketch in CA 7-8R
Houghteling, James L(awrence), Jr. 1920- ..5-6R
Houghton, Bernard 1935- 77-80
Houghton, Diane 1940- 123
Houghton, Elizabeth
See Gilzean, Elizabeth Houghton Blanchet
Houghton, Eric 1930- CANR-2
Earlier sketch in CA 4R
See also SATA 7
Houghton, George William 1905- 13-14R
Houghton, Neal D(oyle) 1895- CAP-2
Earlier sketch in CA 25-28
Houghton, (Charles) Norris 1909- 23-24R
Houghton, Peter 1938- 119
Houghton, Samuel G(ilbert) 1902-1975 65-68
Houghton, (William) Stanley 1881-1913
Brief entry 110
See also DLB 10
Houghton, Walter Edwards 1904-1983 ... CAP-1
Obituary 109
Earlier sketch in CA 9-10
Houlden, J(ames) L(eslie) 1929- 77-80
Houle, Cyril O(rvin) 1913- CANR-3
Earlier sketch in CA 5-6R
Houlehen, Robert J. 1918- 49-52
See also SATA 18
Houlgate, Deke 1930- 61-64
Hoult, Norah 1898-1984 Obituary 112
Hoult, Thomas Ford 1920- Brief entry 116
Houn, Franklin W. 1920- 23-24R
Hounsome, Terry 1944- 109
Houpt, Katherine Albro 1939- 105
Hourani, George F(adlo) 1913-1984 .... CANR-23
Earlier sketch in CA 45-48
Hours, Madeleine 1915- 49-52
Hours-Miedan, Madeleine
See Hours, Madeleine
Hours-Miedan, Magdeleine
See Hours, Madeleine
House, Anne W.
See McCauley, Elfrieda B(abnick)
House, Charles (Albert) 1916- 25-28R
House, Ernest R(obert) 1937- CANR-23
Earlier sketch in CA 45-48
House, Gloria 1941- 117
House, H(ershel) Wayne 1948- 119
House, John William 1919-1984 106
Obituary 112
House, Kurt D(uane) 1947- 104
House, Robert Burton 1892- CAP-1
Earlier sketch in CA 11-12
House, Robert J. 1932- 101
House, Robert W(illiam) 1920- 53-56
House, Ruth Sizemore 1946- 116
House, Victor 1893-1983 Obituary 109
Household, Geoffrey (Edward West)
1900- 77-80
See also SATA 14
See also CLC 11
Houselander, (Frances) Caryll 1901-1954
Brief entry 110
See also SATA 31
Houseman, Barton L(eroy) 1933- 61-64
Houseman, Gerald L. 1935- 108
Houseman, John 1902- Brief entry 110
Housepian, Marjorie
See Dobkin, Marjorie Housepian
Houser, Caroline 115
Housley, Norman (James) 1952- 108
Housman, A(lfred) E(dward) 1859-1936
Brief entry 104
See also DLB 19
See also TCLC 1, 10
Housman, Laurence 1865-1959
Brief entry 106
See also SATA 25
See also DLB 10
See also TCLC 7
Houston, Beverle (Ann) 1936-1988 89-92
Obituary 124
Houston, C(larence) Stuart 1927- 119
Houston, David 1938- 118
Houston, Douglas (Norman) 1947- 123
Houston, James A(rchibald) 1921- 65-68
See also SATA 13
See also CLR 3
Houston, James D. 1933- 25-28R
Houston, James M(ackintosh) 1922- 13-14R
Houston, Jean Brief entry 115
Houston, Jeanne Wakatsuki 1934- 103
Houston, Joan 1928- 19-20R
Houston, John Porter 1933-1987 .... CANR-3
Obituary 123
Earlier sketch in CA 11-12R
Houston, Neal B. 1928- 41-44R
Houston, Peyton (H.) 1910- CANR-1
Earlier sketch in CA 49-52
Houston, R. B.
See Rae, Hugh C(rauford)
Houston, Robert 1935- 37-40R
Houston, W(illiam) Robert, Jr. 1928- .. CANR-18
Earlier sketches in CA 5-6R, CANR-3
Houston, Will
See Paine, Lauran (Bosworth)
Houston, William Neil 1948- 123
Houtart, Francois 1925- 13-14R
Houthakker, Hendrik S(amuel) 1924- 17-18R
Houton, Kathleen
See Kilgore, Kathleen
Houts, Marshall (Wilson) 1919- CANR-13
Earlier sketch in CA 23-24R
Houts, Peter S. 1933- 49-52
Hovannisian, Richard G. 1932- 23-24R
Hovda, Robert W(alker) 1920- CANR-3
Earlier sketch in CA 11-12R
Hovde, A(nnis) J(orgen) 1917- 112
Hovde, Christian A(rneson) 1922- 7-8R
Hovde, Howard 1928- 25-28R
Hovell, Lucille A. (Peterson) 1916- 7-8R
Hovell, Lucy A.
See Hovell, Lucille A. (Peterson)
Hoverland, H. Arthur 1928- 45-48
Hoversten, Chester E. 1922- 7-8R
Hovey, E(lwyn) Paul 1908- CANR-1
Earlier sketch in CA 3R
Hovey, Richard 1864-1900 .... DLB-54
Hovey, Richard B(ennett) 1917- 25-28R
Hovey, Sonya 1898-1960 Obituary 113
Hoveyda, Fereydoun 1924- 101
Hovick, Rose Louise 1914(?)-1970
Obituary 113
Hoving, Thomas 1931- 101
Howald, Reed Anderson 1930- 57-60
Howar, Barbara 1934- 89-92
See also AITN 1, 2
Howard, A(rthur) E(llsworth) Dick 1933- ..15-16R
Howard, Alan 1922- SATA-45
Howard, Alan 1934- CANR-20
Earlier sketch in CA 37-40R
Howard, Alvin Wendell 1922-1975 ....33-36R
Howard, Alyssa
See Buckholtz, Eileen (Garber)
Howard, Alyssa
See Glick, Ruth (Burtnick)
Howard, Alyssa
See Titchener, Louise
Howard, Anthony (Michell) 1934- 109
Howard, Barbara 1930- 53-56
Howard, Ben(jamin Willis) 1944- 73-76
Howard, Bion B. 1912- 15-16R
Howard, Blanche 1923- 101
Howard, C(hester) Jeriel 1939- CANR-14
Earlier sketch in CA 29-32R
Howard, Carleton
See Howe, Charles H(orace)
Howard, Cecil
See Smith, Cecil (Howard III)
Howard, Charles Frederick 1904- 17-18R
Howard, Christopher 1913- 23-24R
Howard, Clark 122
Howard, Clive ?-1974 Obituary 53-56
Howard, Constance (Mildred) 1910- ... CANR-11
Earlier sketch in CA 69-72
Howard, Coralie
See Cogswell, Coralie (Norris)
Howard, D(erek) L(ionel) 1930- CANR-8
Earlier sketch in CA 7-8R
Howard, Daniel F(rancis) 1928- 41-44R
Howard, David M(orris) 1928- CANR-10
Earlier sketch in CA 25-28R
Howard, Deborah (Janet) 1946- 124
Howard, Dick 1943- 77-80
Howard, Don (Marcel) 1940- CANR-22
Earlier sketch in CA 106
Howard, Donald R(oy) 1927-1987 ...... CANR-1
Obituary 121
Earlier sketch in CA 3R
Howard, Dorothy (Arlynne) 1912- 65-68
Howard, Dorothy Gray 1902- 93-96
Howard, Edmund (Bernard Carlo) 1909- ...85-88
Howard, Edward G(arfield) 1918(?)-1972
Obituary 104
Howard, Edwin 1924- 65-68
Howard, Edwin J(ohnston) 1901- CAP-1
Earlier sketch in CA 11-12
Howard, Elizabeth Jane 1923- CANR-8
Earlier sketch in CA 5-6R
See also CLC 7, 29
Howard, Frances Minturn Brief entry 111
Howard, Fred D(avid) 1919- CANR-19
Earlier sketches in CA 3R, CANR-4
Howard, Frederick James 1904- 109
Howard, Gerald J(ohn) 1950- 108
Howard, Gilbert 1934- 49-52
Howard, Harold P. 1905- CAP-2
Earlier sketch in CA 33-36
Howard, Harry Nicholas 1902-1987 49-52
Obituary 123
Howard, Hartley
See Ognall, Leopold Horace
Howard, Helen Addison 1904- CANR-3
Earlier sketch in CA 5-6R
Howard, Ian P. 1927- 23-24R
Howard, J. Woodford, Jr. 1931- 33-36R
Howard, James A(rch) 1922- CANR-8
Earlier sketch in CA 15-16R
Howard, James H(enri) 1925- 41-44R
Howard, James K(enton) 1943- 85-88
Howard, James T(homas) 1934- 101
Howard, Jane (Temple) 1935- CANR-13
Earlier sketch in CA 29-32R
Howard, Jean
See MacGibbon, Jean
Howard, Jessica
See Schere, Monroe
Howard, John (Arnold) 1916- 41-44R

INDEX

Howard, John
See Hewitt, John (Harold)
Howard, John R(obert) 1933- ... 53-56
Howard, John Tasker 1890-1964
Obituary ... 89-92
Howard, Joseph Leon 1917- ... CANR-1
Earlier sketch in CA 1R
Howard, Joyce 1922- ... 7-8R
Howard, Kenneth I(rwin) 1932- ... 115
Howard, Kenneth Samuel 1882-1972 ... 9-10R
Obituary ... 103
Howard, Kez
See Houston, David
Howard, Lee M(ilton) 1922- ... 108
Howard, Leigh
See Lee Howard, Leon Alexander
Howard, Leon 1903-1982 ... 109
Howard, Leon Alexander Lee
See Lee Howard, Leon Alexander
Howard, Leslie G(raham) 1947- ... 114
Howard, Lowell B(ennett) 1925- ... 15-16R
Howard, Mark
See Rigsby, Howard
Howard, Mary
See Mussi, Mary
Howard, Maureen 1930- ... 53-56
See also DLBY 83
See also CLC 5, 14, 46
Howard, Michael (Eliot) 1922- ... CANR-2
Earlier sketch in CA 1R
Howard, Michael S. 1922-1974 Obituary ... 53-56
Howard, Moses L(eon) 1928- ... 109
Howard, Munroe 1913-1974 ... CAP-2
Earlier sketch in CA 23-24
Howard, Nona
See Luxton, Leonora Kathrine
Howard, Oliver Otis 1830-1909 Brief entry ... 109
Howard, Patricia (Lowe) 1937- ... CANR-7
Earlier sketch in CA 17-18R
Howard, Paul Jack 1908-1984 Obituary ... 113
Howard, Peter D(unsmore) 1908-1965 ... CAP-1
Earlier sketch in CA 11-12
Howard, Philip 1933- ... 65-68
Howard, Prosper
See Hamilton, Charles Harold St. John
Howard, Richard 1929- ... 85-88
See also DLB 5
See also CLC 7, 10, 47
See also AITN 1
Howard, Richard C. 1929- ... 53-56
Howard, Robert 1926- ... 41-44R
Howard, Robert Ervin 1906-1936
Brief entry ... 105
See also TCLC 8
Howard, Robert West 1908- ... CANR-1
Earlier sketch in CA 4R
See also SATA 5
Howard, Roger 1938- ... CANR-17
Earlier sketch in CA 93-96
Howard, Ronnalie Roper
See Roper, Ronnalie J.
Howard, Ross 1946- ... 120
Howard, Roy Joseph 1925- ... 112
Howard, Roy Wilson 1883-1964 Obituary ... 89-92
See also DLB 29
Howard, Sidney 1891-1939 ... DLB-7, 26
Howard, Stanley E. 1888(?)-1980
Obituary ... 102
Howard, Ted
See Howard, Theodore Korner
Howard, Theodore Korner 1915- ... 103
Howard, Thomas 1930- ... 37-40R
Howard, Thomas T(rumbull) 1935- ... 111
Howard, Troy
See Paine, Lauran (Bosworth)
Howard, Vechel
See Rigsby, Howard
Howard, Vernon (Linwood) 1918- ... 108
See also SATA 40
Howard, Warren F.
See Pohl, Frederik
Howard, Warren Starkie 1930- ... 7-8R
Howard-Hill, Trevor Howard 1933- ... 85-88
Howard-Williams, Jeremy (Napier)
1922- ... CANR-22
Earlier sketch in CA 106
Howarth, David (Armine) 1912- ... CANR-9
Earlier sketch in CA 13-14R
See also SATA 6
Howarth, Donald 1931- ... 25-28R
Howarth, Pamela 1954- ... 102
Howarth, Patrick (John Fielding) 1916- ... 77-80
Howarth, Stephen (William Russell) 1953- ... 107
Howarth, W(illiam) D(river) 1922- ... 45-48
Howarth, William Louis 1940- ... CANR-20
Earlier sketch in CA 37-40R
Howat, Gerald Malcolm David 1928- ... CANR-16
Earlier sketch in CA 93-96
Howat, John K(eith) 1937- ... 49-52
Howatch, Joseph 1935- ... 65-68
Howatch, Susan 1940- ... CANR-24
Earlier sketch in CA 45-48
See also AITN 1
Howe, Charles H(orace) 1912- ... 53-56
Howe, Charles L. 1932- ... 19-20R
Howe, Christopher (Barry) 1937- ... 121
Howe, Daniel Walker 1937- ... 29-32R
Howe, Deborah 1946-1978 ... 105
See also SATA 29
Howe, Doris Kathleen ... CANR-3
Earlier sketch in CA 49-52
Howe, E. W. 1853-1937 ... DLB-12, 25
Howe, Ellic 1910- ... 25-28R
Howe, Fanny 1940- ... 117
See also CLC 47
Howe, Florence 1929- ... 124
Brief entry ... 109
Howe, G(eorge) Melvyn 1920- ... 101
Howe, George Frederick 1901-1988
Obituary ... 124
Howe, George Locke 1898(?)-1977
Obituary ... 69-72
Howe, Helen 1905-1975 ... CAP-2
Obituary ... 57-60
Earlier sketch in CA 23-24
Howe, Henry 1816-1893 ... DLB-30
Howe, Hubert S(hattuck), Jr. 1942- ... 57-60
Howe, Irving 1920- ... CANR-21
Earlier sketch in CA 9-10R
See also DLB 67
Howe, James 1946- ... CANR-22
Earlier sketch in CA 105
See also SATA 29
See also CLR 9
Howe, James Robinson 1935- ... 69-72
Howe, Jonathan Trumbull 1935- ... 29-32R
Howe, Josephine (Mary) O'Connor
See O'Connor Howe, Josephine (Mary)
Howe, Julia Ward 1819-1910 Brief entry ... 117
See also DLB 1
See also TCLC 21
Howe, Leland W(right) 1940- ... 123
Brief entry ... 118
Howe, Louise Kapp 1934-1984 Obituary ... 111
Howe, Mark Anthony DeWolfe 1864-1960
Obituary ... 89-92
Howe, Nelson 1935- ... 33-36R
Howe, Quincy 1900-1977 ... 49-52
Obituary ... 69-72
Howe, Reuel L(anphier) 1905- ... 23-24R
Howe, Richard J. 1937- ... 77-80
Howe, Russell Warren 1925- ... 49-52
Howe, Tina ... 109
Howe, W(arren) Asquith 1910- ... 29-32R
Howe, William Hugh 1928- ... 65-68
Howell, Barbara 1937- ... 49-52
Howell, Benjamin Franklin 1890-1976
Obituary ... 65-68
Howell, Clark, Sr. 1863-1936 ... DLB-25
Howell, Clinton T. 1913- ... 29-32R
Howell, David Arthur Russell 1936- ... 109
Howell, Elsworth Seaman 1915-1987
Obituary ... 122
Howell, Evan P(ark) 1839-1905
Brief entry ... 119
See also DLB 23
Howell, Helen (Jane) 1934- ... 57-60
Howell, James Edwin 1928- ... CANR-20
Earlier sketch in CA 2R
Howell, John
See Hall, Gus
Howell, John C(hristian) 1924- ... CANR-9
Earlier sketch in CA 21-22R
Howell, John M(ichael) 1933- ... 33-36R
Howell, Joseph T(oy III) 1942- ... CANR-24
Earlier sketch in CA 45-48
Howell, Leon 1936- ... 25-28R
Howell, Michael J. 1932(?)-1986 Obituary ... 118
Howell, Pat 1947- ... SATA-15
Howell, Patricia Hagan 1939- ... 81-84
Howell, Reet 1945- ... 110
Howell, Richard W(esley) 1926- ... 57-60
Howell, Robert Lee 1928- ... 25-28R
Howell, Roger (Jr.) 1936- ... CANR-11
Earlier sketch in CA 21-22R
Howell, S.
See Styles, (Frank) Showell
Howell, Thomas 1944- ... 73-76
Howell, Virginia
See Ellison, Virginia H(owell)
Howell, Wilbur Samuel 1904- ... 33-36R
Howell, William C(arl) 1932- ... 93-96
Howells, J(ames) Harvey 1912- ... 97-100
Howells, John G(wilym) 1918- ... CANR-24
Earlier sketches in CA 23-24R, CANR-9
Howells, Roscoe 1919- ... 104
Howells, William Dean 1837-1920
Brief entry ... 104
See also DLB 12, 64
See also TCLC 7, 17
Howells, William White 1908- ... CANR-19
Earlier sketches in CA 1R, CANR-2
Hower, Edward 1941- ... 106
Hower, Ralph M(erle) 1903-1973 ... 3R
Obituary ... 45-48
Howes, Alan B(arber) 1920- Brief entry ... 112
Howes, Barbara 1914- ... 9-10R
See also CAAS 3
See also SATA 5
See also CLC 15
Howes, Connie B. 1933- ... 89-92
Howes, Frank Stewart 1891-1974
Obituary ... 115
Howes, Michael 1904- ... 61-64
Howes, Paul Griswold 1892-1984 ... 29-32R
Obituary ... 113
Howes, Raymond F(loyd) 1903- ... CAP-1
Earlier sketch in CA 17-18
Howes, Robert Gerard 1919- ... CANR-4
Earlier sketch in CA 1R
Howes, Royce (Bucknam) 1901-1973 ... CAP-2
Obituary ... 41-44R
Earlier sketch in CA 19-20
Howes, Wright 1882-1978 Obituary ... 104
Howick, William Henry 1924- ... 33-36R
Howie, Carl G(ordon) 1920- ... 15-16R
Howith, Harry 1934- ... 25-28R
Howitzer, Bronson
See Hardman, Richards Lynden
Howker, Janni 1957- ... SATA-46
See also CLR 14
Howkins, John 1945- ... CANR-14
Earlier sketch in CA 65-68
Howl, Marcia (Yvonne Hurt) 1947- ... 121
Howland, Bette 1937- ... 85-88
Howland, Harold Edward 1913-1980
Obituary ... 102
Howlett, Duncan 1906- ... 107
Howlett, John (Reginald) 1940- ... CANR-12
Earlier sketch in CA 69-72
Howorth, Beckett 1902- ... 114
Howorth, M. K.
See Black, Margaret K(atherine)
Howorth, Muriel ... CAP-1
Earlier sketch in CA 9-10
Howse, Ernest Marshall 1902- ... 49-52
Howson, Susan 1945- ... 113
Howton, F(rank) William 1925- ... 29-32R
Hoxie, Frederick E(ugene) 1947- ... 117
Hoxie, R(alph) Gordon 1919- ... 103
Hoy, Cyrus H. 1926- ... 21-22R
Hoy, David 1930- ... 17-18R
Hoy, James F(ranklin) 1939- ... 57-60
Hoy, John C. 1933- ... CANR-9
Earlier sketch in CA 21-22R
Hoy, Nina
See Roth, Arthur J(oseph)
Hoye, Anna Scott 1915- ... 15-16R
Hoyem, Andrew 1935- ... 9-10R
See also DLB 5
Hoyer, George W. 1919- ... CANR-4
Earlier sketch in CA 3R
Hoyer, H(arvey) Conrad 1907- ... 33-36R
Hoyer, Mildred N(aeher) ... 57-60
Hoyland, Michael 1925- ... 23-24R
Hoyle, Fred 1915- ... CANR-3
Earlier sketch in CA 7-8R
Hoyle, Geoffrey 1942- ... CANR-6
Earlier sketch in CA 53-56
See also SATA 18
Hoyle, Martha Byrd
See Byrd, Martha
Hoyle, Peter 1939- ... 124
Hoyles, J(ames) Arthur 1908- ... 7-8R
Hoyt, Charles Alva 1931- ... 33-36R
Hoyt, Charles K(ing) 1938- ... 110
Hoyt, Clark 1942- ... 69-72
Hoyt, Edwin P(almer), Jr. 1923- ... CANR-1
Earlier sketch in CA 3R
See also SATA 28
Hoyt, Elizabeth E(llis) 1893- ... 37-40R
Hoyt, Erich 1950- ... 106
Hoyt, Herman A(rthur) 1909- ... 29-32R
Hoyt, Homer 1896-1984 ... CANR-1
Obituary ... 114
Earlier sketch in CA 1R
Hoyt, Jo Wasson 1927- ... 21-22R
Hoyt, Joseph B(ixby) 1913- ... 5-6R
Hoyt, Kenneth B(oyd) 1924- ... CANR-1
Earlier sketch in CA 45-48
Hoyt, Mary Finch 1924(?)- ... 107
Hoyt, Murray 1904- ... 9-10R
Hoyt, Olga (Gruhzit) 1922- ... 25-28R
See also SATA 16
Hoyt, (Edwin) Palmer 1897-1979
Obituary ... 89-92
Hoyt, Robert S(tuart) 1918-1971 Obituary ... 111
Hoyt, Waite (Charles) 1899-1984 Obituary ... 113
Hozeny, Tony 1946- ... 61-64
Hozjusz
See Dobraczynski, Jan
Hrabal, Bohumil 1914- ... 106
See also CLC 13
Hrdy, Sarah Blaffer 1946- ... 107
Hromadka, Josef L(ukl) 1889-1971 ... CAP-1
Earlier sketch in CA 9-10
Hruska-Cortes, Elias 1943- ... 45-48
Hruza, Zdenek 1926- ... 61-64
Hsia, Adrian (Rue Chun) 1938- ... 77-80
Hsia, C(hih)-T(sing) 1921- ... CANR-17
Earlier sketches in CA 2R, CANR-2
Hsia, David Yi-Yung 1925-1972
Obituary ... 33-36R
Hsia, Hsiao
See Liu, Wu-chi
Hsia, Tsi-an 1916-1965 ... CAP-2
Earlier sketch in CA 25-28
Hsiang, Yeh
See Liu, Sydney (Chieh)
Hsiao, Katharine H(uei-Ying Huang)
1923- ... 77-80
Hsiao, Kung-Chuan 1897- ... 3R
Hsiao, Tso-liang 1910- ... 3R
Hsin-Hai, Chang 1898(?)-1972 Obituary ... 37-40R
Hsiung, James Chieh 1935- ... 37-40R
Hsu, Benedict (Pei-Hsiung) 1933- ... 69-72
Hsu, Cho-yun 1930- ... CANR-9
Earlier sketch in CA 17-18R
Hsu, Francis L(ang) K(wang) 1909- ... CANR-16
Earlier sketches in CA 3R, CANR-1
Hsu, Immanuel C. Y. 1923- ... 1R
Hsu, Kai-yu 1922-1982 ... CANR-14
Earlier sketch in CA 21-22R
Hsueh, Chun-tu 1922- ... CANR-15
Earlier sketch in CA 41-44R
Hsun, Lu
See Shu-Jen, Chou
See also TCLC 3
Hsu Ying 1935- ... 124
Htin Aung, U.
See Aung, (Maung) Htin
Hu, Shi Ming
See Hu, Shu Ming
Hu, Shu Ming 1927- ... 85-88
Hu, Sze-Tsen 1914- ... 41-44R
Huaco, George A. 1927- ... 17-18R
Huang, David S(hih-Li) 1930- ... 9-10R
Huang, Parker (Po-fei) 1914- ... CANR-2
Earlier sketch in CA 45-48
Huang, Philip Chung-Chih 1940-
Brief entry ... 105
Huang, Po-fei
See Huang, Parker (Po-fei)
Huang, Ray (Jen-yu) 1918- ... CANR-8
Earlier sketch in CA 61-64
Huang, Stanley S(hang) C(hien) 1923- ... 77-80
Hubach, Robert R(ogers) 1916- ... 1R
Hubartt, Paul L(eroy) 1919- ... 7-8R
Hubbard, Barbara Marx 1929- ... 103
Hubbard, D(onald) L(ee) 1929- ... 21-22R
Hubbard, David Allan 1928- ... CANR-16
Earlier sketch in CA 33-36R
Hubbard, David G(raham) 1920- ... 33-36R
Hubbard, Don 1926- ... 109
Hubbard, Edward (Horton) 1937- ... 124
Hubbard, Frank T. 1921(?)-1976
Obituary ... 65-68
Hubbard, Freeman (Henry) 1894- ... 5-6R
Hubbard, George (Barron) 1884-1958
Brief entry ... 122
Hubbard, J(ake) T(imothy) W(illiam)
1935- ... 124
Hubbard, (Frank Mc)Kin(ney) 1868-1930
Brief entry ... 113
See also DLB 11
Hubbard, L(afayette) Ron(ald)
1911-1986 ... CANR-22
Obituary ... 118
Earlier sketch in CA 77-80
See also CLC 43
Hubbard, Lucien 1889(?)-1971
Obituary ... 33-36R
Hubbard, Margaret Ann
See Priley, Margaret Hubbard
Hubbard, P(hilip) M(aitland) 1910-1980 ... 85-88
Obituary ... 97-100
Hubbard, Paul H. 1900(?)-1983 Obituary ... 109
Hubbard, Preston John 1918- ... 7-8R
Hubbard, (Andrew) Ray 1924- ... 103
Hubbard, Robert Hamilton 1916- ... CANR-21
Earlier sketch in CA 1R
Hubbard, Ruth 1924- ... 116
Hubbard, Thomas Leslie Wallan 1905- ... CAP-1
Earlier sketch in CA 13-14
Hubbard, William 1621(?)-1704 ... DLB-24
Hubbell, Harriet Weed 1909- ... 7-8R
Hubbell, Harry M. 1881-1971 Obituary ... 29-32R
Hubbell, Jay B(roadus) 1885-1979 ... CANR-17
Obituary ... 116
Earlier sketch in CA 1R
Hubbell, John G(erard) 1927- ... 65-68
Hubbell, Lindley Williams 1901- ... CAP-1
Earlier sketch in CA 15-16
Hubbell, Patricia 1928- ... 17-18R
See also SATA 8
Hubbell, Richard Whittaker 1914- ... 13-14R
Hubbell, Sue 1935- ... 120
Hubbs, Carl Leavitt 1894-1979 Obituary ... 89-92
Hubbs, G(uy) Ward 1952- ... 114
Hubenka, Lloyd J(ohn) 1931- ... 49-52
Huber, Jack T(ravis) 1918- ... 23-24R
Huber, Joan 1925- ... CANR-13
Earlier sketch in CA 77-80
Huber, Leonard Victor 1903- ... CANR-6
Earlier sketch in CA 57-60
Huber, Morton Wesley 1923- ... 17-18R
Huber, Richard M(iller) 1922- ... 33-36R
Huber, Thomas 1937- ... 29-32R
Huber, Thomas Michael 1944- ... 112
Huberman, Edward 1910- ... 15-16R
Huberman, Elizabeth Duncan Lyle 1915- ... 15-16R
Huberman, Leo 1903-1968 ... CANR-4
Earlier sketch in CA 1R
Hubert, James Lee 1947- ... 73-76
Hubert, Jim
See Hubert, James Lee
Hubert, Renee Riese 1916- ... 61-64
Hubin, Allen J. 1936- ... 33-36R
Hubka, Betty (Josephine Morgan) 1924- ... 13-14R
Hubler, David 1941- ... 110
Hubler, Edward L(orenzo) 1902-1965 ... CAP-1
Earlier sketch in CA 13-14
Hubler, Herbert Clark 1910- ... 85-88
Hubler, Richard Gibson 1912- ... CANR-2
Earlier sketch in CA 3R
Hubley, Faith Elliot 1924- ... 81-84
See also SATA 48
Hubley, John 1914-1977 ... SATA-24, 48
Huby, Pamela M(argaret Clark) 1922- ... 21-22R
Huch, Friedrich 1873-1913 ... DLB-66
Huch, Ricarda (Octavia) 1864-1947
Brief entry ... 111
See also DLB 66
See also TCLC 13
Huchel, Peter 1903- ... 81-84
Huck, Gabe (Donald Joseph) 1941- ... 112
Huckaby, Elizabeth (Paisley) 1905- ... 106
Huckaby, Gerald 1933- ... 33-36R
Hucker, Charles O(scar) 1919- ... 69-72
Huckins, Wesley C. 1918- ... 23-24R
Huckleberry, E(vermont) R(obbins)
1894- ... CANR-11
Earlier sketch in CA 61-64
Huckshorn, Robert J(ack) 1928- ... 97-100
Hudd, Roy 1936- ... 105
Huddle, David 1942- ... 57-60
Huddle, Frank, Jr. 1943- ... 37-40R
Huddleston, Eugene L(ee) 1931- ... CANR-19
Earlier sketch in CA 102
Huddleston, Lee Eldridge 1935- ... 21-22R
Huddleston, Rodney D(esmond) 1937- ... 33-36R
Huddy, Delia 1934- ... CANR-19
Earlier sketch in CA 25-28R
Hudgens, A(lice) Gayle 1941- ... 37-40R
Hudgins, H(erbert) C(ornelius), Jr.
1932- ... 33-36R
Hudnut, Robert K(ilborne) 1934- ... CANR-17
Earlier sketch in CA 25-28R

Hudoba, Michael 1913-1984 Obituary 113
Hudon, Edward Gerard 1915- 7-8R
Hudson, Alec
See Holmes, W(ilfred) J(ay)
Hudson, Arthur Palmer 1894(?)-1978
Obituary 111
Hudson, Charles M(elvin, Jr.) 1932- 33-36R
Hudson, Danny L. 1940- 122
Hudson, Darril 1931- 45-48
Hudson, Derek (Rommel) 1911- 9-10R
Hudson, Geoffrey Francis 1903-1974
Obituary 49-52
Hudson, Gladys W(atts) 1926- 33-36R
Hudson, Gossie Harold 1930- 93-96
Hudson, Helen
See Lane, Helen
Hudson, Henry Norman 1814-1886 ..... DLB-64
Hudson, Henry T(homas) 1932- 118
Hudson, Herman 1923- 97-100
Hudson, James A(lbert) 1924- 33-36R
Hudson, James J(ackson) 1919- 25-28R
Hudson, James R. 1933- 124
Hudson, Jean B(arlow) 1915- 93-96
Hudson, Jeffery
See Crichton, (John) Michael
Hudson, John A(llen) 1927- 25-28R
Hudson, Kenneth 1916- Brief entry 117
Hudson, (Margaret) Kirsty 1947- 107
See also SATA 32
Hudson, Liam 1933- CANR-12
Earlier sketch in CA 29-32R
Hudson, Lois Phillips 1927- 3R
Hudson, Marc 1947- 116
Hudson, Meg
See Koehler, Margaret Hudson
Hudson, Michael C(raig) 1938- 37-40R
Hudson, Michael Huckleberry 1939- ... CANR-13
Earlier sketch in CA 33-36R
Hudson, (Arthur) Palmer 1892- CAP-2
Earlier sketch in CA 19-20
Hudson, Peggy
See Herz, Peggy
Hudson, R(obert) Lofton 1910- 15-16R
Hudson, Randolph H(oyt) 1927- 19-20R
Hudson, Richard (McLain, Jr.) 1925- 65-68
Hudson, Robert
See Oleksy, Walter
Hudson, Robert P(aul) 1926- 116
Hudson, Robert Vernon 1932- 109
Hudson, Theodore R. 45-48
Hudson, W(illiam) H(enry) 1841-1922
Brief entry 115
See also SATA 35
Hudson, Wilma J(ones) 1916- 33-36R
Hudson, Wilson Mathis 1907- 102
Hudson, Winthrop Still 1911- CANR-2
Earlier sketch in CA 3R
Hudspeth, Robert N. 1936- 103
Huebel, Harry Russell 1943- 77-80
Huebener, Theodore 1895-1983 Obituary ... 111
Huebner, Anna (Ismelda Mathews)
1877(?)-1974 Obituary 53-56
Huegli, A(lbert) G(eorge) 1913- 15-16R
Huelsman, Richard J(oseph) 1921- 111
Huelsmann, Eva 1928- SATA-16
Huerlimann, Bettina 1909-1983 109
Obituary 110
See also SATA 34, 39
Huerlimann, Ruth 1939- 107
See also SATA 31, 32
Huessy, Hans R. 1921- 21-22R
Hueter, John E(dwin) 1918- 114
Huether, Anne Frances
See Freeman, Anne Frances
Huey, F. B., Jr. 1925- CANR-23
Earlier sketch in CA 106
Huey, Lynda 1947- 65-68
Hufana, A(lejandrino) G. 1926- 77-80
Hufbauer, Karl (George) 1937- 109
Huff, Afton (A.) W(alker) 1928- 65-68
Huff, Betty Tracy 25-28R
Huff, Darrell 1913- CANR-5
Earlier sketch in CA 3R
Huff, Robert 1924- CANR-6
Earlier sketch in CA 13-14R
Huff, T(om) E. 1938(?)- 93-96
See also AITN 2
Huff, Vaughn E(dward) 1935- 29-32R
Huffaker, Clair 1927- 113
Huffaker, Sandy 1943- SATA-10
Huffard, Grace Thompson 1892- CAP-1
Earlier sketch in CA 11-12
Huffert, Anton M. 1912- 13-14R
Huffman, Carolyn 1928- 69-72
Huffman, Claire (De Cesare Licari) 116
Huffman, Franklin E(ugene) 1934- CANR-12
Earlier sketch in CA 29-32R
Huffman, James Lamar 1941- 102
Huffman, Laurie 1916- 45-48
Huffman, Tom SATA-24
Hufford, Susan 1940- CANR-9
Earlier sketch in CA 57-60
Hufschmidt, Maynard Michael 1912- ... CANR-15
Earlier sketch in CA 41-44R
Hufton, Olwen H. 1938- 21-22R
Hug, Bernal D(ean) 1896- 57-60
Huggan, Isabel 1943- 119
Huggett, Frank E(dward) 1924- CANR-19
Earlier sketches in CA 9-10R, CANR-3
Huggett, Richard 1929- 53-56
Huggett, William Turner 53-56
Huggins, Alice Margaret 1891-1971 ...... CAP-1
Earlier sketch in CA 17-18
Huggins, Charles B(renton) 1901-
Brief entry 115
Huggins, Nathan Irvin 1927- 29-32R
Hughart, Barry CLC-39
Hughes, Alan 1935- 97-100
Hughes, Alice 1899(?)-1977 Obituary 104
Hughes, Andrew 1937- 61-64
Hughes, Anthony John 1933- 11-12R
Hughes, Arthur Joseph 1928- 17-18R
Hughes, Arthur Montague D'Urban
1873-1974 Obituary 49-52
Hughes, B(asil) P(erronet) 1903- 61-64
Hughes, C(hristopher) J(ohn) 1918- 17-18R
Hughes, C. J. Pennethorne
See Hughes, (Charles James)
Pennethorne
Hughes, Catharine R(achel) 1935-1987 ... 41-44R
Obituary 123
Hughes, Charles C(ampbell) 1929- 41-44R
Hughes, Charles L(loyd) 1933- CANR-11
Earlier sketch in CA 19-20R
Hughes, (John) Cledwyn 1920- 15-16R
Hughes, Colin
See Creasey, John
Hughes, Colin A(nfield) 1930- CANR-9
Earlier sketch in CA 23-24R
Hughes, Daniel 1929- 33-36R
Hughes, Daniel T(homas) 1930- 89-92
Hughes, David (John) 1930- Brief entry 116
See also DLB 14
Hughes, Dean 1943- CANR-22
Earlier sketch in CA 106
See also SATA 33
Hughes, Dean Aubrey 1908(?)-1987
Obituary 122
Hughes, Dorothy (Berry) 1910- CAP-2
Earlier sketch in CA 33-36
Hughes, Dorothy B(elle) 1904- 104
Hughes, Douglas A(llan) 1938- 29-32R
Hughes, Eden
See Butterworth, W(illiam) E(dmund III)
Hughes, Elizabeth
See Zachary, Hugh
Hughes, Emmet John 1920-1982 69-72
Obituary 107
Hughes, Erica 1931- 109
Hughes, Everett Cherrington 1897-1983 103
Obituary 108
Hughes, Felicity 1938- 33-36R
Hughes, G(eorge) E(dward) 1918- 23-24R
Hughes, Gerald (Thomas) 1930- 117
Hughes, Gervase 1905- 9-10R
Hughes, Glyn 1935- CANR-13
Earlier sketch in CA 33-36R
Hughes, Graham 1928- 57-60
Hughes, Gwilym Fielden 1899- 97-100
Hughes, H(enry) Stuart 1916- CANR-2
Earlier sketch in CA 3R
Hughes, Harold K(enneth) 1911- 11-12R
Hughes, Helen (Gintz) 1928- 15-16R
Hughes, Howard (Robard) 1905-1976
Obituary 112
Hughes, Irene Finger 103
Hughes, J(ohnson) Donald 1932- CANR-10
Earlier sketch in CA 65-68
Hughes, James Monroe 1890-1971 .... 1R
Obituary 103
Hughes, James Pennethorne
See Hughes, (Charles James)
Pennethorne
Hughes, James Quentin 1920- CANR-6
Earlier sketch in CA 13-14R
Hughes, James W(ilfred) 1934- 77-80
Hughes, (Robert) John 1930- CANR-4
Earlier sketch in CA 1R
Hughes, John 1950(?)- Brief entry 124
Hughes, John A(nthony) 1941- 41-44R
Hughes, John Jay 1928- 57-60
Hughes, John L(ewis) 1938- 77-80
Hughes, John Paul 1920-1974 .... 1R
Obituary 53-56
Hughes, Jonathan R(oberts) T(yson)
1928- 81-84
Hughes, Judith M(arkham) 1941- 33-36R
Hughes, Judy 1943- 69-72
Hughes, Kathleen W. 1927(?)-1977
Obituary 69-72
Hughes, Ken(neth) 1922- CANR-16
Earlier sketch in CA 7-8R
Hughes, (James) Langston 1902-1967 .. CANR-1
Obituary 25-28R
Earlier sketch in CA 1R
See also SATA 4, 33
See also DLB 4, 7, 48, 51
See also CLC 1, 5, 10, 15, 35, 44
Hughes, Leo 1908- 41-44R
Hughes, Margaret Kelly 1894(?)-1980
Obituary 101
Hughes, Marija Matich 97-100
Hughes, Mary 1951- 122
Hughes, Mary Gray 1930- 61-64
Hughes, Mary Louise 1910- 29-32R
Hughes, Matilda
See MacLeod, Charlotte (Matilda Hughes)
Hughes, Merrit Y(erkes) 1893-1970 ...... CAP-1
Earlier sketch in CA 17-18
Hughes, Monica (Ince) 1925- CANR-23
Earlier sketch in CA 77-80
See also SATA 15
See also CLR 9
Hughes, Nathaniel Cheairs, Jr. 1930- 17-18R
Hughes, Owain (Gardner Collingwood)
1943- 21-22R
Hughes, Patrick 1939- 61-64
Hughes, Paul L(ester) 1915- 9-10R
Hughes, (Charles James) Pennethorne
1907-1967 .... CAP-2
Earlier sketch in CA 21-22
Hughes, Philip 1895-1967 .... CAP-2
Earlier sketch in CA 17-18
Hughes, Philip Edgcumbe 1915- CANR-18
Earlier sketches in CA 9-10R, CANR-3
Hughes, (James) Quentin 1920- 29-32R
Hughes, R(ichard) E(dward) 1927- CANR-6
Earlier sketch in CA 5-6R
Hughes, Richard (Arthur Warren)
1900-1976 .... CANR-4
Obituary 65-68
Earlier sketch in CA 7-8R
See also SATA 8, 25
See also DLB 15
See also CLC 1, 11
Hughes, Richard 1906-1984 Obituary 111
Hughes, Richard 1941- 107
Hughes, Riley 1914-1981 107
Obituary 103
Hughes, Robert 1929(?)-1972 Obituary .. 37-40R
Hughes, Robert (Studley Forrest) 1938(?)- .. 112
Brief entry 110
Hughes, Russell C. 1893(?)-1982
Obituary 108
Hughes, Russell Meriwether 1898(?)-1988
Obituary 124
Hughes, Sam
See Wilks, Brian
Hughes, Shirley 1927- CANR-24
Earlier sketch in CA 85-88
See also SATA 16
Hughes, Stephen Ormsby 1924- 61-64
Hughes, Ted 1930- CANR-1
Earlier sketch in CA 2R
See also SATA 27, 49
See also DLB 40
See also CLC 2, 4, 9, 14, 37
See also CLR 3
Hughes, Terry A. 1933- 65-68
Hughes, Theodore E(rmond) 1942- 116
Hughes, Thomas 1822-1896 .... SATA-31
See also DLB 18
Hughes, Thomas M(ears) 1927- 65-68
Hughes, Thomas Parke 1923- 29-32R
Hughes, Virginia
See Campbell, Hope
Hughes, Walter (Llewellyn) 1910- CANR-1
Earlier sketch in CA 4R
See also SATA 26
Hughes, William J., Jr. 1897(?)-1974
Obituary 45-48
Hughes, Zach
See Zachary, Hugh
Hughes, Zachary
See Zachary, Hugh
Hughey, Ruth Willard 1899- 1R
Hugill, Stan(ley) James 1906- CAP-2
Earlier sketch in CA 23-24
Hugo, Grant
See Cable, James (Eric)
Hugo, Herbert W. 1930(?)-1979
Obituary 89-92
Hugo, Richard F(ranklin) 1923-1982 .... CANR-3
Obituary 108
Earlier sketch in CA 49-52
See also DLB 5
See also CLC 6, 18, 32
Hugo, Victor (Marie) 1802-1885 ...... SATA-47
Huhta, James K(enneth) 1937- 37-40R
Huie, William Bradford 1910-1986 ...... CANR-7
Obituary 121
Earlier sketch in CA 11-12R
See also AITN 1
Huie, William O(rr) 1911- 23-24R
Huisken, Ronald H(erman) 1946- 93-96
Hula, Harold L. 1930- 25-28R
Hulbert, Jack 1892-1978 Obituary 115
Hulet, Claude Lyle 1920- CANR-9
Earlier sketch in CA 53-56
Hulicka, Irene M(ackintosh) 1927- 37-40R
Hulicka, Karel 1913- 41-44R
Huline-Dickens, Frank William 1931- 107
See also SATA 34
Hulke, Malcolm 1924- 81-84
Hull, Cary Schuler 1946- 106
Hull, Charles
See Charles, Gordon H(ull)
Hull, David L(ee) 1935- 77-80
Hull, David Stewart 1938- 25-28R
Hull, Denison Bingham 1897- 37-40R
Hull, Eleanor (Means) 1913- CANR-19
Earlier sketches in CA 11-12R, CANR-4
See also SATA 21
Hull, Eric Traviss
See Harnan, Terry
Hull, Eugene L(eslie) 1928- 37-40R
Hull, George F. 1909(?)-1974 Obituary 53-56
Hull, Gloria T(heresa Thompson) 1944- 108
Hull, H. Braxton
See Jacobs, Helen Hull
Hull, Helen (Rose) 1888(?)-1971 .... CAP-1
Obituary 29-32R
Earlier sketch in CA 9-10
Hull, J(ohn) H(owarth) E(ric) 1923- 25-28R
Hull, Jesse Redding
See Hull, Jessie Redding
Hull, Jessie Redding 1932- 109
Hull, Katharine 1921-1977 .... 29-32R
See also SATA 23
Hull, Marion A(da) 1911- 105
Hull, Opal
See Lehnus, Opal (Hull)
Hull, Oswald 1919- 25-28R
Hull, R(ichard) F(rancis) C(arrington)
1913(?)-1974 Obituary 53-56
Hull, Raymona E. 1907- 116
Hull, Raymond 1919-1985 .... CANR-11
Obituary 116
Earlier sketch in CA 25-28R
Hull, Richard W. 1940- 45-48
Hull, Roger H. 1942- 25-28R
Hull, William (Doyle) 1918- CANR-5
Earlier sketch in CA 13-14R
Hull, William E(dward) 1930- CANR-24
Earlier sketches in CA 17-18R, CANR-7
Hulland, J(ennifer) R(osemary) 1936- 122
Hulley, Clarence C(harles) 1905- 41-44R
Hulme, Hilda Mary 1914- 77-80
Hulme, Kathryn 1900-1981 .... CAP-1
Obituary 104
Earlier sketch in CA 9-10
Hulme, Keri CLC-39
Hulme, T(homas) E(rnest) 1883-1917
Brief entry 117
See also DLB 19
See also TCLC 21
Hulme, William E(dward) 1920- CANR-5
Earlier sketch in CA 13-14R
Hulse, Clark 1947- 106
Hulse, Erroll 1931- CANR-21
Earlier sketch in CA 104
Hulse, James Warren 1930- 11-12R
Hulse, (Herman) LaWayne 1922- 29-32R
Hulse, Michael (William) 1955- 118
Hulse, Stewart H(arding), Jr. 1931- ... CANR-14
Earlier sketch in CA 33-36R
Hult, Ruby El 1912- 57-60
Hulteng, John L. 1921- CANR-13
Earlier sketch in CA 33-36R
Hultgren, Thor 1902- CAP-1
Earlier sketch in CA 17-18
Hultman, Charles W(illiam) 1930- CANR-1
Earlier sketch in CA 1R
Hults, Dorothy Niebrugge 1898- CAP-1
Earlier sketch in CA 9-10
See also SATA 6
Humbaraci, D(emir) Arslan 1923- 49-52
Humbard, (Alpha) Rex (Emmanuel) 1919-
Brief entry 111
Humber, William 1949- 124
Humble, Richard 1945- CANR-17
Earlier sketches in CA 45-48, CANR-2
Humble, William F(rank) 1948- 21-22R
Hume, Arthur W. J. G. Ord
See Ord-Hume, Arthur W. J. G.
Hume, (Alexander) Brit(ton) 1943-
Brief entry 119
Hume, Fergus(on Wright) 1859-1932
Brief entry 109
Hume, John E. N., Jr. 1915-1986
Obituary 118
Hume, John Robert 1939- 106
Hume, Kathryn 1945- 57-60
Hume, Lotta Carswell CAP-1
Earlier sketch in CA 9-10
See also SATA 7
Hume, Martha 1947- 112
Hume, Paul Chandler 1915- 102
Hume, Robert D. 1944- CANR-12
Earlier sketch in CA 29-32R
Hume, Ruth Fox 1922-1980 Obituary 97-100
See also SATA 22, 26
Humes, D(ollena) Joy 1921- 1R
Humes, H(arold) L. 1926- 7-8R
Humes, James C. 1934- CANR-1
Earlier sketch in CA 45-48
Humes, John Portner 1921-1985 Obituary .. 117
Humes, Samuel 1930- 7-8R
Humez, Jean McMahon 1944- 124
Humfrey, C.
See Osborne, C(harles) H(umfrey)
C(aulfeild)
Hummel, Berta 1909-1946 .... SATA-43
Hummel, Charles E. 1923- 19-20R
Hummel, Madeline
See Moore, Madeline (Roberta)
Hummel, Ray O(rvin), Jr. 1909- 33-36R
Hummel, Ruth Stevenson 1929- 7-8R
Hummel, Sister Maria Innocentia
See Hummel, Berta
Humphreville, Frances Tibbetts 1909- 9-10R
Humphrey, David C(hurchill) 1937- 85-88
Humphrey, Henry (III) 1930- 77-80
See also SATA 16
Humphrey, Hubert Horatio 1911-1978 69-72
Obituary 73-76
Humphrey, J(ames) Edward 1918- 93-96
Humphrey, James (Earl) 1939- 45-48
Humphrey, James H(arry) 1911- CANR-23
Earlier sketches in CA 61-64, CANR-8
Humphrey, Michael (Edward) 1926- 29-32R
Humphrey, Paul 1915- 110
Humphrey, Robert L. 1923- 57-60
Humphrey, William 1924- 77-80
See also DLB 6
See also CLC 45
Humphreys, Alexander J(eremiah)
1913- 33-36R
Humphreys, Alice Lee 1893- 7-8R
Humphreys, (Travers) Christmas
1901-1983 77-80
Obituary 109
Humphreys, David 1752-1818 .... DLB-37
Humphreys, Emyr Owen 1919- CANR-24
Earlier sketches in CA 7-8R, CANR-3
See also DLB 15
See also CLC 47
Humphreys, Graham 1945- SATA-32
Humphreys, J(ohn) R(ichard) Adams
1918- CANR-22
Earlier sketch in CA 3R
Humphreys, Josephine 1945- Brief entry ... 121
See also CLC 34
Humphreys, (Robert Allan) Laud 1930- ... 29-32R
Humphreys, Mary Eglantyne Hill 1914- .. CANR-6
Earlier sketch in CA 7-8R
Humphreyville, Theresa R. 1918- 13-14R

INDEX

Humphries, Adelaide M. 1898- CAP-1
Earlier sketch in CA 15-16
Humphries, Helen Speirs Dickie 1915- ... CAP-1
Earlier sketch in CA 9-10
Humphries, (John) Jefferson 1955- 114
Humphries, Mary 1905- 53-56
Humphries, (George) Rolfe 1894-1969 .. CANR-3
Obituary 25-28R
Earlier sketch in CA 5-6R
Humphries, Sydney Vernon 1907- 103
Humphry, Derek 1930- 41-44R
Humphrys, Geoffrey
See Humphrys, Leslie George
Humphrys, Leslie George 1921- 107
Humpstone, Charles Cheney 1931- 49-52
Huncke, Herbert 1915- DLB-16
Hundley, Joan Martin 1921- 45-48
Hundley, Norris (Cecil), Jr. 1935- CANR-8
Earlier sketch in CA 17-18R
Huneryager, S(herwood) G(eorge) 1933- 1R
Hungerford, Cy(rus Cotton) 1889(?)-1983
Obituary 109
Hungerford, Edward Buell 1900- 37-40R
Hungerford, Harold R(alph) 1928- 33-36R
Hungerford, Hesba (Fay) Brinsmead 1922- .. 124
Hungerford, Mary Jane 1913- 77-80
Hungerford, Pixie
See Brinsmead, H(esba) F(ay)
Hungry Wolf, Adolf 1944- 115
Hungry Wolf, Beverly 1950- 117
Hunker, Henry L. 1924- 15-16R
Hunkin, Timothy Mark Trelawney 1950- 102
Hunkins, Francis P(eter) 1938- 57-60
Hunkins, Lee(cynth) 1930- 108
Hunnex, Milton D(eVerne) 1917- 29-32R
Hunnings, Neville March 1929- CANR-12
Earlier sketch in CA 25-28R
Hunnisett, Basil 1923- 119
Hunsaker, David M(alcolm) 1944- 33-36R
Hunsberger, Edith Mae 1927- 109
Hunsberger, Warren S(eabury) 1911- 41-44R
Hunsehe, Raymond W. 1891(?)-1983
Obituary 111
Hunsinger, George 1945- 65-68
Hunsinger, Paul 1919- 33-36R
Hunsinger, Walter (William) 1923- 122
Hunt, Abby Campbell 1933(?)-1985
Obituary 116
Hunt, Barbara
See Watters, Barbara H(unt)
Hunt, Bernice (Kohn) 1920- CANR-21
Earlier sketch in CA 9-10R
Hunt, Charles Butler 1906- 110
Hunt, Charlotte
See Hodges, Doris M(arjorie)
Hunt, Chester L. 1912- CANR-5
Earlier sketch in CA 13-14R
Hunt, Clarence
See Holman, C(larence) Hugh
Hunt, Dave
See Hunt, David C(harles Hadden)
Hunt, David (Wathen Stather) 1913- 102
Hunt, David 1942- 33-36R
Hunt, David C(harles Hadden) 1926- CANR-9
Earlier sketch in CA 57-60
Hunt, David C(urtis) 1935- CANR-16
Earlier sketch in CA 89-92
Hunt, Douglas 1918- 13-14R
Hunt, E(verette) Howard, Jr. 1918- CANR-2
Earlier sketch in CA 45-48
See also CLC 3
See also AITN 1
Hunt, E. K. 1937- 77-80
Hunt, Earl B. 1933- 93-96
Hunt, Earl W(ilbur) 1926- 85-88
Hunt, Edgar H(ubert) 1909- CAP-1
Earlier sketch in CA 9-10
Hunt, Elgin F(raser) 1895-1978 .... 4R
Hunt, Everett Lee 1890(?)-1984 Obituary ... 112
Hunt, Florine E(lizabeth) 1928- 15-16R
Hunt, Francis CAP-2
Earlier sketch in CA 19-20
Hunt, Frazier 1885-1967 Obituary 93-96
Hunt, Garry Edward 1942- 115
Hunt, Geoffrey 1915(?)-1974 Obituary 104
Hunt, George Laird 1918- 49-52
Hunt, George W(illiam) 1937- 120
Hunt, Gill
See Tubb, E(dwin) C(harles)
Hunt, Gladys M. 1926- CANR-13
Earlier sketch in CA 29-32R
Hunt, (Leslie) Gordon 1906-1970 .... CAP-2
Earlier sketch in CA 29-32
Hunt, H(arry) Draper 1935- 37-40R
Hunt, Harrison
See Ballard, (Willis) Todhunter
Hunt, Herbert James 1899-1973 Obituary .. 89-92
Hunt, Hugh 1911- CANR-3
Earlier sketch in CA 5-6R
Hunt, Ignatius 1920- 17-18R
Hunt, Inez Whitaker 1899- CAP-1
Earlier sketch in CA 17-18
Hunt, Irene 1907- CANR-8
Earlier sketch in CA 19-20R
See also SATA 2
See also DLB 52
See also CLR 1
Hunt, J(oseph) McVicker 1906- 37-40R
Hunt, J. William, Jr. 1930- 53-56
Hunt, James Gerald 1932- CANR-14
Earlier sketch in CA 65-68
Hunt, (Henry Cecil) John 1910- 109
Hunt, John
See Paine, Lauran (Bosworth)
Hunt, John Dixon 1936- CANR-17
Earlier sketch in CA 85-88
Hunt, John J. 1929- 33-36R
Hunt, John P(aul) 1915-1988 .... 33-36R
Obituary 124
Hunt, John W(esley) 1927- 21-22R
Hunt, Joyce 1927- CANR-22
Earlier sketch in CA 106
See also SATA 31
Hunt, June 1944- 103
Hunt, Kari (Eleanor B.) 1920- 41-44R
Hunt, Kellogg W(esley) 1912- 7-8R
Hunt, Kenneth E(dward) 1917(?)-1978
Obituary 104
Hunt, Kyle
See Creasey, John
Hunt, Lawrence J. 1920- 7-8R
Hunt, Leon (Gibson) 1931- 65-68
Hunt, Linda 1940- 106
See also SATA 39
Hunt, Mabel Leigh 1892-1971 .... CAP-1
Obituary 106
Earlier sketch in CA 9-10
See also SATA 1, 26
Hunt, Maurice P. 1915- 25-28R
Hunt, Morton M(agill) 1920- CANR-21
Earlier sketch in CA 7-8R
See also SATA 22
Hunt, Nan
See Ray, N(ancy) L(ouise)
Hunt, Nancy (Ridgely) 1927- 103
Hunt, Nigel
See Greenbank, Anthony Hunt
Hunt, Noel Aubrey Bonavia
See Bonavia-Hunt, Noel Aubrey
Hunt, Noreen 1931- 103
Hunt, Norman C.
See Crowther-Hunt, Norman Crowther
Hunt, Norman Crowther Crowther
See Crowther-Hunt, Norman Crowther
Hunt, Patricia 1922(?)-1983 Obituary 120
Hunt, Patricia Joan CANR-21
Earlier sketch in CA 103
Hunt, Penelope
See Napier, Priscilla
Hunt, Peter 1922- 5-6R
Hunt, Peter (Leonard) 1945- 113
Hunt, Ray(mond) C(hamp), Jr. 1919- 122
Hunt, Raymond G(eorge) 1928- CANR-3
Earlier sketch in CA 11-12R
Hunt, Richard (Paul) 1921- 73-76
Hunt, Richard N(orman) 1931- 11-12R
Hunt, Robert C(ushman) 1934- CANR-9
Earlier sketch in CA 21-22R
Hunt, Sam 1946- 110
Hunt, Tim(othy A.) 1949- 121
Hunt, Todd T. 1938- 15-16R
Hunt, V. Daniel 1939- 111
Hunt, Virginia Lloyd 1888(?)-1977
Obituary 73-76
Hunt, William 1934- CANR-3
Earlier sketch in CA 49-52
Hunt, William A(lvin) 1903-1986 Obituary .. 118
Hunt, William Dudley, Jr. 1922-1987 .. CANR-14
Obituary 122
Earlier sketch in CA 33-36R
Hunt, William R(aymond) 1929- 93-96
Hunter, A(rchibald) M(acbride) 1906- ... CANR-6
Earlier sketch in CA 9-10R
Hunter, Alan (James Herbert) 1922- ... CANR-18
Earlier sketches in CA 9-10R, CANR-3
Hunter, Allan A(rmstrong) 1893- 7-8R
Hunter, Anson
See Orrmont, Arthur
Hunter, Beatrice Trum 1918- CANR-22
Earlier sketches in CA 19-20R, CANR-7
Hunter, Bernice Thurman 1922- 119
See also SATA 45
Hunter, Bruce (William) 1952- 123
Hunter, C. Bruce 1917- 61-64
Hunter, Captain Marcy
See Ellis, Edward S(ylvester)
Hunter, Christine
See Hunter, Maud L(ily)
Hunter, Clark 124
Hunter, Clingham, M.D.
See Adams, William Taylor
Hunter, Dard 1883-1966 .... CAP-1
Obituary 25-28R
Earlier sketch in CA 15-16
Hunter, Doris A. 1929- 37-40R
Hunter, Edith Fisher 1919- 107
See also SATA 31
Hunter, Edward 1902-1978 .... 7-8R
Obituary 77-80
Hunter, Evan 1926- CANR-5
Earlier sketch in CA 7-8R
See also SATA 25
See also DLBY 82
See also CLC 11, 31
Hunter, Frederick J(ames) 1916- 33-36R
Hunter, Geoffrey (Basil Bailey) 1925- 33-36R
Hunter, George E.
See Ellis, Edward S(ylvester)
Hunter, Gordon C. 1924- 106
Hunter, Hall
See Marshall, Edison
Hunter, Henry MacGregor 1929-
Brief entry 109
Hunter, Hilda 1921- 49-52
See also SATA 7
Hunter, Howard Eugene 1929- 41-44R
Hunter, J(ames) A(lston) H(ope)
1902- CANR-14
Earlier sketches in CA 9-10, CAP-1
Hunter, J(ohn) F(letcher) M(acGregor)
1924- 37-40R
Hunter, J(ames) Paul 1934- CANR-24
Earlier sketches in CA 21-22R, CANR-9
Hunter, Jack D(ayton) 1921- CANR-6
Earlier sketch in CA 7-8R
Hunter, James H(ogg) 1890- 85-88
Hunter, Jim 1939- CANR-7
Earlier sketch in CA 11-12R
See also DLB 14
Hunter, Joan
See Yarde, Jeanne Betty Frances
Hunter, Joe
See McNeilly, Wilfred Glassford
Hunter, John
See Ballard, (Willis) Todhunter
and Hunter, Maud L(ily)
Hunter, John M(erlin) 1921- 13-14R
Hunter, Kim 1922- 61-64
Hunter, Kristin (Eggleston) 1931- CANR-13
Earlier sketch in CA 13-14R
See also SATA 12
See also DLB 33
See also CLC 35
See also CLR 3
See also AITN 1
Hunter, Leigh
See Etchison, Birdie L(ee)
Hunter, Leslie S(tannard) 1890-1983 ..... CAP-1
Obituary 110
Earlier sketch in CA 19-20
Hunter, Lieutenant Ned
See Ellis, Edward S(ylvester)
Hunter, Louis C. 1898(?)-1984 Obituary 112
Hunter, Louise H(arris) 41-44R
Hunter, Mac
See Hunter, Henry MacGregor
Hunter, Marjorie 1922- 69-72
Hunter, Marvin H(erbert) 1930-
Brief entry 111
Hunter, Mary Vann 1937- 107
Hunter, Maud L(ily) 1910- CANR-4
Earlier sketch in CA 9-10R
Hunter, Mel 1927- 93-96
See also SATA 39
Hunter, Michael (Cyril William) 1949- 104
Hunter, Milton R(eed) 1902-1975
Obituary 104
Hunter, Mollie
See McIlwraith, Maureen Mollie Hunter
See also CLC 21
Hunter, Ned
See Ellis, Edward S(ylvester)
Hunter, Norman (George Lorimer)
1899- CANR-15
Earlier sketch in CA 93-96
See also SATA 26
Hunter, Norman Charles 1908-1971
Obituary 29-32R
See also DLB 10
Hunter, Richard 1923-1981 Obituary 105
Hunter, Robert E(dwards) 1940- CANR-15
Earlier sketch in CA 41-44R
Hunter, Robert Grams 1927- 93-96
Hunter, Rodello
See Calkins, Rodello
Hunter, Sam 1923- CANR-8
Earlier sketch in CA 13-14R
Hunter, Stephen 1946- CANR-19
Earlier sketch in CA 102
Hunter, Thomas 1932- 108
Hunter, Tim 1947- 85-88
Hunter, Valancy
See Meaker, Eloise
Hunter, Vickie
See Hunter, Victoria Alberta
Hunter, Victoria Alberta 1929- 7-8R
Hunter, William A(lbert) 1908- 13-14R
Hunter, William B(ridges), Jr. 1915- 77-80
Hunter Blair, Pauline (Clarke) 1921- 29-32R
See also SATA 3
Hunter Blair, Peter 1912-1982 Obituary 108
Brief entry 107
Hunting, Constance 1925- CANR-23
Earlier sketch in CA 45-48
Huntington, Anna Hyatt 1876-1973
Obituary 45-48
Huntington, (E.) Gale 1902- 11-12R
Huntington, Harriet E(lizabeth) 1909- CANR-5
Earlier sketch in CA 7-8R
See also SATA 1
Huntington, Henry S., Jr. 1892-1981
Obituary 103
Huntington, John (Willard) 1940- 112
Huntington, Samuel P(hillips) 1927- CANR-1
Earlier sketch in CA 1R
Huntington, Thomas W(aterman)
1893-1973 Obituary 45-48
Huntington, Virginia 1889- 21-22R
Huntley, Chester Robert 1911-1974 97-100
Obituary 49-52
See also AITN 1
Huntley, Chet
See Huntley, Chester Robert
Huntley, Frank Livingstone 1902- 33-36R
Huntley, H(erbert) E(dwin) 1892- CAP-1
Earlier sketch in CA 13-14
Huntley, James L(ewis) 1914- 101
Huntley, James Robert 1923- CANR-12
Earlier sketch in CA 29-32R
Huntley, Timothy Wade 1939- 102
Hunton, Mary
See Gilzean, Elizabeth Houghton-Blanchet
Hunton, Richard E(dwin) 1924- 21-22R
Huntress, Keith G(ibson) 1913- 7-8R
Huntsberger, John (Paul) 1931- 5-6R
Huntsberry, William E(mery) 1916- CANR-2
Earlier sketch in CA 3R
See also SATA 5
Hunzicker, Beatrice Plumb 1886- 7-8R
Hupka, Robert 1919- 61-64
Huppe, Bernard F. 1911- CANR-3
Earlier sketch in CA 5-6R
Huppert, George 1934- 29-32R
Hurd, Charles (Wesley Bolick)
1903-1968 .... CAP-1
Earlier sketch in CA 11-12
Hurd, Clement (G.) 1908-1988 .... CANR-24
Obituary 124
Earlier sketches in CA 29-32R, CANR-9
See also SATA 2
Hurd, Douglas (Richard) 1930- CANR-10
Earlier sketch in CA 25-28R
Hurd, Edith (Thacher) 1910- CANR-24
Earlier sketches in CA 13-14R, CANR-9
See also SATA 2
Hurd, Florence 1918- CANR-19
Earlier sketch in CA 103
Hurd, John C(oolidge), Jr. 1928- 17-18R
Hurd, Michael John 1928- CANR-12
Earlier sketch in CA 65-68
Hurd, (John) Thacher 1949- CANR-24
Earlier sketch in CA 106
See also SATA 45, 46
Hure, Anne 1918- 11-12R
Hureau, Jean (Emile Pierre) 1915-
Brief entry 110
Hurewitz, J(acob) C(oleman) 1914- CANR-2
Earlier sketch in CA 1R
hurkey, rooan
See Holzapfel, Rudolf Patrick
Hurlbut, Allen F. 1910-1983 Obituary 110
Hurlbut, Cornelius S(earle), Jr. 1906- .. CANR-11
Earlier sketch in CA 25-28R
Hurlbutt, Robert H(arris), III 1924- 15-16R
Hurley, Alfred F(rancis) 1928- 97-100
Hurley, Doran 1900-1964 .... 5-6R
Hurley, F(orrest) Jack 1940- 45-48
Hurley, Jane (Hezel) 1928- 15-16R
Hurley, John 1928- CANR-13
Earlier sketch in CA 33-36R
Hurley, John J(erome) 1930- 104
Hurley, Kathy 1947- 109
Hurley, Leslie J(ohn) 1911- 49-52
Hurley, Mark J(oseph, Jr.) 1919- 53-56
Hurley, Neil 1925- 29-32R
Hurley, Vic 1898-1978 .... 3R
Obituary 103
Hurley, W(illiam) Maurice 1916- 37-40R
Hurley, Wilfred G(eoffrey) 1895-1973 .... CAP-2
Obituary 45-48
Earlier sketch in CA 17-18
Hurley, William James, Jr. 1924- 9-10R
Hurlimann, Bettina
See Huerlimann, Bettina
See also SATA 34, 39
Hurlimann, Ruth
See Huerlimann, Ruth
See also SATA 31, 32
Hurlock, Elizabeth B. 1898- 41-44R
Hurlow, (Wilma) Janet 1939- 118
Hurm, Ken 1934- 106
Hurne, Ralph 1932- 21-22R
Hurok, Sol(omon) 1888-1974 Obituary 49-52
Hursch, Carolyn J(udge) 41-44R
Hurst, A(lexander) A(nthony) 1917- 5-6R
Hurst, Charles G., Jr. 1928- 37-40R
Hurst, Fannie 1889-1968 .... CAP-1
Obituary 25-28R
Earlier sketch in CA 15-16
Hurst, G(eorge) Cameron III 1941- 85-88
Hurst, James M(arshall) 1924- 29-32R
Hurst, M(ichael) E(liot) Eliot
See Eliot Hurst, M(ichael) E(liot)
Hurst, Michael (Charles) 1931- 23-24R
Hurst, Norman 1944- 53-56
Hurst, Richard Maurice 1938- 101
Hurst, Virginia Radcliffe 1914(?)-1976
Obituary 69-72
Hurstfield, Joel 1911-1980 .... CANR-6
Obituary 102
Earlier sketch in CA 53-56
Hurston, Zora Neale 1903-1960 85-88
See also DLB 51
See also CLC 7, 30
Hurt, Freda M(ary) E(lizabeth) 1911- 103
Hurt, Henry 1942- 106
Hurt, James (Riggins) 1934- CANR-23
Earlier sketch in CA 45-48
Hurtgen, Andre O(scar) 1932- 81-84
Hurvitz, Leon Nahum 1923- 106
Hurwitz, Abraham B. 1905- 29-32R
Hurwitz, Edith F(arber) 1941- 108
Hurwitz, Howard L(awrence) 1916- 37-40R
Hurwitz, Johanna 1937- CANR-10
Earlier sketch in CA 65-68
See also SATA 20
Hurwitz, Ken 1948- 33-36R
Hurwitz, Samuel J(ustin) 1912-1972 ..... CAP-2
Earlier sketch in CA 25-28
Hurwitz, Stephan 1901-1981 Obituary 103
Hurwood, Bernhardt J. 1926-1987 ...... 25-28R
Obituary 121
See also SATA 12, 50
Husar, John 1937- 81-84
Husband, William Hollow 1899(?)-1978
Obituary 81-84
Huse, Dennis P(aul) 1944- 115
Huseman, Richard C. 1939- Brief entry 109
Husen, Torsten 1916- CANR-9
Earlier sketch in CA 23-24R
Huser, (La)Verne (Carl) 1931- CANR-22
Earlier sketch in CA 106
Huson, Paul (Anthony) 1942- CANR-12
Earlier sketch in CA 29-32R
Huss, Roy 1927- 25-28R
Hussein, Taha 1889-1973 Obituary 45-48

Husserl, Edmund (Gustav Albrecht)
1859-1938 Brief entry 116
Hussey, David Edward 1934- CANR-9
Earlier sketch in CA 57-60
Hussey, John A(dam) 1913- 61-64
Hussey, Maurice Percival 1925- 9-10R
Hussman, Lawrence Eugene, Jr. 1932- 115
Huste, Annemarie 1943- 57-60
Husted, Darrell 1931- 81-84
Huston, Anne Marshall 116
Huston, Fran
See Miller, R. S.
Huston, James Alvin 1918- CANR-15
Earlier sketch in CA 41-44R
Huston, John (Marcellus) 1906-1987 73-76
Obituary 123
See also DLB 26
See also CLC 20
Huston, Luther A. 1888- CAP-2
Earlier sketch in CA 21-22
Huston, Mervyn James 1912- CANR-8
Earlier sketch in CA 61-64
Hustvedt, Lloyd (Merlyn) 1922- 21-22R
Huszar, George B(ernard) de 1919-19(?) . CAP-2
Earlier sketch in CA 19-20
Hutchcroft, Vera 1923- 102
Hutchens, Eleanor Newman 1919- 15-16R
Hutchens, John Kennedy 1905- 65-68
Hutchens, Paul 1902-1977 61-64
See also SATA 31
Hutcheson, Richard G(ordon), Jr. 1921- 107
Hutchin, Kenneth Charles 1908- 110
Hutchings, Alan Eric 1910- 4R
Hutchings, Arthur (James Bramwell)
1906- CANR-6
Earlier sketch in CA 7-8R
Hutchings, Bill
See Hutchings, William Bruce
Hutchings, Margaret (Joscelyne) 1918- .. CANR-3
Earlier sketch in CA 9-10R
Hutchings, Monica Mary 1917- 11-12R
Hutchings, Patrick A(elfred) 1929- CANR-4
Earlier sketch in CA 53-56
Hutchings, Raymond 1924- CANR-12
Earlier sketch in CA 33-36R
Hutchings, William Bruce 1948- 111
Hutchins, Carleen Maley 1911- 17-18R
See also SATA 9
Hutchins, Charles R. 1928- 123
Hutchins, Francis Gilman 1939- 21-22R
Hutchins, Hazel J. 1952- 123
Hutchins, Maude (Phelps McVeigh) 61-64
Hutchins, Myldred Flanigan 1910- 112
Hutchins, Pat 1942- CANR-15
Earlier sketch in CA 81-84
See also SATA 15
Hutchins, Robert Maynard 1899-1977 69-72
Hutchins, Ross Elliott 1906- CANR-5
Earlier sketch in CA 9-10R
See also SATA 4
Hutchinson, Arthur Stuart Menteth
1879-1971 Obituary 29-32R
Hutchinson, C(ecil) Alan 1914- 29-32R
Hutchinson, David (Christopher) 1960- 119
Hutchinson, Eliot Dole 1900- 61-64
Hutchinson, G(eorge) Evelyn 1903- CANR-14
Earlier sketches in CA 13-14, CAP-1
Hutchinson, George 1920-1980
Obituary 97-100
Hutchinson, H(ugh) Lester 1904- 17-18R
Hutchinson, John 1921- 45-48
Hutchinson, Joseph (Burtt) 1902-1988 109
Obituary 124
Hutchinson, Margaret Massey 1904- CAP-1
Earlier sketch in CA 15-16
Hutchinson, Mary Jane 1924- 106
Hutchinson, Michael E. 1925- 17-18R
Hutchinson, (William Patrick Henry) Pearse
1927- 103
Hutchinson, Peter 1943- CANR-8
Earlier sketch in CA 61-64
Hutchinson, Ray Coryton 1907-1975 .... CANR-3
Obituary 61-64
Earlier sketch in CA 4R
Hutchinson, Richard Wyatt 1894-1970 .....7-8R
Obituary 89-92
Hutchinson, Robert 1924- 15-16R
Hutchinson, Thomas 1711-1780 .... DLB-30, 31
Hutchinson, Vernal 1922- 49-52
Hutchinson, Veronica S(omerville)
1895-1961 Obituary 111
Hutchinson, Warner Alton, Jr. 1929- 110
Hutchinson, William K(enneth) 1945- 102
Hutchinson, William M(iller) 1916- 112
Hutchison, (William) Bruce 1901- 103
Hutchison, Chester Smith 1902- CAP-2
Earlier sketch in CA 17-18
Hutchison, (Dorothy) Dwight
1890(?)-1975 Obituary 57-60
Hutchison, E(arl) R. 1926- CANR-10
Earlier sketch in CA 25-28R
Hutchison, Emery 1919(?)-1985 Obituary ... 116
Hutchison, Harold Frederick 1900- CANR-4
Earlier sketch in CA 2R
Hutchison, Jane Campbell 1932- 37-40R
Hutchison, John Alexander 1912- 69-72
Hutchison, Sidney C(harles) 1912- 25-28R
Hutchison, William Robert 1930- 21-22R
Huth, Angela 1938- CANR-20
Earlier sketch in CA 85-88
Huth, Marta 1898- Brief entry 106
Huth, Mary Jo(sephine) 1929- 103
Huth, Tom 1941- 97-100
Huthmacher, J. Joseph 1929- 21-22R
See also SATA 5
Hutmacher (MacLean), Barbara Anne
1926- 112
Hutman, Norma Louise 1935- 25-28R
Hutschnecker, Arnold A. 1898- 81-84
Hutson, Anthony Brian Austen 1934- 93-96
Hutson, James H(oward) 1937- 85-88
Hutson, Jan 1932- 106
Hutson, Joan 1929- 89-92
Hutt, Maurice George 1928- 15-16R
Hutt, Max L. 1908- 57-60
Hutt, W(illiam) H(arold) 1899- 57-60
Huttenback, Robert A. 1928- 25-28R
Huttig, Jack W(ilfred) 1919- 53-56
Huttner, Matthew 1915-1975 Obituary 104
Hutto, Nelson (Allen) 1904- CAP-1
Earlier sketch in CA 9-10
See also SATA 20
Hutton, Ann 1929- 108
Hutton, Clarke 1898- 107
Hutton, Geoffrey 1928- 41-44R
Hutton, Ginger
See Hutton, Virginia Carol
Hutton, Harold 1912- 102
Hutton, J(oseph) Bernard 1911-? CANR-14
Earlier sketch in CA 21-22R
Hutton, J(ohn) H(enry) 1885-1968 ...... CAP-1
Earlier sketch in CA 13-14
Hutton, James 1902- 77-80
Hutton, John (Harwood) 1928- 107
Hutton, Malcolm 1921- CANR-24
Earlier sketch in CA 107
Hutton, Richard 1949- 109
Hutton, Richard Holt 1826-1897 .... DLB-57
Hutton, Virginia Carol 1940- 77-80
Hutton, Warwick 1939- CANR-9
Earlier sketch in CA 61-64
See also SATA 20
Huus, Helen 1913- CANR-1
Earlier sketch in CA 3R
Huvos, Kornel 1913- 49-52
Huws, Daniel 1932- 81-84
Huxhold, Harry N(orman) 1922- 61-64
Huxley, Aldous Leonard 1894-1963 85-88
See also DLB 36
See also CLC 1, 3, 4, 5, 8, 11, 18, 35
Huxley, Anthony J(ulian) 1920- CANR-22
Earlier sketches in CA 9-10R, CANR-7
Huxley, Elspeth Josceline 1907- 77-80
Huxley, George 1932- 23-24R
Huxley, Herbert H(enry) 1916- 7-8R
Huxley, Judith 1927(?)-1983 Obituary 111
Huxley, Julian (Sorell) 1887-1975 ...... CANR-7
Obituary 57-60
Earlier sketch in CA 11-12R
Huxley, Laura Archera 15-16R
Huxley, T. H. 1825-1895 .... DLB-57
Huxley-Blythe, Peter J(ames) 1925- 17-18R
Huxtable, Ada Louise (Landman) 1921- 120
Huxtable, (William) John (Fairchild)
1912- 13-14R
Huyck, Dorothy Boyle 1925(?)-1979
Obituary 89-92
Huyck, Margaret Hellie 1939- 49-52
Huyck, Peter H(azelwood) 1940- 107
Huyck, Willard 1945(?)- Brief entry 111
Huygen, Wil(librord Joseph) 1922- CANR-15
Earlier sketch in CA 81-84
Huyghe, Rene (Louis) 1906- CANR-20
Earlier sketch in CA 81-84
Huyler, Jean Wiley 1935- CANR-13
Earlier sketch in CA 69-72
Huynh, Quang Nhuong 1946- 107
Huysmans, Charles Marie Georges
1848-1907 Brief entry 104
Huysmans, Joris-Karl
See Huysmans, Charles Marie Georges
See also TCLC 7
Huzar, Eleanor G(oltz) 1922- 85-88
Hy, Ronald John 1942- 115
Hyam, Ronald 1936- 97-100
Hyams, Barry 1911- 15-16R
Hyams, Edward (Solomon) 1910-1975 ... CANR-8
Obituary 61-64
Earlier sketch in CA 5-6R
Hyams, Joe
See Hyams, Joseph
Hyams, Joseph 1923- CANR-22
Earlier sketches in CA 17-18R, CANR-7
Hyatt, Carole S. 1935- 93-96
Hyatt, I. Ralph 1927- 115
Hyatt, J(ames) Philip 1909- 9-10R
Hyatt, Richard Herschel 1944- 101
Hybels, Saundra 1938- 57-60
Hyde, Anthony 1946(?)- CLC-42
Hyde, Charles K(eith) 1945- 116
Hyde, Dayton O(gden) 25-28R
See also SATA 9
Hyde, Douglas (Arnold) 1911- Brief entry ... 109
Hyde, Elisabeth 1953- 122
Hyde, Fillmore 1896(?)-1970 Obituary 104
Hyde, George E. 1882- 7-8R
Hyde, Harford M(ontgomery) 1907- 5-6R
Hyde, Hawk
See Hyde, Dayton O(gden)
Hyde, Janet Shibley 1948- CANR-10
Earlier sketch in CA 65-68
Hyde, L(ouis) K(epler, Jr.) 1901- CAP-1
Earlier sketch in CA 13-14
Hyde, Laurence 1914- 17-18R
Hyde, Margaret Oldroyd 1917- CANR-1
Earlier sketch in CA 1R
See also SATA 1, 42
See also CLC 21
Hyde, Mary Morley Crapo 1912- 49-52
Hyde, Shelley
See Reed, Kit
Hyde, Simeon, Jr. 1919- 21-22R
Hyde, Stuart W(allace) 1923- 61-64
Hyde, Tracy Elliot
See Venning, Corey
Hyde, W. Lewis 1945- 104
Hyde, Wayne Frederick 1922- 4R
See also SATA 7
Hyden, (Sten Gustav Vilhelm) Goeran
1938- CANR-20
Earlier sketch in CA 103
Hyder, Clyde Kenneth 1902- 33-36R
Hyder, O(liver) Quentin 1930- Brief entry ... 105
Hyer, James Edgar 1923- 77-80
Hyer, Paul Van 1926- 104
Hyers, M. Conrad 1933- 33-36R
Hyett, Barbara Helfgott 1945- 120
Hygen, Johan B(ernitz) 1911- 23-24R
Hyink, Bernard L(ynn) 1913- 45-48
Hyland, Douglas K(irk) S(amuel) 1949- 124
Hyland, Drew A(lan) 1939- CANR-15
Earlier sketch in CA 89-92
Hyland, Jean Scammon 1926- 49-52
Hyland, Paul 1947- 121
Hyland, (Henry) Stanley 1914- 9-10R
Hylander, Clarence J(ohn) 1897-1964 ......7-8R
See also SATA 7
Hylton, Delmer P(aul) 1920- 17-18R
Hyma, Albert 1893- 19-20R
Hyman, Alan 1910- 102
Hyman, Ann 1936- 53-56
Hyman, David N(eil) 1943- CANR-22
Earlier sketches in CA 57-60, CANR-7
Hyman, Dick 1904- CANR-7
Earlier sketch in CA 19-20R
Hyman, Frieda Clark 1913- 5-6R
Hyman, Harold M(elvin) 1924- 5-6R
Hyman, Helen Kandel 1920- 105
Hyman, Herbert H(iram) 1918-1985 .....23-24R
Obituary 118
Hyman, Irwin A(braham Meltzer) 1935- 93-96
Hyman, Jackie Diamond 1949- 108
Hyman, Lawrence W. 1919- 41-44R
Hyman, Paula 1946- 89-92
Hyman, Richard J(oseph) 1921- CANR-1
Earlier sketch in CA 45-48
Hyman, Robin P(hilip) 1931- CANR-15
Earlier sketch in CA 41-44R
See also SATA 12
Hyman, Ronald T. 1933- CANR-9
Earlier sketch in CA 23-24R
Hyman, Sidney 1917- 102
Hyman, Stanley Edgar 1919-1970 85-88
Obituary 25-28R
Hyman, Trina Schart 1939- CANR-2
Earlier sketch in CA 49-52
See also SATA 7, 46
See also DLB 61
Hymans, Jacques Louis 1937- 57-60
Hymes, Dell H(athaway) 1927- 15-16R
Hymes, Lucia M(anley) 1907- 5-6R
See also SATA 7
Hymoff, Edward 1924- 17-18R
Hynd, Alan 1904(?)-1974 Obituary 45-48
Hyndman, Donald W(illiam) 1936- 57-60
Hyndman, Jane Andrews Lee
1912-1978 .... CANR-5
Obituary 89-92
Earlier sketch in CA 7-8R
See also SATA 1, 23, 46
Hyndman, Robert Utley 1906-1973 97-100
See also SATA 18
Hynds, Frances Jane 1929- 77-80
Hyne, C(harles) J(ohn) Cutcliffe (Wright)
1865-1944 Brief entry 111
Hynek, J(osef) Allen 1910-1986 81-84
Obituary 119
Hyneman, Charles S(hang) 1900-1985 ... CAP-1
Obituary 114
Earlier sketch in CA 13-14
Hynes, Samuel (Lynn) 1924- 105
Hyslop, Beatrice F. 1900(?)-1973
Obituary 45-48
Hyslop, James H(ervey) 1854-1920
Brief entry 123
Hyslop, Lois Boe 1908- 41-44R
Hysom, John L(eland, Jr.) 1934- 115
Hytier, Jean (Pierre) 1899-1983 Obituary ... 109

I

Iacone, Salvatore J(oseph) 1945- CANR-15
Earlier sketch in CA 85-88
Iacuzzi, Alfred 1896-1977 Obituary 73-76
Ian, Janis 1951- Brief entry 105
See also CLC 21
Iannelli, Richard 1949- 118
Ianni, Francis A(nthony) J(ames) 1926- ...45-48
Ianniello, Lynne Young 1925- 19-20R
Iannone, Jeanne
See Balzano, Jeanne (Koppel)
See also SATA 7
Iannone, Ron(ald Vincent) 1940- 53-56
Iannuzzi, John Nicholas 1935- 93-96
Iatrides, John O(restes) 1932- CANR-10
Earlier sketch in CA 25-28R
Ibanez, Carlos G. Velez
See Velez-Ibanez, Carlos G(uillermo)
Ibanez, Vicente Blasco
See Blasco Ibanez, Vicente
Ibarguengoitia, Jorge 1928-1983 124
Obituary 113
See also CLC 37
Ibarra, Crisostomo
See Yabes, Leopoldo Y(abes)
Ibbotson, Eva 1925- CANR-15
Earlier sketch in CA 81-84
See also SATA 13
Ibbotson, M. C(hristine) 1930- 25-28R
See also SATA 5
Ibele, Oscar Herman 1917- Brief entry 106
Ibingira, G(race) S(tuart) K(atebarirwe)
1932- 103
Ibrahim, Abdel-Sattar 1939- 69-72
Ibrahim, Ibrahim Abdelkader 1923- 15-16R
Ibsen, Henrik (Johan) 1828-1906
Brief entry 104
See also TCLC 2, 8, 16
Ibuka, Masaru 1908- 102
Ibuse, Masuji 1898- CLC-22
Icaza Coronel, Jorge 1906-1978 89-92
Obituary 85-88
Ice, Jackson Lee 1925- 25-28R
Icenhower, Joseph Bryan 1913- CANR-5
Earlier sketch in CA 7-8R
Ichikawa, Kon 1915- 121
See also CLC 20
Ichikawa, Satomi 1949- Brief entry 116
See also SATA 36, 47
Icks, Robert J(oseph) 1900- 41-44R
Icolari, Daniel Leonardo 1942- 17-18R
Iddon, Don 1913(?)-1979 Obituary 89-92
Ide, Richard S(myth) 1943- 120
Idelsohn, Abraham Zevi 1882-1938
Brief entry 109
Iden, William
See Green, William M(ark)
Idle, Eric 1943- 116
See also CLC 21
Idone, Christopher 1937- 122
Idriess, Ion L. 1891(?)-1979 Obituary 89-92
Iduarte (Foucher), Andres 1907- 33-36R
Idyll, C(larence) P(urvis) 1916- CANR-8
Earlier sketch in CA 11-12R
Ierardi, Francis B. 1886-1970 Obituary 104
Ifft, James B(rown) 1935- 53-56
Ifkovic, Edward 1943- CANR-8
Earlier sketch in CA 61-64
Iggers, Georg G(erson) 1926- 25-28R
Iggers, Wilma Abeles 1921- 25-28R
Iggulden, John Manners 1917- 11-12R
Iglauer, Edith
See Daly, Edith Iglauer
Iglehart, Alfreda P(aulette) 1950- 109
Iglehart, Louis Tillman 1915-1981
Obituary 104
Iglesias, Mario 1924- 45-48
Iglitzin, Lynne 1931- 41-44R
Ignatieff, George 1913- 119
Ignatow, David 1914- 9-10R
See also CAAS 3
See also DLB 5
See also CLC 4, 7, 14, 40
Ignotus, Paul 1901-1978 .... CANR-8
Obituary 77-80
Earlier sketch in CA 7-8R
Igo, John N., Jr. 1927- 15-16R
Igoe, James (Thomas) 1935- 108
Igoe, (Lesly) Lynn Moody 1937- 108
Ihde, Don 1934- CANR-13
Earlier sketch in CA 33-36R
Ihimaera, Witi 1944- 77-80
See also CLC 46
Ihnat, Steve 1935(?)-1972 Obituary 33-36R
Iiams, Thomas M. Jr. 1928- 11-12R
Iino, (David) Norimoto 1918- 61-64
Ike, Nobutaka 1916- 21-22R
Ikeda, Daisaku 1928- 85-88
Ikeda, Kiyoshi 1928- Brief entry 104
Ikejiani, Okechukwu 1917- 17-18R
Ikenberry, Oliver Samuel 1908- 53-56
Ikerman, Ruth C. (Percival) 1910- 15-16R
Ikle, Fred Charles 1924- 45-48
Iko, Momoko 1940- CANR-14
Earlier sketch in CA 77-80
Ilardi, Vincent 1925- 29-32R
Ilardo, Joseph A(nthony) 1944- 89-92
Ilchman, Warren Frederick 1934- CANR-1
Earlier sketch in CA 2R
Iles, Bert
See Ross, Zola Helen
Iles, Francis
See Cox, A(nthony) B(erkeley)
Ilf, Ilya
See Fainzilberg, Ilya Arnoldovich
See also TCLC 21
Ilg, Frances L(illian) 1902-1981 107
Obituary 104
Ilgen, Thomas
See Ilgen, Thomas L.
Ilgen, Thomas L. 1946- 120
Ilich, John 1933- 106
Ilie, Paul 1932- CANR-10
Earlier sketch in CA 25-28R
Illan, Jose M(anuel) 1924- 45-48
Illes, Robert E(noch) 1914- 103
Illiano, Antonio 1934- 41-44R
Illich, Ivan D. 1926- CANR-10
Earlier sketch in CA 53-56
See also AITN 2
Illick, Joseph E. 1934- 17-18R
Illingworth, Frank (M. B.) 1908- CANR-5
Earlier sketch in CA 7-8R
Illingworth, John 1904(?)-1980
Obituary 97-100
Illingworth, Neil 1934- 15-16R
Illingworth, Ronald Stanley 1909- CANR-3
Earlier sketch in CA 9-10R
Illwitzer, Elinor G. 1934- 29-32R
Illyes, Gyula 1902-1983 114
Obituary 109
Ilowite, Sheldon A. 1931- 106
See also SATA 27
Ilsey, Dent
See Chapman, John Stanton Higham

Ilsley, Dent
See Chapman, John Stanton Higham
Ilsley, Velma (Elizabeth) 1918- ... CANR-3
Earlier sketch in CA 11-12R
See also SATA 12
Ilson, Robert (Frederick) 1937- ... 124
Iltinger, Paula 1944- ... 124
Ilyin, Mikhail Andreyevich 1878-1942
Brief entry ... 119
Imamura, Shigeo 1922- ... 77-80
Imber, Gerald 1941- ... 89-92
Imbrie, John 1925- Brief entry ... 107
Imbrie, Katherine P(almer) 1952- ... 104
Imbs, Bravig (Wilbur Eugene) 1904-1946
Brief entry ... 107
See also DLB 4
Imerti, Arthur D. 1915- ... 37-40R
Imfeld, Al 1935- ... CANR-13
Earlier sketch in CA 69-72
Imhoof, Maurice Lee 1930- Brief entry ... 108
Immaculata, Sister
See Maxwell, Sister Mary
Immel, Mary Blair 1930- ... CANR-6
Earlier sketch in CA 15-16R
See also SATA 28
Immerman, Leon Andrew 1952- ... 103
Immerwahr, Sara Anderson 1914-
Brief entry ... 108
Immoos, Thomas 1918- ... CANR-15
Earlier sketch in CA 85-88
Immroth, John Phillip 1936-1976 ... CAP-2
Earlier sketch in CA 33-36
Imperato, Pascal James 1937- Brief entry ... 106
Impey, Oliver (Richard) 1936- ... 108
Imrie, Richard
See Pressburger, Emeric
Inada, Lawson Fusao 1938- ... 33-36R
Inalcik, Halil 1916- ... 49-52
Inayat-Khan, Pir Vilayat 1916- ... 93-96
Inbau, Fred E. 1909- ... CANR-1
Earlier sketch in CA 2R
Inber, Vera Mikhailovna 1893-1972
Obituary ... 37-40R
Ince, Basil A(ndre) 1933- ... 57-60
Ince, Martin (Jeffrey) 1952- ... 110
Inch, Morris Alton 1925- ... CANR-11
Earlier sketch in CA 29-32R
Inchbald, Elizabeth 1753-1821 ... DLB-39
Inciardi, James A(nthony) 1939- ... CANR-8
Earlier sketch in CA 61-64
Inclan, Ramon (Maria) del Valle
See Valle-Inclan, Ramon (Maria) del
Incogniteau, Jean-Louis
See Kerouac, Jean-Louis Lebrid de
Ind, Allison 1903-1974 ... CAP-1
Earlier sketch in CA 15-16
Indelman, Elchanan Chonon 1908(?)-1983
Obituary ... 109
Indelman-Yinnon, Moshe 1895(?)-1977
Obituary ... 73-76
Inderlied, Mary Elizabeth 1945- ... 49-52
Indik, Bernard P(aul) 1932- ... 33-36R
Inez, Colette 1931- ... 37-40R
Infield, Glenn (Berton) 1920-1981 ... CANR-5
Obituary ... 103
Earlier sketch in CA 7-8R
Ing, Dean 1931- ... CANR-23
Earlier sketch in CA 106
Ingalls, Daniel H(enry) H(olmes) 1916- ... 17-18R
Ingalls, David Sinton 1899-1985 Obituary ... 116
Ingalls, Jeremy 1911- ... 4R
Ingalls, Rachel 1941(?)- Brief entry ... 123
See also CLC 42
Ingalls, Robert Paul 1941- ... 110
Brief entry ... 107
Ingard, K(arl) Uno 1921- ... 33-36R
Ingarden, Roman Witold 1893-1970
Obituary ... 113
Ingate, Mary 1912- ... 73-76
Ingbar, Mary Lee 1926- ... 41-44R
Inge, M(ilton) Thomas 1936- ... CANR-9
Earlier sketch in CA 17-18R
Inge, W. R.
See Inge, William Ralph
Inge, William Motter 1913-1973 ... 9-10R
See also DLB 7
See also CDALB 1941-1968
See also CLC 1, 8, 19
Inge, William Ralph 1860-1954
Brief entry ... 116
Ingelfinger, Franz Joseph 1910-1980
Obituary ... 97-100
Ingelow, Jean 1820-1897 ... SATA-33
See also DLB 35
Ingermann, Helena Antonia Maria Elisabeth
Dermout
See Dermout-Ingermann, Helena Antonia
Maria Elisabeth
Ingersol, Jared
See Paine, Lauran (Bosworth)
Ingersoll, David E(dward) 1939- ... 41-44R
Ingersoll, John H. 1925- ... 73-76
Ingersoll, Ralph (McAllister) 1900-1985 ... CAP-1
Obituary ... 115
Earlier sketch in CA 13-14
Ingersoll, Robert Franklin 1933- ... 104
Ingham, Colonel Frederic
See Hale, Edward Everett
Ingham, Daniel
See Lambot, Isobel
Ingham, Jennie 1944- ... 108
Ingham, Kenneth 1921- ... 110
Brief entry ... 108
Ingham, (Ann) Mary 1947- ... 120
Ingham, Richard Arnison 1935- ... 104
Ingham, Robert E(dward) 1934- ... 108
Ingilby, Joan Alicia 1911- ... 9-10R
Ingle, Clifford 1915- ... 29-32R
Ingle, Dwight Joyce 1907- ... CAP-1
Earlier sketch in CA 9-10
Ingleby, Terry 1901- ... 106
Ingles, G(lenn) Lloyd 1901- ... CAP-1
Earlier sketch in CA 19-20
Inglis, Brian (St. John) 1916- ... CANR-23
Earlier sketches in CA 19-20R, CANR-7
Inglis, David Rittenhouse 1905- ... CANR-5
Earlier sketch in CA 7-8R
Inglis, James 1927- ... 21-22R
Inglis, John K(enneth) 1933- ... 106
Inglis, R(obert) M(orton) G(all)
1910-1975 ... CANR-8
Earlier sketch in CA 13-14R
Inglis, Ruth Langdon 1927- ... CANR-1
Earlier sketch in CA 49-52
Inglis, Stuart J(ohn) 1923- ... 41-44R
Ingold, Gerard (Antoine Hubert) 1922- ... CANR-23
Earlier sketch in CA 106
Ingold, Klara (Schmid) 1913- ... 61-64
Ingraham, Barton L(ee) 1930- ... 119
Ingraham, Joseph Holt 1809-1860 ... DLB-3
Ingraham, Leonard W(illiam) 1913- ... 25-28R
See also SATA 4
Ingraham, Mark H(oyt) 1896-1982 ... 61-64
Obituary ... 109
Ingraham, Vernon L. 1924- ... 33-36R
Ingram, Anne (Whitten) Bower 1937- ... 102
Ingram, (Mildred Rebecca) Bowen
(Prewett) ... 37-40R
Ingram, Collingwood 1880-1981 ... 61-64
Obituary ... 103
Ingram, Derek (Thynne) 1925- ... 9-10R
Ingram, Forrest L(eo) 1938- ... 53-56
Ingram, Gregory Keith 1944- ... 77-80
Ingram, Helen Moyer 1937- ... CANR-22
Earlier sketch in CA 105
Ingram, James C(arlton) 1922- ... 5-6R
Ingram, (Archibald) Kenneth 1882-1965 ... CAP-1
Earlier sketch in CA 13-14
Ingram, Thomas Henry 1924- ... CANR-2
Earlier sketch in CA 49-52
Ingram, Tom
See Ingram, Thomas Henry
Ingram, William 1930- ... 41-44R
Ingram, Willis J.
See Harris, Mark
Ingrams, Doreen 1906- ... CANR-12
Earlier sketch in CA 33-36R
See also SATA 20
Ingrams, Richard (Reid) 1937- ... 103
Ingrao, Charles W(illiam) 1948- ... 101
Ingstad, Helge Marcus 1899- ... 65-68
Ingwersen, Faith 1934- ... CANR-15
Earlier sketch in CA 69-72
Ingwersen, Niels 1935- ... CANR-15
Earlier sketch in CA 69-72
Inkeles, Alex 1920- ... CANR-1
Earlier sketch in CA 3R
Inkiow, (Janakiev) Dimiter 1932- ... 101
Inkster, Ian 1949- ... 113
Inlow, Gail M(aurice) 1910- ... CANR-4
Earlier sketch in CA 5-6R
Inman, Arthur Crew 1895-1963 ... 122
Inman, Billie (Jo) Andrew 1929- ... CANR-12
Earlier sketch in CA 29-32R
Inman, Jack (Ingles) 1919- ... 25-28R
Inman, Robert (Anthony) 1931- ... 17-18R
Inman, Will 1923- ... CANR-12
Earlier sketch in CA 25-28R
Inmerito
See Javitch, Daniel Gilbert
Inmon, W(illiam) H(arvey) 1945- ... 110
Innaurato, Albert (F.) 1948(?)- ... 122
Brief entry ... 115
See also CLC 21
Innerhofer, Franz 1944- ... 101
Innes, Brian 1928- ... CANR-14
Earlier sketch in CA 23-24R
Innes, C(atherine) L(ynette) 1940- ... 123
Innes, Christopher David 1941- ... 107
Innes, Frank C. 1934- ... 45-48
Innes, Hammond
See Hammond Innes, Ralph
Innes, Jean
See Saunders, Jean
Innes, Michael
See Stewart, J(ohn) I(nnes) M(ackintosh)
Innes, Ralph Hammond
See Hammond Innes, Ralph
Innes, Rosemary E(lizabeth Jackson) ... 25-28R
Innes, Stephen 1946- ... 116
Innis, Donald Quayle 1924- ... 41-44R
Innis, Pauline B. (Coleman) 1918- ... CANR-4
Earlier sketch in CA 4R
Inoue, Yukitoshi 1945- ... 25-28R
Inouye, Daniel K(en) 1924- ... 25-28R
Insall, Donald W(illiam) 1926- ... 61-64
Insana, Tino 1948- ... 123
Insel, Deborah (June) 1949- ... 110
Insight, James
See Coleman, Robert William Alfred
Insingel, Mark 1935- Brief entry ... 110
Insolia, Anthony Edward 1926- ... 120
Intriligator, Michael D(avid) 1938- ... 53-56
Inwood, M(ichael) J(ames) 1944- ... 117
Inyart, Gene
See Namovicz, Gene Inyart
See also SATA 6
Ionesco, Eugene 1912- ... 9-10R
See also SATA 7
See also CLC 1, 4, 6, 9, 11, 15, 41
Ionescu, Ghita G. 1913- ... 103
Iongh, Mary (Dows Herter Norton) Crena de
See Crena de Iongh, Mary (Dows Herter
Norton)
Iorio, James 1921- ... 61-64
Iorio, John 1925- ... 49-52
Iorizzo, Luciano J(ohn) 1930- ... 73-76
Ipcar, Dahlov (Zorach) 1917- ... CANR-9
Earlier sketch in CA 19-20R
See also SATA 1, 49
Ippolito, Donna 1945- ... 104
Ipsen, D(avid) C(arl) 1921- ... 33-36R
Iqbal, Afzal 1919- ... CANR-10
Earlier sketch in CA 61-64
Iqbal, Sabiha 1950- ... 111
Iranek-Osmecki, Kazimierz 1897-1984 ... 49-52
Obituary ... 113
Irby, Kenneth (Lee) 1936- ... CANR-22
Earlier sketch in CA 69-72
Ireland, David 1927- ... 25-28R
Ireland, Earl (Crowell) 1928- ... 7-8R
Ireland, Joe C. 1936- ... 73-76
Ireland, Kevin (Mark) 1933- ... 73-76
Ireland, Norma Olin 1907- ... CANR-3
Earlier sketch in CA 9-10R
Ireland, Patrick
See O'Doherty, Brian
Ireland, Robert M(ichael) 1937- ... 45-48
Iremonger, Lucille (d'Oyen) ... CANR-6
Earlier sketch in CA 9-10R
Iremonger, Valentin 1918- ... 101
Ireson, Barbara (Francis) 1927- ... CANR-21
Earlier sketch in CA 5-6R
Ireton, Rollo
See Shirley, Ralph
Irfani, Suroosh 1947- ... 118
Irgang, Jacob 1930- ... 85-88
Iribarne, Louis 1940- ... 123
Irion, Mary Jean 1922- ... 23-24R
Irion, Paul E(rnst) 1922- ... 23-24R
Irion, Ruth (Hershey) 1921- ... 65-68
Irish, Donald P(aul) 1919- ... 49-52
Irish, Marian D(oris) 1909- ... 9-10R
Irish, Richard K. 1932- ... 65-68
Irish, William
See Hopley-Woolrich, Cornell George
Iriye, Akira 1934- ... CANR-11
Earlier sketch in CA 25-28R
Irland, David
See Green, Julien (Hartridge)
Iron, Ralph
See Schreiner, Olive (Emilie Albertina)
Ironmaster, Maximus
See Wilkinson, John (Donald)
Ironside, Henry Allan 1876-1951
Brief entry ... 115
Ironside, Virginia 1944- ... 120
Irsfeld, John H(enry) 1937- ... 65-68
Irvin, Bob
See Irvin, Robert W.
Irvin, Fred 1914- ... SATA-15
Irvin, Rea 1881-1972 Obituary ... 93-96
Irvin, Robert W. 1933-1980 Obituary ... 103
Irvine, Betty Jo 1943- ... 77-80
Irvine, Demar (Buel) 1908- ... 33-36R
Irvine, John Henry 1951- ... 119
Irvine, Keith 1924- ... 29-32R
Irvine, Lucy 1956- ... 118
Irvine, R(obert) R(alstone) 1936- ... CANR-15
Earlier sketch in CA 81-84
Irvine, Sidney H(erbert) 1931- Brief entry ... 106
Irvine, William 1906-1964 Obituary ... 106
Irving, Alexander
See Hume, Ruth Fox
Irving, Blanche M(cDaniel) 1904- ... 114
Irving, Brian William 1932- ... 53-56
Irving, Clifford Michael 1930- ... CANR-2
Earlier sketch in CA 2R
See also AITN 1
Irving, Clive 1933- ... CANR-22
Earlier sketch in CA 85-88
Irving, David (John Cawdell) 1938- ... 13-14R
Irving, Edward B(urroughs), Jr. 1923-
Brief entry ... 112
Irving, Gordon 1918- ... 25-28R
Irving, Henry
See Kanter, Hal
Irving, John (Winslow) 1942- ... 25-28R
See also DLB 6
See also DLBY 82
See also CLC 13, 23, 38
Irving, R(obert) L(ock) Graham
1877-1969 ... CAP-1
Earlier sketch in CA 15-16
Irving, Robert
See Adler, Irving
Irving, T(homas) B(allantine) 1914- ... 37-40R
Irving, Washington 1783-1859 ... YABC-2
See also DLB 3, 11, 30, 59
See also CDALB 1640-1865
Irwin, Ann(abelle Bowen) 1915- ... CANR-19
Earlier sketch in CA 101
See also SATA 38, 44
Irwin, Constance Frick 1913- ... CANR-5
Earlier sketch in CA 4R
See also SATA 6
Irwin, Cynthia C.
See Irwin-Williams, Cynthia (Cora)
Irwin, David 1933- ... 53-56
Irwin, Francis William 1905- Brief entry ... 105
Irwin, G. H.
See Palmer, Raymond A.
Irwin, George 1910-1971 ... 41-44R
Irwin, Grace (Lilian) 1907- ... 17-18R
Irwin, Graham W(ilkie) 1920- ... 121
Brief entry ... 118
Irwin, Hadley
See Hadley, Lee
and Irwin, Ann(abelle Bowen)
Irwin, Inez Haynes 1873-1970 ... 102
Irwin, James W. 1891(?)-1977 Obituary ... 73-76
Irwin, John T(homas) 1940- ... 53-56
Irwin, John V(aleur) 1915- ... CANR-1
Earlier sketch in CA 45-48
Irwin, Keith Gordon 1885-1964 ... 7-8R
See also SATA 11
Irwin, Margaret 1889-1967 Obituary ... 93-96
Irwin, P. K.
See Page, P(atricia) K(athleen)
Irwin, (Joseph) Paul 1940- ... 107
Irwin, Raymond 1902- ... CAP-1
Earlier sketch in CA 9-10
Irwin, Robert (Graham) 1946- ... 121
Irwin, Ruth Beckey 1906- ... 29-32R
Irwin, Theodore 1907- ... 65-68
Irwin, Vera Rushforth 1913- ... 33-36R
Irwin, W(illiam) R(obert) 1915- ... 65-68
Irwin, Will(iam Henry) 1873-1948
Brief entry ... 117
See also DLB 25
Irwin-Williams, Cynthia (Cora) 1936- ... CANR-1
Earlier sketch in CA 45-48
Isaac, Erich 1928- ... 45-48
Isaac, Glynn Llewelyn 1937-1985
Obituary ... 117
Isaac, Joanne 1934- ... 25-28R
See also SATA 21
Isaac, Joseph Ezra 1922- ... 115
Isaac, Paul E(dward) 1926- ... 19-20R
Isaac, Rael Jean (Isaacs) 1933- ... 17-18R
Isaac, Rhys L(lywelyn) 1937- ... 113
Isaac, Stephen 1925- ... 33-36R
Isaacs, Alan 1925- ... CANR-3
Earlier sketch in CA 11-12R
Isaacs, Bernard 1924- ... 107
Isaacs, E. Elizabeth 1917- ... 7-8R
Isaacs, Edith Somborn 1884-1978
Obituary ... 77-80
Isaacs, Harold Robert 1910-1986 ... CANR-2
Obituary ... 119
Earlier sketch in CA 3R
Isaacs, Jacob
See Kranzler, George G(ershon)
Isaacs, Neil D. 1931- ... CANR-9
Earlier sketch in CA 7-8R
Isaacs, Norman Ellis 1908- ... 81-84
Isaacs, Stan 1929- ... 15-16R
Isaacs, Stephen D(avid) 1937- ... 81-84
Isaacs, Susan (Sutherland Fairhurst)
1885-1948 Brief entry ... 120
Isaacs, Susan 1943- ... CANR-20
Earlier sketch in CA 89-92
See also CLC 32
Isaacson, Joel 1930- Brief entry ... 114
Isaacson, Robert L. 1928- ... CANR-7
Earlier sketch in CA 17-18R
Isaacson, Walter (Seff) 1952- ... 112
Isaak, Robert A(llen) 1945- ... CANR-13
Earlier sketch in CA 61-64
Isadora, Rachel Brief entry ... 111
See also SATA 32
See also CLR 7
Isais, Juan M. 1926- ... 29-32R
Isakovsky, Mikhail Vasilyevich 1900-1973
Obituary ... 41-44R
Isaksson, Ulla (Margareta Lundberg)
1916- Brief entry ... 109
Isard, Walter 1919- ... 114
Brief entry ... 112
Isban, Samuel 1905- ... CANR-2
Earlier sketch in CA 49-52
Isbister, Clair
See Isbister, Jean Sinclair
Isbister, Jean Sinclair 1915- ... CANR-18
Earlier sketches in CA 3R, CANR-1
Ise, John 1885-196(?) ... CAP-1
Earlier sketch in CA 13-14
Isely, Flora Kunigunde Duncan
See Duncan, Kunigunde
Isely, Helen Sue (Pearson) 1917-1978 ... 7-8R
Obituary ... 120
Iseminger, Gary 1937- ... 37-40R
Isenberg, Irwin M. 1931-1979 ... CANR-11
Earlier sketch in CA 19-20R
Isenberg, Seymour 1930- ... 33-36R
Isenhour, Thomas Lee 1939- ... 57-60
Iser, Wolfgang 1926- ... 57-60
Ishak, Fayek (Matta) 1922- ... 41-44R
Ishak, Yusof bin 1910(?)-1970 Obituary ... 104
Isham, Charlotte H(ickock) 1912- ... 73-76
See also SATA 21
Isham, Linda (Rose) 1938- Brief entry ... 107
Ishee, John A. 1934- ... CANR-18
Earlier sketch in CA 25-28R
Isherwood, Christopher (William Bradshaw)
1904-1986 ... 13-14R
Obituary ... 117
See also DLB 15
See also DLBY 86
See also CLC 1, 9, 11, 14, 44
Ishida, Takeshi 1923- ... CANR-16
Earlier sketch in CA 97-100
Ishigo, Estelle 1899- ... 61-64
Ishiguro, Kazuo 1954- ... 120
See also CLC 27
Ishikawa Takuboku 1886(?)-1912
Brief entry ... 113
See also TCLC 15
Ishino, Iwao 1921- ... 19-20R
Ish-Kishor, Judith 1892-1972 ... 3R
Obituary ... 103
See also SATA 11
Ish-Kishor, Sulamith 1896-1977 ... 73-76
Obituary ... 69-72
See also SATA 17
Ishlon, Deborah 1925- ... 4R
Ishmael, Woodi 1914- ... SATA-31
Ishmole, Jack 1924- ... 49-52

Ishwaran, K(arigoudar) 1922- 49-52
Isichei, Elizabeth 1939- CANR-5
Earlier sketch in CA 53-56
Isis
See Torbett, Harvey Douglas Louis
Iskander, Fazil 1929- 102
See also CLC 47
Islam, A(bul) K(hair) M(uhammed) Aminul
1933- 41-44R
Islam, Kazi Nazrul 1899(?)-1976
Obituary 69-72
Isle, Walter (Whitfield) 1933- 25-28R
Isler, Betty
See Isler, Elizabeth
Isler, Elizabeth 1915- 114
Ismach, Arnold H(arvey) 1930- 85-88
Ismail, A. H. 1923- 25-28R
Isogai, Hiroshi 1940- 102
Ispahani, Mirza Abol Hassan 1902-1981
Obituary 108
Israel, Abby 1942- 107
Israel, Charles E(dward) 1920- 3R
Israel, Elaine 1945- CANR-9
Earlier sketch in CA 53-56
See also SATA 12
Israel, Fred L. 1934- CANR-12
Earlier sketch in CA 19-20R
Israel, Gerard 1928- 81-84
Israel, Jerry (Michael) 1941- 29-32R
Israel, John (Warren) 1935- 21-22R
Israel, Jonathan I. 1946- 109
Israel, Marion Louise 1882-1973 .... 3R
Obituary 103
See also SATA 26
Israel, Martin 1927- 109
Israel, Saul 1910- CAP-1
Earlier sketch in CA 15-16
Israeloff, Roberta 1952- 118
Israelowitz, Oscar 1949- 113
Issachar
See Stanford, J(ohn) K(eith)
Issawi, Charles Philip 1916- CANR-20
Earlier sketches in CA 7-8R, CANR-4
Isser, Natalie 1927- 53-56
Issler, Anne Roller 1892- 49-52
Iswolsky, Helene 1896-1975 .... 7-8R
Obituary 61-64
Italiaander, Rolf (Bruno Maximilian)
1913- CANR-23
Earlier sketches in CA 7-8R, CANR-6
Iterson, S(iny) R(ose) Van
See Van Iterson, S(iny) R(ose)
Itse, Elizabeth M(yers) 1930- CANR-1
Earlier sketch in CA 49-52
Itzin, Catherine 1944- CANR-14
Earlier sketch in CA 77-80
Itzkoff, Seymour W(illiam) 1928- 33-36R
Ivan, Martha Miller Pfaff 1909- CAP-2
Earlier sketch in CA 19-20
Ivancevich, John M(ichael) 1939- 29-32R
Ivanov, Miroslav 1929- 81-84
Ivanov, Vsevolod Vyacheslavovich
1895-1963 Obituary 93-96
Ivanov, Vyacheslav Ivanovich 1866-1949
Brief entry 122
Ivask, George 1910-1986 Obituary 118
Ivask, Ivar Vidrik 1927- CANR-24
Earlier sketch in CA 37-40R
See also CLC 14
Ivens, Michael 1924- 7-8R
Ivens, Virginia R(uth) 1922- 105
Ivers, Larry E(dward) 1936- 77-80
Iversen, Gudmund R(agnvaldsson)
1934- CANR-4
Earlier sketch in CA 53-56
Iversen, Nick 1951- 73-76
Iverson, Genie 1942- CANR-9
Earlier sketch in CA 65-68
Iverson, Jeffrey (James) 1934- 105
Iverson, Lucille K(arin) 1925- 61-64
Iverson, Peter James 1944- 106
Ives, Burl (Icle Ivanhoe) 1909- 103
Ives, Charles Edward 1874-1954
Brief entry 113
Ives, Colta Feller 1943- 118
Ives, Edward D(awson) 1925- 25-28R
Ives, Lawrence
See Woods, Frederick
Ives, Morgan
See Bradley, Marion Zimmer
Ives, Sandy
See Ives, Edward D(awson)
Ives, Sumner 1911- 11-12R
Ivey, Allen E(ugene) 1933- CANR-2
Earlier sketch in CA 49-52
Ivey, Donald 1918- 89-92
Ivey, James Burnett 1925- 119
Ivey, Jim
See Ivey, James Burnett
Ivie, Robert L(ynn) 1945- 115
Ivie, Robert M. 1930- 9-10R
Ivnev, Riurik
See Kovalev, Mikhail A(leksandrovich)
Ivory, James (Francis) 1928- Brief entry 109
Ivry, Alfred Lyon 1935- CANR-1
Earlier sketch in CA 45-48
Ivy, Ralph 1938- 120
Iwamatsu, Jun Atsushi 1908- 73-76
See also SATA 14
Iwaszkiewicz, Jaroslaw 1894-1980
Obituary 97-100
Iwata, Masakazu 1917- 17-18R
Iyengar, B(ellur) K(rishnamachar)
S(undararaja) 1918- 97-100
Iyengar, K(odaganallur) R(amaswami)
Srinivasa 1908- CANR-8
Earlier sketch in CA 7-8R
Iyengar, S. Kesava 1894- 19-20R
Iyer, Raghavan (Narasimhan) 1930- CANR-22
Earlier sketches in CA 57-60, CANR-6
Izant, Grace Goulder 1893- CAP-1
Earlier sketch in CA 9-10
Izard, Barbara 1926- 29-32R
Izard, Carroll E(llis) 1923- CANR-4
Earlier sketch in CA 49-52
Izban, Samuel
See Isban, Samuel
Izenberg, Gerald N(athan) 1939- 105
Izenour, George Charles 1912- 93-96
Izzo, Herbert J(ohn) 1928- 41-44R

J

"J"
See Garrity, Joan Terry
J. L.-M.
See Lees-Milne, James
Jaanus, Maire 1940- 120
Jabay, Earl 1925- 21-22R
Jabber, Fuad 1943- 49-52
Jabber, Paul 1943- 113
Jabez
See Nicol, Eric (Patrick)
Jablon, Howard 1939- 116
Jablonski, Edward 1922- CANR-18
Earlier sketches in CA 2R, CANR-2
Jablonski, Ronald E. 1929- Brief entry 104
Jablow, Martha M(oraghan) 1944- 112
Jabs, Carolyn 1950- 110
Jac, Lee
See Morton, Lee Jack, Jr.
Jaccottet, Philippe 1925- Brief entry 116
Jack, Daniel Thomson 1901-1984
Obituary 115
Jack, Donald Lamont 1924- CANR-3
Earlier sketch in CA 2R
Jack, Homer A(lexander) 1916- CANR-14
Earlier sketch in CA 41-44R
Jack, Ian 1923- 57-60
Jack, R. D. S.
See Jack, Ronald D(yce) S(adler)
Jack, R(obert) Ian 1935- CANR-3
Earlier sketch in CA 49-52
Jack, Ronald D(yce) S(adler) 1941- 120
Jackendoff, Ray S. 1945- CANR-6
Earlier sketch in CA 53-56
Jacker, Corinne L(itvin) 1933- 19-20R
Jackins, Harvey 1916- CANR-17
Earlier sketches in CA 49-52, CANR-1
Jacklin, Anthony 1944- 85-88
Jacklin, Tony
See Jacklin, Anthony
Jackman, E(dwin) R(ussell) 1894-19(?) .. CAP-1
Earlier sketch in CA 15-16
Jackman, Jarrell C(lark) 1943- 120
Jackman, Leslie (Arthur James) 1919- ... 29-32R
Jackman, Michael R. 1952- 120
Jackman, Robert W(illiam) 1946- 124
Jackman, Stuart 1922- CANR-18
Earlier sketch in CA 101
Jackman, Sydney W(ayne) 1925- CANR-19
Earlier sketches in CA 3R, CANR-1
Jackowska, Nicki 1942- 119
Jacks, L(awrence) P(earsall) 1860-1955
Brief entry 113
Jacks, Oliver
See Gandley, Kenneth Royce
Jackson, A(lexander) B(rooks) 1925- 104
Jackson, Alan 1938- 101
Jackson, Albert 1943- 93-96
Jackson, Albina
See Geis, Richard E(rwin)
Jackson, Allan 1905(?)-1976 Obituary 65-68
Jackson, Angela 1951- DLB-41
Jackson, Anna J. 1926- 103
Jackson, Anne 1896(?)-1984 .... SATA-37
Jackson, Anne
See Jackson, Anna J.
Jackson, Anthony 1926- CANR-11
Earlier sketch in CA 69-72
Jackson, Archibald Stewart 1922- 61-64
Jackson, Arlene M(arjorie) 1938- 118
Jackson, Arthur 1921- Brief entry 104
Jackson, B(erkley) R. 1937- 25-28R
Jackson, Barbara (Ward) 1914-1981 .... CANR-6
Obituary 103
Earlier sketch in CA 45-48
Jackson, Barbara Garvey Seagrave
1929- 21-22R
Jackson, Basil 1920- CANR-8
Earlier sketch in CA 57-60
Jackson, Blyden 1910- 57-60
Jackson, Brian 1933(?)-1983 Obituary 110
Jackson, Brooks 1941- 97-100
Jackson, Bruce 1936- 89-92
Jackson, C(hester) O(scar) 1901- CAP-1
Earlier sketch in CA 15-16
Jackson, C(aary) Paul 1902- CANR-6
Earlier sketch in CA 7-8R
See also SATA 6
Jackson, Caary
See Jackson, C(aary) Paul
Jackson, Carlton (Luther) 1933- 21-22R
Jackson, Carole 104
Jackson, Charles (Reginald) 1903-1968 101
Obituary 25-28R
Jackson, Charles O. 1935- Brief entry 112
Jackson, Christine E(lisabeth) 1936- 121
Jackson, Clarence J.-L.
See Bulliet, Richard W(illiams)
Jackson, Dave
See Jackson, J. David
Jackson, David Cooper 1931- 109
Jackson, Derrick 1939- 77-80
Jackson, Diane 1938- 115
Jackson, Don(ald) D(e Avila) 1920-1968 .. CAP-1
Earlier sketch in CA 11-12
Jackson, Donald (Dean) 1919-1987 ...... 19-20R
Obituary 124
Jackson, Donald Dale 1935- CANR-19
Earlier sketches in CA 49-52, CANR-1
Jackson, Dorothy Virginia Steinhauer
1924- 13-14R
Jackson, Douglas N. 1929- 37-40R
Jackson, E. F.
See Tubb, E(dwin) C(harles)
Jackson, Edgar (Newman) 1910- CANR-13
Earlier sketch in CA 77-80
Jackson, Ellen B. 1943- 110
Jackson, Elmore 1910- 112
Jackson, Esther Merle 1922- 15-16R
Jackson, Everatt
See Muggeson, Margaret Elizabeth
Jackson, Frank 1951- 120
Jackson, Franklin Jefferson
See Watkins, Mel
Jackson, Gabriel 1921- 21-22R
Jackson, Gabriele Bernhard 1934- 29-32R
Jackson, Geoffrey (Holt Seymour)
1915-1987 61-64
Obituary 123
Jackson, George (Lester) 1941-1971 120
Obituary 111
Jackson, George D. 1929- 81-84
Jackson, George S(tuyvesant) 1906-1976 . CAP-1
Obituary 61-64
Earlier sketch in CA 17-18
Jackson, Gordon 1934- 104
Jackson, Graham 1949- 112
Jackson, Guida M. 1930- CANR-16
Earlier sketch in CA 93-96
Jackson, Harvey H(ardaway III) 1943- 119
Jackson, Helen Hunt 1830-1885 .... DLB-42, 47
Jackson, Henry Martin 1912-1983
Obituary 110
Jackson, Herbert C(ross) 1917- 9-10R
Jackson, Herbert G., Jr. 1928- 37-40R
Jackson, J. David 1944- CANR-18
Earlier sketch in CA 81-84
Jackson, J. P.
See Atkins, (Arthur) Harold
Jackson, Jacqueline 1928- 45-48
Jackson, Jacquelyne Johnson 1932- 37-40R
Jackson, James Charles 1936-1979
Obituary 117
Jackson, James P(ierre) 1925- CANR-14
Earlier sketch in CA 77-80
Jackson, Jesse 1908-1983 .... 25-28R
Obituary 109
See also SATA 2, 29, 48
See also CLC 12
Jackson, John Archer 1929- 13-14R
Jackson, John E(dgar) 1942- 101
Jackson, John Howard 1932- 41-44R
Jackson, John N(icholas) 1925- CANR-14
Earlier sketch in CA 37-40R
Jackson, Jon A(nthony) 1938- 81-84
Jackson, Jonathan (Charles) 1966- 116
Jackson, Joseph 1924-1987 .... CANR-11
Obituary 122
Earlier sketches in CA 9-10, CAP-1
Jackson, Joseph Hollister 1912- 120
Jackson, Joy J(uanita) 1928- 29-32R
Jackson, Julia A(ndreasen) 1939- 119
Jackson, Karl (Dion) 1942- 102
Jackson, Katherine Gauss 1904-1975
Obituary 57-60
Jackson, (William) Keith 1928- CANR-8
Earlier sketch in CA 61-64
Jackson, Kenneth T. 1939- 21-22R
Jackson, Kevin Goldstein
See Goldstein-Jackson, Kevin
Jackson, Laura (Riding) 1901- 65-68
See also DLB 48
See also CLC 7
Jackson, Louise A(llen) 1937- 93-96
Jackson, Lowell G(eorge) 1934- 118
Jackson, Lucille
See Strauss, (Mary) Lucille Jackson
Jackson, Lydia 1900(?)-1983 Obituary 110
Jackson, Mae 1946- 81-84
Jackson, Mahalia 1901-1972 Obituary ... 33-36R
Jackson, Margaret Weymouth 1895-1974
Obituary 115
See also AITN 1
Jackson, Mark
See Kurz, Ron
Jackson, Martin A(lan) 1941- 89-92
Jackson, Mary 1924- 61-64
Jackson, Melvin H. 1914(?)-1983
Obituary 111
Jackson, Miles M(errill) 1929- 41-44R
Jackson, Neta J. 1944- CANR-18
Earlier sketch in CA 89-92
Jackson, Neville
See Glaskin, G(erald) M(arcus)
Jackson, Nora
See Tennant, Nora Jackson
Jackson, Norman 1932- CANR-17
Earlier sketch in CA 25-28R
Jackson, O. B.
See Jackson, C(aary) Paul
Jackson, Paul R. 1905- CAP-1
Earlier sketch in CA 15-16
Jackson, Percival Ephrates 1891-1970 .. CANR-3
Earlier sketch in CA 2R
Jackson, Philip W(esley) 1928- 23-24R
Jackson, R. E.
See Innes, Rosemary E(lizabeth Jackson)
Jackson, R(ichard) Eugene 1941- 109
Jackson, R(ichard) W(illiam) 1939- 119
Jackson, Reggie
See Jackson, Reginald Martinez
Jackson, Reginald Martinez 1946-
Brief entry 112
Jackson, Richard 1946- 110
Jackson, Robert 1911- 9-10R
Jackson, Robert B(lake) 1926- CANR-6
Earlier sketch in CA 7-8R
See also SATA 8
Jackson, Robert J. 1936- 25-28R
Jackson, Robert L(owell) 1935- 73-76
Jackson, Robert Louis 1923- 109
Jackson, Robert S(umner) 1926- 29-32R
Jackson, Ruth A. 45-48
Jackson, Sally
See Kellogg, Jean (Defrees)
Jackson, Sam
See Trumbo, Dalton
Jackson, Sara
See Thomas, Sara (Sally)
Jackson, Scoop
See Jackson, Henry Martin
Jackson, Shirley 1919-1965 .... CANR-4
Obituary 25-28R
Earlier sketch in CA 1R
See also SATA 2
See also DLB 6
See also CDALB 1941-1968
See also CLC 11
Jackson, Stanley W(ebber) 1920- 124
Jackson, Stephanie
See Werner, Vivian
Jackson, Teague 1938- 93-96
Jackson, W(illiam) A(rthur) Douglas
1923- 45-48
Jackson, W(illiam) G(odfrey) F(othergill)
1917- 25-28R
Jackson, W(illiam) T(homas) H(obdell)
1915-1983 .... CANR-1
Obituary 117
Earlier sketch in CA 3R
Jackson, W(illiam) Turrentine 1915- 13-14R
Jackson, Wallace 1930- 114
Jackson, Wes 1936- CANR-22
Earlier sketches in CA 49-52, CANR-3
Jackson, William Vernon 1926- CANR-13
Earlier sketch in CA 23-24R
Jackson, Wilma 1929- CANR-12
Earlier sketch in CA 73-76
Jackson-Haight, Mabel V. 1912- 25-28R
Jaco, E(gbert) Gartly 1923- CANR-1
Earlier sketch in CA 1R
Jacob, Alaric 1909- 7-8R
Jacob, Charles E. 1931- CANR-5
Earlier sketch in CA 15-16R
Jacob, Ernest Fraser 1894-1971 .... CANR-3
Earlier sketch in CA 4R
Jacob, Francois 1920- 102
Jacob, Fred E. 1899- 105
Jacob, Gordon (Percival Septimus)
1895-1984 Obituary 113
Jacob, Helen Pierce 1927- 69-72
See also SATA 21
Jacob, Herbert 1933- 77-80
Jacob, Margaret C(andee) 1943- CANR-16
Earlier sketch in CA 65-68
Jacob, (Cyprien-)Max 1876-1944
Brief entry 104
See also TCLC 6
Jacob, Nancy L. 1943- 29-32R
Jacob, Naomi Ellington 1884(?)-1964
Obituary 115
Jacob, Paul 1940- 103
Jacob, Philip E(rnest) 1914- CANR-4
Earlier sketch in CA 53-56
Jacob, Piers A(nthony) D(illingham)
1934- 23-24R
Jacobi, Carl (Richard) 1908- CAP-1
Earlier sketch in CA 13-14
Jacobi, Jolande (Szekacs) 1890- 9-10R
Jacobi, Kathy SATA-42
Jacobowitz, Ellen 1948- 121
Jacobs, Al(bert T.) 1903-1985 Obituary 115
Jacobs, Arthur (David) 1922- CANR-21
Earlier sketches in CA 7-8R, CANR-4
Jacobs, Barry (Douglas) 1932- 101
Jacobs, Bradford (McElderry) 1920- 121
Jacobs, Clyde E(dward) 1925- 37-40R
Jacobs, Dan(iel) N(orman) 1924- CANR-4
Earlier sketch in CA 7-8R
Jacobs, David Michael 1942- 57-60
Jacobs, Diane 1948- 73-76
Jacobs, Donald M(artin) 1937- 110
Jacobs, Flora Gill 1918- CANR-21
Earlier sketch in CA 1R
See also SATA 5
Jacobs, Francine 1935- CANR-18
Earlier sketches in CA 49-52, CANR-1
See also SATA 42, 43
Jacobs, Frank 1929- CANR-6
Earlier sketch in CA 13-14R
See also SATA 30
Jacobs, G(enevieve) Walker 1948- 49-52
Jacobs, Garry (Lawrence) 1946- 120
Jacobs, Glenn 1940- 29-32R
Jacobs, Harold 1941- 45-48
Jacobs, Harvey (Collins) 1915- 21-22R
Jacobs, Harvey 1930- 29-32R
Jacobs, Hayes B(enjamin) 1919- 11-12R
Jacobs, Helen Hull 1908- 9-10R
See also SATA 12
Jacobs, Herbert (Austin) 1903-1987 ..... 15-16R
Obituary 122
Jacobs, Howard 1908- 65-68

Jacobs, James B. 1947- ... CANR-18
Earlier sketch in CA 101
Jacobs, Jane 1916- ... CANR-15
Earlier sketch in CA 21-22R
Jacobs, Jerome L. 1931- ... 89-92
Jacobs, Jerry 1932- ... CANR-11
Earlier sketch in CA 29-32R
Jacobs, Jill
See Bharti, Ma Satya
Jacobs, Jim 1942- ... 97-100
See also CLC 12
Jacobs, John (Kedzie) 1918- ... 23-24R
Jacobs, Joseph 1854-1916 Brief entry ... 111
See also SATA 25
Jacobs, Laurence Wile 1939- ... 53-56
Jacobs, Leah
See Gellis, Roberta L(eah Jacobs)
Jacobs, Leland Blair 1907- ... 73-76
See also SATA 20
Jacobs, Lewis 1906- ... 77-80
Jacobs, Linda C. 1943- ... 29-32R
See also SATA 21
Jacobs, Lou(is), Jr. 1921- ... CANR-9
Earlier sketch in CA 23-24R
See also SATA 2
Jacobs, Louis 1920- ... CANR-17
Earlier sketches in CA 3R, CANR-1
Jacobs, Melville 1902-1971 ... 4R
Obituary ... 103
Jacobs, Michael (Stephen) 1955- ... 123
Jacobs, Milton 1920- ... 37-40R
Jacobs, Norman (Gabriel) 1924- ... 77-80
Jacobs, Paul 1918-1978 ... 13-14R
Obituary ... 73-76
Jacobs, Pepita Jimenez 1932- ... 19-20R
Jacobs, Philip E. 1914(?)-1985 Obituary ... 116
Jacobs, Robert D(urene) 1918- ... 41-44R
Jacobs, Roderick A(rnold) 1934- ... 23-24R
Jacobs, Ruth Harriet 1924- ... CANR-15
Earlier sketch in CA 89-92
Jacobs, Sheldon 1931- ... 106
Jacobs, Sophia Yarnall 1902- ... 106
Jacobs, Sue-Ellen 1936- ... 111
Jacobs, Susan
See Quinn, Susan
See also SATA 30
Jacobs, T. C. H.
See Pendower, Jacques
Jacobs, Travis Beal 1936- Brief entry ... 113
Jacobs, Vernon K(enneth) 1936- ... 117
Jacobs, Vivian 1916(?)-1981 Obituary ... 103
Jacobs, W(illiam) W(ymark) 1863-1943
Brief entry ... 121
See also TCLC 22
Jacobs, Walter Darnell 1922- ... 19-20R
Jacobs, Wilbur R(ipley) 1918- ... 15-16R
Jacobs, William Jay 1933- ... CANR-7
Earlier sketch in CA 57-60
See also SATA 28
Jacobsen, Hans Jacob 1901-1987
Obituary ... 122
Jacobsen, Josephine 1908- ... CANR-23
Earlier sketch in CA 33-36R
Jacobsen, Lydik S. 1897(?)-1976
Obituary ... 69-72
Jacobsen, Lyle E. 1929- ... 15-16R
Jacobsen, Marion Leach 1908- ... 61-64
Jacobsen, O(le) Irving 1896- ... CAP-2
Earlier sketch in CA 25-28
Jacobsen, Phebe R(obinson) 1922- ... 73-76
Jacobsen, Thorkild 1904- Brief entry ... 105
Jacobsohn, Gary J. 1946- ... 89-92
Jacobson, Bernard Isaac 1936- ... 109
Jacobson, Beverly 1927- ... 113
Jacobson, Boyd 1942- ... 118
Jacobson, Cliff 1940- ... 85-88
Jacobson, Dan 1929- ... CANR-2
Earlier sketch in CA 2R
See also DLB 14
See also CLC 4, 14
Jacobson, Daniel 1923- ... 53-56
See also SATA 12
Jacobson, David B(ernard) 1928- ... 53-56
Jacobson, Edith 1897(?)-1978 Obituary ... 85-88
Jacobson, Edmund 1888- ... 11-12R
Jacobson, Ethel ... 37-40R
Jacobson, Frederick L(awrence) 1938- ... 49-52
Jacobson, Gary Charles 1944- ... 109
Jacobson, Gerald F. 1922-1987 Obituary ... 123
Jacobson, Harold Karan 1929- ... CANR-19
Earlier sketches in CA 11-12R, CANR-3
Jacobson, Helen S(altz) 1921- ... CANR-6
Earlier sketch in CA 57-60
Jacobson, Howard Boone 1925- ... 2R
Jacobson, Jon 1938- ... 61-64
Jacobson, Julius 1922- ... 45-48
Jacobson, Marcia 1941- ... 115
Jacobson, Michael F. 1943- ... CANR-13
Earlier sketch in CA 77-80
Jacobson, Morris K(arl) 1906- ... CANR-3
Earlier sketch in CA 45-48
See also SATA 21
Jacobson, Nils Olof 1937- Brief entry ... 110
Jacobson, Nolan Pliny 1909- ... CANR-23
Earlier sketches in CA 21-22R, CANR-8
Jacobson, Robert (Marshall) 1940-1987 ... 89-92
Obituary ... 122
Jacobson, Rodolfo 1915- ... 41-44R
Jacobson, Sheldon A(lbert) 1903- ... 37-40R
Jacobson, Sibyl C(hafer) 1942- ... 65-68
Jacobson, Stephen A. 1934- ... 97-100
Jacobson, Steve
See Jacobson, Stephen A.
Jacobstein, J(oseph) Myron 1920- ... 53-56
Jacobus, Donald L(ines) 1887-1970 ... CANR-4
Earlier sketch in CA 5-6R
Jacobus, Elaine Wegener 1908- ... 33-36R
Jacobus, Lee A. 1935- ... CANR-13
Earlier sketch in CA 33-36R
Jacobus, Mary 1944- ... 105
Jacoby, Henry 1905- ... 77-80
Jacoby, Joseph E. 1944- ... 97-100
Jacoby, Neil H(erman) 1909-1979 ... CANR-10
Obituary ... 89-92
Earlier sketch in CA 23-24R
Jacoby, Oswald 1902-1984 ... 107
Obituary ... 113
Jacoby, Russell 1945- ... CANR-15
Earlier sketch in CA 77-80
Jacoby, Stephen M(ichael) 1940- ... 57-60
Jacoby, Susan ... 108
Jacopetti, Alexandra
See Hart, Alexandra
See also SATA 14
Jacot, B. L.
See Jacot de Boinod, Bernard Louis
Jacot, Michael 1924- ... 104
Jacot de Boinod, Bernard Louis
1898-1977 ... 11-12R
Obituary ... 77-80
Jacoway, Elizabeth 1944- ... 110
Jacqueline
See Carpentier (y Valmont), Alejo
Jacqueney, Mona G(raubart) ... 41-44R
Jacqueney, Theodore 1943(?)-1979
Obituary ... 89-92
Jacques, David (Lawson) 1948- ... 123
Jacques, Robin 1920- ... SATA-30, 32
See also SAAS 5
Jacquet, Constant Herbert, Jr. 1925- ... 106
Jaded Observer
See Zolf, Larry
Jados, Stanley S. 1912-1977 ... 33-36R
Jaediker, Kermit 1912(?)-1986 Obituary ... 118
Jaeger, Cyril Karel Stuart 1912- ... 3R
Jaeger, Edmund C(arroll) 1887-1983 ... CAP-2
Obituary ... 110
Earlier sketch in CA 23-24
Jaeger, Harry J., Jr. 1919(?)-1979
Obituary ... 85-88
Jaeger, Lorenz Cardinal 1892-1975
Obituary ... 57-60
Jaeger, Walter H(enry) E(dward)
1902(?)-1982 Obituary ... 108
Jaen, Didier Tisdel 1933- ... 29-32R
Jaenen, Cornelius John 1927- ... CANR-15
Earlier sketch in CA 85-88
Jaffa, George
See Wallace-Clarke, George
Jaffa, Harry V(ictor) 1918- ... 33-36R
Jaffe, A(bram) J. 1912- ... 5-6R
Jaffe, Bernard 1896-1986 ... 5-6R
Obituary ... 121
Jaffe, Dan 1933- ... CANR-17
Earlier sketch in CA 25-28R
Jaffe, Dennis T(heodore) 1946- ... CANR-15
Earlier sketch in CA 89-92
Jaffe, Elsa
See Bartlett, Elsa Jaffe
Jaffe, Eugene D. 1937- ... 37-40R
Jaffe, Frederick S. 1925-1978 ... CANR-5
Earlier sketch in CA 9-10R
Jaffe, Gabriel Vivian 1923- ... 15-16R
Jaffe, Harold 1938- ... 29-32R
Jaffe, Hilde 1927- ... 105
Jaffe, Irma B(lumenthal) ... CANR-1
Earlier sketch in CA 45-48
Jaffe, Joseph 1924- Brief entry ... 113
Jaffe, Louis Leventhal 1905- ... 21-22R
Jaffe, (Andrew) Michael 1923- ... 23-24R
Jaffe, Nora Crow 1944- ... 106
Jaffe, Rona 1932- ... CANR-24
Earlier sketch in CA 73-76
See also AITN 1
Jaffe, Sam(uel Adason) 1929(?)-1985
Obituary ... 115
Jaffe, Sandra Sohn 1943- ... 101
Jaffe, Sherril 1945- ... CANR-19
Earlier sketch in CA 103
Jaffe, William 1898-1980 ... 57-60
Obituary ... 122
Jaffee, Al(lan) 1921- Brief entry ... 116
See also SATA 37
Jaffee, Dwight M. 1943- ... 57-60
Jaffin, David 1937- ... CANR-15
Earlier sketch in CA 65-68
Jagel, Beatrice Hawley 1944(?)-1985
Obituary ... 116
Jagendorf, Moritz (Adolf) 1888-1981 ... 5-6R
Obituary ... 102
See also SATA 2, 24
Jager, Okke 1928- ... CANR-23
Earlier sketches in CA 61-64, CANR-8
Jager, Ronald (Albert) 1932- ... 41-44R
Jaggard, Geoffrey (William) 1902-1970 ... CAP-2
Earlier sketch in CA 21-22
Jagger, John Hubert 1880- ... CAP-1
Earlier sketch in CA 9-10
Jagger, Mick 1944- ... CLC-17
Jagger, Peter (John) 1938- ... CANR-21
Earlier sketch in CA 103
Jagoda, Robert 1923- ... 73-76
Jahan, Rounaq 1944- ... 49-52
Jaher, Frederic Cople 1934- ... 9-10R
Jahn, Ernst A(dalbert) 1929- ... 69-72
Jahn, Janheinz 1918-1973 Obituary ... 111
Jahn, Joseph C. 1914(?)-1984 Obituary ... 113
Jahn, Joseph Michael 1943- ... CANR-5
Earlier sketch in CA 49-52
See also SATA 28
Jahn, Melvin E(dward) 1938- ... 9-10R
Jahn, Michael
See Jahn, Joseph Michael
Jahn, Mike
See Jahn, Joseph Michael
Jahnn, Hans Henny 1894-1959 ... DLB-56
Jahoda, Gloria (Adelaide Love)
1926-1980 ... CANR-4
Obituary ... 104
Earlier sketch in CA 1R
See also AITN 1
Jahoda, Gustav 1920- Brief entry ... 114
Jahsmann, Allan Hart 1916- ... 106
See also SATA 28
Jain, Girilal 1922- ... 11-12R
Jain, Ravindra Kumar 1937- ... 29-32R
Jain, Sagar C. 1930- ... CANR-10
Earlier sketch in CA 25-28R
Jain, Sharad Chandra 1933- ... CANR-21
Earlier sketch in CA 25-28R
Jaini, Padmanabh S. 1923- ... 103
Jakes, John (William) 1932- ... CANR-10
Earlier sketch in CA 57-60
See also DLBY 83
See also CLC 29
Jakle, John Allais 1939- ... 107
Jakobovits, Immanuel 1921- ... 108
Jakobovits, Leon Alex 1938- ... 25-28R
Jakobson, Roman 1896-1982 ... 77-80
Obituary ... 107
Jaksch, Wenzel 1896-1966 ... CAP-1
Earlier sketch in CA 13-14
Jakubauskas, Edward B(enedict) 1930- ... 57-60
Jakubowski, Patricia (Ann) 1941- ... 65-68
James, Alan Geoffrey 1943- ... 104
James, Allen
See Allen, James L(ovic), Jr.
James, Amalia
See Neggers, Carla A(malia)
James, Andrew
See Kirkup, James
James, Anne Eleanor Scott
See Scott-James, Anne Eleanor
James, Anthony
See Hanna, David
James, (Eliot) Antony Brett
See Brett-James, (Eliot) Antony
James, Bernard (Joseph) 1922-
Brief entry ... 110
James, Bessie (Williams) Rowland
1895-1974 ... 107
James, Bill
See James, George W(illiam)
James, Brian
See Thomas, Gordon
and Tierney, John Lawrence
James, Bruno S(cott) 1906- ... 5-6R
James, (David) Burnett (Stephen)
1919-1987 ... 7-8R
Obituary ... 122
James, C. B.
See Coover, James B(urrell)
James, C(yril) L(ionel) R(obert) 1901-
Brief entry ... 117
See also CLC 33
James, C. W.
See Cumes, J(ames) W(illiam) C(rawford)
James, Cary A(mory) 1935- ... 29-32R
James, Charles J(oseph) 1944- ... CANR-5
Earlier sketch in CA 53-56
James, Charles L(yman) 1934- ... 29-32R
James, Clive 1939- Brief entry ... 105
James, Coy Hilton 1915- ... 103
James, Cy
See Watts, Peter Christopher
James, Cynthia
See Cresswell, Jasmine (Rosemary)
James, D(orris) Clayton 1931- ... 29-32R
James, D(avid) G(wilym) 1905-1968 ... CANR-4
Earlier sketch in CA 4R
James, David 1955- ... 119
James, David
See Hagberg, David J(ames)
James, Denise ... 29-32R
James, Diana
See Gunn, Diana Maureen
James, Don(ald H.) 1905- ... CANR-2
Earlier sketch in CA 4R
James, Dorothy Buckton 1937-
Brief entry ... 109
James, Dynely
See Mayne, William (James Carter)
James, Edgar C. 1933- ... CANR-5
Earlier sketch in CA 15-16R
James, Edward (Frank Willis) 1907-1984
Obituary ... 115
James, Edward
See Masur, Harold Q.
James, Edward T(opping) 1917- ... 33-36R
James, Edwin
See Gunn, James E(dwin)
James, Edwin Oliver 1889-1972 ... CAP-1
Earlier sketch in CA 15-16
James, Eleanor 1912- ... 41-44R
James, Elizabeth 1942- ... 121
See also SATA 39, 45
James, Eric Arthur 1925- ... CAP-1
Earlier sketch in CA 9-10
James, Estelle 1935- ... 37-40R
James, F(rank) Cyril 1903-1973 Obituary ... 114
James, Fleming, Jr. 1904- ... CAP-1
Earlier sketch in CA 17-18
James, Gene Gray 1934- ... 114
James, George W(illiam) 1949- ... 109
James, H(enry) Thomas 1915- ... 25-28R
James, Harry Clebourne 1896-1978 ... CANR-4
Earlier sketch in CA 7-8R
See also SATA 11
James, Heather 1914- ... 45-48
James, Henry 1843-1916 Brief entry ... 104
See also DLB 12
See also TCLC 2, 11, 24
James, Howard (Anthony, Jr.) 1935-
Brief entry ... 111
James, Hunter 1932- ... 114
James, Jean Rosemary Haughton
See Haughton-James, Jean Rosemary
James, (David) John ... 45-48
James, John 1633(?)-1729 ... DLB-24
James, Josef C. 1916(?)-1973 Obituary ... 45-48
James, Joseph B. 1912- ... 19-20R
James, Josephine
See Sterne, Emma Gelders
James, Judith
See Jennings, Leslie Nelson
James, Kristin
See Camp, Candace P(auline)
James, Leigh Franklin
See Little, Paul H(ugo)
James, Leonard F(rank) 1904- ... 49-52
James, Lloyd E.
See Laughlin, Tom
James, (William) Louis (Gabriel) ... CANR-6
Earlier sketch in CA 13-14R
James, M. R. 1940- ... 57-60
James, Marlise Ann 1945- ... 57-60
James, Matthew
See Lucey, James D(ennis)
James, Michael 1922(?)-1981 Obituary ... 104
James, Monica
See Nonhebel, Clare
James, Montague (Rhodes) 1862-1936
Brief entry ... 104
See also TCLC 6
James, Muriel ... 85-88
James, Naomi 1949- ... 102
James, Noel David Glaves 1911- ... 107
James, Norah C(ordner) ... 29-32R
James, P. D.
See White, Phyllis Dorothy James
See also CLC 18, 46
James, Paul
See Warburg, James Paul
James, Peter N. 1940- ... 57-60
James, Philip
See del Rey, Lester
and Moorcock, Michael (John)
James, Philip S(eaforth) 1914- ... CAP-1
Earlier sketch in CA 9-10
James, Preston E(verett) 1899- ... 45-48
James, Rebecca
See Elward, James (Joseph)
James, Robert A. 1946-1983 Obituary ... 109
James, Robert C(larke) 1918- ... 5-6R
James, Robert (Vidal) Rhodes
See Rhodes James, Robert (Vidal)
James, Robin (Irene) 1953- ... SATA-50
James, Ronald
See Preston, James
James, Simon
See Kunen, James Simon
James, Stanton
See Flemming, Nicholas Coit
James, Susan
See Griffin, Arthur J.
James, Sydney V(incent, Jr.) 1929- ... CANR-21
Earlier sketch in CA 4R
James, Thelma Gray 1899-1988 ... 7-8R
Obituary ... 124
James, Theodore E(arle) 1913- ... 57-60
James, Theodore, Jr. 1934- ... 33-36R
James, Thomas N.
See Neal, James T(homas)
James, Trevor
See Constable, Trevor James
James, (Arthur) Walter 1912- ... 7-8R
James, Walter S.
See Sheldon, Walter J.
James, Warren E(dward) 1922- ... 45-48
James, Weldon (Bernard) 1912- ... 1R
James, Will(iam Roderick) 1892-1942 ... SATA-19
James, William 1842-1910 Brief entry ... 109
See also TCLC 15
James, William
See Craddock, William J(ames)
James, William M.
See Harknett, Terry
James, William Milbourne 1881- ... CAP-1
Earlier sketch in CA 11-12
James, Wilma Roberts 1905- ... 105
Jameson, Eric
See Trimmer, Eric J.
Jameson, Fredric 1934- ... DLB-67
Jameson, J. Franklin 1859-1937 ... DLB-17
Jameson, Judith
See Neyland, James (Elwyn)
Jameson, Kenneth (Ambrose) 1913- ... 77-80
Jameson, Kenneth P(eter) 1942- ... 112
Jameson, Samuel H(aig) 1896- ... 45-48
Jameson, (Margaret) Storm 1891-1986 ... 81-84
Obituary ... 120
See also DLB 36
Jameson, Vic(tor Loyd) 1924- ... 19-20R
Jamieson, Bob
See Jamieson, Robert John
Jamieson, Paul F(letcher) 1903- ... CAP-1
Earlier sketch in CA 9-10
Jamieson, Robert John 1943- ... 116
Brief entry ... 110
Jamison, A(lbert) Leland 1911- ... 89-92
Jamison, Andrew 1948- ... 29-32R
Jamme, Albert (Joseph) 1916- ... 7-8R
Jampolsky, Gerald G(ershan) 1925- ... 111
Jan
See Noble, John (Appelbe)

Jan, Emerson
See Bixby, Jerome Lewis
Jan, George P(okung) 1925- ... 21-22R
Janas, Frankie-Lee 1908- ... CANR-24
Earlier sketch in CA 106
Jancar, Barbara Wolfe 1935- Brief entry ... 111
Jance, J. A.
See Jance, Judith A(nn)
Jance, Judith A(nn) 1944- ... 118
See also SATA 50
Janda, Kenneth (Frank) 1935- ... 15-16R
Jandl, Ernst 1925- ... CLC-34
Jandl, H(enry) Ward 1946- ... 121
Jandt, Fred E(dmund) 1944- ... 53-56
Jandy, Edward Clarence 1899-1980
Obituary ... 97-100
Jane, Mary Childs 1909- ... CANR-4
Earlier sketch in CA 1R
See also SATA 6
Jane, Nancy 1946- ... 89-92
Janeczko, Paul B(ryan) 1945- ... CANR-22
Earlier sketch in CA 104
Janes, Edward C. 1908- ... 93-96
See also SATA 25
Janes, J(oseph) Robert 1935- ... 123
See also SATA 50
Janes, Percy 1922- ... 113
Janes, Regina (Mary) 1946- ... 120
Janeshutz, Patricia M(arie) 1947- ... 121
Janeshutz, Trish
See Janeshutz, Patricia M(arie)
Janeway, Eliot 1913- Brief entry ... 112
Janeway, Elizabeth (Hall) 1913- ... CANR-2
Earlier sketch in CA 45-48
See also SATA 19
See also AITN 1
Janger, Allen R(obert) 1932- ... CANR-12
Earlier sketch in CA 29-32R
Janice
See Brustlein, Janice Tworkov
Janifer, Laurence M(ark) 1933- ... CANR-5
Earlier sketch in CA 9-10R
Janik, Allan (Stanley Peter) 1941- ... 53-56
Janik, Carolyn 1940- ... CANR-15
Earlier sketch in CA 89-92
Janik, Del Ivan 1945- ... 117
Janik, Phyllis 1944- ... 111
Janis, Irving L(ester) 1918- ... CANR-23
Earlier sketches in CA 19-20R, CANR-8
Janis, J(ack) Harold 1910- ... 15-16R
Jankelevitch, Vladimir 1903-1985
Obituary ... 117
Janko, Richard 1955- ... 111
Jankowsky, Kurt Robert 1928- ... 37-40R
Janner, Greville Ewan 1928- ... CANR-8
Earlier sketch in CA 13-14R
Janos, Andrew C(saba) 1934- ... 106
Janosch
See Eckert, Horst
Janov, Arthur 1924- ... 116
Janovy, John, Jr. 1937- ... CANR-19
Earlier sketch in CA 97-100
Janowitz, Morris 1919- ... 13-14R
Janowitz, Phyllis ... 93-96
Janowitz, Tama 1957- ... 106
See also CLC 43
Janowski, Tadeus M(arian) 1923- ... 53-56
Janowsky, Oscar Isaiah 1900- ... CANR-5
Earlier sketch in CA 7-8R
Janrup, (Ruth) Birgit 1931- ... 97-100
Jans, Zephyr
See Zekowski, Arlene
Jansen, Clifford J. 1935- ... 33-36R
Jansen, G(odfrey) H(enry) 1919- ... 114
Jansen, Godfrey
See Jansen, G(odfrey) H(enry)
Jansen, Jared
See Cebulash, Mel
Jansen, John Frederick 1918- ... 23-24R
Jansen, Robert B(ruce) 1922- ... 81-84
Janson, Anthony F(rederick) 1943- ... 121
Janson, Donald 1921- ... 5-6R
Janson, Dora Jane (Heineberg) 1916- ... 106
See also SATA 31
Janson, H(orst) W(oldemar) 1913-1982 . CANR-4
Obituary ... 107
Earlier sketch in CA 1R
See also SATA 9
Janson, Hank
See Hobson, Harry
and Norwood, Victor G(eorge) C(harles)
Janson-Smith, Celina 1909-1985 Obituary .. 118
Janssen, Al(fred Guthrie) 1949- ... 121
Janssen, Lawrence H(arm) 1921- ... 15-16R
Janssens, Paul Mary ... 53-56
Jansson, Tove Marika 1914- ... 17-18R
See also SATA 3, 41
See also CLR 2
Janta, Alexander 1908-1974 ... 101
Obituary ... 53-56
Jantsch, Erich 1929-1980 ... CANR-10
Earlier sketch in CA 65-68
Jantscher, Gerald R. 1939(?)-1987
Obituary ... 123
Jantzen, Hans 1881-1967 Obituary ... 111
Jantzen, Steven L(loyd) 1941- ... 77-80
Janus
See Clery, (Reginald) Val(entine)
Janus, Grete
See Hertz, Grete Janus
Janus, Sam Shep 1930- Brief entry ... 111
Januz, Lauren Robert 1939- ... 108
Janzen, John M(arvin) 1937- ... 81-84
Jaques, Elliott 1917- ... CANR-6
Earlier sketch in CA 13-14R
Jaques, Faith 1923- ... CANR-20
Earlier sketch in CA 103
See also SATA 21
Jaques, Florence Page 1890-1972 ... 103
Obituary ... 104
Jaques, Francis Lee 1887-1969 ... SATA-28
Jaquette, Jane Stallmann 1942-
Brief entry ... 105
Jaquin, Noel 1894(?)-1974 Obituary ... 112
Jaquith, Priscilla 1908- ... 121
Jaramillo, Samuel 1925- ... 41-44R
Jarchow, Merrill E(arl) 1910- ... CANR-14
Earlier sketch in CA 41-44R
Jardim, Anne 1936- ... 107
Jardim, Vasco S. 1900(?)-1983 Obituary ... 111
Jardine, Alice (Ann) 1951- ... 117
Jardine, Jack 1931- ... 23-24R
Jareed
See Faridi, Shah Nasiruddin Mohammad
Jares, Joe 1937- ... CANR-12
Earlier sketch in CA 33-36R
Jarmain, W. Edwin 1938- ... 13-14R
Jarman, Cosette C(otterell) 1909- ... CAP-2
Earlier sketch in CA 21-22
Jarman, Mark Anthony 1955- ... 118
Jarman, Rosemary Hawley 1935- ... CANR-2
Earlier sketch in CA 49-52
See also SATA 7
Jarman, Thomas Leckie 1907- ... CANR-4
Earlier sketch in CA 7-8R
Jarman, Walton Maxey 1904-1980
Obituary ... 108
Jarmuth, Sylvia L. 1912- ... 25-28R
Jarnow, Jeannette 1909- ... 53-56
Jaroch, F(rancis) A(nthony) Randy 1947- .. 89-92
Jaroch, Randy
See Jaroch, F(rancis) A(nthony) Randy
Jarolimek, John 1921- Brief entry ... 114
Jaron, Lou
See Spender, Lynne
Jarreau, Al(wyn Lopez) 1940- ... 117
Brief entry ... 116
Jarrell, John W. 1908(?)-1978 Obituary ... 81-84
Jarrell, Mary Von Schrader 1914- ... 77-80
See also SATA 35
Jarrell, Randall 1914-1965 ... CANR-6
Obituary ... 25-28R
Earlier sketch in CA 7-8R
See also CABS 2
See also SATA 7
See also DLB 48, 52
See also CDALB 1941-1968
See also CLC 1, 2, 6, 9, 13
See also CLR 6
Jarrett, (John) Derek 1928- ... 57-60
Jarrett, H(arold) Reginald 1916- ... CANR-3
Earlier sketch in CA 9-10R
Jarrett, James Louis 1917- ... 53-56
Jarrett, Marjorie 1923- ... 105
Jarrett, Roxanne
See Werner, Herma
Jarriel, Thomas Edwin 1934- ... 120
Brief entry ... 109
Jarriel, Tom
See Jarriel, Thomas Edwin
Jarrott, Mattie L. 1881(?)-1973
Obituary ... 41-44R
Jarry, Alfred 1873-1907 Brief entry ... 104
See also TCLC 2, 14
Jarvie, Clodagh Gibson
See Gibson-Jarvie, Clodagh
Jarvie, I(an) C(harles) 1937- ... 53-56
Jarvis, Ana C(ortesi) 1936- ... CANR-14
Earlier sketch in CA 65-68
Jarvis, Charles E(fthemios) 1921- ... 111
Jarvis, E. K.
See Bloch, Robert (Albert)
and Ellison, Harlan
and Fairman, Paul W.
and Silverberg, Robert
Jarvis, F(rank) Washington 1939- ... 37-40R
Jarvis, Fred(erick) G(ordon, Jr.) 1930- ... 33-36R
Jarvis, Howard (Arnold) 1902(?)-1986 ... 122
Obituary ... 120
Brief entry ... 111
Jarvis, Jennifer M(ary) 1935- ... 13-14R
Jarvis, Martin 1941- ... 105
Jarvis, Rupert Charles 1899- ... 103
Jarvis, Sharon 1943- ... 119
Jarvis, William Don(ald) 1913- ... CAP-1
Earlier sketch in CA 15-16
Jasen, David A(lan) 1937- ... 29-32R
Jasenas, Michael 1912- Brief entry ... 113
Jashemski, Wilhelmina Feemster 1910- ... CAP-1
Earlier sketch in CA 15-16
Jasmin, Claude 1930- ... 123
See also DLB 60
Jasner, W. K.
See Watson, Jane Werner
Jasny, Naum 1883- ... CAP-1
Earlier sketch in CA 9-10
Jason
See Munro, (Macfarlane) Hugh
and Stannus, (James) Gordon (Dawson)
Jason, Johnny
See Glut, Donald F(rank)
Jason, Philip K(enneth) 1941- ... 114
Jason, Stuart
See Avallone, Michael (Angelo), Jr.
and Floren, Lee
Jason, Stuart
See Floren, Lee
Jaspan, Norman ... 103
Jaspers, Karl (Theodor) 1883-1969 ... 122
Obituary ... 25-28R
Jaspersohn, William 1947- ... 102
Jassal, Harjinder (Singh) 1938- ... 111
Jassy, Marie-France Perrin
See Perrin Jassy, Marie-France
Jastak, Joseph Florian 1901-1979 ... CANR-4
Obituary ... 85-88
Earlier sketch in CA 7-8R
Jastrow, Robert 1925- ... CANR-18
Earlier sketch in CA 23-24R
Jauch, Lawrence R. 1943- ... 112
Jauncey, James H(enry) 1916- ... CANR-20
Earlier sketches in CA 1R, CANR-5
Jauss, Anne Marie 1907- ... CANR-4
Earlier sketch in CA 1R
See also SATA 10
Jauss, David 1951- ... 121
Jaussi, Laureen Richardson 1934- ... 73-76
Javitch, Daniel Gilbert 1941- ... 103
Javits, Benjamin A(braham) 1894-1973
Obituary ... 41-44R
Javits, Eric Moses 1931- ... 1R
Javits, Jacob K(oppel) 1904-1986 ... CANR-17
Obituary ... 118
Earlier sketches in CA 1R, CANR-1
Jawien, Andrzej
See John Paul II, Pope
Jaworska, Wladyslawa Jadwiga 1910- ... 53-56
Jaworski, Leon 1905-1982 ... CAP-1
Obituary ... 108
Earlier sketch in CA 15-16
Jaworskyj, Michael 1921- ... 61-64
Jaxon, Milt
See Kimbro, John M.
Jay, Antony (Rupert) 1930- ... 25-28R
Jay, Bill 1940- Brief entry ... 117
Jay, Charlotte
See Halls, Geraldine (Mary)
Jay, Donald
See Meyer, Charles R(obert)
Jay, Douglas (Patrick Thomas) 1907- .. CANR-12
Earlier sketch in CA 65-68
Jay, Elisabeth 1947- ... 124
Jay, Eric George 1907- ... 7-8R
Jay, G. S.
See Halls, Geraldine (Mary)
Jay, Hilda L(ease) 1921- ... 117
Jay, James M(onroe) 1927- ... 53-56
Jay, John 1745-1829 ... DLB-31
Jay, Karla 1947- ... 85-88
Jay, M(argaret) Ellen 1946- ... 118
Jay, Marion
See Spalding, Ruth
Jay, Martin (Evan) 1944- ... 53-56
Jay, Mel
See Fanthorpe, R(obert) Lionel
Jay, Peter 1937- ... 109
Jay, Peter (Anthony Charles) 1945- ... 97-100
Jay, Peter A. 1940- ... 101
Jay, Robert Ravenelle 1925- Brief entry ... 106
Jay, Ruth I(ngrid) 1920- ... 93-96
Jay, Ruth Johnson
See Jay, Ruth I(ngrid)
Jay, Simon
See Alexander, Colin James
Jayawardena, Visakha Kumari 1931- ... 45-48
Jayme, William North 1925- ... 9-10R
Jayne, Lieutenant R. H.
See Ellis, Edward S(ylvester)
Jayne, Sears 1920- ... 13-14R
Jaynes, Clare
See Mayer, Jane Rothschild
Jaynes, Julian 1923- ... 41-44R
Jaynes, Richard A(ndrus) 1935- ... 65-68
Jaynes, Roger W. 1946- ... 85-88
Jaynes, Ruth 1899- ... CAP-2
Earlier sketch in CA 25-28
Jazayery, M(ohammad) Ali 1924- ... CANR-9
Earlier sketch in CA 21-22R
Jeake, Samuel, Jr.
See Aiken, Conrad (Potter)
Jeal, Tim 1945- ... CANR-9
Earlier sketch in CA 21-22R
Jean, Gabrielle (Lucille) 1924- ... CANR-14
Earlier sketch in CA 37-40R
Jean, Marcel 1900- ... 25-28R
Jean-Louis
See Kerouac, Jean-Louis Lebrid de
Jeannerat, Pierre Gabriel 1902- ... 7-8R
Jeanniere, Abel 1921- ... 49-52
Jeans, Marylu Terral 1914- ... 89-92
Jeansonne, Glen 1946- ... 122
Jebb, (Hubert Miles) Gladwyn 1900- ... 21-22R
Jedamus, Paul 1923- ... 37-40R
Jedlitzka, Maria
See Jeritza, Maria
Jedrey, Christopher M(ichael) 1949- ... 101
Jedrzejewicz, Waclaw 1893- ... 25-28R
Jeef, Kalle
See Tshiamala, Kabasele
Jeeves, Malcolm A(lexander) 1926- ... CANR-12
Earlier sketch in CA 29-32R
Jeffares, A(lexander) Norman 1920- ... CANR-16
Earlier sketch in CA 85-88
Jeffer, Marsha 1940- ... 41-44R
Jefferds, Vincent H(arris) 1916- ... SATA-49
Jefferies, (John) Richard 1848-1887 ... SATA-16
Jefferies, Susan Herring 1903- ... CAP-1
Earlier sketch in CA 13-14
Jefferis, Barbara (Tarlton) 1917- ... 81-84
Jeffers, H(arry) Paul 1934- ... 93-96
Jeffers, Jo
See Johnson, Joan Helen
Jeffers, Lance 1919-1985 ... 65-68
See also DLB 41
Jeffers, (John) Robinson 1887-1962 ... 85-88
See also DLB 45
See also CLC 2, 3, 11, 15
Jeffers, Susan ... 97-100
See also SATA 17
Jefferson, Alan 1921- ... CANR-13
Earlier sketch in CA 33-36R
Jefferson, Blanche (Waugaman) 1909- ... 5-6R
Jefferson, Carter (Alfred) 1927- ... 17-18R
Jefferson, Ian
See Davies, L(eslie) P(urnell)
Jefferson, Omar Xavier
See Jefferson, Xavier T(homas)
Jefferson, Roland S. 1939- ... 111
Jefferson, Sarah
See Farjeon, (Eve) Annabel
Jefferson, Thomas 1743-1826 ... DLB-31
See also CDALB 1640-1865
Jefferson, Xavier T(homas) 1952- ... CANR-13
Earlier sketch in CA 73-76
Jeffery, Grant 1924- ... 1R
Jeffery, Ransom 1943- ... 23-24R
Jefferys, Allan ... 93-96
Jefford, Bat
See Bingley, David Ernest
Jeffress, Philip W. 1941- Brief entry ... 111
Jeffrey, Adi-Kent Thomas 1916- ... 37-40R
Jeffrey, Christopher
See Leach, Michael
Jeffrey, David Lyle 1941- ... CANR-24
Earlier sketches in CA 57-60, CANR-7
Jeffrey, Julie Roy 1941- ... 93-96
Jeffrey, L(illian) H(amilton) 1915- ... 4R
Jeffrey, Lloyd Nicholas 1918- ... 37-40R
Jeffrey, Mildred (Mesurac) ... 7-8R
Jeffrey, Richard Carl 1926- ... 103
Jeffrey, Ruth
See Bell, Louise Price
Jeffrey, William
See Pronzini, Bill
and Wallmann, Jeffrey M(iner)
Jeffrey, William P., Jr. 1919- ... 57-60
Jeffreys, Harold 1891- ... 109
Jeffreys, J. G.
See Healey, Ben (James)
Jeffreys, Montagu Vaughan Castelman
1900-1985 ... CANR-4
Obituary ... 117
Earlier sketch in CA 7-8R
Jeffreys-Jones, Rhodri 1942- ... CANR-13
Earlier sketch in CA 77-80
Jeffries, Charles Joseph 1896-1972 ... CANR-4
Earlier sketch in CA 7-8R
Jeffries, Derwin J(ames) 1915- ... 57-60
Jeffries, Graham Montague 1900-1982 ... 77-80
Jeffries, John Worthington 1942- ... 103
Jeffries, Lewis I(ngles) 1942- ... 103
Jeffries, Ona (Griffin) 1893(?)-1973
Obituary ... 41-44R
Jeffries, Roderic (Graeme) 1926- ... CANR-9
Earlier sketch in CA 19-20R
See also SATA 4
Jeffries, Virginia M(urrill) 1911- ... 5-6R
Jeffs, Julian 1931- ... 37-40R
Jeffs, Rae 1921- ... 25-28R
Jefkins, Frank William 1920- ... CANR-9
Earlier sketch in CA 13-14R
Jehlen, Myra 1940- ... 101
Jelagin, Juri 1910-1987 Obituary ... 123
Jelakowitch, Ivan
See Heijermans, Herman
Jelavich, Barbara 1923- ... 53-56
Jelenski, Constantin 1922- ... 101
Jelinek, Estelle C. 1935- ... 102
Jelinek, Hena Maes
See Maes-Jelinek, Hena
Jellema, Roderick 1927- ... 41-44R
Jellicoe, (Patricia) Ann 1927- ... 85-88
See also DLB 13
See also CLC 27
Jellicoe, Geoffrey Alan 1900- ... 13-14R
Jellicoe, Sidney 1906-1973 ... CAP-2
Earlier sketch in CA 33-36
Jellinek, George 1919- ... 89-92
Jellinek, J(oseph) Stephan 1930- ... 81-84
Jellinek, Paul 1897- ... 13-14R
Jellison, Charles Albert, Jr. 1924- ... 3R
Jelly, George Oliver 1909- ... 103
Jemie, Onwuchekwa 1940- ... 89-92
Jemyma
See Holley, Marietta
Jena, Ruth Michaelis
See Ratcliff, Ruth
Jencks, Charles 1939- ... CANR-2
Earlier sketch in CA 49-52
Jencks, Christopher 1936- ... CANR-2
Earlier sketch in CA 49-52
Jencks, Harlan W(ardell) 1941- ... 111
Jenison, Don P. 1897- ... CANR-7
Earlier sketch in CA 19-20R
Jenkin, A(lfred) K(enneth) Hamilton
1900-1980 Obituary ... 102
Jenkins, Alan 1914- ... CANR-6
Earlier sketch in CA 57-60
Jenkins, Cecil 1927- ... 107
Jenkins, Clive 1926- ... CANR-5
Earlier sketch in CA 13-14R
Jenkins, Dan (Thomas B.) 1929-
Brief entry ... 111
Jenkins, David 1928- ... 97-100
Jenkins, David E(dward) 1925- Brief entry .. 114
Jenkins, Dorothy Helen 1907-1972
Obituary ... 37-40R
Jenkins, (Margaret) Elizabeth (Heald)
1905- ... CANR-13
Earlier sketch in CA 73-76
Jenkins, Emyl 1941- ... 114
Jenkins, Ferrell 1936- ... CANR-6
Earlier sketch in CA 57-60
Jenkins, Frances Briggs 1905- ... CAP-2
Earlier sketch in CA 25-28

Jenkins, Geoffrey 1920- ... CANR-16
Earlier sketch in CA 7-8R
Jenkins, (Thomas) Gilmour 1894-1981
Obituary ... 108
Jenkins, Gladys Gardner 1901- ... CANR-4
Earlier sketch in CA 3R
Jenkins, Gordon (Hill) 1910-1984
Obituary ... 112
Jenkins, Gwyn 1919- ... 2R
Jenkins, Hal
See Jenkins, Harold L.
Jenkins, Harold 1909- ... 9-10R
Jenkins, Harold L. 1909(?)-1987 Obituary .. 124
Jenkins, Holt M. 1920- ... 19-20R
Jenkins, Hugh (Gater) 1908- ... 104
Jenkins, Iredell 1909- ... 106
Jenkins, James J(erome) 1923- ... 15-16R
Jenkins, Jerry B(ruce) 1949- ... CANR-20
Earlier sketches in CA 49-52, CANR-5
Jenkins, John (Robert Graham) 1928- ... 45-48
Jenkins, John Geraint 1929- ... 21-22R
Jenkins, John H(olmes III) 1940- ... CANR-10
Earlier sketch in CA 65-68
Jenkins, Kenneth V(incent) 1930- ... 53-56
Jenkins, Linda Walsh 1944- ... 111
Jenkins, Louis 1942- ... CANR-4
Earlier sketch in CA 53-56
Jenkins, Marie M(agdalen) 1909- ... 41-44R
See also SATA 7
Jenkins, Michael (Romilly Heald) 1936- ... 25-28R
Jenkins, Nancy (Harmon) 1937- ... 109
Jenkins, Patricia 1927-1982 ... 106
Jenkins, Peter 1951- ... 89-92
Jenkins, Phyllis
See Schwalberg, Carol(yn Ernestine Stein)
Jenkins, Ray(mond Leonard) 1935- ... 103
Jenkins, Reese V(almer) 1938- ... 65-68
Jenkins, (John) Robin 1912- ... CANR-1
Earlier sketch in CA 4R
See also DLB 14
Jenkins, Romilly James Heald
1907-1969 ... CANR-5
Earlier sketch in CA 7-8R
Jenkins, Roy Harris 1920- ... CANR-13
Earlier sketch in CA 9-10R
Jenkins, Simon 1943- ... 81-84
Jenkins, Will(iam) F(itzgerald)
1896-1975 ... CANR-4
Obituary ... 57-60
Earlier sketch in CA 9-10R
Jenkins, William A(twell) 1922- ... 61-64
See also SATA 9
Jenkins, William Marshall, Jr. 1918-
Brief entry ... 105
Jenkinson, Edward B(ernard) 1930- ... 23-24R
Jenkinson, Michael 1938- ... 25-28R
Jenks, Almet 1892-1966 ... CAP-1
Earlier sketch in CA 13-14
Jenks, C(larence) Wilfred 1909-1973 ... CANR-4
Earlier sketch in CA 11-12R
Jenks, George C(harles) 1850-1929
Brief entry ... 119
Jenks, James M. 1922- ... 122
Jenks, Randolph 1912- ... 11-12R
Jenkyns, Richard (Henry Austen) 1949- ... 108
Jenner, Bruce 1949- ... 110
Jenner, Chrystie 1950- ... 77-80
Jenner, Delia 1944- ... 23-24R
Jenner, Heather
See James, Heather
Jenner, Philip Norman 1921- ... 89-92
Jenner, W(illiam) J(ohn) F(rancis)
1940- ... CANR-12
Earlier sketch in CA 29-32R
Jenness, Aylette 1934- ... 25-28R
Jennifer, Susan
See Hoskins, Robert
Jennings, Coleman A(lonzo) 1933- ... 124
Jennings, Dana Close 1923- ... 53-56
Jennings, Dean Southern 1905-1969
Obituary ... 89-92
Jennings, Edward M(orton III) 1936- ... 29-32R
Jennings, Elizabeth (Joan) 1926- ... CANR-8
Earlier sketch in CA 61-64
See also CAAS 5
See also DLB 27
See also CLC 5, 14
Jennings, Gary (Gayne) 1928- ... CANR-9
Earlier sketch in CA 7-8R
See also SATA 9
Jennings, (William) Ivor 1903-1965 ... 5-6R
Jennings, James M(urray) 1924- ... 37-40R
Jennings, Jerry (Edward) 1935- ... CANR-7
Earlier sketch in CA 53-56
Jennings, Jesse David 1909- ... CANR-13
Earlier sketch in CA 33-36R
Jennings, John (Edward, Jr.) 1906-1973 . CAP-1
Obituary ... 45-48
Earlier sketch in CA 13-14
Jennings, Lane (Eaton) 1944- ... CANR-19
Earlier sketch in CA 102
Jennings, Leslie Nelson 1890-1972 ... CAP-1
Earlier sketch in CA 9-10
Jennings, Marianne Moody 1953- ... 118
Jennings, Michael Glenn 1931- ... CANR-24
Earlier sketch in CA 69-72
Jennings, Patrick
See Mayer, S(ydney) L(ouis)
Jennings, Paul (Francis) 1918- ... CANR-19
Earlier sketches in CA 9-10R, CANR-4
Jennings, Peter (Charles) 1938-
Brief entry ... 114
Jennings, Raymond P(olson) 1924- ... 110
Jennings, Richard (Wormington) 1907- ... 19-20R
Jennings, Robert
See Hamilton, Charles Harold St. John
Jennings, Robert E(dward) 1931- ... CANR-11
Earlier sketch in CA 61-64
Jennings, S. M.
See Meyer, Jerome Sydney
Jennings, Talbot 1895(?)-1985 Obituary ... 116
Jennings, Ted C(harles) 1949- ... 81-84
Jennings, Vivien ... 61-64
Jennings, Waylon 1937- ... CLC-21
Jennings, William Dale 1917- ... 25-28R
Jennison, C. S.
See Starbird, Kaye
Jennison, Christopher 1938- ... 53-56
Jennison, Keith Warren 1911- ... 73-76
See also SATA 14
Jennison, Peter S(axe) 1922- ... CANR-4
Earlier sketch in CA 9-10R
Jenny, Hans H(einrich) 1922- ... 103
Jenoff, Marvyne 1942- ... 117
Jens, Walter 1923- ... CANR-15
Earlier sketch in CA 89-92
Jensen, Ad(olph) E. 1899-1965 ... CAP-2
Earlier sketch in CA 19-20
Jensen, Alan F(rederick) 1938- ... 53-56
Jensen, Albert C(hristian) 1924- ... 85-88
Jensen, Andrew F(rederick), Jr. 1929- ... 57-60
Jensen, Ann ... 23-24R
Jensen, Arthur R(obert) 1923- ... CANR-2
Earlier sketch in CA 4R
Jensen, Clayne R. 1930- ... CANR-8
Earlier sketch in CA 17-18R
Jensen, De Lamar 1925- ... CANR-7
Earlier sketch in CA 11-12R
Jensen, Dwight 1934- ... 85-88
Jensen, Frede 1926- ... 57-60
Jensen, Gordon Duff 1926- Brief entry ... 106
Jensen, Gwendolyn Evans 1936- ... 57-60
Jensen, H. James 1933- ... 25-28R
Jensen, Irene K(hin Khin Myint) 1925- ... 69-72
Jensen, Irving L. 1920- ... CANR-7
Earlier sketch in CA 19-20R
Jensen, J(ohn) Vernon 1922- ... 49-52
Jensen, Jo
See Pelton, Beverly Jo
Jensen, John H(jalmar) 1929- ... 23-24R
Jensen, John Martin 1893- ... CAP-1
Earlier sketch in CA 15-16
Jensen, Julie
See McDonald, Julie
Jensen, Larry Cyril 1938- ... 106
Jensen, Laura (Linnea) 1948- ... 103
See also CLC 37
Jensen, Lawrence N(eil) 1924- ... 17-18R
Jensen, Lloyd 1936- ... 61-64
Jensen, Margaret Ann 1948- ... 123
Jensen, Marlene 1947- ... 81-84
Jensen, Mary Ten Eyck Bard 1904-1970 ... 5-6R
Obituary ... 29-32R
Jensen, Maxine Dowd 1919- ... 65-68
Jensen, Merrill (Monroe) 1905-1980 ... 77-80
Obituary ... 112
See also DLB 17
Jensen, Michael C(ole) 1939- ... 49-52
Jensen, Niels 1927- ... 49-52
See also SATA 25
Jensen, Ole Klindt
See Klindt-Jensen, Ole
Jensen, Oliver (Ormerod) 1914- ... CANR-10
Earlier sketch in CA 25-28R
Jensen, Paul K. 1916- ... 19-20R
Jensen, Paul M(orris) 1944- ... 53-56
Jensen, Pauline Marie (Long) 1900- ... CAP-2
Earlier sketch in CA 17-18
Jensen, Peter
See Wallmann, Jeffrey M(iner)
Jensen, Richard C(arl) 1936- ... 49-52
Jensen, Richard J. 1941- ... 33-36R
Jensen, Robert (Earl) 1938- ... 111
Jensen, Rolf (Arthur) 1912- ... 21-22R
Jensen, Rosalie (Seymour) 1938- ... 57-60
Jensen, Vernon H(ortin) 1907- ... 106
Jensen, Virginia Allen 1927- ... CANR-1
Earlier sketch in CA 45-48
See also SATA 8
Jensi, Muganwa Nsiku
See Shorter, Aylward
Jenson, Robert W(illiam) 1930- ... CANR-9
Earlier sketch in CA 7-8R
Jenson, William R(obert) 1946- ... 101
Jentleson, Bruce W. 1951- ... 124
Jentz, Gaylord A. 1931- ... CANR-14
Earlier sketch in CA 25-28R
Jenyns, R(oger) Soame 1904-1976 ... 73-76
Obituary ... 69-72
Jenyns, Soame
See Jenyns, R(oger) Soame
Jephcott, E(dmund) F(rancis) N(eville)
1938- Brief entry ... 115
Jeppson, J. O.
See Jeppson, Janet O(pal)
Jeppson, Janet O(pal) 1926- ... CANR-19
Earlier sketch in CA 49-52
See also SATA 46
Jepsen, Stanley M(arius) 1912- ... 77-80
Jerdee, Thomas H(arlan) 1927- ... 118
Jeremias, Joachim 1900- ... CANR-11
Earlier sketch in CA 7-8R
Jeremy, Sister Mary ... 7-8R
Jeritza, Maria 1887-1982 Obituary ... 107
Jermain, Clive 1966(?)-1988 Obituary ... 124
Jerman, James (Auguste) 1920- ... 123
Jerman, Sylvia Paul
See Cooper, Sylvia
Jernick, Ruth 1948- ... 107
Jerome, Jerome K(lapka) 1859-1927
Brief entry ... 119
See also DLB 10, 34
See also TCLC 23
Jerome, John 1932- ... CANR-2
Earlier sketch in CA 45-48
Jerome, Joseph
See Sewell, Brocard
Jerome, Judson (Blair) 1927- ... CANR-20
Earlier sketches in CA 9-10R, CANR-4
Jerome, Lawrence E(dmund) 1944- ... 77-80
Jerome, Mark
See Appleman, Mark J(erome)
Jerome, Stuart 1918(?)-1983 Obituary ... 111
Jerrybilt
See Shields, Gerald R.
Jersild, Arthur T(homas) 1902- ... CANR-21
Earlier sketch in CA 4R
Jersild, Paul T(homas) 1931- ... 37-40R
Jervell, Jacob 1925- ... CANR-23
Earlier sketches in CA 61-64, CANR-8
Jeschke, Marlin 1929- ... 45-48
Jeschke, Susan 1942- ... 77-80
See also SATA 27, 42
Jeske, Richard Lee 1936- ... 111
Jesmer, Elaine 1939- ... 49-52
See also AITN 1
Jespersen, James 1934- ... 103
Jesse, F(ryniwyd) Tennyson 1889-1958
Brief entry ... 112
Jesse, Michael
See Baldwin, Michael
Jessel, Camilla (Ruth) 1937- ... CANR-23
Earlier sketch in CA 104
See also SATA 29
Jessel, George (Albert) 1898-1981 ... 89-92
Obituary ... 103
Jessel, John
See Weinbaum, Stanley Grauman
Jessen, Carl A. 1887(?)-1978 Obituary ... 77-80
Jessey, Cornelia
See Sussman, Cornelia Silver
Jessner, Lucie Ney 1896-1979 Obituary ... 93-96
Jessop, Thomas Edmund 1896- ... 9-10R
Jessor, Richard 1924- ... 41-44R
Jessup, Frances
See Van Briggle, Margaret F(rances) Jessup
Jessup, John K(nox) 1907-1979 ... 101
Obituary ... 89-92
Jessup, Michael H(yle) 1937- Brief entry ... 109
Jessup, Paul F(rederick) 1939- ... 111
Jessup, Philip C(aryl) 1897-1986 ... 77-80
Obituary ... 118
Jessup, Richard 1925(?)-1982 Obituary ... 108
Jesty, P(eter) H(ugh) 1948- ... 121
Jeter, Jacky
See Jeter, Jacquelyn I.
Jeter, Jacquelyn I. 1935- ... 25-28R
Jett, Stephen C(linton) 1938- ... CANR-10
Earlier sketch in CA 25-28R
Jette, Fernand 1921- ... 5-6R
Jeune, Paul 1950- ... 101
Jevons, Frederic, Raphael 1929- ... 61-64
Jevons, Marshall
See Breit, William (Leo) and Elzinga, Kenneth G(erald)
Jewell, Derek 1927-1985 ... CANR-20
Earlier sketches in CA 33-36R, CANR-13
Jewell, Edmund F. 1896(?)-1978
Obituary ... 81-84
Jewell, Malcolm E(dwin) 1928- ... CANR-5
Earlier sketch in CA 4R
Jewell, Nancy 1940- ... CANR-7
Earlier sketch in CA 61-64
See also SATA 41
Jewett, Alyce Lowrie (Williams) 1908- ... CAP-1
Earlier sketch in CA 13-14
Jewett, Ann E(lizabeth) 1921- ... 93-96
Jewett, Claudia L(owe) 1939- ... 112
Jewett, Eleanore Myers 1890-1967 ... 7-8R
See also SATA 5
Jewett, Paul King 1919- ... 53-56
Jewett, Robert 1933- ... CANR-2
Earlier sketch in CA 45-48
Jewett, Sarah Orne 1849-1909 Brief entry .. 108
See also SATA 15
See also DLB 12
See also TCLC 1, 22
Jewison, Norman (Frederick) 1926-
Brief entry ... 113
Jewsbury, Geraldine 1812-1880 ... DLB-21
Jezard, Alison 1919- ... 29-32R
See also SATA 34
Jezer, Marty 1940- ... 109
Jezewski, Bohdan O(lgierd) 1900-1980 ... 7-8R
Obituary ... 103
Jha, Akhileshwar 1932- ... 107
Jhabvala, Ruth Prawer 1927- ... CANR-2
Earlier sketch in CA 4R
See also CLC 4, 8, 29
Jianou, Ionel 1905- ... CANR-9
Earlier sketch in CA 23-24R
Jidejian, Nina 1921- ... 29-32R
Jiler, John 1946- ... 114
See also SATA 35, 42
Jiles, Paulette 1943- ... 101
See also CLC 13
Jillson, Joyce 1950- ... 111
Jimenez, Janey (Renee) 1953- ... 77-80
Jimenez (Mantecon), Juan Ramon
1881-1958 Brief entry ... 104
See also TCLC 4
Jinks, William Howard, Jr. 1938- ... 41-44R
Jipson, Wayne R(ay) 1931- ... 45-48
Jiskogo
See Harrington, Mark Raymond
Jo, Yung-Hwan 1932- ... 45-48
Joachim, Leo H. 1898-1985 Obituary ... 117
Joan, Polly 1933- ... 101
Joans, Ted 1928- ... CANR-2
Earlier sketch in CA 45-48
See also DLB 16, 41
Jobb, Jamie 1945- ... 85-88
See also SATA 29
Jobe, Brock (William) 1948- ... 118
Jobes, Gertrude Blumenthal 1907- ... CAP-1
Earlier sketch in CA 11-12
Jobson, Gary Alan 1950- ... 93-96
Jobson, Hamilton 1914- ... 73-76
Jobson, Sandra
See Darroch, Sandra Jobson
Jocelyn, Richard
See Clutterbuck, Richard
Jochnowitz, George 1937- ... 49-52
Joedicke, Juergen 1925- ... 19-20R
Joel, Asher Alexander 1912- ... 108
Joel, Billy
See Joel, William Martin
See also CLC 26
Joel, William Martin 1949- ... 108
Joels, Merrill E. 1915- ... 25-28R
Joelson, Annette 1903-1971 Obituary ... 29-32R
Joerns, Consuelo ... 114
Brief entry ... 111
See also SATA 33, 44
Joers, Lawrence E(ugene) C(laire)
1900- ... 41-44R
Joesting, Edward Henry 1925- ... 103
Jofen, Jean 1922- ... 37-40R
Joffe, Joyce 1940- ... 77-80
Johannes, John R. 1943- ... 111
Johannes, R.
See Moss, Rose
Johannesen, Richard L(ee) 1937- ... 17-18R
Johannesson, Olof
See Alfven, Hannes O(lof) G(oesta)
Johanningmeier, E(rwin) V(irgil) 1937- ... 104
Johannis, Theodore B(enjamin), Jr.
1914- ... 33-36R
Johannsen, Hano D. 1933- ... 29-32R
Johannsen, Robert Walter 1925- ... 1R
Johansen, Bruce Elliott 1950- ... 110
Johansen, Dorothy O. 1904- ... CAP-1
Earlier sketch in CA 13-14
Johanson, Donald C(arl) 1943- ... 107
Johanson, Stanley Morris 1933- ... 45-48
Johansson, Thomas (Hugo) B(ernard)
1943- ... CANR-19
Earlier sketch in CA 102
John, B.
See John, Elizabeth Beaman
John, Betty
See John, Elizabeth Beaman
John, Colin
See Hagan, Chet
John, Dane
See Major, Alan P(ercival)
John, DeWitt 1915-1985 Obituary ... 117
John, Elizabeth Beaman 1907- ... CANR-8
Earlier sketch in CA 5-6R
John, Helen James 1930- ... 61-64
John, Owen 1918- Brief entry ... 117
John, Robert ... 29-32R
John, Sandra D(eanne Thompson) 1951- ... 114
John, Vera P.
See John-Steiner, Vera P(olgar)
Johnn, David
See Engle, John D(avid), Jr.
John Paul I, Pope 1912-1978 ... 81-84
John Paul II, Pope 1920- Brief entry ... 106
Johnpoll, Bernard K(eith) 1918- ... CANR-24
Earlier sketches in CA 21-22R, CANR-9
Johns, Albert Cameron 1914- ... CANR-6
Earlier sketch in CA 49-52
Johns, Avery
See Cousins, Margaret
Johns, Claude J., Jr. 1930- ... 77-80
Johns, Edward Alistair 1936- ... 45-48
Johns, Elizabeth 1937- ... 121
Johns, Eric 1907-1975 Obituary ... 116
Johns, Foster
See Seldes, Gilbert (Vivian)
Johns, Geoffrey
See Warner, (George) Geoffrey John
Johns, Glover S., Jr. 1911(?)-1976
Obituary ... 65-68
Johns, Janetta
See Quin-Harkin, Janet
Johns, John E(dwin) 1921- ... 9-10R
Johns, June 1925- ... 57-60
Johns, Kenneth
See Bulmer, (Henry) Kenneth
Johns, Marston
See Fanthorpe, R(obert) Lionel
Johns, Ray E(arl) 1900- ... 41-44R
Johns, Richard A(lton) 1929- ... 19-20R
Johns, Warren L. 1929- ... 23-24R
Johns, Whitey
See White, John I(rwin)
Johns, William Earle 1893-1968 ... 73-76
Johnsen, Trevor Bernard Meldal
See Meldal-Johnsen, Trevor Bernard
Johnsgard, Karin L(uisa) 1964- ... 118
Johnsgard, Paul A(ustin) 1931- ... CANR-17
Earlier sketches in CA 49-52, CANR-1
Johnson, A.
See Johnson, Annabell Jones
Johnson, A. E.
See Johnson, Annabell Jones and Johnson, Edgar Raymond
Johnson, Alan P(ackard) 1929- ... 19-20R
Johnson, Albert (Franklin) 1904- ... CANR-6
Earlier sketch in CA 9-10R
Johnson, Alden Porter 1914-1972
Obituary ... 104
Johnson, Allen ... 85-88

Johnson, Allison H(eartz) 1910- 41-44R
Johnson, Alvin 1874-1971 Obituary 29-32R
Johnson, Amandus 1877-1974 Obituary ...49-52
Johnson, Andrew N(isseu) 1887-1982 61-64
Obituary 120
Johnson, Ann Cox
See Saunders, Ann Loreille
Johnson, Annabell Jones 1921- 9-10R
See also SATA 2
Johnson, Arno Hollock 1901-1985
Obituary 116
Johnson, Arnold W(aldemar) 1900- CAP-1
Earlier sketch in CA 13-14
Johnson, Arthur Menzies 1921- 21-22R
Johnson, Arthur W(illiam) 1920- 117
Johnson, Aubrey Rodway 1901-1985
Obituary 117
Johnson, Audrey P(ike) 1915- CANR-15
Earlier sketch in CA 93-96
Johnson, B(owen) C(harleston) 1945- 107
Johnson, B(urdetta) F(aye) 1920- CANR-3
Earlier sketch in CA 4R
Johnson, B(asil) L(eonard) C(lyde) 1919- ... 120
Johnson, B(ryan) S(tanley William)
1933-1973 .... CANR-9
Obituary 53-56
Earlier sketch in CA 9-10R
See also DLB 14, 40
See also CLC 6, 9
Johnson, Barbara F(erry) 1923- 73-76
Johnson, Barclay G(iddings) 1909-1985
Obituary 116
Johnson, Barry L(ynn) 1934- 33-36R
Johnson, Barry L(ee) 1943- 61-64
Johnson, Bea ?-1976 Obituary 65-68
Johnson, Ben E(ugene) 1940- CANR-8
Earlier sketch in CA 61-64
Johnson, Benj. F., of Boone
See Riley, James Whitcomb
Johnson, Benjamin A. 1937- CANR-9
Earlier sketch in CA 23-24R
Johnson, Benjamin F., of Boone
See Riley, James Whitcomb
Johnson, Benton 1928- 81-84
Johnson, Bernard 1933- 33-36R
Johnson, Bertha French 1906- 41-44R
Johnson, Beth 1953- 118
Johnson, Bradford 1937- 57-60
Johnson, Brian (Martin) 1925- CANR-23
Earlier sketch in CA 106
Johnson, Bruce 1933- 33-36R
Johnson, Burges 1877-1963 Obituary 89-92
Johnson, Byron Lindberg 1917- 21-22R
Johnson, C. Edward
See Johnson, Carl E(dward)
Johnson, C. F.
See Goulart, Frances Sheridan
Johnson, Carl E(dward) 1937- 25-28R
Johnson, Carl G(raves) 1915- 101
Johnson, Carol Virginia 1928- CANR-6
Earlier sketch in CA 9-10R
Johnson, Carroll B(ernard) 1938- 73-76
Johnson, Cecil Edward 1927- 33-36R
Johnson, Chalmers A(shby) 1931- CANR-6
Earlier sketch in CA 5-6R
Johnson, Charlene
See Crawford, Char
Johnson, Charles (Richard) 1948- 116
See also DLB 33
See also CLC 7
Johnson, Charles Benjamin 1928-1980 .. CANR-4
Earlier sketch in CA 7-8R
Johnson, Charles Ellicott 1920-1969 .... 1R
Obituary 103
Johnson, Charles R. 1925- 65-68
See also SATA 11
Johnson, Charles S.
See Edwards, William B(ennett)
Johnson, Charles Spurgeon 1893-1956 .. DLB-51
Johnson, Charles W(illiam) 1934- 107
Johnson, Charlotte Buel
See von Wodtke, Charlotte Buel Johnson
See also SATA 46
Johnson, Christine 1943- 123
Johnson, Christopher 1931- CANR-8
Earlier sketch in CA 13-14R
Johnson, Christopher Howard 1937-
Brief entry 106
Johnson, Chuck
See Johnson, Charles R.
Johnson, Clair 1915(?)-1980 Obituary ...97-100
Johnson, Claudia Alta (Taylor) 1912- 89-92
Johnson, Claudia D(urst) 1938- 114
Johnson, Clive (White, Jr.) 1930- 29-32R
Johnson, Crockett
See Leisk, David Johnson
Johnson, Curt(is Lee) 1928- 33-36R
Johnson, Curtiss Sherman 1899- 45-48
Johnson, D(onald) Barton 1933- 33-36R
Johnson, D(avid) Bruce 1942- 61-64
Johnson, D(avid) Gale 1916- 19-20R
Johnson, D(ana) William 1945- 97-100
See also SATA 23
Johnson, Dale A(rthur) 1936- 37-40R
Johnson, Dave W(illiam) 1931- 93-96
Johnson, David 1927- CANR-8
Earlier sketch in CA 15-16R
Johnson, David G(eorge) 1906- 9-10R
Johnson, David Lawrence 1943- 114
Johnson, David Ralph 1942- 117
Johnson, Deidre A(nn) 1953- 116
Johnson, Denis 1949- 121
Brief entry 117
Johnson, Diane 1934- CANR-17
Earlier sketch in CA 41-44R
See also DLBY 80
See also CLC 5, 13
Johnson, Don 1934- 116
Johnson, Donald Bruce 1921-1981 .... 1R
Johnson, Donald M(cEwen) 1909- 4R
Johnson, Donald McI(ntosh) 1903- CANR-8
Earlier sketch in CA 7-8R
Johnson, Donna Kay 1935- 106
Johnson, Donovan A(lbert) 1910- CANR-5
Earlier sketch in CA 7-8R
Johnson, Doris McNeely 1941- 111
Johnson, Dorothy Biddle 1887(?)-1974
Obituary 53-56
Johnson, Dorothy E(thel) 1920- 53-56
Johnson, Dorothy M(arie) 1905-1984 ... CANR-6
Obituary 114
Earlier sketch in CA 5-6R
See also SATA 6, 40
Johnson, Dorris 1914- 109
Johnson, Douglas W(ayne) 1934- CANR-21
Earlier sketches in CA 57-60, CANR-6
Johnson, E(dgar) A(ugustus) J(erome)
1900-1972 .... CAP-1
Obituary 37-40R
Earlier sketch in CA 17-18
Johnson, E(arly) Ashby 1917- 33-36R
Johnson, E(ugene) Harper SATA-44
Johnson, E. Ned
See Johnson, Enid
Johnson, E(mil) Richard 1937- 104
Johnson, E(dward) W(arren) 1941- 29-32R
Johnson, Earl, Jr. 1933- CANR-10
Earlier sketch in CA 61-64
Johnson, Earl S.
See Johnson, Earl Shepard
Johnson, Earl Shepard 1894-1986
Obituary 119
Johnson, Edgar 1901- 9-10R
Johnson, Edgar Raymond 1912- 9-10R
See also SATA 2
Johnson, Edward 1598-1672 .... DLB-24
Johnson, Edward A(ndrew) 1915- 37-40R
Johnson, Edwin Clark (Toby) 1945- 107
Johnson, Eleanor
See Seymour, Dorothy Jane Z(ander)
Johnson, Eleanor Murdock 1892-1987
Obituary 123
Johnson, Electa Search 1909- 4R
Johnson, Elizabeth 1911-1984 .... CANR-4
Obituary 117
Earlier sketch in CA 1R
See also SATA 7, 39
Johnson, Ellen Argo 1933-1983 .... CANR-13
Obituary 110
Earlier sketch in CA 73-76
Johnson, Ellen Argo
See Argo, Ellen
Johnson, Ellen H. 1910- CANR-15
Earlier sketch in CA 37-40R
Johnson, Elmer Douglas 1915- CANR-3
Earlier sketch in CA 9-10R
Johnson, Elmer Hubert 1917- 15-16R
Johnson, Enid 1892- 73-76
Johnson, Eola 1909- 49-52
Johnson, Eric W(arner) 1918- CANR-4
Earlier sketch in CA 5-6R
See also SATA 8
Johnson, Evelyne 1922- CANR-21
Earlier sketch in CA 69-72
See also SATA 20
Johnson, Eyvind (Olof Verner)
1900-1976 73-76
Obituary 69-72
See also CLC 14
Johnson, Falk S(immons) 1913- 19-20R
Johnson, Fenton 1888-1958 124
Brief entry 118
See also DLB 45, 50
Johnson, Ferd 1905- 69-72
Johnson, Forrest B(ryant) 1935- 106
Johnson, Franklyn A(rthur) 1921- CANR-4
Earlier sketch in CA 1R
Johnson, Frederick 1932- 73-76
Johnson, Fridolf (Lester) 1905- 103
Johnson, Frosty
See Johnson, Forrest B(ryant)
Johnson, G(eorge) Orville 1915- CANR-4
Earlier sketch in CA 1R
Johnson, Gaylord 1884- CAP-1
Earlier sketch in CA 9-10
See also SATA 7
Johnson, Geoffrey 1893-1966 .... CAP-1
Earlier sketch in CA 13-14
Johnson, George 1917- 7-8R
Johnson, George (Laclede) 1952- 123
Johnson, Georgia Douglas 1886-1966 ... DLB-51
Johnson, Gerald White 1890-1980 85-88
Obituary 97-100
See also SATA 19, 28
See also DLB 29
Johnson, Gertrude F(alk) 1929- 57-60
Johnson, Greer 1920(?)-1974 Obituary 53-56
Johnson, H(arold) B(enjamin), Jr.
1931- 29-32R
Johnson, H(erbert) Webster 1906- CANR-4
Earlier sketch in CA 5-6R
Johnson, Halvard 1936- 33-36R
Johnson, Harold L. 1924- 13-14R
Johnson, Harold Scholl 1929- 37-40R
Johnson, Harold V. 1897- CANR-5
Earlier sketch in CA 4R
Johnson, Harper
See Johnson, E(ugene) Harper
Johnson, Harriett 1908-1987 Obituary 123
Johnson, Harry Alleyn 1921- 45-48
Johnson, Harry G(ordon) 1923-1977 ....5-6R
Obituary 69-72
Johnson, Harry L. 1929- 29-32R
Johnson, Harry Morton 1917- 9-10R
Johnson, Harvey L(eroy) 1904- 37-40R
Johnson, Haynes Bonner 1931- CANR-12
Earlier sketch in CA 7-8R
Johnson, Helen (Louise) Kendrick
1844(?)-1917 Brief entry 123
Johnson, Helene 1907- DLB-51
Johnson, Henry
See Hammond, John (Henry, Jr.)
Johnson, Herbert A(lan) 1934- CANR-4
Earlier sketch in CA 5-6R
Johnson, Herbert J. 1933- 29-32R
Johnson, Hildegard Binder 1908- CANR-3
Earlier sketch in CA 9-10R
Johnson, Howard Albert 1915-1974 .... 1R
Obituary 49-52
Johnson, Hugh 1939- CANR-16
Earlier sketch in CA 93-96
Johnson, Humphrey Wynne 1925-1976
Obituary 61-64
Johnson, Irma Bolan 1903- CANR-1
Earlier sketch in CA 3R
Johnson, Irving McClure 1905- 4R
Johnson, J. R.
See James, C(yril) L(ionel) R(obert)
Johnson, Jack
See Johnson, John Arthur
Johnson, Jalmar Edwin 1905- 7-8R
Johnson, James A(llen) 1932- Brief entry ... 110
Johnson, James Craig 1944- 53-56
Johnson, James E(dgar) 1927- 77-80
Johnson, James H(enry) 1930- CANR-11
Earlier sketch in CA 25-28R
Johnson, James J(ay) 1939- 33-36R
Johnson, James L. 1927- CANR-9
Earlier sketch in CA 21-22R
Johnson, James P(earce) 1937- 81-84
Johnson, James Ralph 1922- CANR-2
Earlier sketch in CA 4R
See also SATA 1
Johnson, James Rosser 1916- 9-10R
Johnson, James Turner 1938- 61-64
Johnson, James Weldon 1871-1938
Brief entry 104
See also SATA 31
See also DLB 51
See also TCLC 3, 19
Johnson, James William 1927- 53-56
Johnson, Jane 1951- 110
See also SATA 48
Johnson, Jane M(axine) 1914- 49-52
Johnson, Jann
See Johnson, Paula Janice
Johnson, Jean Dye 1920- 23-24R
Johnson, Jerry Mack 1927- CANR-4
Earlier sketch in CA 53-56
Johnson, Jim
See Johnson, James A(llen)
Johnson, Jinna
See Johnson, Virginia
Johnson, Joan D. 1929- Brief entry 106
Johnson, Joan Helen 1931- 61-64
Johnson, Joan J. 1942- 122
Johnson, Joe Donald 1943- 57-60
Johnson, John Arthur 1878-1946
Brief entry 115
Johnson, John Bockover, Jr. 1912-1972
Obituary 106
Johnson, John E(mil) 1929- 110
See also SATA 34
Johnson, John J. 1912- 9-10R
Johnson, John M(yrton) 1941- 93-96
Johnson, Johnni 1922- 13-14R
Johnson, Joseph A., Jr. 1914(?)-1979
Obituary 89-92
Johnson, Joseph E(arl) 1946- 37-40R
Johnson, Joseph M. 1883(?)-1973
Obituary 45-48
Johnson, Josephine W(inslow) 1910- 25-28R
Johnson, Joy Duvall 1932- 110
Johnson, Karen 1939- 69-72
Johnson, Kathryn 1929- 33-36R
Johnson, Keith B(arnard) 1933- 29-32R
Johnson, Kendall 1928- 69-72
Johnson, Kenneth G(ardner) 1922- 41-44R
Johnson, Kenneth M(itchell) 1903- 5-6R
Johnson, Kristi Planck 1944- 57-60
Johnson, L. D. 1916- 33-36R
Johnson, La Verne B(ravo) 1925- 65-68
See also SATA 13
Johnson, Lady Bird
See Johnson, Claudia Alta (Taylor)
Johnson, Lemuel A. 1941- 53-56
Johnson, Lewis Kerr 1904- 1R
Johnson, Lincoln F., Jr. 1920- 81-84
Johnson, Lionel (Pigot) 1867-1902
Brief entry 117
See also DLB 19
See also TCLC 19
Johnson, Loch K. 1942- 121
Johnson, Lois Smith 1894- CAP-1
Earlier sketch in CA 9-10
See also SATA 6
Johnson, Lois Walfrid 1936- CANR-6
Earlier sketch in CA 57-60
See also SATA 22
Johnson, Louis 1924- CANR-18
Earlier sketch in CA 101
Johnson, Luke Timothy 1943- Brief entry ... 107
Johnson, Lyndon Baines 1908-1973 ... CANR-23
Obituary 41-44R
Earlier sketch in CA 53-56
Johnson, Lynn Eric 1932- Brief entry 108
Johnson, M. Glen 1936- 41-44R
Johnson, M. L.
See Abercrombie, M(innie) L(ouie)
J(ohnson)
Johnson, Malcolm (Malone) 1904-1976 ...69-72
Obituary 65-68
Johnson, Malcolm L. 1937- 69-72
Johnson, Manly 1920- 89-92
Johnson, Margaret 1926- 37-40R
Johnson, Margaret S(weet) 1893-1964
Obituary 113
See also SATA 35
Johnson, Marilue Carolyn 1931- CANR-1
Earlier sketch in CA 45-48
Johnson, Marion Georgina Wikeley
1912-1980 ....11-12R
Obituary 97-100
Johnson, Mark 1949- 115
Johnson, Marshall D. 1935- 33-36R
Johnson, Mary Anne 1943- 53-56
Johnson, Mary Ellen 1949- 120
Johnson, Mary Frances K. 1929(?)-1979
Obituary 104
See also SATA 27
Johnson, Mary Louise
See King, Mary Louise
Johnson, Mary Ritz 1904- CAP-1
Earlier sketch in CA 9-10
Johnson, Maryanna 1925- 33-36R
Johnson, Maud Battle 1918(?)-1985
Obituary 117
See also SATA 46
Johnson, Maurice (O.) 1913-1978 ..... CANR-20
Earlier sketch in CA 1R
Johnson, Mauritz (Jr.) 1922- 41-44R
Johnson, Mel
See Malzberg, Barry N(athaniel)
Johnson, Mendal W(illiam) 1928-1976 101
Johnson, Merle Allison 1934- 37-40R
Johnson, Michael L(illard) 1943- CANR-19
Earlier sketches in CA 53-56, CANR-4
Johnson, Mike
See Sharkey, John Michael
Johnson, Milton 1932- SATA-31
Johnson, Neil (James) 1955- 123
Johnson, Nicholas 1934- 29-32R
Johnson, Niel M(elvin) 1931- 41-44R
Johnson, Nora 1933- 106
Johnson, Nunnally 1897-1977 81-84
Obituary 69-72
See also DLB 26
Johnson, Olga Weydemeyer 1901- CAP-2
Earlier sketch in CA 29-32
Johnson, Oliver A(dolph) 1923- CANR-12
Earlier sketch in CA 29-32R
Johnson, Pamela Hansford 1912-1981 .. CANR-2
Obituary 104
Earlier sketch in CA 2R
See also DLB 15
See also CLC 1, 7, 27
Johnson, Patrick Spencer 1938- 9-10R
Johnson, Paul (Bede) 1928- 17-18R
Johnson, Paul C(ornelius) 1904- 81-84
Johnson, Paul E(manuel) 1898- 15-16R
Johnson, Paul Victor 1920- 3R
Johnson, Paula Janice 1946- 106
Johnson, Pauline B. 1R
Johnson, Penelope D(elafield) 1938- 124
Johnson, Peter 1930- 65-68
Johnson, Philip A(rthur) 1915- 15-16R
Johnson, Philip Cortelyou 1906-
Brief entry 106
Johnson, Phyllis Anne 1937- Brief entry 108
Johnson, Pierce 1921- 41-44R
Johnson, Quentin G. 1930- 11-12R
Johnson, R(obbin) S(inclair) 1946- 29-32R
Johnson, Rachel H(arris) 1887-1983
Obituary 110
Johnson, Ralph W(hitney) 1923- 77-80
Johnson, Ray(mond Edward) 1927- 17-18R
Johnson, Ray DeForest 1926- 65-68
Johnson, Raynor C(arey) 1901-
Brief entry 115
Johnson, Richard
See Richey, David
Johnson, Richard A(ugust) 1937- 37-40R
Johnson, Richard B(righam) 1914-1977 ..41-44R
Johnson, Richard C. 1919- 33-36R
Johnson, Richard D(avid) 1927- 109
Johnson, Richard N(ewhall) 1900-1971
Obituary 104
Johnson, Richard R(igby) 1942- 116
Johnson, Robert A. 1921- 61-64
Johnson, Robert C(lyde) 1919- 5-6R
Johnson, Robert Erwin 1923- 37-40R
Johnson, Robert I(var) 1933- 53-56
Johnson, Robert J. 1933- 23-24R
Johnson, Robert L. 1919- 33-36R
Johnson, Robert L(eon, Jr.) 1930- 33-36R
Johnson, Robert Owen 1926- 33-36R
Johnson, Robert Sherlaw 1932- 61-64
Johnson, Robert W(illard) 1921- 19-20R
Johnson, Roger N(ylund) 1939- 53-56
Johnson, Ronald 1935- CANR-20
Earlier sketches in CA 9-10R, CANR-4
Johnson, Ronald C. 1927- 81-84
Johnson, Ronald Maberry 1936-
Brief entry 108
Johnson, Rossall J(ames) 1917- 21-22R
Johnson, Ruby Kelley 1928- 33-36R
Johnson, Ruth I.
See Jay, Ruth I(ngrid)
Johnson, (Walter) Ryerson 1901- CANR-2
Earlier sketch in CA 7-8R
See also SATA 10
Johnson, S(amuel) Lawrence
1909-1978 .... CANR-12
Earlier sketch in CA 29-32R
Johnson, Sabina Thorne
See Thorne, Sabina

Johnson, Sam Houston 1914(?)-1978 89-92
Obituary 81-84
Johnson, Samuel 1696-1772 . . . . . DLB-24
Johnson, Samuel 1709-1784 . . . . . DLB-39
Johnson, Samuel 1822-1882 . . . . . DLB-1
Johnson, Samuel A(ugustus) 1895- 17-18R
Johnson, Sherman E(lbridge) 1908- 53-56
Johnson, Sherman Ellsworth 1896-1978
Obituary 77-80
Johnson, Shirley K(ing) 1927- 11-12R
See also SATA 10
Johnson, Siddie Joe 1905-1977 Obituary . . . 106
See also SATA 20
Johnson, Sonia 1936- 118
Johnson, Spencer 1938- 110
See also SATA 38
Johnson, Stanley (Patrick) 1940- CANR-13
Earlier sketch in CA 23-24R
Johnson, Stanley J. F. 1920(?)-1978
Obituary 77-80
Johnson, Stanley L(ewis) 1920- 17-18R
Johnson, (John) Stephen 1947- 107
Johnson, (Edward) Stowers 7-8R
Johnson, Thomas Frank 1920- 9-10R
Johnson, Thomas Herbert 1902-1985 124
Johnson, Thomas William 1946-
Brief entry 110
Johnson, Una E. Brief entry 109
Johnson, Uwe 1934-1984 . . . . . CANR-1
Obituary 112
Earlier sketch in CA 3R
See also CLC 5, 10, 15, 40
Johnson, Van L(oran) 1908- 37-40R
Johnson, Vernon E(dwin) 1920- 93-96
Johnson, Victor Hugo 1912- Brief entry 110
Johnson, Virginia 1914-1975 . . . . . CAP-2
Earlier sketch in CA 33-36
Johnson, Virginia E. 1925- 21-22R
Johnson, Virginia W(eisel) 1910- 19-20R
Johnson, W. Bolingbroke
See Bishop, Morris
Johnson, W(illiam) Branch 1893- CANR-5
Earlier sketch in CA 7-8R
Johnson, W(illiam) E(rnest) 1858-1931
Brief entry 122
Johnson, W(alter) R(alph) 1933- CANR-9
Earlier sketch in CA 65-68
Johnson, W(endell) Stacy 1927- CANR-17
Earlier sketches in CA 1R, CANR-2
Johnson, Walter 1915-1985 89-92
Obituary 116
Johnson, Walter Frank, Jr. 1914- 7-8R
Johnson, Warren Arthur 1937- 33-36R
Johnson, Wayne G(ustave) 1930- 113
Johnson, Wendell (Andrew Leroy)
1906-1965 . . . . . CANR-1
Earlier sketch in CA 2R
Johnson, Willard R(aymond) 1935- 105
Johnson, William Alexander 1932- 7-8R
Johnson, William C(lark, Jr.) 1945- CANR-8
Earlier sketch in CA 61-64
Johnson, William R. CANR-7
Earlier sketch in CA 17-18R
See also SATA 38
Johnson, William Weber 1909- 17-18R
See also SATA 7
Johnson, Winifred (MacNally) 1905- 7-8R
Johnson Abercrombie, M. L.
See Abercrombie, M(innie) L(ouie) J(ohnson)
Johnson-Marshall, Percy E. A. 1915- 23-24R
John-Steiner, Vera P(olgar) 121
Johnston, A(aron) Montgomery 1915- . . CANR-11
Earlier sketch in CA 29-32R
Johnston, Agnes Christine
See Dazey, Agnes J(ohnston)
Johnston, Alan (William) 1942- 103
Johnston, Albert H. 1914- 69-72
Johnston, Angus James II 1916- 11-12R
Johnston, Annie Fellows 1863-1931
Brief entry 116
See also SATA 37
See also DLB 42
Johnston, (William) Arnold 1942- 77-80
Johnston, Arthur 1924- 23-24R
Johnston, Arvin Harry 1906- 2R
Johnston, Basil H. 1929- CANR-11
Earlier sketch in CA 69-72
See also DLB 60
Johnston, Bernard 1934- 19-20R
Johnston, Bernice Houle 1914-1971 . . . . . CAP-2
Earlier sketch in CA 33-36
Johnston, Brenda A(rlivia) 1944- 57-60
Johnston, Brian 1932- 65-68
Johnston, Bruce F(oster) 1919- CANR-14
Earlier sketch in CA 41-44R
Johnston, Charles (Hepburn)
1912-1986 . . . . . CANR-5
Obituary 119
Earlier sketch in CA 15-16R
Johnston, Colin 1946- 108
Johnston, Dan 1912- 123
Johnston, (William) Denis 1901-1984 . . . . CAP-2
Obituary 113
Earlier sketch in CA 21-22
See also DLB 10
Johnston, Dorothy Grunbock 1915- CANR-5
Earlier sketch in CA 7-8R
Johnston, Ellen Turlington 1929- 65-68
Johnston, Fran(ces Jonsson) 1925- 15-16R
Johnston, Francis E. 1931- CANR-4
Earlier sketch in CA 53-56
Johnston, George 1913- CANR-15
Earlier sketch in CA 89-92
Johnston, George (Benson) 1913- CANR-20
Earlier sketches in CA 2R, CANR-5
Johnston, George Burke 1907- CAP-1
Earlier sketch in CA 17-18
Johnston, Gordon (Frederick) 1920-1983 . . . 122
Johnston, H(ugh) A(nthony) S(tephen)
1913-1967 . . . . . CAP-2
Earlier sketch in CA 21-22
See also SATA 14
Johnston, H(ugh) J(ames) M(orton)
1939- 41-44R
Johnston, Hank
See Johnston, Henry
Johnston, Henry 1922- 25-28R
Johnston, Herbert (Leo) 1912- 7-8R
Johnston, Hugh Buckner 1913- 69-72
Johnston, Jennifer 1930- 85-88
See also DLB 14
See also CLC 7
Johnston, Jill 1929- 53-56
Johnston, Johanna 1914(?)-1982 . . . . . CANR-7
Obituary 108
Earlier sketch in CA 57-60
See also SATA 12, 33
Johnston, John H(ubert) 1921- 11-12R
Johnston, John M. 1898(?)-1979
Obituary 89-92
Johnston, Kenneth R(ichard) 1938- 121
Johnston, Leonard 1920- CANR-11
Earlier sketch in CA 15-16R
Johnston, Lynn (Beverley) 1947- 110
Johnston, Mary 1870-1936 Brief entry 109
See also DLB 9
Johnston, Minton C(oyne) 1900- 7-8R
Johnston, Mireille 1940- 49-52
Johnston, Norma 105
See also SATA 29
Johnston, Norman (Bruce) 1921- CANR-18
Earlier sketch in CA 93-96
Johnston, Norman J. 1918- 120
Johnston, Portia
See Takakjian, Portia
Johnston, R(onald) J(ohn) 1941- CANR-18
Earlier sketch in CA 101
Johnston, Randolph W(ardell) 1904- . . . CANR-15
Earlier sketch in CA 85-88
Johnston, Richard W(yckoff) 1915-1981
Obituary 104
Johnston, Robert Kent 1945- 104
Johnston, Ronald 1926- 15-16R
Johnston, Russell G. 1933- 118
Johnston, S(amuel) Paul 1899-1985
Obituary 117
Johnston, Susan Taylor 1942- CANR-15
Earlier sketch in CA 41-44R
Johnston, Terry C(onrad) 1947- 113
Johnston, Thomas 1945- 104
Johnston, Thomas E. 1931- 15-16R
Johnston, Tony
See Johnston, Susan Taylor
See also SATA 8
Johnston, Velma B. 1912(?)-1977
Obituary 69-72
Johnston, William 1924- 85-88
Johnston, William 1925- 33-36R
Johnston, William M(urray) 1936- 37-40R
Johnstone, Charles 1719(?)-1800(?) DLB-39
Johnstone, D(onald) Bruce 1909- 104
Johnstone, Henry W(ebb), Jr. 1920- 1R
Johnstone, Iain 1943- 108
Johnstone, Kathleen Yerger 1906- 9-10R
Johnstone, Lammy Olcott 1949- CANR-14
Earlier sketch in CA 81-84
Johnstone, Parker Lochiel 1903- 69-72
Johnstone, Rex
See Chapman, Frank M(onroe)
Johnstone, Robert 1951- 118
Johnstone, Robert Morton, Jr. 1939- 81-84
Johnstone, T(homas) M(uir) 1924-1983
Obituary 114
Johnstone, Ted
See McDaniel, David (Edward)
Johnstone, William D(avid) G(ordon)
1935- 77-80
Johnston-Saint, Peter 1889-1974
Obituary 53-56
John XXIII, Pope 1881-1963 Obituary 113
Joiner, Charles A(drian) 1932- 77-80
Joiner, Charles W(ycliffe) 1916- CANR-1
Earlier sketch in CA 4R
Joiner, Edward Earl 1924- 49-52
Joiner, Verna J(ones) 1896- 4R
Joki, Virginia (Carville) 1909(?)-1986
Obituary 120
Jolas, Eugene 1894-1952 Brief entry 107
See also DLB 4, 45
Joliat, Eugene 1910- 49-52
Joliffe, John E(dward) A(ustin) 1891-1964 . . 7-8R
Jolin, Stephen Towne 1941- 45-48
Jolivet, R(egis) 1891-1966 . . . . . CAP-1
Earlier sketch in CA 9-10
Joll, (Dowrish) Evelyn (Louis) 1925- 101
Joll, James (Bysse) 1918- CANR-7
Earlier sketch in CA 7-8R
Jolley, Elizabeth 1923- CLC-46
Jolley, (Stephen) Nicholas 1948- 120
Jolliffe, H(arold) R(ichard) 1904-1978 . . . . . 4R
Obituary 103
Jolly, Alison 1937- CANR-15
Earlier sketch in CA 41-44R
Jolly, Clifford J. 1939- Brief entry 108
Jolly, Cyril Arthur 1910- CAP-1
Earlier sketch in CA 9-10
Jolly, Hugh R. 1918-1986 85-88
Obituary 118
Jolly, W(illiam) P(ercy) 1922- CANR-4
Earlier sketch in CA 53-56
Jolly Cholly
See Grimm, Charles John
Jolson, Marvin A(rnold) 1922- CANR-1
Earlier sketch in CA 49-52
Joly, Cyril Bencraft 1918- CAP-1
Earlier sketch in CA 9-10
Jonas, A(dolphe) David 1913- 107
Jonas, Ann 1919- 105
Jonas, Ann 1932- Brief entry 118
See also SATA 42, 50
See also CLR 12
Jonas, Arthur 1930- 13-14R
Jonas, Carl 1913-1976 . . . . . 9-10R
Obituary 69-72
Jonas, Doris F(rances) 1916- CANR-8
Earlier sketch in CA 61-64
Jonas, George 1935- 29-32R
Jonas, Gerald 1935- 65-68
Jonas, Hans 1903- CANR-23
Earlier sketches in CA 61-64, CANR-7
Jonas, Ilsedore B. 1920- 33-36R
Jonas, Klaus W(erner) 1920- CANR-2
Earlier sketch in CA 1R
Jonas, Manfred 1927- CANR-8
Earlier sketch in CA 21-22R
Jonas, Paul 1922- CANR-13
Earlier sketch in CA 73-76
Jonas, Steven 1936- 89-92
Jonassen, Christen T(onnes) 1912- 41-44R
Joncich, Geraldine
See Clifford, Geraldine Joncich
Jones, A(rnold) H(ugh) M(artin)
1904-1970 Obituary 89-92
Jones, A(rthur) Morris 1899- CAP-1
Earlier sketch in CA 13-14
Jones, Adam Mars
See Mars-Jones, Adam
Jones, Adrienne 1915- 33-36R
See also SATA 7
Jones, Alan Griffith 1943- CANR-19
Earlier sketch in CA 103
Jones, Alan Moore, Jr. 1942- 53-56
Jones, Alan William 1940- 117
Jones, Alexander 1906-1970 . . . . . CANR-2
Obituary 103
Earlier sketch in CA 2R
Jones, Allan Gwynne
See Gwynne-Jones, Allan
Jones, Andrew 1921- 93-96
Jones, Andrew (Eric) 1950- 111
Jones, Annabel
See Lewis, Mary (Christianna Milne)
Jones, Antony Armstrong
See Armstrong-Jones, Antony (Charles Robert)
Jones, Archer 1926- CANR-18
Earlier sketches in CA 1R, CANR-4
Jones, Archie N(eff) 1900- CAP-1
Earlier sketch in CA 15-16
Jones, Arthur F(rederick) 1945- 81-84
Jones, Arthur Glyn Prys
See Prys-Jones, Arthur Glyn
Jones, (Alun) Arthur Gwynne 1919-
Brief entry 120
Jones, Arthur Hope
See Hope-Jones, Arthur
Jones, Arthur (Mervyn) Keppel
See Keppel-Jones, Arthur (Mervyn)
Jones, Arthur Llewellyn 1863-1947
Brief entry 104
Jones, Aubrey 1911- 103
Jones, Barbara (Mildred) 1917(?)-1978 . . CANR-4
Obituary 81-84
Earlier sketch in CA 1R
Jones, Bessie 1902-1984 Obituary 114
Jones, Betty Millsaps 1940- 109
Jones, Bill
See Jones, William David Anthony
Jones, Billy M(ac) 1925- CANR-10
Earlier sketch in CA 21-22R
Jones, Bob
See Jones, Robert Reynolds, Jr.
Jones, Bobby
See Jones, Robert Tyre, Jr.
Jones, Brian 1938- Brief entry 119
Jones, Bryan L. 1945- 110
Jones, C(lifton) Clyde 1922- 109
Jones, C. M.
See Jones, Clarence Medlycott
Jones, Calico
See Richardson, Gladwell
Jones, Candy 1925- 107
Jones, Capt. Wilbur
See Edwards, William B(ennett)
Jones, Carolyn (Sue) 1933-1983 . . . . . 29-32R
Obituary 110
Jones, Charles 1910- CAP-1
Earlier sketch in CA 9-10
Jones, Charles Alfred 1921-1982 Obituary . . 107
Jones, Charles C., Jr. 1831-1893 . . . . . DLB-30
Jones, Charles Edwin 1932- CANR-23
Earlier sketch in CA 49-52
Jones, Charles O(scar) 1931- CANR-7
Earlier sketch in CA 19-20R
Jones, Charles W(illiams) 1905- 15-16R
Jones, Christina Hendry 1896- 73-76
Jones, (Audrey) Christine 1937- 61-64
Jones, Christopher 1937- 23-24R
Jones, Clarence Medlycott 1913(?)-1986
Obituary 118
Jones, Clifford M(erton) 1902- 17-18R
Jones, Craig 1945- 81-84
Jones, Cranston E. 1918- 2R
Jones, Cyril Meredith 1904- CAP-2
Earlier sketch in CA 23-24
Jones, D(ennis) F(eltham) Brief entry 111
Jones, D(ouglas) G(ordon) 1929- CANR-13
Earlier sketch in CA 29-32R
See also DLB 53
See also CLC 10
Jones, D(avid) Gareth 1940- 106
Jones, D(onald) L(ewis) 1925- 25-28R
Jones, D(avid) Mervyn 1922- 21-22R
Jones, Daisy (Marvel) 1906- 17-18R
Jones, Dan Burne 1908- 65-68
Jones, Daniel 1881-1967 . . . . . CANR-6
Earlier sketch in CA 5-6R
Jones, David 1895-1974 . . . . . 9-10R
Obituary 53-56
See also DLB 20
See also CLC 2, 4, 7, 13, 42
Jones, David Arthur 1946- CANR-13
Earlier sketch in CA 73-76
Jones, David Pryce
See Pryce-Jones, David
Jones, David Rhodes 1932- 101
Jones, David Robert 1947- 103
Jones, Diana Wynne 1934- CANR-4
Earlier sketch in CA 49-52
See also SATA 9
See also CLC 26
Jones, Dolores Blythe 1947- 120
Jones, (Gene) Donald 1931- CANR-15
Earlier sketch in CA 85-88
Jones, Donald (Lawrence) 1938- 19-20R
Jones, Dorothy Holder 9-10R
Jones, Douglas C(lyde) 1924- CANR-12
Earlier sketch in CA 21-22R
Jones, Duane
See Jones, Dorothy Holder
Jones, DuPre Anderson 1937- 21-22R
Jones, E(li) Stanley 1884-1973 93-96
Obituary 41-44R
Jones, E(ndsley) Terrence 1941- 33-36R
Jones, E(lbert) Winston 1911- 13-14R
Jones, Ebenezer 1820-1860 . . . . . DLB-32
Jones, (Hilary) Edgar 1953- 118
Jones, Edgar A(llen), Jr. 1921- 89-92
Jones, Edward A(llen) 1903- 25-28R
Jones, Edward E(llsworth) 1926- 17-18R
Jones, Edward H(arral), Jr. 1922- 15-16R
Jones, Eldred D(urosimi) 1925- 45-48
Jones, Elizabeth B(rown) 1907- 61-64
Jones, Elizabeth Orton 1910- 77-80
See also SATA 18
Jones, Elwyn 1923-1982 . . . . . CANR-21
Obituary 106
Earlier sketch in CA 69-72
Jones, Emlyn (David) 1912-1975 . . . . . CAP-2
Earlier sketch in CA 23-24
Jones, Emrys 1920- 17-18R
Jones, Enid (Mary) Huws 1911- 49-52
Jones, Eric Lionel 1936- 104
Jones, Ernest 1819-1868 . . . . . DLB-32
Jones, (Alfred) Ernest 1879-1958
Brief entry 121
Jones, Evan 1915- CANR-6
Earlier sketch in CA 9-10R
See also SATA 3
Jones, Evan David 1903-1987 Obituary 122
Jones, Eve (Spiro-John) 1924- 2R
Jones, Everett L(ee) 1915- 15-16R
Jones, Ezra Earl 1939- 57-60
Jones, F(rank) Lancaster 1937- 29-32R
Jones, Faustine Childress 1927- 77-80
Jones, Felix Edward Aylmer 1889- CAP-1
Earlier sketch in CA 9-10
Jones, Francis P(rice) 1890- 9-10R
Jones, Frank 1937- 119
Jones, Frank E(dward) 1917- 15-16R
Jones, Frank Pierce 1905-1975 Obituary . . . 110
Jones, Franklin Ross 1921- 53-56
Jones, Frederick George Hall
See Hall-Jones, Frederick George
Jones, G(eorge) Curtis 1911- CANR-3
Earlier sketch in CA 5-6R
Jones, G(wyn) O(wain) 1917- 25-28R
Jones, G(eorge) William 1931- CANR-11
Earlier sketch in CA 21-22R
Jones, Gareth (Elwyn) 1939- CANR-19
Earlier sketch in CA 102
Jones, Garth N(elson) 1925- 81-84
Jones, Gary M(artin) 1925- 19-20R
Jones, Gayl 1949- 77-80
See also DLB 33
See also CLC 6, 9
Jones, Gene 1928- 21-22R
Jones, Geoffrey (Gareth) 1952- 122
Jones, George Chetwynd Griffith
See Griffith-Jones, George Chetwynd
Jones, George Fenwick 1916- CANR-7
Earlier sketch in CA 13-14R
Jones, George Hilton 1924- 33-36R
Jones, George Thaddeus 1917- 53-56
Jones, Geraldine 1951- SATA-43
Jones, Geraldine
See McCaughrean, Geraldine
Jones, Gillingham
See Hamilton, Charles Harold St. John
Jones, (Morgan) Glyn 1905- CANR-3
Earlier sketch in CA 9-10R
See also DLB 15
Jones, Gordon W(illis) 1915- 45-48
Jones, Goronwy J(ohn) 1915- 11-12R
Jones, Guy Salisbury
See Salisbury-Jones, Guy
Jones, Gwen 1951(?)-1988 Obituary 124
Jones, Gwendolyn 33-36R
Jones, Gwilym Peredur 1892-1975
Obituary 57-60
Jones, Gwyn 1907- 124
Brief entry 117
See also DLB 15

Jones, Gwyneth A. 1952- 107
Jones, H(ouston) G(wynne) 1924- CANR-13
Earlier sketch in CA 33-36R
Jones, H(enry) John F(ranklin) 1924- 9-10R
Jones, Hardin Blair 1914-1978 Obituary 77-80
Jones, Harold 1904- CANR-15
Earlier sketch in CA 85-88
See also SATA 14
Jones, Harold
See Page, Gerald W(ilburn)
Jones, Harriet
See Marble, Harriet Clement
Jones, Harry Lee 1921(?)-1983 Obituary 110
Jones, Helen 1917- 105
Jones, Helen Hinckley 1903- CANR-5
Earlier sketch in CA 7-8R
See also SATA 26
Jones, Helen L(ouise) 1903-1973
Obituary 104
See also SATA 22
Jones, (Max Him) Henri 1921- 41-44R
Jones, Henry Albert 1889-1981 Obituary 103
Jones, Henry Arthur 1851-1929
Brief entry 110
See also DLB 10
Jones, Hettie 1934- 81-84
See also SATA 27, 42
Jones, Hortense P. 1918- 61-64
See also SATA 9
Jones, Howard 1940- 85-88
Jones, Howard Mumford 1892-1980 85-88
Obituary 97-100
Jones, Howard P(alfry) 1899-1973
Obituary 111
Jones, Hugh 1692(?)-1760 .... DLB-24
Jones, Iris Sanderson 1932- 73-76
Jones, J. Farragut
See Levinson, Leonard
and Streib, Dan(iel Thomas)
Jones, J(ohn) Ithel 1911- CAP-2
Earlier sketch in CA 25-28
Jones, Jack 1884-1970 Obituary 115
Jones, Jack 1913-1984 Obituary 113
Brief entry 109
Jones, Jack 1924- 85-88
Jones, Jack
See Jones, James Larkin
Jones, Jacqueline 1948- 122
Jones, James 1921-1977 .... CANR-6
Obituary 69-72
Earlier sketch in CA 2R
See also DLB 2
See also CLC 1, 3, 10, 39
See also AITN 1, 2
Jones, James C(linton) 1922- 69-72
Jones, James Henry 1907(?)-1977
Obituary 73-76
Jones, James Larkin 1913- 109
Jones, James T. 1948- 124
Jones, Jeanie Schmit Kayser
See Kayser-Jones, Jeanie Schmit
Jones, Jeanne 1937- CANR-12
Earlier sketch in CA 61-64
Jones, Jeannette 1944- 110
Jones, Jenkin Lloyd 1911- 9-10R
Jones, Jessie Mae Orton 1887(?)-1983
Obituary 111
See also SATA 37
Jones, Jimmy
See Jones, Clarence Medlycott
Jones, Jo 33-36R
Jones, Joanna
See Burke, John (Frederick)
Jones, Johanna 1909- 118
Jones, John Bush 1940- 33-36R
Jones, John Griffin 1955- 113
Jones, John J.
See Lovecraft, H(oward) P(hillips)
Jones, John Paul, Jr. 1912- CANR-11
Earlier sketch in CA 69-72
Jones, John R(obert) 1926- 116
Jones, Joseph Jay 1908- CANR-16
Earlier sketches in CA 1R, CANR-1
Jones, Joseph L. 1897-1980 Obituary 102
Jones, Judith Paterson 1938- 106
Jones, K. Westcott
See Westcott-Jones, K(enneth)
Jones, Karen Midkiff 1948- 104
Jones, Katharine M(acbeth) 1900- 7-8R
Jones, Kathleen 1922- 81-84
Jones, Kathleen Eve 1944- 102
Jones, Kaylie (Ann) 1960- 123
Jones, Ken D(uane) 1930- 49-52
Jones, Kenley 1935- 69-72
Jones, Kenneth E(ffner) 1920- 57-60
Jones, Kenneth Glyn 1915- 115
Jones, Kenneth LaMar 1931- 53-56
Jones, Kenneth S. 1919- 21-22R
Jones, Kenneth W. 1934- Brief entry 113
Jones, Landon Y(oung) 1943- 105
Jones, Leon 1936- 101
Jones, Leonidas M(onroe), Sr. 1923- 45-48
Jones, (Everett) LeRoi 1934- 21-22R
See also CLC 1, 2, 3, 5, 10, 14
Jones, Leroy P. 1941- 118
Jones, Lewis 1897-1939 .... DLB-15
Jones, Lewis Pinckney 1916- 61-64
Jones, Linda Phillips
See Phillips-Jones, Linda
Jones, Lloyd S(cott) 1931- CANR-4
Earlier sketch in CA 4R
Jones, Louis C(lark) 1908- 5-6R
Jones, Lyndon Hamer 1927- CANR-22
Earlier sketch in CA 103
Jones, M(arjorie) L(ilian) Glynne
See Glynne-Jones, M(arjorie) L(ilian)
Jones, Madeline Adams 1913- 23-24R
Jones, Madison (Percy, Jr.) 1925- CANR-7
Earlier sketch in CA 13-14R
See also CLC 4
Jones, Major J. 1919- 33-36R
Jones, Major Joseph
See Thompson, William Tappan
Jones, Malcolm V(ince) 1940- 103
Jones, Maldwyn Allen 1922- CANR-4
Earlier sketch in CA 1R
Jones, Marc Edmund 1888- 33-36R
Jones, Margaret Boone 25-28R
Jones, Margaret E. W. 1938- 37-40R
Jones, Marvin 1886-1976 Obituary 65-68
Jones, Mary (Elizabeth) 1942- 120
Jones, Mary Alice 1898(?)-1980 .... 19-20R
Obituary 118
See also SATA 6
Jones, Mary Brush 1925- 25-28R
Jones, Mary Voell 1933- 21-22R
Jones, Maxwell (Shaw) 1907- 25-28R
Jones, Maynard Benedict 1904-1972
Obituary 93-96
Jones, McClure 112
See also SATA 34
Jones, Mervyn 1922- CANR-1
Earlier sketch in CA 45-48
See also CAAS 5
See also CLC 10
Jones, Michael (Christopher Emlyn)
1940- CANR-20
Earlier sketch in CA 104
Jones, Michael Owen 1942- 101
Jones, Mick 1956(?)- CLC-30
Jones, Miriam
See Schuchman, Joan
Jones, Morris Val 1914- 7-8R
Jones, Nard
See Jones, Maynard Benedict
Jones, Nettie 19(?)- CLC-34
Jones, Noel 1939- 81-84
Jones, O(wen) R(ogers) 1922- 2R
Jones, Oakah L., Jr. 1930- CANR-8
Earlier sketch in CA 17-18R
Jones, Orlando
See Looker, Antonina (Hansell)
Jones, P(eter) M(ichael) 1949- 122
Jones, Pat
See Jones, Virgil Carrington
Jones, Paul Davis 1940- 49-52
Jones, Paul J. 1897(?)-1974 Obituary 53-56
Jones, Pearl Binder Elwyn
See Elwyn-Jones, Pearl Binder
Jones, Peggy 1947- 109
Jones, Penelope 1938- CANR-14
Earlier sketch in CA 81-84
See also SATA 31
Jones, Peter 1920- 103
Jones, Peter 1921- 7-8R
Jones, Peter (Austin) 1929- CANR-4
Earlier sketch in CA 53-56
Jones, Peter d'Alroy 1931- CANR-20
Earlier sketches in CA 7-8R, CANR-3
Jones, Peter Gaylord 1929- 73-76
Jones, Philip Howard 1937- 102
Jones, Phillip L. 1928(?)-1979 Obituary 89-92
Jones, Pirkle 1914- 29-32R
Jones, Preston 1936-1979 73-76
Obituary 89-92
See also DLB 7
See also CLC 10
Jones, R(ichard) Ben(jamin) 1933- CANR-12
Earlier sketch in CA 25-28R
Jones, Ray O. 1930- 89-92
Jones, Raymond F. 1915- Brief entry 106
Jones, Rebecca C(astaldi) 1947- CANR-22
Earlier sketch in CA 106
See also SATA 33
Jones, Reginald L(anier) 1931- 45-48
Jones, Reginald Victor 1911- 103
Jones, Richard 1926- CANR-2
Earlier sketch in CA 49-52
Jones, Richard 1953- 121
Jones, Richard Allan 1943- 103
Jones, Richard Granville 1926- 112
Jones, Richard H(utton) 1914- 49-52
Jones, Richard M(atthew) 1925- 93-96
Jones, Robert B(rinkley) 1942- 114
Jones, Robert Emmet 1928- CANR-2
Earlier sketch in CA 1R
Jones, Robert Epes 1908- CAP-1
Earlier sketch in CA 13-14
Jones, Robert F(rancis) 1934- CANR-2
Earlier sketch in CA 49-52
See also CLC 7
Jones, Robert H(uhn) 1927- CANR-2
Earlier sketch in CA 5-6R
Jones, Robert O(wen) 1928- 29-32R
Jones, Robert R(ussell) 1927- 69-72
Jones, Robert Reynolds, Jr. 1911- CANR-11
Earlier sketch in CA 25-28R
Jones, Robert Tyre, Jr. 1902-1971
Obituary 113
Jones, Robin Lloyd
See Lloyd-Jones, Robin
Jones, Rodney W(illiam) 1943- 113
Jones, Roger (Winston) 1939- 101
Jones, Roger Stanley 1934- 113
Jones, Royston Oscar 1925-1974 85-88
Jones, Ruby Aileen Hiday 1908- CAP-1
Earlier sketch in CA 11-12
Jones, Russell 1918-1979 106
Obituary 89-92
Jones, Russell Bradley 1894- 3R
Jones, Ruth Ann 1928- 107
Jones, Ruth Dorval 93-96
Jones, Sally Roberts 1935- 102
Jones, Sandy 1943- CANR-15
Earlier sketch in CA 85-88
Jones, Sanford W.
See Thorn, John
Jones, Scott N. 1929- 29-32R
Jones, Seaborn (Gustavus), Jr. 1942- 104
Jones, Stacy V(anderhoof) 1894- 3R
Jones, Stanley L(lewellyn) 1918- 9-10R
Jones, Stephen (Phillip) 1935- CANR-2
Earlier sketch in CA 49-52
Jones, Stephen D(wight) 1948- 112
Jones, T(homas) Anthony 1940- 110
Jones, Terry 1942- 116
Brief entry 112
See also CLC 21
Jones, Thomas B. 1929- 25-28R
Jones, Thomas M(artin) 1916- 29-32R
Jones, Thomas W(arren) 1947- 53-56
Jones, Tim(othy) Wynne
See Wynne-Jones, Tim(othy)
Jones, Tom 1928- CANR-6
Earlier sketch in CA 53-56
Jones, Tony Armstrong
See Armstrong-Jones, Antony (Charles Robert)
Jones, Trevor Arthur 1936- 105
Jones, Trevor David 1908-1984 Obituary 114
Jones, Tristan 1924- 73-76
Jones, Turkel
See McKimmey, James
Jones, Vane A. 1917- 21-22R
Jones, Vernon 1897- 53-56
Jones, (Charles) Victor 1919- 7-8R
Jones, Virgil Carrington 1906- CANR-2
Earlier sketch in CA 2R
Jones, Volcano
See Mitchell, Adrian
Jones, W(alton) Glyn 1928- 49-52
Jones, W(alter) Paul 1891- CAP-1
Earlier sketch in CA 11-12
Jones, W(illiam) T(homas) 1910- 37-40R
Jones, Walter Benton 1893- 2R
Jones, Webb
See Henley, Arthur
Jones, Weyman (B.) 1928- 19-20R
See also SATA 4
Jones, Wilbur Devereux 1916- CANR-2
Earlier sketch in CA 1R
Jones, William Alfred 1817-1900 .... DLB-59
Jones, William David Anthony 1946- 113
Jones, William Glynne
See Glynne-Jones, William
Jones, William H(ugh) 1939-1982 112
Obituary 108
Jones, William M(cKendrey) 1927- CANR-7
Earlier sketch in CA 61-64
Jones, William Monarch
See Guthrie, Thomas Anstey
Jones, William P(owell) 1901- 4R
Jones, William R(onald) 1933- 104
Jones, Willis Knapp 1895- 13-14R
Jones, Zelda
See Schuchman, Joan
Jones-Evans, Eric 1898- 21-22R
Jones-Jackson, Pat
See Jones-Jackson, Patricia
Jones-Jackson, Patricia 1946-1986
Obituary 124
Jones-Ryan, Maureen 1943- 93-96
Jong, Erica 1942- 73-76
See also DLB 2, 5, 28
See also CLC 4, 6, 8, 18
See also AITN 1
Jongeward, Dorothy 1925- CANR-3
Earlier sketch in CA 49-52
Jonk, Clarence 1906- 5-6R
See also SATA 10
Jonnes, Jill 1952- 121
Jonsen, Albert R(upert) 1931- CANR-11
Earlier sketch in CA 25-28R
Jonson, Ben 1572(?)-1637 .... DLB-62
Jonsson, Snaebjorn 1888(?)-1978
Obituary 81-84
Joos, Martin (George) 1907- CAP-1
Earlier sketch in CA 15-16
Joosse, Barbara M(onnot) 1949- 109
Joost, Nicholas (Teynac) 1916-1980 .... 15-16R
Obituary 97-100
Joplin, Scott 1868-1917 Brief entry 123
Jopp, Hal
See Jopp, Harold Dowling, Jr.
Jopp, Harold Dowling, Jr. 1946- 57-60
Joralemon, Ira B(eaman) 1884-1975
Obituary 61-64
Joravsky, David 1925- CANR-2
Earlier sketch in CA 1R
Jordan, Alexis Hill
See Glick, Ruth (Burtnick)
Jordan, Alexis Hill
See Titchener, Louise
Jordan, Alma Theodora 1929- 33-36R
Jordan, Amos A(zariah) 1922- 33-36R
Jordan, Barbara (Charline) 1936- 123
Brief entry 113
Jordan, Bill
See Jordan, William
Jordan, Borimir 1933- 89-92
Jordan, Carrie
See Cudlipp, Edythe
Jordan, Clarence L(eonard) 1912-1969 .... CAP-2
Earlier sketch in CA 23-24
Jordan, Dale R(oderick) 1931- 45-48
Jordan, David K. 1942- 61-64
Jordan, David M(alcolm) 1935- 33-36R
Jordan, David P(aul) 1939- 57-60
Jordan, David William 1940- 93-96
Jordan, Don
See Howard, Vernon (Linwood)
Jordan, Donald A. 1936- 65-68
Jordan, E(mil) L(eopold) 1900- SATA-31
Jordan, Franklin Everard 1904(?)-1983
Obituary 110
Jordan, Gail
See Dern, Erolie Pearl Gaddis
Jordan, Gerald Ray 1896-1964 .... CAP-1
Earlier sketch in CA 13-14
Jordan, Gilbert John 1902- 49-52
Jordan, Gill
See Gilbert, George
Jordan, Grace Edgington CANR-2
Earlier sketch in CA 4R
Jordan, Hope Dahle 1905- CANR-13
Earlier sketch in CA 77-80
See also SATA 15
Jordan, Jael (Michal) 1949- SATA-30
Jordan, John 1930- 103
Jordan, John E(mory) 1919- CANR-20
Earlier sketch in CA 1R
Jordan, June 1936- 33-36R
See also SATA 4
See also DLB 38
See also CLC 5, 11, 23
See also CLR 10
Jordan, Leonard
See Levinson, Leonard
Jordan, Lewis 1912-1983 Obituary 111
Jordan, Lois B(reedlove) 1912- 57-60
Jordan, Mildred 1901- CAP-2
Earlier sketch in CA 25-28
See also SATA 5
Jordan, Mildred Arlene 1918- 110
Jordan, Monica
See Caruba, Alan
Jordan, Neil 1950(?)- Brief entry 124
Jordan, Norman 1938- 33-36R
Jordan, Pascual 1902-1982(?) Obituary 112
Jordan, Pat(rick M.) 1941- 33-36R
See also CLC 37
Jordan, Philip D(ean) 1940- 110
Jordan, Philip Dillon 1903- 11-12R
Jordan, Robert Paul 1921- 29-32R
Jordan, Robert S(mith) 1929- CANR-1
Earlier sketch in CA 45-48
Jordan, Robin 1947- 65-68
Jordan, Ruth 1926- CANR-7
Earlier sketch in CA 57-60
Jordan, Stello 1914- 29-32R
Jordan, Terry G(ilbert) 1938- CANR-9
Earlier sketch in CA 21-22R
Jordan, Thomas E(dward) 1929- 120
Jordan, Thurston C., Jr. 1940- 25-28R
Jordan, Wayne 1903(?)-1979 Obituary 85-88
Jordan, Weymouth T(yree) 1912-1968 .... CAP-2
Earlier sketch in CA 17-18
Jordan, Wilbur K(itchener) 1902-1980 .... CANR-5
Obituary 97-100
Earlier sketch in CA 5-6R
Jordan, William 1941- Brief entry 118
Jordan, William A. 1928- 33-36R
Jordan, William H., Jr. 1944- 114
Jordan, William J(ohnston) 1924- 114
Jordan, William S(tone), Jr. 1917- 15-16R
Jordan, Winthrop D(onaldson) 1931- 25-28R
Jordan, Z(bigniew) A(ntoni) 1911-1977 .... 25-28R
Obituary 89-92
Jordan-Smith, Paul 1885(?)-1971
Obituary 104
Jorden, Eleanor Harz CANR-8
Earlier sketch in CA 7-8R
Jordy, William H(enry) 1917- 3R
Jorgens, Jack J(ohnstone) 1943- 65-68
Jorgensen, Ivar
See Ellison, Harlan
and Fairman, Paul W.
Jorgensen, James (Aleck) 1931- CANR-19
Earlier sketch in CA 103
Jorgensen, James D(ale) 1932- 41-44R
Jorgensen, Joseph G(ilbert) 1934- CANR-7
Earlier sketch in CA 61-64
Jorgensen, Mary Venn CANR-1
Earlier sketch in CA 2R
See also SATA 36
Jorgensen, Neil 1934- 53-56
Jorgenson, Ivar
See Silverberg, Robert
Jorn, Asger 1914-1973 Obituary 41-44R
Jorstad, Erling (Theodore) 1930- CANR-12
Earlier sketch in CA 29-32R
Joscelyn, Archie L. 1899- CANR-5
Earlier sketch in CA 3R
Jose, F(rancisco) Sionil
See Sionil Jose, F(rancisco)
Jose, James R(obert) 1939- 29-32R
Josefowitz, Natasha 1926- 114
Josefsberg, Milt 1911-1987 81-84
Obituary 124
Joselovitz, Ernest A. 1942- 108
Joselow, Beth Baruch 1948- 114
Joseph, Alexander 1907-1976 .... 13-14R
Obituary 120
Joseph, Bertram L(eon) 1915-1981 .... CANR-6
Obituary 104
Earlier sketch in CA 7-8R
Joseph, David I(glauer) 1941- 9-10R
Joseph, Dov 1899-1980 Obituary 93-96
Joseph, Franz
See Schnaubelt, Franz Joseph
Joseph, James (Herz) 1924- CANR-2
Earlier sketch in CA 4R
Joseph, Jenny 1932- 107
See also DLB 40

Joseph, Joan 1939- ... CANR-17
Earlier sketch in CA 25-28R
See also SATA 34
Joseph, John 1923- ... 1R
Joseph, Jonathan
See Fineman, Irving
Joseph, Joseph M(aron) 1903-1979 ... 5-6R
See also SATA 22
Joseph, M(ichael) K(ennedy)
1914-1981 ... CANR-6
Earlier sketch in CA 9-10R
Joseph, Marie ... 109
Joseph, Marjory L(ockwood) 1917- ... 77-80
Joseph, Mark (Chester) 1946- ... 120
Joseph, Richard 1910-1976 ... CANR-6
Obituary ... 69-72
Earlier sketch in CA 3R
Joseph, Stephen 1921-1967 ... 11-12R
Obituary ... 103
Joseph, Stephen M. 1938- ... 25-28R
Joseph, William A(llen) 1947- ... 118
Josephs, Ray 1912- ... 9-10R
Josephs, Stephen
See Dolmatch, Theodore B(ieley)
Josephson, Clifford A. 1922- ... 19-20R
Josephson, Elmer A. 1909- ... 121
Josephson, Halsey D. 1906(?)-1977
Obituary ... 69-72
Josephson, Hannah 1900-1976 ... CAP-2
Obituary ... 69-72
Earlier sketch in CA 29-32
Josephson, Harold 1942- ... 61-64
Josephson, Matthew 1899-1978 ... 81-84
Obituary ... 77-80
See also DLB 4
Josephy, Alvin M., Jr. 1915- ... CANR-8
Earlier sketch in CA 19-20R
Josey, E(lonnie) J(unius) 1924- ... 29-32R
Joshee, O(m) K(umar) 1934- ... 117
Joshi, Irene M(arian) 1934- ... 110
Joshi, Shivkumar 1916- ... 77-80
Joshua, Wynfred 1930- ... 29-32R
Josiah Allen's Wife
See Holley, Marietta
Josipovici, Gabriel 1940- ... 37-40R
See also DLB 14
See also CLC 6, 43
Joskow, Paul L. 1947- ... 124
Joslin, Sesyle
See Hine, Sesyle Joslin
See also SATA 2
Jospe, Alfred 1909- ... 106
Joss, John 1934- ... 101
Josselyn, John ?-1675 ... DLB-24
Josten, Josef 1913-1985 Obituary ... 118
Joubert, Andre J. 1924- ... 49-52
Joubert, Ingrid 1942- ... 110
Joudry, Patricia 1921- ... 65-68
Jouhandeau, Marcel Henri 1888-1979
Obituary ... 85-88
Jourard, Sidney M(arshall) 1926-1974 .. CANR-6
Obituary ... 53-56
Earlier sketch in CA 7-8R
Jourdain, Alice M. 1923- ... 53-56
Jourdain, Rose (Leonora) 1932- ... 89-92
Journet, Charles 1891-1975 ... 65-68
Obituary ... 57-60
Journlet, Marie de
See Little, Paul H(ugo)
Jouve, Pierre Jean 1887-1976 Obituary ... 65-68
See also CLC 47
Jouvenel, Bertrand de
See de Jouvenel des Ursins, Edouard
Bertrand
Jouvet, Jean
See Strich, Christian
Jovanovich, William (Iliya) 1920- ... 107
Jowett, Garth Samuel 1940- ... CANR-10
Earlier sketch in CA 65-68
Jowett, Paul (Melville) 1959- ... 120
Jowitt, Deborah 1934- ... 103
Joy, Barbara Ellen 1898- ... 7-8R
Joy, David Anthony Welton 1942- ... CANR-20
Earlier sketch in CA 103
Joy, Donald Marvin 1928- ... 15-16R
Joy, Edward T(homas) 1909- ... 9-10R
Joy, Kenneth Ernest 1908- ... CAP-2
Earlier sketch in CA 23-24
Joy, Thomas Alfred 1904- ... 102
Joyce, Adrien
See Eastman, Carol
Joyce, Bill
See Joyce, William
Joyce, Brian T(homas) 1938- ... 106
Joyce, Bruce R(ogers) 1930- Brief entry ... 114
Joyce, Ernest 1899-1975 ... CAP-2
Earlier sketch in CA 33-36
Joyce, J(ames) Avery 1902-1987 ... CANR-10
Obituary ... 121
Earlier sketch in CA 65-68
See also SATA 11, 50
Joyce, James (Augustus Aloysius)
1882-1941 Brief entry ... 104
See also DLB 10, 19, 36
See also TCLC 3, 8, 16
Joyce, James Daniel 1921- ... 9-10R
Joyce, Jon L(oyd) 1937- ... CANR-10
Earlier sketch in CA 65-68
Joyce, Julia
See Tetel, Julie
Joyce, Mary Rosera 1930- ... 29-32R
Joyce, R(oger) B(ilbrough) 1924- ... CANR-1
Earlier sketch in CA 45-48
Joyce, Robert E(dward) 1934- ... 29-32R
Joyce, William 1959(?)- ... 124
See also SATA 46
Joyce, William L(eonard) 1942- ... 111
Joyce, William W(alter) 1934- ... CANR-15
Earlier sketch in CA 85-88
Joyner, Charles W. 1935- ... 37-40R
Joyner, Jerry 1938- ... 107
See also SATA 34
Joyner, William T. 1934- ... 23-24R
Joynson, R(obert) B(illington) 1922- ... 57-60
Joynt, Carey Bonthron 1924- ... 124
Joynt, Robert R(ichard) 1915- ... 106
Jozsef, Attila 1905-1937 Brief entry ... 116
See also TCLC 22
Jucker, Sita 1921- ... CANR-12
Earlier sketch in CA 29-32R
See also SATA 5
Jucovy, Milton Edward 1918- ... 109
Juda, L(yon) 1923- ... 11-12R
Judah, Aaron 1923- ... 103
Judah, J(ay) Stillson 1911- ... 21-22R
Judd, Cyril
See Kornbluth, C(yril) M.
and Merril, Judith
and Pohl, Frederik
Judd, Deane B(rewster) 1900-1972 ... CAP-1
Earlier sketch in CA 13-14
Judd, Denis (O'Nan) 1938- ... CANR-13
Earlier sketch in CA 25-28R
See also SATA 33
Judd, Dennis R. 1943- ... CANR-16
Earlier sketch in CA 93-96
Judd, Frances K. ... CAP-2
Earlier sketch in CA 19-20
See also SATA 1
Judd, Frederick Charles 1914- ... CANR-6
Earlier sketch in CA 7-8R
Judd, Gerrit P(armele) 1915-1971 ... 5-6R
Obituary ... 29-32R
Judd, H(oward) Stanley 1936- ... CANR-21
Earlier sketch in CA 69-72
Judd, Harrison
See Daniels, Norman
Judd, Larry R. 1937- ... 45-48
Judd, Margaret Haddican 1906- ... 5-6R
Judd, Robert 1939- ... 85-88
Judd, Sara (Hutton) Bowen
See Bowen-Judd, Sara (Hutton)
Judd, Sylvester 1813-1853 ... DLB-1
Judelle, Beatrice 1908- ... 33-36R
Judge, Harry George 1928- ... 124
Judson, Clara Ingram 1879-1960 ... SATA-27, 38
Judson, David (Malcolm) 1941- ... 93-96
Judson, Horace Freeland 1931- ... 89-92
Judson, John 1930- ... CANR-12
Earlier sketch in CA 13-14R
Judson, Lewis Van Hagen 1893-1973
Obituary ... 41-44R
Judson, Margaret Atwood 1899- ... 102
Judson, Sylvia Shaw 1897- ... 41-44R
Judson, William
See Corley, Edwin (Raymond)
Judy, Marvin T(hornton) 1911- ... 33-36R
Judy, Stephen
See Tchudi, Stephen N.
Judy, Stephen N.
See Tchudi, Stephen N.
Judy, Susan J(ane) 1944- ... 107
Judy, Will(iam Lewis) 1891- ... 7-8R
Juel, Donald H. 1942- ... 114
Juel-Nielsen, Niels 1920- ... 106
Juengel, Eberhard 1934- Brief entry ... 118
Juenger, Ernst 1895- ... CANR-21
Earlier sketch in CA 101
See also DLB 56
Juergens, George Ivar 1932- ... 109
Juergensen, Hans 1919- ... CANR-8
Earlier sketch in CA 21-22R
Juergensmeyer, Jane Stuart
See Stuart, Jane
Juergensmeyer, John Eli 1934- ... 41-44R
Juhasz, Anne McCreary 1922- ... 53-56
Juhasz, Leslie A.
See Shepard, Leslie Albert
Juhasz, Suzanne 1942- ... 85-88
Jukes, (James Thomas) Geoffrey 1928- .. 29-32R
Jukes, Mavis 1947- Brief entry ... 121
See also SATA 43
Jukic, Ilija 1901-1977 ... 49-52
Obituary ... 103
Julesberg, Elizabeth Rider Montgomery
1902-1985 ... CANR-3
Obituary ... 115
Earlier sketch in CA 2R
See also SATA 3, 34
Jules-Rosette, Bennetta (Washington)
1948- ... 112
Juliard, Pierre 1939- ... 41-44R
Julie
See Robbins, June
Julien, Charles-Andre 1891- ... 103
Julie of Colorado Springs
See Robbins, June
Julier, Virginia Cheatham 1918- ... 5-6R
Julin, Joseph R. 1926- ... 37-40R
Juline, Ruth Bishop
See Ritchie, Ruth
Julitte, Pierre (Gaston Louis) 1910- ... 37-40R
Julius
See Curling, Bryan William Richard
Jullian, Philippe 1919-1977 ... 73-76
Julty, Sam 1927- ... 61-64
July, Robert W(illiam) 1918- ... 41-44R
Jumper, Andrew Albert 1927- ... 17-18R
Jumpp, Hugo
See MacPeek, Walter G.
Jun, Jong S(up) 1936- ... 53-56
June, Jennie
See Croly, Jane Cunningham
Jung, C(arl) G(ustav) 1875-1961 ... 117
Jung, Hwa Yol 1932- ... 37-40R
Jung, John A. 1937- ... 17-18R
Jung, Leo 1892-1987 Obituary ... 124
Junge, Mark G(ene) 1943- ... 122
Jungel, Eberhard
See Juengel, Eberhard
Junger, Ernst
See Juenger, Ernst
See also DLB 56
Jungk, Robert 1913- ... 85-88
Jungle Doctor
See White, Paul Hamilton Hume
Jungreis, Esther 1936- ... 110
Juniper, D(ean) F(rancis) 1929- ... CANR-18
Earlier sketch in CA 97-100
Junius
See Luxemburg, Rosa
Junker, Karin Stensland 1916- ... CANR-3
Earlier sketch in CA 11-12R
Junkins, Donald 1931- ... 33-36R
Junor, John 1919- ... 108
Jupo, Frank J. 1904- ... CANR-2
Earlier sketch in CA 7-8R
See also SATA 7
Jupp, James 1932- ... CANR-11
Earlier sketch in CA 23-24R
Jupp, Kenneth 1939- ... 65-68
Juptner, Joseph Paul 1913- ... 7-8R
Jur, Jerzy
See Lerski, George Jan
Jurek, Martin 1942- ... 77-80
Jurgela, Constantine R. 1904-1988
Obituary ... 124
Jurgens, Curt 1912-1982 Obituary ... 107
Jurgens, W(illiam) A(nthony) 1928- ... 41-44R
Jurgensen, Barbara (Bitting) 1928- ... 19-20R
Juris, Hervey A(sher) 1938- ... CANR-5
Earlier sketch in CA 53-56
Jurjevich, Ratibor-Ray (Momchila)
1915- ... 37-40R
Jurji, Edward J. 1907- ... 15-16R
Jurnak, Sheila
See Raeschild, Sheila
Jussim, Estelle 1927- ... 81-84
Just, Ward S(wift) 1935- ... 25-28R
See also CLC 4, 27
Juster, F. Thomas 1926- ... CANR-2
Earlier sketch in CA 45-48
Juster, Norton 1929- ... CANR-13
Earlier sketch in CA 13-14R
See also SATA 3
Justice, Blair 1927- ... CANR-1
Earlier sketch in CA 45-48
Justice, Donald (Rodney) 1925- ... 7-8R
See also DLBY 83
See also CLC 6, 19
Justice, William G(ross), Jr. 1930- ... CANR-20
Earlier sketches in CA 53-56, CANR-5
Justiciar
See Powell-Smith, Vincent (Walter
Francis)
Justus, May 1898- ... 9-10R
See also SATA 1
Juta, Jan 1895- ... 49-52
Juta, Rene
See Juta, Jan
Jutikkala, Eino Kaarlo Ilmari 1907- ... CAP-1
Earlier sketch in CA 9-10
Jutson, Mary Carolyn Hollers
See George, Mary Carolyn Hollers Jutson
Juvenilia
See Taylor, Ann
Juvenis
See Bourne, Randolph S(illiman)
Juviler, Peter H(enry) 1926- ... 77-80
Jwaideh, Nizar 1933(?)-1988 Obituary ... 124

K

Kaapu, Myrtle King 1898-1985 Obituary ... 119
Kaba, Lansine 1941- ... 61-64
Kabadi, Sunder 1898(?)-1983 Obituary ... 111
Kabaphe, Konstantinos Petrou
See Kavafis, Konstantinos Petrou
Kabaphes, Konstantinos Petrou
See Kavafis, Konstantinos Petrou
Kabasele, Joseph
See Tshiamala, Kabasele
Kabdebo, Tamas
See Kabdebo, Thomas
Kabdebo, Thomas 1934- ... CANR-23
Earlier sketches in CA 53-56, CANR-7
See also SATA 10
Kabibble, Osh
See Jobb, Jamie
Kabotie, Fred 1900- ... 118
Kabraji, Fredoon 1897- ... CAP-1
Earlier sketch in CA 13-14
Kac, Arthur W(ayne) 1904- ... 117
Kac, Mark 1914-1984 Obituary ... 114
Kacew, Romain 1914-1980 ... 108
Obituary ... 102
Kacew, Roman
See Kacew, Romain
Kachru, Braj B(ehari) 1932- ... CANR-23
Earlier sketches in CA 61-64, CANR-8
Kaczer, Illes 1887- ... CAP-1
Earlier sketch in CA 9-10
Kadai, Heino Olavi 1931- ... 21-22R
Kadans, Joseph M(ichael) 1912- ... 118
Kadesch, Robert R(udstone) 1922- ... 57-60
See also SATA 31
Kadic, Ante 1910- Brief entry ... 107
Kadish, Ferne 1940- ... 61-64
Kadish, Mortimer Raymond 1916-
Brief entry ... 106
Kadler, Eric H(enry) 1922- ... 29-32R
Kadushin, Alfred 1916- ... 25-28R
Kadushin, Charles 1932- ... 25-28R
Kaegi, Walter Emil, Jr. 1937- ... CANR-10
Earlier sketch in CA 25-28R
Kael, Pauline 1919- ... CANR-6
Earlier sketch in CA 45-48
Kaelbling, Rudolf 1928- ... 19-20R
Kaelin, Eugene F(rancis) 1926- ... 45-48
Kaellberg, Sture 1928- ... 107
Kaempfert, Wade
See del Rey, Lester
Kaempffert, Waldemar (Bernhard)
1877-1956 Brief entry ... 113
Kaeppler, Adrienne Lois 1935- Brief entry ... 107
Kaese, Harold 1909(?)-1975 Obituary ... 57-60
Kaestle, Carl F(rederick) 1940- ... 85-88
Kaestner, Dorothy 1920- ... 61-64
Kaestner, Erich 1899-1974 ... 73-76
Obituary ... 49-52
See also SATA 14
See also DLB 56
See also CLR 4
Kaeuper, Richard W(illiam) 1941-
Brief entry ... 115
Kafe, Joseph Kofi Thompson 1933- ... 49-52
Kafka, Franz 1883-1924 Brief entry ... 105
See also TCLC 2, 6, 13
Kafka, Sherry 1937- ... 21-22R
Kafka, Vincent W(infield) 1924- ... 61-64
Kafker, Frank A. 1931- ... 37-40R
Kafu
See Nagai Sokichi
Kagan, Abram S. 1889(?)-1983 Obituary ... 111
Kagan, Andrew 1947- ... 123
Kagan, Benjamin 1914- ... 21-22R
Kagan, Donald 1932- ... CANR-9
Earlier sketch in CA 23-24R
Kagan, Jerome 1929- ... CANR-24
Earlier sketches in CA 7-8R, CANR-2
Kagan, Richard (Lauren) 1943- ... 57-60
Kagan, Richard C(lark) 1938- ... 53-56
Kagan-Kans, Eva 1928- ... 49-52
Kaganoff, Nathan M. 1926- Brief entry ... 108
Kagy, Frederick D(avid) 1917- ... 15-16R
Kahan, Gerald 1923- ... 33-36R
Kahan, Stanley 1931- ... 7-8R
Kahan, Stuart 1936- ... 93-96
Kahane, Howard 1928- ... CANR-1
Earlier sketch in CA 49-52
Kahane, Meir (David) 1932- Brief entry ... 112
Kahin, Audrey R. 1934- ... 121
Kahl, Ann Hammel 1929- ... 17-18R
Kahl, Joseph A(lan) 1923- Brief entry ... 109
Kahl, M(arvin) P(hilip) 1934- ... 107
See also SATA 37
Kahl, Virginia 1919- ... CANR-2
Earlier sketch in CA 49-52
See also SATA 38, 48
Kahle, Roger (Raymond) 1943- ... 33-36R
Kahlenberg, Mary Hunt 1940- ... CANR-2
Earlier sketch in CA 45-48
Kahler, Erich Gabriel 1885-1970 ... CANR-7
Obituary ... 29-32R
Earlier sketch in CA 5-6R
Kahler, Hugh (Torbert) MacNair
1883-1969 ... 102
Kahler, Woodland 1895- ... 3R
Kahm, H(arold) S. ... 101
Kahn, Albert E(ugene) 1912-1979 ... 118
Obituary ... 89-92
Kahn, Alfred E(dward) 1917- ... 41-44R
Kahn, Alfred J. 1919- ... CANR-15
Earlier sketch in CA 5-6R
Kahn, Alice 1943- ... 119
Kahn, Arnold Dexter 1939- ... 101
Kahn, Balthazar
See Carlisle, Thomas (Fiske)
Kahn, David 1930- ... CANR-12
Earlier sketch in CA 25-28R
Kahn, E(ly) J(acques), Jr. 1916- ... 65-68
Kahn, Ely Jacques 1884-1972 Obituary ... 37-40R
Kahn, Frank J(ules) 1938- ... 33-36R
Kahn, Gilbert 1912-1971 ... CANR-6
Earlier sketch in CA 4R
Kahn, Grace Leboy 1891-1983 Obituary ... 109
Kahn, Hannah 1911- ... CANR-14
Earlier sketch in CA 77-80
See also AITN 2
Kahn, Herman 1922-1983 ... 65-68
Obituary ... 110
Kahn, Herta Hess 1919- ... 25-28R
Kahn, James 1947- ... 109
Kahn, James M. 1903(?)-1978 Obituary ... 77-80
Kahn, Joan 1914- ... 77-80
See also SATA 48
Kahn, Judd 1940- ... 101
Kahn, Kathy 1945- ... 41-44R
Kahn, Lawrence E(dwin) 1937- ... 103
Kahn, Lothar 1922- ... 25-28R
Kahn, Louis I. 1901-1974 Obituary ... 49-52
Kahn, Ludwig W(erner) 1910- ... 41-44R
Kahn, Margaret 1949- ... 101
Kahn, Michael D. 1936- ... 109
Kahn, Peggy
See Katz, Bobbi
Kahn, Richard (Ferdinand Karn) 1905- ... 97-100
Kahn, Robert I(rving) 1910- ... 7-8R
Kahn, Robert L(ouis) 1918- ... CANR-10
Earlier sketch in CA 17-18R
Kahn, Roger 1927- ... 25-28R
See also SATA 37
See also CLC 30
Kahn, Samuel 1897-1981 Obituary ... 106

Kahn, Sanders A(rthur) 1919-1987 89-92
Obituary 121
Kahn, Sandra S(utker) 1942- 106
Kahn, Sholom J(acob) 1918- 102
Kahn, Si(mon) 1944- 33-36R
Kahn, Stephen 1940- 7-8R
Kahn, Steve
See Kahn, Stephen
Kahn, Sy M. 1924- CANR-10
Earlier sketch in CA 25-28R
Kahn, Theodore C(harles) 1912- 33-36R
Kahn-Fogel, Daniel (Mark) 1948- 97-100
Kahn-Freund, Otto 1900-1979 Obituary 108
Kahnweiler, Daniel-Henry 1884-1979 ....29-32R
Obituary 85-88
Kahrl, George M(orrow) 1904- 105
Kahrl, Stanley J. 1931- 11-12R
Kahrl, William L. 1946- 109
Kaid, Lynda Lee 1948- CANR-16
Earlier sketch in CA 89-92
Kaikini, P(rabhakar) R(amrao) 1912- 61-64
Kaiko, Takeshi 1930- 104
Kaim-Caudle, Peter Robert 1916- 23-24R
Kain, John F(orrest) 1935- 29-32R
Kain, Malcolm
See Oglesby, Joseph
Kain, Richard M(organ) 1908- CANR-2
Earlier sketch in CA 7-8R
Kain, Richard Y(erkes) 1936- 37-40R
Kain, Saul
See Sassoon, Siegfried (Lorraine)
Kains, Josephine
See Goulart, Ron(ald Joseph)
Kainz, Howard Paul 1933- 114
Kairys, Anatolijus 1914- 102
Kaisari, Uri 1899(?)-1979 Obituary 85-88
Kaiser, Artur 1943- 97-100
Kaiser, Bill
See Sumner, David (W. K.)
Kaiser, Christopher B(arina) 1941- 114
Kaiser, Edward J(ohn) 1935- 93-96
Kaiser, Edwin George 1893-1984 45-48
Obituary 114
Kaiser, Ernest 1915- CANR-16
Earlier sketches in CA 49-52, CANR-1
Kaiser, Frances E(lkan) 1922- 57-60
Kaiser, Georg 1878-1945 Brief entry 106
See also TCLC 9
Kaiser, Harvey H. 1936- CANR-14
Earlier sketch in CA 81-84
Kaiser, Leo M(ax) 1918- 116
Kaiser, Otto 1924- 85-88
Kaiser, Robert Blair 1930- 9-10R
Kaiser, Robert G(reeley) 1943- 65-68
Kaiser, Walter (Jacob) 1931- CANR-15
Earlier sketch in CA 37-40R
Kaiser, Walter Christian, Jr. 1933- 114
Kaiser, Ward L(ouis) 1923- 53-56
Kaiser Wilhelm II
See Hohenzollern, Friedrich Wilhelm (Victor Albert)
Kaitz, Edward M. 1928- CANR-13
Earlier sketch in CA 29-32R
Kajencki, Francis C(asimir) 1918- 115
Kakapo, Leilani 1939- CANR-9
Earlier sketch in CA 19-20R
Kakar, Sudhir 1938- 33-36R
Kaki
See Heinemann, Katherine
Kakimoto, Kozo 1915- SATA-11
Kakonen, Ulla
See Anobile, Ulla (Kakonen)
Kakonis, Thomas E. 1930- 57-60
Kakonis, Tom E.
See Kakonis, Thomas E.
Kakugawa, Frances H(ideko) 1936- 77-80
Kaland, William J. 1915(?)-1983 Obituary 111
Kalashnikoff, Nicholas 1888-1961 73-76
See also SATA 16
Kalb, Bernard 1932- Brief entry 109
Kalb, Jonah 1926- CANR-4
Earlier sketch in CA 53-56
See also SATA 23
Kalb, Marvin L. 1930- 5-6R
Kalb, S(am) William 1897- 33-36R
Kalberer, Augustine 1917- 61-64
Kalcheim, Lee 1938- 85-88
Kaldor, Mary 1946- 93-96
Kale, Arvind and Shanta
See Gantzer, Hugh
Kalechofsky, Roberta 1931- CANR-2
Earlier sketch in CA 49-52
See also DLB 28
Kaledin, Eugenia 1929- 109
Kalem, T(heodore) E(ustace) 1919-1985
Obituary 116
Kalemkerian, Zarouhi 1874(?)-1971
Obituary 104
Kalenik, Sandra 1945- 73-76
Kaler, James Otis 1848-1912 Brief entry 120
See also SATA 15
See also DLB 42
Kales, Emily Fox 1944- 23-24R
Kaletski, Alexander 1946- Brief entry 118
See also CLC 39
Kalia, Narendra Nath 1942- 112
Kalich, Jacob 1891-1975 Obituary 89-92
Kalich, Robert 1947- 106
Kalicki, Jan H(enryk) 1948- 65-68
Kalijarvi, Thorsten V(alentine) 1897-1980 ....CAP-1
Obituary 97-100
Earlier sketch in CA 19-20
Kalin, Martin (Gregory) 1943- 53-56
Kalin, Robert 1921- CANR-8
Earlier sketch in CA 61-64
Kalin, Rudolf 1938- 45-48
Kalina, Sigmund 1911-1977 ....CANR-3
Earlier sketch in CA 49-52
Kalins, Dorothy (G.) 1942- CANR-17
Earlier sketch in CA 25-28R
Kalinsky, George 1936- CANR-2
Earlier sketch in CA 49-52
Kalish, Betty McKelvey 1913- 45-48
Kalish, Donald 1919- 11-12R
Kalish, Richard A(llan) 1930- CANR-10
Earlier sketch in CA 7-8R
Kalisher, Simpson 1926- 17-18R
Kallas, James (Gus) 1928- CANR-10
Earlier sketch in CA 17-18R
Kallaus, Norman F. 1924- 33-36R
Kallberg,Sture
See Kaellberg, Sture
Kallen, (Marc) Christian 1950- 120
Kallen, Horace M(eyer) 1882-1974 93-96
Obituary 49-52
Kallen, Laurence 1944- 41-44R
Kallen, Lucille 97-100
Kallenbach, Joseph E(rnest) 1903- 77-80
Kallenbach, W(illiam) Warren 1926- 11-12R
Kallesser, Michael 1886(?)-1975
Obituary 61-64
Kallet, Arthur 1902-1972 Obituary 33-36R
Kallet, Marilyn 1946- 104
Kallich, Martin 1918- CANR-2
Earlier sketch in CA 5-6R
Kallifatides, Theodor 1938- CANR-15
Earlier sketch in CA 85-88
Kallir, Jane K(atherine) 1954- 109
Kallir, Otto 1894-1978 49-52
Obituary 81-84
Kallman, Chester (Simon) 1921-1975 ....CANR-3
Obituary 53-56
Earlier sketch in CA 45-48
See also CLC 2
Kallmann, Helmut Max 1922- 108
Kallsen, T(heodore) J(ohn) 1915- 7-8R
Kalman, Harold David 1943- 103
Kalme, Egils 1909- 81-84
Kalmijn, Jo 1905- CAP-2
Earlier sketch in CA 21-22
Kalmus, Ain
See Mand, Ewald
Kalnay, Francis 1899- 49-52
See also SATA 7
Kalnoky, Ingeborg L(ouise) 1909- 61-64
Kalow, Gert 1921- 29-32R
Kalow, Gisela 1946- 107
See also SATA 32
Kalpakian, Laura Anne 1945- CANR-15
Earlier sketch in CA 81-84
Kals, W(illiam) S(teven) 1910- CANR-24
Earlier sketch in CA 45-48
Kalstone, David (Michael) 1932-1986
Obituary 119
Kalstone, Shirlee A(nn) 1932- CANR-8
Earlier sketch in CA 61-64
Kalt, Bryson R. 1934- 33-36R
Kalt, Jeannette Chappell 1898(?)-1976
Obituary 69-72
Kaltenborn, Hans Von 1878-1965
Obituary 93-96
Kalter, Joanmarie 1951- 102
Kalu, Ogbu Uke 1944- 93-96
Kaluger, George 1921- 29-32R
Kaluger, Meriem Fair 1921- 81-84
Kalven, Harry, Jr. 1914-1974 Obituary 53-56
Kalyanaraman, Aiyaswamy 1903- CAP-2
Earlier sketch in CA 33-36
Kamarck, Andrew M(artin) 1914- CANR-10
Earlier sketch in CA 21-22R
Kamarck, Lawrence 1927- 73-76
Kamath, M(adhav) V(ithal) 1921- CANR-21
Earlier sketch in CA 69-72
Kambu, Joseph
See Amamoo, Joseph Godson
Kamen, Betty 1925- 114
Kamen, Gloria 1923- 114
See also SATA 9
Kamen, Henry Arthur 1936- CANR-7
Earlier sketch in CA 7-8R
Kamen, Isai
See Stein, Jess
Kamen, Martin D(avid) 1913- 118
Kamen, Si 1920- 114
Kamenetsky, Ihor 1927- CANR-4
Earlier sketch in CA 2R
Kamenetz, Rodger 1950- 112
Kamenka, Eugene 1928- CANR-2
Earlier sketch in CA 5-6R
Kamerman, Jack B. 1940- 115
Kamerman, Sheila B(rody) 1928- CANR-10
Earlier sketch in CA 65-68
Kamerman, Sylvia E.
See Burack, Sylvia K.
Kamerschen, David R(oy) 1937- 53-56
Kamien, Marcia 1940- CANR-22
Earlier sketch in CA 105
Kamil, Alan C(urtis) 1941- Brief entry 109
Kamil, Jill 1930- CANR-7
Earlier sketch in CA 57-60
Kamin, Leon J. 1927- 103
Kamin, Nick
See Antonick, Robert J.
Kamins, Jeanette 5-6R
Kamins, Robert Martin 1918- Brief entry 105
Kaminska, Ida 1899-1980 Obituary 97-100
Kaminskaya, Dina 1920- 115
Kaminski, Margaret (Joan) 1944- CANR-8
Earlier sketch in CA 61-64
Kaminsky, Alice R. 33-36R
Kaminsky, Howard 1940- 105
Kaminsky, Jack 1922- 23-24R
Kaminsky, Marc 1943- CANR-24
Earlier sketches in CA 53-56, CANR-5
Kaminsky, Melvin 1926- CANR-16
Earlier sketch in CA 65-68
Kaminsky, Peretz 1916- 33-36R
Kaminsky, Stuart M(elvin) 1934- 73-76
Kaminsky, Susan Stanwood 1937- 115
Brief entry 110
Kamisar, Yale 1929- CANR-13
Earlier sketch in CA 69-72
Kamitses, Zoe 1941- 111
Kamm, Antony 1931- 117
Kamm, (Jan) Dorinda 1952- CANR-14
Earlier sketch in CA 37-40R
Kamm, Herbert 1917- 69-72
Kamm, Jacob Oswald 1918- 7-8R
Kamm, Josephine (Hart) 1905- CANR-5
Earlier sketch in CA 11-12R
See also SATA 24
Kamm, Phyllis S. 1918- 112
Kamman, Madeleine M(arguerite Pin)
1930- 85-88
Kamman, William 1930- 25-28R
Kammen, Michael G(edaliah) 1936- CANR-22
Earlier sketch in CA 25-28R
Kammerer, Gladys M. 1909-1970 ....CANR-16
Obituary 103
Earlier sketch in CA 3R
Kammeyer, Kenneth C(arl) W(illiam)
1931- 29-32R
Kamp, Irene Kittle 1910-1985 Obituary 116
Kampelman, Max M. 1920- 41-44R
Kampen, Irene Trepel 1922- CANR-1
Earlier sketch in CA 3R
Kampen, Michael Edwin 1939- Brief entry 110
Kampf, Abraham 1920- 23-24R
Kampf, Avram
See Kampf, Abraham
Kampf, Louis 1929- 33-36R
Kampov, Boris Nikolayevich 1908-1981 108
Obituary 104
Kamrany, Nake M. 1934- CANR-14
Earlier sketch in CA 37-40R
Kamstra, Leslie D. 1920- 69-72
Kanahele, George Sanford 1930- 102
Kanazawa, Masakata 1934- 25-28R
Kanazawa, Roger
See Kanazawa, Masakata
Kandaouroff, Berice 1912- 33-36R
Kandel, Denise Bystryn 1933- 13-14R
Kandel, I(saac) L(eon) 1881-1965 ....CANR-3
Earlier sketch in CA 4R
Kandel, Lenore 1932- DLB-16
Kandel, Thelma E. 1932- 111
Kandell, Alice S. 1938- CANR-13
Earlier sketch in CA 33-36R
See also SATA 35
Kandinsky, Nina 1896(?)-1980 101
Kandinsky, Wassily 1866-1944 Brief entry 118
Kando, Thomas M. 1941- CANR-2
Earlier sketch in CA 49-52
Kane, Aarno
See Kagan, Andrew
Kane, Basil G(odfrey) 1931- CANR-24
Earlier sketch in CA 69-72
Kane, Dennis Cornelius 1918- 41-44R
Kane, E. B. 1944- 57-60
Kane, Edward J(ames) 1935- 41-44R
Kane, Frank 1912-1968 ....7-8R
Obituary 25-28R
Kane, Frank R. 1925- 77-80
Kane, George 1916- 103
Kane, H. Victor 1906- 29-32R
Kane, Harnett T(homas) 1910-1984
Obituary 113
Kane, Henry Bugbee 1902-1971 73-76
See also SATA 14
Kane, J. Herbert 1910- 97-100
Kane, Jack
See Baker, (Allen) Albert
Kane, James
See Germano, Peter B.
Kane, Jim
See Germano, Peter B.
Kane, John Joseph 1909- CAP-2
Earlier sketch in CA 13-14
Kane, Julia
See Robins, Denise (Naomi)
Kane, Pablo
See Zachary, Hugh
Kane, Paul
See Simon, Paul
Kane, Peter E(vans) 1932- 112
Kane, Robert S. 1925- CANR-23
Earlier sketches in CA 9-10R, CANR-7
Kane, Robert W. 1910- SATA-18
Kane, Thomas S. 1925- 114
Kane, William Everett 1943- 49-52
Kane, Wilson
See Bloch, Robert (Albert)
Kanet, Roger E(dward) 1936- CANR-14
Earlier sketch in CA 33-36R
Kanetzke, Howard W(illiam) 1932- 112
See also SATA 38
Kanfer, Allen 1905(?)-1983 Obituary 110
Kanfer, Frederick H. 1925- CANR-15
Earlier sketch in CA 41-44R
Kanfer, Stefan 1933- 103
Kang, Shin T. 1935- 33-36R
Kang, Younghill 1903-1972 Obituary 37-40R
Kanin, Garson 1912- CANR-7
Earlier sketch in CA 7-8R
See also DLB 7
See also CLC 22
See also AITN 1
Kanin, Michael 1910- 61-64
Kanin, Ruth 1920- 107
Kanitz, Walter 1910- 97-100
Kaniuk, Yoram 1930?- CLC-19
Kaniut, Larry (LeRoy) 1942- 114
Kann, Robert A. 1906-1981 Obituary 105
Kannappan, Subbiah 1927- 93-96
Kanner, Catherine 1954- 123
Kanner, Leo 1894-1981 ....17-18R
Obituary 103
Kanof, Abram 1903- 29-32R
Kanovsky, Eliyahu 1922- 33-36R
Kansil, Joli 1943- 81-84
Kantar, Edwin B(ruce) 1932- 41-44R
Kanter, Arnold 1945- 89-92
Kanter, Hal 1918- 81-84
Kanter, Rosabeth Moss 1943- CANR-14
Earlier sketch in CA 77-80
Kanto, Peter
See Zachary, Hugh
Kantonen, T(aito) A(lmar) 1900- 33-36R
Kantor, Hal 1924- 77-80
Kantor, Harry 1911- CANR-2
Earlier sketch in CA 1R
Kantor, Herman I. 1909- 57-60
Kantor, James 1927-1974 ....CAP-2
Earlier sketch in CA 21-22
Kantor, Leonard 1924(?)-1984 Obituary 112
Kantor, MacKinlay 1904-1977 61-64
Obituary 73-76
See also DLB 9
See also CLC 7
Kantor, Marvin 1934- CANR-2
Earlier sketch in CA 49-52
Kantor, Seth 1926- 81-84
Kantor-Berg, Friedrich 1908-1979
Obituary 89-92
Kantorovich, L(eonid) V(italevich)
1912-1986 Obituary 119
Kantowicz, Edward Robert 1943- 114
Kantrowitz, Arnie 1940- 77-80
Kantrowitz, Joanne Spencer 1931- 81-84
Kantzer, Kenneth S(ealer) 1917- 106
Kanwar, Mahfooz A. 1939- 37-40R
Kany, Charles E(mil) 1895-1968 ....CANR-3
Earlier sketch in CA 1R
Kanya-Forstner, A(lexander) S(ydney)
1940- CANR-17
Earlier sketch in CA 25-28R
Kanza, Thomas R. (Nsenga) 1933- CANR-5
Earlier sketch in CA 53-56
Kanzawa, Toshiko
See Furukawa, Toshi
Kanzer, Mark 1908- 37-40R
Kao, Charles C. L. 1932- 85-88
Kapel, Andrew
See Burgess, M(ichael) R(oy)
Kapelner, Alan 7-8R
Kapelrud, Arvid Schou 1912- 102
Kapfer, Miriam B(ierbaum) 1935- 33-36R
Kapfer, Philip G(ordon) 1936- 33-36R
Kapitsa, Pyotr L(eonidovich) 1894-1984
Obituary 112
Kaplan, Abraham 1918- 13-14R
Kaplan, Allan 1932- 33-36R
Kaplan, Anne Bernays 1930- CANR-5
Earlier sketch in CA 3R
See also SATA 32
Kaplan, Arthur 1925- 7-8R
Kaplan, Benjamin 1911- 1R
Kaplan, Bernard 1944- CANR-2
Earlier sketch in CA 49-52
Kaplan, Berton H(arris) 1930- 61-64
Kaplan, Bess 1927- 85-88
See also SATA 22
Kaplan, Boche 1926- CANR-10
Earlier sketch in CA 23-24R
See also SATA 24
Kaplan, Charles 1919- 9-10R
Kaplan, David Gordon 1908- 61-64
Kaplan, Edward 1946- CANR-11
Earlier sketch in CA 69-72
Kaplan, Eugene H(erbert) 1932- 81-84
Kaplan, Flora S(tewart) 109
Kaplan, Fred 1937- CANR-14
Earlier sketch in CA 41-44R
Kaplan, Fred (Michael) 1954- Brief entry 121
Kaplan, Frederick I(srael) 1920- 23-24R
Kaplan, H. Roy 1944- 89-92
Kaplan, Harold 1916- 19-20R
Kaplan, Helen Singer 1929- 102
See also AITN 1
Kaplan, Howard 1950- 69-72
Kaplan, Howard B(ernard) 1932- CANR-22
Earlier sketches in CA 61-64, CANR-8
Kaplan, Hymen R. 1910- 102
Kaplan, Irma 1900- 29-32R
See also SATA 10
Kaplan, Jack A(rnold) 1947- 57-60
Kaplan, Jacob J. 1920- CANR-10
Earlier sketch in CA 23-24R
Kaplan, Janice Ellen 1955- 117
Kaplan, Jean Caryl Korn 1926- 7-8R
See also SATA 10
Kaplan, Johanna 1942- 77-80
See also DLB 28
Kaplan, Joseph 1916(?)-1980 Obituary 97-100
Kaplan, Justin 1925- CANR-8
Earlier sketch in CA 19-20R
Kaplan, Lawrence Jay 1915- 21-22R
Kaplan, Lawrence S(amuel) 1924- 33-36R
Kaplan, Leonard 1918(?)-1977 Obituary 69-72
Kaplan, Martin (Harold) 1950- 65-68
Kaplan, Martin F(rancis) 1940- 93-96
Kaplan, Max 1911- CANR-20
Earlier sketches in CA 4R, CANR-5
Kaplan, Milton 1910- 65-68
Kaplan, Mordecai M(enahem) 1881-1983
Obituary 111

INDEX

Kaplan, Morton A. 1921- CANR-7
Earlier sketch in CA 7-8R
Kaplan, Norman Mayer 1931- 110
Kaplan, Philip 1916- 13-14R
Kaplan, Richard 1929- 73-76
Kaplan, Robert B. 1928- CANR-22
Earlier sketches in CA 13-14R, CANR-7
Kaplan, S(aul) Howard 1938- 25-28R
Kaplan, Samuel 1935- 21-22R
Kaplan, Sidney 1913- 85-88
Kaplan, Stuart R(onald) 1932- CANR-21
Earlier sketches in CA 49-52, CANR-2
Kaplan, Sydney Janet 1939- 110
Kapler, Aleksei (Yaklovlevich)
1904(?)-1979 Obituary 89-92
Kaplon, Morton F(ischel) 1921- 23-24R
Kaplow, Herb(ert Elias) 1927- 119
Brief entry 110
Kaplow, Jeffry 1937- 17-18R
Kapoor, Ashok 1940- 85-88
Kapoor, Sukhbir Singh 1935- 109
Kapp, K(arl) William 1910-1976 .... CANR-8
Obituary 65-68
Earlier sketch in CA 5-6R
Kapp, Reginald Otto 1885-1966 .... 7-8R
Kapp, Yvonne (Mayer) 1903- 103
Kappauf, William Emil (Jr.) 1913- 106
Kappel, Philip 1901- CAP-1
Earlier sketch in CA 15-16
Kappelman, Murray M(artin) 1931- 73-76
Kappel-Smith, Diana 1951- 121
Kappen, Charles Vaughan 1910- 11-12R
Kaprow, Allan 1927- 105
Kapsner, Oliver L(eonard) 1902- 116
Kapstein, I(srael) J(ames) 1904-1983
Obituary 110
Kaptchuk, Ted J(ack) 1947- 110
Kapur, Harish 1929- CANR-15
Earlier sketch in CA 85-88
Kapuscinski, Ryszard 1932- 114
Kapusta, Paul
See Bickers, Richard Leslie Townshend
Karageorge, Michael
See Anderson, Poul (William)
Karageorghis, Vassos 1929- CANR-15
Earlier sketch in CA 81-84
Karan, Pradyumna P(rasad) 1930- 114
Karanikas, Alexander 1916- 33-36R
Karapanou, Margarita 1946- 101
See also CLC 13
Karas, Jim 1949-1981 Obituary 108
Karas, Joza 1926- 124
Karas, Phyllis 1944- 105
Karasu, Toksoz B(yram) 1935- 105
Karasz, Ilonka 1896-1981 .... SATA-29
Karbo, Joe 1925(?)-1980 Obituary 115
Kardiner, Abram 1891-1981 107
Obituary 104
Kardish, Laurence 1945- 49-52
Kardouche, G(eorge) Khalil 1935- 19-20R
Karel, Leonard 1912- 49-52
Karen
See Aldrich, Sandra Picklesimer
Karen, Robert L(e Roy) 1925- 73-76
Karen, Ruth 1922-1987 .... CANR-11
Obituary 123
Earlier sketch in CA 19-20R
See also SATA 9
Karg, Elissa Jane 1951- 23-24R
Karger, Delmar William 1913- CANR-8
Earlier sketch in CA 17-18R
Kargon, Robert Hugh 1938- 45-48
Kariel, Henry S. 1924- 13-14R
Karina
See Goud, Anne
Kariuki, Josiah Mwangi 1929- 107
Kark, Nina Mary (Mabey) 1925- CANR-8
Earlier sketch in CA 17-18R
See also SATA 4
Karkala, John A.
See Alphonso-Karkala, John B.
Karkala, John B.A.
See Alphonso-Karkala, John B.
Karkhanis, Sharad 1935- 110
Karkoschka, Erhard 1923- 45-48
Karl, Barry D(ean) 1927- 102
Karl, Frederick R(obert) 1927- CANR-3
Earlier sketch in CA 5-6R
See also CLC 34
Karl, Jean E(dna) 1927- CANR-12
Earlier sketch in CA 29-32R
See also SATA 34
Karl, Roger
See Trouve, Roger
Karlan, Richard 1919- 17-18R
Karlen, Arno 1937- CANR-5
Earlier sketch in CA 1R
Karlen, Delmar 1912- CANR-2
Earlier sketch in CA 7-8R
Karlgren, (Klas) Bernhard (Johannes)
1889- CAP-1
Earlier sketch in CA 9-10
Karlin, Eugene 1918- SATA-10
Karlin, Jules 1899- CAP-2
Earlier sketch in CA 25-28
Karlin, Muriel S.
See Trachman, Muriel Karlin
Karlin, Robert 1918- 9-10R
Karlins, Marvin 1941- CANR-17
Earlier sketch in CA 25-28R
Karlsson, Elis (Viktor) 1905- CAP-1
Earlier sketch in CA 15-16
Karlsson, T. Edward 1915(?)-1984
Obituary 113
Karman, Mal 1944- 103
Karmel, Alex 1931- 23-24R
Karmel, Roberta S(arah) 1937- 108
Karmel-Wolfe, Henia 1923- 49-52
Karmen, Roman Lazarevich 1906-1978
Obituary 77-80
Karmi, Abdul Karim 1907(?)-1980
Obituary 102
Karmi, Hasan Said 1908- 45-48
Karmin, Monroe William 1929- 101
Karnad, Girish 1938- 65-68
Karnes, Merle B(riggs) 1916- 85-88
Karnes, Thomas L(indas) 1914- 23-24R
Karney, Beulah Mullen 13-14R
Karniewski, Janusz
See Wittlin, Thaddeus (Andrew)
Karno, Bung
See Sukarno, (Ahmed)
Karnow, Stanley 1925- 57-60
Karol, Alexander
See Kent, Arthur William Charles
Karol, K. S.
See Kewes, Karol
Karolevitz, Bob
See Karolevitz, Robert F.
Karolevitz, Robert F. 1922- CANR-22
Earlier sketches in CA 17-18R, CANR-7
Karolides, Nicholas J(ames) 1928- 21-22R
Karolyi, Catherine (Andrassy) 1898-1985
Obituary 116
Karon, Bertram Paul 1930- CANR-7
Earlier sketch in CA 61-64
Karp, Abraham J. 1921- CANR-18
Earlier sketches in CA 5-6R, CANR-3
Karp, Alan 1947- 107
Karp, David 1922- CANR-1
Earlier sketch in CA 1R
Karp, Ivan C. 1926- 17-18R
Karp, Laurence E(dward) 1939- 77-80
Karp, Lila 1933- 25-28R
Karp, Mark 1922- 1R
Karp, Naomi J. 1926- 81-84
See also SATA 16
Karp, Stephen A(rnold) 1928- CANR-6
Earlier sketch in CA 1R
Karpat, Kemal H(asim) 1925- CANR-11
Earlier sketch in CA 69-72
Karpatkin, Marvin M. 1926-1975
Obituary 53-56
Karpau, Uladzimir
See Karpov, Vladimir
Karpel, Bernard 1911-1986 106
Obituary 118
Karpel, Craig S. 1944- 65-68
Karpeles, Maud 1885- 25-28R
Karpf, Holly W. 1946- 37-40R
Karpin, Fred L(eon) 1913-1986 .... CANR-9
Obituary 119
Earlier sketch in CA 15-16R
Karplus, Walter J. 1927- 21-22R
Karpman, Harold L(ew) 1927- 77-80
Karpov, Vladimir 1912(?)-1977 Obituary 73-76
Karr, E(arl) R(alph) 1918- 3R
Karr, Phyllis Ann 1944- CANR-18
Earlier sketch in CA 101
Karras, Alex(ander G.) 1935- 107
Karrass, Chester L. 1923- 101
Karren, Keith J(ohn) 1943- 116
Karrer, Paul 1889-1971 Obituary 113
Karris, Robert J(oseph) 1938- CANR-5
Earlier sketch in CA 53-56
Karsavina, Jean (Faterson) 1908- 101
Karsavina, Tamara 1885-1978 Obituary 77-80
Karsch, Robert F(rederick) 1909- 77-80
Karsen, Sonja (Petra) 1919- 41-44R
Karsh, Bernard 1921- 103
Karsh, Yousuf 1908- 33-36R
Karshner, Roger 1928- 33-36R
Karsten, Peter 1938- CANR-13
Earlier sketch in CA 37-40R
Karta, Nat
See Norwood, Victor G(eorge) C(harles)
Kartiganer, Donald M. 1937- 97-100
Karu, Baruch 1899-1972 Obituary 104
Karve, Dinakar Dhondo 1899-1980 .... 7-8R
Obituary 103
Karve, Irawati (Karmarkar) 1905-1970 .... CAP-1
Earlier sketch in CA 19-20
Kary, Elizabeth N. (a pseudonym) 1947- 122
Kasarda, John Dale 1945- 103
Kaschnitz, Marie Luise
See von Kaschnitz-Weinberg, Marie Luise
Kasdan, Lawrence 1949- 109
Kasdan, Sara (Moskovitz) 1911- 2R
Kasdorf, Hans 1928- 116
Kase, Francis J(oseph) 1910- 23-24R
Kaselow, Joseph 1912-1986 Obituary 119
Kaser, David 1924- 17-18R
Kaser, Michael (Charles) 1926- CANR-10
Earlier sketch in CA 17-18R
Kaser, Paul 1944- 104
Kash, Don E(ldon) 1934- CANR-9
Earlier sketch in CA 23-24R
Kashdan, Isaac 1905-1985 Obituary 115
Kashima, Tetsuden 1940- 81-84
Kashiwagi, Isami 1925- SATA-10
Kashner, Rita 1942- 105
Kaslow, Florence W(hiteman) 1930- CANR-18
Earlier sketches in CA 45-48, CANR-1
Kasper, Sydney H. 1911- 4R
Kasperson, Roger E. 1938- 29-32R
Kasrils, Ronald 1938- 29-32R
Kass, Jerome 1923(?)-1973 Obituary 104
Kass, Jerome 1937- 57-60
Kass, Norman 1934- 29-32R
Kass, Ray 1944- 118
Kassalow, Everett M(alcolm) 1918- 45-48
Kassebaum, Gene G(irard) 1929- 19-20R
Kassewitz, Jack 1914(?)-1984 Obituary 112
Kassof, Allen 1930- 23-24R
Kasson, John F(ranklin) 1944- 81-84
Kassorla, Irene Chamie 1931- 110
Kast, Fremont E. 1926- 23-24R
Kastan, David Scott 1946- 109
Kastein, Shulamith 1903-1983 105
Obituary 110
Kastel, Warren
See Silverberg, Robert
Kastenbaum, Robert (Jay) 1932- CANR-9
Earlier sketch in CA 15-16R
Kaster, Joseph 1912-19(?) CAP-1
Earlier sketch in CA 19-20
Kastl, Albert J(oseph) 1939- 57-60
Kastl, Lena 1942- 61-64
Kastle, Herbert D(avid) 1924-1987 .... CANR-1
Obituary 123
Earlier sketch in CA 1R
Kastner, Erich
See Kaestner, Erich
See also SATA 14
See also DLB 56
See also CLR 4
Kastner, Jonathan 1937- 25-28R
Kastner, Joseph 1907- 85-88
Kastner, Marianna 1940- 25-28R
Kasulis, T(homas) P(atrick) 1948- 124
Kasuya, Masahiro 1937- 110
Kaszner, Kurt
See Serwicher, Kurt
Kaszubski, Marek 1951- 105
Kataev, Evgeny Petrovich 1903-1942
Brief entry 120
Katahn, Martin 1928- 114
Katan, Norma-Jean 1936- 113
Katayev, Valentin (Petrovich) 1897-1986
Obituary 119
Brief entry 117
Katcha, Vahe
See Katchadourian, Vahe
Katchadourian, Herant A(ram) 1933- CANR-20
Earlier sketch in CA 103
Katchadourian, Vahe 1928- 29-32R
Katchen, Carole 1944- 61-64
See also SATA 9
Katchmer, George Andrew 1916- 3R
Kateb, George (Anthony) 1931- 123
Brief entry 118
Katen, Thomas Ellis 1931- 53-56
Kater, Michael H(ans) 1937- 114
Kates, Brian 1946- 119
Kates, Carol A. 1943- 115
Kates, Robert W. 1929- CANR-24
Earlier sketches in CA 17-18R, CANR-8
Kathman, Michael D(ennis) 1943- 109
Kathryn
See Searle, Kathryn Adrienne
Kati
See Rekai, Kati
Katicic, Radoslav 1930- 37-40R
Katkov, George 1903-1985 Obituary 115
Katkov, Norman 1918- 15-16R
Kato, Hidetoshi 1930- 115
Kato, Shuichi 1919- 37-40R
Katona, Edita 1913- 69-72
Katona, George 1901-1981 Obituary 104
Katona, Robert 1949- SATA-21
Katope, Christopher G. 1918- 21-22R
Katoppo, (Henriette) Marianne 1943- 123
Katsarakis, Joan Harries
See Harries, Joan
Katsaros, Thomas 1926- 57-60
Katsh, Abraham I(saac) 1908- CANR-8
Earlier sketch in CA 7-8R
Katsh, Salem M(ichael) 1948- 110
Kattan, Naim 1928- CANR-11
Earlier sketch in CA 69-72
See also DLB 53
Katterjohn, Arthur D. 1930(?)-1980
Obituary 93-96
Katz, Abraham 1926- 49-52
Katz, Albert M(ichael) 1938- 93-96
Katz, Alfred 1938- 77-80
Katz, Alfred
See Allan, Alfred K.
Katz, Arthur M. 1942- 124
Katz, Basho
See Gatti, Arthur Gerard
Katz, Benjamin 1904-1985 Obituary 115
Katz, Bobbi 1933- CANR-16
Earlier sketch in CA 37-40R
See also SATA 12
Katz, Carol 1939- 115
Katz, Daniel 1903- 41-44R
Katz, Elias 1912- 29-32R
Katz, Ellis 1938- 29-32R
Katz, Eve 1938- CANR-1
Earlier sketch in CA 45-48
Katz, Fred(eric Phillip) 1938- 49-52
See also SATA 6
Katz, Fred E(mil) 1927- 77-80
Katz, Friedrich 1927- Brief entry 113
Katz, Gloria 1945(?)- 107
Katz, Herbert Melvin 1930- 103
Katz, Irving I. 1907- 4R
Katz, Jack 1944- 111
Katz, Jacob 1904- CANR-4
Earlier sketch in CA 1R
Katz, Jane B(resler) 1934- 85-88
See also SATA 33
Katz, Jay 1922- 118
Katz, John Stuart 1938- CANR-14
Earlier sketch in CA 37-40R
Katz, Jonathan 1938- 85-88
Katz, Josef 1918- 53-56
Katz, Joseph 1910- CANR-2
Earlier sketch in CA 1R
Katz, Judith Milstein 1943- 106
Katz, Leon 1919- CANR-20
Earlier sketches in CA 49-52, CANR-4
Katz, Leonard 1926- 21-22R
Katz, Lewis R(obert) 1938- 116
Katz, Lilian G(onshaw) 1932- 111
Katz, Marjorie P.
See Weiser, Marjorie P(hillis) K(atz)
Katz, Martin 1929- 23-24R
Katz, Marvin C(harles) 1930- 25-28R
Katz, Menke 1906- CANR-11
Earlier sketch in CA 15-16R
Katz, Michael B(arry) 1939- CANR-13
Earlier sketch in CA 33-36R
Katz, Michael Ray 1944- CANR-18
Earlier sketch in CA 102
Katz, Mickey
See Katz, Myron Meyer
Katz, Milton 1907- CAP-1
Earlier sketch in CA 11-12
Katz, Mort 1925- CANR-11
Earlier sketch in CA 61-64
Katz, Myron Meyer 1909-1985 81-84
Obituary 116
Katz, Robert 1933- CANR-11
Earlier sketch in CA 25-28R
Katz, Robert L. 1917- 9-10R
Katz, Samuel 1914- CANR-12
Earlier sketch in CA 25-28R
Katz, Sanford N. 1933- CANR-13
Earlier sketch in CA 33-36R
Katz, Shmuel
See Katz, Samuel
Katz, Stan
See Chapman, Frank M(onroe)
Katz, Stanley Nider 1934- 11-12R
Katz, Steve 1935- CANR-12
Earlier sketch in CA 25-28R
See also DLBY 83
See also CLC 47
Katz, Susan 1944(?)-1982 Obituary 107
Katz, William 1940- 85-88
Katz, William A(rmstrong) 1924- CANR-10
Earlier sketch in CA 25-28R
Katz, William Loren 1927- CANR-9
Earlier sketch in CA 21-22R
See also SATA 13
Katzander, Howard L. 1911(?)-1983
Obituary 110
Katzenbach, John 1950- 119
Katzenbach, Maria 1953- 77-80
Katzenbach, William E. 1904-1975
Obituary 61-64
Katzenstein, Mary Fainsod 1945- 93-96
Katzenstein, Peter J(oachim) 1945- CANR-17
Earlier sketch in CA 93-96
Ka-Tzetnik 135633 .... 29-32R
Katzman, Allen 1937- 29-32R
Katzman, Anita 1920- 57-60
Katzman, David Manners 1941- CANR-5
Earlier sketch in CA 53-56
Katzman, Martin T(heodore) 1941- 111
Katznelson-Shazar, Rachel 1888-1975
Obituary 61-64
Katzner, Kenneth 1930- 7-8R
Kau, Michael Y. M.
See Kau, Ying-mao
Kau, Ying-mao 1934- Brief entry 114
Kauder, Emil 1901- 17-18R
Kaufelt, David Allan 1939- CANR-16
Earlier sketches in CA 45-48, CANR-1
Kauffeld, Carl F. 1911-1974 Obituary 49-52
Kauffman, Christmas Carol 1902- 1R
Kauffman, Christopher J. 1936- 107
Kauffman, Donald T(homas) 1920- CANR-11
Earlier sketch in CA 25-28R
Kauffman, Dorotha S(trayer) 1925- 17-18R
Kauffman, Draper L. 1946- 108
Kauffman, George B(ernard) 1930- 19-20R
Kauffman, Henry J. 1908- 13-14R
Kauffman, James M(ilton) 1940- CANR-7
Earlier sketch in CA 57-60
Kauffman, Janet 1945- 117
See also DLBY 86
See also CLC 42
Kauffman, Joseph F(rank) 1921- CANR-1
Earlier sketch in CA 45-48
Kauffman, Milo (Franklin) 1898- 89-92
Kauffmann, Georg (Friedrich) 1925- 49-52
Kauffmann, Lane 1921- 19-20R
Kauffmann, Samuel Hay 1898-1971
Obituary 89-92
Kauffmann, Stanley 1916- CANR-6
Earlier sketch in CA 7-8R
Kaufman, Arnold S. 1927- 25-28R
Kaufman, Arthur 1934- 107
Kaufman, Barry Neil 1942- CANR-17
Earlier sketch in CA 97-100
Kaufman, Bel CANR-13
Earlier sketch in CA 15-16R
Kaufman, Bob (Garnell) 1925-1986 .... CANR-22
Obituary 118
Earlier sketch in CA 41-44R
See also DLB 16, 41
Kaufman, Burton I. 1940- 33-36R
Kaufman, Daniel 1949- 85-88
Kaufman, Debra Renee 1941- 109
Kaufman, Donald D(avid) 1933- 29-32R
Kaufman, Edmund George 1891- 73-76
Kaufman, George S. 1889-1961 108
Obituary 93-96
See also DLB 7
See also CLC 38
Kaufman, Gerald (Bernard) 1930- 23-24R
Kaufman, Gershen 1943- 117
Kaufman, Gloria (Shapiro) 1929- 122
Kaufman, Gordon Dester 1925- CANR-7
Earlier sketch in CA 13-14R

Kaufman, H(arold) G(erson) 1939- 69-72
Kaufman, Herbert 1922- Brief entry 115
Kaufman, I(sadore) 1892-1978 Obituary ... 77-80
Kaufman, Irving 1920- 21-22R
Kaufman, Jacob J(oseph) 1914- 41-44R
Kaufman, Joe 1911- 107
See also SATA 33
Kaufman, Lloyd 1927- 93-96
Kaufman, Martin 1940- 109
Kaufman, Mervyn D. 1932- 7-8R
See also SATA 4
Kaufman, Paul 1886-1979 Obituary 89-92
Kaufman, Philip 1936- 121
Brief entry 112
Kaufman, Polly W(elts) 1929- 114
Kaufman, Robert 1931- 17-18R
Kaufman, Roger (Alexander) 1932- CANR-9
Earlier sketch in CA 53-56
Kaufman, Rosamond (Arleen) V(an)
P(oznak) 1923- CANR-7
Earlier sketch in CA 11-12R
Kaufman, Sherwin A. 1920- CANR-10
Earlier sketch in CA 25-28R
Kaufman, Shirley 1923- 49-52
Kaufman, Sidney 1910-1983 Obituary 110
Kaufman, Stuart Bruce 1942- 123
Kaufman, Sue
See Barondess, Sue K(aufman)
See also CLC 3, 8
Kaufman, Wallace 1939- CANR-10
Earlier sketch in CA 25-28R
Kaufman, William I(rving) 1922- CANR-24
Earlier sketches in CA 13-14R, CANR-7
Kaufman, Wolfe 1905(?)-1970 Obituary ..29-32R
Kaufmann, Angelika 1935- SATA-15
Kaufmann, Harry 1927- 45-48
Kaufmann, Helen L(oeb) 1887- CANR-7
Earlier sketch in CA 5-6R
Kaufmann, Henry William 1913- 41-44R
Kaufmann, John 1931- 81-84
See also SATA 18
Kaufmann, Myron S. 1921- 25-28R
Kaufmann, R(alph) James 1924- 13-14R
Kaufmann, U(rlin) Milo 1934- 41-44R
Kaufmann, Ulrich George 1920- 23-24R
Kaufmann, Walter 1921-1980 .... CANR-1
Obituary 101
Earlier sketch in CA 1R
Kaufmann, Walter 1933- 61-64
Kaufmann, William J(ohn) III 1942- 93-96
Kaufmann, William W. 1918- 13-14R
Kaul, Donald 1934- 65-68
Kaula, Edna Mason 1906- 7-8R
See also SATA 13
Kaumeyer, Dorothy 1914- Brief entry 105
Kauper, Paul Gerhardt 1907-1974 ...... CANR-6
Obituary 49-52
Earlier sketch in CA 4R
Kaur, Sardarni Premka 1943- 77-80
Kausler, Donald H(arvey) 1927- 19-20R
Kauth, Benjamin 1914- 7-8R
Kautsky, Karl (Johann) 1854-1938
Brief entry 123
Kauvar, Gerald B(luestone) 1938- 45-48
Kavafis, Konstantinos Petrou 1863-1933
Brief entry 104
Kavaler, Lucy 1930- CANR-22
Earlier sketches in CA 57-60, CANR-7
See also SATA 23
Kavaler, Rebecca 1932- CANR-16
Earlier sketch in CA 89-92
Kavan, Anna 1901-1968 .... CANR-6
Earlier sketch in CA 7-8R
See also CLC 5, 13
Kavanagh, Aidan 1929- 112
Kavanagh, Dan
See Barnes, Julian
Kavanagh, Jennifer 1947- 119
Kavanagh, Michael 1945- 118
Kavanagh, P(atrick) J(oseph Gregory)
1931- 81-84
See also DLB 40
Kavanagh, Patrick (Joseph) 1904-1967 123
Obituary 25-28R
See also DLB 15, 20
See also CLC 22
Kavanaugh, Cynthia
See Daniels, Dorothy
Kavanaugh, Ian
See Webb, Jean Francis
Kavanaugh, James J(oseph) 1934- CANR-17
Earlier sketch in CA 13-14R
Kavanaugh, John F(rancis) 1941- 115
Kavanaugh, Kieran 1928- 25-28R
Kavanaugh, Robert E. 1926- 29-32R
Kavasch, E(lizabeth) Barrie 1942- 110
Kavenagh, W(illiam) Keith 1926- 37-40R
Kavesh, Robert A(llyn) 1927- 19-20R
Kavet, Robert 1924- 37-40R
Kavifis, Konstantinos Petrou
See Kavafis, Konstantinos Petrou
Kavli, Guthorm 1917- CAP-1
Earlier sketch in CA 9-10
Kavner, Richard S. 1936- 93-96
Kavolis, Vytautas 1930- 25-28R
Kawabata, Yasunari 1899-1972 93-96
Obituary 33-36R
See also CLC 2, 5, 9, 18
Kawahito, Kiyoshi 1939- 37-40R
Kawai, Kazuo 1904-1963 .... 1R
Kawakami, Toyo S(uyemoto) 1916- 33-36R
Kawin, Bruce F. 1945- CANR-13
Earlier sketch in CA 37-40R
Kawin, Ethel ?-1969 .... CAP-1
Earlier sketch in CA 11-12
Kay, Barbara Ann 1929- 13-14R
Kay, Brian Ross 1924- 1R
Kay, David A(llen) 1940- Brief entry 114
Kay, Donald 1939- 57-60
Kay, E(lizabeth) Alison 1928- 65-68
Kay, Ellen
See DeMille, Nelson
Kay, Ernest 1915- CANR-24
Earlier sketches in CA 13-14R, CANR-6
Kay, George 1936- 21-22R
Kay, George
See Lambert, Eric
Kay, Harry 1919- 25-28R
Kay, Helen
See Goldfrank, Helen Colodny
Kay, J(ohn) A(nderson) 1948- 119
Kay, Jane Holtz 1938- CANR-22
Earlier sketch in CA 106
Kay, Kenneth (Edmond) 1915- CANR-6
Earlier sketch in CA 9-10R
Kay, Mara CANR-2
Earlier sketch in CA 7-8R
See also SATA 13
Kay, Mary
See Ash, Mary Kay (Wagner)
Kay, Norman (Forber) 1929- 45-48
Kay, (Sydney Francis) Patrick (Chippendall)
Healey
See Healey-Kay, (Sydney Francis) Patrick
(Chippendall)
Kay, Paul 1934- 41-44R
Kay, Reed 1925- 77-80
Kay, Ronald
See Knox-Mawer, Ronald
Kay, Terence 1918- 19-20R
Kay, Teresa
See de Kerpely, Theresa
Kay, Terry (Winter) 1938- 110
Kay, Terry
See Kay, Terence
Kay, Thomas O(bed) 1932- 3R
Kay, (Albert) William 1930-1976 .... CAP-2
Earlier sketch in CA 29-32
Kay, Zell
See Kemp, Roy Z(ell)
Kayal, Joseph M(itchell) 1942- 57-60
Kayal, Philip M(itchell) 1943- 57-60
Kaye, Alan
See Horowitz, Shel Alan
Kaye, Barbara
See Muir, Marie
Kaye, Bruce (Norman) 1939- 93-96
Kaye, Buddy 1918- 81-84
Kaye, Danny 1913-1987 Obituary 121
See also SATA 50
Kaye, Evelyn 1937- 57-60
Kaye, Geraldine (Hughesdon) 1925- CANR-22
Earlier sketches in CA 15-16R, CANR-7
See also SATA 10
Kaye, H. R.
See Knox, Hugh (Randolph)
Kaye, Harvey E(arle) 1927- 101
Kaye, Harvey J(ordan) 1949- 121
Kaye, Hilary 1950- 116
Kaye, Joanne
See Payes, Rachel C(osgrove)
Kaye, Julian B(ertram) 1925- 1R
Kaye, Kenneth Peter 1946- 111
Kaye, Lenny 1946- Brief entry 121
Kaye, M(ary) M(argaret) 1909- CANR-24
Earlier sketch in CA 89-92
See also CLC 28
Kaye, Marilyn 1949- CANR-24
Earlier sketch in CA 107
Kaye, Marvin (Nathan) 1938- CANR-19
Earlier sketches in CA 53-56, CANR-5
Kaye, Mollie
See Kaye, M(ary) M(argaret)
Kaye, Myrna 1930- 57-60
Kaye, Peggy 1948- 116
Kaye, Philip A. 1920- 37-40R
Kaye, Phyllis Johnson 102
Kaye-Smith, Sheila 1887-1956 Brief entry ... 118
See also DLB 36
See also TCLC 20
Kayira, Legson Didimu 1940- 17-18R
Kaysen, Carl 1920- CANR-11
Earlier sketch in CA 19-20R
Kayser, Elmer Louis 1896-1985 ....37-40R
Obituary 116
Kayser, Hugh F. 1926- 107
Kayser-Jones, Jeanie Schmit 1935- 105
Kaysing, Bill
See Kaysing, William C.
Kaysing, William C. 1922- 33-36R
Kayyali, Abdul-Wahhab (Said) 1939-1981
Obituary 108
Kazakov, Yuri Pavlovich 1927- 7-8R
Kazamias, Andreas M. 1927- 19-20R
Kazan, Elia 1909- 21-22R
See also CLC 6, 16
Kazantzakis, Nikos 1883-1957 Brief entry ... 105
See also TCLC 2, 5
Kazarian, Edward A(rshak) 1931- 53-56
Kazdin, Alan E(dward) 1945- 104
Kazee, Buell H(ilton) 1900-1976 Obituary ... 111
Kazemzadeh Firuz 1924- 23-24R
Kazickas, Jurate C(atherine) 1943- 102
Kazimiroff, Theodore L. 1941- 109
Kazin, Alfred 1915- CANR-1
Earlier sketch in CA 4R
See also DLB 67
See also CLC 34, 38
Kazis, Richard 1952- 112
Kazmer, Daniel (Raphael) 1947- 102
Kazmier, Leonard J(ohn) 1930- 107
Kazziha, Walid W. 1941- 65-68
Keach, Richard L(eroy) 1919- 89-92
Kealey, Edward J(oseph) 1936- CANR-14
Earlier sketch in CA 37-40R
Kealy, Sean P(atrick) 1937- 114
Kean, Benjamin Harrison 1912- 103
Kean, Charles Duell 1910-1963 ....5-6R
Kean, Edmund (Stanley) 1915- 102
Keane, Betty Winkler 1914- 93-96
Keane, Bil 1922- CANR-13
Earlier sketch in CA 33-36R
See also SATA 4
Keane, John B. 1928- 29-32R
See also DLB 13
Keane, Mary Nesta (Skrine) 1904- 114
Brief entry 108
Keane, Molly
See Keane, Mary Nesta (Skrine)
See also CLC 31
Keane, Patrick J(oseph) 1939- CANR-1
Earlier sketch in CA 45-48
Keaney, Marian 1944- 103
Kearey, Charles 1916- 45-48
Kearley, F(loyd) Furman 1932- 57-60
Kearney, Hugh Francis 1924- 7-8R
Kearney, James R(obert III) 1929- 25-28R
Kearney, Jean Nylander 1923- 65-68
Kearney, Robert N(orman) 1930- 81-84
Kearney, Ruth Elizabeth
See Carlson, Ruth (Elizabeth) Kearney
Kearns, Doris Helen
See Goodwin, Doris (Helen) Kearns
Kearns, Francis E(dward) 1931- 29-32R
Kearns, Frank 1917(?)-1986 Obituary 119
Kearns, Frank T. 1903-1984 Obituary 111
Kearns, James A(loysius) III 1949- 29-32R
Kearns, Lionel 1937- CANR-11
Earlier sketch in CA 19-20R
Kearns, Martha 1945- 57-60
Kearny, Edward N. III 1936- 29-32R
Kearny, Jillian
See Goulart, Ron(ald Joseph)
Keasey, Carol Tomlinson
See Tomlinson-Keasey, Carol
Keast, James D. 1930- 25-28R
Keast, William R(ea) 1914- 15-16R
Keates, Jonathan 19(?)- CLC-34
Keating, Bern
See Keating, Leo Bernard
Keating, Charlotte Matthews 1927- 33-36R
Keating, Diane 1940- CANR-18
Earlier sketch in CA 101
Keating, Edward M. 1925- 15-16R
Keating, H(enry) R(eymond) F(itzwalter)
1926- CANR-18
Earlier sketch in CA 33-36R
Keating, John J. 1918(?)-1975 Obituary ...61-64
Keating, L(ouis) Clark 1907- 21-22R
Keating, Lawrence A. 1903-1966 ....7-8R
See also SATA 23
Keating, Leo Bernard 1915- 29-32R
See also SATA 10
Keating, Michael (F.) 1932- 49-52
Keating, Tom 1917-1984 Obituary 112
Keaton, Buster 1895-1966 ....CLC-20
Keats, Charles B. 1905- CAP-1
Earlier sketch in CA 15-16
Keats, Ezra Jack 1916-1983 77-80
Obituary 109
See also SATA 14, 34
See also DLB 61
See also CLR 1
See also AITN 1
Keats, John (C.) 1920- 73-76
Keats, Mark 1905- 77-80
Keaveney, Arthur 1951- 124
Keaveney, Sydney Starr 1939- 53-56
Keay, Frederick 1915- 33-36R
Keay, John (Stanley Melville) 1941- 65-68
Kebbe, Charles Maynard 1913- 114
Kebin, Jodi
See Lawrence, Jodi
Keble, John 1792-1866 .... DLB-32, 55
Kebschull, Harvey G(ustav) 1932- 41-44R
Keck, Leander Earl 1928- 104
Keddell, Georgina (Murray) 1913- 25-28R
Keddie, Nikki R(agozin) 1930- CANR-13
Earlier sketch in CA 25-28R
Kedgley, Susan (Jane) 1948- 61-64
Kedourie, Elie 1926- CANR-10
Earlier sketch in CA 21-22R
Kedzie, Daniel Peter 1930- 17-18R
Kee, (Alexander) Alistair 1937- 89-92
Kee, Howard Clark 1920- CANR-10
Earlier sketch in CA 23-24R
Kee, Robert 1919- Brief entry 113
Keeble, John 1944- CANR-14
Earlier sketch in CA 29-32R
See also DLBY 83
Keech, William J(ohn) 1904- CAP-1
Earlier sketch in CA 9-10
Keech, William R(obertson) 1939- 25-28R
Keedy, Mervin L(averne) 1920- CANR-5
Earlier sketch in CA 53-56
Keefe, Carolyn 1928- 57-60
Keefe, Donald Joseph 1924- 37-40R
Keefe, John Edwin 1942- 107
Keefe, Michael 1946- 93-96
Keefe, Robert 1938- 89-92
Keefer, Catherine
See Ogan, George F.
and Ogan, Margaret E. (Nettles)
Keefer, T(ruman) Frederick 1930- 23-24R
Keeffe, Barrie (Colin) 1945- Brief entry 116
See also DLB 13
Keegan, Frank L. 1925- 45-48
Keegan, Marcia 1943- 49-52
See also SATA 9
Keegan, Mary Heathcott 1914- CANR-3
Earlier sketch in CA 7-8R
Keegan, Terence J(ames) 1939- 117
Keegan, Warren J(oseph) 1936- 57-60
Keel, Frank
See Keeler, Ronald F(ranklin)
Keel, John A.
See Kiehle, John Alva
Keele, Kenneth D(avid) 1909- 7-8R
Keele, Reba Lou 1941- Brief entry 106
Keeler, Mary Frear 1904- 77-80
Keeler, Ronald F(ranklin) 1913-1983 107
See also SATA 47
Keeley, Edmund (Leroy) 1928- CANR-22
Earlier sketches in CA 1R, CANR-1
Keeley, James 1867-1934 .... DLB-25
Keeley, Joseph C(harles) 1907- 25-28R
Keeley, Steve 1949- 93-96
Keeling, Clinton Harry 1932- CANR-7
Earlier sketch in CA 11-12R
Keeling, E. B.
See Curl, James Stevens
Keeling, Jill Annette (Shaw) 1923- CANR-12
Earlier sketches in CA 9-10, CAP-1
Keely, Charles C(larke), Jr. 1934-1985
Obituary 116
Keely, Harry Harris 1904- 65-68
Keely, Jane 1922- 107
Keen, Benjamin 1913- Brief entry 114
Keen, (John) Ernest 1937- 33-36R
Keen, Geraldine
See Norman, Geraldine (Lucia)
Keen, M. H.
See Keen, Maurice Hugh
Keen, Martin L. 1913- 33-36R
See also SATA 4
Keen, Maurice
See Keen, Maurice Hugh
Keen, Maurice Hugh 1933- 122
Keen, Tommy 1923- 108
Keenan, Angela Elizabeth 1890-1983 61-64
Obituary 111
Keenan, Boyd R(aymond) 1928- 17-18R
Keenan, Deborah (Anne) 1950- CANR-11
Earlier sketch in CA 69-72
Keenan, Joseph H(enry) 1900-1977
Obituary 73-76
Keenan, Martha 1927- 77-80
Keene, Burt
See Bickers, Richard Leslie Townshend
Keene, Carolyn
See Adams, Harriet S(tratemeyer)
and McFarlane, Leslie
Keene, Donald 1922- CANR-5
Earlier sketch in CA 1R
See also CLC 34
Keene, J(ames) Calvin 1908- CAP-1
Earlier sketch in CA 17-18
Keene, James A(llen) 1932- 109
Keene, R. D.
See Keene, Raymond D(ennis)
Keene, Ray
See Keene, Raymond D(ennis)
Keene, Raymond D(ennis) 1948-
Brief entry 112
Keener, Frederick M(ichael) 1937- CANR-15
Earlier sketch in CA 53-56
Keeney, Charles James 1912- 7-8R
Keeney, Chuck
See Keeney, Charles James
Keeney, Ralph L(yons) 1944- CANR-16
Earlier sketch in CA 97-100
Keeney, William (Echard) 1922- CANR-15
Earlier sketch in CA 41-44R
Keenleyside, Hugh Llewellyn 1898- CAP-1
Earlier sketch in CA 17-18
Keenleyside, T(erence) A(shley) 1940- 77-80
Keep, Carolyn 1940- 65-68
Keep, David (John) 1936- 61-64
Keep, John (Leslie Howard) 1926- 11-12R
Keeping, Charles 1924- CANR-11
Earlier sketch in CA 21-22R
See also SATA 9
Keery, Sam 1929- 124
Kees, Beverly (Ann) 1941- 81-84
Keese, Parton 1926- 109
Keesecker, William Francis 1918- 33-36R
Keeshan, Robert J. 1927- CANR-5
Earlier sketch in CA 7-8R
See also SATA 32
Keesing, Nancy (Florence) 1923- CANR-6
Earlier sketch in CA 11-12R
Keeslar, Oreon 1907- CAP-1
Earlier sketch in CA 13-14
Keeton, Elizabeth B(aker) 1919- 29-32R
Keeton, George Williams 1902- 13-14R
Keeton, Kathy AITN-2
Keeton, Morris Teuton 1917- CANR-4
Earlier sketch in CA 2R
Keeton, Robert E(rnest) 1919- CANR-2
Earlier sketch in CA 5-6R
Keeton, William T(insley) 1933-1980 124
Keeton, William Tinsley 1933-1980
Obituary 105
Keever, Jack 1938- 53-56
Keevill, Henry J(ohn) 1914- CAP-1
Earlier sketch in CA 9-10
Keezer, Dexter Merriam 1895- 1R
Kefferstan, Jean
See Pedrick, Jean
Kegan, Adrienne Koch 1912-1971
Obituary 33-36R
Kegel, Charles H. 1924- 1R
Kegley, Charles W(illiam), Jr. 1944- 114
Kegley, Charles William 1912- CANR-2
Earlier sketch in CA 5-6R
Kehayan, V. Alex 1944- 110

Kehl, D(elmar) G(eorge) 1936- ... 33-36R
Kehl, James Arthur 1922- ... 112
Kehle, Roberta L(unsford) 1936- ... 116
Kehm, Freda (Irma) S(amuels) ... CAP-2
Earlier sketch in CA 29-32
Kehoe, Constance (DeMuzio) 1933- ... 15-16R
Kehoe, Monika 1909- ... 21-22R
Kehoe, Patrick E(mmett) 1941- ... 57-60
Kehoe, William F. 1933- ... 15-16R
Kehrer, Daniel M(ark) 1953- ... 120
Kehrer, James P(aul) 1951- ... 117
Keidel, Eudene 1921- ... 109
Keidel, Levi (Jr.) 1927- ... 115
Keifetz, Norman 1932- ... 89-92
Keightley, David N(oel) 1932- ... 97-100
Keil, (Harold) Bill 1926- ... 81-84
Keil, Sally Van Wagenen 1946- ... 89-92
Keillor, Garrison
See Keillor, Gary (Edward)
See also CLC 40
Keillor, Gary (Edward) 1942- ... 117
Brief entry ... 111
Keim, Charles J. 1921- ... CANR-13
Earlier sketch in CA 33-36R
Keimberg, Allyn
See Kimbro, John M.
Keinzley, Frances 1922- ... 85-88
Keir, Christine
See Popescu, Christine
Keir, David E(dwin) 1906-1969 ... CAP-1
Earlier sketch in CA 9-10
Keir, David Lindsay 1895-1973 ... CAP-2
Earlier sketch in CA 21-22
Keirstead, Burton Seely 1907- ... 7-8R
Keiser, Bea(trice) 1931- ... 97-100
Keiser, Norman F(red) 1930- ... 15-16R
Keislar, Evan R(ollo) 1913- ... 23-24R
Keisling, Bill
See Keisling, William
Keisling, William 1958- ... 113
Keisman, Michael E(dward) 1932- ... 25-28R
Keister, Elinore
See Dobson, Elinore (Lucille)
Keitges, Julie 1940- ... 110
Keith, Agnes Newton 1901- ... 19-20R
Keith, Carlton
See Robertson, Keith (Carlton)
Keith, David
See Steegmuller, Francis
Keith, Donald
See Monroe, Keith
Keith, Elmer (Merrifield) 1899- ... 101
Keith, Eros 1942- ... 114
Keith, Hal 1934- ... SATA-36
Keith, Hamish
See Chapman, James (Keith)
Keith, Harold Verne 1903- ... CANR-2
Earlier sketch in CA 7-8R
See also SATA 2
Keith, Herbert F. 1895- ... 37-40R
Keith, J. Kilmeny
See Malleson, Lucy Beatrice
Keith, Jean E. 1921-1979 Obituary ... 85-88
Keith, Jennie 1942- ... 116
Keith, Judith 1923- ... 49-52
Keith, K. Wymand 1924- ... 33-36R
Keith, Larry Ficquette 1947- ... 97-100
Keith, Lee
See Sunners, William
Keith, Michael
See Hubbard, L(afayette) Ron(ald)
Keith, Noel L. 1903- ... 57-60
Keith, Robert
See Applebaum, Stan
Keith, Ronald (A.) 1914(?)-1985 Obituary ... 117
Keith, Sam 1921- ... 65-68
Keith, W(illiam) J(ohn) 1934- ... CANR-11
Earlier sketch in CA 17-18R
Keithley, Erwin M. 1905- ... 73-76
Keithley, George 1935- ... 37-40R
Keith-Lucas, Alan 1910- ... CANR-20
Earlier sketches in CA 7-8R, CANR-2
Keith-Lucas, Bryan 1912- ... 107
Keith-Spiegel, Patricia 1939- ... 41-44R
Keith X
See Armstrong, Keith F(rancis) W(hitfield)
Kekes, John 1936- ... 65-68
Kekkonen, Sylvi 1900(?)-1974 Obituary ... 53-56
Kelber, Magda 1908- ... 7-8R
Kelch, Ray Alden 1923- ... 85-88
Kelder, Diane 1934- ... CANR-18
Earlier sketch in CA 25-28R
Keldysh, Mstislav V(sevolodovich) 1911-1978 Obituary ... 77-80
Kele, Max H(erschel) 1936- Brief entry ... 114
Keleher, Will(iam Aloysius) 1886-1972
Obituary ... 37-40R
Keleman, Stanley 1931- ... CANR-14
Earlier sketch in CA 81-84
Kelemen, Pal 1894- ... 104
Kelen, Emery 1896-1978 ... 9-10R
Obituary ... 103
See also SATA 13, 26
Kelen, Stephen 1912- ... 107
Kelf-Cohen, Reuben 1895- ... 49-52
Kelikian, Hampar 1899(?)-1983 Obituary ... 110
Kell, Joseph
See Wilson, John (Anthony) Burgess
Kell, Richard (Alexander) 1927- ... CANR-8
Earlier sketch in CA 7-8R
Kellam, Sheppard (Gordon) 1931- ... 73-76
Kelland, Clarence Budington 1881-1964
Obituary ... 89-92
Kellar, Kenneth C(hambers) 1906- ... 45-48
Kellaway, Frank (Gerald) 1922- ... 9-10R
Kellaway, George P(ercival) 1909- ... CAP-2
Earlier sketch in CA 23-24
Kelleam, Joseph E(veridge) 1913-1975 ... 107
See also SATA 31
Kelleher, Catherine McArdle 1939-
Brief entry ... 115
Kelleher, Patrick J(oseph) 1917-1985
Obituary ... 116
Kelleher, Stephen J(oseph) 1915- ... 69-72
Keller, Allan 1904- ... 29-32R
Keller, Betty 1930- ... 121
Keller, Beverly (Lou) ... CANR-17
Earlier sketches in CA 49-52, CANR-1
See also SATA 13
Keller, Charles 1942- ... CANR-2
Earlier sketch in CA 49-52
See also SATA 8
Keller, Clair W(ayne) 1932- ... 53-56
Keller, Dean H(oward) 1933- ... 53-56
Keller, Dick 1923- ... SATA-36
Keller, Dolores Elaine 1926- ... 104
Keller, Edward A(nthony) 1942- ... 73-76
Keller, Frances Richardson 1914- ... 81-84
Keller, Franklin J. 1887(?)-1976 Obituary ... 65-68
Keller, Fred S(immons) 1899- ... CANR-11
Earlier sketch in CA 69-72
Keller, Gail Faithfull
See Faithfull, Gail
Keller, George 1928- ... 123
Keller, Helen (Adams) 1880-1968 ... 101
Obituary ... 89-92
Keller, Holly Brief entry ... 118
See also SATA 42
Keller, Howard H(ughes) 1941- ... 45-48
Keller, Irene (Barron) 1927- ... 116
See also SATA 36
Keller, James Gregory 1900-1977
Obituary ... 69-72
Keller, John E(sten) 1917- ... 45-48
Keller, Karl 1933- ... CANR-12
Earlier sketch in CA 57-60
Keller, Marti 1948- ... 97-100
Keller, Mitzie Stuart ... 111
Keller, Mollie ... SATA-50
Keller, Morton 1929- ... 5-6R
Keller, Suzanne 1930- ... 65-68
Keller, Thomas F(ranklin) 1931- ... CANR-3
Earlier sketch in CA 11-12R
Keller, W(alter) D(avid) 1900- ... 41-44R
Keller, Werner (Rudolf August Wolfgang) 1909-19(?) ... CANR-13
Earlier sketch in CA 23-24R
Kellerman, Barbara 1939- ... 110
Kellerman, Faye 1952- ... 120
Kellerman, Jonathan 1949- ... 106
See also CLC 44
Kellett, Arnold 1926- ... CANR-19
Earlier sketch in CA 103
Kelley, Alden D(rew) 1903- ... 1R
Kelley, Alice van Buren 1944- ... 81-84
Kelley, Allen C(harles) 1937- ... 104
Kelley, Arleon L(eigh) 1935- ... 115
Kelley, (Albert) Ben 1936- ... 45-48
Kelley, Brooks Mather 1929- ... 111
Kelley, Cecil B., Sr. 1911(?)-1987
Obituary ... 123
Kelley, Dean M(aurice) 1926- ... 81-84
Kelley, Donald R(eed) 1931- ... CANR-12
Earlier sketch in CA 29-32R
Kelley, Earl Clarence 1895- ... 5-6R
Kelley, Edith Summers 1884-1956
Brief entry ... 109
See also DLB 9
Kelley, Eugene J(ohn) 1922- ... 13-14R
Kelley, H. N. 1911- ... 45-48
Kelley, Hubert (Williams), Jr. 1926- ... 5-6R
Kelley, J(ohn) Charles 1913- ... 97-100
Kelley, Jane Holden 1928- ... 45-48
Kelley, Joanna (Elizabeth) 1910- ... CAP-2
Earlier sketch in CA 23-24
Kelley, Jonathan ... 107
Kelley, Joseph J(ohn), Jr. 1914- ... CANR-8
Earlier sketch in CA 61-64
Kelley, Kevin J. 1948- ... 120
Kelley, Kitty 1942- ... 81-84
Kelley, Leo P(atrick) 1928- ... CANR-24
Earlier sketch in CA 107
See also SATA 31, 32
Kelley, Mary 1943- ... 124
Kelley, Maurice (Willyle) 1903- ... 119
Kelley, Page H(utto) 1924- ... 25-28R
Kelley, Ray
See Paine, Lauran (Bosworth)
Kelley, Robert 1925- ... 25-28R
Kelley, Robert E(mmett) 1938- ... 53-56
Kelley, Ruby M.
See Johnson, Ruby Kelley
Kelley, Stanley, Jr. 1926- ... 13-14R
Kelley, True (Adelaide) 1946- ... CANR-23
Earlier sketch in CA 105
See also SATA 39, 41
Kelley, William 1929- ... CANR-6
Earlier sketch in CA 7-8R
Kelley, William Melvin 1937- ... 77-80
See also DLB 33
See also CLC 22
Kelley, William T(homas) 1917- ... 37-40R
Kelley, Win 1923- ... 89-92
Kellin, Sally Moffet 1932- ... 61-64
See also SATA 9
Kelling, Furn L. 1914- ... 19-20R
See also SATA 37
Kelling, George W(alton) 1944- ... CANR-9
Earlier sketch in CA 57-60
Kelling, Hans-Wilhelm 1932- ... 37-40R
Kellison, Stephen G. 1942- ... 53-56
Kellman, Steven G. 1947- ... 112
Kellner, Bruce 1930- ... CANR-11
Earlier sketch in CA 29-32R
Kellner, Douglas Mackay 1943- ... 116
Kellner, Esther ... 13-14R
Kellner, L. 1904- ... 5-6R
Kellock, Archibald P.
See Mavor, Osborne Henry
Kellogg, Alfred Latimer 1915- ... 41-44R
Kellogg, Ansel Nash 1832-1886 ... DLB-23
Kellogg, Charles Edwin 1902-1980
Obituary ... 97-100
Kellogg, Charles Flint 1909- ... CAP-2
Earlier sketch in CA 23-24
Kellogg, Gene
See Kellogg, Jean (Defrees)
Kellogg, James C. III 1915-1980 Obituary ... 103
Kellogg, Jean (Defrees) 1916-1978 ... CANR-7
Earlier sketch in CA 9-10R
See also SATA 10
Kellogg, Marion S(chuyler) 1920- ... 120
Kellogg, Marjorie 1922- ... 81-84
See also CLC 2
Kellogg, Mary Alice 1948- ... 81-84
Kellogg, Steven 1941- ... CANR-1
Earlier sketch in CA 49-52
See also SATA 8
See also DLB 61
See also CLR 6
Kellogg, Virginia 1907-1981 Obituary ... 108
Kellogg, Winthrop N(iles) 1898-1971 ... 1R
Kellough, Richard Dean 1935- ... 53-56
Kellow, Kathleen
See Hibbert, Eleanor Burford
Kellow, Norman B. 1914- ... 21-22R
Kellum, D(avid) F(ranklin) 1936- ... 61-64
Kelly, Alfred H. 1907-1976 ... 5-6R
Obituary ... 65-68
Kelly, Alison 1913- ... 105
Kelly, Averill Alison 1913- ... 13-14R
Kelly, Balmer H(ancock) 1914- ... 19-20R
Kelly, C(harles) Brian 1935- ... 89-92
Kelly, C.M.O.
See Gibbs, (Cecilia) May
Kelly, Carla 1947- ... 118
Kelly, Charles E. 1920(?)-1985 Obituary ... 114
Kelly, Charles Patrick Bernard 1891(?)-1971 Obituary ... 29-32R
Kelly, Clarence 1941- ... 61-64
Kelly, Commando
See Kelly, Charles E.
Kelly, Dave
See Kelly, David M(ichael)
Kelly, David M(ichael) 1938- ... CANR-12
Earlier sketch in CA 29-32R
Kelly, Edward H(anford) 1930- ... 37-40R
Kelly, Emmett (Leo) 1898-1979 Obituary ... 85-88
Kelly, Eric Philbrook 1884-1960 Obituary ... 93-96
See also YABC 1
Kelly, Faye L(ucius) 1914- ... 23-24R
Kelly, Frank K. 1914- ... CANR-16
Earlier sketches in CA 1R, CANR-1
Kelly, Frederic Joseph 1922- ... 53-56
Kelly, Gail P(aradise) 1940- ... 81-84
Kelly, Gary F(rank) 1943- ... 89-92
Kelly, George A. 1916- ... CANR-11
Earlier sketch in CA 17-18R
Kelly, George E. 1887-1974 Obituary ... 49-52
See also DLB 7
See also AITN 1
Kelly, George V(incent) 1919- ... 93-96
Kelly, George W. 1894- ... CANR-9
Earlier sketch in CA 65-68
Kelly, Gerald R(ay) 1930- ... 29-32R
Kelly, Grace (Patricia) 1929-1982 Obituary ... 107
Kelly, Guy
See Moore, Nicholas
Kelly, Henry Ansgar 1934- ... 25-28R
Kelly, James B(urton) 1905- ... 49-52
Kelly, James Plunkett 1920- ... 53-56
Kelly, Jeffrey A(llen) 1948- ... 114
Kelly, Joan 1928(?)-1982 Obituary ... 107
Kelly, Joan Berlin 1939- ... 107
Kelly, John 1921- ... 73-76
Kelly, John M., Jr. 1919- ... 13-14R
Kelly, John Maurice 1931- ... 109
Kelly, John N(orman) D(avidson) 1909- ... CANR-5
Earlier sketch in CA 7-8R
Kelly, John Rivard 1939- ... 103
Kelly, Joyce 1933- ... 106
Kelly, Karen 1935- ... 101
Kelly, Kathleen Sheridan White 1945- ... 49-52
Kelly, L(ouis) G(erard) 1935- ... 107
Kelly, Laurence 1933- ... CANR-15
Earlier sketch in CA 81-84
Kelly, Lawrence C(harles) 1932- ... CANR-8
Earlier sketch in CA 23-24R
Kelly, Leo J. 1925- ... 41-44R
Kelly, (Alison) Linda 1936- ... 103
Kelly, M(ilton) T(erry) 1947- ... CANR-19
Earlier sketch in CA 97-100
Kelly, Mahlon (George) 1939- ... 53-56
Kelly, Marguerite (Lelong) 1932- ... 65-68
Kelly, Martha Rose 1914-1983 ... 69-72
See also SATA 37
Kelly, Marty
See Kelly, Martha Rose
Kelly, Mary Coolican 1927- ... CANR-2
Earlier sketch in CA 4R
Kelly, Mary J(osephine) 1944- ... 117
Kelly, Maurice Anthony 1931- ... 53-56
Kelly, Maurice N. 1919- ... 23-24R
Kelly, Nora (Hickson) 1910- ... 101
Kelly, Patrick
See Allbeury, Theodore Edward le Bouthillier
Kelly, Paula 1949- ... 114
Kelly, Pauline Agnes 1936- ... 45-48
Kelly, Philip John 1896-1972 ... 7-8R
Obituary ... 37-40R
Kelly, Ralph
See Geis, Darlene Stern
Kelly, Ray
See Paine, Lauran (Bosworth)
Kelly, Regina Z(immerman) 1898- ... CANR-2
Earlier sketch in CA 4R
See also SATA 5
Kelly, Richard 1937- ... 107
Kelly, Richard J(ohn) 1938- ... 41-44R
Kelly, Rita Mae 1939- ... 81-84
Kelly, Robert 1935- ... 17-18R
See also DLB 5
Kelly, Robert Glynn 1920- ... 1R
Kelly, Rosalie (Ruth) ... CANR-11
Earlier sketch in CA 61-64
See also SATA 43
Kelly, Russell 1949- ... 123
Kelly, Stan
See Kelly-Bootle, Stan
Kelly, Stephen E(ugene) 1919-1978 ... 110
Obituary ... 104
Kelly, Thomas 1909- ... CAP-1
Earlier sketch in CA 9-10
Kelly, Thomas 1929- ... 109
Kelly, Tim 1935- ... 15-16R
Kelly, Walt(er Crawford) 1913-1973 ... 73-76
Obituary ... 45-48
See also SATA 18
Kelly, William Leo 1924- ... 15-16R
Kelly, William W(atkins) 1928- ... 11-12R
Kelly-Bootle, Stan 1929- ... 110
Kelly-Gadol, Joan ... 61-64
Kelm, Karlton 1908(?)-1987 Obituary ... 121
Kelman, Charles D. 1930- ... 110
Kelman, Herbert C(hanoch) 1927- ... 15-16R
Kelman, Mark 1951- ... 93-96
Kelman, Steven 1948- ... CANR-12
Earlier sketch in CA 29-32R
Kelsay, Isabel Thompson 1905- ... 121
Kelsen, Hans 1881-1973 Obituary ... 115
Kelsey, Alice Geer 1896- ... 5-6R
See also SATA 1
Kelsey, Joan Marshall 1907- ... 7-8R
Kelsey, Morton T(rippe) 1917- ... CANR-10
Earlier sketch in CA 23-24R
Kelsey, Robert J(ohn) 1927- ... 103
Kelso, Louis O. 1913- ... 25-28R
Kelso, Ruth 1885-1986 Obituary ... 119
Kelson, Allen H(oward) 1940- ... CANR-13
Earlier sketch in CA 77-80
Keltner, John W(illiam) 1918- ... 29-32R
Kelton, Elmer 1926- ... CANR-12
Earlier sketch in CA 21-22R
See also AITN 1
Kelvin, Norman 1924- Brief entry ... 118
Kemal, Yashar 1923- ... 89-92
See also CLC 14, 29
Kemble, Fanny 1809-1893 ... DLB-32
Kemble, James ... CAP-2
Earlier sketch in CA 29-32
Kemelman, Harry 1908- ... CANR-6
Earlier sketch in CA 11-12R
See also DLB 28
See also CLC 2
See also AITN 1
Kemeny, Jean A(lexander) 1930- ... 117
Kemeny, John G(eorge) 1926- ... 33-36R
Kemeny, Peter 1938-1975 ... 53-56
Obituary ... 89-92
Kemerer, Frank R(obert) 1940- ... CANR-10
Earlier sketch in CA 65-68
Kemmerer, Donald L(orenzo) 1905- ... 4R
Kemp, Anthony 1939- ... 105
Kemp, Arnold 1938- Brief entry ... 110
Kemp, Bernard Peter 1942- ... 107
Kemp, Betty 1916- ... 11-12R
Kemp, Charles F. 1912- ... CANR-5
Earlier sketch in CA 9-10R
Kemp, Diana Moyle 1919- ... CAP-1
Earlier sketch in CA 9-10
Kemp, Edward C. 1929- ... 81-84
Kemp, Gene 1926- ... CANR-12
Earlier sketch in CA 69-72
See also SATA 25
Kemp, Jack (French) 1935- ... 109
Kemp, Jerrold E(dwin) 1921- ... 77-80
Kemp, John C(rocker) 1942- ... 93-96
Kemp, Lysander (Schaffer, Jr.) 1920- ... CANR-1
Earlier sketch in CA 45-48
Kemp, Martin (John) 1942- ... 108
Kemp, Patrick S(amuel) 1932- ... 53-56
Kemp, Peter (Mant Macintyre) 1915- ... 25-28R
Kemp, Robert 1908-1967 ... CAP-1
Earlier sketch in CA 15-16
Kemp, Roy Z(ell) 1910- ... 9-10R
Kemp, Tom 1921- ... 25-28R
Kempe, C(harles) Henry 1922-1984 ... 122
Kemper, Donald J. 1929- ... 21-22R
Kemper, Inez 1906- ... CAP-1
Earlier sketch in CA 13-14
Kemper, Rachel H. 1931- ... 102
Kemper, Robert V(an) 1945- ... 104
Kemperman, Steve (Richard) 1955- ... 108
Kempfer, Lester Leroy 1932- ... 49-52
Kempher, Ruth Moon 1934- ... CANR-17
Earlier sketch in CA 25-28R
Kempner, Mary Jean 1913-1969 ... CAP-2
Earlier sketch in CA 29-32
See also SATA 10
Kempner, S. Marshall 1898- ... 85-88
Kempowski, Walter 1929- Brief entry ... 122
Kempster, Mary Yates 1911- ... CAP-1
Earlier sketch in CA 9-10
Kempster, Norman 1936- ... 77-80

Kempton, James Murray, Jr. 1945(?)-1971 Obituary 33-36R
Kempton, Jean Goldschmidt 1946(?)-1971 Obituary 33-36R
Kempton, Jean Welch 1914- 49-52
See also SATA 10
Kempton, (James) Murray 1918- 97-100
Kempton, Richard 1935- 106
Kemsley, Viscount
See Berry, James Gomer
Kemsley, William George, Jr. 1928- 85-88
Kendal, Geoffrey
See Bragg, Richard Geoffrey
Kendal, Wallis 1937- 107
Kendall, Aubyn 1919- 107
Kendall, Carol (Seeger) 1917- CANR-7
Earlier sketch in CA 5-6R
See also SATA 11
Kendall, David Evan 1944- 29-32R
Kendall, Dorothy Steinbomer 1912- 57-60
Kendall, E(dith) Lorna 1921- 5-6R
Kendall, Edward C(alvin) 1886-1972 Obituary 111
Kendall, Elaine (Becker) 1929- 17-18R
Kendall, Elizabeth B(emis) 1947- 81-84
Kendall, Gordon
See Lewitt, Shariann (N.)
Kendall, Henry Madison 1901-1966 ....7-8R
Kendall, Kenneth E(verett) 1913- 45-48
Kendall, Lace
See Stoutenburg, Adrien (Pearl)
Kendall, Laurel 1947- 121
Kendall, Lisa See 1955- 111
Kendall, Lyle H(arris), Jr. 1919- 17-18R
Kendall, Marjorie 1930- 121
Kendall, Maurice (George) 1907-1983 Obituary 109
Kendall, Paul Murray 1911-1973 .... CAP-1
Earlier sketch in CA 15-16
Kendall, R(obert) T(illman) 1935- 93-96
Kendall, Robert 1934- CANR-6
Earlier sketch in CA 15-16R
Kendall, T(homas) Robert 1935- 69-72
Kendall, Willmoore 1909-1967 .... CANR-6
Earlier sketch in CA 5-6R
Kendle, John Edward 1937- 61-64
Kendler, Howard H(arvard) 1919- 17-18R
Kendrake, Carleton
See Gardner, Erle Stanley
Kendrick, Baynard H(ardwick) 1894-1977 .... CANR-4
Obituary 69-72
Earlier sketch in CA 4R
Kendrick, David Andrew 1937- CANR-9
Earlier sketch in CA 23-24R
Kendrick, Frank J(enness) 1928- 41-44R
Kendrick, John (Stafford) 1917- 121
Kendrick, John W(hitefield) 1917- Brief entry 110
Kendrick, Thomas Downing 1895- 81-84
Kendrick, Walter 1947- 112
Kendricks, James
See Fox, G(ardner) F(rancis)
Kendris, Christopher 1923- CANR-24
Earlier sketches in CA 5-6R, CANR-7
Keneally, Thomas (Michael) 1935- CANR-10
Earlier sketch in CA 85-88
See also CLC 5, 8, 10, 14, 19, 27, 43
Kenealy, James P. 1927- 93-96
See also SATA 29
Kenealy, Jim
See Kenealy, James P.
Keneas, Alexander 1938(?)-1984 Obituary .. 113
Kenelly, John W(illis Jr.) 1935- 25-28R
Kenen, Isaiah Leo 1905- 107
Kenen, Peter B(ain) 1932- CANR-22
Earlier sketches in CA 5-6R, CANR-7
Kenesson, Frank G. 1913(?)-1985 Obituary 119
Kenez, Peter 1937- 29-32R
Kenian, Paul Roger
See Clifford, Martin
Kenin, Richard (Metz) 1947-1983 Obituary 111
Keniston, Kenneth 1930- 25-28R
Kenkel, William F(rancis) 1925- 61-64
Kenna, Peter 1930- 61-64
Kennamer, Lorrin, Jr. 1924- CANR-6
Earlier sketch in CA 5-6R
Kennan, George Frost 1904- CANR-2
Earlier sketch in CA 3R
Kennan, Kent (Wheeler) 1913- 3R
Kennard-Davis, Arthur (Shelley) 1910- ... CAP-1
Earlier sketch in CA 9-10
Kennaway, James (Pebles Ewing) 1928-1968 103
Obituary 89-92
Kennealy (Morrison), Patricia 1946- 120
Kennebeck, Edwin 1924- 41-44R
Kennebeck, Paul 1943- 53-56
Kennecott, G. J.
See Viksnins, George J(uris)
Kennedy, Adam CANR-24
Earlier sketch in CA 107
See also AITN 1
Kennedy, Adrienne (Lita) 1931- 103
See also DLB 38
Kennedy, Andrew (Karpati) 1931- 61-64
Kennedy, Archibald Edmund Clark
See Clark-Kennedy, Archibald Edmund
Kennedy, Betty 1926- 121
Kennedy, Brendan 1970- 123
Kennedy, Bruce M. 1929- 57-60
Kennedy, Carol CANR-21
Earlier sketch in CA 105
Kennedy, Charles J(oseph) 1935-1984 Obituary 114
Kennedy, Chuck
See Kennedy, Charles J(oseph)
Kennedy, D. James 1930- 61-64
Kennedy, David M. 1941- CANR-13
Earlier sketch in CA 29-32R
Kennedy, Dennis (Edward) 1940- 120
Kennedy, Don H(enry) 1911- 61-64
Kennedy, Dorothy M(intzlaff) 1931- 116
Kennedy, Eddie C. 1910- 89-92
Kennedy, Edward Moore 1932- 110
Kennedy, Edward R(idgway) 1923(?)-1975 Obituary 104
Kennedy, Elliot
See Godfrey, Lionel (Robert Holcombe)
Kennedy, Eugene C(ullen) 1928- 25-28R
Kennedy, Gail 1900-1972 Obituary 33-36R
Kennedy, Gavin 1940- CANR-9
Earlier sketch in CA 61-64
Kennedy, George 1899(?)-1977 Obituary ..73-76
Kennedy, George (Alexander) 1928- CANR-2
Earlier sketch in CA 5-6R
Kennedy, Gerald (Hamilton) 1907- CANR-6
Earlier sketch in CA 7-8R
Kennedy, Harold J. 1915(?)-1988 Obituary 124
Kennedy, Hubert (Collings) 1931- 93-96
Kennedy, J(ames) Hardee 1915- 15-16R
Kennedy, James
See Monahan, James (Henry Francis)
Kennedy, James G(ettier) 1932- 81-84
Kennedy, James William 1905- CANR-1
Earlier sketch in CA 4R
Kennedy, James Y(oung) 1916- 77-80
Kennedy, Jimmy 1903(?)-1984 Obituary 112
Kennedy, John Fitzgerald 1917-1963 .... CANR-1
Earlier sketch in CA 1R
See also SATA 11
Kennedy, John J(oseph) 1914- 57-60
Kennedy, John Pendleton 1795-1870 .... DLB-3
Kennedy, Joseph Charles 1929- CANR-4
Earlier sketch in CA 2R
See also SATA 14
See also CLC 8
Kennedy, Judith M(ary) 1935- 41-44R
Kennedy, Kathleen 1947(?)-1975 Obituary 57-60
Kennedy, Kenneth A(drian) R(aine) 1930- CANR-1
Earlier sketch in CA 45-48
Kennedy, Kieran A. 1935- 37-40R
Kennedy, L. D. 1924- 45-48
Kennedy, Leigh 1951- 122
Kennedy, Lena
See Smith, Lena (Kennedy)
Kennedy, Leonard Anthony 1922- 37-40R
Kennedy, Leonard M(ilton) 1925- 73-76
Kennedy, Ludovic Henry Coverley 1919- ...65-68
Kennedy, Malcolm D(uncan) 1895- 11-12R
Kennedy, Margaret 1896-1967 Obituary ..25-28R
See also DLB 36
Kennedy, Marilyn Moats 1943- 109
Kennedy, Mary 102
Kennedy, Michael 1926- CANR-23
Earlier sketches in CA 15-16R, CANR-5
Kennedy, Moorhead 1930- 123
Kennedy, P(eter) J(ohn) 1925- 123
Kennedy, Paul E(dward) 1929- SATA-33
Kennedy, Paul Michael 1945- CANR-9
Earlier sketch in CA 65-68
Kennedy, Ralph Dale 1897-1965 .... 4R
Kennedy, Raymond A. 1934- 5-6R
Kennedy, Richard 1910- 102
Kennedy, (Jerome) Richard 1932- CANR-7
Earlier sketch in CA 57-60
See also SATA 22
Kennedy, Richard S(ylvester) 1920- CANR-3
Earlier sketch in CA 5-6R
Kennedy, Robert E(mmet), Jr. 1937- 37-40R
Kennedy, Robert F(rancis) 1925-1968 ... CANR-1
Earlier sketch in CA 1R
Kennedy, Robert F(rancis), Jr. 1954- 110
Kennedy, Robert L(ee) 1930- 57-60
Kennedy, Robert Woods 1911- 49-52
Kennedy, Roger G(eorge) 1926- 115
Kennedy, Rose (Fitzgerald) 1890- 53-56
Kennedy, Sighle Aileen 1919- 53-56
Kennedy, Stetson 1916- 7-8R
Kennedy, Susan Estabrook 1942- 45-48
Kennedy, T(eresa) A. 1953- 114
See also SATA 35, 42
Kennedy, T(homas) F(illans) 1921- 53-56
Kennedy, Ted
See Kennedy, Edward Moore
Kennedy, Teresa
See Kennedy, T(eresa) A.
Kennedy, Theodore Reginald 1936- 105
Kennedy, Thomas 1920- 116
Kennedy, William 1928- CANR-14
Earlier sketch in CA 85-88
See also DLBY 85
See also CLC 6, 28, 34
Kennedy, William B(ean) 1926- 116
Kennedy, William J(ohn) 1942- 117
Kennedy, X. J.
See Kennedy, Joseph Charles
See also DLB 5
See also CLC 42
Kennedy-Martin, Ian 1936- 101
Kenneggy, Richard
See Nettell, Richard (Geoffrey)
Kennel, LeRoy E(ldon) 1930- 77-80
Kennell, Ruth Epperson 1893-1977 .... CAP-2
Earlier sketch in CA 29-32
See also SATA 6, 25
Kennelly, Brendan 1936- CANR-5
Earlier sketch in CA 9-10R
See also DLB 40
Kenner, Charles Leroy 1933- 25-28R
Kenner, (William) Hugh 1923- 23-24R
See also DLB 67
Kennerly, David Hume 1947- 101
See also AITN 2
Kennerly, Karen 1940- 33-36R
Kennett, (Houn) Jiyu 1924- 93-96
Kennett, Lee 1931- 23-24R
Kennett, Peggy Teresa Nancy
See Kennett, (Houn) Jiyu
Kenney, Alice P(atricia) 1937-1985 .... CANR-10
Obituary 115
Earlier sketch in CA 25-28R
Kenney, Douglas C. 1947(?)-1980 107
Obituary 101
Kenney, Edwin James, Jr. 1942- 53-56
Kenney, George Churchill 1889- CAP-1
Earlier sketch in CA 11-12
Kenney, John Paul 1920- 17-18R
Kenney, Lona B(ronberg) 1921- 115
Kenney, Susan (McIlvaine) 1941- 115
Kenney, Sylvia W. 1922-19(?) CAP-1
Earlier sketch in CA 19-20
Kennick, W(illiam) E(lmer) 1923- 15-16R
Kennington, (Gilbert) Alan 1906-1986 Obituary 121
Kennington, Alice Eve 1935- 119
Kennon, Donald R. 1948- 122
Kenny, Anthony
See Kenny, Anthony John Patrick
Kenny, Anthony John Patrick 1931- CANR-23
Earlier sketch in CA 101
Kenny, Charles J.
See Gardner, Erle Stanley
Kenny, Ellsworth Newcomb 1909-1971 ....5-6R
Obituary 103
See also SATA 26
Kenny, Herbert Andrew 1912- 41-44R
See also SATA 13
Kenny, James Andrew 1933- 107
Kenny, Jean
See Freeman, Jean Kenny
Kenny, John P. 1909- 17-18R
Kenny, John Peter 1916- CANR-1
Earlier sketch in CA 45-48
Kenny, Kathryn
See Bowden, Joan Chase
and Krull, Kathleen
and Sanderlin, Owenita (Harrah)
and Stack, Nicolete Meredith
Kenny, Kevin
See Krull, Kathleen
Kenny, Mary 1936- 108
Kenny, Michael 1923- CANR-5
Earlier sketch in CA 4R
Kenny, Nicholas Napoleon 1895-1975 Obituary 89-92
Kenny, Nick
See Kenny, Nicholas Napoleon
Kenny, Shirley (Elise) Strum 1934- 45-48
Kenny, Vincent 1919- 45-48
Kenny, W. Henry 1918- 37-40R
Kenofer, C(harles) Louis 1923- 69-72
Kenoyer, Natlee Peoples 1907- CANR-5
Earlier sketch in CA 5-6R
Kenrick, Donald Simon 1929- 81-84
Kenrick, Tony 1935- 104
Kenshalo, Daniel R(alph) 1922- 41-44R
Kensinger, George
See Fichter, George S.
Kent, Alexander
See Reeman, Douglas Edward
Kent, Allegra 1938- Brief entry 105
Kent, Allen 1921- CANR-18
Earlier sketches in CA 11-12R, CANR-3
Kent, Arden
See Marion, Frieda
Kent, Arthur William Charles 1925- 102
Kent, Bill
See Kent, Carleton Volney, Jr.
Kent, Carleton Volney, Jr. 1909-1985 Obituary 114
Kent, David
See Lambert, David (Compton)
Kent, Deborah Ann 1948- 103
See also SATA 41, 47
Kent, Donald P(eterson) 1916-1972 ....19-20R
Obituary 120
Kent, Edward Allen 1933- 45-48
Kent, Ernest W(illiam) 1940- 104
Kent, Fortune
See Toombs, John
Kent, Frank (Richardson, Jr.) 1907(?)-1978 Obituary 81-84
Kent, Frank R(ichardson) 1877-1958 Brief entry 121
See also DLB 29
Kent, George O(tto) 1919- 37-40R
Kent, George W. 1928- 25-28R
Kent, Harold W(infield) 1900- 65-68
Kent, Homer A(ustin), Jr. 1926- CANR-3
Earlier sketch in CA 9-10R
Kent, Jack
See Kent, John Wellington
Kent, John Henry Somerset 1923- 9-10R
Kent, John Wellington 1920-1985 .... CANR-16
Obituary 117
Earlier sketch in CA 85-88
See also SATA 24, 45
Kent, Katherine
See Dial, Joan
Kent, Kelvin
See Kuttner, Henry
Kent, Leonard J. 1927- 77-80
Kent, Louise Andrews 1886-1969 .... CANR-4
Obituary 25-28R
Earlier sketch in CA 4R
Kent, Malcolm 1932- 45-48
Kent, Mallory
See Lowndes, Robert A(ugustine) W(ard)
Kent, Margaret 1894- CAP-2
Earlier sketch in CA 25-28
See also SATA 2
Kent, Noel J(ay) 1944- 111
Kent, Nora 1899- CAP-1
Earlier sketch in CA 9-10
Kent, Pete
See Richardson, Gladwell
Kent, Philip
See Bulmer, (Henry) Kenneth
Kent, Rockwell 1882-1971 .... CANR-4
Obituary 29-32R
Earlier sketch in CA 5-6R
See also SATA 6
Kent, Sherman 1903-1986 53-56
Obituary 118
See also SATA 20, 47
Kent, Simon
See Catto, Max(well Jeffrey)
Kent, Stella
See Phillips, Stella
Kent, Tony
See Crechales, Anthony George
Kent, Valerie 1947- 114
Kentfield, Calvin 1924- 7-8R
Kenton, Leslie 1941- 113
Kenton, Maxwell
See Hoffenberg, Mason
and Southern, Terry
Kenton, Warren 1933- 29-32R
Kenward, James (Macara) 1908- 7-8R
Kenward, Jean 1920- 108
See also SATA 42
Kenward, Michael 1945- 103
Kenworthy, Brian J(ohn) 1920- 103
Kenworthy, Leonard S. 1912- CANR-1
Earlier sketch in CA 1R
See also SATA 6
Kenyatta, Jomo 1891(?)-1978 124
Obituary 113
Kenyon, Bernice
See Gilkyson, Bernice Kenyon
Kenyon, Ernest M(onroe) 1920- 85-88
Kenyon, F(rank) W(ilson) 1912- CANR-1
Earlier sketch in CA 3R
Kenyon, J(ohn) P(hilipps) 1927- CANR-3
Earlier sketch in CA 9-10R
Kenyon, James William 1910- CAP-1
Earlier sketch in CA 9-10
Kenyon, Jane 1947- 118
Kenyon, Karen 1938- 106
Kenyon, Kate
See Ransom, Candice F.
Kenyon, Kathleen Mary 1906-1978 .... CANR-13
Earlier sketch in CA 21-22R
Kenyon, Ley 1913- 13-14R
See also SATA 6
Kenyon, Michael 1931- CANR-12
Earlier sketch in CA 15-16R
Kenyon, Mildred Adams 1894-1980 108
Obituary 105
Kenyon, Paul
See Freedland, Nat(haniel)
Kenyon, Robert O.
See Kuttner, Henry
Kenyon, W. A.
See Kenyon, Walter Andrew
Kenyon, Walter
See Kenyon, Walter Andrew
Kenyon, Walter A.
See Kenyon, Walter Andrew
Kenyon, Walter Andrew 1917-1986 Obituary 121
Keogh, James 1916- 45-48
Keogh, Lilian Gilmore 1927- 11-12R
Keohane, Nannerl O(verholser) 1940- 106
Keohane, Robert O. 1941- 45-48
Kepes, Gyorgy 1906- 101
Kepes, Juliet A(ppleby) 1919- 69-72
See also SATA 13
Kephart, Horace 1862-1931 Brief entry 119
Kephart, Newell C. 1911-1973 .... CAP-2
Earlier sketch in CA 17-18
Kephart, William M. 1921- 41-44R
Kepler, Thomas Samuel 1897-1963 .... 4R
Keppel, Sonia 1900-1986 107
Obituary 120
Keppel-Jones, Arthur (Mervyn) 1909- 118
Kepple, Ella Huff 1902- CAP-2
Earlier sketch in CA 17-18
Keppler, Ann B(lystad) 1946- 117
Keppler, C(arl) F(rancis) 1909- 19-20R
Keppler, Herbert 1925- 85-88
Keppler, Victor 1904-1987 Obituary 124
Ker, Neil Ripley 1908-1982 Obituary 107
Ker, William Paton 1855-1923 Brief entry 121
Kerber, August Frank 1917- 23-24R
Kerber, Linda K(aufman) 1940- Brief entry .. 115
Kerby, Bill 1937- 104
Kerby, Joe Kent 1933- 53-56
Kerby, Philip Pearce 1911- Brief entry 116
Kerby, Robert L(ee) 1934- 41-44R
Kerby, Susan Alice
See Burton, (Alice) Elizabeth
Kerckhoff, Alan C(hester) 1924- 113
Kerek, Andrew 1936- 102
Kerekes, Tibor 1893-1969 .... CAP-2
Earlier sketch in CA 17-18
Kerensky, Alexandr Fedorovich 1881-1970 Obituary 113
Kerensky, Oleg 1930- CANR-12
Earlier sketch in CA 29-32R
Kerensky, V(asil) M(ichael) 1930- 53-56

Keres, Paul (Petrovich) 1916-1975
Obituary 57-60
Kerestesi, Michael 1929- 109
Kereszty, Roch A(ndrew) 1933- 29-32R
Kerewsky-Halpern, Barbara 1931- 102
Kerigan, Florence 1896- 29-32R
See also SATA 12
Kerin, Roger A(nthony) 1947- 109
Kerkvliet, Benedict J(ohn) 1943- 93-96
Kerlan, Irvin 1912-1963 .... 7-8R
Kerlinger, Fred N(ichols) 1910- CANR-2
Earlier sketch in CA 49-52
Kerman, Cynthia Earl 1923- 57-60
Kerman, Gertrude Lerner 1909- 7-8R
See also SATA 21
Kerman, Joseph Wilfred 1924- CANR-15
Earlier sketch in CA 65-68
Kerman, Judith (Berna) 1945- 77-80
Kerman, Sheppard 1928- 85-88
Kermani, Taghi Thomas 1929- 25-28R
Kermode, (John) Frank 1919- CANR-1
Earlier sketch in CA 2R
Kern, Alfred 1924- 33-36R
Kern, Canyon
See Raborg, Frederick A(shton), Jr.
Kern, E. R.
See Kerner, Fred
Kern, Edith 1912- 113
Kern, Gary 1938- 65-68
Kern, Gregory
See Tubb, E(dwin) C(harles)
Kern, Janet (Rosalie) 1924- 7-8R
Kern, Jean B(ordner) 1913- 85-88
Kern, Mary Margaret 1906- 101
Kern, Robert W(illiam) 1934- CANR-7
Earlier sketch in CA 61-64
Kern, Seymour 1913- 93-96
Kern, Stephen 1943- 69-72
Kern, Walter O(tto) 1930- 117
Kernaghan, Eileen 1939- 111
Kernan, Alvin B(ernard) 1923- 49-52
Kernan, Jerome B(ernard) 1932- 25-28R
Kernan, Michael 1927- 81-84
Kerner, Fred 1921- CANR-22
Earlier sketches in CA 9-10R, CANR-6
Kernochan, Sarah 1947- 73-76
Kernodle, George R(iley) 1907- 65-68
Kerns, Frances Casey 1937- 81-84
Kerns, J(ames) Alexander 1894-1975
Obituary 104
Kerns, Robert Louis 1929- 77-80
Kerouac, Jack
See Kerouac, Jean-Louis Lebrid de
See also DLB 2, 16
See also DLBD 3
See also CDALB 1941-1968
See also CLC 1, 2, 3, 5, 14, 29
Kerouac, Jan
See Hackett, Jan Michele
See also DLB 16
Kerouac, Jean-Louis Lebrid de 1922-1969 .. 5-6R
Obituary 25-28R
See also AITN 1
Kerouac, John
See Kerouac, Jean-Louis Lebrid de
Kerpelman, Larry C(yril) 1939- 37-40R
Kerr, Alex(ander McBride) 1921- 61-64
Kerr, Barbara 1913- 89-92
Kerr, Ben
See Ard, William (Thomas)
Kerr, Carole
See Carr, Margaret
Kerr, Catherine 1945- 102
Kerr, Clark 1911- CANR-22
Earlier sketches in CA 45-48, CANR-1
Kerr, D(onald) G(ordon) G(rady)
1913-1976 .... CANR-6
Earlier sketch in CA 1R
Kerr, Donna H(anneman) 1944- 112
Kerr, Elizabeth M. 1905- 37-40R
Kerr, Frederick
See Kerner, Fred
Kerr, Graham 1934- 108
Kerr, Harry P(rice) 1928- 7-8R
Kerr, Homer L(ee) 1921- 120
Kerr, Howard Hastings 1931- 103
Kerr, Hugh Thomson 1909- 103
Kerr, James Lennox 1899-1963 102
Kerr, James Stolee 1928- 19-20R
Kerr, Jean 1923- CANR-7
Earlier sketch in CA 7-8R
See also CLC 22
Kerr, Jessica 1901- CAP-2
Earlier sketch in CA 29-32
See also SATA 13
Kerr, Joan P. 1921- 81-84
Kerr, (Anne-) Judith 1923- 93-96
See also SATA 24
Kerr, K(athel) Austin 1938- 25-28R
Kerr, Lois
See Cardozo, Lois S(teinmetz)
Kerr, M. E.
See Meaker, Marijane
See also SAAS 1
See also CLC 12, 35
Kerr, Malcolm (Hooper) 1931-1984 97-100
Obituary 111
Kerr, Norman D.
See Sieber, Sam Dixon
Kerr, Orpheus C.
See Newell, Robert Henry
Kerr, Phyllis Forbes 1942- 120
Kerr, Robert (a pseudonym) 1899- 69-72
Kerr, Rose Netzorg 1892-1974 .... CAP-2
Earlier sketch in CA 23-24
Kerr, Stanley E. 1894(?)-1976 Obituary 69-72
Kerr, Walter (Francis) 1913- CANR-7
Earlier sketch in CA 7-8R
Kerrigan, (Thomas) Anthony 1918- CANR-4
Earlier sketch in CA 49-52
See also CLC 4, 6
Kerrigan, Catherine 1939- 117
Kerrigan, Kate Lowe
See Rickett, Frances
Kerrigan, William J(oseph) CANR-2
Earlier sketch in CA 49-52
Kerry, Frances
See Kerigan, Florence
Kerry, Lois
See Duncan, Lois
Kersell, John E(dgar) 1930- 45-48
Kersey, Katharine C(lark) 1935- 116
Kersh, Cyril 1925- 104
Kersh, Gerald 1911-1968 Obituary 25-28R
Kershaw, Alister (Nasmyth) 1921- CANR-19
Earlier sketches in CA 7-8R, CANR-3
Kershaw, Gordon Ernest 1928- 85-88
Kershaw, John (Hugh D'Allenger) 73-76
Kershner, Howard E(ldred) 1891- 73-76
Kershner, Richard B(randon) 1913-1982
Obituary 110
Kerslake, Susan 1943- CANR-17
Earlier sketch in CA 93-96
Kersnowski, Frank L. 1934- 41-44R
Kertesz, Andre 1894-1985 85-88
Obituary 117
Kertesz, Louise 1939- 102
Kertesz, Stephen D(enis) 1904- CAP-2
Earlier sketch in CA 21-22
Kertzer, David I(srael) 1948- 106
Kertzer, Morris Norman 1910-1983 .... CANR-1
Obituary 111
Earlier sketch in CA 4R
Ker Wilson, Barbara 1929- CANR-7
Earlier sketch in CA 7-8R
See also SATA 20
Kerwood, John R. 1942- 53-56
Kesey, Ken (Elton) 1935- CANR-22
Earlier sketch in CA 4R
See also DLB 2, 16
See also CLC 1, 3, 6, 11, 46
Keshet, Harry F(inkelstein) 1940- 109
Keshishian, John M. 1923- 25-28R
Kesich, Veselin 1921- Brief entry 111
Kesler, (William) Jackson (II) 1938- 102
Kesler, Jay 1935- CANR-8
Earlier sketch in CA 61-64
Kess, Joseph Francis 1942- 65-68
Kessel, Dmitri 1902- 120
Kessel, John (Joseph Vincent) 1950- 120
Kessel, John H(oward) 1928- CANR-21
Earlier sketch in CA 23-24R
Kessel, Joseph (Elie) 1898-1979 105
Obituary 89-92
Kessel, Joyce Karen 1937- 105
See also SATA 41
Kessel, Lipmann 1914- 13-14R
Kessel, Martin 1901- DLB-56
Kessell, John L(ottridge) 1936- 93-96
Kesselman, Judi R.
See K-Turkel, Judi
Kesselman, Louis Coleridge 1919-1974
Obituary 110
Kesselman, Mark J. CANR-14
Earlier sketch in CA 37-40R
Kesselman-Turkel, Judi
See K-Turkel, Judi
Kesselring, Joseph (Otto) 1902-1967 .... CLC-45
Kessen, William 1925- CANR-1
Earlier sketch in CA 1R
Kessler, Diane Cooksey 1947- 57-60
Kessler, Edward 1927- 61-64
Kessler, Ethel 1922- 121
Brief entry 115
See also SATA 37, 44
Kessler, Francis P(aschal) 1944- 109
Kessler, Frank
See Kessler, Francis P(aschal)
Kessler, Gail 1937- 65-68
Kessler, Henry H(oward) 1896-1978
Obituary 73-76
Kessler, Jascha (Frederick) 1929- CANR-8
Earlier sketch in CA 19-20R
See also CLC 4
Kessler, Kaye (Warren) 1923- 112
Kessler, Leonard P. 1921- 77-80
See also SATA 14
Kessler, Milton 1930- CANR-2
Earlier sketch in CA 4R
Kessler, Rod 1949- 117
Kessler, Ronald (Borek) 1943- CANR-13
Earlier sketch in CA 69-72
Kessler, Sheila 57-60
Kessler, Walter R. 1913-1978 Obituary 81-84
Kessner, Lawrence 1957- 109
Kessner, Thomas 1946- CANR-11
Earlier sketch in CA 69-72
Kesteloot, Lilyan 1931- CANR-19
Earlier sketch in CA 73-76
Kesten, Hermann 1900- DLB-56
Kester, Dana R(ay) 1943- 116
Kesterson, David B(ert) 1938- 41-44R
Kesterton, Wilfred (Harold) 1914- 41-44R
Kesteven, G. R.
See Crosher, G. R.
Kestner, Joseph A(loysius) 1943- 89-92
Ketch, Jack
See Tibbetts, John C(arter)
Ketcham, Carl H(untington) 1923- 29-32R
Ketcham, Charles B(rown) 1926- 29-32R
Ketcham, Hank
See Ketcham, Henry King
Ketcham, Henry King 1920- 105
See also SATA 27, 28
Ketcham, Howard 1902-1982 Obituary 106
Ketcham, Katherine 1949- 118
Ketcham, Orman W(eston) 1918- CANR-9
Earlier sketch in CA 23-24R
Ketcham, Ralph (Louis) 1927- CANR-4
Earlier sketch in CA 11-12R
Ketcham, Rodney K(enneth) 1909- CANR-4
Earlier sketch in CA 2R
Ketchum, Carlton Griswold 1892- 85-88
Ketchum, Creston Donald 1922- 11-12R
Ketchum, J.
See Frentzen, Jeffrey
Ketchum, Jack
See Paine, Lauran (Bosworth)
Ketchum, Marshall D(ana) 1905- CAP-1
Earlier sketch in CA 17-18
Ketchum, Richard M(alcolm) 1922- 25-28R
Ketchum, Robert Glenn 1947- CANR-23
Earlier sketch in CA 107
Ketchum, William C(larence), Jr.
1931- CANR-12
Earlier sketch in CA 33-36R
Keteyian, Armen 1953- 122
Kets de Vries, Manfred F. R. 1942- 111
Kett, Joseph F. 1938- 25-28R
Kettelkamp, Larry (Dale) 1933- CANR-16
Earlier sketch in CA 29-32R
See also SATA 2
See also SAAS 3
See also CLC 12
Ketterer, David (Anthony Theodor)
1942- CANR-21
Earlier sketches in CA 53-56, CANR-4
Ketterman, Grace H(orst) 1926- CANR-22
Earlier sketch in CA 106
Kettl, Donald F. 1952- 111
Kettle, Arnold (Charles) 1916-1986 .... CANR-6
Obituary 121
Earlier sketch in CA 11-12R
Kettle, Jocelyn Pamela 1934- 25-28R
Kettle, Pamela
See Kettle, Jocelyn Pamela
Kettle, Peter
See Glover, Denis (James Matthews)
Kettner, Elmer Arthur 1906-1964 .... 3R
Kettner, James H(arold) 1944- 89-92
Ketton-Cremer, Robert Wyndham
1906-1969 Obituary 106
Keucher, William F. 1918- 49-52
Keuls, Eva C(lara) 1928- 123
Keuls, Hans 1910-1985 Obituary 117
Kevan, Martin 1949- 110
Keve, Paul W(illard) 1913- CANR-6
Earlier sketch in CA 11-12R
Kevern, Barbara
See Shepherd, Donald (Lee)
Keveson, Peter 1919-1986 Obituary 118
Kevin, Jodi
See Lawrence, Jodi
Kevles, Bettyann 1938- CANR-11
Earlier sketch in CA 69-72
See also SATA 23
Kevles, Daniel Jerome 1939- 85-88
Kew, Stephen 1947- 103
Kewes, Karol 1924- 9-10R
Key, Alexander (Hill) 1904-1979 .... CANR-6
Obituary 89-92
Earlier sketch in CA 5-6R
See also SATA 8, 23
Key, Jack D(ayton) 1934- 112
Key, Mary Ritchie 1924- CANR-16
Earlier sketches in CA 45-48, CANR-1
Key, Ted
See Key, Theodore
Key, Theodore 1912- 13-14R
Key, V(aldimer) O(rlando), Jr. 1908-1963 .... 4R
Key, William H(enry) 1919- 45-48
Key, Wilson Bryan 1925- CANR-2
Earlier sketch in CA 49-52
Keyes, Daniel 1927- CANR-10
Earlier sketch in CA 19-20R
See also SATA 37
Keyes, Edward 1927- 103
Keyes, Evelyn 1919(?)- 85-88
Keyes, Fenton 1915- 107
See also SATA 34
Keyes, Frances Parkinson 1885-1970 .... CANR-7
Obituary 25-28R
Earlier sketch in CA 5-6R
Keyes, Kenneth S(cofield), Jr. 1921- CANR-24
Earlier sketches in CA 19-20R, CANR-8
Keyes, Langley Carleton, Jr. 1938- 25-28R
Keyes, Margaret Frings 1929- 57-60
Keyes, Noel
See Keightley, David N(oel)
Keyes, Ralph 1945- CANR-3
Earlier sketch in CA 49-52
Keyfitz, Nathan 1913- CANR-10
Earlier sketch in CA 25-28R
Keyishian, Harry 1932- 61-64
Keylock, Leslie R(obert) 1933- 117
Keylor, Arthur (W.) 1920(?)-1981
Obituary 104
Keylor, William R(obert) 1944- 89-92
Keynes, Edward 1940- 120
Keynes, Geoffrey Langdon 1887-1982 103
Obituary 107
Keynes, John Maynard 1883-1946
Brief entry 114
Keynes, Richard Darwin 1919- 114
Keys, Ancel 1904- 61-64
Keys, Donald (Fraser) 1924- 115
Keys, Ivor Christopher Banfield 1919- 103
Keys, John D. 1938- 9-10R
Keys, Thomas Edward 1908- CAP-1
Earlier sketch in CA 11-12
Keyser, Daniel J. 1935- 121
Keyser, (George) Gustave 1910- 77-80
Keyser, Lester Joseph 1943- 105
Keyser, Marcia 1933- 116
See also SATA 42
Keyser, Samuel Jay 1935- 106
Keyser, Sarah
See McGuire, Leslie Sarah
Keyser, William R(ussell) 1916- 69-72
Keyserling, Eduard von 1855-1918 .... DLB-66
Keyserling, Leon H. 1908-1987 61-64
Obituary 123
Keyssar, Alexander 1947- 121
Keyt, David (Alan) 1930- 1R
Kezdi, Paul 1914- 77-80
Kezys, Algimantas 1928- CANR-14
Earlier sketch in CA 81-84
Kgositsile, Keorapetse (William) 1938- 77-80
Khadduri, Majid 1909- CANR-2
Earlier sketch in CA 1R
Khaketla, B. M.
See Khaketla, B(ennett) Makalo
Khaketla, B(ennett) Makalo 1913-
Brief entry 113
Khalatbari, Adel-Sultan 1901(?)-1977
Obituary 69-72
Khan, Hassina
See Ali Khan, Shirley
Khan, Lurey 1927- 97-100
Khan, (Chaudhri) Muhammad Zafrulla
1893-1985 Obituary 117
Khan, Pir Vilayat Inayat
See Inayat-Khan, Pir Vilayat
Khan, Shirley Ali
See Ali Khan, Shirley
Khan, Taidje 1920(?)-1985 Obituary 117
Khan, Zillur Rahman 1938- CANR-14
Earlier sketch in CA 41-44R
Khanna, J(aswant) L(al) 1925- 23-24R
Khanshendel, Chiron
See Rose, Wendy
Kharasch, Robert Nelson 1926- 103
Khare, Narayan Bhaskar 1882- CAP-1
Earlier sketch in CA 11-12
Kharitonov, Yevgeny 1941(?)-1981
Obituary 104
Khatchadourian, Haig 1925- 53-56
Khatena, Joe
See Khatena, Joseph
Khatena, Joseph 1925- 116
Khazzoom, J. Daniel 1932- 17-18R
Khedouri, Franklin 1944- 101
Kher, Inder Nath 1933- 93-96
Khera, S(ucha) S(ingh) 1903- 13-14R
Kherdian, David 1931- 21-22R
See also CAAS 2
See also SATA 16
See also CLC 6, 9
Khlebnikov, Velimir
See Khlebnikov, Viktor Vladimirovich
See also TCLC 20
Khlebnikov, Viktor Vladimirovich
1885-1922 Brief entry 117
Khodasevich, Vladislav (Felitsianovich)
1886-1939 Brief entry 115
See also TCLC 15
Khomaini, Ayatollah Sayyed Ruholla
Mousavi
See Khomeini, Ruhollah (Mussavi)
Khomeini, Ayatollah
See Khomeini, Ruhollah (Mussavi)
Khomeini, Ayatollah Ruhollah
See Khomeini, Ruhollah (Mussavi)
Khomeini, Imam
See Khomeini, Ruhollah (Mussavi)
Khomeini, Ruhollah (Mussavi) 1900(?)- 117
Khornak, Lucille 1953- 110
Khosla, G(opal) D(as) 1901- 113
Khouri, Fred J(ohn) 1916- 25-28R
Khouri, Mounah A(bdallah) 1918- 114
Khrushchev, Nikita Sergeyevich
1894-1971 112
Khumeini, Ruhollah
See Khomeini, Ruhollah (Mussavi)
Kiang, Ying-cheng 19-20R
Kianto, Ilmari 1874-1970 Obituary 29-32R
Kibbee, Roland 1914-1984 Obituary 113
Kibler, James Everett, Jr. 1944- CANR-22
Earlier sketch in CA 105
Kibler, Robert J(oseph) 1934- 29-32R
Kibler, William W. 1942- 37-40R
Kibre, Pearl 1902(?)-1985 Obituary 116
Kicknosway, Faye 1936- CANR-7
Earlier sketch in CA 57-60
Kicza, John E(dward) 1947- 120
Kidd, Aline H(alstead) 1922- 19-20R
Kidd, David Lundy 1926- CANR-1
Earlier sketch in CA 1R
Kidd, Elisabeth
See Triegel, Linda (Jeanette)
Kidd, Harry 1917- 29-32R
Kidd, J(ames) R(obbins) 1915- CANR-3
Earlier sketch in CA 7-8R
Kidd, J. Roby
See Kidd, J(ames) R(obbins)
Kidd, Ronald 1948- 116
See also SATA 42
Kidd, Russ
See Donson, Cyril
Kidd, Virginia 1921- CANR-10
Earlier sketch in CA 65-68
Kidd, Walter E. 1917- 23-24R
Kiddell, John 1922- 29-32R
See also SATA 3

Kiddell-Monroe, Joan 1908- CAP-1
Earlier sketch in CA 13-14
Kidder, Barbara (Ann) 1933- 41-44R
Kidder, J(onathan) Edward (Jr.) 1922- 107
Kidder, Rushworth M(oulton) 1944- 77-80
Kidder, Tracy 1945- 109
Kiddle, Lawrence B(ayard) 1907- 33-36R
Kidner, (Frank) Derek 1913- 41-44R
Kidney, Dorothy Boone 1919- CANR-3
Earlier sketch in CA 11-12R
Kidney, Walter C(urtis) 1932- CANR-19
Earlier sketches in CA 53-56, CANR-4
Kido, Koichi 1890(?)-1977 Obituary 69-72
Kidwell, Carl 1910- SATA-43
Kidwell, Catherine (Arthelia) 1921- 109
Kieckhefer, Richard 1946- 93-96
Kiefer, Bill
See Kiefer, Tillman W.
Kiefer, Christie Weber 1937- 103
Kiefer, Frederick (Paul) 1945- 114
Kiefer, Irene 1926- CANR-11
Earlier sketch in CA 69-72
See also SATA 21
Kiefer, Tillman W. 1898- CAP-2
Earlier sketch in CA 29-32
Kiefer, Warren 1929- 77-80
Kiefer, William Joseph 1925- 1R
Kiehle, John Alva 1930- Brief entry 115
Kiell, Norman 1916- CANR-5
Earlier sketch in CA 13-14R
Kiell, Paul J(acob) 1930- 124
Brief entry 118
Kielland, Alexander Lange 1849-1906
Brief entry 104
See also TCLC 5
Kiely, Benedict 1919- CANR-2
Earlier sketch in CA 3R
See also DLB 15
See also CLC 23, 43
Kiemel, Ann
See Anderson, Ann Kiemel
Kieniewicz, Stefan 1907- 29-32R
Kienzle, William X(avier) 1928- CANR-9
Earlier sketch in CA 93-96
See also CAAS 1
See also CLC 25
Kiepper, Shirley Morgan 1933- 37-40R
Kieran, John Francis 1892-1981 101
Obituary 105
Kieran, Sheila 1930- 97-100
Kierland, Joseph Scott 1937- 61-64
Kiernan, Brian 1937- 107
Kiernan, Robert F(rancis) 1940- 115
Kiernan, Thomas 113
Kiernan, (E.) V(ictor) G(ordon) 1913- .. CANR-11
Earlier sketch in CA 25-28R
Kiernan, Walter 1902-1978 Obituary 73-76
Kies, Cosette (Nell) 1936- 124
Kiesel, Stanley 1925- 104
See also SATA 35
Kieser, Rolf 1936- 77-80
Kiesler, Charles A(dolphus) 1934- CANR-10
Earlier sketch in CA 25-28R
Kiesler, Sara B(eth) 1940- CANR-16
Earlier sketch in CA 25-28R
Kiesling, Christopher (Gerald)
1925-1986 .... CANR-12
Obituary 120
Earlier sketch in CA 29-32R
Kiesling, Herbert J. 1934- 45-48
Kiester, Edwin, Jr. 1927- 110
Kieszak, Kenneth 1939- 89-92
Kiev, Ari 1933- CANR-3
Earlier sketch in CA 11-12R
Kiev, I. Edward 1905-1975 Obituary 104
Kihl, Armand
See Ald, Roy A(llison)
Kihss, Peter (Frederick) 1912(?)-1984
Obituary 114
Kijima Hajime
See Kojima Shozo
Kikel, Rudy (John) 1942- 117
Kiker, B(ill) F(razier) 1937- 61-64
Kiker, Douglas 1930- 65-68
Kikukawa, Cecily H(arder) 1919- 113
See also SATA 35, 44
Kilander, H(olger) Frederick 1900-1969 ... CAP-2
Earlier sketch in CA 17-18
Kilborne, Virginia Wylie 1912- 21-22R
Kilbourn, Jonathan 1916(?)-1976
Obituary 65-68
Kilbourn, William (Morley) 1926- CANR-11
Earlier sketch in CA 21-22R
Kilbracken, John (Raymond Godley) 1920- ..7-8R
Kilburn, Henry
See Rigg, H(enry Hemmingway) K(ilburn)
Kilburn, Robert E(dward) 1931- 17-18R
Kilby, Clyde Samuel 1902-1986 .... CANR-9
Obituary 120
Earlier sketch in CA 13-14R
Kilby, Peter 1935- CANR-17
Earlier sketch in CA 25-28R
Kildahl, John P. 1927- 89-92
Kildahl, Phillip A. 1912- 23-24R
Kildare, Maurice
See Richardson, Gladwell
Kilduff, (Mary) Dorrell 1901- 7-8R
Kiley, Frederick 1932- CANR-15
Earlier sketch in CA 37-40R
Kiley, Jed
See Kiley, John Gerald
See also DLB 4
Kiley, John Gerald 1889-1962 Obituary 112
Kiley, Margaret A(nn) 1921- 53-56
Kilgallen, Dorothy (Mae) 1913-1965
Obituary 89-92
Kilgallen, James L. 1888(?)-1982
Obituary 108
Kilgore, James C(olumbus) 1928- 33-36R
Kilgore, John
See Paine, Lauran (Bosworth)
Kilgore, Kathleen 1946- 109
See also SATA 42
Kilgore, William J(ackson) 1917- 45-48
Kilgour, John Graham 1937- 105
Kilgour, Raymond L(incoln) 1903- CAP-1
Earlier sketch in CA 15-16
Kilian, Crawford 1941- CANR-22
Earlier sketch in CA 105
See also SATA 35
Kilina, Patricia
See Warren, Patricia Nell
Killam, (Gordon) Douglas 1930- CANR-3
Earlier sketch in CA 49-52
Killanin, Lord
See Morris, Michael
Kille, Mary F. 1948- 33-36R
Killeen, Jacqueline 1931- 61-64
Killen, Linda 1945- 118
Killenberg, George A(ndrew) 1917- 77-80
Killens, John Oliver 1916-1987 77-80
Obituary 123
See also CAAS 2
See also DLB 33
See also CLC 10
Killian, Ida F(aith) 1910- 65-68
Killian, James R(hyne), Jr. 1904-1988 ...97-100
Obituary 124
Killian, Larry
See Wellen, Edward (Paul)
Killian, Lewis M(artin) 1919- 9-10R
Killian, Ray A. 1922- 21-22R
Killigrew, Thomas 1612-1683 .... DLB-58
Killilea, Marie (Lyons) 1913- 7-8R
See also SATA 2
Killinger, George G(lenn) 1908- 102
Killinger, John 1933- 81-84
Killingley, Carl A(rthur) 1918- 118
Killingsworth, Frank R. 1873(?)-1976
Obituary 65-68
Killion, Katheryn L. 1936- 17-18R
Killion, Ronald G(ene) 1931- 61-64
Killorin, Joseph I(gnatius) 1926- 111
Killough, (Karen) Lee 1942- CANR-15
Earlier sketch in CA 89-92
Killy, Jean-Claude 1943- Brief entry 115
Kilmann, Peter R(ichard) 1945- 118
Kilmar, (Alfred) Joyce 1886-1918 ...... DLB-45
Kilmartin, Edward J(ohn) 1923- 17-18R
Kilmer, (Alfred) Joyce 1886-1918
Brief entry 120
Kilmer, Kenton 1909- 1R
Kilmister, C(live) W(illiam) 1924- 119
Kilodney, Crad (a pseudonym) 1948- 115
Kilpatrick, Carroll 1913- 69-72
Kilpatrick, F(ranklin) P(eirce) 1920- 21-22R
Kilpatrick, James Jackson 1920- CANR-1
Earlier sketch in CA 1R
See also AITN 1, 2
Kilpatrick, Sarah
See Underwood, Mavis Eileen
Kilpatrick, Terrence 1920- 81-84
Kilreon, Beth
See Walker, Barbara (Jeanne) K(erlin)
Kilroy, Thomas 1934- 53-56
Kilson, Marion 1936- 37-40R
Kilson, Martin Luther, Jr. 1931- 103
Kilvert, B. Cory, Jr. 1930- 45-48
Kim
See Simenon, Georges (Jacques
Christian)
Kim, C(hong-) I(k) Eugene 1930- 37-40R
Kim, Chin W. 1936- 37-40R
Kim, Chong Lim 1937- 114
Kim, Choong Soon 1938- 116
Kim, David U(ngchon) 1932- 109
Kim, Hee-Jin 1927- 106
Kim, Helen 1899-1970 .... CAP-1
Earlier sketch in CA 15-16
Kim, Hyung-chan 1938- 57-60
Kim, Ilpyong J(ohn) 1931- 53-56
Kim, Jung-Gun 1933- 53-56
Kim, K(wan) H(o) 1936- 29-32R
Kim, Kwan-Bong 1936- 37-40R
Kim, Kyung-Won 1936- 29-32R
Kim, Richard C(hong) C(hin) 1923- 29-32R
Kim, Richard E. 1932- 7-8R
Kim, Samuel S(oonki) 1935- 104
Kim, Se-Jin 1933- 53-56
Kim, Seung Hee 1936- 29-32R
Kim, Sung Bok 1932- Brief entry 113
Kim, Yong Choon 1935- 57-60
Kim, Yong-ik 1920- 19-20R
Kim, Yoon Hough 1934-1976 ....33-36R
Kim, Young Hum 1920- 23-24R
Kimball, Arthur G(ustaf) 1927- 41-44R
Kimball, Dean 1912- 69-72
Kimball, Gayle 1943- 107
Kimball, George 1943- 53-56
Kimball, John P. 1941- CANR-2
Earlier sketch in CA 45-48
Kimball, John W(ard) 1931- CANR-15
Earlier sketch in CA 93-96
Kimball, Michael 1949- 120
Kimball, Nancy
See Upson, Norma
Kimball, Penn T(ownsend) 1915- CANR-18
Earlier sketch in CA 102
Kimball, Philip 1941- 117
Kimball, Richard Laurance 1939- CANR-7
Earlier sketch in CA 53-56
Kimball, Robert Eric 1939- Brief entry 106
Kimball, Solon T(oothaker) 1909- 21-22R
Kimball, Spencer L(evan) 1918- CANR-1
Earlier sketch in CA 1R
Kimball, Spencer W(oolley) 1895-1985 45-48
Obituary 117
Kimball, Stanley B(uchholz) 1926- CANR-10
Earlier sketch in CA 17-18R
Kimball, Warren F. 1935- 25-28R
Kimball, Yeffe 1914-1978 .... SATA-37
Kimberley, Hugh
See Morland, Nigel
Kimberly, Gail 81-84
Kimble, Daniel Porter 1934- 41-44R
Kimble, David 1921- 13-14R
Kimble, George H(erbert) T(inley) 1908- 108
Kimble, Gregory A(dams) 1917- 21-22R
Kimbrell, Grady 1933- 33-36R
Kimbro, Harriet 1937- 112
Kimbro, Jean
See Kimbro, John M.
Kimbro, John M. 1929- CANR-2
Earlier sketch in CA 45-48
Kimbrough, Emily 1899- 19-20R
See also SATA 2
Kimbrough, Katheryn
See Kimbro, John M.
Kimbrough, Ralph B(radley) 1922- 73-76
Kimbrough, Richard B(enito) 1931- 41-44R
Kimbrough, Robert (Alexander III)
1929- CANR-6
Earlier sketch in CA 11-12R
Kimbrough, Sara Dodge 1901- 93-96
Kimche, David 103
Kimenye, Barbara 1940(?)- 101
Kimes, Beverly Rae 1939- 122
Brief entry 107
Kimmel, Arthur S(andor) 1930- 41-44R
Kimmel, Douglas C(harles) 1943- 53-56
Kimmel, Eric A. 1946- CANR-3
Earlier sketch in CA 49-52
See also SATA 13
Kimmel, Jo 1931- CANR-4
Earlier sketch in CA 53-56
Kimmel, Margaret Mary 1938- 124
See also SATA 43
Kimmel, Melvin 1930- 25-28R
Kimmel, Stanley (Preston) 1894(?)-1982
Obituary 109
Kimmel, William (Breyfogel) 1908-1982
Obituary 109
Kimmelman, Elaine 1925- 111
Kimmens, Andrew C(harles) 1942- 124
Kimmey, John Lansing 1922- Brief entry ... 108
Kimmich, Christoph M(artin) 1939- 69-72
Kimmich, Flora (Graham Horne) 1939- 106
Kimpel, Ben D(rew) 1915- 57-60
Kimpel, Ben F(ranklin) 1905- 1R
Kimrey, Grace (Evelyn) Saunders
1910- CANR-24
Earlier sketch in CA 45-48
Kim Ronyoung
See Hahn, Gloria
Kimura, Jiro 1949- 85-88
Kincaid, Alan
See Rikhoff, James C.
Kincaid, Jamaica 1949(?)- CLC-43
Kincaid, James R(ussell) 1937- CANR-15
Earlier sketch in CA 65-68
Kincaid, Suzanne (Moss) 1936- 9-10R
Kinch, Sam E., Jr. 1940- 45-48
Kincheloe, Raymond McFarland 1909- 61-64
Kincl, (Gladys) Kay Owens 1955- 106
Kindall, Alva Frederick 1906- 1R
Kinder, Faye 1902- 7-8R
Kinder, Gary 1946- 109
Kinder, James S. 1895- 15-16R
Kinder, Kathleen
See Potter, Kathleen Jill
Kinder, Marsha 1940- CANR-15
Earlier sketch in CA 41-44R
Kinderlehrer, Jane 1913- 106
Kindleberger, Charles P(oor), II 1910- .. CANR-12
Earlier sketch in CA 73-76
Kindred, Alton R(ichard) 1922- 109
Kindred, Leslie W(ithrow) 1905- 41-44R
Kindred, Wendy (Good) 1937- 37-40R
See also SATA 7
Kindregan, Charles P(eter) 1935- CANR-10
Earlier sketch in CA 23-24R
Kineji, Maborushi
See Gibson, Walter B(rown)
Kinert, Reed (Charles) 1911(?)- 107
Kines, Pat Decker 1937- 65-68
See also SATA 12
Kines, Thomas Alvin 1922- 15-16R
Kines, Tom
See Kines, Thomas Alvin
King, Adam
See Hoare, Robert J(ohn)
King, Adele Cockshoot 1932- CANR-8
Earlier sketch in CA 13-14R
King, Alan 1927- 89-92
King, Alec Hyatt
See King, Alexander Hyatt
King, Alexander 1909- 110
King, Alexander Hyatt 1911- 124
King, Alfred M. 1933- 25-28R
King, Algin B(raddy) 1927- CANR-15
Earlier sketch in CA 41-44R
King, Alison
See Martini, Teri
King, Alvy L(eon) 1932- 33-36R
King, Annette 1941- 33-36R
King, Anthony (Stephen) 1934- 17-18R
King, Archdale Arthur 1890-1972 .... CAP-1
Earlier sketch in CA 17-18
King, Ben F(rank) 1937- 57-60
King, Bert T(homas) 1927- 45-48
King, Betty (Alice) 1919- 103
King, Betty Patterson 1925- 11-12R
King, Billi
See Calder, Colline
King, Billie Jean 1943- CANR-10
Earlier sketch in CA 53-56
See also SATA 12
King, Bruce ?-1976 Obituary 61-64
King, Bruce A. 1933- CANR-19
Earlier sketches in CA 53-56, CANR-4
King, C(lyde) Richard 1924- CANR-11
Earlier sketch in CA 69-72
King, Captain Charles
See King, Charles
King, Cecil
See King, Cecil H(armsworth)
King, Cecil H(armsworth) 1901-1987 110
Obituary 122
King, Charles 1844-1933 Brief entry 122
King, Charles (Lester) 1922- 57-60
King, Clarence (Rivers) 1842-1901
Brief entry 110
See also DLB 12
King, Clarence 1884(?)-1974 Obituary 53-56
King, (David) Clive 1924- 104
See also SATA 28
King, Clyde S(tuart) 1919- 17-18R
King, Coretta Scott 1927- 29-32R
King, Cynthia 1925- 29-32R
See also SATA 7
King, Daniel P(atrick) 1942- CANR-4
Earlier sketch in CA 53-56
King, Deborah 1950- 112
King, Donald B. 1913- 15-16R
King, Edith W(eiss) 1930- CANR-14
Earlier sketch in CA 33-36R
King, Edmund J(ames) 1914- CANR-2
Earlier sketch in CA 7-8R
King, Edmund L(udwig) 1914- CANR-13
Earlier sketch in CA 33-36R
King, Edward L. 1928- 81-84
King, Elizabeth A.
See Abravanel, Elizabeth
King, Florence 1936- CANR-7
Earlier sketch in CA 57-60
See also DLBY 85
See also AITN 1
King, Francis Edward 1931- 61-64
King, Francis H(enry) 1923- CANR-1
Earlier sketch in CA 2R
See also DLB 15
See also CLC 8
King, Francis P(aul) 1922- 15-16R
King, Frank A.
See King, Franklin Alexander
King, Frank H(enry) H(aviland) 1926- 119
King, Frank O. 1883-1969 Obituary 89-92
See also SATA 22
King, Franklin Alexander 1923- 45-48
King, Frederick Murl 1916- CANR-2
Earlier sketch in CA 5-6R
King, General Charles
See King, Charles
King, Glen D. 1925- 11-12R
King, Grace (Elizabeth) 1852(?)-1932
Brief entry 116
See also DLB 12
King, Harold 1945- CANR-7
Earlier sketch in CA 57-60
King, Helen H(ayes) 1937- 33-36R
King, Homer W. 1907- CAP-1
Earlier sketch in CA 15-16
King, Horace Maybray
See Maybray-King, Horace
King, Irving H(enry) 1935- 89-92
King, Ivan R(obert) 1927- 89-92
King, Jack
See Dowling, Allen
King, James 1942- 121
King, James Cecil 1924- CANR-14
Earlier sketch in CA 41-44R
King, James G. 1898(?)-1979 Obituary ...89-92
King, James T(errell) 1933- 37-40R
King, James W. 1920- 9-10R
King, Janet Kauffman 1935- Brief entry 110
King, Jere Clemens 1910- 5-6R
King, Jerome Babcock 1927- 103
King, (Frederick) Jerry 1941- 97-100
King, Joan (M.) 1930- 123
King, Joe 1909(?)-1979 Obituary 85-88
King, John
See McKeag, Ernest L(ionel)
King, John Edward 1947- 102
King, John L(afayette) 1917- 41-44R
King, John N. 1945- 113
King, John O(zias) 1923- Brief entry 108
King, John Q. Taylor 1921- 25-28R
King, Josie
See Germany, (Vera) Jo(sephine)
King, K. DeWayne (Dewey) 1925- 13-14R
King, Kathleen (Marie) 1948- 114
King, Kimball 1934- 110
King, Larry 1933- Brief entry 111
King, Larry L. 1929- CANR-24
Earlier sketch in CA 15-16R
King, Leila Pier 1882-1981 Obituary 105
King, Leslie John 1934- Brief entry 106
King, Lester S(now) 1908- 33-36R
King, Louise W(ooster) CANR-7
Earlier sketch in CA 13-14R
King, Marcet (Alice Hines) 1922- 25-28R
King, Margaret L(eah) 1947- 123
King, Marian 1900(?)-1986 .... CANR-2
Obituary 118
Earlier sketch in CA 5-6R
See also SATA 23, 47
King, Marjorie Cameron 1909- 33-36R

King, Mark 1945- 61-64
King, Martha L. 1918- Brief entry 109
King, Martin
See Marks, Stan(ley)
King, Martin Luther, Jr. 1929-1968 ...... CAP-2
Earlier sketch in CA 25-28
See also SATA 14
King, Martin Luther, Sr. 1899-1984
Obituary 117
King, Mary Louise 1911- 23-24R
King, Michael
See Buse, Renee
and Kahane, Meir (David)
King, Michael J(ulius) 1941- 119
King, Morton Brandon 1913- 102
King, Noel Q(uixote) 1922- CANR-19
Earlier sketches in CA 3R, CANR-4
King, Norman A.
See Tralins, S(andor) Robert
King, O. H. P. 1902- 2R
King, Patricia 1930- 7-8R
King, Paul
See Drackett, Phil(ip Arthur)
King, Pauline 1917- 119
King, Peggy Cameron
See King, Marjorie Cameron
King, Philip 1904- 103
King, Philip B(urke) 1903-1987 Obituary ... 122
King, Preston (Theodore) 1936- CANR-10
Earlier sketch in CA 23-24R
King, Ray A(iken) 1933- 21-22R
King, Richard A(ustin) 1929- 23-24R
King, Richard G. 1922- 37-40R
King, Richard H. 1942- 77-80
King, Richard L(ouis) 1937- CANR-1
Earlier sketch in CA 45-48
King, Robert Charles 1928- 19-20R
King, Robert G. 1929- 23-24R
King, Robert H(arlen) 1935- 45-48
King, Robert L. 1950- 77-80
King, Robert R(ay) 1942- CANR-8
Earlier sketch in CA 61-64
King, Robin 1919- 5-6R
King, Roma Alvah, Jr. 1914- CANR-1
Earlier sketch in CA 1R
King, Ronald (Wilfred) 1914- 107
King, Rufus 1917- 25-28R
King, Ruth Rodney
See Manley, Ruth Rodney King
King, Spencer B(idwell), Jr. 1904- CAP-1
Earlier sketch in CA 17-18
King, Stanley H(all) 1921- Brief entry 110
King, Stella 69-72
King, Stephen (Edwin) 1947- CANR-1
Earlier sketch in CA 61-64
See also SATA 9
See also DLBY 80
See also CLC 12, 26, 37
King, Stephen W(illiam) 1947- 61-64
King, T(homas) J(ames) 1925- 37-40R
King, Tabitha 1949- 105
King, Teri 1940- 89-92
King, Terry Johnson 1929-1978 ....17-18R
Obituary 77-80
King, Thomas M(ulvihill) 1929- 57-60
King, Tony 1947- 109
See also SATA 39
King, Veronica
See King, Florence
King, Vincent
See Vinson, Rex Thomas
King, Willard L. 1893-1981 .... 3R
Obituary 103
King, William Donald Aelian 1910- 89-92
King, William R(ichard) 1938- CANR-8
Earlier sketch in CA 23-24R
King, Winston L(ee) 1907- 41-44R
King, Woodie, Jr. 1937- 103
See also DLB 38
Kingdon, Frank 1894-1972 Obituary 33-36R
Kingdon, John W(ells) 1940- 25-28R
Kingdon, Robert M(cCune) 1927- 21-22R
Kingdon, Roger 1891-1984 Obituary 113
Kingery, Robert E(rnest) 1913-1978 .....11-12R
Obituary 103
King-Farlow, John 1932- 111
King-Hall, Magdalen 1904-1971 .... CAP-1
Obituary 29-32R
Earlier sketch in CA 9-10
King-Hall, (William) Stephen (Richard)
1893-1966 ....7-8R
King-Hele, Desmond (George) 1927- ... CANR-14
Earlier sketch in CA 29-32R
Kinghorn, A(lexander) M(anson) 1926- 93-96
Kinghorn, Kenneth Cain 1930- CANR-14
Earlier sketch in CA 41-44R
Kinglake, Alexander William 1809-1891 .. DLB-55
Kingman, Dong (Moy Shu) 1911- 112
See also SATA 44
Kingman, Lee
See Natti, (Mary) Lee
See also SATA 1
See also SAAS 3
See also CLC 17
Kingman, Russ 1917- CANR-17
Earlier sketch in CA 101
Kingry, Philip L. 1942- 53-56
Kingsbury, Arthur 1939- 29-32R
Kingsbury, Donald (MacDonald) 1929- 124
Kingsbury, Jack Dean 1934- 37-40R
Kingsbury, John M(erriam) 1928- CANR-6
Earlier sketch in CA 15-16R
Kingsbury, Robert C(arrick) 1924- CANR-2
Earlier sketch in CA 4R
Kingsland, Leslie William 1912- 69-72
See also SATA 13
Kingsland, Sharon E. 1951- 124
Kingsley, Charles 1819-1875 .... YABC-2
See also DLB 21, 32
Kingsley, Charlotte Mary
See Hanshew, Thomas W.
Kingsley, Daniel T(hain) 1932- 117
Kingsley, Emily Perl 1940- 107
See also SATA 33
Kingsley, Henry 1830-1876 .... DLB-21
Kingsley, Michael J. 1918(?)-1972
Obituary 37-40R
Kingsley, Sidney 1906- 85-88
See also DLB 7
See also CLC 44
Kingsley-Smith, Terence 1940- 57-60
King-Smith, Dick 1922- CANR-22
Earlier sketch in CA 105
See also SATA 38, 47
Kingsnorth, George W(illiam) 1924- 7-8R
Kingston, Albert J(ames) 1917- 23-24R
Kingston, Jeremy Henry Spencer 1931- 103
Kingston, Maxine (Ting Ting) Hong
1940- CANR-13
Earlier sketch in CA 69-72
See also DLBY 80
See also CLC 12, 19
Kingston, Syd
See Bingley, David Ernest
Kingston, (Frederick) Temple 1925- CANR-12
Earlier sketch in CA 33-36R
Kingston-Mann, Esther 112
King-Stoops, Joyce 1923- 81-84
Kininmonth, Christopher 1917- 53-56
Kinkade, Richard P(aisley) 1939- CANR-14
Earlier sketch in CA 37-40R
Kinkaid, Matt
See Adams, Clifton
Kinkaid, Wyatt E.
See Jennings, Michael Glenn
Kinkead, Eugene (Francis) 1906- CANR-1
Earlier sketch in CA 1R
Kinkead-Weekes, Mark 1931- 124
Kinley, Phyllis (Elaine Gillespie) 1930- 3R
Kinloch, A. Murray 1923- 103
Kinmonth, Earl H. 1946- 107
Kinnaird, Clark 1901-1983 .... CANR-1
Obituary 111
Earlier sketch in CA 45-48
Kinnaird, John (William) 1924-1980 124
Kinnaird, John William 1924-1980
Obituary 97-100
Kinnaird, William M(cKee) 1928- 101
Kinnamon, Keneth 1932- 37-40R
Kinnane, John F. 1921-1987 Obituary 123
Kinnard, Douglas 1921- CANR-14
Earlier sketch in CA 77-80
Kinnear, Elizabeth K. 1902- CAP-2
Earlier sketch in CA 33-36
Kinnear, Michael 1937- 37-40R
Kinneavy, James Louis 1920- 69-72
Kinneir, (Richard) Jock 1917- 121
Kinnell, Galway 1927- CANR-10
Earlier sketch in CA 11-12R
See also DLB 5
See also CLC 1, 2, 3, 5, 13, 29
Kinney, Arthur F(rederick) 1933- CANR-14
Earlier sketch in CA 37-40R
Kinney, C. Cle(land) 1915- 11-12R
See also SATA 6
Kinney, Francis S(herwood) 1915- 106
Kinney, Harrison 1921- 1R
See also SATA 13
Kinney, James (Joseph) 1942- 120
Kinney, James R(oser) 1902(?)-1978
Obituary 81-84
Kinney, Jean Stout 1912- 11-12R
See also SATA 12
Kinney, Lucien Blair 1895-1971 .... CAP-2
Earlier sketch in CA 23-24
Kinney, Peter 1943- 73-76
Kinney, Richard 1924(?)-1979 Obituary ...85-88
Kinnicutt, Susan Sibley 1926- 77-80
Kinnison, William A(ndrew) 1932- 23-24R
Kinor, Jehuda
See Rothmuller, Aron Marko
Kinoshita Junji 1914- 124
Kinross, Lord
See Balfour, (John) Patrick Douglas
Kinsbruner, Jay 1939- 25-28R
Kinsel, Paschal 1895(?)-1976 Obituary 69-72
Kinsella, Paul L. 1923- 21-22R
Kinsella, Thomas 1928- CANR-15
Earlier sketch in CA 17-18R
See also DLB 27
See also CLC 4, 19
Kinsella, W(illiam) P(atrick) 1935- CANR-21
Earlier sketch in CA 97-100
See also CLC 27, 43
Kinsey, Alfred C(harles) 1894-1956
Brief entry 115
Kinsey, Barry Allan 1931- 19-20R
Kinsey, Elizabeth
See Clymer, Eleanor
Kinsey-Jones, Brian
See Ball, Brian N(eville)
Kinsley, D(aniel) A(llan) 1939- 45-48
Kinsley, James 1922-1984 .... CANR-2
Obituary 114
Earlier sketch in CA 1R
Kinsolving, Charles McIlvaine 1893-1984
Obituary 114
Kinstler, Everett Raymond 1926- 33-36R
Kinter, Judith 1928- 109
Kintgen, Eugene R(obert), Jr. 1942- 116
Kintner, Earl W(ilson) 1912- CANR-1
Earlier sketch in CA 45-48
Kintner, Robert Edmonds 1909-1980
Obituary 103
Kintner, William R(oscoe) 1915- CANR-6
Earlier sketch in CA 7-8R
Kinton, Jack F(ranklin) 1939- CANR-7
Earlier sketch in CA 57-60
Kintsch, Walter 1932- 29-32R
Kinzer, Betty 1922- 21-22R
Kinzer, Donald Louis 1914- 53-56
Kinzer, H(arless) M(ahlon) 1923(?)-1975
Obituary 57-60
Kinzer, Nora Scott 1936- Brief entry 106
Kiparsky, Valentin (Julius Alexander)
1904- 17-18R
Kiple, Kenneth F(ranklin) 1939- 120
Kipling, (Joseph) Rudyard 1865-1936 120
Brief entry 105
See also YABC 2
See also DLB 19, 34
See also TCLC 8, 17
Kiplinger, Austin H(untington) 1918- 57-60
Kiplinger, Willard Monroe 1891-1967
Obituary 89-92
Kipnis, Claude 1938-1981 107
Obituary 103
Kippax, Janet 1926- 97-100
Kipphardt, Heinar 1922-1982 89-92
Obituary 108
Kippley, John F(rancis) 1930- 29-32R
Kippley, Sheila K. 1939- 61-64
Kipps, Harriet C(lyde) 1926- 124
Kiraly, Bela (Kalman) 1912- CANR-8
Earlier sketch in CA 61-64
Kirby, (George) Blaik 1928- 77-80
Kirby, D(avid) P(eter) 1936- 25-28R
Kirby, David G. 1942- 101
Kirby, David K(irk) 1944- 53-56
Kirby, Douglas J. 1929- 25-28R
Kirby, E(dward) Stuart 1909- CANR-22
Earlier sketches in CA 15-16R, CANR-7
Kirby, Emily B(aruch) 1929- 117
Kirby, F(rank) E(ugene) 1928- 65-68
Kirby, Gilbert W(alter) 1914- 103
Kirby, Jack Temple 1938- 25-28R
Kirby, Jean
See McDonnell, Virginia B(leecker)
Kirby, Jean
See Robinson, Chaille Howard (Payne)
Kirby, John B(yron) 1938- 105
Kirby, M(ary) Sheelah Flanagan 1916- 7-8R
Kirby, Mark
See Floren, Lee
Kirby, Rollin 1875-1952 Brief entry 118
Kirby, Thomas Austin 1904- 5-6R
Kirchhofer, Alfred H. 1892(?)-1985
Obituary 117
Kirchhoff, Frederick (Thomas) 1942- 111
Kirchner, Audrey Burie 1937- CANR-12
Earlier sketch in CA 73-76
Kirchner, Glenn 1930- 29-32R
Kirchner, Walther 1905- CANR-1
Earlier sketch in CA 1R
Kirchwey, Freda 1893-1976 93-96
Obituary 61-64
Kirdar, Uner 1933- 23-24R
Kirk, Alexandra
See Woods, Sherryl
Kirk, Clara M(arburg) 1898-1976 .... CAP-1
Obituary 69-72
Earlier sketch in CA 17-18
Kirk, Cooper 1920- 116
Kirk, David 1935- 29-32R
Kirk, Donald 1938- 37-40R
Kirk, Donald R. 1935- 57-60
Kirk, Elizabeth D(oan) 1937- 53-56
Kirk, G(eoffrey) S(tephen) 1921- CANR-2
Earlier sketch in CA 5-6R
Kirk, George (Eden) 1911- 1R
Kirk, H(enry) David 1918- CANR-11
Earlier sketch in CA 17-18R
Kirk, Irene 1926- CANR-6
Earlier sketch in CA 7-8R
Kirk, Irina
See Kirk, Irene
Kirk, James A(lbert) 1929- 37-40R
Kirk, Jeremy
See Powell, Richard (Pitts)
Kirk, Jerome (Richard) 1937- 49-52
Kirk, John Esben 1905-1975 Obituary 57-60
Kirk, John T(homas) 1933- 49-52
Kirk, Lydia (Chapin) 1896-1984 Obituary 114
Kirk, Mary Wallace 1889- 57-60
Kirk, Michael
See Knox, William
Kirk, Philip
See Levinson, Leonard
Kirk, R.
See Dietrich, Richard V(incent)
Kirk, Richard (Edmund) 1931- 13-14R
Kirk, Robert Warner ?-1980 ....9-10R
Obituary 103
Kirk, Roger E(dward) 1930- 41-44R
Kirk, Russell (Amos) 1918- CANR-20
Earlier sketches in CA 1R, CANR-1
See also AITN 1
Kirk, Ruth (Kratz) 1925- CANR-9
Earlier sketch in CA 15-16R
See also SATA 5
Kirk, Samuel A(lexander) 1904- CANR-1
Earlier sketch in CA 45-48
Kirk, T(homas) H(obson) 1899- CAP-2
Earlier sketch in CA 23-24
Kirk, Ted
See Bank, Theodore P(aul) II
Kirk, Wayne
See Kock, Winston E(dward)
Kirkbride, Norma Jean 1924(?)-1983
Obituary 111
Kirkbride, Ronald (de Levington) 1912- .. CANR-2
Earlier sketch in CA 3R
Kirkconnell, Watson 1895-1977 Obituary ... 108
Kirkendall, Don(ald M.) 1923- 49-52
Kirkendall, Lester A(llen) 1903- CANR-5
Earlier sketch in CA 4R
Kirkendall, Richard Stewart 1928- 77-80
Kirk-Greene, Anthony (Hamilton Millard)
1925- CANR-11
Earlier sketch in CA 61-64
Kirk-Greene, Anthony H. M.
See Kirk-Greene, Anthony (Hamilton
Millard)
Kirk-Greene, Christopher Walter Edward
1926- 13-14R
Kirkham, E. Bruce 1938- 37-40R
Kirkham, George L. 1941- 77-80
Kirkham, Michael 1934- 25-28R
Kirkland, Bryant M(ays) 1914- 21-22R
Kirkland, Caroline 1801-1864 .... DLB-3
Kirkland, Edward Chase 1894-1975 ..... CANR-6
Obituary 104
Earlier sketch in CA 2R
Kirkland, Joseph 1830-1893 .... DLB-12
Kirkland, Wallace W. 1891(?)-1979
Obituary 89-92
Kirkland, Will
See Hale, Arlene
Kirkman, James S(pedding) 1906- 93-96
Kirkpatrick, Diane 1933- 53-56
Kirkpatrick, Donald L(ee) 1924- 41-44R
Kirkpatrick, Doris (Upton) 1902- 93-96
Kirkpatrick, Dow (Napier) 1917- 23-24R
Kirkpatrick, Evron M(aurice) 1911- 57-60
Kirkpatrick, Frank 1924- 108
Kirkpatrick, Ivone Augustine 1897-1964 .. CAP-1
Earlier sketch in CA 9-10
Kirkpatrick, Jean 1923- 81-84
Kirkpatrick, Jeane D(uane) J(ordan)
1926- CANR-7
Earlier sketch in CA 53-56
Kirkpatrick, John 1905- 45-48
Kirkpatrick, Lyman B(ickford), Jr. 1916- ..33-36R
Kirkpatrick, Oliver (Austin) 1911- 49-52
Kirkpatrick, Ralph 1911-1984 49-52
Obituary 112
Kirkpatrick, Samuel A(lexander) III
1943- 41-44R
Kirkpatrick, Smith 1922- 49-52
Kirkup, James 1918- CANR-2
Earlier sketch in CA 3R
See also CAAS 4
See also SATA 12
See also DLB 27
See also CLC 1
Kirkus, Virginia
See Glick, Virginia Kirkus
Kirkwood, Ellen Swan 1904- 25-28R
Kirkwood, G(ordon) M(acdonald) 1916- ...93-96
Kirkwood, James 1930- CANR-6
Earlier sketch in CA 4R
See also CLC 9
See also AITN 2
Kirkwood, Jim
See Kirkwood, James
Kirkwood, Kenneth P. 1899-1968 ....37-40R
Kirn, Ann Minette 1910- 93-96
Kirp, David L(eslie) 1944- 109
Kirsch, Anthony Thomas 1930- 103
Kirsch, Arthur C(lifford) 1932- 15-16R
Kirsch, Charlotte 1942- 109
Kirsch, Herbert 1924(?)-1978 Obituary 104
Kirsch, Leonard Joel 1934-1977 ....37-40R
Kirsch, Paul John 1914- 108
Kirsch, Robert R. 1922-1980 .... CANR-13
Obituary 102
Earlier sketch in CA 33-36R
Kirschen, Leonard 1908-1983 Obituary 109
Kirschenbaum, Aaron 1926- 33-36R
Kirschenbaum, Howard 1944- 89-92
Kirschner, Allen 1930- 29-32R
Kirschner, Fritz
See Bickers, Richard Leslie Townshend
Kirschner, Joseph 1930- 121
Kirschner, Linda Rae 1939- 33-36R
Kirschten, Ernest 1902-1974 .... CAP-1
Obituary 49-52
Earlier sketch in CA 11-12
Kirshenbaum, Jerry 1938- 107
Kirshenblatt-Gimblett, Barbara 1942- ... CANR-15
Earlier sketch in CA 81-84
Kirshner, Gloria Ifland 41-44R
Kirsner, Douglas 1947- 77-80
Kirsner, Robert 1921- 23-24R
Kirst, Hans Hellmut 1914- 104
Kirst, Michael W(eile) 1939- CANR-24
Earlier sketch in CA 45-48
Kirstein, George G(arland) 1909-1986
Obituary 118
Kirstein, Lincoln (Edward) 1907-
Brief entry 117
Kirsten, Grace 1900- 104
Kirtland, G. B.
See Hine, Al(fred Blakelee)
and Hine, Sesyle Joslin
Kirtland, Helen Johns 1890(?)-1979
Obituary 89-92
Kirtland, Kathleen 1945- 65-68
Kirvan, John J. 1932- CANR-10
Earlier sketch in CA 23-24R
Kirwan, Albert D(ennis) 1904-1971 ..... CANR-4
Earlier sketch in CA 4R
Kirwan, Laurence Patrick 1907- 3R
Kirwan, Molly (Morrow) 1906- CAP-1
Earlier sketch in CA 13-14
Kirwin, Harry Wynne 1911-1963 .... 4R

Kirzner, Israel M(ayer) 1930- ... CANR-3
Earlier sketch in CA 1R
Kis, Danilo 1935- ... 118
Brief entry ... 109
Kisamore, Norman D(ale) 1928- ... 5-6R
Kiser, Clyde V(ernon) 1904- ... 25-28R
Kiser, Lisa J. 1949- ... 114
Kish, G. Hobab
See Kennedy, Gerald (Hamilton)
Kish, George 1914- ... CANR-1
Earlier sketch in CA 1R
Kish, Kathleen Vera 1942- ... CANR-12
Earlier sketch in CA 69-72
Kish, Leslie 1910- ... CAP-1
Earlier sketch in CA 19-20
Kishel, Patricia G(unter) 1948- ... 117
Kishida, Eriko 1929- ... CANR-7
Earlier sketch in CA 53-56
See also SATA 12
Kishon, Ephraim 1924- ... CANR-2
Earlier sketch in CA 49-52
Kishtainy, Khalid 1929- ... 115
Kisiel, Marie 1929- ... 112
Kisinger, Grace Gelvin (Maze) 1913-1965 . CAP-1
Earlier sketch in CA 13-14
See also SATA 10
Kisker, George W. 1912- ... 21-22R
Kismaric, Carole 1942- ... CANR-23
Earlier sketches in CA 33-36R, CANR-8
Kisner, James (Martin, Jr.) 1947- ... 113
Kisor, Henry (Du Bois) 1940- ... 73-76
Kissam, Edward 1943- ... 61-64
Kissane, John M(ichael) 1928- ... 53-56
Kissane, Leedice McAnelly 1905- ... CAP-2
Earlier sketch in CA 25-28
Kissen, Fan(ny) 1904- ... CAP-1
Earlier sketch in CA 15-16
Kissick, Gary 1946- ... 118
Kissin, Eva H. 1923- ... 29-32R
See also SATA 10
Kissinger, Henry A(lfred) 1923- ... CANR-2
Earlier sketch in CA 2R
Kissinger, Warren S(tauffer) 1922- ... 116
Kissling, Dorothy (Hight) 1904-1969
Obituary ... 105
Kissling, Fred R., Jr. 1930- ... 23-24R
Kiste, Robert Carl 1936- ... 61-64
Kister, Kenneth F. 1935- ... 25-28R
Kistiakowsky, George B(ogdan)
1900-1982 Obituary ... 108
Kistiakowsky, Vera 1928- ... 23-24R
Kistler, Mark O(liver) 1918- ... 77-80
Kistner, Robert William 1917- ... CANR-13
Earlier sketch in CA 61-64
Kitagawa, Daisuke 1910- ... CAP-2
Earlier sketch in CA 17-18
Kitagawa, Joseph M. 1915- ... CANR-2
Earlier sketch in CA 1R
Kitano, Harry H. L. 1926- ... 29-32R
Kitao, T(imothy) Kaori 1933- ... 106
Kitchel, Denison 1908- ... 105
Kitchen, Helen (Angell) ... CANR-23
Earlier sketches in CA 11-12R, CANR-8
Kitchen, Herminie B(roedel) 1901-1973 ... CAP-1
Earlier sketch in CA 17-18
Kitchen, Martin 1936- ... CANR-10
Earlier sketch in CA 61-64
Kitchen, Paddy 1934- ... CANR-21
Earlier sketch in CA 25-28R
Kitchener, Richard Frank 1941- ... 124
Kitcher, Philip 1947- ... 113
Kitchin, Laurence 1913- ... 104
Kite, Larry
See Schneck, Stephen
Kite, Pat 1940- ... 119
Kitman, Marvin 1929- ... 101
Kitson, Jack William 1940- ... 25-28R
Kitson Clark, George Sydney Roberts
1900-1975 ... CANR-14
Earlier sketch in CA 23-24R
Kitt, Eartha (Mae) 1928- ... 77-80
Kittelson, David James 1931- ... 119
Kittler, Glenn D. 1920(?)-1986 Obituary ... 119
Kitto, Crispin 1951- ... 119
Kitto, H(umphrey) D(avy) F(indley)
1897-1982 ... CAP-1
Obituary ... 105
Earlier sketch in CA 11-12
Kittredge, William 1932- ... 111
Kittrie, Nicholas N(orbert Nehemiah)
1928- ... 81-84
Kituomba
See Odaga, Asenath (Bole)
Kitzinger, Ernst 1912- ... 108
Kitzinger, Sheila 1929- ... 37-40R
Kitzinger, U(we) W(ebster) 1928- ... CANR-1
Earlier sketch in CA 2R
Kivenson, Gilbert 1920- ... 112
Kivy, Peter Nathan 1934- ... 103
Kiyota, Minoru 1923- ... 113
Kizer, Carolyn (Ashley) 1925- ... CANR-24
Earlier sketch in CA 65-68
See also CAAS 5
See also DLB 5
See also CLC 15, 39
Kjelgaard, James Arthur 1910-1959
Brief entry ... 109
See also SATA 17
Kjelgaard, Jim
See Kjelgaard, James Arthur
Kjome, June C(reola) 1920- ... 7-8R
Klaas, Joe 1920- ... CANR-12
Earlier sketch in CA 29-32R
Klaassen, Leo(nardus) H(endrik)
1920- ... CANR-11
Earlier sketch in CA 23-24R
Klaassen, Walter 1926- ... 115
Klabund 1890-1928 ... DLB-66
Kladstrup, Don(ald) 1943- ... 77-80
Klafs, Carl E. 1911- ... 13-14R
Klagsbrun, Francine (Lifton) ... 21-22R
See also SATA 36
Klaiber, Jeffrey L. 1943- ... 85-88
Klaich, Dolores 1936- ... 49-52
Klainikite, Anne
See Gehman, Betsy Holland
Klaits, Barrie 1944- ... 73-76
Klamer, Arjo 1953- ... 116
Klamkin, Charles 1923- ... 61-64
Klamkin, Lynn 1950- ... 45-48
Klamkin, Marian 1926- ... CANR-1
Earlier sketch in CA 49-52
Klann, Margaret L. 1911- ... 77-80
Klaperman, Gilbert 1921- ... 49-52
See also SATA 33
Klaperman, Libby Mindlin 1921-1982 ... 9-10R
Obituary ... 107
See also SATA 31, 33
Klapp, Orrin E. 1915- ... 9-10R
Klapper, Charles F(rederick) 1905- ... CAP-1
Earlier sketch in CA 9-10
Klapper, Joseph T(homas) 1917-1984
Obituary ... 112
Klapper, M(olly) Roxana 1937- ... 53-56
Klapper, Marvin 1922- ... 19-20R
Klappert, Peter 1942- ... 33-36R
See also DLB 5
Klappholz, Kurt 1913-1975 Obituary ... 61-64
Klapthor, Margaret B(rown) 1922- ... 119
Klare, George R(oger) 1922- ... 5-6R
Klare, Hugh J(ohn) 1916- ... 103
Klaren, Peter F(lindell) 1938- ... 57-60
Klarsfeld, Beate 1939- ... 65-68
Klarsfeld, Serge 1935- ... 115
Klass, Allan Arnold 1907- ... 65-68
Klass, Morton 1927- ... CANR-5
Earlier sketch in CA 1R
See also SATA 11
Klass, Philip J. 1919- ... 25-28R
Klass, Shelia Solomon 1927- ... CANR-13
Earlier sketch in CA 37-40R
See also SATA 45
Klass, Sholom 1916- ... 23-24R
Klassen, Frank Roy 1910- ... 113
Klassen, Peter J(ames) 1930- ... CANR-1
Earlier sketch in CA 45-48
Klassen, Randolph Jacob 1933- ... 61-64
Klassen, Walter
See Klaassen, Walter
Klassen, William 1930- ... CANR-10
Earlier sketch in CA 25-28R
Klauber, John 1917-1981 Obituary ... 104
Klauber, Laurence M(onroe) 1883-1968
Obituary ... 105
Klauck, Daniel L. 1947- ... 69-72
Klauder, Francis John 1918- ... 53-56
Klaue, Lola Shelton 1903- ... 5-6R
Klause, John L(ouis) 1943- ... 118
Klausler, Alfred P(aul) 1910- ... 23-24R
Klausmeier, Herbert J. 1915- ... CANR-20
Earlier sketches in CA 3R, CANR-5
Klausner, Abraham J. 1915- ... 108
Klausner, Lawrence D(avid) 1939- ... 110
Klausner, Margot 1905-1976(?) Obituary ... 61-64
Klausner, Samuel Z(undel) 1923- ... 17-18R
Klavans, J(odie) K(ay) 1956- ... 118
Klaw, Spencer 1920- ... 25-28R
Klawans, Harold L(eo) 1937- ... 106
Klayman, Maxwell Irving 1917- ... 29-32R
Klebe, Charles Eugene 1907- ... CAP-2
Earlier sketch in CA 23-24
Klebe, Gene
See Klebe, Charles Eugene
Kleberger, Ilse 1921- ... CANR-15
Earlier sketch in CA 41-44R
See also SATA 5
Klee, James B(utt) 1916- ... 109
Kleeberg, Irene (Flitner) Cumming
1932- ... CANR-12
Earlier sketch in CA 61-64
Kleene, Stephen Cole 1909- ... 41-44R
Klees, Fredric (Spang) 1901- ... CAP-2
Earlier sketch in CA 19-20
Klehr, Harvey 1945- ... 111
Kleiler, Frank Munro 1914- ... 89-92
Kleiman, Robert 1918- ... 15-16R
Klein, A(braham) M(oses) 1909-1972 ... 101
Obituary ... 37-40R
See also CLC 19
Klein, Aaron E. 1930- ... CANR-19
Earlier sketch in CA 25-28R
See also SATA 28, 45
Klein, Alan F(redric) 1911- ... 57-60
Klein, Alexander 1918- ... CANR-14
Earlier sketch in CA 5-6R
Klein, Arnold William 1945- ... 37-40R
Klein, Bernard 1921- ... 17-18R
Klein, Carole (Doreen) 1934- Brief entry ... 118
Klein, Charlotte 1925- ... 101
Klein, Daniel Martin 1939- ... CANR-11
Earlier sketch in CA 61-64
Klein, Dave 1940- ... 89-92
Klein, David 1919- ... CANR-18
Earlier sketches in CA 4R, CANR-1
Klein, David Ballin 1897- ... 41-44R
Klein, Donald C(harles) 1923- ... 25-28R
Klein, Donald W(alker) 1929- Brief entry ... 114
Klein, Doris F.
See Jonas, Doris F(rances)
Klein, Edward 1936- ... 69-72
Klein, Elizabeth 1939- ... 110
Klein, Ernest 1899- ... CAP-2
Earlier sketch in CA 21-22
Klein, Fannie J. 1903-1984 Obituary ... 113
Klein, Fred 1932- Brief entry ... 115
Klein, Frederic Shriver 1904- ... 15-16R
Klein, Gerard 1937- ... 49-52
Klein, Gerda Weissmann 1924- ... 116
See also SATA 44
Klein, H(erbert) Arthur ... 15-16R
See also SATA 8
Klein, Herbert Sanford 1936- ... CANR-17
Earlier sketch in CA 93-96
Klein, Heywood 1954(?)-1984 Obituary ... 111
Klein, Holger Michael 1938- ... 65-68
Klein, Isaac 1905- ... 57-60
Klein, Jeffrey B. 1948- ... 77-80
Klein, Joe
See Klein, Joseph
Klein, John J(acob) 1929- ... 17-18R
Klein, Joseph 1946- ... 85-88
Klein, Josephine (F. H.) 1926- ... 2R
Klein, Julius 1901-1984 Obituary ... 112
Klein, K. K.
See Turner, Robert H(arry)
Klein, Karl
See Sala, Charles
Klein, Lawrence R(obert) 1920-
Brief entry ... 116
Klein, Leonore (Glotzer) 1916- ... CANR-1
Earlier sketch in CA 4R
See also SATA 6
Klein, Marcus 1928- ... 11-12R
Klein, Martin A. 1934- ... 23-24R
Klein, Marymae E. 1917- ... 97-100
Klein, Maury 1939- ... 33-36R
Klein, Maxine 1934- ... CANR-10
Earlier sketch in CA 61-64
Klein, Melanie 1882-1960 Obituary ... 111
Klein, Milton M(artin) 1917- ... 93-96
Klein, Mina C(ooper) ... 37-40R
See also SATA 8
Klein, Muriel Walzer 1920- ... 29-32R
Klein, Norma 1938- ... CANR-15
Earlier sketch in CA 41-44R
See also SATA 7
See also SAAS 1
See also CLC 30
See also CLR 2
Klein, Philip A(lexander) 1927- ... 17-18R
Klein, Philip Shriver 1909- ... CANR-1
Earlier sketch in CA 3R
Klein, Randolph Shipley 1942- ... 73-76
Klein, Richard C. 1916(?)-1983 Obituary ... 111
Klein, Richard G. 1941- ... 120
Klein, Richard M. 1923- ... 108
Klein, Robin 1936- ... 116
See also SATA 45
Klein, Rose (Shweitzer) 1918- ... 21-22R
Klein, Stanley 1930- ... 57-60
Klein, Stanley D. 1936- ... 77-80
Klein, Stuart M(arc) 1932- Brief entry ... 111
Klein, Suzanne Marie 1940- ... 57-60
Klein, T(heodore) E(ibon) D(onald) 1947- ... 119
See also CLC 34
Klein, Ted U. 1926- ... 25-28R
Klein, Thomas D(icker) 1941- ... 61-64
Klein, Walter J(ulian) 1923- ... 69-72
Klein, Woody 1929- ... 15-16R
Kleinbauer, W(alter) Eugene 1937- ... 37-40R
Kleinbaum, Abby Wettan 1943- ... 113
Kleinberg, Seymour 1933- ... 105
Kleine, Glen 1936- ... 73-76
Kleine-Ahlbrandt, W(illiam) Laird 1932- ... 29-32R
Kleiner, Art 1954- ... 124
Kleinfeld, Gerald R. 1936- ... 103
Kleinfeld, Judith S. 1944- ... CANR-15
Earlier sketch in CA 77-80
Kleinfeld, Vincent A. 1907- ... CANR-10
Earlier sketch in CA 19-20R
Kleinfield, N(athan) R(ichard) 1950- ... CANR-18
Earlier sketch in CA 97-100
Kleinfield, Sonny
See Kleinfield, N(athan) R(ichard)
Kleinhans, Theodore John 1924- ... 7-8R
Kleinke, Chris (Lynn) 1944- ... CANR-15
Earlier sketch in CA 89-92
Kleinman, Arthur (Michael) 1941- ... CANR-22
Earlier sketch in CA 105
Kleinmann, Jack H(enry) 1932- ... 21-22R
Kleinmuntz, Benjamin 1930- ... 33-36R
Klejment, Anne M. 1950- ... CANR-17
Earlier sketch in CA 101
Klem, Kaye Wilson 1941- ... 89-92
Klement, Frank L(udwig) 1908- ... 9-10R
Klemer, Richard Hudson 1918-1972 ... CANR-4
Obituary ... 37-40R
Earlier sketch in CA 7-8R
Klemesrud, Judy 1939(?)-1985 ... 89-92
Obituary ... 117
Klemin, Diana ... 49-52
Klemke, E(lmer) D. 1926- ... CANR-10
Earlier sketch in CA 25-28R
Klemm, Edward G., Jr. 1910- ... 57-60
See also SATA 30
Klemm, Roberta K(ohnhorst) 1884- ... 61-64
See also SATA 30
Klemm, W(illiam) R(obert) 1934- ... 93-96
Klemperer, Otto 1885-1973 Obituary ... 116
Klempner, Irving M(ax) 1924- ... 53-56
Klempner, John 1898(?)-1972 Obituary ... 37-40R
Klenbort, Charlotte
See Sempell, Charlotte
Klenicki, Leon 1930- ... 106
Klenk, Robert W(illiam) 1934- ... 29-32R
Klenz, William 1915- ... 7-8R
Klerer, Melvin 1926- ... 21-22R
Klerman, Lorraine V(ogel) 1929- ... CANR-15
Earlier sketch in CA 81-84
Klett, Guy S(oulliard) 1897- ... CAP-1
Earlier sketch in CA 13-14
Kleuser, Louise C(aroline) 1889(?)-1976
Obituary ... 65-68
Klevin, Jill Ross 1935- ... 111
See also SATA 38, 39
Klewin, W(illiam) Thomas 1921- ... 29-32R
Kleyman, Paul (Fred) 1945- ... 57-60
Kliban, B(ernard) 1935- ... 106
See also SATA 35
Klibansky, Raymond 1905- Brief entry ... 117
Kliever, Lonnie D(ean) 1931- ... 29-32R
Kliewer, Evelyn 1933- ... 101
Kliewer, Warren 1931- ... CANR-2
Earlier sketch in CA 45-48
Kligerman, Jack 1938- ... 85-88
Kligman, Ruth 1930- ... 101
Klima, Ivan 1931- ... CANR-17
Earlier sketch in CA 25-28R
Kliman, Gilbert W(allace) 1929- ... 117
Klimas, Antanas 1924- ... 41-44R
Klimas, John E(dward) 1927-1975
Obituary ... 111
Klimek, David E(rnest) 1941- ... 89-92
Klimenko, Michael 1924- ... 73-76
Klimentov, Andrei Platonovich 1899-1951
Brief entry ... 108
Klimisch, Sister Mary Jane 1920- ... 17-18R
Klimo, Jake
See Klimo, Vernon
Klimo, Vernon 1914- ... 101
Klimowicz, Barbara 1927- ... 21-22R
See also SATA 10
Klin, George 1931- ... 53-56
Klinck, Carl Frederick 1908- ... 17-18R
Klinck, George Alfred 1903-1973 ... 9-10R
Obituary ... 103
Klindt-Jensen, Ole 1918-1980 ... CANR-10
Obituary ... 101
Earlier sketch in CA 21-22R
Kline, George L(ouis) 1921- ... CANR-9
Earlier sketch in CA 17-18R
Kline, Lloyd W. 1931- ... 33-36R
Kline, Morris 1908- ... CANR-2
Earlier sketch in CA 5-6R
Kline, Nancy Meadors 1946- ... 57-60
Kline, Nathan S(chellenberg) 1916-1983 ... 81-84
Obituary ... 109
Kline, Peter 1936- ... 25-28R
Kline, Suzy 1943- ... 120
See also SATA 48
Kline, Thomas J(efferson) 1942- ... 85-88
Klineberg, Stephen L(ouis) 1940- ... 77-80
Klinefelter, Walter 1899- ... CANR-3
Earlier sketch in CA 9-10R
Klineman, George A(lfred) 1947- ... 107
Kling, Robert E(dward), Jr. 1920- ... 29-32R
Kling, Simcha 1922- ... 15-16R
Klingelhofer, E(dwin) L(ewis) 1920- ... 124
Klinger, Eric 1933- ... CANR-13
Earlier sketch in CA 33-36R
Klinger, Kurt 1914- ... 19-20R
Klinghoffer, Arthur Jay 1941- ... 65-68
Klingman, Lawrence (Lewis) 1918-1986
Obituary ... 120
Klingstedt, Joe Lars 1938- ... 53-56
Klink, Johanna L. 1918- ... CANR-8
Earlier sketch in CA 61-64
Klinkowitz, Jerome 1943- ... CANR-1
Earlier sketch in CA 45-48
Klipper, Miriam Z(eldner) ... 108
Klise, Eugene Storm 1908- ... 7-8R
Klise, Thomas S. 1928- ... 57-60
Klobuchar, James John 1928- ... 73-76
Klobuchar, Jim
See Klobuchar, James John
Kloepfer, Marguerite (Fonnesbeck)
1916- ... 97-100
Kloesel, Christian Johannes Wilhelm
1942- ... 113
Kloetzli, Walter, (Jr.) 1921- ... 3R
Klonglan, Gerald E(dward) 1936- ... 41-44R
Klonis, N. I.
See Clones, N(icholas) J.
Klonsky, Milton 1921(?)-1981 Obituary ... 105
Kloos, Peter 1936- ... 93-96
Klooster, Fred H. 1922- ... 3R
Klopf, Donald W(illiam) 1923- ... CANR-15
Earlier sketch in CA 89-92
Klopfer, Donald S(imon) 1902-1986
Obituary ... 119
Klopfer, Peter H(ubert) 1930- ... 85-88
Klopfer, Walter G(eorge) 1923- ... 89-92
Kloppenburg, Boaventura 1919- ... CANR-15
Earlier sketch in CA 65-68
Klos, Frank W(illiam), Jr. 1924- ... 15-16R
Klose, Kevin 1940- ... 53-56
Klose, Norma Cline 1936- ... 19-20R
Klosinski, Emil 1922- ... 65-68
Kloss, Phillips 1902- ... CAP-1
Earlier sketch in CA 15-16
Kloss, Robert J(ames) 1935- ... 45-48
Kloss, Robert Marsh 1938- ... 65-68
Klosty, James (Michael) 1943- Brief entry ... 112
Klotman, Phyllis Rauch ... 93-96
Klotman, Robert Howard 1918- ... 53-56
Klots, Alexander Barrett 1903- ... 107
Klotter, James C(hristopher) 1947- ... 77-80
Klotter, John C(harles) 1918- ... 93-96
Klotz, Lynn C(harles) 1940- ... 116
Klubertanz, George Peter 1912- ... 7-8R
Kluckhohn, Frank L. 1907-1970 ... 7-8R
Obituary ... 29-32R
Klueger, Ruth
See Kluger, Ruth
Klug, Eugene F(rederick Adolf) 1917- ... CANR-1
Earlier sketch in CA 45-48

INDEX

Klug, Ron(ald) 1939- CANR-24
Earlier sketch in CA 107
See also SATA 31
Kluge, Alexander 1932- 81-84
Kluge, Eike-Henner W. 1942- 61-64
Kluge, P(aul) F(rederick) 1942- CANR-16
Earlier sketch in CA 73-76
Kluger, James R. 1939- 29-32R
Kluger, Richard 1934- CANR-6
Earlier sketch in CA 9-10R
Kluger, Ruth 1914-1980 116
Obituary 108
Klugh, Henry E(licker, III) 1927- 53-56
Kluwe, Mary Jean 1905-1975 .... CAP-2
Earlier sketch in CA 23-24
Kmoch, Hans 1897(?)-1973 Obituary 41-44R
Knaack, Twila 1944- 119
Knachel, Philip A(therton) 1926- 23-24R
Knack, Martha C(arol) 1948- 118
Knaplund, Paul (Alexander) 1885-1964 ... CAP-1
Earlier sketch in CA 11-12
Knapp, Bettina (Liebowitz) CANR-21
Earlier sketches in CA 13-14R, CANR-6
Knapp, David A(llan) 1938- 41-44R
Knapp, Herbert W. 1931- 105
Knapp, J(ohn) Merrill 1914- 53-56
Knapp, James F(ranklin) 1940- 107
Knapp, John (Allen) II 1940- 116
Knapp, Joseph G(rant) 1900-1983 .... 37-40R
Obituary 110
Knapp, Joseph G(eorge) 1924- 41-44R
Knapp, Lewis M(ansfield) 1894- 23-24R
Knapp, Mark L(ane) 1938- 81-84
Knapp, Mary L. 1931- 105
Knapp, Peggy A(nn) 1937- 119
Knapp, Robert Hampden 1915-1974 ..... CAP-2
Obituary 53-56
Earlier sketch in CA 15-16
Knapp, Ron 1952- 103
See also SATA 34
Knapp, Ronald Gary 1940- 112
Knapp, Ronald J(ames) 1935- 119
Knapp, Samuel Lorenzo 1783-1838 ...... DLB-59
Knapper, Christopher (Kay) 1940- CANR-12
Earlier sketch in CA 29-32R
Knapton, Ernest John 1902- CANR-1
Earlier sketch in CA 4R
Knaub, Richard K. 1928- 41-44R
Knaus, William A. 1946- 105
Knauth, Percy 1914- 57-60
Knauth, Victor W. 1895(?)-1977
Obituary 73-76
Knebel, Fletcher 1911- CANR-1
Earlier sketch in CA 1R
See also CAAS 3
See also SATA 36
See also CLC 14
See also AITN 1
Knecht, R(obert) J(ean) 1926- CANR-13
Earlier sketch in CA 33-36R
Knechtges, David R(ichard) 1942- 65-68
Kneebone, Geoffrey Thomas 1918- 5-6R
Kneese, Allen V(ictor) 1930- CANR-8
Earlier sketch in CA 15-16R
Knef, Hildegard 1925- CANR-4
Earlier sketch in CA 45-48
Kneller, John W(illiam) 1916- 17-18R
Knelman, Fred H. 1919- 102
Knelman, Martin 1943- 73-76
Knepler, Henry (William) 1922- 23-24R
Knezevich, Stephen J(oseph) 1920- CANR-10
Earlier sketch in CA 7-8R
Knickerbocker, Charles H(errick) 1922- ... 13-14R
Knickerbocker, Diedrich
See Irving, Washington
Knickerbocker, Kenneth L(eslie) 1905- 5-6R
Knickmeyer, Steve 1944- 85-88
Knies, Elizabeth 1941- 109
Knifesmith
See Cutler, Ivor
Kniffen, Fred B(owerman) 1900- 2R
Knigge, Robert (R.) 1921(?)-1987
Obituary 121
See also SATA 50
Knight, Adam
See Lariar, Lawrence
Knight, Alanna CANR-15
Earlier sketch in CA 81-84
Knight, Alice Valle 1922- 81-84
Knight, Anne (Katherine) 1946- SATA-34
Knight, Arthur 1916- 41-44R
Knight, Arthur Winfield 1937- CANR-19
Earlier sketches in CA 53-56, CANR-4
Knight, B(etty) Carolyn 1944- 118
Knight, Bernard 1931- CANR-2
Earlier sketch in CA 49-52
Knight, Bertram 1904- 103
Knight, Charles 1910- 109
Knight, Charles Landon AITN-2
Knight, Charles W. 1891- CAP-1
Earlier sketch in CA 9-10
Knight, Clayton 1891-1969 .... CAP-1
Earlier sketch in CA 9-10
Knight, Damon (Francis) 1922- CANR-17
Earlier sketches in CA 49-52, CANR-3
See also SATA 9
See also DLB 8
Knight, David
See Prather, Richard S(cott)
Knight, David C(arpenter) 1925- 73-76
See also SATA 14
Knight, David Marcus 1936- CANR-7
Earlier sketch in CA 57-60
Knight, Doug(las E.) 1925- 85-88
Knight, Douglas M(aitland) 1921- CANR-2
Earlier sketch in CA 49-52
Knight, Eric (Mowbray) 1897-1943 .... SATA-18
Knight, Etheridge 1931- CANR-23
Earlier sketch in CA 23-24R
See also DLB 41
See also CLC 40
Knight, Everett 1919- 33-36R
Knight, Francis Edgar 1905- 73-76
See also SATA 14
Knight, Frank
See Knight, Francis Edgar
Knight, Frank H(yneman) 1885-1972
Obituary 33-36R
Knight, Franklin Willis 1942- 101
Knight, Frida 1910- CANR-2
Earlier sketch in CA 49-52
Knight, G(ilfred) Norman 1891-1978 ... CANR-17
Earlier sketch in CA 25-28R
Knight, G(eorge) Wilson 1897-1985 ... CANR-10
Obituary 115
Earlier sketch in CA 15-16R
Knight, Gareth
See Wilby, Basil Leslie
Knight, Geoffrey Egerton 1921- 122
Knight, George Angus Fulton 1909- 4R
Knight, Glee 1947-1975 57-60
Obituary 120
Knight, H(erbert) Ralph 1895- CAP-2
Earlier sketch in CA 25-28
Knight, Harold V(incent) 1907- 23-24R
Knight, Hattie M. 1908-1976 .... CAP-2
Earlier sketch in CA 29-32
Knight, Hilary 1926- 73-76
See also SATA 15
Knight, Hugh McCown 1905- 5-6R
Knight, Ione Kemp 1922- 37-40R
Knight, Isabel F(rances) 1930- 25-28R
Knight, James
See Schneck, Stephen
Knight, James A(llen) 1918- CANR-6
Earlier sketch in CA 15-16R
Knight, Janet M(argaret) 1940- 93-96
Knight, John S. III AITN-2
Knight, John Shively 1894-1981 93-96
Obituary 103
See also DLB 29
See also AITN 2
Knight, K(enneth) G(raham) 1921- 25-28R
Knight, Karl F. 1930- 17-18R
Knight, Mallory T.
See Hurwood, Bernhardt J.
Knight, Margaret K(ennedy) Horsey
1903- CAP-1
Earlier sketch in CA 9-10
Knight, Max 1909- 93-96
Knight, Maxwell 1900- CAP-1
Earlier sketch in CA 13-14
Knight, Michael E(mery) 1935- 105
Knight, Norman L(ouis) 1895- CAP-2
Earlier sketch in CA 23-24
Knight, Oliver (Holmes) 1919- 21-22R
Knight, Paul Emerson 1925- 13-14R
Knight, R(oy) C(lement) 1907- 15-16R
Knight, Richard S. 1936- 115
Knight, Robin 1943- 73-76
Knight, Roderic C(opley) 1942- 61-64
Knight, Ruth Adams 1898-1974 .... 5-6R
Obituary 49-52
See also SATA 20
Knight, Sarah Kemble 1666-1727 ...... DLB-24
Knight, Stephen 1951-1985 69-72
Obituary 117
Knight, Thomas J(oseph) 1937- 102
Knight, Thomas S(tanley, Jr.) 1921- 17-18R
Knight, Vick R(alph), Jr. 1928- CANR-16
Earlier sketches in CA 45-48, CANR-1
Knight, Vick (Ralph), Sr. 1908-1984
Obituary 112
Knight, W(illiam) Nicholas 1939- 37-40R
Knight, Walker L(eigh) 1924- CANR-13
Earlier sketch in CA 37-40R
Knight, Wallace E(dward) 1926- CANR-11
Earlier sketch in CA 65-68
Knightley, Phillip 1929- 25-28R
Knight-Patterson, W. M.
See Kulski, Wladyslaw Wszebor
Knights, John Keell 1930(?)-1981
Obituary 102
Knights, L(ionel) C(harles) 1906- CANR-3
Earlier sketch in CA 7-8R
Knights, Peter R(oger) 1938- 37-40R
Knights, Ward A(rthur), Jr. 1927- 97-100
Knigin, Michael Jay 1942- 85-88
Kniker, Charles Robert 1936- 77-80
Knipe, Humphry 1941- 37-40R
Knipe, Wayne Bishop III 1946- 53-56
Knipschield, Don(ald Harold) 1940- 5-6R
Kniskern, David Paul 1948- 112
Knist, F(rances) Emma 1948- CANR-5
Earlier sketch in CA 53-56
Knittel, John (Herman Emanuel)
1891-1970 Obituary 104
Knobel, Lance 1956- 121
Knoblauch, C(yril) H. 1945- 124
Knobler, Nathan 1926- 33-36R
Knobler, Peter (Stephen) 1946- 97-100
Knoblock, Edward 1874-1945 Brief entry ... 108
See also DLB 10
Knock, Warren 1932- 65-68
Knoebl, Kuno 1936- 25-28R
Knoepfle, John 1923- CANR-12
Earlier sketch in CA 13-14R
Knoepflmacher, U(lrich) C(amillus)
1931- CANR-10
Earlier sketch in CA 15-16R
Knoerle, Jeanne 1928- 45-48
Knoke, David (Harmon) 1947- CANR-10
Earlier sketch in CA 65-68
Knoles, (Michael Clive) David 1896- 7-8R
Knoles, George Harmon 1907- 7-8R
Knoll, Erwin 1931- 89-92
Knoll, Gerald M. 1942- 29-32R
Knoll, Paul W(endell) 1937- 107
Knoll, Robert Edwin 1922- CANR-5
Earlier sketch in CA 2R
Knollenberg, Bernhard 1892-1973 .... CAP-2
Obituary 41-44R
Earlier sketch in CA 21-22
Knoop, Faith Yingling 1896- 97-100
Knop, Werner 1912(?)-1970 Obituary 29-32R
Knopf, Alfred A. 1892-1984 106
Obituary 113
See also DLBY 84
Knopf, Edwin H. 1899-1982(?) Obituary 105
Knopf, Irwin J(ay) 1924- 119
Knopf, Kenyon A(lfred) 1921- 77-80
Knopf, Terry Ann 1940- CANR-17
Earlier sketch in CA 25-28R
Knopp, Josephine Zadovsky 1941- 103
Knorr, Albert Scofield 1929- 25-28R
Knorr, Dandi 1949- 112
Knorr, Klaus (Eugene) 1911- Brief entry ... 113
Knorr, Marian L(ockwood) 1910- 102
Knott, Bill
See Knott, William C(ecil, Jr.)
Knott, John R(ay), Jr. 1937- 57-60
Knott, Kim 1955- 124
Knott, Leonard L(ewis) 1905- 107
Knott, Will C.
See Knott, William C(ecil, Jr.)
Knott, William C(ecil, Jr.) 1927- CANR-22
Earlier sketches in CA 5-6R, CANR-7
See also SATA 3
Knotts, Howard (Clayton, Jr.) 1922- ... CANR-11
Earlier sketch in CA 69-72
See also SATA 25
Knowland, A(nthony) S(tephen) 1919- 116
Knowland, William Fife 1908-1974
Obituary 89-92
Knowler, John 1933(?)-1979 Obituary 85-88
Knowles, A(lbert) Sidney, Jr. 1926- 101
Knowles, Alison 1933- CANR-8
Earlier sketch in CA 19-20R
Knowles, Anne 1933- 102
See also SATA 37
Knowles, Asa S(mallidae) 1909- 29-32R
Knowles, Clayton 1908-1978 81-84
Obituary 73-76
Knowles, (Michael Clive) David
1896-1974 .... CANR-4
Obituary 53-56
Earlier sketch in CA 7-8R
Knowles, Dorothy 1906- 25-28R
Knowles, Henry P(aine) 1912- 61-64
Knowles, John 1926- 17-18R
See also SATA 8
See also DLB 6
See also CLC 1, 4, 10, 26
Knowles, John H(ilton) 1926-1979 101
Obituary 85-88
Knowles, Joseph W(illiam) 1922- 23-24R
Knowles, Louis L(eonard) 1947- 29-32R
Knowles, Mabel Winifred 1875-1949
Brief entry 122
Knowles, Malcolm Shepherd 1913- CANR-5
Earlier sketch in CA 7-8R
Knowles, Yereth K(ahn) 1920- 93-96
Knowlton, Derrick 1921- CANR-6
Earlier sketch in CA 57-60
Knowlton, Edgar C(olby), Jr. 1921- 41-44R
Knowlton, James 1943- 120
Knowlton, Robert A(lmy) 1914-1968 .... 3R
Obituary 103
Knowlton, William H. 1927- 19-20R
Knox, Alexander 1907- 81-84
Knox, Bernard M(acGregor) W(alker)
1914- Brief entry 117
Knox, Bill
See Knox, William
Knox, Calvin M.
See Silverberg, Robert
Knox, Caroline 1938- 120
Knox, Cleone
See King-Hall, Magdalen
Knox, Collie T. 1897-1977 77-80
Obituary 73-76
Knox, David H., Jr. 1943- 41-44R
Knox, Donald E(dward) 1936-1986 45-48
Obituary 119
Knox, Edmund George Valpy 1881-1971 112
Obituary 29-32R
Knox, (Mary) Eleanor Jessie 1909- SATA-30
Knox, Frank 1874-1944 .... DLB-29
Knox, George A(lbert) 1918- 121
Knox, Henry M(acdonald) 1916- 13-14R
Knox, Hugh (Randolph) 1942- 103
Knox, Israel 1906-1986 Obituary 119
Knox, James
See Brittain, William
Knox, John 1900- 13-14R
Knox, John Armory 1850-1906 .... DLB-23
Knox, John Ballenger 1909- CAP-1
Earlier sketch in CA 9-10
Knox, Katharine McCook 1890(?)-1983
Obituary 110
Knox, (Thomas) Malcolm 1900-1980 103
Obituary 97-100
Knox, Robert Buick 1918- 25-28R
Knox, Ronald A(rbuthnott) 1888-1957
Brief entry 111
Knox, Sanka (Lutins) 1906-1984 Obituary .. 112
Knox, Vera Huntingdon 11-12R
Knox, Warren Barr 1925- 49-52
Knox, William 1928- CANR-1
Earlier sketch in CA 2R
Knox-Johnston, Robin 1939- CANR-15
Earlier sketch in CA 29-32R
Knox-Mawer, Ronald 1925- 123
Knox-Mawer, Ronnie
See Knox-Mawer, Ronald
Knudsen, Hans August Heinrich
1886-1971 Obituary 29-32R
Knudsen, James 1950- 111
See also SATA 42
Knudson, Danny (Alan) 1940- CANR-11
Earlier sketch in CA 61-64
Knudson, R. R.
See Knudson, Rozanne
Knudson, Richard L(ewis) 1930- CANR-20
Earlier sketch in CA 104
See also SATA 34
Knudson, Rozanne 1932- CANR-15
Earlier sketch in CA 33-36R
See also SATA 7
Knuemann, Carl H(einz) 1922- 77-80
Knusel, Jack L(eonard) 1923- 25-28R
Knuth, Helen 1912- 53-56
Knutson, Harold Christian 1928- 112
Knutson, Jeanne N(ickell) 1934- 41-44R
Knutson, Kent S(iguart) 1924-1973 ...... CAP-2
Obituary 41-44R
Earlier sketch in CA 33-36
Knye, Cassandra
See Disch, Thomas M(ichael)
Ko, Kanzein
See Isogai, Hiroshi
Ko, Won 1925- 61-64
Kobal, John 1943- CANR-11
Earlier sketch in CA 61-64
Kobayashi, Masako Matsuno 1935- CANR-13
Earlier sketch in CA 5-6R
Kobayashi, Noritake 1932- 53-56
Kobayashi, Tetsuya 1926- 69-72
Kober, Arthur 1900-1975 .... CAP-1
Obituary 57-60
Earlier sketch in CA 13-14
See also DLB 11
Kobler, Arthur L(eon) 1920- 15-16R
Kobler, (Albert) John (Jr.) 1910- 65-68
Kobler, (Mary) Turner S. 1930- 37-40R
Kobrak, Peter 1936- 104
Kobre, Sidney 1907- 65-68
Kobrin, David 1941- 41-44R
Kobrin, Janet 1942- 57-60
Kobryn, A(llen) P(aul) 1949- 93-96
Koch, C(hristopher) J(ohn) 1932- CLC-42
Koch, Charlotte 85-88
Koch, Claude (F.) 1918- 11-12R
Koch, Dorothy Clarke 1924- 7-8R
See also SATA 6
Koch, Edward I(rving) 1924- 113
Koch, Eric 1919- 69-72
Koch, H(annsjoachim) W(olfgang)
1933- CANR-15
Earlier sketch in CA 93-96
Koch, Hans-Gerhard 1913- 17-18R
Koch, Helen L(ois) 1895- CAP-2
Earlier sketch in CA 21-22
Koch, Howard 1902- 73-76
See also DLB 26
Koch, James Harold 1926- 106
Koch, Joanne 1940- CANR-15
Earlier sketch in CA 69-72
Koch, Kenneth 1925- CANR-6
Earlier sketch in CA 4R
See also DLB 5
See also CLC 5, 8, 44
Koch, Kurt E(mil) 1913-1987 107
Obituary 122
Koch, Lew(is) Z. 1935- 69-72
Koch, Michael 1916(?)-1981 Obituary 103
Koch, Raymond 85-88
Koch, Richard 1921- 29-32R
Koch, Robert 1918- 9-10R
Koch, Stephen 1941- 77-80
Koch, Thilo 1920- CANR-11
Earlier sketch in CA 25-28R
Koch, Thomas J(ohn) 1947- 61-64
Koch, Thomas Walter 1933- 17-18R
Koch, William H., Jr. 1923- 19-20R
Kochan, Lionel 1922- 105
Kochan, Miriam (Louise) 1929- 103
Kochan, Paul C(ranston) 1906- 45-48
Kochan, Thomas A(nton) 1947- 123
Kochanek, Stanley A(nthony) 1934- 116
Kochen, Manfred 1928- 21-22R
Kochenburger, Ralph J. 1919- 53-56
Kocher, Eric 1912- 57-60
Kocher, Paul H(arold) 1907- 65-68
Kochetov, Vsevolod A(nisimovich)
1912-1973 Obituary 45-48
Kochiss, John (Matthew) 1926- 97-100
Kochka, Mary Murray 1894(?)-1984
Obituary 112
Kochman, Thomas 1936- 37-40R
Kock, Winston E(dward) 1909-1982 110
Kockelmans, Joseph J(ohn) 1923- 117
Brief entry 113
Kocsis, J. C.
See Paul, James
Kocsis, Robert
See Kossez, Robes
Kodaly, Zoltan 1882-1967 Obituary 112
Kodama, Sanehide 1932- 120
Kodanda Rao, Pandurangi 1889- 13-14R
Koda Rohan
See Koda Shigeyuki
Koda Shigeyuki 1867-1947 Brief entry 121
Kodera, Takashi James 1945- 111
Koehler, Alan (Robert) 1928- 13-14R
Koehler, G(eorge) Stanley 1915- 37-40R
Koehler, George E. 1930- 25-28R

Koehler, Ludmila 1917- ... 53-56
Koehler, Lyle P(eter) 1944- ... 109
Koehler, Margaret (Hudson) ... 85-88
Koehler, Nikki 1951- ... 25-28R
Koehler, W(illiam) R. 1914- ... 9-10R
Koehler, Wolfgang 1887-1967 Obituary ... 111
Koehn, Ilse
See Van Zwienen, Ilse Charlotte Koehn
Koehn, Lala
See Koehn-Heine, Lala
Koehn-Heine, Lala 1936- ... 112
Koelsch, William Alvin 1933- ... 104
Koen, Ross Y. 1918- ... 3R
Koenig, Allen Edward 1939- ... 23-24R
Koenig, C(lyde) Eldo 1919- ... 21-22R
Koenig, Duane (Walter) 1918- ... 37-40R
Koenig, Franz 1905- ... 101
Koenig, Fritz H(ans) 1940- ... 53-56
Koenig, John (Thomas) 1938- ... 102
Koenig, Laird ... 29-32R
Koenig, Linda Lee 1948- ... 113
Koenig, Louis William 1916- ... 1R
Koenig, Rene 1906- ... CANR-15
Earlier sketch in CA 81-84
Koenig, Samuel 1899-1972 ... CAP-2
Obituary ... 37-40R
Earlier sketch in CA 17-18
Koenig, Walter 1936- ... 104
Koenigsberg, Moses 1879-1945 ... DLB-25
Koenigsberger, H(elmut) G(eorg) 1918- ... 33-36R
Koenigswald, (Gustav Heinrich) Ralph von
See von Koenigswald, (Gustav Heinrich) Ralph
Koenker, Diane 1947- ... 112
Koenker, Ernest Benjamin 1920-
Brief entry ... 106
Koenner, Alfred 1921- ... CANR-18
Earlier sketch in CA 101
Koepf, Michael 1940- ... 81-84
Koepke, Paul 1918- ... 114
Koepke, Wulf 1928- ... CANR-16
Earlier sketch in CA 93-96
Koeppel, Gary 1938- ... 49-52
Koerner, James D. 1923- ... 9-10R
Koerner, Stephan 1913- ... 1R
Koerner, W(illiam) H(enry) D(avid)
1878-1938 ... SATA-21
Koerte, Mary Norbert 1934- ... 103
Koertge, Noretta 1935- ... CANR-22
Earlier sketch in CA 106
Koertge, Ronald 1940- ... CANR-9
Earlier sketch in CA 65-68
Koestenbaum, Peter 1928- ... CANR-13
Earlier sketch in CA 29-32R
Koestenbaum, Phyllis 1930- ... 107
Koester, Helmut 1926- ... 110
Koestler, Arthur 1905-1983 ... CANR-1
Obituary ... 109
Earlier sketch in CA 1R
See also DLBY 83
See also CLC 1, 3, 6, 8, 15, 33
Koestler, Cynthia 1928(?)-1983 Obituary ... 114
Koethe, John (Louis) 1945- ... 49-52
Koff, Richard Myram 1926- ... CANR-15
Earlier sketch in CA 89-92
Kofoed, Jack
See Kofoed, John C.
Kofoed, John C. 1894-1979 ... 5-6R
Obituary ... 93-96
Kofsky, Frank (Joseph) 1935- ... 57-60
Kogan, Bernard Robert 1920- ... 11-12R
Kogan, Deborah
See Kogan Ray, Deborah
See also SATA 50
Kogan, Herman 1914- ... CANR-20
Earlier sketches in CA 9-10R, CANR-5
Kogan, Leonard S(aul) 1919-1976
Obituary ... 65-68
Kogan, Maurice 1930- ... 107
Kogan, Norman 1919- ... 4R
Kogan Ray, Deborah 1940- ... CANR-22
Earlier sketches in CA 57-60, CANR-7
Kogawa, Joy Nozomi 1935- ... CANR-19
Earlier sketch in CA 101
Kogiku, K(iichiro) C(hris) 1927- ... 33-36R
Koginos, Manny T. 1933- ... 21-22R
Kogos, Frederick 1907-1974 ... CAP-2
Obituary ... 53-56
Earlier sketch in CA 29-32
Koh, Byung Chul 1936- ... 17-18R
Koh, Sung Jae 1917- ... 19-20R
Kohak, Erazim V. 1933- ... CANR-14
Earlier sketch in CA 37-40R
Kohake, Rosanne 1951- ... 114
Kohan, Rhea ... 89-92
Kohanski, Alexander S(iskind) 1902-1987 ... 108
Obituary ... 123
Kohavi, Y.
See Stern, Jay B(enjamin)
Kohen-Raz, Reuven 1921- ... 37-40R
Kohfeldt, Mary Lou 1939- ... 119
Kohl, Herbert 1937- ... CANR-14
Earlier sketch in CA 65-68
See also SATA 47
Kohl, Irene C(aistor) 1927- ... 119
Kohl, James (Virgil) 1942- ... 57-60
Kohl, Marvin 1932- ... 85-88
Kohlberg, Lawrence 1927-1987 Obituary ... 122
Kohlenberg, Robert J(oseph) 1937- ... 111
Kohler, Foy D(avid) 1908- ... 29-32R
Kohler, Heinz 1934- ... 23-24R
Kohler, Julilly H(ouse) 1908-1976 ... 77-80
Obituary ... 69-72
See also SATA 20
Kohler, Mary C.
See Kohler, Mary Conway
Kohler, Mary Conway 1903-1986 Obituary ... 119
Kohler, Saul 1928- ... 69-72
Kohler, Sister Mary Hortense 1892- ... 7-8R
Kohler, Wolfgang
See Koehler, Wolfgang
Kohlmeier, Louis M(artin), Jr. 1926- ... 49-52
Kohls, Richard Louis 1921- Brief entry ... 106
Kohlstedt, Sally Gregory 1943- ... 69-72
Kohmescher, Matthew Franklin 1921- ... 113
Kohn, Alexander 1919- ... 123
Kohn, Alfie 1957- ... 122
Kohn, Bernice
See Hunt, Bernice (Kohn)
See also SATA 4
Kohn, Clyde F(rederick) 1911- Brief entry ... 109
Kohn, Eugene 1887-1977 Obituary ... 69-72
Kohn, George C(hilds) 1940- ... CANR-19
Earlier sketch in CA 103
Kohn, Hans 1891-1971 ... CANR-4
Obituary ... 29-32R
Earlier sketch in CA 1R
Kohn, Howard 1947- ... 124
Kohn, Jacob 1881-1968 ... 5-6R
Obituary ... 103
Kohn, John S. (Van E.) 1906-1976
Obituary ... 104
Kohn, Melvin L(ester) 1928- ... 41-44R
Kohn, Richard H(enry) 1940- ... 115
Kohn, Walter S(amuel) G(erst) 1923- ... 107
Kohner, Frederick 1905-1986 ... CANR-1
Obituary ... 119
Earlier sketch in CA 1R
See also SATA 10, 48
Kohout, Pavel 1928- ... CANR-3
Earlier sketch in CA 45-48
See also CLC 13
Kohr, Louise Hannah 1903- ... 41-44R
Kohs, Samuel C(almin) 1890-1984
Obituary ... 111
Koht, Halvdan 1873-1965 ... 85-88
Kohut, Heinz 1913-1981 ... CANR-1
Obituary ... 105
Earlier sketch in CA 45-48
Kohut, Les
See Kohut, Nester C(larence)
Kohut, Nester C(larence) 1925- ... 45-48
Koidahl, Ilona 1924- ... 97-100
Koide, Tan 1938-1986 ... SATA-50
Koi Hai
See Palmer, (Nathaniel) Humphrey
Koilpillai, (Jesudas) Charles ... 41-44R
Koilpillai, Das
See Koilpillai, (Jesudas) Charles
Koinange, Mbiyu (Peter) 1907-1981
Obituary ... 108
Koiner, Richard B. 1929- ... 19-20R
Koizumi, Yakumo
See Hearn, (Patricio) Lafcadio (Tessima Carlos)
Kojecky, Roger 1943- ... 85-88
Kojima, Naomi 1950- ... 109
Kojima, Takashi 1902- ... CAP-1
Earlier sketch in CA 9-10
Kojima Shozo 1928- ... 69-72
Kokoschka, Oskar 1886-1980 ... 109
Obituary ... 93-96
Kokyshev, Lazor 1933(?)-1975 Obituary ... 104
Kolaja, Jiri Thomas 1919- ... 9-10R
Kolakowski, Leszek 1927- ... 49-52
Kolars, Frank 1899-1973 ... 7-8R
Obituary ... 37-40R
Kolasky, John 1915- ... 25-28R
Kolatch, Alfred Jacob 1916- ... 107
Kolatch, Jonathan 1943- ... 41-44R
Kolb, Annette 1870-1967 ... DLB-66
Kolb, Carolyn 1942- ... 89-92
Kolb, David A(llen) 1939- ... CANR-15
Earlier sketch in CA 65-68
Kolb, Erwin J(ohn) 1924- ... 37-40R
Kolb, Gwin Jackson 1919- ... 2R
Kolb, Harold H(utchinson), Jr. 1933- ... CANR-12
Earlier sketch in CA 29-32R
Kolb, John F. 1916(?)-1974 Obituary ... 53-56
Kolb, Ken(neth) 1926- ... 21-22R
Kolb, Lawrence 1911-1972 Obituary ... 37-40R
Kolb, Philip 1907- ... CANR-4
Earlier sketch in CA 53-56
Kolba, St. Tamara ... 97-100
See also SATA 22
Kolbas, Grace Holden 1914- ... 93-96
Kolbe, Henry E(ugene) 1907- ... 5-6R
Kolbenheyer, Erwin Guido 1878-1962 ... DLB-66
Kolbenschlag, Madonna (Claire) 1935-
Brief entry ... 115
Kolbrek, Loyal 1914- ... 29-32R
Kolchin, Peter 1943- ... 41-44R
Kolde, Endel Jakob 1917- ... CANR-1
Earlier sketch in CA 45-48
Kolenda, Konstantin 1923- ... 15-16R
Kolers, Paul A. 1926- ... 97-100
Kolesar, Paul 1927- ... 105
Kolesnik, Walter B(ernard) 1923- ... CANR-2
Earlier sketch in CA 7-8R
Kolevzon, Edward R. 1913(?)-1976
Obituary ... 69-72
Kolin, Philip C(harles) 1945- ... 119
Kolins, William 1926(?)-1973 Obituary ... 104
Kolinski, Charles J(ames) 1916- ... 19-20R
Kolinsky, Martin 1936- ... CANR-8
Earlier sketch in CA 61-64
Koljevic, Svetozar 1930- ... CANR-7
Earlier sketch in CA 19-20R
Kolker, Robert Phillip 1940- ... 112
Kolko, Gabriel 1932- ... CANR-4
Earlier sketch in CA 5-6R
Kolkowicz, Roman 1929- Brief entry ... 116
Kollat, David T(ruman) 1938- ... 41-44R
Kollek, Teddy
See Kollek, Theodore
Kollek, Theodore 1911- ... CAP-2
Earlier sketch in CA 29-32
Koller, Charles W. 1896(?)-1983 ... 61-64
Obituary ... 109
Koller, James 1936- ... CANR-18
Earlier sketches in CA 49-52, CANR-2
See also CAAS 5
Koller, John M. 1938- ... 33-36R
Koller, Larry
See Koller, Lawrence Robert
Koller, Lawrence Robert 1912-1967 ... CANR-6
Earlier sketch in CA 4R
Koller, Marvin Robert 1919- ... 15-16R
Kollmar, Dick
See Kollmar, Richard Tompkins
Kollmar, Richard Tompkins 1910-1971
Obituary ... 89-92
Kollock, Will(iam Raymond) 1940- ... 33-36R
Kollontai, Alexandra (Mikhailovna)
1872-1952 Brief entry ... 112
Kollstedt, Paula Lubke 1946- ... 113
Kolmogorov, Andrei Nikolayevich
1903-1987 Obituary ... 123
Kolnai, Aurel (Thomas) 1900-1973 ... 103
Kolodin, Irving 1908- ... 93-96
Kolodny, Annette 1941- ... CANR-8
Earlier sketch in CA 61-64
See also DLB 67
Kolodny, Ralph (Leonard) 1923- ... 116
Kolodziej, Edward Albert 1935- ... 97-100
Kolon, Nita
See Onadipe, (Nathaniel) Kola(wole)
Kolosimo, Peter 1922- ... CANR-7
Earlier sketch in CA 53-56
Kolson, Clifford J(ohn) 1920- ... 11-12R
Kolstoe, Oliver P(aul) 1920- ... 17-18R
Koltun, Frances Lang ... 69-72
Kolumban, Nicholas 1937- ... 111
Kolve, Carolee Nance 1946- ... 122
Kolyer, John (McNaughton) 1933- ... CANR-11
Earlier sketch in CA 69-72
Komai, Akira 1908(?)-1983 Obituary ... 111
Komaiko, Jean R. 1922(?)-1984 Obituary ... 114
Komarnicki, Tytus 1896- ... CAP-1
Earlier sketch in CA 9-10
Komarovsky, Mirra ... CAP-1
Earlier sketch in CA 17-18
Komatsu Sakyo 1931- Brief entry ... 113
Kome, Penney 1948- ... 116
Komer, Robert W(illiam) 1922- ... 108
Komisar, Lucy 1942- ... 33-36R
See also SATA 9
Kommers, Donald P. 1932- ... 116
Komoda, Beverly 1939- ... 85-88
See also SATA 25
Komoda, Kiyo 1937- ... SATA-9
Komroff, Manuel 1890-1974 ... CANR-4
Obituary ... 53-56
Earlier sketch in CA 4R
See also SATA 2, 20
See also DLB 4
Konadu, Asare
See Konadu, S(amuel) A(sare)
Konadu, S(amuel) A(sare) 1932- ... 23-24R
Konczacki, Zbigniew Andrzej 1917- ... CANR-10
Earlier sketch in CA 21-22R
Kondoleon, Harry 1955- ... 112
Kondracke, Morton 1939(?)- Brief entry ... 119
Kondrashin, Kiril (Petrovich) 1914-1981
Obituary ... 108
Kondrashov, Stanislav (Nikolaevich)
1928- ... 69-72
Konecky, Edith 1922- ... 69-72
Konefsky, Samuel J. 1915-1970
Obituary ... 29-32R
Konek, Carol (Wolfe) 1934- Brief entry ... 114
Koner, Marvin 1921(?)-1983 Obituary ... 109
Kong, Shiu Loon 1934- ... 108
Konick, Marcus 1914- ... 37-40R
Konig, David Thomas 1947- ... 97-100
Konig, Franz
See Koenig, Franz
Konig, Fritz H(ans)
See Koenig, Fritz H(ans)
Konig, Rene
See Koenig, Rene
Konigsberg, Conrad Isidore 1916- ... 23-24R
Konigsburg, E(laine) L(obl) 1930- ... CANR-17
Earlier sketch in CA 21-22R
See also SATA 4, 48
See also DLB 52
See also CLR 1
Koning, Hans
See Koningsberger, Hans
Koningsberger, Hans 1921- ... CANR-2
Earlier sketch in CA 4R
See also SATA 5
Konkel, Wilbur Stanton 1912- ... 111
Konkle, Janet Everest 1917- ... 4R
See also SATA 12
Konner, Alfred
See Koenner, Alfred
Konner, Linda 1951- ... 102
Konner, Melvin Joel 1946- Brief entry ... 116
Konnyu, Leslie 1914- ... CANR-7
Earlier sketch in CA 15-16R
Konopka, Gisela 1910- ... 9-10R
Konovalov, Sergey 1899-1982 Obituary ... 106
Konrad, Evelyn 1930- ... 33-36R
Konrad, George
See Konrad, Gyoergy
Konrad, Gyoergy 1933- ... 85-88
See also CLC 4, 10
Konrad, James
See Maclean, Charles
Konstan, David 1940- ... 113
Kontos, Cecille
See Haddix-Kontos, Cecille P.
Kontos, Peter G(eorge) 1935-1977 ... CANR-17
Obituary ... 115
Earlier sketch in CA 25-28R
Konvitz, Jeffrey 1944- ... CANR-7
Earlier sketch in CA 53-56
Konvitz, Milton Ridvas 1908- ... CANR-4
Earlier sketch in CA 2R
Konwicki, Tadeusz 1926- ... 101
See also CLC 8, 28
Koo, Anthony Y(ing) C(hang) 1918- ... 57-60
Koo, Samuel 1941- ... 77-80
Koo, V(i) K(yuin) Wellington 1888-1985 ... 81-84
Obituary ... 117
Koob, C(harles) Albert 1920- ... 41-44R
Koob, Derry D(elos) 1933- ... 37-40R
Koob, Joseph E. II 1948- ... 121
Koob, Theodora (J. Foth) 1918- ... 5-6R
See also SATA 23
Kooiker, Leonie
See Kooyker-Romijn, Johanna Maria
Kooiman, Gladys 1927- ... 89-92
Kooiman, Helen W.
See Hosier, Helen Kooiman
Koon, George William 1942- ... 116
Koon, Helene Wickham 1924- ... 120
Koonce, Ray F. 1913- ... 11-12R
Koonts, Jones Calvin 1924- ... 49-52
Koontz, Dean R(ay) 1945- ... CANR-19
Earlier sketch in CA 108
Koontz, Harold 1908-1984 ... 41-44R
Obituary ... 112
Koop, Katherine C. 1923- ... 19-20R
Koopman, LeRoy George 1935- ... 101
Koopmans, Tjalling (Charles) 1910-1985
Obituary ... 115
Koopowitz, Harold 1940- ... 114
Kooser, Ted
See Kooser, Theodore
Kooser, Theodore 1939- ... CANR-15
Earlier sketch in CA 33-36R
Kootz, Samuel Melvin 1898-1982
Obituary ... 107
Kooyker-Romijn, Johanna Maria 1927- ... 107
See also SATA 48
Kooyker-Romyn, Johanna Maria
See Kooyker-Romijn, Johanna Maria
Kopal, Zdenek 1914- ... 93-96
Kopelev, Lev (Zinovievich) 1912- ... 123
Kopelev, Raissa (Davydovna) Orlova
See Orlova-Kopelev, Raissa (Davydovna)
Kopelman, Arie 1937- ... 113
Koperwas, Sam 1948- ... CANR-22
Earlier sketch in CA 105
Kopf, David 1930- ... 89-92
Kopff, E(dward) Christian 1946- ... 117
Kopit, Arthur (Lee) 1937- ... 81-84
See also DLB 7
See also CLC 1, 18, 33
See also AITN 1
Kopkind, Andrew D(avid) 1935- ... 29-32R
Koplin, H(arry) T(homas) 1923- ... 33-36R
Koplinka, Charlotte
See Lukas, Charlotte Koplinka
Koplitz, Eugene D(e Vere) 1928- ... 37-40R
Kopman, H(enri Marshall) 1918- ... 89-92
Kopp, Anatole 1915- ... CANR-12
Earlier sketch in CA 29-32R
Kopp, Harriet Green ... 41-44R
Kopp, O(swald) W. 1918- ... 33-36R
Kopp, Richard L. 1934- ... CANR-13
Earlier sketch in CA 33-36R
Kopp, Sheldon B(ernard) 1929- ... 37-40R
Kopp, William LaMarr 1930- ... 65-68
Koppel, Lillian 1926- ... 108
Koppel, Shelley R(uth) 1951- ... 108
Koppel, Ted 1940(?)- ... 103
Kopper, Edward A(nthony), Jr. 1937- ... CANR-15
Earlier sketch in CA 69-72
Kopper, Philip (Dana) 1937- ... 97-100
Kopperman, Paul Edward 1945- ... 69-72
Koppett, Leonard 1923- ... CANR-11
Earlier sketch in CA 25-28R
Koppitz, Elizabeth M(unsterberg)
1919-1983 ... CANR-14
Obituary ... 111
Earlier sketch in CA 13-14R
Koppman, Lionel 1920- ... CANR-6
Earlier sketch in CA 11-12R
Kops, Bernard 1926- ... 5-6R
See also DLB 13
See also CLC 4
Kopulos, Stella 1906- ... 49-52
Kopycinski, Joseph V(alentine) 1923- ... 33-36R
Korach, Mimi 1922- ... SATA-9
Koran, Dennis 1947- ... 120
Korb, Lawrence J(oseph) 1939- ... 77-80
Korbel, John 1918- ... 11-12R
Korbel, Josef 1909-1977 ... 37-40R
Obituary ... 73-76
Korbonski, Andrzej 1927- ... 9-10R
Korbonski, Stefan 1903- ... CANR-5
Earlier sketch in CA 5-6R
Korda, Michael Vincent 1933- ... 107
Kordel, Lelord 1904- ... 106
Koren, Edward 1935- ... CANR-11
Earlier sketch in CA 25-28R
See also SATA 5
Koren, Henry J(oseph) 1912- ... 9-10R
Korenbaum, Myrtle 1915- ... 57-60
Korenblit, Joan B(ravo) 1952- ... 113
Korey, William 1922- Brief entry ... 112
Korfker, Dena 1908- ... CANR-17
Earlier sketch in CA 3R

Korg, Jacob 1922- ... CANR-2
Earlier sketch in CA 5-6R
Korges, James 1930-1975 ... CAP-2
Earlier sketch in CA 25-28
Korinets, Iurii Iosifovich
See Korinetz, Yuri (Iosifovich)
Korinetz, Yuri (Iosifovich) 1923- ... CANR-11
Earlier sketch in CA 61-64
See also SATA 9
See also CLR 4
Korman, A. Gerd 1928- ... 53-56
Korman, Gordon 1963- ... 112
See also SATA 41, 49
Korman, Keith 1956- ... 102
Kormendi, Ferenc 1900-1972 Obituary ... 37-40R
Kormondy, Edward J(ohn) 1926- ... CANR-13
Earlier sketch in CA 33-36R
Korn, Alfons L(udwig) 1906-1986 ... 93-96
Obituary ... 119
Korn, Bertram Wallace 1918-1979 ... CANR-1
Earlier sketch in CA 2R
Korn, Frank J(ames) 1935- ... 115
Korn, Henry James 1945- ... 69-72
Korn, Noel 1923- ... 73-76
Korn, Peggy
See Liss, Peggy K.
Korn, Walter 1908- ... 73-76
Kornai, J(anos) 1928- ... 13-14R
Kornblatt, Joyce (Reiser) 1944- ... 106
Kornbluh, Marvin 1927-1987 Obituary ... 124
Kornblum, Allan 1949- ... 69-72
Kornblum, Cinda 1950- ... 69-72
Kornblum, Sylvan 1927- ... 41-44R
Kornbluth, C(yril) M. 1923-1958
Brief entry ... 105
See also DLB 8
See also TCLC 8
Kornbluth, Jesse 1946- ... CANR-17
Earlier sketch in CA 25-28R
Korneichuk, Aleksandr Y. 1905-1972
Obituary ... 33-36R
Korner, Stephan
See Koerner, Stephan
Kornfeld, Anita Clay 1928- ... 97-100
Kornfeld, Robert J(onathan) 1919- ... 106
Kornhauser, David H(enry) 1918- ... CANR-14
Earlier sketch in CA 41-44R
Kornhauser, William 1925- ... 2R
Kornrich, Milton 1933- ... 19-20R
Korol, Alexander G. 1900- ... 7-8R
Korolenko, V. G.
See Korolenko, Vladimir Galaktionovich
Korolenko, Vladimir
See Korolenko, Vladimir Galaktionovich
Korolenko, Vladimir G.
See Korolenko, Vladimir Galaktionovich
Korolenko, Vladimir Galaktionovich
1853-1921 Brief entry ... 121
See also TCLC 22
Korotkin, Judith 1931- ... 53-56
Korr, Charles Paul 1939- ... 112
Kors, Alan Charles 1943- ... 77-80
Kort, Carol 1945- ... 106
Kort, Wesley A(lbert) 1935- ... 37-40R
Korte, Mary Norbert
See Koerte, Mary Norbert
Korten, David C(raig) 1937- ... CANR-15
Earlier sketch in CA 41-44R
Kortepeter, (Carl) Max 1928- ... 41-44R
Korth, Francis N(icholas) 1912- ... 25-28R
Kortner, Peter 1924- ... 33-36R
Korty, Carol 1937- ... 77-80
See also SATA 15
Korty, John Van Cleave 1936- ... 106
Kory, Robert B(ruce) 1950- ... 65-68
Korzenny, Felipe 1947- ... 116
Korzybski, Alfred (Habdank Skarbek)
1879-1950 Brief entry ... 123
Kos, Erih 1913- Brief entry ... 106
Kosa, John 1914-1972 ... 5-6R
Kosch, Erich
See Kos, Erih
Koschade, Alfred 1928- ... 21-22R
Kosel, Janice E. 1948- ... 116
Koshetz, Herbert 1907(?)-1977 Obituary ... 73-76
Koshi, George M. 1911- ... CAP-2
Earlier sketch in CA 29-32
Koshland, Ellen 1947- ... CANR-13
Earlier sketch in CA 33-36R
Kosinski, Jerzy (Nikodem) 1933- ... CANR-9
Earlier sketch in CA 17-18R
See also DLB 2
See also DLBY 82
See also CLC 1, 2, 3, 6, 10, 15
Kosinski, Leonard V. 1923- ... 25-28R
Koskoff, David E(lihu) 1939- ... 49-52
Koslow, Jules 1916- ... CANR-6
Earlier sketch in CA 3R
Kosmala, Hans 1904(?)-1981 Obituary ... 104
Kosof, Anna 1945- ... 85-88
Koss, Stephen E(dward) 1940-1984 ... 25-28R
Obituary ... 114
Kossez, Robes 1935- ... CANR-12
Earlier sketch in CA 29-32R
Kossin, Sandy (Sanford) 1926- ... SATA-10
Kosslyn, Stephen Michael 1948- ... 117
Kossmann, Rudolf R(ichard) 1934- ... 37-40R
Kossoff, David 1919- ... 61-64
Kost, Mary Lu 1924- ... 45-48
Kost, Robert John 1913- ... 3R
Kostash, Myrna 1944- ... 65-68
Koste, Robert Francis 1933- ... 81-84
Kostelanetz, Andre 1901-1980 Obituary ... 107
Kostelanetz, Richard C(ory) 1940- ... 15-16R
See also CLC 28
Kosten, Andrew 1921- ... 2R
Koster, Donald N(elson) 1910- ... 53-56
Koster, John (Peter, Jr.) 1945- ... CANR-5
Earlier sketch in CA 53-56
Koster, R(ichard) M(orton) 1934- ... 37-40R
Kostich, Dragos D. 1921- ... CANR-10
Earlier sketch in CA 5-6R
Kostis, Nicholas ... 103
Kostiuk, Hryhory 1902- ... 77-80
Kostka, Edmund Karl 1915- ... 17-18R
Kostrowitzki, Wilhelm Apollinaris de
1880-1918 Brief entry ... 104
Kostrubala, Thaddeus 1930- ... 101
Kostyu, Frank A(lexander) 1919- ... CANR-1
Earlier sketch in CA 49-52
Kosygin, Alexei Nikolayevich 1904-1980
Obituary ... 102
Kot, Stanislaw 1886(?)-1976 Obituary ... 65-68
Kotarba, Joseph A(nthony) 1947- ... 111
Kotarbinski, Tadeusz (Marian) 1886-1981
Obituary ... 105
Kotcheff, Ted
See Kotcheff, William Theodore
Kotcheff, William Theodore 1931- ... 115
Kothari, Rajni 1928- ... 33-36R
Kotin, Armine Avakian
See Mortimer, Armine Kotin
Kotker, Norman 1931- ... CANR-10
Earlier sketch in CA 25-28R
Kotker, Zane 1934- ... CANR-3
Earlier sketch in CA 49-52
Kotler, Milton 1935- ... 29-32R
Kotler, Philip 1931- ... CANR-13
Earlier sketch in CA 33-36R
Kotlowitz, Robert 1924- ... 33-36R
See also CLC 4
Kotowska, Monika 1942- ... 93-96
Kotowski, Joanne 1930- ... 57-60
Kotre, John N(icholas) 1940- ... 81-84
Kotrozo, Carol Donnell
See Donnell-Kotrozo, Carol
Kotschevar, Lendal H(enry) 1908- ... CANR-10
Earlier sketch in CA 19-20R
Kotschnig, Walter M(aria) 1901-1985
Obituary ... 117
Kotsilibas-Davis, James 1940- ... 106
Kotsuji, Abraham S(etsuzau) 1899-1973 ... CAP-1
Obituary ... 45-48
Earlier sketch in CA 15-16
Kott, Jan 1914- ... 13-14R
Kottler, Dorothy 1918- ... 97-100
Kottman, Richard N(orman) 1932- ... 25-28R
Kotz, David M(ichael) 1943- ... 81-84
Kotz, Mary Lynn 1936- ... 104
Kotz, Nick 1932- ... 29-32R
Kotz, Samuel 1930- ... CANR-7
Earlier sketch in CA 15-16R
Kotzin, Michael C(harles) 1941- ... 37-40R
Kotzwinkle, William 1938- ... CANR-3
Earlier sketch in CA 45-48
See also SATA 24
See also CLC 5, 14, 35
See also CLR 6
Koubourlis, Demetrius J(ohn) 1938- ... 57-60
Koufax, Sandy
See Koufax, Sanford
Koufax, Sanford 1935- ... 89-92
Kouhi, Elizabeth 1917- ... SATA-49
Koulack, David 1938- ... 102
Koumoulides, John (Thomas Anastassios)
1938- ... 41-44R
Koupernik, Cyrille 1917- ... 57-60
Kourdakov, Sergei 1951-1973 Obituary ... 115
Kousoulas, D(imitrios) George 1923- ... 19-20R
Kousser, J(oseph) Morgan 1943- ... 57-60
Koutoukas, H. M. 1947- ... 69-72
Koutoukas, H.M.
See Rivoli, Mario
Kouts, Anne 1945- ... 29-32R
See also SATA 8
Kouts, Hertha Pretorius 1922-1973 ... 2R
Obituary ... 103
Kouwenhoven, John A(tlee) 1909- ... 1R
Kouyoumdjian, Dikran
See Arlen, Michael
Kovach, Barbara L(usk) Forisha
See Forisha-Kovach, Barbara L(usk)
Kovach, Bill 1932- ... CANR-11
Earlier sketch in CA 69-72
Kovach, Francis J(oseph) 1918- ... 61-64
Kovacs, Alexander 1930(?)-1977
Obituary ... 73-76
Kovacs, Imre 1913-1980 ... 23-24R
Obituary ... 102
Kovaleff, Theodore Philip 1943- ... 116
Kovalev, Mikhail A(leksandrovich)
1893-1981 Obituary ... 108
Kovalik, Nada 1926- ... 25-28R
Kovalik, Vladimir 1928- ... 25-28R
Kovarik, Bill
See Kovarik, William
Kovarik, William 1951- ... 113
Kovarsky, Irving 1918- ... 29-32R
Kovel, Joel S. 1936- ... CANR-14
Earlier sketch in CA 29-32R
Kovel, Ralph ... CANR-23
Earlier sketches in CA 17-18R, CANR-8
Kovel, Terry 1928- ... CANR-23
Earlier sketches in CA 17-18R, CANR-8
Kovner, Aba 1918-1987 Obituary ... 123
Kovner, B.
See Adler, Jacob
Kovrig, Bennett 1940- ... CANR-12
Earlier sketch in CA 29-32R
Kowalewski, David 1943- ... 112
Kowalski, Frank 1907- ... 37-40R
Kowet, Don 1937- ... CANR-10
Earlier sketch in CA 57-60
Kowit, Steve 1938- ... 118
Kowitt, Sylvia
See Crosbie, Sylvia Kowitt
Kowitz, Gerald T(homas) 1928- ... 33-36R
Kownslar, Allan O(wen) 1935- ... 61-64
Koyama, Kosuke 1929- ... CANR-7
Earlier sketch in CA 57-60
Koykka, Arthur S(idney) 1937- ... 116
Koyre, Alexandre 1892-1964 Obituary ... 111
Kozak, Jan B(lahoslav) 1889(?)-1974
Obituary ... 45-48
Kozar, Andrew Joseph 1930- ... 103
Kozelka, Paul 1909- ... CAP-2
Earlier sketch in CA 25-28
Kozer, Jose 1940- ... CANR-2
Earlier sketch in CA 49-52
Kozicki, Henry 1924- ... 103
Kozicki, Richard J(oseph) 1929-
Brief entry ... 118
Koziebrodzki, Leopold B(olesta) 1906- ... 41-44R
Kozintsev, Grigori (Mikhailovich)
1905-1973 ... 53-56
Kozlenko, William 1917- ... 57-60
Kozloff, Max 1933- Brief entry ... 114
Kozlow, Mark J.
See Newton, Michael
Kozlowski, Theodore T(homas) 1917- ... CANR-19
Earlier sketches in CA 9-10R, CANR-4
Kozol, Jonathan 1936- ... CANR-16
Earlier sketch in CA 61-64
See also CLC 17
Kozoll, Michael 1940?- ... CLC-35
Kozulin, Alex 1949- ... 122
Kpomassie, Tete-Michel 1941- ... 123
Kraay, Colin M(ackennal) 1918-1982
Obituary ... 116
Kracmar, John Z. 1916- ... 37-40R
Krader, Lawrence 1919- ... 21-22R
Kraditor, Aileen S. 1928- ... 15-16R
Kraehe, Enno E(dward) 1921- ... 9-10R
Kraemer, Kenneth L(eo) 1936- ... 111
Kraemer, Richard H(oward) 1920- ... CANR-4
Earlier sketch in CA 53-56
Kraenzel, Carl F(rederick) 1906- ... 73-76
Kraenzel, Margaret (Powell) 1899- ... 4R
Kraf, Elaine 1946- ... CANR-11
Earlier sketch in CA 65-68
See also DLBY 81
Krafft, C(onrad) James 1923- ... 119
Krafft, Jim
See Krafft, C(onrad) James
Krafft, Maurice 1946- ... CANR-10
Earlier sketch in CA 65-68
Krafsur, Richard Paul 1940- ... 103
Kraft, Barbara 1939- ... 97-100
Kraft, Betsy Harvey 1937- ... 89-92
Kraft, Charles H(oward) 1932- ... CANR-16
Earlier sketches in CA 45-48, CANR-1
Kraft, Charlotte 1922- ... 103
Kraft, Dean 1950- ... 114
Kraft, Eric (Lance) 1944- ... 108
Kraft, Hy(man Solomon) 1899-1975 ... 41-44R
Obituary ... 57-60
Kraft, Joseph 1924-1986 ... 9-10R
Obituary ... 118
Kraft, Ken(neth) 1907- ... CANR-1
Earlier sketch in CA 4R
Kraft, Kenneth H., Sr. 1896-1983
Obituary ... 111
Kraft, Leo 1922- ... 41-44R
Kraft, Leonard E(dward) 1923- ... 29-32R
Kraft, Robert Alan 1934- ... 37-40R
Kraft, Stephanie (Barlett) 1944- ... 105
Kraft, Virginia 1932- ... 21-22R
Kraft, Walter Andreas
See Friedlander, Walter A(ndreas)
Kraft, William F. 1938- ... 33-36R
Kragen, Jinx
See Morgan, Judith A(dams)
Krahn, Fernando 1935- ... CANR-11
Earlier sketch in CA 65-68
See also SATA 31, 49
See also CLR 3
Kraig, Bruce 1939- ... CANR-18
Earlier sketch in CA 102
Krailsheimer, Alban John 1921- ... CANR-2
Earlier sketch in CA 5-6R
Kraines, Oscar 1916- ... 97-100
Kraines, Samuel H(enry) 1906- ... 77-80
Krajenke, Robert William 1939- ... 29-32R
Krajewski, Frank R. 1938- ... CANR-10
Earlier sketch in CA 65-68
Krajewski, Robert J(oseph) 1940- ... 97-100
Krakel, Dean Fenton 1923- ... 45-48
Krakowski, Lili 1930- ... 85-88
Kramarz, Joachim 1931- ... 25-28R
Kramer, A(lfred) T(heodore) 1892- ... CAP-1
Earlier sketch in CA 11-12
Kramer, Aaron 1921- ... CANR-12
Earlier sketch in CA 23-24R
Kramer, Anthony ... SATA-42
Kramer, Bernard M(ordecai) 1923- ... 77-80
Kramer, Dale 1936- ... CANR-5
Earlier sketch in CA 53-56
Kramer, Daniel C(aleb) 1934- ... 53-56
Kramer, Edith 1916- ... 33-36R
Kramer, Edna E.
See Kramer-Lassar, Edna Ernestine
Kramer, Eugene F(rancis) 1921- ... 37-40R
Kramer, Frank Raymond 1908- ... CAP-1
Earlier sketch in CA 11-12
Kramer, Gene 1927- ... 69-72
Kramer, George
See Heuman, William
Kramer, Hilton 1928- ... 113
Brief entry ... 109
Kramer, Jack 1923- ... 41-44R
Kramer, Jane 1938- ... 102
Kramer, Joel (Herbert) 1937- ... 97-100
Kramer, John Eichholtz, Jr. 1935- ... 108
Kramer, Jonathan M. 1946- ... 121
Kramer, Judith Rita 1933-1970 ... 3R
Obituary ... 103
Kramer, Kathryn 19(?)- ... CLC-34
Kramer, Larry 1935- Brief entry ... 124
See also CLC 42
Kramer, Lawrence (Eliot) 1946- ... 120
Kramer, Leonie Judith 1924- ... CANR-17
Earlier sketch in CA 81-84
Kramer, Mark (William) 1944- ... CANR-17
Earlier sketch in CA 97-100
Kramer, Milton D. 1915-1973 Obituary ... 37-40R
Kramer, Nancy 1942- ... 101
Kramer, Nora 1896(?)-1984 ... 107
Obituary ... 113
See also SATA 26, 39
Kramer, (Simon) Paul 1914- ... 21-22R
Kramer, Paul J(ackson) 1904- ... CANR-1
Earlier sketch in CA 45-48
Kramer, Rita 1929- ... 69-72
Kramer, Roberta 1935- ... 103
Kramer, Roland Laird 1898- ... 7-8R
Kramer, Samuel Noah 1897- ... 11-12R
Kramer, Ted
See Steward, Samuel M(orris)
Kramer, Victor A. 1939- ... CANR-16
Earlier sketch in CA 85-88
Kramer-Lassar, Edna Ernestine 1902-1984 ... 107
Obituary ... 113
Kramish, Arnold 1923- ... CANR-7
Earlier sketch in CA 7-8R
Krammer, Arnold Paul 1941- ... CANR-11
Earlier sketch in CA 61-64
Kramon, Florence 1920- ... 25-28R
Kramrisch, Stella 1898- ... CAP-2
Earlier sketch in CA 21-22
Kranidas, Kathleen
See Collins, Kathleen
Krantz, Hazel Newman 1920- ... CANR-16
Earlier sketches in CA 3R, CANR-1
See also SATA 12
Krantz, Judith 1927- ... CANR-11
Earlier sketch in CA 81-84
Krantz, Les(lie Jay) 1945- ... 120
Kranz, E(dwin) Kirker 1949- ... 33-36R
Kranz, Stewart D(uane) 1924- ... 101
Kranzberg, Melvin 1917- ... CANR-11
Earlier sketch in CA 21-22R
Kranzler, David 1930- ... 93-96
Kranzler, George G(ershon) 1916- ... CANR-12
Earlier sketch in CA 57-60
See also SATA 28
Kranzler, Gershon
See Kranzler, George G(ershon)
Krapf, Norbert 1943- ... 117
Krapp, R. M.
See Adams, Robert Martin
Krar, Stephen Frank 1924- ... CANR-20
Earlier sketches in CA 53-56, CANR-4
Kraselchik, R.
See Dyer, Charles (Raymond)
Krasilovsky, M(arvin) William 1926- ... 61-64
Krasilovsky, Phyllis 1926- ... CANR-11
Earlier sketch in CA 29-32R
See also SATA 1, 38
See also SAAS 5
Kraske, Robert Brief entry ... 116
See also SATA 36
Kraslow, David 1926- ... 29-32R
Krasna, Norman 1909-1984 Obituary ... 114
See also DLB 26
Krasne, Betty
See Levine, Betty K(rasne)
Krasner, Jack Daniel 1921-1978 ... CANR-3
Earlier sketch in CA 49-52
Krasner, Leonard 1924- ... 33-36R
Krasner, Stephen D(avid) 1942- ... CANR-15
Earlier sketch in CA 85-88
Krasner, William 1917- ... CANR-15
Earlier sketch in CA 37-40R
Krasney, Samuel A. 1922- ... 2R
Krasnow, Erwin G(ilbert) 1936- ... 103
Krasovskaya, Vera 1915- Brief entry ... 106
Krass, Alfred C(harles) 1936- ... 116
Krasser, Wilhelm 1925(?)-1979 Obituary ... 89-92
Krassner, Paul 1932- ... CANR-11
Earlier sketch in CA 21-22R
Krasso, Miklos 1929(?)-1986 Obituary ... 118
Kratcoski, Peter C(harles) 1936- ... 111
Kratochvil, Paul 1932- ... 25-28R
Kratos
See Power, Norman S(andiford)
Kratovil, Robert 1910- ... CANR-5
Earlier sketch in CA 5-6R
Kratzenstein, Jossef J. 1904- ... CAP-2
Earlier sketch in CA 17-18
Krauch, Velma 1916- ... 37-40R
Kraues, Judith E. ... 101
Kraus, Albert L(awson) 1920- ... 41-44R
Kraus, Barbara 1929-1977 ... 102
Kraus, Bruce R. 1954- ... 97-100
Kraus, C(lyde) Norman 1924- ... CANR-15
Earlier sketch in CA 41-44R
Kraus, Charles E. 1946- ... 111
Kraus, George 1930- ... 25-28R
Kraus, Hans P(eter) 1907- ... CAP-2
Earlier sketch in CA 29-32
Kraus, Joanna Halpert 1937- ... CANR-21
Earlier sketch in CA 104
Kraus, Joe 1939- ... CANR-15
Earlier sketch in CA 89-92
Kraus, Joseph 1925- ... CANR-4
Earlier sketch in CA 53-56
Kraus, Karl 1874-1936 Brief entry ... 104
See also TCLC 5

Kraus, Michael 1901- ... 5-6R
Kraus, Richard G(ordon) 1923- ... CANR-11
Earlier sketch in CA 13-14R
Kraus, Robert 1925- ... 33-36R
See also SATA 4
Kraus, Sidney 1927- ... CANR-10
Earlier sketch in CA 7-8R
Kraus, W. Keith 1934- ... 21-22R
Krause, Frank H(arold) 1942- ... 104
Krause, Harry D(ieter) 1932- ... 33-36R
Krause, Herbert 1905-1976 ... 49-52
Obituary ... 103
Krause, Lawrence Berle 1929- ... 113
Krause, Pat 1930- ... 114
Krause, Sydney J(oseph) 1925- ... 21-22R
Krause, Walter 1917- ... CANR-1
Earlier sketch in CA 2R
Kraushaar, John L. 1917- ... 45-48
Kraushaar, Otto F(rederick) 1901- ... 37-40R
Krauskopf, Konrad B(ates) 1910- ... 77-80
Krauss, Bob
See Krauss, Robert G.
Krauss, Bruno
See Bulmer, (Henry) Kenneth
Krauss, Ellis S(aunders) 1944- ... CANR-8
Earlier sketch in CA 61-64
Krauss, Herbert Harris 1940- ... 85-88
Krauss, Paul Gerhardt 1905- ... 3R
Krauss, Robert G. 1924- ... CANR-2
Earlier sketch in CA 1R
Krauss, Robert M. 1931- ... 17-18R
Krauss, Rosalind E(pstein) 1940- ... 81-84
Krauss, Ruth (Ida) 1911- ... CANR-13
Earlier sketches in CA 3R, CANR-1
See also SATA 1, 30
See also DLB 52
Krausz, Ernest 1931- ... 104
Krausz, Michael 1942- ... CANR-4
Earlier sketch in CA 53-56
Krausz, Norman G(eorge) P(hilip) 1920- ... 41-44R
Kraut, Benny 1947- ... 113
Krauthammer, Charles 1950- Brief entry ... 121
Krautheimer, Richard 1897- ... 103
Krautter, Elisa (Bialk) ... CANR-1
Earlier sketch in CA 1R
See also SATA 1
Krauze, Andrzej 1947- ... SATA-46
Krauzer, Steven M(ark) 1948- ... 109
Kravetz, Nathan 1921- ... 11-12R
Kravis, Irving B(ernard) 1916- ... CANR-7
Earlier sketch in CA 17-18R
Kravitz, Nathan
See Kravitz, Nathaniel
Kravitz, Nathaniel 1905- ... 49-52
Krawiec, Richard 1952- ... 122
Krawiec, T(heophile) S(tanley) 1913- ... CANR-10
Earlier sketch in CA 25-28R
Krawitz, Henry 1947- ... 45-48
Krawitz, Herman E(verett) 1925- ... 61-64
Krawitz, Ruth (Lifshitz) 1929- ... 9-10R
Kraybill, Donald B(rubaker) 1945- ... 69-72
Krebs, Alfred H. 1920- ... 23-24R
Krebs, Hans (Adolf) 1900-1981 Obituary ... 108
Krech, David 1909-1977 Obituary ... 73-76
Krech, Shepard III 1944- ... 119
Kredel, Fritz 1900-1973 Obituary ... 41-44R
See also SATA 17
Kredenser, Gail 1936- ... 21-22R
Kreeft, Peter 1937- ... CANR-14
Earlier sketch in CA 81-84
Krefetz, Gerald 1932- ... CANR-15
Earlier sketch in CA 33-36R
Krefetz, Ruth 1931-1972 ... CAP-2
Obituary ... 37-40R
Earlier sketch in CA 33-36
Kregel, J(an) A(llen) 1944- ... 41-44R
Kreh, Bernard 1925- ... 57-60
Kreider, Barbara 1942- ... 41-44R
Kreider, Carl 1914- ... 37-40R
Kreider, Jan F(rederick) 1942- ... 111
Kreidl, John Francis 1939- ... 81-84
Kreig, Margaret B. (Baltzell) 1922- ... 13-14R
Krein, David F(rederick) 1942- ... 85-88
Kreindler, Lee (Stanley) 1924- ... 17-18R
Kreingold, Shana 1889(?)-1972
Obituary ... 37-40R
Kreinin, Mordechai 1930- ... 9-10R
Kreisel, Henry 1922- ... 61-64
Kreiser, B(ernard) Robert 1943- ... 116
Kreisler, Fritz 1875-1962 Obituary ... 115
Kreisman, Leonard T(heodore) 1925- ... 15-16R
Kreisman, Marvin 1933(?)-1979(?)
Obituary ... 102
Kreitler, Hans 1916- ... 45-48
Kreitler, Shulamith 1938- ... 45-48
Krejci, Jaroslav 1916- ... CANR-14
Earlier sketch in CA 41-44R
Kremen, Bennett 1936- ... 57-60
Kremenliev, Boris A(ngeloff) 1911- ... 45-48
Krementz, Jill 1940- ... CANR-23
Earlier sketch in CA 41-44R
See also SATA 17
See also CLR 5
See also AITN 1, 2
Kremer, Laura Evelyn 1921- ... 103
Kremer, William F. 1919- ... 69-72
Kreml, Anne Lee 1930- ... 21-22R
Krempel, Daniel S(partakus) 1926- ... 33-36R
Kren, George M. 1926- ... 102
Krenek, Ernst 1900- ... 57-60
Krenkel, John H(enry) 1906- ... CAP-2
Earlier sketch in CA 33-36
Krensky, Stephen (Alan) 1953- ... CANR-13
Earlier sketch in CA 73-76
See also SATA 41, 47
Krentel, Mildred White 1921- ... 5-6R
Krents, Harold Eliot 1944-1987 ... 37-40R
Obituary ... 121
Krentz, Edgar (Martin) 1928- ... 23-24R
Krepps, Robert W(ilson) 1919-1980 ... CANR-1
Earlier sketch in CA 1R
Kresge, George Joseph, Jr.
See Kreskin
Kresh, Paul 1919- ... CANR-13
Earlier sketch in CA 15-16R
Kreskin 1935- ... 101
Kress, Paul F(rederick) 1935- ... 29-32R
Kress, Robert (Lee) 1932- ... CANR-8
Earlier sketch in CA 61-64
Kress, Roy A(lfred) 1916- ... 107
Kress, Stephen W. 1945- ... 122
Kressel, Kenneth 1942- ... 119
Kressy, Michael 1936- ... CANR-8
Earlier sketch in CA 61-64
Kretsch, Robert W. 1913(?)-1979
Obituary ... 89-92
Kretzmann, Adalbert Raphael 1903- ... CAP-1
Earlier sketch in CA 15-16
Kretzmann, Norman 1928- ... 49-52
Kretzmer, Herbert 1925- ... 105
Kreuger, Miles 1934- ... 81-84
Kreusler, Abraham A(rthur) 1897- ... 65-68
Kreuter, Kent 1932- ... 29-32R
Kreuzer, James R. 1913-1971 ... CAP-1
Earlier sketch in CA 11-12
Kreve (Mickevicius), Vincas 1882-1954 ... TCLC-27
Krevitsky, Nathan I. 1914- ... 9-10R
Krevitsky, Nik
See Krevitsky, Nathan I.
Krevolin, Nathan 1927- ... CANR-14
Earlier sketch in CA 41-44R
Krewer, Semyon E(fimovich) 1915- ... 105
Kreyche, Gerald F. 1927- ... 37-40R
Kreyche, Robert J. 1920- ... 13-14R
Kreymborg, Alfred 1883-1966 Obituary ... 25-28R
See also DLB 4, 54
Krich, A. M.
See Krich, Aron
Krich, Aron 1916- ... 120
Krich, Aron M.
See Krich, Aron
Krich, John 1951- ... 108
Krieg, Saul 1917- ... 81-84
Kriegel, Gail 1942- ... 108
Kriegel, Harriet ... 104
Kriegel, Leonard 1933- ... CANR-12
Earlier sketch in CA 33-36R
Krieger, Leonard 1918- ... CANR-7
Earlier sketch in CA 17-18R
Krieger, Murray 1923- ... CANR-2
Earlier sketch in CA 3R
See also DLB 67
Krieghbaum, Hillier (Hiram) 1902- ... CANR-2
Earlier sketch in CA 5-6R
Kriegman, Oscar M(arvin) 1930- ... 9-10R
Kriensky, Morris (Edward) 1917- ... 57-60
Krier, James E(dward) 1939- ... 81-84
Kriesberg, Louis 1926- ... CANR-12
Earlier sketch in CA 29-32R
Krikorian, Yervant H(ovhannes)
1892-1977 ... CANR-2
Obituary ... 73-76
Earlier sketch in CA 45-48
Krim, Seymour 1922- ... CANR-4
Earlier sketch in CA 7-8R
See also DLB 16
Krimerman, Leonard Isaiah 1934- ... 17-18R
Krimsky, Joseph (Hayylm) 1883(?)-1971
Obituary ... 104
Krimsky, Sheldon 1941- ... 113
Kring, Hilda Adam 1921- ... 77-80
Kring, Walter Donald 1916- ... 116
Krinsky, Carol Herselle 1937- ... 37-40R
Kripalani, J(iwatram) B(hagwandas)
1888-1982 Obituary ... 110
Kripke, Dorothy Karp ... 19-20R
See also SATA 30
Krippendorff, Klaus 1932- ... 77-80
Krippner, Stanley (Curtis) 1932- ... CANR-15
Earlier sketch in CA 81-84
Krisch, Henry 1931- Brief entry ... 111
Krise, Raymond (Owens, Jr.) 1949- ... 109
Krisher, Bernard 1931- ... CANR-18
Earlier sketch in CA 77-80
Krishna, Gopi
See Shivpuri, Gopi Krishna
Krishnamurti, Jiddu 1895-1986 ... CANR-11
Obituary ... 118
Earlier sketch in CA 61-64
Krislov, Alexander
See Lee Howard, Leon Alexander
Krislov, Joseph 1927- ... 41-44R
Krislov, Samuel 1929- ... CANR-18
Earlier sketches in CA 9-10R, CANR-3
Krispyn, Egbert 1930- ... 15-16R
Kriss, Ronald P(aul) 1934- ... 69-72
Kristein, Marvin M(ichael) 1926- ... 29-32R
Kristeller, Paul Oskar 1905- ... CANR-6
Earlier sketch in CA 9-10R
Kristian, Hans
See Neerskov, Hans Kristian
Kristof, Jane 1932- ... 29-32R
See also SATA 8
Kristof, Ladis K(ris) D(onabed) 1918- ... 61-64
Kristofferson, Kris 1936- ... 104
See also CLC 26
Kristol, Irving 1920- ... 25-28R
Kritsick, Stephen M(ark) 1951- ... 112
Kritzeck, James 1930- ... 5-6R
Krizay, John 1926- ... 61-64
Krleza, Miroslav 1893-1981 ... 97-100
Obituary ... 105
See also CLC 8
Krmpotic, Vesna 1932- ... CANR-20
Earlier sketch in CA 102
Kroc, Ray(mond Albert) 1902-1984 ... 118
Obituary ... 111
Kroch, Adolph A. 1882-1978 Obituary ... 81-84
Krochmal, Arnold 1919- ... CANR-14
Earlier sketch in CA 69-72
Krochmal, Connie 1949- ... 41-44R
Krock, Arthur 1887-1974 ... CAP-2
Obituary ... 49-52
Earlier sketch in CA 33-36
See also DLB 29
See also AITN 1
Krodel, Gerhard 1926- ... 61-64
Kroeber, A(lfred) L(ouis) 1876-1960
Obituary ... 110
Kroeber, Clifton B(rown) 1921- ... 110
Kroeber, Donald W(alter) 1934- ... 115
Kroeber, Karl 1926- ... 57-60
Kroeber, Theodora (Kracaw) 1897-1979 ... CANR-5
Obituary ... 89-92
Earlier sketch in CA 5-6R
See also SATA 1
Kroeber-Quinn, Theodora
See Kroeber, Theodora (Kracaw)
Kroeger, Arthur 1908- ... 15-16R
Kroeger, Frederick P(aul) 1921- ... 33-36R
Kroepcke, Karol
See Krolow, Karl (Gustav Heinrich)
Kroetsch, Robert 1927- ... CANR-8
Earlier sketch in CA 19-20R
See also DLB 53
See also CLC 5, 23
Kroetz, Franz Xaver 1946- ... CLC-41
Kroger, William S. 1906- ... CAP-1
Earlier sketch in CA 13-14
Krohn, Ernst C(hristopher) 1888-1975 ... 37-40R
See also AITN 1
Krohn, Norman Odya 1920- ... 116
Krohn, Robert 1937- ... 45-48
Kroll, Burt
See Rowland, D(onald) S(ydney)
Kroll, Ernest 1914- ... 97-100
Kroll, Francis Lynde 1904-1973 ... CAP-1
Earlier sketch in CA 15-16
See also SATA 10
Kroll, John (Leon) 1925-1986 Obituary ... 119
Kroll, Judith 1943- ... 65-68
Kroll, Morton 1923- ... 49-52
Kroll, Steven 1941- ... CANR-9
Earlier sketch in CA 65-68
See also SATA 19
Krolow, Karl (Gustav Heinrich) 1915- ... 81-84
Kromer, Helen ... 93-96
Kromminga, John H(enry) 1918- ... 77-80
Kronegger, Maria Elisabeth 1932- ... 25-28R
Kronenberg, Henry Harold 1902- ... 1R
Kronenberg, Maria Elizabeth 1881(?)-1970
Obituary ... 104
Kronenberger, Louis 1904-1980 ... CANR-2
Obituary ... 97-100
Earlier sketch in CA 4R
Kroner, Richard 1884- ... 9-10R
Kronhausen, Eberhard W(ilhelm) 1915- ... CANR-6
Earlier sketch in CA 11-12R
Kronhausen, Phyllis C(armen) 1929- ... CANR-6
Earlier sketch in CA 11-12R
Kronick, David A(braham) 1917- ... 11-12R
Kronick, Joseph G. 1953- ... 122
Kroninger, Robert H(enry) 1923- ... 15-16R
Kronk, Gary (Wayne) 1956- ... 115
Kronman, Anthony T(ownsend) 1945- ... 113
Kronstadt, Henry L(ippin) 1915- ... 73-76
Kronus, Sidney J., Jr. 1937- Brief entry ... 107
Krook, Dorothea 1920- ... 123
Krooss, Herman E. 1912-1975 ... CAP-2
Obituary ... 57-60
Earlier sketch in CA 17-18
Kropf, Linda S(toddart) 1947- ... 49-52
Kropf, Richard W(illiam Bartlett)
1932- ... CANR-10
Earlier sketch in CA 65-68
Kropotkin, Peter (Aleksieevich) 1842-1921
Brief entry ... 119
Kropp, Lloyd ... 25-28R
Kropp, Paul (Stephan) 1948- ... 112
See also SATA 34, 38
Krosby, H(ans) Peter 1929- ... 89-92
Krosney, Mary Stewart 1939- ... 19-20R
Krotki, Karol J(ozef) 1922- ... 41-44R
Krotkov, Yuri 1917- ... 102
See also CLC 19
Krout, John Allen 1896-1979 ... 97-100
Obituary ... 85-88
Kruchkow, Diane 1947- ... 69-72
Kruck, William E(vert) 1942- ... 114
Krueger, Anne O. 1934- ... CANR-15
Earlier sketch in CA 37-40R
Krueger, Christoph 1937- ... 33-36R
Krueger, Hardy 1928- ... 77-80
Krueger, John R(ichard) 1927- ... CANR-10
Earlier sketch in CA 21-22R
Krueger, Ralph R. 1927- ... CANR-2
Earlier sketch in CA 49-52
Krueger, Robert B(lair) 1928- ... 57-60
Krueger, Thomas A. 1936- ... 21-22R
Kruess, James 1926- ... CANR-5
Earlier sketch in CA 53-56
See also SATA 8
See also CLR 9
Krug, Edward August 1911-1980 ... CANR-4
Earlier sketch in CA 5-6R
Krug, Mark M. 1915- Brief entry ... 109
Krug, Samuel E(dward) 1943- ... 121
Kruger, Arthur N(ewman) 1916- ... CANR-1
Earlier sketch in CA 2R
Kruger, Daniel H(erschel) 1922- ... 25-28R
Kruger, Hardy
See Krueger, Hardy
Kruger, Mollee (Coppel) 1929- ... CANR-21
Earlier sketch in CA 69-72
Kruger, Paul
See Sebenthal, R(oberta) E(lizabeth)
Kruger, (Charles) Rayne ... 7-8R
Kruglak, Haym 1909- ... 53-56
Krulewitch, Melvin Levin 1895-1978 ... 103
Krulik, Stephen 1933- ... CANR-8
Earlier sketch in CA 17-18R
Krull, Felix
See White, Stanley
Krull, Kathleen 1952- ... 106
See also SATA 39
Krumb
See Crumb, R(obert)
Krumboltz, John D(wight) 1928-
Brief entry ... 110
Krumgold, Joseph (Quincy) 1908-1980 ... CANR-7
Obituary ... 101
Earlier sketch in CA 11-12R
See also SATA 1, 23, 48
See also CLC 12
Krumm, John McGill 1913- ... 109
Krummel, Donald William 1929- ... 106
Krumpelmann, John T(heodore) 1892- ... 41-44R
Krumwitz
See Crumb, R(obert)
Krupat, Edward 1945- ... 77-80
Krupnik, Baruch
See Karu, Baruch
Krupp, E(dwin) C(harles) 1944- ... CANR-21
Earlier sketch in CA 105
Krupp, Nate 1935- ... CANR-10
Earlier sketch in CA 21-22R
Krupp, Sherman Roy 1926- ... 3R
Krusch, Werner E. 1927- ... 7-8R
Kruschke, Earl R(oger) 1934- ... 41-44R
Kruse, Alexander Z. 1888(?)-1972
Obituary ... 33-36R
Kruse, Harry D(ayton) 1900-1977
Obituary ... 73-76
Kruse, John 1919- ... 114
Krush, Beth 1918- ... SATA-18
Krush, Joe 1918- ... SATA-18
Krusich, Walter S(teve) 1922- ... 49-52
Kruskal, William H(enry) 1919- ... 33-36R
Kruss, James
See Kruess, James
See also CLR 9
Kruszewski, Z. Anthony 1928- Brief entry ... 113
Krutch, Joseph Wood 1893-1970 ... CANR-4
Obituary ... 25-28R
Earlier sketch in CA 2R
See also DLB 63
See also CLC 24
Krutilla, John Vasil 1922- ... CANR-9
Earlier sketch in CA 23-24R
Krutzch, Gus
See Eliot, T(homas) S(tearns)
Kruuk, Hans 1937- ... 61-64
Kruzas, Anthony T(homas) 1914- ... CANR-17
Earlier sketches in CA 1R, CANR-2
Krymow, Virginia P(auline) 1930- ... 69-72
Krypton
See Graham, Lloyd M.
Krysl, Marilyn 1943- ... 105
Krythe, Maymie Richardson ... 19-20R
Krzywan, Jozef
See Krotki, Karol J(ozef)
Krzyzaniak, Marian 1911- ... 11-12R
Krzyzanowski, Jerzy R(oman) 1922- ... 37-40R
Krzyzanowski, Ludwik 1907(?)-1986
Obituary ... 118
Kselman, Thomas A. 1948- ... 110
K-Turkel, Judi 1934- ... CANR-8
Earlier sketch in CA 61-64
Kubal, David L(awrence) 1936- ... 45-48
Kubat, Daniel 1928- Brief entry ... 114
Kubeck, James (Ernest) 1920- ... 17-18R
Kubek, Anthony 1920- ... 104
Kubelka, Susanna 1942- ... 113
Kube-McDowell, Michael P(aul) 1954- ... 119
Kubiak, T(imothy) J(ames) 1942- ... 61-64
Kubiak, William J. 1929- ... 33-36R
Kubicek, Robert V(incent) 1935- ... 29-32R
Kubie, Lawrence S. 1896(?)-1973
Obituary ... 45-48
Kubie, Nora Gottheil Benjamin 1899- ... 7-8R
See also SATA 39
Kubin, Alfred 1877-1959 Brief entry ... 112
See also TCLC 23
Kubinyi, Laszlo 1937- ... 85-88
See also SATA 17
Kubis, Pat 1928- ... 25-28R
Kubler, George (Alexander) 1912- ... 11-12R
Kubler-Ross, Elisabeth
See Kuebler-Ross, Elisabeth
Kublin, Hyman 1919- ... 9-10R
Kubly, Herbert (Oswald Nicholas)
1915- ... CANR-4
Earlier sketch in CA 7-8R
Kubo, Sakae 1926- ... CANR-7
Earlier sketch in CA 57-60
Kubose, Gyomay M(asao) 1905- ... 49-52
Kubota, Akira 1932- ... 37-40R
Kubrick, Stanley 1928- ... 81-84
See also DLB 26
See also CLC 16
Kucera, Henry 1925- ... 21-22R
Kucharek, Casimir (Anthony) 1928- ... 57-60
Kucharski, Kasimir
See Koch, Kurt E(mil)
Kucharsky, David (Eugene) 1931- ... 65-68
Kucherov, Alexander 1927-1985 Obituary ... 117
Kucich, John (Richard) 1952- ... 112

Kuczkir, Mary 1933- 115
Brief entry 111
Kuczynski, Pedro-Pablo 1938- 77-80
Kudian, Mischa 107
Kudrle, Robert Thomas 1942- 112
Kuebler-Ross, Elisabeth 1926- 25-28R
Kuehl, John 1928- 21-22R
Kuehl, Linda 1939(?)-1978 Obituary 104
Kuehl, Warren F(rederick) 1924- CANR-7
Earlier sketch in CA 17-18R
Kuehn, Dorothy Dalton
See Dalton, Dorothy
Kuehn, Thomas James 1950- 116
Kuehnelt-Leddihn, Erik (Maria) Ritter von
1909- CANR-20
Earlier sketches in CA 9-10R, CANR-3
Kuemmerly, Walter 1903- 49-52
Kuen, Alfred (F.) 1921- 107
Kuenan, Philip Henry 1902-1976 Obituary 116
Kueng, Hans 1928- 53-56
Kuenne, Robert E(ugene) 1924- 5-6R
Kuenstler, Morton 1927- SATA-10
Kuenzli, Alfred E(ugene) 1923- 17-18R
Kuesel, Harry N. 1892(?)-1977 Obituary 73-76
Kuester, David 1938- 53-56
Kuether, Edith Lyman 1915- 49-52
Kufeldt, George 1923- 37-40R
Kuffler, Stephen 1913-1980 Obituary 105
Kufner, Herbert L(eopold) 1927- 7-8R
Kugel, James 1945- 29-32R
Kugelman, Richard 1908- 41-44R
Kugelmass, J. Alvin 1910-1972 .... CANR-4
Obituary 33-36R
Earlier sketch in CA 7-8R
Kuh, Charlotte 1892(?)-1985 Obituary 115
See also SATA 43
Kuh, Edwin 1925-1986 .... 23-24R
Obituary 119
Kuh, Frederick Robert 1895-1978
Obituary 89-92
Kuh, Katharine W. 1904- 13-14R
Kuh, Richard H. 1921- 23-24R
Kuhatschek, Jack 1949- 122
Kuhl, Ernest Peter 1881- 41-44R
Kuhlken, Ken(neth Wayne) 1945- 102
Kuhlman, James A(llen) 1941- 85-88
Kuhlman, John M(elville) 1923- 17-18R
Kuhlman, Kathryn 1910(?)-1976 .... CANR-12
Obituary 65-68
Earlier sketch in CA 57-60
Kuhlmann, Susan 1942- 85-88
Kuhn, Alfred 1914- CANR-3
Earlier sketch in CA 11-12R
Kuhn, Annette 1945- 111
Kuhn, Edward, Jr. 1924(?)-1979 102
Obituary 93-96
Kuhn, Ferdinand 1905-1978 .... 5-6R
Obituary 81-84
Kuhn, Harold B(arnes) 1911- 49-52
Kuhn, Irene Corbally CAP-1
Earlier sketch in CA 9-10
Kuhn, Karl F(rancis) 1939- 65-68
Kuhn, Maggie
See Kuhn, Margaret E.
Kuhn, Margaret E. 1905- Brief entry 109
Kuhn, Martin A(rno) 1924- 9-10R
Kuhn, Reinhard 1930- 45-48
Kuhn, Thomas S(amuel) 1922- CANR-11
Earlier sketch in CA 21-22R
Kuhn, Tillo E. 1919- 5-6R
Kuhn, William Ernst 1922- 37-40R
Kuhn, Wolfgang Erasmus 1914- 5-6R
Kuhne, Cecil 1952- 93-96
Kuhne, Marie (Ahnighito Peary)
1893-1978 Obituary 77-80
Kuhner, Herbert 1935- 25-28R
Kuhns, Dennis R(ay) 1947- 113
Kuhns, Dorothy
See Heyward, Dorothy (Hartzell Kuhns)
Kuhns, Grant (Wilson) 1929- 9-10R
Kuhns, Richard (Francis, Jr.) 1924- 37-40R
Kuhns, William 1943- 23-24R
Kuhse, Helga 1940- 122
Kuic, Vukan 1923- 37-40R
Kuiper, Gerard Peter 1905-1973 .... CAP-2
Obituary 45-48
Earlier sketch in CA 17-18
Kuisel, Richard F(rancis) 1935- 23-24R
Kuist, J(ames) M(arquis) 1935- 124
Kuitert, H(arminus) Martinus 1924- 25-28R
Kujawa, Duane 1938- 33-36R
Kujoth, Jean Spealman 1935-1975 .... CAP-2
Earlier sketch in CA 25-28
See also SATA 30
Kukla, Robert J(ohn) 1932- 49-52
Kuklick, Bruce 1941- 41-44R
Kuleshov, Arkady A. 1914-1978 Obituary 77-80
Kulick, John
See Pinchot, Ann (Kramer)
Kulkarni, Hemant B(alvantrao) 1916- CANR-1
Earlier sketch in CA 45-48
Kulkarni, R(amchandra) G(anesh) 1931- 29-32R
Kulkarni, Venkatesh S(rinivas) 1945- 113
Kulkin, Mary-Ellen
See Siegel, Mary-Ellen Kulkin
Kullman, Harry 1919-1982 93-96
See also SATA 35
Kulshrestha, Chirantan 1946- 107
Kulski, Julian (Eugeniusz) 1929- CANR-14
Earlier sketch in CA 21-22R
Kulski, Wladyslaw W(szebor) 1903- 5-6R
Kulstein, David J. 1916-1974 .... CAP-2
Earlier sketch in CA 25-28
Kultermann, Udo 1927- 85-88
Kulukundis, Elias 1937- 21-22R
Kumar, Krishna 1942- 109
Kumar, Satish 1933- 112
Kumar, Shiv K(umar) 1921- CANR-7
Earlier sketch in CA 9-10R
Kumbel,
See Hein, Piet
Kumin, Maxine (Winokur) 1925- CANR-21
Earlier sketches in CA 2R, CANR-1
See also SATA 12
See also DLB 5
See also CLC 5, 13, 28
See also AITN 2
Kummel, Bernhard 1919- 33-36R
Kummerly, Walter
See Kuemmerly, Walter
Kunce, Joseph T(yree) 1928- 41-44R
Kuncewicz, Maria (Szczepanska) 1899- CAP-1
Earlier sketch in CA 9-10
Kuncewiczowa, Maria
See Kuncewicz, Maria (Szczepanska)
Kundera, Milan 1929- CANR-19
Earlier sketch in CA 85-88
See also CLC 4, 9, 19, 32
Kundsin, Ruth Blumfeld 1916- 106
Kunen, James Simon, 1948- 25-28R
Kuner, M(ildred) C(hristophe) 1922- 41-44R
Kung, Hans
See Kueng, Hans
Kung, Shien Woo 1905- 2R
Kunhappa, Murkot 1905- 69-72
Kunhardt, Dorothy (Meserve) 1901-1979 107
Obituary 93-96
See also SATA 22
Kunhardt, Philip B(radish) Jr. 1928- 85-88
Kunhi Krishnan, T(aramal) V(anmeri)
1919- 61-64
Kuniczak, W(iselaw) S(tanislaw) 1930- 85-88
Kuniholm, Bruce Robellet 1942- 93-96
Kuniholm, Whitney 1954- 112
Kunin, Madeleine May 1933- 93-96
Kunin, Richard A(llen) 1932- 107
Kunitz, Joshua 1896(?)-1980 Obituary 97-100
Kunitz, Stanley (Jasspon) 1905- 41-44R
See also DLB 48
See also CLC 6, 11, 14
Kunjufu, Johari M. Amini 1935- 41-44R
Kunkel, Francis L(eo) 1921- 45-48
Kunnes, Richard 1941- 33-36R
Kuno, Susumu 1933- 41-44R
Kunreuther, Howard Charles 1938- 25-28R
Kunst, David W(illiam) 1939- 85-88
Kunstler, James Howard 1948- CANR-18
Earlier sketch in CA 101
Kunstler, Morton
See Kuenstler, Morton
Kunstler, William M(oses) 1919- CANR-5
Earlier sketch in CA 9-10R
Kuntz, J(ohn) Kenneth 1934- CANR-9
Earlier sketch in CA 23-24R
Kuntz, Kenneth A. 1916- 3R
Kuntz, Paul G. 1915- 5-6R
Kuntzleman, Charles T(homas) 1940- CANR-22
Earlier sketches in CA 57-60, CANR-7
Kunz, Marji 1939(?)-1979 Obituary 89-92
Kunz, Phillip Ray 1936- CANR-19
Earlier sketch in CA 37-40R
Kunz, Roxane (Brown) 1932- 121
Kunz, Virginia B(rainard) 1921- 21-22R
Kunze, Reiner 1933- 93-96
See also CLC 10
Kunzle, David Mark 1936- CANR-5
Earlier sketch in CA 53-56
Kunzur, Sheela
See Geis, Richard E(rwin)
Kuo, Ping-chia 1908- 7-8R
Kuo, Shirley W. Y. 1930- 115
Kuo, Ting-yee 1904(?)-1975 Obituary 61-64
Kuo Mo-Jo 1892-1978 Obituary 77-80
Kup, Alexander Peter 1924- CANR-9
Earlier sketch in CA 15-16R
Kup, Karl 1903-1981 Obituary 104
Kuper, Adam (Jonathan) 1941- CANR-20
Earlier sketch in CA 103
Kuper, Hilda Beemer 1911- CANR-2
Earlier sketch in CA 3R
Kuper, Jack 1932- 23-24R
Kuper, Leo 1908- CANR-11
Earlier sketch in CA 21-22R
Kuper, Yuri
See Kuperman, Yuri
Kuperman, Yuri 1940- 102
Kupfer, Fern 1946- 106
Kupferberg, Herbert 1918- 29-32R
See also SATA 19
Kupferberg, Naphtali 1923- CANR-13
Earlier sketch in CA 21-22R
Kupferberg, Tuli
See Kupferberg, Naphtali
See also DLB 16
Kupperman, Joel J. 1936- 33-36R
Kupperman, Karen O(rdahl) 1939- 111
Kuprin, Aleksandr Ivanovich 1870-1938
Brief entry 104
See also TCLC 5
Kuralt, Charles Bishop 1934- 89-92
Kurath, Gertrude Prokosch 1903- 15-16R
Kurath, Hans 1891- 9-10R
Kuratomi, Chizuko 1939- CANR-10
Earlier sketch in CA 21-22R
See also SATA 12
Kurdsen, Stephen
See Noon, Brian
Kurelek, William 1927-1977 .... CANR-3
Earlier sketch in CA 49-52
See also SATA 8, 27
See also CLR 2
Kurian, George 1928- 107
Kurien, C(hristopher) T(homas) 1931- CANR-13
Earlier sketch in CA 33-36R
Kurihara, Kenneth Kenkichi 1910-1972 .... CANR-6
Obituary 37-40R
Earlier sketch in CA 3R
Kurkjian, Stephen A. 1944(?)- Brief entry 116
Kurkul, Edward 1916- 25-28R
Kurland, Gerald 1942- CANR-14
Earlier sketch in CA 41-44R
See also SATA 13
Kurland, Michael (Joseph) 1938- CANR-11
Earlier sketch in CA 61-64
See also SATA 48
Kurland, Philip B. 1921- CANR-7
Earlier sketch in CA 9-10R
Kurman, George 1942- 53-56
Kurnitz, Harry 1909-1968 Obituary 25-28R
Kuroda, Yasumasa 1931- 45-48
Kuropas, Myron B(ohdon) 1932- 45-48
Kurosawa, Akira 1910- 101
See also CLC 16
Kurowski, Eugeniusz
See Dobraczynski, Jan
Kurrik, Maire Jaanus 1940- 101
Kursh, Charlotte Olmsted 1912- 9-10R
Kursh, Harry 1919- 9-10R
Kurten, Bjorn (Olof) 1924- CANR-20
Earlier sketch in CA 25-28R
Kurth-Voigt, Lieselotte E. 1923-
Brief entry 110
Kurtis, Arlene Harris 1927- 25-28R
Kurtis, Bill
See Kurtis, William Horton
Kurtis, William Horton 1940- Brief entry 124
Kurtz, C(larence) Gordon 1902- 65-68
Kurtz, David L(ee) 1941- 41-44R
Kurtz, Donna Carol 1943- 93-96
Kurtz, Ernest 1935- 112
Kurtz, Harold 1913- 17-18R
Kurtz, Irma 1935- 118
Kurtz, Katherine (Irene) 1944- 29-32R
Kurtz, Kenneth H(assett) 1928- 33-36R
Kurtz, Michael L(ouis) 1941- 107
Kurtz, Paul 1925- CANR-5
Earlier sketch in CA 13-14R
Kurtz, Stephen G(uild) 1926- 11-12R
Kurtzman, Jeffrey G(ordon) 1940- 110
Kurtzman, Joel 1947- 29-32R
Kurtz-Phelan, James L(anham) 1946- 49-52
Kurz, Artur R.
See Scortia, Thomas N(icholas)
Kurz, Isolde 1853-1944 .... DLB-66
Kurz, Mordecai 1934- CANR-12
Earlier sketch in CA 29-32R
Kurz, Otto 1908-1975 107
Obituary 104
Kurz, Paul Konrad 1927- 29-32R
Kurz, Ron 1940- CANR-14
Earlier sketch in CA 81-84
Kurzer, Siegmund F. 1907(?)-1973
Obituary 104
Kurzman, Dan 1927- CANR-14
Earlier sketch in CA 69-72
Kurzman, Paul A(lfred) 1938- CANR-13
Earlier sketch in CA 33-36R
Kurzweg, Bernhard F. 1926- 17-18R
Kurzweil, Arthur 1951- 97-100
Kurzweil, Edith 110
Kurzweil, Zvi Erich 1911- CAP-1
Earlier sketch in CA 11-12
Kusan, Ivan 1933- CANR-6
Earlier sketch in CA 9-10R
Kusche, Larry
See Kusche, Lawrence David
Kusche, Lawrence David 1940- CANR-5
Earlier sketch in CA 53-56
Kushel, Gerald 1930- CANR-11
Earlier sketch in CA 25-28R
Kushner, David Z(arkeri) 1935- 53-56
Kushner, Donn 1927- 113
Kushner, Harold S(amuel) 1935- 107
Kushner, Harvey W(olf) 1941- 110
Kushner, Howard Irvin 1943- 81-84
Kushner, Irving 1929- 119
Kushner, Rose 1929- 61-64
Kushner, Sam 1915(?)-1987 Obituary 123
Kusin, Vladimir V(ictor) 1929- CANR-13
Earlier sketch in CA 33-36R
Kuske, Martin 1940- 97-100
Kuskin, Karla (Seidman) 1932- CANR-22
Earlier sketches in CA 3R, CANR-4
See also SATA 2
See also SAAS 3
See also CLR 4
Kuslan, Louis I(saac) 1922- CANR-1
Earlier sketch in CA 45-48
Kusmer, Kenneth Leslie 1945- 102
Kusnick, Barry A. 1910- 53-56
Kusniewicz, Andrzej 1904- 107
Kuspit, Donald B(urton) 1935- 97-100
Kussmaul, Ann (Sturm) 1945- 110
Kustermeir, Rudolf 1893(?)-1977
Obituary 73-76
Kustow, Michael (David) 1939- Brief entry 106
Kutash, Samuel Benjamin 1912-1979 .... CANR-2
Earlier sketch in CA 4R
Kuten, Jay 1935- Brief entry 108
Kuter, Laurence S(herman) 1905-1979
Obituary 113
Kutler, Stanley I. 1934- 23-24R
Kutner, Luis 1908- 109
Kutner, Nanette 1906?-1962 .... 4R
Kutsche, Paul 1927- 114
Kutscher, Charles L(awrence) 1936- 77-80
Kutsky, Roman Joseph 1922- Brief entry 110
Kuttna, Mari 1934-1983 Obituary 109
Kuttner, Henry 1915-1958 Brief entry 107
See also DLB 8
See also TCLC 10
Kuttner, Paul 1931- CANR-13
Earlier sketch in CA 77-80
See also SATA 18
Kutz, LeRoy M. 1922- 15-16R
Kutza, Elizabeth Ann 111
Kuwayama, George 1925- 116
Kuykendall, Eleanor 1938- Brief entry 109
Kuykendall, Jack L(awrence) 1940- 57-60
Kuykendall, Ralph S(impson) 1885-1963 .... 3R
Kuzma, Greg 1944- 33-36R
See also CLC 7
Kuzma, Kay 1941- CANR-23
Earlier sketch in CA 106
See also SATA 39
Kuznets, Simon (Smith) 1901-1985
Obituary 116
Brief entry 108
Kuznetsov, (Edward) 1939- 57-60
Kuznetsov, Anatoli 1929-1979 Obituary 89-92
Kuzniewski, Anthony J(oseph) 1945- 107
Kvale, Velma R(uth) 1898- CAP-2
Earlier sketch in CA 25-28
See also SATA 8
Kvam, Wayne (Eugene) 1938- 45-48
Kvasnicka, Robert M(ichael) 1935- 97-100
Kwabena Nketia, J. H.
See Nketia, J(oseph) H(anson) Kwabena
Kwan, Kian M(oon) 1929- 17-18R
Kwant, R. C.
See Kwant, Remigius C(ornelis)
Kwant, Remigius C(ornelis) 1918- CANR-18
Earlier sketches in CA 9-10R, CANR-3
Kwant, Remy C.
See Kwant, Remigius C(ornelis)
Kwanten, Luc 1944- 93-96
Kwavnick, David 1940- 45-48
Kweder, Adele 1910- 5-6R
Kweder, David James 1905- 5-6R
Kweit, Robert W(illiam) 1946- 112
Kwiatkowska, Hanna Yaxa 1907(?)-1980
Obituary 97-100
Kwitny, Jonathan 1941- CANR-23
Earlier sketches in CA 49-52, CANR-1
Kwolek, Constance
See Porcari, Constance Kwolek
Kyburg, Henry (Guy) E(ly), Jr. 1928- CANR-8
Earlier sketch in CA 5-6R
Kyd, Thomas 1558-1594 .... DLB-62
Kyd, Thomas
See Harbage, Alfred (Bennett)
Kydd, Sam(uel) 1917-1982 109
Obituary 106
Kyemba, Henry 1939- 81-84
Kyes, Robert L(ange) 1933- 49-52
Kyger, Joanne (Elizabeth) 1934- CANR-17
Earlier sketch in CA 101
See also DLB 16
Kyle, Duncan
See Broxholme, John Franklin
Kyle, Elisabeth
See Dunlop, Agnes M. R.
Kyle, Marlaine
See Hager, Jean
Kyle, Robert
See Terrall, Robert
Kyme, Ernest Hector 1906- 103
Kynett, Harold Havelock 1889-1973
Obituary 106
Kyper, Frank 1940- 85-88
Kyprianos, Iossif
See Samarakis, Antonis
Kyre, Joan Randolph 1935- 25-28R
Kyre, Martin (Theodore, Jr.) 1928- 25-28R
Kyrle, Roger (Ernie) Money
See Money-Kyrle, Roger (Ernie)
Kysar, Robert (Dean) 1934- CANR-22
Earlier sketch in CA 69-72
Kyselka, Will 1921- 106
Kyte, Kathy S. 1946- SATA-44, 50
Kytle, Elizabeth 112
Kytle, Ray(mond) 1941- 29-32R
Kyvig, David E(dward) 1944- 101

L

La-Anyane, Seth 1922- 9-10R
Laas, William M. 1910(?)-1975 Obituary 61-64
LaBar, Tom 1937- 25-28R
Labaree, Benjamin Woods 1927- CANR-6
Earlier sketch in CA 9-10R
Labaree, Leonard W(oods) 1897-1980 73-76
Obituary 97-100
Labarge, Margaret Wade 1916- CANR-11
Earlier sketch in CA 25-28R
LaBarge, William Howard 1948- 116
La Barr, Creighton
See von Block, Bela W(illiam)
La Barre, Weston 1911- CANR-22
Earlier sketch in CA 2R
LaBastille, Anne 1938- CANR-8
Earlier sketch in CA 57-60
L'Abate, Luciano 1928- 111
Labatut, Jean 1899-1986 Obituary 121
Labbe, John T. CANR-17
Earlier sketch in CA 97-100
La Beau, Dennis (George) 1941- 97-100
LaBelle, Maurice Marc 1939- 113
Laber, Jeri 1931- CANR-9
Earlier sketch in CA 65-68
Laberge, Marie 1950- DLB-60
LaBier, Douglas 1944- 124
Labin, Suzanne (Devoyon) 1913- CANR-14
Earlier sketch in CA 29-32R
Labor, Earle G. 1928- 21-22R

LaBorde, Rene
  See Neuffer, Irene LaBorde
Labovitz, I(srael) M(ilton) 1907- ... 5-6R
Labrador, James
  See Hamel Dobkin, Kathleen
Labrador, Judy
  See Hamel Dobkin, Kathleen
LaBrecque, Claude X. ... 85-88
La Brie, Henry George III 1946- ... 57-60
Labrie, Roger P(aul) 1952- ... 113
Labroca, Mario 1897(?)-1973 Obituary ... 41-44R
Labus, Marta Haake 1943- ... 109
Labuta, Joseph A(nthony) 1931- ... 57-60
Labuz, Ronald M. 1953- ... 123
Labys, Walter C(arl) 1937- ... 73-76
La Camera, Anthony 1914(?)-1984
  Obituary ... 114
Lacan, Jacques (Marie Emile) 1901-1981 ... 121
  Obituary ... 104
LaCapra, Dominick 1939- ... 109
La Capria, Raffaele 1922- ... CANR-4
  Earlier sketch in CA 9-10R
La Casce, Steward 1935- ... 37-40R
Laccetti, (Silvio) Richard 1941- ... CANR-13
  Earlier sketch in CA 37-40R
Lace, O(live) Jessie 1906- ... 17-18R
Lacerda, Carlos 1914-1977 Obituary ... 69-72
Lacey, A(lan) R(obert) 1926- ... 112
Lacey, Archie L(ouis) 1923- ... 9-10R
Lacey, Douglas R(aymond) 1913- ... 29-32R
Lacey, Jeannette F. ... 77-80
Lacey, John
  See Alexander, Boyd
Lacey, Louise 1940- ... 81-84
Lacey, Paul A. 1934- ... 41-44R
Lacey, Peter 1929- ... 23-24R
Lacey, Robert 1944- ... CANR-16
  Earlier sketch in CA 33-36R
Lacey, W(alter) K(irkpatrick) 1921- ... CANR-11
  Earlier sketch in CA 25-28R
Lach, Donald F(rederick) 1917- ... 102
La Charite, Virginia Anding 1937- ... 29-32R
Lachenbruch, David 1921- ... 89-92
Lachenmeyer, Charles W(illiam) 1943- ... 105
Lachmann, Frank M(ichael) 1929- ... 103
Lachs, John 1934- ... 23-24R
Lack, David Lambert 1910-1973 ... CANR-4
  Obituary ... 89-92
  Earlier sketch in CA 7-8R
Lackey, Douglas Paul 1945- ... 103
Lackmann, Ron(ald) 1934- ... CANR-13
  Earlier sketch in CA 29-32R
Lackner, Stephan 1910- ... CANR-15
  Earlier sketch in CA 29-32R
Lacks, Cecilia 1945- ... 69-72
Lacks, Cissy
  See Lacks, Cecilia
Lacks, Roslyn 1933- ... 102
La Clair, Earl E. 1916- ... 21-22R
La Claustra, Vera Berneicia (Derrick)
  1903- ... 53-56
Lacocque, Andre (Marie) 1927- ... 112
Lacocque, Pierre-Emmanuel 1952- ... 112
La Colere, Francois
  See Aragon, Louis
Lacolere, Francois
  See Aragon, Louis
Lacombe, Gabriel 1905(?)-1973
  Obituary ... 37-40R
Lacoste, Paul 1923- ... CANR-1
  Earlier sketch in CA 45-48
Lacouture, Jean Marie Gerard 1921- ... 101
Lacretelle, Jacques de 1888-1985 ... DLB-65
Lacroix, Louise
  See Swift, Helen C(ecilia)
LaCroix, Mary 1937- ... CANR-22
  Earlier sketch in CA 106
Lacroix, Ramon
  See McKeag, Ernest L(ionel)
LaCrosse, E. Robert 1937- ... 33-36R
Lacy, A(lexander) D(acre) 1894-1969 ... CAP-2
  Earlier sketch in CA 25-28
Lacy, Charles
  See Hippisley Coxe, Antony D(acres)
Lacy, Creighton (Boutelle) 1919- ... 15-16R
Lacy, Dan (Mabry) 1914- ... 37-40R
Lacy, Donald Charles 1933- ... 105
Lacy, Eric Russell 1933- ... 17-18R
Lacy, Gene M(elvin) 1934- ... 53-56
Lacy, Gerald M(orris) 1940- ... 77-80
Lacy, Leslie Alexander 1937- ... 33-36R
  See also SATA 6
Lacy, Mary Lou (Pannill) 1914- ... 17-18R
Lacy, Norris J(oiner) 1940- ... CANR-23
  Earlier sketches in CA 61-64, CANR-8
Ladas, Gerasimos 1937- ... 53-56
Ladas, Stephen P(ericles) 1898-1976 ... 102
Ladd, Bruce 1936- ... 25-28R
Ladd, Edward T(aylor) 1918-1973 ... CANR-4
  Earlier sketch in CA 5-6R
Ladd, Everett Carll, Jr. 1937- ... CANR-11
  Earlier sketch in CA 25-28R
Ladd, George E(ldon) 1911- ... CANR-5
  Earlier sketch in CA 7-8R
Ladd, Helen F. 1945- ... 111
Ladd, John 1917- ... 81-84
Ladd, Joseph Brown 1764-1786 ... DLB-37
Ladd, Veronica
  See Miner, Jane Claypool
Ladenson, Alex 1907- ... 17-18R
Ladenson, Robert Franklin 1943- ... 113
Lader, Lawrence 1919- ... CANR-2
  Earlier sketch in CA 1R
  See also SATA 6
Laderman, Carol (C.) ... 121
Ladner, Joyce A(nn) 1943- ... 124
  Brief entry ... 122
Ladner, Kurt
  See DeMille, Nelson
Ladner, Mildred D. 1918- ... 97-100
Lado, Robert 1915- ... CANR-7
  Earlier sketch in CA 11-12R
Ladurie, Emmanuel Le Roy
  See Le Roy Ladurie, Emmanuel
Lady, A
  See Taylor, Ann
Lady Gregory
  See Gregory, Isabella Augusta (Persse)
Ladyman, Phyllis ... 103
Lady Mears
  See Tempest, Margaret Mary
Lady of Quality, A
  See Bagnold, Enid
Lael, Richard L(ee) 1946- ... 111
Laemmar, Jack W. 1909- ... 1R
Laertes, Joseph
  See Saltzman, Joseph
Laestadius, Lars-Levi 1909-1982 Obituary ... 107
Laeuchli, Samuel 1924- ... CANR-4
  Earlier sketch in CA 5-6R
Laevastu, Taivo 1923- ... CANR-15
  Earlier sketch in CA 41-44R
La Farge, Oliver (Hazard Perry)
  1901-1963 ... 81-84
  See also SATA 19
  See also DLB 9
La Farge, Phyllis ... 73-76
  See also SATA 14
Lafarge, Rene 1902- ... CAP-2
  Earlier sketch in CA 29-32
LaFauci, Horatio M(ichael) 1917- ... 33-36R
Lafayette, Carlos
  See Boiles, Charles Lafayette (Jr.)
Lafayette, Rene
  See Hubbard, L(afayette) Ron(ald)
LaFeber, Walter (Fredrick) 1933- ... CANR-5
  Earlier sketch in CA 11-12R
Laffal, Julius 1920- ... 49-52
Laffan, Kevin (Barry) 1922- ... 37-40R
Lafferty, Perry (Francis) 1917- ... CANR-6
  Earlier sketch in CA 9-10R
Lafferty, R(aphael) A(loysius) 1914- ... CANR-12
  Earlier sketch in CA 57-60
  See also DLB 8
Laffin, John (Alfred Charles) 1922- ... CANR-23
  Earlier sketches in CA 53-56, CANR-7
  See also SATA 31
Laffont, Jean-Pierre 1935- ... 115
LaFitte, Pat Chew 1950- ... 107
LaFleur, William R. 1936- ... 115
La Follette, Marcel (Evelyn) Chotkowski
  1944- ... 114
La Follette, Suzanne 1894(?)-1983
  Obituary ... 109
LaFontaine, Blanche
  See Schwalberg, Carol(yn Ernestine
  Stein)
LaFontaine, Charles Vivian 1936- ... 57-60
La Fontaine, Jean de 1621-1695 ... SATA-18
Lafore, Laurence Davis 1917-1985 ... 13-14R
  Obituary ... 118
LaForte, Robert Sherman 1933- ... 57-60
La Fountaine, George 1934- ... CANR-7
  Earlier sketch in CA 57-60
Lafourcade, Bernard 1934-1986 ... 115
  Obituary ... 118
Lafreniere, Gyslaine F. 1948- ... 116
Lagace, Louise Lambert
  See Lambert-Lagace, Louise
LaGattuta, Margo 1942- ... 115
Lager, Marilyn 1939- ... 121
Lagercrantz, Rose (Elsa) 1947- ... 108
  See also SATA 39
Lagerkvist, Paer (Fabian) 1891-1974 ... 85-88
  Obituary ... 49-52
  See also CLC 7, 10, 13
Lagerkvist, Par
  See Lagerkvist, Paer (Fabian)
Lagerloef, Selma (Ottiliana Lovisa)
  1858-1940 Brief entry ... 108
  See also SATA 15
  See also TCLC 4
  See also CLR 7
Lagerlof, Selma (Ottiliana Lovisa)
  See Lagerloef, Selma (Ottiliana Lovisa)
  See also SATA 15
  See also CLR 7
Lagerwall, Edna ... 45-48
Lagerwerff, Ellen Best 1919- ... 85-88
Lagevi, Bo
  See Blom, Karl Arne
Lagneau-Kesteloot, Lilyan
  See Kesteloot, Lilyan
Lago, Mary M(cClelland) 1919- ... CANR-15
  Earlier sketch in CA 85-88
LaGrand, Louis E. 1935- ... 33-36R
La Grange, Henry Louis De
  See De La Grange, Henry Louis
LaGuardia, David M(ichael) 1943- ... 118
La Guardia, Fiorello Henry 1882-1947
  Brief entry ... 120
Laguerre, Andre 1915(?)-1979 ... 97-100
  Obituary ... 85-88
Laguerre, Michel S(aturnin) 1945- ... 115
La Guma, (Justin) Alex(ander) 1925-1985 .. 49-52
  Obituary ... 118
  See also CLC 19
La Gumina, Salvatore John 1928- ... 77-80
LaHaye, Tim 1926- ... CANR-9
  Earlier sketch in CA 65-68
Lahee, Frederic Henry 1884-1968 ... CAP-2
  Earlier sketch in CA 19-20
Lahey, Edwin A(loysius) 1902-1969
  Obituary ... 115
LaHood, Marvin J(ohn) 1933- ... CANR-10
  Earlier sketch in CA 25-28R
Lahr, John (Henry) 1941- ... CANR-21
  Earlier sketch in CA 25-28R
Lahr, Raymond M(errill) 1914-1973
  Obituary ... 41-44R
Lahue, Kalton C. 1934- ... CANR-7
  Earlier sketch in CA 15-16R
Lai, T'ien-Ch'ang 1921- ... CANR-11
  Earlier sketch in CA 69-72
Lai, Violet Lau 1916- ... 119
Laidlaw, A. K.
  See Grieve, C(hristopher) M(urray)
Laidlaw, Harry Hyde, Jr. 1907- ... 7-8R
Laidlaw, Marc 1960- ... 119
Laidlaw, Ross 1931- ... 118
Laidlaw, W(illiam) A(llison) 1898-1983
  Obituary ... 109
Laidler, Harry W(ellington) 1884-1970 ... CANR-5
  Obituary ... 29-32R
  Earlier sketch in CA 5-6R
Laiken, Deirdre S(usan) 1948- ... 104
  See also SATA 40, 48
Laikin, Paul 1927- ... 7-8R
Laimgruber, Monika 1946- ... SATA-11
Laine, Barry 1951-1987 Obituary ... 123
Laine, Gloria
  See Hanna, David
Lainez, Manuel Mujica
  See Mujica Lainez, Manuel
Laing, Alexander (Kinnan) 1903-1976 ... CANR-4
  Obituary ... 65-68
  Earlier sketch in CA 5-6R
Laing, Anne C.
  See Schachterle, Nancy (Lange)
Laing, Frederick ... 105
Laing, Jennifer 1948- ... 106
Laing, Lloyd (Robert) 1944- ... CANR-5
  Earlier sketch in CA 53-56
Laing, Martha
  See Celestino, Martha Laing
Laing, R(onald) D(avid) 1927- ... 107
Lair, Jacqueline Carey 1930- ... 119
Lair, Jess K. 1926- ... CANR-14
  Earlier sketch in CA 41-44R
Lair, Robert L(eland) 1932- ... 53-56
Laird, Bailey
  See Goodwin, Richard N(aradhof)
Laird, Betty A(nn) 1925- ... CANR-15
  Earlier sketch in CA 33-36R
Laird, Carobeth 1895-1983 ... CANR-8
  Obituary ... 110
  Earlier sketch in CA 61-64
  See also DLBY 82
Laird, Charlton G(rant) 1901- ... 13-14R
Laird, David
  See Laird, W(ilbur) David, Jr.
Laird, Donald A(nderson) 1897-1969 ... 7-8R
  Obituary ... 25-28R
Laird, Dorothy
  See Carr, Dorothy Stevenson Laird
Laird, Dugan 1920- ... CANR-12
  Earlier sketch in CA 73-76
Laird, Eleanor Childs 1908- ... 73-76
Laird, Helen 1933- ... 122
Laird, J(ohn) T(udor) 1921- ... 69-72
Laird, Jean E(louise) 1930- ... CANR-6
  Earlier sketch in CA 11-12R
  See also SATA 38
Laird, Melvin R(obert) 1922- ... 65-68
Laird, Robbin F. 1946- ... 113
Laird, Roy D(ean) 1925- ... CANR-15
  Earlier sketch in CA 33-36R
Laird, W(ilbur) David, Jr. 1937- ... 113
Lait, Robert 1921- ... CANR-2
  Earlier sketch in CA 4R
Laite, Gordon 1925- ... SATA-31
Laite, William Edward, Jr. 1932- ... 37-40R
Laithwaite, Eric Roberts 1921- ... 103
Laitin, Ken 1963- ... 102
Laitin, Lindy 1968- ... 108
Laitin, Steve 1965- ... 102
Lajolo, Davide 1913(?)-1984 Obituary ... 113
Lakatos, Imre 1922-1974 Obituary ... 116
Lake, Carolyn 1932- ... 25-28R
Lake, David J. 1929- ... CANR-10
  Earlier sketch in CA 65-68
Lake, Frank 1914-1982 ... CANR-10
  Earlier sketch in CA 21-22R
Lake, Harriet
  See Taylor, Paula (Wright)
Lake, Kenneth R(obert) 1931- ... CANR-5
  Earlier sketch in CA 53-56
Lakeman, Enid 1903- ... 107
Laken, Bob
  See Holman, Robert
Lakey, George (Russell) 1937- ... CANR-7
  Earlier sketch in CA 17-18R
Lakin, Martin 1925- ... 73-76
Laklan, Carli 1907- ... CANR-1
  Earlier sketch in CA 3R
  See also SATA 5
Lakoff, George 1941- ... 29-32R
Lakoff, Robin Tolmach 1942- ... 103
Lakoff, Sanford A(llan) 1931- ... CANR-1
  Earlier sketch in CA 1R
Lakritz, Esther Himmelman 1928- ... 3R
Lal, Gobind Behari 1890(?)-1982 Obituary ... 106
Lal, Kishori Saran 1920- ... 23-24R
Lal, P. 1929- ... CANR-9
  Earlier sketch in CA 13-14R
Laliberte, Norman 1925- ... 104
Lalicki, Barbara ... 119
Lalley, Joseph M. 1897(?)-1980 Obituary ... 102
Lalli, Judy 1949- ... 110
Lally, Michael 1942- ... CANR-14
  Earlier sketch in CA 77-80
La Londe, Bernard J. 1933- ... 33-36R
Lalonde, Michele 1937- ... DLB-60
Lalonde, Robert 1947- ... 109
Lalumia, Joseph 1916- ... 23-24R
Lam, Charlotte (Dawson) 1924- ... 37-40R
Lam, Truong Buu 1933- ... 25-28R
Laman, Russell 1907- ... CAP-1
  Earlier sketch in CA 9-10
LaMancusa, Katherine C.
  See Koop, Katherine C.
Lamanna, Dolores B. 1930-1980 ... 11-12R
  Obituary ... 97-100
Lamantia, Philip 1927- ... 117
  Brief entry ... 111
  See also DLB 16
Lamar, Howard R(oberts) 1923- ... 19-20R
Lamar, Lavoisier 1907- ... 7-8R
Lamar, Nedra Newkirk ... 69-72
Lamarque, Peter 1948- ... 120
LaMarre, Virgil E. 1910(?)-1985 Obituary ... 115
LaMarsh, Judy
  See LaMarsh, Julia Verlyn
LaMarsh, Julia Verlyn 1924-1980 ... CANR-13
  Obituary ... 105
  Earlier sketch in CA 29-32R
Lamb, Antonia 1943- ... 23-24R
Lamb, Beatrice Pitney 1904- ... 5-6R
  See also SATA 21
Lamb, Charles 1775-1834 ... SATA-17
Lamb, Charles Bentall 1914-1981 ... 102
  Obituary ... 105
Lamb, Charles M(oody) 1945- ... 124
Lamb, Charlotte
  See Holland, Sheila
Lamb, Dana S(torrs) 1900-1986 Obituary ... 120
Lamb, David 1940- ... 110
Lamb, Edward 1902-1987 ... 108
  Obituary ... 122
Lamb, Eleanor 1917- ... 69-72
Lamb, Elizabeth Searle 1917- ... 33-36R
  See also SATA 31
Lamb, F(rank) Bruce 1913- ... 33-36R
Lamb, G(eoffrey) F(rederick) ... CANR-19
  Earlier sketches in CA 53-56, CANR-4
  See also SATA 10
Lamb, H(ubert) H(orace) 1913- ... 23-24R
Lamb, Harold (Albert) 1892-1962 ... 101
  Obituary ... 89-92
Lamb, Helen B.
  See Lamont, Helen Lamb
Lamb, Hugh 1946- ... CANR-1
  Earlier sketch in CA 49-52
Lamb, Karl A(llen) 1933- ... CANR-18
  Earlier sketches in CA 7-8R, CANR-3
Lamb, Lawrence E(dward) 1926- ... 97-100
Lamb, Lynton (Harold) 1907-1977 ... CANR-4
  Earlier sketch in CA 1R
  See also SATA 10
Lamb, Marion M(inerva) 1905- ... 7-8R
Lamb, Mary Ann 1764-1847 ... SATA-17
Lamb, Robert (Boyden) 1941- ... 29-32R
  See also SATA 13
Lamb, Ruth S(tanton) ... CANR-21
  Earlier sketch in CA 45-48
Lamb, Sydney M(acDonald) 1929- ... 33-36R
Lamb, William
  See Jameson, (Margaret) Storm
Lamb, William Kaye 1904- ... 81-84
Lambasa, Frank Slavko 1921-1987
  Obituary ... 123
Lambdin, William 1936- ... 102
Lambec, Zoltan
  See Kimbro, John M.
Lamberg, Robert F(elix) 1929- ... 65-68
Lamberg-Karlovsky, Clifford Charles
  1937- ... 85-88
Lambert, B. Geraldine 1922- ... 41-44R
Lambert, Betty
  See Lambert, Elizabeth (Minnie)
  See also DLB 60
Lambert, Byron Cecil 1923- ... 97-100
Lambert, Christine
  See Albrand, Martha
Lambert, Darwin (Seymour) 1916- ... CANR-2
  Earlier sketch in CA 7-8R
Lambert, David (Compton) 1932- ... 122
  See also SATA 49
Lambert, Derek 1929- ... CANR-17
  Earlier sketch in CA 25-28R
Lambert, Eleanor ... 102
Lambert, Elisabeth
  See Ortiz, Elisabeth Lambert
Lambert, Elizabeth (Minnie) 1933-1983 ... 102
Lambert, Eric 1918-1966 ... CAP-1
  Earlier sketch in CA 13-14
Lambert, Gavin 1924- ... CANR-1
  Earlier sketch in CA 3R
Lambert, Hazel Margaret (?)-1968 ... 2R
Lambert, Herbert H. 1929- ... 69-72
Lambert, J(ack) W(alter) 1917-1986 ... 108
  Obituary ... 120
Lambert, Jacques Edward 1901- ... CAP-2
  Earlier sketch in CA 23-24
Lambert, Janet 1895(?)-1973 Obituary ... 41-44R
  See also SATA 25
Lambert, John (Robin) 1936- ... CANR-8
  Earlier sketch in CA 5-6R
Lambert, Mark 1942- ... 73-76
Lambert, Ronald Dick 1936- ... 108
Lambert, Roy Eugene 1918- ... 37-40R
Lambert, Royston James 1932-1982
  Obituary ... 108
Lambert, Saul 1928- ... 106
  See also SATA 23
Lambert, Sheila 1926- ... 85-88
Lambert, William Wilson 1919- ... 11-12R
Lamberti, Marjorie 1937- ... 103

Lambert-Lagace, Louise 1941- ... 111
Lamberton, Donald McLean 1927- ... 103
Lamberts, J(acob) J. 1910- ... 37-40R
Lambeth, Edmund Barry 1932- ... 123
Lambley, Peter 1946- ... 109
Lambo, Thomas Adeoye 1923- ... 29-32R
Lamborn, LeRoy L(eslie) 1937- ... 23-24R
Lambot, Isobel 1926- ... 73-76
Lambourne, John
See Lamburn, John Battersby Crompton
Lambrick, Hugh Trevor 1904- ... CANR-6
Earlier sketch in CA 9-10R
Lambright, William Henry 1939- ... 103
Lambro, Donald (Joseph) 1940- ... CANR-7
Earlier sketch in CA 57-60
Lambton, Anne (Patricia St. Clair) 1918- ... 85-88
Lamburn, John Battersby Crompton
1893- ... CAP-1
Earlier sketch in CA 9-10
Lamburn, Richmal Crompton 1890-1969 .. CAP-1
Obituary ... 25-28R
Earlier sketch in CA 9-10
See also SATA 5
Lame Deer 1895(?)-1976 Obituary ... 69-72
Lamensdorf, Leonard 1930- ... 29-32R
La Meri
See Hughes, Russell Meriwether
L'Ami, Charles Ernest 1896- ... 102
Lamirande, Emilien 1926- ... CANR-8
Earlier sketch in CA 17-18R
Lamm, Joyce 1933- ... 57-60
Lamm, Maurice 1930- ... 17-18R
Lamm, Norman 1927- ... 49-52
Lamme, Linda Leonard 1942- ... 102
Lamming, George (William) 1927- ... 85-88
See also CLC 2, 4
Lamming, R. M. 1949- Brief entry ... 119
Lamon, Lester C(rawford) 1942- ... 89-92
Lamond, Henry George 1885-1969
Obituary ... 25-28R
Lamont, Corliss 1902- ... CANR-11
Earlier sketch in CA 15-16R
Lamont, Douglas Felix 1937- ... 41-44R
Lamont, Helen Lamb 1906(?)-1975
Obituary ... 61-64
Lamont, Lansing 1930- ... CANR-11
Earlier sketch in CA 17-18R
Lamont, Marianne
See Rundle, Anne
Lamont, N. B.
See Barnitt, Nedda Lemmon
Lamont, Nedda
See Barnitt, Nedda Lemmon
Lamont, Rosette C(lementine) ... 33-36R
Lamont, William D(awson) 1901-1982 ... CAP-1
Obituary ... 108
Earlier sketch in CA 11-12
Lamont-Brown, Raymond 1939- ... CANR-14
Earlier sketch in CA 73-76
Lamorisse, Albert (Emmanuel) 1922-1970 .. 101
See also SATA 23
Lamott, Kenneth (Church) 1923-1979 ... 25-28R
Obituary ... 89-92
Lamotte, Etienne 1904(?)-1983 Obituary ... 109
Lamour, Dorothy
See Kaumeyer, Dorothy
L'Amour, Louis (Dearborn) 1908- ... CANR-3
Earlier sketch in CA 4R
See also DLBY 80
See also CLC 25
See also AITN 2
Lamparski, Richard ... 21-22R
Lampe, David 1923- ... CANR-1
Earlier sketch in CA 4R
Lampedusa, Giuseppe (Tomasi) di
See Tomasi di Lampedusa, Giuseppe
See also TCLC 13
Lampell, Millard 1919- ... 11-12R
Lampert, Emily 1951- ... 121
See also SATA 49
Lamphere, Louise (Anne) 1940- ... 89-92
Lampkin, William R(obert) 1932- ... 106
Lampl, Paul 1915- Brief entry ... 104
Lamplugh, Lois 1921- ... CANR-24
Earlier sketches in CA 13-14R, CANR-9
See also SATA 17
Lampman, Ben Hur 1886-1954 Brief entry .. 111
Lampman, Evelyn Sibley 1907-1980 ... CANR-11
Obituary ... 101
Earlier sketch in CA 15-16R
See also SATA 4, 23
Lampman, Robert James 1920- ... 103
Lampo, Hubert 1920- Brief entry ... 105
Lamport, Felicia 1916- ... 1R
Lamppa, William R(ussell) 1928- ... 53-56
Lamprecht, Sterling P(ower) 1890-1973 .. CAP-1
Earlier sketch in CA 17-18
Lamprey, Louise 1869-1951 Brief entry ... 117
See also YABC 2
Lampson, Robin 1900-1978 Obituary ... 77-80
Lampton, Chris
See Lampton, Christopher
Lampton, Christopher ... SATA-47
Lamsa, George M(amishisho)
1892-1975 ... CANR-9
Earlier sketches in CA 23-24, CAP-2
Lamson, Peggy 1912- ... 25-28R
La Mure, Pierre 1909-1976 Obituary ... 104
Lan, David 1952- ... CANR-24
Earlier sketch in CA 97-100
Lana, Robert E(dward) 1932- ... 33-36R
Lancaster, Bob 1943- ... 111
Lancaster, Bruce 1896-1963 ... CAP-1
Earlier sketch in CA 9-10
See also SATA 9
See also CLC 36
Lancaster, Burt(on Stephen) 1913- ... 122
Brief entry ... 116
Lancaster, Clay 1917- ... CANR-8
Earlier sketch in CA 7-8R
Lancaster, Evelyn
See Sizemore, Chris(tine) Costner
Lancaster, F. Donald
See Fredriksson, Don
Lancaster, F(rederick) Wilfrid 1933- ... CANR-19
Earlier sketches in CA 53-56, CANR-4
Lancaster, Kelvin (John) 1924- ... 33-36R
Lancaster, Lydia
See Meaker, Eloise
Lancaster, Marie-Jaqueline 1922- ... 25-28R
Lancaster, Matthew 1973(?)-1983
Obituary ... 117
See also SATA 45
Lancaster, Osbert 1908-1986 ... 105
Obituary ... 119
Lancaster, Otis Ewing 1909- ... 103
Lancaster, Richard ... 21-22R
Lancaster, Sheila
See Holland, Sheila
Lancaster-Brown, Peter 1927- ... CANR-19
Earlier sketches in CA 53-56, CANR-4
Lance, Derek (Paul) 1932- ... CANR-9
Earlier sketch in CA 15-16R
Lance, H(ubert) Darrell 1935- ... 115
Lance, James Waldo 1926- ... 65-68
Lance, Kathryn 1943- ... 122
Lance, LaBelle D(avid) 1931- ... 81-84
Lance, Leslie
See Swatridge, Charles (John)
Lanchester, Elsa 1902-1986 Obituary ... 121
Lanciano, Claude O(lwen), Jr. 1922- ... CANR-1
Earlier sketch in CA 45-48
Lancour, Gene
See Fisher, Gene L(ouis)
Lancour, (Adlore) Harold 1908-1981 ... 23-24R
Obituary ... 105
Lancy, David F(alcon) 1945- ... 110
Land
See Landry, Robert John
Land, Aubrey C(hristian) 1912- ... 41-44R
Land, Barbara (Neblett) 1923- ... 81-84
See also SATA 16
Land, (Reginald) Brian 1927- ... 101
Land, George T(homas) Lock 1933- ... 53-56
Land, Jane
See Borland, Kathryn Kilby
and Speicher, Helen Ross S(mith)
Land, Jane and Ross
See Borland, Kathryn Kilby
and Speicher, Helen Ross S(mith)
Land, Myrick (Ebben) 1922- ... CANR-11
Earlier sketch in CA 13-14R
See also SATA 15
Landar, Herbert (Jay) 1927- ... 33-36R
Landau, Elaine 1948- ... CANR-5
Earlier sketch in CA 53-56
See also SATA 10
Landau, Genevieve Millet 1927- ... 107
Landau, Jacob 1917- ... SATA-38
Landau, Jacob M. 1924- ... CANR-24
Earlier sketches in CA 19-20R, CANR-8
Landau, Lev Davidovich 1908-1968
Obituary ... 113
Landau, Mark Alexandrovich
See Aldanov, Mark (Alexandrovich)
Landau, Martin 1921- ... 45-48
Landau, Rom 1899-1974 ... CANR-4
Obituary ... 49-52
Earlier sketch in CA 3R
Landau, Sidney I(van) 1933- ... CANR-7
Earlier sketch in CA 57-60
Landau, Sol 1920- ... 49-52
Landau-Aldanov, Mark Alexandrovich
See Aldanov, Mark (Alexandrovich)
Landauer, Carl 1891-1983 ... CANR-21
Earlier sketch in CA 2R
Landauer, Jerry Gerd 1932-1981 ... 109
Obituary ... 103
Lande, Henry F(rank) 1920- ... 29-32R
Lande, Lawrence (Montague) 1906- ... 105
Lande, Nathaniel 1939- ... 104
Landeck, Beatrice 1904- ... 73-76
See also SATA 15
Landecker, Manfred 1929- ... 29-32R
Landeen, William M. 1891-1982 Obituary ... 109
Landeira, Ricardo L(opez) 1917- ... 81-84
Landen, Robert Geran 1930- ... 21-22R
Lander, Ernest McPherson, Jr. 1915- ... CANR-4
Earlier sketch in CA 2R
Lander, Jack Robert 1921- ... 101
Lander, Jeannette 1931- ... 33-36R
Lander, Louise 1938- ... 85-88
Lander, Mamie Stubbs 1891(?)-1975
Obituary ... 53-56
Landers, Ann
See Lederer, Esther Pauline
Landers, Gunnard W(illiam) 1944- ... 93-96
Landes, David S(aul) 1924- ... CANR-22
Earlier sketch in CA 103
Landes, Ruth 1908- ... CAP-2
Earlier sketch in CA 29-32
Landes, Sonia 1925- ... CANR-22
Earlier sketch in CA 104
Landesman, Charles 1932- ... 85-88
Landesman, Fran(ces) 1927- Brief entry ... 120
See also DLB 16
Landesman, Irving Ned
See Landesman, Jay (Irving)
Landesman, Jay (Irving) 1919- Brief entry .. 118
See also DLB 16
Landgren, Marchal E. 1907(?)-1983
Obituary ... 109
Landi, Ferruccio Rossi
See Rossi-Landi, Ferruccio
Landin, Les 1923- ... 5-6R
See also SATA 2
Landis, Benson Y. 1897-1966 ... CAP-1
Earlier sketch in CA 13-14
Landis, Dennis Channing 1947- ... 110
Landis, Fred S(imon) 1943- ... 107
Landis, Jessie Royce 1904-1972
Obituary ... 33-36R
Landis, John 1950- ... 122
Landis, John (David) 1950- Brief entry ... 112
See also CLC 26
Landis, Judson R(ichard) 1935- ... 33-36R
Landis, Lincoln 1922- ... 45-48
Landis, Paul H(enry) 1901- ... CANR-5
Earlier sketch in CA 5-6R
Landman, David 1917- ... CANR-11
Earlier sketch in CA 69-72
Lando, Barry Mitchell 1939- ... 77-80
Landolfi, Tommaso 1908-1979 Obituary ... 117
See also CLC 11
Landon, Donald D. 1930- ... 25-28R
Landon, H(oward) C(handler) Robbins
1926- ... CANR-13
Earlier sketch in CA 77-80
Landon, Lucinda 1950- ... 123
Landon, Margaret (Dorothea Mortenson)
1903- ... CAP-1
Earlier sketch in CA 13-14
See also SATA 50
Landon, Michael de L(aval) 1935- ... 29-32R
Landorf, Joyce 1932- ... 124
See also AITN 1
Landow, George P(aul) 1940- ... CANR-19
Earlier sketches in CA 53-56, CANR-4
Landowska, Wanda (Aleksandra)
1879-1959 Brief entry ... 122
Landreth, Catherine 1899- ... 77-80
Landrith, Harold Fochone 1919- ... 103
Landrum, Phil 1939- ... 81-84
Landry, Hilton (James) 1924- ... 13-14R
Landry, Robert John 1903- ... 69-72
Landsberg, Hans H. 1913- ... CANR-10
Earlier sketch in CA 17-18R
Landsberg, Helmut Erich 1906-1985 ... 107
Obituary ... 118
Landsberg, Michele 1939- ... 123
Landsbergis, Algirdas J. 1924- ... CANR-13
Earlier sketch in CA 33-36R
Landsburg, Alan William 1933- ... 103
Landsburg, Sally (Breit) 1933- ... 57-60
Landshoff, Ursula 1908- ... 29-32R
See also SATA 13
Landstrom, Bjorn O(lof) 1917- ... 15-16R
Landsverk, O(le) G(odfred) 1901- ... 61-64
Landvater, Dorothy 1927- ... 103
Landwehr, Arthur J. II 1934- ... 37-40R
Landwirth, Heinz 1927- ... CANR-7
Earlier sketch in CA 11-12R
Landy, David 1917- ... 77-80
Landy, Eugene E(llsworth) 1934- ... 41-44R
Landynski, Jacob W. 1930- ... 21-22R
Lane, Allen 1902-1970 Obituary ... 29-32R
Lane, Ann J(udith) 1931- Brief entry ... 110
Lane, Anthony 1916- ... 13-14R
Lane, Arthur (Ernest) 1937- ... 41-44R
Lane, Carl D(aniel) 1899- ... 105
Lane, Carolyn 1926- ... CANR-12
Earlier sketch in CA 29-32R
See also SATA 10
Lane, Charles 1800-1870 ... DLB-1
Lane, Charles
See Gatti, Arthur Gerard
Lane, David (Stuart) 1933- ... CANR-17
Earlier sketch in CA 29-32R
Lane, E(ugene Numa) 1936- ... 37-40R
Lane, Frank Walter 1908- ... 9-10R
Lane, Frederic C(hapin) 1900-1984 ... 105
Obituary ... 114
Lane, Gary 1943- ... 37-40R
Lane, Hana Umlauf 1946- ... 118
Lane, Harlan (Lawson) 1936- Brief entry ... 111
Lane, Helen 1920- ... 123
Lane, Helen R(uth) ... CANR-2
Earlier sketch in CA 45-48
Lane, Irving M(ark) 1944- ... 53-56
Lane, Jack C(onstant) 1932- ... CANR-4
Earlier sketch in CA 53-56
Lane, James B(uchanan) 1942- ... 93-96
Lane, Jane
See Dakers, Elaine Kidner
Lane, Jerry
See Martin, Patricia Miles
Lane, John 1932- ... SATA-15
Lane, John (Richard) 1932- ... 106
Lane, Laura Gordon 1913- ... 102
Lane, M(illicent) Travis 1934- ... 112
See also DLB 60
Lane, Marc J(ay) 1946- ... CANR-21
Earlier sketch in CA 105
Lane, Margaret 1907- ... CANR-13
Earlier sketch in CA 25-28R
See also SATA 38
Lane, Mark 1927- ... CANR-21
Earlier sketch in CA 61-64
Lane, Mary (Lois) B(eauchamp) 1911- .. CANR-9
Earlier sketch in CA 15-16R
Lane, Mary D.
See Delaney, Mary Murray
Lane, Michael (John) 1941- ... 85-88
Lane, Patrick 1939- ... 97-100
See also DLB 53
See also CLC 25
Lane, Pinkie Gordon 1923- ... 41-44R
See also DLB 41
Lane, Raymond A. 1894(?)-1974
Obituary ... 53-56
Lane, Richard 1926- ... CANR-10
Earlier sketch in CA 21-22R
Lane, Robert E(dwards) 1917- ... CANR-6
Earlier sketch in CA 1R
Lane, Roger 1934- ... 105
Lane, Ronnie M(ack) 1949- ... 41-44R
Lane, Rose Wilder 1887-1968 ... 102
See also SATA 28, 29
Lane, Roumelia
See Green, Kay
Lane, Sherry
See Smith, Richard Rein
Lane, Sylvia 1916- ... CANR-8
Earlier sketch in CA 5-6R
Lane, Thomas A. 1906- ... 15-16R
Lane, Wheaton J. 1902-1983 Obituary ... 111
Lane, William G(uerrant) 1919- ... 25-28R
Lane, William L. 1931- ... 29-32R
Lane, Yoti ... 2R
Lanegran, David A(ndrew) 1941- ... CANR-16
Earlier sketch in CA 89-92
Lanes, Selma Gordon 1929- ... 25-28R
See also SATA 3
Laney, Al 1896- ... 108
See also DLB 4
Laney, J(ohn) Carl 1948- ... 114
Laney, James Thomas 1927- ... 103
Lanford, H(orace) W(haley) 1919- ... 41-44R
Lang, Allen Kim 1928- ... 17-18R
Lang, Andrew 1844-1912 Brief entry ... 114
See also SATA 16
See also TCLC 16
Lang, Barbara 1935- ... 11-12R
Lang, Berel 1933- ... CANR-15
Earlier sketch in CA 41-44R
Lang, Daniel 1915-1981 ... CANR-4
Obituary ... 105
Earlier sketch in CA 7-8R
Lang, David 1913- ... 106
Lang, David Marshall 1924- ... CANR-17
Earlier sketches in CA 7-8R, CANR-2
Lang, Derek 1913- ... 102
Lang, Frances
See Mantle, Winifred (Langford)
Lang, Fritz 1890-1976 ... 77-80
Obituary ... 69-72
See also CLC 20
Lang, George 1924- ... 101
Lang, Gottfried O(tto) 1919- ... 45-48
Lang, Grace
See Floren, Lee
Lang, Gregor
See Birren, Faber
Lang, H. Jack 1904- ... 115
Lang, Jack (Frederick) 1921- ... 5-6R
Lang, Jovian Peter 1919- ... CANR-15
Earlier sketch in CA 41-44R
Lang, King
See Tubb, E(dwin) C(harles)
Lang, Kurt 1924- ... 33-36R
Lang, Mabel Louise 1917- Brief entry ... 106
Lang, Martin
See Birren, Faber
Lang, Martin A(ndrew) 1930- ... 115
Lang, Maud
See Williams, Claerwen
Lang, Miriam (Milman) 1915- ... 7-8R
Lang, Nancy M.
See Mace, Nancy L(awson)
Lang, Ned
See Sheckley, Robert
Lang, Paul Henry 1901- ... 103
Lang, Robert (Peregrine) 1912- ... 41-44R
Lang, Ronald William 1933- ... 103
Lang, Rupert
See Turner, E(rnest) S(ackville)
Lang, T. T.
See Taylor, Theodore
Lang, William Rawson 1909- ... CANR-21
Earlier sketch in CA 103
Langacker, Ronald W(ayne) 1942- ... 23-24R
Langan, Ruth Ryan 1937- ... CANR-24
Earlier sketch in CA 107
Langan, Thomas 1929- ... CANR-17
Earlier sketch in CA 3R
Langbaum, Robert (Woodrow) 1924- ... CANR-1
Earlier sketch in CA 45-48
Langbein, John H(arriss) 1941- ... 124
Langdale, Eve
See Craig, E(velyn) Quita
Langdon, Charles 1934- ... 77-80
Langdon, Frank C(orriston) 1919- ... 23-24R
Langdon, George D(orland), Jr. 1933- ... 21-22R
Langdon, Grace 1889- ... 2R
Langdon, John 1913- ... 7-8R
Langdon, Margaret Hoffmann (Storms)
1926- Brief entry ... 107
Langdon, Philip 1937- ... 109
Langdon, Robert Adrian 1924- ... CANR-20
Earlier sketch in CA 104
Lange, Dorothea 1895-1965 Obituary ... 107
Lange, Gerald 1946- ... 69-72
Lange, John
See Crichton, (John) Michael
Lange, John Frederick, Jr. 1931- ... CANR-8
Earlier sketch in CA 97-100
Lange, (Leo) Joseph (Jr.) 1932- ... CANR-8
Earlier sketch in CA 17-18R
Lange, Kelly ... 89-92
Lange, Oliver (a pseudonym) 1927- ... CANR-23
Earlier sketch in CA 103
Lange, Oskar (Richard) 1904-1965
Obituary ... 116
Lange, Suzanne 1945- ... 29-32R
See also SATA 5

Lange, (Hermann Walter) Victor 1908- 11-12R
Langendoen, D(onald) Terence 1939- 33-36R
Langer, Elinor 1939- 121
See also CLC 34
Langer, Ellen J(ane) 1947- 49-52
Langer, Jonas 1936- 33-36R
Langer, Lawrence L(ee) 1929- CANR-11
Earlier sketch in CA 65-68
Langer, Marshall J. 1928- 105
Langer, Susanne (Katherina) K(nauth)
1895-1985 41-44R
Obituary 116
Langer, Sydney 1914- 109
Langer, Thomas Edward 1929- 7-8R
Langer, Walter Charles 1899-1981 102
Obituary 104
Langer, William L(eonard) 1896-1977 CANR-14
Obituary 73-76
Earlier sketch in CA 29-32R
Langevin, Andre 1927- DLB-60
Langevin, Sister Jean Marie 1917- 53-56
Langford, Alec J. 1926- 97-100
Langford, Gary R(aymond) 1947- CANR-20
Earlier sketch in CA 103
Langford, George 1939- 53-56
Langford, Gerald 1911- 1R
Langford, James R(ouleau) 1937- 53-56
Langford, Jane
See Mantle, Winifred (Langford)
Langford, Jerome J.
See Langford, James R(ouleau)
Langford, Thomas Anderson 1929- 9-10R
Langford, Walter McCarty 1908- 33-36R
Langgaesser, Elisabeth (Maria) 1899-1950
Brief entry 121
Langgasser, Elisabeth (Maria)
See Langgaesser, Elisabeth (Maria)
Langguth, A(rthur) J(ohn) 1933- 61-64
Langhoff, Severin Peter, Jr. 1910-1987
Obituary 122
Langholm, Neil
See Bulmer, (Henry) Kenneth
Langhorne, Elizabeth 49-52
Langhorne, Richard (Tristan Bailey) 1940- 122
Langiulli, Nino 1932- 53-56
Langland, Elizabeth 1948- 112
Langland, Joseph (Thomas) 1917- CANR-8
Earlier sketch in CA 7-8R
Langley, Adria (Locke) 1899(?)-1983
Obituary 110
Langley, Bob 1936- 85-88
Langley, Dorothy
See Kissling, Dorothy (Hight)
Langley, Harold D. 1925- 21-22R
Langley, Helen
See Rowland, D(onald) S(ydney)
Langley, James Maydon 1916-1983 102
Obituary 109
Langley, Lester D(anny) 1940- CANR-19
Earlier sketch in CA 102
Langley, Michael (John) 1933- 97-100
Langley, Noel 1911-1980 15-16R
Obituary 102
See also SATA 25
Langley, Raymond J. 1935- Brief entry 108
Langley, Roger 1930- 73-76
Langley, Stephen G(ould) 1938- 41-44R
Langley, Tania
See Armstrong, Tilly
Langley, Wright 1935- 57-60
Langlois, Walter G(ordon) 1925- CANR-9
Earlier sketch in CA 23-24R
Langman, Ida Kaplan 1904- CAP-1
Earlier sketch in CA 15-16
Langman, Larry 1930- 109
Langner, Lawrence 1890-1962 Obituary 116
Langner, Nola 1930- CANR-15
Earlier sketch in CA 37-40R
See also SATA 8
Langone, John (Michael) 1929- CANR-1
Earlier sketch in CA 49-52
See also SATA 38, 46
Langsam, Walter Consuelo 1906-1985 CANR-2
Obituary 117
Earlier sketch in CA 3R
Lang-Sims, Lois Dorothy 1917- 106
Langsley, Donald G(ene) 1925- CANR-4
Earlier sketch in CA 53-56
Langstaff, J(ohn) Brett 1889-1985 3R
Obituary 115
Langstaff, John Meredith 1920- CANR-4
Earlier sketch in CA 2R
See also SATA 6
See also CLR 3
Langstaff, Josephine
See Herschberger, Ruth (Margaret)
Langstaff, Launcelot
See Irving, Washington
Langstaff, Nancy 1925- CANR-12
Earlier sketch in CA 73-76
Langton, Clair V(an Norman) 1895- 5-6R
Langton, Daniel J(oseph) 1927- 93-96
Langton, Jane (Gillson) 1922- CANR-18
Earlier sketches in CA 4R, CANR-1
See also SATA 3
See also SAAS 5
Langton, Kenneth P(atrick) 1933- 25-28R
Langwill, Lyndesay Graham 1897- 15-16R
Langworth, Richard M(ichael) 1941- 73-76
Langworthy, Harry W(ells III) 1939- 57-60
Lanham, Charles Trueman 1902-1978
Obituary 81-84
Lanham, Edwin (Moultrie) 1904-1979 9-10R
Obituary 89-92
See also DLB 4
Lanham, Frank W(esley) 1914- CANR-6
Earlier sketch in CA 4R
Lanham, Richard Alan 1936- CANR-10
Earlier sketch in CA 25-28R
Lanham, Url(ess Norton) 1918- 25-28R
Lanier, Alison Raymond 1917- CANR-12
Earlier sketch in CA 19-20R
Lanier, Sidney 1842-1881 SATA-18
See also DLB 64
Lanier, Sterling E(dmund) 1927-
Brief entry 118
Lanigan, Catherine 1947- 108
Laning, Edward 1906- 53-56
Lank, Edith H(andleman) 1926- 109
Lankevich, George J(ohn) 1939- CANR-13
Earlier sketch in CA 77-80
Lankford, John (Errett) 1934- 19-20R
Lankford, Philip Marlin 1945- CANR-7
Earlier sketch in CA 57-60
Lankford, T(homas) Randall 1942- 65-68
Lanks, Herbert C(harles) 1899-1987
Obituary 122
Lanne, William F.
See Leopold, Nathan F.
Lanner, Ronald Martin 1930- 107
Lanning, Edward P(utnam) 1930- 17-18R
Lanning, George (William), Jr. 1925- 11-12R
Lanning, John Tate 1902-1976 Obituary 108
Lanoil, Georgia Hope Witkin
See Witkin-Lanoil, Georgia Hope
Lanoue, Fred Richard 1908-1965 CAP-1
Earlier sketch in CA 13-14
La Noue, George R(ichard) 1937- 73-76
Lanoux, Armand 1913-1983 Obituary 109
Lansbury, Angela 1946- 81-84
Lansdale, Edward Geary 1908-1987
Obituary 121
Lansdale, Joe R(ichard) 1951- 113
Lansdale, Robert Tucker 1900-1980
Obituary 103
Lansdowne, J(ames) F(enwick) 1937- 49-52
Lanser, Susan Sniader 107
Lansing, Alfred 1921-1975 13-14R
Obituary 61-64
See also SATA 35
Lansing, Elisabeth Hubbard 1911- 7-8R
Lansing, Gerrit (Yates) 1928- 73-76
Lansing, Henry
See Rowland, D(onald) S(ydney)
Lansing, John B(elcher) 1919-1970
Obituary 108
Lansky, Bruce 1941- 109
Lansky, Vicki 1942- 81-84
Lanson, Lucienne (Therese) 1930-
Brief entry 108
Lant, Harvey
See Rowland, D(onald) S(ydney)
Lant, Jeffrey Ladd 1947- 109
Lanterman, Ray(mond E.) 1916- 106
Lantis, David W(illiam) 1917- 13-14R
Lantis, Margaret (Lydia) 1906- CAP-2
Earlier sketch in CA 29-32
Lantry, Mike
See Tubb, E(dwin) C(harles)
Lantz, Fran
See Lantz, Francess L(in)
Lantz, Francess L(in) 1952- 115
Lantz, Herman R. 1919-1987 37-40R
Obituary 122
Lantz, Louise K. 1930- 45-48
Lantz, Paul 1908- SATA-45
Lantz, Walter 1900- Brief entry 108
See also SATA 37
Lanyon, Carla 1906-1971 CAP-1
Earlier sketch in CA 13-14
Lanzillotti, Robert F(ranklin) 1921- 77-80
Lao, Kan 1907- 41-44R
Lao She
See Shu Ch'ing-ch'un
Lapage, Geoffrey 1888- CAP-1
Earlier sketch in CA 9-10
La Palombara, Joseph 1925- CANR-6
Earlier sketch in CA 3R
Lapaquellerie, Yvon
See Bizardel, Yvon
Lapati, Americo D. 1924- CANR-1
Earlier sketch in CA 3R
La Patra, Jack W(illiam) 1927- 93-96
Lape, Esther Everett 1881-1981 Obituary 108
Lape, Fred 1900- 102
Lapedes, Daniel N. 1913(?)-1979
Obituary 93-96
LaPenta, Anthony V(incent), Jr. 1943- 69-72
Lapeza, David (Henry) 1950- 73-76
Lapham, Arthur L(owell) 1922- 49-52
Lapham, Lewis H(enry) 1935- 77-80
Lapham, Maxwell E(dward) 1900(?)-1983
Obituary 110
Lapham, Samuel, Jr. 1892-1972 Obituary 106
Lapide, Phinn E.
See Lapide, Pinchas E.
Lapide, Pinchas E. 1922- CANR-13
Earlier sketch in CA 23-24R
Lapidus, Elaine 1939- 21-22R
Lapidus, Jacqueline (Anita) 1941- 97-100
Lapidus, Morris 1902- 77-80
Lapierre, Dominique 1931- CANR-19
Earlier sketch in CA 69-72
LaPierre, Laurier L. 1929- Brief entry 107
La Pietra, Mary 1929- 61-64
Lapin, Howard S(idney) 1922- 19-20R
Lapin, Jackie 1951- 85-88
Lapine, James (Elliot) 1949- Brief entry 123
See also CLC 39
Lapinski, Susan 1948- 115
La Place, John 1922- 103
LaPointe, Frank 1936- 93-96
Lapointe, Paul-Marie 1929- Brief entry 109
Laponce, Jean Antoine 1925- 53-56
Laporte, Jean 1924- 41-44R
Laporte, Maurice 1901(?)-1987 Obituary 123
LaPorte, Robert, Jr. 1940- 41-44R
Lapp, Charles (Leon) 1914- CANR-1
Earlier sketch in CA 45-48
Lapp, Chuck
See Lapp, Charles (Leon)
Lapp, Eleanor J. 1936- 69-72
Lapp, Eunice Willis Bodine 1905- 123
Lapp, John Allen 1933- 41-44R
Lapp, John Clarke 1917-1977 85-88
Lapp, Ralph Eugene 1917- 81-84
Lapp, Rudolph M(athew) 1915- 113
Lappe, Frances Moore 1944- 37-40R
Lappin, Ben
See Lappin, Bernard William
Lappin, Bernard William 1916- 9-10R
Lappin, Peter 1911- CANR-7
Earlier sketch in CA 57-60
See also SATA 32
Lapping, Brian 1937- 25-28R
Laprade, William Thomas 1883-1975
Obituary 89-92
LaPray, (Margaret) Helen 1916- CANR-7
Earlier sketch in CA 53-56
Lapsley, James N(orvell) 1930- 25-28R
Laqueur, Walter (Ze'ev) 1921- CANR-23
Earlier sketch in CA 7-8R
Laquian, Aprodicio A(rcilla) 1935- 29-32R
Lara
See Griffith-Jones, George Chetwynd
Lara, Agustin 1900-1970 Obituary 104
Laramore, Darryl 1928- 101
Larbaud, Valery (Nicolas) 1881-1957
Brief entry 106
See also TCLC 9
Larco, Isabel Granda 1911(?)-1983
Obituary 109
Lardas, Konstantinos 1927- 13-14R
Lardner, George, Jr. 1934- 73-76
Lardner, James 1948- 118
Lardner, John (Abbott) 1912-1960
Obituary 93-96
Lardner, Ring(gold Wilmer) 1885-1933
Brief entry 104
See also DLB 11, 25
See also TCLC 2, 14
Lardner, Ring(gold Wilmer), Jr. 1915- CANR-13
Earlier sketch in CA 25-28R
See also DLB 26
Lardner-Burke, Desmond William
1909-1984 Obituary 114
Laredo, Betty
See Codrescu, Andrei
Laredo, Johnny
See Caesar, (Eu)Gene (Lee)
La Reyniere
See Courtine, Robert
Large, Peter Somerville
See Somerville-Large, Peter
Large, R(ichard) Geddes 1901- 102
Large, Stephen S(toker) 1942- 120
Largo, Michael 1950- 73-76
Lariar, Lawrence 1908- CAP-1
Earlier sketch in CA 9-10
Larimore, Bertha B(urnham) 1915- 61-64
La Rivers, Ira II 1915-1977 41-44R
Larkey, Patrick Darrel 1943- 85-88
Larkin, Amy
See Burns, Olive Ann
Larkin, Emmet 1927- CANR-9
Earlier sketch in CA 15-16R
Larkin, John A(lan) 1936- 41-44R
Larkin, John Day 1897-1986 Obituary 118
Larkin, Maia
See Wojciechowska, Maia (Teresa)
Larkin, Maurice (John Milner) 1932- 102
Larkin, Miriam Therese 1930- Brief entry 108
Larkin, Oliver Waterman 1896-1970 4R
Obituary 29-32R
Larkin, Philip (Arthur) 1922-1985 CANR-24
Obituary 117
Earlier sketch in CA 7-8R
See also DLB 27
See also CLC 3, 5, 8, 9, 13, 18, 33, 39
Larkin, R. T.
See Larkin, Rochelle
Larkin, Rochelle 1935- CANR-13
Earlier sketch in CA 33-36R
Larkin, Sarah
See Loening, Sarah (Elizabeth) Larkin
Larlham, Hattie 1914- 113
Larminie, Margaret Beda 1924- CANR-18
Earlier sketches in CA 7-8R, CANR-2
Larmore, Lewis 1915- 45-48
Larn, Richard (James Vincent) 1930- CANR-20
Earlier sketch in CA 103
Larnach, Rupert
See Nevill, Barry St-John
Larner, Christina (Ross) ?-1983 Obituary 115
Larner, Jeremy 1937- 11-12R
Larner, John (Patrick) 1930- 81-84
Larneuil, Michel
See Batbedat, Jean
Laroche, Rene
See McKeag, Ernest L(ionel)
Larock, Bruce Edward 1940- 53-56
La Rocque, Gilbert 1943-1984 DLB-60
Larom, Henry V. 1903(?)-1975 Obituary 61-64
See also SATA 30
La Rosa, Paul (Frank) 1953- 113
Larose, Paul 1947- 114
LaRouche, Lyndon H(ermyle), Jr. 1922-
Brief entry 124
Larrabee, Carroll Burton 1896-1983
Obituary 110
Larrabee, Eric 1922- CANR-1
Earlier sketch in CA 1R
Larrabee, Harold A(tkins) 1894-1979 CAP-1
Obituary 85-88
Earlier sketch in CA 11-12
Larranaga, Robert O. 1940- 49-52
Larrea, Jean-Jacques 1960- 45-48
Larrecq, John M(aurice)
1926-1980 SATA-25, 44
Larrick, Nancy 1910- CANR-1
Earlier sketch in CA 1R
See also SATA 4
See also DLB 61
Larrie, Reginald R. 1928- 123
Brief entry 118
Larrison, Earl J(unior) 1919- CANR-9
Earlier sketch in CA 57-60
Larrowe, Charles P(atrick) 1916- 41-44R
Larry
See Parkes, Terence
Larsen, Beverly (Namen) 1929- 17-18R
Larsen, Carl 1934- 77-80
Larsen, Charles E(dward) 1923- 33-36R
Larsen, David C(harles) 1944- 73-76
Larsen, E(gner) John 1926- CANR-16
Earlier sketch in CA 25-28R
Larsen, Egon 1904- CANR-3
Earlier sketch in CA 9-10R
See also SATA 14
Larsen, Elyse 1957- 41-44R
Larsen, Erik 1911- 41-44R
Larsen, Erling 1909- 13-14R
Larsen, Ernest 1946- 106
Larsen, Gaylord 1932- 112
Larsen, J(akob) A(ll) O(tteson)
1888-1974 Obituary 111
Larsen, Kalee 1952- 41-44R
Larsen, Knud S(onderhede) 1938- 53-56
Larsen, Lawrence H. 1931- 21-22R
Larsen, Nella 1891-1964 DLB-51
See also CLC 37
Larsen, Otto N. 1922- CANR-2
Earlier sketch in CA 3R
Larsen, Paul E(manuel) 1933- 93-96
Larsen, Peter 1933- CANR-22
Earlier sketch in CA 29-32R
Larsen, Rebecca 1944- 122
Larsen, Ronald J(ames) 1948- 41-44R
Larsen, Roy E(dward) 1899-1979
Obituary 89-92
Larsen, Stephen 1941- 69-72
Larsen, Tony 1949- 107
Larsen, Wendy Wilder 1940- 120
Larsen, William E(dward) 1936- 17-18R
Larsgaard, Mary L(ynette) 1946- 122
Larson, Albert J. 1934- 112
Larson, Andrew Karl 1899- CAP-2
Earlier sketch in CA 33-36
Larson, Arthur 1910- CANR-1
Earlier sketch in CA 2R
Larson, Bob 1944- CANR-5
Earlier sketch in CA 53-56
Larson, Bruce 1925- CANR-13
Earlier sketch in CA 57-60
Larson, Bruce L(lewellyn) 1936- 85-88
Larson, Calvin J. 1933- 49-52
Larson, Carl M. 1916- 41-44R
Larson, Cedric Arthur 1908- 65-68
Larson, Charles 1922- 25-28R
Larson, Charles R(aymond) 1938- CANR-4
Earlier sketch in CA 53-56
See also CLC 31
Larson, Charles U(rban) 1940- 97-100
Larson, Clinton F(oster) 1919- 57-60
Larson, Donald (Norman) 1925- 57-60
Larson, Doran 1957- 124
Larson, E. Richard 1944- 105
Larson, Esther Elisabeth 17-18R
Larson, Eve
See St. John, Wylly Folk
Larson, Gary 1950- 118
Larson, Gary O(tto) 1949- 115
Larson, George C(harles) 1942- CANR-9
Earlier sketch in CA 65-68
Larson, Gerald James 1938- 93-96
Larson, Glen A. 1937(?)- Brief entry 115
Larson, Gustive O. 1897- 29-32R
Larson, Harold J. 1934- 53-56
Larson, Henrietta M(elia) 1894-1983 CAP-2
Obituary 110
Earlier sketch in CA 23-24
Larson, James F(rederick) 1947- 115
Larson, Janet Karsten 1945- 104
Larson, Jean Russell 1930- 21-22R
Larson, Jeanne 1920- 57-60
Larson, Knute (G.) 1919- 9-10R
Larson, Kris 1953- 77-80
Larson, Magali Sarfatti 1936- 97-100
Larson, Martin Alfred 1897- CANR-2
Earlier sketch in CA 7-8R
Larson, Mel(vin Gunnard) 1916- 7-8R
Larson, Muriel 1924- CANR-24
Earlier sketches in CA 23-24R, CANR-9
Larson, Norita D(ittberner) 1944- 105
See also SATA 29
Larson, Orvin Prentiss 1910- 77-80
Larson, P(aul) Merville 1903- 41-44R
Larson, Peggy (Ann Pickering) 1931- 81-84
Larson, Richard Francis 1931- CANR-15
Earlier sketch in CA 41-44R
Larson, Robert H(erbert) 1942- 113
Larson, Robert W. 1927- 85-88
Larson, Simeon 1925- 61-64
Larson, T(aft) A(lfred) 1910- 33-36R
Larson, Thomas B(ryan) 1914- 25-28R
Larson, Victor E. 1898- 25-28R

Larson, William H. 1938- ... 23-24R
See also SATA 10
Larsson, Carl (Olof) 1853-1919
Brief entry ... 115
See also SATA 35
Larsson, Flora (Benwell) 1904- ... 93-96
Lartigue, Jacques-Henri 1894-1986 ... 33-36R
Obituary ... 120
La Rue, Daniel Wolford, Jr. 1878-1969
Obituary ... 116
Larue, Gerald A(lexander) 1916- ... 23-24R
LaRusso, Dominic A(nthony) 1924- ... 33-36R
Lary, N(ikita) M(ichael) 1940- ... 61-64
Lasagna, Louis (Cesare) 1923- Brief entry .. 106
LaSalle, Charles A.
See Ellis, Edward S(ylvester)
LaSalle, Charles E.
See Ellis, Edward S(ylvester)
La Salle, Donald (Philip) 1933- ... 29-32R
LaSalle, Dorothy (Marguerite) ... 5-6R
LaSalle, Peter 1947- ... 103
La Salle, Victor
See Fanthorpe, R(obert) Lionel
Lasater, Alice E(lizabeth) 1936- ... 57-60
Lasby, Clarence G(eorge) 1933- ... 105
Lasch, Christopher 1932- ... 73-76
Lasch, Robert 1907- ... 102
Laschever, Barnett D. 1924- ... CANR-6
Earlier sketch in CA 4R
LaScola, Ray(mond) L. 1915- ... 3R
Lasdun, Susan 1929- ... 111
Lasell, Elinor H. 1929- ... CANR-7
Earlier sketch in CA 7-8R
See also SATA 19
Lasell, Fen H.
See Lasell, Elinor H.
Laser, Marvin 1914- ... 9-10R
Lash, Joseph P. 1909-1987 ... CANR-16
Obituary ... 123
Earlier sketch in CA 17-18R
See also SATA 43
Lasher, Albert C. 1928- ... 25-28R
Lasher, Faith B. 1921- ... 37-40R
See also SATA 12
Laska
See Laska, P(eter) J(erome)
Laska, P(eter) J(erome) 1938- ... CANR-15
Earlier sketch in CA 65-68
Laska, Vera
See Laska, Vera O(ravec)
Laska, Vera O(ravec) 1923- ... 119
Lasker, David 1950- ... 112
See also SATA 38
Lasker, Edward 1885-1981 ... 5-6R
Obituary ... 103
Lasker, Gabriel Ward 1912- ... 2R
Lasker, Joe 1919- ... CANR-1
Earlier sketch in CA 49-52
See also SATA 9
Lasker-Schueler, Else 1869-1945 ... DLB-66
Laski, Marghanita 1915-1988 ... 105
Obituary ... 124
Laskin, Bora 1912-1984 Obituary ... 112
Laskowski, Jerzy 1919- ... 77-80
Lasky, Betty 1927- ... 119
Lasky, Jesse Louis, Jr. 1910- ... CANR-20
Earlier sketches in CA 2R, CANR-4
See also AITN 1
Lasky, Kathryn 1944- ... CANR-11
Earlier sketch in CA 69-72
See also SATA 13
See also CLR 11
Lasky, Melvin J(onah) 1920- ... 53-56
Lasky, Victor 1918- ... CANR-10
Earlier sketch in CA 5-6R
See also AITN 1
Lasky, William R(aymond) 1921- ... 97-100
Laslett, John H(enry) M(artin) 1933- ... CANR-12
Earlier sketch in CA 29-32R
Laslett, Peter 1915- ... CANR-12
Earlier sketch in CA 73-76
Lasley, Jack
See Lasley, John Wayne III
Lasley, John Wayne III 1925- ... 19-20R
LaSor, William Sanford 1911- ... CANR-21
Earlier sketches in CA 4R, CANR-2
La Sorte, A(ntonio) Michael 1931- ... 15-16R
La Spina, (Fanny) Greye 1880- ... CAP-1
Earlier sketch in CA 13-14
Lass, Abraham H(arold) 1907- ... 11-12R
Lass, Betty (Lipschitz) 1908(?)-1976
Obituary ... 69-72
Lass, William E(dward) 1928- ... CANR-2
Earlier sketch in CA 4R
Lass, William M. 1910(?)-1975 Obituary ... 104
Lassalle, C. E.
See Ellis, Edward S(ylvester)
Lassam, Robert (Errington) 1914- ... 112
Lassen-Willems, James
See Willems, J. Rutherford
Lassers, Willard J. 1919- ... 17-18R
Lassimonne, Denise ... 25-28R
Lassiter, Isaac Steele 1941- ... 33-36R
Lassiter, (Albin) Perry (Jr.) 1935- ... 97-100
Lassiter, Roy L(eland), Jr. 1927- ... 21-22R
Lassner, Jacob 1935- ... CANR-20
Earlier sketch in CA 29-32R
Lasson, Kenneth (Lee) 1943- ... CANR-13
Earlier sketch in CA 33-36R
Lasswell, Harold D. 1902-1978 Obituary ... 104
Lasswell, Marcia 1927- ... 97-100
Lasswell, Thomas Ely 1919- ... 17-18R
Last, Jef
See Last, Josephus Carel Franciscus
Last, Joan 1908- ... 107
Last, Josephus Carel Franciscus
1898-1972 ... CAP-2
Earlier sketch in CA 33-36
Laster, Ann A(ppleton) 1936- ... 29-32R
Laszlo, Ervin 1932- ... 41-44R
Laszlo, Miklos 1904(?)-1973 Obituary ... 41-44R
Latane, Bibb 1937- ... 37-40R
Latch, William 1950(?)-1985 Obituary ... 117
Latchaw, Marjorie Elizabeth 1914- ... 5-6R
Latham, Aaron 1943- ... 33-36R
Latham, Barbara 1896- ... SATA-16
Latham, Donald Crawford 1932- ... 11-12R
Latham, Earl Ganson 1907- ... 103
Latham, Frank B(rown) 1910- ... 49-52
See also SATA 6
Latham, Harold Strong 1887-1969 ... CAP-1
Earlier sketch in CA 9-10
Latham, Ian 1956- ... 109
Latham, Jean Lee 1902- ... CANR-7
Earlier sketch in CA 7-8R
See also SATA 2
See also CLC 12
See also AITN 1
Latham, John H. 1917- ... 5-6R
Latham, Joyce 1943- ... 73-76
Latham, Lenn Learner 1901-197(?) ... 2R
Latham, Lorraine 1948- ... 65-68
Latham, Marte Hooper 1924- ... 9-10R
Latham, Mavis
See Clark, Mavis Thorpe
Latham, Peter 1910- ... CAP-1
Earlier sketch in CA 11-12
Latham, Philip
See Richardson, Robert S(hirley)
Latham, Roger M. 1914(?)-1979
Obituary ... 85-88
Lathen, Emma
See Hennissart, Martha
and Latsis, Mary J(ane)
See also CLC 2
Lathrop, Dorothy P(ulis) 1891-1980 ... 73-76
Obituary ... 102
See also SATA 14, 24
See also DLB 22
Lathrop, Francis
See Leiber, Fritz (Reuter, Jr.)
Lathrop, Irvin T(unis) 1927- ... CANR-22
Earlier sketch in CA 45-48
Lathrop, JoAnna 1931- ... 61-64
Lathrop, John, Jr. 1772-1820 ... DLB-37
Latimer, H(enry) C. 1893- ... 29-32R
Latimer, Jonathan (Wyatt) 1906-1983
Obituary ... 110
Latman, Alan 1930-1984 Obituary ... 113
Latner, Helen (Stambler) 1918- ... 106
Latner, Pat Wallace
See Strother, Pat Wallace
Latorre, Dolores L(aguarta Blasco) 1903- .. 65-68
Latorre, Felipe A(ugusto) 1907- ... 65-68
La Tour du Pin, Patrice de 1911-1975
Obituary ... 115
La Tourette, Aileen 1946- ... 119
Latourette, Kenneth Scott 1884-1967 ... CAP-2
Earlier sketch in CA 23-24
La Tourrette, Jacqueline 1926- ... 49-52
Latow, (Muriel) Roberta 1931- ... 116
Latsis, Mary J(ane) ... 85-88
Latta, Richard 1946- ... CANR-19
Earlier sketches in CA 53-56, CANR-4
Latta, William (Charlton, Jr.) 1929- ... 115
Lattimer, John Kingsley 1914- ... 106
Lattimore, Eleanor Frances 1904-1986 .. CANR-6
Obituary ... 119
Earlier sketch in CA 9-10R
See also SATA 7, 48
Lattimore, Owen 1900- ... 97-100
Lattimore, Richmond (Alexander)
1906-1984 ... CANR-1
Obituary ... 112
Earlier sketch in CA 4R
See also CLC 3
Lattin, Ann
See Cole, Lois Dwight
Lattin, Harriet Pratt 1898- ... 33-36R
Latukefu, Sione 1927- ... 73-76
Latzer, Beth Good 1911- ... 65-68
Lau, Charles Richard 1933-1984 Obituary .. 112
Lau, Charley
See Lau, Charles Richard
Lau, Joseph S(hui) M(ing) 1934- ... 77-80
Laub, (Martin) Julian 1929- ... 37-40R
Laubach, Frank Charles 1884-1970 ... CAP-1
Earlier sketch in CA 9-10
Laube, Clifford J(ames) 1891-1974
Obituary ... 53-56
Laubenthal, Sanders Anne 1943- ... 61-64
Lauber, Patricia (Grace) 1924- ... CANR-24
Earlier sketches in CA 9-10R, CANR-6
See also SATA 1, 33
Laubin, Gladys (Winifred) ... 111
Laubin, Reginald K(arl) ... 111
Laucanno, Christopher Sawyer
See Sawyer-Laucanno, Christopher
Lauck, Carol 1934- ... 93-96
Lauder, George
See Dick-Lauder, George (Andrew)
Lauder, George (Andrew) Dick
See Dick-Lauder, George (Andrew)
Lauder, Phyllis 1898- ... 93-96
Lauderdale, Pat 1944- ... 101
Laudicina, Paul A(ndrew) 1949- ... 93-96
Laudin, Harvey 1922- ... 77-80
Laue, Max Theodor Felix von 1879-1960
Obituary ... 113
Lauer, Evelyn G(erda) 1938- ... 29-32R
Lauer, Jeanette C(arol) 1935- ... CANR-19
Earlier sketch in CA 104
Lauer, Jean-Philippe 1902- ... 85-88
Lauer, Robert H(arold) 1933- ... CANR-19
Earlier sketches in CA 53-56, CANR-4
Lauer, Rosemary Zita 1919- ... 5-6R
Lauer, Theodore E. 1931- ... 37-40R
Lauerman, David A(nthony) 1931- ... 19-20R
Lauersen, Niels H(elth) 1939- ... CANR-15
Earlier sketch in CA 85-88
Lauf, Detlef I. Charles 1936- ... 103
Laufe, Abe 1906- ... 17-18R
Laufer, Leopold 1925- ... 21-22R
Lauffer, Armand A(lbert) 1933- ... CANR-19
Earlier sketches in CA 53-56, CANR-5
Laugesen, Mary E(akin) 1906- ... CAP-2
Earlier sketch in CA 29-32
See also SATA 5
Laughbaum, Steve 1945- ... SATA-12
Laughlin, Clarence John 1905-1985
Obituary ... 114
Laughlin, Florence Young 1910- ... 9-10R
See also SATA 3
Laughlin, Henry Prather 1916- ... CANR-8
Earlier sketch in CA 61-64
Laughlin, James 1914- ... CANR-9
Earlier sketch in CA 21-22R
See also DLB 48
Laughlin, Ledlie Irwin 1890-1977 ... 37-40R
Laughlin, Tom 1938(?)- Brief entry ... 116
Laughton, Tom 1904(?)-1984 Obituary ... 112
Laugier, Odile 1956- ... 108
Laugier, R.
See Cumberland, Marten
Laumann, Edward O. 1938- ... 33-36R
Laumer, (John) Keith 1925- ... CANR-7
Earlier sketch in CA 11-12R
See also DLB 8
Launay, Andre (Joseph) 1930- ... 25-28R
Launay, Droo
See Launay, Andre (Joseph)
Laune, Paul Sidney 1899- ... 19-20R
Launitz-Schurer, Leopold (Sidney), Jr.
1942- ... 103
Laurance, Alfred D.
See Tralins, S(andor) Robert
Laurance, Alice (a pseudonym) 1938- ... 101
Laure, Ettagale
See Blauer, Ettagale
Laure, Jason 1940- ... 104
See also SATA 44, 50
Laurel, Alicia Bay 1949- ... 41-44R
Lauren, Linda
See Bunce, Linda Susan (Staines)
Laurence, Dan H. 1920- ... CANR-13
Earlier sketch in CA 17-18R
Laurence, Ester Hauser 1935- ... 29-32R
See also SATA 7
Laurence, John 1939- ... 69-72
Laurence, (Jean) Margaret (Wemyss)
1926-1987 ... 7-8R
Obituary ... 121
See also SATA 50
See also DLB 53
See also CLC 3, 6, 13
Laurence, Michael M(arshall) 1940- ... 33-36R
Laurence, Will
See Smith, Willard L(aurence)
Laurence, William Leonard 1888-1977 ... 77-80
Obituary ... 69-72
Laurent, Lawrence (Bell) 1925- ... 69-72
Laurenti, Joseph L(ucian) 1931- ... 49-52
Laurentin, Rene 1917- ... 106
Laurents, Arthur 1918- ... CANR-8
Earlier sketch in CA 15-16R
See also DLB 26
Lauria, Frank (Jonathan) 1935- ... 103
Laurie, Annie
See Black, Winifred
Laurie, Bruce 1943- ... 115
Laurie, Edward J(ames) 1925- ... CANR-8
Earlier sketch in CA 19-20R
Laurie, Harry C.
See Cahn, Zvi
Laurie, James 1947- ... 69-72
Laurie, Rona ... CANR-15
Earlier sketch in CA 85-88
Laurin, Anne
See McLaurin, Anne
Lauritsen, John (Phillip) 1939- ... 57-60
Lauritzen, Elizabeth Moyes 1909- ... CAP-1
Earlier sketch in CA 15-16
Lauritzen, Jonreed 1902- ... 5-6R
See also SATA 13
Lauri-Volpi, Giacomo 1893(?)-1979
Obituary ... 85-88
Laury, Jean Ray 1928- ... 77-80
Lauscher, Hermann
See Hesse, Hermann
Lautenbach, Renee 1932- ... 110
Lauter
See Chamson, Andre J(ules) L(ouis)
Lauter, Geza Peter 1932- ... 41-44R
Lauter, Paul 1932- ... 15-16R
Lauterbach, Albert 1904- ... CANR-1
Earlier sketch in CA 3R
Lauwerys, Joseph (Albert) 1902-1981 ... 15-16R
Obituary ... 104
Laux, Dorothy 1920- ... 61-64
See also SATA 49
Laux, James M(ichael) 1927- ... 33-36R
Laux, P(eter) J(ohn) 1922- ... 25-28R
Lavagnino, Allessandra 1927- ... CANR-2
Earlier sketch in CA 45-48
LaValle, Irving H(oward) 1939- ... 33-36R
Lavan, Spencer 1937- ... CANR-8
Earlier sketch in CA 57-60
Lave, Lester B(ernard) 1939- ... CANR-15
Earlier sketch in CA 41-44R
Lavelle, Mike 1933- ... 65-68
Lavelle, Sheila 1939- ... 109
Lavender, David (Sievert) 1910- ... CANR-18
Earlier sketches in CA 4R, CANR-2
Lavender, William 1921- ... CANR-10
Earlier sketch in CA 65-68
Lavenson, James H. 1919- ... 103
Lavenson, Jim
See Lavenson, James H.
Laver, James 1899-1975 ... CANR-3
Obituary ... 57-60
Earlier sketch in CA 2R
Laver, Michael 1949- ... CANR-23
Earlier sketch in CA 107
Laver, Rod(ney George) 1938- Brief entry .. 112
La Verdiere, Eugene Armand 1936- ... CANR-19
Earlier sketch in CA 102
Lavers, Norman 1935- ... 104
Laverty, Carroll D(ee) 1906- ... 77-80
Laverty, Donald
See Blish, James (Benjamin)
and Knight, Damon (Francis)
Lavery, Emmet (Godfrey) 1902-1986
Obituary ... 118
Laves, Walter H(erman) C(arl) 1902-1983
Obituary ... 111
La Vey, Anton Szandor 1930- Brief entry ... 109
Lavin, David E(dwin) 1931- ... CANR-2
Earlier sketch in CA 2R
Lavin, Henry St. C. 1921-1985 Obituary ... 114
Lavin, J(oseph) A(nthony) 1932- ... 33-36R
Lavin, Marilyn Aronberg 1925- ... 106
Lavin, Mary 1912- ... 9-10R
See also DLB 15
See also CLC 4, 18
Lavine, David 1928- ... SATA-31
Lavine, Harold 1915-1984 ... 41-44R
Obituary ... 113
Lavine, Richard A. 1917- ... 23-24R
Lavine, Sigmund Arnold 1908- ... CANR-19
Earlier sketches in CA 3R, CANR-4
See also SATA 3
Lavington, H(arold) Dude 1907- ... 117
Lavinson, Joseph
See Kaye, Marvin (Nathan)
Laviolette, Emily A. 1923(?)-1975 ... SATA-49
Lavond, Paul Dennis
See Kornbluth, C(yril) M.
and Lowndes, Robert A(ugustine) W(ard)
and Pohl, Frederik
Lavori, Nora 1950- ... 93-96
Lavrin, Janko Matthew 1887-1986 ... 9-10R
Obituary ... 120
Law, Carol Russell ... 106
Law, Howard W(illiam) 1919- ... 23-24R
Law, Janice
See Trecker, Janice Law
Law, Marie Hamilton 1884-1981 Obituary ... 106
Law, Richard 1901-1980 Obituary ... 105
Law, Virginia W.
See Shell, Virginia Law
Lawder, Douglas W(ard) 1934- ... CANR-1
Earlier sketch in CA 45-48
Lawford, J(ames) P(hilip) 1915- ... 33-36R
Lawhead, Victor B(ernard) 1919- ... 41-44R
Lawhorne, Clifton O. 1927-1983 ... 104
Obituary ... 110
Lawler, Donald L(ester) 1935- ... 105
Lawler, James R. 1929- ... 57-60
Lawler, Lillian B. 1898- ... 15-16R
Lawler, Philip F(rederick) 1950- ... 110
Lawler, Raymond Evenor 1922- ... 103
Lawler, Ronald (David) 1926- Brief entry ... 110
Lawless, Anthony
See MacDonald, Philip
Lawless, Bettyclare Hamilton 1915- ... 61-64
Lawless, Dorothy (Mae) Kennedy 1906- ... 7-8R
Lawless, Edward W(illiam) 1931- ... 114
Lawless, Gary 1951- ... CANR-13
Earlier sketch in CA 73-76
Lawlor, Florine 1925- ... 65-68
Lawlor, John (James) 1918- ... 5-6R
Lawlor, Monica (Mary) 1926- ... 9-10R
Lawlor, Pat
See Lawlor, Patrick Anthony
Lawlor, Patrick Anthony 1893- ... CAP-1
Earlier sketch in CA 9-10
Lawner, Lynne 1935- ... 9-10R
Lawrence, A. R.
See Foff, Arthur R(aymond)
Lawrence, Alexander Atkinson 1906-1979 ... 102
Lawrence, Ann (Margaret) 1942- ... 104
See also SATA 41
Lawrence, Berta ... 73-76
Lawrence, Bill 1930- ... 25-28R
Lawrence, D. Baloti 1950- ... 113
Lawrence, D(avid) H(erbert Richards)
1885-1930 ... 121
Brief entry ... 104
See also DLB 10, 19, 36
See also TCLC 2, 9, 16
Lawrence, Daniel 1940- ... 57-60
Lawrence, David 1888-1973 ... 102
Obituary ... 41-44R
See also DLB 29
Lawrence, David, Jr. 1942- ... 73-76
Lawrence, E. S.
See Bradburne, E(lizabeth) S.
Lawrence, Eddie
See Eisler, Lawrence
Lawrence, Edward
See Eisler, Lawrence
Lawrence, Elizabeth L. 1904-1985 ... 124
Lawrence, Emeric Anthony 1908- ... CANR-5
Earlier sketch in CA 3R
Lawrence, Francis L(eo) 1937- ... 49-52

Lawrence, George H(ill Mathewson)
1910-1978 Obituary 81-84
Lawrence, H(enry) L(ionel) 1908- CAP-1
Earlier sketch in CA 9-10
Lawrence, Helen M(ary) 1925- 111
Lawrence, Isabelle (Wentworth) SATA-29
Lawrence, J(ames) D(uncan) 1918- 17-18R
Lawrence, J. T.
See Rowland-Entwistle, (Arthur) Theodore (Henry)
Lawrence, Jack
See Fitzgerald, Lawrence P(ennybaker)
Lawrence, Jerome 1915- 41-44R
Lawrence, Jock
See Lawrence, Justus Baldwin
Lawrence, Jodi 1938- CANR-3
Earlier sketch in CA 45-48
Lawrence, John (Waldemar) 1907- 81-84
Lawrence, John 1933- CANR-24
Earlier sketch in CA 107
See also SATA 30
Lawrence, John
See Lawrence, Jodi
Lawrence, John A. 1908-1976 Obituary 65-68
Lawrence, John S(helton) 1938- 123
Lawrence, John Shelton 1938- Brief entry 107
Lawrence, Josephine 1890(?)-1978 77-80
See also SATA 24
Lawrence, Justus Baldwin 1903-1987
Obituary 122
Lawrence, Karl
See Foff, Arthur R(aymond)
Lawrence, Kenneth G.
See Ringgold, Gene
Lawrence, Lesley
See Lewis, Lesley
Lawrence, Louise
See Holden, Elizabeth Rhoda
See also SATA 38
Lawrence, Louise de Kiriline 1894- 25-28R
See also SATA 13
Lawrence, Margaret Morgan 1914- 33-36R
Lawrence, Marjorie 1907-1979 Obituary 85-88
Lawrence, Martin
See Greif, Martin and Grow, Lawrence
Lawrence, Mary Margaret 1920- 93-96
Lawrence, Merle 1915- 21-22R
Lawrence, Michael
See Lariar, Lawrence
Lawrence, Mildred Elwood 1907- CANR-5
Earlier sketch in CA 1R
See also SATA 3
Lawrence, Nathaniel (Morris)
1917-1986 CANR-22
Earlier sketch in CA 45-48
Lawrence, P.
See Tubb, E(dwin) C(harles)
Lawrence, Peter 1921-1988 Obituary 124
Lawrence, R(onald) D(ouglas) 1921- CANR-11
Earlier sketch in CA 65-68
Lawrence, Richard A.
See Leopold, Nathan F.
Lawrence, Robert 1912(?)-1981 Obituary 105
Lawrence, Robert
See Beum, Robert (Lawrence)
Lawrence, Robert A(llen) 1948- 118
Lawrence, Roy 1930- 45-48
Lawrence, Samuel A. 1928- 21-22R
Lawrence, Sharon 1945- 65-68
Lawrence, Steven C.
See Murphy, Lawrence A(gustus)
Lawrence, T(homas) E(dward) 1888-1935
Brief entry 115
See also TCLC 18
Lawrence, Thomas
See Roberts, Thom(as Sacra)
Lawrence, Vera Brodsky 1909- Brief entry 109
Lawrence, William Howard 1916-1972
Obituary 33-36R
Lawrence, William J(ohn) C(ooper)
1899(?)-1985 Obituary 118
Lawrence Of Arabia
See Lawrence, T(homas) E(dward)
Lawrenson, Helen 1907-1982 117
Obituary 106
Lawrenson, Thomas Edward 1918-1982
Obituary 106
Lawry, Jon Sherman 1924- 7-8R
Laws, G(eorge) Malcolm, Jr. 1919- 37-40R
Laws, Priscilla W(atson) 1940- 73-76
Lawshe, C(harles) H(ubert) 1908- CAP-2
Earlier sketch in CA 23-24
Lawson, (Richard) Alan 1934- 53-56
Lawson, Annetta 1939- 116
Lawson, Carol (Antell) 1946- SATA-42
Lawson, Chet
See Tubb, E(dwin) C(harles)
Lawson, David 1927- 57-60
Lawson, Don(ald Elmer) 1917- CANR-2
Earlier sketch in CA 1R
See also SATA 9
Lawson, Donna Roberta 1937- 41-44R
Lawson, E(verett) LeRoy 1938- CANR-19
Earlier sketches in CA 53-56, CANR-4
Lawson, Evelyn 1917- 57-60
Lawson, F(loyd) Melvyn 1907- 53-56
Lawson, Frederick Henry 1897-1983
Obituary 109
Lawson, H(orace) L(owe) 1900- 5-6R
Lawson, H. Lowe
See Lawson, H(orace) L(owe)
Lawson, Henry (Archibald Hertzberg)
1867-1922 Brief entry 120
See also TCLC 27
Lawson, Jacob
See Burgess, M(ichael) R(oy)
Lawson, James 1938- 65-68
Lawson, Joan 1906- 103
Lawson, John 1909- CANR-3
Earlier sketch in CA 2R
Lawson, John ?-1711 DLB-24
Lawson, John Howard 1894-1977 CAP-1
Obituary 73-76
Earlier sketch in CA 15-16
Lawson, Kay 1933- 104
Lawson, Lewis A. 1931- 21-22R
Lawson, M. C.
See Lawson, H(orace) L(owe)
Lawson, Marion Tubbs 1896- CAP-1
Earlier sketch in CA 9-10
See also SATA 22
Lawson, Michael
See Ryder, M(ichael) L(awson)
Lawson, Philip J. 1908(?)-1978 Obituary 77-80
Lawson, (Phillippe) Reed 1929- 7-8R
Lawson, Richard H(enry) 1919- CANR-8
Earlier sketch in CA 17-18R
Lawson, Robert 1892-1957 Brief entry 118
See also YABC 2
See also DLB 22
See also CLR 2
Lawson, Robert G. 1938- 118
Lawson, Ruth C(atherine) 1911- 9-10R
Lawson, S. Alexander 1912- 57-60
Lawson, Sarah (Anne) 1943- 120
Lawson, Steve
See Turner, Robert (Harry)
Lawson, Steven F(red) 1945- 122
Lawson, Victor F. 1850-1925 DLB-25
Lawson, W. B.
See Jenks, George C(harles)
Lawton, Charles
See Heckelmann, Charles N(ewman)
Lawton, Dennis
See Faust, Frederick (Shiller)
Lawton, Harry Wilson 1927- 33-36R
Lawton, Manny
See Lawton, Marion R(ussell)
Lawton, Marion R(ussell) 1918-1986 118
Lawton, Sherman P(axton) 1908- CAP-2
Earlier sketch in CA 19-20
Lawyer, Annabel Glenn 1906(?)-1974
Obituary 53-56
Law Yone, Edward Michael 1911(?)-1980
Obituary 101
Lax, Robert 1915- CANR-11
Earlier sketch in CA 25-28R
Laxalt, Robert P(eter) 1923- 13-14R
Laxness, Halldor
See Gudjonsson, Halldor Kiljan
See also CLC 25
Lay, Bennett 1910- CAP-1
Earlier sketch in CA 11-12
Lay, Bierne, Jr. 1909-1982 Obituary 107
Lay, Daniel W(ayne) 1914- 118
Lay, Nancy Duke S. 1938- CANR-21
Earlier sketch in CA 105
Lay, Norvie L(ee) 1940- 49-52
Lay, S(amuel) Houston 1912- 33-36R
Lay, Shawn 1953- 124
Laybourne, Lawrence E. 1914(?)-1976
Obituary 65-68
Laycock, Ellen (Mae) 1921- 112
Laycock, George (Edwin) 1921- CANR-19
Earlier sketches in CA 7-8R, CANR-4
See also SATA 5
Laycock, Harold R. (I. O.) 1916- 7-8R
Laye, Camara 1928-1980 85-88
Obituary 97-100
See also CLC 4, 38
Layman, Constance 1943- 111
Layman, Emma McCloy 1910- 81-84
Layman, Richard 1947- 65-68
Laymon, Charles Martin 1904- CANR-7
Earlier sketch in CA 11-12R
Layne, Bobby
See Layne, Robert Lawrence
Layne, Laura
See Knott, William C(ecil, Jr.)
Layne, Robert Lawrence 1927-1986
Obituary 121
Layton, Andrea
See Bancroft, Iris (May Nelson)
Layton, Aviva 1933- 116
Layton, Edwin T(homas), Jr. 1928- 29-32R
Layton, Felix 1910- CAP-2
Earlier sketch in CA 23-24
Layton, Irving (Peter) 1912- CANR-2
Earlier sketch in CA 3R
See also CLC 2, 15
Layton, Marilyn Smith 1941- 114
Layton, Robert 1930- 21-22R
Layton, Thomas Arthur 1910- 9-10R
Layton, Wilbur L. 1922- Brief entry 106
Layton, William (Isaac) 1913- 19-20R
Lazar, Wendy 1939- 104
Lazare, Gerald John 1927- SATA-44
Lazare, Jerry
See Lazare, Gerald John
Lazareff, Pierre 1907-1972 Obituary 33-36R
Lazareth, William Henry 1928- CANR-16
Earlier sketches in CA 3R, CANR-1
Lazarevich, Mila 1942- SATA-17
Lazaron, Hilda R(othschild) 1895- 49-52
Lazarre, Jane D(eitz) 1943- 101
Lazarsfeld, Paul F(elix) 1901-1976 73-76
Obituary 69-72
Lazarus, A(rnold) L(eslie) 1914- CANR-11
Earlier sketch in CA 25-28R
Lazarus, Arnold A(llan) 1932- CANR-14
Earlier sketch in CA 41-44R
Lazarus, Arthur 1892(?)-1978 Obituary 77-80
Lazarus, Edward H. 1959- 122
Lazarus, Felix
See Cable, George Washington
Lazarus, Harold 1927- 23-24R
Lazarus, Keo Felker 1913- 41-44R
See also SATA 21
Lazarus, Marguerite 1916- 106
Lazarus, Mell 1927- CANR-11
Earlier sketch in CA 19-20R
Lazarus, Richard S(tanley) 1922- CANR-5
Earlier sketch in CA 3R
Lazarus, Simon 1941- 57-60
LaZebnik, Edith 1897- 85-88
Lazell, James Draper, Jr. 1939- 65-68
Lazenby, Walter S(ylvester), Jr. 1930- 65-68
Lazer, William 1924- CANR-19
Earlier sketches in CA 3R, CANR-4
Lazere, Donald 1935- 105
Lazerowitz, Alice Ambrose 1906- CANR-17
Earlier sketches in CA 49-52, CANR-1
Lazerowitz, Morris 1907- CANR-17
Earlier sketches in CA 11-12R, CANR-3
Lazlo, Kate
See Angus, Sylvia
Lazo, Hector 1899-1965 CANR-3
Earlier sketch in CA 3R
Lazreg, Marnia 1941- 69-72
Lea, Alec 1907- 73-76
See also SATA 19
Lea, David A(lexander) M(aclure)
1934- CANR-10
Earlier sketch in CA 21-22R
Lea, F(rank) A(lfred) 1915-1977 CANR-3
Earlier sketch in CA 4R
Lea, Frederick (Measham) 1900-1984
Obituary 113
Lea, Henry Charles 1825-1909 Brief entry 122
See also DLB 47
Lea, Joan
See Neufeld, John (Arthur)
Lea, John Sedgwick 1910(?)-1987
Obituary 124
Lea, Kathleen M(arguerite) 1903- 119
Lea, Sydney (L. Wright, Jr.) 1942- CANR-22
Earlier sketch in CA 106
Lea, Timothy
See Wood, Christopher (Hovelle)
Lea, Tom 1907- Brief entry 115
See also DLB 6
Leab, Daniel Josef 1936- CANR-11
Earlier sketch in CA 29-32R
Leabo, Dick A. 1921- 9-10R
Leacacos, John P. 1908-1986 25-28R
Obituary 121
Leach, Aroline Beecher 1899- 61-64
Leach, Barry Arthur 1930- 102
Leach, Bernard Howell 1887-1979 97-100
Obituary 85-88
Leach, Douglas Edward 1920- 19-20R
Leach, Eleanor Winsor 1937- 103
Leach, Gerald Adrian 1933- CANR-21
Earlier sketch in CA 7-8R
Leach, Graham (John) 1948- 122
Leach, John Robert 1922- 23-24R
Leach, Joseph (Lee) 1921- 29-32R
Leach, Maria 1892-1977 53-56
Obituary 69-72
See also SATA 28, 39
Leach, (Richard) Max(well) 1909- 41-44R
Leach, Michael 1940- 73-76
Leach, Paul Roscoe 1890-1977 Obituary 73-76
Leach, Penelope (Jane) 1937- CANR-21
Earlier sketch in CA 97-100
Leach, Richard H(eald) 1922- Brief entry 113
Leach, Robert J. 1916- 29-32R
Leach, (Carson) Wilford 1932- CANR-2
Earlier sketch in CA 45-48
Leachman, Robert Briggs 1921- 104
Leacock, Eleanor Burke 1922-1987 CANR-15
Obituary 122
Earlier sketch in CA 37-40R
Leacock, John 1729-1802 DLB-31
Leacock, Ruth 1926- 37-40R
Leacock, Stephen (Butler) 1869-1944
Brief entry 104
See also TCLC 2
Leacroft, Helen (Mabel Beal) 1919- CANR-2
Earlier sketch in CA 5-6R
See also SATA 6
Leacroft, Richard (Vallance Becher)
1914- CANR-2
Earlier sketch in CA 5-6R
See also SATA 6
Leadbetter, Eric 1892(?)-1971 Obituary 104
Leadbitter, Mike 1942- 41-44R
Leader, (Evelyn) Barbara (Blackburn)
1898- 61-64
Leader, Charles
See Smith, Robert Charles
Leader, Mary (Bartelt) 85-88
Leader, Ninon 1933- 21-22R
Leader, Shelah Gilbert 1943- 110
Leaf, David 1952- 117
Leaf, Margaret P. 1909(?)-1988 Obituary 124
Leaf, (Wilbur) Munro 1905-1976 73-76
Obituary 69-72
See also SATA 20
Leaf, Murray J(ohn) 1939- CANR-1
Earlier sketch in CA 45-48
Leaf, Russell C(harles) 1935- 21-22R
Leaf, VaDonna Jean 1929- 57-60
See also SATA 26
Leagans, John Paul 1911- 103
Leahy, Syrell Rogovin 1935- CANR-12
Earlier sketch in CA 57-60
Leake, Chauncey D(epew) 1896-1978 CANR-3
Obituary 73-76
Earlier sketch in CA 49-52
Leake, Jane Acomb 1928- 21-22R
Leakey, Louis S(eymour) B(azett)
1903-1972 97-100
Obituary 37-40R
Leakey, Mary (Douglas Nicol) 1913- CANR-18
Earlier sketch in CA 97-100
Leakey, Richard E(rskine Frere) 1944- CANR-18
Earlier sketch in CA 93-96
See also SATA 42
Leaman, David R(ay) 1947- 115
Leamer, Edward E(mery) 1944- 29-32R
Leamer, Laurence Allen 1941- CANR-13
Earlier sketch in CA 65-68
Leaming, Barbara 107
Lean, Arthur E(dward) 1909- 73-76
Lean, David 1908- Brief entry 111
Lean, E(dward) Tangye 1911-1974
Obituary 53-56
Lean, Garth Dickinson 1912- CANR-17
Earlier sketch in CA 29-32R
Leander, Ed
See Richelson, Geraldine
Leaney, Alfred Robert Clare 1909- CANR-2
Earlier sketch in CA 7-8R
Leap, Harry P(atrick) 1908-1976 3R
Obituary 103
Leapman, Michael 1938- 109
Lear, Edward 1812-1888 SATA-18
See also DLB 32
See also CLR 1
Lear, Floyd Seyward 1895- CAP-1
Earlier sketch in CA 17-18
Lear, John 1909- 37-40R
Lear, Martha Weinman 1930- CANR-9
Earlier sketch in CA 9-10R
Lear, Melva Gwendoline Bartlett 1917- 7-8R
Lear, Norman (Milton) 1922- 73-76
See also CLC 12
Lear, Peter
See Lovesey, Peter
Leard, G(eorge) Earl 1918- 9-10R
Leard, John E. 1916- 73-76
Learmonth, Andrew Thomas Amos
1916- 15-16R
Learned, Edmund Philip 1900- 104
Leary, David E. 1945- 124
Leary, Edward A(ndrew) 1913- CANR-12
Earlier sketch in CA 29-32R
Leary, John P(atrick) 1919- 11-12R
Leary, Lewis (Gaston) 1906- CANR-4
Earlier sketch in CA 1R
Leary, Paris 1931- 17-18R
Leary, Timothy (Francis) 1920- 107
See also DLB 16
Leary, William G(ordon) 1915- 49-52
Leary, William M., Jr. 1934- 93-96
Leas, Speed 1937- 49-52
Lease, Benjamin 1917- Brief entry 114
Lease, Gary 1940- 45-48
Leasher, Evelyn M(arie) 1941- 115
Leaska, Mitchell A(lexander) 1934- CANR-13
Earlier sketch in CA 77-80
Leasor, (Thomas) James 1923- CANR-2
Earlier sketch in CA 4R
Least Heat Moon, William
See Trogdon, William (Lewis)
Leasure, Robert E. 1921- 112
Leather, Edwin (Hartley Cameron) 1919- 97-100
Leather, George
See Swallow, Norman
Leatherman, LeRoy 1922-1984 23-24R
Obituary 112
Leautaud, Paul 1872-1956 DLB-65
Leavell, Landrum P(inson) II 1926- 89-92
Leavenworth, Carol 1940- CANR-14
Earlier sketch in CA 81-84
Leavenworth, James Lynn 1915- 21-22R
Leaver, Robin Alan 1939- CANR-9
Earlier sketch in CA 61-64
Leavis, F(rank) R(aymond) 1895-1978 21-22R
Obituary 77-80
See also CLC 24
Leavis, Q(ueenie) D(orothy) 1906-1981 97-100
Obituary 108
Leavitt, David 1961- 122
Brief entry 116
See also CLC 34
Leavitt, Harold J(ack) 1922- Brief entry 117
Leavitt, Hart Day 1909- 15-16R
Leavitt, Harvey R(obert) 1934- 65-68
Leavitt, Jack 1931- 97-100
Leavitt, Jerome E(dward) 1916- CANR-17
Earlier sketches in CA 4R, CANR-1
See also SATA 23
Leavitt, Judith A(nn) 1947- 110
Leavitt, Richard Freeman 1929- 89-92
Leavitt, Ruby R.
See Rohrlich, Ruby
Leavitt, William J. 1928-1984 Obituary 112
Leavy, Stanley A(rnold) 1915- 120
LeBar, Lois E. 1907- 21-22R
LeBar, Mary E(velyn) 1910-1982 107
See also SATA 35
LeBaron, Charles W. 1943- CANR-9
Earlier sketch in CA 61-64
Lebeaux, Richard 1946- CANR-12
Earlier sketch in CA 73-76
Leber, George L. 1917(?)-1976 Obituary 61-64
Lebergott, Stanley 1918- 103
Lebert, Randy
See Brannon, William T.
Lebeson, Anita Libman 1896-1987 29-32R
Obituary 121
Leblanc, Maurice (Marie Emile)
1864-1941 Brief entry 110
LeBlanc, Rena Dictor 1938- 104
Leblon, Jean (Marcel Jules) 1928- 41-44R

Lebo, Dell 1922- 57-60
LeBoeuf, Michael 1942- CANR-15
Earlier sketch in CA 93-96
Le Boutillier, Cornelia Geer 1894(?)-1973
Obituary 45-48
Lebovich, William Louis 1948- 115
Lebovitz, Harold Paul 1916- 77-80
Lebow, Victor 1902- 37-40R
Lebowitz, Alan 1934- 25-28R
Lebowitz, Albert 1922- 73-76
Lebowitz, Fran(ces Ann) 1951(?)- CANR-14
Earlier sketch in CA 81-84
See also CLC 11, 36
Lebowitz, Naomi 1932- 37-40R
Leboyer, Frederick 1918- 106
Lebra, Joyce C(hapman) CANR-1
Earlier sketch in CA 45-48
Lebra, Takie Sugiyama 1930- 77-80
Lebra, William P(hilip) 1922- 33-36R
Lebrecht, Norman 1948- 117
Lebreo, Steward
See Weiner, Stewart
Lebreo, Stewart
See Weiner, Stewart
Le Breton, Auguste
See Montfort, Auguste
Le Brown, Andreas
See Brown, Andreas Le
LeBrun, Gautier
See Gibson, Walter B(rown)
LeBrun, George P. 1862-1966 5-6R
Lebrun, Richard Allen 1931- 41-44R
Le Cain, Errol John 1941- CANR-13
Earlier sketch in CA 33-36R
See also SATA 6
Lecale, Errol
See McNeilly, Wilfred Glassford
Lecar, Helene Lerner 1938- 25-28R
le Carre, John
See Cornwell, David (John Moore)
See also CLC 3, 5, 9, 15, 28
Lecavele, Roland
See Dorgeles, Roland
Le Chanois, Jean-Paul
See Drefus, Jean-Paul Etienne
Lechlitner, Ruth N. 1901- 105
See also DLB 48
Lechner, Robert F(irman) 1918- 33-36R
Lecht, Charles Philip 1933- 21-22R
Lecht, Leonard A. 1920- CANR-11
Earlier sketch in CA 25-28R
Lecker, Robert 1951- 111
Leckey, Dolores (Conklin) 1933- 109
Leckie, Robert (Hugh) 1920- 13-14R
Leckie, William H. 1915- 23-24R
LeClair, Thomas 1944- 113
LeClair, Tom
See LeClair, Thomas
LeClaire, Gordon 1905- 69-72
Leclerc, Felix 1914- DLB-60
Leclerc, Ivor 1915- 33-36R
Leclerc, Victor
See Parry, Albert
Le Clercq, Jacques Georges Clemenceau
1898-1972 Obituary 37-40R
Le Clezio, J(ean) M(arie) G(ustave) 1940-
Brief entry 116
See also CLC 31
Le Cocq, Rhoda P(riscilla) 1921- 73-76
Lecoin, Louis 1888(?)-1971 Obituary 33-36R
Lecomber, Brian 1945- CANR-13
Earlier sketch in CA 73-76
Lecompte, Janet 1923- 122
Le Comte, Edward (Semple) 1916- CANR-5
Earlier sketch in CA 4R
Lecomte du Nouey
See Lecomte du Nouey, Pierre
(-Andre-Leon)
Lecomte du Nouey, P.
See Lecomte du Nouey, Pierre
(-Andre-Leon)
Lecomte du Nouey, Pierre (-Andre-Leon)
1883-1947 Brief entry 119
Lecomte du Nouy, Pierre (-Andre-Leon)
See Lecomte du Nouey, Pierre
(-Andre-Leon)
LeCroy, Anne K(ingsbury) 1930- CANR-16
Earlier sketch in CA 41-44R
LeCroy, Ruth Brooks 45-48
Ledbetter, J(ack) T(racy) 1934- 73-76
Ledbetter, Jack Wallace 1930- 5-6R
Ledbetter, Joe O(verton) 1927- 45-48
Ledbetter, Ken(neth Lee) 1931- 117
Ledbetter, Les 1941(?)-1985 Obituary 116
Ledbetter, Virgil C. 1918-19(?) CAP-1
Earlier sketch in CA 15-16
Ledderose, Lothar 1942- 85-88
Leder, Jane Mersky 1945- 117
Leder, Lawrence H. 1927- 25-28R
Lederer, Charles 1910-1976 Obituary 65-68
See also DLB 26
Lederer, Chloe 1915- 77-80
Lederer, Edith Madelon 1943- 97-100
Lederer, Esther Pauline 1918- 89-92
Lederer, Ivo J(ohn) 1929- 11-12R
Lederer, Jiri 1922-1983 Obituary 111
Lederer, Joseph 1927- 73-76
Lederer, Lajos 1904-1985 Obituary 118
Lederer, Laura 1951- 121
Lederer, Muriel 1929- 77-80
See also SATA 48
Lederer, Paul Joseph 1944- 111
Lederer, Rhoda Catharine (Kitto)
1910- CANR-22
Earlier sketches in CA 9-10R, CANR-6
Lederer, William J(ulius) 1912- CANR-5
Earlier sketch in CA 4R
Lederman, Leonard L(awrence) 1931- 61-64
Ledermann, Erich Kurt 1908- 107
Ledermann, Walter 1911- 49-52
Ledesert, (Dorothy) Margaret 1916- 45-48
Ledesert, R(ene) P(ierre) L(ouis)
1913-1984 45-48
Obituary 114
Le Duan 1908(?)-1986 Obituary 119
Le Duc, Don R(aymond) 1933- 49-52
Leduc, Violette 1907-1972 CAP-1
Obituary 33-36R
Earlier sketch in CA 13-14
See also CLC 22
Ledwidge, Francis 1887(?)-1917
Brief entry 123
See also DLB 20
See also TCLC 23
Ledwidge, William (Bernard) John 1915- 103
Ledwith, Frank 1907- 103
Ledyard, Gleason H(ines) 1919- 7-8R
Lee, A. R.
See Ash, Rene Lee
Lee, Addison E(arl) 1914- 9-10R
Lee, Adrian Iselin, Jr. 1920- 89-92
Lee, Al(fred Matthew) 1938- 45-48
Lee, Alfred McClung 1906- CANR-19
Earlier sketches in CA 1R, CANR-3
Lee, Alvin A. 1930- 33-36R
Lee, Amanda
See Baggett, Nancy
and Buckholtz, Eileen (Garber)
and Glick, Ruth (Burtnick)
Lee, Amber
See Baldwin, Faith
Lee, Andrea 1953- CLC-36
Lee, Andrea
See Toona, Elin(-Kai)
Lee, Andrew
See Auchincloss, Louis (Stanton)
Lee, Arthur M(atthias) 1918- 41-44R
Lee, Asher 1909- 73-76
Lee, Audrey 25-28R
Lee, Austin 1904-19(?) CAP-1
Earlier sketch in CA 15-16
Lee, Barbara 1932- 109
Lee, Barbara (Moore) 1934- CANR-9
Earlier sketch in CA 53-56
Lee, Benjamin 1921- 104
See also SATA 27
Lee, Betsy 1949- 106
See also SATA 37
Lee, Betty 1921- 103
Lee, Betty
See Lambert, Elizabeth (Minnie)
Lee, Bill
See Lee, William Saul
Lee, Bob
See McGrath, Robert L(ee)
Lee, Brother Basil Leo 1909-1974
Obituary 53-56
Lee, C(harles) Nicholas 1933- 49-52
Lee, C(larence) P(endleton) 1913- 49-52
Lee, Calvin B. T. 1934- 33-36R
Lee, Carol
See Fletcher, Helen Jill
Lee, Carolina
See Dern, Erolie Pearl Gaddis
Lee, Carvel (Bigham) 1910- CAP-1
Earlier sketch in CA 13-14
Lee, Charles 1913- 33-36R
Lee, Charles Robert, Jr. 1929- 7-8R
Lee, Charlotte I(rene) 1909- 23-24R
Lee, Chong-Sik 1931- CANR-15
Earlier sketch in CA 41-44R
Lee, Christine Eckstrom 1952- 110
Lee, Christopher Frank Carandini 1922- 73-76
Lee, C(hin)-Y(ana) 1917- 11-12R
Lee, David 1944- 111
Lee, David Dale 1948- 117
Lee, Deemer 1905-1979 111
Lee, Dennis (Beynon) 1939- CANR-11
Earlier sketch in CA 25-28R
See also SATA 14
See also DLB 53
See also CLR 3
Lee, Derek 1937- 107
Lee, (Henry) Desmond (Pritchard) 1908- 102
Lee, Devon
See Pohle, Robert W(arren), Jr.
Lee, Don L.
See Madhubuti, Haki R.
See also CLC 2
Lee, Doris Emrick 1905-1983 Obituary 110
See also SATA 35, 44
Lee, Dorris M(ay Potter) 1905- 13-14R
Lee, Douglas A(llen) 1932- 53-56
Lee, Dwight E(rwin) 1898- 7-8R
Lee, Eddie H. 1917- 69-72
Lee, Edward Edson AITN-1
Lee, Edward N(icholls) 1935- 29-32R
Lee, Elizabeth Briant 1908- 37-40R
Lee, Elsie 1912- 85-88
Lee, Eric
See Lee, Fleming
and Page, Gerald W(ilburn)
Lee, Essie E. 1920- CANR-4
Earlier sketch in CA 49-52
Lee, Eugene (Huey) 1941- 49-52
Lee, Fleming 1933- CANR-7
Earlier sketch in CA 9-10R
Lee, Florence Henry 1910- CAP-1
Earlier sketch in CA 17-18
Lee, Francis Nigel 1934- CANR-8
Earlier sketch in CA 57-60
Lee, Frank F(reeman) 1920- 2R
Lee, Fred 1927- 109
Lee, G. Avery 1916- 104
Lee, George J. 1920(?)-1976 Obituary 65-68
Lee, George Leslie
See Lee, Brother Basil Leo
Lee, George W(ashington) 1894-1976 DLB-51
Lee, Gerard (Majella) 1951- 93-96
Lee, Ginffa 1900(?)-1976 Obituary 69-72
Lee, Gordon C(anfield) 1916- 13-14R
Lee, Gypsy Rose
See Hovick, Rose Louise
Lee, H. Alton 1942- 81-84
Lee, Hahn-Been 1921- CANR-11
Earlier sketch in CA 25-28R
Lee, Harold N(ewton) 1899- 37-40R
Lee, (Nelle) Harper 1926- 15-16R
See also SATA 11
See also DLB 6
See also CDALB 1941-1968
See also CLC 12
Lee, Harriet 1757-1851 DLB-39
Lee, Harry J., Jr. 1914-1985 Obituary 118
Lee, Hector (Haight) 1908- 97-100
Lee, Helen Clara 1919- 49-52
Lee, Helen Jackson 1908- 81-84
Lee, Henry (Walsh) 1911- 5-6R
Lee, Henry F(oster) 1913- 89-92
Lee, Herbert d'H.
See Kastle, Herbert D(avid)
Lee, Hermione 1948- CANR-15
Earlier sketch in CA 73-76
Lee, Howard
See Goulart, Ron(ald Joseph)
Lee, Irvin H. 1932- 21-22R
Lee, J(erry) W(allace) 1932- 93-96
Lee, James F. 1905(?)-1975 Obituary 61-64
Lee, James Michael 1931- CANR-13
Earlier sketch in CA 19-20R
Lee, James W. 1931- 25-28R
Lee, Janice (Jeanne) 1944- 33-36R
Lee, Joe Won 1921- 41-44R
Lee, John (Darrell) 1931- CANR-9
Earlier sketch in CA 25-28R
Lee, John A(lexander) 1891- CANR-7
Earlier sketch in CA 53-56
Lee, John Eric 1919- 33-36R
Lee, John Michael 1932- CANR-6
Earlier sketch in CA 13-14R
Lee, John R(obert) 1923-1976 57-60
Obituary 120
See also SATA 27
Lee, Judy
See Carlson, Judith Lee
Lee, Julian
See Latham, Jean Lee
Lee, Jung Young 1935- 33-36R
Lee, Kay
See Kelly, Karen
Lee, L(awrence) L(ynn) 1924- 73-76
Lee, Lamar, Jr. 1911- 17-18R
Lee, Lance 1942- CANR-13
Earlier sketch in CA 77-80
Lee, Laurel 1945(?)- Brief entry 113
Lee, Laurie 1914- 77-80
See also DLB 27
Lee, Lawrence 1903- 25-28R
See also CLC 34
Lee, (Enoch) Lawrence 1912- 15-16R
Lee, Leo Ou-fan 1939- 102
Lee, Lincoln 1922- 9-10R
Lee, Linda 1947- CANR-13
Earlier sketch in CA 77-80
Lee, Loyd Ervin 1939- 102
Lee, Lucy
See Talbot, Charlene Joy
Lee, M(ark) Owen 1930- 33-36R
Lee, Mabel Barbee 1886(?)-1978
Obituary 85-88
Lee, Malka 1905(?)-1976 Obituary 65-68
Lee, Manfred B(ennington) 1905-1971 CANR-2
Obituary 29-32R
Earlier sketch in CA 1R
See also CLC 11
Lee, Manning de Villeneuve 1894-1980
Obituary 104
See also SATA 22, 37
Lee, Maria Berl 1924- CANR-9
Earlier sketch in CA 61-64
Lee, Marian
See Clish, (Lee) Marian
Lee, Marjorie 1921- CANR-4
Earlier sketch in CA 4R
Lee, Mark W. 1923- CANR-18
Earlier sketches in CA 11-12R, CANR-3
Lee, Martin A. 1954- 121
Lee, Mary 1949- 29-32R
Lee, Mary Price 1934- CANR-24
Earlier sketches in CA 57-60, CANR-9
See also SATA 8
Lee, Maryat 25-28R
Lee, Maurice (duPont), Jr. 1925- CANR-21
Earlier sketch in CA 45-48
Lee, Meredith 1945- 93-96
Lee, Mildred
See Scudder, Mildred Lee
See also SATA 6
Lee, Molly K(yung) S(ook) C(hang) 1934- 53-56
Lee, Muna 1895-1965 Obituary 25-28R
Lee, Nata
See Frackman, Nathaline
Lee, Norma E. 1924- 65-68
Lee, Oliver M(inseem) 1927- 41-44R
Lee, Parker
See Turner, Robert H(arry)
Lee, Patricia 1941- 115
Lee, Patrick C(ornelius) 1936- 65-68
Lee, Peter H(acksoo) 1929- CANR-3
Earlier sketch in CA 9-10R
Lee, Philip J. 1932- 124
Lee, Polly Jae 1929- CANR-13
Earlier sketch in CA 29-32R
Lee, R(oy) Alton 1931- 21-22R
Lee, Raymond 1910(?)-1974 Obituary 49-52
Lee, Raymond L(awrence) 1911- 41-44R
Lee, Rebecca Smith 1894- 5-6R
Lee, Rensselaer W(right) 1898-1984
Obituary 114
Lee, Richard
See Lee, Richard B(orshay)
Lee, Richard B(orshay) 1937- CANR-20
Earlier sketch in CA 45-48
Lee, Robert 1929- CANR-3
Earlier sketch in CA 5-6R
Lee, Robert
See Fairman, Paul W.
Lee, Robert C. 1931- CANR-10
Earlier sketch in CA 25-28R
See also SATA 20
Lee, Robert E(arl) 1906- 53-56
See also AITN 1
Lee, Robert E(dwin) 1918- CANR-2
Earlier sketch in CA 45-48
Lee, Robert E. A. 1921- 11-12R
Lee, Robert Edson 1921- 25-28R
Lee, Robert Edward 1912- 111
Lee, Robert Greene 1886-19(?) CANR-3
Earlier sketch in CA 2R
Lee, Robert J. 1921- SATA-10
Lee, Roberta
See McGrath, Robert L(ee)
Lee, Ronald 1934- 37-40R
Lee, Rowena
See Bartlett, Marie (Swan)
Lee, Roy
See Hopkins, Clark
Lee, Roy Stuart 1899- CAP-1
Earlier sketch in CA 9-10
Lee, Russel V(an Arsdale) 1895-1982
Obituary 110
Lee, Ruth (Wile) 1892- CAP-2
Earlier sketch in CA 23-24
Lee, S(amuel) E(dgar) 1894- 73-76
Lee, S(idney) G(illmore) M(cKenzie)
1920-1973 CAP-2
Earlier sketch in CA 33-36
Lee, Samuel J(ames) 1906- CAP-2
Earlier sketch in CA 29-32
Lee, Sherman Emery 1918- CANR-1
Earlier sketch in CA 2R
Lee, Sophia 1750-1824 DLB-39
Lee, Stan 1922- 111
Brief entry 108
See also CLC 17
Lee, Stewart M(unro) 1925- 57-60
Lee, Susan 1944- 110
Lee, Susan Dye 1939- 85-88
Lee, Tanith 1947- 37-40R
See also SATA 8
See also CLC 46
Lee, Terence R(ichard) 1938- 29-32R
Lee, Tom(my L.) 1950- 65-68
Lee, Vernon
See Paget, Violet
See also DLB 57
See also TCLC 5
Lee, Virginia 1905(?)-1981 Obituary 105
Lee, Virginia (Yew) 1927- 9-10R
Lee, W. Storrs
See Lee, William Storrs
Lee, Walt(er William, Jr.) 1931- 61-64
Lee, Warren M. 1908- 77-80
Lee, Wayne C. 1917- CANR-17
Earlier sketches in CA 4R, CANR-2
Lee, William
See Burroughs, William S(eward)
Lee, William R(owland) 1911- CANR-19
Earlier sketches in CA 9-10R, CANR-4
Lee, William Saul 1938- 104
Lee, William Storrs 1906- CANR-1
Earlier sketch in CA 4R
Lee, Willy
See Burroughs, William S(eward)
Lee, Yur Bok 1934- 29-32R
Leech, Alfred B. 1918(?)-1974 Obituary 49-52
Leech, Bryan Jeffery 1931- 93-96
Leech, Clifford 1909-1977 CANR-4
Earlier sketch in CA 4R
Leech, Geoffrey N(eil) 1936- CANR-12
Earlier sketch in CA 29-32R
Leech, Kenneth 1939- 103
Leech, Margaret (Kernochan) 1893-1974 93-96
Obituary 49-52
Leecing, Walden A. 1932- 33-36R
Leed, Eric J. 1942- 89-92
Leed, Jacob R. 1924- CANR-7
Earlier sketch in CA 17-18R
Leed, Richard L. 1929- 15-16R
Leed, Theodore William 1927- Brief entry 106
Leedham, Charles 1926- 15-16R
Leedham, John 1912- CANR-13
Earlier sketch in CA 23-24R
Leeds, Anthony 1925- 19-20R
Leeds, Barry H. 1940- 29-32R
Leeds, Morton (Harold) 1921- 15-16R
Leeds, Patricia (Miriam) 1920(?)-1985
Obituary 114
Leedy, Jack J. 1921- 23-24R
Leedy, Loreen (Janelle) 1959- 122
See also SATA 50
Leedy, Paul D. 1908- CANR-1
Earlier sketch in CA 3R
Leefeldt, Christine 1941- 93-96
Lee-Hamilton, Eugene (Jacob) 1845-1907
Brief entry 117
See also TCLC 22

Lee Howard, Leon Alexander
  1914-1979(?) Obituary ... 104
Leek, Sybil 1923-1982 ... 102
  Obituary ... 108
Leekley, Richard N. 1912-1976 Obituary .. 69-72
Leekley, Thomas B(riggs) 1910- ... 5-6R
  See also SATA 23
Leeman, Wayne A(lvin) 1924- ... 15-16R
Leeming, David Adams 1937- ... 49-52
Leeming, Donald 1944- ... 114
Leeming, Glenda 1943- ... CANR-4
  Earlier sketch in CA 53-56
Leeming, Jo Ann
  See Leeming, Joseph
Leeming, John F(ishwick) 1900- ... CAP-1
  Earlier sketch in CA 9-10
Leeming, Joseph 1897-1968 ... 73-76
  See also SATA 26
Leeming, Owen (Alfred) 1930- ... CANR-15
  Earlier sketch in CA 65-68
Leenhouts, Keith J(ames) 1925- ... 61-64
Leepa, Allen 1919- ... 45-48
Leeper, Sarah H(ammond) 1912- ... 57-60
Leepson, Marc 1945- ... 111
Leer, Norman Robert 1937- ... 19-20R
Leerburger, Benedict A., Jr. 1932- ... 11-12R
Lees, Andrew 1940- ... 122
Lees, Carlton Brown 1924- ... 103
Lees, Charles J. 1919- ... 25-28R
Lees, Dan 1927- ... CANR-13
  Earlier sketch in CA 33-36R
Lees, Francis A(nthony) 1931- ... CANR-9
  Earlier sketch in CA 65-68
Lees, Gene 1928- ... CANR-24
  Earlier sketches in CA 23-24R, CANR-9
Lees, Hannah
  See Fetter, Elizabeth Head
Lees, Hilda Frances 1900-1983 Obituary ... 111
Lees, John D(avid) 1936- ... 53-56
Lees, John G(arfield) 1931- ... 57-60
Lees, Lynn Hollen 1941- ... 113
Lees, Ray 1931- ... CANR-8
  Earlier sketch in CA 61-64
Lees, Richard 1948- ... 108
Leese, Elizabeth 1937- ... 85-88
Lees-Milne, James 1908- ... CANR-13
  Earlier sketch in CA 9-10R
Leeson, C(harles) Roland 1926- ... 93-96
Leeson, Howard A(lfred) 1942- ... 118
Leeson, R. A.
  See Leeson, Robert (Arthur)
Leeson, Robert (Arthur) 1928- ... CANR-22
  Earlier sketch in CA 105
  See also SATA 42
Leet, Judith 1935- ... CLC-11
Le Fanu, Joseph Sheridan 1814-1873 ... DLB-21
Lefco, Helene 1922- ... 53-56
Lefcoe, George 1938- ... 21-22R
Lefcowitz, Barbara F(reedgood) 1935- ... 104
Lefebure, Marcus 1933- ... 113
Lefebure, Molly ... 57-60
Lefebvre, Henri 1901- ... CANR-11
  Earlier sketch in CA 25-28R
Lefebvre d'Argence, Rene-Yvon 1928- .. CANR-11
  Earlier sketch in CA 23-24R
Le Feuvre, Amy ?-1929 Brief entry ... 111
Lefever, D(avid) Welty 1901- ... 49-52
Lefever, Ernest W(arren) 1919- ... CANR-1
  Earlier sketch in CA 1R
LeFevre, Adam 1950- ... 81-84
Lefevre, Carl A(nthony) 1913- ... CANR-7
  Earlier sketch in CA 11-12R
Lefevre, Gui
  See Bickers, Richard Leslie Townshend
Lefevre, Helen (Elveback) ... 19-20R
LeFevre, Perry D(eyo) 1921- ... CANR-10
  Earlier sketch in CA 21-22R
LeFevre, Robert (Thomas) 1911-1986 ... CANR-9
  Obituary ... 119
  Earlier sketch in CA 57-60
Leff, Arthur A(llen) 1935-1981 Obituary ... 105
Leff, Gordon 1926- ... CANR-3
  Earlier sketch in CA 11-12R
Leff, Nathaniel H. 1938- ... 25-28R
Leffelaar, Hendrik Louis 1929- ... 5-6R
Lefferts, George 1921- ... CANR-14
  Earlier sketch in CA 69-72
Leffland, Ella 1931- ... 29-32R
  See also DLBY 84
  See also CLC 19
Leffler, Melvyn Paul 1945- ... 89-92
Lefkoe, Morty R. 1937- ... 29-32R
Lefkowitz, Annette S(arah) 1922- ... 19-20R
Lefkowitz, Bernard 1937- ... 29-32R
Lefkowitz, Joel M. 1940- ... 45-48
Lefkowitz, Mary Rosenthal 1935- ... CANR-19
  Earlier sketch in CA 103
Lefkowitz, R(obert) J. 1942- ... 45-48
Leflar, Robert A(llen) 1901- ... 29-32R
Le Fleming, Christopher (Kaye) 1908-1985
  Obituary ... 117
Lefler, Hugh Talmage 1901- ... 7-8R
Lefler, Irene (Whitney) 1917- ... CANR-1
  Earlier sketch in CA 45-48
  See also SATA 12
LeFlore, Ron(ald) 1948(?)- Brief entry ... 115
Le Fontaine, Joseph (Raymond) 1927- ... 106
le Fort, Gertrud (Petrea) von 1876-1971 ... 69-72
  Obituary ... 33-36R
  See also DLB 66
Lefranc, Pierre 1927- ... 41-44R
Lefrancois, Guy R(enald) 1940- ... CANR-18
  Earlier sketches in CA 45-48, CANR-2
Lefton, Robert Eugene 1931- ... 49-52
Leftwich, James (Adolf) 1902- ... CANR-15
  Earlier sketch in CA 41-44R
Leftwich, Joseph 1892-1983 ... 7-8R
  Obituary ... 109
Leftwich, Richard Henry 1920- ... CANR-5
  Earlier sketch in CA 13-14R
LeGalley, Donald P(aul) 1901- ... CAP-2
  Earlier sketch in CA 17-18
Le Galliene, Eva 1899- ... 45-48
  See also SATA 9
Le Gallienne, Richard 1866-1947
  Brief entry ... 107
  See also DLB 4
Legare, Hugh Swinton 1797-1843 ... DLB-3, 59
Legare, James Mathewes 1823-1859 ... DLB-3
Legaret, Jean 1913-1976 ... CAP-2
  Earlier sketch in CA 29-32
Legarreta, Dorothy 1926- ... 118
Legat, Michael (Ronald) 1923- ... 122
Legault, Albert 1938- ... 53-56
Leger, (Marie-Rene) Alexis Saint-Leger
  1887-1975 ... 13-14R
  Obituary ... 61-64
  See also CLC 11
Leger, Fernand 1881-1955 Brief entry ... 123
Leger, Saintleger
  See Leger, (Marie-Rene) Alexis
    Saint-Leger
Legeza, (Ireneus) Laszlo 1934- ... 65-68
Legg, Sarah Martha Ross Bruggeman
  ?-1982 ... SATA-40
Leggatt, Alexander (Maxwell) 1940- ... 97-100
Legge, Elisabeth Schwarzkopf
  See Schwarzkopf-Legge, Elisabeth
Legge, J(ohn) D(avid) 1921- ... CANR-2
  Earlier sketch in CA 2R
Legge, M(ary) Dominica 1905-1986
  Obituary ... 121
Legge-Bourke, (Edward Alexander) Henry
  1914-1973 ... CAP-1
  Earlier sketch in CA 9-10
Leggett, B(obby) J(oe) 1938- ... 53-56
Leggett, Eric
  See Rimel, Duane (Weldon)
Leggett, Glenn 1918- ... CANR-5
  Earlier sketch in CA 13-14R
Leggett, John (Ward) 1917- ... CANR-2
  Earlier sketch in CA 1R
Leggett, John C. 1930- ... 25-28R
Leggett, Linda 1941- ... 108
Leggett, Stephen 1949- ... 77-80
Leggitt, (Samuel) Hunter (Jr.) 1935- ... 65-68
Legh, Kathleen Louise Wood
  See Wood-Legh, Kathleen Louise
Legler, Henry M. 1897- ... 97-100
Legler, Philip 1928- ... 9-10R
Legman, G(ershon) 1917- ... CANR-15
  Earlier sketch in CA 21-22R
LeGrand
  See Henderson, LeGrand
Legrand, Lucien 1926- ... 7-8R
Legrand, Michel (Jean) 1932- Brief entry ... 114
Legters, Lyman H(oward) 1928- ... CANR-15
  Earlier sketch in CA 33-36R
Le Guin, Ursula K(roeber) 1929- ... CANR-9
  Earlier sketch in CA 21-22R
  See also SATA 4
  See also DLB 8, 52
  See also CLC 8, 13, 22, 45
  See also CLR 3
  See also AITN 1
Legum, Colin 1919- ... CANR-4
  Earlier sketch in CA 1R
  See also SATA 10
Legvold, Robert 1940- ... 85-88
Lehan, Richard (D'Aubin Daniel) 1930- ... 21-22R
Lehane, Brendan 1936- ... CANR-10
  Earlier sketch in CA 23-24R
Lehiste, Ilse 1922- ... 37-40R
Lehman, Anita Jacobs 1920- ... 23-24R
Lehman, Celia 1928- ... CANR-1
  Earlier sketch in CA 49-52
Lehman, Chester K. 1895-1980 ... CANR-1
  Earlier sketch in CA 4R
Lehman, Dale 1920- ... 11-12R
Lehman, David 1948- ... CANR-24
  Earlier sketches in CA 57-60, CANR-8
Lehman, Ernest Paul 1915- ... 85-88
  See also DLB 44
Lehman, F(rederick) K. 1924- ... 9-10R
Lehman, Godfrey ... 25-28R
Lehman, Harold D(aniel) 1921- ... 81-84
Lehman, John F(rancis), Jr. 1942- ... 15-16R
Lehman, Milton 1917-1966 ... CAP-1
  Earlier sketch in CA 13-14
Lehman, Peter 1944- ... 115
Lehman, Sam 1899- ... 49-52
Lehman, Warren (Winfred, Jr.) 1930- ... 21-22R
Lehman, Yvonne 1936- ... CANR-12
  Earlier sketch in CA 29-32R
Lehmann, A(ndrew) George 1922- ... CANR-4
  Earlier sketch in CA 4R
Lehmann, Arno 1901- ... CAP-2
  Earlier sketch in CA 29-32
Lehmann, Geoffrey (John) 1940-
  Brief entry ... 107
Lehmann, Irving J(ack) 1927- ... 53-56
Lehmann, Johannes 1929- ... CANR-14
  Earlier sketch in CA 37-40R
Lehmann, (Rudolph) John (Frederick)
  1907-1987 ... CANR-8
  Obituary ... 122
  Earlier sketch in CA 9-10R
  See also DLB 27
Lehmann, Linda 1906- ... 85-88
Lehmann, Lotte 1888-1976 ... 73-76
  Obituary ... 69-72
Lehmann, Martin Ernest 1915- ... 7-8R
Lehmann, Michael Boas 1941- ... 119
Lehmann, Paul Louis 1906- ... 85-88
Lehmann, Peter 1938- ... 57-60
Lehmann, Robert A(rthur) 1932- ... 57-60
Lehmann, Rosamond (Nina) 1901- ... CANR-8
  Earlier sketch in CA 77-80
  See also DLB 15
  See also CLC 5
Lehmann, Theo 1934- ... 41-44R
Lehmann, Wilhelm 1882-1968 ... DLB-56
Lehmann, Winfred P(hilipp) 1916- ... 33-36R
Lehmann-Haupt, Christopher (Charles
  Herbert) 1934- ... 109
Lehmann-Haupt, Hellmut 1903- ... 9-10R
Lehmberg, Paul 1946- ... 102
Lehmberg, Stanford Eugene 1931- ... CANR-2
  Earlier sketch in CA 2R
Lehn, Cornelia 1920- ... CANR-12
  Earlier sketch in CA 29-32R
  See also SATA 46
Lehner, Christine (Reine) 1952- ... 109
Lehnert, Herbert (Hermann) 1925- ... 41-44R
Lehning, James R(obert) 1947- ... 105
Lehninger, Albert L(ester) 1917-1986
  Obituary ... 119
Lehnus, Donald James 1934- ... CANR-9
  Earlier sketch in CA 57-60
Lehnus, Opal (Hull) 1920- ... 9-10R
Lehovich, Eugenie Ouroussow
  See Ouroussow, Eugenie
Lehr, Delores 1920- ... 19-20R
  See also SATA 10
Lehr, Paul E(dwin) 1918- ... 65-68
Lehrer, Adrienne (Joyce) 1937- ... 29-32R
Lehrer, James (Charles) 1934- ... 114
  Brief entry ... 109
Lehrer, Keith 1936- ... 17-18R
Lehrer, Robert N(athaniel) 1922- ... 61-64
Lehrer, Stanley 1929- ... CANR-2
  Earlier sketch in CA 5-6R
Lehrer, Thomas Andrew 1928- ... 123
Lehrer, Tom
  See Lehrer, Thomas Andrew
Lehrman, Liza
  See Williams, Liza
Lehrman, Nat 1929- ... 93-96
Lehrman, Robert L(awrence) 1921- ... CANR-7
  Earlier sketch in CA 5-6R
Lehrman, Simon Maurice 1900- ... CAP-1
  Earlier sketch in CA 9-10
Lehrmann, Chanan
  See Lehrmann, Charles C(uno)
Lehrmann, Charles C(uno) 1905-1977 ... 33-36R
Lehrmann, Cuno Chanan
  See Lehrmann, Charles C(uno)
Leib, Amos Patten 1917- ... 45-48
Leibbrand, Kurt 1914- ... 45-48
Leibel, Charlotte P(ollack) 1899- ... 33-36R
Leibenguth, Charla Ann
  See Banner, Charla Ann Leibenguth
Leibenstein, Harvey 1922- ... 103
Leiber, Fritz (Reuter, Jr.) 1910- ... CANR-2
  Earlier sketch in CA 45-48
  See also SATA 45
  See also DLB 8
  See also CLC 25
Leiber, Justin Fritz 1938- ... CANR-17
  Earlier sketch in CA 97-100
Leibert, Julius A(mos) 1888- ... CAP-2
  Earlier sketch in CA 17-18
Leibold, Jay 1957- ... 123
Leibold, (William) John 1926- ... 37-40R
Leibowitz, Herbert A. 1935- ... 25-28R
Leibowitz, Herschel W. 1925- ... CANR-8
  Earlier sketch in CA 17-18R
Leibowitz, Irving 1922-1979 ... 11-12R
  Obituary ... 85-88
Leibowitz, Rene 1913-1972 Obituary ... 37-40R
Leibson, Jacob J. 1883(?)-1971
  Obituary ... 33-36R
Leiby, Adrian C(oulter) 1904-1976 ... CAP-1
  Obituary ... 65-68
  Earlier sketch in CA 9-10
Leiby, James 1924- ... 33-36R
Leichman, Seymour 1933- ... 25-28R
  See also SATA 5
Leichter, Otto 1898(?)-1973 Obituary ... 41-44R
Leiden, Carl 1922- ... 7-8R
Leider, Emily Wortis 1937- ... 81-84
Leider, Frida 1888-1975 Obituary ... 57-60
Leigh, Carolyn 1926-1983 Obituary ... 111
Leigh, Egbert Giles, Jr. 1940- ... 57-60
Leigh, Eugene
  See Seltzer, Leon E(ugene)
Leigh, James L(eighton) 1930- ... 9-10R
Leigh, Michael 1914- ... 13-14R
Leigh, Mike 1943- ... 109
Leigh, Palmer
  See Palmer, Pamela Lynn
Leigh, Ralph Alexander 1915-1987
  Obituary ... 124
Leigh, Spencer 1945- ... 102
Leigh, Susannah 1938- ... CANR-15
  Earlier sketch in CA 81-84
Leigh, Tom 1947- ... SATA-46
Leigh Fermor, Patrick Michael
  See Fermor, Patrick Leigh
Leigh-Pemberton, John 1911- ... 108
  See also SATA 35
Leight, Robert L(ewis) 1932- ... 110
Leighton, Albert C(hester) 1919- ... 37-40R
Leighton, Alexander H(amilton) 1908- ... 41-44R
Leighton, Ann
  See Smith, Isadore Leighton Luce
Leighton, Clare (Veronica Hope) 1899- ... 108
  See also SATA 37
Leighton, David S(truan) R(obertson)
  1928- ... CANR-2
  Earlier sketch in CA 5-6R
Leighton, Frances Spatz ... 81-84
Leighton, Jack Richard 1918- ... 3R
Leighton, Lauren G(ray) 1934- ... 118
Leighton, Lee
  See Overholser, Wayne D.
Leighton, Margaret (Carver) 1896-1987 ... 9-10R
  Obituary ... 123
  See also SATA 1
Leikind, Morris C. 1906(?)-1976
  Obituary ... 65-68
Leimbach, Patricia Penton 1927- ... 57-60
Leimberg, Stephan R(obert) 1943- ... 117
Leimert, Lucille 1895(?)-1983 Obituary ... 110
Leinbach, Esther V(ashti) 1924- ... 61-64
Leinfellner, Werner (Hubertus) 1921- ... CANR-5
  Earlier sketch in CA 53-56
Leininger, Madeleine M. 1925- ... 33-36R
Leino, Eino
  See Loennbohm, Armas Eino Leopold
  See also TCLC 24
Leinsdorf, Erich 1912- ... 119
  Brief entry ... 112
Leinster, Murray
  See Jenkins, Will(iam) F(itzgerald)
  See also DLB 8
Leinwand, Gerald 1921- ... CANR-9
  Earlier sketch in CA 7-8R
Leip, Hans 1893-1983 Obituary ... 110
Leipart, Charles 1944- ... 108
Leiper, Henry Smith 1891-1975 Obituary .. 53-56
Leipold, L. Edmond 1902- ... 69-72
  See also SATA 16
Leiris, Michel (Julien) 1901- Brief entry ... 119
Leiser, Burton M. 1930- ... CANR-12
  Earlier sketch in CA 29-32R
Leiser, Erwin (Moritz) 1923- ... CANR-14
  Earlier sketch in CA 29-32R
Leiserson, Michael 1939- ... 37-40R
Leishman, J(ames) Blair 1902-1963 ... CANR-6
  Earlier sketch in CA 7-8R
Leishman, Thomas L. 1900-1978
  Obituary ... 81-84
Leisk, David Johnson 1906-1975 ... 9-10R
  Obituary ... 57-60
  See also SATA 1, 26, 30
Leiss, William 1939- ... 41-44R
Leister, Mary 1917- ... CANR-11
  Earlier sketch in CA 65-68
  See also SATA 29
Leistritz, F(redrick) Larry 1945- ... 104
Leisy, James (Franklin) 1927- ... CANR-20
  Earlier sketches in CA 11-12R, CANR-4
Leitch, Adelaide 1921- ... 101
Leitch, D(avid) B(ruce) 1940- ... 57-60
Leitch, Maurice 1933- ... 102
  See also DLB 14
Leitch, Patricia 1933- ... CANR-9
  Earlier sketch in CA 61-64
  See also SATA 11
Leitch, Vincent Barry 1944- ... 113
Leitenberg, Milton 1933- ... CANR-19
  Earlier sketch in CA 101
Leiter, Louis (Henry) 1921- ... 37-40R
Leiter, Marcia 1942- ... 116
Leiter, Robert D(avid) 1922-1976 ... CANR-4
  Obituary ... 69-72
  Earlier sketch in CA 7-8R
Leiter, Samuel Louis 1940- ... 93-96
Leiter, Sharon 1942- ... 57-60
Leites, Nathan Constantin 1912-1987
  Obituary ... 122
Leith, (James) Andrew 1931- ... CANR-20
  Earlier sketch in CA 45-48
Leith, J(ames) Clark 1937- ... 57-60
Leith, John H. 1919- ... CANR-3
  Earlier sketch in CA 5-6R
Leithauser, Brad 1953- ... 107
  See also CLC 27
Leithauser, Gladys Garner 1925- ... 15-16R
Leitmann, George 1925- ... 53-56
Leitner, Moses J. 1908- ... CAP-1
  Earlier sketch in CA 15-16
Leivick, H.
  See Halpern, Leivick
Leivick, Halper
  See Halpern, Leivick
Lekachman, Robert 1920- Brief entry ... 106
Lekai, J(ulius) Louis 1916- ... 33-36R
Lekis, Lisa 1917- ... 11-12R
Lekson, Stephen H(enry) 1950- ... 122
Leland, Charles G(odfrey) 1824-1903
  Brief entry ... 118
  See also DLB 11
Leland, Christopher Towne 1951- ... 108
Leland, Henry 1923- ... CANR-18
  Earlier sketch in CA 89-92
Leland, Jeremy (Francis David) 1932- .. CANR-13
  Earlier sketch in CA 33-36R
Leland, Timothy 1937- ... 102
Lelchuk, Alan 1938- ... CANR-1
  Earlier sketch in CA 45-48
  See also CLC 5
Lele, Uma 1941- ... 73-76
Leliaert, Richard Maurice 1940- ... 101
Lelouch, Claude (Barruck Joseph) 1937-
  Brief entry ... 113
LeLoup, Lance T. 1949- ... 110
Lelyveld, Arthur J(oseph) 1913- ... 25-28R
Lelyveld, Joseph (Salem) 1937-
  Brief entry ... 117
Lem, Stanislaw 1921- ... 105
  See also CAAS 1
  See also CLC 8, 15, 40
LeMahieu, D(an) L(loyd) 1945- ... 69-72

LeMair, H(enriette) Willebeek 1889-1966 ... SATA-29
LeMaire, H. Paul 1933- ... 113
Lemaitre, Georges E(douard) 1898-1972 .. CAP-2
Obituary ... 37-40R
Earlier sketch in CA 25-28
Lemann, Bernard 1905- ... CANR-21
Earlier sketch in CA 41-44R
Lemann, Nancy 1956- Brief entry ... 118
See also CLC 39
Lemarchand, Elizabeth (Wharton) 1906- ... CANR-10
Earlier sketch in CA 25-28R
Lemarchand, Rene 1932- ... 15-16R
LeMaster, J(immie) R(ay) 1934- ... CANR-13
Earlier sketch in CA 33-36R
LeMay, Alan 1899-1964 Obituary ... 115
Lemay, Harding 1922- ... CANR-21
Earlier sketches in CA 45-48, CANR-1
Lemay, J(oseph) A(lberic) Leo 1935- ... CANR-24
Earlier sketches in CA 19-20R, CANR-9
le May, Reginald Stuart 1885- ... 7-8R
Lembeck, Ruth (Louise) 1919- ... 105
Lembke, Janet (Nutt) 1933- ... 45-48
Lembo, Diana L.
See Spirt, Diana L(ouise)
Lembo, John M(ario) 1937- ... 29-32R
Lembourn, Hans Joergen 1923- ... 105
Lemelle, Wilbert J. 1931- ... 45-48
Lemert, Charles C(lay) 1937- ... 111
Lemert, Edwin M(cCarty) 1912- ... 93-96
Lemert, James B(olton) 1935- ... 73-76
Lemert, Jim
See Lemert, James B(olton)
Lemesurier, Peter
See Britton, Peter Ewart
Lemieux, Joanne (Hero) 1946- ... 114
Lemieux, Lucien 1934- ... 41-44R
Lemieux, Marc 1948- ... 102
Lemir, Andre
See Rimel, Duane (Weldon)
Le Mire, Eugene D(ennis) 1929- ... 41-44R
Lemire, Robert A(rthur) 1933- ... 101
Lemish, John 1921- ... 7-8R
Lemke, Horst 1922- ... 107
See also SATA 38
Lemme, Janet E(llen) 1941- ... 29-32R
Lemmon, Kenneth 1911- ... 65-68
Lemmon, Sarah McCulloh 1914- ... 21-22R
Lemoine, Ernest
See Roy, Ewell Paul
LeMon, Cal 1945- ... 53-56
Lemon, James Thomas 1929- ... 37-40R
Lemon, Lee T(homas) 1931- ... 17-18R
LeMon, Lynn
See Wert, Lynette L(emon)
LeMond, Alan 1938- ... CANR-9
Earlier sketch in CA 61-64
Lemonnier, (Antoine Louis) Camille 1844-1913 Brief entry ... 121
See also TCLC 22
Lemons, J. Stanley 1938- ... 37-40R
Lemont, George 1927- ... 65-68
Lemos, Ramon M(arcelino) 1927- ... 37-40R
Lenanton, Carola Mary Anima Oman
See Oman, Carola (Mary Anima)
Lenarcic, R(aymond) J(ames) 1942- ... 49-52
Lenard, Alexander 1910-1972 ... CANR-4
Obituary ... 89-92
Earlier sketch in CA 7-8R
See also SATA 21
Lenard, Yvone 1921- ... CANR-7
Earlier sketch in CA 53-56
Lenardon, Robert J(oseph) 1928- ... 33-36R
Lenburg, Greg 1956- ... 105
Lenburg, Jeff 1956- ... CANR-20
Earlier sketch in CA 104
Lenczowski, George 1915- ... CANR-4
Earlier sketch in CA 3R
Lendon, Kenneth Harry 1928- ... 9-10R
Lendvai, Paul 1929- ... CANR-15
Earlier sketch in CA 85-88
Lenehan, William T. 1930- ... 23-24R
L'Enfant, Julie 1944- ... 109
Lengel, Frances
See Trocchi, Alexander
Lengle, James I(rvin) 1949- ... 106
L'Engle, Madeleine 1918- ... CANR-21
Earlier sketches in CA 3R, CANR-3
See also SATA 1, 27
See also DLB 52
See also CLC 12
See also CLR 1, 14
See also AITN 2
Lengyel, Alfonz 1921- ... 116
Lengyel, Cornel Adam 1915- ... CANR-24
Earlier sketches in CA 4R, CANR-1
See also SATA 27
Lengyel, Emil 1895-1985 ... CANR-3
Obituary ... 115
Earlier sketch in CA 9-10R
See also SATA 3, 42
Lengyel, Jozsef 1896-1975 ... 85-88
Obituary ... 57-60
See also CLC 7
Lengyel, Melchior 1879(?)-1974 Obituary .. 53-56
Lenhoff, Alan (Stuart) 1951- ... 73-76
Lenier, Sue 1957- ... 120
Lenihan, John (Howard) 1941- ... 105
Lenihan, Kenneth J. 1928- ... 97-100
Lenin 1870-1924 Brief entry ... 121
Lenin, N.
See Lenin
Lenin, Nikolai
See Lenin
Lenin, V. I.
See Lenin
Lenin, Vladimir I.
See Lenin
Lenin, Vladimir Ilyich
See Lenin
Lenn, Theodore I. 1914- ... 45-48
Lennart, Isobel 1915-1971 Obituary ... 29-32R
See also DLB 44
Lenneberg, Eric H. 1921-1975 ... CANR-7
Obituary ... 57-60
Earlier sketch in CA 53-56
Lennig, Arthur 1933- ... 57-60
Lennon, Florence Becker (Tanenbaum) 1895- ... 15-16R
Lennon, Helen M.
See Goulart, Frances Sheridan
Lennon, John (Ono) 1940-1980 ... 102
See also CLC 12, 35
Lennon, Joseph Luke 1919- ... 33-36R
Lennon, Nigey 1954- ... 109
Lennon, Sister M. Isidore 1901- ... 41-44R
Lennox, Charlotte 1729(?)-1804 ... DLB-39
Lennox-Short, Alan 1913- ... 102
Lens, Sidney 1912-1986 ... CANR-17
Obituary ... 119
Earlier sketches in CA 4R, CANR-1
See also SATA 13, 48
Lensen, George Alexander 1923-1980 ... CANR-2
Earlier sketch in CA 1R
Lenski, Gerhard Emmanuel, Jr. 1924- ... 2R
Lenski, Lois 1893-1974 ... CAP-1
Obituary ... 53-56
Earlier sketch in CA 13-14
See also SATA 1, 26
See also DLB 22
Lenson, David (Rollar) 1945- ... 73-76
Lent, Blair ... CANR-11
Earlier sketch in CA 21-22R
See also SATA 2
Lent, D(ora) Geneva 1904- ... 5-6R
Lent, Henry Bolles 1901-1973 ... 73-76
See also SATA 17
Lent, John A(nthony) 1936- ... CANR-12
Earlier sketch in CA 29-32R
Lentfoehr, Therese 1902- ... 97-100
Lentilhon, Robert Ward 1925- ... 11-12R
Lentin, Antony 1941- ... 103
Lentner, Howard H(enry) 1931- ... 106
Lenton, Henry Trevor 1924- ... 103
Lentricchia, Frank (Jr.) 1940- ... CANR-19
Earlier sketch in CA 25-28R
See also CLC 34
Lentz, Donald A. 1910- ... 19-20R
Lentz, Harold H(erbert) 1910- ... 57-60
Lentz, Perry 1943- ... 23-24R
Lenz, Carolyn Ruth Swift
See Swift, Carolyn Ruth
Lenz, Frederick 1950- ... 97-100
Lenz, Siegfried 1926- ... 89-92
See also CLC 27
Lenz, William E(rnest) 1950- ... 118
Leodhas, Sorche Nic
See Alger, Leclaire (Gowans)
LeoGrande, William M(ark) 1949- ... 122
Leokum, Arkady 1916(?)- ... 116
See also SATA 45
Leon, Frances
See Swadesh, Frances Leon
Leon, Henry Cecil 1902-1976 Obituary ... 115
Leon, Pierre R. 1926- ... CANR-17
Earlier sketches in CA 45-48, CANR-1
Leonard, Calista V(erne) 1919- ... 21-22R
Leonard, Charlene M(arie) 1928- ... 33-36R
Leonard, Constance (Brink) 1923- ... 49-52
See also SATA 40, 42
Leonard, Edith Marian ... CAP-1
Earlier sketch in CA 15-16
Leonard, Elmore 1925- ... CANR-12
Earlier sketch in CA 81-84
See also CLC 28, 34
See also AITN 1
Leonard, Eugenie Andruss 1888-1980 ... CAP-2
Obituary ... 97-100
Earlier sketch in CA 17-18
Leonard, Frank G. 1935(?)-1974 Obituary ... 49-52
Leonard, George (Jay) 1946- ... 112
Leonard, George B(urr) 1923- ... CANR-20
Earlier sketches in CA 9-10R, CANR-3
Leonard, George E(dward) 1931- ... 23-24R
Leonard, George H. 1921- ... 65-68
Leonard, George K., Jr. 1915- ... 17-18R
Leonard, Gladys Osborne 1882-1968 Obituary ... 112
Leonard, Graham Douglas 1921- ... 103
Leonard, Hugh
See Byrne, John Keyes
See also DLB 13
Leonard, Irving A(lbert) 1896- ... CANR-5
Earlier sketch in CA 5-6R
Leonard, Jason
See Escott, Jonathan
Leonard, John 1939- ... CANR-12
Earlier sketch in CA 13-14R
Leonard, Jonathan N(orton) 1903-1975 ... 61-64
Obituary ... 57-60
See also SATA 36
Leonard, Joseph T. 1916- ... 9-10R
Leonard, Justin W(ilkinson) 1909- ... CAP-1
Earlier sketch in CA 19-20
Leonard, Lawrence ... 121
Leonard, Leo D(onald) 1938- ... CANR-5
Earlier sketch in CA 53-56
Leonard, Maurice 1939- ... 107
Leonard, Neil 1927- ... 4R
Leonard, Phyllis B. 1929- ... 117
Leonard, Phyllis G(rubbs) 1924- ... CANR-12
Earlier sketch in CA 69-72
Leonard, Richard Anthony 1900(?)-1979 Obituary ... 85-88
Leonard, Robert 1928-1984 Obituary ... 112
Leonard, Robert C(arl) 1928- ... 45-48
Leonard, Roger Ashley 1940- ... 25-28R
Leonard, Ruth S(haw) 1906- ... CAP-2
Earlier sketch in CA 23-24
Leonard, Thomas C(harles) 1944- ... 77-80
Leonard, Thomas M. 1937- ... 122
Leonard, Tom 1944- ... CANR-13
Earlier sketch in CA 77-80
Leonard, V. A. 1898- ... CANR-15
Earlier sketch in CA 37-40R
Leonard, William Ellery 1876-1944 ... DLB-54
Leonard, William N. 1912- ... 37-40R
Leonard, William Torbert 1918- ... 107
Leondes, Cornelius Thomas 1927- ... 17-18R
Leone, Bruno 1939- ... 110
Leone, Leonard 1914- ... 115
Leone, Mark P(aul) 1940- ... 93-96
Leone, Robert A. 1945- ... 122
Leone, Sergio 1929- ... 123
Leong, Charles L. 1911(?)-1984 Obituary ... 112
Leong, Gor Yun
See Ellison, Virginia H(owell)
Leonhard, Charles 1915- ... 5-6R
Leonhardt, Fritz 1909- ... 123
Leonhardt, Rudolf Walter 1921- ... CANR-3
Earlier sketch in CA 9-10R
Leon-Portilla, Miguel 1926- ... CANR-11
Earlier sketch in CA 21-22R
Leontiades, Milton 1932- ... 110
Leontief, Wassily 1906- ... CAP-1
Earlier sketch in CA 17-18
Leontyev, Lev Abramovich 1901-1974 Obituary ... 49-52
Leopold, A(ldo) Starker 1913-1983 Obituary ... 110
Leopold, Allison Kyle 1955- ... 112
Leopold, Carolyn Clugston 1923- ... 73-76
Leopold, Luna B(ergere) 1915- ... 49-52
Leopold, Nathan F. 1904-1971 ... CAP-1
Obituary ... 29-32R
Earlier sketch in CA 15-16
Leopold, Richard William 1912- ... CANR-2
Earlier sketch in CA 3R
Leopold, Werner F. 1896- ... 45-48
Leopold III 1901-1983 Obituary ... 110
Le Pan, Douglas (Valentine) 1914- Brief entry ... 117
Le Patourel, John Herbert 1909-1981 ... CAP-1
Obituary ... 104
Earlier sketch in CA 9-10
Lepawsky, Albert 1908- ... 45-48
Le Pelley, Guernsey 1910- ... 81-84
Lepetit, Charles
See Sala, Charles
Lepidus, Henry 1916(?)-1983 Obituary ... 110
Lepko, E.
See Kopelev, Lev (Zinovievich)
Lepley, Jean Elizabeth 1934- ... 69-72
Lepley, Paul M(ichael) 1933- ... 53-56
Le Poer Trench, (William Francis) Brinsley 1911- Brief entry ... 116
Lepore, D(ominick) J(ames) 1911- ... 45-48
Lepp, Henry 1922- ... 53-56
Leppmann, Peter K. 1931- ... 25-28R
Leppmann, Wolfgang Arthur 1922- ... 3R
Leppzer, Robert 1958- ... 105
Leprohon, Pierre 1903- ... CANR-1
Earlier sketch in CA 45-48
Le Quesne, A(lfred) L(aurence) 1928- ... 116
Le Quesne, Laurence
See Le Quesne, A(lfred) L(aurence)
Le Queux, William (Tufnell) 1864-1927 Brief entry ... 109
Lerbinger, Otto 1925- ... 23-24R
Lerche, Charles O(lsen), Jr. 1918-1966 ... 7-8R
Le Reveler
See Artaud, Antonin
le Riche, William Harding 1916- ... 107
Lerman, Eleanor 1952- ... 85-88
See also CLC 9
Lerman, Leo 1914- ... 45-48
Lerman, Paul 1926- ... 97-100
Lerman, Rhoda 1936- ... 49-52
Lerner, Aaron Bunsen 1920- ... 108
See also SATA 35
Lerner, Abba P(tachya) 1903-1982 ... CANR-2
Obituary ... 108
Earlier sketch in CA 3R
Lerner, Alan Jay 1918-1986 ... 77-80
Obituary ... 119
Lerner, Arthur 1915- ... 102
Lerner, Carol 1927- ... 102
See also SATA 33
Lerner, Daniel 1917-1980 ... CANR-6
Obituary ... 97-100
Earlier sketch in CA 1R
Lerner, Eugene Max 1928- ... 17-18R
Lerner, Gerda 1920- ... 25-28R
Lerner, Herbert J. 1933- ... 53-56
Lerner, I. Michael 1910- ... 41-44R
Lerner, Janet W(eiss) 1926- ... CANR-7
Earlier sketch in CA 57-60
Lerner, Joel J. 1936- ... 53-56
Lerner, Laurence (David) 1925- ... CANR-20
Earlier sketches in CA 7-8R, CANR-3
Lerner, Lily Gluck 1928- ... 117
Lerner, Linda ... 73-76
Lerner, Louis A. 1935-1984 Obituary ... 114
Lerner, Marguerite Rush 1924-1987 ... 13-14R
Obituary ... 122
See also SATA 11
Lerner, Maura 1953- ... 97-100
Lerner, Max(well Alan) 1902- ... 13-14R
See also DLB 29
See also AITN 1
Lerner, Michael G(ordon) 1943- ... 49-52
Lerner, Michael P(hillip) 1943- ... 45-48
Lerner, Richard E(dward) 1941- ... 73-76
Lerner, Richard M(artin) 1946- ... 93-96
Lerner, Robert E. 1940- ... CANR-8
Earlier sketch in CA 23-24R
Lerner, Sharon (Ruth) 1938-1982 ... CANR-3
Obituary ... 106
Earlier sketch in CA 7-8R
See also SATA 11, 29
Lerner, Warren 1929- ... 29-32R
Lernet-Holenia, Alexander 1898(?)-1976 Obituary ... 65-68
Lernoux, Penny (Mary) 1940- ... 77-80
Leroe, Ellen W(hitney) 1949- ... 116
Le Roi, David (de Roche) 1905- ... CANR-3
Earlier sketch in CA 11-12R
Leroi-Gourhan, Andre (Georges Leandre) 1911-1986 Obituary ... 118
Leroux, Etienne
See Leroux, S(tephanus) P(etrus) D(aniel)
Leroux, Gaston 1868-1927 Brief entry ... 108
See also TCLC 25
Leroux, S(tephanus) P(etrus) D(aniel) 1922- ... CANR-2
Earlier sketch in CA 49-52
Le Roy, Bruce Murdock 1920- Brief entry ... 106
LeRoy, Dave
See LeRoy, (Lemuel) David
LeRoy, (Lemuel) David 1920- ... 81-84
LeRoy, Douglas 1943- ... CANR-18
Earlier sketches in CA 49-52, CANR-3
LeRoy, Gaylord C. 1910- ... 37-40R
LeRoy, Gen Brief entry ... 115
See also SATA 36
Leroy, Maurice (A. L.) 1909- ... 25-28R
LeRoy, Mervyn 1900-1987 Obituary ... 123
Brief entry ... 108
Le Roy Ladurie, Emmanuel 1929- ... 113
Lerrigo, Marion Olive 1898-1968 Obituary .. 109
See also SATA 29
Lerro, Anthony Joseph 1932- ... 33-36R
Lerski, George Jan 1917- ... 73-76
Lerteth, Oban
See Fanthorpe, R(obert) Lionel
Lerude, Warren (Leslie) 1937- Brief entry ... 122
Le Sage, Laurent 1913- ... 3R
Lescoe, Francis J(oseph) 1916- ... 61-64
Lescroart, John T. 1948- ... 122
Lesesne, J(oab) Mauldin 1899- ... CAP-2
Earlier sketch in CA 33-36
LeShan, Eda J(oan) 1922- ... CANR-21
Earlier sketch in CA 15-16R
See also SATA 21
See also CLR 6
LeShan, Lawrence L(ee) 1920- ... CANR-21
Earlier sketch in CA 19-20R
Le Shana, David C(harles) 1932- ... 29-32R
Lesher, Phyllis A(senath Bayers) 1912- ... CANR-17
Earlier sketch in CA 25-28R
Lesher, Stephan 1935- ... 103
LeSieg, Theo.
See Geisel, Theodor Seuss
Lesieur, Henry R(ichard) 1946- ... 77-80
Lesikar, Raymond Vincent 1922- ... CANR-2
Earlier sketch in CA 1R
Lesikin, Joan 1947- ... 93-96
Lesins, Knuts 1909- ... 73-76
Lesko, George 1932- ... 19-20R
Lesko, Leonard Henry 1938- ... CANR-8
Earlier sketch in CA 61-64
Lesky, Albin (Hans) 1896- ... 85-88
Leslau, Wolf 1906- ... 104
Lesley, Blake
See Duckworth, Leslie Blakey
Lesley, Cole
See Cole, Leonard Leslie
Leslie, A. L.
See Lazarus, A(rnold) L(eslie)
Leslie, Aleen ... 5-6R
Leslie, Anita 1914-1985 ... 49-52
Obituary ... 117
Leslie, Cecilie 1914- ... 17-18R
Leslie, Charles M. 1923- ... 7-8R
Leslie, Clare Walker 1947- ... 108
Leslie, Conrad 1923- ... 29-32R
Leslie, Desmond 1921- ... 9-10R
Leslie, Donald Daniel 1922- ... 102
Leslie, Doris
See Fergusson Hannay, Doris
Leslie, F(rederic) Andrew 1927- ... CANR-7
Earlier sketch in CA 17-18R
Leslie, Frank 1821-1880 ... DLB-43
Leslie, Gerald R(onnell) 1925- ... 17-18R
Leslie, Jane
See Coade, Jessie
Leslie, John Andrew 1940- ... 112
Leslie, Josephine Aimee Campbell 1898-1979 ... 85-88
Leslie, Kenneth 1892-1974 ... 93-96
Obituary ... 53-56
Leslie, Michael 1952- ... 118
Leslie, O. H.
See Slesar, Henry
Leslie, Robert B.
See Wooley, John (Steven)
Leslie, Robert C(ampbell) 1917- ... 33-36R
Leslie, Robert Franklin 1911- ... 49-52
See also SATA 7
Leslie, Rochelle
See Diamond, Graham
Leslie, Roy F. 1922- ... 41-44R

Leslie, S(amuel) Clement 1898- 85-88
Leslie, San
See Crook, Bette (Jean)
Leslie, Sarah
See McGuire, Leslie Sarah
Leslie, Seymour 1890(?)-1979 Obituary ... 89-92
Leslie, (John Randolph) Shane 1885-1971
Obituary 33-36R
Leslie, Sir Shane
See Leslie, (John Randolph) Shane
Leslie, Ward S.
See Ward, Elizabeth Honor (Shedden)
Leslie, Warren III 1927- 9-10R
Leslie-Melville, Betty 1929- 81-84
Leslie-Melville, Jock
See Leslie-Melville, John D.
Leslie-Melville, John D. 1933-1984 81-84
Obituary 112
Lesly, Philip 1918- CANR-14
Earlier sketch in CA 81-84
Lesnoff-Caravaglia, Gari 41-44R
LeSourd, Catherine
See Marshall, (Sarah) Catherine (Wood)
Lesowitz, Robert I(rwin) 1939- 57-60
L'Esperance, Wilford L(ouis) III 1930- 33-36R
Lessa, William A(rmand) 1908- 61-64
Lessac, Arthur 1910- Brief entry 110
Lessard, Michel 1942- 104
Lessel, William M. 1906- CAP-2
Earlier sketch in CA 33-36
Lesser, Alexander 1902-1982 49-52
Obituary 107
Lesser, Charles H(uber) 1944- 73-76
Lesser, Eugene (Bernard) 1936- 49-52
Lesser, Gerald S(amuel) 1926- 97-100
Lesser, Margaret 1899(?)-1979 Obituary .. 93-96
See also SATA 22
Lesser, Michael 1939- 102
Lesser, Milton
See Marlowe, Stephen
Lesser, R(oger) H(arold) 1928- CANR-14
Earlier sketch in CA 73-76
Lesser, Rika 1953- 118
Lesser, Robert C. 1933- 104
Lessere, Samuel E. 1892- CAP-2
Earlier sketch in CA 21-22
Lessing, Bruno 1870-1940 .... DLB-28
Lessing, Doris (May) 1919- 9-10R
See also DLB 15
See also DLBY 85
See also CLC 1, 2, 3, 6, 10, 15, 22, 40
Lessler, Richard Sigmund 1924- 2R
Lessmann, Paul G. 1919- 17-18R
LesStrang, Jacques 1926- CANR-17
Earlier sketch in CA 65-68
Lester, Alison 1952- SATA-50
Lester, Andrew D(ouglas) 1939- 109
Lester, Anthony 1936- 37-40R
Lester, David 1942- CANR-12
Earlier sketch in CA 33-36R
Lester, Frank
See Usher, Frank (Hugh)
Lester, Gene
See Mercer, Jean
Lester, Godfrey Allen 1943- 111
Lester, Helen 1936- 115
See also SATA 46
Lester, James
See Blake, L(eslie) J(ames)
Lester, James D. 1935- CANR-15
Earlier sketch in CA 89-92
Lester, James P(inkney) 1944- 114
Lester, John
See Werner, Vivian
Lester, Julius (Bernard) 1939- CANR-23
Earlier sketches in CA 17-18R, CANR-8
See also SATA 12
See also CLR 2
Lester, Mark
See Russell, Martin
Lester, Reginald Mounstephens 1896- CAP-1
Earlier sketch in CA 9-10
Lester, Richard 1932- CLC-20
Lester, Richard A. 1908- 102
Lester, Robert C(arlton) 1933- 73-76
Lester, William 57-60
Lester-Rands, A.
See Judd, Frederick Charles
LeStourgeon, Diana E. 1927- 15-16R
L'Estrange, Anna
See Ellerbeck, Rosemary (Anne L'Estrange)
Le Sueur, Lucille 1908(?)-1977 Obituary ... 111
Le Sueur, Meridel 1900- CANR-2
Earlier sketch in CA 49-52
See also SATA 6
Lesure, Francois 1923- Brief entry 108
Lesure, Thomas B(arbour) 1923- 102
Leszlei, Marta
See Dosa, Marta Leszlei
L'Etang, Hugh J(oseph) C(harles) J(ames) 1917- 45-48
LeTarte, Clyde E(dward) 1938- 53-56
Leterman, Elmer G. 1897- 25-28R
Lethbridge, Rex
See Meyers, Roy (Lethbridge)
Lethbridge, T(homas) C(harles) 1901-1971 .... CAP-2
Earlier sketch in CA 29-32
Letiche, John M(arion) 1918- 49-52
Le Tord, Bijou 1945- 65-68
See also SATA 49
LeTourneau, Richard (Howard) 1925- .. CANR-23
Earlier sketches in CA 53-56, CANR-7
Letrusco
See Martini, Virgilio
Lettau, Reinhard 1929- CANR-9
Earlier sketch in CA 17-18R
Letterman, Edward John 1926- 29-32R
Lettis, Richard 1928- 7-8R
Lettvin, Maggie 1927- 73-76
Letwin, Shirley Robin 1924- 17-18R
Letwin, William L(ouis) 1922- 11-12R
Leuba, Clarence J(ames) 1899- 37-40R
Leubsdorf, Carl P(hilipp) 1938- 73-76
Leuchtenburg, William E(dward) 1922- CANR-12
Earlier sketch in CA 7-8R
Leukel, Francis 1922- 53-56
Leuthold, David Allen 1932- 23-24R
Leutscher, Alfred (George) 1913- 73-76
See also SATA 23
Lev, Daniel S(aul) 1933- 41-44R
Levack, Brian P(aul) 1943- 53-56
Levai, Blaise 1919- 108
See also SATA 39
Levant, Howard 1929- 89-92
Levant, Oscar 1906-1972 Obituary 37-40R
Levantrosser, William F(rederick) 1925- .. 21-22R
Levanway, Russell W(ilford) 1919-
Brief entry 107
Levarie, Siegmund 1914- 13-14R
Le Vay, David 1915- 89-92
Levell, Byrd 1911(?)-1979 Obituary 89-92
Leven, Charles L(ouis) 1928- CANR-14
Earlier sketch in CA 41-44R
Leven, Jeremy 1941- 102
Levendosky, Charles (Leonard) 1936- .. CANR-12
Earlier sketch in CA 29-32R
Levene, Malcolm 1937- 45-48
Levenkron, Steven 1941- 109
Levenson, Alan Ira 1935- 45-48
Levenson, Christopher 1934- 29-32R
Levenson, Dorothy (Perkins) 1927- 9-10R
Levenson, Edgar A. 1924- Brief entry 108
Levenson, J(acob) C(lavner) 1922- 25-28R
Levenson, Jordan 1936- CANR-23
Earlier sketches in CA 57-60, CANR-7
Levenson, Joseph Richmond 1920-1969 .... CANR-6
Earlier sketch in CA 1R
Levenson, Myron H(erbert) 1926-1974 53-56
Levenson, Sam(uel) 1911-1980 65-68
Obituary 101
See also AITN 1
Levenson, William B. 1907- CAP-2
Earlier sketch in CA 25-28
Levenstein, Aaron 1910-1986 .... CAP-1
Obituary 119
Earlier sketch in CA 19-20
Levenstein, Harvey A(llan) 1938- 106
Levenstein, Sidney 1917- 11-12R
Leventhal, Albert Rice 1907-1976 65-68
Obituary 61-64
Leventhal, Donald B(ecker) 1930- 45-48
Leventhal, Fred Marc 1938- Brief entry 109
Leventhal, Herbert 1941- 69-72
Leventhal, Lance A. 1945- 110
Leventman, Seymour 1930- CANR-1
Earlier sketch in CA 2R
Lever, Charles 1806-1872 .... DLB-21
Lever, J(ulius) W(alter) 1913-1975 ...... CAP-2
Obituary 61-64
Earlier sketch in CA 23-24
Lever, Janet 1946- 85-88
Lever, Judy 1947- 107
Lever, Katherine 1916- 17-18R
Lever, Tresham (Joseph Philip) 1900-1975 .... 13-16R
Obituary 57-60
Lever, Walter
See Lever, J(ulius) W(alter)
Leverence, William John 1946- 102
Levering, Frank (Graham) 1952- 119
Levering, Ralph (Brooks) 1947- 85-88
Leverson, Ada 1865(?)-1936(?)
Brief entry 117
See also TCLC 18
LeVert, (William) John 1946- 122
Levertov, Denise 1923- CANR-3
Earlier sketch in CA 2R
See also DLB 5
See also CLC 1, 2, 3, 5, 8, 15, 28
Levey, Martin 1913-1970 .... CANR-10
Earlier sketch in CA 15-16R
Levey, Michael (Vincent) 1927- CANR-4
Earlier sketch in CA 7-8R
Levey, Samuel 1932- CANR-2
Earlier sketch in CA 45-48
Levi, Albert William 1911- Brief entry 107
Levi, Anthony H(erbert) T(igar) 1929- .. CANR-24
Earlier sketches in CA 15-16R, CANR-9
Levi, Carlo 1902-1975 .... CANR-10
Obituary 53-56
Earlier sketch in CA 65-68
Levi, Edward H(irsch) 1911- CANR-2
Earlier sketch in CA 49-52
Levi, Hans 1935- 41-44R
Levi, Helen I(sabel) 1929- 117
Levi, Isaac 1930- 97-100
Levi, Julian (Edwin) 1900-1982 Obituary ... 106
Levi, Lennart 1930- CANR-8
Earlier sketch in CA 19-20R
Levi, Leo 1926- 114
Levi, Maurice 1945- 111
Levi, Peter (Chad Tigar) 1931- 7-8R
See also DLB 40
See also CLC 41
Levi, Primo 1919-1987 .... CANR-12
Obituary 122
Earlier sketch in CA 15-16R
See also CLC 37
Levi, Vicki Gold 1941- 101
Levi, Werner 1912- CANR-16
Earlier sketch in CA 25-28R
Levi D'Ancona, Mirella
See D'Ancona, Mirella Levi
Levien, Sonya
See Hovey, Sonya
See also DLB 44
Levin, Alexandra Lee 1912- 11-12R
Levin, Alfred 1908- 15-16R
Levin, Alvin Irving 1921- CANR-1
Earlier sketch in CA 45-48
Levin, Beatrice Schwartz 1920- CANR-18
Earlier sketches in CA 11-12R, CANR-3
Levin, Benjamin H. 49-52
Levin, Betty 1927- CANR-9
Earlier sketch in CA 65-68
See also SATA 19
Levin, Bob
See Levin, Robert A.
Levin, Dan 1914- Brief entry 108
Levin, David 1924- CANR-8
Earlier sketch in CA 7-8R
Levin, Gail 1948- 102
Levin, Gerald H(enry) 1929- CANR-15
Earlier sketch in CA 33-36R
Levin, Harold L(eonard) 1929- 93-96
Levin, Harry (Tuchman) 1912- CANR-2
Earlier sketch in CA 2R
Levin, Harry 1925- 109
Levin, Harvey J(oshua) 1924- 11-12R
Levin, Henry M(ordecai) 1938- 122
Levin, Ira 1929- CANR-17
Earlier sketch in CA 21-22R
See also CLC 3, 6
Levin, Jack 1941- CANR-19
Earlier sketches in CA 53-56, CANR-4
Levin, James (Benesch) 1940- 111
Levin, Jane Whitbread 1914- Brief entry 106
Levin, Jenifer 1955- 108
Levin, John 1944- 107
Levin, Jonathan V(ictor) 1927- 11-12R
Levin, Kenneth 1944- Brief entry 115
Levin, Kim 73-76
Levin, Kristine Cox 1944- 65-68
Levin, Marcia Obrasky 1918- 13-14R
See also SATA 13
Levin, Marlin 1921- CANR-9
Earlier sketch in CA 65-68
Levin, Meyer 1905-1981 .... CANR-15
Obituary 104
Earlier sketch in CA 11-12R
See also SATA 21, 27
See also DLB 9, 28
See also DLBY 81
See also CLC 7
See also AITN 1
Levin, Milton 1925- 25-28R
Levin, Molly Apple 61-64
Levin, N. Gordon, Jr. 1935- 25-28R
Levin, Nora 1916- 25-28R
Levin, Richard Louis 1922- 4R
Levin, Robert A. 1942- 81-84
Levin, Robert J. 1921(?)-1976 Obituary ... 65-68
Levin, Saul 1921- 13-14R
Levin, William C. 1946- 105
Levine, A(aron) L(awrence) 1925- 23-24R
Levine, Adeline 1925- 49-52
Levine, Andrew 1944- 65-68
Levine, Arthur E(lliott) 1948- 73-76
Levine, Barry B(ernard) 1941- 101
Levine, Bernard 1934- 29-32R
Levine, Betty K(rasne) 1933- 93-96
Levine, Bob
See Levine, Robert
Levine, Caroline Anne 1942- 89-92
Levine, Charles H(oward) 1939- CANR-15
Earlier sketch in CA 89-92
Levine, Daniel 1934- 15-16R
Levine, Daniel H(arris) 1942- 73-76
Levine, Daniel Urey 1935- 57-60
Levine, David 1926- 116
Brief entry 113
See also SATA 35, 43
Levine, David 1928- 17-18R
Levine, David O(scar) 1955- 124
Levine, Donald N(athan) 1931- 53-56
Levine, Edna S(imon) 85-88
See also SATA 35
Levine, Edward M(onroe) 1924- 21-22R
Levine, Edwin Burton 1920- 25-28R
Levine, Ellen 1939- CANR-22
Earlier sketch in CA 69-72
Levine, Erwin L(eon) 1926- 11-12R
Levine, Faye (Iris) 1944- CANR-3
Earlier sketch in CA 49-52
Levine, Frederick S(pencer) 1945- 120
Levine, Gary 1938- 61-64
Levine, Gene N(orman) 1930- 7-8R
Levine, George 1931- CANR-20
Earlier sketch in CA 25-28R
Levine, George R. 1929- 23-24R
Levine, Herbert S(amuel) 1928-
Brief entry 107
Levine, I(srael) E. 1923- CANR-1
Earlier sketch in CA 3R
See also SATA 12
Levine, Irving R(askin) 1922- 15-16R
Levine, Isaac Don 1892-1981 .... CANR-11
Obituary 103
Earlier sketch in CA 13-14R
Levine, Isidore N. 1909-1972 .... 41-44R
Levine, Joan Goldman 61-64
See also SATA 11
Levine, Joseph 1910- 108
See also SATA 33
Levine, Laurence William 1931- 103
Levine, Lawrence 1916- 9-10R
Levine, Lawrence W(illiam) 1933-
Brief entry 115
Levine, Lois (Elaine) L. 1931- 106
Levine, Louis 1921- Brief entry 116
Levine, Mark Lee 1943- CANR-2
Earlier sketch in CA 49-52
Levine, Marvin J. 1930- CANR-21
Earlier sketch in CA 45-48
Levine, Maurice 1902-1971 85-88
Levine, Michael 1954- 89-92
Levine, Milton I(sra) 1902- 109
Levine, Miriam 1939- 116
Levine, Mortimer 1922- 19-20R
Levine, Murray 1928- 49-52
Levine, Norman 1924- CANR-14
Earlier sketch in CA 73-76
Levine, Norman D(ion) 1912- 85-88
Levine, Philip 1928- CANR-9
Earlier sketch in CA 9-10R
See also DLB 5
See also CLC 2, 4, 5, 9, 14, 33
Levine, Rhoda 73-76
See also SATA 14
Levine, Robert 1944- 121
LeVine, Robert A(lan) 1932- CANR-13
Earlier sketch in CA 21-22R
Levine, Robert M. 1910(?)-1981 Obituary .. 108
Levine, Robert M. 1941- CANR-11
Earlier sketch in CA 21-22R
Levine, Saul V. 1938- 123
Levine, Sol 1914-1987 .... 9-10R
Obituary 124
Levine, Solomon B. 1920- 104
Levine, Stephen 1937- 45-48
Levine, Stuart (George) 1932- 19-20R
Levine, Suzanne Jill 1946- CANR-13
Earlier sketch in CA 49-52
LeVine, Victor T(heodore) 1928- 15-16R
Levine-Shneidman, Conalee 1930- 119
Levinger, George 1927- CANR-2
Earlier sketch in CA 49-52
Levins, Richard 1930- 119
Levinson, Barry (Michael) 1932-
Brief entry 112
Levinson, Boris M(ayer) 1907-1984 .... CANR-13
Obituary 112
Earlier sketch in CA 33-36R
Levinson, Charles 1920- CANR-21
Earlier sketch in CA 45-48
Levinson, Daniel Jacob 1920- 102
Levinson, Deirdre 1931- 73-76
Levinson, Harold M(yer) 1919- 21-22R
Levinson, Harry 1922- CANR-1
Earlier sketch in CA 4R
Levinson, Henry Samuel 1948- 109
Levinson, Horace C(lifford) 1895-19(?) ... CAP-1
Earlier sketch in CA 19-20
Levinson, Irene
See Zahava, Irene
Levinson, Leonard 1935- CANR-14
Earlier sketch in CA 77-80
Levinson, Leonard L. 1905(?)-1974
Obituary 45-48
Levinson, Nancy Smiler 1938- CANR-23
Earlier sketch in CA 107
See also SATA 33
Levinson, Olga May 103
Levinson, Richard (Leighton) 1934-1987 .... CANR-13
Obituary 121
Earlier sketch in CA 73-76
Levinson, Riki 121
See also SATA 49
Levinthal, Israel Herbert 1888- 13-14R
Levis, Donald J(ames) 1936- 41-44R
Levis, Larry 1946- 77-80
Levison, Andrew 1948- 93-96
Levi-Strauss, Claude 1908- CANR-6
Earlier sketch in CA 4R
See also CLC 38
Levit, Herschel 1912- 111
Levit, Martin 1918- 45-48
Levit, Rose 1922- 73-76
Levitan, Donald 1928- 104
Levitan, Max 1921- 53-56
Levitan, Sar A. 1914- CANR-3
Earlier sketch in CA 11-12R
Levitan, Tina (Nellie) 1928- 11-12R
Levitas, Gloria B(arach) 1931- CANR-21
Earlier sketch in CA 45-48
Levitas, Maurice 1917- 77-80
Levitch, Joel A. 1942- 37-40R
Levith, Murray J(ay) 1939- 81-84
Levitin, Sonia (Wolff) 1934- CANR-14
Earlier sketch in CA 29-32R
See also SATA 4
See also SAAS 2
See also CLC 17
Levitine, George 1916- 41-44R
Levitsky, David A(aron) 1942- 116
Levitt, I(srael) M(onroe) 1908- 45-48
Levitt, Jesse 1919- 45-48
Levitt, Leonard 1941- 104
Levitt, Morris J(acob) 1938- CANR-15
Earlier sketch in CA 41-44R
Levitt, Mortimer 1907- 118
Levitt, Morton 1920- 61-64
Levitt, Morton P(aul) 1936- 111
Levitt, Saul 1911-1977 81-84
Obituary 73-76
Levitzky, Sergei A. 1909-1983 Obituary 110
Levon, Fred
See Ayvazian, L. Fred
Levoy, Myron CANR-18
Earlier sketch in CA 93-96
See also SATA 37, 49

Levtzion, Nehemia 1935- ... CANR-4
Earlier sketch in CA 53-56
Levy, Alan 1932- ... CANR-21
Earlier sketches in CA 9-10R, CANR-6
Levy, Babette May 1907-1977 ... 81-84
Obituary ... 73-76
Levy, Benn W(olfe) 1900-1973 ... 101
Obituary ... 45-48
See also DLB 13
See also DLBY 81
Levy, Bernard 1907- ... 61-64
Levy, Bernard-Henri 1949- ... 122
Levy, Bill
See Levy, William V.
Levy, Charles K(ingsley) 1924- ... 120
Levy, D(arryl) A(llen) 1942-1968 ... CAP-2
Earlier sketch in CA 19-20
Levy, Darline Gay Shapiro 1939- ... 102
Levy, David 1913- ... 13-14R
Levy, David A(rthur) 1955- ... 108
Levy, David M(ordecai) 1892-1977 ... 73-76
Obituary ... 69-72
Levy, David N(eil) L(aurence) 1945- ... 119
Levy, David W(illiam) 1937- ... 41-44R
Levy, Elizabeth 1942- ... CANR-15
Earlier sketch in CA 77-80
See also SATA 31
Levy, Emanuel 1947- ... 108
Levy, Eugene Donald 1933- ... 102
Levy, Fred D(avid), Jr. 1937- ... CANR-14
Earlier sketch in CA 37-40R
Levy, G(ertrude) Rachel 1883-1966 ... 7-8R
Levy, Harold B(ernard) 1918- ... 73-76
Levy, Harry L(ouis) 1906-1981 ... 33-36R
Obituary ... 103
Levy, Herta Hess
See Kahn, Herta Hess
Levy, Howard S(eymour) 1923- ... CANR-10
Earlier sketch in CA 17-18R
Levy, Hyman 1889-1975 Obituary ... 57-60
Levy, Isaac Jack 1928- ... 41-44R
Levy, Jack Steven 1948- ... 115
Levy, Jonathan 1935- ... CANR-10
Earlier sketch in CA 61-64
Levy, Joseph V(ictor) 1928- ... 106
Levy, Julien 1906-1981 Obituary ... 103
Levy, Leonard W(illiams) 1923- ... CANR-20
Earlier sketches in CA 1R, CANR-1
Levy, Lester S(tern) 1896- ... 61-64
Levy, Lillian (Rae Berliner) 1918-1986 ... 17-18R
Obituary ... 120
Levy, Lorelei
See Schwalberg, Carol(yn Ernestine Stein)
Levy, Marion Joseph, Jr. 1918- ... 73-76
Levy, Michael E(rnst) 1929- ... CANR-2
Earlier sketch in CA 5-6R
Levy, Michael R(ichard) 1946- ... 77-80
Levy, Morton 1930- ... 77-80
Levy, Owen 1948- ... 118
Levy, Raphael 1900-1969 ... CAP-1
Earlier sketch in CA 15-16
Levy, Reynold 1945- ... 97-100
Levy, Richard C. 1947- ... 73-76
Levy, Robert 1926- ... 77-80
Levy, Robert Calmann
See Calmann-Levy, Robert
Levy, Robert J(oseph) 1931- ... 37-40R
Levy, Rosalie Marie 1889- ... CAP-1
Earlier sketch in CA 9-10
Levy, S Jay 1922- ... 108
Levy, Sidney Jay 1921- Brief entry ... 106
Levy, Stephen 1947- ... 105
Levy, Sue 1936- ... CANR-8
Earlier sketch in CA 57-60
Levy, Wilbert J. 1917- ... CANR-6
Earlier sketch in CA 57-60
Levy, William Turner 1922- ... 25-28R
Levy, William V. 1930- ... 9-10R
Levytskyj, Borys 1915- ... 65-68
Lewald, H(erald) Ernest 1922-1982 ... 23-24R
Obituary ... 114
Lewald, (Theo) Roon 1942- ... 93-96
Lewallen, John 1942- ... 69-72
Lewalski, Barbara Kiefer 1931- ... 104
Lewandowski, Dan 1947- ... 77-80
Lewandowski, Stephen 1947- ... 93-96
Lewanski, Richard C(asimir) 1918- ... 19-20R
LeWarne, Charles P(ierce) 1930- ... 57-60
Lewbin, Hyman J(oseph) 1894- ... 61-64
Lewcock, Ronald (B.) 1929- ... 121
Lewellen, T(ed) C(harles) 1940- ... CANR-6
Earlier sketch in CA 13-14R
Lewels, Francisco J(ose), Jr. 1944- ... 104
Lewenstein, Morris R. 1923- ... 13-14R
Lewes, George Henry 1817-1878 ... DLB-55
Lewes, Lettie
See Cleveland, Philip Jerome
Lewesdon, John
See Daniell, Albert Scott
Lewin, Bertram D(avid) 1896-1971 ... 65-68
Lewin, Betsy 1937- ... 104
See also SATA 32
Lewin, C. L.
See Brister, Richard
Lewin, Elsa ... 118
Lewin, Esther 1922- ... 61-64
Lewin, Hugh 1939- ... 113
See also SATA 40
See also CLR 9
Lewin, L(eonard) 1919- ... 49-52
Lewin, Leonard C(ase) 1916- ... 19-20R
Lewin, Michael Zinn 1942- ... 73-76
Lewin, Nathan 1936- ... 101
Lewin, (George) Ronald 1914-1984 ... CANR-13
Obituary ... 111
Earlier sketch in CA 25-28R
Lewin, Ted 1935- ... 69-72
See also SATA 21
Lewine, Richard 1910- ... 81-84
Lewing, Anthony Charles 1933- ... 81-84
LeWinter, Oswald 1931- ... 3R
Lewis, A(rthur) J(ames) 1914- ... 7-8R
Lewis, A(drian) S(teven) 1945- ... 116
Lewis, Adele
See Corwin, Adele Beatrice Lewis
Lewis, Albert 1885(?)-1978 Obituary ... 77-80
Lewis, Alfred Allan 1929- ... CANR-15
Earlier sketch in CA 73-76
Lewis, Alfred E. 1912-1968 Obituary ... 111
See also SATA 32
Lewis, Alfred Henry 1857-1914
Brief entry ... 120
See also DLB 25
Lewis, Alice C. 1936- ... SATA-46
Lewis, Alice Hudson 1895(?)-1971
Obituary ... 109
See also SATA 29
Lewis, Allan 1905- ... 15-16R
Lewis, Alun 1915-1944 Brief entry ... 104
See also DLB 20
See also TCLC 3
Lewis, (Joseph) Anthony 1927- ... 11-12R
See also SATA 27
Lewis, Anthony Carey 1915-1983
Obituary ... 110
Lewis, Archibald Ross 1914- ... 81-84
Lewis, Arthur H. 1906- ... CANR-1
Earlier sketch in CA 1R
Lewis, Arthur O(rcutt), Jr. 1920- ... 9-10R
Lewis, Arthur William 1905-1970 ... CAP-1
Earlier sketch in CA 9-10
Lewis, Barbara 1928-1984 Obituary ... 113
Lewis, Benjamin F. 1918- ... 45-48
Lewis, Bernard 1916- ... 118
Brief entry ... 113
Lewis, Beth Irwin 1934- ... 33-36R
Lewis, Bill
See Lewis, William
Lewis, Bill H. 1927- ... 3R
Lewis, C. Day
See Day Lewis, C(ecil)
Lewis, C(larence) I(rving) 1883-1964 ... 7-8R
Lewis, C(live) S(taples) 1898-1963 ... 81-84
See also SATA 13
See also DLB 15
See also CLC 1, 3, 6, 14, 27
See also CLR 3
Lewis, Charles
See Dixon, Roger
Lewis, Charles Bertrand 1842-1924
Brief entry ... 114
See also DLB 11
Lewis, Claude A. 1934- ... 11-12R
Lewis, Claudia (Louise) 1907- ... CANR-6
Earlier sketch in CA 7-8R
See also SATA 5
Lewis, Clay(ton Wilson) 1936- ... 101
Lewis, D. B.
See Bixby, Jerome Lewis
Lewis, D(ominic) B(evan) Wyndham 1894-1969 Obituary ... 25-28R
Lewis, Dave
See Lewis, David V.
Lewis, David 1909-1981 ... 104
Lewis, David 1922- ... 41-44R
Lewis, David 1942- ... CANR-12
Earlier sketch in CA 69-72
Lewis, David B(enjamin) 1965- ... 111
Lewis, David Kellogg 1941- ... CANR-15
Earlier sketch in CA 81-84
Lewis, David L(anier) 1927- ... 69-72
Lewis, David L(evering) 1936- ... CANR-2
Earlier sketch in CA 45-48
Lewis, David Marshall
See Cook, Michael Lewis
Lewis, David T(revor) 1920- ... 45-48
Lewis, David V. 1923- ... 7-8R
Lewis, Donald Earle 1925- ... 5-6R
Lewis, Dorothy Roe 1904-1985 Obituary ... 115
Lewis, E. M. ... 69-72
See also SATA 20
Lewis, Edith 1882(?)-1972 Obituary ... 111
Lewis, Edward W(illiams) 1899-1986
Obituary ... 118
Lewis, Edwin C(lark) 1933- ... 25-28R
Lewis, Eils Moorhouse 1919- ... 106
Lewis, Elizabeth Foreman 1892-1958 ... YABC-2
Lewis, Elliott (Bruce) 1917- ... CANR-22
Earlier sketch in CA 104
Lewis, Eugene 1940- ... CANR-4
Earlier sketch in CA 53-56
Lewis, (E.) Faye (Cashatt) 1896- ... 25-28R
Lewis, Felice (Elizabeth) Flanery 1920- ... 73-76
Lewis, Finlay 1938- ... 101
Lewis, Flora Brief entry ... 119
Lewis, Francine
See Wells, Helen
Lewis, Francis Ames
See Ames-Lewis, Francis
Lewis, Freeman 1908-1976 Obituary ... 69-72
Lewis, Fulton, Jr. 1903-1966 Obituary ... 89-92
Lewis, G(ranville) Douglass 1934- ... 106
Lewis, Gene D. 1931- ... 45-48
Lewis, Geoffrey (Lewis) 1920- ... 13-14R
Lewis, George 1941- ... 29-32R
Lewis, George 1943- ... 77-80
Lewis, George H(allam) 1943- ... 53-56
Lewis, George L. 1916- ... CANR-3
Earlier sketch in CA 45-48
Lewis, George Q. 1916- ... 21-22R
Lewis, Gordon R(ussell) 1926- ... CANR-10
Earlier sketch in CA 21-22R
Lewis, Grover Virgil 1934- ... 106
Lewis, H(ywel) D(avid) 1910- ... CANR-3
Earlier sketch in CA 9-10R
Lewis, H. Warren 1924- ... 29-32R
Lewis, Harold M. 1891(?)-1973 Obituary ... 45-48
Lewis, Harry 1917- ... 109
Lewis, Harry 1942- ... CANR-3
Earlier sketch in CA 49-52
Lewis, Helen (Lillian) Block 1913-1987 ... 110
Obituary ... 121
Lewis, Henry Clay 1825-1850 ... DLB-3
Lewis, Henry T(rickey) 1928- ... 73-76
Lewis, Herbert S(amuel) 1934- ... 17-18R
Lewis, Hilda (Winifred) 1896-1974 ... 93-96
Obituary ... 49-52
See also SATA 20
Lewis, Horacio D(elano) 1944- ... 57-60
Lewis, Howard R(obert) 1934- ... CANR-10
Earlier sketch in CA 25-28R
Lewis, Hunter 1947- ... 109
Lewis, I(oan) M(yrddin) 1930- ... CANR-21
Earlier sketches in CA 11-12R, CANR-5
Lewis, Ian
See Bensman, Joseph
Lewis, J. R.
See Lewis, (John) Roy(ston)
Lewis, Jack P(earl) 1919- ... 37-40R
Lewis, James 1935- ... 65-68
Lewis, James, Jr. 1930- ... CANR-12
Earlier sketch in CA 29-32R
Lewis, Jan (Ellen) 1949- ... 115
Lewis, Janet
See Winters, Janet Lewis
See also CLC 41
Lewis, Jean 1924- ... CANR-11
Earlier sketch in CA 23-24R
Lewis, Jerry 1926- ... 121
Brief entry ... 113
Lewis, John 1889- ... CANR-5
Earlier sketch in CA 5-6R
Lewis, John (Noel Claude) 1912- ... CANR-19
Earlier sketch in CA 102
Lewis, John D(onald) 1905-1988 ... 65-68
Obituary ... 124
Lewis, John E(arl) 1931- ... CANR-21
Earlier sketches in CA 57-60, CANR-6
Lewis, John P(rior) 1921- ... 9-10R
Lewis, John Parry 1927- ... 107
Lewis, John W(ilson) 1930- ... 11-12R
Lewis, Joseph 1889-1968 ... CAP-1
Earlier sketch in CA 13-14
Lewis, Judith Mary 1921- ... 97-100
Lewis, June E(thelyn) 1905- ... CAP-2
Earlier sketch in CA 29-32
Lewis, Lange
See Brandt, Jane Lewis
Lewis, Larry L(ynn) 1935- ... 115
Lewis, Lawrence E(dwin) 1928- ... 69-72
Lewis, Leon 1904- ... CAP-1
Earlier sketch in CA 15-16
Lewis, Leon Ray 1883- ... CAP-1
Earlier sketch in CA 9-10
Lewis, Lesley 1909- ... 102
Lewis, Linda 1927- ... 93-96
Lewis, Lionel Stanley 1933- ... CANR-5
Earlier sketch in CA 53-56
Lewis, Lucia Z.
See Anderson, Lucia (Lewis)
Lewis, Margie M. 1923- ... 101
Lewis, Marianna Olmstead 1923- ... 9-10R
Lewis, Marjorie 1929- ... 108
See also SATA 35, 40
Lewis, Martha E(llen) 1941- ... CANR-10
Earlier sketch in CA 25-28R
Lewis, Marvin 1923-1971 ... CAP-2
Earlier sketch in CA 21-22
Lewis, Mary (Christianna Milne) 1907- ... CANR-13
Earlier sketch in CA 77-80
Lewis, Mary F. W.
See Bond, Mary Fanning Wickham
Lewis, Matthew Gregory 1775-1818 ... DLB-39
Lewis, Maynah 1919- ... CANR-16
Earlier sketch in CA 25-28R
Lewis, Mervyn
See Frewer, Glyn (M.)
Lewis, Michael 1937- ... CANR-1
Earlier sketch in CA 45-48
Lewis, Michael Arthur 1890-1970 ... CANR-5
Obituary ... 29-32R
Earlier sketch in CA 7-8R
Lewis, Mildred D. 1912- ... 13-14R
Lewis, Mort(imer) R(eis) 1908- ... 105
Lewis, Naphtali 1911- ... 110
Lewis, Nigel (Stephen) 1948- ... 116
Lewis, Nolan D(on) C(arpenter) 1889- ... 7-8R
Lewis, Norman Brief entry ... 112
Lewis, Norman 1912- ... CANR-3
Earlier sketch in CA 11-12R
Lewis, Oren Ritter 1902-1983 Obituary ... 110
Lewis, Oscar 1893- ... 5-6R
Lewis, Oscar 1914-1970 ... CAP-1
Obituary ... 29-32R
Earlier sketch in CA 19-20
Lewis, Patricia Ann 1933- ... 112
Lewis, Paul
See Gerson, Noel Bertram
Lewis, Paul H. 1937- ... 73-76
Lewis, Peirce F(ee) 1927- ... 41-44R
Lewis, Peter 1922- ... 9-10R
Lewis, Peter 1938- ... CANR-21
Earlier sketch in CA 45-48
Lewis, Philip 1913- ... 3R
Lewis, R. Duffy 1908- ... CAP-1
Earlier sketch in CA 11-12
Lewis, R(ichard) W(arrington) B(aldwin) 1917- ... 102
Lewis, Ralph F(erguson) 1918-1979 ... 29-32R
Obituary ... 89-92
Lewis, Ralph L(oren) 1919- ... 117
Lewis, Richard 1700(?)-1734 ... DLB-24
Lewis, Richard 1935- ... CANR-5
Earlier sketch in CA 11-12R
See also SATA 3
Lewis, Richard S. 1916- ... CANR-9
Earlier sketch in CA 57-60
Lewis, Robert 1932- ... 97-100
Lewis, Robert T(urner) 1923- ... 85-88
Lewis, Roger
See Zarchy, Harry
Lewis, Ronello B. 1909- ... CAP-1
Earlier sketch in CA 17-18
Lewis, (Ernest Michael) Roy 1913- ... CANR-3
Earlier sketch in CA 7-8R
Lewis, (John) Roy(ston) 1933- ... 105
Lewis, Samella S(anders) 1924-
Brief entry ... 112
Lewis, Sasha Gregory 1947- ... CANR-15
Earlier sketch in CA 85-88
Lewis, Saunders 1893-1985 Obituary ... 117
Lewis, Selma S. 1921- ... 123
Lewis, Shari 1934- ... CANR-19
Earlier sketch in CA 89-92
See also SATA 30, 35
Lewis, (Harry) Sinclair 1885-1951
Brief entry ... 104
See also DLB 9
See also DLBD 1
See also TCLC 4, 13, 23
Lewis, Stephen 1947(?)-1981 Obituary ... 103
See also AITN 1
Lewis, Stephen Richmond, Jr. 1939- ... 41-44R
Lewis, Sylvan R.
See Aronson, Virginia
Lewis, T(heodore) G(yle) 1941- ... 111
Lewis, Ted
See Lewis, Edward W(illiams)
Lewis, Therese 1912(?)-1984 Obituary ... 113
Lewis, Thomas P(arker) 1936- ... 29-32R
See also SATA 27
Lewis, Thomas S(pottswood) W(ellford) 1942- ... 49-52
Lewis, Tom 1940- ... 105
Lewis, Tony 1938- ... 122
Lewis, Voltaire
See Ritchie, Edwin
Lewis, W(illiam) Arthur 1915- ... CANR-13
Brief entry ... 111
Earlier sketch in CA 19-20R
Lewis, W(alter) David 1931- ... CANR-9
Earlier sketch in CA 15-16R
Lewis, Walker 1904- ... CAP-2
Earlier sketch in CA 19-20
Lewis, Warren 1940- ... 115
Lewis, William 1946- ... 120
Lewis, William Hubert 1928- ... 13-14R
Lewis, Willie Newbury 1891-1985 ... 93-96
Obituary ... 116
Lewis, Wilmarth Sheldon 1895-1979 ... CANR-15
Obituary ... 89-92
Earlier sketch in CA 65-68
Lewis, (Percy) Wyndham 1884(?)-1957
Brief entry ... 104
See also DLB 15
See also TCLC 2, 9
Lewisohn, Ludwig 1883-1955 Brief entry ... 107
See also DLB 4, 9, 28
See also TCLC 19
Lewiston, Robert R(ueben) 1909- ... CAP-2
Earlier sketch in CA 23-24
Lewis-Williams, J(ames) David 1934- ... 117
Lewiton, Mina 1904-1970 ... CAP-2
Obituary ... 29-32R
Earlier sketch in CA 23-24
See also SATA 2
Lewitt, Shariann (N.) 1954- ... 119
Lewittes, Mordecai Henry
See Lewittes, Morton H(enry)
Lewittes, Morton H(enry) 1911- ... 25-28R
Lewontin, Richard Charles 1929- ... 104
Lewsen, Phyllis 1916- ... 109
Lewton-Brain, James 1923- ... 97-100
Lewty, Marjorie 1906- ... CAP-1
Earlier sketch in CA 9-10
Lewy, Guenter 1923- ... CANR-21
Earlier sketches in CA 11-12R, CANR-3
Lexau, Joan M. ... CANR-11
Earlier sketch in CA 19-20R
See also SATA 1, 36
Ley, Alice Chetwynd 1913- ... CANR-21
Earlier sketches in CA 15-16R, CANR-6
Ley, Arthur Gordon 1911-1968 Obituary ... 102
Ley, Charles David 1913- ... 9-10R
Ley, Ralph 1929- ... 41-44R
Ley, Robert Arthur
See Ley, Arthur Gordon
Ley, Sandra 1944- ... 57-60
Ley, Willy 1906-1969 ... 9-10R
Obituary ... 25-28R
See also SATA 2
Leyburn, Ellen Douglass 1907-1966 ... CAP-2
Earlier sketch in CA 25-28
Leyburn, James G(raham) 1902- ... 5-6R
Leyda, Jay 1910-1988 ... 108
Obituary ... 124
Leydet, Francois G(uillaume) 1927- ... 9-10R
Leydon, Rita (Floden) 1949- ... SATA-21
Leyhart, Edward
See Edwards, Elwyn Hartley
Leyland, Eric (Arthur) 1911- ... SATA-37
Leyland, Mal(colm Rex) 1944- ... 108
Leyland, Winston 1940- ... 107
Leynard, Martin
See Berger, Ivan (Bennett)
Leyner, Mark 1956- ... 110

Leypoldt, Martha M. 1918-1975 CAP-2
Earlier sketch in CA 23-24
Leys, Mary Dorothy Rose 1890- 7-8R
Leys, Simon
See Ryckmans, Pierre
Leys, Wayne A(lbert) R(isser) 1905-1973 CAP-1
Earlier sketch in CA 17-18
Leyser, Karl Joseph 1920- 112
Leyton, Elliott (Hastings) 1939- 120
Leyton, Sophie
See Walsh, Sheila
Leyva, Ricardo
See Valdes, Nelson P.
Lezama Lima, Jose 1910-1976 77-80
See also CLC 4, 10
Lezra, Grizzella Paull 1934- 61-64
Lhamon, W(illiam) T(aylor), Jr. 1945- 65-68
L'Heureux, Bill
See L'Heureux, W(illard) J(oseph)
L'Heureux, John (Clarke) 1934- CANR-23
Earlier sketch in CA 15-16R
L'Heureux, W(illard) J(oseph) 1918- 7-8R
L'Hommedieu, Dorothy Keasley
1885-1961 Obituary 109
See also SATA 29
Li, C(hing) C(hun) 1912- 19-20R
Li, Chiang-Kwang 1915- 73-76
Li, Choh-Ming 1912- 2R
Li, David H(siang-fu) 1928- 15-16R
Li, Fang Kuei 1902- 112
Li, Hui-Lin 1911- CANR-15
Earlier sketch in CA 85-88
Li, Shu Hua 1890(?)-1979 Obituary 89-92
Li, Tien-yi 1915- 37-40R
Li, Tze-chung 1927- CANR-14
Earlier sketch in CA 41-44R
Li, Yao-wen 1924- 106
Liang, Chin-tung 1893- 81-84
Liang, Yen 1908- 5-6R
Liao, David C. E. 1925- 41-44R
Lias, Edward J(ohn) 1934- 120
Lias, Godfrey 7-8R
Libbey, Elizabeth 1947- 110
Libbey, James K(eith) 1942- 81-84
Libby, Anthony 1942- 118
Libby, Bill
See Libby, William M.
Libby, Leona Marshall 1919-1986 101
Obituary 121
Libby, Violet K(elway) 1892(?)-1981
Obituary 105
Libby, Willard F(rank) 1908-1980
Obituary 113
Libby, William C(harles) 104
Libby, William M. 1927-1984 CANR-10
Obituary 113
Earlier sketch in CA 25-28R
See also SATA 5, 39
Liberace
See Liberace, Wladziu Valentino
Liberace, Wladziu Valentino
1919-1987 CANR-22
Obituary 121
Earlier sketch in CA 89-92
Liberman, Alexander 1912- Brief entry 113
Liberman, Anatoly 1937- 116
Liberman, Evsei Grigorevich 1897-1983
Obituary 109
Liberman, Judith 1929- 73-76
Liberman, M(yron) M(andell) 1921- 57-60
Liberman, Robert Paul 1937- CANR-22
Earlier sketches in CA 61-64, CANR-7
Liberman, Yevsei Grigorievich
See Liberman, Evsei Grigorevich
Libersat, Henry 1934- 53-56
Liberty, Gene 1924- CANR-8
Earlier sketch in CA 7-8R
See also SATA 3
Libin, Laurence (Elliot) 1944- 119
Liblit, Jerome 15-16R
Libman, Carol 1928- 113
Libo, Kenneth (Harold) 1937- Brief entry 109
Libo, Lester M(artin) 1923- 77-80
Librach, Jan 1904(?)-1973 Obituary 41-44R
LiBretto, Ellen V. 1947- 110
Lichello, Robert 1926- 15-16R
Lichine, Alexis 1913- 9-10R
Licht, Fred (Stephen) 1928- 101
Licht, Sidney Herman 1907-1979 Obituary 108
Lichtblau, Myron Ivor 1925- 17-18R
Lichtenberg, Elisabeth Jacoba 1913- 13-14R
Lichtenberg, Jacqueline 1942- 73-76
Lichtenberg, Philip 1926- CANR-13
Earlier sketch in CA 37-40R
Lichtenstadter, Ilse 1907- CANR-13
Earlier sketch in CA 33-36R
Lichtenstein, Aharon 1933- 19-20R
Lichtenstein, Grace 1941- CANR-22
Earlier sketches in CA 49-52, CANR-2
Lichtheim, George 1912-1973 Obituary 41-44R
Lichtman, Allan J. 1947- 124
Lichtman, Celia S(chmukler) 1932- 41-44R
Lichtman, Wendy 1946- 114
Lichty, George M(aurice) 1905-1983 104
Obituary 110
Lichty, Lawrence W(ilson) 1937- 53-56
Lichty, Ron 1950- CANR-18
Earlier sketch in CA 101
Licklider, Roy E(ilers) 1941- 33-36R
Lickona, Thomas Edward 1943- 113
Lida, Denah (Levy) 1923- 23-24R
Liddell, Brendan E(dwin) A(lexander)
1927- 29-32R
Liddell, C. H.
See Kuttner, Henry
Liddell, (John) Robert 1908- 13-14R
Liddell Hart, Basil Henry 1895-1970 103
Obituary 89-92
Lidderdale, Halliday Adair 1917- 21-22R
Liddicoat, Richard T., Jr. 1918- 45-48
Liddle, Peter Hammond 1934- CANR-18
Earlier sketch in CA 102
Liddle, William 1925- 77-80
Liddy, G(eorge) Gordon (Battle) 1930- 114
Liddy, James (Daniel Reeves) 1934- CANR-20
Earlier sketches in CA 13-14R, CANR-5
See also AITN 2
Lidman, David 1905- 69-72
Lidoff, Joan (Ilene) 1944- 115
Lidtke, Vernon L. 1930- 23-24R
Lidz, Theodore 1910- 29-32R
Lie, Jonas (Lauritz Idemil) 1833-1908(?)
Brief entry 115
See also TCLC 5
Lie, Trygve (Halvdan) 1896-1968 Obituary 113
Lieb, Fred(erick George) 1888-1980 69-72
Obituary 97-100
Lieb, Irwin Chester 1925- Brief entry 105
Lieb, Michael 1940- 65-68
Lieb, Robert C. 1944- 37-40R
Lieb, Sandra 112
Liebenow, J. Gus 1925- 45-48
Lieber, Arnold L(ou) 1937- Brief entry 113
Lieber, Joel 1937-1971 73-76
Obituary 29-32R
See also CLC 6
Lieber, Robert J(ames) 1941- CANR-12
Earlier sketch in CA 29-32R
Lieber, Stanley Martin
See Lee, Stan
Lieber, Todd M(ichael) 1944- 45-48
Lieberg, Owen S. 1896-1973 CAP-2
Earlier sketch in CA 25-28
Lieberman, Arnold (Leo) 1903- CAP-1
Earlier sketch in CA 19-20
Lieberman, Donald 1927- 111
Lieberman, E(dwin) James 1934- CANR-22
Earlier sketch in CA 45-48
Lieberman, Elias 1883- 7-8R
Lieberman, Fredric 1940- CANR-7
Earlier sketch in CA 53-56
Lieberman, Gerald F. 1923-1986 85-88
Obituary 119
Lieberman, Herbert (Henry) 1933- CANR-19
Earlier sketches in CA 11-12R, CANR-5
Lieberman, J. Ben 1914-1984 Obituary 113
Lieberman, Jethro K(oller) 1943- CANR-10
Earlier sketch in CA 21-22R
Lieberman, Joseph I. 1942- 19-20R
Lieberman, Laurence 1935- CANR-8
Earlier sketch in CA 17-18R
See also CLC 4, 36
Lieberman, Mark 1942- 29-32R
Lieberman, Mendel Halliday 1913- 106
Lieberman, Morton A(lexander) 1931- 41-44R
Lieberman, Myron 1919- CANR-8
Earlier sketch in CA 5-6R
Lieberman, Philip 1934- 93-96
Lieberman, Robert (Howard) 1941- CANR-10
Earlier sketch in CA 57-60
See also AITN 1
Lieberman, Rosalie 11-12R
Lieberman, Samuel 1911- 17-18R
Lieberman, Saul 1898-1983 Obituary 109
Liebers, Arthur 1913- CANR-3
Earlier sketch in CA 5-6R
See also SATA 12
Liebers, Ruth 1910- CAP-1
Earlier sketch in CA 9-10
Lieberson, Goddard 1911- CAP-2
Earlier sketch in CA 25-28
Lieberson, Stanley 1933- CANR-17
Earlier sketches in CA 4R, CANR-1
Lieberstein, Stanley H. 1934- 105
Liebert, Burt 1925- 33-36R
Liebert, Doris 1934- 105
Liebert, Robert M. 1942- 41-44R
Lieberthal, Milton M(orton) 1911- 117
Liebeschuetz, Hans 1893(?)-1978(?)
Obituary 85-88
Liebhafsky, Herbert Hugo 1919- 5-6R
Liebhafsky, Herman A(lfred) 1905- 53-56
Lieblich, Amia 1939- 93-96
Lieblich, Irene 1923- SATA-22
Liebling, A(bbott) J(oseph) 1904-1963 104
Obituary 89-92
See also DLB 4
Liebman, Arthur 1926- CANR-6
Earlier sketch in CA 57-60
Liebman, Charles S(eymour) 1934- 61-64
Liebman, Marcel 1930(?)-1986 Obituary 118
Liebman, Ron(ald S.) 1943- 120
Liebman, Seymour B(ertrand)
1907-1986 CANR-7
Obituary 120
Earlier sketch in CA 17-18R
Liebow, Averill A(braham) 1911-1978
Obituary 111
Liederbach, Clarence Andrew 1910- 93-96
Liederman, Judith 1927- 85-88
Liedholm, Carl (Edward) 1940- 41-44R
Liedloff, Jean 81-84
Liedtke, Kurt E(rnst) H(einrich) 1919- 19-20R
Lief, N. H.
See Bayes, Ronald H(omer)
Lief, Nina R. 1907- 118
Lief, Philip 1947- 107
Liehm, Antonin J. 1924- 102
Lieksman, Anders
See Haavikko, Paavo Juhani
Liem, Nguyen Dang 1936- 57-60
Lien, Arnold J. 1920-1979 23-24R
Obituary 122
Lienhard, John H(enry IV) 1930- CANR-4
Earlier sketch in CA 53-56
Lientz, Bennet Price 1942- CANR-8
Earlier sketch in CA 61-64
Liepolt, Werner 1944- 25-28R
Liers, Emil E(rnest) 1890-1975 107
See also SATA 37
Liesner, Hans Hubertus (Karl Kurt Otto)
1929- 104
Lietaer, Bernard A(rthur) 1942- 33-36R
Lietaert Peerbolte, Maarten 1905- 102
Lietz, Gerald S. 1918- SATA-11
Lieuwen, Edwin 1923- CANR-5
Earlier sketch in CA 2R
Liew, Kit Siong 1932- 77-80
Lifar, Serge 1905-1986 Obituary 121
Lifchitz, Boris 1895-1984 Obituary 114
Li Fei-kan 1904- 105
See also CLC 18
Liffring, Joan Louise 1929- 19-20R
Lifshin, Lyn (Diane) 1944- CANR-8
Earlier sketch in CA 33-36R
Lifson, David S. 1908- 33-36R
Lifton, Betty Jean CANR-12
Earlier sketch in CA 5-6R
See also SATA 6
Lifton, Robert Jay 1926- 17-18R
Lifton, Walter M. 1918- CANR-16
Earlier sketch in CA 33-36R
Liggero, John 1921- 25-28R
Liggett, Clayton E(ugene) 1930- 29-32R
Liggett, Hunter
See Paine, Lauran (Bosworth)
Liggett, John 1923- 57-60
Liggett, Thomas 1918- 5-6R
Light, Albert 1927- 93-96
Light, Ivan 1941- 73-76
Light, James F. 1921- CANR-1
Earlier sketch in CA 3R
Light, Martin 1927- 53-56
Light, Patricia Kahn 1939- 61-64
Lightbody, Charles Wayland 1904- 5-6R
Lightbody, Donna Mae 1920-1976
Obituary 110
Lightbown, Ronald William 1932- 104
Lightfoot, Alfred 1936- CANR-4
Earlier sketch in CA 53-56
Lightfoot, Claude M. 1910- 123
Lightfoot, David (William) 1945- 116
Lightfoot, Gordon 1938- Brief entry 109
See also CLC 26
Lightfoot, Neil R(oland) 1929- 81-84
Lightfoot, Paul 1946- 110
Lightman, Bernard 1950- 116
Lightner, A. M.
See Hopf, Alice (Martha) L(ightner)
Lightner, Alice
See Hopf, Alice (Martha) L(ightner)
Lightner, Robert P(aul) 1931- CANR-16
Earlier sketches in CA 49-52, CANR-1
Lightner, Theodore 1893(?)-1981
Obituary 113
Lightwood, Martha B. 1923- 33-36R
Lignell, Lois 1911- SATA-37
Ligomenides, Panos A. 1928- 29-32R
Ligon, Ernest M(ayfield) 1897- CAP-1
Earlier sketch in CA 9-10
Ligotti, Thomas 1953- 123
See also CLC 44
Liguori, Frank E. 1917- 21-22R
Lihani, John 1927- CANR-14
Earlier sketch in CA 37-40R
Lihn, Enrique 1929- 104
Lijphart, Arend 1936- CANR-10
Earlier sketch in CA 21-22R
Likeness, George C(lark) 1927- 17-18R
Likert, Rensis 1903- 93-96
Likhovski, Eliahou 1927- 45-48
Liles, Bruce (Lynn) 1934- 53-56
Liley, Helen Margaret Irwin 1928- 25-28R
Liliencron, (Friedrich Adolf Axel) Detlev von
1844-1909 Brief entry 117
See also TCLC 18
Lilienfeld, Abraham M(orris) 1920-1984
Obituary 113
Lilienfeld, Robert Henry 1927- CANR-1
Earlier sketch in CA 3R
Lilienthal, Alfred M(orton) 1913- 37-40R
Lilienthal, David E(li) 1899-1981 CANR-3
Obituary 102
Earlier sketch in CA 7-8R
Li Ling-Ai 77-80
Lilje, Hanns 1899-1977 Obituary 69-72
Lillard, Charles (Marion) 1944- CANR-8
Earlier sketch in CA 61-64
Lillard, Paula Polk 1931- 73-76
Lillard, Richard G(ordon) 1909- 21-22R
Lilley, Dorothy B(race) 1914- 113
Lilley, Peter 1943- 77-80
Lillibridge, G(eorge) D(onald) 1921- 13-14R
Lillich, Meredith Parsons 1932-
Brief entry 105
Lillich, Richard B(onnot) 1933- 119
Lillie, Helen 1915- 65-68
Lillie, John Adam 1884-1983 Obituary 110
Lillie, Ralph D(ougall) 1896-1979
Obituary 89-92
Lillie, William 1899- 5-6R
Lillington, Kenneth (James) 1916- CANR-3
Earlier sketch in CA 7-8R
See also SATA 39
Lilly, Charles SATA-33
Lilly, Doris 1926- CANR-11
Earlier sketch in CA 29-32R
Lilly, Eli 1885-1977 Obituary 69-72
Lilly, John C(unningham) 1915- CANR-1
Earlier sketch in CA 4R
Lilly, Ray
See Curtis, Richard (Alan)
Lim, Genny 1946- 116
Lim, John 1932- 116
See also SATA 43
Lim, Paul Stephen 1944- 108
Lima, Carolyn W(omack) 1938- 118
Lima, Frank 1939- 73-76
Lima, Robert 1935- 9-10R
Lima Barreto, Afonso Henrique de
1881-1922 Brief entry 117
See also TCLC 23
Liman, Claude Gilbert 1943- 57-60
Liman, Ellen (Fogelson) 1936- CANR-13
Earlier sketch in CA 61-64
See also SATA 22
Limb, Sue 1946- 115
Limbacher, James L. 1926- CANR-17
Earlier sketches in CA 5-6R, CANR-2
Limburg, James 1935- 112
Limburg, Peter R(ichard) 1929- 33-36R
See also SATA 13
Limentani, Uberto 1913- 19-20R
Limerick, Jeffrey W. 1948- 102
Limmer, Ruth 1927- CANR-1
Earlier sketch in CA 45-48
Limpert, John A. 1934- 77-80
Lin, Adet J(usu) 1923- 5-6R
Lin, Florence (Shen) CANR-12
Earlier sketch in CA 61-64
Lin, Frank
See Atherton, Gertrude (Franklin Horn)
Lin, Julia C(hang) 1928- 73-76
Lin, Nan 1938- 73-76
Lin, Robert K(wan-Hwan) 1937- CANR-10
Earlier sketch in CA 65-68
Lin, San-su C(hen) 1916- 19-20R
Lin, Tai-yi 1926- 11-12R
Lin, Yu-sheng 1934- 89-92
Lin, Yutang 1895-1976 CANR-2
Obituary 65-68
Earlier sketch in CA 45-48
Linamen, Harold Frederick 1921- 17-18R
Linck, Orville F. 1906- 7-8R
Lincke, Jack 1909- CAP-2
Earlier sketch in CA 29-32
Lincoff, Gary Henry 1942- 112
Lincoln, Alan Jay 1945- 123
Lincoln, Bruce 1948- CANR-22
Earlier sketch in CA 105
Lincoln, C(harles) Eric 1924- CANR-1
Earlier sketch in CA 2R
See also SATA 5
Lincoln, Edith Maas 1891-1977 Obituary 73-76
Lincoln, G(eorge) Gould 1880-1974
Obituary 113
See also AITN 1
Lincoln, George Arthur 1907-1975 3R
Obituary 57-60
Lincoln, Harry B. 1922- 25-28R
Lincoln, Henry 110
Lincoln, James Finney 1883-1965 2R
Lincoln, James H. 1916- 25-28R
Lincoln, Kenneth Robert 1943- 114
Lincoln, Murray D. 1892-1966 CAP-2
Earlier sketch in CA 19-20
Lincoln, Roger J(ohn) 1942- 117
Lincoln, Victoria 1904-1981 CAP-1
Obituary 104
Earlier sketch in CA 17-18
Lincoln, W(illiam) Bruce 1938- 85-88
Lind, Alan R(obert) 1940- CANR-12
Earlier sketch in CA 61-64
Lind, Andrew W(illiam) 1901- CANR-21
Earlier sketch in CA 45-48
Lind, Jakov
See Landwirth, Heinz
See also CAAS 4
See also CLC 1, 2, 4, 27
Lind, L(evi) R(obert) 1906- CANR-4
Earlier sketch in CA 5-6R
Lind, Millard C. 1918- 115
Lind, Sidney Edmund 1914- 37-40R
Lind, William S(turgiss) 1947- 123
Lindaman, Edward B. 1920-1982 77-80
Obituary 107
Lindars, Barnabas 1923- CANR-11
Earlier sketch in CA 25-28R
Lindauer, John Howard 1937- 23-24R
Lindauer, Lois Lyons 1933- 49-52
Lindauer, Martin 1918- 7-8R
Linday, Ryllis Elizabeth Paine 1919- 13-14R
Lindbeck, (K.) Assar (E.) 1930- 37-40R
Lindberg, Carter 1937- 112
Lindberg, David C. 1935- CANR-11
Earlier sketch in CA 69-72
Lindberg, Gary H(ans) 1941- 65-68
Lindberg, Leon N. 1932- 33-36R
Lindberg, Lucile 1913- 37-40R
Lindberg, Paul M(artin) 1905- 5-6R
Lindberg, Richard 1953- 110
Lindberg, Stanley W(illiam) 1939- 112
Lindbergh, Anne
See Sapieyevski, Anne Lindbergh
Lindbergh, Anne (Spencer) Morrow
1906- CANR-16
Earlier sketch in CA 17-18R
See also SATA 33
Lindbergh, Charles A(ugustus, Jr.)
1902-1974 CANR-16
Obituary 53-56
Earlier sketch in CA 93-96
See also SATA 33
Lindberg-Seyersted, Brita 1923- 111
Lindblom, Charles E(dward) 1917- CANR-1
Earlier sketch in CA 3R

Lindblom, (Christian) Johannes
1882-1974 Obituary ... 53-56
Lindblom, Steven (Winther) 1946- ... CANR-23
Earlier sketch in CA 106
See also SATA 39, 42
Linde, Gunnel 1924- ... CANR-11
Earlier sketch in CA 21-22R
See also SATA 5
Linde, Shirley Motter 1929- ... CANR-18
Earlier sketches in CA 45-48, CANR-1
Lindeburg, Franklin Alfred 1918- ... 5-6R
Lindeman, Jack 1924- ... 23-24R
Lindemann, Albert S(hirk) 1938- ... 49-52
Lindemann, Constance 1923- ... 61-64
Lindemann, Herbert Fred 1909- ... 29-32R
Linden, Catherine 1939- ... 110
Linden, George William 1938- ... 65-68
Linden, Kathryn (Wolaver) 1925- ... 37-40R
Linden, Sara
See Bartlett, Marie (Swan)
Lindenau, Judith Wood 1941- ... 77-80
Lindenberger, Herbert (Samuel) 1929- ... CANR-3
Earlier sketch in CA 7-8R
Lindenfeld, David Frank 1944- ... 106
Lindenfeld, Frank 1934- ... 33-36R
Lindenmeyer, Otto J. 1936- ... 77-80
Linder, Bertram L. 1931- ... CANR-2
Earlier sketch in CA 49-52
Linder, Bill R. 1937- ... 112
Linder, Darwyn E(llsworth) 1939- ... 57-60
Linder, Erich 1925(?)-1983 Obituary ... 109
Linder, Ivan H. 1894- ... CAP-1
Earlier sketch in CA 9-10
Linder, Leslie ?-1973 Obituary ... 41-44R
Linder, Mark 1944- ... 120
Linder, Norma West 1928- ... 97-100
Linder, Robert D(ean) 1933- ... 41-44R
Linder, Staffan B(urenstam) 1931-
Brief entry ... 105
Linder, Steven 1953- ... 112
Linderman, Earl W. 1931- ... 33-36R
Linderman, Gerald F(loyd) 1934- ... 85-88
Linderman, Winifred B. ... CAP-2
Earlier sketch in CA 25-28
Lindesmith, Alfred Ray 1905- ... CAP-1
Earlier sketch in CA 9-10
Lindfors, Judith Wells 1937- ... 117
Lindgren, Alvin J. 1917- ... CANR-8
Earlier sketch in CA 17-18R
Lindgren, Astrid 1907- ... 13-14R
See also SATA 2, 38
See also CLR 1
Lindgren, Barbro 1937- ... SATA-46
Lindgren, Ernest H. 1910-1973 ... CAP-1
Earlier sketch in CA 13-14
Lindgren, Henry Clay 1914- ... CANR-1
Earlier sketch in CA 2R
Lindheim, Irma Levy 1886-1978 ... 5-6R
Obituary ... 77-80
Lindholm, Richard W(adsworth) 1914- ... CANR-5
Earlier sketch in CA 4R
Lindley, Betty G(rimes) 1900(?)-1976
Obituary ... 65-68
Lindley, Denver 1904-1982 Obituary ... 106
Lindley, Erica
See Quigley, Aileen
Lindley, Ernest K(idder) 1899-1979
Obituary ... 89-92
Lindley, Hilda 1919(?)-1980 Obituary ... 102
Lindley, Kenneth (Arthur) 1928- ... CANR-10
Earlier sketch in CA 7-8R
Lindman, Maj (Jan) 1886-1972 ... SATA-43
Lindner, D. Berry
See Du Breuil, (Elizabeth) L(or)inda
Lindner, Edgar T(heodore) 1911- ... 57-60
Lindop, Audrey (Beatrice Noel) Erskine
See Erskine-Lindop, Audrey (Beatrice Noel)
Lindop, Edmund 1925- ... CANR-17
Earlier sketches in CA 5-6R, CANR-2
See also SATA 5
Lindop, Grevel 1948- ... CANR-13
Earlier sketch in CA 61-64
Lindow, John Frederick 1946- ... 113
Lindow, Wesley 1910- ... 45-48
Lindquist, Donald 1930- ... 65-68
Lindquist, E(veret) F(ranklin) 1901-1978
Obituary ... 77-80
Lindquist, Emory Kempton 1908- ... 49-52
Lindquist, Jennie Dorothea 1899-1977 ... 73-76
Obituary ... 69-72
See also SATA 13
Lindquist, John H(enry) 1931- ... 41-44R
Lindquist, Ray (Irving) 1941- ... 45-48
Lindquist, Willis 1908- ... 73-76
See also SATA 20
Lindsay, Catherine Brown 1928- ... 23-24R
Lindsay, Cressida 1934- ... 23-24R
Lindsay, David 1878-1945 Brief entry ... 113
See also TCLC 15
Lindsay, Dorothy 1902(?)-1983 Obituary ... 110
Lindsay, Frank Whiteman 1909- ... 104
Lindsay, Harold Arthur 1900- ... 7-8R
Lindsay, Howard 1889-1968 Obituary ... 25-28R
Lindsay, Ian G(ordon) 1906-1966 ... CAP-1
Earlier sketch in CA 9-10
Lindsay, Inabel (Frances) B(urns)
1900-1983 Obituary ... 110
Lindsay, J(ohn) Robert 1925- ... 13-14R
Lindsay, Jack 1900- ... CANR-11
Earlier sketch in CA 9-10R
See also DLBY 84
Lindsay, James Martin 1924- ... 29-32R
Lindsay, Jean 1926- ... CANR-11
Earlier sketch in CA 25-28R
Lindsay, Jeanne Warren 1929- ... CANR-22
Earlier sketch in CA 106
Lindsay, John Vliet 1921- ... 101
Lindsay, Kenneth C(lement) 1919- ... 112
Lindsay, Martin Alexander 1905-1981
Obituary ... 103
Lindsay, Mary
See Nonhebel, Clare
Lindsay, (John) Maurice 1918- ... CANR-22
Earlier sketches in CA 9-10R, CANR-6
Lindsay, Merrill K(irk) 1915-1985 ... 73-76
Obituary ... 115
Lindsay, Michael Francis Morris 1909- ... CANR-1
Earlier sketch in CA 45-48
Lindsay, Norman Alfred William
1879-1969 ... 102
See also CLR 8
Lindsay, Perry
See Dern, Erolie Pearl Gaddis
Lindsay, R(obert) Bruce 1900- ... CANR-8
Earlier sketch in CA 15-16R
Lindsay, Rae ... 109
Lindsay, Robert 1924- ... 77-80
Lindsay, Thomas Fanshawe 1910- ... 23-24R
Lindsay, (Nicholas) Vachel 1879-1931
Brief entry ... 114
See also SATA 40
See also DLB 54
See also TCLC 17
Lindsay, Zaidee 1923- ... 29-32R
Lindsell, Harold 1913- ... CANR-5
Earlier sketch in CA 13-14R
Lindsey, Alfred J. 1931- ... 41-44R
Lindsey, Almont 1906- ... 2R
Lindsey, David 1914- ... 11-12R
Lindsey, George R(oy) 1920- ... 65-68
Lindsey, Hal ... CANR-22
Earlier sketch in CA 104
Lindsey, Jim 1957- ... 65-68
Lindsey, (Helen) Johanna 1952- ... CANR-18
Earlier sketch in CA 73-76
Lindsey, Karen 1944- ... 73-76
Lindsey, Robert (Hughes) 1935- ... CANR-22
Earlier sketch in CA 97-100
Lindskoog, Kathryn (Ann) 1934- ... CANR-10
Earlier sketch in CA 65-68
Lindsley, Mary F(rances) ... CANR-9
Earlier sketch in CA 61-64
Lindstrom, Carl E(inar) 1896-1969 ... 3R
Obituary ... 103
Lindstrom, Naomi (Eva) 1950- ... 112
Lindstrom, Thais (Stakhy) 1917- ... 23-24R
Lindt, Gillian 1932- ... 107
Line, Les 1935- ... 73-76
See also SATA 27
Line, Maurice Bernard 1928- ... 107
Lineaweaver, Thomas H(astings) III
1926- ... 73-76
Lineback, Richard H(arold) 1936- ... 29-32R
Linebarger, J(ames) M(orris) 1934- ... CANR-2
Earlier sketch in CA 49-52
Linebarger, Paul M(yron) A(nthony)
1913-1966 ... CANR-6
Earlier sketch in CA 5-6R
Lineberry, John H(arvey) 1926- ... 4R
Lineberry, Robert L(eon) 1942- ... CANR-18
Earlier sketch in CA 73-76
Linecar, Howard (Walter Arthur) 1912- ... 110
Linedecker, Clifford L. 1931- ... 73-76
Linen, James A., III 1912-1988 Obituary ... 124
Linenthal, Edward Tabor 1947- ... 112
Linet, Beverly 1929- ... CANR-22
Earlier sketch in CA 89-92
Linett, Deena 1938- ... 113
Linfield, Esther ... 112
See also SATA 40
Ling, Arthur (William) 1901- ... 7-8R
Ling, Cyril Curtis 1936- ... 17-18R
Ling, Dwight L(eroy) 1923- ... CANR-11
Earlier sketch in CA 21-22R
Ling, H(sien) C(hang) 1910- ... 57-60
Ling, Hung-hsun 1894(?)-1981 Obituary ... 105
Ling, Jack (Chieh Sheng) 1930- ... 25-28R
Ling, Mona ... 9-10R
Ling, Roger (John) 1942- ... CANR-19
Earlier sketch in CA 103
Ling, Trevor 1920- ... CANR-11
Earlier sketch in CA 21-22R
Lingard, Joan 1932- ... CANR-18
Earlier sketch in CA 41-44R
See also SATA 8
See also SAAS 5
Lingeman, Richard R(oberts) 1931- ... CANR-11
Earlier sketch in CA 17-18R
Lingenfelter, Richard Emery 1934- ... CANR-5
Earlier sketch in CA 15-16R
Lingenfelter, Sherwood Galen 1941- ... 53-56
Lingis, Alphonso Frank 1933- ... CANR-15
Earlier sketch in CA 37-40R
Lings, Martin 1909- ... 57-60
Linington, Elizabeth 1921- ... CANR-20
Earlier sketches in CA 2R, CANR-1
Link, Arthur S(tanley) 1920- ... CANR-3
Earlier sketch in CA 1R
See also DLB 17
Link, Edwin A(lbert) 1904-1981 Obituary ... 108
Link, Eugene P(erry) 1907- ... 37-40R
Link, Frederick M(artin) 1930- ... CANR-4
Earlier sketch in CA 53-56
Link, (S.) Gordden 1907-1986 ... 120
Link, John R(einhardt) 1907- ... 19-20R
Link, Mark J(oseph) 1924- ... CANR-20
Earlier sketches in CA 15-16R, CANR-5
Link, Martin 1934- ... 106
See also SATA 28
Link, (Eugene) Perry (Jr.) 1944- ... 105
Link, Robert G(rant) 1918-1984 Obituary ... 113
Link, Ruth 1923- ... 29-32R
Link, Theodore Carl 1905(?)-1974
Obituary ... 104
Link, William 1933- ... CANR-13
Earlier sketch in CA 73-76
Linke, Maria (Zeitner) 1908- ... 65-68
Linke-Poot
See Doeblin, Alfred
Linker, Robert White 1905- ... 104
Linklater, Eric (Robert Russell)
1899-1974 ... CAP-2
Obituary ... 53-56
Earlier sketch in CA 13-14
Linkletter, Art(hur Gordan) 1912- ... CANR-4
Earlier sketch in CA 9-10R
Linkletter, John A(ustin) 1923-1985 ... 69-72
Obituary ... 115
Links, J(oseph) G(luckenstein) 1904- ... 81-84
Linkugel, Wil(mer) A(lbert) 1929- ... CANR-13
Earlier sketch in CA 17-18R
Linley, John (William) 1916- ... 41-44R
Linn, Bill
See Linn, William J(oseph)
Linn, Charles F. 1930- ... 85-88
Linn, Edward Allen 1922- ... 97-100
Linn, John Blair 1777-1804 ... DLB-37
Linn, John Gaywood 1917- ... 25-28R
Linn, William J(oseph) 1943- ... 117
Linnell, Charles Lawrence Scruton 1915- ... 7-8R
Linnell, Robert H(artley) 1922- ... 53-56
Linneman, Robert E. 1928- ... 29-32R
Linneman, William R(ichard) 1926-
Brief entry ... 118
Linner, Birgitta 1920- ... CANR-10
Earlier sketch in CA 23-24R
Linney, Romulus 1930- ... 2R
Linowes, David F(rancis) 1917- ... 49-52
Lins, Osman 1924- Brief entry ... 105
Linsenmeyer, Helen Walker 1906- ... CANR-1
Earlier sketch in CA 45-48
Linsky, Leonard 1922- Brief entry ... 112
Linsley, William A(llan) 1933- ... 25-28R
Linstone, Harold A(drian) 1924- ... 112
Linstrum, Derek 1925- ... 107
Linthicum, Robert Charles 1936- ... 65-68
Lintner, John (Virgil) 1916-1983 ... 104
Obituary ... 110
Linton, Barbara Leslie 1945- ... 33-36R
Linton, Calvin D(arlington) 1914- ... CANR-5
Earlier sketch in CA 15-16R
Linton, David (Hector) 1923- ... 11-12R
Linton, Eliza Lynn 1822-1898 ... DLB-18
Linton, James M(ichael) 1946- ... 123
Linton, Robert R. 1909(?)-1979 Obituary ... 89-92
Linton, Ron(ald) M. 1929- ... 41-44R
Linton, William James 1812-1897 ... DLB-32
Lintott, Andrew (William) 1936- ... 116
Lintz, Harry McCormick ... 3R
Linzee, David (Augustine Anthony) 1952- ... 73-76
Linzey, Donald Wayne 1939- ... CANR-13
Earlier sketch in CA 61-64
Lionberger, Herbert F(rederick) 1912- ... 73-76
Lionel, Robert
See Fanthorpe, R(obert) Lionel
Lionni, Leo 1910- ... 53-56
See also SATA 8
See also DLB 61
See also CLR 7
Lipe, Dewey 1933- ... 85-88
Lipetz, Ben-Ami 1927- ... 33-36R
Lipez, Richard 1938- ... CANR-18
Earlier sketch in CA 101
Lipham, James Maurice 1927- ... 81-84
Lipinsky de Orlov, Lino S. 1908- ... SATA-22
Lipkin, Gladys B(albus) 1925- ... CANR-2
Earlier sketch in CA 49-52
Lipkin, Mack, Jr. 1943- ... CANR-18
Earlier sketch in CA 101
Lipkina, Lawrence (Irwin) 1934- ... 41-44R
Lipkind, William 1904-1974 ... 101
Obituary ... 53-56
See also SATA 15
Lipman, Aaron 1925- ... 21-22R
Lipman, Burton E(llis) 1931- ... 109
Lipman, David 1931- ... 23-24R
See also SATA 21
Lipman, Eugene Jay 1919- ... 9-10R
Lipman, Ira A 1940- ... 65-68
Lipman, Jean ... CANR-10
Earlier sketch in CA 21-22R
Lipman, Marilyn 1938- ... 69-72
Lipman, Matthew 1923- ... CANR-13
Earlier sketch in CA 33-36R
See also SATA 14
Lipman, Samuel 1934- ... 77-80
Lipman, Vivian David 1921- ... 9-10R
Lipmann, Fritz Albert 1899-1986 Obituary ... 119
Lipp, Frederick (John) 1916- ... 106
Lipp, Martin R(obert) 1940- ... 106
Lipp, Solomon 1913- Brief entry ... 111
Lippard, Lucy R. 1937- ... CANR-20
Earlier sketch in CA 25-28R
Lippert, Clarissa Start 1917- ... 77-80
Lipphard, William B(enjamin) 1886-1971 ... CAP-2
Earlier sketch in CA 29-32
Lippincott, Bertram 1898(?)-1985
Obituary ... 115
See also SATA 42
Lippincott, David (McCord) 1925- ... CANR-9
Earlier sketch in CA 61-64
Lippincott, Joseph W(harton) 1887-1976 ... 73-76
Obituary ... 69-72
See also SATA 17
Lippincott, Sara Jane Clarke 1823-1904
Brief entry ... 120
See also DLB 43
Lippincott, Sarah Lee 1920- ... 17-18R
See also SATA 22
Lippitt, Gordon L(eslie) 1920- ... CANR-12
Earlier sketch in CA 29-32R
Lippitt, Ronald O. 1914- ... 37-40R
Lippman, Edward A. 1920- ... 122
Lippman, Leopold 1919- ... 49-52
Lippman, Peter J. 1936- ... 108
See also SATA 31
Lippman, Theo, Jr. 1929- ... 33-36R
Lippmann, Walter 1889-1974 ... CANR-6
Obituary ... 53-56
Earlier sketch in CA 9-10R
See also DLB 29
See also AITN 1
Lipschutz, Ilse Hempel 1923- ... 41-44R
Lipscomb, Commander F. W.
See Lipscomb, F(rank) W(oodgate)
Lipscomb, David M(ilton) 1935- ... CANR-1
Earlier sketch in CA 49-52
Lipscomb, Elizabeth J(ohnston) 1938- ... 115
Lipscomb, F(rank) W(oodgate) 1903- ... 29-32R
Lipscomb, James 1926- ... 85-88
Lipsen, Charles B. 1925- ... 73-76
Lipset, Seymour Martin 1922- ... CANR-1
Earlier sketch in CA 3R
Lipsett, Laurence Cline 1915- ... 11-12R
Lipsey, Richard A(llan) 1930- ... CANR-23
Earlier sketch in CA 107
Lipsey, Richard G(eorge) 1928- ... CANR-17
Earlier sketch in CA 97-100
Lipsey, Robert E(dward) 1926- ... CANR-18
Earlier sketches in CA 7-8R, CANR-2
Lipsitz, George R(aymond) 1947- ... 113
Lipsitz, Lou 1938- ... CANR-18
Earlier sketch in CA 101
Lipski, Alexander 1919- ... 49-52
Lipsky, David Bruce 1939- ... 103
Lipsky, Eleazar 1911- Brief entry ... 115
Lipsky, Michael 1940- ... 61-64
Lipsky, Mortimer 1915- ... 73-76
Lipson, Charles 1948- ... 123
Lipson, Goldie 1905- ... 33-36R
Lipson, Harry A(aron, Jr.) 1919- ... 61-64
Lipson, Leon Samuel 1921- ... 104
Lipson, Leslie (Michel) 1912- ... 106
Lipson, Milton 1913- ... 65-68
Lipson, Shelley 1948- ... 119
Lipstadt, Deborah E(sther) 1947- ... 111
Lipstein, Kurt 1909- ... 117
Lipstreu, Otis 1919-1970 ... CAP-1
Earlier sketch in CA 15-16
Lipsyte, Marjorie (Rubin) 1932- ... 105
Lipsyte, Robert (Michael) 1938- ... CANR-8
Earlier sketch in CA 19-20R
See also SATA 5
See also CLC 21
Lipton, David R(obert) 1947- ... 97-100
Lipton, Dean 1919- ... 29-32R
Lipton, Lawrence 1898-1975 ... 93-96
Obituary ... 57-60
See also DLB 16
Lipton, Lenny 1940- ... 101
Liptzin, Sol(omon) 1901- ... 11-12R
Liroff, Richard A(lan) 1948- ... CANR-11
Earlier sketch in CA 69-72
Lisagor, Peter 1915-1976 Obituary ... 69-72
Lisca, Peter 1925- ... 37-40R
Lischer, Richard 1943- ... 101
Lisci, Leonardo Ginori
See Ginori Lisci, Leonardo
Lish, Gordon (Jay) 1934- ... 117
Brief entry ... 113
See also CLC 45
Lishka, Gerald R 1949- ... 89-92
Lisi, Albert 1929- ... 25-28R
Lisio, Donald J(ohn) 1934- ... 124
Lisk, Jill 1938- ... 25-28R
Liska, Edward G. 1914(?)-1984 Obituary ... 113
Liska, George 1922- ... 104
Lisker, Sonia O. 1933- ... CANR-2
Earlier sketch in CA 49-52
See also SATA 44
Lisle, Janet Taylor ... SATA-47
Lisle, Seward D.
See Ellis, Edward S(ylvester)
Lison-Tolosana, Carmelo 1929- ... CANR-13
Earlier sketch in CA 21-22R
Lisowski, Gabriel 1946- ... 97-100
See also SATA 31, 47
Lispector, Clarice 1925-1977 Obituary ... 116
See also CLC 43
Liss, Howard 1922- ... CANR-16
Earlier sketch in CA 25-28R
See also SATA 4
Liss, Jerome 1938- ... 53-56
Liss, Peggy K(orn) 1927- ... 41-44R
Liss, Robert E. 1945(?)-1979 Obituary ... 115
Liss, Sheldon B. 1936- ... 23-24R
Lissak, Moshe (Avraham) 1928- ... 97-100
Lissim, Simon 1900-1981 Obituary ... 109
See also SATA 28
Lissitzyn, Oliver J(ames) 1912- ... 45-48
Lissner, Will 1908- ... 101
List, Ilka Katherine 1935- ... 37-40R
See also SATA 6
List, Jacob Samuel 1896-1967 ... CAP-1
Earlier sketch in CA 19-20
List, Robert Stuart 1903-1983 Obituary ... 109
Lister, Hal
See Lister, Harold
Lister, Harold 1922- ... 73-76
Lister, Laurier L. 1907-1986 Obituary ... 120
Lister, R(ichard) P(ercival) 1914- ... CANR-5
Earlier sketch in CA 9-10R
Lister, Raymond (George) 1919- ... CANR-24
Earlier sketches in CA 13-14R, CANR-8
Liston, Jack
See Maloney, Ralph Liston

Liston, Mary Dawn 1936- 53-56
Liston, Robert A. 1927- CANR-12
Earlier sketch in CA 19-20R
See also SATA 5
Listowel, Judith (de Marffy-Mantuano)
1904- 15-16R
Litchfield, Ada B(assett) 1916- CANR-10
Earlier sketch in CA 25-28R
See also SATA 5
Litchfield, Harry R(obert) 1898-1973
Obituary 41-44R
Litchfield, Robert O(rbin) ?-1977
Obituary 73-76
Lite, Jams
See Schneck, Stephen
Lithwick, Norman Harvey 1938- 61-64
Litoff, Judy Barrett 1944- 85-88
Litowinsky, Olga (Jean) 1936- 81-84
See also SATA 26
Litsey, Sarah 5-6R
Littauer, Florence 1928- 115
Littauer, Raphael (Max) 1925- Brief entry ... 109
Littell, Franklin H(amlin) 1917- Brief entry .. 112
Littell, Robert 1896-1963 Obituary 93-96
Littell, Robert 1935(?)- 112
Brief entry 109
See also CLC 42
Litterer, Joseph A(ugust) 1926- CANR-3
Earlier sketch in CA 9-10R
Littke, Lael J. 1929- CANR-15
Earlier sketch in CA 85-88
Little, A. Edward
See Klein, Aaron E.
Little, Alan M(acNaughton) G(ordon)
1901-1987 Obituary 124
Little, Bryan (Desmond Greenway)
1913- CANR-22
Earlier sketch in CA 104
Little, David 1933- 29-32R
Little, Elbert L(uther), Jr. 1907- 57-60
Little, Elbert Payson 1912(?)-1983
Obituary 110
Little, Geraldine C(linton) 109
Little, Ian M(alcolm) D(avid) 1918- CANR-15
Earlier sketch in CA 21-22R
Little, Jack
See Little, John D(utton)
Little, Jane Sneddon 1942- Brief entry 113
Little, (Flora) Jean 1932- 23-24R
See also SATA 2
See also CLR 4
Little, John D(utton) 1894- 65-68
Little, Kenneth
See Scotland, James
Little, Kenneth L(indsay) 1908- 17-18R
Little, Lawrence Calvin 1897-1976 ...... CANR-3
Earlier sketch in CA 2R
Little, Lessie Jones 1906-1986 101
Obituary 121
See also SATA 50
Little, Lester Knox 1935- 103
Little, Loyd (Harry), Jr. 1940- 81-84
Little, Malcolm 1925-1965 Obituary 111
Little, Mary E. 1912- 105
See also SATA 28
Little, Nina Fletcher 1903- Brief entry 106
Little, Paul E. 1928-1975 .... CAP-2
Earlier sketch in CA 21-22
Little, Paul H(ugo) 1915-1987 .... CANR-13
Obituary 122
Earlier sketch in CA 17-18R
Little, Paula
See Little, Paul H(ugo)
Little, Pippa 1958- 123
Little, Ray 1918(?)-1980 Obituary 102
Little, Richard 1944- 114
Little, Roger W(illiam) 1922- 29-32R
Little, Royal 1896- 106
Little, S. George 1903-1974 Obituary 49-52
Little, Sara (Pamela) 1919- 116
Little, Stuart W. 1921- CANR-1
Earlier sketch in CA 45-48
Little, Thomas Russell 1911- 13-14R
Little, Tom
See Little, Thomas Russell
Little, William Alfred
See Little, Wm. A.
Little, Wm. A. 1929- 57-60
Littleboy, Sheila M.
See Ary, Sheila M(ary Littleboy)
Littledale, Freya (Lota) CANR-10
Earlier sketch in CA 23-24R
See also SATA 2
Littledale, Harold (Aylmer) 1927- 5-6R
Littlefair, Duncan (Elliot) 1912- 45-48
Littlefield, David Joseph 1928- 41-44R
Littlefield, James Edward 1932- 53-56
Littlejohn, (Cameron) Bruce 1913- 61-64
Littlejohn, David 1937- CANR-14
Earlier sketch in CA 41-44R
Littleton, C(ovington) Scott 1933- 23-24R
Littleton, Harvey K(line) 1922- 53-56
Littlewit, Humphrey, Gent.
See Lovecraft, H(oward) P(hillips)
Littlewood, Joan (Maud) 1914- Brief entry .. 116
See also DLB 13
Littlewood, Robert Percy 1910- 7-8R
Littlewood, Thomas B. 1928- 29-32R
Littman, Robert J. 1943- 81-84
Litto, Fredric M. 1939- 25-28R
Litto, Gertrude 1929- 69-72
Litvag, Irving 1928- 57-60
Litvak, Isaiah A(llan) 1936- 15-16R
Litvinoff, Barnet 1917- 17-18R
Litvinoff, Emanuel 1915- Brief entry 117
Litvinoff, Saul 1925- 41-44R
Litvinov, Ivy 1890(?)-1977 Obituary 69-72
Litvinov, Pavel 1940- 89-92
Litwack, Leon F(rank) 1929- CANR-1
Earlier sketch in CA 4R
Litwak, Eugene 1925- Brief entry 114
Litwak, Leo (E.) 1924- CANR-22
Earlier sketch in CA 7-8R
Litwos
See Sienkiewicz, Henryk (Adam Aleksander Pius)
Litz, A(rthur) Walton (Jr.) 1929- 33-36R
Litzel, Otto 1901- 57-60
Litzinger, Boyd (A., Jr.) 1929- CANR-20
Earlier sketches in CA 13-14R, CANR-5
Liu, Aimee 1953- 89-92
Liu, Alan P(ing-) L(in) 1937- 61-64
Liu, Da 1910- 85-88
Liu, James J(o) Y(u) 1926- CANR-7
Earlier sketch in CA 7-8R
Liu, James T(zu) C(hien) 1919- 21-22R
Liu, Jung-Chao 1929- 29-32R
Liu, Leo Yueh-yun 1940- 41-44R
Liu, Sarah 1943- 115
Liu, Sydney (Chieh) 1920- 103
Liu, Tzu-chien
See Liu, James T(zu) C(hien)
Liu, William T(homas) 1930- CANR-13
Earlier sketch in CA 23-24R
Liu, Wu-chi 1907- CANR-10
Earlier sketch in CA 15-16R
Liu, Yong
See Liu, William T(homas)
Liu E 1857-1909 Brief entry 115
See also TCLC 15
Liu Zongren 1940- 116
Livant, Rose Adleman 1899(?)-1986
Obituary 120
Lively, Penelope 1933- 41-44R
See also SATA 7
See also DLB 14
See also CLC 32
See also CLR 7
Lively, Walter
See Elliott, Bruce (Walter Gardner Lively Stacy)
Liverani, Giuseppe 1903- CANR-6
Earlier sketch in CA 5-6R
Liverani, Mary Rose 1939- 104
Livergood, Norman D(avid) 1933- 37-40R
Livermore, Jean
See Sanville, Jean
Livermore, Seward W. 1901(?)-1984
Obituary 112
Livermore, Shaw 1902- CAP-2
Earlier sketch in CA 19-20
Liversidge, (Henry) Douglas 1913- CAP-1
Earlier sketch in CA 9-10
See also SATA 8
Liversidge, Joan (Eileen Annie)
1915(?)-1984 103
Obituary 112
Liverton, Joan 1913- CAP-1
Earlier sketch in CA 9-10
Livesay, Dorothy 1909- 25-28R
See also CLC 4, 15
See also AITN 2
Livesey, Claire Warner 1927- 29-32R
Livgren, Kerry 1949- 114
Livia, Anna 1955- 119
Livie-Noble, Frederick Stanley 1899-1970 . CAP-1
Earlier sketch in CA 9-10
Livingood, James W(eston) 1910- CANR-8
Earlier sketch in CA 17-18R
Livings, Henry 1929- 15-16R
See also DLB 13
Livingston, A(lfred) D(elano) 1932- CANR-13
Earlier sketch in CA 17-18R
Livingston, Anne Home 1763-1841 ..... DLB-37
Livingston, Bernard 1911- 81-84
Livingston, Carole 1941- 105
See also SATA 42
Livingston, Dorothy Michelson 1906- 49-52
Livingston, Elizabeth J(ane) 1952- 113
Livingston, George Herbert 1916- 53-56
Livingston, Harold 1924- 2R
Livingston, J(oseph) A(rnold) 1905- 1R
Livingston, James C(raig) 1930- CANR-21
Earlier sketch in CA 45-48
Livingston, Jane S(helton) 1944- 107
Livingston, Jon 1944- 49-52
Livingston, M. Jay
See Livingston, Myran Jabez, Jr.
Livingston, Martha 1945- 115
Livingston, Myra Cohn 1926- CANR-1
Earlier sketch in CA 3R
See also SATA 5
See also SAAS 1
See also DLB 61
See also CLR 7
Livingston, Myran Jabez, Jr. 1934- CANR-22
Earlier sketch in CA 105
Livingston, Peter Van Rensselaer
See Townsend, James B(arclay) J(ermain)
Livingston, Richard R(oland) 1922- 45-48
See also SATA 8
Livingston, Robert B(urr) 1918- 97-100
Livingston, William 1723-1790 .... DLB-31
Livingston, William S. 1920- CANR-3
Earlier sketch in CA 11-12R
Livingstone, Angela 1934- 119
Livingstone, Bernard L. 1907(?)-1984
Obituary 112
Livingstone, Douglas (James) 1932- ... CANR-20
Earlier sketches in CA 15-16R, CANR-5
Livingstone, Harrison Edward 1937- 33-36R
Livingstone, J(ohn) Leslie 1932- 73-76
Livingstone, Leon 1912- 33-36R
Livingstone, Marco (Eduardo) 1952- ... CANR-24
Earlier sketch in CA 107
Livo, Norma J. 1929- 123
Livoni, Cathy 1956- 113
Livsey, Clara G(rabois) 1924- 107
Livson, Norman 1924- 49-52
Liyong, Taban lo 1938- 105
Ljoka, Daniel J. 1935- 49-52
Lleo, Manuel Urrutia
See Urrutia Lleo, Manuel
Llerena, Mario 1913- 81-84
Llerena Aguirre, Carlos (Antonio) 1952- ...77-80
See also SATA 19
Llewellyn, D(avid) W(illiam) Alun 1903- 57-60
Llewellyn, Edward
See Llewellyn-Thomas, Edward
Llewellyn, Richard
See Llewellyn Lloyd, Richard Dafydd Vivian
See also DLB 15
See also CLC 7
Llewellyn-Jones, Derek 1923- CANR-15
Earlier sketch in CA 37-40R
Llewellyn Lloyd, Richard Dafydd Vivian
1906-1983 .... CANR-7
Obituary 111
Earlier sketch in CA 53-56
See also SATA 11, 37
Llewellyn-Thomas, Edward 1917- 104
Llewelyn, T. Harcourt
See Hamilton, Charles Harold St. John
Llewelyn-Davies, Richard 1912-1981 .....13-14R
Obituary 105
Llorens, Vicente 1906-1979 Obituary 89-92
Lloret, Antoni 1935- 29-32R
Llosa, Ricardo Pau
See Pau-Llosa, Ricardo
Lloyd, Alan C(hester) 1915- CANR-1
Earlier sketch in CA 2R
Lloyd, Albert Lancaster 1908-1982
Obituary 107
Lloyd, Charles
See Birkin, Charles (Lloyd)
Lloyd, (Charles) Christopher 1906-1986
Obituary 119
Lloyd, Christopher 1921- 120
Lloyd, Craig 1940- 61-64
Lloyd, Cynthia B(rown) 1943- CANR-8
Earlier sketch in CA 61-64
Lloyd, David 1946- 89-92
Lloyd, David Demarest 1911-1962 .... CAP-1
Earlier sketch in CA 11-12
Lloyd, Dennis 1915- 13-14R
Lloyd, E. James
See James, Elizabeth
Lloyd, Errol 1943- 101
See also SATA 22
Lloyd, Francis V(ernon), Jr. 1908- CAP-2
Earlier sketch in CA 21-22
Lloyd, G(eoffrey) E(rnest) R(ichard)
1933- 57-60
Lloyd, Howell Arnold 1937- 103
Lloyd, Hugh (Pughe) 1894-1981 Obituary .. 108
Lloyd, J. Ivester 1905- 13-14R
Lloyd, Jack Ivester
See Lloyd, J. Ivester
Lloyd, James
See James, Elizabeth
Lloyd, James Barlow 1945- 112
Lloyd, John Ivester
See Lloyd, J. Ivester
Lloyd, John S. B. Selwyn
See Selwyn-Lloyd, John S. B.
Lloyd, Marjorie 1909- CANR-8
Earlier sketch in CA 7-8R
Lloyd, Norman 1909-1980 ....37-40R
Obituary 101
See also SATA 23
Lloyd, (Mary) Norris 1908- CANR-1
Earlier sketch in CA 3R
See also SATA 10
Lloyd, Peter C(utt) 1927- CANR-11
Earlier sketch in CA 25-28R
Lloyd, Peter Edward 1938- 107
Lloyd, Robin 1925- 73-76
Lloyd, Ronald
See Friedland, Ronald Lloyd
Lloyd, Rosemary (Helen) 1949- 116
Lloyd, Stephanie
See Golding, Morton J(ay)
Lloyd, Trevor (Owen) 1934- 25-28R
Lloyd Evans, Barbara 1924- 93-96
Lloyd Evans, Gareth 1923-1984 Obituary ... 117
Lloyd George (of Dwyor), Frances (Louise Stevenson) 1888(?)-1972 Obituary 37-40R
Lloyd-Jones, Esther McDonald 1901- 15-16R
Lloyd-Jones, (Peter) Hugh (Jefferd)
1922- CANR-21
Earlier sketches in CA 7-8R, CANR-4
Lloyd-Jones, Robin 1934- 111
Lloyd Owen, David Lanyon 1917- 117
Lloyd-Thomas, Catherine 1917- 65-68
Lloyd Webber, Andrew 1948- Brief entry 116
Llywelyn, Morgan 1937- CANR-16
Earlier sketch in CA 81-84
Llywelyn-Williams, Alun 1913- CAP-1
Earlier sketch in CA 9-10
Lo, Irving Yucheng 1922- 57-60
Lo, Ruth Earnshaw 1910- 106
Lo, Samuel E. 1931- 29-32R
Loader, William Reginald 1916- 4R
Loades, David Michael 1934- 19-20R
Loane, Marcus L(awrence) 1911- CANR-2
Earlier sketch in CA 3R
Loasby, Brian John 1930- 93-96
Lobb, Charlotte 1935- CANR-15
Earlier sketch in CA 65-68
Lobb, Ebenezer
See Upward, Allen
Lobdell, Helen 1919- 11-12R
Lobdell, Jared C(harles) 1937- 49-52
Lobel, Anita (Kempler) 1934- CANR-9
Earlier sketch in CA 53-56
See also SATA 6
Lobel, Arnold Stark 1933-1987 .... CANR-2
Obituary 124
Earlier sketch in CA 4R
See also SATA 6
See also DLB 61
See also CLR 5
See also AITN 1
Lobel, Brana 1942- 97-100
Lobel, Edgar 1889-1982 Obituary 107
Lobel, Stanley 1937- 111
Lo Bello, Nino 1921- CANR-12
Earlier sketch in CA 29-32R
Loberg, Mary Alice 1943- 29-32R
Lobkowicz, Nicholas 1931- CANR-10
Earlier sketch in CA 21-22R
Lobley, Robert (John) 1934- 29-32R
Lobo, Anthony S(avio) 1937- 49-52
Lobsenz, Amelia 13-14R
See also SATA 12
Lobsenz, Norman M(itchell) 1919- CANR-4
Earlier sketch in CA 9-10R
See also SATA 6
Loch, Joice N(anKivell) 1893-1982 ......25-28R
Obituary 108
Lochak, Michele 1936- 106
See also SATA 39
Lochard, Metz T(ullus) P(aul) 1896-1984
Obituary 112
Lochbiler, Don 1908- 49-52
Locher, Dick
See Locher, Richard (Earl)
Locher, Frances C(arol) CANR-17
Earlier sketch in CA 97-100
Locher, Richard (Earl) 1929- CANR-16
Earlier sketch in CA 85-88
Lochhead, Douglas (Grant) 1922- CANR-16
Earlier sketches in CA 45-48, CANR-1
Lochhead, Liz 1947- 81-84
Lochhead, Marion Cleland 1902-1985 101
Obituary 115
Lochlons, Colin
See Jackson, C(aary) Paul
Lochman, Jan Milic 1922- CANR-12
Earlier sketch in CA 29-32R
Lochner, Louis P(aul) 1887-1975 65-68
Obituary 53-56
Lochridge, Betsy Hopkins
See Fancher, Betsy
Lochte, Dick
See Lochte, Richard S(amuel)
Lochte, Richard S(amuel) 1944- CANR-23
Earlier sketch in CA 105
LoCicero, Donald 1937- 25-28R
Lock, C(lara) B(eatrice) Muriel 1914- 49-52
Lock, Dennis (Laurence) 1929- CANR-14
Earlier sketch in CA 41-44R
Lock, F(rederick) P(eter) 1948- 118
Lock, Fred
See Lock, F(rederick) P(eter)
Lockard, Craig Alan 1942- 122
Lockard, (Walter) Duane 1921- 17-18R
Lockard, Leonard
See Thomas, Theodore L.
Locke, Alain (Le Roy) 1886-1954 124
Brief entry 106
See also DLB 51
Locke, Charles O. 1896(?)-1977 Obituary ..69-72
Locke, Clinton W. CAP-2
Earlier sketch in CA 19-20
See also SATA 1
Locke, David M(illard) 1929- 41-44R
Locke, David Ross 1833-1888 ...... DLB-11, 23
Locke, Duane CANR-1
Earlier sketch in CA 49-52
Locke, Edwin A. III 1938- 15-16R
Locke, Elsie 1912- CANR-11
Earlier sketch in CA 25-28R
Locke, Frederick W. 1918- 13-14R
Locke, Hubert G. 1934- 29-32R
Locke, Louis G(lenn) 1912- 33-36R
Locke, Lucie 1904- 53-56
See also SATA 10
Locke, Martin
See Duncan, W(illiam) Murdoch
Locke, Michael (Stephen) 1943- 73-76
Locke, Peter
See McCutchan, J(ohn) Wilson
Locke, R. E.
See Raffelock, David
Locke, Ralph P(aul) 1949- 124
Locke, Richard Adams 1800-1871 ...... DLB-43
Locke, Wende 1945- 33-36R
Locke-Elliott, Sumner
See Elliott, Sumner Locke
Locker, Thomas 1937- CLR-14
Lockerbie, D(onald) Bruce 1935- CANR-14
Earlier sketch in CA 37-40R
Lockerbie, Jeanette W. Honeyman CANR-5
Earlier sketch in CA 11-12R
Lockerbie, Jeannie 1938- CANR-13
Earlier sketch in CA 73-76
Locker-Lampson, Frederick 1821-1895 .. DLB-35
Lockert, (Charles) Lacy (Jr.) 1888-1974 .. CAP-2
Earlier sketch in CA 25-28
Lockert, Lucia (Alicia Ungaro Fox)
1928- CANR-14
Earlier sketch in CA 73-76
Lockhart, (Jeanne) Aileene Simpson
1911- 15-16R

Lockhart, Freda Bruce 1909-1987
Obituary 124
Lockhart, Jack Herbert 1909-1985
Obituary 117
Lockhart, Robert (Hamilton) Bruce
1886-1970 Obituary 89-92
Lockhart, Russell A(rthur) 1938- CANR-21
Earlier sketch in CA 45-48
Locklair, Wriston 1924(?)-1984 Obituary 112
Lockley, Lawrence Campbell 1899-1969 .. CAP-1
Earlier sketch in CA 11-12
Lockley, Ronald M(athias) 1903- CANR-22
Earlier sketches in CA 9-10R, CANR-5
Locklin, Gerald (Ivan) 1941- CANR-14
Earlier sketch in CA 37-40R
Locklin, (David) Philip 1897- 2R
Lockmann, Ronald F(rederick) 1942- 117
Lockmiller, David A(lexander) 1906- 77-80
Lockridge, Ernest (Hugh) 1938- 25-28R
See also AITN 1
Lockridge, Frances Louise ?-1963
Obituary 93-96
Lockridge, Hildegarde (Dolson)
1908-1981 .... CANR-3
Obituary 102
Earlier sketch in CA 5-6R
Lockridge, Kenneth A(lan) 1940-
Brief entry 107
Lockridge, Norman
See Roth, Samuel
Lockridge, Richard 1898-1982 85-88
Obituary 107
Lockridge, Ross (Franklin), Jr. 1914-1948
Brief entry 108
See also DLBY 80
Lockspeiser, Edward 1905-1973 .... CANR-6
Earlier sketch in CA 7-8R
Lockwood, Allison 1920- 115
Lockwood, C. C. 1949- 117
Lockwood, Charles Andrews 1890-1967 .... 2R
Lockwood, Douglas (Wright) 1918- 21-22R
Lockwood, Guy C. 1943- 65-68
Lockwood, Lee 1932- 37-40R
Lockwood, Margo 1939- 117
Lockwood, Mary
See Spelman, Mary
Lockwood, Michael 1944- 122
Lockwood, Theodore Davidge 1924- CANR-1
Earlier sketch in CA 4R
Lockwood, W(illiam) B(urley) 1917- 29-32R
Lockwood, William W(irt) 1906- CAP-2
Earlier sketch in CA 23-24
Lockyer, Herbert 1888(?)-1984 Obituary 115
Lockyer, Roger 1927- CANR-12
Earlier sketch in CA 19-20R
Lode, Rex
See Goldstein, William Isaac
Loden, Barbara (Ann) 1937-1980 Obituary .. 101
Lodge, Bernard 1933- 107
See also SATA 33
Lodge, David (John) 1935- CANR-19
Earlier sketch in CA 17-18R
See also DLB 14
See also CLC 36
Lodge, George Cabot 1873-1909
Brief entry 123
See also DLB 54
Lodge, George Cabot 1927- 17-18R
Lodge, Henry Cabot 1850-1924 .... DLB-47
Lodge, Henry Cabot (Jr.) 1902-1985 53-56
Obituary 115
Lodge, Oliver (Joseph) 1851-1940
Brief entry 117
Lodge, Orlan Robert 1917-1975 Obituary .. 57-60
Lodrick, Deryck O(scar) 1942- 106
Loeb, Catherine (Roberta) 1949- 89-92
Loeb, Gerald M(artin) 1899-1974 .... CAP-1
Obituary 49-52
Earlier sketch in CA 15-16
Loeb, Harold A(lbert) 1891-1974 106
Obituary 45-48
See also DLB 4
Loeb, Jeffrey 1946- 123
Loeb, Madeleine H. 1905(?)-1974
Obituary 45-48
Loeb, Marshall Robert 1929- 23-24R
Loeb, Paul Rogat 1952- 109
Loeb, Robert F(rederick) 1895-1973
Obituary 45-48
Loeb, Robert H., Jr. 1917- CANR-12
Earlier sketch in CA 29-32R
See also SATA 21
Loeb, William 1905-1981 93-96
Obituary 104
Loebl, Eugen 1907-1987 Obituary 123
Loebl, Suzanne 69-72
Loefgren, Ulf 1931- CANR-16
Earlier sketch in CA 25-28R
See also SATA 3
Loefstedt, Bengt 1931- CANR-1
Earlier sketch in CA 45-48
Loehlin, John C(linton) 1926- 23-24R
Loemker, Leroy E(arl) 1900- 41-44R
Loening, Grover C. 1889(?)-1976
Obituary 65-68
Loening, Sarah (Elizabeth) Larkin
1896-1988 .... CANR-21
Obituary 124
Earlier sketch in CA 45-48
Loennbohm, Armas Eino Leopold
1878-1926 Brief entry 123
Loeoef, Jan 1940- 81-84
Loeper, John J(oseph) 1929- CANR-12
Earlier sketch in CA 29-32R
See also SATA 10
Loesch, Juli(anne) 1951- 89-92
Loescher, Ann Dull 1942- CANR-9
Earlier sketch in CA 61-64
See also SATA 20
Loescher, Gil(burt Damian) 1945- CANR-9
Earlier sketch in CA 61-64
See also SATA 20
Loeschke, Maravene Sheppard 1947- 115
Loeser, Herta 1921- 57-60
Loeser, Katinka 1913- 17-18R
Loesser, Francis Henry 1910-1969
Obituary 112
Loesser, Frank
See Loesser, Francis Henry
Loether, Herman J(ohn) 1930- 21-22R
Loetscher, Lefferts A(ugustine) 1904- 5-6R
Loevinger, Jane 1918- 41-44R
Loevinger, Lee 1913- CANR-15
Earlier sketch in CA 81-84
Loew, Ralph William 1907- CAP-1
Earlier sketch in CA 19-20
Loew, Sebastian 1939- CANR-19
Earlier sketch in CA 103
Loewald, Hans W. 1906- 101
Loewe, Ralph E. 1923- 23-24R
Loewe, Raphael J(ames) 1919- 118
Loewen, James W. 1942- CANR-14
Earlier sketch in CA 37-40R
Loewenberg, Bert James 1905-1974 .... CANR-5
Earlier sketch in CA 11-12R
Loewenberg, Frank M(eyer) 1925- CANR-2
Earlier sketch in CA 45-48
Loewenberg, Gerhard 1928- CANR-9
Earlier sketch in CA 23-24R
Loewenberg, J(orn) Joseph 1933- 33-36R
Loewenberg, Peter J(acob) 1933- 109
Loewenberg, Robert J(ames) 1938-
Brief entry 114
Loewenfeld, Claire 1899-1974 .... CAP-2
Earlier sketch in CA 23-24
Loewenstein, Bernice SATA-40
Loewenstein, Hubertus Prinz zu
See
Loewenstein(-Wertheim-Freudenberg),
Hubertus (Friedrich Maria Johannes
Leopold Ludwig) zu
Loewenstein(-Wertheim-Freudenberg),
Hubertus (Friedrich Maria Johannes
Leopold Ludwig) zu 1906-1984 .... CANR-4
Obituary 114
Earlier sketch in CA 7-8R
Loewenstein, Joseph 1952- 124
Loewenstein, Karl 1891-1973 Obituary .. 41-44R
Loewenstein, Louis Klee 1927- 37-40R
Loewenstein, Prince Hubertus (zu)
See
Loewenstein(-Wertheim-Freudenberg),
Hubertus (Friedrich Maria Johannes
Leopold Ludwig) zu
Loewenstein, Rudolph M(aurice)
1898-1976 .... CAP-2
Obituary 65-68
Earlier sketch in CA 21-22
Loewenstein-Wertheim-Freudenberg,
Hubertus Prinz zu
See
Loewenstein(-Wertheim-Freudenberg),
Hubertus (Friedrich Maria Johannes
Leopold Ludwig) zu
Loewenthal, L(eonard) J(oseph) A(lfonso) ... 61-64
Loewinsohn, Ron(ald William) 1937- 25-28R
Loewith, Karl 1897-1973 Obituary 116
Loewy, Ariel G(ideon) 1925- 89-92
Loewy, Raymond Fernand 1893-1986 104
Obituary 119
Lofaro, Michael Anthony 1948- 89-92
Lofland, John (Franklin) 1936- CANR-12
Earlier sketch in CA 33-36R
Lofland, Lyn (Hebert) 1937- 61-64
Lofstedt, Bengt
See Loefstedt, Bengt
Loftas, Tony 1940- 21-22R
Lofthouse, Jessica 1916- 29-32R
Lofthus, Myrna 1935- 115
Lofting, Hugh (John) 1886-1947
Brief entry 109
See also SATA 15
Loftis, Anne 1922- 45-48
Loftis, John (Clyde, Jr.) 1919- CANR-3
Earlier sketch in CA 2R
Lofton, John (Marion) 1919- CANR-6
Earlier sketch in CA 11-12R
Lofts, Norah (Robinson) 1904-1983 .... CANR-6
Obituary 110
Earlier sketch in CA 7-8R
See also SATA 8, 36
See also AITN 2
Loftus, Elizabeth F. 1944- 105
Loftus, Ernest Achey 1884-1987 Obituary ... 123
Loftus, John (Joseph) 1950- 117
Loftus, Richard J. 1929- 15-16R
Logan, Albert Boyd 1909- 53-56
Logan, Daniel 1936- 25-28R
Logan, Don
See Crawford, William (Elbert)
Logan, Elizabeth D(ulaney) 1914- 61-64
Logan, F(rancis) Donald 1930- 45-48
Logan, Ford
See Newton, D(wight) B(ennett)
Logan, Frank A(nderson) 1924- 41-44R
Logan, Gene A(dams) 1922- CANR-7
Earlier sketch in CA 11-12R
Logan, Gerald E(lton) 1924- 73-76
Logan, Jake
See Knott, William C(ecil, Jr.)
and Krepps, Robert W(ilson)
and Pearl, Jacques Bain
and Riefe, Alan
and Rifkin, Shepard
and Smith, Martin Cruz
Logan, James 1674-1751 .... DLB-24
Logan, James Phillips 1921- 37-40R
Logan, Jane
See Gardner, Virginia (Marberry)
Logan, John (Burton) 1923-1987 77-80
Obituary 124
See also DLB 5
See also CLC 5
Logan, John A(rthur), Jr. 1923- 2R
Logan, Joshua Lockwood 1908- 89-92
See also AITN 1
Logan, Lillian M(ay) 1909- CANR-1
Earlier sketch in CA 2R
Logan, Rayford W(hittingham)
1897-1982 .... CANR-1
Obituary 108
Earlier sketch in CA 2R
Logan, Sara
See Haydon, June
and Simpson, Judith H(olroyd)
Logan, Sister Mary Francis Louise 1928- .. 7-8R
Logan, Spencer 1912(?)-1980 Obituary ... 93-96
Logan, Terence P(atrick) 1936- 57-60
Logan, Virgil G(lenn) 1904- 21-22R
Loganbill, G. Bruce 1938- 37-40R
Logelin, Warren E. 1940(?)-1985
Obituary 117
Loggins, Vernon 1893-1968 .... 7-8R
Loggins, William Kirk 1946- 77-80
Logsdon, John M(ortimer III) 1937-
Brief entry 115
Logsdon, Joseph 1938- 25-28R
Logsdon, Richard Henry 1912- CANR-2
Earlier sketch in CA 5-6R
Logsdon, Thomas S(tanley) 1937- CANR-21
Earlier sketches in CA 57-60, CANR-6
Logsdon, Tom
See Logsdon, Thomas S(tanley)
Logue, Cal(vin McLeod) 1935- Brief entry .. 105
Logue, Christopher 1926- CANR-3
Earlier sketch in CA 11-12R
See also SATA 23
See also DLB 27
Logue, Jeanne 1921- 89-92
Logue, William (Herbert) 1934- 45-48
Loh, Jules 1931- 33-36R
Loh, Pichon P(ei) Y(ung) 1928- 17-18R
Loh, Robert 1924- 19-20R
Lohf, Kenneth A. 1925- CANR-3
Earlier sketch in CA 9-10R
Lohman, Joseph D(ean) 1910-1968 .... CAP-2
Earlier sketch in CA 23-24
Lohnes, Walter F. W. 1925- 49-52
Lohr, Thomas F. 1926- 77-80
Lohrer, M(ary) Alice 1907- 17-18R
Lohrli, Anne 1906- 111
Lohrman, Paul
See Fairman, Paul W.
Lohse, Eduard 1924- 107
Loisy, Alfred (Firmin) 1857-1940
Brief entry 120
Lo-Johansson, (Karl) Ivar 1901- CANR-20
Earlier sketch in CA 102
Loken, Newton Clayton 1919- 3R
See also SATA 26
Loki
See Pearson, Karl
Lokken, Roy N(orman) 1917- 53-56
Lokos, Lionel 1928- 25-28R
Loll, Leo M(arius), Jr. 1923-1968 .... CAP-2
Earlier sketch in CA 25-28
Lollar, Coleman Aubrey (Jr.) 1946- 49-52
Lolli, Giorgio 1905-1979 .... CANR-2
Obituary 85-88
Earlier sketch in CA 4R
Lollis, Lorraine 1911- CAP-2
Earlier sketch in CA 29-32
Lolos, Kimon 1917- 4R
Lomas, Charles W(yatt) 1907- CAP-1
Earlier sketch in CA 13-14
Lomas, Derek 1933- 29-32R
Lomas, Geoffrey (Robert) 1950- 93-96
Lomas, Peter 1923- 23-24R
Lomas, Steve
See Brennan, Joseph Lomas
Lomask, Milton (Nachman) 1909- CANR-1
Earlier sketch in CA 3R
See also SATA 20
Lomax, Alan 1915- CANR-1
Earlier sketch in CA 4R
Lomax, Bliss
See Drago, Harry Sinclair
Lomax, John A(lbert) 1930- 61-64
Lomax, Louis E(manuel) 1922-1970 .... CAP-2
Earlier sketch in CA 25-28
Lomax, Pearl Cleage 1948- 41-44R
Lombard, C(harles) M(orris) 1920- CANR-1
Earlier sketch in CA 49-52
Lombard, Helen
See Vischer, Helen (Cassin Lombard)
Carusi
Lombard, Lawrence Brian 1944- 124
Lombard, Nap
See Johnson, Pamela Hansford
Lombardi, John V(incent) 1942- CANR-20
Earlier sketches in CA 53-56, CANR-5
Lombardi, Mary 1940- 61-64
Lombardo, Josef Vincent 1908- 7-8R
LoMedico, Brian T.
See Monteleone, Thomas F(rancis)
Lommasson, Robert C(urtis) 1917- 41-44R
Lomosia, Andrew
See Stern, Jay B(enjamin)
Lomupo, Brother Robert 1939- 15-16R
London, Artur 1915-1986 .... CANR-12
Obituary 120
Earlier sketch in CA 65-68
London, Carolyn 1918- 57-60
London, H(oyt) H(obson) 1900- 49-52
London, Hannah R. 1894- 29-32R
London, Herbert I(ra) 1939- CANR-12
Earlier sketch in CA 33-36R
London, Jack 1915- 89-92
London, Jack
See London, John Griffith
See also SATA 18
See also DLB 8, 12
See also TCLC 9, 15
See also AITN 2
London, Jane
See Geis, Darlene Stern
London, Joan 1901-1971 .... CAP-2
Earlier sketch in CA 25-28
London, John Griffith 1876-1916 119
Brief entry 110
London, Julius 1917- 118
London, Kurt L(udwig) 1900- CANR-6
Earlier sketch in CA 3R
London, Laura
See Curtis, Sharon
and Curtis, Thomas (Dale)
London, Mel 1923- CANR-24
Earlier sketch in CA 107
London, Perry 1931- 45-48
London, Roy 1946- 108
Londre, Felicia Hardison 1941- CANR-21
Earlier sketch in CA 105
Lonergan, Bernard J(oseph) F(rancis)
1904-1984 .... CANR-11
Obituary 114
Earlier sketch in CA 53-56
Lonergan, (Pauline) Joy (MacLean) 1909- 3R
See also SATA 10
Lonesome Cowboy
See White, John I(rwin)
Lone Star Ranger
See White, John I(rwin)
Lonette, Reisie (Dominee) 1924- SATA-43
Loney, Glenn (Meredith) 1928- CANR-14
Earlier sketch in CA 33-36R
Loney, Martin 1944- CANR-18
Earlier sketch in CA 102
Long, A(nthony) A(rthur) 1937- CANR-13
Earlier sketch in CA 33-36R
Long, Ann Marie
See Jensen, Pauline Marie (Long)
Long, Charles 1938- 65-68
Long, Charles R(ussell) 1904- CAP-1
Earlier sketch in CA 11-12
Long, Chester, Clayton 1932- 25-28R
Long, Clayton
See Long, Chester Clayton
Long, David E(dwin) 1937- 89-92
Long, David F(oster) 1917- CANR-8
Earlier sketch in CA 61-64
Long, E(verette) B(each) 1919-1981 .... CANR-1
Obituary 103
Earlier sketch in CA 3R
Long, Earlene (Roberta) 1938- SATA-50
Long, Edward LeRoy, Jr. 1924- CANR-22
Earlier sketches in CA 5-6R, CANR-7
Long, Emmett
See Leonard, Elmore
Long, Esmond R(ay) 1890-1979
Obituary 89-92
Long, Eugene Thomas (III) 1935- 25-28R
Long, Father Valentine W. 1902- 19-20R
Long, Fern CAP-2
Earlier sketch in CA 23-24
Long, Frank Belknap 1903- CANR-16
Earlier sketch in CA 81-84
Long, Frederick Lawrence 1917- 11-12R
Long, Haniel (Clark) 1888-1956
Brief entry 122
See also DLB 45
Long, Helen Beecher CAP-2
Earlier sketch in CA 19-20
See also SATA 1
Long, Howard Rusk 1906- CANR-3
Earlier sketch in CA 7-8R
Long, Huey P(ierce) 1893-1935
Brief entry 115
Long, J(ohn) C(uthbert) 1892- CAP-1
Earlier sketch in CA 9-10
Long, James M. 1907-1979 Obituary 85-88
Long, John D(ouglas) 1920- 17-18R
Long, John H(enderson) 1916- 13-14R
Long, John L(atham) 1932- 111
Long, Judith Elaine 1953- 65-68
See also SATA 20
Long, Judy
See Long,Judith Elaine
Long, Laura Mooney 1892-1967 Obituary ... 109
See also SATA 29
Long, Lois 1901-1974 Obituary 104
Long, Louise 37-40R
Long, Lucile
See Brandt, Lucile (Long Strayer)
Long, Luman H(arrison) 1907-1971 108
Obituary 104
Long, M(olly) 1916- 23-24R
Long, Naomi Cornelia
See Madgett, Naomi Long
Long, Norton E. 1910- 45-48
Long, Priscilla 1943- 29-32R
Long, Ralph B(ernard) 1906- 5-6R

Long, Richard A(lexander) 1927- CANR-24
Earlier sketch in CA 37-40R
Long, Robert 1954- 110
Long, Robert Emmet 1934- 122
Long, T(heodore) Dixon 1933- 121
Brief entry 118
Long, Thomas (Joseph) 1938- 119
Long, William Stuart
See Stuart, (Violet) Vivian (Finlay)
Longacre, Edward G(eorge) 1946- CANR-22
Earlier sketches in CA 53-56, CANR-5
Longacre, Robert E(dmondson) 1922- .. CANR-19
Earlier sketches in CA 53-56, CANR-4
Longacre, William A(tlas) II 1937- CANR-12
Earlier sketch in CA 29-32R
Longaker, Richard P(ancoast) 1924- CANR-1
Earlier sketch in CA 3R
Longbeard, Frederick
See Longyear, Barry Brookes
Longeaux y Vasquex, Enriqueta 1930- 57-60
Longenecker, Justin G. 1917- CANR-1
Earlier sketch in CA 2R
Longenecker, Richard N(orman) 1930- ...15-16R
Longest, George C(alvin) 1938- 107
Longfellow, Henry Wadsworth
1807-1882 .... SATA-19
See also DLB 1, 59
See also CDALB 1640-1865
Longfellow, Samuel 1819-1892 .... DLB-1
Longford, Elizabeth Harmon 1906- 7-8R
Longgood, William (Frank) 1917- CANR-17
Earlier sketch in CA 2R
Longhurst, Henry Carpenter 1909-1978 85-88
Obituary 81-84
Longino, Charles F(reeman), Jr.
1938- CANR-24
Earlier sketches in CA 53-56, CANR-7
Longland, Jean R(ogers) 1913- CANR-10
Earlier sketch in CA 21-22R
Longleigh, Peter J., Jr.
See Korges, James
Longley, John Lewis, Jr. 1920- 7-8R
Longley, Lawrence D(ouglas) 1939- 41-44R
Longley, Michael 1939- 102
See also DLB 40
See also CLC 29
Longley, Richmond W(ilberforce) 1907- ...73-76
Longley, W. B.
See Randisi, Robert J(oseph)
Longman, Harold S. 1919- 25-28R
See also SATA 5
Longman, Lester Duncan 1905-1987
Obituary 121
Longman, Mark Frederic Kerr 1916-1972
Obituary 37-40R
Longmate, Norman Richard 1925- CANR-6
Earlier sketch in CA 9-10R
Longmore, Laura 7-8R
Long-Neck Woman
See Cheatham, K(aryn) Follis
Longo, Lucas 1919- 25-28R
Longrigg, Jane Chichester 1929- 9-10R
Longrigg, Roger (Erskine) 1929- CANR-3
Earlier sketch in CA 4R
Longrigg, Stephen Hemsley 1893-1979
Obituary 89-92
Longstreet, Augustus Baldwin
1795-1870 .... DLB-3, 11
Longstreet, Stephen 1907- CANR-7
Earlier sketch in CA 9-10R
Longstreet, Wilma S. 1935- 93-96
Longstreth, Edward 1894-19(?) CAP-1
Earlier sketch in CA 15-16
Longstreth, T(homas) Morris 1886- 7-8R
Longsword, John
See Long, John Frederick Lawrence
Longsworth, Polly 1933- 106
See also SATA 28
Longsworth, Robert M. 1937- 21-22R
Longtemps, Kenneth 1933- SATA-17
Longway, A. Hugh
See Lang, Andrew
Longworth, Alice Lee (Roosevelt)
1884-1980 Obituary 93-96
Longworth, I(an) H(eaps) 1935- 120
Longworth, Philip 1933- CANR-10
Earlier sketch in CA 23-24R
Longworth, Richard C(ole) 1935- 85-88
Longyear, Barry Brookes 1942- 102
Longyear, Christopher R(udston) 1929- 105
Longyear, Marie Marcia Bernstein 1928- 115
Longyear, Rey M(organ) 1930- CANR-22
Earlier sketch in CA 45-48
Lonnbohm, Armas Eino Leopold
See Loennbohm, Armas Eino Leopold
Lonsdale, Adrian L. 1927- 15-16R
Lonsdale, Frederick 1881-1954 Brief entry .. 109
See also DLB 10
Lonsdale, Gordon Arnold 1923(?)-1970
Obituary 104
Lonsdale, Kathleen (Yardley) 1903-1971 ....7-8R
Obituary 33-36R
Lonsdale, Richard E. 1926- CANR-13
Earlier sketch in CA 23-24R
Lonsdale, Steven (Hancock) 1952- 114
Look, Al 1893- 57-60
Look, Dennis 1949- 73-76
Looker, Antonina (Hansell) 29-32R
Looker, (Reginald) Earle 1895-1976 ..... CAP-2
Obituary 65-68
Earlier sketch in CA 29-32
Lookout
See Noble, John (Appelbe)
Lookstein, Haskel 1932- 119
Loomba, N(arendra) Paul 1927- 57-60
Loomes, Brian 1938- CANR-12
Earlier sketch in CA 69-72
Loomie, Albert Joseph 1922- 5-6R
Loomis, Albertine (G.) 1895-1985 93-96
Obituary 117
Loomis, Charles P(rice) 1905- CANR-13
Earlier sketch in CA 21-22R
Loomis, Chauncey C(hester), Jr. 1930- ...33-36R
Loomis, Edward 1924- CANR-2
Earlier sketch in CA 1R
Loomis, Noel M(iller) 1905-1969 .... 3R
Obituary 25-28R
Loomis, Rae
See Steger, Shelby
Loomis, Robert D. 19-20R
See also SATA 5
Loomis, Roger Sherman 1887-1966 .... CANR-8
Earlier sketch in CA 7-8R
Loomis, Stanley 1922-1972 .... CAP-1
Obituary 37-40R
Earlier sketch in CA 11-12
Loomis, Zona Kemp 1911- 45-48
Looney, Robert E(dward) 1941- 104
Loory, Stuart H. 1932- 25-28R
Loos, Anita 1893(?)-1981 ....21-22R
Obituary 104
See also DLB 11, 26
See also DLBY 81
See also AITN 1
Loos, Mary AITN-1
Loose, Gerhard 1907- 45-48
Loose, H.
See Lourie, Dick
Loots, Barbara Kunz 1946- 57-60
Loovis, David (Mactavish) 1926- CANR-1
Earlier sketch in CA 2R
Lopata, Helena Znaniecka 1925- 104
Lopate, Carol
See Ascher, Carol
Lopate, Phillip 1943- 97-100
See also DLBY 80
See also CLC 29
Lopatin, Judy 1954- 124
Loper, William C. 1927- 15-16R
Lopes, Michael 1943- 57-60
Lopez, Adalberto 1943- 103
Lopez, Andrew 1910-1986 Obituary 120
Lopez, Barry Holstun 1945- CANR-23
Earlier sketches in CA 65-68, CANR-7
Lopez, Cecilia L(uisa) 1941- 53-56
Lopez, Claude-Anne 1920- 104
Lopez, Ella B. 1900(?)-1978 Obituary 81-84
Lopez, Enrique 1921(?)-1985 Obituary 117
Lopez, Felix Manuel, Jr. 1917- 15-16R
Lopez, Manuel Dennis 1934- CANR-22
Earlier sketch in CA 105
Lopez, Nancy (Marie) 1957- Brief entry 113
Lopez, Robert S(abatino) 1910-1986
Obituary 119
Brief entry 112
Lopez, Vincent (Joseph) 1895-1975
Obituary 61-64
Lopez-Morillas, Juan 1913- CANR-1
Earlier sketch in CA 2R
Lopez Portillo (y Pacheco), Jose 1920- ...CLC-46
Lopez-Rey, Jose 1905- 37-40R
Lopez-Rey (y Arrojo), Manuel
1902-1987 ....29-32R
Obituary 124
Lopez y Fuentes, Gregorio 1897-1966 ....CLC-32
Lopez Y Rivas, Gilberto 1943- 97-100
LoPiccolo, Joseph 1943- CANR-15
Earlier sketch in CA 81-84
Lo Pinto, Maria 1900(?)-1970 Obituary 104
Lopreato, Joseph 1928- 33-36R
Lopshire, Robert M(artin) 1927- CANR-8
Earlier sketch in CA 5-6R
See also SATA 6
Lopukhov, Fyodor V(asilevich) 1886-1973
Obituary 41-44R
Lora, Josephine
See Alexander, Josephine
Lora, Ronald 1938- 41-44R
Lorac, E. C. R.
See Rivett, Edith Caroline
Loram, Ian Craig 1917- 5-6R
Loran, Martin
See Baxter, John
Lorand, (Alexander) Sandor
1893(?)-1987 .... CAP-1
Obituary 123
Earlier sketch in CA 9-10
Lorang, Ruth Mary
See Lorang, Sister Mary Corde
Lorang, Sister Mary Corde 1904- 49-52
Lorant, Stefan 1901- CANR-9
Earlier sketch in CA 5-6R
See also AITN 1
Lorayne, Harry 1926- 41-44R
Lorberg, Aileen Dorothy 1910- CANR-2
Earlier sketch in CA 5-6R
Lorca, Federico Garcia
See Garcia Lorca, Federico
Lorch, Robert Stuart 1925- 73-76
Lord, Albert Bates 1912- 103
Lord, Athena V. 1932- 109
See also SATA 39
Lord, Beman 1924- 33-36R
See also SATA 5
Lord, Bette Bao 1938- 107
See also CLC 23
Lord, Clifford L(ee) 1912-1980 .... CANR-8
Obituary 102
Earlier sketch in CA 15-16R
Lord, Donald Charles 1930- 37-40R
Lord, (Doreen Mildred) Douglas 1904- ... CAP-1
Earlier sketch in CA 13-14
See also SATA 12
Lord, Douglas
See Cooper, Douglas
Lord, Eda 1907-1976 Obituary 104
Lord, Edith Elizabeth 1907- 41-44R
Lord, Eugene Hodgdon 1894- 4R
Lord, Francis A. 1911- 19-20R
Lord, Frederic Mather 1912- 37-40R
Lord, Gabrielle 1946- 106
Lord, George deF(orest) 1919- CANR-10
Earlier sketch in CA 65-68
Lord, Graham 1943- CANR-4
Earlier sketch in CA 53-56
Lord, Jeffrey
See Nelson, R. Faraday
Lord, Jeremy
See Redman, Ben Ray
Lord, Jess R. 1911- 65-68
Lord, John Vernon 1939- 53-56
See also SATA 21
Lord, Mary Stinson Pillsbury 1904-1978 ...85-88
Obituary 81-84
Lord, Nancy
See Titus, Eve
Lord, Phillips H.
See Yolen, Will (Hyatt)
Lord, Priscilla Sawyer 1908- 9-10R
Lord, Robert (Needham) 1945- 61-64
Lord, Shirley
See Anderson, Shirley Lord
Lord, Vivian
See Strother, Pat Wallace
Lord, Walter 1917- CANR-22
Earlier sketches in CA 3R, CANR-5
See also SATA 3
Lord, William Jackson, Jr. 1926- 7-8R
Lord Altrincham
See Grigg, John (Edward Poynder)
Lord Astor of Hever
See Astor, Gavin
Lord Auch
See Bataille, Georges
Lord Beveridge
See Beveridge, William (Henry)
Lord Blake
See Blake, Robert (Norman William)
Lord Boyle of Handsworth
See Boyle, Edward Charles Gurney
Lord Brooke
See Greville, Fulke
Lord Butler of Saffron Walden
See Butler, Richard Austen
Lord Chalfont
See Jones, (Alun) Arthur Gwynne
Lord Crowther-Hunt
See Crowther-Hunt, Norman Crowther
Lord Denning
See Denning, Alfred Thompson
Lord Dunsany
See Dunsany, Edward John Moreton
Drax Plunkett
See also TCLC 2
Lorde, Audre (Geraldine) 1934- CANR-16
Earlier sketch in CA 25-28R
See also DLB 41
See also CLC 18
Lord Energlyn
See Evans, William David
Lord Evans of Hungershall
See Evans, Benjamin Ifor
Lord Francis Williams
See Williams, Edward Francis
Lord George-Brown
See George-Brown, George Alfred
Lord Hailsham of St. Marylebone
See Hogg, Quintin McGarel
Lord Home
See Home, Alexander Frederick
Lord Houghton
See Milnes, Richard Monckton
Lordi, Robert J(oseph) 1923- 89-92
Lord Killanin
See Morris, Michael
Lord Moran
See Wilson, (Richard) John (McMoran)
Lord Rhyl
See Birch, (Evelyn) Nigel (Chetwode)
Lord Snowdon
See Armstrong-Jones, Antony (Charles
Robert)
Lord Strange
See Drummond, John
Lord Thomas
See Thomas, (William) Miles (Webster)
Lord Windlesham
See Hennessy, David James George
Loree, Kate (Lambie) 1920- 21-22R
Lorek, Daniel N. 1958(?)-1983 Obituary 110
Loren, Sophia 1934- Brief entry 111
Lorenz, Alfred Lawrence 1937- 45-48
Lorenz, J(ames) D(ouglas) 1938- 102
Lorenz, Konrad Zacharias 1903- 61-64
Lorenz, Lee (Sharp) 1932- Brief entry 124
See also SATA 39
Lorenz, Sarah E.
See Winston, Sarah
Lorenzen, Coral Elsie 1925- 113
Lorenzen, David N(eal) 1940- 33-36R
Lorenzini, Carlo 1826-1890 .... SATA-29
Lorenzo, Carol Lee 1939- 53-56
Loria, Jeffrey H. 1940- 19-20R
Lorie, James Hirsch 1922- 103
Lorig, Kate R. 1942- 117
Lorimer, Frank 1894-1985 Obituary 116
Lorimer, James 1942- 123
Lorimer, Lawrence T(heodore) 1941- ... CANR-6
Earlier sketch in CA 57-60
Lorimer, Scat
See Fuentes, Martha Ayers
Loring, Ann 1915- 97-100
Loring, J. M.
See Warner-Crozetti, R(uth G.)
Loring, Murray 1917- CANR-22
Earlier sketch in CA 45-48
Lorion, R(aymond) P(aul) 1946- 85-88
Loris
See Hofmannsthal, Hugo von
Lornquest, Olaf
See Rips, Ervine M(ilton)
Lorrah, Jean CANR-19
Earlier sketch in CA 103
Lorraine, Walter (Henry) 1929- SATA-16
Lorrance, Arleen 1939- 85-88
Lorrimer, Claire
See Robins, Patricia (Denise)
Lorsch, Jay William 1932- 97-100
Lorsch, Susan E. 1950- 116
Lortie, Dan C(lement) 1926- 115
Lortz, Richard 1917-1980 .... CANR-11
Obituary 102
Earlier sketch in CA 57-60
Lorwin, Val Rogin 1907-1982 Obituary 111
Lory, Robert (Edward) 1936- CANR-10
Earlier sketch in CA 53-56
Los, George
See Amabile, George
Losang, Rato Khyongla Ngawang 1923- ...81-84
Lose, M(argaret) Phyllis 1925- CANR-18
Earlier sketch in CA 101
Losey, Joseph (Walton) 1909-1984
Obituary 113
Loshak, David (Leslie Ivor) 1933- 41-44R
Losoncy, Lawrence J. 1941- CANR-14
Earlier sketch in CA 37-40R
Losoncy, Mary Jan 1942- 37-40R
los Rios, Francisco Giner de
See Giner de los Rios, Francisco
Loss, Joan 1933- SATA-11
Loss, Louis 1914- CANR-2
Earlier sketch in CA 5-6R
Loss, Richard (Archibald John) 1938- 65-68
Lossing, Benson J. 1813-1891 .... DLB-30
Lossky, Andrew 1917- 93-96
Lossy, Rella 1934- 81-84
Loth, Calder 1943- 73-76
Loth, David 1899- CANR-1
Earlier sketch in CA 3R
Lothian, John Maule 1896-1970 .... CAP-1
Earlier sketch in CA 9-10
Lothringen, Geza Louis Eusebius Gebhard
Ralphael Albert Maria von Habsburg
See von Habsburg-Lothringen, Geza
Louis Eusebius Gebhard Ralphael
Albert Maria
Lothrop, Harriet Mulford Stone
1844-1924 .... SATA-20
See also DLB 42
Loti, Pierre
See Viaud, (Louis Marie) Julien
See also TCLC 11
Lott, Arnold S(amuel) 1912- 15-16R
Lott, Davis Newton 1913- CANR-10
Earlier sketch in CA 21-22R
Lott, Milton 1919- 19-20R
Lott, Monroe
See Howard, Edwin
Lott, Robert E(ugene) 1926- CANR-4
Earlier sketch in CA 5-6R
Lottich, Kenneth V(erne) 1904- 19-20R
Lottie
See Grimke, Charlotte L(ottie) Forten
Lottinville, Savoie 1906- 105
Lottman, Eileen 1927- CANR-12
Earlier sketch in CA 57-60
Lottman, Herbert R. 1927- 105
Lotz, David W(alter) 1937- Brief entry 115
Lotz, James Robert 1929- CANR-14
Earlier sketch in CA 37-40R
Lotz, Jim
See Lotz, James Robert
Lotz, John 1913-1973 Obituary 45-48
Lotz, Wolfgang 1912- 81-84
Louch, A(lfred) R(ichard) 1927- 19-20R
Louchheim, Kathleen 1903- 21-22R
Louchheim, Katie
See Louchheim, Kathleen
Loucks, William Negele 1899- 2R
Loud, Pat(ricia Russell) 1926- Brief entry .. 114
Louden, Robert Stuart 1912- 7-8R
Lougee, Robert Wayne 1919- 5-6R
Loughary, John W(illiam) 1930- 41-44R
Loughhead, LaRue A(lvin) 1927- 61-64
Loughlin, Richard L(awrence) 1907- ... CANR-21
Earlier sketch in CA 45-48
Loughmiller, Campbell 1906- CANR-13
Earlier sketch in CA 77-80
Loughran, Bernice B(ingham) 1919- 7-8R
Loughran, Peter 1938- 25-28R
Lougy, Robert E. 1940- 118
Louie, Ai-Ling 1949- 112
See also SATA 34, 40
Louis, Arthur M(urray) 1938- 106
Louis, Debbie 1945- 29-32R
Louis, Father M.
See Merton, Thomas
Louis, J(ack) C(harles), Jr. 1949- 105
Louis, Joe
See Barrow, Joseph Louis
Louis, Pat
See Francis, Dorothy Brenner
Louis, Paul P(anickavede) 1918- CANR-12
Earlier sketch in CA 61-64
Louis, Pierre(-Felix) 1870-1925 Brief entry .. 105
Louis, Ray Baldwin 1949- 65-68

Louis, Tobi 1940- ... 57-60
Louisburgh, Sheila Burnford
See Burnford, Sheila (Philip Cochrane Every)
Louisell, David William 1913-1977 ... CANR-4
Obituary ... 73-76
Earlier sketch in CA 2R
Loukes, Harold 1912- ... 17-18R
Lounsbury, Myron O. 1940- ... 37-40R
Loup, Jacques 1942- ... 120
Louria, Donald B(ruce) 1928- ... 107
Lourie, Dick 1937- ... 33-36R
Lourie, Helen
See Storr, Catherine (Cole)
Lousley, J(ob) E(dward) 1907-1976
Obituary ... 104
Louthan, Robert 1951- ... 109
Louviere, Vernon Ray 1920- ... 108
Louvish, Misha 1909- ... CANR-1
Earlier sketch in CA 45-48
Louvish, Simon 1947- ... 121
Louw, Nicholaas Petrus Van Wyk
1906-1970 Obituary ... 89-92
Loux, Michael Joseph 1942- ... 103
Louys, Pierre
See Louis, Pierre(-Felix)
Lovaas, O(le) Ivar 1927- ... CANR-22
Earlier sketch in CA 45-48
Lovasik, Lawrence George 1913- ... CANR-20
Earlier sketches in CA 3R, CANR-1
Lovatt, Edwin A(lbert) 1944- ... 119
Love, Alan C(arson) 1937- ... 53-56
Love, Barbara J. 1937- ... 37-40R
Love, Charles (Ross) 1932- ... 25-28R
Love, Charles K.
See Swicegood, Thomas L. P.
Love, Edmund G(eorge) 1912- ... CANR-4
Earlier sketch in CA 4R
Love, Glen A. 1932- ... 29-32R
Love, Iris Cornelia 1933- ... 29-32R
Love, Janet
See Ferrier, Janet Mackay
Love, Jean O. 1920- ... 29-32R
Love, Joseph L., (Jr.) 1938- ... 29-32R
Love, Katherine (Isabel) 1907- ... SATA-3
Love, Kennett 1924- ... 77-80
Love, Philip H(ampton) 1905-1977 ... 77-80
Obituary ... 73-76
Love, Richard S. 1923- ... 81-84
Love, Sandra (Weller) 1940- ... CANR-11
Earlier sketch in CA 69-72
See also SATA 26
Love, Sydney F(rancis) 1923- ... 81-84
Love, Thomas Teel 1931- ... 15-16R
Lovecraft, H(oward) P(hillips) 1890-1937
Brief entry ... 104
See also TCLC 4, 22
Lovegrove, Philip
See Ray, John (Philip)
Lovehill, C. B.
See Beaumont, Charles
Lovejoy, Bahija Fattuhi 1914- ... 5-6R
Lovejoy, Clarence Earle 1894-1974 ... 5-6R
Obituary ... 45-48
Lovejoy, David Sherman 1919- ... 103
Lovejoy, Elijah P(arish) 1940- ... 45-48
Lovejoy, Jack 1937- ... 114
Lovejoy, L(awrence) C(lark) 1893- ... 3R
Lovejoy, Paul E(llsworth) 1943- ... 115
Lovelace, Delos Wheeler 1894-1967 ... 7-8R
Obituary ... 25-28R
See also SATA 7
Lovelace, Earl 1935- ... 77-80
Lovelace, Linda
See Marciano, Linda Boreman
Lovelace, Marc Hoyle 1920- ... 37-40R
Lovelace, Maud Hart 1892-1980 ... 7-8R
Obituary ... 104
See also SATA 2, 23
Lovelace, Richard Franz 1930- ... 101
Loveland, Anne C(arol) 1938- Brief entry ... 114
Loveless, E(dward) E. 1919- ... 57-60
Lovell, Ann 1933- ... CANR-19
Earlier sketch in CA 97-100
Lovell, (Alfred Charles) Bernard 1913- ... CANR-6
Earlier sketch in CA 13-14R
Lovell, Colin Rhys 1917- ... 5-6R
Lovell, Ernest J(ames), Jr. 1918-1975 ... 4R
Obituary ... 103
Lovell, Ingraham
See Bacon, Josephine Dodge (Daskam)
Lovell, John, Jr. 1907-1974 ... CAP-2
Obituary ... 49-52
Earlier sketch in CA 33-36
Lovell, John P(hilip) 1932- ... CANR-15
Earlier sketch in CA 29-32R
Lovell, Marc
See McShane, Mark
Lovell, Mark 1934- ... CANR-8
Earlier sketch in CA 61-64
Lovell, Michael Christopher 1930- ... 33-36R
Lovell, Ronald P. 1937- ... CANR-13
Earlier sketch in CA 73-76
Lovell, Stanley P(latt) 1890- ... 5-6R
Lovelock, J. E.
See Lovelock, James (Ephraim)
Lovelock, James (Ephraim) 1919- ... 123
Loveman, Brian E(lliot) 1944- ... CANR-17
Earlier sketch in CA 89-92
Loveman, Samuel 1885(?)-1976 Obituary .. 65-68
Lovenstein, Meno 1909- ... CANR-3
Earlier sketch in CA 7-8R
Lovequist, Gwendlelynn
See Stafford, Linda (Crying Wind)
Loverde, Lorin (James Bell) 1943- ... 45-48
Loveridge, Ronald O. 1938- ... 33-36R
Lovering, Joseph Paul 1921- ... 104
Lovesey, Peter 1936- ... 41-44R
Lovestrand, Harold 1925- ... 21-22R
Lovett, A(lbert) W(inston) 1944- ... 124
Lovett, Clara Maria 1939- ... CANR-16
Earlier sketch in CA 93-96
Lovett, Gabriel H(arry) 1921- ... 65-68
Lovett, Margaret (Rose) 1915- ... 61-64
See also SATA 22
Lovett, Robert W. 1913- ... 33-36R
Lovin, Clifford R(amsey) 1937- ... 37-40R
Lovin, Roger Robert 1941- ... CANR-6
Earlier sketch in CA 57-60
Loving, Jerome MacNeill 1941- ... 112
Lovins, Amory B(loch) 1947- ... 69-72
Lovoll, Odd Sverre 1934- ... CANR-7
Earlier sketch in CA 61-64
Lovoos, Janice
See Garbutt, Janice (D.) Lovoos
Low, Alfred D(avid) 1913- ... 33-36R
Low, Alice 1926- ... CANR-8
Earlier sketch in CA 61-64
See also SATA 11
Low, Ann Marie 1912- ... 118
Low, Anthony 1935- ... CANR-13
Earlier sketch in CA 37-40R
Low, D(onald) A(nthony) 1927- ... 73-76
Low, David (Alexander Cecil) 1891-1963
Obituary ... 89-92
Low, Dorothy Mackie
See Low, Lois Dorothea
Low, Elizabeth Hammond 1898- ... CAP-2
Earlier sketch in CA 19-20
See also SATA 5
Low, Francis 1893-1972 Obituary ... 115
Low, Gardner
See Rodda, Charles
Low, George M(ichael) 1926-1984
Obituary ... 113
Low, Ivy
See Litvinov, Ivy
Low, Joseph 1911- ... CANR-15
Earlier sketch in CA 85-88
See also SATA 14
Low, Lois Dorothea 1916- ... CANR-15
Earlier sketch in CA 37-40R
Low, Samuel 1765-? ... DLB-37
Low, Victor N. 1931- ... CANR-1
Earlier sketch in CA 49-52
Lowance, Mason I(ra), Jr. 1938- ... 57-60
Lowbury, Edward (Joseph Lister)
1913- ... CANR-12
Earlier sketch in CA 29-32R
Lowden, Desmond 1937- ... 53-56
Lowder, Jerry 1932- ... 65-68
Lowder, Paul D(aniel) 1929- ... 93-96
Lowdermilk, W(alter) C(lay) 1888-1974
Obituary ... 49-52
Lowe, Alfonso
See Loewenthal, L(eonard) J(oseph) A(lfonso)
Lowe, C(arrington) Marshall 1930- ... 29-32R
Lowe, Corke
See Pepper, Choral
Lowe, David (Garrard) 1933- ... CANR-22
Earlier sketch in CA 104
Lowe, David A(llan) 1948- ... 111
Lowe, Donald M. 1928- ... 21-22R
Lowe, Gordon R(obb) 1928- ... 49-52
Lowe, Gustav E. 1901- ... CAP-2
Earlier sketch in CA 23-24
Lowe, Henry Paget
See Lovecraft, H(oward) P(hillips)
Lowe, Jay, Jr.
See Loeper, John J(oseph)
Lowe, Jeanne R. 1924(?)-1972
Obituary ... 33-36R
Lowe, John (Evelyn) 1928- ... 123
Lowe, John W(esley) G(uinn) 1946- ... 121
Lowe, Judah
See Lyon, Christopher (Leslie)
Lowe, Marjorie G(riffiths) Lowe 1909- ... 4R
Lowe, Richard Barrett 1902-1972
Obituary ... 33-36R
Lowe, Richard G. 1942- ... 123
Lowe, Robert W. 1910- ... CAP-1
Earlier sketch in CA 13-14
Lowe, Roberta (Justine) 1940- ... CANR-24
Earlier sketches in CA 61-64, CANR-8
Lowe, Sue Davidson 1922- ... 118
Lowe, Victor (Augustus) 1907- ... 17-18R
Lowe, Victoria Lincoln
See Lincoln, Victoria
Lowe, William T(ebbs) 1929- ... 73-76
Lowell, Amy 1874-1925 Brief entry ... 104
See also DLB 54
See also TCLC 1, 8
Lowell, C. Stanley 1909- ... CANR-6
Earlier sketch in CA 5-6R
Lowell, James Russell
1819-1891 ... DLB-1, 11, 64
See also CDALB 1640-1865
Lowell, Jon 1938- ... 97-100
Lowell, Juliet 1901- ... CANR-1
Earlier sketch in CA 3R
Lowell, Mildred Hawksworth 1905-1974 .. CAP-2
Earlier sketch in CA 33-36
Lowell, Robert (Traill Spence, Jr.)
1917-1977 ... 9-10R
Obituary ... 73-76
See also CABS 2
See also DLB 5
See also CLC 1, 2, 3, 4, 5, 8, 9, 11, 15, 37
Lowell, Tex
See Turner, George E(ugene)
Lowen, Alexander 1910- ... 19-20R
Lowenfeld, Andreas F(rank) 1930- ... CANR-8
Earlier sketch in CA 61-64
Lowenfeld, Berthold 1901- ... 17-18R
Lowenfels, Walter 1897-1976 ... CANR-3
Obituary ... 65-68
Earlier sketch in CA 1R
See also DLB 4
Lowenfish, Lee (Elihu) 1942- ... 106
Lowenkopf, Shelly A(lan) 1931- ... CANR-4
Earlier sketch in CA 49-52
Lowens, Irving 1916-1983 ... CANR-11
Obituary ... 111
Earlier sketch in CA 17-18R
Lowenstein, Dyno 1914- ... 9-10R
See also SATA 6
Lowenstein, Hubertus (Prinz) zu
See
Loewenstein(-Wertheim-Freudenberg), Hubertus (Friedrich Maria Johannes Leopold Ludwig) zu
Lowenstein, Ralph Lynn 1930- ... 17-18R
Lowenstein, Sharon R. 1937- ... 122
Lowenstein, Tom 1941- ... 93-96
Lowenthal, David 1923- ... 115
Lowenthal, Leo 1900- ... CANR-20
Earlier sketches in CA 2R, CANR-5
Lowenthal, Marjorie Fiske
See Fiske, Marjorie
Lower, Arthur R(eginald) M(arsden)
1889-1988 ... CANR-4
Obituary ... 124
Earlier sketch in CA 11-12R
Lower, J(oseph) Arthur 1907- ... 23-24R
Lowery, Bruce Arlie 1931- ... CANR-1
Earlier sketch in CA 2R
Lowery, Daniel L(orne) 1929- ... 113
Lowery, James L(incoln), Jr. 1932- ... 45-48
Lowery, Lynn 1949- ... 93-96
Lowery, Thomas V(incent) 1919- ... 37-40R
Lowi, Theodore J(ay) 1931- ... 37-40R
Lowing, Anne
See Geach, Christine
Lowinsky, Edward E(lias) 1908-1985 ... CAP-1
Obituary ... 117
Earlier sketch in CA 13-14
Lowith, Karl
See Loewith, Karl
Lowitz, Anson C. 1901(?)-1978 ... 81-84
Obituary ... 73-76
See also SATA 18
Lowitz, Sadyebeth Heath 1901-1969 ... 85-88
See also SATA 17
Lowman, Charles LeRoy 1880(?)-1977
Obituary ... 69-72
Lowman, Eleanor B(arry) 1906-1983
Obituary ... 110
Lowman, Josephine (Cherry)
1899(?)-1983 Obituary ... 110
Lowndes, Betty 1929- ... 61-64
Lowndes, George Alfred Norman 1897- ... 7-8R
Lowndes, Marie Adelaide (Belloc)
1868-1947 Brief entry ... 107
See also TCLC 12
Lowndes, Robert A(ugustine) W(ard)
1916- Brief entry ... 113
Lowndes, William 1914- ... 13-14R
Lowney, Paul Benjamin 1922- ... CANR-17
Earlier sketch in CA 93-96
Lowrey, Janette Sebring 1892- ... 13-14R
See also SATA 43
Lowrey, Kathleen 1943- ... 57-60
Lowrey, P(errin) H(olmes) 1923-1965 ... CAP-1
Earlier sketch in CA 11-12
Lowrey, Sara 1897- ... 17-18R
Lowrie, Donald A(lexander) 1889-1974 ... 5-6R
Obituary ... 53-56
Lowrie, Jean E(lizabeth) 1918- ... 45-48
Lowry, Albert J(ames) 1927- Brief entry ... 118
Lowry, Bates 1923- ... CANR-1
Earlier sketch in CA 3R
Lowry, Beverly (Fey) 1938- ... 101
Lowry, Charles W(esley) 1905- ... 37-40R
Lowry, Fern 1896(?)-1983 Obituary ... 111
Lowry, Joan (Catlow) 1911- ... 13-14R
Lowry, Lois 1937- ... CANR-13
Earlier sketch in CA 69-72
See also SATA 23
See also SAAS 3
See also DLB 52
See also CLR 6
Lowry, (Clarence) Malcolm 1909-1957
Brief entry ... 105
See also DLB 15
See also TCLC 6
Lowry, Martin John Clement 1940- ... 107
Lowry, Mina Gertrude 1882-1966 ... 113
Lowry, Nan
See MacLeod, Ruth
Lowry, Peter 1953- ... 49-52
See also SATA 7
Lowry, Ritchie P(eter) 1926- ... 17-18R
Lowry, Robert (James Collas) 1919- ... 61-64
Lowry, Shirley Park 1933- ... 109
Lowry, Thomas P. 1932- ... 21-22R
Lowther, George F. 1913-1975 Obituary ... 57-60
See also SATA 30
Lowther, Kevin G(eorge) 1941- ... 81-84
Lowther, Pat 1935-1975 ... DLB-53
Lowy, George 1924- ... 17-18R
Loxmith, John
See Brunner, John (Kilian Houston)
Loxton, (Charles) Howard 1934- ... CANR-11
Earlier sketch in CA 25-28R
Loy, J(ohn) Robert 1918- Brief entry ... 108
Loy, Jane M.
See Rausch, Jane M(eyer)
Loy, Mina
See Lowry, Mina Gertrude
See also DLB 4, 54
See also CLC 28
Loyd, Marianne 1955- ... 115
Loye, David (Elliot) 1925- ... 33-36R
Loyn, H(enry) R(oyston) 1922- ... 117
Loyn, Henry
See Loyn, H(enry) R(oyston)
Loyn, Henry R.
See Loyn, H(enry) R(oyston)
Loyson-Bridet
See Schwob, (Mayer Andre) Marcel
Lozano, Wendy 1941- ... 102
Lozier, Herbert 1915- ... 49-52
See also SATA 26
Lozowick, Louis 1892-1973 Obituary ... 107
Lu, David J(ohn) 1928- ... CANR-5
Earlier sketch in CA 9-10R
Lu, K'uan-yu
See Luk, Charles
Lu, Paul Hsien 1926- ... 41-44R
Luard, (David) Evan (Trant) 1926- ... CANR-1
Earlier sketch in CA 4R
Luard, Nicholas 1937- ... 85-88
Lubalin, Herb(ert Frederick) 1918-1981
Obituary ... 104
Lubans, John, Jr. 1941- ... 57-60
Lubar, Joel F. 1938- ... 37-40R
Lubar, Robert 1920- ... 73-76
Lubbe, Catherine Case ... AITN-1
Lubbock, (Mary Katherine) Adelaide
1906- ... 29-32R
Lubbock, Mark Hugh 1898-1986 Obituary .. 121
Lubbock, Percy 1879-1965 ... 85-88
Lubeck, Steven G. 1944- ... 29-32R
Lubell, Cecil 1912- ... CANR-4
Earlier sketch in CA 9-10R
See also SATA 6
Lubell, Harold 1925- ... 9-10R
Lubell, Samuel 1911-1987 ... 15-16R
Obituary ... 123
Lubell, Winifred (A. Milius) 1914- ... CANR-4
Earlier sketch in CA 49-52
See also SATA 6
Lubenow, William (Cornelius) 1939-
Brief entry ... 107
Luber, Philip 1948- ... 124
Lubetski, Edith 1940- ... 112
Lubetski, Meir 1938- ... 112
Lubin, Bernard 1923- ... CANR-9
Earlier sketch in CA 21-22R
Lubin, David M. 1950- ... 120
Lubin, Ernest 1916-1977 ... 41-44R
Lubin, Isador 1896-1978 Obituary ... 77-80
Lubin, Leonard B. 1943- Brief entry ... 115
See also SATA 37, 45
Lubis, Mochtar 1922- ... 29-32R
Lubitz, Raymond 1937-1984 Obituary ... 113
Lubove, Roy 1934- ... 23-24R
Lubow, Robert E. 1932- ... 77-80
Lubowe, Irwin I(rville) 1905- ... 53-56
Lubrano, Linda L. 1943- Brief entry ... 108
Lucas, Alec 1913- ... 101
Lucas, Barbara
See Wall, Barbara
Lucas, Bryan Keith
See Keith-Lucas, Bryan
Lucas, C. Payne 1933- ... 85-88
Lucas, Carol 1929- ... 17-18R
Lucas, Celia 1938- ... CANR-24
Earlier sketch in CA 107
Lucas, Christopher J(ohn) 1940- ... 25-28R
Lucas, D(onald) W(illiam) 1905-1985 ... CAP-1
Obituary ... 116
Earlier sketch in CA 13-14
Lucas, Darrel B(laine) 1902- ... CAP-1
Earlier sketch in CA 9-10
Lucas, Dione (Narnona Margaris Wilson)
1909-1971 Obituary ... 104
Lucas, E(dna) Louise 1899-1970 ... CAP-2
Earlier sketch in CA 25-28
Lucas, E(dward) V(errall) 1868-1938 ... SATA-20
Lucas, F(rank) L(aurence) 1894-1967 ... CANR-4
Obituary ... 25-28R
Earlier sketch in CA 4R
Lucas, George 1944- ... 77-80
See also CLC 16
Lucas, Hans
See Godard, Jean-Luc
Lucas, Henry C(ameron), Jr. 1944- ... 109
Lucas, J. K.
See Paine, Lauran (Bosworth)
Lucas, J(ohn) R(andolph) 1929- ... CANR-11
Earlier sketch in CA 23-24R
Lucas, J(ames) R(aymond) 1950- ... 118
Lucas, Jason 1904- ... CAP-1
Earlier sketch in CA 9-10
Lucas, Jeremy 1953- ... 108
Lucas, Jerry 1940- ... 108
See also SATA 33
Lucas, Jim Griffing 1914-1970 Obituary ... 104
Lucas, John 1937- ... CANR-14
Earlier sketch in CA 37-40R
Lucas, Joseph 1928- ... 69-72
Lucas, Joyce 1927- ... 57-60
Lucas, Lawrence E(dward) 1933- ... 65-68
Lucas, Marion B(runson) 1935- ... 81-84
Lucas, Martin 1944- ... 111
Lucas, N. B. C. 1901- ... 81-84
Lucas, Noah 1927- ... 57-60
Lucas, Robert 1904-1984 ... 101
Obituary ... 111
Lucas, Robert Emerson, Jr. 1937- ... 107
Lucas, Robert Harold 1933- ... 37-40R
Lucas, Ruth (Baxendale) 1909- ... CAP-2
Earlier sketch in CA 19-20

Lucas, Scott 1937- 93-96
Lucas, T(homas) E(dward) 1919- 77-80
Lucas, Victoria
 See Plath, Sylvia
Lucas, W(ilmer) F(rancis, Jr.) 1927- 77-80
Lucash, Frank S. 1938- 120
Lucas Phillips, C(ecil) E(rnest)
 1897-1984 .... CANR-3
 Obituary 112
 Earlier sketch in CA 4R
Lucchesi, Aldo
 See von Block, Bela W(illiam)
Luce, Celia (Geneva Larsen) 1914- 61-64
 See also SATA 38
Luce, Clare Boothe 1903-1987 45-48
 Obituary 123
Luce, Don 1934- CANR-12
 Earlier sketch in CA 29-32R
Luce, Gay Gaer 1930- 103
Luce, Henry R(obinson) 1898-1967 104
 Obituary 89-92
Luce, J(ohn) V(ictor) 1920- 61-64
Luce, Willard (Ray) 1914- 61-64
 See also SATA 38
Luce, William (Aubert) 1931- CANR-11
 Earlier sketch in CA 65-68
Lucente, Gregory L. 1948- 120
Lucentini, Mauro 1924- 69-72
Lucero, Roberto
 See Meredith, Robert C(hidester)
Lucey, James D(ennis) 1923- 25-28R
Lu-ch'iao
 See Wu, Nelson I(kon)
Luchins, Abraham S(amuel) 1914- CANR-11
 Earlier sketch in CA 69-72
Luchins, Edith H(irsch) 1921- CANR-11
 Earlier sketch in CA 19-20R
Luchsinger, Elaine King 1902- CAP-2
 Earlier sketch in CA 17-18
Lucia, Ellis (Joel) 1922- CANR-22
 Earlier sketches in CA 2R, CANR-4
Lucia, Salvatore Pablo 1901-1984 .... 13-14R
 Obituary 112
Luciani, Vincent 1906- 61-64
Lucid, Robert F(rancis) 1930- 25-28R
Lucie-Smith, (John) Edward (McKenzie)
 1933- CANR-7
 Earlier sketch in CA 15-16R
 See also DLB 40
Luck, David Johnston 1912- CANR-4
 Earlier sketch in CA 53-56
Luck, G(eorge) Coleman 1913- 15-16R
Luck, George Hans 1926- 7-8R
Luck, Thomas Jefferson 1922- 5-6R
Luckert, Karl W(ilhelm) 1934- 81-84
Luckett, Hubert Pearson 1916- 77-80
Luckett, Karen Beth 1944- 77-80
Luckey, Eleanore Braun 1915- 33-36R
Luckhardt, C(harles) Grant 1943- 93-96
Luckhardt, Mildred Corell 1898- 15-16R
 See also SATA 5
Luckless, John
 See Burkholz, Herbert
 and Irving, Clifford Michael
Luckmann, Thomas 1927- CANR-19
 Earlier sketch in CA 101
Luckock, Elizabeth 1914- 21-22R
Luckyj, George S(tephen) N(estor)
 1919- CANR-21
 Earlier sketch in CA 45-48
Ludden, Allen (Ellsworth) 1918(?)-1981
 Obituary 104
 See also SATA 27
Ludel, Jacqueline 1945- 111
Luder, William Fay 1910- 29-32R
Ludington, (Charles) Townsend 1936- ... CANR-9
 Earlier sketch in CA 45-48
Ludlam, Charles 1943-1987 85-88
 Obituary 122
 See also CLC 46
Ludlow, Geoffrey
 See Meynell, Laurence Walter
Ludlow, George
 See Kay, Ernest
Ludlow, Howard T(homas) 1921- 23-24R
Ludlow, James Minor 1917-1974
 Obituary 53-56
Ludlum, Mabel Cleland
 See Widdemer, Mabel Cleland
Ludlum, Robert 1927- 33-36R
 See also DLBY 82
 See also CLC 22, 43
Ludlum, Robert P(hillips) 1909-1987 ..... CAP-1
 Obituary 122
 Earlier sketch in CA 15-16
Ludmerer, Kenneth M. 1947- 45-48
Ludovici, Anthony M(ario) 1882-19(?) CAP-1
 Earlier sketch in CA 11-12
Ludovici, L. J.
 See Ludovici, Lorenz James
Ludovici, Laurence James
 See Ludovici, Lorenz James
Ludovici, Lorenz James 1910- CANR-10
 Earlier sketch in CA 23-24R
Ludowyk, E(velyn) F(rederick) C(harles)
 1906-1985 .... CAP-1
 Obituary 117
 Earlier sketch in CA 11-12
Ludtke, James Buren 1924- 2R
Ludvigsen, Karl (Eric- 1934- 73-76
Ludvigson, Susan 1942- CANR-7
 Earlier sketch in CA 57-60
Ludwig, Charles Shelton 1918- CANR-20
 Earlier sketches in CA 9-10R, CANR-5
Ludwig, Ed(ward William) 1920- 97-100
Ludwig, Eric
 See Grunwald, Stefan
Ludwig, Frederic
 See Grunwald, Stefan
Ludwig, Helen SATA-33
Ludwig, Jack 1922- CANR-1
 Earlier sketch in CA 4R
 See also DLB 60
Ludwig, Jerry 1934- 81-84
Ludwig, Lyndell 1923- 115
Ludwig, Myles Eric 1942- 25-28R
Ludwig, Richard M(ilton) 1920- 19-20R
Ludwigson, Kathryn Romaine 1921- CANR-6
 Earlier sketch in CA 53-56
Luebke, Frederick Carl 1927- CANR-12
 Earlier sketch in CA 33-36R
Luecke, Janemarie 1924- CANR-21
 Earlier sketch in CA 104
Lueders, Edward (George) 1923- CANR-5
 Earlier sketch in CA 15-16R
 See also SATA 14
Luedtke, Kurt (Mamre) 1939- 111
 Brief entry 109
Lueker, Erwin L(ouis) 1914- CANR-23
 Earlier sketches in CA 17-18R, CANR-8
Luening, Otto 1900- 102
Luenn, Nancy 1954- 116
Lueschen, Guenther R(udolf) 1930- CANR-4
 Earlier sketch in CA 53-56
Luescher, Max 1923- 101
Luetgen, Kurt (Bodo Heinrich) 1911- 108
Luethi, Max 1909- 29-32R
Luetzelschwab, John (William) 1940- 121
 Brief entry 118
Lufburrow, William 1931(?)-1986
 Obituary 118
Luff, S(tanley) G(eorge) A(nthony) 1921- .. 9-10R
Lufkin, Raymond H. 1897- SATA-38
Luft, David Sheers 1944- 106
Lugard, Flora Louisa Shaw 1852-1929 . SATA-21
Luger, Harriett Mandelay 1914- CANR-1
 Earlier sketch in CA 45-48
 See also SATA 23
Lugg, George Wilson 1902- 105
Lugo, Ariel E(milio) 1943- 41-44R
Lugo, James O. 1928- 29-32R
Lugones, Leopoldo 1874-1938 Brief entry .. 116
 See also TCLC 15
Lugt, Herbert Vander
 See Vander Lugt, Herbert
Luhr, William 1946- 106
Luhrmann, Winifred B(ruce) 1934- 61-64
 See also SATA 11
Lu Hsun 1881-1936 .... TCLC-3
Luick, John F(rancis) 1920- 25-28R
Luis, Earlene W. 1929- 61-64
 See also SATA 11
Luisada, Aldo A(ugusto) 1901-1987
 Obituary 124
Luisi, Billie M(eisner) 1940- 73-76
Luk, Charles 1898- 9-10R
Luka, Ronald 1937- 61-64
Lukach, Joan M(ickelson) 1935- 118
Lukacher, Ned 1950- 120
Lukacs, Georg
 See Lukacs, Gyorgy
Lukacs, George
 See Lukacs, Gyorgy
 See also CLC 24
Lukacs, Gyorgy 1885-1971 101
 Obituary 29-32R
Lukacs, John (Adalbert) 1923- CANR-17
 Earlier sketches in CA 3R, CANR-1
Lukaczer, Moses 1911-1984 Obituary 112
Lukas, Charlotte Koplinka 1954- 93-96
Lukas, Ellen 97-100
Lukas, J(ay) Anthony 1933- CANR-19
 Earlier sketches in CA 49-52, CANR-2
Lukas, Mary 101
Lukas, Richard C. 1937- 33-36R
Lukas, Susan 1940- 53-56
Lukashevich, Stephen 1931- 33-36R
Luke, Hugh J(ay) 1932- 89-92
Luke, Mary M. 1919- CANR-14
 Earlier sketch in CA 23-24R
Luke, Peter (Ambrose Cyprian) 1919- 81-84
 See also DLB 13
 See also CLC 38
Luke, Thomas
 See Masterton, Graham
Lukenbill, Willis B(ernard) 1939- 103
Luker, Kristin Carol 1946- 61-64
Lukes, Steven (Michael) 1941- CANR-16
 Earlier sketch in CA 93-96
Lukodianov, Isai (Borisovich) 1913- 101
Lukonin, Mikhail K. 1920(?)-1977
 Obituary 69-72
Lum, Peter
 See Crowe, Bettina Lum
Lumian, Norman C. 1928- 29-32R
Lumiansky, R(obert) M(ayer) 1913-1987
 Obituary 122
Lumley, Brian 1937- Brief entry 120
Lummis, Keith 1904- 104
Lumpkin, Angela 1950- 112
Lumpkin, Grace 69-72
Lumpkin, Henry H(ope) 1913- 122
Lumpkin, William Latane 1916- CANR-4
 Earlier sketch in CA 2R
Lumsden, Charles J(ohn) 1949- 111
Lumsden, D(an) Barry 1939- CANR-21
 Earlier sketch in CA 45-48
Lunan, Duncan (Alasdair) 1945- 107
Lunar, Dennis
 See Mungo, Raymond
Lunch, Lydia (a pseudonym) 1959- 115
Lund, A. Morten 1926- 13-14R
Lund, Doris Herold 1919- 17-18R
 See also SATA 12
Lund, Gerald N. 1939- CANR-13
 Earlier sketch in CA 33-36R
Lund, Gilda E. 1909- 7-8R
Lund, Herb(ert Frederick) 1926- 45-48
Lund, James
 See Stonehouse, John (Thomson)
Lund, Philip R(eginald) 1938- 57-60
Lund, Robert P. 1915- 2R
Lund, Thomas A. 1922- 33-36R
Lundahl, Gene 1933- 21-22R
Lundberg, Dan
 See Lundberg, Daniel
Lundberg, Daniel 1912-1986 114
 Obituary 119
Lundberg, Donald E(mil) 1916- CANR-12
 Earlier sketch in CA 33-36R
Lundberg, Erik F(ilip) 1907- CANR-17
 Earlier sketch in CA 25-28R
Lundberg, (Edgar) Ferdinand 1905- CAP-1
 Earlier sketch in CA 9-10
Lundberg, Margaret (Jessie) 1919- 61-64
Lundborg, Louis B(illings) 1906- 81-84
Lunde, Donald T(heodore) 1937- 101
Lunde, Karl (Roy) 1931- 122
Lunden, Walter A(lbin) 1899- 21-22R
Lundgren, Paul Arthur 1925-1981
 Obituary 103
Lundgren, William R. 1918- 13-14R
Lundin, Robert W(illiam) 1920- 2R
Lundkvist, Artur (Nils) 1906- Brief entry 117
Lundquist, James (Carl) 1941- 65-68
Lundsgaarde, Henry P(eder) 1938- CANR-14
 Earlier sketch in CA 73-76
Lundsteen, Sara W. 109
Lundwall, Sam J(errie) 1941- CANR-17
 Earlier sketches in CA 49-52, CANR-1
Lundy, Robert F(ranklin) 1937- 7-8R
Lunenfeld, Marvin C. 1934- 61-64
Lunin, Lois F(ranklin) 102
Lunn, Arnold 1888-1974 81-84
 Obituary 49-52
Lunn, Eugene 1941- 45-48
Lunn, Janet (Louise Swoboda) 1928- .. CANR-22
 Earlier sketch in CA 33-36R
 See also SATA 4
Lunn, John Edward 1930- 41-44R
Lunsford, Cin Forshay
 See Forshay-Lunsford, Cin
Lunt, Elizabeth Graves 1922- 33-36R
Lunt, Horace Gray 1918- Brief entry 107
Lunt, James D(oiran) 1917- CANR-3
 Earlier sketch in CA 3R
Lunt, Lois
 See Metz, Lois Lunt
Lunt, Richard D(eForest) 1933- 15-16R
Luomala, Katharine 1907- 37-40R
Luongo, C. Paul 1930- 105
Luper, Harold L(ee) 1924- 17-18R
Lupo, Alan 1938- 41-44R
Lupoff, Dick
 See Lupoff, Richard A(llen)
Lupoff, Richard A(llen) 1935- CANR-9
 Earlier sketch in CA 23-24R
Lupul, Manoly Robert 1927- Brief entry 106
Lurgan, Lester
 See Knowles, Mabel Winifred
Luria, Alexander R(omanovich)
 1902-1977 .... 25-28R
 Obituary 73-76
Luria, Maxwell Sidney 1932- 37-40R
Luria, S(alvador) E(dward) 1912- 61-64
Lurie, Alison 1926- CANR-17
 Earlier sketches in CA 3R, CANR-2
 See also SATA 46
 See also DLB 2
 See also CLC 4, 5, 18, 39
Lurie, Edward 1927- CANR-7
 Earlier sketch in CA 9-10R
Lurie, Harry L. 1892(?)-1973 Obituary ... 41-44R
Lurie, Nancy Oestreich 1924- CANR-16
 Earlier sketch in CA 2R
Lurie, Ranan R(aymond) 1932- 57-60
Lurie, Richard G. 1919- 23-24R
Lurie, Toby 1925- 45-48
Luriya, Aleksander Romanovich
 See Luria, Alexander R(omanovich)
Luschei, Eugene C(harles) 1928- 37-40R
Luscher, Max
 See Luescher, Max
Luscombe, David Edward 1938- 41-44R
Luscombe, William 1912- 7-8R
Lusinchi, Victor 1912-1985 Obituary 115
Luskin, Bernard J(ay) 1937- 33-36R
Luskin, John 1908- 45-48
Lussier, (Joseph) Ernest 1911-1979 .... CANR-9
 Earlier sketch in CA 57-60
Lussu, Joyce (Salvadori) 1912- CANR-14
 Earlier sketch in CA 29-32R
Lust, John (Benedict) 1920- 116
Lust, Peter 1911- 103
Lustbader, Eric Van 1946- CANR-14
 Earlier sketch in CA 85-88
Lustgarten, Edgar (Marcus)
 1907-1978 .... CANR-22
 Earlier sketch in CA 25-28R
Lustgarten, Karen 1944- 85-88
Lustick, Ian Steven 1949- 117
Lustig, Arnost 1926- 69-72
Lustig, Loretta 1944- SATA-46
Lustig, R(ichard) Jeffrey 1943- 112
Lustig-Arecco, Vera 1942- 101
Lutes, Catherine Urell 1900(?)-1983
 Obituary 110
Lutetius
 See Stearns, Harold Edmund
Lutgen, Kurt
 See Luetgen, Kurt (Bodo Heinrich)
Luthans, Fred 1939- 29-32R
Luther, Edward T(urner) 1928- 77-80
Luther, Frank 1905-1980 Obituary 102
 See also SATA 25
Luther, James W(allace) 1940- 69-72
Luther, Jim
 See Luther, James W(allace)
Luther, Ray
 See Ley, Arthur Gordon
Luthi, Max
 See Luethi, Max
Luthuli, A. J.
 See Luthuli, Albert John
Luthuli, Albert John 1898(?)-1967
 Obituary 113
Lutin, Michael 1940- 89-92
Luttbeg, Norman R. 1938- CANR-10
 Earlier sketch in CA 25-28R
Luttrell, Guy L. 1938- 97-100
 See also SATA 22
Luttrell, Ida 1934- 110
 See also SATA 35, 40
Luttrell, Mark H. 1914- 97-100
Luttwak, Edward N(icholae) 1942- CANR-11
 Earlier sketch in CA 25-28R
Lutwack, Leonard 1917- 41-44R
Lutyens, (Agnes) Elisabeth 1906-1983
 Obituary 109
Lutyens, Mary 1908- 25-28R
Lutz, Alma 1890-1973 .... CAP-1
 Obituary 45-48
 Earlier sketch in CA 9-10
Lutz, Charles P(aul) 1931- 115
Lutz, Cora Elizabeth 1906-1985 102
 Obituary 115
Lutz, Frank W. 1928- 33-36R
Lutz, Gertrude May 1899- 33-36R
Lutz, Harley L. 1882-1975 Obituary 53-56
Lutz, Jerry 1939- 89-92
Lutz, Jessie Gregory 1925- 15-16R
Lutz, John (Thomas) 1939- CANR-24
 Earlier sketches in CA 65-68, CANR-9
Lutz, Paul E(ugene) 1934- 61-64
Lutz, William D. 1940- 33-36R
Lutz, William W(alter) 1919- 49-52
Lutze, Karl E(rnst) 1920- 89-92
Lutzer, Erwin W(esley) 1941- CANR-2
 Earlier sketch in CA 45-48
Lutzker, Edythe 1904- 37-40R
 See also SATA 5
Luvaas, Jay 1927- 15-16R
Luvaas, William 1945- 121
Lux, Thomas 1946- 41-44R
Luxemburg, Rosa 1870(?)-1919
 Brief entry 118
Luxenburg, Norman 1927- 41-44R
Luxton, Leonora Kathrine 1895- 85-88
Luxton, Richard (Neil) 1950- 110
Luyben, Helen L. 1932- 17-18R
Luytens, David (Edwin) Bulwer 1929- 13-14R
Luza, Radomir 1922- CANR-24
 Earlier sketches in CA 11-12R, CANR-9
Luzbetak, Louis J(oseph) 1918- 33-36R
Luzi, Mario 1914- CANR-9
 Earlier sketch in CA 61-64
 See also CLC 13
Luzwick, Dierdre 1945- 65-68
Luzzati, Emanuele 1921- 29-32R
 See also SATA 7
Luzzatto, Paola Caboara 1938- 112
 See also SATA 38
Lyall, Gavin T(udor) 1932- CANR-4
 Earlier sketch in CA 9-10R
Lyall, Katharine Elizabeth 1928- CANR-7
 Earlier sketch in CA 7-8R
Lyall, Leslie T(heodore) 1905- 15-16R
Lycan, Gilbert L(ester) 1909- CAP-2
 Earlier sketch in CA 33-36
Lyday, Leon F(aidherbee) III 1939- 33-36R
Lydecker, Beatrice 1938- 106
Lyden, Fremont J(ames) 1926- 25-28R
Lydenberg, John 1913- 37-40R
Lydolph, Paul E. 1924- 13-14R
Lydon, James Gavin 1927- Brief entry 105
Lydon, Michael 1942- 85-88
 See also SATA 11
Lyfick, Warren
 See Reeves, Lawrence F.
Lyford, Joseph Philip 1918- 37-40R
Lyford-Pike, Margaret (Prudence) 1911- 109
Lygre, David G(erald) 1942- 93-96
Lykiard, Alexis (Constantine) 1940- 81-84
Lykken, David Thoreson 1928- 105
Lyle, Albert Walter 1944- 124
 Brief entry 117
Lyle, David 1927- 118
Lyle, Guy R(edvers) 1907- 61-64
Lyle, Jack 1929- 13-14R
Lyle, Jerolyn R(oss) 1937- 89-92
Lyle, Katie Letcher 1938- 49-52
 See also SATA 8
Lyle, Sparky
 See Lyle, Albert Walter
Lyles, Vina Honish 1935- 11-12R
Lyles, William H(using) 1946- 111
Lyle-Smythe, Alan 1914- 103
Lyly, John 1554(?)-1606 .... DLB-62
Lyman, Albert Robison 1880-1973 ...... CAP-1
 Earlier sketch in CA 15-16
Lyman, Helen (Lucille) Huguenor 1910- ... 65-68
Lyman, Howard B(urbeck) 1920- 41-44R
Lyman, Irene (Vera) Ponting 7-8R
Lyman, Lauren D(wight) 1891-1972
 Obituary 89-92
Lyman, Marilyn F(lorence) 1925- 93-96
Lyman, Mary Ely 1887-1975 Obituary 53-56

Lyman, Stanford M(orris) 1933- ... CANR-12
Earlier sketch in CA 29-32R
Lyman, Susan Elizabeth 1906-1976
Obituary ... 69-72
Lymington, John
See Chance, John Newton
Lynch, Brian
See Liddy, James (Daniel Reeves)
Lynch, David 1946- Brief entry ... 124
Lynch, Edith M. (Carstensen) 1912-1986 ... 105
Obituary ... 119
Lynch, Eric
See Bingley, David Ernest
Lynch, Etta Lee 1924- ... 69-72
Lynch, Frances
See Compton, D(avid) G(uy)
Lynch, Hayden Wood 1927(?)-1979
Obituary ... 89-92
Lynch, Henry T(homson) 1928- ... 89-92
Lynch, Hollis Ralph 1935- ... CANR-1
Earlier sketch in CA 45-48
Lynch, J(ohn) Joseph 1894-1987
Obituary ... 123
Lynch, James 1936- ... CANR-18
Earlier sketch in CA 101
Lynch, James
See Andreyev, Leonid (Nikolaevich)
Lynch, James F. 1919(?)-1985 Obituary ... 117
Lynch, James J(oseph) 1938- ... 73-76
Lynch, John 1927- ... 85-88
Lynch, Kathleen M(artha) 1898- ... 73-76
Lynch, Kevin (Andrew) 1918-1984 ... CANR-3
Obituary ... 112
Earlier sketch in CA 5-6R
Lynch, Lorenzo 1932- ... 29-32R
See also SATA 7
Lynch, Malcolm 1922- ... 119
Lynch, Marietta 1947- ... 106
See also SATA 29
Lynch, Marilyn 1938- ... 89-92
Lynch, Owen M(artin) 1931- ... CANR-11
Earlier sketch in CA 29-32R
Lynch, Patricia (Nora) 1898-1972 ... CAP-1
Earlier sketch in CA 11-12
See also SATA 9
Lynch, Patrick B(eavis) 1927- ... 9-10R
Lynch, Thomas Francis 1938- ... 45-48
Lynch, W(illiam) E(dward) 1930- ... CANR-10
Earlier sketch in CA 19-20R
Lynch, William F. 1908-1987 ... CANR-3
Obituary ... 121
Earlier sketch in CA 1R
Lynch Davis, B.
See Bioy Casares, Adolfo
and Borges, Jorge Luis
Lynch-Fraser, Diane 1953- ... 111
Lynch-Watson, Janet 1936- ... 93-96
Lynd, Helen Merrell 1896-1982 Obituary ... 105
Lynd, Robert S. 1892-1970 Obituary ... 29-32R
Lynd, Staughton (Craig) 1929- Brief entry ... 112
Lynde, Stan 1931- ... 65-68
Lynden, Patricia 1937- ... 73-76
Lyndon, Amy
See Radford, Richard F(rancis), Jr.
Lyndon, Diana
See Anthony, Diana
Lynds, Dennis 1924- ... CANR-22
Earlier sketches in CA 3R, CANR-6
See also SATA 37, 47
Lyne, John Alexander 1909- ... 97-100
Lyneis, Richard George 1935- ... 81-84
Lynen, John Fairbanks 1924- ... CANR-2
Earlier sketch in CA 4R
Lynes, (Joseph) Russell (Jr.) 1910- ... CANR-3
Earlier sketch in CA 2R
Lyngseth, Joan
See Davies, Joan
Lyngstad, Alexandra Halina 1925- ... 37-40R
Lyngstad, Sverre 1922- ... CANR-16
Earlier sketch in CA 37-40R
Lynn
See Brown, Velma Darbo
Lynn, Arthur D(ellert), Jr. 1921- ... CANR-10
Earlier sketch in CA 25-28R
Lynn, Conrad J. 1908- ... CAP-2
Earlier sketch in CA 23-24
Lynn, David B(randon) 1925- ... 57-60
Lynn, Edward S(hird) 1919- ... 57-60
Lynn, Edwin Charles 1935- ... 45-48
Lynn, Elizabeth A. 1946- ... 81-84
Lynn, Frank
See Leisy, James (Franklin)
Lynn, Irene
See Rowland, D(onald) S(ydney)
Lynn, Janet
See Salomon, Janet Lynn (Nowicki)
Lynn, Jeannette Murphy 1905- ... CAP-2
Earlier sketch in CA 21-22
Lynn, Jonathan 1943- ... 104
Lynn, Kenneth S(chuyler) 1923- ... CANR-3
Earlier sketch in CA 1R
Lynn, Laurence Edwin, Jr. 1937- ... 105
Lynn, Loretta (Webb) 1932(?)- ... 81-84
Lynn, Margaret
See Battye, Gladys Starkey
Lynn, Mary
See Brokamp, Marilyn
Lynn, Naomi B. 1933- ... 61-64
Lynn, Patricia
See Watts, Mabel Pizzey
Lynn, Richard 1930- ... 37-40R
Lynn, Roa 1937- ... 101
Lynn, Robert A(than) 1930- ... 17-18R
Lynn, Robert Wood 1925- ... 23-24R
Lynn, Ruth Nadelman 1948- ... 103
Lynne, Becky
See Zawadsky, Patience
Lynne, James Broom 1920- ... 77-80
Lynskey, Winifred 1904- ... CAP-2
Earlier sketch in CA 23-24
Lynton, Ann
See Rayner, Claire (Berenice)
Lynton, Harriet Ronken 1920- ... 73-76
Lynx
See West, Rebecca
Lyon, Bryce Dale 1920- Brief entry ... 106
Lyon, Buck
See Paine, Lauran (Bosworth)
Lyon, Christopher (Leslie) 1949-
Brief entry ... 118
Lyon, E(lijah) Wilson 1904- ... 97-100
Lyon, Elinor 1921- ... 25-28R
See also SATA 6
Lyon, Eugene 1929- ... 106
Lyon, George Ella 1949- ... 120
Lyon, Harold C(lifford), Jr. 1935- ... 41-44R
Lyon, James K(arl) 1934- ... CANR-1
Earlier sketch in CA 45-48
Lyon, Jessica
See DeLeeuw, Cateau
Lyon, John 1932- ... CANR-15
Earlier sketch in CA 41-44R
Lyon, Katherine
See Mix, Katherine Lyon
Lyon, Lyman R.
See de Camp, L(yon) Sprague
Lyon, Matthew 1749-1822 ... DLB-43
Lyon, Melvin (Ernest) 1927- ... 33-36R
Lyon, Peter 1915- ... CANR-5
Earlier sketch in CA 7-8R
Lyon, Peyton V(aughan) 1921- ... CANR-3
Earlier sketch in CA 11-12R
Lyon, Quinter M(arcellus) 1898- ... CAP-1
Earlier sketch in CA 19-20
Lyon, Thomas Edgar, Jr. 1939- ... 37-40R
Lyon, William Henry 1926- ... 15-16R
Lyon, Winston
See Woolfolk, William
Lyons, Arthur (Jr.) 1946- ... CANR-12
Earlier sketch in CA 29-32R
Lyons, Augusta Wallace ... 85-88
Lyons, Barbara (Baldwin) 1912- ... 93-96
Lyons, Catherine 1944- ... 85-88
Lyons, Daniel 1920- ... 41-44R
Lyons, David (Barry) 1935- ... 33-36R
Lyons, Delphine C.
See Smith, Evelyn E.
Lyons, Dorothy M(arawee) 1907- ... CANR-24
Earlier sketch in CA 2R
See also SATA 3
Lyons, Elena
See Fairburn, Eleanor
Lyons, Enid (Muriel) 1897-1981 ... 23-24R
Obituary ... 108
Lyons, Eugene 1898-1985 ... 9-10R
Obituary ... 114
Lyons, F(rancis) S(tewart) L(eland)
1923-1983 ... 29-32R
Obituary ... 110
Lyons, Grant 1941- ... CANR-15
Earlier sketch in CA 41-44R
See also SATA 30
Lyons, Ivan 1934- ... CANR-19
Earlier sketch in CA 101
Lyons, J. B. 1922- ... CANR-17
Earlier sketch in CA 97-100
Lyons, James
See Loewen, James W.
Lyons, John O(rmsby) 1927- ... 4R
Lyons, John T. 1926- ... 29-32R
Lyons, Joseph 1918- ... 13-14R
Lyons, Len 1942- ... 93-96
Lyons, Leonard 1906-1976 Obituary ... 69-72
Lyons, Louis M. 1897-1982 Obituary ... 106
Lyons, Marcus
See Blish, James (Benjamin)
Lyons, Mark Joseph 1910- ... 7-8R
Lyons, Nan 1935- ... CANR-19
Earlier sketch in CA 101
Lyons, Nick 1932- ... CANR-4
Earlier sketch in CA 53-56
Lyons, Richard D(aniel) 1928- ... 69-72
Lyons, Richard E(ugene) 1920- ... CANR-21
Earlier sketch in CA 45-48
Lyons, Sister Jeanne Marie 1904- ... CAP-1
Earlier sketch in CA 11-12
Lyons, Thomas Tolman 1934- ... CANR-3
Earlier sketch in CA 11-12R
Lyons, Timothy J(ames) 1944- ... 73-76
Lyons, Tom W(allace) 1943- ... 116
Ly-Qui, Chung 1940- ... 29-32R
Lyre, Pinchbeck
See Sassoon, Siegfried (Lorraine)
Lys, Daniel 1924- ... 23-24R
Lysaght, Averil M(argaret) ... 85-88
Lysaught, Jerome Paul 1930- ... CANR-6
Earlier sketch in CA 7-8R
Lysenko, T(rofim) D(enisovich) 1898-1976
Obituary ... 69-72
Lysons, Kenneth 1923- ... CANR-15
Earlier sketch in CA 85-88
Lystad, Mary (Hanemann) 1928- ... CANR-10
Earlier sketch in CA 65-68
See also SATA 11
Lystad, Robert A(rthur) 1920- ... 15-16R
Lyte, Charles 1935- ... 104
Lyte, Richard
See Whelpton, (George) Eric
Lytle, Andrew (Nelson) 1902- ... 9-10R
See also DLB 6
See also CLC 22
Lytle, Clifford M(erle) 1932- ... 93-96
Lytle, Guy Fitch (III) 1944- ... 118
Lytle, Ruby (Coker) 1917-19(?) ... CAP-1
Earlier sketch in CA 15-16
Lyttelton, Humphrey (Richard Adeane)
1921- Brief entry ... 118
Lyttle, Charles Harold 1885(?)-1980 ... 109
Obituary ... 97-100
Lyttle, G(erald) R(oland) 1908- ... CAP-1
Earlier sketch in CA 9-10
Lyttle, Jean
See Garrett, Eileen J(eanette)
Lyttle, Richard B(ard) 1927- ... CANR-13
Earlier sketch in CA 33-36R
See also SATA 23
Lytton, Edward G(eorge) E(arle) L(ytton)
Bulwer-Lytton, Baron 1803-1873 ... SATA-23
Lytton, Edward Robert Bulwer
1831-1891 ... DLB-32
Lytton, Hugh 1921- ... 45-48
Lytton, Noel (Anthony Scawen)
1900-1985 ... CAP-1
Obituary ... 115
Earlier sketch in CA 9-10
Lytton-Sells, Iris (Esther) 1903- ... 29-32R
Lyudvinskaya, Tatyana 1885(?)-1976
Obituary ... 65-68

M

M
See Stone, Susan Berch
M. C.
See Cook, Mabel Collins
M. G.
See Giergielewicz, Mieczyslaw F.
Ma, John T(a-jen) 1920- ... 49-52
Ma, Nancy Chih 1919- ... CANR-10
Earlier sketch in CA 65-68
Maar, Leonard (Frank, Jr.) 1927- ... 106
See also SATA 30
Maas, Audrey Gellen 1936-1975 ... CAP-2
Obituary ... 57-60
Earlier sketch in CA 23-24
Maas, Henry 1929- ... 25-28R
Maas, Jeremy 1928- ... 29-32R
Maas, Peter 1929- ... 93-96
See also CLC 29
Maas, Selve ... 69-72
See also SATA 14
Maas, Virginia H(argrave) 1913- ... 105
Maas, Willard 1911-1971 ... CAP-1
Obituary ... 29-32R
Earlier sketch in CA 13-14
Maasarani, Aly Mohamed 1927- ... 49-52
Maass, Arthur 1917- Brief entry ... 105
Maass, Joachim 1901-1972 Obituary ... 37-40R
Maass, John 1918- Brief entry ... 108
Mabberley, D(avid) J(ohn) 1948- ... 122
Mabbett, I(an) W(illiam) 1939- ... 29-32R
Mabbott, John David 1898-1988 ... 13-14R
Obituary ... 124
Mabee, Carleton 1914- ... CANR-21
Earlier sketch in CA 1R
Maberly, Allan 1922-1977 ... 103
Maberly, Norman C(harles) 1926- ... 33-36R
Mabery, D. L. 1953- ... 121
Mabey, Richard (Thomas) 1941- ... CANR-9
Earlier sketch in CA 23-24R
Mabley, Edward (Howe) 1906-1984 ... 29-32R
Obituary ... 114
Mabley, Jack 1915- ... 105
Mabogunje, Akin(lawon) L(adipo)
1931- ... CANR-16
Earlier sketch in CA 77-80
Mabon, John Scott 1910(?)-1980
Obituary ... 104
Mabry, Bevars Dupre 1928- ... 45-48
Mabry, Donald J(oseph) 1941- ... 49-52
Mac
See MacManus, Seumas
Mac, Carm
See Armstrong, Keith F(rancis)
W(hitfield)
MacAdam, Eve
See Leslie, Cecilie
MacAdams, Lewis (Perry, Jr.) 1944- ... 97-100
MacAfee, Norman 1943- ... 122
MacAgy, Douglas G(uernsey) 1913-1973 ... 102
Macainsh, Noel Leslie 1926- ... 103
MacAlan, Peter
See Ellis, Peter Berresford
MacAlpin, Rory
See Mackinnon, Charles Roy
MacAlpine, Margaret H(esketh Murray)
1907- ... CAP-1
Earlier sketch in CA 11-12
Macan, T(homas) T(ownley) 1910- ... 107
Macao, Marshall
See Tuleja, Thaddeus F(rancis)
MacAodhagain, Eamon
See Egan, E(dward) W(elstead)
MacApp, C. C.
See Capps, Carroll M.
Macarov, David 1918- ... CANR-12
Earlier sketch in CA 29-32R
MacArthur, Charles 1895-1956 Brief entry ... 108
See also DLB 7, 25, 44
MacArthur, D(avid) Wilson 1903- ... CANR-5
Earlier sketch in CA 11-12R
MacArthur, Douglas 1880-1964 Obituary ... 113
MacArthur, John F., Jr. 1939- ... 81-84
MacArthur, Robert H(elmer) 1930-1972
Obituary ... 37-40R
MacArthur-Onslow, Annette Rosemary
1933- ... 102
See also SATA 26
Macartney, (Carlile) Aylmer 1895- ... 19-20R
Macaulay, David (Alexander) 1946- ... CANR-5
Earlier sketch in CA 53-56
See also SATA 27, 46
See also DLB 61
See also CLR 3, 14
Macaulay, John (Ure) 1925- ... 107
Macaulay, Neill (Webster, Jr.) 1935- ... 21-22R
Macaulay, Rose 1881-1958 Brief entry ... 104
See also DLB 36
See also TCLC 7
Macaulay, Stewart 1931- ... 77-80
Macaulay, Susan Schaeffer 1941- ... 120
Macaulay, Thomas Babington
1800-1859 ... DLB-32, 55
Macauley, Robie Mayhew 1919- ... CANR-3
Earlier sketch in CA 3R
MacAusland, Earle R(utherford)
1893-1980 Obituary ... 101
MacAvoy, Paul W(ebster) 1934-
Brief entry ... 105
MacAvoy, Roberta Ann 1949- ... 113
MacBean, Dilla Whittemore 1895- ... 5-6R
MacBeth, George (Mann) 1932- ... 25-28R
See also SATA 4
See also DLB 40
See also CLC 2, 5, 9
Macbeth, Norman 1910- ... CAP-2
Earlier sketch in CA 33-36
MacBride, Robert O(liver) 1926- ... 19-20R
MacBride, Roger Lea 1929- ... 81-84
MacBride, Sean 1904-1988 Obituary ... 124
MacCaffrey, Isabel Gamble 1924-1978 ... 81-84
Obituary ... 77-80
MacCaffrey, Wallace T(revethic) 1920-
Brief entry ... 112
Mac Caig, Norman (Alexander) 1910- ... CANR-3
Earlier sketch in CA 9-10R
See also DLB 27
See also CLC 36
MacCall, Libby
See Machol, Libby
MacCallum Scott, John H. 1911- ... 25-28R
MacCampbell, James C(urtis) 1916- ... 9-10R
MacCann, Donnarae 1931- ... CANR-1
Earlier sketch in CA 45-48
MacCann, Richard Dyer 1920- ... CANR-5
Earlier sketch in CA 9-10R
MacCarthy, Fiona 1940- ... 105
MacCarthy, J(oseph) A(idan) 1913- ... 107
MacCauley, Sister Rose Agnes 1911- ... 37-40R
Macciocchi, Maria Antoinetta 1922- ... 73-76
MacClintock, Dorcas 1932- ... CANR-6
Earlier sketch in CA 57-60
See also SATA 8
MacCloskey, Monro 1902- ... CANR-5
Earlier sketch in CA 11-12R
Maccoby, Eleanor E(mmons) 1917-
Brief entry ... 113
Maccoby, Michael 1933- ... CANR-14
Earlier sketch in CA 33-36R
MacCollam, Joel A(llan) 1946- ... 105
MacCombie, John 1932- ... 37-40R
MacCorkle, Stuart A(lexander) 1903- ... 19-20R
MacCormac, Earl Ronald 1935- ... 85-88
MacCormack, Sabine G(abriele) 1941- ... 106
MacCormick, Austin H(arbutt) 1893-1979
Obituary ... 93-96
MacCorquodale, Patricia (Lee) 1950- ... 101
MacCracken, Calvin D(odd) 1919- ... 116
MacCracken, Henry Noble 1880-1970 ... CAP-1
Obituary ... 29-32R
Earlier sketch in CA 19-20
MacCracken, Mary 1926- ... 49-52
MacCraig, Hugh
See Ward, Craig
MacCurdy, Raymond R(alph, Jr.) 1916- ... 41-44R
MacDermott, Mercia 1927- ... 106
MacDiarmid, Hugh
See Grieve, C(hristopher) M(urray)
See also DLB 20
See also CLC 2, 4, 11, 19
MacDonagh, Donagh 1912-1968
Obituary ... 93-96
MacDonald, Aeneas
See Thomson, George Malcolm
MacDonald, Anne Elizabeth Campbell Bard
1908-1958 Brief entry ... 121
MacDonald, Anson
See Heinlein, Robert A(nson)
MacDonald, Bernell 1948- ... 113
MacDonald, Betty
See MacDonald, Anne Elizabeth Campbell
Bard
See also YABC 1
Macdonald, Blackie
See Emrich, Duncan (Black Macdonald)
MacDonald, Bonnie 1941- ... 117
MacDonald, Charles B(rown) 1922- ... CANR-23
Earlier sketches in CA 9-10R, CANR-6
Macdonald, Coll 1924- ... 19-20R
MacDonald, Craig 1949- ... CANR-9
Earlier sketch in CA 57-60
Macdonald, Cynthia 1928- ... CANR-4
Earlier sketch in CA 49-52
See also CLC 13, 19
Macdonald, David W(hyte) 1951- ... 106
MacDonald, Dennis Ronald 1946- ... 111
Macdonald, Dwight 1906-1982 ... 29-32R
Obituary ... 108
See also SATA 29, 33
MacDonald, Edgar E(dgeworth) 1919- ... 115
MacDonald, Edwin A(nderson) 1907- ... 41-44R
Macdonald, Eleanor 1910- ... CAP-1
Earlier sketch in CA 9-10
Macdonald, Elisabeth 1926- ... 65-68

MacDonald, George 1824-1905
Brief entry 106
See also SATA 33
See also DLB 18
See also TCLC 9
Macdonald, Gerard 1940- 119
MacDonald, Golden
See Brown, Margaret Wise
Macdonald, Gordon A(ndrew)
1911-1978 .... CANR-15
Earlier sketch in CA 65-68
Macdonald, H(enry) Malcolm 1914- 19-20R
MacDonald, J. Fred(erick) 1941-
Brief entry 117
Macdonald, John (Barfoot) 1918- CANR-1
Earlier sketch in CA 49-52
Macdonald, John
See Millar, Kenneth
MacDonald, John D(ann) 1916-1986 .... CANR-19
Obituary 121
Earlier sketches in CA 2R, CANR-1
See also DLB 8
See also DLBY 86
See also CLC 3, 27, 44
Macdonald, John M. CANR-2
Earlier sketch in CA 4R
Macdonald, John Ross
See Millar, Kenneth
Macdonald, Julie 1926- 19-20R
Macdonald, Kenneth 1905- 73-76
Macdonald, Malcolm
See Ross-Macdonald, Malcolm J(ohn)
MacDonald, Malcolm John 1901-1981 .... 11-12R
Obituary 102
MacDonald, Malcolm M(urdoch) 1935- 41-44R
Macdonald, Marcia
See Hill, Grace Livingston
MacDonald, Margaret Read 1940- 110
Macdonald, Mary
See Gifford, Griselda
Macdonald, Neil (William) 1936- 89-92
Macdonald, Nina Hansell
See Looker, Antonina (Hansell)
MacDonald, Philip 1896(?)- 81-84
Macdonald, R. Ross 1923(?)-1983
Obituary 110
Macdonald, Robert M(unro) 1923- 11-12R
Macdonald, Robert S. 1925- 15-16R
Macdonald, Robert W. 1922- 19-20R
Macdonald, Ronald St. John 1928- 103
Macdonald, Ross
See Millar, Kenneth
See also CLC 1, 2, 3, 14, 34, 41
MacDonald, Ruby (DeAngelo Norton)
1930- 115
MacDonald, Sandy 1949- 103
Macdonald, Shelagh 1937- 97-100
See also SATA 25
MacDonald, Simon G(avin) G(eorge)
1923- 53-56
MacDonald, Timothy I(gnatius) 1941- 121
MacDonald, William L. 1921- 23-24R
Macdonald, Zillah K(atherine) 1885- CAP-1
Earlier sketch in CA 9-10
See also SATA 11
Macdonnell, James Edmond 1917- CANR-8
Earlier sketch in CA 7-8R
MacDonnell, Kevin 1919- 45-48
MacDonnell, Megan
See Stevens, Serita (Deborah)
MacDouall, Robertson
See Mair, George Brown
MacDougal, John
See Blish, James (Benjamin)
and Lowndes, Robert A(ugustine) W(ard)
MacDougall, A(llan) Kent 1931- 45-48
MacDougall, Curtis D(aniel) 1903-1985 53-56
Obituary 117
MacDougall, (George) Donald (Alastair)
1912- 106
MacDougall, Fiona
See MacLeod, Robert F.
MacDougall, Malcolm D(ouglas) 1928-
Brief entry 110
MacDougall, Mary Katherine CANR-12
Earlier sketch in CA 29-32R
MacDougall, Ruth Doan 1939- CANR-8
Earlier sketch in CA 19-20R
MacDowell, Douglas M(aurice) 1931- CANR-6
Earlier sketch in CA 5-6R
Mace, C(ecil) Alec 1894- CAP-1
Earlier sketch in CA 13-14
Mace, Carroll Edward 1926- 41-44R
Mace, David Robert 1907- CANR-23
Earlier sketches in CA 57-60, CANR-7
Mace, Don 1899(?)-1983 Obituary 109
Mace, Elisabeth 1933- CANR-23
Earlier sketch in CA 77-80
See also SATA 27
Mace, Myles L(a Grange) 1911-
Brief entry 110
Mace, Nancy L(awson) 1941- 119
Mace, Varian 1938- SATA-49
Mace, Vera C(hapman) 1902- 113
MacEoin, Gary 1909- CANR-2
Earlier sketch in CA 4R
Macer-Story, E(ugenia) 1945- CANR-23
Earlier sketch in CA 107
Macesich, George 1927- 15-16R
MacEwan, J(ohn) W(alter) Grant 1902- 41-44R
MacEwan, Paul W. 1943- CANR-7
Earlier sketch in CA 61-64
MacEwen, Gwendolyn (Margaret)
1941-1987 .... CANR-22
Obituary 124
Earlier sketches in CA 9-10R, CANR-7
See also SATA 50
See also DLB 53
See also CLC 13
MacEwen, Malcolm 1911- 110
Macey, Samuel L(awson) 1922- 102
Macfadden, Bernarr 1868-1955 .... DLB-25
MacFall, Russell P(atterson) 1903-1983 .... CAP-1
Obituary 110
Earlier sketch in CA 11-12
Macfarlan, Allan A. 1892-1982 107
See also SATA 35
Macfarlane, (Robert) Gwyn 1907-1987
Obituary 122
MacFarlane, Iris 1922- 89-92
See also SATA 11
MacFarlane, Kenneth
See Walker, Kenneth Macfarlane
Macfarlane, Leslie John 1924- 21-22R
MacFarlane, Louise 1917(?)-1979
Obituary 89-92
MacFarlane, Stephen
See Cross, John Keir
MacFarquhar, Roderick 1930- CANR-13
Earlier sketch in CA 21-22R
MacFee, Maxwell
See Rennie, James Alan
MacGaffey, Wyatt 1932- 73-76
MacGibbon, Jean 1913- 97-100
MacGill, Patrick 1890(?)-1963 116
MacGillivray, John H(enry) 1899- CAP-2
Earlier sketch in CA 25-28
MacGorman, J(ohn) W(illiam) 1920- 102
Macgowan, Kenneth 1888-1963 Obituary 93-96
MacGregor, Alasdair Alpin (Douglas)
1899-1970 .... CAP-1
Obituary 29-32R
Earlier sketch in CA 11-12
MacGregor, Bruce (Alan) 1945- 77-80
MacGregor, David Roy 1925- 93-96
MacGregor, Ellen 1906-1954 Brief entry 111
See also SATA 27, 39
Macgregor, Frances Cooke CANR-1
Earlier sketch in CA 1R
MacGregor, (John) Geddes 1909- CANR-21
Earlier sketches in CA 3R, CANR-2
Macgregor, James (Murdoch) 1925- CANR-5
Earlier sketch in CA 13-14R
MacGregor, James G(rierson) 1905- CANR-10
Earlier sketch in CA 25-28R
MacGregor, Malcolm D(ouglas) 1945- 102
MacGregor, Robert Mercer 1911-1974
Obituary 104
MacGregor, T. J.
See Janeshutz, Patricia M(arie)
MacGregor-Hastie, Roy (Alasdhair Niall)
1929- CANR-20
Earlier sketches in CA 4R, CANR-2
See also SATA 3
Macgregor-Morris, Pamela 1925- 29-32R
MacGuigan, Mark R(udolph) 1931- 23-24R
Machado (y Ruiz), Antonio 1875-1939
Brief entry 104
See also TCLC 3
Machado, Manuel Anthony, Jr. 1939- 29-32R
Machado de Assis, Joaquim Maria
1839-1908 Brief entry 107
See also TCLC 10
Machan, Tibor R(ichard) 1939- CANR-1
Earlier sketch in CA 45-48
MacHardy, Charles 1926- 104
Machen, Arthur
See Jones, Arthur Llewellyn
See also DLB 36
See also TCLC 4
Machetanz, Frederick 1908- SATA-34
Machetanz, Sara Burleson 1918- 4R
Machiavelli
See McCready, Warren T(homas)
Machin, G(eorge) Ian T(hom) 1937- 15-16R
Machin Goodall, Daphne (Edith) CANR-7
Earlier sketch in CA 7-8R
See also SATA 37
Machlin, Milton Robert 1924- CANR-2
Earlier sketch in CA 4R
Machlis, Joseph 1906- CANR-22
Earlier sketches in CA 2R, CANR-2
Machlowitz, Marilyn M(arcia) 1952- 101
Machlup, Fritz 1902-1983 .... CANR-6
Obituary 109
Earlier sketch in CA 3R
Machol, Libby 1916- 23-24R
Machol, Robert E(ngel) 1917- 37-40R
Macholtz, James Donald 1926- 53-56
Machorton, Ian (Duncan) 1923- CANR-8
Earlier sketch in CA 19-20R
MacHorton, Ian
See Machorton, Ian (Duncan)
Machotka, Otakar (Richard) 1899-1970 .... CAP-1
Obituary 29-32R
Earlier sketch in CA 15-16
Macht, Joel 1938- 57-60
Macia, Rafael 1946- 97-100
Maciel, Judi(th Anne) 1942- 33-36R
MacInnes, Colin 1914-1976 .... CANR-21
Obituary 65-68
Earlier sketch in CA 69-72
See also DLB 14
See also CLC 4, 23
MacInnes, Helen (Clark) 1907-1985 .... CANR-1
Obituary 117
Earlier sketch in CA 1R
See also SATA 22, 44
See also CLC 27, 39
MacInnis, Donald E(arl) 1920- 41-44R
MacIntosh, J(ohn) J(ames) 1934- 37-40R
MacIntosh, Joan 1924- 107
MacIntosh, Keitha 1954- 112
MacIntyre, Alasdair (Chalmers) 1929-
Brief entry 118
Macintyre, Angus (Donald) 1935- 118
MacIntyre, Christine Melba 1939-1987
Obituary 123
Macintyre, Donald George (Frederick
Wyville) 1904- 7-8R
MacIntyre, Elisabeth 1916- CANR-5
Earlier sketch in CA 11-12R
See also SATA 17
MacIre, Esor B.
See Ambrose, Eric (Samuel)
MacIsaac, David 1935- CANR-14
Earlier sketch in CA 77-80
MacIsaac, Sharon 57-60
Maciuszko, Jerzy J. 1913- 25-28R
Maciuszko, Kathleen L(ynn) 1947- 113
MacIver, Robert M(orrison) 1882-1970 .... CAP-1
Obituary 25-28R
Earlier sketch in CA 11-12
Mack, Edward C. 1905(?)-1973 Obituary 45-48
Mack, Evalina
See McNamara, Lena Brooke
Mack, Gerstle 1894-1983 Obituary 109
Mack, J. A. 1906- 65-68
Mack, James D(ecker) 1916- 21-22R
Mack, Jerry
See Johnson, Jerry Mack
Mack, John E(dward) 1929- 106
Mack, Karin E(ileen) 1946- 97-100
Mack, Kirby
See McEvoy, Harry K(irby)
Mack, Marjorie
See Dixon, Marjorie (Mack)
Mack, Mary Peter 1927-1973 .... 4R
Obituary 103
Mack, Max Noble 1916- 61-64
Mack, Maynard 1909- 9-10R
Mack, Raymond (Wright) 1927- 13-14R
Mack, Stan(ley) 85-88
See also SATA 17
Mack, Walter Staunton 1895- 109
Mackal, Roy P(aul) 1925- 73-76
Mackaman, Frank H(indes) II 1950- 111
Mackarness, Richard 1916- 103
MacKay, Alfred F(arnum) 1938- 104
MacKay, Alistair McColl 1931- 81-84
Mackay, Barbara E. 1944- 77-80
Mackay, Claire 1930- CANR-22
Earlier sketch in CA 105
See also SATA 40
Mackay, Constance D'Arcy (?)-1966 102
MacKay, D(onald) I(ain) 1937- CANR-24
Earlier sketch in CA 29-32R
MacKay, Donald M(acCrimmon)
1922-1987 .... CANR-13
Obituary 121
Earlier sketch in CA 29-32R
Mackay, James (Alexander) 1936- CANR-23
Earlier sketches in CA 53-56, CANR-7
Mackay, John Alexander 1889-1983
Obituary 110
MacKay, Joy 1918- 65-68
Mackay, Malcolm George 1919- 108
Mackay, Mary 1855-1924 Brief entry 118
Mackay, Mercedes (Isabelle) 1906- CAP-1
Earlier sketch in CA 11-12
MacKay, Robert A(lexander) 1894- 11-12R
Mackay, Ruddock F(inlay) 1922- 102
Mackay, Shena 1944- 104
MacKay, William 1943(?)- Brief entry 110
MacKaye, Benton 1879-1975 Obituary 61-64
MacKaye, Milton 1901-1979 93-96
Obituary 85-88
MacKaye, Percy (Wallace) 1875-1956
Brief entry 113
See also SATA 32
See also DLB 54
MacKaye, William Ross 1934- Brief entry 109
MacKeever, Maggie
See Clark, Gail
MacKeith, Ronald Charles 1908-1977
Obituary 77-80
MacKellar, William 1914- CANR-13
Earlier sketch in CA 33-36R
See also SATA 4
Mackelworth, R(onald) W(alter) 1930- 29-32R
Macken, Walter 1915-1967 .... CAP-1
Obituary 25-28R
Earlier sketch in CA 13-14
See also SATA 36
See also DLB 13
Mackendrick, John 1946- 81-84
MacKendrick, Paul Lachlan 1914- CANR-1
Earlier sketch in CA 1R
Mackensen, Heinz Friedrich 1921-
Brief entry 107
Mackenzie, Alastair (Ian Folliott) 1933- 118
MacKenzie, Andrew 1911- 49-52
Mackenzie, Basil William Sholto
1900-1983 Obituary 111
MacKenzie, Christine Butchart 1917- 15-16R
Mackenzie, Compton (Edward Montague)
1883-1972 .... CAP-2
Obituary 37-40R
Earlier sketch in CA 21-22
See also DLB 34
See also CLC 18
MacKenzie, David 1927- 21-22R
MacKenzie, Donald 1918- CANR-21
Earlier sketch in CA 25-28R
MacKenzie, Fred 1905- CAP-2
Earlier sketch in CA 25-28
MacKenzie, Garry 1921- SATA-31
Mackenzie, Henry 1745-1831 .... DLB-39
MacKenzie, Jean 1928- 93-96
MacKenzie, (Daisy) Jeanne 1922-1986
Obituary 120
MacKenzie, Joan Finnigan 1925- CANR-13
Earlier sketch in CA 17-18R
MacKenzie, John P(ettibone) 1930- 65-68
Mackenzie, Kathleen Guy 1907- 7-8R
Mackenzie, Kenneth (Ivo) 1913-1955
Brief entry 122
Mackenzie, Kenneth Donald 1937- 37-40R
Mackenzie, Locke L. 1900(?)-1977
Obituary 69-72
MacKenzie, Louise (Wilks) 1920- 29-32R
Mackenzie, Manfred 1934- 65-68
MacKenzie, Norman H(ugh) 1915- 23-24R
MacKenzie, Ossian 1907-1980 .... 25-28R
Obituary 120
MacKenzie, R(oderick) A(ndrew) F(rancis)
1911- 7-8R
Mackenzie, R. Alec
See Mackenzie, Richard Alexander
MacKenzie, Rachel 1909-1980 102
Obituary 97-100
Mackenzie, Richard Alexander 1923- 109
Mackenzie, Seaforth
See Mackenzie, Kenneth (Ivo)
Mackenzie, W(illiam) J(ames) M(illar)
1909- 104
Mackenzie, Willard, Dr.
See Stratemeyer, Edward L.
Mackenzie-Grieve, Averil (Salmond)
1903- 9-10R
Mackerras, Colin Patrick 1939- CANR-15
Earlier sketch in CA 85-88
Mackesy, Piers G(erald) 1924- CANR-3
Earlier sketch in CA 9-10R
MacKethan, Lucinda Hardwick 1945- 102
Mackey, Ernan
See McInerny, Ralph
Mackey, Helen T. 1918- 5-6R
Mackey, J(ames) P(atrick) 1934- CANR-9
Earlier sketch in CA 65-68
Mackey, Louis H(enry) 1926- 33-36R
Mackey, Mary 1945- CANR-15
Earlier sketch in CA 77-80
Mackey, William Francis 1918- 37-40R
Mackey, William J., Jr. 1902(?)-1972
Obituary 37-40R
Mackey, William Wellington 1937- 124
Brief entry 120
See also DLB 38
Mackie, Alastair 1925- 19-20R
Mackie, Albert D(avid) 1904- CAP-1
Earlier sketch in CA 9-10
Mackie, J(ohn) L(eslie) 1917- CANR-7
Earlier sketch in CA 57-60
Mackie, (Benjamin) James 1932- 41-44R
Mackie, John
See Levinson, Leonard
Mackie, Margaret Davidson 1914- 102
Mackie, Maron
See McNeely, Jeannette
Mackie, Philip 1918-1985 103
Obituary 118
Mackiewicz, Jozef 1902-1985 Obituary 116
MacKillop, James (John) 1939- 113
Mackin, Anita
See Donson, Cyril
Mackin, Catherine (Patricia) 1939-1982 109
Obituary 108
Mackin, Cooper R(icherson) 1933- 41-44R
Mackin, Dorothy (May Mabee) 1917- 107
Mackin, John H(oward) 1921- 33-36R
Mackin, Theodore 1922- 116
Mackinlay, Leila Antoinette Sterling
1910- CANR-24
Earlier sketches in CA 11-12, CAP-1
Mackinlock, Duncan
See Watts, Peter Christopher
Mackinnon, Charles Roy 1924- CANR-7
Earlier sketch in CA 9-10R
MacKinnon, Edward M(ichael) 1928- CANR-12
Earlier sketch in CA 61-64
MacKinnon, Frank 1919- 49-52
MacKinnon, John Ramsay 1947- 103
MacKinnon, Stephen Robert 1940- 107
MacKinstry, Elizabeth 1879-1956 .... SATA-42
Mackintosh, Athole S(palding) 1926- 7-8R
Mackintosh, Elizabeth 1896(?)-1952
Brief entry 110
MacKintosh, Ian 1940- 73-76
Mackintosh, John (Pitcairn) 1929-1978 103
Mackintosh, (John) Malcolm 1921- 7-8R
Mackintosh, N(icholas) J(ohn) 1935- 124
Mackintosh, Prudence 1944- 124
Mackle, Jeff
See McLeod, John F(reeland)
Mackler, Bernard 1934- 23-24R
Mackley, George 1900-1983 Obituary 109
Macklin, Barbara J(une) 1925- Brief entry 118
Macklin, June
See Macklin, Barbara J(une)
MacKnight, Nancy (Margaret) 1940- 118
Mackowski, Richard M(artin) 1929- 106
Macksey, (Catherine Angela) Joan 1925- 65-68
Macksey, Kenneth J. 1923- CANR-11
Earlier sketch in CA 25-28R
Macksey, Major K. J.
See Macksey, Kenneth J.
Macksey, Richard (Alan) 1930- 101
Mack Smith, Denis 1920- CANR-17
Earlier sketch in CA 23-24R
Mackworth, Cecily 57-60
Mackworth, Jane F. 1917- 37-40R
Macky, Peter W(allace) 1937- 53-56

MacLachlan, James Angell 1891-1967 ... CAP-2
Earlier sketch in CA 19-20
Maclachlan, Lewis 1894-1980 ... CANR-6
Earlier sketch in CA 7-8R
MacLachlan, Patricia 1938- Brief entry ... 118
See also SATA 42
See also CLR 14
Maclagan, Bridget
See Borden, Mary
Maclagan, Michael 1914- ... 7-8R
MacLaine, Allan H(ugh) 1924- ... 15-16R
MacLaine, Shirley
See Beaty, Shirley MacLean
MacLaren, A. Allan 1938- ... 106
Maclaren, Colin Shaw 1898-1985
Obituary ... 116
MacLaren, James
See Grieve, C(hristopher) M(urray)
MacLaren, Sherrill M. 1939- ... 124
Mac Laverty, Bernard 1942- ... 118
Brief entry ... 116
See also CLC 31
Maclay, George 1943- ... 45-48
Maclay, Joanna Hawkins 1938- ... 112
Maclean, Alasdair 1926- Brief entry ... 113
MacLean, Alistair (Stuart) 1922(?)-1987 ... 57-60
Obituary ... 121
See also SATA 23, 50
See also CLC 3, 13
Maclean, Arthur
See Tubb, E(dwin) C(harles)
MacLean, Barbara Anne Hutmacher
See Hutmacher (MacLean), Barbara Anne
Maclean, Charles 1946- ... 109
Maclean, Donald Duart 1913-1983
Obituary ... 109
Maclean, Fitzroy (Hew) 1911- ... CANR-14
Earlier sketch in CA 29-32R
MacLean, Jane 1935- ... 101
MacLean, Janet Rockwood 1917- ... 33-36R
MacLean, Katherine 1925- ... 33-36R
See also DLB 8
Maclean, Norman 1902- ... 102
Maclean, Una 1925- ... 69-72
MacLeish, Andrew 1923- ... 19-20R
MacLeish, Archibald 1892-1982 ... 9-10R
Obituary ... 106
See also DLB 4, 7, 45
See also DLBY 82
See also CLC 3, 8, 14
MacLeish, Kenneth 1917-1977 ... 81-84
Obituary ... 73-76
MacLeish, Rod(erick) 1926- ... 41-44R
MacLeish, William H(itchcock) 1928- ... 120
MacLennan, David Alexander
1903-1978 ... CANR-2
Earlier sketch in CA 3R
MacLennan, (John) Hugh 1907- ... 7-8R
See also CLC 2, 14
MacLennan, Toby 1939- ... 115
Macleod, Alison 1920- ... 53-56
MacLeod, Alistair 1936- ... 123
See also DLB 60
MacLeod, Beatrice (Beach) 1910- ... CAP-1
Earlier sketch in CA 19-20
See also SATA 10
MacLeod, Celeste (Lipow) 1931- ... 105
MacLeod, Charlotte (Matilda Hughes)
1922- ... CANR-18
Earlier sketch in CA 23-24R
See also SATA 28
Macleod, David I(rving, Jr.) 1943- ... 123
Macleod, Donald 1914- ... 19-20R
MacLeod, Doug 1959- ... 112
MacLeod, Duncan J(ohn) 1939- ... 61-64
MacLeod, Earle Henry 1907- ... CAP-1
Earlier sketch in CA 9-10
MacLeod, Ellen Jane (Anderson) 1916- ... CANR-3
Earlier sketch in CA 7-8R
See also SATA 14
MacLeod, Jean Sutherland 1908- ... CANR-3
Earlier sketch in CA 11-12R
Macleod, Jennifer Selfridge 1929- ... 102
Macleod, Joseph (Todd Gordon)
1903-1984(?) ... 65-68
Obituary ... 112
Macleod, Norman (Wicklund) 1906-1985 ... 73-76
Obituary ... 116
See also DLB 4
MacLeod, Robert
See Knox, William
MacLeod, Robert F. 1917- ... 77-80
MacLeod, Roderick 1892(?)-1984
Obituary ... 113
MacLeod, Ruth 1903- ... 93-96
Mac Liammhoir, Micheal
See Mac Liammoir, Micheal
Mac Liammhoir, Micheal
See Mac Liammoir, Micheal
Mac Liammoir, Micheal 1899-1978 ... CANR-3
Obituary ... 77-80
Earlier sketch in CA 45-48
Mac Low, Jackson 1922- ... 81-84
Maclure, (John) Stuart 1926- ... 61-64
MacLysaght, Edward Anthony
1887-1986 ... CANR-1
Obituary ... 118
Earlier sketch in CA 3R
Macmahon, Arthur W(hittier) 1890- ... 19-20R
MacMahon, Bryan (Michael) 1909- ... CANR-23
Earlier sketch in CA 41-44R
MacMahon, Candace W(addell) 1950- ... 112
Macmann, Elaine
See Willoughby, Elaine Macmann
MacManus, James
See MacManus, Seumas
MacManus, Seumas 1869-1960 ... 102
Obituary ... 93-96
See also SATA 25
Macmanus, Sheila 1946- ... 111
MacManus, Susan A(nn) 1947- ... 116
MacManus, Yvonne 1931- ... CANR-11
Earlier sketch in CA 25-28R
MacMaster, Eve (Ruth) B(owers) 1942- ... 112
See also SATA 46
MacMaster, Richard Kerwin 1935- ... 115
Mac Master, Robert E(llsworth) 1919- ... 33-36R
MacMillan, Annabelle
See Quick, Annabelle
Macmillan, C(harles) J(ames) B(arr)
1935- ... 21-22R
MacMillan, Cecile 1898(?)-1986 Obituary ... 120
Macmillan, David S(tirling) 1925- ... 113
MacMillan, Donald L(ee) 1940- ... 57-60
Macmillan, Gail 1944- ... 97-100
Macmillan, (Maurice) Harold 1894-1986
Obituary ... 121
Brief entry ... 113
Macmillan, Maurice Victor 1921-1984
Obituary ... 112
Macmillan, Mona 1908- ... 33-36R
Macmillan, Norman 1892-1976 ... CAP-1
Obituary ... 69-72
Earlier sketch in CA 11-12
Macmillan, William Miller 1885-1974 ... CANR-9
Obituary ... 53-56
Earlier sketches in CA 11-12, CAP-1
MacMullan, Charles Walden Kirkpatrick
1889-1973 Obituary ... 89-92
MacMullen, Ramsay 1928- ... CANR-13
Earlier sketch in CA 21-22R
Macnab, Francis Auchline 1931- ... 25-28R
MacNab, P(eter) A(ngus) 1903- ... 33-36R
Macnab, Roy 1923- ... 65-68
MacNalty, Arthur (Salusbury)
1880-1969 ... CANR-5
Earlier sketch in CA 7-8R
MacNamara, Brinsley
See Weldon, John
See also DLB 10
Mac Namara, Donal E(oin) J(oseph)
1916- ... CANR-14
Earlier sketch in CA 33-36R
Macnamara, Ellen 1924- ... 103
Macnamara, John (Theodore) 1929- ... CANR-13
Earlier sketch in CA 21-22R
Macnaughton, William R(obert) 1939- ... 119
MacNeice, Jill 1956- ... 115
MacNeice, (Frederick) Louis 1907-1963 ... 85-88
See also DLB 10, 20
See also CLC 1, 4, 10
MacNeil, Duncan
See McCutchan, Philip (Donald)
Macneil, Ian R(oderick) 1929- ... 33-36R
MacNeil, Neil 1891-1969 ... CAP-1
Obituary ... 29-32R
Earlier sketch in CA 19-20
MacNeil, Neil
See Ballard, (Willis) Todhunter
MacNeil, Robert (Breckenridge Ware)
1931- ... 114
Brief entry ... 108
MacNeill, Dand
See Fraser, George MacDonald
MacNeill, Earl S(chwom) 1893-1972
Obituary ... 37-40R
Macneill, Janet
See McNeely, Jeannette
Macneill, Norma 1922- ... 117
MacNeish, Richard S(tockton) 1918- ... 37-40R
Macnell, James
See Macdonnell, James Edmond
MacNelly, C(larence) L(amont)
1920(?)-1986 Obituary ... 118
MacNelly, Jeff(rey Kenneth) 1947- ... 102
MacNib
See Mackie, Albert D(avid)
MacNicholas, John (Malcolm) 1943- ... 123
Brief entry ... 118
Macnicol, Eona K(athleen) Fraser 1910- ... 9-10R
MacNutt, Francis S. 1925- ... CANR-12
Earlier sketch in CA 73-76
Macomber, Daria
See Robinson, Patricia Colbert
Macomber, William (Butts, Jr.) 1921- ... 61-64
Mac Orlan, Pierre
See Dumarchais, Pierre
MacPeek, Walter G. 1902-1973 ... CAP-2
Obituary ... 41-44R
Earlier sketch in CA 29-32
See also SATA 4, 25
Macpherson, C(rawford) Brough
1911-1987 ... CANR-2
Obituary ... 123
Earlier sketch in CA 7-8R
Macpherson, (Jean) Jay 1931- ... 5-6R
See also DLB 53
See also CLC 14
Macpherson, Jeanie 1884-1946
Brief entry ... 123
See also DLB 44
Macpherson, Kenneth 1903(?)-1971
Obituary ... 29-32R
MacPherson, Malcolm C(ook) 1943- ... CANR-24
Earlier sketch in CA 102
MacPherson, Margaret 1908- ... 49-52
See also SATA 9
See also SAAS 4
MacPherson, Thomas George
1915-1976 ... CANR-4
Earlier sketch in CA 4R
See also SATA 30
Macquarrie, Alan (Denis) 1954- ... 122
Macquarrie, Heath Nelson 1919- ... CANR-20
Earlier sketch in CA 41-44R
Macquarrie, John 1919- ... CANR-1
Earlier sketch in CA 3R
Macqueen, James G(alloway) 1932- ... 19-20R
MacQuitty, William ... CANR-7
Earlier sketch in CA 19-20R
MacRae, C(hristopher) Fred(erick) 1909- ... 45-48
MacRae, Donald E. 1907- ... 93-96
MacRae, Donald G. 1921- ... 15-16R
MacRae, Duncan (Jr.) 1921- ... 23-24R
MacRae, George W(insor) 1928-1985
Obituary ... 117
Macrae, John, Jr. 1898(?)-1983 Obituary ... 111
Macrae, Marjorie Knight ?-1973
Obituary ... 41-44R
Macrae, Norman 1923- ... CANR-22
Earlier sketch in CA 106
Macrae, Travis
See Feagles, Anita M(acRae)
Macridis, Roy C(onstantine) 1918- ... 115
Macro, Eric 1920- ... 29-32R
Macrorie, Ken(neth) 1918- ... 65-68
Macrow, Brenda G(race Joan) Barton
1916- ... 11-12R
MacShane, Denis 1948- ... 109
MacShane, Frank 1927- ... CANR-3
Earlier sketch in CA 11-12R
See also CLC 39
MacStiofain, Sean
See Stephenson, John Edward Drayton
MacSweeney, Barry 1948- ... CANR-20
Earlier sketch in CA 25-28R
MacTaggart, Morna Doris
See Brown, Morna Doris
MacThomais, Ruaraidh
See Thomson, Derick S(mith)
Macumber, Mari
See Sandoz, Mari(e Susette)
Macura, Paul 1924- ... CANR-8
Earlier sketch in CA 19-20R
MacVane, John (Franklin) 1912-1984 ... CANR-16
Obituary ... 111
Earlier sketch in CA 65-68
MacVeagh, Lincoln 1890-1972 Obituary ... 33-36R
Macvey, John W(ishart) 1923- ... CANR-7
Earlier sketch in CA 19-20R
MacVicar, Angus 1908- ... CANR-10
Earlier sketch in CA 13-14R
Macy, Helen 1904(?)-1978 Obituary ... 81-84
Macy, John W(illiams), Jr. 1917-1986 ... 33-36R
Obituary ... 121
Macy, Mike 1951- ... 122
Madachy, Joseph S(teven) 1927- ... 5-6R
Madame Simone
See Porche, Simone (Benda)
Madan, T(riloki) N(ath) 1931- ... CANR-7
Earlier sketch in CA 19-20R
Madaras, Area 1969- ... 116
Madaras, Lynda 1947- ... 107
Madariaga, Isabel de
See de Madariaga, Isabel
Madariaga (Y Rojo), Salvador de
1886-1978 ... CANR-6
Obituary ... 81-84
Earlier sketch in CA 9-10R
Maday, Bela C(harles) 1912- ... 41-44R
Madden, Arthur Gerard 1911- ... 1R
Madden, Betty I(senbarger) 1915- ... 57-60
Madden, Carl H(alford) 1920-1978 ... 41-44R
Obituary ... 81-84
Madden, Cecil (Charles) 1902-1987
Obituary ... 122
Madden, Charles F(rank) 1921- ... 25-28R
Madden, Daniel Michael 1916- ... 65-68
Madden, (Jerry) David 1933- ... CANR-4
Earlier sketch in CA 3R
See also CAAS 3
See also DLB 6
See also CLC 5, 15
Madden, Don 1927- ... 25-28R
See also SATA 3
Madden, Donald L(eo) 1937- ... CANR-4
Earlier sketch in CA 53-56
Madden, E(dward) S(tanislaus) 1919- ... 11-12R
Madden, Edward H. 1925- ... CANR-1
Earlier sketch in CA 1R
Madden, Henry Miller 1912-1982 Obituary ... 108
Madden, Myron C(rowson) 1918- ... 115
Madden, Peter 1939- ... 115
Madden, Richard Raymond 1924- ... 5-6R
Madden, Warren
See Cameron, Kenneth Neill
Madden, William A. 1923- ... 23-24R
Maddern, Al(an)
See Ellison, Harlan
Madderom, Gary 1937- ... 45-48
Maddex, Jack P(endleton), Jr. 1941-
Brief entry ... 111
Maddi, Salvatore R(ichard) 1933- ... 13-14R
Maddison, Angela Mary 1923- ... 53-56
See also SATA 10
Maddison, Angus 1926- ... CANR-10
Earlier sketch in CA 13-14R
Maddison, Carol Hopkins 1923- ... 19-20R
Maddock, Brent 1950- ... 81-84
Maddock, Kenneth ?-1971 Obituary ... 104
Maddock, Larry
See Jardine, Jack
Maddock, Mary (Denise Catharine Majdak)
1951- ... 116
Maddock, Reginald (Bertram) 1912- ... 81-84
See also SATA 15
Maddocks, Margaret (Kathleen Avern)
1906- ... 116
Maddocks, Morris Henry St. John 1928- ... 116
Maddow, Ben 1909- ... DLB-44
Maddox, Brenda 1932- ... CANR-22
Earlier sketch in CA 97-100
Maddox, Carl
See Tubb, E(dwin) C(harles)
Maddox, Conroy 1912- ... 101
Maddox, Gaynor ... 9-10R
Maddox, George L(amar), Jr. 1925- ... 19-20R
Maddox, James G(ray) 1907-1973 ... CAP-2
Obituary ... 45-48
Earlier sketch in CA 21-22
Maddox, Jerrold (Warren) 1932- ... 19-20R
Maddox, Lester (Garfield) 1915-
Brief entry ... 112
Maddox, Marion Errol 1910- ... 23-24R
Maddox, Robert James 1931- ... 33-36R
Maddox, Russell W(ebber), Jr. 1921- ... 3R
Maddox, Sara Higgins Sturm
See Sturm-Maddox, Sara Higgins
Maddux, Rachel 1912- ... CANR-5
Earlier sketch in CA 4R
Madeleva, Sister Mary
See Wolff, Mary Evaline
Madelung, A. Margaret (Arent) 1926- ... 15-16R
Mader, (Stanley) Chris(topher, Jr.)
1943(?)-1980 Obituary ... 103
Madge, Charles Henry 1912- ... 97-100
Madge, John (Hylton) 1914-1968 ... CAP-1
Earlier sketch in CA 9-10
Madge, Violet 1916-19(?) ... CAP-2
Earlier sketch in CA 21-22
Madgett, Naomi Long 1923- ... CANR-13
Earlier sketch in CA 33-36R
Madgwick, P(eter) J(ames) 1925- ... CANR-24
Earlier sketch in CA 29-32R
Madhubuti, Haki R. 1942- ... CANR-24
Earlier sketch in CA 73-76
See also DLB 5, 41
See also CLC 6
Madian, Jon 1941- ... 61-64
See also SATA 9
Madigan, Marian East 1898- ... CAP-2
Earlier sketch in CA 19-20
Madigan, Mary Jean Smith 1941- ... 110
Madison, Arnold 1937- ... CANR-9
Earlier sketch in CA 21-22R
See also SATA 6
Madison, Charles A(llan) 1895- ... CANR-1
Earlier sketch in CA 3R
Madison, Frank
See Hutchins, Francis Gilman
Madison, Hank
See Rowland, D(onald) S(ydney)
Madison, James 1751-1836 ... DLB-37
Madison, Jane
See Horne, Hugh Robert
Madison, Joyce
See Mintz, Joyce Lois
Madison, Peter 1918- ... 9-10R
Madison, Russ 1929- ... 25-28R
Madison, Thomas A(lvin) 1926- ... 57-60
Madison, Tom
See Madison, Thomas A(lvin)
Madison, Winifred ... 37-40R
See also SATA 5
Madle, Dorothy
See Madlee, Dorothy (Haynes)
Madlee, Dorothy (Haynes) 1917-1980 ... CANR-10
Earlier sketch in CA 19-20R
Madott, Darlene (Patrice) 1952- ... 123
Madow, Leo 1915- ... CANR-13
Earlier sketch in CA 33-36R
Madow, Pauline (Reichberg) ... 11-12R
See also CLC 1
Madrigal, Margarita 1912(?)-1983
Obituary ... 110
Madruga, Lenor 1942- ... 102
Madsen, Axel 1930- ... 25-28R
Madsen, Borge Gedso 1920- ... 1R
Madsen, Brigham Dwaine 1914- ... 103
Madsen, David Lawrence 1929- ... 23-24R
Madsen, Richard (Paul) 1941- ... 123
Madsen, Roy Paul 1928- ... 89-92
Madsen, Truman Grant 1926- Brief entry ... 106
Maduell, Charles Rene, Jr. 1918- ... 73-76
Mae, Eydie
See Hunsberger, Edith Mae
Maedke, Wilmer O(tto) 1922- ... 57-60
Maehl, William H(arvey) 1915- ... 89-92
Maehl, William Henry, Jr. 1930- ... 23-24R
Maehlqvist, (Karl) Stefan 1943- ... CANR-24
Earlier sketch in CA 107
See also SATA 30
Maenchen, Otto John 1894-1969 Obituary ... 109
Maenchen-Helfen, Otto J.
See Maenchen, Otto John
Maend, Evald
See Mand, Ewald
Maepenn, Hugh
See Kuttner, Henry
Maepenn, K. H.
See Kuttner, Henry
Maeroff, Gene I(rving) 1939- ... 61-64
Maertz, Richard Charles 1935- ... 73-76
Maes-Jelinek, Hena 1929- ... 107
Maestro, Betsy C. 1944- ... CANR-23
Earlier sketches in CA 61-64, CANR-8
See also SATA 30
Maestro, Giulio 1942- ... CANR-23
Earlier sketches in CA 57-60, CANR-8
See also SATA 8
Maeterlinck, Maurice 1862-1949
Brief entry ... 104
See also TCLC 3
Maffei, Paolo 1926- ... 108
Magalaner, Marvin 1920- ... CANR-1
Earlier sketch in CA 1R
Magaret, Helene 1906- ... 4R

Magarshack, David 1899- 7-8R
Magary, Alan 1944- CANR-8
Earlier sketch in CA 61-64
Magary, James F(rederick) 1933- 25-28R
Magary, Kerstin Fraser 1947- CANR-12
Earlier sketch in CA 61-64
Magdalany, Philip 1936(?)-1985 Obituary ... 117
Magdol, Edward 1918- CANR-9
Earlier sketch in CA 21-22R
Magee, Bryan 1930- CANR-2
Earlier sketch in CA 7-8R
Magee, David (Bickersteth) 1905-1977 81-84
Obituary 73-76
Magee, John 1901-1987 Obituary 122
Magee, Wes 1939- CANR-23
Earlier sketch in CA 107
Mager, George C(lyde) 1937- 49-52
Mager, Nathan H. 1912-1986 .... CANR-18
Earlier sketches in CA 45-48, CANR-2
Maggal, Moshe M(orris) 1908- CAP-2
Earlier sketch in CA 23-24
Maggin, Elliot S. 1950- 102
Maggio, Joe 1938- CANR-1
Earlier sketch in CA 45-48
Maggiolo, Walter A(ndrew) 1908- 85-88
Maggs, Peter B(lount) 1936- CANR-23
Earlier sketches in CA 19-20R, CANR-8
Maggs, Will(iam) Colston 1912- 13-14R
Magidoff, Robert 1905-1970 .... CAP-1
Earlier sketch in CA 19-20
Magidson, Herbert (Adolph) 1906-1986
Obituary 118
Magill, Frank N(orthen) 1907- CANR-6
Earlier sketch in CA 7-8R
Magill, Kathleen 1948- 116
Magill, Marcus
See Hill, Brian (Merrikin)
Magill, Robert S(amuel) 1941- 89-92
Maginnis, Andrew Francis 1923- 45-48
Magister, Joseph
See Grant, Louis T(heodore)
Magloire-Saint-Aude, Clement 1912- 15-16R
Magnarella, Paul J(oseph) 93-96
Magner, James A. 1901- CAP-1
Earlier sketch in CA 13-14
Magner, James Edmund, Jr. 1928- CANR-7
Earlier sketch in CA 19-20R
Magner, Thomas F(reeman) 1918- 19-20R
Magnin, Cyril I. 1899- 107
Magnus, Philip
See Magnus-Allcroft, Sir Philip (Montefiore)
Magnus, Samuel Woolf 1910- CAP-1
Earlier sketch in CA 9-10
Magnus-Allcroft, Sir Philip (Montefiore) 1906- CAP-1
Earlier sketch in CA 11-12
Magnuson, Don(ald Hammer) 1911-1979
Obituary 89-92
Magnuson, Edward F. 1926- 102
Magnuson, Keith (Arlen) 1947- 93-96
Magnuson, Paul 1939- 69-72
Magnuson, Paul Budd 1884-1968
Obituary 106
Magnuson, Warren G(rant) 1905- 85-88
Magnussen, Daniel Osar 1919- 65-68
Magnusson, Magnus 1929- CANR-23
Earlier sketch in CA 105
Magog, Paul Dowsey
See Dowsey-Magog, Paul
Magoon, Robert A(rnold) 1922- CANR-24
Earlier sketch in CA 107
Magorian, Christopher 1959- 111
Magorian, James 1942- CANR-18
Earlier sketch in CA 102
See also SATA 32
Magoun, F(rederick) Alexander 1896- CAP-2
Earlier sketch in CA 17-18
Magoun, Francis P(eabody), Jr. 1895-1979(?) 107
Magowan, Robin 1936- CANR-20
Earlier sketches in CA 9-10R, CANR-4
Magrath, C(laude) Peter 1933- 19-20R
Magrid, Henry M. 1918(?)-1979 Obituary ..89-92
Magruder, Jeb Stuart 1934- 101
Magsam, Charles Michael 1907- CAP-1
Earlier sketch in CA 15-16
Magubane, Bernard (Makhosezwe) 1930- ..93-96
Maguen, David
See Markish, David
Maguinness, W(illiam) Stuart 1903-1982 . CAP-1
Obituary 108
Earlier sketch in CA 15-16
Maguire, Anne
See Nearing, Penny
Maguire, Daniel Charles 1931- 49-52
Maguire, Francis T(homas) 1911-1976
Obituary 69-72
Maguire, Gregory 1954- 81-84
See also SATA 28
Maguire, Henry Pownall 1943- 111
Maguire, Jack 1920- 81-84
Maguire, John David 1932- CANR-9
Earlier sketch in CA 21-22R
Maguire, John T(homas) 1917- 2R
Maguire, Michael 1945- 104
Maguire, R(obert) A(gustine) J(oseph) 1898- 7-8R
Maguire, Robert A(lan) 1930- 73-76
Magwood, John McLean 1912- 106
Mahajan, Vidya Dhar 1913- CANR-11
Earlier sketch in CA 25-28R
Mahajani, Usha 1933- 53-56
Mahan, Alfred Thayer 1840-1914 .... DLB-47
Mahan, Bill
See Mahan, William Allen
Mahan, Pat
See Wheat, Patte
Mahan, Patte Wheat
See Wheat, Patte
Mahan, William Allen 1930- CANR-15
Earlier sketch in CA 85-88
Mahapatra, Jayanta 1928- CANR-15
Earlier sketch in CA 73-76
See also CLC 33
Mahar, J. Michael 1929- 13-14R
Mahdi, Muhsin S(ayyid) 1926- CANR-3
Earlier sketch in CA 1R
Maher, Brendan A(rnold) 1924- 25-28R
Maher, James T(homas) 1917- 65-68
Maher, John E. 1925- 19-20R
Maher, Ramona 1934- CANR-9
Earlier sketch in CA 21-22R
See also SATA 13
Maher, Robert F. 1922- 19-20R
Maher, Trafford P(atrick) 1914- 21-22R
Maheshwari, Shriram 1931- CANR-11
Earlier sketch in CA 23-24R
Maheux-Forcier, Louise 1929- DLB-60
Mahin, John Lee 1902(?)-1984 Obituary ... 112
See also DLB 44
Mahl, George F(ranklin) 1917- 93-96
Mahl, Mary R. 1914- 25-28R
Mahlendorf, Ursula R. 1929- 49-52
Mahler, Gregory S. 1950- 123
Mahler, Jane Gaston 1906- 37-40R
Mahler, Margaret S(choenberger) 1897-1985 103
Obituary 117
Mahlqvist, (Karl) Stefan
See Maehlqvist, (Karl) Stefan
See also SATA 30
Mahmood, Mamdani 1946- 105
Maholick, Leonard T(homas) 1921- CANR-1
Earlier sketch in CA 4R
Mahon, Derek 1941- Brief entry 113
See also DLB 40
See also CLC 27
Mahon, John K(eith) 1912- 19-20R
Mahon, Julia C(unha) 1916- 61-64
See also SATA 11
Mahon, Thomas (Cavan) 1944- 119
Mahoney, Irene 1921- 61-64
Mahoney, J. Daniel 1931- 61-64
Mahoney, John (Francis) 1929- 41-44R
Mahoney, John Leo 1928- CANR-14
Earlier sketch in CA 33-36R
Mahoney, John Thomas 1905-1981 ...... CAP-1
Obituary 104
Earlier sketch in CA 11-12
Mahoney, Michael J(ohn) 1946- CANR-8
Earlier sketch in CA 53-56
Mahoney, Patrick 1927- 81-84
Mahoney, Robert F. 1914- 15-16R
Mahoney, Thomas Arthur 1928- 1R
Mahoney, Thomas H(enry) D(onald) 1913- 13-14R
Mahoney, Tim 1947- 123
Mahoney, Tom
See Mahoney, John Thomas
Mahony, Elizabeth Winthrop 1948- 41-44R
See also SATA 8
Mahony, Patrick
See O'Mahony, Patrick
Mahony, Peter (Bernard) 1931- 118
Mahood, Kenneth 1930- 103
See also SATA 24
Mahood, Ruth I. 1908- CAP-1
Earlier sketch in CA 19-20
Mahrer, Alvin R(aymond) 1927- 23-24R
Mahy, Margaret 1936- CANR-13
Earlier sketch in CA 69-72
See also SATA 14
See also CLR 7
Mai, Ludwig H(ubert) 1898- 73-76
Maibaum, Richard 1909- 102
Maiden, Cecil (Edward) 1902- 73-76
Maidoff, Ilka
See List, Ilka Katherine
Maier, Charles S(teven) 1939- 69-72
Maier, Ernest L(ouis) 1938- 105
Maier, Howard 1906(?)-1983 Obituary 109
Maier, Joseph (Ben) 1911- 23-24R
Maier, Norman R(aymond) F(rederick) 1900-1977 .... CANR-4
Obituary 73-76
Earlier sketch in CA 1R
Maier, Paul L(uther) 1930- CANR-2
Earlier sketch in CA 5-6R
Maier, Pauline (Rubbelke) 1938- 37-40R
Maier, (Henry) William (Jr.) 1901- 2R
Maik, Henri
See Hecht, Henri Joseph
Mailer, Norman 1923- 11-12R
See also CABS 1
See also DLB 2, 16, 28
See also DLBY 80, 83
See also DLBD 3
See also CLC 1, 2, 3, 4, 5, 8, 11, 14, 28, 39
See also AITN 2
Maillard, Keith 1942- 93-96
Maillet, Antonine 1929- 120
Brief entry 115
See also DLB 60
Mailloux, Steven 1950- 107
Mails, Thomas E. 1920(?)- Brief entry 111
Maimon, Morton A. 1931- 33-36R
Main, Gloria (Jean) L(und) 1933- 112
Main, Jackson Turner 1917- CANR-1
Earlier sketch in CA 1R
Main, Mildred Miles 1898- CAP-1
Earlier sketch in CA 15-16
Maine, Charles Eric
See McIlwain, David
Maine, David
See Avice, Claude (Pierre Marie)
Maingot, Rodney 1893-1982 Obituary 105
Mainprize, Don 1930- CANR-7
Earlier sketch in CA 19-20R
Mains, David R(andall) 1936- 93-96
Mainstone, Rowland J(ohnson) 1923- .. CANR-23
Earlier sketch in CA 107
Mainwaring, Daniel 1902-1977 .... DLB-44
Mainwaring, Marion CANR-3
Earlier sketch in CA 4R
Maiolo, Joseph 1938- 49-52
Maiorano, Robert 1946- 116
See also SATA 43
Mair, Alistair 1924- 11-12R
Mair, (Alexander) Craig 1948- 102
Mair, George Brown 1914- CANR-12
Earlier sketch in CA 13-14R
Mair, George F(isk) 1922-1978 Obituary 111
Mair, Lucy Philip 1901-1986 Obituary 119
Mair, Margaret
See Crompton, Margaret (Norah Mair)
Mair, Victor H(enry) 1943- 113
Mairowitz, David Zane 1943- 122
Mais, Roger 1905-1955 124
Brief entry 105
See also TCLC 8
Mais, S(tuart) P(etre) B(rodie) 1885-1975 ..69-72
Obituary 57-60
Maisel, Herbert 1930- 53-56
Maisel, Louis Sandy 1945- 117
Maisel, Sherman J(oseph) 1918- CANR-19
Earlier sketches in CA 5-6R, CANR-4
Maisels, Maxine S. 1939- 49-52
Maisky, Ivan (Mikhailovich) 1884-1975 65-68
Obituary 61-64
Maison, Della
See Katz, Bobbi
Maison, Margaret M(ary Bowles) 1920- ...17-18R
Maissi, Elie 1911(?)-1983 Obituary 110
Maital, Shlomo 1942- 108
Maitland, Antony Jasper 1935- 101
See also SATA 25
Maitland, David J(ohnston) 1922- 116
Maitland, Derek 1943- CANR-23
Earlier sketch in CA 29-32R
Maitland, Margaret
See Du Breuil, (Elizabeth) L(or)inda and Wallmann, Jeffrey M(iner)
Maitland, Sara (Louise) 1950- CANR-13
Earlier sketch in CA 69-72
Maitra, Priyatosh 1930- 107
Maizel, C. L.
See Maizel, Clarice Matthews
Maizel, Clarice Matthews 1919- 11-12R
Maizel, Leah
See Maizel, Clarice Matthews
Majault, Joseph 1916- 101
Majerus, Janet 1936- 65-68
Majeski, Bill
See Majeski, William
Majeski, William 1927- CANR-18
Earlier sketch in CA 25-28R
Majka, Linda C. 1947- 124
Majonica, Ernst 1920- 29-32R
Major, Alan P(ercival) 1929- CANR-7
Earlier sketch in CA 57-60
Major, Andre 1942- DLB-60
Major, Clarence 1936- CANR-13
Earlier sketch in CA 23-24R
See also CAAS 6
See also DLB 33
See also CLC 3, 19
Major, Geraldyn Hodges 1894-1984 85-88
Obituary 113
Major, Gerri
See Major, Geraldyn Hodges
Major, H. M.
See Jarvis, Sharon
Major, Henriette 1933- 109
Major, J(ames) Russell 1921- CANR-2
Earlier sketch in CA 7-8R
Major, Jean-Louis 1937- CANR-18
Earlier sketches in CA 49-52, CANR-2
Major, John M(cClellan) 1918- 13-14R
Major, Kevin (Gerald) 1949- CANR-21
Earlier sketch in CA 97-100
See also SATA 32
See also DLB 60
See also CLC 26
See also CLR 11
Major, Mabel 1893- 45-48
Major, Mark Imre 1923- 65-68
Major, Ralph Hermon 1884-1970 .... CAP-1
Earlier sketch in CA 9-10
Major, Reginald W. 1926- 29-32R
Major-General of Marsland
See Duncan, Ronald
Major-Poetzl, Pamela 1943- 116
Majumdar, R(amesh) C(handra) 1888- ...33-36R
Majumder, Sanat K(umer) 1929- 33-36R
Makanowitzky, Barbara
See Norman, Barbara
Makarova, Marina 1942- 120
Makarova, Natalia 1940- 113
Makary
See Iranek-Osmecki, Kazimierz
Makeba, (Zensi) Miriam 1932- 104
Makely, William O(rson) 1932- 53-56
Makemie, Francis 1658(?)-1708 .... DLB-24
Makepeace, Joanna
See York, Margaret Elizabeth
Makepeace, R(oyston) W(illiam) 1950- 116
Makerney, Edna Smith 1921- 61-64
Maki, James
See Ozu, Yasujiro
Maki, John M(cGilvrey) 1909- 109
Makie, Pam 1943- SATA-37
Makin, Peter (Julian) 1946- 93-96
Makino, Seiichi 1935- 113
Makins, Roger Mellor 1904- 111
Makkai, Adam 1935- CANR-10
Earlier sketch in CA 57-60
Makkreel, Rudolf A. 1939- 122
Makow, Henry 1949- 7-8R
Makower, Addie (Gertrude Leonaura) 1906- 65-68
Makower, Joel 1952- 124
Makowsky, Veronica A(nn) 1954- 116
Maksimov, Vladimir (Yemelyanovich)
See Maximov, Vladimir (Yemelyanovich)
Maktari, Abdulla M. A. 1936- 37-40R
Maktos, John 1902-1977 Obituary 69-72
Mal
See Hancock, Malcolm
Malabaila, Damianos
See Levi, Primo
Malabre, Alfred L(eopold, Jr.) 1931- ... CANR-12
Earlier sketch in CA 65-68
Malamud, Bernard 1914-1986 ....7-8R
Obituary 118
See also CABS 1
See also DLB 2, 28
See also DLBY 80, 86
See also CDALB 1941-1968
See also CLC 1, 2, 3, 5, 8, 9, 11, 18, 27, 44
Malan, Roy Mark 1911- 41-44R
Maland, David 1929- 103
Malanga, Gerard (Joseph) 1943-
Brief entry 112
Malanos, George J(ohn) 1919-1962 .... 3R
Obituary 103
Malarek, Victor 1948- 123
Malavie, M. J. 1920- 29-32R
Malbin, Michael J(acob) 1943- CANR-17
Earlier sketch in CA 73-76
Malcolm, Andrew (Ian) 1927- 97-100
Malcolm, Andrew H(ogarth) 1943- 53-56
Malcolm, Dan
See Silverberg, Robert
Malcolm, Donald 1932(?)-1975 Obituary ... 104
Malcolm, Ian
See Malcolm, Andrew (Ian)
Malcolm, Janet 123
Malcolm, John
See Andrews, John Malcolm
Malcolm, Margaret
See Kuether, Edith Lyman
Malcolm, Norman 1911- 37-40R
Malcolmson, Anne
See von Storch, Anne B.
Malcolmson, David 1899- 7-8R
See also SATA 6
Malcolmson, Robert W(illiam) 1943- ... CANR-19
Earlier sketch in CA 103
Malcolm X
See Little, Malcolm
Malcom, Robert E. 1933- 19-20R
Malcomson, R(osalie) M(ary) 1925- 119
Malcomson, William L. 1932- 25-28R
Malcoskey, Edna Walker 19-20R
Maldonado-Denis, Manuel 1933-
Brief entry 113
Male, David Arthur 1928- 57-60
Male, Roy R(aymond) 1919- 104
Malecki, Edward S(tanley) 1938- 41-44R
Malefakis, Edward E(manuel) 1932- 29-32R
Malefijt, Annemarie de Waal
See de Waal Malefijt, Annemarie
Malek, Frederic Vincent 1937- 81-84
Malek, James S(tanley) 1941- 57-60
Malenbaum, Wilfred 1913- CANR-1
Earlier sketch in CA 3R
Malerich, Edward P. 1940- 33-36R
Maleska, Eugene Thomas 1916- CANR-1
Earlier sketch in CA 4R
Malet, B(aldwyn) Hugh G(renville) 1928- 19-20R
Malgonkar, Manohar (Dattatray) 1913- . CANR-18
Earlier sketches in CA 2R, CANR-1
Malherbe, Abraham J(ohannes) 1930- ... CANR-1
Earlier sketch in CA 49-52
Malherbe, Ernst Gideon 1895- CAP-1
Earlier sketch in CA 13-14
Malherbe, Janie Antonia (Nel) 1897- CAP-1
Earlier sketch in CA 15-16
Malhotra, Ashok Kumar 1940- 110
Mali, Jane Lawrence 1937- 114
See also SATA 44
Mali, Paul 1926- CANR-8
Earlier sketch in CA 57-60
Malick, Terrence 1943- 101
Malick, Terry
See Malick, Terrence
Malickson, David L. 1928- 110
Malik, Charles Habib 1906-1987 .... CANR-7
Obituary 124
Earlier sketch in CA 45-48
Malik, Hafeez 1930- CANR-21
Earlier sketch in CA 77-80
Malik, Yogendra K(umar) 1929- 81-84
Malikin, David 1913- 77-80
Malin, David (Frederick) 1941- 118
Malin, Irving 1934- CANR-6
Earlier sketch in CA 13-14R
Malin, James Claude 1893-1979 Obituary ... 113
Malin, Peter
See Conner, Patrick Reardon
Malina, Bruce J(ohn) 1933- 112

Malina, Frank J(oseph) 1912-1981 ... 93-96
Obituary ... 108
Malina, Judith 1926- ... CANR-18
Earlier sketch in CA 102
Maling, Arthur (Gordon) 1923- ... CANR-22
Earlier sketches in CA 49-52, CANR-3
Malinin, Theodore I 1933- ... 93-96
Malino, Frances 1940- ... 115
Malinowski, Bronislaw (Kasper)
1884-1942 Brief entry ... 114
Malins, Edward (Greenway) 1910- ... 103
Malipiero, Gian Francesco 1882-1973
Obituary ... 45-48
Malkiel, Burton Gordon 1932- ... 49-52
Malkiel, Yakov 1914- ... 25-28R
Malkiewicz, J(an) Kris 1931- ... 57-60
Malkin, Maurice L. 1900- ... 49-52
Malkin, Sol(omon) M. 1910-1986
Obituary ... 118
Malkoff, Karl 1938- ... 19-20R
Malkus, Alida Wright 1899- ... 5-6R
Mall, E. Jane 1920- ... CANR-13
Earlier sketch in CA 23-24R
Mall, Viktor
See Beskow, Bo
Mallaby, (Howard) George 1902-1978
Obituary ... 108
Mallalieu, John Percival William
1908-1980 Obituary ... 97-100
Mallan, Lloyd 1914- ... 5-6R
Malle, Louis 1932- ... 101
Mallea, Eduardo 1903-1982(?) Obituary ... 114
Mallen, Bruce E. 1937- ... CANR-14
Earlier sketch in CA 21-22R
Mallery, David 1923- ... 5-6R
Malleson, Andrew (Graeme) 1931-
Brief entry ... 112
Malleson, Lucy Beatrice 1899-1973 ... 97-100
Obituary ... 49-52
Mallet-Joris, Francoise 1930- ... CANR-17
Earlier sketch in CA 65-68
See also CLC 11
Mallett, Anne 1913- ... 49-52
Malley, Ern
See McAuley, James Phillip
Mallin, Jay 1927- ... 19-20R
Mallin, Tom 1927(?)-1978 Obituary ... 89-92
Mallinson, George Greisen 1918- ... CANR-1
Earlier sketch in CA 3R
Mallinson, Jeremy (John Crosby)
1937- ... CANR-6
Earlier sketch in CA 57-60
Mallinson, Vernon 1910- ... 7-8R
Malliol, William
See McInenly, William T(homas)
Mallis, Jackie
See Mallis, Jacqueline
Mallis, Jacqueline 1922- ... 113
Malloch, Peter
See Duncan, W(illiam) Murdoch
Mallock, W. H. 1849-1923 ... DLB-18, 57
Mallon, Bill 1952- ... 119
Mallon, Thomas 1951- ... 110
Mallone, George 1944- ... 115
Mallone, Ronald Stephen 1916- ... CAP-1
Earlier sketch in CA 9-10
Mallonee, Richard C(arvel) II 1923- ... 109
Mallory, Bob F(ranklin) 1932- ... 89-92
Mallory, Enid Lorraine 1938- ... 105
Mallory, Kenneth 1945- ... 124
Mallory, Mark
See Reynolds, Dallas McCord
Mallory, Walter Hampton 1892-1980 ... 11-12R
Obituary ... 101
Mallough, Don 1914- ... 23-24R
Mallowan, Agatha Christie
See Christie, Agatha (Mary Clarissa)
Mallowan, Max (Edgar Lucien)
1904-1978 ... CANR-21
Obituary ... 81-84
Earlier sketch in CA 69-72
Mallows, (Edward) Wilfrid (Nassau) 1905- ... 119
Malloy, Ruth Lor 1932- ... CANR-22
Earlier sketch in CA 69-72
Malloy, Terry 1950- ... 69-72
Mally, E(mma) Louise 1908- ... 33-36R
Malm, F(inn) T(heodore) 1919- ... 19-20R
Malm, William P(aul) 1928- ... 9-10R
Malmberg, Carl 1904- ... 33-36R
See also SATA 9
Malmgren, Harald B(ernard) 1935- ... 45-48
Malmo, Robert Beverley 1912- ... 61-64
Malmstroem, Vincent H(erschel)
See Malmstrom, Vincent H(erschel)
Malmstrom, Jean 1908- ... 53-56
Malmstrom, Vincent H(erschel) 1926- ... 112
Malo, John W. 1911- ... CANR-12
Earlier sketch in CA 33-36R
See also SATA 4
Malocsay, Zoltan 1946- ... 81-84
Malof, Joseph F(etler) 1934- ... 29-32R
Maloff, Saul 1922- ... 33-36R
See also CLC 5
Malone, Bill C(harles) 1934- ... 65-68
Malone, Colonel Dick
See Malone, Richard S(ankey)
Malone, Dick
See Malone, Richard S(ankey)
Malone, Dumas 1892-1986 ... CANR-2
Obituary ... 121
Earlier sketch in CA 1R
See also DLB 17
Malone, Elmer Taylor, Jr. 1943- ... CANR-17
Earlier sketches in CA 49-52, CANR-1
Malone, Joseph James 1924-1983
Obituary ... 111
Malone, Kemp 1889-1971 Obituary ... 89-92
Malone, Louis
See MacNeice, (Frederick) Louis
Malone, Margaret Gay 1939- ... 112
Malone, Mary ... CANR-2
Earlier sketch in CA 1R
Malone, Michael (Christopher) 1942- ... CANR-14
Earlier sketch in CA 77-80
See also CLC 43
Malone, Michael P. 1940- ... CANR-12
Earlier sketch in CA 29-32R
Malone, R. S.
See Malone, Richard S(ankey)
Malone, Richard S(ankey) 1909-1985
Obituary ... 116
Brief entry ... 107
Malone, Ruth 1918- ... 93-96
Malone, Ted
See Malone, Elmer Taylor, Jr.
Malone, Wex S(mathers) 1906- ... 11-12R
Maloney, Frank E(dward) 1918-1980 ... 73-76
Obituary ... 97-100
Maloney, George A(nthony) 1924- ... CANR-8
Earlier sketch in CA 23-24R
Maloney, J(oseph) J(ohn) 1940- ... 109
Maloney, Joan M(arie) 1931- ... 37-40R
Maloney, Pat
See Markun, Patricia Maloney
Maloney, Ralph Liston 1927-1973 ... CANR-3
Obituary ... 45-48
Earlier sketch in CA 2R
Malony, H(enry) Newton 1931- ... 104
Malory, (Sir) Thomas 1410(?)-1471(?) . SATA-33
Malouf, (George Joseph) David 1934- ... 124
Malouf, David 1934- ... CLC-28
Malouf, Pyrrha 1929- ... 117
Malpass, E(ric) L(awson) 1910- ... CANR-18
Earlier sketches in CA 9-10R, CANR-3
Malpass, Leslie F(rederick) 1922- ... CANR-8
Earlier sketch in CA 19-20R
Malpede, Karen
See Taylor, Karen Malpede
Malraux, (Georges-) Andre 1901-1976 ... CAP-2
Obituary ... 69-72
Earlier sketch in CA 21-22
See also CLC 1, 4, 9, 13, 15
Malraux, Clara (Goldschmidt)
1897(?)-1982 Obituary ... 108
Malraux-Goldschmidt, Clara
See Malraux, Clara (Goldschmidt)
Malta, Demetrio Aguilera
See Aguilera Malta, Demetrio
Maltby, Arthur 1935- ... CANR-10
Earlier sketch in CA 25-28R
Maltby, William S(aunders) 1940-
Brief entry ... 113
Malten, William 1902- ... CAP-2
Earlier sketch in CA 23-24
Maltese, Michael 1909(?)-1981 Obituary ... 103
See also SATA 24
Maltin, Leonard 1950- ... CANR-12
Earlier sketch in CA 29-32R
Maltman, Kim 1950- ... 112
Maltz, Albert 1908-1985 ... 41-44R
Obituary ... 115
Maltz, Maxwell 1899-1975 ... 65-68
Obituary ... 57-60
Maltz, Stephen 1932- ... 57-60
Maluf, Chafic 1905(?)-1976 Obituary ... 69-72
Malveaux, Julianne M(arie) 1953- ... CANR-23
Earlier sketch in CA 105
Malvern, Corinne 1905-1956 Brief entry ... 115
See also SATA 34
Malvern, Gladys ?-1962 ... 73-76
See also SATA 23
Malville, J. McKim
See Malville, John McKim
Malville, John McKim 1934- ... 120
Malville, Kim
See Malville, John McKim
Maly, Eugene H. 1920-1981 ... CANR-14
Earlier sketch in CA 23-24R
Malz, Betty 1929- ... 113
Malzberg, Barry N(athaniel) 1939- ... CANR-16
Earlier sketch in CA 61-64
See also CAAS 4
See also DLB 8
See also CLC 7
Malzberg, Benjamin 1893-1975 ... CAP-1
Obituary ... 57-60
Earlier sketch in CA 15-16
Mama G.
See Davis, Grania
Mamalakis, Markos J(ohn) 1932- ... 45-48
Maman, Andre 1927- ... 73-76
Mamatey, Victor S(amuel) 1917- ... 9-10R
Mamet, David (Alan) 1947- ... CANR-15
Earlier sketch in CA 81-84
See also DLB 7
See also CLC 9, 15, 34, 46
Mamis, Justin E. 1929- ... 11-12R
Mamleev, Yury
See Mamleyev, Yuri
Mamleyev, Yuri 1931- ... 85-88
Mamonova, Tatyana 1943- ... 114
Mamoulian, Rouben (Zachary)
1897-1987 ... 25-28R
Obituary ... 124
See also CLC 16
Man, Felix H.
See Baumann, Hans Felix S(iegismund)
Man, John 1941- ... CANR-16
Earlier sketch in CA 93-96
Manach, Jorge 1898(?)-1961 Obituary ... 111
Manard, Barbara Bolling 1945- ... 121
Manarin, Louis H(enry) 1932- ... 23-24R
Mana-Zucca
See Cassel, Mana-Zucca
Mancewicz, Bernice Winslow 1917- ... 37-40R
Manch, Joseph (Rodman) 1910- ... 53-56
Manchee, Fred B. 1903(?)-1981 Obituary ... 105
Manchel, Frank 1935- ... CANR-14
Earlier sketch in CA 37-40R
See also SATA 10
Manchester, Harland 1898-1977 ... 4R
Obituary ... 73-76
Manchester, Paul T(homas) 1893- ... 61-64
Manchester, William 1922- ... CANR-3
Earlier sketch in CA 1R
See also AITN 1
Mancini, Anthony 1939- ... 73-76
Mancini, Pat McNees
See McNees, Pat
Mancke, Richard B(ell) 1943- ... 81-84
Mancroft, Stormont Mancroft Samuel
1914- ... 49-52
Mancusi-Ungaro, Harold R(aymond), Jr.
1947- ... 97-100
Mancuso, Joe
See Mancuso, Joseph R.
Mancuso, Joseph R. 1941- ... 93-96
Mand, Ewald 1906- ... 19-20R
Mandel, Adrienne Schizzano 1934- ... 37-40R
Mandel, Benjamin 1891(?)-1973 Obituary ... 45-48
Mandel, Bernard 1920- ... 4R
Mandel, Eli(as Wolf) 1922- ... CANR-15
Earlier sketch in CA 73-76
See also DLB 53
Mandel, Ernest 1923- ... CANR-15
Earlier sketch in CA 37-40R
Mandel, George 1920- ... 2R
Mandel, Jerome 1937- ... 37-40R
Mandel, Leon 1928- ... CANR-13
Earlier sketch in CA 77-80
Mandel, Loring 1928- ... 73-76
Mandel, Morris 1911- ... CANR-6
Earlier sketch in CA 7-8R
Mandel, Oscar 1926- ... CANR-21
Earlier sketches in CA 1R, CANR-2
Mandel, Ruth Blumenstock 1938- ... 105
Mandel, Sally Elizabeth 1944- ... 102
Mandel, Sheila 1930(?)-1987 Obituary ... 124
Mandel, Sidney Albert 1923- ... 93-96
Mandel, Siegfried 1922- ... CANR-20
Earlier sketches in CA 4R, CANR-5
Mandel, William M(arx) 1917- ... 11-12R
Mandelbaum, Allen ... 111
Mandelbaum, David G(oodman)
1911-1987 ... 41-44R
Obituary ... 122
Mandelbaum, Maurice (H.) 1908-1987
Obituary ... 121
Brief entry ... 113
Mandelbaum, Michael 1946- ... 101
Mandelbaum, Seymour J. 1936- ... 19-20R
Mandelker, Daniel Robert 1926- ... CANR-20
Earlier sketches in CA 3R, CANR-5
Mandelkorn, Eugenia Miller 1916- ... 11-12R
Mandell, Arnold Joseph 1934- ... 101
Mandell, Betty Reid 1924- ... CANR-8
Earlier sketch in CA 61-64
Mandell, Fran Gare 1939- ... 115
Mandell, Gail Porter 1940- ... 123
Mandell, Maurice I(ra) 1925- ... CANR-11
Earlier sketch in CA 25-28R
Mandell, Mel 1926- ... 41-44R
Mandell, Muriel (Hortense Levin) 1921- ... 9-10R
Mandell, Richard Donald 1929- ... CANR-10
Earlier sketch in CA 25-28R
Mandelshtam, Nadezhda
See Mandelstam, Nadezhda (Yakovlevna)
Mandelstam, Nadezhda (Yakovlevna)
1899-1980 ... 110
Obituary ... 102
Mandelstam, Osip (Emilievich)
1891(?)-1938(?) Brief entry ... 104
See also TCLC 2, 6
Mandelstamm, Allan B(eryle) 1928- ... 41-44R
Mander, A(lfred) E(rnest) 1894- ... CAP-1
Earlier sketch in CA 11-12
Mander, Anica Vesel 1934- ... CANR-8
Earlier sketch in CA 61-64
Mander, Gertrud 1927- ... 93-96
Mander, Jerry 1936- ... 81-84
Mander, Raymond (Josiah Gale)
1911(?)-1983 ... 101
Obituary ... 111
Mander, Rosalie Grylls ... 7-8R
Mandiargues, Andre Pieyre de
See Pieyre de Mandiargues, Andre
See also CLC 41
Mandino, Og 1923- ... 103
Mandler, George 1924- ... CANR-19
Earlier sketches in CA 1R, CANR-4
Mandler, Jean Matter 1929- ... CANR-19
Earlier sketch in CA 15-16R
Mandrake, Ethel Belle
See Thurman, Wallace (Henry)
Mandrepelias, Loizos
See Hartocollis, Peter
Mane, Robert 1926- ... 37-40R
Manella, Raymond L(awrence) 1917- ... 19-20R
Manes, Stephen 1949- ... 97-100
See also SATA 40, 42
Manfred, Frederick (Feikema) 1912- ... CANR-5
Earlier sketch in CA 9-10R
See also SATA 30
See also DLB 6
Manfred, Freya 1944- ... 69-72
Manfred, Robert
See Marx, Erica Elizabeth
Manfredi, John Francis 1920- ... 109
Manfredi, V.
See Musciano, Walter A.
Mang, Karl 1922- ... 101
Mangalam, J(oseph) J(oseph) 1924- ... 37-40R
Mangan, James Thomas 1896- ... CAP-2
Earlier sketch in CA 19-20
Mangan, (John Joseph) Sherry 1904-1961
Obituary ... 112
See also DLB 4
Manganiello, Dominic 1951- ... 124
Mangat, J(agjit) S(ingh) 1937- ... 73-76
Mangione, Jerre 1909- ... CANR-16
Earlier sketch in CA 15-16R
See also SATA 6
Mango, Cyril (Alexander) 1928- ... 109
Mango, Karin N. 1936- ... 123
Mangold, Tom 1934- ... 69-72
Mangum, Garth L(eroy) 1926- ... 81-84
Mangurian, David 1938- ... CANR-10
Earlier sketch in CA 57-60
See also SATA 14
Manhattan, Avro 1914- ... CANR-5
Earlier sketch in CA 11-12R
Manheim, Jarol B(ruce) 1946- ... CANR-21
Earlier sketches in CA 57-60, CANR-6
Manheim, Leonard (Falk) 1902- ... CAP-2
Earlier sketch in CA 21-22
Manheim, Michael 1928- ... 81-84
Manheim, Ralph 1907(?)- Brief entry ... 115
Manheim, Sylvan D. 1897-1977 Obituary ... 73-76
Manheim, Theodore 1921- Brief entry ... 108
Manheim, Werner 1915- ... 53-56
Manhire, Bill 1946- ... CANR-20
Earlier sketch in CA 103
Manhoff, Bill
See Manhoff, Wilton
Manhoff, Wilton 1919-1974 Obituary ... 49-52
Maniates, Maria Rika 1937- ... 113
Maniaty, Anthony 1949- ... 119
Maniaty, Tony
See Maniaty, Anthony
Manicas, Peter T(heodore) 1934- ... 53-56
Maniere, J.-E.
See Giraudoux, (Hippolyte) Jean
Manifold, J(ohn) S(treeter) 1915- ... CANR-24
Earlier sketch in CA 69-72
Manigault, Edward 1897(?)-1983 Obituary ... 109
Manilla, James ... 97-100
Manis, Jerome G. 1917- ... 25-28R
Manis, Melvin 1931- ... 21-22R
Maniscalco, Joseph 1926- ... CANR-8
Earlier sketch in CA 5-6R
See also SATA 10
Manjon, Maite
See Manjon-Alonso, Maria Teresa
Manjon-Alonso, Maria Teresa 1931- ... 116
Mank, Gregory William 1950- ... 89-92
Mankekar, D. R. 1910- ... CANR-13
Earlier sketch in CA 21-22R
Mankiewicz, Don M(artin) 1922- ... 13-14R
Mankiewicz, Frank (Fabian) 1924- ... 89-92
Mankiewicz, Herman (Jacob) 1897-1953
Brief entry ... 120
See also DLB 26
Mankiewicz, Joseph L(eo) 1909- ... 73-76
See also DLB 44
Mankiewicz, Thomas F. 1942- Brief entry ... 124
Mankiewicz, Tom
See Mankiewicz, Thomas F.
Mankin, Paul A. 1924- ... 37-40R
Mankoff, Allan H. 1935- ... 45-48
Mankowitz, Wolf 1924- ... CANR-5
Earlier sketch in CA 7-8R
See also DLB 15
Mankowska, Joyce Kells Batten 1919- ... CAP-1
Earlier sketch in CA 9-10
Manley, Deborah 1932- ... CANR-22
Earlier sketch in CA 105
See also SATA 28
Manley, Delariviere 1672(?)-1724 ... DLB-39
Manley, Frank 1930- ... 5-6R
Manley, John F(rederick) 1939- ... 77-80
Manley, Lawrence (Gordon) 1949- ... 109
Manley, Michael Norman 1923- ... 85-88
Manley, Ruth Rodney King 1907(?)-1973
Obituary ... 41-44R
Manley, Seon 1921- ... 85-88
See also SATA 15
See also SAAS 2
See also CLR 3
Manley-Tucker, Audrie 1924(?)-1983(?)
Obituary ... 108
Manlove, Colin Nicholas 1942- ... 113
Mann, A. Philo
See Ald, Roy A(llison)
Mann, Abby 1927- ... 109
See also DLB 44
Mann, Abel
See Creasey, John
Mann, (Francis) Anthony 1914- ... CAP-1
Earlier sketch in CA 9-10
Mann, Arthur 1922- ... 109
Mann, Avery
See Breetveld, Jim Patrick
Mann, Bob 1948- ... 61-64
Mann, Charles W., Jr. 1929- ... 41-44R
Mann, (Robert Francis) Christopher Stephen
1917- ... 89-92
Mann, D. J.
See Freeman, James Dillet
Mann, Dale 1938- ... 61-64
Mann, David Douglas 1934- ... 49-52
Mann, Dean Edson 1927- ... CANR-5
Earlier sketch in CA 11-12R
Mann, Deborah
See Bloom, Ursula
Mann, Donald Nathaniel 1920-1985
Obituary ... 114
Mann, Edward
See Fried, Emanuel

Mann, Edward Andrew 1932- 103
Mann, Erika 1905-1969 Obituary 25-28R
Mann, Esther Kingston
See Kingston-Mann, Esther
Mann, Floyd C(hristopher) 1917- 1R
Mann, Georg K(arl) F(riedrich) 1913- 1R
Mann, Golo 1909- 97-100
Mann, Harold W(ilson) 1925- 19-20R
Mann, (Luiz) Heinrich 1871-1950
Brief entry 106
See also DLB 66
See also TCLC 9
Mann, Horace 1796-1859 .... DLB-1
Mann, Jessica CANR-24
Earlier sketches in CA 49-52, CANR-2
Mann, John H. 1928- 85-88
Mann, Josephine
See Pullein-Thompson, Josephine (Mary Wedderburn)
Mann, Julia de Lacy 1891-1985 Obituary ... 116
Mann, Katharina 1883(?)-1980 Obituary ..97-100
Mann, Kenneth Walker 1914- 29-32R
Mann, Klaus 1906-1949 .... DLB-56
Mann, Lucile Q.
See Mann, Lucile Quarry
Mann, Lucile Quarry 1897(?)-1986
Obituary 121
Mann, Marty 1904-1980 103
Obituary 101
Mann, Michael 1919-1977 .... CANR-3
Obituary 69-72
Earlier sketch in CA 49-52
Mann, Michael 1943(?)- Brief entry 120
Mann, Milton B(ernard) 1937- 45-48
Mann, Patrick,
See Waller, Leslie
Mann, Peggy CANR-10
Earlier sketch in CA 25-28R
See also SATA 6
Mann, Peter (Clifford) 1948- 93-96
Mann, Peter H. 1926- CANR-12
Earlier sketch in CA 25-28R
Mann, Philip A(lan) 1934- 73-76
Mann, Ralph 1943- 112
Mann, Richard G(eorge) 1949- 124
Mann, Thomas 1875-1955 Brief entry 104
See also DLB 66
See also TCLC 2, 8, 14, 21
Mann, W(illiam) Edward 1918- 49-52
Mann, William S(omervell) 1924- 109
Mann, Zane B. 1924- 101
Manne, Henry G. 1928- 33-36R
Mannello, George Jr. 1913- 33-36R
Mannering, Julia
See Bingham, Madeleine (Mary Ebel)
Manners, Alexandra
See Rundle, Anne
Manners, Ande Miller 1923(?)-1975
Obituary 57-60
Manners, David X. 1912- 106
Manners, Elizabeth (Maude) 1917- 49-52
Manners, Gerald 1932- 37-40R
Manners, John (Errol) 1914- 106
Manners, Julia
See Greenaway, Gladys
Manners, Robert A(lan) 1913- 33-36R
Manners, William 1907- 65-68
Mannes, Marya 1904- CANR-3
Earlier sketch in CA 2R
Manngian, Peter
See Monger, (Ifor) David
Mannheim, Grete (Salomon) 1909- 11-12R
See also SATA 10
Manniche, Lise 1943- 107
See also SATA 31
Mannin, Ethel (Edith) 1900-1984 .... CANR-8
Obituary 114
Earlier sketch in CA 53-56
Manning, Ambrose N(uel) 1922- 114
Manning, Bayless Andrew 1923- CANR-9
Earlier sketch in CA 13-14R
Manning, Beverley J(ane) 1942- 109
Manning, Clarence A(ugustus) 1893-1972
Obituary 37-40R
Manning, David
See Faust, Frederick (Shiller)
Manning, David John 1938- 103
Manning, Frank E(dward) 1944- CANR-7
Earlier sketch in CA 53-56
Manning, Frederic 1887(?)-1935
Brief entry 124
See also TCLC 25
Manning, Harvey (Hawthorne) 1925- 112
Manning, Helen Taft 1891(?)-1987
Obituary 121
Manning, Jack 1920- 69-72
Manning, Margaret Raymond 1921-1984
Obituary 114
Manning, Marie 1873(?)-1945 .... DLB-29
Manning, Marsha
See Grimstead, Hettie
Manning, Martin
See Smith, R(eginald) D(onald)
Manning, Mary Louise
See Cameron, Lou
Manning, Matthew 1955- Brief entry 111
Manning, Michael 1940- 65-68
Manning, Olivia 1915-1980 ....5-6R
Obituary 101
See also CLC 5, 19
Manning, Paul 1912- 107
Manning, Peter K(irby) 1940- CANR-14
Earlier sketch in CA 37-40R
Manning, Philip 1930(?)-1983 Obituary 110
Manning, Phyllis A(nne) Sergeant 1903- 5-6R
Manning, Reg(inald West) 1905-1986
Obituary 118
Manning, Robert (Joseph) 1919- 69-72
Manning, Rosemary 1911- CANR-1
Earlier sketch in CA 3R
See also SATA 10
Manning, Rosemary
See Cole, Margaret Alice
Manning, Stanley Arthur 1921- 110
Manning, Sylvia 1943- 81-84
Manning, Thomas Davys 1898-1972 ..... CAP-1
Earlier sketch in CA 19-20
Manning-Sanders, Ruth 1895- 73-76
See also SATA 15
Mannion, John J(oseph) 1941- 73-76
Mannix, Edward 1928- 15-16R
Mannon, James M(onroe) 1942- 110
Mannon, Warwick
See Hopkins, Kenneth
Mannoni, Octave 1899- 102
Mano, D. Keith 1942- 25-28R
See also CAAS 6
See also DLB 6
See also CLC 2, 10
Mano, M(oshe) Morris 1927- 103
Manocchia, Benito 1934- 69-72
Manogaran, Chelvadurai 1935- 124
Manolson, Frank 1925- 19-20R
Manoni, Mary H(allahan) 1924- CANR-4
Earlier sketch in CA 49-52
Manoogian, Haig P. 1916(?)-1980
Obituary 97-100
Manor, Jason
See Hall, Oakley (Maxwell)
Manos, Charley 1923-1985 ....29-32R
Obituary 116
Manosevitz, Martin 1938- 29-32R
Manross, William Wilson 1905- 57-60
Manry, Robert 1918-1971 .... CAP-2
Obituary 29-32R
Earlier sketch in CA 21-22
Mansbach, Richard W(allace) 1943- 53-56
Mansbridge, John 1901(?)-1981 Obituary .. 105
Manschreck, Clyde Leonard 1917- CANR-5
Earlier sketch in CA 9-10R
Mansell, Darrel (Lee, Jr.) 1934- 57-60
Manser, Martin H(ugh) 1952- 118
Mansergh, (Philip) Nicholas (Seton) 1910- .. 105
Mansfield, Bruce Edgar 1926- 103
Mansfield, Comins 1896-1984 Obituary 112
Mansfield, Edwin 1930- CANR-18
Earlier sketches in CA 11-12R, CANR-3
Mansfield, Elizabeth
See Schwartz, Paula
Mansfield, Harold H. 1912- 19-20R
Mansfield, Harvey C(laflin) 1905- 1R
Mansfield, John M(aurice) 1936- 29-32R
Mansfield, Katherine
See Beauchamp, Kathleen Mansfield
See also TCLC 2, 8
Mansfield, Libby
See Schwartz, Paula
Mansfield, Norman
See Gladden, E(dgar) Norman
Mansfield, Peter 1928- 65-68
Mansfield, Roger (Ernest) 1939- CANR-11
Earlier sketch in CA 25-28R
Manship, David 1927- 25-28R
Manso, Peter 1940- 29-32R
See also CLC 39
Manson, Beverlie 1945- 113
See also SATA 44
Manson, Richard 1939- 29-32R
Mansoor, Menahem 1911- CANR-15
Earlier sketch in CA 41-44R
Mansur, Ina 1910- 116
Mantague, John 1929- 11-12R
Mantel, Samuel J(oseph), Jr. 1921- 15-16R
Mantell, Leroy H. 1919- 37-40R
Mantell, Martin E(den) 1936- 45-48
Manternach, Janaan 1927- 116
Mantey, Julius Robert 1890- CAP-1
Earlier sketch in CA 11-12
Mantle, Mickey (Charles) 1931- 89-92
Mantle, Winifred (Langford) CANR-6
Earlier sketch in CA 13-14R
Manton, Jo
See Gittings, Jo (Grenville) Manton
Manton, Peter
See Creasey, John
Manuel, E(spiridion) Arsenio 1909- 118
Manuel, Frank Edward 1910- CANR-6
Earlier sketch in CA 11-12R
Manuel, George 1921- 107
Manus, Mavis 1929- 116
Manus, Willard 1930- 108
Manushkin, Fran 1942- CANR-1
Earlier sketch in CA 49-52
See also SATA 7
Manvell, (Arnold) Roger 1909-1987 .... CANR-23
Obituary 124
Earlier sketches in CA 4R, CANR-6
Manville, W(illiam) H(enry) 1930- 93-96
Manwell, Reginald D. 1897- 37-40R
Man Without A Spleen
See Chekhov, Anton (Pavlovich)
Man Without a Spleen, A
See Chekhov, Anton (Pavlovich)
Many, Seth E(dward) 1939- 97-100
Manyan, Gladys 1911- 57-60
Manzalaoui, Mahmoud (Ali) 1924- CANR-12
Earlier sketch in CA 29-32R
Manzella, David (Bernard) 1924- 5-6R
Manzini, Gianna 1899-1974 Obituary 53-56
Manzoni, Pablo Michelangelo 1939-
Brief entry 106
Mao, James C. T. 1925- 37-40R
Mao Tse-tung 1893-1976 73-76
Obituary 69-72
Mapel, William 1902-1984 Obituary 112
Mapes, Arthur Franklin 1913-1986
Obituary 118
Mapes, Mary A.
See Ellison, Virginia H(owell)
Maple, Eric William 1915- CANR-6
Earlier sketch in CA 53-56
Maple, Terry 1946- CANR-1
Earlier sketch in CA 49-52
Maples, Evelyn Palmer 1919- CANR-17
Earlier sketches in CA 7-8R, CANR-2
Mapp, Alf J(ohnson), Jr. 1925- CANR-1
Earlier sketch in CA 4R
Mapp, Edward C(harles) 33-36R
Maquet, Jacques Jerome Pierre 1919- ... CANR-8
Earlier sketch in CA 61-64
Mara, Barney
See Roth, Arthur J(oseph)
Mara, Jeanette
See Cebulash, Mel
Mara, Thalia 1911- 11-12R
Marable, Manning 1950- 110
Maraini, Dacia 1936- CANR-11
Earlier sketch in CA 7-8R
Maraini, Fosco 1912- Brief entry 116
Marais, Josef 1905-1978 Obituary 77-80
See also SATA 24
Maran, Rene 1887-1960 Obituary 107
Maran, Stephen P(aul) 1938- 57-60
Maranda, Elli Kongas 1932- Brief entry 107
Maranda, Pierre 1930- 37-40R
Maranell, Gary M. 1932- 37-40R
Marangell, Virginia J(ohnson) 1924- 93-96
Maras, Karl
See Bulmer, (Henry) Kenneth
Marasmus, Seymour
See Rivoli, Mario
Marath, Laurie
See Roberts, Suzanne
Marath, Sparrow
See Roberts, Suzanne
Maravich, Pete(r Press) 1947(?)-1988
Obituary 124
Marazzi, Rich(ard Thomas) 1943- 102
Marberry, M. M(arion) 1905-1968 .... CAP-2
Earlier sketch in CA 21-22
Marble, Harriet Clement 1903-1975 73-76
Marble, Samuel D(avey) 1915- 106
Marbrook, Del
See Marbrook, Djelloul
Marbrook, Djelloul 1934- 73-76
Marbut, F(rederick) B(rowning) 1905- 33-36R
Marcal, Annette B.
See Callaway, Bernice (Anne)
Marcatante, John 1930- CANR-10
Earlier sketch in CA 25-28R
Marceau, Felicien
See Carette, Louis
Marceau, LeRoy 1907- CAP-1
Earlier sketch in CA 19-20
Marceau, Marcel 1923- 85-88
Marcel, Gabriel Honore 1889-1973 102
Obituary 45-48
See also CLC 15
Marcelin, Pierre 1908- 106
Marcelino
See Agnew, Edith J(osephine)
Marcell, David Wyburn 1937- 41-44R
March, Andrew Lee 1932- 110
March, Anthony 1912-1973 Obituary 45-48
March, Hilary
See Adcock, Almey St. John
March, James Gardner 1928- 13-14R
March, Joseph 1899(?)-1977 Obituary 69-72
March, Josie
See Titchener, Louise
March, Robert H(erbert) 1934- 61-64
March, William
See Campbell, William Edward March
See also DLB 9
March, William J. 1915- 13-14R
Marchaj, C(zeslaw) A(ntony) 1918- CANR-5
Earlier sketch in CA 11-12R
Marchak, M(aureen) Patricia 1936- 111
Marchak, Maureen
See Marchak, M(aureen) Patricia
Marcham, Frederick George 1898- 13-14R
Marchand, C(harles) Roland 1933-
Brief entry 110
Marchand, Leslie A(lexis) 1900- CANR-12
Earlier sketch in CA 65-68
Marchant, Anyda 1911- 15-16R
Marchant, Bessie 1862-1941 .... YABC-2
Marchant, Catherine
See Cookson, Catherine (McMullen)
Marchant, Herbert S(tanley) 106
Marchant, Leslie R(onald) 1924-
Brief entry 110
Marchant, Maurice P(eterson) 1927- 110
Marchant, R(ex) A(lan) 1933- 15-16R
Marchant, William 1923- 69-72
Marchbanks, Samuel
See Davies, (William) Robertson
Marchenko, Anatoly (Timofeevich)
1938-1986 ....25-28R
Obituary 121
Marcher, Marion Walden 1890- 1R
See also SATA 10
Marchessault, Jovette 1938- DLB-60
Marchetti, Albert 1947- 89-92
Marchetti, Victor Brief entry 108
Marchi, Giacomo
See Bassani, Giorgio
Marchione, Margherita (Frances)
1922- CANR-15
Earlier sketch in CA 37-40R
Marciano, Linda Boreman 1949(?)-
Brief entry 114
Marciniak, Ed(ward) 1917- 29-32R
Marckwardt, Albert H(enry) 1903-1975 .. CANR-4
Obituary 61-64
Earlier sketch in CA 2R
Marco
See Mountbatten, Louis (Francis Albert Victor Nicholas)
Marco, Anton N(icholas) 1943- 110
Marco, Barbara (Starkey) 1934- 11-12R
Marco, Guy A(nthony) 1927- 118
Marco, Lou
See Gottfried, Theodore Mark
Marcombe, Edith Marion
See Shiffert, Edith (Marcombe)
Marcosson, Isaac Frederick 1877-1961
Obituary 89-92
Marcovich, Miroslav 1919- 115
Marcson, Simon 1910- 49-52
Marcum, John A(rthur) 1927- CANR-14
Earlier sketch in CA 25-28R
Marcus, Aaron 1943- 53-56
Marcus, Adrianne 1935- CANR-1
Earlier sketch in CA 45-48
Marcus, Alfred A(llen) 1950- 118
Marcus, Anne M(ulkeen) 1927- 73-76
Marcus, Betty Blum 1923-1984 Obituary ... 113
Marcus, David 1926- Brief entry 110
Marcus, Edward 1918- CANR-14
Earlier sketch in CA 21-22R
Marcus, Frank 1928- CANR-2
Earlier sketch in CA 45-48
See also DLB 13
Marcus, Fred H(arold) 1921- 104
Marcus, Genevieve Grafe 1932- 111
Marcus, George E. 1946- 124
Marcus, George H. 1939- 120
Marcus, Greil (Gerstley) 1945- 122
Marcus, Harold G. 1936- 37-40R
Marcus, Irwin M. 1919- 45-48
Marcus, Jacob Rader 1896- 23-24R
Marcus, Jerry 1924- 97-100
Marcus, Joanna
See Andrews, Lucilla Mathew
Marcus, Joe 1933- 65-68
Marcus, Maeva 1941- Brief entry 108
Marcus, Martin 1933- 25-28R
Marcus, Mildred Rendl 1928- CANR-2
Earlier sketch in CA 1R
Marcus, Mordecai 1925- CANR-17
Earlier sketch in CA 77-80
Marcus, Morton 1936- 105
Marcus, Phillip L. 1941- Brief entry 111
Marcus, Rebecca B(rian) 1907- CANR-1
Earlier sketch in CA 5-6R
See also SATA 9
Marcus, Robert D. 1936- Brief entry 110
Marcus, Ruth Barcan 1921- 41-44R
Marcus, Sheldon 1937- Brief entry 106
Marcus, Stanley 1905- 53-56
Marcus, Steven 1928- 41-44R
Marcuse, F(rederick) L(awrence) 1916- ...11-12R
Marcuse, Herbert 1898-1979 Obituary 89-92
Marcuse, Ludwig 1894-1971 Obituary 33-36R
Marden, Charles F(rederick) 1902- 37-40R
Marden, William (Edward) 1947- 61-64
Marder, Arthur (Jacob) 1910-1980 105
Obituary 102
Marder, Daniel 1923- 21-22R
Marder, Herbert 1934- 69-72
Marder, Louis 1915- 7-8R
Mardock, Robert W(inston) 1921- 19-20R
Mardon, Michael (Claude) 1919- 13-14R
Mardor, Munya Meir 1913- 19-20R
Mardus, Elaine Bassler 1914- 9-10R
Mare, W(illiam) Harold 1918- 105
Marei, Sayed (Ahmed) 1913- 73-76
Marein, Shirley 1926- CANR-1
Earlier sketch in CA 45-48
Marek, George R(ichard) 1902-1987 .... CANR-1
Obituary 121
Earlier sketch in CA 49-52
Marek, Hannelore M(arie) C(harlotte)
1926- 15-16R
Marek, Kurt W(illi) 1915-1972 .... CAP-2
Obituary 33-36R
Earlier sketch in CA 17-18
Marek, Margot L. 1934(?)-1987 Obituary ... 123
Marelli, Leonard R(ussell) 1933-1973 .... CAP-1
Earlier sketch in CA 15-16
Maremaa, Thomas 1945- 85-88
Marenco, Ethne (Elsie) K(aplan) 1925- 103
Marer, Paul 1936- 105
Mares, F(rancis) H(ugh) 1925- 25-28R
Maresca, Thomas Edward 1938- 85-88
Mareth, Glenville
See Gilbert, Willie
Marett, Robert Hugh Kirk 1907- 25-28R
Marevna
See Vorobeva, Maria
Margadant, Ted W(inston) 1941- 93-96
Margalith, Pinhas Z(alman) 1926- 110
Margaret, Karla
See Andersdatter, Karla M(argaret)
Margenau, Henry 1901- CANR-14
Earlier sketch in CA 37-40R
Marger, Mary Ann 1934- 93-96
Margerson, David
See Davies, David Margerison
Margetson, Stella 1912- CANR-13
Earlier sketch in CA 33-36R
Marghieri, Clotilde 1901(?)-1981 Obituary .. 105
Margold, Stella 81-84
Margolies, Edward 1925- CANR-11
Earlier sketch in CA 65-68

INDEX

Margolies, Joseph A(aron) 1889-1982
Obituary ... 108
Margolies, Luise 1945- ... 102
Margolies, Marjorie 1942- ... CANR-13
Earlier sketch in CA 65-68
Margolin, Edythe ... 69-72
Margolin, Judith B(elle) 1946- ... 117
Margolin, Malcolm 1940- ... 57-60
Margolin, Victor 1941- ... 65-68
Margolis, Diane Rothbard 1933- ... 97-100
Margolis, Ellen (Edelman) 1934- ... 2R
Margolis, Gary 1945- ... 73-76
Margolis, Jack S 1934- ... 69-72
Margolis, John D(avid) 1941- Brief entry ... 113
Margolis, Joseph 1924- ... 37-40R
Margolis, Julius 1920- Brief entry ... 109
Margolis, Maxine L(uanna) 1942- ... 53-56
Margolis, Michael (Stephen) 1940- ... 93-96
Margolis, Richard J(ules) 1929- ... 29-32R
See also SATA 4
Margolis, Susan Spector 1941- ... 81-84
Margolis, Susanna 1944- ... 107
Margolis, Vivienne 1922- ... SATA-46
Margolius, Sidney (Senier) 1911-1980 . CANR-11
Obituary ... 93-96
Earlier sketch in CA 21-22R
Margon, Lester 1892- ... CAP-1
Earlier sketch in CA 15-16
Margoshes, Dave 1941- ... 111
Margulies, Harry D. 1907(?)-1980
Obituary ... 97-100
Margulies, Herbert F(elix) 1928- ... 77-80
Margulies, Leo 1900-1975 Obituary ... 61-64
Margulies, Newton 1932- ... 61-64
Margulis, Lynn 1938- ... CANR-4
Earlier sketch in CA 53-56
Margull, Hans J(ochen) 1925- ... 9-10R
Marhoefer, Barbara (McGeary) 1936- ... 61-64
Maria Del Rey, Sister 1908- ... 5-6R
Mariah, Paul 1937- ... CANR-4
Earlier sketch in CA 53-56
Mariana
See Foster, Marian Curtis
Mariani, John Francis 1945- ... 117
Mariani, Paul L(ouis) 1940- ... CANR-12
Earlier sketch in CA 29-32R
Mariano, Frank 1931(?)-1976 Obituary ... 69-72
Marias (Aguilera), Julian 1914- ... CANR-22
Earlier sketches in CA 9-10R, CANR-5
Marie, Beverly Sainte
See Sainte-Marie, Beverly
Marie, Buffy Sainte
See Sainte-Marie, Beverly
Marie, Geraldine (a pseudonym) 1949- ... 108
Marie, Jeanne
See Wilson, Marie B(eatrice)
Marie-Andre du Sacre-Coeur, Sister 1899- .. 7-8R
Marien, Michael 1938- ... CANR-16
Earlier sketches in CA 49-52, CANR-1
Marier, Captain Victor
See Griffith, D(avid Lewelyn) W(ark)
Marie Therese, Mother 1891- ... CAP-1
Earlier sketch in CA 13-14
Maril, Nadja 1954- ... CANR-17
Earlier sketch in CA 85-88
Marill, Alvin H(erbert) 1934- ... CANR-12
Earlier sketch in CA 73-76
Marilla, E(smond) L(inworth) 1900- ... CAP-2
Earlier sketch in CA 23-24
Marilue
See Johnson, Marilue Carolyn
Marimow, William K. 1947- ... 93-96
Marin, A. C.
See Coppel, Alfred
Marin, Cheech
See Marin, Richard Anthony
Marin, Diego 1914- ... 19-20R
Marin, Luis Munoz
See Munoz Marin, Luis
Marin, Richard Anthony 1946- Brief entry .. 112
Marinacci, Barbara 1933- ... CANR-9
Earlier sketch in CA 21-22R
Marinaccio, Anthony 1912- ... 53-56
Marine, David 1880(?)-1976 Obituary ... 69-72
Marine, Gene 1926- ... 65-68
Marine, Nick
See Oursler, Will(iam Charles)
Marinelli, Peter V(incent) 1933- ... 41-44R
Mariner, David
See Smith, David MacLeod
Mariner, Scott
See Pohl, Frederik
Marinetti, Filippo Tommaso 1876-1944
Brief entry ... 107
See also TCLC 10
Maring, Joel M(arvin) 1935- ... 49-52
Maring, Norman H(ill) 1914- ... 19-20R
Marini, Frank N(ick) 1935- ... 45-48
Marino, Carolyn Fitch 1942- ... 110
Marino, Dorothy Bronson 1912- ... 73-76
See also SATA 14
Marino, John J. 1948- ... 106
Marino, Joseph D. 1912(?)-1983 Obituary .. 109
Marino, Trentino J(oseph) 1917- ... 65-68
Marinoni, Rosa Zagnoni 1888-1970 ... CAP-1
Earlier sketch in CA 13-14
Marion, Frances 1886-1973 Obituary ... 41-44R
See also DLB 44
Marion, Frieda 1912- ... CANR-8
Earlier sketch in CA 61-64
Marion, Henry
See del Rey, Lester
Marion, John Francis 1922- ... CANR-3
Earlier sketch in CA 7-8R
Mariotti, (Raffaello) Marcello 1938- ... 29-32R
Marique, Joseph M(arie-) F(elix) 1899- ... 33-36R
Maris, Roger (Eugene) 1934-1985
Obituary ... 118
Maris, Ron ... SATA-45
Marisa
See Nucera, Marisa Lonette
Mariscal, Richard N(orth) 1935- ... 53-56
Maritain, Jacques 1882-1973 ... 85-88
Obituary ... 41-44R
Maritano, Nino 1919- ... 13-14R
Marius, Richard 1933- ... 25-28R
See also DLBY 85
Marjolin, Robert (Ernest) 1911-1986
Obituary ... 119
Marjoram, J.
See Mottram, R(alph) H(ale)
Mark, Charles Christopher 1927- ... CANR-1
Earlier sketch in CA 1R
Mark, David 1922- ... 2R
Mark, Edwina
See Fadiman, Edwin, Jr.
Mark, Irving 1908-1987 ... CAP-1
Obituary ... 121
Earlier sketch in CA 19-20
Mark, Jan 1943- ... CANR-17
Earlier sketch in CA 93-96
See also SATA 22
See also CLR 11
Mark, Jon
See Du Breuil, (Elizabeth) L(or)inda
Mark, Julius 1898-1977 ... 81-84
Obituary ... 73-76
Mark, Matthew
See Babcock, Frederic
Mark, Max 1910- ... 73-76
Mark, Michael L(aurence) 1936- ... 93-96
Mark, Norman (Barry) 1939- ... 113
Mark, Pauline (Dahlin) 1913- ... CANR-7
Earlier sketch in CA 19-20R
See also SATA 14
Mark, Polly
See Mark, Pauline (Dahlin)
Mark, Robert 1930- ... 110
Mark, Shelley M(uin) 1922- ... CANR-1
Earlier sketch in CA 1R
Mark, Steven Joseph 1913- ... 19-20R
Mark, Ted
See Gottfried, Theodore Mark
Mark, Theonie Diakidis 1938- ... 69-72
Mark, Yudel 1897-1975 Obituary ... 61-64
Mark-Alan, Roy
See Malan, R(enato) M(arco)
Markandaya, Kamala
See Taylor, Kamala (Purnaiya)
See also CLC 8, 38
Markbreit, Jerry 1935- ... 49-52
Marke, Julius J(ay) 1913- ... 19-20R
Markel, Geraldine (Ponte) 1939- ... 108
Markel, Lester 1894-1977 ... 37-40R
Obituary ... 73-76
Markels, Julian 1925- ... 25-28R
Marken, Jack W(alter) 1922- ... 49-52
Marker, Frederick (Joseph, Jr.) 1936- .. CANR-16
Earlier sketch in CA 41-44R
Marker, Lise-Lone (Christensen) 1934- .. CANR-8
Earlier sketch in CA 61-64
Market Man
See Lake, Kenneth R(obert)
Markevitch, Igor 1912-1983 Obituary ... 109
Markey, Gene 1895-1980 ... CAP-1
Obituary ... 97-100
Earlier sketch in CA 11-12
Markfield, Wallace 1926- ... 69-72
See also CAAS 3
See also DLB 2, 28
See also CLC 8
Markgraf, Carl 1928- ... 49-52
Markham, Beryl 1902-1986 Obituary ... 119
Markham, Clarence M(atthew), Jr. 1911- .. 69-72
Markham, Dewey 1904-1981 Obituary ... 108
Markham, Edwin 1852-1940 ... DLB-54
Markham, Felix (Maurice Hippisley)
1908- ... CAP-1
Earlier sketch in CA 11-12
Markham, James M(orris) 1943- ... 93-96
Markham, James W(alter) 1910-1972 ... CAP-2
Earlier sketch in CA 21-22
Markham, Jesse William 1916- ... 9-10R
Markham, Meeler 1914- ... CANR-12
Earlier sketch in CA 25-28R
Markham, Pigmeat
See Markham, Dewey
Markham, Reed 1957- ... 110
Markham, Robert
See Amis, Kingsley (William)
Marki, Ivan 1934- ... 97-100
Markides, Kyriacos (Costa) 1942- ... 81-84
Markie, Peter J(oseph) 1950- ... 123
Markins, W. S.
See Jenkins, Marie M(agdalen)
Markish, David 1938- ... 69-72
Markle, Joyce B(onners) 1942- ... 69-72
Markle, Sandra L(ee) 1946- ... 111
See also SATA 41
Markley, Kenneth A(lan) 1933- ... 61-64
Markley, R(ayner) W(are) 1934- ... 111
Markman, Howard (Joel) 1950- ... 69-72
Markman, Sherwin J. 1929- ... 104
Markman, Sidney David 1911- ... CAP-2
Earlier sketch in CA 33-36
Markmann, Charles Lam 1913- ... 15-16R
Marko, Katherine D(olores) ... CANR-15
Earlier sketch in CA 29-32R
See also SATA 28
Markoe, Karen 1942- ... 81-84
Markoosie
See Patsauq, Markoosie
Markov, Georgi 1929(?)-1978 Obituary ... 104
Markov, Vladimir 1920- ... 19-20R
Markova, Alicia 1910- ... CAP-2
Earlier sketch in CA 19-20
Markovic, Miroslav
See Marcovich, Miroslav
Markovic, Vida E. 1916- ... 33-36R
Markovitz, Irving Leonard 1934- ... 33-36R
Markowitz, Norman Daniel 1943- ... 45-48
Marks, Alfred H(arding) 1920- ... CANR-23
Earlier sketch in CA 45-48
Marks, Barry A(lan) 1926- ... 19-20R
Marks, Bayly Ellen 1943- ... 115
Marks, Burton 1930- ... 107
See also SATA 43, 47
Marks, Charles 1922- ... CANR-5
Earlier sketch in CA 53-56
Marks, Claude (Mordecai) 1915- ... 61-64
Marks, Edith Bobroff 1924- ... 17-18R
Marks, Edward S(tanford) 1936- ... 45-48
Marks, Elaine 1930- ... CANR-23
Earlier sketches in CA 19-20R, CANR-7
Marks, Eli S(amplin) 1911- ... 85-88
Marks, Frederick (William III) 1940- ... 97-100
Marks, Geoffrey 1906- ... 33-36R
Marks, Hannah K.
See Trivelpiece, Laurel
Marks, Henry S(eymour) 1933- ... 73-76
Marks, J
See Highwater, Jamake (Mamake)
Marks, J(ames) M(acdonald) 1921- ... 61-64
See also SATA 13
Marks, James R(obert) 1932- ... 19-20R
Marks, Jane (A. Steinberg) 1943- ... 113
Marks, John 1943- ... 110
Marks, John David 1909-1985 Obituary ... 117
Marks, John H(enry) 1923- ... 19-20R
Marks, Johnny
See Marks, John David
Marks, Margaret L. 1911(?)-1980
Obituary ... 101
See also SATA 23
Marks, Mickey Klar ... CANR-6
Earlier sketch in CA 2R
See also SATA 12
Marks, Norton E(lliott) 1932- ... 23-24R
Marks, Pat R.
See Feinman, Jeffrey
Marks, Peter
See Smith, Robert Kimmel
Marks, Rita 1938- ... 106
See also SATA 47
Marks, Sally (Jean) 1931- ... 102
Marks, Sema 1942- ... 29-32R
Marks, Stan(ley) 1929- ... CANR-12
Earlier sketch in CA 29-32R
See also SATA 14
Marks, Stuart A. 1939- ... 69-72
Marks, Vic(tor James) 1955- ... 118
Marksberry, Mary Lee ... 15-16R
Markson, David M(errill) 1927- ... CANR-1
Earlier sketch in CA 49-52
Markstein, David L. 1920- ... 29-32R
Markstein, George 1929-1987 Obituary ... 121
Markun, Alan Fletcher 1925- ... 45-48
Markun, Patricia Maloney 1924- ... CANR-4
Earlier sketch in CA 5-6R
See also SATA 15
Markus, Julia 1939- ... 105
Markus, R(obert) A(ustin) 1924- ... CANR-16
Earlier sketch in CA 65-68
Marland, Edward Allen 1912- ... 19-20R
Marland, Michael 1934- ... 103
Marland, Sidney P(ercy, Jr.) 1914- ... 53-56
Marlatt, Daphne (Buckle) 1942- ... CANR-17
Earlier sketch in CA 25-28R
See also DLB 60
Marlborough
See Oaksey, John
Marley, Augusta Anne ?-1973 Obituary ... 41-44R
Marley, Bob
See Marley, Robert Nesta
See also CLC 17
Marley, Robert Nesta 1945-1981 ... 107
Obituary ... 103
Marlin, Alice Tepper 1944- ... 123
Marlin, Henry
See Giggal, Kenneth
Marlin, Hilda
See Van Stockum, Hilda
Marlin, Jeffrey 1940- ... 45-48
Marlin, John Tepper 1942- ... 124
Marling, William 1951- ... 123
Marling, Yvonne Rodd
See Rodd-Marling, Yvonne
Marlo, John A. 1934- ... 29-32R
Marlor, Clark Strang 1922- ... 37-40R
Marlot, Raymond
See Angremy, Jean-Pierre
Marlow, Cecilia Ann 1952- ... 121
Marlow, David 1943- ... 107
Marlow, Edwina
See Huff, T(om) E.
Marlow, Joyce
See Connor, Joyce Mary
Marlow, Louis
See Wilkinson, Louis (Umfreville)
Marlowe, Alan Stephen 1937- ... 23-24R
Marlowe, Amy Bell ... CAP-2
Earlier sketch in CA 19-20
See also SATA 1
Marlowe, Christopher 1564-1593 ... DLB-62
Marlowe, Dan J(ames) 1914- ... CANR-1
Earlier sketch in CA 2R
Marlowe, Derek 1938- ... CANR-11
Earlier sketch in CA 19-20R
Marlowe, Don ... 61-64
Marlowe, Hugh
See Patterson, Henry
Marlowe, Kenneth 1926- ... 13-14R
Marlowe, Stephen 1928- ... CANR-6
Earlier sketch in CA 13-14R
Marlowe, Webb
See McComas, J(esse) Francis
Marlyn, John 1912- ... 11-12R
Marmion, Harry A. 1931- ... 25-28R
Marmion, Shakerley 1603-1639 ... DLB-58
Marmon, William F., Jr. 1942- ... 77-80
Marmor, J(udd) 1910- ... CANR-12
Earlier sketch in CA 25-28R
Marmor, T(heodore) R(ichard) 1939- ... 29-32R
Marmur, Dow 1935- ... 121
Marmur, Jacland 1901- ... 9-10R
Marmur, Mildred 1930- ... 7-8R
Marnell, William H. 1907- ... 23-24R
Marney, (Leonard) Carlyle 1916- ... 57-60
Marney, Dean 1952- ... 110
Marney, John 1933- ... 69-72
Marnham, Patrick 1943- ... 102
Marokvia, Artur 1909- ... SATA-31
Marokvia, Mireille (Journet) 1918- ... 29-32R
See also SATA 5
Maron, Margaret ... 122
Marossi, Ruth
See Krefetz, Ruth
Marot, Marc
See Koch, Kurt E(mil)
Marple, Allen Clark 1901(?)-1968
Obituary ... 106
Marple, Hugo D(ixon) 1920- ... 53-56
Marples, William F(rank) 1907- ... CAP-1
Earlier sketch in CA 15-16
Marquand, John P(hillips) 1893-1960 ... 85-88
See also DLB 9
See also CLC 2, 10
Marquand, Josephine
See Gladstone, Josephine
Marquard, Leo(pold) 1897- ... 7-8R
Marquardt, Dorothy Ann 1921- ... 15-16R
Marques, Rene 1919-1979 ... 97-100
Obituary ... 85-88
Marquess, Harlan E(arl) 1931- ... 49-52
Marquess of Anglesey
See Paget, George Charles Henry Victor
Marquez, Gabriel Garcia
See Garcia Marquez, Gabriel (Jose)
Marquez, Robert 1942- ... 53-56
Marquis, Arnold ... 57-60
Marquis, Dave 1951- ... 113
Marquis, Don(ald Robert Perry)
1878-1937 Brief entry ... 104
See also DLB 11, 25
See also TCLC 7
Marquis, Donald G(eorge) 1908-1973
Obituary ... 45-48
Marquis, G(eorge) Welton 1916- ... 19-20R
Marr, David G. 1937- ... 33-36R
Marr, James Pratt 1898-1986 Obituary ... 121
Marr, John S(tuart) 1940- ... 81-84
See also SATA 48
Marranca, Bonnie 1947- ... CANR-9
Earlier sketch in CA 65-68
Marreco, Anne
See Wignall, Anne
Marric, J. J.
See Creasey, John
Marrin, Albert 1936- ... 49-52
See also SATA 43
Marriner, Ernest (Cummings)
1891-1983 ... 37-40R
Obituary ... 109
Marrington, Pauline 1921- ... CANR-10
Earlier sketch in CA 65-68
Marriott, Alice Lee 1910- ... 57-60
See also SATA 31
Marriott, (Joyce) Anne 1913- ... CANR-18
Earlier sketch in CA 102
Marriott, Pat(ricia) 1920- ... SATA-35
Marriott, William H. 1909(?)-1986
Obituary ... 118
Marriott-Watson, Nan 1899-1982 Obituary .. 107
Marris, Peter (Horsey) 1927- ... 111
Marris, Robin Lapthorn 1924- ... CANR-8
Earlier sketch in CA 5-6R
Marris, Ruth 1948- ... 106
Marrison, L(eslie) W(illiam) 1901- ... 29-32R
Marr-Johnson, Diana (Maugham) 1908- .. 13-14R
Marrocco, W(illiam) Thomas 1909- ... 11-12R
Marrone, Robert 1941- ... 77-80
Marroquin, Patricio
See Markun, Patricia Maloney
Marrow, Alfred J. 1905-1978 ... 81-84
Obituary ... 77-80
Marrow, Stanley B. 1931- ... CANR-10
Earlier sketch in CA 25-28R
Marrs, Edwin W(ilson), Jr. 1928- ... 25-28R
Marrus, Michael R(obert) 1941- ... CANR-12
Earlier sketch in CA 33-36R
Marryat, Frederick 1792-1848 ... DLB-21
Mars, Alastair 1915-1985 Obituary ... 116
Mars, Florence L. 1923- ... 101
Mars, Jean Price
See Price-Mars, Jean
Mars, W. T.
See Mars, Witold Tadeusz J.
Mars, Witold Tadeusz J. 1912- ... 25-28R
See also SATA 3
Marsano, Ramon
See Dinges, John (Charles)
Marsden, George (Mish) 1939- ... CANR-12
Earlier sketch in CA 73-76
Marsden, James
See Creasey, John
Marsden, Lorna R(uth) 1942- ... 85-88

Marsden, Malcolm Morse 1922- 7-8R
Marsden, Peter (Richard Valentine)
1940- CANR-14
Earlier sketch in CA 77-80
Marsden, Philip Kitson 1916-1984
Obituary 113
Marsden-Smedley, Hester 1901-1982
Obituary 107
Marsh, Analyticus
See Morrison, Marsh
Marsh, Andrew
See O'Donovan, John
Marsh, Clifton E. 1946- 77-80
Marsh, Dave 1950- CANR-17
Earlier sketch in CA 97-100
Marsh, David Charles 1917- 103
Marsh, Edwin
See Schorb, E(dwin) M(arsh)
Marsh, George Perkins 1801-1882 ... DLB-1, 64
Marsh, Henry
See Saklatvala, Beram
Marsh, Irving T. 1907-1982 ....11-12R
Obituary 107
Marsh, J. E.
See Marshall, Evelyn
Marsh, James 1794-1842 .... DLB-1, 59
Marsh, Jean
See Marshall, Evelyn
Marsh, Jeanne C(ay) 1948- 111
Marsh, Jeri 1940- 85-88
Marsh, John 1904- CAP-1
Earlier sketch in CA 9-10
Marsh, John 1907- CAP-1
Earlier sketch in CA 15-16
Marsh, John L(eslie) 1927- CANR-1
Earlier sketch in CA 45-48
Marsh, Leonard (Charles) 1906- 37-40R
Marsh, Leonard (George) 1930- CANR-13
Earlier sketch in CA 73-76
Marsh, Margaret Sammartino 1945- 106
Marsh, Mary Val 1925- CANR-11
Earlier sketch in CA 69-72
Marsh, Meredith 1946- 77-80
Marsh, (Edith) Ngaio 1899-1982 ...... CANR-6
Earlier sketch in CA 11-12R
See also CLC 7
Marsh, Norman Stayner 1913- 117
Marsh, Patrick O(tis) 1928- 25-28R
Marsh, Paul
See Hopkins, Kenneth
Marsh, Peter T(imothy) 1935- 33-36R
Marsh, Philip M(errill) 1893- 11-12R
Marsh, Rebecca
See Neubauer, William Arthur
Marsh, Robert (Harrison) 1926- 19-20R
Marsh, Robert C(harles) 1924- 15-16R
Marsh, Robert M(ortimer) 1931- CANR-2
Earlier sketch in CA 1R
Marsh, Ronald (James) 1914- 13-14R
Marsh, Spencer 1931- 61-64
Marsh, Susan (Sherry Raymond) 1914- ...9-10R
Marsh, U(lysses) Grant 1911- 57-60
Marsh, Willard 1922-1970 .... CAP-2
Earlier sketch in CA 25-28
Marshak, Robert Eugene 1916- 107
Marshak, Samuil Yakovlevich 1887-1964
Obituary 111
Marshall, Alan 1902- 85-88
Marshall, Alfred 1884-1965 ....7-8R
Marshall, Annie Jessie 1922- CAP-1
Earlier sketch in CA 9-10
Marshall, Anthony D(ryden) 1924- 29-32R
See also SATA 18
Marshall, Bill 1937- CANR-17
Earlier sketch in CA 65-68
Marshall, Bruce 1899-1987 ....5-6R
Obituary 123
Marshall, Burke 1922- 15-16R
Marshall, Byron K. 1936- 33-36R
Marshall, (Sarah) Catherine (Wood)
1914-1983 .... CANR-8
Obituary 109
Earlier sketch in CA 19-20R
See also SATA 2, 34
Marshall, Charles Burton 1908- 37-40R
Marshall, Charles Wheeler 1906- 110
Marshall, D(onald) Bruce 1931- 65-68
Marshall, David F(ranklin) 1938- 25-28R
Marshall, Don
See Marshall, Donovan
Marshall, Donald R. 1934- 93-96
Marshall, Donald S(tanley) 1919- 29-32R
Marshall, Donovan 1908- 117
Marshall, Dorothy 1900- CAP-1
Earlier sketch in CA 13-14
Marshall, Douglas
See McClintock, Marshall
Marshall, E(dmund) Jesse 1888- CAP-1
Earlier sketch in CA 11-12
Marshall, Edison 1894-1967 .... CAP-1
Obituary 29-32R
Earlier sketch in CA 9-10
Marshall, Edmund
See Hopkins, Kenneth
Marshall, Edward 1932- DLB-16
Marshall, Emily
See Hall, Bennie Caroline (Humble)
Marshall, Evelyn 1897- CANR-18
Earlier sketches in CA 7-8R, CANR-2
See also SATA 11
Marshall, F(reddie) Ray 1928- CANR-8
Earlier sketch in CA 19-20R
Marshall, Garry 1934- 111
See also CLC 17
Marshall, George (Nichols) 1920- 77-80
Marshall, George C(atlett), Jr. 1880-1959
Brief entry 115
Marshall, George O(ctavius), Jr. 1922- ...19-20R
Marshall, H.H.
See Jahn, Joseph Michael
Marshall, Helen E(dith) 1899- 37-40R
Marshall, Helen Lowrie 1904-1975 103
Marshall, Herbert (Percival James)
1906- 25-28R
Marshall, Herbert Hedley 1909(?)-1982
Obituary 112
Marshall, Hermine H(alprin) 1935- CANR-14
Earlier sketch in CA 41-44R
Marshall, Howard D(rake) 1924-1972 .... CAP-2
Obituary 37-40R
Earlier sketch in CA 23-24
Marshall, Howard Wight 1944- 107
Marshall, Hubert (Ray) 1920- 23-24R
Marshall, I(an) Howard 1934- 122
Marshall, J(ohn) D(uncan) 1919- 73-76
Marshall, Jack 1937- 97-100
Marshall, James 1896-1986 ....41-44R
Obituary 120
Marshall, James 1942- 41-44R
See also SATA 6
See also DLB 61
Marshall, James M(orse) 1924- 120
Marshall, James Vance 1887-1964 ...... CAP-1
Earlier sketch in CA 11-12
Marshall, James Vance
See Payne, Donald Gordon
Marshall, Jeff
See Laycock, George (Edwin)
Marshall, Joanne
See Rundle, Anne
Marshall, John 1905(?)-1985(?) Obituary ... 116
Marshall, John 1922- CANR-15
Earlier sketch in CA 89-92
Marshall, John David 1928- CANR-19
Earlier sketches in CA 9-10R, CANR-3
Marshall, John Ross 1912- 109
Marshall, John S(edberry) 1898- CAP-1
Earlier sketch in CA 19-20
Marshall, Joyce 1913- 102
Marshall, Kathryn 1951- 57-60
See also AITN 1
Marshall, Kim
See Marshall, Michael (Kimbrough)
Marshall, Lenore Guinzburg 1899-1971 ... CAP-2
Obituary 33-36R
Earlier sketch in CA 25-28
Marshall, Lovat
See Duncan, W(illiam) Murdoch
Marshall, Margaret 1901(?)-1974
Obituary 104
Marshall, Margaret Wiley 1908- CAP-1
Earlier sketch in CA 9-10
Marshall, Martin V(ivan) 1922- 2R
Marshall, Max Lawrence 1922- 19-20R
Marshall, Max S(kidmore) 1897- CAP-1
Earlier sketch in CA 13-14
Marshall, Megan 1954- 124
Marshall, Mel(vin D.) 1911- CANR-12
Earlier sketch in CA 29-32R
Marshall, Michael (Kimbrough) 1948- ... CANR-3
Earlier sketch in CA 49-52
See also SATA 37
Marshall, Muriel 106
Marshall, Natalie J(unemann) 1929- 41-44R
Marshall, Norman 1901-1980 Obituary 108
Marshall, Paule 1929- 77-80
See also DLB 33
See also CLC 27
Marshall, Percy
See Young, Percy M(arshall)
Marshall, Peter 1902-1949 Brief entry 112
Marshall, Ray
See Marshall, F(reddie) Ray
Marshall, Raymond
See Raymond, Rene (Brabazon)
Marshall, Robert G. 1919- 37-40R
Marshall, Robert L(ewis) 1939- 104
Marshall, Roderick 1903-1975 Obituary ...53-56
Marshall, Ronald 1905- CAP-2
Earlier sketch in CA 33-36
Marshall, Rosalind Kay 1939- CANR-19
Earlier sketches in CA 53-56, CANR-4
Marshall, S(amuel) L(yman) A(twood)
1900-1977 81-84
Obituary 73-76
See also SATA 21
Marshall, Shirley E(velyn) 1925- 21-22R
Marshall, Sybil Mary (Edwards) 1913- ... CANR-1
Earlier sketch in CA 4R
Marshall, T(homas) H(umphrey)
1893-1981 109
Obituary 105
Marshall, Thomas Archibald 1938- CANR-17
Earlier sketches in CA 49-52, CANR-1
Marshall, Thomas F(rederic) 1908- CAP-2
Earlier sketch in CA 23-24
Marshall, Thomas R. 1949- 115
Marshall, Tom
See Marshall, Thomas Archibald
See also DLB 60
Marshall, William H(arvey) 1925-1968 .... CAP-1
Earlier sketch in CA 11-12
Marshall-Cornwall, James (Handyside)
1887-1985 107
Obituary 118
Marshburn, Joseph Hancock 1890-1975 109
Obituary 106
Marshner, Connaught Coyne 1951- CANR-16
Earlier sketch in CA 93-96
Mars-Jones, Adam 1954- 109
Marsland, Amy 1924- CANR-19
Earlier sketch in CA 103
Marsoli, Lisa Ann 1958- 120
Marson, Philip 1892- 11-12R
Marsteller, Bill
See Marsteller, William A.
Marsteller, William A. 1914-1987 Obituary .. 123
Marsten, Richard
See Hunter, Evan
Marston, Elsa 1933- 113
Marston, Hope Irvin 1935- 101
See also SATA 31
Marston, John 1576-1634 .... DLB-58
Marston, John E. 1911- 5-6R
Marston, Philip Bourke 1850-1887 ..... DLB-35
Marston, Thomas Ewart 1904-1984
Obituary 112
Marszalek, John F(rancis, Jr.) 1939- ... CANR-14
Earlier sketch in CA 37-40R
Martchenko, Michael 1942- SATA-50
Marteka, Vincent (James) 1936- 15-16R
Martel, Jane G. 1926- 57-60
Martell, James
See Bingley, David Ernest
Martell, Paul 1921(?)-1985 Obituary 116
Martellaro, Joseph A. 1924- 19-20R
Martens, Kurt 1870-1945 .... DLB-66
Marter, Joan M. 1946- 124
Marth, Del 1925- 61-64
Martha, Henry
See Harris, Mark
Marti, Fritz 1894- 107
Martianoff, Nicholas 1893-1984 Obituary ... 112
Martignoni, Margaret E. 1908(?)-1974
Obituary 104
See also SATA 27
Marti-Ibanez, Felix 1912(?)-1972
Obituary 33-36R
Martin, Albert
See Nussbaum, Al(bert F.)
and Mehan, Joseph Albert
Martin, Albro 1921- 77-80
Martin, Alfred 1916- 117
Martin, Alfred Manuel 1928- 108
Martin, Allie Beth 1914-1976 Obituary 65-68
Martin, Anamae 1919- 9-10R
Martin, Andre
See Jacoby, Henry
Martin, Andrew 1906-1985 Obituary 115
Martin, Ann Bodenhamer 1927- CANR-11
Earlier sketch in CA 69-72
Martin, Ann M(atthews) 1955- 111
See also SATA 41, 44
Martin, April
See Sherrill, Dorothy
Martin, Arlan Stone 1932- 69-72
Martin, Augustine 1935- 93-96
Martin, Barclay (Cluck) 1923- 73-76
Martin, Ben(jamin S.) 1921- 1R
Martin, Benjamin F(ranklin, Jr.) 1947- 89-92
Martin, Bernard (Davis) 1897- CAP-1
Earlier sketch in CA 9-10
Martin, Bernard 1905- CAP-1
Earlier sketch in CA 11-12
Martin, Bernard 1928- CANR-4
Earlier sketch in CA 53-56
Martin, Betty
See Martin, Elizabeth DuVernet
Martin, Bill, Jr.
See Martin, William Ivan
Martin, Billy
See Martin, Alfred Manuel
Martin, Boyd A(rcher) 1911- 37-40R
Martin, Brian P(hilip) 1947- 116
Martin, Bruce
See Paine, Lauran (Bosworth)
Martin, C(arol) Dianne 1943- 113
Martin, C(harles) Leslie 1897- 5-6R
Martin, C. Lewis 1915- 25-28R
Martin, Calvin (L.) 1948- Brief entry 113
Martin, Carter W(illiams) 1933- 25-28R
Martin, Charles 1906- 3R
Martin, Charles B(asil) 1930- 93-96
Martin, Charles Burton 1924- 25-28R
Martin, Charles E.
See Mastrangelo, Charles E.
Martin, Charles-Noel 1923- 29-32R
Martin, Chip
See Martin, Stoddard (Hammond), Jr.
Martin, Christopher
See Hoyt, Edwin P(almer), Jr.
Martin, Claire 1914- DLB-60
Martin, Cort
See Sherman, Jory (Tecumseh)
Martin, Curtis 1915- 53-56
Martin, David 1915- CANR-24
Earlier sketch in CA 103
Martin, David 1946- 89-92
Martin, David Alfred 1929- 107
Martin, David C(lark) 1943- 102
Martin, David Grant 1939- 65-68
Martin, David L(incoln) 1947- 119
Martin, David Stone 1913- SATA-39
Martin, Don 1931- 101
Martin, Donald Franklin 1944- 65-68
Martin, Donald L(loyd) 1939- 111
Martin, Dorothy 1921- CANR-6
Earlier sketch in CA 57-60
See also SATA 47
Martin, Dwight 1921-1978 Obituary 77-80
Martin, E(rnest) W(alter) 1914- CANR-20
Earlier sketches in CA 11-12R, CANR-5
Martin, Earl S(auder) 1944- 102
Martin, Edward A(lexander) 1927- 120
Martin, Elizabeth DuVernet 1910- 103
Martin, Ellis
See Ryan, Marah Ellis
Martin, Esmond Bradley 1941- CANR-16
Earlier sketch in CA 93-96
Martin, Eugene CAP-2
Earlier sketch in CA 19-20
See also SATA 1
Martin, F(rancis) David 1920- 33-36R
Martin, F(rancis) X(avier) 1922- CANR-13
Earlier sketch in CA 23-24R
Martin, Frances M(cEntee) 1906- 61-64
See also SATA 36
Martin, Francis
See Reid, Charles (Stuart)
Martin, Frederick M(orris) 1923-1985
Obituary 115
Martin, Fredric
See Christopher, Matt(hew F.)
Martin, G(eoffrey H(oward) 1928- 5-6R
Martin, Gary M. 1936- 89-92
Martin, Ged
See Martin, Gerald Warren
Martin, Geoffrey John 1934- CANR-14
Earlier sketch in CA 37-40R
Martin, George (Whitney) 1926- CANR-21
Earlier sketches in CA 9-10R, CANR-3
Martin, George R(aymond) R(ichard)
1948- 81-84
Martin, Gerald Warren 1945- CANR-17
Earlier sketches in CA 45-48, CANR-1
Martin, Graham Dunstan 1932- CANR-23
Earlier sketch in CA 106
Martin, Greg
See Miller, George Louquet
Martin, Harold Clark 1917- 9-10R
Martin, Harold Harber 1910- CANR-7
Earlier sketch in CA 61-64
Martin, Harold S(heaffer) 1930- 57-60
Martin, Herbert 1913- 29-32R
Martin, Herbert Woodward 1933- 73-76
Martin, Hubert M., Jr. 1932- 103
Martin, Ian Kennedy
See Kennedy-Martin, Ian
Martin, Ira Jay III 1911- 53-56
Martin, J(ohn) P(ercival) 1880(?)-1966 81-84
See also SATA 15
Martin, Jack
See Etchison, Dennis (William)
Martin, James 1921- 119
Martin, James (Thomas) 1933- Brief entry .. 112
Martin, James Alfred, Jr. 1917- 73-76
Martin, James Gilbert 1926- 11-12R
Martin, James J(oseph) 1916- CANR-8
Earlier sketch in CA 5-6R
Martin, James L. 1948- 81-84
Martin, James Perry 1923- 5-6R
Martin, Jane Roland 1929- 119
Martin, Janet
See Garfinkel, Bernard Max
Martin, Jay (Herbert) 1935- CANR-21
Earlier sketch in CA 5-6R
Martin, Jay
See Golding, Morton J(ay)
Martin, Jeremy
See Levin, Marcia Obrasky
Martin, John 1893-1985 Obituary 116
Martin, John Bartlow 1915-1987 .... CANR-8
Obituary 121
Earlier sketch in CA 15-16R
Martin, John Hanbury 1892-1983
Obituary 109
Martin, John Henry 1915- 102
Martin, John Rupert 1916- 19-20R
Martin, John Sayre 1921- 103
Martin, John Stuart 1900-1977 ....9-10R
Obituary 69-72
Martin, Jose L(uis) 1921- CANR-12
Earlier sketch in CA 61-64
Martin, Joseph George 1915-1981 108
Obituary 102
Martin, Joy 1922- 57-60
Martin, Judith (Sylvia) 1938- CANR-12
Earlier sketch in CA 97-100
Martin, June Hall
See McCash, June Hall
Martin, Kathryn 1908- 108
Martin, Ken
See Hubbard, L(afayette) Ron(ald)
Martin, Kenneth R(obert) 1938- CANR-17
Earlier sketches in CA 45-48, CANR-1
Martin, Kevin
See Pelton, Robert W(ayne)
Martin, (Basil) Kingsley 1897-1969 .... CANR-11
Obituary 25-28R
Earlier sketch in CA 7-8R
Martin, L(eslie) John 1921- CANR-22
Earlier sketches in CA 57-60, CANR-6
Martin, Laura C(oogle) 1952- 117
Martin, Laurence W(oodward) 1928- CANR-7
Earlier sketch in CA 5-6R
Martin, Lawrence 1895- CAP-1
Earlier sketch in CA 9-10
Martin, Lee
See Wingate, (Martha) Anne (Guice)
Martin, Lee Nicholson 1916(?)-1987
Obituary 124
Martin, Les
See Schulman, L(ester) M(artin)
Martin, Lucien
See Gabel, Joseph
Martin, Luther H(oward), Jr. 1937- 124
Martin, Lynne 1923- 65-68
See also SATA 21
Martin, M(arilynn) Kay 1942- 65-68
Martin, Malachi 81-84
See also AITN 1
Martin, Marcia
See Levin, Marcia Obrasky
Martin, Margaret Joan 1928- 69-72
Martin, Marie-Louise 1912- 69-72

Martin, Mario, Jr.
See Monteleone, Thomas F(rancis)
Martin, Marjorie 1942- 53-56
Martin, Marta San
See San Martin, Marta
Martin, Mary 1913(?)- 113
Brief entry 111
Martin, Mary Steichen
See Calderone, Mary S(teichen)
Martin, Maurice 1946- 115
Martin, Michael L. 1932- 19-20R
Martin, Michael William 1946- 121
Martin, Michelle 1957- 119
Martin, Mike W.
See Martin, Michael William
Martin, Milward Wyatt 1895-1974 .... CAP-1
Earlier sketch in CA 19-20
Martin, Morgan 1921- 19-20R
Martin, Murray S(impson) 1928- 112
Martin, Nancy
See Salmon, Annie Elizabeth
Martin, Noah S(ensenig) 1940- 69-72
Martin, Norma F(rances) 1936- 113
Martin, Oliver
See Smith, R(eginald) D(onald)
Martin, Ovid A. 1904-1979 Obituary 89-92
Martin, Patricia Miles 1899-1986 .... CANR-2
Obituary 119
Earlier sketch in CA 4R
See also SATA 1, 43, 48
Martin, Paul
See Deale, Kenneth Edwin Lee
Martin, Paul Sidney 1899-1974 .... CANR-8
Earlier sketch in CA 7-8R
Martin, Pete
See Martin, William Thorton
Martin, (Roy) Peter 1931- Brief entry 120
Martin, Peter
See Chaundler, Christine
Martin, Peter W(illiam) 1939- 89-92
Martin, Philip (John Talbot) 1931- CANR-24
Earlier sketches in CA 61-64, CANR-9
Martin, Phyllis Cook 1908- 5-6R
Martin, Quinn 1922-1987 Obituary 123
Martin, R. Johnson
See Mehta, Rustam Jehangir
Martin, R(ichard) M(ilton) 1916- CANR-15
Earlier sketch in CA 41-44R
Martin, Ralph 1942- CANR-9
Earlier sketch in CA 57-60
Martin, Ralph C. 1924- 9-10R
Martin, Ralph G. 1920- 5-6R
Martin, Ralph P(hilip) CANR-9
Earlier sketch in CA 65-68
Martin, Rene 1891-1977 .... SATA-20, 42
Martin, Renee C(ohen) 1928- 49-52
Martin, Rhona 1922- 121
Brief entry 116
Martin, Richard 1946- 124
Martin, Richard
See Creasey, John
Martin, Robert (Lee) 1908-1976 .... 2R
Obituary 103
Martin, Robert A(llen) 1930- 110
Martin, Robert Bernard 1918- CANR-2
Earlier sketch in CA 4R
Martin, Robert K(essler) 1941- 102
Martin, Robert Sidney 1949- 122
Martin, Robert W.
See Pelton, Robert W(ayne)
Martin, Roderick 1940- CANR-12
Earlier sketch in CA 29-32R
Martin, Ron 1941- 122
Martin, Ronald E(dward) 1933- 19-20R
Martin, Roscoe C(oleman) 1903-1972 .... CAP-1
Obituary 33-36R
Earlier sketch in CA 19-20
Martin, Rupert (Claude) 1905- SATA-31
Martin, Ruth
See Rayner, Claire (Berenice)
Martin, Sam
See Moskowitz, Sam
Martin, Samuel Elmo 1924- Brief entry 105
Martin, Stefan 1936- SATA-32
Martin, Stella
See Heyer, Georgette
Martin, Steve 1945(?)- 97-100
See also CLC 30
Martin, Stoddard (Hammond), Jr. 1948- 117
Martin, Susan Ehrlich 1940- 124
Martin, Sylvia (Pass) 1913- 19-20R
Martin, Thom(as) Francis 1934- 7-8R
Martin, Thomas Lyle, Jr. 1921- 11-12R
Martin, Tom
See Paine, Lauran (Bosworth)
Martin, Tony 1942- CANR-6
Earlier sketch in CA 57-60
Martin, Valerie 1948- 85-88
Martin, Vance G(regory) 1949- 114
Martin, Vernon N(orthfleet) 1930- 45-48
Martin, Vicky
See Storey, Victoria Carolyn
Martin, Wallace 1933- 122
Martin, Walter T(ilford) 1917- 11-12R
Martin, Warren Bryan 1925- CANR-20
Earlier sketch in CA 41-44R
Martin, Webber
See Silverberg, Robert
Martin, Wendy 1940- 37-40R
Martin, Wendy
See Martini, Teri
Martin, Wilfred B(enjamin) W(eldon) 1940- 116
Martin, William C. 1937- CANR-14
Earlier sketch in CA 77-80
Martin, William Ivan 1916- Brief entry 117
See also SATA 40
Martin, William Keble 1877-1969 Obituary .. 104
Martin, William Thorton 1901(?)-1980
Obituary 102
Martinco, John P. 1917(?)-1986 Obituary .. 118
Martindale, Charles (Anthony) 1949- 124
Martindale, Colin (Eugene) 1943- 61-64
Martindale, Don (Albert) 1915- CANR-6
Earlier sketch in CA 13-14R
Martin du Gard, Roger 1881-1958
Brief entry 118
See also DLB 65
See also TCLC 24
Martine
See Woolfolk, Joanna Martine
Martine, James J(ohn) 1937- 57-60
Martineau, Gilbert CANR-17
Earlier sketch in CA 29-32R
Martineau, Harriet 1802-1876 .... YABC-2
See also DLB 21, 55
Martineau, James 1805-1900 Brief entry ... 122
Martineau, Robert Arnold Schurhoff 1913- .. 106
Martine-Barnes, Adrienne 1942- 110
Martinelli, Ricardo
See Brandon, Johnny
Martines, Julia
See O'Faolain, Julia
Martines, Lauro 1927- CANR-12
Earlier sketch in CA 25-28R
Martinet, Andre 1908- CAP-1
Earlier sketch in CA 11-12
Martinetti, Ronald 1945- 57-60
Martinetz, V(ivian) L. 1927- 61-64
Martinez, Al 1929- 57-60
Martinez, Elizabeth Sutherland 1925- 121
Martinez, Jacinto Benavente y
See Benavente (y Martinez), Jacinto
Martinez, Julio A(ntonio) 1931- CANR-18
Earlier sketch in CA 101
Martinez, Oscar J(aquez) 1943- 120
Martinez, Rafael V. 1923- 11-12R
Martinez, Raymond J(oseph) 1889- 61-64
Martinez, S(ally) A. 1938- 81-84
Martinez Ruiz, Jose 1873-1969 93-96
Martinez Sierra, Gregorio 1881-1947
Brief entry 115
See also TCLC 6
Martinez Sierra, Maria (de la O'LeJarraga) 1874-1974 Obituary 115
Martinez Sierra, Maria (de la O'LeJarraga) 1880(?)-1974 .... TCLC-6
Martini, Teri 1930- CANR-2
Earlier sketch in CA 5-6R
See also SATA 3
Martini, Therese
See Martini, Teri
Martini, Virgilio 1903- 37-40R
Martino, Bill 1933- 57-60
Martino, Joseph P(aul) 1931- 61-64
Martino, Rocco L(eonard) 1929- 15-16R
Martins, Maria 1898(?)-1973 Obituary 41-44R
Martins, Maria Isabel Barreno de Faria 1939- 105
Martins, Peter 1946- 113
Martins, Wilson 1921- 19-20R
Martinsen, Ella Barbara Lung 1901-1977 103
Martinsen, Martin
See Follett, Ken(neth Martin)
Martinson, David (Keith) 1946- CANR-1
Earlier sketch in CA 45-48
Martinson, Floyd M(ansfield) 1916- 93-96
Martinson, Harry (Edmund) 1904-1978 77-80
See also CLC 14
Martinson, Robert M. 1927- 41-44R
Martinson, Ruth A(lice) 1915- CANR-17
Earlier sketch in CA 25-28R
Martinson, Tom L. 1941- 77-80
Martinson, William D. 1924- 23-24R
Martland, Thomas R(odolphe) 1926- 5-6R
Marton, Beryl M(itchell) 1922- CANR-11
Earlier sketch in CA 69-72
Marton, Endre 1910- 37-40R
Marton, George 1900- 29-32R
Martone, Michael 1955- 124
Brief entry 118
Martos, Borys 1879-1977 Obituary 73-76
Martos, Joseph (John) 1943- 105
Marty, Martin E(mil) 1928- CANR-21
Earlier sketch in CA 5-6R
Marty, Myron A. 1932- CANR-11
Earlier sketch in CA 25-28R
Marty, Sid 1944- 108
Martyn, Edward 1859-1923 .... DLB-10
Martyn, Howe 1906- 11-12R
Martyn, James Louis 1925- Brief entry 105
Martyn, Kenneth A(lfred) 1926- 23-24R
Martynov, Leonid (Nikolaevich) 1905-
Brief entry 116
Martz, John D(anhouse) 1934- CANR-1
Earlier sketch in CA 45-48
Martz, Lawrence J. 1933- 69-72
Martz, Louis L(ohr) 1913- CANR-5
Earlier sketch in CA 13-14R
Martz, William J. 1928- CANR-9
Earlier sketch in CA 21-22R
Marut, Ret
See Traven, B.
Marut, Robert
See Traven, B.
Maruyama, Masao 1914- 13-14R
Marvel, Tom 1901-1970 Obituary 104
Marvick, Elizabeth Wirth 1925- 117
Marvin, Burton Wright 1913-1979
Obituary 85-88
Marvin, David Keith 1921- 15-16R
Marvin, Dorothy Betts 1894(?)-1975
Obituary 57-60
Marvin, Harold Myers 1893-1977 .... 7-8R
Obituary 73-76
Marvin, John R(obert) 1923- 117
Marvin, John T. 1906- 19-20R
Marvin, Philip (Roger) 1916- CANR-13
Earlier sketch in CA 37-40R
Marvin, Richard
See Ellis, Julie
Marvin, Susan
See Ellis, Julie
Marvin, W. R.
See Cameron, Lou
Marvin X
See El Muhajir
See also DLB 38
Marwell, Gerald 1937- 41-44R
Marwick, Arthur 1936- CANR-13
Earlier sketch in CA 29-32R
Marwick, Helen
See Lillie, Helen
Marwick, Lawrence 1909-1981 Obituary 106
Marwick, M(axwell) G(ay) 1916- 37-40R
Marwil, Jonathan L(evy) 1940- 114
Marx, Anne CANR-12
Earlier sketch in CA 29-32R
Marx, Arthur 1893-1964 Obituary 113
Marx, Arthur 1921- CANR-24
Earlier sketch in CA 81-84
Marx, Erica Elizabeth 1909-1967 .... CAP-1
Earlier sketch in CA 13-14
Marx, Gary T. 1938- CANR-14
Earlier sketch in CA 37-40R
Marx, Groucho
See Marx, Julius Henry
Marx, Harpo
See Marx, Arthur
Marx, Herbert L(ewis), Jr. 1922- CANR-6
Earlier sketch in CA 9-10R
Marx, Jenifer (Grant) 1940- 101
Marx, Jerry
See Bernstein, Jerry Marx
Marx, Julius Henry 1890-1977 81-84
Obituary 73-76
Marx, Kenneth S(amuel) 1939- 69-72
Marx, Melvin H(erman) 1919- CANR-6
Earlier sketch in CA 5-6R
Marx, Paul 1920- 37-40R
Marx, Robert F(rank) 1936- CANR-6
Earlier sketch in CA 11-12R
See also SATA 24
Marx, Samuel 1902- 103
Marx, Werner 1910- 81-84
Marx, Wesley 1934- CANR-12
Earlier sketch in CA 23-24R
Marxhausen, Joanne G. 1935- 37-40R
Mary Agnes Therese, Sister 1910- 2R
Mary Francis, Mother
See Aschmann, Alberta
Mary Kay
See Ash, Mary Kay (Wagner)
Mary Madeleine, Sister 1916-1974 .... CAP-1
Earlier sketch in CA 15-16
Marzan, Julio 1946- Brief entry 113
Marzani, Carl (Aldo) 1912- 61-64
See also SATA 12
Marzials, Theo 1850-1920 .... DLB-35
Marzolf, Marion (Tuttle) 1930- Brief entry .. 114
Marzolf, Marion Tuttle 1930- 124
Marzollo, Jean 1942- CANR-15
Earlier sketch in CA 81-84
See also SATA 29
Masani, Shakuntala 112
Masani, Zareer 1947- 97-100
Masannat, George S. 1933- 25-28R
Masao, Maruyama 1914- 107
Masaoka Shiki
See Masaoka Tsunenori
See also TCLC 18
Masaoka Tsunenori 1867-1902 Brief entry .. 117
Mascall, Eric L(ionel) 1905- 7-8R
Mascott, Trina 81-84
Masefield, Geoffrey Bussell 1911- 7-8R
Masefield, John (Edward) 1878-1967 .... CAP-2
Obituary 25-28R
Earlier sketch in CA 19-20
See also SATA 19
See also DLB 10
See also CLC 11, 47
Masefield, (John) Richard (William) 1943- .. 119
Maser, Edward A(ndrew) 1923- 45-48
Maser, Jack D(avid) 1937- 57-60
Masey, Mary Lou(ise) 1932- 21-22R
Masha
See Stern, Marie
Masheck, Joseph (Daniel) 1942- 105
Masia, Seth 1948- 110
Masinton, Charles G(erald) 1938- 77-80
Maslach, Christina 1946- 111
Maslenikov, Oleg A(lexander) 1907-1972
Obituary 111
Maslin, Alice 1914(?)-1981 Obituary 104
Maslin, Bonnie L(ynn) 1947- 107
Maslow, Abraham H. 1908-1970 .... CANR-4
Obituary 29-32R
Earlier sketch in CA 2R
Maslowski, Peter 1944- 97-100
Maslowski, Raymond M(arion) 1931- 93-96
Maslowski, Stanley 1937- 21-22R
Masnata, Albert 1900- 93-96
Maso, Carole 19(?)- CLC-44
Mason, Alpheus Thomas 1899- 1R
Mason, Betty (Oxford) 1930- 37-40R
Mason, Bobbie Ann 1940- CANR-11
Earlier sketch in CA 53-56
See also CLC 28, 43
Mason, Bruce B(onner) 1923- 11-12R
Mason, Bruce Edward George 1921-1982
Obituary 110
Mason, Carola
See Zentner, Carola
Mason, Chuck
See Rowland, D(onald) S(ydney)
Mason, Clarence (Eugene), Jr. 1904- 57-60
Mason, David E(rnest) 1928- 21-22R
Mason, Douglas R(ankine) 1918- CANR-17
Earlier sketches in CA 49-52, CANR-1
Mason, Edmund (John) 1911- 103
Mason, Edward S(agendorph) 1899- 73-76
Mason, Edwin A. 1905-1979 .... CAP-2
Obituary 89-92
Earlier sketch in CA 25-28
See also SATA 32
Mason, Ernst
See Pohl, Frederik
Mason, Eudo C(olecestra) 1901-1969 .... CAP-1
Earlier sketch in CA 9-10
Mason, F(rancis) van Wyck 1901-1978 .. CANR-8
Obituary 81-84
Earlier sketch in CA 5-6R
See also SATA 3, 26
Mason, Francis K(enneth) 1928- 103
Mason, Frank Earl 1893-1979 Obituary 89-92
Mason, Frank W.
See Mason, F(rancis) van Wyck
Mason, Gabriel Richard 1884-1979
Obituary 85-88
Mason, Gene (William) 1928- 89-92
Mason, George E(van) 1932- CANR-12
Earlier sketch in CA 29-32R
Mason, George Frederick 1904- 73-76
See also SATA 14
Mason, Haydn T(revor) 1929- CANR-3
Earlier sketch in CA 11-12R
Mason, Herbert Molloy, Jr. 1927- CANR-6
Earlier sketch in CA 15-16R
Mason, Herbert Warren, Jr. 1932- CANR-16
Earlier sketch in CA 85-88
Mason, James (Neville) 1909-1984
Obituary 113
Mason, John Brown 1904- 49-52
Mason, Julian D(ewey) Jr. 1931- 37-40R
Mason, Lee W.
See Malzberg, Barry N(athaniel)
Mason, Lowell Blake 1893-1983 Obituary ... 110
Mason, Madeline 1913- 9-10R
Mason, Michael 1939- 120
Mason, Michael Henry 1900-1982
Obituary 108
Mason, Miriam E(vangeline) 1900-1973 .... CANR-15
Obituary 103
Earlier sketch in CA 2R
See also SATA 2, 26
Mason, Nicholas (Charles Sheppard) 1938- CANR-24
Earlier sketch in CA 104
Mason, Nick 1945- CLC-35
Mason, Pamela 1918- Brief entry 105
Mason, Paul T(aylor) 1937- 33-36R
Mason, Peter (Geoffrey) 1914- 114
Mason, Philip 1906- CANR-3
Earlier sketch in CA 9-10R
Mason, Philip (Parker) 1927- 19-20R
Mason, R(ichard) A(nthony) 1932- 119
Mason, R(onald) A(lison) K(ells) 1905-1971 Obituary 89-92
Mason, Raymond 1926- 9-10R
Mason, Richard (Lakin) 1919- 11-12R
Mason, Robert E(mmett) 1914- CANR-17
Earlier sketch in CA 1R
Mason, Ronald (Charles) 1912- CANR-24
Earlier sketch in CA 13-14R
Mason, Ronald M. 1949- 111
Mason, Ruth Fitch 1890-1974 Obituary ... 53-56
Mason, Tally
See Derleth, August (William)
Mason, Ted
See Mason, Theodore C(harles)
Mason, Theodore C(harles) 1921- 109
Mason, Thomas A(lexander) 1944- 120
Mason, Tyler
See Mason, Madeline
Mason, Van Wyck
See Mason, F(rancis) van Wyck
Mason, Will Edwin 1912- 5-6R
Masotti, Louis H(enry) 1934- 41-44R
Mass, Jeffrey P(aul) 1940- Brief entry 111
Mass, William
See Gibson, William
Massa, Ann 1940- 29-32R
Massa, Richard W(ayne) 1932- 57-60
Massanari, Jared (Dean) 1943- 65-68
Massaquoi, Hans J(urgen) 1926- 69-72
Massarik, Fred 1926- 4R
Massel, Mark S. 1910- CAP-1
Earlier sketch in CA 11-12
Masselink, Ben 1919- 19-20R
Masselman, George 1897-1971 .... 9-10R
See also SATA 19
Masserman, Jules H(oman) 1905- 69-72
Massey, Ellen Gray 1921- 118
Massey, Erika 1900- 61-64
Massey, Floyd, Jr. 1915- 65-68
Massey, Gerald 1828-1907 .... DLB-32
Massey, Gerald J. 1934- 89-92
Massey, Harrie Stewart Wilson 1908-1983
Obituary 111
Massey, Irving (Joseph) 1924- 77-80
Massey, James A(ldege) 1939- 121
Massey, James Earl 1930- CANR-12
Earlier sketch in CA 29-32R
Massey, Joseph Earl 1897- 29-32R

Massey, Mary Elizabeth 1915-197(?) CAP-2
Earlier sketch in CA 23-24
Massey, Raymond (Hart) 1896-1983 104
Obituary 110
Massey, Reginald 1932- 23-24R
Massialas, Byron G. 1929- CANR-8
Earlier sketch in CA 21-22R
Massie, Diane Redfield 81-84
See also SATA 16
Massie, Joseph Logan 1921- CANR-2
Earlier sketch in CA 3R
Massie, Robert K(inloch) 1929- CANR-14
Earlier sketch in CA 77-80
Massine, Leonide
See Myassin, Leonid Fedorovich
Massing, Hede 1899-1981 Obituary 108
Massinger, Philip 1583-1640 .... DLB-58
Massingham, Harold William 1932- 65-68
Massis, Henri 1886-1970 Obituary 29-32R
Massman, Patti 1945- 117
Massman, Virgil Frank 1929- 37-40R
Masson, Andre (Aime Rene) 1896-1987
Obituary 124
Masson, David I. 1915- 25-28R
Masson, Georgina
See Johnson, Marion Georgina Wikeley
Masson, J. Moussaieff
See Masson, Jeffrey Moussaieff
Masson, Jeffrey M.
See Masson, Jeffrey Moussaieff
Masson, Jeffrey Moussaieff 1941- 122
Masson, Loyes 1915-1969 .... CAP-1
Earlier sketch in CA 13-14
Massow, Rosalind 89-92
Massy, William F(rancis) 1934- 41-44R
Mast, Gerald 1940- CANR-12
Earlier sketch in CA 69-72
Mast, Russell L. 1915- 13-14R
Masterman, John Cecil 1891-1977 ..... CANR-6
Obituary 69-72
Earlier sketch in CA 9-10R
Masterman-Smith, Virginia 1937- 110
Masters, Anthony 25-28R
Masters, Anthony 1948(?)-1985 Obituary ... 115
Masters, Brian 1939- 118
Masters, Edgar Lee 1869(?)-1950
Brief entry 104
See also DLB 54
See also TCLC 2, 25
Masters, Elaine 1932- 57-60
Masters, G(eorge) Mallary 1936- 25-28R
Masters, Hardin (Wallace) 1899(?)-1979
Obituary 89-92
Masters, Hilary 1928- CANR-13
Earlier sketch in CA 25-28R
Masters, John 1914-1983 110
Brief entry 108
Masters, Kelly R. 1897- 3R
See also SATA 3
Masters, Mildred 1932- 110
See also SATA 42
Masters, Nicholas A. 1929- 13-14R
Masters, Olga 1919- 121
Masters, Roger D(avis) 1933- 21-22R
Masters, William
See Cousins, Margaret
Masters, William H(owell) 1915- 21-22R
See also AITN 1
Masters, Zeke
See Bensen, Donald R.
and Goulart, Ron(ald Joseph)
Masterson, Dan 1934- 81-84
Masterson, Dave 1951- 118
Masterson, J. B.
See Edmondson, G. C.
Masterson, James F(rancis) 1925- 69-72
Masterson, Patrick 1936- 73-76
Masterson, Thomas R(obert) 1915- 25-28R
Masterson, Whit
See Miller, (H.) Bill(y)
and Wade, Robert (Allison)
Masterson, William Henry 1914-1983 123
Masterton, Elsie (Lipstein) 1914-1966 ......5-6R
Masterton, Graham 1946- CANR-22
Earlier sketch in CA 105
Mastny, Vojtech 1936- CANR-13
Earlier sketch in CA 33-36R
Maston, T(homas) B(ufford) 1897- CANR-18
Earlier sketches in CA 5-6R, CANR-2
Mastrangelo, Charles E. 1910- 113
Mastro, Susan (Duff) 1945- 69-72
Mastrosimone, William 19(?)- CLC-36
Masuda, Takeshi 1944- 123
Masuda, Yoneji 1909- 109
Masur, Gerhard Strassman 1901-1975 .. CANR-4
Earlier sketch in CA 3R
Masur, Harold Q. 1909- CANR-13
Earlier sketch in CA 77-80
Masur, Jenny 1948- 65-68
Mata, Daya 1914- 77-80
Matanzo, Jane Brady 1940- 103
Matarazzo, James M. 1941- CANR-14
Earlier sketch in CA 37-40R
Matarazzo, Joseph D(ominic) 1925- 57-60
Matcha, Jack 1919- CANR-2
Earlier sketch in CA 2R
Matchett, William H(enry) 1923- 13-14R
Matchette, Katharine E. 1941- 53-56
See also SATA 38
Matczak, Sebastian A(lexander) 1914- 9-10R
Matejic, Mateja 1924- 112
Matejka, Ladislav 1919- 73-76
Matejko, Alexander J. 1924- CANR-22
Earlier sketches in CA 57-60, CANR-6
Matek, Ord 1922- 89-92
Matenko, Percy 1901- CANR-1
Earlier sketch in CA 45-48
Mateosian, S. Richard 1941- 111
Materer, Timothy (John) 1940- 89-92
Mates, Julian 1927- 1R
Matesky, Ralph 1913- 7-8R
Math, Irwin 1940- 112
See also SATA 42
Mathai, M. O. 1909-1981 Obituary 108
Mathay, Francis 1925- 57-60
Mathe, Albert
See Camus, Albert
Mather, Berkely
See Davies, John Evan Weston
Mather, Bertrand 1914- CAP-1
Earlier sketch in CA 9-10
Mather, Bob
See Mather, Robert E(dward)
Mather, Cotton 1663-1728 .... DLB-24, 30
See also CDALB 1640-1865
Mather, Eleanore Price 1910- 116
Mather, Increase 1639-1723 .... DLB-24
Mather, Jean 1946- 115
Mather, June 1924- 107
Mather, Kirtley F(letcher) 1888- 19-20R
Mather, Melissa
See Brown, Melissa Mather
Mather, Richard 1596-1669 .... DLB-24
Mather, Richard B(urroughs) 1913- 73-76
Mather, Robert E(dward) 1945- 115
Mathers, Michael 1945- 65-68
Mathers, Peter 1931- Brief entry 116
Mathes, J(ohn) C(harles) 1931- 49-52
Mathes, W(illiam) Michael 1936- CANR-8
Earlier sketch in CA 61-64
Matheson, Joan (Transue) 1924- 97-100
Matheson, John Ross 1917- CANR-23
Earlier sketch in CA 106
Matheson, Richard Burton 1926- 97-100
See also DLB 8, 44
See also CLC 37
Matheson, Sylvia A.
See Schofield, Sylvia Anne
Matheson, William H(oward) 1929- 23-24R
Matheus, John F(rederick) 1887-1983 124
See also DLB 51
Mathew, David 1902-1975 .... CAP-2
Earlier sketch in CA 25-28
Mathew, (Anthony) Gervase 1905- 11-12R
Mathew, Ray(mond Frank) 1929- 19-20R
Mathews, Anthony Stuart 1930- 93-96
Mathews, Arthur 1903(?)-1980 Obituary 102
Mathews, Cornelius 1817(?)-1889 .... DLB-3, 64
Mathews, Denise
See Mathews, Patricia J.
Mathews, Donald G. 1932- 19-20R
Mathews, Donald K(enneth) 1923- 57-60
Mathews, Eleanor Muth 1923- 15-16R
Mathews, Evelyn Craw 1906- CAP-2
Earlier sketch in CA 19-20
Mathews, F(rancis) X. 1935- 25-28R
Mathews, H(arry) Lee 1939- 37-40R
Mathews, Harry 1930- CANR-18
Earlier sketch in CA 21-22R
See also CAAS 6
See also CLC 6
Mathews, J(oseph) Howard 1881-1970 ....9-10R
Obituary 103
Mathews, Jackson 1907(?)-1978 Obituary ... 104
Mathews, Jane DeHart 1936- 23-24R
Mathews, Janet 1914- 115
See also SATA 41
Mathews, John Joseph 1895- CAP-2
Earlier sketch in CA 19-20
Mathews, Louise
See Tooke, Louise Mathews
Mathews, Marcia Mayfield 9-10R
Mathews, Mitford M(cLeod) 1891-1985
Obituary 115
Mathews, Patricia J. 1929(?)-1983
Obituary 109
Mathews, Richard (Barrett) 1944- CANR-1
Earlier sketch in CA 45-48
Mathews, Russell Lloyd 1921- 109
Mathews, Thomas G(eorge) 1925- 49-52
Mathews, Virginia H(opper) 1925- 121
Mathews, Walter M(ichael) 1942- 110
Mathewson, Rufus Wellington, Jr.
1919(?)-1978 Obituary 81-84
Mathewson, William (Glen, Jr.) 1940- 106
Mathias, Frank Furlong 1925- CANR-12
Earlier sketch in CA 61-64
Mathias, Peter 1928- 19-20R
Mathias, Roland (Glyn) 1915- CANR-19
Earlier sketch in CA 97-100
See also DLB 27
See also CLC 45
Mathiesen, Egon 1907-1976 Obituary 109
See also SATA 28
Mathiesen, Thomas J(ames) 1947- 113
Mathieson, John A(ndrew) 1949- 111
Mathieson, Theodore 1913- 11-12R
Mathieu, Beatrice 1904-1976 Obituary 65-68
Mathieu, Bertrand 1936- 73-76
Mathieu, Joe
See Mathieu, Joseph P.
Mathieu, Joseph P. 1949- Brief entry 117
See also SATA 36, 43
Mathieu, Noel Jean 1916-1984 Obituary 113
Mathis, (Byron) Claude 1927- 45-48
Mathis, Cleopatra 1947- 104
Mathis, (Luster) Doyle 1936- 45-48
Mathis, Edward 1927- 119
Mathis, F(erdinand) John 1941- 37-40R
Mathis, James L. 1925- 105
Mathis, June 1892-1927 .... DLB-44
Mathis, (Gerald) Ray 1937-1981 ....37-40R
Obituary 113
Mathis, Sharon Bell 1937- 41-44R
See also SATA 7
See also SAAS 3
See also DLB 33
See also CLR 3
Mathison, Richard Randolph
1919-1980 .... CANR-3
Earlier sketch in CA 3R
Mathison, Stuart L. 1942- 29-32R
Mathur, Dinesh C(handra) 1918- 41-44R
Mathur, Y. B. 1930- 49-52
Matias, Waldemar 1934- 7-8R
Matilal, Bimal Krishna 1935- CANR-13
Earlier sketch in CA 23-24R
Matisoff, James A(lan) 1937- 103
Matisoff, Susan 1940- 104
Matisse, Henri (Emile Benoit) 1869-1954
Brief entry 122
Matlaw, Myron 1924- 33-36R
Matlin, Margaret White 1944- 119
Matloff, Maurice 1915- CANR-6
Earlier sketch in CA 13-14R
Matney, Bill
See Matney, William C., Jr.
Matney, William C., Jr. 1924- 69-72
Matossian, Nouritza 1945- 124
Matrat, Jean 1915- 61-64
Matschat, Cecile H. 1895(?)-1976
Obituary 65-68
Matsen, Herbert Stanley 1926- 57-60
Matson, Albert Thomas 1915(?)-1987
Obituary 124
Matson, Emerson N(els) 1926- 45-48
See also SATA 12
Matson, Floyd W(illiam) 1921- 15-16R
Matson, Theodore E. 1906- 3R
Matson, Virginia (Mae) Freeberg 1914- ...33-36R
Matson, Wallace I(rving) 1921- 13-14R
Matsuba, Moshe 1917- 37-40R
Matsui, Tadashi 1926- 41-44R
See also SATA 8
Matsumoto, Toru 1914(?)-1979 Obituary ..89-92
Matsunaga, Alicia 1936- 29-32R
Matsunaga, Daigan Lee 1941- 41-44R
Matsuno, Masako
See Kobayashi, Masako Matsuno
See also SATA 6
Matsutani, Miyoko 1925- 69-72
Matt, Daniel C(hanan) 1950- 116
Matt, Paul R(obert) 1926- 33-36R
Mattam, Donald 1909- 45-48
Matte, (Encarnacion) L'Enc 1936- SATA-22
Matte, Robert G., Jr. 1948- CANR-16
Earlier sketch in CA 65-68
Matteo, P. B., Jr.
See Ringgold, Gene
Matter, Joseph Allen 1901- 29-32R
Mattersdorf, Leo 1903-1985 Obituary 117
Mattes, Merrill J(ohn) 1910- 41-44R
Matteson, Michael T(ownsend) 1943- .. CANR-16
Earlier sketch in CA 89-92
Mattessich, Richard V(ictor) 1922- CANR-9
Earlier sketch in CA 15-16R
Matthaei, Julie Ann 1951- 110
Mattheson, Rodney
See Creasey, John
Matthew, Christopher C(harles) F(orrest)
1939- Brief entry 116
Matthew, Donald J(ames) A(lexander)
1930- CANR-15
Earlier sketch in CA 7-8R
Matthew, Henry Colin Gray 1941- 53-56
Matthews, Anthony
See Barker, Dudley
Matthews, Brad
See DeMille, Nelson
Matthews, C(onstance) M(ary) 1908- 25-28R
Matthews, Carola 1937- 25-28R
Matthews, Carole Smith 1943- 111
Matthews, Clayton (Hartley) 1918- CANR-9
Earlier sketch in CA 53-56
Matthews, Clyde 1917- 103
Matthews, (Robert) Curt(is, Jr.) 1934- 73-76
Matthews, Denis (James) 1919- 103
Matthews, Desmond S. 1922- 23-24R
Matthews, Donald Rowe 1925- CANR-2
Earlier sketch in CA 1R
Matthews, Ellen 1950- 89-92
See also SATA 28
Matthews, Elmora Messer 1925- 21-22R
Matthews, Geoffrey M. 1920-1984
Obituary 115
Matthews, Greg 1949- CLC-45
Matthews, Harry G(len) 1939- 73-76
Matthews, Herbert Lionel 1900-1977 .... CANR-2
Obituary 73-76
Earlier sketch in CA 1R
Matthews, Honor 1901- CAP-2
Earlier sketch in CA 23-24
Matthews, J(ohn) H(erbert) 1930- CANR-20
Earlier sketches in CA 15-16R, CANR-5
Matthews, Jack 1917- 11-12R
Matthews, Jack
See Matthews, John H(arold)
See also DLB 6
Matthews, Jacklyn Meek
See Meek, Jacklyn O'Hanlon
Matthews, Jessie 1907-1981 Obituary 108
Matthews, Joan E(thel) 1914- 21-22R
Matthews, John (Pengwerne) 1927- 118
Matthews, John H(arold) 1925- CANR-15
Earlier sketch in CA 33-36R
Matthews, Kathy 1949- 110
Matthews, Kevin
See Fox, G(ardner) F(rancis)
Matthews, L(eonard) Harrison
1901-1986 .... CANR-4
Obituary 121
Earlier sketch in CA 53-56
Matthews, Patricia (Anne) 1927- CANR-9
Earlier sketch in CA 29-32R
See also SATA 28
Matthews, Ralph 1904(?)-1978 85-88
Obituary 81-84
Matthews, Richard K(evin) 1952- 117
Matthews, Robert J(ames) 1926- 65-68
Matthews, Roy A(nthony) 1927- CANR-13
Earlier sketch in CA 33-36R
Matthews, Roy T(homas) 1932- 109
Matthews, Rupert O(liver) 1961- 118
Matthews, Stanley 1915- Brief entry 115
Matthews, Stanley G(oodwin) 1924- 21-22R
Matthews, T(homas) S(tanley) 1901- ... CANR-18
Earlier sketches in CA 11-12, CAP-1
Matthews, Tom
See Klewin, W(illiam) Thomas
Matthews, Victor Monroe 1921- 93-96
Matthews, Walter Robert 1881-1973 ..... CAP-1
Earlier sketch in CA 13-14
Matthews, William (Richard) 1905-1975 ...61-64
Obituary 57-60
Matthews, William 1942- CANR-12
Earlier sketch in CA 29-32R
See also DLB 5
See also CLC 40
Matthews, William Henry III 1919- 9-10R
See also SATA 28, 45
Matthias, Catherine 1945- 110
See also SATA 41
Matthias, John (Edward) 1941- 33-36R
See also CLC 9
Matthiessen, F. O. 1902-1950 .... DLB-63
Matthiessen, Peter 1927- CANR-21
Earlier sketch in CA 11-12R
See also SATA 27
See also DLB 6
See also CLC 5, 7, 11, 32
Matthis, Raimund Eugen 1928- 37-40R
Mattick, Paul 1904-1981 Obituary 115
Mattil, Edward La Marr 1918- Brief entry ... 106
Mattill, A(ndrew) J(acob), Jr. 1924- ... CANR-14
Earlier sketch in CA 37-40R
Mattingley, Christobel (Rosemary)
1931- CANR-20
Earlier sketch in CA 97-100
See also SATA 37
Mattingly, Garrett 1900-1962 Obituary 111
Mattingly, George E. 1950- 105
Mattioli, Raffaele 1895-1973 Obituary 45-48
Mattis, George 1905- CAP-2
Earlier sketch in CA 29-32
Mattison, Alice 1942- 110
Mattison, Judith 1939- CANR-24
Earlier sketches in CA 61-64, CANR-8
Mattlin, Paula Plotnick 1934(?)-1981
Obituary 104
Mattson, George E(dward) 1937- 7-8R
Mattson, Lloyd 1923- CANR-17
Earlier sketch in CA 93-96
Matulay, Laszlo 1912- SATA-43
Matulka, Jan 1890-1972 .... SATA-28
Matura, Mustapha 1939- CANR-12
Earlier sketch in CA 65-68
Matus, Greta 1938- 93-96
See also SATA 12
Matute, Ana Maria 1925- 89-92
See also CLC 11
Mau, Ernest E(ugene) 1945- 112
Mau, James A. 1935- 25-28R
Mauchline, Mary 1915- 53-56
Maud, John Redcliffe
See Redcliffe-Maud, John
Maude, George 1931- 113
Maude, H(enry) E(vans) 1906- 103
Maududi, Maulana Abdul Ala
1903(?)-1979 Obituary 89-92
Maue, Kenneth 1947- 97-100
Mauermann, Mary Anne 1927- 33-36R
Maugham, Diana
See Marr-Johnson, Diana (Maugham)
Maugham, Robert Cecil Romer
1916-1981 .... 9-10R
Obituary 103
Maugham, Robin
See Maugham, Robert Cecil Romer
Maugham, W(illiam) Somerset 1874-1965 ..5-6R
Obituary 25-28R
See also DLB 10, 36
See also CLC 1, 11, 15
Maughan, A(nne) M(argery) 53-56
Mauldin, Bill
See Mauldin, William Henry
Mauldin, William Henry 1921- Brief entry ... 111
Maule, Christopher J(ohn) 1934- 37-40R
Maule, Hamilton Bee 1915- CANR-3
Earlier sketch in CA 1R
Maule, Harry E(dward) 1886-1971
Obituary 104
Maule, Tex
See Maule, Hamilton Bee
Maultsby, Maxie C(larence), Jr. 1932- 81-84
Maund, Alfred (Thomas, Jr.) 1923- 4R
Maunder, Elwood R(ondeau) 1917- 85-88
Maunder, W(illiam) J(ohn) 1932- 33-36R
Maung, Mya 1933- 37-40R
Maupassant, (Henri Rene Albert) Guy de
1850-1893 .... SSC-1
Maura, Sister
See Eichner, Maura
Maureen, Sister Mary 1924- 23-24R
Maurer, Armand A(ugustine) 1915- 21-22R
Maurer, Charles Benes 1933- 33-36R

INDEX

Maurer, David J(oseph) 1935- ... 102
Maurer, David W(arren) 1906-1981 ... 19-20R
Obituary ... 104
Maurer, Joan Howard 1927- ... 119
Maurer, John G. 1937- ... 37-40R
Maurer, Otto
See Mason, Eudo C(olecestra)
Maurer, Rose
See Somerville, Rose M(aurer)
Maurhut, Richard
See Traven. B.
Mauriac, Claude 1914- ... 89-92
See also CLC 9
Mauriac, Francois (Charles) 1885-1970 ... CAP-2
Earlier sketch in CA 25-28
See also DLB 65
See also CLC 4, 9
Maurice, David (John Kerr) 1899- ... CAP-1
Earlier sketch in CA 11-12
Maurice, Frederick Denison 1805-1872 .. DLB-55
Maurice, Roger
See Asselineau, Roger (Maurice)
Mauricio, Victoria Courtney 1928- ... 106
Maurina, Zenta 1897-1978 Obituary ... 85-88
Maurois, Andre 1885-1967 ... CAP-2
Obituary ... 25-28R
Earlier sketch in CA 21-22
See also DLB 65
Mauron, Charles (Paul) 1899-1966 ... CAP-1
Earlier sketch in CA 9-10
Maury, Inez 1909- ... 61-64
Maury, James 1718-1769 ... DLB-31
Maury, Reuben 1899-1981 Obituary ... 103
Mauser, Ferdinand F. 1914- ... CANR-2
Earlier sketch in CA 1R
Mauser, Patricia Rhoads 1943- ... CANR-22
Earlier sketch in CA 106
See also SATA 37
Mauskopf, Seymour Harold 1938- ... 104
Mauss, Armand L(ind) 1928- ... 111
Mautner, Franz H(einrich) 1902- ... CANR-12
Earlier sketch in CA 61-64
Mauzey, Merritt 1897-1975 ... 102
Maves, Carl (Edwin) 1940- ... 69-72
Maves, Karl
See Maves, Carl E(dwin)
Maves, Mary Carolyn 1916- ... 49-52
See also SATA 10
Maves, Paul B(enjamin) 1913- ... CANR-17
Earlier sketches in CA 45-48, CANR-1
See also SATA 10
Mavin, John
See Rickword, (John) Edgell
Mavis, Walter Curry 1905- ... 5-6R
Mavor, Elizabeth (Osborne) 1927- ... 107
See also DLB 14
Mavor, Osborne Henry 1888-1951
Brief entry ... 104
Mavrodes, George I(on) 1926- ... 21-22R
Mavrogordato, J(ohn) G(eorge)
1905-1987 Obituary ... 122
Mavrogordato, Jack G.
See Mavrogordato, J(ohn) G(eorge)
Mavrogordatos, George T(hemistocles)
1945- ... 115
Mawby, Janet
See Garton, Janet
Mawdsley, Norman
See Hargreaves-Mawdsley, W(illiam)
Norman
Mawer, Ronald Knox
See Knox-Mawer, Ronald
Mawer, Ronnie Knox
See Knox-Mawer, Ronald
Mawicke, Tran 1911- ... SATA-15
Max, Nicholas
See Asbell, Bernard
Max, Peter 1939- ... 116
See also SATA 45
Maxa, Rudolph Joseph, Jr. 1949- ... 65-68
Maxa, Rudy
See Maxa, Rudolph Joseph, Jr.
Maxcy, Spencer J. 1939- ... 110
Maxey, Chester Collins 1890- ... CAP-1
Earlier sketch in CA 15-16
Maxey, David R(oy) 1936-1984 ... 73-76
Obituary ... 112
Maxfield, Elizabeth
See Miller, Elizabeth Maxfield
Maxhim, Tristan
See Jones, (Max Him) Henri
Maxim, John R. 1937- ... 118
Maximov, Vladimir (Yemelyanovich) 1930- .. 104
Maxmen, Jerrold S(amuel) 1942- ... 106
Maxon, Anne
See Best, (Evangel) Allena Champlin
Maxon, John 1916-1977 Obituary ... 69-72
Maxon, Lou R(ussell) 1900-1971 Obituary .. 116
Maxtone Graham, James Anstruther
1924- ... 69-72
Maxtone-Graham, John 1929- ... 69-72
Maxwell, A(lbert) E(rnest) 1916- ... 7-8R
Maxwell, A. E.
See Maxwell, Ann (Elizabeth)
Maxwell, Ann (Elizabeth) 1944- ... 105
Maxwell, Arthur S. 1896-1970 ... CAP-1
Earlier sketch in CA 9-10
See also SATA 11
Maxwell, Cassandre 1942- ... 117
Maxwell, D(esmond) E(rnest) S(tewart)
1925- ... 33-36R
Maxwell, Edith 1923- ... 49-52
See also SATA 7
Maxwell, Edward
See Allan, Ted
Maxwell, Elsa 1883-1963 Obituary ... 89-92
Maxwell, Gavin 1914-1969 ... 7-8R
Obituary ... 25-28R
Maxwell, Gilbert 1910-1979 ... CAP-1
Obituary ... 93-96
Earlier sketch in CA 9-10
Maxwell, Grant
See Richardson, Gladwell
Maxwell, Grover (Edward) 1918-1981 ... CANR-9
Earlier sketch in CA 7-8R
Maxwell, Jack
See McKeag, Ernest L(ionel)
Maxwell, James A. 1912- ... 13-14R
Maxwell, John
See Freemantle, Brian Harry
Maxwell, Kenneth (Robert) 1941- ... CANR-15
Earlier sketch in CA 85-88
Maxwell, Kenneth E(ugene) 1908- ... 73-76
Maxwell, Margaret F(inlayson) 1927- ... 109
Maxwell, Maurice 1910-1982 Obituary ... 107
Maxwell, Neville (George Anthony)
1926- ... CANR-4
Earlier sketch in CA 49-52
Maxwell, Nicole (Hughes) ... 3R
Maxwell, Patricia 1942- ... CANR-12
Earlier sketch in CA 29-32R
Maxwell, Rhonda 1950- ... 112
Maxwell, Richard C(allender) 1919- ... 41-44R
Maxwell, (Ian) Robert 1923- ... 11-12R
Maxwell, Robert S(idney) 1911- ... 57-60
Maxwell, Ronald
See Smith, Ronald Gregor
Maxwell, Sister Mary 1913- ... 37-40R
Maxwell, Vicky
See Worboys, Anne(tte Isobel) Eyre
Maxwell, W(illiam) David 1926- ... 61-64
Maxwell, William (Keepers, Jr.) 1908- ... 93-96
See also DLBY 80
See also CLC 19
Maxwell-Hudson, (Rachel) Clare 1946- ... 69-72
Maxwell-Lefroy, Cecil Anthony 1907- ... CAP-1
Earlier sketch in CA 15-16
May, Allan 1923- ... 85-88
May, Arthur James 1899-1968 ... CAP-1
Earlier sketch in CA 11-12
May, Charles E(dward) 1941- ... 117
May, Charles Paul 1920- ... CANR-5
Earlier sketch in CA 1R
See also SATA 4
May, Dean E(dward) 1944- ... 57-60
May, Derwent (James) 1930- ... CANR-11
Earlier sketch in CA 25-28R
May, Edgar 1929- ... 9-10R
May, Elaine 1932- Brief entry ... 124
See also DLB 44
See also CLC 16
May, Elaine Tyler 1947- ... 111
May, Elizabeth 1907- ... CAP-2
Earlier sketch in CA 19-20
May, Ernest R(ichard) 1928- ... CANR-22
Earlier sketches in CA 1R, CANR-6
May, Eugene 1906- ... 4R
May, Florissa
See Green, Kay
May, Francis Barns 1915- ... 9-10R
May, George S(mith) 1924- ... 65-68
May, Georges Claude 1920- ... CANR-6
Earlier sketch in CA 15-16R
May, Gerald G(ordon) 1940- Brief entry ... 112
May, Gita 1929- ... CANR-13
Earlier sketch in CA 29-32R
May, H(enry) J(ohn) 1903- ... 13-14R
May, Henry F(arnham) 1915- ... 11-12R
May, Herbert Gordon 1904-1977 ... CANR-6
Obituary ... 89-92
Earlier sketch in CA 5-6R
May, Irvin M(arion), Jr. 1939- ... 123
May, J. C.
See May, Julian
May, Jacques M. 1896-1975 Obituary ... 57-60
May, James Boyer 1904- ... CAP-1
Earlier sketch in CA 11-12
May, John D(ickinson) 1932- ... 45-48
May, John R(ichard) 1931- ... CANR-18
Earlier sketches in CA 45-48, CANR-2
May, Judy Gail 1943- ... 57-60
May, Julian 1931- ... CANR-6
Earlier sketch in CA 2R
See also SATA 11
May, Kenneth Ownsworth 1915-1977
Obituary ... 73-76
May, Lawrence Alan 1948- ... 106
May, Philip Radford 1928- ... 45-48
May, Robert E(van) 1943- ... 57-60
May, Robert Lewis 1905-1976 Obituary ... 104
See also SATA 27
May, Robert M(cCredie) 1936- ... 69-72
May, Robert Stephen 1929- ... CANR-13
Earlier sketch in CA 29-32R
See also SATA 46
May, Robin
See May, Robert Stephen
May, Rollo (Reece) 1909- ... 111
May, Sophie
See Clarke, Rebecca Sophia
May, Stephen 1946- ... 124
May, Thomas 1595(?)-1650 ... DLB-58
May, Timothy C(laude) 1940- ... 73-76
May, William E(ugene) 1928- ... CANR-14
Earlier sketch in CA 41-44R
Mayakovski, Vladimir (Vladimirovich)
1893-1930 Brief entry ... 104
See also TCLC 4, 18
Mayall, David 1953- ... 119
Mayall, R(obert) Newton 1904- ... CAP-1
Earlier sketch in CA 11-12
Maybaum, Ignaz 1897- ... CAP-1
Earlier sketch in CA 9-10
Mayberry, Florence V(irginia) Wilson ... 9-10R
See also SATA 10
Mayberry, Genevieve 1900- ... CAP-1
Earlier sketch in CA 19-20
Maybray-King, Horace 1901-1986 ... 29-32R
Obituary ... 120
Maybury, Anne
See Buxton, Anne (Arundel)
Maybury-Lewis, David H(enry) P(eter)
1929- ... 19-20R
Maye, Patricia 1940- ... 53-56
Mayer, Adrian C(urtius) 1922- ... 4R
Mayer, Agatha
See Maher, Ramona
Mayer, Albert 1897-1981 ... 73-76
Obituary ... 105
Mayer, Albert Ignatius, Jr. 1906-1960
Obituary ... 109
See also SATA 29
Mayer, Alfred 1903(?)-1984 Obituary ... 114
Mayer, (Henri) Andre (Van Huysen) 1946- .. 110
Mayer, Ann M(argaret) 1938- ... 57-60
See also SATA 14
Mayer, Arno J. 1926- ... 85-88
Mayer, Arthur L(oeb) 1886-1981 Obituary .. 108
Mayer, Bernadette 1945- ... 33-36R
Mayer, Carl J. 1959- ... 122
Mayer, Charles Leopold 1881- ... CANR-6
Earlier sketch in CA 3R
Mayer, Christa Charlotte
See Thurman, Christa C(harlotte) Mayer
Mayer, Clara Woollie 1895- ... CAP-2
Earlier sketch in CA 19-20
Mayer, Debby
See Mayer, Deborah Anne
Mayer, Deborah Anne 1946- ... 109
Mayer, Ellen Moers
See Moers, Ellen
Mayer, Fanny (Alice) Hagin 1899- ... 118
Mayer, Gary (Richard) 1945- ... 53-56
Mayer, Gerda (Kamilla) 1927- ... 106
Mayer, Hannelore Valencak 1929- ... 116
Mayer, Hans (Heinrich) 1907- Brief entry ... 113
Mayer, Harold M(elvin) 1916- ... 41-44R
Mayer, Harry F(rederick) 1912- ... 101
Mayer, Henry 1941- ... 122
Mayer, Herbert Carleton 1893-1978 ... 41-44R
Mayer, Herbert T. 1922- ... 33-36R
Mayer, Jane Rothschild 1903- ... 9-10R
See also SATA 38
Mayer, Jean 1920- Brief entry ... 117
Mayer, Lawrence C(lark) 1936- ... 97-100
Mayer, Leo V. 1936- ... 73-76
Mayer, Lynne Rhodes 1926- ... 73-76
Mayer, Marianna 1945- ... 93-96
See also SATA 32
Mayer, Martin (Prager) 1928- ... 5-6R
Mayer, Mercer 1943- ... 85-88
See also SATA 16, 32
See also DLB 61
See also CLR 11
Mayer, Michael F. 1917- ... 15-16R
Mayer, Milton (Sanford) 1908-1986 ... 37-40R
Obituary ... 119
Mayer, Orlando Benedict 1818-1891 ... DLB-3
Mayer, Philip 1910- ... 49-52
Mayer, Ralph 1895-1979 ... 29-32R
Obituary ... 89-92
Mayer, Raymond Richard 1924- ... 4R
Mayer, Robert 1879-1985 Obituary ... 115
Mayer, S(ydney) L(ouis) 1937- ... 103
Mayer, Sigrid 1933- ... 121
Mayer, Thomas 1927- ... CANR-9
Earlier sketch in CA 23-24R
Mayer, Tom 1943- ... 9-10R
Mayers, Lewis 1890-1975 Obituary ... 61-64
Mayers, Marvin K(eene) 1927- ... 41-44R
Mayerson, Charlotte Leon ... 13-14R
See also SATA 36
Mayerson, Evelyn Wilde 1935- ... 101
Mayerson, Philip 1918- ... 41-44R
Mayer-Thurman, Christa C.
See Thurman, Christa C(harlotte) Mayer
Mayes, Edythe Beam 1902- ... CANR-7
Earlier sketch in CA 53-56
Mayes, Frances ... 81-84
Mayes, Herbert R(aymond) 1900-1987 ... 105
Obituary ... 124
Mayes, Stanley (Herbert) 1911- ... 1R
Mayes, Wendell 1919- ... 103
See also DLB 26
Mayeux, Peter E(dmond) 1942- ... 119
Mayfair, Bertha
See Raborg, Frederick A(shton), Jr.
Mayfair, Franklin
See Mendelsohn, Felix, Jr.
Mayfield, Chris 1951- ... 107
Mayfield, Guy 1905-1976 ... 7-8R
Obituary ... 122
Mayfield, Jack
See Cooper, Parley J(oseph)
Mayfield, James Bruce 1934- ... 69-72
Mayfield, John S. 1904-1983 Obituary ... 109
Mayfield, Julia
See Hastings, Phyllis (Dora Hodge)
Mayfield, Julian (Hudson) 1928-1984 ... 13-14R
Obituary ... 114
See also DLB 33
See also DLBY 84
Mayfield, L(afayette) H(enry) II 1910- ... CAP-2
Earlier sketch in CA 19-20
Mayfield, Marlys
See Frey, Marlys
Mayfield, Robert C(harles) 1928- ... 37-40R
Mayfield, Sara (Martin) 1905-1979 ... 25-28R
Obituary ... 85-88
Mayhall, Jane (Francis) 1921- ... CANR-8
Earlier sketch in CA 19-20R
Mayhall, Mildred P(ickle) 1902- ... CANR-1
Earlier sketch in CA 4R
Mayhar, Ardath 1930- ... CANR-19
Earlier sketch in CA 103
See also SATA 38
Mayhew, Christopher Paget 1915-
Brief entry ... 106
Mayhew, David R(aymond) 1937- ... 19-20R
Mayhew, Edgar deNoailles 1913- ... 37-40R
Mayhew, Elizabeth
See Bear, Joan
Mayhew, Henry 1812-1887 ... DLB-18, 55
Mayhew, Jonathan 1720-1766 ... DLB-31
Mayhew, Lenore 1924- ... 49-52
Mayhew, Lewis B. 1917- ... CANR-4
Earlier sketch in CA 2R
Mayhue, Richard L(ee) 1944- ... 116
Ma Yinchu 1882-1982 Obituary ... 110
Mayleas, William 1927- ... 120
Mayman, Martin 1924- ... 11-12R
Maynard, Alan (Keith) 1944- ... CANR-7
Earlier sketch in CA 57-60
Maynard, Chris
See Maynard, Christopher
Maynard, Christopher 1949- Brief entry ... 118
See also SATA 43
Maynard, Fredelle (Bruser) 1922- ... 85-88
Maynard, Geoffrey W(alter) 1921- ... 5-6R
Maynard, Harold Bright 1902-1975 ... 11-12R
Obituary ... 103
Maynard, John (Rogers) 1941- ... 65-68
Maynard, Joyce 1953- Brief entry ... 111
See also CLC 23
Maynard, Olga 1920- ... 114
See also SATA 40
Maynard, Richard Allen 1942- ... 33-36R
Maynard, Robert C(lyve) 1937- ... 115
Brief entry ... 110
Mayne, Richard (John) 1926- ... CANR-6
Earlier sketch in CA 13-14R
Mayne, Seymour 1944- ... CANR-18
Earlier sketch in CA 101
See also DLB 60
Mayne, William (James Carter) 1928- ... 11-12R
See also SATA 6
See also CLC 12
Maynes, E(dwin) Scott 1922- ... 45-48
Maynes, J. O. Rocky, Jr.
See Maynes, J. Oscar, Jr.
Maynes, J. Oscar, Jr. 1929- ... 115
See also SATA 38
Mayo, Bernard 1902-1979 Obituary ... 89-92
Mayo, Charles G(eorge) 1931-1985
Obituary ... 116
Mayo, E(dward) L(eslie) 1904- ... 97-100
Mayo, James
See Coulter, Stephen
Mayo, Janet 1949- ... 121
Mayo, Lida (Smith) 1904-1978 Obituary ... 112
Mayo, Lucy Graves 1909-1963 ... 5-6R
Mayo, Margaret (Mary) 1935- ... 107
See also SATA 38
Mayo, Margot 1910- ... CAP-1
Earlier sketch in CA 15-16
Mayo, Mark
See Lane, Yoti
Mayo, Nick 1922-1983 ... 103
Obituary ... 110
Mayo, Patricia Elton 1915- ... 103
Mayo, William L. 1931- ... 19-20R
Mayor, A(lpheus) Hyatt 1901-1980 ... CANR-1
Obituary ... 97-100
Earlier sketch in CA 45-48
Mayor, Alfred Hyatt 1934- ... 65-68
Mayor, Beatrice ?-1971 ... CAP-1
Earlier sketch in CA 9-10
Mayor, Flora Macdonald 1872-1932 ... DLB-36
Mayor, Stephen (Harold) 1927- ... 23-24R
Mayr, Ernst 1904- ... CANR-2
Earlier sketch in CA 5-6R
Mayrant, Drayton
See Simons, Katherine Drayton Mayrant
Mays, Benjamin E(lijah) 1894-1984 ... 45-48
Obituary ... 112
Mays, Buddy (Gene) 1943- ... CANR-12
Earlier sketch in CA 73-76
Mays, Cedric Wesley 1907- ... 29-32R
Mays, James A(rthur) 1939- ... 57-60
Mays, John Barron 1914-1987 Obituary ... 123
Mays, Lucinda L(a Bella) 1924- ... 101
See also SATA 49
Mays, Spike
See Mays, Cedric Wesley
Mays, (Lewis) Victor (Jr.) 1927- ... 25-28R
See also SATA 5
Mays, Willie (Howard, Jr.) 1931- ... 105
Mayshark, Cyrus 1926- ... 19-20R
Maysi, Kadra
See Simons, Katherine Drayton Mayrant
Maysles, Albert 1926- ... 29-32R
See also CLC 16
Maysles, David 1932- ... CLC-16
Maytham, Thomas N(orthrup) 1931- ... 103
Maza, Regino Sainz de la
See Sainz de la Maza, Regino
Maze, Edward 1925- ... 7-8R
Mazer, Harry 1925- ... 97-100
See also SATA 31
Mazer, Milton 1911- ... 85-88
Mazer, Norma Fox 1931- ... CANR-12
Earlier sketch in CA 69-72
See also SATA 24
See also SAAS 1
See also CLC 26

Mazia, Marjorie
See Guthrie, Marjorie (Greenblatt Mazia)
Maziarz, Edward A(nthony) 1915- ... 37-40R
Mazlish, Bruce 1923- ... CANR-2
Earlier sketch in CA 7-8R
Mazmanian, Arthur B(arkev) 1931- ... 77-80
Mazmanian, Daniel (Aram) 1945- ... CANR-5
Earlier sketch in CA 53-56
Mazo, Earl 1919- ... 37-40R
Mazo, Joseph H(enry) 1938- ... 69-72
Mazonowicz, Douglas 1920- ... 57-60
Mazour, Anatole G. 1900- ... 13-14R
Mazow, Julia Wolf 1937- ... 103
Mazrui, Ali A(l'Amin) 1933- ... CANR-13
Earlier sketch in CA 21-22R
Mazur, Allan Carl 1939- ... 105
Mazur, Gail 1937- ... 77-80
Mazur, Paul M(yer) 1892-1979 ... 102
Obituary ... 89-92
Mazur, Ronald Michael 1934- ... 25-28R
Mazurkiewicz, Albert J. 1926- ... CANR-3
Earlier sketch in CA 11-12R
Mazursky, Paul 1930- ... CANR-24
Earlier sketch in CA 77-80
See also DLB 44
Mazza, Adriana 1928- ... CANR-4
Earlier sketch in CA 3R
See also SATA 19
Mazzaro, Jerome 1934- ... CANR-13
Earlier sketch in CA 33-36R
Mazze, Edward M(ark) 1941- ... CANR-5
Earlier sketch in CA 13-14R
Mazzei, George 1941- ... 117
Mazzeo, Guido E(ttore) 1914-1984 ... 45-48
Obituary ... 113
Mazzeo, Joseph Anthony 1923- ... 19-20R
Mazzetti, Lorenza 1933- ... 11-12R
Mazzotta, Giuseppe 1942- ... CANR-16
Earlier sketch in CA 93-96
Mazzulla, Fred 1903- ... CAP-2
Earlier sketch in CA 29-32
Mberi, Antar Sudan Katara 1949- ... 81-84
Mbiti, John S(amuel) 1931- ... CANR-11
Earlier sketch in CA 23-24R
McAdam, Charles Vincent 1892-1985
Obituary ... 116
Mc Adam, Robert E(verett) 1920- ... 81-84
McAdoo, Henry Robert 1916- ... 107
McAfee, (James) Thomas 1928- ... CANR-1
Earlier sketch in CA 45-48
McAfee, Ward M(erner) 1939- ... 57-60
McAleavey, David 1946- ... 65-68
McAleavy, Henry 1912-1968 ... CAP-2
Earlier sketch in CA 21-22
McAleer, John J(oseph) 1923- ... CANR-13
Earlier sketch in CA 21-22R
McAleer, Neil 1942- ... 119
McAlester, A(rcie) Lee 1933- ... 118
McAlester, Lee
See McAlester, A(rcie) Lee
McAlester, Virginia 1943- ... 120
McAlindon, Thomas 1932- ... 97-100
McAlister, Neil Harding 1952- ... 110
McAlister, W(alter) Robert 1930- ... 69-72
McAllaster, Elva 1922- ... 33-36R
McAllister, Alister 1877-1943 Brief entry ... 121
McAllister, Amanda
See Dowdell, Dorothy (Florence) Karns
and Hager, Jean
and Meaker, Eloise
McAllister, Annie Laurie
See Cassiday, Bruce (Bingham)
McAllister, Bruce (Hugh) 1946- ... 33-36R
McAllister, Harry E(dward) ... 5-6R
McAllister, Lester G(rover) 1919- ... 41-44R
McAlmon, Robert (Menzies) 1895-1956
Brief entry ... 107
See also DLB 4, 45
McAlpin, Heller 1955- ... 109
McAnally, Mary E(llen) 1939- ... CANR-21
Earlier sketch in CA 105
McAndrew, John 1904-1978 Obituary ... 77-80
McAndrews, John
See Steward, Samuel M(orris)
McAnelly, James R. 1932- ... 57-60
McArdle, Catherine
See Kelleher, Catherine McArdle
McArdle, Hugh M(c Lure) 1905- ... 107
McArdle, William D(aniel) 1939- ... 110
McArthur, Charles C(ampbell) 1920- ... 41-44R
McArthur, Edwin Douglas 1907-1987 ... 19-20R
Obituary ... 121
McArthur, Harvey K(ing) 1912- ... 25-28R
McArthur, John
See Wise, Arthur
McAulay, John D(avid) 1912- ... 15-16R
McAuley, James J(ohn) 1936- ... 77-80
McAuley, James Phillip 1917-1976 ... 97-100
See also CLC 45
McAuley, Patricia Ann Calistro
See Calistro McAuley, Patricia Ann
McAuliffe, Clarence 1903- ... CAP-2
Earlier sketch in CA 19-20
McAuliffe, Kevin Michael 1949- ... 81-84
McAuliffe, Mary Sperling 1943- ... 81-84
McAvoy, Thomas T(imothy)
1903-1969 ... CANR-15
Earlier sketch in CA 3R
McBain, Donald J(ames) 1945- ... 45-48
McBain, Ed
See Hunter, Evan
McBain, Gordon D(uncan) III 1946- ... 106
McBain, John M(aurice) 1921- ... 41-44R
McBain, Laurie 1949- ... 97-100
McBath, James Harvey 1922- ... 19-20R
McBee, Mary Louise 1924- ... 103
McBrearty, James C(onnell) 1941-
Brief entry ... 113
McBriar, Alan M(arne) 1918- ... 7-8R
McBride, Alfred 1928- ... CANR-6
Earlier sketch in CA 15-16R
McBride, (Mary) Angela Barron 1941- ... CANR-1
Earlier sketch in CA 49-52
McBride, Chris(topher James) 1941- ... 81-84
McBride, David P(aul) 1947- ... 116
McBride, Donald O(pie) 1903-1978
Obituary ... 77-80
McBride, Earl Duwain 1891- ... CAP-1
Earlier sketch in CA 13-14
McBride, James H(ubert) 1924- ... 25-28R
McBride, John Cosgrove 1911-1983
Obituary ... 110
McBride, John G. 1919- ... 9-10R
McBride, Joseph (Pierce) 1947- ... 41-44R
McBride, Katharine 1904-1976 Obituary ... 65-68
McBride, Mary Margaret 1899-1976 ... 69-72
Obituary ... 65-68
McBride, Patricia
See Bartz, Patricia McBride
McBride, Richard William 1928- ... 19-20R
McBride, Robert 1941- Brief entry ... 116
McBride, Robert H(enry) 1918-1983 ... 107
Obituary ... 111
McBride, Theresa Marie 1947- ... 112
McBride, William Leon 1938- ... CANR-6
Earlier sketch in CA 57-60
McBrien, Richard P(eter) 1936- ... CANR-10
Earlier sketch in CA 19-20R
McBrien, William Augustine 1930- ... 107
See also CLC 44
McBroom, R. Curtis 1910- ... CAP-2
Earlier sketch in CA 21-22
McBurney, James H(oward) 1905- ... 19-20R
McCabe, Bernard P(atrick), Jr. 1933- ... 53-56
McCabe, Cameron
See Borneman, Ernest
McCabe, Charles B. 1899-1970 Obituary ... 89-92
McCabe, Charles Raymond 1915-1983
Obituary ... 109
McCabe, Cynthia Jaffee 1943-1986 ... 117
Obituary ... 120
McCabe, David Aloysius 1884(?)-1974
Obituary ... 45-48
McCabe, Herbert 1926- ... 13-14R
McCabe, James P(atrick) 1937- ... 101
McCabe, John Charles III 1920- ... CANR-1
Earlier sketch in CA 1R
McCabe, Joseph E. 1912- ... 19-20R
McCabe, Sybil Anderson 1902- ... CAP-1
Earlier sketch in CA 15-16
McCabe, Victoria 1948- ... 29-32R
McCafferty, Lawrence ... 25-28R
McCaffery, Janet 1936- ... SATA-38
McCaffery, John K(erwin) M(ichael)
1914(?)-1983 Obituary ... 111
McCaffery, Larry 1946- ... 115
McCaffery, Margo (Smith) 1938- ... 37-40R
McCaffrey, Anne (Inez) 1926- ... CANR-15
Earlier sketch in CA 25-28R
See also SATA 8
See also DLB 8
See also CLC 17
See also AITN 2
McCaffrey, Donald W. 1926- Brief entry ... 114
McCaffrey, Joseph A. 1940- ... 37-40R
McCaffrey, Lawrence John 1925- ... 25-28R
McCaffrey, Mary
See Szudek, Agnes S(usan) P(hilomena)
McCaffrey, Phillip 1945- ... CANR-15
Earlier sketch in CA 77-80
McCagg, William O., Jr. 1930- ... 93-96
McCaghy, Charles H(enry) 1934- ... 25-28R
McCague, James (P.) 1909-1977 ... CANR-2
Earlier sketch in CA 2R
McCahill, Thomas 1907(?)-1975 Obituary ... 104
McCaig, Donald 1940- ... CANR-14
Earlier sketch in CA 104
McCaig, Robert Jesse 1907- ... CANR-1
Earlier sketch in CA 1R
McCaig, Snee
See McCaig, Donald
McCain, Murray (David, Jr.)
1926-1981 ... CANR-15
Obituary ... 105
Earlier sketch in CA 4R
See also SATA 7, 29
McCaleb, Robert Bruce 1950- ... 111
McCaleb, Walter Flavius 1873-1967 ... CAP-1
Earlier sketch in CA 9-10
McCall, Dan (Elliott) 1940- Brief entry ... 113
McCall, Daniel F(rancis) 1918- ... 19-20R
McCall, Dorothy Lawson 1889(?)-1982 ... 109
Obituary ... 106
McCall, Edith (Sansom) 1911- ... CANR-19
Earlier sketches in CA 1R, CANR-4
See also SATA 6
McCall, George J(ohn) 1939- ... CANR-9
Earlier sketch in CA 21-22R
McCall, Grant 1943- ... 107
McCall, John Corey
See Morland, Nigel
McCall, John R(obert) 1920- ... CANR-1
Earlier sketch in CA 45-48
McCall, Marsh H(oward), Jr. 1939- ... 29-32R
McCall, Mary C(aldwell), Jr. 1904-1986
Obituary ... 118
McCall, Robert B(ooth) 1940- ... CANR-14
Earlier sketch in CA 33-36R
McCall, Storrs 1930- ... 11-12R
McCall, Thomas (Lawson) 1913-1983
Obituary ... 108
McCall, Thomas S(creven) 1936- ... CANR-1
Earlier sketch in CA 49-52
McCall, Tom
See McCall, Thomas (Lawson)
McCall, Vincent
See Morland, Nigel
McCall, Virginia Nielsen 1909- ... CANR-17
Earlier sketches in CA 2R, CANR-1
See also SATA 13
McCall, William A(nderson) 1891- ... CAP-1
Earlier sketch in CA 19-20
McCalley, John W(allace) 1916-1983 ... 110
McCallum, George E(dward) 1931- ... 37-40R
McCallum, Ian R(obert) M(ore)
1919-1987 ... 13-14R
Obituary ... 124
McCallum, James Dow 1893-1971
Obituary ... 104
McCallum, John D(ennis) 1924- ... CANR-4
Earlier sketch in CA 53-56
McCallum, Neil 1916- ... 13-14R
McCallum, Phyllis 1911- ... CANR-4
Earlier sketch in CA 53-56
See also SATA 10
McCallum, Ronald Buchanan 1898-1973 ... 7-8R
Obituary ... 89-92
McCamant, John F. 1933- ... 25-28R
McCammon, Robert R(ick) 1952- ... 81-84
McCampbell, James M. 1924- ... 49-52
McCamy, James L(ucian) 1906- ... 5-6R
McCandless, Hugh (Douglas) 1907- ... 7-8R
McCandless, Perry 1917- ... CANR-1
Earlier sketch in CA 49-52
McCandlish, George E(dward) 1914-1975 ... 65-68
Obituary ... 61-64
McCanles, Michael (Frederick) 1936- ... 69-72
McCann, Arthur
See Campbell, John W(ood)
McCann, Coolidge
See Fawcett, F(rank) Dubrez
McCann, Dennis P(atrick) 1945- ... 115
McCann, Eamonn 1943- Brief entry ... 117
McCann, Edson
See del Rey, Lester
and Pohl, Frederik
McCann, Francis Daniel, Jr. 1938- ... 117
McCann, Frank D., Jr.
See McCann, Francis Daniel, Jr.
McCann, Gerald 1916- ... SATA-41
McCann, Kevin 1904-1981 Obituary ... 103
McCann, Sean 1929- Brief entry ... 115
McCann, Thomas 1934- ... 73-76
McCannon, Dindga ... 114
See also SATA 41
McCants, Olga 1901- ... CANR-14
Earlier sketch in CA 73-76
McCants, Sister Dorothea Olga
See McCants, Olga
McCardell, John (Malcolm, Jr.) 1949- ... 101
McCardle, Carl W(esley) 1904(?)-1972 ... 37-40R
McCardle, Dorothy Bartlett 1904-1978 ... 85-88
Obituary ... 81-84
McCarr, Ken(neth George) 1903-1977 ... 109
Obituary ... 106
McCarrick, Earlean M. 1930- ... 103
McCarroll, Marion C(lyde) 1893(?)-1977
Obituary ... 73-76
McCarroll, Tolbert (Henry) 1931- ... 110
McCarry, Charles 1930- ... 103
McCarten, John (Bernard Francis James)
1916(?)-1974 Obituary ... 115
McCarter, Alan 1943- ... 107
McCarter, Neely Dixon 1929- ... 109
See also SATA 47
McCarter, P(ete) Kyle (Jr.) 1945- ... 105
McCarthy, Agnes 1933- ... 19-20R
See also SATA 4
McCarthy, Barry (Wayne) 1943- ... 113
McCarthy, Cavan 1943- ... 61-64
McCarthy, Charlene B(arbara) 1929- ... 41-44R
McCarthy, Clarence F. 1909- ... 29-32R
McCarthy, Cormac 1933- ... CANR-10
Earlier sketch in CA 15-16R
See also DLB 6
See also CLC 4
McCarthy, Darry 1930- ... 7-8R
McCarthy, David (Edgar) 1925- ... 3R
McCarthy, David Seymour 1935- ... 115
McCarthy, Dennis John 1924- ... 23-24R
McCarthy, E(dmund) Jerome 1928-
Brief entry ... 112
McCarthy, Edward V., Jr. 1924- ... 93-96
McCarthy, Emily J(eannette) 1945- ... 113
McCarthy, Eugene J(oseph) 1916- ... CANR-2
Earlier sketch in CA 4R
McCarthy, Gary 1943- ... CANR-22
Earlier sketch in CA 69-72
McCarthy, James J(erome) 1927- ... 41-44R
McCarthy, Joe
See McCarthy, Joseph Weston
McCarthy, John 1898- ... 45-48
McCarthy, John P(atrick) 1938- ... 97-100
McCarthy, Joseph M(ichael) 1940- ... 97-100
McCarthy, Joseph Raymond 1909-1957
Brief entry ... 111
McCarthy, Joseph Weston 1915-1980 ... CANR-1
Obituary ... 97-100
Earlier sketch in CA 2R
McCarthy, Kevin M. 1940- ... 120
McCarthy, Martha M(ay) 1945- ... 111
McCarthy, Marvin 1902-1983 Obituary ... 110
McCarthy, Mary (Therese) 1912- ... CANR-16
Earlier sketch in CA 7-8R
See also DLB 2
See also DLBY 81
See also CLC 1, 3, 5, 14, 24, 39
McCarthy, Patrick Joseph 1922- ... 11-12R
McCarthy, Paul Eugene 1921- ... 103
McCarthy, R. Delphina (Polley) 1894- ... CAP-1
Earlier sketch in CA 15-16
McCarthy, Ray 1920(?)-1984 Obituary ... 112
McCarthy, Richard D(ean Max) 1927- ... 41-44R
McCarthy, Shaun (Lloyd) 1928- ... CANR-6
Earlier sketch in CA 9-10R
McCarthy, Teresa
See Anderson, Teresa
McCarthy, Thomas N. 1927- ... 37-40R
McCarthy, Thomas P. 1920- ... 13-14R
McCarthy, (Daniel) Todd 1950- ... 105
McCarthy, William E(dward) J(ohn)
1925- ... CANR-6
Earlier sketch in CA 11-12R
McCartney, Christine Maye 1949- ... 116
McCartney, James H(arold) 1925- ... 73-76
McCartney, Mike
See McCartney, Peter Michael
McCartney, (James) Paul 1942- ... CLC-12, 35
McCartney, Peter Michael 1944- ... 109
McCarty, Clifford 1929- ... 19-20R
McCarty, Doran Chester 1931- ... CANR-10
Earlier sketch in CA 65-68
McCarty, Maclyn 1911- ... 120
McCarty, Norma
See Crandall, Norma
McCarty, Rega Kramer 1904- ... 7-8R
See also SATA 10
McCary, James Leslie 1919-1978 ... 85-88
McCash, June Hall 1938- ... 37-40R
McCasland, S(elby) Vernon 1896- ... 5-6R
McCaslin, Nellie 1914- ... 33-36R
See also SATA 12
McCaughey, Ellen
See Koshland, Ellen
McCaughey, Robert A(nthony) 1939- ... 77-80
McCaughrean, Geraldine 1951- ... 117
McCaughrean, Geraldine
See Jones, Geraldine
McCauley, Carole Spearin 1939- ... CANR-8
Earlier sketch in CA 57-60
McCauley, Elfrieda B(abnick) 1915- ... 9-10R
McCauley, Leon 1908(?)-1984 Obituary ... 112
McCauley, Martin 1934- ... CANR-23
Earlier sketch in CA 107
McCauley, Michael F(rederick) 1947- ... CANR-9
Earlier sketch in CA 61-64
McCaull, M. E.
See Bohlman, (Mary) Edna McCaull
McCaw, Kenneth Malcolm 1907- ... 109
McCaw, Mabel Niedermeyer 1899- ... CAP-2
Earlier sketch in CA 19-20
McCay, Winsor 1871-1934 ... SATA-41
See also DLB 22
McChesney, Kathryn 1936- ... 115
McClain, Alva J. 1888-? ... 65-68
McClain, Carl S. 1899- ... 37-40R
McClain, John O. 1942- ... 110
McClain, Leanita 1952(?)-1984 Obituary ... 112
McClain, Russell H(arding) 1910- ... CAP-2
Earlier sketch in CA 21-22
McClane, Albert Jules 1922- Brief entry ... 106
McClane, Kenneth Anderson, Jr.
1951- ... CANR-21
Earlier sketches in CA 57-60, CANR-6
McClary, Andrew 1927- ... 61-64
McClary, Ben Harris 1931- ... CANR-3
Earlier sketch in CA 11-12R
McClary, Jane Stevenson 1919- ... CANR-1
Earlier sketch in CA 2R
McClatchy, C. K. 1858-1936 ... DLB-25
McClatchy, Eleanor Grace 1895(?)-1980
Obituary ... 102
McClatchy, J(oseph) D(onald, Jr.) 1945- ... 105
McClaurin, Irma Pearl 1952- ... 57-60
McClean, Joseph Lucius 1919- ... CAP-1
Earlier sketch in CA 9-10
McCleary, Elliott H(arold) 1927- ... 57-60
McCleary, Robert A(ltwig) 1923- ... 19-20R
McCleary, William J(ames) 1938- ... 119
McCleery, William (Thomas) 1911- ... CANR-5
Earlier sketch in CA 1R
McClellan, A(rchibald) W(illiam) 1908- ... 77-80
McClellan, Albert (Alfred) 1922- ... 122
McClellan, Edwin 1925- Brief entry ... 115
McClellan, George Marion 1860-1934 ... DLB-50
McClellan, Grant S(amuel) 1914-
Brief entry ... 114
McClellan, James (Paul) 1937- ... 23-24R
McClellan, James Edward, Jr. 1922- ... 25-28R
McClellan, Norris 1905-1984 Obituary ... 116
McClellan, Robert F., Jr. 1934- ... 33-36R
McClelland, Charles A. 1917- ... 85-88
McClelland, Charles E(dgar III) 1940- ... 33-36R
McClelland, David C(larence) 1917- ... 25-28R
McClelland, Diane Margaret 1931- ... 105
McClelland, Doug 1934- ... CANR-14
Earlier sketch in CA 41-44R
McClelland, Ivy Lilian 1908- ... 29-32R
McClelland, Lucille Hudlin 1920- ... 23-24R
McClelland, Vincent Alan 1933- ... 103
McClendon, James William, Jr. 1924- ... CANR-5
Earlier sketch in CA 11-12R
McClendon, Sarah 1910- ... 73-76
McClennen, Sandra Elaine 1942- ... 103
McClintock, Marshall 1906-1967 ... CAP-1
Earlier sketch in CA 9-10
See also SATA 3
McClintock, Mike
See McClintock, Marshall
McClintock, Robert (Mills) 1909- ... CAP-2
Earlier sketch in CA 21-22
McClintock, Theodore 1902-1971 ... 73-76
Obituary ... 33-36R
See also SATA 14
McClinton, Katharine Morrison 1899- ... CANR-5
Earlier sketch in CA 4R

INDEX

McClinton, Leon 1933- 65-68
See also SATA 11
McClory, Robert J(oseph) 1932- CANR-13
Earlier sketch in CA 77-80
McCloskey, Donald N(ansen) 1942- CANR-8
Earlier sketch in CA 57-60
McCloskey, Eunice (Loncoske) 1906- 11-12R
McCloskey, H(enry) J(ohn) 1925- 110
McCloskey, Mark 1938- CANR-1
Earlier sketch in CA 45-48
McCloskey, Maxine E(laine) 1927- 33-36R
McCloskey, Patrick 1948- 115
McCloskey, Paul N., Jr. 1927- 37-40R
McCloskey, (John) Robert 1914- 11-12R
See also SATA 2, 39
See also DLB 22
See also CLR 7
McCloskey, William B(ertine), Jr. 1928- 101
McCloy, Helen (Worrell Clarkson) 1904- 25-28R
McCloy, James F(loyd) 1941- 103
McCloy, Shelby Thomas 1898-19(?) CAP-2
Earlier sketch in CA 23-24
McClung, Floyd, Jr. 1945- 61-64
McClung, Patricia A. 1950- 119
McClung, Robert M(arshall) 1916- CANR-21
Earlier sketches in CA 13-14R, CANR-6
See also SATA 2
See also CLR 11
See also AITN 2
McClung, William Alexander 1944- 113
McClure, Arthur F(rederick) II 1936- CANR-10
Earlier sketch in CA 65-68
McClure, Charles R(obert) 1949- 111
McClure, Gillian Mary 1948- 103
See also SATA 31
McClure, Grace 1918- 123
McClure, Hal 1921- 81-84
McClure, James (Howe) 1939- 69-72
McClure, Joanna 1930- Brief entry 116
See also DLB 16
McClure, Larry 1941- 69-72
McClure, Michael (Thomas) 1932- CANR-17
Earlier sketch in CA 21-22R
See also DLB 16
See also CLC 6, 10
McClure, Ron 1941- 37-40R
McClure, Ruth Koonz 107
McCluskey, John (A.), Jr. 1944- CANR-24
Earlier sketches in CA 57-60, CANR-7
See also DLB 33
McCluskey, Neil Gerard 1921- CANR-12
Earlier sketch in CA 25-28R
McCollam, James Graham 1913- CANR-4
Earlier sketch in CA 45-48
McCollam, Jim
See McCollam, James Graham
McColley, Robert (McNair) 1933- 15-16R
McCollough, Albert W. 1917- 102
McCollough, Celeste 1926- 13-14R
McCollough, Charles R(andolph) 1934- 118
McCollum, Audrey T(almage) 1924- 107
McCollum, Elmer Verner 1879-1967 ..... CAP-1
Earlier sketch in CA 13-14
McComas, Annette Peltz 1911- 109
McComas, J(esse) Francis 1911-1978
Obituary 104
McComb, David G(lendinning) 1934- CANR-12
Earlier sketch in CA 29-32R
McComb, K(atherine Woods) 1895- 13-14R
McCombs, Don 1948- 115
McCombs, Judith 1939- 102
McCombs, Maxwell E(lbert) 1938- CANR-12
Earlier sketch in CA 73-76
McCombs, Philip A(lgie) 1944- 49-52
McConagha, Alan 1932- 77-80
McConahay, John B. 1938- 110
McCondach, J. P. 1912- 117
McCone, R(obert) Clyde 1915- 77-80
McConica, James Kelsey 1930- CANR-13
Earlier sketch in CA 33-36R
McConkey, Clarence 1925- 29-32R
McConkey, Dale Durant 1928- 93-96
McConkey, James (Rodney) 1921- 19-20R
McConkie, Bruce R(edd) 1915-1985
Obituary 115
McConnell, Allen 1923- 77-80
McConnell, Campbell R(obertson) 1928- 7-8R
McConnell, Frank D(eMay) 1942- 104
McConnell, Grant 1915- 65-68
McConnell, James Douglas Rutherford
1915- CANR-22
Earlier sketches in CA 11-12R, CANR-6
See also SATA 40
McConnell, James V(ernon) 1925- 5-6R
McConnell, Jean 1928- CANR-16
Earlier sketch in CA 85-88
McConnell, John Lithgow Chandos 1918- 53-56
McConnell, John W(ilkinson) 1907- 107
McConnell, Jon Patrick 1928- 21-22R
McConnell, Malcolm 1939- 106
McConnell, Raymond A(rnott) 1915-1979
Obituary 89-92
McConnell, Roland C(alhoun) 1910- 73-76
McConnell, T. R.
See McConnell, Thomas Raymond
McConnell, Terrance C(allihan) 1948- 110
McConnell, Thomas Raymond 1901- 118
McConnell, Virginia (McCorison) 1928- 13-14R
McConnell, William T(ate) 1941- 115
McConnor, Vincent CANR-23
Earlier sketch in CA 106
McCord, Anne 1942- 109
See also SATA 41
McCord, Arline F(ujii) 1934- CANR-1
Earlier sketch in CA 45-48
McCord, David (Thompson Watson)
1897- 73-76
See also SATA 18
See also DLB 61
See also CLR 9
McCord, Guy
See Reynolds, Dallas McCord
McCord, Howard 1932- CANR-18
Earlier sketches in CA 11-12R, CANR-4
McCord, James I(ley) 1919- 23-24R
McCord, James W(alter), Jr. 1918?- AITN-1
McCord, Jean 1924- 49-52
See also SATA 34
McCord, John H(arrison) 1934- CANR-17
Earlier sketch in CA 25-28R
McCord, Whip
See Norwood, Victor G(eorge) C(harles)
McCord, William Maxwell 1930- CANR-1
Earlier sketch in CA 3R
McCorduck, Pamela 1940- CANR-15
Earlier sketch in CA 81-84
McCorison, Marcus Allen 1926- 33-36R
McCorkle, Chester O(liver), Jr. 1925- 110
McCorkle, Jill (Collins) 1958- 121
McCorkle, Samuel Eusebius 1746-1811 ..... DLB-37
McCormac, John W. 1926- 41-44R
McCormack, Arthur Gerard 1911- 7-8R
McCormack, Gavan Patrick 1937- CANR-22
Earlier sketch in CA 105
McCormack, Mark H(ume) 1930- CANR-17
Earlier sketch in CA 49-52
McCormack, S(usan) Allison 1943- 111
McCormack, William A. 1932- 25-28R
McCormick, Anne (Elizabeth) O'Hare
1882(?)-1954 Brief entry 118
See also DLB 29
McCormick, Brooks
See Adams, William Taylor
McCormick, Claire
See Labus, Martha Haake
McCormick, Dell J. 1892-1949 ..... SATA-19
McCormick, Diana Festa
See Festa-McCormick, Diana
McCormick, (George) Donald (King)
1911- CANR-14
Earlier sketch in CA 73-76
See also SATA 14
McCormick, E(dward) Allen 1925- 107
McCormick, E(ric) H(all) 1906- 103
McCormick, Edgar L(indsley) 1914- 5-6R
McCormick, Edith (Joan) 1934- SATA-30
McCormick, Ernest J(ames) 1911- 93-96
McCormick, Jack (Sovern) 1929-1979 ..... CANR-5
Obituary 85-88
Earlier sketch in CA 9-10R
McCormick, James (Phillip) 1920- 25-28R
McCormick, John O(wen) 1918- 19-20R
McCormick, Mary
See McCormick, Sister Rose M(atthew)
McCormick, Merla Jean 1938- 97-100
McCormick, Mona 77-80
McCormick, Peter J(oseph) 1940- 112
McCormick, Richard Arthur 1922- CANR-22
Earlier sketch in CA 105
McCormick, Richard P(atrick) 1916- 11-12R
McCormick, Robert (K.) 1911-1985 115
Obituary 117
McCormick, Robert R. 1880-1955 ..... DLB-29
McCormick, Scott, Jr. 1929- 19-20R
McCormick, Sister Rose M(atthew)
1914- 23-24R
McCormick, Wilfred 1903- CANR-1
Earlier sketch in CA 2R
McCormmach, Russell (Keith) 1933- 118
Brief entry 112
McCorquodale, Barbara
See Cartland, Barbara (Hamilton)
McCorquodale, Robin (Hunt) 121
McCourt, Edward (Alexander)
1907-1972 ..... 11-12R
Obituary 103
See also SATA 28
McCourt, James 1941- 57-60
See also CLC 5
McCowen, George S(mith), Jr. 1935- 89-92
McCown, James H. 1911- 89-92
McCown, Wayne (Gordon) 1942- 111
McCoy, Alfred W. 1945- CANR-17
Earlier sketch in CA 29-32R
McCoy, Andrew 117
McCoy, Arch
See Miller, Victor (Brooke)
McCoy, Charles A(llan) 1920- CANR-16
Earlier sketch in CA 65-68
McCoy, D(onald) E(dward) 1923- 37-40R
McCoy, Donald R(ichard) 1928- CANR-2
Earlier sketch in CA 5-6R
McCoy, Elaine 1945- 119
McCoy, F(lorence) N(ina) 1925- 65-68
McCoy, Horace (Stanley) 1897-1955
Brief entry 108
See also DLB 9
McCoy, Iola Fuller 13-14R
See also SATA 3
McCoy, J(oseph) J(erome) 1917- CANR-6
Earlier sketch in CA 13-14R
See also SATA 8
McCoy, John P(leasant) 1906(?)-1974
Obituary 49-52
McCoy, Joseph A(loysius) 1911- 4R
McCoy, Kathleen 1945- CANR-22
Earlier sketch in CA 81-84
McCoy, Kathy
See McCoy, Kathleen
McCoy, Lois (Rich) 1941- CANR-22
Earlier sketch in CA 101
See also SATA 38
McCoy, Malachy
See Caulfield, Malachy Francis
McCoy, Marjorie Casebier 1934-1985
Obituary 114
McCoy, Maureen 1949- 119
McCoy, Ralph E(dward) 1915- 37-40R
McCoy, Ronald 1947- 81-84
McCoy, Roy 1935- 29-32R
McCoy, Samuel (Duff) 1882-1964
Obituary 93-96
McCoy, Tim(othy John Fitzgerald)
1891-1978 81-84
Obituary 77-80
McCracken, (James) David 1939- 119
McCracken, Esther 1902-1971 Obituary 33-36R
McCracken, George E(ngler) 1904- 19-20R
McCracken, Glenn 1908- 7-8R
McCracken, Harold 1894- 107
McCracken, J(ohn) L(eslie) 1914- 25-28R
McCracken, Karen Harden 1905- 122
McCracken, Kay
See McCracken, Karen Harden
McCracken, Kenneth David 1901-1983
Obituary 109
McCracken, Mary Lou 1943- 61-64
McCracken, Paul Winston 1915- CANR-6
Earlier sketch in CA 7-8R
McCracken, Samuel 111
McCrackin, Mark (Owens) 1949- 107
McCrady, Lady 1951- 93-96
See also SATA 16
McCrae, John 1872-1918 Brief entry 109
See also TCLC 12
McCrank, Lawrence J(oseph) 1945- 110
McCrary, (James) Peyton 1943- 85-88
McCraw, James Edward 1943- 101
McCraw, Louise Harrison 1893-1975 ..... 2R
Obituary 103
McCraw, Thomas K(incaid) 1940- CANR-17
Earlier sketch in CA 33-36R
McCrea, James (Craig, Jr.) 1920- CANR-8
Earlier sketch in CA 7-8R
See also SATA 3
McCrea, Joan Marie Ryan 1922- 57-60
McCrea, Ruth (Pirman) 1921- CANR-8
Earlier sketch in CA 7-8R
See also SATA 3
McCrea, William Hunter 1904- 107
McCreadie, Marsha A. 1943- 111
McCready, Jack
See Powell, Talmage
McCready, Warren T(homas) 1915- 21-22R
McCreary, Alf(red) 1940- 69-72
McCreary, W. Burgess 1894- CAP-1
Earlier sketch in CA 19-20
McCreery, Charles (Anthony Selby)
1942- 25-28R
McCreigh, James
See Pohl, Frederik
McCrimmon, Barbara (Smith) 1918- 108
McCrimmon, James M(cNab) 1908- 9-10R
McCrindle, Joseph F(eder) 1923- 29-32R
McCrohan, Donna 1947- 111
McCrorey, Sanders
See Counselman, Mary Elizabeth
McCroskey, James C(layborne) 1936- CANR-13
Earlier sketch in CA 77-80
McCrossen, V(incent) A(loysius) 1918- 53-56
McCrosson, Doris Ross 1923- 19-20R
McCrum, Robert 1953- 101
McCuaig, Ronald 1908- 114
McCue, George R(obert) 1910- 110
McCue, Lillian Bueno 1902- CANR-2
Earlier sketch in CA 2R
McCuen, Jo Ray 1929- 85-88
McCuen, John J(oachim) 1926- 21-22R
McCullagh, Joseph B. 1842-1896 ..... DLB-23
McCullagh, Sheila K(athleen) 1920- 110
McCullar, Michael 1951- 122
McCullers, (Lula) Carson (Smith)
1917-1967 ..... CANR-18
Obituary 25-28R
Earlier sketch in CA 5-6R
See also CABS 1
See also SATA 27
See also DLB 2, 7
See also CDALB 1941-1968
See also CLC 1, 4, 10, 12
McCulley, Johnston 1883-1958
Brief entry 115
McCullin, Donald 1935- Brief entry 106
McCulloch, Alan McLeod 1907- 104
McCulloch, Derek (Ivor Breashur)
1897-1967 Obituary 109
See also SATA 29
McCulloch, Frank E(lliot) 1898- 112
McCulloch, John I(rvin) B(eggs)
1909(?)-1983 Obituary 110
McCulloch, Sarah
See Ure, Jean
McCulloch, Warren S(turgis) 1898-1969 ..... CAP-2
Earlier sketch in CA 21-22
McCulloh, William Ezra 1931- 49-52
McCullough, Bonnie Runyan 1944- CANR-18
Earlier sketch in CA 102
McCullough, Colleen 1938(?)- CANR-17
Earlier sketch in CA 81-84
McCullough, Constance Mary 1912- CANR-5
Earlier sketch in CA 3R
McCullough, David (Gaub) 1933- CANR-2
Earlier sketch in CA 49-52
McCullough, Edo
See McCullough, Edward Joseph Tilyou
McCullough, Edward Joseph Tilyou
1901(?)-1987 Obituary 123
McCullough, Frances Monson 1938- 41-44R
See also SATA 8
McCullough, John Gerard 1917-1984
Obituary 111
McCullough, Ken(neth Douglas) 1943- CANR-22
Earlier sketch in CA 45-48
McCullough, W(illiam) Stewart 1902- 23-24R
McCully, Emily Arnold
See Arnold, Emily
See also SATA 5
McCully, Ethel Walbridge 1896-1980
Obituary 103
McCully, Helen 1902(?)-1977 81-84
Obituary 73-76
McCully, Robert (Stephen) 1921- 53-56
McCune, Shannon 1913- CANR-13
Earlier sketch in CA 77-80
McCunn, Ruthanne Lum 1946- 119
McCurdy, Charles Robert 1926- 7-8R
McCurdy, Frances Lea 1906- 41-44R
McCurdy, Harold Grier 1909- CANR-7
Earlier sketch in CA 19-20R
McCurdy, Howard E(arl) 1941- 81-84
McCurdy, Jack 1933- 69-72
McCurdy, Michael 1942- 69-72
See also SATA 13
McCurley, Foster R., Jr. 1937- Brief entry 107
McCusker, John J(ames) 1939- 102
McCutchan, J(ohn) Wilson 1909- 7-8R
McCutchan, Philip (Donald) 1920- CANR-22
Earlier sketches in CA 11-12R, CANR-5
McCutchen, Samuel Proctor 1909-1966 ..... CAP-1
Earlier sketch in CA 9-10
McCutcheon, Hugh Davie-Martin 1909- CANR-5
Earlier sketch in CA 9-10R
McCutcheon, James
See Lundgren, Paul Arthur
McCutcheon, James M(iller) 1932- 45-48
McCutcheon, John Tinney, Jr. 1917- 69-72
McCutcheon, Lynn E(llis) 1944- 57-60
McCutcheon, W(illiam) A(lan) 1934- 53-56
McCutcheon, W(illiam) J(ohn) 1928- 41-44R
McDade, Thomas M. 1907- CAP-1
Earlier sketch in CA 15-16
McDaniel, Becky Bring 1953- 117
McDaniel, C. Yates 1907(?)-1983
Obituary 109
McDaniel, David (Edward) 1939-1977 ..... CANR-10
Earlier sketch in CA 23-24R
McDaniel, Elsiebeth 65-68
McDaniel, Eugene B(arker) 1931- 65-68
McDaniel, George William 1944- 116
McDaniel, Gerald G(reen) 1945- 122
McDaniel, Herman 1938- 111
McDaniel, John N(oble) 1941- 57-60
McDaniel, Joseph Milton, Jr. 1902-1980
Obituary 97-100
McDaniel, Roderick D. 1927- 37-40R
McDaniel, Ruel 1896- CAP-1
Earlier sketch in CA 13-14
McDaniel, Walton Brooks 1871-1978 77-80
Obituary 81-84
McDaniels, Carl 1930- 93-96
McDarrah, Fred W(illiam) 1926- CANR-24
Earlier sketch in CA 81-84
McDavid, John E., Jr. 1934- 37-40R
McDavid, John W(alter, Jr.) 1933- 41-44R
McDavid, Raven I(oor), Jr. 1911-1984 ..... 41-44R
Obituary 114
McDavid, Virginia (Glenn) 1926- 37-40R
McDearmon, Kay CANR-11
Earlier sketch in CA 69-72
See also SATA 20
McDermott, A(gnes) Charlene Senape
1937- 77-80
McDermott, Alice 1953- 109
McDermott, Beatrice Schmulling 19-20R
McDermott, Beverly Brodsky 1941- CANR-16
Earlier sketch in CA 65-68
See also SATA 11
McDermott, Charles J(ames) 1905- CAP-1
Earlier sketch in CA 15-16
McDermott, Geoffrey (Lyster) 1912- 73-76
McDermott, Gerald 1941- 85-88
See also SATA 16
See also CLR 9
See also AITN 2
McDermott, John F(rancis), Jr. 1929-
Brief entry 114
McDermott, John Francis (III)
1902-1981 ..... CANR-6
Earlier sketch in CA 5-6R
McDermott, John J(oseph) 1932- 73-76
McDermott, John R(alph) 1921-1977
Obituary 69-72
McDermott, Robert
See Hawley, Donald Thomas
McDermott, Robert A(nthony) 1939- 57-60
McDermott, Sister Maria Concepta
1913- 19-20R
McDermott, Thomas J. 1915- 11-12R
McDermott, Walsh 1909-1981 Obituary 105
McDill, Edward L. 1930- 77-80
McDole, Carol
See Farley, Carol
McDonagh, Don(ald Francis) 1932- CANR-1
Earlier sketch in CA 49-52
McDonagh, Enda 1930- 101
McDonagh, John Michael 1944- 109
McDonald, Alan (Patrick) 1949- 124
McDonald, Angus W(illiam), Jr. 1941- 105
McDonald, Archie P(hilip) 1935- CANR-15
Earlier sketch in CA 81-84
McDonald, Claude C(omstock), Jr.
1925- 29-32R
McDonald, David J(ohn) 1902- 45-48
McDonald, Dianna
See Shomaker, Dianna

McDonald, Elvin 1937- ... CANR-8
Earlier sketch in CA 7-8R
McDonald, Erwin L(awrence) 1907- ... 73-76
McDonald, Eva (Rose) ... CANR-6
Earlier sketch in CA 15-16R
McDonald, Forrest 1927- ... CANR-5
Earlier sketch in CA 11-12R
See also DLB 17
McDonald, Frank J(ames) 1941- ... 97-100
McDonald, Gerald D(oan) 1905-1970 ... CAP-1
Earlier sketch in CA 11-12
See also SATA 3
McDonald, Gregory 1937- ... CANR-3
Earlier sketch in CA 7-8R
McDonald, Hugh C(hisholm) 1913- ... 65-68
McDonald, Hugh Dermot 1910- ... CANR-3
Earlier sketch in CA 11-12R
McDonald, Ian A(rchie) 1933- ... 29-32R
McDonald, James Robert 1934- ... 41-44R
McDonald, Jamie
See Heide, Florence Parry
McDonald, Jerry N(ealon) 1944- ... 105
McDonald, Jill (Masefield) 1927-1982 .. CANR-12
Obituary ... 105
Earlier sketch in CA 65-68
See also SATA 13, 29
McDonald, John D(ennis) 1906- ... CAP-2
Earlier sketch in CA 19-20
McDonald, Julie 1929- ... CANR-12
Earlier sketch in CA 29-32R
McDonald, Kay L(aureen) 1934- ... 57-60
McDonald, Lee Cameron 1925- ... 7-8R
McDonald, Linda 1939- ... CANR-4
Earlier sketch in CA 49-52
McDonald, Lucile Saunders 1898- ... CANR-18
Earlier sketches in CA 3R, CANR-4
See also SATA 10
McDonald, (Mary) Lynn 1940- ... 101
McDonald, Mary Reynolds 1888- ... CAP-1
Earlier sketch in CA 15-16
McDonald, Nicholas 1923- ... 15-16R
McDonald, Paula 1939?- ... AITN-1
McDonald, Pauline 1907- ... 33-36R
McDonald, (Duncan) Peter 1962- ... 124
McDonald, Richard C. 1935?- ... AITN-1
McDonald, Robert 1943- ... 115
McDonald, Roger 1941- ... 101
McDonald, Stephen L(ee) 1924- ... 89-92
McDonald, Walter (Robert) 1934- ... CANR-12
Earlier sketch in CA 73-76
McDonald, William Andrew 1913- ... 41-44R
McDonald, William Francis 1898-1976 ... 37-40R
McDonald, William U(lma), Jr. 1927- ... 19-20R
McDonnell, Christine 1949- ... CANR-23
Earlier sketch in CA 107
See also SATA 34
McDonnell, Helen M(argaret) 1923- ... CANR-13
Earlier sketch in CA 33-36R
McDonnell, Jinny
See McDonnell, Virginia B(leecker)
McDonnell, Kilian (Perry) 1921- ... 33-36R
McDonnell, Lois Eddy 1914- ... 7-8R
See also SATA 10
McDonnell, Robert F. 1928- ... 19-20R
McDonnell, Virginia B(leecker) 1917- ... CANR-8
Earlier sketch in CA 21-22R
McDonough, George Edward 1924- ... 41-44R
McDonough, James Lee 1934- ... 73-76
McDonough, Jerome 1946- ... 109
McDonough, Jerry
See McDonough, Jerome
McDonough, Nancy 1935- ... 57-60
McDonough, Sheila 1928- ... 77-80
McDonough, Thomas E(dmund) 1929- ... 21-22R
McDonough, William K. 1900- ... CAP-1
Earlier sketch in CA 9-10
McDormand, Thomas Bruce 1904- ... CAP-1
Earlier sketch in CA 19-20
McDougal, Myres Smith 1906- ... CANR-6
Earlier sketch in CA 5-6R
McDougal, Stan
See Diamant, Lincoln
McDougal, Stuart Y(eatman) 1942- ... CANR-13
Earlier sketch in CA 73-76
McDougall, Anne 1926- ... 104
McDougall, Donald 1907- ... 81-84
McDougall, John Lorne 1900- ... 37-40R
McDougall, Joyce 1926- ... CANR-11
Earlier sketch in CA 25-28R
McDougall, Marina 1945- ... 97-100
McDougall, Walter A(llan) 1946-
Brief entry ... 121
McDow, Gerald
See Scortia, Thomas N(icholas)
McDowall, Robert William 1914-1987
Obituary ... 123
McDowell, (Ho)Bart (Kelliston, Jr.)
1923- ... 25-28R
McDowell, Charles (Rice), Jr. 1926- ... 2R
McDowell, Crosby
See Freeman, John Crosby
McDowell, David 1918(?)-1985 Obituary ... 115
McDowell, Dimmes 1925(?)-1976
Obituary ... 69-72
McDowell, Edward Allison, Jr. 1898- ... CAP-2
Earlier sketch in CA 21-22
McDowell, Edwin (Stewart) 1935- ... 11-12R
McDowell, Elizabeth Tibbals 1912- ... 5-6R
McDowell, Frank 1911- ... 53-56
McDowell, Frederick P(eter) W(oll)
1915- ... CANR-5
Earlier sketch in CA 3R
McDowell, John (Henry) 1942- ... 103
McDowell, John Holmes 1946- ... 97-100
McDowell, Margaret B(laine) 1923- ... 69-72
McDowell, Michael 1950- ... 93-96
McDowell, Michael P(aul) Kube
See Kube-McDowell, Michael P(aul)
McDowell, Robert Emmett 1914-1975 ... 3R
Obituary ... 103
McDowell, Virginia (Duncan) H(ecker)
1933- ... 85-88
McEachern, Theodore 1928- ... 23-24R
McElaney, (Joseph) Paul 1922- ... 11-12R
McElderry, Bruce R., Jr. 1900-1970 ... CAP-1
Earlier sketch in CA 13-14
McEldowney, (Richard) Dennis 1926- ... 103
McEleney, Neil Joseph 1927- ... 115
McElfresh, (Elizabeth) Adeline 1918- ... 4R
McElhaney, James W(illson) 1937- ... 85-88
McElhanon, K(enneth) A(ndrew) 1939- .. CANR-5
Earlier sketch in CA 53-56
McEllhenney, John Galen 1934- ... 53-56
McElrath, Damian (Edmund) 1928-
Brief entry ... 111
McElrath, Dennis Cornealius 1929- ... 45-48
McElrath, Joseph R(ichard), Jr. 1945- ... 65-68
McElrath, William N. 1932- ... 77-80
McElroy, Bernard (Patrick, Jr.) 1938- ... 61-64
McElroy, Colleen J(ohnson) 1935- ... CANR-17
Earlier sketches in CA 49-52, CANR-2
McElroy, Davis Dunbar 1917- ... 37-40R
McElroy, Elam E. 1922- ... 57-60
McElroy, John Alexander 1913- ... 19-20R
McElroy, Joseph 1930- ... 19-20R
See also CLC 5, 47
McElroy, Lee
See Kelton, Elmer
McElroy, Paul Simpson 1902- ... 5-6R
McElroy, Thomas P(arker), Jr. 1914- ... 73-76
McElvaine, Robert S(tuart) 1947- ... 114
McElwee, William (Lloyd) 1907-1979 ... 57-60
Obituary ... 104
McEntee, Dorothy (Layng) 1902- ... SATA-37
McEvedy, Colin (Peter) 1930- ... 97-100
McEvoy, Dennis 1918- ... 73-76
McEvoy, Harry K(irby) 1910- ... 19-20R
McEvoy, Hubert 1899- ... 7-8R
McEvoy, James III 1940-1976 ... CAP-2
Earlier sketch in CA 33-36
McEvoy, Marjorie Harte ... CANR-18
Earlier sketches in CA 7-8R, CANR-2
McEwan, Ian (Russell) 1948- ... CANR-14
Earlier sketch in CA 61-64
See also DLB 14
See also CLC 13
McEwan, Jenny 1951- ... 124
McEwan, Keith 1926- ... 21-22R
McEwan, Peter J(ames) M(ichael)
1924- ... CANR-17
Earlier sketch in CA 25-28R
McEwen, Robert (Lindley) 1926-1980
Obituary ... 101
See also SATA 23
McFadden, Charles Joseph 1909- ... 77-80
McFadden, Cyra 1937- ... 77-80
McFadden, David 1940- ... 104
See also DLB 60
McFadden, Dorothy Loa 1902- ... 19-20R
McFadden, George 1916- ... 111
McFadden, James A., Jr. 1913- ... 19-20R
McFadden, Maggie
See McFadden, Margaret
McFadden, Margaret 1941- ... 115
McFadden, Robert D(ennis) 1937- ... CANR-15
Earlier sketch in CA 85-88
McFadden, Roy 1921- Brief entry ... 111
McFadden, Thomas M(ore) 1935- ... 89-92
McFague, Sallie 1933- ... CANR-11
Earlier sketch in CA 21-22R
McFall, Christie 1918- ... 7-8R
See also SATA 12
McFarlan, Donald M(aitland) 1915- ... CANR-10
Earlier sketch in CA 65-68
McFarlan, F. Warren 1937- ... 19-20R
McFarland, Andrew S(tuart) 1940- ... CANR-13
Earlier sketch in CA 25-28R
McFarland, C(harles) K(eith) 1934- ... 29-32R
McFarland, Carl 1904-1979 Obituary ... 85-88
McFarland, Dalton E(dward) 1919- ... CANR-2
Earlier sketch in CA 5-6R
McFarland, Dorothy Tuck 1938- ... 11-12R
McFarland, Ernest W(illiam) 1894-1984
Obituary ... 114
McFarland, Gerald Ward 1938- ... 85-88
McFarland, John 1943- ... 116
McFarland, Keith D(onavon) 1940- ... 57-60
McFarland, Kenton D(ean) 1920- ... 61-64
See also SATA 11
McFarland, M(alcolm) Carter 1912- ... 85-88
McFarland, Marvin W(ilks) 1919-1985
Obituary ... 115
McFarland, Philip (James) 1930- ... CANR-12
Earlier sketch in CA 73-76
McFarland, Ronald E(arl) 1942- ... 113
McFarland, Ross A(rmstrong) 1901- ... CAP-2
Earlier sketch in CA 21-22
McFarland, Thomas (Alfred, Jr.) 1926- ... 41-44R
McFarlane, Brian 1931- ... 122
McFarlane, Bruce John 1936- ... CANR-16
Earlier sketch in CA 81-84
McFarlane, I(an) D(alrymple) 1915- ... 107
McFarlane, James Walter 1920- ... CANR-5
Earlier sketch in CA 3R
McFarlane, K. B. 1903-1966 Obituary ... 114
McFarlane, Leslie 1902-1977 ... 112
See also SATA 31
McFate, Patricia Ann 1932- ... 103
McFather, Nelle 1936- ... CANR-4
Earlier sketch in CA 49-52
McFeat, Tom Farrar Scott 1919- ... 103
McFee, June King 1917- ... CANR-16
Earlier sketch in CA 81-84
McFee, Michael 1954- ... 112
McFee, Oonah 1922- ... 116
McFee, William (Morley Punshon)
1881-1966 Obituary ... 116
McFeely, Mary Drake 1932- ... 110
McFeely, William S(hield) 1930- ... CANR-15
Earlier sketch in CA 33-36R
McFerran, Ann
See Townsend, Doris McFerran
McFerran, Doris
See Townsend, Doris McFerran
McFerran, Douglass David 1934- ... 65-68
McGaa, Ed 1936- ... 97-100
McGaffin, William 1910-1975 ... CAP-2
Earlier sketch in CA 25-28
McGahern, John 1935- ... 19-20R
See also DLB 14
See also CLC 5, 9
McGahey, Michael J(oseph) 1948- ... 116
McGann, George T(homas) 1913- ... 93-96
McGann, Jerome J(ohn) 1937- ... CANR-14
Earlier sketches in CA 45-48, CANR-1
McGann, Thomas F. 1920- ... 13-14R
McGannon, J(ohn) Barry 1924- ... 13-14R
McGarey, Gladys T(aylor) 1920- ... 57-60
McGarey, William A. 1919- ... 57-60
McGarrigle, Francis Joseph 1888- ... 5-6R
McGarrity, Mark 1943- ... CANR-17
Earlier sketches in CA 45-48, CANR-1
McGarry, Daniel D(oyle) 1907- ... CAP-1
Earlier sketch in CA 11-12
McGarry, Kevin J(ohn) 1935- ... 102
McGarry, Michael B(rett) 1948- ... 102
McGarvey, Robert 1948- ... 113
McGaugh, James L(afayette) 1931- ... CANR-7
Earlier sketch in CA 57-60
McGaughey, (Florence) Helen 1904- ... 37-40R
McGavin, E(lmer) Cecil 1900- ... CAP-1
Earlier sketch in CA 11-12
McGavran, Donald 1897- ... 13-14R
McGaw, Charles James 1910-1978
Obituary ... 106
McGaw, Jessie Brewer 1913- ... 1R
See also SATA 10
McGaw, Naomi Blanche Thoburn 1920- .. 11-12R
McGaw, William C(ochran) 1914- ... 101
McGeachy, D(aniel) P(atrick) III 1929- .. CANR-8
Earlier sketch in CA 61-64
McGear, Mike
See McCartney, Peter Michael
McGee, Barbara 1943- ... 25-28R
See also SATA 6
McGee, (Doctor) Frank 1921-1974 ... 105
Obituary ... 89-92
McGee, Harold 1951- ... 118
McGee, Reece (Jerome) 1929- ... CANR-17
Earlier sketches in CA 5-6R, CANR-2
McGee, Robert W(illiam) 1947- ... 112
McGee, T. D.
See Savage, Teresa
McGee, T(erence) G(ary) 1936- ... CANR-10
Earlier sketch in CA 21-22R
McGee, Victor (Errol) 1935- ... 41-44R
McGeehan, Robert 1933- ... 33-36R
McGeehan, W. O. 1879-1933 ... DLB-25
McGeeney, Patrick John 1918- ... 7-8R
McGehee, Ralph W(alter) 1928- ... 112
McGeown, Patrick 1897- ... CAP-2
Earlier sketch in CA 23-24
McGerr, Patricia 1917-1985 ... CANR-1
Obituary ... 116
Earlier sketch in CA 2R
See also AITN 1
McGhan, Barry (Robert) 1939- ... 69-72
McGhie, Andrew 1926- ... 97-100
McGiffert, Michael 1928- ... 13-14R
McGiffert, Robert C(arnahan) 1922- ... 49-52
McGiffin, (Lewis) Lee (Shaffer) 1908- ... CAP-1
Earlier sketch in CA 15-16
See also SATA 1
McGill, Dan M(ays) 1919- Brief entry ... 107
McGill, Ian
See Allegro, John Marco
McGill, Leonard J(ames) 1956- ... 115
McGill, Ormond 1913- ... CANR-2
Earlier sketch in CA 49-52
McGill, Ralph (Emerson) 1898-1969 ... 7-8R
Obituary ... 25-28R
See also DLB 29
McGill, Thomas E(merson) 1930- ... 19-20R
McGilligan, Patrick (Michael) 1951- ... CANR-10
Earlier sketch in CA 65-68
McGilvery, Laurence 1932- ... 33-36R
McGimsey, Charles Robert III 1925- ... 37-40R
McGinley, Patrick (Anthony) 1937-
Brief entry ... 120
See also CLC 41
McGinley, Phyllis 1905-1978 ... CANR-19
Obituary ... 77-80
Earlier sketch in CA 11-12R
See also SATA 2, 24, 44
See also DLB 11, 48
See also CLC 14
McGinn, Bernard John 1937- ... 113
McGinn, Donald Joseph 1905- ... CAP-2
Earlier sketch in CA 23-24
McGinn, John T. 1900(?)-1972
Obituary ... 33-36R
McGinn, Matt 1928-1977 ... 106
McGinn, Maureen Ann
See Sautel, Maureen Ann
McGinn, Noel F(rancis) 1934- ... 73-76
McGinnies, Elliott M(orse) 1921- ... 77-80
McGinnies, W(illiam) G(rovenor) 1899- ... CANR-7
Earlier sketch in CA 57-60
McGinnis, Bruce 1941- ... 97-100
McGinnis, Dorothy Jean 1920- ... 29-32R
McGinnis, Duane
See Niatum, Duane
McGinnis, K. K.
See Page, Grover, Jr.
McGinnis, Lila S(prague) 1924- ... 93-96
See also SATA 44
McGinnis, Marilyn 1939- ... 57-60
McGinnis, Robert 1927- ... 45-48
McGinnis, Thomas C(harles) 1925-1987 ... 65-68
Obituary ... 123
McGinniss, Joe 1942- ... 25-28R
See also CLC 32
See also AITN 2
McGirt, James E. 1874-1930 ... DLB-50
McGivering, John H. 1923- ... 25-28R
McGivern, Maureen Daly ... 11-12R
McGivern, William P(eter) 1922-1982 ... CANR-7
Obituary ... 108
Earlier sketch in CA 49-52
McGlade, Francis S(tanley) 1930- ... 41-44R
McGlamry, Beverly 1932- ... 119
McGlashan, Alan (Fleming) 1898- ... 41-44R
McGlennon, John J(oseph) 1949- ... 119
McGlinchee, Claire ... CAP-2
Earlier sketch in CA 23-24
McGlinn, Dwight
See Brannon, William T.
McGloin, John Bernard 1912- ... 33-36R
McGloin, Joseph T(haddeus) 1917- ... CANR-18
Earlier sketches in CA 4R, CANR-1
McGlone, Edward Leon 1941- Brief entry ... 108
McGlothlin, William J(oseph) 1908- ... CAP-2
Earlier sketch in CA 19-20
McGlynn, Christopher
See Ginder, Richard
McGlynn, James V(incent) 1919-1973 ... 2R
Obituary ... 103
McGoey, John Heck 1915- ... CANR-21
Earlier sketches in CA 11-12R, CANR-6
McGoldrick, Desmond Francis 1919- ... 19-20R
McGoldrick, Edward J., Jr. 1909-1967 ... CAP-1
Earlier sketch in CA 19-20
McGoldrick, Joseph D. 1901-1978
Obituary ... 97-100
McGoldstein, Paddy
See Page, William
McGoon, Clifford D. 1939- ... 113
McGough, Elizabeth (Hemmes) 1934- ... 107
See also SATA 33
McGough, Roger 1937- ... 105
See also DLB 40
McGovern, Ann ... CANR-2
Earlier sketch in CA 49-52
See also SATA 8
McGovern, Arthur F(rancis) 1929- ... 116
McGovern, Constance M(adeline) 1938- ... 120
McGovern, George S(tanley) 1922- ... CANR-8
Earlier sketch in CA 45-48
McGovern, James 1923- ... CANR-7
Earlier sketch in CA 19-20R
McGovern, James R(ichard) 1928- ... 108
McGovern, John P(hillip) 1921- ... CANR-13
Earlier sketch in CA 21-22R
McGovern, Robert 1927- ... 49-52
McGowan, Jack 1896(?)-1977 Obituary ... 69-72
McGowan, James A(lfred) 1932- ... 97-100
McGowan, John J. 1936(?)-1982
Obituary ... 106
McGowan, Margaret M(ary) ... 69-72
McGowen, Charles H(ammond) 1936- ... 69-72
McGowen, Thomas 1927- ... CANR-8
Earlier sketch in CA 23-24R
See also SATA 2
McGowen, Tom
See McGowen, Thomas
McGrade, Arthur Stephen 1934- ... 25-28R
McGrady, Donald Lee 1935- ... 25-28R
McGrady, Mike 1933- ... CANR-2
Earlier sketch in CA 49-52
See also SATA 6
McGrady, Patrick M(ichael), Jr. 1932- .. CANR-12
Earlier sketch in CA 29-32R
McGrady, Patrick Michael, Sr. 1908-1980 ... 103
Obituary ... 97-100
McGrail, Joie 1922(?)-1977 Obituary ... 69-72
McGrath, Alice (Greenfield) 1917- ... 112
McGrath, Doyle
See Schorb, E(dwin) M(arsh)
McGrath, Earl James 1902- ... CAP-1
Earlier sketch in CA 19-20
McGrath, Edward G(orham) 1917- ... 25-28R
McGrath, Francis E. 1903(?)-1976
Obituary ... 61-64
McGrath, J. H. 1923- ... 29-32R
McGrath, James Bernard, Jr. 1917- ... 5-6R
McGrath, Joan Rosita (Torr)
1895(?)-1967 Obituary ... 116
McGrath, John (Peter) 1935- Brief entry ... 112
McGrath, Lee Parr 1933- ... 29-32R
McGrath, Robert L(ee) 1920- ... 97-100
McGrath, Roger D. 1947- ... 118
McGrath, Sean
See Douglas, John (Frederick James)
McGrath, Susan 1955- ... 121
McGrath, Sylvia Wallace 1937- ... 61-64
McGrath, Thomas 1916- ... CANR-6
Earlier sketch in CA 9-10R
See also SATA 41
See also CLC 28
McGrath, William J(ames) 1937- ... 85-88
McGrath, William Thomas 1917- ... 103
McGratty, Arthur R. 1909-1975 Obituary ... 53-56
McGraw, Eloise Jarvis 1915- ... CANR-19
Earlier sketches in CA 7-8R, CANR-4
See also SATA 1
McGraw, Harold Whittlesey, Sr.
1890(?)-1970 Obituary ... 29-32R

McGraw, James (Paul) 1913-1977 ... 4R
McGraw, James R. 1935- ... 93-96
McGraw, Walter John, Jr. 1919(?)-1978
Obituary ... 81-84
McGraw, William Corbin 1916- ... 29-32R
See also SATA 3
McGreal, Elizabeth
See Yates, Elizabeth
McGreal, Ian Philip 1919- ... 77-80
McGreevey, William Paul 1938- ... CANR-11
Earlier sketch in CA 69-72
McGregor
See Hurley, Doran
McGregor, Craig 1933- ... CANR-13
Earlier sketch in CA 23-24R
See also SATA 8
McGregor, Iona 1929- ... 105
See also SATA 25
McGregor, John C(harles) 1905- ... CAP-1
Earlier sketch in CA 19-20
McGregor, Malcolm Francis 1910- ... 45-48
McGregor, Rob Roy, Jr. 1929- ... 108
McGrew, William W. 1933- ... 122
McGrory, Mary 1918- ... 106
See also AITN 2
McGuane, Thomas (Francis III) 1939- ... CANR-24
Earlier sketches in CA 49-52, CANR-5
See also DLB 2
See also DLBY 80
See also CLC 3, 7, 18, 45
See also AITN 2
McGuckian, Medbh 1950- ... DLB-40
McGuffey, William Holmes 1800-1863 ... DLB-42
McGuffie, Tom H(enderson) 1902- ... CAP-2
Earlier sketch in CA 19-20
McGuigan, Dorothy Gies 1914-1982 ... CANR-11
Earlier sketch in CA 21-22R
McGuigan, F(rank) J(oseph) 1924- ... CANR-8
Earlier sketch in CA 5-6R
McGuinness, Arthur E(dward) 1936- ... 25-28R
McGuire, E(dward) Patrick 1932- ... 25-28R
McGuire, Edna 1899- ... CANR-2
Earlier sketch in CA 7-8R
See also SATA 13
McGuire, Frances Margaret (Cheadle) ... CAP-1
Earlier sketch in CA 9-10
McGuire, James Dean 1936- ... 21-22R
McGuire, Jerry 1934- ... 93-96
McGuire, Joseph William 1925- ... 9-10R
McGuire, Leslie Sarah 1945- ... 107
See also SATA 45
McGuire, Martin C. 1933- ... 37-40R
McGuire, Martin Rawson Patrick
1897-1969 Obituary ... 111
McGuire, Meredith Anne (Black) 1944- ... 118
McGuire, Michael Terrance 1929- ... 41-44R
McGuire, Richard L(en) 1940- ... 57-60
McGuire, Robert G. (III) 1938(?)-1975
Obituary ... 61-64
McGuire, Thomas (Vertin) 1945- ... 73-76
McGuire, Thomas G. 1950- ... 111
McGurk, Patrick (Maurice) 1928- ... 118
McGurk, Slater
See Roth, Arthur J(oseph)
McGurn, Barrett 1914- ... CANR-1
Earlier sketch in CA 4R
McHale, John 1922-1978 ... CANR-17
Earlier sketch in CA 61-64
McHale, Philip John 1928- ... 103
McHale, Tom 1942(?)-1982 ... 77-80
Obituary ... 106
See also CLC 3, 5
See also AITN 1
McHale, Vincent E(dward) 1939- ... 112
McHam, David 1933- ... 73-76
McHaney, Thomas L(afayette) 1936- ... CANR-24
Earlier sketches in CA 65-68, CANR-9
McHarg, Ian L(ennox) 1920- ... 29-32R
McHargue, Georgess 1941- ... CANR-24
Earlier sketch in CA 25-28R
See also SATA 4
See also SAAS 5
See also CLR 2
McHenry, Dean E(ugene) 1910- ... 109
McHenry, Paul G(raham), Jr. 1924- ... 61-64
McHugh, Arona 1924- ... 7-8R
McHugh, Edna ... 69-72
McHugh, (Berit) Elisabet 1941- ... 113
See also SATA 44
McHugh, Heather 1948- ... CANR-11
Earlier sketch in CA 69-72
McHugh, John (Francis) 1927- ... 103
McHugh, Leroy 1891(?)-1975 Obituary ... 104
McHugh, Mary 1928- ... 85-88
McHugh, Maxine Davis 1899(?)-1978
Obituary ... 77-80
McHugh, P(atrick) J(oseph) 1922- ... 23-24R
McHugh, Roger Joseph 1908- ... 7-8R
McHugh, Roland 1945- ... CANR-10
Earlier sketch in CA 65-68
McHugh, Ruth Nelson
See Nelson, Ruth
McHugh, Stuart
See Rowland, D(onald) S(ydney)
McHugh, Thomas Cannell 1926- ... 103
McHugh, Tom
See McHugh, Thomas Cannell
McHugh, Vincent 1904-1983 Obituary ... 109
McIlhany, William H(erbert) II 1951- ... CANR-6
Earlier sketch in CA 57-60
McIlroy, Thad 1956- ... 122
McIlvaine, Betsy 1945- ... 123
McIlvaine, Jane
See McClary, Jane Stevenson
McIlvanney, William 1936- ... 25-28R
See also DLB 14
See also CLC 42
McIlwain, Charles Howard 1871-1968 ... 102
McIlwain, David 1921- ... 109
McIlwain, William (Franklin, Jr.) 1925- ... CANR-1
Earlier sketch in CA 1R
McIlwraith, Maureen Mollie Hunter
1922- ... 29-32R
See also SATA 2
McInenly, William T(homas) 1932- ... 124
McInerney, Jay 1955- ... 123
Brief entry ... 116
See also CLC 34
McInerney, Judith W(hitelock) 1945- ... 118
See also SATA 46, 49
McInerny, Dennis Q(uentin) 1936- ... 97-100
McInerny, Ralph 1929- ... CANR-12
Earlier sketch in CA 21-22R
McInnes, Edward 1935- ... 109
McInnes, Graham (Campbell) 1912-1970 ... CAP-2
Earlier sketch in CA 25-28
McInnes, Ian (Andrew Stuart Fraser)
1925- ... 25-28R
McInnes, Neil 1924- ... 77-80
McInnis, Edgar Wardwell 1899- ... 7-8R
McInnis, Noel F. 1936- ... CANR-14
Earlier sketch in CA 33-36R
McInnis, Raymond G(eorge) 1936- ... 110
McIntire, Roger W(arren) 1935- ... 53-56
McIntosh, Alexander 1947- ... CANR-2
Earlier sketch in CA 45-48
McIntosh, Carey 1934- ... 77-80
McIntosh, Christopher 1943- ... 33-36R
McIntosh, Donal W. 1919- ... 69-72
McIntosh, Douglas M. 1909- ... CAP-1
Earlier sketch in CA 13-14
McIntosh, E. 1894(?)-1970 Obituary ... 104
McIntosh, J. T.
See Macgregor, James (Murdoch)
McIntosh, James (Henry) 1934- ... 104
McIntosh, John 1930-1970 ... CAP-2
Earlier sketch in CA 21-22
McIntosh, Kinn Hamilton ... 25-28R
McIntosh, Louis
See Johnson, Christopher
McIntosh, Michael (Scott) 1945- ... 107
McIntosh, Peter Chisholm 1915- ... 102
McIntosh, Sandy
See McIntosh, Alexander
McInturff, Roy A(rthur) 1905- ... 53-56
McIntyre, John A(rmin) 1920- ... 57-60
McIntyre, Kenneth E. 1918- ... CANR-9
Earlier sketch in CA 21-22R
McIntyre, Michael P(erry) 1921- ... 41-44R
McIntyre, O. O. 1884-1938 ... DLB-25
McIntyre, Thomas (Alfred) 1952- ... 120
McIntyre, Thomas J(ames) 1915-
Brief entry ... 114
McIntyre, Vonda N(eel) 1948- ... CANR-17
Earlier sketch in CA 81-84
See also CLC 18
McIntyre, W(illiam) David 1932- ... CANR-10
Earlier sketch in CA 21-22R
McIntyre, William (Alexander) 1916- ... 37-40R
McIver, J(ohn) R(abie) 1931- ... 25-28R
McIver, Ray 1913- ... 25-28R
McIver, Stuart B(etts) 1921- ... 69-72
McJimsey, George T(ilden) 1936- ... 93-96
McJimsey, Harriet Tilden 1902- ... 7-8R
McKain, David W. 1937- ... CANR-5
Earlier sketch in CA 11-12R
McKale, Donald M(arshall) 1943- ... CANR-5
Earlier sketch in CA 53-56
McKane, William 1921- ... 117
McKay, Alexander G(ordon) 1924- ... 37-40R
McKay, (Herbert) Alwyn (Cochrane) 1913- ... 119
McKay, Arthur R(aymond) 1918- ... 5-6R
McKay, Claude 1890-1948 Brief entry ... 104
See also DLB 4, 45, 51
See also TCLC 7
McKay, Claude
See McKay, Festus Claudius
McKay, Derek 1942- ... 81-84
McKay, Don(ald) 1932- ... 33-36R
McKay, Donald 1895- ... SATA-45
McKay, Douglas R(ich) 1936- ... CANR-7
Earlier sketch in CA 57-60
McKay, Ernest A. 1918- ... 21-22R
McKay, Festus Claudius 1889-1948 ... 124
McKay, George Frederick 1899-1970
Obituary ... 106
McKay, Jim
See McManus, James Kenneth
McKay, John H(arvey) 1923- Brief entry ... 115
McKay, John P(atrick) 1938- ... 29-32R
McKay, Quinn G(unn) 1926- ... 57-60
McKay, Robert B(udge) 1919- ... 57-60
McKay, Robert W. 1921- ... CANR-10
Earlier sketch in CA 15-16R
See also SATA 15
McKay, Vernon 1912- ... 7-8R
McKay, William Paul 1951- ... 116
McKeachie, Wilbert J(ames) 1921- ... 21-22R
McKeag, Ernest L(ionel) 1896- ... CAP-1
Earlier sketch in CA 15-16
McKean, Dayton D(avid) 1904- ... CAP-1
Earlier sketch in CA 19-20
McKean, Gil(bert S.) 1918- ... 7-8R
McKean, Hugh Ferguson 1908- ... 102
McKean, John (Maule) 1943- ... 107
McKean, John Richard 1939- ... 33-36R
McKean, Keith F. 1915- ... 37-40R
McKean, Margaret A(nne) 1946- ... 108
McKean, Robert C(laud) 1920- ... 13-14R
McKean, Roland N(eely) 1917- ... 33-36R
McKean, William V. 1820-1903 ... DLB-23
McKeating, Henry 1932- ... 37-40R
McKeay, Eileen
See McKeag, Ernest L(ionel)
McKee, Alexander (Paul Charrier)
1918- ... CANR-11
Earlier sketch in CA 11-12R
McKee, Barbara H(astings) 1902- ... 57-60
McKee, Christopher (Fulton) 1935- ... 77-80
McKee, Edwin D(inwiddie) 1906- ... 57-60
McKee, Eric
See McKee, J. E. G.
McKee, J. E. G. ?-1983 Obituary ... 111
McKee, John DeWitt 1919- ... 41-44R
McKee, Louis 1951- ... 110
McKee, Paul Gordon 1897- ... CAP-1
Earlier sketch in CA 11-12
McKeefery, William James 1918-1987
Obituary ... 123
McKeever, James Ross 1909(?)-1986
Obituary ... 120
McKeever, Marcia
See Laird, Jean E(louise)
McKelvey, Blake F. 1903- ... 19-20R
McKelvey, James Lee 1934- ... 45-48
McKelvey, John J(ay), Jr. 1917- ... CANR-8
Earlier sketch in CA 61-64
McKelway, Alexander J(effery) 1932- ... 15-16R
McKelway, Benjamin M. 1895-1976
Obituary ... 69-72
McKelway, St. Clair 1905-1980 ... 5-6R
Obituary ... 93-96
McKemy, Kay 1924- ... 29-32R
McKendrick, (Hector) Fergus 1933- ... 115
McKendrick, Melveena (Christine)
1941- ... CANR-17
Earlier sketch in CA 93-96
McKendry, John (Joseph) 1933-1975
Obituary ... 61-64
McKenna, A. Daniel
See Corson-Finnerty, Adam Daniel
McKenna, Evelyn
See Joscelyn, Archie L.
McKenna, F(rancis) E(ugene) 1921-1978
Obituary ... 85-88
McKenna, George 1937- ... CANR-14
Earlier sketch in CA 81-84
McKenna, J(ane) J(essica) 1945- ... 93-96
McKenna, J(ohn) W(illiam) 1938- ... 37-40R
McKenna, Marian Cecilia 1926- ... CANR-22
Earlier sketch in CA 1R
McKenna, Michael C(layton) 1947- ... 116
McKenna, Patricia
See Goedicke, Patricia (McKenna)
McKenna, Richard (Milton) 1913-1964 ... CANR-13
Earlier sketch in CA 5-6R
McKenna, Sister Margaret Mary 1930- ... 23-24R
McKenna, Sister Mary Lawrence
See McKenna, Sister Margaret Mary
McKenna, Stephen 1888-1967 ... CAP-1
Earlier sketch in CA 9-10
McKenna, Terry 1949- ... 109
McKenney, Kenneth 1929- ... 69-72
McKenney, Mary 1946- ... 61-64
McKenney, Ruth 1911-1972 ... 93-96
Obituary ... 37-40R
McKennon, Joe
See McKennon, Joseph W(esley)
McKennon, Joseph W(esley) 1907- ... CANR-2
Earlier sketch in CA 49-52
Mc Kenny, Margaret ... 73-76
McKenzie, Barbara 1934- ... 21-22R
McKenzie, Dorothy Clayton 1910-1981 ... SATA-28
McKenzie, Doug
See Thomas, Dave
McKenzie, Garry D(onald) 1941- ... 41-44R
McKenzie, George W(ashington) 1939- ... 69-72
McKenzie, John L(awrence) 1910- ... 9-10R
McKenzie, Leon R(oy) 1932- ... 29-32R
McKenzie, Paige
See Blood, Marje
McKenzie, Robert T(relford) 1917-1981 ... 19-20R
Obituary ... 105
McKeon, Richard P(eter) 1900-1985
Obituary ... 115
McKeown, James E(dward) 1919- ... 15-16R
McKeown, Tom 1937- ... CANR-20
Earlier sketches in CA 45-48, CANR-2
McKercher, Berneth N(oble) 1915- ... 53-56
McKern, Sharon S(mith) 1941- ... 37-40R
McKernan, John J(oseph) 1942- ... 110
McKersie, R. B.
See McKersie, Robert Bruce
McKersie, Robert Bruce 1929- Brief entry ... 116
McKhann, Charles Fremont 1930- ... 112
McKibbin, Alma E(stelle Baker)
1871-1974 ... CAP-1
Earlier sketch in CA 19-20
McKibbin, Frank L(owell) 1917- ... 65-68
McKibbin, Jean 1919- ... 65-68
McKie, Ronald (Cecil Hamlyn) 1909- ... CANR-6
Earlier sketch in CA 11-12R
McKillip, Patricia A(nne) 1948- ... CANR-18
Earlier sketches in CA 49-52, CANR-4
See also SATA 30
McKillop, Alan D(ugald) 1892-1974 ... CAP-1
Obituary ... 53-56
Earlier sketch in CA 19-20
McKillop, Menzies 1929- ... 77-80
McKillop, Norman 1892-1974 ... 7-8R
McKillop, Susan Regan 1929- ... CANR-8
Earlier sketch in CA 61-64
McKim, Audrey Margaret 1909- ... CANR-4
Earlier sketch in CA 4R
See also SATA 47
McKim, Donald K(eith) 1950- ... CANR-17
Earlier sketch in CA 93-96
McKimmey, James 1923- ... CANR-22
Earlier sketch in CA 85-88
McKinlay, Brian John 1933- ... CANR-19
Earlier sketch in CA 103
McKinley, Daniel (Lawson) 1924- ... 25-28R
McKinley, David Hopwood 1906- ... CAP-2
Earlier sketch in CA 33-36
McKinley, James (Courtright) 1935- ... 69-72
McKinley, (Jennifer Carolyn) Robin 1952- ... 107
See also SATA 32, 50
See also DLB 52
See also CLR 10
McKinnell, James 1933- ... CANR-12
Earlier sketch in CA 61-64
McKinnell, Robert Gilmore 1926- ... 102
McKinney, D. J.
See Cooper, Parley J(oseph)
McKinney, David Walter, Jr. 1920- ... 37-40R
McKinney, Don(ald Lee) 1923- ... 73-76
McKinney, Donald 1909- ... CANR-7
Earlier sketch in CA 57-60
McKinney, Eleanor Ruth 1918- ... 33-36R
McKinney, Eugene 1922- ... CANR-15
Earlier sketch in CA 73-76
McKinney, Fred 1908- ... 19-20R
McKinney, Gene
See McKinney, Eugene
McKinney, George Dallas, Jr. 1932- ... 7-8R
McKinney, George W(esley), Jr. 1922- ... 57-60
McKinney, Gordon B(artlett) 1943- ... 85-88
McKinney, H(enry) Lewis 1935- ... 41-44R
McKinney, John William 1908- ... 3R
McKinney, Virginia (Marie) 1940- ... 57-60
McKinney, William 1946- ... 121
McKinnon, Alastair Thomson 1925- ... 102
McKinnon, Robert Scott 1937- ... 37-40R
McKinzie, Richard D. 1936- ... 77-80
McKisack, May 1900-1981 ... 107
Obituary ... 103
McKissack, Fredrick L(emuel) 1939- ... 120
McKissack, Patricia (L'Ann) C(arwell)
1944- ... 118
McKissick, Floyd Bixler 1922- ... 49-52
McKitrick, Eric Louis 1919- ... 23-24R
McKittrick, David 1938- ... 61-64
McKivigan, John R(aymond) 1949- ... 119
McKnight, Allan Douglas 1918- ... 104
McKnight, Brian Emerson 1938- ... 106
McKnight, C(olbert) A(ugustus)
1916-1986 Obituary ... 120
McKnight, C. A.
See Russell, Rosalind
McKnight, Edgar V(ernon) 1931- ... 21-22R
McKnight, Gerald 1919- ... 15-16R
McKnight, John P(roctor) 1908(?)-1987
Obituary ... 123
McKnight, Thomas Lee
See McKnight, Tom Lee
McKnight, Tom Lee 1928- ... CANR-5
Earlier sketch in CA 9-10R
McKowen, Clark 1929- ... 41-44R
McKown, Dave Ross 1895- ... 97-100
McKown, Robert 1908-1973 Obituary ... 104
McKown, Robin ?-1976 ... CANR-1
Earlier sketch in CA 3R
See also SATA 6
McKuen, Rod 1933- ... 41-44R
See also CLC 1, 3
See also AITN 1
McKusick, Marshall Bassford 1930- ... CANR-9
Earlier sketch in CA 13-14R
McLachlan, Ian 1938- ... 69-72
McLanathan, Richard 1916- ... 81-84
McLandress, Herschel
See Galbraith, John Kenneth
McLane, Charles B(ancroft) 1919- ... 25-28R
McLane, Helen J. ... CANR-4
Earlier sketch in CA 11-12R
McLane, John R. 1935- ... 97-100
McLane, Paul Elliott 1907- ... CAP-1
Earlier sketch in CA 9-10
McLaren, Colin Andrew 1940- ... 106
McLaren, Homer D. 1887- ... CAP-2
Earlier sketch in CA 29-32
McLaren, Ian A. 1928- ... 103
McLaren, Ian Francis 1912- ... CANR-24
Earlier sketch in CA 106
McLaren, John (David) 1932- ... 29-32R
McLaren, Moray (David Shaw) 1901-1971 ... 103
McLaren, N(orman) Loyall 1892(?)-1977
Obituary ... 73-76
McLaren, Robert Bruce 1923- ... 29-32R
McLarry, Newman R(ay) 1923- ... 15-16R
McLaughlin, Arthur Leo 1921- ... 19-20R
McLaughlin, Bill
See Phillips, James W.
McLaughlin, Charles Bernard 1937- ... 61-64
McLaughlin, Curtis P. 1932- ... CANR-5
Earlier sketch in CA 53-56
McLaughlin, David J(ohn) 1936- ... 73-76
McLaughlin, Dean (Jr.) 1931- ... 9-10R
McLaughlin, Elizabeth Taylor 1923- ... 93-96
McLaughlin, Emma Maude 1901- ... 65-68
McLaughlin, Joseph 1940- ... CANR-20
Earlier sketches in CA 45-48, CANR-4
McLaughlin, Joseph F., Jr. 1919-1978
Obituary ... 77-80
McLaughlin, Lorrie (Bell) 1924-1971 ... CANR-5
Earlier sketch in CA 7-8R
McLaughlin, Mignon ... 11-12R
McLaughlin, Robert (Emmet) 1908-1973 ... 3R
Obituary ... 45-48
McLaughlin, Robert William 1900- ... 1R
McLaughlin, Samuel Clarke 1924- ... 89-92
McLaughlin, Sister Raymond 1897- ... 25-28R
McLaughlin, Ted J(ohn) 1921- ... 15-16R
McLaughlin, Terence (Patrick) 1928- ... 33-36R
McLaughlin, Virginia Yans
See Yans-McLaughlin, Virginia
McLaughlin, William (DeWitt) 1918- ... 107

McLaughlin, William Raffian Davidson
1908- CAP-1
Earlier sketch in CA 11-12
McLaurin, Anne 1953- 106
See also SATA 27
McLaurin, Melton Alonza 1941- 81-84
McLaurin, R(onald) D(e) 1944- CANR-17
Earlier sketch in CA 65-68
McLaverty, Michael 1904- CAP-1
Earlier sketch in CA 13-14
See also DLB 15
McLean, Albert F(orbes), Jr. 1928- 19-20R
McLean, Allan Campbell 1922- CANR-4
Earlier sketch in CA 3R
McLean, Anne (Julia) 1951- 120
McLean, Beth Bailey 1892- CAP-2
Earlier sketch in CA 19-20
McLean, Don(ald George) 1932- 122
McLean, Donald 1905-1975 .... CANR-4
Earlier sketch in CA 2R
McLean, George 1905(?)-1983 Obituary 109
McLean, George F(rancis) 1929- CANR-6
Earlier sketch in CA 15-16R
McLean, Gordon R(onald) 1934- CANR-2
Earlier sketch in CA 49-52
McLean, Hugh 1925- 65-68
McLean, J. Sloan
See Gillette, Virginia M(ary)
and Wunsch, Josephine (McLean)
McLean, Janice W(alker) 1944- 119
McLean, John R. 1848-1916 .... DLB-23
McLean, Joseph E(rigina) 1915-1985
Obituary 118
McLean, Kathryn (Anderson) 1909-1966 .. CAP-2
Obituary 25-28R
Earlier sketch in CA 21-22
See also SATA 9
McLean, Malcolm Dallas 1913- CANR-16
Earlier sketch in CA 93-96
McLean, Robert 1891-1980 Obituary 103
McLean, Robert Colin 1927- 19-20R
McLean, Ruari 1917- CANR-10
Earlier sketch in CA 21-22R
McLean, Sammy Kay 1929- 37-40R
McLean, Susan 1937- 106
McLean, William L. 1852-1931 .... DLB-25
McLeave, Hugh George 1923- CANR-6
Earlier sketch in CA 7-8R
McLeavy, Gus 1951- 105
McLeish, Garen
See Stine, Whitney Ward
McLeish, John 1917- CANR-7
Earlier sketch in CA 57-60
McLeish, Kenneth 1940- CANR-13
Earlier sketch in CA 29-32R
See also SATA 35
McLellan, David 1940- CANR-15
Earlier sketch in CA 33-36R
McLellan, David S(tanley) 1924- 103
McLellan, Diana 1937- 114
McLellan, Robert 1907-1985 .... 41-44R
Obituary 115
McLemore, Richard Aubrey 1903-1976 49-52
Obituary 103
McLemore, S(amuel) Dale 1928- 9-10R
McLendon, Gloria H(ouston) 1940- 112
McLendon, Gordon (Barton) 1921-1986
Obituary 120
McLendon, James (Nelson) 1942-1982 .... 41-44R
Obituary 106
McLendon, Jonathon C(ollins) 1919- 19-20R
McLendon, Will L(oving) 1925- 9-10R
McLendon, Winzola Poole 93-96
McLenighan, Valjean 1947- 108
See also SATA 40, 46
McLennan, Barbara N(ancy) 1940- 85-88
McLeod, Alan L(indsey) 1928- 11-12R
McLeod, Emilie Warren 1926-1982 .... 33-36R
Obituary 108
See also SATA 23, 31
McLeod, Enid Devoge 1896-1985
Obituary 116
McLeod, James R(ichard) 1942- 41-44R
McLeod, John F(reeland) 1917- 69-72
McLeod, Kirsty
See Hudson, (Margaret) Kirsty
McLeod, Malcolm Donald 1941- 110
McLeod, Margaret Vail
See Holloway, Teresa (Bragunier)
McLeod, Mary Alice 1937- 112
McLeod, Raymond, Jr. 1932- CANR-19
Earlier sketches in CA 49-52, CANR-3
McLeod, Ross
See Feldman, Herbert (H. S.)
McLeod, Wallace (Edmond) 1931- CANR-14
Earlier sketch in CA 37-40R
McLin, Jon (Blythe) 1938- 102
McLin, Ruth (Arlene) 1924- 61-64
McLoughlin, John C. 1949- 108
See also SATA 47
McLoughlin, William G. 1922- CANR-6
Earlier sketch in CA 13-14R
McLouth, Gary (Michael) 1944- 119
McLowery, Frank
See Keevill, Henry J(ohn)
McLuhan, (Herbert) Marshall
1911-1980 .... CANR-12
Obituary 102
Earlier sketch in CA 11-12R
See also CLC 37
McLure, Charles E., Jr. 1940- CANR-8
Earlier sketch in CA 57-60
McMahan, Ian SATA-45
McMahon, Bob 1943- 111
McMahon, Bryan T(homas) 1950- 45-48
McMahon, Charles P. 1916(?)-1983
Obituary 109
McMahon, Dorothy 1912-1984 Obituary 112
McMahon, Ed(ward Leo Peter, Jr.) 1923- 89-92
McMahon, Francis E(lmer) 1906-1987
Obituary 123
McMahon, Jeremiah 1919- 109
McMahon, Joseph H(enry) 1930-1987 .... 11-12R
Obituary 124
McMahon, Michael 1943- 69-72
McMahon, Pat
See Hoch, Edward D(entinger)
McMahon, Robert
See Weverka, Robert
McMahon, Robert J. 1949- 109
McMahon, Thomas 1923(?)-1972
Obituary 37-40R
McMahon, Thomas (Arthur) 1943- CANR-15
Earlier sketch in CA 33-36R
McManis, Douglas R. 69-72
McManners, John 1916- CANR-14
Earlier sketch in CA 37-40R
McManus, Edgar J. 1924- 97-100
McManus, Frederick R(ichard) 1923- 2R
McManus, James 1951- 117
McManus, James Kenneth 1921- 85-88
McManus, Marjorie 1950- 73-76
McManus, Patrick (Francis) 1933- 105
See also SATA 46
McMaster, Beth 1935- 112
McMaster, John Bach 1852-1932 .... DLB-47
McMaster, Juliet 1937- 37-40R
McMeekin, Clark
See McMeekin, Isabel McLennan
McMeekin, Isabel McLennan 1895- 5-6R
See also SATA 3
McMenemey, William Henry 1905- CAP-1
Earlier sketch in CA 11-12
McMenemy, Nickie 1925- 97-100
McMichael, George 1927- 103
McMichael, James 1939- 69-72
McMichael, Joan K(atharine) 1906- 107
McMillan, Bruce 1947- CANR-13
Earlier sketch in CA 73-76
See also SATA 22
McMillan, Colin 1923- 29-32R
McMillan, Constance (VanBrunt Johnson)
1949- 85-88
McMillan, George 1913-1987 102
Obituary 123
McMillan, James B. 1907- 85-88
McMillan, James F(rancis) 1948- 122
McMillan, Polly Miller 1920- 4R
McMillan, Priscilla Johnson 1928- 41-44R
McMillan, Roddy 1923-1979 Obituary 109
McMillen, Howard 1938- 57-60
McMillen, Neil R(aymond) 1939- 33-36R
McMillen, S(im) I. (Socrates) 1898- 7-8R
McMillen, Wheeler 1893- 33-36R
McMillin, (Joseph) Laurence (Jr.) 1923- 33-36R
McMillion, Bonner 1921- 15-16R
McMorran, Susan
See Beattie, Susan
McMorrow, Fred 1925- 57-60
McMullan, Frank (Alonzo) 1907- 7-8R
McMullan, Kate (Hall) 1947- SATA-48
McMullan, Kate
See McMullan, Kate Hall
McMullan, Kate Hall 1947- 123
McMullen, Catherine
See Cookson, Catherine (McMullen)
McMullen, Jay L. 1921- 118
Brief entry 114
McMullen, Jeremy (John) 1948- 103
McMullen, Lorraine 1926- 117
McMullen, Mary
See Reilly, Mary
McMullen, Roy 1911-1984 .... 25-28R
Obituary 113
McMullin, Ernan 1924- CANR-22
Earlier sketches in CA 13-14R, CANR-6
McMullin, Ruth R(oney) 1942- 61-64
McMurdie, Annie Laurie
See Cassiday, Bruce (Bingham)
McMurray, George R(ay) 1925- 103
McMurray, Nancy A(rmistead) 1936- 41-44R
McMurrin, Sterling M(oss) 1914- 29-32R
McMurry, James Burton 1941- 69-72
McMurry, Linda O. 1945- 106
McMurry, Robert N(oleman) 1901- 19-20R
McMurry, Sarah L. 1944- 123
McMurtrey, Martin A(loysias) 1921- 69-72
See also SATA 21
McMurtry, Jo 1937- 89-92
McMurtry, Larry (Jeff) 1936- CANR-19
Earlier sketch in CA 7-8R
See also DLB 2
See also DLBY 80
See also CLC 2, 3, 7, 11, 27, 44
See also AITN 2
McMurtry, Robert Gerald 1906- CAP-1
Earlier sketch in CA 11-12
McNab, Thomas 1933- 108
McNab, Tom
See McNab, Thomas
McNail, Eddie Gathings 1905- CANR-6
Earlier sketch in CA 57-60
McNair, Kate 19-20R
See also SATA 3
McNair, Malcolm P(errine) 1894-1985 .... CAP-1
Obituary 117
Earlier sketch in CA 11-12
McNair, Philip Murray Jourdan 1924- 23-24R
McNair, Sylvia 1924- 121
McNair Scott, Ronald (Guthrie) 1906- 111
McNairy, Philip F(rederick) 1911- 19-20R
McNall, P(reston) E(ssex) 1888- 29-32R
McNall, Scott G(rant) 1941- CANR-11
Earlier sketch in CA 25-28R
McNally, Curtis
See Birchall, Ian H(arry)
McNally, Dennis 1949- 103
McNally, Gertrude Bancroft 1908(?)-1985
Obituary 115
McNally, John 1914- 19-20R
McNally, Raymond T. 1931- CANR-14
Earlier sketch in CA 37-40R
McNally, Robert 1946- 107
McNally, Robert E(dward) 1917-1978 .. CANR-11
Earlier sketch in CA 23-24R
McNally, Terrence 1939- CANR-2
Earlier sketch in CA 45-48
See also DLB 7
See also CLC 4, 7, 41
McNally, Tom 1923- 85-88
McNamara, Brooks 1937- 25-28R
McNamara, Eugene (Joseph) 1930- CANR-10
Earlier sketch in CA 21-22R
McNamara, Jo Ann 1931- CANR-15
Earlier sketch in CA 85-88
McNamara, John J(oseph), Jr.
1932-1986 .... 41-44R
Obituary 120
McNamara, John S. 1908(?)-1977
Obituary 69-72
McNamara, Kevin (John) 1926-1987 .... 25-28R
Obituary 122
McNamara, Lena Brooke 1891- CAP-1
Earlier sketch in CA 11-12
McNamara, Margaret C(raig)
1915-1981 .... SATA-24
McNamara, Michael M. 1940-1979
Obituary 89-92
McNamara, Robert S(trange) 1916-
Brief entry 112
McNamara, Sister Marie Aquinas
See Schaub, Marilyn McNamara
McNamara, William E. 1926- CANR-4
Earlier sketch in CA 4R
McNamee, James 1904- 7-8R
McNamee, Lawrence F. 1917- 25-28R
McNamee, Maurice B(asil) 1909- 5-6R
McNaspy, Clement James 1915- CANR-2
Earlier sketch in CA 7-8R
McNaught, Brian Robert 1948- 105
McNaught, Harry 106
See also SATA 32
McNaught, Kenneth (William Kirkpatrick)
1918- 29-32R
McNaughton, Arnold 1930- 57-60
McNaughton, Colin 1951- 112
See also SATA 39
McNaughton, Frank 1906(?)-1978
Obituary 81-84
McNaughton, Howard (Douglas) 1945- 57-60
McNaughton, Wayne L. 1902- 1R
McNaughton, William (Frank) 1933- 41-44R
McNeal, Robert H(atch) 1930- 11-12R
McNear, Robert 1930(?)-1985 Obituary 117
McNeely, Jeannette 1918- 41-44R
See also SATA 25
McNeely, Jerry Clark 1928- Brief entry 115
McNeer, May CANR-2
Earlier sketch in CA 7-8R
See also SATA 1
McNees, Pat 1940- CANR-7
Earlier sketch in CA 57-60
McNeil, Art 1944- 124
McNeil, Barbara L(aurie) 1951- 97-100
McNeil, Elton B(urbank) 1924-1974 .... CAP-2
Earlier sketch in CA 25-28
McNeil, Florence 1940- 116
See also DLB 60
McNeill, Anthony 1941- 97-100
McNeill, Donald P(aul) 1936- 107
McNeill, Janet
See Alexander, Janet
See also SATA 1
McNeill, John J. 1925- 65-68
McNeill, John Thomas 1885-1975 .... CANR-10
Obituary 57-60
Earlier sketches in CA 11-12, CAP-1
McNeill, Robert B(lakely) 1915- 19-20R
McNeill, Stuart 1942- 65-68
McNeill, William H(ardy) 1917- CANR-2
Earlier sketch in CA 7-8R
McNeilly, Wilfred Glassford 1921- 29-32R
McNeir, Waldo F(orest) 1908- 19-20R
McNeish, James 1931- CANR-12
Earlier sketch in CA 69-72
McNelly, Theodore (Hart) 1919- 7-8R
McNelly, Willis E(verett) 1920- 107
McNew, Ben(nie) B(anks) 1931- CANR-3
Earlier sketch in CA 11-12R
McNickle, (William) D'Arcy 1904-1977 .. CANR-5
Obituary 85-88
Earlier sketch in CA 9-10R
See also SATA 22
McNicoll, Alan (Wedel Ramsay)
1908-1987 Obituary 124
McNicoll, Robert E. 1907- 37-40R
McNiece, Harold Francis 1923-1972
Obituary 37-40R
McNierney, Mary Alice 11-12R
McNiff, William John 1899-1987 Obituary .. 122
McNitt, Gale 1921- 57-60
McNiven, Malcolm A(lbert) 1929- 29-32R
McNown, John S(tephenson) 1916- 57-60
McNulty, Edward N. 1936- CANR-10
Earlier sketch in CA 65-68
McNulty, Faith 1918- CANR-1
Earlier sketch in CA 49-52
See also SATA 12
McNulty, James Edmund, Jr. 1924-1965 .... 3R
Obituary 103
McNulty, James Francis 1934-1979
Obituary 113
McNutt, Dan James 1938- 61-64
McNutt, James (Allen) 1944- 49-52
McOwan, Rennie 1933- 115
McPhail, David M(ichael) 1940- CANR-22
Earlier sketch in CA 85-88
See also SATA 32, 47
McPharlin, Paul 1903-1948 Brief entry 110
See also SATA 31
McPhaul, Jack
See McPhaul, John J.
McPhaul, John J. 1904-1983 .... 9-10R
Obituary 110
McPhee, Arthur G(ene) 1945- Brief entry 116
McPhee, John (Angus) 1931- CANR-20
Earlier sketch in CA 65-68
See also CLC 36
McPhee, Richard B(yron) 1934- 111
See also SATA 41
McPhee, William N(orvell) 1921- 19-20R
McPherson, Anna Talbott 1904- CANR-19
Earlier sketches in CA 4R, CANR-4
McPherson, Gertrude H(untington) 1923- .. 45-48
McPherson, Harry Cummings, Jr. 1929- 104
McPherson, Holt 1907(?)-1979 Obituary .. 89-92
McPherson, Hugo (Archibald) 1921- 29-32R
McPherson, James Alan 1943- CANR-24
Earlier sketch in CA 25-28R
See also DLB 38
See also CLC 19
McPherson, James Lowell 1921- 15-16R
McPherson, James M. 1936- 11-12R
See also SATA 16
McPherson, John 1925- 119
McPherson, Sandra 1943- CANR-12
Earlier sketch in CA 29-32R
See also DLBY 86
McPherson, Thomas Herdman 1925- 19-20R
McPherson, William (Alexander) 1933- 69-72
See also CLC 34
McPherson, William 1939- 57-60
McPhie, Walter E(van) 1926- 29-32R
McPolk, Andre (Hans) 1935- 93-96
McQuade, Ann Aikman 1928- 1R
McQuade, De Rosset Morrissey
1934(?)-1978 Obituary 81-84
McQuade, Donald A(nthony) 1941- CANR-16
Earlier sketch in CA 65-68
McQuade, Walter 1922- 103
McQuaid, Kim 1947- CANR-24
Earlier sketch in CA 107
McQuaig, Jack Hunter 11-12R
McQueen, Ian 1930- 104
McQueen, Lucinda SATA-48
McQueen, Mildred Hark 1908- CAP-1
Earlier sketch in CA 9-10
See also SATA 12
McQueen, William A. 1926- 23-24R
McQuigg, R. Bruce 1927- 19-20R
McQuilkin, Frank 1936- CANR-13
Earlier sketch in CA 33-36R
McQuiston, Joanne W(orth) 1922(?)-1985
Obituary 117
McQuown, F(rederic) R(ichard) 1907- 11-12R
McQuown, Judith H(ershkowitz) 1941- 107
McQuown, Norman Anthony 1914-
Brief entry 106
McRae, Hamish (Malcolm Donald) 1943- .. 57-60
McRae, Kenneth D(ouglas) 1925- CANR-17
Earlier sketch in CA 2R
McRae, Lindsay
See Sowerby, A(rthur) L(indsay) M(cRae)
McRae, Robert (Forbes) 1914- 77-80
McRae, William John 1933- 106
McReynolds, David 1929- 29-32R
McReynolds, Edwin C(larence)
1890-1967 .... CAP-1
Earlier sketch in CA 19-20
McReynolds, Ronald W(eldon) 1934- 49-52
McRoberts, Agnesann
See Meek, Pauline Palmer
McRoberts, R(obert) Lewis 1944- 33-36R
McShan, James 1937- 69-72
McShane, Mark 1930- CANR-22
Earlier sketches in CA 19-20R, CANR-7
McShane, Philip 1932- 69-72
McShean, Gordon 1936- 108
See also SATA 41
McSherry, Frank D(avid), Jr. 1927- CANR-23
Earlier sketch in CA 107
McSherry, James E(dward) 1920- 49-52
McShine, Kynaston (Leigh) 1935-
Brief entry 115
McSorley, Joseph 1874-1963 .... CAP-1
Earlier sketch in CA 15-16
McSweeney, Kerry CLC-34
McSweeny, Maxine 1905- 61-64
Mc Swigan, Marie 1907-1962 73-76
See also SATA 24
McTaggart, Fred 1939- 65-68
McTaggart, J. McT. Ellis
See McTaggart, John McTaggart Ellis
McTaggart, John McTaggart Ellis
1866-1925 Brief entry 120
McTaggart, Lynne (Ann) 1951- Brief entry .. 113
McTeer, Wilson 1905- 41-44R
McVay, Gordon 1941- 73-76
McVean, James
See Luard, Nicholas
McVeigh, Malcolm J(ames) 1931- 61-64
McVey, Ruth T(homas) 1930- 109
McVickar, Elinor Guthrie 1902(?)-1982
Obituary 106
McVicker, Charles (Taggart) 1930- SATA-39
McVicker, Chuck
See McVicker, Charles (Taggart)

McVicker, Daphne Alloway 1895-1979
Obituary ... 85-88
McWaters, Barry 1937- ... 108
McWhiney, Grady 1928- ... CANR-6
Earlier sketch in CA 7-8R
McWhinney, Edward 1926- ... CANR-12
Earlier sketch in CA 29-32R
McWhinnie, Donald 1920-1987 Obituary ... 123
McWhirter, A(lan) Ross 1925-1975 ... 19-20R
Obituary ... 61-64
See also SATA 31, 37
McWhirter, George 1939- ... CANR-13
Earlier sketch in CA 77-80
See also DLB 60
McWhirter, Glenna S. 1929- ... 89-92
McWhirter, Nickie
See McWhirter, Glenna S.
McWhirter, Norris Dewar 1925- ... 13-14R
See also SATA 37
McWilliams, Carey 1905-1980 ... CANR-2
Obituary ... 101
Earlier sketch in CA 45-48
McWilliams, John P(robasco), Jr. 1940- ... 49-52
McWilliams, Margaret (Ann Edgar)
1929- ... CANR-8
Earlier sketch in CA 19-20R
McWilliams, Peter 1949- ... 41-44R
McWilliams, Wilson Carey 1933- ... CANR-19
Earlier sketch in CA 103
Meacham, Ellis K. 1913- ... 25-28R
Meacham, Harry M(onroe) 1901-1975 ... CAP-2
Earlier sketch in CA 25-28
Meacham, Margaret 1952- ... 118
Meacham, Standish (Jr.) 1932-
Brief entry ... 110
Meacher, Michael Hugh 1939- ... 109
Mead, D(onald) Eugene 1934- ... 65-68
Mead, Edgar T(horn), Jr. 1922- ... 113
Mead, Frank Spencer 1898-1982 ... CANR-9
Obituary ... 107
Earlier sketches in CA 19-20, CAP-1
Mead, G(eorge) R(obert) S(tow)
1863-1933 Brief entry ... 122
Mead, Harold C(harles) H(ugh) 1910- ... CAP-1
Earlier sketch in CA 13-14
Mead, Jude 1919- ... 25-28R
Mead, Margaret 1901-1978 ... CANR-4
Obituary ... 81-84
Earlier sketch in CA 3R
See also SATA 20
See also CLC 37
See also AITN 1
Mead, Matthew 1924- ... 101
See also DLB 40
Mead, Peter (Willan) 1911- ... 116
Mead, Robert Douglas 1928-1983 ... 41-44R
Obituary ... 110
Mead, Russell (M., Jr.) 1935- ... 11-12R
See also SATA 10
Mead, Russell
See Koehler, Margaret Hudson
Mead, (Edward) Shepherd 1914- ... 9-10R
Mead, Sidney E(arl) 1904- ... CAP-1
Earlier sketch in CA 9-10
Mead, Sidney Moko 1927- ... CANR-23
Earlier sketch in CA 106
Mead, Stella ?-1981 Obituary ... 103
See also SATA 27
Mead, Taylor 1931(?)- Brief entry ... 116
See also DLB 16
Mead, Walter B(ruce) 1934- ... 37-40R
Mead, William B(owmar) 1934- ... CANR-15
Earlier sketch in CA 85-88
Mead, William Richard 1915- ... 103
Meade, Bill C.
See Rogers, Paul T(aylor)
Meade, Dorothy (Joan Sampson) 1923- ... 9-10R
Meade, Elizabeth Thomasina
1854(?)-1914(?) Brief entry ... 112
Meade, Ellen
See Roddick, Ellen
See also SATA 5
Meade, Everard 1914- ... 25-28R
Meade, James Edward 1907- ... CANR-2
Earlier sketch in CA 1R
Meade, L. T.
See Meade, Elizabeth Thomasina
Meade, Marion 1934- ... CANR-1
Earlier sketch in CA 49-52
See also SATA 23
Meade, Mary
See Church, Ruth Ellen (Lovrien)
Meade, Richard
See Haas, Ben(jamin) L(eopold)
Meade, Richard A(ndrew) 1911- ... 45-48
Meade, Robert Douthat 1903-197(?) ... CAP-2
Earlier sketch in CA 25-28
Meader, Stephen W(arren) 1892- ... 5-6R
See also SATA 1
Meador, Roy 1929- ... CANR-11
Earlier sketch in CA 69-72
Meadow, Charles T(roub) 1929- ... CANR-15
Earlier sketch in CA 29-32R
See also SATA 23
Meadow, Kathryn Pendleton 1929- ... CANR-7
Earlier sketch in CA 57-60
Meadowcroft, Enid LaMonte
See Wright, Enid Meadowcroft (LaMonte)
Meadowes, Alicia
See Burak, Linda (Gallina)
and Zieg, Joan (Gallina)
Meadows, Eddie S(pencer) 1939- ... 109
Meadows, Edward 1944- ... 101
Meadows, Paul 1913- ... 41-44R
Meadows, Peter
See Lindsay, Jack

Meagher, John C. 1935- ... CANR-11
Earlier sketch in CA 19-20R
Meagher, Paul Kevin 1907-1976 Obituary ... 69-72
Meagher, Robert E(mmett) 1943- ... CANR-10
Earlier sketch in CA 25-28R
Meagher, Robert F. 1927- ... 41-44R
Meaker, Eloise 1915- ... 105
Meaker, M. J.
See Meaker, Marijane
Meaker, Marijane 1927- ... 107
See also SATA 20
Meakin, David 1943- ... 69-72
Means, Florence Crannell 1891-1980 ... 4R
Obituary ... 103
See also SATA 1, 25
Means, Gardiner C(oit) 1896-1988
Obituary ... 124
Means, Gordon P(aul) 1927- ... 33-36R
Means, John Barkley 1939- ... 33-36R
Means, Louis Edgar 1902- ... CANR-2
Earlier sketch in CA 5-6R
Means, Marianne Hansen 1934- ... 11-12R
Means, Richard K(eith) 1929- ... CANR-17
Earlier sketches in CA 7-8R, CANR-2
Meany, George 1894-1980 Obituary ... 97-100
Meara, (Mary) Jane (Frances) Cavolina
1954- ... 120
Meara, Mary Jane Frances Cavolina
See Meara, (Mary) Jane (Frances)
Cavolina
Meares, Ainslie Dixon 1910- ... CANR-11
Earlier sketch in CA 25-28R
Mearian, Judy Frank 1936- ... 101
See also SATA 49
Mearns, David Chambers 1899-1981 ... 2R
Obituary ... 104
Mears, Brainerd, Jr. 1921- ... 53-56
Mears, Richard Chase 1935- ... 101
Mears, Walter R(obert) 1935- ... 113
Brief entry ... 111
Mearsheimer, John J(oseph) 1947- ... 117
Measday, George
See Soderberg, Percy Measday
Measham, D(onald) C. 1932- ... 21-22R
Measures, (William) Howard 1894- ... CAP-1
Earlier sketch in CA 13-14
Mebane, John (Harrison) 1909- ... 15-16R
Mebane, Mary E(lizabeth) 1933- ... 73-76
Mech, Dave
See Mech, L(ucyan) David
Mech, L(ucyan) David 1937- ... CANR-14
Earlier sketch in CA 33-36R
Mecham, John Lloyd 1893- ... 2R
Mechanic, David 1936- ... CANR-19
Earlier sketches in CA 5-6R, CANR-3
Mechanic, Sylvia (Gertrude) 1920- ... 69-72
Mechin, Jacques Benoist
See Benoist-Mechin, Jacques
Meckier, Jerome (Thomas) 1941- ... 33-36R
Meckler, Alan Marshall 1945- ... 57-60
Meckley, Richard F(rederick) 1928- ... 37-40R
Mecklin, John Martin 1918-1971
Obituary ... 33-36R
Meckstroth, Jacob A. 1887(?)-1985
Obituary ... 115
Meckstroth, Jake
See Meckstroth, Jacob A.
Medalia, Leon S. 1881- ... 85-88
Medary, Marjorie 1890- ... 73-76
See also SATA 14
Medawar, Peter Brian 1915-1987 ... 97-100
Obituary ... 123
Medd, Patrick 1919- ... 25-28R
Meddaugh, Susan 1944- ... 106
See also SATA 29
Meddis, Ray 1944- ... 77-80
Medea, Andra 1953- ... 57-60
Medearis, Mary 1915- ... 69-72
See also SATA 5
Medeiros, Earl Caton 1933- ... 89-92
Medhin, Tsegaye (Kawessa) Gabre
See Gabre-Medhin, Tsegaye (Kawessa)
Medhurst, Joan
See Liverton, Joan
Medicus II
See Philipp, Elliot Elias
Medill, Joseph 1823-1899 ... DLB-43
Medina, Jeremy T(yler) 1942- ... CANR-11
Earlier sketch in CA 69-72
Medina, William A.
See Medina, William Antonio
Medina, William Antonio 1935-1985
Obituary ... 117
Medley, Anne
See Borchard, Ruth (Berendsohn)
Medley, (Rachel) Margaret 1918- ... 15-16R
Medley, Morris L(ee) 1942- ... 57-60
Medlicott, Alexander G(uild), Jr. 1927- ... 37-40R
Medlicott, Margaret P(aget) 1913- ... 29-32R
Medlicott, William Norton 1900-1987 ... 9-10R
Obituary ... 123
Medlin, Virgil D(ewain) 1943- ... 57-60
Mednick, Murray 1939- ... 21-22R
Medoff, Mark (Howard) 1940- ... CANR-5
Earlier sketch in CA 53-56
See also DLB 7
See also CLC 6, 23
See also AITN 1
Medsger, Betty (Louise) 1942- ... 113
Medsker, Leland L. 1905- ... CANR-2
Earlier sketch in CA 3R
Medved, Harry 1961(?)- ... 93-96
Medved, Michael 1948- ... CANR-11
Earlier sketch in CA 65-68
Medvedev, Pavel
See Bakhtin, Mikhail (Mikhailovich)
Medvedev, Roy (Alexandrovich) 1925- ... 81-84

Medvedev, Zhores A(leksandrovich)
1925- ... 69-72
Mee, Charles L., Jr. 1938- ... CANR-3
Earlier sketch in CA 45-48
See also SATA 8
Mee, Fiona 1946(?)-1978 Obituary ... 104
Mee, John F(ranklin) 1908- ... CAP-1
Earlier sketch in CA 9-10
Meechan, Hugh L(awrence) 1933- ... 19-20R
Meehan, Daniel Joseph 1930-1978
Obituary ... 77-80
Meehan, Danny
See Meehan, Daniel Joseph
Meehan, Eugene J(ohn) 1923- ... CANR-14
Earlier sketch in CA 37-40R
Meehan, Francis X(avier) 1937- ... 116
Meehan, Richard Lawrence 1939- ... 107
Meehan, Thomas Edward 1932- ... 29-32R
Meehl, Paul E(verett) 1920- ... 93-96
Meek, Alexander Beaufort 1814-1865 ... DLB-3
Meek, Forrest B(urns) 1928- ... 110
Meek, Jacklyn O'Hanlon 1933- ... 77-80
See also SATA 34
Meek, Jay 1937- ... 107
Meek, Lois Hayden
See Stolz, Lois Meek
Meek, Loyal George 1918- ... 73-76
Meek, Margaret
See Meek Spencer, Margaret (Diston)
Meek, Pauline Palmer 1917- ... 106
Meek, Ronald L(indley) 1917-1978 ... CANR-6
Earlier sketch in CA 9-10R
Meek, S(terner St.) P(aul) 1894-1972 ... 4R
Obituary ... 103
See also SATA 28
Meeker, Alice (MacCutcheon) 1904- ... CAP-2
Earlier sketch in CA 25-28
Meeker, Joseph W(arren) 1932- ... 49-52
Meeker, Mary Nacol 1928- ... 53-56
Meeker, Oden 1919(?)-1976 ... 73-76
Obituary ... 65-68
See also SATA 14
Meeker, Richard Kilburn 1925-19(?) ... CAP-2
Earlier sketch in CA 19-20
Meeks, Esther MacBain ... 4R
See also SATA 1
Meeks, John E. ... 33-36R
Meeks, Linda A.
See Brower, Linda A.
Meeks, M(errill) Douglas 1941- ... 93-96
Meeks, Wayne A. 1932- ... CANR-5
Earlier sketch in CA 15-16R
Meek Spencer, Margaret (Diston)
1925- ... CANR-21
Earlier sketch in CA 105
Meen, Victor Ben 1910-1971 Obituary ... 106
Meenan, James F(rancis) 1910-1987 ... 124
Meer, Fatima 1929- ... 73-76
Meerhaeghe, M(arcel) A(lfons) G(ilbert) Van
See Van Meerhaeghe, M(arcel) A(lfons)
G(ilbert)
Meerloo, Joost A(braham) M(aurits)
1903-1976 ... CANR-4
Obituary ... 69-72
Earlier sketch in CA 1R
Meeropol, Abel 1903(?)-1986 Obituary ... 121
Meese, Elizabeth Ann 1943- ... 122
Meeter, Glenn 1934- ... CANR-12
Earlier sketch in CA 33-36R
Meeth, Louis Richard 1934- ... 19-20R
Meeuse, Bastiaan (Jacob Dirk) 1916- ... 119
Meezan, William 1947- ... 117
Megargee, Edwin I(nglee) 1937- ... CANR-7
Earlier sketch in CA 19-20R
Meged, Aharon
See Megged, Aharon
Meged, Aron
See Megged, Aharon
Megged, Aharon 1920- ... CANR-1
Earlier sketch in CA 49-52
See also CLC 9
Meggendorfer, Lothar 1847-1925
Brief entry ... 115
See also SATA 36
Meggers, Betty J(ane) 1921- ... 19-20R
Meggitt, M(ervyn) J(ohn) 1924- ... 15-16R
Meggs, Brown (Moore) 1930- ... CANR-7
Earlier sketch in CA 61-64
Meggs, Philip B(axter) 1942- ... 116
Meggyesy, Dave
See Meggyesy, David M.
Meggyesy, David M. 1941- ... 33-36R
Megill, Kenneth Alden 1939- Brief entry ... 106
Meglin, Nick 1935- ... CANR-21
Earlier sketch in CA 69-72
Meglitsch, Paul A(llen) 1914- ... 53-56
Mego, Al
See Roberts, Arthur O.
Megrah, Maurice Henry 1896-1985
Obituary ... 116
Megson, Barbara 1930- ... 29-32R
Mehaffy, Robert E(ugene) 1935- ... 113
Mehan, Joseph Albert 1929- ... 101
Mehdevi, Alexander (Sinclair) 1947- ... 49-52
See also SATA 7
Mehdevi, Anne (Marie) Sinclair 1947- ... 5-6R
See also SATA 8
Mehdi, M(ohammed) T(aki) 1928- ... CANR-8
Earlier sketch in CA 19-20R
Mehegan, John (Francis) 1920(?)-1984 ... 7-8R
Obituary ... 112
Meher Baba
See Baba, Meher
Mehl, Roger 1912- ... CANR-21
Earlier sketches in CA 11-12R, CANR-6
Mehlinger, Howard D(ean) 1931- ... CANR-6
Earlier sketch in CA 11-12R

Mehlmann, Marilyn 1939- ... 119
Mehnert, Klaus 1906-1984 ... CANR-2
Obituary ... 111
Earlier sketch in CA 2R
Mehr, Joseph (John) 1941- Brief entry ... 113
Mehrabian, Albert 1939- ... 33-36R
Mehrens, William A(rthur) 1937- ... 37-40R
Mehring, Walter 1896-1981 Obituary ... 105
Mehrotra, S(ri) Ram 1931- ... CANR-8
Earlier sketch in CA 15-16R
Mehrtens, Susan E(mily) 1945- ... 53-56
Mehta, Gaganvihari L(allubhai) 1900-1974
Obituary ... 49-52
Mehta, Rustam Jehangir 1912- ... 11-12R
Mehta, Shahnaz ... 106
Mehta, Ved (Parkash) 1934- ... CANR-23
Earlier sketches in CA 3R, CANR-2
See also CLC 37
Mei, Ko-Wang 1918- ... CANR-2
Earlier sketch in CA 45-48
Meiden, Walter 1907- ... CANR-8
Earlier sketch in CA 13-14R
Meier, August 1923- ... CANR-3
Earlier sketch in CA 11-12R
Meier, Gerald M(arvin) 1923- ... 112
Meier, Heinz K(arl) 1929- ... 61-64
Meier, Joel F(rancis) 1940- ... 109
Meier, Matt S(ebastian) 1917- ... CANR-14
Earlier sketch in CA 41-44R
Meier, Richard L(ouis) 1920- ... 19-20R
Meierhenry, Wesley Carl 1915- ... 41-44R
Meiggs, Russell 1902- ... 103
Meighan, Donald Charles 1929- ... CANR-24
Earlier sketch in CA 107
See also SATA 30
Meigs, Alexander James 1921- ... 104
Meigs, Cornelia Lynde 1884-1973 ... 9-10R
Obituary ... 45-48
See also SATA 6
Meigs, Peveril 1903- ... 37-40R
Meigs, Walter B(erkeley) 1912- ... 23-24R
Meij, Jacob L(ouis) 1900- ... 7-8R
Meijer, M(arinus) J(ohan) 1912- ... 69-72
Meikle, Clive
See Brooks, Jeremy
Meikle, Jeffrey L(ee) 1949- ... 101
Meiklejohn, Alexander 1872-1964
Obituary ... 111
Meilach, Dona Z(weigoron) 1926- ... CANR-22
Earlier sketches in CA 11-12R, CANR-5
See also SATA 34
Meilach, Michael D(avid) 1932- ... CANR-2
Earlier sketch in CA 7-8R
Meilaender, Gilbert 1946- ... 109
Meilen, Bill 1932- ... 69-72
Meillassoux, Claude 1925- ... 25-28R
Mein, Margaret ... 61-64
Meiners, R(oger) K(eith) 1932- ... CANR-3
Earlier sketch in CA 7-8R
Meiners, Roger Evert 1948- ... 110
Meinig, Donald William 1924- ... 112
Meinke, Peter 1932- ... 25-28R
See also DLB 5
Meinkoth, Norman A(ugust) 1913- ... 113
Meintjes, Johannes 1923-1980 ... CANR-8
Earlier sketch in CA 19-20R
Meir, Golda 1898-1978 ... 89-92
Obituary ... 81-84
Meiring, Desmond
See Rice, Desmond Charles
Meiring, Jane (Muriel) 1920- ... CANR-20
Earlier sketch in CA 103
Meisch, Lynn A. 1945- ... 105
Meisch, Richard A(lden) 1943- ... 33-36R
Meisel, Anthony C(lark) 1943- ... 105
Meisel, Gerald Stanley 1937- ... 9-10R
Meisel, John 1923- ... 19-20R
Meisel, Martin 1931- ... CANR-15
Earlier sketch in CA 5-6R
Meisel, Perry 1949- ... 102
Meisel, Tony
See Meisel, Anthony C(lark)
Meiselas, Susan 1948- ... 106
Meiselman, David I(srael) 1924- ... 13-14R
Meisenholder, Robert 1915- ... 37-40R
Meisler, Richard 1940- ... 124
Meisler, Stanley 1931- ... 73-76
Meisner, Maurice 1931- ... 21-22R
Meiss, Millard (Lazare) 1904-1975 ... 61-64
Obituary ... 57-60
Meissner, Hans-Otto 1909- ... CANR-2
Earlier sketch in CA 49-52
Meissner, Kurt 1885-1976 ... CAP-2
Earlier sketch in CA 29-32
Meissner, W(illiam) W. 1931- ... CANR-13
Earlier sketch in CA 33-36R
Meister, Anton D(iderik) 1944- ... 118
Meister, Barbara 1932- ... 102
Meister, Richard J(ulius) 1938- ... 57-60
Meister, Robert 1926- ... CANR-9
Earlier sketch in CA 7-8R
Meixner, John A(lbert) 1925- ... 5-6R
Mejia, Arthur, Jr. 1934- ... 81-84
Mekas, Jonas 1922- Brief entry ... 113
Melady, John 1938- ... 122
See also SATA 49
Melady, Thomas Patrick 1927- ... CANR-5
Earlier sketch in CA 9-10R
Melahn, Martha 1924- ... 107
Melamid, Alexander 1914- ... 45-48
Melancon, Robert 1947- ... DLB-60
Meland, Bernard Eugene 1899- ... 19-20R
Melanson, Richard A(llen) 1944- ... 113
Melanter
See Blackmore, R(ichard) D(oddridge)
Melaro, Constance L(oraine) 1929- ... 17-18R
Melas, Evi 1930- ... 65-68

Melber, Jehuda 1916- ... 29-32R
Melbin, Murray 1927- ... 45-48
Melbo, Irving Robert 1908- ... 49-52
Melby, Ernest O(scar) 1891-1987
  Obituary ... 121
Melby, John Fremont 1913- Brief entry ... 106
Melcher, Daniel 1912-1985 ... 33-36R
  Obituary ... 116
  See also SATA 43
Melcher, Frederic Gershom 1879-1963
  Obituary ... 89-92
  See also SATA 22
Melcher, Marguerite Fellows 1879-1969 ... 7-8R
  See also SATA 10
Melcher, Robert Augustus 1910- ... 19-20R
Melchert, Norman Paul 1933- ... 25-28R
Melchinger, Siegfried 1906- ... 81-84
Melchior, Ib (Jorgen) 1917- ... CANR-22
  Earlier sketches in CA 45-48, CANR-2
Meldal-Johnsen, Trevor Bernard
  1944- ... CANR-19
  Earlier sketch in CA 101
Melden, A(braham) I(rving) 1910- ... 19-20R
Melder, Keith E(ugene) 1932- ... 81-84
Mele, Frank Michael 1935- ... 53-56
Mele, Jim 1950- ... 113
Melendy, H(oward) Brett 1924- ... CANR-23
  Earlier sketches in CA 19-20R, CANR-8
Meleski, Patricia F(erguson) 1935- ... 61-64
Melezh, Ivan 1921(?)-1976 Obituary ... 69-72
Melfi, Leonard 1935- ... 73-76
Melfi, Mary 1951- ... 113
Melford, Austin (Alfred) 1884-1971
  Obituary ... 115
Melhem, D(iana) H(elen) ... CANR-2
  Earlier sketch in CA 49-52
Melhorn, Charles M(ason) 1918-1983 ... 57-60
  Obituary ... 111
Melhuish, George (William Seymour)
  1916-1985 Obituary ... 117
Melick, Arden Davis 1940- ... 106
Melikow, Loris
  See Hofmannsthal, Hugo von
Melin, Grace Hathaway 1892-1973 ... CAP-2
  Obituary ... 45-48
  Earlier sketch in CA 21-22
  See also SATA 10
Mell
  See Lazarus, Mell
Mell, Donald C(harles), Jr. 1931- ... 115
Mellaart, James 1925- Brief entry ... 118
Mellan, Eleanor 1905- ... 7-8R
Mellan, Ibert 1901- ... 5-6R
Mellanby, Kenneth 1908- ... 85-88
Mellander, Gustavo Adolfo 1935- ... 33-36R
Mellard, James Milton 1938- ... 105
Mellen, Ida M(ay) 1877- ... 7-8R
Mellen, Joan 1941- ... CANR-11
  Earlier sketch in CA 65-68
Mellencamp, Virginia Lynn 1917- ... 9-10R
Meller, Norman 1913- ... 25-28R
Mellers, Wilfrid (Howard) 1914- ... CANR-4
  Earlier sketch in CA 7-8R
Mellersh, H(arold) E(dward) L(eslie)
  1897- ... CANR-9
  Earlier sketch in CA 53-56
  See also SATA 10
Mellert, Robert B(oros) 1937- ... 61-64
Mellichamp, Josephine 1923- ... 93-96
Mellin, Jeanne 1929- ... CANR-24
  Earlier sketch in CA 49-52
Mellini, Peter 1935- ... 93-96
Mellinkoff, David 1914- ... 13-14R
Mellinkoff, Ruth 1924- ... CANR-14
  Earlier sketch in CA 37-40R
Mellins, Thomas 1957- ... 122
Mellon, Constance A. 1938- ... 123
Mellon, James R(oss) 1942- ... 69-72
Mellon, John C(raig) 1933- Brief entry ... 107
Mellon, Knox
  See Mellon, William Knox, Jr.
Mellon, Matthew T(aylor) 1897- ... 29-32R
Mellon, Stanley 1927- Brief entry ... 108
Mellon, William Knox, Jr. 1925- ... 37-40R
Mellor, Anne Kostelanetz 1941- ... 45-48
Mellor, J(ohn) Leigh 1928- ... 19-20R
Mellor, John W(illiams) 1928- ... 33-36R
Mellor, William Bancroft 1906- ... 61-64
Mellors, John (Parkin) 1920- ... 65-68
Mellors, Samantha
  See Lottman, Eileen
Mellow, James R(obert) 1926- ... 105
Mellown, Elgin W(endell, Jr.) 1931- ... 19-20R
Mellows, Joan ... 77-80
Melly, George 1926- ... 81-84
Melman, Seymour 1917- ... CANR-4
  Earlier sketch in CA 1R
Melmoth, Sebastian
  See Wilde, Oscar (Fingal O'Flahertie
  Wills)
Melnick, Donald 1926-1977 Obituary ... 69-72
Melnick, Jack 1929- ... 89-92
Melnyk, Z(inowii) Lew 1928- ... 41-44R
Meloan, Taylor Wells 1919- ... 45-48
Melone, Albert P(hilip) 1942- ... 109
Melone, Joseph J(ames) 1931- ... 13-14R
Meloney, William Brown 1905-1971
  Obituary ... 104
Meloon, Marion 1921- ... 65-68
Melosi, Martin Victor 1947- ... CANR-13
  Earlier sketch in CA 77-80
Melrose, Andrea La Sonde
  See Anastos, Andrea La Sonde (Melrose)
Melsa, James L(ouis) 1938- ... 104
Melson, Robert 1937- ... 85-88
Melton, David 1934- ... CANR-22
  Earlier sketch in CA 69-72
Melton, J(ohn) Gordon 1942- ... 110
Melton, John L. 1920- ... 11-12R
Melton, Julius W(emyss), Jr. 1933- ... 23-24R
Melton, William 1920- ... 37-40R
Meltsner, Arnold J(erry) 1931- ... 57-60
Meltsner, Michael (Charles) 1937-
  Brief entry ... 108
Meltzer, Allan H. 1928- ... CANR-18
  Earlier sketches in CA 5-6R, CANR-3
Meltzer, Bernard N(athan) 1916- ... 23-24R
Meltzer, David 1937- ... CANR-6
  Earlier sketch in CA 9-10R
  See also DLB 16
Meltzer, Jack 1921- ... 119
Meltzer, Milton 1915- ... 13-14R
  See also SATA 1, 50
  See also SAAS 1
  See also DLB 61
  See also CLC 26
  See also CLR 13
Meltzer, Morton F. 1930- ... 23-24R
Meltzer, Peter D. 1951- ... 120
Meltzoff, Julian 1921- ... 23-24R
Meltzoff, Nancy 1952- ... 93-96
Meluch, R(ebecca) M. 1956- ... 109
Melvill, Harald 1895- ... 7-8R
Melville, Alan
  See Caverhill, William Melville
Melville, Annabelle McConnell 1910- ... 7-8R
Melville, Anne
  See Potter, Margaret (Newman)
Melville, Herman 1819-1891 ... DLB-3
  See also CDALB 1640-1865
  See also SSC 1
Melville, J. Keith 1921- ... 53-56
Melville, James
  See Martin, (Roy) Peter
Melville, Jennie
  See Butler, Gwendoline Williams
Melville, Jock Leslie
  See Leslie-Melville, John D.
Melville, John D. Leslie
  See Leslie-Melville, John D.
Melville, Joy 1932- ... 85-88
Melville, Keith 1945- ... 41-44R
Melvin, A(rthur) Gordon 1894- ... 9-10R
Melvin, Ann (Patricia) Skene
  See Skene-Melvin, Ann (Patricia)
Melvin, (Lewis) David (St. Columb) Skene
  See Skene-Melvin, (Lewis) David (St.
  Columb)
Melvin, Herman 1819-1891 ... DLB-3
Melwani, Murli Das 1939- ... 61-64
Melwood, Mary
  See Lewis, E. M.
Melzack, Ronald 1929- ... CANR-15
  Earlier sketch in CA 41-44R
  See also SATA 5
Melzer, John Henry 1908-1967 ... CAP-1
  Earlier sketch in CA 13-14
Melzi, Robert C. 1915- ... 37-40R
Memling, Carl 1918-1969 ... CANR-4
  Earlier sketch in CA 4R
  See also SATA 6
Memmi, Albert 1920- ... CANR-14
  Earlier sketch in CA 81-84
Mena, Janet Gonzalez
  See Gonzalez-Mena, Janet
Menacker, Julius 1933- ... 41-44R
Menaker, Daniel 1941- ... 65-68
Menard, H(enry) William 1920-1986 ... 37-40R
  Obituary ... 118
Menard, Jean 1930(?)-1977 Obituary ... 69-72
Menard, Orville D. 1933- ... 23-24R
Menasco, Norman
  See Guin, Wyman (Woods)
Menashe, Louis 1935- ... 21-22R
Menashe, Samuel 1925- ... 115
  Brief entry ... 111
Mencher, Melvin 1927- ... 73-76
Menchin, Robert S(tanley) 1923- ... CANR-13
  Earlier sketch in CA 21-22R
Mencken, H(enry) L(ouis) 1880-1956
  Brief entry ... 105
  See also DLB 11, 29, 63
  See also TCLC 13
Menczer, Bela 1902-1983 Obituary ... 110
Mendel, Arthur 1905-1979 ... 41-44R
  Obituary ... 89-92
Mendel, Arthur P(aul) 1927-1988 ... 13-14R
  Obituary ... 124
Mendel, Douglas H(eusted), Jr. 1921- ... 19-20R
Mendel, Jo
  See Bond, Gladys Baker
  and Gilbertson, Mildred Geiger
Mendel, Sydney 1925- Brief entry ... 109
Mendel, Werner M(ax) 1927- ... CANR-11
  Earlier sketch in CA 21-22R
Mendele mocher seforim
  See Abramowitz, Shalom Jacob
Mendell, Clarence W(hittlesey)
  1883-1970 ... CAP-1
  Earlier sketch in CA 19-20
Mendeloff, Henry 1917-1984 Obituary ... 113
Mendelowitz, Daniel M(arcus) 1905- ... 11-12R
Mendels, Joseph 1937- ... 29-32R
Mendels, Ora 1936- ... 124
Mendelsohn, Allan R(obert) 1928- ... 45-48
Mendelsohn, Everett (Irwin) 1931- ... CANR-11
  Earlier sketch in CA 19-20R
Mendelsohn, Felix, Jr. 1906- ... 29-32R
Mendelsohn, Harold 1923- ... 49-52
Mendelsohn, Jack 1918- ... CANR-1
  Earlier sketch in CA 4R
Mendelsohn, Martin 1935- ... CANR-13
  Earlier sketch in CA 33-36R
Mendelsohn, Michael John 1931- ... 85-88
Mendelsohn, Oscar (Adolf) 1896-1978 ... CANR-22
  Earlier sketch in CA 9-10R
Mendelsohn, Pamela 1944- ... 101
Mendelsohn, Stefan 1930(?)-1987(?)
  Obituary ... 122
Mendelson, Edward 1946- ... CANR-11
  Earlier sketch in CA 65-68
Mendelson, Lee 1933- ... 33-36R
Mendelson, Mary Adelaide (Jones) 1917- ... 85-88
Mendelson, Morris 1922- ... CANR-2
  Earlier sketch in CA 7-8R
Mendelson, Wallace 1911- ... 3R
Mendelssohn, Kurt (Alfred Georg)
  1906-1980 ... CANR-7
  Obituary ... 105
  Earlier sketch in CA 53-56
Mendenhall, George E(mery) 1916- ... 33-36R
Mendenhall, James Edgar 1903-1971
  Obituary ... 33-36R
Mendenhall, John D(ale) 1911(?)-1983
  Obituary ... 110
Mendenhall, Ruth Dyar 1912- ... 65-68
Mendenhall, Thomas C(orwin II) 1910- ... 115
Mendes-France, Pierre 1907-1982 ... 81-84
  Obituary ... 108
Mendez, Charlotte (Walker) 1935- ... 120
Mendl, Robert William Sigismund
  1892-1983 Obituary ... 111
Mendlovitz, Saul H. 1925- ... 23-24R
Mendonca, Susan
  See Smith, Susan Vernon
  See also SATA 45
Mendonsa, Eugene L(ouis) 1942- ... 109
Mendoza, George 1934- ... 73-76
  See also SATA 39, 41
Mendoza, Manuel G. 1936- ... 53-56
Mendras, Henri 1927- ... CANR-13
  Earlier sketch in CA 73-76
Mendus, Susan 1951- ... 123
Menen, (Salvator) Aubrey (Clarence)
  1912- ... CANR-2
  Earlier sketch in CA 2R
Menendez, Albert J(ohn) 1942- ... CANR-22
  Earlier sketches in CA 53-56, CANR-7
Menendez Pidal, Ramon 1869-1968
  Obituary ... 116
Meneses, Enrique 1929- ... CANR-11
  Earlier sketch in CA 25-28R
Meng, Heinz (Karl) 1924- ... 69-72
  See also SATA 13
Meng, John J(oseph) 1906-1988 Obituary ... 124
Menges, Karl (Heinrich) 1908- ... 37-40R
Menhennet, Alan 1933- ... 97-100
Menikoff, Barry 1939- ... 37-40R
Menkiti, Ifeanyi 1940- ... 65-68
Menkus, Belden 1931- ... 19-20R
Mennel, Robert McKisson 1938-
  Brief entry ... 109
Mennell, Stephen (John) 1944- ... 107
Menning, J(ack) H(arwood) 1915- ... 23-24R
Menninger, Edwin A(rnold) 1896- ... 11-12R
Menninger, Karl A. 1893- ... 19-20R
Menninger, W(illiam) Walter 1931- ... 111
Menninger, Walt
  See Menninger, W(illiam) Walter
Menninger, William C(laire) 1899-1966
  Obituary ... 25-28R
Mennis, Bernard 1938- ... 41-44R
Menolascino, Frenk J(oseph) 1930- ... 73-76
Menon, K(umara) P(admanabha)
  S(ivasankara) 1898-1982 ... CANR-5
  Obituary ... 108
  Earlier sketch in CA 7-8R
Menon, R(amakrishna) Rabindranath
  1927- ... CANR-11
  Earlier sketch in CA 65-68
Menotti, Gian Carlo 1911- ... 104
  See also SATA 29
Menshikov, Marina 1928(?)-1979
  Obituary ... 93-96
Mensoian, Michael G(eorge), Jr. 1927- ... 85-88
Menton, Seymour 1927- ... 45-48
Mentor
  See Lake, Kenneth R(obert)
Mentschikoff, Soia 1915-1984 Obituary ... 113
Mentzer, Michael J(ohn) 1949- ... 118
Menuhin, Hephzibah 1920-1981 Obituary ... 108
Menuhin, Yehudi 1916- ... CANR-2
  Earlier sketch in CA 45-48
  See also SATA 40
Menut, Albert D. 1894- ... 25-28R
Menville, Douglas 1935- ... 57-60
Menyuk, Paula 1929- ... 37-40R
Menzel, Barbara Jean 1946- ... 114
Menzel, Donald H(oward) 1901-1976 ... CAP-2
  Obituary ... 69-72
  Earlier sketch in CA 21-22
Menzel, Johanna
  See Meskill, Johanna Menzel
Menzel, Paul T(heodore) 1942- ... 53-56
Menzel, Roderich 1907- ... 93-96
Menzies, Edna O(live) 1921- ... 116
Menzies, Elizabeth G(rant) C(ranbrook)
  1915- ... 19-20R
Menzies, Robert Gordon 1894-1978 ... 81-84
  Obituary ... 77-80
Menzies, William W(atson) 1931-
  Brief entry ... 110
Meo, Lucy Dorothy 1920- ... 25-28R
Meras, Phyllis 1931- ... CANR-16
  Earlier sketch in CA 41-44R
Merbaum, Michael 1933- ... 65-68
Mercatante, Anthony Stephen 1940- ... 41-44R
Mercer, Blaine (Eugene) 1921- ... CANR-2
  Earlier sketch in CA 2R
Mercer, Cecil William 1885-1960 Obituary ... 114
Mercer, Charles (Edward) 1917- ... CANR-2
  Earlier sketch in CA 1R
  See also SATA 16
Mercer, Colin 1952- ... 117
Mercer, David 1928-1980 ... CANR-23
  Obituary ... 102
  Earlier sketch in CA 11-12R
  See also DLB 13
  See also CLC 5
Mercer, James L(ee) 1936- ... 112
Mercer, Jane R. ... 45-48
Mercer, Jean 1941- ... CANR-13
  Earlier sketch in CA 33-36R
Mercer, Jessie ... CANR-2
  Earlier sketch in CA 2R
Mercer, Joan Bodger 1923- ... 101
Mercer, John 1704-1768 ... DLB-31
Mercer, Johnny 1906-1976 Obituary ... 65-68
Mercer, Marilyn 1923- Brief entry ... 107
Mercer, Paul 1950- ... 111
Mercer, Virginia Fletcher 1916- ... 7-8R
Mercey, Arch Andrew 1906-1980 Obituary ... 102
Merchant, Carolyn 1936- ... 113
Merchant, Jane (Hess) 1919-1972 ... CANR-4
  Obituary ... 33-36R
  Earlier sketch in CA 3R
Merchant, Larry 1931- ... 102
Merchant, Paul
  See Ellison, Harlan
Mercie, Jean-Luc Henri 1939- ... 49-52
Mercier, Jean Doyle 1916- ... 4R
Mercier, Vivian (Herbert Samuel) 1919- ... 81-84
Mercouri, Melina 1925- Brief entry ... 106
Mercury
  See Allen, Cecil J(ohn)
Meredith, Anne
  See Malleson, Lucy Beatrice
Meredith, Arnold
  See Hopkins, Kenneth
Meredith, Char(lotte) 1921- ... 106
Meredith, David William
  See Miers, Earl Schenck
Meredith, Dean
  See Dean, Edith M(ae)
Meredith, Don 1938- ... 102
Meredith, George 1828-1909 Brief entry ... 117
  See also DLB 18, 35, 57
  See also TCLC 17
Meredith, George (Marlor) 1923- ... CANR-4
  Earlier sketch in CA 11-12R
Meredith, George Patrick 1904-1978
  Obituary ... 108
Meredith, James Howard 1933- ... 77-80
Meredith, Joel L(yman) 1935- ... 116
Meredith, Joseph C(harlton) 1914- ... 53-56
Meredith, Nicolete
  See Stack, Nicolete
Meredith, Owen
  See Lytton, Edward Robert Bulwer
Meredith, Richard C(arlton) 1937- ... 85-88
Meredith, Robert (King) 1923- ... 5-6R
Meredith, Robert C(hidester) 1921- ... 7-8R
Meredith, Roy 1914(?)-1984 Obituary ... 111
Meredith, Scott 1923- ... CANR-3
  Earlier sketch in CA 11-12R
Meredith, William (Morris) 1919- ... CANR-6
  Earlier sketch in CA 9-10R
  See also DLB 5
  See also CLC 4, 13, 22
Merewitz, Leonard (Alan) 1943- ... 69-72
Merezhkovsky, Zinaida
  See Gippius, Zinaida (Nikolayevna)
Mergen, Bernard 1937- ... 112
Merick, Wendell S. 1928(?)-1988
  Obituary ... 124
Merideth, Robert 1935- ... 49-52
Merillat, Herbert C(hristian) L(aing)
  1915- ... 29-32R
Merin, Peter
  See Bihalji-Merin, Oto
Meringoff, Laurene Krasny
  See Brown, Laurene Krasny
Meritt, Lucy Shoe 1906- ... 37-40R
Merivale, Patricia 1934- ... 29-32R
Meriwether, James B. 1928- ... 15-16R
Meriwether, Lee 1862-1966 Obituary ... 116
Meriwether, Louise ... 77-80
  See also SATA 31
  See also DLB 33
Merk, Frederick 1887-1977 ... 41-44R
  Obituary ... 73-76
Merkel, Miles Adair 1929- ... 53-56
Merkin, Daphne 1954- ... 123
  See also CLC 44
Merkin, Donald H. 1945- ... 69-72
Merkin, Robert (Bruce) 1947- ... 109
Merkl, Peter H(ans) 1932- ... CANR-24
  Earlier sketches in CA 7-8R, CANR-7
Merkle, Edgar A. 1900(?)-1984 Obituary ... 113
Merkle, Judith A(stria) 1942- ... 105
Merklinghaus, Michele 1965- ... 116
Merle, Robert (Jean Georges) 1908- ... 93-96
Merleau-Ponty, Maurice 1908-1961 ... 114
  Obituary ... 89-92
Merli, Frank J(ohn) 1929- Brief entry ... 113
Merlin, Arthur
  See Blish, James (Benjamin)
Merlin, Christina
  See Heaven, Constance
Merlin, David
  See Moreau, David Merlin
Merlin, Jan 1925- ... 108
Merlin, Mark D(avid) ... 118
Merlin, Samuel 1910- ... 115
Merlis, George 1940- ... 33-36R
Merliss, Reuben 1915- ... 19-20R

Merman, Ethel
See Zimmermann, Ethel Agnes
Mermin, Samuel 1912- 53-56
Merne, Oscar James 1943- 102
Mernit, Susan 1953- 69-72
Meroff, Deborah 1948- 89-92
Merrell, James L(ee) 1930- 19-20R
Merrell, Jo Ann 1945- 113
Merrell, Karen Dixon 1936- CANR-6
Earlier sketch in CA 13-14R
Merrell, V(ictor) Dallas 1936- 11-12R
Merrens, H(arry) Roy 1931- 11-12R
Merrett, Robert James 1944- 111
Merriam, Alan P(arkhurst) 1923-1980 ... CANR-1
Earlier sketch in CA 2R
Merriam, Eve 1916- 5-6R
See also SATA 3, 40
See also DLB 61
See also CLR 14
Merriam, Harold G(uy) 1883-1981 ..... CANR-10
Earlier sketch in CA 61-64
Merriam, Robert E(dward) 1918- 7-8R
Merrick, Gordon 1916- CANR-11
Earlier sketch in CA 13-14R
Merrick, Hugh
See Meyer, H(arold) A(lbert)
Merrick, William 1916-1969 .... CAP-1
Earlier sketch in CA 11-12
Merril, Judith 1923- CANR-15
Earlier sketch in CA 15-16R
Merrill, Antoinette June 1912- 45-48
Merrill, Arch 1895(?)-1974 Obituary 49-52
Merrill, Boynton, Jr. 1925- 69-72
Merrill, David W. 1928- 108
Merrill, Dean 1943- CANR-8
Earlier sketch in CA 61-64
Merrill, Dick
See Merrill, Henry Tindall
Merrill, Edward C(lifton), Jr. 1920- 23-24R
Merrill, Edward H. 1903- CAP-1
Earlier sketch in CA 15-16
Merrill, Francis E(llsworth) 1904-1969 .... CAP-1
Earlier sketch in CA 19-20
Merrill, Frederick Thayer 1905-1974
Obituary 53-56
Merrill, Harwood F(erry) 1904-1984
Obituary 114
Merrill, Henry Tindall 1897-1982 Obituary .. 108
Merrill, James (Ingram) 1926- CANR-10
Earlier sketch in CA 13-14R
See also DLB 5
See also DLBY 85
See also CLC 2, 3, 6, 8, 13, 18, 34
Merrill, James M(ercer) 1920- 11-12R
Merrill, Jane 1946- SATA-42
Merrill, Jean (Fairbanks) 1923- CANR-4
Earlier sketch in CA 1R
See also SATA 1
Merrill, John Calhoun 1924- CANR-13
Earlier sketch in CA 73-76
Merrill, John N(igel) 1943- CANR-22
Earlier sketch in CA 103
Merrill, M. David 1937- CANR-16
Earlier sketch in CA 41-44R
Merrill, P. J.
See Roth, Holly
Merrill, Phil
See Filstrup, Jane (Merrill)
Merrill, Robert 1919- 81-84
Merrill, Robert 1944- 89-92
Merrill, Thomas F. 1932- 29-32R
Merrill, Toni
See Merrill, Antoinette June
Merrill, Walter M. 1915- CANR-13
Earlier sketch in CA 23-24R
Merrill, Wilfred K. 1903- 11-12R
Merrill, William C. 1934- 29-32R
Merriman, Alex
See Silverberg, Robert
Merriman, Ann Lloyd 1934- 77-80
Merriman, Beth
See Taylor, Demetria
Merriman, Jerry Johnson 1939- 25-28R
Merriman, John 1924-1974 Obituary 104
Merriman, Pat
See Atkey, Philip
Merritt, A.
See Merritt, Abraham (P.)
Merritt, Abraham (P.) 1884-1943
Brief entry 120
Merritt, Dixon Lanier 1879-1972
Obituary 33-36R
Merritt, Don 1945- CANR-22
Earlier sketch in CA 106
Merritt, E. B.
See Waddington, Miriam
Merritt, Helen Henry 1920- 19-20R
Merritt, James D. 1934- 33-36R
Merritt, LeRoy Charles 1912-1970 .... CAP-2
Earlier sketch in CA 33-36
Merritt, Miriam 1925- 19-20R
Merritt, Muriel 1905- 69-72
Merritt, Ray E(merson), Jr. 1948- 73-76
Merritt, Raymond H(arland) 1936- 85-88
Merritt, Richard L(awrence) 1933- 41-44R
Merry, Henry J(ohn) 1908- 37-40R
Mersand, Joseph 1907- CANR-1
Earlier sketch in CA 3R
Mersereau, John, Jr. 1925- CANR-2
Earlier sketch in CA 1R
Mersky, Roy M. 1925- 37-40R
Mersmann, James Frederick 1938- 61-64
Mertens, Lawrence E(dwin) 1929- 85-88
Mertens, Thomas R(obert) 1930- CANR-6
Earlier sketch in CA 57-60
Mertins, Herman, Jr. 1931- 41-44R
Mertins, (Marshall) Louis 1885-1973 .....41-44R
Merton, Andrew H(arris) 1944- 107
Merton, Giles
See Curran, Mona (Elisa)
Merton, Robert K(ing) 1910- 41-44R
Merton, Stephen 1912- 21-22R
Merton, Thomas 1915-1968 .... CANR-22
Obituary 25-28R
Earlier sketch in CA 5-6R
See also DLB 48
See also DLBY 81
See also CLC 1, 3, 11, 34
Mertz, Barbara (Gross) 1927- CANR-11
Earlier sketch in CA 21-22R
See also SATA 49
Mertz, Richard R(olland) 1927- 23-24R
Merwe, A. v.d.
See Geyl, Pieter (Catharinus Arie)
Merwin, Decie 1894-1961 Obituary 111
See also SATA 32
Merwin, W(illiam) S(tanley) 1927- CANR-15
Earlier sketch in CA 15-16R
See also DLB 5
See also CLC 1, 2, 3, 5, 8, 13, 18, 45
Mery, Fernand 1897- 105
Merz, Charles 1893-1977 Obituary 73-76
Merzer, Meridee 1947- 102
Mesa-Lago, Carmelo 1934- CANR-10
Earlier sketch in CA 25-28R
Meserve, Walter Joseph, Jr. 1923- CANR-1
Earlier sketch in CA 2R
Meshack, B(illie) A(ugusta) 1922- 93-96
Meshenberg, Michael J(ay) 1942- CANR-16
Earlier sketch in CA 93-96
Meske, Eunice Boardman 1926- CANR-4
Earlier sketch in CA 11-12R
Meskill, Johanna Menzel 1930- 19-20R
Meskill, Robert 1918(?)-1970 Obituary 104
Mesquita, Bruce James Bueno de
See Bueno de Mesquita, Bruce James
Messager, Charles 1882-1971 Obituary 93-96
Messdeck Annie
See Coade, Jessie
Messegue, Maurice 1921- 103
Messel, Harry 1922- CANR-21
Earlier sketch in CA 103
Messenger, Charles (Rynd Milles)
1941- CANR-13
Earlier sketch in CA 73-76
Messenger, Elizabeth Margery (Esson)
1908- CAP-1
Earlier sketch in CA 11-12
Messent, Peter Ronald 1949- 106
Messer, Alfred A(mes) 1922- 29-32R
Messer, Ronald Keith 1942- 57-60
Messer, Sarah Carlin 1924(?)-1984
Obituary 112
Messer, Thomas M. 1920- 111
Brief entry 106
Messerer, Asaf Mikhailovich 1903- 104
Messerli, Douglas 1947- 116
Messerli, Jonathan C. 1926- 41-44R
Messick, Dale 1906- SATA-48
Messick, Hank
See Messick, Henry H(icks)
Messick, Henry H(icks) 1922- CANR-2
Earlier sketch in CA 45-48
Messieres, Nicole de
See de Messieres, Nicole
Messing, Shep 1949- Brief entry 111
Messing, Simon D(avid) 1922- 57-60
Messinger, C. F. 1913- 21-22R
Messinger, Sheldon L(eopold) 1925- 25-28R
Messmer, Otto 1892(?)-1983 Obituary 111
See also SATA 37
Messner, Fred(rick) R(ichard) 1926- 13-14R
Messner, Gerald 1935- 29-32R
Messner, Johannes 1891-1984 Obituary 112
Messner, Reinhold 1944- CANR-15
Earlier sketch in CA 81-84
Messner, Stephen Dale 1936- 23-24R
Mesta, Perle 1893(?)-1975 Obituary 57-60
Mesthene, Emmanuel George 1920- 77-80
Meston, John 1915(?)-1979 Obituary 85-88
Meszaros, Istvan 1930- CANR-9
Earlier sketch in CA 57-60
Meta
See Tomkiewicz, Mina
Metalious, Grace (de Repentigny)
1924-1964 .... CAP-2
Earlier sketch in CA 21-22
Metaxas, B(asil) N(icolas) 1925- 37-40R
Metcalf, E(ugene) W(esley) 1945- 65-68
Metcalf, George R. 1914- 25-28R
Metcalf, John 1938- 113
See also DLB 60
See also CLC 37
Metcalf, Kenneth N(olan) 1923-1965 ....5-6R
Metcalf, Keyes DeWitt 1889-1983 ....19-20R
Obituary 111
Metcalf, Lawrence E(ugene) 1915- 21-22R
Metcalf, Paul 1917- CANR-17
Earlier sketches in CA 45-48, CANR-1
Metcalf, Peter 116
Metcalf, Suzanne
See Baum, L(yman) Frank
Metcalf, Thomas R. 1934- 15-16R
Metcalf, Vicky 1901- 89-92
Metcalfe, John Wallace 1901-1982
Obituary 107
Metcalfe, Steve 1953- 108
Metereau, Rebecca Bell
See Bell-Metereau, Rebecca
Metesky, George
See Hoffman, Abbie
Methold, Kenneth (Walter) 1931- 13-14R
Methvin, Eugene H. 1934- 29-32R
Metos, Thomas H(arry) 1932- 93-96
See also SATA 37
Metraux, Guy S(erge) 1917- 9-10R
Metraux, Rhoda 1914- 57-60
Metress, James F(rancis)
See Metress, Seamus P.
Metress, Seamus P. 1933- CANR-21
Earlier sketches in CA 57-60, CANR-6
Metropolis, Nicholas Constantine 1915- 110
Mets, David Raymond 1928- 118
Mettler, George B(arry) 1934- 93-96
Metwally, M(okhtar) M(ohamed)
1939- CANR-15
Earlier sketch in CA 65-68
Metz, Donald L(ehman) 1935- 21-22R
Metz, Donald S(hink) 1916- 45-48
Metz, Jerred 1943- CANR-22
Earlier sketch in CA 104
Metz, Leon C(laire) 1930- CANR-16
Earlier sketches in CA 45-48, CANR-1
Metz, Lois Lunt 1906- CAP-1
Earlier sketch in CA 9-10
Metz, Mary (Seawell) 1937- 53-56
Metz, Mary Haywood 1939- CANR-15
Earlier sketch in CA 85-88
Metz, Robert (Henry) 1928- CANR-13
Earlier sketch in CA 61-64
Metz, William 1918- 77-80
Metzdorf, Robert F(rederic) 1912-1975
Obituary 57-60
Metzger, Barbara 1944- 110
Metzger, Bruce Manning 1914- CANR-4
Earlier sketch in CA 9-10R
Metzger, Charles R(eid) 1921- 25-28R
Metzger, Erika A(lma) 1933- 33-36R
Metzger, H(owell) Peter 1931- Brief entry ... 107
Metzger, Michael M(oses) 1935- 21-22R
Metzger, Norman 1924- CANR-9
Earlier sketch in CA 53-56
Metzger, Philip W. 1931- 45-48
Metzger, Robert 1950- 117
Metzger, Stanley D. 1916- 9-10R
Metzger, Thomas A(lbert) 1933- 97-100
Metzger, Walter P. 1922- CANR-17
Earlier sketch in CA 61-64
Metzker, Isaac 1901- 45-48
Metzler, Ken(neth Theodore) 1929- CANR-4
Earlier sketch in CA 53-56
Metzler, Lloyd A(ppleton) 1913- 104
Metzler, Paul 1914- CANR-6
Earlier sketch in CA 57-60
Metzner, Ralph 1936- 69-72
Metzner, Seymour 1924- 23-24R
Meudt, Edna Kritz 1906- CANR-9
Earlier sketch in CA 15-16R
Meurice, Blanca
See von Block, Bela W(illiam)
Meux, Milton O(tto) 1930- 45-48
Meves, Christa 1925- CANR-24
Earlier sketch in CA 93-96
Mew, Charlotte (Mary) 1870-1928
Brief entry 105
See also DLB 19
See also TCLC 8
Mewburn, Martin
See Hitchin, Martin Mewburn
Mewhinney, Bruce 1949- 118
Mews, Hazel 1909-1975 .... CAP-2
Earlier sketch in CA 29-32
Mews, Siegfried 1933- CANR-22
Earlier sketches in CA 57-60, CANR-7
Mewshaw, Michael 1943- CANR-7
Earlier sketch in CA 53-56
See also DLBY 80
See also CLC 9
Mey, Jacob Lovis
See Meij, Jacob Lovis
Meyen, Edward L. 1937- 33-36R
Meyendorff, John 1926- CANR-9
Earlier sketch in CA 21-22R
Meyer, Agnes E(lizabeth Ernst) 1887-1970
Obituary 29-32R
Meyer, Albert Julius 1919-1983 Obituary ... 111
Meyer, Alfred (Herman) 1893- CAP-1
Earlier sketch in CA 13-14
Meyer, Alfred George 1920- 19-20R
Meyer, Armin Henry 1914- 85-88
Meyer, Ben F. 1927- CANR-14
Earlier sketch in CA 37-40R
Meyer, Bernard C. 1910- 73-76
Meyer, Bernard F. 1891(?)-1975
Obituary 57-60
Meyer, Carl S(tamm) 1907-1972 .... CAP-1
Earlier sketch in CA 15-16
Meyer, Carol H. 1924- CANR-13
Earlier sketch in CA 73-76
Meyer, Carolyn 1935- CANR-2
Earlier sketch in CA 49-52
See also SATA 9
Meyer, Charles R. 1920- 33-36R
Meyer, Charles R(obert) 1926- 69-72
Meyer, Clarence 1903- 97-100
Meyer, D. Swing 1938- 19-20R
Meyer, David R. 1943- 65-68
Meyer, Donald (Burton) 1923- 23-24R
Meyer, Donald H(arvey) 1935- Brief entry ... 113
Meyer, Doris 1942- 89-92
Meyer, Duane Gilbert 1926- 5-6R
Meyer, Edith Patterson 1895- CANR-1
Earlier sketch in CA 2R
See also SATA 5
Meyer, Elizabeth C(ooper) 1958- 69-72
Meyer, Ellen Hope 1928- 119
Meyer, Erika 1904- 73-76
Meyer, Eugene 1875-1959 .... DLB-29
Meyer, F(ranklyn) E(dward) 1932- 4R
See also SATA 9
Meyer, Frank S(traus) 1909-1972 .... CAP-1
Obituary 33-36R
Earlier sketch in CA 9-10
Meyer, Fred(erick Robert) 1922-1985 57-60
Obituary 117
Meyer, George H(erbert) 1928- 116
Meyer, Gladys (Eleanor) 1908-1986
Obituary 118
Meyer, H(arold) A(lbert) 1898-1980 ..... CANR-4
Obituary 102
Earlier sketch in CA 7-8R
Meyer, H. K. Houston
See Meyer, Heinrich
Meyer, Harold D(iedrich) 1892-1974(?) ... CAP-2
Earlier sketch in CA 19-20
Meyer, Harold G. 1909(?)-1986 Obituary ... 118
Meyer, Heinrich 1904-1977 49-52
Obituary 85-88
Meyer, Herbert W(alter) 1892- CAP-2
Earlier sketch in CA 33-36
Meyer, Herman 1911- 23-24R
Meyer, Howard N(icholas) 1914- 13-14R
Meyer, Jean Shepherd SATA-11
Meyer, Jerome Sydney 1895-1975 ...... CANR-4
Obituary 57-60
Earlier sketch in CA 2R
See also SATA 3, 25
Meyer, Joachim-Ernst 1917- 57-60
Meyer, John Robert 1927- CANR-9
Earlier sketch in CA 13-14R
Meyer, June
See Jordan, June
Meyer, Karl E(rnest) 1928- CANR-1
Earlier sketch in CA 3R
Meyer, Kathleen Allan 1918- 123
See also SATA 46
Meyer, Lawrence R(obert) 1941- 73-76
Meyer, Leonard B. 1918- 13-14R
Meyer, Lillian Nicholson 1917(?)-1983
Obituary 109
Meyer, Linda D(oreen) 1948- CANR-16
Earlier sketch in CA 93-96
Meyer, Louis A(lbert) 1942- 37-40R
See also SATA 12
Meyer, Mabel H. 1890(?)-1976 Obituary ..61-64
Meyer, Marie-Louise 1936- 97-100
Meyer, Mary Keysor 1919- 102
Meyer, Michael (Leverson) 1921- CANR-13
Earlier sketch in CA 25-28R
Meyer, Michael A. 1937- 21-22R
Meyer, Michael C. 1935- CANR-10
Earlier sketch in CA 21-22R
Meyer, Nicholas 1945- CANR-7
Earlier sketch in CA 49-52
Meyer, Philip (Edward) 1930- CANR-10
Earlier sketch in CA 65-68
Meyer, Renate 1930- 53-56
See also SATA 6
Meyer, Robert H. 1934- 37-40R
Meyer, Roy W(illard) 1925- 19-20R
Meyer, Ruth F(ritz) 1910- CAP-2
Earlier sketch in CA 23-24
Meyer, Stewart (Martin) 1947- 118
Meyer, Susan E. 1940- CANR-19
Earlier sketches in CA 45-48, CANR-2
Meyer, Thomas 1947- CANR-1
Earlier sketch in CA 49-52
Meyer, William Eugene 1923- 45-48
Meyer, William R(obert) 1949- 77-80
Meyerhoff, Arthur E(dward) 1895-1986
Obituary 120
Meyerhoff, Howard A(ugustus) 1899- CAP-2
Earlier sketch in CA 19-20
Meyering, Ralph A. 1930- 29-32R
Meyer-Meyrink, Gustav 1868-1932
Brief entry 117
Meyerowitz, Eva (Leonie) L(ewin-)
R(ichter) 11-12R
Meyerowitz, Patricia 1933- 23-24R
Meyers, Albert L. 1904(?)-1981 Obituary ... 102
Meyers, Bert(ram) 1928-1979 101
Meyers, Carlton R(oy) 1922- 57-60
Meyers, Carol L(yons) 1942- 113
Meyers, Carole Terwilliger 1945- 69-72
Meyers, Cecil H(arold) 1920- 29-32R
Meyers, David W. 1942- 29-32R
Meyers, Edward 1934- 101
Meyers, Eric M(ark) 1940- 110
Meyers, Gertrude Barlow 1902- 3R
Meyers, Jeffrey 1939- 73-76
See also CLC 39
Meyers, Joan Simpson 1927- CANR-14
Earlier sketch in CA 19-20R
Meyers, Lawrence Stanley 1943- 57-60
Meyers, Marvin 1921- Brief entry 108
Meyers, Mary Ann 1937- 116
Meyers, Michael Jay 1946- 65-68
Meyers, Robert Rex 1923- 19-20R
Meyers, Roy (Lethbridge) 1910-1974 .... CAP-2
Earlier sketch in CA 25-28
Meyers, Ruth S(chlaff) 1923- 117
Meyers, Susan 1942- CANR-13
Earlier sketch in CA 21-22R
See also SATA 19
Meyers, Susan
See Falk, Susan Meyers
Meyers, Walter E(arl) 1939- CANR-6
Earlier sketch in CA 53-56
Meyerson, Edward L(eon) 1904-1980 .. CANR-12
Earlier sketch in CA 61-64
Meyerson, Martin 1922- Brief entry 115
Meynell, Alice (Christina Gertrude
Thompson) 1847-1922 Brief entry 104
See also DLB 19
See also TCLC 6

Meynell, Francis Meredith Wilfrid
1891-1975 .... CAP-2
Obituary 57-60
Earlier sketch in CA 19-20
Meynell, Laurence Walter 1899- CANR-15
Earlier sketch in CA 81-84
Meyners, J. Robert 1922- 104
Meynier, Yvonne (Pollet) 1908- 73-76
See also SATA 14
Meyrink, Gustav
See Meyer-Meyrink, Gustav
See also TCLC 21
Meyrink, Gustav Meyer
See Meyer-Meyrink, Gustav
Meza, Pedro Thomas 1941- 37-40R
Mezerick, Avrahm G. 1901-1986 Obituary .. 119
Mezey, Michael L(loyd) 1943- 118
Mezey, Robert 1935- CANR-7
Earlier sketch in CA 57-60
See also SATA 33
Mezvinsky, Edward M. 1937- 103
Mezzrow, Mezz
See Mezzrow, Milton
Mezzrow, Milton 1890(?)-1972 ....37-40R
Miall, Robert
See Burke, John (Frederick)
Mian, Mary (Lawrence Shipman)
1902- SATA-47
Micale, Albert 1913- SATA-22
Micallef, Benjamin A(nthony) 1925-1980 ...53-56
Obituary 103
Micallef, John 1923- 25-28R
Micaud, Charles Antoine 1910- 5-6R
Miceli, Frank 1932- 57-60
Miceli, Vincent P(eter) 1915- Brief entry 114
Michael, David J. 1944- 29-32R
Michael, Franz H(enry) 1907- CANR-4
Earlier sketch in CA 7-8R
Michael, George 1919- 41-44R
Michael, Henry N(athaniel) 1913- 33-36R
Michael, Ian (Lockie) 1915- 104
Michael, James
See Scagnetti, Jack
Michael, Manfred
See Winterfeld, Henry
Michael, Paul Martin 1934- CANR-10
Earlier sketch in CA 19-20R
Michael, Phyllis C(allender) 1908- CANR-2
Earlier sketch in CA 7-8R
Michael, S(tanley) T(heodore) 1912- 13-14R
Michael, Thomas A. 1933- 33-36R
Michael, Tom
See Michael, Thomas A.
Michael, William B(urton) 1922- 45-48
Michael, Wolfgang F(riedrich) 1909- ... CANR-14
Earlier sketch in CA 41-44R
Michaeles, M. M.
See Golding, Morton J(ay)
Michaelides, Constantine E. 1930- 25-28R
Michaelis, David (Tead) 1957- 114
Michaelis, John U(dell) 1912- 69-72
Michaelis-Jena, Ruth
See Ratcliff, Ruth
Michaels, Barbara
See Mertz, Barbara (Gross)
Michaels, Carolyn Leopold
See Leopold, Carolyn Clugston
Michaels, Dale
See Rifkin, Shepard
Michaels, Fern
See Anderson, Roberta
and Kuczkir, Mary
Michaels, J. Ramsey 1931- 116
Michaels, Joanne 1950- CANR-23
Earlier sketch in CA 107
Michaels, Joanne Louise
See Teitelbaum, Michael
Michaels, Joe
See Saltzman, Joseph
Michaels, Kasey
See Seidick, Kathryn A(melia)
Michaels, Kristin
See Williams, Jeanne
Michaels, Leonard 1933- CANR-21
Earlier sketch in CA 61-64
See also CLC 6, 25
Michaels, Lynn
See Strongin, Lynn
Michaels, Neal
See Teitelbaum, Michael
Michaels, Norman 97-100
Michaels, Philip
See van Rjndt, Philippe
Michaels, Ralph
See Filicchia, Ralph
Michaels, Sidney R(amon) 1927- 19-20R
Michaels, Ski
See Pellowski, Michael (Joseph)
Michaels, Steve
See Avallone, Michael (Angelo), Jr.
Michaelson, L(ouis) W. 1917- CANR-14
Earlier sketch in CA 77-80
Michaely, Michael 1928- 103
Michalczyk, John Joseph 1941- 104
Michalopoulos, Andre 1897- CAP-2
Earlier sketch in CA 23-24
Michalos, Alex C. 1935- 37-40R
Michalowski, Kazimierz 1901-1981
Obituary 108
Michalski, John 1934- 25-28R
Michalson, Carl (Donald, Jr.) 1915-1965 .... 4R
Michaud, Charles Regis 1910- CAP-2
Earlier sketch in CA 19-20
Michaud, Stephen G(age) 1948- 109
Michaux, Henri 1899-1984 85-88
Obituary 114
See also CLC 8, 19
Michaux, William W(hitehead) 1919- 41-44R
Miche, Giuseppe
See Bochenski, Joseph M.
Micheaux, Oscar 1884-1951 .... DLB-50
Michel, Anna 1943- 85-88
See also SATA 40, 49
Michel, Beth
See Dubus, Elizabeth Nell
Michel, Georges 1926- 25-28R
Michel, Henri (Jules) 1907- CANR-19
Earlier sketches in CA 53-56, CANR-4
Michel, Joseph 1922- CANR-13
Earlier sketch in CA 25-28R
Michel, Michel Georges
See Georges-Michel, Michel
Michel, Pierre 1934- 57-60
Michel, Sandra (Seaton) 1935- 77-80
Michel, Sandy
See Michel, Sandra (Seaton)
Michel, (Milton) Scott 1916- 4R
Michel, Walter 1922- 81-84
Micheli, Lyle Joseph 1940- CANR-20
Earlier sketch in CA 97-100
Micheline, Jack 1929- 122
Brief entry 114
See also DLB 16
Michell, John (F.) 1933- CANR-23
Earlier sketch in CA 107
Michelman, Herbert 1913-1980 Obituary ... 102
Michelman, Irving S(imon) 1917- 69-72
Michelmore, Peter 1930- CANR-7
Earlier sketch in CA 5-6R
Michelon, L. C. 1918- CANR-1
Earlier sketch in CA 45-48
Michels, Caroll Chesy 1943- 117
Michelson, Edward J(ulias) 1915- 77-80
Michelson, Florence B. CAP-2
Earlier sketch in CA 21-22
Michelson, Peter 1937- CANR-1
Earlier sketch in CA 45-48
Michelson, Stephan 1938- 93-96
Michelson, William M. 1940- 33-36R
Michener, Charles D(uncan) 1918- 117
Michener, Charles Thomson 1940- 104
Michener, James A(lbert) 1907(?)- CANR-21
Earlier sketch in CA 5-6R
See also DLB 6
See also CLC 1, 5, 11, 29
See also AITN 1
Michie, Allan (Andrew) 1915-1973
Obituary 45-48
Michie, Donald 1923- 121
Michie, James 1927- Brief entry 116
Michman, Ronald D(avid) 1931- CANR-7
Earlier sketch in CA 57-60
Mickel, Emanuel John, Jr. 1937- 37-40R
Mickelsen, A(nton) Berkeley 1920- 9-10R
Mickelsen, Olaf 1912- 19-20R
Mickelson, Sig 1913- 111
Micken, Charles M. 1918- 13-14R
Mickey, Paul A(lbert) 1937- CANR-1
Earlier sketch in CA 49-52
Mickiewicz, Ellen Propper 1938- CANR-24
Earlier sketches in CA 23-24R, CANR-9
Micklejohn, George 1717(?)-1818 ...... DLB-31
Micklem, Nathaniel 1888-1976 103
Micklish, Rita 1931- 49-52
See also SATA 12
Mickolus, Edward F(rancis) 1950- 106
Micks, Marianne H(offman) 1923- CANR-12
Earlier sketch in CA 19-20R
Micunovic, Veljko 1916-1982 109
Obituary 107
Middeldorf, Ulrich Alexander 1901-1983
Obituary 109
Middendorf, John Harlan 1922- 104
Middlebrook, David
See Rosenus, Alan (Harvey)
Middlebrook, Diane Wood 1939- CANR-15
Earlier sketch in CA 81-84
Middlebrook, Jonathan 1940- 65-68
Middlebrook, (Norman) Martin 1932- .. CANR-14
Earlier sketch in CA 37-40R
Middlekauff, Robert (Lawrence) 1929-
Brief entry 112
Middleman, Ruth J. Rosenbloom 1923- 104
Middlemas, Keith
See Middlemas, Robert Keith
Middlemas, Robert Keith 1935- CANR-12
Earlier sketch in CA 29-32R
Middlemiss, Robert (William) 1938- ... CANR-12
Earlier sketch in CA 73-76
Middleton, Bernard C(hester) 1924- 41-44R
Middleton, Christopher 1926- 15-16R
See also DLB 40
See also CLC 13
Middleton, David L. 1940- 37-40R
Middleton, Drew 1914(?)- Brief entry 110
Middleton, George 1880-1967 Obituary ..25-28R
Middleton, Michael (Humfrey) 1917- 124
Middleton, Nigel (Gordon) 1918- 45-48
Middleton, O(sman) E(dward) 1925- 81-84
Middleton, Richard 1945- 109
Middleton, Stanley 1919- CANR-21
Earlier sketch in CA 25-28R
See also DLB 14
See also CLC 7, 38
Middleton, Thomas 1580-1627 .... DLB-58
Middleton-Murry, Colin
See Middleton-Murry, John (Jr.)
Middleton-Murry, John (Jr.) 1926- CANR-3
Earlier sketch in CA 7-8R
Middleton Murry, Mary
See Murry, Mary Middleton
Midelfort, H(ans) C(hristian) Erik 1942- 45-48
Midgett, Elwin W. 1911- CAP-2
Earlier sketch in CA 29-32
Midgett, Wink
See Midgett, Elwin W.
Midgley, David A(lan) 1898- 19-20R
Midgley, E(rnest) B(rian) F(rancis) 1927- ..93-96
Midgley, Graham 1923- 73-76
Midgley, Louis C(asper) 1931- 41-44R
Midgley, Mary 1919- CANR-20
Earlier sketch in CA 89-92
Midlarsky, Manus I(ssacher) 1937- 57-60
Midler, Bette 1945- 106
Midtlyng, Joanna 1927- 61-64
Midwinter, E(ric) C(lare) 1932- 29-32R
Mieczkowski, Bogdan 1924- 111
Miegel, Agnes 1879-1964 .... DLB-56
Miel, Alice Marie 1906- CANR-20
Earlier sketches in CA 3R, CANR-5
Mielke, Arthur W(illard) 1912-1978 ..... CANR-4
Earlier sketch in CA 2R
Mielziner, Jo 1901-1976 45-48
Obituary 65-68
Miernyk, William Henry 1918- 19-20R
Miers, Earl Schenck 1910-1972 .... CANR-2
Obituary 37-40R
Earlier sketch in CA 3R
See also SATA 1, 26
Miers, Suzanne (Doyle) 1922- 61-64
Mierzenski, Stanislaw 1903-1964 .... 2R
Miethe, Terry Lee 1948- 105
Miewald, Robert D(ale) 1938- 117
Migdal, Joel S(amuel) 1945- CANR-6
Earlier sketch in CA 57-60
Migdalski, Edward C(harles) 1918- CANR-4
Earlier sketch in CA 9-10R
Migliore, R. Henry 1940- 110
Migliorini, Bruno 1896-1975 Obituary 116
Miglis, John 1950- CANR-20
Earlier sketch in CA 81-84
Mignani, Rigo 1921- 37-40R
Migueis, Jose Rodrigues 1901- CLC-10
Miguez-Bonino, Jose 1924- 49-52
Mihailovich, Vasa D. 1926- CANR-14
Earlier sketch in CA 41-44R
Mihajlov, Mihajlo 1934- Brief entry 105
Mihalas, Dimitri M(anuel) 1939- CANR-4
Earlier sketch in CA 53-56
Mihaly, Mary E(llen) 1950- 97-100
Mihanovich, Clement Simon 1913- 7-8R
Mikan, Baron
See Barba, Harry
Mikdashi, Zuhayr 1933- CANR-17
Earlier sketch in CA 89-92
Mikes, George 1912-1987 .... CANR-6
Obituary 123
Earlier sketch in CA 11-12R
Mikesell, Arthur M. 1932- 13-14R
Mikesell, John L(ee) 1942- 102
Mikesell, Marvin Wray 1930- CANR-4
Earlier sketch in CA 3R
Mikesell, Raymond F(rech) 1913- CANR-19
Earlier sketches in CA 4R, CANR-4
Mikesell, Rufus Merrill 1893-1972 .... CAP-2
Earlier sketch in CA 25-28
Mikesell, William H(enry) 1887-1969 ..... CAP-2
Earlier sketch in CA 19-20
Mikhail, E(dward) H(alim) 1928- CANR-14
Earlier sketch in CA 37-40R
Mikhalkov, Sergei Vladimirovich 1913-
Brief entry 116
Miki, Chihan
See Naruse, Mikio
Mikkelsen, Ejnar 1881(?)-1971 Obituary ..29-32R
Miklowitz, Gloria D. 1927- CANR-10
Earlier sketch in CA 25-28R
See also SATA 4
Mikolaycak, Charles 1937- CANR-23
Earlier sketches in CA 61-64, CANR-8
See also SATA 9
See also SAAS 4
Mikulas, William Lee 1942- 53-56
Mikus, Joseph A(ugust) 1909- 61-64
Milberg, Warren H(oward) 1941- 109
Milbrath, Lester W(alter) 1925- CANR-4
Earlier sketch in CA 11-12R
Milburn, George 1906-1966 Obituary 109
Milburn, Josephine F(ishel) 1928- CANR-13
Earlier sketch in CA 21-22R
Milburn, Joyce 1953- 114
Milch, Robert J(effrey) 1938- 25-28R
Milcsik, Margie 1950- 110
Mild, Warren (Paul) 1922- CANR-8
Earlier sketch in CA 23-24R
See also SATA 41
Mildo, Albert 1945- CANR-21
Earlier sketch in CA 73-76
Mileck, Joseph 1922- 107
Milenkovitch, Michael M. 1932- 37-40R
Miles, Angela R(ose) 1946- 122
Miles, (Louise) Bebe 1924-1980 .... CANR-9
Earlier sketch in CA 61-64
Miles, Betty 1928- CANR-20
Earlier sketches in CA 3R, CANR-5
See also SATA 8
Miles, Beverly Parkhurst 1940- 107
Miles, Charles 1894- 5-6R
Miles, David H(olmes) 1940- 57-60
Miles, Dorien K(lein) 1915- CANR-8
Earlier sketch in CA 61-64
Miles, Edwin A(rthur) 1926- 1R
Miles, Elliot
See Ludvigsen, Karl (Eric)
Miles, Elton (Roger) 1917- 37-40R
Miles, Gary Britten 1940- 102
Miles, George C(arpenter) 1904-1975
Obituary 61-64
Miles, Herbert J(ackson) 1907- 23-24R
Miles, Ian (Douglas) 1948- 115
Miles, John
See Bickham, Jack M(iles)
Miles, Josephine 1911-1985 .... CANR-2
Obituary 116
Earlier sketch in CA 3R
See also DLB 48
See also CLC 1, 2, 14, 34, 39
Miles, Joyce C(rudgington) 1927- 105
Miles, Judith Mary (Huhta) 1937- 65-68
Miles, Keith
See Tralins, S(andor) Robert
Miles, Leland, (Weber, Jr.) 1924- 15-16R
Miles, Margaret R(uth) 1937- 117
Miles, Mary Lillian (Brown) 1908- 15-16R
Miles, Matthew B(ailey) 1926- CANR-15
Earlier sketch in CA 81-84
Miles, Michael W. 1945- 33-36R
Miles, Miska
See Martin, Patricia Miles
Miles, O. Thomas 1923- 21-22R
Miles, (Mary) Patricia 1930- CANR-11
Earlier sketch in CA 69-72
See also SATA 29
Miles, Peter
See Miles, Richard
Miles, Richard 1938- 105
Miles, Robert H. 1944- 118
Miles, Robert L(ee) 1939- 107
Miles, Russell Hancock 1895- CAP-1
Earlier sketch in CA 9-10
Miles, Stanley 1911-1987 Obituary 123
Miles, Sylva
See Miles, Dorien K(lein)
and Mularchyk, Sylva
Miles, T(homas) R(ichard) 1923- CANR-17
Earlier sketches in CA 49-52, CANR-1
Milestone, Lewis 1895-1980 Obituary 101
Miletus, Rex
See Burgess, M(ichael) R(oy)
Milford, D(avid) S(umner) 1905-1984
Obituary 113
Milford, Nancy 1938- 29-32R
Milgate, Rodney Armour 1934- 107
Milgram, Gail Gleason 1942- 29-32R
Milgram, Morris 1916- 73-76
Milgram, Stanley 1933-1984 105
Obituary 114
Milgrom, Harry 1912- CANR-3
Earlier sketch in CA 4R
See also SATA 25
Milgrom, Jacob 1923- 53-56
Milhaud, Darius 1892-1974 Obituary 49-52
Milhaven, John Giles 1927- 29-32R
Milhous, Katherine 1894-1977 Obituary 104
See also SATA 15
Milhouse, Paul W(illiam) 1910- CANR-11
Earlier sketch in CA 25-28R
Mili, Gjon 1904-1984 Obituary 112
Milic, Louis T(onko) 1922- 23-24R
Milio, Nancy 1938- CANR-13
Earlier sketch in CA 29-32R
Militant
See Sandburg, Carl (August)
Militello, Pietro
See Natali, Alfred Maxim
Milius, John 1945- 101
See also DLB 44
Milkomane, George Alexis Milkomanovich
1903- CANR-20
Earlier sketch in CA 104
Milks, Harold Keith 1908-1979 108
Obituary 93-96
Mill, C. R.
See Crnjanski, Milos
Mill, John Stuart 1806-1873 .... DLB-55
Milland, Jack
See Milland, Ray
Milland, Ray 1908(?)-1986 Obituary 118
Brief entry 113
Millar, Barbara F. 1924- 25-28R
See also SATA 12
Millar, Fergus 1935- CANR-20
Earlier sketches in CA 13-14R, CANR-5
Millar, George Reid 1910- 73-76
Millar, Gilbert John 1939- 104
Millar, J(ohn) Halket 1899- 11-12R
Millar, James Primrose Malcolm 1893- ... CAP-1
Earlier sketch in CA 9-10
Millar, James R(obert) 1936- 29-32R
Millar, Jeff(ery Lynn) 1942- CANR-11
Earlier sketch in CA 69-72
Millar, (Minna Henrietta) Joy 1914- 93-96
Millar, Kenneth 1915-1983 .... CANR-16
Obituary 110
Earlier sketch in CA 9-10R
See also DLB 2
See also DLBY 83
See also CLC 14
Millar, Margaret (Ellis Sturm) 1915- ... CANR-16
Earlier sketch in CA 13-14R
Millar, Ronald (Graeme) 1919- 73-76
Millar, T(homas) B(ruce) 29-32R
Millard, A(lan) R(alph) 1937- CANR-11
Earlier sketch in CA 25-28R
Millard, Charles W(arren III) 1932-
Brief entry 115
Millard, Gregory B. 1947(?)-1984
Obituary 114
Millard, Joe
See Millard, Joseph (John)
Millard, Joseph (John) 1908- 15-16R
Millay, Edna St. Vincent 1892-1950
Brief entry 104
See also DLB 45
See also TCLC 4
Millbank, Captain H. R.
See Ellis, Edward S(ylvester)

INDEX

Millburn, Cynthia
See Brooks, Anne Tedlock
Milldyke, (John) William 1937-1983 ... 77-80
Obituary ... 111
Millen, Clifford H. 1901(?)-1972 Obituary ... 104
Millender, Dharathula H(ood) 1920- ... 19-20R
Miller, Abraham H(irsh) 1940- ... 104
Miller, Al 1936- ... 65-68
Miller, Alan Robert 1929- ... 73-76
Miller, Alan W. 1926- ... 29-32R
Miller, Albert G(riffith) 1905-1982 ... CANR-1
Obituary ... 107
Earlier sketch in CA 3R
See also SATA 12, 31
Miller, Albert Jay 1928- ... CANR-1
Earlier sketch in CA 45-48
Miller, Alden D(ykstra) 1940(?)-1984
Obituary ... 113
Miller, Alden Holmes 1906-1965 Obituary ... 109
Miller, Alfred W. 1893(?)-1983 Obituary ... 111
Miller, Alice P(atricia McCarthy) ... 29-32R
See also SATA 22
Miller, Anita 1926- ... 111
Miller, Ann
See Collier, Lucille Ann
Miller, Arthur 1915- ... CANR-2
Earlier sketch in CA 2R
See also DLB 7
See also CDALB 1941-1968
See also CLC 1, 2, 6, 10, 15, 26, 47
See also AITN 1
Miller, Arthur B(urton) 1922- ... 37-40R
Miller, Arthur R(aphael) 1934- Brief entry ... 114
Miller, Arthur S(elwyn) 1917- ... CANR-11
Earlier sketch in CA 69-72
Miller, Barbara D(iane) 1948- ... CANR-23
Earlier sketch in CA 106
Miller, Barbara S(toler) 1940- ... CANR-11
Earlier sketch in CA 25-28R
Miller, Barry 1946- ... 33-36R
Miller, Benj.
See Loomis, Noel M(iller)
Miller, Benjamin F(rank) 1907-1971 ... CANR-4
Obituary ... 29-32R
Earlier sketch in CA 3R
Miller, Bernard S. 1920- ... 106
Miller, Beulah Montgomery 1917- ... 61-64
Miller, (H.) Bill(y) 1920-1961 ... 108
Miller, Bill D. 1936- ... 102
Miller, Brent C(arlton) 1947- ... 112
Miller, (Harvey) Brown 1943- ... 101
Miller, Byron Strongman 1912(?)-1978
Obituary ... 77-80
Miller, C(larence) William 1914- ... 53-56
Miller, Calvin 1936- ... CANR-13
Earlier sketch in CA 21-22R
Miller, Caroline 1903- ... DLB-9
Miller, Carroll H(iram) 1907-197(?) ... CAP-1
Earlier sketch in CA 19-20
Miller, Casey (Geddes) 1919- ... 69-72
Miller, Cecilia Parsons 1909- ... CANR-12
Earlier sketch in CA 23-24R
Miller, Cecille (Boyd) 1908- ... 11-12R
Miller, Char
See Miller, Frank L(ubbock) IV
Miller, Charles 1918- ... 77-80
Miller, Charles A. 1937- ... 29-32R
Miller, Charles D(avid) 1942- ... 69-72
Miller, Charles E. 1929- ... 33-36R
Miller, Charles Henderson 1905- ... CAP-2
Earlier sketch in CA 19-20
Miller, Charles Leslie 1908- ... 49-52
Miller, Christian 1920- ... 108
Miller, Clarence H(arvey) 1930- ... 102
Miller, Clarence J(ohn) 1916- ... CANR-13
Earlier sketch in CA 23-24R
Miller, Clement (Albin) 1915- ... 41-44R
Miller, Conrad
See Strung, Norman
Miller, D(ean) A(rthur) 1931- ... 23-24R
Miller, Daniel Adlai II 1918- ... 37-40R
Miller, David E(ugene) 1909-1978 ... 45-48
Obituary ... 103
Miller, David Harry 1938- ... 57-60
Miller, David L(eroy) 1936- ... 49-52
Miller, David Lee 1951- ... 122
Miller, David Louis 1903-1986 ... 23-24R
Obituary ... 118
Miller, David Merlin 1934- ... 93-96
Miller, David W. 1940- ... 49-52
Miller, Deborah Uchill 1944- ... 116
Miller, Delbert C(harles) 1913- ... 25-28R
Miller, Don 1923- ... SATA-15
Miller, Donald 1893-1986 Obituary ... 119
Miller, Donald 1934- ... 97-100
Miller, Donald C(urtis) 1933- ... CANR-6
Earlier sketch in CA 57-60
Miller, Donald Eugene 1929- ... CANR-24
Earlier sketch in CA 106
Miller, Donald George 1909- ... CANR-4
Earlier sketch in CA 5-6R
Miller, Donald L(ane) 1918- ... 19-20R
Miller, Doris R.
See Mosesson, Gloria R(ubin)
Miller, Dorothy (Ryan)
See Ryan, Dorothy (Barger)
Miller, Douglas T(aylor) 1937- ... 21-22R
Miller, E. Ethelbert 1950- ... DLB-41
Miller, E. F.
See Pohle, Robert W(arren), Jr.
Miller, E(dwin) S(hepard) 1904- ... 45-48
Miller, E(ugene) Willard 1915- ... CANR-17
Earlier sketches in CA 5-6R, CANR-2
Miller, Ed(die) L(eRoy) 1937- ... 37-40R
Miller, Eddie
See Miller, Edward
Miller, Edna Anita 1920- ... 112
See also SATA 29
Miller, Edward 1905-1974 ... CAP-2
Earlier sketch in CA 25-28
See also SATA 8
Miller, Edwin Haviland 1918- ... 110
Miller, Elizabeth 1933- ... 117
See also SATA 41
Miller, Elizabeth Kubota 1932- ... 15-16R
Miller, Elizabeth Maxfield 1910- ... 45-48
Miller, Ella May 1915- ... CANR-11
Earlier sketch in CA 23-24R
Miller, Elwood E. 1925- ... 122
Miller, Ethel Prince 1893- ... CAP-1
Earlier sketch in CA 13-14
Miller, Eugene 1925- ... 101
See also SATA 33
Miller, Eugenia
See Mandelkorn, Eugenia Miller
Miller, F(rederick) W(alter) G(ascoyne)
1904- ... CANR-11
Earlier sketch in CA 25-28R
Miller, Florence B. 1895(?)-1976
Obituary ... 69-72
Miller, Floyd C. 1912- ... CANR-2
Earlier sketch in CA 4R
Miller, Forrestt A. 1931- ... 25-28R
Miller, Frances A. 1937- ... 123
See also SATA 46
Miller, Francis Pickens 1895- ... 69-72
Miller, Frank 1925-1983 Obituary ... 109
Miller, Frank
See Loomis, Noel M(iller)
Miller, Frank L(ubbock) IV 1951- ... 113
Miller, G. R.
See Judd, Frederick Charles
Miller, Gabriel 1948- ... 115
Miller, Gary M(ichael) 1941- ... 113
Miller, Gene Edward 1928- ... 97-100
Miller, Genevieve 1914- ... 19-20R
Miller, Geoffrey 1921-1984 Obituary ... 112
Miller, Geoffrey Samuel 1945- ... 104
Miller, George (Eric) 1943- ... CANR-14
Earlier sketch in CA 73-76
Miller, George A(rmitage) 1920- ... CANR-1
Earlier sketch in CA 4R
Miller, George H(all) 1919- ... 33-36R
Miller, George Louquet 1934- ... 89-92
Miller, Gerald 1928(?)-1970 Obituary ... 104
Miller, Gerald R(aymond) 1931- ... CANR-16
Earlier sketch in CA 93-96
Miller, Glenn T(homas) 1942- Brief entry ... 110
Miller, Gordon W(esley) 1918- ... 89-92
Miller, Gus
See Miller, Gustavus Hindman
Miller, Gustavus Hindman 1857-1929
Brief entry ... 120
Miller, Haskell M(orris) 1910- ... CAP-2
Earlier sketch in CA 23-24
Miller, Heather Ross 1939- ... CANR-5
Earlier sketch in CA 13-14R
Miller, Helen Hill 1899- ... 11-12R
Miller, Helen M(arkley) ... CANR-2
Earlier sketch in CA 2R
See also SATA 5
Miller, Helen Topping 1884-1960 Obituary ... 109
See also SATA 29
Miller, Henry (Valentine) 1891-1980 ... 9-10R
Obituary ... 97-100
See also DLB 4, 9
See also DLBY 80
See also CLC 1, 2, 4, 9, 14, 43
Miller, Henry Knight 1920- ... CANR-2
Earlier sketch in CA 3R
Miller, Herbert E(lmer) 1914- ... CANR-11
Earlier sketch in CA 19-20R
Miller, Hope Ridings ... 25-28R
Miller, Howard S(mith) 1936- ... 29-32R
Miller, Hubert John 1927- ... 37-40R
Miller, Hugh 1897(?)-1979 Obituary ... 89-92
Miller, Hugh 1937- ... CANR-12
Earlier sketch in CA 61-64
Miller, Hugh Milton 1908- ... 33-36R
Miller, Isabel
See Routsong, Alma
Miller, J(ohn) D(onald) B(ruce) 1922- ... CANR-13
Earlier sketch in CA 73-76
Miller, J. Dale 1923- ... 105
Miller, J(oseph) Hillis 1928- ... 85-88
See also DLB 67
Miller, J. Innes 1892-1976 ... CAP-2
Earlier sketch in CA 29-32
Miller, J(ames) Maxwell 1937- ... 110
Miller, J(ames) P. 1919- ... 25-28R
See also AITN 1, 2
Miller, J(ohn) Robert 1913- ... 45-48
Miller, James C(lifford) III 1942- ... CANR-10
Earlier sketch in CA 25-28R
Miller, James Edwin (Jr.) 1920- ... CANR-1
Earlier sketch in CA 3R
Miller, James G(rier) 1916- ... 23-24R
Miller, Jane (Judith) 1925- ... CANR-13
Earlier sketch in CA 77-80
See also SATA 15
Miller, Jason 1939(?)- ... 73-76
See also DLB 7
See also CLC 2
See also AITN 1
Miller, Jay W(ilson) 1893- ... CAP-1
Earlier sketch in CA 13-14
Miller, Jean Baker 1927- Brief entry ... 108
Miller, Jerome K. 1931- ... 105
Miller, Jim Wayne 1936- ... CANR-20
Earlier sketches in CA 49-52, CANR-1
Miller, Joan (Irene) 1944- ... 117
Miller, Joan M(ary) 1941- ... 108
Miller, John (Laurence) 1947- ... 93-96
Miller, John
See Samachson, Joseph
Miller, John C. 1916(?)-1979 Obituary ... 89-92
Miller, John Chester 1907- ... 73-76
Miller, John Harold 1925- ... 7-8R
Miller, John N. 1933- ... 33-36R
Miller, John P(earse, Jr.) 1943- ... 69-72
Miller, Johnny
See Miller, John (Laurence)
Miller, Jolonda 1945- ... 108
Miller, Jon (Gordon) 1921- ... 53-56
Miller, Jonathan (Wolfe) 1934- ... 115
Brief entry ... 110
Miller, Jordan Y(ale) 1919- ... CANR-2
Earlier sketch in CA 3R
Miller, Joseph C(alder) 1939- ... 93-96
Miller, Judi 1941- ... 106
Miller, Judith von Daler 1940- ... 69-72
Miller, Julian M. 1922-1976 Obituary ... 69-72
Miller, June 1923- ... 89-92
Miller, K(eith) Bruce 1927- ... 33-36R
See also AITN 1
Miller, Karl (Fergus Connor) 1931-
Brief entry ... 107
Miller, Kenneth Dexter 1887- ... CAP-1
Earlier sketch in CA 13-14
Miller, Kenneth E(ugene) 1926- ... 23-24R
Miller, Kent S(amuel) 1927- Brief entry ... 109
Miller, Lanora 1932- ... 61-64
Miller, Lenore 1924- ... 107
Miller, Leon Gordon 1917- ... 104
Miller, Levi 1944- ... 113
Miller, Lewis (Ames) 1928- ... 93-96
Miller, Liam 1924(?)-1987 Obituary ... 122
Miller, Libuse (Lukas) 1915-1973 ... 3R
Obituary ... 103
Miller, Lillian B(eresnack) 1923- ... CANR-9
Earlier sketch in CA 21-22R
Miller, Linda B. 1937- ... 21-22R
Miller, Linda Lael 1949- ... 110
Miller, Luree 1926- ... 93-96
Miller, Lyle L. 1919- ... CANR-6
Earlier sketch in CA 13-14R
Miller, Lynn F(ieldman) 1938- ... 109
Miller, Lynn H(ellwarth) 1937- ... 37-40R
Miller, Lynne (Ellen) 1945- ... 89-92
Miller, Madelaine Hemingway 1904- ... 103
See also AITN 2
Miller, Madge 1918- ... 123
Brief entry ... 117
Miller, Mara (Jayne) 1944- ... 97-100
Miller, Marc S(cott) 1947- ... 105
Miller, Margaret J.
See Dale, Margaret J(essy) Miller
Miller, Margery
See Welles, Margery Miller
Miller, Marilyn (Jean) 1925- ... SATA-33
Miller, Marilyn McMeen
See Brown, Marilyn McMeen Miller
Miller, Marjorie M. 1922- ... 101
Miller, Marshall Lee 1942- ... CANR-9
Earlier sketch in CA 57-60
Miller, Martha
See Ivan, Martha Miller Pfaff
Miller, Martha Porter 1897(?)-1983
Obituary ... 109
Miller, Martin A. 1938- ... 65-68
Miller, Mary
See Northcott, (William) Cecil
Miller, Mary Agnes 1888(?)-1973
Obituary ... 45-48
Miller, Mary Beth 1942- ... 61-64
See also SATA 9
Miller, Mary Britton 1883-1975 ... CANR-16
Obituary ... 57-60
Earlier sketch in CA 2R
Miller (Riis), Maurine 1910- ... 118
Miller, Max (Carlton) 1899-1967 ... CANR-16
Obituary ... 25-28R
Earlier sketch in CA 3R
Miller, May 1899- ... DLB-41
Miller, Melvin H(ull) 1920- ... 15-16R
Miller, Merl Kem 1942- ... 111
Miller, Merle 1919-1986 ... CANR-4
Obituary ... 119
Earlier sketch in CA 9-10R
See also AITN 1
Miller, Merton Howard 1923- Brief entry ... 109
Miller, Michael M. 1910(?)-1977
Obituary ... 73-76
Miller, Milt 1916- ... 117
Miller, Minnie M. 1899-1983 ... CAP-2
Obituary ... 110
Earlier sketch in CA 21-22
Miller, Morris 1914- ... 19-20R
Miller, Muriel
See Minor, Muriel Miller
Miller, N(ewton) Edd 1920- ... 25-28R
Miller, Naomi 1928- ... 111
Miller, Natalie 1917-1976 ... SATA-35
Miller, Nathan 1927- ... CANR-4
Earlier sketch in CA 53-56
Miller, Neal E(lgar) 1909- ... 81-84
Miller, Nicole Puleo 1944- ... 49-52
Miller, Nina Hull 1894-1974 ... CAP-1
Earlier sketch in CA 9-10
Miller, Nolan 1912- ... 11-12R
Miller, Norman 1933- ... 37-40R
Miller, Norman C(harles) 1934- ... 37-40R
Miller, Nyle H. 1907- ... CAP-2
Earlier sketch in CA 23-24
Miller, Olga K(omarkova) 1908- ... 107
Miller, Orson K., Jr. 1930- Brief entry ... 110
Miller, Osborn (Maitland) 1896(?)-1979
Obituary ... 89-92
Miller, Oscar J. 1913- ... 37-40R
Miller, Patrick Dwight, Jr. 1935- ... 112
Miller, Paul Martin 1914- ... CANR-10
Earlier sketch in CA 19-20R
Miller, Paul R(ichard) 1929- ... 21-22R
Miller, Paul William 1926- ... 41-44R
Miller, Perry (Gilbert Eddy) 1905-1963
Obituary ... 93-96
See also DLB 17, 63
Miller, (Mitchell) Peter 1934- ... 37-40R
Miller, Peter M(ichael) 1942- ... 69-72
Miller, Philip L(ieson) 1906- ... CAP-1
Earlier sketch in CA 11-12
Miller, R(onald) Baxter 1948- ... 115
Miller, R(ay Stephans) June 1923- ... 65-68
Miller, R. S. 1936- ... 45-48
Miller, Randall Martin 1945- ... CANR-15
Earlier sketch in CA 81-84
Miller, Randolph Crump 1910- ... CANR-1
Earlier sketch in CA 3R
Miller, Raymond W(iley) 1895-1988
Obituary ... 124
Miller, Rene Fueloep
See Fueloep-Miller, Rene
Miller, Rene Fulop
See Fueloep-Miller, Rene
Miller, Rex 1929- ... 110
Miller, Richard (Connelly) 1925- ... 19-20R
Miller, Richard
See Pietschmann, Richard John III
Miller, Richard I(rwin) 1924- ... 41-44R
Miller, Richard S(herwin) 1930- ... 23-24R
Miller, Richard Ulric 1932- ... CANR-17
Earlier sketch in CA 41-44R
Miller, Rob(ert) Hollis 1944- ... 37-40R
Miller, Robert A(llen) 1932- ... 33-36R
Miller, Robert H(enry) 1889- ... 33-36R
Miller, Robert Henry 1938- ... 110
Miller, Robert Keith 1949- ... 114
Miller, Robert L. 1928- ... 25-28R
Miller, Robert Moats 1924- Brief entry ... 105
Miller, Robert Ryal 1923- ... 41-44R
Miller, Roger LeRoy 1943- Brief entry ... 107
Miller, Ron 1947- ... 117
Miller, Ronald E(ugene) 1933- ... 5-6R
Miller, Roy Andrew 1924- ... CANR-18
Earlier sketches in CA 7-8R, CANR-2
Miller, Ruby 1890(?)-1976 Obituary ... 65-68
Miller, Russell E(lliott) 1916- Brief entry ... 117
Miller, Ruth 1921- Brief entry ... 106
Miller, Ruth
See Jacobs, Ruth Harriet
Miller, Ruth White
See White, Ruth C.
Miller, S(eymour) M(ichael) 1922- ... 19-20R
Miller, Sally M. 1937- ... 45-48
Miller, Samuel Jefferson 1919- ... 53-56
Miller, Sandra (Peden) 1948- ... 115
Miller, Sandy
See Miller, Sandra (Peden)
See also SATA 35, 41
Miller, Shane 1907- ... CAP-2
Earlier sketch in CA 21-22
Miller, Shirley 1920- ... 93-96
Miller, Sigmund Stephen 1917- ... CANR-4
Earlier sketch in CA 3R
Miller, Stanley 1916(?)-1977 Obituary ... 69-72
Miller, Stanley L(loyd) 1930- ... 45-48
Miller, Stanley S. 1924- ... 13-14R
Miller, Stephen J(ohn) 1936- ... 33-36R
Miller, Stuart 1937- ... 41-44R
Miller, Stuart Creighton 1927- ... 33-36R
Miller, Sue 19(?)- ... CLC-44
Miller, Susan 1944- ... 107
Miller, Teresa 1952- ... 105
Miller, Thomas Lloyd 1913- ... 25-28R
Miller, Tom 1947- ... CANR-14
Earlier sketch in CA 73-76
Miller, Vassar 1924- ... CANR-4
Earlier sketch in CA 11-12R
Miller, Victor (Brooke) 1940- ... 107
Miller, Wade
See Miller, (H.) Bill(y)
and Wade, Robert (Allison)
Miller, Walter James 1918- ... 81-84
Miller, Walter M(ichael, Jr.) 1923- ... 85-88
See also DLB 8
See also CLC 4, 30
Miller, Warren 1921-1966 Obituary ... 25-28R
Miller, Warren E. 1924- ... CANR-11
Earlier sketch in CA 15-16R
Miller, Wayne Charles 1939- ... CANR-1
Earlier sketch in CA 45-48
Miller, Webb 1892-1940 ... DLB-29
Miller, William (Moseley) 1909- ... 81-84
Miller, William Alvin 1931- ... CANR-17
Earlier sketches in CA 49-52, CANR-1
Miller, William D. 1916- ... 15-16R
Miller, William Hugh 1905-1975 ... 2R
Miller, William McElwee 1892- ... CANR-6
Earlier sketch in CA 57-60
Miller, William Robert 1927-1970 ... CAP-1
Obituary ... 29-32R
Earlier sketch in CA 11-12
Miller, Wilma H(ildruth) 1936- ... CANR-12
Earlier sketch in CA 33-36R
Miller, Wright (Watts) 1903-1974 ... 19-20R
Obituary ... 120
Miller, Zane L. 1934- ... CANR-12
Earlier sketch in CA 25-28R
Millerson, Geoffrey L. 1931- ... 19-20R
Millet, Stanton 1931- ... 25-28R
Millett, Allan R(eed) 1937- ... 23-24R
Millett, Fred B(enjamin) 1890-1976
Obituary ... 61-64
Millett, John (Antill) 1922- ... CANR-20
Earlier sketch in CA 103
Millett, John D(avid) 1912- ... 104

Millett, Kate 1934- 73-76
See also AITN 1
Millett, Richard L(eroy) 1938- 117
Millgate, Jane 1937- 57-60
Millgate, Michael (Henry) 1929- 29-32R
Millgram, Abraham E(zra) 1901- 33-36R
Millham, C(harles) B(lanchard) 1936- 37-40R
Millhauser, Milton 1910- CAP-1
Earlier sketch in CA 15-16
Millhauser, Steven 1943- 111
Brief entry 110
See also DLB 2
See also CLC 21
Millhiser, Marlys (Joy) 1938- 53-56
Millican, Arthenia Jackson Bates 1920- 105
See also DLB 38
Millicent
See Jordan, Mildred Arlene
Millichap, Joseph R(obert) 1940- 116
Millies, Suzanne 1943- 49-52
Milligan, Edward Archibald 1903-1977 41-44R
Milligan, Spike
See Milligan, Terence Alan
Milligan, Terence Alan 1918- CANR-4
Earlier sketch in CA 9-10R
See also SATA 29
Milliken, Ernest Kenneth 1899- 7-8R
Milliken, Stephen F(rederick) 1928- 93-96
Milliken, William Mathewson 1889- CAP-2
Earlier sketch in CA 23-24
Millimaki, Robert H. 1931- 57-60
Millin, Sarah Gertrude 1889-1968 102
Obituary 93-96
Millington, Barry 1951- 119
Millington, Frances Ryan 1899-1977
Obituary 69-72
Millington, Patrick 1910-1982 Obituary 107
Millington, Roger 1939- 65-68
Million, Elmer M(ayse) 1912- 41-44R
Millis, Walter 1899-1968 CAP-1
Obituary 37-40R
Earlier sketch in CA 9-10
Millman, Lawrence 1946- CANR-17
Earlier sketch in CA 93-96
Millon, Henry (Armand) 1927- 97-100
Millon, Rene 1921- 116
Brief entry 113
Millon, Robert Paul 1932- 23-24R
Millon, Theodore 1929- 57-60
Mills, Alison 1951- 53-56
Mills, Barriss 1912- CANR-12
Earlier sketch in CA 25-28R
Mills, Belen Collantes 1930- 37-40R
Mills, Betty (Lidstrom) 1926- 11-12R
Mills, Brenda J. 1940- 120
Mills, C(harles) Wright 1916-1962
Obituary 107
Mills, Carley 1897-1962 2R
Obituary 103
Mills, Clarence A(lonzo) 1891-1974 CAP-1
Obituary 53-56
Earlier sketch in CA 15-16
Mills, Claudia 1954- 109
See also SATA 41, 44
Mills, Constance (Quinby) 1898-1987
Obituary 122
Mills, Daniel Quinn 1941- 112
Mills, David Harlow 1932- 104
Mills, Dorothy
See Howard, Dorothy Gray
Mills, Edward D(avid) 1915- CANR-19
Earlier sketches in CA 7-8R, CANR-4
Mills, G(len) E(arl) 1908- CAP-1
Earlier sketch in CA 13-14
Mills, Gary B(ernard) 1944- 81-84
Mills, George S(torginne) 1906- 97-100
Mills, Gordon H(arrison) 1914-1978
Obituary 117
Mills, Helen 1923- CANR-16
Earlier sketch in CA 97-100
Mills, Hilary (Paterson) 1950- 115
Mills, Irving 1894-1985 Obituary 115
Mills, J(anet) M(elanie) A(ilsa) 1894- 69-72
Mills, James R(obert) 1927- 85-88
Mills, Jeannie 1939- 93-96
Mills, John 1908- 108
Mills, John 1930- 81-84
Mills, John FitzMaurice 1917- 103
Mills, John W(illiam) 1933- 69-72
Mills, Leonard Russell 1917- 45-48
Mills, Liston O. 1928- 107
Mills, (William) Mervyn 1906- CAP-1
Earlier sketch in CA 11-12
Mills, Ralph J(oseph), Jr. 1931- CANR-18
Earlier sketches in CA 9-10R, CANR-3
Mills, Richard W. 1945- Brief entry 112
Mills, Robert P(ark) 1920-1986 97-100
Obituary 118
Mills, Terry Kenneth 1949- 107
Mills, Theodore M(ason) 1920- 23-24R
Mills, Watson Early 1939- 57-60
Mills, William 1935- Brief entry 118
Mills, William Donald 1925- 33-36R
Mills, Yaroslava Surmach 1925- SATA-35
Millstead, Thomas E. 106
See also SATA 30
Millstein, Rose Silverman 1903(?)-1975
Obituary 61-64
Millum, Trevor 1945- CANR-21
Earlier sketch in CA 104
Millward, Celia M(cCullough) 1935- 53-56
Millward, Eric (Geoffrey William) 1935- 65-68
Millward, John S(candrett) 1924- 13-14R
Milman, Donald S. 1924- Brief entry 111
Milman, Miriam 1928- 112
Milne, A(lan) A(lexander) 1882-1956
Brief entry 104
See also YABC 1
See also DLB 10
See also TCLC 6
See also CLR 1
Milne, Antony 1942- 101
Milne, Christopher (Robin) 1920- CANR-11
Earlier sketch in CA 61-64
See also AITN 2
Milne, Edward James 1915-1983 Obituary 109
Milne, Evander Mackay 1920- 7-8R
Milne, (Charles) Ewart 1903-1987 CANR-16
Obituary 121
Earlier sketch in CA 97-100
Milne, (William) Gordon 1921- 21-22R
Milne, Jean (Killgrove) 1920- 19-20R
Milne, Lorus J. CANR-14
Earlier sketch in CA 33-36R
See also SATA 5
Milne, Margery CANR-14
Earlier sketch in CA 33-36R
See also SATA 5
Milne, Roseleen 1945- CANR-13
Earlier sketch in CA 73-76
Milner, Christina 1942- 49-52
Milner, Clyde A. II 1948- 108
Milner, Esther 1918- 23-24R
Milner, Ian Frank George 1911- 104
Milner, Jay (Dunston) 1926- 4R
Milner, Lucille Bernheimer 1888(?)-1975
Obituary 61-64
Milner, Marion (Blackett) 1900- 11-12R
Milner, Michael
See Cooper, Saul
Milner, Murray, Jr. 1935- 41-44R
Milner, Neal A(lan) 1941- Brief entry 112
Milner, Richard B(ruce) 1941- 49-52
Milner, Ron(ald) 1938- CANR-24
Earlier sketch in CA 73-76
See also DLB 38
See also AITN 1
Milnes, Eric Charles 1912-1984 Obituary 112
Milnes, Richard Monckton 1809-1885 DLB-32
Milns, R(obert) D(avid) 1938- 33-36R
Milo, Ronald D(mitri) 1935- 25-28R
Milonas, Rolf
See Myller, Rolf
Miloradovich, Milo 1901(?)-1972
Obituary 37-40R
Milosh, Joseph E(dmund) 1936- 21-22R
Miloslavsky, Nikolai Dimitrievich Tolstoy
See Tolstoy (-Miloslavsky), Nikolai (Dimitrievich)
Milosz, Czeslaw 1911- CANR-23
Earlier sketch in CA 81-84
See also CLC 5, 11, 22, 31
Milotte, Alfred G(eorge) 1904- CAP-1
Earlier sketch in CA 19-20
See also SATA 11
Milsen, Oscar
See Mendelsohn, Oscar (Adolf)
Milson, Fred(erick William) 1912- 73-76
Milstead, Jessica L(ee) 1939- CANR-14
Earlier sketch in CA 33-36R
Milstead, John 1924- 49-52
Milstein, Mike M(yron) 1937- 81-84
Milton, Arthur 1922- 109
Milton, Charles R(udolph) 1925- 53-56
Milton, David Scott 1934- CANR-13
Earlier sketch in CA 73-76
Milton, Hilary (Herbert) 1920- CANR-21
Earlier sketches in CA 57-60, CANR-6
See also SATA 23
Milton, Jack
See Kimbro, John M.
Milton, John R(onald) 1924- 33-36R
See also SATA 24
Milton, Joyce 1946- 106
See also SATA 41
Milton, Mark
See Pelton, Robert W(ayne)
Milton, Oliver
See Hewitt, Cecil Rolph
Milunsky, Aubrey 1936- 103
Milverton, Charles A.
See Penzler, Otto
Milward, Alan S. 1935- 45-48
Milward, Peter 1925- 101
Mims, Forrest M(arion) III 1944- CANR-16
Earlier sketch in CA 97-100
Mims, Lambert C. 1930- 29-32R
Mims, Roddey Earl 1936(?)-1982
Obituary 108
Minadeo, Richard (William) 1929- 25-28R
Minahan, John 1933- CANR-2
Earlier sketch in CA 45-48
Minale, Marcello 1938- 108
Minar, David W(illiam) 1925-1973
Obituary 111
Minarik, Else Holmelund 1920- 73-76
See also SATA 15
Minarik, John Paul 1947- CANR-13
Earlier sketch in CA 73-76
Mincer, Jacob 1922- Brief entry 114
Minchinton, W(alter) E(dward) 1921- CANR-12
Earlier sketch in CA 29-32R
Mincieli, Rose Laura 1912- CANR-4
Earlier sketch in CA 5-6R
Minckler, (Sherwood) Leon 1906- 57-60
Mindel, Eugene D. 1934- 41-44R
Mindell, Earl L(awrence) 1940- 105
Mindlin, Murray 1924(?)-1987 Obituary 122
Mindszenty, Jozsef 1892-1975 65-68
Obituary 57-60
Mindt, Heinz R. 1940- Brief entry 115
Minear, Paul Sevier 1906- CANR-3
Earlier sketch in CA 4R
Minear, Richard H(offman) 1938- 33-36R
Minehaha, Cornelius
See Wedekind, (Benjamin) Frank(lin)
Mineka, Francis Edward 1907- Brief entry 106
Miner, Caroline Eyring 1907- CANR-11
Earlier sketch in CA 25-28R
Miner, Charles S(ydney) 1906- CAP-1
Earlier sketch in CA 19-20
Miner, Dwight Carroll 1904-1978
Obituary 81-84
Miner, Earl (Roy) 1927- CANR-1
Earlier sketch in CA 2R
Miner, H. Craig 1944- CANR-16
Earlier sketches in CA 45-48, CANR-1
Miner, (Opal) Irene Sevrey (Frazine) 1906- 5-6R
Miner, Jane Claypool 1933- 106
See also SATA 37, 38
Miner, John B(urnham) 1926- CANR-20
Earlier sketches in CA 11-12R, CANR-5
Miner, Joshua L. 1920- 106
Miner, Lewis S. 1909- CAP-1
Earlier sketch in CA 11-12
See also SATA 11
Miner, Mary Green 1928- 69-72
Miner, Matthew
See Wallmann, Jeffrey M(iner)
Miner, Valerie 1947- 97-100
See also CLC 40
Miner, Ward L(ester) 1916- 9-10R
Mines, Jeanette (Marie) 1948- 119
Mines, Samuel 1909- CANR-1
Earlier sketch in CA 45-48
Mines, Stephanie 1944- 77-80
Minetree, Harry 1935- 93-96
Mingay, G(ordon) E(dmund) 1923- CANR-11
Earlier sketch in CA 19-20R
Minge, Ward Alan 1924- 97-100
Minghi, Julian V(incent) 1933- 29-32R
Mingus, Charles 1922-1979 93-96
Obituary 85-88
Minick, Michael 1945- 65-68
Minier, Nelson
See Stoutenburg, Adrien (Pearl)
Minifie, James MacDonald 1900-1974 49-52
Minihan, Janet
See Oppenheim, Janet
Minimo, Duca
See D'Annunzio, Gabriele
Minio-Paluello, Lorenzo 1907-1986
Obituary 119
Minium, Edward W(headon) 1917- 29-32R
Mink, Louis Otto, Jr. 1921-1983 104
Obituary 109
Mink, Nelson G. 1907- 123
Minkovitz, Moshe
See Shokeid, Moshe
Minnelli, Vincente 1913(?)-1986 Obituary 119
Brief entry 117
Minney, R(ubeigh) J(ames) 1895- CANR-5
Earlier sketch in CA 7-8R
Minnich, Helen Benton 1892- CAP-1
Earlier sketch in CA 9-10
Minnick, Wayne C. 1915- 25-28R
Minnigerode, Meade 1887-1967 Obituary 116
Minogue, Kenneth R(obert) 1930- 7-8R
Minor, Andrew Collier 1918- 15-16R
Minor, Anthropopagus
See Conniff, James C(lifford) G(regory)
Minor, Audax
See Ryall, George (Francis Trafford)
Minor, Edward Orville 1920- 9-10R
Minor, Marz 1928- 103
Minor, Muriel Miller 1908-1987 Obituary 122
Minor, Nono 1932- 103
Minot, Stephen 1927- CANR-17
Earlier sketch in CA 13-14R
Minot, Susan 1956- CLC-44
Minott, Rodney G(lisan) 1928- 11-12R
Minow, Newton N(orman) 1926- 15-16R
Minrath, William R(ichard) 1900-1971 CAP-1
Obituary 89-92
Earlier sketch in CA 9-10
Minshall, Merlin (Theodore) 1906-1987
Obituary 123
Minshall, Vera (Wild) 1924- 13-14R
Minshull, Evelyn 1929- 37-40R
Minshull, Roger (Michael) 1935- 21-22R
Minsky, Betty Jane (Toebe) 1932- 7-8R
Minsky, Hyman P(hilip) 1919- 85-88
Minsky, Marvin (Lee) 1927- 23-24R
Minsky, Morton 1902(?)-1987 Obituary 122
Minter, David L. 1935- CANR-12
Earlier sketch in CA 25-28R
Minter, William 1942- 124
Minters, Arthur Herman 1932- 102
Minto-Cowen, Frances
See Munthe, Frances
Minton, Lynn 107
Minton, Madge Rutherford 1920- 45-48
Minton, Paula
See Little, Paul H(ugo)
Minton, Robert 1918- 57-60
Minton, Sherman A(nthony), Jr. 1919- 45-48
Mintonye, Grace 25-28R
See also SATA 4
Minturn, Leigh 1928- 23-24R
Minty, Judith 1937- CANR-21
Earlier sketches in CA 49-52, CANR-2
Mintz, Barbara 1931- 110
Mintz, Donald E(dward) 1932- 19-20R
Mintz, Elizabeth E. 1913- 73-76
Mintz, Joyce Lois 1933- 65-68
Mintz, Leigh W(ayne) 1939- 57-60
Mintz, Max M. 1919- 33-36R
Mintz, Morton A. 1922- 15-16R
Mintz, Norman N(elson) 1934- 41-44R
Mintz, Ruth Finer 1919- 15-16R
Mintz, Samuel I(saiah) 1923- 5-6R
Mintz, Sidney W(ilfred) 1922- CANR-21
Earlier sketches in CA 3R, CANR-5
Mintz, Steven (Harry) 1953- 118
Mintz, Thomas 1931- 108
Mintzberg, Henry 1939- CANR-1
Earlier sketch in CA 45-48
Mintzer, Yvette 1947- 77-80
Minus, Ed 1938- CLC-39
Minus, Paul M(urray, Jr.) 1935- 118
Minyard, John Douglas 1943- 120
Mirabehn
See Slade, Madeleine
Mirabelli, Eugene (Jr.) 1931- 25-28R
Miracle, Gordon E. 1930- 33-36R
Miracle, Marvin P(reston) 1933- 19-20R
Miranda, Javier
See Bioy Casares, Adolfo
Mirande, Alfredo M(anuel) 1940- 115
Mireaux, Emile 1885(?)-1969 Obituary 104
Mireles, Marina 1927(?)-1986 Obituary 119
Mirenburg, Barry (Leonard Steffan) 1952- 101
Mirepoix, Camille 1926- 105
Miro (Ferrer), Gabriel (Francisco Victor) 1879-1930 Brief entry 104
See also TCLC 5
Miro, Joan 1893-1983 121
Obituary 111
Miron, Dan 1934- 77-80
Miron, Gaston 1928- DLB-60
Miron, Murray S(amuel) 1932- 81-84
Mirsky, Jeannette 1903-1987 CAP-2
Obituary 122
Earlier sketch in CA 19-20
See also SATA 8
Mirsky, Mark Jay 1939- 25-28R
Mirsky, Reba Paeff 1902-1966 2R
See also SATA 1
Mirsky, Stanley 1929- 110
Mirvish, Robert Franklin 1921- 2R
Miscall, Peter D(arwin) 1943- 111
Misch, Robert J(ay) 1905- 23-24R
Mische, Gerald F(rederick) 1926- 97-100
Mische, Patricia M(ary) 1939- CANR-16
Earlier sketch in CA 93-96
Mischke, Bernard Cyril 1926- 13-14R
Mischke, Fridolin 1916- 117
Mischke, Fritz
See Mischke, Fridolin
Mises, Ludwig (Edler) von 1881-1973 CANR-19
Obituary 45-48
Earlier sketch in CA 7-8R
Mises, Margit von 1896- CANR-19
Earlier sketch in CA 89-92
Mish, Charles C(arroll) 1913- 33-36R
Mishael, Bert
See Mishael, Herbert Stanley
Mishael, Herbert Stanley 1900(?)-1985
Obituary 117
Mishan, E(zra) J(oshua) 1917- CANR-13
Earlier sketch in CA 73-76
Misheiker, Betty Fairly 1919- 11-12R
Mishima, Yukio
See Hiraoka, Kimitake
See also CLC 2, 4, 6, 9, 27
Mishkin, Paul J. 1927- 19-20R
Mishra, Vishwa Mohan 1937- 61-64
Misiak, Henryk 1911- CANR-5
Earlier sketch in CA 2R
Misiunas, Romauld John 1945- 109
Miskimin, Harry A(lvin, Jr.) 1932-
Brief entry 109
Miskovits, Christine 1939- 53-56
See also SATA 10
Misner, Arthur J(ack) 1921- 21-22R
Misra, Bankey Bihari 1909- 104
Miss C. L. F.
See Grimke, Charlotte L(ottie) Forten
Missen, Leslie R(obert) 1897-1983
Obituary 110
Miss Frances
See Horwich, Frances R(appaport)
Missildine, (Whitney) Hugh 1915- 77-80
Missinne, Leo E(miel) 1927- 116
Missiroli, Mario 1886-1974 Obituary 53-56
Miss Lou
See Bennett-Coverley, Louise
Miss Manners
See Martin, Judith (Sylvia)
Miss Read
See Saint, Dora Jessie
Mister Rogers
See Rogers, Fred McFeely
Mister X
See Hoch, Edward D(entinger)
Mistral, Frederic 1830-1914 Brief entry 122
Mistral, Gabriela
See Godoy Alcayaga, Lucila
See also TCLC 2
Mitcalfe, Barry 1930- 110
Mitcham, Carl 1941- CANR-16
Earlier sketch in CA 85-88
Mitcham, Gilroy
See Newton, William Simpson
Mitcham, Samuel W(ayne), Jr. 1949- 106
Mitchel, Jonathan 1624-1668 DLB-24
Mitchell, Adam
See Pyle, Hilary
Mitchell, Adrian 1932- 33-36R
See also DLB 40
Mitchell, Alan 1922- CANR-8
Earlier sketch in CA 57-60
Mitchell, Alexander Ross Kerr 1934- 73-76
Mitchell, Allan 1933- 102

Mitchell, Allison
See Butterworth, W(illiam) E(dmund III)
Mitchell, Andrew W. 1953- ... 124
Mitchell, Arthur A(ustin) 1926- ... 11-12R
Mitchell, Austin (Vernon) 1934- ... CANR-12
Earlier sketch in CA 25-28R
Mitchell, B(rian) R(edman) 1929- ... 49-52
Mitchell, Barbara 1941- ... 117
Mitchell, Barbara A. 1939- ... 25-28R
Mitchell, Basil George 1917- ... 104
Mitchell, Betty L(ou) 1947- ... 107
Mitchell, Bonner 1929- ... 25-28R
Mitchell, Breon 1942- ... 112
Mitchell, Broadus 1892- ... CANR-5
Earlier sketch in CA 4R
Mitchell, Burroughs 1914(?)-1979
Obituary ... 89-92
Mitchell, Carlton
See Marshall, Mel(vin D.)
Mitchell, Charles 1912- ... 11-12R
Mitchell, Clyde
See Ellison, Harlan
and Silverberg, Robert
Mitchell, Colin W(are) 1927- ... 73-76
Mitchell, Curtis Cornelius, Jr. 1927- ... 105
Mitchell, Cynthia 1922- ... 106
See also SATA 29
Mitchell, Daniel J(esse) B(rody) 1942- ... 123
Mitchell, David (John) 1924- ... CANR-12
Earlier sketch in CA 53-56
Mitchell, Don(ald Earl) 1947- ... CANR-14
Earlier sketch in CA 33-36R
Mitchell, Donald (Charles Peter) 1925- ... 103
Mitchell, Donald Grant 1822-1908 ... DLB-1
Mitchell, Edgar D(ean) 1930- ... 53-56
Mitchell, Edward B. 1937- ... 23-24R
Mitchell, Elizabeth P(ryse) 1946- ... 101
Mitchell, (Sibyl) Elyne (Keith) 1913- ... CANR-21
Earlier sketches in CA 53-56, CANR-5
See also SATA 10
Mitchell, Emerson Blackhorse Barney
1945- ... 45-48
Mitchell, Erica
See Posner, Richard
Mitchell, Ewan
See Janner, Greville Ewan
Mitchell, Fay Langellier 1884-1964 ... 5-6R
Mitchell, Frank
See Mitchell, George Francis
Mitchell, Frank Vincent 1919-19(?) ... 9-10R
Mitchell, Franklin D. 1932- Brief entry ... 118
Mitchell, G(eoffrey) Duncan 1921- ... CANR-11
Earlier sketch in CA 29-32R
Mitchell, George Francis 1912- ... 77-80
Mitchell, Giles 1928- ... 93-96
Mitchell, Gladys (Maude Winifred)
1901-1983 ... CANR-9
Obituary ... 110
Earlier sketch in CA 11-12R
See also SATA 35, 46
Mitchell, Greg 1947- ... 73-76
Mitchell, Harold P(aton) 1900-1983 ... 11-12R
Obituary ... 109
Mitchell, (Arthur) Harris 1916- ... 119
Mitchell, Helen S(wift) 1895-1984 ... 25-28R
Obituary ... 114
Mitchell, Henry H(eywood) 1919- ... CANR-10
Earlier sketch in CA 57-60
Mitchell, (William) Hobart 1908- ... 119
Mitchell, Howard E(still) 1921- ... 108
Mitchell, J(ames) Clyde 1918- ... CANR-9
Earlier sketch in CA 13-14R
Mitchell, Jack 1925- ... 11-12R
Mitchell, Jackson
See Matcha, Jack
Mitchell, James 1926- ... CANR-12
Earlier sketch in CA 13-14R
Mitchell, James (Alexander Hugh)
1939-1985 Obituary ... 115
Mitchell, James Leslie 1901-1935
Brief entry ... 104
See also DLB 15
Mitchell, Jay
See Roberson, Jennifer
Mitchell, Jeremy 1929- ... 41-44R
Mitchell, Jerome 1935- ... 25-28R
Mitchell, Jerry 1905(?)-1972 Obituary ... 33-36R
Mitchell, Joan Cattermole 1920- ... CAP-1
Earlier sketch in CA 9-10
Mitchell, John D(ietrich) 1917- ... 49-52
Mitchell, John D(avid) B(awden)
1917-1980 Obituary ... 105
Mitchell, John Howard 1921- ... 11-12R
Mitchell, John J(oseph) 1941- ... CANR-1
Earlier sketch in CA 45-48
Mitchell, Joni 1943- ... 112
See also CLC 12
Mitchell, Joseph (Quincy) 1908- ... 77-80
Mitchell, Joseph B(rady) 1915- ... 11-12R
Mitchell, Joyce Slayton 1933- ... CANR-15
Earlier sketch in CA 65-68
See also SATA 43, 46
Mitchell, Judith Paige ... CANR-18
Earlier sketch in CA 85-88
Mitchell, (Charles) Julian 1935- ... CANR-5
Earlier sketch in CA 7-8R
See also DLB 14
Mitchell, Juliet 1940- ... 45-48
Mitchell, K. L.
See Lamb, Elizabeth Searle
Mitchell, Ken(neth Ronald) 1940- ... CANR-16
Earlier sketch in CA 93-96
See also DLB 60
Mitchell, Kenneth R. 1930- ... 19-20R
Mitchell, Kerry
See Wilkes-Hunter, R(ichard)
Mitchell, Lane 1907- ... CAP-1
Earlier sketch in CA 19-20
Mitchell, Langdon (Elwyn) 1862-1935
Brief entry ... 120
See also DLB 7
Mitchell, Lee M(ark) 1943- ... CANR-1
Earlier sketch in CA 49-52
Mitchell, Leeds 1912- ... 89-92
Mitchell, Leonel Lake 1930- ... 89-92
Mitchell, Leslie 1905-1985 Obituary ... 118
Mitchell, Lionel H. 1942- ... 106
Mitchell, Loften 1919- ... 81-84
See also DLB 38
Mitchell, Marcia L(ouise) 1942- ... 113
Mitchell, Margaret (Munnerlyn) 1900-1949
Brief entry ... 109
See also DLB 9
See also TCLC 11
Mitchell, Margaretta K. 1935- ... CANR-14
Earlier sketch in CA 29-32R
Mitchell, Marianne Helen 1937- ... 85-88
Mitchell, Memory F(armer) 1924- ... 37-40R
Mitchell, Otis C. 1935- ... CANR-13
Earlier sketch in CA 37-40R
Mitchell, P(hilip) M(arshall) 1916- ... CANR-20
Earlier sketch in CA 104
Mitchell, Paige
See Mitchell, Judith Paige
Mitchell, Pamela Holsclaw 1940- ... CANR-6
Earlier sketch in CA 57-60
Mitchell, Peggy
See Mitchell, Margaret (Munnerlyn)
Mitchell, Peter M(cQuilkin) 1934- ... 85-88
Mitchell, Richard H(anks) 1931- ... 23-24R
Mitchell, Robert H(ughes) 1921- ... 117
Mitchell, Roger (Sherman) 1935- ... 25-28R
Mitchell, Ruth K. ... 33-36R
Mitchell, S. Valentine
See Gammell, Susanna Valentine Mitchell
Mitchell, Sally 1937- ... 110
Mitchell, Scott
See Godfrey, Lionel (Robert Holcombe)
Mitchell, Sidney Alexander 1895- ... 7-8R
Mitchell, Stephen Arnold 1903-1974
Obituary ... 49-52
Mitchell, Stephen O. 1930- ... 15-16R
Mitchell, Thomas N(oel) 1939- ... 103
Mitchell, W.J.T. 1942- ... CANR-14
Earlier sketch in CA 81-84
Mitchell, W(illiam) O(rmond) 1914- ... CANR-15
Earlier sketch in CA 77-80
See also CLC 25
Mitchell, William E(dward) 1927- ... 81-84
Mitchell, William E. 1936- ... 93-96
Mitchell, William Hamilton 1907(?)-1982
Obituary ... 107
Mitchell, Yvonne 1925-1979 ... CANR-10
Obituary ... 85-88
Earlier sketch in CA 19-20R
See also SATA 24
Mitchelson, Marvin M. 1928- ... 104
Mitchenson, Francis Joseph Blackett ... 101
Mitchenson, Joe
See Mitchenson, Francis Joseph Blackett
Mitchison, (Sonja) Lois ... 2R
Mitchison, Naomi Margaret (Haldane)
1897- ... CANR-15
Earlier sketch in CA 77-80
See also SATA 24
Mitchison, Rosalind (Mary) 1919- ... 33-36R
Mitchner, Stuart 1938- ... 61-64
Mitchnik, Helen 1901- ... 117
See also SATA 35, 41
Mitchum, Hank
See Knott, William C(ecil, Jr.)
and Newton, D(wight) B(ennett)
and Sherman, Jory (Tecumseh)
Mitelman, Bonnie Cossman 1941- ... 111
Mitford, Jessica 1917- ... CANR-1
Earlier sketch in CA 2R
Mitford, Nancy 1904-1973 ... 9-10R
See also CLC 44
Mitgang, Herbert 1920- ... CANR-4
Earlier sketch in CA 11-12R
Mitgang, Lee D. 1949- ... 77-80
Mitrany, David 1888-1975 ... 65-68
Obituary ... 61-64
Mitscherlich, Alexander Joseph 1908-1982
Obituary ... 107
Mitson, Eileen N(ora) 1930- ... 25-28R
Mitsuhashi, Yoko ... SATA-33, 45
Mittelholzer, Edgar Austin 1909-1965 ... CAP-1
Earlier sketch in CA 13-14
Mittelman, James H(oward) 1944- ... CANR-13
Earlier sketch in CA 73-76
Mitterling, Philip Ira 1926- ... 102
Mittermeyer, Helen (Hayton Monteith)
1930- ... 124
Mittlebeeler, Emmet V(aughn) 1915- ... 57-60
Mitton, Bruce H(arold) 1950- ... 108
Mitton, Charles Leslie 1907- ... CANR-4
Earlier sketch in CA 4R
Mitton, Jacqueline 1948- ... 97-100
Mitton, Simon 1946- ... 97-100
Mittra, S(id) 1930- ... 41-44R
Mitzman, Arthur Benjamin 1931- ... 104
Mitzman, Max E. 1908- ... 97-100
Miura, Akira 1927- ... 117
Miura, Ayako 1922- ... 73-76
Mix, C(larence) Rex 1935- ... 29-32R
Mix, Katherine Lyon ... 53-56
Mix, Paul E(merson) 1934- ... 45-48
Mix, Susan Shank 1943- ... 29-32R
Mixter, Elisabeth W.
See Morss, Elisabeth W.
Mixter, Keith Eugene 1922- ... 41-44R
Mixter, Russell Lowell 1906- ... CAP-1
Earlier sketch in CA 15-16
Miyakawa, T(etsuo) Scott 1906- ... 19-20R
Miyamoto, Kazuo 1900- ... CAP-1
Earlier sketch in CA 11-12
Miyoshi, Masao 1928- ... 29-32R
Mizener, Arthur (Moore) 1907-1988 ... CANR-5
Obituary ... 124
Earlier sketch in CA 5-6R
Mizner, Elizabeth Howard 1907- ... 13-14R
See also SATA 27
Mizruchi, Ephraim H(arold) 1926- ... 41-44R
Mizruchi, Mark S(heldon) 1953- ... 110
Mizumura, Kazue ... 85-88
See also SATA 18
Mjelde, Michael Jay 1938- ... 69-72
Mnacko, Ladislav 1919- ... 29-32R
Mo, Timothy 1953- ... 117
See also CLC 46
Moak, Lennox L. 1912- ... 23-24R
Moak, Samuel K(uhn) 1929- ... 37-40R
Moan, Terrence 1947- ... 97-100
Moat, John 1936- ... CANR-13
Earlier sketch in CA 33-36R
Moats, Alice-Leone ... CAP-1
Earlier sketch in CA 15-16
Moberg, David O(scar) 1922- ... CANR-18
Earlier sketches in CA 2R, CANR-2
Moberg, (Carl Arthur) Vilhelm
1898-1973 ... 97-100
Obituary ... 45-48
Moberly, R(obert) B(asil) 1920- ... 29-32R
Moberly, Walter (Hamilton) 1881-1974 ... CAP-2
Earlier sketch in CA 29-32
Moberly-Bell, Enid 1881- ... 7-8R
Mobley, Harris W(itsel) 1929- ... 37-40R
Mobley, Tony Allen 1938- ... 102
Mobley, Walt
See Burgess, M(ichael) R(oy)
Moche, Dinah (Rachel) L(evine) 1936- ... 89-92
See also SATA 40, 44
Mochi, Ugo (A.) 1889-1977 ... SATA-38
Mock, Edward J(oseph) 1934- ... 21-22R
Mocker, Donald W(ilbur) 1935- ... 102
Mockler, Anthony 1937- ... 69-72
Mockler, Mike 1945- ... 109
Mockler, Robert J. 1932- ... 33-36R
Mockridge, Norton 1915- Brief entry ... 110
Mocsy, Andras 1929- ... 65-68
Modak, Manorama Ramkrishna 1895- ... 97-100
Modarressi, Taghi (M.) 1931- Brief entry ... 121
See also CLC 44
Mode, Heinz (Adolf) 1913- Brief entry ... 111
Model, Lisette 1906-1983 Obituary ... 109
Modell, Frank B. 1917- ... 116
See also SATA 36, 39
Modell, John 1941- ... 93-96
Modell, Judith Schachter 1941- ... 111
Modelski, George 1926- ... CANR-2
Earlier sketch in CA 49-52
Modesitt, L(eland) E(xton), Jr. 1943- ... 109
Modgil, Celia 1937- ... 124
Modgil, Sohan (Lal) 1938- ... 124
Modiano, Patrick (Jean) 1945- ... CANR-17
Earlier sketch in CA 85-88
See also CLC 18
Modigliani, Andre 1940- ... 53-56
Modigliani, Jeanne 1918(?)-1984 Obituary ... 113
Modisane, Bloke
See Modisane, William
Modisane, William 1923-1986 Obituary ... 118
Modley, Rudolph 1906-1976 Obituary ... 69-72
Modras, Ronald E(dward) 1937- ... CANR-9
Earlier sketch in CA 23-24R
Moe, Barbara 1937- ... 69-72
See also SATA 20
Moe, Christian (Hollis) 1929- ... 41-44R
Moe, Edith Monroe 1896(?)-1987
Obituary ... 122
Moehlman, Arthur H(enry) 1907- ... 11-12R
Moehlmann, F. Herbert 1893- ... 93-96
Moelleken, Wolfgang W. 1934- ... 33-36R
Moeller, Charles 1912- ... 73-76
Moeller, Dorothy W(ilson) 1902- ... 45-48
Moeller, Helen (Elaine) 1921- ... CANR-13
Earlier sketch in CA 23-24R
Moellering, Ralph L(uther) 1923- ... 15-16R
Moenkemeyer, Heinz 1914- ... 102
Moenssens, Andre A. 1930- ... 29-32R
Moerck, Paal
See Roelvaag, O(le) E(dvart)
Moeri, Louise 1924- ... CANR-9
Earlier sketch in CA 65-68
See also SATA 24
Moerman, Daniel E(llis) 1941- ... 105
Moerman, Michael (Harris) 1934- ... 25-28R
Moers, Ellen 1928-1979 ... 9-10R
Obituary ... 89-92
Moes, Joh(a)n E(rnst) 1926- ... 3R
Moeser, John V(ictor) 1942- ... 116
Moffat, Abbot Low 1901- ... 4R
Moffat, Alexander W(hite) 1891- ... 69-72
Moffat, Anne Simon 1947- ... 107
Moffat, Frances 1912- ... 97-100
Moffat, Gwen 1924- ... CANR-10
Earlier sketch in CA 13-14R
Moffat, John Lawrence 1916- ... 103
Moffat, Mary Jane 1933- ... CANR-17
Earlier sketch in CA 97-100
Moffatt, Doris 1919- ... 105
Moffatt, (Marston) Michael 1944- ... CANR-20
Earlier sketch in CA 85-88
Moffett, Eileen Flower 1928- ... 123
Moffett, George D(inwiddie) III 1943- ... 118
Moffett, Hugh (Oliver) 1910-1985 ... 73-76
Obituary ... 115
Moffett, Judith 1942- ... CANR-14
Earlier sketch in CA 69-72
Moffett, Kenworth W(illiam) 1934-
Brief entry ... 118
Moffett, Martha (Leatherwood) 1934- ... 37-40R
See also SATA 8
Moffett, Samuel Hugh 1916- ... CANR-5
Earlier sketch in CA 9-10R
Moffett, (Anthony) Toby 1944- ... 85-88
Moffitt, Donald (Anthony) 1936-
Brief entry ... 111
Moffitt, John 1908- ... CANR-10
Earlier sketch in CA 25-28R
Moffitt, Phillip 1946- ... 114
Brief entry ... 110
Moffitt, William J. 1930- ... 57-60
Mofolo, Thomas (Mokopu) 1875(?)-1948
Brief entry ... 121
See also TCLC 22
Mofsie, Louis B. 1936- ... SATA-33
Mogal, Doris P(ick) 1918- ... 69-72
Mogan, Joseph J(ohn), Jr. 1924- ... 49-52
Mogel, Leonard Henry 1922- ... 104
Moger, Allen W(esley) 1905- ... CAP-2
Earlier sketch in CA 25-28
Moger, Art 1911- ... 120
Moggach, Deborah 1948- ... CANR-18
Earlier sketch in CA 89-92
Moggridge, D(onald) E(dward) 1943- ... 29-32R
Moglen, Helene 1936- ... 65-68
Mogulof, Melvin B(ernard) 1926- ... 105
Mohammed Riza Pahlevi
See Pahlevi, Mohammed Riza
Mohan, Beverly Moffett 1918- ... 7-8R
Mohan, Brij 1939- ... 110
Mohan, Peter John 1930- ... CANR-10
Earlier sketch in CA 61-64
Mohan, Robert Paul 1920- ... 41-44R
Mohanty, Jitendra N(ath) 1928- ... 117
Mohl, Raymond A(llen) 1939- ... CANR-13
Earlier sketch in CA 33-36R
Mohl, Ruth 1891- ... CAP-1
Earlier sketch in CA 15-16
Mohlenbrock, Robert H. 1931- ... CANR-5
Earlier sketch in CA 53-56
Mohler, Charles 1913- ... 29-32R
Mohler, James A(ylward) 1923- ... CANR-23
Earlier sketches in CA 23-24R, CANR-8
Mohn, Peter B(urnet) 1934- ... 106
See also SATA 28
Mohn, Viola Kohl 1914- ... SATA-8
Mohr, Gordon 1916- ... CANR-12
Earlier sketch in CA 25-28R
Mohr, Jack
See Mohr, Gordon
Mohr, James C(rail) 1943- ... 73-76
Mohr, Nicholasa 1935- ... CANR-1
Earlier sketch in CA 49-52
See also SATA 8
See also CLC 12
Mohrenschildt, Dimitri Sergius Von
See Von Mohrenschildt, Dimitri Sergius
Mohrhardt, Foster E(dward) 1907- ... CAP-1
Earlier sketch in CA 15-16
Mohrmann, Christine A(ndrina) E(lisabeth)
M(aria) 1903- ... CAP-1
Earlier sketch in CA 9-10
Mohrt, Michel 1914- ... 13-14R
Moir, Alfred 1924- ... CANR-24
Earlier sketches in CA 21-22R, CANR-9
Moir, Duncan Wilson 1930-1983 Obituary ... 110
Moir, John S(argent) 1926- ... 41-44R
Moir, May A(rstad) 1907- ... 111
Moir, Ronald Eugene 1928- ... 29-32R
Moise, Lotte E(lla) 1917- ... 103
Mojica, Jose 1896-1974 Obituary ... 53-56
Mojtabai, A(nn) G(race) 1938- ... 85-88
See also CLC 5, 9, 15, 29
Mok, Paul P. 1934- ... 11-12R
Mokashi-Punekar, Shankar 1925- ... 97-100
Mokgatle, (Monyadio Moreleba) Naboth
1911-1985 ... CAP-2
Obituary ... 115
Earlier sketch in CA 33-36
Mokgatle, Naboth Nyadioe
See Mokgatle, (Monyadio Moreleba)
Naboth
Mokgatle, Nyadioe Naboth
See Mokgatle, (Monyadio Moreleba)
Naboth
Mokres, James A(llen) 1945- ... 49-52
Mol, Hans
See Mol, J(ohannis) J(acob)
Mol, J(ohannis) J(acob) 1922- ... CANR-18
Earlier sketches in CA 49-52, CANR-2
Molan, Dorothy L(ennon) 1911- ... 9-10R
Molan, Pat Carlson 1941- ... 112
Molarsky, Osmond 1909- ... 25-28R
See also SATA 16
Moldafsky, Annie 1930- ... 61-64
Moldea, Dan E. 1950- ... 122
Moldenhauer, Hans 1906- ... CANR-3
Earlier sketch in CA 3R
Moldenhauer, Joseph J(ohn) 1934- ... 33-36R
Moldenhauer, Rosaleen 1926- ... 97-100
Moldon, Peter L(eonard) 1937- ... 121
See also SATA 49
Moldovsky, Joel S(amuel) 1939- ... 97-100
Mole, John 1941- ... CANR-18
Earlier sketch in CA 101
See also SATA 36
Mole, Robert L. 1923- ... 29-32R
Molen, Ronald Lowry 1929- ... 65-68
Molenaar, Dee 1918- ... 37-40R
Moler, Kenneth Lloyd 1938- ... 89-92
Molesworth, Charles 1941- ... CANR-18
Earlier sketch in CA 77-80

Molette, Barbara Jean 1940- 45-48
Molette, Carlton W(oodard) II 1939- CANR-1
Earlier sketch in CA 45-48
Moley, Raymond (Charles) 1886-1975 61-64
Molho, Anthony 1939- Brief entry 106
Molin, Sven Eric 1929- 19-20R
Molinaro, Julius A(rthur) 1918- 41-44R
Molinaro, Ursule 69-72
Moline, Jon Nelson 1937- 111
Moline, Mary 1932- CANR-7
Earlier sketch in CA 57-60
Molinsky, Joan Sandra 1933- 123
Brief entry 116
Moll, Elick 1907- CANR-2
Earlier sketch in CA 2R
Molland, Einar 1908- 53-56
Mollegen, Albert Theodore 1906-1984
Obituary 111
Mollegen, Anne Rush
See Smith, Anne Mollegen
Mollenhoff, Clark R(aymond) 1921- CANR-13
Earlier sketch in CA 19-20R
Mollenkott, Virginia R(amey) 1932- CANR-12
Earlier sketch in CA 33-36R
Moller, Richard Jay 1952- 106
Mollinger, Robert N. 1945- 106
Mollo, Andrew 1940- CANR-15
Earlier sketch in CA 65-68
Mollo, Terry (Madeline) 1949- 102
Mollo, Victor 1909-1987 .... CANR-20
Obituary 123
Earlier sketches in CA 11-12R, CANR-5
Molloy, Anne Baker 1907- 13-14R
See also SATA 32
Molloy, John T. 1937(?)- 81-84
Molloy, Julia Sale 1905-1983 .... CANR-1
Obituary 110
Earlier sketch in CA 2R
Molloy, M(ichael) J(oseph) 1917- 103
Molloy, Paul (George) 1924- CANR-17
Earlier sketch in CA 2R
See also SATA 5
Molloy, Robert (William) 1906-1977 ..... CAP-2
Obituary 69-72
Earlier sketch in CA 29-32
Molloy, Tom 1948- 107
Molnar, Ferenc 1878-1952 Brief entry 109
See also TCLC 20
Molnar, Imre
See Lakatos, Imre
Molnar, Maria 1910(?)-1985 Obituary 117
Molnar, Thomas 1921- CANR-19
Earlier sketches in CA 3R, CANR-3
Molody, Konan Trofimovich
See Lonsdale, Gordon Arnold
Molotch, Harvey L(uskin) 1940- CANR-15
Earlier sketch in CA 41-44R
Molotov, V.
See Molotov, Viacheslav Mikhailovich
Molotov, V. M.
See Molotov, Viacheslav Mikhailovich
Molotov, Viacheslav Mikhailovich
1890-1986 Obituary 121
Moltmann, Juergen 1926- 93-96
Molumby, Lawrence E. 1932- 23-24R
Molz, (Redmond) Kathleen 1928- 49-52
Momaday, N(avarre) Scott 1934- CANR-14
Earlier sketch in CA 25-28R
See also SATA 30, 48
See also CLC 2, 19
Momboisse, Raymond M. 1927- 29-32R
Momen, Moojan 1950- 122
Moment, David 1925- 11-12R
Momigliano, Arnaldo (Dante) 1908-1987
Obituary 123
Mommsen, Katharina 1925- 69-72
Mommsen, Wolfgang J(ustin) 1930- 101
Monaco, James 1942- CANR-15
Earlier sketch in CA 69-72
Monaco, Richard 1940- CANR-15
Earlier sketch in CA 65-68
Monad, Jacques 1910-1976 Obituary 65-68
Monagan, Charles A(ndrew) 1950- 109
Monaghan, E(dith) Jennifer 1933- 115
Monaghan, (James) Jay (IV) 1891-1981 ..41-44R
Obituary 103
Monaghan, (Mary) Patricia 1946- CANR-23
Earlier sketch in CA 107
Monaghan, Patrick C. 1903(?)-1972
Obituary 37-40R
Monahan, Arthur P(atrick) 1928- 57-60
Monahan, Brent J(effrey) 1948- 93-96
Monahan, James (Henry Francis)
1912-1985 Obituary 118
Monahan, John
See Burnett, W(illiam) R(iley)
Monahan, Kaspar AITN-1
Monas, Sidney 1924- 13-14R
Monath, Elizabeth 1907- 5-6R
Monbeck, Michael E(ugene) 1942- CANR-2
Earlier sketch in CA 49-52
Moncreiffe, (Rupert) Iain (Kay) 1919-1985
Obituary 115
Moncrieff, David (William Hardy) Scott
See Scott-Moncrieff, David (William
Hardy)
Moncrieff, Earnest
See Chi, Richard Hu See-Yee
Moncrieff, Martha Christian Scott
See Scott Moncrieff, Martha Christian
Moncure, Jane Belk 1926- CANR-6
Earlier sketch in CA 11-12R
See also SATA 23
Mondadori, Alberto 1914(?)-1976
Obituary 65-68
Mondadori, Arnoldo 1889-1971
Obituary 29-32R
Mondale, Joan Adams 1930- 41-44R
Mondale, Walter F(rederick) 1928- 65-68
Monday, James 1951- 61-64
Monday, Michael
See Ginder, Richard
Mondey, David (Charles) 1917- 93-96
Mondor, Henri 1885(?)-1962 Obituary 111
Monegal, Emir Rodriguez
See Rodriguez Monegal, Emir
Monelli, Paolo 1894(?)-1984 Obituary 114
Monet, Dorothy 1927- 81-84
Monet, Jacques 1930- CANR-11
Earlier sketch in CA 65-68
Money, David Charles 1918- 107
Money, John (William) 1921- CANR-18
Earlier sketches in CA 45-48, CANR-1
Money, Keith 1935- 107
Moneyhon, Carl H. 1944- 120
Money-Kyrle, Roger (Ernie) 1898-1980
Obituary 101
Monfalcone, Wesley R. 1942- 109
Monfolo, Rodolpho 1899(?)-1976
Obituary 69-72
Monger, (Ifor) David 1908- 7-8R
Monguio, Luis 1908- 5-6R
Monheim, Leonard M. 1911-1971
Obituary 33-36R
Monhoff, June Hildegarde Flanner
1899-1987 Obituary 122
Monie, Willis J. 1945- 112
Monier-Williams, Randall Herbert
1892(?)-1984 Obituary 113
Monig, Christopher
See Crossen, Kendell Foster
Monjo, F(erdinand) N. 1924-1978 81-84
See also SATA 16
See also CLR 2
Monk, Alan
See Kendall, Willmoore
Monk, Galdo
See Riseley, Jerry B(urr, Jr.)
Monk, Janice J(ones) 1937- 93-96
Monk, Lorraine (Althea Constance) 101
Monk, Robert C(larence) 1930- 21-22R
Monka, Paul 1935- 29-32R
Monkhouse, Alan 1858-1936 .... DLB-10
Monkhouse, Francis John 1914-1975 ... CANR-10
Obituary 57-60
Earlier sketch in CA 13-14R
Monkkonen, Eric H(enry) 1942- 61-64
Monmonier, Mark Stephen 1943- 109
Monnet, Jean (Omer Marie) 1888-1979 102
Monninger, Joseph 1953- 121
Monnow, Peter
See Croudace, Glynn
Monod, Jacques 1910-1976 69-72
Monod, Rene
See Koch, Kurt E(mil)
Monod, Sylvere 1921- 21-22R
Monod, (Andre) Theodore 1902- 65-68
Monongo
See Clytus, John
Monro, Gavin
See Monro-Higgs, Gertrude
Monro, Harold 1879-1932 .... DLB-19
Monro, Isabel S(tevenson) 1884- CAP-2
Earlier sketch in CA 19-20
Monro, Kate M. 1883-19(?) CAP-2
Earlier sketch in CA 19-20
Monroe, Alan D(ouglas) 1944- 57-60
Monroe, Alan Houston 1903- 5-6R
Monroe, Bill
See Monroe, William Blanc, Jr.
Monroe, Carole 1944- 105
Monroe, Charles R(exford) 1905- 73-76
Monroe, Elizabeth 1905-1986 ....13-14R
Obituary 118
Monroe, Frank
See Chapman, Frank M(onroe)
Monroe, Harriet 1860-1936 Brief entry 109
See also DLB 54
See also TCLC 12
Monroe, Keith 1917- CANR-2
Earlier sketch in CA 5-6R
Monroe, Lyle
See Heinlein, Robert A(nson)
Monroe, (Marilyn) Lynn Lee 1935- 53-56
Monroe, Margaret Ellen 1914- 5-6R
Monroe, Marilyn
See Baker, Norma Jean
Monroe, Marion
See Cox, Marion Monroe
See also SATA 34
Monroe, Ruskyn Y. (a pseudonym) 1958- .. 116
Monroe, William Blanc, Jr. 1920- 108
Monro-Higgs, Gertrude 1905- 105
Monsarrat, Ann Whitelaw 1937- 73-76
Monsarrat, Nicholas (John Turney)
1910-1979 .... CANR-3
Earlier sketch in CA 2R
See also DLB 15
Monsell, Helen Albee 1895-1971 .... CAP-1
Earlier sketch in CA 9-10
See also SATA 24
Monsen, R(aymond) Joseph, Jr. 1931- 9-10R
Monsey, Derek 1921-1979 .... CANR-2
Obituary 85-88
Earlier sketch in CA 4R
Monsky, Mark 1941- 65-68
Monsma, James E. 1929- 29-32R
Monsma, Stephen V(os) 1936- 33-36R
Monsman, Gerald Cornelius 1940- CANR-8
Earlier sketch in CA 21-22R
Monson, Charles H., Jr. 1924- 5-6R
Monson, Karen Ann 1945-1988 .... CANR-20
Obituary 124
Earlier sketch in CA 97-100
Monsour, Sally A. 1929- 23-24R
Montag, Thomas 1947- 103
Montag, Tom
See Montag, Thomas
Montagnes, Ian 1932- 45-48
Montagu, Ashley 1905- CANR-5
Earlier sketch in CA 5-6R
Montagu, Elizabeth 1917- 11-12R
Montagu, Ewen (Edward Samuel)
1901-1985 77-80
Obituary 116
Montagu, Ivor (Goldsmid Samuel)
1904-1984 ....15-16R
Obituary 114
Montagu, Jeremy (Peter Samuel) 1927- ...93-96
Montague, Gene Bryan 1928- 93-96
Montague, Jeanne
See Yarde, Jeanne Betty Frances
Montague, Joel B(enjamin), Jr. 1912- 5-6R
Montague, John (Patrick) 1929- CANR-9
Earlier sketch in CA 11-12R
See also DLB 40
See also CLC 13, 46
Montague, Lisa
See Shulman, Sandra (Dawn)
Montague, Peter Gunn 1938- 85-88
Montague-Smith, Patrick Wykeham 1920- ... 107
Montagu of Beaulieu, Edward John
Barrington 1926- CANR-6
Earlier sketch in CA 9-10R
Montaigne, Sanford H(oward) 1935- 65-68
Montalbano, William D(aniel) 1940- CANR-22
Earlier sketch in CA 105
Montale, Eugenio 1896-1981 ....19-20R
Obituary 104
See also CLC 7, 9, 18
Montana, Bob 1920-1975 Obituary 89-92
See also SATA 21
Montana, Patrick J(oseph) 1937- CANR-10
Earlier sketch in CA 25-28R
Montanari, A(delio) J(oseph) 1917- 104
Montandon, Pat 57-60
Montapert, Alfred Armand 1906- 108
Montapert, William D(avid) 1930- 107
Montclair, Dennis
See Sladen, Norman St. Barbe
Monteilhet, Hubert 1928- Brief entry 117
Monteiro, George 1932- CANR-7
Earlier sketch in CA 19-20R
Monteiro, Luis (Infante de la Cerda) de
Sttau 1926- CANR-10
Earlier sketch in CA 15-16R
Monteith, Hayton
See Mittermeyer, Helen (Hayton
Monteith)
Monteleone, Thomas F(rancis) 1946- 113
Brief entry 109
Montell, William Lynwood 1931- CANR-11
Earlier sketch in CA 29-32R
Monter, E. William 1936- 23-24R
Montero, Darrel Martin 1946- 101
Monterosso, Carlo 1921- 29-32R
Montes, Antonio Llano 1924- CANR-14
Earlier sketch in CA 69-72
Montes de Oca, Marco Antonio 1932- 114
Montesi, Albert Joseph 1921- 37-40R
Montessori, Maria 1870-1952 Brief entry ... 115
Monteux, Doris (Hodgkins) 1894-1984 .... CAP-2
Obituary 112
Earlier sketch in CA 19-20
Montey, Vivian M(arie) 1956- 105
Montfort, Auguste 1913- CANR-18
Earlier sketch in CA 101
Montgomerie, Norah (Mary) 1913- 105
See also SATA 26
Montgomery, Albert A. 1929- 13-14R
Montgomery, Bernard Law 1887-1976 69-72
Obituary 65-68
Montgomery, Brian (Frederick) 1903- 53-56
Montgomery, (Robert) Bruce 1921-1978
Obituary 104
Montgomery, Charles F(ranklin)
1910-1978 81-84
Obituary 77-80
Montgomery, Constance
See Cappel, Constance
Montgomery, David 1927- 81-84
Montgomery, David Bruce 1938- 29-32R
Montgomery, Edward F(inley) 1918- 9-10R
Montgomery, Elizabeth
See Julesberg, Elizabeth Rider
Montgomery
Montgomery, Elizabeth Rider
See Julesberg, Elizabeth Rider
Montgomery
See also SATA 3, 34, 41
Montgomery, Elizabeth Wakefield 1891- ..41-44R
Montgomery, Helen
See Gunn, Helen Montgomery
Montgomery, Herbert J. 1933- CANR-18
Earlier sketches in CA 49-52, CANR-3
Montgomery, Horace 1906- 11-12R
Montgomery, John (McVey) 1919- 25-28R
See also DLB 16
Montgomery, John D(ickey) 1920- CANR-18
Earlier sketches in CA 7-8R, CANR-3
Montgomery, John Warwick 1931- CANR-10
Earlier sketch in CA 21-22R
Montgomery, L(ucy) M(aud) 1874-1942
Brief entry 108
See also YABC 1
See also CLR 8
Montgomery, Marion H., Jr. 1925- CANR-3
Earlier sketch in CA 2R
See also DLB 6
See also CLC 7
See also AITN 1
Montgomery, Max
See Davenport, Guy (Mattison, Jr.)
Montgomery, Michael B. 1950- 122
Montgomery, Nancy S(chwinn) 93-96
Montgomery, Raymond A. (Jr.) 1936- . CANR-16
Earlier sketch in CA 97-100
See also SATA 39
Montgomery, Robert 1904-1981 Obituary ... 108
Montgomery, Robert L(angford), Jr.
1927- 5-6R
Montgomery, Ruth Shick CANR-17
Earlier sketches in CA 4R, CANR-2
See also AITN 1
Montgomery, Rutherford George 1894- 9-10R
See also SATA 3
Montgomery, Thomas (Andrew) 1925- 49-52
Montgomery, Tommie Sue 1942- 112
Montgomery, Vivian 102
See also SATA 36
Monthan, Doris Born 1924- 115
Montherlant, Henry (Milon) de
1896-1972 85-88
Obituary 37-40R
See also CLC 8, 19
Monti, Laura V(irginia) 1930- 111
Montias, John Michael 1928- CANR-2
Earlier sketch in CA 3R
Monticone, Ronald Charles 1937- 73-76
Montini, Giovanni Battista (Enrico Antonio
Maria)
See Paul VI, Pope
Montresor, Beni 1926- 29-32R
See also SATA 3, 38
See also SAAS 4
Montrose, Graham
See Mackinnon, Charles Roy
Montrose, James St. David
See Appleman, John Alan
Montross, David
See Backus, Jean L(ouise)
Monty, Jeanne R(uth) 1935- 49-52
Monty Python
See Chapman, Graham
and Cleese, John (Marwood)
and Gilliam, Terry (Vance)
and Idle, Eric
and Jones, Terry
and Palin, Michael
See also CLC 21
Mood, Alexander M(cFarlane) 1913- 53-56
Mood, John J(ordan) L(indemann) 1932- ..57-60
Moodie, Graeme C(ochrane) 1924- CANR-2
Earlier sketch in CA 3R
Moodie, T(homas) Dunbar 1940- 77-80
Moody, Anne 1940- 65-68
Moody, Dale 1915- 19-20R
Moody, Eric N(elson) 1946- 116
Moody, Ernest A(ddison) 1903-1975 .....15-16R
Obituary 61-64
Moody, G. F.
See Hamel Dobkin, Kathleen
Moody, J. Carroll 1934- 33-36R
Moody, Jess C. 1925- 23-24R
Moody, Joseph Nestor 1904- CANR-1
Earlier sketch in CA 49-52
Moody, Joshua 1633(?)-1697 .... DLB-24
Moody, Paul Amos 1903- 53-56
Moody, Paul E(lliot) 1936- 118
Moody, Peter R(ichard, Jr.) 1943-
Brief entry 107
Moody, R. Bruce 1933- 19-20R
Moody, Ralph Owen 1898- CAP-1
Earlier sketch in CA 9-10
See also SATA 1
Moody, Raymond Avery, Jr. 1944- 93-96
Moody, Richard 1911- 33-36R
Moody, Ron 1924- 108
Moody, T(heodore) W(illiam) 1907- 13-14R
Moody, William Vaughn 1869-1910
Brief entry 110
See also DLB 7, 54
Moolb, Leinad
See Bloom, Daniel Halevi
Moolson, Melusa
See Solomon, Samuel
Moomaw, Ira W. 1894- CAP-1
Earlier sketch in CA 13-14
Moon, Carl 1879-1948 Brief entry 111
See also SATA 25
Moon, Douglas Mark 1937- 19-20R
Moon, G(eoff) J. H. 1915- 105
Moon, Grace Purdie 1877(?)-1947
Brief entry 113
See also SATA 25
Moon, Harold K(ay) 1932- 53-56
Moon, Henry Lee 1901-1985 Obituary 116
Moon, Michael E(lliott) 1948- 85-88
Moon, (Edward) Penderel 1905-1987
Obituary 122
Moon, Rexford G(eorge), Jr. 1922- 41-44R
Moon, Robert 1925- 73-76
Moon, Sheila (Elizabeth) 1910- 25-28R
See also SATA 5
Moonblood, Q.
See Stallone, Sylvester (Enzio)
Mooney, Bill
See Mooney, William F.
Mooney, Booth 1912-1977 .... CANR-3
Obituary 69-72
Earlier sketch in CA 49-52
Mooney, Canice (Albert James)
1911-1963 ....7-8R
Mooney, Chase C(urran) 1913-1972 ..... CAP-2
Earlier sketch in CA 19-20
Mooney, Christopher F(rancis) 1925- .. CANR-14
Earlier sketch in CA 37-40R

Mooney, Elizabeth C(omstock)
1918-1986 .... CANR-9
Obituary 119
Earlier sketch in CA 61-64
See also SATA 48
Mooney, Eugene F. 1930- 19-20R
Mooney, George A(ustin) 1911-1979
Obituary 89-92
Mooney, Harry J(ohn), Jr. 1927- 7-8R
Mooney, Michael M.
See Mooney, Michael Macdonald
Mooney, Michael Macdonald
1930-1985 .... CANR-21
Obituary 117
Earlier sketch in CA 65-68
Mooney, Patrick 1937- 115
Mooney, Ted 1951- CLC-25
Mooney, William F. 1919(?)-1985
Obituary 116
Mooneyham, W(alter) Stanley 1926- CANR-6
Earlier sketch in CA 13-14R
Moonitz, Maurice 1910- CANR-2
Earlier sketch in CA 5-6R
Moonman, Eric 1929- 103
Mooradian, Karlen 1935- 97-100
Moorcock, Michael (John) 1939- CANR-17
Earlier sketches in CA 45-48, CANR-2
See also CAAS 5
See also DLB 14
See also CLC 5, 27
Moore, Acel 1940- 69-72
Moore, Alan 1960- 123
Moore, Alice Ruth
See Nelson, Alice Ruth Moore Dunbar
Moore, Alma Chesnut 1901- CAP-1
Earlier sketch in CA 13-14
Moore, Amos
See Hubbard, George (Barron)
Moore, Andrew
See Binder, Frederick Moore
Moore, Anne Carroll 1871-1961 73-76
See also SATA 13
Moore, Archie Lee 1916- 33-36R
Moore, Arthur 1906(?)-1977 Obituary 69-72
Moore, Arthur James 1888-1974 .... 7-8R
Obituary 49-52
Moore, Austin
See Muir, (Charles) Augustus
Moore, Barbara
See Lee, Barbara (Moore)
Moore, Barrington, Jr. 1913- 117
Moore, Basil John 1933- 23-24R
Moore, Bernard 1904- CANR-13
Earlier sketch in CA 69-72
Moore, Bidwell 1917- 33-36R
Moore, Bob 1948- 61-64
Moore, Brian 1921- CANR-1
Earlier sketch in CA 2R
See also CLC 1, 3, 5, 7, 8, 19, 32
Moore, C(atherine) L(ucile) 1911- 104
See also DLB 8
Moore, Carey Armstrong 1930- 37-40R
Moore, Carl L(eland) 1921- CANR-15
Earlier sketch in CA 5-6R
Moore, Carman L(eroy) 1936- 61-64
Moore, Charles
See Moore, Reg(inald Charles Arthur)
Moore, Charles A(lexander) 1901-1967 .. CANR-3
Earlier sketch in CA 3R
Moore, Charles Garrett Ponsonby 1910- 108
Moore, Chauncey O. 1895-1965 .... CAP-1
Earlier sketch in CA 11-12
Moore, Christopher (Hugh) 1950- 119
Moore, Clayton
See Brandner, Gary
and Granbeck, Marilyn
Moore, Clement Clarke 1779-1863 ..... SATA-18
See also DLB 42
Moore, Clyde B. 1886-1973 .... CANR-4
Earlier sketch in CA 3R
Moore, Colleen 1902(?)-1988 Obituary 124
Moore, Cora R. 1902- CAP-2
Earlier sketch in CA 25-28
Moore, Cory
See Sturgeon, Wina
Moore, Dan Tyler 1908- 7-8R
Moore, Daniel G(eorge) 1899- 57-60
Moore, David G. 1918- CANR-2
Earlier sketch in CA 4R
Moore, David Moresby 1933- 112
Moore, Deborah Dash 1946- 108
Moore, Dick
See Moore, John Richard, Jr.
Moore, Don W. 1905(?)-1986 Obituary 119
See also SATA 48
Moore, Donald Joseph 1929- 57-60
Moore, Doris Langley CANR-1
Earlier sketch in CA 1R
Moore, Dorothea (Mary) 1881-1933
Brief entry 121
Moore, Dorothy N(elson) 1915- CANR-21
Earlier sketch in CA 89-92
Moore, Douglas Stuart 1893-1969 .... CAP-1
Earlier sketch in CA 15-16
Moore, E(velyn) Garth 1906- CAP-1
Earlier sketch in CA 11-12
Moore, Edmund A(rthur) 1903- 5-6R
Moore, Edward
See Muir, Edwin
Moore, Edward C(arter) 1917- CANR-5
Earlier sketch in CA 2R
Moore, Edward J(ames) 1935- 65-68
Moore, Edward M(umford) 1940- 57-60
Moore, Elizabeth
See Atkins, Meg Elizabeth
Moore, Ethel Pauline Perry 1902- CAP-1
Earlier sketch in CA 11-12
Moore, Eva 1942- 45-48
See also SATA 20
Moore, Everett T(homson) 1909- CAP-1
Earlier sketch in CA 11-12
Moore, Fenworth CAP-2
Earlier sketch in CA 19-20
Moore, Francis D(aniels) 1913- Brief entry .. 113
Moore, Francis Edward 1898- CAP-1
Earlier sketch in CA 9-10
Moore, Frank Harper 1920- 5-6R
Moore, Frank Ledlie 1923- 7-8R
Moore, Franklin G. 1905- 2R
Moore, G(ranville) Alexander Jr. 1937- ... 21-22R
Moore, Gary T(homas) 1945- CANR-15
Earlier sketch in CA 85-88
Moore, Gene D. 1919- 23-24R
Moore, Geoffrey H(oyt) 1914- CANR-19
Earlier sketch in CA 81-84
Moore, Geoffrey Herbert 1920- 109
Moore, George Augustus 1852-1933
Brief entry 104
See also DLB 10, 18, 57
See also TCLC 7
Moore, George Ellis 1916- 7-8R
Moore, Gerald 1899-1987 .... CANR-5
Obituary 122
Earlier sketch in CA 4R
Moore, Glover 1911- 107
Moore, (David) Harmon 1911- 15-16R
Moore, Harold A. 1913- 33-36R
Moore, Harris
See Harris, Alf(red)
Moore, Harry Estill 1897- CAP-1
Earlier sketch in CA 13-14
Moore, Harry T(hornton) 1908-1981 .... CANR-3
Obituary 103
Earlier sketch in CA 7-8R
Moore, Henry (Spencer) 1898-1986
Obituary 121
Moore, Honor 1945- 85-88
Moore, J(ohn) Preston 1906- 65-68
Moore, J(ohn) William 1928- 5-6R
Moore, Jack (William) 1941- 112
See also SATA 32, 46
Moore, Jack B(ailey) 1933- 33-36R
Moore, Jack L(ynne) 1920- 89-92
Moore, James 1928- 97-100
Moore, James R(ichard) 1947- CANR-22
Earlier sketch in CA 105
Moore, James T. III 1939- 29-32R
Moore, James Tice 1945- 73-76
Moore, Jane Ann 1931- 37-40R
Moore, Janet Gaylord 1905- 77-80
See also SATA 18
Moore, Jenny 1923-1973 Obituary 45-48
Moore, Jerome (Aaron) 1903- 81-84
Moore, Jerrold Northrup 1934- 104
Moore, Jessie Eleanor 1886-19(?) CAP-1
Earlier sketch in CA 19-20
Moore, Jim 1946- SATA-42
Moore, Jimmy
See Moore, James T. III
Moore, John (Cecil) 1907- 7-8R
Moore, John A(lexander) 1915- 45-48
Moore, John A(ndrew) 1918-1972
Obituary 37-40R
Moore, John A.
See Moore, John Allen
Moore, John Allen 1912- 119
Moore, John C(lare) 1933- 49-52
Moore, John H. 1935- 118
Moore, John Hammond 1924- 57-60
Moore, John Hebron 1920- 21-22R
Moore, John Michael 1935- 104
Moore, John Norton 1937- CANR-14
Earlier sketch in CA 37-40R
Moore, John R(obert) 1928- CANR-3
Earlier sketch in CA 2R
Moore, John Rees 1918- 33-36R
Moore, John Richard, Jr. 1925- 19-20R
Moore, John Robert 1890-1973 .... CAP-1
Earlier sketch in CA 9-10
Moore, John Travers 1908- CANR-3
Earlier sketch in CA 5-6R
See also SATA 12
Moore, Julia A. (Davis) 1847-1920
Brief entry 116
Moore, Katharine 1898- CANR-20
Earlier sketch in CA 89-92
Moore, Katherine Davis 1915- 13-14R
Moore, Keith L(eon) 1925- 69-72
Moore, Kenneth Clark 1943- 102
Moore, Kenneth E(ugene) 1930- 73-76
Moore, Kenny
See Moore, Kenneth Clark
Moore, L(ittleton) Hugh 1935- 49-52
Moore, L. Silas (Jr.) 1936- 41-44R
Moore, Lamont 1909- SATA-29
Moore, Lander
See Fensch, Thomas
Moore, Lester L(ee) 1924- 33-36R
Moore, Lilian 103
Moore, Lillian 1917-1967 .... CANR-2
Earlier sketch in CA 2R
Moore, Linda Perigo 1946- 107
Moore, Lisa
See Chater, Elizabeth (Eileen)
Moore, Lorrie
See Moore, Marie Lorena
See also CLC 39, 45
Moore, Madeline (Roberta) 1934- 124
Moore, Marcia 1928- CANR-13
Earlier sketch in CA 61-64
Moore, Margaret R(umberger) 1903- 9-10R
See also SATA 12
Moore, Marianne (Craig) 1887-1972 .... CANR-3
Obituary 33-36R
Earlier sketch in CA 4R
See also SATA 20
See also DLB 45
See also CLC 1, 2, 4, 8, 10, 13, 19, 47
Moore, Marie Drury 1926- 33-36R
Moore, Marie Lorena 1957- 116
Moore, Marna
See Reynolds, (Marjorie) Moira Davison
Moore, (Georgina) Mary (Galbraith) 1930-
Brief entry 112
Moore, Maxine 1927- 73-76
Moore, Michael
See Harris, Herbert
Moore, Nicholas 1918- 69-72
Moore, P(eter) G(erald) 1928- 45-48
Moore, Pamela 1937-1964 .... 4R
Moore, Patrick (Alfred) 1923- CANR-8
Earlier sketch in CA 13-14R
See also SATA 39, 49
Moore, Paul, Jr. 1919- 89-92
Moore, Paul L. 1917-1976 .... 4R
Obituary 103
Moore, R(obert) Laurence 1940- 29-32R
Moore, Ray (S.) 1905(?)-1984 Obituary 111
See also SATA 37
Moore, Rayburn Sabatzky 1920- CANR-17
Earlier sketches in CA 4R, CANR-2
Moore, Raylyn 1928- 29-32R
Moore, Raymond Arthur, Jr. 1925- 5-6R
Moore, Raymond S. 1915- CANR-21
Earlier sketch in CA 29-32R
Moore, Reg(inald Charles Arthur) 1930- 104
Moore, Regina
See Dunne, Mary Collins
Moore, Richard (Thomas) 1927- CANR-20
Earlier sketch in CA 33-36R
Moore, Richard B. 1893(?)-1978
Obituary 81-84
Moore, Richard H(arlan) 1945- 121
Moore, Richard R. 1934- 105
Moore, Robert (Samuel) 1936- CANR-11
Earlier sketch in CA 25-28R
Moore, Robert
See Williams, Robert Moore
Moore, Robert E(verett) 1914- 57-60
Moore, Robert Etheridge 1919- 61-64
Moore, Robert Hamilton 1913-1984
Obituary 114
Moore, Robert L(owell), Jr. 1925- 15-16R
See also AITN 1
Moore, Robin
See Moore, Robert L(owell), Jr.
Moore, Roger George 1927- 109
Moore, Rosalie (Gertrude) 1910- CANR-3
Earlier sketch in CA 5-6R
Moore, Russell Franklin 1920- CANR-6
Earlier sketch in CA 11-12R
Moore, Ruth CANR-6
Earlier sketch in CA 4R
See also SATA 23
Moore, Ruth Nulton 1923- CANR-15
Earlier sketch in CA 81-84
See also SATA 38
Moore, S(arah) E. CANR-2
Earlier sketch in CA 49-52
See also SATA 23
Moore, Sally Falk 1924- CANR-6
Earlier sketch in CA 57-60
Moore, Samuel Taylor 1893-1974
Obituary 53-56
Moore, Sebastian 1917- 23-24R
Moore, Sonia 1902- CANR-2
Earlier sketch in CA 45-48
Moore, Steven 1951- 123
Moore, Susanna 1948- 109
Moore, T(om) Inglis 1901- 21-22R
Moore, T(homas) Sturge 1870-1944
Brief entry 118
See also DLB 19
Moore, Tara 1950- 116
Moore, Thomas Gale 1930- CANR-12
Earlier sketch in CA 29-32R
Moore, Tom 1950- CANR-18
Earlier sketch in CA 101
Moore, Trevor Wyatt 1924- CANR-12
Earlier sketch in CA 29-32R
Moore, Tui De Roy 1953- 107
Moore, Vardine (Russell) 1906- 41-44R
Moore, Virginia Dryden 1911- 19-20R
Moore, W(illiam) Glenn 1925- 49-52
Moore, Walter Lane 1905- CAP-1
Earlier sketch in CA 19-20
Moore, Ward 1903-1978 .... CAP-2
Obituary 113
Earlier sketch in CA 29-32
See also DLB 8
Moore, Warren (M., Jr.) 1923- 25-28R
Moore, Wilbert E(llis) 1914- CANR-5
Earlier sketch in CA 4R
Moore, Wilfred George 1907- CANR-4
Earlier sketch in CA 11-12R
Moore, William Howard 1942- 73-76
Moore, William L(eonard, Jr.) 1943- 93-96
Moorehead, Agnes 1906-1974 Obituary ... 49-52
Moorehead, Alan (McCrae) 1910-1983 .. CANR-6
Obituary 110
Earlier sketch in CA 7-8R
Moorehead, Caroline 1944- CANR-18
Earlier sketch in CA 101
Moore-Rinvolucri, Mina Josephine 1902- ... 107
Moores, Dick
See Moores, Richard (Arnold)
Moores, Richard (Arnold) 1909-1986 69-72
Obituary 119
See also SATA 48
Moorhead, Diana 1940- 105
Moorhead, James H(owell) 1947- 124
Moorhead, Max L(eon) 1914- 23-24R
Moorhouse, Charles Edmund 1911- 108
Moorhouse, Frank 1938- 118
Moorhouse, Geoffrey 1931- 25-28R
Moorhouse, Hilda Vansittart CAP-1
Earlier sketch in CA 11-12
Moorman, Charles (Wickliffe) 1925-
Brief entry 114
Moorman, John Richard Humpidge
1905- CANR-2
Earlier sketch in CA 4R
Moorshead, Henry
See Pine, Leslie Gilbert
Moorsom, Sasha 1931- CANR-14
Earlier sketch in CA 69-72
Moorsteen, Richard H. 1926(?)-1975
Obituary 57-60
Moos, Malcolm C(harles) 1916-1982 ..... 37-40R
Obituary 105
Moos, Rudolf H. 1934- CANR-1
Earlier sketch in CA 49-52
Moose, Ruth 1938- 101
Mooser, Stephen 1941- CANR-15
Earlier sketch in CA 89-92
See also SATA 28
Moote, A(lanson) Lloyd 1931- 33-36R
Moquin, Wayne-(Francis) 1930- 33-36R
Mora, Carl J(ose) 1936- 109
Mora, George 1923- CANR-1
Earlier sketch in CA 45-48
Morace, Robert A(nthony) 1947- 113
Moraes, Dom(inic F.) 1938- 25-28R
Moraes, Frank Robert 1907-1974 .... CAP-1
Obituary 49-52
Earlier sketch in CA 13-14
Moraes, (Marcus) Vinicius (Cruz) de (Mello)
1913-1980 Obituary 101
Morain, Lloyd L. 1917- 69-72
Morais, Vamberto 1921- 69-72
Morales, Angel Luis 1919- 49-52
Moramarco, Fred Stephen 1938- 57-60
Moran, Barbara B. 1944- 124
Moran, Charles McMoran Wilson
See Wilson, Charles McMoran
Moran, Emilio F(ederico) 1946- 117
Moran, Gabriel 1935- CANR-4
Earlier sketch in CA 53-56
Moran, George 1942- 115
Moran, Hugh Anderson 1881-1977
Obituary 73-76
Moran, James Sterling 1909- CANR-12
Earlier sketch in CA 9-10R
Moran, Jim
See Moran, James Sterling
Moran, John 1930- 45-48
Moran, John C(harles) 1942- 110
Moran, Mike
See Ard, William (Thomas)
Moran, Patrick Alfred Pierce 1917- 11-12R
Moran, Richard (Jerome) 1942- 121
Moran, Ronald (Wesson, Jr.) 1936- 37-40R
Moran, Tom 1943- 111
Moran, William E(dward), Jr. 1916- 13-14R
Morand, Paul 1888-1976 Obituary 69-72
See also DLB 65
See also CLC 41
Morano, Donald V(ictor) 1934- 45-48
Morante, Elsa 1918-1985 85-88
Obituary 117
See also CLC 8, 47
Morantz, Regina Markell
See Morantz-Sanchez, Regina (Ann)
Markell
Morantz-Sanchez, Regina (Ann) Markell
1943- 124
Morasky, Robert Louis 1940- 105
Moraud, Marcel I(an) 1917- 53-56
Moravia, Alberto
See Pincherle, Alberto
See also CLC 2, 7, 11, 27, 46
Morawetz, Thomas H(ubert) 1942- 101
Morawski, Stefan T(adeusz) 1921- 81-84
Moray, Helga 89-92
Moray, Neville (Peter) 1935- 29-32R
Moray Williams, Ursula 1911- 111
Morcom, John Brian 1925- 7-8R
Mordden, Ethan (Christopher) 1947- 73-76
Mordechai, Ben
See Gerber, Israel J(oshua)
Mordock, John B. 1938- 61-64
Mordvinoff, Nicolas 1911-1973 73-76
Obituary 41-44R
See also SATA 17
More, Caroline
See Cone, Molly Lamken
and Strachan, Margaret Pitcairn
More, Daphne 1929- 65-68
More, Harry W(illiam) 1929- CANR-20
Earlier sketches in CA 53-56, CANR-4
More, Jasper 1907-1987 .... CAP-1
Obituary 124
Earlier sketch in CA 9-10
More, Kenneth 1914-1982 Obituary 107
Moreas, Jean
See Papadiamantopoulos, Johannes
See also TCLC 18
Moreau, David Merlin 1927- 93-96
Moreau, John Adam 1938- 37-40R
Moreau, Jules Laurence 1917-1971 .... 3R
Obituary 103
Moreau, Reginald E(rnest) 1897-1970
Obituary 104
Morecambe, Eric 1926-1984 Obituary 112
Morehead, Albert H(odges) 1909-1966 ... CAP-1
Earlier sketch in CA 13-14

Morehead, Joe
See Morehead, Joseph H., Jr.
Morehead, Joseph H., Jr. 1931- CANR-6
Earlier sketch in CA 57-60
Morehouse, Clifford P(helps) 1904- 11-12R
Morehouse, Laurence E(nglemohr)
1913- CANR-4
Earlier sketch in CA 11-12R
Morehouse, Thomas A(lvin) 1937- 124
Morehouse, Ward 1899(?)-1966
Obituary 25-28R
Morel, Dighton
See Warner, Kenneth (Lewis)
Moreland, Lois B. 45-48
Morell, David 1939- 110
Morella, Joseph (James) 1949- 104
Moremen, Grace E(llen Partin) 1930- CANR-1
Earlier sketch in CA 45-48
Moren, Sally M(oore) 1947- 97-100
Morency, Pierre 1942- DLB-60
Moreno, Antonio Elosequi 1918- 33-36R
Moreno, Francisco Jose 1934- 29-32R
Moreno, Jacob L. 1892-1974 ..... CAP-2
Obituary 49-52
Earlier sketch in CA 19-20
Moreno, Jose A. 1928- 25-28R
Moreno, Martin
See Swartz, Harry (Felix)
Moreno, Pedro R. 1947- 69-72
Morentz, Ethel Irene 29-32R
Morentz, Pat
See Morentz, Ethel Irene
Morenus, Constance Gay 1895(?)-1985
Obituary 117
Moreton, John
See Cohen, Morton N(orton)
Moretti, Marino 1885(?)-1979 Obituary ... 89-92
Morewedge, Parviz 1934- 93-96
Morey, Charles
See Fletcher, Helen Jill
Morey, Robert A(lbert) 1946- 113
Morey, Roy D. 1937- 19-20R
Morey, Walt(er Nelson) 1907- 29-32R
See also SATA 3
Morford, Mark P(ercy) O(wen) 1929-
Brief entry 111
Morgan, Al(bert Edward) 1920- CANR-1
Earlier sketch in CA 45-48
Morgan, Alfred P(owell) 1889-1972 107
See also SATA 33
Morgan, Alison Mary 1930- CANR-18
Earlier sketches in CA 49-52, CANR-1
See also SATA 30
Morgan, Alyssa
See Delatush, Edith G.
Morgan, Angela
See Paine, Lauran (Bosworth)
Morgan, Anne Hodges 1940- 117
Morgan, Arlene
See Paine, Lauran (Bosworth)
Morgan, Arthur Ernest 1878-1975 ..... CANR-3
Obituary 61-64
Earlier sketch in CA 5-6R
Morgan, B(ayard) Q(uincy) 1883-1967 ... CAP-1
Earlier sketch in CA 11-12
Morgan, Barton 1889- CAP-1
Earlier sketch in CA 9-10
Morgan, Berry 1919- 49-52
See also DLB 6
See also CLC 6
Morgan, Bill 1949- 110
Morgan, Brian 1919- 7-8R
Morgan, Bryan S(tanford) 1923-1976 ... CANR-9
Earlier sketch in CA 7-8R
Morgan, Charles 1894-1958 ..... DLB-34
Morgan, Charles H(ill) 1902-1984 ..... 37-40R
Obituary 112
Morgan, Charles, Jr. 1930- CANR-13
Earlier sketch in CA 19-20R
Morgan, Chester A(lan) 1914- 19-20R
Morgan, Christopher 1952- 105
Morgan, Claire
See Highsmith, (Mary) Patricia
Morgan, Clifford T(homas) 1915-1976 .. CANR-4
Obituary 65-68
Earlier sketch in CA 2R
Morgan, Dale L. 1914-1971 Obituary 104
Morgan, Dan 1925- CANR-14
Earlier sketch in CA 37-40R
Morgan, Daniel C(roxton), Jr. 1931- 19-20R
Morgan, Darold H. 1924- 23-24R
Morgan, Davd (Rhys) 1937- 45-48
Morgan, David P(age) 1927- 123
Brief entry 118
Morgan, David T(aft, Jr.) 1937- 69-72
Morgan, Dewi (Lewis) 1916- CANR-1
Earlier sketch in CA 2R
Morgan, Donald G(rant) 1911- 19-20R
Morgan, Donn F(arley) 1943- 113
Morgan, Edmund S(ears) 1916- CANR-4
Earlier sketch in CA 11-12R
See also DLB 17
Morgan, Edward James Ranembe
1900-1978 Obituary 108
Morgan, Edward P. 1910- CAP-1
Earlier sketch in CA 19-20
Morgan, Edwin (George) 1920- CANR-3
Earlier sketch in CA 7-8R
See also DLB 27
See also CLC 31
Morgan, Elaine (Neville) 1920- 41-44R
Morgan, Elizabeth 1947- 108
Morgan, Ellen
See Bumstead, Kathleen Mary
Morgan, Emanuel
See Bynner, Witter
Morgan, Frank
See Paine, Lauran (Bosworth)
Morgan, Fred Bruce, Jr. 1919-1975 65-68
Obituary 61-64
Morgan, Fred Troy 1926- 89-92
Morgan, (George) Frederick 1922- CANR-21
Earlier sketch in CA 19-20R
See also CLC 23
Morgan, G. J.
See Rowland, D(onald) S(ydney)
Morgan, Geoffrey 1916- 23-24R
See also SATA 46
Morgan, Gerald 1925- 41-44R
Morgan, Glenn G(uy) 1926- 9-10R
Morgan, Gwen 101
Morgan, Gwyneth
See Beal, Gwyneth
Morgan, H(oward) Wayne 1934- CANR-18
Earlier sketches in CA 5-6R, CANR-2
Morgan, Hal
See Morgan, Henry A.
Morgan, Helen (Gertrude Louise) 1921- ... 57-60
See also SATA 29
Morgan, Henry
See von Ost, Henry Lerner
Morgan, Henry A. 1954- 112
Morgan, Hilda Campbell 1892-1985
Obituary 118
Morgan, Irvonwy 1907-1982 Obituary 107
Morgan, James N(ewton) 1918- 21-22R
Morgan, Jane
See Moren, Sally M(oore)
and Cooper, James Fenimore
Morgan, Janet 1945- 65-68
See also CLC 39
Morgan, Jean (Werner) 1922- 102
Morgan, (Walter) Jefferson 1940- CANR-12
Earlier sketch in CA 73-76
Morgan, Jim 1950- 45-48
Morgan, Joan 1905- 7-8R
Morgan, Joe Warner 1912- 9-10R
Morgan, John
See Paine, Lauran (Bosworth)
Morgan, John A(ndrew), Jr. 1935- 49-52
Morgan, John S. 1921- 15-16R
Morgan, Joy Elmer 1889-1986 Obituary 119
Morgan, Judith A(dams) 1939- 49-52
Morgan, Kathryn L. 117
Morgan, Kay Summersby 1909-1975
Obituary 53-56
Morgan, Kenneth Owen 1934- CANR-23
Earlier sketches in CA 15-16R, CANR-7
Morgan, Kenneth R(emsen) 1916- 13-14R
Morgan, Lael 1936- CANR-5
Earlier sketch in CA 53-56
Morgan, Lenore H. 1908-1976 ..... CAP-2
Earlier sketch in CA 33-36
See also SATA 8
Morgan, Louise 9-10R
Morgan, Lucy 1940- 108
Morgan, M(argaret) Ruth 1942(?)-1983
Obituary 109
Morgan, Marabel 1937- CANR-2
Earlier sketch in CA 49-52
See also AITN 1
Morgan, Marion (Nora Eluned) 1942- 120
Morgan, Marjorie
See Chibnall, Marjorie (McCallum)
Morgan, Mark
See Overholser, Wayne D.
Morgan, McKayla
See Basile, Gloria Vitanza
Morgan, Memo
See Avallone, Michael (Angelo), Jr.
Morgan, Michael Croke 1911- 93-96
Morgan, Michaela
See Basile, Gloria Vitanza
Morgan, Murray 1916- 107
Morgan, Neil 1924- CANR-2
Earlier sketch in CA 5-6R
Morgan, Nicholas
See Morgan, Thomas Bruce
Morgan, Patricia 1944- 89-92
Morgan, Patrick M. 1940- 37-40R
Morgan, Paul 1928- 61-64
Morgan, Peter F(rederick) 1930- 113
Morgan, Raleigh, Jr. 1916- 41-44R
Morgan, Richard E(rnest) 1937- CANR-15
Earlier sketch in CA 41-44R
Morgan, Robert 1921- CANR-20
Earlier sketch in CA 103
Morgan, Robert (R.) 1944- CANR-21
Earlier sketch in CA 33-36R
Morgan, Robert
See Turner, Robert (Harry)
Morgan, Roberta 1953- CANR-15
Earlier sketch in CA 93-96
Morgan, Robin 1941- 69-72
See also CLC 2
Morgan, Roger P(earce) 1932- CANR-12
Earlier sketch in CA 19-20R
Morgan, Roy A(mos) 1916- 41-44R
Morgan, Ruth P. 1934- 37-40R
Morgan, Sarah (Williams) 1901- CAP-1
Earlier sketch in CA 9-10
Morgan, Scott
See Kuttner, Henry
Morgan, Sharon A(ntonia) 1951- 61-64
Morgan, Shirley
See Kiepper, Shirley Morgan
See also SATA 10
Morgan, Speer 1946- 97-100
Morgan, Stanley 1929- 69-72
Morgan, Steven Michael 1942- 115
Morgan, Ted 1932- CANR-3
Earlier sketch in CA 45-48
See also CAAS 4
Morgan, (Joseph) Theodore 1910- 19-20R
See also CAAS 3
Morgan, Thomas (Bruce) 1885(?)-1972
Obituary 37-40R
Morgan, Thomas Bruce 1926- 13-14R
Morgan, Tom 1942- 108
See also SATA 42
Morgan, Valerie
See Paine, Lauran (Bosworth)
Morgan, Virginia
See Mundis, Hester
Morgan, Wesley
See Bennett, Isadora
Morgan, William 1944- 109
Morgan-Grenville, Gerard (Wyndham)
1931- 57-60
Morgan Witts, Max 1931- 29-32R
Morgello, Clemente Frank 1923- 103
Morgenroth, Barbara Brief entry 117
See also SATA 36
Morgenstein, Gary 1952- 116
Morgenstern, Christian 1871-1914
Brief entry 105
See also TCLC 8
Morgenstern, Dan Michael 1929-
Brief entry 111
Morgenstern, Julian 1881-1976 ..... CAP-1
Obituary 89-92
Earlier sketch in CA 19-20
Morgenstern, Oskar 1902-1977 ..... CANR-5
Obituary 73-76
Earlier sketch in CA 9-10R
Morgenstern, Soma 1891(?)-1976
Obituary 65-68
Morgenthau, Hans Joachim 1904-1980 .... 9-10R
Obituary 101
Morgenthau, Henry, Jr. 1891-1967
Obituary 116
Morghen, Raffaello 1896-1983 Obituary 109
Morgulas, Jerrold 1934- CANR-13
Earlier sketch in CA 23-24R
Morhaim, Victoria Kelrich 1937- 2R
Mori, Kyozo 1907(?)-1984 Obituary 112
Mori, Toshio 1910- Brief entry 116
Moriarty, Alice Marie Ewell 1917- 23-24R
Moriarty, Christopher 1936- 81-84
Moriarty, Florence Jarman 104
Moriarty, Frederick Leo 1913- CANR-2
Earlier sketch in CA 7-8R
Moriarty, Tim 1923- 61-64
Morice, Anne
See Shaw, Felicity
Morice, Dave 1946- 109
Morich, Stanton
See Griffith-Jones, George Chetwynd
Morick, Harold 1933- 25-28R
Morin, Claire
See Dore, Claire (Morin)
Morin, Edgar 1921- 107
Morin, Relman George 1907-1973 ..... CANR-4
Obituary 41-44R
Earlier sketch in CA 3R
Morin, William J(ames) 1939- 111
Morine, Hoder
See Conroy, John Wesley
Morini, Simona 1932- 110
Mori Ogai
See Mori Rintaro
See also TCLC 14
Mori Rintaro 1862-1922 Brief entry 110
Morisey, A. Alexander 1913-1979
Obituary 89-92
Morison, David Lindsay 1920- 15-16R
Morison, Samuel Eliot 1887-1976 ..... CANR-4
Obituary 65-68
Earlier sketch in CA 2R
See also DLB 17
Morisseau, James J(oseph) 1929- 41-44R
Morita, James R. 1931- 103
Morita, Yuzo 1940- CANR-1
Earlier sketch in CA 45-48
Moritz, A(lbert) F(rank) 1947- 110
Moritz, Charles Fredric 1917- 118
Morken, Lucinda Oakland 1906- 61-64
Morkovin, Bela V.
See Morkovin, Boris V(ladimir)
Morkovin, Boris V(ladimir) 1882-1968 .... CAP-1
Earlier sketch in CA 19-20
Morlan, George K(olmer) 1904- 29-32R
Morlan, John E(dmund) 1930- 11-12R
Morlan, Robert L(oren) 1920-1985 ..... 19-20R
Obituary 118
Morland, Dick
See Hill, Reginald (Charles)
Morland, Howard 1942- 107
Morland, (John) Kenneth 1916- 41-44R
Morland, Nigel 1905-1986 53-56
Obituary 119
Morland, Peter Henry
See Faust, Frederick (Shiller)
Morle, Albert Henry George 1919- 7-8R
Morley, Brian
See Bradley, Marion Zimmer
Morley, Christopher (Darlington)
1890-1957 Brief entry 112
See also DLB 9
Morley, David 1923- 108
Morley, Don 1937- 108
Morley, Felix M. 1894-1982 Obituary 106
Morley, Frank V(igor) 1899-1980 105
Morley, Frank Vigor 1899-1980 Obituary ... 102
Morley, (John) Geoffrey (Nicholson)
1905-1983 Obituary 109
Morley, Hugh 1908(?)-1978 Obituary 77-80
Morley, James William 1921- 13-14R
Morley, John 1838-1923 ..... DLB-57
Morley, Patricia (Ann) 1929- 73-76
Morley, Robert 1908- Brief entry 113
Morley, S(ylvanus) Griswold 1878- 5-6R
Morley, Samuel A. 1934- 37-40R
Morley, Sheridan 1941- 29-32R
Morley, Susan
See Cross, John Keir
Morley, Wilfred Owen
See Lowndes, Robert A(gustine) W(ard)
Morman, Jean Mary 1925- 61-64
Morn, Frank T(homas) 1937- 107
Morneau, Robert Fealey 1938- 113
Morningstar, Connie 1927- 69-72
Moroney, John R. 1939- CANR-17
Earlier sketch in CA 41-44R
Morowitz, Harold Joseph 1927- 104
Morpurgo, J(ack) E(ric) 1918- CANR-4
Earlier sketch in CA 9-10R
Morra, Marion Eleanor 104
Morra, Umberto ?-1981 Obituary 105
Morrah, Dave
See Morrah, David Wardlaw, Jr.
Morrah, David Wardlaw, Jr. 1914- 4R
See also SATA 10
Morrah, Dermot (Michael Macgregor)
1896-1974 ..... CAP-2
Obituary 53-56
Earlier sketch in CA 29-32
Morrall, John B. 1923- 25-28R
Morray, Joseph Parker 1916- 5-6R
Morreale, Ben 1924- 57-60
Morrell, David 1943- CANR-7
Earlier sketch in CA 57-60
Morrell, David C. 1929- 81-84
Morrell, Robert E(llis) 1930- 121
Morrell, William Parker 1899- CANR-1
Earlier sketch in CA 3R
Morren, Theophil
See Hofmannsthal, Hugo von
Morressy, John 1930- CANR-8
Earlier sketch in CA 23-24R
See also SATA 23
Morrice, J(ames) K(enneth) W(att) 1924- ... 118
Morrice, Ken
See Morrice, J(ames) K(enneth) W(att)
Morrie
See Turner, Morris
Morrill, Allen C(onrad) 1904- 101
Morrill, Claire 1900(?)-1981 Obituary 103
Morrill, Eleanor D(unlap) 1907- 101
Morrill, George Percival 1920- 33-36R
Morrill, Leslie H(olt) 1934- SATA-33, 48
Morrill, Richard
See Schreck, Everett M.
Morrill, Richard L(eland) 1934- 29-32R
Morris, A(ndrew) J(ames) A(nthony)
1936- CANR-12
Earlier sketch in CA 73-76
Morris, Adalaide K(irby) 1942- 57-60
Morris, Aldyth V. 1901- 29-32R
Morris, Alton C(hester) 1903- 15-16R
Morris, Ben(jamin Stephen) 1910- 113
Morris, Bernadine (Taub) 1925- 102
Morris, Bertram 1908- CANR-18
Earlier sketch in CA 2R
Morris, Brian 1930- CANR-18
Earlier sketch in CA 29-32R
Morris, Bruce R(obert) 1909- 5-6R
Morris, Charles (William) 1901- 13-14R
Morris, Charles Lee 1943(?)-1986
Obituary 118
Morris, Christopher 1938- 21-22R
Morris, Clyde M(cMahon) 1921- 93-96
Morris, (Edward) Craig 1939- 123
Morris, Cynthia Taft 1928- 25-28R
Morris, Dan (H.) 1912- 21-22R
Morris, David 1945- 85-88
Morris, David Brown 1942- CANR-22
Earlier sketch in CA 105
Morris, Desmond (John) 1928- CANR-18
Earlier sketches in CA 45-48, CANR-2
See also SATA 14
Morris, Donald R. 1924- 19-20R
Morris, Edgar Poe
See Kinnaird, Clark
Morris, Edita (deToll) CANR-1
Earlier sketch in CA 3R
Morris, Edmund 1940- 89-92
Morris, (Murrell) Edward 1935- CANR-14
Earlier sketch in CA 69-72
Morris, Edwin Bateman 1881-1971
Obituary 112
Morris, Eric 1940- 81-84
Morris, Everett B. 1899-1967 ..... CAP-1
Earlier sketch in CA 9-10
Morris, Freda 1933- CANR-4
Earlier sketch in CA 53-56
Morris, Gilbert (Leslie) 1929- 117
Morris, Grant Harold 1940- 29-32R
Morris, Gregory L(ynn) 1950- 119
Morris, Harry (Caesar) 1924- 11-12R
Morris, Helen 1909- CANR-18
Earlier sketch in CA 101
Morris, Henry M(adison, Jr.) 1918- CANR-13
Earlier sketch in CA 37-40R
Morris, Herbert 1928- CANR-1
Earlier sketch in CA 2R
Morris, Ira (Victor) 1903- 9-10R
Morris, Ivan (Ira Esme) 1925-1976 .... CANR-11
Obituary 65-68
Earlier sketch in CA 9-10R
Morris, J(ohn) H(umphrey) C(arlile) 1910- .. 7-8R
Morris, J(ames) Kenneth 1896- 5-6R
Morris, J. R. 1914(?)-1977 Obituary 73-76
Morris, Jackson E(dgar) 1918- 19-20R
Morris, James (Humphrey)
See Morris, Jan
Morris, James A(lvin) 1938- 120

Morris, James E(lliot) 1942- ... 112
Morris, James M(atthew) 1935- ... 89-92
Morris, Jan 1926- ... CANR-1
Earlier sketch in CA 3R
Morris, Jane
See Ardmore, Jane Kesner
Morris, Janet E(llen) 1946- ... CANR-13
Earlier sketch in CA 73-76
Morris, (Margaret) Jean 1924- Brief entry ... 116
Morris, Jerrold 1911- ... CANR-11
Earlier sketch in CA 23-24R
Morris, Joan 1901- ... 45-48
Morris, Joe A(lex) 1904- ... 65-68
Morris, Joe Alex, Jr. 1927- ... 73-76
Morris, John 1895-1980 Obituary ... 102
Morris, John
See Hearne, John (Edgar Caulwell)
Morris, John D(avid) 1946- ... 111
Morris, John N(elson) 1931- ... 33-36R
Morris, John O(sgood) 1918- ... 41-44R
Morris, John W(esley) 1907- ... CANR-6
Earlier sketch in CA 15-16R
Morris, Jonas 1933- ... 117
Morris, Judy K. 1936- ... 116
Morris, Julian
See West, Morris L(anglo)
Morris, Katharine ... CAP-1
Earlier sketch in CA 15-16
Morris, Kenneth T(hompson) 1941- ... 57-60
Morris, Leon (Lamb) 1914- ... CANR-20
Earlier sketches in CA 9-10R, CANR-4
Morris, Lewis 1833-1907 ... DLB-35
Morris, Loverne Lawton 1896- ... 7-8R
Morris, M.
See Thibaudeau, Colleen
Morris, Margaret 1891-1980 Obituary ... 97-100
Morris, Margaret Francine 1938- ... 57-60
Morris, Mary (Elizabeth Davis)
1913-1986 ... 53-56
Obituary ... 121
Morris, Mary Lee ... 120
Morris, Max 1913- ... 109
Morris, Mel (Merrill) 1930- ... 69-72
Morris, Michael 1914- ... CANR-5
Earlier sketch in CA 7-8R
Morris, Michael (Spence Lowdell)
1940- ... CANR-23
Earlier sketch in CA 107
Morris, Michelle 1941- ... 108
Morris, Milton D(onald) 1939- ... 57-60
Morris, Monica B. 1928- Brief entry ... 113
Morris, Nobuko
See Albery, Nobuko
Morris, Norman S. 1931- ... 33-36R
Morris, Norval 1923- ... 37-40R
Morris, Phyllis 1894-1982 Obituary ... 106
Morris, Phyllis Sutton 1931- ... 104
Morris, R(oger) J(ohn) B(owring) 1946- ... 93-96
Morris, Raymond N. 1936- ... 25-28R
Morris, Raymond Philip 1904- ... 45-48
Morris, Richard (Ward) 1939- ... CANR-18
Earlier sketches in CA 45-48, CANR-1
Morris, Richard B(randon) 1904- ... CANR-2
Earlier sketch in CA 49-52
See also DLB 17
Morris, Richard J(ules) 1942- ... CANR-16
Earlier sketch in CA 89-92
Morris, Richard K(nowles) 1915- ... 21-22R
Morris, Robert 1910- ... CANR-16
Earlier sketch in CA 89-92
Morris, Robert (Lyle) 1942- Brief entry ... 116
Morris, Robert A(da) 1933- ... 49-52
See also SATA 7
Morris, Robert Kerwin 1933- ... 33-36R
Morris, Ruby Turner 1908- ... CANR-1
Earlier sketch in CA 2R
Morris, Ruth
See Webb, Ruth Enid Borlase Morris
Morris, Sara
See Burke, John (Frederick)
Morris, Sarah M(iller) 1906- ... 81-84
Morris, Scot 1942- ... 101
Morris, Stephen 1935- ... CANR-20
Earlier sketch in CA 103
Morris, Steveland Judkins 1950(?)-
Brief entry ... 111
Morris, Suzanne 1944- ... CANR-17
Earlier sketch in CA 89-92
Morris, T(homas) B(aden) 1900- ... CANR-2
Earlier sketch in CA 7-8R
Morris, Taylor 1923- ... 103
Morris, Terry Lesser 1914- ... 9-10R
Morris, Thomas D(ean) 1938- Brief entry ... 112
Morris, Thomas Victor 1952- ... 120
Morris, Tina 1941- ... CANR-12
Earlier sketch in CA 29-32R
Morris, W. R. 1936- ... 77-80
Morris, William 1834-1896 ... DLB-18, 35, 57
Morris, William 1913- ... CANR-12
Earlier sketch in CA 19-20R
See also SATA 29
Morris, William E(dgar) 1926- ... 9-10R
Morris, William O. 1922- ... 37-40R
Morris, William T(homas) 1928- ... 19-20R
Morris, Willie 1934- ... CANR-13
Earlier sketch in CA 19-20R
See also DLBY 80
See also AITN 2
Morris, Wright 1910- ... CANR-21
Earlier sketch in CA 9-10R
See also DLB 2
See also DLBY 81
See also CLC 1, 3, 7, 18, 37
Morrisey, George L(ewis) 1926- ... CANR-14
Earlier sketch in CA 73-76
Morris-Goodall, Vanne 1909- ... 29-32R
Morrish, (Ernest) Ivor (James) 1914- ... 33-36R
Morris-Jones, W(yndraeth) H(umphreys)
1918- ... CANR-11
Earlier sketch in CA 21-22R
Morrison, Arnold Telford 1928- ... 110
Morrison, Arthur 1863-1945 Brief entry ... 120
Morrison, Bill 1935- Brief entry ... 115
See also SATA 37
Morrison, Bruce 1904(?)-1983 Obituary ... 109
Morrison, Carl V(incent) 1908- ... 93-96
Morrison, Charles Clayton 1874-1966
Obituary ... 89-92
Morrison, Cheryl 1947- ... 107
Morrison, Chloe Anthony Wofford
See Morrison, Toni
Morrison, Claudia C(hristopherson)
1936- ... 29-32R
Morrison, Clinton (Dawson, Jr.) 1924- ... 15-16R
Morrison, David (Douglas) 1940- ... 112
Morrison, Denton E(dward) 1932- ... CANR-6
Earlier sketch in CA 57-60
Morrison, Donald George 1938- ... 85-88
Morrison, Dorothy Nafus ... CANR-24
Earlier sketches in CA 61-64, CANR-8
See also SATA 29
Morrison, Edward
See Humphrey, Paul
Morrison, Eleanor S(helton) 1921- ... CANR-1
Earlier sketch in CA 49-52
Morrison, Eula Atwood 1911- ... 25-28R
Morrison, Frank G. 1894(?)-1983
Obituary ... 111
Morrison, Frank M. 1914- ... 37-40R
Morrison, Fred L. 1939- Brief entry ... 112
Morrison, G.F.
See Bernstein, Gerry
Morrison, Gert W.
See Stratemeyer, Edward L.
Morrison, Hobe 1904- ... 77-80
Morrison, Howard A(lexander) 1955- ... 118
Morrison, Ida Edith ... 2R
Morrison, J. S.
See Morrison, John (Sinclair)
Morrison, Jack 1912- ... 105
Morrison, James (Harris) 1918- ... 73-76
Morrison, James (Ryan) 1924- ... 105
Morrison, James Douglas 1943-1971 ... 73-76
Morrison, James F(rederic) 1937- ... 25-28R
Morrison, James L(unsford), Jr. 1923- ... 57-60
Morrison, James R(oy) 1940- ... 123
Morrison, James R. 1940- Brief entry ... 118
Morrison, Jim
See Morrison, James Douglas
See also CLC 17
Morrison, John (Sinclair) 1913- ... 122
Morrison, John Gordon 1904- ... 103
Morrison, Joseph L(ederman) 1918-1970 ... 5-6R
Obituary ... 122
Morrison, Kristin (Diane) 1934- ... CANR-14
Earlier sketch in CA 37-40R
Morrison, Lester M. 1907- ... CAP-1
Earlier sketch in CA 15-16
Morrison, Lillian 1917- ... CANR-22
Earlier sketches in CA 11-12R, CANR-7
See also SATA 3
Morrison, Lucile Phillips 1896- ... SATA-17
Morrison, Margaret Mackie 19(?)-1973
Obituary ... 41-44R
Morrison, Marsh 1902- ... CANR-10
Earlier sketch in CA 61-64
Morrison, N(ancy Agnes) Brysson (Inglis)
?-1986 ... 15-16R
Obituary ... 118
Morrison, Paul Fix 1902-1983 Obituary ... 111
Morrison, Peggy
See Morrison, Margaret Mackie
Morrison, Philip 1915- Brief entry ... 106
Morrison, Phylis 1927- ... 117
Morrison, Richard
See Lowndes, Robert A(ugustine) W(ard)
Morrison, Robert
See Lowndes, Robert A(ugustine) W(ard)
Morrison, Robert H(aywood) 1927- ... 5-6R
Morrison, Robert S(tanley) 1909- ... 65-68
Morrison, Roberta
See Webb, Jean Francis
Morrison, Susan Dudley 1949- ... 119
Morrison, Theodore 1901- ... CANR-1
Earlier sketch in CA 4R
Morrison, Toni 1931- ... 29-32R
See also DLB 6, 33
See also DLBY 81
See also CLC 4, 10, 22
Morrison, Tony 1936- ... 81-84
Morrison, Van 1945- Brief entry ... 116
See also CLC 21
Morrison, Velma Ford 1909- ... 9-10R
See also SATA 21
Morrison, Victor
See Glut, Donald F(rank)
Morrison, Wilbur Howard 1915- ... CANR-1
Earlier sketch in CA 3R
Morrison, William
See Samachson, Joseph
Morrison, William R(obert) 1942- ... 124
Morrison-Reed, Mark D(ouglas) 1949- ... 116
Morriss, Frank 1923- ... CANR-3
Earlier sketch in CA 5-6R
Morriss, J. H.
See Ghnassia, Maurice (Jean-Henri)
Morriss, James E(dward) 1932- ... 57-60
See also SATA 8
Morriss, Mack 1920(?)-1976 Obituary ... 65-68
Morrissette, Bruce A(rcher) 1911- ... 19-20R
Morrissey, Charles Thomas 1933- ... 108
Morrissey, L(eroy) J(ohn) 1935- ... CANR-1
Earlier sketch in CA 49-52
Morrissey, Leonard E., Jr. 1925- ... 11-12R
Morrissey, Stephen 1950- ... 115
Morris-Suzuki, Tessa 1951- ... 123
Morritt, Hope 1930- ... CANR-16
Earlier sketch in CA 97-100
Morrow, Betty
See Bacon, Elizabeth
Morrow, Bradford 1951- ... 113
Morrow, Charlotte
See Kirwan, Molly (Morrow)
Morrow, E(verett) Frederic 1909- ... CANR-2
Earlier sketch in CA 7-8R
Morrow, Felix 1906- ... 107
Morrow, Glenn R(aymond) 1895-197(?) ... CAP-1
Earlier sketch in CA 19-20
Morrow, James 1947- ... 108
Morrow, John Howard 1910- ... 25-28R
Morrow, John Howard, Jr. 1944- ... 113
Morrow, Lance 1939- Brief entry ... 119
Morrow, Mable 1892-1977 Obituary ... 106
Morrow, Mary Lou 1926- ... 61-64
Morrow, Patrick David 1940- ... CANR-8
Earlier sketch in CA 61-64
Morrow, Stephen 1939- ... 73-76
Morrow, William L(ockhart) 1935- ... 33-36R
Mors, Victor
See Roeseler, W(olfgang) G(uenter)
Mors, Wallace P. 1911- ... 19-20R
Morsberger, Katharine M. 1931- ... 105
Morsberger, Robert Eustis 1929- ... CANR-3
Earlier sketch in CA 5-6R
Morscher, Betsy 1939- ... 115
Morse, A. Reynolds 1914- ... CANR-7
Earlier sketch in CA 19-20R
Morse, Anne Christensen 1915- ... 4R
Morse, Arthur David 1920-1971
Obituary ... 29-32R
Morse, B. J. ?-1977 Obituary ... 73-76
Morse, Carol
See Yeakley, Marjory Hall
Morse, Chandler 1906- ... 5-6R
Morse, Charles A. 1898- ... CAP-1
Earlier sketch in CA 19-20
Morse, David 1940- ... 37-40R
Morse, Donald E. 1936- ... 37-40R
Morse, Donald R(oy) 1931- ... CANR-21
Earlier sketch in CA 105
Morse, Dorothy B(ayley) 1906-1979 ... SATA-24
Morse, Edward Lewis 1942- ... CANR-7
Earlier sketch in CA 57-60
Morse, Flo 1921- ... 106
See also SATA 30
Morse, Grant W(esley) 1926- ... 19-20R
Morse, H(enry) Clifton Iv 1924- ... 9-10R
Morse, Harold Marston 1892-1977
Obituary ... 69-72
Morse, Hermann Nelson 1887-1977
Obituary ... 73-76
Morse, J(osiah) Mitchell 1912- ... 65-68
Morse, Jedidiah 1761-1826 ... DLB-37
Morse, John D. 1906- ... 104
Morse, John T., Jr. 1840-1937 ... DLB-47
Morse, L(arry) A(lan) 1945- ... 107
Morse, Peter 1935- ... CANR-14
Earlier sketch in CA 73-76
Morse, Philip M(cCord) 1903-1985 ... 108
Obituary ... 117
Morse, Richard M(cGee) 1922- ... CANR-10
Earlier sketch in CA 15-16R
Morse, Roger A(lfred) 1927- ... CANR-23
Earlier sketches in CA 57-60, CANR-8
Morse, Samuel French 1916- ... CANR-4
Earlier sketch in CA 9-10R
Morse, Theresa Adler 1901-1980 ... 89-92
Obituary ... 97-100
Morse, Thomas S(purr) 1925- ... 109
Morse, Wayne (Lyman) 1900-1974
Obituary ... 49-52
Morse-Boycott, Desmond (Lionel)
1892-1979 ... 107
Obituary ... 104
Morsey, Royal J(oseph) 1910- ... 73-76
Morshead, Ian 1922- ... 111
Morshiel, George
See Shiels, George
Morson, Gary S(aul) 1948- ... 121
Morss, Elisabeth W. 1918- ... 41-44R
Mort, Vivian
See Cromie, Alice Hamilton
Mortensen, Ben(jamin) F. 1928- ... 104
Mortensen, C. David 1939- ... 37-40R
Mortimer, Anthony 1936- ... 116
Mortimer, Armine Kotin 1943- ... 117
Mortimer, Chapman
See Chapman-Mortimer, William Charles
Mortimer, John (Clifford) 1923- ... CANR-21
Earlier sketch in CA 13-14R
See also DLB 13
See also CLC 28, 43
Mortimer, John L(ynn) 1908- ... 69-72
Mortimer, Mary H.
See Coury, Louise Andree
Mortimer, Penelope (Ruth) 1918- ... 57-60
See also CLC 5
Mortimer, Peter
See Roberts, Dorothy James
Mortimore, Olive 1890- ... 49-52
Morton, A(rthur) L(eslie) 1903-1987 ... 11-12R
Obituary ... 124
Morton, A(ndrew) Q(ueen) 1919- ... 105
Morton, Alexander C(lark) 1936- ... CANR-12
Earlier sketch in CA 25-28R
Morton, Anthony
See Creasey, John
Morton, C(lement) Manly 1884-1976 ... CAP-2
Earlier sketch in CA 29-32
Morton, Carlos 1947- ... 73-76
Morton, Desmond 1937- ... CANR-15
Earlier sketch in CA 29-32R
Morton, Donald E(dward) 1938- ... 57-60
Morton, Frederic 1924- ... CANR-20
Earlier sketches in CA 2R, CANR-3
Morton, Gregory 1911-1986 ... 102
Obituary ... 118
Morton, H(enry Canova) V(ollam)
1892-1979 ... 103
Obituary ... 89-92
Morton, Harry 1925- ... CANR-15
Earlier sketch in CA 81-84
Morton, Henry W(alter) 1929- ... 13-14R
Morton, Jane 1931- ... 93-96
See also SATA 50
Morton, Jocelyn 1912- ... 73-76
Morton, John (Cameron Andrieu) Bingham
(Michael) 1893-1979 ... 93-96
Obituary ... 85-88
Morton, Joseph
See Richmond, Al
Morton, Lee Jack, Jr. 1928- ... SATA-32
Morton, Lena Beatrice 1901- ... 19-20R
Morton, Leopold 1922- ... 110
Morton, Louis 1913-1976 ... CANR-21
Obituary ... 65-68
Earlier sketch in CA 69-72
Morton, Lucie T. 1950- ... 118
Morton, Lynne 1952- ... 106
Morton, Marcia Colman 1927- ... 73-76
Morton, Marian J(ohnson) 1937- ... 77-80
Morton, Miriam 1918(?)-1985 ... CANR-2
Obituary ... 117
Earlier sketch in CA 49-52
See also SATA 9, 46
Morton, Nathaniel 1613-1685 ... DLB-24
Morton, Newton 1901-1967 ... CAP-1
Earlier sketch in CA 19-20
Morton, Patricia
See Golding, Morton J(ay)
Morton, Phyllis Digby ?-1984 Obituary ... 113
Morton, R(obert) S(teel) 1917- ... 49-52
Morton, Richard (Everett) 1930- ... 37-40R
Morton, Richard Lee 1889-1974 ... CANR-16
Obituary ... 53-56
Earlier sketch in CA 2R
Morton, Robert 1934- ... 69-72
Morton, Robert L(ee) 1889- ... 45-48
Morton, Sarah Wentworth 1759-1846 ... DLB-37
Morton, T(homas) Ralph 1900- ... 29-32R
Morton, Thomas 1579(?)-1647(?) ... DLB-24
Morton, W(illiam) L(ewis) 1908- ... CAP-1
Earlier sketch in CA 19-20
Morton, W(illiam) Scott 1908- ... 81-84
Morton, Ward McKinnon 1907- ... 2R
Morton, William C(uthbert) 1875-1971 ... CAP-2
Earlier sketch in CA 25-28
Morwood, James 1943- ... 124
Moscati, Sabatino 1922- ... 77-80
Mosco, Vincent 1948- ... 114
Moscotti, Albert D(ennis) 1920- ... 65-68
Moscovitch, Allan 1946- ... 111
Moscovitz, Judy 1942- ... 123
Moscow, Alvin 1925- ... CANR-4
Earlier sketch in CA 2R
See also SATA 3
Moscow, Henry (I.) 1904(?)-1983
Obituary ... 108
Moscow, Warren 1908- ... 23-24R
Moscowitz, Raymond 1938- ... 111
Mosel, Arlene (Tichy) 1921- ... 49-52
See also SATA 7
Mosel, Tad 1922- ... 73-76
Moseley, David (Victor) 1939- ... 97-100
Moseley, Edwin M(aurice) 1916-1978 ... CANR-8
Earlier sketch in CA 5-6R
Moseley, George (V. H. III) 1931- ... 49-52
Moseley, J(oseph) Edward 1910-1973 ... 37-40R
Moseley, James G(wyn) 1946- ... 116
Moseley, Ray 1932- ... 85-88
Moseley, Spencer A(ltemont) 1925- ... 93-96
Moseley, Virginia D(ouglas) 1917- ... 23-24R
Mosely, Philip Edward 1905-1972
Obituary ... 33-36R
Moser, Charles A. 1935- ... 29-32R
Moser, Don(ald Bruce) 1932- ... 106
See also SATA 31
Moser, Lawrence E. 1939- ... 33-36R
Moser, Mary Beck 1924- ... 122
Moser, Norman Calvin 1931- ... CANR-10
Earlier sketch in CA 57-60
Moser, Reta C(arol) 1936- ... 15-16R
Moser, Shia 1906- ... CAP-2
Earlier sketch in CA 25-28
Moser, Thomas (Colborn) 1923- ... 7-8R
Moses, Anna Mary Robertson 1860-1961
Obituary ... 93-96
Moses, Claire Goldberg 1941- ... 113
Moses, Elbert R(aymond), Jr. 1908- ... CAP-1
Earlier sketch in CA 15-16
Moses, Gerald Robert 1938- ... 57-60
Moses, Grandma
See Moses, Anna Mary Robertson
Moses, Joel C(harles) 1944- ... CANR-10
Earlier sketch in CA 65-68
Moses, Robert 1888-1981 ... 45-48
Obituary ... 104
Moses, W(illiam) R(obert) 1911- ... 11-12R
Moses, Wilson Jeremiah 1942- ... 85-88
Mosesson, Gloria R(ubin) ... 41-44R
See also SATA 24
Mosey, Anne Cronin 1938- ... 49-52
Moshe, David
See Winkelman, Donald M.
Mosher, Arthur Theodore 1910- ... 85-88
Mosher, Frederick C(amp) 1913- ... 37-40R

Mosher, Ralph Lamont 1928- CANR-7
Earlier sketch in CA 19-20R
Mosher, Steven W(estley) 1948- 116
Mosher, (Christopher) Terry 1942- 93-96
Moshier, W(illiam) Franklyn 1929- 97-100
Mosiman, Billie Sue (Stahl) 1947- 119
Mosk
See Moskowitz, Gene
Moskin, J(ohn) Robert 1923- 19-20R
Moskin, Marietta D(unston) 1928- CANR-13
Earlier sketch in CA 73-76
See also SATA 23
Moskof, Martin Stephen 1930- 29-32R
See also SATA 27
Moskos, Charles C. 1934- CANR-10
Earlier sketch in CA 25-28R
Moskow, Michael H. 1938- CANR-14
Earlier sketch in CA 37-40R
Moskowitz, Gene 1921(?)-1982 Obituary ... 108
Moskowitz, Ira 1912- 102
Moskowitz, Moses 1911- Brief entry 114
Moskowitz, Robert 1946- 109
Moskowitz, Sam 1920- CANR-4
Earlier sketch in CA 7-8R
Moskvitin, Jurij 1938- 93-96
Mosley, Diana 1910- 106
Mosley, Jean Bell 1913- 9-10R
Mosley, Leonard O(swald) 1913- 109
Brief entry 108
Mosley, Nicholas 1923- 69-72
See also DLB 14
See also CLC 43
Mosley, Oswald (Ernald) 1896-1980 ..... CAP-2
Obituary 102
Earlier sketch in CA 25-28
Moss, Arthur 1889-1969 Obituary 112
See also DLB 4
Moss, Barbara 1946- 116
Moss, Bernard H(aym) 1943- Brief entry ... 115
Moss, Bobby Gilmer 1932- 49-52
Moss, C(laude) Scott 1924- CANR-8
Earlier sketch in CA 19-20R
Moss, Cynthia J(ane) 1940- CANR-12
Earlier sketch in CA 65-68
Moss, Don(ald) 1920- SATA-11
Moss, Elaine (Dora) 1924- Brief entry 110
See also SATA 31
Moss, Frank Edward 1911- CANR-13
Earlier sketch in CA 61-64
Moss, Gordon E(rvin) 1937- 57-60
Moss, Howard 1922-1987 .... CANR-1
Obituary 123
Earlier sketch in CA 2R
See also DLB 5
See also CLC 7, 14, 45
Moss, J. Joel 1922- 45-48
Moss, James A(llen) 1920- 33-36R
Moss, John 1940- CANR-17
Earlier sketch in CA 97-100
Moss, Leonard (Jerome) 1931- 25-28R
Moss, Michael (Stanley) 1947- 108
Moss, Nancy
See Moss, Robert (Alfred)
Moss, Norman 1928- 49-52
Moss, (Victor) Peter (Cannings) 1921- .. CANR-2
Earlier sketch in CA 49-52
Moss, Ralph W(alter) 1943- 101
Moss, Robert (Alfred) 1903- CAP-1
Earlier sketch in CA 11-12
Moss, Robert (John) 1946- Brief entry 118
Moss, Robert F. 1942- CANR-20
Earlier sketch in CA 81-84
Moss, Roberta
See Moss, Robert (Alfred)
Moss, Roger 1951- 124
Moss, Rose 1937- 49-52
Moss, Sanford Alexander III 1939- 118
Moss, Sidney P(hil) 1917- 5-6R
Moss, Stanley 1925- 97-100
Moss, Stephen Joseph 1935- 103
Moss, Stirling 1929- 7-8R
Moss, Walter (Gerald) 1938- 65-68
Mosse, George L(achmann) 1918- CANR-12
Earlier sketch in CA 5-6R
Mosse, Werner E(ugen Emil) 1918- 9-10R
Mossiker, Frances (Sanger) 1906-1985 ...11-12R
Obituary 116
Mossman, Dow 1943- 45-48
Mossman, Frank H(omer) 1915- CANR-5
Earlier sketch in CA 3R
Mossman, Jennifer 1944- CANR-17
Earlier sketch in CA 97-100
Mossner, Ernest C(ampbell) 1907-1986 123
Mossner, Ernest Campbell 1907-1986
Obituary 120
Mossop, D(eryk) J(oseph) 1919- 3R
Mossop, Irene
See Swatridge, Irene Maude (Mossop)
Most, Bernard 1937- 104
See also SATA 40, 48
Most, Glenn W(arren) 1952- 112
Most, William G(eorge) 1914- 49-52
Mostel, Kate
See Mostel, Kathryn Harkin
Mostel, Katherine Harkin
See Mostel, Kathryn Harkin
Mostel, Kathryn Harkin 1918-1986 81-84
Obituary 118
Mostel, Samuel Joel 1915-1977 89-92
Mostel, Zero
See Mostel, Samuel Joel
Mosteller, (Charles) Frederick 1916- ... CANR-23
Earlier sketches in CA 19-20R, CANR-7
Mostert, Noel 1929- 105
Mostofsky, David I(saac) 1931- 19-20R
Mota, Avelino Teixeira da
See Teixeira da Mota, Avelino
Mother Mary Anthony
See Weinig, Jean Maria
Mothershead, Harmon Ross 1931- 33-36R
Mothner, Ira S(anders) 1932- CANR-13
Earlier sketch in CA 21-22R
Motion, Andrew 1952- DLB-40
See also CLC 47
Motley, Arthur H(arrison) 1900-1984
Obituary 112
See also AITN 2
Motley, John Lothrop
1814-1877 ....DLB-1, 30, 59
Motley, Mary
See De Reneville, Mary Margaret Motley
Sheridan
Motley, Mary Penick 1920- 73-76
Motley, Red
See Motley, Arthur H(arrison)
Motley, Willard (Francis) 1912-1965 117
Obituary 106
See also CLC 18
Motley, Wilma E(lizabeth) 1912- 41-44R
Motmot, Snik P.
See Tompkins, Everett Thomas
Motoyama, Hiroshi 1925- 110
Mott, Frank Luther 1886-1964 .... 4R
Mott, George Fox 1907-1987 ....13-14R
Obituary 123
Mott, Michael (Charles Alston) 1930- ... CANR-7
Earlier sketch in CA 7-8R
See also CLC 15, 34
Mott, Paul E. 103
Mott, Stephen Charles 1940- 116
Mott, Vincent Valmon 1916- 41-44R
Motta, Dick 1931- Brief entry 111
Mottahedeh, Roy Parviz 1940- CANR-21
Earlier sketch in CA 104
Motter, Alton M(yers) 1907- CAP-1
Earlier sketch in CA 11-12
Motto, Anna Lydia 41-44R
Motto, Carmine J. 1914- 33-36R
Mottram, Anthony John 1920- 7-8R
Mottram, (Vernon) Henry 1882-19(?) CAP-1
Earlier sketch in CA 11-12
Mottram, R(alph) H(ale) 1883-1971 108
Obituary 29-32R
See also DLB 36
Mottram, Tony
See Mottram, Anthony John
Motz, Lloyd 1909- CANR-4
Earlier sketch in CA 9-10R
See also SATA 20
Mouat, Kit 1920- 113
Mould, Daphne D(esiree) C(harlotte) Pochin
1920- CANR-4
Earlier sketch in CA 9-10R
Mould, George 1894- 57-60
Moule, C(harles) F(rancis) D(igby)
1908- CANR-5
Earlier sketch in CA 4R
Moulier, (Antoine) Fernand 1913- 81-84
Moult, Edward (Walker) 1926-1986
Obituary 120
Moult, Ted
See Moult, Edward (Walker)
Moult, Thomas 1895-1974 Obituary 89-92
Moulton, Edward C. 1936- 77-80
Moulton, Eugene R(ussell) 1916-1981 .. CANR-11
Earlier sketch in CA 23-24R
Moulton, Gary E(van) 1942- 115
Moulton, Harland B. 1925- 37-40R
Moulton, J(ames) L(ouis) 1906- 23-24R
Moulton, Nancy 1946- 116
Moulton, Phillips P(rentice) 1909- 37-40R
Moulton, William G(amwell) 1914- 9-10R
Mouly, George J(oseph) 1915- CANR-17
Earlier sketch in CA 3R
Mounce, R(obert H.) 1921- CANR-2
Earlier sketch in CA 3R
Mount, Charles Merrill 1928- 13-14R
Mount, Elisabeth
See Dougherty, Betty
Mount, Ellis 1921- 116
Mount, (William Robert) Ferdinand
1939- CANR-11
Earlier sketch in CA 21-22R
Mount, Marshall Ward 1927- 73-76
Mountain, Julian
See Cowie, Donald
Mountain, Marian
See Wisberg, Marian Aline
Mountain, Robert
See Montgomery, Raymond A. (Jr.)
Mountbatten, Louis (Francis Albert Victor
Nicholas) 1900-1979 Obituary 113
Mountbatten, Richard
See Wallmann, Jeffrey M(iner)
Mountfield, David
See Grant, Neil
Mountfield, Stuart 1903(?)-1984 Obituary .. 115
Mountfort, Guy 1905- 19-20R
Mountjoy, Roberta Jean
See Sohl, Jerry
Mountsier, Robert 1888(?)-1972
Obituary 37-40R
Mourant, John A(rthur) 1903- CAP-1
Earlier sketch in CA 9-10
Moure, Erin 1955- 113
See also DLB 60
Mourelatos, Alexander P(hoebus)
D(ionysiou) 1936- 29-32R
Mourier, Marguerite
See Boulton, Marjorie
Moursund, David G. 1936- CANR-12
Earlier sketch in CA 25-28R
Moursund, Janet (Peck) 1936- 45-48
Moussa, Pierre L(ouis) 1922- 13-14R
Moussard, Jacqueline 1924- CANR-8
Earlier sketch in CA 61-64
See also SATA 24
Mouton, Jane Srygley 1930- 123
Moutoux, John T. 1901(?)-1979
Obituary 89-92
Mouzelis, Nicos P. 1939- 33-36R
Mouzon, Olin T(errell) 1912- 7-8R
Mow, Anna Beahm 1893- CANR-3
Earlier sketch in CA 9-10R
Mowat, C(harles) L(och) 1911-1970 ..... CAP-1
Earlier sketch in CA 15-16
Mowat, David 1943- 77-80
Mowat, Farley (McGill) 1921- CANR-24
Earlier sketches in CA 3R, CANR-4
See also SATA 3
See also CLC 26
Mowat, R(obert) C(ase) 1913- 29-32R
Mowatt, Ian 1948- 41-44R
Mowitz, Robert J(ames) 1920- CANR-3
Earlier sketch in CA 5-6R
Mowrer, Edgar Ansel 1892-1977 .... CAP-1
Obituary 69-72
Earlier sketch in CA 15-16
See also DLB 29
Mowrer, Lilian Thomson 65-68
Mowrer, O(rval) Hobart 1907- CANR-1
Earlier sketch in CA 4R
Mowrer, Paul Scott 1887-1971 .... CANR-4
Obituary 29-32R
Earlier sketch in CA 5-6R
See also DLB 29
Mowry, George E(dwin) 1909-1984 .... CANR-17
Earlier sketch in CA 2R
Mowshowitz, Abbe 1939- 109
Moxham, Robert Morgan 1919-1978
Obituary 77-80
Moyer, Claire B. (Inch) 1905- CAP-2
Earlier sketch in CA 19-20
Moyer, Elgin Sylvester 1890- 5-6R
Moyer, Kenneth E(van) 1919- CANR-13
Earlier sketch in CA 33-36R
Moyers, Bill 1934- 61-64
See also AITN 2
Moyes, John Stoward 1884- CAP-1
Earlier sketch in CA 13-14
Moyes, Norman Barr 1931- 37-40R
Moyes, Patricia
See Haszard, Patricia Moyes
Moyler, Alan (Frank Powell) 1926- SATA-36
Moyles, R(obert) Gordon 1939- CANR-17
Earlier sketch in CA 65-68
Moynahan, John F. 1912-1985 Obituary 115
Moynahan, Julian (Lane) 1925- CANR-1
Earlier sketch in CA 2R
Moyne, Ernest J(ohn) 1916-1976 .... CAP-2
Earlier sketch in CA 25-28
Moynihan, Daniel P(atrick) 1927- 7-8R
Moynihan, John Dominic 1932- 103
Moynihan, Maurice (Gerard) 1902- 107
Moynihan, Ruth B(arnes) 1933- 117
Moynihan, William T. 1927- 23-24R
Moyse-Bartlett, Hubert 1902(?)-1973(?)
Obituary 104
Mozley, Charles 1915- SATA-32, 43
Mphahlele, Ezekiel 1919- 81-84
See also CLC 25
Mqhayi, S(amuel) E(dward) K(rune Loliwe)
1875-1945 ....TCLC-25
Mr. Cleveland
See Seltzer, Louis B(enson)
Mr. Kenneth
See Marlowe, Kenneth
Mr. Martin
See Burroughs, William (Seward)
Mr. McGillicuddy
See Abisch, Roslyn Kroop
Mr. Metropolitan Opera
See Robinson, Francis (Arthur)
Mr. Sniff
See Abisch, Roslyn Kroop
Mr. Wizard
See Herbert, Don
Mrabet, Mohammed
See el Hajjam, Mohammed ben Chaib
Mrazek, James E(dward) 1914- 33-36R
Mrozek, Donald J(ohn) 1945- 107
Mrozek, Slawomir 1930- 13-14R
See also CLC 3, 13
Mrs. Belloc-Lowndes
See Lowndes, Marie Adelaide (Belloc)
Mrs. Bishop
See Bishop, Isabella Lucy (Bird)
Mrs. Fairstar
See Horne, Richard Henry
Mrs. G.
See Griffiths, Kitty Anna
Mrs. Miggy
See Krentel, Mildred White
Mrs. R.F.D.
See Peden, Rachel (Mason)
M'Taggart, John M'Taggart Ellis
See McTaggart, John McTaggart Ellis
M'Timkulu, Donald (Guy Sidney) 1910- ...97-100
Mtwa, Percy 19(?)- CLC-47
Mu, Yang
See Wang, C(hing) H(sien)
Mucha, Jiri 1915- CANR-11
Earlier sketch in CA 23-24R
Muchnic, Helen (Lenore) 1903- CANR-5
Earlier sketch in CA 2R
Mudd, Emily Hartshorne 1898- 15-16R
Mudd, Roger H(arrison) 1928- 105
Mudd, Stuart 1893-1975 ....11-12R
Obituary 57-60
Mude, O
See Gorey, Edward (St. John)
Mudge, Jean McClure 1933- CANR-6
Earlier sketch in CA 7-8R
Mudge, Lewis Seymour 1929- 89-92
Mudgeon, Apeman
See Mitchell, Adrian
Mudgett, Herman W.
See White, William A(nthony) P(arker)
Mudie, Ian (Mayelston) 1911- 25-28R
Mudrick, Marvin 1921- CANR-20
Earlier sketch in CA 25-28R
Muecke, D(ouglas) C(olin) 1919- 53-56
Muehl, Lois Baker 1920- CANR-18
Earlier sketch in CA 3R
Muehl, (Ernest) William 1919- 45-48
Muehlen, Norbert 1909-1981 69-72
Obituary 104
Muehsam, Gerd 1913(?)-1979 Obituary ...93-96
Muelder, Walter George 1907- CAP-1
Earlier sketch in CA 13-14
Mueller, Amelia 1911- 57-60
Mueller, Barbara R(uth) 1925- 11-12R
Mueller, Charles S(teinkamp) 1929- CANR-20
Earlier sketches in CA 13-14R, CANR-5
Mueller, Claus 1941- 65-68
Mueller, David L. 1929- 29-32R
Mueller, Dennis C(ary) 1940- 116
Mueller, Dorothy 1901- 102
Mueller, Erwin W. 1911-1977 Obituary 69-72
Mueller, Gerald F(rancis) 1927- 15-16R
Mueller, Gerhard G(ottlob) 1930- CANR-12
Earlier sketch in CA 25-28R
Mueller, Gerhard O. W. 1926- CANR-20
Earlier sketches in CA 2R, CANR-5
Mueller, Gerhardt
See Bickers, Richard Leslie Townshend
Mueller, Gustav Emil 1898- CANR-7
Earlier sketch in CA 19-20R
Mueller, James W(illiam) 1941- 57-60
Mueller, John E(rnest) 1937- CANR-14
Earlier sketch in CA 37-40R
Mueller, Kate Hevner 1898- 41-44R
Mueller, Klaus Andrew 1921- CANR-4
Earlier sketch in CA 49-52
Mueller, Lisel 1924- 93-96
See also CLC 13
Mueller, M(ax) G(erhard) 1925- 19-20R
Mueller, Marlies K(uhfuss) 1937- 114
Mueller, Merrill 1916-1980 Obituary 103
Mueller, Red
See Mueller, Merrill
Mueller, Reuben Herbert 1897-1982
Obituary 107
Mueller, Robert E(mmett) 1925- 4R
Mueller, Robert Kirk 1913- CANR-12
Earlier sketch in CA 73-76
Mueller, Virginia 1924- CANR-10
Earlier sketch in CA 65-68
See also SATA 28
Mueller, Willard Fritz 1925- 19-20R
Mueller, William R(andolph) 1916- CANR-2
Earlier sketch in CA 3R
Muenchen, Al(fred) 1917- 49-52
Muesing, Edith E(lizabeth)
See Muesing-Ellwood, Edith E(lizabeth)
Muesing-Ellwood, Edith E(lizabeth) 1947- ... 114
Muffett, D(avid) J(oseph) M(ead) 1919- ... 45-48
Muggeridge, Malcolm (Thomas) 1903- 101
See also AITN 1
Muggeson, Margaret Elizabeth 1942- 103
Muhajir, Nazzam Al Fitnah
See El Muhajir
Muheim, Harry Miles 1920- 85-88
Muhlen, Norbert
See Muehlen, Norbert
Muhlenfeld, Elisabeth 1944- CANR-24
Earlier sketch in CA 108
Muhlhausen, John Prague 1940- 61-64
Muhlstein, Anka 1935- 114
Mui, Hoh-cheung 1916- 45-48
Muileman, Kathryn Saltzman 1946- 85-88
Muilenburg, Grace (Evelyn) 1913- 61-64
Muir, (Charles) Augustus 13-14R
Muir, Barbara K(enrick Gowing) 1908- ...11-12R
Muir, Dexter
See Gribble, Leonard (Reginald)
Muir, Edwin 1887-1959 Brief entry 104
See also DLB 20
See also TCLC 2
Muir, Frank 1920- 81-84
See also SATA 30
Muir, Helen AITN-2
Muir, Helen 1937- DLB-14
Muir, Jane
See Petrone, Jane Muir
Muir, Jean 1906-1973 .... CAP-2
Obituary 41-44R
Earlier sketch in CA 29-32
Muir, Kenneth (Arthur) 1907- CANR-4
Earlier sketch in CA 2R
Muir, Lynette R(oss) 1930- 122
Muir, Malcolm 1885-1979 93-96
Obituary 85-88
Muir, Malcolm, Jr. 1915-1984 Obituary 113
Muir, Marie 1904- CANR-5
Earlier sketch in CA 4R
Muir, Percival H(orace) 1894-1979 ..... CANR-5
Obituary 97-100
Earlier sketch in CA 11-12R
Muir, Percy H.
See Muir, Percival H(orace)
Muir, Richard 1943- CANR-23
Earlier sketch in CA 106
Muir, William Ker, Jr. 1931- 53-56
Muirhead, Ian A(dair) 1913- 15-16R
Muirhead, Thorburn 1899- 7-8R

Mujica Lainez, Manuel 1910-1984 81-84
Obituary 112
See also CLC 31
Mukerji, Chandra 1945- 113
Mukerji, Dhan Gopal 1890-1936
Brief entry 119
See also SATA 40
See also CLR 10
Mukerji, Kshitimohon 1920- 19-20R
Mukherjee, Bharati 1940- 107
See also DLB 60
Mukherjee, Meenakshi 1937- 65-68
Mukherjee, Ramkrishna 1919- CANR-7
Earlier sketch in CA 57-60
Mulac, Margaret E(lizabeth) 1912- CANR-2
Earlier sketch in CA 7-8R
Mulaisho, Dominic (Chola) 1933- 97-100
Mularchyk, Sylva 93-96
Mulay, Larry L. 1904(?)-1987 Obituary 122
Mulcahy, Lucille Burnett 5-6R
See also SATA 12
Mulchrone, Vincent 1919(?)-1977
Obituary 73-76
Mulder, John M(ark) 1946- Brief entry 112
Muldoon, Paul 1951- Brief entry 113
See also DLB 40
See also CLC 32
Muldoon, Roland W. 1941- 105
Mule, Marty 1944- 108
Mulesko, Angelo
See Oglesby, Joseph
Mulford, David Campbell 1937- 11-12R
Mulford, Philippa G(reene) 1948- 116
See also SATA 43
Mulgan, Catherine 1931- CANR-11
Earlier sketch in CA 25-28R
Mulgrew, Peter David 1927- 15-16R
Mulhauser, Ruth (Elizabeth) 1913-1980 .. CANR-7
Earlier sketch in CA 7-8R
Mulhearn, John 1932- 65-68
Mulholland, Jim 1949- 61-64
Mulholland, John 1898-1970 ....7-8R
Obituary 89-92
Mulholland, John F(ield) 1903- 41-44R
Mulisch, Harry 1927- CANR-6
Earlier sketch in CA 9-10R
See also CLC 42
Mulkeen, Anne
See Marcus, Anne M(ulkeen)
Mulkeen, Thomas P(atrick) 1923- 85-88
Mulkerne, Donald James Dennis 1921- ...11-12R
Mull, Martin 1943- 105
See also CLC 17
Mullally, Frederic 1920- CANR-1
Earlier sketch in CA 4R
Mullaly, Edward (Joseph) 1941- 41-44R
Mullan, Bob 1947- 123
Mullan, Fitzhugh 1942- 69-72
Mullaney, Marie Marmo 1953- 112
Mullaney, Thomas E. 1922(?)-1978 93-96
Obituary 81-84
Mullard, Chris(topher Paul) 1944-
Brief entry 112
Mullarky, Taylor 1922- 103
Mullen, Barbara 1914-1979 Obituary 85-88
Mullen, C.J.J.
See Mullen, Cyril J.
Mullen, Cyril J. 1908- 61-64
Mullen, Dore
See Mullen, Dorothy
Mullen, Dorothy 1933- 104
Mullen, Edward John, Jr. 1942- CANR-17
Earlier sketches in CA 49-52, CANR-2
Mullen, Harris H. 1924- 69-72
Mullen, James H. 1924- 3R
Mullen, Michael 1937- 116
Mullen, Robert R(odolph) 1908- CAP-1
Earlier sketch in CA 19-20
Mullen, Thomas J(ames) 1934- CANR-5
Earlier sketch in CA 11-12R
Mullen, William Charles 1944- 73-76
Mullendore, William Clinton 1892-1983
Obituary 111
Muller, Alexander V(ilhelm) 1932- 45-48
Muller, Billex
See Ellis, Edward S(ylvester)
Muller, Charles G(eorge Geoffrey)
1897- CANR-2
Earlier sketch in CA 1R
Muller, Charles Geoffrey
See Muller, Charles G(eorge Geoffrey)
Muller, Dorothy
See Mueller, Dorothy
Muller, Edward John 1916- 57-60
Muller, Gilbert H(enry) 1941- CANR-14
Earlier sketch in CA 41-44R
Muller, H(erman) J(oseph) 1890-1967
Obituary 106
Muller, Herbert J(oseph) 1905- CANR-1
Earlier sketch in CA 2R
Muller, Herman J(oseph) 1909- 73-76
Muller, Hilgard 1914-1985 Obituary 117
Muller, John E.
See Fanthorpe, R(obert) Lionel
Muller, John P(aul) 1940- 103
Muller, Leo C., Jr. 1924- 7-8R
Muller, Marcia 1944- 81-84
Muller, Peter O. 1942- 110
Muller, Priscilla E(lkow) 1930- 61-64
Muller, Robert George 1923- 103
Muller, Ronald E(rnst) 1939- 107
Muller, Siegfried H(ermann) 1902-1965 .. CAP-1
Earlier sketch in CA 11-12
Mulligan, Hugh A. 1925- CANR-11
Earlier sketch in CA 23-24R
Mulligan, James J. 1936- 45-48
Mulligan, John Joseph 1918- 33-36R
Mulligan, Raymond A(lexander) 1914- 37-40R
Mulligan, Robert S(mith) 1941- 65-68
Mulliken, Robert Sanderson 1896-1986 109
Obituary 120
Mullin, Michael 1944- 103
Mullin, Robert N(orville) 1893- 89-92
Mullin, Willard 1902-1978 Obituary 89-92
Mullings, Llewellyn M. 1932- 37-40R
Mullins, (George) Aloysius 1910- CAP-1
Earlier sketch in CA 13-14
Mullins, Ann
See Dally, Ann Mullins
Mullins, Carolyn J(ohns) 1940- CANR-10
Earlier sketch in CA 65-68
Mullins, Claud 1887-1968 .... CAP-1
Earlier sketch in CA 13-14
Mullins, Edward S(wift) 1922- 19-20R
See also SATA 10
Mullins, Edwin (Brandt) 1933- CANR-22
Earlier sketches in CA 53-56, CANR-4
Mullins, Helene 1899- 77-80
Mullins, Larry E(dward) 1935- 117
Mullins, Nicholas C(reed) 1939- 33-36R
Mullins, Vera (Annie) Cooper 1903- 61-64
Mulloy, Elizabeth D(ibert) 1945- 93-96
Mulock, Dinah Maria
See Craik, Dinah Maria (Mulock)
Multhauf, Robert P(hilip) 1919- 93-96
Mulvanity, George 1903(?)-1976
Obituary 69-72
Mulvey, Ruth Watt
See Harmer, Ruth Mulvey
Mulvihill, Edward Robert 1917- 11-12R
Mulvihill, William Patrick 1923- 3R
See also SATA 8
Mulville, Frank 1924- 107
Mumey, Glen A(llen) 1933- 73-76
Mumford, Bob 1930- 103
Mumford, Emily (Hamilton)
1920(?)-1987 57-60
Obituary 123
Mumford, Lewis 1895- CANR-5
Earlier sketch in CA 2R
See also DLB 63
Mummery, David R. 1932- 23-32R
Mumms, Hardee
See McLellan, Diana
Munari, Bruno 1907- 73-76
See also SATA 15
See also CLR 9
Munby, A(lan) N(oel) L(atimer) 1913-1974
Obituary 53-56
Munby, Arthur Joseph 1828-1910 ...... DLB-35
Munby, D(enys) L(awrence) 1919-1976 . CANR-2
Earlier sketch in CA 4R
Munce, Ruth Hill 1898- CAP-1
Earlier sketch in CA 9-10
See also SATA 12
Munch, Peter A(ndreas) 1908-1984 ......29-32R
Obituary 111
Munch, Theodore W(illiam) 1919- 57-60
Muncy, Raymond Lee 1928- 49-52
Mund, Vernon A(rthur) 1906- CANR-20
Earlier sketch in CA 2R
Munday, Anthony 1560-1633 .... DLB-62
Mundel, Marvin E(verett) 1916- 21-22R
Mundell, Robert A(lexander) 1932- CANR-2
Earlier sketch in CA 45-48
Mundell, William Daniel 1913- 73-76
Mundis, Hester 1938- CANR-15
Earlier sketch in CA 69-72
Mundis, Jerrold 1941- CANR-11
Earlier sketch in CA 69-72
Mundlak, Max 1899- CAP-1
Earlier sketch in CA 9-10
Mundy, John Hine 1917- 45-48
Mundy, Max
See Schofield, Sylvia Anne
Munford, Robert 1737(?)-1783 .... DLB-31
Munford, W(illiam) A(rthur) 1911- 116
Mungello, David Emil 1943- 110
Munger, Al
See Unger, Maurice Albert
Munger, Frank James 1929-1981 .... CANR-1
Obituary 116
Earlier sketch in CA 3R
Munger, Hortense Roberta
See Roberts, Hortense Roberta
Munger, Robert Boyd 1910- 77-80
Mungo, Raymond 1946- CANR-2
Earlier sketch in CA 49-52
Munholland, John K(im) 1934- 29-32R
Munir, Muhammad 1895-1981 Obituary 108
Munitz, Milton K(arl) 1913- CANR-16
Earlier sketch in CA 93-96
Munk, Arthur W. 1909- CANR-7
Earlier sketch in CA 15-16R
Munk, Christian
See Weisenborn, Guenther
Munk, Erika 1939- 19-20R
Munn, Geoffrey C(harles) 1953- 118
Munn, Glenn (Gaywaine) 1890(?)-1977
Obituary 73-76
Munn, H(arold) Warner 1903-1981 .... CANR-11
Earlier sketch in CA 21-22R
Munn, Hart
See Hardy, C. Colburn
Munnecke, Wilbur C(heney) 1906-1984
Obituary 112
Munnell, Alicia H(aydock) 1942- CANR-13
Earlier sketch in CA 73-76
Munonye, John 1929- 103
Munowitz, Ken 1935-1977 .... SATA-14
Munoz, Braulio 1946- 110
Munoz, Heraldo 1948- 111
Munoz, William 1949- SATA-42
Munoz Marin, Luis 1898-1980 Obituary ..97-100
Munro, Alice 1931- 33-36R
See also SATA 29
See also DLB 53
See also CLC 6, 10, 19
See also AITN 2
Munro, Bertha 1887-1983 45-48
Munro, C. K.
See MacMullan, Charles Walden
Kirkpatrick
Munro, Dana Gardner 1892- 3R
Munro, David
See Devine, D(avid) M(cDonald)
Munro, Duncan H.
See Russell, Eric Frank
Munro, Eleanor 1928- 4R
See also SATA 37
Munro, Hector Hugh 1870-1916
Brief entry 104
See also DLB 34
Munro, (Macfarlane) Hugh 11-12R
Munro, Ian S. 29-32R
Munro, James
See Cave, Roderick (George James
Munro)
and Mitchell, James
Munro, Jane 1943- 112
Munro, John (Henry Alexander) 1938- ...41-44R
Munro, John M(urchinson) 1932- CANR-11
Earlier sketch in CA 69-72
Munro, Leslie Knox 1901-1974 Obituary ... 49-52
Munro, Mary
See Howe, Doris Kathleen
Munro, Thomas 1897-1974 .... CANR-3
Earlier sketch in CA 5-6R
Munroe, Elizabeth L(ee) 1900- CANR-2
Earlier sketch in CA 19-20R
Munroe, John A(ndrew) 1914- 49-52
Munroe, Kirk 1850-1930 Brief entry 123
See also DLB 42
Munrow, David John 1942-1976 103
Obituary 106
Munsch, Robert (Norman) 1945- 121
See also SATA 48, 50
Munsey, Cecil (Richard, Jr.) 1935- CANR-17
Earlier sketch in CA 41-44R
Munsey, Frank A(ndrew) 1854-1925
Brief entry 116
See also DLB 25
Munshi, Kiki Skagen 1943- CANR-15
Earlier sketch in CA 37-40R
Munshi, Shehnaaz
See Munshi, Kiki Skagen
Munshower, Suzanne 1945- 97-100
Munsinger, Harry 1935- 45-48
Munsinger, Lynn 1951- SATA-33
Munslow, Barry 1950- 117
Munson, Amelia H. (?)-1972 Obituary ...33-36R
Munson, Byron Edwin 1921- 41-44R
Munson, Charlie E(llis) 1877-1975 57-60
Munson, Don 1908- 73-76
Munson, Fred C(aleb) 1928- 33-36R
Munson, Gorham B(ert) 1896-1969 ...... CAP-1
Earlier sketch in CA 11-12
Munson, Harold L(ewis) 1923- 29-32R
Munson, Henry (Lee), Jr. 1946- 115
Munson, James (Edward Bradbury) 1944- .. 124
Munson, Kenneth (George) 1929-
Brief entry 111
Munson, Lou
See Munson, Mary Lou (Easley)
Munson, Mary Lou (Easley) 1935- 11-12R
Munson, Thomas N(olan) 1924- CANR-20
Earlier sketch in CA 2R
Munson, Thurman (Lee) 1947-1979 108
Obituary 89-92
Munson-Benson, Tunie 1946- 77-80
See also SATA 15
Munsterberg, Hugo 1916- CANR-2
Earlier sketch in CA 7-8R
Munsterhjelm, Erik 1905- 49-52
Munter, Robert (L.) 1926- 23-24R
Munthe, Adam John 1946- 107
Munthe, Frances 1915- 11-12R
Munthe, Malcolm Grane 1920- 7-8R
Munthe, Nelly 1947- 117
Munton, Alan (Guy) 1945- CANR-24
Earlier sketch in CA 107
Muntyan, Miodrag 1914-1985 Obituary 117
Muntz, (Isabelle) Hope 1907- 15-16R
Muntz, James
See Crowcroft, Peter
Munves, James (Albert) 1922- CANR-3
Earlier sketch in CA 5-6R
See also SATA 30
Munz, Peter 1921- 15-16R
Munz, Philip Alexander 1892- 7-8R
Munzer, Martha E. 1899- CANR-4
Earlier sketch in CA 2R
See also SATA 4
Murad, Anatol 1904- 73-76
Murad, Gauhar-i
See Sa'Idi, Ghulam Husayn
Murari, Timeri N(rupendra) 1941- 102
Muravin, Victor 1929- 85-88
Murawski, Benjamin J(oseph) 1926- 45-48
Murbarger, Nell Lounsberry 1909- CAP-1
Earlier sketch in CA 15-16
Murch, Edward (William Lionel) 1920- 61-64
Murch, James DeForest 1892-1973 ..... CANR-4
Earlier sketch in CA 7-8R
Murchie, Guy 1907- 2R
Murchison, Thomas Moffat 1907-1984
Obituary 111
Murchland, Bernard 1929- 112
Murden, Forrest D(ozier), Jr. 1921-1977
Obituary 73-76
Murdick, Robert Gordon 1920- CANR-6
Earlier sketch in CA 7-8R
Murdin, Paul 1942- CANR-23
Earlier sketch in CA 106
Murdoch, (Henry) Derrick 1909-1985 89-92
Obituary 116
Murdoch, (Jean) Iris 1919- CANR-8
Earlier sketch in CA 13-14R
See also DLB 14
See also CLC 1, 2, 3, 4, 6, 8, 11, 15,
22, 31
Murdoch, Joseph S(impson) F(erguson)
1919- 102
Murdoch, (Keith) Rupert 1931- Brief entry .. 111
Murdock, Eugene C(onverse) 1921- CANR-13
Earlier sketch in CA 33-36R
Murdock, George Peter 1897- CAP-1
Earlier sketch in CA 13-14
Murdock, Kenneth Ballard 1895-1975 65-68
Obituary 61-64
Murdock, Laurette P. 1900- 101
Murdock, M(elinda) S(eabrooke) 1947- 113
Murdock, Myrtle Cheney 1886(?)-1980
Obituary 97-100
Murdy, Louise Baughan 1935- 33-36R
Mure, David William Alexander
1912-1986(?) Obituary 120
Mure, G(eoffrey) R(eginald) G(ilchrist)
1893-1979 107
Murfin, James Vernon 1930(?)-1987
Obituary 122
Murfree, Mary Noailles 1850-1922
Brief entry 122
See also DLB 12
Murie, Margaret Elizabeth 1902- 110
Murnau, Friedrich Wilhelm
See Plumpe, Friedrich Wilhelm
Murnion, Philip (Joseph) 1938- 116
Muro, Diane Patricia 1940- 65-68
Muro, James J(oseph) 1934- 33-36R
Murphet, Howard 1906- 61-64
Murphey, Murray Griffin 1928- CANR-6
Earlier sketch in CA 5-6R
Murphey, Rhoads 1919- 33-36R
Murphey, Robert W(entworth) 1916- 15-16R
Murphy, Agnes Louise Keating 1912- 3R
Murphy, Arthur Lister 1906- 77-80
Murphy, Arthur Richard, Jr. 1915-1987
Obituary 123
Murphy, Barbara Beasley 1933- CANR-20
Earlier sketch in CA 41-44R
See also SATA 5
Murphy, Beatrice M. 1908- CANR-9
Earlier sketch in CA 53-56
Murphy, Brenda C(arol) 1950- 120
Murphy, Brian (Michael) 1931- CANR-13
Earlier sketch in CA 21-22R
Murphy, Brian 1939- 108
Murphy, Buck
See Whitcomb, Ian
Murphy, C. L.
See Murphy, Charlotte A(lice)
and Murphy, Lawrence A(gustus)
Murphy, Charles J(ohn) V(incent)
1904-1987 Obituary 124
Murphy, Charlotte A(lice) 1924- 105
Murphy, Cornelius Francis, Jr. 1933- 89-92
Murphy, Dervla (Mary) 1931- CANR-21
Earlier sketch in CA 103
Murphy, Dorothy Dey 1911(?)-1983
Obituary 110
Murphy, E(mmett) Jefferson 1926- 25-28R
See also SATA 4
Murphy, Earl Finbar 1928- 13-14R
Murphy, Ed
See Murphy, Edward Francis
Murphy, Edward Francis 1914- 102
Murphy, Edward J. 1927- 37-40R
Murphy, Emmy Lou Osborne 1910- 5-6R
Murphy, Francis 1932- CANR-7
Earlier sketch in CA 13-14R
Murphy, Frank Hughes 1940- 61-64
Murphy, Fred P. 1889-1979 Obituary 89-92
Murphy, Gardner 1895-1979 93-96
Obituary 85-88
Murphy, George E(dward), Jr. 1948- .. CANR-13
Earlier sketch in CA 77-80
Murphy, George G(regory) S(tanislaus)
1924- 21-22R
Murphy, George Lloyd 1902- 45-48
Murphy, Grace E. Barstow 1888-1975
Obituary 57-60
Murphy, Hazel
See Thurston, Hazel (Patricia)
Murphy, Herta A(lbrecht) 1908- 49-52
Murphy, Irene L(yons) 1920- 53-56
Murphy, J(ohn) Carter 1921- 15-16R
Murphy, James F(redrick) 1943- CANR-8
Earlier sketch in CA 61-64
Murphy, James J(erome) 1923- CANR-12
Earlier sketch in CA 33-36R
Murphy, James M(artin) 1917- 29-32R
Murphy, James M(aurice) 1932-1966(?) .. CAP-1
Earlier sketch in CA 11-12
Murphy, Jane Brevoort Walden
1902(?)-1980 Obituary 97-100
Murphy, Jeffrie G(uy) 1940- Brief entry 118
Murphy, Jill 1949- 105
See also SATA 37
Murphy, Jim 1947- 111
See also SATA 32, 37
Murphy, John
See Grady, Ronan Calistus, Jr.
Murphy, John L(awrence) 1924- CANR-20
Earlier sketch in CA 2R
Murphy, John W(illiam) 1948- 112
Murphy, Karen A(lee) 1945- 115

Murphy, Larry
See Murphy, Lawrence R(ichard)
Murphy, Lawrence A(gustus) 1924- ... 104
Murphy, Lawrence R(ichard) 1942- ... 105
Murphy, Lois Barclay 1902- ... CANR-19
Earlier sketches in CA 4R, CANR-4
Murphy, Louis J.
See Hicks, Tyler Gregory
Murphy, Mario
See Edmondson, G. C.
Murphy, Marion Fisher 1902- ... 53-56
Murphy, Michael 1930- ... 73-76
Murphy, Nonie Carol
See Caroll, Nonie
Murphy, Pat
See Murphy, E(mmett) Jefferson
Murphy, Patrick T(homas) 1939- ... 108
Murphy, Patrick V(incent) 1920- ... 105
Murphy, Paul 1917(?)-1983 Obituary ... 111
Murphy, Paul J(ames) 1943- ... 112
Murphy, Paul L(loyd) 1923- ... CANR-7
Earlier sketch in CA 19-20R
Murphy, Raymond E(dward) 1898- ... 41-44R
Murphy, Reg 1934- ... 33-36R
Murphy, Richard 1927- ... 29-32R
See also DLB 40
See also CLC 41
Murphy, Richard T. A. 1908- ... CANR-1
Earlier sketch in CA 3R
Murphy, Robert (William) 1902-1971 ... CAP-1
Obituary ... 29-32R
Earlier sketch in CA 9-10
See also SATA 10
Murphy, Robert Cushman 1887-1973 ... CAP-2
Obituary ... 41-44R
Earlier sketch in CA 23-24
Murphy, Robert D(aniel) 1894-1978 ... CAP-1
Obituary ... 73-76
Earlier sketch in CA 9-10
Murphy, Robert F(rancis) 1924- ... 118
Murphy, Roland Edmund 1917- ... CANR-6
Earlier sketch in CA 5-6R
Murphy, Romaine 1941- ... 77-80
Murphy, Sharon M. 1940- ... 77-80
Murphy, Shirley Rousseau 1928- ... CANR-13
Earlier sketch in CA 21-22R
See also SATA 36
Murphy, Sylvia 19(?)- ... CLC-34
Murphy, Sylvia 1937- ... 121
Murphy, Terrence J. 1921- ... 7-8R
Murphy, Thomas (Bernard) 1935- ... 101
Murphy, Thomas Basil, Jr. 1935- ... CANR-11
Earlier sketch in CA 69-72
Murphy, Thomas P(atrick) 1931- ... CANR-16
Earlier sketch in CA 41-44R
Murphy, Tom
See Murphy, Thomas Basil, Jr.
Murphy, Vi 1924(?)-1987 Obituary ... 124
Murphy, Walter F(rancis) 1929- ... CANR-2
Earlier sketch in CA 2R
Murphy, Warren B. 1933- ... 33-36R
Murphy, William Francis 1906- ... 19-20R
Murphy, William M(ichael) 1916- ... 85-88
Murphy-O'Connor, Jerome James
1935- ... CANR-5
Earlier sketch in CA 15-16R
Murra, John V(ictor) 1916- ... CANR-1
Earlier sketch in CA 45-48
Murrah, David Joe 1941- ... 106
Murray, Adrian
See Curran, Mona (Elisa)
Murray, Albert 1916- ... 49-52
See also DLB 38
Murray, Andrew Evans 1917- ... 25-28R
Murray, Beatrice
See Posner, Richard
Murray, Bruce C(hurchill) 1931- ... 103
Murray, Christopher 1940- ... 117
Murray, Clara Elizabeth 1894- ... CAP-1
Earlier sketch in CA 9-10
Murray, Cromwell
See Morgan, Murray
Murray, D. Stark
See Murray, David Stark
Murray, Daniel E(dward) 1925- ... 45-48
Murray, David Stark 1900-1977 Obituary ... 111
Murray, Dick 1924- ... 106
Murray, Donald M(orison) 1924- ... CANR-17
Earlier sketch in CA 4R
Murray, Dorothy Garst 1915- ... 21-22R
Murray, Edmund P(atrick) 1930- ... 81-84
Murray, Edna
See Rowland, D(onald) S(ydney)
Murray, Edward (James, Jr.) 1928- ... CANR-1
Earlier sketch in CA 49-52
Murray, Edward J(ames) 1928- ... 15-16R
Murray, Elwood 1897- ... 73-76
Murray, Eugene Bernard 1927- ... 104
Murray, Frances
See Booth, Rosemary Frances
Murray, G(erald) E(dward, Jr.) 1945- ... CANR-5
Earlier sketch in CA 53-56
Murray, George (McIntosh) 1900-1970 ... CAP-1
Earlier sketch in CA 13-14
Murray, (Jesse) George 1909- ... 19-20R
Murray, (George) Gilbert (Aime)
1866-1957 Brief entry ... 110
See also DLB 10
Murray, Hallard T(homas), Jr. 1937- ... 19-20R
Murray, Henry A(lexander) 1893-
Brief entry ... 116
Murray, Irene
See Witherspoon, Irene Murray
Murray, J(ohn) Alex ... 41-44R
Murray, J. Harley 1910(?)-1977 Obituary ... 73-76
Murray, J(ohn) Joseph 1915- ... CANR-4
Earlier sketch in CA 7-8R
Murray, James 1946- ... CANR-1
Earlier sketch in CA 49-52
Murray, James Patrick 1919- ... CANR-15
Earlier sketch in CA 65-68
Murray, Jean Shaw 1927(?)-1985
Obituary ... 116
Murray, Jerome T(homas) 1928- ... 33-36R
Murray, Jim
See Murray, James Patrick
Murray, Joan 1943- ... 124
Murray, Joan 1945- ... 77-80
Murray, Joan E. 1941- ... 81-84
Murray, Jocelyn (Margaret) 1929- ... 113
Murray, John 1923- ... CANR-19
Earlier sketches in CA 7-8R, CANR-4
See also SATA 39
Murray, John Bernard 1915- ... 41-44R
Murray, John Courtney 1904-1967
Obituary ... 106
Murray, John E(dward), Jr. 1932- ... 45-48
Murray, John F(rancis) 1923-1977 ... CAP-2
Obituary ... 69-72
Earlier sketch in CA 29-32
Murray, John L(arry) 1937- ... 108
Murray, John MacDougall 1910- ... 33-36R
Murray, Judith Sargent 1751-1820 ... DLB-37
Murray, K. F.
See Carlisle, Fred
Murray, K(atherine) M(aud) Elisabeth
1909- ... 77-80
Murray, Keith A. 1910- ... CAP-2
Earlier sketch in CA 33-36
Murray, Ken
See Turner, Robert H(arry)
Murray, Les(lie) A(llan) 1938- ... CANR-11
Earlier sketch in CA 23-24R
See also CLC 40
Murray, Linda Charlton 1936(?)-1986
Obituary ... 118
Murray, Lois Smith 1906- ... 37-40R
Murray, Margaret Alice 1863-1963 ... 7-8R
Murray, Marian ... 41-44R
See also SATA 5
Murray, Mary (Morrison) 1925- ... 25-28R
Murray, Maynard 1911(?)-1983 Obituary ... 110
Murray, Merrill G. 1900(?)-1976
Obituary ... 69-72
Murray, Michael
See McLaren, Moray (David Shaw)
Murray, Michael V(ivian) 1906- ... 7-8R
Murray, (Judith) Michele (Freedman)
1933-1974 ... 49-52
See also SATA 7
Murray, Ossie 1938- ... SATA-43
Murray, (Anna) Pauli(ne) 1910-1985
Obituary ... 116
See also DLB 41
Murray, Peter (John) 1920- ... CANR-10
Earlier sketch in CA 13-14R
Murray, Philip 1924- ... 65-68
Murray, Ralph L(a Verne) 1921- ... 15-16R
Murray, Rebecca (Jean) 1936- ... 57-60
Murray, Robert A. 1929- ... 29-32R
Murray, Robert Keith 1922- ... 53-56
Murray, Roger N(icholas) 1932- ... 23-24R
Murray, Ruth Lovell 1900- ... 103
Murray, Sister Mary Verona 1909- ... 19-20R
Murray, Sonia Bennett 1936- ... 65-68
Murray, Thomas J(oseph) 1943- ... 77-80
Murray, W(illiam) H(utchison) 1913- ... CANR-4
Earlier sketch in CA 11-12R
Murray, Walter I(saiah) 1910-1978 ... 85-88
Obituary ... 73-76
Murray, William Cotter 1929- ... 53-56
Murray, William J(oseph) III 1946- ... 110
Murray-Brown, Jeremy 1932- ... 77-80
Murray-Smith, Stephen 1922- ... 103
Murrell, Elsie Kathleen Seth-Smith 1883- . CAP-1
Earlier sketch in CA 9-10
Murrell, K(eith) F(rank) H(ywel)
1908(?)-1984 Obituary ... 112
Murrett, John Charles 1892- ... 4R
Murrow, Casey 1945- ... 97-100
Murrow, Edward R(oscoe) 1908-1965 ... 103
Obituary ... 89-92
Murry, J. Middleton
See Murry, John Middleton
Murry, John Middleton 1889-1957
Brief entry ... 118
See also TCLC 16
Murry, Mary Middleton 1897-1983
Obituary ... 110
Murstein, Bernard I(rving) 1929- ... CANR-3
Earlier sketch in CA 11-12R
Murtagh, John M(artin) 1911-1976 ... 19-20R
Obituary ... 61-64
Murtagh, William J. 1923- ... 25-28R
Murton, Jessie Wilmore ... 7-8R
Murton, Mary 1933- ... 117
Musa, Mark 1934- ... 15-16R
Musafir
See Tagore, Amitendranath
Musaphia, Joseph 1935- ... CANR-17
Earlier sketch in CA 97-100
Muscat, Robert J. 1931- ... 19-20R
Muscatine, Charles 1920- ... 21-22R
Muscatine, Doris (Corn) 1926- ... 9-10R
Muschamp, Thomas
See Lloyd-Thomas, Catherine
Muschenheim, Carl 1905-1977 Obituary ... 69-72
Muschenheim, William 1902- ... CAP-1
Earlier sketch in CA 15-16
Musciano, Walt
See Musciano, Walter A.
Musciano, Walter A. 1922- ... 121
Muse, Beatriz de Regil 1901(?)-1983
Obituary ... 109
Muse, Benjamin 1898- ... CANR-1
Earlier sketch in CA 3R
Muse, Clarence 1889-1979 Obituary ... 104
Muse, Daphne P. 1944- ... 112
Muse, Ken 1925- ... 111
Muse, Patricia (Alice) 1923- ... 69-72
Muses, C. A.
See Muses, Charles Arthur
Muses, Charles Arthur 1919- Brief entry ... 115
Musetto, Andrew P(aul) 1945- ... 111
Musgrave, Barbara S(tewart) 1913- ... 5-6R
Musgrave, Clifford 1904-1982 Obituary ... 107
Musgrave, Florence 1902- ... CAP-1
Earlier sketch in CA 13-14
See also SATA 3
Musgrave, Richard Abel 1910- ... 113
Musgrave, Susan 1951- ... 69-72
See also CLC 13
Musgraves, Don 1935- ... 65-68
Musgrove, Frank 1922- ... CANR-6
Earlier sketch in CA 15-16R
Musgrove, Margaret Wynkoop 1943- ... 65-68
See also SATA 26
Musgrove, Philip 1940- ... CANR-11
Earlier sketch in CA 29-32R
Musgrove, Stanley (E.) 1924-1986 ... 108
Obituary ... 118
Mushabac, Jane 1944- ... 108
Mushkat, Jerome 1931- ... 81-84
Mushkat, Mari'on 1919- ... 120
Mushkin, Selma J. 1913-1979 Obituary ... 93-96
Musial, Joe 1905(?)-1977 Obituary ... 69-72
Musial, Stan(ley Frank) 1920- ... 93-96
Musicant, Elke (Alice) 1919- ... 107
Musicant, Tobias (Ted) 1921- ... 108
Musiker, Reuben 1931- ... 57-60
Musil, Robert (Edler von) 1880-1942
Brief entry ... 109
See also TCLC 12
Muske, Carol 1945- ... 65-68
Muske, Irmgard (Gertrud) 1912- ... CANR-18
Earlier sketch in CA 25-28R
Muskie, Edmund S(ixtus) 1914- ... CANR-2
Earlier sketch in CA 49-52
Musmanno, Michael A(ngelo) ?-1968 ... CAP-1
Earlier sketch in CA 9-10
Musolf, Lloyd D(aryl) 1919- ... CANR-9
Earlier sketch in CA 19-20R
Musselman, George Paul 1895-1987
Obituary ... 123
Musselman, Vernon A(rmor) 1912- ... 37-40R
Mussen, Paul Henry 1922- Brief entry ... 114
Musser, Joe
See Musser, Joseph L.
Musser, Joseph L. 1936- ... CANR-12
Earlier sketch in CA 29-32R
Mussey, Virginia Howell
See Ellison, Virginia H(owell)
Mussey, Virginia T.H.
See Ellison, Virginia H(owell)
Mussi, Mary 1907- ... CANR-6
Earlier sketch in CA 53-56
Mussoff, Lenore 1927- ... 21-22R
Mussolini, Benito (Amilcare Andrea)
1883-1945 Brief entry ... 116
Mussolini, Rachele Guidi 1890-1979
Obituary ... 111
Mussulman Joseph A(gee) 1928- ... 37-40R
Mustafa, Zaki 1934- ... 41-44R
Muste, John M(artin) 1927- ... 21-22R
Musteikis, Antanas 1914- ... 45-48
Musto, Barry 1930- ... 106
Musto, David Franklin 1936- ... 104
Musurillo, Herbert (Anthony Peter)
1917-1974 ... CAP-1
Obituary ... 49-52
Earlier sketch in CA 13-14
Mutchler, David E(dward) 1941- ... 33-36R
Muth, John F(raser) 1930- ... 13-14R
Muth, Richard F(erris) 1927- ... 13-14R
Mutharika, B(rightson) W(ebster) T(hom)
1934- ... 41-44R
Muthesius, Stefan 1939- ... 61-64
Mutke, Peter H(ans) C(hristoph) 1927- ... 93-96
Muto, Susan Annette 1942- ... 110
Mutton, Alice F. A. 1908- ... 5-6R
Mutz
See Kuenstler, Morton
Muus, Bent J(oergen) 1926- ... 103
Muus, Flemming B(ruun) 1907-1982
Obituary ... 110
Muuss, Rolf E(duard Helmut) 1924- ... 9-10R
Muzumdar, Ammu Menon 1919- ... 21-22R
Mwanga
See Stark, Claude Alan
Myassin, Leonid Fedorovich 1895-1979 ... 97-100
Obituary ... 85-88
My Brother'S Brother
See Chekhov, Anton (Pavlovich)
My Brother's Brother
See Chekhov, Anton (Pavlovich)
Mycue, Edward 1937- ... CANR-4
Earlier sketch in CA 53-56
Mydans, Carl ... 97-100
Mydans, Shelley Smith 1915- Brief entry ... 105
Myddleton, Robert
See Hebblethwaite, Peter
Myer, Dillon S(eymour) 1891-1982 ... CAP-2
Obituary ... 116
Earlier sketch in CA 29-32
Myer, John Colby 1912- ... 45-48
Myer, John Randolph 1927- ... 7-8R
Myerhoff, Barbara G. 1936(?)-1985
Obituary ... 114
Myers, A(lexander) J(ohn) William 1877- . CAP-1
Earlier sketch in CA 11-12
Myers, Albert M(orris) 1917- ... 118
Myers, Alec Reginald
See Myers, Alexander Reginald
Myers, Alexander Reginald 1912-1980 . CANR-10
Earlier sketch in CA 13-14R
Myers, Alonzo F(ranklin) 1895-1970
Obituary ... 104
Myers, Andrew Breen 1920- ... 61-64
Myers, Arthur 1922- ... CANR-7
Earlier sketch in CA 19-20R
See also SATA 35
Myers, Arthur Sim 1928-1984 Obituary ... 113
Myers, Bernard S(amuel) 1908- ... 65-68
Myers, Bernice ... CANR-8
Earlier sketch in CA 61-64
See also SATA 9
Myers, Bettye (Blanche) 1926- Brief entry ... 107
Myers, C. F.
See Fairbanks, Carol
Myers, C(hauncie) Kilmer 1916-1981
Obituary ... 108
Myers, Carol Fairbanks
See Fairbanks, Carol
Myers, Caroline Elizabeth Clark
1887-1980 ... 29-32R
See also SATA 28
Myers, Charles A(ndrew) 1913- ... 85-88
Myers, Charles B(ennett) 1939- ... 57-60
Myers, David G. 1942- ... CANR-22
Earlier sketch in CA 106
Myers, (Eugene Victor) Debs 1911-1971
Obituary ... 104
Myers, Desaix B. III 1945- ... 104
Myers, Edward 1950- ... 116
Myers, Elisabeth P(erkins) 1918- ... CANR-3
Earlier sketch in CA 5-6R
See also SATA 36
Myers, Eugene A(braham) 1910- ... 45-48
Myers, Francis Milton 1917- ... 7-8R
Myers, Gail E(ldridge) 1923- ... CANR-1
Earlier sketch in CA 49-52
Myers, Garry Cleveland 1884-1971 ... CAP-2
Earlier sketch in CA 29-32
Myers, Gay Nagle 1943- ... 102
Myers, George (Francis), Jr. 1953- ... 119
Myers, Gerald E(ugene) 1923- ... 29-32R
Myers, Gustavus 1872-1942 Brief entry ... 123
See also DLB 47
Myers, Harriet Kathryn
See Whittington, Harry (Benjamin)
Myers, (Mary) Hortense (Powner)
1913-1987 ... CANR-2
Obituary ... 123
Earlier sketch in CA 4R
See also SATA 10
Myers, Irma A(shley) 1924- ... 112
Myers, J(ohn) William 1919- ... CANR-12
Earlier sketch in CA 33-36R
Myers, (Elliott) Jack 1941- ... 73-76
Myers, Jacob M(artin) 1904- ... 19-20R
Myers, John Bernard 1920(?)-1987
Obituary ... 123
Myers, John H(olmes) 1915- ... 11-12R
Myers, John Myers 1906- ... CANR-1
Earlier sketch in CA 3R
Myers, Katherine 1952- ... 110
Myers, L. H. 1881-1944 ... DLB-15
Myers, L(ouis) M(cCorry) 1901- ... 21-22R
Myers, Lonny 1922- ... 65-68
Myers, M(arvin) Scott 1922- ... 69-72
Myers, Martin 1927- ... CANR-20
Earlier sketch in CA 29-32R
Myers, Mary Ruth 1947- ... CANR-16
Earlier sketch in CA 85-88
Myers, Neil 1930- ... 105
Myers, Norma 1929- ... 61-64
Myers, Norman 1934- ... CANR-20
Earlier sketches in CA 49-52, CANR-1
Myers, Patricia 1929- ... 37-40R
Myers, Paul 1932- ... 123
Myers, R(obert) E(ugene) 1924- ... CANR-23
Earlier sketch in CA 77-80
Myers, Ramon H. 1929- ... 113
Myers, Raymond E(dward) 1902- ... CAP-1
Earlier sketch in CA 15-16
Myers, Robert J(ulius) 1912- ... CANR-6
Earlier sketch in CA 15-16R
Myers, Robert J(ohn) 1924- ... 107
Myers, Robert Manson 1921- ... 37-40R
Myers, Rollo Hugh 1892-1984(?) ... 19-20R
Obituary ... 115
Myers, Samuel 1897(?)-1983 Obituary ... 109
Myers, Walter Dean 1937- ... CANR-20
Earlier sketch in CA 33-36R
See also SATA 27, 41
See also SAAS 2
See also DLB 33
See also CLC 35
See also CLR 4
Myers, Walter M.
See Myers, Walter Dean
Myerscough-Walker, Raymond 1912-1984
Obituary ... 113
Myerson, Bess 1924- ... 108
Myerson, Joel 1945- ... CANR-19
Earlier sketch in CA 102
Myerson, Michael 1940- ... 73-76
Myhers, John 1921- ... 105
Myhill, Henry (James) 1925-1977 ... 103
Mykle, Agrar 1915- ... 15-16R
Mylander, Maureen 1937- ... CANR-5
Earlier sketch in CA 53-56
Myler, Joseph L. 1905(?)-1973
Obituary ... 41-44R
Myles, Eugenie Louise (Butler) 1905- ... CAP-1
Earlier sketch in CA 11-12
Myles, Symon
See Follett, Ken(neth Martin)

Myller, Rolf 1926- CANR-8
Earlier sketch in CA 7-8R
See also SATA 27
Mynors, Roger A(ubrey) B(askerville) 1903- 7-8R
Myra, Harold L(awrence) 1939- CANR-8
Earlier sketch in CA 61-64
See also SATA 42, 46
Myrdal, Alva Reimer 1902-1986 69-72
Obituary 118
Myrdal, (Karl) Gunnar 1898-1987 CANR-4
Obituary 122
Earlier sketch in CA 9-10R
Myrdal, Jan 1927- Brief entry 117
Myrer, Anton 1922- CANR-3
Earlier sketch in CA 2R
Myres, J(ohn) N(owell) L(inton) 1902- 123
Myres, Sandra Lynn 1933- CANR-14
Earlier sketch in CA 33-36R
Myrick, David F. CANR-6
Earlier sketch in CA 13-14R
Myrick, Robert D(eWayne) 1935- CANR-17
Earlier sketch in CA 41-44R
Myrick, William J(ennings, Jr.) 1932- 73-76
Myrland, Doug 1952- 117
Myron, Robert 1926- 15-16R
Myrsiades, Kostas J. 1940- 109
Myrus, Donald (Richard) 1927- CANR-4
Earlier sketch in CA 4R
See also SATA 23

N

Naamani, Israel T(arkow) 1913(?)- 124
Naamani, Israel Tarkow 1913(?)- Brief entry 106
Naar, Jon 1920- 102
Nabbes, Thomas 1605(?)-1641 DLB-58
Nabholtz, John R(obert) 1931- 65-68
Nabokov, Nicolas 1903-1978 85-88
Obituary 77-80
Nabokov, Peter (Francis) 1940- CANR-9
Earlier sketch in CA 21-22R
Nabokov, Vladimir (Vladimirovich) 1899-1977 CANR-20
Obituary 69-72
Earlier sketch in CA 7-8R
See also DLB 2
See also DLBY 80
See also DLBD 3
See also CDALB 1941-1968
See also CLC 1, 2, 3, 6, 8, 11, 15, 23, 44, 46
Nacci, Chris (Natale) 1909- 41-44R
Nachbar, Herbert 1930(?)-1980 Obituary 97-100
Nachbar, Jack 1941- 53-56
Nachman, Gerald 1938- CANR-16
Earlier sketch in CA 65-68
Nachtigal, Paul M. 1930- 112
Nachtigall, Lila Ehrenstein 1934- Brief entry 105
Nachtmann, Francis Weldon 1913- 37-40R
Nadan, Paul 1933(?)-1978 Obituary 104
Naddor, Eliezer 1920- 21-22R
Nadeau, Maurice 1911- 49-52
Nadeau, R(aymond) E(rnest) 1913- Brief entry 107
Nadeau, Ray E.
See Nadeau, R(aymond) E(rnest)
Nadeau, Remi A(llen) 1920- CANR-2
Earlier sketch in CA 1R
Nadeau, Roland 1928- CANR-4
Earlier sketch in CA 53-56
Nadel, Frances 1905(?)-1977 Obituary 69-72
Nadel, Gerald H. 1944-1977 81-84
Obituary 73-76
Nadel, Ira Bruce 1943- CANR-18
Earlier sketch in CA 102
Nadel, Mark V(ictor) 1943- 33-36R
Nadel, Norman (Sanford) 1915- 106
Nader, George 1921- Brief entry 109
Nader, George Albert 1940- 111
Nader, Laura 1930- CANR-7
Earlier sketch in CA 19-20R
Nader, Ralph 1934- 77-80
Nadler, Harvey 1933- 15-16R
Nadler, Leonard 1922- CANR-20
Earlier sketches in CA 53-56, CANR-5
Nadler, Paul S(tephen) 1930- 25-28R
Nadler, Susan
See Gantry, Susan Nadler
Nadler, Zeace 1925- 121
Naef, Weston J(ohn) 1942- Brief entry 111
Naeslund, Erik 1948- 103
Naess, Harald Sigurd 1925- 41-44R
Naether, Carl (Albert) 1892- 25-28R
Nafziger, E(stel) Wayne 1938- 85-88
Nag
See Grauer, Neil A(lbert)
Nag, Moni 1925- 41-44R
Nagai Berthrong, Evelyn 1946- 115
Nagai Kafu
See Nagai Sokichi
Nagai Sokichi 1879-1959 Brief entry 117
Nagara, Susumu 1932- CANR-3
Earlier sketch in CA 45-48
Nagatsu, Toshiharu 1930- 107
na gCopaleen, Myles
See O Nuallain, Brian
Nagel, Andreas Fischer
See Fischer-Nagel, Andreas
Nagel, Ernest 1901-1985 93-96
Obituary 117
Nagel, Heiderose Fischer
See Fischer-Nagel, Heiderose
Nagel, James (Edward) 1940- 29-32R
Nagel, Otto 1894-1967 Obituary 106
Nagel, Paul C(hester) 1926- CANR-22
Earlier sketches in CA 11-12R, CANR-5
Nagel, Shirley 1922- 93-96
Nagel, Stuart S(amuel) 1934- CANR-14
Earlier sketch in CA 33-36R
Nagel, Thomas 1937- CANR-4
Earlier sketch in CA 53-56
Nagel, William G(eorge) 1916- 49-52
Nagenda, Musa
See Howard, Moses L(eon)
Nagera, Humberto 1927- 57-60
Nagi, Mostafa H. 1934- 33-36R
Nagi, Saad Z. 1925- 29-32R
Nagle, James J. 1909-1978 85-88
Obituary 81-84
Naglee, David Ingersoll 1930- 53-56
Nagler, Alois Maria 1907- CANR-19
Earlier sketch in CA 103
Nagler, Barney 1912- 19-20R
Nagler, Michael N(icholas) 1937- CANR-13
Earlier sketch in CA 73-76
na Gopaleen, Myles
See O Nuallain, Brian
Nagorski, Andrew 1947- 93-96
Nagorski, Zygmunt 1885(?)-1973 Obituary 41-44R
Nagorski, Zygmunt, Jr. 1912- 73-76
Nagourney, Peter (Jon) 1940- 37-40R
Naguib, Mohammed 1902(?)-1984 Obituary 113
Nagy, Ferenc 1903-1979 Obituary 89-92
Nagy, Gil D. 1933- 25-28R
Nagy, Gregory 1942- 102
Nagy, Imre 1895(?)-1958 Brief entry 118
Nagy, Laszlo 1925-1978 Obituary 112
See also CLC 7
Nagy-Talavera, Nicholas M(anuel) 1929- 33-36R
Naha, Ed 1950- 109
Nahal, Chaman 1927- CANR-17
Earlier sketch in CA 37-40R
Nahas, Gabriel G(eorges) 1920- CANR-17
Earlier sketches in CA 49-52, CANR-1
Nahas, Rebecca 1946- 69-72
Nahem, Joseph 1917- 113
Nahm, Milton C(harles) 1903- 15-16R
Nahum, Lucien 1930(?)-1983 Obituary 111
Naidis, Mark 1918- 33-36R
Naifeh, Steven Woodward 1952- 102
Naik, Madhukar Krishna 1926- CANR-10
Earlier sketch in CA 21-22R
Naim, C(houdhri) M(ohammed) 1936- Brief entry 112
Naiman, Arthur 1941- 108
Naimy, Mikhail 1889-1988 Obituary 124
Naipaul, Shiva(dhar Srinivasa) 1945-1985 112
Obituary 116
Brief entry 110
See also DLBY 85
See also CLC 32, 39
Naipaul, V(idiadhar) S(urajprasad) 1932- CANR-1
Earlier sketch in CA 4R
See also DLBY 85
See also CLC 4, 7, 9, 13, 18, 37
Nairn, Ian (Douglas) 1930-1983 Obituary 110
Nairn, Ronald C(harles) 1922- 21-22R
Naisawald, L. Van Loan 1920- CANR-6
Earlier sketch in CA 5-6R
Naisbitt, John 1929(?)- Brief entry 113
Naismith, Grace (Akin) 1904-1983 CANR-20
Obituary 111
Earlier sketch in CA 65-68
Naismith, Helen 1929- 69-72
Naismith, Horace
See Helmer, William J.
Naismith, James 1861-1939 Brief entry 118
Naismith, Marion (Overend) 1922- 29-32R
Naismith, Robert J. 1916- 121
Najafi, Najmeh 25-28R
Najarian, Nevart 1901(?)-1985 Obituary 117
Najder, Zdzislaw 1930- 19-20R
Najemy, John Michael 1943- 118
Nakadate, Neil Edward 1943- 115
Nakae, Noriko 1940- 49-52
Nakamura, Hajime 1912- CANR-10
Earlier sketch in CA 53-56
Nakamura, James I. 1919- 21-22R
Nakamura, Yasuo 1919- 45-48
Nakanishi, Don T(oshiaki) 1949- 114
Nakanishi, Marsha
See Hirano-Nakanishi, Marsha J(oyce)
Nakanishi, Marsha J(oyce) Hirano
See Hirano-Nakanishi, Marsha J(oyce)
Nakano, Hirotaka 1942- 33-36R
Nakarai, Toyozo W(ada) 1898- 41-44R
Nakashima, George Katsutoshi 1905- 106
Nakatani, Chiyoko 1930- 77-80
See also SATA 40
Nakayama, Shigeru 1928- 29-32R
Nakhleh, Emile A. 1938- 77-80
Nakhnikian, George 1920- CANR-2
Earlier sketch in CA 2R
Nakos, Lilika 1899(?)- CLC-29
Nalder, Eric C(hristopher) 1946- 89-92
Nale, Sharon Anne 1944- 108
Nall, Hiram Abiff 1950- 57-60
Nall, T(orney) Otto 1900- 19-20R
Nallin, Walter E. 1917(?)-1978 Obituary 77-80
Nalty, Bernard Charles 1931- CANR-18
Earlier sketch in CA 102
Nam, Charles B(enjamin) 1926- CANR-10
Earlier sketch in CA 65-68
Nam, Koon Woo 1928- 61-64
Namath, Joe
See Namath, Joseph William
Namath, Joseph William 1943- 89-92
Namba, Toshio 1910-1987 Obituary 124
Nambiar, O. K. 1910- 13-14R
Nameroff, Rochelle 1943- 41-44R
Namias, June 1941- 81-84
Namier, Julia 1893-1977 61-64
Obituary 120
Namier, Lewis Bernstein 1888-1960 Obituary 113
Namikawa, Banri 1931- CANR-8
Earlier sketch in CA 53-56
Namikawa, Ryo 1905- 93-96
Namioka, Lensey 1929- CANR-11
Earlier sketch in CA 69-72
See also SATA 27
Namir, Mordecai 1897-1975 Obituary 57-60
Namjoshi, Suniti 1941- 113
Namovicz, Gene Inyart 1927- 19-20R
Nanassy, Louis C(harles) 1913- CANR-19
Earlier sketches in CA 53-56, CANR-4
Nance, Guinevera Ann 1939- 106
Nance, James Clark 1893(?)-1984 Obituary 113
Nance, Joseph Milton 1913- CANR-1
Earlier sketch in CA 4R
Nanda, B(al) R(am) 1917- CANR-23
Earlier sketches in CA 13-14R, CANR-7
Nandakumar, Prema 1939- 9-10R
Nandy, Pritish 1947- CANR-12
Earlier sketch in CA 65-68
Nangia, Sudesh 1942- CANR-22
Earlier sketches in CA 53-56, CANR-4
NanKivell, Joice M.
See Loch, Joice N(anKivell)
Nannes, Caspar Harold 1906-1978 11-12R
Obituary 81-84
Nanry, Charles (Anthony) 1938- 73-76
Nanus, Burt 1936- 115
Napier, B(unyan) Davie 1915- CANR-4
Earlier sketch in CA 2R
Napier, Mark
See Laffin, John (Alfred Charles)
Napier, Mary
See Wright, (Mary) Patricia
Napier, Priscilla 1908- 23-24R
Napier, William
See Seymour, William Napier
Napjus, Alice James 1913- 21-22R
Napjus, James
See Napjus, Alice James
Napoleon, Art
See Sudhalter, Richard M(errill)
Napolitan, Joseph 1929- 37-40R
Napolitane, Catherine A(nn) Durrum 1936- 85-88
Narain, Jai Prakash
See Narayan, Jayaprakash
Narang, Gopi Chand 1931- CANR-14
Earlier sketch in CA 29-32R
Narasimha Char, K. T. 1903- CANR-5
Earlier sketch in CA 53-56
Narasimhachar, K. T.
See Narasimha Char, K. T.
Narasimhan, Chakravarthi V. 1915- 19-20R
Narayan, Jayaprakash 1902-1979 97-100
Obituary 89-92
Narayan, Ongkar 1926- 103
Narayan, R(asipuram) K(rishnaswami) 1906- 81-84
See also CLC 7, 28, 47
Narayn, Deane 1929- 1R
Nardin, Terry 1942- 41-44R
Narell, Irena 1923- CANR-1
Earlier sketch in CA 3R
Naremore, James 1941- CANR-11
Earlier sketch in CA 69-72
Naroll, Raoul 1920-1985 33-36R
Obituary 116
Narramore, Stanley Bruce 1941- 57-60
Naruse, Mikio 1905-1969 118
Narveson, Jan F(redric) 1936- CANR-24
Earlier sketches in CA 23-24R, CANR-9
Nasatir, A(braham) P(hineas) 1904- CANR-5
Earlier sketch in CA 11-12R
Nasatir, David 1934- 41-44R
Nasaw, David 1945- 116
Nasaw, Jonathan Lewis 1947- 61-64
Nasby, A(sher Gordon) 1909-1983 Obituary 109
Nasby, Petroleum Vesuvius
See Locke, David Ross
Nash, Allan N(ylin) 1932- 41-44R
Nash, Bruce M(itchell) 1947- CANR-15
Earlier sketch in CA 85-88
See also SATA 34
Nash, Daniel
See Loader, William Reginald
Nash, David T(heodore) 1929- 93-96
Nash, Eno
See Stevens, Austin N(eil)
Nash, Ethel Miller 1909- CAP-1
Earlier sketch in CA 15-16
Nash, Father Stephen
See Kavanaugh, James J(oseph)
Nash, Gary B. 1933- 37-40R
Nash, Gerald D(avid) 1928- CANR-8
Earlier sketch in CA 23-24R
Nash, Howard P(ervear), Jr. 1900- 73-76
Nash, J(essie) Madeleine 1943- 69-72
Nash, James E(dward) 1933- 29-32R
Nash, Jay Robert 1937- 21-22R
Nash, June (Caprice) 1927- 29-32R
Nash, Lee (Marten) 1927- 41-44R
Nash, Linell
See Smith, Linell Nash
Nash, Manning 1924- 19-20R
Nash, Mary (Hughes) 1925- 5-6R
See also SATA 41
Nash, N. Richard 1913- CANR-14
Earlier sketch in CA 85-88
Nash, Nancy 1943- 21-22R
Nash, Newlyn
See Howe, Doris Kathleen
and Howe, Muriel
Nash, (Fredric) Ogden 1902-1971 CAP-1
Obituary 29-32R
Earlier sketch in CA 13-14
See also SATA 2, 46
See also DLB 11
See also CLC 23
Nash, Padder
See Sewart, Alan
Nash, Paul 1924- 19-20R
Nash, Ralph (Lee) 1925- 19-20R
Nash, Ray 1905-1982 Obituary 106
Nash, Robert 1902- CAP-1
Earlier sketch in CA 9-10
Nash, Roderick 1939- 19-20R
Nash, Ronald H. 1936- CANR-23
Earlier sketches in CA 5-6R, CANR-8
Nash, Simon
See Chapman, Raymond
Nash, William (Wray), Jr. 1928- 85-88
Naske, Claus-M(ichael) 1935- CANR-13
Earlier sketch in CA 77-80
Naslund, Erik
See Naeslund, Erik
Nason, Alvin 1919-1978 Obituary 77-80
Nason, Donna 1944- 97-100
Nason, Leonard H(astings) 1895-1970 Obituary 114
Nason, Leslie J. 7-8R
Nasr, Seyyed Hossein 1933- CANR-10
Earlier sketch in CA 23-24R
Nass, Elyse (Linda) 1947- 111
Nass, Stanley 1940- 115
Nassaar, Christopher S(uhayl) 1944- 97-100
Nassar, Eugene Paul 1935- 33-36R
Nassau, Wilhelmina Helena Pauline Maria 1880-1962 Obituary 113
Nassauer, Rudolf 1924- 105
Nasser, Gamal Abdel 1918-1970 Obituary 113
Nassivera, John 1950- 109
Nassour, Ellis (Michael) 1941- 119
Nast, Elsa Ruth
See Watson, Jane Werner
Nast, Thomas 1840-1902 Brief entry 112
See also SATA 33
Nastick, Sharon 1954- 114
See also SATA 41
Natale, Samuel M(ichael) 1943- 116
Natali, Alfred Maxim 1915- 57-60
Natanson, George 1928- 73-76
Natanson, Maurice (Alexander) 1924- CANR-12
Earlier sketch in CA 19-20R
Natchez, Gladys W. 1915- CANR-4
Earlier sketch in CA 11-12R
Natella, Arthur A(ristides), Jr. 1941- CANR-15
Earlier sketch in CA 89-92
Nathan, Adele (Gutman) 1900(?)-1986 73-76
Obituary 119
See also SATA 48
Nathan, Andrew J(ames) 1943- 65-68
Nathan, Daniel
See Dannay, Frederic
Nathan, David 1926- CANR-12
Earlier sketch in CA 29-32R
Nathan, Dorothy (Goldeen) ?-1966 81-84
See also SATA 15
Nathan, George Jean 1882-1958 Brief entry 114
See also TCLC 18
Nathan, Hans 1910- CANR-1
Earlier sketch in CA 3R
Nathan, James A. 1942- CANR-16
Earlier sketch in CA 85-88
Nathan, Joan 1943- 61-64
Nathan, Joe 1948- 115
Nathan, Leonard E(dward) 1924- CANR-7
Earlier sketch in CA 5-6R
Nathan, Norman 1915- CANR-1
Earlier sketch in CA 1R
Nathan, Otto 1893-1987 Obituary 121
Nathan, Paul S. 1913- Brief entry 116
Nathan, Peter E. 1935- 73-76
Nathan, Richard P(erle) 1935- CANR-7
Earlier sketch in CA 57-60
Nathan, Robert (Gruntal) 1894-1985 CANR-6
Obituary 116
Earlier sketch in CA 15-16R
See also SATA 6, 43
See also DLB 9
Nathan, Robert Stuart 1948- 81-84
Nathanson, Jerome 1908-1975 Obituary 57-60
Nathanson, Laura Walther 1941- 123
Nathanson, Leonard 1933- 23-24R
Nathanson, Nathaniel L(ouis) 1908-1983 89-92
Obituary 111
Nathanson, Yale S(amuel) 1895- 77-80
Nations, Opal (Louis) 1941- 112
Natow, Annette 1933- 114
Natsume, Kinnosuke 1867-1916 Brief entry 104
Natsume, Soseki
See Natsume, Kinnosuke
See also TCLC 2, 10
Natta, Giulio 1903-1979 Obituary 113
Natti, (Mary) Lee 1919- CANR-2
Earlier sketch in CA 7-8R
Natti, Susanna 1948- SATA-32
Natusch, Sheila (Ellen) 1926- CANR-20
Earlier sketch in CA 103

Natwar-Singh, K. 1931- ...13-14R
Nau, Erika S(chwager) 1918- ...65-68
Naude, (Aletta) Adele da Fonseca-Wollheim 1910- ...11-12R
Nauer, Barbara Joan 1932- Brief entry ... 105
Naughton, Bill 1910- ... 105
See also DLB 13
Naughton, John 1933- ...57-60
Naugle, Helen Harrold 1920- ...53-56
Naugle, John E(arl) 1923- ...65-68
Nauheim, Ferd(inand Alan) 1909- ... CANR-16
Earlier sketches in CA 49-52, CANR-1
Nauman, St. Elmo, Jr. 1935- ...53-56
Naumann, Anthony Frank 1921-1971 ...21-22R
Obituary ...89-92
Naumann, Marina 1938- ...93-96
Naumann, Oscar E(dward) 1912- ...77-80
Naumann, Rose 1919- ...65-68
Naumburg, Margaret 1890-1983 Obituary ... 109
Nauticus
See Waltari, Mika (Toimi)
Nava, Julian 1927- ...61-64
Nava, Michael 1954- ... 124
Nava, Roberto 1906(?)-1983 Obituary ... 111
Navarra, Fernand Jean 1915- ... 108
Navarra, John Gabriel 1927- ...41-44R
See also SATA 8
Navarro, Antonio 1922- ... 107
Navarro (Gerassi), Marysa 1934- ... 106
Navarro, Peter 1949- ... 118
Navas, Deborah 1943- ... 112
Navasky, Victor S. 1932- ... CANR-10
Earlier sketch in CA 21-22R
Navas-Ruiz, Ricardo 1932- Brief entry ... 107
Navone, John J(oseph) 1930- ... CANR-10
Earlier sketch in CA 23-24R
Navrozov, Lev 1928- ...61-64
Naydler, Merton 1920- ...45-48
Naylor, Chris(topher Michael) 1947- ... 118
Naylor, Eric W(oodfin) 1936- ...45-48
Naylor, Gloria 1950- ... 107
See also CLC 28
Naylor, Harriet H. 1915- ... CANR-9
Earlier sketch in CA 21-22R
Naylor, James C(harles) 1932- ... CANR-1
Earlier sketch in CA 45-48
Naylor, John 1920- ...93-96
Naylor, Margot (Ailsa) Lodge 1907- ...11-12R
Naylor, Penelope 1941- ...37-40R
See also SATA 10
Naylor, Phyllis (Reynolds) 1933- ... CANR-24
Earlier sketches in CA 21-22R, CANR-8
See also SATA 12
Nazareth, Peter 1940- ... 101
Nazarian, Nikki
See Nichols, Cecilia Fawn
Nazaroff, Alexander I. 1898- ...33-36R
See also SATA 4
Nazzaro, Anthony M. 1927- Brief entry ... 106
Neagle, Anna 1904-1986 Obituary ... 119
Neagley, Ross Linn 1907- ... 106
Neagoe, Anna (Frankel) 1885(?)-1986
Obituary ... 120
Neagoe, Peter 1881-1960 ... 105
See also DLB 4
Neal, Alfred C. 1912- ... 121
Neal, Ann Parker 1934- Brief entry ... 114
Neal, Arminta Pearl 1921- ...85-88
Neal, Bruce W(alter) 1931- ...21-22R
Neal, Charles Dempsey 1908- ... CANR-5
Earlier sketch in CA 5-6R
Neal, Emily Gardiner ... CANR-3
Earlier sketch in CA 5-6R
Neal, Ernest G(ordon) 1911- ...13-14R
Neal, Fred Warner 1915- ... CANR-2
Earlier sketch in CA 7-8R
Neal, Harry
See Bixby, Jerome Lewis
Neal, Harry Edward 1906- ... CANR-2
Earlier sketch in CA 5-6R
See also SATA 5
Neal, Helen Keating 1907-1987 ... 124
Obituary ... 122
Neal, Hilary
See Norton, Olive (Claydon)
Neal, James M(adison) 1925- ...73-76
Neal, James T(homas) 1936- ...57-60
Neal, John 1793-1876 ... DLB-1, 59
Neal, Joseph C. 1807-1847 ... DLB-11
Neal, Julia 1905- ...69-72
Neal, Larry
See Neal, Lawrence (P.)
See also DLB 38
Neal, Lawrence (P.) 1937-1981 ...81-84
Obituary ... 102
Neal, Marie Augusta 1921- ... 114
Neal, Michael
See Teitelbaum, Michael
Neal, Nelson 1921(?)-1983 Obituary ... 109
Neal, Patsy 1938- ...61-64
Neal, Sister Marie Augusta 1921- ...29-32R
Neale, Gay Weeks 1935- ... 113
Neale, John E(rnest) 1890-1975 ...65-68
Obituary ...61-64
Neale, Robert George 1919- Brief entry ... 108
Neale, Walter Castle 1925- ... CANR-7
Earlier sketch in CA 5-6R
Neale-Silva, Eduardo 1905- Brief entry ... 106
Nealon, Eleanor ... 103
Nealon, Thomas E. 1933- ...33-36R
Neaman, Judith S(ilverman) 1936- ...61-64
Neame, Alan John 1924- ... CANR-2
Earlier sketch in CA 4R
Nearing, Guy 1890-1986 Obituary ... 118
Nearing, Helen K(nothe) 1904- ... CANR-11
Earlier sketch in CA 29-32R
Nearing, Penny 1916- ...81-84
See also SATA 42, 47
Nearing, Scott 1883-1983 ... CANR-11
Obituary ... 110
Earlier sketch in CA 41-44R
Neary, John (Anthony, Jr.) 1937-
Brief entry ... 107
Neatby, H(erbert) Blair 1924- Brief entry ... 111
Neatby, Leslie Hamilton 1902- ... CANR-3
Earlier sketch in CA 7-8R
Neate, Frank Anthony 1928- ... 105
Neave, Airey (Middleton Sheffield)
1916-1979 ...85-88
Neavles, Janet Talmadge 1919- ...5-6R
Nebel, Gustave E. ... SATA-33, 45
Nebel, Mimouca
See Nebel, Gustave E.
Nebenzahl, Kenneth 1927- ... 111
Brief entry ... 109
Nebrensky, Alex
See Cooper, Parley J(oseph)
Nebylitsyn, Vladimir Dmitrievich
1930(?)-1972 Obituary ...37-40R
Necheles, Ruth F. 1936- ...41-44R
Necker, Claire (Kral) 1917- ...33-36R
Nederhood, Joel H(oman) 1930- ...29-32R
Nee, Brett de Bary 1943- ... 101
Nee, Kay Bonner ... CANR-2
Earlier sketch in CA 49-52
See also SATA 10
Needham, David C. 1929- ... 118
Needham, (Noel) Joseph (Terence
Montgomery) 1900- ... CANR-5
Earlier sketch in CA 11-12R
Needham, Richard (John) 1912- ... 101
Needham, Rodney 1923- ... CANR-15
Earlier sketch in CA 81-84
Needham, (Amy) Violet 1876-1967
Obituary ... 116
Needle, Jan 1943- ... 106
See also SATA 30
Needleman, Jacob 1934- ... CANR-12
Earlier sketch in CA 29-32R
See also SATA 6
Needleman, Morriss H. 1907- ...25-28R
Needler, Howard I(an) 1937- ... 111
Needler, Martin C(yril) 1933- ... CANR-18
Earlier sketches in CA 7-8R, CANR-2
Needles, Robert Johnson 1903- ... CAP-1
Earlier sketch in CA 11-12
Neef, Elton T.
See Fanthorpe, R(obert) Lionel
Neel, (Louis) Boyd 1905-1981 Obituary ... 108
Neel, Joanne Loewe 1920- ...25-28R
Neely, Bill 1930- ... CANR-13
Earlier sketch in CA 33-36R
Neely, Carol Thomas 1939- Brief entry ... 107
Neely, James C. 1926- ... 109
Neely, Mark E(dward), Jr. 1944- ... 106
Neely, Martina 1939- ...61-64
Neely, Richard (Forlani) 1941- ... 107
Neenan, William B(raunger) 1929- ...41-44R
Neeper, Carolyn 1937- ...57-60
Neeper, Cary
See Neeper, Carolyn
Neerskov, Hans Kristian 1932- ...65-68
Nef, Evelyn Stefansson 1913- ... CANR-20
Earlier sketch in CA 49-52
Nef, John Ulric 1899- ... CANR-20
Earlier sketch in CA 2R
Neff, Alan (Henry) 1949- ... 117
Neff, Donald 1930- ...77-80
Neff, Emery E. 1892-1983 ...5-6R
Obituary ... 109
Neff, H(arry) Richard 1933- ...33-36R
Neff, Hildegard
See Knef, Hildegard
Neff, John C. 1913- ...19-20R
Neff, Miriam 1945- ... 115
Neff, Renfreu (de St. Laurence) 1938- ...29-32R
Neff, Robert W(ilbur) 1936- ... 106
Neff, Walter S(cott) 1910- ... CAP-2
Earlier sketch in CA 25-28
Neff, William Lee 1906-1973 ... 2R
Obituary ... 103
Neft, David S(amuel) 1937- ...41-44R
Negandhi, A(nant) R(anchoddas) 1933- ...33-36R
Neggers, Carla A(malia) 1955- ... 112
Negley, Glenn (Robert) 1907- ...19-20R
Negri, Rocco 1932- ... SATA-12
Negroponte, Nicholas Peter 1943- ...29-32R
Negus, Arthur George 1903-1985
Obituary ... 116
Negus, Kenneth George 1927- ...19-20R
Neher, Andre 1914- ... 109
Neher, Clark D(umont) 1938- ... 118
Neher, Jack 1918- ... 118
Nehrling, Arno H. 1886-1974 ...11-12R
Obituary ...53-56
Nehrling, Irene Dahlberg 1900- ...11-12R
Nehrt, Lee Charles 1926- ... CANR-13
Earlier sketch in CA 23-24R
Nehru, Jawaharlal 1889-1964 ...85-88
Neiburg, Gladys Eudas 1898- ...61-64
Neider, Charles 1915- ... CANR-24
Earlier sketch in CA 19-20R
Neiderman, Andrew 1940- ... CANR-13
Earlier sketch in CA 33-36R
Neidermyer, Dan 1947- ... CANR-24
Earlier sketch in CA 45-48
Neidhardt, W(ilfried) S(teffen) 1941- ...65-68
Neidpath, James
See Charteris, James Donald
Neier, Aryeh 1937- ...57-60
Neighbour, Ralph W(ebster) 1906- ... CANR-1
Earlier sketch in CA 2R
Neighbour, Rhona M.
See Martin, Rhona
Neighbours, Kenneth Franklin 1915- ...61-64
Neigoff, Anne ...41-44R
See also SATA 13
Neigoff, Mike 1920- ... CANR-2
Earlier sketch in CA 5-6R
See also SATA 13
Neihardt, John Gneisenau 1881-1973 ... CAP-1
Earlier sketch in CA 13-14
See also DLB 9, 54
See also CLC 32
Neikirk, William (Robert) 1938- ... 117
Neil, Hugh Michael 1930- Brief entry ... 109
Neil, J. Meredith 1937- ...33-36R
Neil, Randolph L. 1941- ...93-96
Neil, Randy
See Neil, Randolph L.
Neil, William 1909-1979 ... CANR-6
Obituary ...93-96
Earlier sketch in CA 11-12R
Neilan, Sarah ...69-72
Neilands, J(ohn) B(rian) 1921- ...97-100
Neill, A(lexander) S(utherland) 1883-1973 ... 101
Obituary ...45-48
Neill, Christopher Harry Douglas 1955- ... 117
Neill, Stephen Charles 1900-1984 ... CANR-7
Obituary ... 113
Earlier sketch in CA 11-12R
Neill, Thomas Patrick 1915-1970 ... CANR-3
Earlier sketch in CA 7-8R
Neilson, Andrew 1946- ... 110
Neilson, Frances Fullerton (Jones) 1910- ...73-76
See also SATA 14
Neilson, James Warren 1933- ... 4R
Neilson, Marguerite
See Tompkins, Julia (Marguerite Hunter Manchee)
Neilson, N(eils) P. 1895- ... CANR-2
Earlier sketch in CA 5-6R
Neiman, David 1921- ...69-72
Neiman, Fraser 1911- ...25-28R
Neimark, Anne E. 1935- ... CANR-16
Earlier sketch in CA 29-32R
See also SATA 4
Neimark, Edith D(eborah) 1928- ...41-44R
Neimark, Paul G. 1934- Brief entry ... 115
See also SATA 37
Neipris, Janet
See Wille, Janet Neipris
Neisser, Hans P(hilip) 1895-1975 ... CAP-1
Obituary ...53-56
Earlier sketch in CA 15-16
Neisser, Ulric 1928- ... 108
Nekrasov, Viktor (Platonovich) 1911-1987
Obituary ... 123
Nekrich, Aleksandr M(oisei) 1920- ...81-84
Neligan, David 1899- ... CAP-2
Earlier sketch in CA 29-32
Nelkin, Dorothy 1933- ... CANR-14
Earlier sketch in CA 41-44R
Nell, Edward John 1935- ...65-68
Nelles, Henry Vivian 1942- ... 103
Nelli, Humbert S(teven) 1930- ... CANR-14
Earlier sketch in CA 41-44R
Nelligan, Emile 1879-1941 Brief entry ... 114
See also TCLC 14
Nellis, Muriel ... 102
Nellist, John B(owman) 1923- ...25-28R
Nelms, C(larice) E. 1919- ...25-28R
Nelms, Henning C(unningham) 1900-1986
Obituary ... 119
Nelsen, Anne Kusener 1942- ...97-100
Nelsen, Hart M(ichael) 1938- ... CANR-8
Earlier sketch in CA 53-56
Nelson, A(ndrew) Thomas 1933- ...7-8R
Nelson, Alan H(olm) 1938- ... 104
Nelson, Alice Fray 1911(?)-1983 Obituary ... 110
Nelson, Alice Ruth Moore Dunbar
1875-1935 ... 124
Brief entry ... 122
See also DLB 50
Nelson, Alvin F(redolph) 1917-1973 ... CAP-2
Earlier sketch in CA 25-28
Nelson, Amirtharaj 1934- ...57-60
Nelson, Andrew N(athaniel) 1893-1975 ... CANR-3
Earlier sketch in CA 7-8R
Nelson, Anne 1954- ... 123
Nelson, Benjamin N. 1911-1977 ...81-84
Obituary ...73-76
Nelson, Benjamin N(athaniel) 1935- ... CANR-1
Earlier sketch in CA 2R
Nelson, Beth
See Nelson, Mary Elizabeth
Nelson, Bryan 1932- ... 103
Nelson, C(arl) Ellis 1916- ... 108
Nelson, Carl Leroy 1910- ... 104
Nelson, Carnot E(dward) 1941- ...37-40R
Nelson, Cary (Robert) 1946- ...49-52
Nelson, Charles Lamar 1917- ...69-72
Nelson, Charles R(owe) 1942- ...37-40R
Nelson, Cholmondeley M. 1903- ...5-6R
Nelson, Clifford Ansgar 1906- ... CAP-1
Earlier sketch in CA 11-12
Nelson, Conny E(dwin) 1933- Brief entry ... 108
Nelson, Cordner (Bruce) 1918- ...29-32R
See also SATA 29
Nelson, Dalmas H(ildor) 1925- ... 119
Nelson, Daniel 1941- ...25-28R
Nelson, David Moir 1920- ... CANR-17
Earlier sketch in CA 2R
Nelson, Donald F. 1929- ...37-40R
Nelson, E(ugene) Clifford 1911- ...13-14R
Nelson, Edna Deu Pree ...5-6R
Nelson, Elof G. 1924- ...23-24R
Nelson, Eric Hilliard 1940-1985 Obituary ... 118
Nelson, Esther L. 1928- ... CANR-11
Earlier sketch in CA 69-72
See also SATA 13
Nelson, Ethel Florence 1913- ... CANR-6
Earlier sketch in CA 53-56
Nelson, Eugene 1929- ...61-64
Nelson, F(rancis) William 1922- ...13-14R
Nelson, Geoffrey K(enneth) 1923- ... CANR-24
Earlier sketch in CA 29-32R
Nelson, George (H.) 1908-1986 ...81-84
Obituary ... 118
Nelson, George (Carl) E(dward)
1900-1982 ... CANR-24
Earlier sketch in CA 45-48
Nelson, Gideon E(dmund, Jr.) 1924- ...53-56
Nelson, Harold A(lfred) 1932- ... 114
Nelson, Harold L(ewis) 1917- ...93-96
Nelson, Herbert B(enjamin) 1903- ... CAP-2
Earlier sketch in CA 19-20
Nelson, Indiana 1940- ...97-100
Nelson, J. Bryan 1932- ... CANR-10
Earlier sketch in CA 25-28R
Nelson, J(oseph) Raleigh 1873-1961
Obituary ... 110
Nelson, J(ohn) Robert 1920- ... CANR-19
Earlier sketches in CA 11-12R, CANR-3
Nelson, Jack
See Nelson, John Howard
Nelson, Jack L. 1932- ... CANR-10
Earlier sketch in CA 25-28R
Nelson, James B(ruce) 1930- ... CANR-17
Earlier sketches in CA 49-52, CANR-1
Nelson, James C(ecil) 1908- ... CANR-13
Earlier sketch in CA 77-80
Nelson, James G(raham) 1929- ...11-12R
Nelson, Jan Alan 1935- ...41-44R
Nelson, Jane Armstrong 1927- Brief entry ... 105
Nelson, Janet 1930- ... 115
Nelson, Jean Erichsen
See Erichsen-Nelson, Jean
Nelson, John Charles 1925- ...49-52
Nelson, John Howard 1929- ...29-32R
Nelson, John Oliver 1909- ...37-40R
Nelson, Joseph Bryan 1932- ... 105
Nelson, Joseph Schieser 1937- ...73-76
Nelson, June Kompass 1920- ...73-76
Nelson, Katherine Shaw 1926- ... 110
Nelson, Kay Shaw
See Nelson, Katherine Shaw
Nelson, Keith L(ebahn) 1932- Brief entry ... 113
Nelson, Kent 1943- ...77-80
Nelson, L(ester) Ivar 1941- ... 119
Nelson, Lawrence E(rnest) 1928-1977 ...53-56
Obituary ... 103
See also SATA 28
Nelson, Lawrence Emerson 1893- ...19-20R
Nelson, Lois (Ney) 1930- ...61-64
Nelson, Lowry, Jr. 1926- ...5-6R
Nelson, Malcolm A. 1934- ...45-48
Nelson, Marg (Raibley) 1899- ... CANR-2
Earlier sketch in CA 2R
Nelson, Marguerite
See Floren, Lee
Nelson, Marion Harvey 1925- ...11-12R
Nelson, Martha 1923- ...29-32R
Nelson, Mary Carroll 1929- ... CANR-16
Earlier sketches in CA 49-52, CANR-1
See also SATA 23
Nelson, Mary Elizabeth 1926- ...93-96
Nelson, Michael Harrington 1921- ... CANR-2
Earlier sketch in CA 7-8R
Nelson, Nina
See Nelson, Ethel Florence
Nelson, Oliver W(endell) 1904- ...29-32R
Nelson, Oswald George 1907-1975 ...93-96
Obituary ...57-60
Nelson, Ozzie
See Nelson, Oswald George
Nelson, Paul David 1941- ... 120
Nelson, Peter 1940- ... CANR-12
Earlier sketch in CA 61-64
Nelson, Peter
See Solow, Martin
Nelson, Philip Bradford 1951- ... 113
Nelson, R. Faraday 1931- ...69-72
Nelson, Rachel W(est) 1955- ... 117
Nelson, Ralph 1916-1987 ...49-52
Obituary ... 124
Nelson, Ralph C(arl) 1927- ...53-56
Nelson, Randy F(ranklin) 1948-
Brief entry ... 110
Nelson, Ray
See Nelson, R. Faraday
Nelson, Raymond S(tanley) 1921- ... CANR-16
Earlier sketches in CA 45-48, CANR-1
Nelson, Richard 1950- Brief entry ... 123
Nelson, Richard K(ing) 1941- ... CANR-12
Earlier sketch in CA 29-32R
Nelson, Richard R(obinson) 1930- ... CANR-16
Earlier sketch in CA 97-100
Nelson, Rick
See Nelson, Eric Hilliard
Nelson, Ricky
See Nelson, Eric Hilliard
Nelson, Robert James 1925- ... CANR-8
Earlier sketch in CA 5-6R
Nelson, Rosanne E(ierdanz) 1939- ...49-52
Nelson, Rowland Whiteway 1902-1979
Obituary ... 105
Nelson, Roy Paul 1923- ... CANR-22
Earlier sketches in CA 19-20R, CANR-7
Nelson, Ruben F(rederick) W(erthenbach)
1939- ... 112
Nelson, Ruth 1914- ...41-44R
Nelson, Ruth Youngdahl 1904(?)-1984
Obituary ... 112
Nelson, Severing E. 1896- ...7-8R

Nelson, Sharon H. 1948- 113
Nelson, Stanley 1933- CANR-18
Earlier sketches in CA 49-52, CANR-1
Nelson, Thomas P. 1925(?)-1983
Obituary 110
Nelson, Truman (John Seymour)
1911-1987 .... CANR-1
Obituary 123
Earlier sketch in CA 2R
Nelson, W(esley) Dale 1927- 77-80
Nelson, Walter Henry 1928- CANR-7
Earlier sketch in CA 15-16R
Nelson, Warren L. 1940- 89-92
Nelson, William 1908-1978 49-52
Obituary 103
Nelson, William R(ichard) 1924- 25-28R
Nelson, William Rockhill 1841-1915 .... DLB-23
Nelson, Willie 1933- 107
See also CLC 17
Nelton, Sharon (Lee) 1937- 123
Nemanic, Gerald Carl 1941- 107
Nemec, David 1938- CANR-2
Earlier sketch in CA 49-52
Nemerov, Howard 1920- CANR-1
Earlier sketch in CA 3R
See also CABS 2
See also DLB 6
See also DLBY 83
See also CLC 2, 6, 9, 36
Nemeth, Laszlo 1901-1975 93-96
Obituary 57-60
Nemir, Alma 1902-1971 .... CAP-2
Earlier sketch in CA 29-32
Nemiro, Beverly Anderson 1925- CANR-5
Earlier sketch in CA 53-56
Nemiroff, Robert Brief entry 116
See also AITN 2
Nemirow, Steven 1949- 110
Nemmers, Erwin Esser 1916- 11-12R
Nemser, Cindy 1937- 61-64
Nenni, Pietro 1891-1980 Obituary 105
Nerbovig, Marcella H. 1919- 89-92
Nere, Jacques 1917- 57-60
Nerhood, Harry W(arren) 1910- 29-32R
Nerlich, Graham 73-76
Nerlove, Marc L(eon) 1933- 104
Nerlove, Miriam 1959- 121
See also SATA 49
Neruda, Pablo 1904-1973 .... CAP-2
Obituary 45-48
Earlier sketch in CA 19-20
See also CLC 1, 2, 5, 7, 9, 28
Nerval, Gaston
See Diez de Medina, Raul
Nervi, Pier Luigi 1891-1979 Obituary 113
Nervo, Amado (Ruiz de) 1870-1919
Brief entry 109
See also TCLC 11
Nesbin, Esther W(inter) 1910- 41-44R
Nesbit, E(dith) 1858-1924 Brief entry 118
See also YABC 1
See also CLR 3
Nesbit, Robert C(arrington) 1917- 45-48
Nesbit, Troy
See Folsom, Franklin (Brewster)
Nesbitt, Cathleen 1888-1982 Obituary 107
Nesbitt, Elizabeth 1897(?)-1977 Obituary 73-76
Nesbitt, George L(yman) 1903- 41-44R
Nesbitt, Paul H(omer) 1904- 77-80
Nesbitt, Ralph Beryl 1891(?)-1975
Obituary 61-64
Nesbitt, Rosemary (Sinnett) 1924- 81-84
Neshamith, Sara
See Dushnitzky-Shner, Sara
Nesmith, Robert I. 1891-1972 .... CANR-15
Obituary 103
Earlier sketch in CA 3R
Nespojohn, Katherine V(eronica) 1912- 37-40R
See also SATA 7
Ness, Evaline (Michelow) 1911-1986 .... CANR-5
Obituary 120
Earlier sketch in CA 7-8R
See also SATA 1, 26, 49
See also SAAS 1
See also DLB 61
See also CLR 6
Ness, Gayl D(eForrest) 1929- 29-32R
Ness, John H., Jr. 1919- 21-22R
Nessen, (Lewis) Robert 1932- 107
Nessen, Ron(ald Harold) 1934-
Brief entry 106
Nessi, Pio Baroja y
See Baroja (y Nessi), Pio
Nestle, John Francis 1912- 89-92
Nestor, William P(rodromos) 1947- 109
See also SATA 49
Nesvadba, Josef 1926- 97-100
Netanyahu, Benzion 1910- 61-64
Netanyahu, Jonathan 1946(?)-1976
Obituary 114
Netanyahu, Yonatan
See Netanyahu, Jonathan
Netboy, Anthony 1906- CANR-7
Earlier sketch in CA 19-20R
Neter, John 1923- 53-56
Netherclift, Beryl (Constance) 1911- 93-96
Nethercot, Arthur H(obart) 1895- 2R
Netland, Dwayne 1932- 110
Neto, Antonio Agostinho 1922-1979 101
Obituary 89-92
Nettel, Reginald 1899- 13-14R
Nettelbeck, F(red) A(rthur) 1950- 118
Nettell, Richard (Geoffrey) 1907- CAP-2
Earlier sketch in CA 25-28
Nettels, Curtis Putnam 1898- CANR-1
Earlier sketch in CA 2R
Nettels, Elsa 1931- 77-80
Netter, (Jean) Patrick 1952- 119
Netting, Robert M(cCorkle) 1934- 61-64
Nettis, Joseph 1928- 11-12R
Nettl, Bruno 1930- 19-20R
Nettl, J(ohn) P(eter) 1926-1968 .... CAP-2
Earlier sketch in CA 23-24
Nettl, Paul 1889-1972 .... CAP-1
Obituary 33-36R
Earlier sketch in CA 9-10
Nettleford, Rex M. 37-40R
Nettler, Gwynn 1913- 33-36R
Nettles, Thomas Julian 1946- 117
Nettles, Tom
See Nettles, Thomas Julian
Netzer, Dick 1928- Brief entry 112
Netzer, Lanore A. 1916- 19-20R
Neu, Charles E. 1936- 21-22R
Neubauer, David William 1944- 65-68
Neubauer, John 1933- 101
Neubauer, William Arthur 1916- 9-10R
Neubeck, Gerhard 1918- 41-44R
Neuberger, Egon 1925- 25-28R
Neuberger, Richard Lewis 1912-1960
Obituary 89-92
Neubert, Christopher J. 1948- 106
Neuburg, Paul 1939- 45-48
Neuburg, Victor E. 1924- 33-36R
Neuenschwander, John A. 1941-
Brief entry 113
Neufeld, John (Arthur) 1938- CANR-11
Earlier sketch in CA 25-28R
See also SATA 6
See also SAAS 3
See also CLC 17
Neufeld, Maurice Frank 1910- 4R
Neufeld, Peter Lorenz 1931- 25-28R
Neufeld, Rose 1924- 29-32R
Neufelder, Jerome M(ichael) 1929- 115
Neufeldt, Leonard N(ick) 1937- 108
Neufer Emswiler, Sharon
See Emswiler, Sharon Neufer
Neuffer, Claude Henry 1911- 41-44R
Neuffer, Irene LaBorde 1919- 61-64
Neugeboren, Jay (Michael) 1938- CANR-21
Earlier sketch in CA 19-20R
See also DLB 28
Neuharth, Allen AITN-2
Neuhaus, Richard (John) 1936- 33-36R
Neuhaus, Ruby (Hart) 1932- 103
Neulinger, John 1924- CANR-16
Earlier sketch in CA 41-44R
Neuls-Bates, Carol 1939- 114
Neuman, Abraham A(aron) 1890-1970
Obituary 104
Neuman, Betty Mavine 1924- 33-36R
Neuman, Fredric (Jay) 1934- CANR-20
Earlier sketch in CA 97-100
Neuman, Ladd A. 1942- 97-100
Neuman, Shirley Carol 1946- 121
Neuman, William Frederick 1919-1981
Obituary 103
Neumann, Alfred 1895-1952 .... DLB-56
Neumann, Emanuel 1893-1980 Obituary 105
Neumann, Gareth William 1930- 61-64
Neumann, John von
See von Neumann, John
Neumann, Jonathan 1950- 85-88
Neumann, Robert 1897-1975 103
Obituary 89-92
Neumann, Robert G(erhard) 1916- 7-8R
Neumann, William Louis 1915-1971 .... CAP-1
Obituary 33-36R
Earlier sketch in CA 11-12
Neumeyer, Alfred 1900(?)-1973
Obituary 41-44R
Neumeyer, Ken(neth Walter) 1953- 107
Neumeyer, M(artin) Henry 1892- CAP-2
Earlier sketch in CA 19-20
Neumeyer, Peter F(lorian) 1929- 33-36R
See also SATA 13
Neurath, Marie (Reidemeister) 1898- 13-14R
See also SATA 1
Neurath, Otto 1882-1945 Brief entry 117
Neuschel, Richard F(rederick) 1915- 15-16R
Neuschuetz, Karin 1946- 116
Neuschutz, Karin
See Neuschuetz, Karin
Neuse, Erna Kritsch 1923- 105
Neusner, Jacob 1932- CANR-22
Earlier sketches in CA 15-16R, CANR-7
See also SATA 38
Neustadt, Bertha C(ummings)
1921(?)-1984 Obituary 112
Neustadt, Egon 1898(?)-1984 Obituary 112
Neustadt, Richard Elliott 1919- 11-12R
Neustadt, Richard M(itchells) 1948- 45-48
Neutra, Richard Joseph 1892-1970 .... CANR-5
Obituary 29-32R
Earlier sketch in CA 7-8R
Neutrelle, Dale 1937- 61-64
Neuville, H(enry) Richmond, Jr. 1937- 23-24R
Neve, Herbert T(heodore) 1931- 25-28R
Neve, Lloyd 1923- 53-56
Nevell, Dick
See Nevell, Richard (William Babcock)
Nevell, Richard (William Babcock) 1947- 102
Nevelson, Louise 1900- 108
Neveux, Georges 1900-1982 Obituary 108
Nevill, Barry St-John 1941- 119
Neville, Anna
See Fairburn, Eleanor
Neville, B(arbara) Alison (Boodson)
1925- CANR-11
Earlier sketch in CA 7-8R
Neville, Charles
See Bodsworth, (Charles) Fred(erick)
Neville, Emily Cheney 1919- CANR-3
Earlier sketch in CA 7-8R
See also SATA 1
See also SAAS 2
See also CLC 12
Neville, Gwen Kennedy 1938- 114
Neville, Heather Buckley
See Buckley Neville, Heather
Neville, James Edmund Henderson
1897-1982 Obituary 107
Neville, Jill 1932- 21-22R
Neville, Joyce 115
Neville, Kris (Ottman) 1925-1980 Obituary 117
Neville, Mary
See Woodrich, Mary Neville
Neville, Pauline 1924- 29-32R
Neville, Richard F. 1931- 85-88
Neville, Robert 1905-1970 Obituary 104
Neville, Robert C(ummings) 1939- CANR-11
Earlier sketch in CA 25-28R
Neville, Susan 1951- 119
Nevin, David 1927- 121
Nevin, Evelyn C. 1910- 19-20R
Nevins, Albert J. 1915- CANR-19
Earlier sketches in CA 5-6R, CANR-5
See also SATA 20
Nevins, (Joseph) Allan 1890-1971 .... 5-6R
Obituary 29-32R
See also DLB 17
Nevins, Deborah 1947- 105
Nevins, Edward M(ichael) 1938- 29-32R
Nevins, Francis M(ichael), Jr. 1943- CANR-16
Earlier sketch in CA 41-44R
Nevinson, C(hristopher) R(ichard) W(ynne)
1889-1946 Brief entry 120
Nevitt, H(enry) J(ohn) Barrington
1908- CANR-14
Earlier sketch in CA 37-40R
Nevius, Blake (Reynolds) 1916- 19-20R
Nevo, Ruth 1924- 61-64
New, Anthony (Sherwood Brooks)
1924- CANR-23
Earlier sketch in CA 107
New, Christopher 116
New, William Herbert 1938- Brief entry 114
Newall, Venetia 1935- 37-40R
Newberry, Clare Turlay 1903-1970 .... CAP-2
Earlier sketch in CA 19-20
See also SATA 1, 26
Newberry, Lida 1909- 97-100
Newberry, Wilma (Jean) 1927- 73-76
Newbery, John 1713-1767 .... SATA-20
Newbigin, (James Edward) Lesslie
1909- CANR-10
Earlier sketch in CA 13-14R
Newbill, James Guy 1931- 61-64
Newbold, H(erbert) L(eon, Jr.) 1921- CANR-5
Earlier sketch in CA 2R
Newbold, Robert T(homas, Jr.) 1920- 89-92
Newbold, Stokes
See Adams, Richard N(ewbold)
Newbolt, Henry (John) 1862-1938
Brief entry 118
See also DLB 19
Newbound, Bernard Slade 1930- 81-84
Newbury, Colin (Walter) 1929- CANR-8
Earlier sketch in CA 7-8R
Newbury, Will 1912- 45-48
Newby, Eric 1919- 7-8R
Newby, I(dus) A. 1931- 19-20R
Newby, James R(ichard) 1949- 112
Newby, Leroy Winfred 1921- 114
Newby, P(ercy) H(oward) 1918- 7-8R
See also DLB 15
See also CLC 2, 13
Newcomb, Benjamin H. 1938- 45-48
Newcomb, Charles King 1820-1894 .... DLB-1
Newcomb, Covelle 1908- CAP-2
Earlier sketch in CA 19-20
Newcomb, Duane G(raham) 1929- CANR-5
Earlier sketch in CA 53-56
Newcomb, Ellsworth
See Kenny, Ellsworth Newcomb
Newcomb, Franc(es Lynette) J(ohnson)
1887- 17-18R
Newcomb, John (Robert) 1937- 123
Newcomb, Kerry 1946- CANR-10
Earlier sketch in CA 65-68
Newcomb, Norma
See Neubauer, William Arthur
Newcomb, Richard F(airchild) 1913- 1R
Newcomb, Robert N(orman) 1925- 21-22R
Newcomb, Simon 1835-1909 Brief entry 108
Newcomb, Theodore Mead 1903-1984 .... 33-36R
Obituary 114
Newcomb, Wilburn Wendell 1935- 19-20R
Newcomb, William W(ilmon), Jr. 1921- 102
Newcombe, Jack 113
See also SATA 33, 45
Newcombe, John (David) 1944- 69-72
Newcombe, Park Judson 1930- 106
Newcomer, James (William) 1912- CANR-15
Earlier sketch in CA 41-44R
Newell, Allen 1927- 104
Newell, Arlo F(rederic) 1926- 114
Newell, Barbara Warne 1929- 2R
Newell, Crosby
See Bonsall, Crosby Barbara (Newell)
Newell, D. A.
See Musciano, Walter A.
Newell, David McCheyne 1898(?)-1986
Obituary 120
Newell, Edythe W(eatherford) 1910- 65-68
See also SATA 11
Newell, Fred D(elmer) 1912- 97-100
Newell, Gordon 1913- CANR-20
Earlier sketches in CA 9-10R, CANR-4
Newell, Helen M(arie) 1909- 93-96
Newell, Homer E(dward) 1915-1983 97-100
Obituary 110
Newell, Hope Hockenberry 1896-1965 73-76
See also SATA 24
Newell, Kenneth B(ernard) 1930- 41-44R
Newell, Norman Dennis 1909- CANR-21
Earlier sketch in CA 104
Newell, Peter (Sheaf Hersey) 1862-1924
Brief entry 122
See also DLB 42
Newell, Peter F(rancis) 1915- 13-14R
Newell, Richard S. 1933- Brief entry 112
Newell, Robert Henry 1836-1901
Brief entry 111
See also DLB 11
Newell, Rosemary 1922- 49-52
Newell, William H(are) 1922- 103
Newell, William T(hrift) 1929- 37-40R
Newfeld, Frank 1928- 105
See also SATA 26
Newfield, Jack 1939- CANR-13
Earlier sketch in CA 21-22R
Newhafer, Richard L. 1922- 15-16R
Newhall, Beaumont 1908- 11-12R
Newhall, Nancy 1908-1974 Obituary 49-52
Newhall, Richard A. 1888-1973
Obituary 41-44R
Newhouse, Edward 1911- 97-100
Newhouse, Joseph P. 1942- 111
Newhouse, Neville H. 1919- 23-24R
Newhouse, Samuel I(rving) 1895-1979
Obituary 89-92
Newick, John 1919- CAP-1
Earlier sketch in CA 11-12
Newkirk, Glen A. 1931- 37-40R
Newland, Kathleen 1951- 97-100
Newland, T. Ernest 1903- 105
Newley, Anthony (George) 1931- 105
Newlin, Dika 1923- 107
Newlin, Margaret Rudd 1925- CANR-1
Earlier sketch in CA 49-52
Newlon, (Frank) Clarke 1905(?)-1982 .... CANR-10
Obituary 108
Earlier sketch in CA 49-52
See also SATA 6, 33
Newlove, Donald 1928- 29-32R
See also CLC 6
Newlove, John (Herbert) 1938- CANR-9
Earlier sketch in CA 23-24R
See also CLC 14
Newlyn, Walter T(essier) 1915- 21-22R
Newman, Adrien Ann 1941- 102
Newman, Albert H. 1913(?)-1987
Obituary 122
Newman, Alyse 1953- 107
Newman, Andrea 1938- 73-76
Newman, Arthur J. 1939- 117
Newman, Aubrey N(orris) 1927- 29-32R
Newman, Barbara
See Newman, Mona Alice Jean
Newman, Barclay M., Jr. 1931- CANR-9
Earlier sketch in CA 19-20R
Newman, Bernard (Charles) 1897-1968 97-100
Obituary 25-28R
Newman, Charles 1938- 21-22R
See also CLC 2, 8
Newman, Charles L. 1923- CANR-6
Earlier sketch in CA 13-14R
Newman, Christina McCall 1935- 112
Newman, Coleman J. 1935- 77-80
Newman, Daisy 1904- 37-40R
See also SATA 27
Newman, David 1937- 102
See also DLB 44
Newman, E. J. 1943- 61-64
Newman, Edwin (Harold) 1919- CANR-5
Earlier sketch in CA 69-72
See also CLC 14
See also AITN 1
Newman, Elmer S(imon) 1919- 106
Newman, Eric P. 1911- 7-8R
Newman, Ernest
See Roberts, William
Newman, Frances 1883(?)-1928
Brief entry 110
See also DLBY 80
Newman, Frank
See Abrams, Sam(uel)
Newman, G(ordon) F. 1942- 104
Newman, George 1936- 106
Newman, Gerald 1939- 101
See also SATA 42, 46
Newman, Greatrex 1892-1984(?) Obituary 112
Newman, Harold 1899- CANR-10
Earlier sketch in CA 65-68
Newman, Harold 1927- 53-56
Newman, Herbert Ellis 1914- 25-28R
Newman, Howard 1911-1977 57-60
Obituary 73-76
Newman, Jacob 1914- 11-12R
Newman, Jay Hartley 1951- CANR-9
Earlier sketch in CA 65-68
Newman, Jeremiah Joseph 1926- CANR-8
Earlier sketch in CA 5-6R
Newman, John Henry
1801-1890 .... DLB-18, 32, 55
Newman, John Kevin 1928- 123
Newman, Jon O(rmond) 1932- 23-24R
Newman, Joseph 1912- CANR-17
Earlier sketch in CA 89-92
Newman, Joseph W(illiam) 1918- 37-40R
Newman, Judie 1950- 117
Newman, Katharine D. 1911- 37-40R
Newman, Kim (James) 1959- 119
Newman, L(eonard) Hugh 1909- 11-12R
Newman, Lea Bertani Vozar 1926- 120

Newman, Lee Scott 1953- CANR-15
Earlier sketch in CA 65-68
Newman, Loretta Marie 1911- 45-48
Newman, Louis Israel 1893-1972 .... CAP-1
Obituary 33-36R
Earlier sketch in CA 19-20
Newman, Michael 1946- 116
Newman, Mona Alice Jean 102
Newman, Oscar 1935- 102
Newman, P(aul) B(aker) 1919- 33-36R
Newman, Parley Wright 1923- Brief entry ... 106
Newman, Peter (Kenneth) 1928- 17-18R
Newman, Peter C(harles) 1929- CANR-3
Earlier sketch in CA 11-12R
Newman, Philip L(ee) 1931- 17-18R
Newman, Ralph Abraham 1892- CANR-6
Earlier sketch in CA 3R
Newman, Ralph G(eoffrey) 1911- 45-48
Newman, Randolph H. 1904-1975
Obituary 61-64
Newman, Richard (Alan) 1930- 110
Newman, Robert (Howard) 1909- CANR-19
Earlier sketches in CA 2R, CANR-4
See also SATA 4
Newman, Robert Chapman 1941- 115
Newman, Robert D(ouglas) 1951- 120
Newman, Robert P(reston) 1922- 2R
Newman, Robert S. 1935- 65-68
Newman, Ruth (May) G(allert) 1914- 105
Newman, Sharan 1949- 106
Newman, Shirlee Petkin 1924- 5-6R
See also SATA 10
Newman, Shirley S. 1924- 123
Newman, Stephen A(aron) 1946- 97-100
Newman, Stewart A(lbert) 1907- CAP-2
Earlier sketch in CA 23-24
Newman, Terence 1927- 7-8R
Newman, Terry
See Newman, Terence
Newman, Thelma R(ita) 1925-1978 ..... CANR-7
Obituary 81-84
Earlier sketch in CA 15-16R
Newman, Walter (Brown) 1920-
Brief entry 110
Newman, William H(erman) 1909- CANR-19
Earlier sketches in CA 5-6R, CANR-3
Newman, William Mark 1943- 57-60
Newman, William S(tein) 1912- CANR-3
Earlier sketch in CA 4R
Newmar, Rima
See Wagman, Naomi
Newmark, Joseph 1943- 53-56
Newmark, Leonard 1929- 19-20R
Newmyer, R. Kent 1930- 77-80
Newport, John P(aul) 1917- CANR-13
Earlier sketch in CA 33-36R
Newquist, Jerreld L. 1919- 19-20R
Newquist, Roy 1925- 13-14R
Newsham, Ian (Alan) 1953- 115
Newsham, Wendy (Elizabeth) 1952- 117
Newsom, Carol 1948- SATA-40
Newsom, Carroll V(incent) 1904- CAP-2
Earlier sketch in CA 17-18
Newsom, Doug(las Ann) 1934- 73-76
Newsome, Arden J(eanne) 1932- 29-32R
Newsome, David Hay 1929- CANR-17
Earlier sketch in CA 89-92
Newsome, George L(ane), Jr. 1923- 29-32R
Newsome, Walter L(ee) 1941- 105
Newson, Elizabeth (Palmer) 1929- CANR-5
Earlier sketch in CA 11-12R
Newson, John 1925- 11-12R
Newson, Tony 1953- 124
Newth, Rebecca 1940- 33-36R
Newton, Brian 1928- 49-52
Newton, Byron Louis 1913- 53-56
Newton, D(wight) B(ennett) 1916- CANR-17
Earlier sketches in CA 7-8R, CANR-2
Newton, David C.
See Chance, John Newton
Newton, Derek A(rnold) 1930- 120
Newton, Douglas 1920- 104
Newton, Earle Williams 1917- 41-44R
Newton, Eric 1893-1965 .... CAP-1
Earlier sketch in CA 15-16
Newton, Ethel (de la Bete) 1921- 101
Newton, Francis
See Hobsbawm, Eric J(ohn Ernest)
Newton, Huey P(ercy) 1942- Brief entry 114
Newton, Ian 1940- 123
Newton, Ivor 1892-1981 Obituary 108
Newton, James R(obert) 1935- 101
See also SATA 23
Newton, Kenneth 1940- CANR-16
Earlier sketch in CA 29-32R
Newton, Macdonald
See Newton, William Simpson
Newton, Michael 1951- 108
Newton, Norman (Lewis) 1929- 11-12R
Newton, Norman Thomas 1898- 104
Newton, Peter 1906- CAP-1
Earlier sketch in CA 9-10
Newton, Peter A(nthony) 1935-1987
Obituary 124
Newton, Ray C(lyde) 1935- 77-80
Newton, Robert (Henry) G(erald) 1903- ... CAP-1
Earlier sketch in CA 9
Newton, Robert P(arr) 1929- 113
Newton, Roy 1904(?)-1974 Obituary 104
Newton, Stu
See Whitcomb, Ian
Newton, Suzanne 1936- CANR-14
Earlier sketch in CA 41-44R
See also SATA 5
See also CLC 35
Newton, Virgil Miller, Jr. 1904-1977 .... 3R
Obituary 103
Newton, William Simpson 1923- CANR-7
Earlier sketch in CA 53-56
Ney, James W(alter) 1932- CANR-15
Earlier sketch in CA 41-44R
Ney, John 1923- 115
See also SATA 33, 43
Ney, Patrick
See Bolitho, (Henry) Hector
Ney, Richard 1917?- AITN-1
Ney, Virgil 1905-1979 Obituary 85-88
Neyland, James (Elwyn) 1939- 103
Neyman, Jerzy 1899-1981 Obituary 108
Nezval, Vitezslav 1900-1958 Brief entry 123
Ng, David 1934- 115
Ng, Larry K. Y. 1940- CANR-9
Earlier sketch in CA 17-18R
Ngagoyeanes, Nicholas 1939- 49-52
Ngara, Emmanuel 1947- 109
Ngubane, Jordan K(hush) 1917- 121
Ngugi, James T(hiong'o) 1938- 81-84
See also CLC 3, 7, 13, 36
Nguyen, Dinh Hoa 1924- CANR-10
Earlier sketch in CA 23-24R
Nguyen, Vuong Hung 1922(?)-1985
Obituary 118
Nguyen Ngoc Bich 1937- CANR-15
Earlier sketch in CA 81-84
Niall, Sean
See Mangan, (John Joseph) Sherry
Nias, D(avid) K(enneth) B(oydell) 1940- 105
Niatum, Duane 1938- CANR-21
Earlier sketch in CA 41-44R
Niblett, W(illiam) R(oy) 1906- CANR-3
Earlier sketch in CA 2R
Niccolini, Dianora 1936- 113
Nicely, Thomas S(hryock), Jr. 1939- 93-96
Nicely, Tom
See Nicely, Thomas S(hryock), Jr.
Nichelson, F(loyd) Patrick 1942- 33-36R
Nichol, B(arrie) P(hillip) 1944- 53-56
See also DLB 53
See also CLC 18
Nichol, John Thomas 1928- 19-20R
Nicholas, Anna Katherine 1917- 93-96
Nicholas, Barry 1919- 7-8R
Nicholas, David M(ansfield) 1939- 49-52
Nicholas, Donald 1909- 7-8R
Nicholas, Elizabeth 1915-1985 Obituary 117
Nicholas, Herbert George 1911- 3R
Nicholas, John (Morton) 1944- 118
Nicholas, Leslie 1913- 81-84
Nicholas, Robert L(eon) 1937- 53-56
Nicholas, Ted
See Peterson, Ted Nicholas
Nicholas, Tracy (Christine) 1952- 121
Nicholas, William
See Thimmesch, Nicholas Palen
Nicholds, Elizabeth (Beckwith) CAP-1
Earlier sketch in CA 11-12
Nicholl, Louise Townsend 1890(?)-1981 ..97-100
Obituary 105
Nicholls, David 1948- 97-100
Nicholls, F(rederick) F(rancis) 1926- 7-8R
Nicholls, Judith (Ann) 1941- 121
Nicholls, Mark
See Frewin, Leslie Ronald
Nicholls, Peter (Douglas) 1939- 105
Nicholls, (C. G.) William 1921- 17-18R
Nichols, Albert L. 1951- 122
Nichols, (John) Beverley 1898-1983 ... CANR-17
Obituary 110
Earlier sketch in CA 93-96
Nichols, Bill
See Nichols, William James
Nichols, Cecilia Fawn 1906- CAP-1
Earlier sketch in CA 15-16
See also SATA 12
Nichols, Charles H(arold) 1919- CANR-6
Earlier sketch in CA 53-56
Nichols, Dale (William) 1904- CAP-2
Earlier sketch in CA 17-18
Nichols, Dave
See Frost, Helen
Nichols, David A(llen) 1939- 104
Nichols, Dudley 1895-1960 Obituary 89-92
See also DLB 26
Nichols, Edward J(ay) 1900- 7-8R
Nichols, Fred Joseph 1939- 114
Nichols, Frederick Adams 1907-1983
Obituary 111
Nichols, Harold 1903- CAP-1
Earlier sketch in CA 15-16
Nichols, Irby C(oghill), Jr. 1926- 41-44R
Nichols, J(ohn) G(ordon) 1930- 33-36R
See also CAAS 2
Nichols, Jack 1938- 41-44R
Nichols, James Hastings 1915- Brief entry .. 114
Nichols, James R(ichard) 1938- 105
Nichols, Jeannette 1931- 77-80
Nichols, Jeannette Paddock 1890-1982 ...11-12R
Obituary 107
Nichols, John (Treadwell) 1940- CANR-6
Earlier sketch in CA 11-12R
See also CAAS 2
See also DLBY 82
See also CLC 38
Nichols, Joseph C. 1905(?)-1984
Obituary 114
Nichols, Leigh
See Koontz, Dean R(ay)
Nichols, Lewis 1903-1982 Obituary 106
Nichols, Maggie
See Nichols, Margaret
Nichols, Margaret 1931- 81-84
Nichols, Marie Hochmuth 1908-1978 103
Nichols, Marion 1921- 102
Nichols, Mary Sargeant (Neal) Gove
1810-1884 .... DLB-1
Nichols, Nina (Marianna) da Vinci
1932- CANR-14
Earlier sketch in CA 73-76
Nichols, Paul D(yer) 1938- 109
Nichols, Peter 1927- 104
See also DLB 13
See also CLC 5, 36
Nichols, Peter
See Youd, Samuel
Nichols, R(oy) Eugene 1914- 29-32R
Nichols, Robert (Molise Bowyer) 1919- 93-96
Nichols, Roger 1939- 108
Nichols, Roger L(ouis) 1933- CANR-5
Earlier sketch in CA 15-16R
Nichols, Roy F(ranklin) 1896-1973 ..... CANR-3
Obituary 37-40R
Earlier sketch in CA 5-6R
See also DLB 17
Nichols, (Joanna) Ruth 1948- CANR-16
Earlier sketch in CA 25-28R
See also SATA 15
See also DLB 60
Nichols, Scott
See Scortia, Thomas N(icholas)
Nichols, Stephen G(eorge, Jr.) 1936- 45-48
Nichols, Sue 11-12R
Nichols, William James 1942- 93-96
Nichols, William Thomas 1927- 41-44R
Nicholsen, Margaret E(sther) 1904- 29-32R
Nicholson, Arnold 1902- CAP-2
Earlier sketch in CA 19-20
Nicholson, Ben 1894-1982 Obituary 110
Nicholson, C(harles) A. III 1922- 41-44R
Nicholson, Dorothy Nelis 1923-
Brief entry 109
Nicholson, Geoffrey (George) 1929- CANR-8
Earlier sketch in CA 7-8R
Nicholson, Gerald W(illiam) L(ingen)
1902-1980 101
Nicholson, Hubert 1908- 13-14R
Nicholson, Jack 1937(?)- Brief entry 116
Nicholson, Jane
See Steen, Marguerite
Nicholson, Joe
See Nicholson, Joseph Hugh, Jr.
Nicholson, John Greer 1929- 45-48
Nicholson, Joseph Hugh, Jr. 1943- 81-84
Nicholson, Joyce Thorpe 1919- CANR-5
Earlier sketch in CA 11-12R
See also SATA 35
Nicholson, (Edward) Max 1904-
Brief entry 106
Nicholson, Norman (Cornthwaite)
1914-1987 .... CANR-24
Obituary 122
Earlier sketches in CA 9-10R, CANR-3
See also DLB 27
Nicholson, Norman L(eon) 1919- CANR-3
Earlier sketch in CA 9-10R
Nicholson, Patrick J(ames) 1920- 120
Nicholson, Paul (Joseph), Jr. 1937- 73-76
Nicholson, Ranald (George) 1931- 37-40R
Nicholson, Robert Lawrence 1908-1985 53-56
Obituary 117
Nicholson, Shirley J. 1925- 29-32R
Nicholson, Simon 1934- 114
Nicholson, W(illiam) G(eorge) 1935- 93-96
Nichter, Rhoda 1926- 81-84
Nichtern, Sol 1920- 17-18R
Ni Chuilleanain, Eilean 1942- DLB-40
Nickel, Herman 1928- 73-76
Nickel, Mildred L(ucille) 1912- 108
Nickell, Joe 1944- 110
Nickell, Lesley J(acqueline) 1944- 103
Nickels, William G(eorge) 1939- 108
Nickelsburg, George W(illiam) E(lmer), Jr.
1934- CANR-19
Earlier sketches in CA 53-56, CANR-5
Nickelsburg, Janet 1893- 65-68
See also SATA 11
Nickerson, Betty 1922- 77-80
Nickerson, Clarence B(entley) 1906- 5-6R
Nickerson, Elizabeth
See Nickerson, Betty
See also SATA 14
Nickerson, Jan ?-19(?) 4R
Nickerson, Jane Soames (Bon)
1900-1988 77-80
Obituary 124
Nickerson, John Mitchell 1937- 53-56
Nickerson, Roy 1927- 114
Nickerson, Sheila B(unker) 1942- 118
Nickerson, William (Ernest) 1908- 2R
Nicklanovich, Michael David 1941- 107
Nicklaus, Carol SATA-33
Nicklaus, (Charles) Frederick 1936- 37-40R
Nicklaus, Jack (William) 1940- CANR-16
Earlier sketch in CA 89-92
Nickle, Keith Fullerton 1933- 115
Nickless, Will 1902- 81-84
Niclas, Yolla 1900- 25-28R
Nic Leodhas, Sorche
See Alger, Leclaire (Gowans)
Nicol, Abioseh
See Nicol, Davidson (Sylvester Hector
Willoughby)
Nicol, Ann
See Turnbull, Ann (Christine)
Nicol, Charles (David) 1940- 115
Nicol, D(onald) M(acGillivray) 1923- CANR-4
Earlier sketch in CA 53-56
Nicol, Davidson (Sylvester Hector
Willoughby) 1924- 61-64
Nicol, Eric (Patrick) 1919- CANR-16
Earlier sketches in CA 49-52, CANR-1
Nicol, Jean 1919- 21-22R
Nicolaeff, Ariadne 1915- 57-60
Nicolas
See Mordvinoff, Nicolas
Nicolas, Claire
See White, Claire Nicolas
Nicolas, F. R. E.
See Freeling, Nicolas
Nicolay, Helen 1866-1954 Brief entry 121
See also YABC 1
Nicolay, John G(eorge) 1832-1901
Brief entry 122
See also DLB 47
Nicolaysen, Bruce 1934- 105
Nicole, Christopher Robin 1930- 13-14R
See also SATA 5
Nicoll, (John Ramsay) Allardyce
1894-1976 .... CANR-5
Obituary 65-68
Earlier sketch in CA 9-10R
Nicoll, Bruce H. 1913(?)-1983 Obituary 111
Nicoll, Helen 1937- 122
Nicolle, Jacques Maurice Raoul 1901- 9-10R
Nicoloff, Philip Loveless 1926- 3R
Nicolson, (Lionel) Benedict 1914-1978 .. CANR-6
Earlier sketch in CA 13-14R
Nicolson, Catherine 121
Nicolson, Harold George 1886-1968 ..... CAP-1
Earlier sketch in CA 15-16
Nicolson, I(an) F(erguson) 1921- 29-32R
Nicolson, James R(obert) 1934- CANR-9
Earlier sketch in CA 65-68
Nicolson, Marjorie Hope 1894-1981 ......9-10R
Obituary 103
Nicolson, Nigel 1917- 101
Nicolson, Victoria Mary
See Sackville-West, V(ictoria Mary)
Nicosia, Francesco M(ichael) 1933- 81-84
Nicosia, Franco M.
See Nicosia, Francesco M(ichael)
Nicosia, Gerald (Martin) 1949- 115
Nida, Eugene A(lbert) 1914- CANR-17
Earlier sketches in CA 4R, CANR-1
Nidditch, Peter (Harold) 1928-1983
Obituary 109
Niddrie, David Lawrence 1917- 25-28R
Nideffer, Robert M(orse) 1942- CANR-9
Earlier sketch in CA 65-68
Nidetch, Jean 1923- 89-92
Nie, Norman H. 1943- CANR-15
Earlier sketch in CA 65-68
Niebuhr, H(elmut) Richard 1894-1962
Obituary 116
Niebuhr, Reinhold 1892-1971 ....41-44R
Obituary 29-32R
See also DLB 17
Niebuhr, Richard R. 1926- 77-80
Niebuhr, Ursula 1907- 89-92
Nieburg, H(arold) L. 1927- 11-12R
Niedecker, Lorine 1903-1970 .... CAP-2
Earlier sketch in CA 25-28
See also DLB 48
See also CLC 10, 42
Niederauer, David J(ohn) 1924- 45-48
Niederhoffer, Arthur 1917-1981 Obituary 103
Niederland, William G(ugliemo) 1904- 81-84
Niedzielski, Henri 1931- 49-52
Nieh, Hualing 1925- 81-84
Niehoff, Arthur H. 1921- 21-22R
Nielander, William Ahlers 1901- 7-8R
Nielsen, Aage Rosendal 1921- 25-28R
Nielsen, Dulcimer 1943- 93-96
Nielsen, Eduard 1923- 29-32R
Nielsen, Gary (Elton) 1939- 97-100
Nielsen, Helen Berniece 1918- CANR-1
Earlier sketch in CA 2R
Nielsen, Jean Sarver 1922- 5-6R
Nielsen, Kay (Rasmus) 1886-1957 ..... SATA-16
Nielsen, Knut Schmidt
See Schmidt-Nielsen, Knut
Nielsen, Margaret A(nne) 105
Nielsen, Niels Christian, Jr. 1921- CANR-3
Earlier sketch in CA 11-12R
Nielsen, Niels Juel
See Juel-Nielsen, Niels
Nielsen, Oswald 1904- CAP-2
Earlier sketch in CA 19-20
Nielsen, Robert F. 1937- 122
Nielsen, Sven Sigurd 1901-1976 Obituary .. 104
Nielsen, Torben 1918- Brief entry 114
Nielsen, Veneta Leatham 1909- 89-92
Nielsen, Virginia
See McCall, Virginia Nielsen
Nielsen, Waldemar August 1917- 103
Nielssen, Eric
See Ludvigsen, Karl (Eric)
Nieman, Egbert William 1909- CAP-1
Earlier sketch in CA 11-12
Nieman, Lucius W. 1857-1935 .... DLB-25
Niemeier, Jean (Gilbreath) 1912- 25-28R
Niemeyer, Eberhardt Victor, Jr. 1919- 102
Niemeyer, Gerhart 1907- 2R
Niemeyer, Roy K(urt) 1922- 2R
Niemi, Albert (William), Jr. 1942- 73-76
Niemi, John A. 1932- 77-80
Niemi, Richard G(ene) 1941- 41-44R
Niemoeller, (Friedrich Gustav Emil) Martin
1892-1984 Obituary 112
Niemoller, Ara
See Llerena, Mario
Niemoller, (Friedrich Gustav Emil) Martin
See Niemoeller, (Friedrich Gustav Emil)
Martin
Nierenberg, Gerard I. 1923- 25-28R
Nierman, M. Murray 1918- 3R
Nies, Judith 1941- 77-80

Niesewand, Peter 1944-1983 101
  Obituary 109
Niess, Robert Judson 1911- CAP-2
  Earlier sketch in CA 29-32
Niethammer, Carolyn 1944- 85-88
Nietz, John Alfred 1888- 4R
Nietzke, Ann 1945- 105
Nietzsche, Friedrich (Wilhelm) 1844-1900 ... 121
  Brief entry 107
  See also TCLC 10, 18
Nievergelt, Jurg 1938- 29-32R
Niewyk, Donald L. 1940- 33-36R
Nigg, Joe
  See Nigg, Joseph E(ugene)
Nigg, Joseph E(ugene) 1938- 114
Niggli, Josefina CAP-2
  Earlier sketch in CA 21-22
  See also DLBY 80
Nightingale, Anne Redmon 1943- 103
Nightingale, Elena O(ttolenghi) 1932- 123
Nightingale, Sir Geoffrey (Slingsby)
  1904- CAP-1
  Earlier sketch in CA 13-14
Nightrate, Emil
  See Spielmann, Peter James
Nigro, Felix A(nthony) 1914- CANR-14
  Earlier sketch in CA 37-40R
Nihal Singh, Surendra 1929- 93-96
Nihilo, Arthur X. 1938- 105
Niizaka, Kazuo 1943- 77-80
Nijinska, Bronislava 1891-1972 117
Nijinsky, Romola Flavia 1891-1978
  Obituary 81-84
Nijinsky, Vaslav (Fomitch) 1890-1950
  Brief entry 115
Nik.T.O.
  See Annensky, Innokenty Fyodorovich
Nikelly, Arthur G(eorge) 1927- 19-20R
Niklas, Gerald R. 1933- 118
Niklaus, Robert 1910- 9-10R
Niklaus, Thelma (Jones) 1912- 11-12R
Nikolay, Michael 1941- 97-100
Niland, D'Arcy Francis 1920-1967 .... CANR-3
  Earlier sketch in CA 3R
Niland, Deborah 1951- 106
  See also SATA 27
Niland, Powell 1919- 23-24R
Nile, Dorothea
  See Avallone, Michael (Angelo), Jr.
Niles, D(aniel) T(hambyrajah) 1908-1970
  Obituary 29-32R
Niles, Gwendolyn 1914- 11-12R
Niles, Hezekiah 1777-1839 .... DLB-43
Niles, John Jacob 1892-1980 .... 41-44R
  Obituary 97-100
Nill, Michael 1942- 124
Nilles, Jack M(athias) 1932- 108
Nilsen, Alleen Pace 1936- 112
Nilsen, Don L(ee) F(red) 1934- CANR-15
  Earlier sketch in CA 41-44R
Nilsson, Usha Saksena 1930- 41-44R
Nimble, Jack B.
  See Burgess, M(ichael) R(oy)
Nimeth, Albert J. 1918-1984 .... 25-28R
  Obituary 114
Nimitz, Chester W(illiam) 1885-1966
  Obituary 113
Nimmer, Melville B(ernard) 1923-1985 49-52
  Obituary 117
Nimmo, Dan D(ean) 1933- CANR-7
  Earlier sketch in CA 15-16R
Nimmo, Derek (Robert) 1933- 109
Nimmo, Jenny 1942- 108
Nimnicht, Nona 1930- 73-76
Nimocks, Walter 1930- 41-44R
Nimoy, Leonard 1931- 57-60
Nims, Charles F(rancis) 1906- 17-18R
Nims, John Frederick 1913- CANR-6
  Earlier sketch in CA 15-16R
  See also DLB 5
Nin, Anais 1903-1977 .... CANR-22
  Obituary 69-72
  Earlier sketch in CA 13-14R
  See also DLB 2, 4
  See also CLC 1, 4, 8, 11, 14
  See also AITN 2
Nineham, Dennis (Eric) 1921- 85-88
Nininger, H(arvey) H(arlow) 1887-1986 ... 23-24R
  Obituary 118
Nioche, Brigitte 109
Nir, Yehuda 1930- 107
Nirenberg, Jesse S(tanley) 1921- 69-72
Nirmala-Kumara, V
  See Bose, N(irmal) K(umar)
Nirodi, Hira 1930- 5-6R
Nisbet, Ada Blanche 1907- 41-44R
Nisbet, Robert A(lexander) 1913- CANR-17
  Earlier sketch in CA 25-28R
Nisbet, Stanley (Donald) 1912- CAP-1
  Earlier sketch in CA 13-14
Nisbett, (Thomas) Alec 1930- CANR-22
  Earlier sketch in CA 81-84
Nisbett, Richard E. 1941- 37-40R
Nisetich, Frank Joseph 1942- 97-100
Nish, Ian Hill 1926- CANR-17
  Earlier sketch in CA 21-22R
Nishihara, Masashi 1937- CANR-12
  Earlier sketch in CA 69-72
Nishio, Suehiro 1891-1981 Obituary 108
Nishiwaki, Junzaburo 1894-1982 Obituary ... 107
Nishiyama, Chiaki 1924- Brief entry 110
Niskanen, William Arthur, Jr. 1933- 41-44R
Nissen, Lowell A(llen) 1932- 33-36R
Nissenbaum, Stephen 1941- 77-80
Nissenson, Hugh 1933- 17-18R
  See also DLB 28
  See also CLC 4, 9
Nissman, Albert 1930- 37-40R
Nissman, Blossom S. 1928- CANR-19
  Earlier sketch in CA 37-40R
Nist, John (Albert) 1925-1981 .... CANR-11
  Earlier sketch in CA 21-22R
Nitchie, George W(ilson) 1921- 11-12R
Nitske, W(illiam) Robert 1909- CANR-5
  Earlier sketch in CA 15-16R
Nittler, Alan H(opkins) 1918- CANR-13
  Earlier sketch in CA 61-64
Nityanandan, P(erumpilavil) M(adhava
  Menon) 1926- 11-12R
Nitzsche, Jane Chance 1945- CANR-8
  Earlier sketch in CA 57-60
Niven, Alastair 1944- CANR-16
  Earlier sketch in CA 81-84
Niven, Alexander Curt 1920- CANR-2
  Earlier sketch in CA 5-6R
Niven, (James) David (Graham)
  1910-1983 77-80
  Obituary 110
Niven, John 1921- 65-68
Niven, Larry
  See Niven, Laurence Van Cott
  See also DLB 8
  See also CLC 8
Niven, Laurence Van Cott 1938- CANR-14
  Earlier sketch in CA 21-22R
Niven, Marian
  See Alston, Mary Niven
Niven, (Cecil) Rex 1898- 120
Niven, Vern
  See Grier, Barbara G(ene Damon)
Nivens, Beatryce 1948- 114
Nivison, David Shepherd 1923- 103
Niwa, Tamako 1922- Brief entry 106
Nixon, Agnes Eckhardt 1927- 110
  See also CLC 21
Nixon, Allan 1918- 17-18R
Nixon, Edna (Mary) 5-6R
Nixon, George 1924- 49-52
Nixon, Hershell Howard 1923- 89-92
  See also SATA 42
Nixon, Howard Millar 1909-1983 Obituary .. 109
Nixon, Ivor Gray 1905- CAP-2
  Earlier sketch in CA 29-32
Nixon, Joan Lowery 1927- CANR-24
  Earlier sketches in CA 11-12R, CANR-7
  See also SATA 8, 44
Nixon, John Erskine 1917- 101
Nixon, K.
  See Nixon, Kathleen Irene (Blundell)
Nixon, Kathleen Irene (Blundell) 73-76
  See also SATA 14
Nixon, Lucille M. 1908-1963 .... 5-6R
Nixon, Marion 1930- 49-52
Nixon, Richard M(ilhous) 1913- 73-76
Nixon, Robert E(arl, Jr.) 1918- 5-6R
Nixon, St. John Cousins 1885- 7-8R
Nixon, William R(ussell) 1918- 29-32R
Nixson, Frederick Ian 1943- CANR-20
  Earlier sketch in CA 104
Nizer, Louis 1902- 53-56
Njururi, Ngumbu 1930- 19-20R
Nketia, J(oseph) H(anson) Kwabena
  1921- CANR-7
  Earlier sketch in CA 11-12R
Nkosi, Lewis 1936- 65-68
  See also CLC 45
Nkrumah, Kwame 1909-1972 Obituary 113
Noad, Frederick (McNeill) 1929- CANR-4
  Earlier sketch in CA 11-12R
Noah, Harold J(ulius) 1925- CANR-13
  Earlier sketch in CA 33-36R
Noah, Joseph W(atson) 1928- 81-84
Noakes, Jeremy 1941- 101
Noakes, Vivien 1937- 65-68
Noall, Roger 1935- 11-12R
Nobile, Umberto 1885-1978 Obituary 81-84
Noble, Allen G(eorge) 1930- 116
Noble, Charles
  See Pawley, Martin Edward
Noble, David Watson 1925- CANR-1
  Earlier sketch in CA 49-52
Noble, Dudley (Henry) 1893(?)-1970
  Obituary 104
Noble, Elizabeth Marian 1945- CANR-9
  Earlier sketch in CA 65-68
Noble, G(eorge) Bernard 1892-1972 .... CAP-2
  Obituary 37-40R
  Earlier sketch in CA 33-36
Noble, Iris (Davis) 1922-1986 .... CANR-2
  Obituary 120
  Earlier sketch in CA 3R
  See also SATA 5, 49
Noble, J(ames) Kendrick 1896(?)-1978
  Obituary 104
Noble, J(ames) Kendrick, Jr. 1928- 19-20R
Noble, Jeanne L(aveta) 1926- Brief entry ... 112
Noble, John (Appelbe) 1914- CANR-1
  Earlier sketch in CA 45-48
Noble, John 1923- 45-48
Noble, John Wesley 1913- 9-10R
Noble, Joseph Veach 1920- 61-64
Noble, June (Solveig) 1924-1984 .... CANR-18
  Earlier sketch in CA 97-100
Noble, Marguerite (Buchanan) 1910- 105
Noble, Stanley R(odman) 1904(?)-1977
  Obituary 104
Noble, Trinka Hakes Brief entry 116
  See also SATA 37
Noble, William Charles 1935- 107
Noble, William P(arker) 1932- CANR-18
  Earlier sketch in CA 101
Nochlin, Linda Weinberg 1931- CANR-6
  Earlier sketch in CA 11-12R
Nock, Albert Jay 1870(?)-1945 Brief entry .. 122
Nock, Francis J. 1905-1969 .... CAP-1
  Earlier sketch in CA 13-14
Nock, O(swald) S(tevens) 1905- CANR-16
  Earlier sketch in CA 85-88
Nockolds, Harold 1907-1982 Obituary 108
Noddings, Nel 1929- 115
Noddings, Thomas C. 1933- CANR-2
  Earlier sketch in CA 49-52
Nodel, Sol 1912-1976 Obituary 107
Nodset, Joan L.
  See Lexau, Joan M.
Noe, Thomas R. 1947- 112
Noe, Tom
  See Noe, Thomas R.
Noel, Daniel C(alhoun) 1936- 101
Noel, Hilda Bloxton, Jr.
  See Schroetter, Hilda Noel
Noel, John
  See Bird, Dennis L(eslie)
Noel, John V(avasour), Jr. 1912- CANR-15
  Earlier sketch in CA 21-22R
Noel, Roden 1834-1894 .... DLB-35
Noel, Ruth (Swycaffer) 1947- 69-72
Noel, Sterling 1903-1984 Obituary 114
Noel, Thomas Jacob 1945- CANR-24
  Earlier sketch in CA 107
Noel-Baker, Philip John 1889-1982
  Obituary 108
Noel Hume, Ivor 1927- CANR-12
  Earlier sketch in CA 13-14R
Noer, Thomas John 1944- 102
Noestlinger, Christine 1936- 123
  Brief entry 115
  See also SATA 37
  See also CLR 12
Noether, Emiliana P. 101
Nofi, Albert A(urelio) 1944- 112
Nofziger, Margaret 1946- 110
Nogee, Joseph Lippman 1929- 17-18R
Noggle, Burl L. 1924- Brief entry 107
Noguere, Suzanne 1947- 107
  See also SATA 34
Nohl, Frederick 1927- CANR-3
  Earlier sketch in CA 7-8R
Nohrnberg, James (Carson) 1941- 69-72
Nojiri, Kiyohiko 1897-1973 93-96
  Obituary 41-44R
Nokes, Gerald Dacre 1899-1971 Obituary ... 104
Nolan, Alan T. 1923- 1R
Nolan, Albert 1934- 117
Nolan, Bob 1908(?)-1980 Obituary 101
Nolan, Brian
  See O Nuallain, Brian
Nolan, Carroll A(nthony) 1906- 17-18R
Nolan, Christopher 1965- 111
Nolan, Chuck
  See Edson, J(ohn) T(homas)
Nolan, Dennis 1945- 112
  See also SATA 34, 42
Nolan, Edward Francis 1915- Brief entry 108
Nolan, James 1947- CANR-5
  Earlier sketch in CA 53-56
Nolan, Jeannette Covert 1897-1974 .... CANR-4
  Obituary 53-56
  Earlier sketch in CA 7-8R
  See also SATA 2, 27
Nolan, Keith W(illiam) 1964- 114
Nolan, Madeena Spray 1943- 89-92
Nolan, Paul T(homas) 1919- CANR-2
  Earlier sketch in CA 5-6R
  See also SATA 48
Nolan, Richard Thomas 1937- CANR-10
  Earlier sketch in CA 25-28R
Nolan, Tom 1948- 77-80
Nolan, William F(rancis) 1928- CANR-1
  Earlier sketch in CA 4R
  See also SATA 28
  See also DLB 8
Nolan, Winefride (Bell) 1913- 13-14R
Noland, C. F. M. 1810(?)-1858 .... DLB-11
Noland, Ronald G(ene) 1936- 41-44R
Nolde, O(tto) Frederick 1899-1972 .... CAP-2
  Obituary 37-40R
  Earlier sketch in CA 29-32
Nolen, Barbara 1902- 104
Nolen, Claude H. 1921- 21-22R
Nolen, William A(nthony) 1928-1986 ... CANR-15
  Obituary 121
  Earlier sketch in CA 77-80
Nolin, Bertil 1926- 65-68
Noling, A(lfred) W(ells) 1899- CAP-2
  Earlier sketch in CA 29-32
Noll, Bink
  See Noll, Lou Barker
Noll, Lou Barker 1927- 7-8R
Noll, Mark A(llan) 1946- 115
Noll, Martin David
  See Buxbaum, Martin
Noll, Roger G(ordon) 1940- CANR-8
  Earlier sketch in CA 53-56
Nollau, Gunther 1911- 7-8R
Nollen, Stanley D(ale) 1940- 110
Nolte, Carl William 1933- 77-80
Nolte, Elleta 1919- 61-64
Nolte, M(ervin) Chester 1911- 11-12R
Nolte, William H(enry) 1928- 33-36R
Nolting, Orin F(rederyc) 1903- 29-32R
Noltingk, B(ernard) E(dward) 1918- 17-18R
Noma, Koremichi 1938(?)-1987 Obituary ... 122
Nomad, Max 1880(?)-1973 Obituary 41-44R
Noma Shoichi 1911-1984 Obituary 113
Nonas, Elisabeth 1949- 119
Nonet, Philippe 1939- 57-60
Nonhebel, Clare 1953- 119
Noon, Brian 1919- 49-52
Noon, William T(homas) 1912-1975 65-68
  Obituary 53-56
Noonan, John Ford 1943- 85-88
Noonan, John T(homas), Jr. 1926- CANR-13
  Earlier sketch in CA 15-16R
Noonan, Julia 1946- 33-36R
  See also SATA 4
Noonan, Lowell G(erald) 1922- 29-32R
Noonan, Michael John 1921- 21-22R
Noone, Edwina
  See Avallone, Michael (Angelo), Jr.
Noone, John 1936- Brief entry 109
  See also DLB 14
Noone, Richard 1918(?)-1973 Obituary 104
Noorbergen, Rene 1928- 77-80
Nooteboom, Cees 1933- Brief entry 124
Nora, James Jackson 1928- CANR-20
  Earlier sketch in CA 104
Norback, Craig T(homas) 1943- 113
Norbeck, Edward 1915- CANR-1
  Earlier sketch in CA 2R
Norberg-Schulz, Christian 1926- 81-84
Norbu, Thubten Jigme
  See Thubten Sigme Norbu
Norcross, John
  See Conroy, John Wesley
Norcross, Lisabet
  See Gladstone, Arthur M.
Norcutt, Bill
  See Norcutt, William E.
Norcutt, William E. 1946- Brief entry 118
Nord, Ole C. 1935- 13-14R
Nord, Paul 1900(?)-1981 Obituary 103
Nord, Walter R(obert) 1939- 37-40R
Nordan, Lewis 1939- 117
Nordberg, H(arold) Orville 1916- 2R
Nordberg, Robert B. 1921- 15-16R
Nordby, Vernon James 1945- 57-60
Nordell, (Hans) Roderick 1925- 104
Norden, Albert 1904-1982 Obituary 107
Norden, Charles
  See Durrell, Lawrence (George)
Norden, Denis 1922- 104
Norden, Heinz 1905- 53-56
Norden, Helen Brown
  See Lawrenson, Helen
Nordham, George Washington 1929- ... CANR-23
  Earlier sketch in CA 106
Nordhaus, William D(awbney) 1941- 97-100
Nordhoff, Charles (Bernard) 1887-1947
  Brief entry 108
  See also SATA 23
  See also DLB 9
  See also TCLC 23
Nordholm, Harriet 1912- 29-32R
Nordicus
  See Snyder, Louis L.
Nordin, D(ennis) Sven 1942- 61-64
Nordland, Gerald John 1927- 104
Nordland, Rod(ney Lee) 1949- 118
Nordlicht, Lillian 105
  See also SATA 29
Nordlinger, Eric A. 1939- 77-80
Nordmann, Joseph (Behrens) 1922- 25-28R
Nordness, Lee 1924- 9-10R
Nordoff, Paul 1909-1977 102
Nordquist, Barbara K(ay) 1940- 77-80
Nordskog, John Eric 1893-1974 .... 2R
  Obituary 120
Nordstrom, Ursula 13-14R
  See also SATA 3
Nordtvedt, Matilda 1926- 124
Nordyke, Eleanor C(ole) 1927- 107
Nordyke, James W(alter) 1930- 49-52
Noreen, Robert Gerald 1938- 77-80
Norelli, Martina R(oudabush) 1942- 73-76
Noren, Catherine (Hanf) 1938- CANR-16
  Earlier sketch in CA 65-68
Noren, Paul Harold Andreas 1910- CAP-1
  Earlier sketch in CA 11-12
Norfleet, Barbara P. 1926- Brief entry 107
Norfleet, Mary Crockett 1919- 4R
Norgate, Matthew 1901- 103
Norgay, Tenzing 1914-1986 Obituary 119
Nori, Claude 1949- CANR-18
  Earlier sketch in CA 101
Norland, Howard Bernett 1932- 49-52
Norling, Bernard 1924- 29-32R
Norling, Jo(sephine Stearns) 2R
Norling, Rita 61-64
Norman, Adrian R(oger) D(udley) 1938- .. 29-32R
Norman, Alexander Vesey Bethune
  1930- CANR-9
  Earlier sketch in CA 21-22R
Norman, Barbara 33-36R
Norman, Bruce 1936- 61-64
Norman, C. J.
  See Barrett, Norman (S.)
Norman, Cecilia 1927- CANR-23
  Earlier sketches in CA 57-60, CANR-7
Norman, Charles 1904- 107
  See also SATA 38
Norman, Don(ald) Cleveland 1909(?)-1979
  Obituary 89-92
Norman, Donald A(rthur) 1935- CANR-1
  Earlier sketch in CA 49-52
Norman, Dorothy 1905- 25-28R
Norman, E.D.
  See Goodwin, Bennie Eugene
Norman, Edward (Robert) 1938- CANR-10
  Earlier sketch in CA 17-18R
Norman, Frank 1930-1980 .... CANR-6
  Obituary 102
  Earlier sketch in CA 2R
Norman, Geraldine (Lucia) 1940- 93-96
Norman, James
  See Schmidt, James Norman
Norman, Jillian 1940- 25-28R

Norman, Joe
See Heard, J(oseph) Norman
Norman, John 1912- 19-20R
Norman, John
See Lange, John Frederick, Jr.
Norman, Joyce Ann 1937- 65-68
Norman, Kerry
See Le Pelley, Guernsey
Norman, Lilith 1927- CANR-1
Earlier sketch in CA 45-48
Norman, Lloyd (Henry) 1913-1987 102
Obituary 124
Norman, Louis
See Whittemore, Don
Norman, Marc 1941- 49-52
Norman, Marsha 1947- 105
See also DLBY 84
See also CLC 28
Norman, Mary 1931- SATA-36
Norman, Maxwell H(erbert) 1917- 29-32R
Norman, Nicole
See Cudlipp, Edythe
Norman, Ruth 1903(?)-1977 Obituary 73-76
Norman, Steve
See Pashko, Stanley
Norman, Sylva 1901- CAP-1
Earlier sketch in CA 13-14
Norman, Theodore 1910-1987 124
Obituary 122
Norman, Vesey
See Norman, Alexander Vesey Bethune
Norman, W. S.
See Wilson, N(orman) Scarlyn
Norman, Yvonne
See Seely, Norma
Normyx
See Douglas, (George) Norman
Norodom Sihanouk (Varman), Samdech Preah 1922- Brief entry 106
Norquest, Carrol 1901- 41-44R
Norquist, Richard F(ranklin) 1933- 113
Norrie, Ian 1927- CANR-23
Earlier sketch in CA 106
Norris, Benjamin Franklin, Jr. 1870-1902
Brief entry 110
See also TCLC 24
Norris, Charles G(ilman Smith) 1881-1945
Brief entry 118
See also DLB 9
Norris, Christopher (Charles) 1947- 111
Norris, Christopher Neil Foxley
See Foxley-Norris, Christopher Neil
Norris, Donald F(ranklin) 1942- CANR-2
Earlier sketch in CA 49-52
Norris, Dorothy E. Koch 1907- CAP-2
Earlier sketch in CA 21-22
Norris, Edgar Poe
See Kinnaird, Clark
Norris, Francis Hubert 1909- 7-8R
Norris, Frank
See Norris, Benjamin Franklin, Jr.
See also DLB 12
Norris, Frank C(allan) 1907-1967
Obituary 25-28R
Norris, Gunilla Brodde 1939- 93-96
See also SATA 20
Norris, Harold 1918- 108
Norris, Hoke 1913-1977 ....11-12R
Obituary 73-76
Norris, J(ames) A(lfred) 1929- 25-28R
Norris, James Donald 1930- 19-20R
Norris, Joan 1943- 73-76
Norris, John 1925- 11-12R
Norris, Kathleen (Thompson) 1880-1966
Obituary 25-28R
Norris, Kathleen 1947- 33-36R
Norris, Katrin 19-20R
Norris, Ken 1951- 113
Norris, Kenneth S(tafford) 1924- 77-80
Norris, Leslie 1921- CANR-14
Earlier sketches in CA 11-12, CAP-1
See also DLB 27
See also CLC 14
Norris, Louanne 1930- CANR-20
Earlier sketch in CA 53-56
Norris, Louis William 1906- CAP-1
Earlier sketch in CA 9-10
Norris, Maureen
See Cudlipp, Edythe
Norris, Nigel (Harold) 1943- 65-68
Norris, Richard A(lfred), Jr. 1930- 19-20R
Norris, Ronald V. 1940- 116
Norris, Ruby Turner
See Morris, Ruby Turner
Norris, Russell Bradner (Jr.) 1942- 53-56
Norris, Theo L. 1926- 23-24R
Norse, Harold (George) 1916- CANR-4
Earlier sketch in CA 53-56
See also DLB 16
North, Alvin J(ohn) 1917- 49-52
North, Andrew
See Norton, Alice Mary
North, Anthony
See Koontz, Dean R(ay)
North, Captain George
See Stevenson, Robert Louis (Balfour)
North, Charles W.
See Bauer, Erwin A.
North, Christopher R(ichard) 1888-1975
Obituary 61-64
North, Colin
See Bingley, David Ernest
North, Edmund H(all) 1911- 121
North, Eleanor B(eryl) 1898- 49-52
North, Elizabeth 1932- 81-84
North, Gary 1942- CANR-16
Earlier sketch in CA 65-68
North, Gil
See Horne, Geoffrey
North, Helen Florence 1921- 104
North, Joan 1920- 13-14R
See also SATA 16
North, John (Francis Allen) 1894-1973 107
Obituary 104
North, Joseph 1904-1976 .... CANR-4
Obituary 69-72
Earlier sketch in CA 2R
North, Mark
See Miller, Wright (Watts)
North, Morgan 1915(?)-1978 Obituary 104
North, Robert
See Withers, Carl A.
North, Robert Carver 1914- CANR-4
Earlier sketch in CA 5-6R
North, Robert Grady 1916- 17-18R
North, Sara
See Bonham, Barbara Thomas and Hager, Jean
North, Sterling 1906-1974 ....5-6R
Obituary 53-56
See also SATA 1, 26, 45
North, Wheeler James 1922- 101
Northam, Ray M(ervyn) 1929- 73-76
Northart, Leo J(oseph) 1929- 69-72
Northcote, Peter
See Cotes, Peter
Northcott, (William) Cecil 1902-1987 ......9-10R
Obituary 124
Northcott, Kenneth J(ames) 1922- 45-48
Northedge, Frederick Samuel 1918-1985 104
Obituary 115
Northen, Helen 1914- CANR-13
Earlier sketch in CA 33-36R
Northen, Henry T(heodore) 1908-1979 ...97-100
Northen, Rebecca Tyson 1910- 105
Northgrave, Anne
See Tibble, Anne
Northmore, Elizabeth Florence
1906-1974 .... CAP-2
Earlier sketch in CA 19-20
Northouse, Cameron (George) 1948- 81-84
Northrop, Filmer S(tuart) C(uckow)
1893- CANR-17
Earlier sketch in CA 4R
Northrop, J. H.
See Northrop, John H(oward)
Northrop, John H(oward) 1891-1987
Obituary 123
Northrup, B. A.
See Hubbard, L(afayette) Ron(ald)
Northrup, Herbert Roof 1918- 9-10R
North Staffs
See Hulme, T(homas) E(rnest)
Northumbrian Gentleman, The
See Tegner, Henry (Stuart)
Northway, Mary L(ouise) 1909- 45-48
Northwood, Lawrence K(ing) 1917- 15-16R
Norton, Alan (Lewis) 1926- CANR-15
Earlier sketch in CA 81-84
Norton, Alden H(olmes) 1903- 101
Norton, Alice 1926- 33-36R
Norton, Alice Mary 1912- CANR-2
Earlier sketch in CA 4R
See also SATA 1, 43
Norton, Andre
See Norton, Alice Mary
See also DLB 8, 52
See also CLC 12
Norton, Andrews 1786-1853 .... DLB-1
Norton, Augustus Richard 1946- 113
Norton, Bess
See Norton, Olive (Claydon)
Norton, Bettina A(ntonia) 1936- 93-96
Norton, Boyd 1936- 37-40R
Norton, Bram
See Bramesco, Norton J.
Norton, Browning
See Norton, Frank R. B(rowning)
Norton, Caroline 1808-1877 .... DLB-21
Norton, Charles A(lbert) 1920- 109
Norton, Charles Eliot 1827-1908 ..... DLB-1, 64
Norton, David Fate 1937- 107
Norton, David L. 1930- 37-40R
Norton, (William) Elliot 1903- Brief entry 109
Norton, Frank R. B(rowning) 1909- 61-64
See also SATA 10
Norton, Frederick H. 1896- 61-64
Norton, Glyn P(eter) 1941- 122
Norton, Herman A. 1921- CANR-7
Earlier sketch in CA 5-6R
Norton, Howard Melvin 1911- CANR-3
Earlier sketch in CA 4R
Norton, Hugh S(tanton) 1921- 11-12R
Norton, John 1606-1663 .... DLB-24
Norton, Joseph L(ouis) 1918- 29-32R
Norton, M. D. Herter
See Crena de Iongh, Mary (Dows Herter Norton)
Norton, Mary 1903- 97-100
See also SATA 18
See also CLR 6
Norton, Mary Beth 1943- CANR-5
Earlier sketch in CA 49-52
Norton, Mary E(lizabeth) 1913- 41-44R
Norton, Olive (Claydon) 1913-1973 ......11-12R
Norton, Paul Foote 1917- 41-44R
Norton, Perry L. 1920- 15-16R
Norton, Peter (John) 1913- 13-14R
Norton, Roger C(ecil) 1921- 114
Norton, Thomas 1532-1584 .... DLB-62
Norton, Thomas Elliot 1942- 61-64
Norton, Victor 1906-1983 Obituary 109
Norton, Wesley 1923- 114
Norton-Smith, John 1931- 107
Norton-Taylor, Duncan 1904-1982 102
Obituary 107
Norvil, Manning
See Bulmer, (Henry) Kenneth
Norville, Warren 1923- 73-76
Norwak, Mary 1929- 109
Norway, Kate
See Norton, Olive (Claydon)
Norway, Nevil Shute 1899-1960 102
Obituary 93-96
Norwich, John Julius (Cooper) 1929- ... CANR-5
Earlier sketch in CA 49-52
Norwood, Fred W(ayland) 1920-
Brief entry 112
Norwood, Frederick Abbott 1914- CANR-20
Earlier sketches in CA 4R, CANR-5
Norwood, Gilbert 1880-1954 Brief entry 116
Norwood, John
See Stark, Raymond
Norwood, Paul
See Nettl J(ohn) P(eter)
Norwood, Victor G(eorge) C(harles)
1920- CANR-10
Earlier sketch in CA 21-22R
Norwood, Warren C. 1945- 112
Nosco, Peter 1950- 93-96
Nosille, Nabrah
See Ellison, Harlan
Noss, John Boyer 1896- 85-88
Noss, Luther (Melancthon) 1907- 5-6R
Nossack, Hans Erich 1901-1978 93-96
Obituary 85-88
See also CLC 6
Nossal, Frederick (Christian) 1927-1979 ....7-8R
Obituary 89-92
Nossal, Gustav Joseph Victor 1931- 109
Nossiter, Bernard D(aniel) 1926- 41-44R
Nostlinger, Christine
See Noestlinger, Christine
See also SATA 37
See also CLR 12
Nostrand, Howard Lee 1910- 9-10R
Nosu, Chuji
See Ozu, Yasujiro
Notar, Stephen 1926- 119
Notarius
See Martin, Andrew
Notehelfer, F(red) G(eorge) 1939- 81-84
Notestein, Frank Wallace 1902-1983
Obituary 109
Notestein, Wallace 1878-1969 .... CAP-1
Earlier sketch in CA 9-10
Noth, Martin D. 1902-1968 .... CAP-2
Earlier sketch in CA 21-22
Nothing Venture
See Finney, Humphrey S.
Notlep, Robert
See Pelton, Robert W(ayne)
Notley, Alice 1945- Brief entry 124
Nott, David 1928- 45-48
Nott, Kathleen Cecilia CANR-3
Earlier sketch in CA 4R
Notterman, Joseph M(elvin) 1923- 17-18R
Nottingham, Elizabeth K. 1900- 93-96
Nottingham, William Jesse 1927- 25-28R
Notz, Rebecca Love 1888-1974 Obituary ... 104
Nourissier, Francois 1927- 81-84
Nourse, Alan E(dward) 1928- CANR-21
Earlier sketches in CA 1R, CANR-3
See also SATA 48
See also DLB 8
Nourse, Edwin G(riswold) 1883-1974
Obituary 49-52
Nourse, Hugh O(liver) 1933- Brief entry 107
Nourse, James G(regory) 1947- 105
Nourse, Joan Thellusson 1921- 11-12R
Nourse, Mary Augusta 1880(?)-1971
Obituary 33-36R
Nourse, Robert Eric Martin 1938- 23-24R
Nouveau, Arthur
See Whitcomb, Ian
Nouwen, Henri J(osef Machiel) 1932- 73-76
Nova, Craig 1945- CANR-2
Earlier sketch in CA 45-48
See also CLC 7, 31
Novack, Evelyn Reed 1906(?)-1979
Obituary 85-88
Novack, George (Edward) 1905- 49-52
Novak, Barbara 97-100
Novak, Bogdan C(yril) 1919- 33-36R
Novak, David 1941- 93-96
Novak, Jane Dailey 1917- 105
Novak, Joe
See Novak, Joseph
Novak, Joseph 1898- CAP-1
Earlier sketch in CA 11-12
Novak, Joseph
See Kosinski, Jerzy (Nikodem)
Novak, Lorna 1927- 19-20R
Novak, Maximillian E(rwin) 1930- CANR-12
Earlier sketch in CA 33-36R
Novak, Michael 1933- CANR-1
Earlier sketch in CA 2R
Novak, Michael Paul 1935- 49-52
Novak, Robert
See Levinson, Leonard
Novak, Robert D(avid) 1931- CANR-12
Earlier sketch in CA 13-14R
Novak, Rose 1940- CANR-22
Earlier sketch in CA 105
Novak, Stephen R(obert) 1922- 85-88
Novak, William (Arnold) 1948- 93-96
Novarr, David 1917- 19-20R
Nove, Alec 1915- CANR-3
Earlier sketch in CA 4R
Novelli, Florence 1931- 112
Novello, Don 1943- 107
Nover, Barnet 1899-1973 Obituary 41-44R
Noverr, Douglas A(rthur) 1942- 102
Novick, David 1906- 33-36R
Novick, Julius Lerner 1939- 103
Novick, Marian 1951- 123
Novik, Mary 1945- 61-64
Novitski, Joseph (W. D.) 1940- 124
Novitz, Charles R. 1934- 69-72
Novo, Salvador 1904-1974 Obituary 110
Novoa, John David Bruce
See Bruce-Novoa, John David
Novoa, Juan Bruce
See Bruce-Novoa, John David
Novogrod, R(eevan) Joseph 1916- 29-32R
Novomesky, Ladislav 1904-1976
Obituary 69-72
Novotny, Ann M. 1936-1982 ....25-28R
Obituary 108
Novotny, Fritz 1903-19(?) CANR-18
Earlier sketch in CA 65-68
Novotny, Louise Miller 1889- CAP-2
Earlier sketch in CA 23-24
Novy, Marianne (Lucille) 1945- 118
Nowacki, Walenty 1906- 37-40R
Nowak, Mariette 1941- 102
Nowakowski, Marek 1935- 119
Nowell, Elizabeth Cameron CANR-1
Earlier sketch in CA 2R
See also SATA 12
Nowlan, Alden (Albert) 1933-1983 ...... CANR-5
Earlier sketch in CA 9-10R
See also DLB 53
See also CLC 15
Nowlan, James Dunlap 1941- Brief entry ... 105
Nowlan, Philip Francis 1888-1940
Brief entry 108
Nowlan, Robert Anthony, Jr. 1934- 113
Nowlis, Helen H(oward) 1913- Brief entry ... 111
Noxon, James Herbert 1924- 85-88
Noyce, Gaylord B. 1926- CANR-13
Earlier sketch in CA 37-40R
Noyes, Alfred 1880-1958 Brief entry 104
See also DLB 20
See also TCLC 7
Noyes, Charles Edmund 1904-1972 ......37-40R
Noyes, Crosby S. 1825-1908 .... DLB-23
Noyes, David 1898(?)-1981 Obituary 104
Noyes, James H(oyt) 1927- 118
Noyes, Jeanice W. 1914- 25-28R
Noyes, Joan 1935- 115
Noyes, Kathryn Johnston 1930- 17-18R
Noyes, Morgan Phelps 1891-1972 .... CAP-1
Obituary 37-40R
Earlier sketch in CA 11-12
Noyes, Nell Braly 1921- 37-40R
Noyes, Nicholas 1647-1717 .... DLB-24
Noyes, Peter R. 1930- 49-52
Noyes, Russell 1901- 25-28R
Noyes, Stanley 1924- CANR-1
Earlier sketch in CA 45-48
Noyes, Theodore W. 1858-1946 .... DLB-29
Noyes-Kane, Dorothy 1906- CAP-1
Earlier sketch in CA 13-14
Noyle, Ken(neth Alfred Edward) 1922- 85-88
Nozick, Martin 1917- 37-40R
Nozick, Robert 1938- 61-64
Nsarkoh, J. K(wasi) 1931- 15-16R
Nucera, Marisa Lonette 1959- 17-18R
Nuchtern, Jean 1939- 25-28R
Nuckolls, James L(awton) 1938-1987
Obituary 123
Nudel, Adele Rice 1927- 124
Nudelman, Jerrold 1942- 33-36R
Nuechterlein, Donald Edwin 1925- CANR-1
Earlier sketch in CA 2R
Nuelle, Helen S(hearman) 1923- CANR-12
Earlier sketch in CA 61-64
Nuernberger, Phil 1942- 114
Nuessel, Frank H(enry) 1943- 111
Nuetzel, Charles (Alexander) 1934- 105
Nugent, Donald G(ene) 1930- 45-48
Nugent, Elliott (John) 1899-1980 ....5-6R
Obituary 101
Nugent, Frances Roberts 1904-1964(?) 5-6R
Nugent, Frank 1908-1965 .... DLB-44
Nugent, Jeffrey B(ishop) 1936- 93-96
Nugent, John Peer 1930- 15-16R
Nugent, Nancy 1938- CANR-16
Earlier sketch in CA 65-68
Nugent, Richard Bruce 1906- DLB-51
Nugent, Robert 1920- 61-64
Nugent, Tom 1943- 49-52
Nugent, Vincent Joseph 1913- 41-44R
Nugent, Walter T(erry) K(ing) 1935- CANR-5
Earlier sketch in CA 7-8R
Null, Gary CANR-17
Earlier sketch in CA 65-68
Nulman, Macy 1923- 57-60
Numbers, Ronald L(eslie) 1942- CANR-18
Earlier sketch in CA 101
Numeroff, Laura Joffe 1953- 106
See also SATA 28
Nummi, Seppo (Antero Yrjoepoika)
1932-1981 Obituary 108
Nunan, Desmond J. 1927- 19-20R
Nunes, Claude 1924- Brief entry 112
Nunes, Rhoda (Gwylleth) 1938-
Brief entry 113
Nunez, Ana Rosa 1926- CANR-14
Earlier sketch in CA 69-72
Nunis, Doyce B(lackman), Jr. 1924- ... CANR-19
Earlier sketches in CA 5-6R, CANR-3
Nunley, Maggie Rennert
See Rennert, Maggie
Nunn, Frederick M. 1937- 33-36R
Nunn, G(odfrey) Raymond 1918- CANR-13
Earlier sketch in CA 33-36R

Nunn, Henry L(ightfoot) 1878-1972
Obituary ... 37-40R
Nunn, John 1955- ... 115
Nunn, Kem 19(?)- ... CLC-34
Nunn, Marshall E(arl) 1928- ... 112
Nunn, Walter (Harris) 1942- ... CANR-23
Earlier sketch in CA 45-48
Nunn, William Curtis 1908- ... CANR-1
Earlier sketch in CA 3R
Nunnerley, (Gould) David 1947- ... 45-48
Nuquist, Andrew E(dgerton) 1905-1975
Obituary ... 61-64
Nuraini
See Sim, Katharine (Thomasset)
Nurcombe, Barry 1933- ... 65-68
Nurenberg, Thelma
See Greenhaus, Thelma Nurenberg
Nurge, Ethel 1920- ... 33-36R
Nurmi, Martin Karl 1920- ... CANR-17
Earlier sketch in CA 2R
Nurnberg, Maxwell 1897-1984 ... CANR-2
Obituary ... 114
Earlier sketch in CA 7-8R
See also SATA 27, 41
Nurnberg, Walter 1907- ... 13-14R
Nurse, Malcolm Ivan Meredith 1903-1959
Brief entry ... 119
Nurse, Peter H(arold) 1926- ... 11-12R
Nusbaum, N. Richard
See Nash, N. Richard
Nusbaum, Rosemary 1907- ... 113
Nussbaum, Aaron 1910-1981 ... 49-52
Obituary ... 104
Nussbaum, Al(bert F.) 1934- ... 85-88
Nussbaumer, Paul (Edmund) 1934- ... 93-96
See also SATA 16
Nusser, J(ames) L(ivingston) 1925- ... 3R
Nutini, Hugo G(ino) 1928- Brief entry ... 109
Nutt, Grady 1934- ... 97-100
Nuttall, A(nthony) D(avid) 1937- ... CANR-11
Earlier sketch in CA 23-24R
Nuttall, Geoffrey Fillingham 1911- ... CANR-10
Earlier sketch in CA 15-16R
Nuttall, Jeff 1933- ... CANR-14
Earlier sketch in CA 29-32R
Nuttall, Kenneth 1907- ... 17-18R
Nuttall-Smith, Margaret Emily Noel 1919- ... 104
Nutter, G(ilbert) Warren 1923-1979 ... CANR-2
Obituary ... 85-88
Earlier sketch in CA 4R
Nutting, (Harold) Anthony 1920- ... CANR-7
Earlier sketch in CA 5-6R
Nutting, Willis D(wight) 1900-1975 ... CAP-2
Earlier sketch in CA 25-28
Nwankwo, Nkem 1936- ... 65-68
Nwoauau, Edwin Ifeanyichukwu 1933- ... 19-20R
Nyabongo, Akiki K. 1905-1975 Obituary ... 61-64
Nyad, Diana 1949- Brief entry ... 111
Nyanaponika 1901- ... CAP-1
Earlier sketch in CA 9-10
Nybakken, Elizabeth I. 1940- ... 114
Nybakken, Oscar Edward 1904- ... 93-96
Nyberg, David (Alan) 1943- ... 107
Nyberg, Kathleen Neill 1919- ... 21-22R
Nyce, (Nellie) Helene von Strecker
1885-1969 ... SATA-19
Nyce, Vera 1862-1925 ... SATA-19
Nye, Bill
See Nye, Edgar Wilson
See also DLB 11
Nye, Doug(las Charles) 1945- Brief entry ... 114
Nye, Edgar Wilson 1850-1896 ... DLB-23
Nye, F(rancis) Ivan 1918- ... CANR-21
Earlier sketches in CA 11-12R, CANR-6
Nye, Hermes 1908- ... CAP-2
Earlier sketch in CA 19-20
Nye, Joseph S(amuel), Jr. 1937- ... CANR-12
Earlier sketch in CA 25-28R
Nye, Loyal 1921- ... 106
Nye, Miriam (Maurine Hawthorn) Baker
1918- ... 85-88
Nye, Nelson C(oral) 1907- ... CANR-4
Earlier sketch in CA 7-8R
Nye, Robert 1939- ... 33-36R
See also SATA 6
See also DLB 14
See also CLC 13, 42
Nye, Robert D(onald) 1934- ... 73-76
Nye, Robert Evans 1911- ... CANR-1
Earlier sketch in CA 4R
Nye, Russel B(laine) 1913- ... CANR-4
Earlier sketch in CA 3R
Nye, Vernice Trousdale 1913- ... CANR-1
Earlier sketch in CA 4R
Nye, Wilbur S. 1898-1970 ... CANR-15
Obituary ... 103
Earlier sketch in CA 2R
Nyenhuis, Jacob E(ugene) 1935-
Brief entry ... 117
Nyerere, Julius K(ambarage) 1922-
Brief entry ... 105
Nygaard, Anita 1934- ... 65-68
Nygaard, Norman E. 1897-1971 ... CANR-2
Earlier sketch in CA 3R
Nygard, Roald 1935- ... 103
Nygren, Anders T(heodor) S(amuel)
1890- ... 9-10R
Nykoruk, Barbara (Christine) 1949-
Brief entry ... 115
Nylander, Carl 1932- ... 33-36R
Nynych, Stephanie J.
See Caulder, Colline
Nyquist, Ewald B(erger) 1914- Brief entry ... 113
Nyquist, Thomas E. 1931- ... 41-44R
Nyren, Dorothy Elizabeth 1927- ... CANR-5
Earlier sketch in CA 2R
Nyro, Laura 1947- ... CLC-17
Nystrom, Carolyn 1940- ... 114
Nzimiro, Ikenna 1927- ... CANR-2
Earlier sketch in CA 45-48

O

O(rdonez), Jaime E(dmundo) Rodriguez
See Rodriguez O(rdonez), Jaime E(dmundo)
Oak, Liston M. 1895-1970 Obituary ... 104
Oakes, James 1953- ... 107
Oakes, John Bertram 1913- ... 15-16R
Oakes, Philip (Barlow) 1928- ... CANR-4
Earlier sketch in CA 53-56
Oakes, Urian 1631(?)-1681 ... DLB-24
Oakes, Vanya 1909-1983 ... 33-36R
Obituary ... 111
See also SATA 6, 37
Oakeshott, Michael 1901- ... 4R
Oakeshott, Walter (Fraser) 1903-1987 ... 13-14R
Obituary ... 123
Oakie, Jack
See Offield, Lewis Delaney
Oakland, Thomas David 1939- ... 53-56
Oakley, Ann (Rosamund) 1944- ... CANR-6
Earlier sketch in CA 57-60
Oakley, Barry K(ingham) 1931- ... 104
Oakley, Charles Allen 1900- ... 108
Oakley, Don(ald G.) 1927- ... 29-32R
See also SATA 8
Oakley, Eric Gilbert 1916- ... 9-10R
Oakley, Francis (Christopher) 1931- ... 15-16R
Oakley, Giles (Francis) 1946- ... 103
Oakley, Graham 1929- ... 106
See also SATA 30
See also CLR 7
Oakley, Helen (McKelvey) 1906- ... 17-18R
See also SATA 10
Oakley, J. Ronald 1941- ... 121
Oakley, Josephine 1903(?)-1978
Obituary ... 81-84
Oakley, K. P.
See Oakley, Kenneth Page
Oakley, Kenneth P.
See Oakley, Kenneth Page
Oakley, Kenneth Page 1911-1981 ... 122
Obituary ... 108
Oakley, Mary Ann B. 1940- ... 45-48
Oakley, Stewart P(hilip) 1931- ... 21-22R
Oakman, Barbara F(rances) 1931- ... 57-60
Oaks, Dallin H(arris) 1932- ... 25-28R
Oaksey, John 1929- ... 105
Oana, Katherine 1929- ... 108
See also SATA 37
Oates, Jeannette 1912(?)-1984 Obituary ... 112
Oates, John (Frederick) 1944- ... 69-72
Oates, John F. 1934- ... 19-20R
Oates, Joyce Carol 1938- ... 7-8R
See also DLB 2, 5
See also DLBY 81
See also CLC 1, 2, 3, 6, 9, 11, 15, 19, 33
See also AITN 1
Oates, Stephen B. 1936- ... CANR-4
Earlier sketch in CA 11-12R
Oates, Wallace Eugene 1937- ... CANR-14
Earlier sketch in CA 37-40R
Oates, Wayne Edward 1917- ... 85-88
Oates, Whitney J(ennings) 1904-1973 ... CANR-3
Obituary ... 45-48
Earlier sketch in CA 5-6R
Oathout, John D(avid) 1913- ... 111
Oatley, Keith 1939- ... 45-48
Oatman, Eric F(urber) 1939- ... CANR-19
Earlier sketch in CA 103
Oatts, Balfour
See Oatts, Lewis Balfour
Oatts, Henry Augustus 1898-1980 ... 7-8R
Obituary ... 103
Oatts, Lewis Balfour 1902- ... 110
Obach, Robert 1939- ... 106
Obaldia, Rene de 1918- Brief entry ... 116
O'Ballance, Edgar 1918- ... CANR-7
Earlier sketch in CA 7-8R
O'Banion, Terry 1936- ... 33-36R
O'Barr, William M(cAlston) 1942- ... 49-52
O'Beirne, T(homas) H(ay) 1915-1982 ... 17-18R
Obituary ... 120
Obele, Norma Taylor 1933- ... 104
Obenchain, Anne DeCroes 1914(?)-1984
Obituary ... 112
Obenhaus, Victor 1903- ... CAP-1
Earlier sketch in CA 13-14
Ober, Stuart Alan 1946- ... 103
Ober, Warren U(pton) 1925- ... 15-16R
Oberg, Arthur K. 1938-1977 Obituary ... 112
Oberg, James E(dward) 1944- ... 108
Oberhansli, Trudi
See Schlapbach-Oberhansli, Trudi
Oberhelman, Harley D(ean) 1928- ... 53-56
Oberholtzer, Ellis Paxton 1868-1936 ... DLB-47
Oberholtzer, Peter
See Brannon, William T.
Oberholtzer, W(alter) Dwight 1939- ... 101
Oberholzer, Emil, Jr. 1926(?)-1981
Obituary ... 102
Oberman, Heiko Augustinus 1930- ... CANR-7
Earlier sketch in CA 5-6R
Obermann, C. Esco 1904- ... 53-56
Obermayer, Herman J. 1924- ... 65-68
Obermeyer, Barrett John 1937- ... 5-6R
Obermeyer, Henry 1899- ... CAP-2
Earlier sketch in CA 29-32
Obermeyer, Marion Barrett ... 7-8R
Oberschall, Antony R. 1936- ... 97-100
Obert, John C. 1924-1987 Obituary ... 122
Oberth, Hermann Julius 1894-1979(?)
Obituary ... 113
Obey, Andre 1892-1975 ... 97-100
Obituary ... 57-60
Obichere, Boniface Ihewunwa 1932- ... 41-44R
Obiechina, Emmanuel Nwanonye
1933- ... CANR-15
Earlier sketch in CA 41-44R
Obligado, Lilian (Isabel) 1931- ... SATA-45
Oboe, Peter
See Jacobs, Walter Darnell
Obojski, Robert 1929- ... CANR-24
Earlier sketch in CA 108
Obolensky, Dimitri 1918- ... 45-48
Oboler, Arch 1909(?)-1987 Obituary ... 122
Brief entry ... 105
Oboler, Eli M(artin) 1915-1983 ... CANR-6
Obituary ... 110
Earlier sketch in CA 57-60
Obourn, Ellsworth Scott 1897- ... CAP-2
Earlier sketch in CA 17-18
O'Brady, Frederic Michel Maurice
1903- ... CANR-3
Earlier sketch in CA 9-10R
Obrant, Susan 1946- ... SATA-11
O'Brawes, Tarnel
See La Barre, Weston
Obregon, Mauricio 1921- ... CANR-1
Earlier sketch in CA 45-48
O'Brian, Frank
See Garfield, Brian (Wynne)
O'Brian, Jack 1921- ... 103
O'Brian, John Lord 1874-1973 Obituary ... 41-44R
O'Briant, Walter H(erbert) 1937- ... 25-28R
O'Brien, Andrew William 1910- ... CANR-17
Earlier sketch in CA 25-28R
O'Brien, Andy
See O'Brien, Andrew William
O'Brien, Anne Sibley 1952- ... 122
See also SATA 48
O'Brien, Conor Cruise 1917- ... 65-68
O'Brien, Cyril C(ornelius) 1906- ... 53-56
O'Brien, Darcy 1939- ... CANR-8
Earlier sketch in CA 21-22R
O'Brien, David J(oseph) 1938- ... 25-28R
O'Brien, Dean D.
See Binder, Otto, O(scar)
O'Brien, Dee
See Bradley, Marion Zimmer
O'Brien, Des(mond John) 1930- ... 114
O'Brien, E. G.
See Clarke, Arthur C(harles)
O'Brien, Edna 1936- ... CANR-6
Earlier sketch in CA 3R
See also DLB 14
See also CLC 3, 5, 8, 13, 36
O'Brien, Edward C.
See Schrodt, Philip A(ndrew)
O'Brien, Elmer 1911- ... 19-20R
O'Brien, Esse Forrester 1895(?)-1975
Obituary ... 61-64
See also SATA 30
O'Brien, Flann
See O Nuallain, Brian
See also CLC 1, 4, 5, 7, 10, 47
O'Brien, Frances (Kelly) 1906- ... CAP-2
Earlier sketch in CA 17-18
O'Brien, Francis J(oseph) 1903- ... 81-84
O'Brien, Geoffrey 1948- ... 106
O'Brien, George Dennis 1931- ... 103
O'Brien, Gregory (C., Jr.) 1945- ... 117
O'Brien, J(ohn) W(ilfrid) 1931- ... 15-16R
O'Brien, Jacqueline Robin 1949- ... 105
O'Brien, James A(loysius) 1936-
Brief entry ... 110
O'Brien, James J. 1929- ... CANR-9
Earlier sketch in CA 17-18R
O'Brien, John Anthony 1893-1980 ... CANR-1
Obituary ... 97-100
Earlier sketch in CA 4R
O'Brien, John J(oseph) 1937- ... 111
O'Brien, Justin (McCortney) 1906-1968 ... CANR-5
Earlier sketch in CA 5-6R
O'Brien, K.
See O'Brien, Katherine
O'Brien, Kate 1897-1974 ... 93-96
Obituary ... 53-56
See also DLB 15
O'Brien, Katherine 1915-1982 Obituary ... 118
O'Brien, Kevin P. 1922- ... 53-56
O'Brien, Lawrence Francis 1917- ... 57-60
O'Brien, Lee 1948- ... 61-64
O'Brien, Marian P(lowman) 1915- ... 53-56
O'Brien, Michael 1948- ... 121
O'Brien, Michael J. 1920- ... 25-28R
O'Brien, (William Joseph) Pat(rick)
1899-1983 Obituary ... 111
O'Brien, Patrick 1932- ... 23-24R
O'Brien, Richard 19(?)- ... CLC-17
O'Brien, Richard 1934- ... 73-76
O'Brien, Richard 1942- ... 124
O'Brien, Robert C.
See Conly, Robert Leslie
See also CLR 2
O'Brien, Robert W(illiam) 1907- ... 45-48
O'Brien, Saliee
See Janas, Frankie-Lee
O'Brien, Sister Mary Celine 1922- ... 21-22R
O'Brien, Thomas C(lement) 1938- ... 106
See also SATA 29
O'Brien, Tim 1946- ... 85-88
See also DLBY 80
See also CLC 7, 19, 40
O'Brien, Vincent 1916- ... 9-10R
O'Brien, William V(incent) 1923- ... 15-16R
O'Broin, Leon 1902- ... CANR-8
Earlier sketch in CA 61-64
O'Brynt, Jon
See Barnum, W(illiam) Paul
Observer
See Velikovsky, Immanuel
Obst, Frances Melanie ... 19-20R
Obstfeld, Raymond 1952- ... 116
Obstfelder, Sigbjoern 1866-1900
Brief entry ... 123
See also TCLC 23
Obstfelder, Sigbjorn
See Obstfelder, Sigbjoern
See also TCLC 23
O'Callaghan, Denis F(rancis) 1931- ... 17-18R
O'Callaghan, Joseph F(rancis) 1928- ... 81-84
O'Callaghan, Julie 1954- ... 117
Ocampo, Victoria 1891-1979 ... 105
Obituary ... 85-88
O'Carroll, Ryan
See Markun, Patricia Maloney
O'Casey, Eileen (Reynolds) 1904(?)-
Brief entry ... 112
O'Casey, Sean 1880-1964 ... 89-92
See also DLB 10
See also CLC 1, 5, 9, 11, 15
O'Cathasaigh, Donal
See Casey, Daniel J(oseph)
O'Cathasaigh, Sean
See O'Casey, Sean
Occomy, Marita Bonner 1899-1971 ... DLB-51
Ocean, Julian
See de Mesne, Eugene (Frederick Peter Cheshire)
O Ceithearnaigh, Seumas
See Carney, James (Patrick)
Ochester, Ed(win Frank) 1939- ... 45-48
Ochiltree, Thomas H 1912- ... 77-80
Ochojski, Paul M(aximilian)
1916-1983 ... CANR-20
Earlier sketch in CA 25-28R
Ochorowicz, Julian 1850-1917 Brief entry ... 114
Ochs, Adolph S(imon) 1858-1935
Brief entry ... 118
See also DLB 25
Ochs, Carol (Rebecca) 1939- ... 114
Ochs, Donovan J(oseph) 1938- ... 45-48
Ochs, Michael 1943- ... 119
Ochs, Phil 1940-1976 Obituary ... 65-68
See also CLC 17
Ochs, Robert J. 1930- ... 29-32R
Ochse, Orpha Caroline 1925- ... 93-96
Ochsenschlager, Edward L(loyd) 1932- ... 19-20R
Ochsner, (Edward William) Alton
1896-1981 ... 17-18R
Obituary ... 105
Ochsner, Jeffrey Karl 1950- ... 111
Ockenga, Harold John 1905-1985 ... CANR-1
Obituary ... 115
Earlier sketch in CA 4R
O'Clair, Robert M. 1923- ... 77-80
O'Clery, Helen (Gallagher) 1910- ... 11-12R
O'Collins, Gerald Glynn 1931- ... CANR-15
Earlier sketch in CA 85-88
O'Connell, Brian (Vincent) J(ohn) 1923-
Brief entry ... 113
O'Connell, Daniel Patrick 1924-1979 ... 29-32R
Obituary ... 89-92
O'Connell, David 1940- ... 102
O'Connell, Frank 1892- ... 5-6R
O'Connell, Jeffrey 1928- ... CANR-11
Earlier sketch in CA 25-28R
O'Connell, Jeremiah Joseph 1932- ... CANR-7
Earlier sketch in CA 13-14R
O'Connell, John James III 1921-1982
Obituary ... 107
O'Connell, Margaret F(orster) 1935-1977 ... 73-76
See also SATA 30, 49
O'Connell, Marvin R(ichard) 1930-
Brief entry ... 111
O'Connell, Maurice R. 1922- ... 17-18R
O'Connell, Michael (William) 1943- ... 101
O'Connell, Peg
See Ahern, Margaret McCrohan
O'Connell, Richard L(eo), Jr.
1912-1975 ... 41-44R
O'Connell, Timothy E(dward) 1943- ... CANR-12
Earlier sketch in CA 73-76
O'Connell, Walter E(dward) 1925- ... 41-44R
O'Conner, R(ay) L. 1928- ... 17-18R
O'Connor, A(nthony) M(ichael) 1939- ... CANR-11
Earlier sketch in CA 21-22R
O'Connor, Anthony ?-1983(?) Obituary ... 109
O'Connor, Clint
See Paine, Lauran (Bosworth)
O'Connor, Daniel William 1925- ... 33-36R
O'Connor, David 1949- ... 110
O'Connor, Dick 1930- ... 97-100
O'Connor, Edward Dennis 1922- ... 41-44R
O'Connor, Edwin (Greene) 1918-1968 ... 93-96
Obituary ... 25-28R
See also CLC 14
O'Connor, Egan 1937- ... 119
O'Connor, Elizabeth Anita 1921- ... 25-28R
O'Connor, (Mary) Flannery 1925-1964 ... CANR-3
Earlier sketch in CA 1R
See also DLB 2
See also DLBY 80
See also CDALB 1941-1968
See also CLC 1, 2, 3, 6, 10, 13, 15, 21
See also SSC 1
O'Connor, Francine M(arie) 1930- ... 111
O'Connor, Francis V(alentine) 1937- ... CANR-13
Earlier sketch in CA 21-22R
O'Connor, Frank
See O'Donovan, Michael John
See also CLC 23

O'Connor, Garry 1938- CANR-20
Earlier sketch in CA 89-92
O'Connor, Harvey 1897-1987 .... 7-8R
Obituary 123
O'Connor, Jack
See O'Connor, John Woolf
O'Connor, James I(gnatius) 1910- CAP-1
Earlier sketch in CA 15-16
O'Connor, Jane 1947- 124
See also SATA 47
O'Connor, John (Morris) 1937- 29-32R
O'Connor, John E. 1943- Brief entry 109
O'Connor, John J(oseph) 1918- 73-76
O'Connor, John Joseph 1904-1978
Obituary 77-80
O'Connor, John P. 1892-1986 Obituary 119
O'Connor, John Woolf 1902-1978 ...... CANR-3
Obituary 77-80
Earlier sketch in CA 7-8R
O'Connor, June (Elizabeth) 1941- 114
O'Connor, Karen 1938- SATA-34
O'Connor, Liam
See Liddy, James (Daniel Reeves)
O'Connor, Lillian M. 1894(?)-1987
Obituary 122
O'Connor, M.
See O'Connor, Michael Patrick
O'Connor, Mark 1945- CANR-11
Earlier sketch in CA 65-68
O'Connor, Michael Patrick 1950- 113
O'Connor, Patricia Walker 1931- CANR-17
Earlier sketch in CA 37-40R
O'Connor, Patrick 77-80
O'Connor, Patrick
See Wibberley, Leonard (Patrick O'Connor)
O'Connor, Patrick J(oseph) 1947- 113
O'Connor, Patrick Joseph 1924- 53-56
O'Connor, Philip Francis 1932- 33-36R
O'Connor, Philip Marie Constant Bancroft
1916- 11-12R
O'Connor, Raymond G(ish) 1915- CANR-4
Earlier sketch in CA 7-8R
O'Connor, Richard 1915-1975 61-64
Obituary 57-60
See also SATA 21
O'Connor, Rory 1951- 109
O'Connor, Sister Mary Catharine CAP-2
Earlier sketch in CA 17-18
O'Connor, Thomas Henry 1922- 33-36R
O'Connor, Ulick 1928- CANR-4
Earlier sketch in CA 11-12R
O'Connor, William E(dmund) 1922- 37-40R
O'Connor, William P., Jr. 1916- 11-12R
O'Connor, William Van 1915-1966 ...... CANR-1
Obituary 25-28R
Earlier sketch in CA 1R
O'Connor Howe, Josephine (Mary) 1924- ... 119
O'Conor, John F(rancis) 1918- 33-36R
October, John
See Portway, Christopher (John)
Octopus
See Drachman, Julian M(oses)
Ocvirk, Otto G(eorge) 1922- 61-64
Odaga, Asenath (Bole) 1937- 124
Odahl, Charles Matson 1944- 37-40R
Odajnyk, Walter 1938- 15-16R
O Danachair, Caoimhin
See Danaher, Kevin
O'Daniel, Janet 1921- 29-32R
See also SATA 24
O'Daniel, Therman B(enjamin) 1908- 45-48
O'Day, Cathy
See Crane, Barbara (Joyce)
O'Day, Edward Francis 1925- 29-32R
O'Day, Rey 1947- 105
Odd, Gilbert E(dward) 1902- 110
Oddo, Gilbert L. 1922- CANR-1
Earlier sketch in CA 1R
Oddo, Sandra (Schmidt) 1937- 65-68
O'Dea, Agnes C. 1911- 124
O'Dea, Thomas F(rancis) 1915-1974 ..... CAP-2
Obituary 53-56
Earlier sketch in CA 23-24
Odegaard, Charles Edwin 1911-
Brief entry 106
Odegard, Douglas Andrew 1935- 108
Odegard, Holtan Peter 1923- 61-64
O'Dell, Andrew C(harles) 1909-1966 ..... CAP-1
Earlier sketch in CA 15-16
Odell, Gill
See Gill, Traviss
Odell, Jonathan 1737-1818 .... DLB-31
Odell, Ling Chung 1945- 45-48
O'Dell, M(ary) E(lise) 11-12R
Odell, Peter R(andon) 1930- 97-100
Odell, Rice 1928- 77-80
Odell, Robin 1935- CANR-12
Earlier sketch in CA 73-76
O'Dell, Scott 1903- CANR-12
Earlier sketch in CA 61-64
See also SATA 12
See also DLB 52
See also CLC 30
See also CLR 1
O'Dell, William F(rancis) 1909- CANR-12
Earlier sketch in CA 25-28R
Odem, J.
See Rubin, Jacob A.
Oden, Clifford 1916- 65-68
Oden, Gloria (Catherine) 1923- 108
Oden, Marilyn Brown 1937- 33-36R
Oden, Thomas C(lark) 1931- CANR-19
Earlier sketches in CA 11-12R, CANR-5
Oden, William E(ugene) 1923- 37-40R
Odenwald, Robert P(aul) 1899-1965 .... 2R
See also SATA 11
Odescalchi, Esther Kando 1938- 69-72
Odets, Clifford 1906-1963 85-88
See also DLB 7, 26
See also CLC 2, 28
Odgers, Merle Middleton 1900-1983
Obituary 110
Odier, Daniel 1945- 29-32R
Odiorne, George Stanley 1920- CANR-1
Earlier sketch in CA 1R
Odishaw, Hugh 1916-1984 Obituary 112
Odle, Joe T(aft) 1908-1980 ....33-36R
Obituary 97-100
Odling-Smee, John (Charles) 1943- 112
Odlum, Doris Maude 1890-1985 .... CAP-1
Obituary 118
Earlier sketch in CA 13-14
O'Doherty, Brian 1934- 105
O'Doherty, E(amonn) F(elchin) 1918- 37-40R
O'Doire, Annraoi
See Beechhold, Henry F(rank)
Odom, William E(ldridge) 1932- 73-76
O'Donnell, Bernard 1929- 41-44R
O'Donnell, Cyril 1900- CAP-1
Earlier sketch in CA 11-12
O'Donnell, Dick
See Lupoff, Richard A(llen) and Thompson, Don(ald Arthur)
O'Donnell, Donat
See O'Brien, Conor C(ruise)
O'Donnell, Elliott 1872-1965 .... CAP-1
Earlier sketch in CA 15-16
O'Donnell, Francis ?-1984 Obituary 114
O'Donnell, Harry J(ames) 1914-1985
Obituary 117
O'Donnell, James H(owlett) III 1937- 45-48
O'Donnell, James J(oseph, Jr.) 1950- .. CANR-16
Earlier sketch in CA 89-92
O'Donnell, James Kevin 1951- CANR-6
Earlier sketch in CA 57-60
O'Donnell, Jim
See O'Donnell, James Kevin
O'Donnell, John A. 1916- 19-20R
O'Donnell, John P. 1923- 19-20R
O'Donnell, K. M.
See Malzberg, Barry N(athaniel)
O'Donnell, (Philip) Kenneth 1924-1977 81-84
Obituary 73-76
O'Donnell, Kenneth P.
See O'Donnell, (Philip) Kenneth
O'Donnell, Kevin, Jr. 1950- CANR-23
Earlier sketch in CA 106
O'Donnell, Lawrence
See Kuttner, Henry and Moore, C(atherine) L(ucile)
O'Donnell, Lawrence F(rancis), Jr. 1951- ... 117
O'Donnell, Lillian Udvardy 1926- CANR-18
Earlier sketches in CA 7-8R, CANR-3
O'Donnell, Margaret Jane 1899- 7-8R
O'Donnell, Mark 1954- CANR-21
Earlier sketch in CA 104
O'Donnell, Patrick (James) 1948- 114
O'Donnell, Peadar 1893-1986 Obituary 119
O'Donnell, Peter 1920- 117
Brief entry 114
O'Donnell, Red
See O'Donnell, Francis
O'Donnell, Thomas Francis 1915- CANR-1
Earlier sketch in CA 1R
O'Donnell, Thomas J(oseph) 1918- 65-68
O'Donnevan, Finn
See Sheckley, Robert
O'Donoghue, Bryan 1921- 77-80
O'Donoghue, Gregory 1951- 114
Brief entry 109
O'Donoghue, Joseph 1931- 23-24R
O'Donovan, John 1921- CANR-11
Earlier sketch in CA 25-28R
O'Donovan, Katherine 1942- 123
O'Donovan, Michael John 1903-1966 93-96
See also CLC 14
Odor, Ruth Shannon 1926- 120
See also SATA 44
O'Dowd, Liam 1947- 116
O'Driscoll, Robert 1938- 53-56
O'Dwyer, James F. 1939- 33-36R
O'Dwyer, Paul 1907- 97-100
Odysseus
See Johnson, Donald McI(ntosh)
Oe, Kenzaburo 1935- 97-100
See also CLC 10, 36
Oechsli, Kelly 1918- CANR-16
Earlier sketch in CA 97-100
See also SATA 5
Oehmke, T(homas) H(arold) 1947- CANR-11
Earlier sketch in CA 65-68
Oehser, Paul H(enry) 1904- CANR-12
Earlier sketch in CA 29-32R
Oeksenholt, Svein 1925- Brief entry 106
Oenslager, Donald (Mitchell) 1902-1975 ...61-64
Obituary 57-60
Oepik, Ernst Julius 1893-1985 Obituary 118
Oerkeny, Istvan
See Orkeny, Istvan
Oerum, Poul (Erik) 1919- CANR-13
Earlier sketch in CA 65-68
Oesterle, John A(rthur) 1912- 5-6R
Oesterreicher, John M. 1904- 29-32R
Oettinger, Anthony Gervin 1929- 1R
Oettinger, Elmer R(osenthal, Jr.) 1913- ...29-32R
O'Faolain, Julia 1932- CANR-12
Earlier sketch in CA 81-84
See also CAAS 2
See also DLB 14
See also CLC 6, 19, 47
O'Faolain, Sean 1900- CANR-12
Earlier sketch in CA 61-64
See also DLB 15
See also CLC 1, 7, 14, 32
Ofari, Earl 1945- 41-44R
O'Farrell, Patrick (James) 1933- CANR-20
Earlier sketch in CA 103
Ofek, Uriel 1926- CANR-18
Earlier sketch in CA 101
See also SATA 36
Offen, Karen Marie Stedtfeld 1939- 113
Offen, Neil 1946- 49-52
Offen, Ron 1930- 45-48
Offer, Daniel 1930- CANR-11
Earlier sketch in CA 21-22R
Offerle, Mildred 1912- 77-80
Offield, Lewis Delaney 1903-1978
Obituary 111
Offiong, Daniel A(sukwo) 1942- 118
Offit, Avodah K(omito) 1931- CANR-13
Earlier sketch in CA 77-80
Offit, Sidney 1928- CANR-1
Earlier sketch in CA 4R
See also SATA 10
Offner, Arnold A. 1937- 25-28R
Offner, Eric D(elmonte) 1928- CANR-9
Earlier sketch in CA 19-20R
Offord, Lenore Glen 1905- 77-80
Offutt, Andrew J(efferson V) 1934(?)- .. CANR-15
Earlier sketch in CA 41-44R
O Fiaich, Tomas 1923- 103
O'Finn, Thaddeus
See McGloin, Joseph T(haddeus)
O'Flaherty, James C(arneal) 1914- 21-22R
O'Flaherty, Liam 1896-1984 101
Obituary 113
See also DLB 36
See also DLBY 84
See also CLC 5, 34
O'Flaherty, Louise 1920- CANR-6
Earlier sketch in CA 57-60
O'Flaherty, Terrence 1917- 73-76
O'Flaherty, Wendy Doniger 1940- CANR-23
Earlier sketch in CA 65-68
O'Flinn, Peter
See Fanthorpe, R(obert) Lionel
O'Flynn, Peter
See Fanthorpe, R(obert) Lionel
Ofomata, G(odfrey) E(zediaso) K(ingsley)
1936- 93-96
Ofosu-Appiah, L(awrence) H(enry)
1920- 33-36R
See also SATA 13
Ofshe, Richard 1941- 89-92
Og, Liam
See O'Neill, William
O'Gallagher, Liam 1917- 45-48
Ogan, George F. 1912- CANR-4
Earlier sketch in CA 9-10R
See also SATA 13
Ogan, M. G.
See Ogan, George F. and Ogan, Margaret E. (Nettles)
Ogan, Margaret E. (Nettles) 1923-1979 .. CANR-4
Earlier sketch in CA 11-12R
See also SATA 13
O'Gara, James Vincent, Jr. 1918-1979 69-72
Obituary 85-88
Ogata, Sadako (Nakamura) 1927- CANR-9
Earlier sketch in CA 19-20R
Ogawa, Dennis Masaaki 1943- 37-40R
Ogawa, Tetsuro 1912-1978 ....41-44R
Ogbu, John U(zor) 1939- 93-96
Ogburn, Charlton (Jr.) 1911- CANR-3
Earlier sketch in CA 5-6R
See also SATA 3
Ogburn, W. F.
See Ogburn, William Fielding
Ogburn, William F.
See Ogburn, William Fielding
Ogburn, William Fielding 1886-1959
Brief entry 122
Ogden, Daniel M(iller), Jr. 1922- 11-12R
Ogden, Dunbar H. 53-56
Ogden, Gina 1935- 81-84
Ogden, Margaret Sinclair 1909-
Brief entry 107
Ogden, (John) Michael (Hubert) 1923- ...13-14R
Ogden, Samuel R(obinson) 1896- 29-32R
Ogden, Schubert Miles 1928- CANR-21
Earlier sketch in CA 104
Ogg, Oscar (John) 1908-1971 .... CAP-1
Obituary 33-36R
Earlier sketch in CA 11-12
Ogilvie, Elisabeth May 1917- CANR-19
Earlier sketch in CA 103
See also SATA 29, 40
Ogilvie, Gordon (Bryant) 1934- CANR-8
Earlier sketch in CA 61-64
Ogilvie, Lloyd John 1930- 73-76
Ogilvie, Mardel 1910- 1R
Ogilvie, Robert Maxwell 1932-1981 ..... CANR-6
Obituary 105
Earlier sketch in CA 15-16R
Ogilvy, C(harles) Stanley 1913- CANR-4
Earlier sketch in CA 5-6R
Ogilvy, David Mackenzie 1911- Brief entry .. 105
Ogilvy, Stewart Marks 1914-1985(?)
Obituary 118
Oglanby, Elva
See Clairmont, Elva
Ogle, James Lawrence 1911- 7-8R
Ogle, Jim
See Ogle, James Lawrence
Ogle, Robert 1926(?)-1984 Obituary 112
Oglesby, Joseph 1931- CANR-17
Earlier sketch in CA 97-100
Oglesby, Richard E(dward) 1931- CANR-6
Earlier sketch in CA 11-12R
Oglesby, William B(arr), Jr. 1916- 25-28R
Ogletree, Earl Joseph 1930- CANR-10
Earlier sketch in CA 65-68
Ogletree, Thomas W(arren) 1933- 19-20R
Ognall, Leopold Horace 1908-1979 .... CANR-12
Earlier sketch in CA 9-10R
Ognibene, Peter J(ohn) 1941- 110
O'Gorman, Edward Charles 1929- 81-84
O'Gorman, Frank 1940- 61-64
O'Gorman, Gerald 1916- 21-22R
O'Gorman, James F(rancis) 1933- 53-56
O'Gorman, John
See MacGill, Patrick
O'Gorman, Ned
See O'Gorman, Edward Charles
O'Gorman, Richard F. 1928- 37-40R
O'Gorman, Samuel F.
See Cusack, Michael J.
O'Grada, Sean
See O'Grady, John (Patrick)
O'Grady, Anne 53-56
O'Grady, Desmond (James Bernard)
1935- CANR-14
Earlier sketch in CA 25-28R
See also DLB 40
O'Grady, Francis Dominic 1909- CAP-1
Earlier sketch in CA 9-10
O'Grady, Frank
See O'Grady, Francis Dominic
O'Grady, John (Patrick) 1907- 104
O'Grady, John F(rancis) 1939- 93-96
O'Grady, Joseph P(atrick) 1934- 41-44R
O'Grady, Rohan
See Skinner, June O'Grady
O'Grady, Ron 1930- 114
O'Grady, Standish James 1846-1928
Brief entry 104
See also TCLC 5
Ogram, Ernest W(illiam), Jr. 1928- 57-60
O'Green, Jennifer
See Roberson, Jennifer
Ogul, Morris S(amuel) 1931- 15-16R
Oh, John Kie-chiang 1930- 29-32R
O'Hagan, Caroline 1946- 111
See also SATA 38
O'Hagan, Howard 1902- 3R
O'Hair, Madalyn (Mays) Murray 1919- .. CANR-12
Earlier sketch in CA 61-64
O'Hanlon, Daniel John 1919- 61-64
O'Hanlon, Jacklyn
See Meek, Jacklyn O'Hanlon
O'Hanlon, Redmond (Douglas) 1947- 123
O'Hanlon, Thomas J(oseph) 1933- 61-64
O'Hara, Charles E. 1912- 29-32R
O'Hara, Dale
See Gillese, John Patrick
O'Hara, Frank 1926-1966 ....9-10R
Obituary 25-28R
See also DLB 5, 16
See also CLC 2, 5, 13
O'Hara, Frederic James 1917- 103
O'Hara, John (Henry) 1905-1970 ....5-6R
Obituary 25-28R
See also DLB 9
See also DLBD 2
See also CLC 1, 2, 3, 6, 11, 42
O'Hara, Kenneth
See Morris, (Margaret) Jean
O'Hara, Kevin
See Cumberland, Marten
O'Hara, Mary
See Alsop, Mary O'Hara
Ohashi, Wataru 1944- 73-76
O'Hayre, John 1923-1986 Obituary 121
O'hearn, Peter J(oseph) T(homas)
1917- 17-18R
O'Heffernan, Patrick 1944- 117
O Hehir, Diana 1922- 93-96
See also CLC 41
O'Higgins, Donal Peter 1922-1984 77-80
Obituary 112
Ohira, Masayoshi 1910-1980 Obituary 105
Ohkawa, Kazushi 1908- 85-88
Ohl, (Mary) Suzanne Sickler 1923- 69-72
Ohles, John Ford 1920- 57-60
Ohlig, Karl-Heinz 1938- CANR-13
Earlier sketch in CA 69-72
Ohlin, Bertil 1899(?)-1979 Obituary 89-92
Ohlin, Lloyd E(dgar) 1918- 104
Ohlinger, Gustavus 1877-1972 Obituary ..37-40R
Ohlsen, Merle M(arvel) 1914- CANR-15
Earlier sketch in CA 37-40R
Ohlsson, Ib 1935- SATA-7
Ohman, Jack 1960- 110
Brief entry 108
Ohmann, Richard (Malin) 1931- 15-16R
Ohmer, Merlin M(aurice) 1923- 57-60
Ohon
See Barba, Harry
Ohsberg, H(arry) Oliver 1926- 114
Ohtomo, Yasuo 1946- SATA-37
Oinas, Felix J(ohannes) 1911- CANR-13
Earlier sketch in CA 33-36R
Ojany, Francis Frederick 1935- 77-80
Ojo, G. J. Afolabi 1930- 25-28R
Okamoto, Shumpei 1932- 29-32R
Okara, Gabriel Imomotimi Gbaingbain
1921- 105
Okasha, Elisabeth 1942- 45-48
Oke, Janette 1935- 111
O'Keefe, Bernard J(oseph) 1919- 120
O'Keefe, Daniel Lawrence 1928-
Brief entry 116
O'Keefe, M(aurice) Timothy 1943- 77-80

O'Keefe, Patrick E.
See Grace, John Patrick
O'Keefe, Paul 1900(?)-1976 Obituary ... 65-68
O'Keefe, Richard R(obert) 1934- ... 57-60
O'Keefe, Sister Maureen 1917- ... 5-6R
O'Keeffe, Georgia 1887-1986 ... 110
Obituary ... 118
O'Keeffe, Laurence 1931- ... 122
Okeke, Uchefuna 1933- ... 97-100
O'Kelley, Mattie Lou 1908- ... 116
See also SATA 36
O'Kelly, Charlotte G. 1946- ... 111
O'Kelly, Elizabeth 1915- ... CANR-20
Earlier sketch in CA 103
Oken, Alan C(harles) 1944- ... 45-48
O'Key
See Radwanski, Pierre A(rthur)
Okigbo, Christopher (Ifenayichukwu)
1932-1967 ... 77-80
See also CLC 25
Okigbo, P(ius) N(wabufo) C. 1924- ... 19-20R
Okihiro, Gary Y(ukio) 1945- ... 120
Okimoto, Jean Davies 1942- ... CANR-16
Earlier sketch in CA 97-100
See also SATA 34
Okin, Susan Moller 1946- ... 93-96
Oklahoma Peddler
See Gilles, Albert S(imeon), Sr.
Okner, Benjamin A. 1936- ... 21-22R
Okonjo, Chukuka 1928- ... 29-32R
Okpaku, Joseph (Ohiomogben) 1943- ... 29-32R
Okpewho, Isidore 1941- ... CANR-3
Earlier sketch in CA 49-52
Okrent, Daniel 1948- ... CANR-22
Earlier sketch in CA 105
Oksenberg, Michel Charles 1938- ... 111
Oksenholt, Svein
See Oeksenholt, Svein
Okubo, Genji 1915- ... 25-28R
Okudzhava, Bulat Shalvovich 1924-
Brief entry ... 116
Okun, Arthur M. 1928-1980 ... CANR-11
Obituary ... 97-100
Earlier sketch in CA 61-64
Okun, Lawrence E(ugene) 1929- ... 101
Olafson, Frederick A(rlan) 1924- ... 17-18R
Olan, Ben 1923- ... 111
Olan, Levi Arthur 1903- ... 109
O'Laoghaire, Liam
See O'Leary, Liam
Olbricht, Thomas H. 1929- ... 33-36R
Olby, Robert C(ecil) 1933- ... 23-24R
Olcheski, Bill 1925- ... CANR-8
Earlier sketch in CA 61-64
Olcott, Anthony 1950- ... 106
Olcott, Frances Jenkins 1872(?)-1963 ... SATA-19
Olcott, Henry Steel 1832-1907 Brief entry ... 118
Olcott, Jack 1932- ... 53-56
Old, Bruce S(cott) 1913- ... CANR-17
Earlier sketch in CA 4R
Old Boy
See Hughes, Thomas
Oldenburg, Claes (Thure) 1929- ... 121
Brief entry ... 117
Oldenburg, E(gbert) William 1936-1974 ... 105
See also SATA 35
Older, Fremont 1856-1935 ... DLB-25
Older, Julia 1941- ... CANR-14
Earlier sketch in CA 73-76
Olderman, Murray 1922- ... CANR-1
Earlier sketch in CA 45-48
Olderman, Raymond M. 1937- ... 41-44R
Old Fag
See Bell, Robert S(tanley) W(arren)
Oldfeld, Peter
See Bartlett, Vernon
Oldfield, A(rthur) Barney 1909- ... 105
Oldfield, James E(dmund) 1921- ... 89-92
Oldfield, R(ichard) C(harles) 1909-1972 ... CAP-2
Earlier sketch in CA 25-28
Oldfield, Ruth L(atzer) 1922- ... 15-16R
Oldham, Frank 1903- ... 9-10R
Oldham, Mary 1944- ... 109
Oldham, Perry (Donald) 1943- ... 107
Oldham, W(illiam) Dale 1903- ... 11-12R
Oldman, Oliver 1920- ... 33-36R
Oldroyd, Harold 1913- ... 77-80
Olds, Elizabeth 1896- ... 5-6R
See also SATA 3
Olds, Elizabeth Fagg 1913- ... 123
Olds, Helen Diehl 1895-1981 ... CANR-3
Obituary ... 103
Earlier sketch in CA 4R
See also SATA 9, 25
Olds, Sally Wendkos 1933- ... CANR-18
Earlier sketches in CA 45-48, CANR-1
Olds, Sharon 1942- ... CANR-18
Earlier sketch in CA 101
See also CLC 32, 39
Oldsey, Bernard 1923- ... CANR-7
Earlier sketch in CA 7-8R
Oldson, William O(rville) 1940- ... 53-56
Old Stager
See Gore, John Francis
Oldstyle, Jonathan
See Irving, Washington
Olea, Maria Florencia Varas 1938- ... 105
O'Leary, Brian (Todd) 1940- ... CANR-20
Earlier sketch in CA 33-36R
See also SATA 6
O'Leary, Chester F.
See Kuehnelt-Leddihn, Erik (Maria) Ritter von
O'Leary, Frank(lin) J. 1922- ... 7-8R
O'Leary, K. Daniel 1940- ... 41-44R
O'Leary, Liam 1910- ... 109
O'Leary, Thomas V(incent) 1910- ... 5-6R
Oleck, Howard L(eoner) 1911- ... CANR-4
Earlier sketch in CA 9-10R
Oleksy, Walter 1930- ... CANR-17
Earlier sketches in CA 45-48, CANR-1
Olen, Jeffrey 1946- ... 112
Olendorf, William 1924- ... 117
Olesha, Yuri (Karlovich) 1899-1960 ... 85-88
See also CLC 8
Oleszek, Walter J(oseph) 1941- ... 120
O'Levenson, Jordan
See Levenson, Jordan
Oleyar, Rita Balkey 1922- ... 111
Olford, Stephen F(rederick) 1918- ... 17-18R
Olfson, Lewy 1937- ... 93-96
Olgyay, Victor 1910-1970 ... 7-8R
Obituary ... 103
Olien, Diana Davids 1943- ... 113
Olien, Michael D(avid) 1937- ... CANR-3
Earlier sketch in CA 49-52
Olien, Roger M. 1938- ... 113
Olin, Spencer C(arl), Jr. 1937- ... 93-96
Olin, William 1929- ... 106
Olins, Wally 1930- ... 120
Oliphant, J(ames) Orin 1894-1979
Obituary ... 85-88
Oliphant, Laurence 1829(?)-1888 ... DLB-18
Oliphant, Margaret 1828-1897 ... DLB-18
Oliphant, Patrick (Bruce) 1935- ... 101
Oliphant, Robert (Thompson) 1924- ... 102
Oliva, L(awrence) Jay 1933- ... 13-14R
Oliva, Leo E. 1937- ... CANR-24
Earlier sketches in CA 21-22R, CANR-9
Olivares, Julian (Jr.) 1940- ... 118
Oliveira, Antonio Ramos
See Ramos-Oliveira, Antonio
Oliveira Salazar, Antonio de
See Salazar, Antonio de Oliveira
Oliven, John F. 1915(?)-1975 Obituary ... 53-56
Oliver, A. Richard 1912- ... 15-16R
Oliver, Amy Roberta
See Ruck, Amy Roberta
Oliver, Andrew 1906-1981 ... 109
Obituary ... 105
Oliver, Anthony 1923- ... CANR-20
Earlier sketch in CA 103
Oliver, Bernard John Jr. 1918-1966 ... 7-8R
Oliver, Burton
See Burt, Olive Woolley
Oliver, Carl Russell 1941- ... 106
Oliver, Chad 1928- ... DLB-8
Oliver, Chad
See Oliver, Symmes C(hadwick)
Oliver, Covey T(homas) 1913- ... 111
Oliver, Dawn 1942- ... 123
Oliver, Douglas Llewellyn 1913- ... 97-100
Oliver, E(dward) J(ames) 1911- ... 11-12R
Oliver, Egbert S(amuel) 1902- ... 103
Oliver, G(uillaume) Raymond 1909- ... CAP-2
Earlier sketch in CA 25-28
Oliver, H(arold) J(ames) 1916-1982
Obituary ... 111
Oliver, Herman 1885- ... CAP-1
Earlier sketch in CA 11-12
Oliver, James A(rthur) 1914-1981
Obituary ... 106
Oliver, James Henry 1905- ... CANR-17
Earlier sketch in CA 1R
Oliver, Jane
See Rees, Helen Christina Easson (Evans)
Oliver, John Edward 1933- ... 33-36R
See also SATA 21
Oliver, Kenneth A(rthur) 1912- ... 53-56
Oliver, Mark
See Tyler-Whittle, Michael Sidney
Oliver, Mary 1935- ... CANR-9
Earlier sketch in CA 21-22R
See also DLB 5
See also CLC 19, 34
Oliver, Mary Hempstone 1885(?)-1973
Obituary ... 41-44R
Oliver, Paul (Hereford) 1927- ... CANR-1
Earlier sketch in CA 4R
Oliver, R(ichard) A(lexander) C(avaye)
1904- ... CAP-1
Earlier sketch in CA 11-12
Oliver, Raymond (Davies) 1936- ... 109
Oliver, Revilo P(endleton) 1910- ... 121
Oliver, Richard (Bruce) 1942-1985 ... 116
Oliver, Robert (Shelton) 1934- ... 105
Oliver, Robert T(arbell) 1909- ... CANR-19
Earlier sketches in CA 7-8R, CANR-4
Oliver, Roland Anthony 1923- ... CANR-12
Earlier sketch in CA 73-76
Oliver, Rupert
See Matthews, Rupert O(liver)
Oliver, Smith Hempstone 1912- ... 25-28R
Oliver, Symmes C(hadwick) 1928- ... 113
Oliver, W. Andrew 1941- ... 37-40R
Oliver, William Irvin 1926- ... 19-20R
Olivera, Otto 1919- ... 49-52
Oliveri, Mario 1944- ... 107
Olivier, Charles P(ollard) 1884-1975
Obituary ... 61-64
Olivier, Laurence (Kerr) 1907- Brief entry ... 111
See also CLC 20
Olivier, Robert L(ouis) 1903- ... 93-96
Olivova, Vera 1926- ... 81-84
Olkowski, Helga 1931- ... 85-88
Olkowski, William 1941- ... 97-100
Ollard, Richard (Laurence) 1923- ... CANR-20
Earlier sketch in CA 93-96
Oller, John W(illiam), Jr. 1943- ... CANR-5
Earlier sketch in CA 53-56
Ollerenshaw, Kathleen (Mary) 1912-
Brief entry ... 107
Ollestad, Norman (Tennyson) 1935- ... 21-22R
Olli, John B. 1893(?)-1984 Obituary ... 112
Ollier, Cliff(ord) David 1931- ... 61-64
Ollif, Lorna (Anne) 1918- ... 93-96
Olliff, Donathan C(arnes) 1933- ... 115
Ollman, Bertell 1935- ... CANR-16
Earlier sketch in CA 85-88
Olm, Kenneth W(illiam) 1924- ... 21-22R
Olmstead, Alan H. 1907(?)-1980 Obituary ... 101
Olmstead, Clifton Earl 1926-1962 ... 2R
Olmsted, Charlotte
See Kursh, Charlotte Olmsted
Olmsted, Frederick Law 1822-1903
Brief entry ... 120
Olmsted, John Charles 1942- ... 93-96
Olmsted, Lorena Ann 1890- ... 29-32R
See also SATA 13
Olmsted, Robert W(alsh) 1936- ... 41-44R
Olmsted, Sterling P(itkin) 1915- ... 25-28R
Olney, James 1933- ... 77-80
Olney, Ross R. 1929- ... CANR-7
Earlier sketch in CA 15-16R
See also SATA 13
Olorunsola, Victor A. 1939- ... CANR-7
Earlier sketch in CA 57-60
O'Loughlin, Carleen ... CAP-2
Earlier sketch in CA 25-28
Olscamp, Paul James 1937- ... 104
Olschewski, Alfred 1920- ... 41-44R
See also SATA 7
Olschki, G. Cesare 1890-1971 Obituary ... 104
Olsen, Alfa-Betty 1947- ... 103
Olsen, Alfred Johannes, Jr. 1884-1956
Brief entry ... 113
Olsen, Bob
See Olsen, Alfred Johannes, Jr.
Olsen, Donald J(ames) 1929- ... 15-16R
Olsen, Edward G(ustave) 1908- ... CANR-11
Earlier sketches in CA 9-10, CAP-1
Olsen, Hans Christian, Jr. 1929-
Brief entry ... 106
Olsen, Ib Spang 1921- ... CANR-3
Earlier sketch in CA 49-52
See also SATA 6
Olsen, Jack
See Olsen, John Edward
Olsen, James 1933- ... 49-52
Olsen, John Edward 1925- ... CANR-9
Earlier sketch in CA 19-20R
Olsen, Larry Dean 1939- ... 69-72
Olsen, Marvin E(lliott) 1936- ... 29-32R
Olsen, Otto H(arald) 1925- ... 33-36R
Olsen, R(obert) Arthur 1910- ... CAP-2
Earlier sketch in CA 23-24
Olsen, Richard E(llison) 1941- ... 81-84
Olsen, T(heodore) V(ictor) 1932- ... CANR-18
Earlier sketches in CA 2R, CANR-3
Olsen, Tillie 1913- ... CANR-1
Earlier sketch in CA 4R
See also DLB 28
See also DLBY 80
See also CLC 4, 13
Olsen, V(iggo) Norskov 1916- ... 53-56
Olsen, Violet 1922- ... 113
Olshaker, Bennett 1921- Brief entry ... 108
Olshaker, Mark 1951- ... 73-76
Olshaker, Thelma ... 114
Olshan, Neal H(ugh) 1947- ... 119
Olshen, Barry N(eil) 1944- ... 89-92
Olshewsky, Thomas M(ack) 1934- ... 37-40R
Olson, Alan M(elvin) 1939- ... CANR-8
Earlier sketch in CA 61-64
Olson, Alison Gilbert 1931- Brief entry ... 109
Olson, Arnold O(rville) 1917- ... 45-48
Olson, Bernhard Emanuel 1910-1975 ... CANR-24
Obituary ... 61-64
Earlier sketch in CA 45-48
Olson, Carl 1941- ... 114
Olson, Charles (John) 1910-1970 ... CAP-1
Obituary ... 25-28R
Earlier sketch in CA 15-16
See also CABS 2
See also DLB 5, 16
See also CLC 1, 2, 5, 6, 9, 11, 29
Olson, Clair C(olby) 1901-1972 ... 41-44R
Olson, (Carl Bernard) David 1904- ... 61-64
Olson, David F. 1938- ... 49-52
Olson, David John 1941- ... 53-56
Olson, David R(ichard) 1935- ... 33-36R
Olson, Donald 1938- ... 65-68
Olson, Elder (James) 1909- ... CANR-6
Earlier sketch in CA 7-8R
See also DLB 48, 63
Olson, Eric 1944- ... 53-56
Olson, Everett C. 1910- ... 53-56
Olson, Gene 1922- ... 106
See also SATA 32
Olson, Harry E(dwin), Jr. 1932- ... 61-64
Olson, Harry F(erdinand) 1901- ... 37-40R
Olson, Harvey S(tuart) 1908-1985 ... CANR-1
Obituary ... 118
Earlier sketch in CA 4R
Olson, Helen Kronberg ... CANR-12
Earlier sketch in CA 29-32R
See also SATA 48
Olson, Herbert Waldo 1927- ... 1R
Olson, James C(lifton) 1917- ... 37-40R
Olson, James R(obert) 1938- ... 49-52
Olson, Jane Virginia 1916- ... 89-92
Olson, Keith W(aldemar) 1931- ... 49-52
Olson, Ken(neth John) 1930- ... 97-100
Olson, Lawrence Alexander 1918-
Brief entry ... 110
Olson, Lois Ellen 1941- ... 105
Olson, Mancur, Jr. 1932- ... 13-14R
Olson, McKinley C(lar) 1931- ... 110
Olson, Merle Theodore
See Olson, Toby
Olson, Mildred Thompson 1922- ... 23-24R
Olson, Paul R(ichard) 1925- ... 21-22R
Olson, Philip G(ilbert) 1934- ... 11-12R
Olson, Richard G(eorge) 1940- ... CANR-17
Earlier sketch in CA 89-92
Olson, Richard Paul 1934- ... CANR-24
Earlier sketches in CA 61-64, CANR-8
Olson, Robert G(oodwin) 1924- ... 29-32R
Olson, Sidney 1908- ... CAP-1
Earlier sketch in CA 11-12
Olson, Sigurd F(erdinand) 1899-1982 ... CANR-1
Obituary ... 105
Earlier sketch in CA 3R
Olson, Stanley 1948- ... 89-92
Olson, Ted
See Olson, Theodore B.
Olson, Theodore B. 1899- ... 49-52
Olson, Toby 1937- ... CANR-9
Earlier sketch in CA 65-68
See also CLC 28
Olson, Willard Clifford 1899-1978
Obituary ... 111
Olsson, Axel Adolf 1889-1977 Obituary ... 73-76
Olsson, Karl A(rthur) 1913- ... CANR-4
Earlier sketch in CA 7-8R
Olsson, Nils 1909- ... 73-76
Olstad, Charles (Frederick) 1932- ... 17-18R
Olthuis, James H(erman) 1938- ... 61-64
Oltmans, Willem L(eonard) 1925- ... 57-60
Olton, Charles S(haw) 1938- Brief entry ... 108
Olton, Roy 1922- ... 103
Olugebefola, Ademole 1941- ... SATA-15
Olyesha, Yuri
See Olesha, Yuri (Karlovich)
Olzendam, Roderic Marble 1892-1986
Obituary ... 121
O'Mahoney, Rich
See Warner-Crozetti, R(uth G.)
O'Mahony, Patrick 1911- ... 15-16R
O'Malley, Brian (Jack Morgan)
1918(?)-1980 Obituary ... 101
O'Malley, Charles Donald 1907-1970
Obituary ... 109
O'Malley, Frank
See O'Rourke, Frank
O'Malley, J(ohn) Steven 1942- ... 53-56
O'Malley, John W(illiam) 1927-
Brief entry ... 114
O'Malley, Joseph James 1930- ... 37-40R
O'Malley, Kevin
See Hossent, Harry
O'Malley, Mary Brief entry ... 110
O'Malley, Mary Dolling (Sanders)
1889-1974 ... 65-68
O'Malley, Michael (Anthony) ... 4R
O'Malley, Patrick
See O'Rourke, Frank
O'Malley, Richard K(ilroy) 1911- ... 97-100
O'Malley, Suzanne 1951- ... 110
O'Malley, William J(ohn) 1931- ... CANR-12
Earlier sketch in CA 73-76
Oman, Carola (Mary Anima) 1897-1978 ... CANR-4
Earlier sketch in CA 7-8R
See also SATA 35
Oman, Charles Chichele 1901-1982 ... 103
Obituary ... 105
Omansky, Dorothy Linder 1905(?)-1977
Obituary ... 73-76
O Maolain, Ciaran 1958- ... 123
O'Maonaigh, Cainneach
See Mooney, Canice (Albert James)
Omari, T(hompson) Peter 1930- ... 29-32R
Omarr, Sydney Brief entry ... 116
O'Meara, John J. 1915- ... CANR-3
Earlier sketch in CA 4R
O'Meara, Patrick 1938- ... 113
O'Meara, Thomas F(ranklin) 1935- ... 110
O'Meara, Walter (Andrew) 1897- ... 13-14R
Omer, Garth St.
See St. Omer, Garth
Ommanney, F(rancis) D(ownes)
1903-1980 ... CANR-7
Obituary ... 101
Earlier sketch in CA 13-14R
See also SATA 23
O'More, Peggy
See Blocklinger, Peggy O'More
O'Morrison, Kevin ... CANR-9
Earlier sketch in CA 53-56
O Mude
See Gorey, Edward (St. John)
Onacewicz, Wlodzimierz 1893(?)-1986
Obituary ... 120
Onadipe, (Nathaniel) Kola(wole) 1922- ... 101
O'Nair, Mairi
See Evans, Constance May
Onate, Andres David 1940- Brief entry ... 112
Ondaatje, Christopher 1933- ... 49-52
Ondaatje, Michael 1943- ... 77-80
See also DLB 60
See also CLC 14, 29
O'Neal, Bill
See O'Neal, John W(illiam)
O'Neal, Charles E. 1904- ... CAP-2
Earlier sketch in CA 19-20
O'Neal, Cothburn M(adison) 1907- ... 2R
Oneal, Elizabeth 1934- ... 106
See also SATA 30
O'Neal, Forest Hodge 1917- ... 7-8R
O'Neal, Glenn (Franklin) 1919- ... 49-52
O'Neal, John W(illiam) 1942- ... 89-92
O'Neal, William B(ainter) 1907- ... 73-76
Oneal, Zibby
See Oneal, Elizabeth
See also CLC 30
See also CLR 13
O'Neil, Daniel J. 1936- ... 89-92

O'Neil, Dennis 1939- 97-100
O'Neil, Eric
See Barnum, W(illiam) Paul
O'Neil, Isabel MacDonald 1908(?)-1981
Obituary 105
O'Neil, Robert M(archant) 1934- 106
O'Neil, Terry 1949- 61-64
O'Neil, W(illiam) M(atthew) 1912- 113
O'Neil, Will(iam Daniel III) 1938- 101
O'Neill, Archie
See Henaghan, Jim
O'Neill, Barbara Powell 1929- 19-20R
O'Neill, Carlota 1918- 101
O'Neill, Carlotta Monterey 1888-1970
Obituary 29-32R
O'Neill, Charles Edwards 1927- CANR-9
Earlier sketch in CA 23-24R
O'Neill, Cherry Boone 1954- 112
O'Neill, Daniel Joseph 1905- Brief entry 106
O'Neill, David P(atrick) 1918- 19-20R
O'Neill, Dennis (Bernard) 1947- 114
O'Neill, E. Bard 1941- 85-88
O'Neill, Egan
See Linington, Elizabeth
O'Neill, Eugene (Gladstone) 1888-1953
Brief entry 110
See also DLB 7
See also TCLC 1, 6, 27
See also AITN 1
O'Neill, Eugene 1922- 77-80
O'Neill, Frank (Quale) 1943- 120
O'Neill, Frank F. 1926(?)-1983 Obituary 109
O'Neill, George 1921(?)-1980 Obituary 102
See also AITN 1
O'Neill, Gerard (Michael) 1942- 69-72
O'Neill, Gerard K(itchen) 1927- CANR-21
Earlier sketch in CA 93-96
O'Neill, James E(dward) 1929-1987 117
Obituary 121
O'Neill, John 1933- 53-56
O'Neill, John Joseph 1920- 23-24R
O'Neill, Joseph Harry 1915- 13-14R
O'Neill, Judith (Beatrice) 1930- 109
See also SATA 34
O'Neill, Mary L(e Duc) 1908- CANR-4
Earlier sketch in CA 5-6R
See also SATA 2
O'Neill, Michael J. 104
O'Neill, Michael J. 1913- 15-16R
O'Neill, Michael J(ames) 1922- 112
O'Neill, Michael J. 1922- Brief entry 108
O'Neill, Nena AITN-1
O'Neill, Olivia
See Barstow, Phyllida
O'Neill, Patrick Geoffrey 1924- 21-22R
O'Neill, Paul 1928- 107
O'Neill, Reginald F. 1915- 2R
O'Neill, Richard W(inslow) 1925-
Brief entry 107
O'Neill, Robert J(ohn) 1936- 25-28R
O'Neill, Shane
See O'Neill, William
O'Neill, Terence Marne 1914- 108
O'Neill, Tim 1918- 2R
O'Neill, Timothy P. 1941- 85-88
O'Neill, William 1927- 37-40R
O'Neill, William F. 1931- 29-32R
O'Neill, William L. 1935- CANR-12
Earlier sketch in CA 21-22R
O'Neill Of The Maine, Baron of Ahoghill
See O'Neill, Terence Marne
O'Nell, Carl William 1925- 73-76
Onetti, Juan Carlos 1909- 85-88
See also CLC 7, 10
Ong, Walter J(ackson) 1912- CANR-21
Earlier sketches in CA 2R, CANR-4
Ongaro, Alberto 1925- 25-28R
O'Niell, C. M.
See Wilkes-Hunter, R(ichard)
Onions, Charles Talbut 1873-1965
Obituary 107
Onley, David C(harles) 1950- 112
Onlooker
See Grange, Cyril
Ono, Chiyo 1941- CANR-12
Earlier sketch in CA 29-32R
Onoda, Hiroo 1922(?)- Brief entry 108
O'Nolan, Brian
See O Nuallain, Brian
Onopa, Robert 1943- 112
Onorato, Richard James 1933- Brief entry .. 108
Onslow, Annette Rosemary MacArthur
See MacArthur-Onslow, Annette
Rosemary
Onslow, John 1906-1985 Obituary 118
See also SATA 47
Onstott, Kyle 1887- 7-8R
O Nuallain, Brian 1911-1966 .... CAP-2
Obituary 25-28R
Earlier sketch in CA 21-22
Ooi Jin-Bee 1931- 73-76
Ooiman, Jo Ann
See Robinson, Jo Ann Ooiman
Oost, Stewart Irvin 1921- 29-32R
Oosterman, Gordon 1927- 49-52
Oosterwal, Gottfried 1930- 93-96
Oosthuizen, Gerhardus C(ornelis) 1922- .. 29-32R
Oparin, Aleksandr (Ivanovich) 1894-1980
Obituary 108
Opdahl, Keith Michael 1934- 61-64
Opdahl, Richard D(ean) 1924- 21-22R
Opgenoorth, Winfried 1939- SATA-50
Ophuls, Max 1902-1957 Brief entry 113
Opie, Iona 1923- 61-64
See also SATA 3
Opie, John 1934- 29-32R
Opie, Peter (Mason) 1918-1982 .... CANR-2
Obituary 106
Earlier sketch in CA 7-8R
See also SATA 3, 28
Opie, Redvers 1900-1984 Obituary 112
Opik, E.
See Oepik, Ernst Julius
Opik, Ernst
See Oepik, Ernst Julius
Opik, Ernst J.
See Oepik, Ernst Julius
Opik, Ernst Julius
See Oepik, Ernst Julius
Opitz, Edmund A. 1914- 29-32R
Opland, Jeff 1943- 106
Opler, Marvin K(aufmann) 1914- 23-24R
Opler, Morris E(dward) 1907- 45-48
Opotowsky, Stan 1923- CANR-1
Earlier sketch in CA 1R
Oppen, George 1908-1984 .... CANR-8
Obituary 113
Earlier sketch in CA 15-16R
See also DLB 5
See also CLC 7, 13, 34
Oppen, Mary 1908- 119
Oppenheim, A(dolph) Leo 1904-1974
Obituary 49-52
Oppenheim, E(dward) Phillips 1866-1946
Brief entry 111
Oppenheim, Felix E(rrera) 1913- 2R
Oppenheim, Frank Mathias 1925- 116
Oppenheim, Irene 1928- 77-80
Oppenheim, James 1882-1932 .... DLB-28
Oppenheim, Janet 1948- 117
Oppenheim, Joanne 1934- CANR-9
Earlier sketch in CA 23-24R
See also SATA 5
Oppenheim, Paul 1885(?)-1977 Obituary .. 69-72
Oppenheim, S(aul) Chesterfield 1897-1988
Obituary 124
Oppenheim, Shulamith (Levey) 1930- 73-76
Oppenheimer, Evelyn 1907- CANR-3
Earlier sketch in CA 3R
Oppenheimer, George 1900-1977 .... 15-16R
Obituary 73-76
Oppenheimer, Harold L. 1919- 17-18R
Oppenheimer, J(ulius) Robert 1904-1967 ... 103
Oppenheimer, Joan L(etson) 1925- CANR-17
Earlier sketch in CA 37-40R
See also SATA 28
Oppenheimer, Joe A(llan) 1941- 111
Oppenheimer, Joel (Lester) 1930- CANR-21
Earlier sketches in CA 9-10R, CANR-4
See also DLB 5
Oppenheimer, Martin 1930- 29-32R
Oppenheimer, Max, Jr. 1917- 17-18R
Oppenheimer, Paul 1939- 21-22R
Oppenheimer, Samuel P(hilip) 1903- 33-36R
Opper, F.
See Opper, Frederick (Burr)
Opper, Frederick (Burr) 1857-1937
Brief entry 118
See also AITN 1
Opper, Jacob 1935- 49-52
Opperby, Preben 1924- 110
Oppitz, Rene 1905(?)-1976 Obituary 65-68
Oppong, Christine 1940- CANR-7
Earlier sketch in CA 57-60
Optic, Oliver
See Adams, William Taylor
and Stratemeyer, Edward L.
Opton, Edward M., Jr. 1936- CANR-11
Earlier sketch in CA 21-22R
Opuls, Max
See Ophuls, Max
O'Quill, Scarlett
See Mossman, Dow
O'Quinn, Garland 1935- 23-24R
O'Quinn, Hazel Hedick 37-40R
Orage, A(lfred) R(ichard) 1873-1934
Brief entry 122
Oraison, Marc 1914- 85-88
Oram, Hiawyn 1946- 106
Oram, Malcolm 1944(?)-1976 Obituary 104
O'Ramus, Seamus
See O'Neill, William
O'Rand, Angela M(etropulos) 1945- 104
Oras, Ants 1900- CAP-1
Earlier sketch in CA 15-16
Orbaan, Albert F. CANR-8
Earlier sketch in CA 5-6R
Orbach, Ruth Gary 1941- 65-68
See also SATA 21
Orbach, Susie 1946- CANR-19
Earlier sketch in CA 85-88
Orbach, William W(olf) 1946- 73-76
Orben, Robert 1927- 81-84
Orbis, Victor
See Powell-Smith, Vincent (Walter
Francis)
Orcutt, Georgia 1949- 112
Orczy, Emma Magdalena Rosalia Maria
Josefa Barbara 1865-1947 Brief entry 104
See also SATA 40
Orczy, Emmuska
See Orczy, Emma Magdalena Rosalia
Maria Josefa Barbara
See also SATA 40
Ord, John E. 1917- 81-84
Orde, Lewis 1943- 109
Ord-Hume, Arthur W. J. G. 101
Ordish, George 1908- CANR-9
Earlier sketch in CA 61-64
Ordway, Frederick I(ra) III 1927- CANR-20
Earlier sketches in CA 7-8R, CANR-5
Ordway, Roger
See Pauker, John
Ordway, Sally 1939- 57-60
O'Regan, Richard Arthur 1919- 73-76
O'Reilly, Don 1913- 111
O'Reilly, Jane 1936- 73-76
O'Reilly, John (Thomas) 1945- 29-32R
O'Reilly, Montagu
See Andrews, Wayne
O'Reilly, Robert P. 1936- 29-32R
O'Reilly, Timothy 1954- CANR-23
Earlier sketch in CA 106
Orel, Harold 1926- CANR-19
Earlier sketches in CA 7-8R, CANR-3
O'Relley, Z(oltan) Edward 1940- 119
Orem, R(eginald) C(alvert) 1931- 17-18R
Oren, Uri 1931- 65-68
Orengo, Charles 1913(?)-1974 Obituary 104
Orenstein, Denise Gosliner 1950- 110
Orenstein, Frank (Everett) 1919- 111
Orenstein, Gloria Feman 1938- 65-68
Orenstein, Henry 1924- 15-16R
Orent, Norman B. 1920- 17-18R
Oreshnik, A. F.
See Nussbaum, Al(bert F.)
Oresick, Peter (Michael) 1955- CANR-13
Earlier sketch in CA 73-76
Orest
See Bedrij, Orest (John)
Orewa, George Oka 1928- 7-8R
Orff, Carl 1895-1982 Obituary 106
Orfield, Olivia 1922- 103
Orga, Ates 1944- 93-96
Organ, John 1925- CANR-7
Earlier sketch in CA 7-8R
Organ, Troy Wilson 1912- 37-40R
Organski, A(bramo) F(imo) K(enneth)
1923- 103
Orgel, Doris 1929- CANR-2
Earlier sketch in CA 45-48
See also SATA 7
See also AITN 1
Orgel, Joseph Randolph 1902-1987 .... CAP-1
Obituary 123
Earlier sketch in CA 11-12
Orgel, Stephen (Kitay) 1933- CANR-14
Earlier sketch in CA 73-76
Orgill, Douglas 1922- 81-84
Orgill, Michael (Thomas) 1946- 61-64
Orians, George H(arrison) 1900- 49-52
Orians, Gordon H(owell) 1932- 45-48
Oriard, Michael (Vincent) 1948- 110
Origo, Iris (Margaret Cutting) 1902- 105
O'Riley, Warren
See Richardson, Gladwell
Oring, Elliott 1945- 111
Oriolo, Joe
See Oriolo, Joseph D.
Oriolo, Joseph D. 1913-1985 Obituary 118
See also SATA 46
Orion
See Naylor, John
O'Riordan, Robert (Garrett) 1943- 119
Orjuela, Hector H(ugo) 1930- CANR-2
Earlier sketch in CA 45-48
Orkeny, Istvan 1912-1979 103
Obituary 89-92
Orkin, Harvey 1918(?)-1975 Obituary 61-64
Orkin, Ruth 1921-1985 119
Obituary 114
Orlans, Harold 1921- CANR-15
Earlier sketch in CA 33-36R
Orleans, Ilo 1897-1962 .... CANR-15
Earlier sketch in CA 2R
See also SATA 10
Orleans, Leo A(nton) 1924- CANR-15
Earlier sketch in CA 41-44R
Orledge, Robert (Nicholas) 1948- 113
Orlen, Steve 1942- 101
Orlev, Uri 1931- 101
Orlich, Donald C(harles) 1931- CANR-22
Earlier sketches in CA 15-16R, CANR-7
Orlick, Terrance D(ouglas) 1945- CANR-21
Earlier sketches in CA 57-60, CANR-6
Orlick, Terry
See Orlick, Terrance D(ouglas)
Orlicky, Joseph A. 1922- 25-28R
Orlier, Blaise
See Sylvestre, (Joseph Jean) Guy
Orlinsky, Harry M(eyer) 1908- 85-88
Orlob, Helen Seaburg 1908- 7-8R
Orlock, Carol (Ellen) 1947- 122
Orloff, Ed(gar Sam) 1923-1983 69-72
Obituary 110
Orloff, Max
See Crowcroft, Peter
Orlofsky, Myron 1928(?)-1976 Obituary ... 69-72
Orloski, Richard J(ohn) 1947- 97-100
Orlova, R.
See Orlova-Kopelev, Raissa (Davydovna)
Orlova, R. D.
See Orlova-Kopelev, Raissa (Davydovna)
Orlova, Raisa
See Orlova-Kopelev, Raissa (Davydovna)
Orlova-Kopelev, Raissa (Davydovna)
1918- 123
Orlovitz, Gil 1918-1973 77-80
Obituary 45-48
See also DLB 2, 5
See also CLC 22
Orlovsky, Peter 1933- CANR-9
Earlier sketch in CA 15-16R
See also DLB 16
Orlow, Dietrich 1937- 65-68
Ormai, Stella SATA-48
Orme, Antony R(onald) 1936- 73-76
Ormerod, Jan(ette Louise) 1946- 113
See also SATA 44
Ormerod, Roger 1920- CANR-15
Earlier sketch in CA 77-80
Ormes, Jackie
See Ormes, Zelda J.
Ormes, Robert M. 1904- CAP-1
Earlier sketch in CA 11-12
Ormes, Robert Verner 1921-1984
Obituary 112
Ormes, Zelda J. 1914-1986 Obituary 118
See also SATA 47
Ormesson, Jean (Bruno Waldemar
Francois-de-Paule Lefevre) d'
See d'Ormesson, Jean (Bruno Waldemar
Francois-de-Paule Lefevre)
Ormesson, Wladimir d' 1888-1973
Obituary 45-48
Ormiston, Roberta
See Fletcher, Adele (Whitely)
Ormond, (Willard) Clyde 1906-1985 .... 9-10R
Obituary 115
Ormond, Frederic
See Dey, Frederic (Merrill) Van
Rensselaer
Ormond, John 1923- 65-68
See also DLB 27
Ormond, Leonee (Jasper) 1940- 85-88
Ormond, Richard (Louis) 1939- CANR-15
Earlier sketch in CA 41-44R
Ormondroyd, Edward 1925- 73-76
See also SATA 14
Ormont, Louis Robert 1918- 13-14R
Ormrod, Richard (James) 1946- 119
Ormsbee, David
See Longstreet, Stephen
Ormsby, Frank 1947- CANR-23
Earlier sketch in CA 107
Ormsby, Virginia H(aire) 11-12R
See also SATA 11
Ormsby, William (George) 1921- 73-76
Orna, Mary Virginia 1934- 29-32R
Ornati, Oscar A(braham) 1922- CANR-14
Earlier sketch in CA 37-40R
Ornis
See Winchester, Clarence
Ornitz, Samuel (Badisch) 1890-1957
Brief entry 117
See also DLB 28, 44
Ornstein, Allan C(harles) 1941- CANR-4
Earlier sketch in CA 53-56
Ornstein, Dolph 1947- 77-80
Ornstein, J. L.
See Ornstein-Galicia, J(acob) L(eonard)
Ornstein, Jack H(ervey) 1938- 103
Ornstein, Norman J(ay) 1948- 93-96
Ornstein, Robert 1925- 2R
Ornstein, Robert E. 1942- 53-56
Ornstein-Galicia, J(acob) L(eonard) 1915- .. 93-96
O'Rourke, Edward William 1917- 112
O'Rourke, Frank 1916- 118
Brief entry 114
O'Rourke, John James Joseph 1926- .. 33-36R
O'Rourke, John T(homas) 1900-1983
Obituary 111
O'Rourke, Lawrence Michael 1938- 69-72
O'Rourke, P. J. 1947- CANR-13
Earlier sketch in CA 77-80
O'Rourke, Terrence James 1932- 41-44R
O'Rourke, Timothy G(erald) 1949- 111
O'Rourke, William (Andrew) 1945- CANR-1
Earlier sketch in CA 45-48
Orpaz, Yitzhak 1923- 101
Orpen, Eve 1926(?)-1978 Obituary 104
Orpen, Neil (Newton D'Arcy) 1913- 120
Orpen, Neil D.
See Orpen, Neil (Newton D'Arcy)
Orr, Bobby
See Orr, Robert Gordon
Orr, Daniel 1933- 29-32R
Orr, David 1929- 33-36R
Orr, Gregory 1947- CANR-22
Earlier sketch in CA 105
Orr, J(ames) Edwin 1912- CANR-4
Earlier sketch in CA 11-12R
Orr, John Boyd 1880-1971 Obituary 113
Orr, Linda 1943- 97-100
Orr, Mary
See Denham, Mary Orr
Orr, Mary E. E. McCombe 1917- 7-8R
Orr, Oliver H(amilton), Jr. 1921- 2R
Orr, Robert Gordon 1948- 112
Orr, Robert R(ichmond) 1930- 25-28R
Orr, Robert T. 1908- 33-36R
Orr, William F(ridell) 1907- 108
Orrell, John (Overton) 1934- CANR-15
Earlier sketch in CA 37-40R
Orris
See Ingelow, Jean
Orrmont, Arthur 1922- CANR-4
Earlier sketch in CA 2R
Orsborn, Carol 1948- 124
Orsini, Gian Napoleone Giordano
1903-19(?) 5-6R
Orsini, Joseph E(mmanuel) 1937- 37-40R
Orso, Kathryn Wickey 1921-1979 57-60
Obituary 85-88
Orsy, Ladislas M. 1921- 25-28R
Orszagh, Laszlo 1907-1984 Obituary 112
Ort, Ana
See Andrews, Arthur (Douglas, Jr.)
Ortega y Gasset, Jose 1883-1955
Brief entry 106
See also TCLC 9
Orth, Charles D., III 1921- 7-8R
Orth, Penelope 1938- 45-48
Orth, Ralph H(arry) 1930- 21-22R
Orth, Richard
See Gardner, Richard (M.)

Orthwine, Rudolf 1900(?)-1970 Obituary ... 104
Ortiz, Alfonso A(lex) 1939- ... 29-32R
Ortiz, Elisabeth Lambert 1928- ... 97-100
Ortiz, Simon J. 1941- ... CLC-45
Ortiz, Victoria 1942- ... 107
Ortiz y Pino, Jose III 1932- ... 112
Ortlund, Anne 1923- ... 106
Ortlund, Raymond C(arl) 1923- ... 114
Ortman, E(lmore) Jan 1884- ... CAP-2
Earlier sketch in CA 25-28
Ortman, Elmer John
See Ortman, E(lmore) Jan
Ortner, Donald John 1938- ... 117
Ortner-Zimmerman, Toni 1941- ... CANR-19
Earlier sketches in CA 53-56, CANR-5
Orton, Alvin E. 1906-1987 Obituary ... 122
Orton, Barry 1949- ... 111
Orton, Harold 1898-1975 Obituary ... 57-60
Orton, Joe
See Orton, John Kingsley
See also DLB 13
See also CLC 4, 13, 43
Orton, John Kingsley 1933-1967 ... 85-88
Orton, Lawrence D(wayne) 1941-
Brief entry ... 118
Orton, Vrest 1897-1986 ... 33-36R
Obituary ... 121
Ortzen, Len
See Ortzen, Leonard Edwin
Ortzen, Leonard Edwin 1912-1979 ... 118
Brief entry ... 114
Orum, Anthony M(endl) 1939- ... 41-44R
Orvell, Miles 1944- ... 41-44R
Orwell, George
See Blair, Eric Hugh
See also DLB 15
See also TCLC 2, 6, 15
Orwell, Sonia 1919(?)-1980 Obituary ... 102
Orwen, (Phillips) Gifford ... 37-40R
Ory, Edward 1886-1973 Obituary ... 41-44R
Ory, Kid
See Ory, Edward
Orzeck, Arthur Z(alman) 1921- ... CANR-1
Earlier sketch in CA 45-48
Osanka, Franklin Mark 1936- ... 5-6R
Osaragi, Jiro
See Nojiri, Kiyohiko
Osbeck, Kenneth W. 1924- ... CANR-19
Earlier sketches in CA 3R, CANR-3
Osbon, B. S. 1827-1912 ... DLB-43
Osborn, Albert D. 1896(?)-1972 Obituary ... 104
Osborn, Alex(ander) F(aickney) 1888-1966
Obituary ... 106
Osborn, Arthur W(alter) 1891- ... 23-24R
Osborn, Barbara M(onroe)
See Henkel, Barbara Osborn
Osborn, Carolyn 1934- ... 93-96
Osborn, Catherine B. 1914- ... 29-32R
Osborn, David (D.) 1923- Brief entry ... 109
Osborn, Eric (Francis) 1922- ... 65-68
Osborn, Frederic J(ames) 1885-1978 ... CANR-5
Earlier sketch in CA 7-8R
Osborn, Frederick (Henry) 1889-1981 ... 25-28R
Obituary ... 102
Osborn, George C(oleman) 1904-1982 . CANR-19
Earlier sketch in CA 25-28R
Osborn, James M(arshall) 1906-1976 ... CAP-2
Obituary ... 69-72
Earlier sketch in CA 25-28
Osborn, John Jay, Jr. 1945- ... CANR-6
Earlier sketch in CA 57-60
Osborn, Lois D(orothy) 1915- ... 116
Osborn, Mary Elizabeth 1898- ... 7-8R
Osborn, Merton B(idwell) 1908- ... 25-28R
Osborn, Paul 1901- ... 112
Brief entry ... 108
Osborn, Percy George 1899(?)-1972
Obituary ... 104
Osborn, Robert (Chesley) 1904- ... 15-16R
Osborn, Robert T(appan) 1926- ... 21-22R
Osborn, Ronald E(dwin) 1917- ... 15-16R
Osborn, Thomas Noel II 1940- ... 114
Osborne, Adam 1939- ... 109
Osborne, (Reginald) Arthur 1906- ... 19-20R
Osborne, Betsy
See Boswell, Barbara (S.)
Osborne, C(harles) H(umfrey) C(aufeild)
1891- ... 7-8R
Osborne, Cecil G. 1904- ... CANR-1
Earlier sketch in CA 45-48
Osborne, Charles 1927- ... CANR-13
Earlier sketch in CA 13-14R
Osborne, Chester G. 1915- ... CANR-9
Earlier sketch in CA 21-22R
See also SATA 11
Osborne, Dan 1948(?)-1983 Obituary ... 110
Osborne, David
See Silverberg, Robert
Osborne, Dorothy (Gladys) Yeo 1917- ... 9-10R
Osborne, Elsie L(etitia) 1924- ... 118
Osborne, Ernest (Glenn) 1903-1963 ... 7-8R
Osborne, G(erald) S(tanley) 1926- ... 23-24R
Osborne, Geoffrey 1930- ... 110
Osborne, George
See Silverberg, Robert
Osborne, George E(dward) 1893- ... CAP-2
Earlier sketch in CA 23-24
Osborne, Harold 1905-1987 ... CANR-6
Obituary ... 122
Earlier sketch in CA 13-14R
Osborne, Harold W(ayne) 1930- ... 57-60
Osborne, Helena
See Moore, (Georgina) Mary (Galbraith)
Osborne, J(ulius) K(enneth) 1941- ... 33-36R
Osborne, John (Franklin) 1907-1981 ... CANR-10
Obituary ... 108
Earlier sketch in CA 61-64
Osborne, John (James) 1929- ... CANR-21
Earlier sketch in CA 13-14R
See also DLB 13
See also CLC 1, 2, 5, 11, 45
Osborne, John W(alter) 1927- ... 33-36R
Osborne, Juanita Tyree 1916- ... CANR-23
Earlier sketches in CA 61-64, CANR-8
Osborne, Leone Neal 1914- ... 23-24R
See also SATA 2
Osborne, Linda Barrett 1949- ... 65-68
Osborne, Maggie
See Osborne, Margaret Ellen
Osborne, Margaret 1909- ... 13-14R
Osborne, Margaret Ellen 1941- ... CANR-18
Earlier sketch in CA 102
Osborne, Martha Lee 1928- ... 113
Osborne, Mary Pope 1949- ... 111
See also SATA 41
Osborne, Maureen 1924- ... 109
Osborne, Milton Edgeworth 1936- ... CANR-9
Earlier sketch in CA 15-16R
Osborne, Richard 1943- ... 123
Osborne, Richard Horsley 1925- ... 21-22R
Osborne, William (Terry, Jr.) 1934- ... 25-28R
Osborne, William A(udley) 1919- ... 61-64
Osborne, William S(tewart) 1923- ... 53-56
Osbourn, R(ichard) A(lton) 1930- ... 120
Osbourne, Ivor Livingstone 1951- ... 108
Osburn, Charles B(enjamin) 1939- ... CANR-13
Earlier sketch in CA 33-36R
Osceola
See Blixen, Karen (Christentze Dinesen)
Osen, Lynn M(oses) 1920- ... 65-68
Osenenko, John 1918-1983 Obituary ... 109
Oser, Jacob 1915- ... CANR-2
Earlier sketch in CA 5-6R
Osgood, Charles
See Wood, Charles Osgood III
Osgood, Charles E(gerton) 1916- ... 19-20R
Osgood, Charles Grosvenor 1871-1964 .. CANR-4
Earlier sketch in CA 7-8R
Osgood, Cornelius 1905-1985 Obituary ... 114
Osgood, David William 1940- ... 89-92
Osgood, Don(ald W.) 1930- ... CANR-11
Earlier sketch in CA 61-64
Osgood, Ernest S(taples) 1888- ... CAP-1
Earlier sketch in CA 11-12
Osgood, Herbert L(evi) 1855-1918
Brief entry ... 122
See also DLB 47
Osgood, Lawrence 1929- ... 85-88
Osgood, Robert Endicott 1921-1986 ... CANR-3
Obituary ... 121
Earlier sketch in CA 1R
Osgood, Samuel M(aurice) 1920-1975 ... 33-36R
Osgood, William E(dward) 1926- ... 33-36R
See also SATA 37
O'Shaughnessy, Arthur 1844-1881 ... DLB-35
O'Shea, (Martin) Lester 1938- ... 108
O'Shea, Sean
See Tralins, S(andor) Robert
Oshima, Nagisa 1932- ... 121
Brief entry ... 116
See also CLC 20
Osiek, Betty Tyree 1931- ... 45-48
O Siochain, P(adraig) A(ugustine) 1905- .. CAP-2
Earlier sketch in CA 17-18
Osipow, Samuel H(erman) 1934- ... CANR-1
Earlier sketch in CA 49-52
Osis, Karlis 1917- ... 85-88
Oskam, Bob
See Oskam, Robert T(heo)
Oskam, Robert T(heo) 1945- ... 108
Oskamp, Stuart 1930- ... CANR-12
Earlier sketch in CA 29-32R
Oski, Frank A(ram) 1932- ... 119
Osler, Robert Willard 1911-1984 ... CANR-17
Obituary ... 114
Earlier sketch in CA 2R
Osman, Betty B(arshad) 1929- ... 93-96
Osman, Jack D(ouglas) 1943- ... CANR-11
Earlier sketch in CA 61-64
Osman, John 1907(?)-1978 Obituary ... 77-80
Osmer, Margaret ... 93-96
Osmond, Andrew 1938- ... 25-28R
Osmond, Edward 1900- ... CAP-1
Earlier sketch in CA 13-14
See also SATA 10
Osmond, Humphrey (Fortescue) 1917- ... 23-24R
Osmond, Marie 1959- Brief entry ... 112
Osmond-Smith, David 1946- ... 120
Osmun, Mark 1952- ... 93-96
Osmunson, Robert Lee 1924- ... 11-12R
Osofsky, Gilbert 1935-1974 ... 65-68
Obituary ... 53-56
Osserman, Richard A. 1930- ... 29-32R
Osslinger, Kurt
See Allen, Bob
Ossman, David (H.) 1936- ... 9-10R
Ossoli, Sarah Margaret (Fuller marchesa d')
1810-1850 ... SATA-25
Ossorgin, Mikhail
See Ilyin, Mikhail Andreyevich
Ossowska, Maria 1896- ... 29-32R
Ossowski, Stanislaw 1897-1963 ... CAP-1
Earlier sketch in CA 13-14
Ost, David H(arry) 1940- ... CANR-6
Earlier sketch in CA 53-56
Ost, John William Philip 1931- ... 37-40R
Osten, Gar 1923- ... 65-68
Ostendorf, (Arthur) Lloyd (Jr.) 1921- ... CANR-6
Earlier sketch in CA 2R
Ostenso, Martha 1900-1963 ... CAP-1
Earlier sketch in CA 15-16
Oster, Jerry 1943- ... 77-80
Oster, Ludwig (Friedrich) 1931- ... 53-56
Osterburg, James W(illiam) 1917- ... 45-48
Ostergaard, G(eoffrey) N(ielsen) 1926- ... 25-28R
Osterhaven, M(aurice) Eugene 1915- ... 49-52
Osterhoudt, Robert G(erald) 1942- ... 53-56
Osterlund, Steven 1943- ... 77-80
Osterritter, John F. 1923- ... 45-48
Osterweis, Rollin G(ustav)
1907-1982(?) ... 41-44R
Obituary ... 106
Ostheimer, John 1938- ... 41-44R
Ostle, Bernard 1921- ... 7-8R
Ostlere, Gordon (Stanley) 1921- ... 107
Ostling, Richard N(eil) 1940- ... 53-56
Ostow, Mortimer 1918- ... 49-52
Ostrander, Gilman Marston 1923- ... 65-68
Ostriker, Alicia 1937- ... CANR-10
Earlier sketch in CA 25-28R
Ostrinsky, Meir Simha 1906- ... CAP-2
Earlier sketch in CA 29-32
Ostroff, Anthony J(ames) 1923-1978 ... CANR-3
Obituary ... 77-80
Earlier sketch in CA 7-8R
Ostrom, Alan (Baer) 1925- ... 21-22R
Ostrom, John Ward 1903- ... 1R
Ostrom, Thomas M. 1936- ... 37-40R
Ostrom, Vincent (Alfred) 1919- Brief entry .. 113
Ostrov, Eric 1941- ... 113
Ostrow, Joanna 1938- ... 29-32R
Ostrower, Alexander 1901-1979 ... 17-18R
Obituary ... 120
Ostrowsky
See Holmquist, Anders
Ostry, Sylvia 1927- ... CANR-15
Earlier sketch in CA 41-44R
Ostwald, Martin 1922- ... 33-36R
Ostwald, Peter F. 1928- ... 17-18R
O Suilleabhain, Sean 1903- ... CANR-18
Earlier sketch in CA 25-28R
O'Sullivan, Joan (D'Arcy) ... 77-80
O'Sullivan, John J. 1939- Brief entry ... 114
O'Sullivan, Judith 1942- ... 120
O'Sullivan, P. Michael 1940- ... 93-96
O'Sullivan, Sean
See O Suilleabhain, Sean
O'Sullivan, Vincent (Gerard) 1937- ... 97-100
Osusky, Stefan 1889-1973 Obituary ... 45-48
Oswald, Eleazer 1755-1795 ... DLB-43
Oswald, Ian 1929- ... CANR-13
Earlier sketch in CA 19-20R
Oswald, J(oseph) Gregory 1922- ... 104
Oswald, Russell G. 1908- ... 45-48
Oswalt, John N(ewell) 1940- ... 117
Oswalt, Sabine
See MacCormack, Sabine G(abriele)
Oswalt, Wendell H(illman) 1927- ... CANR-12
Earlier sketch in CA 19-20R
Otake, Sadao 1913(?)-1983 Obituary ... 109
Otchis, Ethel (Herberg) 1920- ... 15-16R
Otero, Blas de 1916- ... 89-92
See also CLC 11
Otis, George
See Mellen, Ida M(ay)
Otis, Jack 1923- ... 2R
Otis, James
See Kaler, James Otis
Otis, James, Jr. 1725-1783 ... DLB-31
O'Toole, Rex
See Tralins, S(andor) Robert
O'Trigger, Sir Lucius
See Horne, Richard Henry
Ott, Attiat F(arag) 1935- ... CANR-10
Earlier sketch in CA 21-22R
Ott, David Jackson 1934-1975 ... CANR-8
Earlier sketch in CA 5-6R
Ott, Maggie Glen
See Ott, Virginia
Ott, Peter
See von Hildebrand, Dietrich
Ott, Thomas O(liver) III 1938- ... 49-52
Ott, Virginia 1917- ... 77-80
Ott, William Griffith 1909- ... CANR-1
Earlier sketch in CA 2R
Ottemiller, John H(enry) 1916-1968 ... CAP-2
Earlier sketch in CA 17-18
Otten, Anna ... 21-22R
Otten, C. Michael 1934- ... 33-36R
Otten, Charlotte M(arie) 1915- ... 29-32R
Otten, Terry (Ralph) 1938- ... CANR-15
Earlier sketch in CA 37-40R
Ottenberg, Miriam 1914-1982 ... CANR-10
Obituary ... 108
Earlier sketch in CA 7-8R
Ottenberg, Simon 1923- ... 33-36R
Ottendorfer, Oswald 1826-1900
Brief entry ... 123
See also DLB 23
Otter, Anthony 1896-1986 Obituary ... 118
Otterbein, Keith Frederick 1936- ... 21-22R
Ottersen, (John) Ottar 1918- ... 33-36R
Ottesen, Thea Tauber 1913- ... 5-6R
Otteson, Schuyler Franklin 1917-
Brief entry ... 106
Ottley, Reginald Leslie ... 93-96
See also SATA 26
Ottley, Roi (Vincent) 1906-1960 Obituary .. 89-92
Ottlik, Geza 1912- ... 19-20R
Ottman, Robert W(illiam) 1914- ... CANR-3
Earlier sketch in CA 1R
Otto, Calvin P. 1930- ... 29-32R
Otto, Henry J. 1901- ... CAP-2
Earlier sketch in CA 15-16
Otto, Herbert Arthur 1922- ... CANR-1
Earlier sketch in CA 45-48
Otto, Margaret Glover 1909-1976
Obituary ... 61-64
See also SATA 30
Otto, Wayne (R.) 1931- ... CANR-11
Earlier sketch in CA 29-32R
Ottum, Bob
See Ottum, Robert K., Jr.
Ottum, Robert K., Jr. 1925(?)-1986
Obituary ... 119
Otwell, John H(erbert) 1915- ... 73-76
Ouellette, Fernand 1930- ... CANR-17
Earlier sketches in CA 49-52, CANR-2
See also DLB 60
Oughton, Frederick 1923- ... 2R
Ouida
See De La Ramee, (Marie) Louise
See also DLB 18
Ouimette, Victor 1944- ... 73-76
Oulahan, Richard 1918-1985 ... 33-36R
Obituary ... 117
Oulanoff, Hongor 1929- ... 25-28R
Ouologuem, Yambo 1940- Brief entry ... 111
Ouroussoff, Peter Sergeievich
1900(?)-1984 Obituary ... 114
Ouroussow, Eugenie 1908-1975 Obituary .. 53-56
Oursler, (Charles) Fulton 1893-1952
Brief entry ... 108
Oursler, Fulton, Jr. 1932- Brief entry ... 116
Oursler, Will(iam Charles) 1913-1985 ... CANR-2
Obituary ... 115
Earlier sketch in CA 7-8R
Ousby, Ian (Vaughan Kenneth) 1947- ... 89-92
Ousley, Odille 1896- ... CAP-1
Earlier sketch in CA 11-12
See also SATA 10
Ousmane, Sembene 1923- Brief entry ... 117
Outerbridge, David E(ugene) 1933- ... CANR-16
Earlier sketch in CA 93-96
Outhwaite, Leonard 1892- ... 53-56
Outka, Gene 1937- ... 41-44R
Outland, Charles 1910- ... 11-12R
Outler, Albert C(ook) 1908- ... CANR-1
Earlier sketch in CA 3R
Ouverson, Marlin D(ean) 1952- ... 111
Ovard, Glen F. 1928- ... 33-36R
Overacker, Louise 1891- ... CAP-2
Earlier sketch in CA 29-32
Overbeck, Pauletta 1915- ... 97-100
Overbeek, J(ohannes) 1932- ... 73-76
Overberg, Kenneth R(ichard) 1944- ... 114
Overbury, Stephen 1954- ... 119
Overholser, Stephen 1944- ... CANR-16
Earlier sketch in CA 97-100
Overholser, Wayne D. 1906- ... CANR-16
Earlier sketches in CA 7-8R, CANR-2
Overholt, William H. 1945- ... 117
Overman, Michael 1920- ... 108
Overstreet, Bonaro (Wilkinson) 1902-1985
Obituary ... 117
Overstreet, Harry Allen 1875-1970 ... CAP-1
Obituary ... 29-32R
Earlier sketch in CA 15-16
Overton, Jenny (Margaret Mary) 1942- ... 57-60
See also SATA 36
Overton, Richard Cleghorn 1907- ... 108
Overton, Robert
See Knox-Mawer, Ronald
Overy, Paul 1940- ... 29-32R
Overy, R(ichard) J(ames) 1947- ... 119
Ovesen, Ellis
See Smith, Shirley M(ae)
Owen, Alan Robert George 1919- ... 11-12R
Owen, Alun Davies 1926- ... 7-8R
Owen, Bob
See Geis, Richard E(rwin)
Owen, Bruce M(anning) 1943- ... 57-60
Owen, Caroline Dale
See Snedeker, Caroline Dale (Parke)
Owen, Charles A(braham), Jr. 1914- ... 53-56
Owen, Clifford
See Hamiltlon, Charles Harold St. John
Owen, D(enis) F(rank) 1931- ... CANR-4
Earlier sketch in CA 53-56
Owen, David (Edward) 1898-1968 ... CAP-1
Earlier sketch in CA 15-16
Owen, David E(lystan) 1912-1987 ... 124
Owen, David Lanyon Lloyd
See Lloyd Owen, David Lanyon
Owen, Dilys
See Gater, Dilys
Owen, Dolores B(ullock) ... 53-56
Owen, Douglas David Roy 1922- ... 89-92
Owen, Edmund
See Teller, Neville
Owen, (Benjamin) Evan 1918-1984 ... 109
See also SATA 38
Owen, Frank 1907(?)-1979 Obituary ... 85-88
Owen, G(ail) L(ee) 1937- ... 45-48
Owen, G(eorge) Vale 1869-1931
Brief entry ... 119
Owen, George Earle 1908- ... 77-80
Owen, Guy (Jr.) 1925-1981 ... CANR-3
Obituary ... 104
Earlier sketch in CA 2R
See also DLB 5
Owen, Gwilym Ellis Lane 1922-1982
Obituary ... 107
Owen, (William) Harold 1897-1971 ... 15-16R
Obituary ... 89-92
Owen, Henry 1920- Brief entry ... 111
Owen, Hugh
See Faust, Frederick (Shiller)
Owen, Irvin 1910- ... 97-100
Owen, Jack 1929- ... 33-36R
Owen, Jennifer 1936- ... 116
Owen, John E. 1919- ... CANR-4
Earlier sketch in CA 11-12R
Owen, Lewis 1915- ... 29-32R
Owen, Lewis J(ames) 1925- Brief entry ... 116
Owen, Marsha
See Stanford, Sally
Owen, Oliver S. 1920- ... 104

Owen, Philip
See Philips, Judson (Pentecost)
Owen, Reginald 1887-1972 Obituary 37-40R
Owen, Robert N.
See Geis, Richard E(rwin)
Owen, Roderic
See Fenwick-Owen, Roderic (Franklin Rawnsley)
Owen, Roderic (Franklin Rawnsley) Fenwick
See Fenwick-Owen, Roderic (Franklin Rawnsley)
Owen, Roger C(orey) 1928- 77-80
Owen, Thomas Richard 1918- CANR-10
Earlier sketch in CA 23-24R
Owen, Tobias Chant 1936- 111
Owen, Tom
See Watts, Peter Christopher
Owen, W(arwick) J(ack) B(urgoyne) 1916-
Brief entry 111
Owen, Wilfred 1893-1918 Brief entry 104
See also DLB 20
See also TCLC 5, 27
Owen, Wilfred 1912- 37-40R
Owen, William Vern 1894- CAP-2
Earlier sketch in CA 17-18
Owen, Wyn F(oster) 1923- Brief entry 115
Owendoff, Robert S(cott) 1945- 19-20R
Owens, Bill 1938- 73-76
Owens, Carole (Ehrlich) 1942- 116
Owens, Carolyn 1946- 109
Owens, Edgar (Leonard) 1924-1987
Obituary 124
Owens, Gary 1936- 97-100
Owens, Jesse 1913-1980 110
Owens, Joan (Margaret) Llewelyn 1919- ..15-16R
Owens, John R(obert) 1926- 77-80
Owens, Joseph 1908- CANR-20
Earlier sketches in CA 7-8R, CANR-5
Owens, Pat(rick) J. 1929- 73-76
Owens, Richard Meredith 1944- 61-64
Owens, Robert Goronwy 1923- 29-32R
Owens, Rochelle 1936- 17-18R
See also CAAS 2
See also CLC 8
Owens, Thelma 1905- 69-72
Owens, Virginia Stem 1941- CANR-14
Earlier sketch in CA 81-84
Owens, William A. 1905- 11-12R
Ower, John 1942- 77-80
Owings, Loren C(lyde) 1928- 37-40R
Owings, Mark (Samuel) 1945- Brief entry ... 114
Owings, Nathaniel Alexander 1903-1984 ...61-64
Obituary 113
Owomoyela, Oyekan 1938- 112
Owsley, Frank L(awrence) 1890-1956
Brief entry 116
See also DLB 17
Owsley, Harriet Chappell 1901- 81-84
Oxenbury, Helen 1938- 25-28R
See also SATA 3
Oxenham, Elsie J.
See Dunkerley, Elsie Jeanette
Oxenhandler, Neal 1926- CANR-6
Earlier sketch in CA 13-14R
Oxley, Dorothy (Anne) 1948- 116
Oxley, William 1939- 73-76
Oxnam, Robert B(romley) 1942- CANR-5
Earlier sketch in CA 53-56
Oxnard, Charles (Ernest) 1933- CANR-16
Earlier sketches in CA 45-48, CANR-1
Oxorn, Harry 1920- 111
Oxtoby, Willard Gurdon 1933- 49-52
Oyle, Irving 1925- CANR-6
Earlier sketch in CA 57-60
Oyler, Philip (Tom) 1879- CAP-1
Earlier sketch in CA 9-10
Oy-Vik
See Holmvik, Oyvind
Oz, Amos 1939- 53-56
See also CLC 5, 8, 11, 27, 33
Ozaki, Robert S(higeo) 1934- 49-52
Ozawa, Terutomo 1935- 85-88
Ozer, Jerome S. 1927- 107
Ozer, Mark N(orman) 1932- 112
Ozick, Cynthia 1928- CANR-23
Earlier sketch in CA 17-18R
See also DLB 28
See also DLBY 82
See also CLC 3, 7, 28
Ozinga, James Richard 1932- 97-100
Ozment, Robert V. 1927- 17-18R
Ozment, Steven E(dgar) 1939- 108
Ozmon, Howard A. 25-28R
Ozu, Yasujiro 1903-1963 112
See also CLC 16
Ozy
See Rosset, B(enjamin) C(harles)

P

P. L. K.
See Kirk-Greene, Anthony (Hamilton Millard)
P.Q.
See Quennell, Peter (Courtney)
P. W.
See Strasser, Bernard Paul
Paak, Carl Erich 1922- 106
Paananen, Eloise (Katherine) 1923- CANR-18
Earlier sketches in CA 2R, CANR-2
Paananen, Victor Niles 1938- 73-76
Paarlberg, Don 1911- 23-24R
Paasche, Carol L(evine) 1937- 5-6R
Paauw, Douglas Seymour 1921- 103
Pab
See Blooman, Percy A.
Paca, Lillian Grace (Baker) 1883- CAP-1
Earlier sketch in CA 11-12
Pacaut, Marcel 1920- 29-32R
Pace, C(harles) Robert 1912- 81-84
Pace, Denny F. 1925- 49-52
Pace, Donald Metcalf 1906-1982 Obituary .. 108
Pace, Eric 1936- 45-48
Pace, J. Blair 1916- 69-72
Pace, Mildred Mastin 1907- CANR-5
Earlier sketch in CA 7-8R
See also SATA 29, 46
Pace, Nathaniel 1925- 110
Pace, Peter
See Burnett, David (Benjamin Foley)
Pace, R(alph) Wayne 1931- CANR-1
Earlier sketch in CA 45-48
Pace, Robert Lee 1924- 4R
Pacernick, Gary 1941- 73-76
Pacey, (William Cyril) Desmond
1917-1975 ..... CANR-4
Earlier sketch in CA 7-8R
Pachai, Bridglal 1927- CANR-17
Earlier sketch in CA 93-96
Pacheco, Ferdie 1927- 81-84
Pacheco, Henry L(uis) 1947- 49-52
Pacheco, Jose Emilio 1939- Brief entry 111
Pa Chin
See Li Fei-kan
Pachmuss, Temira 1927- CANR-20
Earlier sketches in CA 11-12R, CANR-4
Pachter, Henry M(aximilian) 1907- 9-10R
Pacifici, Sergio 1925- CANR-3
Earlier sketch in CA 3R
Pacifico, Carl 1921- 23-24R
Pack, Robert 1929- CANR-3
Earlier sketch in CA 3R
See also DLB 5
See also CLC 13
Pack, Roger A(mbrose) 1907- CAP-1
Earlier sketch in CA 15-16
Pack, S(tanley) W(alter) C(roucher)
1904- 13-14R
Packard, Andrew 1929- 2R
Packard, Cindy
See Richmond, Cindy Packard
Packard, Edward 1931- 114
See also SATA 47
Packard, Frederick Clifton, Jr. 1899-1985
Obituary 116
Packard, George R(andolph) III 1932-
Brief entry 112
Packard, Jerrold M(ichael) 1943- CANR-23
Earlier sketch in CA 106
Packard, Karl 1911(?)-1977 Obituary 69-72
Packard, Reynolds 1903-1976 73-76
Obituary 69-72
Packard, Robert G(eorge) 1933- 57-60
Packard, Rosa Covington 1935- 97-100
Packard, Rosalie 1R
Packard, Russell C. 1946- 119
Packard, Sidney R(aymond) 1893- 61-64
Packard, Vance (Oakley) 1914- CANR-7
Earlier sketch in CA 11-12R
See also AITN 1
Packard, William 1933- CANR-7
Earlier sketch in CA 13-14R
Packenham, Robert Allen 1937- 73-76
Packer, Arnold H. 1935- 37-40R
Packer, Bernard J(ules) 1934- CANR-19
Earlier sketch in CA 65-68
Packer, David W(illiam) 1937- 11-12R
Packer, Herbert L(eslie) 1925-1972 .....37-40R
Packer, J(ames) I(nnell) 1926- CANR-16
Earlier sketches in CA 49-52, CANR-1
Packer, Joy (Petersen) 1905-1977 ..... CANR-3
Earlier sketch in CA 4R
Packer, Lady
See Packer, Joy (Petersen)
Packer, Nancy Huddleston 1925- 65-68
Packer, Rod Earle 1931- 109
Packer, Vin
See Meaker, Marijane
Packman, David 1949- 123
Pacosz, Christina V(ivian) 1946- 77-80
Padberg, Daniel I(van) 1931- 33-36R
Padberg, John W(illiam) 1926- 25-28R
Padden, R(obert) C(harles) 1922- 21-22R
Paddison, Ronan 1945- 117
Paddleford, Clementine Haskin 1900-1967
Obituary 89-92
Paddock, John 1918- 17-18R
Paddock, Paul (Ezekiel, Jr.) 1907-1975 ... CAP-2
Obituary 61-64
Earlier sketch in CA 21-22
Paddock, William (Carson) 1921- 21-22R
Pade, Victoria 1953- 113
Paden, William D(oremus, Jr.) 1941- 124
Padfield, Harland (Irvine) 1926-
Brief entry 112
Padfield, Peter 1932- 101
Padgett, Desmond
See von Block, Bela W(illiam)
Padgett, Dora 1893(?)-1976 Obituary 61-64
Padgett, Lewis
See Kuttner, Henry
and Moore, C(atherine) L(ucile)
Padgett, Ron 1942- CANR-12
Earlier sketch in CA 25-28R
See also DLB 5
Padilla (Lorenzo), Heberto 1932-
Brief entry 123
See also CLC 38
See also AITN 1
Padilla, Victoria 1907-1986 103
Obituary 120
Padley, Walter Ernest 1916-1984 Obituary .. 112
Padmore, George
See Nurse, Malcolm Ivan Meredith
Padovano, Anthony T(homas) 1934- ... CANR-22
Earlier sketches in CA 17-18R, CANR-7
Padover, Saul K(ussiel) 1905-1981 ..... CANR-2
Obituary 103
Earlier sketch in CA 49-52
Padwick, E(ric) W(illiam) 1923- 119
Paetro, Maxine 1946- 123
Paffard, Michael Kenneth 1928- 103
Pafford, John Henry Pyle 1900- CANR-21
Earlier sketch in CA 104
Pagden, Anthony 1945- 101
Page, Benjamin I(ngrim) 1940- 112
Page, Carole Gift 1942- 117
Page, Charles H(unt) 1909- CANR-4
Earlier sketch in CA 7-8R
Page, Curtis C(arling) 1914- 21-22R
Page, Drew 1905- 105
Page, Eileen
See Heal, Edith
Page, Eleanor
See Coerr, Eleanor (Beatrice)
Page, Ellis Batten 1924- 15-16R
Page, Emma
See Tirbutt, Honoria
Page, Evelyn 1902- 7-8R
Page, G. S.
See Galbraith, Georgie Starbuck
Page, Gerald W(ilburn) 1939- 93-96
Page, Grover, Jr. 1918- 17-18R
Page, Harry Robert 1915- 11-12R
Page, Homer (Gordon) 1918-1985
Obituary 117
Page, Jake
See Page, James K(eena), Jr.
Page, James A(llen) 1918- 107
Page, James D. 1910- 73-76
Page, James K(eena), Jr. 1936- 97-100
Page, Jimmy 1944- CLC-12
Page, Joseph A(nthony) 1934- CANR-14
Earlier sketch in CA 81-84
Page, Lorna
See Rowland, D(onald) S(ydney)
Page, Lou Williams 1912- CANR-5
Earlier sketch in CA 5-6R
See also SATA 38
Page, Louise 1955- CLC-40
Page, Malcolm 1935- 45-48
Page, Marian 69-72
Page, Martin 1938- CANR-12
Earlier sketch in CA 19-20R
Page, Mary
See Heal, Edith
Page, Norman 1930- CANR-8
Earlier sketch in CA 61-64
Page, P(atricia) K(athleen) 1916- CANR-22
Earlier sketches in CA 53-56, CANR-4
See also CLC 7, 18
Page, Robert Collier 1908-1977 Obituary ..73-76
Page, Robert J(effress) 1922- 17-18R
Page, Robert Morris 1903- CAP-2
Earlier sketch in CA 17-18
Page, Robin 1943- 103
Page, Roch 1939- 33-36R
Page, Russell 1906-1985 Obituary 114
Page, Stanton
See Fuller, Henry Blake
Page, Thomas 1942- 81-84
Page, Thomas Nelson 1853-1922
Brief entry 118
See also DLB 12
Page, Thornton (Leigh) 1913- CANR-2
Earlier sketch in CA 5-6R
Page, Vicki
See Avey, Ruby
Page, Warren (Kempton) 1910-1977
Obituary 111
Page, William 1929- 114
Page, William 1946- 115
Page, William Roberts 1904- 21-22R
Pagel, Walter T. U. 1898-1983 Obituary 109
Pagels, Elaine Hiesey 1943- CANR-24
Earlier sketches in CA 45-48, CANR-2
Pagels, Heinz R(udolf) 1939- CANR-23
Earlier sketch in CA 107
Pages, Pedro
See Alba, Victor
Paget, George Charles Henry Victor
1922- 17-18R
Paget, John
See Aiken, John (Kempton)
Paget, Julian 1921- 23-24R
Paget, Margaret
See Medlicott, Margaret P(aget)
Paget, Violet 1856-1935 Brief entry 104
Paget-Fredericks, Joseph E. P.
Rous-Marten 1903-1963 ..... SATA-30
Paget-Lowe, Henry
See Lovecraft, H(oward) P(hillips)
Paglin, Morton 1922- 97-100
Pagnol, Marcel 1895-1974 Obituary 49-52
Paher, Stanley W(illiam) 1940- 29-32R
Pahl, R(aymond) E(dward) 1935- 25-28R
Pahlavi, Mohammed Riza
See Pahlevi, Mohammed Riza
Pahlen, Kurt 1907- CANR-7
Earlier sketch in CA 15-16R
Pahlevi, Mohammed Riza 1919-1980
Obituary 106
Pahz, (Anne) Cheryl Suzanne 1949- CANR-8
Earlier sketch in CA 53-56
See also SATA 11
Pahz, James Alon 1943- CANR-8
Earlier sketch in CA 53-56
See also SATA 11
Pai, Anna C(hao) 1935- 89-92
Pai, Young 1929- 33-36R
Paice, Margaret 1920- CANR-20
Earlier sketch in CA 29-32R
See also SATA 10
Paier, Robert (David) 1943- 89-92
Paige, Glenn D(urland) 1929- 25-29R
Paige, Harry W(orthington) 1922- 113
See also SATA 35, 41
Paige, Leo
See Cochrane, William E.
Paige, Leroy Robert 1907(?)-1982
Obituary 107
Paige, Richard
See Koontz, Dean R(ay)
Paige, Richard E(aton) 1904- 111
Paige, Satchel
See Paige, Leroy Robert
Pain, Barry (Eric Odell) 1864-1928
Brief entry 109
Pain, Philip ?-1666(?) DLB-24
Paine, Albert Bigelow 1861-1937
Brief entry 108
Paine, J. Lincoln
See Kramish, Arnold
Paine, Lauran (Bosworth) 1916- CANR-7
Earlier sketch in CA 45-48
Paine, Philbrook 1910- CAP-1
Earlier sketch in CA 11-12
Paine, R(ussell) Howard 1922- 7-8R
Paine, Robert Treat, Jr. 1773-1811 ..... DLB-37
Paine, Roberta M. 1925- 33-36R
See also SATA 13
Paine, Roger W(arde) III 1942- 65-68
Paine, Stephen William 1908- 3R
Paine, Thomas 1737-1809 ..... DLB-31, 43
See also CDALB 1640-1865
Painter, Charlotte CANR-3
Earlier sketch in CA 2R
Painter, Daniel
See Burgess, M(ichael) R(oy)
Painter, George D(uncan) 1914- 101
Painter, Helen W(elch) 1913- 33-36R
Painter, Nell Irvin 1942- CANR-19
Earlier sketch in CA 65-68
Painter, Pamela 1941- 122
Pairault, Pierre 1922- 53-56
Pais, Abraham 1918- 109
Paish, F(rank) W(alter) 1898- 17-18R
Paisley, Tom 1932- CANR-15
Earlier sketch in CA 61-64
Paisner, Milton 1915- 113
Pak Chong-Hui
See Park Chung Hee
Pakenham, Edward Arthur Henry
1902-1961 Obituary 114
Pakenham, Francis Aungier 1905- 109
Pakenham, Frank, Seventh Earl of Longford
See Pakenham, Francis Aungier
Pakenham, Simona Vere 1916- CANR-3
Earlier sketch in CA 4R
Pakenham, Thomas (Frank Dermot) 1933- .. 109
Pakula, Alan J(ay) 1928- Brief entry 124
Pakula, Marion Broome 1926- CANR-7
Earlier sketch in CA 57-60
Pal, Pratapaditya 1935- 37-40R
Palamas, Kostes 1859-1943 Brief entry 105
See also TCLC 5
Palamountain, Joseph Cornwall, Jr.
1920-1987 45-48
Obituary 124
Palandri, Angela (Chin-ying) Jung 1926- ..37-40R
Palange, Anthony (Jr.) 1942- 37-40R
Palau, Luis (Jr.) 1934- 116
Palazzeschi, Aldo 1885-1974 89-92
Obituary 53-56
See also CLC 11
Palazzo, Anthony D.
See Palazzo, Tony
Palazzo, Tony 1905-1970 ..... CANR-4
Obituary 29-32R
Earlier sketch in CA 7-8R
See also SATA 3
Palder, Edward L. 1922- SATA-5
Paleckis, Justas (Ignovich) 1899-1980
Obituary 105
Palen, J(oseph) John 1939- CANR-15
Earlier sketch in CA 41-44R
Palen, Jennie M. 7-8R
Palermo, David Stuart 1929- 19-20R
Palestrant, Simon S. 1907- CAP-1
Earlier sketch in CA 9-10
Paley, Alan L(ouis) 1943- 69-72
Paley, Grace 1922- CANR-13
Earlier sketch in CA 25-28R
See also DLB 28
See also CLC 4, 6, 37
Paley, Maggie 1939- 121
Paley, Morton D(avid) 1935- CANR-13
Earlier sketch in CA 33-36R
Paley, Nicholas M(iroslav) 1911- CANR-15
Earlier sketch in CA 41-44R
Paley, Vivian Gussin 1929- 93-96
Paley, William S(amuel) 1901- 110
Palffy-Alpar, Julius 1908- CAP-2
Earlier sketch in CA 23-24
Palfrey, John Gorham 1796-1881 ..... DLB-1, 30
Palfrey, Thomas R(ossman) 1895- 61-64
Palgrave, Francis Turner 1824-1897 ..... DLB-35
Palin, Michael 107
See also CLC 21
Palinchak, Robert S(tephen) 1942- 49-52
Palinurus
See Connolly, Cyril (Vernon)
Palisca, Claude V. 1921- 17-18R
Pall, Ellen Jane 1952- 93-96
Palladini, David (Mario) 1946- SATA-32, 40

INDEX

Pallas, Dorothy Constance 1933-1971
 Obituary ... 33-36R
Pallas, Norvin 1918- ... CANR-3
 Earlier sketch in CA 2R
 See also SATA 23
Pallavera, Franco
 See Soldati, Mario
Palle, Albert 1916- ... 13-14R
Pallenberg, Corrado 1912- ... 15-16R
Palley, Julian I(rving) 1925- ... 73-76
Palley, Marian Lief 1939- ... CANR-8
 Earlier sketch in CA 61-64
Palli, Pitsa
 See Hartocollis, Peter
Pallidini, Jodi
 See Robbin, (Jodi) Luna
Pallis, Alexander (Anastasius) 1883-1975
 Obituary ... 61-64
Pallister, Janis L(ouise) 1926- ... CANR-14
 Earlier sketch in CA 41-44R
Pallister, John C(lare) 1891-1980 ... 7-8R
 Obituary ... 103
 See also SATA 26
Pallone, Nathaniel John 1935- ... CANR-10
 Earlier sketch in CA 21-22R
Palm, Goeran 1931- ... 29-32R
Palm, Goran
 See Palm, Goeran
Palm, John Daniel 1924- Brief entry ... 106
Palmatier, Robert Allen 1926- ... 37-40R
Palmedo, Roland 1895-1977 ... 53-56
 Obituary ... 69-72
Palmer, Alan Warwick 1926- ... CANR-6
 Earlier sketch in CA 13-14R
Palmer, Archie M(acInnes) 1896-1985 ... 13-14R
 Obituary ... 116
Palmer, Arnold (Daniel) 1929- ... 85-88
Palmer, B. C.
 See Schmidt, Laura M(arie)
Palmer, Bernard 1914- ... CANR-12
 Earlier sketches in CA 57-60, CANR-7
 See also SATA 26
Palmer, Brooks 1900(?)-1974 Obituary ... 45-48
Palmer, Bruce (Hamilton) 1932- ... CANR-3
 Earlier sketch in CA 3R
Palmer, C(yril) Everard 1930- ... 41-44R
 See also SATA 14
Palmer, C(edric) King 1913- ... 13-14R
Palmer, (Ruth) Candida 1926- ... 61-64
 See also SATA 11
Palmer, (John) Carey (Bowden) 1943- ... 103
Palmer, Charles Earl 1919- ... 15-16R
Palmer, (Thomas) Cruise 1917- ... 69-72
Palmer, Dave Richard 1934- ... CANR-1
 Earlier sketch in CA 45-48
Palmer, David 1928- ... 21-22R
Palmer, Donald C. 1934- ... 53-56
Palmer, Dorothy Ann 1935- ... 57-60
Palmer, E(dgar) P(oole), Jr. 1938- ... 116
Palmer, Earl Frank 1931- ... 113
Palmer, Edgar Z(avitz) 1898- ... 21-22R
Palmer, Edward L. 1938- ... 101
Palmer, Elsie Pavitt 1922- ... 7-8R
Palmer, Eve 1916- ... 23-24R
Palmer, Everett W(alter) 1906-1970 ... CAP-2
 Earlier sketch in CA 17-18
Palmer, Frank R. 1922- ... 17-18R
Palmer, George 1915(?)-1986 Obituary ... 119
Palmer, George E. 1908- ... 1R
Palmer, George Herbert 1842-1933
 Brief entry ... 121
Palmer, Gerald Eustace Howell 1904-1984
 Obituary ... 112
Palmer, (James) Gregory 1938- ... 121
Palmer, Heidi 1948- ... SATA-15
Palmer, Helen H. 1911- ... 21-22R
Palmer, Helen Marion
 See Geisel, Helen
Palmer, Henry R(obinson), Jr. 1911- ... 23-24R
Palmer, (Nathaniel) Humphrey 1930- ... CANR-12
 Earlier sketch in CA 29-32R
Palmer, James B. 1929- ... 25-28R
Palmer, Jerome Robert 1904- ... 45-48
Palmer, Jim
 See Palmer, James B.
Palmer, John (Leslie) 1885-1944
 Brief entry ... 121
Palmer, John A. 1926- ... 29-32R
Palmer, John L(ogan) 1943- ... 73-76
Palmer, Joseph (Mansergh) 1912- ... 7-8R
Palmer, Juliette 1930- ... 81-84
 See also SATA 15
Palmer, Kenneth T. 1937- ... 77-80
Palmer, L(eonard) R(obert) 1906-1984 ... 25-28R
 Obituary ... 114
Palmer, Larry Garland 1938- ... 19-20R
Palmer, Laura
 See Schmidt, Laura M(arie)
Palmer, Lilli
 See Peiser, Maria Lilli
Palmer, Lynn
 See Palmer, Pamela Lynn
Palmer, Madelyn 1910- ... 103
Palmer, Marian 1930- ... 53-56
Palmer, Marjorie 1919- ... CANR-12
 Earlier sketch in CA 57-60
Palmer, Michael (Stephen) 1942- ... 114
Palmer, Michael D. 1933- ... 37-40R
Palmer, Nicholas 1950- ... CANR-15
 Earlier sketch in CA 89-92
Palmer, Norman D(unbar) 1909- ... CANR-19
 Earlier sketches in CA 3R, CANR-3
Palmer, Pamela Lynn 1951- ... CANR-4
 Earlier sketch in CA 53-56
Palmer, Parker J. 1939- ... 115
Palmer, Pete
 See Palmer, E(dgar) P(oole), Jr.
Palmer, Peter
 See Palmer, Elsie Pavitt
Palmer, Peter John 1932- ... CANR-20
 Earlier sketch in CA 103
Palmer, R(obert) R(oswell) 1909- ... 13-14R
Palmer, Ralph Simon 1914- ... 73-76
Palmer, Raymond A. 1910-1977 Obituary ... 111
Palmer, Raymond Edward 1927- ... 77-80
Palmer, Richard 1904- ... 97-100
Palmer, Richard Edward 1933- ... CANR-1
 Earlier sketch in CA 45-48
Palmer, Richard Phillips 1921- ... 57-60
Palmer, Robert (Franklin, Jr.) 1945-
 Brief entry ... 121
Palmer, Robert C(harles) 1947- ... 113
Palmer, Robert E(verett) A(llen) 1932-
 Brief entry ... 114
Palmer, Robin 1911- ... 109
 See also SATA 43
Palmer, Roy (Ernest) 1932- ... CANR-23
 Earlier sketches in CA 61-64, CANR-8
Palmer, Spencer J(ohn) 1927- ... CANR-10
 Earlier sketch in CA 61-64
Palmer, Stuart 1924- ... CANR-3
 Earlier sketch in CA 1R
Palmer, Thomas 1955- ... 109
Palmer, Tim 1948- ... 121
Palmer, Tobias
 See Weathers, Winston
Palmer, Tony 1941- Brief entry ... 111
Palmer, Winthrop Bushnell 1899- ... 65-68
Palmieri, Anthony Francis 1920- ... 114
Palmore, Erdman B. 1930- ... 37-40R
Palms, Roger C(urtis) 1936- ... CANR-17
 Earlier sketch in CA 93-96
Paloczi-Horvath, George 1908-1973 ... 7-8R
 Obituary ... 37-40R
Palombo, Stanley R(obert) 1934- ... 122
Palomo, G(aspar) J(esus) 1952- ... 61-64
Palovic, Clara Lora 1918- ... 25-28R
Paltenghi, Madeleine
 See Anderson, Madeleine Paltenghi
Paltock, Robert 1697-1767 ... DLB-39
Paltrowitz, Donna (Milman) 1950- ... 119
 See also SATA 50
Paltrowitz, Stuart 1946- ... 118
 See also SATA 50
Paludan, (Stig Henning) Jacob (Puggaard)
 1896-1975 Obituary ... 115
Paludan, Phillip S(haw) 1938- ... 73-76
Paluello, Lorenzo Minio
 See Minio-Paluello, Lorenzo
Palumbo, Dennis J(ames) 1929- ... 29-32R
Palusci, Larry 1916- ... 29-32R
Paluszny, Maria Janina 1939- ... 103
Palyi, Melchior 1892(?)-1970 Obituary ... 104
Pan, Peter
 See Bartier, Pierre
Pan, Stephen C(hao) Y(ing) 1915- ... 45-48
Panagopoulos, Epaminondas Peter
 1915- ... 13-14R
Panama, Norman 1920- ... 104
 See also DLB 26
Panassie, Hugues (Louis Marie Henri)
 1912-1974 ... 97-100
 Obituary ... 53-56
Panati, Charles 1943- ... 81-84
Pancake, Breece Dexter 1952-1979 ... 123
Pancake, Breece D'J 1952(?)-1979
 Obituary ... 109
 See also CLC 29
Pancake, Breece D'J
 See Pancake, Breece Dexter
Pancake, John S(ilas) 1920- ... 53-56
Pandey, B(ishwa) N(ath) 1929-1982 ... CANR-20
 Obituary ... 108
 Earlier sketch in CA 25-28R
Pandit, Vijaya Lakshmi 1900- ... 104
Panek, LeRoy Lad 1943- ... 113
Panella, Vincent 1939- ... 97-100
Panetta, George 1915-1969 ... 81-84
 See also SATA 15
Panetta, Leon Edward 1938- ... 101
Pang, May 1950- ... 118
Pangborn, Edgar 1909-1976 ... CANR-4
 Earlier sketch in CA 1R
 See also DLB 8
Panger, Daniel 1926- ... 93-96
Panglaykim, J(usuf Pangestu) 1922- ... CANR-15
 Earlier sketch in CA 23-24R
Pangle, Thomas L(ee) 1944- ... CANR-1
 Earlier sketch in CA 49-52
Pangrazzi, Arnaldo 1947- ... 115
Paniagua Bermudez, Domingo
 1880(?)-1973 Obituary ... 41-44R
Panichas, George A(ndrew) 1930- ... CANR-10
 Earlier sketch in CA 25-28R
Panikkar, K(avalam) Madhava 1895-1963 ... CAP-1
 Earlier sketch in CA 15-16
Panikkar, Raimundo 1918- ... 81-84
Panin, Dimitri (Mikhailovich) 1911-1987
 Obituary ... 124
Panitch, Leo (Victor) 1945- ... 119
Panitt, Merrill 1917- ... 106
Panitz, Esther L(eah) ... 116
Pankey, Eric 1959- ... 120
Pankhurst, Emmeline (Goulden)
 1858-1928 Brief entry ... 116
Pankhurst, Richard (Keir Pethick)
 1927- ... CANR-21
 Earlier sketches in CA 9-10R, CANR-6
Pankin, Robert M. 1935- ... 114
Pannabecker, Samuel Floyd 1896- ... 65-68
Pannell, Anne Gary 1910- ... CAP-2
 Earlier sketch in CA 23-24
Pannenberg, Wolfhart (Ulrich) 1928- ... CANR-11
 Earlier sketch in CA 25-28R
Pannor, Reuben 1922- ... 61-64
Pannwitz, Rudolf 1881-1969 Obituary ... 89-92
Pano, Nicholas C(hristopher) 1934- ... 37-40R
Panofsky, Erwin 1892-1968 ... 117
 Obituary ... 113
Panos, Chris(tos) 1935- ... 65-68
Panov, Valery (Shulman) 1938- ... 102
Panova, Vera (Fedorovna) 1905-1973 ... 102
 Obituary ... 89-92
Panowski, Eileen Thompson 1920- ... 5-6R
 See also SATA 49
Panshin, Alexei 1940- ... 57-60
 See also DLB 8
Panshin, Cory (Seidman) 1947-
 Brief entry ... 112
Pansy
 See Alden, Isabella (Macdonald)
Pantell, Dora (Fuchs) ... 111
 See also SATA 39
Panter, Carol 1936- ... 49-52
 See also SATA 9
Panter, Gideon G. 1935- ... 77-80
Panter-Downes, Mollie Patricia 1906- ... 101
Panting, Phyllis
 See Morton, Phyllis Digby
Panzarella, Andrew 1940- ... 25-28R
Panzarella, Joseph John, Jr. 1919- ... 85-88
Panzer, Pauline (Richman) 1911(?)-1972
 Obituary ... 37-40R
Pao, Ping-Nie 1922- ... 103
Paoletti, John T(homas) 1939- ... 112
Paoli, Pia 1930- ... 25-28R
Paolini, Gilberto 1928- ... CANR-22
 Earlier sketch in CA 45-48
Paolucci, Anne ... 73-76
Paolucci, Henry 1921- ... 102
Paone, Anthony J(oseph) 1913- ... 5-6R
Paor, Richard de
 See Power, Richard
Papachristou, Judy 1930- ... 93-96
Papadiamantopoulos, Johannes
 1856-1910 Brief entry ... 117
Papaleo, Joseph 1925- ... 25-28R
Papandreou, Andreas G(eorge) 1919- ... 37-40R
Papandreou, Margaret C. 1923- ... 29-32R
Papanek, Ernst 1900-1973 ... CANR-4
 Earlier sketch in CA 2R
Papanek, Gustav F(ritz) 1926- ... CANR-1
 Earlier sketch in CA 45-48
Papas, William 1927- ... CANR-12
 Earlier sketch in CA 25-28R
 See also SATA 50
Papashvily, George 1898-1978 ... 81-84
 Obituary ... 77-80
 See also SATA 17
Papashvily, Helen (Waite) 1906- ... 81-84
 See also SATA 17
Papazian, Dennis R(ichard) 1931- ... 45-48
Pape, D. L.
 See Pape, Donna (Lugg)
Pape, Donna (Lugg) 1930- ... CANR-9
 Earlier sketch in CA 23-24R
 See also SATA 2
Pape, Gordon 1936- ... 105
Pape, Greg 1947- ... 113
Papenfuse, Edward C(arl), Jr. 1943- ... CANR-8
 Earlier sketch in CA 57-60
Paper, Herbert H(arry) 1925- ... CANR-1
 Earlier sketch in CA 45-48
Paper, Lewis J(ay) 1946- Brief entry ... 114
Paperny, Myra (Green) 1932- ... 69-72
 See also SATA 33
Papert, Emma N. 1926- ... 101
Papi, G(iuseppe) Ugo 1893- ... 25-28R
Papich, Stephen 1925- ... 69-72
Papier, Judith Barnard 1932- ... 21-22R
Papin, Joseph 1914- ... 65-68
Papini, Giovanni 1881-1956 Brief entry ... 121
 See also TCLC 22
Papp, Charles Steven 1917- ... CANR-15
 Earlier sketch in CA 41-44R
Pappageotes, George C(hristos)
 1926-1963 ... CANR-2
 Earlier sketch in CA 1R
Pappas, George 1929- ... 29-32R
Pappas, Lou Seibert 1930- ... CANR-23
 Earlier sketches in CA 61-64, CANR-8
Pappworth, M(aurice) H(enry) 1910- ... 23-24R
Paprika
 See Holmvik, Oyvind
Papus
 See Encausse, Gerard (Anaclet Vincent)
Paquet, Alfons 1881-1944 ... DLB-66
Paradis, Adrian A(lexis) 1912- ... CANR-18
 Earlier sketches in CA 4R, CANR-3
 See also SATA 1
Paradis, James G(ardiner) 1942- ... 93-96
Paradis, Marjorie Bartholomew
 1886(?)-1970 ... 73-76
 Obituary ... 29-32R
 See also SATA 17
Paradis, Suzanne 1936- ... DLB-53
Paradise, Louis V(incent) 1946- ... 114
Parakh, Jal Sohrab 1932- Brief entry ... 105
Parandowski, Jan 1895- ... CAP-1
 Earlier sketch in CA 11-12
Parasol, Peter
 See Stevens, Wallace
Parasuram, T(attamangalam) V(iswanatha
 Iyer) 1923- ... 106
Paratore, Angela 1912- ... 13-14R
Parchman, William E(ugene) 1936- ... 93-96
Pardee, Michael 1945- ... 113
Pardey, Larry
 See Pardey, Lawrence Fred
Pardey, Lawrence Fred 1939- ... 93-96
Pardey, (Mary) Lin 1944- ... 93-96
Paredes, Americo 1915- ... 37-40R
Pareek, Udai (Narain) 1925- ... CANR-11
 Earlier sketch in CA 21-22R
Parelius, Ann Parker 1943- ... 81-84
Parelius, Robert J. 1941- ... 81-84
Parens, Henri 1928- ... 89-92
Parent, David J(oseph) 1931- ... CANR-9
 Earlier sketch in CA 57-60
Parent, Gail 1940- ... 101
Parent, Ronald 1937-1982 Obituary ... 107
Parente, Pascal P(rosper) 1890-1971 ... CAP-1
 Obituary ... 33-36R
 Earlier sketch in CA 17-18
Parente, Sarah (Eleanor) 1913- ... CANR-16
 Earlier sketch in CA 41-44R
Parenteau, Shirley Laurolyn 1935- ... CANR-15
 Earlier sketch in CA 85-88
 See also SATA 40, 47
Parenti, Michael 1933- ... 73-76
Pares, Marion (Stapylton) 1914- ... CANR-12
 Earlier sketch in CA 17-18R
Paret, Peter 1924- Brief entry ... 114
Paretti, Sandra ... CANR-7
 Earlier sketch in CA 53-56
Parezo, Nancy Jean 1951- ... 114
Parfit, Michael 1947- ... 119
Parfitt, George (Albert Ekins) 1939- ... 109
Parfitt, Tudor (Vernon) 1944- ... 123
Pargeter, Edith Mary 1913- ... CANR-24
 Earlier sketches in CA 4R, CANR-4
Parham, Joseph Byars 1919- ... 65-68
Parham, Robert Randall 1943- ... 57-60
Parham, William 1914- ... 103
Parham, William Thomas 1913- ... CANR-20
 Earlier sketch in CA 103
Parini, Jay (Lee) 1948- ... 97-100
Parins, James William 1939- ... 109
Paris, Bernard J. 1931- ... CANR-7
 Earlier sketch in CA 17-18R
Paris, Erna 1938- ... 105
Paris, Ginette 1946- ... 123
Paris, Jeanne 1918- ... 1R
Parise, Goffredo 1929-1986 Obituary ... 120
Pariseau, Earl J(oseph) 1928- ... 11-12R
Parish, Charles 1927- ... 25-28R
Parish, David 1932- ... CANR-14
 Earlier sketch in CA 73-76
Parish, Helen Rand 1912- Brief entry ... 115
Parish, James 1904-1973 Obituary ... 114
Parish, James Robert 1944- ... 33-36R
Parish, Margaret Cecile 1927- ... CANR-18
 Earlier sketch in CA 73-76
Parish, Margaret Holt
 See Holt, Margaret
Parish, Peggy
 See Parish, Margaret Cecile
 See also SATA 17
Parish, Peter J(oseph) 1929- ... 57-60
Parish, Townsend
 See Pietschmann, Richard John III
Parisi, Joseph 1944- ... 93-96
Parizeau, Alice 1930- ... DLB-60
Park, Barbara 1947- ... 113
 See also SATA 35, 40
Park, Bill
 See Park, W(illiam) B(ryan)
 See also SATA 22
Park, Charles F(rederick), Jr. 1903- ... 57-60
Park, Clara Claiborne 1923- ... 23-24R
Park, D. U.
 See Woods, Clee
Park, David 1919- ... 105
Park, Ed 1930- ... 73-76
Park, Edwards 1917- ... 123
Park, Elm
 See Dunbar, Charles Stuart
Park, George 1925- ... 77-80
Park, James (Robert) 1956- ... 120
Park, James William 1936- ... 121
Park, Joe 1913- ... 23-24R
Park, Jordan
 See Kornbluth, C(yril) M.
 and Pohl, Frederik
Park, Joseph H. 1890(?)-1979 Obituary ... 89-92
Park, Maeva
 See Dobner, Maeva Park
Park, O'Hyun 1940- ... 53-56
Park, Peter 1929- ... 29-32R
Park, Richard L(eonard) 1920- ... 77-80
Park, Robert E(zra) 1864-1944 Brief entry ... 122
Park, Robert L. 1932- ... 89-92
Park, (Rosina) Ruth ... 105
 See also SATA 25
Park, Sung-Bae 1933- ... 115
Park, W(illiam) B(ryan) 1936- ... CANR-17
 Earlier sketch in CA 97-100
 See also SATA 22
Park, William John 1930- ... 49-52
Park Chung Hee 1917-1979 ... CANR-10
 Obituary ... 97-100
 Earlier sketch in CA 61-64
Parke, Herbert William 1903- ... 105
Parke, John 1754-1789 ... DLB-31
Parke, Margaret Bittner 1901- ... 89-92
Parke, Ross D(uke) 1938- ... CANR-16
 Earlier sketches in CA 45-48, CANR-1
Parker, Adrian David 1947- ... 103
Parker, Alexander A(ugustine) 1908- ... CANR-16
 Earlier sketch in CA 23-24R
Parker, Alfred Browning 1916- ... 17-18R
Parker, Ann
 See Neal, Ann Parker
Parker, Arthur C(aswell) 1881-1955
 Brief entry ... 115
Parker, Barry (Richard) 1935- ... 112
Parker, Beatrice
 See Huff, T(om) E.

Parker, Bert
See Ellison, Harlan
Parker, Bertha Morris 1890-1980 .... CANR-5
Obituary 102
Earlier sketch in CA 7-8R
Parker, Betty June 1929- CANR-22
Earlier sketches in CA 57-60, CANR-7
Parker, Beulah 1912- 81-84
Parker, Brant Julian 1920- Brief entry 114
Parker, Clifford S(tetson) 1891- 7-8R
Parker, Clyde A. 1927- 41-44R
Parker, David L(ambert) 1935- 108
Parker, David Marshall 1929- 77-80
Parker, Dee
See Parker, David L(ambert)
Parker, (William George) Derek 1932- .. CANR-23
Earlier sketch in CA 29-32R
Parker, Don(ald) H(enry) 1912- CANR-6
Earlier sketch in CA 7-8R
Parker, Donald Dean 1899- 37-40R
Parker, Donn B(lanchard) 1929- CANR-9
Earlier sketch in CA 65-68
Parker, Dorothy (Rothschild) 1893-1967 .. CAP-2
Obituary 25-28R
Earlier sketch in CA 19-20
See also DLB 11, 45
See also CLC 15
Parker, Dorothy 1922- 93-96
Parker, Dorothy Mills CANR-11
Earlier sketch in CA 21-22R
Parker, Douglas Hugh 1926- 1R
Parker, Edna Jean 1935- 101
Parker, Edwin B(urke) 1932- 15-16R
Parker, Elinor Milnor 1906- CANR-3
Earlier sketch in CA 4R
See also SATA 3
Parker, Elliott S(evern) 1939- 103
Parker, Francis H(oward) 1920- 21-22R
Parker, Frank J(oseph) 1940- 49-52
Parker, Franklin 1921- CANR-22
Earlier sketches in CA 33-36R, CANR-7
Parker, Franklin D(allas) 1918- 13-14R
Parker, Gail Thain 1943- 104
Parker, Geoffrey 1933- 49-52
Parker, Gordon 1940- 103
Parker, H(enry) M(ichael) D(enne)
1896(?)-1971 Obituary 104
Parker, Harold T(albot) 1907- CANR-9
Earlier sketch in CA 23-24R
Parker, Hershel 1935- CANR-13
Earlier sketch in CA 33-36R
Parker, Howard J(ohn) 1948- 57-60
Parker, J(ohn) Carlyle 1931- CANR-24
Earlier sketches in CA 57-60, CANR-7
Parker, Jack Horace 1914- 113
Parker, James 1714(?)-1770 .... DLB-43
Parker, James
See Newby, Eric
Parker, James Reid 1909-1984 Obituary 111
Parker, Jean
See Sharat Chandra, G(ubbi) S(hankara Chetty)
Parker, Joan H. 1932- 85-88
Parker, (Herbert) John (Harvey)
1906-1987 ....7-8R
Obituary 124
Parker, John 1923- CANR-5
Earlier sketch in CA 5-6R
Parker, John
See Wyatt, John
Parker, John Thomas 1950- 118
Parker, Julia (Louise) 1932- CANR-23
Earlier sketch in CA 101
Parker, Laura
See Castoro, Laura A(nn)
Parker, Lois M(ay) 1912- CANR-11
Earlier sketch in CA 69-72
See also SATA 30
Parker, Margot M. 1937- 122
Parker, Marsha Zurich 1952- 107
Parker, Nancy Winslow 1930- CANR-22
Earlier sketches in CA 49-52, CANR-1
See also SATA 10
Parker, Nathan Carlyle 1960- 102
Parker, Pat 1944- 57-60
Parker, Percy Spurlark 1940- 53-56
Parker, Richard 1915- 73-76
See also SATA 14
Parker, Robert 1920- CANR-13
Earlier sketch in CA 77-80
Parker, Robert
See Boyd, Waldo T.
Parker, Robert Allerton 1889(?)-1970
Obituary 29-32R
Parker, Robert B(rown) 1932- CANR-1
Earlier sketch in CA 49-52
See also CLC 27
Parker, Robert Miles 1939- 118
Parker, Robert Stewart 1915- 103
Parker, Rolland (Sandau) 1928- CANR-2
Earlier sketch in CA 45-48
Parker, Ron
See Parker, Ronald B(ruce)
Parker, Ronald B(ruce) 1932- 117
Parker, Ronald K(eith) 1939- 108
Parker, Rowland 1912- CANR-10
Earlier sketch in CA 65-68
Parker, Sanford S. 1919(?)-1980
Obituary 97-100
Parker, Scott 1950- 113
Parker, Stanley R(obert) 1927- CANR-19
Earlier sketch in CA 103
Parker, Stephen Jan 1939- 118
Parker, Stewart 1941- 103
Parker, T(homas) H(enry) L(ouis)
1916- CANR-6
Earlier sketch in CA 7-8R
Parker, Theodore 1810-1860 .... DLB-1
Parker, Thomas F(rancis) 1932- 73-76
Parker, Thomas Maynard 1906- CAP-2
Earlier sketch in CA 17-18
Parker, Tom
See Parker, John Thomas
Parker, W(illiam) H(enry) 1912- CANR-13
Earlier sketch in CA 33-36R
Parker, W(ilford) Oren 1911- 41-44R
Parker, Watson 1924- 106
Parker, William Riley 1906-1968 .... CAP-2
Earlier sketch in CA 17-18
Parker, Willie J. 1924- 77-80
Parker, Wyman W(est) 1912- 15-16R
Parkerson, John 1885(?)-1978 Obituary ...77-80
Parkes, Colin Murray 1928- 81-84
Parkes, Henry B. 1904-1972 Obituary 33-36R
Parkes, James William 1896-1981
Obituary 104
Parkes, Lucas
See Harris, John (Wyndham Parkes Lucas) Beynon
Parkes, (Grahem) Roger 1933- 53-56
Parkes, Terence 1927- 104
Parket, I(rwin) Robert 1931- 114
Parkhill, Forbes 1892- 4R
Parkhill, John
See Cox, William (Robert)
Parkhill, Wilson 1901- 5-6R
Parkhurst, Helen 1887-1973 Obituary 41-44R
Parkhurst, Louis Gifford, Jr. 1946- 113
Parkhurst, Winthrop 1892(?)-1983
Obituary 110
Parkin, Alan 1934- 29-32R
Parkin, David 1940- CANR-13
Earlier sketch in CA 25-28R
Parkin, Frank 1940- CLC-43
Parkin, G(eorge) Raleigh 1896-1977(?)
Obituary 106
Parkin, Molly 1932- 104
Parkin, Peter Hubert 1917-1984 Obituary ... 113
Parkinson, C(yril) Northcote 1909- CANR-5
Earlier sketch in CA 7-8R
Parkinson, (Frederick) Charles Douglas
1916- CAP-1
Earlier sketch in CA 11-12
Parkinson, Claire L(ucille) 1948- 120
Parkinson, Cornelia M. 1925- CANR-15
Earlier sketch in CA 81-84
Parkinson, Ethelyn M(inerva) 1906- CANR-1
Earlier sketch in CA 49-52
See also SATA 11
Parkinson, J(ohn) R(ichard) 1922- 102
Parkinson, Kathryn N. 1954- 120
Parkinson, Kathy
See Parkinson, Kathryn N.
Parkinson, Michael 1944- 29-32R
Parkinson, Roger 1939-1978 106
Parkinson, Thomas (Francis) 1920- CANR-3
Earlier sketch in CA 7-8R
Parkinson, Thomas P(aul) 102
Parkinson, Tom
See Parkinson, Thomas P(aul)
Parkman, Francis, Jr. 1823-1893 ..... DLB-1, 30
Parks, Aileen Wells 1901- 5-6R
Parks, Arva Moore 1939- 103
Parks, David 1944- 25-28R
Parks, Douglas R(ichard) 1942- 111
Parks, Edd Winfield 1906-1968 ....7-8R
See also SATA 10
Parks, Edmund 1911- 69-72
Parks, Edna D(orintha) 1910- 15-16R
Parks, Gordon (Alexander Buchanan)
1912- 41-44R
See also SATA 8
See also DLB 33
See also CLC 1, 16
See also AITN 2
Parks, Joseph Howard 1903- 4R
Parks, Lloyd Clifford 1922- 57-60
Parks, Pat 1918- 61-64
Parks, Robert James 1940- 65-68
Parks, Stephen Robert 1940- 65-68
Parks, William 1698(?)-1750 .... DLB-43
Parksmith, George
See Bush, George S(idney)
Parlato, Salvatore J(oseph), Jr. 1936- 73-76
Parlett, David (Sidney) 1939- CANR-20
Earlier sketch in CA 103
Parley, Peter
See Goodrich, Samuel Griswold
Parlin, Bradley W(illiam) 1938- 69-72
Parlin, John
See Graves, Charles Parlin
Parma, Clemens
See Menzel, Roderich
Parman, Donald L(ee) 1932- 65-68
Parmelee, Alice 1903- CAP-2
Earlier sketch in CA 21-22
Parmenter, Ross 1912- 17-18R
Parmer, J(ess) Norman 1925- 7-8R
Parmet, Herbert S. 1929- CANR-11
Earlier sketch in CA 21-22R
Parmet, Robert D(avid) 1938- 77-80
Parmet, Simon 1897- CAP-1
Earlier sketch in CA 13-14
Parnaby, Owen Wilfred 1921- 11-12R
Parnall, Peter 1936- 81-84
See also SATA 16
Parnas, Raymond I. 1937- 33-36R
Parnes, Herbert S(aul) 1919- CANR-15
Earlier sketch in CA 41-44R
Parnes, Sidmore 1928-1984 Obituary 113
Parnes, Sidney J. 1922- CANR-10
Earlier sketch in CA 21-22R
Paroissien, David (Harry) 1939- 111
Parque, Richard (Anthony) 1935- 124
Parr, Charles McKew 1884- CAP-1
Earlier sketch in CA 11-12
Parr, James A(llan) 1936- 49-52
Parr, John (Lloyd) 1928- 102
Parr, Letitia (Evelyn) 1906- 103
See also SATA 37
Parr, Lucy 1924- 29-32R
See also SATA 10
Parr, Michael 1927- 17-18R
Parra, Nicanor 1914- 85-88
See also CLC 2
Parramore, Thomas C(ustis) 1932- 112
Parrinder, E(dward) Geoffrey 1910- CANR-10
Earlier sketch in CA 23-24R
Parrington, Vernon L(ouis) 1871-1929
Brief entry 113
See also DLB 17, 63
Parrini, Carl P. 1933- Brief entry 107
Parrino, John J(oseph) 1942- 101
Parrino, Michael 1915(?)-1976 Obituary ...65-68
Parriott, Sara 1953- 107
Parris, Addison W(ilson) 1923-1975 ..... CAP-2
Earlier sketch in CA 25-28
Parris, Guichard 1903- 81-84
Parris, Judith (Ann) H(eimlich) 1939- 57-60
Parrish, Anne 1888-1957 Brief entry 115
See also SATA 27
Parrish, Bernard P. 1936- 103
Parrish, Bernie
See Parrish, Bernard P.
Parrish, Carl (George) 1904-1965 ....7-8R
Parrish, Eugene
See Harding, Donald Edward
Parrish, John A(lbert) 1939- 37-40R
Parrish, Louis 1927- Brief entry 107
Parrish, Mary
See Cousins, Margaret
Parrish, Mary Frances
See Fisher, M(ary) F(rances) K(ennedy)
Parrish, (Frederick) Maxfield
1870-1966 .... SATA-14
Parrish, Michael E. 1942- 29-32R
Parrish, Patt
See Bucheister, Patt
Parrish, Robert (Reese) 1916- 81-84
Parrish, Stephen Maxfield 1921- 104
Parrish, Thomas (Douglas) 1927- 93-96
Parrish, Wayland Maxfield 1887-? CAP-2
Earlier sketch in CA 23-24
Parrish, Wendy 1950- 73-76
Parrish, William E(arl) 1931- CANR-3
Earlier sketch in CA 2R
Parrott, Cecil (Cuthbert) 1909-1984 103
Obituary 113
Parrott, Fred J(ames) 1913- 41-44R
Parrott, Ian 1916- CANR-2
Earlier sketch in CA 7-8R
Parrott, (Alonzo) Leslie 1922- 97-100
Parrott, Lindesay 1901-1987 Obituary 123
Parrott, Lora Lee 1923- 25-28R
Parry, Albert 1901- CANR-6
Earlier sketch in CA 4R
Parry, Clive 1917-1982 Obituary 107
Parry, David 1908- 113
Parry, Ellwood C(omly) III 1941- 93-96
Parry, Hugh J(ones) 1916- 13-14R
Parry, J(ohn) H(orace) 1914- CANR-6
Earlier sketch in CA 5-6R
Parry, John
See Whelpton, (George) Eric
Parry, Linda (Alberta) 1945- 111
Parry, Marian 1924- 41-44R
See also SATA 13
Parry, Michael Patrick 1947- 101
Parry, Thomas H. 1904-1985 Obituary 116
Parry-Jones, Daniel 1891- 15-16R
Parseghian, Ara (Raoul) 1923- Brief entry .. 105
Parsegian, V(ozcan) Lawrence 1908- 57-60
Parsifal
See Curl, James Stevens
Parsloe, Guy Charles 1900- CAP-1
Earlier sketch in CA 13-14
Parson, Ruben L(eRoy) 1907- 15-16R
Parson Lot
See Kingsley, Charles
Parsons, C(hristopher) J(ames) 1941- 103
Parsons, Charles (Dacre) 1933- 45-48
Parsons, Coleman O(scar) 1905- CAP-1
Earlier sketch in CA 15-16
Parsons, Cynthia 1926- CANR-21
Earlier sketch in CA 45-48
Parsons, Denys 1914- CANR-12
Earlier sketch in CA 15-16R
Parsons, Ellen
See Dragonwagon, Crescent
Parsons, Elmer E. 1919- 25-28R
Parsons, Geoffrey 1908-1981 Obituary 105
Parsons, Harriet Oettinger
1906(?)-1983(?) Obituary 108
Parsons, Howard L(ee) 1918- CANR-17
Earlier sketches in CA 49-52, CANR-1
Parsons, Ian (Macnaghten) 1906-1980 ...97-100
Obituary 102
Parsons, Jack 1920- 104
Parsons, James Bunyan 1921- 29-32R
Parsons, John (Anthony) 1938- 120
Parsons, Kermit Carlyle 1927- 29-32R
Parsons, Kitty ?-1976 ....15-16R
Obituary 120
Parsons, Louella (Oettinger) 1881-1972 ...93-96
Obituary 37-40R
Parsons, Malcolm Barningham 1919-
Brief entry 108
Parsons, Martin 1907- 53-56
Parsons, R(ichard) A(ugustus) 101
Parsons, Stanley B., Jr. 1927- CANR-21
Earlier sketch in CA 45-48
Parsons, Talcott 1902-1979 .... CANR-4
Obituary 85-88
Earlier sketch in CA 7-8R
Parsons, Thornton H(arris) 1921- 73-76
Parsons, Tom
See MacPherson, Thomas George
Parsons, William Edward, Jr. 1936- 21-22R
Parsons, William T(homas) 1923- 65-68
Partain, Floydene 1924- 114
Partch, Virgil Franklin II 1916-1984 108
Obituary 113
See also SATA 39, 45
Partington, F. H.
See Yoxall, Harry W(aldo)
Partington, Martin 1944- 124
Partington, Susan Trowbridge 1924- 11-12R
Partlow, Vern 1910(?)-1987 Obituary 121
Partner, Peter (David) 1924- 85-88
Parton, James 1822-1891 .... DLB-30
Parton, Margaret 1915- 97-100
Parton, Sara Payson Willis 1811-1872 .. DLB-43
Partridge, Anthony
See Oppenheim, E(dward) Phillips
Partridge, Astley Cooper 1901- 103
Partridge, Benjamin W(aring), Jr. 1915- ..25-28R
See also SATA 28
Partridge, Edward B(ellamy) 1916- 65-68
Partridge, Elinore Hughes 1937- 115
Partridge, Eric (Honeywood)
1894-1979 .... CANR-3
Obituary 85-88
Earlier sketch in CA 4R
Partridge, Ernest 1935- 115
Partridge, Frances 1900- 29-32R
Partridge, Jenny (Lilian) 1947- 109
See also SATA 37
Partridge, Larry (Harold) 1949- 114
Partridge, William L(ee) 1944- CANR-1
Earlier sketch in CA 45-48
Parulski, George R(ichard), Jr. 1954- .. CANR-17
Earlier sketch in CA 97-100
Parvin, Betty 1916- CANR-17
Earlier sketch in CA 97-100
Parx, C. C.
See Gilmore, Christopher Cook
Parzen, Herbert 1896- 25-28R
Pasachoff, Jay M(yron) 1943- 117
Pasamanik, Luisa 1930- 101
Pascal, Anthony H(enry) 1933- CANR-16
Earlier sketch in CA 29-32R
Pascal, David 1918- 11-12R
See also SATA 14
Pascal, Francine 1938- 123
Brief entry 115
See also SATA 37
Pascal, Gerald Ross 1907- 37-40R
Pascal, John Robert 1932(?)-1981
Obituary 102
Pascal, Paul 1925- 23-24R
Pascal, Roy 1904-1980 .... CANR-6
Earlier sketch in CA 7-8R
Pascale, Richard Tanner 1938- 53-56
Pascarella, Perry (James) 1934- 93-96
Paschal, George H., Jr. 1925- 29-32R
Paschal, Nancy
See Trotter, Grace V(iolet)
Paschall, H. Franklin 1922- 25-28R
Pascoe, Elaine 1946- 124
Pascoe, Elizabeth Jean 69-72
Pascoe, John (Dobree) 1908-1972 .... CAP-1
Earlier sketch in CA 13-14
Pascu, Stefan 1914- 117
Pascudniak, Pascal
See Lupoff, Richard A(llen)
Pasewark, William R(obert) 1924- CANR-15
Earlier sketch in CA 33-36R
Pashko, Stanley 1913- 97-100
See also SATA 29
Pasinetti, P(ier-) M(aria) 1913- 73-76
Pask, Gordon 1928- 111
Pask, Raymond (Frank) 1944- CANR-22
Earlier sketch in CA 105
Paskowicz, Patricia
See Molan, Pat Carlson
Pasley, Virginia Schmitz 1905-1986
Obituary 119
Pasmanik, Wolf 1924- 101
Pasolini, Pier Paolo 1922-1975 93-96
Obituary 61-64
See also CLC 20, 37
Pasquier, Marie-Claire 1933- 29-32R
Pass, Gail 1940- 65-68
Passage, Charles Edward 1913-1983 .....33-36R
Obituary 110
Passailaigue, Thomas E.
See Paisley, Tom
Passantino, Gretchen 1953- 110
Passantino, Robert Louis 1951- 108
Passel, Anne W(onders) 1918- CANR-11
Earlier sketch in CA 29-32R
Passell, Peter 1944- CANR-2
Earlier sketch in CA 45-48
Passerin D'Entreves, Alessandro 1902- 69-72
Passeron, Rene (Jean) 1920- CANR-17
Earlier sketch in CA 97-100
Passes(-Pazolski), Alan 1943- 85-88
Passin, Herbert 1916- CANR-20
Earlier sketches in CA 45-48, CANR-1
Passman, Brian 1934- 25-28R
Passmore, John (Arthur) 1914- CANR-6
Earlier sketch in CA 13-14R
Passmore, Richard E. (?)-1982 Obituary ... 107
Passonneau, Joseph Russell 1921- 19-20R
Passow, A(aron) Harry 1920- CANR-3
Earlier sketch in CA 3R
Passwater, Richard (Albert) 1937- CANR-19
Earlier sketch in CA 97-100

Past, Ray(mond Edgar) 1918- 29-32R
Pastan, Linda (Olenik) 1932- CANR-18
Earlier sketch in CA 61-64
See also DLB 5
See also CLC 27
Pasternack, Stefan Alan 1939- Brief entry ... 108
Pasternak, Boris (Leonidovich) 1890-1960
Obituary 116
See also CLC 7, 10, 18
Pasternak, Burton 1933- Brief entry 109
Pasternak, Velvel 1933- 73-76
Pastine, Maureen (Diane) 1944- CANR-8
Earlier sketch in CA 57-60
Paston, Herbert S. 1928- 49-52
Pastor, Robert (Alan) 1947- 105
Pastore, Arthur R(alph), Jr. 1922- 19-20R
Pastore, Nicholas 1916- 29-32R
Pastorius, Francis Daniel 1651-1720(?) .. DLB-24
Pastor X
See Johnson, Merle Allison
Patai, Daphne 1943- 113
Patai, Raphael 1910- CANR-20
Earlier sketch in CA 29-32R
Pataky, Denes 1921- 15-16R
Patanne, Maria
See La Pietra, Mary
Patapoff, Elizabeth 1917- 29-32R
Patchen, Kenneth 1911-1972 .... CANR-3
Obituary 33-36R
Earlier sketch in CA 4R
See also DLB 16, 48
See also CLC 1, 2, 18
Patchen, Martin 1932- 57-60
Patchett, Mary (Osborne) Elwyn 1897- .. CANR-3
Earlier sketch in CA 7-8R
Pate, Billie 1932- 61-64
Pate, Martha B. Lucas 1912-1983
Obituary 110
Patel, Harshad C(hhotabhia) 1934- 53-56
Pateman, Carole 1940- 85-88
Pateman, Kim
See Levin, Kim
Pateman, Trevor 1947- 49-52
Patent, Dorothy Hinshaw 1940- CANR-24
Earlier sketches in CA 61-64, CANR-9
See also SATA 22
Pater, Walter 1839-1894 .... DLB-57
Paterson, Alistair (Ian Hughes) 1929- 107
Paterson, Allen P(eter) 1933- 93-96
Paterson, Ann 1916- 33-36R
Paterson, Barbara (Olive) 1933- 112
Paterson, Diane (R. Cole) 1946- 101
See also SATA 33
Paterson, George W(illiam) 1931- 103
Paterson, Huntley
See Ludovici, Anthony M(ario)
Paterson, John 1887- CAP-1
Earlier sketch in CA 13-14
Paterson, John Harris 1923- CANR-6
Earlier sketch in CA 7-8R
Paterson, Judith
See Jones, Judith Paterson
Paterson, Katherine (Womeldorf) 1932- .. 23-24R
See also SATA 13
See also DLB 52
See also CLC 12, 30
See also CLR 7
Paterson, (James Edmund) Neil 1916- ... 13-14R
Paterson, R(onald) W(illiam) K(eith)
1933- 33-36R
Paterson, Thomas G(raham) 1941- CANR-16
Earlier sketches in CA 45-48, CANR-1
Paterson, William E(dgar) 1941- CANR-13
Earlier sketch in CA 61-64
Paterson-Jones, Judith
See Jones, Judith Paterson
Patinkin, Don 1922- CANR-10
Earlier sketch in CA 19-20R
Patka, Frederick 1922- 11-12R
Patman, (John William) Wright 1893-1976 .. 109
Obituary 107
Patmore, Coventry 1823-1896 .... DLB-35
Patmore, Derek Coventry 1908-1972 .... 7-8R
Obituary 103
Patmore, John Allan 1931- 104
Paton, Alan (Stewart) 1903- CANR-22
Earlier sketches in CA 15-16, CAP-1
See also SATA 11
See also CLC 4, 10, 25
Paton, David Macdonald 1913- 114
Paton, George (Whitecross) 1902- CAP-1
Earlier sketch in CA 11-12
Paton, Herbert James 1887-1969 .... CAP-1
Earlier sketch in CA 13-14
Paton, Jane (Elizabeth) 1934- SATA-35
Paton, Joseph Noel 1821-1901 .... DLB-35
Paton, Steven C. 1928(?)-1980
Obituary 97-100
Patoski, Margaret (Nancy Pearson) 1930- .. 69-72
Patra, Atul Chandra 1915- 57-60
Patras, Louis 1931- CANR-15
Earlier sketch in CA 85-88
Patrice, Ann
See Galbraith, Georgie Starbuck
Patrick, Alison (Mary Houston) 1921- 49-52
Patrick, Clarence H(odges) 1907- 33-36R
Patrick, Cuthbert Melvin 1914-1985
Obituary 116
Patrick, Douglas Arthur 1905- 17-18R
Patrick, Hugh 1930- 41-44R
Patrick, J(ohn) Max 1911- CANR-5
Earlier sketch in CA 7-8R
Patrick, James (Arthur) 1933- CANR-20
Earlier sketch in CA 104
Patrick, John 1905- 89-92
See also DLB 7
Patrick, Johnstone G(illespie) 1918- CANR-2
Earlier sketch in CA 5-6R
Patrick, Leal
See Stone, Patti
Patrick, Lilian
See Keogh, Lilian Gilmore
Patrick, Martha 1956- 109
Patrick, Maxine
See Maxwell, Patricia
Patrick, Q.
See Wheeler, Hugh (Callingham)
Patrick, Rembert Wallace 1909- 7-8R
Patrick, Robert 1937- CANR-1
Earlier sketch in CA 45-48
See also AITN 2
Patrick, Vincent 1935- CANR-22
Earlier sketch in CA 104
Patrick, Walton Richard 1909- 37-40R
Patrides, C(onstantinos) A(postolos)
1930- CANR-20
Earlier sketches in CA 15-16R, CANR-5
Patrikeyev
See Healey-Kay, (Sydney Francis) Patrick (Chippendall)
Patrouch, Joseph F(rancis), Jr. 1935- 49-52
Patsauq, Markoosie 1942- 101
Patsouras, Louis
See Patras, Louis
Pattee, Howard Hunt, Jr. 1926-
Brief entry 109
Pattemore, Arnel W(ilfred) 1934- 53-56
Patten, Bebe H(arrison) 1913- 61-64
Patten, Brian 1946- 25-28R
See also SATA 29
Patten, Lewis B(yford) 1915-1981 .... CANR-21
Obituary 103
Earlier sketch in CA 25-28R
Patten, Nigel 1940- 25-28R
Patten, Priscilla C(arla) 1950- 117
Patten, (Bebe) Rebecca 1950- 117
Patten, Robert L(owry) 1939- 109
Patten, Thomas H., Jr. 1929- 21-22R
Patterson, A(lfred) Temple 1902-1983 103
Obituary 111
Patterson, Alicia Brooks 1906-1963
Obituary 89-92
Patterson, Barbara 1944- 110
Patterson, Benton Rain 1929- 122
Patterson, C(ecil) H(olden) 1912- CANR-16
Earlier sketch in CA 23-24R
Patterson, Carolyn Bennett 1921- 106
Patterson, Charles 1935- 117
Patterson, Charles D(arold) 1928- 122
Patterson, Charles E(dwin), Jr. 1934- 41-44R
Patterson, Charles H(enry) 1896- 37-40R
Patterson, Charlotte (Buist) 1942- 29-32R
Patterson, Craig E(ugene) 1945- 93-96
Patterson, David S(ands) 1937- 65-68
Patterson, Edwin W(ilhite) 1889-1965 .... 3R
Patterson, Eleanor Medill 1881(?)-1948
Brief entry 118
See also DLB 29
Patterson, Elinor Josephine
See Patterson, Eleanor Medill
Patterson, Elizabeth C. 29-32R
Patterson, Emma L. 1904- CAP-2
Earlier sketch in CA 25-28
Patterson, Eric James 1891-1972 .... CAP-1
Earlier sketch in CA 11-12
Patterson, Evelyn Roelofs 1917- 5-6R
Patterson, Frank Harmon 1912-
Brief entry 109
Patterson, Frank M(organ) 1931- 45-48
Patterson, Franklin (Kessel) 1916- 45-48
Patterson, Gardner 1916- Brief entry 106
Patterson, Geoffrey 1943- 103
See also SATA 44
Patterson, Gerald R. 1926- 41-44R
Patterson, Harriet-Louise H(olland) 1903- . CAP-1
Earlier sketch in CA 15-16
Patterson, Harry
See Patterson, Henry
Patterson, Henry 1929- 15-16R
Patterson, James (Tyler) 1935- 21-22R
Patterson, Jane
See Britton, Mattie Lula Cooper
Patterson, Janet McFadden 1915- 89-92
Patterson, Jefferson 1891-1977 Obituary ... 115
Patterson, Jerry E(ugene) 1931-
Brief entry 107
Patterson, John McCready 1913-1983
Obituary 109
Patterson, Joseph Medill 1879-1946
Brief entry 118
See also DLB 29
Patterson, K(arl) David 1941- 65-68
Patterson, L(loyd) G(eorge), Jr. 1929- ... 41-44R
Patterson, L(yman) Ray 1929- 33-36R
Patterson, Lawrence Thomas II 1937- 104
Patterson, Letha L(emon) 1913- 5-6R
Patterson, Lillie G. 73-76
See also SATA 14
Patterson, Lindsay 1942- 77-80
Patterson, Margaret C(leveland) 1923- .. CANR-7
Earlier sketch in CA 57-60
Patterson, Mary H(agelin) 1928-1973
Obituary 37-40R
Patterson, Michael 1939- 111
Patterson, (James) Milton 1927- 53-56
Patterson, Olive
See Rowland, D(onald) S(ydney)
Patterson, (Horace) Orlando (Lloyd)
1940- 65-68
Patterson, (Leighton) Paige 1942- CANR-10
Earlier sketch in CA 25-28R
Patterson, Paul 1909- 85-88
Patterson, Peter
See Terson, Peter
Patterson, Raymond R. 1929- 29-32R
Patterson, Rebecca Elizabeth Coy
1911-1975 103
Patterson, Richard 1908(?)-1976
Obituary 69-72
Patterson, Richard North 1947- 85-88
Patterson, Robert B(enjamin) 1934- 73-76
Patterson, Robert Leet 1893- 19-20R
Patterson, Ruth P(olk) 1930- 119
Patterson, Samuel C(harles) 1931- CANR-22
Earlier sketches in CA 19-20R, CANR-7
Patterson, Samuel White 1883-1975 .... CAP-2
Obituary 61-64
Earlier sketch in CA 17-18
Patterson, Sheila Caffyn 1918- 9-10R
Patterson, Sylvia W(iese) 1940- 61-64
Patterson, Virginia 1931- 102
Patterson, W. M(acLean) 1912(?)-1976
Obituary 69-72
Patterson, W. Morgan 1925- 65-68
Patterson, Walter C(ram) 1936- CANR-20
Earlier sketch in CA 103
Patterson, Ward L(amont) 1933- CANR-23
Earlier sketches in CA 57-60, CANR-8
Patterson, Wayne 1946- CANR-16
Earlier sketch in CA 85-88
Patterson, Webster T. 1920- 25-28R
Patterson, William Dudley 1910-1986
Obituary 119
Patterson, William L(orenzo) 1890-1980 .. 41-44R
Obituary 97-100
Patti, Archimedes L(eonida) A(ttilio) 1913- .. 106
Patti, Ercole 1904(?)-1976 Obituary 69-72
Pattie, Alice 1906- CAP-2
Earlier sketch in CA 29-32
Pattillo, Henry 1726-1801 .... DLB-37
Pattillo, James W(ilson) 1937- CANR-11
Earlier sketch in CA 19-20R
Pattillo, Manning M., Jr. 1919- 21-22R
Pattinson, Nancy Evelyn Brief entry 117
Pattison, O(live) R(uth) B(rown) 1916- ... 29-32R
Pattison, Walter Thomas 1903- 81-84
Patton, Alva Rae 1908- 5-6R
Patton, Arch 1908- CAP-1
Earlier sketch in CA 15-16
Patton, Bobby R(ay) 1935- CANR-17
Earlier sketches in CA 45-48, CANR-1
Patton, Brian (Lee) 1943- 123
Patton, Frances Gray 1906- 101
Patton, Frank
See Palmer, Raymond A.
Patton, Gerald W(ilson) 1947- 112
Patton, James W(elch) 1900- CAP-1
Earlier sketch in CA 11-12
Patton, Kenneth L(eo) 1911- CANR-7
Earlier sketch in CA 19-20R
Patton, Oliver B(eirne) 1920- 81-84
Patton, Rob(ert Warren) 1943- 37-40R
Pattullo, George 1879-1967 Obituary 115
Patty, C. Robert 1925- CANR-10
Earlier sketch in CA 25-28R
Patty, Ernest N(ewton) 1894-1976 .... CAP-2
Earlier sketch in CA 25-28
Patty, James S(ingleton) 1925- 53-56
Paturi, Felix R.
See Mindt, Heinz R.
Pauck, Wilhelm 1901-1981 81-84
Obituary 104
Pauk, Walter 1914- CANR-18
Earlier sketches in CA 5-6R, CANR-2
Pauker, Guy J(ean) 1916- CANR-1
Earlier sketch in CA 45-48
Pauker, John 1920- 25-28R
Pauker, Ted
See Conquest, (George) Robert (Acworth)
Paul, Aileen 1917- CANR-19
Earlier sketch in CA 41-44R
See also SATA 12
Paul, Anthony (Marcus) 1937- 77-80
Paul, (John) Anthony 1941- 77-80
Paul, Auren
See Uris, Auren
Paul, Charles B. 1931- 105
Paul, Charlotte 1916- CANR-7
Earlier sketch in CA 5-6R
Paul, Daniel
See Kessel, Lipmann
Paul, Danielle
See Mittermeyer, Helen (Hayton Monteith)
Paul, David W(arren) 1944- 107
Paul, Elizabeth
See Crow, Donna Fletcher
Paul, Elliot (Harold) 1891-1958
Brief entry 107
See also DLB 4
Paul, Emily
See Eicher, (Ethel) Elizabeth
Paul, F. W.
See Fairman, Paul W.
Paul, Florrie 1928- 61-64
Paul, Geoffrey John 1921-1983 Obituary ... 110
Paul, Gordon L. 1935- CANR-7
Earlier sketch in CA 19-20R
Paul, Grace 1908- 19-20R
Paul, Hugo
See Little, Paul H(ugo)
Paul, I(rving) H. 1928- 103
Paul, James 1936- SATA-23
Paul, Jordan 1936- 97-100
Paul, Judith Edison 1939- CANR-16
Earlier sketch in CA 29-32R
Paul, Leslie (Allen) 1905-1985 .... CANR-3
Obituary 117
Earlier sketch in CA 4R
Paul, Louis
See Placet, Leroi
Paul, Margaret 1939- 97-100
Paul, Norman L(eo) 1926- 61-64
Paul, Raymond 1940- 106
Paul, Robert
See Roberts, John G(aither)
Paul, Robert S(idney) 1918- CANR-3
Earlier sketch in CA 1R
Paul, Rodman Wilson 1912-1987 .... CANR-3
Obituary 122
Earlier sketch in CA 2R
Paul, Roland A(rthur) 1937- 41-44R
Paul, Sheri
See Resnick, Sylvia (Safran)
Paul, Sherman 1920- CANR-3
Earlier sketch in CA 7-8R
Paul, William
See Eicher, (Ethel) Elizabeth
Paulden, Sydney (Maurice) 1932- CANR-12
Earlier sketch in CA 29-32R
Paulding, James Kirke 1778-1860 .... DLB-3, 59
Pauley, Barbara Anne 1925- 89-92
Pauley, Bruce F. 1937- 41-44R
Pauley, (Margaret) Jane 1950- 106
Paulhan, Jean 1884-1968 Obituary 25-28R
Pauli, Hertha (Ernestine) 1909-1973 .... CANR-2
Obituary 41-44R
Earlier sketch in CA 2R
See also SATA 3, 26
Paulin, Thomas Neilson 1949- Brief entry ... 123
Paulin, Tom
See Paulin, Thomas Neilson
See also DLB 40
See also CLC 37
Pauling, Linus (Carl) 1901- 116
Brief entry 110
Paull, Grace A. 1898- SATA-24
Paull, Raymond Allan 1906-1972 .... CAP-1
Earlier sketch in CA 9-10
Pau-Llosa, Ricardo 1954- 111
Paulon, Flavia 1907(?)-1987 Obituary 122
Pauls, John P. 1916- 45-48
Paulsell, William Oliver 1935- 111
Paulsen, F(rank) Robert 1922- 21-22R
Paulsen, Gary 1939- 73-76
See also SATA 22, 50
Paulsen, Lois (Thompson) 1905- CAP-2
Earlier sketch in CA 19-20
Paulsen, Wolfgang 1910- CANR-11
Earlier sketch in CA 19-20R
Paulson, Belden 1927- 21-22R
Paulson, Jack
See Jackson, C(aary) Paul
Paulson, Morton C. 1923- 111
Paulson, Ronald (Howard) 1930- CANR-15
Earlier sketch in CA 19-20R
Paulsson, Bjoern 1932- 61-64
Paulsson, Thomas A(lfred) 1923- 11-12R
Paulston, Christina Bratt CANR-10
Earlier sketch in CA 65-68
Paulston, Rolland G(lenn) 1929- CANR-13
Earlier sketch in CA 33-36R
Paulu, Burton 1910- 15-16R
Paulus, John Douglas 1917- 69-72
Paul VI, Pope 1897-1978 81-84
Obituary 77-80
Pauly, Thomas H(arry) 1940- 115
Paun, Maggie
See Voysey, Margaret
Pauquet, Gina Ruck
See Ruck-Pauquet, Gina
Paustovsky, Konstantin (Georgievich)
1892-1968 93-96
Obituary 25-28R
See also CLC 40
Pautler, Albert J., Jr. 1935- 33-36R
Pauw, Berthold Adolf 1924- 9-10R
Pauwels, Louis 1920- Brief entry 111
Pavalko, Ronald M(ichael) 1934- 57-60
Pavarotti, Luciano 1935- Brief entry 112
Pavel, Frances 1907- 21-22R
See also SATA 10
Pavenstedt, Eleanor 1903- 21-22R
Pavese, Cesare 1908-1950 Brief entry 104
See also TCLC 3
Pavey, Don 1922- 107
Pavitranda, Swami 1896(?)-1977
Obituary 73-76
Pavlakis, Christopher 1928- 73-76
Pavletich, Aida 101
Pavlik, Evelyn Marie 1954- 97-100
Pavlov, Ivan Petrovich 1849-1936
Brief entry 118
Pavlowitch, Stevan K. 1933- CANR-13
Earlier sketch in CA 33-36R
Pavord, Anna 1940- 115
Pawelczynska, Anna 1922- 101
Pawle, Gerald 1913- 5-6R
Pawley, Bernard C(linton) 1911-1981 .... 25-28R
Obituary 105
Pawley, Martin Edward 1938- 101
Pawley, Thomas Desire III 1917- 29-32R
Pawlick, Thomas F(rancis) 1941- 119
Pawlicki, T(homas) B(ert) 1930- 109
Pawlikowski, John T. 1940- CANR-24
Earlier sketches in CA 21-22R, CANR-9
Pawlowicz, Sala Kaminska 1925- 7-8R
Pawlowski, Gareth L. 1939- 29-32R
Pawson, G(eoffrey) P(hilip) H(enry) 1904- .. 7-8R
Pax, Clyde 1928- 49-52
Paxman, Jeremy Dickson 1950- 108
Paxson, Ethel 1885- 25-28R

Paxton, Dr. John
See Lawton, Sherman P(axton)
Paxton, Jack 1939-1985 Obituary 117
Paxton, Jack
See Lawton, Sherman P(axton)
Paxton, John 1911-1985 Obituary 114
See also DLB 44
Paxton, Lois
See Low, Lois Dorothea
Paxton, Mary Jean Wallace 1930- 109
Paxton, Robert O(wen) 1932- 73-76
Paxton, Thomas R. 1937- 105
Paxton, Tom
See Paxton, Thomas R.
Payack, Paul J. J. 1950- 69-72
Paye, Robert
See Campbell, (Gabrielle) Margaret (Vere)
Payelle, Raymond-Gerard 1898-1971
Obituary 33-36R
Payer, Cheryl Ann 1940- 61-64
Payes, Rachel C(osgrove) 1922- CANR-16
Earlier sketches in CA 49-52, CANR-1
Payn, James 1830-1898 .... DLB-18
Payne, Alan
See Jakes, John (William)
Payne, Alma Smith
See Ralston, Alma (Smith Payne)
Payne, B(en) Iden 1888-1976 73-76
Obituary 65-68
Payne, Basil 1928- 81-84
Payne, Bruce 1911- 11-12R
Payne, Charles 1909- 103
Payne, David A(llen) 1935- 25-28R
Payne, Donald Gordon 1924- CANR-24
Earlier sketches in CA 15-16R, CANR-9
See also SATA 37
Payne, Emmy
See West, Emily Govan
Payne, Eric Francis Jules 1895- 57-60
Payne, Ernest A(lexander) 1902-1980 ... CANR-9
Obituary 105
Earlier sketch in CA 11-12R
Payne, F(rances) Anne 1932- 73-76
Payne, J(ohn) Barton 1922- CANR-3
Earlier sketch in CA 1R
Payne, J(ames) Gregory 1949- 123
Payne, Jack 1926- 33-36R
Payne, James L. 1939- 33-36R
Payne, Joan Balfour (?)-1973 Obituary ... 41-44R
Payne, John 1842-1916 .... DLB-35
Payne, John Howard 1791-1852 .... DLB-37
Payne, Karen 1951- 111
Payne, Ladell 1933- Brief entry 111
Payne, Laurence 1919- 7-8R
Payne, LaVeta Maxine 1916- 37-40R
Payne, Leanne 1932- 115
Payne, Michael 1941- CANR-12
Earlier sketch in CA 29-32R
Payne, Mildred Y(ounger) 1906- 41-44R
Payne, Richard A. 1934- 97-100
Payne, (Pierre Stephen) Robert
1911-1983 .... 25-28R
Obituary 109
Payne, Robert O. 1924- 97-100
Payne, Ronald 1926- 97-100
Payne, Stanley G(eorge) 1934- CANR-3
Earlier sketch in CA 1R
Paynter, Will(iam) 1903-1984 Obituary 115
Paynter, William Henry 1901- 15-16R
Paynton, Clifford T. 1929- 37-40R
Payson, Dale 1943- CANR-3
Earlier sketch in CA 49-52
See also SATA 9
Payson, Herb(ert III) 1927- 115
Payzant, Charles SATA-18
Paz, A.
See Pahz, James Alon
Paz, Carlos F(ernando) 1937- 109
Paz, Gil
See Lugones, Leopoldo
Paz, Octavio 1914- 73-76
See also CLC 3, 4, 6, 10, 19
Paz, Zan
See Pahz, (Anne) Cheryl Suzanne
Pazder, Lawrence Henry 1936- 107
p'Bitek, Okot 1931-1982 124
Obituary 107
Peabody, Barbara 1933- 122
Peabody, Elizabeth Palmer 1804-1894 .... DLB-1
Peabody, Oliver William Bourn
1799-1848 .... DLB-59
Peabody, Robert Lee 1931- 11-12R
Peabody, Velton 1936- 53-56
Peace, Richard 1938- CANR-14
Earlier sketch in CA 25-28R
Peace, Roger Craft 1899-1968 Obituary ... 89-92
Peach, Lawrence du Garde 1890-1974 101
Peach, William Nelson 1912- 23-24R
Peacher, Georgiana M(elicent) 1919- 25-28R
Peachey, Laban 1927- 19-20R
Peacock, Alan T(urner) 1922- CANR-3
Earlier sketch in CA 4R
Peacock, Basil 1898- 103
Peacock, D(avid) P(hilip) S(pencer) 1939- ... 123
Peacock, Dick
See Peacock, Richard
Peacock, James Craig 1888(?)-1977
Obituary 73-76
Peacock, James L(owe) 1937- Brief entry ... 113
Peacock, L(elon) J(ames) 1928- 21-22R
Peacock, Mary (Willa) 1942- 69-72
Peacock, Mary Reynolds (Bradshaw)
1916- 57-60
Peacock, Molly 1947- 103
Peacock, Richard 1933- 107
Peacock, Ronald 1907- CANR-5
Earlier sketch in CA 53-56
Peacock, Wilbur Scott 1915(?)-1979
Obituary 89-92
Peacocke, A(rthur) R(obert) 1924- 41-44R
Peacocke, Christopher 1950- 124
Peacocke, Isabel Maud 1881-1973
Obituary 116
Pead, Deuel ?-1727 .... DLB-24
Peairs, Lillian Gehrke 1925- 103
Peairs, Richard Hope 1929- Brief entry 105
Peake, C(harles) H. 1920(?)-1988
Obituary 124
Peake, Lilian (Margaret) 1924- Brief entry .. 115
Peake, Mervyn 1911-1968 .... CANR-3
Obituary 25-28R
Earlier sketch in CA 7-8R
See also SATA 23
See also DLB 15
See also CLC 7
Peake, Miriam Morrison 1901- 57-60
Peaker, G(ilbert) F. 1903(?)-1983(?)
Obituary 109
Peale, Norman Vincent 1898- 81-84
See also SATA 20
See also AITN 1
Peale, Ruth Stafford 1906- 73-76
Pear, Lillian Myers 73-76
Pearce, Ann Philippa
See Christie, (Ann) Philippa
Pearce, Arthur Williams 1913(?)-1983
Obituary 111
Pearce, Brian Louis 1933- CANR-19
Earlier sketch in CA 103
Pearce, Charles A. 1906-1970 Obituary 104
Pearce, Dick
See Pearce, Richard Elmo
Pearce, Donald R(oss) 1917- 119
Pearce, Donn 1928- 15-16R
Pearce, Frank 1909- 109
Pearce, J(ohn) Kenneth 1898- 45-48
Pearce, J. Winston 1907- Brief entry 106
Pearce, Janice 1931- 61-64
Pearce, John Kingston 1925- 118
Pearce, Kenneth 1921- 120
Pearce, Mary E(mily) 1932- 69-72
Pearce, Moira 103
Pearce, Philippa
See Christie, (Ann) Philippa
See also SATA 1
See also CLC 21
See also CLR 9
Pearce, Richard 1932- 41-44R
Pearce, Richard Elmo 1909- 1R
Pearce, Roy Harvey 1919- CANR-3
Earlier sketch in CA 1R
Pearce, Thomas Matthews 1902- CANR-7
Earlier sketch in CA 19-20R
Pearce, William M(artin) 1913- 11-12R
Pearcy, G(eorge) Etzel 1905-1980 ...... CANR-3
Earlier sketch in CA 1R
Peardon, Thomas Preston 1899-1985
Obituary 116
Peare, Catherine Owens 1911- 5-6R
See also SATA 9
Pearl, Arthur 1922- 13-14R
Pearl, Chaim 1919- 49-52
Pearl, Cyril (Altson) 1906-1987(?)
Obituary 122
Pearl, Eric
See Elman, Richard
Pearl, Esther Elizabeth
See Ritz, David
Pearl, Hal 1914(?)-1975 Obituary 61-64
Pearl, Jack
See Pearl, Jacques Bain
Pearl, Jacques Bain 1923- CANR-23
Earlier sketch in CA 7-8R
Pearl, Joseph L. 1886(?)-1974 Obituary ... 53-56
Pearl, Leon 1922- 7-8R
Pearl, Leonard 1911- CAP-2
Earlier sketch in CA 33-36
Pearl, Ralph 1910- 73-76
Pearl, Richard M(axwell) 1913- CANR-3
Earlier sketch in CA 11-12R
Pearl, Virginia L(ou) 1930- 61-64
Pearlman, Daniel (David) 1935- CANR-24
Earlier sketches in CA 61-64, CANR-9
Pearlman, Maurice 1911- CANR-6
Earlier sketch in CA 7-8R
Pearlman, Moshe
See Pearlman, Maurice
Pearlstein, Howard J. 1942- 57-60
Pearman, Jean R(ichardson) 1915- 49-52
Pears, Charles 1873-1958 Brief entry 114
See also SATA 30
Pears, David Francis 1921- 65-68
Pearsall, Derek (Albert) 1931- CANR-24
Earlier sketch in CA 107
Pearsall, Robert Brainard 1920- CANR-2
Earlier sketch in CA 45-48
Pearsall, Ronald 1927- CANR-14
Earlier sketch in CA 21-22R
Pearsall, Thomas E. 1925- 25-28R
Pearsall, William Harold 1891-1964
Obituary 106
Pearson, Andrew Russell 1897-1969 .... CANR-6
Obituary 25-28R
Earlier sketch in CA 5-6R
Pearson, B(enjamin) H(arold) 1893- 65-68
Pearson, Bill
See Pearson, William Harrison
Pearson, Bruce L. 1932- 73-76
Pearson, Carol 1944- 57-60
Pearson, Diane
See McClelland, Diane Margaret
Pearson, Drew
See Pearson, Andrew Russell
Pearson, Frederic S(tephen) 1944- 113
Pearson, Gayle 1947- 122
Pearson, (Edward) Hesketh (Gibbons)
1887-1964 .... 5-6R
Pearson, James Larkin 1879-1981
Obituary 104
Pearson, Jim Berry 1924- 19-20R
Pearson, John 1934- CANR-4
Earlier sketch in CA 49-52
Pearson, Karl 1857-1936 Brief entry 119
Pearson, Lester B(owles) 1897-1972 121
Obituary 37-40R
Pearson, (Edith) Linnea 1942- 65-68
Pearson, Lionel (Ignatius Cusack) 1908- 1R
Pearson, Lon
See Pearson, Milo Lorentz
Pearson, M(ichael) N(aylor) 1941-
Brief entry 118
Pearson, Michael 102
Pearson, Milo Lorentz 1939- 73-76
Pearson, Neville P(ershing) 1917- 45-48
Pearson, Norman Holmes 1909-1975 .... CAP-1
Obituary 61-64
Earlier sketch in CA 15-16
Pearson, Richard Joseph 1938- 65-68
Pearson, Robert Paul 1938- 65-68
Pearson, Ronald Hooke 1915- 13-14R
Pearson, Roy 1914- 3R
Pearson, Scott Roberts 1938- CANR-11
Earlier sketch in CA 29-32R
Pearson, Susan 1946- CANR-14
Earlier sketch in CA 65-68
See also SATA 27, 39
Pearson, T(homas) R(eid) 1956-
Brief entry 120
See also CLC 39
Pearson, William Harrison 1922- 57-60
Peary, Dannis 1949- 109
Peary, Danny
See Peary, Dannis
Peary, Marie Ahnighito
See Kuhne, Marie (Ahnighito Peary)
Peascod, Bill
See Peascod, William
Peascod, William 1920(?)-1985 Obituary ... 116
Pease, Dorothy Wells 1896- 7-8R
Pease, Howard 1894-1974 .... 7-8R
Obituary 106
See also SATA 2, 25
Pease, Jane H(anna) 1929- CANR-4
Earlier sketch in CA 11-12R
Pease, Victor Philip 1938- 107
Pease, William H(enry) 1924- CANR-4
Earlier sketch in CA 11-12R
Peaston, Monroe 1914- 49-52
Peate, Iorwerth C.
See Peate, Iorwerth Cyfeiliog
Peate, Iorwerth Cyfeiliog 1901-1982 120
Obituary 108
Peate, Patricia Flynn 1911(?)-1983
Obituary 111
Peatman, John Gray 1904- 7-8R
Peattie, Donald Culross 1898-1964 102
Peattie, Lisa Redfield 1924- CANR-10
Earlier sketch in CA 25-28R
Peattie, Mark R(obert) 1930- CANR-8
Earlier sketch in CA 61-64
Peavy, Charles D(ruery) 1931- 25-28R
Peavy, John W(esley) III 1944- 119
Peavy, Linda 1943- 109
Pebworth, Ted-Larry 1936- 121
Peccei, Aurelio 1908-1984 Obituary 112
Peccorini, Francisco L(etona) 1915- 45-48
Pech, Stanley Z. 1924- 33-36R
Pechman, Joseph Aaron 1918- 85-88
Pechter, Edward 1941- 85-88
Peck, Abe 1945- 73-76
Peck, Anne Merriman 1884- 77-80
See also SATA 18
Peck, David W(arner) 1902- 1R
Peck, Ellen 1942- Brief entry 113
Peck, Frederic Taylor 1920(?)-1983
Obituary 110
Peck, George W(ilbur) 1840-1916
Brief entry 115
See also DLB 23, 42
Peck, Helen E(stelle) 1910- 7-8R
Peck, Ira 1922- 77-80
Peck, John 1941- CANR-3
Earlier sketch in CA 49-52
See also CLC 3
Peck, John B. 1918(?)-1973 Obituary 104
Peck, Kathryn Blackburn 1904-1975 ..... CAP-2
Earlier sketch in CA 25-28
Peck, Leonard
See Hardy, C. Colburn
Peck, M(organ) Scott 1936- CANR-20
Earlier sketch in CA 89-92
Peck, Merton J(oseph) 1925- 13-14R
Peck, Paula 1927(?)-1972 Obituary 104
Peck, Ralph H(arold-Henry) 1926- CANR-22
Earlier sketch in CA 69-72
Peck, Richard 1934- CANR-19
Earlier sketch in CA 85-88
See also SATA 18
See also SAAS 2
See also CLC 21
Peck, Richard E(arl) 1936- 81-84
Peck, Robert F. 1919- 13-14R
Peck, Robert McCracken 1952- 112
Peck, Robert Newton 1928- 81-84
See also SATA 21
See also SAAS 1
See also CLC 17
Peck, Russell A(lbert) 1933- 108
Peck, Ruth L. 1915- 29-32R
Peck, Seymour 1917-1985 Obituary 114
Peck, Sidney M. 1926- 5-6R
Peck, Stacey 1925- 123
Peck, Theodore P(arker) 1924- 103
Peckenpaugh, Angela J(ohnson) 1942- 104
Peckham, Howard Henry 1910- 11-12R
Peckham, James O. 1903(?)-1984
Obituary 113
Peckham, Lawton (Parker Greenman)
1904-1979 Obituary 89-92
Peckham, Morse 1914- CANR-1
Earlier sketch in CA 1R
Peckham, Richard
See Holden, Raymond (Peckham)
Peckinpah, (David) Sam(uel) 1925-1984 109
Obituary 114
See also CLC 20
Pecsok, Mary Bodell 1919- 7-8R
Peden, Margaret Sayers 1927- CANR-14
Earlier sketch in CA 37-40R
Peden, Rachel (Mason) 1901- 110
Peden, William (Harwood) 1913- 23-24R
Pedersen, Elsa Kienitz 1915- CANR-2
Earlier sketch in CA 4R
Pedersen, (Thelma) Jean J(orgenson)
1934- CANR-21
Earlier sketches in CA 57-60, CANR-6
Pedersen, Knut 1859-1952 119
Brief entry 104
Pedersen, Paul B(odholdt) 1936- 41-44R
Pederson, Kern O(wen) 1910- 102
Pedicord, Harry William 1912- 33-36R
Pedler, Christopher Magnus Howard
1927- 97-100
Pedler, Frederick Johnson 1908- 107
Pedler, Kit
See Pedler, Christopher Magnus Howard
Pedley, Robin 1914- 11-12R
Pedoe, Daniel 1910- 65-68
Pedolsky, Andrea 1951- 115
Pedrick, Jean 1922- CANR-6
Earlier sketch in CA 57-60
Peebles, Anne
See Galloway, Priscilla
Peebles, Dick 1918-1980 77-80
Obituary 97-100
Peek, Bertrand Meigh 1891-1964 Obituary .. 111
Peek, Merle 1938- CANR-22
Earlier sketch in CA 105
See also SATA 39
Peek, Walter W(illiam) 1922- 45-48
Peel, Bruce Braden 1916- 19-20R
Peel, Colin D(udley) 1936- 119
Peel, Edwin A(rthur) 1911- 13-14R
Peel, H(azel) M(ary) 1930- CANR-4
Earlier sketch in CA 9-10R
Peel, J(ohn) D(avid) Y(eadon) 1941- 33-36R
Peel, John Donald 1908- 33-36R
Peel, Kendal J(ohn) 1940- 116
Peel, Malcolm Lee 1936- 29-32R
Peel, Norman Lemon
See Hirsch, Phil
Peel, Robert 1909- 77-80
Peel, Ronald Francis (Edward Waite)
1912-1985 Obituary 117
Peel, Wallis
See Peel, H(azel) M(ary)
Peele, David A(rnold) 1929-1985 102
Obituary 118
Peele, George 1556-1596 .... DLB-62
Peele, Stanton 1946- 57-60
Peelor, Harry N. 1922- 19-20R
Peeples, Edwin A(ugustus, Jr.) 1915- 11-12R
See also SATA 6
Peer, Lyndon A. 1899(?)-1977 Obituary ... 73-76
Peerbolte, Maarten Lietaert
See Lietaert Peerbolte, Maarten
Peerce, Jan 1904-1984 101
Obituary 114
Peerman, Dean G(ordon) 1931- 13-14R
Peers, William R(aymond) 1914-1984 ..... 15-16R
Obituary 112
Peery, Paul D(enver) 1906- CAP-2
Earlier sketch in CA 29-32
Peeslake, Gaffer
See Durrell, Lawrence (George)
Peet, Bill
See Peet, William Bartlett
See also CLR 12
Peet, C(harles) Donald, Jr. 1927- 15-16R
Peet, Creighton B. 1899-1977 106
Obituary 69-72
See also SATA 30
Peet, Louise Jenison 1885- 7-8R
Peet, William Bartlett 1915- 19-20R
See also SATA 2, 41
Peffer, Randall S(cott) 1948- 101
Pegge, C(ecil) Denis 1902- CAP-1
Earlier sketch in CA 15-16
Pegis, Anton Charles 1905- Brief entry 106
Pegis, Jessie Corrigan 1907- CAP-1
Earlier sketch in CA 13-14
Pegler, (James) Westbrook 1894-1969 103
Obituary 89-92
Pegram, Marjorie Anne (Dykes) 1925- ... 11-12R
Pegrum, Dudley F(rank) 1898- 33-36R
Pegues, Franklin J(ohnson) 1924- 7-8R
Peguy, Charles Pierre 1873-1914
Brief entry 107
See also TCLC 10
Pehnt, Wolfgang 1931- CANR-24
Earlier sketch in CA 107
Pehrson, Justine Davis Randers
See Randers-Pehrson, Justine Davis
Pei, Mario A(ndrew) 1901-1978 .... CANR-5
Obituary 77-80
Earlier sketch in CA 5-6R
Peifer, Claude J(ohn) 1927- 19-20R
Peikoff, Leonard 1933- 108

Peil, Margaret 1929- ... CANR-8
Earlier sketch in CA 61-64
Peirce, J(ames) F(ranklin) 1918- ... 41-44R
Peirce, Neal R. 1932- ... CANR-21
Earlier sketch in CA 25-28R
Peirce, Waldo 1884-1970 ... SATA-28
Peiris, Denzil 1918(?)-1985 Obituary ... 116
Peiser, Maria Lilli 1914-1986 ... 116
Obituary ... 118
Brief entry ... 110
Peissel, Michel (Francois) 1937- ... CANR-12
Earlier sketch in CA 25-28R
Peitchinis, Stephen G(abriel) 1925- ... CANR-24
Earlier sketch in CA 45-48
Pejovich, Svetozar 1931- ... CANR-12
Earlier sketch in CA 19-20R
Pekarik, Andrew J(oseph) 1946- ... 112
Pekic, Borislav 1930- ... 69-72
Peladeau, Marius B(eaudoin) 1935- ... 73-76
Pelaez, Jill 1924- ... 33-36R
See also SATA 12
Pelavin, Cheryl 1946- ... 106
Pelenski, Jaroslaw 1929- Brief entry ... 111
Pelfrey, William 1947- ... 33-36R
Pelger, Lucy J. 1913-1971 ... CAP-2
Earlier sketch in CA 21-22
Pelikan, Jaroslav Jan 1923- ... CANR-1
Earlier sketch in CA 2R
Pelissier, Roger 1924-1972 ... CAP-2
Obituary ... 37-40R
Earlier sketch in CA 23-24
Pell, Arthur R. 1920- ... CANR-11
Earlier sketch in CA 29-32R
Pell, Claiborne (de Borda) 1918- ... 49-52
Pell, Derek 1947- ... 77-80
Pell, Eve 1937- ... 33-36R
Pell, John (Howland Gibbs) 1904-1987
Obituary ... 123
Pell, Olive Bigelow 1886-1980 Obituary ... 103
Pell, Robert
See Hagberg, David J(ames)
Pell, Walden II 1902-1983 Obituary ... 109
Pella, Milton O(rville) 1914- ... 19-20R
Pellegreno, Ann Holtaren ... 33-36R
Pellegrini, Angelo M. 1904- ... 19-20R
Pellegrini, Anthony D(avid) 1949- ... 117
Pellegrino, Victoria Y(urasits) 1944- ... 107
Peller, Sigismund 1890-1985 Obituary ... 116
Pelletier, Ingrid 1912- ... 29-32R
Pelletier, Kenneth R. 1946- ... CANR-11
Earlier sketch in CA 69-72
Pelletreau, John 1925(?)-1983 Obituary ... 111
Pellew, Jill (Hosford) 1942- ... 109
Pellicer, Carlos 1900(?)-1977 Obituary ... 69-72
Pelling, Henry Mathison 1920- ... 61-64
Pellow, Deborah 1945- ... CANR-13
Earlier sketch in CA 73-76
Pellowski, Anne 1933- ... CANR-9
Earlier sketch in CA 23-24R
See also SATA 20
Pellowski, Michael (Joseph) 1949- ... 110
See also SATA 48
Pells, Richard Henry 1941- ... 53-56
Pelly, David F. 1948- ... 124
Pelshe, Arvid Yanovich 1899-1983
Obituary ... 109
Pelta, Kathy 1928- ... 85-88
See also SATA 18
Peltason, J(ack) W(alter) 1923- ... CANR-4
Earlier sketch in CA 3R
Peltier, Leslie C(opus) 1900- ... 19-20R
See also SATA 13
Pelto, Bert
See Pelto, Pertti J(uho)
Pelto, Pertti J(uho) 1927- ... 97-100
Pelton, Barry C(lifton) 1935- ... 61-64
Pelton, Beverly Jo 1939- ... 49-52
Pelton, Joseph N(eal) 1943- ... 107
Pelton, Robert D(oane) 1935- ... 103
Pelton, Robert Stuart 1921- ... 7-8R
Pelton, Robert W(ayne) 1934- ... 29-32R
Peltz, Mary Ellis 1896-1981 ... 85-88
Obituary ... 105
Peluso, Joseph L(ouis) 1929- ... 97-100
Pelz, Lotte A(uguste) Hensl 1924- ... 11-12R
Pelz, Stephen Ernest 1942- ... 114
Brief entry ... 110
Pelz, Werner 1921- ... 11-12R
Peman, Jose Maria 1897-1981 Obituary ... 104
Pemberton, John E(dward) 1930- ... 33-36R
Pemberton, John Leigh
See Leigh-Pemberton, John
Pemberton, Madge 188(?)-1970
Obituary ... 29-32R
Pemberton, Margaret 1943- ... CANR-17
Earlier sketch in CA 93-96
Pemberton, Max 1863-1950 Brief entry ... 120
Pemberton, William Baring 1897- ... 7-8R
Pemberton, William E(rwin) 1940- ... 97-100
Pembrook, Linda 1942- ... 61-64
Pembrooke, Kenneth
See Page, Gerald W(ilburn)
Pembury, Bill
See Groom, Arthur William
Pempel, T. J. 1942- ... 112
Pen, Jan 1921- ... CANR-17
Earlier sketch in CA 1R
Pena, Humberto J(ose) 1928- ... 73-76
Pena, Ramon del Valle y
See Valle-Inclan, Ramon (Maria) del
Pendar, Kenneth 1906-1972 Obituary ... 37-40R
Pendell, Elmer 1894- ... CAP-1
Earlier sketch in CA 11-12
Pendennis, Arthur, Esquire
See Thackeray, William Makepeace
Pender, Lex
See Pendower, Jacques
Pender, Lydia Podger 1907- ... CANR-2
Earlier sketch in CA 5-6R
Pender, Marilyn
See Pendower, Jacques
Pendergast, Charles 1950- ... 65-68
Pendergast, Chuck
See Pendergast, Charles
Pendergast, Richard J. 1927- ... 93-96
Penderwhistle, Judith (Blair) 1952- ... CANR-22
Earlier sketch in CA 81-84
Pendery, Rosemary (Schmitz) ... 53-56
See also SATA 7
Pendle, Alexy 1943- ... SATA-29
Pendle, George 1906-1977 ... 7-8R
Obituary ... 103
See also SATA 28
Pendlebury, B(evis) J(ohn) 1898- ... CAP-2
Earlier sketch in CA 33-36
Pendleton, Conrad
See Kidd, Walter E.
Pendleton, Don(ald Eugene) 1927- ... 33-36R
Pendleton, Don
See Obstfeld, Raymond
Pendleton, James D(udley) 1930- ... 107
Pendleton, Mary ... 65-68
Pendleton, Winston K. 1910- ... CAP-1
Earlier sketch in CA 15-16
Pendo, Stephen 1947- ... 65-68
Pendower, Jacques 1899-1976 ... 9-10R
Obituary ... 89-92
Pendray, Edward
See Pendray, George Edward
Pendray, G. Edward
See Pendray, George Edward
Pendray, George Edward 1901-1987
Obituary ... 123
Penfield, Thomas 1903- ... 5-6R
Penfield, Wilder (Graves) 1891-1976 ... CANR-3
Obituary ... 65-68
Earlier sketch in CA 7-8R
Pengelley, Eric T. 1919- ... 89-92
Penick, James (Lal), Jr. 1932- ... 33-36R
Penn, Anne
See Pendower, Jacques
Penn, Arthur (Hiller) 1922- Brief entry ... 112
Penn, Asher 1908(?)-1979 Obituary ... 93-96
Penn, Audrey 1950- ... CANR-13
Earlier sketch in CA 77-80
Penn, Christopher
See Lawlor, Patrick Anthony
Penn, John
See Harcourt, Palma
Penn, Margaret ?-1981 Obituary ... 105
Penn, Ruth Bonn
See Rosenberg, Ethel (Clifford)
Penn, William 1644-1718 ... DLB-24
Pennage, E. M.
See Finkel, George (Irvine)
Pennar, Jaan 1924- Brief entry ... 115
Pennekamp, John (David) 1897-1978
Obituary ... 89-92
See also AITN 2
Penner, Jonathan 1940- ... CANR-17
Earlier sketch in CA 97-100
See also DLBY 83
Penney, Annette Culler 1916- ... 45-48
Penney, Grace Jackson 1904- ... 5-6R
See also SATA 35
Penney, J(ames) C(ash) 1875-1971
Obituary ... 29-32R
Penney, Jennifer 1946- ... 122
Pennick, Nigel Campbell 1946- ... 110
Penniman, Clara 1914- Brief entry ... 111
Penniman, Howard R(ae) 1916- ... CANR-12
Earlier sketch in CA 13-14R
Penniman, Thomas Kenneth 1896(?)-1977
Obituary ... 69-72
Penninger, F(rieda) Elaine 1927- ... 57-60
Penningroth, Paul W(illiam) 1901-1974 ... 49-52
Obituary ... 103
Pennington, Albert Joe 1950- ... 57-60
Pennington, Anne (Elizabeth) 1934-1981
Obituary ... 114
Pennington, Chester Arthur 1916- ... 104
Pennington, Donald Henshaw 1919- ... 7-8R
Pennington, Eunice 1923- ... 57-60
See also SATA 27
Pennington, Howard (George) 1923- ... 49-52
Pennington, John Selman 1924(?)-1980
Obituary ... 102
Pennington, Lee 1939- ... 69-72
See also DLBY 82
Pennington, Lillian Boyer 1904- ... SATA-45
Pennington, Lucinda 1945- ... 117
Pennington, M. (Robert John) Basil
1931- ... CANR-16
Earlier sketch in CA 93-96
Pennington, Penny
See Galbraith, Georgie Starbuck
Pennington, Robert (Roland) 1927- ... 73-76
Pennington, Stuart
See Galbraith, Georgie Starbuck
Pennington, W(eldon) J(erry) 1919-1985
Obituary ... 115
Pennink, (John Jacob) Frank 1913- ... 7-8R
Pennock, J(ames) Roland 1906- ... CANR-13
Earlier sketch in CA 33-36R
Penny, Julie 1945- ... 117
Penny, Prudence
See Goldberg, Hyman
Penny, Ruthanna (Merrick) 1914- ... 19-20R
Pennycuick, John 1943- ... 97-100
Penrod, James 1934- ... 77-80
Penrose, Boies 1902-1976 Obituary ... 65-68
Penrose, Edith Tilton 1914- ... 25-28R
Penrose, Harald ... CANR-21
Earlier sketches in CA 13-14R, CANR-6
Penrose, Margaret ... CAP-2
Earlier sketch in CA 19-20
Penrose, Roland (Algernon) 1900-1984 ... 85-88
Obituary ... 112
Pentecost, Edward C(lyde) 1917- ... 57-60
Pentecost, Hugh
See Philips, Judson (Pentecost)
Pentecost, J(ohn) Dwight 1915- ... CANR-2
Earlier sketch in CA 5-6R
Pentecost, Martin
See Hearn, John
Pentony, DeVere Edwin 1924- ... CANR-8
Earlier sketch in CA 5-6R
Pentreath, A(rthur Godolphin) Guy
C(arleton) 1902-1985 ... CAP-1
Obituary ... 118
Earlier sketch in CA 13-14
Pentz, Croft Miner ... CANR-9
Earlier sketch in CA 7-8R
Pentz, Lundy H(urd) 1951- ... 116
Penuel, Arnold M(cCoy) 1936- ... 57-60
Penuelas, Marcelino C. 1916- ... 25-28R
Penzel, Frederick 1948- ... 85-88
Penzik, Irena
See Narell, Irena
Penzl, Herbert 1910- ... CANR-24
Earlier sketch in CA 45-48
Penzler, Otto 1942- ... 81-84
See also SATA 38
Pepe, John Frank 1920- ... 11-12R
Pepe, Phil(ip) 1935- ... CANR-18
Earlier sketch in CA 25-28R
See also SATA 20
Pepelasis, Adam(antios) A. 1923- ... CANR-2
Earlier sketch in CA 2R
Peper, George Frederick 1950- ... 108
Pepin, Jacques (Georges) 1935- ... 103
Pepinsky, Harold E(ugene) 1945- ... 119
Pepitone, Albert (Davison) 1923- ... 11-12R
Pepitone, Joe 1940- Brief entry ... 109
Pepitone, Joseph Anthony
See Pepitone, Joe
Peppard, Murray B(isbee) 1917-1974 ... CAP-2
Obituary ... 53-56
Earlier sketch in CA 21-22
Peppe, Rodney 1934- ... 33-36R
See also SATA 4
Pepper, Adeline ... 41-44R
Pepper, Art(hur Edward) 1925-1982
Obituary ... 107
Pepper, Choral 1918- ... 25-28R
Pepper, Curtis Bill
See Pepper, Curtis G.
Pepper, Curtis G. 1920- ... CANR-10
Earlier sketch in CA 23-24R
Pepper, Joan
See Wetherell-Pepper, Joan Alexander
Pepper, John 1942- ... 117
Pepper, Martin
See Krich, John
Pepper, Stephen Coburn 1891-1972 ... 3R
Obituary ... 103
Pepper, Thomas 1939- ... CANR-16
Earlier sketch in CA 97-100
Pepper, William M(ullin), Jr. 1903-1975 ... 97-100
Obituary ... 57-60
Peppercorn, David 1931- ... 118
Peppiatt, Michael 1941- ... 118
Peppin, Brigid (Mary) 1941- ... 65-68
Peppler, Alice Stolper 1934- ... 53-56
Peradotto, John Joseph 1933- ... 41-44R
Perceval-Maxwell, M(ichael) 1933- ... 53-56
Percival, Alicia C(onstance) 1903- ... 11-12R
Percival, John 1927- ... 33-36R
Percival, Walter 1896- ... CAP-1
Earlier sketch in CA 11-12
Percy, Charles H(arting) 1919- ... 65-68
Percy, Charles Henry
See Smith, Dodie
Percy, Douglas Cecil 1914- ... CANR-3
Earlier sketch in CA 7-8R
Percy, Herbert R(oland) 1920- ... 7-8R
Percy, Walker 1916- ... CANR-23
Earlier sketches in CA 3R, CANR-1
See also DLB 2
See also DLBY 80
See also CLC 2, 3, 6, 8, 14, 18, 47
Percy, William A., Jr. 1933- ... 29-32R
Perdue, Theda 1949- ... CANR-16
Earlier sketch in CA 93-96
Perdurabo, Frater
See Crowley, Edward Alexander
Pereda (y Sanchez de Porrua), Jose Maria
de 1833-1906 Brief entry ... 117
See also TCLC 16
Pereda y Porrua, Jose Maria de
See Pereda (y Sanchez de Porrua), Jose
Maria de
Peregrine
See Deutscher, Isaac
Pereira, Harold Bertram 1890- ... 9-10R
Pereira, Sam 1949- ... 111
Pereira, W(ilfred) D(ennis) 1921- ... CANR-20
Earlier sketch in CA 104
Pereira Carneiro, Maurina 1899(?)-1983
Obituary ... 111
Perel, William M. 1927- ... 33-36R
Perella, Nicholas James 1927- ... 73-76
Perelman, Chaim 1912- ... 103
Perelman, Lewis J(oel) 1946- ... 73-76
Perelman, Michael 1939- ... 111
Perelman, S(idney) J(oseph)
1904-1979 ... CANR-18
Obituary ... 89-92
Earlier sketch in CA 73-76
See also DLB 11, 44
See also CLC 3, 5, 9, 15, 23, 44
See also AITN 1, 2
Perenyi, Eleanor (Spencer Stone) 1918-
Brief entry ... 113
Perera, Gretchen G(ifford) 1940- ... 93-96
Perera, Thomas Biddle 1938- ... CANR-21
Earlier sketch in CA 37-40R
See also SATA 13
Perera, Victor 1934- ... 29-32R
Peres, Richard 1947- ... 93-96
Peres, Shimon 1923- ... 85-88
Peret, Benjamin 1899-1959 Brief entry ... 117
See also TCLC 20
Peretz, Don 1922- ... CANR-19
Earlier sketches in CA 11-12R, CANR-4
Peretz, Isaac Loeb 1851(?)-1915
Brief entry ... 109
See also TCLC 16
Peretz, Yitzkhok Leibush
See Peretz, Isaac Loeb
Pereyra, Lillian A(nita) 1920- ... 21-22R
Perez, Joseph F(rancis) 1930- ... CANR-16
Earlier sketch in CA 29-32R
Perez, Louis A., Jr. 1943- ... 121
Perez, Louis C(elestino) 1923- ... 77-80
Perez de Ayala, Ramon 1881-1962
Obituary ... 93-96
Perez-Firmat, Gustavo (Francisco) 1949- ... 123
Perez Galdos, Benito 1843-1920 ... TCLC-27
Perez Lopez, Francisco 1916- ... 49-52
Perham, Margery (Freda) 1895-1982 ... CANR-1
Obituary ... 106
Earlier sketch in CA 1R
Pericoli, Ugo 1923- ... 97-100
Perigoe, J. Rae 1910- ... 61-64
Perillo, Joseph M. 1933- ... 19-20R
Perin, Constance ... 29-32R
Perinbanayagam, Robert S(idharthan)
1934- ... 109
Perino, Joseph 1946- ... 106
Perino, Sheila C. 1948- ... 106
Peripatus
See Whittington-Egan, Richard
Peristiany, John G(eorge) 1911-1987 ... 19-20R
Obituary ... 124
Peritz, Rene 1933- ... 45-48
Perkes, Dan 1931- ... CANR-21
Earlier sketch in CA 69-72
Perkin, Harold (James) 1926- ... CANR-14
Earlier sketch in CA 77-80
Perkin, J(ames) R(ussell) C(onway) 1928- ... 113
Perkin, Robert L(yman) 1914-1978
Obituary ... 77-80
Perkins, Agnes (Regan) 1926- ... CANR-10
Earlier sketch in CA 57-60
Perkins, Al(bert Rogers) 1904-1975 ... 107
Obituary ... 57-60
See also SATA 30
Perkins, Ann (Louise) 1915- Brief entry ... 113
Perkins, Bradford 1925- ... 1R
Perkins, Carl (Lee) 1932- ... 102
Perkins, David 1928- ... 77-80
Perkins, David (Lee) 1939- ... CANR-13
Earlier sketch in CA 73-76
Perkins, Dexter 1889-1984 ... 7-8R
Obituary ... 113
Perkins, Dwight Heald 1934- ... CANR-22
Earlier sketches in CA 19-20R, CANR-7
Perkins, E(rnest) Benson 1881- ... 7-8R
Perkins, Edward A., Jr. 1928- ... CANR-14
Earlier sketch in CA 21-22R
Perkins, Edwin Judson 1939- ... 106
Perkins, Eugene 1932- ... DLB-41
Perkins, Faith
See Bramer, Jennie (Perkins)
Perkins, George (Burton, Jr.) 1930- ... 15-16R
Perkins, Hugh V(ictor) 1918-1988 ... 93-96
Obituary ... 124
Perkins, James Alfred 1911- ... 108
Perkins, James Ashbrook 1941- ... 73-76
Perkins, James Oliver Newton 1924- ... 11-12R
Perkins, James S(cudday) 1899- ... 89-92
Perkins, John (William) 1935- ... CANR-13
Earlier sketch in CA 73-76
Perkins, John Allen 1919- ... 114
Perkins, John Bryan Ward
See Ward-Perkins, John Bryan
Perkins, Lawrence A. 1917(?)-1979
Obituary ... 89-92
Perkins, Lucy Fitch 1865-1937 Brief entry ... 122
Perkins, (Richard) Marlin 1905-1986 ... 103
Obituary ... 119
See also SATA 21, 48
Perkins, Merle Lester 1919- ... 45-48
Perkins, Michael 1942- ... CANR-8
Earlier sketch in CA 19-20R
Perkins, Newton Stephens 1925- ... 49-52
Perkins, Ralph 1913- ... 15-16R
Perkins, Robert L(ee) 1930- ... 25-28R
Perkins, Rollin M(orris) 1889- ... 53-56
Perkins, Steve
See Perkins, Newton Stephens
Perkins, Van L. 1930- Brief entry ... 106
Perkins, Virginia Chase 1902- ... CAP-2
Earlier sketch in CA 33-36
Perkins, Whitney Trow 1921- ... 106
Perkins, William H(ughes) 1923- ... 53-56
Perkins, Wilma Lord 1897-1976 Obituary ... 104
Perkinson, Henry J(oseph) 1930- ... CANR-12
Earlier sketch in CA 19-20R
Perkoff, Stuart Z. 1930-1974 Obituary ... 113
See also DLB 16

Perkowski, Jan Louis 1936- ... CANR-2
Earlier sketch in CA 45-48
Perl, Arnold 1914-1971 Obituary ...33-36R
Perl, Lila ...33-36R
See also SATA 6
Perl, Ruth June 1929- ...25-28R
Perl, Susan 1922-1983 ... CANR-11
Obituary ... 110
Earlier sketch in CA 19-20R
See also SATA 22, 34
Perl, Teri (Hoch) 1926- ... CANR-19
Earlier sketch in CA 93-96
Perlberg, Deborah 1948- ... 118
Perlberg, Mark 1929- ...37-40R
Perle, George 1915- ... CANR-3
Earlier sketch in CA 2R
Perles, Benjamin Max 1922- ...45-48
Perley, Michael 1946- ... 114
Perlin, Seymour 1925- ... 121
Perlinski, Jerome 1940- ... 112
Perlis, Vivian 1928- ...85-88
Perlman, Bennard B(loch) 1928- ...89-92
Perlman, Helen Harris 1905- ... CANR-3
Earlier sketch in CA 4R
Perlman, Janice E(laine) 1943- ...61-64
Perlman, Jess 1891- ...89-92
Perlman, John N(iels) 1946- ... CANR-12
Earlier sketch in CA 33-36R
Perlman, Mark 1923- ... CANR-19
Earlier sketches in CA 1R, CANR-3
Perlman, Samuel 1905-1975 ... CAP-2
Earlier sketch in CA 33-36
Perlmutter, Emanuel 1907(?)-1986
Obituary ... 118
Perlmutter, Jerome H. 1924- ...19-20R
Perlmutter, Nathan 1923-1987 ...15-16R
Obituary ... 123
Perlmutter, O(scar) William 1920-1975 ...57-60
See also SATA 8
Perlmutter, Ruth Ann 1924- ... 109
Perlo, Victor 1912- ... CANR-2
Earlier sketch in CA 5-6R
Perloff, Harvey S(tephen) 1915-1983
Obituary ... 110
Perloff, Marjorie G(abrielle) 1931- ... CANR-22
Earlier sketches in CA 57-60, CANR-7
Perlongo, Bob 1933- ... 112
Perls, Eugenia Soderberg 1904(?)-1973
Obituary ...37-40R
Perls, Frederick S(alomon) 1893-1970 ... 101
Perls, Frederick S(alomon) 1894(?)-1970
Obituary ...29-32R
Perls, Fritz
See Perls, Frederick S(alomon)
Perls, Hugo 1886(?)-1977 Obituary ...73-76
Perlstein, Gary R(obert) 1940- ...57-60
Perman, Dagmar Horna 1926(?)-1978
Obituary ...77-80
Perman, Michael 1942- Brief entry ... 113
Pernet, A(nn) 1940- ... 107
Perniciaro, Tony 1917- ...41-44R
Pernoud, Regine 1909- ... 102
Peroff, Nicholas C(arl) 1944- ... 113
Peron, Juan (Domingo) 1895-1974
Obituary ...49-52
Perosa, Sergio 1933- ... CAP-1
Earlier sketch in CA 15-16
Peroutka, Ferdinand 1895(?)-1978
Obituary ...77-80
Perowne, Barry
See Atkey, Philip
Perowne, Stewart Henry 1901- ... CANR-3
Earlier sketch in CA 4R
Perrault, Charles 1628-1703 ... SATA-25
Perreard, Suzanne Louise Butler 1919- . SATA-29
Perreault, John 1937- ... CANR-1
Earlier sketch in CA 45-48
Perreault, William D(aniel), Jr. 1948- ... 110
Perrella, Robert 1917- ...61-64
Perrenod, Virginia Marion (Lacy) 1928- ... 117
Perret, Gene 1937- ... 117
Brief entry ... 114
Perrett, Bryan 1934- ... CANR-20
Earlier sketch in CA 29-32R
Perrett, Geoffrey 1940- ... CANR-4
Earlier sketch in CA 53-56
Perrigo, Lynn I(rwin) 1904- ...33-36R
Perrin, Blanche Chenery 1894-1973 ...5-6R
Obituary ...41-44R
Perrin, Noel 1927- ...13-14R
Perrin, (Horace) Norman 1920-1976 ... CANR-11
Earlier sketch in CA 15-16R
Perrin, Porter Gale 1896-1962 Obituary ... 113
Perrin, Robert 1939- ...97-100
Perrin, Robert G(eorge) 1945- ... 111
Perrin, Ursula 1935- ... 101
Perrine, Laurence 1915- ... CANR-3
Earlier sketch in CA 1R
Perrine, Mary 1913- ...25-28R
See also SATA 2
Perrin Jassy, Marie-France 1942- ...93-96
Perrins, Lesley 1953- ... 123
Perrottet, Philippe (Louis Gaston)
1921-1982 ...25-28R
Obituary ... 122
Perroy, Edouard (Marie Joseph)
1901-1974 Obituary ...53-56
Perrucci, Robert 1931- ... CANR-15
Earlier sketch in CA 85-88
Perruchot, Henri 1917-1967 ... CAP-1
Earlier sketch in CA 9-10
Perry, Anne 1938- ... CANR-22
Earlier sketch in CA 101
Perry, Barbara Fisher
See Fisher, Barbara
Perry, Ben Edwin 1892-1968 ... CAP-2
Earlier sketch in CA 23-24
Perry, Bernard (Berenson) 1910-1985
Obituary ... 117
Perry, Brighton
See Sherwood, Robert E(mmet)
Perry, Carmen ... AITN-2
Perry, Charles 1941- ... 124
Perry, Charles Edward ... AITN-2
Perry, Charner M(arquis) 1902-1985
Obituary ... 117
Perry, Collin 1949- ... 108
Perry, David L. 1931- ...33-36R
Perry, David Thomas 1946- ...37-40R
Perry, Dick 1922- ...13-14R
Perry, Edgar C(loud) 1900- ... 117
Perry, Eleanor (Rosenfeld Bayer)
1915(?)-1981 ... 111
Obituary ... 103
See also DLB 44
Perry, Elisabeth Israels 1939- ... 111
Perry, Elizabeth Jean 1948- ... 104
Perry, Erma (Jackson McNeil) ...89-92
Perry, Gaylord (Jackson) 1938-
Brief entry ... 113
Perry, George 1935- ... 103
Perry, Gordon Arthur 1914- ... 108
Perry, Grace 1927- ... CANR-20
Earlier sketch in CA 102
Perry, Henry Ten Eyck 1890-1973 ... CAP-2
Earlier sketch in CA 19-20
Perry, Huey 1936- ...49-52
Perry, James M(oorhead) 1927- ...15-16R
Perry, Jim (Angelo) 1942- ...53-56
Perry, John 1914- ... CANR-6
Earlier sketch in CA 5-6R
Perry, John Curtis 1930- ... 104
Perry, John D(elbert), Jr. 1940- ...25-28R
Perry, John Oliver 1929- ...93-96
Perry, Joseph M(cGarity) 1936- ...37-40R
Perry, Kenneth F(rederick) 1902-1974 ... CAP-2
Earlier sketch in CA 19-20
Perry, Kenneth I. 1929- ...29-32R
Perry, Kenneth W(ilbur) 1919- ...57-60
Perry, Lewis (Curtis) 1938- ... CANR-1
Earlier sketch in CA 45-48
Perry, Linette (Purbi) ... 108
Perry, Lloyd M(erle) 1916- ... CANR-9
Earlier sketch in CA 23-24R
Perry, Louis B(arnes) 1918- ... CAP-1
Earlier sketch in CA 13-14
Perry, Margaret 1933- ...89-92
Perry, Michael (Charles) 1933- ... 101
Perry, Milton F(reeman) 1926- ...15-16R
Perry, Nicolette E. 1949- ... 119
Perry, Octavia Jordan 1894- ... CAP-1
Earlier sketch in CA 13-14
Perry, Patricia 1949- ... 106
See also SATA 30
Perry, Peter John 1937- ...49-52
Perry, Phillip M. 1948- ...29-32R
Perry, Ralph Barton 1876-1957
Brief entry ... 123
Perry, Richard ...41-44R
Perry, Richard 1944- ... 115
Perry, Richard S. 1924- ...13-14R
Perry, Ritchie (John Allen) 1942- ... CANR-21
Earlier sketches in CA 45-48, CANR-1
Perry, Robin 1917- ...65-68
Perry, Roger 1933- ... CANR-14
Earlier sketch in CA 77-80
See also SATA 27
Perry, Rosalie Sandra 1945- ...53-56
Perry, Rufus
See Gibson, Walter B(rown)
Perry, Ruth 1943- ... 118
Perry, Shauneille 1930- ... 113
Perry, Stewart E(dmond) 1928- ...19-20R
Perry, (Charles) Stuart 1908- ... 107
Perry, Susan
See Perry, Susan M.
Perry, Susan M. 1950- ... 124
Perry, T. Anthony 1938- ...81-84
Perry, Thomas Brief entry ... 123
Perry, Thomas Whipple 1925- ...11-12R
Perry, Troy D(eroy) 1940- Brief entry ... 109
Perry, Walter (Laing Macdonald) 1921- ... 113
Perry, Will 1933- ...65-68
Perry, William E(dward) 1931- ... 111
Perry, Wilma I. 1912- ... 105
Perse, St.-John
See Leger, (Marie-Rene) Alexis
Saint-Leger
See also CLC 4, 11, 46
Pershing, Marie
See Schultz, Pearle Henriksen
Persichetti, Vincent 1915-1987 Obituary ... 124
Persico, Joseph E(dward) 1930- ... CANR-21
Earlier sketch in CA 93-96
Persinger, Michael A. 1945- ...69-72
Persis
See Haime, Agnes Irvine Constance
(Adams)
Perske, Robert 1927- ... 106
Persky, Mordecai 1931- ...81-84
Persky, Mort
See Persky, Mordecai
Persky, Stan 1941- ... CANR-18
Earlier sketch in CA 101
Person, Amy L. 1896- ... CAP-2
Earlier sketch in CA 23-24
Person, Bernard 1895(?)-1981 Obituary ... 103
Person, Peter P. 1889- ... CAP-1
Earlier sketch in CA 11-12
Persons, Robert H(odge), Jr. 1922- ... CANR-13
Earlier sketch in CA 19-20R
Persons, Stow Spaulding 1913- ... 103
Pertinax
See Geraud, (Charles Joseph) Andre
and Haws, Duncan
Pertschuk, Michael 1933- ... 109
Pertwee, Michael (Henry Roland) 1916-
Brief entry ... 124
Pertwee, Roland 1885-1963 Obituary ...93-96
Perutz, Kathrin 1939- ... CANR-3
Earlier sketch in CA 3R
Pervin, Lawrence A. 1936- ... CANR-8
Earlier sketch in CA 23-24R
Peschel, Enid Rhodes 1943- ... 110
Pescow, Jerome K(enneth) 1929- ...45-48
Pesek, Boris P(eter) 1926- ...23-24R
Pesek, Ludek 1919- ...29-32R
Pesetsky, Bette 1932- ...CLC-28
Peshkin, Alan 1931- ...81-84
Peshkov, Alexei Maximovich 1868-1936
Brief entry ... 105
Pesin, Harry 1919- ...29-32R
Peskin, Allan 1933- Brief entry ... 109
Pesnot, Patrick 1943- ... 101
Pessen, Beth 1943- ...97-100
Pessen, Edward 1920- ... CANR-14
Earlier sketch in CA 37-40R
Pessina, Giorgio 1902(?)-1977 Obituary ...73-76
Pessino, Clara Park 1899(?)-1985
Obituary ... 116
Pesso, Albert 1929- ...73-76
Pessoa, Fernando (Antonio Nogueira)
1888-1935 ...TCLC-27
Pestelli, Giorgio 1938- ... 124
Pestieau, Phyllis Smith 1946- ...97-100
Petacco, Arrigo 1929- ... CANR-21
Earlier sketch in CA 103
Petaja, Emil (Theodore) 1915- ...25-28R
Peter, Armistead (III) 1896(?)-1983
Obituary ... 111
Peter, James (Fletcher) 1919- ...19-20R
Peter, John (Desmond) 1921- ... CANR-3
Earlier sketch in CA 1R
Peter, Laurence J. 1919- ... CANR-17
Earlier sketch in CA 19-20R
See also DLB 53
Peterfreund, Sheldon P(aul) 1917- ...21-22R
Peterfreund, Stuart (Samuel) 1945- ... CANR-13
Earlier sketch in CA 33-36R
Peterkiewicz, Jerzy 1916- ... CANR-5
Earlier sketch in CA 7-8R
Peterkin, Julia Mood 1880-1961 ... 102
See also DLB 9
See also CLC 31
Peterman, Michael A(lan) 1942- ... 111
Peterman, Ruth 1924- ...57-60
Peters, Alexander
See Hollander, Zander
Peters, Arthur Anderson 1913-1979
Obituary ...93-96
Peters, Arthur King 1919- ... 104
Peters, Barney
See Bauer, Erwin A.
Peters, Caroline
See Betz, Eva Kelly
Peters, Charles (Given, Jr.) 1926- ... 122
Brief entry ... 116
Peters, Christina 1942- ...85-88
Peters, Daniel (James) 1948- ... CANR-15
Earlier sketch in CA 85-88
Peters, David A(lexander) 1923- ...25-28R
Peters, Donald L. 1925- ...21-22R
Peters, Edward (Murray) 1936- ... CANR-18
Earlier sketch in CA 101
Peters, Elizabeth
See Mertz, Barbara (Gross)
Peters, Ellis
See Pargeter, Edith Mary
Peters, Eugene H(erbert) 1929- ...41-44R
Peters, F(rancis) E(dward) 1927- ... CANR-12
Earlier sketch in CA 73-76
Peters, Frederick George 1935- ... 104
Peters, Fritz
See Peters, Arthur Anderson
Peters, Geoffrey
See Palmer, Madelyn
Peters, George W(illiam) 1907- ... CANR-24
Earlier sketch in CA 45-48
Peters, H. Frederick 1910- ...73-76
Peters, J. Ross 1936- ...29-32R
Peters, Jean (Rae) 1935- ... 116
Peters, Joan K. 1945- ...CLC-39
Peters, Ken(neth Walter) 1929- ...19-20R
Peters, Lane
See Lapidus, Elaine
Peters, Lawrence
See Davies, L(eslie) P(urnell)
Peters, Lenrie (Wilfred Leopold) 1932- ... 108
Peters, Leslie
See Peters, Donald L.
Peters, Ludovic
See Brent, Peter (Ludwig)
Peters, Marcia
See Gouled, Vivian G(loria)
Peters, Margaret Evelyn 1936- ...53-56
Peters, Margot 1933- ... CANR-12
Earlier sketch in CA 73-76
Peters, Maureen 1935- ...33-36R
Peters, Max S(tone) 1920- ...57-60
Peters, Michael Bartley 1943- ... 110
Brief entry ... 108
Peters, Mike
See Peters, Michael Bartley
Peters, Natasha
See Cleaver, Anastasia N.
Peters, R(ichard) S(tanley) 1919- ... CANR-16
Earlier sketch in CA 23-24R
Peters, Richard Dorland 1910-1984
Obituary ... 114
Peters, Robert Anthony 1926- ...49-52
Peters, Robert L(ouis) 1924- ...15-16R
See also CLC 7
Peters, Ronald M., Jr. 1947- ...85-88
Peters, Ruth Marie 1913(?)-1978
Obituary ... 104
Peters, S. H.
See Porter, William Sydney
Peters, S. T.
See Brannon, William T.
Peters, Steven
See Geiser, Robert L(ee)
Peters, Ted
See Peters, Theodore F(rank)
Peters, Theodore F(rank) 1941- ...81-84
Peters, Thomas J. 1942- Brief entry ... 123
Peters, Tom
See Peters, Thomas J.
Peters, Victor 1915- ...19-20R
Peters, Virginia Bergman 1918- ...93-96
Peters, William 1921- ... CANR-20
Earlier sketches in CA 11-12R, CANR-3
Petersen, Arnold 1885-1976 Obituary ...65-68
Petersen, Carol Otto 1914- ...57-60
Petersen, Clarence G. 1933- ...77-80
Petersen, David M(uir) 1939- ...41-44R
Petersen, Donald 1928- ...13-14R
Petersen, E. Allen 1903(?)-1987 Obituary ... 122
Petersen, Gwenn Boardman 1924- ... CANR-2
Earlier sketch in CA 45-48
Petersen, James R(eeve) 1948- ... 114
Petersen, Karen Daniels 1910- ...73-76
Petersen, Mark E. 1900-1984 Obituary ... 111
Petersen, Melba F(rances) Runtz 1919- ...5-6R
Petersen, P(eter) J(ames) 1941- ... 112
See also SATA 43, 48
Petersen, Peter (Barron) 1932- ...57-60
Petersen, Sigurd Damskov 1904- ...11-12R
Petersen, William 1912- ... CANR-3
Earlier sketch in CA 1R
Petersen, William J. 1929- ... CANR-9
Earlier sketch in CA 21-22R
Petersen, William John 1901- ...7-8R
Petersham, Maud (Fuller) 1890-1971 ...73-76
Obituary ...33-36R
See also SATA 17
See also DLB 22
Petersham, Miska 1888-1960 ...73-76
See also SATA 17
See also DLB 22
Peterson, A(lexander) D(uncan) C(ampbell)
1908- ... 108
Peterson, Agnes F(ischer) 1923- ...29-32R
Peterson, Arthur L(aVerne) 1926- ...11-12R
Peterson, Brent D(an) 1942- ... 120
Peterson, Carl 1896(?)-1983 Obituary ... 110
Peterson, Carolyn Sue 1938- ... CANR-12
Earlier sketch in CA 73-76
Peterson, Carroll V(alleen) 1929- ...45-48
Peterson, Charles 1900(?)-1976 Obituary ..69-72
Peterson, Charles S. 1927- ...49-52
Peterson, Christmas
See Christmas, Joyce
Peterson, Dale 1944- ... 109
Peterson, Donald R(obert) 1923- ...25-28R
Peterson, Douglas L(ee) 1924- ...41-44R
Peterson, Edward N(orman) 1925- ...29-32R
Peterson, Edwin (Lewis) 1904-1972
Obituary ...37-40R
Peterson, Edwin Loose 1915- ...7-8R
Peterson, Eldridge 1905(?)-1977
Obituary ...73-76
Peterson, Eleanor M. 1912- ...25-28R
Peterson, Elmer 1930- ...37-40R
Peterson, Esther (Allen) 1934- ... CANR-16
Earlier sketch in CA 89-92
See also SATA 35
Peterson, Evan T(ye) 1925- ...45-48
Peterson, F. Ross 1941- ...97-100
Peterson, Forrest H(arold) 1912- ...45-48
Peterson, Franklynn 1938- ... 110
Peterson, Frederick Alvin 1920- ...49-52
Peterson, Gilbert Allan 1935- ... 114
Peterson, Hans 1922- ... CANR-1
Earlier sketch in CA 49-52
See also SATA 8
Peterson, Harold 1939- ...29-32R
Peterson, Harold F(erdinand) 1900- ...5-6R
Peterson, Harold L(eslie) 1922-1978 ... CANR-4
Obituary ...73-76
Earlier sketch in CA 3R
See also SATA 8
Peterson, Helen Stone 1910- ...37-40R
See also SATA 8
Peterson, Houston 1897-1981 ... 107
Obituary ... 103
Peterson, James
See Zeiger, Henry A(nthony)
Peterson, James Alfred 1913- ... 104
Peterson, James Allan 1932- ...29-32R
Peterson, Jeanne Whitehouse
See Whitehouse, Jeanne
Peterson, Jim
See Crawford, William (Elbert)
Peterson, John Eric 1933- ...53-56
Peterson, John J. 1918- ...53-56
Peterson, John W(illard) 1921- ...97-100
Peterson, Kenneth G(erard) 1927- ...33-36R
Peterson, Levi S(avage) 1933- ... 109
Peterson, Linda H(aenlein) 1948- ... 121
Peterson, Lloyd R(ichard) 1922-
Brief entry ... 107
Peterson, Lorraine 1940- ... 113
See also SATA 44
Peterson, M(ildred) Jeanne 1937- ... 103
Peterson, Marilyn Ann 1933- ...57-60

Peterson, Martin Severin 1897- ... CANR-3
Earlier sketch in CA 2R
Peterson, Mendel (Lazear) 1918- ... 73-76
Peterson, Merrill D(aniel) 1921- ... CANR-19
Earlier sketches in CA 1R, CANR-3
Peterson, Nancy L(ee) 1939- ... 105
Peterson, Norma Lois 1922- ... 15-16R
Peterson, Ottis 1907- ... 23-24R
Peterson, Owen M. 1924- ... 108
Peterson, Paul E(lliott) 1940- ... CANR-24
Earlier sketch in CA 45-48
Peterson, R(odney) D(elos) 1932- ... 41-44R
Peterson, Reona 1941- ... 73-76
Peterson, Richard A(ustin) 1932- ... 25-28R
Peterson, Robert 1924- ... CANR-17
Earlier sketch in CA 25-28R
Peterson, Robert E(ugene) 1928- ... 15-16R
Peterson, Robert W. 1925- ... 33-36R
Peterson, Roger Tory 1908- ... CANR-1
Earlier sketch in CA 4R
Peterson, Russell Arthur 1922- ... 33-36R
Peterson, Simone
See Thomson, Daisy H(icks)
Peterson, Susan (Annette) H(arnly) 1925- .. 57-60
Peterson, Ted Nicholas 1934- ... 121
Peterson, Theodore (Bernard) 1918- ... 11-12R
Peterson, Trudy H(uskamp) 1945- ... 116
Peterson, Virgilia 1904-1966 Obituary ... 25-28R
Peterson, Wallace Carroll 1921- ... 7-8R
Peterson, Walter Scott 1944- ... 23-24R
Peterson, Wilferd Arlan 1900- ... CANR-6
Earlier sketch in CA 11-12R
Peterson, Willard James 1938- ... 103
Peterson, William S(amuel) 1939- ... CANR-11
Earlier sketch in CA 29-32R
Petersson, Robert T. 1918- ... 45-48
Peterzell, Jay 1952- ... 118
Petesch, Natalie L(evin) M(aines) ... CANR-21
Earlier sketches in CA 57-60, CANR-6
Petgen, Dorothea 1903(?)-1985 Obituary ... 115
Petgen, Dorothy
See Petgen, Dorothea
Pethybridge, Roger 1934- ... 5-6R
Petie, Haris
See Petty, Roberta
See also SATA 10
Petievich, Gerald 1944- ... 105
Petiot, Henri Jules Charles 1901-1965
Obituary ... 114
Petit, Gaston 1930- ... 73-76
Petitclerc, Denne Bart 1929- ... 93-96
Petite, Irving (Laurence) 1920- Brief entry ... 113
Petkas, Peter (James) 1945- ... 37-40R
Petmecky, Ben (Joe) 1922- ... 3R
Peto
See White, Stanley
Peto, James
See White, Stanley
Petrakis, Harry Mark 1923- ... CANR-4
Earlier sketch in CA 11-12R
See also CLC 3
Petras, James Frank 1937- ... CANR-22
Earlier sketches in CA 61-64, CANR-7
Petras, John W. 1940- ... 29-32R
Petratur, Joyce 1939- Brief entry ... 111
Petrement, Simone 1907- ... 77-80
Petres, Robert E(van) 1939- ... 104
Petrich, Patricia Barrett 1942- ... 61-64
Petrides, Avra ... 123
Petrides, George Athan 1916- Brief entry ... 106
Petrides, Heidrun 1944- ... SATA-19
Petrie, Alexander 1881- ... CAP-1
Earlier sketch in CA 15-16
Petrie, Asenath 1914- ... 23-24R
Petrie, Catherine 1947- ... 109
See also SATA 41
Petrie, Charles (Alexander) 1895-1977 .. CANR-8
Obituary ... 89-92
Earlier sketch in CA 19-20R
Petrie, Mildred McClary 1912- ... 21-22R
Petrie, Paul J(ames) 1928- ... CANR-18
Earlier sketches in CA 9-10R, CANR-3
Petrie, Rhona
See Buchanan, Marie
Petrie, Sidney 1923- ... 23-24R
Petrinovich, Lewis 1930- ... 41-44R
Petro, Sylvester 1917- ... 1R
Petrocelli, Orlando R(alph) 1930- ... CANR-1
Earlier sketch in CA 45-48
Petrone, Jane Muir 1929- ... 7-8R
Petroni, Frank A. 1936- ... 85-88
Petropulos, John A(nthony) 1929- ... 25-28R
Petroski, Catherine (Ann Groom)
1939- ... CANR-22
Earlier sketch in CA 106
See also SATA 48
Petrou, David Michael 1949- ... 73-76
Petrov, Evgeny
See Kataev, Evgeny Petrovich
See also TCLC 21
Petrov, Fyodor 1877(?)-1973 Obituary ... 41-44R
Petrov, Victor P. 1907- ... CANR-10
Earlier sketch in CA 23-24R
Petrov, Vladimir 1915- ... 21-22R
Petrova, Olga 1884(?)-1977 Obituary ... 73-76
Petrovich, Michael B(oro) 1922- ... 108
See also SATA 40
Petrovska, Marija 1926- ... 107
Petrovskaya, Kyra
See Wayne, Kyra Petrovskaya
Petrovsky, N.
See Poltoratzky, N(ikolai) P(etrovich)
Petrucci, Kenneth R(occo) 1947- ... 57-60
Petry, Ann (Lane) 1908- ... CANR-4
Earlier sketch in CA 7-8R
See also CAAS 6
See also SATA 5
See also CLC 1, 7, 18
See also CLR 12
Petry, Carl Forbes 1943- ... 106
Petry, R(ay) C. 1903- ... 5-6R
Pettas, Mary 1918- ... 25-28R
Petterson, Henry William 1922- ... 11-12R
Petterssen, Sverre 1898-1974 Obituary ... 53-56
Pettersson, Karl-Henrik 1937- ... 65-68
Pettes, Dorothy E. ... CANR-12
Earlier sketch in CA 25-28R
Pettigrew, Thomas Fraser 1931- ... CANR-13
Earlier sketch in CA 33-36R
Pettingill, Amos
See Harris, William Bliss
Pettingill, Olin Sewall, Jr. 1907- ... CANR-1
Earlier sketch in CA 45-48
Pettit, Arthur G. 1938- ... 53-56
Pettit, Clyde Edwin 1932- ... 65-68
Pettit, Henry (Jewett) 1906- ... 2R
Pettit, Lawrence K. 1937- ... 33-36R
Pettit, Michael (Edwin) 1950- ... 114
Pettit, Norman 1929- ... 19-20R
Pettit, Philip 1945- ... CANR-17
Earlier sketch in CA 97-100
Pettitt, George A(lbert) 1901-1976 ... CAP-2
Earlier sketch in CA 29-32
Pettoello, Decio (Egberto Saadi)
1886-1984 Obituary ... 113
Petty, Anne C(otton) 1945- ... 115
Petty, Mary 1899-1976 Obituary ... 65-68
Petty, Norman 1927(?)-1984 Obituary ... 113
Petty, Roberta 1915- ... CANR-10
Earlier sketch in CA 61-64
Petty, Walter T. 1918- ... CANR-9
Earlier sketch in CA 23-24R
Petty, William Henry 1921- ... 65-68
Petuchowski, Jakob Josef 1925- ... CANR-18
Earlier sketches in CA 1R, CANR-3
Petulla, Joseph M. 1932- ... CANR-9
Earlier sketch in CA 23-24R
Petzold, Paul 1940- ... CANR-9
Earlier sketch in CA 61-64
Petzoldt, Paul Kiesow 1908- ... 57-60
Petzoldt, Richard 1907-1974 Obituary ... 111
Pevsner, Nikolaus (Bernhard Leon)
1902-1983 ... CANR-7
Obituary ... 110
Earlier sketch in CA 9-10R
Pevsner, Stella ... 57-60
See also SATA 8
Peyo
See Culliford, Pierre
Peyre, Henri (Maurice) 1901- ... CANR-3
Earlier sketch in CA 7-8R
Peyrefitte, Alain Antoine 1925- ... 85-88
Peyrefitte, (Pierre) Roger 1907- ... 65-68
Peyser, Joan 1931- Brief entry ... 112
Peyton, K. M.
See Peyton, Kathleen Wendy
See also CLR 3
Peyton, Karen (Hansen) 1897-196(?) ... CAP-1
Earlier sketch in CA 9-10
Peyton, Kathleen Wendy 1929- ... 69-72
See also SATA 15
Peyton, Myron A(lvin) 1909- Brief entry ... 114
Peyton, Patrick J(oseph) 1909- ... CAP-2
Earlier sketch in CA 23-24
Pezzulo, Ted 1936(?)-1979 Obituary ... 89-92
Pezzuti, Thomas Alexander 1936- ... 61-64
Pfadt, Robert Edward 1915- ... 73-76
Pfaff, William (Wendle III) 1928- ... CANR-24
Earlier sketch in CA 7-8R
Pfaffenberger, Bryan 1949- ... 118
Pfaffenberger, Clarence J. 1889-1967 ... CAP-1
Earlier sketch in CA 13-14
Pfahl, John K(erch) 1927- ... CANR-1
Earlier sketch in CA 1R
Pfaltz, Marilyn 1933- ... 103
Pfaltzgraff, Robert L., Jr. 1934- ... CANR-24
Earlier sketches in CA 23-24R, CANR-9
Pfanner, Helmut Franz 1933- ... 57-60
Pfarrer, Donald 1934- ... 111
Pfatteicher, Philip H(enry) 1935- ... 114
Pfau, Hugo 1908- ... 29-32R
Pfau, Richard Anthony 1942- ... 120
Pfeffer, J(ay) Alan 1907- ... CANR-3
Earlier sketch in CA 4R
Pfeffer, Jeffrey 1946- ... 109
Pfeffer, Leo 1910- ... CANR-22
Earlier sketches in CA 13-14R, CANR-7
Pfeffer, Rose 1908-1985 Obituary ... 115
Pfeffer, Susan Beth 1948- ... 29-32R
See also SATA 4
See also CLR 11
Pfeffermann, Guy 1941- ... 25-28R
Pfeifer, Carl J(ames) 1929- ... 49-52
Pfeifer, Luanne 1928- ... CANR-16
Earlier sketch in CA 89-92
Pfeiffer, Bruce Brooks 1930- ... 121
Pfeiffer, C(urtis) Boyd 1937- ... 57-60
Pfeiffer, Carl Curt 1908- ... 101
Pfeiffer, Charles F. 1919-1976 ... CANR-4
Obituary ... 65-68
Earlier sketch in CA 2R
Pfeiffer, Eric 1935- ... CANR-10
Earlier sketch in CA 13-14R
Pfeiffer, John E(dward) 1914- ... 101
Pfeiffer, Karl G(raham) ... 3R
Pfeiffer, Marcella
See Syracuse, Marcella Pfeiffer
Pfeilschifter, Boniface 1900- ... CAP-2
Earlier sketch in CA 19-20
Pferd, William (III) 1922(?)-1987 Obituary .. 121
Pfiffner, John M(cDonald) 1893- ... 7-8R
Pfingston, Roger 1940- ... CANR-20
Earlier sketch in CA 104
Pfister, Arthur 1949- ... 45-48
Pflanze, Otto (Paul) 1918- ... 7-8R
Pflaum, Irving Peter 1906-1985 ... 15-16R
Obituary ... 115
Pflaum, Melanie L(oewenthal) 1909- ... CANR-6
Earlier sketch in CA 13-14R
Pflaum, Susanna Whitney 1937- ... 110
Brief entry ... 106
Pflaum-Connor, Susanna
See Pflaum, Susanna Whitney
Pflieger, Elmer F. 1908- ... 19-20R
Pflum, John (Edward) 1934- Brief entry ... 107
Pfordresher, John 1943- ... 65-68
Pfouts, Ralph W(illiam) 1920- ... 41-44R
Pfoutz, Shirley Eclov 1922- ... 2R
Pfriem, John E. 1923(?)-1983 Obituary ... 110
Pfuetze, Paul E(ugene) 1904-1985 ... 3R
Obituary ... 118
Phair, Judith Turner 1946- ... 61-64
Phalle, Thibaut de Saint
See de Saint Phalle, Thibaut
Phan, Peter C(ho) 1943- ... 114
Phares, Donald 1942- ... 81-84
Phares, Ross (Oscar) 1908- ... CAP-1
Earlier sketch in CA 11-12
Phares, Timothy B. 1954- ... 97-100
Pharr, Emory Charles 1896(?)-1981
Obituary ... 104
Pharr, Robert D(eane) 1916- ... 49-52
See also DLB 33
Pharr, Susan J(ane) 1944- ... 105
Phelan, Francis Joseph 1925- ... 7-8R
Phelan, James Pius X 1951- ... 114
Phelan, John Leddy 1924-1976 ... CANR-12
Earlier sketch in CA 23-24R
Phelan, John Martin 1932- ... 73-76
Phelan, Josephine 1905- ... SATA-30
Phelan, Mary Kay 1914- ... CANR-4
Earlier sketch in CA 4R
See also SATA 3
Phelan, Mary Michenfelder 1936- ... 97-100
Phelan, Nancy 1913- ... 101
Phelan, Terry Wolfe 1941- ... 97-100
Phelge, Nanker
See Richards, Keith
Phelps, Arthur Warren 1909- ... 49-52
Phelps, Ashton 1913-1983 Obituary ... 109
Phelps, D(udley) Maynard 1897- ... CAP-2
Earlier sketch in CA 25-28
Phelps, Digger
See Phelps, Richard
Phelps, Donald (Norman) 1929- ... 45-48
Phelps, Ethel Johnston 1914- ... 106
See also SATA 35
Phelps, Frederic
See McCulley, Johnston
Phelps, Gilbert (Henry, Jr.) 1915- ... CANR-7
Earlier sketch in CA 7-8R
Phelps, Humphrey 1927- ... 111
Phelps, Jack 1926- ... 29-32R
Phelps, O(rme) Wheelock 1906- ... 2R
Phelps, Phelps 1897-1981 Obituary ... 104
Phelps, Richard ... 103
Phelps, Robert 1922- ... CANR-19
Earlier sketch in CA 19-20R
Phelps, Roger P(aul) 1920- ... 49-52
Phelps, Thomas Ross 1929- ... 61-64
Phenix, Philip Henry 1915- ... 5-6R
Pheto, Molefe 1935- ... 118
Phialas, Peter George 1914- ... 25-28R
Phibbs, Brendan (Pearse) 1916- ... 33-36R
Phifer, Kenneth G. 1915- ... 19-20R
Philbrick, Allen Kellogg 1914- ... 117
Philbrick, Charles (Horace) II
1922-1971 ... CANR-4
Earlier sketch in CA 4R
Philbrick, Helen L. 1910- ... 103
Philbrick, Joseph Lawrence 1927- ... 45-48
Philbrook, Clem(ent E.) 1917- ... 104
See also SATA 24
Philip, Cynthia Owen 1928- ... 49-52
Philip, J(ames) A(llenby) 1901- ... CAP-2
Earlier sketch in CA 23-24
Philip, John Robert 1927- ... 108
Philip, Lotte Brand
See Foerster, Lotte B(rand)
Philipp, Elliot Elias 1915- ... CANR-3
Earlier sketch in CA 9-10R
Philippatos, George Crito 1938-
Brief entry ... 106
Philippe, Charles-Louis 1874-1909 ... DLB-65
Philippi, Donald L. 1930- ... 108
Philips, Cyril Henry 1912- ... 103
Philips, G(eorge) Edward 1926- ... 41-44R
Philips, Judson (Pentecost) 1903- ... CANR-14
Earlier sketch in CA 89-92
See also AITN 1
Philips, Thomas
See Davies, L(eslie) P(urnell)
Philipson, Morris H. 1926- ... CANR-4
Earlier sketch in CA 1R
Philipson, Susan Sacher 1934- ... 11-12R
Philliber, William W(esley) 1943- ... 111
Phillifent, John Thomas 1916-1976
Obituary ... 102
Phillippi, Wendell Crane 1918- ... 77-80
Phillips, Aileen Paul
See Paul, Aileen
Phillips, Alan
See Stauderman, Albert P(hilip)
Phillips, Alan Meyrick Kerr 1916- ... 7-8R
Phillips, Alice H(erz) 1909- ... 114
Phillips, Allen
See Allen, (Evelyn) Elizabeth
Phillips, Almarin 1925- ... CANR-1
Earlier sketch in CA 2R
Phillips, Anne G(arvey) 1929- ... 73-76
Phillips, (Elizabeth Margaret Ann) Barty
1933- ... CANR-24
Earlier sketches in CA 61-64, CANR-8
Phillips, Beeman N(oal) 1927- ... 122
Phillips, Bernard S. 1931- ... CANR-12
Earlier sketch in CA 25-28R
Phillips, Bernice Maxine 1925- ... 45-48
Phillips, Betty Lou
See Phillips, Elizabeth Louise
Phillips, Billie M(cKindra) 1925- ... 102
Phillips, Bob 1940- ... 69-72
Phillips, C(ecil) E(rnest) Lucas
See Lucas Phillips, C(ecil) E(rnest)
Phillips, Cabell (Beverly Hatchett)
1904-1975 ... 97-100
Obituary ... 61-64
Phillips, Carole 1938- ... 108
Phillips, Cecil R(andolph) 1933- ... 15-16R
Phillips, Celeste R(ose Nagel) 1933- ... 110
Phillips, Charles F(ranklin, Jr.) 1910- ... 85-88
Phillips, Charles F(ranklin), Jr. 1934- ... CANR-2
Earlier sketch in CA 7-8R
Phillips, Claude S., Jr. 1923- ... 11-12R
Phillips, Clifton J(ackson) 1919- ... 37-40R
Phillips, (Preswly) Craig 1922- ... 11-12R
Phillips, D(ennis) J(ohn Andrew)
1924- ... CANR-10
Earlier sketch in CA 15-16R
Phillips, David Atlee 1922- ... CANR-12
Earlier sketch in CA 69-72
Phillips, David Graham 1867-1911
Brief entry ... 108
See also DLB 9, 12
Phillips, Debora R(othman) 1939- ... 93-96
Phillips, Derek L(ee) 1934- ... CANR-18
Earlier sketch in CA 33-36R
Phillips, Dewi Zephaniah 1934- ... CANR-9
Earlier sketch in CA 19-20R
Phillips, Dorothy S(anborn) 1893-1972
Obituary ... 37-40R
Phillips, Dorothy W. 1906-1977 Obituary .. 73-76
Phillips, E(lmo) Bryant 1905-1975 ... CANR-6
Earlier sketch in CA 5-6R
Phillips, E(wing) Lakin 1915- ... 37-40R
Phillips, E(ugene) Lee 1941- ... 115
Phillips, Edward O. 1931- ... 124
Phillips, Edwin A(llen) 1915- ... 53-56
Phillips, Elizabeth C(row) 1906- ... 41-44R
Phillips, Elizabeth Louise ... SATA-48
Phillips, Emma Julia 1900- ... CAP-1
Earlier sketch in CA 13-14
Phillips, Frances Lucas 1896-1986
Obituary ... 119
Phillips, Frank
See Nowlan, Philip Francis
Phillips, Gene D(aniel) 1935- ... CANR-17
Earlier sketches in CA 45-48, CANR-1
Phillips, George H(oward) 1907- ... 112
Phillips, Gerald M. 1928- ... CANR-13
Earlier sketch in CA 33-36R
Phillips, Gordon Lewis 1911-1982
Obituary ... 108
Phillips, Herbert P. 1929- ... 15-16R
Phillips, Hiram Stone 1912(?)-1979 ... 85-88
Phillips, Irv(ing W.) 1908- ... 65-68
See also SATA 11
Phillips, J(ohn) B(ertram) 1906-1982 ... 106
Obituary ... 108
Phillips, Jack
See Sandburg, Carl (August)
Phillips, James E(merson, Jr.) 1912-1979
Obituary ... 89-92
Phillips, James Emerson, Jr. 1912-1979 ... 101
Phillips, James M(cJunkin) 1929- ... 106
Phillips, James W. 1922- ... 33-36R
Phillips, Jayne Anne 1952- ... CANR-24
Earlier sketch in CA 101
See also DLBY 80
See also CLC 15, 33
Phillips, Jerome C.
See Cleveland, Philip Jerome
Phillips, Jewell Cass 1900- ... CAP-2
Earlier sketch in CA 33-36
Phillips, Jill (Meta) 1952- ... CANR-14
Earlier sketch in CA 65-68
Phillips, John L(awrence), Jr. 1923- ... 33-36R
Phillips, Josephine E(lvira Frye)
1896-1975 ... 5-6R
Obituary ... 61-64
Phillips, Julien L(ind) 1945- ... 77-80
Phillips, Kathleen C(oleman) 1920- ... 116
Phillips, Keith W(endall) 1946- ... 102
Phillips, Kevin Price 1940- ... 65-68
Phillips, Klaus (Peter) 1947- ... 116
Phillips, L(ouis) C(hristopher) 1939- ... 57-60
Phillips, Laughlin 1924- ... 102
Phillips, Leon
See Gerson, Noel Bertram
Phillips, Leona Rasmussen 1925- ... CANR-14
Earlier sketch in CA 65-68
Phillips, Lois (Elisabeth) 1926- Brief entry .. 114
Phillips, Loretta (Hosey) 1893- ... CAP-1
Earlier sketch in CA 15-16
See also SATA 10
Phillips, Louis 1942- ... CANR-20
Earlier sketches in CA 49-52, CANR-3
See also SATA 8
Phillips, Mac
See Phillips, Maurice J(ack)
Phillips, Margaret 1892(?)-1985 Obituary ... 116
Phillips, Margaret Mann 1906-1987 ... 15-16R
Obituary ... 123
Phillips, Margaret McDonald
1910(?)-1978 Obituary ... 77-80

Phillips, Marjorie (Fell) 7-8R
Phillips, Mark
See Janifer, Laurence M(ark)
Phillips, Mary Geisler 1881-1964 ....5-6R
See also SATA 10
Phillips, Mary L. 1930- 116
Phillips, Maurice J(ack) 1914-1976 ....7-8R
Obituary 103
Phillips, Michael 1938- 108
Phillips, Michael
See Nolan, William F(rancis)
Phillips, Michael Joseph 1937- CANR-18
Earlier sketches in CA 49-52, CANR-3
Phillips, Michael R(ay) 1946- 114
Phillips, Mickey
See Phillips, Alan Meyrick Kerr
Phillips, Mike
See Phillips, Michael R(ay)
Phillips, O(wen) Hood 1907- CANR-2
Earlier sketch in CA 7-8R
Phillips, O(wen) M(artin) 1930- 89-92
Phillips, Osborne
See Barcynski, Leon Roger
Phillips, Patricia 1935- 103
Phillips, Paul 1938- CANR-14
Earlier sketch in CA 73-76
Phillips, Pauline (Esther Friedman)
1918- CANR-19
Earlier sketch in CA 1R
Phillips, Prentice 1894- CAP-1
Earlier sketch in CA 15-16
See also SATA 10
Phillips, R. Hart
See Phillips, Ruby Hart
Phillips, Rachel 1934- 49-52
Phillips, Ray C. 1922- CANR-10
Earlier sketch in CA 25-28R
Phillips, Richard
See Dick, Philip K(indred)
Phillips, Richard C(laybourne) 1934- 65-68
Phillips, Robert (Schaeffer) 1938- CANR-8
Earlier sketch in CA 19-20R
See also CLC 28
Phillips, Robert L(eRoy), Jr. 1940- 77-80
Phillips, Ruby Hart 1902-1985 Obituary 117
Phillips, Samantha
See Gelles-Cole, Sandi
Phillips, Stella 1927- CANR-11
Earlier sketch in CA 21-22R
Phillips, Stephen 1864-1915 Brief entry 111
See also DLB 10
Phillips, Steve
See Whittington, Harry (Benjamin)
Phillips, Steven 1947- 103
Phillips, Tom
See Drotning, Phillip T(homas)
Phillips, Ulrich B. 1877-1934 .... DLB-17
Phillips, Velma 1894- CAP-2
Earlier sketch in CA 19-20
Phillips, Ward
See Lovecraft, H(oward) P(hillips)
Phillips, Warren (Henry) 1926- 107
Phillips, Wendell 1921-1975 .... CAP-2
Obituary 61-64
Earlier sketch in CA 23-24
Phillips, Willard 1784-1873 .... DLB-59
Phillips, William 29-32R
Phillips-Birt, Douglas Hextall Chedzey
1920-1977 .... CANR-1
Earlier sketch in CA 4R
Phillips-Jones, Linda 1943- 109
Phillipson, David 1930- 57-60
Phillipson, David W(alter) 1942- 107
Phillpotts, (Mary) Adelaide Eden 1896- 115
Phillpotts, Eden 1862-1960 102
Obituary 93-96
See also SATA 24
See also DLB 10
Philmus, Robert M. 1943- 33-36R
Philomythes
See Dewart, Leslie
Philp, Howard Littleton 1902- 7-8R
Philp, Kenneth R(oy) 1941- 65-68
Philp, (Dennis Alfred) Peter 1920- 7-8R
Philp, Richard Nilson 1943- CANR-11
Earlier sketch in CA 69-72
Philpott, David G(oodwin) 1927- 123
Philpott, Kent 1942- 61-64
Phin
See Thayer, Ernest Lawrence
Phipps, Christine 1945- 123
Phipps, Frances (Lucille Walker)
1924(?)-1986 Obituary 119
Phipps, Grace May Palk 1901- CANR-4
Earlier sketch in CA 11-12R
Phipps, Joyce 1942- 49-52
Phipps, Nicholas 1913-1980 Obituary 97-100
Phipps, William E(ugene) 1930- CANR-12
Earlier sketch in CA 29-32R
Phipson, Joan
See Fitzhardinge, Joan Margaret
See also SAAS 3
See also CLR 5
Phiz
See Browne, Hablot Knight
Phleger, Fred B. 1909- CANR-21
Earlier sketch in CA 2R
See also SATA 34
Phleger, Marjorie Temple 1908(?)-1986 ..11-12R
Obituary 118
See also SATA 1, 47
Phoenix, John
See Derby, George Horatio
Phoenix, Pat
See Pilkington, Pat
Phypers, David (John) 1939- 114
Physick, John Frederick 1923- 114
Phythian, B(rian) A(rthur) 1932- CANR-10
Earlier sketch in CA 23-24R
Piaf, Edith 1915-1963 Obituary 113
Piaget, Jean 1896-1980 ....21-22R
Obituary 101
See also SATA 23
Pian, Rulan Chao 1922- 23-24R
Piano, Celeste
See Lykiard, Alexis (Constantine)
Piasecki, Bruce 1955- CANR-12
Earlier sketch in CA 69-72
Piatigorsky, Alexander 1929- 124
Piatigorsky, Gregor 1903-1976 Obituary ...69-72
Piatti, Celestino 1922- 73-76
See also SATA 16
Piazza, Ben 1934- 11-12R
Picano, Felice 1944- CANR-11
Earlier sketch in CA 69-72
Picard, Barbara Leonie 1917- CANR-2
Earlier sketch in CA 7-8R
See also SATA 2
Picasso, Pablo (Ruiz) 1881-1973 97-100
Obituary 41-44R
Picazo, Jose 1910- CAP-1
Earlier sketch in CA 13-14
Piccard, Auguste 1884-1962 Obituary 113
Piccard, Betty
See Piccard, Elizabeth J(ane)
Piccard, Elizabeth J(ane) 1925- 65-68
Piccard, Jacques 1922- 65-68
Piccard, Joan Russell 29-32R
Picchio, Riccardo 1923- CANR-24
Earlier sketch in CA 45-48
Piccolo, Lucio 1901-1969 97-100
See also CLC 13
Pichaske, David Richard 1943- CANR-1
Earlier sketch in CA 45-48
Pick, J(ohn) B(arclay) 1921- CANR-5
Earlier sketch in CA 3R
Pick, John 1911- CAP-2
Earlier sketch in CA 33-36
Pick, (Frederick) Michael 1949- 123
Pick, Robert 1898-1978 .... CANR-8
Obituary 77-80
Earlier sketch in CA 19-20R
Pickard, Charles 1932- SATA-36
Pickard, Dorothea Wilgus 1902- 23-24R
Pickard, John Benedict 1928- 2R
Pickard, Tom 1946- 81-84
See also DLB 40
Pickell, Charles N(orman) 1927- 19-20R
Pickem, Peter
See Stearns, Harold Edmund
Picken, Mary Brooks 1886(?)-1981
Obituary 103
Picken, Stuart D(onald) B(lair) 1942- 106
Pickens, Donald Kenneth 1934- 53-56
Pickens, Robert S. 1900(?)-1978
Obituary 81-84
Pickens, Roy 1939- 57-60
Picker, Fred 1927- 81-84
Picker, Ingrid 1932- 25-28R
Picker, Martin 1929- CANR-7
Earlier sketch in CA 19-20R
Pickerell, Albert G(eorge) 1912- 25-28R
Pickerill, Don 1928- 77-80
Pickering, Ernest 1893(?)-1974 Obituary ..53-56
Pickering, Frederick Pickering 1909- 105
Pickering, George (White) 1904-1980 73-76
Obituary 105
Pickering, James H(enry) 1937- CANR-13
Earlier sketch in CA 33-36R
Pickering, James Sayre 1897-1969 .... CANR-16
Obituary 103
Earlier sketch in CA 1R
See also SATA 28, 36
Pickering, Jerry V(ane) 1931- 57-60
Pickering, Percival
See Stirling, Anna Maria Diana
Wilhelmina (Pickering)
Pickering, R(obert) E(aston) 1934- 21-22R
Pickering, Samuel Francis, Jr. 1941- 104
Pickering, Stephen 1947- 57-60
Pickersgill, J(ohn) W(hitney) 1905- 45-48
Pickett, Calder M. 1921- 53-56
Pickett, Carla 1944- 37-40R
Pickett, J(arrell) Waskom 1890- CAP-1
Earlier sketch in CA 15-16
Pickett, Robert S. 1931- 33-36R
Pickford, Cedric Edward 1926-1983 107
Obituary 109
Pickford, Mary 1893-1979 Obituary 85-88
Pickle, Hal B(rittain) 1929- CANR-21
Earlier sketches in CA 57-60, CANR-6
Pickles, (Maud) Dorothy 1903- 77-80
Pickles, M(abel) Elizabeth 1902- CAP-1
Earlier sketch in CA 9-10
Pickles, Wilfred 1904-1978(?) 108
Pickoff, David 1930(?)-1986 Obituary 118
Pickrel, Paul (Murphy) 1917- 9-10R
Pickthall, Marjorie L(owry) C(hristie)
1883-1922 Brief entry 107
See also TCLC 21
Pickthorn, Helen 1927- 25-28R
Pico, Rafael 1912- 45-48
Picon, Molly 1898- 104
Picton, Bernard
See Knight, Bernard
Pidal, Ramon Menendez
See Menendez Pidal, Ramon
Pidgeon, Mary E. 1890(?)-1979 Obituary ..89-92
Piechocki, Joachim von Lang
See von Lang-Piechocki, Joachim
Piediscalzi, Nicholas 1931- 122
Brief entry 112
Piehl, Mel (Willis) 1946- 111
Piehler, Paul 1929- Brief entry 111
Piekalkiewicz, Jaroslaw A. 1926- 81-84
Piel, Gerard 1915- 57-60
Pienkowski, Jan 1936- CANR-11
Earlier sketch in CA 65-68
See also SATA 6
See also CLR 6
Pieper, Josef 1904- 119
Piepkorn, Arthur Carl 1907-1973 ....41-44R
Pier, Arthur Stanhope 1874(?)-1966
Obituary 25-28R
Pierard, Richard Victor 1934- CANR-17
Earlier sketch in CA 29-32R
Pieratt, Asa B. 1938- 77-80
Pierce, Arthur Dudley 1897-1967 .... 1R
Obituary 103
Pierce, Bessie Louise 1888-1974
Obituary 53-56
Pierce, E(ugene) 1924- 15-16R
Pierce, Edith Gray 1893-1977 61-64
See also SATA 45
Pierce, Edward T. 1917(?)-1978 Obituary ..77-80
Pierce, George Gilbert 1923- 7-8R
Pierce, Gerald S(wetnam) 1933- 45-48
Pierce, Glenn
See Dumke, Glenn S.
Pierce, James Smith 1930- 21-22R
Pierce, Janis V(aughn) 1934- 45-48
Pierce, Joe E. 1924- 33-36R
Pierce, John Leonard, Jr. 1921- 11-12R
Pierce, John Robinson 1910- 17-18R
Pierce, Katherine
See St. John, Wylly Folk
Pierce, Lawrence C(olman) 1936- 85-88
Pierce, Meredith Ann 1958- 108
See also SATA 48
Pierce, Milton Plotz 1933- 106
Pierce, Ovid Williams 1910- CANR-4
Earlier sketch in CA 1R
Pierce, Patricia (May) 1943- 120
Pierce, Paul 1910- 69-72
Pierce, Philip E(arly) 1912- 110
Pierce, Richard A(ustin) 1918- CANR-2
Earlier sketch in CA 7-8R
Pierce, Robert N(ash) 1931- 104
Pierce, Roy 1923- 37-40R
Pierce, Ruth (Ireland) 1936- 29-32R
See also SATA 5
Pierce, Tamora 1954- 118
See also SATA 49
Pierce, Willard Bob 1914- 13-14R
Piercy, Josephine Ketcham 1895- CAP-1
Earlier sketch in CA 15-16
Piercy, Marge 1936- CANR-13
Earlier sketch in CA 23-24R
See also CAAS 1
See also CLC 3, 6, 14, 18, 27
Pierik, Robert 1921- 37-40R
See also SATA 13
Pierman, Carol J 1947- 77-80
Pierotti, John 1911-1987 Obituary 122
Pierpoint, Robert (Charles) 1925- 107
Pierre, Andrew J. 1934- CANR-1
Earlier sketch in CA 45-48
Pierre, Clara 1939- 65-68
Pierrot, George Francis 1898-1980 ....7-8R
Obituary 103
See also AITN 2
Piers, Maria W(eigl) 1911- CANR-8
Earlier sketch in CA 23-24R
Pierson, Frank
See Pierson, Frank R(omer)
Pierson, Frank R(omer) 1925- 123
Brief entry 114
Pierson, G(eorge) W(ilson) 1904- CANR-3
Earlier sketch in CA 9-10R
Pierson, Howard 1922- 49-52
Pierson, Jan 1937- 112
Pierson, John H(erman) G(roesbeck)
1906- CANR-4
Earlier sketch in CA 11-12R
Pierson, Paul Everett 1927- 108
Pierson, Peter O'Malley 1932- 97-100
Pierson, Robert H. 1911- 21-22R
Pierson, Stanley 1925- 85-88
Pierson, William H(arvey), Jr. 1911- 122
Piet, John H(enry) 1914- 29-32R
Pietri, Pedro Juan 1943- 97-100
Pietrofesa, John J(oseph) 1940- 57-60
Pietropinto, Anthony 1938- 89-92
Pietsch, Paul Andrew 1929- 104
Pietschmann, Richard John III 1940- 69-72
Pieyre de Mandiargues, Andre 1909- ... CANR-22
Earlier sketch in CA 103
Pifer, Ellen 1942- CANR-23
Earlier sketch in CA 106
Pig, Edward
See Gorey, Edward (St. John)
Piggott, C. M.
See Guido, (Cecily) Margaret
Piggott, (Alan) Derek 1923- 115
Pigman, William Ward 1910-1977
Obituary 73-76
Pigney, Joseph Pape 1908- 3R
Pihera, Larry 1933- CANR-1
Earlier sketch in CA 45-48
Pihl, Marshall R(alph) 1933- 49-52
Pijewski, John 1952- 111
Piji
See Williams, Ann, Jr.
Pike, Burton 1930- 2R
Pike, Charles R.
See Bulmer, (Henry) Kenneth
and Harknett, Terry
Pike, Dag 1933- 69-72
Pike, Diane Kennedy 1938- 37-40R
Pike, E(dgar) Royston 1896- 9-10R
See also SATA 22
Pike, Eunice V(ictoria) 1913- CANR-20
Earlier sketch in CA 97-100
Pike, James A(lbert) 1913-1969 .... CANR-4
Obituary 25-28R
Earlier sketch in CA 4R
Pike, Kenneth Lee 1912- 120
Pike, Margaret (Prudence) Lyford
See Lyford-Pike, Margaret (Prudence)
Pike, Nelson C. 1930- Brief entry 111
Pike, Norman 1901- CAP-2
Earlier sketch in CA 25-28
Pike, Robert E(vording) 1905- 7-8R
Pike, Robert L.
See Fish, Robert L.
Pike, Ruth 1931- Brief entry 112
Pike, William H. 1943- 115
Pikelny, Philip S. 1951- 107
Pikoulis, John 1941- 115
Pikunas, Justin 1920- 25-28R
Pilapil, Vicente R. 1941- 37-40R
Pilarski, Laura 1926- 29-32R
See also SATA 13
Pilat, O. R.
See Pilat, Oliver (Ramsay)
Pilat, Oliver (Ramsay) 1903-1987 ....7-8R
Obituary 123
Pilbrow, Richard (Hugh) 1933- 29-32R
Pilcer, Sonia 1949- CANR-13
Earlier sketch in CA 89-92
Pilch, John J(oseph) 1936- 108
Pilch, Judah 1902- CANR-6
Earlier sketch in CA 7-8R
Pilcher, George William 1935- 105
Pilcher, Rosamunde 1924- 57-60
Pilcher, William W. 1930- 45-48
Pilditch, James (George Christopher)
1929- 11-12R
Pile, John F(rederick) 1924- CANR-16
Earlier sketch in CA 93-96
Pileggi, Nicholas 1933- 124
Pilgrim, Anne
See Allan, Mabel Esther
Pilgrim, David 1950- 120
Pilgrim, David
See Palmer, John (Leslie)
and Saunders, Hilary Aidan St. George
Pilgrim, Geneva Hanna 1914- 25-28R
Pilgrim, Walter E(dward) 1934- 113
Piliawsky, Monte 1944- 111
Pilinszky, Janos 1921-1981 Obituary 104
Pilio, Gerone
See Whitfield, John Humphreys
Pilisuk, Marc 1934- 29-32R
Pilk, Henry
See Campbell, Ken
Pilkey, Orrin H. 1934- 97-100
Pilkington, Betty 69-72
Pilkington, Cynthia
See Horne, Cynthia Miriam
Pilkington, E(dward) C(ecil) A(rnold)
1907- CAP-2
Earlier sketch in CA 25-28
Pilkington, Francis Meredyth 1907- CAP-2
Earlier sketch in CA 25-28
See also SATA 4
Pilkington, John, Jr. 1918- 19-20R
Pilkington, Pat 1923-1986 123
Obituary 120
Pilkington, Roger (Windle) 1915- CANR-5
Earlier sketch in CA 3R
See also SATA 10
Pilkington, Walter ?-1983 Obituary 109
Pilkington, William T(homas, Jr.)
1939- CANR-8
Earlier sketch in CA 61-64
Pill, Virginia 1922- 61-64
Pillai, Karnam Chengalvaroya 1901- 7-8R
Pillar, James Jerome 1928- 15-16R
Pillin, William 1910-1985 ....11-12R
Obituary 116
Pilling, Arnold R(emington) 1926- CANR-3
Earlier sketch in CA 1R
Pilling, Christopher Robert 1936- CANR-19
Earlier sketch in CA 101
Pillinger, Douglass 1906(?)-1983 Obituary .. 111
Pillon, Nancy Bach 1917- 110
Pilnyak, Boris
See Vogau, Boris Andreyevich
See also TCLC 23
Pilo, Giuseppe Maria 1929- CANR-5
Earlier sketch in CA 9-10R
Pilon, Jean-Guy 1930- DLB-60
Pilon, Juliana Geran 1947- 97-100
Pilou
See Bardot, Louis
Pilpel, Harriet F(leischl) CAP-2
Earlier sketch in CA 21-22
Pilpel, Robert H(arry) 1943- CANR-9
Earlier sketch in CA 65-68
Pimsleur, Meira Goldwater
1905(?)-1979 ....13-14R
Obituary 89-92
Pimsleur, Paul 1927-1976 .... CAP-2
Obituary 65-68
Earlier sketch in CA 33-36
Pina, Laura ?-1984 Obituary 113
Pinar, William 1947- 57-60
Pinard, (J. L.-M.) Maurice 1929- 41-44R
Pincher, H(enry) Chapman 1914- CANR-12
Earlier sketch in CA 15-16R
Pincherle, Alberto 1907- 25-28R
See also CLC 11, 18
Pincherle, Marc 1888-1974 Obituary 49-52
Pinchin, Jane Lagoudis 1942- 69-72
Pinchot, Ann (Kramer) CANR-4
Earlier sketch in CA 4R

Pinchot, David 1914(?)-1983 Obituary 109
See also SATA 34
Pinckney, Catherine L(arkum) 19-20R
Pinckney, Cathey
See Pinckney, Catherine L(arkum)
Pinckney, Edward R(obert) 1924- 19-20R
Pinckney, Josephine (Lyons Scott)
1895-1957 Brief entry 107
See also DLB 6
Pincus, Edward R. 1938- CANR-12
Earlier sketch in CA 33-36R
Pincus, Gregory Goodwin 1903-1967
Obituary 113
Pincus, Harriet 1938- 102
See also SATA 27
Pincus, Joseph 1919- 25-28R
Pincus, Lily 1898-1981 .... CANR-5
Obituary 105
Earlier sketch in CA 53-56
Pinder, John H(umphrey) M(urray) CANR-18
Earlier sketches in CA 9-10R, CANR-3
Pindyck, Robert (Stephen) 1945- 89-92
Pine, Leslie Gilbert 1907-1987 ....13-14R
Obituary 122
Pine, Theodore
See Petaja, Emil (Theodore)
Pine, Tillie S(chloss) 1896- 69-72
See also SATA 13
Pine, William
See Harknett, Terry
Pineau, Roger 1916- 25-28R
Pineda, Cecile 1942- 118
See also CLC 39
Pinero, Arthur Wing 1855-1934
Brief entry 110
See also DLB 10
Pinero, Miguel (Gomez) 1946- 61-64
See also CLC 4
Pines, Maya 15-16R
Pines, Paul (Andre) 1941- 112
Ping, Charles J. 1930- 19-20R
Pinget, Robert 1919- 85-88
See also CLC 7, 13, 37
Pinion, F(rancis) B(ertram) 1908- CANR-12
Earlier sketch in CA 25-28R
Pinkerton, Edward C(askin) 1911- 108
Pinkerton, James R(onald) 1932- CANR-24
Earlier sketch in CA 45-48
Pinkerton, Jan 1934- Brief entry 112
Pinkerton, Joan Trego 1928- 107
Pinkerton, Kathrene Sutherland (Gedney)
1887-1967 .... 2R
Obituary 103
See also SATA 26
Pinkerton, Marjorie Jean 1934- 45-48
Pinkerton, Robert E(ugene) 1882-1970
Obituary 29-32R
Pinkerton, Todd 1917- 69-72
Pinkerton, W. Anson
See Steele, Henry
Pinkett, Harold T(homas) 1914- 29-32R
Pink Floyd
See Barrett, (Roger) Syd
and Gilmour, David
and Mason, Nick
and Waters, Roger
and Wright, Rick
See also CLC 35
Pinkham, Mary Ellen 101
Pinkney, Alphonso 1929- 25-28R
Pinkney, David H(enry) 1914- 11-12R
Pinkney, Jerry 1939- SATA-32, 41
Pinkowski, Edward 1916- 9-10R
Pinkston, Joe M. 1931- 7-8R
Pinkus, Oscar 1927- 7-8R
Pinkus, Philip 1922- Brief entry 113
Pinkwater, Daniel Manus 1941- CANR-12
Earlier sketch in CA 29-32R
See also SATA 46
See also SAAS 3
See also CLC 35
See also CLR 4
Pinkwater, Manus
See Pinkwater, Daniel Manus
See also SATA 8
Pinna, Giovanni 1939- CANR-4
Earlier sketch in CA 49-52
Pinner, David 1940- CANR-19
Earlier sketch in CA 25-28R
Pinner, Erna 1896- CAP-1
Earlier sketch in CA 11-12
Pinner, Joma
See Werner, Herma
Pinney, Peter (Patrick) 1922- 25-28R
Pinney, Roy 1911- CANR-6
Earlier sketch in CA 7-8R
Pinney, Thomas 1932- CANR-21
Earlier sketch in CA 85-88
Pinney, Wilson G(ifford) 1929- 45-48
Pino, E.
See Wittermans, Elizabeth (Pino)
Pino, Jose Ortiz y III
See Ortiz y Pino, Jose III
Pinoak, Justin Willard
See Prosser, H(arold) L(ee)
Pinsdorf, Marion K(atheryn) 1932- 124
Pinsent, Arthur 1888- CAP-2
Earlier sketch in CA 29-32
Pinsent, Gordon (Edward) 1930- 106
Pinsker, Sanford 1941- CANR-12
Earlier sketch in CA 33-36R
Pinsky, Robert 1940- 29-32R
See also CAAS 4
See also DLBY 82
See also CLC 9, 19, 38
Pinson, William M(eredith), Jr. 1934- ... CANR-9
Earlier sketch in CA 19-20R
Pintauro, Joseph 1930- 81-84
Pintel, Gerald 1922- CANR-4
Earlier sketch in CA 49-52
Pinter, Harold 1930- 7-8R
See also DLB 13
See also CLC 1, 3, 6, 9, 11, 15, 27
Pinter, Walter S. 1928- 102
Pintner, Walter McKenzie 1931- 23-24R
Pinto, David 1937- 61-64
Pinto, Edward Henry 1901-1972 .... CAP-1
Earlier sketch in CA 13-14
Pinto, Peter
See Berne, Eric (Lennard)
Pinto, Vivian de Sola 1895-1969 ...... CANR-10
Earlier sketch in CA 5-6R
Pintoff, Ernest 1931- 19-20R
Pintoro, John 1947- 103
Pioneer
See Yates, Raymond F(rancis)
Piontek, Heinz 1925- CANR-13
Earlier sketch in CA 25-28R
Piotrow, Phyllis Tilson 1933- 122
Piovene, Guido 1907-1974 97-100
Obituary 53-56
Piowaty, Kim Kennelly 1957- 115
See also SATA 49
Pipa, Arshi 1920- CANR-10
Earlier sketch in CA 25-28R
Piper, Anson C(onant) 1918- 41-44R
Piper, Don Courtney 1932- CANR-15
Earlier sketch in CA 41-44R
Piper, Eileen 1906- 122
Piper, H(enry) Beam 1904-1964 117
Obituary 110
See also DLB 8
Piper, H(erbert) W(alter) 1915- 7-8R
Piper, Henry Dan 1918- 19-20R
Piper, Jim 1937- 97-100
Piper, Otto A. 1891- 5-6R
Piper, Roger
See Fisher, John (Oswald Hamilton)
Piper, Watty
See Bragg, Mabel Caroline
See also DLB 22
Piper, William Bowman 1927- CANR-12
Earlier sketch in CA 61-64
Pipes, Richard (Edgar) 1923- 23-24R
Pippert, Wesley Gerald 1934- 53-56
Pippett, (Winifred) Aileen 1895- CAP-1
Earlier sketch in CA 13-14
Pippin, Frank Johnson 1906-1968 .... CAP-2
Earlier sketch in CA 19-20
Pipping, Ella (Geologica) 1897- 61-64
Piquet, Howard S(amuel) 1903-1983 ... CANR-16
Obituary 111
Earlier sketches in CA 19-20, CAP-2
Piquet-Wicks, Eric 1915- 7-8R
Pirages, Dennis (Clark) 1942- 116
Pirandello, Luigi 1867-1936 Brief entry 104
See also TCLC 4
Pires, Joe
See Stout, Robert Joe
Pirie, David (Tarbat) 1946- CANR-21
Earlier sketch in CA 97-100
Pirie, N(orman) W(ingate) 1907- 29-32R
Pirie-Gordon, (Charles) Harry (Clinton)
1883(?)-1969 Obituary 104
Pirmantgen, Pat
See Pirmantgen, Patricia H.
Pirmantgen, Patricia H. 1933- 45-48
Piro, Richard 1934- 49-52
See also SATA 7
Pirogov, Peter A. 1920-1987 Obituary 121
Pirone, Pascal P(ompey) 1907- 11-12R
Pirsig, Robert M(aynard) 1928- 53-56
See also SATA 39
See also CLC 4, 6
Pirson, Sylvain J. 1905- 5-6R
Pirtle, Caleb (Jackson) III 1941- CANR-11
Earlier sketch in CA 69-72
Pisano, Ronald G(eorge) 1948- CANR-20
Earlier sketch in CA 102
Pisar, Samuel 1929- 29-32R
See also DLBY 83
Piserchia, Doris (Elaine) 1928- Brief entry .. 107
Pishkin, Vladimir 1931- CANR-24
Earlier sketch in CA 45-48
Pisk, Paul A(madeus) 1893- CAP-1
Earlier sketch in CA 13-14
Pismire, Osbert
See Hivnor, Robert
Pisor, Robert (Louis) 1939- 109
Pistole, Elizabeth (Smith) 1920- CANR-8
Earlier sketch in CA 19-20R
Piston, Walter 1894-1976 Obituary 69-72
Pitavy, Francois L(ouis) 1934- 73-76
Pitcairn, Frank
See Cockburn, (Francis) Claud
Pitcairn, Leonora 1912- 23-24R
Pitcher, Evelyn G(oodenough) 1915- 19-20R
Pitcher, George (Willard) 1925- 23-24R
Pitcher, Gladys 1890- CAP-1
Earlier sketch in CA 9-10
Pitcher, Harvey (John) 1936- CANR-3
Earlier sketch in CA 45-48
Pitcher, Robert W(alter) 1918- 29-32R
Pitchford, Kenneth S(amuel) 1931- 104
Pitkin, Dorothy (Horton) 1899(?)-1972
Obituary 37-40R
Pitkin, Hanna Fenichel 1931- 122
Brief entry 111
Pitkin, Thomas M(onroe) 1901- 19-20R
Pitkin, Timothy 1766-1847 ....DLB-30
Pitkin, Walter, Jr. 1913- 15-16R
Pitman, (Isaac) James 1901-1985 .... CAP-2
Obituary 117
Earlier sketch in CA 29-32
See also SATA 46
Pitrone, Jean Maddern 1920- CANR-8
Earlier sketch in CA 19-20R
See also SATA 4
Pitseolak, Peter 1902-1973 93-96
Pitt, Barrie (William Edward) 1918- CANR-20
Earlier sketch in CA 5-6R
Pitt, David C(harles) 1938- CANR-16
Earlier sketch in CA 29-32R
Pitt, Jeremy
See Wynne-Tyson, (Timothy) Jon
(Lyden)
Pitt, Peter (Clive Crawford) 1933- 33-36R
Pitt, Valerie Joan 1925- 7-8R
Pittenger, W(illiam) Norman 1905- CANR-20
Earlier sketches in CA 4R, CANR-5
Pitter, Ruth 1897- CAP-1
Earlier sketch in CA 13-14
See also DLB 20
Pittman, David J(oshua) 1927- CANR-6
Earlier sketch in CA 7-8R
Pittock, Joan (Hornby) 1930- 107
Pitt-Rivers, Julian Alfred 1919- 101
Pitts, Denis 1930- 65-68
Pitts, Robert F. 1908-1977 Obituary 69-72
Pitz, Henry C(larence) 1895-1976 .... CANR-9
Obituary 69-72
Earlier sketch in CA 9-10R
See also SATA 4, 24
Pitzer, Sara 1938- 107
Pivar, David J. 1933- 45-48
Piven, Frances Fox 1932- 49-52
Pixley, Jorge V. 1937- CANR-16
Earlier sketches in CA 45-48, CANR-1
Pizer, Donald 1929- 11-12R
Pizer, Harry F(rancis) 1947- 101
Pizer, Vernon 1918- CANR-4
Earlier sketch in CA 4R
See also SATA 21
Pizzat, Frank J(oseph) 1924- 49-52
Pizzey, Erin 1939- 81-84
Pizzo, Peggy 1946- 118
Pla, Josep 1897-1981 Obituary 103
Place, Irene Magdaline (Glazik) 1912- ... CANR-1
Earlier sketch in CA 1R
Place, Janey Ann 1946- 73-76
Place, Marian T(empleton) 1910- CANR-20
Earlier sketches in CA 1R, CANR-5
See also SATA 3
Placere, Morris N.
See Gupta, S(ushil) (Kumar)
Placet, Leroi 1901-1970 Obituary 29-32R
Placksin, Sally 1948- 111
Placzek, Adolf Kurt 1913- 112
Plagemann, Bentz 1913- CANR-4
Earlier sketch in CA 1R
Plagens, Peter (L.) 1941- Brief entry 107
Plager, Sheldon J. 1931- 25-28R
Plaidy, Jean
See Hibbert, Eleanor Burford
Plain, Belva 1919- CANR-14
Earlier sketch in CA 81-84
Plaine, Alfred R. 1898(?)-1981 Obituary 105
See also SATA 29
Plaister, Theodore H. 1923- Brief entry 113
Plaja, Guillermo Diaz
See Diaz Plaja, Guillermo
Plamenatz, John Petrov 1912-1975 ..... CANR-5
Earlier sketch in CA 13-14R
Planck, Carolyn H(eine) 1910- 73-76
Planck, Charles Evans 1896-1987 73-76
Obituary 121
Planck, Max (Karl Ernst Ludwig)
1858-1947 Brief entry 115
Plank, Emma N(uschi) 1905- CAP-2
Earlier sketch in CA 33-36
Plank, Robert 1907-1983 .... CANR-12
Earlier sketch in CA 25-28R
Plano, Jack Charles 1921- CANR-17
Earlier sketches in CA 7-8R, CANR-2
Plant, Marcus L. 1911- 1R
Plant, Raymond 1945- CANR-21
Earlier sketch in CA 29-32R
Plant, Robert 1948- CLC-12
Plante, David 1940- CANR-12
Earlier sketch in CA 37-40R
See also DLBY 83
See also CLC 7, 23, 38
Plante, (Joseph) Jacques (Omer)
1929-1986 Obituary 118
Brief entry 108
Plante, Julian G(erard) 41-44R
Plantinga, Alvin C. 1932- CANR-11
Earlier sketch in CA 23-24R
Plantinga, Leon B(rooks) 1935- 23-24R
Planz, Allen 1937- 53-56
Plaskow, Judith Ellen 1947- Brief entry 108
Plastaras, James C(onstantine) 1931- 21-22R
Plate, Robert 1918- 19-20R
Plate, Thomas 1944- CANR-23
Earlier sketch in CA 69-72
Plater, Alan (Frederick) 1935- 85-88
Plater, William M(armaduke) 1945- 85-88
Plath, David W(illiam) 1930- CANR-3
Earlier sketch in CA 11-12R
Plath, Sylvia 1932-1963 .... CAP-2
Earlier sketch in CA 19-20
See also DLB 5, 6
See also CDALB 1941-1968
See also CLC 1, 2, 3, 5, 9, 11, 14, 17
Platig, E(mil) Raymond 1924- 37-40R
Platonov, Andrei
See Klimentov, Andrei Platonovich
See also TCLC 14
Platov, Mariquita (Villard) 1905- 7-8R
Platt, Anthony M. 1942- 25-28R
Platt, Charles 1945- CANR-24
Earlier sketch in CA 23-24
Platt, D(esmond) C(hristopher St.) M(artin)
1934- Brief entry 109
Platt, Eugene Robert 1939- CANR-3
Earlier sketch in CA 49-52
Platt, Frederick 1946- 61-64
Platt, Gerald M. 1933- CANR-17
Earlier sketch in CA 97-100
Platt, Harlan D. 1950- 123
Platt, Harrison Gray 1902- 41-44R
Platt, Jennifer (Ann) 1937- 29-32R
Platt, John (Rader) 1918- 19-20R
Platt, Kin 1911- CANR-11
Earlier sketch in CA 19-20R
See also SATA 21
See also CLC 26
Platt, Lyman De 1943- 102
Platt, Michael 1942- 122
Platt, Rutherford 1894-1975 Obituary 61-64
Platt, Washington 1890-1965 .... 2R
Obituary 120
Platten, Thomas George 1899- CAP-1
Earlier sketch in CA 11-12
Platts, Beryl 1918- 61-64
Plauger, P(hillip) J(ames) 1944- 57-60
Plaut, Allene Talmey 1903-1986 Obituary ... 118
Plaut, Thomas F(ranz) A(lfred) 1925- 25-28R
Plaut, W(olf) Gunther 1912- CANR-17
Earlier sketches in CA 7-8R, CANR-2
Plawin, Paul 1938- 89-92
Player, Gary (Jim) 1935- 101
Player, Ian 1927- 49-52
Playfair, Guy Lyon 1935- CANR-23
Earlier sketch in CA 106
Playfellow, Robin
See Ellis, Edward S(ylvester)
Playsted, James
See Wood, James Playsted
Pleasants, Henry 1910- 107
Pleasants, Henry, Jr. 1884-1963 .... 4R
Pleasants, Samuel A(ugustus III) 1918- ...77-80
Pleck, Elizabeth Hafkin 1945- Brief entry ... 115
Pleck, Joseph H(ealy) 1946- CANR-23
Earlier sketches in CA 57-60, CANR-7
Plekker, Robert J(ohn) 1929- 69-72
Plendello, Leo
See Saint, Andrew (John)
Plender, Richard O(wen) 1945- 101
Plesset, Isabel R(osahoff) 1912- 103
Plesur, Milton 1927-1987 .... CANR-24
Earlier sketch in CA 45-48
Pletcher, Barbara A. 1946- 123
Pletcher, David M(itchell) 1920- 3R
Pleydell, Susan
See Senior, Isabel J(anet Couper Syme)
Plick et Plock
See Simenon, Georges (Jacques
Christian)
Plimmer, Charlotte 1916- 104
Plimmer, Denis 1914- 104
Plimpton, George (Ames) 1927- 21-22R
See also SATA 10
See also CLC 36
See also AITN 1
Plimpton, Ruth Talbot 1916- 13-14R
Plischke, Elmer 1914- CANR-18
Earlier sketches in CA 2R, CANR-2
Plochmann, George Kimball 1914- 5-6R
Ploeg, Johannes P(etrus) M(aria) van der
See Van Der Ploeg, Johannes P(etrus)
M(aria)
Plog, Fred (Thomas III) 1944- CANR-12
Earlier sketch in CA 25-28R
Plog, Stanley C. 1930- CANR-15
Earlier sketch in CA 41-44R
Ploghoft, Milton E(rnest) 1923- 104
Plomer, William Charles Franklin
1903-1973 .... CAP-2
Earlier sketch in CA 21-22
See also SATA 24
See also DLB 20
See also CLC 4, 8
Plomley, Roy 1914-1985 Obituary 116
Brief entry 107
Plommer, (William) Hugh ?-1983
Obituary 109
Plopper, Julie Jynelle 1916- 69-72
Ploscowe, Morris 1904-1975 .... CANR-2
Obituary 61-64
Earlier sketch in CA 45-48
Ploss, Sidney I. 1932- 15-16R
Plossl, George W. 1918- 21-22R
Plotnick, Alan R(alph) 1926- 19-20R
Plotnick, Charles K(eith) 1931- 114
Plotnicov, Leonard 1930- 23-24R
Plotnik, Arthur 1937- CANR-20
Earlier sketch in CA 69-72
Plotz, Helen Ratnoff 1913- CANR-8
Earlier sketch in CA 11-12R
See also SATA 38
Plowden, Alison 1931- CANR-15
Earlier sketch in CA 33-36R
Plowden, David 1932- 33-36R
Plowden, G(eoffrey) F(rank) C(hichele)
1929- 116
Plowden, Gene 1906-1985 ....21-22R
Obituary 117
Plowhead, Ruth Gipson 1877-1967 .... SATA-43
Plowman, E(dward) Grosvenor 1899- 13-14R
Plowman, Edward E(arl) 1931- 37-40R
Plowman, Piers
See Kavanagh, Patrick (Joseph)

Plowman, Stephanie 1922- ... CANR-5
Earlier sketch in CA 53-56
See also SATA 6
Pluckrose, Henry (Arthur) 1931- ... 33-36R
See also SATA 13
Pluff, Barbara Littlefield 1926- ... 5-6R
Plum, J.
See Wodehouse, P(elham) G(renville)
Plum, Jennifer
See Kurland, Michael (Joseph)
Plum, Lester Virgil 1906-1972 ... 1R
Obituary ... 37-40R
Plumb, Barbara Louise Brown 1934- ... CANR-15
Earlier sketch in CA 89-92
Plumb, Beatrice
See Hunzicker, Beatrice Plumb
Plumb, Charles P. 1900(?)-1982 Obituary ... 105
See also SATA 29
Plumb, Charlie
See Plumb, Joseph Charles, Jr.
Plumb, J(ohn) H(arold) 1911- ... CANR-3
Earlier sketch in CA 7-8R
Plumb, Joseph Charles, Jr. 1942- ... CANR-3
Earlier sketch in CA 49-52
Plume, Ilse ... SATA-43
Plumly, Stanley (Ross) 1939- ... 110
Brief entry ... 108
See also DLB 5
See also CLC 33
Plummer, Alfred 1896- ... 29-32R
Plummer, Ben
See Bingley, David Ernest
Plummer, Beverly J. 1918- ... 29-32R
Plummer, Catharine 1922- ... 23-24R
Plummer, Clare (Emsley) 1912- ... 25-28R
Plummer, Kenneth 1946- ... 73-76
Plummer, L. Gordon 1904- ... CAP-2
Earlier sketch in CA 33-36
Plummer, Margaret 1911- ... CAP-2
Earlier sketch in CA 25-28
See also SATA 2
Plummer, Mark A(llen) 1929- ... 37-40R
Plummer, William (Halsey Jr.) 1945- ... 102
Plummer, William J(oseph) 1927- ... 53-56
Plumpe, Friedrich Wilhelm 1888-1931
Brief entry ... 112
Plumpp, Sterling D(ominic) 1940- ... CANR-24
Earlier sketch in CA 45-48
See also DLB 41
Plumptre, Arthur Fitzwalter Wynne
1907-1977 ... 109
Obituary ... 106
Plumstead, A(rthur) William 1933- ... CANR-11
Earlier sketch in CA 25-28R
Plunket, Robert 1945- ... 115
Plunkett, James
See Kelly, James Plunkett
See also DLB 14
Plunkett, Thomas J. 1921- ... 33-36R
Plutchik, Robert 1927- ... CANR-11
Earlier sketch in CA 21-22R
Pluto, Terry 1955- ... 107
Plutonius
See Mehta, Rustam Jehangir
Plutschow, Herbert Eugen 1939- ... CANR-18
Earlier sketch in CA 102
Plutzik, Roberta Ann 1948- ... 110
Plymell, Charles 1935- ... CANR-11
Earlier sketch in CA 21-22R
See also DLB 16
Plympton, Bill
See Plympton, William M.
Plympton, William M. 1946- ... 110
Poag, James F(itzgerald) 1934-
Brief entry ... 107
Poage, Godfrey Robert 1920- ... 5-6R
Poage, Scott T(abor) 1931- ... 53-56
Poague, Leland A(llen) 1948- ... CANR-6
Earlier sketch in CA 57-60
Pobo, Kenneth 1954- ... 104
Pochmann, Henry A(ugust) 1901-1973 ... 37-40R
Pochmann, Ruth Fouts 1903- ... CAP-2
Earlier sketch in CA 25-28
Pocock, H(ugh) R(aymond) S(pilsbury)
1904- ... 25-28R
Pocock, Nick 1934- ... 53-56
Pocock, Thomas Allcot Guy 1925- ... CANR-23
Earlier sketch in CA 103
Pocock, Tom
See Pocock, Thomas Allcot Guy
Podbielski, Gisele 1918- ... 53-56
Podell, Janet 1954- ... 124
Podendorf, Illa E. 1903(?)-1983 ... 81-84
Obituary ... 110
See also SATA 18, 35
Podeschi, John B(attista) 1942- ... 110
Podhajsky, Alois 1898-1973 ... 69-72
Podhoretz, Norman 1930- ... CANR-7
Earlier sketch in CA 9-10R
Podhradsky, Gerhard 1929- ... 23-24R
Podlecki, Anthony J(oseph) 1936- ... CANR-3
Earlier sketch in CA 49-52
Podmarsh, Rollo
See Salter, Donald P. M.
Podoliak, Boris
See Kostiuk, Hryhory
Podulka, Fran 1933- ... 49-52
Poduschka, Walter 1922- ... 107
Poe, Charlsie 1909- ... CAP-2
Earlier sketch in CA 23-24
Poe, Edgar Allan 1809-1849 ... SATA-23
See also DLB 3, 59
See also CDALB 1640-1865
See also SSC 1
Poe, James 1921-1980 ... 113
Obituary ... 93-96
See also DLB 44
Poen, Monte Mac 1930- ... 107
Poern, Ingmar 1935- ... 33-36R
Poetker, Frances Jones 1912- ... 85-88
Poetzl, Pamela Major
See Major-Poetzl, Pamela
Poewe, Karla 1941- ... 124
Poganski, Donald J(ohn) 1928- ... 25-28R
Pogany, Andras H(enrik) 1919- ... 23-24R
Pogany, Hortenzia Lers ... 23-24R
Pogany, William Andrew 1882-1955 ... SATA-44
Pogany, Willy
See Pogany, William Andrew
See also SATA 30
Poggi, Emil J. 1928- ... 29-32R
Poggi, Gianfranco 1934- ... 85-88
Poggi, Jack
See Poggi, Emil J.
Poggie, John J(oseph), Jr. 1937-
Brief entry ... 107
Poggioli, Renato 1907-1963 ... CANR-2
Earlier sketch in CA 1R
Pogrebin, Letty Cottin 1939- ... CANR-15
Earlier sketch in CA 29-32R
Pogue, Forrest Carlisle 1912- ... CANR-3
Earlier sketch in CA 7-8R
Poh, Caroline (Anne) 1938- ... 61-64
Pohl, Frederick Julius 1889- ... CANR-5
Earlier sketch in CA 1R
Pohl, Frederik 1919- ... CANR-11
Earlier sketch in CA 61-64
See also CAAS 1
See also SATA 24
See also DLB 8
See also CLC 18
Pohle, Linda C(arol) 1947- ... 45-48
Pohle, Robert W(arren), Jr. 1949- ... 81-84
Pohlman, Edward 1933- ... 33-36R
Pohlmann, Lillian (Grenfell) 1902- ... 11-12R
See also SATA 11
Pohndorf, Richard Henry 1916-1977
Obituary ... 73-76
Poignant, Raymond 1917- ... 29-32R
Poincelot, Raymond P. 1944- ... 122
Poindexter, Clarence Albert 1902(?)-1984
Obituary ... 111
Poindexter, David 1929- ... 29-32R
Poindexter, Hally Beth Walker 1927-
Brief entry ... 110
Poindexter, Marian J(ean) 1929- ... 29-32R
Poinsett, Alex(ander) Ceasar 1926- ... 29-32R
Pointer, Larry 1940- ... 101
Pointer, Michael 1927- ... 57-60
Pointon, Marcia R(achel) 1943- ... 33-36R
Pointon, Robert
See Rooke, Daphne (Marie)
Poirier, Frank E(ugene) 1940- ... CANR-3
Earlier sketch in CA 49-52
Poirier, Louis 1910- Brief entry ... 122
Poirier, Normand 1928(?)-1981 Obituary ... 102
Poirier, Philip P. 1920- Brief entry ... 113
Poirier, Richard 1925- ... CANR-3
Earlier sketch in CA 1R
Pois, Joseph 1905- ... CAP-1
Earlier sketch in CA 15-16
Poitier, Sidney 1927- ... 117
See also CLC 26
Pok Chong-Hui
See Park Chung Hee
Pokrovsky, Boris Aleksandrovich 1912-
Brief entry ... 109
POLA
See Watson, Pauline
Polach, Jaroslav G(eorge) 1914- ... 9-10R
Polack, Albert Isaac 1892- ... CAP-1
Earlier sketch in CA 9-10
Polak, Ada Buch 1914- Brief entry ... 111
Polak, Jacques Jacobus 1914- ... 104
Polakoff, Keith Ian 1941- ... 49-52
Polakoff, Murray Emanuel 1922-
Brief entry ... 114
Polakow, Valerie (Suransky) 1950- ... 111
Poland, Dorothy (Elizabeth Hayward)
1937- ... CANR-20
Earlier sketch in CA 103
Poland, Larry 1939- ... 101
Polanski, Roman 1933- ... 77-80
See also CLC 16
Polansky, Norman A. 1918- ... 85-88
Polanyi, Michael 1891-1976 ... 81-84
Obituary ... 65-68
Polatnick, Florence T. 1923- ... 29-32R
See also SATA 5
Polcher, Egon
See Anschel, Eugene
Polder, Markus
See Kruess, James
Poldervaart, Arie 1909-1969 ... 3R
Obituary ... 103
Pole, J(ack) R(ichon) 1922- ... CANR-8
Earlier sketch in CA 19-20R
Polebaum, Elliot E(dward) 1950- ... 107
Poleman, Thomas T(heobald) 1928- ... 15-16R
Polenberg, Richard 1937- ... 21-22R
Polese, Marcia Ann 1949- ... 65-68
Polette, Nancy (Jane) 1930- ... CANR-21
Earlier sketches in CA 57-60, CANR-6
See also SATA 42
Polevoi, Boris
See Kampov, Boris Nikolayevich
Polhamus, Jean Burt 1928- ... 103
See also SATA 21
Poli, Bernard 1929- ... 21-22R
Poliakoff, Stephen 1952- ... 106
See also DLB 13
See also CLC 38
Poliakov, Leon 1910- ... 104
Police
See Copeland, Stewart (Armstrong)
and Summers, Andrew James
and Sumner, Gordon Matthew
See also CLC 26
Polier, Justine Wise 1903-1987 ... 104
Obituary ... 123
Polin, Raymond 1918- ... 37-40R
Poling, Daniel Alfred 1884-1968 Obituary ... 93-96
Poling, David 1928- ... 85-88
Polinger, Elliot Hirsch 1898-1970
Obituary ... 104
Polis, A(lbert) Richard 1937- ... CANR-6
Earlier sketch in CA 57-60
Polisensky, Josef V. 1915- Brief entry ... 107
Polish, David 1910- ... 13-14R
Polishook, Irwin H. 1935- ... 21-22R
Polite, Carlene Hatcher 1932- ... 23-24R
See also DLB 33
Politella, Dario 1921- ... 13-14R
Politella, Joseph 1910- ... CAP-2
Earlier sketch in CA 21-22
Politi, Leo 1908- ... CANR-13
Earlier sketch in CA 19-20R
See also SATA 1, 47
Politicus
See Kilski, Wladyslaw W(szebor)
Politzer, Heinrich 1910-1978 ... CANR-3
Obituary ... 81-84
Earlier sketch in CA 5-6R
Politzer, Heinz
See Politzer, Heinrich
Politzer, Robert L. 1921- ... 5-6R
Polivy, Janet 1951- ... 115
Poljanski, Hristo Andonov
See Andonov-Poljanski, Hristo
Polk, Cara Saylor 1945- ... 116
Polk, Dora (Beale) 1923- ... 49-52
Polk, Edwin Weiss 1916- ... 37-40R
Polk, James 1939- ... CANR-23
Earlier sketch in CA 105
Polk, James R. 1937- ... 69-72
Polk, Judd (Knox) 1913(?)-1975
Obituary ... 57-60
Polk, Kenneth 1935- ... CANR-1
Earlier sketch in CA 2R
Polk, Mary 1898- ... CAP-1
Earlier sketch in CA 11-12
Polk, Noel E(arl) 1943- ... 123
Polk, Ralph Lane, Jr. 1940-1985 Obituary ... 118
Polk, Ralph Weiss 1890-1978 ... 37-40R
Obituary ... 77-80
Polk, Stella Gipson 1901- ... CANR-16
Earlier sketch in CA 93-96
Polk, William R(oe) 1929- ... 25-28R
Polking, Kirk 1925- ... CANR-12
Earlier sketch in CA 29-32R
See also SATA 5
Polkinghorn, Anne T(oogood) 1937- ... 109
Poll, Richard Douglas 1918- ... 101
Pollack, Cecelia 1909- ... 29-32R
Pollack, Ervin H(arold) 1913-1972 ... CAP-1
Earlier sketch in CA 15-16
Pollack, (Wilburt) Erwin 1935- ... 49-52
Pollack, Harvey 1913- ... 7-8R
Pollack, Herman 1907- ... 69-72
Pollack, Jack H(arrison) 1915(?)-1984
Obituary ... 113
Pollack, Merrill S. 1924-1988 ... 7-8R
Obituary ... 124
Pollack, Norman 1933- ... 13-14R
Pollack, Peter 1911-1978 ... 81-84
Obituary ... 77-80
Pollack, Reginald 1924- ... 37-40R
Pollack, Robert H(arvey) 1927- ... 49-52
Pollack, Sandra (Barbara) 1937- ... 119
Pollack, Seymour V(ictor) 1933- ... 25-28R
Pollak, Felix 1909- ... CANR-10
Earlier sketch in CA 25-28R
Pollak, Kurt 1919- ... 29-32R
Pollak, Louis Heilprin 1922- ... 19-20R
Pollak, Michael 1918- ... 122
Pollak, Richard 1934- Brief entry ... 111
Polland, Barbara K(ay) 1939- ... 73-76
See also SATA 44
Polland, Madeleine A(ngela Cahill)
1918- ... CANR-3
Earlier sketch in CA 5-6R
See also SATA 6
Pollard, David 1942- ... 123
Pollard, Edward A. 1832-1872 ... DLB-30
Pollard, (Henry) Graham 1903-1976
Obituary ... 69-72
Pollard, Jack 1926- ... 29-32R
Pollard, James E(dward) 1894-1979 ... CAP-1
Obituary ... 89-92
Earlier sketch in CA 15-16
Pollard, John (Richard Thornhill) 1914- ... 7-8R
Pollard, Sidney 1925- ... CANR-13
Earlier sketch in CA 19-20R
Pollard, T(homas) E(van) 1921- ... 29-32R
Pollard, William G(rosvenor) 1911- ... CANR-6
Earlier sketch in CA 13-14R
Polley, Robert L. 1933- ... 19-20R
Pollinger, Kenneth Joseph 1933- ... 57-60
Pollini, Francis 1930- ... CANR-1
Earlier sketch in CA 2R
Pollio, Howard R. 1937- ... 37-40R
Pollitt, Jerome J(ordan) 1934- ... 21-22R
Pollitt, Katha 1949- ... 122
Brief entry ... 120
See also CLC 28
Pollitt, Ronald 1939- ... 122
Pollock, Bruce 1945- ... CANR-23
Earlier sketches in CA 57-60, CANR-7
See also SATA 46
Pollock, David H(arold) 1922- ... 49-52
Pollock, George 1938- ... 61-64
Pollock, Harry 1920- ... 89-92
Pollock, James K(err) 1898-1968 ... CAP-2
Obituary ... 29-32R
Earlier sketch in CA 21-22
Pollock, John (Charles) 1923- ... CANR-18
Earlier sketches in CA 5-6R, CANR-2
Pollock, John L(eslie) 1940- ... 37-40R
Pollock, Linda A(nne) 1955- ... 116
Pollock, Mary
See Blyton, Enid (Mary)
Pollock, Norman H(all), Jr. 1909- ... CAP-2
Earlier sketch in CA 33-36
Pollock, Penny 1935- ... 101
See also SATA 42, 44
Pollock, Robert 1930- ... 45-48
Pollock, Seton 1910- ... 7-8R
Pollock, Sharon 1936- ... DLB-60
Pollock, Ted 1929- ... 85-88
Pollock, Thomas Clark 1902- ... CAP-2
Earlier sketch in CA 21-22
Pollock, William 1899-1982 Obituary ... 110
Pollowitz, Melinda Kilborn 1944- ... CANR-13
Earlier sketch in CA 77-80
See also SATA 26
Polmar, Norman 1938- ... 49-52
Polnaszek, Frank P(aul) 1947- ... 107
Polner, Murray 1928- ... CANR-23
Earlier sketches in CA 13-14R, CANR-5
Poloma, Margaret Mary 1943- ... 111
Polome, Edgar (Ghislain) C(harles)
1920- ... CANR-13
Earlier sketch in CA 29-32R
Polon, Linda Beth 1943- ... CANR-20
Earlier sketch in CA 103
Polonsky, Abraham (Lincoln) 1910- ... 104
See also DLB 26
Polonsky, Antony Barry 1940- ... 73-76
Polonsky, Arthur 1925- ... SATA-34
Polony, Raymond
See Machan, Tibor R(ichard)
Polos, Nicholas C(hristopher) 1917- ... 19-20R
Pols, Edward 1919- ... 11-12R
Polsby, Nelson W(oolf) 1934- ... CANR-23
Earlier sketches in CA 53-56, CANR-5
Polselli, Joseph 1950- ... 122
Polseno, Jo ... 81-84
See also SATA 17
Polsky, Abe 1935- ... 109
Polsky, Howard W. 1928- ... 25-28R
Polsky, Ned 1928- ... 25-28R
Poltoratzky, N(ikolai) P(etrovich) 1921- ... 73-76
Poltroon, Milford
See Bascom, David
Polunin, Nicholas (Vladimir) 1909- ... 65-68
Polunin, Oleg 1914-1985 ... 85-88
Obituary ... 117
Polya, George 1887-1985 Obituary ... 117
Polya, Gyorgy
See Polya, George
Pomada, Elizabeth 1940- ... CANR-8
Earlier sketch in CA 61-64
Pomerance, Bernard 1940- ... 101
See also CLC 13
Pomerantz, Charlotte 1930- ... CANR-16
Earlier sketch in CA 85-88
See also SATA 20
Pomerantz, Edward 1934- ... 65-68
Pomerantz, Joel 1930- ... 29-32R
Pomerantz, Sidney I(rving) 1909-1975
Obituary ... 61-64
Pomeranz, Virginia E. 1925(?)-1986
Obituary ... 120
Pomerleau, Cynthia S(todola) 1943- ... 73-76
Pomerleau, Ovide F(elix) 1940- ... CANR-13
Earlier sketch in CA 73-76
Pomeroy, Charles A. 1930- ... 25-28R
Pomeroy, Earl 1915- ... 19-20R
Pomeroy, Elizabeth W(right) 1938- ... 113
Pomeroy, Florence Mary
See Powley, Florence Mary Pomeroy
Pomeroy, Hub(bard)
See Claassen, Harold
Pomeroy, John H(oward) 1918-1985
Obituary ... 115
Pomeroy, Kenneth B(rownridge)
1907-1975 Obituary ... 61-64
Pomeroy, Pete
See Roth, Arthur J(oseph)
Pomeroy, Sarah B(erman) 1938- ... 65-68
Pomeroy, Wardell B. 1913- ... CANR-1
Earlier sketch in CA 1R
Pomeroy, William J(oseph) 1916- ... 85-88
Pomfret, Baron
See Dame, Lawrence
Pomfret, John Edwin 1898-1981 ... CANR-3
Obituary ... 105
Earlier sketch in CA 3R
Pomfret, Richard 1948- ... 112
Pommer, Henry F(rancis) 1918- ... CANR-20
Earlier sketch in CA 1R
Pommery, Jean 1932- ... 101
Pomorska, Krystyna 1928- ... 41-44R
Pompa, Leon 1933- ... CANR-7
Earlier sketch in CA 57-60
Pomper, Gerald M(arvin) 1935- ... CANR-19
Earlier sketches in CA 11-12R, CANR-5
Pomper, Philip 1936- ... 77-80
Pompian, Richard O(wen) 1935- ... CANR-11
Earlier sketch in CA 29-32R
Pompidou, Georges (Jean Raymond)
1911-1974 Obituary ... 49-52
Pomrenke, Norman E. 1930- ... 23-24R
Pomroy, Martha 1943- ... 101
Ponce de Leon, Jose Luis S. 1931- ... 49-52

Pond, Alonzo W(illiam) 1894- ... CANR-1
Earlier sketch in CA 4R
See also SATA 5
Pond, Grace (Isabelle) 1910- ... CANR-5
Earlier sketch in CA 13-14R
Pond, L. W.
See Chute, Robert M.
Ponder, Catherine 1927- ... CANR-17
Earlier sketches in CA 4R, CANR-1
Ponder, James A(lton) 1933- ... 69-72
Ponder, Patricia
See Maxwell, Patricia
Pondrom, Cyrena N(orman) 1938-
Brief entry ... 111
Ponge, Francis (Jean Gaston Alfred)
1899- ... 85-88
See also CLC 6, 18
Poniatowska, Elena 1933- ... 101
Ponicsan, Darryl 1938- ... CANR-21
Earlier sketch in CA 29-32R
Ponnamperuma, Cyril A. 1923- ... 101
Pons, Maurice 1927- ... CANR-5
Earlier sketch in CA 53-56
Ponsonby, D(oris) A(lmon) ... CANR-2
Earlier sketch in CA 7-8R
Ponsonby, Frederick Edward Neuflize
1913- ... 13-14R
Ponsot, Marie Birmingham ... 11-12R
Pont, Clarice Holt 1907- ... 5-6R
Ponte, Lowell (Alton) 1946- ... 57-60
Ponte, Pierre Viansson
See Viansson-Ponte, Pierre
Pontes, Paulo 1941(?)-1976 Obituary ... 69-72
Pontiero, Giovanni 1932- ... 29-32R
Pontiflet, Ted 1932- ... 105
See also SATA 32
Ponting, Kenneth 1913-1983 Obituary ... 109
Pontney, Jack A(rthur) 1931- ... 23-24R
Ponty, Maurice Merleau
See Merleau-Ponty, Maurice
Pool, David de Sola 1885-1970
Obituary ... 29-32R
Pool, Elizabeth 1914- ... 114
Pool, Eugene (Hillhouse) 1943- ... 85-88
Pool, Ithiel de Sola 1917-1984 ... CANR-14
Obituary ... 112
Earlier sketch in CA 19-20R
Pool, Phoebe Dorothy 1913- ... 7-8R
Pool, Tamar de Sola 1891(?)-1981
Obituary ... 104
Poole, Ernest 1880-1950 Brief entry ... 109
See also DLB 9
Poole, Frederick King 1934- ... 25-28R
Poole, Gary Thomas 1931- ... 107
Poole, Gray Johnson 1906- ... CANR-6
Earlier sketch in CA 7-8R
See also SATA 1
Poole, Herbert (Leslie) ... 103
Poole, Herbert Edmund 1912-1984
Obituary ... 115
Poole, Josephine
See Helyar, Jane Penelope Josephine
See also SATA 5
See also SAAS 2
See also CLC 17
Poole, Lynn 1910-1969 ... 7-8R
See also SATA 1
Poole, Peggy 1925- ... CANR-24
Earlier sketch in CA 107
See also SATA 39
Poole, Peter A(ndrews) ... 113
Poole, Robert W(illiam), Jr. 1944- ... 112
Poole, Roger 1939- ... 102
Poole, Seth
See Riemer, George
Poole, Susan 1926- ... 114
Poole, Victoria (Simes) 1927- ... 102
Pooler, Victor H(erbert), Jr. 1924- ... 15-16R
Pooley, Beverley J(ohn) 1934- ... 45-48
Pooley, Robert C(ecil) 1898-1978 ... CANR-7
Earlier sketch in CA 5-6R
Pooley, Roger 1947- ... 115
Poolla, Tirupati Raju
See Raju, Poolla Tirupati
Poor, Harold Lloyd 1935- ... 45-48
Poor, Henry Varnum 1914(?)-1972
Obituary ... 37-40R
Poore, Benjamin Perley 1820-1887 ... DLB-23
Poore, Charles (Graydon) 1902-1971
Obituary ... 29-32R
Poorman, Paul Arthur 1930- ... 106
Poortvliet, Marien
See Poortvliet, Rien
Poortvliet, Rien 1933(?)- ... SATA-37
Poots-Booby, Edna
See Larsen, Carl
Poovey, W(illiam) A(rthur) 1913- ... CANR-10
Earlier sketch in CA 23-24R
Popa, Vasko 1922- Brief entry ... 112
See also CLC 19
Pope, Arthur Upham 1881-1969
Obituary ... 25-28R
Pope, Carl 1945- ... 113
Pope, Clifford Hillhouse 1899-1974 ... 3R
Obituary ... 103
Pope, Daniel 1946- ... 111
Pope, Dudley (Bernard Egerton) 1925- ... CANR-2
Earlier sketch in CA 7-8R
Pope, Edwin 1928- ... 73-76
Pope, Elizabeth Marie 1917- ... 49-52
See also SATA 36, 38
Pope, Harrison (Graham), Jr. 1947- ... 41-44R
Pope, James S., Sr. 1900(?)-1985
Obituary ... 118
Pope, John Alexander 1906-1982
Obituary ... 107
Pope, Joya 1943- ... 124
Pope, Katherine Victoria 1939- ... 111
Pope, Maurice (Wildon Montague) 1926- ... 69-72
Pope, Michael James 1940- ... 101
Pope, Phyllis Ackerman 1894(?)-1977
Obituary ... 69-72
Pope, Ray 1924- ... 29-32R
Pope, Richard Martin 1916- ... 19-20R
Pope, Robert G(ardner) 1936- ... 29-32R
Pope, Robert H. 1925- ... 33-36R
Pope, Thomas Harrington 1913- ... 73-76
Pope, Whitney 1935- ... 69-72
Pope-Hennessy, James 1916-1974 ... 97-100
Obituary ... 45-48
Pope-Hennessy, John W(yndham)
1913- ... CANR-1
Earlier sketch in CA 1R
Popenoe, David 1932- ... CANR-12
Earlier sketch in CA 29-32R
Popenoe, Paul 1888- ... 4R
Popescu, Christine 1930- ... CANR-20
Earlier sketches in CA 13-14R, CANR-7
Popescu, D. R.
See Popescu, Dumitru Radu
Popescu, Dumitru Radu 1935- Brief entry ... 122
Popescu, Julian (John Hunter) 1928- ... CANR-20
Earlier sketches in CA 2R, CANR-1
Popham, Arthur Ewart 1889-1970
Obituary ... 111
Popham, Estelle I. 1906- ... CANR-5
Earlier sketch in CA 1R
Popham, Hugh 1920- ... CANR-6
Earlier sketch in CA 7-8R
Popham, Margaret Evelyn 1895(?)-1982
Obituary ... 106
Popham, Melinda 1944- ... 49-52
Popham, Peter (Nicholas Home) 1952- ... 121
Popiel, Elda S(taver) 1915- ... 57-60
Popkin, Debra 1944- ... 118
Popkin, Jeremy D(avid) 1948- ... 102
Popkin, John William 1909- ... CAP-1
Earlier sketch in CA 13-14
Popkin, Richard H(enry) 1923- ... 77-80
Popkin, Roy 1921- ... 25-28R
Popkin, Zelda F. 1898-1983 ... 25-28R
Obituary ... 109
Popov, Dusko 1912(?)-1981 Obituary ... 105
Popov, Haralan Ivanov 1907- ... 21-22R
Popovic, Nenad D(ushan) 1909- ... CAP-2
Earlier sketch in CA 29-32
Popovsky, Mark 1922- ... CANR-19
Earlier sketch in CA 102
Popowski, Bert (John) 1904- ... CANR-17
Earlier sketch in CA 4R
Poppe, Fred C(hristoph) 1923- ... 114
Poppe, Nicholas N. 1897- ... 73-76
Popper, Frank J. 1944- ... CANR-12
Earlier sketch in CA 29-32R
Popper, Karl R(aimund) 1902- ... CANR-20
Earlier sketches in CA 7-8R, CANR-3
Popperwell, Ronald ?-1983 Obituary ... 111
Poppino, Rollie E(dward) 1922- ... 15-16R
Popple, James 1927- ... 107
Poppleton, Marjorie 1895- ... CAP-1
Earlier sketch in CA 13-14
Popplewell, Jack 1911- ... 11-12R
Porada, Edith 1912- ... 103
Porath, Jonathan David 1944- ... 118
Porcari, Constance Kwolek 1933- ... 33-36R
Porch, Douglas 1944- ... 107
Porche, Simone (Benda) 1877(?)-1985
Obituary ... 118
Porcher, Mary F. Wickham
See Bond, Mary Fanning Wickham
Porcino, Jane 1923- ... 116
Pore, Renate (Elfriede) 1943- ... 113
Porell, Bruce 1947- ... 102
Porges, Paul Peter 1927- ... 124
Poriss, Martin 1948- ... 81-84
Porlock, Martin
See MacDonald, Philip
Porosky, P. H. ... 45-48
Porqueras-Mayo, Alberto 1930- ... CANR-24
Earlier sketch in CA 45-48
Porsche, Ferdinand 1909- ... 89-92
Porsche, Ferry
See Porsche, Ferdinand
Port, M(ichael) H. 1930- ... 69-72
Port, Wymar
See Judy, Will(iam Lewis)
Portal, Colette 1936- ... 53-56
See also SATA 6
Portal, Ellis
See Powe, Bruce
Portal, Francis Spencer 1903-1984
Obituary ... 114
Porte, Barbara Ann ... SATA-45
Porte, Joel (Miles) 1933- ... CANR-24
Earlier sketches in CA 19-20R, CANR-8
Porten, Bezalel 1931- ... CANR-11
Earlier sketch in CA 25-28R
Porteous, (Leslie) Crichton 1901- ... 7-8R
Porter, Alan
See Clark, Ruth C(ampbell)
Porter, Alan L(eslie) 1945- ... 115
Porter, Albert Wright 1923- ... 107
Porter, Alvin
See Rowland, D(onald) S(ydney)
Porter, Andrew 1928- ... CANR-23
Earlier sketches in CA 53-56, CANR-5
Porter, Arthur T(homas) 1924- ... 7-8R
Porter, Bern(ard Harden) 1911- ... CANR-24
Earlier sketches in CA 21-22R, CANR-9
Porter, Bernard (John) 1941- ... CANR-24
Earlier sketch in CA 107
Porter, Brian (Ernest) 1928- ... 25-28R
Porter, Bruce 1938- ... 124
Porter, Burton F(rederick) 1936- ... 106
Porter, C(edric) L(ambert) 1905- ... CAP-2
Earlier sketch in CA 23-24
Porter, Charles A(llan) 1932- ... 21-22R
Porter, Cole 1893-1964 Obituary ... 93-96
Porter, Darwin (Fred) 1937- ... CANR-13
Earlier sketch in CA 69-72
Porter, David L(indsey) 1941- ... CANR-24
Earlier sketch in CA 107
Porter, David T. 1928- ... 19-20R
Porter, Donald 1939- ... CANR-19
Earlier sketch in CA 103
Porter, Edward A. 1936- ... 23-24R
Porter, Eleanor H(odgman) 1868-1920
Brief entry ... 108
See also DLB 9
Porter, Elias H(ull) 1914- ... 11-12R
Porter, Eliot (Furness) 1901- ... 7-8R
Porter, Ernest Graham 1889- ... 3R
Porter, Ethel K. 1901- ... CAP-2
Earlier sketch in CA 21-22
Porter, Fairfield 1907-1975 Obituary ... 61-64
Porter, Frank W(illiam) III 1947- ... 97-100
Porter, Gene L. 1935- ... 25-28R
Porter, Gene(va Grace) Stratton
1863(?)-1924 Brief entry ... 112
See also TCLC 21
Porter, George 1920- ... 107
Porter, Glenn 1944- ... 73-76
Porter, H(arry) Boone 1923- ... CANR-8
Earlier sketch in CA 7-8R
Porter, H(arry) C(ulverwell) 1927- ... 33-36R
Porter, Hal 1911-1984 ... CANR-3
Obituary ... 114
Earlier sketch in CA 9-10R
Porter, Henry ... DLB-62
Porter, J(ene) M(iles) 1937- ... CANR-21
Earlier sketch in CA 103
Porter, J(oshua) R(oy) 1921- ... CANR-5
Earlier sketch in CA 53-56
Porter, Jack Nusan 1944- ... CANR-20
Earlier sketch in CA 41-44R
Porter, James A(rmer), Jr. 1922- ... 121
Porter, Joe Ashby 1942- ... CANR-12
Earlier sketch in CA 73-76
Porter, John 1919- ... 23-24R
Porter, Jonathan 1938- ... 77-80
Porter, Joseph C(harles) 1946- ... 116
Porter, Joyce 1924- ... CANR-8
Earlier sketch in CA 19-20R
Porter, Judith D(eborah) R(evitch) 1940- ... 81-84
Porter, Katherine Anne 1890-1980 ... CANR-1
Obituary ... 101
Earlier sketch in CA 2R
See also SATA 23, 39
See also DLB 4, 9
See also DLBY 80
See also CLC 1, 3, 7, 10, 13, 15, 27
See also AITN 2
Porter, Kathryn
See Swinford, Betty (June Wells)
Porter, Kenneth Wiggins 1905- ... CANR-2
Earlier sketch in CA 7-8R
Porter, Laurence M(inot) 1936- ... CANR-23
Earlier sketch in CA 107
Porter, Lyman W(illiam) 1930- ... 21-22R
Porter, Margaret Eudine 1905-1975 ... CANR-8
Earlier sketch in CA 57-60
Porter, Mark
See Leckie, Robert (Hugh)
and Cox, James Anthony
Porter, McKenzie 1911- ... 69-72
Porter, Michael E. 1947- ... CANR-22
Earlier sketch in CA 105
Porter, Michael Leroy 1947- ... 118
Porter, Monica 1952- ... 107
Porter, Peter (Neville Frederick) 1929- ... 85-88
See also DLB 40
See also CLC 5, 13, 33
Porter, Philip W(iley) 1900-1985 ... 69-72
Obituary ... 116
Porter, R(obert) Russell 1908-1986
Obituary ... 120
Porter, Raymond J(ames) 1935- ... 85-88
Porter, Richard C(orbin) 1931- ... 11-12R
Porter, Robert 1946- ... 122
Porter, Sheena 1935- ... 81-84
See also SATA 24
Porter, Sue
See Limb, Sue
Porter, Sylvia F(ield) 1913- ... 81-84
Porter, Theodore M(ark) 1953- ... 123
Porter, Thomas E. 1928- ... 29-32R
Porter, W(alter) Thomas, Jr. 1934- ... 29-32R
Porter, Willard H(all) 1920- ... 57-60
Porter, William E. 1918- ... CANR-13
Earlier sketch in CA 69-72
Porter, William Sydney 1862-1910
Brief entry ... 104
See also YABC 2
See also DLB 12
Porter, William Trotter 1809-1858 ... DLB-3, 43
Porterfield, Bruce 1925- ... 23-24R
Porterfield, Nolan 1936- ... 33-36R
Portes, Alejandro 1944- ... CANR-16
Earlier sketch in CA 93-96
Porteus, Stanley D(avid) 1883- ... CANR-17
Earlier sketch in CA 4R
Portis, Charles (McColl) 1933- ... CANR-1
Earlier sketch in CA 45-48
See also DLB 6
Portisch, Hugo 1927- ... 21-22R
Portman, David N(athan) 1937- ... 45-48
Portnoy, Howard N. 1946- ... 81-84
Portoghesi, Paolo 1931- ... 108
Portteus, Eleanora Marie Manthei
?-1983 ... SATA-36
Portugal, Franklin H. 1940- Brief entry ... 116
Portuges, Paul 1945- ... 77-80
Portway, Christopher (John) 1923- ... 57-60
Porush, David H(illel) 1952- ... CANR-17
Earlier sketch in CA 93-96
Porzelt, Paul 1902- ... 108
Posell, Elsa Z. ... CANR-20
Earlier sketches in CA 2R, CANR-4
See also SATA 3
Posey, Carl A(lfred, Jr.) 1933- ... 111
Posey, Sam 1944- ... 93-96
Posey, Walter B(rownlow) 1900- ... CAP-1
Earlier sketch in CA 15-16
Posin, Daniel Q. 1909- ... CAP-1
Earlier sketch in CA 13-14
Posin, Jack A. 1900- ... 15-16R
Posner, Alice
See Fins, Alice
Posner, Barry Z(ane) 1949- ... 111
Posner, David Louis 1938-1985 ... 106
Obituary ... 117
Posner, Donald 1931- Brief entry ... 115
Posner, Ernst (Maximilian) 1892-1980 ... 41-44R
Obituary ... 97-100
Posner, Mitchell Jay 1949- ... 110
Posner, Richard 1944- ... CANR-20
Earlier sketches in CA 53-56, CANR-5
Pospelov, Pyotr Nikolayevich 1898-1979
Obituary ... 85-88
Pospesel, Howard Andrew 1937- ... 73-76
Pospielovsky, Dimitry V. 1935- ... 29-32R
Pospisil, J(aroslav) Leopold 1923- ... 13-14R
Possony, Stefan T(homas) 1913-
Brief entry ... 117
Post, Austin 1922- ... 85-88
Post, C(harles) Gordon 1903- ... CAP-1
Earlier sketch in CA 11-12
Post, Elizabeth L(indley) 1920- ... 49-52
Post, Emily Price 1873-1960 ... 103
Obituary ... 89-92
Post, Felix 1913- ... 21-22R
Post, Gaines 1902- ... CAP-1
Earlier sketch in CA 13-14
Post, Gaines, Jr. 1937- ... CANR-12
Earlier sketch in CA 73-76
Post, Henry 1948- ... 61-64
Post, Homer A(very) 1888- ... CAP-2
Earlier sketch in CA 25-28
Post, J(eremiah) B(enjamin) 1937- ... 97-100
Post, Jonathan F(rench) S(cott) 1947- ... 115
Post, Joyce A(rnold) 1939- ... CANR-8
Earlier sketch in CA 61-64
Post, Marie J. 1919- ... 111
Post, Melville Davisson 1869-1930
Brief entry ... 110
Post, Steve(n A.) 1944- ... 103
Postal, Bernard 1905-1981 ... CANR-2
Obituary ... 103
Earlier sketch in CA 5-6R
Postan, Michael Moissey 1899-1981
Obituary ... 105
Posten, Margaret L(ois) 1915- ... 29-32R
See also SATA 10
Poster, Carol 1956- ... 118
Poster, Cyril D(ennis) 1924- ... CANR-7
Earlier sketch in CA 15-16R
Poster, John B. 1939- ... 29-32R
Poster, Mark 1941- ... 33-36R
Posteuca, Vasile 1912-1972 Obituary ... 37-40R
Postgate, Raymond (William)
1896-1971 ... CANR-3
Obituary ... 89-92
Earlier sketch in CA 5-6R
Posthumus, Cyril 1918- ... 104
Postlethwait, S(amuel) N(oel) 1918- ... CANR-8
Earlier sketch in CA 19-20R
Postma, Lidia 1952- ... 101
Postma, Magdalena Jacomina 1908- ... 65-68
Postma, Minnie
See Postma, Magdalena Jacomina
Postman, Neil ... 102
Poston, Richard W(averly) 1914- ... 65-68
Poston, Ted
See Poston, Theodore Roosevelt
Augustus Major
See also DLB 51
Poston, Theodore Roosevelt Augustus
Major 1906-1974 Obituary ... 104
Posvar, Wesley W(entz) 1925- ... 19-20R
Posy, Arnold 1894- ... 9-10R
Potash, Betty 1933- ... 122
Potash, Robert A(aron) 1921- ... CANR-19
Earlier sketch in CA 102
Poteet, G(eorge) Howard 1935- ... CANR-13
Earlier sketch in CA 33-36R
Pothan, Kap 1929- ... 29-32R
Potholm, Christian Peter II 1940- ... 29-32R
Potichnyj, Peter J(oseph) 1930- ... 41-44R
Potiphar
See Hern, (George) Anthony
Potok, Chaim 1929- ... CANR-19
Earlier sketch in CA 19-20R
See also SATA 33
See also DLB 28
See also CLC 2, 7, 14, 26
See also AITN 1, 2
Potoker, Edward M(artin) 1931- ... 33-36R
Pottebaum, Gerald A. 1934- ... CANR-5
Earlier sketch in CA 11-12R
Potter, A(lfred) Neal 1915- ... 15-16R
Potter, Beatrice
See Webb, (Martha) Beatrice (Potter)
Potter, (Helen) Beatrix 1866-1943
Brief entry ... 108
See also YABC 1
See also CLR 1
Potter, Beverly A(nn) 1944- ... 119
Potter, Carole A. 1940- ... 123

Potter, Charles E(dward) 1916- 61-64
Potter, Clare J. 1946- 122
Potter, Dan (Scott) 1932- 33-36R
Potter, David 1915- 29-32R
Potter, David Morris 1910-1971 108
See also DLB 17
Potter, Dennis (Christopher George) 1935- .. 107
Potter, E. B. 1908- 37-40R
Potter, Eloise Fretz 1931- CANR-21
Earlier sketch in CA 105
Potter, Faith
See Toperoff, Sam
Potter, G(eorge) W(illiam, Jr.) 1930- 3R
Potter, Gail M(ac Leod) 1914- 25-28R
Potter, George Richard 1900- 7-8R
Potter, J(im) 1922- 23-24R
Potter, Jack M(ichael) 1936- 41-44R
Potter, James Gerrard 1944- 97-100
Potter, James H(arry) 1912-1978
Obituary 77-80
Potter, James L(ane) 1922- 107
Potter, Jeremy 1922- 53-56
Potter, John Mason 1907- CAP-1
Earlier sketch in CA 11-12
Potter, Joy Hambuechen 1935- 123
Potter, Karl Harrington 1927- 5-6R
Potter, Kathleen 1929(?)-1987 Obituary 122
Potter, Kathleen Jill 1932- 104
Potter, Lois 1941- CANR-15
Earlier sketch in CA 41-44R
Potter, Loren D(avid) 1918- 121
Potter, M(aurice) David 1900- CAP-2
Earlier sketch in CA 23-24
Potter, Margaret (Newman) 1926- CANR-21
Earlier sketches in CA 13-14R, CANR-6
See also SATA 21
Potter, Marian 1915- CANR-1
Earlier sketch in CA 49-52
See also SATA 9
Potter, Miriam Clark 1886-1965 ....5-6R
See also SATA 3
Potter, Robert Alonzo 1934- CANR-1
Earlier sketch in CA 45-48
Potter, Robert D(ucharme) 1905-1978
Obituary 77-80
Potter, Simeon 1898-1976 .... CANR-4
Earlier sketch in CA 7-8R
Potter, Stephen 1900-1969 101
Obituary 25-28R
Potter, Sulamith Heins 1944- 81-84
Potter, Van Rensselaer 1911- 37-40R
Potter, Vincent G. 1928- 25-28R
Potter, William Hotchkiss 1914- 2R
Potterton, Gerald 1931- 49-52
Potterton, Homan 1946- 108
Pottker, Janice Marie 1948- 118
Pottle, Frederick A(lbert) 1897-1987 .... CANR-3
Obituary 122
Earlier sketch in CA 7-8R
Potts, Albert M(intz) 1914- 116
Potts, Charles 1943- 105
Potts, E(li) Daniel 1930- 25-28R
Potts, Eve 1929- 103
Potts, George Chapman 1898- CAP-1
Earlier sketch in CA 11-12
Potts, Jean 1910- CANR-2
Earlier sketch in CA 5-6R
Potts, Ralph Bushnell 1901- 57-60
Potts, Richard 1938- 103
Potts, Willard (Charles) 1929- 123
Potvin, Denis (Charles) 1953- Brief entry ... 113
Potvin, Georges C. 1928- 45-48
Potvin, Raymond H(erve) 1924- 21-22R
Pou, Genevieve Long 1919- Brief entry 114
Poucher, William Arthur 1891- CAP-1
Earlier sketch in CA 11-12
Pough, Frederick Harvey 1906- 81-84
Pouillon, Fernand 1912- 29-32R
Poulakidas, Andreas K. 1934- 45-48
Poulet, Georges 1902- 13-14R
Poulin, A(lfred A.), Jr. 1938- CANR-12
Earlier sketch in CA 23-24R
Poulin, Jacques 1937- DLB-60
Poullada, Leon B(aqueiro) 1913-1987
Obituary 123
Poulos, Constantine 1916(?)-1986
Obituary 119
Poulter, S(cott) L(arry) 1943- 49-52
Poulton, Edith Eleanor (Diana) Chloe
1903- 85-88
Poulton, Helen Jean 1920-1971 .... CAP-2
Earlier sketch in CA 33-36
Poulton, Richard (Christopher) 1938- 107
Pound, Arthur 1884-1966 Obituary 89-92
Pound, Ezra (Loomis) 1885-1972 ....7-8R
Obituary 37-40R
See also DLB 4, 45, 63
See also CLC 1, 2, 3, 4, 5, 7, 10, 13,
18, 34
Pound, Merritt B(loodworth) 1898-1970 .. CAP-2
Earlier sketch in CA 19-20
Pound, Omar S(hakespear) 1926- CANR-16
Earlier sketches in CA 49-52, CANR-1
Pound, Roscoe 1870-1964 Obituary 111
Pounds, Norman John Greville 1912- ... CANR-4
Earlier sketch in CA 3R
Pounds, Ralph Linnaeus 1910- 7-8R
Pournelle, Jerry (Eugene) 1933- 77-80
See also SATA 26
Poussaint, Alvin F(rancis) 1934- 53-56
Povenmire, (Edward) King(sley) 1904- 61-64
Poverman, C. E. 1944- Brief entry 115
Povey, John F. 1929- 85-88
Povod, Reinaldo 1959- CLC-44
Powdermaker, Hortense 1900-1970 ...... CAP-1
Obituary 29-32R
Earlier sketch in CA 13-14
Powe, Bruce 1925- 53-56
Powell, A. M.
See Morgan, Alfred P(owell)
Powell, Adam Clayton, Jr. 1908-1972 102
Obituary 33-36R
Powell, Anthony (Dymoke) 1905- CANR-1
Earlier sketch in CA 4R
See also DLB 15
See also CLC 1, 3, 7, 9, 10, 31
Powell, Barbara 1929- 119
Powell, Brian S(harples) 1934- 25-28R
Powell, Cecil Frank 1903-1969 Obituary 113
Powell, Clarence Alva 1905- CAP-1
Earlier sketch in CA 11-12
Powell, Clilan B. 1894-1977 Obituary 73-76
Powell, (John) Craig 1940- 77-80
Powell, Dawn 1897-1965 ....5-6R
Powell, Donald M. 1914- 13-14R
Powell, Dorothy Baden
See Baden-Powell, Dorothy
Powell, Dorothy M. 1914- 106
Powell, (Drexel) Dwane (Jr.) 1944- 89-92
Powell, Elwin H(umphreys) 1925- 81-84
Powell, Eric F(rederick) W(illiam) 1899- . CANR-6
Earlier sketch in CA 7-8R
Powell, Evan Arnold 1937- CANR-21
Earlier sketch in CA 69-72
Powell, Fern 1942- 25-28R
Powell, G. Bingham, Jr. 1942- CANR-11
Earlier sketch in CA 29-32R
Powell, Geoffrey Stewart 1914- 61-64
Powell, Gordon (George) 1911- 2R
Powell, Ivor 1910- CANR-17
Earlier sketch in CA 4R
Powell, J(ohn) Enoch 1912- 97-100
Powell, James 1932- 107
Powell, James M(atthew) 1930- CANR-8
Earlier sketch in CA 7-8R
Powell, James V(irgil) 1938- 104
Powell, John Roland 1889- CAP-1
Earlier sketch in CA 13-14
Powell, L(awrence) F(itzroy) 1881-1975
Obituary 57-60
Powell, Larson Merrill 1932- 103
Powell, Lawrence Clark 1906- CANR-8
Earlier sketch in CA 21-22R
Powell, Lawrence N(elson) 1943- 104
Powell, Marcia (Leonora) 108
Powell, Margaret 1907(?)-1984 .... CANR-15
Obituary 112
Earlier sketch in CA 29-32R
Powell, Marvin 1924- CANR-8
Earlier sketch in CA 21-22R
Powell, Meredith (Ann) 1936- 37-40R
Powell, Milton Bryan 1934- 23-24R
Powell, Neil 1948- CANR-15
Earlier sketch in CA 85-88
Powell, Neil
See Innes, Brian
Powell, (Caryll) Nicolas (Peter) 1920- .. CANR-12
Earlier sketch in CA 61-64
Powell, Norman J(ohn) 1908-1974 ...... CAP-2
Obituary 49-52
Earlier sketch in CA 21-22
Powell, Padgett 1952- CLC-34
Powell, Paul W. 1933- 116
Powell, Peter 1908-1985 Obituary 116
Powell, Peter John 1928- 33-36R
Powell, Philip Wayne 1913- 85-88
Powell, Ralph L. 1917-1975 Obituary 57-60
Powell, Raymond P(ark) 1922-1980
Obituary 97-100
Powell, Reed M(adsen) 1921- 29-32R
Powell, Richard (Pitts) 1908- CANR-4
Earlier sketch in CA 1R
Powell, Richard Stillman
See Barbour, Ralph Henry
Powell, Robert (Stephenson Smyth) Baden
See Baden-Powell, Robert (Stephenson
Smyth)
Powell, Robert Richard 1909- 7-8R
Powell, Ronald R(owe) 1944- 114
Powell, Shirley 1931- 106
Powell, Sidney W. 7-8R
Powell, Sumner Chilton 1924- 7-8R
Powell, Talmage 1920- CANR-2
Earlier sketch in CA 7-8R
Powell, Terry 1949- 103
Powell, Theodore 1919- 1R
Powell, Thomas F. 1933- 25-28R
Powell, Victor M(organ) 1919- 45-48
Powell, Violet Georgiana 1912- 103
Powell, William S(tevens) 1919- 69-72
Powell-Smith, Vincent (Walter Francis)
1939- 25-28R
Powelson, John Palen 1920- CANR-19
Earlier sketches in CA 1R, CANR-4
Power, Arthur
See Dudden, Arthur P(ower)
Power, Catherine
See Du Breuil, (Elizabeth) L(or)inda
Power, Edward John 1921- CANR-2
Earlier sketch in CA 7-8R
Power, Francis C. 1909(?)-1987 Obituary ... 124
Power, John 1927- 61-64
Power, Jonathan 1941- 107
Power, Michael 1933- CAP-1
Earlier sketch in CA 11-12
Power, Norman S(andiford) 1916- CANR-10
Earlier sketch in CA 65-68
Power, Paul F(rederick) 1925- 41-44R
Power, Rex
See Langley, John
Power, Richard 1928-1970 .... CAP-1
Earlier sketch in CA 9-10
Power, Tyrone
See Guthrie, (William) Tyrone
Power, (Patrick) Victor 1930- CANR-13
Earlier sketch in CA 77-80
Power-Ross, Robert W. 1922- 102
Powers, Andy 1896- CANR-6
Earlier sketch in CA 57-60
Powers, Anne
See Schwartz, Anne Powers
Powers, Barbara Hudson
See Dudley, Barbara Hudson
Powers, Bill 1931- 77-80
See also SATA 31
Powers, Bob
See Powers, Robert L(eroy)
and Repp, William
Powers, David Guy 1911-1967 .... CAP-2
Earlier sketch in CA 19-20
Powers, Doris Cooper 1918- 105
Powers, Edward A(lvin) 1941- 77-80
Powers, Edward Alton 1927- 53-56
Powers, Edward D(oyle) 1900- 45-48
Powers, Edwin 1896- 73-76
Powers, Francis Gary 1929-1977 Obituary .. 109
Powers, George
See Infield, Glenn (Berton)
Powers, Helen 1925- 97-100
Powers, J(ames) F(arl) 1917- CANR-2
Earlier sketch in CA 3R
See also CLC 1, 4, 8
Powers, Jeffrey W(ells) 1950- 61-64
Powers, John J(ames) 1945- 69-72
Powers, John R.
See Powers, John J(ames)
Powers, Joseph M(ichael) 1926- 85-88
Powers, Lyall H(arris) 1924- Brief entry 115
Powers, M. L.
See Tubb, E(dwin) C(harles)
Powers, Margaret
See Heal, Edith
Powers, Mark James 1940- 110
Powers, Patrick W(illiam) 1924- 13-14R
Powers, Richard M. Gorman 1921- 21-22R
Powers, Robert L(eroy) 1924- 93-96
Powers, Robert M(aynard) 1942- CANR-14
Earlier sketch in CA 77-80
Powers, Ron(ald Dean) 1941- 97-100
Powers, Thomas (Moore) 1940- CANR-17
Earlier sketch in CA 37-40R
Powers, William 1930- 45-48
Powers, William Edwards 1902- CAP-2
Earlier sketch in CA 19-20
Powers, William K(eegan) 1934- 25-28R
Powers, William T(reval) 1926- 111
Power-Waters, Alma Shelley
1896-1983 .... CANR-18
Earlier sketch in CA 3R
Power-Waters, Brian 1922- CANR-18
Earlier sketch in CA 93-96
Powicke, Michael Rhys 1920- CANR-8
Earlier sketch in CA 7-8R
Powledge, Fred 1935- CANR-9
Earlier sketch in CA 23-24R
See also SATA 37
Powley, Edward Barzillai 1887-1968 ..... CAP-1
Earlier sketch in CA 13-14
Powley, Florence Mary Pomeroy 1892- ... CAP-1
Earlier sketch in CA 15-16
Powling, Chris 1943- 121
Pownall, David 1938- 89-92
See also DLB 14
See also CLC 10
Powrie, Peter James 1927- 21-22R
Powys, John Cowper 1872-1963 85-88
See also DLB 15
See also CLC 7, 9, 15, 46
Powys, T(heodore) F(rancis) 1875-1953
Brief entry 106
See also DLB 36
See also TCLC 9
Poyer, David 1949- 111
Poyer, Joe
See Poyer, Joseph John (Jr.)
Poyer, Joseph John (Jr.) 1939- CANR-17
Earlier sketches in CA 49-52, CANR-1
Poynter, Dan(iel Frank) 1938- CANR-24
Earlier sketch in CA 89-92
Poynter, Margaret 1927- CANR-16
Earlier sketch in CA 93-96
See also SATA 27
Poynter, Nelson 1903-1978 Obituary 77-80
Pozzetta, George Enrico 1942- 111
Prabhavananda, Swami 1893-1976 ..... CANR-8
Obituary 65-68
Earlier sketch in CA 19-20R
Prabhu, Pandharinath H. 1911- CANR-7
Earlier sketch in CA 13-14R
Prabhupada, A. C. Bhaktivedanta
1896-1977 .... CANR-14
Earlier sketch in CA 73-76
Prabhupada, A. C. Bhaktivedanta Swami
See Prabhupada, A. C. Bhaktivedanta
Prada Oropeza, Renato 1937- 41-44R
Prado, C(arlos) G(onzalez) 1937- 110
Prados, John 1951- 106
Prager, Arthur CANR-12
Earlier sketch in CA 29-32R
See also SATA 44
Prager, Jonas 1938- 105
Prager, Karsten 1936- 73-76
Prago, Albert 1911- 29-32R
Prain, Ronald (Lindsay) 1907- 109
Prall, Stuart E(dward) 1929- 23-24R
Prance, Claude A(nnett) 1906- CANR-20
Earlier sketch in CA 89-92
Prance, June E(lizebeth) 1929- 69-72
Prandy, K(en) 1938- 117
Prange, Erwin (Edward) 1917- 113
Prange, Gordon W(illiam) 1910-1980
Obituary 97-100
Pranger, Robert J(ohn) 1931- CANR-10
Earlier sketch in CA 25-28R
Prasad, S(rinivas) Benjamin 1929- CANR-5
Earlier sketch in CA 53-56
Prassel, Frank Richard 1937- CANR-1
Earlier sketch in CA 49-52
Prather, Hugh 1938- CANR-2
Earlier sketch in CA 45-48
Prather, Richard S(cott) 1921- CANR-5
Earlier sketch in CA 2R
Pratley, Gerald 1923- 112
Pratney, William Alfred 1944- 124
Pratney, Winkie
See Pratney, William Alfred
Pratson, Frederick John 1935- 101
Pratt, Allan D(aniel) 1933- 112
Pratt, Charles 1926-1976 .... CANR-21
Obituary 65-68
Earlier sketch in CA 69-72
Pratt, Chris (James) 1950- 118
Pratt, (Mildred) Claire 1921- 103
Pratt, Dallas 1914- 106
Pratt, Edwin John 1883-1964 Obituary 93-96
See also CLC 19
Pratt, (Murray) Fletcher 1897-1956
Brief entry 113
Pratt, J(oseph) Gaither 1910-1979 ...... CANR-6
Obituary 89-92
Earlier sketch in CA 11-12R
Pratt, James Norwood 1942- 112
Pratt, John 1931- CANR-1
Earlier sketch in CA 3R
Pratt, John Clark 1932- CANR-17
Earlier sketch in CA 13-14R
Pratt, John Lowell 1906-1968 .... CANR-3
Earlier sketch in CA 2R
Pratt, Julius W(illiam) 1888- CAP-1
Earlier sketch in CA 11-12
Pratt, Keith L(eslie) 1938- 29-32R
Pratt, Norman T(wombly), Jr. 1911- 118
Pratt, Robert Cranford 1926- 101
Pratt, Samuel Jackson 1749-1814 ...... DLB-39
Pratt, Theodore 1901-1969 .... CANR-4
Earlier sketch in CA 3R
Pratt, William C(rouch, Jr.) 1927- CANR-6
Earlier sketch in CA 13-14R
Pratt, Willis Winslow 1908- Brief entry 105
Pratt-Butler, Grace Kipp 1916- 103
Pratte, Richard (Norman) 1929- 93-96
Prattis, Percival L. 1895-1980 Obituary ..97-100
Prawer, Joshua 1917- 41-44R
Prawer, S(iegbert) S(alomon) 1925- 103
Pray, Lawrence M. 1947- 113
Praz, Mario 1896-1982 101
Obituary 106
Prchal, Mildred 1895-1983 Obituary 109
Prebble, John Edward Curtis 1915- CANR-3
Earlier sketch in CA 7-8R
Prebble, Marjorie Mary Curtis 1912- ... CANR-15
Earlier sketch in CA 19-20R
Prebish, Charles S(tuart) 1944- 57-60
Preble, Duane 1936- 61-64
Preble, Robert Curtis 1897-1983 Obituary .. 111
Predmore, Michael 1938- 45-48
Predmore, Richard L. 1911- 19-20R
Preece, Harold 1906- 7-8R
Preece, Rod(ney John) 1939- 113
Preedy, George
See Campbell, (Gabrielle) Margaret (Vere)
Preeg, Ernest H. 1934- 33-36R
Prefontaine, Yves 1937- DLB-53
Pregel, Boris 1893-1976 Obituary 106
Preger, Paul D(aniel), Jr. 1926- 49-52
Preheim, Marion Keeney 1934- 25-28R
Preil, Gabriel 1911- CANR-1
Earlier sketch in CA 49-52
Preiser, Wolfgang F(riedrich) E(rnst)
1941- CANR-7
Earlier sketch in CA 57-60
Preiss, Byron (Cary) CANR-14
Earlier sketch in CA 69-72
See also SATA 42, 47
Preiss, David (Lee) 1935- 69-72
Prelinger, Ernst 1926- 11-12R
Prelutsky, Jack 1940- 93-96
See also SATA 22
See also DLB 61
See also CLR 13
Prem, Dhani 1904(?)-1979 Obituary 93-96
Premacanda
See Srivastava, Dhanpat Rai
Premack, Ann J(ames) 1929- 57-60
Premchand
See Srivastava, Dhanpat Rai
See also TCLC 21
Prem Chand, Munshi
See Srivastava, Dhanpat Rai
Premchand, Munshi
See Srivastava, Dhanpat Rai
Preminger, Alex 1915- 15-16R
Preminger, Marion Mill 1913-1972
Obituary 33-36R
Preminger, Otto (Ludwig) 1906(?)-1986
Obituary 119
Brief entry 110
Premont, Brother Jeremy
See Willett, Brother Franciscus
Prendergast, Alan 1956- 124
Prendergast, Karen A(nn) 1951- 117
Prentice, Amy
See Kaler, James Otis
Prentice, Ann E(thelynd) 1933- CANR-6
Earlier sketch in CA 57-60
Prentice, Charlotte
See Platt, Charles

INDEX

Prentice, George D. 1802-1870 ... DLB-43
Prenting, Theodore O(tto) 1933- ... 57-60
Prentis, Steve ?-1987 Obituary ... 122
Prentiss, Augustin M. 1890-1977
 Obituary ... 69-72
Presberg, Miriam Goldstein 1919-1978 .. CANR-3
 Earlier sketch in CA 2R
 See also SATA 38
Prescott, Allen 1904(?)-1978 Obituary ... 73-76
Prescott, Caleb
 See Bingley, David Ernest
Prescott, David M(arshall) 1926-
 Brief entry ... 113
Prescott, J(ohn) R(obert) V(ictor)
 1931- ... CANR-23
 Earlier sketch in CA 107
Prescott, John Brewster 1919- ... 5-6R
Prescott, Kenneth W(ade) 1920- ... CANR-8
 Earlier sketch in CA 57-60
Prescott, Orville 1906- ... 41-44R
Prescott, Peter S(herwin) 1935- ... CANR-14
 Earlier sketch in CA 37-40R
Prescott, William Hickling
 1796-1859 ... DLB-1, 30, 59
Preshing, W(illiam) A(nthony) 1929- ... 85-88
Preslan, Kristina 1945- ... 106
Presland, John
 See Bendit, Gladys Williams
Presley, Delma E(ugene) 1939- ... 112
Presley, James (Wright) 1930- ... CANR-10
 Earlier sketch in CA 21-22R
Presnell, Robert (Jr.) 1915(?)-1986
 Obituary ... 119
Press, (Otto) Charles 1922- ... CANR-6
 Earlier sketch in CA 13-14R
Press, John (Bryant) 1920- ... CANR-3
 Earlier sketch in CA 9-10R
Press, Simone Juda 1943- ... 111
Press, Toni 1949- ... 108
Pressau, Jack Renard 1933- ... 77-80
Pressburger, Emeric 1902-1988 ... 104
 Obituary ... 124
Presseisen, Ernst L(eopold) 1928- ... 15-16R
Presser, (Gerrit) Jacob 1899-1970 ... CAP-2
 Earlier sketch in CA 25-28
Presser, Janice 1946- ... CANR-24
 Earlier sketch in CA 107
Pressly, Thomas J(ames) 1919- ... 19-20R
Pressman, David 1937- ... 89-92
Pressman, Jeffrey L(eonard) 1943- ... CANR-3
 Earlier sketch in CA 45-48
Prest, Alan Richmond 1919-1985 ... 93-96
 Obituary ... 115
Prest, Wilfred 1907-1985 ... 111
 Obituary ... 117
Prest, Wilfrid R(obertson) 1940- ... 112
Prestbo, John A(ndrew) 1941- ... CANR-2
 Earlier sketch in CA 49-52
Prestera, Hector A(nthony) 1932- ... 65-68
Presthus, Robert 1917- ... CANR-20
 Earlier sketches in CA 1R, CANR-5
Prestidge, Pauline 1922- ... 103
Preston, Dickson J(oseph) 1914-1985 ... CANR-8
 Obituary ... 114
 Earlier sketch in CA 61-64
Preston, Edna Mitchell ... 111
 See also SATA 40
Preston, Edward
 See Guess, Edward Preston
Preston, Florence (Margaret) 1905- ... 103
Preston, Frances I(sabella) 1898- ... 61-64
Preston, Harry 1923- ... CANR-23
 Earlier sketch in CA 57-60
Preston, Ivan L. 1931- ... 57-60
Preston, Ivy (Alice) Kinross 1914- ... CANR-12
 Earlier sketches in CA 9-10, CAP-1
Preston, James 1913- ... CAP-1
 Earlier sketch in CA 9-10
Preston, James
 See Unett, John
Preston, James J(ohn) 1941- ... 109
Preston, John Hyde 1906-1980 Obituary ... 102
Preston, Lee E. 1930- ... CANR-11
 Earlier sketch in CA 23-24R
Preston, Lillian Elvira 1918- ... 108
 See also SATA 47
Preston, Nathaniel Stone 1928- ... 29-32R
Preston, Ralph C(lausius) 1908- ... CANR-6
 Earlier sketch in CA 13-14R
Preston, Richard
 See Lindsay, Jack
Preston, Richard Arthur 1910- ... CANR-18
 Earlier sketches in CA 7-8R, CANR-3
Preston, Thomas 1537-1598 ... DLB-62
Preston, Thomas A(rthur) 1933- ... 112
Preston, Thomas R(onald) 1936-
 Brief entry ... 109
Preston, William L(ee) 1949- ... 105
Prestwich, Menna 1917- ... 23-24R
Pretorius, Hertha
 See Kouts, Hertha Pretorius
Preto-Rodas, Richard (Anthony) 1936- ... 49-52
Prettyman, E(lijah) Barrett, Jr. 1925- ... 11-12R
Preus, Anthony 1936- ... 49-52
Preus, Herman Amberg 1896- ... 85-88
Preus, Jacob A(all) O(ttesen) 1920- ... 33-36R
Preus, Johan Carl Keyser 1881-1983
 Obituary ... 111
Preus, Robert 1924- ... 33-36R
Preussler, Otfried 1923- ... 77-80
 See also SATA 24
 See also CLC 17
Prevelakis, Pandelis 1909-1986 Obituary ... 118
Prevert, Jacques (Henri Marie)
 1900-1977 ... 77-80
 Obituary ... 69-72
 See also SATA 30
 See also CLC 15
Previn, Andre (George) 1929- ... 115
Previn, Dor(oth)y (Langan) 1929(?)- ... 111
Prevost, Alain 1930(?)-1971 Obituary ... 33-36R
Prevost, Marcel 1862-1941 Brief entry ... 116
Prewitt, Kenneth 1936- ... CANR-12
 Earlier sketch in CA 29-32R
Preziosi, Donald 1941- ... 93-96
Prezzolini, Giuseppi 1882-1982 Obituary ... 107
Pribam, Karl 1878(?)-1973 Obituary ... 41-44R
Pribichevich, Stoyan 1905(?)-1976
 Obituary ... 65-68
Price, Alfred 1936- ... CANR-24
 Earlier sketches in CA 23-24R, CANR-9
Price, Anthony 1928- ... CANR-15
 Earlier sketch in CA 77-80
Price, Archibald Grenfell 1892- ... 9-10R
Price, Arnold H(ereward) 1912- ... 45-48
Price, Barbara Anne Ellvinger
 1946(?)-1987 Obituary ... 122
Price, Barbara Pradal ... 103
Price, Beverley Joan 1931- ... CANR-24
 Earlier sketch in CA 106
Price, Bruce D(eitrick) 1941- ... 25-28R
Price, Byron 1891-1981 Obituary ... 104
Price, Cecil (John Layton) 1915- ... 21-22R
Price, Charles 1925- ... 11-12R
Price, Charles C(oale) 1913- ... 107
Price, Charles P(hilip) 1920- ... 115
Price, Christine (Hilda) 1928-1980 ... CANR-4
 Obituary ... 93-96
 Earlier sketch in CA 5-6R
 See also SATA 3, 23
Price, Daniel O('Haver) 1918- ... 21-22R
Price, David Deakins 1902-1983 Obituary ... 110
Price, Derek (John) de Solla
 1922-1983 ... CANR-3
 Obituary ... 110
 Earlier sketch in CA 1R
Price, Don C(ravens) 1937- ... 81-84
Price, Don K(rasher, Jr.) 1910- ... 73-76
Price, E(dgar) Hoffmann 1898- ... CANR-10
 Earlier sketch in CA 61-64
Price, Emerson 1902(?)-1977 Obituary ... 104
Price, Eugenia 1916- ... CANR-18
 Earlier sketches in CA 7-8R, CANR-2
Price, Evadne 1896-1985 Obituary ... 116
Price, Frances Brown 1895- ... 49-52
Price, Francis Wilson 1895-1974 ... CAP-1
 Earlier sketch in CA 13-14
Price, Frank James 1917- ... 104
Price, Frank W.
 See Price, Francis Wilson
Price, Garrett 1896-1979 Obituary ... 85-88
 See also SATA 22
Price, George 1901- ... 103
Price, George (Henry) 1910-19(?) ... CAP-1
 Earlier sketch in CA 13-14
Price, George R(ennie) 1909- ... CANR-4
 Earlier sketch in CA 1R
Price, Glenn W(arren) 1918- ... 23-24R
Price, Harry 1881-1948 Brief entry ... 119
Price, Henry Habberley 1899-1984
 Obituary ... 114
Price, J(oseph) H(enry) 1924- ... 25-28R
Price, Jacob M(yron) 1925- ... CANR-1
 Earlier sketch in CA 45-48
Price, James Ligon, Jr. 1915- ... 3R
Price, Jennifer
 See Hoover, Helen (Drusilla Blackburn)
Price, Jimmie
 See White, John I(rwin)
Price, Joan 1931- ... 111
Price, John A(ndrew) 1933- ... CANR-7
 Earlier sketch in CA 57-60
Price, John Valdimir 1937- ... 19-20R
Price, Jonathan (Reeve) 1941- ... CANR-19
 Earlier sketches in CA 45-48, CANR-3
 See also SATA 46
Price, Kenneth M(arsden) 1954- ... 115
Price, Kingsley Blake 1917- ... 23-24R
Price, Larkin B(url) 1927- Brief entry ... 112
Price, Leo 1941- ... 77-80
Price, Lucie Locke
 See Locke, Lucie
Price, Margaret (Evans) 1888-1973
 Obituary ... 109
 See also SATA 28
Price, Marion E(lizabeth) 1947- ... 111
Price, Marjorie 1929- ... 53-56
Price, Martin 1920- ... CANR-13
 Earlier sketch in CA 19-20R
Price, Miles O(scar) 1890-1968 ... CAP-1
 Earlier sketch in CA 15-16
Price, Molly 1903(?)-1984 Obituary ... 114
Price, Morgan Philips 1885-1973 ... CAP-1
 Earlier sketch in CA 13-14
Price, (Lilian) Nancy (Bache) 1880-1970
 Obituary ... 111
Price, Nelson Lynn 1931- ... CANR-24
 Earlier sketches in CA 61-64, CANR-8
Price, Olive 1903- ... 41-44R
 See also SATA 8
Price, Paul 1912(?)-1985 Obituary ... 116
Price, R(onald) F(rancis) 1926- ... 29-32R
Price, R(ichard) G(eoffrey) G(eorge)
 1910- ... CAP-1
 Earlier sketch in CA 13-14
Price, Ray(mond John) 1931- ... 25-28R
Price, Ray Glenn 1903- ... CANR-2
 Earlier sketch in CA 7-8R
Price, Raymond (Kissam, Jr.) 1930- ... 105
Price, (Edward) Reynolds 1933- ... CANR-1
 Earlier sketch in CA 2R
 See also DLB 2
 See also CLC 3, 6, 13, 43
Price, Rhys
 See Price, George (Henry)
Price, Richard 1941- ... 105
Price, Richard 1949- ... CANR-3
 Earlier sketch in CA 49-52
 See also DLBY 81
 See also CLC 6, 12
Price, Robert 1900- ... 33-36R
Price, Robert W. 1925(?)-1979 Obituary ... 89-92
Price, Roger 1921- ... 11-12R
Price, Roger (David) 1944- ... 107
Price, S(eymour) Stephen 1919- ... 25-28R
Price, Sally 1943- ... 106
Price, Stanley 1931- ... 13-14R
Price, Steven D(avid) 1940- ... CANR-16
 Earlier sketches in CA 49-52, CANR-1
Price, Susan 1955- ... 105
 See also SATA 25
Price, V(incent) B(arrett) 1940- ... 69-72
Price, Victor 1930- ... 11-12R
Price, Vincent 1911- ... 89-92
Price, Walter K(leber) 1924- ... CANR-7
 Earlier sketch in CA 19-20R
Price, Willadene Anton 1914- ... 5-6R
Price, Willard 1887-1983 ... CANR-1
 Earlier sketch in CA 4R
 See also SATA 38, 48
Price, William 1938- ... 37-40R
Price, Wilson T(itus) 1931- ... 37-40R
Price-Mars, Jean 1875-1969 Obituary ... 113
Prichard, Caradog 1904-1980 ... 103
 Obituary ... 97-100
Prichard, Doris (Smith) 1947- ... 116
Prichard, James W(illiam) 1925- ... 15-16R
Prichard, Katharine Susannah 1883-1969 . CAP-1
 Earlier sketch in CA 11-12
 See also CLC 46
Prichard, Nancy S(awyer) 1924- ... 29-32R
Prichard, Robert Williams 1923- ... 89-92
Prichard, Susan Perez 1953- ... 108
Prickett, (Alexander Thomas) Stephen
 1939- ... 29-32R
Priddy, Fran(ces Rosaleen) 1931- ... CANR-17
 Earlier sketch in CA 3R
Pride, Cletis 1925- ... 41-44R
Pride, J(ohn) B(ernard) 1929- Brief entry ... 110
Prideaux, Tom 1908- ... 108
 See also SATA 37
Pridham, Geoffrey 1942- ... CANR-17
 Earlier sketch in CA 97-100
Pridham, Radost 1922- ... 23-24R
Pries, Nancy R(uth) 1944- ... 118
Priesand, Sally J(ane) 1946- ... 65-68
Priest, Alice L. 1931- ... 102
Priest, Christopher 1943- ... 33-36R
 See also DLB 14
Priest, Harold Martin 1902- ... 73-76
Priest, Robert 1951- ... 118
Priestley, Barbara 1937- ... 33-36R
Priestley, F(rancis) E(thelbert) L(ouis)
 1905- ... 21-22R
Priestley, Harold E(dford) 1901- ... 73-76
Priestley, J(ohn) B(oynton) 1894-1984 ... 9-10R
 Obituary ... 113
 See also DLB 10, 34
 See also DLBY 84
 See also CLC 2, 5, 9, 34
Priestley, Lee (Shore) 1904- ... CANR-2
 Earlier sketch in CA 5-6R
 See also SATA 27
Priestley, Mary 1925- ... 61-64
Priestley, Philip 1939- ... 123
Prieto, Mariana Beeching 1912- ... CANR-5
 Earlier sketch in CA 5-6R
 See also SATA 8
Prigmore, Charles S(amuel) 1919- ... 45-48
Priley, Margaret Hubbard 1909- ... 2R
Prill, Felician 1904- ... 103
Primack, Joel (Robert) 1945- ... 61-64
Primavera, Elise 1954- ... SATA-48
Prime, Benjamin Young 1733-1791 ... DLB-31
Prime, C(ecil) T(homas) 1909-1979 ... CANR-3
 Earlier sketch in CA 49-52
Prime, Derek (James) 1931- ... 108
 See also SATA 34
Primeau, Ronald 1946- ... 108
Primeaux, Walter J(oseph) Jr. 1928- ... 41-44R
Primm, Brother Orrin
 See Willett, Brother Franciscus
Primm, James Neal 1918- ... 45-48
Primmer, Phyllis (Cora Griesbach) 1926- ... 7-8R
Primo, Albert T. 1935- ... 73-76
Primrose, William 1904-1982 ... 116
 Obituary ... 106
Prince (Rogers Nelson) 1958?- ... CLC-35
Prince, Alison 1931- ... 29-32R
 See also SATA 28
Prince, Carl E. 1934- ... CANR-14
 Earlier sketch in CA 21-22R
Prince, (Peter) Derek 1915- ... 113
Prince, Don 1905(?)-1983 Obituary ... 110
Prince, F(rank) T(empleton) 1912- ... 101
 See also DLB 20
 See also CLC 22
Prince, Gary Michael 1948- ... 89-92
Prince, Gerald (Joseph) 1942- ... 57-60
Prince, J(ack) H(arvey) 1908- ... 81-84
 See also SATA 17
Prince, Melvin 1932- ... 116
Prince, Morton 1854-1929 Brief entry ... 121
Prince, Suzan D(enise) 1957- ... 111
Prince, Thomas 1687-1758 ... DLB-24
Prince, Thomas Richard 1934- ... 15-16R
Prince Ibis
 See Randi, James
Prince Kropotkin
 See Kropotkin, Peter (Aleksieevich)
Princess Grace
 See Kelly, Grace (Patricia)
Prindl, A(ndreas) R(obert) 1939- ... 69-72
Pring, Julian Talbot 1913- ... 7-8R
Pring, Martin J(ohn) 1943- ... 111
Pringle, J(ohn) M(artin) Douglas 1912- ... 13-14R
Pringle, Laurence P. 1935- ... CANR-14
 Earlier sketch in CA 29-32R
 See also SATA 4
 See also CLR 4
Pringle, Mia (Lilly) Kellmer 1920(?)-1983 ... 65-68
 Obituary ... 109
Pringle, Peter 1940- ... 69-72
Pring-Mill, Robert D(uguid) F(orrest)
 1924- ... 9-10R
Printz, Peggy 1945- ... 73-76
Prinz, Joachim 1902- ... CAP-1
 Earlier sketch in CA 11-12
Priolo, Pauline Pizzo 1907- ... 2R
Prior, A(rthur) N(orman) 1914-1969 ... CANR-3
 Earlier sketch in CA 1R
Prior, Allan 1922- ... CANR-10
 Earlier sketch in CA 65-68
Prior, Andrew 1940- ... 112
Prior, Ann 1949- ... 25-28R
Prior, Kenneth Francis William 1926- ... 19-20R
Prisco, Michele 1920- ... 53-56
Prisco, Salvatore III 1943- ... CANR-12
 Earlier sketch in CA 61-64
Prising, Robin 1933- ... 57-60
Pritchard, Arnold 1949- ... 97-100
Pritchard, J(ohn) Harris 1923- ... 21-22R
Pritchard, James Bennett 1909- ... 5-6R
Pritchard, John Paul 1902- ... 11-12R
Pritchard, John Wallace 1912- ... 81-84
Pritchard, Leland J(ames) 1908- ... CAP-1
 Earlier sketch in CA 11-12
Pritchard, Norman Henry II 1939- ... 77-80
Pritchard, R(onald) E(dward) 1936- ... 37-40R
Pritchard, R(obert) John 1945- ... 116
Pritchard, Sheila (Edwards) 1909- ... CAP-1
 Earlier sketch in CA 15-16
Pritchard, William H(arrison) 1932- ... CANR-23
 Earlier sketch in CA 65-68
 See also CLC 34
Pritchett, C(harles) Herman 1907- ... CANR-18
 Earlier sketches in CA 2R, CANR-3
Pritchett, Elaine H(illyer) 1920- ... 108
 See also SATA 36
Pritchett, John Perry 1902- ... 2R
Pritchett, Price 1941- ... 123
Pritchett, V(ictor) S(awdon) 1900- ... 61-64
 See also DLB 15
 See also CLC 5, 13, 15, 41
Pritchett, W(illiam) Kendrick 1909- ... 97-100
Pritikin, Nathan 1915-1985 ... 89-92
 Obituary ... 114
Pritikin, Robert C(harles) 1929- ... 104
Prittie, Terence Cornelius Farmer
 1913-1985 ... CANR-4
 Obituary ... 116
 Earlier sketch in CA 2R
Private 19022
 See Manning, Frederic
Priyamvada, Usha
 See Nilsson, Usha Saksena
Prizzia, Ross 1942- ... 119
Probert, Walter 1925- ... 77-80
Probst, Leonard 1921-1982 ... 65-68
 Obituary ... 106
Prochnau, William W. 1937- ... 33-36R
Prochnow, Herbert V. 1897- ... CANR-4
 Earlier sketch in CA 2R
Prochnow, Herbert V(ictor), Jr. 1931- ... 110
Procktor, Richard (Edward Christopher)
 1933- ... 53-56
Procopio, Mariellen
 See Grutz, Mariellen Procopio
Procter, Adelaide Anne 1825-1864 ... DLB-32
Procter, Ben H. 1927- ... CANR-9
 Earlier sketch in CA 5-6R
Procter, Maurice 1906-1973 ... 7-8R
 Obituary ... 122
Proctor, Charles S(heridan) 1925- ... 29-32R
Proctor, (Philip) Dennis 1905-1983
 Obituary ... 110
Proctor, Dorothea Hardy 1910- ... 61-64
Proctor, E(velyn) E(mma) S(tefanos)
 1897-1980 ... 103
 Obituary ... 97-100
Proctor, Elsie 1902- ... 29-32R
Proctor, Everitt
 See Montgomery, Rutherford George
Proctor, Lillian Cummins 1900- ... CAP-2
 Earlier sketch in CA 23-24
Proctor, Priscilla 1945- ... 65-68
Proctor, Raymond L(ambert) 1920- ... 45-48
Proctor, Samuel 1919- ... CANR-3
 Earlier sketch in CA 11-12R
Proctor, Samuel D(eWitt) 1921-
 Brief entry ... 118
Proctor, Thelwall 1912- ... 29-32R
Proctor, William (Gilbert, Jr.) 1941- ... CANR-16
 Earlier sketch in CA 37-40R
Prodan, Mario 1911- ... 11-12R
Proface, Dom
 See Sheehy, Maurice S(tephen)
Proffer, Carl R(ay) 1938-1984 ... 41-44R
 Obituary ... 113
Proffer, Ellendea 1944- ... CANR-1
 Earlier sketch in CA 45-48
Proffitt, Charles G. 1896-1982 Obituary ... 108

Proger, Samuel (Herschel) 1906-
Brief entry 106
Prohias, Antonio 1921- 104
Prokasy, William F(rederick) 1930- 49-52
Prokhovnik, Simon Jacques 1920- 107
Prokofiev, Aleksandr Andreyevich
1900-1971 Obituary 33-36R
Prokofiev, Camilla Gray 1938(?)-1971
Obituary 33-36R
Prokofiev, Sergei (Sergeevich) 1891-1953
Brief entry 112
Prokop, Phyllis Stillwell 1922- CANR-9
Earlier sketch in CA 21-22R
Prokopczyk, Czeslaw 1935- 108
Prokosch, Frederic 1908- 73-76
See also DLB 48
See also CLC 4
Prole, Lozania
See Bloom, Ursula
Pronin, Alexander 1927- 49-52
Pronko, Leonard Cabell 1927- CANR-1
Earlier sketch in CA 1R
Pronko, N(icholas) Henry 1908- 11-12R
Pronzini, Bill 1943- CANR-14
Earlier sketches in CA 49-52, CANR-1
Proosdii, Cornelis Van
See Van Proosdy, Cornelis
Propes, Stephen Charles 1942- CANR-1
Earlier sketch in CA 49-52
Propes, Steve
See Propes, Stephen Charles
Propper, Dan 1937- 104
See also DLB 16
Prosch, Harry 1917- 13-14R
Prose, Francine 1947- 112
Brief entry 109
See also CLC 45
Proske, Beatrice (Irene) Gilman 1899- CAP-1
Earlier sketch in CA 9-10
Proskouriakoff, Tatiana (Avenivovna)
1909-1985 Obituary 117
Prosper, John (joint pseudonym)
See Farrar, John C(hipman)
Prosper, Lincoln
See Cannon, Helen
Prosser, Eleanor 1922- 3R
Prosser, H(arold) L(ee) 1944- CANR-15
Earlier sketch in CA 77-80
Prosser, Michael H. 1936- CANR-17
Earlier sketch in CA 25-28R
Prostano, Emanuel Theodore, Jr. 1931- .. 29-32R
Prosterman, Roy L. 1935- 57-60
Prothero, R(alph) Mansell 1924- 41-44R
Prothro, Edwin Terry 1919- 53-56
Prothro, James W(arren) 1922- CANR-8
Earlier sketch in CA 5-6R
Protopapas, George 1917- 57-60
Prou, Suzanne (Marcelle Henriette)
1920- CANR-20
Earlier sketch in CA 33-36R
Proud, Robert 1728-1813 .... DLB-30
Proudfoot, J(ohn) J(ames) 1918- 21-22R
Proudhon
See Cunha, Euclides (Rodrigues Pimenta)
da
Proujan, Carl 1929- 81-84
Proussis, Costas M(ichael) 1911- CANR-15
Earlier sketch in CA 41-44R
Proust,
(Valentin-Louis-George-Eugene-)Marcel
1871-1922 120
Brief entry 104
See also DLB 65
See also TCLC 7, 13
Prout, W(illiam) Leslie 1922- 9-10R
Prouty, L. Fletcher 1917- 45-48
Prouty, Morton D(ennison), Jr. 1918- 3R
Prouty, Olive Higgins 1882(?)-1974 ...... 11-12R
Obituary 49-52
Prouvost, Jean 1885-1978 Obituary 89-92
Provan, Jill E(llen) 1948- 117
Provence, Marcel
See Jouhandeau, Marcel Henri
Provensen, Alice 1918- CANR-5
Earlier sketch in CA 53-56
See also SATA 9
See also CLR 11
Provensen, Martin (Elias) 1916-1987 .... CANR-5
Obituary 122
Earlier sketch in CA 53-56
See also SATA 9
See also CLR 11
Provo, Frank 1913(?)-1975 Obituary 61-64
Provus, Malcolm M. 1928- Brief entry 108
Prowe, Diethelm (Manfred-Hartmut)
1941- 57-60
Prowler, Don(ald) 1950- 121
Prowler, Harley
See Masters, Edgar Lee
Prown, Jules David 1930- 29-32R
Proxmire, William 1915- 29-32R
Prpic, George J(ure) 1920- CANR-17
Earlier sketch in CA 25-28R
Prucha, Francis Paul 1921- CANR-17
Earlier sketches in CA 5-6R, CANR-2
Prudden, Bonnie 1914- CANR-14
Earlier sketch in CA 77-80
Prude, Agnes George 1905- 65-68
Pruden, (James) Wesley, Jr. 1935- 19-20R
Prueitt, Melvin L(ewis) 1932- 118
Pruett, John H(aywood) 1947- 102
Prugh, Jeff(ery Douglas) 1939- 41-44R
Pruitt, Evelyn L(ord) 1918- 5-6R
Pruitt, Ida 1888-1985 Obituary 116
Pruitt, William O(badiah), Jr. 1922- 21-22R
Pruner, Leonora 1931- 114
Prunty, Merle C(harles) 1917-1983 ...... 37-40R
Obituary 109
Prunty, (Eugene) Wyatt 1947- 110
Prusek, Jaroslav 1906- Brief entry 117
Prusina, Katica 1935- 69-72
Pruthi, Surinder P(aul) S(ingh) 1934- 61-64
Pruyser, Paul W(illem) 1916- CANR-9
Earlier sketch in CA 23-24R
Prybyla, Jan S(tanislaw) 1927- 23-24R
Pryce, Roy 1928- 29-32R
Pryce-Jones, David 1936- CANR-14
Earlier sketch in CA 13-14R
Pryde, Philip Rust 1938- 61-64
Pryer, Pauline
See Roby, Mary Linn
Prynne, J. H. 1936- 97-100
See also DLB 40
Pryor, Adel
See Wasserfall, Adel
Pryor, Frederic L(eRoy) 1933- CANR-2
Earlier sketch in CA 7-8R
Pryor, Helen Brenton 1897-1972 .... CAP-2
Earlier sketch in CA 33-36
See also SATA 4
Pryor, Karen 1932- 119
Pryor, Larry
See Pryor, Lawrence A(llderdice)
Pryor, Lawrence A(llderdice) 1938- 85-88
Pryor, Richard (Franklin Lenox Thomas)
1940- Brief entry 122
See also CLC 26
Prys-Jones, Arthur Glyn 1888- 104
Przybyszewski, Stanislaw 1868-1927 .... DLB-66
Psathas, George 1929- 23-24R
Pteleon
See Grieve, C(hristopher) M(urray)
Puccetti, Roland (Peter) 1924- 93-96
Pucci, Albert John 1920- SATA-44
Pucciani, Oreste F(rancesco) 1916- 23-24R
Puche, Jose Luis Castillo
See Castillo Puche, Jose Luis
Puck, Wolfgang 1949- 124
Puck, Y. U.
See Andre, (Kenneth) Michael
Puckett, Lute
See Masters, Edgar Lee
Puckett, Robert Hugh 1935- 41-44R
Puckett, (William) Ronald 1936- 33-36R
Puckett, Ruby Parker 1932- 57-60
Puckey, Walter (Charles) 1899-1983 ..... CAP-2
Obituary 111
Earlier sketch in CA 29-32
Pudaite, Rochunga 1927- 120
Puddepha, Derek (Noel) 1930- 61-64
Pudney, John (Sleigh) 1909-1977 ...... CANR-5
Obituary 77-80
Earlier sketch in CA 9-10R
See also SATA 24
Pudovkin, V(sevolod) I(llarionovich)
1893-1953 Brief entry 112
Puechner, Ray 1935- 25-28R
Puette, William J(oseph) 1946- 77-80
Puffer, K(enneth) Hart 1910- 7-8R
Pugh, Anthony (Roy) 1931- 53-56
Pugh, Charles 1948- 81-84
Pugh, Ellen (Tiffany) 1920- 49-52
See also SATA 7
Pugh, Griffith T(hompson) 1908- 7-8R
Pugh, J(ohn) W(ilbur) 1912- 21-22R
Pugh, John Charles 1919- 110
Pugh, L(eslie) P(enrhys) 1895-1983
Obituary 110
Pugh, Ralph B(ernard) 1910-1982 .... 25-28R
Obituary 108
Pugh, Rod(erick) W(ellington) 1919- 45-48
Pugh, Samuel F(ranklin) 1904- CAP-1
Earlier sketch in CA 13-14
Pugh, Wynette 1942- Brief entry 111
Pugin, A. Welby 1812-1852 .... DLB-55
Pugliese, Anthony J(ulian) 1912-1985
Obituary 117
Pugsley, Clement H. 1908- CAP-1
Earlier sketch in CA 13-14
Pugsley, John A. 1934- CANR-19
Earlier sketch in CA 103
Puharich, Henry (Andrija) Karl 1918- 85-88
Puhvel, Jaan 1932- 29-32R
Puig, Manuel 1932- CANR-2
Earlier sketch in CA 45-48
See also CLC 3, 5, 10, 28
Pulaski, Mary Ann Spencer 1916- CANR-10
Earlier sketch in CA 25-28R
Pulay, George 1923- 45-48
Puleo, Nicole
See Miller, Nicole Puleo
Pulgram, Ernst 1915- 49-52
Puligandla, Ramakrishna 1930- CANR-7
Earlier sketch in CA 61-64
Pulis, Clifford A(lton) 1916- 116
Pulitzer, Joseph 1847-1911 Brief entry 114
See also DLB 23
Pulitzer, Joseph, Jr. 1885-1955 .... DLB-29
Pulkingham, Betty (Jane) 1928- CANR-8
Earlier sketch in CA 61-64
Pulkingham, W(illiam) Graham 1926- 53-56
Pullapilly, Cyriac K(alapura) 1932- 61-64
Pullar, Philippa 1935- Brief entry 116
Pullein-Thompson, Christine
See Popescu, Christine
See also SATA 3
Pullein-Thompson, Denis
See Cannan, Denis
Pullein-Thompson, Diana
See Farr, Diana (Pullein-Thompson)
See also SATA 3
Pullein-Thompson, Joanna Maxwell
1898-1961 106
Pullein-Thompson, Josephine (Mary
Wedderburn) CANR-20
Earlier sketches in CA 7-8R, CANR-7
See also SATA 3
Pullen, John James 1913- 19-20R
Pulliam, Eugene C(ollins) 1889-1975
Obituary 89-92
See also AITN 2
Pulliam, H(oward) Ronald 1945- 114
Pulliam, Myrta 1947- 97-100
Pullias, Earl V(ivon) 1907- CAP-1
Earlier sketch in CA 11-12
Pulling, Albert Van Siclen 1891- 53-56
Pulling, Christopher Robert Druce 1893- .. CAP-1
Earlier sketch in CA 13-14
Pulling, Pierre
See Pulling, Albert Van Siclen
Pulman, Jack 1928(?)-1979 Obituary 85-88
Pulman, Michael Barraclough 1933- 33-36R
Pulos, William L(eroy) 1920- 45-48
Pulsipher, Gerreld L(ewis) 1939- 101
Pulzer, Peter George Julius 1929- 15-16R
Pumphrey, H(enry) George 1912- 13-14R
Pumroy, Donald K(eith) 1925- 49-52
Punch, Maurice 1941- 65-68
Pundeff, Marin 1921- 11-12R
Pundt, Helen Marie 7-8R
Punekar, Shankar Mokashi
See Mokashi-Punekar, Shankar
Puner, Helen W(alker) 1915- CANR-2
Earlier sketch in CA 7-8R
See also SATA 37
Puner, Morton 1921- 73-76
Punnett, R(obert) M(alcolm) 1936- 25-28R
Purcal, John T(homas) 1931- 33-36R
Purcell, Arthur Henry 1944- 102
Purcell, Donald 1916- 122
Purcell, Gillis Philip 1904-1987 Obituary 124
Purcell, H(ugh) D(ominic) 1932- CANR-17
Earlier sketch in CA 25-28R
Purcell, Mary 1906- CANR-2
Earlier sketch in CA 7-8R
Purcell, Roy E(verett) 1936- CANR-6
Earlier sketch in CA 57-60
Purcell, Sally 1944- 49-52
Purcell, Susan Kaufman 1942- Brief entry .. 114
Purcell, Theodore V(incent) 1911-1984 ... 41-44R
Obituary 112
Purcell, Victor 1896-1965 .... 5-6R
Purchase, Elspeth (Sandilands) 1940- 108
Purdom, Charles B(enjamin) 1883-1965 .. CAP-1
Earlier sketch in CA 9-10
Purdom, P(aul) Walton 1917- 57-60
Purdom, Thomas E. 1936- 15-16R
Purdom, Tom
See Purdom, Thomas E.
Purdon, Eric (Sinclaire) 1913- 93-96
Purdue, A(rthur) W(illiam) 1941- 124
Purdue, Bill
See Purdue, A(rthur) W(illiam)
Purdy, A(lfred) W(ellington) 1918- 81-84
See also CLC 3, 6, 14
Purdy, Al
See Purdy, A(lfred) W(ellington)
Purdy, Alexander 1890-1976 Obituary 65-68
Purdy, Anne S. 1902(?)-1987 Obituary 122
Purdy, (Charles) Anthony 1932- 19-20R
Purdy, Captain Jim
See Gillelan, G(eorge) Howard
Purdy, James (Amos) 1923- CANR-19
Earlier sketch in CA 33-36R
See also CAAS 1
See also DLB 2
See also CLC 2, 4, 10, 28
Purdy, John David 1946- 122
Purdy, Ken W(illiam) 1913-1972
Obituary 37-40R
Purdy, Susan Gold 1939- CANR-10
Earlier sketch in CA 15-16R
See also SATA 8
Purdy, Theodore Martindale 1903-1979
Obituary 89-92
Pure, Simon
See Swinnerton, Frank Arthur
Purkey, Roy (Delbert) 1905- CAP-2
Earlier sketch in CA 23-24
Purkey, William Watson 1929- 29-32R
Purkis, John 1933- 97-100
Purkiser, W(estlake) T(aylor) 1910- CAP-1
Earlier sketch in CA 15-16
Purl, Sandy M. 1953- 122
Purnell, Idella 1901- 61-64
Purpel, David E(dward) 1932- 49-52
Purrington, Robert Daniel 1936- 122
Purscell, Phyllis 1934- 25-28R
See also SATA 7
Pursell, Carroll W(irth), Jr. 1932- 77-80
Purser, John Whitley 1942- 103
Purser, Philip John 1925- CANR-21
Earlier sketch in CA 104
Purtill, Richard L. 1931- 37-40R
Purton, Rowland W(illiam Crisby)
1925- CANR-4
Earlier sketch in CA 53-56
Purves, Alan C(arroll) 1931- CANR-9
Earlier sketch in CA 21-22R
Purvis, Charles C. 1902(?)-1985 Obituary .. 115
Puryear, Alvin N(elson) 1937- Brief entry ... 115
Puryear, Edgar F., Jr. 1930- 115
Pusey, Edward Bouverie 1800-1882 .... DLB-55
Pusey, Merlo John 1902-1985 .... 11-12R
Obituary 117
Pusey, Nathan Marsh 1907- 109
Pushkarev, Boris S. 1929- CANR-6
Earlier sketch in CA 7-8R
Pushkarev, Sergei Germanovich 1888- .. CANR-6
Earlier sketch in CA 7-8R
Pustay, John S(tephen) 1931- 19-20R
Putcamp, Luise, jr. 1924- 29-32R
Puthoff, Harold E(dward) 1936-
Brief entry 113
Putnam, Alice 1916- 112
Putnam, Arnold Oscar 1922- 11-12R
Putnam, Arthur Lee
See Alger, Horatio, Jr.
Putnam, Carleton 1901- 65-68
Putnam, Donald F(ulton) 1903- CAP-2
Earlier sketch in CA 29-32
Putnam, George Palmer 1814-1872 ...... DLB-3
Putnam, George Palmer 1887-1950
Brief entry 109
Putnam, Hilary 1926- 61-64
Putnam, J. Wesley
See Drago, Harry Sinclair
Putnam, Jackson K(eith) 1929- 29-32R
Putnam, John
See Beckwith, Burnham Putnam
Putnam, John Fay 1924(?)-1982 Obituary .. 106
Putnam, Michael Courtney Jenkins 1933- ... 105
Putnam, Peter B(rock) 1920- 85-88
See also SATA 30
Putnam, Robert D(avid) 1941- CANR-10
Earlier sketch in CA 65-68
Putnam, Robert E. 1933- CANR-19
Earlier sketches in CA 53-56, CANR-5
Putnam, Roy Clayton 1928- 69-72
Putnam, Samuel Whitehall 1892-1950
Brief entry 107
See also DLB 4
Putney, Gail J.
See Fullerton, Gail Jackson
Putra, Kerala
See Panikkar, K(avalam) Madhava
Putt, Robert C. 1938- 120
Putt, S(amuel) Gorley 1913- CANR-6
Earlier sketch in CA 7-8R
Putter, Irving 1917- 65-68
Putter, Polly
See Adomeit, Ruth E(lizabeth)
Putterman, Ron 1946- 108
Puttfarken, Thomas 1943- 122
Putz, Louis J. 1909- CAP-1
Earlier sketch in CA 13-14
Putzar, Edward (David) 1930- 41-44R
Putzel, Max 1910- 11-12R
Putzel, Michael 1942- 73-76
Puxon, Grattan 1939- 81-84
Puzo, Mario 1920- CANR-4
Earlier sketch in CA 65-68
See also DLB 6
See also CLC 1, 2, 6, 36
Pybus, Rodney 1938- 107
Pye, (John) David 1932- 25-28R
Pye, Lloyd (Anthony, Jr.) 1946- 77-80
Pye, Lucian W(ilmot) 1921- 23-24R
Pye, Norman 1913- 109
Pyk, Ann Phillips 1937- 77-80
Pyke, Helen Godfrey 1941- 29-32R
Pyke, Magnus 1908- CANR-6
Earlier sketch in CA 13-14R
Pyle, A(lbert) M(offett) 1945- 123
Pyle, Ernest Taylor 1900-1945 Brief entry .. 115
Pyle, Ernie
See Pyle, Ernest Taylor
See also DLB 29
Pyle, (William) Fitzroy 1907- CAP-2
Earlier sketch in CA 29-32
Pyle, Hilary 1936- 77-80
Pyle, Howard 1853-1911 Brief entry 109
See also SATA 16
See also DLB 42
Pyles, Aitken
See McDavid, Raven I(oor), Jr.
Pyles, Thomas 1905- 15-16R
Pylyshyn, Zenon W(alter) 1937- 29-32R
Pym, Barbara (Mary Crampton)
1913-1980 .... CANR-13
Obituary 97-100
Earlier sketches in CA 13-14, CAP-1
See also DLB 14
See also CLC 13, 19, 37
Pym, Christopher 1929- 13-14R
Pym, Denis 1936- 25-28R
Pym, Dora Olive (Ivens) 1890- CAP-1
Earlier sketch in CA 13-14
Pym, Michael 1890(?)-1983 Obituary 109
Pynchon, Thomas 1937- CANR-22
Earlier sketch in CA 19-20R
See also DLB 2
See also CLC 2, 3, 6, 9, 11, 18, 33
Pyne, Mable Mandeville 1903-1969 .... 4R
Obituary 103
See also SATA 9
Pyne, Stephen J(oseph) 1949- 106
Pynn, Ronald 1942- 85-88
Pyrnelle, Louise-Clarke 1850-1907 ...... DLB-42
Pyros, John 1931- 77-80
Pytchely, R. F. St. B.
See Cowie, Donald

Q

Q
See Quiller-Couch, Arthur Thomas
Qadar, Basheer
See Alexander, C(harles) K(halil)
Qazzaz, Ayad (Sayyid Ali) Al
See Al-Qazzaz, Ayad (Sayyid Ali)
Qian Hao 1925- 111
Qoboza, Percy 1938-1988 Obituary 124
Qroll
See Dagerman, Stig (Halvard)

INDEX

Quackenbush, Margery (Carlson) 1943- ... 73-76
Quackenbush, Robert M(ead) 1929- ... CANR-17
Earlier sketches in CA 45-48, CANR-2
See also SATA 7
Quad, M.
See Lewis, Charles Bertrand
Quade, Quentin Lon 1933- Brief entry ... 106
Quaife, Milo Milton 1880-1959 Brief entry ... 114
Quain, Edwin A. 1906(?)-1975 Obituary ... 61-64
Quale, G(ladys) Robina 1931- ... 23-24R
Qualey, Carlton C(hester) 1904- ... 77-80
Qualter, Terence H(all) 1925- ... 37-40R
Quammen, David 1948- ... 29-32R
See also SATA 7
Quanbeck, Philip A. 1927- ... 25-28R
Quandt, B. Jean 1932- ... 33-36R
Quandt, Richard E(meric) 1930- ... 45-48
Quandt, William B. 1941- ... 29-32R
Quantrill, Malcolm 1931- ... 13-14R
Quarles, Benjamin 1904- ... CANR-16
Earlier sketches in CA 2R, CANR-1
See also SATA 12
Quarles, John R(hodes), Jr. 1935- ... CANR-15
Earlier sketch in CA 65-68
Quarm, Daisy 1948- ... 122
Quarmby, Arthur 1934- ... 45-48
Quarrie, Bruce (Roy Bryant) 1947- ... 103
Quartermain, James
See Lynne, James Broom
Quartermain, Peter (Allan) 1934- ... 117
Quasimodo, Salvatore 1901-1968 ... CAP-1
Obituary ... 25-28R
Earlier sketch in CA 15-16
See also CLC 10
Quastel, J. H.
See Quastel, Juda Hirsch
Quastel, Juda Hirsch 1899-1987 Obituary ... 123
Quasten, Johannes 1900- ... 9-10R
Quay, Herbert C. 1927- ... 13-14R
Quayle, Eric 1921- ... 21-22R
Qubain, Fahim I(ssa) 1924- ... 3R
Quebedeaux, Richard (Anthony) 1944- . CANR-12
Earlier sketch in CA 73-76
Queen, Ellery
See Dannay, Frederic
and Lee, Manfred B(ennington)
See also CLC 3, 11
Queen, Ellery, Jr.
See Dannay, Frederic
and Holding, James (Clark Carlisle, Jr.)
and Lee, Manfred B(ennington)
Queen, Stuart Alfred 1890- ... 23-24R
Queen Wilhelmina
See Nassau, Wilhelmina Helena Pauline Maria
Quelch, John A(nthony) 1951- ... 112
Queller, Donald E(dward) 1925- ... CANR-4
Earlier sketch in CA 53-56
Queneau, Raymond 1903-1976 ... 77-80
Obituary ... 69-72
See also CLC 2, 5, 10, 42
Quenelle, Gilbert 1914- ... 25-28R
Quennell, Marjorie Courtney 1884-1972 ... 73-76
See also SATA 29
Quennell, Peter (Courtney) 1905- ... 115
Brief entry ... 113
Quentin, Patrick
See Wheeler, Hugh (Callingham)
Querry, Ronald B(urns) 1943- ... 117
Query, William T(heodore), Jr. 1929- ... 41-44R
Quesnell, John G(eorge) 1936- ... CANR-1
Earlier sketch in CA 45-48
Quesnell, Quentin 1927- ... 120
Quest, Linda (Gerber) 1935- ... 77-80
Quest, (Edna) Olga W(ilbourne) Hall
See Hall-Quest, (Edna) Olga W(ilbourne)
Quest, Rodney ... CAP-2
Earlier sketch in CA 29-32
Quester, George H. 1936- ... CANR-10
Earlier sketch in CA 25-28R
Quezada, Abel 1920- ... 7-8R
Quichot, Dona
See Tomkiewicz, Mina
Quick, Annabelle 1922- ... 23-24R
See also SATA 2
Quick, Armand James 1894-1978
Obituary ... 73-76
Quick, Philip
See Strage, Mark
Quick, Thomas L(ee) 1929- ... 41-44R
Quickel, Stephen (Woodside) 1936- ... 73-76
Quie, Gretchen 1927- ... 117
Quiery, William H. 1926- ... 23-24R
Quigg, Jane (Hulda) ?-1986 Obituary ... 120
See also SATA 49
Quigg, Philip W. 1920- ... 11-12R
Quigless, Helen Gordon 1944- Brief entry ... 105
Quigley, Aileen 1930- ... 124
Brief entry ... 104
Quigley, Austin E(dmund) 1942- ... 101
Quigley, Carroll 1910-1977 ... 37-40R
Obituary ... 69-72
Quigley, Eileen Elliott
See Vivers, Eileen Elliott
Quigley, Ellen 1955- ... 111
Quigley, Harold Scott 1889-1968 ... 3R
Obituary ... 103
Quigley, Joan ... 29-32R
Quigley, John 1927- ... 19-20R
Quigley, John M(ichael) 1942- ... 110
Brief entry ... 107
Quigley, Martin (Peter) 1913- ... CANR-18
Earlier sketch in CA 19-20R
Quigley, Martin, Jr. 1917- ... CANR-17
Earlier sketch in CA 4R
Quilici, Folco 1930- ... 105
Quill
See Grange, Cyril
Quill, Barnaby
See Brandner, Gary
Quill, Monica
See McInerny, Ralph
Quiller, Andrew
See Bulmer, (Henry) Kenneth
Quiller-Couch, Arthur Thomas 1863-1944
Brief entry ... 118
Quilligan, Maureen 1944- ... CANR-16
Earlier sketch in CA 89-92
Quimber, Mario
See Alexander, C(harles) K(halil)
Quimby, George Irving 1913- ... 57-60
Quimby, Myron J. ... 25-28R
Quimby, Myrtle 1891- ... CAP-2
Earlier sketch in CA 25-28
Quin, Ann (Marie) 1936-1973 ... 11-12R
Obituary ... 45-48
See also DLB 14
See also CLC 6
Quin, Mike
See Ryan, Paul William
Quince, Peter
See Day, George Harold
Quince, Peter Lum
See Ritchie, (Harry) Ward
Quincunx, Ramona J.
See Borgmann, Dmitri A(lfred)
Quincy, Samuel 1734-1789 ... DLB-31
Quinderpunte, Raoul (Cornelius)
1907- ... CANR-15
Earlier sketch in CA 85-88
Quine, Willard Van Orman 1908- ... CANR-16
Earlier sketches in CA 4R, CANR-1
Quin-Harkin, Janet 1941- ... CANR-15
Earlier sketch in CA 81-84
See also SATA 18
Quinlan, Red
See Quinlan, Sterling C(arroll)
Quinlan, Sterling C(arroll) 1916- ... CANR-8
Earlier sketch in CA 5-6R
Quinley, Harold E(arl) 1942- ... 61-64
Quinn, A(lexander) James 1932- ... 29-32R
Quinn, Anthony (Rudolph Oaxaca) 1915-
Brief entry ... 111
Quinn, Arthur 1942- ... 110
Quinn, (Mary) Bernetta 1915- ... 105
Quinn, Charles (Nicholas) 1930- ... 123
Quinn, Charles Nicholas 1930- Brief entry ... 110
Quinn, David B(eers) 1909- ... CANR-15
Earlier sketch in CA 77-80
Quinn, Edward 1932- ... 77-80
Quinn, Elisabeth 1881-1962 ... SATA-22
Quinn, Esther Casier 1922- ... 7-8R
Quinn, Francis X. 1932- ... CANR-4
Earlier sketch in CA 11-12R
Quinn, Herbert F(urlong) 1910- ... CAP-1
Earlier sketch in CA 19-20
Quinn, James 1919- ... 15-16R
Quinn, James Brian 1928- ... 13-14R
Quinn, Jane Bryant 1939- ... 93-96
Quinn, John Francis 1925- Brief entry ... 115
Quinn, John M(ichael) 1922- ... 45-48
Quinn, John Paul 1943- ... 33-36R
Quinn, John R. 1938- ... 97-100
Quinn, Kenneth (Fleming) 1920- ... CANR-17
Earlier sketch in CA 25-28R
Quinn, Martin
See Smith, Martin Cruz
Quinn, Michael A(lan) 1945- ... 45-48
Quinn, Niall 1943- ... 108
Quinn, R(obert) M(acLean) 1920- ... 23-24R
Quinn, Sally 1941- ... 65-68
See also AITN 2
Quinn, Seabury (Grandin) 1889-1969 ... 108
Obituary ... 104
Quinn, Simon
See Smith, Martin Cruz
Quinn, Sister Bernetta
See Quinn, (Mary) Bernetta
Quinn, Susan 1940- ... 103
Quinn, Terry 1945- ... CANR-18
Earlier sketch in CA 101
Quinn, Vernon
See Quinn, Elisabeth
Quinn, Vincent 1926- ... 23-24R
Quinn, William Arthur 1920- ... 7-8R
Quinn, Zdenka (Hodbodova) 1942- ... 33-36R
Quinnett, Paul G(uthrie) 1939- ... 114
Quinney, Richard 1934- ... CANR-9
Earlier sketch in CA 57-60
Quinones, Ricardo J(oseph) 1935-
Brief entry ... 112
Quint, Barbara Gilder 1928- ... 103
Quint, Bert 1930- ... 69-72
Quint, Howard H. 1917- ... 97-100
Quint, Jeanne
See Benoliel, Jeanne Quint
Quintal, Claire 1930- ... 15-16R
Quintana, Bertha B(eatrice) 1924-
Brief entry ... 113
Quintana, Frances
See Swadesh, Frances Leon
Quintana, Ricardo (Beckwith) 1898- ... 25-28R
Quintanilla, Maria Aline Griffith y Dexter,
Condesa de 1921- ... 11-12R
Quinto, Leon 1926- ... 37-40R
Quinton, Anthony Meredith 1925- ... CANR-10
Earlier sketch in CA 23-24R
Quirarte, Jacinto 1931- ... 45-48
Quirin, G(eorge) David 1931- ... CANR-9
Earlier sketch in CA 21-22R
Quirin, William L(ouis) 1942- ... 93-96
Quirk, James P(atrick) 1926- ... CANR-7
Earlier sketch in CA 57-60
Quirk, John E(dward) 1920- ... 5-6R
Quirk, Lawrence J. 1923- ... CANR-12
Earlier sketch in CA 25-28R
Quirk, Paul J. 1949- ... 108
Quirk, Randolph 1920- ... CANR-2
Earlier sketch in CA 7-8R
Quirk, Robert E. 1918- ... 2R
Quirk, Thomas Vaughan 1946- ... 122
Quirk, Tom
See Quirk, Thomas Vaughan
Quiroga, Horacio 1878-1937 Brief entry ... 117
See also TCLC 20
Quispel, Gilles 1916- ... 89-92
Quist, Susan 1944- ... 57-60
Quitslund, Sonya A(ntoinette) 1935- ... CANR-1
Earlier sketch in CA 49-52
Quoirez, Francoise 1935- ... CANR-6
Earlier sketch in CA 49-52
See also CLC 9
Quoist, Michel 1921- ... 65-68
Quong, Rose Lanu 1879(?)-1972
Obituary ... 37-40R
Qureshi, Ishtiaq Husain 1903- ... CAP-1
Earlier sketch in CA 11-12

R

R
See Rees, (Morgan) Goronwy
R. R.
See Iyengar, K(odaganallur)
R(amaswami) Srinivasa
Ra, Jong Oh 1945- ... 85-88
Raab, Lawrence 1946- ... 65-68
Raab, Menachem 1923- ... 114
Raab, Robert Allen 1924- ... 29-32R
Raab, Selwyn 1934- ... 73-76
Raack, R(ichard) C(harles) 1928- ... 41-44R
Ra'Anan, Gavriel D. 1954(?)-1983
Obituary ... 110
Ra'Anan, H. F. Frischwasser
See Ra'Anan, Uri
Ra'Anan, Uri 1926- ... 108
Raat, W(illiam) Dirk 1939- ... CANR-23
Earlier sketch in CA 106
Rabalais, Maria 1921- ... 61-64
Raban, Jonathan 1942- ... CANR-17
Earlier sketch in CA 61-64
Rabassa, Gregory 1922- ... CANR-2
Earlier sketch in CA 45-48
Rabasseire, Henri
See Pachter, Henry M(aximilian)
Rabb, Theodore K. 1937- ... CANR-10
Earlier sketch in CA 21-22R
Rabbie
See Towers, Maxwell
Rabbitt, Thomas 1943- ... 57-60
Rabdau, Marianne
See Bakker-Rabdau, Marianne K(atherine)
Rabe, Berniece (Louise) 1928- ... CANR-1
Earlier sketch in CA 49-52
See also SATA 7
Rabe, David (William) 1940- ... 85-88
See also DLB 7
See also CLC 4, 8, 33
Rabe, Olive H(anson) ?-1968 ... CAP-2
Earlier sketch in CA 19-20
See also SATA 13
Rabe, Stephen G(eorge) 1948- ... 108
Raben, Joseph 1924- ... CANR-12
Earlier sketch in CA 69-72
Rabie, Jan 1920- ... 29-32R
Rabikovitz, Dalia 1936- Brief entry ... 108
Rabikovitz, Dalyah
See Rabikovitz, Dalia
Rabil, Albert, Jr. 1934- ... CANR-10
Earlier sketch in CA 25-28R
Rabin, A(lbert) I(srael) 1912- ... CANR-19
Earlier sketches in CA 53-56, CANR-4
Rabin, Chaim 1915- ... 105
Rabin, Edward H(arold) 1937- ... 49-52
Rabin, Yitzhak 1922- Brief entry ... 111
Rabinovich, Abraham 1933- ... 61-64
Rabinovich, Isaiah 1904-1972 ... CAP-2
Earlier sketch in CA 25-28
Rabinovitch, Sholem 1859-1916
Brief entry ... 104
Rabinovitz, Rubin 1938- ... 21-22R
Rabinow, Paul 1944- ... CANR-13
Earlier sketch in CA 61-64
Rabinowich, Ellen 1946- ... 106
See also SATA 29
Rabinowicz, Mordka Harry 1919- ... 5-6R
Rabinowitch, Alexander 1934- ... 23-24R
Rabinowitch, Eugene 1901-1973 ... 77-80
Obituary ... 41-44R
Rabinowitz, Alan 1927- ... 29-32R
Rabinowitz, Ezekiel 1892- ... 25-28R
Rabinowitz, Howard Neil 1942- ... 105
Rabinowitz, Louis Isaac 1906-1984
Obituary ... 113
Rabinowitz, Peter MacGarr 1956- ... 104
Rabinowitz, Sandy 1954- ... 103
See also SATA 39
Rabinowitz, Solomon
See Rabinovitch, Sholem
Rabins, Peter V(incent) 1947- ... 109
Rabkin, Brenda 1945- ... 101
Rabkin, Eric S. 1946- ... CANR-4
Earlier sketch in CA 49-52
Rabkin, Gerald Edward 1930- Brief entry ... 105
Rabkin, Norman C. 1930- ... CANR-4
Earlier sketch in CA 3R
Rabkin, Richard 1932- ... 33-36R
Rable, George C(alvin) 1950- ... 116
Raboff, Ernest Lloyd ... SATA-37
Raborg, Frederick A(shton), Jr. 1934- .. CANR-20
Earlier sketch in CA 103
Rabow, Gerald 1928- ... 25-28R
Rabushka, Alvin 1940- Brief entry ... 116
Rabuzzi, Kathryn Allen 1938- ... 113
Raby, Derek Graham 1927- ... 103
Raby, William L(ouis) 1927- ... CANR-23
Earlier sketches in CA 19-20R, CANR-8
Race, Jeffrey 1943- ... 37-40R
Race, Robert Russell 1907-1984 Obituary .. 113
Racevskis, Karlis 1939- ... 117
Rachleff, Owen S(pencer) 1934- ... CANR-14
Earlier sketch in CA 21-22R
Rachlin, Carol K(ing) 1919- ... 57-60
Rachlin, Harvey (Brant) 1951- ... 107
See also SATA 47
Rachlin, Nahid ... CANR-14
Earlier sketch in CA 81-84
Rachlis, Eugene (Jacob) 1920-1986 ... 5-6R
Obituary ... 121
See also SATA 50
Rachman, David Jay 1928- ... 57-60
Rachman, Stanley Jack 1934- ... 89-92
Rachow, Louis A(ugust) 1927- ... 57-60
Racina, Thom 1946- ... CANR-12
Earlier sketch in CA 73-76
Rack, Henry D(enman) 1931- ... 15-16R
Racker, Efraim 1913- ... 89-92
Rackham, Arthur 1867-1939 ... SATA-15
Rackham, John
See Phillifent, John Thomas
Rackham, Thomas W(illiam) 1919- ... 25-28R
Rackin, Phyllis 1933- ... 85-88
Rackman, Emanuel 1910- ... 29-32R
Rackowe, Alec 1897- ... 25-28R
Rad, Gerhard von
See von Rad, Gerhard
Radan, G. T.
See Radan, George T(ivadar)
Radan, George T(ivadar) 1923- ... 116
Radbill, Samuel X. 1901- ... 49-52
Radcliff, Alan L(awrence) 1920- ... 49-52
Radcliff, Peter (Edward, Jr.) 1932- ... 21-22R
Radcliffe, Ann 1764-1823 ... DLB-39
Radcliffe, George L. 1878(?)-1974
Obituary ... 53-56
Radcliffe, Janette
See Roberts, Janet Louise
Radcliffe, Lynn J. 1896- ... 2R
Radcliffe, Philip (Fitzhugh) 1905-1986
Obituary ... 120
Radcliffe, Virginia
See Hurst, Virginia Radcliffe
Radcliffe-Brown, A(lfred) R(eginald)
1881-1955 Brief entry ... 114
Radcliff-Umstead, Douglas 1944- ... CANR-13
Earlier sketch in CA 33-36R
Raddall, Thomas Head 1903- ... 2R
Raddysh, Garry
See Radison, Garry
Radel, John J(oseph) 1934- ... 29-32R
Radelet, Louis A(ugust) 1917- ... 89-92
Rader, Benjamin G(ene) 1935- ... 21-22R
Rader, Dotson 1942- ... CANR-11
Earlier sketch in CA 61-64
Rader, Melvin (Miller) 1903-1981 ... CANR-5
Earlier sketch in CA 13-14R
Rader, Ralph Wilson 1930- ... 13-14R
Rader, Randall R(ay) 1949- ... 121
Rader, Rosemary 1931- ... 112
Rader, (John) Trout (III) 1938- ... 37-40R
Radest, Howard B(ernard) 1928- ... 41-44R
Radford, Edwin Isaac 1891- ... 104
Radford, John 1901-1967 ... CAP-2
Earlier sketch in CA 21-22
Radford, Richard F(rancis), Jr. 1939- .. CANR-20
Earlier sketch in CA 104
Radford, Ruby L(orraine) 1891-1971 ... CANR-4
Earlier sketch in CA 3R
See also SATA 6
Radha, Sivananda 1911- ... 114
Radhakrishnan, C(hakkorayil) 1939- ... 57-60
Radhakrishnan, Sarvepalli 1888-1975 ... CAP-1
Obituary ... 57-60
Earlier sketch in CA 15-16
Radice, Betty 1912-1985 ... CANR-12
Obituary ... 115
Earlier sketch in CA 25-28R
Radice, Giles 1936- ... CANR-17
Earlier sketch in CA 25-28R
Radiguet, Raymond 1903-1923 ... DLB-65
Radimsky, Ladislaw 1898-1970
Obituary ... 29-32R
Radin, Edward D(avid) 1909-1966
Obituary ... 114
Radin, George 1896-1981 Obituary ... 102
Radin, Paul 1883-1959 Brief entry ... 120
Radin, Ruth Yaffe 1938- ... 124
Radison, Garry 1949- ... 117
Radke, Don 1940- ... 57-60
Radl, Shirley L(ouise) 1935- ... CANR-12
Earlier sketch in CA 69-72
Radlauer, David 1952- ... 106
See also SATA 28
Radlauer, Edward 1921- ... CANR-13
Earlier sketch in CA 69-72
See also SATA 15
Radlauer, Ruth Shaw 1926- ... CANR-13
Earlier sketch in CA 81-84
See also SATA 15
Radler, D(on) H. 1926- ... 13-14R
Radley, Eric John 1917- ... 109
Radley, Gail 1951- ... CANR-16
Earlier sketch in CA 89-92
See also SATA 25
Radley, Paul John 1962- ... 121

Radley, Virginia L. 1927- 25-28R
Radner, Roy 1927- 49-52
Radnoti, Miklos 1909-1944 Brief entry 118
See also TCLC 16
Rado, Alexander
See Rado, Sandor
Rado, James 1939- 105
See also CLC 17
Rado, Sandor 1900-1981 109
Obituary 105
Radoff, Morris L(eon) 1905-1978 85-88
Obituary 81-84
Radom, Matthew 1905- 57-60
Radosh, Ronald 1937- 101
Radtke, Guenter 1920- 110
Radtke, Gunter
See Radtke, Guenter
Radvanyi, Janos 1922- 41-44R
Radvanyi, Netty 1900-1983 85-88
Obituary 110
Radwanski, Pierre A(rthur) 1903- CAP-2
Earlier sketch in CA 23-24
Radwanski-Szinagel, Dr. Pierre A.
See Radwanski, Pierre A(rthur)
Radway, Ann
See Geis, Richard E(rwin)
Radway, Janice A(nne) 1949- 121
Radyr, Tomos
See Haldane-Stevenson, James Patrick
Radzinowicz, Leon 1906- 106
Rae, Daphne 1933- 109
Rae, (Margaret) Doris 1907- CANR-15
Earlier sketches in CA 11-12, CAP-1
Rae, Douglas W(hiting) 1939- 77-80
Rae, Evonne 1928-1974 Obituary 104
Rae, Gwynedd 1892-1977 65-68
See also SATA 37
Rae, Hugh C(rauford) 1935- CANR-8
Earlier sketch in CA 19-20R
Rae, John B(ell) 1911- 13-14R
Rae, John Malcolm 1931- CANR-4
Earlier sketch in CA 2R
Rae, Milford Andersen 1946- CANR-8
Earlier sketch in CA 61-64
Rae, Rusty
See Rae, Milford Andersen
Rae, Walter 1916- 57-60
Rae, Wesley D(ennis) 1932- 23-24R
Raebeck, Lois 1921- 13-14R
See also SATA 5
Raeburn, Antonia 1934- 101
Raeburn, John (Hay) 1941- 57-60
See also CLC 34
Raeburn, Michael 1940- 107
Raeburn, Michael 1943- 103
Raef, Laura (Gladys) C(auble) CANR-11
Earlier sketch in CA 29-32R
Raeff, Marc 1923- 61-64
Rael, Leyla 1948- 106
Raeschild, Sheila 1936- CANR-22
Earlier sketch in CA 105
Rafael, Gideon 1913- Brief entry 106
Rafelson, Bob 1933(?)- Brief entry 112
Raffa, Frederick Anthony 1944- 53-56
Raffaele, Joseph A(ntonio) 1916- CANR-8
Earlier sketch in CA 7-8R
Raffel, Burton 1928- CANR-7
Earlier sketch in CA 11-12R
Raffelock, David 1897- CAP-2
Earlier sketch in CA 25-28
See also AITN 1
Rafferty, Kathleen Kelly 1915-1981
Obituary 103
Rafferty, Max L. 1917-1982 .... CANR-1
Obituary 107
Earlier sketch in CA 2R
Rafferty, Milton 1932- 101
Rafferty, S.S.
See Hurley, John J(erome)
Raffini, James O. 1941- 117
Raftery, Gerald (Bransfield) 1905- CAP-1
Earlier sketch in CA 13-14
See also SATA 11
Ragan, David 1925- 65-68
Ragan, Sam(uel Talmadge) 1915- 15-16R
Ragan, William Burk 1896-1973 .... CANR-2
Earlier sketch in CA 3R
Ragaway, Martin A(rnold) 1928- CANR-12
Earlier sketch in CA 61-64
Ragen, Joseph E(dward) 1897-1971 ..... CAP-2
Obituary 33-36R
Earlier sketch in CA 21-22
Raghavan, Manayath D. 1892- CAP-2
Earlier sketch in CA 19-20
Ragins, Sanford 117
Raglan, Baron
See Raglan, FitzRoy
Raglan, FitzRoy 1885-1964 ....7-8R
Ragni, Gerome 1942- 105
See also CLC 17
Rago, Henry Anthony 1915-1969 .... CAP-2
Earlier sketch in CA 25-28
Rago, Louis J(oseph von) 1924- 9-10R
Ragosta, Millie J(ane) 1931- CANR-12
Earlier sketch in CA 73-76
Ragsdale, Ray W(aldo) 1909- 45-48
Ragsdale, W(arner) B(ernice) 1898-1986 ..73-76
Obituary 121
Raguin, Yves (Emile) 1912- 81-84
Ragusa, Olga (M.) 1922- 122
Rahill, Peter J(ames) 1910- 5-6R
Rahim, Enayetur 1938- 107
Rahl, James A(ndrew) 1917- 77-80
Rahm, David A. 1931- 57-60
Rahman, Abdul
See Wayman, Tony Russell
Rahn, Joan Elma 1929- CANR-13
Earlier sketch in CA 37-40R
See also SATA 27
Rahner, Karl 1904-1984 109
Obituary 112
Rahner, Raymond M. 101
Rahsepar
See Yar-Shater, Ehsan O(llah)
Rahtjen, Bruce D(onald) 1933- 21-22R
Rahv, Betty T(homas) 1931- 105
Rahv, Philip
See Greenberg, Ivan
See also CLC 24
Rai, Kul B(husan) 1937- 105
Rai, Navab
See Srivastava, Dhanpat Rai
Raia, Anthony P(aul) 1928- 61-64
Raible, Alton (Robert) 1918- SATA-35
Raiff, Stan 1930- 61-64
See also SATA 11
Railton, Esther P(auline) 1929- 101
Raimi, Sam(uel M.) 1959- 123
Raimond, C. E.
See Robins, Elizabeth
Raimy, Eric 1942- 93-96
Raimy, Victor 1913- 81-84
Rainbird, George (Meadus) 1905-1986
Obituary 120
Rainbow-Wind, Shandor
See Weiss, (Paul) Shandor
Raine, Craig 1944- 108
See also DLB 40
See also CLC 32
Raine, Kathleen (Jessie) 1908- 85-88
See also DLB 20
See also CLC 7, 45
Raine, Norman Reilly 1895-1971
Obituary 33-36R
Raine, Richard
See Sawkins, Raymond H(arold)
Rainer, George
See Greenburger, Ingrid Elisabeth
Rainer, Julia
See Goode, Ruth
Raines, Howell (Hiram) 1943- 73-76
Raines, John C. 1933- 73-76
Raines, Robert A(rnold) 1926- CANR-7
Earlier sketch in CA 13-14R
Raines, Shirley (Carol) 1945- 113
Rainey, Bill G. 1926- 89-92
Rainey, Buck
See Rainey, Bill G.
Rainey, Gene E(dward) 1934- 25-28R
Rainey, Homer Price 1896-1985 Obituary ... 118
Rainey, Patricia Ann 1937- 49-52
Rainey, W. B.
See Blassingame, Wyatt Rainey
Rainham, Thomas
See Barren, Charles (MacKinnon)
Rainsberger, Todd J(effrey) 1951- 106
Rainsford, George Nichols 1928- 49-52
Raintree, Lee
See Sellers, Con(nie Leslie, Jr.)
Rainwater, (Mary) Catherine 1953- 119
Rainwater, Dorothy T(hornton) 1918- ... CANR-1
Earlier sketch in CA 45-48
Rainwater, Lee 1928- 53-56
Raistrick, Arthur 1896- CANR-3
Earlier sketch in CA 11-12R
Raisz, Erwin J(osephus) 1893-1968 .... 4R
Obituary 103
Raitt, A(lan) W(illiam) 1930- 29-32R
Raizis, M(arios) Byron 1931- 41-44R
Rajan, Balachandra 1920- 69-72
Rajan, M(annarswamighala) S(reeranga)
1920- CANR-13
Earlier sketch in CA 13-14R
Rajan, Tilottama 1951- 107
Rajanen, Aini 109
Rajaram
See Iyengar, K(odaganallur)
R(amaswami) Srinivasa
Rajasekharaiah, T(umkur) R(udraradhya)
1926- 33-36R
Rajec, Elizabeth M(olnar) 1931- 109
Rajneesh, Acharya 1931- 93-96
Rajneesh, Bhagwan Shree
See Rajneesh, Acharya
Rajski, Raymond B. 1917- 23-24R
Raju, Poolla Tirupati 1904- 33-36R
Rakel, Robert E(dwin) 1932- 107
Raknes, Ola 1887-1975 .... CAP-2
Earlier sketch in CA 29-32
Rako, Susan Mandell 1939- 117
Rakoff, Alvin 1927- 102
Rakosi, Carl
See Rawley, Callman
See also CAAS 5
See also CLC 47
Rakosi, Matyas 1892-1971 Obituary 29-32R
Rakove, Jack N(orman) 1947- 93-96
Rakove, Milton L(eon) 1918-1983 ..... CANR-15
Obituary 111
Earlier sketch in CA 65-68
Rakowski, James Peter 1945- 105
Rakowski, John 1922- 106
Rakstis, Ted J(ay) 1932- 101
Ralbovsky, Martin Paul 1942- 49-52
Rale, Nero
See Burgess, M(ichael) R(oy)
Raleigh, John Henry 1920- CANR-3
Earlier sketch in CA 2R
Raleigh, Richard
See Lovecraft, H(oward) P(hillips)
Raley, Harold (Cecil) 1934- 41-44R
Raley, Patricia E(ward) 1940- 73-76
Raley, Rowena
See McCulley, Johnston
Rallentando, H. P.
See Sayers, Dorothy L(eigh)
Ralph, David Clinton 1922- CANR-2
Earlier sketch in CA 5-6R
Ralph, Elizabeth K(ennedy) 1921- 33-36R
Ralph, Julian 1853-1903 .... DLB-23
Ralph, Margaret Nutting 1941- 121
Ralphs, Sheila 1923- 106
Ralston, Alma (Smith Payne) CANR-11
Earlier sketch in CA 19-20R
Ralston, Gilbert A(lexander) 1912- CANR-2
Earlier sketch in CA 45-48
Ralston, James Kenneth 1896- 49-52
Ralston, Jan
See Dunlop, Agnes M. R.
Ralston, Leonard F. 1925- 45-48
Ralston, Melvin B. 1937- 49-52
Ram, Immanuel
See Velikovsky, Immanuel
Rama
See Gupta, Ram Chandra
Rama, Swami
See Swami Rama
Ramacharaka, Yogi
See Atkinson, William Walker
Ramage, Edwin S(tephen) 1929- 65-68
Ramage, James A(lfred) 1940- 61-64
Ramal, Walter
See de la Mare, Walter (John)
Ramamurty, K(otamraju) Bhaskara 1924- ..53-56
Raman, Chandrasekhara Venkata
1888-1970 Obituary 113
Ramanujan, A(ttipat) K(rishnaswami)
1929- CANR-24
Earlier sketches in CA 19-20R, CANR-8
Ramanujan, Molly 1932- CANR-24
Earlier sketch in CA 29-32R
Ramanujan, Shouri
See Ramanujan, Molly
Rama Rau, Dhanvanthi (Handoo)
1893-1987 Obituary 123
Brief entry 106
Rama Rau, Santha
See Wattles, Santha Rama Rau
Ramaswamy, Mysore 1902- CAP-1
Earlier sketch in CA 13-14
Ramati, Alexander 1921- CANR-7
Earlier sketch in CA 13-14R
Ramati, Yohanan (Joseph) 1921- 111
Ramazani, Rouhollah K(aregar) 1928- .. CANR-10
Earlier sketch in CA 13-14R
Rambam, Cyvia
See Rambert, Marie
Rambam, Myriam
See Rambert, Marie
Rambeau, James (Morris) 1938- 117
Ramberg, Bennett 1946- 111
Rambert, Marie 1888-1982 103
Obituary 107
Rambo, Lewis Ray 1943- 109
Rame, David
See Divine, Arthur Durham
Rameh, Clea 1927- 53-56
Ramey, James W(alter) 1928- 112
Ramge, Sebastian Victor 1930- 11-12R
Ramirez, Carolyn H(olmes) 1933- CANR-2
Earlier sketch in CA 5-6R
Ramirez de Arellano, Diana 1919- 45-48
Ramis, Harold (Allen) 1944- Brief entry 124
Ramke, Bin 1947- CANR-14
Earlier sketch in CA 81-84
Ramm, Bernard L(awrence) 1916-
Brief entry 112
Rammelkamp, Julian S(turtevant) 1917- ..19-20R
Ramo, Simon 1913- Brief entry 111
Ramond, Charles K(night) 1930- 101
Ramos, Suzanne 1942- 101
Ramos-Oliveira, Antonio 1907-1973
Obituary 104
Ramp, Eugene A(ugust) 1942- 49-52
Rampa, Tuesday Lobsang
See Hoskin, Cyril Henry
Rampersad, Arnold CLC-44
Ramquist, Grace (Bess) Chapman
1907- CANR-3
Earlier sketch in CA 11-12R
Ramrus, Al 1930- 105
Rams, Edwin M(arion) 1922- 19-20R
Ramsaur, Ernest Edmondson, Jr. 1915- ..41-44R
Ramsay, David 1749-1815 .... DLB-30
Ramsay, J(ames) A(rthur) 1909-1988
Obituary 124
Ramsay, Raymond (Henry) 1927- 77-80
Ramsay, William M(cDowell) 1922- CANR-12
Earlier sketch in CA 15-16R
Ramsbottom, John 1885-1974 Obituary ...53-56
Ramsden, E. H. 102
Ramsden, Herbert 1927- 108
Ramsden, John Andrew 1947- 108
Ramsell, Donald 1926(?)-1983 Obituary 110
Ramsett, David E. 1942- 29-32R
Ramsey, Charles E(ugene) 1923- 15-16R
Ramsey, Dan(ny Clarence) 1945- 101
Ramsey, Eric
See Hagberg, David J(ames)
Ramsey, (Charles) Frederic, Jr. 1915- 7-8R
Ramsey, G(ordon) C(lark) 1941- CANR-9
Earlier sketch in CA 21-22R
Ramsey, George Wilson 1937- 113
Ramsey, Ian T(homas) 1915-1972 ...... CANR-4
Earlier sketch in CA 7-8R
Ramsey, Jackson E. 1938- 122
Ramsey, Jarold 1937- 33-36R
Ramsey, John F(raser) 1907- 49-52
Ramsey, Lee C(arter) 1935- 120
Ramsey, (Arthur) Michael 1904- CANR-14
Earlier sketch in CA 77-80
Ramsey, (Robert) Paul 1913-1988 ...... CANR-1
Obituary 124
Earlier sketch in CA 2R
Ramsey, Paul 1924- 41-44R
Ramsey, Paul W. 1905-1976 Obituary 69-72
Ramsey, Robert D. 1934- 25-28R
Ramsey, Roy S. 1920(?)-1976 Obituary ...65-68
Ramsey, Russell W. 1935- 124
Ramseyer, John A(lvin) 1908-1968 ..... CANR-4
Earlier sketch in CA 7-8R
Ramseyer, Lloyd L. 1899- CAP-2
Earlier sketch in CA 19-20
Ramskill, Valerie Patricia Roskams CAP-1
Earlier sketch in CA 9-10
Ramson, W(illiam) S(tanley) 1933- 45-48
Ramundo, Bernard A. 1925- 21-22R
Rana, J.
See Bhatia, Jamunadevi
Ranadive, Gail 1944- 53-56
See also SATA 10
Rand, Ann (Binkley) 106
See also SATA 30
Rand, Austin Loomer 1905- 89-92
Rand, Ayn 1905-1982 ....15-16R
Obituary 105
See also CLC 3, 30, 44
Rand, Brett
See Norwood, Victor G(eorge) C(harles)
Rand, Christopher 1912-1968 77-80
Rand, Clayton (Thomas) 1891-1971 ....5-6R
Obituary 29-32R
Rand, Earl (James) 1933- 23-24R
Rand, Frank Prentice 1889- CAP-1
Earlier sketch in CA 11-12
Rand, J. H.
See Holland, James R.
Rand, James S.
See Attenborough, Bernard George
Rand, Paul 1914- 23-24R
See also SATA 6
Rand, Peter 1942- 77-80
Rand, Willard J., Jr. 1913- 11-12R
Randal, Beatrice (a pseudonym) 1916- 61-64
Randal, Vera 1922- 11-12R
Randall, Belle 1940- 118
Randall, Bob 1937- 106
Randall, Charles Edgar 1897- 41-44R
Randall, Clarence Belden 1891-1967 ...... CAP-1
Earlier sketch in CA 13-14
Randall, Clay
See Adams, Clifton
Randall, Dale B(ertrand) J(onas) 1929- .. CANR-2
Earlier sketch in CA 5-6R
Randall, David A(nton) 1905-1975
Obituary 57-60
Randall, Diane
See Ross, W(illiam) E(dward) D(aniel)
Randall, Donald A. 1933- 61-64
Randall, Dudley (Felker) 1914- CANR-23
Earlier sketch in CA 25-28R
See also DLB 41
See also CLC 1
Randall, Florence Engel 1917- 41-44R
See also SATA 5
Randall, Francis Ballard 1931- 11-12R
Randall, Henry S. 1811-1876 .... DLB-30
Randall, J. G.
See Randall, James Garfield
Randall, James G.
See Randall, James Garfield
See also DLB 17
Randall, James Garfield 1881-1953
Brief entry 118
Randall, Janet
See Young, Janet Randall
and Young, Robert W(illiam)
Randall, Jo Anne Yarus 1942- 118
Randall, John E(rnest, Jr.) 1924- 65-68
Randall, John Herman, Jr. 1899-1980 .. CANR-1
Obituary 102
Earlier sketch in CA 3R
Randall, John L(eslie) 1933- 107
Randall, Joseph Hungerford 1897- 3R
Randall, Julia (Sawyer) 1923- 33-36R
Randall, Laura 1935- 37-40R
Randall, Lillian M. C. 1931- 23-24R
Randall, Margaret 1936- 41-44R
Randall, Marta 107
Randall, Mary
See Colver, Alice Mary (Ross)
Randall, Mercedes M. 1895-1977 ....15-16R
Obituary 69-72
Randall, Monica 1944- 97-100
Randall, Randolph C. 1900- 19-20R
Randall, Robert
See Silverberg, Robert
Randall, Ruth (Elaine) Painter 1892-1971 .... 1R
Obituary 103
See also SATA 3
Randall, Steven
See Andrews, Clarence A(delbert)
Randall, Willard Sterne 1942- 69-72
Randall-Mills, Elizabeth West 1906- 15-16R
Randel, William (Peirce) 1909- 13-14R
Randell, Beverley
See Price, Beverley Joan
Randell, John Bulmer 1918-1982 109
Obituary 106
Randers-Pehrson, Justine Davis 1910- 111
Randhawa, Mohinder Singh 1909- 29-32R
Randi, James 1928- 117
Randisi, Robert J(oseph) 1951- 116
Randles, Anthony V(ictor), Jr. 1942- 65-68
Randles, Slim
See Randles, Anthony V(ictor), Jr.

Randoll, Anthony
See Blacking, John (Anthony Randoll)
Randolph, A(sa) Philip 1889-1979
Obituary ... 85-88
Randolph, Arthur C.
See Greene, A(lvin) C(arl)
Randolph, Boynton, M.D.
See Ellis, Edward S(ylvester)
Randolph, David James 1934- ... CANR-3
Earlier sketch in CA 49-52
Randolph, Ellen
See Ross, W(illiam) E(dward) D(aniel)
Randolph, Geoffrey
See Ellis, Edward S(ylvester)
Randolph, Georgiana Ann 1908-1957
Brief entry ... 116
Randolph, Gordon
See von Block, Bela W(illiam)
and von Block, Sylvia
Randolph, J. H.
See Ellis, Edward S(ylvester)
Randolph, John 1915- ... 45-48
Randolph, Lieutenant J. H.
See Ellis, Edward S(ylvester)
Randolph, Marion
See Rodell, Marie F(reid)
Randolph, Melanie
See Ragosta, Millie J(ane)
Randolph, Nancy
See Robb, Inez (Callaway)
Randolph, Thomas 1605-1635 ... DLB-58
Randolph, Vance 1892- ... 105
Random, Alan
See Kay, Ernest
Random, Alex
See Rowland, D(onald) S(ydney)
Rands, William Brighty 1823-1882 ... SATA-17
Ranga, N. G. 1900- ... 29-32R
Ranganathan, S(hiyali) R(amamrita)
1892-1972 ... CANR-5
Earlier sketch in CA 5-6R
Range, Willard Edgar Allen 1910- ... 2R
Rangel, Carlos 1929-1988 ... 104
Obituary ... 124
Rangell, Leo 1913- ... 105
Ranger, Ken
See Creasey, John
Ranger, Paul 1933- ... 37-40R
Ranger, T(erence) O(sborn) 1929- ... CANR-19
Earlier sketch in CA 25-28R
Ranis, Gustav 1929- ... CANR-3
Earlier sketch in CA 11-12R
Ranis, Peter 1935- ... 41-44R
Ranjee
See Shahani, Ranjee
Rank, Benjamin (Keith) 1911- ... 109
Rank, Hugh (Duke) 1932- ... CANR-12
Earlier sketch in CA 73-76
Rank, Maureen Joy 1947- ... 117
Ranki, Gyoergy 1930-1988 Obituary ... 124
Rankin, Daniel S(tanislaus) 1895-1972 ... CAP-1
Earlier sketch in CA 15-16
Rankin, David J. 1945- ... 108
Rankin, Herbert David 1931- ... 103
Rankin, Hugh F(ranklin) 1913- ... CANR-1
Earlier sketch in CA 2R
Rankin, Jeannette 1880-1973 Obituary ... 41-44R
Rankin, Judith Torluemke 1945-
Brief entry ... 107
Rankin, Judy
See Rankin, Judith Torluemke
Rankin, Karl Lott 1898- ... CAP-1
Earlier sketch in CA 15-16
Rankin, Paula C(lark) 1945- ... CANR-21
Earlier sketch in CA 104
Rankin, Robert 1915- Brief entry ... 108
Rankin, Robert P(arks) 1912- ... 77-80
Rankin, Ruth (DeLone) I(rvine) 1924- ... 61-64
Rankine, John
See Mason, Douglas R(ankine)
Rankine, Paul Scott 1909(?)-1983
Obituary ... 109
Ranly, Ernest W. 1930- ... 37-40R
Ranney, Agnes V. 1916- ... 5-6R
See also SATA 6
Ranney, (Joseph) Austin 1920- ... 77-80
Rannit, Aleksis 1914-1985 Obituary ... 114
Brief entry ... 109
Ranous, Charles A. 1912- ... 15-16R
Ransel, David L(orimer) 1939- ... 73-76
Ransford, Oliver 1914- ... CANR-10
Earlier sketch in CA 21-22R
Ransley, Peter 1931- ... CANR-21
Earlier sketch in CA 69-72
Ransohoff, Paul M(artin) 1948- ... 103
Ransom, Bill 1945- ... CANR-19
Earlier sketch in CA 101
Ransom, Candice F. 1952- ... 121
See also SATA 49
Ransom, Harry Howe 1922- ... 11-12R
Ransom, Jay Ellis 1914- ... CANR-20
Earlier sketches in CA 9-10R, CANR-3
Ransom, John Crowe 1888-1974 ... CANR-6
Obituary ... 49-52
Earlier sketch in CA 7-8R
See also DLB 45, 63
See also CLC 2, 4, 5, 11, 24
Ransom, William Michael 1945-
Brief entry ... 108
Ransom, William R. 1876-1973
Obituary ... 37-40R
Ransome, Arthur Michell 1884-1967 ... 73-76
See also SATA 22
See also CLR 8
Ransome, Eleanor 1915- ... 93-96
Ransome, Stephen
See Davis, Frederick C(lyde)
Ransome-Davies, Basil
See Colley, Iain
Ransone, Coleman B(ernard), Jr. 1920- ... 45-48
Rant, Tol E.
See Longyear, Barry Brookes
Ranum, Orest Allen 1933- ... CANR-8
Earlier sketch in CA 11-12R
Ranum, Patricia M(cGroder) 1932- ... 45-48
Ranz, James 1921- ... 11-12R
Ranz, Jim
See Ranz, James
Ranzini, Addis Durning 1909-1983
Obituary ... 110
Rao, B. Shiva 1900(?)-1975 Obituary ... 61-64
Rao, C. H. Hanumantha 1929- ... CANR-7
Earlier sketch in CA 19-20R
Rao, R(anganatha) P(admanabha)
1924- ... 13-14R
Rao, Raja 1909- ... 73-76
See also CLC 25
Raoul, Anthony
See Wilmot, Anthony
Rapaport, Herman 1947- ... 114
Rapaport, Ionel F. 1909(?)-1972
Obituary ... 37-40R
Rapaport, Stella F(read) ... 4R
Raper, Arthur F(ranklin) 1899-1979 ... CANR-12
Obituary ... 89-92
Earlier sketch in CA 61-64
Raper, J(ulius) R(owan) 1938- ... 33-36R
Raper, Jack
See Raper, J(ulius) R(owan)
Raphael, Bertram 1936- ... 97-100
Raphael, Beverley 1934- ... 117
Raphael, Chaim 1908- ... CANR-16
Earlier sketch in CA 85-88
Raphael, Dan 1952- ... 104
Raphael, Dana ... 61-64
Raphael, David D(aiches) 1916- ... CANR-20
Earlier sketches in CA 7-8R, CANR-2
Raphael, Elaine
See Bolognese, Elaine Raphael
(Chionchio)
See also SATA 23
Raphael, Frederic (Michael) 1931- ... CANR-1
Earlier sketch in CA 4R
See also DLB 14
See also CLC 2, 14
Raphael, Jay
See Josephs, Ray
Raphael, Marc Lee 1942(?)- Brief entry ... 113
Raphael, Phyllis 1940- ... 45-48
Raphael, Rick 1919- ... CANR-10
Earlier sketch in CA 21-22R
Raphael, Robert 1927- ... 45-48
Raphael, Sandra (Joan) 1939- ... 104
Raphaelson, Elliot 1937- ... 124
Raphaelson, Samson 1896-1983 ... 65-68
Obituary ... 110
See also DLB 44
Rapkin, Chester 1918- ... 19-20R
Rapoport, Amos 1929- ... 65-68
Rapoport, Anatol 1911- ... 41-44R
Rapoport, Janis 1946- ... CANR-18
Earlier sketch in CA 101
Rapoport, Louis (Harvey) 1942- ... 117
Rapoport, Rhona (Ross) 1927- ... CANR-8
Earlier sketch in CA 61-64
Rapoport, Robert Norman 1924- ... CANR-17
Earlier sketches in CA 7-8R, CANR-2
Rapoport, Roger 1946- ... 33-36R
Rapoport, Ron 1940- ... 89-92
Rapp, Doris Jean 1929- ... CANR-21
Earlier sketch in CA 37-40R
Rapp, Joel ... AITN-1
Rapp, Lynn ... AITN-1
Rappaport, Alfred 1932- Brief entry ... 110
Rappaport, Armin H. 1916- Brief entry ... 111
Rappaport, David 1907- ... CAP-2
Earlier sketch in CA 19-20
Rappaport, Eva 1924- ... 29-32R
See also SATA 6
Rappaport, Julian 1942- Brief entry ... 112
Rappaport, Roy A(braham) 1926- ... 41-44R
Rappaport, Sheldon R(aphael) 1926- ... 29-32R
Rappole, John H(ilton) 1946- ... 123
Rappoport, Ken 1935- ... CANR-20
Earlier sketches in CA 53-56, CANR-4
Rappoport, Leon 1932- ... 41-44R
Rapson, Richard L(awrence) 1937- ... CANR-10
Earlier sketch in CA 23-24R
Rarick, Carrie 1911- ... 115
See also SATA 41
Rasberry, Robert W. 1945- ... 110
Rasberry, Salli 1940- ... CANR-23
Earlier sketch in CA 107
Rasch, Sunna Cooper 1925- ... 105
Raschke, Carl A(llan) 1944- ... 104
Rascoe, Jesse Ed
See Bartholomew, Ed(ward Ellsworth)
Rascoe, Judith 1941(?)- ... 107
Rascovich, Mark 1918(?)-1976 Obituary ... 69-72
Rasey, Ruth M.
See Simpson, Ruth Mary Rasey
Rash, Dora Eileen Agnew (Wallace)
1897- ... CANR-2
Earlier sketch in CA 7-8R
Rash, J(esse) Keogh 1906- ... 93-96
Rashidof, Sharif Rashidovich
See Rashidov, Sharaf Rashidovich
Rashidov, Sharaf Rashidovich
1917(?)-1983 Obituary ... 111
Rashke, Richard L. 1936- ... CANR-24
Earlier sketch in CA 107
Raskin, A(braham) H(enry) 1911- ... 104
Raskin, Edith Lefkowitz 1908- ... CANR-3
Earlier sketch in CA 11-12R
See also SATA 9
Raskin, Ellen 1928-1984 ... 23-24R
Obituary ... 113
See also SATA 2, 38
See also DLB 52
See also CLR 1, 12
Raskin, Eugene 1909- ... 33-36R
Raskin, Herbert A(lfred) 1919-1979 ... 29-32R
Obituary ... 122
Raskin, Jonah 1942- ... 81-84
Raskin, Joseph 1897-1982 ... CANR-13
Obituary ... 105
Earlier sketch in CA 33-36R
See also SATA 12, 29
Raskin, Marcus G. 1934- ... 37-40R
Rasky, Frank (John) 1923- Brief entry ... 107
Rasky, Harry 1928- ... 105
Rasmusen, Henry N(eil) 1909- ... 5-6R
Rasmussen, David (William) 1942- ... 53-56
Rasmussen, Douglas B(ruce) 1948- ... 119
Rasmussen, John Peter 1933- Brief entry ... 110
Rasmussen, Knud Johan Victor
1879-1933 Brief entry ... 113
See also SATA 34
Rasmussen, Larry L. 1939- ... 118
Rasmussen, Louis J(ames, Jr.) 1921- ... 73-76
Rasmussen, R. Kent 1943- ... 93-96
Rasmussen, Wayne D(avid) 1915- ... 33-36R
Rasof, Henry 1946- ... 113
Rasor, Eugene L(atimer) 1936- ... 89-92
Raspberry, William J(ames) 1935- ... 122
Brief entry ... 110
Rasponi, Lanfranco 1914-1983 ... 19-20R
Obituary ... 109
Rasputin, Maria
See Bern, Maria Rasputin Soloviev
Rasputin, Valentin (Grigorevich) 1937-
Brief entry ... 108
Rass, Rebecca 1936- ... 105
Rast, Walter E(mil) 1930- ... 73-76
Ratch, Jerry 1944- ... 118
Ratcliff, Carter 1941- ... CANR-13
Earlier sketch in CA 61-64
Ratcliff, John Drury 1903-1973 ... 108
Obituary ... 106
Ratcliff, Ruth 1905- ... 121
Ratcliffe, Barrie M(ichael) 1940- ... 114
Ratcliffe, James M(axwell) 1925- ... 21-22R
Ratcliffe, T(om) A(rundel) 1910- ... CAP-2
Earlier sketch in CA 25-28
Ratermanis, J(anis) B(ernhards) 1904- ... 9-10R
Rath, Frederick L(ouis), Jr. 1913- ... 41-44R
Rath, Patricia M(ink) ... 19-20R
Rath, R. John 1910- ... 37-40R
Rath, Sara 1941- ... 108
Rathbone, Julian 1935- ... 101
See also CLC 41
Rathbone, Lucy 1896- ... 7-8R
Rathbone, Ouida Bergere 1886(?)-1974
Obituary ... 53-56
Rathbone, Robert Reynolds 1916- ... 21-22R
Rathe, Alex W(erner) 1912- ... 19-20R
Rathenau, Walther 1867-1922 Brief entry ... 121
Rather, Dan (Irvin) 1931- ... CANR-9
Earlier sketch in CA 53-56
See also AITN 1
Rather, L(elland) J(oseph) 1913- ... 77-80
Rathjen, Carl Henry 1909- ... CANR-2
Earlier sketch in CA 7-8R
See also SATA 11
Rathjen, Frederick W(illiam) 1929- ... 41-44R
Rathlesberger, James (H.) 1948-
Brief entry ... 114
Rathmell, J(ohn) C. A. 1935- ... 11-12R
Rathmell, Neil 1947- ... 104
Ratigan, Eleanor Eldridge 1916- ... 5-6R
Ratigan, William 1910- ... 29-32R
Ratiu, Ion 1917- ... 7-8R
Ratliff, Charles Edward, Jr. 1926- ... CANR-1
Earlier sketch in CA 4R
Ratliff, Gerald Lee 1944- ... 107
Ratliff, Richard C(harles) 1922- ... 65-68
Ratliffe, Sharon A(nn) 1939- ... 61-64
Ratner, Joseph 1901(?)-1979 Obituary ... 85-88
Ratner, Leonard G(ilbert) 1916- ... 21-22R
Ratner, Lorman 1932- ... CANR-10
Earlier sketch in CA 25-28R
Ratner, Marc L. 1926- ... 45-48
Ratner, Rochelle 1948- ... CANR-12
Earlier sketch in CA 33-36R
Ratner, Sidney 1908- ... 23-24R
Ratner, Stanley C(harles) 1925- ... 15-16R
Rattenbury, Arnold (Foster) 1921- ... 29-32R
Ratti, John 1933- ... 73-76
Ratti, Oscar ... 41-44R
Rattigan, Terence (Mervyn) 1911-1977 ... 85-88
Obituary ... 73-76
See also DLB 13
See also CLC 7
Rattner, David S(amuel) 1916- ... 69-72
Rattray, Everett T(ennant) 1932-1980 ... 89-92
Obituary ... 97-100
Rattray, Simon
See Trevor, Elleston
Ratzan, Scott C. 1962- ... 124
Rau, Dhanvanthi (Handoo) Rama
See Rama Rau, Dhanvanthi (Handoo)
Rau, Dhanvanthi Rama
See Rama Rau, Dhanvanthi (Handoo)
Rau, Margaret 1913- ... CANR-8
Earlier sketch in CA 61-64
See also SATA 9
See also CLR 8
Rauch, Basil 1908-1986 ... CAP-2
Obituary ... 119
Earlier sketch in CA 19-20
Rauch, Constance 1937- ... 57-60
Rauch, Earl Mac 1950(?)- Brief entry ... 118
Rauch, Georg Von
See Von Rauch, Georg
Rauch, Irmengard 1933- ... CANR-11
Earlier sketch in CA 21-22R
Rauch, Leo 1927- ... 110
Rauch, Mabel Thompson 1888-1972 ... 7-8R
Obituary ... 103
See also SATA 26
Rauch, Rufus William, Jr. 1929-1977
Obituary ... 113
Raucher, Alan R(ichard) 1939- ... 118
Raucher, Herman 1928- ... 29-32R
See also SATA 8
Raudive, Konstantin 1909- ... 29-32R
Rauf, Abdur 1924- ... CANR-13
Earlier sketch in CA 73-76
Rauf, Muhammad Abdul
See Abdul-Rauf, Muhammad
Raulston, J(ames) Leonard 1905- ... 89-92
Rault, Walter
See Gorham, Maurice Anthony Coneys
Rauner, Robert M(cKenzie) 1925- ... CANR-1
Earlier sketch in CA 2R
Raunikar, Robert 1931- ... 124
Raup, H(allock) F(loyd) 1901- ... 37-40R
Raup, Robert 1888(?)-1976 Obituary ... 65-68
Rausch, Edward N. 1919- ... CANR-7
Earlier sketch in CA 15-16R
Rausch, Jane M(eyer) 1940- ... 119
Rauschenberg, Roy A(nthony) 1929- ... 45-48
Rauscher, Donald J. 1921- ... 11-12R
Rauschning, Hermann 1887-1982
Obituary ... 109
Raush, Harold L(ester) 1921- Brief entry ... 110
Raushenbush, Esther (Mohr) 1898- ... CAP-1
Earlier sketch in CA 15-16
Ravel, Aviva 1928- ... 119
Raven, Frithjof Andersen 1907-1966 ... CAP-1
Earlier sketch in CA 15-16
Raven, J(ohn) E(arle) 1914-1980 ... 103
Obituary ... 97-100
Raven, Ronald William 1904- ... CANR-23
Earlier sketch in CA 107
Raven, Simon (Arthur Noel) 1927- ... 81-84
See also CLC 14
Ravenal, Earl C(edric) 1931- ... 33-36R
Ravenel, Shannon 1938- ... 108
Ravenscroft, Arthur 1924- ... 110
Ravetch, Irving 1915(?)- Brief entry ... 110
Ravetz, Alison 1930- ... 116
Ravetz, Jerome R(aymond) 1929- ... 97-100
Ravetz, Jerry
See Ravetz, Jerome R(aymond)
Ravich, Robert A(lan) 1920- Brief entry ... 113
Ravielli, Anthony 1916- ... CANR-11
Earlier sketch in CA 29-32R
See also SATA 3
Ravikovitch, Dahlia
See Rabikovitz, Dalia
Ravikovitz, Dalia
See Rabikovitz, Dalia
Ravin, Neil 1947- ... 105
Ravindra, Ravi 1939- ... 114
Ravitch, Diane 1938- ... CANR-4
Earlier sketch in CA 53-56
Ravitch, Norman 1936- ... 37-40R
Ravitz, Abe Carl 1927- ... 9-10R
Ravitz, Shlomo 1885-1980 Obituary ... 103
Raw, Isaias 1927- ... 57-60
Rawcliffe, (John) Michael 1934- ... 115
Rawford, W. C.
See Crawford, William (Elbert)
Rawick, George P(hilip) 1929- ... 61-64
Rawles, Beverly A(rcher) 1930- ... 107
Rawley, Callman 1903- ... CANR-12
Earlier sketch in CA 23-24R
Rawley, James A. 1916- ... 21-22R
Rawling, Thomas Jackson 1916- ... 114
Rawling, Tom
See Rawling, Thomas Jackson
Rawlings, Hunter Ripley III 1944- ... 103
Rawlings, John 1930(?)-1981(?) Obituary ... 102
Rawlings, Louisa
See Baumgarten, Sylvia
Rawlings, Marjorie Kinnan 1896-1953
Brief entry ... 104
See also YABC 1
See also DLB 9, 22
See also TCLC 4
Rawlings, Maurice S(kaggs) 1922- ... 108
Rawlins, Clive Leonard 1940- ... CANR-22
Earlier sketch in CA 105
Rawlins, Dennis 1937- ... 45-48
Rawlins, Eustace Robert
See Barton, Eustace Robert
Rawlins, Jack P. 1946- ... 57-60
Rawlins, Jennie Brown 1910- ... CAP-2
Earlier sketch in CA 23-24
Rawlins, Winifred 1907- ... 9-10R
Rawlinson, A(rthur) R(ichard) 1894-1984
Obituary ... 113
Rawlinson, Dick
See Rawlinson, A(rthur) R(ichard)
Rawls, Eugene S. 1927- ... 11-12R
Rawls, James J(abus) 1945- ... 112
Rawls, John Bordley 1921- Brief entry ... 114
Rawls, Philip
See Levinson, Leonard
Rawls, Walter Cecil, Jr. 1928- ... 111
Rawls, Walton (Hendry) 1933- ... 121
Rawls, Wendell L(ee), Jr. 1941- ... CANR-22
Earlier sketch in CA 73-76

Rawls, (Woodrow) Wilson 1913- ... CANR-5
Earlier sketch in CA 3R
See also SATA 22
See also AITN 1
Rawlyk, George Alexander 1935- ... 109
Raworth, Thomas Moore 1938- ... 29-32R
Raworth, Tom
See Raworth, Thomas Moore
See also DLB 40
Rawski, Conrad H(enry) 1914- ... 73-76
Rawski, Evelyn S(akakida) 1939- ... 89-92
Rawson, Beryl 1933- ... 121
Rawson, C(laude) J(ulien) 1935- ... 25-28R
Rawson, Clayton 1906-1971 ... CANR-4
Obituary ... 29-32R
Earlier sketch in CA 5-6R
Rawson, Elizabeth (Donata) 1934-
Brief entry ... 115
Rawson, Margaret B(yrd) 1899- ... 25-28R
Rawson, Philip Stanley 1924- ... CANR-21
Earlier sketches in CA 5-6R, CANR-6
Rawson, Wyatt Trevelyan Rawson
1894-1980 ... 7-8R
Obituary ... 103
Ray, Ann 1937- ... 114
Ray, Cyril 1908- ... CANR-21
Earlier sketches in CA 7-8R, CANR-5
Ray, D(avid) Michael 1935- ... CANR-9
Earlier sketch in CA 19-20R
Ray, David 1932- ... CANR-5
Earlier sketch in CA 11-12R
See also DLB 5
Ray, Deborah
See Kogan Ray, Deborah
See also SATA 8
Ray, Dorothy Jean 1919- ... CANR-12
Earlier sketch in CA 25-28R
Ray, George McNeill 1910- ... 2R
Ray, Gordon N(orton) 1915-1986 ... 57-60
Obituary ... 121
Ray, H(enrietta) Cordelia 1849(?)-1916 ... 124
Brief entry ... 122
See also DLB 50
Ray, Irene
See Sutton, Margaret Beebe
Ray, JoAnne 1935- ... 61-64
See also SATA 9
Ray, John (Philip) 1929- ... CANR-11
Earlier sketch in CA 25-28R
Ray, John B(ernard) 1930- ... 61-64
Ray, John R(obert) 1921- ... 37-40R
Ray, Joseph M(alchus) 1907- ... 41-44R
Ray, (Suzanne) Judy 1939- ... 111
Ray, Karen 1956- ... 108
Ray, Kenneth Clark 1901- ... CAP-2
Earlier sketch in CA 19-20
Ray, Man 1890-1976 ... 77-80
Obituary ... 69-72
Ray, Mary (Eva Pedder) 1932- ... CANR-12
Earlier sketch in CA 29-32R
See also SATA 2
Ray, Michele S. 1938- ... 25-28R
Ray, N(ancy) L(ouise) 1918- ... 109
Ray, Oakley S(tern) 1931- ... 45-48
Ray, Paul C(harles) 1926- ... 104
Ray, Philip A(lexander) 1911-1970 ... CAP-2
Earlier sketch in CA 23-24
Ray, Russell
See Strait, Raymond
Ray, Satyajit 1921- ... 114
See also CLC 16
Ray, Sibnarayan 1921- ... CANR-15
Earlier sketch in CA 23-24R
Ray, Talton F. 1939- ... 29-32R
Ray, Trevor 1934- ... 107
Ray, Wesley
See Gaulden, Ray
Ray, Wilbert S(cott) 1901- ... CAP-2
Earlier sketch in CA 25-28
Rayback, Joseph G(eorge) 1914- ... 7-8R
Rayburn, James Chalmers III 1945- ... 121
Rayburn, Jim III
See Rayburn, James Chalmers III
Rayburn, Robert G(ibson) 1915- ... 25-28R
Raycraft, Donald R(obert) 1942- ... 41-44R
Rayfield, David 1940- ... 45-48
Rayfield, (Patrick) Donald 1942- ... 103
Rayfield, Stanley C. 1901(?)-1983(?)
Obituary ... 108
Raygor, Alton Lamon 1922- ... 49-52
Rayman, Paula Marian 1947- ... 107
Raymond, Agnes G. 1916- ... 25-28R
Raymond, Alex(ander Gillespie)
1909-1956 Brief entry ... 112
Raymond, Charles
See Koch, Charlotte
and Koch, Raymond
Raymond, Diana (Joan) 1916- ... 89-92
Raymond, E.V.
See Gallun, Raymond Z(inke)
Raymond, Ellsworth (Lester) 1912- ... 37-40R
Raymond, Ernest 1888-1974 Obituary ... 89-92
Raymond, Father M.
See Flanagan, Joseph David Stanislaus
Raymond, G. Alison
See Lanier, Alison Raymond
Raymond, Harold 1887-1975 Obituary ... 104
Raymond, Henry 1820-1869 ... DLB-43
Raymond, James (Charles) 1940- ... 119
Raymond, James Crossley 1917-1981
Obituary ... 105
See also SATA 29
Raymond, Janice G. 1943- ... 89-92
Raymond, Joseph H.
See Le Fontaine, Joseph (Raymond)
Raymond, Lee
See Hill, Mary Raymond
Raymond, Margaret E(lmendorf) 1912- ... 104
Raymond, Mary
See Keegan, Mary Heathcott
Raymond, P. L.
See Gibson, Walter B(rown)
Raymond, Patrick (Ernest) 1924- ... 102
Raymond, Rene (Brabazon) 1906-1985
Obituary ... 115
Raymond, Robert
See Alter, Robert Edmond
Raymond, Steve 1940- ... 49-52
Raymond, Walter J(ohn) 1930- ... 53-56
Raymond, William O. 1880-1970 ... CAP-2
Earlier sketch in CA 19-20
Raymond de Jesus, Mother
See Dion, Sister Anita
Raynal, Paul 1885(?)-1971 Obituary ... 33-36R
Rayne, Alan
See Tobin, James Edward
Rayner, Claire (Berenice) 1931- ... CANR-13
Earlier sketch in CA 21-22R
Rayner, E(dgar) G(eoffrey) 1927- ... CANR-10
Earlier sketch in CA 23-24R
Rayner, John Desmond 1924- ... 103
Rayner, Mary 1933- ... CANR-12
Earlier sketch in CA 69-72
See also SATA 22
Rayner, Ray
See Rahner, Raymond M.
Rayner, Richard
See McIlwain, David
Rayner, William 1929- ... 77-80
See also SATA 36
Raynor, David R(alph) 1948- ... 111
Raynor, Dorka ... 106
See also SATA 28
Raynor, Henry (Broughton) 1917- ... 85-88
Rayside, Betty 1931- ... 57-60
Rayson, Paul
See Jennings, Leslie Nelson
Rayson, Steven 1932- ... 106
See also SATA 30
Rayward, W(arden) Boyd 1939- ... 102
Raywid, Mary Anne ... 7-8R
Razaf, Andy 1895-1973 Obituary ... 41-44R
Razik, Taher A. 1924- ... CANR-19
Earlier sketch in CA 25-28R
Razor Saltboy
See Louis, Ray Baldwin
Razran, Gregory 1901-1973 ... 41-44R
Obituary ... 45-48
Razzell, Arthur (George) 1925- ... 85-88
See also SATA 11
Razzi, James 1931- ... CANR-5
Earlier sketch in CA 53-56
See also SATA 10
Re, Edward D(omenic) 1920- ... CANR-12
Earlier sketch in CA 21-22R
Rea, Frederick B(eatty) 1908- ... 9-10R
Rea, Gardner 1892-1966 Obituary ... 93-96
Rea, K(enneth) J(ohn) 1932- Brief entry ... 107
Rea, Kenneth Wesley 1944- ... 107
Rea, Robert R(ight) 1922- ... 4R
Reach, James 1910(?)-1970 Obituary ... 29-32R
Read, Al 1919-1987 Obituary ... 123
Read, Anthony 1935- ... 107
Read, Bill 1917- ... 13-14R
Read, Brian (Ahier) 1927- ... 108
Read, Cecil B(yron) 1901-1972 ... CAP-1
Earlier sketch in CA 15-16
Read, David Haxton Carswell 1910- ... CANR-3
Earlier sketch in CA 3R
Read, Donald 1930- ... CANR-1
Earlier sketch in CA 4R
Read, Elfreida 1920- ... CANR-9
Earlier sketch in CA 23-24R
See also SATA 2
Read, Forrest 1926-1980 Obituary ... 112
Read, Gardner 1913- ... CANR-6
Earlier sketch in CA 15-16R
Read, Hadley 1918- ... 81-84
Read, Helen Appleton 1887(?)-1974
Obituary ... 53-56
Read, Herbert Edward 1893-1968 ... 85-88
Obituary ... 25-28R
See also DLB 20
See also CLC 4
Read, Jan
See Read, John Hinton
Read, John Hinton 1917- ... CANR-15
Earlier sketch in CA 77-80
Read, Kenneth E(yre) 1917- ... 101
Read, Leonard Edward 1898-1983 ... CANR-11
Obituary ... 109
Earlier sketch in CA 19-20R
Read, Maureen Hay 1937- ... 113
Read, Opie 1852-1939 ... DLB-23
Read, Piers Paul 1941- ... 23-24R
See also SATA 21
See also DLB 14
See also CLC 4, 10, 25
Read, R. B. 1916-1982 ... CANR-13
Earlier sketch in CA 61-64
Read, Ritchard 1914- ... 57-60
Read, Sylvia Joan ... 103
Read, William M(erritt) 1901- ... 33-36R
Reade, B(rian) Edmund 1913- ... 23-24R
Reade, Charles 1814-1884 ... DLB-21
Reade, Hamish
See Gray, Simon
Reade, Lang
See Carter, David C(harles)
Reader, Dennis Joel 1939- ... 106
Reader, Desmond H. 1920- ... 21-22R
Reader, W(illiam) J(oseph) 1920- ... CANR-16
Earlier sketch in CA 37-40R
Reading, Peter 1946- ... 103
See also DLB 40
See also CLC 47
Ready, Kirk L(ewis) 1943- ... 114
See also SATA 39
Ready, William B(ernard) 1914-1981 ... CANR-22
Earlier sketch in CA 25-28R
Reagan, Charles E(llis) 1942- ... 53-56
Reagan, Michael D(aniel) 1927- ... 49-52
Reagan, Nancy Davis 1923- ... 110
Reagan, Ronald 1911- ... 85-88
Reagan, Sydney C(handler) 1916- ... 41-44R
Reagan, Thomas (James) B(utler)
1916- ... 37-40R
Reagen, Edward P(aul) 1924- ... 49-52
Reagen, Michael V. 1942- ... 81-84
Reagin, Ewell Kerr 1900- ... 41-44R
Reaman, George Elmore 1889-1969 ... CAP-1
Earlier sketch in CA 11-12
Reams, Bernard D(insmore), Jr.
1943- ... CANR-16
Earlier sketch in CA 93-96
Reamy, Tom 1935-1977 ... 81-84
Reaney, James 1926- ... 41-44R
See also SATA 43
See also CLC 13
Rearden, Jim 1925- ... 65-68
Reardon, B(ernard) M(orris) G(arvin)
1914- ... CANR-2
Earlier sketch in CA 7-8R
Reardon, Dennis J(oseph) 1944- ... 113
Brief entry ... 110
Reardon, Joan 1930- ... 116
Reardon, John J(oseph) 1926- ... 61-64
Reardon, William R. 1920- ... CANR-2
Earlier sketch in CA 2R
Rearick, Charles Walter 1942- ... 102
Reaske, Christopher R(ussell) 1941- ... 23-24R
Reason, James T(ootle) 1938- ... 104
Reasoner, Harry 1923- ... 111
See also AITN 1
Reaver, J(oseph) Russell 1915- ... 33-36R
Reaves, Philip
See Kiester, Edwin, Jr.
Reaves, Wendy Wick 1950- ... 114
Reavey, George 1907-1976 Obituary ... 69-72
Reavey, Jean (Bullowa) 1917(?)-1987
Obituary ... 123
Reb, Paul 1924- ... 49-52
Rebatet, Lucien 1903-1972 Obituary ... 37-40R
Rebay, Luciano 1928- ... 45-48
Rebbot, Olivier 1951(?)-1981 Obituary ... 103
Rebelsky, Freda Gould 1931- ... 41-44R
Rebert, M. Charles 1920- ... 53-56
Rebeta-Burditt, Joyce ... 81-84
Rebholz, Ronald A(lexander) 1932- ... 111
Rebischung, James A. 1928- ... 53-56
Rebuffat, Gaston (Louis Simon)
1921-1985 ... 21-22R
Obituary ... 116
Rechcigl, Miloslav, Jr. 1930- ... CANR-12
Earlier sketch in CA 19-20R
Rechy, John (Francisco) 1934- ... CANR-6
Earlier sketch in CA 7-8R
See also CAAS 4
See also DLBY 82
See also CLC 1, 7, 14, 18
Reck, Alma Kehoe 1901- ... 4R
Reck, Andrew J(oseph) 1927- ... CANR-6
Earlier sketch in CA 13-14R
Reck, David 1935- ... 73-76
Reck, Franklin Mering 1896-1965
Obituary ... 109
See also SATA 30
Reck, Rima Drell 1933- ... 21-22R
Reck, W(aldo) Emerson 1903- ... 61-64
Recker, Colane 1940- ... 113
Reckless, Walter Cade 1899- ... 37-40R
Reckord, Barry ... 77-80
Record, Cy Wilson 1916- ... 11-12R
Record, Jane Cassels 1915-1981 ... CANR-5
Earlier sketch in CA 13-14R
Rector, Frank ... 106
Reday, Ladislaw 1913- ... 112
Red Butterfly
See Lauritsen, John (Phillip)
Redcam, Tom 1870-1933 ... TCLC-25
Redcliffe-Maud, John 1906-1982 Obituary ... 108
Redd, (Newton) Lawrence 1941- ... 57-60
Reddan, Harold J. 1926- ... 15-16R
Reddaway, Peter (Brian) 1939- ... CANR-10
Earlier sketch in CA 23-24R
Reddaway, W(illiam) Brian 1913- ... 17-18R
Redden, James Erskine 1928- ... 41-44R
Redder, George
See Drummond, Jack
Reddick, DeWitt Carter 1904- ... 7-8R
Reddick, L(awrence) D(unbar) 1910- ... 61-64
Reddin, W(illiam) J(ames) 1930- ... 29-32R
Redding, Bud
See Redding, Edward C.
Redding, David A. 1923- ... CANR-3
Earlier sketch in CA 4R
Redding, Edward C. 1917-1984 Obituary ... 113
Redding, Robert Hull 1919- ... CANR-11
Earlier sketch in CA 23-24R
See also SATA 2
Redding, (Jay) Saunders 1906-1988
Obituary ... 124
Redding (Jay) Saunders 1906-1988 ... CANR-5
Earlier sketch in CA 4R
See also DLB 63
Reddish, Bessie Braid 1905-1974 ... 25-28R
Reddy, John F. X. 1912(?)-1975
Obituary ... 53-56
Reddy, Michael 1933- ... 61-64
Reddy, T. J. 1945- ... 45-48
Reddy, T(hammaiahgari) Ramakrishna
1937- ... 45-48
Redekop, Calvin Wall 1925- ... CANR-10
Earlier sketch in CA 25-28R
Redekop, John Harold 1932- ... 21-22R
Reder, Philip 1924-1983 Obituary ... 110
Redfern, George B. 1910- ... 11-12R
Redfern, W(alter) D(avid) 1936- ... 21-22R
Redfield, Alden 1941- ... 77-80
Redfield, Alfred Clarence 1890-1983
Obituary ... 109
Redfield, Clark
See McMorrow, Fred
Redfield, Jennifer
See Hoskins, Robert
Redfield, Malissa
See Elliott, Malissa Childs
Redfield, Margaret Park 1899(?)-1977
Obituary ... 69-72
Redfield, Robert 1897-1958 Brief entry ... 121
Redfield, William 1927-1976 Obituary ... 69-72
Redford, Emmette Shelburn 1904- ... 112
Redford, Polly 1925-1972 ... CAP-2
Earlier sketch in CA 33-36
Redford, (Charles) Robert (Jr.) 1937- ... 107
Red Fox, William 1871(?)-1976 Obituary ... 65-68
Redgate, John
See Kennedy, Adam
Redgrave, Michael (Scudamore)
1908-1985 Obituary ... 115
Redgrave, Paul 1920- ... 7-8R
Redgrove, Peter (William) 1932- ... CANR-3
Earlier sketch in CA 4R
See also DLB 40
See also CLC 6, 41
Redinger, Ruby V(irginia) 1915-1981 ... 65-68
Obituary ... 120
Redish, Bessie Braid 1905-1974 ... CAP-2
Earlier sketch in CA 25-28
Redkey, Edwin S(torer) 1931- ... 29-32R
Redlich, Frederick Carl 1910- Brief entry ... 106
Redman, Ben Ray 1896-1961 Obituary ... 93-96
Redman, Eric 1948- ... 49-52
Redman, L(ister) A(ppleton) 1933- ... 108
Redmayne, John
See Wood, Herbert Fairlie
Redmayne, Paul (Brewis) 1900- ... 7-8R
Redmon, Anne
See Nightingale, Anne Redmon
See also DLBY 86
See also CLC 22
Redmond, Eugene B. 1937- ... CANR-12
Earlier sketch in CA 25-28R
See also DLB 41
Redmond, Gerald 1934- ... 37-40R
Redmond, Howard A(lexander) 1925- ... 15-16R
Redmond, Juanita
See Hipps, Juanita Redmond
Redmont, Bernard Sidney 1918- ... 73-76
Redmont, Dennis Foster 1942- ... 77-80
Redner, Harry 1937- ... 110
Redpath, (Robert) Theodore (Holmes)
1913- ... 104
Redpath, William 1893(?)-1985 Obituary ... 116
Redstone, Louis G(ordon) 1903- ... CANR-2
Earlier sketch in CA 49-52
Redway, Ralph
See Hamilton, Charles Harold St. John
Redway, Ridley
See Hamilton, Charles Harold St. John
Redwood, Alec
See Milkomane, George Alexis
Milkomanovich
Redwood, John (Alan) 1951- ... CANR-19
Earlier sketch in CA 102
Ree, Jonathan 1948- ... 57-60
Reece, Benny R(amon) 1930- ... 41-44R
Reece, Jack Eugene 1941- ... 101
Reeck, Darrell (Lauren) 1939- ... 104
Reed, A(lfred) H(amish) 1875-1975 ... CANR-4
Obituary ... 57-60
Earlier sketch in CA 9-10R
Reed, A(lexander) W(yclif) 1908-1979 ... CANR-4
Earlier sketch in CA 9-10R
Reed, Alison Touster 1952- ... 105
Reed, Barry
See Reed, Barry C(lement)
Reed, Barry C(lement) 1927- ... CANR-23
Earlier sketch in CA 29-32R
Reed, Betty Jane 1921- ... 29-32R
See also SATA 4
Reed, Bobbie (Butler) 1944- ... 77-80
Reed, Carroll E(dward) 1914- ... 103
Reed, Daniel 1892(?)-1978 Obituary ... 77-80
Reed, Don C(harles) 1945- ... 106
Reed, Donald A(nthony) 1935- ... 103
Reed, Douglas 1895-1976 ... 103
Obituary ... 89-92
Reed, Edward W(ilson) 1913- ... 29-32R
Reed, Eliot
See Ambler, Eric
Reed, Elizabeth Liggett 1895- ... 77-80
Reed, Elizabeth Stewart 1914- ... 2R
Reed, Emmett X.
See King, Florence
Reed, Evelyn 1905-1979 ... 102
Reed, Graham 1923- ... CANR-24
Earlier sketch in CA 45-48
Reed, Gwendolyn E(lizabeth) 1932- ... 25-28R
See also SATA 21
Reed, H(erbert) Owen 1910- ... CANR-19
Earlier sketches in CA 53-56, CANR-4
Reed, Harold W(illiam) 1909- ... 118
Reed, Harrison Merrick, Jr. 1898-19(?) ... 4R
Reed, Henry 1808-1854 ... DLB-59

INDEX

Reed, Henry 1914-1986 ... 104
Obituary ... 121
See also DLB 27
Reed, Henry Clay 1899-1972 Obituary ... 111
Reed, Howard Alexander 1920- ... 15-16R
Reed, Ishmael 1938- ... 23-24R
See also DLB 2, 5, 33
See also CLC 2, 3, 5, 6, 13, 32
Reed, J(ames) D(onald) 1940- ... 33-36R
Reed, James 1922- ... 102
Reed, James F(red) 1909- ... CAP-1
Earlier sketch in CA 11-12
Reed, James Wesley 1944- ... 112
Reed, John (Silas) 1887-1920 Brief entry ... 106
See also TCLC 9
Reed, John F(ord) 1911- ... 15-16R
Reed, John L(incoln) 1938- ... 57-60
Reed, John P(lume) 1921- ... 65-68
Reed, John Q(uincy) 1918-1978 ... 45-48
Obituary ... 103
Reed, John R(obert) 1938- ... CANR-8
Earlier sketch in CA 19-20R
Reed, John Shelton (Jr.) 1942- ... CANR-5
Earlier sketch in CA 53-56
Reed, Joseph Verner 1902-1973
Obituary ... 45-48
Reed, Joseph W(ayne), Jr. 1932- ... 37-40R
Reed, Kenneth 1944- ... 57-60
Reed, Kenneth T(errence) 1937- ... 73-76
Reed, Kit 1932- ... CANR-16
Earlier sketches in CA 2R, CANR-1
See also SATA 34
Reed, Lawrence
See Reday, Ladislaw
Reed, Lou
See Firbank, Louis
See also CLC 21
Reed, Louis S(chultz) 1902-1975
Obituary ... 61-64
Reed, Luther D(otterer) 1873- ... 7-8R
Reed, M(athilda) N(ewman) 1905-19(?) ... 4R
Reed, Macon, Jr. 1911(?)-1986 Obituary ... 121
Reed, Marcia 1929- ... 120
Reed, Mark D(ouglas) Morrison
See Morrison-Reed, Mark D(ouglas)
Reed, Mark L(afayette) III 1935- ... 93-96
Reed, Mary Jane (Pobst) 1920- ... 25-28R
Reed, Michael 1930- ... 123
Reed, (Fred) Mort(on) 1912- ... 61-64
Reed, Nelson A. 1926- ... 11-12R
Reed, Paul 1956- ... 113
Reed, Peter J. 1935- ... 53-56
Reed, Philip G. 1908- ... SATA-29
Reed, Rex (Taylor) 1938- ... CANR-9
Earlier sketch in CA 53-56
See also AITN 1
Reed, Robert C(arroll) 1937- ... CANR-10
Earlier sketch in CA 65-68
Reed, Robert Rentoul, Jr. 1911- ... 33-36R
Reed, Ronald F. 1945- ... 116
Reed, S(amuel) Kyle 1922- ... 41-44R
Reed, Sampson 1800-1880 ... DLB-1
Reed, Thomas (James) 1947- ... 103
See also SATA 34
Reed, Thomas Harrison 1881-1971
Obituary ... 110
Reed, Thomas Thornton 1902- ... 107
Reed, Victor (Brenner) 1926- ... 33-36R
Reed, Walter Logan 1943- ... 102
Reed, William Maxwell 1871-1962 ... SATA-15
Reed, Willis 1942- ... 104
Reeder, Colonel Red
See Reeder, Russell P., Jr.
Reeder, John P., Jr. 1937- ... 101
Reeder, Russell P., Jr. 1902- ... CANR-5
Earlier sketch in CA 3R
See also SATA 4
Reedstrom, Ernest Lisle 1928- ... 89-92
Reedy, George E(dward) 1917- ... 29-32R
Reedy, Jerry Edward 1936- ... 119
Reedy, John Louis 1925-1983 Obituary ... 111
Reedy, William A. 1916(?)-1975
Obituary ... 61-64
Reedy, William James 1921- ... 15-16R
Reefe, Thomas Q(uentin) 1943- ... 123
Brief entry ... 116
Reel, A(dolf) Frank 1907- ... 93-96
Reeman, Douglas Edward 1924- ... CANR-3
Earlier sketch in CA 2R
See also SATA 28
Reems, Harry 1947- ... 61-64
Reens, Mary
See Singleton, Betty
Reep, Edward 1918- ... 33-36R
Rees, Alan M(axwell) 1929- ... 106
Rees, Albert (Everett) 1921- ... CANR-12
Earlier sketch in CA 29-32R
Rees, Barbara (Elizabeth) 1934- ... CANR-9
Earlier sketch in CA 53-56
Rees, Clair (Francis) 1938- ... 117
Rees, David 1928- ... CANR-11
Earlier sketch in CA 11-12R
Rees, David Bartlett 1936- ... 105
See also SATA 36
See also SAAS 5
Rees, David Morgan 1904- ... 104
Rees, Dilwyn
See Daniel, Glyn (Edmund)
Rees, Ennis (Samuel, Jr.) 1925- ... CANR-2
Earlier sketch in CA 2R
See also SATA 3
Rees, (Morgan) Goronwy 1909- ... CANR-3
Earlier sketch in CA 45-48
Rees, Helen Christina Easson (Evans)
1903-1970 ... 7-8R
Obituary ... 89-92
Rees, Henry 1916- ... 107
Rees, Ioan Bowen 1929- ... 29-32R
Rees, Jean A(nglin) 1912- ... CANR-1
Earlier sketch in CA 2R
Rees, Joan 1927- ... CANR-12
Earlier sketch in CA 25-28R
Rees, Joan Alice Gladys
See Rees, Joan
Rees, (George) Leslie (Clarence) 1905- ... 104
Rees, Lucy 1943- ... 107
Rees, Margaret A(nn) 1933- ... CANR-18
Earlier sketch in CA 101
Rees, Meriel
See Lambot, Isobel
Rees, Paul Stromberg 1900- ... 7-8R
Rees, Richard (Lodowick Edward Montagu)
1900-1970 ... CANR-4
Obituary ... 89-92
Earlier sketch in CA 7-8R
Rees, Robert A(lvin) 1935- ... 81-84
Rees, (Margaret) Una 1920- ... 124
Rees, William 1887-1978(?) ... 7-8R
Obituary ... 104
Reese, Alexander 1881-1969 ... 97-100
Reese, Algernon B(everly) 1896-1981
Obituary ... 105
Reese, Bob
See Reese, Robert A.
Reese, Carolyn Johnson 1938- ... 112
Reese, Curtis W(illiford) 1887-1961
Obituary ... 110
Reese, Edward, Jr. 1928- ... 113
Reese, Francesca Gardner 1940- ... 65-68
Reese, Gustave 1899-1977 Obituary ... 73-76
Reese, Heloise (Bowles) 1919-1977 ... 11-12R
Obituary ... 73-76
Reese, Jim E(anes) 1912- ... 15-16R
Reese, John (Henry) ... 102
Reese, Lizette Woodworth 1856-1935 ... DLB-54
Reese, Lyn
See Reese, Carolyn Johnson
Reese, M(ax) M(eredith) 1910-1987 ... CANR-3
Obituary ... 123
Earlier sketch in CA 9-10R
Reese, Mason 1966- ... 97-100
Reese, Robert A. 1938- ... 114
Reese, Sammy
See Reese, Samuel Pharr
Reese, Samuel Pharr 1930-1985 ... 49-52
Obituary ... 117
Reese, (John) Terence 1913- ... 109
Reese, Thomas 1742-1796 ... DLB-37
Reese, Thomas J(oseph) 1945- ... 106
Reese, Thomas R. 1890(?)-1974
Obituary ... 53-56
Reese, Trevor Richard 1929- ... 11-12R
Reese, William Lewis 1921- ... CANR-8
Earlier sketch in CA 19-20R
Reese, William S(herman) 1955- ... 111
Reese, Willis L(ivingston) M(esier) 1913- ... 57-60
Reesink, Maryke 1919- ... 25-28R
Reeve, Clara 1729-1807 ... DLB-39
Reeve, F(ranklin) D(olier) 1928- ... 77-80
Reeve, Frank D(river) 1899-1967 ... CAP-1
Earlier sketch in CA 11-12
Reeve, G. Joan (Price) 1901- ... 15-16R
Reeve, Joel
See Cox, William (Robert)
Reeve, Richard M(ark) 1935- ... 37-40R
Reeve, Wilfred D. 1895- ... CAP-1
Earlier sketch in CA 13-14
Reeve, William Charles 1943- ... 93-96
Reeves, Alexander Stuart Frere
See Frere-Reeves, Alexander Stuart
Reeves, Amber
See Blanco White, Amber
Reeves, (Richard) Ambrose 1899-1980
Obituary ... 105
Reeves, Bruce Douglas 1940- ... CANR-11
Earlier sketch in CA 21-22R
Reeves, Charles Everand 1889- ... 7-8R
Reeves, Donald 1952- ... 37-40R
Reeves, Dorothea D(resser) 1901- ... CAP-1
Earlier sketch in CA 11-12
Reeves, Earl J(ames, Jr.) 1933- ... 61-64
Reeves, Elton T(raver) 1912- ... 29-32R
Reeves, Fionnuala 1943- ... 112
Reeves, Floyd (Wesley) 1890-1979
Obituary ... 89-92
Reeves, Gareth 1947- ... 119
Reeves, Gene (Arthur) 1933- ... 61-64
Reeves, Gregory Shaw 1950- ... 77-80
Reeves, James 1909- ... 7-8R
See also SATA 15
Reeves, Joan Wynn 1910-1972 ... CAP-2
Earlier sketch in CA 21-22
Reeves, John 1926- ... 113
Reeves, John K(night) 1907- ... CAP-2
Earlier sketch in CA 25-28
Reeves, Joyce 1911- ... CANR-12
Earlier sketch in CA 73-76
See also SATA 17
Reeves, Lawrence F. 1926- ... 105
See also SATA 29
Reeves, Marjorie E(thel) 1905- ... CANR-20
Earlier sketches in CA 13-14R, CANR-5
Reeves, Martha Emilie 1941- ... 65-68
Reeves, Mavis Mann 1921- ... 45-48
Reeves, Nancy 1913- ... 33-36R
Reeves, Paschal 1917-1976 ... 81-84
Reeves, Richard 1936- ... 69-72
Reeves, Rosser 1910-1984 ... 89-92
Obituary ... 111
Reeves, Ruth Ellen
See Ranney, Agnes V.
Reeves, Thomas C(harles) 1936- ... CANR-9
Earlier sketch in CA 57-60
Reeves, Thomas Carl 1939- ... 33-36R
Reff, Theodore Franklin 1930- ... 89-92
Refregier, Anton 1905- ... 5-6R
Regalado, Nancy Freeman 1935- ... 19-20R
Regan, Brad
See Norwood, Victor G(eorge) C(harles)
Regan, Cronan 1925- ... 45-48
Regan, Donald Thomas 1918- Brief entry ... 106
Regan, Richard Joseph 1930- ... 7-8R
Regan, Robert (Charles) 1930- ... 19-20R
Regan, Thomas Howard 1938- ... 104
Regan, Tom
See Regan, Thomas Howard
Regardie, (Francis) Israel 1907- ... 85-88
Regehr, Lydia 1903- ... 45-48
See also SATA 37
Regelski, Thomas A(dam) 1941- ... 57-60
Regenstein, Lewis 1943- ... 57-60
Regensteiner, Else (Friedsam) 1906-
Brief entry ... 111
Reger, Roger 1933- ... 23-24R
Reggiani, Renee 1925- ... 85-88
See also SATA 18
Reghaby, Heydar 1932- ... 29-32R
Regin, Deric (Wagenvort) ... 37-40R
Reginald
See Burgess, M(ichael) R(oy)
Reginald, R(obert)
See Burgess, M(ichael) R(oy)
Regis, Sister Mary 1908- ... CAP-1
Earlier sketch in CA 13-14
Register, Willie Raymond 1937- ... 45-48
Regnery, Henry 1912- ... 101
Regoli, Robert M. 1950- ... 116
Regosin, Richard L(loyd) 1937-
Brief entry ... 109
Regueiro, Helen 1943- ... 104
Rehak, Peter (Stephen) 1936- ... 77-80
Rehder, Helmut 1905-1977 ... CANR-4
Earlier sketch in CA 7-8R
Rehder, Jessie Clifford 1908-1967 ... CAP-1
Earlier sketch in CA 9-10
Rehfuss, John Alfred 1934- ... 85-88
Rehrauer, George 1923- ... 53-56
Reibel, Paula
See Schwartz, Paula
Reich, Ali
See Katz, Bobbi
Reich, Bernard 1941- ... CANR-14
Earlier sketch in CA 81-84
Reich, Charles Alan 1928- ... 108
Reich, Edward 1903(?)-1983 Obituary ... 109
Reich, Ilse Ollendorff 1909- ... 49-52
Reich, John Theodore 1906-1988
Obituary ... 124
Reich, Kenneth 1938- ... 69-72
Reich, Peter M(aria) 1929- ... 85-88
Reich, Sheldon 1931- ... 112
Reich, Steve 1936- ... CANR-8
Earlier sketch in CA 61-64
Reich, Tova Rachel 1942- ... 103
Reichard, Gary Warren 1943- ... CANR-10
Earlier sketch in CA 61-64
Reichard, Robert S. 1923- ... 23-24R
Reichardt, Jasia 1933- ... CANR-2
Earlier sketch in CA 7-8R
Reichart, Walter A(lbert) 1903- ... 5-6R
Reiche, Reimut 1941- ... 41-44R
Reichek, Morton A(rthur) 1924- ... 85-88
Reichel, O. Asher 1921- ... 45-48
Reichenbach, Bruce R. 1943- ... 33-36R
Reichenberger, Arnold G(ottfried) 1903- ... 19-20R
Reichert, Herbert W(illiam) 1917-1978 ... CANR-24
Earlier sketch in CA 45-48
Reichert, Victor Emanuel 1897- ... 15-16R
Reichl, Ernst 1900-1980 Obituary ... 102
Reichl, Ruth 1948- ... 61-64
Reichler, Joseph Lawrence 1918- ... 103
Reichley, (Anthony) James 1929- ... 2R
Reichmann, Felix 1899- ... 104
Reicke, Bo I(var) 1914- ... 15-16R
Reid, Alan 1915(?)-1987 Obituary ... 123
Reid, Alastair 1926- ... CANR-3
Earlier sketch in CA 7-8R
See also SATA 46
See also DLB 27
Reid, Albert Clayton 1894- ... 53-56
Reid, Alfred S(andlin) 1924-1976 ... CANR-2
Earlier sketch in CA 45-48
Reid, Anthony 1916- ... 29-32R
Reid, B(enjamin) L(awrence) 1918- ... 19-20R
Reid, Barbara 1922- ... CANR-12
Earlier sketch in CA 25-28R
See also SATA 21
Reid, Charles (Stuart) 1900-1987 ... 101
Obituary ... 121
Reid, Charles K(er) II 1912-19(?) ... CAP-1
Earlier sketch in CA 19-20
Reid, Charles L(loyd) 1927- ... 37-40R
Reid, Charles R(obert) 1926- ... 114
Reid, Christopher 1949- ... DLB-40
See also CLC 33
Reid, Clyde H. 1928- ... CANR-12
Earlier sketch in CA 25-28R
Reid, Desmond
See McNeilly, Wilfred Glassford
and Moorcock, Michael (John)
Reid, Donald (Matthew) 1952- ... 124
Reid, Dorothy M(arion) ?-1974 Obituary ... 109
See also SATA 29
Reid, E. Emmet 1872-1973 Obituary ... 45-48
Reid, Ela 1907-1982 Obituary ... 107
Reid, Escott (Meredith) 1905- ... CANR-20
Earlier sketch in CA 101
Reid, Esmond 1945- ... 123
Reid, Eugenie Chazal 1924- ... 15-16R
See also SATA 12
Reid, Frances P(ugh) 1910- ... CANR-2
Earlier sketch in CA 7-8R
Reid, H. 1925- ... 19-20R
Reid, Helen Rogers 1882-1970 Obituary ... 115
See also DLB 29
Reid, Hilda (Stewart) 1898-1982 Obituary ... 106
Reid, Ian 1915-1984 Obituary ... 113
Reid, Inez Smith ... 49-52
Reid, J(ohn) C(owie) 1916-1972 ... 11-12R
Obituary ... 103
Reid, James ... DLB-31
Reid, James Macarthur 1900-1970 ... CAP-1
Earlier sketch in CA 9-10
Reid, James Malcolm 1902-1982 ... 7-8R
Obituary ... 107
Reid, James W. 1912-197(?) ... CAP-2
Earlier sketch in CA 25-28
Reid, Jan 1945- ... 61-64
Reid, Jim 1929- ... 61-64
Reid, John Calvin ... CANR-11
Earlier sketch in CA 25-28R
See also SATA 21
Reid, John Kelman Sutherland 1910- ... CANR-3
Earlier sketch in CA 4R
Reid, John Phillip 1930- ... CANR-19
Earlier sketch in CA 25-28R
Reid, John T(urner) 1908-1978 ... 81-84
Reid, Leslie Hartley 1895- ... CAP-1
Earlier sketch in CA 13-14
Reid, Loren (Dudley) 1905- ... CANR-1
Earlier sketch in CA 3R
Reid, Louis Arnaud 1895- ... CAP-1
Earlier sketch in CA 13-14
Reid, Malcolm 1941- ... 53-56
Reid, (Thomas) Mayne 1818-1883 ... SATA-24
See also DLB 21
Reid, Meta Mayne ... 13-14R
See also SATA 36
Reid, Mildred I. 1908- ... 23-24R
Reid, Philip
See Ingrams, Richard (Reid)
and Osmond, Andrew
Reid, R(obert) W(illiam) 1933- ... 29-32R
Reid, Randall 1931- ... 25-28R
Reid, Robert G(eorge) B(urnside) 1939- ... 119
Reid, Seerley 1909(?)-1972 Obituary ... 37-40R
Reid, Sue Titus 1939- ... CANR-14
Earlier sketch in CA 37-40R
Reid, Tim
See Reid, Timothy E. H.
Reid, Timothy E. H. 1936- ... 19-20R
Reid, Vic(tor Stafford) 1913- ... CANR-16
Earlier sketch in CA 65-68
Reid, W(illiam) Stanford 1913- ... CANR-18
Earlier sketches in CA 49-52, CANR-1
Reid, Whitelaw 1837-1912 ... DLB-23
Reid, William 1926- ... 85-88
Reid, William H(oward) 1945- ... CANR-16
Earlier sketch in CA 93-96
Reid, William J(ames) 1928- ... CANR-17
Earlier sketch in CA 77-80
Reida, Bernice 1915- ... 93-96
Reid Banks, Lynne 1929- ... CANR-22
Earlier sketches in CA 1R, CANR-6
See also SATA 22
Reidel, Carl Hubert 1937- ... 107
Reidel-Geubtner, Virginia 1921- ... 116
Reidenbaugh, Lowell (Henry) 1919- ... 121
Reidy, John Patrick 1930- ... 19-20R
Reidy, Joseph 1920- ... 53-56
Reierson, Gary B(ruce) 1948- ... 114
Reif, Rita 1929- ... 41-44R
Reifen, David 1911- ... 93-96
Reiff, Henry 1899-1983 Obituary ... 110
Reiff, Robert (Frank) 1918- ... 19-20R
Reiff, Stephanie Ann 1948- ... 93-96
See also SATA 28, 47
Reiffel, Leonard 1927- ... 101
Reifler, Samuel 1939- ... 93-96
Reifsnyder, William E(dward) 1924- ... 65-68
Reig, June 1933- ... 105
See also SATA 30
Reigelman, Milton Monroe 1942- ... 65-68
Reiger, George (Wesley) 1939- ... CANR-18
Earlier sketch in CA 101
Reiger, John F(ranklin) 1943- ... 57-60
Reiger, Kurt (Edward) 1956- ... 116
Reigle, Donald W(ayne), Jr. 1938- ... 61-64
Reigot, Betty Polisar 1924- ... 111
See also SATA 41
Reigstad, Paul (Matthew) 1921- ... 81-84
Reik, Theodor 1888-1969 ... CANR-5
Obituary ... 25-28R
Earlier sketch in CA 5-6R
Reile, Louis 1925- ... 29-32R
Reill, Peter Hanns 1938- ... 101
Reilly, Catherine W(inifred) 1925- ... 118
Reilly, Christopher T(homas) 1924- ... 101
Reilly, D(avid) Robin 1928- ... CANR-8
Earlier sketch in CA 7-8R
Reilly, Edward R(andolph) 1929- ... 93-96
Reilly, Edwin David, Jr. 1932- ... 111
Reilly, Esther H(untington) 1917- ... 33-36R
Reilly, Francis E(agan) 1922- ... 29-32R
Reilly, Harold J. 1895(?)-1987 Obituary ... 123
Reilly, John H(urford) 1934- ... 77-80
Reilly, John M(arsden) 1933- ... 104
Reilly, Judith G(ladding) 1935- ... 61-64
Reilly, Mary 1920- Brief entry ... 114
Reilly, Mary Lonan 1926- ... 33-36R
Reilly, Michael (Francis) 1910(?)-1973
Obituary ... 41-44R
Reilly, Patrick 1932- ... 115
Reilly, Patrick D.
See Rogers, Peter D(amien)
Reilly, Robert Thomas 1922- ... CANR-2
Earlier sketch in CA 5-6R

Reilly, Robin 1928- CANR-5
Earlier sketch in CA 53-56
Reilly, William J(ohn) 1899- CAP-2
Earlier sketch in CA 19-20
Reilly, William K.
See Creasey, John
Reiman, Donald H(enry) 1934- CANR-14
Earlier sketch in CA 33-36R
Reiman, Jeffrey H. 1942- 93-96
Reimann, Guenter Hans 1904- 25-28R
Reimann, Lewis C. 1890-1961 Obituary 113
Reimann, Viktor 1915- 69-72
Reimer, Bennett 1932- CANR-3
Earlier sketch in CA 45-48
Reimers, David 1931- 115
Rein, Irving J. 1937- 25-28R
Rein, Martin 1928- 93-96
Rein, Richard
See Smith, Richard Rein
Reina, Ruben E. 1924- 49-52
Reinach, Jacquelyn (Krasne) 1930- CANR-22
Earlier sketch in CA 105
See also SATA 28
Reincheld, Bill 1946- 57-60
Reindorp, George E(dmund) 1911- CANR-5
Earlier sketch in CA 7-8R
Reindorp, Reginald C(arl) 1907- 25-28R
Reinecke, Ian 1945- 117
Reinemer, Vic 1923- 21-22R
Reiner, Carl 1922- Brief entry 112
Reiner, Joseph H. 1912(?)-1983 Obituary .. 111
Reiner, Laurence E(rwin) 102
Reiner, Max
See Caldwell, (Janet Miriam) Taylor (Holland)
Reiner, William B(uck) 1910-1976 ...... CANR-3
Obituary 61-64
Earlier sketch in CA 45-48
See also SATA 30, 46
Reinerman, Alan J(erome) 1935- 114
Reinert, Paul C(lare) 1910- 85-88
Reines, Alvin J. 1926- 53-56
Reinfeld, Fred 1910-1964 .... CAP-1
Earlier sketch in CA 9-10
See also SATA 3
Reinhard, David W(illiam) 1952- 118
Reinhard, Ernst
See Frank, Rudolf
Reinhardt, Ad(olph Frederick) 1913-1967
Obituary 111
Reinhardt, Gottfried 1913- 93-96
Reinhardt, James Melvin 1894-1974 .... CANR-4
Obituary 49-52
Earlier sketch in CA 2R
Reinhardt, Jon M(c Ewen) 1936- 41-44R
Reinhardt, Kurt F(rank) 1896- CANR-1
Earlier sketch in CA 4R
Reinhardt, Richard 1927- CANR-13
Earlier sketch in CA 25-28R
Reinhart, Bruce Aaron 1926- 5-6R
Reinhart, Charles (Franklin) 1946- 104
Reinhartz, Dennis 1944- 123
Reinharz, Jehuda 1944- CANR-24
Earlier sketches in CA 65-68, CANR-9
Reinhold, Meyer 1909- CANR-5
Earlier sketch in CA 7-8R
Reiniger, Lotte 1899-1981 Obituary 108
See also SATA 33, 40
Reining, Conrad C(opeland) 1918-1984 ...21-22R
Obituary 114
Reinitz, Richard (Martin) 1934- 89-92
Reinke, William A(ndrew) 1928- CANR-24
Earlier sketch in CA 45-48
Reinmuth, Oscar William 1900- 37-40R
Reinsmith, Richard
See Smith, Richard Rein
Reis, Claire Raphael 1889-1978 Obituary ..77-80
Reis, Richard H(erbert) 1930- 41-44R
Reisch, Walter 1903-1983 Obituary 109
See also DLB 44
Reischauer, August Karl 1879-1971 ...... CAP-2
Earlier sketch in CA 19-20
Reischauer, Edwin O(ldfather) 1910- 19-20R
Reiser, Martin 1927- 53-56
Reiser, Morton F(rancis) 1919- 124
Reiser, Oliver Leslie 1895-1974 .... CANR-4
Obituary 49-52
Earlier sketch in CA 3R
Reiser, William (Edward) 1943- 114
Reisfeld, Bert 1906- 112
Reising, Robert W(illiam) 1933- 89-92
Reisman, Arnold 1934- CANR-12
Earlier sketch in CA 33-36R
Reisman, George Gerald 1937- 104
Reisman, John M(ark) 1930- CANR-8
Earlier sketch in CA 21-22R
Reisner, George
See Ben-Ephraim, Gavriel
Reisner, Robert George 1921- 11-12R
Reisner, Thomas Andrew 1935- 113
Reiss, Albert J(ohn), Jr. 1922- CANR-24
Earlier sketches in CA 23-24R, CANR-9
Reiss, Alvin 1932- 61-64
Reiss, Alvin H(erbert) 1930- 81-84
Reiss, Barbara Eve 1941- CANR-15
Earlier sketch in CA 41-44R
Reiss, David S. 1953- 108
Reiss, Edmund (Allan) 1934- CANR-10
Earlier sketch in CA 23-24R
Reiss, Ira L(eonard) 1925- 15-16R
Reiss, James 1941- 33-36R
Reiss, Johanna (de Leeuw) 1929(?)- 85-88
See also SATA 18
Reiss, John J. 106
See also SATA 23
Reiss, Stephen (Charles) 1918- 57-60
Reiss, Timothy James 1942- 107
Reissig, Herman F. 1899(?)-1985
Obituary 116
Reissman, Leonard 1921-1975 .... CANR-4
Obituary 53-56
Earlier sketch in CA 5-6R
Reister, Floyd Nester 1919- 69-72
Reit, Seymour (V.) 1918- CANR-16
Earlier sketch in CA 93-96
See also SATA 21
Reit, Sy
See Reit, Seymour (V.)
Reitan, E(arl) A(aron) 1925- 19-20R
Reitci, John G(eorge) 1922-1983 Obituary .. 109
Reitci, Rita Krohne 1930- 5-6R
Reitemeyer, John Reinhart 1898-1979
Obituary 85-88
Reiter, Charles Jules 1928- 25-28R
Reiter, Robert E. 1932- 25-28R
Reiter, Seymour 1921- 101
Reiterman, Carl 1921- 49-52
Reiterman, Tim 1947- 109
Reith, Charles C. 1953- 122
Reith, J.C.W.
See Reith, John Charles Walsham
Reith, John Charles Walsham 1889-1971
Obituary 113
Reither, Joseph 1903- 109
Reitlinger, Gerald R. 1900(?)-1978
Obituary 104
Reitmeister, Louis Aaron 1903-1975 49-52
Obituary 61-64
Reitsch, Hanna 1912(?)-1979 Obituary 89-92
Reitz, Donald J(oseph) 1932- 25-28R
Reitze, Arnold W(infred), Jr. 1938- 49-52
Rejai, Mostafa 1931- CANR-13
Earlier sketch in CA 37-40R
Rejaunier, Jeanne 1934- 29-32R
Rekai, Kati 1921- 105
Rekers, George A(lan) 1948- 119
Relgis, Eugene 1895- 81-84
Relis, Harry
See Endore, (Samuel) Guy
Relyea, Suzanne 1945- 77-80
Remak, Henry H. H. 1916- 19-20R
Remak, Joachim 1920- CANR-3
Earlier sketch in CA 1R
Remarque, Erich Maria 1898-1970 77-80
Obituary 29-32R
See also DLB 56
See also CLC 21
Rembar, Charles 1915- 25-28R
Remen, (Rachelle) Naomi 1938- 122
Brief entry 118
Remenih, Maurine 1916(?)-1985 Obituary .. 118
Remer, Theodore G. 1899- CAP-1
Earlier sketch in CA 15-16
Remi, Georges 1907-1983 69-72
Obituary 109
See also SATA 13, 32
Remington, Ella-Carrie 1914- 69-72
Remington, Frederic 1861-1909
Brief entry 108
See also SATA 41
See also DLB 12
Remington, Mark
See Bingley, David Ernest
Remington, Robin Alison 1938- CANR-12
Earlier sketch in CA 33-36R
Remini, Robert V(incent) 1921- CANR-20
Earlier sketches in CA 11-12R, CANR-3
Remizov, Alexey (Mikhailovich)
1877-1957 ....TCLC-27
Remley, David A. 1931- 45-48
Remley, Mary L(ouise) 1930- 102
Remmers, H(ermann) H(enry) 1892-1969 .... 2R
Obituary 103
Remmling, Gunter W(erner) 1929- 41-44R
Remoff, Heather T(rexler) 1938- 117
Remonda-Ruibal, Jorge Silvestre 1928- 108
Remsberg, Bonnie K(ohn) 1937- 69-72
Remsberg, Charles A(ndruss) 1936- CANR-7
Earlier sketch in CA 57-60
Remson, Irwin 1923- 53-56
Remy
See Renault, Gilbert (Leon Etienne Theodore)
Remy, Georges
See Remi, Georges
Remy, Pierre-Jean
See Angremy, Jean-Pierre
Remy, Richard C. 1942- 111
Rena, Sally
See Rena, Sarah Mary
Rena, Sarah Mary 1941- 103
Renan, Sheldon (Jackson) 1941- CANR-14
Earlier sketch in CA 23-24R
Renard, Alexandre Charles 1906-1983
Obituary 111
Renard, Jules 1864-1910 Brief entry 117
See also TCLC 17
Renaud, Jacques 1943- DLB-60
Renault, Gilbert (Leon Etienne Theodore)
1904-1984 Obituary 113
Renault, Mary
See Challans, Mary
See also DLBY 83
See also CLC 3, 11, 17
Renault, Rick
See Wallmann, Jeffrey M(iner)
Renay, Liz 1926- 33-36R
Rendall, Ted S. 101
Rendel, George William 1889-1979 ....7-8R
Obituary 103
Rendel, John 1906(?)-1978 Obituary 104
Rendell, Joan CANR-23
Earlier sketches in CA 61-64, CANR-7
See also SATA 28
Rendell, Ruth 1930- 109
See also CLC 28
Render, Sylvia Lyons 1913- CANR-15
Earlier sketch in CA 41-44R
Rendina, Laura (Jones) Cooper 1902- 11-12R
See also SATA 10
Rendleman, Danny L(ee) 1945- 65-68
Rendon, Armando B. 1939- 37-40R
Rene, Leon (T.) 1902-1982 Obituary 107
Rene, Natalia 1908(?)-1977 Obituary 69-72
Renehan, Robert (Francis Xavier) 1935-
Brief entry 108
Renetzky, Alvin 1940- 101
Renfield, Richard L. 1932- 29-32R
Renfrew, Jane Margaret 1942- 49-52
Renfroe, Martha Kay 1938- CANR-9
Earlier sketch in CA 65-68
Renich, Fred C. 1916-1979 115
Renich, Jill 1916- 25-28R
Renick, Marion (Lewis) 1905- CANR-1
Earlier sketch in CA 3R
See also SATA 1
Renier, Elizabeth
See Baker, Betty D(oreen Flook)
Renken, Aleda 1907- CANR-12
Earlier sketch in CA 21-22R
See also SATA 27
Renkiewicz, Frank 1935- 45-48
Renlie, Frank H. 1936- SATA-11
Renn, Casey
See Crim, Keith R(enn)
Renn, Ludwig
See Vieth von Golssenau, Arnold Friedrich
Renn, Thomas E(dward) 1939- 29-32R
Renne, Roland Roger 1905- 2R
Renner, Al G. 1912- 89-92
Renner, Beverly Hollett 1929- 85-88
Renner, Bruce 1944- 33-36R
Renner, John Wilson 1924- 41-44R
Renner, K(enneth) Edward 1936- 101
Renner, Thomas C(hoate) 1928- 73-76
Renner, Tom
See Renner, Thomas C(hoate)
Rennert, Maggie 1922- CANR-13
Earlier sketch in CA 61-64
Rennick, Robert M(orris) 1932- 122
Rennie, Christopher
See Ambrose, Eric (Samuel)
Rennie, Eric 1947- 45-48
Rennie, James Alan 1899-1969 .... CAP-1
Earlier sketch in CA 11-12
Rennie, Ysabel Fisk 1918- CANR-2
Earlier sketch in CA 7-8R
Reno, Clint
See Ballard, (Willis) Todhunter
Reno, Marie R(oth) CANR-10
Earlier sketch in CA 65-68
Reno, Ottie W(ayne) 1929- 41-44R
Reno, Philip 1913-1981 Obituary 111
Renoir, Alain 1921- 77-80
Renoir, Jean 1894-1979 Obituary 85-88
See also CLC 20
Renouf, Alan 1919- 108
Rensberger, Boyce 1942- 81-84
Rensch, Bernhard (Carl Emmanuel) 1900- .. 102
Renshaw, Domeena C(ynthia) 1929- 89-92
Renshaw, Patrick (Richard George)
1936- 21-22R
Renshaw, Samuel 1892- 77-80
Renshon, Stanley Allen 1943- Brief entry ... 109
Rensie, Willis
See Eisner, Will(iam Erwin)
Renton, Cam
See Armstrong, Richard
Renton, Julia
See Cole, Margaret Alice
Rentschler, Eric 1949- 118
Renvoize, Jean 41-44R
See also SATA 5
Renwick, Ethel Hulbert 1910- 7-8R
Renwick, Fred B(lackwell) 1930- 33-36R
Renzulli, L(ibero) Marx, Jr. 1934-
Brief entry 108
Replansky, Naomi 1918- 33-36R
Repp, Arthur C(hristian) 1906- CAP-1
Earlier sketch in CA 15-16
Repp, Ed Earl 1900(?)-1979 Obituary 85-88
Repp, William 1936- 110
Reps, John W(illiam) 1921- CANR-18
Earlier sketches in CA 45-48, CANR-1
Reps, (Saladin) Paul 1895- CANR-6
Earlier sketch in CA 7-8R
ReQua, Eloise Gallup 1902- CAP-1
Earlier sketch in CA 15-16
Resch, John Phillips 1940- Brief entry 108
Rescher, Nicholas 1928- CANR-12
Earlier sketch in CA 21-22R
Rescoe, A(ntoine) Stan(ley) 1910- 7-8R
Reshetar, John S(tephen) Jr. 1924- 7-8R
Reshevsky, Samuel Herman 1911- 65-68
Resick, Matthew C(larence) 1916- 57-60
Reske, Hermann 1911- 45-48
Reskind, John
See Wallmann, Jeffrey M(iner)
Resnais, Alain 1922- CLC-16
Resnick, H(arvey) L(ewis) P(aul) 1930- ...23-24R
Resnick, Marvin D. 1933- 21-22R
Resnick, Michael D(iamond) 1942- CANR-24
Earlier sketch in CA 107
See also SATA 38
Resnick, Mike
See Resnick, Michael D(iamond)
Resnick, Nathan 1910-1977 .... CAP-2
Obituary 73-76
Earlier sketch in CA 19-20
Resnick, Rose 61-64
Resnick, Seymour 1920- 73-76
See also SATA 23
Resnick, Sylvia (Safran) 1927- 93-96
Resnik, H(arvey) L(ewis) P(aul) 1930- .. CANR-10
Earlier sketch in CA 23-24R
Resnik, Henry S. 1940- 29-32R
Resnik, Michael D(avid) 1938- 116
Resposo, Epifania R. Castro 1922-1974
Obituary 113
Ressler, Alice 1918- 53-56
Ressner, Phil(ip) 1922- 15-16R
Rest, Friedrich Otto 1913- CANR-17
Earlier sketches in CA 5-6R, CANR-2
Rest, Karl H(einrich) A(lbert) 1908- 7-8R
Restak, Richard M(artin) 1942- CANR-24
Earlier sketches in CA 61-64, CANR-8
Restivo, Sal 1940- 112
Restle, Frank 1927- 41-44R
Reston, James (Barrett) 1909- 65-68
See also AITN 1, 2
Reston, James B(arrett), Jr. 1941- 37-40R
Reston, Jody AITN-2
Reston, Richard AITN-2
Retla, Robert
See Alter, Robert Edmond
Retner, Beth A.
See Brown, Beth
Rettig, Edward B(ertram) 1940- 57-60
Rettig, Jack L(ouis) 1925- 57-60
Reuben, David 1933- 41-44R
See also AITN 1
Reuber, Grant L(ouis) 1927- CANR-3
Earlier sketch in CA 49-52
Reul, R(ose) Myrtle 1919- 21-22R
Reuman, Robert E(verett) 1923- 37-40R
Reumann, John 1927- CANR-5
Earlier sketch in CA 2R
Reuss, Carl F(rederick) 1915- 41-44R
Reuss, Frederick G(ustav) 1904- CAP-1
Earlier sketch in CA 11-12
Reuss, Henry S(choellkopf) 1912- CANR-6
Earlier sketch in CA 11-12R
Reuter, Carol (Joan) 1931- 23-24R
See also SATA 2
Reuter, Frank T. 1926- 21-22R
Reuter, Gabriele 1859-1941 .... DLB-66
Reuther, David L(ouis) 1946- 112
Reuther, Ruth E. 1917- CANR-12
Earlier sketch in CA 33-36R
Reuther, Victor G(eorge) 1912- 77-80
Rev, B.
See Eisner, Betty Grover
Reval, Jacques
See Laver, James
Revankar, Ratna G. 1937- 33-36R
Revard, Stella Purce 1933- 97-100
Reve, Karel van het
See van het Reve, Karel
Revel, Jean-Francois
See Ricard, Jean-Francois
Reveley, Edith 1930- 123
Revell, Donald 1954- 116
Revell, J(ohn) R(obert) S(tephen)
1920- CANR-11
Earlier sketch in CA 25-28R
Revell, Jack
See Revell, J(ohn) R(obert) S(tephen)
Revell, Peter 1929-1983 .... CANR-13
Earlier sketch in CA 29-32R
ReVelle, Charles S. 1938- 45-48
ReVelle, Penelope 1941- 49-52
Revena
See Wright, Betty Ren
Reventlow, Franziska Graefin zu
1871-1918 .... DLB-66
Reverdy, Pierre 1889-1960 97-100
Obituary 89-92
Reverend Mandju
See Su Chien
Reves, Emery 1904-1981 Obituary 105
Rewald, John 1912- CANR-5
Earlier sketch in CA 9-10R
Rewoldt, Stewart H(enry) 1922- 37-40R
Rex, Barbara (Clayton) 1904- 77-80
Rex, John A(rderne) 1925- CANR-24
Earlier sketches in CA 5-6R, CANR-6
Rex, Walter E(dwin) 1927- 45-48
Rexine, John E(fstratios) 1929- CANR-15
Earlier sketch in CA 37-40R
Rexroth, Kenneth 1905-1982 .... CANR-14
Obituary 107
Earlier sketch in CA 5-6R
See also DLB 16, 48
See also DLBY 82
See also CDALB 1941-1968
See also CLC 1, 2, 6, 11, 22
Rey, H(ans) A(ugusto) 1898-1977 ...... CANR-6
Obituary 73-76
Earlier sketch in CA 5-6R
See also SATA 1, 26
See also DLB 22
See also CLR 5
Rey, Margret (Elisabeth) 1906- 105
See also SATA 26
See also CLR 5
Rey, Michael Stephan 1946- 113
Reyam
See Mayer, Charles Leopold
Reybold, Malcolm 1911(?)-1988 Obituary .. 124
Reyburn, Wallace (Macdonald) 1913- ... CANR-1
Earlier sketch in CA 49-52
Reyes, Carlos 1935- CANR-3
Earlier sketch in CA 49-52
Reyes y Basoalto, Ricardo Eliecer Neftali
See Neruda, Pablo
Reyher, Becky
See Reyher, Rebecca Hourwich

Reyher, Rebecca Hourwich 1897-1987
Obituary ... 121
See also SATA 18, 50
Reymont, Wladyslaw (Stanislaw) 1868(?)-1925 Brief entry ... 104
See also TCLC 5
Reynolds, Alan 1942- ... 61-64
Reynolds, Ann
See Bly, Carol(yn)
Reynolds, Anne
See Steinke, Ann (Elizabeth)
Reynolds, Barbara 1914- ... 9-10R
Reynolds, Barbara (Ann) 1942- ... 73-76
Reynolds, Barrie (Gordon Robert) 1932- ... 13-14R
Reynolds, Bart
See Emblen, D(onald) L(ewis)
Reynolds, Bertha Capen 1885- ... CAP-2
Earlier sketch in CA 19-20
Reynolds, Charles O. 1921- ... 9-10R
Reynolds, (Alfred) Christopher 1911- ... 104
Reynolds, Clark G(ilbert) 1939- ... CANR-12
Earlier sketch in CA 25-28R
Reynolds, Clark Winton 1934- ... CANR-8
Earlier sketch in CA 23-24R
Reynolds, Dallas McCord 1917- ... CANR-9
Earlier sketch in CA 7-8R
Reynolds, David K(ent) 1940- ... CANR-9
Earlier sketch in CA 65-68
Reynolds, David S(pencer) 1948- ... 124
Reynolds, Dickson
See Reynolds, Helen Mary Greenwood Campbell
Reynolds, Donald E. 1931- ... 33-36R
Reynolds, Elizabeth
See Steinke, Ann (Elizabeth)
Reynolds, Ernest (Randolph) 1910- ... CANR-6
Earlier sketch in CA 3-14R
Reynolds, Frank 1923-1983 ... 114
Obituary ... 109
Reynolds, G. Scott 1925- ... 29-32R
Reynolds, G. W. M. 1814-1879 ... DLB-21
Reynolds, (Arthur) Graham 1914- ... CANR-17
Earlier sketch in CA 13-14R
Reynolds, Harry W., Jr. 1924- ... 15-16R
Reynolds, Helen Mary Greenwood Campbell 1884-1969 ... 7-8R
Obituary ... 103
See also SATA 26
Reynolds, Jack
See Jones, Jack
Reynolds, Joe
See Steward, Samuel M(orris)
Reynolds, John 1901- ... 11-12R
Reynolds, John
See Whitlock, Ralph
Reynolds, John J(oseph) 1924- ... 37-40R
Reynolds, Jonathan 1942- ... 65-68
See also CLC 6, 38
Reynolds, Julia Louise 1883(?)-1980
Obituary ... 102
Reynolds, Larry T(homas) 1938-
Brief entry ... 107
Reynolds, Lloyd George 1910- ... CANR-15
Earlier sketch in CA 23-24R
Reynolds, Louis B. 1917- ... 41-44R
Reynolds, Mack
See Reynolds, Dallas McCord
See also DLB 8
Reynolds, Madge
See Whitlock, Ralph
Reynolds, Malvina 1900-1978 ... 114
Obituary ... 105
See also SATA 24, 44
Reynolds, Marie E. 1912- ... 19-20R
Reynolds, Marjorie Harris 1903- ... 7-8R
Reynolds, Mary Trackett 1914- ... 109
Reynolds, Michael Shane 1937- ... CANR-9
Earlier sketch in CA 65-68
See also CLC 44
Reynolds, (Marjorie) Moira Davison 1915- ... CANR-21
Earlier sketch in CA 105
Reynolds, Morgan O(wen) 1942- ... 117
Reynolds, Pamela 1923- ... 103
See also SATA 34
Reynolds, Paul Davidson 1938- ... CANR-12
Earlier sketch in CA 33-36R
Reynolds, Paul R(evere) 1904- ... 102
Reynolds, Peter C(arlton) 1943- ... 105
Reynolds, Philip Alan 1920- ... CANR-3
Earlier sketch in CA 7-8R
Reynolds, Quentin (James) 1902-1965 ... 73-76
Reynolds, Robert Leonard 1902-1966 ... 2R
Obituary ... 103
Reynolds, Roger 1934- ... 53-56
Reynolds, Ruth Sutton 1890(?)-1977
Obituary ... 69-72
Reynolds, Susan (Mary Grace) 1929- ... 117
Reynolds, Terry S(cott) 1946- ... 117
Reynolds, Timothy (Robin) 1936- ... CANR-8
Earlier sketch in CA 9-10R
Reynolds, Valrae 1944- ... 93-96
Reynolds, William Howard 1922-1972
Obituary ... 107
Reynolds, William J. 1956- ... 123
Reynolds, William Jensen 1920- ... CANR-7
Earlier sketch in CA 7-8R
Rezits, Joseph 1925- ... 107
Rezler, Julius 1911- ... 25-28R
Rezmerski, John Calvin 1942- ... 29-32R
Rezneck, Samuel 1897-1983 ... CANR-24
Obituary ... 110
Earlier sketch in CA 45-48

Reznikoff, Charles 1894-1976 ... CAP-2
Obituary ... 61-64
Earlier sketch in CA 33-36
See also DLB 28, 45
See also CLC 9
Rezny, Arthur A(dolph) 1910- ... CAP-2
Earlier sketch in CA 19-20
Rezzori (d'Arezzo), Gregor von 1914-
Brief entry ... 122
See also CLC 25
Rhea, Claude H(iram), Jr. 1927- ... 103
Rhea, Nicholas
See Walker, Peter N.
Rhein, Francis Bayard 1915- ... 19-20R
Rhein, Phillip H(enry) 1923- ... 81-84
Rheinstein, Max 1899-1977 Obituary ... 73-76
Rhenisch, Harold (Arthur) 1958- ... 113
Rhett, Robert Barnwell 1800-1876 ... DLB-43
Rhie, Schi-Zhin 1936- ... 77-80
Rhine, J(oseph) B(anks) 1895-1980 ... CANR-4
Obituary ... 93-96
Earlier sketch in CA 7-8R
Rhine, Louisa (Weckesser) E. 1891- ... CANR-4
Earlier sketch in CA 3R
Rhinehart, Luke
See Cockcroft, George Powers
Rhinehart, Susan Oneacre 1938- ... 4R
Rhoades, Jonathan
See Olsen, John Edward
Rhoades, Judith G(rubman) 1935- ... 97-100
Rhoads, Dorothy M(ary) 1895- ... CAP-2
Earlier sketch in CA 19-20
Rhoads, Edward J(ohn) M(ichael) 1938- ... 33-36R
Rhoads, Jonathan E(vans) 1907- ... 104
Rhode, Austen
See Francis, Basil (Hoskins)
Rhode, Eric 1934- ... 21-22R
Rhode, Irma 1900-1982 Obituary ... 106
Rhode, Robert B(artlett) 1916- ... 19-20R
Rhode, Robert D(avid) 1911- ... 93-96
Rhode, Winslow
See Roe, F(rederic) Gordon
Rhodehamel, Josephine DeWitt 1901- ... 61-64
Rhodes, Albert 1916-1977 ... CANR-14
Earlier sketch in CA 21-22R
Rhodes, Anthony (Richard Ewart) 1916- ... 9-10R
Rhodes, Arnold Black 1913- ... 15-16R
Rhodes, Bennie (Loran) 1927- ... 108
See also SATA 35
Rhodes, Carolyn Hodgson 1925- ... 122
Rhodes, Clifford Oswald 1911-1985 ... 65-68
Obituary ... 118
Rhodes, David 1946- ... 57-60
Rhodes, Dennis Everard 1923- ... 15-16R
Rhodes, Ernest Lloyd 1915- ... 119
Rhodes, Evan H. 1929- ... CANR-10
Earlier sketch in CA 57-60
Rhodes, Frank Harold Trevor 1926- ... 107
See also SATA 37
Rhodes, Hari 1932- ... 19-20R
Rhodes, Irwin Seymour 1901- ... 73-76
Rhodes, James Allen 1909- Brief entry ... 105
Rhodes, James Ford 1848-1927 ... DLB-47
Rhodes, James M. 1940- ... 89-92
Rhodes, John J(acob) 1916- ... 103
Rhodes, Laura
See Robinson, Lisa
Rhodes, Margaret 1915- ... 45-48
Rhodes, Philip 1922- ... 107
Rhodes, Richard (Lee) 1937- ... CANR-20
Earlier sketches in CA 45-48, CANR-1
Rhodes, Robert E(dward) 1927- ... 122
Rhodes, Robert I. 1942- ... 69-72
Rhodes, William C(onley) 1918- ... 81-84
Rhodes James, Robert (Vidal) 1933- ... CANR-14
Earlier sketch in CA 101
Rhodin, Eric Nolan 1916- ... CANR-3
Earlier sketch in CA 3R
Rhue, Morton
See Strasser, Todd
Rhydderch, Ieuan
See Jones, Evan David
Rhymer, Joseph 1927- ... CANR-9
Earlier sketch in CA 23-24R
Rhys, Frank
See Rees, Clair (Francis)
Rhys, Ioan
See Rees, Ioan Bowen
Rhys, J(ohn) Howard W(inslow) 1917- ... 19-20R
Rhys, Jean 1894-1979 ... 25-28R
Obituary ... 85-88
See also DLB 36
See also CLC 2, 4, 6, 14, 19
Rhys, Kate
See Donald, Anabel
Rhys, Keidrych 1915-1987 Obituary ... 122
Riasanovsky, Nicholas V(alentine) 1923- ... CANR-3
Earlier sketch in CA 5-6R
Ribal, Joseph E(dward) 1931- ... 61-64
Ribalow, Harold U(riel) 1919-1982 ... CANR-2
Obituary ... 108
Earlier sketch in CA 5-6R
Ribar, Joe 1943- ... 77-80
Ribbons, Ian 1924- ... 108
See also SATA 30, 37
See also SAAS 3
Ribeiro, Aileen 1944- ... 124
Ribeiro, Darcy 1922- ... 33-36R
See also CLC 34
Ribeiro, Joao Ubaldo (Osorio Pimentel) 1941- ... 81-84
See also CLC 10
Ribicoff, Abraham (Alexander) 1910- ... 108
Ribman, Ronald (Burt) 1932- ... 21-22R
See also CLC 7

Ribner, Irving 1921-1972 ... CANR-3
Obituary ... 37-40R
Earlier sketch in CA 2R
Riboud, Barbara (Dewayne Tosi) Chase
See Chase-Riboud, Barbara (Dewayne Tosi)
Ribuffo, Leo P(aul) 1945- ... 118
Ricard, Jean-Francois 1924- Brief entry ... 109
Ricardo, Harry R(alph) 1885-1974
Obituary ... 114
Ricardo-Campbell, Rita ... CANR-8
Earlier sketch in CA 57-60
Ricart, Josep Gudiol i
See Gudiol i Ricart, Josep
Riccards, Michael P(atrick) 1944- ... 61-64
Ricchiuti, Paul B(urton) 1925- ... 107
Ricci, Larry J. 1948- ... 109
Ricciardi, Lorenzo 1930- ... 109
Ricciuti, Edward R(aphael) 1938- ... 41-44R
See also SATA 10
Rice, A(lbert) Kenneth 1908- ... 7-8R
Rice, Albert
See Leventhal, Albert Rice
Rice, Allan Lake 1905- ... 37-40R
Rice, Anne 1941- ... CANR-12
Earlier sketch in CA 65-68
See also CLC 41
Rice, Arnold Sanford 1928- ... 113
Rice, Berkeley 1937- ... 21-22R
Rice, C(harles) David 1941- ... 118
Rice, C(harles) Duncan 1942- ... CANR-10
Earlier sketch in CA 57-60
Rice, Charles D(uane) 1910-1971
Obituary ... 104
See also SATA 27
Rice, Charles E. 1931- ... CANR-1
Earlier sketch in CA 4R
Rice, Charles L(ynvel) 1936- ... 65-68
Rice, Craig
See Randolph, Georgiana Ann
Rice, Cy 1905-1971 ... CAP-1
Obituary ... 33-36R
Earlier sketch in CA 11-12
Rice, Dale R(ichard) 1948- ... 116
See also SATA 42
Rice, David G(ordon) 1938- ... 101
Rice, David Talbot 1903-1972 ... CANR-5
Earlier sketch in CA 9-10R
Rice, Desmond Charles 1924- ... CANR-21
Earlier sketches in CA 11-12R, CANR-5
Rice, Donald L. 1938- ... CANR-14
Earlier sketch in CA 37-40R
Rice, Dorothy Mary 1913- ... 11-12R
Rice, Edmund C. 1910(?)-1982 Obituary ... 106
Rice, Edward E(arl) 1909- ... 41-44R
Rice, Edward E. 1918- ... CANR-1
Earlier sketch in CA 49-52
See also SATA 42, 47
Rice, Elinor
See Hays, Elinor Rice
Rice, Elizabeth 1913- ... 23-24R
See also SATA 2
Rice, Elmer 1892-1967 ... CAP-2
Obituary ... 25-28R
Earlier sketch in CA 21-22
See also DLB 4, 7
See also CLC 7
Rice, Eugene F(ranklin), Jr. 1924- ... 29-32R
Rice, Eve (Hart) 1951- ... CANR-4
Earlier sketch in CA 53-56
See also SATA 34
Rice, Frank M(artin) 1908- ... 45-48
Rice, George H(all), Jr. 1923- ... 53-56
Rice, Grantland 1880-1954 Brief entry ... 114
See also DLB 29
Rice, Homer C(ranston) 1927- ... 73-76
Rice, Inez 1907- ... 29-32R
See also SATA 13
Rice, James 1934- ... CANR-8
Earlier sketch in CA 61-64
See also SATA 22
Rice, John R(ichard) 1895-1980 ... CANR-5
Earlier sketch in CA 5-6R
Rice, Joseph Peter 1930- ... 29-32R
Rice, Julius 1923- ... 41-44R
Rice, Keith A(lan) 1954- ... 109
Rice, Lawrence D. 1929- ... 33-36R
Rice, Martin P(aul) 1938- ... 57-60
Rice, Max M(cGee) 1928- ... 93-96
Rice, Otis K(ermit) 1919- ... 29-32R
Rice, R. B.
See Chapman, Frank M(onroe)
Rice, Ross R(ichard) 1922- ... 45-48
Rice, Stan 1942- ... 77-80
Rice, Tamara (Abelson) Talbot 1904-
Brief entry ... 111
Rice, Thomas Jackson 1945- ... CANR-18
Earlier sketch in CA 101
Rice, Tim 1944- ... 103
See also CLC 21
Rice, Wayne 1945- ... 89-92
Rice, William (Edward) 1938- ... 118
Rice, William C(arroll) 1911- ... 11-12R
Rich, Adrienne (Cecile) 1929- ... CANR-20
Earlier sketch in CA 11-12R
See also DLB 5, 67
See also CLC 3, 6, 7, 11, 18, 36
Rich, Alan 1924- ... 11-12R
Rich, Daniel Catton 1904-1976 ... 73-76
Obituary ... 69-72
Rich, Edwin Ernest 1904-1979 Obituary ... 89-92
Rich, Elaine Sommers 1926- ... CANR-24
Earlier sketches in CA 19-20R, CANR-9
See also SATA 6
Rich, Elizabeth 1935- ... 29-32R
Rich, (Ora) Everett 1900- ... CAP-1
Earlier sketch in CA 11-12

Rich, Frank 1949- ... 73-76
Rich, Gerry
See Brandon, Johnny
Rich, (David) Gibson 1936- ... 57-60
Rich, Joe 1935- ... 57-60
Rich, John H., Jr. 1917- ... 81-84
Rich, John Martin 1931- ... 21-22R
Rich, Josephine Bouchard 1912- ... 5-6R
See also SATA 10
Rich, Louise Dickinson 1903- ... 73-76
Rich, Michael B(enjamin) 1935- ... 29-32R
Rich, Norman 1921- ... 45-48
Rich, Paul B(enjamin) 1950- ... 124
Rich, Robert
See Trumbo, Dalton
Rich, Russell R(ogers) 1912- ... 101
Richard, Adrienne 1921- ... 29-32R
See also SATA 5
Richard, Arthur Windsor
See Windsor-Richards, Arthur (Bedlington)
Richard, Betty Byrd 1922- ... 106
Richard, James Robert
See Bowen, Robert Sydney
Richard, John 1954- ... 106
Richard, Keith
See Richards, Keith
Richard, Lee
See Le Pelley, Guernsey
Richard, Lionel (Camille Paul) 1938- ... 93-96
Richard, Lucien J(oseph) 1931- ... 105
Richard, Marthe 1889-1982 Obituary ... 110
Richard, Michel Paul 1933- ... 45-48
Richard, Olga 1914- ... 103
Richards, Alayna
See Posner, Richard
Richards, Alfred (Luther) 1939- ... 45-48
Richards, Allen
See Rosenthal, Richard A.
Richards, Alun 1929- ... CANR-17
Earlier sketch in CA 65-68
Richards, Arlene Kramer 1935- ... CANR-11
Earlier sketch in CA 65-68
Richards, Audrey I(sabel) 1899-1984 ... 23-24R
Obituary ... 113
Richards, Blair P(atton) 1940- ... 69-72
Richards, Cara E(lizabeth) 1927- ... CANR-1
Earlier sketch in CA 49-52
Richards, Carl Edward, Jr. 1933- ... CANR-24
Earlier sketch in CA 45-48
Richards, Caroline 1939- ... 77-80
Richards, Charles
See Marvin, John T.
Richards, Clare
See Titchener, Louise
Richards, Clay
See Crossen, Kendell Foster
Richards, David
See Bickers, Richard Leslie Townshend
Richards, David Adams 1950- ... 93-96
See also DLB 53
Richards, Denis (George) 1910- ... 11-12R
Richards, Dennis L(ee) 1938- ... 102
Richards, Dorothy B(urney) 1894- ... 85-88
Richards, Duane
See Hurley, Vic
Richards, E. B.
See Bayley, Edwin Richard
Richards, Frank
See Hamilton, Charles Harold St. John
Richards, Fred
See Richards, Alfred (Luther)
Richards, George 1760(?)-1814 ... DLB-37
Richards, Guy 1905-1979 ... CANR-11
Obituary ... 81-84
Earlier sketch in CA 61-64
Richards, H(arold) M(arshall) S(ylvester) 1894-1985 ... CAP-2
Obituary ... 116
Earlier sketch in CA 23-24
Richards, Hilda
See Hamilton, Charles Harold St. John
Richards, Horace G(ardiner) 1906- ... 5-6R
Richards, I(vor) A(rmstrong) 1893-1979 ... 41-44R
Obituary ... 89-92
See also DLB 27
See also CLC 14, 24
Richards, J(ohn) Howard 1916- ... CANR-18
Earlier sketches in CA 45-48, CANR-2
Richards, J(ames) M(aude) 1907- ... CANR-5
Earlier sketch in CA 5-6R
Richards, Jack W(esley) 1933- ... 33-36R
Richards, James O(lin) 1936- ... 37-40R
Richards, Jane 1934- ... 33-36R
Richards, Jeffrey (Michael) 1945- ... CANR-13
Earlier sketch in CA 73-76
Richards, Jock 1918- ... 107
Richards, Joe 1909- ... CAP-1
Earlier sketch in CA 9-10
Richards, John 1939- ... 57-60
Richards, John F(olsom) 1938- ... 115
Richards, John Marvin 1929- ... 15-16R
Richards, Kathleen
See Dale, Kathleen
Richards, Kay
See Baker, Susan (Catherine)
Richards, Keith 1943- ... 107
Richards, Kenny
See Broderick, Richard L(awrence)
Richards, Kent David 1938- ... 104
Richards, Larry
See Richards, Lawrence O.
Richards, Laura E(lizabeth Howe) 1850-1943 Brief entry ... 120
See also YABC 1
See also DLB 42

Richards, Lawrence O. 1931- CANR-20
Earlier sketch in CA 29-32R
Richards, Lewis A(lva) 1925- 45-48
Richards, M(ary) C(aroline) 1916- 108
Richards, Mark
See Ra'Anan, Uri
Richards, Martin P(aul) M(eredith)
1940- CANR-23
Earlier sketches in CA 61-64, CANR-8
Richards, Max D(eVoe) 1923- CANR-16
Earlier sketch in CA 23-24R
Richards, Nat
See Richardson, James Nathaniel
Richards, Norman 1932- 112
See also SATA 48
Richards, Owain Westmacott 1901-1984
Obituary 114
Richards, Pamela Spence 1941- 111
Richards, Peter
See Monger, (Ifor) David
Richards, Peter Godfrey 1923-1987 108
Obituary 123
Richards, Phyllis
See Auty, Phyllis
Richards, R(onald) C(harles) W(illiam)
1923- CANR-10
Earlier sketch in CA 21-22R
See also SATA 43
Richards, Stanley 1918-1980 .... 25-28R
Obituary 101
Richards, Todd
See Sutphen, Richard Charles
Richards, Victor 1918- 57-60
Richardson, Alan 1923- 29-32R
Richardson, Ann 1942- 119
Richardson, Anne
See Roiphe, Anne Richardson
Richardson, Arleta 1923- CANR-16
Earlier sketch in CA 93-96
Richardson, Beth
See Gutcheon, Beth R(ichardson)
Richardson, Betty 1935- 53-56
Richardson, Bradley M. 1928- 49-52
Richardson, C.
See Munsey, Cecil (Richard, Jr.)
Richardson, Cecil Antonio 1928- 121
Brief entry 115
Richardson, Charles E(verett) 1928- 57-60
Richardson, Cyril Charles 1909-1976 ..... 37-40R
Obituary 69-72
Richardson, Don(ald MacNaughton)
1935- CANR-9
Earlier sketch in CA 65-68
Richardson, Donald P(orter) 1932- 119
Richardson, Dorothy Lee 1900-1986 106
Obituary 121
Richardson, Dorothy Miller 1873-1957
Brief entry 104
See also DLB 36
See also TCLC 3
Richardson, Dorsey 1896-1981 Obituary ... 105
Richardson, Edgar Preston 1902-1985 110
Obituary 115
Richardson, Elliot L(ee) 1920- Brief entry ... 111
Richardson, Elmo (R.) 1930- CANR-11
Earlier sketch in CA 13-14R
Richardson, Ethel Florence (Lindesay)
1870-1946 Brief entry 105
Richardson, Evelyn M(ay Fox) 1902- CAP-1
Earlier sketch in CA 13-14
Richardson, Frank Howard 1882-1970
Obituary 104
See also SATA 27
Richardson, Frank McLean 1904- CANR-20
Earlier sketch in CA 103
Richardson, Gayle E(lwin) 1911- 11-12R
Richardson, George Barclay 1924- 4R
Richardson, Gladwell 1903-1980 123
Richardson, Grace Lee
See Dickson, Naida
Richardson, H(arold) Edward 1929- CANR-15
Earlier sketch in CA 29-32R
Richardson, Harry V(an Buren) 1901- 69-72
Richardson, Harry W(ard) 1938- 29-32R
Richardson, Henrietta
See Richardson, Ethel Florence
(Lindesay)
Richardson, Henry Handel
See Richardson, Ethel Florence
(Lindesay)
See also TCLC 4
Richardson, Henry V(okes) M(ackey)
1923- 25-28R
Richardson, Howard (Dixon) 1917-1984 .. 41-44R
Obituary 114
Richardson, Isla Paschal 1886-1971 ..... CAP-1
Earlier sketch in CA 9-10
Richardson, Ivan L(eRoy) 1920- 101
Richardson, Ivor Lloyd Morgan 1930- 11-12R
Richardson, Jack (Carter) 1935- 7-8R
See also DLB 7
Richardson, James 1950- 77-80
Richardson, James F(rancis) 1931- 29-32R
Richardson, James L(ongden) 1933- 21-22R
Richardson, James Nathaniel 1942- 53-56
Richardson, James R. 1911- 2R
Richardson, Jeremy John 1942- 29-32R
Richardson, Joanna CANR-10
Earlier sketch in CA 13-14R
Richardson, Joe M(artin) 1934- 45-48
Richardson, John Adkins 1929- 57-60
Richardson, John Martin, Jr. 1938- ... CANR-12
Earlier sketch in CA 33-36R
Richardson, Justin 1900(?)-1975
Obituary 61-64
Richardson, Kenneth Ridley 1934- 29-32R
Richardson, Laurel 1938- 111
Richardson, Laurence E(aton) 1893- CAP-1
Earlier sketch in CA 11-12
Richardson, (Stewart) Lee (Jr.) 1940- ... CANR-9
Earlier sketch in CA 21-22R
Richardson, Leopold John Dixon
1893-1979(?) Obituary 104
Richardson, Malcolm 1947- 120
Richardson, Midge Turk 1930- 33-36R
Richardson, Miles (Edward) 1932- 33-36R
Richardson, Mozelle Groner 1914- 33-36R
Richardson, Neil R(yan) 1944- 103
Richardson, Nola 1936- 57-60
Richardson, (George) Peter 1935- 114
Richardson, R(alph) Daniel 1931- 109
Richardson, Richard C(olby), Jr.
1933- CANR-13
Earlier sketch in CA 77-80
Richardson, Richard Judson 1935- 29-32R
Richardson, Robert (Dale, Jr.) 1934- .. CANR-12
Earlier sketch in CA 29-32R
Richardson, Robert Galloway 1926- CANR-7
Earlier sketch in CA 15-16R
Richardson, Robert S(hirley) 1902- 49-52
See also SATA 8
Richardson, Rupert Norval 1891- 19-20R
Richardson, S(tanley) D(ennis) 1925- .. CANR-10
Earlier sketch in CA 21-22R
Richardson, Samuel 1689-1761 .... DLB-39
Richardson, Stephen A. 1920- 61-64
Richardson, Thomas Dow 1887- 7-8R
Richardson, Tony
See Richardson, Cecil Antonio
Richardson, Vokes
See Richardson, Henry V(okes) M(ackey)
Richardson, W(alter) C(ecil) 1902- CANR-1
Earlier sketch in CA 2R
Richardson, William John 1920- 21-22R
Richardson, Willis 1889-1977 124
See also DLB 51
Richason, Benjamin F(ranklin, Jr.)
1922- 41-44R
Richberg, Donald R(andall) 1881-1960
Obituary 113
Riche, Pierre 1921- 123
Riche, Robert 1925- 108
Riche, William Harding le
See le Riche, William Harding
Richelieu, Peter
See Robinson, P. W.
Richelson, Geraldine 1922- 106
See also SATA 29
Richelson, Jeffrey T(albot) 1949- 119
Richens, Richard Hook 1919-1984
Obituary 114
Riches, John (Kenneth) 1939- 117
Riches, Pierre 1927- 118
Richette, Lisa Aversa 1928- 25-28R
Richetti, John J(oseph) 1938- 110
Richey, David 1939- CANR-10
Earlier sketch in CA 57-60
Richey, Dorothy Hilliard CANR-6
Earlier sketch in CA 9-10R
Richey, Elinor 1920- 45-48
Richey, Margaret Fitzgerald 1883(?)-1974
Obituary 53-56
Richey, Robert W(illiam) 1912-1978 ... CANR-17
Obituary 116
Earlier sketch in CA 25-28R
Richey, Russell Earle 1941- 69-72
Richie, Donald (Steiner) 1924- CANR-24
Earlier sketches in CA 19-20R, CANR-8
Richland, W(ilfred) Bernard 1909- 102
Richler, Mordecai 1931- 65-68
See also SATA 27, 44
See also DLB 53
See also CLC 3, 5, 9, 13, 18, 46
See also AITN 1
Richman, Barry M(artin) 1936-1978 ... CANR-17
Earlier sketch in CA 23-24R
Richman, Milton (Saul) 1922-1986 69-72
Obituary 119
Richman, Phyllis C. 1939- 89-92
Richman, Robert (Maxwell) 1914-1987
Obituary 124
Richman, Saul 1917(?)-1979 Obituary 85-88
Rich-McCoy, Lois
See McCoy, Lois (Rich)
Richmond, Al 1913-1987 .... 41-44R
Obituary 124
Richmond, Anthony H(enry) 1925- 23-24R
Richmond, Cindy Packard 1948- 112
Richmond, Dick 1933- 61-64
Richmond, Douglas W(ertz) 1946- 111
Richmond, Grace
See Marsh, John
Richmond, H(ugh) M(acrae) 1932- CANR-3
Earlier sketch in CA 9-10R
Richmond, Ian Archibald 1902-1965
Obituary 111
Richmond, John C(hristopher) B(lake)
1909- Brief entry 106
Richmond, Julius B(enjamin) 1916- 29-32R
Richmond, Lee 1943- 49-52
Richmond, Lee J(oyce) 1934- 113
Richmond, Leigh (Tucker) 1911- 23-24R
Richmond, Roaldus Frederick 1910- 114
Richmond, Robert P. 1914- 21-22R
Richmond, Robert W(illiam) 1927- 53-56
Richmond, Rod
See Glut, Donald F(rank)
Richmond, Roe
See Richmond, Roaldus Frederick
Richmond, Samuel B(ernard) 1919- 41-44R
Richmond, Sandra 1948- 117
Richmond, (John) Stanley 1906- 45-48
Richmond, Velma E. B(ourgeois) 1931- ... 61-64
Richmond, W(illiam) Kenneth 1910- ... CANR-10
Earlier sketch in CA 25-28R
Richmond, Walt(er F.) 1922-1977 .... 23-24R
Obituary 117
Richoux, Pat(ricia) 1927- 25-28R
See also SATA 7
Richstatter, Thomas 1939- 112
Richter, Alice 1941- 105
See also SATA 30
Richter, C(harles) F(rancis) 1900-1985
Obituary 117
Richter, Conrad (Michael) 1890-1968 .. CANR-23
Obituary 25-28R
Earlier sketch in CA 7-8R
See also SATA 3
See also DLB 9
See also CLC 30
Richter, David H. 1945- 101
Richter, Derek 1907- 101
Richter, Dorothy 1906- 29-32R
Richter, Gerard R(ichard) 1905- 5-6R
Richter, Gisela M(arie) A(ugusta)
1882-1972 .... CANR-4
Earlier sketch in CA 7-8R
Richter, Hans 1888-1976 73-76
Obituary 65-68
Richter, Hans Peter 1925- CANR-2
Earlier sketch in CA 45-48
See also SATA 6
Richter, Hans Werner 1908- 97-100
Richter, Harvena 1919- CANR-3
Earlier sketch in CA 7-8R
Richter, Horst-Eberhard 1923- CANR-20
Earlier sketches in CA 53-56, CANR-5
Richter, Irving 1911- 57-60
Richter, J. H(ans) 1901- CAP-1
Earlier sketch in CA 15-16
Richter, Joan 1930- 101
Richter, Lin 1936- 73-76
Richter, Linda K. 1942- 117
Richter, Maurice N(athaniel), Jr. 1930- 49-52
Richter, Melvin 1921- Brief entry 110
Richter, Valentin
See Pick, Robert
Richter, Vernon
See Hutchcroft, Vera
Rickard, Bob
See Rickard, Robert J(ohn) M(oberley)
Rickard, Robert J(ohn) M(oberley) 1945- ... 106
Rickards, Colin (William) 1937- 25-28R
Rickards, Maurice 1919- 103
Rickel, Annette U. 1941- 123
Rickels, Karl 1924- CANR-1
Earlier sketch in CA 45-48
Rickels, Milton H. 1920- 5-6R
Rickenbacker, Eddie
See Rickenbacker, Edward Vernon
Rickenbacker, Edward Vernon 1890-1973 ... 101
Obituary 41-44R
Ricker, George Marvin 1922- CANR-20
Earlier sketch in CA 89-92
Rickert, Corinne Holt
See Sawyer, Corinne Holt
Rickert, John E(arl) 1923- CANR-24
Earlier sketch in CA 45-48
Rickett, Frances 1921- 107
Rickett, Harold William 1896- 19-20R
Ricketts, C(arl) E(verett) 1906- 57-60
Ricketts, Ralph Robert 1902- 116
Ricketts, Viva Leone (Harris) 1900- CAP-1
Earlier sketch in CA 11-12
Rickey, Don, Jr. 1925- CANR-9
Earlier sketch in CA 7-8R
Rickey, George Warren 1907- 65-68
Rickey, Mary Ellen 1929- 23-24R
Rickman, Geoffrey (Edwin) 1932- 29-32R
Rickman, H(ans) P(eter) 1918- CANR-14
Earlier sketch in CA 19-20R
Rickover, H. G.
See Rickover, Hyman George
Rickover, Hyman George 1900-1986
Obituary 119
Ricks, Chip
See Ricks, Nadine
Ricks, Christopher (Bruce) 1933- CANR-23
Earlier sketches in CA 11-12R, CANR-7
Ricks, David F(rank) 1927- CANR-10
Earlier sketch in CA 21-22R
Ricks, David Trulock 1936- 25-28R
Ricks, Don(ald) M(ax) 1936- 25-28R
Ricks, Nadine 1925- CANR-13
Earlier sketch in CA 77-80
Rickword, (John) Edgell 1898-1982 101
Obituary 106
See also DLB 20
Rico, Don(ato) 1917-1985 81-84
Obituary 115
See also SATA 43
Rico, Gabriele Lusser 1937- 110
Ricoeur, Paul 1913- CANR-10
Earlier sketch in CA 61-64
Ricou, Laurence (Rodger) 1944- CANR-8
Earlier sketch in CA 61-64
Riday, George E(mil) 1912- 15-16R
Riddel, Frank S(tephen) 1940- 85-88
Riddel, Joseph N(eill) 1931- CANR-5
Earlier sketch in CA 9-10R
Riddell, Alan 1927- 104
Ridder, Bernard J. 1913-1983 Obituary 110
Ridder, Marie 1925- 73-76
Ridderbos, Herman N(icolaas) 1909- 57-60
Riddle, Donald H(usted) 1921- 11-12R
Riddle, John M(arion) 1937- 45-48
Riddle, Kenneth Wilkinson 1920- 3R
Riddle, Maxwell 1907- CANR-3
Earlier sketch in CA 7-8R
Riddle, Thomas Wilkinson 1886-1983
Obituary 110
Riddleberger, Patrick Williams 1915- 21-22R
Ridenour, Fritz 1932- 108
Ridenour, George M(eyer) 1928- 93-96
Ridenour, Ron 1939- 69-72
Rider, Alice Damon 1895- 69-72
Rider, (Arthur) Fremont 1885-1962
Obituary 89-92
Rider, John R. 1923- 25-28R
Ridge, Antonia (Florence) ?-1981 .... 9-10R
Obituary 104
See also SATA 7, 27
Ridge, George Ross 1931- 3R
Ridge, Julie 1956- 120
Ridge, Lola 1873-1941 .... DLB-54
Ridge, Martin 1923- 121
See also SATA 43
Ridgely, Beverly S(ellman) 1920- CANR-17
Earlier sketch in CA 25-28R
Ridgely, Joseph Vincent 1921- 7-8R
Ridgeway, James Fowler 1936- 106
Ridgeway, Jason
See Marlowe, Stephen
Ridgeway, Marian E(lizabeth) 1913- 33-36R
Ridgeway, Rick 1949- 93-96
Ridgway, Brunilde Sismondo 1929- CANR-1
Earlier sketch in CA 45-48
Ridgway, John M. 1938- 25-28R
Ridgway, Judith 1939- 109
Ridgway, Judy
See Ridgway, Judith
Ridgway, Ronald S(idney) 1923- 45-48
Ridgway, Whitman H(awley) 1941- 101
Riding, Alan 1943- 122
Riding, Laura
See Jackson, Laura (Riding)
See also CLC 3, 7
Ridle, Julia Brown 1923- 4R
Ridler, Anne Barbara 1912- CANR-3
Earlier sketch in CA 5-6R
See also DLB 27
Ridley, Anthony 1933- 107
Ridley, Arnold 1896-1984 Obituary 112
Ridley, B(rian) K(idd) 1931- 104
Ridley, Charles P(rice) 1933- 73-76
Ridley, Jasper (Godwin) 1920- CANR-22
Earlier sketches in CA 13-14R, CANR-6
Ridley, Nat, Jr. CAP-2
Earlier sketch in CA 19-20
Ridlon, Marci
See Balterman, Marcia Ridlon
See also SATA 22
Ridout, Albert K(ilburn) 1905- CAP-2
Earlier sketch in CA 19-20
Ridout, Ronald 1916- CANR-20
Earlier sketch in CA 103
Ridpath, Ian (William) 1947- 77-80
Ridruejo, Dionisio 1913(?)-1975
Obituary 57-60
Rieber, Alfred J(oseph) 1931- 11-12R
Rieber, R(obert) W(olff) 1932- CANR-3
Earlier sketch in CA 45-48
Riedel, Eunice 1931(?)-1986 Obituary 120
Riedel, Richard Langham 1908- CAP-2
Earlier sketch in CA 29-32
Riedel, Walter E(rwin) 1936- CANR-24
Earlier sketch in CA 45-48
Riedesel, C(lark) Alan 1930- 25-28R
Riedl, John O(rth) 1905- CAP-2
Earlier sketch in CA 21-22
Riedman, Sarah R(egal) 1902- CANR-1
Earlier sketch in CA 4R
See also SATA 1
Riefe, Alan 1925- CANR-9
Earlier sketch in CA 61-64
Riefe, Barbara
See Riefe, Alan
Riefenstahl, Berta Helene Amalia 1902- 108
Riefenstahl, Leni
See Riefenstahl, Berta Helene Amalia
See also CLC 16
Rieff, Philip 1922- 49-52
Riegel, Robert Edgar 1897- 5-6R
Rieger, James H(enry) 1936- 93-96
Rieger, Shay 1929- 29-32R
Riegert, Eduard Richard 1932- 69-72
Riegert, Ray 1947- 105
Riely, John (Cabell) 1945- 113
Riemer, George 1920-1973 .... CAP-2
Obituary 41-44R
Earlier sketch in CA 25-28
Riemer, Neal 1922- 21-22R
Rienits, Rex 1909-1971 .... CAP-1
Obituary 29-32R
Earlier sketch in CA 13-14
Rienow, Leona Train 1903(?)-1983 111
Rienow, Robert 1909- 21-22R
Rienstra, Ellen Walker 1940- 123
Riepe, Dale (Maurice) 1918- 37-40R
Ries, Al 1929- 120
Ries, Estelle H. 1896- 25-28R
Ries, John C(harles) 1930- 15-16R
Ries, Lawrence R(obert) 1940- 65-68
Riese, Walther 1890- 49-52
Rieseberg, Harry E(arl) 1892- 5-6R
Rieselbach, Leroy N(ewman) 1934- CANR-24
Earlier sketches in CA 23-24R, CANR-9
Riesenberg, Felix, Jr. 1913-1962 101
See also SATA 23
Riesenberg, Saul H(erbert) 1911- 49-52
Rieser, Dolf 1898-1983 Obituary 109
Riesman, David 1909- 7-8R
Riesman, Evelyn Thompson 1912- 21-22R
Riess, Claudia 1937- 110
Riess, Oswald George Lorenz 1896- 7-8R
Riess, Steven A(llan) 1947- 112

INDEX

Riess, Walter 1925- ... 19-20R
Riessen, Martin Clare 1941- ... 41-44R
Riessman, Frank 1924- ... CANR-6
Earlier sketch in CA 2R
Riesterer, Berthold P(hillip) 1935- ... 41-44R
Rieth, Marian
See Amft, M(arian) J(anet)
Rietz, Sandra A. 1943- ... 123
Rieu, E(mile) V(ictor) 1887-1972 ... CANR-15
Obituary ... 103
Earlier sketch in CA 4R
See also SATA 26, 46
Riewald, J(acobus) G(erhardus) 1910- . CANR-21
Earlier sketches in CA 57-60, CANR-6
Rifaat, Alifa
See Rifaat, Fatma Abdallah
Rifaat, Fatma Abdallah 1930- ... 123
Rifbjerg, Klaus (Thorvald) 1931-
Brief entry ... 124
Rife, J(ohn) Merle 1895- ... 61-64
Rife, Joanne 1932- ... 110
Rife, Rosemary
See Nusbaum, Rosemary
Riffaterre, Michael 1924- ... DLB-67
Riffe, Ernest
See Bergman, (Ernst) Ingmar
Riffel, Herman H(arold) 1916- ... 112
Rifkin, Jeremy 1945- Brief entry ... 121
Rifkin, Shepard 1918- ... CANR-1
Earlier sketch in CA 3R
Rifkind, Carole 1935- ... 85-88
Rifkind, Simon H(irsch) 1901- ... 109
Rift, Valerie
See Bartlett, Marie (Swan)
Riga, Frank P(eter) 1936- ... 89-92
Riga, Peter J(ohn) 1933- ... 5-6R
Rigault, Andre 1922- ... 45-48
Rigby, Andrew 1944- ... 61-64
Rigby, Ida Katherine 1944- ... CANR-10
Earlier sketch in CA 65-68
Rigby, Paul H(erbert) 1924- ... 19-20R
Rigby, T(homas) H(enry Richard)
1925- ... CANR-10
Earlier sketch in CA 19-20R
Rigdon, Raymond M. 1919- ... 29-32R
Rigdon, Walter 1930- ... 15-16R
Rigelhof, T(errance) F(rederick) 1944- ... 112
Rigg, A(rthur) G(eorge) 1937- ... 37-40R
Rigg, H(enry Hemmingway) K(ilburn)
1911-1980 ... 29-32R
Obituary ... 93-96
Rigg, John Linton 1894- ... 7-8R
Rigg, Robinson P(eter) 1918- ... 33-36R
Riggan, (John) Rob(inson) 1943- ... 115
Riggan, William (Edward, Jr.) 1946- ... 103
Riggio, Thomas P(asquale) 1943- ... 109
Riggs, Dionis Coffin 1898- ... CAP-2
Earlier sketch in CA 29-32
Riggs, Fred(erick) W(arren) 1917- ... CANR-16
Earlier sketch in CA 25-28R
Riggs, James (Lear) 1929- ... 33-36R
Riggs, John R(aymond) 1945- ... 115
Riggs, Robert E. 1927- ... CANR-8
Earlier sketch in CA 15-16R
Riggs, Sidney Noyes 1892-1975 ... 2R
Obituary ... 103
See also SATA 28
Riggs, William (George) 1938- ... 61-64
Righter, Carroll 1900- ... 93-96
Righter, James H(aslam) 1916-1984
Obituary ... 113
Righter, Robert Willms 1933- ... 108
Right Honourable Lord Denning
See Denning, Alfred Thompson
Rigoni, Orlando (Joseph) 1897- ... CANR-11
Earlier sketch in CA 15-16R
Rigsby, Howard 1909- ... 11-12R
Riha, Thomas 1929- ... 11-12R
Riis, Jacob A(ugust) 1849-1914
Brief entry ... 113
See also DLB 23
Riker, John H. 1943- ... 111
Riker, Leigh 1941- ... 119
Riker, Tom L. 1936- ... 104
Riker, William H(arrison) 1920- ... CANR-24
Earlier sketch in CA 4R
Rikhoff, James C. 1931- ... 13-14R
Rikhoff, Jean 1928- ... 61-64
See also SATA 9
Rikhye, Indar Jit 1920- ... CANR-17
Earlier sketch in CA 93-96
Rikki
See Ducornet, Erica
Rikon, Irving 1931- ... 29-32R
Riley, Carroll L(averne) 1923- ... CANR-10
Earlier sketch in CA 25-28R
Riley, Clara (Mae Deatherage) 1931- ... 25-28R
Riley, Dick 1946- ... 101
Riley, E(dward) C(alverley) 1923- ... 11-12R
Riley, G. Micheal 1934- ... 45-48
Riley, Glenda 1938- ... CANR-23
Earlier sketch in CA 106
Riley, James F. 1912- ... 29-32R
Riley, James Whitcomb 1849-1916
Brief entry ... 118
See also SATA 17
Riley, Jocelyn (Carol) 1949- ... 115
See also SATA 50
Riley, John 1937-1978 ... DLB-40
Riley, Lawrence 1897(?)-1975 Obituary ... 61-64
Riley, Madeleine 1933- ... 25-28R
Riley, Matilda White 1911- Brief entry ... 114
Riley, Miles O'Brien 1937- ... CANR-21
Earlier sketch in CA 104
Riley, (Thomas) Nord 1914- ... 13-14R
Riley, R. David 1944(?)-1983 Obituary ... 111
Riley, (Hugh) Ridge(ly, Jr.) 1907-1976 ... 101
Riley, Roy, Jr. 1943(?)-1977 Obituary ... 73-76
Riley, Sandra 1938- ... 104
Riley, Tex
See Creasey, John
Riley, Thomas J. 1901(?)-1977 Obituary ... 73-76
Riley-Smith, Jonathan (Simon Christopher)
1938- ... 23-24R
Riling, Raymond L. J. 1896(?)-1974
Obituary ... 53-56
Rilke, Rainer Maria 1875-1926 Brief entry ... 104
See also TCLC 1, 6, 19
Rilla, Wolf 1925- ... 49-52
Rils
See Bohr, R(ussell) L(eRoi)
Rima, I(ngrid) H(ahne) 1925- ... 23-24R
Rimanoczy, Richard Stanton 1902- ... 73-76
Rimberg, John 1929- ... 57-60
Rimel, Duane (Weldon) 1915- ... 29-32R
Rimington, Critchell 1907-1976 Obituary ... 61-64
Rimland, Bernard 1928- ... CANR-6
Earlier sketch in CA 15-16R
Rimland, Ingrid 1936- ... 61-64
Rimlinger, Gaston V. 1926- ... 37-40R
Rimmer, C(harles) Brandon 1918- ... CANR-12
Earlier sketch in CA 61-64
Rimmer, Douglas 1927- ... 111
Rimmer, Robert H(enry) 1917- ... CANR-20
Earlier sketches in CA 11-12R, CANR-4
Rimmer, W. J.
See Rowland, D(onald) S(ydney)
Rimmington, Gerald T(horneycroft)
1930- ... 19-20R
Rinaldi, Ann 1934- ... 111
See also SATA 50
Rinaldi, Nicholas M. 1934- ... CANR-22
Earlier sketch in CA 104
Rinaldini, Angiolo
See Battisti, Eugenio
Rinard, Judith E(llen) 1947- ... 97-100
See also SATA 44
Rinchen, Byambyn 1905(?)-1977
Obituary ... 69-72
Rinder, Walter (Murray) 1934- ... CANR-11
Earlier sketch in CA 69-72
Rindfleisch, Norval (William) 1930- ... 65-68
Rinehart, Frederick Roberts 1903(?)-1981
Obituary ... 104
Rinehart, Mary Roberts 1876-1958
Brief entry ... 108
Rinehart, Stanley Marshall, Jr. 1897-1969
Obituary ... 29-32R
Ring, Alfred A. 1905- ... 29-32R
Ring, Daniel F(rank) 1945- ... 113
Ring, Douglas
See Prather, Richard S(cott)
Ring, Elizabeth 1912- ... 103
Ring, Malvin E. 1919- ... 120
Ringdalh, Mark
See Longyear, Barry Brookes
Ringe, Donald A(rthur) 1923- ... 3R
Ringenbach, Paul T(homas) 1936- ... 45-48
Ringer, Alexander L(othar) 1921- ... CANR-24
Earlier sketch in CA 45-48
Ringer, Barbara Alice 1925- ... 11-12R
Ringer, Fritz (Franz) K(laus) 1934- ... 73-76
Ringer, Robert J. ... 81-84
Ringgold, Gene 1918- ... 25-28R
Ringgren, (Karl Vilhelm) Helmer 1917- ... CANR-3
Earlier sketch in CA 7-8R
Ringi, Kjell (Arne Soerensen) 1939- ... CANR-1
Earlier sketch in CA 45-48
See also SATA 12
Ringkamp, Jonathan 1929-1986 Obituary ... 120
Ringler, William A(ndrew), Jr.
1912-1987(?) ... 5-6R
Obituary ... 121
Ringo, Johnny
See Keevill, Henry J(ohn)
Ringold, Clay
See Hogan, (Robert) Ray
Ringold, May Spencer 1914- ... 21-22R
Ringrose, David R. 1938- ... 53-56
Ringwald, Donald C(harles) 1917-1987 ... 21-22R
Obituary ... 122
Ringwood, Gwen(dolyn Margaret) Pharis
1910-1984 Obituary ... 112
Rinhart, Floyd (Lincoln) 1915- ... CANR-10
Earlier sketch in CA 25-28R
Rinhart, Marion (Hutchinson) 1916- ... CANR-10
Earlier sketch in CA 25-28R
Rinker, Rosalind Beatrice 1906- ... CANR-5
Earlier sketch in CA 7-8R
Rinkoff, Barbara Jean (Rich) 1923-1975 ... CAP-2
Obituary ... 57-60
Earlier sketch in CA 19-20
See also SATA 4, 27
Rinpoche
See Chogyam Trungpa
Rintels, David 1939- ... 73-76
Rinvolucri, Mario (Francesco Giuseppe)
1940- ... CANR-10
Earlier sketch in CA 23-24R
Rinvolucri, Mina Josephine Moore
See Moore-Rinvolucri, Mina Josephine
Rinzema, Jakob 1931- ... 102
Rinzler, Alan 1938- ... CANR-12
Earlier sketch in CA 21-22R
Rinzler, Carol Eisen 1941- ... 49-52
Rio, Michel 19(?)- ... CLC-43
Riols, Noreen 1926- ... 124
Riopelle, Arthur J. 1920- ... 37-40R
Riordan, James 1936- ... CANR-11
Earlier sketch in CA 69-72
See also SATA 28
Riordan, James 1949- ... 111
Riordan, Mary Marguerite 1931- ... 106
Riordan, Michael 1946- ... 106
Rios, Alberto (Alvaro) 1952- ... 113
Rios, Francisco Giner de los
See Giner de los Rios, Francisco
Rios, Tere
See Versace, Marie Teresa Rios
Riotte, Louise 1909- ... 57-60
Riotto, Guy Michael 1943- ... 73-76
Riou, Roger 1909- ... 61-64
Ripa, Karol 1895-1983 Obituary ... 109
Ripley, Alexandra 1934- ... 119
Ripley, Arthur 1895-1961 ... DLB-44
Ripley, (Sidney) Dillon 1913- ... 57-60
Ripley, Elizabeth Blake 1906-1969 ... CANR-3
Earlier sketch in CA 4R
See also SATA 5
Ripley, Francis Joseph 1912- ... CANR-18
Earlier sketches in CA 3R, CANR-3
Ripley, George 1802-1880 ... DLB-1, 64
Ripley, Jack
See Wainwright, John
Ripley, Randall B(utler) 1938- ... CANR-19
Earlier sketches in CA 53-56, CANR-5
Ripley, Sheldon N(ichols) 1925- ... 7-8R
Ripley, Stephens 1901(?)-1984 Obituary ... 111
Ripley, Theresa M(argaret) 1944- ... 85-88
Ripley, (William Young) Warren 1921- . CANR-15
Earlier sketch in CA 33-36R
Rippa, S(ol) Alexander 1925- ... 53-56
Ripper, Charles L(ewis) 1929- ... CANR-1
Earlier sketch in CA 4R
See also SATA 3
Ripper, Chuck
See Ripper, Charles L(ewis)
Ripperger, Helmut Lothar 1897-1974
Obituary ... 53-56
Ripperger, Henrietta
See Hawley, Henrietta Ripperger
Rippey, Mari 1939- ... 112
Rippey, Robert (Max) 1926- ... 45-48
Ripple, Paula ... 112
Ripple, Richard E. 1931- ... CANR-22
Earlier sketch in CA 33-36R
Rippley, La Vern J. 1935- ... 33-36R
Rippon, Marion E(dith) 1921- ... CANR-1
Earlier sketch in CA 49-52
Rippy, Frances (Marguerite) Mayhew
1929- ... 89-92
Rips, Ervine M(ilton) 1921- ... 101
Rips, Geoffrey 1950- ... 108
Rips, Rae Elizabeth 1914-1970 Obituary ... 104
Riq
See Atwater, Richard Tupper
Riquelme, John Paul 1946- ... 119
Risatti, Howard A(nthony) 1943- ... 49-52
Rischin, Moses 1925- ... CANR-3
Earlier sketch in CA 11-12R
Riseley, Jerry B(urr, Jr.) 1920- ... CANR-13
Earlier sketch in CA 23-24R
Riseling, John J. W. 1888(?)-1977
Obituary ... 73-76
Risenhoover, Morris 1940- ... 65-68
Riser, Wayne H. 1909- ... CAP-1
Earlier sketch in CA 13-14
Risjord, Norman K. 1931- ... CANR-22
Earlier sketches in CA 19-20R, CANR-7
Riskin, Robert 1897-1955 ... DLB-26
Riskind, Mary 1944- ... 108
Riss, Richard 1952- ... 81-84
Rissi, Mathias 1920- ... 45-48
Rissman, Art
See Sussman, Susan
Rissman, Susan
See Sussman, Susan
Rissover, Fredric 1940- ... 33-36R
Rist, John M(ichael) 1936- ... CANR-18
Earlier sketch in CA 101
Rist, Ray C(harles) 1944- ... CANR-3
Earlier sketch in CA 49-52
Rist Arnold, Elisabeth 1950- ... 65-68
Riste, Olav 1933- ... CANR-12
Earlier sketch in CA 29-32R
Ristic, Dragisha N. 1909- ... CAP-2
Earlier sketch in CA 21-22
Ristow, Walter W(illiam) 1908- ... 19-20R
Ritcheson, Charles R(ay) 1925-
Brief entry ... 112
Ritchey, John A(rthur) 1919- ... 23-24R
Ritchie, (John) Andrew 1943- ... 85-88
Ritchie, Andrew Carnduff 1907-1978
Obituary ... 81-84
Ritchie, Anna Cora (Ogden) Mowatt
1819-1870 ... DLB-3
Ritchie, Anne Thackeray 1837-1919 ... DLB-18
Ritchie, Barbara Gibbons ... 73-76
See also SATA 14
Ritchie, Bill
See Edgar, Frank Terrell Rhoades
Ritchie, C(icero) T(heodore) 1914- ... 11-12R
Ritchie, Donald A(rthur) 1945- ... 122
Brief entry ... 106
Ritchie, Donald D(irk) 1914- ... 112
Ritchie, Edwin 1931- ... 29-32R
Ritchie, Elisavietta (Yurievna Artamonoff) .. CANR-2
Earlier sketch in CA 49-52
Ritchie, G(eorge) Stephen 1914- ... 13-14R
Ritchie, Jack
See Reitci, John G(eorge)
Ritchie, James McPherson 1927- ... 25-28R
Ritchie, James T. R. 1908- ... CAP-2
Earlier sketch in CA 19-20
Ritchie, John C(ollins) 1927- ... 49-52
Ritchie, M(iller) A(lfred) F(ranklin) 1909- .. CAP-2
Earlier sketch in CA 29-32
Ritchie, Paul 1923- ... 23-24R
Ritchie, Rita
See Reitci, Rita Krohne
Ritchie, Ruth 1900- ... CANR-2
Earlier sketch in CA 4R
Ritchie, Thomas 1778-1854 ... DLB-43
Ritchie, (Harry) Ward 1905- ... CANR-22
Earlier sketches in CA 57-60, CANR-7
Ritchie, William A(ugustus) 1903- ... CANR-24
Earlier sketch in CA 45-48
Ritchie-Calder, Peter Ritchie 1906-1982 . CANR-4
Obituary ... 105
Earlier sketch in CA 1R
Ritner, Peter Vaughn 1927(?)-1976 ... 77-80
Obituary ... 69-72
Ritschl, Dietrich 1929- ... CANR-24
Earlier sketches in CA 21-22R, CANR-9
Ritsos, Giannes
See Ritsos, Yannis
Ritsos, Yannis 1909- ... 77-80
See also CLC 6, 13, 31
Rittenhouse, Mignon 1904- ... 41-44R
Ritter, Alan 1937- ... 117
Brief entry ... 113
Ritter, Ed 1917- ... 19-20R
Ritter, Felix
See Kruess, James
Ritter, Gerhard 1888-1967 Obituary ... 111
Ritter, Henry, Jr. 1920- ... 93-96
Ritter, Jess(e P., Jr.) 1930- ... 37-40R
Ritter, Lawrence S(tanley) 1922- ... CANR-22
Earlier sketch in CA 23-24R
Ritterbush, Philip C. 1936- ... CANR-6
Earlier sketch in CA 11-12R
Ritts, Paul 1920(?)-1980 Obituary ... 102
See also SATA 25
Ritvala, M.
See Waltari, Mika (Toimi)
Ritvo, Harriet 1946- ... 124
Ritz, Charles 1891-1976 Obituary ... 65-68
Ritz, David 1943- ... 85-88
Ritz, Jean-Georges 1906- ... 7-8R
Ritz, Joseph P. 1929- ... 21-22R
Ritzenthaler, Pat 1914- ... 25-28R
Ritzer, George 1940- ... CANR-20
Earlier sketches in CA 53-56, CANR-5
Rivas, Gilberto Lopez y
See Lopez Y Rivas, Gilberto
Rive, Richard 1931- ... 15-16R
Rivel, Isade
See Cuevas, Clara
Rivenburgh, Viola K(leinke) 1897- ... 19-20R
Rivera, Feliciano (Moreno) 1932- ... CANR-24
Earlier sketch in CA 45-48
Rivera, Geraldo (Miguel) 1943- ... 108
See also SATA 28
Rivera, Tomas 1935- ... 49-52
Rivere, Alec
See Nuetzel, Charles (Alexander)
Rivero, Eliana Suarez 1942- ... 41-44R
Rivers, Caryl 1937- ... CANR-22
Earlier sketches in CA 49-52, CANR-4
Rivers, Clarence Joseph 1931- ... 77-80
Rivers, Conrad Kent 1933-1968 ... 85-88
See also DLB 41
See also CLC 1
Rivers, Elfrida
See Bradley, Marion Zimmer
Rivers, Elias L(ynch) 1924- ... 19-20R
Rivers, Joan
See Molinsky, Joan Sandra
Rivers, Julian Alfred Pitt
See Pitt-Rivers, Julian Alfred
Rivers, Larry 1923- ... 124
Brief entry ... 117
Rivers, William L. 1925- ... CANR-7
Earlier sketch in CA 19-20R
Rivers-Coffey, Rachel 1943- ... 73-76
Riverside, John
See Heinlein, Robert A(nson)
Rives, Leigh
See Seward, William W(ard), Jr.
Rives, Stanley G(ene) 1930- ... CANR-11
Earlier sketch in CA 23-24R
Rives, William T. 1911(?)-1983 Obituary ... 111
Rivet, A(lbert) L(ionel) F(rederick)
1915- ... CANR-24
Earlier sketches in CA 23-24R, CANR-9
Rivett, Carol
See Rivett, Edith Caroline
Rivett, Edith Caroline 1894-1958
Brief entry ... 110
Rivett, Rohan (Deakin) 1917- ... 25-28R
Rivett-Carnac, Charles Edward 1901- ... CAP-2
Earlier sketch in CA 19-20
Rivette, Marc 1916- ... 7-8R
Riviere, Bill
See Riviere, William Alexander
Riviere, Claude 1932- ... 102
Riviere, Peter Gerard 1934- ... 103
Riviere, William Alexander 1916- ... CANR-8
Earlier sketch in CA 5-6R
Rivington, James 1724(?)-1802 ... DLB-43
Rivkin, Allen (Erwin) 1903- ... CANR-11
Earlier sketch in CA 65-68
See also DLB 26
Rivkin, Ann 1920- ... 112
See also SATA 41
Rivkin, Arnold 1919-1968 ... CANR-3
Earlier sketch in CA 3R
Rivkin, Ellis 1918- ... 33-36R
Rivlin, Alice M(itchell) 1931- ... 33-36R
Rivlin, Harry N. 1904- ... 19-20R
Rivoire, Jean 1929- ... CANR-21
Earlier sketches in CA 9-10R, CANR-5
Rivoli, Mario 1943- ... SATA-10
Rix, Donna
See Rowland, D(onald) S(ydney)
Rizzo, Betty 1926- ... 111
Rizzo, Mario 1948- ... 124

Rizzoli, Andrea 1914-1983 Obituary 109
Rizzoli, Angelo 1889-1970 Obituary 104
Rizzuto, Anthony 1937- 106
Rizzuto, James J(oseph) 1939- 107
Rizzuto, Jim
See Rizzuto, James J(oseph)
Roa (y Garcia), Raul 1908-1982 Obituary ... 107
Roa Bastos, Augusto 1917- CLC-45
Roach, Helen P(auline) 1903- CAP-1
Earlier sketch in CA 11-12
Roach, Hildred 1937- 57-60
Roach, Jack L. 1925- Brief entry 109
Roach, James P. 1907-1978 Obituary 77-80
Roach, Joyce Gibson 1935- CANR-18
Earlier sketch in CA 101
Roach, Marilynne K(athleen) 1946- CANR-12
Earlier sketch in CA 57-60
See also SATA 9
Roach, Marion 1956- 120
Roach, Mary Ellen 1921- 19-20R
Roach, Portia
See Takajian, Portia
Roadarmel, Gordon 1932-1972 Obituary 104
Roadarmel, Paul 1942- 93-96
Roaden, Arliss L. 1930- 37-40R
Roadstrum, William H(enry) 1915- 25-28R
Roalfe, William R(obert) 1896- 93-96
Roam, Pearl (Sovern) 1920- 3R
Roark, Albert E(dward) 1933- 85-88
Roark, Dallas M(organ) 1931- 37-40R
Roark, Garland 1904-1985 .... CANR-1
Obituary 115
Earlier sketch in CA 2R
Roark, James L. 1941- CANR-19
Earlier sketch in CA 85-88
Roazen, Paul 1936- 25-28R
Roback, A(braham) A(aron) 1890-1965 .....5-6R
Robacker, Earl Francis 1904- 53-56
Robana, Abderrahman 1938- 65-68
Robard, Jackson
See Wallmann, Jeffrey M(iner)
Robards, Karen 1954- 122
Robards, Sherman M(arshall) 1939- 61-64
Robards, Terry
See Robards, Sherman M.
Robathan, Dorothy M(ae) 1898- 41-44R
Robb, Brian 1913-1979 113
Robb, David M(etheny) 1903- Brief entry ... 113
See also AITN 1
Robb, (George) Douglas 1899-1974
Obituary 114
Robb, Frank Thomson 1908- 57-60
Robb, Inez (Callaway) 1901(?)-1979 97-100
Obituary 85-88
Robb, J(ohn) Wesley 1919- 7-8R
Robb, James H(arding) 1920- 9-10R
Robb, James Willis 1918- 41-44R
Robb, Mary K(unkle) 1908- CAP-2
Earlier sketch in CA 19-20
Robb, Nesca A(deline) 1905- 9-10R
Robbe-Grillet, Alain 1922- 9-10R
See also CLC 1, 2, 4, 6, 8, 10, 14, 43
Robben, John 1930- 93-96
Robbert, Louise Buenger 1925- 41-44R
Robbin, (Jodi) Luna 1936- 103
Robbins, Brother Gerald 1940- 15-16R
Robbins, Caroline 1903- 107
Robbins, Ceila Dame 1943- 118
Robbins, Daniel 1933- CANR-3
Earlier sketch in CA 45-48
Robbins, Frank 1917- 109
See also SATA 32, 42
Robbins, Glaydon Donaldson 1908- 7-8R
Robbins, Harold 1916- 73-76
See also CLC 5
Robbins, Henry 1928(?)-1979 Obituary ...89-92
Robbins, Horace 1909-1982 Obituary 107
Robbins, Ira A(braham) 1954- 123
Robbins, J(ohn) Albert 1914- 19-20R
Robbins, Jane
See Robbins-Carter, Jane (Borsch)
Robbins, June 61-64
Robbins, Kay
See Hooper, Kay
Robbins, Keith (Gilbert) 1940- CANR-11
Earlier sketch in CA 25-28R
Robbins, Lionel (Charles) 1898-1984
Obituary 112
Robbins, Martin 1931- CANR-12
Earlier sketch in CA 29-32R
Robbins, Marty
See Robinson, Martin David
Robbins, Matthew Brief entry 110
Robbins, Mildred Brown CAP-2
Earlier sketch in CA 33-36
Robbins, Millie
See Robbins, Mildred Brown
Robbins, Paul R(ichard) 1930- 114
Robbins, Raleigh
See Hamilton, Charles Harold St. John
Robbins, Richard G., Jr. 1939- 53-56
Robbins, Rossell Hope 1912- CANR-2
Earlier sketch in CA 45-48
Robbins, Roy M(arvin) 1904- 65-68
Robbins, Ruth 1917(?)- 73-76
See also SATA 14
Robbins, S(allie) A(nn) 1940- 23-24R
Robbins, Sam
See Potter, Carole A.
Robbins, Thomas Eugene 1936- 81-84
Robbins, Tom
See Robbins, Thomas Eugene
See also DLBY 80
See also CLC 9, 32
Robbins, Tony
See Pashko, Stanley
Robbins, Trina 1938- CLC-21
Robbins, Vesta O(rdelia) 1891- 53-56
Robbins, Wayne
See Cox, William (Robert)
Robbins-Carter, Jane (Borsch) 1939- 116
Robe, Stanley L(inn) 1915- CANR-6
Earlier sketch in CA 7-8R
Robeck, Mildred C(oen) 1915- 57-60
Roberge, Earl 1918- 85-88
Roberson, (Charles) Ed(win) 1939- 77-80
Roberson, Jennifer 1953- 117
Roberson, Marie
See Hamm, Marie Roberson
Roberson, Ricky James 1956- 101
Roberson, William H(oward) 1952- 110
Robert, Marc 1927- 114
Robert, Marika Barna 11-12R
Robert, Paul 1911(?)-1980 Obituary 101
Robert, Paul A.
See Roubiczek, Paul (Anton)
Robertiello, Richard C. 1923- CANR-3
Earlier sketch in CA 9-10R
Roberto, Brother
See Mueller, Gerald F(rancis)
Roberts, (Edward) Adam 1940- CANR-9
Earlier sketch in CA 21-22R
Roberts, Allen 1914- 29-32R
Roberts, Anthony
See Watney, John B(asil)
Roberts, Archibald Edward 1915- CANR-6
Earlier sketch in CA 57-60
Roberts, Arthur O. 1923- 25-28R
Roberts, Arthur Sydney 1905(?)-1978 85-88
Obituary 81-84
Roberts, Ben
See Eisenberg, Benjamin
Roberts, Benjamin Charles 1917- 102
Roberts, Bill 1914(?)-1978 Obituary 81-84
Roberts, Bleddyn J(ones) 1906- CAP-1
Earlier sketch in CA 13-14
Roberts, Brian 1930- CANR-12
Earlier sketch in CA 29-32R
Roberts, Bruce (Stuart) 1930- CANR-6
Earlier sketch in CA 9-10R
See also SATA 39, 47
Roberts, C(atherine) 1917- 23-24R
Roberts, Carey 1935- 106
Roberts, Carol A. 1933- 37-40R
Roberts, Cecil (Edric Mornington)
1892-1976 .... CAP-2
Obituary 69-72
Earlier sketch in CA 29-32
Roberts, Chalmers M(cGeagh) 1910- 41-44R
Roberts, Charles G(eorge) D(ouglas)
1860-1943 Brief entry 105
See also SATA 29
See also TCLC 8
Roberts, Charles Wesley 1916- 19-20R
Roberts, (Ray) Clayton 1923- 21-22R
Roberts, Clete 1910(?)-1984 Obituary 113
Roberts, Colette Jacqueline 1910-1971
Obituary 115
Roberts, Dan
See Ross, W(illiam) E(dward) D(aniel)
Roberts, Daniel (Frank) 1922- CANR-6
Earlier sketch in CA 11-12R
Roberts, David
See Cox, John Roberts
Roberts, David Arthur 1924-1987
Obituary 122
Roberts, David D(ion) 1943- 101
Roberts, David S(tuart) 1943- 33-36R
Roberts, Dell
See Fendell, Bob
Roberts, Dennis W(ayne) 1947- 109
Roberts, Denys (Tudor Emil) 1923- CAP-1
Earlier sketch in CA 9-10
Roberts, Denys Kilham 1904(?)-1976
Obituary 65-68
Roberts, Derrell C(layton) 1927- 29-32R
Roberts, Donald Alfred 1897-1978
Obituary 77-80
Roberts, Donald Frank, Jr. 1939- 107
Roberts, Doreen 1922- 108
Roberts, Dorothy James 1903- CAP-1
Earlier sketch in CA 13-14
Roberts, Edgar V. 1928- 23-24R
Roberts, Edward B(aer) 1935- CANR-9
Earlier sketch in CA 21-22R
Roberts, Edward Barry 1900-1972 ...... CAP-2
Earlier sketch in CA 19-20
Roberts, Edwin A(lbert), Jr. 1932- 23-24R
Roberts, Elizabeth H. 1913- 61-64
Roberts, Elizabeth Madox 1886-1941
Brief entry 111
See also SATA 27, 33
See also DLB 9, 54
Roberts, Elizabeth (Allan) Mauchline
1936- Brief entry 114
Roberts, Ellen Elizabeth Mayhew 1946- 108
Roberts, Elliott B. 1899- 4R
Roberts, Eric 1914- 7-8R
Roberts, Estelle (Wills) 1889-1970
Obituary 112
Roberts, Eugene (L., Jr.) 1932- 97-100
Roberts, Evelyn Lutman 1917- 65-68
Roberts, F(rederick) David 1923- 5-6R
Roberts, Florence Bright 1941- 65-68
Roberts, Frances C(abaniss) 1916- 11-12R
Roberts, Francis Warren 1916- 13-14R
Roberts, Geoffrey R(ansford) 1924- 101
Roberts, Grant
See Wallmann, Jeffrey M(iner)
Roberts, Harold 1896(?)-1982 Obituary 108
Roberts, Harold S(elig) 1911-1970 ...... CAP-2
Earlier sketch in CA 23-24
Roberts, Henry L(ithgow) 1916-1972
Obituary 37-40R
Roberts, Hortense Roberta 89-92
Roberts, Howard R(adclyffe) 1906- 109
Roberts, I.
See Roberts, Irene
Roberts, I(olo) F(rancis) 1925- 29-32R
Roberts, I. M.
See Roberts, Irene
Roberts, Irene 1925- CANR-21
Earlier sketches in CA 13-14R, CANR-6
Roberts, Ivor
See Roberts, Irene
Roberts, J(ohn) A(lexander) Fraser
1899-1987 Obituary 121
Roberts, J(ohn) Kimberley 1935- 117
Roberts, J. R.
See Randisi, Robert J(oseph)
Roberts, James Deotis 1927- CANR-15
Earlier sketch in CA 33-36R
Roberts, James Hall
See Duncan, Robert L(ipscomb)
Roberts, Jane
See Butts, Jane Roberts
Roberts, Janet Louise 1925- CANR-13
Earlier sketch in CA 61-64
Roberts, Jason
See Bock, Fred
Roberts, Jeanne Addison 89-92
Roberts, Jim
See Bates, Barbara S(nedeker)
Roberts, Joan Ila 1935- 29-32R
Roberts, Joe
See Saltzman, Joseph
Roberts, John
See Bingley, David Ernest
Roberts, John G(aither) 1913- 49-52
See also SATA 27
Roberts, John M(ilton) 1916- 37-40R
Roberts, John M(orris) 1928- CANR-16
Earlier sketch in CA 85-88
Roberts, John R. 1934- CANR-12
Earlier sketch in CA 33-36R
Roberts, John Storm 1936- CANR-12
Earlier sketch in CA 25-28R
Roberts, Joseph B(oxley), Jr. 1918- 41-44R
Roberts, Julian
See Bardens, Dennis (Conrad)
Roberts, K.
See Lake, Kenneth R(obert)
Roberts, Kate 1891-1985 107
Obituary 116
See also CLC 15
Roberts, Keith (John Kingston) 1935- 25-28R
See also CLC 14
Roberts, Keith 1937(?)-1979 Obituary 85-88
Roberts, Ken
See Lake, Kenneth R(obert)
Roberts, Kenneth (Lewis) 1885-1957
Brief entry 109
See also DLB 9
See also TCLC 23
Roberts, Kenneth H(arris) 1930- 33-36R
Roberts, Kevin E(rnest) A(lbert) 1940- 113
Roberts, Lee
See Martin, Robert (Lee)
Roberts, Len
See Roberts, Leonard
Roberts, Leonard 1947- 113
Roberts, Leonard W(ard) 1912- 33-36R
Roberts, Leslie 1896-1980 103
Roberts, Lionel
See Fanthorpe, R(obert) Lionel
Roberts, Lisa
See Turner, Robert H(arry)
Roberts, MacLennan
See Terrall, Robert
Roberts, Mary D(uffy) 1925- 4R
Roberts, Mervin F(rancis) 1922- CANR-24
Earlier sketches in CA 65-68, CANR-9
Roberts, Michael 1945- 69-72
Roberts, Michele (B.) 1949- 115
Roberts, Myron 1923- 29-32R
Roberts, Nancy Correll 1924- CANR-6
Earlier sketch in CA 11-12R
See also SATA 28
Roberts, Nora 1950- 123
Roberts, Oral 1918- 41-44R
Roberts, (Thomas) Patrick 1920- 61-64
Roberts, Paul Craig 1939- CANR-22
Earlier sketch in CA 33-36R
Roberts, Paul McHenry 1917-1967 .... 3R
Obituary 103
Roberts, Percival R(udolph) III 1935- 41-44R
Roberts, Philip Davies 1938- 109
Roberts, Phyllis Barzillay 1932- 41-44R
Roberts, Rachel 1927-1980 Obituary 115
Roberts, Rand
See Parham, Robert Randall
Roberts, Richard J(erome) 1928- 7-8R
Roberts, Richard W. 1935-1978 Obituary ..73-76
Roberts, Rinalda
See Cudlipp, Edythe
Roberts, Robert B. 1911- 117
Roberts, Robert C(ampbell) 1942- CANR-14
Earlier sketch in CA 69-72
Roberts, Ron E. 1939- 33-36R
Roberts, Roy Allison 1887-1967 Obituary ..89-92
Roberts, Rufus Putnam 1926- 2R
Roberts, Sally
See Jones, Sally Roberts
Roberts, Sheila 1942- 102
Roberts, Spencer Eugene 1920- 89-92
Roberts, Steven V(ictor) 1943- 61-64
Roberts, Susan F. 1919- 104
Roberts, Suzanne 1931- 106
Roberts, Sydney (Castle) 1887-1966 ..... CAP-1
Earlier sketch in CA 15-16
Roberts, Terence
See Sanderson, Ivan T(erence)
Roberts, Thom(as Sacra) 1940- CANR-15
Earlier sketch in CA 81-84
Roberts, Thomas J(ohn) 1925- 41-44R
Roberts, Tom
See Thomas, R(obert) Murray
Roberts, Trev
See Trevathan, Robert E.
Roberts, Vera Mowry 1918- 19-20R
Roberts, Virginia
See Dean, Nell Marr
Roberts, Walter R(onald) 1916- CANR-1
Earlier sketch in CA 49-52
Roberts, Warren (Errol) 1933- 73-76
Roberts, Warren Aldrich 1901- CAP-1
Earlier sketch in CA 11-12
Roberts, Wayne
See Overholser, Wayne D.
Roberts, William 1868-1959 Brief entry 122
Roberts, William P(utnam) 1931- 113
Roberts, Willo Davis 1928- CANR-19
Earlier sketches in CA 49-52, CANR-3
See also SATA 21
Robertshaw, (James) Denis 1911- 65-68
Robertson, Alec
See Robertson, Alexander Thomas Parke
Anthony Cecil
Robertson, Alexander Thomas Parke
Anthony Cecil 1892-1982 104
Obituary 105
Robertson, Andrew 1921-1986 Obituary 120
Robertson, Arthur Henry 1913-1984 ......9-10R
Obituary 113
Robertson, Barbara (Anne) 1931- 25-28R
See also SATA 12
Robertson, Brian 1951- 101
Robertson, Carol P. 1934- 123
Robertson, Charles L(angner) 1927- 23-24R
Robertson, Charles Martin 1911- 104
Robertson, Colin 1906- 11-12R
Robertson, Constance (Pierrepont Noyes)
1896(?)-1985 ....29-32R
Obituary 116
Robertson, Cordelia Biddle 1898(?)-1984
Obituary 114
Robertson, D(onald) J(ames)
1926-1970 .... CANR-10
Earlier sketch in CA 5-6R
Robertson, D(urant) W(aite), Jr. 1914- .. CANR-9
Earlier sketch in CA 61-64
Robertson, Dale 1923- Brief entry 107
Robertson, David (Allan, Jr.) 1915- 81-84
Robertson, Dede 1927- 114
Robertson, Don 1929- CANR-23
Earlier sketches in CA 9-10R, CANR-7
See also SATA 8
Robertson, Donald S. 1918- 123
Robertson, Dorothy Lewis 1912- 25-28R
See also SATA 12
Robertson, Dougal 1924- 61-64
Robertson, Durant Waite, Jr. 1914- 109
Robertson, E(smonde) M(anning)
1923-1987 ....29-32R
Obituary 121
Robertson, Edith Anne (Stewart)
1883-19(?) CAP-1
Earlier sketch in CA 11-12
Robertson, Elizabeth Chant 1899- 49-52
Robertson, Ellis
See Ellison, Harlan
and Silverberg, Robert
Robertson, Eric Desmond 1914-1987
Obituary 122
Robertson, Frank C(hester) 1890-1969 .. CANR-4
Earlier sketch in CA 2R
Robertson, H(ector) M(enteith) 1905-1984
Obituary 113
Robertson, Heather Margaret 1942- CANR-17
Earlier sketch in CA 93-96
Robertson, Howard Stephen 1931- 41-44R
Robertson, James 1911- 7-8R
Robertson, James Douglas 1904- 7-8R
Robertson, James (Irvin), Jr. 1930- CANR-6
Earlier sketch in CA 11-12R
Robertson, James Louis 1907- CAP-2
Earlier sketch in CA 29-32
Robertson, James Oliver 1932- 111
Brief entry 106
Robertson, James Wilson 1899-1983 109
Obituary 110
Robertson, Jennifer Sinclair 1942- CANR-5
Earlier sketch in CA 53-56
See also SATA 12
Robertson, Jenny
See Robertson, Jennifer Sinclair
Robertson, John (Charles) 1951- 124
Robertson, Keith (Carlton) 9-10R
See also SATA 1
Robertson, Leon S(purgeon) 1936- 41-44R
Robertson, M(arion) G(ordon) 1930- 111
Robertson, Marian 1921- 111
Robertson, Martin
See Robertson, Charles Martin
Robertson, Mary D(emmond) 1927- 102
Robertson, Mary Elsie 1937- CANR-15
Earlier sketch in CA 81-84
Robertson, Nan 1926- 121
Robertson, Olivia (Melian) 1917- 9-10R
Robertson, Pat
See Robertson, M(arion) G(ordon)
Robertson, Patrick 1940- 61-64
Robertson, Priscilla (Smith) 1910- CAP-2
Earlier sketch in CA 23-24
Robertson, Roland 1938- 29-32R
Robertson, Thomas Anthony 1897- CAP-1
Earlier sketch in CA 15-16

Robertson, Wally
See Robertson, Walter
Robertson, Walter 1892-1983 Obituary ... 109
Robertson, Wilfrid 1892- ... 7-8R
Roberts-Wray, Kenneth (Owen) 1899- ... CAP-2
Earlier sketch in CA 25-28
Robeson, Gerald B(yron) 1938- ... 65-68
Robeson, Kenneth
See Dent, Lester
and Goulart, Ron(ald Joseph)
Robeson, Paul (Leroy Bustill) 1898-1976 ... 124
Obituary ... 109
Robey, Daniel 1944- ... 111
Robey, Edward George (Haydon)
1900-1983 Obituary ... 109
Robey, Harriet 1900- ... 107
Robey, Ralph W(est) 1899-1972
Obituary ... 37-40R
Robhs, Dwight
See Monaco, Richard
Robichaud, Gerald A(laric) 1912-1979
Obituary ... 85-88
Robichaud, Gerard 1908- ... CAP-2
Earlier sketch in CA 17-18
Robichon, Jacques 1920- ... 101
Robie, Edward H(odges) 1886- ... CAP-2
Earlier sketch in CA 19-20
Robilliard, Eileen Dorothy 1921- ... 23-24R
Robilliard, St. John Anthony 1953- ... 124
Robin
See Roberts, Eric
Robin, Arthur de Quetteville 1929- ... 104
Robin, Leo 1900(?)-1984 Obituary ... 114
Robin, Ralph 1914- ... 65-68
Robin, Richard S(hale) 1926- ... 23-24R
Robinet, Harriette Gillem 1931- ... 69-72
See also SATA 27
Robinett, Betty Wallace 1919- ... 41-44R
Robinett, Stephen (Allen) 1941- ... 101
Robins, Corinne 1934- ... 118
Robins, Denise (Naomi) 1897(?)-1985 . CANR-19
Obituary ... 116
Earlier sketches in CA 65-68, CANR-10
Robins, Dorothy B.
See Robins-Mowry, Dorothy B(ernice)
Robins, Eli 1921- ... 109
Robins, Elizabeth 1862(?)-1952
Brief entry ... 116
Robins, Harry Franklin 1915- ... 5-6R
Robins, Lee N(elken) 1922- ... CANR-14
Earlier sketch in CA 23-24R
Robins, Natalie S. 1938- ... 19-20R
Robins, Patricia (Denise) 1921- ... CANR-19
Earlier sketch in CA 89-92
Robins, Robert Henry 1921- ... 7-8R
Robins, Rollo, Jr.
See Ellis, Edward S(ylvester)
Robins, Seelin
See Ellis, Edward S(ylvester)
Robins-Mowry, Dorothy B(ernice) 1921- .. 25-28R
Robinson, A(ntony) M(eredith) Lewin
1916- ... CANR-9
Earlier sketch in CA 21-22R
Robinson, A(rthur) N(apoleon) R(aymond)
1926- ... 33-36R
Robinson, Abby 1947- ... 117
Robinson, Adjai 1932- ... 45-48
See also SATA 8
Robinson, Alan R(onald) 1920- ... CAP-1
Earlier sketch in CA 11-12
Robinson, Albert J(ohn) 1926- ... 53-56
Robinson, Alice Gram 1896(?)-1984
Obituary ... 111
Robinson, Alice M(erritt) 1920-1983 ... 108
Obituary ... 109
Robinson, Anthony (Christopher) 1931- . CANR-1
Earlier sketch in CA 3R
Robinson, Archie W. 1906(?)-1987
Obituary ... 123
Robinson, B(asil) W(illiam) 1912- ... CANR-3
Earlier sketch in CA 7-8R
Robinson, Barbara Webb 1927- ... 3R
See also SATA 8
Robinson, Barry (James) 1938- ... 25-28R
Robinson, Betsy Julia 1951- ... 109
Robinson, Bill
See Robinson, William Wheeler
Robinson, Blackwell P(ierce) 1916- ... CANR-24
Earlier sketch in CA 45-48
Robinson, Brooks (Calbert, Jr.) 1937- ... 116
Robinson, Budd
See Robinson, David
Robinson, C(harles) A(lexander), Jr.
1900-1965 ... CANR-4
Earlier sketch in CA 1R
See also SATA 36
Robinson, Casey 1903-1979 ... DLB-44
Robinson, Cecil 1921- ... 15-16R
Robinson, Cervin 1928- ... 61-64
Robinson, Chaille Howard (Payne) ... 13-14R
Robinson, Charles 1870-1937 ... SATA-17
Robinson, Charles 1931- ... CANR-2
Earlier sketch in CA 49-52
See also SATA 6
Robinson, Charles E(dward) 1941- ... CANR-13
Earlier sketch in CA 77-80
Robinson, Charles Knox (Jr.) 1909-1980 ... 103
Obituary ... 97-100
Robinson, Charles M. III 1949- ... 120
Robinson, Corinne H(ogden) 1909- ... 93-96
Robinson, Daniel N. 1937- ... 33-36R
Robinson, Daniel Sommer 1888- ... 29-32R
Robinson, David 1915- ... 81-84
Robinson, David A. 1925- ... 17-18R
Robinson, Dean (Stewart) 1946- ... 114
Robinson, Derek 1932- ... 77-80
Robinson, Donald 1913- ... 25-28R
Robinson, Donald H(oy) 1910- ... CAP-2
Earlier sketch in CA 33-36
Robinson, Donald L(eonard) 1936- ... 41-44R
Robinson, Donald W(ittmer)
1911-1980 ... CANR-12
Earlier sketch in CA 23-24R
Robinson, Douglas Hill 1918- ... CANR-8
Earlier sketch in CA 7-8R
Robinson, E(dwin) A(rlington) 1869-1935
Brief entry ... 104
See also DLB 54
See also TCLC 5
Robinson, Earl (Hawley) 1910- ... CANR-2
Earlier sketch in CA 45-48
Robinson, Edgar Eugene 1887-1977
Obituary ... 73-76
Robinson, Edward G. 1893-1973
Obituary ... 45-48
Robinson, Edward L(ouis) 1921- ... 41-44R
Robinson, Elwyn B(urns) 1905- ... CAP-2
Earlier sketch in CA 19-20
Robinson, Eric 1924- ... 49-52
Robinson, Forrest G(len) 1940- ... 41-44R
Robinson, Francis (Arthur) 1910-1980
Obituary ... 97-100
Robinson, Francis (Christopher Rowland)
1944- ... 112
Robinson, Frank M(alcolm) 1926- ... CANR-19
Earlier sketches in CA 49-52, CANR-3
Robinson, Frank M(elvin), Jr. 1928- ... 57-60
Robinson, Frank S(teven) 1947- ... 97-100
Robinson, Fred Colson 1930- ... 37-40R
Robinson, Fred Miller 1942- ... 107
Robinson, Godfrey Clive 1913- ... 13-14R
Robinson, Gustavus H. 1881-1972
Obituary ... 37-40R
Robinson, Haddon W. 1931- ... 73-76
Robinson, Halbert B(enefiel)
1925-1981 ... CANR-9
Earlier sketch in CA 19-20R
Robinson, Helen Caister 1899- ... CANR-16
Earlier sketch in CA 93-96
Robinson, Helen Mansfield 1906- ... 13-14R
Robinson, Helene M. ... 15-16R
Robinson, Henry Morton 1898-1961
Obituary ... 116
Robinson, Herbert Spencer ... 93-96
Robinson, Horace W(illiam) 1909- ... 93-96
Robinson, Howard 1885- ... CAP-1
Earlier sketch in CA 13-14
Robinson, Hubbell 1905-1974 Obituary ... 53-56
Robinson, Ira E(dwin) 1927- ... 81-84
Robinson, J(ohn) Lewis 1918- ... 107
Robinson, J(ohn) W(illiam) 1934- ... 17-18R
Robinson, James A(rthur) 1932- ... 17-18R
Robinson, James Harvey 1863-1936 ... DLB-47
Robinson, James K(eith) 1916- ... 17-18R
Robinson, James M(cConkey) 1924- ... 15-16R
Robinson, Jan M. 1933- ... 61-64
See also SATA 6
Robinson, Janet O(live) 1939- ... 33-36R
Robinson, Janice S(tevenson) 1941- ... 111
Robinson, Jay (Luke) 1932- ... 41-44R
Robinson, Jean O. 1934- ... 29-32R
See also SATA 7
Robinson, Jeffrey 1945- ... 121
Robinson, Jerry 1922- Brief entry ... 112
See also SATA 34
Robinson, Jill 1936- ... 102
See also CLC 10
Robinson, Jo Ann Ooiman 1942- ... 111
Robinson, Joan (Mary) G(ale Thomas)
1910- ... CANR-5
Earlier sketch in CA 7-8R
See also SATA 7
Robinson, Joan Violet 1903-1983 ... CANR-6
Obituary ... 110
Earlier sketch in CA 9-10R
Robinson, John A(rthur) T(homas)
1919-1983 ... CANR-6
Obituary ... 111
Earlier sketch in CA 7-8R
Robinson, John W(esley) 1929- ... CANR-2
Earlier sketch in CA 49-52
Robinson, Joseph 1927- ... 45-48
Robinson, Joseph Frederick 1912- ... 13-14R
Robinson, Joseph William 1908- ... CAP-2
Earlier sketch in CA 25-28
Robinson, Karl Frederic 1904-1967 ... CANR-5
Earlier sketch in CA 5-6R
Robinson, Kathleen
See Robinson, Chaille Howard (Payne)
Robinson, Kenneth Ernest 1914- ... 7-8R
Robinson, Kim Stanley 1952- ... CLC-34
Robinson, L(eonard) W(allace) 1912- ... 69-72
Robinson, (Esme Stuart) Lennox
1886-1958 Brief entry ... 120
See also DLB 10
Robinson, Leonard A. 1904(?)-1980 ... 97-100
Robinson, Lisa 1936- ... 93-96
Robinson, Lloyd
See Silverberg, Robert
Robinson, Logan Gilmore 1949- ... 108
Robinson, Louie, Jr. 1926- ... 107
Robinson, Lytle W(ebb) 1913- ... 61-64
Robinson, Mabel Louise 1874-1962
Obituary ... 113
See also DLB 22
Robinson, Mairi 1945- ... 123
Robinson, Margaret A(twood) 1937- ... 107
Robinson, Marguerite S. 1935- ... 49-52
Robinson, Marileta 1942- ... 101
See also SATA 32
Robinson, Marilynne 1944- ... 116
See also CLC 25
Robinson, Martin David 1925-1982
Obituary ... 108
Robinson, Matt(hew) 1937- ... 45-48
Robinson, Maudie Millian Oller 1914- ... CANR-8
Earlier sketch in CA 61-64
See also SATA 11
Robinson, Maurice R(ichard) 1895-1982
Obituary ... 106
See also SATA 29
Robinson, Max 1939- Brief entry ... 110
Robinson, Max (C.) 1939- ... 124
Robinson, Michael J(ay) 1945- ... 113
Robinson, Nancy K(onheim) 1942- ... CANR-24
Earlier sketch in CA 106
See also SATA 31, 32
Robinson, Nancy (Lou) M(ayer) 1930- ... 61-64
Robinson, Norman H(amilton) G(alloway)
1912- ... 13-14R
Robinson, O(liver) Preston 1903- ... 13-14R
Robinson, (Frances) Olvis 1923- ... 53-56
Robinson, P. W. 1893- ... 103
Robinson, Patricia
See Goedicke, Patricia (McKenna)
Robinson, Patricia Colbert 1923- ... 77-80
Robinson, Paul 1940- ... 81-84
Robinson, Philip (Bedford) 1926- ... CANR-16
Earlier sketch in CA 21-22R
Robinson, Ras 1935- ... 105
Robinson, Ray(mond Kenneth) 1920- ... 77-80
See also SATA 23
Robinson, Ray Charles 1932- Brief entry ... 115
Robinson, Raymond Henry 1927- ... 41-44R
Robinson, Richard 1945- ... CANR-13
Earlier sketch in CA 57-60
Robinson, Richard Dunlop 1921- ... 7-8R
Robinson, Robert 1886-1975 Obituary ... 113
Robinson, Robert (Reginald) 1922- ... CANR-14
Earlier sketch in CA 41-44R
Robinson, Robert 1927- ... 11-12R
Robinson, Robert H(ouston) 1936- ... CANR-6
Earlier sketch in CA 7-8R
Robinson, Roland Inwood 1907- ... CANR-1
Earlier sketch in CA 4R
Robinson, Rollo S(mith) 1915- ... 41-44R
Robinson, Rose ... 77-80
Robinson, Selma 1899(?)-1977 Obituary .. 73-76
Robinson, Shari
See McGuire, Leslie Sarah
Robinson, Sidney K. 1943- ... 113
Robinson, Sister Marian Dolores 1916- ... 11-12R
Robinson, Smokey
See Robinson, William, Jr.
See also CLC 21
Robinson, Sondra Till 1931- ... CANR-7
Earlier sketch in CA 53-56
Robinson, Spider 1948- ... CANR-11
Earlier sketch in CA 65-68
Robinson, T(homas) H(eath)
1869-1950 ... SATA-17
Robinson, T(homas) M(ore) 1936- ... 29-32R
Robinson, Terry 1916- ... 108
Robinson, Therese 1797-1870 ... DLB-59
Robinson, Thomas W. 1935- ... 33-36R
Robinson, Trevor 1929- ... 53-56
Robinson, (Wanda) Veronica 1926- ... 105
See also SATA 30
Robinson, Vince
See Newton, Michael
Robinson, Virgil E. 1908- ... 23-24R
Robinson, W(illiam) Gordon 1903-1977 . CANR-5
Earlier sketch in CA 7-8R
Robinson, W(illiam) Heath 1872-1944 .. SATA-17
Robinson, W(illiam) R(onald) 1927- ... 23-24R
Robinson, W(alter) Stitt 1917- Brief entry .. 105
Robinson, Wayne 1916- ... 2R
Robinson, Wayne A(ustin) 1937- ... 73-76
Robinson, Wilhelmena S(impson) 1912- .. 25-28R
Robinson, Willard B(ethurem) 1935- ... 57-60
Robinson, William Childs 1897-1982 ... 4R
Obituary ... 116
Robinson, William F(rank) 1946- ... 118
Robinson, William H. 1912-1984 Obituary .. 111
Robinson, William H(enry) 1922- ... 37-40R
Robinson, William, Jr. 1940- Brief entry ... 116
Robinson, William P(owell) 1910- ... 5-6R
Robinson, William Wheeler 1918- ... CANR-18
Earlier sketches in CA 7-8R, CANR-3
Robison, Bonnie 1924- ... 57-60
See also SATA 12
Robison, David V. 1911(?)-1978 ... 93-96
Obituary ... 81-84
Robison, Mabel Otis 1891- ... CAP-1
Earlier sketch in CA 11-12
Robison, Mary 1949- ... 116
Brief entry ... 113
See also CLC 42
Robison, Nancy L(ouise) 1934- ... 93-96
See also SATA 32
Robison, Sophia Moses 1888-1969 ... 7-8R
Obituary ... 103
Robitscher, Jonas B(ondi, Jr.)
1920-1981 ... CANR-19
Obituary ... 103
Earlier sketch in CA 21-22R
Robles, Emmanuel 1914- ... 81-84
Robles, Mireya 1934- ... 81-84
Robley, Grace 1918- ... 61-64
Robley, Rob
See Robley, Wendell
Robley, Wendell 1916- ... 61-64
Robo, Etienne 1879- ... CAP-1
Earlier sketch in CA 11-12
Robock, Stefan H. 1915- ... 19-20R
Robottom, John 1934- ... CANR-16
Earlier sketch in CA 29-32R
See also SATA 7
Robsjohn-Gibbings, Terence Harold
1905-1976 Obituary ... 69-72
Robson, B(rian) T(urnbull) 1939- ... 29-32R
Robson, D(erek) I(an) 1935- ... 25-28R
Robson, Dirk
See Robinson, Derek
Robson, E(manuel) W(alter) 1897- ... 65-68
Robson, Elizabeth 1942- ... 101
Robson, Ernest (Mack) 1902- ... CANR-24
Earlier sketch in CA 45-48
Robson, James 1890- ... 7-8R
Robson, Jeremy 1939- ... CANR-4
Earlier sketch in CA 7-8R
Robson, John M(ercel) 1927- ... 29-32R
Robson, Lucia St. Clair 1942- ... 108
Robson, Marion M. 1908- ... 89-92
Robson, William Alexander 1895-1980 ... 103
Obituary ... 97-100
Robson, William N. ... AITN-1
Roby, Kinley E. 1929- ... 77-80
Roby, Mary Linn ... CANR-7
Earlier sketch in CA 15-16R
Roby, Pamela A. 1942- ... 29-32R
Roby, Robert C(urtis) 1922- ... 7-8R
Robyns, Gwen 1917- ... 93-96
Roca-Pons, Josep 1914- ... 49-52
Roccapriore, Marie 1933- ... 115
Roch, John H(enry) 1916- ... 102
Rochard, Henri
See Charlier, Roger H(enri)
Rochberg-Halton, Eugene 1950- ... 111
Roche, A. K.
See Abisch, Roslyn Kroop
and Kaplan, Boche
Roche, Alphonse Victor 1895- ... 104
Roche, Douglas J. 1929- ... 101
Roche, George Charles III 1935- ... 29-32R
Roche, J. Jeffrey 1916(?)-1975 Obituary .. 61-64
Roche, John
See Le Roi, David (de Roche)
Roche, John P(earson) 1923- ... 69-72
Roche, Kennedy Francis 1911- ... 61-64
Roche, Orion 1948- ... 61-64
Roche, Owen I. A. 1911(?)-1973
Obituary ... 41-44R
Roche, P(atricia) K. Brief entry ... 112
See also SATA 34
Roche, Paul 1928- ... CANR-4
Earlier sketch in CA 7-8R
Roche, T(homas) W(illiam) E(dgar)
1919-197(?) ... CAP-2
Earlier sketch in CA 21-22
Roche, Terry
See Poole, Peggy
Roche, Thomas P(atrick), Jr. 1931- ... 106
Rochelle, Jay C. 1938- ... 53-56
Rocher, Guy 1924- ... CANR-24
Earlier sketch in CA 45-48
Rocher, Ludo 1926- Brief entry ... 106
Rochester, Devereaux 1917- ... 105
Rochester, Harry A(rthur) 1897(?)-1983
Obituary ... 109
Rochester, J. Martin 1945- ... 37-40R
Rochester, Jack B. 1944- ... 122
Rochlin, Gregory 1912- ... 49-52
Rochlin, Harriet 1924- ... 117
Rochmis, Lyda N(onne) 1912- ... 29-32R
Rock, David (Peter) 1945- ... CANR-19
Earlier sketch in CA 101
Rock, Gail Brief entry ... 111
See also SATA 32
Rock, Irvin 1922- ... CANR-10
Earlier sketch in CA 21-22R
Rock, James M(artin) 1935- ... 102
Rock, John 1890-1984 Obituary ... 114
Rock, Maxine 1940- ... 113
Rock, Milton L(ee) 1921- ... 49-52
Rock, Phillip 1927- ... 101
Rock, Richard
See Mainprize, Don
Rock, Stanley A(rthur) 1937- ... 101
Rock, William R(ay) 1930- ... 41-44R
Rockas, Leo 1928- ... 15-16R
Rockcastle, Verne N(orton) 1920- ... 73-76
Rocke, Russell 1945- ... 33-36R
Rockefeller, John D(avison, Sr.)
1839-1937 Brief entry ... 116
Rockefeller, John Davison III 1906-1978 ... 81-84
Obituary ... 77-80
Rockefeller, John William, Jr.
1899(?)-1987 Obituary ... 122
Rocker, Fermin 1907- ... SATA-40
Rockingham, Montague
See Nye, Nelson C(oral)
Rockland, Mae Shafter 1937- ... 65-68
Rockland, Michael Aaron 1935- ... 37-40R
Rockley, L(awrence) E(dwin) 1916- ... 29-32R
Rocklin, Ross Louis 1913- ... 61-64
Rocklynne, Ross
See Rocklin, Ross Louis
Rockne, Dick 1939- ... 61-64
Rockowitz, Murray 1920- ... 25-28R
Rocks, Lawrence 1933- ... 85-88
Rockwell, Anne (F.) 1934- ... CANR-22
Earlier sketch in CA 21-22R
See also SATA 33
Rockwell, F(rederick) F(rye) 1884-1976 ... 49-52
Obituary ... 103
Rockwell, Gail ... SATA-36
Rockwell, Harlow ... CANR-22
Earlier sketch in CA 109
See also SATA 33
Rockwell, Jane 1929- ... 65-68
Rockwell, John (Sargent) 1940-
Brief entry ... 114
Rockwell, Kiffin Ayres 1917- ... 37-40R
Rockwell, Matt
See Rowland, D(onald) S(ydney)

Rockwell, Norman (Percevel) 1894-1978 ... 89-92
Obituary ... 81-84
See also SATA 23
Rockwell, Thomas 1933- ... 29-32R
See also SATA 7
See also CLR 6
Rockwell, Wilson (Miller) 1909- ... CAP-2
Earlier sketch in CA 19-20
Rockwood, Joyce 1947- ... CANR-6
Earlier sketch in CA 57-60
See also SATA 39
Rockwood, Louis G. 1925- ... 45-48
Rockwood, Roy ... CAP-2
Earlier sketch in CA 19-20
See also SATA 1
Rockwood, Roy
See McFarlane, Leslie
Rodahl, Kaare 1917- ... 9-10R
Rodale, J(erome) I(rving) 1898-1971
Obituary ... 29-32R
Rodale, Robert 1930- ... 53-56
Rodan, Paul N. Rosenstein
See Rosenstein-Rodan, Paul N.
Rodaway, Angela 1918- ... 120
Rodberg, Leonard S(idney) 1932- ... CANR-24
Earlier sketch in CA 45-48
Rodberg, Lillian 1936- ... 29-32R
Rodd, Kathleen Tennant 1912-1988 ... CANR-5
Obituary ... 124
Earlier sketch in CA 5-6R
Rodda, Charles 1891- ... 7-8R
Rodda, Peter (Gordon) 1937- ... 81-84
Roddenberry, Eugene Wesley 1921- ... 110
See also SATA 45
Roddenberry, Gene
See Roddenberry, Eugene Wesley
See also CLC 17
Roddick, Alan (Melven) 1937- ... CANR-15
Earlier sketch in CA 77-80
Roddick, Ellen 1936- ... 41-44R
Roddis, Louis Harry 1887- ... 7-8R
Roddis, Roland J. 1908- ... 7-8R
Rodd-Marling, Yvonne 1912-1982
Obituary ... 107
Roddy, Lee 1921- ... 123
Rodefer, Stephen 1940- ... CANR-23
Earlier sketch in CA 107
Rodell, Fred 1907-1980 Obituary ... 97-100
Rodell, Marie F(reid) 1912-1975 Obituary .. 61-64
Rodenberg, Julius 1884-1970 Obituary ... 104
Roder, Wolf 1932- ... 17-18R
Roderus, Frank 1942- ... CANR-17
Earlier sketch in CA 89-92
Rodes, John E(dward) 1923- ... 15-16R
Rodes, Robert Emmet, Jr. 1927- ... 112
Rodewyk, Adolf 1894- ... 65-68
Rodger, Alec
See Rodger, Thomas Alexander
Rodger, Anne 1910-1983 Obituary ... 111
Rodger, Ian (Graham) 1926- ... CANR-4
Earlier sketch in CA 7-8R
Rodger, Thomas Alexander 1907-1982
Obituary ... 106
Rodgers, Betsy (Aikin-Sneath) 1907- ... CAP-1
Earlier sketch in CA 13-14
Rodgers, Betty June (Flint) 1921- ... 11-12R
Rodgers, Brian 1910- ... 29-32R
Rodgers, Buck
See Rodgers, Francis G.
Rodgers, Carolyn M. ... CANR-2
Earlier sketch in CA 45-48
See also DLB 41
Rodgers, Daniel T(racy) 1942- ... 124
Rodgers, Dorothy F(einer) 1909- ... 89-92
Rodgers, Francis G. 1926- ... 123
Rodgers, Frank
See Infield, Glenn (Berton)
Rodgers, Frank P(eter) 1924- ... 11-12R
Rodgers, Harrell R(oss), Jr. 1939- ... CANR-7
Earlier sketch in CA 53-56
Rodgers, Joann Ellison 1941- ... 77-80
Rodgers, John (Charles) 1906- ... CAP-1
Earlier sketch in CA 11-12
Rodgers, Mary 1931- ... CANR-8
Earlier sketch in CA 49-52
See also SATA 8
See also CLC 12
Rodgers, Raboo 1945- ... 119
Rodgers, Richard (Charles) 1902-1979 ... 89-92
Rodgers, Stanley 1928-1977 Obituary ... 106
Rodgers, W(illiam) R(obert) 1909-1969 ... 85-88
See also DLB 20
See also CLC 7
Rodgers, William H. 1918- ... 19-20R
Rodgers, William Henry 1947- ... 101
Rodick, Burleigh Cushing 1889- ... 5-6R
Rodimer, Eva 1895- ... CAP-2
Earlier sketch in CA 21-22
Rodimstev, Aleksandr 1905(?)-1977
Obituary ... 69-72
Rodin, Alvin E(li) 1926- ... 119
Rodin, Arnold W. 1917- ... 89-92
Rodini, Robert J(oseph) 1936- ... 29-32R
Rodinson, Maxime 1915- ... CANR-4
Earlier sketch in CA 53-56
Roditi, Edouard Herbert 1910- ... 101
Rodli, Agnes Sylvia 1921- ... 11-12R
Rodman, Bella (Kashin) 1903- ... CAP-2
Earlier sketch in CA 19-20
Rodman, Emerson
See Ellis, Edward S(ylvester)
Rodman, Eric
See Silverberg, Robert
Rodman, F(rancis) Robert 1934- ... 122
Brief entry ... 117
Rodman, Howard 1920(?)-1985 Obituary ... 118
Rodman, Hyman 1931- ... CANR-8
Earlier sketch in CA 17-18R
Rodman, Maia
See Wojciechowska, Maia (Teresa)
Rodman, Selden 1909- ... CANR-5
Earlier sketch in CA 5-6R
See also SATA 9
Rodney, Bob
See Rodrigo, Robert
Rodney, Robert M(orris) 1911- ... 77-80
Rodney, William 1923- ... 25-28R
Rodnick, David 1908- ... 33-36R
Rodnitzky, Jerome Leon 1936- ... 41-44R
Rodolph, Utto
See Ouologuem, Yambo
Rodowsky, Colby (F.) 1932- ... CANR-23
Earlier sketch in CA 69-72
See also SATA 21
Rodrigo, Robert 1928- ... 13-14R
Rodrigues, Jose Honorio 1913- ... CANR-13
Earlier sketch in CA 29-32R
Rodriguez, Claudio 1934- ... CLC-10
Rodriguez, Judith Green 1936- ... CANR-23
Earlier sketch in CA 107
Rodriguez, Mario 1922- ... 17-18R
Rodriguez, Richard 1944- ... 110
Rodriguez-Alcala, Hugo (Rosendo)
1917- ... CANR-14
Earlier sketch in CA 21-22R
Rodriguez-Alcala, Sally 1938- ... 23-24R
Rodriguez Cepeda, Enrique 1939- ... 45-48
Rodriguez Delgado, Jose M(anuel)
See Delgado, Jose Manuel R(odriguez)
Rodriguez Monegal, Emir 1921-1985
Obituary ... 117
Brief entry ... 115
Rodriguez O(rdonez), Jaime E(dmundo)
1940- ... 110
Rodway, Allan 1919- ... 13-14R
Rodwin, Lloyd 1919- ... CANR-19
Earlier sketches in CA 5-6R, CANR-4
Rodwin, Victor G(eorge) 1950- ... 120
Rodzinski, Halina 1904- ... 69-72
Roe, Anne 1904- ... 17-18R
Roe, Daphne A(nderson) 1923- ... 93-96
Roe, Derek A(rthur) 1937- ... CANR-23
Earlier sketch in CA 107
Roe, Dorothy
See Lewis, Dorothy Roe
Roe, F(rederic) Gordon 1894-1985 ... 9-10R
Obituary ... 115
Roe, Gerald 1940- ... 117
Roe, Harry Mason ... CAP-2
Earlier sketch in CA 19-20
Roe, Kathleen Robson 1910- ... 93-96
Roe, Richard L(ionel) 1936- ... CANR-15
Earlier sketch in CA 65-68
Roe, W(illiam) G(ordon) 1932- ... 21-22R
Roe, William Henry 1918- ... 5-6R
Roeber, Edward C(harles) 1913-1969 ... CANR-5
Earlier sketch in CA 5-6R
Roebuck, Carl Angus 1914- Brief entry ... 105
Roebuck, Derek 1935- ... 111
Roebuck, Janet 1943- ... 49-52
Roebuck, Julian B(aker) 1920- ... 101
Roebuck, Peter (Michael) 1956- ... 119
Roeburt, John 1909(?)-1972 Obituary ... 33-36R
Roecker, W(illiam) A. 1942- ... 61-64
Roeder, Bill 1922-1982 Obituary ... 107
Roeder, Ralph Leclerq 1890-1969
Obituary ... 104
Roehr, George L. 1931(?)-1983 Obituary ... 110
Roehrs, Walter R(obert) 1901- ... 103
Roeiker, Nancy Lyman 1915- ... 11-12R
Roelofs, H. Mark 1923- ... 111
Roelvaag, O(le) E(dvart) 1876-1931
Brief entry ... 117
See also DLB 9
See also TCLC 17
Roemer, Kenneth Morrison 1945- ... 112
Roemer, Michael 1937- ... 111
Roemer, Milton I(rwin) 1916- ... CANR-21
Earlier sketches in CA 57-60, CANR-6
Roemer, Norma H. 1905-1973 ... CAP-2
Earlier sketch in CA 19-20
Roeming, Robert Frederick 1911- ... 29-32R
Roepke, Wilhelm (Theodor) 1899-1966 ... CAP-1
Earlier sketch in CA 9-10
Roer, Berniece Marie ... 9-10R
Roes, Nicholas 1926- ... 29-32R
Roes, Nicholas A. 1952- ... 124
Roesch, Roberta F(leming) 1919- ... CANR-2
Earlier sketch in CA 5-6R
Roesch, Ronald 1947- ... 106
Roeseler, Robert O. 1882- ... CAP-2
Earlier sketch in CA 17-18
Roeseler, W(olfgang) G(uenter) 1925- ... 111
Roesler, Robert Harry 1927- ... 120
Roessel-Waugh, C. C.
See Waugh, Carol-Lynn Roessel
and Waugh, Charles G(ordon)
Roessel-Waugh, C. C.
See Waugh, Charles G(ordon)
Roessler, Carl (Fred) 1933- ... 117
Roethenmund, Robert 1956- ... 103
Roethke, Theodore (Huebner) 1908-1963 .. 81-84
See also CABS 2
See also DLB 5
See also CDALB 1941-1968
See also CLC 1, 3, 8, 11, 19, 46
Roett, Riordan Joseph Allenby III 1938- ... 57-60
Roetter, Charles Frederick 1919- ... 61-64
Roetzel, Calvin J. 1931- ... 112
Roever, J(oan) M(arilyn) 1935- ... 105
See also SATA 26
Rofe, (Fevzi) Husein 1922- ... CAP-1
Earlier sketch in CA 9-10
Rofes, Eric Edward 1954- ... 106
Roff, William R(obert) 1929- ... 57-60
Roffey, Maureen 1936- ... 108
See also SATA 33
Roffman, Howard 1953- ... 61-64
Roffman, Roger A. 1942- ... 110
Roffman, Sara
See Hershman, Morris
Rogal, Samuel J. 1934- ... CANR-17
Earlier sketch in CA 25-28R
Rogaly, (Henry) Joseph 1935- ... 104
Rogan, Barbara 1951- ... 124
Rogan, Donald L(ynn) 1930- ... 29-32R
Roger, Mae Durham ... 57-60
Rogers, A(mos) Robert 1927- ... CANR-8
Earlier sketch in CA 61-64
Rogers, Agnes
See Allen, Agnes Rogers
Rogers, Alan 1933- ... CANR-11
Earlier sketch in CA 21-22R
Rogers, (Thomas) Alan (Stinchcombe)
1937- ... CANR-18
Earlier sketch in CA 25-28R
See also SATA 2
Rogers, Augustus James III 1929- ... 33-36R
Rogers, Barbara 1945- ... CANR-17
Earlier sketch in CA 65-68
Rogers, Berto 1903-1974 ... CAP-2
Earlier sketch in CA 29-32
Rogers, Bruce 1870-1957 Brief entry ... 123
Rogers, Carl R(ansom) 1902-1987 ... CANR-18
Obituary ... 121
Earlier sketches in CA 3R, CANR-1
Rogers, (Grenville) Cedric (Harry)
1915- ... CANR-1
Earlier sketch in CA 4R
Rogers, Charles B. 1911- ... 89-92
Rogers, Clara Coltman
See Vyvyan, Clara C(oltman Rogers)
Rogers, Cyril A(lfred) 1923- ... 5-6R
Rogers, Cyril H(arold) 1907- ... CANR-20
Earlier sketches in CA 11-12R, CANR-5
Rogers, Dale Evans 1912- ... 103
Rogers, David 1930- ... 29-32R
Rogers, David C(harles) D(rummond)
1931- ... CANR-5
Earlier sketch in CA 11-12R
Rogers, Donald I(rwin) 1918-1980 ... 57-60
Obituary ... 102
Rogers, Dorothy 1914-1986 ... CANR-1
Obituary ... 118
Earlier sketch in CA 3R
Rogers, Edith R(andam) 1924- ... 117
Rogers, Elizabeth F(rances) 1892-1974 ... 5-6R
Obituary ... 53-56
Rogers, Elyse M(acFadyen) 1932- ... 102
Rogers, Florence K(atherine) 1936- ... 101
Rogers, Floyd
See Spence, William John Duncan
Rogers, Frances 1888-1974 ... 5-6R
See also SATA 10
Rogers, Francis M(illet) 1914- ... CANR-1
Earlier sketch in CA 3R
Rogers, Franklin R(obert) 1921- ... 2R
Rogers, Fred B(aker) 1926- ... 109
Rogers, Fred McFeely 1928- ... 107
See also SATA 33
Rogers, Garet ... 2R
Rogers, Gayle 1923- ... 69-72
Rogers, George Calvin, Jr. 1922- ... CANR-1
Earlier sketch in CA 4R
Rogers, George W(illiam) 1917- ... CANR-1
Earlier sketch in CA 1R
Rogers, H(ugh) C(uthbert) Basset
1905- ... CANR-14
Earlier sketch in CA 73-76
Rogers, Henry C. 1914- ... 102
Rogers, Ingrid 1951- ... 116
Rogers, Jack 1934- ... 93-96
Rogers, James Allen 1929- ... 13-14R
Rogers, James T(racy) 1921- ... 45-48
Rogers, Jane 1952- ... 113
Rogers, Jean 1919- ... 115
See also SATA 47
Rogers, Jeanne F. 1926(?)-1984 Obituary .. 113
Rogers, JoAnn V. 1940- ... 89-92
Rogers, Joel Townsley 1896-1984
Obituary ... 114
Rogers, John 1906- ... 7-8R
Rogers, Josephine 1925- ... 61-64
Rogers, Kate Ellen 1920- ... 13-14R
Rogers, Katharine M(unzer) 1932- ... CANR-8
Earlier sketch in CA 21-22R
Rogers, Keith
See Harris, Marion Rose (Young)
Rogers, Kenneth Paul 1940- ... 53-56
Rogers, Kenneth Ray 1938- ... 85-88
Rogers, Kenny
See Rogers, Kenneth Ray
Rogers, Linda (Hall) 1944- ... 77-80
Rogers, Matilda 1894-1976 ... CAP-2
Earlier sketch in CA 29-32
See also SATA 5, 34
Rogers, Max Gray 1932- ... 53-56
Rogers, Michael 1950- ... CANR-1
Earlier sketch in CA 49-52
Rogers, Mick
See Glut, Donald F(rank)
Rogers, Millard F(oster), Jr. 1932- ... 101
Rogers, Neville William 1908- ... 108
Rogers, Pamela 1927- ... CANR-4
Earlier sketch in CA 49-52
See also SATA 9
Rogers, Pat 1938- ... 85-88
Rogers, Pattiann 1940- ... 109
Rogers, Paul (Patrick) 1900- ... 41-44R
Rogers, Paul 1950- ... 123
Rogers, Paul T(aylor) 1936-1984 ... 119
Obituary ... 113
Rogers, Peter 1934- ... 101
Rogers, Peter D(amien) 1942- ... 116
Rogers, Raymond A(rthur) 1911- ... 21-22R
Rogers, Robert
See Hamilton, Charles Harold St. John
Rogers, Rolf E(rnst) 1931- ... 57-60
Rogers, Rosemary 1932- ... CANR-23
Earlier sketches in CA 49-52, CANR-3
See also AITN 1
Rogers, Roy 1912- ... 112
Rogers, Rutherford D(avid) 1915-
Brief entry ... 109
Rogers, Sarah F. 1923(?)-1976 Obituary .. 69-72
Rogers, Thomas Hunton 1927- ... 89-92
Rogers, Timothy (John Godfrey) 1927- .. CANR-1
Earlier sketch in CA 45-48
Rogers, (George) Truett 1931- ... 69-72
Rogers, Tyler Stewart 1895- ... 7-8R
Rogers, Vincent R(obert) 1926-
Brief entry ... 115
Rogers, W(illiam) G(arland) 1896-1978 ... 11-12R
Obituary ... 77-80
See also SATA 23
Rogers, Wade
See Madlee, Dorothy (Haynes)
Rogers, Warren (Joseph, Jr.) 1922- ... CANR-13
Earlier sketch in CA 77-80
Rogers, Warren
See Brucker, Roger W(arren)
Rogers, Will(iam Penn Adair) 1879-1935
Brief entry ... 105
See also DLB 11
See also TCLC 8
Rogers, William C(ecil) 1919- ... 19-20R
Rogers, William D(ill) 1927- ... 41-44R
Rogers, William Elford 1944- ... 113
Rogers, William R(aymond) 1932- ... 104
Rogers, William Warren 1929- Brief entry ... 112
Rogerson, J(ohn) W(illiam) 1935- ... 115
Rogerson, John
See Rogerson, J(ohn) W(illiam)
Rogg, Eleanor H(ertha) Meyer 1942- ... 57-60
Rogg, Sanford G. 1917- ... 19-20R
Rogge, Oetje John 1903-1981 ... 4R
Obituary ... 103
Rogin, Gilbert 1929- ... CANR-15
Earlier sketch in CA 65-68
See also CLC 18
Rogin, Michael Paul 1937- ... 101
Roginski, J(ames) W. 1945- ... 119
Roginski, Jim
See Roginski, J(ames) W.
Rogler, Lloyd H(enry) 1930- ... 17-18R
Roglieri, John Louis 1939- ... 105
Rogness, Alvin N. 1906- ... CANR-8
Earlier sketch in CA 21-22R
Rogness, Michael 1935- ... 101
Rogo, D. Scott 1950- ... CANR-13
Earlier sketch in CA 33-36R
Rogoff, Barbara 1950- ... 118
Rogoff, Harry 1882-1971 Obituary ... 33-36R
Rogosin, (William) Donn 1947- ... 123
Rogovin, Anne 1918- ... 97-100
Rogow, Arnold Austin 1924- ... CANR-1
Earlier sketch in CA 3R
Roh, Jae Min 1927- ... 117
Rohan, Koda
See Koda Shigeyuki
See also TCLC 22
Rohatyn, Dennis 1949- ... 69-72
Rohatyn, Felix G(eorge) 1928- ... 118
Rohen, Edward 1931- ... CANR-4
Earlier sketch in CA 53-56
Rohlen, Tom 1940- ... 85-88
Rohmer, Eric
See Scherer, Jean-Marie Maurice
See also CLC 16
Rohmer, Richard 1924- ... CANR-19
Earlier sketch in CA 103
Rohmer, Sax
See Ward, Arthur Henry Sarsfield
Rohn, Arthur H(enry, Jr.) 1929- ... 45-48
Rohner, Ronald P(reston) 1935- ... 37-40R
Rohr, John A. 1934- ... 33-36R
Rohrbach, Peter Thomas 1926- ... CANR-1
Earlier sketch in CA 2R
Rohrbaugh, Joanna Bunker 1943- ... 101
Rohrberger, Mary 1929- ... CANR-1
Earlier sketch in CA 45-48
Rohrbough, Malcolm J(ustin) 1932- ... 29-32R
Rohrer, Alyce Stevens 1922- ... 123
Rohrer, Daniel M(organ) 1941- ... 33-36R
Rohrer, Norman B(echtel) 1929- ... CANR-16
Earlier sketch in CA 93-96
Rohrer, Wayne C(urry) 1920- ... 21-22R
Rohrl, Vivian J. (Lober) ... 110
Rohrlich, Chester 1900(?)-1974 Obituary .. 53-56
Rohrlich, George F(riedrich) 1914- ... CANR-14
Earlier sketch in CA 37-40R
Rohrlich, Ruby ... CANR-5
Earlier sketch in CA 53-56
Rohrlich-Leavitt, Ruby
See Rohrlich, Ruby
Rohrlick, Paula 1955- ... 111
Rohrman, Nicholas L(eroy) 1937- ... 29-32R
Rohwer, Juergen 1924- ... 65-68
Rohwer, Jurgen
See Rohwer, Juergen
Roider, Karl A(ndrew), Jr. 1943- ... 111
Roiphe, Anne Richardson 1935- ... 89-92
See also DLBY 80
See also CLC 3, 9
Rojan
See Rojankovsky, Feodor Stephanovich

Rojankovsky, Feodor Stepanovich
1891-1970 77-80
See also SATA 21
Rojas, Carlos 1928- CANR-22
Earlier sketches in CA 19-20R, CANR-7
Rojko, Anthony J. 1918(?)-1978
Obituary 77-80
Rojo, Ricardo 1923- 25-28R
Rokeach, Milton 1918- CANR-5
Earlier sketch in CA 3R
Rokeby-Thomas, Anna E(lma) 1911- 77-80
See also SATA 15
Rokes, Willis Park 1926- 25-28R
Roland, Albert 1925- 61-64
See also SATA 11
Roland, Betty 1903- 103
Roland, Charles P(ierce) 1918- 41-44R
Roland, Mary
See Lewis, Mary (Christianna Milne)
Roland, Nicholas
See Walmsley, Arnold Robert
Roland Smith, Gordon 1931- 102
Rolant, Rene
See Fanthorpe, R(obert) Lionel
Roldos Aguilera, Jaime 1940-1981
Obituary 108
Roleder, George 1928- CANR-21
Earlier sketch in CA 105
Rolerson, Darrell A(llen) 1946- 49-52
See also SATA 8
Rolfe, Bari 1916- 113
Rolfe, Eugene (Edward Musgrave)
1914- 13-14R
Rolfe, Franklin P(rescott) 1902-1985
Obituary 117
Rolfe, Frederick (William Serafino Austin
Lewis Mary) 1860-1913 Brief entry 107
See also DLB 34
See also TCLC 12
Rolfe, Lionel (Menuhin) 1942- 110
Rolfe, Sheila Constance 1935- 102
Rolfe, Sidney 1921-1976 69-72
Obituary 65-68
Rolfsrud, Erling Nicolai 1912- 65-68
Roll, Charles W(eissert), Jr. 1928- CANR-1
Earlier sketch in CA 45-48
Roll, Eric 1907- 102
Roll, Richard J(effrey) 1952- 124
Roll, Samuel 1942- 124
Roll, William George, Jr. 1926- 81-84
Roll, Winifred 1909- 49-52
See also SATA 6
Rolland, Barbara J(une) 1929- 77-80
Rolland, Romain 1866-1944 Brief entry 118
See also DLB 65
See also TCLC 23
Rolle, Andrew Frank 1922- CANR-3
Earlier sketch in CA 4R
Roller, David C(harles) 1937- 107
Roller, Duane H(enry) D(uBose) 1920- 61-64
Rolleston, James Lancelot 1939- 85-88
Rollin, Bernard Elliot 1943- 108
Rollin, Betty 1936- CANR-22
Earlier sketches in CA 15-16R, CANR-7
Rollin, Roger Best 1930- CANR-8
Earlier sketch in CA 17-18R
Rollins, Alfred Brooks, Jr. 1921- 5-6R
Rollins, Bryant 1937- 49-52
Rollins, C(alvin) D(wight) 1918- 41-44R
Rollins, Charlemae Hill 1897-1979 .... 11-12R
Obituary 104
See also SATA 3, 26
Rollins, Judith 122
Rollins, Kelly (a pseudonym) 1924- 106
Rollins, Peter C(ushing) 1942- 108
Rollins, Richard M(eryl) 1945- 121
Rollins, Royce
See Pepper, Choral
Rollins, Steed 1916-1985 Obituary 118
Rollins, Wayne G(ilbert) 1929- CANR-3
Earlier sketch in CA 11-12R
Rollison, William D(ewey) 1897-1971 .... CAP-2
Earlier sketch in CA 19-20
Rollo, Vera Foster 1924- 81-84
Rolls, Anthony
See Vulliamy, Colwyn Edward
Rolls, Charles J(ubilee) 1887- 107
Rolls, Eric C(harles) 1923- CANR-13
Earlier sketch in CA 33-36R
Rolo, Charles J(acques) 1916-1982 101
Obituary 108
Rolo, Paul Jacques Victor 1917- 21-22R
Roloff, Leland Harold 1927- 49-52
Rolph, C. H.
See Hewitt, Cecil Rolph
Rolph, Earl R(obert) 1910- CAP-2
Earlier sketch in CA 23-24
Rolston, Holmes 1900-1977 .... CANR-3
Earlier sketch in CA 3R
Rolston, Holmes III 1932- 113
Rolt, L(ionel) T(homas) C(aswall)
1910-1974 .... CANR-1
Earlier sketch in CA 4R
Rolt-Wheeler, Francis William 1876-1960
Obituary 89-92
Rolvaag, O(le) E(dvart)
See Roelvaag, O(le) E(dvart)
Rom, M. Martin 1946- 81-84
Romagnoli, G(ian) Franco 1926- 73-76
Romagnoli, Margaret O'Neill 1922- 73-76
Romain Arnaud, Saint
See Aragon, Louis
Romaine, Lawrence B. 1900- CAP-1
Earlier sketch in CA 13-14
Romaine, Paul
See Bleamer, Burton
Romains, Jules 1885-1972 85-88
See also DLB 65
See also CLC 7
Roman, Daniel (David) 1921- 41-44R
Roman, Eric 1926- CANR-1
Earlier sketch in CA 1R
Roman, Murray 1920-1984 Obituary 112
Roman, Stephen B(oleslav) 1921-
Brief entry 112
Romanell, Patrick 1912- 23-24R
Romanelli, Charles S. 1930- 15-16R
Romano, Clare 1922- CANR-24
Earlier sketch in CA 41-44R
Romano, Deane Louis 1927- 25-28R
Romano, Don
See Turner, Robert (Harry)
Romano, Louis G. 1921- CANR-8
Earlier sketch in CA 19-20R
See also SATA 35
Romanoff, Alexis Lawrence 1892-1980 .. CANR-5
Earlier sketch in CA 11-12R
Romanoff, Harry 1892(?)-1970 Obituary 104
Romans, J(ohn) Thomas 1933- 15-16R
Romanucci-Ross, Lola 1928- CANR-18
Earlier sketch in CA 101
Romanus, Charles Franklin 1915-1983 .... 23-24R
Obituary 111
Romanyshyn, Robert Donald 1942- 108
Romasco, Albert U(go) 1930- 110
Romberger, Judy 1940- 106
Rome, Anthony
See Albert, Marvin H.
Rome, Beatrice K(aufman) 1913- 13-14R
Rome, Florence 1910- 33-36R
Romein, J. M.
See Romein, Jan (Marius)
Romein, Jan (Marius) 1893-1962
Obituary 111
Romer, Alfred 1906- 37-40R
Romer, (Louis) John 1941- 110
Romero, George A. 1940(?)- Brief entry 116
Romero, Gerry
See Neyland, James (Elwyn)
Romero, Jose Ruben 1890-1952
Brief entry 114
See also TCLC 14
Romero, Luis 1916- Brief entry 111
Romero, Orlando 1945- 69-72
Romero, Patricia W.
See Curtin, Patricia (W.) Romero
Romerstein, Herbert 1931- 11-12R
Romey, Bill
See Romey, William D(owden)
Romey, William D(owden) 1930- 57-60
Romig, Edna Davis 1889-1978 45-48
Obituary 103
Romig, Walter 1903-1977 Obituary 109
Romijn, Johanna Maria Kooyker
See Kooyker-Romijn, Johanna Maria
Romm, Ethel Grodzins 1925- 33-36R
Romm, Sharon 1942- 118
Rommel, (Mimi) Dayton 7-8R
Rommetveit, Ragnar 1924- 57-60
Romney, George W(ilcken) 1907-
Brief entry 106
Romney, Rodney Ross 1931- 102
Romney, Ronna 1943- 116
Romney, Steve
See Bingley, David Ernest
Romo, Ricardo 1943- 111
Romoser, George K(enneth) 1929- 41-44R
Rompkey, Ronald (George) 1943- 118
Romulo, Carlos P(ena) 1899(?)-1985 .. CANR-10
Obituary 118
Earlier sketch in CA 15-16R
Romyn, Johanna Maria Kooyker
See Kooyker-Romijn Johanna Maria
Rona, Peter A(rnold) 1934- 108
Ronald, Ann 1939- 124
Ronald, David William 1937- 65-68
Ronald, Hugh 1912(?)-1983 Obituary 109
Ronalds, Mary Teresa 1946- 25-28R
Ronaldson, Agnes S. 1916- 17-18R
Ronan, Colin A(listair) 1920- CANR-6
Earlier sketch in CA 7-8R
Ronan, Georgia
See Crampton, Georgia Ronan
Ronan, Margaret 1918- 102
Ronan, Thomas Matthew 1907- CAP-1
Earlier sketch in CA 9-10
Ronan, Tom
See Ronan, Thomas Matthew
Ronan, William W. 1917- 33-36R
Ronay, Gabriel Ernest 1930- 85-88
Roncali, Angelo Giuseppe
See John XXIII, Pope
Ronck, Ronn 1946- 121
Ronda, James P(aul) 1943- Brief entry 113
Rondell, Florence 1907- 57-60
Ronder, Paul 1940(?)-1977 Obituary 73-76
Rondinelli, Dennis A(ugust) 1943- 111
Rondthaler, Edward 1905- 15-16R
Ronen, Dov 1933- CANR-10
Earlier sketch in CA 57-60
Roney, Ruth Anne
See McMullin, Ruth R(oney)
Rongen, Bjoern 1906- CAP-2
Earlier sketch in CA 29-32
See also SATA 10
Rongen, Bjorn
See Rongen, Bjoern
Rongione, Louis Anthony 1912- 57-60
Ronken, Harriet
See Lynton, Harriet Ronken
Ronne, Finn 1899-1980 .... CANR-1
Obituary 97-100
Earlier sketch in CA 3R
Ronnie, Art(hur William) 1931- 41-44R
Ronning, C. Neale 1927- 7-8R
Ronning, Chester A. 1894-1984 Obituary 114
Ronns, Edward
See Aarons, Edward S(idney)
Ronsheim, Sally B(ober) 57-60
Ronsin, Jean
See Rodinson, Maxime
Ronsley, Joseph 1931- CANR-10
Earlier sketch in CA 25-28R
Ronsman, M. M.
See Nowak, Mariette
Ronson, Mark
See Alexander, Marc
Rood, Allan 1894- CAP-1
Earlier sketch in CA 13-14
Rood, John (Hiram) 1902-1974 .... 5-6R
Obituary 120
Rood, Karen Lane 1946- 102
Rood, Robert Thomas 1942- 107
Rood, Ronald (N.) 1920- CANR-24
Earlier sketches in CA 23-24R, CANR-9
See also SATA 12
Roodenburg, Nancy McKee 1909-1972
Obituary 104
Roof, Wade Clark 1939- 114
Rook, (William) Alan 1909- 97-100
Rook, Earnest Robert 1917- 104
Rook, Tony 1932- 69-72
Rooke, Daphne (Marie) 1914- 53-56
See also SATA 12
Rooke, Leon 1934- CANR-23
Earlier sketch in CA 25-28R
See also CLC 25, 34
Rookmaaker, Hendrik Roelof 1922-1977 57-60
Rooks, George (M.) 1951- CANR-22
Earlier sketch in CA 105
Room, Adrian 1933- CANR-16
Earlier sketch in CA 97-100
Roome, Katherine Ann Davis 1952- 85-88
Rooney, Andrew A(itken) 1919- CANR-9
Earlier sketch in CA 5-6R
Rooney, Andy
See Rooney, Andrew A(itken)
Rooney, David Douglas 1924- CANR-11
Earlier sketch in CA 21-22R
Rooney, Elmo
See Perry, Charles
Rooney, James 1938- 101
Rooney, James R(owell) 1927- 61-64
Rooney, Jim
See Rooney, James
Rooney, John F(rancis), Jr. 1939- 101
Rooney, Miriam Theresa 81-84
Rooney, Patrick C. 1937- 29-32R
Rooney, William Richard 1938- 102
Roop, Connie
See Roop, Constance Betzer
Roop, Constance Betzer 1951- 122
See also SATA 49
Roop, Peter (G.) 1951- 122
See also SATA 49
Roos, Audrey Kelley 1912-1982 Obituary 108
Roos, Charles A. 1914(?)-1974 Obituary 53-56
Roos, Hans
See Meissner, Hans-Otto
Roos, Hans Dietrich 1919- 19-20R
Roos, Kelley
See Roos, Audrey Kelley
Roos, Leslie L(eon), Jr. 1940- 33-36R
Roos, Murphre (joint pseudonym)
See Mele, Jim
Roos, Noralou P(reston) 1942- 33-36R
Roos, Stephen (Kelley) 1945- 112
See also SATA 41, 47
Roosa, Robert V(incent) 1918- 25-28R
Roose, Ronald 1945- 81-84
Roose-Evans, James 1927- 29-32R
Roosen, William (James) 1940- 117
Roosenburg, Henriette 1920-1972
Obituary 37-40R
Roosevelt, Edith Kermit 1926- 69-72
Roosevelt, (Anna) Eleanor 1884-1962
Obituary 89-92
See also SATA 50
Roosevelt, Elliott 1910- 105
See also AITN 1
Roosevelt, Felicia Warburg 1927- 57-60
Roosevelt, Franklin Delano 1882-1945
Brief entry 116
Roosevelt, James 1907- CANR-12
Earlier sketch in CA 69-72
Roosevelt, Nicholas 1893-1982 Obituary 106
Roosevelt, Theodore 1858-1919
Brief entry 115
See also DLB 47
Root, Deane L(eslie) 1947- CANR-23
Earlier sketch in CA 107
Root, E(dward) Merrill 1895-1973 .... CAP-1
Earlier sketch in CA 15-16
Root, Franklin Russell 1923- 7-8R
Root, Judith C(arol) 65-68
Root, Lin (Segal) 69-72
Root, Oren 1911- 85-88
Root, Phyllis SATA-48
Root, Phyllis 1949- 123
Root, Waverley (Lewis) 1903-1982 .... 25-28R
Obituary 108
See also DLB 4
Root, William Pitt 1941- CANR-12
Earlier sketch in CA 25-28R
Rooth, Gerhard Theodore 1898(?)-1983
Obituary 110
Rootham, Jasper (St. John) 1910- CANR-19
Earlier sketches in CA 7-8R, CANR-4
Roots, Clive (George) 1935- Brief entry 111
Roots, Ivan Alan 1921- 11-12R
Rooze, Gene E(dward) 1934- 120
Rope, Henry Edward George 1880-1978 .... 7-8R
Obituary 103
Roper, Gayle G(ordinier) 1940- 97-100
Roper, H(ugh) R(edwald) Trevor
See Trevor-Roper, H(ugh) R(edwald)
Roper, John Stephen 1924(?)-1980
Obituary 102
Roper, Lanning 1912-1983 Obituary 109
Roper, Laura Wood 1911- 57-60
See also SATA 34
Roper, Robert 1946- 73-76
Roper, Ronnalie J. 1936- 41-44R
Roper, Steve 1941- 103
Roper, Susan Bonthron 1948- 81-84
Roper, William L(eon) 1897- 33-36R
Ropke, Wilhelm (Theodor)
See Roepke, Wilhelm (Theodor)
Ropp, Theodore 1911- 5-6R
Roppolo, Joseph Patrick 1913- 15-16R
Rops, Daniel
See Petiot, Henri Jules Charles
Roquemore, Kathleen (Ann) 1941- 61-64
Rorabaugh, William Joseph 1945- 101
Rorem, Ned 1923- 17-18R
Roripaugh, A(lan) Robert 1930- 13-14R
Rorke, Margaret (Curry) 1915- 110
Rorty, Amelie Oksenberg 1932- 107
Rorty, James 1891(?)-1973 Obituary 41-44R
Rorty, Richard M(cKay) 1931- CANR-9
Earlier sketch in CA 23-24R
Rorty, Winifred Raushenbush
1894(?)-1979 Obituary 93-96
Rorvik, David M(ichael) 1946- 85-88
Rosa, Alfred F(elix) 1942- 41-44R
Rosa, Joao Guimaraes 1908-1967
Obituary 89-92
See also CLC 23
Rosa, Joseph G. 1932- 15-16R
Rosa, Nicholas 1926- 110
Rosage, David E. 1913- CANR-21
Earlier sketches in CA 13-14R, CANR-6
Rosaldo, Michelle Z(imbalist) 1944-1981 101
Obituary 108
Rosaldo, Renato I(gnacio), Jr. 1941- 89-92
Rosand, David 1938- 111
Rosa-Nieves, Cesareo 1901-1974 57-60
Rosbottom, Ronald C(arlisle) 1942- 61-64
Roscoe, A(drian) A(lan) 1939- 49-52
Roscoe, Charles
See Rowland, D(onald) S(ydney)
Roscoe, D(onald) T(homas) 1934- 113
See also SATA 42
Roscoe, Edwin Scott 1896-1978 .... 7-8R
Obituary 103
Roscoe, George B(oggs) 1907- 65-68
Rosdail, Jesse Hart 1914(?)-1977
Obituary 73-76
Rose, A(rthur) James 1927- 19-20R
Rose, Ada Campbell 1902(?)-1976
Obituary 65-68
Rose, Al 1916- 97-100
Rose, Alan Henry 1938- 93-96
Rose, Albert H(enry) 1903- 41-44R
Rose, Alvin E(manuel) 1903-1983
Obituary 109
Rose, Anna Perrott
See Wright, Anna (Maria Louisa Perrott)
Rose
Rose, Anne CANR-2
Earlier sketch in CA 49-52
See also SATA 8
Rose, Anthony Lewis 1939- 101
Rose, Arnold 1916-1983 Obituary 109
Rose, Arnold M(arshall) 1918-1968 .... 7-8R
Rose, Barbara E. 1937- Brief entry 111
Rose, Betsy
See Rose, Elizabeth
Rose, Billy 1899-1966 Obituary 116
Rose, Brian Waldron 1915- 97-100
Rose, Camille Davied 1893- CAP-2
Earlier sketch in CA 21-22
Rose, Carl 1903-1971 Obituary 29-32R
See also SATA 31
Rose, Clarkson 1890-1968 .... 7-8R
Rose, Clive (Martin) 1921- 121
Rose, Constance Hubbard 1934- CANR-16
Earlier sketch in CA 29-32R
Rose, Daniel M. 1940- 33-36R
Rose, David S. 1947- 121
Rose, Elinor K(iess) 1920- 29-32R
Rose, Elizabeth 1915- 73-76
Rose, Elizabeth (Jane Pretty) 1933- CANR-9
Earlier sketch in CA 7-8R
See also SATA 28
Rose, (Edward) Elliot 1928- 65-68
Rose, Ernst A(ndreas) G(ottlieb) 1899- .. CANR-4
Earlier sketch in CA 7-8R
Rose, Florella
See Carlson, Vada F.
Rose, Frank 1949- 103
Rose, Gerald (Hembdon Seymour)
1935- CANR-9
Earlier sketch in CA 65-68
See also SATA 30
Rose, Gilbert J(acob) 1923- 103
Rose, (Arthur) Gordon 1920-1975 .... CANR-4
Earlier sketch in CA 1R
Rose, Grace B(erne) 1914- 108
Rose, Hannah T. 1909(?)-1976 Obituary 69-72
Rose, Harold 1921-1967 .... 7-8R
Obituary 103
Rose, Harold Wickliffe 1896- CAP-1
Earlier sketch in CA 9-10
Rose, Helen 1904(?)-1985 Obituary 117
Rose, Hilary
See Mackinnon, Charles Roy

Rose, Homer C. 1909-1967 .... CAP-1
Earlier sketch in CA 15-16
Rose, James M. 1941- 102
Rose, Jeanne 1940- CANR-16
Earlier sketch in CA 93-96
Rose, Jennifer
See Weber, Nancy
Rose, Jerome G. 1926- CANR-8
Earlier sketch in CA 15-16R
Rose, Jerry D. 1933- 33-36R
Rose, Kenneth (Vivian) 1924- Brief entry ... 123
Rose, Kenneth Jon 1954- 115
Rose, Leo E. 1926- 85-88
Rose, Lisle A(bbott) 1936- CANR-10
Earlier sketch in CA 65-68
Rose, Lynn Edmondson 1934- Brief entry .. 105
Rose, Marcia
See Kamien, Marcia
and Novak, Rose
Rose, Marilyn Gaddis 1930- 33-36R
Rose, Mark 1939- CANR-10
Earlier sketch in CA 25-28R
Rose, Nancy (Ann) 1934- 37-40R
Rose, Nancy A.
See Sweetland, Nancy A(nn)
Rose, Norman Anthony 1934- 104
Rose, Paul (Bernard) 1935- 103
Rose, Pete(r Edward) 1942- Brief entry 113
Rose, Peter I(saac) 1933- CANR-5
Earlier sketch in CA 13-14R
Rose, Phyllis
See Thompson, Phyllis Hoge
Rose, R(obert) B(arrie) 1929- 61-64
Rose, Ralph 1911(?)-1984 Obituary 112
Rose, Reginald 1920- 73-76
See also DLB 26
Rose, Richard 1933- CANR-10
Earlier sketch in CA 21-22R
Rose, Stuart 1899(?)-1975 Obituary 61-64
Rose, Susan (Phyllida) 1938- 111
Rose, Thomas 1938- 33-36R
Rose, Wendy 1948- CANR-5
Earlier sketch in CA 53-56
See also SATA 12
Rose, Will(iam Palen) 1889- 57-60
Rose, William 1920(?)-1987 Obituary 121
Rose, Willie Lee (Nichols) 1927- 13-14R
Rose-Ackerman, Susan 1942- 111
Roseberry, Cecil R. 1902- 21-22R
Roseboom, Eugene Holloway 1892- 5-6R
Roseboro, John 1933- 102
Rosebrock, Ellen Fletcher 1947- CANR-10
Earlier sketch in CA 57-60
Rosebury, Theodor 1904-1976 .... CAP-2
Obituary 69-72
Earlier sketch in CA 25-28
Rosecrance, Francis Chase 1897- 7-8R
Rosecrance, Richard (Newton) 1930-
Brief entry 111
Rosedale, Valerie
See Harron, Don(ald)
Rosefielde, Steven 1942- 45-48
Roseliep, Raymond 1917- CANR-6
Earlier sketch in CA 9-10R
Roselle, Daniel 1920- 13-14R
Roseller, David
See Timms, E(dward) V(ivian)
Roseman, Ellen Barbara 1947- 124
Roseman, Kenneth David 1939- 110
Rosemeyer, Nita (Mary) 1907- 119
Rosemond, John K(irk) 1947- 110
Rosemont, Henry, Jr. 1934- 41-44R
Rosen, Barbara 1929- 37-40R
Rosen, Benson 1942- 120
Rosen, Carol (Cynthia) 1950- 119
Rosen, Dorothy 1916- 119
Rosen, Edward 1906-1985 ....23-24R
Obituary 115
Rosen, Elliot A(lfred) 1928- 93-96
Rosen, Frederick 1938- 120
Rosen, George 1910-1977 81-84
Obituary 73-76
Rosen, George 1920- 57-60
Rosen, Gerald 1938- 33-36R
Rosen, Haiim B(aruch) 1922- CANR-20
Earlier sketch in CA 1R
Rosen, Hjalmar 1922- 19-20R
Rosen, Ira 1954- 114
Rosen, James Alan 1908(?)-1972
Obituary 37-40R
Rosen, Joe
See Rosen, Joseph
Rosen, Joseph 1937- CANR-9
Earlier sketch in CA 65-68
Rosen, Laura 1948- 116
Rosen, Lawrence R(onald) 1938- 57-60
Rosen, Lillian (Diamond) 1928- 108
Rosen, Martin Meyer
See Rosen, Moishe (Martin)
Rosen, Marvin J(erold) 1929- 69-72
Rosen, Michael 1946- CANR-15
Earlier sketch in CA 25-28R
See also SATA 40, 48
Rosen, Moishe (Martin) 1932- CANR-4
Earlier sketch in CA 49-52
Rosen, Mortimer (Gilbert) 1931- 101
Rosen, Norma (Gangel) 1925- 33-36R
See also DLB 28
Rosen, Paul L(yon) 1939- 61-64
Rosen, R(ichard) D(ean) 1949- 77-80
See also CLC 39
Rosen, Robert C(harles) 1947- 106
Rosen, S. McKee 1902(?)-1978 Obituary ..77-80
Rosen, Sam 1920- 7-8R
Rosen, Samuel 1897-1981 Obituary 108
Rosen, Seymour Michael 1924- 33-36R
Rosen, Sheldon 1943- 109
Rosen, Shirley 1933- 105
Rosen, Sidney 1916- 11-12R
See also SATA 1
Rosen, Stanley H. 1929- 25-28R
Rosen, Stephen 1934- 65-68
Rosen, Trix 1947- 116
Rosen, Winifred 1943- 29-32R
See also SATA 8
Rosenast, Eleanor S(trauss) 1929- 97-100
Rosenau, Helen 101
Rosenau, James N(athan) 1924- CANR-18
Earlier sketches in CA 1R, CANR-2
Rosenauer, Johnnie L(ee) 1951- 110
Rosenbaum, Alan S(helby) 1941- 124
Rosenbaum, Alan Shelby 1941-
Brief entry 106
Rosenbaum, Alvin 1945- 113
Rosenbaum, Bernard L. 1937- 107
Rosenbaum, Eileen 1936- 21-22R
Rosenbaum, Ernest H. 1929- 97-100
Rosenbaum, H. Jon 1941- 41-44R
Rosenbaum, Jean 1927- 19-20R
Rosenbaum, Kurt 1926- 15-16R
Rosenbaum, Maurice 1907- 17-18R
See also SATA 6
Rosenbaum, Max 1923- 41-44R
Rosenbaum, Nathan 1897- CAP-2
Earlier sketch in CA 23-24
Rosenbaum, Patricia L(eib) 1932- 105
Rosenbaum, Peter S. 1940- CANR-14
Earlier sketch in CA 23-24R
Rosenbaum, S(tanford) P(atrick) 1929- ...15-16R
Rosenbaum, Samuel R(awlins) 1888-1972
Obituary 37-40R
Rosenbaum, Veryl 1936- CANR-1
Earlier sketch in CA 49-52
Rosenbaum, Walter A(nthony) 1937- 21-22R
Rosenberg, Arthur D(onald) 1939- 61-64
Rosenberg, Betty 1916- 113
Rosenberg, Bruce A(lan) 1934- 29-32R
Rosenberg, Charles E(rnest) 1936- 97-100
Rosenberg, Claude N(ewman), Jr.
1928- CANR-5
Earlier sketch in CA 4R
Rosenberg, David A(aron) 1940- 93-96
Rosenberg, Dorothy 1906- CANR-18
Earlier sketches in CA 45-48, CANR-2
See also SATA 40
Rosenberg, Edgar 1925- 13-14R
Rosenberg, Ellis Howard 1936(?)-1986
Obituary 121
Rosenberg, Emily S(chlaht) 1944- 108
Rosenberg, Ethel (Clifford) 1915- CANR-16
Earlier sketch in CA 29-32R
See also SATA 3
Rosenberg, George S(tanley) 1930- 29-32R
Rosenberg, Harold 1906-1978 ....21-22R
Obituary 77-80
Rosenberg, Harry E. 1932- 57-60
Rosenberg, Isaac 1890-1918 Brief entry 107
See also DLB 20
See also TCLC 12
Rosenberg, Israel 1909- 49-52
Rosenberg, J(ehiol) Mitchell 1906- 37-40R
Rosenberg, Jakob 1893-1980 Obituary ... 97-100
Rosenberg, James L. 1921- 15-16R
Rosenberg, Jane 1949- 121
Rosenberg, Janet 1930- 117
Rosenberg, Jerome Roy 1926- 104
Rosenberg, Jerry M. 1935- CANR-24
Earlier sketches in CA 23-24R, CANR-9
Rosenberg, Jessie 1941- 23-24R
Rosenberg, Joel 1954- 115
Rosenberg, John D(avid) 1929- CANR-5
Earlier sketch in CA 3R
Rosenberg, John J.
See Ramati, Yohanan (Joseph)
Rosenberg, Joseph
See Ramati, Yohanan (Joseph)
Rosenberg, Judith K(aren) 1945- 57-60
Rosenberg, Kenyon Charles 1933- 57-60
Rosenberg, Marvin 1912- 1R
Rosenberg, Maurice 1919- 81-84
Rosenberg, Maxine B(erta) 1939- 117
See also SATA 47
Rosenberg, Morris 1922- CANR-2
Earlier sketch in CA 7-8R
Rosenberg, Nancy (Sherman) 1931- ... CANR-22
Earlier sketches in CA 1R, CANR-5
See also SATA 4
Rosenberg, Nathan 1927- Brief entry 113
Rosenberg, Neil V. 1939- 122
Rosenberg, Norman J(ack) 1930- 57-60
Rosenberg, Norman L(ewis) 1942- 122
Rosenberg, Philip 1942- 103
Rosenberg, Rosalind 1946- 108
Rosenberg, Samuel 1912- 53-56
Rosenberg, Sharon 1942- CANR-10
Earlier sketch in CA 57-60
See also SATA 8
Rosenberg, Shirley Sirota 1925- CANR-12
Earlier sketch in CA 21-22R
Rosenberg, Stephen N(icholas) 1941- 111
Rosenberg, Stuart E. 1922- CANR-9
Earlier sketch in CA 5-6R
Rosenberg, William Gordon 1938- 61-64
Rosenberg, Wolfgang 1915- CANR-9
Earlier sketch in CA 65-68
Rosenberger, Francis Coleman 1915- .. CANR-15
Earlier sketch in CA 41-44R
Rosenberger, Harleigh M. 1913- 21-22R
Rosenberger, Homer Tope 1908- CANR-8
Earlier sketch in CA 19-20R
Rosenblatt, Arthur S. 1938- SATA-45
Rosenblatt, Bernard A. 1886- CAP-1
Earlier sketch in CA 13-14
Rosenblatt, Fred 1914- 41-44R
Rosenblatt, Gary 1947- 77-80
Rosenblatt, Joe
See Rosenblatt, Joseph
See also CLC 15
Rosenblatt, Jon M(ichael) 1947- 89-92
Rosenblatt, Joseph 1933- 89-92
Rosenblatt, Louise M(ichelle) 1904- 49-52
Rosenblatt, Milton B. 1908(?)-1975
Obituary 53-56
Rosenblatt, Roger 1940- 85-88
Rosenblatt, Samuel 1902- 53-56
Rosenblatt, Stanley M. 1936- 29-32R
Rosenblatt, Suzanne Maris 1937- 69-72
Rosenblith, Judy F(rancis) 1921- 25-28R
Rosenbloom, Bert 1944- 109
Rosenbloom, David H(arry) 1943- 73-76
Rosenbloom, David L. 1944- 45-48
Rosenbloom, Jerry S(amuel) 1939-
Brief entry 110
Rosenbloom, Joseph 1928- CANR-21
Earlier sketches in CA 57-60, CANR-6
See also SATA 21
Rosenbloom, Joseph R. 1928- 29-32R
Rosenbloom, Noah H. 1915- CANR-14
Earlier sketch in CA 37-40R
Rosenblum, Art 1927- 57-60
Rosenblum, Davida 1927- 93-96
Rosenblum, Gershen 1924- 41-44R
Rosenblum, Helen Faye 1941- 121
Rosenblum, Joseph 1947- 111
Rosenblum, Leonard A. 1936- CANR-11
Earlier sketch in CA 57-60
Rosenblum, Marc J. 1936- 29-32R
Rosenblum, Martin J(ack) 1946- CANR-18
Earlier sketches in CA 45-48, CANR-2
Rosenblum, Mort 1943- 73-76
Rosenblum, Richard 1928- CANR-9
Earlier sketch in CA 65-68
See also SATA 11
Rosenblum, Robert H. 1927- CANR-5
Earlier sketch in CA 3R
Rosenbluth, Gideon 1921- 61-64
Rosenburg, John M. 1918- 23-24R
See also SATA 6
Rosenburg, Robert K(emper) 1920- CANR-4
Earlier sketch in CA 7-8R
Rosendall, Betty 1916- 49-52
Rosenfarb, Chawa 1923- 53-56
Rosenfeld, Albert (Hyman) 1920- CANR-11
Earlier sketch in CA 65-68
Rosenfeld, Alvin 1919- 73-76
Rosenfeld, Alvin H(irsch) 1938- CANR-24
Earlier sketches in CA 49-52, CANR-4
Rosenfeld, Arnold (Solomon) 1933- 65-68
Rosenfeld, Edward J(ulius) 1943- 41-44R
Rosenfeld, Harry M(orris) 1929- 69-72
Rosenfeld, Harvey 1939- 110
Rosenfeld, Isaac 1918-1956 .... DLB-28
Rosenfeld, Isadore 1926- 81-84
Rosenfeld, Jeffrey P(hilip) 1946- 115
Rosenfeld, Lulla 1914- 85-88
Rosenfeld, Marthe 1928- 45-48
Rosenfeld, Sam 1920- 11-12R
Rosenfeld, Samuel 1896-1963 Obituary ...89-92
Rosenfeld, Sybil (Marion) 1903- 119
Rosenfield, Isadore 1893-1980 Obituary ..97-100
Rosenfield, James A(lexander) 1943- 49-52
Rosenfield, John M(ax) 1924- CANR-14
Earlier sketch in CA 23-24R
Rosenfield, Leonora Cohen 1909-1982 ...41-44R
Obituary 105
Rosengart, Oliver A. 1941- 49-52
Rosengarten, Frank 1927- 73-76
Rosengarten, Frederic (Jr.) 1916- 118
Rosengarten, Theodore 1944- 103
Rosengren, William R(udolph) 1929-
Brief entry 114
Rosenhaupt, Hans 1911-1985 Obituary 116
Rosenheim, Edward W(eil), Jr. 1918- 25-28R
Rosenhouse, Archie 1878- CAP-2
Earlier sketch in CA 21-22
Rosenkrantz, Linda 1934- CANR-11
Earlier sketch in CA 25-28R
Rosenkranz, Richard S. 1942- 37-40R
Rosenman, John B(rown) 1941- 106
Rosenman, Ray H(arold) 1920- 97-100
Rosenman, Samuel I(rving) 1896-1973
Obituary 41-44R
Rosenmeyer, Thomas Gustav 1920- 111
Rosenn, Keith S(amuel) 1938- 111
Rosenof, Theodore 1943- CANR-10
Earlier sketch in CA 65-68
Rosenow, John E(dward) 1949- 97-100
Rosenquist, Carl M(artin) 1895-1973 ..... CAP-2
Earlier sketch in CA 29-32
Rosenrauch, Heinz Erich
See Rosen, Haiim B(aruch)
Rosensaft, Menachem Z. 1948- 23-24R
Rosenstein-Rodan, Paul N. 1902-1985 107
Obituary 116
Rosenstiel, Annette 1911- 115
Rosenstiel, Leonie 1947- 85-88
Rosenstock, (Patricia) Janet (Stearns)
1933- 108
Rosenstock-Huessy, Eugen 1888-1973 ... CAP-1
Obituary 41-44R
Earlier sketch in CA 15-16
Rosenstone, Robert A(llan) 1936- 29-32R
Rosenstone, Steven J(ay) 1952- 104
Rosenthal, A(braham) M(ichael) 1922- ...21-22R
Rosenthal, Alan 1936- 105
Rosenthal, Albert H(arold) 1914- 23-24R
Rosenthal, Andrew 1918(?)-1979
Obituary 89-92
Rosenthal, Bernard G(ordon) 1922- ... CANR-11
Earlier sketch in CA 29-32R
Rosenthal, Bernice (Glatzer) 1938- 121
Rosenthal, David 1916- 41-44R
Rosenthal, Donald B. 1937- CANR-14
Earlier sketch in CA 37-40R
Rosenthal, Douglas E(urico) 1940- 57-60
Rosenthal, Earl E(dgar) 1921- 41-44R
Rosenthal, Edwin Stanley 1914- 77-80
Rosenthal, Eric 1905- CANR-6
Earlier sketch in CA 9-10R
Rosenthal, Erwin Isak Jacob 1904- 102
Rosenthal, F(rank) F(ranz) 1911(?)-1979
Obituary 89-92
Rosenthal, Harold 1914- 111
See also SATA 35
Rosenthal, Harold (David) 1917-1987 ......7-8R
Obituary 122
Rosenthal, Harry F(rederick) 1927- 65-68
Rosenthal, Harry Kenneth 1941- 57-60
Rosenthal, Henry Moses 1906-1977
Obituary 73-76
Rosenthal, Joe
See Rosenthal, Joseph J.
Rosenthal, Joel T(homas) 1934- 57-60
Rosenthal, Joseph J. 1911- 69-72
Rosenthal, Jules M. 1924- 19-20R
Rosenthal, M(acha) L(ouis) 1917- CANR-4
Earlier sketch in CA 4R
See also CAAS 6
See also DLB 5
See also CLC 28
Rosenthal, Mitchell S(tephen) 1935- 104
Rosenthal, Peggy 1944- 121
Rosenthal, Renee ?-1975 Obituary 57-60
Rosenthal, Richard A. 1925- 3R
Rosenthal, Ricky 1930(?)-1984 Obituary ... 114
Rosenthal, Robert 1933- CANR-16
Earlier sketch in CA 41-44R
Rosenthal, Stuart 1934- 117
Rosenthal, Sylvia 1911- 109
Rosenus, Alan (Harvey) 1940- 73-76
Rosenwald, Henry M(artin) 1905- 33-36R
Rosenwasser, Dorothy Eckmann 1917- 2R
Rosenzweig, Michael L(eo) 1941- 101
Rosenzweig, Norman 1924- CANR-6
Earlier sketch in CA 57-60
Rosenzweig, Robert Myron 1931- 113
Rosenzweig, Roy 1950- 113
Rosett, Arthur (Irwin) 1934- 69-72
Rosette, Bennetta Jules
See Jules-Rosette, Bennetta
(Washington)
Roseveare, Helen Margaret 1925- 73-76
Rosewell, Paul Truman 1926- 17-18R
Roseyear, John 1936- 21-22R
Roshco, Bernard 1929- 7-8R
Rosher, Grace ?-1980 Obituary 111
Roshwalb, Irving 1924- 45-48
Roshwald, Mordecai Marceli 1921- 1R
Rosi, Eugene J(oseph) 1931- 61-64
Rosichan, Richard H(arry) 1941- 45-48
Rosie, George 1941- 120
Rosier, Bernard 1931- CANR-12
Earlier sketch in CA 29-32R
Rosier, James L(ouis) 1932- CANR-22
Earlier sketch in CA 2R
Rosillo-Calle, Francisco 1945- 121
Rositzke, Harry A(ugust) 1911- 45-48
Roskamp, Karl Wilhelm 1923- 15-16R
Roske, Ralph Joseph 1921- 122
Roskies, David G(regory) 1948- 120
Roskies, Ethel 1933- 45-48
Roskill, Mark W(entworth) 1933- CANR-6
Earlier sketch in CA 5-6R
Roskill, Stephen W(entworth)
1903-1982 .... CANR-6
Obituary 108
Earlier sketch in CA 15-16R
Rosko, Milt 1930- 41-44R
Roskolenko, Harry 1907-1980 .... CANR-17
Obituary 101
Earlier sketch in CA 15-16R
Roslavleva, Natalia
See Rene, Natalia
Rosman, Abraham 1930- 89-92
Rosmond, Babette 1921- CANR-6
Earlier sketch in CA 7-8R
Rosner, David K(arl) 1947- 112
Rosner, Fred 1935- 113
Rosner, Joseph 1914- 57-60
Rosner, Lynn 1944- 61-64
Rosner, Stanley 1928- 41-44R
Rosnow, Ralph L. 1936- CANR-10
Earlier sketch in CA 23-24R
Rosochacki, Daniel 1942- 45-48
Rosoff, Sidney D. 1924- 1R
Rosovsky, Henry 1927- Brief entry 105
Rosow, Irving 1921- 85-88
Rosow, Jerome M(orris) 1919- 81-84
Rosowski, Susan J(ean) 1942- 111
Ross, Alan 1922- CANR-21
Earlier sketches in CA 11-12R, CANR-6
Ross, Alan
See Warwick, Alan R(oss)
Ross, Alan O(tto) 1921- 41-44R
Ross, Alan Strode Campbell 1907-1980 ..11-12R
Obituary 102
Ross, Alec 1926- 29-32R
Ross, Alex(ander) 1909- SATA-29
Ross, Alf (Niels Christian Hansen) 1899- ..53-56
Ross, Angus 1911- 21-22R
Ross, Angus
See Giggal, Kenneth
Ross, Barnaby
See Dannay, Frederic
and Lee, Manfred B(ennington)
Ross, Bernard H(arvey) 1934- 102
Ross, Bernard L.
See Follett, Ken(neth Martin)

INDEX

Ross, Bette M. 1932- ... 106
Ross, Betty ... 69-72
Ross, Bill D. 1921- ... 123
Ross, Billy I(rvan) 1925- ... 57-60
Ross, Brian Elliott 1948- Brief entry ... 119
Ross, Caroline
See Nicolson, Catherine
Ross, Catherine
See Beaty, Betty
Ross, Charles (Derek) 1924(?)-1986
Obituary ... 118
Ross, Charlotte (Brand) 1921- ... 117
Ross, Clare
See Romano, Clare
See also SATA 48
Ross, Clarissa
See Ross, W(illiam) E(dward) D(aniel)
Ross, Colin
See Roskolenko, Harry
Ross, Corinne Madden 1931- ... 106
Ross, Dallas
See Reynolds, Dallas McCord
Ross, Dan
See Ross, W(illiam) E(dward) D(aniel)
Ross, Dana
See Ross, W(illiam) E(dward) D(aniel)
Ross, Dave
See Ross, David
See also SATA 32
Ross, David 1896-1975 ... 65-68
Obituary ... 61-64
See also SATA 20, 49
Ross, David 1949- ... 111
Ross, David O(liver), Jr. 1936- Brief entry ... 117
Ross, David P(reston), Jr. 1908-1984
Obituary ... 112
Ross, Davis R. B. 1934- ... 33-36R
Ross, Diana
See Denney, Diana
Ross, Donald K. 1943- ... 49-52
Ross, Elizabeth Irvin 1942- ... 121
Ross, Emory 1887-1973 Obituary ... 41-44R
Ross, Eric (De Witt) 1929- ... 29-32R
Ross, Eulalie Steinmetz 1910- ... 17-18R
Ross, Eva J(eany) 1903-1969 ... CAP-2
Earlier sketch in CA 23-24
Ross, Floyd H(iatt) 1910- ... 73-76
Ross, Frances Aileen 1909- ... CAP-1
Earlier sketch in CA 9-10
Ross, Frank E. 1925- ... 19-20R
Ross, Frank (Xavier), Jr. 1914- ... CANR-16
Earlier sketch in CA 93-96
See also SATA 28
Ross, Gary 1948- ... 115
Ross, George
See Morgan-Grenville, Gerard (Wyndham)
Ross, H(ugh) Laurence 1934- ... CANR-13
Earlier sketch in CA 77-80
Ross, Hal 1941- ... 65-68
Ross, Harold Raymond 1904- ... CAP-2
Earlier sketch in CA 19-20
Ross, Harold W(allace) 1892-1951
Brief entry ... 119
Ross, Helaine
See Daniels, Dorothy
Ross, Helen 1890(?)-1978 ... 85-88
Obituary ... 81-84
Ross, Ian
See Rossmann, John F(rancis)
Ross, Ian Simpson 1930- ... CANR-3
Earlier sketch in CA 45-48
Ross, Irwin 1919- ... 97-100
Ross, Ishbel 1897-1975 ... 93-96
Obituary ... 61-64
Ross, Ivan T.
See Rossner, Robert
Ross, J. H.
See Lawrence, T(homas) E(dward)
Ross, James Davidson 1924- ... 49-52
Ross, James F(rancis) 1931- ... CANR-11
Earlier sketch in CA 21-22R
Ross, James Frederick Stanley 1886- ... 11-12R
Ross, James S(tiven) 1892-1975
Obituary ... 57-60
Ross, Janet 1914- ... 37-40R
Ross, Joel E(lmore, Jr.) 1922- ... 29-32R
Ross, John 1921- ... 108
See also SATA 45
Ross, John A(ddison) 1919- ... 19-20R
Ross, John O'C(onnell) 1916- ... 25-28R
Ross, Jonathan
See Rossiter, John
Ross, Joseph
See Wrzos, Joseph Henry
Ross, Judith Wilson 1937- ... 114
Ross, K. G. M. ?-1985 Obituary ... 116
Ross, Katherine
See Walter, Dorothy Blake
Ross, Kenneth (Michael Andrew) 1941- ... 107
Ross, Kenneth N(eedham) 1908-1970 ... CANR-5
Earlier sketch in CA 7-8R
Ross, Lanson Clifford, Jr. 1936- ... 120
Ross, Laura
See Mincieli, Rose Laura
Ross, Leah 1938- ... 61-64
Ross, Leonard
See Rosten, Leo C(alvin)
Ross, Leonard M(ichael) 1945-1985 ... 29-32R
Obituary ... 116
Ross, Leonard Q.
See Rosten, Leo C(alvin)
Ross, Lillian 1927- ... 11-12R
Ross, Lola Romanucci
See Romanucci- Ross, Lola
Ross, Mabel (Irene) H(ughes) 1909- ... 81-84
Ross, Malcolm
See Ross-Macdonald, Malcolm J(ohn)
Ross, Marc H(ansen) 1928- ... 114
Ross, Marilyn
See Ross, W(illiam) E(dward) D(aniel)
Ross, Marilyn (Ann) Heimberg 1939- ... CANR-14
Earlier sketch in CA 81-84
Ross, Marjorie Drake Rhoades 1901- ... 3R
Ross, Martha 1951- ... 103
Ross, Martin J. 1912- ... 53-56
Ross, Marvin C(hauncey) 1904-1977 ... CAP-2
Obituary ... 69-72
Earlier sketch in CA 19-20
Ross, Mary Adelaide Eden
See Phillpotts, (Mary) Adelaide Eden
Ross, Michael 1905- ... 85-88
Ross, Michael W(allis) 1952- ... 118
Ross, Mitchell S(cott) 1953- ... 81-84
Ross, Murray George 1912- ... 19-20R
Ross, Nancy
See DeRoin, Nancy
Ross, Nancy Wilson 1910-1986 ... 97-100
Obituary ... 118
Ross, Nathaniel 1904- ... 21-22R
Ross, Pat 1943- ... SATA-48
Ross, Patricia
See Baxter, Patricia E. W.
Ross, Paul
See Crawford, William (Elbert)
Ross, Philip 1939- ... 69-72
Ross, Phyllis (Freedman) 1926-1970 ... CAP-2
Earlier sketch in CA 17-18
Ross, Ralph 1911- ... 13-14R
Ross, Raymond S(amuel) 1925- ... CANR-8
Earlier sketch in CA 21-22R
Ross, Robert H(enry), Jr. 1916- ... 15-16R
Ross, Robert Horace ... 106
Ross, Robert S(amuel) 1940- ... 57-60
Ross, Robert W.
See Power-Ross, Robert W.
Ross, Russell M. 1921- ... 21-22R
Ross, Ruth 1930(?)-1986 Obituary ... 119
Ross, Sam 1912- ... 15-16R
Ross, Sheila Muriel 1925- ... 106
Ross, (James) Sinclair 1908- ... 73-76
See also CLC 13
Ross, Stanley R(obert) 1921- ... CANR-7
Earlier sketch in CA 17-18R
Ross, Stanley Ralph 1940- ... CANR-20
Earlier sketch in CA 97-100
Ross, Stephen David 1935- ... CANR-17
Earlier sketch in CA 41-44R
Ross, Steven Thomas 1937- ... 41-44R
Ross, Sutherland
See Callard, Thomas Henry
Ross, T(heodore) J(ohn) 1924- ... 57-60
Ross, Terrence 1947- ... 103
Ross, Thomas B. 1929- ... 29-32R
Ross, Thomas W(ynne) 1923- ... 41-44R
Ross, Timothy A(rrowsmith) 1936- ... 57-60
Ross, Tony 1938- ... 77-80
See also SATA 17
Ross, Veronica 1946- ... 113
Ross, W(illiam) E(dward) D(aniel)
1912- ... CANR-14
Earlier sketch in CA 81-84
Ross, W(illiam) Gordon 1900- ... 45-48
Ross, Wilda 1915- ... 85-88
See also SATA 39
Ross, William
See Dewart, Leslie
Ross, William B. 1915- ... 25-28R
Ross, Z. H.
See Ross, Zola Helen
Ross, Zola Helen 1912- ... 53-56
Rossabi, Morris 1941- ... 102
Rossbach, Richard M. 1915(?)-1987
Obituary ... 123
Rossbacher, Lisa A(nn) 1952- ... 117
Rossberg, Robert H. 1926- ... 45-48
Rosse, Ian
See Straker, J(ohn) F(oster)
Rosse, Susanna
See Connolly, Vivian
Rossel, Seymour 1945- ... CANR-21
Earlier sketches in CA 53-56, CANR-5
See also SATA 28
Rossel, Sven H(akon) 1943- ... CANR-22
Earlier sketch in CA 105
Rossellini, Roberto 1906-1977 Obituary ... 69-72
Rossel-Waugh, C. C.
See Waugh, Carol-Lynn Roessel
Rossen, Robert 1908-1966 Obituary ... 113
See also DLB 26
Rosser, Neill A(lbert) 1916-1973 ... CAP-1
Earlier sketch in CA 15-16
Rosset, B(enjamin) C(harles)
1910-1974 ... 11-12R
Obituary ... 103
Rosset, Barnet Lee, Jr. 1922- ... 97-100
Rosset, Barney
See Rosset, Barnet Lee, Jr.
Rossetti, Christina (Georgina)
1830-1894 ... SATA-20
See also DLB 35
Rossetti, Dante Gabriel 1828-1882 ... DLB-35
Rossetti, Minerva
See Rowland, D(onald) S(ydney)
Rossi, Aga
See Agarossi, Elena
Rossi, Alfred 1935- ... 29-32R
Rossi, Alice S(chaerr) 1922- ... CANR-17
Earlier sketches in CA 45-48, CANR-1
Rossi, Bruno
See Levinson, Leonard
Rossi, Ernest Lawrence 1933- ... CANR-14
Earlier sketch in CA 37-40R
Rossi, Ino ... 89-92
Rossi, Lino 1923- ... 104
Rossi, Mario 1916- ... CANR-8
Earlier sketch in CA 5-6R
Rossi, Nicholas Louis, Jr. 1924- ... CANR-6
Earlier sketch in CA 15-16R
Rossi, Nick
See Rossi, Nicholas Louis, Jr.
Rossi, Paul A. 1929- Brief entry ... 110
Rossi, Peter Henry 1921- ... CANR-19
Earlier sketches in CA 3R, CANR-4
Rossi, Philip Joseph 1943- ... 115
Rossi, Sanna Morrison Barlow 1917- ... 93-96
Rossi, William A(nthony) 1916- ... 65-68
Rossie, Jonathan Gregory 1935-
Brief entry ... 106
Rossi-Landi, Ferruccio 1921- ... 114
Rossini, Frederick A(nthony) 1939- ... CANR-12
Earlier sketch in CA 73-76
Rossit, Edward A. 1921- ... 17-18R
Rossiter, Clinton (Lawrence) 1917-1970
Obituary ... 25-28R
Rossiter, Frank R(aymond) 1937- ... 61-64
Rossiter, Ian
See Ross Williamson, Hugh
Rossiter, Jane
See Ross, W(illiam) E(dward) D(aniel)
Rossiter, John 1916- ... 33-36R
Rossiter, Margaret W(alsh) 1944- ... CANR-13
Earlier sketch in CA 77-80
Rossiter, (Percival) Stuart (Bryce) 1923- ... 85-88
Rosskam, Edwin 1903(?)-1985 Obituary ... 115
Rosskopf, Myron Frederick 1907-1973 ... CANR-5
Obituary ... 41-44R
Earlier sketch in CA 5-6R
Ross-Macdonald, Malcolm J(ohn)
1932- ... CANR-13
Earlier sketch in CA 65-68
Rossman, Charles Raymond 1938- ... 113
Rossman, Evelyn
See Rothchild, Sylvia
Rossman, Jack E(ugene) 1936- ... 49-52
Rossman, Marlene L. 1948- ... 124
Rossman, Michael Dale 1939- ... 101
Rossman, (George) Parker 1919- ... 69-72
Rossmann, John F(rancis) 1942- ... 101
Rossner, Judith (Perelman) 1935- ... CANR-18
Earlier sketch in CA 19-20R
See also DLB 6
See also CLC 6, 9, 29
See also AITN 2
Rossner, Robert 1932- ... CANR-1
Earlier sketch in CA 2R
Rossoff, Martin 1910- ... 11-12R
Rossomando, Frederic William 1924- ... 49-52
Ross-Robertson, Lynne Nannen 1936- ... 107
Ross Williamson, Hugh 1901-1978 ... CANR-8
Earlier sketch in CA 17-18R
Rostand, Edmond (Eugene Alexis)
1868-1918 Brief entry ... 104
See also TCLC 6
Rostand, Jean 1894-1977 Brief entry ... 124
Rostand, Robert
See Hopkins, Robert S(ydney)
Rosten, Leo C(alvin) 1908- ... CANR-6
Earlier sketch in CA 7-8R
See also DLB 11
Rosten, Norman 1914- ... CANR-21
Earlier sketch in CA 77-80
Rostenberg, Leona 1908- ... CANR-5
Earlier sketch in CA 7-8R
Roston, Murray 1928- ... CANR-5
Earlier sketch in CA 53-56
Rostow, Eugene Victor 1913- ... 7-8R
Rostow, Walt W(hitman) 1916- ... CANR-8
Earlier sketch in CA 15-16R
Rostvold, Gerhard N(orman) 1919- ... CANR-10
Earlier sketch in CA 21-22R
Roszak, Betty 1933- ... 29-32R
Roszak, Theodore 1933- ... 77-80
Rotarius
See Kerekes, Tibor
Rotberg, Robert I. 1935- ... CANR-21
Earlier sketches in CA 15-16R, CANR-6
Rotblat, Joseph 1908- ... 109
Rotchstein, Janice 1944- ... 106
Rote, Kyle 1928- ... 23-24R
Rotella, Guy Louis 1947- ... 115
Rotenstreich, Nathan 1914- ... CANR-23
Earlier sketches in CA 61-64, CANR-8
Roth, Alexander
See Dunner, Joseph
Roth, Andrew 1919- ... 53-56
Roth, Arlen 1952- ... 103
Roth, Arnold 1929- ... 21-22R
See also SATA 21
Roth, Arthur 1920- ... 3R
Roth, Arthur J(oseph) 1925- ... CANR-7
Earlier sketch in CA 53-56
See also SATA 28, 43
Roth, Audrey J. 1927- ... 23-24R
Roth, Cecil 1899-1970 ... CANR-13
Obituary ... 25-28R
Earlier sketch in CA 9-10R
Roth, Charles E(dmund) 1934- ... 111
Roth, Claire Jarett 1923- ... 7-8R
Roth, David 1940- ... 106
See also SATA 36
Roth, David F(rancisco) 1939- ... 41-44R
Roth, David M. 1874(?)-1971 Obituary ... 104
Roth, David M(orris) 1935- ... 57-60
Roth, Don A. 1927- ... 25-28R
Roth, Ernst 1896-1971 ... CAP-2
Earlier sketch in CA 25-28
Roth, Eugen 1895-1976 Obituary ... 65-68
Roth, Geneen 1951- ... 111
Roth, Hal 1927- ... 37-40R
Roth, Harold ... SATA-49
Roth, Harold L(eo) 1919-1982 Obituary ... 108
Roth, Harry 1903(?)-1976 Obituary ... 65-68
Roth, Henry 1906- ... CAP-1
Earlier sketch in CA 11-12
See also DLB 28
See also CLC 2, 6, 11
Roth, Herbert (Otto) 1917- ... 61-64
Roth, Herrick S. 1916- ... 77-80
Roth, Holly 1916-1964 ... CANR-6
Earlier sketch in CA 4R
Roth, Jack J(oseph) 1920- ... 23-24R
Roth, John K(ing) 1940- ... CANR-10
Earlier sketch in CA 25-28R
Roth, Julius A(lfred) 1924- ... 21-22R
Roth, June (Spiewak) 1926- ... CANR-19
Earlier sketches in CA 11-12R, CANR-5
Roth, Leland M(artin) 1943- ... CANR-16
Earlier sketch in CA 93-96
Roth, (Hyam) Leon 1896-1963 Obituary ... 106
Roth, Lillian 1910-1980 Obituary ... 97-100
Roth, Mark J(oseph) 1941- ... 77-80
Roth, Mary Jane ... 21-22R
Roth, Moira 1933- ... 121
Roth, Peggy (Meehan) ?-1973 Obituary ... 104
Roth, Philip (Milton) 1933- ... CANR-22
Earlier sketches in CA 2R, CANR-1
See also DLB 2, 28
See also DLBY 82
See also CLC 1, 2, 3, 4, 6, 9, 15, 22, 31, 47
Roth, Richard H(enry) 1949- ... 77-80
Roth, Robert Howard 1933- ... CANR-14
Earlier sketch in CA 41-44R
Roth, Robert J. 1920- ... 17-18R
Roth, Robert Paul 1919- ... 61-64
Roth, Samuel 1894-1974 Obituary ... 49-52
Roth, Sister Mary Augustine 1926- ... CANR-3
Earlier sketch in CA 9-10R
Roth, Sol 1927- ... 65-68
Roth, Theodore W(illiam) 1916- ... 57-60
Roth, William 1942- ... 101
Roth, Wolfgang M(ax) W(ilhelm) 1930- ... 41-44R
Rotha, Paul 1907-1984 ... 9-10R
Obituary ... 112
Rothafel, Roxy
See Rothafel, Samuel L(ionel)
Rothafel, Samuel L(ionel)
1881(?)-1936(?) Brief entry ... 123
Rothbard, Murray N(ewton) 1926- ... CANR-22
Earlier sketches in CA 7-8R, CANR-6
Rothbart, Harold A(rthur) 1917- ... 111
Rothbaum, Melvin 1926- ... 7-8R
Rothberg, Abraham 1922- ... 33-36R
Rothblatt, Ben 1924- ... 25-28R
Rothblatt, Donald N(oah) 1935- ... CANR-23
Earlier sketches in CA 61-64, CANR-8
Rothblatt, Henry B(arnett) 1916-1985 ... CANR-19
Obituary ... 117
Earlier sketch in CA 25-28R
Rothchild, Donald (Sylvester) 1928- ... CANR-14
Earlier sketch in CA 41-44R
Rothchild, Sylvia 1923- ... 77-80
Rothel, David 1936- ... CANR-10
Earlier sketch in CA 65-68
Rothenberg, Alan B(aer) 1907-1977
Obituary ... 73-76
Rothenberg, Albert 1930- ... CANR-8
Earlier sketch in CA 57-60
Rothenberg, B(arbara) Annye 1940- ... 107
Rothenberg, Diane Brodatz 1932- ... 115
Rothenberg, Gunther Eric 1923- ... CANR-8
Earlier sketch in CA 21-22R
Rothenberg, Jerome 1924- ... 29-32R
Rothenberg, Jerome 1931- ... CANR-1
Earlier sketch in CA 45-48
See also DLB 5
See also CLC 6
Rothenberg, Joshua 1911- ... 37-40R
Rothenberg, Lillian 1922- ... 11-12R
Rothenberg, Marc 1949- ... 115
Rothenberg, Polly 1916- ... 85-88
Rothenberg, Randall 1956- ... 118
Rothenberg, Robert E(dward) 1908- ... 37-40R
Rothenstein, John K(newstub) M(aurice)
1901- ... CANR-1
Earlier sketch in CA 1R
Rothermere, Viscount
See Harmsworth, Esmond Cecil
Rothery, Brian 1934- ... CANR-1
Earlier sketch in CA 49-52
Rothfork, John 1946- ... 110
Rothkopf, Carol Z. 1929- ... 25-28R
See also SATA 4
Rothman, Barbara Katz 1948- ... 111
Rothman, Charles Warren 1952- ... 120
Rothman, Chuck
See Rothman, Charles Warren
Rothman, David B. 1956- ... 111
Rothman, David J. 1937- ... 33-36R
Rothman, Esther P. 1919- ... 37-40R
Rothman, Joel 1938- ... 37-40R
See also SATA 7
Rothman, Judith
See Peters, Maureen
Rothman, Milton A. 1919- ... 41-44R
Rothman, Stanley 1927- ... 93-96
Rothman, Theodore 1907- ... CAP-2
Earlier sketch in CA 29-32
Rothman, Tony 1953- ... CANR-15
Earlier sketch in CA 85-88
Rothmuller, Aron Marko 1908- ... 73-76
Rothrock, George A(bel) 1932- ... 61-64
Rothschild, Alfred 1894(?)-1972 ... 37-40R
Rothschild, Fritz A(lexander) 1919-
Brief entry ... 106

Rothschild, J(acquard) H(irshorn) 1907- .. CAP-2
Earlier sketch in CA 17-18
Rothschild, Joseph 1931- CANR-3
Earlier sketch in CA 11-12R
Rothschild, Kurt Wilhelm 1914- CANR-23
Earlier sketch in CA 102
Rothschild, Lincoln 1902-1983 .... CANR-12
Obituary 109
Earlier sketch in CA 45-48
Rothschild, Norman 1913- 103
Rothschild, Richard Charles 1895-1986
Obituary 118
Rothstein, Arthur 1915-1985 .... CANR-6
Obituary 117
Earlier sketch in CA 57-60
Rothstein, Eric 1936- 73-76
Rothstein, Samuel 1902(?)-1978
Obituary 77-80
Rothstein, Samuel 1921- 61-64
Rothstein, Stanley William 1929- 120
Rothstein, William G(ene) 1937- 73-76
Rothweiler, Paul Roger 1931- CANR-10
Earlier sketch in CA 65-68
Rothwell, Bruce 1923(?)-1984 Obituary 114
Rothwell, Kenneth J(ames) 1925- CANR-14
Earlier sketch in CA 23-24R
Rothwell, Kenneth S(prague) 1921- 33-36R
Rothwell, Talbot (Nelson Conn)
1916-1981 Obituary 103
Rothwell, V(ictor) H(oward) 1945- 37-40R
Rotimi, E. G. O.
See Rotimi, (Emmanuel Gladstone)
Ola(wale)
Rotimi, (Emmanuel Gladstone) Ola(wale)
1938(?)- 124
Rotimi, Olawale
See Rotimi, (Emmanuel Gladstone)
Ola(wale)
Rotkin, Charles E. 1916- 7-8R
Rotmans, Elmer A. 1896- 7-8R
Rotondi, Cesar 1926- 97-100
Rotsler, William 1926- CANR-4
Earlier sketch in CA 53-56
Rotstein, Abraham 1929- 104
Rottenberg, Dan(iel) 1942- CANR-19
Earlier sketch in CA 102
Rottenberg, Isaac C. 1925- 15-16R
Rottensteiner, Franz 1942- CANR-15
Earlier sketch in CA 81-84
Rotter, Julian B(ernard) 1916- 33-36R
Rotter, Marion 1940(?)-1973 Obituary 104
Roubiczek, Paul (Anton) 1898-1972
Obituary 115
Roubinek, Darrell L(eRoy) 1935- 57-60
Roucek, Joseph S. 1902- 11-12R
Roudiez, Leon S(amuel) 1917- 37-40R
Roudybush, Alexandra (Brown) 1911- 65-68
Roueche, Berton 1911- CANR-1
Earlier sketch in CA 2R
See also SATA 28
Roueche, John E(dward) 1938- 49-52
Rougemont, Denis de
See de Rougemont, Denis
Roughsey, Dick 1921(?)- 109
See also SATA 35
Rougier, Louis (Auguste Paul)
1889-1982 .... CANR-13
Earlier sketch in CA 29-32R
Rougier, Nicole 1929- 29-32R
Rouhani, Fuad 1907- 37-40R
Roukes, Nicholas 1925- 25-28R
Roulac, Stephen E. 1945- 104
Rouleau, Raymond (Edgard Marie)
1904-1981 Obituary 108
Roulston, Marjorie Hillis 1890-1971
Obituary 104
Roumain, Jacques 1907-1944 Brief entry ... 117
See also TCLC 19
Rounds, David 1930-1983 Obituary 111
Rounds, Glen (Harold) 1906- CANR-22
Earlier sketches in CA 53-56, CANR-7
See also SATA 8
Rouner, Arthur A(cy), Jr. 1929- CANR-5
Earlier sketch in CA 11-12R
Rouner, Leroy S(tephens) 1930- 73-76
Rountree, Owen
See Kittredge, William
and Krauzer, Steven M(ark)
Rountree, Thomas J. 1927- 25-28R
Rourke, Constance (Mayfield) 1885-1941
Brief entry 107
See also YABC 1
See also TCLC 12
Rourke, Francis E(dward) 1922- CANR-6
Earlier sketch in CA 2R
Rous, Stanley (Ford) 1895- 108
Rousculp, Charles G(ene) 1923- 29-32R
Rouse, (Hubert) Blair 1912- 4R
Rouse, (Benjamin) Irving, (Jr.) 1913- 11-12R
Rouse, John E(vans) 1892- 73-76
Rouse, John E(dward), Jr. 1942- 89-92
Rouse, Parke (Shepherd), Jr. 1915- 17-18R
Rouse, Richard H(unter) 1933- 29-32R
Rouse, Russell 1913(?)-1987 Obituary 123
Rouse Jones, Lewis 1907- CAP-1
Earlier sketch in CA 13-14
Roush, Barbara 1940- 109
Roush, John H., Jr. 1923- 37-40R
Rousmaniere, John 1944- CANR-17
Earlier sketch in CA 93-96
Rousseau, George Sebastian 1941- CANR-11
Earlier sketch in CA 29-32R
Rousseau, Richard W(ilfred) 1924- 110
Roussel, Raymond 1877-1933 Brief entry .. 117
See also TCLC 20
Roussin, Andre (Jean Paul Marie)
1911-1987 Obituary 124
Rout, Leslie B(rennan), Jr. 1936-1987 57-60
Obituary 122
Routh, C(harles) R(ichard) N(airne)
1896- CAP-1
Earlier sketch in CA 13-14
Routh, Donald K(ent) 1937- 57-60
Routh, Francis John 1927- 13-14R
Routh, Jonathan 110
Routh, Porter W(roe) 1911- 77-80
Routley, Erik (Reginald) 1917-1982 ..... CANR-5
Obituary 108
Earlier sketch in CA 3R
Routsong, Alma 1924- 49-52
Routt, Mary Patterson 1890(?)-1986
Obituary 119
Routtenberg, Max Jonah 1909- 77-80
Rouverol, Jean
See Butler, Jean Rouverol
Roux, Edward R(udolph) 1903- 13-14R
Roux, Georges 1914- 17-18R
Roux, Willan Charles 1902- CAP-2
Earlier sketch in CA 17-18
Rover, Constance (Mary) 1910- 23-24R
Rovere, Richard H(alworth) 1915-1979 .. CANR-3
Obituary 89-92
Earlier sketch in CA 49-52
Rovin, Ben
See Clevenger, Ernest Allen, Jr.
Rovin, Jeff 1951- 77-80
Rovit, Earl (Herbert) 1927- CANR-12
Earlier sketch in CA 7-8R
See also CLC 7
Rowan, Andrew N(icholas) 1946- 124
Rowan, Carl Thomas 1925- 89-92
Rowan, Deirdre
See Williams, Jeanne
Rowan, Ford 1943- 69-72
Rowan, Helen 1927(?)-1972 Obituary 37-40R
Rowan, Richard Lamar 1931- 11-12R
Rowan, Stephen A(nthony) 1928- 45-48
Rowan, Steven William 1943- 116
Rowans, Virgina
See Tanner, Edward Everett III
Rowat, Donald C(ameron) 1921- CANR-20
Earlier sketches in CA 11-12R, CANR-5
Rowbotham, David (Harold) 1924-
Brief entry 112
Rowbotham, Sheila 1943- 101
Rowdon, Maurice 1922- Brief entry 110
Rowe, A(lbert) W(ard) 1915- CANR-14
Earlier sketch in CA 23-24R
Rowe, Clarence J(ohn), Jr. 1916- 104
Rowe, David Knox 77-80
Rowe, David Nelson 1905- CANR-2
Earlier sketch in CA 7-8R
Rowe, Elizabeth 1674-1737 .... DLB-39
Rowe, Erna (Dirks) 1926- 93-96
Rowe, Frank 1921-1985 Obituary 115
Rowe, Frederick William 1912- 101
Rowe, G(ail) S(tuart) 1936- 112
Rowe, George E(rnest), Jr. 1947- 93-96
Rowe, H. Edward 1927- 69-72
Rowe, James L(ester), Jr. 1948- 69-72
Rowe, James N(icholas) 1938- 37-40R
Rowe, Jeanne A. 1938- 29-32R
Rowe, John Carlos 1945- 114
Rowe, John L. 1914- 19-20R
Rowe, John Seymour 1936- 109
Rowe, Margaret (Kevin) 1920- 15-16R
Rowe, Mary Budd 1925- 113
Rowe, Robert 1920- 17-18R
Rowe, Terry AITN-2
Rowe, Viola Carson 1903-1969 .... 2R
Obituary 103
See also SATA 26
Rowe, Vivian C(laud) 1902-1978 .... CANR-2
Earlier sketch in CA 3R
Rowe, William D(avid) 1930- 114
Rowe, William L. 1931- Brief entry 108
Rowell, Galen 1940- CANR-18
Earlier sketch in CA 65-68
Rowell, George (Rignall) 1923- CANR-18
Earlier sketches in CA 7-8R, CANR-2
Rowell, Henry T(hompson) 1904- CAP-1
Earlier sketch in CA 13-14
Rowell, John W(illiam) 1914- 33-36R
Rowen, Betty Jane Rose 1920- Brief entry .. 109
Rowen, Henry S(tanislaus) 1925- 123
Brief entry 118
Rowen, Herbert H(arvey) 1916- CANR-3
Earlier sketch in CA 11-12R
Rowen, Hobart 1918- 11-12R
Rowen, Lilian 1925- 108
Rowen, Ruth Halle 1918- 33-36R
Rowes, Barbara Gail 101
Rowland, Arthur R(ay) 1930- CANR-21
Earlier sketches in CA 13-14R, CANR-6
Rowland, Benjamin, Jr. 1904-1972
Obituary 37-40R
Rowland, Beryl 89-92
Rowland, Christopher (Charles) 1947- 116
Rowland, Claude K. 1943- 112
Rowland, D(onald) S(ydney) 1928- 21-22R
Rowland, Diana 1950- 122
Rowland, Florence Wightman 1900- CANR-5
Earlier sketch in CA 5-6R
See also SATA 8
Rowland, Iris
See Roberts, Irene
Rowland, J(ohn) R(ussell) 1925- 101
Rowland, Judith 1944- 124
Rowland, Peter (Kenneth) 1938- 25-28R
Rowland, Stanley J., Jr. 1928- 15-16R
Rowland, Virgil K(enneth) 1909- 5-6R
Rowland-Entwistle, (Arthur) Theodore
(Henry) 1925- CANR-24
Earlier sketch in CA 107
See also SATA 31
Rowlands, John Robert 1947- 109
Rowlands, Peter
See Lovell, Mark
Rowlandson, Mary 1635(?)-1678(?) DLB-24
Rowlatt, Mary 1908- 5-6R
Rowley, Ames Dorrance
See Lovecraft, H(oward) P(hillips)
Rowley, Anthony 1939- 61-64
Rowley, Brian A(lan) 1923- 7-8R
Rowley, Charles (Dunford) 1906-1985 103
Obituary 117
Rowley, Peter 1934- 65-68
Rowley, Peter T(empleton) 1929-
Brief entry 112
Rowley, Thomas
See Pauker, John
Rowley, William 1585(?)-1626 .... DLB-58
Rowley, William Dean 1939- 112
Rowling, Marjorie A(lice Thexton) 1900- 7-8R
Rowlingson, Donald T(aggart) 1907- CANR-6
Earlier sketch in CA 2R
Rowney, Don Karl 1936- 108
Rowse, A(lfred) L(eslie) 1903- CANR-1
Earlier sketch in CA 4R
Rowsome, Frank (Howard), Jr.
1914-1983 112
See also SATA 36
Rowson, Susanna Haswell
1762(?)-1824 .... DLB-37
Rowthorn, Anne W(heeler) 1939- 113
Roxas, Savina A. 37-40R
Roxborough, Henry Hall 1891- 7-8R
Roxon, Lillian 1933(?)-1973 Obituary 111
Roy, Archibald Edmiston 1924- 102
Roy, Archie E.
See Roy, Archibald Edmiston
Roy, David Tod 1933- 41-44R
Roy, Emil L. 1933- 25-28R
Roy, Ewell Paul 1929- 11-12R
Roy, G(eorge) Ross 1924- 77-80
Roy, Gabrielle 1909-1983 .... CANR-5
Obituary 110
Earlier sketch in CA 53-56
See also CLC 10, 14
Roy, Gregor 1929- 23-24R
Roy, Jack
See Dangerfield, Rodney
Roy, James A(lexander) 1884- CAP-1
Earlier sketch in CA 11-12
Roy, Jessie Hailstalk 1895-1986 Obituary ... 121
Roy, Joaquin 1943- 77-80
Roy, John (Flint) 1913- 93-96
Roy, Katherine (Morris) 1906- 3R
Roy, Liam
See Scarry, Patricia (Murphy)
Roy, Michael 1913-1976 .... CANR-10
Obituary 65-68
Earlier sketch in CA 61-64
Roy, Mike
See Roy, Michael
Roy, Reginald H(erbert) 1922- 49-52
Roy, Robert L(ouis) 1947- 106
Roy, Robin 1946- 114
Roy, Ron(ald) 1940- 114
See also SATA 35, 40
Roy, Rustum 1924- 113
Royal, Claudia Smith 1904- 7-8R
Royal, D.
See Du Breuil, (Elizabeth) L(or)inda
Royal, Denise 1935- 25-28R
Royal, William Robert 1905- 101
Royall, Anne 1769-1854 .... DLB-43
Royall, Vanessa
See Hinkemeyer, Michael T(homas)
Royce, Anya Peterson 1940- 101
Royce, James E(mmet) 1914- 3R
Royce, Kenneth
See Gandley, Kenneth Royce
Royce, Patrick M(ilan) 1922- 15-16R
Royce, R(ussell) Joseph 1921- CANR-9
Earlier sketch in CA 23-24R
Royds, Caroline 1953- 123
Royer, Fanchon 1902- 7-8R
Royko, Mike 1932- 89-92
Roylance, William H(erbert) 1927- 61-64
Royle, Edward 1944- 61-64
Royle, Selena 1904-1983 Obituary 109
Royle, Trevor 1945- 112
Royster, Charles 1944- 101
Royster, Philip M. 1943- CANR-13
Earlier sketch in CA 65-68
Royster, Salibelle 1895-1975 .... CAP-2
Earlier sketch in CA 25-28
Royster, Vermont (Connecticut) 1914- ... 21-22R
Royston, Olive 1904- 102
Rozeboom, William W(arren) 1928- 17-18R
Rozek, Evalyn Robillard 1941- 61-64
Rozental, Alek A(ron) 1920- 33-36R
Rozewicz, Tadeusz 1921- 108
See also CLC 9, 23
Rozhdestvensky, Vsevolod A.
1895(?)-1977 Obituary 73-76
Rozier, John W(iley) 1918- 107
Rozin, Skip 1941- 89-92
Rozman, Deborah 1949- 115
Rozman, Gilbert Friedell 1943- 109
Rozovsky, Lorne Elkin 1942- CANR-24
Earlier sketch in CA 108
Rozwenc, Edwin C(harles) 1915-1974 .... CAP-1
Earlier sketch in CA 13-14
Ruane, Gerald P(atrick) 1934- 69-72
Ruano, Argimiro 1924- 33-36R
Ruano, Nazario
See Ruano, Argimiro
Ruark, Gibbons 1941- CANR-14
Earlier sketch in CA 33-36R
See also CLC 3
Ruark, Robert (Chester) 1915-1965 ...... CAP-2
Obituary 25-28R
Earlier sketch in CA 19-20
Ruas, Charles (Edward) 1938- 124
Rubadeau, Duane O. 1927- 29-32R
Rubashov, Schneor Zalman
See Shazar, (Schneor) Zalman
Rubashov, Zalman
See Shazar, (Schneor) Zalman
Rubbra, Edmund 1901-1986 Obituary 119
Rubel, Arthur J. 1924- CANR-15
Earlier sketch in CA 41-44R
Rubel, Marc (Reid) 1949- 123
Rubel, Maximilien 1905- CAP-1
Earlier sketch in CA 11-12
Rubel, Nicole 1953- SATA-18
Rubel, Paula G(licksman) 1933- 89-92
Ruben, Brent David 1944- 41-44R
Ruben, Harvey L. 1941- 119
Rubens, Bernice 1923- 25-28R
See also DLB 14
See also CLC 19, 31
Rubens, Jeff(rey Peter) 1941- CANR-17
Earlier sketch in CA 25-28R
Rubenson, Sven (Abel) 1921- 115
Rubenstein, Boris B. 1907(?)-1974
Obituary 53-56
Rubenstein, Joshua 1949- 103
Rubenstein, Richard E(dward) 1938- 29-32R
Rubenstein, Richard L(owell) 1924- CANR-17
Earlier sketch in CA 21-22R
Rubenstein, (Clarence) Robert 1926- 21-22R
Rubenstein, Roberta 1944- 89-92
Rubenstone, Jessie 1912- 69-72
Rubia Barcia, Jose 1914- CANR-19
Earlier sketch in CA 103
Rubicam, Harry Cogswell, Jr. 1902- CAP-2
Earlier sketch in CA 17-18
Rubicon
See Lunn, Arnold
Rubin, Alan (Michael) 1936- 113
Rubin, Amy Kateman 1945- 106
Rubin, Arnold P(erry) 1946- 69-72
Rubin, Barry (M.) 1950- 108
Rubin, Benny 1899-1986 Obituary 119
Rubin, Charles J. 1950- 101
Rubin, Cynthia Elyce 1944- 97-100
Rubin, David Lee 1939- CANR-15
Earlier sketch in CA 41-44R
Rubin, David M. 1945- 77-80
Rubin, Dorothy 1932- CANR-19
Earlier sketch in CA 101
Rubin, Duane R(oger) 1931- 57-60
Rubin, Eli Z(under) 1922- 17-18R
Rubin, Ernest 1915-1978 Obituary 81-84
Rubin, Eva Johanna 1925- SATA-38
Rubin, Eva R(edfield) 1926- 113
Rubin, Frederick 1926- 33-36R
Rubin, Ida Ely 1923- 107
Rubin, Isadore 1912-1970 .... CAP-1
Obituary 29-32R
Earlier sketch in CA 15-16
Rubin, Israel 1923- 37-40R
Rubin, Jacob A. 1910-1972 .... CAP-1
Obituary 37-40R
Earlier sketch in CA 11-12
Rubin, James Henry 1944- 106
Rubin, Jerry 1938- 69-72
Rubin, Joan 1932- 102
Rubin, Julia Danielle 1944- 113
Rubin, Larry (Jerome) 1930- 5-6R
Rubin, Leona G(reenstone) 1920- 49-52
Rubin, Lillian Breslow 1924- 65-68
Rubin, Louis D(ecimus), Jr. 1923- CANR-21
Earlier sketches in CA 3R, CANR-6
Rubin, Mann 1927- 119
Rubin, Mark 1946- CANR-9
Earlier sketch in CA 53-56
Rubin, Michael 1935- CANR-1
Earlier sketch in CA 1R
Rubin, Morris H(arold) 1911-1980
Obituary 101
Rubin, Morton 1923- 41-44R
Rubin, Stanley 1928- 107
Rubin, Steven Jay 1951- 110
Rubin, Steven Joel 1943- 107
Rubin, Theodore Isaac 1923- 110
Brief entry 108
See also AITN 1
Rubin, Vera (Dourmashkin) 1911-1985
Obituary 115
Rubin, Vitalii 1923-1981 69-72
Obituary 105
Rubin, William 1927- 77-80
Rubin, Zick 1944- CANR-1
Earlier sketch in CA 49-52
Rubinfeld, William A. 1914(?)-1984
Obituary 113
Rubington, Earl 1923- 73-76
Rubinoff, (M.) Lionel 1930- 25-28R
Rubinow, Sol (Isaac) 1923-1981 Obituary .. 103
Rubins, Harriett 1942- 120
Rubins, Jack L(awrence) 1916-1982 85-88
Obituary 107
Rubinstein, Alvin Zachary 1927- CANR-18
Earlier sketches in CA 9-10R, CANR-3
Rubinstein, Amnon 1931- CANR-7
Earlier sketch in CA 15-16R
Rubinstein, Arthur 1887(?)-1982 113
Obituary 108
Rubinstein, Daryl Reich 1938(?)-1981
Obituary 102

Rubinstein, David H(ugh) 1915- 109
Rubinstein, David M(ichael) 1942- 93-96
Rubinstein, E(lliott) 1936- 41-44R
Rubinstein, Erna F(erber) 1922- 120
Rubinstein, H(arold) F(rederick) 1891-1975 Obituary 115
Rubinstein, Helena 1871(?)-1965 Obituary 113
Rubinstein, Hilary 1926- 57-60
Rubinstein, Moshe F(ajwel) 1930- 57-60
Rubinstein, Paul (Arthur) CANR-7
Earlier sketch in CA 61-64
Rubinstein, Robert E(dward) 1943- 106
See also SATA 49
Rubinstein, S(amuel) Leonard 1922- 45-48
Rubinstein, Stanley (Jack) 1890-1975 CAP-2
Earlier sketch in CA 29-32
Rubinstein, W(illiam) D(avid) 1946- 114
Rublowsky, John M(artin) 1928- 17-18R
Rubsamen, Walter H. 1911- 13-14R
Rubulis, Aleksis 1922- 37-40R
Ruby, Kathryn 1947- 65-68
Ruby, Lois F. 1942- CANR-18
Earlier sketch in CA 97-100
See also SATA 34, 35
Ruby, Robert Holmes 1921- CANR-7
Earlier sketch in CA 19-20R
Ruchames, Louis 1917-1976 CANR-2
Obituary 65-68
Earlier sketch in CA 2R
Ruchelman, Leonard I. 1933- 29-32R
Ruchlis, Hy(man) 1913- CANR-2
Earlier sketch in CA 4R
See also SATA 3
Ruck, Amy Roberta 1878-1978 CANR-5
Earlier sketch in CA 7-8R
Ruck, Berta
See Ruck, Amy Roberta
Ruck, Carl A(nton) P(aul) 1935- 25-28R
Ruck, Peter F(rederick) Carter
See Carter-Ruck, Peter F(rederick)
Rucker, Bryce W(ilson) 1921- 11-12R
Rucker, (Egbert) Darnell 1921- 41-44R
Rucker, Frank Warren 1886-1975 4R
Obituary 103
Rucker, Helen (Bornstein) 1R
Rucker, Rudolf v(on) B(itter) 1946- 124
Brief entry 119
Rucker, Rudy
See Rucker, Rudolf v(on) B(itter)
Rucker, W(infred) Ray 1920- 13-14R
Ruckman, Ivy 1931- 111
See also SATA 37
Ruck-Pauquet, Gina 1931- 122
Brief entry 116
See also SATA 37, 40
Rudd, Enid 108
Rudd, Hughes (Day) 1921- 73-76
Rudd, Margaret
See Newlin, Margaret Rudd
Rudd, Margaret T(homas) 1907- 19-20R
Rudd, Robert D(ean) 1924- 93-96
Rudd, Robert L. 1921- 117
Rudd, Steele
See Davis, Arthur Hoey
Ruddell, Robert B(yron) 1937- 93-96
Rudder, Robert S(ween) 1937- CANR-5
Earlier sketch in CA 53-56
Rudder, Virginia L. 1941- 65-68
Ruddick, Sara 1935- 77-80
Ruddock, Ralph 1913- 53-56
Ruddy, Frank C.
See Frank, Rudolf
Ruddy, T(homas) Michael 1946- 124
Rude, George F. E(lliot) 1910- CANR-24
Earlier sketches in CA 7-8R, CANR-5
Rudeen, Kenneth Brief entry 117
See also SATA 36
Rudel, Hans-Ulrich 1916-1982 Obituary 110
Rudelius, William 1931- 45-48
Rudenstine, Neil Leon 1935- Brief entry 105
Ruder, William 1921- 19-20R
Rudhart, Alexander 1930- 61-64
Rudhyar, Dane 1895-1985 CANR-21
Obituary 117
Earlier sketch in CA 29-32R
Rudin, Jacob Philip 1902-1982 Obituary 107
Rudin, Marcia Ruth 1940- 102
Rudinsky, Joseph F(rancis) 1891- 5-6R
Rudis, Al 1943- 77-80
Rudisill, D(orus) P(aul) 1902- 45-48
Rudkin, (James) David 1936- 89-92
See also DLB 13
See also CLC 14
Rudley, Stephen 1946- 106
See also SATA 30
Rudloe, Jack 1943- 97-100
Rudman, Mark 1948- 119
Rudman, Masha Kabakow 1933- 110
Rudnick, Hans H(einrich) 1935- 41-44R
Rudnick, Lois Palken 1944- 121
Rudnick, Milton Leroy 1927- CANR-3
Earlier sketch in CA 2R
Rudnik, Raphael 1933- 29-32R
See also CLC 7
Rudofsky, Bernard 1905- 17-18R
Rudolf, Anthony 1942- CANR-24
Earlier sketches in CA 61-64, CANR-9
Rudolph, Albert
See Frank, Rudolf
Rudolph, Donna Keyse 1934- 33-36R
Rudolph, Erwin Paul 1916- 33-36R
Rudolph, Frederick 1920- 11-12R
Rudolph, L(avere) C(hristian) 1921- CANR-2
Earlier sketch in CA 7-8R
Rudolph, Lee (Norman) 1948- CANR-7
Earlier sketch in CA 57-60
Rudolph, Lloyd I(rving) 1927- 57-60
Rudolph, Marguerita 1908- CANR-13
Earlier sketch in CA 33-36R
See also SATA 21
Rudolph, Nancy 1923- 57-60
Rudolph, Robert S. 1937- 41-44R
Rudolph, Susanne Hoeber 1930- 25-28R
Rudomin, Esther
See Hautzig, Esther Rudomin
Rudrum, Alan (William) 1932- 25-28R
Rudwick, Elliot M. 1927-1986(?) 104
Obituary 118
Rudy, Ann 1927- 101
Rudy, Peter 1922- 53-56
Rudy, Willis 1920- 37-40R
Rue, John E. 1924- 21-22R
Rue, Leonard Lee III 1926- CANR-1
Earlier sketch in CA 4R
See also SATA 37
Rue, Leslie W(aits) 1944- 110
Rue, Nancy Naylor 1951- 122
Ruebsaat, Helmut J(ohannes) 1920- 61-64
Ruechelle, Randall C(ummings) 1920- 41-44R
Rueckert, William H(owe) 1926- 23-24R
Ruedi, Norma Paul
See Ainsworth, Norma
Ruef, John S. 1927- 37-40R
Rueff, Jacques (Leon) 1896-1978 CANR-12
Obituary 77-80
Earlier sketch in CA 65-68
Ruege, Klaus 1934- CANR-11
Earlier sketch in CA 65-68
Ruehle, Juergen 1924- 25-28R
Ruehlmann, William 1946- 105
Ruell, Patrick
See Hill, Reginald (Charles)
Ruesch, Hans 1913- 15-16R
Ruesch, Jurgen 1909- 73-76
Rueschemeyer, Marilyn 1938- 122
Rueschhoff, Phil H. 1924- 29-32R
Ruether, Rosemary Radford 1936- 97-100
Rueveni, Uri 1933- 102
Ruff, Ann 1930- 120
Ruff, Howard J. 93-96
Ruffell, Ann 1941- CANR-23
Earlier sketch in CA 107
See also SATA 30
Ruffell, Thomas
See Laslett, Peter
Ruffian, M.
See Hasek, Jaroslav (Matej Frantisek)
Ruffin, C(avlbert) Bernard III 1947- 109
Ruffini, (Jacopo) Remo 1942- 57-60
Ruffins, Reynold 1930- 112
See also SATA 41
Ruffle, The
See Tegner, Henry (Stuart)
Ruffner, Budge
See Ruffner, Lester Ward
Ruffner, Lester Ward 1918- 89-92
Ruffo, Vinnie 25-28R
Ruffridge, Frank(lin James) 1931- CANR-12
Earlier sketch in CA 25-28R
Rugel, Miriam 1911- 101
Rugg, Dean S(prague) 1923- 41-44R
Ruggiero, Guido 1944- 118
Ruggiers, Paul G(eorge) 1918- CANR-24
Earlier sketch in CA 25-28R
Ruggles, Eleanor 1916- 7-8R
Ruggles, Henry Joseph 1813-1906 DLB-64
Ruggles, Joanne Beaule 1946- 73-76
Ruggles, Philip (Kent) 1944- 73-76
Rugh, Belle Dorman 1908- CAP-1
Earlier sketch in CA 15-16
Rugh, Roberts 1903-1978 93-96
Obituary 81-84
Rugoff, Milton 1913- 21-22R
See also SATA 30
Ruhen, Olaf 1911- CANR-20
Earlier sketches in CA 4R, CANR-5
See also SATA 17
Ruhlen, Merritt 1944- 122
Ruibal, Jorge Silvestre Remonda
See Remonda-Ruibal, Jorge Silvestre
Ruihley, Glenn Richard 107
Ruitenbeek, Hendrik M(arinus) 1928-1983 CANR-8
Obituary 109
Earlier sketch in CA 7-8R
Ruiz, Jose Martinez
See Martinez Ruiz, Jose
See also CLC 11
Ruiz, Ramon Eduardo 1921- CANR-11
Earlier sketch in CA 25-28R
Ruiz, Ricardo Navas
See Navas-Ruiz, Ricardo
Ruiz, Roberto 1925- 41-44R
Ruiz-De-Conde, Justina (Malaxechevarria) 1909- 73-76
Ruiz-Fornells, Enrique 1925- 33-36R
Ruja, Harry 1912- 41-44R
Rukeyser, Louis 1933- 65-68
Rukeyser, Merryle Stanley 1897-1974 CAP-2
Earlier sketch in CA 23-24
Rukeyser, Muriel 1913-1980 7-8R
Obituary 93-96
See also SATA 22
See also DLB 48
See also CLC 6, 10, 15, 27
Rukeyser, William Simon 1939- 69-72
Ruksenas, Algis 1942- 49-52
Ruland, Richard (Eugene) 1932- 21-22R
Ruland, Vernon Joseph 1931- 19-20R
Rule, Gordon Wade 1906-1982 Obituary 107
Rule, James B(ernard) 1943- 73-76
Rule, Jane (Vance) 1931- CANR-12
Earlier sketch in CA 25-28R
See also DLB 60
See also CLC 27
Rulfo, Juan 1918-1986 85-88
Obituary 118
See also CLC 8
Rulon, Philip Reed 1934- CANR-14
Earlier sketch in CA 37-40R
Rumaker, Michael 1932- CANR-2
Earlier sketch in CA 3R
See also DLB 16
Rumanes, George N(icholas) 1925- 45-48
Rumbelow, Donald 1940- 49-52
Rumberger, Russell W(illiam) 1949- 109
Rumble, Thomas C(lark) 1919- 15-16R
Rumble, Wilfrid E., Jr. 1931- 25-28R
Rumbold-Gibbs, Henry St. John Clair 1913- CANR-3
Earlier sketch in CA 1R
Rumens, Carol 1944- DLB-40
Rummel, J(osiah) Francis 1911- 19-20R
Rummel, R(udolph) J(oseph) 1932- 65-68
Rumpleforeskin
See Krassner, Paul
Rumscheidt, H(ans) Martin 1935- 57-60
Rumsey, Marian (Barritt) 1928- 21-22R
See also SATA 16
Runcie, Robert Alexander Kennedy 1921- 108
Runciman, (James Cochran) Steven(son) 1903- CANR-3
Earlier sketch in CA 3R
Rundell, Walter, Jr. 1928- CANR-3
Earlier sketch in CA 11-12R
Rundle, Anne CANR-12
Earlier sketch in CA 57-60
Runes, Dagobert D(avid) 1902-1982 25-28R
Obituary 108
Runge, C(arlisle) Ford 1953- 122
Runge, William H(arry) 1927- 2R
Runia, Klaas 1926- CANR-20
Earlier sketches in CA 7-8R, CANR-5
Runkel, Philip J(ulian) 1917- CANR-11
Earlier sketch in CA 29-32R
Runkle, Gerald 1924- CANR-14
Earlier sketch in CA 37-40R
Running, Leona Glidden 1916- 89-92
Runte, Alfred 1947- CANR-19
Earlier sketch in CA 102
Runyan, Harry (John) 1913-(?) CAP-2
Earlier sketch in CA 23-24
Runyan, John
See Palmer, Bernard
Runyan, Thora J. 1931- 69-72
Runyon, A(lfred) Milton 1905-1983
Obituary 109
Runyon, Catherine 1947- 61-64
Runyon, Charles W. 1928- 17-18R
Runyon, (Alfred) Damon 1884(?)-1946
Brief entry 107
See also DLB 11
See also TCLC 10
Runyon, Daniel V. 1954- 120
Runyon, John H(arold) 1945- 33-36R
Runyon, Richard P(orter) 1925- CANR-3
Earlier sketch in CA 45-48
Ruoff, James E. 1925- 41-44R
Ruotolo, Andrew K(eogh) 1926(?)-1979 103
Obituary 89-92
Ruotolo, Lucio P(eter) 1927- 41-44R
Rupert, Hoover 1917- CANR-3
Earlier sketch in CA 2R
Rupert, Raphael Rudolph 1910- CAP-2
Earlier sketch in CA 19-20
Ruple, Wayne Douglas 1950- 53-56
Rupp, E. G.
See Rupp, E(rnest) Gordon
Rupp, E(rnest) Gordon 1910-1986 124
Brief entry 113
Rupp, Gordon
See Rupp, E(rnest) Gordon
Rupp, Leila J(ane) 1950- 81-84
Rupp, Richard H(enry) 1934- 29-32R
Ruppenthal, Karl M. 1917- 19-20R
Ruppersburg, Hugh Michael 1950- 124
Ruppli, Michel 1934- 101
Ruprecht, Mary M(argaret Wyant) 1934- 118
Rus, Vladimir 1931- 17-18R
Rusalem, Herbert 1918- 41-44R
Rusch, Hermann G. 1907- 61-64
Rusch, John J(ay) 1942- 106
Rusco, Elmer R(itter) 1928- 65-68
Ruscoe, (Steuart) James (Bailey) 1947- 116
Ruse, Gary Alan 1946- CANR-12
Earlier sketch in CA 61-64
Ruse, Michael E. 1940- 107
Rush, Alison 1951- 115
See also SATA 41
Rush, Anne Kent 1945- CANR-8
Earlier sketch in CA 61-64
Rush, Benjamin 1746-1813 DLB-37
Rush, Christopher 1944- 122
Rush, Elizabeth 1918- 115
Rush, James J. 1929- 120
Rush, Joseph H(arold) 1911- 5-6R
Rush, Joshua
See Pearlstein, Howard J.
Rush, Michael (David) 1937- 61-64
Rush, Myron 1922- 45-48
Rush, N(ixon) Orwin 1907- 45-48
Rush, Norman 1933- Brief entry 121
See also CLC 44
Rush, Peter 1937- 111
See also SATA 32
Rush, Philip 1908- 104
Rush, Philip
See Lardner, Ring(gold Wilmer), Jr.
Rush, Ralph E(ugene) 1903-1965 7-8R
Rush, Richard Henry 1915- CANR-6
Earlier sketch in CA 5-6R
Rush, Robert
See Barber, D(ulan) F(riar Whilberton)
Rush, Theressa Gunnels 1945- 104
Rushbrook Williams, L(aurence) F(rederic) 1890-1978 97-100
Rushdie, (Ahmed) Salman 1947- 111
Brief entry 108
See also CLC 23, 31
Rushdoony, R(ousas) J(ohn) 1916- 93-96
Rusher, William Allen 1923- 103
Rushford, Patricia H(elen) 1943- 115
Rushforth, Peter (Scott) 1945- 101
See also CLC 19
Rushing, Francis W(illard) 1939- 112
Rushing, Jane Gilmore 1925- 49-52
Rushing, William A. 1930- 81-84
Rushmer, Robert F(razer) 1914-
Brief entry 111
Rushmore, Helen 1898- 25-28R
See also SATA 3
Rushmore, Robert (William) 1926-1986 25-28R
Obituary 120
See also SATA 8, 49
Rusholm, Peter
See Powell, Eric F(rederick) W(illiam)
Rushton, J(ohn) Philippe 1943- 111
Rushton, William Faulkner 1947- CANR-22
Earlier sketch in CA 101
Rusinek, Alla 1949- 45-48
Rusinow, Dennison I. 1930- 85-88
Rusk, Howard A(rchibald) 1901- 103
Rusk, Ralph Leslie 1888-1962 5-6R
Ruskay, Joseph A. 1910- CAP-2
Earlier sketch in CA 29-32
Ruskay, Sophie 1887-1980 69-72
Obituary 97-100
Ruskin, Ariane
See Batterberry, Ariane Ruskin
Ruskin, John 1819-1900 Brief entry 114
See also SATA 24
See also DLB 55
See also TCLC 20
Ruskin, Ronald 1944- 115
Russ, Joanna 1937- CANR-11
Earlier sketch in CA 25-28R
See also DLB 8
See also CLC 15
Russ, Laurence 1943- 114
Russ, Lavinia 1904- 25-28R
Russ, Martin 1931- 106
Russ, William Adam, Jr. 1903- 3R
Russel, Robert R(oyal) 1890- 15-16R
Russell, Albert
See Bixby, Jerome Lewis
Russell, Allan Melvin 1930- 122
Russell, Amanda
See Feldman, Ellen (Bette)
Russell, Andy 1915- CANR-10
Earlier sketch in CA 21-22R
Russell, Annie V(est) 1880(?)-1974
Obituary 49-52
Russell, Arthur (Wolseley) 1908- CANR-16
Earlier sketches in CA 13-14, CAP-1
Russell, Benjamin 1761-1845 DLB-43
Russell, Bertrand (Arthur William) 1872-1970 CAP-1
Obituary 25-28R
Earlier sketch in CA 15-16
Russell, Bill
See Russell, William Felton
Russell, C(harles) Allyn 1920- 65-68
Russell, Carroll Mason 1898(?)-1983
Obituary 111
Russell, Charles 1944- 111
Russell, Charles Edward 1860-1941 DLB-25
Russell, Charlotte
See Rathjen, Carl Henry
Russell, Claude Vivian 1919- 17-18R
Russell, Clifford S(pringer) 1938- CANR-12
Earlier sketch in CA 73-76
Russell, Colin Archibald 1928- 45-48
Russell, Conrad 1937- 33-36R
Russell, D(iana) E(lizabeth) H(amilton) 1938- CANR-8
Earlier sketch in CA 61-64
Russell, D(avid) S(yme) 1916- 15-16R
Russell, Daniel 1937- 41-44R
Russell, Diarmuid 1902(?)-1973 Obituary 45-48
Russell, Don(ald Bert) 1899-1986 CANR-1
Obituary 118
Earlier sketch in CA 2R
See also SATA 47
Russell, Donald Andrew (Frank Moore) 1920- 110
Russell, Dora (Winifred Black) 1894-1986
Obituary 119
Russell, Douglas A(ndrew) 1927- CANR-16
Earlier sketch in CA 41-44R
Russell, Edward (Frederick Langley) 1895-1981 107
Obituary 103
Russell, Eric Frank 1905-1978 124
Obituary 102
Russell, Foster Meharry 1907- 111
Russell, Francis 1910- 25-28R
Russell, Franklin (Alexander) 1926- CANR-11
Earlier sketch in CA 19-20R
See also SATA 11
Russell, Frederick Stratten 1897-1984
Obituary 113
Russell, George William 1867-1935
Brief entry 104
Russell, Gertrude Barrer
See Barrer-Russell, Gertrude

Russell, (Sydney) Gordon 1892- CAP-2
Earlier sketch in CA 29-32
Russell, Gordon 1930(?)-1981 Obituary 102
Russell, H. Diane 1936- 110
Russell, Helen Ross 1915- 33-36R
See also SATA 8
Russell, Howard S(ymmes) 1887-1980 105
Russell, I(saac) Willis 1903-1985 118
Russell, Ivy E(thel Southern) 1909- 7-8R
Russell, J.
See Bixby, Jerome Lewis
Russell, J(effrey) P(eter) 1954- 112
Russell, James
See Harknett, Terry
Russell, James E. 1916-1975 Obituary 57-60
Russell, Jeffrey Burton 1934- CANR-11
Earlier sketch in CA 25-28R
Russell, Jeremy Longmore 1935- 110
Russell, Joan Mercedes 1921- 102
Russell, John 1919- 13-14R
Russell, John David 1928- 11-12R
Russell, John L(eonard) 1906- 13-14R
Russell, John L(owry), Jr. 1921- 11-12R
Russell, Josiah Cox 1900- 41-44R
Russell, (Henry) Ken(neth Alfred) 1927- 105
See also CLC 16
Russell, Ken(neth Victor) 1929- CANR-11
Earlier sketch in CA 25-28R
Russell, Letty M(andeville) 1929- CANR-8
Earlier sketch in CA 57-60
Russell, Lois Ann 1931- 113
Russell, Mariann Barbara 1935- 109
Russell, Mark 1932- 113
Brief entry 108
Russell, Martin 1934- 73-76
Russell, Maurin
See Russell, Maurine (Fletcher)
Russell, Maurine (Fletcher) 1899- CAP-1
Earlier sketch in CA 9-10
Russell, Norma Hull Lewis 1902- 7-8R
Russell, Norman H(udson), Jr. 1921- 49-52
Russell, O(liver) Ruth 1897- 57-60
Russell, P(eggy) J(ean) 1934- 97-100
Russell, Pamela Redford 1950- 81-84
Russell, Patrick
See Sammis, John
Russell, (Irwin) Peter 1921- 97-100
Russell, Ray 1924- CANR-6
Earlier sketch in CA 3R
Russell, Robert (William) 1924- 2R
Russell, Ronald (Stanley) 1904-1974 ..... CAP-1
Earlier sketch in CA 11-12
Russell, Ronald 1924- 102
Russell, Rosalind 1911-1976 116
Obituary 111
Russell, Ross 1909- 2R
Russell, Roy 1918- 107
Russell, Sarah
See Laski, Marghanita
Russell, Shane
See Norwood, Victor G(eorge) C(harles)
Russell, Solveig Paulson 1904- CANR-5
Earlier sketch in CA 3R
See also SATA 3
Russell, Thomas 1902(?)-1984 Obituary 114
Russell, Victor L. 1948- 117
Russell, William Felton 1934- 108
Russell, William H. 1911- 61-64
Russell Taylor, Elisabeth 1930- CANR-15
Earlier sketch in CA 81-84
Russell-Wood, A(nthony) J(ohn) R(ussell)
1939- CANR-7
Earlier sketch in CA 57-60
Russett, Bruce M(artin) 1935- CANR-2
Earlier sketch in CA 7-8R
Russett, Cynthia Eagle 1937- 21-22R
Russo, Anthony 1933- 61-64
Russo, Giuseppe Luigi 1884- CAP-1
Earlier sketch in CA 9-10
Russo, John Paul 1944- 41-44R
Russo, Joseph Louis
See Russo, Giuseppe Luigi
Russo, Sarett Rude 1918(?)-1976
Obituary 65-68
Russo, Susan 1947- 106
See also SATA 30
Russo, Vito 1946- 107
Russon, Allien R. 1905- 105
Russon, L(eslie) J(ohn) 1907- 19-20R
Rust, Brian Arthur Lovell 1922- CANR-2
Earlier sketch in CA 45-48
Rust, Claude 1916- 109
Rust, Doris (Dibblin) 13-14R
Rust, Eric C(harles) 1910- 15-16R
Rust, Richard Dilworth 1937- 29-32R
Rusticus
See Martin, Brian P(hilip)
Rustin, Bayard 1910(?)-1987 53-56
Obituary 123
Rustomji, Nari Kaikhosru 1919- 101
Rustow, Dankwart A(lexander) 1924- ... CANR-1
Earlier sketch in CA 3R
Rutberg, Sidney 1924- 69-72
Rutenber, Culbert G(erow) 1909- CAP-2
Earlier sketch in CA 17-18
Rutgers van der Loeff, An
See Rutgers van der Loeff-Basenau,
An(na) Maria Margaretha
Rutgers van der Loeff-Basenau, An(na)
Maria Margaretha 1910- CANR-7
Earlier sketch in CA 9-10R
See also SATA 22
Ruth, Babe
See Ruth, George Herman (Jr.)
Ruth, Claire (Merritt) 1900-1976
Obituary 69-72
Ruth, George Herman (Jr.) 1895-1948
Brief entry 116
Ruth, John L(andis) 1930- 73-76
Ruth, Kent Ringelman 1916- CANR-2
Earlier sketch in CA 5-6R
Ruth, Rod 1912- SATA-9
Rutherford, Andrew 1929- CANR-9
Earlier sketch in CA 5-6R
Rutherford, Douglas
See McConnell, James Douglas
Rutherford
Rutherford, Malcolm 1939- 119
Rutherford, Margaret 1882-1972
Obituary 33-36R
Rutherford, Mark
See White, William Hale
See also DLB 18
See also TCLC 25
Rutherford, Meg 1932- 29-32R
See also SATA 34
Rutherford, Michael (Andrew) 1946- 45-48
Rutherford, Phillip Roland 1939- 37-40R
Rutherford, Ward 1927- CANR-14
Earlier sketch in CA 77-80
Ruthin, Margaret SATA-4
Ruthstrom, Dorotha 1936- 107
Ruthven, K(enneth) K(nowles) 1936- 25-28R
Rutkoff, Peter M. 1942- 116
Rutkowski, Edwin H(enry) 1923- 37-40R
Rutland, Dodge
See Singleton, Betty
Rutland, Robert A(llen) 1922- CANR-2
Earlier sketch in CA 45-48
Rutledge, Aaron L(eslie) 1919- 45-48
Rutledge, Albert J(ohn) 1934- 33-36R
Rutledge, Archibald (Hamilton)
1883-1973 .... CANR-5
Obituary 45-48
Earlier sketch in CA 5-6R
Rutledge, Brett
See Paul, Elliot (Harold)
Rutledge, Dom Denys
See Rutledge, Edward William
Rutledge, Edward William 1906- 7-8R
Rutledge, Harley Dean 1926- 107
Rutledge, Howard Elmer 1929(?)-1984
Obituary 113
Rutman, Darrett B(ruce) 1929- CANR-6
Earlier sketch in CA 15-16R
Rutman, Gilbert L(ionel) 1935- 25-28R
Rutman, Leo 1935- 45-48
Rutsala, Vern 1934- CANR-20
Earlier sketches in CA 11-12R, CANR-6
Rutstein, David D(avis) 1909-1986 ......33-36R
Obituary 118
Rutstein, Harry Sidney 1929- 108
Rutstein, Nat(han) 1930- 53-56
Rutstrum, Calvin 1895-1982 .... CANR-1
Obituary 106
Earlier sketch in CA 3R
Rutt, M. E.
See Shah, Amina
Rutt, Richard 1925- CANR-6
Earlier sketch in CA 11-12R
Ruttan, Vernon W(esley) 1924- 41-44R
Ruttenberg, Joseph 1889-1983 Obituary 109
Ruttenberg, Stanley H(arvey) 1917- 33-36R
Rutter, Barbara A. 1943- 118
Rutter, Eileen Joyce 1945- CANR-10
Earlier sketch in CA 61-64
Rutter, Michael (Llewellyn) 1933- 109
Ruttkowski, Wolfgang Victor 1935- CANR-15
Earlier sketch in CA 41-44R
Ruttle, Lee 1909- 81-84
Rutz, Viola Larkin 1932- 23-24R
See also SATA 12
Rutzebeck, Hjalmar 1889- 11-12R
Ruud, Charles A(rthur) 1933- 121
Ruud, Josephine Bartow 1921- 73-76
Ruuth, Marianne 1937- CANR-21
Earlier sketches in CA 57-60, CANR-6
Ruxin, Robert H(arris) 1953- 110
Ruyerson, James Paul
See Rothweiler, Paul Roger
Ruyslinck, Ward
See Belser, Reimond Karel Maria de
Ruz, Fidel Castro
See Castro, Fidel
Ruzic, Neil P. 1930- CANR-8
Earlier sketch in CA 17-18R
Ruzicka, Rudolph 1883-1978 Obituary 81-84
See also SATA 24
Ryall, Edward W(illiam) 1902- 61-64
Ryall, George (Francis Trafford)
1887(?)-1979 103
Obituary 89-92
Ryalls, Alan 1919- 102
Ryals, Clyde de L(oache) 1928- 23-24R
Ryan, Alan 1940- 29-32R
Ryan, Allan A(ndrew), Jr. 1945- 124
Ryan, Alvan Sherman 1912- 19-20R
Ryan, Bernard, Jr. 1923- CANR-6
Earlier sketch in CA 7-8R
Ryan, Betsy
See Ryan, Elizabeth (Anne)
Ryan, Bob 1946- CANR-4
Earlier sketch in CA 49-52
Ryan, Bryce F(inley) 1911- 81-84
Ryan, Charles W(illiam) 1929- 57-60
Ryan, Charles W(illiam) 1932- 93-96
Ryan, Cheli Duran 102
See also SATA 20
Ryan, Claude 1925- Brief entry 111
Ryan, Cornelius John 1920-1974 69-72
Obituary 53-56
See also CLC 7
Ryan, Desmond 1893-1964 Obituary 113
Ryan, Dorothy (Barger) 1942- CANR-13
Earlier sketch in CA 73-76
Ryan, Edwin 1916- 5-6R
Ryan, Elizabeth (Anne) 1943- CANR-7
Earlier sketch in CA 61-64
See also SATA 30
Ryan, Herbert J(oseph) 1931- 41-44R
Ryan, James H(erbert) 1928- 53-56
Ryan, Jeanette Mines
See Mines, Jeanette (Marie)
Ryan, Jessica Cadwalader 1915(?)-1972
Obituary 33-36R
Ryan, John (Gerald Christopher)
1921- CANR-16
Earlier sketches in CA 49-52, CANR-1
See also SATA 22
Ryan, John Barry 1933- CANR-7
Earlier sketch in CA 57-60
Ryan, John Fergus 1931- 73-76
Ryan, John J. 1922(?)-1977 Obituary 69-72
Ryan, John Julian 1898- 73-76
Ryan, John K(enneth) 1897-1981 ..... CANR-16
Earlier sketch in CA 13-14R
Ryan, Joseph J. 1910(?)-1976 Obituary ...69-72
Ryan, Juanita 1949- 120
Ryan, Kathryn Morgan 1925- 102
Ryan, Kevin 1932- CANR-12
Earlier sketch in CA 29-32R
Ryan, Lawrence Vincent 1923- 5-6R
Ryan, Leonard Eames 1930- 11-12R
Ryan, Marah Ellis 1866(?)-1934
Brief entry 122
Ryan, Marleigh Grayer 1930- 19-20R
Ryan, Mary P(atricia) 1945- Brief entry 113
Ryan, Maureen Jones
See Jones-Ryan, Maureen
Ryan, Michael 1946- 49-52
See also DLBY 82
Ryan, Milo 1907- 5-6R
Ryan, Neil Joseph 1930- 13-14R
Ryan, Pat M(artin) 1928- CANR-13
Earlier sketch in CA 33-36R
Ryan, Patrick J. 1902- CAP-1
Earlier sketch in CA 11-12
Ryan, Paul B(rennan) 1913- CANR-15
Earlier sketch in CA 81-84
Ryan, Paul William 1906-1947 Brief entry .. 114
Ryan, Peter (Charles) 1939- 61-64
See also SATA 15
Ryan, Peter Allen 1923- 109
Ryan, Regina (Claire) 1938- 118
Ryan, Regina S(ara) 1945- 119
Ryan, Robert Michael 1934- 29-32R
Ryan, Sister Joseph Eleanor 61-64
Ryan, T. Antoinette 1924- 41-44R
Ryan, Thomas Arthur 1911- 41-44R
Ryan, Thomas Richard 1897-1981 ....29-32R
Obituary 122
Ryan, Tim
See Dent, Lester
Ryan, Tom 1938- CANR-10
Earlier sketch in CA 57-60
Ryan, William (Howard) 1914- 104
Ryan, William (Michael) 1948- 122
Ryan, William H. 1928(?)-1986 Obituary ... 121
Ryan, William M(artin) 1918- 33-36R
Ryans, David Garriott 1909- 7-8R
Ryans, John K(elley), Jr. 1932- 61-64
Ryback, Eric 1952- 37-40R
Rybak, Nathan 1913-1978(?) Obituary 81-84
Rybakov, Anatoli 1911(?)- CLC-23
Rybalka, Michel 1933- 41-44R
Rybczynski, Witold Marian 1943- 110
Rybka, Edward F(rank) 1928- 33-36R
Rybot, Doris
See Ponsonby, D(oris) A(lmon)
Rychlak, Joseph F(rank) 1928- CANR-14
Earlier sketch in CA 37-40R
Ryckmans, Pierre 1935- CANR-16
Earlier sketch in CA 85-88
Rycroft, Charles (Frederick) 1914- CANR-11
Earlier sketch in CA 21-22R
Rydberg, Ernest E(mil) 1901- 15-16R
See also SATA 21
Rydberg, Lou(isa Hampton) 1908- 69-72
See also SATA 27
Rydel, Christine A(nn) 1944- 118
Rydell, Forbes
See Forbes, DeLoris (Florine) Stanton
Rydell, Wendell
See Rydell, Wendy
Rydell, Wendy 33-36R
See also SATA 4
Ryden, Ernest Edwin 1886-1981 Obituary ... 102
Ryden, Hope CANR-14
Earlier sketch in CA 33-36R
See also SATA 8
Ryder, A(rthur) J(ohn) 1913- 21-22R
Ryder, Eileen 1908- 117
Ryder, Ellen 1913- 29-32R
Ryder, Frank G(lessner) 1916- 7-8R
Ryder, Joanne Brief entry 112
See also SATA 34
Ryder, John 1917- CANR-5
Earlier sketch in CA 7-8R
Ryder, Jonathan
See Ludlum, Robert
Ryder, M(ichael) L(awson) 1927- 102
Ryder, Meyer S. 1909- 21-22R
Ryder, Norman B(urston) 1923- 37-40R
Ryder, Ron 1904- 61-64
Ryder, Rowland (Vint) 1914- 85-88
Ryder, T(homas) A(rthur) 1902- 7-8R
Ryding, William W. 1924- 77-80
Rye, Anthony
See Youd, Samuel
Rye, Bjoern Robinson 1942- 61-64
Ryerson, Martin 1907- CANR-8
Earlier sketch in CA 15-16R
Ryf, Robert S. 1918-1985 ....17-18R
Obituary 117
Ryga, George 1932-1987 101
Obituary 124
See also DLB 60
See also CLC 14
Ryken, Leland 1942- CANR-12
Earlier sketch in CA 29-32R
Rykwert, Joseph 1926- CANR-11
Earlier sketch in CA 69-72
Ryland, Lee
See Arlandson, Leone
Rylant, Cynthia 1954- SATA-44, 50
Ryle, Anthony 1927- 107
Ryle, Gilbert 1900-1976 73-76
Obituary 69-72
Rylski, Aleksander Scibor
See Scibor-Rylski, Aleksander
Rymer, Alta May 1925- CANR-1
Earlier sketch in CA 49-52
See also SATA 34
Rymes, Thomas Kenneth 1932- 37-40R
Rynearson, Edward H(arper) 1901-1987
Obituary 121
Rynew, Arden N. 1943- 37-40R
Ryrie, Charles C(aldwell) 1925- CANR-18
Earlier sketches in CA 11-12R, CANR-3
Ryskamp, Charles (Andrew) 1928- 104
Ryskind, Morrie 1895-1985 Obituary 117
Brief entry 109
See also DLB 26
Rystrom, Kenneth 1932- 110
Rywell, Martin 1905-1971 .... CAP-2
Earlier sketch in CA 19-20
Rywkin, Michael 1925- 13-14R
Ryzl, Milan 1928- 29-32R
Rzhevsky, Leonid 1905- CANR-14
Earlier sketch in CA 41-44R
Rzhevsky, Nicholas 1943- 115

S

S. S. E.
See Sperry, (Sally) Baxter
Saab, E(velyn) Ann Pottinger 1934- 107
Saab, Edouard 1929-1976 Obituary 65-68
Saadawi, Nawal El
See El Saadawi, Nawal
Saal, Jocelyn
See Sachs, Judith
Saalman, Howard 1928- CANR-1
Earlier sketch in CA 1R
Saarinen, Aline B(ernstein Louchheim)
1914-1972 Obituary 37-40R
Saarinen, Eero 1910-1961 Obituary 113
Saaty, Thomas L(orie) 1926- CANR-8
Earlier sketch in CA 57-60
Saavedra, Luis Spota
See Spota Saavedra, Luis
Sabais, Heinz Winfried 1922-1981
Obituary 114
Sabaliunas, Leonas 1934- 61-64
Sabar, Yona 1939- 112
Sabaroff, Rose Epstein 1918- 85-88
Sabatier, Robert 1923- CANR-18
Earlier sketch in CA 102
Sabato, Ernesto 1911- 97-100
See also CLC 10, 23
Sabato, Larry (J.) 1952- 108
Sabbag, Robert 1946- 101
Sabbah, Hassan i
See Butler, William Huxford
Saberhagen, Fred (Thomas) 1930- CANR-7
Earlier sketch in CA 57-60
See also SATA 37
See also DLB 8
Sabiad
See White, Stanhope
Sabin, Edwin L(egrand) 1870-1952 ..... YABC-2
Sabin, Francene CANR-11
Earlier sketch in CA 69-72
See also SATA 27
Sabin, Katharine Cover 1910- 57-60
Sabin, Lou
See Sabin, Louis
Sabin, Louis 1930- CANR-11
Earlier sketch in CA 69-72
See also SATA 27
Sabin, Mark
See Fox, Norman A(rnold)
Sabine, B.E.V. 1914- 97-100
Sabine, Ellen S. (Borcherding) 1908- CAP-1
Earlier sketch in CA 17-18
Sabine, Gordon Arthur 1917- 117
Sabine, Waldo
See Sabine, William H(enry) W(aldo)
Sabine, William H(enry) W(aldo) 1903- .. CANR-4
Earlier sketch in CA 53-56
Sabini, John Anthony 1921- 9-10R
Sabki, Hisham M. 1934- Brief entry 106
Sable, Martin Howard 1924- CANR-12
Earlier sketch in CA 33-36R
Sabloff, Jeremy A(rac) 1944- CANR-8
Earlier sketch in CA 61-64
Sablosky, Irving L. 1924- 124
Sabom, Michael Bruce 1944- 109
Sabourin, Anne Winifred 1910- 101
Sabourin, Justine
See Sabourin, Anne Winifred
Sabourin, Leopold 1919- CANR-11
Earlier sketch in CA 65-68
Sabre, Dirk
See Laffin, John (Alfred Charles)

Sabri-Tabrizi, Gholam-Reza 1934- ... 61-64
Sacastru, Martin
See Bioy Casares, Adolfo
Saccio, Peter (Churchill) 1941- ... 61-64
Sach, Nathan
See Zach, Nathan
Sachar, Abram Leon 1899- ... 97-100
Sachar, Howard Morley 1928- ... CANR-6
Earlier sketch in CA 7-8R
Sachar, Louis 1954- ... CANR-15
Earlier sketch in CA 81-84
See also SATA 50
Sacharoff, Shanta Nimbark 1945- ... 61-64
Sachdev, Paul ... 115
Sachem, E. B.
See Creel, Stephen Melville
Sacher, Jack, Jr. 1931- ... 57-60
Sacher-Masoch, Alexander 1902(?)-1972
Obituary ... 37-40R
Sachs, Albert Louis 1935- ... CANR-14
Earlier sketch in CA 21-22R
Sachs, Albie
See Sachs, Albert Louis
Sachs, Alexander 1893-1973 Obituary ... 41-44R
Sachs, Elizabeth-Ann 1946- ... 111
See also SATA 48
Sachs, Georgia
See Adams, Georgia Sachs
Sachs, (Stewart) Harvey 1946- ... 85-88
Sachs, Herbert L. 1929- ... 25-28R
Sachs, Judith 1947- ... 122
Sachs, Lewis Benjamen 1938- ... 61-64
Sachs, Margaret 1948- Brief entry ... 115
Sachs, Marianne 1945- ... 114
Sachs, Marilyn (Stickle) 1927- ... CANR-13
Earlier sketch in CA 19-20R
See also SATA 3
See also SAAS 2
See also CLC 35
See also CLR 2
Sachs, Mary P(armly) K(oues)
1882(?)-1973 Obituary ... 45-48
Sachs, Mendel 1927- ... CANR-12
Earlier sketch in CA 29-32R
Sachs, Michael L(eo) 1951- ... 115
Sachs, Murray 1924- ... CANR-14
Earlier sketch in CA 37-40R
Sachs, Nelly 1891-1970 ... CAP-2
Obituary ... 25-28R
Earlier sketch in CA 17-18
See also CLC 14
Sachse, William L(ewis) 1912- ... 25-28R
Sack, James J(ohn) 1944- ... 101
Sack, John 1930- ... CANR-14
Earlier sketch in CA 21-22R
Sack, Saul 1912- ... 53-56
Sackerman, Henry
See Kahm, H(arold) S.
Sackett, L(eyland) H(ugh) 1928- ... 119
Sackett, S(amuel) J(ohn) 1928- ... CANR-6
Earlier sketch in CA 1R
See also SATA 12
Sackett, Susan 1943- ... CANR-22
Earlier sketch in CA 106
Sackett, Theodore Alan 1940- ... 89-92
Sackett, Walter W(allace), Jr. 1905-1985 ... 5-6R
Obituary ... 117
Sackheim, Maxwell 1890-1982 Obituary ... 108
Sackler, Howard (Oliver) 1929-1982 ... 61-64
Obituary ... 108
See also DLB 7
See also CLC 14
Sackman, Harold 1927- ... CANR-12
Earlier sketch in CA 23-24R
Sackrey, Charles 1936- ... 77-80
Sacks, Benjamin 1903- ... CAP-2
Earlier sketch in CA 23-24
Sacks, Claire
See Sprague, Claire S(acks)
Sacks, Karen 1941- ... 109
Sacks, Norman P(aul) 1914- ... 45-48
Sacks, Oliver W(olf) 1933- ... 53-56
Sacks, Peter
See Sacks, Peter M.
Sacks, Peter M. 1950- ... 124
Sacks, Sheldon 1930-1979 ... 17-18R
Obituary ... 122
Sackson, Sid 1920- ... CANR-12
Earlier sketch in CA 69-72
See also SATA 16
Sackton, Alexander H(art) 1911- ... 37-40R
Sackville, Thomas 1536-1608 ... DLB-62
Sackville-West, V(ictoria Mary) 1892-1962 ... 104
Obituary ... 93-96
See also DLB 34
(el-)Sadat, Anwar 1918-1981 ... 101
Obituary ... 104
Sadd, Susan 1951- ... 103
Saddhatissa, Hammalawa 1914- ... CANR-17
Earlier sketch in CA 97-100
Saddlemyer, E(leanor) Ann 1932- ... 17-18R
Saddler, Allen
See Richards, R(onald) C(harles) W(illiam)
Saddler, K. Allen
See Richards, R(onald) C(harles) W(illiam)
Sadecky, Petr Milos 1943- ... 41-44R
Sadeh, Pinhas 1929- ... CANR-13
Earlier sketch in CA 25-28R
Sadie, Stanley (John) 1930- ... CANR-9
Earlier sketch in CA 19-20R
See also SATA 14
Sadiq, Muhammad 1898-1984 ... CANR-18
Earlier sketch in CA 19-20R
Sadker, Myra Pollack 1943- ... CANR-22
Earlier sketches in CA 53-56, CANR-5
Sadler, Arthur Lindsay 1882- ... 7-8R
Sadler, Catherine Edwards ... SATA-45
Sadler, Christine 1908-1983 ... CAP-1
Obituary ... 110
Earlier sketch in CA 11-12
Sadler, Ella Jo 1942- ... 57-60
Sadler, Glenn Edward 1935- ... 97-100
Sadler, Julius Trousdale, Jr. 1923- ... 65-68
Sadler, Mark
See Lynds, Dennis
Sadler, William A(lan), Jr. 1931- ... 25-28R
Sadock, Benjamin James 1933-
Brief entry ... 105
Sadoff, Ira 1945- ... CANR-21
Earlier sketches in CA 53-56, CANR-5
See also CLC 9
Sadun, Elvio H. 1918(?)-1974 Obituary ... 49-52
Saerchinger, Cesar 1884-1971 Obituary ... 33-36R
Saetone
See Camus, Albert
Safa, Helen Icken 1930- ... CANR-1
Earlier sketch in CA 45-48
Safarian, Albert Edward 1924- ... 105
Safarik, Allan 1948- ... 114
Safdie, Moshe 1938- ... 69-72
Safer, Daniel J. 1934- ... CANR-11
Earlier sketch in CA 69-72
Safer, Elaine Berkman 1937- ... 41-44R
Safer, Morley 1931- ... 93-96
See also AITN 2
Saffell, David C(lyde) 1941- ... CANR-11
Earlier sketch in CA 61-64
Saffin, John 1626(?)-1710 ... DLB-24
Saffron, Morris Harold 1905- ... 45-48
Saffron, Robert 1918(?)-1985 Obituary ... 114
Safian, Jill
See Bharti, Ma Satya
Safilios-Rothschild, Constantina 1936- ... 45-48
Safir, Leonard 1921- ... 109
Safire, William 1929- ... 19-20R
See also CLC 10
Safran, Claire 1930- ... 101
Safran, Nadav 1925- ... 5-6R
Safran, William 1930- ... 113
Sagall, Elliot L. 1918- ... 29-32R
Sagan, Carl (Edward) 1934- ... CANR-11
Earlier sketch in CA 25-28R
See also CLC 30
Sagan, Eli 1927- ... 124
Sagan, Francoise
See Quoirez, Francoise
See also CLC 3, 6, 9, 17, 36
Sagan, Leonard A. 1928- ... 49-52
Sagan, Miriam 1954- ... 77-80
Sagar, Keith (Milsom) 1934- ... CANR-14
Earlier sketch in CA 21-22R
Sagarin, Edward 1913- ... CANR-4
Earlier sketch in CA 7-8R
Sagarin, Mary 1903- ... 81-84
Sagarra, Eda 1933- ... CANR-11
Earlier sketch in CA 65-68
Sage, George Harvey 1929- ... 61-64
Sage, Joe
See Sage, Joseph
Sage, Joseph 1921-1987 Obituary ... 122
Sage, Juniper
See Brown, Margaret Wise and Hurd, Edith (Thacher)
Sage, Leland L(ivingston) 1899- ... 61-64
Sage, Robert 1899-1962 ... 106
See also DLB 4
Sagendorf, Bud
See Sagendorf, Forrest C(owles)
Sagendorf, Forrest C(owles) 1915-
Brief entry ... 112
Sagendorph, Robb Hansell 1900-1970 ... CANR-7
Obituary ... 29-32R
Earlier sketch in CA 7-8R
Sager, Clifford J. 1916- ... CANR-12
Earlier sketch in CA 29-32R
Sager, Samuel 1923- ... 123
Sageser, A(delbert) Bower 1902- ... 29-32R
Saggs, Henry W(illiam) F(rederick) 1920- ... 7-8R
Saghir, Marcel T(awfic) 1937- ... 49-52
Sagnier, Thierry (Bright) 1946- ... 53-56
Sagsoorian, Paul 1923- ... SATA-12
Sagstetter, Karen 1941- ... 105
Sahakian, Lucille 1894- ... 53-56
Sahakian, Mabel Lewis 1921- ... 21-22R
Sahakian, William S(ahak) 1921- ... CANR-8
Earlier sketch in CA 17-18R
Sahgal, Nayantara (Pandit) 1927- ... CANR-11
Earlier sketch in CA 11-12R
See also CLC 41
Sahl, Mort(on Lyon) 1927- Brief entry ... 113
Sahlins, Marshall (David) 1930-
Brief entry ... 114
Sahn, Seung 1927- ... 113
Sahni, Balbir S. 1934- ... CANR-3
Earlier sketch in CA 45-48
Said, Abdul Aziz 1930- ... 81-84
Said, Edward W. 1935- ... 21-22R
See also DLB 67
Saida
See LeMair, H(enriette) Willebeek
Saidel, Rochelle G. 1942- ... 121
Sa'Idi, Ghulam Husayn 1936-1985
Obituary ... 119
Saidy, Anthony Fred 1937- ... 89-92
Saidy, Fareed Milhem 1907-1982 Obituary ... 106
Saidy, Fred M.
See Saidy, Fareed Milhem
Sailor, Charles 1947- ... 97-100
Sailor, Merlin F(orrest) 1906- ... CAP-1
Earlier sketch in CA 15-16
Saine, Thomas P(rice) 1941- ... 41-44R
Sainer, Arthur 1924- ... CANR-3
Earlier sketch in CA 49-52
Saini, B(alwant) S(ingh) 1930- ... 107
Sainsbury, Eric (Edward) 1925- ... CANR-13
Earlier sketch in CA 33-36R
Sainsbury, Maurice Joseph 1927- ... 108
Saint, Andrew (John) 1946- ... 65-68
Saint, Dora Jessie 1913- ... CANR-22
Earlier sketches in CA 13-14R, CANR-7
See also SATA 10
Saint, Phil(ip) 1912- ... 61-64
St. Andre, Lucien
See Mott, Vincent Valmon
St. Angelo, Douglas 1931- ... 45-48
St. Antoine, Theodore J(oseph) 1929- ... 41-44R
St. Aubin de Teran, Lisa 1953- Brief entry ... 118
St. Aubyn, F(rederic) C(hase) 1921- ... 25-28R
St. Aubyn, Fiona 1952- ... CANR-23
Earlier sketch in CA 106
St. Aubyn, Giles 1925- ... CANR-19
Earlier sketches in CA 7-8R, CANR-4
St. Bruno, Albert Francis 1909- ... CAP-1
Earlier sketch in CA 9-10
St. Clair, (Howard) Barry 1945- ... 120
St. Clair, Byrd Hooper 1905-1976 ... 3R
Obituary ... 103
See also SATA 28
St. Clair, Clovis
See Skarda, Patricia Lyn
St. Clair, David 1932- ... 33-36R
St. Clair, Elizabeth
See Cohen, Susan
St. Clair, Katherine
See Huff, T(om) E.
St. Clair, Leonard 1916-1986 ... 101
Obituary ... 118
St. Clair, Margaret 1911- ... 49-52
St. Clair, Philip
See Howard, Munroe
St. Clair, Robert James 1925- ... 11-12R
St. Clair, William ... 77-80
St. Cyr, Cyprian
See Berne, Eric (Lennard)
St. Cyr, Margaret 1920- ... 29-32R
Saint-Denis, Michel Jacques 1897-1971 ... CAP-2
Obituary ... 33-36R
Earlier sketch in CA 19-20
Saint Dorliae
See Dorliae, Peter Gondro
Saint-Eden, Dennis
See Foster, Don(ald)
Sainte-Marie, Beverly 1941- ... 107
Sainte-Marie, Buffy
See Sainte-Marie, Beverly
Saint-Exupery, Antoine (Jean Baptiste Marie Roger) de 1900-1944 Brief entry ... 108
See also SATA 20
See also TCLC 2
See also CLR 10
Saint-Gall, Auguste Amedee de
See Strich, Christian
St. George, Arthur
See Paine, Lauran (Bosworth)
St. George, David
See Markov, Georgi
St. George, Edith
See Delatush, Edith G.
St. George, George 1904- ... 25-28R
St. George, Judith 1931- ... CANR-14
Earlier sketch in CA 69-72
See also SATA 13
St. George, Margaret
See Osborne, Margaret Ellen
St. Germain, Gregory
See Wallmann, Jeffrey M(iner)
St. Hereticus
See Brown, Robert McAfee
Saint-Jacques, Bernard 1928- ... CANR-16
Earlier sketch in CA 41-44R
St. James, Bernard
See Treister, Bernard W(illiam)
St. James, Blakely
See Gottfried, Theodore Mark and Platt, Charles
St. John, Beth
See John, Elizabeth Beaman
St. John, Bob (J.) 1937- Brief entry ... 122
St. John, Bruce (Carlisle) 1923- ... 107
St. John, David
See Hunt, E(verette) Howard, Jr.
St. John, Elizabeth
See John, Elizabeth Beaman
St. John, John 1917- ... CANR-5
Earlier sketch in CA 7-8R
St. John, Leonie
See Bayer, William and Jenkins, Nancy (Harmon)
St. John, Nicole
See Johnston, Norma
St. John, Patricia Mary 1919- ... CANR-3
Earlier sketch in CA 7-8R
St. John, Philip
See del Rey, Lester
St. John, Primus 1939- ... 113
St. John, Robert 1902- ... CANR-5
Earlier sketch in CA 2R
St. John, Wylly Folk 1908-1985 ... 21-22R
Obituary ... 117
See also SATA 10, 45
St-John Nevill, Barry
See Nevill, Barry St-John
Saint-John Perse
See Leger, (Marie-Rene) Alexis Saint-Leger
St. Johns, Adela Rogers 1894- ... 108
See also DLB 29
See also AITN 1
St. John-Stevas, Norman Anthony Francis 1929- ... CANR-4
Earlier sketch in CA 49-52
St. Max, E. S.
See Ellis, Edward S(ylvester)
St. Mox, E. A.
See Ellis, Edward S(ylvester)
St. Myer, Ned
See Stratemeyer, Edward L.
St. Omer, Garth ... 73-76
Saint Phalle, Thibaut de
See de Saint Phalle, Thibaut
St. Pierre, Dorothy
See Nyren, Dorothy Elizabeth
St. Pierre, Paul 1923- ... 113
Saintsbury, George 1845-1933 ... DLB-57
St. Tamara
See Kolba, St. Tamara
St. Vivant, M.
See Bixby, Jerome Lewis
Sainty, John Christopher 1934- ... 93-96
Sainz de la Maza, Regino 1896-1981
Obituary ... 108
Saisselin, Remy G(ilbert) 1925- ... 11-12R
Sait Faik
See Abasiyanik, Sait Faik
See also TCLC 23
Saito, Fred
See Saito, Hiroyuki
Saito, Hiroyuki 1917- ... 61-64
Saito, Michiko
See Fujiwara, Michiko
Sakamaki, Shunzo 1906-1973 ... 4R
Obituary ... 103
Sakell, Achilles Nicholas 1906-1987 ... 4R
Obituary ... 123
Sakers, George 1950- ... 108
Sakharov, Andrei Dimitrievich 1921-
Brief entry ... 105
Saki
See Munro, Hector Hugh
See also TCLC 3
Saklatvala, Beram 1911-1976 ... 89-92
Sakoian, Frances 1912- ... 65-68
Sakol, Jeannie 1928- ... CANR-11
Earlier sketch in CA 7-8R
Sakran, Frank Charles 1895(?)-1983
Obituary ... 111
Saks, Elmer Eliot
See Fawcett, F(rank) Dubrez
Saks, Katia 1939- ... 29-32R
Sala, Charles 1924- ... 116
Salaam, Kalamu ya 1947- ... DLB-38
Saladino, Salvatore 1922- ... 33-36R
Salaff, Janet W. 1940- ... 112
Salama, Hannu 1936- ... CLC-18
Salaman, Esther 1900- ... 61-64
Salaman, Nicholas 1936- Brief entry ... 116
Salamanca, J(ack) R(ichard) 1922- ... 25-28R
See also CLC 4, 15
Salamanca, Lucy
See del Barco, Lucy Salamanca
Salamatullah
See Ullah, Salamat
Salamon, Lester M(ilton) 1943- ... 89-92
Salant, Nathan N(athaniel) 1955- ... 106
Salant, Walter S. 1911- ... CANR-2
Earlier sketch in CA 7-8R
Salas, Floyd Francis 1931- ... 119
Salas, Rafael M(ontinola) 1928-1987
Obituary ... 121
Salassi, Otto R(ussell) 1939- ... 106
See also SATA 38
Salazar, Antonio de Oliveira 1889-1970
Obituary ... 113
Salazar, Fred A. 1942- ... 23-24R
Salazar, Rachel 1954- ... 123
Salazar, Ruben 1928-1970 Obituary ... 115
Saldutti, Denise 1953- ... SATA-39
Sale, J. Kirkpatrick
See Sale, Kirkpatrick
Sale, Kirkpatrick 1937- ... CANR-10
Earlier sketch in CA 13-14R
Sale, Larry L(owell) 1939- Brief entry ... 113
Sale, Richard (Bernard) 1911- ... 9-10R
Sale, Roger 1932- ... 21-22R
Sale, William (Merritt III) 1929- ... 45-48
Saleh, Dennis 1942- ... CANR-13
Earlier sketch in CA 33-36R
Salem, Elie Adib 1930- ... 49-52
Salem, James M. 1937- ... 23-24R
Salemme, Lucia (Autorino) 1919- ... 89-92
Salemson, Harold J(ason) 1910- ... 110
Brief entry ... 108
See also DLB 4
Salerno, Lynn M(cCormick) 1926- ... 119
Sales, Grover 1919- ... 65-68
Sales, Jane M(agorian) 1931- ... 49-52
Sales, M(ary) E(ileen) 1936- ... 29-32R
Sales, M(illard) Vance 1929- ... 53-56
Saletore, Bhasker Anand 1900- ... 7-8R
Salgado, Gamini 1929- ... 102
Salgado, Maria Antonia 1933- ... 41-44R
Saliba, John A. 1937- ... 114
Saliers, Don E(arl) 1937- ... 119
Salih, H(alil) Ibrahim 1939- ... 93-96
Salin, Mary Wolff
See Wolff-Salin, Mary
Salinas (y Serrano), Pedro 1891(?)-1951
Brief entry ... 117
See also TCLC 17
Salinger, Herman 1905- ... CAP-1
Earlier sketch in CA 13-14
Salinger, J(erome) D(avid) 1919- ... 5-6R
See also DLB 2
See also CDALB 1941-1968
See also CLC 1, 3, 8, 12

Salinger, Margaretta 1908(?)-1985
 Obituary 115
Salinger, Pierre (Emil George) 1925- CANR-14
 Earlier sketch in CA 19-20R
Salisbury, Carola (Isobel Julien) 1943- 89-92
Salisbury, Dorothy (Kendall Cleveland)
 1891(?)-1976 Obituary 69-72
Salisbury, Edward J(ames) 1886- CAP-1
 Earlier sketch in CA 13-14
Salisbury, Frank 1930- 108
Salisbury, Frank B(oyer) 1926- CANR-8
 Earlier sketch in CA 17-18R
Salisbury, Harrison E(vans) 1908- CANR-3
 Earlier sketch in CA 2R
Salisbury, Ralph 1926- CANR-15
 Earlier sketch in CA 41-44R
Salisbury, Ray(mond Eric) 1942- 110
Salisbury, Richard Frank 1926- CANR-9
 Earlier sketch in CA 7-8R
Salisbury, Robert H(olt) 1930- 11-12R
Salisbury, Ruth 1921- 73-76
Salisbury-Jones, Guy 1896-1985 Obituary 115
Salivarova, Zdena
 See Skvorecka, Zdena Salivarova
Salk, Erwin Arthur 1918- 81-84
Salk, Jonas Edward 1914- 49-52
Salk, Lee 1926- 104
 See also AITN 1
Salkeld, Robert J. 1932- 29-32R
Salkever, Louis R(omov) 1914- 19-20R
Salkey, (Felix) Andrew (Alexander)
 1928- CANR-13
 Earlier sketch in CA 7-8R
 See also SATA 35
Sallada, Logan Henry 1942-1987 Obituary 123
Sallaska, Georgia 1933- 25-28R
Sallaway, George H(enry) 1930- 21-22R
Sallis, James 1944- 33-36R
Sallis, John C(leveland) 1938- 41-44R
Salls, Betty Ruth 1926- 49-52
Salm, Peter 1919- 41-44R
Salma, Abu
 See Karmi, Abdul Karim
Salmon, Annie Elizabeth 1899- CANR-12
 Earlier sketch in CA 69-72
 See also SATA 13
Salmon, Charles Gerald 1930- 49-52
Salmon, Edward T(ogo) 1905- CANR-2
 Earlier sketch in CA 7-8R
Salmon, H. Morrey 1892(?)-1985
 Obituary 116
Salmon, J(ohn) B(rynmor) 1942- 118
Salmon, J(ohn) H(earsey) M(cMillan)
 1925- 25-28R
Salmon, James F(rancis) 1925- 111
Salmon, John Tenison 1910- 13-14R
Salmon, Margaret Belais 1921- CANR-8
 Earlier sketch in CA 17-18R
Salmon, Nathan Ucuzoglu 1951- 109
Salmon, Wesley C(harles) 1925- CANR-23
 Earlier sketches in CA 17-18R, CANR-8
Salmond, John A(lexander) 1937- 114
Salmonson, Jessica Amanda 1950- 114
Salmonson, R(oland) F(rank) 1922- CANR-17
 Earlier sketch in CA 25-28R
 See also SATA 3
Saloma, John S. III 1935(?)-1983
 Obituary 110
Salomon, Albert 1891-1966 7-8R
Salomon, Herman Prins 1930- 41-44R
Salomon, I(sidore) L(awrence)
 1899-1985 73-76
 Obituary 116
Salomon, Irving 1897-1979 Obituary 85-88
Salomon, Janet Lynn (Nowicki) 1953- 61-64
Salomon, Julian Harris 1896-1987
 Obituary 123
Salomon, Roger Blaine 1928- 1R
Salomon, Sir Walter
 See Salomon, Walter (Hans)
Salomon, Walter (Hans) 1906-1987
 Obituary 123
Salomone, A(rcangelo) William 1915- 15-16R
Salop, Lynne
 See Hawes, Lynne Gusikoff Salop
Salot, Lorraine 1914- 17-18R
Saloutos, Theodore 1910- 11-12R
Salper, Roberta Linda 1940- 105
Salpeter, Eliahu (Arnost) 1927- 93-96
Salsbury, Barbara G(race) 1937- 121
 Brief entry 118
Salsbury, Edith Colgate 1907-1971 CAP-2
 Earlier sketch in CA 17-18
Salsbury, Kathryn H(errick) 1924- 107
Salsbury, Stephen 1931- CANR-11
 Earlier sketch in CA 23-24R
Salsini, Paul E(dward) 1935- 77-80
Salt, Beryl (Winifred) 1931- 110
Salt, Waldo 1914-1987 111
 Obituary 121
 See also DLB 44
Salten, Felix
 See Salzmann, Siegmund
Salter, Cedric
 See Knight, Francis Edgar
Salter, Donald P. M. 1942- 93-96
Salter, Elizabeth 1918-1981 CANR-9
 Obituary 103
 Earlier sketch in CA 53-56
Salter, Elizabeth 1925-1980 105
 Obituary 97-100
Salter, James 1925- 73-76
 See also CLC 7
Salter, Lionel (Paul) 1914- CANR-3
 Earlier sketch in CA 7-8R
Salter, Margaret Lennox
 See Donaldson, Margaret
Salter, Mary D.
 See Ainsworth, Mary D(insmore) Salter
Salter, Mary Jo 1954- 119
Salter, Paul Sanford 1926- 61-64
Salter, Robbie
 See Salter, Robina
Salter, Robina 123
Salter, Stefan 1908(?)-1985 Obituary 115
Salter, W(illiam) H(enry) 1880-1970
 Obituary 112
Salter-Mathieson, Nigel Cedric Stephen
 1932- 4R
Salthe, Stanley N(orman) 1930- 53-56
Saltman, Juliet 1923- 101
Saltonstall, Richard, Jr. 1937-1981 33-36R
 Obituary 103
Saltus, Edgar (Everton) 1855-1921
 Brief entry 105
 See also TCLC 8
Saltz, Donald 1933- 102
Saltz, Eli 1926- Brief entry 108
Saltzgaber, Jan M. 1933- 115
Saltzman, Joe
 See Saltzman, Joseph
Saltzman, Joseph 1939- 81-84
Saltzman, Marvin L(ouis) 1922- 85-88
Salu, Mary 1919- 93-96
Salvadori, Joyce
 See Lussu, Joyce (Salvadori)
Salvadori, Mario (George) 1907- 108
 See also SATA 40
Salvadori, Massimo
 See Salvadori-Paleotti, Massimo
Salvadori, Max (William)
 See Salvadori-Paleotti, Massimo
Salvadori-Paleotti, Massimo 1908- CANR-7
 Earlier sketch in CA 11-12R
Salvan, Jacques-Leon 1898- 2R
Salvato, Larry 1948- 118
Salvato, Sharon 1938- CANR-15
 Earlier sketch in CA 65-68
Salvatore, Nicholas 1943- 109
Salvatore, Nick
 See Salvatore, Nicholas
Salvendy, Gavriel 1938- 49-52
Salzano, F(rancisco) M(auro) 1928- CANR-12
 Earlier sketch in CA 29-32R
Salzer, Felix 1904-1986 109
 Obituary 120
Salzer, L. E.
 See Wilson, Lionel
Salzer, Linda P(arsons) 1951- 122
Salzinger, Kurt 1929- Brief entry 107
Salzman, Eric 1933- CANR-13
 Earlier sketch in CA 25-28R
Salzman, Jack 1937- CANR-11
 Earlier sketch in CA 25-28R
Salzman, Yuri SATA-42
Salzmann, Siegmund 1869-1945
 Brief entry 108
 See also SATA 25
Salzmann, Zdenek 1925- CANR-16
 Earlier sketch in CA 97-100
Samachson, Dorothy (Mirkin) 1914- 11-12R
 See also SATA 3
Samachson, Joseph 1906-1980 17-18R
 Obituary 122
 See also SATA 3
Samarakis, Antonis 1919- 25-28R
 See also CLC 5
Samarin, William J. 1926- 93-96
Samartha, S(tanley) J(edidiah) 1920- CAP-1
 Earlier sketch in CA 11-12
Samay, Sebastian 1926- 37-40R
Sambrook, Arthur James 1931- 13-14R
Sambrot, William 1920- 25-28R
Samelson, William 1928- CANR-17
 Earlier sketch in CA 25-28R
Sametz, Arnold W(illiam) 1919- CANR-1
 Earlier sketch in CA 4R
Samford, Clarence D(ouglas) 1905- CAP-2
 Earlier sketch in CA 19-20
Samford, Doris E. 1923- 21-22R
Samhaber, Ernst Marzell 1901-1974 11-12R
 Obituary 122
Samigli, E.
 See Schmitz, Aron Hector
Samkange, Stanlake (John Thompson)
 1922- 29-32R
Samli, A. Coskun 1931- CANR-22
 Earlier sketch in CA 105
Sammartino, Peter 1904- CANR-7
 Earlier sketch in CA 57-60
Sammis, John 1942- 29-32R
 See also SATA 4
Sammons, David 1938- 73-76
Sammons, Jeffrey L(eonard) 1936- CANR-19
 Earlier sketch in CA 23-24R
Samoiloff, Louise Cripps
 See Cripps, L(ouise) L(ilian)
Samolin, William 1911- 61-64
Samora, Julian 1920- 37-40R
Samore, Theodore 1924- Brief entry 108
Sampedro, Jose Luis 1917- CANR-11
 Earlier sketch in CA 23-24R
Sampford, Michael 1924(?)-1983
 Obituary 109
Sampley, Arthur M(cCullough)
 1903-1975 41-44R
Sampley, J(ohn) Paul 1935- 105
Sampson, A(lywin) A(rthur) 1926- 117
Sampson, Anthony 1926- CANR-3
 Earlier sketch in CA 1R
Sampson, Edward C(oolidge) 1920- 57-60
Sampson, Edward E. 1934- CANR-14
 Earlier sketch in CA 37-40R
Sampson, Fay (Elizabeth) 1935- CANR-18
 Earlier sketch in CA 101
 See also SATA 40, 42
Sampson, Geoffrey 1944- 97-100
Sampson, H(erbert) Grant 1932- 45-48
Sampson, Henry T(homas) 1934- 117
Sampson, R. Neil 1938- 106
Sampson, R(onald) V(ictor) 1918- CANR-5
 Earlier sketch in CA 11-12R
Sampson, Robert C. 1909- 21-22R
Sampson, Roy J(ohnson) 1919- CANR-1
 Earlier sketch in CA 4R
Samra, Cal 1931- 37-40R
Sams, Eric 1926- 123
Sams, Jonathan Carter 1942- Brief entry 110
Samsell, R(ay) L(ane) 1925- 69-72
Samson, Anne S(tringer) 1933- 25-28R
 See also SATA 2
Samson, Jack
 See Samson, John Gadsden
Samson, Joan 1937-1976 73-76
 See also SATA 13
Samson, John Gadsden 1936- Brief entry 109
Samsonov, Leon
 See Maximov, Vladimir (Yemelyanovich)
Samstag, Nicholas 1903-1968 7-8R
 Obituary 25-28R
Samter, Linda Bantel
 See Bantel, Linda
Samtur, Susan J(oy) 1944- 97-100
Samuel, Alan E(douard) 1932- CANR-17
 Earlier sketch in CA 73-76
Samuel, Athanasius Y.
 See Samuel, Yeshue
Samuel, Dorothy T(ucker) 1918- 45-48
Samuel, Edwin Herbert 1898-1978 CANR-2
 Earlier sketch in CA 2R
Samuel, Irene 1915- 17-18R
Samuel, Maurice 1895-1972 102
 Obituary 33-36R
Samuel, Yeshue 1907- CAP-2
 Earlier sketch in CA 21-22
Samuels, Charles 1902-1982 CANR-5
 Obituary 106
 Earlier sketch in CA 4R
 See also SATA 12
Samuels, Charles Thomas 1936-1974 41-44R
 Obituary 49-52
Samuels, E. A.
 See Tiffany, E. A.
Samuels, Ernest 1903- CAP-1
 Earlier sketch in CA 11-12
Samuels, Gertrude CANR-6
 Earlier sketch in CA 11-12R
 See also SATA 17
Samuels, Harold 1917- 93-96
Samuels, Harry 1893- 13-14R
Samuels, Lesser 1894(?)-1980 Obituary 102
Samuels, M(ichael) L(ouis) 1920- 41-44R
Samuels, Peggy 1922- 97-100
Samuels, Warren J. 1933- CANR-14
 Earlier sketch in CA 23-24R
Samuelson, Arnold 1912(?)-1981
 Obituary 116
Samuelson, Paul A(nthony) 1915- 5-6R
Samway, Patrick H(enry) 1939- CANR-21
 Earlier sketch in CA 105
Sanborn, B. X.
 See Ballinger, William Sanborn
Sanborn, Duane 1914- CANR-1
 Earlier sketch in CA 4R
 See also SATA 38
Sanborn, Franklin Benjamin 1831-1917 DLB-1
Sanborn, Margaret 1915- CANR-4
 Earlier sketch in CA 53-56
Sanborn, Patricia F. 1937- 25-28R
Sanborn, Ruth Cummings 1917- 29-32R
Sancha, Sheila 1924- CANR-11
 Earlier sketch in CA 69-72
 See also SATA 38
Sanchez, Federico
 See Semprun, Jorge
Sanchez, Jose M(ariano) 1932- 11-12R
Sanchez, Luis Rafael 1936- CLC-23
Sanchez, Ramiro Guerra y
 See Guerra y Sanchez, Ramiro
Sanchez, Ricardo 1941- 73-76
Sanchez, Sonia 1934- CANR-24
 Earlier sketch in CA 33-36R
 See also SATA 22
 See also DLB 41
 See also CLC 5
Sanchez, Thomas 1944- CANR-2
 Earlier sketch in CA 45-48
Sanchez Albornoz, Claudio 1893-1984
 Obituary 113
Sanchez-Hidalgo, Efrain Sigisfredo
 1918-1974 57-60
Sanchez-Silva, Jose Maria 1911- 73-76
 See also SATA 16
 See also CLR 12
Sanctuary, Gerald 1930- CANR-12
 Earlier sketch in CA 29-32R
Sand, George X. 15-16R
 See also SATA 45
Sand, Margaret 1932- 85-88
Sand, Richard E(ugene) 1924- 33-36R
Sandak, Cass R(obert) 1950- 108
 See also SATA 37
Sandars, N(ancy) K(atharine) 1914- 61-64
Sandbach, Francis Henry 1903- 93-96
Sandbach, Mary (Warburton) 1901- 25-28R
Sandberg, (Karin) Inger 1930- CANR-11
 Earlier sketch in CA 65-68
 See also SATA 15
Sandberg, John H(ilmer) 1930- 49-52
Sandberg, Karl C. 1931- 49-52
 See also SATA 35
Sandberg, Larry 1944- 77-80
Sandberg, Lars G(unnarsson) 1939- 53-56
Sandberg, Lasse (E. M.) 1924- SATA-15
Sandberg, Margaret M(ay) 1919- 61-64
Sandberg, Peter Lars 1934- CANR-24
 Earlier sketches in CA 61-64, CANR-9
Sandbrook, K(eith) R(ichard) J(ames)
 1943- CANR-16
 Earlier sketch in CA 97-100
Sandburg, Carl (August) 1878-1967 7-8R
 Obituary 25-28R
 See also SATA 8
 See also DLB 17, 54
 See also CLC 1, 4, 10, 15, 35
Sandburg, Charles A.
 See Sandburg, Carl (August)
Sandburg, Helga 1918- CANR-5
 Earlier sketch in CA 4R
 See also SATA 3
Sande, Theodore Anton 1933- CANR-12
 Earlier sketch in CA 65-68
Sandeen, Ernest (Emanuel) 1908- 15-16R
Sandeen, Ernest Robert 1931- CANR-1
 Earlier sketch in CA 45-48
Sandelowski, Margarete J. 1946- 116
Sander, (Jane) Ellen 1944- 41-44R
Sander, Joseph Lincoln 1926- Brief entry 108
Sander, Volkmar 1929- 113
Sanderlin, David 1943- 123
Sanderlin, George 1915- 13-14R
 See also SATA 4
Sanderlin, Owenita (Harrah) 1916- CANR-7
 Earlier sketch in CA 17-18R
 See also SATA 11
Sanders, Albert
 See Davidson, David
Sanders, Ann(a Pearl Goodman) 1935- 7-8R
Sanders, Buck
 See Frentzen, Jeffrey
Sanders, Byrne Hope
 See Sperry, Byrne Hope
Sanders, Charles 1935- 25-28R
Sanders, D(onald) G(len) 1899- 85-88
Sanders, Daphne
 See Randolph, Georgiana Ann
Sanders, David (Scott, Jr.) 1926- 25-28R
Sanders, (Franklin) David 1934- 41-44R
Sanders, Dennis 1949- 108
Sanders, Donald 1915(?)-1979 Obituary 89-92
Sanders, Donald H. 1932- CANR-10
 Earlier sketch in CA 25-28R
Sanders, Dorothy Lucie 1917- 33-36R
Sanders, (James) Ed(ward) 1939- CANR-13
 Earlier sketch in CA 15-16R
 See also DLB 16
Sanders, Ed Parish 1937- 105
Sanders, Frederick K(irkland) 1936- 65-68
Sanders, Gerald D(eWitt) 1895- CAP-1
 Earlier sketch in CA 13-14
Sanders, Harland 1890-1980 114
 Obituary 102
Sanders, Herbert H(arvey) 1909- 15-16R
Sanders, Ivan 1944- 119
Sanders, J(ohn) Oswald 1902- CANR-21
 Earlier sketches in CA 15-16R, CANR-6
Sanders, Jack T(homas) 1935- 37-40R
Sanders, Jacquin 1922- 3R
Sanders, James A(lvin) 1927- CANR-14
 Earlier sketch in CA 21-22R
Sanders, James Bernard 1924- 41-44R
Sanders, James Edward 1911- 103
Sanders, Jeanne
 See Rundle, Anne
Sanders, Jennings B(ryan) 1901- CAP-2
 Earlier sketch in CA 25-28
Sanders, Joan Allred 1924- 11-12R
Sanders, Joseph Lee 1940- 105
Sanders, Kent
 See Wilkes-Hunter, R(ichard)
Sanders, Lawrence 1920- 81-84
 See also CLC 41
Sanders, Leonard 1929- CANR-3
 Earlier sketch in CA 11-12R
Sanders, Margaret 7-8R
Sanders, Marion K. 1905-1977 33-36R
 Obituary 73-76
Sanders, Marlene 1931- 65-68
Sanders, Noah
 See Blount, Roy (Alton), Jr.
Sanders, Norman (Joseph) 1929- 11-12R
Sanders, Peter B(asil) 1938- 105
Sanders, Pieter 1912- CANR-12
 Earlier sketch in CA 29-32R
Sanders, (Charles) Richard 1904- 53-56
Sanders, Ronald 1932- CANR-20
 Earlier sketch in CA 23-24R
Sanders, Scott Russell 1945- CANR-15
 Earlier sketch in CA 85-88
Sanders, Sol (Witner) 1926- CANR-2
 Earlier sketch in CA 49-52
Sanders, Stephen (Jesse, Jr.) 1919- 29-32R
Sanders, Thomas E. 1926- 21-22R
Sanders, Thomas Griffin 1932- 11-12R
Sanders, Tobi Gillian
 See Hammes, Tobi Gillian Sanders
Sanders, William B(rauns) 1944- CANR-10
 Earlier sketch in CA 65-68
Sanders, William T(imothy) 1926- CANR-3
 Earlier sketch in CA 45-48
Sanders, Winston P.
 See Anderson, Poul (William)
Sanderson, Isabel S(aunders) 1913-1987
 Obituary 123

Sanderson, Ivan T(erence) 1911-1973 ....37-40R
Obituary 41-44R
See also SATA 6
Sanderson, James L(ee) 1926- Brief entry .. 111
Sanderson, Jayne 1943- 23-24R
Sanderson, Milton W(illiam) 1910- CANR-9
Earlier sketch in CA 11-12R
Sanderson, Peter (Crawshaw) 1929- 33-36R
Sanderson, Ruth (L.) 1951- SATA-41
Sanderson, Sabina W(arren) 1931- CANR-3
Earlier sketch in CA 11-12R
Sanderson, Stewart (Forson) 1924- 108
Sanderson, Warren 1931- 105
Sandford, Cedric Thomas 1924- 113
Sandford, Christopher 1902-1983
Obituary 109
Sandford, John 1929- 101
Sandford, Nell Mary 1936- 81-84
Sandford, Paula 1931- 101
Sandford, William P(hillips) 1896-1975 ... CAP-2
Earlier sketch in CA 17-18
Sandhaus, Paul 1923- 25-28R
Sandifer, Durward Valdamir 1900-1981
Obituary 108
Sandifer, Linda P(rophet) 1951- 120
Sandin, Joan 1942- SATA-12
Sandin, Robert T(heodore) 1927- 111
Sandison, Alan 1932- 23-24R
Sandison, Janet
See Cameron, Elizabeth Jane
Sandle, Floyd Leslie 1913- Brief entry 106
Sandler, Benjamin P. 1902(?)-1979
Obituary 85-88
Sandler, Irving (Harry) 1925- 29-32R
Sandler, Lucy Freeman 1930- Brief entry ... 113
Sandler, Stanley Lawrence 1937- 113
Sandlin, Joann S(chepers) De Lora
1935- CANR-4
Earlier sketch in CA 53-56
Sandlin, John L(ewis) 1908- CANR-4
Earlier sketch in CA 3R
Sandman, Peter M(ark) 1945- 25-28R
Sandmel, Samuel 1911-1979 .... CANR-2
Earlier sketch in CA 1R
Sando, Joe S. 1923- 123
Sandon, Henry 1928- 81-84
Sandor, Bela I(mre) 1935- 102
Sandor, Gyorgy 108
Sandoz, (George) Ellis (Jr.) 1931- CANR-14
Earlier sketch in CA 37-40R
Sandoz, Mari(e Susette) 1896-1966 .... CANR-17
Obituary 25-28R
Earlier sketch in CA 2R
See also SATA 5
See also DLB 9
See also CLC 28
Sandrof, Ivan 1912(?)-1979 93-96
Obituary 85-88
Sandroff, Ronni 1943- 102
Sandrow, Edward T. 1906-1975 Obituary ..61-64
Sands, Donald B. 1920- 15-16R
Sands, Dorothy 1893-1980 Obituary 102
Sands, Edith Sylvia (Abeloff) 1912- 23-24R
Sands, John Edward 1930- 15-16R
Sands, Kathleen M.
See Sands, Kathleen Mullen
Sands, Kathleen Mullen 118
Sands, Leo G(eorge) 1912-1984 ....19-20R
Obituary 114
Sands, Martin
See Burke, John (Frederick)
Sands, Melissa 1949- 109
Sandusky, Annie Lee 1900(?)-1976
Obituary 69-72
Sandved, Arthur O. 1931- 33-36R
Sandy, Max
See Saunders, Carl Maxon
Sandy, Stephen 1934- CANR-22
Earlier sketches in CA 49-52, CANR-5
Sandys, Elspeth
See Purchase, Elspeth (Sandilands)
Sandys, George 1578-1644 .... DLB-24
Saner, Reg(inald Anthony) 1931- 65-68
See also CLC 9
Sanfield, Steve 1937- 124
Sanfilip, Thomas 1952- 57-60
Sanford, Agnes (White) 1897- 17-18R
Sanford, Charles B(elding) 1920- 113
Sanford, Charles Le Roy 1920- 5-6R
Sanford, David (Boyer) 1943- Brief entry ... 114
Sanford, Fillmore H(argrave) 1914-1967 ..... 4R
Obituary 103
Sanford, George 1943- 118
Sanford, Harry Allen 1929- 3R
Sanford, Jack D(onald) 1925- 7-8R
Sanford, John 1904- 123
Sanford, John A. 1929- CANR-10
Earlier sketch in CA 25-28R
Sanford, John B.
See Sanford, John
Sanford, John B.
See Shapiro, Julian L.
Sanford, Leda 1933- CANR-12
Earlier sketch in CA 65-68
Sanford, Terry 1917- 17-18R
Sanford, Thomas K(yle), Jr. 1921-1977 ...73-76
Sanger, Andrew 1948- 123
Sanger, Clyde 1928- 114
Sanger, Margaret (Higgins) 1883-1966
Obituary 89-92
Sanger, Marjory Bartlett 1920- 37-40R
See also SATA 8
Sanger, Richard H. 1905(?)-1979
Obituary 85-88
Sangiuliano, Iris (Agatha) 1923-
Brief entry 114
Sangrey, Dawn 1942- CANR-15
Earlier sketch in CA 85-88
Sangster, Ian 1934- 61-64
Sangster, Jimmy 1927- CANR-14
Earlier sketch in CA 23-24R
Sangster, Margaret E(lizabeth) 1894-1981
Obituary 105
Sanguinetti, Elise Ayers 1926- CANR-1
Earlier sketch in CA 2R
Saniel, Josefa M. 1925- 13-14R
Sanjian, Avedis K(rikor) 1921- 33-36R
San Juan, Epifanio, Jr. 1938- CANR-10
Earlier sketch in CA 25-28R
Sankar, D(evarakonda) V(enkata) Siva
1927- 53-56
Sankey, Alice (Ann-Susan) 1910- 61-64
See also SATA 27
Sankhala, Kailash S. 1925- 101
San Martin, Marta 1942- 102
Sann, Paul 1914-1986 .... CANR-5
Obituary 120
Earlier sketch in CA 13-14R
Sannebeck, Norvelle 1909- 97-100
Sansom, Arthur B(aldwin) 1920- 112
Sansom, Clive 1910- 104
Sansom, William 1912-1976 ....7-8R
Obituary 65-68
See also CLC 2, 6
Sansone, Sam J(ohn) 1915- 115
San Souci, Robert D. 1946- 108
See also SATA 40
Sansweet, Stephen Jay 1945- 61-64
Santa Maria
See Powell-Smith, Vincent (Walter
Francis)
Santas, Joan Foster 1930- 19-20R
Santayana, George 1863-1952 Brief entry ... 115
See also DLB 54
Santee, Ross 1889(?)-1965 108
Santesson, Hans Stefan 1914(?)-1975 93-96
Obituary 57-60
See also SATA 30
Santi, Enrico Mario 1950- 116
Santiago, Danny 1911- CLC-33
Santini, Rosemarie 81-84
Santmire, H(arold) Paul 1935- 53-56
Santmyer, Helen Hooven 1895-1986 ... CANR-15
Obituary 118
Earlier sketch in CA 4R
See also DLBY 84
See also CLC 33
Santoli, Al 1949- 105
Santoni, Georges V. 1938- 103
Santoni, Ronald E(rnest) 1931- 7-8R
Santos, Bienvenido N(uqui) 1911- CANR-19
Earlier sketch in CA 101
See also CLC 22
Santos, Eduardo 1888-1974 Obituary 89-92
Santostefano, Sebastiano 1929- 41-44R
Santrey, Louis
See Sabin, Louis
Sanville, Jean 1918- 89-92
Sanwal, B(hairava) D(at) 1917- 19-20R
Saperstein, Alan 103
Saphier, Michael 1911- 25-28R
Saphire, Saul 1896(?)-1974 Obituary 53-56
Sapiets, Janis 1921-1983(?) Obituary 109
Sapieyevski, Anne Lindbergh 1940- 115
Brief entry 113
See also SATA 35
Sapinsley, Alvin 1921- CANR-21
Earlier sketch in CA 104
Sapir, Richard (Ben) 1936-1987 .... CANR-13
Obituary 121
Earlier sketch in CA 69-72
Sapori, Armando 1892- 33-36R
Saporta, Marc(el) 1923- 21-22R
Saporta, Sol 1925- 17-18R
Saposnik, Irving Seymour 1936- 97-100
Saposs, David Joseph 1886-1968 .... CANR-15
Obituary 103
Earlier sketch in CA 4R
Sapp, Phyllis Woodruff 1908- CANR-1
Earlier sketch in CA 3R
Sappington, Roger E(dwin) 1929- 15-16R
Sara
See Blake, Sally Mirliss
Sara, Dorothy 1897(?)-1976 Obituary 69-72
Sarac, Roger
See Caras, Roger A(ndrew)
Saracevic, Tefko 1930- 37-40R
Sarah, Robyn 1949- 112
Sarano, Jacques 1920- 29-32R
Sarant, P(eter) C. 1933(?)-1979 Obituary ..89-92
Sarasin, Jennifer
See Sachs, Judith
Sarason, Seymour Bernard 1919- 120
Sarasy, Phyllis Powell 1930- 13-14R
Sarat, Austin Dean 1947- 106
SarDesai, D(amodar) R. 1931- CANR-11
Earlier sketch in CA 25-28R
Sardeson, Charles T. 1921- 7-8R
Sarducci, Father Guido
See Novello, Don
Sarduy, Severo 1937- 89-92
See also CLC 6
Sarett, Alma (Johnson) 1908- CAP-2
Earlier sketch in CA 17-18
Sarett, Morton R(euben) 1916- 93-96
Sarf, Wayne M(ichael) 1957- 114
Sarg, Anthony Frederick
See Sarg, Tony
Sarg, Tony 1880-1942 .... YABC-1
Sargant, Norman 1909-1982 Obituary 107
Sargant, William (Walters) 1907- 65-68
Sargeant, Howland H(ill) 1911-1984
Obituary 112
Sargeant, Winthrop 1903-1986 ....29-32R
Obituary 120
Sargent, Alice G(oldstein) 1939- 110
Sargent, Alvin 121
Brief entry 111
Sargent, Ben 1948- 118
Brief entry 113
Sargent, Brian (Lawrence) 1927- 97-100
Sargent, Daniel 1890-1987 Obituary 121
Sargent, David R(utledge) 1920- 93-96
Sargent, Frederic O(berlin) 1919- 41-44R
Sargent, Jean Vieth 1918- 106
Sargent, John Richard 1925- 13-14R
Sargent, Lyman Tower 1940- CANR-15
Earlier sketch in CA 29-32R
Sargent, Pamela CANR-8
Earlier sketch in CA 61-64
See also SATA 29
See also DLB 8
Sargent, Ralph M(illard) 1904-1985 ....37-40R
Obituary 116
Sargent, Robert 1933- 23-24R
See also SATA 2
Sargent, Ruth (Sexton) 1920- 112
Sargent, Sarah 1937- 106
See also SATA 41, 44
Sargent, Shirley 1927- CANR-2
Earlier sketch in CA 4R
See also SATA 11
Sargent, (Francis) William (Jr.) 1946- 106
Sargent, Wyn 49-52
Sargeson, Frank 1903-1982 ....25-28R
Obituary 106
See also CLC 31
Sarhan, Samir 1941- 103
Sari
See Fleur, Anne
Saricks, Ambrose 1915- 17-18R
Sariego, Patricia Treece
See Treece, Patricia
Sariola, Sakari 1919- 41-44R
Sarjeant, William A(ntony) S(within) 1935- .. 105
Sarkar, Asoke 1911(?)-1983 Obituary 109
Sarkar, (Anvil) Kumar 1912- 37-40R
Sarkesian, Sam C(harles) 1927- 57-60
Sarlos, Robert Karoly 1931- 109
Sarma, G. V. L. N. 1925- 19-20R
Sarmiento, Felix Ruben Garcia 1867-1916
Brief entry 104
Sarna, Jonathan D(aniel) 1955- 109
Sarna, Nahum M(attathias) 1923- 19-20R
Sarnat, Marshall 1929- CANR-10
Earlier sketch in CA 21-22R
Sarndal, Carl Erik 1937- 105
Sarner, Harvey 1934- 19-20R
Sarno, Arthur D. 1921(?)-1982 Obituary ... 106
Sarno, Ronald A(nthony) 1941- CANR-12
Earlier sketch in CA 29-32R
Sarnoff, David 1891-1971 Obituary 113
Sarnoff, Dorothy 1917- 33-36R
Sarnoff, Irving 1922- CANR-8
Earlier sketch in CA 19-20R
Sarnoff, Jane 1937- CANR-9
Earlier sketch in CA 53-56
See also SATA 10
Sarnoff, Paul 1918- CANR-18
Earlier sketches in CA 7-8R, CANR-2
Sarnoff, Suzanne 1928- 97-100
Saroyan, Aram 1943- 21-22R
See also CAAS 5
Saroyan, Arshalyus 1923-1974 Obituary ...53-56
Saroyan, William 1908-1981 ....7-8R
Obituary 103
See also SATA 23, 24
See also DLB 7, 9
See also DLBY 81
See also CLC 1, 8, 10, 29, 34
Sarrantonio, Al 1952- 120
Sarratt, Reed 1918(?)-1986 Obituary 118
Sarraute, Nathalie 1900- CANR-23
Earlier sketch in CA 9-10R
See also CLC 1, 2, 4, 8, 10, 31
Sarre, Winifred Turner 1931- 29-32R
Sarri, Rosemary C(onzemius) 1926- 111
Sarris, Andrew 1928- 21-22R
Sarsfield, C. P.
See Marshner, Connaught Coyne
Sartain, Aaron Quinn 1905- 4R
Sarti, Roland 1937- 37-40R
Sarto, Ben
See Fawcett, F(rank) Dubrez
Sarton, (Eleanor) May 1912- CANR-1
Earlier sketch in CA 4R
See also SATA 36
See also DLB 48
See also DLBY 81
See also CLC 4, 14
Sartori, Giovanni 1924- CANR-17
Earlier sketches in CA 7-8R, CANR-2
Sartre, Jean-Paul 1905-1980 .... CANR-21
Obituary 97-100
Earlier sketch in CA 9-10R
See also CLC 1, 4, 7, 9, 13, 18, 24, 44
Sarvepalli, Gopal 1923- 81-84
Sarver, Hannah
See Nielsen, Jean Sarver
Sasaki, Tazu 1932- CANR-10
Earlier sketch in CA 25-28R
Sasek, Lawrence A(nton) 1923- CANR-1
Earlier sketch in CA 1R
Sasek, Miroslav 1916-1980 73-76
Obituary 101
See also SATA 16, 23
See also CLR 4
Saslow, Helen 1926- 105
Sasnett, Martena T(enney) 1908- 53-56
Saso, Michael R. 1930- 112
Sass, Lorna Janet 1945- 102
Sass, Steven A(rthur) 1949- 116
Sasser, Charles W(ayne) 1942- 122
Sassoon, Beverly Adams 65-68
Sassoon, Rosemary 1931- 118
Sassoon, Siegfried (Lorraine) 1886-1967 ... 104
Obituary 25-28R
See also DLB 20
See also CLC 36
Sassoon, Vidal 1928- CANR-15
Earlier sketch in CA 65-68
Sasuly, Richard 1913- 109
Satchidananda, Swami
See Dharmi, Santana
Satchwell, John SATA-49
Sater, William F(rederick) 1937- 118
Sather, Julia Coley Duncan 1940- 103
Satin, Joseph 1922- 11-12R
Satin, Mark 1946- 41-44R
Satiricus
See Roetter, Charles Frederick
Sato, Esther Masako Tateishi 1915- 108
Satprem 1923- CANR-15
Earlier sketch in CA 85-88
Satran, Pamela Redmond 1953- 110
Satterfield, Archie 1933- CANR-14
Earlier sketch in CA 57-60
Satterfield, Charles
See del Rey, Lester
and Pohl, Frederik
Satterlund, Donald R(obert) 1928- 53-56
Satterly, Weston
See Sunners, William
Sattler, Helen Roney 1921- CANR-14
Earlier sketch in CA 33-36R
See also SATA 4
Sattler, Henry V(ernon) 1917- CANR-7
Earlier sketch in CA 5-6R
Sattler, Jerome M(urray) 1931- 49-52
Sattler, Warren 1934- 65-68
Sattley, Helen R(owland) 2R
Satz, Paul 1932- 61-64
Satz, Ronald Norman 1944- CANR-8
Earlier sketch in CA 61-64
Saucy, Robert L(loyd) 1930- 123
Brief entry 118
Sauer, Carl Ortwin 1889-1975 .... CANR-9
Earlier sketch in CA 61-64
Sauer, Julia Lina 1891-1983 81-84
See also SATA 32, 36
Sauer, Muriel Stafford 13-14R
Sauer, Val John, Jr. 1938- 107
Sauerhaft, Stan 1926- 85-88
Sauerlaender, Willibald 1924- 118
Sauerlander, Willibald
See Sauerlaender, Willibald
Sauers, Richard James 1930- 53-56
Sauers, Wendy 1958- 116
Saul, George Brandon 1901-1986 .... CANR-6
Obituary 120
Earlier sketch in CA 13-14R
Saul, John (W. III) 1942- CANR-16
Earlier sketch in CA 81-84
See also CLC 46
Saul, Leon J(oseph) 1901- CANR-10
Earlier sketch in CA 21-22R
Saul, Mary 105
Saul, Nigel Edward 1952- 117
Saul, Norman E(ugene) 1932- 53-56
Saul, Oscar
See Halpern, Oscar Saul
Saul, (Ellen) Wendy 1946- 114
See also SATA 42
Saulnier, Raymond Joseph 1908- 7-8R
Sauls, Roger 1944- 33-36R
Saunders, Allen 1899-1986 69-72
Obituary 118
Saunders, Ann Loreille 1930- 103
Saunders, Aretas (Andrews) 1884- CAP-1
Earlier sketch in CA 11-12
Saunders, B(ernard) C(harles) 1903-1983
Obituary 115
Saunders, Beatrice 49-52
Saunders, Blanche 1906- CAP-1
Earlier sketch in CA 13-14
Saunders, Caleb
See Heinlein, Robert A(nson)
Saunders, Carl Maxon 1890-1974
Obituary 89-92
Saunders, Charles B(askerville), Jr.
1928- 61-64
Saunders, Christopher T(homas) 1907- 119
Saunders, David
See Sontup, Dan(iel)
Saunders, Doris E(vans) 1921- 77-80
Saunders, E. Dale 1919- 5-6R
Saunders, Ernest 1901(?)-1983 Obituary ... 109
Saunders, Helen E(lizabeth) 1912- 25-28R
Saunders, Hilary Aidan St. George
1898-1951 Brief entry 121
Saunders, Ione
See Cole, Margaret Alice
Saunders, J(ohn) W(hiteside) 1920- 116
Saunders, James (Arthur) 1925- DLB-13
Saunders, James (Arthur) 1925-
Brief entry 124
Saunders, Jason Lewis 1922- Brief entry ... 106
Saunders, Jean 1932- CANR-19
Earlier sketch in CA 102
Saunders, John Monk 1897-1940 .... DLB-26
Saunders, John Turk 1929-1974 .... CAP-2
Earlier sketch in CA 21-22
Saunders, Keith 1910- 57-60
See also SATA 12
Saunders, Peter 1950- 114
Saunders, Richard 1947- CANR-21
Earlier sketch in CA 105

Saunders, Roy 1911- ... CAP-1
Earlier sketch in CA 11-12
Saunders, Rubie (Agnes) 1929- ... 49-52
See also SATA 21
Saunders, Susan 1945- ... 106
See also SATA 41, 46
Saunders, Thomas 1909- ... CANR-12
Earlier sketch in CA 73-76
Saura, Carlos 1932- Brief entry ... 114
See also CLC 20
Sauro, Regina Calderone 1924- ... 11-12R
Sause, George G(abriel) 1919- ... 41-44R
Sauser-Hall, Frederic 1887-1961 ... 102
Obituary ... 93-96
See also CLC 18
Saussure, Eric de
See de Saussure, Eric
Sautel, Maureen Ann 1951- ... 61-64
Sauter, Edwin Charles Scott, Jr. 1930- ... 15-16R
Sauter, Eric 1948- ... 117
Sauter, Van Gordon 1935- ... 73-76
Sauvage, Franck
See Horn, Maurice
Sauvage, Roger 1917-1977 Obituary ... 73-76
Sauvageau, Juan 1917- ... CANR-11
Earlier sketch in CA 65-68
Sauvain, Philip Arthur 1933- ... CANR-21
Earlier sketch in CA 104
Sauvant, Karl P(eter) 1944- ... 77-80
Sauvy, Jean (Maurice Paul) 1916- ... 65-68
Sauvy, Simonne 1922- ... 65-68
Sava, George
See Milkomane, George Alexis Milkomanovich
Savacool, John K(enneth) 1917- ... 45-48
Savage, Blake
See Goodwin, Harold Leland
Savage, Brian 1933- ... 41-44R
Savage, Candace (M.) 1949- ... 123
Savage, Catharine
See Brosman, Catharine Savage
Savage, Charles 1918- ... 53-56
Savage, Christina
See Newcomb, Kerry
and Schaefer, Frank
Savage, Christopher I(vor) 1924-1969 ... CANR-6
Earlier sketch in CA 7-8R
Savage, D(ouglas) J(oseph) 1950- ... 118
Savage, D(erek) S(tanley) 1917- ... 104
Savage, Elizabeth Fitzgerald 1918- ... CANR-1
Earlier sketch in CA 3R
Savage, Ernest 1918- ... 112
Savage, Frances Higginson (Fuller) 1898- . CAP-1
Earlier sketch in CA 19-20
Savage, (Leonard) George (Gimson) 1909- ... CANR-5
Earlier sketch in CA 11-12R
Savage, Helen 1915- ... 97-100
Savage, Henry, Jr. 1903- ... CAP-2
Earlier sketch in CA 25-28
Savage, James 1784-1873 ... DLB-30
Savage, James F(rancis) 1939- ... 73-76
Savage, Joseph P. 1895(?)-1977
Obituary ... 69-72
Savage, Katharine James 1905- ... 15-16R
Savage, Lee 1928- ... 101
Savage, Leonard J(immie) 1917-1971 ... CAP-2
Obituary ... 33-36R
Earlier sketch in CA 17-18
Savage, Marc 1945- ... 65-68
Savage, Marmion 1803(?)-1872 ... DLB-21
Savage, Michael D(onald) 1946- ... 101
Savage, Mildred (Spitz) 1919- ... 11-12R
Savage, Minot Judson 1841-1918
Brief entry ... 115
Savage, Robert L(ynn) 1939- ... 109
Savage, Roth
See Kehrer, Daniel M(ark)
Savage, Teresa 1950- ... 113
Savage, Thomas 1915- ... CLC-40
Savage, Thomas Gerard 1926- ... 49-52
Savage, W(illiam) Sherman 1890- ... 69-72
Savage, William W(oodrow) 1914- ... 37-40R
Savage, William W(oodrow), Jr. 1943- ... 57-60
Savain, Petion ?-1973 Obituary ... 41-44R
Savan, Bruce (Sheldon) 1927-1987 ... 5-6R
Obituary ... 122
Savarese, Julia ... 37-40R
Savarin
See Courtine, Robert
Savary, Louis M(ichael) 1936- ... CANR-24
Earlier sketches in CA 23-24R, CANR-9
Savas, E(manuel) S(tephen) 1931- ... 17-18R
Saveland, Robert N(elson) 1921- ... 41-44R
Savell, Don P(atrick) 1939- ... 119
Savelle, Max(well) 1896- ... 21-22R
Savery, Constance (Winifred) 1897- ... CANR-7
Earlier sketch in CA 11-12R
See also SATA 1
Savery, Ranald 1903(?)-1974 Obituary ... 104
Saveson, John E(dward) 1923- ... 41-44R
Saveth, Edward N(orman) 1915- ... 21-22R
Saville, Eugenia (Curtis) 1913- ... 41-44R
Saville, Lloyd (Blackstone) 1913- ... 21-22R
Saville, (Leonard) Malcolm 1901-1982 ... 101
Obituary ... 107
See also SATA 23, 31
Savin, Marc 1948- ... 106
Saviozzi, Adriana
See Mazza, Adriana
Savitch, Jessica 1948-1983 ... 108
Obituary ... 110
Savitt, Ronald 1939- ... 33-36R
Savitt, Sam ... CANR-17
Earlier sketches in CA 4R, CANR-1
See also SATA 8
Savitt, Todd Lee 1943- ... 102
Savitz, Harriet May 1933- ... CANR-14
Earlier sketch in CA 41-44R
See also SATA 5
Savitz, Leonard D. 1926- ... CANR-8
Earlier sketch in CA 23-24R
Savoie, Donald J(oseph) 1947- ... 112
Savoie, Paul 1946- ... 113
Savory, Alan Forsyth 1905- ... 11-12R
Savory, Hubert Newman 1911- ... CANR-10
Earlier sketch in CA 25-28R
Savory, Jerold 1933- ... CANR-10
Earlier sketch in CA 25-28R
Savory, Teo ... 29-32R
Savory, Theodore Horace 1896-1980 ... CANR-6
Earlier sketch in CA 5-6R
Savours, Ann (Margaret) 1927- ... 57-60
Savoy, Mark
See Turner, Robert H(arry)
Sawai, Gloria Ostrem ... 113
Saward, Michael 1932- ... 97-100
Sawatsky, Harry Leonard 1931- ... 89-92
Sawer, Geoffrey 1910- ... 19-20R
Sawey, Orlan (Lester) 1920- ... CANR-12
Earlier sketch in CA 29-32R
Sawicki, Marianne 1950- ... 114
Sawin, Martica 1927- ... 124
Sawkins, Raymond H(arold) 1923- ... 103
Sawyer, Albert E(rnest) 1898- ... 7-8R
Sawyer, Charles 1887-1979 ... CAP-2
Obituary ... 85-88
Earlier sketch in CA 25-28
Sawyer, Corinne Holt ... 17-18R
Sawyer, Diane K. 1946(?)- ... 115
Brief entry ... 109
Sawyer, Jack 1931- ... 61-64
Sawyer, Jesse O. 1918- ... 17-18R
Sawyer, John
See Foley, (Cedric) John
Sawyer, Mark
See Greenhood, (Clarence) David
Sawyer, P(eter) H(ayes) 1928- ... CANR-6
Earlier sketch in CA 11-12R
Sawyer, R(obert) McLaran 1929- ... 45-48
Sawyer, Ralph Alanson 1895-1978
Obituary ... 81-84
Sawyer, Roger 1931- ... 123
Sawyer, Ruth 1880-1970 ... 73-76
See also SATA 17
See also DLB 22
Sawyer, W(alter) W(arwick) 1911- ... 53-56
Sawyer-Laucanno, Christopher 1951- ... 114
Sawyerr, Harry (Alphonso Ebun) 1909-1986 ... 37-40R
Obituary ... 120
Sax, Gilbert 1930- ... 23-24R
Sax, Joseph L. 1936- ... 33-36R
Sax, Karl 1892-1973 Obituary ... 45-48
Sax, Saville 1924- ... 97-100
Saxberg, Borje O(svald) 1928- ... 41-44R
Saxe, Isobel
See Rayner, Claire (Berenice)
Saxe, Richard W(arren) 1923- ... 49-52
Saxe, Thomas E., Jr. 1903-1975
Obituary ... 61-64
Saxon, A(rthur) H(artley) 1935- ... CANR-16
Earlier sketch in CA 25-28R
Saxon, Alex
See Pronzini, Bill
Saxon, Antonia
See Sachs, Judith
Saxon, Bill
See Wallmann, Jeffrey M(iner)
Saxon, Charles D(avid) 1920- Brief entry ... 118
Saxon, Gladys Relyea ... 7-8R
Saxon, John
See Rumbold-Gibbs, Henry St. John Clair
Saxon, Lyle 1891-1946 Brief entry ... 119
Saxon, Van
See Granbeck, Marilyn
Saxon, William
See Mayleas, William
Saxton, Alexander P(laisted) 1919- ... 105
Saxton, Josephine (Mary) 1935- ... 29-32R
Saxton, Judith 1936- ... 105
Saxton, Lloyd 1919- ... 29-32R
Saxton, Mark 1914-1988 ... 93-96
Obituary ... 124
Saxton, Martha 1945- ... 81-84
Say, Allen 1937- ... 29-32R
See also SATA 28
Saya, Peter
See Peterson, Robert E(ugene)
Sayce, Richard Anthony 1917- ... 61-64
Saydah, J. Roger 1939-1976 ... 25-28R
Obituary ... 120
Saye, Albert B(erry) 1912- ... CANR-5
Earlier sketch in CA 7-8R
Sayeed, Khalid B. 1926- ... 25-28R
Sayegh, Fayez A(bdullah) 1922-1980 ... 11-12R
Obituary ... 102
Sayer, Angela 1935- ... 89-92
Sayers, Dorothy L(eigh) 1893-1957 ... 119
Brief entry ... 104
See also DLB 10, 36
See also TCLC 2, 15
Sayers, Frances Clarke 1897- ... 19-20R
See also SATA 3
Sayers, Gale 1943- ... 73-76
Sayers, Peig 1873-1958 Brief entry ... 113
Sayers, Raymond S. 1912- ... CANR-10
Earlier sketch in CA 25-28R
Sayles, E(dwin) B(ooth) 1892- ... CAP-2
Earlier sketch in CA 25-28
Sayles, George O(sborne) 1901- ... CANR-4
Earlier sketch in CA 53-56
Sayles, John Thomas 1950- ... 57-60
See also DLB 44
See also CLC 7, 10, 14
Sayles, Leonard Robert 1926- ... CANR-1
Earlier sketch in CA 3R
Sayles, Nettie Leitch Major 1903(?)-1984
Obituary ... 113
Sayles, Ted
See Sayles, E(dwin) B(ooth)
Saylor, David J(onathan) 1945- ... 89-92
Saylor, Irene 1932- ... 33-36R
Saylor, J(ohn) Galen 1902- ... CANR-9
Earlier sketch in CA 19-20R
Saylor, Neville 1922- ... 61-64
Sayre, Anne 1923- ... 61-64
Sayre, Eleanor Axson 1916- ... 25-28R
Sayre, Henry M(arshall) 1948- ... 119
Sayre, J(ohn) Woodrow 1913- ... CANR-5
Earlier sketch in CA 11-12R
Sayre, Joel 1900-1979 Obituary ... 89-92
Sayre, John L(eslie) 1924- ... 53-56
Sayre, Kenneth Malcolm 1928- ... CANR-3
Earlier sketch in CA 11-12R
Sayre, Leslie C. 1907- ... CAP-1
Earlier sketch in CA 11-12
Sayre, Nora 1932- ... 118
Sayre, Robert F(reeman) 1933- ... 11-12R
Sayre, Wallace S. 1905-1972 Obituary ... 33-36R
Sayres, Alfred Nevin 1893-19(?) ... CAP-1
Earlier sketch in CA 17-18
Sayres, William C(ortlandt) 1927- ... 17-18R
Sayrs, Henry John 1904- ... 7-8R
Saywell, John T(upper) 1929- ... 13-14R
Sazer, Nina 1949- ... 69-72
See also SATA 13
Scabrini, Janet 1953- ... SATA-13
Scacco, Anthony M., Jr. 1939- ... 109
Scaduto, Anthony ... 104
Scaduto, Tony
See Scaduto, Anthony
Scaer, David P(aul) 1936- ... CANR-12
Earlier sketch in CA 33-36R
Scaglione, Aldo D(omenico) 1925- ... CANR-21
Earlier sketches in CA 13-14R, CANR-6
Scaglione, Cecil F(rank) 1934- ... 81-84
Scagnetti, Jack 1924- ... CANR-4
Earlier sketch in CA 49-52
See also SATA 7
Scala, James 1934- ... 124
Scalapino, Leslie 1947- ... 123
Scalapino, Robert A(nthony) 1919- ... CANR-18
Earlier sketches in CA 1R, CANR-2
Scales, James Ralph 1919- ... 120
Scales, Pat(sy) R. 1944- ... 122
Scali, John (Alfred) 1918- ... 65-68
Scally, M. A.
See Scally, Sister (Mary) Anthony
Scally, Robert James 1937- ... 61-64
Scally, Sister (Mary) Anthony 1905- ... 110
Scally, Sister Mary Anthony
See Scally, Sister (Mary) Anthony
Scalzo, Joe 1941- ... 49-52
Scamehorn, H(oward) Lee 1926- ... 69-72
Scammell, Michael ... CLC-34
Scammell, William McConnell 1920- ... CANR-6
Earlier sketch in CA 7-8R
Scammon, John H(umphrey) 1905- ... 53-56
Scammon, Richard M(ontgomery) 1915- ... 61-64
Scandura, Joseph M(ichael) 1931- ... CANR-5
Earlier sketch in CA 53-56
Scanlan, James P(atrick) 1927- ... 11-12R
Scanlan, Michael 1931- ... CANR-23
Earlier sketches in CA 57-60, CANR-7
Scanlan, Patrick F. 1895(?)-1983
Obituary ... 109
Scanlan, Thomas J. 1934- ... 114
Scanlon, David G. 1921- ... 15-16R
Scanlon, Kathryn I(da) 1909- ... CAP-1
Earlier sketch in CA 11-12
Scanlon, Marion Stephany ... 7-8R
See also SATA 11
Scannell, Vernon 1922- ... CANR-24
Earlier sketches in CA 7-8R, CANR-8
See also DLB 27
Scanzoni, John H. 1935- ... CANR-24
Earlier sketches in CA 23-24R, CANR-9
Scanzoni, Letha Dawson 1935- ... CANR-14
Earlier sketch in CA 57-60
Scarborough, Alma May C. 1913- ... 5-6R
Scarborough, Elizabeth (Ann) 1947- ... 120
Scarborough, John 1940- ... CANR-15
Earlier sketch in CA 41-44R
Scarborough, Ruth 1904- ... 115
Scarborough, William Kauffman 1933- ... 19-20R
Scarbrough, George (Addison) 1915- ... CANR-16
Earlier sketch in CA 77-80
Scardino, Albert 1948- Brief entry ... 119
Scaretti, Marjorie ?-1982 Obituary ... 107
Scarf, Maggi
See Scarf, Maggie
Scarf, Maggie 1932- ... CANR-22
Earlier sketch in CA 29-32R
See also SATA 5
Scarfe, Allan (John) 1931- ... CANR-13
Earlier sketch in CA 25-28R
Scarfe, Francis Harold 1911-1986
Obituary ... 118
Scarfe, Wendy (Elizabeth) 1933- ... CANR-13
Earlier sketch in CA 25-28R
Scargall, Jeanne Anna 1928- ... 93-96
Scargill, (David) Ian 1935- ... CANR-12
Earlier sketch in CA 61-64
Scarisbrick, J(ohn) J(oseph) 1928- ... CANR-18
Earlier sketch in CA 25-28R
Scarlett, Roger
See Page, Evelyn
Scarlett, Susan
See Streatfeild, (Mary) Noel
Scarne, John 1903-1985 Obituary ... 116
Scarpitti, Frank R(oland) 1936- ... CANR-14
Earlier sketch in CA 41-44R
Scarr, Dee 1948- ... 122
Scarrott, Michael
See Fisher, A(rthur) Stanley T(heodore)
Scarrow, Howard A(lbert) 1928- ... 110
Scarry, Huck
See Scarry, Richard, Jr.
Scarry, Patricia (Murphy) 1924- ... 19-20R
See also SATA 2
Scarry, Patsy
See Scarry, Patricia (Murphy)
Scarry, Richard (McClure) 1919- ... CANR-18
Earlier sketch in CA 19-20R
See also SATA 2, 35
See also DLB 61
See also CLR 3
Scarry, Richard, Jr. 1953- ... SATA-35
Scavullo, Francesco 1929- ... 102
Schaaf, C(arl) Hart 1912- ... 7-8R
Schaaf, Martha Eckert 1911- ... CANR-1
Earlier sketch in CA 4R
Schaaf, Peter 1942- ... 106
Schaafsma, Polly 1935- ... 57-60
Schaal, John H. 1908- ... 73-76
Schaap, Dick
See Schaap, Richard J(ay)
Schaap, James C(alvin) 1948- ... 118
Schaap, Richard J(ay) 1934- ... CANR-5
Earlier sketch in CA 11-12R
Schaar, John H(omer) 1928- ... 3R
Schaarwaechter, Georg 1929- ... 25-28R
Schabert, Kyrill S. 1909(?)-1983 Obituary ... 109
Schachner, Nat(han) 1895-1955
Brief entry ... 120
Schacht, Al(exander) 1894(?)-1984
Obituary ... 113
Schacht, Hjalmar (Horace Greeley) 1877-1970 Obituary ... 113
Schacht, Richard (Lawrence) 1941- ... 29-32R
Schachtel, Ernest G(eorge) 1903-1975 ... 37-40R
Schachtel, Hyman Judah 1907- ... 49-52
Schachtel, Roger (Bernard) 1949- ... 106
See also SATA 38
Schachter, Gustav 1926- ... 17-18R
Schachter, Michael 1941- ... 102
Schachter, Oscar 1915- ... 65-68
Schachter, Stanley 1922- ... 37-40R
Schachterle, Nancy (Lange) 1925- ... 101
Schachtman, Max 1903-1972 Obituary ... 37-40R
Schackne, Stewart 1905-1975 Obituary ... 61-64
Schad, Jasper G(ripper) 1932- ... 110
Schad, Wilhelm
See Reichert, Herbert W(illiam)
Schaechter, Mordkhe 1927- ... 41-44R
Schaedel, Richard P. 1920- ... 45-48
Schaef, Anne Wilson 1934- ... 118
Schaefer, Charles E. 1933- ... 37-40R
Schaefer, Claude 1913- ... 33-36R
Schaefer, Frank 1936- ... CANR-10
Earlier sketch in CA 65-68
Schaefer, Jack Warner 1907- ... CANR-15
Earlier sketches in CA 11-12, CAP-1
See also SATA 3
Schaefer, John H(arrison) 1937- ... 57-60
Schaefer, Josephine O'Brien 1929- ... 37-40R
Schaefer, Leah Cahan 1920- ... 49-52
Schaefer, Nicola Caroline 1939- ... 104
Schaefer, Ted 1939- ... 77-80
Schaefer, Vincent J(oseph) 1906- ... 120
Schaefer, Walter Erich 1901-1982(?)
Obituary ... 106
Schaeffer, Albrecht 1885-1950 ... DLB-66
Schaeffer, Claude Frederic Armand 1898-1982 Obituary ... 108
Schaeffer, Edith (Seville) 1914- ... 77-80
Schaeffer, Elizabeth 1939- ... 45-48
Schaeffer, Francis A(ugust) 1912-1984 ... 77-80
Obituary ... 112
Schaeffer, K(laus) H(eymann) 1921- ... 61-64
Schaeffer, Mead 1898- ... SATA-21
Schaeffer, Neil 1940- ... 107
Schaeffer, Norma 1924-1985 ... 119
Schaeffer, Susan Fromberg 1941- ... CANR-18
Earlier sketch in CA 49-52
See also SATA 22
See also DLB 28
See also CLC 6, 11
Schaeffer-Forrer, Claude F. A.
See Schaeffer, Claude Frederic Armand
Schaeling, Marianne
See Amft, M(arian) J(anet)
Schaeper, Thomas J(erome) 1948- ... 109
Schaeren, Beatrix 1941- ... 29-32R
Schaetzel, J(oseph) Robert 1917- ... 65-68
Schafer, Charles (Louis) 1916- ... 61-64
Schafer, Edward Hetzel 1913- ... CANR-1
Earlier sketch in CA 1R
Schafer, Grant C. 1926- ... 23-24R
Schafer, R(aymond) Murray 1933- ... 77-80
Schafer, Robert 1942- ... 108
Schafer, Stephen 1911-1976 ... 37-40R
Schafer, Violet (Christine) 1910- ... 61-64
Schafer, William J. 1937- ... 49-52
Schaff, Adam 1913- ... CANR-12
Earlier sketch in CA 25-28R
Schaff, David 1943- ... 33-36R
Schaffer, (Benjamin) Bernard 1925-1984
Obituary ... 113
Schaffer, Daniel 1950- ... 114
Schaffer, Frank 1910- ... 103
Schaffer, Jeff(rey P.) 1943- ... CANR-22
Earlier sketch in CA 105
Schaffer, Lewis A(dam) 1934- ... 101

Schaffer, Marion 1931- ... 111
Schaffer, Ulrich 1942- ... 69-72
Schaffner, Cynthia V. A. 1947- ... 121
Schaffner, Kenneth 1939- ... 45-48
Schaffner, Nicholas 1953- ... CANR-15
Earlier sketch in CA 85-88
Schaffner, Val(entine) 1951- ... 107
Schaflander, Gerald M(aurice) 1920- ... 37-40R
Schagrin, Morton L(ouis) 1930- ... 25-28R
Schaie, K(laus) Warner 1928- ... CANR-15
Earlier sketch in CA 41-44R
Schakne, Robert 1926- ... 65-68
Schakovskoy, Zinaida 1908- ... CANR-8
Earlier sketch in CA 17-18R
Schaldenbrand, Mary 1922- ... 49-52
Schaleben, Arville Orman 1907- ... CANR-1
Earlier sketch in CA 3R
Schalk, Adolph F(rancis) 1923- ... 33-36R
Schalk, David L(ouis) 1936- ... 89-92
Schall, James V(incent) 1928- ... CANR-20
Earlier sketches in CA 11-12R, CANR-6
Schaller, George B(eals) 1933- ... CANR-9
Earlier sketch in CA 7-8R
See also SATA 30
Schaller, Michael 1947- Brief entry ... 110
Schalm, Bernard 1928-1974 ... 3R
Obituary ... 103
Scham, Alan (Myron) 1937- ... 29-32R
Schama, Simon Michael 1945- ... 105
Schanberg, Sydney H(illel) 1934- ... 69-72
Schanche, Don A. 1926- ... CANR-6
Earlier sketch in CA 5-6R
Schandler, Herbert Y(ale) 1928- ... 69-72
Schang, Frederick C. 1893- ... CANR-13
Earlier sketch in CA 33-36R
Schanz, John P(hilip) 1924- ... 107
Schanzer, George O(swald) 1914- ... 41-44R
Schapiro, J(acob) Salwyn 1879-1973 ... CANR-5
Obituary ... 45-48
Earlier sketch in CA 7-8R
Schapiro, Leonard (Bertram)
1908-1983 ... CANR-13
Obituary ... 111
Earlier sketch in CA 65-68
Schapiro, Meyer 1904- ... 97-100
Schapper, Beatrice Aronson 1906-1974 ... 11-12R
Obituary ... 45-48
Schappes, Morris U(rman) 1907- ... 49-52
Schapsmeier, Edward L(ewis) 1927- ... 29-32R
Schapsmeier, Frederick H(erman) 1927- ... 29-32R
Schara, Ron 1942- ... 69-72
Scharbach, (John) Alexander 1909- ... 114
Scharbach, J. Alexander
See Scharbach, (John) Alexander
Scharf, Bertram 1931- ... 53-56
Scharf, J. Thomas 1843-1898 ... DLB-47
Scharfenberg, Doris 1925- ... 108
Scharff, Edward E. 1946- ... 123
Scharfstein, Ben-Ami 1919- ... 101
Scharfstein, Zevi 1884-1972 Obituary ... 37-40R
Scharine, Richard (G.) 1938- Brief entry ... 118
Scharine, Richard G. 1938- ... 123
Scharlatt, Hal 1936(?)-1974 Obituary ... 104
Scharlemann, Dorothy Hoyer 1912- ... 65-68
Scharlemann, Martin H(enry) 1910- ... 15-16R
Scharlemann, Robert Paul 1929- ... 11-12R
Scharnhorst, Gary (Francis) 1950- ... 119
Scharper, Phillip (Jenkins) 1919-1985 ... 73-76
Obituary ... 116
Schary, Dore 1905-1980 ... CANR-1
Obituary ... 101
Earlier sketch in CA 3R
Schary, Jill
See Robinson, Jill
Schatell, Brian ... 124
See also SATA 47
Schatkin, Margaret 1944- ... 118
Schatkin, Sidney B. 1903- ... 25-28R
Schatt, Stanley 1943- ... 69-72
Schatten, Fritz (Max Robert) 1930- ... 15-16R
Schatten, Robert 1911-1977 Obituary ... 73-76
Schatz, Mark N(orton) 1929- ... 113
Schatz, Sayre P(erry) 1922- ... 41-44R
Schatzki, Walter 1899- ... SATA-31
Schau, Michael 1945- ... 85-88
Schaub, Marilyn McNamara 1928- ... 19-20R
Schaub, Thomas Hill 1947- ... 105
Schauer, Frederick Franklin 1946- ... 112
Schauf, George Edward 1925- ... 41-44R
Schaufele, William E., Jr. 1923- ... 111
Scheader, Catherine 1932- ... 85-88
Schealer, John M(ilton) 1920- ... 5-6R
Schechner, Richard 1934- ... CANR-17
Earlier sketches in CA 45-48, CANR-1
Schechter, Alan H(enry) 1936- ... 11-12R
Schechter, Betty (Goodstein) 1921- ... 7-8R
See also SATA 5
Schechter, Harold 1948- ... 108
Schechter, Ruth Lisa 1927- ... 33-36R
Schechter, William 1934- ... 23-24R
Schechtman, Joseph B. 1891-1970 ... CANR-3
Earlier sketch in CA 4R
Schecter, Jerrold L. 1932- ... 23-24R
Scheel, J(oergen) D(itlev) 1918- ... 11-12R
Scheele, Adele M. 1938- ... CANR-18
Earlier sketch in CA 97-100
Scheele, Carl H(arry) 1928- ... 85-88
Scheer, George F(abian) 1917- ... 15-16R
Scheer, Julian (Weisel) 1926- ... 49-52
See also SATA 8
Scheer, Robert 1936- ... 106
Scheer, Wilbert E. 1909- ... CANR-17
Earlier sketch in CA 25-28R
Scheff, Thomas Joel 1929- ... 105
Scheffer, Nathalie P. 1890(?)-1981
Obituary ... 105
Scheffer, Victor B(lanchard) 1906- ... CANR-11
Earlier sketch in CA 29-32R
See also SATA 6
Scheffler, Harold W(alter) 1932- ... 19-20R
Scheffler, Israel 1923- ... CANR-1
Earlier sketch in CA 1R
Scheflen, Albert E. 1920-1980 ... CANR-3
Obituary ... 101
Earlier sketch in CA 45-48
Schefter, Jim 1940- ... 89-92
Scheibe, Karl E(dward) 1937- ... CANR-11
Earlier sketch in CA 29-32R
Scheiber, Harry N(oel) 1935- ... CANR-1
Earlier sketch in CA 3R
Scheiber, Jane L(ang) 1937- ... 93-96
Scheibla, Shirley 1919- ... 41-44R
Scheick, William J(oseph) 1941- ... CANR-17
Earlier sketches in CA 49-52, CANR-1
Scheid, Francis J(ames) 1920- ... 17-18R
Scheidler, Joseph M. 1927- ... 122
Scheier, Ivan Henry 1926- ... CANR-7
Earlier sketch in CA 5-6R
Scheier, Michael 1943- ... 115
See also SATA 36, 40
Scheimann, Eugene 1897- ... 33-36R
Schein, Clarence J(acob) 1918- ... 65-68
Schein, James Arns 1920(?)-1983
Obituary ... 110
Schein, Jerome D(aniel) 1923- ... 118
Scheiner, Seth M(ordecai) 1933- ... 17-18R
Scheinfeld, Aaron 1899-1970 ... CAP-2
Earlier sketch in CA 29-32
Scheinfeld, Amram 1897-1979 ... 17-18R
Obituary ... 89-92
Scheingold, Stuart A(llen) 1931- ... 53-56
Scheleen, Joseph C(arl) 1904-1985
Obituary ... 116
Schell, Bunny
See Schell, Rolfe F(inch)
Schell, Edgar T(homas) 1931- ... 45-48
Schell, Herbert S(amuel) 1899- ... CANR-21
Earlier sketch in CA 2R
Schell, Jonathan 1943- ... CANR-12
Earlier sketch in CA 73-76
See also CLC 35
Schell, Maximilian 1930- Brief entry ... 116
Schell, Mildred 1922- ... 113
See also SATA 41
Schell, Orville H. 1940- ... 25-28R
See also SATA 10
Schell, Rolfe F(inch) 1916- ... CANR-7
Earlier sketch in CA 57-60
Schellenberg, Helene Chambers ... 13-14R
Schellenberg, James A. 1932- ... 37-40R
Schellenberg, Theodore R. 1903-19(?) ... CAP-1
Earlier sketch in CA 17-18
Schellie, Don 1932- ... 101
See also SATA 29
Schelling, Thomas Crombie 1921- ... 1R
Schelly, William 1951- ... 114
Schemering, (Crien) Christopher 1956- ... 123
Schemm, Mildred Walker 1905- ... CANR-1
Earlier sketch in CA 3R
See also SATA 21
Schemmer, Benjamin Franklin 1932- ... 61-64
Schemmer, Kenneth E(dwin) 1936- ... 110
Schenck, Anita A(llen) 1909- ... 89-92
Schenck, Janet Daniels 1883(?)-1976
Obituary ... 69-72
Schendler, Sylvan 1925- ... 25-28R
Schenk, H(ans) G(eorg) 1912- ... 23-24R
Schenken, Howard 1904(?)-1979 ... 93-96
Obituary ... 85-88
Schenker, Alexander M(arian) 1924- ... 33-36R
Schenker, Eric 1931- ... 37-40R
Scheper, Nancy
See Scheper-Hughes, Nancy
Scheper-Hughes, Nancy 1944- ... 89-92
Schepers, Maurice B. 1928- ... 13-14R
Scheps, Clarence 1915- ... 33-36R
Scher, Helene L(enz) 1935- ... 123
Scher, Helene Lenz 1935- Brief entry ... 118
Scher, Les 1946- ... 101
Scher, Paula 1948- ... 115
See also SATA 47
Scher, Steven Paul 1936- ... CANR-3
Earlier sketch in CA 49-52
Schere, Monroe 1913- ... 85-88
Scherer, F(rederic) M(ichael) 1932- ... CANR-12
Earlier sketch in CA 29-32R
Scherer, Frances Schlosser 1912- ... 69-72
Scherer, Jack F(ranklin) 1939- ... 69-72
Scherer, Jacqueline Rita 1931- ... 53-56
Scherer, Jean-Marie Maurice 1920- ... 110
Scherer, Joanna Cohan 1942- ... 107
Scherer, Klaus R(ainer) 1943- ... 101
Scherer, Paul (Ehrman) 1892- ... 5-6R
Scherer, Priscilla 1948- ... 119
Scherer, Raymond Lewis 1919- ... 104
Scherer, William F(rederick) 1939- ... 41-44R
Scherf, Margaret 1908-1979 ... CANR-6
Earlier sketch in CA 7-8R
See also SATA 10
Scherle, Victor 1935- ... 25-28R
Scherman, Bernadine Kielty 1890(?)-1973
Obituary ... 45-48
Scherman, David E(dward) 1916- ... 102
Scherman, Katharine 1915- ... CANR-11
Earlier sketch in CA 5-6R
Scherman, Thomas K(ielty) 1917-1979
Obituary ... 106
Schermer, Judith (Denise) 1941- ... 106
See also SATA 30
Schermerhorn, Richard A(lonzo) 1903- ... 37-40R
Scherr, George Harry 1920- ... 114
Scherr, Max 1916(?)-1981 Obituary ... 105
Schertenleib, Charles 1905-1972
Obituary ... 37-40R
Schertle, Alice 1941- ... CANR-23
Earlier sketch in CA 107
See also SATA 36
Scherzer, Carl John 1901- ... 4R
Scheub, Harold 1931- ... 61-64
Scheuer, Joseph F(rancis) 1918-1975
Obituary ... 61-64
Scheuer, Philip K(atz) 1902-1985
Obituary ... 115
Scheuerle, William H(oward) 1930- ... 33-36R
Scheuerman, Richard D(ean) 1951- ... 57-60
Scheuring, Lyn 1937- ... 73-76
Scheuring, Tom 1942- ... 73-76
Schevill, James (Erwin) 1920- ... 7-8R
See also CLC 7
Schevitz, Jeffrey M(orrie) 1941- ... 65-68
Scheyer, Ernst 1900- ... 15-16R
Schiaparelli, Elsa 1890-1973 Obituary ... 113
Schiappa, Barbara D(ublin) 1943- ... 109
Schiavone, James 1933- ... CANR-9
Earlier sketch in CA 7-8R
Schick, Alice 1946- ... CANR-15
Earlier sketch in CA 81-84
See also SATA 27
Schick, Eleanor 1942- ... CANR-19
Earlier sketches in CA 49-52, CANR-4
See also SATA 9
Schick, George B(aldwin Powell) 1903- ... 41-44R
Schick, Joel 1945- ... 107
See also SATA 30, 31
Schickel, Julia Whedon 1936- ... 49-52
Schickel, Richard (Warren) 1933- ... CANR-1
Earlier sketch in CA 3R
See also AITN 1
Schickele, Peter 1935- ... 85-88
Schickele, Rene 1883-1940 ... DLB-66
Schiddel, Edmund 1909-1982 ... 7-8R
Obituary ... 107
Schiefelbusch, Richard L. 1918- ... CANR-11
Earlier sketch in CA 25-28R
Schieffer, Bob 1937- ... 69-72
Schier, Donald (Stephen) 1914- ... 29-32R
Schier, Ernest L. 1918- ... 77-80
Schiff, Dorothy 1903- ... 121
Brief entry ... 114
Schiff, Harold (Irvin) 1923- ... 89-92
Schiff, Irwin A(llan) 1928- ... 65-68
Schiff, Jacqui Lee 1934- ... 37-40R
Schiff, Ken(neth Roy) 1942- ... 49-52
See also SATA 7
Schiff, Michael 1915- ... 15-16R
Schiffer, Irvine 1917- Brief entry ... 114
Schiffer, Michael 1948- ... 106
Schiffer, Michael B(rian) 1947- ... 110
Schifferes, Justus J(ulius) 1907- ... CANR-5
Earlier sketch in CA 5-6R
Schiffhorst, Gerald J. 1940- ... 19-20R
Schiffman, Jack 1921- ... 49-52
Schiffman, Joseph Harris 1914- ... 19-20R
Schiffrin, Harold Z. 1922- ... 29-32R
Schiler, Marc (Eugene) 1951- ... 106
Schillaci, Anthony
See Schillaci, Peter Paul
Schillaci, Peter Paul 1929- ... 29-32R
Schillebeeckx, Edward (Cornelis Florentius
Alfons) 1914- Brief entry ... 111
Schiller, A. Arthur 1902-1977 ... 37-40R
Obituary ... 73-76
Schiller, Andrew 1919- ... 41-44R
See also SATA 21
Schiller, Barbara (Heyman) 1928- ... 17-18R
See also SATA 21
Schiller, Bob
See Schiller, Robert Achille
Schiller, Bradley R(obert) 1943- ... 57-60
Schiller, Craig 1951- ... 81-84
Schiller, Dorothea E. 1898(?)-1987
Obituary ... 123
Schiller, Herbert I(rving) 1919- ... 29-32R
Schiller, Jerome P(aul) 1934- ... 25-28R
Schiller, Justin G. 1943- Brief entry ... 110
See also SATA 31
Schiller, Lee Virginia Chambers
See Chambers-Schiller, Lee Virginia
Schiller, Mayer
See Schiller, Craig
Schiller, Robert Achille 1918- ... 123
Brief entry ... 118
Schiller, Rose Leiman
See Goldemberg, Rose Leiman
Schilling, Betty 1925- ... 106
Schilling, S. Paul 1904- ... CANR-16
Earlier sketches in CA 2R, CANR-1
Schilling, Warner R(oller) 1925-
Brief entry ... 112
Schilpp, Madelon Golden ... 117
Schilpp, Paul A(rthur) 1897- ... CANR-19
Earlier sketches in CA 4R, CANR-4
Schimel, John L(ouis) 1916- ... 25-28R
Schimmel, Annemarie (Brigitte) 1922-
Brief entry ... 120
Schimmel, Herbert D(avid) 1927- ... 117
Schimmels, Cliff 1937- ... 115
Schinagl, Mary S(onora) 1914- ... 17-18R
Schindeler, Fred(erick) Fernand 1934- ... 41-44R
Schindelman, Joseph 1923- ... SATA-32
Schindler, Marvin Samuel 1932-
Brief entry ... 106
Schindler, S(tephen) D. ... SATA-50
Schinhan, Jan Philip 1887-1975 ... CAP-2
Obituary ... 61-64
Earlier sketch in CA 23-24
Schioetz, Aksel 1906-1975 Obituary ... 111
Schiotz, Aksel
See Schioetz, Aksel
Schipf, Robert G(eorge) 1923- ... 61-64
Schirmer, Daniel B(oone) 1915- ... 41-44R
Schirmer, Gregory A(lan) 1944- ... 117
Schirmer, Henry W. 1922- ... 107
Schirmer, Jennifer G(ay) 1947- ... 113
Schirmerhorn, Clint
See Riemer, George
Schirokauer, Conrad M(ax) 1929- ... 107
Schisgal, Murray (Joseph) 1926- ... 21-22R
See also CLC 6
Schisgall, Oscar 1901-1984 ... CANR-9
Obituary ... 112
Earlier sketch in CA 53-56
See also SATA 12, 38
Schivelbusch, Wolfgang 1941- ... 105
Schjeldahl, Peter 1942- Brief entry ... 113
Schkade, Lawrence L. 1930- ... CANR-7
Earlier sketch in CA 17-18R
Schlabach, Theron F(rederick) 1933- ... 25-28R
Schlabrendorff, Fabian von
See von Schlabrendorff, Fabian
Schlachter, Gail Ann 1943- ... CANR-14
Earlier sketch in CA 77-80
Schlachter, Susan
See Thaler, Susan
Schlafly, Phyllis 1924- ... 25-28R
See also AITN 1
Schlain, Bert H(oward) 1898- ... 19-20R
Schlamm, William S(iegmund)
1904-1978 ... 93-96
Obituary ... 81-84
Schlanger, Henry 1918(?)-1984 Obituary ... 113
Schlant, Ernestine 1935- ... 81-84
Schlapbach-Oberhansli, Trudi 1944- ... 23-24R
Schlatter, Richard 1912-1987 ... 23-24R
Obituary ... 123
Schlauch, Margaret 1898-1986 ... CAP-1
Obituary ... 119
Earlier sketch in CA 13-14
Schlebecker, John T(homas) 1923- ... 11-12R
Schleck, Charles A. 1925- ... CANR-6
Earlier sketch in CA 7-8R
Schlee, Ann 1934- ... 101
See also SATA 36, 44
See also CLC 35
Schlee, Susan 1940- ... 93-96
Schlegel, Dorothy B(adders) 1910- ... 37-40R
Schlegel, Richard 1913- ... 65-68
Schlegel, Stuart A(llen) 1932- ... 61-64
Schlegelmann, V. E.
See Hartz, Fred R.
Schleicher, Charles P. 1907- ... 11-12R
Schleier, Curt 1944- ... 89-92
Schleier, Gertrude 1933- ... 3R
Schleifer, James T(homas) 1942- ... 97-100
Schleifer, Ronald 1948- ... 118
Schlein, Miriam 1926- ... CANR-2
Earlier sketch in CA 4R
See also SATA 2
Schleiner, Winfried 1938- ... 29-32R
Schlem
See Prevost, Marcel
Schlender, William E(lmer) 1920- ... CANR-14
Earlier sketch in CA 17-18R
Schlenker, Elizabeth D. (Wallace) 1912- ... 17-18R
Schlenther, Boyd (Stanley) 1936- ... 41-44R
Schlepp, Wayne Allen 1931- ... 29-32R
Schlereth, Howard (Hewitt) 1936- ... 57-60
Schlereth, Thomas J(ohn) 1941- ... 97-100
Schlesinger, Alfred Cary 1900- ... CAP-1
Earlier sketch in CA 13-14
Schlesinger, Arthur (Meier), Jr. 1917- ... CANR-1
Earlier sketch in CA 4R
See also DLB 17
See also AITN 1
Schlesinger, Arthur Meier 1888-1965 ... CANR-5
Obituary ... 25-28R
Earlier sketch in CA 5-6R
Schlesinger, Benjamin 1928- ... CANR-22
Earlier sketches in CA 19-20R, CANR-7
Schlesinger, Bruno Walter 1876-1962 ... 116
Obituary ... 111
Schlesinger, Elizabeth Bancroft 1886-1977
Obituary ... 69-72
Schlesinger, Hilde S(tephanie) ... CANR-6
Earlier sketch in CA 53-56
Schlesinger, Joseph A(braham) 1922- ... 61-64
Schlesinger, Lawrence E(rwin) 1921- ... 41-44R
Schlesinger, Marian Cannon 1912- ... 89-92
Schlesinger, Stephen C(annon) 1942- ... 57-60
Schlesinger, Thomas O(tto) 1925- ... 41-44R
Schlessinger, Philip J. 1914- ... 7-8R
Schleunes, Karl A(lbert) 1937- ... 29-32R
Schley, Jim 1956- ... 118
Schlichting, Harold E(ugene, Jr.) 1926- ... 112
Schlimbach, Alice (Paula) 1898- ... CAP-1
Earlier sketch in CA 15-16
Schlink, Frederick John 1891- ... 65-68
Schlink, Klara 1904- ... 101
Schlink, M. Basilea
See Schlink, Klara
Schlink, Mother Basilea
See Schlink, Klara
Schlissel, Lillian 1930- ... CANR-13
Earlier sketch in CA 25-28R
Schlitzer, Albert Lawrence 1902- ... 2R
Schloat, G. Warren, Jr. 1914- ... 23-24R
See also SATA 4
Schlobin, Roger Clark 1944- ... CANR-18
Earlier sketch in CA 102
Schlosberg, H. J.
See May, H(enry) J(ohn)
Schloss, Arthur David
See Waley, Arthur (David)
Schlossberg, Dan 1948- ... CANR-19
Earlier sketch in CA 101

Schlossberg, Edwin (Arthur) 1945-
Brief entry ... 112
Schlossberg, Herbert 1935- ... 111
Schlossman, Beryl 1955- ... 124
Schlossman, Steven L(awrence)
1947- ... CANR-16
Earlier sketch in CA 81-84
Schlossstein, Steven 1941- ... 122
Schlueter, June 1942- ... 101
Schlueter, Paul (George) 1933- ... CANR-11
Earlier sketch in CA 15-16R
Schlumberger, Daniel 1904-1972
Obituary ... 37-40R
Schlumberger, Jean 1877-1968 Obituary ... 116
See also DLB 65
Schmalenbach, Werner 1917- ... CANR-13
Earlier sketch in CA 73-76
Schmandt, Henry J. 1918- ... CANR-9
Earlier sketch in CA 7-8R
Schmandt, Raymond H(enry, Jr.) 1925- ... 11-12R
Schmandt-Besserat, Denise 1933- ... CANR-20
Earlier sketch in CA 69-72
Schmeck, Harold M(arshall), Jr. 1923- ... 17-18R
Schmeidler, Gertrude Raffel 1912- ... 37-40R
Schmeiser, Douglas Albert 1934- ... CANR-3
Earlier sketch in CA 11-12R
Schmeling, Gareth L(on) 1940- ... 73-76
Schmeling, Marianne 1930- ... 101
Schmeltz, Susan Alton ... 111
Schmeltz, Susan M.
See Schmeltz, Susan Alton
Schmeltz, William Frederick 1924- ... 41-44R
Schmemann, Alexander 1921-1983 ... 117
Obituary ... 111
Schmertz, Herb(ert) 1930- ... 120
Schmid, A. Allan 1935- ... 37-40R
Schmid, Carlo 1896-1979 Obituary ... 97-100
Schmid, Carol L(ouise) 1946- ... 105
Schmid, Claus-Peter 1942- ... 61-64
Schmid, Eduard 1890-1966 Obituary ... 113
Schmid, Elenore 1939- ... CANR-21
Earlier sketches in CA 53-56, CANR-5
See also SATA 12
Schmid, Mark J(oseph) 1901-19(?) ... CAP-1
Earlier sketch in CA 13-14
Schmiderer, Dorothy 1940- ... 85-88
See also SATA 19
Schmidgall, Gary 1945- ... 77-80
Schmidhauser, John R(ichard) 1922- ... CANR-1
Earlier sketch in CA 45-48
Schmidt, Albert J(ohn) 1925- ... 37-40R
Schmidt, Alice M(ahany) 1925- ... 65-68
Schmidt, Alvin J(ohn) 1932- ... CANR-1
Earlier sketch in CA 45-48
Schmidt, Arno (Otto) 1914-1979 Obituary ... 109
Schmidt, Charles T., Jr. 1934- ... 25-28R
Schmidt, Claire Harman 1957- ... 109
Schmidt, Dana Adams 1915- ... 11-12R
Schmidt, Dolores Barracano 1931- ... 41-44R
Schmidt, Dorothea
See Wender, Dorothea
Schmidt, Elizabeth 1915- ... SATA-15
Schmidt, Emerson Peter 1899-1976
Obituary ... 111
Schmidt, Fred H(artz) 1918- ... 85-88
Schmidt, Frederick G. 1924- ... 49-52
Schmidt, Hans 1938- ... 61-64
Schmidt, Helmut Dan 1915- ... 11-12R
Schmidt, Hubert (Glasgow) 1905-1980
Obituary ... 112
Schmidt, J(akob) E(dward) 1906- ... 13-14R
Schmidt, James Norman 1912- ... CANR-1
Earlier sketch in CA 1R
See also SATA 21
Schmidt, James W. 1947- ... 121
Schmidt, Jerry A(rthur) 1945- ... 69-72
Schmidt, John 1905-1969 ... CAP-1
Earlier sketch in CA 19-20
Schmidt, Karl M. (Jr.) 1917- ... 13-14R
Schmidt, Laura M(arie) 1952- ... CANR-16
Earlier sketch in CA 65-68
Schmidt, Lyle D(arrel) 1933- ... 61-64
Schmidt, Margaret Fox 1925- ... 65-68
Schmidt, Michael Norton 1947- ... CANR-2
Earlier sketch in CA 49-52
See also DLB 40
Schmidt, Nancy Jeanne 1936- ... CANR-7
Earlier sketch in CA 57-60
Schmidt, Paul Frederic 1925- ... CANR-1
Earlier sketch in CA 1R
Schmidt, Peggy Jeanne 1951- ... 109
Schmidt, Rick
See Schmidt, William R(ichard) III
Schmidt, Robert Milton 1930- ... 7-8R
Schmidt, Royal Jae (Jr.) 1915- ... 41-44R
Schmidt, Sandra
See Oddo, Sandra Schmidt
Schmidt, Stanley (Albert) 1944- ... CANR-24
Earlier sketches in CA 61-64, CANR-8
Schmidt, Steven (Thomas) 1927- ... 33-36R
Schmidt, Warren H(arry) 1920- ... CANR-1
Earlier sketch in CA 45-48
Schmidt, Werner Felix 1923- ... 11-12R
Schmidt, William E. 1947- ... 73-76
Schmidt, William R(ichard) III 1949- ... 110
Schmidt, Wilson Emerson 1927- ... 103
Schmidt-Nielsen, Knut 1915- ... 106
Schmier, Louis Eugene 1940- ... 112
Schmithals, Walter 1923- ... CANR-9
Earlier sketch in CA 65-68
Schmitt, Abraham 1927- ... CANR-17
Earlier sketch in CA 97-100
Schmitt, Albert R(ichard) 1929- ... 73-76
Schmitt, Bernadotte Everly 1886-1969 ... 2R
Obituary ... 103
Schmitt, Charles 1934(?)-1986 Obituary ... 119
Schmitt, David (Edward) 1940- ... 53-56
Schmitt, Gladys 1909-1972 ... CANR-2
Obituary ... 37-40R
Earlier sketch in CA 2R
Schmitt, Hans A. 1921- ... CANR-5
Earlier sketch in CA 4R
Schmitt, Heinrich 1894-1976 Obituary ... 115
Schmitt, Karl Michael 1922- ... 41-44R
Schmitt, Marshall L. 1919- ... 13-14R
Schmitt, Martin (Ferdinand) 1917-1978 ... CANR-9
Earlier sketch in CA 53-56
Schmitt, Raymond L(ouis) 1936- ... 93-96
Schmitt, Richard 1927- ... 118
Schmitter, Dean Morgan 1917- ... 41-44R
Schmitter, Phillipe Charles 1936- ... 115
Schmitthoff, Clive M(acmillan) 1903- ... CANR-18
Earlier sketches in CA 7-8R, CANR-3
Schmittroth, John 1924- ... 49-52
Schmittroth, John (William), Jr.
1949- ... CANR-19
Earlier sketch in CA 97-100
Schmitz, Aron Hector 1861-1928 ... 122
Brief entry ... 104
Schmitz, Carl August 1920-1966 Obituary ... 116
Schmitz, Charles Henry 1904- ... 7-8R
Schmitz, Dennis 1937- ... 29-32R
Schmitz, Ettore
See Schmitz, Aron Hector
Schmitz, James H(enry) 1911- ... 103
See also DLB 8
Schmitz, Joseph William 1905-1966 ... 7-8R
Schmitz, Michael J. 1934- ... 23-24R
Schmitz, Virginia
See Pasley, Virginia Schmitz
Schmokel, Wolfe W(illiam) 1933- ... 11-12R
Schmoller, Hans 1916-1985 Obituary ... 117
Schmuck, Richard A(llen) 1936- ... 15-16R
Schmucke, Anne
See Strich, Christian
Schmuller, Aaron 1910- ... 53-56
Schnabel, Billie H(agen) 1944(?)-1980
Obituary ... 101
Schnabel, Truman Gross, Jr. 1919- ... 105
Schnacke, Dick
See Schnacke, Richard N(ye)
Schnacke, Richard N(ye) 1919- ... 61-64
Schnackenberg, Gjertrud 1953-
Brief entry ... 116
See also CLC 40
Schnackenburg, Rudolf 1914- ... CANR-12
Earlier sketch in CA 29-32R
Schnall, Maxine (Swartz) 1934- ... 19-20R
Schnaubelt, Franz Joseph 1914- ... 65-68
Schneck, Jerome M. 1920- ... 17-18R
Schneck, Stephen 1933- ... CANR-10
Earlier sketch in CA 13-14R
Schneebaum, Tobias 1921- ... CANR-15
Earlier sketch in CA 29-32R
Schneede, Uwe M(ax) 1939- Brief entry ... 111
Schneewind, Elizabeth Hughes 1940- ... CANR-2
Earlier sketch in CA 45-48
Schneewind, J(erome) B(orges) 1930- ... 25-28R
Schneidau, Herbert N. 1935- ... 29-32R
Schneider, Anna
See Sequoia, Anna
Schneider, Ben Ross, Jr. 1920- ... 37-40R
Schneider, Benjamin 1938- ... 41-44R
Schneider, Carl D(avid) 1942- ... 69-72
Schneider, Clement J(oseph)
1927-1972 ... 41-44R
Schneider, Daniel J(ohn) 1927- ... 61-64
Schneider, David 1918- ... 114
Schneider, David M(urray) 1918-
Brief entry ... 112
Schneider, Delwin Byron 1926- ... 37-40R
Schneider, Dick
See Schneider, Richard H(enry)
Schneider, Duane 1937- ... 103
Schneider, Elisabeth Wintersteen 1897- ... CAP-1
Earlier sketch in CA 11-12
Schneider, Elizabeth (Susan) 1943- ... CANR-16
Earlier sketch in CA 93-96
Schneider, Hans J(uergen) 1935- ... 73-76
Schneider, Harold K(enneth) 1925- ... 33-36R
Schneider, Herbert Wallace 1892-1984 ... 13-14R
Obituary ... 114
Schneider, Herman 1905- ... CANR-16
Earlier sketch in CA 29-32R
See also SATA 7
Schneider, Howie ... AITN-2
Schneider, Isidor 1896-1977 ... CAP-1
Obituary ... 73-76
Earlier sketch in CA 13-14
Schneider, John C(harles) 1945- ... 102
Schneider, Joyce Anne 1942- ... 107
Schneider, Kenneth Ray 1927- ... 49-52
Schneider, Lambert 1900-1970 Obituary ... 104
Schneider, Laurence Allen 1937- ... 81-84
Schneider, Laurie
See Adams, Laurie
Schneider, Leo 1916- ... 5-6R
Schneider, Leonard Alfred 1925-1966 ... 89-92
Schneider, Louis 1915-1979 ... CANR-13
Earlier sketch in CA 57-60
Schneider, Myles J(ay) 1943- ... 116
Schneider, Myra 1936- ... CANR-24
Earlier sketch in CA 107
Schneider, Nicholas A. 1930- ... 25-28R
Schneider, Nina 1913- ... CANR-15
Earlier sketch in CA 29-32R
See also SATA 2
Schneider, Rex 1937- ... 122
See also SATA 44
Schneider, Richard H(enry) 1922- ... 97-100
Schneider, Robert G. 1930- ... 112
Schneider, Robert T(homas) 1925- ... 7-8R
Schneider, Robert W. 1933- ... 15-16R
Schneider, Rolf 1932- Brief entry ... 112
Schneider, Ronald M(ilton) 1932- ... 53-56
Schneider, Stanley D(ale) 1921- ... 17-18R
Schneider, Stephen H(enry) 1945- ... CANR-12
Earlier sketch in CA 69-72
Schneider, Steven A. 1952- ... 120
Schneider, Susan Weidman 1944- ... 118
Schneider, William, Jr. 1941- ... CANR-19
Earlier sketch in CA 29-32R
Schneiderman, Beth Kline ... 97-100
Schneiderman, Harry 1885-1975
Obituary ... 61-64
Schneiderman, L(awrence) J(erome)
1932- ... 57-60
Schneiderman, Stuart (Alan) 1943- ... 114
Schneiders, Alexander A(loysius)
1909-1968 ... CAP-1
Earlier sketch in CA 17-18
Schneier, Edward V(incent), Jr. 1939- ... 29-32R
Schneir, Miriam 1933- ... 77-80
Schnell, George A(dam) 1931- ... CANR-12
Earlier sketch in CA 29-32R
Schnell, R(odolph) L(eslie) 1931- ... 113
Schnell, William J(acob) ... 7-8R
Schnelle, Kenneth E(dward) 1914- ... 23-24R
Schnepper, Jeff A(lan) 1947- ... CANR-21
Earlier sketch in CA 85-88
Schneps, Maurice 1917- ... 2R
Schnessel, S. Michael 1947- ... CANR-14
Earlier sketch in CA 73-76
Schneyder, J. F.
See Taylor, (Frank Herbert) Griffin
Schnirel, James R. 1931- ... 69-72
See also SATA 14
Schnitzer, Martin C(olby) 1925-
Brief entry ... 110
Schnitzler, Arthur 1862-1931 Brief entry ... 104
See also TCLC 4
Schnore, Leo F(rancis) 1927- ... 19-20R
Schob, David Eugene 1941- ... 61-64
Schochet, Gordon J(oel) 1937- ... 45-48
Schochet, J(acob) Immanuel 1935- ... CANR-1
Earlier sketch in CA 45-48
Schock, Pauline 1928- ... 111
See also SATA 45
Schocken, Theodore 1914-1975 Obituary ... 104
Schoder, Raymond V(ictor) 1916-1987 ... CANR-1
Obituary ... 122
Earlier sketch in CA 3R
Schoeck, Richard J(oseph) 1920- ... CANR-5
Earlier sketch in CA 4R
Schoeffler, Oscar E(dmund) 1899-1979 ... 73-76
Obituary ... 85-88
Schoeman, Karel 1939- ... 101
Schoen, Barbara 1924- ... 21-22R
See also SATA 13
Schoen, Elin 1945- ... 101
Schoen, Juliet P. 1923- ... 69-72
Schoenbach, Carrie 1928- ... 120
Schoenbaum, S(amuel) 1927- ... 107
Schoenbaum, Thomas John 1939- ... 104
Schoenberg, Arnold 1874-1951
Brief entry ... 109
Schoenberg, B(ernhardt) Mark 1928- ... 97-100
Schoenberg, Bernard 1927-1979 ... CANR-2
Obituary ... 85-88
Earlier sketch in CA 45-48
Schoenberg, Wilfred Paul 1915- ... 11-12R
Schoenberger, Guido L. 1891-1974
Obituary ... 53-56
Schoenberger, Walter Smith 1920- ... 29-32R
Schoenberner, Franz 1892-1970 Obituary ... 104
Schoenbohm, Wilko B. 1913- ... 19-20R
Schoenbrun, David (Franz) 1915- ... CANR-3
Earlier sketch in CA 49-52
Schoendoerffer, Pierre 1928- Brief entry ... 111
Schoenfeld, Clarence Albert 1918- ... CANR-6
Earlier sketch in CA 1R
Schoenfeld, David 1923- ... CANR-12
Earlier sketch in CA 19-20R
Schoenfeld, Eugene 1935- Brief entry ... 118
Schoenfeld, Hanns Martin W(alter)
1928- ... CANR-6
Earlier sketch in CA 57-60
Schoenfeld, Maxwell Philip 1936- ... 33-36R
Schoenfield, Allen 1896(?)-1979 Obituary ... 85-88
Schoenherr, John (Carl) 1935- ... SATA-37
Schoenherr, Richard Anthony 1935- ... CANR-21
Earlier sketch in CA 29-32R
Schoenholtz, Larry 1948- ... 57-60
Schoenman, Ralph 1935- ... 25-28R
Schoenstein, Paul 1902-1974 Obituary ... 89-92
Schoenstein, Ralph 1933- ... 13-14R
Schoenwald, Richard L. 1927- ... 17-18R
Schoep, Arthur Paul 1920- ... 53-56
Schoepfer, Virginia B. 1934- ... 33-36R
Schoepflin, George A. 1939- ... 29-32R
Schoeps, Hans-Joachim 1909- Brief entry ... 106
Schoeps, Karl-Heinz 1935- ... CANR-24
Earlier sketch in CA 107
Schoer, Lowell A(ugust) 1931- ... 29-32R
Schoettle, Lynn ... 49-52
Schofer, Lawrence 1940- ... 77-80
Schofield, B(rian) B(etham) 1895-1984 ... 23-24R
Obituary ... 114
Schofield, J(ohn) N(oel) 1899-1986
Obituary ... 120
Schofield, Jonathan
See Streib, Dan(iel Thomas)
Schofield, Mary Anne 1948- ... 124
Schofield, Michael 1919- ... CANR-14
Earlier sketch in CA 41-44R
Schofield, Paul
See Tubb, E(dwin) C(harles)
Schofield, Sylvia Anne 1918- ... CANR-13
Earlier sketch in CA 73-76
Schofield, William 1921- ... 11-12R
Schofield, William G(reenough) 1909- ... CANR-2
Earlier sketch in CA 7-8R
Scholastica, Sister Mary
See Jenkins, Marie M(agdalen)
Scholberg, Henry 1921- ... 77-80
Scholderer, Victor 1880-1971 Obituary ... 104
Scholefield, Alan 1931- ... 97-100
Scholefield, Edmund O.
See Butterworth, W(illiam) E(dmund III)
Scholem, Gershom (Gerhard) 1897-1982 ... 45-48
Obituary ... 106
Scholer, David M(ilton) 1938- ... 101
Scholes, Katherine 1959- ... 123
Scholes, Marie V(ielmetti) 1916- ... 29-32R
Scholes, Robert (Edward) 1929- ... CANR-14
Earlier sketch in CA 11-12R
Scholes, Walter V(inton) 1916-1975 ... CAP-2
Earlier sketch in CA 29-32
Scholey, Arthur 1932- ... 93-96
See also SATA 28
Scholl, John 1922- ... 11-12R
Scholl, Lisette 1945- ... 89-92
Scholl, Sharon L. 1932- ... 41-44R
Scholl, William M(athias) 1882-1968
Obituary ... 113
Scholt, Grayce 1925- ... 104
Scholtz, William 1916- ... 7-8R
Scholz, Albert A(ugust) 1899-19(?) ... CAP-2
Earlier sketch in CA 29-32
Scholz, Carter 1953- ... 119
Scholz, Jackson Volney 1897-1986 ... 7-8R
Obituary ... 120
See also SATA 49
Scholz, William 1916- ... 7-8R
Schomaker, Mary Zimmeth 1928- ... 108
Schomp, Gerald 1937- ... 29-32R
Schon, Donald A(lan) 1930- ... 19-20R
Schon, Isabel 1940- ... 110
Schonberg, Arnold
See Schoenberg, Arnold
Schonberg, Harold C(harles) 1915- ... 112
Schonberg, Rosalyn Krokover
1913(?)-1973 Obituary ... 41-44R
Schonberger, Richard J. 1937- ... 110
Schonborg, Virginia 1913- ... 77-80
Schone, Virginia ... 97-100
See also SATA 22
Schonell, Fred(erick) Joyce 1900-1969 ... CANR-2
Earlier sketch in CA 4R
Schonfeld, William R(ost) 1942- ... CANR-17
Earlier sketch in CA 37-40R
Schonfield, Hugh J(oseph) 1901-1988 ... 9-10R
Obituary ... 124
Schongut, Emanuel ... SATA-36
Schooler, Carmi 1933- ... 114
Schooler, (Seward) Dean, Jr. 1941- ... 73-76
Schoolfield, George C(larence) 1925- ... CANR-6
Earlier sketch in CA 1R
Schoolland, Marian M(argaret) 1902- ... CANR-2
Earlier sketch in CA 5-6R
Schoonhoven, Calvin R(obert) 1931- ... 21-22R
Schoonmaker, Alan N. 1936- ... 25-28R
Schoonmaker, Ann 1928- ... 73-76
Schoonmaker, Frank 1905-1976 Obituary ... 61-64
Schoonover, Frank (Earle) 1877-1972 ... 106
See also SATA 24
Schoonover, Lawrence Lovell
1906-1980 ... CANR-4
Obituary ... 97-100
Earlier sketch in CA 1R
Schoonover, Melvin E(ugene) 1926-
Brief entry ... 114
Schoonover, Shirley 1936- ... 77-80
Schoonover, Thelma I(rene) 1907- ... 41-44R
Schoonover, Thomas D(avid) 1936- ... 120
Schoor, Gene 1921- ... 29-32R
See also SATA 3
Schopflin, George A.
See Schoepflin, George A.
Schor, Amy 1954- ... 105
Schor, Lynda 1938- ... 73-76
Schor, Naomi 1943- ... CANR-16
Earlier sketch in CA 89-92
Schorb, E(dwin) M(arsh) 1940- ... 61-64
Schorer, Mark 1908-1977 ... CANR-7
Obituary ... 73-76
Earlier sketch in CA 5-6R
See also CLC 9
Schorr, Alan Edward 1945- ... 85-88
Schorr, Alvin L. 1921- ... CANR-15
Earlier sketch in CA 29-32R
Schorr, Daniel (Louis) 1916- ... 65-68
See also AITN 2
Schorr, Jerry 1934- ... 29-32R
Schorr, Mark 1953- ... 122
Schorsch, Ismar 1935- Brief entry ... 115
Schorske, Carl E(mil) 1915- ... 85-88
Schosberg, Paul A. 1938- ... 13-14R
Schossberger, Emily Maria 1905-1979
Obituary ... 104
Schott, John R(obert) 1936- ... CANR-7
Earlier sketch in CA 57-60
Schott, Penelope Scambly 1942- ... 77-80
Schott, Richard Lockwood 1939- ... 117
Schott, Webster 1927- ... 49-52
Schottland, Charles Irwin 1906- ... 13-14R
Schouler, James 1839-1920 ... DLB-47
Schowalter, John E(rwin) 1936- ... 109
Schoyer, B. Preston 1912(?)-1978
Obituary ... 77-80
Schrader, Constance 1933- ... CANR-18
Earlier sketch in CA 101
Schrader, George A(lfred), Jr. 1917- ... 23-24R
Schrader, Paul Joseph 1946- ... 37-40R
See also DLB 44
See also CLC 26
Schrader, Richard James 1941- ... 85-88

Schrader, Robert F(ay) 1931- 119
Schraff, Anne E(laine) 1939- CANR-17
Earlier sketches in CA 49-52, CANR-1
See also SATA 27
Schraff, Francis Nicholas 1937- 101
Schraffenberger, Nancy 1933- CANR-16
Earlier sketch in CA 93-96
Schrag, Adele Frisbie 1921- 105
Schrag, Calvin Orville 1928- CANR-1
Earlier sketch in CA 1R
Schrag, Oswald O. 1916- 49-52
Schrag, Peter 1931- CANR-8
Earlier sketch in CA 15-16R
Schrag, Philip G(ordon) 1943- 102
Schram, Martin 1942- CANR-13
Earlier sketch in CA 69-72
Schram, Stuart R(eynolds) 1924- 97-100
Schramm, Percy Ernst 1894-1970
Obituary 104
Schramm, Richard (Howard) 1934- 41-44R
Schramm, Sarah Slavin 1942- 93-96
Schramm, Wilbur (Lang) 1907-1987 .... CANR-22
Obituary 124
Earlier sketch in CA 105
Schrank, Jeffrey 1944- 29-32R
Schrank, Joseph 1900-1984 .... CANR-20
Obituary 112
Earlier sketch in CA 5-6R
See also SATA 38
Schreck, Alan (Edward) 1951- 124
Schreck, Everett M. 1897- CAP-2
Earlier sketch in CA 33-36
Schrecker, John (Ernest) 1937-
Brief entry 112
Schreiber, Daniel 1909-1981 .... CAP-1
Obituary 103
Earlier sketch in CA 13-14
Schreiber, Elizabeth Anne (Ferguson)
1947- 69-72
See also SATA 13
Schreiber, Flora Rheta 1918- CANR-11
Earlier sketch in CA 53-56
See also AITN 1
Schreiber, Georges 1904-1977 Obituary 109
See also SATA 29
Schreiber, Hermann 1920- 25-28R
Schreiber, Jan 1941- 65-68
Schreiber, Jean-Jacques Servan
See Servan-Schreiber, Jean-Jacques
Schreiber, Mark 1960- 116
Schreiber, Michael 1937- 116
Schreiber, Ralph W(alter) 1942- 69-72
See also SATA 13
Schreiber, Ron 1934- 41-44R
Schreiber, Ted
See Schreiber, V. Theodore
Schreiber, V. Theodore 1905-1986 124
Schreiber, Vernon R(oy) 1925- 61-64
Schreiber-Wicke, Edith 1943- 123
Schreider, Frank(lin David) 1924- 7-8R
Schreiner, George F(rederic) 1949- 117
Schreiner, Lee
See Schreiner, George F(rederic)
Schreiner, Olive (Emilie Albertina)
1855-1920 Brief entry 105
See also DLB 18
See also TCLC 9
Schreiner, Samuel A(gnew), Jr. 1921- .. CANR-9
Earlier sketch in CA 65-68
Schreiner-Mann, Joan 1939- 45-58
Schreiter, Rick 1936- 21-22R
Schreivogel, Paul A. 1930- 25-28R
Schrepfer, Susan R(ita) 1941- 117
Schreuder, D(eryck) M(arshall) 1942- 120
Schreyer, George M(aurice) 1913- 5-6R
Schrier, Arnold 1925- 49-52
Schrier, Nettie Vander
See Vander-Schrier, Nettie
Schrier, William 1900-1973 .... 41-44R
Schrift, Shirley 1922(?)- 113
Brief entry 110
Schriftgiesser, Karl 1903- CAP-1
Earlier sketch in CA 11-12
Schrire, Theodore 1906- 21-22R
Schrock, Simon 1938- 113
Schroder, Amund A. Schulze 1925- CANR-5
Earlier sketch in CA 13-14R
Schroder, John Henry Erle 1895- CAP-1
Earlier sketch in CA 13-14
Schrodinger, Erwin
See Schroedinger, Erwin
Schrodt, Philip A(ndrew) 1951- 111
Schroedel, Jean Reith 1951- 122
Schroeder, Albert H(enry) 1914- CANR-14
Earlier sketch in CA 41-44R
Schroeder, Andreas (Peter) 1946- CANR-16
Earlier sketch in CA 93-96
See also DLB 53
Schroeder, David 1924- 23-24R
Schroeder, Eric 1904- CAP-1
Earlier sketch in CA 13-14
Schroeder, Fred E(rich) H(arald) 1932- 41-44R
Schroeder, Frederick W(illiam) 1896- 3R
Schroeder, Henry A(lfred) 1906-1975 .... CAP-2
Earlier sketch in CA 25-28
Schroeder, John H(erman) 1943- 49-52
Schroeder, Mary 1903- 73-76
Schroeder, Oliver Charles, Jr. 1916- 110
Schroeder, Paul Walter 1927- 7-8R
Schroeder, Ted 1931(?)-1973 .... SATA-20
Schroeder, W(illiam) Widick 1928-
Brief entry 111
Schroedinger, Erwin 1887-1961 Obituary 113
Schroeter, James 1927- 21-22R
Schroeter, Louis C(larence) 1929- 29-32R
Schroetter, Hilda Noel 1917- 29-32R
Schroll, Herman T(heodore III) 1946- 33-36R
Schruben, Francis W(illiam) 1918- 45-48
Schruth, Peter Elliott 1917-1979
Obituary 89-92
Schubart, Mark Allen 1918- 105
Schubert, Delwyn George 1919- 11-12R
Schubert, Dieter 1947- 111
Schubert, Glendon 1918- CANR-21
Earlier sketches in CA 5-6R, CANR-6
Schubert, Kurt 1923- 7-8R
Schubert-Gabrys, Ingrid 1953- 111
Schuberth, Christopher J. 1933- CANR-18
Earlier sketch in CA 25-28R
Schuchman, Joan 1934- 101
Schudson, Michael 1946- CANR-19
Earlier sketch in CA 101
Schueler, Donald G(ustave) 1929- 106
Schuerer, Ernst 1933- CANR-17
Earlier sketches in CA 45-48, CANR-1
Schuessler, Hermann E. 1929(?)-1975
Obituary 61-64
Schuessler, Karl F(rederick) 1915- 105
Schuettinger, Robert Lindsay 1936- 33-36R
Schuetz, John Howard 1933- 97-100
Schuetze, Armin William 1917- 57-60
Schug, Willis E(rvin) 1924- 49-52
Schuh, Dwight R(aymond) 1945- 101
Schuh, G(eorge) Edward 1930- 29-32R
Schuker, Stephen Alan 1939- 69-72
Schul, Bill D(ean) 1928- CANR-8
Earlier sketch in CA 61-64
Schulberg, Budd (Wilson) 1914- CANR-19
Earlier sketch in CA 25-28R
See also DLB 6, 26, 28
See also DLBY 81
See also CLC 7
Schulberg, Herbert C(harles) 1934- CANR-8
Earlier sketch in CA 61-64
Schulberg, Stuart 1922-1979 Obituary 89-92
Schulder, Diane Blossom 1937- 37-40R
Schuler, Carol Ann 1946- 106
Schuler, Edgar A(lbert) 1905- CAP-2
Earlier sketch in CA 23-24
Schuler, Stanley Carter 1915- CANR-5
Earlier sketch in CA 7-8R
Schulke, Flip Phelps Graeme 1930- CANR-22
Earlier sketch in CA 105
Schulkind, Eugene (Walter) 1923- 97-100
Schull, (John) Joseph 1916-1980 .... CANR-8
Earlier sketch in CA 53-56
Schuller, Gunther 1925- 69-72
Schuller, Robert (Harold) 1926- CANR-14
Earlier sketch in CA 11-12R
Schullery, Paul (David) 1948- 111
Schulman, Arnold 1925- 103
Schulman, Bob
See Schulman, Robert
Schulman, Grace 65-68
Schulman, J(oseph) Neil 1953- 89-92
Schulman, Janet 1933- 101
See also SATA 22
Schulman, L(ester) M(artin) 1934- CANR-12
Earlier sketch in CA 33-36R
See also SATA 13
Schulman, Robert 1916- 77-80
Schulman, Rosalind 1914- 41-44R
Schulman, Sam 1924- 45-48
Schulman, Sarah 1958- 118
Schulmerich, Alma 1902(?)-1985
Obituary 115
Schulte, Elaine L(ouise) 1934- CANR-12
Earlier sketch in CA 73-76
See also SATA 36
Schulte, Henry F(rank) 1924- 25-28R
Schulte, Paul C(larence) 1890-1984
Obituary 112
Schulte, Rainer 23-24R
Schultes, Richard Evans 1915- 108
Schultheis, Rob 1943- 111
Schulthess, Emil 1913- 65-68
Schults, Raymond L. 1926- 105
Schultz, Barbara 1923- 21-22R
Schultz, Barbara A. 117
Schultz, Dodi 1930- CANR-16
Earlier sketches in CA 45-48, CANR-1
Schultz, Donald O. 1939- CANR-17
Earlier sketch in CA 25-28R
Schultz, Duane P(hilip) 1934- 29-32R
Schultz, Ed 1933- 45-48
Schultz, Edna Moore 1912- 13-14R
Schultz, Edward W(illiam) 1936- CANR-1
Earlier sketch in CA 45-48
Schultz, George F(ranklin) 1908- CAP-2
Earlier sketch in CA 19-20
Schultz, George J(oseph) 1932-
Brief entry 109
Schultz, Gerard 1902-1974 Obituary 110
Schultz, Gladys Denny 1896(?)-1984
Obituary 113
Schultz, Gwendolyn 65-68
See also SATA 21
Schultz, Harold John 1923- 103
Schultz, Harry D. CANR-14
Earlier sketch in CA 23-24R
Schultz, James Willard 1859-1947
Brief entry 121
See also YABC 1
Schultz, John (Ludwig) 1932- CANR-15
Earlier sketch in CA 41-44R
Schultz, Joseph P(enn) 1928- 113
Schultz, Mark 1935- 116
Schultz, Mort(on) J(oel) 1930- CANR-12
Earlier sketch in CA 73-76
Schultz, Pearle Henriksen 1918- CANR-1
Earlier sketch in CA 49-52
See also SATA 21
Schultz, Philip 1945- 104
Schultz, Samuel J(acob) 1914- CANR-12
Earlier sketch in CA 25-28R
Schultz, Sigrid (Lillian) 1893-1980
Obituary 97-100
Schultz, Stanley K(enton) 1938-
Brief entry 116
Schultz, Terri 1946- CANR-10
Earlier sketch in CA 65-68
Schultz, Theodore William 1902- 85-88
Schultz, Vernon B(urdette) 1924- 11-12R
Schultze, Charles L(ouis) 1924-
Brief entry 114
Schultze, William Andrew 1937- 37-40R
Schulz, Ann Tibbitts 1938- 116
Schulz, Anne Markham 1938- 121
Schulz, Bruno 1892-1942 123
Brief entry 115
See also TCLC 5
Schulz, Charles M(onroe) 1922- CANR-6
Earlier sketch in CA 9-10R
See also SATA 10
See also CLC 12
Schulz, Clare Elmore 1924- 15-16R
Schulz, David A. 1933- 29-32R
Schulz, Ernst B(ernhard) 1896- 73-76
Schulz, Florence 1908- CAP-2
Earlier sketch in CA 21-22
Schulz, James Henry 1936- 89-92
Schulz, John E. 1939- 29-32R
Schulz, Juergen 1927- 41-44R
Schulz, Max F(rederick) 1923- 7-8R
Schulz, Phillip Stephen 1946- 123
Schulz-Behrend, George 1913- 45-48
Schulze, Franz 1927- 41-44R
Schulze, Gene 1912- 85-88
Schulze, Hertha 1935- 122
Schulzinger, Robert D(avid) 1945- 61-64
Schumacher, Alvin J. 1928- 15-16R
Schumacher, Ernst Friedrich
1911(?)-1977 81-84
Obituary 73-76
Schuman, Ben N. 1923- 17-18R
Schuman, David Feller 1942- CANR-17
Earlier sketch in CA 97-100
Schuman, Frederick Lewis 1904- 45-48
Schuman, Howard 1928- 124
Schuman, Patricia Glass 1943- CANR-14
Earlier sketch in CA 33-36R
Schumann, Elizabeth Creighton 1907- CAP-1
Earlier sketch in CA 11-12
Schumann, Paul L. 1955- 112
Schuon, Frithjof 1907- CANR-13
Earlier sketch in CA 73-76
Schuon, Karl Albert 1913-1984 .... 15-16R
Obituary 114
Schur, Edwin M(ichael) 1930- CANR-7
Earlier sketch in CA 13-14R
Schur, Maxine 1948- SATA-49
Schur, Norman W(arren) 1907- CANR-17
Earlier sketch in CA 41-44R
Schurer, Ernst
See Schuerer, Ernst
Schurer, Leopold (Sidney) Launitz, Jr.
See Launitz-Schurer, Leopold (Sidney), Jr.
Schurfranz, Vivian 1925- 61-64
See also SATA 13
Schurmacher, Emile C. 1903(?)-1976
Obituary 69-72
Schurman, D(onald) M. 1924- 37-40R
Schurr, Cathleen 11-12R
Schurz, Carl 1829-1906 .... DLB-23
Schuschnigg, Kurt von
See von Schuschnigg, Kurt
Schusky, Ernest L(ester) 1931- CANR-8
Earlier sketch in CA 17-18R
Schuster, George 1873-1972 Obituary 37-40R
Schuster, George 1881-1982 Obituary 107
Schuster, Louis A. 1916- 15-16R
Schuster, Max Lincoln 1897-1970
Obituary 29-32R
Schutte, William Metcalf 1919- 5-6R
Schutz, Anton Friedrich Joseph
1894-1977 81-84
Obituary 73-76
Schutz, Benjamin Merrill 1949- 107
Schutz, John Adolph 1919- 7-8R
Schutz, John Howard
See Schuetz, John Howard
Schutz, Susan Polis 1944- 105
Schutz, Wilhelm Wolfgang 1911- 25-28R
Schutz, William C(arl) 1925- CANR-10
Earlier sketch in CA 25-28R
Schutze, Gertrude 1917- 17-18R
Schutze, Jim 1946- 123
Schutzer, A. I. 1922- 25-28R
See also SATA 13
Schutzman, Steven 1947- 114
Schuyler, George Samuel 1895-1977 81-84
Obituary 73-76
See also DLB 29, 51
Schuyler, James Marcus 1923- 101
See also DLB 5
See also CLC 5, 23
Schuyler, Jane 1943- 65-68
Schuyler, Joseph B(ernard) 1921- 3R
Schuyler, Judy
See Eshbach, Lloyd Arthur
Schuyler, Keith C. 1919- CANR-12
Earlier sketch in CA 29-32R
Schuyler, Pamela R. 1948- 106
See also SATA 30
Schuyler, Philippa Duke 1934-1967 .... 5-6R
Schuyler, Robert Livingston 1883-1966 .... CAP-1
Earlier sketch in CA 11-12
Schvaneveldt, Jay D. 1937- 103
Schwab, Arnold T. 1922- 11-12R
Schwab, George 1931- CANR-16
Earlier sketches in CA 45-48, CANR-1
Schwab, John J. 1923- 85-88
Schwab, Joseph J(ackson) 1909- CANR-5
Earlier sketch in CA 5-6R
Schwab, Paul Josiah 1894-1966 .... 7-8R
Obituary 103
Schwab, Peter 1940- CANR-14
Earlier sketch in CA 41-44R
Schwabacher, Ethel K(remer) 1903-1984
Obituary 114
Schwabe, William
See Cassidy, William L(awrence Robert)
Schwaber, Paul 1936- 13-14R
Schwadron, Abraham A(be) 1925-1987
Obituary 123
Schwalberg, Carol(yn Ernestine Stein)
1930- 69-72
Schwamm, Ellen 1934- 122
Schwartz, Alfred 1922- 19-20R
Schwartz, Alvin 1927- CANR-24
Earlier sketches in CA 13-14R, CANR-7
See also SATA 4
See also CLR 3
Schwartz, Amy 1954- 110
See also SATA 41, 47
Schwartz, Anne Powers 1913- CANR-1
Earlier sketch in CA 1R
See also SATA 10
Schwartz, Arthur Nathaniel 1922- CANR-8
Earlier sketch in CA 61-64
Schwartz, Audrey James 1928- 89-92
Schwartz, Barry 1938- 77-80
Schwartz, Barry N. 1942- 33-36R
Schwartz, Benjamin I. 1916- 13-14R
Schwartz, Bernard 1923- Brief entry 117
Schwartz, Bernard (Sherman) 1945- 106
Schwartz, Bertie G. 1901(?)-1976
Obituary 69-72
Schwartz, Betty 1927- 93-96
Schwartz, Charles 73-76
Schwartz, Charles W(alsh) 1914- 13-14R
See also SATA 8
Schwartz, Daniel (Bennet) 1929- SATA-29
Schwartz, David C. 1939- 37-40R
Schwartz, David J(oseph), Jr. 1927- CANR-13
Earlier sketch in CA 19-20R
Schwartz, David M(artin) 1951- 118
Schwartz, Delmore 1913-1966 .... CAP-2
Obituary 25-28R
Earlier sketch in CA 17-18
See also DLB 28, 48
See also CLC 2, 4, 10, 45
Schwartz, Douglas W(right) 1929- CANR-17
Earlier sketch in CA 25-28R
Schwartz, Eleanor Brantley 1937- 57-60
Schwartz, Eli 1921- 4R
Schwartz, Elias 1923- 41-44R
Schwartz, Elizabeth Reeder 1912- 15-16R
See also SATA 8
Schwartz, Elkanah 1937- 23-24R
Schwartz, Elliott S. 1936- 15-16R
Schwartz, Emanual K. 1912-1973 .... 37-40R
Obituary 41-44R
Schwartz, Ernst
See Ozu, Yasujiro
Schwartz, Eugene M. 1927- 13-14R
Schwartz, Gail Garfield 117
Schwartz, George 1908-1974 Obituary 104
Schwartz, George Leopold 1891-1983
Obituary 109
Schwartz, George R. 1942- CANR-17
Earlier sketch in CA 97-100
Schwartz, Gerald 1932- 120
Schwartz, Harry W. 1903(?)-1984
Obituary 114
Schwartz, Helen 1935- 111
Schwartz, Helene E(nid) 1941- 65-68
Schwartz, Hillel 1948- CANR-20
Earlier sketch in CA 102
Schwartz, Howard 1945- CANR-22
Earlier sketches in CA 49-52, CANR-5
Schwartz, Israel J(acob) 1885-1971
Obituary 33-36R
Schwartz, Jerome
See Lawrence, Jerome
Schwartz, Joel L. 1940- 121
Schwartz, Jonathan 1938- 97-100
See also DLBY 82
Schwartz, Joseph 1925- 33-36R
Schwartz, Julius 1907- 109
See also SATA 45
Schwartz, K(arlene) V. 1936- 104
Schwartz, Kessel 1920- CANR-6
Earlier sketch in CA 4R
Schwartz, Larry 1922- 53-56
Schwartz, Leon 1922- 113
Schwartz, Lester J(erome) 1927- 113
Schwartz, Lewis M(arvin) 1935- 45-48
Schwartz, Lita Linzer 1930- 29-32R
Schwartz, Lloyd 1941- 112
Schwartz, Lois C. 1935- 33-36R
Schwartz, Loretta 1943- 97-100
Schwartz, Louis B. 1913- 23-24R
Schwartz, Lynne Sharon 1939- 103
See also CLC 31
Schwartz, Martin D(avid) 1945- 118
Schwartz, Michael 1942- 113
Schwartz, Mildred A(nne) 1932- CANR-9
Earlier sketch in CA 21-22R
Schwartz, Morris S. 1916- 17-18R
Schwartz, Mortimer (Donald) 1922- 116
Schwartz, Muriel A.
See Eliot, T(homas) S(tearns)
Schwartz, Murray M. 1942- 116
Schwartz, Nancy Lynn 1952-1978 107
Schwartz, Ned 1948- 107

Schwartz, Norman B(oris) 1932- 111
Schwartz, Paula 1925- CANR-18
Earlier sketch in CA 85-88
Schwartz, Pedro 1935- CANR-24
Earlier sketch in CA 107
Schwartz, Pepper 1945- 33-36R
Schwartz, Richard B. 1941- CANR-15
Earlier sketch in CA 85-88
Schwartz, Richard D(erecktor) 1925- CANR-6
Earlier sketch in CA 1R
Schwartz, Ronald 1937- 65-68
Schwartz, S.
See Starr, S(tephen) Frederick
Schwartz, Sheila (Ruth) 1929- CANR-11
Earlier sketch in CA 25-28R
See also SATA 27
Schwartz, Stephen (Lawrence) 1948- 85-88
See also SATA 19
Schwartz, Steven 1950- 118
Schwartz, Stuart B. 1940- Brief entry 108
Schwartz, William 1916-1982 Obituary 107
Schwartzberg, Julie 1943- 29-32R
Schwartzman, Aaron 1900(?)-1981
Obituary 102
Schwartzman, David 1924- 41-44R
Schwartzman, Edward 1927- 73-76
Schwartzman, Sylvan D(avid) 1913- CANR-21
Earlier sketch in CA 41-44R
Schwartzmann, Mischa 1919- 29-32R
Schwarz, Alfred 1925- Brief entry 118
Schwarz, Boris 1906-1983 37-40R
Obituary 111
Schwarz, Egon 1922- 57-60
Schwarz, Fred(erick) Charles 1913- 1R
Schwarz, Hans 1939- 41-44R
Schwarz, Henry G(uenter) 1928- 37-40R
Schwarz, Jack
See Schwarz, Jacob
Schwarz, Jacob 1924- 103
Schwarz, Jordan A(braham) 1937- 105
Schwarz, Leo W(alder) 1906-1967 7-8R
Schwarz, Richard W(illiam) 1925- CANR-12
Earlier sketch in CA 29-32R
Schwarz, Robert 1921- 77-80
Schwarz, Solomon M. 1882(?)-1973
Obituary 45-48
Schwarz, Ted
See Schwarz, Theodore R., Jr.
Schwarz, Theodore R., Jr. 1945- CANR-10
Earlier sketch in CA 65-68
Schwarz, Walter 1930- 13-14R
Schwarz, Wilhelm Johannes 1929- 65-68
Schwarz-Bart, Andre 1928- 89-92
See also CLC 2, 4
Schwarz-Bart, Simone 1938- 97-100
See also CLC 7
Schwarzenberger, Georg 1908- 13-14R
Schwarzenegger, Arnold 1947- CANR-21
Earlier sketch in CA 81-84
Schwarzkopf, LeRoy C(arl) 1920- 115
Schwarzkopf-Legge, Elisabeth 1915- 109
Schwarzschild, Bettina 1925- 29-32R
Schwarzschild, Stuart 1918- 7-8R
Schwarzweller, Harry K(arl) 1929- 37-40R
Schwebel, Milton 1914- 19-20R
Schwebel, Stephen M(yron) 1929- 77-80
Schwebell, Gertrude C(lorius) 9-10R
Schwed, Peter 1911- CANR-13
Earlier sketch in CA 57-60
Schweid, Eliezer 1929- CANR-18
Earlier sketches in CA 45-48, CANR-1
Schweid, Richard M. 1946- 106
Schweik, Robert C(harles) 1927- 45-48
Schweitzer, Albert 1875-1965 Obituary 93-96
Schweitzer, Arthur 1905- 11-12R
Schweitzer, Byrd Baylor
See Baylor, Byrd
Schweitzer, Christoph E(ugen) 1922-
Brief entry 107
Schweitzer, Darrell 1952- 116
Schweitzer, George K(eene) 1924- 17-18R
Schweitzer, Gertrude 1909- 85-88
Schweitzer, Iris Brief entry 117
See also SATA 36
Schweitzer, Jerome William 1908- 41-44R
Schweitzer, John C. 1934- 19-20R
Schweizer(-Hanhart), Eduard 1913- CANR-20
Earlier sketches in CA 13-14R, CANR-5
Schwendeman, J(oseph) R(aymond)
1897- 81-84
Schweninger, Ann 1951- 107
See also SATA 29
Schweninger, Loren (Lance) 1941- 101
Schwerin, Doris H(alpern) 1922- CANR-9
Earlier sketch in CA 65-68
Schwerin, Kurt 1902- 45-48
Schwerner, Armand 1927- 11-12R
Schwiebert, Ernest G(eorge) 1895- CAP-1
Earlier sketch in CA 15-16
Schwieder, Dorothy 1933- 89-92
Schwitzgebel, Robert L. 1934- 41-44R
Schwob, (Mayer Andre) Marcel
1867-1905 Brief entry 117
See also TCLC 20
Schwoerer, Lois G(reen) 1927- CANR-15
Earlier sketch in CA 77-80
Schydlowsky, Daniel M(oses) 1940- 45-48
Scialiano, Robert (G.) 1925- 11-12R
Sciascia, Leonardo 1921- 85-88
See also CLC 8, 9, 41
Scibor-Rylski, Aleksander 1927(?)-1983
Obituary 109
Scicluna, Hannibal Publius 1880-1981(?)
Obituary 106
Scifres, Bill(y N.) 1925- 103
Scipio
See Watson, (John Hugh) Adam
Scire
See Gardner, G(erald) B(rosseau)
Scism, Carol K. 1931- 41-44R
Scithers, George H(arry) 1929- 57-60
Scitovsky, Tibor 1910- 104
Scoales, William 1933- 33-36R
Scobel, Donald N. 1929- 122
Scobey, Joan 1927- CANR-7
Earlier sketch in CA 57-60
Scobey, Mary-Margaret 1915- CANR-1
Earlier sketch in CA 4R
Scobie, James R(alston) 1929-1981 CANR-6
Obituary 104
Earlier sketch in CA 11-12R
Scobie, Stephen 1943- 111
Scoby, Donald R(ay) 1931- 33-36R
Scofield, Jonathan
See Levinson, Leonard
and Rothweiler, Paul Roger
and Toombs, John
Scofield, Norma Margaret Cartwright
1924- 103
Scofield, William H. 1915- 19-20R
Scoggin, Margaret C(lara)
1905-1968 SATA-28, 47
Scoggins, James (Lawrence) 1934- 21-22R
Scoles, Eugene F(rancis) 1921- CANR-15
Earlier sketch in CA 37-40R
Scollan, E. A.
See O'Grady, Anne
Scolnick, Sylvan 1930(?)-1976 Obituary 69-72
Scopes, John T. 1900-1970 Obituary 29-32R
Scoppettone, Sandra 1936- 7-8R
See also SATA 9
See also CLC 26
Scorer, Richard 1919- 77-80
Scorsese, Martin 1942- 114
Brief entry 110
See also CLC 20
Scortia, Thomas N(icholas) 1926-1986 CANR-6
Obituary 119
Earlier sketch in CA 3R
Scorza, Manuel 1928-1983 Obituary 113
Scot, Chesman
See Bulmer, (Henry) Kenneth
Scotford, John Ryland 1888-1976 7-8R
Obituary 103
Scotland, Andrew 1905- 7-8R
Scotland, James 1917-1983 33-36R
Obituary 110
Scotland, Jay
See Jakes, John (William)
Scotson, John L(loyd) 1928- 21-22R
Scott, A(dolphe) C(larence) 1909- CANR-2
Earlier sketch in CA 7-8R
Scott, Alexander 1920- 105
Scott, Allen John 1938- 97-100
Scott, Amoret (Scudamore) 1930- CANR-10
Earlier sketch in CA 21-22R
Scott, Andrew M(acKay) 1922- 19-20R
Scott, Ann Herbert 1926- 21-22R
See also SATA 29
Scott, Anne Firor 1921- 33-36R
Scott, Anthony
See Dresser, Davis
Scott, Anthony Dalton 1923- CANR-11
Earlier sketch in CA 65-68
Scott, Arthur Finley 1907- CANR-18
Earlier sketches in CA 7-8R, CANR-2
Scott, Arthur L(incoln) 1914- 23-24R
Scott, Austin (Wakeman) 1885(?)-1981
Obituary 103
Scott, Bill 1920(?)-1985 Obituary 117
See also SATA 46
Scott, Bonnie Kime 1944- 119
Scott, C(atharine) A(my) Dawson
See Dawson-Scott, C(atharine) A(my)
Scott, C(ecil) Winfield 1905- 7-8R
Scott, Casey
See Kubis, Pat
Scott, Cecil Alexander 1902(?)-1981
Obituary 104
Scott, Charles R(alph), Jr. 1914- CANR-16
Earlier sketch in CA 89-92
Scott, Charles T. 1932- 21-22R
Scott, Charles W(esley) 1932- 116
Scott, Christopher 1930- 21-22R
Scott, Claudia 1948-1979 Obituary 114
Scott, Clinton Lee 1890- CAP-2
Earlier sketch in CA 19-20
Scott, Cora Annett (Pipitone) 1931- 17-18R
See also SATA 11
Scott, Cyril (Meir) 1879-1970 Obituary 111
Scott, Dan CAP-2
Earlier sketch in CA 19-20
Scott, Dan
See Barker, S. Omar
Scott, Dana
See Robertson, Constance (Pierrepont
Noyes)
Scott, David (Aubrey) 1919- 109
Scott, David W(infield) 1916- 109
Scott, Denise 114
Scott, Donald F(letcher) 1930- 89-92
Scott, Dorothea Hayward 93-96
Scott, Duncan Campbell 1862-1947
Brief entry 104
See also TCLC 6
Scott, Edward M. 1919- 33-36R
Scott, Elaine 1940- CANR-21
Earlier sketch in CA 105
See also SATA 36
Scott, Eleanor 1921- 61-64
Scott, Ellis L(averne) 1915- 49-52
Scott, Eve
See Rodgers, Joann Ellison
Scott, Evelyn 1893-1963 104
Obituary 112
See also DLB 9, 48
See also CLC 43
Scott, F(rancis) R(eginald) 1899-1985 101
Obituary 114
See also CLC 22
Scott, Frances V.
See Wing, Frances (Scott)
Scott, Frank
See Scott, F(rancis) R(eginald)
Scott, Franklin D(aniel) 1901- CANR-5
Earlier sketch in CA 7-8R
Scott, Gavin 1936- 77-80
Scott, Geoffrey 1952- 106
Scott, George (Edwin) 1925- 29-32R
Scott, George Walton 1921- 23-24R
Scott, Harold George 1925- 61-64
Scott, Harold Richard 1887- 7-8R
Scott, Harold W(illiam) 1906- 118
Scott, Harvey W. 1838-1910 DLB-23
Scott, Helen G. 1915(?)-1987 Obituary 124
Scott, Herbert 1931- CANR-6
Earlier sketch in CA 53-56
Scott, Hilda 1915- 124
Scott, Ira O(scar), Jr. 1918- 19-20R
Scott, J(ohn) D(ick) 1917-1980 77-80
Obituary 97-100
Scott, J(ohn) Irving E(lias) 73-76
Scott, J(ames) M(aurice) 1906-1986 105
Obituary 118
Scott, Jack B(rown) 1928- 77-80
Scott, Jack Denton 1915- 108
See also SATA 31
Scott, Jack S.
See Escott, Jonathan
Scott, James A. 1946- 123
Scott, James B(urton) 1926- 85-88
Scott, James C(ampbell) 1936- 29-32R
Scott, James Frazier 1934- CANR-22
Earlier sketch in CA 77-80
Scott, Jane
See McElfresh, (Elizabeth) Adeline
Scott, Jean
See Muir, Marie
Scott, Jeffrey
See Usher, Shaun
Scott, Jeremy
See Dick, Kay
Scott, Jody 81-84
Scott, John 1912-1976 CANR-6
Obituary 69-72
Earlier sketch in CA 7-8R
See also SATA 14
Scott, John Anthony 1916- CANR-23
Earlier sketches in CA 11-12R, CANR-6
See also SATA 23
Scott, John M(artin) 1913- CANR-10
Earlier sketch in CA 65-68
See also SATA 12
Scott, Johnie Harold 1946- CANR-14
Earlier sketch in CA 33-36R
Scott, (Henry) Joseph 1917- 57-60
Scott, Joseph Reid 1926- 41-44R
Scott, Judith Unger 1916- 5-6R
Scott, Justin 104
Scott, Kenneth 1900- CANR-11
Earlier sketch in CA 69-72
Scott, Kenneth J. 1933(?)-1983 Obituary 111
Scott, Lalla (McIntosh) 1893- CAP-2
Earlier sketch in CA 21-22
Scott, Latayne Colvett 1952- CANR-17
Earlier sketch in CA 97-100
Scott, Lauren
See Frentzen, Jeffrey
Scott, Laurence Prestwich 1909-1983
Obituary 110
Scott, Lloyd
See Turner, George E(ugene)
Scott, Lloyd F. 1926- 23-24R
Scott, Louise Binder 1910- CANR-4
Earlier sketch in CA 4R
Scott, Marcia (Adele Morse) 1943- 97-100
Scott, Margaret B(rodie) ?-1976 Obituary 61-64
Scott, Martin
See Gehman, Richard (Boyd)
Scott, Marvin B(ailey) 1944- Brief entry 118
Scott, Mel(lier Goodin) 1906- 29-32R
Scott, (Guthrie) Michael 1907-1983
Obituary 110
Scott, Natalie Anderson 1906- CAP-2
Earlier sketch in CA 23-24
Scott, Nathan A(lexander), Jr. 1925- CANR-20
Earlier sketches in CA 9-10R, CANR-5
Scott, Nerissa
See Ring, Elizabeth
Scott, Norford
See Rowland, D(onald) S(ydney)
Scott, Otto J. 1918- 85-88
Scott, Owen Le Grand 1898-1985
Obituary 117
Scott, P. T.
See Poage, Scott T(abor)
Scott, Patrick (Greig) 1945- 112
Scott, Paul (Mark) 1920-1978 81-84
Obituary 77-80
See also DLB 14
See also CLC 9
Scott, Peter (Markham) 1909- 101
Scott, Peter Dale 1929- CANR-9
Earlier sketch in CA 21-22R
Scott, Peter Graham
See Graham Scott, Peter
Scott, R(obert) B(algarnie) Y(oung)
1899-1987 Obituary 124
Scott, Rachel (Ann) 1947- 103
Scott, Ralph S(amuel) 1927- 41-44R
Scott, Richard A(llen) 1931- 25-28R
Scott, Robert A. 1936- 89-92
Scott, Robert Adrian 1901(?)-1972
Obituary 37-40R
Scott, Robert E(dwin) 1923- CANR-1
Earlier sketch in CA 1R
Scott, Robert F(alcon) 1868-1912
Brief entry 115
Scott, Robert Haney 1927- 17-18R
Scott, Robert Ian 1931- 106
Scott, Robert Lee 1928- CANR-3
Earlier sketch in CA 5-6R
Scott, Robert Lee, Jr. 1908- CAP-1
Earlier sketch in CA 11-12
Scott, Robin
See Wilson, Robin Scott
Scott, Roger (Dennis) 1939- 97-100
Scott, Ronald Bodley 1906-1982 109
Obituary 106
Scott, Ronald (Guthrie) McNair
See McNair Scott, Ronald (Guthrie)
Scott, Roney
See Gault, William Campbell
Scott, Roy Vernon 1927- CANR-1
Earlier sketch in CA 4R
Scott, Sally 1909-1978 116
See also SATA 43
Scott, Sally (Elisabeth) 1948- SATA-44
Scott, Sarah 1723-1795 DLB-39
Scott, Sheila 1927- 53-56
Scott, Sir Walter 1771-1832 YABC-2
Scott, Stanley
See Fagerstrom, Stan
Scott, Stephen E. 1948- 119
Scott, Steve
See Crawford, William (Elbert)
Scott, Stuart
See Aitken, W(illiam) R(ussell)
Scott, Tirsa Saavedra 1920- 13-14R
Scott, Tom 1918- 9-10R
See also DLB 27
Scott, Valerie
See Rowland, D(onald) S(ydney)
Scott, Virgil (Joseph) 1914- CANR-2
Earlier sketch in CA 7-8R
Scott, Virginia M(uhleman) 1945- 121
Scott, W(illiam) E(dgar), Jr. 1929- 49-52
Scott, W(illiam) Richard 1932- 19-20R
Scott, Warwick
See Trevor, Elleston
Scott, Willard H., Jr. 1934- 109
Scott, William Abbott 1926- CANR-9
Earlier sketch in CA 7-8R
Scott, William Bell 1811-1890 DLB-32
Scott, William C(lyde) 1937- 119
Scott, William G(eorge) 1926- CANR-11
Earlier sketch in CA 23-24R
Scott, William R(eese) 1907- 77-80
Scott, William R(alph) 1918- 101
Scott, Wilson L(udlow) 1909-1983 45-48
Obituary 111
Scott, Winfield H(arker) 1932- 21-22R
Scott, Winfield Townley 1910-1968 CANR-7
Obituary 25-28R
Earlier sketch in CA 7-8R
Scott-Giles, C(harles) W(ilfred)
1893-1982(?) Obituary 106
Scott-Heron, Gil 1949- 45-48
See also DLB 41
Scott-Heron, Gil 1952- CANR-24
Scotti, Paul C(arl) 1943- 118
Scotti, R. A. 1946- 122
Scott-James, Anne Eleanor 1913- 105
Scott-Moncrieff, David (William Hardy)
1907-1987 Obituary 123
Scott-Moncrieff, George (Irving) 1910- CAP-1
Earlier sketch in CA 11-12
Scott Moncrieff, Martha Christian 1897- 61-64
Scotto, Robert M(ichael) 1942- 57-60
Scott-Stokes, Henry J.M. Brief entry 117
Scott-Taggart, John 1897-1979 Obituary 104
Scott Thorn, Ronald
See Wilkinson, Ronald
Scout, Ted
See Brand, Kurt
Scouten, Arthur Hawley 1910- CANR-11
Earlier sketches in CA 13-14, CAP-1
Scovel, Myra (Scott) 1905- CANR-2
Earlier sketch in CA 7-8R
Scovell, Jane (Frances) 1934- 116
Scoville, Herbert, Jr. 1915-1985 29-32R
Obituary 116
Scoville, James G(riffin) 1940- 29-32R
Scoville, Warren Candler 1913-1969 CANR-2
Earlier sketch in CA 4R
Scowcroft, Richard P(ingree) 1916- 11-12R
Scriabine, Helen (Gorstrine) 1906- CANR-14
Earlier sketch in CA 23-24R
Scribner, Charles, Jr. 1921- 69-72
See also SATA 13
Scribner, Joanne L. 1949- SATA-33
Scrimgeour, Gary J(ames) 1934- 108
Scrimshaw, Nevin Stewart 1918- 89-92
Scrimsher, Lila Gravatt 1897-1974 4R
Obituary 103
See also SATA 28
Scripps, E(dward) W(yllis) 1854-1926
Brief entry 118
See also DLB 25
Scripps, James G. 1911-1986 Obituary 121
Scriven, Michael (John) 1928- CANR-14
Earlier sketch in CA 21-22R
Scriver, Bob
See Scriver, Robert MacFie
Scriver, Robert MacFie 1914- 115
Scrivner, Wilma Possien 1915- 107
Scroggins, Daniel C(oy) 1937- 33-36R

Scroggs, Robin (Jerome) 1930- 116
Scruggs, C(harles) Eugene 1937- 113
Scrum, R.
See Crumb, R(obert)
Scruton, Roger 1944- CANR-16
Earlier sketch in CA 89-92
Scudder, C(leo) W(ayne) 1915- CANR-3
Earlier sketch in CA 1R
Scudder, Horace E(lisha) 1838-1902
Brief entry 119
See also DLB 42
Scudder, Kenyon J. 1890-1977 Obituary .. 73-76
Scudder, Mildred Lee 1908- 9-10R
Scudder, Rogers V(aughn) 1912- 19-20R
Scudder, Thayer 1930- Brief entry 106
Sculatti, (Eu)Gene 1947- 110
Scull, Andrew 1947- CANR-15
Earlier sketch in CA 81-84
Scull, Florence Doughty 1905- CAP-1
Earlier sketch in CA 11-12
Scullard, Howard Hayes 1903-1983 ..... CANR-3
Obituary 109
Earlier sketch in CA 11-12R
Scully, Frank 1892-1964 .... 7-8R
Scully, Gerald William 1941- 65-68
Scully, James 1937- CANR-11
Earlier sketch in CA 25-28R
Scully, Julia S(ilverman) 1929- 103
Scully, Vincent (Joseph, Jr.) 1920-
Brief entry 113
Scum
See Crumb, R(obert)
Scumbag, Little Bobby
See Crumb, R(obert)
Scuorzo, Herbert E(rnest) 1928- 23-24R
Scupham, John Peter 1933- CANR-9
Earlier sketch in CA 65-68
See also DLB 40
Scuro, Vincent 1951- CANR-5
Earlier sketch in CA 53-56
See also SATA 21
Scutt, Ronald 1916- 97-100
Seaberg, Stanley 1929- 21-22R
Seaborg, Glenn T(heodore) 1912- CANR-2
Earlier sketch in CA 49-52
Seabough, Ed(ward Ellis) 1932- 29-32R
Seabrook, Jeremy 1939- 108
Seabrook, John
See Hubbard, L(afayette) Ron(ald)
Seabrook, William B(uehler) 1886-1945
Brief entry 107
See also DLB 4
Seabrooke, Brenda 1941- 107
See also SATA 30
Seabury, Paul 1923- Brief entry 115
Seabury, Samuel 1729-1796 .... DLB-31
Seagears, Clayton B. 1902(?)-1983
Obituary 110
Seager, Allan 1906-1968 .... 7-8R
Obituary 25-28R
Seager, Ralph William 1911- CANR-6
Earlier sketch in CA 11-12R
Seager, Robert II 1924- CANR-6
Earlier sketch in CA 7-8R
Seager, Walter H(arold) T(ennant) 1938- 120
Seagle, Janet 1924- 102
Seagle, William 1898-1977 .... 7-8R
Obituary 73-76
Seagoe, May V(iolet) 1906-1980 ...... CANR-10
Earlier sketch in CA 15-16R
Seagroatt, Margaret 1920- CANR-13
Earlier sketch in CA 73-76
Seagull, Louis Martin 1941- 112
Seal, Anil 1938- 25-28R
Seale, Bobby
See Seale, Robert George
Seale, Patrick 1930- 97-100
Seale, Robert George 1936- 110
Seale, William 1939- CANR-7
Earlier sketch in CA 19-20R
Sealey, Bruce
See Sealey, D(onald) Bruce
Sealey, D(onald) Bruce 1929- 121
Sealey, Danguole 1931- 33-36R
Sealey, Leonard (George William) 1923- 103
Sealey, (Bertram) Raphael (Izod) 1927- 65-68
Sea-Lion
See Bennett, Geoffrey (Martin)
Sealock, Richard Burl 1907- CAP-2
Earlier sketch in CA 23-24
Sealts, Merton M(iller), Jr. 1915- 13-14R
Seaman, Augusta Huiell 1879-1950
Brief entry 110
See also SATA 31
Seaman, Barbara 1935- 29-32R
Seaman, (A.) Barrett 1945- 73-76
Seaman, Don F(erris) 1935- 77-80
Seaman, Donald (Peter) 1922- Brief entry .. 114
Seaman, Elizabeth Cochrane
See Cochrane, Elizabeth
Seaman, Gerald Roberts 1934- 25-28R
Seaman, John E(ugene) 1932- 89-92
Seaman, L(ewis) C(harles) B(ernard)
1911- 57-60
Seaman, Sylvia S(ybil) CAP-2
Earlier sketch in CA 23-24
Seaman, William M(illard) 1907- 41-44R
Seamands, John Thompson 1916- 11-12R
Seamands, Ruth 1916- 45-48
See also SATA 9
Sear, Frank 1944- 121
Seara Vazquez, M(odesto) 1931- CANR-14
Earlier sketch in CA 17-18R
Search-Light
See Frank, Waldo (David)
Searcy, Margaret Zehmer 1926- 81-84
See also SATA 39
Seare, Nicholas
See Whitaker, Rod
Searight, Mary W(illiams) 1918- 29-32R
See also SATA 17
Searing, Helen E. 1933- 111
Searing, Susan Ellis 1950- 122
Searle, Humphrey 1915-1982 .... 9-10R
Obituary 106
Searle, John R(ogers) 1932- 25-28R
Searle, Kathryn Adrienne 1942- 29-32R
See also SATA 10
Searle, Leroy F(rank) 1942- 73-76
Searle, Mark 1941- 114
Searle, Ronald (William Fordham) 1920- ... 9-10R
See also SATA 42
Searles, (William) Baird 1934- 123
Searles, Herbert L(eon) 1891- 45-48
Searls, Hank
See Searls, Henry Hunt, Jr.
Searls, Henry Hunt, Jr. 1922- 15-16R
Sears, David O'Keefe 1935- 29-32R
Sears, Deane
See Rywell, Martin
Sears, Donald A(lbert) 1923- CANR-6
Earlier sketch in CA 7-8R
Sears, Francis W. 1898-1975 Obituary 61-64
Sears, Hal D(on) 1942- 122
Sears, Paul Bigelow 1891- 17-18R
Sears, Paul M(cCutcheon) 1920- 1R
Sears, Pauline Snedden 1908- 29-32R
Sears, Peter 1937- 110
Sears, Robert R(ichardson) 1908- 17-18R
Sears, Sallie 1932- 41-44R
Sears, Stephen W. 1932- 33-36R
See also SATA 4
Sears, Val 1927- 73-76
Sears, William P(aul), Jr. 1902-1976
Obituary 61-64
Seary, E(dgar) R(onald) 1908- 41-44R
Seashore, Stanley E. 1915- CANR-24
Earlier sketch in CA 33-36R
Seasoltz, R(obert) Kevin 1930- 11-12R
Seasongood, Murray 1878-1983 Obituary ... 109
Seat, William R(obert), Jr. 1920- 13-14R
Seaton, Beryl
See Platts, Beryl
Seaton, Don Cash(ius) 1902- CAP-1
Earlier sketch in CA 9-10
Seaton, Douglas P(aul) 1947- 107
Seaton, Frederick Andrew 1909-1974
Obituary 89-92
Seaton, George 1911-1979 105
Obituary 89-92
See also DLB 44
Seaton, Mary Ethel ?-1974 Obituary 53-56
Seaton, William Winston 1785-1866 .... DLB-43
Seaver, George (Fenn) 1890- CAP-1
Earlier sketch in CA 13-14
Seaver, Paul S(iddall) 1932- 29-32R
Seay, James 1939- 29-32R
Seay, Thomas A(ustin) 1942- 97-100
Sebald, Hans 1929- 73-76
Sebald, William J(oseph) 1901-1980 ..... CAP-1
Obituary 101
Earlier sketch in CA 15-16
Sebastian, Jeanne
See Newsome, Arden J(eanne)
Sebastian, Lee
See Silverberg, Robert
Sebastian, Margaret
See Gladstone, Arthur M.
Sebastian Owl
See Thompson, Hunter S(tockton)
Sebenthall, R(oberta) E(lizabeth) 1917- ... 33-36R
Sebeok, Thomas A(lbert) 1920- 11-12R
Seberg, Jean 1938-1979 Obituary 89-92
Sebesta, Sam L(eaton) 1930- 85-88
Sebestyen, Gyorgy 1930- CANR-6
Earlier sketch in CA 9-10R
Sebestyen, Ouida 1924- 107
See also SATA 39
See also CLC 30
Seboldt, Roland H(enry) A(ugust) 1924- 7-8R
Sebree, Charles 1914-1985 Obituary 117
Sebrey, Mary Ann 1951- 116
Secher, Bjorn 1929- 33-36R
Sechrest, Lee 1929- 19-20R
Sechrist, Elizabeth Hough 1903- 7-8R
See also SATA 2
Seckel, Al 1958- 122
Seckler, David William 1935- 115
Secombe, Harry (Donald) 1921- 57-60
Secondari, John Hermes 1919-1975 61-64
Obituary 57-60
Secor, Robert 1939- CANR-15
Earlier sketch in CA 89-92
Secrest, Meryle
See Beveridge, Meryle Secrest
Secrist, Margaret C(rystal) 1915- 111
Secunda, Sholom 1894-1974 Obituary 49-52
Sedaka, Neil 1939- 103
Sederberg, Arelo Charles 1930- 37-40R
Sederberg, Peter C(arl) 1943- 65-68
Sedges, John
See Buck, Pearl S(ydenstricker)
Sedgewick, Ellery 1872-1960 Obituary 89-92
Sedgwick, Alexander 1930- 19-20R
Sedgwick, Arthur George 1844-1915 .... DLB-64
Sedgwick, Catharine Maria 1789-1867 .... DLB-1
Sedgwick, Jeffrey Leigh 1951- 116
Sedgwick, Michael Carl 1926-1983 89-92
Obituary 111
Sedgwick, Peter 1934-1983 Obituary 110
Sedgwick, Walter (Bradbary) 1885- CAP-1
Earlier sketch in CA 13-14
Sedlacek, William E(dward) 1939- 69-72
Sedler, Robert Allen 1935- 41-44R
Seduro, Vladimir 1910- 41-44R
Sedwick, B(enjamin) Frank 1924- 9-10R
Sedych, Andrei
See Zwibak, Jacques
See, Carolyn 1934- 29-32R
See, (Nadine) Ingram 1904- 112
See, Ruth Douglas 1910- CANR-1
Earlier sketch in CA 4R
Seeber, Edward Derbyshire 1904- 15-16R
Seeber, Gerd Christian 1941- 113
Seebohm, Caroline 1940- 102
Seebord, G. R.
See Soderberg, Percy Measday
Seed, Cecile Eugenie 1930- CANR-10
Earlier sketch in CA 21-22R
Seed, Jenny
See Seed, Cecile Eugenie
See also SATA 8
Seed, Sheila Turner 1937(?)-1979
Obituary 89-92
See also SATA 23
Seedman, Albert A. 1918- Brief entry 112
Seeger, Alan 1888-1916 .... DLB-45
Seeger, Charles Louis 1886-1979 101
Obituary 85-88
Seeger, Elizabeth 1889-1973 Obituary 45-48
See also SATA 20
Seeger, Pete(r R.) 1919- 69-72
See also SATA 13
Seegers, Kathleen Walker 1915- 23-24R
Seeley, John R(onald) 1913- 25-28R
Seelhammer, Ruth 1917- 41-44R
Seelig, Sharon Cadman 1941- 119
Seely, Gordon M. 1930- 37-40R
Seely, Norma 1942- 113
Seely, Rebecca Z(ahm) 1935- 104
Seelye, H(ugh) Ned 1934- 102
Seelye, John 1931- CLC-7
Seelye, John (Douglas) 1931- 97-100
Seeman, Bernard 1911- 23-24R
Seeman, Elizabeth (Brickel) 1904- CAP-1
Earlier sketch in CA 19-20
Seeman, Ernest Albright 1887- 85-88
Seers, Dudley 1920-1983 Obituary 109
Seese, Ethel Gray 1903- 89-92
Seever, R.
See Reeves, Lawrence F.
Seferiades, Giorgos Stylianou
1900-1971 .... CANR-5
Obituary 33-36R
Earlier sketch in CA 5-6R
Seferis, George
See Seferiades, Giorgos Stylianou
See also CLC 5, 11
Sefler, George Francis 1945- 81-84
Sefton, Catherine
See Waddell, Martin
Sefton, James E(dward) 1939- 21-22R
Segal, Abraham 1911(?)-1977 Obituary ... 69-72
Segal, Alan F(ranklin) 1945- 119
Segal, Charles Paul 1936- CANR-16
Earlier sketch in CA 41-44R
Segal, David I. 1928(?)-1970 Obituary 104
Segal, David R(obert) 1941- 111
Segal, Elliot A(lan) 1938- 93-96
Segal, Erich (Wolf) 1937- CANR-20
Earlier sketch in CA 25-28R
See also DLBY 86
See also CLC 3, 10
Segal, Fred 1924(?)-1976 69-72
Obituary 65-68
Segal, Gerald 1953- 117
Segal, Geraldine R(osenbaum) 1908- 113
Segal, Hanna M(aria) 1918- 101
Segal, Harold S. 1903- 29-32R
Segal, Harriet 1931- 123
Segal, Harvey H(irst) 1922- 4R
Segal, Henry 1901(?)-1985 Obituary 116
Segal, Jeanne (Sandra) 1939- 108
Segal, Joyce 1940- 101
See also SATA 35
Segal, Julius 1924- Brief entry 112
Segal, Lore (Groszmann) 1928- CANR-5
Earlier sketch in CA 15-16R
See also SATA 4
Segal, Marilyn 1927- CANR-23
Earlier sketches in CA 19-20R, CANR-8
Segal, Martin CANR-1
Earlier sketch in CA 4R
Segal, Melvin J(ames) 1910- 37-40R
Segal, Mendel 1914- 49-52
Segal, Muriel 1913- 121
Segal, Robert M. 1925- 29-32R
Segal, Ronald (Michael) 1932- CANR-14
Earlier sketch in CA 21-22R
Segal, S(tanley) S. 1919- 25-28R
Segalman, Ralph 1916- 106
Segel, Harold B(ernard) 1930- 23-24R
Segel, Thomas D(onald) 1931- 93-96
Seger, Bob 1945- CLC-35
Segerberg, Osborn, Jr. 1924- 115
Segger, Sydney Walter 1902-19(?) CAP-1
Earlier sketch in CA 15-16
Seghers
See Radvanyi, Netty
Seghers, Anna
See Radvanyi, Netty
See also CLC 7
Segler, Franklin Morgan 1907- 19-20R
Segovia, Andres 1893(?)-1987 Obituary 122
Brief entry 111
Segrave, Edmond 1904-1971 Obituary ... 29-32R
Segraves, Kelly L(ee) 1942- CANR-13
Earlier sketch in CA 61-64
Segre, Claudio Giuseppe 1937- 53-56
Segre, Dan V(ittorio) 1922- 104
Segre, Emilio (Gino) 1905- CANR-13
Earlier sketch in CA 33-36R
Segundo, Bart
See Rowland, D(onald) S(ydney)
Segy, Ladislas 1904- 45-48
Seib, Kenneth Allen 1938- 29-32R
Seibel, C(lifford) W(inslow) 1890- CAP-2
Earlier sketch in CA 25-28
Seibel, Hans Dieter 1941- CANR-11
Earlier sketch in CA 65-68
Seid, Ruth 1913- 5-6R
Seide, Diane 1930- CANR-14
Earlier sketch in CA 73-76
Seide, Michael 1911- 111
Seidel, Frederick (Lewis) 1936- CANR-8
Earlier sketch in CA 15-16R
See also DLBY 84
See also CLC 18
Seidel, George J(oseph) 1932- 15-16R
Seidel, Ina 1885-1974 Obituary 116
See also DLB 56
Seidel, Kathleen G(illes) 1951- 112
Seidel, Michael Alan 1943- 93-96
Seidelman, James Edward 1926- 25-28R
See also SATA 6
Seiden, Art(hur) SATA-42
Seiden, Martin H. 1934- 15-16R
Seiden, Morton Irving 1921- 19-20R
Seidenbaum, Art(hur) 1930- 29-32R
Seidenberg, Robert 1920- 25-28R
Seidenberg, Roderick 1890(?)-1973
Obituary 45-48
Seidensticker, Edward G. 1921- 89-92
Seidick, Kathryn A(melia) 1943- 108
Seidler, Ann (G.) 1925- 25-28R
Seidler, Grzegorz Leopold 1913- CANR-12
Earlier sketch in CA 29-32R
Seidler, Lee J. 1935- 73-76
Seidler, Murray Benjamin 1924- 5-6R
Seidler, Tor 1952- 123
See also SATA 46
Seidlin, Oskar 1911- 41-44R
Seidman, Ann (Willcox) 1926- 81-84
Seidman, Harold 1911- 29-32R
Seidman, Hugh 1940- 29-32R
Seidman, Jerome M(artin) 1911- 45-48
Seidman, Joel 1906- CANR-9
Earlier sketch in CA 5-6R
Seidman, Laurence Ivan 1925- 77-80
See also SATA 15
Seidman, Robert J(erome) 1941- 73-76
Seidner, Diane
See Seide, Diane
Seifert, Anne 1943- 105
Seifert, Elizabeth
See Gasparotti, Elizabeth Seifert
Seifert, Harvey (J.D.) 1911- CANR-3
Earlier sketch in CA 11-12R
Seifert, Jaroslav 1901-1986 .... CLC-34, 44
Seifert, Shirley L(ouise) 1888-1971 ..... CANR-2
Obituary 33-36R
Earlier sketch in CA 4R
Seifman, Eli 1936- 37-40R
Seigel, Jerrold (Edward) 1936- 85-88
Seigel, Jules 1931- 93-96
Seigel, Kalman 1917- 25-28R
See also SATA 12
Seigenthaler, John (Lawrence) 1927-
Brief entry 113
Seignobosc, Francoise 1897-1961 73-76
See also SATA 21
Seignolle, Claude 1917- 23-24R
Seiler, John A(ndrew) 1927- 23-24R
Seiler, Robert E. 1925- 19-20R
Seilhamer, Frank Henry 1933- 85-88
Seim, Richard K(nudt) 1928- 102
Seimer, Stanley J(ames) 1918- 2R
Seinfel, Ruth
See Goode, Ruth
Seip, Terry Lee 1944- 113
Seitlin, Charlotte 1907(?)-1979 Obituary ... 89-92
Seitz, Georg J(osef) 1920- 13-14R
Seitz, Jacqueline 1931- SATA-50
Seitz, Nick 1939- 97-100
Seitz, William Chapin 1914-1974 .... CANR-2
Obituary 53-56
Earlier sketch in CA 3R
Seixas, Judith S. 1922- 85-88
See also SATA 17
Sejima, Yoshimasa 1913- 33-36R
See also SATA 8
Sejour, Victor 1817-1874 .... DLB-50
Sejour Marcou et Ferrand, Juan Victor
See Sejour, Victor
Sekers, Simone 1945- 119
Sekler, Eduard F(ranz) 1920- 69-72
Sekora, John 1939- Brief entry 106
Selavy, Rrose
See Duchamp, (Henri-Robert) Marcel
Selbourne, David 1937- CANR-16
Earlier sketch in CA 89-92
Selby, Bettina 1934- 117
Selby, Donald Joseph 1915- CANR-24
Earlier sketch in CA 1R
Selby, Edward B(urford), Jr. 1938- 45-48
Selby, Hazel Barrington 1889-1972 ...... CAP-2
Earlier sketch in CA 17-18
Selby, Henry A. 1934- 37-40R
Selby, Hubert, Jr. 1928- 15-16R
See also DLB 2
See also CLC 1, 2, 4, 8
Selby, James Winford III 1947- 108
Selby, John (Allen) 1897-1980 .... 1R
Obituary 97-100
Selby, John M(illin) 1905- 25-28R
Selcamm, George
See Machlis, Joseph

Selcher, Wayne A(lan) 1942- CANR-10
Earlier sketch in CA 65-68
Selden, George
See Thompson, George Selden
See also DLB 52
See also CLR 8
Selden, Mark 1938- 81-84
Selden, Neil R(oy) 1931- 106
Selden, Samuel 1899-1979 .... CANR-3
Earlier sketch in CA 1R
Selden, William K(irkpatrick) 1911- 3R
Seldes, George (Henry) 1890- CANR-2
Earlier sketch in CA 7-8R
Seldes, Gilbert (Vivian) 1893-1970 .... 7-8R
Obituary 29-32R
Seldes, Marian (Hall) 1928- CANR-19
Earlier sketch in CA 85-88
Seldin, Maury 1931- CANR-15
Earlier sketch in CA 29-32R
Seldis, Henry 1925-1978 Obituary 77-80
Seldon, James R(alph) 1944- 112
Seldon, Mary Elisabeth 1921- 37-40R
Seldon-Truss, Leslie 1892- 7-8R
Selegen, Galina V(assily) 1899- 41-44R
Selement, George Joseph 1946- 113
Self, Carolyn Shealy 1931- CANR-16
Earlier sketch in CA 93-96
Self, Edwin F(orbes) 1920- 69-72
Self, Huber 1914- 73-76
Self, Jerry M(arvin) 1938- 61-64
Self, Margaret Cabell 1902- CANR-3
Earlier sketch in CA 7-8R
See also SATA 24
Self, Peter J(ohn) O(tter) 1919- 120
Self, William L(ee) 1932- 122
Selg, Herbert 1935- 69-72
Selig, Elaine Booth 1935- 104
Selig, Sylvie 1942- SATA-13
Seligman, Barnard 1923- 113
Seligman, Ben B(aruch) 1912-1970 .... CANR-2
Obituary 29-32R
Earlier sketch in CA 4R
Seligman, Daniel 1924- Brief entry 113
Seligman, Edwin R. A. 1861-1939 .... DLB-47
Seligman, Eustace 1889(?)-1976
Obituary 69-72
Seligman, Germain 1893-1978 Obituary 77-80
Seligman, Lester George 1918- 13-14R
Seligman, Linda H(elen Goldberg) 1944- 114
Seligman, Susan Meilach 1950- 105
Seligmann, G(ustav) L(eonard) Jr. 1934- 45-48
Seligmann, Herbert J(acob) 1891-1984
Obituary 112
Seligmann, Nancy 1948- 57-60
Seligson, Mitchell A(llan) 1945- 119
Seligson, Tom 1946- 33-36R
Selimovic, Mehmed 1910-1982 Obituary 108
Selimovic, Mesa
See Selimovic, Mehmed
Selkirk, Jane
See Chapman, John Stanton Higham
Sell, Betty (Marie) H(aas) 1928- 102
Sell, Charles M(urray) 1933- 113
Sell, DeWitt E(llsworth) 1915- 4R
Sell, Francis Edmund 1902- 7-8R
Sell, Henry Blackman 1889-1974
Obituary 89-92
Sell, Joseph
See Haley, William (John)
Sell, Kenneth D(aniel) 1928- 102
Sell, Roger D(avid) 1944- 116
Sell, Ted 1928- 69-72
Sellen, Robert W(alker) 1930- 45-48
Seller, Maxine Schwartz 1935- 104
Sellers, Bettie M(ixon) 1926- 77-80
Sellers, Charles Coleman 1903-1980 .... CANR-11
Earlier sketch in CA 17-18R
Sellers, Con(nie Leslie, Jr.) 1922- 97-100
Sellers, James Earl 1926- 113
Sellers, Naomi
See Flack, Naomi John White
Sellers, Robert Victor 1894-1973 .... CAP-1
Obituary 89-92
Earlier sketch in CA 13-14
Sellers, Ronnie 1948- 115
Sellery, C. Morley 1894- CAP-2
Earlier sketch in CA 21-22
Sellew, Gladys 1887- CAP-1
Earlier sketch in CA 11-12
Sellin, Eric 1933- CANR-22
Earlier sketches in CA 17-18R, CANR-7
Sellin, Paul R(oland) 1930- 45-48
Sellings, Arthur
See Ley, Arthur Gordon
Sellman, Hunton Dade 1900- 7-8R
Sellman, Roger R(aymond) 1915- CANR-1
Earlier sketch in CA 4R
Sells, Arthur Lytton 1895- CANR-6
Earlier sketch in CA 7-8R
Sells, Iris (Esther) Lytton
See Lytton-Sells, Iris (Esther)
Sells, S(aul) B. 1913- CANR-19
Earlier sketches in CA 3R, CANR-4
Selltiz, Claire (Alice) 1914- 7-8R
Selmark, George
See Seldon-Truss, Leslie
Selness, Craig A(lan) 1955- 119
Selormey, Francis 1927- 21-22R
Selsam, Howard 1903-1970 Obituary 29-32R
Selsam, Millicent Ellis 1912- CANR-5
Earlier sketch in CA 11-12R
See also SATA 1, 29
See also CLR 1
Seltzer, Alvin J(ay) 1939- 65-68
Seltzer, Daniel 1933-1980 89-92
Obituary 97-100
Seltzer, David 1920(?)- Brief entry 110
Seltzer, George 1924- 73-76
Seltzer, Leon E(ugene) 1918-1988 89-92
Obituary 124
Seltzer, Leon F(rancis) 1940- 33-36R
Seltzer, Louis B(enson) 1897-1980
Obituary 97-100
Seltzer, Meyer 1932- SATA-17
Seltzer, Richard (Warren, Jr.) 1946- 105
See also SATA 41
Selver, (Percy) Paul 1888-1970 .... CAP-2
Earlier sketch in CA 29-32
Selvin, David F(rank) 1913- 25-28R
Selvin, Hanan C(harles) 1921- 11-12R
Selvon, Sam
See Selvon, Samuel (Dickson)
Selvon, Samuel (Dickson) 1923-
Brief entry 117
Selwyn-Clarke, Selwyn 1893-1976
Obituary 65-68
Selwyn-Lloyd, John S. B. 1904-1978
Obituary 110
Selye, Hans 1907-1982 .... CANR-2
Obituary 108
Earlier sketch in CA 7-8R
Selz, Peter (Howard) 1919- 2R
Selzer, Joae Graham 1926- 53-56
Selzer, Michael (I.) 1940- CANR-9
Earlier sketch in CA 53-56
Selzer, Richard 1928- CANR-14
Earlier sketch in CA 65-68
Selznick, David O(liver) 1902-1965
Obituary 110
Semaan, Khalil I. H. 1920- 37-40R
Sembene, Ousmane
See Ousmane, Sembene
Semeiks, Jonna Gormely 1944- 109
Semenov, Julian Semenovich 1931- 85-88
Semkiw, Virlyana
See Bishop, Tania Kroitor
Semloh
See Holmes, Peggy
Semmel, Bernard 1928- 77-80
Semmelroth, Otto 1912-1979 .... CANR-10
Earlier sketch in CA 13-14R
Semmens, James P(ike) 1919- 61-64
Semmler, Clement (William) 1914- CANR-14
Earlier sketch in CA 23-24R
Semonche, John E(rwin) 1933- 45-48
Sempell, Charlotte 1909- 41-44R
Semple, Gordon
See Neubauer, William Arthur
Semprun, Jorge 1920(?)- Brief entry 111
Sen, Ela
See Reid, Ela
Sen, Sudhir 1906- 33-36R
Sena, John F(rancis) 1940- 110
Sencourt, Robert
See George, Robert Esmonde Gordon
Sencourt, Robert Esmonde
See George, Robert Esmonde Gordon
Sendak, Jack 77-80
See also SATA 28
Sendak, Maurice (Bernard) 1928- CANR-11
Earlier sketch in CA 7-8R
See also SATA 1, 27
See also DLB 61
See also CLR 1
Sender, Ramon (Jose) 1902-1982 .... CANR-8
Obituary 105
Earlier sketch in CA 7-8R
See also CLC 8
Sendler, David A. 1938- 65-68
Sendrey, A(ladar) Alfred 1884- 15-16R
Sendy, Jean 1910-1978 .... CANR-12
Earlier sketch in CA 53-56
Senelick, Laurence P(hilip) 1942- CANR-22
Earlier sketch in CA 106
Senesh, Hannah 1921-1944 Brief entry 119
Senesi, Mauro 1931- 19-20R
Seng, Peter J. 1922- 19-20R
Senghor, Leopold Sedar 1906- Brief entry 116
Sengler, Johanna 1924- SATA-18
Sengstacke, John H(erman Henry) 1912- 101
Sen Gupta, Pranati 1938- 102
Sen Gupta, Rajeswar 1908- CAP-1
Earlier sketch in CA 9-10
Senick, Gerard J(oseph) 1953- 97-100
Senior, Clarence (Ollson) 1903-1974 65-68
Obituary 53-56
Senior, Donald 1940- CANR-13
Earlier sketch in CA 77-80
Senior, Isabel J(anet Couper Syme) CANR-9
Earlier sketch in CA 7-8R
Senior, Michael 1940- 103
Senior, Nancy 1941- 119
Senkevitch, Anatole, Jr. 1942- CANR-19
Earlier sketch in CA 101
Senn, Alfred Erich 1932- Brief entry 112
Senn, Frank C(olvin) 1943- 115
Senn, Fritz 1928- 41-44R
Senn, Milton J(ohn) E(dward) 1902- 81-84
Senn, Peter R(ichard) 1923- 33-36R
Senn, Steve 1950- 105
See also SATA 48
Senna, Carl 1944- CANR-19
Earlier sketches in CA 49-52, CANR-4
Sennett, Richard 1943- 73-76
Sennett, Ted 1928- 33-36R
Sennholz, Hans F. 1922- 120
Brief entry 118
Sensabaugh, George Frank 1906- CAP-1
Earlier sketch in CA 13-14
Senser, Robert A(nton) 1921- 5-6R
Senter, Florence H.
See Ellis, Florence Hawley
Senter, Sylvia 1921- 113
Sentner, David P. 1898-1975 Obituary 57-60
Sentner, Mary Steele 1900(?)-1983
Obituary 110
Seoane, Rhoda 1905- CAP-2
Earlier sketch in CA 25-28
Sepetys, Jonas 1901- 57-60
Sepheriades, Georgios
See Seferiades, Giorgos Stylianou
Sepia
See Holmvik, Oyvind
Sequoia, Anna 109
Serafian, Michael
See Martin, Malachi
Serafini, Anthony Louis 1945- 112
Serage, Nancy 1924- 65-68
See also SATA 10
Serb, Ann Toland 1937- 81-84
Serban, William M(ichael) 1949- 102
Serebryakova, Galina Iosifovna 1905-1980
Obituary 102
Seredy, Kate 1899-1975 .... 7-8R
Obituary 57-60
See also SATA 1, 24
See also DLB 22
See also CLR 10
Sereni, Vittorio 1913-1983 Obituary 109
Sereny, Gitta
See Serenyi, Gitta
Serenyi, Gitta 1923- 119
Serenyi, Peter 1931- 61-64
Serfaty, Simon 1940- CANR-10
Earlier sketch in CA 25-28R
Sergeant, (Herbert) Howard
1914-1987 .... CANR-20
Obituary 121
Earlier sketches in CA 7-8R, CANR-5
Sergievsky, Orest 1911-1984 Obituary 114
Sergio, Lisa 1905- 61-64
Seriel, Jerome
See Vallee, Jacques F.
Serif, Med 1924- 17-18R
Serig, Beverly J. 1934- 101
Serle, (Alan) Geoffrey 1922- 13-14R
Serling, Robert J(erome) 1918- CANR-1
Earlier sketch in CA 45-48
Serling, (Edward) Rod(man) 1924-1975 65-68
Obituary 57-60
See also DLB 26
See also CLC 30
See also AITN 1
Serna-Maytorena, Manuel Antonio
1932- CANR-3
Earlier sketch in CA 45-48
Sernett, Milton C(harles) 1942- 61-64
Seroff, Victor I(lyitch) 1902-1979 .... 25-28R
Obituary 85-88
See also SATA 12, 26
Seroka, James H. 1950- 124
Seroka, Jim
See Seroka, James H.
Serpieres
See Guillevic, (Eugene)
Serra, Diana
See Cary, Peggy-Jean Montgomery
Serraillier, Ian (Lucien) 1912- CANR-1
Earlier sketch in CA 1R
See also SATA 1
See also SAAS 3
See also CLR 2
Serrano, Napoleon Diestro Valeriano
See Valeriano, Napoleon D(iestro)
Serrano Plaja, Arturo 1909-1979 .... CANR-13
Earlier sketch in CA 29-32R
Serrifile, F. O. O.
See Holmes, William Kersley
Serron, Luis A(ugusto) 1930- 102
Sert, Josep Lluis 1902-1983 Obituary 109
Servadio, Gaia 1938- CANR-11
Earlier sketch in CA 25-28R
Servan-Schreiber, Jean-Jacques 1924- 102
Servello, Joe 1932- SATA-10
Serventy, Vincent (Noel) CANR-10
Earlier sketch in CA 65-68
Service, Elman Rogers 1915- 112
Service, John S(tewart) 1909- Brief entry 113
Service, Pamela F. 1945- 120
Service, Robert
See Service, Robert W(illiam)
Service, Robert W(illiam) 1874(?)-1958
Brief entry 115
See also SATA 20
See also TCLC 15
Servin, Manuel P(atrick) 1920- 37-40R
Serviss, Garrett P(utnam) 1851-1929
Brief entry 119
Serwadda, W(illiam) Moses 1931- 107
See also SATA 27
Serwer, Blanche L. 1910- 65-68
See also SATA 10
Serwicher, Kurt 1912-1979 Obituary 89-92
Seskin, Eugene P(aul) 1948- 89-92
Sesonske, Alexander 1917- 15-16R
Sessions, Kyle Cutler 1934- Brief entry 106
Sessions, Roger Huntington 1896-1985 93-96
Obituary 115
Sessions, Will 1905- 1R
Sessoms, H(anson) Douglas 1931- 41-44R
Seth, Ronald (Sydney) 1911-1985 106
Obituary 115
Seth, Vikram 1952- Brief entry 121
See also CLC 43
Sethi, Narendra Kumar 1935- CANR-14
Earlier sketch in CA 37-40R
Sethi, S. Prakash 1934- 41-44R
Sethna, Jehangir Minocher 1941- 37-40R
Sethna, Minocher Jehangirji 1911- 11-12R
Seth-Smith, Elsie K.
See Murrell, Elsie Kathleen Seth-Smith
Seth-Smith, Leslie James 1923- 104
Seth-Smith, Michael 1928- CANR-16
Earlier sketch in CA 29-32R
Seton, Anya 17-18R
See also SATA 3
Seton, Cynthia Propper 1926-1982 .... CANR-7
Obituary 108
Earlier sketch in CA 5-6R
See also CLC 27
Seton, Ernest (Evan) Thompson
1860-1946 Brief entry 109
See also SATA 18
Seton, Marie 1910- 105
Seton-Thompson, Ernest
See Seton, Ernest (Evan) Thompson
Seton-Watson, Christopher 1918- CANR-11
Earlier sketch in CA 23-24R
Seton-Watson, (George) Hugh (Nicholas)
1916-1984 117
Obituary 114
Settel, Gertrude S. 17-18R
Settel, Irving 1916- 17-18R
Settel, Trudy S.
See Settel, Gertrude S.
Settle, Edith
See Andrews, (William) Linton
Settle, Mary Lee 1918- 89-92
See also CAAS 1
See also DLB 6
See also CLC 19
Setton, Kenneth M. 1914- CANR-18
Earlier sketches in CA 11-12R, CANR-3
Setzekorn, William David 1935- 65-68
Setzler, Frank M(aryl) 1902-1975
Obituary 57-60
Seufert, Karl Rolf 1923- 9-10R
Seuling, Barbara 1937- CANR-8
Earlier sketch in CA 61-64
See also SATA 10
Seung, Thomas Kaehao 1930- 108
Seuphor, Michel
See Arp, Jean
Seuren, Pieter A. M. 1934- 49-52
Seuss, Dr.
See Geisel, Theodor Seuss
See also CLR 9
Sevareid, (Arnold) Eric 1912- 69-72
See also AITN 1
Sevela, Efraim 1928- 69-72
Severin, Mark (Fernand) 1906- 107
Severin, (Giles) Timothy 1940- CANR-10
Earlier sketch in CA 23-24R
Severino, Alexandrino E(usebio) 1931- 41-44R
Severn, Bill
See Severn, William Irving
Severn, David
See Unwin, David S(torr)
Severn, Sue 1918- 5-6R
Severn, William Irving 1914- CANR-16
Earlier sketches in CA 4R, CANR-1
See also SATA 1
Severo, Richard 1932- 73-76
Severs, Jerome
See Wooley, John (Steven)
Severs, Vesta-Nadine 1935- CANR-15
Earlier sketch in CA 89-92
Severson, John H(ugh) 1933- 15-16R
Sewall, Joseph 1688-1769 .... DLB-24
Sewall, Marcia 1935- CANR-18
Earlier sketches in CA 45-48, CANR-1
See also SATA 37
Sewall, Mary Franklin 1884-19(?) CAP-2
Earlier sketch in CA 21-22
Sewall, Richard B(enson) 1908- 93-96
Sewall, Samuel 1652-1730 .... DLB-24
Seward, Desmond 1935- Brief entry 114
Seward, Jack
See Seward, John Neil
Seward, James H(odson) 1928- 65-68
Seward, John Neil 1924- CANR-8
Earlier sketch in CA 23-24R
Seward, Prudence 1926- SATA-16
Seward, William W(ard), Jr. 1913- 11-12R
Sewart, Alan 1928- 108
Sewel, John 1946- 103
Sewell, Anna 1820-1878 .... SATA-24
Sewell, Brocard 1912- 107
Sewell, (Margaret) Elizabeth 1919- 49-52
Sewell, Helen (Moore) 1896-1957
Brief entry 123
See also SATA 38
Sewell, J. Leslie 1923- 21-22R
Sewell, James Patrick 1930- 73-76
Sewell, Richard H(erbert) 1931-
Brief entry 117
Sewell, W. R. Derrick 1931- CANR-9
Earlier sketch in CA 23-24R
Sewell, William H(amilton) 1909- 45-48
Sewell, Winifred 1917- 102
Sewny, Kathryn Wiehe 1909- CAP-1
Earlier sketch in CA 15-16
Sewter, Albert Charles 1912- 89-92
Sexton, A(da) Jeanette 1924- 65-68
Sexton, Anne (Harvey) 1928-1974 .... CANR-3
Obituary 53-56
Earlier sketch in CA 4R
See also CABS 2
See also SATA 10
See also DLB 5
See also CDALB 1941-1968
See also CLC 2, 4, 6, 8, 10, 15
Sexton, James D(ean) 1942- 113
Sexton, Linda Gray 1953- 101
Sexton, Michael J(oseph) 1939- 45-48
Sexton, Richard J(oseph) 1912- 45-48
Sexton, Virgil Wesley 1918- 33-36R
Sexton, Virginia Staudt 1916- 29-32R

Seybolt, Peter J(ordan) 53-56
Seydel, Mildred Woolley 1890(?)-1988 ...37-40R
Obituary 124
Seydell, Mildred
See Seydel, Mildred Woolley
Seydor, Paul 1947- 97-100
Seyer, Philip C. 1941- 119
Seyersted, Brita Lindberg
See Lindberg-Seyersted, Brita
Seyersted, Per 1921- CANR-15
Earlier sketch in CA 29-32R
Seyfert, Carl K(eenan) 1938- 57-60
Seyler, Dorothy U(pton) 1938- 109
Seymour, A(rthur) J(ames) 1914- 97-100
Seymour, Alan 1927- 53-56
Seymour, Alta Halverson CAP-1
Earlier sketch in CA 11-12
See also SATA 10
Seymour, Anne
See Morton, Phyllis Digby
Seymour, Charles, Jr. 1912-1977 ....11-12R
Obituary 69-72
Seymour, Digby G. 1923- 19-20R
Seymour, Dorothy Jane Z(ander) 1928- ...89-92
Seymour, Emery W. 1921- 13-14R
Seymour, Forrest W. 1905-1983 Obituary ..111
Seymour, (William Herschel Kean) Gerald
1941- 101
Seymour, Henry
See Hartmann, Helmut Henry
Seymour, John 1914- CANR-9
Earlier sketch in CA 13-14R
Seymour, Miranda
See Sinclair, Miranda
Seymour, Raymond B(enedict) 1912- ..CANR-13
Earlier sketch in CA 73-76
Seymour, Rogers James 1942- 110
Seymour, Stephan A(ndrew) 1920- 21-22R
Seymour, W(illiam) Douglas 1910- 49-52
Seymour, Whitney North, Jr. 1923- ...CANR-14
Earlier sketch in CA 81-84
Seymour, William Kean 1887- 9-10R
Seymour, William Napier 1914- 77-80
Seymour-Smith, Martin 1928- 7-8R
Seymour-Ure, Colin K. 1938- CANR-18
Earlier sketch in CA 25-28R
Seyton, Marion
See Saxon, Gladys Relyea
Seznec, Jean J. 1905-1983 Obituary 111
Sgroi, Peter Philip 1936- 57-60
Sgroi, Suzanne M(ary) 1943- 108
Shaaber, M. A.
See Shaaber, Matthias A(dam)
Shaaber, Matthias A(dam) 1897-1979
Obituary 111
Shaara, Michael (Joseph) 1929- 102
See also DLBY 83
See also CLC 15
See also AITN 1
Shabad, Theodore 1922-1987 ....CANR-10
Obituary 122
Earlier sketch in CA 25-28R
Shachtman, Tom 1942- 89-92
See also SATA 49
Shack, William A(lfred) 1923- 113
Shackelford, Jean 1946- 105
Shacket, Sheldon R(ubin) 1941- 102
Shackford, Martha Hale 1875-1963 ....3R
Shackford, R(oland) H(erbert) 1908- 3R
Shackle, G(eorge) L(ennox) S(harman)
1903- CANR-2
Earlier sketch in CA 7-8R
Shackleford, Bernard L. 1889-1975 ....CAP-2
Earlier sketch in CA 29-32
Shackleford, Ruby P(aschall) 1913- 57-60
Shackleton, C. C.
See Aldiss, Brian W(ilson)
Shackleton, Doris (Cavell) 1918- 93-96
Shackleton, Edward Arthur Alexander
1911- 13-14R
Shackleton, Ernest Henry 1874-1922
Brief entry 118
Shackleton, Keith Hope 1923- 7-8R
Shackleton, Philip 1923- 101
Shackleton, Robert 1919-1986 ....3R
Obituary 120
Shackleton Bailey, D(avid) R(oy)
1917- CANR-19
Earlier sketches in CA 7-8R, CANR-3
Shackley, Myra (Lesley) 1949- 115
Shackley, Theodore (George, Jr.) 1927-
Brief entry 117
Shacochis, Bob 1951- Brief entry 119
See also CLC 39
Shacochis, Bob
See Shacochis, Robert G.
Shacochis, Robert G. 1951- 124
Shadbolt, Maurice (Francis Richard)
1932- CANR-5
Earlier sketch in CA 13-14R
See also CAAS 3
Shade, Rose (Marian) 1927- 57-60
Shade, William G(erald) 1939- 41-44R
Shade, William L(eonard) 1945-
Brief entry 113
Shadegg, Stephen C. 1909- 13-14R
Shadi, Dorothy Clotelle Clarke 1908- 13-14R
Shadily, Hassan 1920- 105
Shadlick, Harold (Ernest) 1902- 41-44R
Shadoian, Jack 1940- 105
Shadow, Slim
See Shepard, Sam
Shadowitz, Albert 1915- 69-72
Shaearman, John 1931- 15-16R
Shaevitz, Marjorie Hansen 1943- 101
Shaevitz, Morton H(erbert) 1935- 102
Shafarevich, Igor Rostislavovich 1923- 105
Shafer, Boyd Carlisle 1907- 17-18R
Shafer, Neil 1933- 33-36R
Shafer, Robert E(ugene) 1925- CANR-10
Earlier sketch in CA 57-60
See also SATA 9
Shafer, Robert Jones 1920- 37-40R
Shafer, Ronald G. 1939- CANR-10
Earlier sketch in CA 65-68
Shafer, Thomas 1910(?)-1986 Obituary 119
Shaff, Albert L(averne) 1937- 29-32R
Shaffer, Anthony (Joshua) 1926- 116
Brief entry 110
See also DLB 13
See also CLC 19
Shaffer, Betty
See Shaffer, Elizabeth (Nickerson)
Shaffer, Dale Eugene 1929- 37-40R
Shaffer, Elizabeth (Nickerson) 1925- 113
Shaffer, Harry George 1919- CANR-6
Earlier sketch in CA 7-8R
Shaffer, Helen B. 1909(?)-1978 85-88
Obituary 81-84
Shaffer, Jerome A(rthur) 1929- 37-40R
Shaffer, K(atherine) Stevenson 1902- CAP-2
Earlier sketch in CA 17-18
Shaffer, Kenneth R(aymond) 1914- 5-6R
Shaffer, Laurance Frederic 1903-1976
Obituary 65-68
Shaffer, Peter (Levin) 1926- 25-28R
See also DLB 13
See also CLC 5, 14, 18, 37
Shaffer, Samuel 1910- 104
Shaffer, Thomas Lindsay 1934- 37-40R
Shaffer, Wilma L. 1916- 19-20R
Shafritz, Jay M(ichael) 1944- 117
Shaftel, Oscar 1912- 57-60
Shaftner, Dorothy 1918- 25-28R
Shagan, Steve 1927- CANR-6
Earlier sketch in CA 53-56
Shaginyan, Marietta Sergeyevna
1888-1982 Obituary 106
Shah, A(ruind) M(anilal) 1931- 73-76
Shah, Amina 1918- 49-52
Shah, Diane K(iver) 1945- 73-76
Shah, (Sayed) Idries 1924- CANR-22
Earlier sketches in CA 17-18R, CANR-7
Shah, Krishna B. 1933- 17-18R
Shaha, Rishikesh 1925- 69-72
Shahan, Lynn 1941- 106
Shahane, Vasant Anant 1923- CANR-12
Earlier sketch in CA 25-28R
Shahani, Ranjee 1904-1968 ....CANR-2
Earlier sketch in CA 2R
Shahar, David 1926- 65-68
Shaheen, Jack G(eorge) 1935- 124
Shaheen, Naseeb 1931- 65-68
Shahn, Ben(jamin) 1898-1969 121
Obituary 89-92
See also SATA 21
Shahn, Bernarda Bryson
See Bryson, Bernarda
Shah Of Iran
See Pahlevi, Mohammed Riza
Shain, Henry 1941- 57-60
Shain, Merle 1935- 61-64
See also AITN 1
Shainmark, Eliezer L. 1900-1976 Obituary ..104
Shainmark, Lou
See Shainmark, Eliezer L.
Shairp, (Alexander) Mordaunt 1887-1939
Brief entry 110
See also DLB 10
Shakabpa, Tsepon W(angchuk) D(edan)
1907- CAP-2
Earlier sketch in CA 23-24
Sha'Ked, Ami 1945- 101
Shakesby, Paul S(tewart) 1946- 57-60
Shakespeare, Geoffrey (Hithersay)
1893-1980 Obituary 105
Shakespeare, William 1564-1616 ....DLB-62
Shakey, Bernard
See Young, Neil
Shakow, David 1901-1981 Obituary 108
Shalamov, Varlam (Tikhonovich)
1907(?)-1982 Obituary 105
See also CLC 18
Shale, Richard 1947- 89-92
Shales, Thomas William 1948- 112
Brief entry 110
Shales, Tom
See Shales, Thomas William
Shalett, Anita Effron 1917(?)-1984
Obituary 114
Shalhope, Robert E. 1941- 85-88
Shallcrass, John James 1922- CANR-20
Earlier sketch in CA 103
Shallow, Robert
See Atkinson, Frank
Shaloff, Stanley 1939- 29-32R
Shalom, Stephen Rosskamm 1948- 112
Shalvey, Thomas (Joseph) 1937- 105
Shamburger, (Alice) Page 9-10R
Shames, Laurence 1951- 124
Shamlu, Ahmad 1925- CLC-10
Shamon, Albert Joseph 1915- 15-16R
Shan, Yeh
See Wang, C(hing) H(sien)
Shanahan, Eileen 1924- 102
Shanahan, William J. 1935- 29-32R
Shands, Harley C. 1916-1981 Obituary 105
Shands, Harley Cecil 1916-1981 109
Shane, Alex M(ichael) 1933- 45-48
Shane, C(harles) Donald 1895-1983
Obituary 109
Shane, Don (Graves) 1933- 53-56
Shane, Harold Gray 1914- CANR-21
Earlier sketches in CA 11-12R, CANR-3
See also SATA 36
Shane, John
See Durst, Paul
Shane, Mark
See Norwood, Victor G(eorge) C(harles)
Shane, Maxwell 1905(?)-1983 Obituary 111
Shane, Rhondo
See Norwood, Victor G(eorge) C(harles)
Shaner, Madeleine 1932- 73-76
Shange, Ntozake 1948- 85-88
See also DLB 38
See also CLC 8, 25, 38
Shank, Alan 1936- 53-56
Shank, David Arthur 1924- 29-32R
Shank, Joseph E(lmer) 1892- CAP-2
Earlier sketch in CA 25-28
Shank, Margarethe Erdahl 1910- CAP-2
Earlier sketch in CA 19-20
Shankel, George Edgar 1894- CAP-2
Earlier sketch in CA 23-24
Shankland, Peter Macfarlane 1901- CANR-16
Earlier sketches in CA 11-12, CAP-1
Shankle, Ralph O(tis) 1933- 11-12R
Shanklin, William L(eslie) 1941- 120
Shankman, Florence V(ogel) 1912- 41-44R
Shankman, Paul (Andrew) 1943- 93-96
Shanks, Ann Zane (Kushner) 53-56
See also SATA 10
Shanks, Bob 1932- 101
Shanks, Bruce AITN-1
Shanks, Hershel 1930- Brief entry 106
Shanks, Michael (James) 1927-1984 ....CANR-8
Obituary 111
Earlier sketch in CA 5-6R
Shann, Renee 1907(?)-1979 Obituary 89-92
Shannon, David Allen 1920- 1R
Shannon, Dell
See Linington, Elizabeth
Shannon, Doris 1924- CANR-23
Earlier sketches in CA 61-64, CANR-8
Shannon, Edgar F(inley), Jr. 1918- 11-12R
Shannon, Ellen 1927- 77-80
Shannon, Foster (Houts) 1930- 106
Shannon, Fred Albert 1893-1963 Obituary ..111
Shannon, George (William Bones)
1952- CANR-23
Earlier sketch in CA 106
See also SATA 35
Shannon, Jasper Berry 1903-1984 ....2R
Obituary 114
Shannon, John 1943- 57-60
Shannon, Lyle William 1920- 61-64
Shannon, M.
See Geddie, John
Shannon, Monica 1905(?)-1965 Obituary ...109
See also SATA 28
Shannon, Richard 1945- 73-76
Shannon, Robert
See Wieder, Robert S(hannon)
Shannon, Robert C. 1930- 15-16R
Shannon, Robert L(eroy) 1926- 93-96
Shannon, Terry
See Mercer, Jessie
See also SATA 21
Shannon, Thomas A(nthony) 1940- CANR-20
Earlier sketches in CA 53-56, CANR-5
Shannon, William H(enry) 1917- 45-48
Shannon, William V(incent) 1927- CANR-6
Earlier sketch in CA 11-12R
Shanor, Donald Read 1927- CANR-12
Earlier sketch in CA 61-64
Shanwa
See Haarer, Alec Ernest
Shao, Stephen P(inyee) 1924- CANR-11
Earlier sketch in CA 23-24R
Shapcott, Thomas William 1935- 69-72
See also CLC 38
Shapell, Nathan 1922- 49-52
Shapere, Dudley 1928- 17-18R
Shapiro, Cecile 85-88
Shapiro, Charles K. 1926- 7-8R
Shapiro, David (Joel) 1947- 15-16R
Shapiro, David S(idney) 1923-1983 ....CANR-1
Obituary 109
Earlier sketch in CA 4R
Shapiro, Deborah 1923- 106
Shapiro, Dolph
See Sharp, Dolph
Shapiro, Edward 1920- 19-20R
Shapiro, Elizabeth Klein
See Klein, Elizabeth
Shapiro, Fred(eric) C(harles) 1931- 19-20R
Shapiro, Harold I(srael) 1931- 45-48
Shapiro, Harry L(ionel) 1902- 49-52
Shapiro, Harvey 1924- CANR-15
Earlier sketch in CA 41-44R
Shapiro, Henry D(avid) 1937- CANR-3
Earlier sketch in CA 11-12R
Shapiro, Herbert 1929- 37-40R
Shapiro, Herman 1922- 15-16R
Shapiro, Howard I(ra) 1937- 73-76
Shapiro, Irving 1917- 29-32R
Shapiro, Irwin 1911- 81-84
See also SATA 32
Shapiro, James E(rnest) 1946- 108
Shapiro, Jane P.
See Zacek, Jane Shapiro
Shapiro, Jim
See Shapiro, James E(rnest)
Shapiro, Joan Hatch 1928- 33-36R
Shapiro, Julian L. 1904- Brief entry 117
Shapiro, Julian L.
See Sanford, John
Shapiro, Karl (Jay) 1913- CANR-1
Earlier sketch in CA 4R
See also CAAS 6
See also DLB 48
See also CLC 4, 8, 15
Shapiro, Kenneth A(llan) 1942- 118
Shapiro, Lillian L(adman) 1913- 102
Shapiro, Linda Gaye 1953- 65-68
Shapiro, Marianne (Goldner) 1940- 123
Brief entry 118
Shapiro, Martin M(athew) 1933- 102
Shapiro, Max 1912(?)-1981 Obituary 105
Shapiro, Mel 1937- 101
Shapiro, Milton J. 1926- 81-84
See also SATA 32
Shapiro, Nat(haniel M.) 1922-1983 ....CANR-15
Obituary 111
Earlier sketch in CA 29-32R
Shapiro, Norman R(ichard) 1930- 93-96
Shapiro, Robert 1935- 113
Shapiro, Samuel 1927- CANR-1
Earlier sketch in CA 3R
Shapiro, Sue A. 1947- 109
Shapiro, William E. 1934- CANR-20
Earlier sketch in CA 25-28R
Shaplen, June Herman 1924(?)-1982
Obituary 108
Shaplen, Robert M. 1917- 9-10R
Shapley, Fern Rusk 1890-1984 ....41-44R
Obituary 114
Shapley, Harlow 1885-1972 Obituary 37-40R
Shapley, John 1890(?)-1978 Obituary 81-84
Shapo, Marshall S(chambelan) 1936- ..CANR-15
Earlier sketch in CA 41-44R
Shapp, Charles M(orris) 1906- 57-60
Shapp, Martha Glauber 1910- CANR-2
Earlier sketch in CA 1R
See also SATA 3
Shappiro, Herbert (Arthur) 1899(?)-1975 .CAP-2
Obituary 57-60
Earlier sketch in CA 21-22
Sharabi, H(isham) B(ashir) 1927- CANR-2
Earlier sketch in CA 7-8R
Sharat Chandra, G(ubbi) S(hankara Chetty)
1938- 53-56
Sharfman, Amalie 73-76
See also SATA 14
Sharif, M(ohammad) Nawaz 1942- 114
Sharif, Omar
See Chalhoub, Michael
Sharkansky, Ira 1938- 29-32R
Sharkey, Bernarda 1934- 33-36R
Sharkey, Jack
See Sharkey, John Michael
Sharkey, John Michael 1931- CANR-3
Earlier sketch in CA 3R
Sharkey, (Neil) Owen 1917- 61-64
Sharlet, Robert (Stewart) 1935- 37-40R
Sharlin, Harold I(ssadore) 1925- 11-12R
Sharma, Chandradhar 1920- 13-14R
Sharma, Govind Narain 1927- 45-48
Sharma, Jagdish Prasad 1934- 81-84
Sharma, Partap 1939- CANR-14
Earlier sketch in CA 77-80
See also SATA 15
Sharma, Ravindra N(ath) 1944- 110
Sharma, Shripad Rama 1879- CAP-2
Earlier sketch in CA 29-32
Sharman, Maisie
See Bolton, Maisie Sharman
Sharman, Miriam
See Bolton, Maisie Sharman
Sharmat, Marjorie Weinman 1928- CANR-12
Earlier sketch in CA 25-28R
See also SATA 4, 33
Sharmat, Mitchell 1927- 104
See also SATA 33
Sharon, Donna Haye
See Scharlemann, Dorothy Hoyer
Sharon, Rose
See Merril, Judith
Sharon, Sylvia
See Little, Paul H(ugo)
Sharot, Stephen 1943- 109
Sharp, Aaron John 1904- 11-12R
Sharp, Alan 1934- 15-16R
Sharp, Andrew 1906-1974 ....CANR-3
Earlier sketch in CA 2R
Sharp, Ann Margaret 1942- 81-84
Sharp, Ansel M(iree) 1924- 77-80
Sharp, Buchanan 1942- 105
Sharp, Clifford Henry 1922- 108
Sharp, Daniel A(sher) 1932- 49-52
Sharp, Dolph 1914- 29-32R
Sharp, Donald Bruce 1938- 29-32R
Sharp, Doreen Maud 1920- 108
Sharp, Dorothea Elizabeth 21-22R
Sharp, Edith Lambert 1917- 5-6R
Sharp, Ernest Jack
See Sharpsteen, Ernest Jack
Sharp, Francis Michael 1941- 106
Sharp, Hal
See Sharp, Harold W(ilson)
Sharp, Harold S(pencer) 1909- CANR-3
Earlier sketch in CA 11-12R
Sharp, Harold W(ilson) 1914- 93-96
Sharp, Helen
See Paine, Lauran (Bosworth)
Sharp, James
See Kinghorn, A(lexander) M(anson)
Sharp, James Roger 1936- 29-32R
Sharp, John Kean 1892-1979 Obituary 93-96
Sharp, John R. 1921- 17-18R
Sharp, Laure M(etzger) 1921- 29-32R
Sharp, Margery 1905- CANR-18
Earlier sketch in CA 21-22R
See also SATA 1, 29

Sharp, Martin 1900(?)-1987 Obituary ... 124
Sharp, Roger (William) 1935-1986 ... 73-76
Obituary ... 119
Sharp, Ronald A(lan) 1945- ... 123
Sharp, Saundra 1942- ... 45-48
Sharp, Shirley I. 1934- ... 45-48
Sharp, Sister Mary Corona 1922- ... 13-14R
Sharp, Zerna A. 1889-1981 Obituary ... 104
See also SATA 27
Sharpe, Genell J(ackson) Subak
See Subak-Sharpe, Genell J(ackson)
Sharpe, Grant W(illiam) 1925- ... 69-72
Sharpe, J(ames) A(nthony) 1946- ... 117
Sharpe, Jon
See Knott, William C(ecil, Jr.)
Sharpe, Lawrence A(lbright) 1920- ... 49-52
Sharpe, Lucretia
See Burgess, M(ichael) R(oy)
Sharpe, Mitchell R(aymond) 1924- ... 29-32R
See also SATA 12
Sharpe, Roger Carter 1948- ... 93-96
Sharpe, Thomas Ridley 1928- ... 122
Brief entry ... 114
Sharpe, Tom
See Sharpe, Thomas Ridley
See also DLB 14
See also CLC 36
Sharpe, William D(onald) 1927- ... 19-20R
Sharpes, Donald K(enneth) 1934- ... CANR-1
Earlier sketch in CA 45-48
Sharples, Win(ston S.), Jr. 1932- ... 45-48
Sharpless, F(rancis) Parvin 1929- ... 25-28R
Sharpsteen, Ernest Jack 1880-1976
Obituary ... 110
Sharpton, Robert E(arl) 1936- ... 104
Sharrock, Roger (Ian) 1919- ... CANR-2
Earlier sketch in CA 7-8R
Sharwood Smith, Bryan Evers
1899-1983 ... CAP-2
Obituary ... 111
Earlier sketch in CA 29-32
Shatto, Gloria M. 1931- ... 41-44R
Shattock, Ernest (Henry) 1904- ... 102
Shattuck, Charles H(arlen) 1910- ... CANR-2
Earlier sketch in CA 7-8R
Shattuck, Roger (Whitney) 1923- ... CANR-7
Earlier sketch in CA 7-8R
Shatzkin, Leonard 1919- ... 109
Shaughnessy, Edward J(oseph, Jr.) 1934- .. 110
Shaul, Frank
See Rowland, D(onald) S(ydney)
Shaull, (Millard) Richard 1919- ... CANR-11
Earlier sketch in CA 21-22R
Shave, Gordon A(shton) 1922- ... 101
Shavelson, Melville 1917- ... CANR-4
Earlier sketch in CA 53-56
Shaver, James P. 1933- ... CANR-7
Earlier sketch in CA 19-20R
Shaver-Crandell, Anne (Elizabeth) 1941- ... 113
Shaver-Crandell, Annie
See Shaver-Crandell, Anne (Elizabeth)
Shavin, Norman 1926- ... 81-84
Shaw, Alan George Lewers 1916- ... CANR-9
Earlier sketch in CA 23-24R
Shaw, Arnold 1909- ... CANR-1
Earlier sketch in CA 3R
See also SATA 4
Shaw, B(iswanath) N. 1923- ... 37-40R
Shaw, Barton C(arr) 1947- ... 123
Shaw, Bernard 1940- ... 119
Brief entry ... 109
Shaw, Bob 1931- ... CANR-19
Earlier sketches in CA 49-52, CANR-1
Shaw, Brian
See Tubb, E(dwin) C(harles)
Shaw, Bruce 1941- ... 119
Shaw, Bruno 1905-1984 Obituary ... 114
Shaw, Bynum (Gillette) 1923- ... CANR-4
Earlier sketch in CA 3R
Shaw, Carleton Ford 1908- ... CAP-1
Earlier sketch in CA 15-16
Shaw, Carolyn Hagner 1903(?)-1977
Obituary ... 69-72
Shaw, Charles (Green) 1892-1974 ... CAP-1
Earlier sketch in CA 17-18
See also SATA 13
Shaw, Charles R(aymond) 1921- ... CANR-14
Earlier sketch in CA 21-22R
Shaw, Chester Lee 1898(?)-1985 Obituary .. 118
Shaw, David 1943- ... 49-52
Shaw, Dawn
See Shaw, Thelma
Shaw, Donald Lewis 1936- ... 61-64
Shaw, Earl Bennett 1889- ... CAP-1
Earlier sketch in CA 17-18
Shaw, Edward P(ease) 1911-1986 ... 21-22R
Obituary ... 118
Shaw, Elizabeth
See Prance, June E(lizebeth)
Shaw, Ellen Torgerson
See Torgerson Shaw, Ellen
Shaw, Evelyn S. 1927- ... 104
See also SATA 28
Shaw, Felicity 1918- ... 104
Shaw, Flora Louisa
See Lugard, Flora Louisa Shaw
Shaw, Fred ?-1972 Obituary ... 104
Shaw, Frederick 1912- ... CANR-1
Earlier sketch in CA 45-48
Shaw, Frederick W. 1916(?)-1983
Obituary ... 111
Shaw, Gaylord 1942- ... 81-84
Shaw, George
See Bickham, Jack M(iles)
Shaw, George Bernard 1856-1950
Brief entry ... 104
See also DLB 10, 57
See also TCLC 3, 9, 21
Shaw, Graham 1944- ... 118
Shaw, Harold 1916(?)-1986 Obituary ... 118
Shaw, Harry (Lee, Jr.) 1905- ... 81-84
Shaw, Harry Edmund 1946- ... 114
Shaw, Helen 1913-1985 ... CANR-20
Earlier sketch in CA 103
Shaw, Henry I(var), Jr. 1926- ... 33-36R
Shaw, Henry Wheeler 1818-1885 ... DLB-11
Shaw, Howard 1934- ... 106
Shaw, Irene
See Roberts, Irene
Shaw, Irwin 1913-1984 ... CANR-21
Obituary ... 112
Earlier sketch in CA 15-16R
See also DLB 6
See also DLBY 84
See also CDALB 1941-1968
See also CLC 7, 23, 34
See also AITN 1
Shaw, J(oseph) Thomas 1919- ... 17-18R
Shaw, John Bennett 1913- ... 21-22R
Shaw, John Mackay 1897-1984 ... CANR-13
Earlier sketch in CA 29-32R
Shaw, Lau
See Shu Ch'ing-ch'un
Shaw, Lawrence H(ugh) 1940- ... 69-72
Shaw, Leroy R(obert) 1923- ... 13-14R
Shaw, Linda 1938- ... CANR-23
Earlier sketch in CA 106
Shaw, Luci N(orthcote) 1928- ... CANR-17
Earlier sketch in CA 101
Shaw, Malcolm Edwin 1926- ... CANR-1
Earlier sketch in CA 1R
Shaw, Marvin E(vert) 1919- ... 23-24R
Shaw, Maxine 1945- ... 57-60
Shaw, Nancy Stoller 1942- ... 57-60
Shaw, Peter 1936- ... CANR-9
Earlier sketch in CA 65-68
Shaw, Priscilla Washburn 1930- ... 13-14R
Shaw, Ralph R(obert) 1907-1972
Obituary ... 37-40R
Shaw, Ray ... 33-36R
See also SATA 7
Shaw, Richard 1923- ... 37-40R
See also SATA 12
Shaw, Robert 1927-1978 ... CANR-4
Obituary ... 81-84
Earlier sketch in CA 1R
See also DLB 13, 14
See also CLC 5
See also AITN 1
Shaw, Robert Byers 1916- ... 37-40R
Shaw, Ronald D. M. 1883- ... CAP-1
Earlier sketch in CA 13-14
Shaw, Ronald E. 1923- ... 19-20R
Shaw, Russell B(urnham) 1935- ... CANR-3
Earlier sketch in CA 3R
Shaw, Stanford Jay 1930- ... CANR-6
Earlier sketch in CA 7-8R
Shaw, Steven John 1918- ... 19-20R
Shaw, T. D. W.
See Shaw, Thelma
Shaw, T. E.
See Lawrence, T(homas) E(dward)
Shaw, Thelma ... 25-28R
Shaw, Thurstan 1914- ... 103
Shaw, Timothy Milton 1945- ... 112
Shaw, Vivian
See Seldes, Gilbert (Vivian)
Shaw, W. David 1937- ... 29-32R
Shaw, (Harold) Watkins 1911- ... 4R
Shaw, Wayne E(ugene) 1932- ... 53-56
Shaw, William Harlan 1922- ... CANR-15
Earlier sketch in CA 41-44R
Shawcross, John T. 1924- ... 15-16R
Shawcross, William 1946- ... 105
Shawn, Edwin Meyers 1891-1972
Obituary ... 33-36R
Shawn, Frank S.
See Goulart, Ron(ald Joseph)
Shawn, Ted
See Shawn, Edwin Meyers
Shawn, Wallace 1943- ... 112
See also CLC 41
Shawn, William 1907- ... 108
Shay, Arthur 1922- ... 33-36R
See also SATA 4
Shay, Lacey
See Shebar, Sharon Sigmond
Shayne, Gordon
See Winter, Bevis (Peter)
Shayon, Robert Lewis ... 49-52
Shayon, Samuel 1904(?)-1984 Obituary ... 112
Shazar, Rachel
See Katznelson-Shazar, Rachel
Shazar, (Schneor) Zalman 1889-1974 ... 101
Obituary ... 53-56
Shea, Donald F(rancis) 1925- ... 73-76
Shea, George 1940- ... 108
See also SATA 42
Shea, George E., Jr. 1902-1980
Obituary ... 97-100
Shea, James J. 1890(?)-1977 Obituary ... 69-72
Shea, John 1941- ... 73-76
Shea, John Gerald 1906- ... 11-12R
Shea, John Gilmary 1824-1892 ... DLB-30
Shea, John S. 1933- ... 21-22R
Shea, Michael 1946- ... 112
Shea, Robert (Joseph) 1933- ... 101
Shea, Shirley 1924- ... 121
Sheaffer, Louis
See Slung, Louis Sheaffer
Sheaffer, Robert M(errill) 1949- ... 106
Sheagren, Thomas G(eorge) 1949- ... 118
Sheahan, John 1923- ... 19-20R
Sheahan, Richard T(homas) 1942- ... CANR-15
Earlier sketch in CA 65-68
Shealy, C(lyde) Norman 1932- ... CANR-7
Earlier sketch in CA 57-60
Shean, Glenn (Daniel) 1939- ... 53-56
Sheard, Kevin 1916- ... 41-44R
Shearer, John 1947- ... SATA-27, 43
Shearer, Ronald A(lexander) 1932- ... 77-80
Shearer, Ted 1919- ... SATA-43
Shearing, Joseph
See Campbell, (Gabrielle) Margaret (Vere)
Shearman, Hugh (Francis) 1915- ... 13-14R
Shearman, John 1931- ... 15-16R
Shears, Billie
See Watson, O(scar) Michael
Sheats, Mary Boney 1918- ... 15-16R
Sheats, Paul Douglas 1932- ... 101
Shebar, Sharon Sigmond 1945- ... CANR-19
Earlier sketch in CA 103
See also SATA 36
Shebbeare, John 1709-1788 ... DLB-39
Shebl, James M(ichael) 1942- ... CANR-23
Earlier sketches in CA 61-64, CANR-8
Shechner, Mark E. 1940- ... 124
Sheckley, Robert 1928- ... CANR-2
Earlier sketch in CA 3R
See also DLB 8
Shecter, Ben 1935- ... 81-84
See also SATA 16
Shecter, Leonard 1926-1974 Obituary ... 45-48
Shedd, Charlie W. 1915- ... 19-20R
Shedd, Clarence Prouty 1887-1973
Obituary ... 45-48
Shedd, Margaret Cochran 1900-1986
Obituary ... 118
Shedd, William G. T. 1820-1894 ... DLB-64
Shedley, Ethan I.
See Beizer, Boris
Shean, Diana 1915(?)-1987 Obituary ... 124
Sheean, (James) Vincent 1899-1975 ... 61-64
Sheed, Francis Joseph 1897-1981
Obituary ... 105
Sheed, Frank
See Sheed, Francis Joseph
Sheed, Wilfrid (John Joseph) 1930- ... 65-68
See also DLB 6
See also CLC 2, 4, 10
Sheedy, Alexandra Elizabeth 1962- ... 85-88
See also SATA 19, 39
Sheehan, Arthur 1910(?)-1975 Obituary ... 61-64
Sheehan, Bernard W(illiam) 1934- ... 41-44R
Sheehan, Donald Henry 1917-1974 ... CANR-2
Earlier sketch in CA 4R
Sheehan, Ethna 1908- ... 61-64
See also SATA 9
Sheehan, George (Augustine) 1918- ... CANR-13
Earlier sketch in CA 73-76
Sheehan, James J(ohn) 1937- ... CANR-11
Earlier sketch in CA 19-20R
Sheehan, John F(rancis) X(avier) 1933- ... 122
Brief entry ... 118
Sheehan, Joseph Green 1918-1983
Obituary ... 111
Sheehan, Margaret A(nne) 1956- ... 111
Sheehan, Neil 1936- ... 29-32R
Sheehan, Patrick Augustine
See O Siochain, P(adraig) A(ugustine)
Sheehan, Paul V(incent) 1904- ... 33-36R
Sheehan, Sister Helen 1904- ... CAP-1
Earlier sketch in CA 17-18
Sheehan, Susan 1937- ... CANR-12
Earlier sketch in CA 21-22R
Sheehan, Thomas 1941- ... 122
Sheehan, Valerie Harms
See Harms, Valerie
Sheehy, Eugene P(aul) 1922- ... 9-10R
Sheehy, Gail ... CANR-1
Earlier sketch in CA 49-52
Sheehy, Jeanne 1939- ... 110
Sheehy, Maurice S(tephen) 1898-1972
Obituary ... 111
Sheekman, Arthur 1901-1978 ... 81-84
Obituary ... 73-76
Sheen, Fulton J(ohn) 1895-1979 ... CANR-5
Obituary ... 89-92
Earlier sketch in CA 5-6R
Sheeran, James Jennings 1932- ... 65-68
Sheerin, John Basil 1906- ... CANR-4
Earlier sketch in CA 2R
Sheets, Elva (Darah) 1898- ... 57-60
Sheets, John R(ichard) 1922- ... 25-28R
Sheetz, Ann Kindig 1934- ... 101
Shefelman, Janice Jordan 1930- ... 120
Sheffer, H. R.
See Abels, Harriette S(heffer)
Sheffer, Isaiah 1935- ... 17-18R
Sheffield, James Rockwell 1936-
Brief entry ... 106
Sheffield, Janet N. 1926- ... 65-68
See also SATA 26
Sheffy, Lester Fields 1887- ... CAP-1
Earlier sketch in CA 13-14
Shefter, Harry 1910- ... 11-12R
Shefts, Joelle ... SATA-49
Shehan, Lawrence Joseph 1898-1984 ... 117
Shein, Brian 1947- ... 110
Shein, Louis J(ulius) 1914- ... 25-28R
Sheiness, (Lee) Marsha 1940- ... CANR-15
Earlier sketch in CA 89-92
Sheinwold, Alfred 1912- ... 61-64
Sheinwold, Patricia
See Fox-Sheinwold, Patricia
Shek, Ben-Zion 1927- ... 110
Shekerjian, Regina Tor ... SATA-16
Shelbourne, Cecily
See Goodwin, Suzanne
Shelby, Brit
See Grady, James (Thomas)
Shelby, Carroll Hall 1923- ... 19-20R
Shelby, Graham 1940- ... 102
Shelby, Susan
See Kinnicutt, Susan Sibley
Sheldon, Alan 1933- ... 114
Sheldon, Alice Hastings Bradley
1915(?)-1987 ... 108
Obituary ... 122
Sheldon, Ann ... CAP-2
Earlier sketch in CA 19-20
See also SATA 1
Sheldon, Aure 1917-1976 ... 61-64
See also SATA 12
Sheldon, Charles Harvey 1929- ... 107
Sheldon, Charles S(tuart) II 1917-1981
Obituary ... 105
Sheldon, Deyan ... 53-56
Sheldon, Edward 1886-1946 ... DLB-7
Sheldon, Eleanor Bernert 1920- ... 85-88
Sheldon, Esther K. 1906- ... 37-40R
Sheldon, George E.
See Stahl, Le Roy
Sheldon, John
See Bloch, Robert (Albert)
Sheldon, Lee
See Lee, Wayne C.
Sheldon, Michael 1918- ... 19-20R
Sheldon, Muriel 1926- ... CANR-18
Earlier sketch in CA 101
See also SATA 39, 45
Sheldon, Peter 1922- ... 25-28R
Sheldon, Raccoona
See Sheldon, Alice Hastings Bradley
Sheldon, Richard (Robert) 1932- ... 33-36R
Sheldon, Roy ... AITN-1
Sheldon, Roy
See Tubb, E(dwin) C(harles)
Sheldon, Scott
See Wallmann, Jeffrey M(iner)
Sheldon, Sidney 1917- ... 29-32R
See also AITN 1
Sheldon, Suzanne Eaton 1928(?)-1985
Obituary ... 117
Sheldon, Walt
See Sheldon, Walter J.
Sheldon, Walter J. 1917- ... CANR-10
Earlier sketch in CA 25-28R
See also AITN 1
Sheldon, William (Herbert) 1898-1977 ... 25-28R
Obituary ... 116
Sheldon, William Denley 1915- ... 17-18R
Sheldrick, Daphne 1934- ... CANR-3
Earlier sketch in CA 49-52
Shell, Virginia Law 1923- ... 21-22R
Shelley, Bruce L(eon) 1927- ... CANR-9
Earlier sketch in CA 23-24R
Shelley, Dolores 1937- ... 122
Shelley, Florence D(ubroff) 1921- ... 65-68
Shelley, Frances
See Wees, Frances Shelley
Shelley, Lillian
See Koppel, Lillian
and Koppel, Shelley R(uth)
Shelley, Louise I(sabel) 1952- ... 108
Shelley, Mary Wollstonecraft (Godwin)
1797-1851 ... SATA-29
Shelley, Noreen 1920- ... 104
Shelley, Rebecca 1887(?)-1984 Obituary ... 111
Shelly, (Michael) Bruce 1929- ... 57-60
Shelly, Judith A(llen) 1944- ... 115
Shelly, Maynard W(olfe) 1928- ... CANR-7
Earlier sketch in CA 15-16R
Shelly, Peter
See Dresser, Davis
Shelmerdine, Cynthia Wright 1949- ... 117
Shelp, Earl E(dward) 1947- ... 116
Shelton, Barrett C(linton) 1903(?)-1984
Obituary ... 112
Shelton, (Austin) Jess(e), Jr. 1926- ... 3R
Shelton, Lola
See Klaue, Lola Shelton
Shelton, Regina Maria 1927- ... 112
Shelton, Richard 1933- ... CANR-13
Earlier sketch in CA 33-36R
Shelton, Suzanne
See Buckley, Suzanne Shelton
Shelton, William Roy 1919- ... CANR-11
Earlier sketch in CA 5-6R
See also SATA 5
See also AITN 1
Shemin, Margaretha (Hoeneveld) 1928- ... 13-14R
See also SATA 4
Shen, Peter ... 110
Shenk, David W(itmer) 1937- ... 106
Shenk, Lois (Landis) 1944- ... 114
Shenk, Marcia Ann 1953- ... 73-76
Shenk, Wilbert R. 1935- ... 23-24R
Shenkin, Elizabeth Shoemaker ?-1975
Obituary ... 61-64
Shennan, Joseph Hugh 1933- ... 103
Shenoy, B(ellikoth) R(aghunath) 1905- ... 77-80
Shenton, Edward 1895-1977 ... SATA-45
Shenton, Edward H(eriot) 1932- ... CANR-17
Earlier sketch in CA 25-28R
Shenton, James P(atrick) 1925- ... CANR-2
Earlier sketch in CA 5-6R
Shepard, David W. 1922- ... 93-96
Shepard, Elaine (Elizabeth) 1923- ... 21-22R
Shepard, Ernest Howard 1879-1976 ... CANR-23
Obituary ... 65-68
Earlier sketch in CA 9-10R
See also SATA 3, 24, 33
Shepard, Francis P(arker) 1897- ... 13-14R

INDEX

Shepard, Gary 1939- ...97-100
Shepard, Jean H(eck) 1930- ...49-52
Shepard, Jim 19??- ...CLC-36
Shepard, Jon M(ax) 1939- ...CANR-7
Earlier sketch in CA 57-60
Shepard, Leslie (Alan) 1917- ...CANR-8
Earlier sketch in CA 19-20R
Shepard, Leslie Albert 1929- ...29-32R
Shepard, Lucius 19(?)- ...CLC-34
Shepard, Martin 1934- ...33-36R
Shepard, Mary
See Knox, (Mary) Eleanor Jessie
Shepard, Odell 1884-1967 ...CANR-3
Obituary ...25-28R
Earlier sketch in CA 5-6R
Shepard, Paul (Howe) 1925- ...CANR-10
Earlier sketch in CA 23-24R
Shepard, Richard F. 1922- ...115
Shepard, Richmond 1929- ...29-32R
Shepard, Sam 1943- ...CANR-22
Earlier sketch in CA 69-72
See also DLB 7
See also CLC 4, 6, 17, 34, 41, 44
Shepard, Thomas I 1604(?)-1649 ...DLB-24
Shepard, Thomas II 1635-1677 ...DLB-24
Shepard, Thomas Rockwell, Jr. 1918- ...105
Shepardson, Mary (Thygeson) 1906- ...29-32R
Shephard, Esther 1891-1975 ...CAP-2
Obituary ...57-60
Earlier sketch in CA 25-28
See also SATA 5, 26
Shephard, John (Brownlow) 1900- ...CAP-1
Earlier sketch in CA 13-14
Shephard, Roy J(esse) 1929- ...CANR-11
Earlier sketch in CA 29-32R
Shepherd, (Richard) David 1931- ...65-68
Shepherd, David Gwynne 1924- ...5-6R
Shepherd, Donald (Lee) 1932- ...61-64
Shepherd, Elizabeth ...33-36R
See also SATA 4
Shepherd, Geoffrey (Seddon) 1898- ...CANR-20
Earlier sketch in CA 4R
Shepherd, George W., Jr. 1926- ...CANR-6
Earlier sketch in CA 4R
Shepherd, Gordon
See Brook-Shepherd, (Fred) Gordon
Shepherd, J(ohn) Barrie 1935- ...111
Shepherd, Jack 1937- ...57-60
Shepherd, James L(eftwich) III 1921- ...21-22R
Shepherd, Jean (Parker) 1929- ...77-80
See also AITN 2
Shepherd, Joan
See Buchanan, Betty (Joan)
Shepherd, John
See Ballard, (Willis) Todhunter
Shepherd, L. P. ...53-56
Shepherd, Massey H., Jr.
See Shepherd, Massey Hamilton, Jr.
Shepherd, Massey Hamilton
See Shepherd, Massey Hamilton, Jr.
Shepherd, Massey Hamilton, Jr. 1913- ...122
Shepherd, Nan 1893- ...105
Shepherd, Neal
See Morland, Nigel
Shepherd, Robert Henry Wishart
1888-1971 ...CAP-1
Earlier sketch in CA 13-14
Shepherd, Simon 1951- ...120
Shepherd, Walter Bradley 1904- ...105
Shepherd, William C(hauncey) 1942- ...CANR-18
Earlier sketch in CA 25-28R
Shepley, James R(obinson) 1917-
Brief entry ...112
Sheppard, Barry 1937- ...61-64
Sheppard, Cynthia A(nne) 1955- ...108
Sheppard, David Stuart 1929- ...103
Sheppard, Eugenia (Benbow)
1900(?)-1984 ...103
Obituary ...114
Sheppard, Francis Henry Wollaston
1921- ...21-22R
Sheppard, Harold L(loyd) 1922- ...CANR-1
Earlier sketch in CA 45-48
Sheppard, Joseph 1930- ...CANR-23
Earlier sketches in CA 61-64, CANR-8
Sheppard, Lancelot C(apel) 1906- ...CANR-5
Earlier sketch in CA 7-8R
Sheppard, Lila (Brooks) 1906- ...CAP-1
Earlier sketch in CA 13-14
Sheppard, Mary ...29-32R
Sheppard, Roger 1939- ...77-80
Sheppard, Sally 1917- ...69-72
Sheppard, Stephen 1945- ...105
Sheppard, Thomas F(rederick) 1935- ...73-76
Sheppard, Walter Lee, Jr. 1911- ...69-72
Sheppard-Jones, Elisabeth 1920- ...13-14R
Shepperson, Wilbur Stanley 1919- ...CANR-6
Earlier sketch in CA 1R
Sheps, Cecil G(eorge) 1913- ...11-12R
Sheps, Mindel (Cherniack) 1913-1973
Obituary ...37-40R
Sher, Eva ...CAP-2
Earlier sketch in CA 23-24
Sher, Gerson S(amuel) 1947- ...81-84
Sher, Zelig 1888-1971 Obituary ...104
Shera, Jesse Hauk 1903-1982 ...CANR-2
Obituary ...106
Earlier sketch in CA 7-8R
Sherar, Mariam G(hose) 1924- ...45-48
Sherashevski, Boris
See Brown, John J.
Sheraton, Neil
See Smith, Norman Edward Mace
Sheratsky, Rodney E(arl) 1933- ...25-28R
Sherbo, Arthur 1918- Brief entry ...113
Sherburne, Donald W(ynne) 1929- ...1R
Sherburne, James (Robert) 1925- ...33-36R
Sherburne, Zoa (Morin) 1912- ...CANR-3
Earlier sketch in CA 3R
See also SATA 3
See also CLC 30
Sherby, Linda B(arbara) 1946- ...108
Shercliff, Jose 1902(?)-1985 Obituary ...115
Sherdeman, Ted 1910(?)-1987 Obituary ...123
Shere, Dennis 1940- ...77-80
Sherek, Henry 1900-1967 ...CAP-1
Earlier sketch in CA 15-16
Sherer, Mary Louise 1901- ...101
Sherer, Robert G(lenn, Jr.) 1940- ...69-72
Sheret, Rene (Dundee) 1933- ...29-32R
Sherfey, Mary Jane 1933-1983 Obituary ...109
Shergold, N(orman) D(avid) 1925- ...25-28R
Sheridan, Adora
See Hong, Jane Fay
and Pavlik, Evelyn Marie
Sheridan, Anne-Marie 1948- ...85-88
Sheridan, Dorothy Elizabeth 1948- ...116
Sheridan, Eugene Robert 1945- ...CANR-23
Earlier sketch in CA 107
Sheridan, Frances 1724-1766 ...DLB-39
Sheridan, James E(dward) 1922- ...23-24R
Sheridan, James F(rancis), Jr. 1927- ...29-32R
Sheridan, Jane
See Winslow, Pauline Glen
Sheridan, John V. 1915- ...CANR-3
Earlier sketch in CA 9-10R
Sheridan, L(ionel) A(stor) 1927- ...CANR-9
Earlier sketch in CA 21-22R
Sheridan, Lane
See Winslow, Pauline Glen
Sheridan, Lee
See Lee, Elsie
Sheridan, Marion Campbell ...17-18R
Sheridan, Martin 1914- ...104
Sheridan, Polly
See Oates, Jeannette
Sheridan, Richard B. 1918- ...45-48
Sheridan, Thomas 1938- ...61-64
Sheridan, Thomas L. 1926- ...37-40R
Sherif, Carolyn W(ood) 1922- ...17-18R
Sherif, Muzafer 1906- ...CAP-1
Earlier sketch in CA 13-14
Sheriff, John K(eith) 1944- ...120
Sherlock, John 1932- ...CANR-3
Earlier sketch in CA 11-12R
Sherlock, Philip Manderson 1902- ...CANR-6
Earlier sketch in CA 5-6R
Sherman, A(lan) Robert 1942- ...57-60
Sherman, Allan 1924-1973 ...101
Obituary ...45-48
Sherman, Arnold 1932- ...CANR-14
Earlier sketch in CA 33-36R
Sherman, Arthur W(esley), Jr. 1917- ...CANR-21
Earlier sketch in CA 3R
Sherman, Barbara H(ayes) 1942- ...25-28R
Sherman, Bernard 1929- ...29-32R
Sherman, Cecil E(dwin) 1927- Brief entry ...110
Sherman, Charles Bezalel 1896-1971 ...2R
Obituary ...103
Sherman, Charlotte A.
See Sherman, Jory (Tecumseh)
Sherman, Claire Richter 1930- ...106
Sherman, Constance D(enise) 1909- ...45-48
Sherman, D(enis) R(onald) 1934- ...CANR-8
Earlier sketch in CA 15-16R
See also SATA 29, 48
Sherman, Dan(iel Michael) 1950- ...77-80
Sherman, Diane (Finn) 1928- ...CANR-5
Earlier sketch in CA 11-12R
See also SATA 12
Sherman, Eileen Bluestone 1951- ...119
Sherman, Eleanor Rae 1929- ...15-16R
Sherman, Elizabeth
See Friskey, Margaret (Richards)
Sherman, Eric 1947- ...69-72
Sherman, Franklin (Eugene) 1928- ...57-60
Sherman, G(eorge) W(itters) 1903- ...117
Sherman, Harold (Morrow) 1898- ...77-80
See also SATA 37
Sherman, (Marcus) Harvey 1917-1985 ...21-22R
Obituary ...114
Sherman, Howard J. 1931- ...CANR-10
Earlier sketch in CA 15-16R
Sherman, Ingrid 1919- ...103
Sherman, James E(dward) 1939- ...25-28R
Sherman, Jane 1908- ...CANR-12
Earlier sketch in CA 73-76
Sherman, Jerry 1924- ...97-100
Sherman, Joan
See Dern, Erolie Pearl Gaddis
Sherman, Jory (Tecumseh) 1932- ...CANR-11
Earlier sketch in CA 69-72
Sherman, Julia A(nn) 1934- ...37-40R
Sherman, Kenneth 1950- ...117
Sherman, L. L.
See Armentrout, Fred S(herman)
Sherman, Lawrence W(illiam) 1949- ...CANR-7
Earlier sketch in CA 57-60
Sherman, Martin Brief entry ...116
See also CLC 19
Sherman, Martin 1941(?)- ...123
Sherman, Michael
See Lowndes, Robert A(ugustine) W(ard)
Sherman, Michele 1945- ...114
Sherman, Murray H(erbert) 1922- ...19-20R
Sherman, Nancy
See Rosenberg, Nancy (Sherman)
Sherman, Patrick 1928- ...103
Sherman, Peter Michael
See Lowndes, Robert A(ugustine) W(ard)
Sherman, Philip M(artin) 1930- ...29-32R
Sherman, Ray W(esley) 1884-1971
Obituary ...33-36R
Sherman, Richard B. 1929- ...29-32R
Sherman, Richard M(orton) 1928-
Brief entry ...107
Sherman, Robert B(ernard) 1925-
Brief entry ...108
Sherman, Roger 1930- ...37-40R
Sherman, Spencer E. 1936- ...112
Sherman, Steve (Barry) 1938- ...37-40R
Sherman, Susan Jean 1939- ...1R
Sherman, T. P. 1917-1976 ...CAP-2
Earlier sketch in CA 29-32
Sherman, Theodore A(llison) 1901- ...17-18R
Sherman, William David 1940- ...CANR-21
Earlier sketch in CA 105
Sherman, William Lewis 1927- ...105
Shero, Fred (Alexander) 1925- ...105
Sherover, Charles M. ...25-28R
Sherr, Lynn Beth 1942- Brief entry ...109
Sherr, Paul C(linton) 1920- ...77-80
Sherrard, Philip (Owen Arnould) 1922- ...CANR-7
Earlier sketch in CA 13-14R
Sherriff, R(obert) C(edric) 1896-1975 ...85-88
Obituary ...61-64
See also DLB 10
Sherriffs, Ronald E(verett) 1934-
Brief entry ...112
Sherrill, Dorothy 1901- ...69-72
Sherrill, Elizabeth 1928- ...110
Sherrill, Henry Knox 1890-1980
Obituary ...97-100
Sherrill, John L. 1923- ...110
Sherrill, Robert G(lenn) 1925- ...CANR-15
Earlier sketch in CA 21-22R
Sherrill, Suzanne
See Woods, Sherryl
Sherrin, Edward George 1931- ...CANR-15
Earlier sketch in CA 23-24R
Sherrin, Ned
See Sherrin, Edward George
Sherrington, Richard (Wallace) 1940-1977 ...108
Sherrod, Blackie ...AITN-2
Sherrod, Drury 1943- ...109
Sherrod, Jane
See Singer, Jane Sherrod
Sherrod, Robert (Lee) 1909- ...77-80
Sherry, James 1946- ...112
Sherry, John (Olden) 1923- ...119
Sherry, John E(rnest) H(orwath)
1932- ...CANR-16
Earlier sketch in CA 89-92
Sherry, Michael S(tephen) 1945- ...73-76
Sherry, Norman 1925- ...49-52
Sherry, Pearl Andelson 1899- ...109
Sherry, (Dulcie) Sylvia ...49-52
See also SATA 8
Sherry, Vincent B(ernard), Jr. 1948- ...116
Shershow, Scott Cutler 1953- ...123
Shertzer, Bruce E(ldon) 1928- ...CANR-3
Earlier sketch in CA 11-12R
Sherwan, Earl 1917- ...7-8R
See also SATA 3
Sherwin, Byron L(ee) 1946- ...123
Sherwin, Judith Johnson 1936- ...25-28R
See also CLC 7, 15
Sherwin, Martin J(ay) 1937- Brief entry ...110
Sherwin, Oscar 1902-1976 ...3R
Obituary ...65-68
Sherwin, Richard E(lliott) 1933- ...69-72
Sherwin, Sidney 1920- ...65-68
Sherwin, Sterling
See Hagen, John Milton
Sherwin-White, A(drian) N(icholas) 1911- ...119
Sherwood, Debbie
See Sherwood, Deborah
Sherwood, Deborah ...25-28R
Sherwood, Frank Persons 1920- ...CANR-9
Earlier sketch in CA 7-8R
Sherwood, Hugh C. 1928- ...29-32R
Sherwood, John (Herman Mulso)
1913- ...CANR-21
Earlier sketches in CA 7-8R, CANR-6
Sherwood, John C(ollingwood) 1918- ...13-14R
Sherwood, John J(oseph) 1933- ...29-32R
Sherwood, Martin (Anthony) 1942- ...CANR-19
Earlier sketch in CA 102
Sherwood, Michael 1938-1976 ...CAP-2
Earlier sketch in CA 29-32
Sherwood, Morgan B(ronson) 1929- ...CANR-6
Earlier sketch in CA 15-16R
Sherwood, Nelson
See Bulmer, (Henry) Kenneth
Sherwood, Robert D(an) 1949- ...118
Sherwood, Robert E(mmet) 1896-1955
Brief entry ...104
See also DLB 7, 26
See also TCLC 3
Sherwood, William Robert 1929- ...21-22R
Shesgreen, Sean N(icholas) 1939- ...45-48
Shestack, Alan 1938- ...33-36R
Shestack, Jerome J(oseph) 1925- ...118
Shestack, Melvin (Bernard) 1931- ...120
Sheth, Jagdish N(anchand) 1938- ...CANR-11
Earlier sketch in CA 61-64
Shetter, William Z(eiders, Jr.) 1927- ...81-84
Shetterly, Will(iam Howard) 1955- ...119
Shettles, Landrum Brewer 1909- ...CANR-13
Earlier sketch in CA 77-80
Shetty, C(handrashekar) M(ajur)
1927- ...CANR-10
Earlier sketch in CA 13-14R
Shetty, Sharat 1940- ...73-76
Shev, Edward E(lmer) 1919- ...93-96
Shevchuk, Tetiana
See Bishop, Tania Kroitor
Shevelove, Burt 1915-1982 Obituary ...106
Shevin, David (Avram) 1951- ...77-80
Shew, E(dward) Spencer 1908-1977 ...CANR-3
Obituary ...69-72
Earlier sketch in CA 1R
Shewbridge, Edythe A(nne) 1943- ...41-44R
Shewell-Cooper, W(ilfred) E(dward)
1900- ...CANR-7
Earlier sketch in CA 9-10R
Shewmaker, Kenneth E. 1936- ...33-36R
Shi, David Emory 1951- ...106
Shiarella, Robert 1936- ...57-60
Shibles, Warren 1933- ...CANR-12
Earlier sketch in CA 29-32R
Shibutani, Tamotsu 1920- ...17-18R
Shideler, John C(lement) 1949- ...118
Shideler, Mary McDermott 1917- ...25-28R
Shidle, Norman G(lass) 1895- ...17-18R
Shiefman, Vicky 1942- ...57-60
See also SATA 22
Shieh, Francis S(hih-hoa) 1926- ...37-40R
Shiel, M(atthew) P(hipps) 1865-1947
Brief entry ...106
See also TCLC 8
Shield, Renee Rose 1948- ...115
Shields, Allan (Edwin) 1919- ...65-68
Shields, Brenda Desmond (Armstrong)
1914- ...7-8R
See also SATA 37
Shields, Carol 1935- ...81-84
Shields, Charles 1944- ...SATA-10
Shields, Currin Vance 1918- ...3R
Shields, David 1956- ...124
Shields, Donald J(ames) 1937- ...53-56
Shields, Gerald R. 1925- ...110
Shields, Joyce Farley 1930- Brief entry ...109
Shiels, Frederick L(ambert) 1949- ...118
Shiels, George 1886-1949 Brief entry ...111
See also DLB 10
Shiels, W(illiam) Eugene 1897- ...CAP-1
Earlier sketch in CA 9-10
Shiers, George 1908- ...73-76
Shiff, Nathan A. 1914- ...25-28R
Shiffert, Edith (Marcombe) 1916- ...CANR-6
Earlier sketch in CA 13-14R
Shiffrin, Nancy 1944- ...81-84
Shiflet, Kenneth E(lwood) 1918-1978 ...CANR-2
Obituary ...81-84
Earlier sketch in CA 2R
Shiflett, Lee
See Shiflett, Orvin Lee
Shiflett, Orvin Lee 1947- ...115
Shiga, Naoya 1883-1971 ...101
Obituary ...33-36R
See also CLC 33
Shigley, Forrest Dwight 1930- ...4R
Shih, Chung-wen ...81-84
Shih, Vincent Y(u) C(hung) 1903- ...77-80
Shih Hsio-Yen 1933- ...119
Shikes, Ralph E. 1912- ...CANR-12
Earlier sketch in CA 29-32R
Shillaber, Benjamin Penhallow
1814-1890 ...DLB-1, 11
Shiller, Jack G(erald) 1928- ...73-76
Shilling, Dana 1953- ...109
Shilling, N(ed) 1924- ...29-32R
Shillinglaw, Gordon 1925- ...CANR-7
Earlier sketch in CA 17-18R
Shillony, Ben-Ami 1937- ...73-76
Shiloh, Ailon 1924- ...33-36R
Shils, Edward B. 1915- ...CANR-6
Earlier sketch in CA 7-8R
Shilton, Lance(lot) R(upert) 1921- ...7-8R
Shilts, Randy 1952(?)- Brief entry ...115
Shimazaki, Haruki 1872-1943 Brief entry ...105
Shimazaki, Toson
See Shimazaki, Haruki
See also TCLC 5
Shimberg, Benjamin 1918- ...45-48
Shimberg, Elaine Fantle 1937- ...112
Shimer, Dorothy Blair 1911- ...45-48
Shimin, Symeon 1902- ...81-84
See also SATA 13
Shimoniak, Wasyl 1923- Brief entry ...108
Shimota, Helen
See Gross, Helen Shimota
Shinagel, Michael 1934- ...25-28R
Shindell, Sidney 1923- ...15-16R
Shine, Deborah 1932- ...110
Shine, Frances L(ouise) 1927- ...25-28R
Shine, Ted 1931- ...CANR-24
Earlier sketches in CA 77-80, CANR-13
See also DLB 38
Shiner, Larry (Ernest) 1934- ...21-22R
Shiner, Roger A(lfred) 1940- Brief entry ...109
Shingleton, John D. ...115
Shingleton, Royce (Gordon, Sr.)
1935- ...CANR-12
Earlier sketch in CA 29-32R
Shinkle, James D. 1897(?)-1973 Obituary ...104
Shinkle, Tex
See Shinkle, James D.
Shinn, Everett 1876-1953 ...SATA-21
Shinn, Larry Dwight 1942- ...107
Shinn, Roger L(incoln) 1917- ...CANR-18
Earlier sketch in CA 4R
Shinnie, Peter Lewis 1915- ...103
Shinoda, Minoru 1915- ...7-8R
Shinwell, Emanuel 1884-1986 Obituary ...119
Shipler, David K(arr) 1942- ...CANR-21
Earlier sketch in CA 103
Shiplett, June Lund 1930- ...CANR-16
Earlier sketch in CA 81-84
Shipley, David
See Holden, David (Shipley)
Shipley, David O. 1925- ...37-40R
Shipley, Joseph T(wadell) 1893- ...CANR-9
Earlier sketch in CA 15-16R
Shipley, Nan (Sommerville) ...11-12R

Shipley, Peter (Samuel) 1946- CANR-20
Earlier sketch in CA 103
Shipley, (Howard) Thorne 1927- 7-8R
Shipman, David 1932- CANR-12
Earlier sketch in CA 29-32R
Shipman, Harry L(ongfellow) 1948- CANR-10
Earlier sketch in CA 65-68
Shipp, Nelson 1892- 57-60
Shipp, Thomas J. 1918- 13-14R
Shippen, Katherine B(inney) 1892-1980 ....7-8R
Obituary 93-96
See also SATA 1, 23
Shipper, Frank M(artin) 1945- 119
Shippey, Frederick Alexander 1908- CAP-1
Earlier sketch in CA 13-14
Shippey, (Henry) Lee 1884-1969
Obituary 89-92
Shippey, Thomas Alan 1943- 108
Shippy, Richard W. 1927- 81-84
Shipton, Clifford K(enyon) 1902-1973 .... CAP-2
Earlier sketch in CA 17-18
Shipton, Eric Earle 1907-1977 65-68
Obituary 69-72
See also SATA 10
Shipway, George 1908- 25-28R
Shirakawa, Yoshikazu 1935- CANR-14
Earlier sketch in CA 73-76
Shire, Helena (Mary) Mennie 1912- 29-32R
Shirer, William L(awrence) 1904- CANR-7
Earlier sketch in CA 9-10R
See also SATA 45
See also DLB 4
Shires, Henry M(illis) 1913- 19-20R
Shires, Linda M(arguerite) 1950- 118
Shirk, Evelyn Urban 1918- 17-18R
Shirk, George H(enry) 1913- 17-18R
Shirk, Susan L(ee) 1945- 108
Shirkey, Albert P(atterson) 1904- CAP-2
Earlier sketch in CA 17-18
Shirley, Frances A(nn) 1931- CANR-2
Earlier sketch in CA 7-8R
Shirley, Glenn 1916- 89-92
Shirley, Hardy L(omax) 1900- 37-40R
Shirley, James 1596-1666 .... DLB-58
Shirley, John William 1908- Brief entry 114
Shirley, Ralph 1865-1946 Brief entry 117
Shirley-Smith, Hubert 1901-1981 Obituary .. 113
Shirreffs, Gordon D(onald) 1914- CANR-21
Earlier sketches in CA 15-16R, CANR-6
See also SATA 11
Shirts, Morris A(lpine) 1922- 73-76
Shissler, Barbara J(ohnson) 1931- 29-32R
Shivanandan, Mary 1932- CANR-12
Earlier sketch in CA 73-76
Shively, Donald H(oward) 1921-
Brief entry 115
Shively, George Jenks 1893(?)-1980
Obituary 97-100
Shivers, Alfred Samuel 1929- 41-44R
Shivers, Jay S(anford) 1930- CANR-12
Earlier sketch in CA 33-36R
Shivers, Samuel A.
See Shivers, Alfred Samuel
Shivpuri, Gopi Krishna 1903-1984 101
Obituary 113
Shklovsky, Iosif Samuilovitch 1916-1985
Obituary 115
Shklovsky, Viktor Borisovich 1893-1984
Obituary 114
Shlemon, Barbara Leahy 1936- 112
Shlonsky, Abraham 1898(?)-1973
Obituary 41-44R
Shmueli, Adi 1941- CANR-1
Earlier sketch in CA 45-48
Shneerson, Grigory Mikhailovich
1901-1982 Obituary 106
Shneiderman, Ben A. 1947- 115
Shneiderman, Samuel L(oeb) 1906- 97-100
Shneidman, Conalee Levine
See Levine-Shneidman, Conalee
Shneidman, Edwin S. 1918- 29-32R
Shneidman, J(erome) Lee 1929- 37-40R
Shneour, Elie A(lexis) 1925- 37-40R
Shoaf, Richard Allen 1948- 119
Shoben, Edward Joseph, Jr. 1918- 21-22R
Shober, Joyce Lee 1932- 4R
Shoberg, Lore 1949- 33-36R
Shobin, David 1945- CANR-20
Earlier sketch in CA 104
Shoblad, Richard H(anson) 1937- 41-44R
Shock, Julian
See Williamson, Gerald Neal
Shock, Nathan W(etherill) 1906- 7-8R
Shockley, Ann Allen 1927- CANR-1
Earlier sketch in CA 49-52
See also DLB 33
Shockley, Donald G(rady) 1937- 103
Shockley, William (Bradford) 1910-
Brief entry 113
Shoe, Lucy T.
See Meritt, Lucy Shoe
Shoemaker, Don(ald) C(leavenger)
1912- 97-100
Shoemaker, Donald J(ay) 1927- 37-40R
Shoemaker, Leonard Calvin 1881- CAP-1
Earlier sketch in CA 15-16
Shoemaker, Lynn Henry 1939- CANR-9
Earlier sketch in CA 65-68
Shoemaker, Richard H(eston) 1907-1970 . CAP-1
Earlier sketch in CA 11-12
Shoemaker, Robert John 1919- 15-16R
Shoemaker, Robin 1949- 108
Shoemaker, William H(utchinson) 1902- ..15-16R
Shoemaker, William Lee 1931- Brief entry .. 115
Shoemaker, Willie
See Shoemaker, William Lee
Shoenight, Aloise 1914- 77-80
Shoesmith, Kathleen A(nne) 1938- CANR-17
Earlier sketches in CA 49-52, CANR-1
Shofner, Jerrell H(arris) 1929- 57-60
Shofner, Robert D(ancey) 1933- 57-60
Shokeid, Moshe 1936- CANR-16
Earlier sketch in CA 41-44R
Sholinsky, Jane 1943- 89-92
Sholokhov, Mikhail (Aleksandrovich)
1905-1984 101
Obituary 112
See also SATA 36
See also CLC 7, 15
Shomaker, Dianna 1934- 109
Shomon, Joseph James 1914- 73-76
Shomroni, Reuven
See von Block, Bela W(illiam)
Shone, Patric
See Hanley, James
Shone, Robert 1906- 109
Shone, Ronald 1946- CANR-20
Earlier sketch in CA 103
Shonfield, Andrew (Akiba) 1917-1981 105
Obituary 102
Shontz, Franklin C(urtis) 1926- 19-20R
Shook, Karel 1920-1985 Obituary 117
Shook, Laurence K(ennedy) 1909- 73-76
Shook, Robert L. 1938- CANR-23
Earlier sketches in CA 61-64, CANR-8
Shoolbred, C(laude) F(rederick) 1901- CAP-2
Earlier sketch in CA 25-28
Shor, Elizabeth N(oble) 1930- 110
Shor, Franc(is Marion Luther) 1914-1974
Obituary 111
Shor, Joel 1919- 89-92
Shor, Pekay 1923- 45-48
Shor, Ronald (Edwin) 1930- 61-64
Shorb, Wil(bert Hanson, Jr.) 1938- 45-48
Shore, Bernard (Alexander Royle)
1896-1985 Obituary 116
Shore, Jane 1947- 77-80
Shore, June Lewis 105
See also SATA 30
See also AITN 1
Shore, Norman
See Smith, Norman Edward Mace
Shore, Paul J(ohn) 1956- 118
Shore, Philippa
See Holbeche, Philippa Jack
Shore, Robert 1924- SATA-39
Shore, Sidney 1921-1981 Obituary 103
Shore, William B(urton) 1925- 53-56
Shore, Wilma 1913- 15-16R
Shores, David L(ee) 1933- 123
Brief entry 118
Shores, Louis 1904-1981 .... CANR-8
Obituary 104
Earlier sketch in CA 15-16R
Shorris, Earl 1936- CANR-10
Earlier sketch in CA 65-68
Shorrock, William I(rwin) 1941- 65-68
Short, Alan Lennox
See Lennox-Short, Alan
Short, Alison 1920- 61-64
Short, Bobby
See Short, Robert Waltrip
Short, (Charles) Christopher (Dudley)
(?)-1978 .... CANR-2
Earlier sketch in CA 4R
Short, Clarice 1910-1977 45-48
Obituary 103
Short, Edmund C(oen) 1931- 25-28R
Short, Howard E(lmo) 1907- 61-64
Short, Jackson 53-56
Short, James F(ranklin, Jr.) 1924- CANR-8
Earlier sketch in CA 5-6R
Short, James R. 1922(?)-1980 Obituary 103
Short, Luke
See Glidden, Frederick D(illey)
Short, Michael 1937- 117
Short, Philip 1945- 105
Short, Robert L(ester) 1932- 77-80
Short, Robert Stuart 1938- 29-32R
Short, Robert Waltrip 1924(?)- Brief entry .. 107
Short, Roger
See Arkin, Alan (Wolf)
Short, Roger, Jr.
See Eyen, Tom
Short, Roy Hunter 1902- 120
Short, Ruth Gordon CANR-6
Earlier sketch in CA 3R
Short, Thayne R(edford) 1929- 108
Short, Wayne 1926- 11-12R
Shortall, Leonard W. 81-84
See also SATA 19
Shorter, Aylward 1932- 81-84
Shorter, Carl
See Schwalberg, Carol(yn Ernestine
Stein)
Shorter, Edward 1941- 73-76
Shorthouse, Joseph Henry 1834-1903
Brief entry 121
See also DLB 18
Shorto, Harry L(eonard) 1919- 7-8R
Shortt, Terence Michael 1911- 77-80
Shostak, Arthur B. 1937- 108
Shostak, Jerome 1913- CANR-7
Earlier sketch in CA 19-20R
Shostak, Stanley 1938- 117
Shostakovich, Dmitri 1906-1975 Obituary ... 113
Shosteck, Robert 1910-1979 .... CANR-11
Obituary 85-88
Earlier sketch in CA 61-64
Shotwell, Louisa Rossiter 1902- CANR-4
Earlier sketch in CA 3R
See also SATA 3
Shouksmith, George A. 1931- 49-52
Shoumatoff, Alex(ander) 1946- CANR-9
Earlier sketch in CA 53-56
Shoup, Carl S(umner) 1902- 49-52
Shoup, Laurence H(enry) 1943- 102
Shoup, Paul Snedden 1929- 106
Shover, John L. 1927- 21-22R
Showalter, Dennis 1942- 89-92
Showalter, Elaine 1941- 57-60
See also DLB 67
Showalter, English, Jr. 1935- 53-56
Showalter, Jean B(reckinridge) 21-22R
See also SATA 12
Showalter, Ronda Kerr 1942- 37-40R
Showell, Ellen Harvey 1934- 85-88
See also SATA 33
Showers, Paul C. 1910- CANR-4
Earlier sketch in CA 1R
See also SATA 21
See also CLR 6
Showers, Renald E(dward) 1935- CANR-13
Earlier sketch in CA 77-80
Showers, Victor 1910- 53-56
Shoy, Lee Ang
See Sheridan, L(ionel) A(stor)
Shrady, Maria 1924- 49-52
Shragin, Boris 1926- 102
Shrake, Bud
See Shrake, Edwin
Shrake, Edwin 1931- Brief entry 116
Shreve, L(evin) G(ale) 1910- 101
Shreve, Susan Richards 1939- CANR-5
Earlier sketch in CA 49-52
See also CAAS 5
See also SATA 41, 46
See also CLC 23
Shriber, Ione Sandberg 1911-1987
Obituary 121
Shrimpton, Gordon Spencer 1941- 115
Shrimsley, Anthony 1934-1984 Obituary 114
Shrimsley, Bernard 1931- 103
Shriver, Donald W(oods), Jr. 1927- CANR-1
Earlier sketch in CA 45-48
Shriver, George H(ite), Jr. 1931- 21-22R
Shriver, Harry C(lair) 1904- CANR-10
Earlier sketch in CA 65-68
Shriver, Peggy (Ann) L(eu) 1931- 107
Shriver, Phillip Raymond 1922- 15-16R
Shriver, Rosalia (Oliver) 1927- 115
Shroder, Maurice Z(orensky) 1933- 1R
Shrodes, Caroline 1908- CANR-4
Earlier sketch in CA 4R
Shropshire, W(alter), Jr. 1932- 118
Shrout, Thomas R(euben) 1919- 41-44R
Shroyer, Frederick B(enjamin)
1916-1983 .... CANR-13
Earlier sketch in CA 13-14R
Shryock, (Edwin) Harold 1906- CANR-8
Earlier sketch in CA 23-24R
Shryock, Richard Harrison 1893-1972 .... CAP-2
Obituary 33-36R
Earlier sketch in CA 17-18
Shtainmets, Leon 105
See also SATA 32
Shtemenko, Sergei Matveyevich
1907-1976 103
Shternfeld, Ari A(bramovich) 1905-1980
Obituary 105
Shu, Austin Chi-wei 1915- 29-32R
Shub, Beth
See Pessen, Beth
Shub, David 1887-1973 Obituary 41-44R
Shub, Elizabeth CANR-15
Earlier sketch in CA 41-44R
See also SATA 5
Shubik, Martin 1926- CANR-2
Earlier sketch in CA 7-8R
Shubin, Seymour 1921- 3R
Shucard, Alan R(obert) 1935- 61-64
Shu Ch'ing-ch'un 1899-1966 Obituary 109
Shuchman, Abraham 1919-1978
Obituary 77-80
Shue, Larry 1946-1985 Obituary 117
Shuffelton, Frank 1940- 115
Shuford, Cecil Eugene 1907- 13-14R
See also AITN 1
Shuford, Gene
See Shuford, Cecil Eugene
Shugrue, Michael F(rancis) 1934- 21-22R
Shu-Jen, Chou 1881-1936 Brief entry 104
Shukman, Harold 1931- 53-56
Shula, Don(ald Francis) 1930- Brief entry ... 106
Shulberg, Alan
See Wilkes-Hunter, R(ichard)
Shulevitz, Uri 1935- CANR-3
Earlier sketch in CA 11-12R
See also SATA 3, 50
See also DLB 61
See also CLR 5
Shull, Fremont Adam, Jr. 1924- CANR-1
Earlier sketch in CA 3R
Shull, Margaret Anne Wyse 1940- 77-80
Shull, Peg
See Shull, Margaret Anne Wyse
Shulman, Albert M(aimon) 1902- 49-52
Shulman, Alix Kates 1932- 29-32R
See also SATA 7
See also CLC 2, 10
Shulman, Arnold 1914- 29-32R
Shulman, Bernard H. 1922- 108
Shulman, Charles E. 1904-1968 .... CAP-1
Earlier sketch in CA 13-14
Shulman, David Dean 1949- 102
Shulman, Frank Joseph 1943- CANR-12
Earlier sketch in CA 29-32R
Shulman, Harry 1903-1955 Brief entry 112
Shulman, Harry Manuel 1899- 4R
Shulman, Irving 1913- CANR-6
Earlier sketch in CA 4R
See also SATA 13
Shulman, Marshall Darrow 1916- 3R
Shulman, Max 1919- 89-92
See also DLB 11
Shulman, Milton 1913- 103
Shulman, Morton 1925- CANR-14
Earlier sketch in CA 23-24R
See also AITN 1
Shulman, Neil B(arnett) 1945- CANR-9
Earlier sketch in CA 65-68
Shulman, Sandra (Dawn) 1944- CANR-9
Earlier sketch in CA 21-22R
Shultz, George P(ratt) 1920- 104
Shultz, Gladys Denny 1895- 49-52
Shultz, William J(ohn) 1902-1970 ..... CANR-16
Obituary 103
Earlier sketch in CA 2R
Shulvass, Moses A. 1909- 15-16R
Shumaker, Wayne 1910- 7-8R
Shuman, Bruce A(lan) 1941- 110
Shuman, James B(urrow) 1932- 61-64
Shuman, Nicholas R(oman) 1921- 109
Shuman, R(obert) Baird 1929- CANR-4
Earlier sketch in CA 4R
Shuman, Samuel I(rving) 1925- CANR-3
Earlier sketch in CA 11-12R
Shumsky, Zena
See Hampson, Zena
Shumway, Floyd M(allory, Jr.) 1917- 29-32R
Shumway, George (Alfred, Jr.) 1928- 9-10R
Shumway, Mary L. 1926- CANR-7
Earlier sketch in CA 17-18R
Shupp, Mike 1946- 121
Shura, Mary Francis
See Craig, Mary (Francis)
Shurden, Walter B(yron) 1937- CANR-21
Earlier sketch in CA 69-72
Shurkin, Joel N. 1938- CANR-14
Earlier sketch in CA 69-72
Shurr, William H(oward) 1932- CANR-18
Earlier sketch in CA 41-44R
Shurter, Robert L(e Fevre) 1907-1974 ... CANR-2
Earlier sketch in CA 1R
Shurtleff, Malcolm C., Jr. 1922- 7-8R
Shurtleff, Michael 1930- 41-44R
Shurtleff, William 1941- CANR-16
Earlier sketch in CA 93-96
Shuseki, Hayashi
See Hubbell, Lindley Williams
Shuster, Albert H., Jr. 1917- 19-20R
Shuster, Alvin 1930- Brief entry 113
Shuster, George Nauman 1894-1977 77-80
Obituary 69-72
Shuster, Joe 1914- CLC-21
Shuster, Ronald L(owell) 1927- 45-48
Shusterman, David 1912- 25-28R
Shute, Alberta V(an Horn) 1906- CANR-7
Earlier sketch in CA 57-60
Shute, Gary Brana
See Brana-Shute, Gary
Shute, Henry A. 1856-1943 .... DLB-9
Shute, Nerina 101
Shute, Nevil
See Norway, Nevil Shute
See also CLC 30
Shute, R(eginald) Wayne 1933- 29-32R
Shute, Wallace B. 1911- 29-32R
Shute, Wilfred Eugene 1907- 105
Shuttle, Penelope (Diane) 1947- 93-96
See also DLB 14, 40
See also CLC 7
Shuttlesworth, Dorothy Edwards CANR-4
Earlier sketch in CA 1R
See also SATA 3
Shuttleworth, John 1937- AITN-1
Shuval, Judith T(annenbaum) 1925- 45-48
Shuy, Roger W(ellington) 1931- CANR-13
Earlier sketch in CA 61-64
Shwadran, Benjamin 1907- CANR-20
Earlier sketches in CA 13-14R, CANR-5
Shwartz, Susan Martha 1949- 109
Shwayder, David S(amuel) 1926- 106
Shy, John W(illard) 1931- CANR-3
Earlier sketch in CA 5-6R
Shyer, Marlene Fanta CANR-11
Earlier sketch in CA 69-72
See also SATA 13
Shyne, Ann W(entworth) 1914- 115
Shyre, Paul 1929- 103
Siano, Mary M(artha) 1924- 77-80
Siberell, Anne 104
See also SATA 29
Siberry, (Jane) Elizabeth 1957- 122
Sibley, Agnes M(arie) 1914- 61-64
Sibley, Celestine 1917- 85-88
Sibley, Don 1922- SATA-12
Sibley, Elbridge 1903- CAP-1
Earlier sketch in CA 13-14
Sibley, Marilyn McAdams 1923- 21-22R
Sibley, Mulford Quickert 1912- CANR-6
Earlier sketch in CA 7-8R
Sibley, Patricia (Hayles) 1928- 97-100
Sibley, Susan
See Kinnicutt, Susan Sibley
Sibly, John 1920- 2R
Sices, David 1933- 25-28R
Sichel, Peter M(ax) F(erdinand) 1922- 65-68
Sichel, Pierre (Laugier) 1915- 1R
Sichel, Werner 1934- CANR-23
Earlier sketches in CA 23-24R, CANR-8
Sichov, Vladimir 1945- 108
Sicignano, Robert 1946- 116
Siciliano, Vincent Paul 1911- CAP-2
Earlier sketch in CA 29-32
Sicinski, Andrzej 1924- 115

Sickels, Robert J(udd) 1931- 41-44R
Sicker, Philip 1951- 103
Sickles, William Russell 1913- 57-60
Sickman, Laurence C(halfant) S(tevens) 1906- CAP-1
Earlier sketch in CA 11-12
Siculan, Daniel 1922- SATA-12
Siddall, William R(ichard) 1928- 41-44R
Siddiqi, Akhtar Husain 1925- 61-64
Siddiqui, Ashraf (Hossain) 1927- CANR-2
Earlier sketch in CA 7-8R
Siddons, Anne Rivers 101
Siddons, Robert 1952- 119
Sidel, Victor W(illiam) 1931- CANR-9
Earlier sketch in CA 65-68
Sider, Don 1933- 77-80
Sider, Robert Dick 1932- CANR-16
Earlier sketch in CA 37-40R
Sider, Ronald J(ames) 1939- CANR-17
Earlier sketch in CA 93-96
Siders, Ellis L(eroy) 1920- 17-18R
Sidetracked Home Executives
See Jones, Peggy
and Young, Pam
Sidey, Hugh (Swanson) 1927- 124
Brief entry 111
Sidgwick, Henry 1838-1900 Brief entry 120
Sidhwa, Bapsy (N.) 1938- 108
Sidhwa, Keki R(attanshah) 1926- 69-72
Sidjakov, Nicolas 1924- SATA-18
Sidley, Nathan T(heodore) 1929- 113
Sidnell, Michael John 1935- 113
Sidney, Frank
See Warwick, Alan R(oss)
Sidney, Jonathan
See Cooper, Emmanuel
Sidney, Kathleen M(arion) 1944- 103
Sidney, Margaret
See Lothrop, Harriet Mulford Stone
Sidney, Neilma
See Gantner, Neilma
Sidney-Fryer, Donald 1934- 45-48
Sidowski, Joseph B(oleslaus) 1925- 21-22R
Sidran, Ben H. 1943- 102
Siebel, Fritz (Frederick) 1913- SATA-44
Siebenheller, Norma 1937- 107
Siebenschuh, William R(obert) 1942- 89-92
Sieber, Joan E. 1937- 114
Sieber, Roy 1923- 102
Sieber, Sam Dixon 1931- 13-14R
Siebert, Fred(rick) Seaton 1901- 21-22R
Siedel, Frank 1914- 25-28R
Siedel, James M. 1937- 25-28R
Siegal, Aranka 1930- 112
See also SATA 37
Siegal, Mordecai 1934- 102
Siegal, Sanford (Sherwin) 1928- 105
Siegan, Bernard H(erbert) 1924- 65-68
Siegel, Adrienne 1936- CANR-12
Earlier sketch in CA 61-64
Siegel, Beatrice CANR-18
Earlier sketch in CA 101
See also SATA 36
Siegel, Ben 1925- 77-80
Siegel, Benjamin 1914- CANR-4
Earlier sketch in CA 3R
Siegel, Bernie S(hepard) 1932- 123
Siegel, Bertram M. 1936- 25-28R
Siegel, Dorothy (Schainman) 1932- 11-12R
Siegel, Eli 1902-1978 .... CANR-9
Obituary 81-84
Earlier sketch in CA 19-20R
Siegel, Ernest 1922- 73-76
Siegel, Esther 1949- 102
Siegel, Gonnie McClung 1928- 110
Siegel, Helen
See Siegl, Helen
Siegel, Irving H(erbert) 1914- CANR-9
Earlier sketch in CA 21-22R
Siegel, Jack
See Siegel, Jacob
Siegel, Jacob 1913- 17-18R
Siegel, James T. 1937- Brief entry 113
Siegel, Jerome 1914- Brief entry 116
See also CLC 21
Siegel, Jerry
See Siegel, Jerome
Siegel, June 1929- 77-80
Siegel, Marcia B. 1932- 69-72
Siegel, Mark Richard 1949- 110
Siegel, Martin 1933- 33-36R
Siegel, Mary-Ellen
See Siegel, Mary-Ellen Kulkin
Siegel, Mary-Ellen Kulkin 1932- 116
Siegel, Max 1904-1972 Obituary 104
Siegel, Maxwell E(dward) 1933- 101
Siegel, Paul N. 1916- 37-40R
Siegel, Richard L(ewis) 1940- 73-76
Siegel, Robert (Harold) 1939- CANR-21
Earlier sketches in CA 53-56, CANR-5
See also SATA 39
Siegel, Seymour 1927-1988 Obituary 124
Siegel, Stanley E(lliott) 1928- 41-44R
Siegel-Gorelick, Bryna 1954- 115
Siegelman, James Howard 1951- 81-84
Siegelman, Jim
See Siegelman, James Howard
Siegener, Ray 1931- Brief entry 118
Siegener, Ray(mond) 1931- 123
Siegl, Helen 1924- SATA-34
Siegle, Bernard A(ndrew) 1914- 89-92
Siegler, Frederick Adrian 1932- 49-52
Siegler, Ilene C. 1946- 114
Siegman, Gita 1939- 112
Siegmeister, Elie 1909- CANR-1
Earlier sketch in CA 3R
Siegner, C(larence) Vernon, Jr. 1920- 4R
Sielaff, Theodore J. 1920- 13-14R
Sieller, William Vincent 1917- 29-32R
Siemanowski, Richard F. 1922(?)-1981
Obituary 104
Siemens, Reynold Gerrard 1932- 41-44R
Siemon, James Ralph 1948- 121
Siemon, Jeff 1950- 103
Sienkiewicz, Henryk (Adam Aleksander Pius) 1846-1916 Brief entry 104
See also TCLC 3
Sienko, Michell J. 1923-1983 Obituary 111
Siepmann, Charles Arthur 1899-1985 .... 1R
Obituary 115
Sierra, Gregorio Martinez
See Martinez Sierra, Gregorio
Sierra, Maria (de la O'LeJarraga) Martinez
See Martinez Sierra, Maria (de la O'LeJarraga)
Sies, Luther F(rank) 1927- 111
Siev, Asher 1913- 57-60
Sievers, Allen M. 1918- 89-92
Sievers, Harry J(oseph) 1920-1977 .... 25-28R
Obituary 73-76
Sievers, W(ieder) David 1919-1966 .... 1R
Obituary 103
Siewert, Frances E. (Cornelius) 1881- CAP-1
Earlier sketch in CA 11-12
Sifakis, G(regory) M(ichael) 1935- 25-28R
Siffert, Robert S(pencer) 1918- 109
Sifford, (Charles) Darrell 1931- CANR-15
Earlier sketch in CA 77-80
Sifton, Claire 1897(?)-1980 Obituary 93-96
Sifton, Paul F. 1893(?)-1972 Obituary 33-36R
Sigal, Clancy 1926- 3R
See also CLC 7
Sigal, Leon V(ictor) 1942- Brief entry 114
Sigband, Norman Bruce 1920- CANR-17
Earlier sketches in CA 7-8R, CANR-2
Sigel, Efrem 1943- 121
Sigelschiffer, Saul 1902- 81-84
Sigler, Jay A(drian) 1933- 25-28R
Sigmund, Paul E(ugene) 1929- CANR-18
Earlier sketches in CA 7-8R, CANR-2
Signoret, Simone 1921-1985 Obituary 117
Sigourney, Lydia Howard (Huntley) 1791-1865 .... DLB-1, 42
Sigurjonsson, Johann 1880-1919 .... TCLC-27
Sigworth, Oliver F(rederic) 1921- 15-16R
Sihanouk, Norodom
See Norodom Sihanouk (Varman), Samdech Preah
Siirala, Aarne 1919- 13-14R
Sik, Endre 1891-1978 Obituary 77-80
Sikes, Herschel Moreland 1928- 17-18R
Sikes, Walter W(allace) 1925- 57-60
Sikora, Frank J(oseph) 1936- 115
Sikora, Joseph (John) 1932-1967 .... CAP-2
Earlier sketch in CA 17-18
Sikora, Stefan
See Rey, Michael Stephan
Sikorsky, Igor (Ivan) 1889-1972 Obituary 113
Siks, Geraldine Brain 1912- 25-28R
Sikula, Andrew F(rank) 1944- CANR-2
Earlier sketch in CA 49-52
Silangan, Manuel
See Yabes, Leopoldo Y(abes)
Silbajoris, Frank
See Silbajoris, Rimvydas
Silbajoris, Rimvydas 1926- 25-28R
Silber, Evelyn (Ann) 1949- 124
Silber, Irwin 1925- 11-12R
Silber, Joan 1945- CANR-20
Earlier sketch in CA 104
Silber, Kate 1902- 77-80
Silber, Mark 1946- 45-48
Silber, Norman I. 1951- 114
Silber, William L. 1942- 29-32R
Silberg, Moshe 1900-1975 Obituary 61-64
Silberg, Richard 1942- 23-24R
Silberger, Julius 1929- CANR-21
Earlier sketch in CA 105
Silberkleit, Louis Horace 1905-1986
Obituary 118
Silberman, Charles E(liot) 1925- CANR-7
Earlier sketch in CA 9-10R
Silberman, Jerome 1935(?)- Brief entry 116
Silberman, Neil Asher 1950- 108
Silbermann, Eileen Z(ieget) 1925- 114
Silbersack, John (Walter) 1954- 107
Silberschlag, Eisig 1903- CANR-17
Earlier sketches in CA 4R, CANR-1
Silberschmidt, Max 1899- 65-68
Silberstang, Edwin 1930- CANR-3
Earlier sketch in CA 49-52
Silberstein, Gerard Edward 1926- 37-40R
Silberstein, Howard E. 1907(?)-1984
Obituary 112
Silberstein, Warren P(aul) 1948- 110
Silberstein-Storfer, Muriel (Rosoff) 111
Silbey, Joel H. 1933- 21-22R
Silcock, Sara Lesley 1947- SATA-12
Silcock, Thomas H(enry) 1910- 11-12R
Silcox, David Phillips 1937- 109
Silen, Juan Angel 1938- 33-36R
Silet, Charles L(oring) P(rovine) 1942- CANR-17
Earlier sketch in CA 93-96
Silitch, Clarissa MacVeagh 1930- 112
Silk, Andrew 1953(?)-1981 Obituary 106
Silk, Leonard S(olomon) 1918- CANR-4
Earlier sketch in CA 2R
Silkin, Jon 1930- 7-8R
See also CAAS 5
See also DLB 27
See also CLC 2, 6, 43
Silko, Leslie Marmon 1948- 122
Brief entry 115
See also CLC 23
Sill, Geoffrey M(ichael) 1944- 111
Sill, Gertrude Grace 69-72
Sill, Sterling Welling 1903- CANR-6
Earlier sketch in CA 57-60
Sillanpaa, Frans Eemil 1888-1964
Obituary 93-96
See also CLC 19
Sillem, Edward 1916-1964 .... 5-6R
Sillen, Samuel 1911(?)-1973 Obituary 41-44R
Sillery, Anthony 1903-1976 .... CANR-5
Obituary 65-68
Earlier sketch in CA 7-8R
Silliman, Ron(ald Glenn) 1946- 45-48
Silliphant, Stirling (Dale) 1918- CANR-14
Earlier sketch in CA 73-76
See also DLB 26
Sillitoe, Alan 1928- CANR-8
Earlier sketch in CA 11-12R
See also CAAS 2
See also DLB 14
See also CLC 1, 3, 6, 10, 19
See also AITN 1
Sillman, Leonard (Dexter) 1908-1982
Obituary 105
Sills, Beverly 1929- 89-92
Sills, David Lawrence 1920- 33-36R
Sills, Frank D(reyer) 1914- 4R
Sills, Jennifer
See Lewis, Stephen
Sills, Ruth C(urtis) 29-32R
Silman, Roberta 1934- 101
See also DLB 28
Silone, Ignazio 1900-1978 .... CAP-2
Obituary 81-84
Earlier sketch in CA 25-28
See also CLC 4
Siluriensis, Leolinus
See Jones, Arthur Llewellyn
Silva, Eduardo Neale
See Neale-Silva, Eduardo
Silva, Joseph
See Goulart, Ron(ald Joseph)
Silva, Julian 1927- 115
Silva, Julio A(lberto) 1933- 17-18R
Silva, Ruth C. 13-14R
Silvanus
See Strasser, Bernard Paul
Silvaroli, Nicholas J. 1930- CANR-12
Earlier sketch in CA 29-32R
Silver, A(aron) David 1941- 124
Silver, A(aron) Henry 1891-1986 Obituary 121
Silver, Abba Hillel 1893-1963 .... 2R
Silver, Alain (Joel) 1947- CANR-10
Earlier sketch in CA 57-60
Silver, Alfred 1951- CANR-15
Earlier sketch in CA 85-88
Silver, Daniel Jeremy 1928- CANR-3
Earlier sketch in CA 7-8R
Silver, Gary (Thomas) 1944- 89-92
Silver, Gerald A(lbert) 1932- CANR-13
Earlier sketch in CA 33-36R
Silver, Harold 1928- CANR-10
Earlier sketch in CA 23-24R
Silver, Isidore 1934- 53-56
Silver, James W(esley) 1907- 9-10R
Silver, Joan Micklin 1935- 121
Brief entry 114
See also CLC 20
Silver, Jody 1942- 109
Silver, Marjorie A. 1948- 93-96
Silver, Nathan 1936- CANR-11
Earlier sketch in CA 21-22R
Silver, Nicholas
See Faust, Frederick (Shiller)
Silver, Philip Warnock 1932- 106
Silver, Richard
See Bulmer, (Henry) Kenneth
Silver, Rollo G(abriel) 1909- CAP-1
Earlier sketch in CA 19-20
Silver, Roy R. 1918-1979 Obituary 89-92
Silver, Ruth
See Chew, Ruth
Silver, Samuel 1915(?)-1976 Obituary 69-72
Silver, Samuel M. 1912- CANR-11
Earlier sketch in CA 23-24R
Silver, Warren A. 1914- 65-68
Silvera, Alain 1930- 23-24R
Silverberg, Robert 1935- CANR-20
Earlier sketches in CA 3R, CANR-1
See also CAAS 3
See also SATA 13
See also DLB 8
See also CLC 7
Silverlock, Anne
See Titchener, Louise
Silverman, Al 1926- 11-12R
Silverman, Alvin Michaels 1912- 11-12R
Silverman, Burt(on Philip) 1928- 103
Silverman, Corinne 1930- 7-8R
Silverman, David 1907- CAP-2
Earlier sketch in CA 21-22
Silverman, Harold M(artin) 1945- 112
Silverman, Hillel E. 1924- CANR-11
Earlier sketch in CA 21-22R
Silverman, Hirsch Lazaar 1915- 45-48
Silverman, Hugh J(erald) 1945- 118
Silverman, Jason H(oward) 1952- 110
Silverman, Jerry 1931- CANR-7
Earlier sketch in CA 15-16R
Silverman, Joseph H(erman) 1924- 104
Silverman, Judith 1933- 103
Silverman, Kenneth 1936- CANR-17
Earlier sketch in CA 57-60
Silverman, Mel(vin Frank) 1931-1966 .... 5-6R
See also SATA 9
Silverman, Milton J. 1944- 108
Silverman, Morris 1894-1972 Obituary 33-36R
Silverman, Oscar Ansell 1903-1977
Obituary 69-72
Silverman, Robert A(llan) 1943- 57-60
Silverman, Robert E(ugene) 1924- 41-44R
Silverman, Robert J(ay) 1940- 101
Silverman, Rose
See Millstein, Rose Silverman
Silverman, S(ol) Richard 1911- 107
Silverman, Samuel AITN-1
Silverman, Sydel 1933- 77-80
Silverman, William B. 1913- 49-52
Silvern, Leonard C. 1919- CANR-7
Earlier sketch in CA 17-18R
Silvers, Phil
See Silversmith, Philip
Silvers, Vicki 1941- 93-96
Silversmith, Philip 1912-1985 Obituary 117
Brief entry 111
Silverstein, Alvin 1933- CANR-2
Earlier sketch in CA 49-52
See also SATA 8
See also CLC 17
Silverstein, Charles 1935- 73-76
Silverstein, Josef 1922- CANR-14
Earlier sketch in CA 37-40R
Silverstein, Mel(vin Jerome) 1940- 101
Silverstein, Norman 1922-1974 .... 37-40R
Obituary 49-52
Silverstein, Shel(by) 1932- 107
See also SATA 27, 33
See also CLR 5
Silverstein, Theodore 1904- 106
Silverstein, Virginia B(arbara Opshelor) 1937- CANR-2
Earlier sketch in CA 49-52
See also SATA 8
See also CLC 17
Silverstone, Lou 1928- 108
Silverstone, Paul H. 1931- 21-22R
Silvert, Kalman H(irsch) 1921-1976 .... CANR-6
Obituary 65-68
Earlier sketch in CA 13-14R
Silverthorn, J(ames) E(dwin) 1906- CAP-1
Earlier sketch in CA 15-16
Silverthorne, Elizabeth 1930- 89-92
See also SATA 35
Silverton, Michael 1935- 65-68
Silverwood, Jane
See Titchener, Louise
Silvester, Frank
See Bingley, David Ernest
Silvester, Victor CAP-1
Earlier sketch in CA 13-14
Silvestri, Richard 1944- 81-84
Silving, Helen 1906- 41-44R
Silvius, G(eorge) Harold 1908-1981 .... CANR-3
Obituary 104
Earlier sketch in CA 7-8R
Sim, Georges
See Simenon, Georges
Sim, John Cameron 1911- 25-28R
Sim, Katharine (Thomasset) 1913- 13-14R
Sim, Myre 1915- 61-64
Sim, Yawsoon 1937- 108
Simak, Clifford D(onald) 1904- CANR-1
Earlier sketch in CA 4R
See also DLB 8
See also CLC 1
Simbari, Nicola 1927- CANR-1
Earlier sketch in CA 4R
Simckes, L(azarre) S(eymour) 1937- 9-10R
Simcox, George Augustus 1841-1905 .... DLB-35
Sime, Mary 1911- 53-56
Simenon, Georges (Jacques Christian) 1903- 85-88
See also CLC 1, 2, 3, 8, 18, 47
Simeon, Mother Mary 1888- CAP-1
Earlier sketch in CA 13-14
Simeon, Richard 1943- CANR-9
Earlier sketch in CA 61-64
Simeone, Diane A. 1953(?)-1983 Obituary 109
Simic, Andrei 1930- 93-96
Simic, Charles 1938- CANR-12
Earlier sketch in CA 29-32R
See also CAAS 4
See also CLC 6, 9, 22
Simini, Joseph Peter 1921- CANR-8
Earlier sketch in CA 17-18R
Simirenko, Alex 1931- 15-16R
Simister, Florence Parker 1913- CANR-2
Earlier sketch in CA 7-8R
Simkin, C(olin) G(eorge) F(rederick) 1915- 29-32R
Simkin, Penny 1938- 116
Simkin, William E(dward) 1907- 45-48
Simkins, Lawrence D(avid) 1933- 41-44R
Simley, Anne 1891- 5-6R
Simmel, Edward C(lemens) 1932- 45-48
Simmel, Johannes M(ario) 1924- 81-84
Simmel, Marianne L(enore) 1923- 21-22R
Simmie, James Martin 1941- 115
Simmonds, A(ndrew) J(effrey) 1943- 81-84
Simmonds, George W. 1929- 21-22R
Simmonds, James D(udley) 1933- 104
Simmonds, Walter H(enry) C(live) 1917- 118
Simmons, A(lan) John 1950- 106
Simmons, Anthony 1922- 103
Simmons, Billy E. 1931- CANR-10
Earlier sketch in CA 23-24R
Simmons, Blake
See Wallmann, Jeffrey M(iner)
Simmons, Charles (Paul) 1924- 89-92
Simmons, D(avid) R(oy) 1930- 110
Simmons, Dan CLC-44
Simmons, David
See Gold, Alan R(obert)
Simmons, Dawn Langley 29-32R

Simmons, Edwin Howard 1921- 89-92
Simmons, Ernest J(oseph) 1903-1972 .. CANR-3
Earlier sketch in CA 2R
Simmons, Geoffrey 1943- 104
Simmons, Gloria Mitchell 1932- 37-40R
Simmons, Henry T. 1927(?)-1986
Obituary 120
Simmons, Herbert A(lfred) 1930- 3R
See also DLB 33
Simmons, Ian 1937- 106
Simmons, J(oseph) Edgar (Jr.) 1921- 21-22R
Simmons, J(erry) L(aird) 1933- 29-32R
Simmons, Jack 1915- CANR-2
Earlier sketch in CA 7-8R
Simmons, James (Stewart Alexander)
1933- 105
See also DLB 40
See also CLC 43
Simmons, James E(dwin) 1923- 41-44R
Simmons, James W(illiam) 1936- CANR-12
Earlier sketch in CA 17-18R
Simmons, John Edwards 1918-1986
Obituary 121
Simmons, Joseph Larry 1935- 65-68
Simmons, Judy Dothard 1944- 77-80
Simmons, Mabel Clark 1899-1988
Obituary 124
Simmons, Marc 1937- CANR-10
Earlier sketch in CA 25-28R
Simmons, Mary Kay 1933- 81-84
Simmons, Matty 1926- 29-32R
Simmons, Merle Edwin 1918- CANR-2
Earlier sketch in CA 7-8R
Simmons, Otis D(avis) 1928- 57-60
Simmons, Ozzie Gordon 1919- 11-12R
Simmons, Patricia A. 1930- 93-96
Simmons, Paul D(ewayne) 1936- 45-48
Simmons, Robert R. 1940- 97-100
Simmons, S. H.
See Simmons, Sylvia
Simmons, Sylvia 49-52
Simmons, William S(cranton) 1938- 121
Simms, D(enton) Harper 1912- 29-32R
Simms, Eric Arthur 1921- 101
Simms, George (Otto) 1910- 108
Simms, Peter (F. J.) 1925- 21-22R
Simms, Ruth P. 1937- 17-18R
Simms, Willard S. 1943- 29-32R
Simms, William Gilmore
1806-1870 ....DLB-3, 30, 59
Simon, Alfred 1907- 41-44R
Simon, Andre (Louis) 1877-1970
Obituary 29-32R
Simon, Anne W(ertheim) 1914- 105
Simon, Arthur 1930- 33-36R
Simon, Bennett 1933- 101
Simon, Boris-Jean 1913(?)-1972
Obituary 33-36R
Simon, Carl P(aul) 1945- 107
Simon, Carly 1945- 105
See also CLC 26
Simon, Charlie May
See Fletcher, Charlie May Hogue
Simon, Christopher Fitz
See Fitz-Simon, Christopher
Simon, Claude 1913- 89-92
See also CLC 4, 9, 15, 39
Simon, Disney 1927- 23-24R
Simon, Eckehard 1939- 61-64
Simon, Edith 1917- 13-14R
Simon, George T(homas) 1912- CANR-17
Earlier sketch in CA 25-28R
Simon, Henry W(illiam) 1901-1970 ..... CANR-4
Obituary 29-32R
Earlier sketch in CA 5-6R
Simon, Herbert 1898(?)-1974 Obituary 53-56
Simon, Herbert A(lexander) 1916- CANR-9
Earlier sketch in CA 13-14R
Simon, Hilda Rita 1921- 77-80
See also SATA 28
Simon, Howard 1903-1979 ....33-36R
Obituary 89-92
See also SATA 21, 32
Simon, Hubert K. 1917- 15-16R
Simon, James E(dward) 1954- 119
Simon, Jo Ann 1946- 106
Simon, Joan L. 1921- 15-16R
Simon, Joe
See Simon, Joseph H.
Simon, John (Ivan) 1925- 21-22R
Simon, John G. 1928- 37-40R
Simon, John Y. 1933- CANR-12
Earlier sketch in CA 25-28R
Simon, Joseph H. 1913- 29-32R
See also SATA 7
Simon, Julian L. 1932- 33-36R
Simon, Kate (Grobsmith) Brief entry 115
Simon, Leonard 1922- 11-12R
Simon, Linda 1946- CANR-13
Earlier sketch in CA 73-76
Simon, Lorena Cotts 1897- 5-6R
Simon, Louis M(ortimer) 1906- 77-80
Simon, Marcia L. 1939- 93-96
Simon, Martin P(aul William) 1903-1969 . CAP-1
Earlier sketch in CA 11-12
See also SATA 12
Simon, Mary of the Angels 1897(?)-1985
Obituary 116
Simon, Matila 1908- 17-18R
Simon, Michael A(rthur) 1936- CANR-13
Earlier sketch in CA 33-36R
Simon, Mina Lewiton
See Lewiton, Mina
Simon, Morton J. 1913- 19-20R
Simon, (Marvin) Neil 1927- 21-22R
See also DLB 7
See also CLC 6, 11, 31, 39
See also AITN 1
Simon, Norma (Feldstein) 1927- CANR-21
Earlier sketches in CA 7-8R, CANR-6
See also SATA 3
Simon, Paul 1928- 81-84
Simon, Paul 1942(?)- Brief entry 116
See also CLC 17
Simon, Pierre-Henri 1903-1972
Obituary 37-40R
Simon, Rita James 1931- CANR-8
Earlier sketch in CA 21-22R
Simon, Robert
See Musto, Barry
Simon, Robert A. 1897(?)-1981 Obituary ... 103
Simon, Roger David 1943- 109
Simon, Samuel A(lan) 1945- 117
Simon, Seymour 1931- CANR-11
Earlier sketch in CA 25-28R
See also SATA 4
See also CLR 9
Simon, Sheldon W(eiss) 1937- CANR-10
Earlier sketch in CA 25-28R
Simon, Shirley (Schwartz) 1921- CANR-16
Earlier sketches in CA 4R, CANR-1
See also SATA 11
Simon, Sidney B(lair) 1927- 101
Simon, Solomon 1895-1970 Obituary 104
See also SATA 40
Simon, (Edward) Ted 1931- 105
Simon, Tony 1921- 5-6R
Simon, Ulrich E(rnst) 1913- 29-32R
Simon, Walter G(old) 1924- 19-20R
Simon, William 1927- 11-12R
Simon, William E(dward) 1927- 81-84
Simonds, John Ormsbee 1913- 77-80
Simonds, Roger (Tyrrell) 1929- 93-96
Simonds, Rollin Head 1910- 1R
Simonds, William Adams 1887-19(?) CAP-1
Earlier sketch in CA 11-12
Simone
See Porche, Simone (Benda)
Simone, Albert Joseph 1935- 17-18R
Simone, Charles B(rian) 1949- 116
Simonelli, Maria Picchio 1921- 49-52
Simonet, Thomas Solon 1942- 116
Simonetta, Linda 1948- 77-80
See also SATA 14
Simonetta, Sam 1936- 77-80
See also SATA 14
Simonhoff, Harry 1891- 7-8R
Simoni, John Peter 1911- Brief entry 106
Simonin, Albert (Charles) 1905-1980
Obituary 104
Simonini, R(inaldo) C(harles), Jr.
1922-1967 .... CAP-1
Earlier sketch in CA 11-12
Simonon, Paul 1956(?)- CLC-30
Simonov, Konstantin (Kirill) Mikhailovich
1915-1979 Obituary 89-92
Simons, Barbara B(rooks) 1934- 108
See also SATA 41
Simons, Beverley 1938- 104
Simons, David G(oodman) 1922- 19-20R
Simons, Elwyn LaVerne 1930- CANR-22
Earlier sketch in CA 105
Simons, Eric N(orman) 1896- 15-16R
Simons, Hans 1893-1972 Obituary 33-36R
Simons, Harry 1912- 3R
Simons, Howard, 1929- 65-68
Simons, James Marcus 1939- 106
Simons, Jim
See Simons, James Marcus
Simons, John D(onald) 1935- 41-44R
Simons, Joseph 1933- 81-84
Simons, Katherine Drayton Mayrant
1892(?)-1969 ....9-10R
Obituary 112
See also DLBY 83
Simons, Lewis M(artin) 1939- Brief entry ... 123
Simons, Myron (Bud) 1920- 113
Simons, Robin 1951- 65-68
Simons, Thomas G(erald) 1950- 111
Simons, William Edward 1927- 17-18R
Simonson, Conrad 1931- 49-52
Simonson, Harold P(eter) 1926- 33-36R
Simonson, Lee 1888-1967 ....9-10R
Simonson, Mary Jane
See Wheeler, Mary Jane
Simonson, Solomon S. 1914- 23-24R
Simont, Marc 1915- 61-64
See also SATA 9
Simonton, Dean Keith 1948- 119
Simoons, Frederick J. 1922- CANR-23
Earlier sketch in CA 1R
Simos, Miriam 1951- 104
Simper, Robert 1937- CANR-23
Earlier sketches in CA 61-64, CANR-8
Simpich, Frederick, Jr. 1911-1975 61-64
Obituary 57-60
Simpkin, Richard E(velyn) 1921-1986 124
Simpson, A(lfred) W. Brian 1931- 5-6R
Simpson, Alan 1912- 3R
Simpson, Cedric Keith 1907-1985 111
Obituary 117
Simpson, Claude M(itchell), Jr.
1910-1976 ....5-6R
Obituary 65-68
Simpson, Colin 1908- CANR-5
Earlier sketch in CA 53-56
See also SATA 14
Simpson, Craig M(ichael) 1942- 119
Simpson, D(avid) P(enistan) 1917- 11-12R
Simpson, Dick 1940- CANR-13
Earlier sketch in CA 33-36R
Simpson, Dorothy 1933- 107
Simpson, E(rvin) P(eter) Y(oung) 1911- ..19-20R
Simpson, Elizabeth Leonie 33-36R
Simpson, Ethel 1937- 117
Simpson, (John) Evan 1940- 97-100
Simpson, George E(dward) 1944- 101
Simpson, George Eaton 1904- 77-80
Simpson, George Gaylord 1902-1984 .. CANR-16
Obituary 114
Earlier sketches in CA 19-20, CAP-1
Simpson, Harold Brown 1917- CANR-4
Earlier sketch in CA 11-12R
Simpson, Harriette
See Arnow, Harriette (Louisa) Simpson
Simpson, Hassell A(lgernon) 1930- 41-44R
Simpson, Helen (De Guerry) 1897-1940
Brief entry 109
Simpson, Howard Russell 1925- CANR-1
Earlier sketch in CA 1R
Simpson, Ian J(ames) 1895- CAP-1
Earlier sketch in CA 13-14
Simpson, Ida Harper 1928- 19-20R
Simpson, Jacqueline (Mary) 1930- CANR-5
Earlier sketch in CA 15-16R
Simpson, Jacynth Hope
See Hope Simpson, Jacynth
Simpson, James B(easley) 1926- CANR-9
Earlier sketch in CA 7-8R
Simpson, Jean I(rwin) 1896- 7-8R
Simpson, Joan Murray 1918-1977
Obituary 89-92
Simpson, John (Andrew) 1953- 122
Simpson, John L(iddle) 11-12R
Simpson, Judith H(olroyd) 1941- 110
Simpson, Kemper 1893- CAP-1
Earlier sketch in CA 11-12
Simpson, Kirke L(arue) 1882(?)-1972
Obituary 37-40R
Simpson, Leo 1934- 101
See also AITN 2
Simpson, Lewis P(earson) 1916- CANR-8
Earlier sketch in CA 19-20R
Simpson, Louis (Aston Marantz) 1923- .. CANR-1
Earlier sketch in CA 4R
See also CAAS 4
See also DLB 5
See also CLC 4, 7, 9, 32
Simpson, Michael Andrew 1944- 89-92
Simpson, Mona (Elizabeth) 1957-
Brief entry 122
See also CLC 44
Simpson, Myrtle L(illias) 1931- CANR-11
Earlier sketch in CA 23-24R
See also SATA 14
Simpson, N(orman) F(rederick) 1919- 13-14R
See also DLB 13
See also CLC 29
Simpson, O(renthal) J(ames) 1947- 103
Simpson, R(onald) A(lbert) 1929- CANR-14
Earlier sketch in CA 77-80
Simpson, Ray H. 1907- 4R
Simpson, Richard L(ee) 1929- 11-12R
Simpson, Robert (Wilfred Levick) 1921- 103
Simpson, Robert 1924- 49-52
Simpson, Robert H. 1912- 108
Simpson, Ruth 1926- 73-76
Simpson, Ruth Mary Rasey 1902- CANR-1
Earlier sketch in CA 4R
Simpson, (Robert) Smith 1906- CAP-2
Earlier sketch in CA 21-22
Simpson, Stanhope Rowton 1903- 73-76
Simpson, W. W.
See Simpson, William Wynn
Simpson, William Hays 1903- 41-44R
Simpson, William Kelly 1928- 105
Simpson, William Wynn 1907-1987
Obituary 123
Sims, Bernard John 1915- 13-14R
Sims, Bobbi 1931- 117
Sims, Charles A(gustus) 1901-1983
Obituary 111
Sims, Edward H. 1923- CANR-6
Earlier sketch in CA 1R
Sims, Edward J(ames) 1927- 41-44R
Sims, George (Frederick Robert)
1923- CANR-12
Earlier sketch in CA 25-28R
Sims, George R. 1847-1922 .... DLB-35
Sims, Harold D(ana) 1935- 41-44R
Sims, James H(ylbert) 1924- 1R
Sims, Janet L.
See Sims-Wood, Janet L(ouise)
Sims, Lois Dorothy Lang
See Lang-Sims, Lois Dorothy
Sims, Mary Sophia Stephens 1886-1976
Obituary 65-68
Sims, Naomi 1949- 69-72
Sims, Patsy 1938- Brief entry 110
Sims, Patterson 1947- 124
Sims, Phillip L(eon) 1940- 105
Simson, Eve 1937- 73-76
Simsova, Sylva 1931- CANR-12
Earlier sketch in CA 29-32R
Sims-Wood, Janet L(ouise) 1945- 108
Sinai, I(saac) Robert 1924- CANR-10
Earlier sketch in CA 23-24R
Sinclair, Andrew (Annandale) 1935- CANR-14
Earlier sketch in CA 9-10R
See also CAAS 5
See also DLB 14
See also CLC 2, 14
Sinclair, Bennie Lee 1939- CANR-1
Earlier sketch in CA 49-52
Sinclair, Bruce A. 1929- Brief entry 106
Sinclair, Clover
See Gater, Dilys
Sinclair, Donna 1943- CANR-23
Earlier sketch in CA 106
Sinclair, Emil
See Hesse, Hermann
Sinclair, (Allan) Gordon 1900-1984 102
Obituary 112
See also AITN 1
Sinclair, Grace
See Wallmann, Jeffrey M(iner)
Sinclair, Grant
See Drago, Harry Sinclair
Sinclair, Harold (Augustus) 1907-1966 .....7-8R
Sinclair, Heather
See Johnston, William
Sinclair, Ian
See Foley, (Cedric) John
Sinclair, Irene
See Griffith, D(avid Lewelyn) W(ark)
Sinclair, James
See Staples, Reginald Thomas
Sinclair, Jo
See Seid, Ruth
See also DLB 28
Sinclair, John L(eslie) 1902- 105
Sinclair, Julian
See Sinclair, Mary Amelia St. Clair
Sinclair, Keith 1922- 17-18R
Sinclair, Lister (Shedden) 1921- 105
Sinclair, Mary Amelia St. Clair
1865(?)-1946 Brief entry 104
Sinclair, Max 1945- 113
Sinclair, May
See Sinclair, Mary Amelia St. Clair
See also DLB 36
See also TCLC 3, 11
Sinclair, Miranda 1948- 77-80
Sinclair, Murray 1950- 108
Sinclair, Olga 1923- CANR-11
Earlier sketch in CA 61-64
Sinclair, Rose
See Smith, Susan Vernon
Sinclair, Roy
See Griffith, D(avid Lewelyn) W(ark)
Sinclair, Sandra 1940- 120
Sinclair, Upton (Beall) 1878-1968 ...... CANR-7
Obituary 25-28R
Earlier sketch in CA 5-6R
See also SATA 9
See also DLB 9
See also CLC 1, 11, 15
Sinclair-Stevenson, Christopher 1939- 102
Sincoff, Michael Z(olman) 1943- 85-88
Sindler, Allan Paul 1928- 97-100
Sinel, Allen 1936- 45-48
Siner, Howard W(alter) 1946- 117
Sinfield, Alan 1941- 113
Singer, Adam
See Karp, David
Singer, Amanda
See Brooks, Janice Young
Singer, Armand Edwards 1914- CANR-14
Earlier sketch in CA 41-44R
Singer, Benjamin D. 1931- 37-40R
Singer, Beth J(udith) 1927- 113
Singer, Burns
See Singer, James Hyman
Singer, C(harles) Gregg 1910- CANR-12
Earlier sketch in CA 73-76
Singer, David L(in) 1937- 73-76
Singer, Fred J. 1931- 23-24R
Singer, Irving 1925- 23-24R
Singer, Isaac
See Singer, Isaac Bashevis
Singer, Isaac Bashevis 1904- CANR-1
Earlier sketch in CA 1R
See also SATA 3, 27
See also DLB 6, 28, 52
See also CDALB 1941-1968
See also CLC 1, 3, 6, 9, 11, 15, 23, 38
See also CLR 1
See also AITN 1, 2
Singer, J(oel) David 1925- CANR-6
Earlier sketch in CA 4R
Singer, Jack W(olfe) 1942- 104
Singer, James Hyman 1928-1964 102
Obituary 89-92
Singer, Jane Sherrod 1917-1985 ...... CANR-17
Obituary 115
Earlier sketch in CA 25-28R
See also SATA 4, 42
Singer, Joe
See Singer, Joseph
Singer, Joseph 1923-19? CANR-2
Earlier sketch in CA 45-48
Singer, Joseph I.
See Singer, Joseph
Singer, Joy Daniels 1928- 29-32R
Singer, Judith 1926- 61-64
Singer, Julia 1917- 65-68
See also SATA 28
Singer, June (Kurlander) 1918- CANR-10
Earlier sketch in CA 41-44R
Singer, June Flaum 1933- 106
Singer, Kurt D(eutsch) 1911- CANR-2
Earlier sketch in CA 49-52
See also SATA 38
Singer, Marcus George 1926- CANR-3
Earlier sketch in CA 2R
Singer, Marilyn 1948- CANR-9
Earlier sketch in CA 65-68
See also SATA 38, 48
Singer, Marshall R. 1932- 41-44R
Singer, Michael A(lan) 1947- 57-60
Singer, Milton Borah 1912- CANR-23
Earlier sketch in CA 105
Singer, Neil M(ichael) 1939- 93-96
Singer, Norman 1925- 41-44R

Singer, Peter (Albert David) 1946- ... CANR-8
Earlier sketch in CA 57-60
Singer, Phylis
See Morrison, Phylis
Singer, Ray 1916- ... 105
Singer, Richard G. 1943- ... 89-92
Singer, (Dennis) Robert 1931- ... 49-52
Singer, Robert N. ... CANR-5
Earlier sketch in CA 53-56
Singer, Rochelle 1939- ... CANR-20
Earlier sketch in CA 104
Singer, S(iegfried) Fred 1924- Brief entry ... 118
Singer, Samuel L(oewenberg) 1911- ... 65-68
Singer, Sarah 1915- ... 81-84
Singer, Shelley
See Singer, Rochelle
Singer, Sholom A. 1924-1987 Obituary ... 123
Singer, Susan (Mahler) 1941- ... 61-64
See also SATA 9
Singerman, Robert 1942- ... 110
Singh, Ajit 1940- ... 109
Singh, Amritjit 1945- ... 102
Singh, Arjan 1917- ... 49-52
Singh, Avtar 1929- ... 65-68
Singh, Baliit 1929- ... 41-44R
Singh, Bawa Satinder 1932- ... 101
Singh, G(han Shyam) 1926- ... CANR-20
Earlier sketches in CA 11-12R, CANR-5
Singh, Harbans 1921- ... 19-20R
Singh, Karan 1931- ... 15-16R
Singh, Khushwant 1915- ... CANR-6
Earlier sketch in CA 9-10R
See also CLC 11
Singh, Lalita Prasad 1936- ... 23-24R
Singh, Madanjeet 1924- ... 19-20R
Singh, Nagendra 1914- ... CANR-7
Earlier sketch in CA 19-20R
Singh, R. K. Janmeja 1932- ... 37-40R
Singh, St. Nihal 1884- ... 105
Singh, Surender 1932- ... 49-52
Singh, Surendra Nihal
See Nihal Singh, Surendra
Singh, Vijai Pratap 1939- Brief entry ... 106
Singhal, D(amodar) P(rasad) 1925- ... 49-52
Singing Nun, The
See Deckers, Jeanine
Singletary, Otis Arnold, Jr. 1921- ... 45-48
Singleton, Betty 1910- ... CAP-2
Earlier sketch in CA 25-28
Singleton, Charles S(outhward)
1909-1985 Obituary ... 117
Brief entry ... 113
Singleton, Frederick Bernard 1926- ... 89-92
Singleton, Ira C(uster) 1920- ... 7-8R
Singleton, Jack 1911- ... 13-14R
Singleton, John 1930- ... 23-24R
Singleton, M(arvin) K(enneth) 1933- ... 3R
Singleton, Mary Ann 1934- ... 57-60
Singleton, Ralph Herbert 1900- ... 15-16R
Singleton, Rebecca (Jane) 1948- ... 121
Singleton, V(ernon) L(eRoy) 1923- ... 25-28R
Singmaster, Elsie 1879-1958 Brief entry ... 110
See also DLB 9
Sinha, Krishna N(andan) 1924- ... 15-16R
Sinha, Sasadhar 1901- ... 17-18R
Sinibaldi, Fosco
See Kacew, Romain
Sinick, Daniel 1913- ... 45-48
Sinicropi, Giovanni Andrea 1924- ... 45-48
Sinisgalli, Leonardo 1908-1981 Obituary ... 103
Sinjohn, John
See Galsworthy, John
Sinjun
See John, Elizabeth Beaman
Sinkankas, John 1915- ... CANR-6
Earlier sketch in CA 4R
Sinkler, George 1927- ... 85-88
Sinnema, John R(alph) 1911- ... 41-44R
Sinnen, Jeanne 1926-1976 Obituary ... 104
Sinnigen, William G. 1928- ... 15-16R
Sinning, Wayne E. 1931- ... 77-80
Sinor, Denis 1916- ... CANR-6
Earlier sketch in CA 3R
Sinor, John 1930- ... CANR-11
Earlier sketch in CA 69-72
Sinyavsky, Andrei (Donatevich) 1925- ... 85-88
See also CLC 8
Siodmak, Curt 1902- ... 113
Brief entry ... 111
See also DLB 44
Sionil Jose, F(rancisco) 1924- ... CANR-10
Earlier sketch in CA 23-24R
Sions, Harry 1906-1974 Obituary ... 104
Siotis, Jean 1931- ... 25-28R
Sippl, Charles J. 1924- ... CANR-18
Earlier sketch in CA 21-22R
Siracusa, Joseph 1929- ... CANR-1
Earlier sketch in CA 45-48
Siracusa, Joseph M(arcus) 1944- ... CANR-12
Earlier sketch in CA 73-76
Sirageldin, Ismail A(bdel-Hamid)
1930- ... CANR-16
Earlier sketch in CA 29-32R
Sirc, Ljubo 1920- ... 103
Sire, James W(alter) 1933- ... CANR-11
Earlier sketch in CA 29-32R
Sirica, John J(oseph) 1904- ... 110
Sirin, V.
See Nabokov, Vladimir (Vladimirovich)
Siris, Peter 1944- ... 117
Sirjamaki, John 1911- ... 15-16R
Sirkin, Gerald 1920- ... 25-28R
Sirkis, Nancy 1936- ... 102
Sirluck, Ernest 1918- ... 25-28R
Sirof, Harriet 1930- ... CANR-20
Earlier sketch in CA 104
See also SATA 37

Sirrom, Wes
See Weiss, Morris S(amuel)
Sisco, John I(sodore) 1931- ... 41-44R
Sisk, Dorothy Poole 1897-1983 Obituary ... 111
Sisk, Frank A., Jr. 1915-1985 Obituary ... 115
Sisk, Henry L(ybran) 1914- ... 49-52
Sisk, John P(aul) 1914- ... 29-32R
Siskel, Eugene Kal 1946- ... 113
Brief entry ... 110
Siskel, Gene
See Siskel, Eugene Kal
Sisler, Harry Hall 1917- ... 109
Sisler, Rebecca 1932- ... 104
Sisley, Emily L(ucretia) 1930- Brief entry ... 113
Sissle, Noble 1889-1975 Obituary ... 112
Sissman, L(ouis) E(dward) 1928-1976 . CANR-13
Obituary ... 65-68
Earlier sketch in CA 21-22R
See also DLB 5
See also CLC 9, 18
Sisson, A(lbert) F(ranklin) 1901- ... 5-6R
Sisson, C(harles) H(ubert) 1914- ... CANR-3
Earlier sketch in CA 2R
See also CAAS 3
See also DLB 27
See also CLC 8
Sisson, Rosemary Anne 1923- ... CANR-12
Earlier sketch in CA 13-14R
See also SATA 11
Sister Luc-Gabrielle
See Deckers, Jeanine
Sister M. Victoria
See Maria Del Rey, Sister
Sister Mary Annette
See Buttimer, Anne
Sister Mary Terese
See Donze, Mary Terese
Sister Maura
See Eichner, Maura
Sister Smile
See Deckers, Jeanine
Sister Teresa Margaret
See Rowe, Margaret (Kevin)
Sisyphus
See Barthelmes, (Albert) Wes(ley, Jr.)
Sitaram, K(ondavagil) S(urya) 1935- ... 69-72
Sitarz, Paula (Gaj) 1955- ... 122
Sitchin, Zecharia 1920- ... CANR-22
Earlier sketch in CA 69-72
Sites, James N(eil) 1924- ... 4R
Sites, Paul 1926- ... 53-56
Sithole, Ndabaningi 1920- Brief entry ... 110
Sitomer, Harry 1903- ... 101
See also SATA 31
Sitomer, Mindel 1903- ... 101
See also SATA 31
Sitter, John E(dward) 1944- Brief entry ... 114
Sittler, Joseph 1904-1987 Obituary ... 124
Sitton, Claude (Fox) 1925- Brief entry ... 122
Sitwell, Dame Edith 1887-1964 ... 11-12R
See also DLB 20
See also CLC 2, 9
Sitwell, (Francis) Osbert (Sacheverell)
1892-1969 ... CAP-2
Obituary ... 25-28R
Earlier sketch in CA 21-22
Sitwell, Sacheverell 1897- ... 21-22R
Sitzfleisch, Vladimir
See Spirer, Herbert F(rederick)
Siu, Helen 1950- ... 114
Siu, R(alph) G(un) H(oy) 1917- ... CANR-10
Earlier sketch in CA 25-28R
Sive, Helen R(obinson) 1951- ... 107
See also SATA 30
Sive, Mary Robinson 1928- ... CANR-10
Earlier sketch in CA 65-68
Siviero, Rodolpho 1912(?)-1983 Obituary ... 111
Sivulich, Sandra (Jeanne) Stroner 1941- ... 61-64
See also SATA 9
Siwek, Manuel 1908-1976 Obituary ... 65-68
Siwundhla, Alice Msumba 1928- ... 45-48
Sixsmith, Eric Keir Gilborne 1904-1986 ... 33-36R
Obituary ... 118
Siy, Robert Y(oung), Jr. 1955- ... 119
Sizemore, Burlan A. 1933- ... 45-48
Sizemore, Chris(tine) Costner 1927- ... 81-84
Sizemore, Margaret D(avidson) ... CAP-2
Earlier sketch in CA 19-20
Sizer, John 1938- ... CANR-12
Earlier sketch in CA 29-32R
Sizer, Nancy F(aust) 1935- ... 45-48
Sizer, Theodore R(yland) 1932- ... CANR-13
Earlier sketch in CA 33-36R
Sjoeberg, Leif 1925- ... 65-68
Sjoewall, Maj 1935- ... 65-68
See also CLC 7
Sjowall, Maj
See Sjoewall, Maj
Skaar, Grace Brown 1903- ... 69-72
Skaer, Peter M(acKall) 1953- ... 103
Skagen, Kiki
See Munshi, Kiki Skagen
Skaggs, David Curtis (Jr.) 1937- ... 41-44R
Skaggs, Jimmy M(arion) 1940- ... CANR-1
Earlier sketch in CA 45-48
Skaggs, Merrill Maguire 1937- ... 45-48
Skala, John J. 1923- ... 19-20R
Skaldaspillir, Sigfridur
See Broxon, Mildred Downey
Skallerup, Harry R(obert) 1927- ... 73-76
Skard, Sigmund 1903- ... CANR-22
Earlier sketches in CA 19-20R, CANR-7
Skarda, Patricia Lyn 1946- ... 106
Skardon, Dorothy Burton 1922- ... 61-64
Skardon, Alvin W(ilson, Jr.) 1912- ... 53-56
Skarsten, Malvin O. 1892- ... CAP-1
Earlier sketch in CA 15-16

Skartvedt, Dan (L.) 1945- ... 77-80
Skates, John R(ay) 1934- ... 97-100
Skeaping, John Rattenbury 1901-1980 ... 108
Obituary ... 97-100
Skeaping, Mary 1902-1984 Obituary ... 112
Skedgell, Marian Jay 1921- ... CANR-14
Earlier sketch in CA 17-18R
Skeel, Dorothy J(une) ... CANR-8
Earlier sketch in CA 61-64
Skeen, Carl Edward 1937- ... 113
Skehan, James W(illiam) 1923- ... 57-60
Skei, Allen B(ennet) 1935- ... 108
Skellings, Edmund 1932- ... 77-80
Skelly, James R(ichard) 1927- ... 85-88
See also SATA 17
Skelly, Madge 1903- ... 41-44R
Skelton, Eugene (Lamar) 1914- ... CANR-1
Earlier sketch in CA 45-48
Skelton, Geoffrey (David) 1916- ... CANR-18
Earlier sketches in CA 49-52, CANR-1
Skelton, John E. 1934- ... 37-40R
Skelton, Peter 1928- ... 13-14R
Skelton, Red 1913- ... 104
Skelton, Robin 1925- ... 7-8R
See also CAAS 5
See also DLB 27, 53
See also CLC 13
See also AITN 2
Skelton, Roger
See Horn, Peter (Rudolf Gisela)
Skemp, Joseph Bright 1910- ... 106
Skemp, Richard R(owland) 1919- ... 107
Skendi, Stavro 1906- ... 25-28R
Skene-Melvin, Ann (Patricia) 1936- ... 108
Skene-Melvin, (Lewis) David (St. Columb)
1936- ... 108
Skibbe, Eugene M(oritz) 1930- ... 23-24R
Skidelsky, Robert 1939- ... CANR-11
Earlier sketch in CA 25-28R
Skidmore, Ian 1929- ... CANR-10
Earlier sketch in CA 61-64
Skidmore, Max J(oseph, Sr.) 1933- ... CANR-12
Earlier sketch in CA 29-32R
Skidmore, Rex A(ustin) 1914- ... 15-16R
Skidmore, Thomas E. 1932- ... 21-22R
Skiles, Jacqueline D(ean) 1937- ... 108
Skilken, Patricia S(tout) 1943- ... 119
Skilling, H(arold) Gordon 1912- ... CANR-7
Earlier sketch in CA 15-16R
Skillings, R(oger) D(eering) 1937- ... 61-64
Skilliter, S(usan) A. 1931(?)-1985
Obituary ... 117
Skilton, John H. 1906- ... 37-40R
Skimin, Robert (Elwayne) 1929- ... 108
Skinner, Ainslie
See Gosling, Paula
Skinner, B(urrhus) F(rederic) 1904- ... CANR-18
Earlier sketch in CA 11-12R
Skinner, Charles Edward 1891- ... CAP-1
Earlier sketch in CA 17-18
Skinner, Constance Lindsay 1882-1939 .. YABC-1
Skinner, Cornelia Otis 1901-1979 ... 19-20R
Obituary ... 89-92
See also SATA 2
Skinner, Elliott P(ercival) 1924- ... 13-14R
Skinner, G(eorge) William 1925- ... CANR-2
Earlier sketch in CA 49-52
Skinner, Gordon S(weetland) 1924- ... 13-14R
Skinner, John Emory 1925- ... 7-8R
Skinner, June O'Grady 1922- ... 5-6R
Skinner, Knute (Rumsey) 1929- ... CANR-24
Earlier sketches in CA 17-18R, CANR-9
Skinner, Rulon Dean 1931- ... 61-64
Skinner, Thomas Edward 1909- ... 109
Skinner, Tom 1942- ... 25-28R
Skiold, Birgit ?-1982 Obituary ... 107
Skipp, Victor (Henry Thomas) 1925- ... 123
Brief entry ... 118
Skipper, Betty
See Barr, Betty
Skipper, G. C. 1939- ... CANR-14
Earlier sketch in CA 77-80
See also SATA 38, 46
Skipper, James K(inley), Jr. 1934- ... CANR-12
Earlier sketch in CA 17-20R
Skipsey, Joseph 1832-1903 ... DLB-35
Skipwith, Sofka 1907- ... 29-32R
Skira, Albert 1904-1973 Obituary ... 104
Skirpa, Kazys 1895(?)-1979 Obituary ... 89-92
Skjei, Eric William 1947- ... 97-100
Sklansky, Morris Aaron 1919- ... 17-18R
Sklar, Dusty 1928- ... 65-68
Sklar, George 1908- ... 1R
Sklar, Kathryn Kish 1939- ... CANR-18
Earlier sketches in CA 45-48, CANR-3
Sklar, Lawrence 1938- ... 105
Sklar, Michael Joel 1945(?)-1984
Obituary ... 112
Sklar, Morty 1935- ... CANR-13
Earlier sketch in CA 77-80
Sklar, Richard L(awrence) 1930- ... 9-10R
Sklar, Robert 1936- ... CANR-8
Earlier sketch in CA 21-22R
Sklare, Arnold B(eryl) 1924- ... 17-18R
Sklare, Marshall 1921- ... CANR-12
Earlier sketch in CA 23-24R
Sklarew, Myra 1934- ... 109
Sklarewitz, Norman 1924- ... 69-72
Skocpol, Theda Ruth 1947- Brief entry ... 105
Skofield, James ... SATA-44
Skoglund, Elizabeth 1937- ... CANR-15
Earlier sketch in CA 41-44R
Skoglund, Goesta 1904- ... 65-68
Skoglund, John Egnar 1912- ... 11-12R
Skold, Betty Westrom 1923- ... 112
See also SATA 41
Skolimowski, Jerzy 1938- ... CLC-20

Skolnick, Jerome H(erbert) 1931-
Brief entry ... 114
Skolnik, Alfred 1920(?)-1977 Obituary ... 69-72
Skolnik, Peter L(aurence) 1944- ... 57-60
Skolnikoff, Eugene B. 1928- ... 21-22R
Skolsky, Sidney 1905-1983 ... 103
Obituary ... 109
Skornia, Harry J(ay) 1910- ... CAP-2
Earlier sketch in CA 17-18
Skorpen, Liesel Moak 1935- ... 25-28R
See also SATA 3
Skotheim, Robert Allen 1933- ... 21-22R
Skou-Hansen, Tage 1925- ... CANR-6
Earlier sketch in CA 13-14R
Skousen, Mark ... 104
Skousen, W(illard) Cleon 1913- ... CANR-5
Earlier sketch in CA 7-8R
Skowronski, JoAnn ... 108
Skoyles, John 1949- ... 104
Skrade, Carl 1935- ... 65-68
Skram, Amalie (Bertha) 1847-1905 ... TCLC-25
Skrivanek, John M(arion) 1913- ... 49-52
Skulicz, Matthew V. 1944- ... 37-40R
Skulsky, Harold Lawrence 1935- ... 107
Skura, Meredith Anne 1944- ... 117
Skurdenis, Juliann V.
See Skurdenis-Smircich, Juliann V(eronica)
Skurdenis-Smircich, Juliann V(eronica)
1942- ... 77-80
Skurnik, W. A. E. 1926- ... 41-44R
Skurzynski, Gloria (Joan) 1930- ... CANR-13
Earlier sketch in CA 33-36R
See also SATA 8
Skutch, Alexander F(rank) 1904- ... CANR-21
Earlier sketch in CA 33-36R
Skutch, Margaret F. 1932- ... 105
Skvorecka, Zdena Salivarova 1933- ... 41-44R
Skvorecky, Josef (Vaclav) 1924- ... CANR-10
Earlier sketch in CA 61-64
See also CAAS 1
See also CLC 15, 39
Sky, Kathleen
See Goldin, Kathleen Mckinney
Skyrms, Brian 1938- ... 108
Slaatte, Howard A(lexander) 1919- ... CANR-14
Earlier sketch in CA 41-44R
Slaby, Andrew Edmund 1942- ... CANR-7
Earlier sketch in CA 57-60
Slack, Adrian (Charles) ... 104
Slack, Charles W(illiam) 1929- ... 61-64
Slack, Kenneth 1917-1987 Obituary ... 123
Slack, Robert C(harles) 1914- ... 81-84
Slack, Walter H. 1932- ... 23-24R
Slackman, Charles B. 1934- ... SATA-12
Slade, Afton 1919- ... 89-92
Slade, Bernard
See Newbound, Bernard Slade
See also DLB 53
See also CLC 11, 46
Slade, Caroline (Beach) 1886-1975
Obituary ... 61-64
Slade, Jack
See Ballard, (Willis) Todhunter
and Germano, Peter B.
Slade, Joseph W(arren) 1941- ... 89-92
Slade, Madeleine 1892-1982 Obituary ... 115
Slade, Peter 1912- ... 13-14R
Slade, Richard 1910-1971 ... CAP-2
Earlier sketch in CA 23-24
See also SATA 9
Slade, Tony 1936- ... 33-36R
Sladek, John 1937- ... 25-28R
Sladen, Kathleen 1904- ... 69-72
Sladen, Norman St. Barbe ?-1969 ... CAP-1
Earlier sketch in CA 13-14
Slaght, Lawrence T(ownsend) 1912- ... 73-76
Slakter, Malcolm J(ulian) 1929- ... 41-44R
Slamecka, Vladimir 1928- ... 7-8R
Slaney, George Wilson 1884- ... CAP-1
Earlier sketch in CA 13-14
Slappey, Sterling G(reene) 1917- ... 65-68
Slate, Joseph 1927- ... 45-48
Slate, Joseph (Frank) 1928- ... 110
See also SATA 38
Slate, Sam J(ordan) 1909- ... 49-52
Slaten, Yeffe Kimball 1914(?)-1978
Obituary ... 77-80
Slater, Charlotte (Wolpers) 1944- ... 65-68
Slater, Eliot (Trevor Oakeshott) 1904- ... 53-56
Slater, Ian 1941- ... 85-88
Slater, Jerome N(orman) 1935- ... 17-18R
Slater, Jim 1929- Brief entry ... 112
See also SATA 34
Slater, Layton Ernest Alfred 1916-1984
Obituary ... 114
Slater, Leonard 1920- ... 15-16R
Slater, Mariam K(reiselman) 1922- ... 123
Brief entry ... 118
Slater, Mary Louise 1923- ... 29-32R
Slater, Maya 1941- ... 119
Slater, Miriam 1931- ... 120
Slater, Nigel 1944- ... CANR-18
Earlier sketch in CA 102
Slater, Peter Gregg 1940- ... 81-84
Slater, Philip E(lliot) 1927- ... 23-24R
Slater, Ralph P(hipps) 1915- ... 23-24R
Slater, Ray
See Lansdale, Joe R(ichard)
Slater, Robert 1943- ... 119
Slater, Robert (Henry) Lawson 1896- ... CAP-1
Earlier sketch in CA 13-14
Slater, Veronica
See Sullivan, Victoria
Slatkin, Charles Eli 1907-1977 Obituary ... 73-76
Slatoff, Walter J(acob) 1922- ... 11-12R
Slattery, Timothy Patrick 1911- ... 25-28R

Slattery, William J(ames) 1930- 101
Slatzer, Robert F(ranklin) 1927-
Brief entry 113
Slaughter, Carolyn 1946- 85-88
Slaughter, Eugene Edward 1909- 37-40R
Slaughter, Frank G(ill) 1908- CANR-5
Earlier sketch in CA 7-8R
See also CLC 29
See also AITN 2
Slaughter, Howard K(ey) 1927- 45-48
Slaughter, Jane M(undy) 1908- 73-76
Slaughter, Jean
See Doty, Jean Slaughter
Slaughter, Jim
See Paine, Lauran (Bosworth)
Slavens, Thomas P(aul) 1928- CANR-22
Earlier sketch in CA 104
Slavet, Joseph S. 1920- 61-64
Slavic, Rosalind Welcher
See Welcher, Rosalind
Slavick, William H(enry) 1927- 104
Slavin, Arthur Joseph 1933- CANR-3
Earlier sketch in CA 11-12R
Slavin, Morris 1913- 118
Slavin, Stephen L(oren) 1939- 111
Slavitt, David R. 1935- 21-22R
See also CAAS 3
See also DLB 5, 6
See also CLC 5, 14
Slavson, Samuel R(ichard) 1891- 17-18R
Slavutych, Yar 1918- CANR-17
Earlier sketches in CA 45-48, CANR-2
Slawson, William David 1931- 110
Slaymaker, R(edsecker) Samuel II 1923- 65-68
Slayton, Mariette (Elizabeth) Paine 1908- 65-68
Sleator, William (Warner III) 1945- 29-32R
See also SATA 3
Sledd, James Hinton 1914- 19-20R
Sledge, Linda Ching 1944- 108
Sleigh, Barbara 1906-1982 .... CANR-6
Obituary 106
Earlier sketch in CA 13-14R
See also SATA 3, 30
Sleigh, (Brocas) Linwood 1902- 7-8R
Sleigh, Robert Collins, Jr. 1932- 37-40R
Sleight, Robert B(enton) 1922- 41-44R
Slepian, Jan(ice B.) 1921- SATA-45
Slesar, Henry 1927- CANR-1
Earlier sketch in CA 2R
Slesin, Suzanne 1944- 123
Slesinger, Doris P(eyser) 1927- 113
Slesinger, Reuben E. 1916- 5-6R
Slesinger, Tess 1905-1945 Brief entry 107
See also TCLC 10
Slesinger, Warren 1933- 33-36R
Slesser, Malcolm 1926- 19-20R
Slessor, Kenneth 1901-1971 102
Obituary 89-92
See also CLC 14
Sletholt, Erik 1919- 77-80
Slezak, Walter 1902-1983 Obituary 109
Slicer, Margaret O. 1920- 25-28R
See also SATA 4
Slide, Anthony 1944- CANR-12
Earlier sketch in CA 33-36R
Slim, William Joseph 1891-1970 Obituary 107
Slimming, John 1927-1979 .... 25-28R
Obituary 89-92
Slitor, Richard Eaton 1911- 45-48
Slive, Seymour 1920- 103
Sliwa, Curtis 1954- 111
Sljivic-Simsic, Biljana 1933- 41-44R
Sloan, Alfred P(ritchard), Jr. 1875-1966
Obituary 113
Sloan, Allan 1944- 118
Sloan, Edward William III 1931- 37-40R
Sloan, Harold Stephenson 1887- CAP-1
Earlier sketch in CA 17-18
Sloan, Irving J. 1924- CANR-7
Earlier sketch in CA 17-18R
Sloan, James Park (Jr.) 1944- 29-32R
Sloan, Kay 1951- 108
Sloan, Pat(rick Alan) 1908- 65-68
Sloan, Phillip R(eid) 1938- 109
Sloan, Raymond Paton 1893-1983 .... CAP-1
Obituary 109
Earlier sketch in CA 19-20
Sloan, Ruth Catherine 1898(?)-1976
Obituary 65-68
Sloan, Stephen 1936- 33-36R
Sloan, Thomas 1928- 93-96
Sloan, William Wilson 1901- 1R
Sloane, Arthur A(llan) 1931- 33-36R
Sloane, Eric 1910(?)-1985 108
Obituary 115
See also SATA 42
Sloane, Eugene A(nthony) 1926- 65-68
Sloane, Howard N(orman) 1932- 81-84
Sloane, Joseph C(urtis) 1909- CAP-1
Earlier sketch in CA 11-12
Sloane, Leonard 1932- 21-22R
Sloane, Peter J(ames) 1942- 108
Sloane, R(obert) Bruce 1923- 53-56
Sloane, Sara
See Bloom, Ursula
Sloane, Thomas O. 1929- 37-40R
Sloane, William M. 1906-1974 Obituary 53-56
Sloate, Daniel 1931- 113
Slobin, Dan Isaac 1939- CANR-11
Earlier sketch in CA 65-68
Slobin, Mark 1943- 93-96
Slobodin, Richard 1915- 102
Slobodkin, Florence Gersh 1905- 4R
See also SATA 5
Slobodkin, Louis 1903-1975 .... 13-14R
Obituary 57-60
See also SATA 1, 26
Slobodkina, Esphyr 1908- CANR-1
Earlier sketch in CA 1R
See also SATA 1
Slochower, Harry 1900- CANR-2
Earlier sketch in CA 49-52
Slocum, Bill
See Slocum, William J(oseph Michael), Jr.
Slocum, Donald Barclay 1911-1983
Obituary 110
Slocum, John W(esley), Jr. 1940- 112
Slocum, Michael
See Slocum, William J(oseph Michael), Jr.
Slocum, Robert Bigney 1922- 11-12R
Slocum, Walter L(ucius) 1910- 21-22R
Slocum, William J(oseph Michael), Jr.
1912(?)-1974 Obituary 53-56
Sloggatt, Arthur H(astings) 1917(?)-1975
Obituary 61-64
Sloggett, Nellie 1851-1923 .... SATA-44
Sloma, Richard Stanley 1929- CANR-19
Earlier sketch in CA 103
Sloman, Albert Edward 1921- 7-8R
Sloman, Larry 1948- CANR-20
Earlier sketch in CA 81-84
Slomovitz, Philip 1896- 81-84
Slone, Dennis 1930-1982 Obituary 106
Slone, Verna Mae 1914- 89-92
Slonim, Marc 1894-1976 Obituary 65-68
Slonim, Morris J(ames) 1909- 3R
Slonim, Reuben 1914- 97-100
Slonim, Ruth 1918- 19-20R
Slonimski, Antoni 1895-1976 Obituary 65-68
Slonimsky, Nicolas 1894- 17-18R
Slonimsky, Yuri 1902-1978 Obituary 77-80
Slosberg, Mike 1934- 69-72
Slosberg, Myron
See Slosberg, Mike
Slosser, Bob G(ene) 1929- CANR-10
Earlier sketch in CA 65-68
Slosson, Preston (William) 1892- CANR-8
Earlier sketch in CA 61-64
Slote, Alfred 1926- SATA-8
See also CLR 4
Slote, Bernice D. 1915(?)-1983 Obituary 109
Slote, Michael A(nthony) 1941- 61-64
Slote, Stanley J(ames) 1917- 61-64
Slotkin, Richard S. 1942- 102
Slotnick, Daniel L(eonid) 1931-1985
Obituary 117
Slovenko, Ralph 1926- 19-20R
Sloyan, Gerard Stephen 1919- CANR-18
Earlier sketches in CA 5-6R, CANR-2
Sluckin, W(ladyslaw) 1919-1985 .... 21-22R
Obituary 116
Slung, Louis Sheaffer 1912- 53-56
Slung, Michele (Beth) 1947- 102
Slusher, Howard S. 1937- 25-28R
Slusser, Dorothy M. 1922- 33-36R
Slusser, George Edgar 1939- CANR-13
Earlier sketch in CA 69-72
Slusser, Gerald H(erbert) 1920- 15-16R
Slusser, Robert M(elville) 1916- CANR-3
Earlier sketch in CA 3R
Slye, Leonard
See Rogers, Roy
Small, Bertrice 1937- CANR-13
Earlier sketch in CA 77-80
Small, David 1937- 108
Small, David 1945- SATA-46, 50
Small, Dwight Hervey 1919- CANR-8
Earlier sketch in CA 61-64
Small, Ernest
See Lent, Blair
Small, George L(eroy) 1924- 85-88
Small, George Raphael 1918- 57-60
Small, Kenneth A(lan) 1945- 112
Small, Melvin 1939- CANR-12
Earlier sketch in CA 29-32R
Small, Miriam Rossiter 1899- 4R
Small, Norman M. 1944- 41-44R
Small, William
See Eversley, D(avid) E(dward) C(harles)
Smallenburg, Harry W. 1907- CAP-1
Earlier sketch in CA 13-14
Smalley, Barbara Martin 1926- 105
Smalley, Beryl 1905-1984 103
Obituary 112
Smalley, Donald (Arthur) 1907- 17-18R
Smalley, Ruth E(lizabeth) 1903- CAP-2
Earlier sketch in CA 21-22
Smalley, Stephen Stewart 1931- 103
Smalley, William A. 1923- CANR-1
Earlier sketch in CA 45-48
Smallwood, Carol 1939- 122
Smallwood, Frank(lin) 1927- 123
Brief entry 118
Smallwood, James (Milton) 1944- 115
Smallwood, Joseph R(oberts) 1900- 105
Smallwood, Norah (Evelyn) 1910(?)-1984
Obituary 114
See also SATA 41
Smaridge, Norah (Antoinette) 1903- 37-40R
See also SATA 6
Smart, (Peter) Alastair (Marshall) 1922- 37-40R
Smart, Barry 1946- 117
Smart, Carol 1948- CANR-16
Earlier sketch in CA 73-76
Smart, Carolyn (Alexandra) 1952- 116
Smart, Charles Allen 1904-1967 .... CAP-1
Earlier sketch in CA 11-12
Smart, Elizabeth 1913-1986 81-84
Obituary 118
Smart, Graydon F. 1906(?)-1984 Obituary 111
Smart, Harold R(obert) 1892- CAP-1
Earlier sketch in CA 9-10
Smart, J(ohn) J(amieson) C(arswell)
1920- CANR-7
Earlier sketch in CA 13-14R
Smart, James D(ick) 1906-1982 .... CANR-8
Obituary 105
Earlier sketch in CA 57-60
Smart, Mollie S(tevens) 1916- 61-64
Smart, (Roderick) Ninian 1927- CANR-12
Earlier sketch in CA 29-32R
Smart, William (Edward, Jr.) 1933- CANR-7
Earlier sketch in CA 15-16R
Smead, (Edwin) Howard 1953- 124
Smedes, Lewis B. 1921- CANR-11
Earlier sketch in CA 69-72
Smedley, Hester Marsden
See Marsden-Smedley, Hester
Smeds, Dave 1955- 118
Smee, John (Charles) Odling
See Odling-Smee, John (Charles)
Smeeton, Miles (Richard) 1906- 13-14R
Smellie, K.
See Smellie, Kingsley Bryce (Speakman)
Smellie, K. B.
See Smellie, Kingsley Bryce (Speakman)
Smellie, Kingsley Bryce (Speakman)
1897-1987 .... 5-6R
Obituary 124
Smelser, Marshall 1912- 17-18R
Smelser, Neil J(oseph) 1930- CANR-8
Earlier sketch in CA 19-20R
Smelser, William T. 1924- 29-32R
Smeltzer, C(larence) H(arry)
1900-19(?) CANR-15
Earlier sketch in CA 4R
Smelyakov, Yaroslav 1913(?)-1972
Obituary 37-40R
Smerk, George M(artin) 1933- 107
Smertenko, Johan J. 1897(?)-1983
Obituary 109
Smerud, Warren D(ouglas) 1928- 49-52
Smetana, Josette 1928- 93-96
Smethurst, William (Knowles) 1945- 117
Smidt, Kristian 1916- 17-18R
Smigel, Erwin O. 1917-1973 .... 41-44R
Obituary 45-48
Smil, Vaclav 1943- 112
Smiles, Samuel 1812-1904 .... DLB-55
Smiley, Charles W(esley) 1940- 113
Smiley, David L(eslie) 1921- 5-6R
Smiley, Jane (Graves) 1949- 104
Smiley, Sam Max 1931- 105
Smiley, Virginia Kester 1923- CANR-12
Earlier sketch in CA 29-32R
See also SATA 2
Smirnov, Sergei Sergeevich 1915-1976
Obituary 65-68
Smith, A(nthony) C(harles) H(ockley)
1935- 119
Brief entry 116
Smith, A(lexander) G(raham) Cairns
See Cairns-Smith, A(lexander) G(raham)
Smith, A(lbert) H(ugh) 1903- 7-8R
Smith, A(lbert) J(ames) 1924- 65-68
Smith, A(rthur) J(ames) M(arshall)
1902-1980 .... CANR-4
Obituary 102
Earlier sketch in CA 2R
See also CLC 15
Smith, A. Robert 1925- 73-76
Smith, A. Weston 1900(?)-1975 Obituary 57-60
Smith, Abbot E(merson) 1906-1983
Obituary 109
Smith, Ada Beatrice Queen Victoria Louisa
Virginia 1894-1984 Obituary 111
Smith, Adam
See Goodman, George J(erome) W(aldo)
Smith, Alan M(cKinley) 1937- 41-44R
Smith, Alexander 1829-1867 .... DLB-32, 55
Smith, Alfred Edward 1895-1969 .... CAP-1
Earlier sketch in CA 11-12
Smith, Alfred G(oud) 1921- CANR-4
Earlier sketch in CA 11-12R
Smith, Alice Upham 1908- 45-48
Smith, Allen William 1938- 61-64
Smith, Alson Jesse 1908-1965 .... 4R
Obituary 103
Smith, Alton E. 1917- 19-20R
Smith, Angel
See Masterton, Graham
Smith, Anna H(ester) 1912- CANR-6
Earlier sketch in CA 57-60
Smith, Anna Piszczan-Czaja 1920- 110
Smith, Anne Mollegen 1940- 81-84
Smith, Anne Warren 1938- 111
See also SATA 34, 41
Smith, Anthony (John Francis) 1926- CANR-3
Earlier sketch in CA 11-12R
Smith, Anthony 1938- CANR-10
Earlier sketch in CA 53-56
Smith, Anthony D(avid) 1939- 101
Smith, Anthony Peter 1912-1980 Obituary 105
Smith, Arnold Cantwell 1915- 109
Smith, Arthur 1948- 120
Smith, Arthur C. 1916- 21-22R
Smith, Arthur L(ee)
See Asante, Molefi K(ete)
Smith, Arthur L(ee), Jr. 1927- 37-40R
Smith, Arthur M(umford) 1903- CAP-2
Earlier sketch in CA 17-18
Smith, Audrey D(owling) 1930- 119
Smith, Barbara Clark 1951- 124
Smith, Barbara Herrnstein 1932- 13-14R
Smith, Bardwell L(eith) 1925- 41-44R
Smith, Barry S(ecker) 1940- 29-32R
Smith, Beatrice S(chillinger) CANR-10
Earlier sketch in CA 57-60
See also SATA 12
Smith, Ben A(rwood) 1916- 4R
Smith, Benjamin Franklin 1902- 41-44R
Smith, Bernard (William) 1916- CANR-17
Earlier sketches in CA 1R, CANR-1
Smith, Bert Kruger 1915- CANR-11
Earlier sketch in CA 15-16R
Smith, Betsy Covington 1937- 111
See also SATA 43
Smith, Betty (Wehner) 1896-1972 .... 5-6R
Obituary 33-36R
See also SATA 6
See also DLBY 82
See also CLC 19
Smith, Beulah Fenderson 1915- 15-16R
Smith, Bonnie G(ene) 1940- 108
Smith, Boyd M. 1888(?)-1973 Obituary 41-44R
Smith, Bradford 1909-1964 .... CANR-16
Earlier sketch in CA 2R
See also SATA 5
Smith, Bradley 1910- CANR-19
Earlier sketches in CA 5-6R, CANR-2
Smith, Bradley F. 1931- 108
Smith, Brian (Clive) 1938- 110
Smith, Bromley K(eables) 1911-1987
Obituary 121
Smith, Bruce 1949- 108
Smith, Bryan Evers Sharwood
See Sharwood Smith, Bryan Evers
Smith, C. Busby
See Smith, John (Charles)
Smith, C. Pritchard
See Hoyt, Edwin P(almer), Jr.
Smith, C. Ray 1929- 109
Smith, C(lifford) T(horpe) 1924- 23-24R
Smith, C. U. 1901- 41-44R
Smith, C(hristopher) U(pham) M(urray)
1930- 33-36R
Smith, C(harles) W(illiam) 1940- 61-64
Smith, C. Willard 1899(?)-1979 Obituary 89-92
Smith, Caesar
See Trevor, Elleston
Smith, Carleton 1910-1984 Obituary 112
Smith, Carlton
See Rocklin, Ross Louis
Smith, Carmichael
See Linebarger, Paul M(yron) A(nthony)
Smith, Carol H(ertzig) 1929- 7-8R
Smith, Carol Sturm 1938- 25-28R
See also DLBY 81
Smith, Carole 1935- 101
Smith, (Charles) Carter (Jr.) 1930- 107
Smith, Catherine C. 1929- 29-32R
Smith, Cecil (Howard III) 1917- 69-72
Smith, Celina Janson
See Janson-Smith, Celina
Smith, Chard Powers 1894-1977 .... 7-8R
Obituary 73-76
Smith, Charles E(dward) 1904-1970
Obituary 29-32R
Smith, Charles Harvard Gibbs
See Gibbs-Smith, Charles Harvard
Smith, Charles Henry 1826-1903
Brief entry 119
See also DLB 11
Smith, Charles Merrill ?-1985 Obituary 115
Smith, Charles W(illiam) (Frederick)
1905- 13-14R
Smith, Charlotte 1749-1806 .... DLB-39
Smith, Cherry 1931- 120
Smith, Clagett G. 1930- 37-40R
Smith, Clark Ashton 1893-1961 .... CLC-43
Smith, Clifford Neal 1923- 41-44R
Smith, Clodus R(ay) 1928- CANR-8
Earlier sketch in CA 21-22R
Smith, (Christopher) Colin 1927- 102
Smith, Cordelia Titcomb 1902- CAP-1
Earlier sketch in CA 11-12
Smith, Cordwainer
See Linebarger, Paul M(yron) A(nthony)
See also DLB 8
Smith, Cornelius C(ole, Jr.) 1913- CANR-22
Earlier sketch in CA 23-24R
Smith, Courtland L(ester) 1939- 81-84
Smith, Craig R(alph) 1944- 81-84
Smith, Curt 1951- 81-84
Smith, Cynthia S. 1924- 106
Smith, Cyril 1928- 109
Smith, Cyril James 1909-1974 Obituary 53-56
Smith, D(avid) Howard 1900-1987 .... 25-28R
Obituary 123
Smith, D. MacLeod
See Smith, David MacLeod
Smith, D(wight) Moody, Jr. 1931- CANR-20
Earlier sketch in CA 41-44R
Smith, D(onald) V(incent) 1933-1978 .... 25-28R
Obituary 117
Smith, D(avid) W(arner) 1932- CANR-12
Earlier sketch in CA 19-20R
Smith, Dale O(rville) 1911- 73-76
Smith, Dan Throop 1908-1982 Obituary 106
Smith, Dana Prom 1927- 49-52
Smith, Daniel M(alloy) 1922-1976 .... CANR-8
Earlier sketch in CA 19-20R
Smith, Darren L. 1958- 124
Smith, Datus C(lifford), Jr. 1907- CANR-11
Earlier sketches in CA 11-12, CAP-1
See also SATA 13
Smith, Dave
See Smith, David (Jeddie)
See also DLB 5
See also CLC 22, 42
Smith, David 1906-1965 Obituary 113
Smith, David (Jeddie) 1942- CANR-1
Earlier sketch in CA 49-52
Smith, David C(layton) 1929- 49-52
Smith, David C. 1931- 69-72
Smith, David C. 1952- 120

Smith, David Elvin 1939- 29-32R
Smith, David Fay 1939- 112
Smith, David H. 1939- 93-96
Smith, David Horton 1939- CANR-7
Earlier sketch in CA 57-60
Smith, David M(arshall) 1936- CANR-12
Earlier sketch in CA 29-32R
Smith, David MacLeod 1920- CANR-5
Earlier sketch in CA 53-56
Smith, David Osmond
See Osmond-Smith, David
Smith, David Shiverick 1918- 108
Smith, David T. 1935- 53-56
Smith, David W. 1921-1981 110
Obituary 108
Smith, Dean E(llis) 1923- CANR-4
Earlier sketch in CA 9-10R
Smith, Delos Owen 1905-1973 Obituary .. 41-44R
Smith, Denison Langley 1924- 15-16R
Smith, Dennis 1940- CANR-10
Earlier sketch in CA 61-64
Smith, Desmond 1927- 103
Smith, Dian G. 1946- 120
Smith, Diana Kappel
See Kappel-Smith, Diana
Smith, Dick 1908-1974 .... CAP-1
Earlier sketch in CA 19-20
Smith, Dick King
See King-Smith, Dick
Smith, Dodie 33-36R
See also SATA 4
See also DLB 10
Smith, Don(ald Taylor) 1909- 49-52
Smith, Don Ian 1918- 45-48
Smith, Donal Ian Bryce 1934- 41-44R
Smith, Donald Eugene 1927- 9-10R
Smith, Donald G. 1927- 13-14R
Smith, Doris Buchanan 1934- CANR-11
Earlier sketch in CA 69-72
See also SATA 28
See also DLB 52
Smith, Doris E(dna Elliott) 1919- CANR-18
Earlier sketch in CA 25-28R
Smith, Dorothy Stafford 1905- 23-24R
See also SATA 6
Smith, Dorothy Valentine 1908- 29-32R
Smith, Douglas 1918- 73-76
Smith, Douglas 1949- 113
Smith, Duane A(llan) 1937- CANR-23
Earlier sketches in CA 23-24R, CANR-8
Smith, Dwight C(hichester), Jr. 1930- 77-80
Smith, Dwight L. 1918- CANR-24
Earlier sketch in CA 33-36R
Smith, Dwight R. 1921- 106
Smith, E(lmer) Boyd 1860-1943 .... YABC-1
Smith, E(dric) Brooks 1917- 5-6R
See also SATA 40
Smith, E(ric) D(avid) 1923- 118
Smith, E. E.
See Smith, Edward Elmer
Smith, E. E. "Doc"
See Smith, Edward Elmer
Smith, Edgar H(erbert) 1934- 25-28R
Smith, Edna Hopkins 1932(?)-1979
Obituary 89-92
Smith, Edward Conrad 1891- 45-48
Smith, Edward E.
See Smith, Edward Elmer
Smith, Edward E. "Doc"
See Smith, Edward Elmer
Smith, Edward Ellis 1921- 25-28R
Smith, Edward Elmer 1890-1965 118
Obituary 102
See also DLB 8
Smith, Edward W(illiam) 1920-1975
Obituary 57-60
Smith, Edwin H. 1920- 15-16R
Smith, Elbert B(enjamin) 1920- 23-24R
Smith, Eleanor Touhey 1910- 25-28R
Smith, Elihu Hubbard 1771-1798 .... DLB-37
Smith, Elinor Goulding 1917- CANR-3
Earlier sketch in CA 2R
Smith, Eliot Fremont
See Fremont-Smith, Eliot
Smith, Elizabeth Oakes (Prince)
1806-1893 .... DLB-1
Smith, Elliott Dunlap 1890(?)-1976
Obituary 61-64
Smith, Elsdon C(oles) 1903- CANR-6
Earlier sketch in CA 2R
Smith, Elske v(an)P(anhuys) 1929- 77-80
Smith, Elton E(dward) 1915- CANR-14
Earlier sketch in CA 15-16R
Smith, Elva Sophronia 1871-1965
Obituary 107
See also SATA 31
Smith, Elwyn Allen 1919- CANR-9
Earlier sketch in CA 5-6R
Smith, Emma 1923- 73-76
See also SATA 36
Smith, Ernest A(llyn) 1911-1977 .... 3R
Obituary 103
Smith, Ethel Sabin 1887- CAP-1
Earlier sketch in CA 15-16
Smith, Eugene L(ewis) 1912-1986 .... 23-24R
Obituary 118
Smith, Eugene Waldo 1905- CAP-1
Earlier sketch in CA 9-10
Smith, (Katherine) Eunice (Young)
1902- CANR-2
Earlier sketch in CA 7-8R
See also SATA 5
Smith, Evelyn E. 1927- Brief entry 113
Smith, F(rederick) G(eorge) Walton 1909- .. 45-48
Smith, F. Joseph 1925- CANR-2
Earlier sketch in CA 45-48
Smith, Fay Jackson 1912- 25-28R
Smith, Florence Margaret 1902-1971 .... CAP-2
Obituary 29-32R
Earlier sketch in CA 17-18
See also CLC 8
Smith, Frances C(hristine) 1904- CANR-1
Earlier sketch in CA 2R
See also SATA 3
Smith, Frances Scott Fitzgerald Lanahan
1921-1986 Obituary 119
Smith, Frank (Arthur) 1917- 69-72
Smith, Frank E(llis) 1918- 17-18R
Smith, Frank E. 1919-1984 Obituary 114
Smith, Frank Kingston 1919- CANR-18
Earlier sketch in CA 102
Smith, Frank O. M. ?-1983 Obituary 109
Smith, Frank Seymour 1898-1972 .... 9-10R
Obituary 89-92
Smith, (David) Fred(erick) 1898(?)-1976
Obituary 69-72
Smith, Frederick E(screet) 1922- CANR-19
Earlier sketches in CA 7-8R, CANR-3
Smith, Frederick W(illiam) 1920- 73-76
Smith, Frederick William Robin 1936-1985
Obituary 115
Smith, Frederick Winston Furneaux
1907-1975 65-68
Obituary 57-60
Smith, Fredrika Shumway 1877-1968
Obituary 109
See also SATA 30
Smith, G(eorge) E(verard) Kidder 1913- .. 11-12R
Smith, Gaddis 1932- 23-24R
Smith, Garry (Van Dorn) 1933- 5-6R
Smith, Gary (Milton) 1943- 97-100
Smith, Gary R. 1932- 69-72
See also SATA 14
Smith, Gary V(incent) 1943- 101
Smith, Gene 1924- 77-80
Smith, Gene 1929- 81-84
Smith, Genevieve Love 1917- 21-22R
Smith, Geoffrey (John) 1943- 120
Smith, Geoffrey (Francis) Hattersley
See Hattersley-Smith, Geoffrey (Francis)
Smith, Geoffrey Sutton 1941- 49-52
Smith, George (Henry) 1922- 103
Smith, George E. 1938- 37-40R
Smith, George Harmon 1920- 49-52
See also SATA 5
Smith, George Ivan 1915- 121
Smith, George O(liver) 1911-1981 97-100
Obituary 103
See also DLB 8
Smith, Gerald A(lfred) 1921- 37-40R
Smith, Gerald B. 1909- CAP-2
Earlier sketch in CA 25-28
Smith, Gerald L(yman) K(enneth)
1898-1976 Obituary 65-68
Smith, Gerald Stanton 1938- 123
Smith, Glenn C. 1924- 123
Smith, Godfrey 1926- 9-10R
Smith, Goldwin (Albert) 1912- 41-44R
Smith, Gordon Roland
See Roland Smith, Gordon
Smith, Gordon Ross 1917- 7-8R
Smith, Grahame 1933- 25-28R
Smith, Gretchen L. ?-1972 Obituary 104
Smith, Grover C(leveland) 1923- 33-36R
Smith, Gudmund J(ohn) W(ilhelm) 1920- ... 102
Smith, Guy-Harold 1895- CAP-2
Earlier sketch in CA 19-20
Smith, H(arry) Allen 1907-1976 .... CANR-5
Obituary 65-68
Earlier sketch in CA 7-8R
See also SATA 20
See also DLB 11, 29
See also AITN 2
Smith, H(arold) Wendell 1923- 111
Smith, Hale G(illiam) 1918- 61-64
Smith, Hallett (Darius) 1907- 23-24R
Smith, Harmon L. 1930- 29-32R
Smith, Harold Ivan 1947- 121
Smith, Harris (Gordon) 1921- 49-52
Smith, (Oliver) Harrison 1888-1971
Obituary 29-32R
Smith, Harry 1936- CANR-13
Earlier sketch in CA 77-80
Smith, Harry E(dmund) 1928- 25-28R
Smith, Harry W(illiam) 1937- 112
Smith, Harvey K(ennedy) 1904-1968 .... CAP-1
Earlier sketch in CA 13-14
Smith, Hedrick (Laurence) 1933- CANR-11
Earlier sketch in CA 65-68
Smith, Helen Zenna
See Price, Evadne
Smith, Henry 1905-1988 Obituary 124
Smith, Henry
See Smith, Henry DeWitt II
Smith, Henry Clay 1913- 2R
Smith, Henry DeWitt II 1940- 119
Smith, Henry Lee, Jr. 1913-1972
Obituary 37-40R
Smith, Henry Nash 1906-1986 .... CANR-2
Obituary 119
Earlier sketch in CA 4R
Smith, Henry Peter 1910-1968 .... 4R
Obituary 103
Smith, Herbert F(rancis) 1922- CANR-13
Earlier sketch in CA 77-80
Smith, Herbert F. A. 1915-1969 .... CAP-1
Earlier sketch in CA 15-16
Smith, Hermon Dunlap 1900-1983
Obituary 109
Smith, Hilda Worthington 1889(?)-1984
Obituary 112
Smith, Hobart M(uir) 1912- CANR-9
Earlier sketch in CA 65-68
Smith, Hope M(ayhew) 1916- 2R
Smith, Howard E(verett), Jr. 1927- CANR-21
Earlier sketch in CA 25-28R
See also SATA 12
Smith, Howard K(ingsbury) 1914- CANR-2
Earlier sketch in CA 45-48
Smith, Howard R(oss) 1917- 4R
Smith, Howard Van 1910(?)-1986 .... 5-6R
Obituary 120
Smith, Hubert Shirley
See Shirley-Smith, Hubert
Smith, Hugh L(etcher) 1921-1968 .... CAP-2
Earlier sketch in CA 25-28
See also SATA 5
Smith, Huston (Cummings) 1919- 61-64
Smith, I(rving) Norman 1909- 107
Smith, Iain Crichton 1928- 23-24R
See also DLB 40
Smith, Imogene Henderson 1922- 7-8R
See also SATA 12
Smith, Irene 1903- 73-76
Smith, Irving H(arold) 1932- 49-52
Smith, Irwin 1892-1977 .... 7-8R
Obituary 73-76
Smith, Isadore Leighton Luce 1901-1985 ... 101
Obituary 118
Smith, J. Allen 1860-1924 .... DLB-47
Smith, J.C.S.
See Smith, Jane S.
Smith, J(ohn) Holland 1932- 17-18R
Smith, J(ames) L(eonard) B(rierley)
1897-1968 .... CAP-1
Earlier sketch in CA 13-14
Smith, J(ohn) Malcolm 1921- 49-52
Smith, J(oseph) Russell 1874-1966 .... CAP-1
Earlier sketch in CA 13-14
Smith, J(oe) W(illiam) Ashley 1914- 7-8R
Smith, Jack (Clifford) 1916- CANR-12
Earlier sketch in CA 69-72
Smith, Jackie M. 1930- 93-96
Smith, Jackson Algernon 1917-
Brief entry 105
Smith, Jacqueline B. 1937- SATA-39
Smith, James 1904-1972 85-88
Smith, James A. 1914- 23-24R
Smith, James D(ale) 1940- 121
Smith, James L(eslie Clarke) 1936- 25-28R
Smith, James Morton 1919- 103
Smith, James R. 1941- 101
Smith, James Roy 1920- 23-24R
Smith, Jane F(rances) 1916- 123
Brief entry 117
Smith, Jane I(dleman) 1937- 107
Smith, Jane S. 1947- 118
Smith, Janet (Buchanan) Adam
See Adam Smith, Janet (Buchanan)
Smith, Jean
See Smith, Frances C(hristine)
Smith, Jean DeMouthe 1949- 65-68
Smith, Jean Edward 1932- 37-40R
Smith, Jean Pajot 1945- 53-56
See also SATA 10
Smith, Jerome F(ranken) 1928- 107
Smith, Jessica 1895- CANR-2
Earlier sketch in CA 49-52
Smith, Jessie Carney 1930- CANR-17
Earlier sketch in CA 89-92
Smith, Jessie Willcox 1863-1935 .... SATA-21
Smith, Jim 1920- Brief entry 115
See also SATA 36
Smith, Joan 1933- SATA-46
Smith, Joan 1935- 61-64
Smith, Joan K(aren) 1939- 93-96
Smith, Joanmarie 1932- CANR-16
Earlier sketch in CA 85-88
Smith, Jody Brant 1943- 113
Smith, John 1580(?)-1631 .... DLB-24, 30
Smith, John (Charles) 1924- 103
Smith, John
See Herrick, Marvin Theodore
Smith, John Chabot 1915- 69-72
Smith, John Coventry 1903-1984 115
Smith, John David 1949- 111
Smith, John Edwin 1921- 103
Smith, John F(erris) 1934- 81-84
Smith, John H(azel) 1928- 11-12R
Smith, John Norton
See Norton-Smith, John
Smith, Johnston
See Crane, Stephen (Townley)
Smith, Jon R(ichard) 1946- 77-80
Smith, Jordan 1954- 110
Smith, Joseph B(urkholder) 1921- 65-68
Smith, Joseph Fielding 1876-1972
Obituary 37-40R
Smith, Joseph H(enry) 1913-1981
Obituary 105
Smith, Josiah 1704-1781 .... DLB-24
Smith, Julia Floyd 1914- 85-88
Smith, Julian 1937- 61-64
Smith, Julian W. 1901- 13-14R
Smith, Julie 1944- 112
Smith, K(ermit) Wayne 1938- 29-32R
Smith, Karl U(lrich) 1907- CANR-9
Earlier sketch in CA 61-64
Smith, Kate
See Smith, Kathryn Elizabeth
Smith, Kathleen J(oan) 1929- 103
Smith, Kathryn Elizabeth 1907(?)-1986
Obituary 119
Smith, Kay
See Smith, Catherine C.
Smith, Kay Nolte 1932- CANR-18
Earlier sketch in CA 101
Smith, Keith V(an) 1937- 112
Smith, Ken(neth Danforth) 1902- CANR-1
Earlier sketch in CA 45-48
Smith, Ken(neth John) 1938- 33-36R
See also DLB 40
Smith, Kenneth Lee 1925- 77-80
Smith, Kenneth M(anley) 1892-1981
Obituary 108
Smith, L(eonard) Glenn 1939- 93-96
Smith, Lacey Baldwin 1922- CANR-6
Earlier sketch in CA 5-6R
Smith, Lafayette
See Higdon, Hal
Smith, Larry 1940- 49-52
Smith, Laura I(vory) 1902- 19-20R
Smith, Laurence D. 1950- 123
Smith, Lavon B(enson) 1921- 23-24R
Smith, Lawrence Berk 1939- CANR-13
Earlier sketch in CA 73-76
Smith, Lawrence R(ichard) 1945- 117
Smith, Lee 1937- 73-76
Smith, Lee 1944- 119
Brief entry 114
See also DLBY 83
See also CLC 25
Smith, Lee
See Albion, Lee Smith
Smith, Lee L. 1930- 29-32R
Smith, Lena (Kennedy) 1914- 93-96
Smith, Lendon H(oward) 1921- 81-84
Smith, LeRoi Tex 1934- 29-32R
Smith, Leslie F(rancis) 1901- CAP-1
Earlier sketch in CA 19-20
Smith, Leslie James Seth
See Seth-Smith, Leslie James
Smith, Leslie R(aymond) 1904- 4R
Smith, Lew
See Floren, Lee
Smith, Lillian (Eugenia) 1897-1966 .... CAP-2
Obituary 25-28R
Earlier sketch in CA 17-18
Smith, Lillian H(elena) 1887-1983
Obituary 111
See also SATA 32
Smith, Linell Nash 1932- 5-6R
See also SATA 2
Smith, Liz 1923- 65-68
Smith, Lou 1918- 73-76
Smith, Louis
See Barzini, Luigi (Giorgio, Jr.)
Smith, Louis M(ilde) 1929- 19-20R
Smith, Lucia B. 1943- 108
See also SATA 30
Smith, Lynnette 1951- 116
Smith, M(ahlon) Brewster 1919- 61-64
Smith, M. Estellie 1935- CANR-8
Earlier sketch in CA 61-64
Smith, M. Weston
See Weston-Smith, M.
Smith, Malcolm 1938- 97-100
Smith, Malcom N(orman) 1919(?)-1985
Obituary 116
Smith, Manuel (Juan) 1934- 105
Smith, Marcus J(oel) 1918- 73-76
Smith, Margaret Chase 1897- 73-76
Smith, Margaret Emily Noel Nuttall
See Nuttall-Smith, Margaret Emily Noel
Smith, Margaret F(oltz) 1915- 102
Smith, Margaret Mary 1916- 108
Smith, Margaret Ruth 1902- CAP-1
Earlier sketch in CA 19-20
Smith, Margarita G. 1923(?)-1983
Obituary 109
Smith, Marie D. 13-14R
Smith, Marilyn Cochran
See Cochran-Smith, Marilyn
Smith, Marion Hagens 1913- 17-18R
See also SATA 12
Smith, Marion Jaques 1899- CANR-11
Earlier sketch in CA 69-72
See also SATA 13
Smith, Mark (Richard) 1935- CANR-10
Earlier sketch in CA 15-16R
See also DLBY 82
Smith, Marny 1932- 108
Smith, Martin
See Smith, Martin Cruz
Smith, Martin Cruz 1942- CANR-23
Earlier sketches in CA 85-88, CANR-6
See also CLC 25
Smith, Mary Benton 1903- CAP-2
Earlier sketch in CA 17-18
Smith, Mary Elizabeth 1932- 41-44R
Smith, Mary Ellen 69-72
See also SATA 10
Smith, Mary-Ann Tirone 1944- Brief entry .. 118
See also CLC 39
Smith, Mason McCann 1952- 108
Smith, Maxwell A(ustin) 1894- 37-40R
Smith, (Albert) Merriman 1913-1970 .... CANR-2
Obituary 29-32R
Earlier sketch in CA 2R
Smith, Merritt Roe 1940- 77-80
Smith, Michael 1698-1771(?) DLB-31
Smith, Michael (Townsend) 1935- CANR-11
Earlier sketch in CA 21-22R
Smith, Michael A(nthony) 1942- 102
Smith, Michael P(eter) 1942- 65-68
Smith, Michael Stephen 1944- 103
Smith, Mike
See Smith, Mary Ellen
Smith, Mildred C(atharine) 1891-1973 101
Obituary 45-48
Smith, Mildred Nelson 1918- 69-72
Smith, Mortimer B(rewster) 1906-1981 107
Obituary 104
Smith, Morton 1915- CANR-6
Earlier sketch in CA 5-6R
Smith, Morton Howison 1923- 45-48

Smith, Murphy D(ewitt) 1920- CANR-13
Earlier sketch in CA 37-40R
Smith, Murray G(ordon) 1952- 120
Smith, Myron J(ohn), Jr. 1944- CANR-16
Earlier sketches in CA 45-48, CANR-1
Smith, N(orman) J(ames) 1930- CANR-20
Earlier sketch in CA 103
Smith, Nancy Covert 1935- CANR-10
Earlier sketch in CA 57-60
See also SATA 12
Smith, Nancy Taylor 57-60
Smith, Neil Homer 1909(?)-1972
Obituary 37-40R
Smith, Nigel J(ohn) H(arwood) 1949- 109
Smith, Nila Banton 1890-1976 .... 21-22R
Obituary 120
Smith, Nina Slingsby 1928- 119
Smith, Norman Edward Mace 1914- 103
Smith, Norman F. 1920- 29-32R
See also SATA 5
Smith, Norman Lewis 1941- 77-80
Smith, Norris Kelly 1917- 21-22R
Smith, Ophia D(elilah) Smith 1891- 5-6R
Smith, Oswald J(effrey) 1889-1986
Obituary 119
Smith, P(eter) J(ohn) 1931- 41-44R
Smith, (Charles) Page 1917- CANR-2
Earlier sketch in CA 4R
Smith, Patricia Jean Adam
See Adam-Smith, Patricia Jean
Smith, Patrick 1936- 77-80
Smith, Patrick D(avis) 1927- 77-80
Smith, Patrick J(ohn) 1932- 41-44R
Smith, Patrick Wykeham Montague
See Montague-Smith, Patrick Wykeham
Smith, Patti 1946- 93-96
See also CLC 12
Smith, Pattie Sherwood 1909(?)-1974
Obituary 53-56
Smith, Paul CANR-2
Earlier sketch in CA 2R
Smith, Paul B(rainerd) 1921- CANR-10
Earlier sketch in CA 13-14R
Smith, Paul C. 1908-1976 Obituary 65-68
Smith, Paul F. 1919- 57-60
Smith, Paul H(ubert) 1931- 89-92
Smith, Paul Jordan
See Jordan-Smith, Paul
Smith, Pauline (Urmson) 1882-1959 .... TCLC-25
Smith, Pauline C(oggeshall) 1908- 29-32R
See also SATA 27
Smith, Percival Gardner
See Gardner-Smith, Percival
Smith, Perry McCoy 1934- 29-32R
Smith, Peter 1897-1982 Obituary 107
Smith, Peter C(harles Horstead) 1940- .. CANR-7
Earlier sketch in CA 57-60
Smith, Peter H(opkinson) 1940- 41-44R
Smith, Peter J(ohn) 1931- 114
Smith, Philip Chadwick Foster 1939- 77-80
Smith, Philip E(dward II) 1943- 25-28R
Smith, Philip L. 1943- 108
Smith, Philip Warren 1936- SATA-46
Smith, R(ichard) A(lbert) N(ewton) 1908- .. 9-10R
Smith, R(eginald) C(harles) 1907- 65-68
Smith, R(eginald) D(onald) 1914- 117
Smith, R(obert) Philip 1907- 81-84
Smith, R(ichard) Selby 1914- 108
Smith, Ralph (Bernard) 1939- 33-36R
Smith, Ralph Alexander 1929- 77-80
Smith, Ralph B. 1894(?)-1985 Obituary 115
Smith, Ralph Carlisle 1910- 124
Smith, Ralph Lee 1927- CANR-1
Earlier sketch in CA 4R
Smith, Ray 1915- CANR-11
Earlier sketch in CA 15-16R
Smith, Ray 1941- CANR-18
Earlier sketch in CA 101
Smith, Ray Winfield 1897-1982 Obituary ... 110
Smith, Red
See Smith, Walter W(ellesley)
See also DLB 29
Smith, Rex Alan 1921- 61-64
Smith, Rhea Marsh 1907- CAP-1
Earlier sketch in CA 17-18
Smith, Richard 1941- 81-84
Smith, Richard A(ustin) 1911- 19-20R
Smith, Richard C(hristopher) 1948- 81-84
Smith, Richard Harris 1946- 41-44R
Smith, Richard Joseph 1944- CANR-20
Earlier sketch in CA 97-100
Smith, Richard K(ent) 1936- 41-44R
Smith, Richard M(ills) 1946- 73-76
Smith, Richard N. 1937- 23-24R
Smith, Richard P(aul) 1949- 111
Smith, Richard Rein 1930- 97-100
Smith, Robert A(rthur) 1944- 69-72
Smith, Robert Allan 1909-1980 Obituary 105
Smith, Robert C(hester) 1912-1975
Obituary 114
Smith, Robert C(harles) 1947- 111
Smith, Robert Charles 1938- 65-68
Smith, Robert D. 1937- 37-40R
Smith, Robert Dickie 1928- 9-10R
Smith, Robert Eliot 1899- 37-40R
Smith, Robert Ellis 1940- CANR-16
Earlier sketch in CA 89-92
Smith, Robert Freeman 1930- CANR-1
Earlier sketch in CA 3R
Smith, Robert G(illen) 1913- 45-48
Smith, Robert G(ordon) 1947- 102
Smith, Robert Griffin, Jr. 1920- 41-44R
Smith, Robert Houston 1931- 105
Smith, Robert J(ohn) 1927- 53-56
Smith, Robert Kimmel 1930- CANR-8
Earlier sketch in CA 61-64
See also SATA 12
Smith, Robert Lee 1928- 111
Smith, Robert Paul 1915-1977 73-76
Obituary 69-72
See also SATA 30
Smith, Robert S(idney) 1904-1969 ...... CAP-1
Earlier sketch in CA 15-16
Smith, Robert W(ayne) 1926- 45-48
Smith, Robert W(illiam) 1926- 15-16R
Smith, Robin Baird
See Baird-Smith, Robin
Smith, Rockwell Carter 1908- 53-56
Smith, Rodney P(ennell), Jr. 1930- 29-32R
Smith, Roger H(askell) 1932-1980 69-72
Obituary 101
Smith, Roger Montgomery 1915(?)-1975
Obituary 57-60
Smith, Rogers M(ood) 1953- 120
Smith, Roland B(eatcher) 1909- 2R
Smith, Ronald Gregor 1913-1968 .... CAP-1
Earlier sketch in CA 9-10
Smith, Ronald L(ande) 1952- 110
Smith, Rowland (James) 1938- 45-48
Smith, Roy C(yrus) 1896- 124
Smith, Roy H(armon) III 1936- 25-28R
Smith, Russell E. 1932- 77-80
Smith, Russell F. W. 1915(?)-1975
Obituary 61-64
Smith, Ruth Leslie 1902- CAP-2
Earlier sketch in CA 29-32
See also SATA 2
Smith, Ruth Schluchter 1917- CANR-11
Earlier sketch in CA 69-72
Smith, S(idney) G(erald) Denis 1932- 103
Smith, Sally Liberman 1929- CANR-11
Earlier sketch in CA 21-22R
Smith, Sam(uel Frederic Houston) 1937- .. 73-76
Smith, Samantha 1972-1985 Obituary 117
See also SATA 45
Smith, Samuel 1904- CANR-11
Earlier sketch in CA 29-32R
Smith, Samuel Harrison 1772-1845 ..... DLB-43
Smith, Samuel Stanhope 1751-1819 .... DLB-37
Smith, Sandra 1940- 122
Smith, Sarah 1832-1911 Brief entry 112
Smith, Sarah Stafford
See Smith, Dorothy Stafford
Smith, Scottie
See Smith, Frances Scott Fitzgerald Lanahan
Smith, Scottie Fitzgerald
See Smith, Frances Scott Fitzgerald Lanahan
Smith, Seba 1792-1868 .... DLB-1, 11
Smith, Sharon 1947- 77-80
Smith, Sheila Kaye
See Kaye-Smith, Sheila
Smith, Shelley
See Bodington, Nancy H(ermione) and Shelley, Dolores and Smith, Sandra
Smith, Sherwin 1924(?)-1985 Obituary 116
Smith, Shirley M(ae) 1923- CANR-4
Earlier sketch in CA 53-56
Smith, Stan(ley William) 1943- 120
Smith, Stan(ley Roger) 1946- 85-88
Smith, Stephen Murray
See Murray-Smith, Stephen
Smith, Steve(n R.) 1947- 118
Smith, Steven A(lbert) 1939- 57-60
Smith, Steven Phillip 1943- CANR-10
Earlier sketch in CA 57-60
Smith, Stevie
See Smith, Florence Margaret
See also DLB 20
See also CLC 3, 8, 25, 44
Smith, Susan Carlton 1923- SATA-12
Smith, Susan Mathias 1950- 114
See also SATA 35, 43
Smith, Susan Vernon 1950- CANR-19
Earlier sketch in CA 102
See also SATA 48
Smith, Susy 1911- CANR-6
Earlier sketch in CA 5-6R
Smith, Sydney Goodsir 1915-1975 101
Obituary 57-60
See also DLB 27
Smith, T(ed) C. 1915- 49-52
Smith, T(homas) E(dward) 1916- 15-16R
Smith, T(homas) Lynn 1903- 7-8R
Smith, Talbot 1899- CAP-1
Earlier sketch in CA 11-12
Smith, Terence (Fitzgerald) 1938- 73-76
Smith, Thomas B(ell) 1923- 122
Smith, Thomas G. 1945- 123
Smith, Thomas Malcolm 1921- Brief entry .. 106
Smith, Tilman R(ay) 1903- 113
Smith, Timothy Dudley
See Dudley-Smith, Timothy
Smith, Timothy L(awrence) 1924- 116
Smith, Toby 1946- 119
Smith, Tony 93-96
Smith, Tony
See Smith, Anthony Peter
Smith, V(incent) Kerry 1945- 111
Smith, Varrel Lavere 1925- 29-32R
Smith, Verla Lee 1927(?)-1982 Obituary 106
Smith, Vernon Lomax 1927- CANR-6
Earlier sketch in CA 4R
Smith, Vesta (Henderson) 1933- 5-6R
Smith, Vian (Crocker) 1920-1969 .... CANR-3
Earlier sketch in CA 4R
See also SATA 11
Smith, Victor C(lyde) 1902- 7-8R
Smith, Vincent E(dward) 1915-1972
Obituary 33-36R
Smith, Virginia Carlson 1944- 49-52
Smith, Virginia Masterman
See Masterman-Smith, Virginia
Smith, Vivian (Brian) 1933- CANR-23
Earlier sketches in CA 61-64, CANR-8
Smith, W(illiam) David 1928- 77-80
Smith, W. Eugene 1918(?)-1978
Obituary 81-84
Smith, Walter W(ellesley) 1905-1982 77-80
Obituary 105
Smith, Ward
See Goldsmith, Howard
Smith, Warren L(ounsbury) 1914-1972 ... CAP-2
Earlier sketch in CA 21-22
Smith, Warren Sylvester 1912- 21-22R
Smith, Warren T(homas) 1923-1986 117
Obituary 119
Smith, Webster
See Coleman, Clayton W(ebster)
Smith, Wendell 1914-1972 Obituary 104
Smith, Wendell I(rving) 1921- 13-14R
Smith, Wesley D(ale) 1930- Brief entry 111
Smith, Wesley E. 1938- 29-32R
Smith, Whitney, Jr. 1940- 97-100
Smith, Wilbur A(ddison) 1933- CANR-7
Earlier sketch in CA 13-14R
See also CLC 33
Smith, Wilbur M(oorehead) 17-18R
Smith, Wilford E(mery) 1916- 49-52
Smith, Wilfred Cantwell 1916- CANR-7
Earlier sketch in CA 13-14R
Smith, Wilfred R(obert) 1915- 13-14R
Smith, Willard L(aurence) 1927- 7-8R
Smith, William 1727-1803 .... DLB-31
Smith, William 1728-1793 .... DLB-30
Smith, William A. 1918- SATA-10
Smith, William A. 1929- 45-48
Smith, William Allen 1904- 45-48
Smith, William C(harles) 1881-1972
Obituary 111
Smith, William Dale 1929- 49-52
Smith, William E(rnest) 1892- 5-6R
Smith, William Frank 1925- 103
Smith, William Gardner 1926-1974 65-68
Obituary 53-56
Smith, William I. 1932- 29-32R
Smith, William J. 1907(?)-1986 Obituary ... 118
Smith, William Jay 1918- 7-8R
See also SATA 2
See also DLB 5
See also CLC 6
Smith, William Martin 1911- 105
Smith, William S. 1917- 15-16R
Smith, William Scott 1926- 117
Smith, William Stevenson 1907-1969 .... CAP-2
Earlier sketch in CA 21-22
Smith, (Francis) Wilson 1922- 81-84
Smith, Winsome 1935- 115
See also SATA 45
Smith, Woodrow Wilson
See Kuttner, Henry
Smith, Woodruff D(onald) 1946- 85-88
Smith, Z. Z.
See Westheimer, David
Smith Brindle, Reginald 1917- 89-92
Smithdas, Robert Joseph 1925- 17-18R
Smithells, Roger (William) 1905- CAP-1
Earlier sketch in CA 13-14
Smither, Elizabeth 1941- 107
Smitherman, P(hilip) H(enry) 1910- 21-22R
Smithers, Don LeRoy 1933- 45-48
Smithers, Peter Henry Berry Otway
1913- 29-32R
Smithgall, Elizabeth
See Watts, Elizabeth (Bailey) Smithgall
Smithies, Arthur 1907-1981 Obituary 104
Smithies, Richard H(ugo) R(ipman)
1936- 23-24R
Smithson, Alison (Margaret) 1928- CANR-5
Earlier sketch in CA 25-28R
Smithson, Norman 1931- 33-36R
Smithson, Peter (Denham) 1923- CANR-5
Earlier sketch in CA 53-56
Smithson, Rulon N(ephi) 1927- 45-48
Smithyman, (William) Kendrick 1922- 101
Smits, Teo
See Smits, Theodore R(ichard)
Smits, Theodore R(ichard) 1905- 77-80
See also SATA 28, 45
Smitten, Jeffrey Roger 1941- 105
Smoke, Jim 109
Smoke, Richard 1944- CANR-10
Earlier sketch in CA 65-68
Smolansky, Oles M. 1930- CANR-1
Earlier sketch in CA 45-48
Smolar, Boris (Ber) 1897-1986 .... 41-44R
Obituary 118
Smolich, Yurik K. 1899(?)-1976 Obituary .. 69-72
Smolin, C. Roger 1948- 110
Smoll, Frank L(ouis) 1941- 115
Smolla, Rodney A(lan) 1953- 121
Smoller, Bruce M. 1944- 113
Smoller, Sanford J(erome) 1937- 57-60
Smollett, Tobias 1721-1771 .... DLB-39
Smooha, Sammy 1941- 101
Smoot, Dan 1913- CANR-1
Earlier sketch in CA 4R
Smothers, Frank A(lbert) 1901-1981
Obituary 104
Smout, T(homas) C(hristopher) 1933- ... CANR-9
Earlier sketch in CA 21-22R
Smucker, Barbara (Claassen) 1915- CANR-23
Earlier sketch in CA 106
See also SATA 29
See also CLR 10
Smucker, Leonard 1928- 23-24R
Smullyan, Arthur Francis 1912- 4R
Smullyan, Raymond M(errill) 1919-
Brief entry 120
Smurl, James F(redrick) 1934- 45-48
Smurr, John Welling 1922- 3R
Smurthwaite, Ronald 1918-1975 .... CAP-2
Earlier sketch in CA 21-22
Smyer, Richard 1935- 102
Smykay, Edward W(alter) 1924- CANR-12
Earlier sketch in CA 19-20R
Smylie, James H(utchinson) 1925- CANR-14
Earlier sketch in CA 37-40R
Smylie, Mark A. 1954- 111
Smyrl, Frank H(erbert) 1938- 113
Smyser, Adam A(lbert) 1920- 77-80
Smyser, H(amilton) M(artin) 1901- CAP-1
Earlier sketch in CA 15-16
Smyser, Jane Worthington 1914-1975 65-68
Obituary 61-64
Smyth, Alice M.
See Hadfield, Alice M(ary)
Smyth, David 1929- CANR-12
Earlier sketch in CA 61-64
Smyth, H. D.
See Smyth, Henry DeWolf
Smyth, H(arriet) Rucker (Crowell) 1926- 2R
Smyth, Henry DeWolf 1898-1986
Obituary 120
Smyth, Howard McGaw 1901-1975
Obituary 61-64
Smyth, Jacqui (Marie) 1960- 124
Smyth, John (George) 1893-1983 ..... CANR-11
Obituary 109
Earlier sketch in CA 61-64
Smyth, Paul 1944- CANR-8
Earlier sketch in CA 61-64
Smyth, R(obert) L(eslie) 1922- CANR-10
Earlier sketch in CA 9-10R
Smythe, Colin 1942- CANR-16
Earlier sketch in CA 97-100
Smythe, Daniel Webster 1908- 15-16R
Smythe, David Mynders 1915- 3R
Smythe, Donald 1927- 41-44R
Smythe, Hugh H(eyne) 1913-1977 .... 11-12R
Obituary 69-72
Smythe, Mabel M(urphy) 1918- 37-40R
Smythe, Reginald 1918?- AITN-1
Smythe, Ted Curtis 1932- 101
Smythies, J(ohn) R(aymond) 1922- 37-40R
Snadowsky, Alvin M. 1938- 61-64
Snailham, (George) Richard 1930- 37-40R
Snaith, Norman Henry 1898-1982
Obituary 106
Snaith, William Theodore 1908-1974 110
Obituary 106
Snape, H(enry) Currie 1902- 9-10R
Snape, R(ichard) H(al) 1936- 29-32R
Snapes, Joan 1925- 107
Snavely, Adam A. 1930- 25-28R
Snavely, Ellen Bartow 1910- CAP-2
Earlier sketch in CA 21-22
Snavely, Guy Everett 1881-1974 .... 5-6R
Obituary 49-52
Snavely, Tipton Ray 1890- 19-20R
Snavely, William P(ennington) 1920- 17-18R
Snead, Rodman Eldredge 1931- 73-76
Snead, Sam(uel Jackson) 1912-
Brief entry 114
Snedeker, Bonnie 1947- 119
Snedeker, Caroline Dale (Parke)
1871-1956 .... YABC-2
Sneed, Joseph Donald 1938- 49-52
Sneed, Joseph Tyree 1920- 23-24R
Sneider, Vern(on) John 1916-1981 .... CANR-13
Obituary 103
Earlier sketch in CA 7-8R
Snell, Bruno 1896- CAP-1
Earlier sketch in CA 15-16
Snell, David 1936- 77-80
Snell, Foster Dee 1898-1980 Obituary 108
Snell, Frank 1920- 1R
Snell, George Davis 1903- 106
Snell, John Leslie, Jr. 1923-1972 ...... CANR-3
Obituary 33-36R
Earlier sketch in CA 7-8R
Snell, John Nicholas Blashford
See Blashford-Snell, John Nicholas
Snell, Nigel (Edward Creagh) 1936- 111
See also SATA 40
Snell, Tee Loftin 1922- 105
Sneller, Delwyn Lee 1945- 111
Snellgrove, David L(lewellyn) 1920-
Brief entry 115
Snellgrove, L(aurence) E(rnest) 1928- .. CANR-23
Earlier sketches in CA 9-10R, CANR-3
Snellgrove, Louis 1928- 45-48
Snelling, Lois 7-8R
Snelling, O(swald) F(rederick) 1916- 17-18R
Snelling, W(illiam) Rodman 1931- 93-96
Snellings, Rolland
See Toure, Askia Muhammad
Snellings, Rolland
See Toure, Askia Muhammad Abu Bakr el
Snepp, Frank (Warren III) 1943- 105
Snetsinger, John (Goodall) 1941- 73-76
Snetsinger, Robert 1928- 107
Sneve, Virginia Driving Hawk 1933- CANR-3
Earlier sketch in CA 49-52
See also SATA 8
See also CLR 2
Snider, Delbert A(rthur) 1914- 2R
Snider, Lewis W. 119
Sniderman, Florence (Lama) 1915- 33-36R
Snipes, Wilson Currin 1924- 29-32R
Snively, Susan 1945- 117
Snively, W(illiam) D(aniel), Jr. 1911- 29-32R

Snodgrass, A(nthony) M(cElrea)
1934- ... CANR-10
Earlier sketch in CA 21-22R
Snodgrass, Donald R(ay) 1935- ... 112
Snodgrass, Joan Gay 1934- ... 77-80
Snodgrass, Jon 1941- ... 113
Snodgrass, Milton M(oore) 1931- ... 29-32R
Snodgrass, Thomas Jefferson
See Clemens, Samuel Langhorne
Snodgrass, W(illiam) D(e Witt) 1926- ... CANR-6
Earlier sketch in CA 2R
See also DLB 5
See also CLC 2, 6, 10, 18
Snoek, J(aap) Diedrick 1931- ... 49-52
Snook, Barbara (Lillian) 1913-1976 ... 109
See also SATA 34
Snook, I(van) A(ugustine) 1933- ... CANR-14
Earlier sketch in CA 77-80
Snook, John B. 1927- ... 106
Snortum, Niel K(lendenon) 1928- ... 23-24R
Snow, C(harles) P(ercy) 1905-1980 ... 7-8R
Obituary ... 101
See also DLB 15
See also CLC 1, 4, 6, 9, 13, 19
Snow, Charles Ernest 1910-1967 Obituary ... 116
Snow, D(avid) W(illiam) 1924- ... 65-68
Snow, Davis W. 1913(?)-1975 Obituary ... 61-64
Snow, Don(ald Merritt) 1943- ... 106
Snow, Donald Clifford 1917- ... 85-88
See also SATA 16
Snow, Donald M. 1943- ... 124
Snow, Dorothea J(ohnston) 1909- ... CANR-3
Earlier sketch in CA 4R
See also SATA 9
Snow, Dorothy Mary Barter 1897- ... CAP-1
Earlier sketch in CA 13-14
Snow, Edgar Parks 1905-1972 ... 81-84
Obituary ... 33-36R
Snow, Edward Rowe 1902-1982 ... CANR-6
Obituary ... 106
Earlier sketch in CA 9-10R
Snow, Frances Compton
See Adams, Henry (Brooks)
Snow, George (D'Oyly) 1903- ... 7-8R
Snow, Helen Foster 1907- ... 57-60
Snow, John Hall 1924- ... 37-40R
Snow, Karen (a pseudonym) 1923- ... 120
Snow, Kathleen 1944- ... 81-84
Snow, Keith Ronald 1943- ... 110
Snow, Lois Wheeler 1920- ... 57-60
Snow, Lucy
See Aubert, Rosemary
Snow, Peter G(ordon) 1933- ... 23-24R
Snow, Philip Albert 1915- ... 9-10R
Snow, Richard F(olger) 1947- ... 106
See also SATA 37
Snow, Roslyn 1936- ... CANR-9
Earlier sketch in CA 23-24R
Snow, Russell E(lwin) 1938- ... 65-68
Snow, Sinclair 1909-1972 ... CAP-2
Earlier sketch in CA 25-28
Snow, Vernon F. 1924- ... 37-40R
Snow, (Charles) Wilbert 1884-1977 ... 9-10R
Obituary ... 73-76
Snow, William George Sinclair 1908- ... 7-8R
Snowden, Frank M(artin), Jr. 1911- ... 41-44R
Snowdon
See Armstrong-Jones, Antony (Charles Robert)
Snowman, Daniel 1938- ... CANR-4
Earlier sketch in CA 53-56
Snukal, Robert (Martin) 1942- ... 45-48
Snyder, Anne 1922- ... CANR-14
Earlier sketch in CA 37-40R
See also SATA 4
Snyder, Bernadette McCarver 1930- ... 115
Snyder, Carl Dean 1921- Brief entry ... 113
Snyder, Carol 1941- ... 85-88
See also SATA 35
Snyder, Cecil K., Jr. 1927- ... 29-32R
Snyder, Charles M. 1909- ... 49-52
Snyder, Charles Royce 1924- ... 105
Snyder, Chuck 1933- ... 122
Snyder, E(ugene) V(incent) 1943- ... 41-44R
Snyder, Eldon E. 1930- ... 49-52
Snyder, Eloise C(olleen) 1928- ... 29-32R
Snyder, Francis Gregory 1942- ... CANR-22
Earlier sketches in CA 19-20R, CANR-7
Snyder, Fred A. 1931- ... 37-40R
Snyder, Gary 1930- ... 17-18R
See also DLB 5, 16
See also CLC 1, 2, 5, 9, 32
Snyder, George Sergeant 1952- ... 122
Snyder, Gerald S(eymour) 1933- ... CANR-12
Earlier sketch in CA 61-64
See also SATA 34, 48
Snyder, Glenn Herald 1924- ... CANR-18
Earlier sketch in CA 3R
Snyder, Graydon F. 1930- ... 15-16R
Snyder, Guy (Eugene, Jr.) 1951- ... 57-60
Snyder, Henry Leonard 1929- ... 41-44R
Snyder, Howard A(lbert) 1940- ... 113
Snyder, James E(dward) 1928- ... 123
Brief entry ... 117
Snyder, Jerome 1916-1976 Obituary ... 65-68
See also SATA 20
Snyder, Joan 1943- ... 41-44R
Snyder, John P(arr) 1926- ... 41-44R
Snyder, John William 1924- ... 2R
Snyder, Laura (Lillie) 1940- ... 120
Snyder, Leslie 1945- ... 114
Snyder, Louis L. 1907- ... CANR-2
Earlier sketch in CA 3R
Snyder, Marilyn 1936- ... 120
Snyder, (Donald) Paul 1933- ... CANR-1
Earlier sketch in CA 45-48
Snyder, Rachel 1924- ... 9-10R
Snyder, Richard C(arlton) 1916- ... 61-64
Snyder, Robert Edward 1943- ... 120
Snyder, Robert L. 1928- ... 25-28R
Snyder, Solomon H(albert) 1938- ... CANR-14
Earlier sketch in CA 37-40R
Snyder, Susan 1934- ... 93-96
Snyder, Tom 1936- ... 121
Brief entry ... 109
Snyder, William 1951- ... 104
Snyder, William P(aul) 1928- ... 15-16R
Snyder, William S(tover) 1927- ... 123
Brief entry ... 118
Snyder, Zilpha Keatley 1927- ... 11-12R
See also SATA 1, 28
See also SAAS 2
See also CLC 17
Snyderman, Reuven K. 1922- ... 29-32R
See also SATA 5
Soames, Mary 1922- ... 111
Soares, Anthony T(homas) 1923- ... 45-48
Sobel, B. Z. 1933- ... 77-80
Sobel, Bernard 1887-1964 ... 5-6R
Sobel, Brian M. 1954- ... 107
Sobel, Harold W(illiam) 1933- ... 61-64
Sobel, Irwin Philip 1901- ... 45-48
Sobel, Lester A(lbert) 1919- ... CANR-9
Earlier sketch in CA 21-22R
Sobel, Robert 1931- ... CANR-8
Earlier sketch in CA 7-8R
Sobell, Morton 1917- ... 53-56
Soberman, Richard M. 1937- ... CANR-10
Earlier sketch in CA 25-28R
Sobh, A.
See Shamlu, Ahmad
Sobieski, Carol 1939- Brief entry ... 124
Sobiloff, Hy(man J.) 1912-1970
Obituary ... 29-32R
See also DLB 48
Sobin, A. G.
See Sobin, Anthony
Sobin, Anthony 1944- ... 116
Sobin, Gustaf 1935- ... 115
Soble, Alan 1947- ... 122
Soble, Jennie
See Cavin, Ruth (Brodie)
Sobol, Donald J. 1924- ... CANR-18
Earlier sketches in CA 1R, CANR-1
See also SATA 1, 31
See also CLR 4
Sobol, Harriet Langsam 1936- ... CANR-8
Earlier sketch in CA 61-64
See also SATA 34, 47
Sobol, Louis 1896-1986 ... CAP-2
Obituary ... 118
Earlier sketch in CA 29-32
Sobol, Rose 1931- ... 101
Sobolev, Leonid (Sergeevich) 1898-1971
Obituary ... 29-32R
Soboul, Albert Marius 1914-1982
Obituary ... 107
Sobrino, Josephine 1915- ... 45-48
Soby, James Thrall 1906-1979 ... 103
Socarides, Charles W(illiam) 1922-
Brief entry ... 118
Sochen, June 1937- ... CANR-14
Earlier sketch in CA 41-44R
Sockman, Ralph W(ashington) 1889-1970 ... 5-6R
Obituary ... 89-92
Socolofsky, Homer E(dward) 1922- ... CANR-1
Earlier sketch in CA 4R
Socolow, Robert H(arry) 1937- ... 37-40R
Sodaro, Craig 1948- ... CANR-18
Earlier sketch in CA 101
Soderberg, Paul Stephen 1949- ... CANR-19
Earlier sketch in CA 103
Soderberg, Percy Measday 1901-1969 ... CAP-1
Earlier sketch in CA 9-10
Soderholm, Marjorie Elaine 1923- ... 13-14R
Soderlind, Arthur E(dwin) 1920- ... 69-72
See also SATA 14
Soderstrom, Edward Jonathan 1954- ... 111
Soekarno
See Sukarno, (Ahmed)
Soelle, Dorothee 1929- ... CANR-11
Earlier sketch in CA 69-72
Soeur Sourire
See Deckers, Jeanine
Sofen, Edward 1919- ... 9-10R
Sofer, Cyril 1921- ... 5-6R
Soffer, Reba N(usbaum) 1934- ... 85-88
Softly, Barbara Frewin 1924- ... CANR-2
Earlier sketch in CA 5-6R
See also SATA 12
Softly, Edgar
See Lovecraft, H(oward) P(hillips)
Softly, Edward
See Lovecraft, H(oward) P(hillips)
Soglow, Otto 1900-1975 ... 93-96
Obituary ... 57-60
See also SATA 30
Sohl, Frederic J(ohn) 1916- ... 21-22R
See also SATA 10
Sohl, Jerry 1913- ... CANR-15
Earlier sketch in CA 81-84
Sohl, Robert (Allen) 1941- ... 103
Sohn, David A. 1929- ... CANR-6
Earlier sketch in CA 11-12R
Sohn, Louis B(runo) 1914- ... 101
Sokel, Walter H(erbert) 1917- ... CANR-6
Earlier sketch in CA 7-8R
Sokol, Anthony E. 1897- ... 37-40R
Sokol, Bill
See Sokol, William
Sokol, David M(artin) 1942- ... CANR-16
Earlier sketches in CA 49-52, CANR-1
Sokol, William 1923- ... SATA-37
Sokoloff, Alice Hunt 1912- ... 25-28R
Sokoloff, Boris Theodore 1889- ... 89-92
Sokoloff, Kiril 1947- ... 108
Sokoloff, Natalie B.
See Scott, Natalie Anderson
Sokoloff, Natalie J(ean) 1944- ... 113
Sokolov, Alexander V(sevolodovich)
1943- ... 73-76
Sokolov, Kirill 1930- ... SATA-34
Sokolov, Raymond 1941- ... 85-88
See also CLC 7
Sokolov, Sasha
See Sokolov, Alexander V(sevolodovich)
Sokolov, Valentin 1925(?)-1984 Obituary ... 114
Sokolow, Jayme Aaron 1946- ... 113
Sokolowski, Robert (Stanley) 1934- ... 89-92
Sokolski, Alan 1931- ... 15-16R
Sokolsky, George Ephraim 1893-1962
Obituary ... 89-92
Solano, Solita 1888-1975 ... 117
Obituary ... 61-64
See also DLB 4
Solaun, Mauricio 1935- Brief entry ... 106
Solberg, Carl 1915- ... CANR-12
Earlier sketch in CA 73-76
Solberg, Carl Edward 1940- ... 61-64
Solberg, Gunard 1932- ... 29-32R
Solberg, Richard W. 1917- ... CANR-3
Earlier sketch in CA 11-12R
Solberg, S(ammy) E(dward) 1930- ... 21-22R
Solberg, Winton U(dell) 1922- ... 41-44R
Solbert, Romaine G. 1925- ... 29-32R
See also SATA 2
Solbert, Ronni
See Solbert, Romaine G.
Solbrig, Otto T(homas) 1930- ... CANR-9
Earlier sketch in CA 21-22R
Soldati, Mario 1906- ... 108
Soldo, John J(oseph) 1945- ... CANR-14
Earlier sketch in CA 77-80
Soldofsky, Robert Melvin 1920- ... CANR-1
Earlier sketch in CA 2R
Sole, Carlos A(lberto) 1938- ... 53-56
Solecki, Ralph S(tefan) 1917- Brief entry ... 109
Solem, (George) Alan 1931- ... 57-60
Solensten, John M(artin) 1929- ... 110
Soleri, Paolo 1919- ... 106
Soliday, Gerald Lyman 1939- ... CANR-12
Earlier sketch in CA 61-64
Solinger, Dorothy J(ane) 1945- ... 113
Soll, Ivan 1938- ... 29-32R
Solle, Dorothee
See Soelle, Dorothee
Solley, Charles Marion, Jr. 1925- ... 2R
Sollors, Werner 1943- ... 119
Solman, Paul 1944- Brief entry ... 119
Solmon, Lewis C(alvin) 1942- ... 41-44R
Solmsen, Friedrich (Rudolf Heinrich)
1904- ... 53-56
Solnick, Bruce B. 1933- ... 29-32R
Solnit, Albert J. 1919- ... 103
Solo, Jay
See Ellison, Harlan
Solo, Robert A(lexander) 1916- ... CANR-17
Earlier sketches in CA 45-48, CANR-1
Sologub, Fyodor
See Teternikov, Fyodor Kuzmich
See also TCLC 9
Solomon, Barbara H. 1936- ... CANR-13
Earlier sketch in CA 73-76
Solomon, Barbara Probst 1928- ... 5-6R
Solomon, Bernard S(imon) 1924- ... 61-64
Solomon, (Neal) Brad(ley) 1945- ... 103
Solomon, Brad 1945- ... 101
Solomon, Carl 1928- ... 21-22R
See also DLB 16
Solomon, Charles J. 1906(?)-1975
Obituary ... 61-64
Solomon, Daniel 1933- ... 11-12R
Solomon, David J. 1925- ... 19-20R
Solomon, Dorothy Allred 1949- ... 119
Solomon, Esther Riva 1921- ... 7-8R
Solomon, Ezra 1920- ... CANR-17
Earlier sketch in CA 85-88
Solomon, Flora 1895(?)-1984 Obituary ... 114
Solomon, George 1940- ... 45-48
Solomon, Goody L(ove) ... 57-60
Solomon, Henry A. 1937- ... 123
Solomon, Irving I. 1922- ... CANR-16
Earlier sketch in CA 21-22R
Solomon, Janis Little 1938- ... CANR-15
Earlier sketch in CA 41-44R
Solomon, Joan 1930- ... 109
See also SATA 40
Solomon, Kenneth Ira 1942- ... 49-52
Solomon, Leonard 1930- ... 45-48
Solomon, Margaret C(laire) 1918- ... 29-32R
Solomon, Maynard (Elliott) 1930- ... 41-44R
Solomon, Michael M(aurice) 1909- ... 97-100
Solomon, Morris J. 1919- ... 13-14R
Solomon, Neil 1937- ... 65-68
Solomon, Norman 1951- ... CANR-9
Earlier sketch in CA 57-60
Solomon, Richard H(arvey) 1937- ... 103
Solomon, Robert 1921- ... 108
Solomon, Robert C(harles) 1942- ... CANR-15
Earlier sketch in CA 41-44R
Solomon, Ruth (Freeman) 1908- ... 23-24R
Solomon, Samuel 1904- ... 53-56
Solomon, Shirl 1928- ... 93-96
Solomon, Stanley J. 1937- ... 41-44R
Solomon, Stephen D(avid) 1950- ... 69-72
Solomon, Steve 1942- ... 117
Solomons, David 1912- ... 13-14R
Solomons, Ikey, Esquire, Jr.
See Thackeray, William Makepeace
Solon, Gregory Kent 1923(?)-1985
Obituary ... 117
Solonevich, George 1915- ... SATA-15
Solot, Mary Lynn 1939- ... 49-52
See also SATA 12
Solotaroff, Robert David 1937- ... 57-60
Solotaroff, Ted
See Solotaroff, Theodore
See also CAAS 2
Solotaroff, Theodore 1928- ... CANR-8
Earlier sketch in CA 11-12R
Soloukhin, Vladimir (Alekseevich) 1924-
Brief entry ... 111
Solow, Martin 1920- ... 81-84
Soloway, Richard Allen 1934- ... 118
Solt, Mary Ellen (Bottom) 1920- ... 17-18R
Soltau, T(heodore) Stanley 1890- ... 7-8R
Soltis, Andrew (Eden, Jr.) 1947- ... CANR-4
Earlier sketch in CA 49-52
Soltis, Andy
See Soltis, Andrew (Eden, Jr.)
Soltis, Jonas F(rancis) 1931- ... CANR-14
Earlier sketch in CA 37-40R
Soltow, James H(arold) 1924- ... 109
Soltow, Lee 1923- ... 108
Soltow, Martha-Jane 1924- ... 110
Solway, David 1941- ... 112
See also DLB 53
Solwoska, Mara
See French, Marilyn
Solyn, Paul 1951- ... 77-80
Solzhenitsyn, Aleksandr I(sayevich) 1918- ... 69-72
See also CLC 1, 2, 4, 7, 9, 10, 18, 26, 34
See also AITN 1
Soman, Alfred 1934- ... 45-48
Soman, Jean Powers 1949- ... 122
Soman, Shirley Camper ... CANR-3
Earlier sketch in CA 9-10R
Somekh, Emile 1915- ... 53-56
Somer, John (Laddie) 1936- ... 37-40R
Somerlott, Robert 1928- ... 105
Somers, Albert B(ingham) 1939- ... 115
Somers, Gerald G(eorge) 1922-1977 ... CANR-5
Earlier sketch in CA 13-14R
Somers, Herman Miles 1911- ... CANR-1
Earlier sketch in CA 3R
Somers, Paul
See Winterton, Paul
Somers, Robert H(ough) 1929- ... 45-48
Somers, Suzanne
See Daniels, Dorothy
Somerset, FitzRoy Richard
See Raglan, FitzRoy
Somerset, Henry Hugh Arthur FitzRoy
1900-1984 Obituary ... 112
Somerset Fry, (Peter George Robin)
Plantagenet 1931- ... 104
Somerville, (James) Hugh (Miller) 1922- ... 9-10R
Somerville, John 1905- ... 45-48
Somerville, (Henry) Lee 1915- ... 69-72
Somerville, Mollie ... CANR-12
Earlier sketch in CA 29-32R
Somerville, Rose M(aurer) 1908- ... 45-48
Somerville-Large, Peter 1928- ... CANR-20
Earlier sketch in CA 97-100
Somes, Jethro
See Pauker, John
Somit, Albert 1919- ... 81-84
Somkin, Fred 1924- ... 25-28R
Sommer, Elyse 1929- ... CANR-2
Earlier sketch in CA 49-52
See also SATA 7
Sommer, Joellen 1957- ... 45-48
Sommer, John 1941- ... 29-32R
Sommer, Richard J(erome) 1934- ... CANR-1
Earlier sketch in CA 45-48
Sommer, Robert 1929- ... CANR-18
Earlier sketches in CA 11-12R, CANR-3
See also SATA 12
Sommer, Scott 1951- ... 106
See also CLC 25
Sommerfeld, Ray(nard) M(athias) 1933- ... 105
Sommerfeld, Richard Edwin 1928- ... 15-16R
Sommerfeldt, John R(obert) 1933- ... CANR-3
Earlier sketch in CA 49-52
Sommerfelt, Aimee 1892- ... 37-40R
See also SATA 5
Sommerness, Martin David 1954- ... 116
Sommers, David
See Smith, Howard Van
Sommers, Fred(eric Tamler) 1923- ... 113
Sommers, Jay 1917(?)-1985 Obituary ... 117
Sommers, Joseph 1924- ... 25-28R
Sommers, Tish 1914(?)-1985 Obituary ... 117
Somorjai, Gabor Arpad 1935- ... 105
Somtow, S. P.
See Sucharitkul, Somtow
Sondak, Norman E(dward) 1931- ... 112
Sondermann, Fred A. 1923- ... 49-52
Sondheim, Stephen (Joshua) 1930- ... 103
See also CLC 30, 39
Sondrup, Steven P(reece) 1944- ... 103
Sonenblick, Jerry 1931- ... 104
Sonenblum, Sidney 1924- ... 29-32R
Sonenscher, Michael 1947- ... 118
Sonero, Devi
See Pelton, Robert W(ayne)
Song, Ben (Chunho) 1937- ... 37-40R
Song, C(hoan-)S(eng) 1929- ... 115
Songe, Alice Heloise 1914- ... 102
Sonkin, Robert 1911(?)-1980 Obituary ... 97-100
Sonneborn, Harry L(ee) 1919- ... 77-80
Sonneborn, Ruth (Cantor) 1899-1974 ... CAP-2
Obituary ... 49-52
Earlier sketch in CA 21-22
See also SATA 4, 27
Sonneborn, Tracy Morton 1905-1981
Obituary ... 108

Sonnenfeld, Marion (Wilma) 1928- 37-40R
Sonnichsen, C. L. 1901- CANR-17
Earlier sketches in CA 2R, CANR-2
Sonntag, Jacob 1905-1984 Obituary 113
Son Of The Soil
See Fletcher, J(oseph) S(mith)
Sonstegard, Manford Aldrich 1911- CANR-2
Earlier sketch in CA 49-52
Sonstroem, David 1936- 29-32R
Sontag, Alan 1946- 85-88
Sontag, Frederick (Earl) 1924- CANR-1
Earlier sketch in CA 2R
Sontag, Frederick H(erman) 1924- 81-84
Sontag, Raymond J(ames) 1897-1972
Obituary 37-40R
Sontag, Susan 1933- 19-20R
See also DLB 2, 67
See also CLC 1, 2, 10, 13, 31
Sontheimer, Morton 101
Sontup, Dan(iel) 1922- 4R
Soong Ching-ling 1890-1981 Obituary 108
Soper, Alexander Coburn 1904- 105
Soper, Donald Oliver 1903- 109
Soper, Eileen A(lice) 1905- 9-10R
Soper, Eileen Louise 1900- 103
Soper, Fred L. 1894(?)-1977 Obituary 69-72
Soper, Paul L(eon) 1906- 7-8R
Soper, Tony 1939- CANR-22
Earlier sketch in CA 105
Sopher, Sharon Isabel 1945- 101
Sorauf, Francis Joseph 1928- 11-12R
Sorauf, Frank J.
See Sorauf, Francis Joseph
Sorden, L(eland) G(eorge) 1898- CANR-1
Earlier sketch in CA 1R
Sorel, Byron
See Yatron, Michael
Sorel, Edward 1929- 9-10R
See also SATA 37
Sorel, Georges 1847-1922 Brief entry 118
Sorel, Julia
See Drexler, Rosalyn
Sorel, Nancy Caldwell 1934- 37-40R
Sorell, Walter 1905- 21-22R
Sorensen, Andrew Aaron 1938- 65-68
Sorensen, Chris 1942- 107
Sorensen, Jacki 1942- 110
Sorensen, Robert C(haikin) 1923- 45-48
Sorensen, Theodore C(haikin) 1928- CANR-2
Earlier sketch in CA 45-48
Sorensen, Thomas C. 1926- 23-24R
Sorensen, Virginia 1912- CANR-22
Earlier sketch in CA 15-16R
See also SATA 2
Sorenson, Herbert 1898- 23-24R
Sorenson, Marian 1925-1968 .... CAP-1
Earlier sketch in CA 11-12
Sorestad, Glen 1937- 112
Sorgman, Mayo 1912- 15-16R
Sorin, Gerald 1940- 77-80
Sorine, Stephanie Riva 1954- 105
Sorkin, Alan Lowell 1941- CANR-14
Earlier sketch in CA 41-44R
Sorley, Lewis 1934- 117
Sorley Walker, Kathrine CANR-6
Earlier sketch in CA 7-8R
See also SATA 41
Sorokin, Boris 1922- 116
Sorokin, Elena 1894(?)-1975 Obituary 61-64
Sorokin, Pitirim A(lexandrovitch)
1889-1968 .... CANR-5
Obituary 25-28R
Earlier sketch in CA 7-8R
Sorrell, Alan 1904-1974 93-96
Sorrells, Dorothy C. 9-10R
Sorrells, Helen 1908- 37-40R
Sorrentino, Gilbert 1929- CANR-14
Earlier sketch in CA 77-80
See also DLB 5
See also DLBY 80
See also CLC 3, 7, 14, 22, 40
Sorrentino, Joseph N. 1937- CANR-3
Earlier sketch in CA 49-52
See also SATA 6
Sorsby, Arnold 1900- 85-88
Sortor, June Elizabeth 1939- 61-64
See also SATA 12
Sortor, Toni
See Sortor, June Elizabeth
Sorum, Paul Clay 1943- 103
Sosa, Ernest 1940- 53-56
Sosa de Quesada, Aristides V. 1908- 53-56
Soskice, Janet Martin 1951- 124
Soskin, V.H.
See Ellison, Virginia H(owell)
Sosna, Morton 1945- 102
Sosnick, Stephen H(oward) 1930- 45-48
Sosnow, Eric 1910-1987 Obituary 121
Sossaman, Stephen 1944- 77-80
Soth, Lauren (Kephart) 1910- CAP-1
Earlier sketch in CA 17-18
Soto, Gary 1952- Brief entry 119
See also CLC 32
Soto, Pedro Juan 1928- Brief entry 114
Sotomayor, Antonio 1902- 73-76
See also SATA 11
Sotter, Fred
See Lake, Kenneth R(obert)
Souci, Robert D. San
See San Souci, Robert D.
Soucy, Robert J(oseph) 1933- 45-48
Soudley, Henry
See Wood, James Playsted
Souerwine, Andrew H(arry) 1924- CANR-19
Earlier sketch in CA 81-84
Soukup, James R(udolph) 1928- 11-12R
Soule, Gardner (Bosworth) 1913- CANR-2
Earlier sketch in CA 5-6R
See also SATA 14
Soule, George (Henry, Jr.) 1887-1970 ... CAP-2
Obituary 29-32R
Earlier sketch in CA 21-22
Soule, George (Alan) 1930- 57-60
Soule, Isabel Walker 1898(?)-1972
Obituary 37-40R
Soule, Jean Conder 1919- 7-8R
See also SATA 10
Soupault, Philippe 1897- Brief entry 116
Soupcoff, Murray 1943- 101
Souper, Patrick Charles 1928- 110
Sour, Robert B(andler) 1905-1985
Obituary 115
Sourian, Peter 1933- 1R
Sourkes, Theodore L(ionel) 1919- 17-18R
Sours, John Appling 1931-1983 .... CANR-9
Obituary 110
Earlier sketch in CA 21-22R
Sousa, Marion 1941- 65-68
Souster, (Holmes) Raymond 1921- CANR-13
Earlier sketch in CA 13-14R
See also CLC 5, 14
South, Clark
See Swain, Dwight V(reeland)
South, Cris 1950- 118
South, Grace
See Clark, Gail
South, Malcolm Hudson 1937- 107
Southall, Aidan (William) 1920- 77-80
Southall, Ivan (Francis) 1921- CANR-7
Earlier sketch in CA 9-10R
See also SATA 3
See also SAAS 3
See also CLR 2
Southam, B(rian) C(harles) 1931- CANR-10
Earlier sketch in CA 15-16R
Southard, Frank Allan, Jr. 1907- 107
Southard, Helen Fairbairn 1906- 5-6R
Southard, Samuel 1925- CANR-3
Earlier sketch in CA 4R
Southerington, F(rank) R(odney) 1938- 57-60
Southerland, Ellease 1943- 107
See also DLB 33
Southern, David W. 1938- 25-28R
Southern, Eileen 1920- CANR-14
Earlier sketch in CA 37-40R
Southern, Richard William 1912- 9-10R
Southern, Terry 1926- CANR-1
Earlier sketch in CA 1R
See also DLB 2
See also CLC 7
Southgate, Vera 109
Southgate, W(yndham) M(ason) 1910- ... CAP-2
Earlier sketch in CA 23-24
Southwell, Eugene A. 1928- 17-18R
Southwell, Samuel B(eall) 1922- 19-20R
Southwick, Charles H(enry) 1928- 65-68
Southworth, Herbert Rutledge 1908- 85-88
Southworth, Horton C. 1926- 17-18R
Southworth, James G(ranville) 1896- CAP-2
Earlier sketch in CA 33-36
Southworth, John Van Duyn
1904-1986 .... CANR-6
Obituary 118
Earlier sketch in CA 7-8R
Southworth, Louis
See Grealey, Thomas Louis
Southworth, Warren H(ilbourne) 1912- ...37-40R
Soutter, Fred
See Lake, Kenneth R(obert)
Souvarine, Boris
See Lifchitz, Boris
Souza, Ernest
See Scott, Evelyn
Souza, Raymond D(ale) 1936- CANR-13
Earlier sketch in CA 69-72
Souza, Steven M. 1953- 49-52
Souza Filho, Henrique de 1945(?)-1988
Obituary 124
Sovik, E(dward) A(nders) 1918-
Brief entry 112
Sowards, J(esse) K(elley) 1924- 73-76
Sowden, Lewis 1905-1974 .... CAP-1
Earlier sketch in CA 9-10
Sowell, Thomas 1930- 41-44R
Sowerby, A(rthur) L(indsay) M(cRae)
1899- CAP-1
Earlier sketch in CA 9-10
Sowerby, E(mily) Millicent 1883-1977 .... CAP-2
Obituary 73-76
Earlier sketch in CA 25-28
Sowers, Miriam R. 1922- 89-92
Sowers, Robert (Watson) 1923- 17-18R
Sowers, Sidney Gerald, Jr. 1935- 17-18R
Sox, (Harold) David 1936- 124
Soyer, Raphael 1899-1987 81-84
Obituary 124
Soyinka, Wole 1934- 15-16R
See also CLC 3, 5, 14, 36, 44
Spaak, Paul-Henri 1899-1972 Obituary ...37-40R
Spaatz, Carl A(ndrew) 1891-1974
Obituary 49-52
Spach, John Thom 1928- 29-32R
Spache, Evelyn B(ispham) 1929- 29-32R
Spache, George D(aniel) 1909- CANR-6
Earlier sketch in CA 7-8R
Spackman, Doc
See Spackman, Robert R., Jr.
Spackman, Robert R., Jr. 1917-1984 ....15-16R
Obituary 111
Spackman, W(illiam) M(ode) 1905- 81-84
See also CLC 46
Spacks, Barry 1931- 29-32R
See also CLC 14
Spacks, Patricia Meyer 1929- CANR-1
Earlier sketch in CA 3R
Spada, James 1950- CANR-7
Earlier sketch in CA 57-60
Spade, Mark
See Balchin, Nigel (Marlin)
Spade, Rupert
See Pawley, Martin Edward
Spaeth, David A(nthony) 1941- 119
Spaeth, Eloise O'Mara 1904- 104
Spaeth, Gerold 1939- CANR-24
Earlier sketches in CA 65-68, CANR-9
Spaeth, Harold J(oseph) 1930- 45-48
Spaeth, Robert L(ouis) 1935- 119
Spaeth, Sigmund 1885-1965 ....5-6R
Spahn, Mary Attea 1929- CANR-7
Earlier sketch in CA 57-60
Spain, Daphne 1949- 111
Spain, David H. 1939- 57-60
Spain, James W(illiam) 1926- 7-8R
Spain, John
See Adams, Cleve F(ranklin)
Spain, Rufus B(uin) 1923- 21-22R
Spake, Amanda 1947- 77-80
Spalatin, Christopher 1909- 49-52
Spalding, Frances 1950- 104
Spalding, Graydon (Edward) 1911- 89-92
Spalding, Henry D(aniel) 1915- CANR-11
Earlier sketch in CA 25-28R
Spalding, Jack 1913- 69-72
Spalding, Lucile
See Spalding, Ruth
Spalding, P(hilip) A(nthony) 1911- 7-8R
Spalding, (Billups) Phinizy 1930- CANR-16
Earlier sketch in CA 41-44R
Spalding, R(onald) W(olcott) 1904- 81-84
Spalding, Ruth 104
Spalek, John M. 1928- 104
Spalter, Max 1929- 21-22R
Spanfeller, James J(ohn) 1930- SATA-19
Spangenberg, Judith Dunn 1942- CANR-12
Earlier sketch in CA 29-32R
See also SATA 5
Spangler, Earl 1920- CANR-5
Earlier sketch in CA 7-8R
Spanidou, Irini 1946- CLC-44
Spanier, David 1932- CANR-18
Earlier sketch in CA 101
Spanier, John W(inston) 1930- CANR-2
Earlier sketch in CA 4R
Spann, Edward K(enneth) 1931- 45-48
Spann, Gloria Carter 1926- 77-80
Spann, Meno 1903- CANR-21
Earlier sketch in CA 1R
Spann, Weldon O(ma) 1924- 17-18R
Spano, Charles 1948- 93-96
Spanos, William V(aios) 1925- CANR-11
Earlier sketch in CA 21-22R
Spar, Jerome 1918- 25-28R
See also SATA 10
Sparano, Vin(cent) T(homas) 1934- CANR-22
Earlier sketch in CA 45-48
Spargo, John 1876-1966 Obituary 89-92
Spark, Debra (Alison) 1962- 122
Spark, Muriel (Sarah) 1918- CANR-12
Earlier sketch in CA 7-8R
See also DLB 15
See also CLC 2, 3, 5, 8, 13, 18, 40
Sparke, (George) Archibald 1871-1970 ... CAP-2
Earlier sketch in CA 21-22
Sparkes, Ivan G(eorge) 1930- 115
Sparkia, Roy (Bernard) 1924- 77-80
Sparkman, Brandon B(uster) 1929- CANR-13
Earlier sketch in CA 61-64
Sparkman, G(rady) Temp 1932- CANR-15
Earlier sketch in CA 89-92
Sparkman, William
See Roger, William L(eon)
Sparks, Asa H(oward) 1937- CANR-19
Earlier sketch in CA 97-100
Sparks, Beatrice Mathews 1918- 97-100
See also SATA 28, 44
Sparks, Bertel M(ilas) 1918- 21-22R
Sparks, Donald B. 1931- 124
Sparks, Edgar H(erndon) 1908- 13-14R
Sparks, Fred 1916(?)-1981 Obituary 103
Sparks, Jack Norman 1928- 102
Sparks, James Allen 1933- 109
Sparks, Jared 1789-1866 .... DLB-1, 30
Sparks, John 1939- 103
Sparks, Mary W. 1920- SATA-15
Sparks, Merla Jean
See McCormick, Merla Jean
Sparks, Merrill 1922- 23-24R
Sparks, Will (R.) 1924-1987 ....37-40R
Obituary 124
Sparrow, (John Walter) Gerald 1903- 49-52
Sparrow, John (Hanbury Angus) 1906- 103
Sparrow, Phil
See Steward, Samuel M(orris)
Sparrow, Philip
See Steward, Samuel M(orris)
Sparse Grey Hackle
See Miller, Alfred W.
Sparshott, F. E.
See Sparshott, Francis (Edward)
Sparshott, Francis (Edward) 1926- CANR-10
Earlier sketch in CA 25-28R
See also DLB 60
Spartacus, Deutero
See Fanthorpe, R(obert) Lionel
Spartacus, Tertius
See Burgess, M(ichael) R(oy)
Spate, O(skar) H(ermann) K(hristian)
1911- CANR-10
Earlier sketch in CA 25-28R
Spater, George (Alexander) 1909-1984
Obituary 113
Spath, Gerold
See Spaeth, Gerold
Spatz, (Kenneth) Chris(topher, Jr.)
1940- 37-40R
Spatz, Jonas 1935- 29-32R
Spaulding, Dayton M(athewson) 1922- 61-64
Spaulding, Douglas
See Bradbury, Ray (Douglas)
Spaulding, Leonard
See Bradbury, Ray Douglas
Spaulding, Robert K(ilburn) 1898- 7-8R
Spaulding, William E(llsworth) 1898-1979
Obituary 93-96
Spaull, Hebe (Fanny Lily) 1893- 9-10R
Speaight, George Victor 1914- CANR-12
Earlier sketch in CA 29-32R
Speaight, Robert (William) 1904-1976 .. CANR-12
Earlier sketch in CA 13-14R
Spear, Allan Henry 1937- 21-22R
Spear, Benjamin
See Henisch, Heinz K.
Spear, George E(lliott) 1925- 102
Spear, Hilda D(oris) 1926- CANR-23
Earlier sketch in CA 107
Spear, (Thomas George) Percival
1901-1982 106
Obituary 108
Spear, Richard E(dmund) 1940- 45-48
Spear, Roberta 1948- 113
Speare, Elizabeth George 1908- 2R
See also SATA 5
See also CLR 8
Spearing, Judith (Mary Harlow) 1922- ... CANR-3
Earlier sketch in CA 49-52
See also SATA 9
Spearman, Arthur Dunning 1899- CAP-2
Earlier sketch in CA 21-22
Spearman, Walter (Smith) 1908- CAP-2
Earlier sketch in CA 29-32
Spears, Betty (Mary) 1918- CANR-6
Earlier sketch in CA 2R
Spears, Dorothea (Johnson) 1901- CAP-1
Earlier sketch in CA 13-14
Spears, Edward (Louis) 1886-1974 ...... CAP-2
Obituary 45-48
Earlier sketch in CA 23-24
Spears, Jack 1919- 29-32R
Spears, Monroe K(irk) 1916- CANR-2
Earlier sketch in CA 5-6R
Spears, Richard A(lan) 1939- CANR-21
Earlier sketch in CA 104
Spears, Ross 1947- 122
Spears, Woodridge 1913- 13-14R
Specht, Ernst Konrad 1926- 29-32R
Specht, Harry 1929- CANR-8
Earlier sketch in CA 53-56
Specht, Robert 1928- 103
Specht, Walter F(rederick) 1912- 97-100
Speck, Gordon 1898- CAP-2
Earlier sketch in CA 17-18
Speck, Ross V. 1927- Brief entry 107
Specking, Inez 1890-196? 7-8R
See also SATA 11
Spectator
See Popovic, Nenad D(ushan)
Spector, Debra 1953- 109
Spector, Irwin 1916- 45-48
Spector, Ivar 1898- 3R
Spector, Jack J. 1925- 29-32R
Spector, Leonard S. 1945- 122
Spector, Marshall 1936- 45-48
Spector, Robert Donald 1922- 15-16R
Spector, Ronald (Harvey) 1943- 57-60
Spector, Samuel I(ra) 1924- 77-80
Spector, Sherman David 1927- CANR-22
Earlier sketch in CA 1R
Spector, Shushannah 1903- 11-12R
Spector, Stanley 1924- 9-10R
Spectorsky, A(uguste) C(omte)
1910-1972 .... CAP-2
Obituary 33-36R
Earlier sketch in CA 17-18
Spedding, C(olin) R(aymond) W(illiam)
1925- 53-56
Speed, F(rederick) Maurice 1912- 107
Speed, Frank Warren 104
Speed, (Herbert) Keith 1934- 115
Speelman, Arlene 1916- 41-44R
Speer, Albert 1905-1981 65-68
Obituary 104
Speer, David G(ordon) 1913- 45-48
Speer, Michael L. 1934- 93-96
Speeth, Kathleen Riordan 1937- 89-92
Spehar, Betty M. 1924- 45-48
Speicher, Helen Ross S(mith) 1915- CANR-4
Earlier sketch in CA 5-6R
See also SATA 8
Speicher, John 1934(?)-1986 Obituary 119
Speidel, Hans 1897-1984 Obituary 114
Speidel, Michael P(aul) 1937- 108
Speier, Hans 1905- CANR-9
Earlier sketch in CA 23-24R
Speight, Harold 1916- 7-8R
Speight, Johnny 1921(?)- Brief entry 117
Speirs, John (Hastie) 1906- 61-64
Speirs, Logan 1938- 37-40R
Speirs, Russell 1901-1975 .... CANR-4
Obituary 61-64
Earlier sketch in CA 45-48
Speiser, Jean 69-72
Speiser, Stuart Marshall 1923- Brief entry .. 106
Speitel, H. H.
See Speitel, Hans(-Henning)
Speitel, Hans(-Henning) 1937- 123
Speizman, Morris 1905- 77-80

INDEX

Spekke, Arnolds 1887-1972 Obituary 37-40R
Spelios, Thomas 1930- 25-28R
Spellman, Alfred B. 1935- 97-100
See also DLB 41
Spellman, Cathy Cash 1941- 121
Spellman, Francis (Joseph) 1889-1967
Obituary 113
Spellman, Francis Cardinal
See Spellman, Francis (Joseph)
Spellman, John W(illard) 1934- 13-14R
See also SATA 14
Spellman, Roger G.
See Cox, William (Robert)
Spelman, Mary 1934- CANR-13
Earlier sketch in CA 77-80
See also SATA 28
Spelvin, George
See Phillips, David Atlee
Spence, Bill
See Spence, William John Duncan
Spence, Clark C(hristian) 1923- CANR-6
Earlier sketch in CA 1R
Spence, Donald P(ond) 1926- Brief entry ... 109
Spence, Duncan
See Spence, William John Duncan
Spence, Eleanor (Rachel) 1928- CANR-3
Earlier sketch in CA 49-52
See also SATA 21
Spence, Gerald Leonard 1929- 118
Spence, Geraldine 1931- SATA-47
Spence, Gerry
See Spence, Gerald Leonard
Spence, Gordon William 1936- 25-28R
Spence, Hartzell 1908- 7-8R
Spence, J. A. D.
See Eliot, T(homas) S(tearns)
Spence, J(ohn) E(dward) 1931- 25-28R
Spence, James R(obert) 1927- 25-28R
Spence, Jonathan D(ermot) 1936- CANR-23
Earlier sketch in CA 21-22R
Spence, (James) Lewis (Thomas Chalmers)
1874-1955 Brief entry 115
Spence, Mary Lee 1927- 45-48
Spence, Vernon Gladden 1924- 37-40R
Spence, William John Duncan 1923- ... CANR-20
Earlier sketch in CA 103
Spencer
See Herz, Jerome Spencer
Spencer, Ann 1918- 29-32R
See also SATA 10
Spencer, Anne 1882-1975 .... DLB-51, 54
Spencer, Benjamin T(ownley) 1904- 124
Spencer, (Charles) Bernard 1909-1963
Obituary 115
Spencer, Bonnell 1909- 106
Spencer, Charles 1920- 49-52
Spencer, Christopher 1930- 13-14R
Spencer, Colin 1933- CANR-12
Earlier sketch in CA 21-22R
Spencer, Cornelia
See Yaukey, Grace S(ydenstricker)
Spencer, Dale R(ay) 1925- 57-60
Spencer, Donald D(ean) 1931- 108
See also SATA 41
Spencer, Edgar Winston 1931- 41-44R
Spencer, Elizabeth 1921- 13-14R
See also SATA 14
See also DLB 6
See also CLC 22
Spencer, Harold (Edwin) 1920- CANR-23
Earlier sketch in CA 45-48
Spencer, Herbert 1820-1903 .... DLB-57
Spencer, J(oseph) E(arle) 1907-1984 .. CANR-22
Earlier sketch in CA 45-48
Spencer, James 1932- 109
Spencer, Jean E(lizabeth) 1933- 19-20R
Spencer, Jeffry Withers B(urress) 1927- ...45-48
Spencer, John (Walter) 1922- 9-10R
Spencer, John Hall 1928- 7-8R
Spencer, John Hathaway 1907- 112
Spencer, LaVyrle 1943- 102
Spencer, Leonard G.
See Silverberg, Robert
Spencer, Lloyd Neville 1955- 121
Spencer, Margaret 1916- 21-22R
Spencer, Metta Wells 1931- 69-72
Spencer, Michael (Clifford) 1936- 57-60
Spencer, Milton Harry 1926- CANR-6
Earlier sketch in CA 1R
Spencer, Robert Allan 1920- 7-8R
Spencer, Robert F(rancis) 1917-
Brief entry 108
Spencer, Ross (Harrison) 1921- 101
Spencer, Scott 1945- 113
See also DLBY 86
See also CLC 30
Spencer, Sharon Dougherty 1933- CANR-13
Earlier sketch in CA 7-8R
Spencer, Sidney 7-8R
Spencer, Steven M. 1905- CAP-1
Earlier sketch in CA 13-14
Spencer, Stewart 1949- 121
Spencer, Terence (John Bew) 1915-1978
Obituary 77-80
Spencer, Warren F(rank) 1923- 29-32R
Spencer, William 1922- CANR-23
Earlier sketches in CA 19-20R, CANR-8
See also SATA 9
Spencer, Zane A(nn) 1935- 89-92
See also SATA 35
Spender, Dale 1943- Brief entry 120
Spender, Lynne 1946- 119
Spender, Stephen (Harold) 1909- 11-12R
See also DLB 20
See also CLC 1, 2, 5, 10, 41
Spengemann, William Charles 1932- 102
Spengler, Edwin H(arold) 1906-1981
Obituary 104
Spengler, Oswald (Arnold Gottfried)
1880-1936 Brief entry 118
See also TCLC 25
Sperber, Al E(lias) 1916- 65-68
Sperber, Manes 1905-1984 124
Obituary 112
Sperber, Murray A(rnold) 1940- CANR-12
Earlier sketch in CA 61-64
Sperber, Perry Arthur 1907- 37-40R
Sperber, Philip 1944- 109
Spergel, Irving A. 1924- CANR-11
Earlier sketch in CA 23-24R
Sperka, Joshua S. 1905- 49-52
Sperlich, Peter W. 1934- 37-40R
Sperling, Dan(iel Lee) 1949- 112
Sperling, John G(len) 1921- 49-52
Spero, Sterling D. 1896-1976 65-68
Obituary 61-64
Speroni, Charles 1911-1984 93-96
Obituary 113
Sperry, Armstrong W. 1897-1976 .... CAP-1
Obituary 107
Earlier sketch in CA 9-10
See also SATA 1, 27
Sperry, (Sally) Baxter 1914- CANR-16
Earlier sketches in CA 49-52, CANR-1
Sperry, Byrne Hope 1902- 69-72
Sperry, J. E.
See Eisenstat, Jane Sperry
Sperry, Kip 1940- CANR-19
Earlier sketch in CA 101
Sperry, Len 1943- CANR-12
Earlier sketch in CA 61-64
Sperry, Margaret 1905- 37-40R
Sperry, Ralph A(ddison) 1944- 106
Sperry, Raymond, Jr. CAP-2
Earlier sketch in CA 19-20
See also SATA 1
Sperry, Stuart M(ajor) 1929- 49-52
Speshock, Phyllis (Nieboer) 1925- 19-20R
Spewack, Samuel 1899-1971 Obituary ...33-36R
Spice, Marjorie Davis 1924- 11-12R
Spicehandler, Daniel 1923- 2R
Spicer, Bart 1918- 103
Spicer, Dorothy Gladys CANR-4
Earlier sketch in CA 4R
See also SATA 32
Spicer, Jack 1925-1965 85-88
See also DLB 5, 16
See also CLC 8, 18
Spicer, James 1928(?)-1979 Obituary 85-88
Spicker, Stuart Francis 1937- 65-68
Spiegel, Don(ald Elwin) 1926- 41-44R
Spiegel, Henry William 1911- 3R
Spiegel, John P(aul) 1911- 103
Spiegel, Joseph 1928- 9-10R
Spiegel, Richard Alan 1947- 104
Spiegel, Robert H. 1922- 81-84
Spiegel, Shalom 1899-1984 Obituary 112
Spiegel, Steven L(ee) 1941- 77-80
Spiegel, Ted 1934- Brief entry 105
Spiegelberg, Herbert 1904- 9-10R
Spiegelman, J(oseph) Mavvin 1926- 57-60
Spiegelman, Judith 1942- 101
Spiegelman, Judith M. 23-24R
See also SATA 5
Spiegler, Charles G. 1911- CANR-3
Earlier sketch in CA 9-10R
Spiegler, Michael D(avid) 1943- 61-64
Spiel, Hilde (Maria) 1911- CANR-14
Earlier sketches in CA 9-10, CAP-1
Spielberg, Peter 1929- CANR-4
Earlier sketch in CA 5-6R
See also DLBY 81
See also CLC 6
Spielberg, Steven 1947- 77-80
See also SATA 32
See also CLC 20
Spielberger, Charles D(onald) 1927- 102
Spielberger, Walter Jakob 1925- CANR-16
Earlier sketch in CA 21-22R
Spielman, Patrick E. 1936- CANR-22
Earlier sketches in CA 15-16R, CANR-7
Spielmann, Peter James 1952- 97-100
Spier, Peter (Edward) 1927- 7-8R
See also SATA 4
See also DLB 61
See also CLR 5
Spier, Robert F(orest) G(ayton) 1922- 41-44R
Spier, William H. 1907(?)-1973
Obituary 41-44R
Spiering, Frank 1938- CANR-10
Earlier sketch in CA 25-28R
Spiers, Edward M(ichael) 1947- 119
Spies, Werner 1937- 37-40R
Spigel, Irwin M(yron) 1926- 17-18R
Spigelgass, Leonard 1908-1985 103
Obituary 115
Spike, Paul 1947- 120
Spikes, Brian S. J. 101
Spilhaus, Athelstan (Frederick) 1911- 17-18R
See also SATA 13
Spilka, Arnold 1917- 49-52
See also SATA 6
Spilka, Mark 1925- 81-84
Spilke, Francine S. 101
Spillane, Frank Morrison 1918- 25-28R
Spillane, John D(avid) 1909(?)-1985
Obituary 117
Spillane, Mickey
See Spillane, Frank Morrison
See also CLC 3, 13
Spiller, Burton L(owell) 1886- 7-8R
Spiller, Earl A(lexander), Jr. 1934- 21-22R
Spiller, Robert E. 1896- CANR-4
Earlier sketch in CA 7-8R
Spillmann, Betty Evelyn 1920- 53-56
Spilsbury, Richard J(oy) 1919-1984 104
Obituary 113
Spina, Tony 1914- 69-72
Spinage, Clive A(lfred) 1933- 15-16R
Spindler, Arthur 1918- 104
Spindler, George Dearborn 1920- 21-22R
Spindler, Louise Schaubel 1917- 49-52
Spindler, Michael (James) 1948- 116
Spinelli, Altiero 1907-1986 .... CANR-16
Obituary 119
Earlier sketch in CA 23-24R
Spinelli, Eileen 1942- 107
See also SATA 38
Spinelli, Jerry 1941- 111
See also SATA 39
Spinelli, Marcos 1904-1970 Obituary 29-32R
Sping, Dan
See Spalding, Henry D(aniel)
Spingarn, Lawrence P(erreira) 1917- ... CANR-23
Earlier sketches in CA 3R, CANR-6
Spingarn, Natalie Davis 1922- 85-88
Spinifex
See Martin, David
Spink, Ian 1932- Brief entry 113
Spink, John Stephenson 1909-1985
Obituary 116
Spink, Reginald (William) 1905- CANR-19
Earlier sketches in CA 53-56, CANR-4
See also SATA 11
Spink, Walter M. 1928- 61-64
Spinka, Matthew 1890-1972 .... CANR-2
Obituary 37-40R
Earlier sketch in CA 1R
Spinks, G(eorge) Stephens 1903- CAP-2
Earlier sketch in CA 23-24
Spinks, John William Tranter 1908- 109
Spinner, Stephanie 1943- 45-48
See also SATA 38
Spinner, Thomas J(ohn), Jr. 1929- 45-48
Spinney, David
See Spinney, J(ohn) D(avid)
Spinney, J(ohn) D(avid) 1912- 29-32R
Spinossimus
See White, William, Jr.
Spinrad, Norman (Richard) 1940- CANR-20
Earlier sketch in CA 37-40R
See also DLB 8
See also CLC 46
Spinrad, William 1917- 29-32R
Spira, Ruth Rodale 1928- 61-64
Spirer, Herbert F(rederick) 1925- CANR-16
Earlier sketch in CA 93-96
Spires, Elizabeth 1952- 106
Spiro, Edward 1908- 25-28R
Spiro, Herbert J(ohn) 1924- CANR-6
Earlier sketch in CA 2R
Spiro, Herzl Robert 1935- 104
Spiro, Jack D. 1933- CANR-6
Earlier sketch in CA 11-12R
Spiro, Melford E(lliot) 1920- CANR-1
Earlier sketch in CA 45-48
Spirt, Diana L(ouise) 1925- 19-20R
Spisak, James W(illiam) 1951- 117
Spit, Sam
See Schneck, Stephen
Spittel, Richard Lionel 1881-1969 .... CAP-1
Earlier sketch in CA 13-14
Spitteler, Carl (Friedrich Georg)
1845-1924 Brief entry 109
See also TCLC 12
Spitz, A. Edward 1923- 73-76
Spitz, Allan A(ugust) 1928- 13-14R
Spitz, David 1916-1979 ....41-44R
Obituary 85-88
Spitz, Lewis W(illiam) 1922- CANR-6
Earlier sketch in CA 4R
Spitz, Mark (Andrew) 1950- Brief entry 115
Spitzer, Abe 1912(?)-1984 Obituary 112
Spitzer, E(rwin) E(dwin) 1910- CAP-2
Earlier sketch in CA 21-22
Spitzer, Herbert Frederick 1906- CAP-1
Earlier sketch in CA 13-14
Spitzer, John 1956- CANR-18
Earlier sketch in CA 102
Spitzer, Leo 1939- 61-64
Spitzer, Lyman (Jr.) 1914- 116
Spitzer, Morton Edward 41-44R
Spitzer, Robert J(ames) 1953- 112
Spitzer, Robert S(idney) 1926- 61-64
Spivack, Charlotte K(esler) 1926- 23-24R
Spivack, Ellen Sue 1937- 106
Spivack, George 1927- Brief entry 109
Spivack, Kathleen (Romola Drucker)
1938- 49-52
See also CLC 6
Spivack, Robert (Gerald) 1915-1970
Obituary 104
Spivak, Gayatri Chakravorty 1942-
Brief entry 110
Spivak, John L(ouis) 1897-1981 Obituary ... 105
Spivak, Mel 1937- 57-60
Spivak, Talbot 1937- 77-80
Spivakovsky, Erika 1909- 49-52
Spivey, Richard L. 1937- 115
Spivey, Robert Atwood 1931- Brief entry ... 106
Spivey, Ted R(ay) 1927- 105
Splane, Richard B. 1916- 17-18R
Splaver, Sarah 85-88
See also SATA 28
Spletter, Mary 1946- 111
Spock, Benjamin (McLane) 1903- 21-22R
See also AITN 1
Spodek, Bernard 1931- CANR-22
Earlier sketches in CA 17-18R, CANR-7
Spoehr, Alexander 1913- 109
Spoelstra, Nyle (Ray) 1939- 29-32R
Spofford, Walter O(smon), Jr. 1936- 107
Spollen, Christopher 1952- SATA-12
Spolsky, Bernard 1932- CANR-1
Earlier sketch in CA 45-48
Spolsky, Ellen 1943- 119
Spong, John Shelby 1931- 104
Spooner, Frank (Clyffurde) 1924- 85-88
Spooner, Frederick Percy 1898- CAP-1
Earlier sketch in CA 13-14
Spooner, Jane R(oss) 1922- 5-6R
Spooner, John D. 1937- 23-24R
Spooner, (Glenda) Victoria Maude (Graham)
1897- CAP-1
Earlier sketch in CA 9-10
Spores, Ronald 1931- 21-22R
Spot, Ryhen
See Post, Henry
Spota, Luis
See Spota Saavedra, Luis
Spota Saavedra, Luis 1925-1985 Obituary .. 114
Spotnitz, Hyman 1908- CANR-6
Earlier sketch in CA 4R
Spoto, Donald 1941- CANR-11
Earlier sketch in CA 65-68
See also CLC 39
Spotte, Stephen 1942- CANR-1
Earlier sketch in CA 45-48
Spottiswoode, Raymond J. 1913-1970
Obituary 104
Spotts, Charles D(ewey) 1899-1974(?) ... CAP-2
Earlier sketch in CA 19-20
Spotts, Frederic 1930- 101
Spradley, James P(hillip) 1933-1982 ... CANR-13
Earlier sketch in CA 29-32R
Spradling, Mary Elizabeth Mace 1911- 104
Spragens, Thomas A(rthur), Jr. 1942- 85-88
Spragens, William C(lark) 1925- 41-44R
Spraggett, Allen (Frederick) 1932- CANR-18
Earlier sketch in CA 25-28R
Sprague, Arthur Colby 1895- 89-92
Sprague, Charles Arthur 1887-1969
Obituary 89-92
Sprague, Claire S(acks) 1926- 25-28R
Sprague, Gretchen (Burnham) 1926- 15-16R
See also SATA 27
Sprague, Howard B(ennet) 1898- 41-44R
Sprague, Irvine H(enry, Jr.) 1921- 123
Sprague, Ken 1945- 108
Sprague, Marshall 1909- CANR-1
Earlier sketch in CA 4R
Sprague, Richard E. 1921- 29-32R
Sprague, Rosamond Kent 1922- CANR-2
Earlier sketch in CA 5-6R
Sprague, Rosemary 19-20R
Sprague, W. D.
See von Block, Bela W(illiam)
and von Block, Sylvia
Spraos, John 1926- 5-6R
Spratt, Hereward Philip 1902- 7-8R
Spray, Pauline 1920- CANR-10
Earlier sketch in CA 25-28R
Spray, Sherrad L(ee) 1935- 104
Spreiregen, Paul D. 1931- 21-22R
Sprengel, Donald P(hilip) 1938- 53-56
Spriegel, William R(obert) 1893- 7-8R
Sprigel, Olivier
See Avice, Claude (Pierre Marie)
Sprigg, C(hristopher) St. John 1907-1937
Brief entry 120
Sprigg, June 1953- 65-68
Sprigge, Elizabeth (Miriam Squire)
1900-1974 ....13-14R
See also SATA 10
Sprigge, Timothy L(auro) S(quire) 1932- ..57-60
Sprinchorn, Evert Manfred 1923- 107
Spring, Bob
See Spring, Robert W(alton)
Spring, David 1918- 81-84
Spring, Gerald M(ax) 1897- 61-64
Spring, (Robert) Howard 1889-1965 ...... CAP-1
Earlier sketch in CA 9-10
See also SATA 28
Spring, Ira L. 1918- CANR-7
Earlier sketch in CA 57-60
Spring, Joel Henry 1940- CANR-3
Earlier sketch in CA 49-52
Spring, Norma 1917- 61-64
Spring, Robert W(alton) 1918- CANR-7
Earlier sketch in CA 57-60
Springborg, Robert 1944- 119
Springer, Axel 1912-1985 Obituary 117
Springer, Bernhard J. 1907(?)-1970
Obituary 29-32R
Springer, E(ustace) Laurence 1903- 21-22R
Springer, Haskell S(aul) 1939- 111
Springer, John 1916- 53-56
Springer, John L(awrence) 1915- 2R
Springer, L(ois) Elsinore 1911- 69-72
Springer, Marilyn Harris 1931- CANR-9
Earlier sketch in CA 21-22R
See also SATA 47
Springer, Marlene Ann 1937- 107
Springer, Mary Doyle 1918- 116
Springer, Nancy 1948- CANR-18
Earlier sketch in CA 101
Springer, Nelson P(aul) 1915- 115
Springer, Nesha Bass 1930- 81-84
Springer, Otto 1905- CAP-1
Earlier sketch in CA 13-14
Springer, Sally P(earl) 1947- 108
Springfield
See Kelly, Maurice Anthony
Springfield, David
See Lewis, (John) Roy(ston)
Springsted, Eric Osmon 1951- 113

Springsteen, Bruce (F.) 1949- 111
See also CLC 17
Springstubb, Tricia 1950- CANR-21
Earlier sketch in CA 105
See also SATA 40, 46
Sprinkel, Beryl W(ayne) 1923- 11-12R
Sprinthall, Richard C(lark) 1930- 45-48
Sproat, John G(erald) 1921- 25-28R
Sproston, John
See Scott, Peter Dale
Sprott, W(alter) John Herbert 1897-1971 CANR-16
Obituary 103
Earlier sketch in CA 4R
Sproul, Barbara Chamberlain 1945- 105
Sproul, Dorothy Noyes
See Noyes-Kane, Dorothy
Sproul, R(obert) C(harles) 1939- 111
Sprouse, Mary L. 1948- 108
Sprout, Harold 1901-1980 CANR-6
Obituary 102
Earlier sketch in CA 3R
Spruch, Grace Marmor 1926- 57-60
Spruch, Larry 1923- 102
Sprug, Joseph W(illiam) 1922- 23-24R
Spruill, Charles R(ay) 1946- 117
Spruill, Steven G(regory) 1946- 73-76
Sprunger, Keith L(a Verne) 1935- 41-44R
Sprunt, Alexander, Jr. 1898-1973
Obituary 37-40R
Spuhler, J(ames) N(orman) 1917- CANR-3
Earlier sketch in CA 1R
Spulber, Nicolas 1915- CANR-3
Earlier sketch in CA 11-12R
Spuler, Bertold 1911- 81-84
Spungen, Deborah 1937- 119
Spurling, Hilary 1940- 104
See also CLC 34
Spurling, John 1936- CANR-1
Earlier sketch in CA 45-48
Spurr, Clinton
See Rowland, D(onald) S(ydney)
Spurr, David Anton 1949- 118
Spurr, Stephen Hopkins 1918- 81-84
Spurr, William A(lfred) 1905- 7-8R
Spurrier, William A(twell) 1916- 53-56
Spyers-Duran, Peter 1932- CANR-23
Earlier sketches in CA 19-20R, CANR-8
Spyker, John Howland 1918- 101
Spykman, E(lizabeth) C(hoate) 1896-1965 101
See also SATA 10
Spyri, Johanna (Heusser) 1827-1901 SATA-19
See also CLR 13
Spyridakis, Stylianos 1937- 89-92
Squibob
See Derby, George Horatio
Squier, Charles L(a Barge) 1931- 17-18R
Squier, Susan Merrill 1950- 120
Squire, Elizabeth 1919- 13-14R
Squire, Jason E(dward) 1948- CANR-23
Earlier sketch in CA 45-48
Squire, Norman 1907- CANR-3
Earlier sketch in CA 9-10R
Squire, Robin 1937- 105
Squire, Russel Nelson 1908- 3R
Squire, Susan 1950- 112
Squires, Eric
See Ball, Sylvia Patricia
Squires, James (David) 1943- 119
Squires, James Duane 1904- 7-8R
Squires, Michael (George) 1941- 61-64
Squires, Patricia
See Ball, Sylvia Patricia
Squires, Phil
See Barker, S. Omar
Squires, Radcliffe 1917- CANR-21
Earlier sketches in CA 1R, CANR-6
Sraffa, Piero 1898-1983 45-48
Obituary 110
Srere, Benson M. 1928- 77-80
S-Ringi, Kjell
See Ringi, Kjell (Arne Soerensen)
Srivastava, Dhanpat Rai 1880(?)-1936
Brief entry 118
Srivastava, Jane Jonas 1941- 119
See also SATA 37
Srole, Leo 1908- Brief entry 107
Staaf, Robert J(ames) 1939- 93-96
Staal, Cyril 1912- Brief entry 113
Staal, J(ohan) F(rederik) 1930- 45-48
Staal, Julius D(irk) W(illem) 1917-1986
Obituary 120
Staar, Richard F(elix) 1923- CANR-16
Earlier sketches in CA 4R, CANR-1
Staats, Arthur (Wilbur) 1924- 15-16R
Stabb, Martin S(anford) 1928- 23-24R
Stabile, Toni 85-88
Stableford, Brian M. 1948- 57-60
Stablein, Marilyn 1946- 120
Stabler, Arthur P(hillips) 1919- CANR-14
Earlier sketch in CA 41-44R
Stabley, Fred(erick) W(illiam) 1915- 112
Stace, Christopher 1942- 97-100
Stace, Walter Terence 1886-1967 CANR-2
Earlier sketch in CA 1R
Stacey, C(harles) P(erry) 1906- CANR-19
Earlier sketch in CA 101
Stacey, Frank Arthur 1923- 57-60
Stacey, Margaret 1922- CANR-17
Earlier sketch in CA 29-32R
Stacey, Nicholas Anthony Howard 1920- 7-8R
Stacey, Roy 1919- 9-10R
Stacey, Thomas Charles Gerard 1930- CANR-21
Earlier sketch in CA 9-10R
Stacey, Tom
See Stacey, Thomas Charles Gerard
Stachow, Hasso G(ert) 1924- 109
Stachys, Dimitris
See Constantelos, Demetrios J.
Stack, Edward MacGregor 1919- 1R
Stack, Frank H(untington) 1937- CANR-9
Earlier sketch in CA 61-64
Stack, George J. 1931- 37-40R
Stack, Herbert James 1893-1967 CANR-3
Earlier sketch in CA 2R
Stack, Nicolete Meredith 1896- 13-14R
Stackhouse, Max L. 1935- 23-24R
Stackhouse, Reginald 1925- 21-22R
Stackpole, Edouard Alexander 1903- CANR-16
Earlier sketches in CA 4R, CANR-1
Stackpole, Edward J(ames) 1894-1967 4R
Obituary 103
Stacks, John F(ultz) 1942- 113
Stacton, David (Derek) 1925-1968 CANR-6
Obituary 25-28R
Earlier sketch in CA 7-8R
Stacy, Bruce
See Elliott, Bruce (Walter Gardner Lively Stacy)
Stacy, Donald L. 1925- 29-32R
Stacy, Pat(ricia A.) 1941- 118
Stacy, R(obert) H(arold) 1919- 73-76
Stacy, Walter
See Elliott, Bruce (Walter Gardner Lively Stacy)
Stade, George 1933- 29-32R
Stadelman, S(ara) L(ee) 1917- 81-84
Stadler, Karl R(udolph) 1913- 23-24R
Stadler, Pat (Anna May Gough) 1918-
Brief entry 114
Stadt, Ronald W(ilmer) 1935- CANR-16
Earlier sketch in CA 93-96
Stadter, Philip A(ustin) 1936- 104
Stadtfeld, Curtis K(arl) 1935- 49-52
Stadtler, Bea 1921- 65-68
See also SATA 17
Stadtman, Verne A. 1926- 29-32R
Staebler, Edna 101
Staebler, Neil 1905- 77-80
Staebler, Warren 1912- 45-48
Staehle, Albert 1899-1974 AITN-1
Staender, Gilbert F(rank) 1930- 104
Staender, Vivian 1923- 97-100
Staff, Adrienne 1947- 123
Staff, Frank 1908- 25-28R
Stafford, Caroline
See Watjen, Carolyn L. T.
Stafford, David (Christopher) 1943- 103
Stafford, David Alexander Tetlow 1942- CANR-21
Earlier sketch in CA 104
Stafford, Gilbert Wayne 1938- 112
Stafford, Irvin G. 1936- 114
Stafford, Jean 1915-1979 CANR-3
Obituary 85-88
Earlier sketch in CA 4R
See also SATA 22
See also DLB 2
See also CLC 4, 7, 19
Stafford, Kenneth R(ay) 1922- 17-18R
Stafford, Kim R(obert) 1949- CANR-22
Earlier sketch in CA 69-72
Stafford, Linda (Crying Wind) 1943- 108
Stafford, Muriel
See Sauer, Muriel Stafford
Stafford, Peter
See Tabori, Paul
Stafford, William (Edgar) 1914- CANR-22
Earlier sketches in CA 7-8R, CANR-5
See also CAAS 3
See also DLB 5
See also CLC 4, 7, 29
Stafford, William B(utler) 1931- 53-56
Stafford, William T(almadge) 1924- 1R
Stafford-Clark, David 1916- 21-22R
Staffordshire Knot
See Wrottesley, A(rthur) J(ohn) F(rancis)
Stageberg, Norman C(lifford) 1905- CAP-1
Earlier sketch in CA 11-12
Stagg, Albert 1903- 85-88
Stagg, Evelyn 1914- 85-88
Stagg, Frank 1911- CANR-18
Earlier sketches in CA 4R, CANR-1
Stagg, James Martin 1900-1975 Obituary 61-64
Stagg, Paul L. 1914- 23-24R
Stagge, Jonathan
See Wheeler, Hugh (Callingham)
Stagner, Lloyd Ernest 1923- 101
Stagner, Ross 1909- CANR-5
Earlier sketch in CA 5-6R
Stahl, Ben(jamin) 1910-1987 29-32R
Obituary 123
See also SATA 5
Stahl, Donald 1935- 25-28R
Stahl, Fred Alan 1944- 45-48
Stahl, Gustav Richard 1888(?)-1978
Obituary 81-84
Stahl, Hilda 1938- 116
See also SATA 48
Stahl, Le Roy 1908- CAP-1
Earlier sketch in CA 11-12
Stahl, Lesley R(ene) 1941- 107
See also AITN 2
Stahl, Nancy 1937- 104
Stahl, Norman 1931- 85-88
Stahl, O(scar) Glenn 1910- CANR-14
Earlier sketch in CA 41-44R
Stahl, William Harris 1908-1969 Obituary 111
Stahlecker, Lotar V(ictor) 1915- 23-24R
Stahlman, James Geddes 1893-1976
Obituary 89-92
Stahnke, Arthur A(llan) 1935- 65-68
Stahnke, Astrida B. 1935- 123
Stahr, John W. 1904-1981 Obituary 104
Staib, Bjorn O. 1938- 17-18R
Staicar, Thomas Edward 1946- 108
Staicar, Tom
See Staicar, Thomas Edward
Staiger, Janet 1946- 123
Stainback, Susan Bray 1947- CANR-14
Earlier sketches in CA 57-60, CANR-7
Stainback, William (Clarence) 1943- CANR-14
Earlier sketch in CA 77-80
Staines, Trevor
See Brunner, John (Kilian Houston)
Stainsby, Charles 1925-1985 Obituary 118
Stair, Gobin (John) 1912- SATA-35
Stairs, Denis (Winfield) 1939- Brief entry 114
Stairs, Gordon
See Austin, Mary (Hunter)
Stalder, Valerie 41-44R
See also SATA 27
Staley, Allen 1935- Brief entry 115
Staley, Charles E(arl) 1927- 45-48
Staley, (Alvah) Eugene 1906- 77-80
Staley, Thomas F(abian) 1935- CANR-13
Earlier sketch in CA 77-80
Stallard, John (Richard) 1935-1985 49-52
Obituary 116
Stalley, Rodney E(dward) 1930- 116
Stalley, Roger 1945- 101
Stallibrass, (Helen) Alison 1916- 104
Stallings, Constance L(ee) 1932- CANR-17
Earlier sketch in CA 97-100
Stallings, James O. 1938- CANR-19
Earlier sketch in CA 103
Stallings, Laurence 1894-1968 Obituary 89-92
See also DLB 7, 44
Stallman, Robert Wooster 1911- CANR-3
Earlier sketch in CA 4R
Stallone, Sylvester (Enzio) 1946- 77-80
Stallworth, Anne Nall 1935- 85-88
Stallworthy, Jon (Howie) 1935- CANR-8
Earlier sketch in CA 11-12R
See also DLB 40
Stallybrass, Oliver (George Weatherhead) 1925-1978 CANR-24
Earlier sketch in CA 29-32R
Stalvey, Lois Mark 1925- CANR-14
Earlier sketch in CA 29-32R
Stam, James H(enry) 1937- 49-52
Stam, Robert 1941- 115
Stamaty, Mark Alan 1947- CANR-15
Earlier sketch in CA 61-64
See also SATA 12
Stambaugh, Joan 1932- 89-92
Stambaugh, Sara 1936- 119
Stamberg, Susan 1938- 103
Stambler, Helen
See Latner, Helen (Stambler)
Stambler, Irwin 1924- CANR-2
Earlier sketch in CA 5-6R
See also SATA 5
Stambolian, George 1938- 41-44R
Stambuk, George 1927- 7-8R
Stames, Ward
See Steward, Samuel M(orris)
Stamm, Keith R(oman) 1941- 116
Stamm, Martin L. 1917- CANR-19
Earlier sketch in CA 37-40R
Stammers, Neil 1950- 119
Stamp, L(aurence) Dudley 1898-1966 CAP-1
Earlier sketch in CA 13-14
Stamper, Alexander
See Kent, Arthur William Charles
Stampfer, Judah (Leon) 1923- 25-28R
Stampfle, Felice 1912- 105
Stampp, Kenneth M. 1912- 13-14R
See also DLB 17
Stanbury, David 1933- 104
Stanbury, Walter A. 1910-1976 Obituary 65-68
Stancliffe, Michael (Staffurth) 1916-1987 124
Stancu, Zaharia 1902-1974 97-100
Obituary 53-56
Standard, William L. 1900(?)-1978
Obituary 77-80
Stander, Siegfried 1935- CANR-19
Earlier sketches in CA 9-10R, CANR-4
Standiford, Lester A(lan) 1945- 77-80
Standing, Edwin (Mortimer) 1887- CAP-1
Earlier sketch in CA 9-10
Standing, Sue 1952- 119
Standing Bear, Luther 1868(?)-1939(?)
Brief entry 113
Standish, Buck
See Paine, Lauran (Bosworth)
Standish, Robert 1898(?)-1981 Obituary 105
Standley, Fred L(loyd) 1932- 41-44R
Standon, Anna (Slater) 1929- 17-18R
Standring, Gillian 1935- 69-72
Stanek, Carolyn 1951- 107
Stanek, Muriel (Novella) 1915- Brief entry 112
See also SATA 34
Stanev, Emilian
See Stanev, Nikola (Stoyanov)
Stanev, Nikola (Stoyanov) 1907-1979 108
Stanfield, Nancy Fisher Clay 1905- CAP-1
Earlier sketch in CA 9-10
Stanfield, Vernon Latrelle 1920- 97-100
Stanford, Alfred (Boller) 1900-1985 CAP-1
Obituary 115
Earlier sketch in CA 17-18
Stanford, Ann 1916-1987 CANR-4
Obituary 123
Earlier sketch in CA 9-10R
See also DLB 5
Stanford, Barbara Dodds 1943- 37-40R
Stanford, Derek 1918- 9-10R
Stanford, Don(ald Kent) 1918- 53-56
Stanford, Don
See Stanford, Donald E(lwin)
Stanford, Donald E(lwin) 1913- CANR-5
Earlier sketch in CA 13-14R
Stanford, Edward V(alentine) 1897-1966 7-8R
Stanford, Gene 1944- 37-40R
Stanford, J(ohn) K(eith) 1892- 7-8R
Stanford, Melvin Joseph 1932- CANR-16
Earlier sketch in CA 89-92
Stanford, Miles J(oseph) 1914- 65-68
Stanford, Quentin Hunt 1935- 45-48
Stanford, Sally 1903-1982 Obituary 105
Stanford, William Bedell 1910-1984 85-88
Obituary 115
Stanforth, Deirdre 1924- 102
Stang, Judit 1921-1977 CANR-8
Earlier sketch in CA 5-6R
See also SATA 29
Stang, Judy
See Stang, Judit
Stange, G(eorge) Robert 1919- 23-24R
Stanger, Frank Bateman 1914- 109
Stanger, Ila (Ann) 1940- 65-68
Stanhope, Eric
See Hamilton, Charles Harold St. John
Stanier, Maida Euphemia Kerr 1909- 101
Staniforth, (John Hamilton) Maxwell 1893- CAP-2
Earlier sketch in CA 25-28
Stanislavsky, Constantin (Sergeivich) 1863(?)-1938 Brief entry 118
Stanislawski, Dan 1903- CANR-3
Earlier sketch in CA 7-8R
Stanislawski, Michael 1952- 119
Stanke, Alain 1934- 81-84
Stanke, Don E(dward) 1929- 61-64
Stankevich, Boris 1928- 23-24R
See also SATA 2
Stankiewicz, Edward 1920- 45-48
Stankiewicz, Marketa Goetz
See Goetz-Stankiewicz, Marketa
Stankiewicz, W(ladyslaw) J(ozef) 1922- CANR-1
Earlier sketch in CA 45-48
Stanko, Elizabeth Anne 1950- 116
Stanley, Alexander O. 1910- 7-8R
Stanley, Bennett
See Hough, S(tanley), B(ennett)
Stanley, C(laude) Maxwell 1904-1984 114
Stanley, Carol
See White, Carol
Stanley, Dave
See Dachs, David
Stanley, David 1944- 115
Stanley, David T(aylor) 1916- Brief entry 107
Stanley, Diana 1909- SATA-30
Stanley, Diane 1943- 112
See also SATA 32, 37
Stanley, Fay Grissom (Shulman) 1925- 101
Stanley, George 1934- Brief entry 114
Stanley, George Edward 1942- CANR-17
Earlier sketch in CA 97-100
Stanley, George F(rancis) G(ilman) 1907- CANR-15
Earlier sketch in CA 41-44R
Stanley, John 1940- 21-22R
Stanley, John L(angley) 1937- 45-48
Stanley, Julian C(ecil), Jr. 1918- CANR-8
Earlier sketch in CA 21-22R
Stanley, Leo Leonidas 1886- 69-72
Stanley, Liz 1947- 119
Stanley, Marge
See Weinbaum, Stanley Grauman
Stanley, Nora Kathleen Begbie Strange 1885- CAP-1
Earlier sketch in CA 11-12
Stanley, Peter (Alan) 1956- 118
Stanley, Phil
See Ind, Allison
Stanley, Robert
See Hamilton, Charles Harold St. John
Stanley, Robert Henry 1940- 101
Stanley, Roy M. II 1936- 114
Stanley, Steven M(itchell) 1941- 109
Stanley, Timothy Wadsworth 1927- 77-80
Stanley, Warwick
See Hilton, John Buxton
Stanley, William O(liver), Jr. 1902- CANR-1
Earlier sketch in CA 1R
Stanley-Brown, Katherine (Oliver) 1893(?)-1972 Obituary 33-36R
Stanley-Jones, D(ouglas) 1905- 9-10R
Stanley-Wrench, Margaret 1916- 11-12R
Stanli, Sue
See Meilach, Dona Z(weigoron)
Stanlis, Peter J(ames) 1919- 101
Stanmeyer, William A(nthony) 1934- 118
Stann, Francis E. 1912(?)-1987 Obituary 124
Stannard, David E(dward) 1941- 65-68
Stannard, Martin CLC-44
Stannard, Neville (George) 1949- 118
Stannard, Una 1927- 73-76
Stanner, W(illiam) E(dward) H(anley) 1905-1981 Obituary 108
Stannus, (James) Gordon (Dawson) 1902- 65-68
Stanovich, Betty Jo 1954- 118
Stans, Maurice H(ubert) 1908- Brief entry 113
Stansberger, Richard 1950- CANR-18
Earlier sketch in CA 101
Stansbury, Donald L. 1929- 37-40R
Stansfield, Richard Habberton 1921- 107
Stansgate, Caroline DeCamp Wedgwood Benn
See Benn, Caroline DeCamp Wedgwood
Stansky, Peter (David Lyman) 1932- CANR-12
Earlier sketch in CA 17-18R
Stanstead, John
See Groom, Arthur William

INDEX

Stanton, Dorothy
See Kaumeyer, Dorothy
Stanton, Edward F(eagler) 1942- ... 89-92
Stanton, Frank L. 1857-1927 ... DLB-25
Stanton, Gerald B(arry) 1918- ... 9-10R
Stanton, Graham N(orman) 1940- ... 61-64
Stanton, Jessie Earl 1887-1976 Obituary ... 65-68
Stanton, Maura 1946- ... CANR-15
Earlier sketch in CA 89-92
See also CLC 9
Stanton, Paul
See Beaty, (Arthur) David
Stanton, Peggy Smeeton 1939- ... 61-64
Stanton, Phoebe B(aroody) 1914- ... 37-40R
Stanton, Royal (Waltz) 1916- ... 37-40R
Stanton, Schuyler
See Baum, L(yman) Frank
Stanton, Vance
See Avallone, Michael (Angelo), Jr.
Stanton, Will 1918- ... 85-88
Stanton, William 1925- ... 3R
Stanton, William J(ohn, Jr.) 1919-
Brief entry ... 115
Stanwood, Brooks
See Kaminsky, Howard
and Kaminsky, Susan Stanwood
Stanwood, Brooks
See Kaminsky, Susan Stanwood
Stanwood, P(aul) G(rant) 1933- ... 49-52
Stanyer, Jeffrey 1936- ... 61-64
Stapledon, (William) Olaf 1886-1950
Brief entry ... 111
See also DLB 15
See also TCLC 22
Stapler, Harry (Bascom) 1919- ... CANR-13
Earlier sketch in CA 61-64
Staples, Reginald Thomas 1911- ... CANR-14
Earlier sketch in CA 69-72
Staples, Robert (Eugene) 1942- ... CANR-2
Earlier sketch in CA 49-52
Stapleton, Constance 1930- ... 104
Stapleton, G(eorge) Brian 1922- ... 25-28R
Stapleton, Jean 1942- ... 69-72
Stapleton, (Katharine) Laurence 1911- ... 17-18R
Stapleton, Margaret (Lucy) 1903- ... 57-60
Stapleton, Marjorie (Winifred) 1932- ... 106
See also SATA 28
Stapleton, Richard John 1940- ... 89-92
Stapleton, Ruth Carter 1929-1983 ... 81-84
Obituary ... 110
Stapp, Arthur D(onald) 1906-1972 ... CANR-2
Obituary ... 33-36R
Earlier sketch in CA 4R
See also SATA 4
Stapp, William B. 1929- ... CANR-22
Earlier sketches in CA 45-48, CANR-2
Stappenbeck, Herb(ert) Louis (Jr.) 1935- ... 65-68
Star, Angel
See Quigley, Joan
Star, Cima 1939- ... 110
Star, Jack 1920- ... 73-76
Star, Max 1890(?)-1986 Obituary ... 121
Star, Shirley A(nn) 1918-1976 ... 41-44R
Obituary ... 65-68
Starbird, Kaye ... 17-18R
See also SATA 6
Starbuck, George (Edwin) 1931- ... CANR-23
Earlier sketch in CA 21-22R
Starbuck, William H(aynes) 1934- ... CANR-7
Earlier sketch in CA 57-60
Starch, Daniel 1883- ... 37-40R
Starchild, Adam (Aristotle) 1946- ... 123
Starchuk, Orest 1915- ... 5-6R
Stardust, Alvin 1942- ... 123
Starenko, Ronald C(harles) 1930- ... 93-96
Stargell, Willie
See Stargell, Wilver Dornel
Stargell, Wilver Dornel 1941- Brief entry ... 118
Starhawk
See Simos, Miriam
Stark, Bradford 1948-1979 ... CANR-3
Earlier sketch in CA 49-52
Stark, Claude Alan 1935- ... 57-60
Stark, Freya (Madeline) 1893- ... CANR-5
Earlier sketch in CA 5-6R
Stark, Gary Duane 1948- ... CANR-21
Earlier sketch in CA 105
Stark, George Washington 1884-1966
Obituary ... 89-92
Stark, Harry 1895- ... 2R
Stark, Irwin 1912- ... 9-10R
Stark, Jack
See Stark, John H.
Stark, James
See Goldston, Robert (Conroy)
Stark, John
See Godwin, John
Stark, John H. 1914- ... 49-52
Stark, John Olsen 1939- ... CANR-5
Earlier sketch in CA 53-56
Stark, Joshua
See Olsen, T(heodore) V(ictor)
Stark, Michael
See Lariar, Lawrence
Stark, Paul C. 1891(?)-1974 Obituary ... 53-56
Stark, R. J.
See Kikel, Rudy (John)
Stark, Raymond 1919- ... 73-76
Stark, Richard
See Westlake, Donald E(dwin)
Stark, Werner 1909- ... CANR-10
Earlier sketch in CA 21-22R
Starke, Aubrey (Harrison) 1905(?)-1972
Obituary ... 37-40R
Starke, Catherine Juanita 1913- ... 37-40R
Starke, J(oseph) G(abriel) 1911- ... 115
Starke, Roland ... 53-56
Starkey, Lycurgus M(onroe), Jr. 1928- ... 5-6R
Starkey, Marion L(ena) 1901- ... CANR-1
Earlier sketch in CA 2R
See also SATA 13
Starkie, Enid 1903(?)-1970 ... CANR-2
Obituary ... 29-32R
Earlier sketch in CA 3R
Starkie, Walter F(itzwilliam) 1894-1976 ... 77-80
Obituary ... 69-72
Starkins, Edward 1946- ... 120
Starkloff, Carl F. 1933- ... 53-56
Starkman, Miriam K(osh) 1916- ... 65-68
Starkman, Moshe 1906-1975 Obituary ... 57-60
Starks, Richard 1947- ... 113
Starkweather, David 1935- ... 97-100
See also DLB 7
Starling, Thomas
See Hayton, Richard Neil
Star-Man's Padre
See Patrick, Johnstone G(illespie)
Starn, Randolph 1939- ... 45-48
Starnes, Richard 1922- Brief entry ... 114
Starobin, Joseph R(obert) 1913-1976 ... 45-48
Obituary ... 69-72
Starobin, Rosalind Gould 1912(?)-1983
Obituary ... 111
Starr, Cecile 1921- ... 65-68
Starr, Chauncey 1912- ... 109
Starr, Chester G. 1914- ... CANR-16
Earlier sketches in CA 2R, CANR-1
Starr, Edward Caryl 1911- ... 13-14R
Starr, Frank 1938- ... 69-72
Starr, Henry
See Bingley, David Ernest
Starr, Herbert F(rederick) 1932- ... 116
Starr, Isidore 1911- ... CANR-7
Earlier sketch in CA 15-16R
Starr, Jerold M. 1941- ... 77-80
Starr, John 1914(?)-1980 Obituary ... 101
Starr, John
See Counselman, Mary Elizabeth
Starr, John A.
See Gillese, John Patrick
Starr, John Bryan 1939- ... 77-80
Starr, Judy
See Gelfman, Judith S(chlein)
Starr, Kevin 1940- ... 120
Starr, Louis M(orris) 1917-1980 ... 53-56
Obituary ... 97-100
Starr, Mark 1894-1985 Obituary ... 116
See also AITN 1
Starr, Martin Kenneth 1927- ... CANR-8
Earlier sketch in CA 17-18R
Starr, Paul 1949- Brief entry ... 123
Starr, Penelope
See Gelles-Cole, Sandi
Starr, Raymond 1937- ... 65-68
Starr, Roger 1918- ... CANR-11
Earlier sketch in CA 21-22R
Starr, Roland
See Rowland, D(onald) S(ydney)
Starr, S(tephen) Frederick 1940- ... CANR-17
Earlier sketch in CA 85-88
Starr, Stephen Z. 1909-1985 ... CANR-17
Earlier sketch in CA 37-40R
Starr, William Thomas 1910- ... 41-44R
Starr, Wilmarth Holt 1913- ... 17-18R
Starratt, Alfred B(yron) 1914- ... 17-18R
Starret, William
See McClintock, Marshall
Starrett, (Charles) Vincent (Emerson)
1886-1974 ... 73-76
Obituary ... 45-48
Starrs, James E(dward) 1930- ... 118
Starry, Donn Albert 1925- ... 109
Start, Clarissa
See Lippert, Clarissa Start
Stasch, Stanley F. 1931- ... 41-44R
Stasheff, Christopher 1944- ... CANR-10
Earlier sketch in CA 65-68
Stasheff, (Adolph) Edward 1909- ... 7-8R
Stasiak, Krystyna ... SATA-49
Stasio, Marilyn L(ouise) 1940- ... 33-36R
Stassinopoulos, Arianna 1950- Brief entry ... 114
Stasz, Clarice ... CANR-7
Earlier sketch in CA 61-64
Staten, Patricia S. 1945- ... 53-56
Statera, Gianni 1943- ... CANR-8
Earlier sketch in CA 57-60
States, Bert O(len) 1929- ... 73-76
Statham, Frances P(atton) 1931- ... 101
Statham, Jane 1917- ... 15-16R
Statler, Oliver Hadley 1915- ... 7-8R
Staton, Knofel L. 1934- ... 114
Staton, Thomas Felix 1917- ... 7-8R
Staub, August W(illiam) 1931- ... CANR-2
Earlier sketch in CA 45-48
Staubach, Charles N(eff) 1906- ... CANR-4
Earlier sketch in CA 5-6R
Staubach, Roger (Thomas) 1942- ... 104
Staudacher, Joseph M. 1914- ... 25-28R
Staudacher, Rosemarian V(alentiner)
1918- ... 5-6R
Staudenraus, P(hilip) J(ohn) 1928-1971 ... 2R
Obituary ... 103
Stauder, Jack 1939- ... 37-40R
Stauderman, Albert P(hilip) 1910- ... CANR-18
Earlier sketch in CA 77-80
Staudinger, Hermann 1881-1965 Obituary ... 113
Staudt, Virginia
See Sexton, Virginia Staudt
Stauffer, Don
See Berkebile, Fred D(onovan)
Stauffer, Donald Barlow 1930- ... 57-60
Stauffer, Helen Winter 1922- ... 109
Staum, Martin Sheldon 1943- ... 103
Staunton, Schuyler
See Baum, L(yman) Frank
Stauter, (Justin) Jay 1907-1986 Obituary ... 118
Stave, Bruce M(artin) 1937- ... CANR-12
Earlier sketch in CA 29-32R
Staveley, Gaylord L(ee) 1931- ... 37-40R
Stavenhagen, Lee 1933- ... 104
Stavenhagen, Rodolfo 1932- ... CANR-12
Earlier sketch in CA 29-32R
Stavis, Barrie 1906- ... 49-52
Stavis, Ben(edict) 1941- ... 29-32R
Stavrianos, Leften Stavros 1913- ... CANR-6
Earlier sketch in CA 7-8R
Stavros, Niko
See King, Florence
Stavrou, Theofanis G. 1934- ... 45-48
Stayer, James M(entzer) 1935- ... 45-48
Stead, Christian Karlson 1932- ... CANR-6
Earlier sketch in CA 57-60
Stead, Christina (Ellen) 1902-1983 ... 15-16R
Obituary ... 109
See also CLC 2, 5, 8, 32
Stead, Philip John 1916- ... 108
Stead, Thistle Yolette 1902- ... 107
Steadman, David (Wilton) 1936- ... 107
Steadman, John M(arcellus III) 1918- ... 25-28R
Steadman, Mark 1930- ... 37-40R
See also DLB 6
Steadman, Ralph (Idris) 1936- ... 107
See also SATA 32
Steahly, Vivian Eugenia Emrick 1915- ... 61-64
Steakley, John 1951- ... 120
Stealingworth, Slim
See Wesselmann, Tom
Steamer
See Nason, Leonard H(astings)
Steamer, Robert J(ulius) 1920- ... 41-44R
Steane, J(ohn) B(arry) 1928- ... 11-12R
Steanson, Karen E(lizabeth) 1942- ... 116
Stearn, Gerald E. 1934(?)-1982 Obituary ... 108
Stearn, Jess ... 97-100
Stearns, Harold Edmund 1891-1943
Brief entry ... 107
See also DLB 4
Stearns, Marshall Winslow 1908-1966
Obituary ... 110
Stearns, Martha Genung 1886- ... 11-12R
Stearns, Monroe (Mather) 1913-1987 ... CANR-2
Obituary ... 124
Earlier sketch in CA 5-6R
See also SATA 5
Stearns, Pamela Fujimoto 1935- ... 65-68
Stearns, Peter N. 1936- ... CANR-10
Earlier sketch in CA 21-22R
Stearns, Raymond Phineas 1904-1970 ... CAP-1
Earlier sketch in CA 11-12
Stebbins, G(eorge) Ledyard 1906- ... 45-48
Stebbins, Richard P(oate) 1913- ... CANR-2
Earlier sketch in CA 5-6R
Stebbins, Robert A(lan) 1938- ... CANR-12
Earlier sketch in CA 29-32R
Stebbins, Robert C(yril) 1915- ... 49-52
Stebbins, Theodore Ellis, Jr. 1938- ... 89-92
Stebel, S(idney) L(eo) 1924- ... 29-32R
Steber, A. R.
See Palmer, Raymond A.
Stecher, Miriam B(rodie) 1917- ... 106
Stechow, Wolfgang 1896-1974 ... CANR-9
Obituary ... 53-56
Earlier sketch in CA 65-68
Steck, James S(perow) 1911- ... 41-44R
Steckel, William Reed 1915- ... 17-18R
Steckler, Arthur 1921- ... 108
Steckler, Doug(las) 1948- ... 107
Steckler, Phyllis B. (Schwartzbard)
1933- ... 11-12R
Stedman, Edmund Clarence 1833-1908 ... DLB-64
Stedman, James Murphy 1938- ... 77-80
Stedman, Jane W(infred) 1920- ... 37-40R
Stedman, Murray S(alisbury), Jr. 1917- ... 17-18R
Stedman, R(aymond) William 1930- ... 29-32R
Stedman, Ray C. 1917- ... 104
Stedman Jones, Gareth 1942- ... 45-48
Stedmond, John Mitchell 1916- ... 103
Stedwell, Paki 1945- ... 103
Steed, Gitel P. 1914-1977 ... 41-44R
Steed, Thomas Jefferson 1904-1983
Obituary ... 110
Steed, Tom
See Steed, Thomas Jefferson
Steedman, Marguerite Couturier 1908- ... CANR-1
Earlier sketch in CA 4R
Steefel, Lawrence D. 1894- ... CAP-2
Earlier sketch in CA 21-22
Steeger, Henry 1903- ... 41-44R
Steeger, Henry 1929(?)-1978 Obituary ... 77-80
Steegmuller, Francis 1906- ... CANR-2
Earlier sketch in CA 49-52
Steel, Anthony Bedford 1900-1973 ... 7-8R
Obituary ... 89-92
Steel, Byron
See Steegmuller, Francis
Steel, Danielle ... CANR-19
Earlier sketch in CA 81-84
Steel, Edward M(arvin), Jr. 1918- ... 11-12R
Steel, Eric M. 1904- ... 89-92
Steel, Flora Annie (Webster) 1847-1929
Brief entry ... 116
Steel, Ronald (Lewis) 1931- ... CANR-7
Earlier sketch in CA 11-12R
Steel, Tex
See Ross, W(illiam) E(dward) D(aniel)
Steele, A(rchibald) T(rojan) 1903- ... CAP-2
Earlier sketch in CA 19-20
Steele, Addison II
See Lupoff, Richard A(llen)
Steele, Alan 1905-1985 Obituary ... 115
Steele, Arthur R(obert) 1916- ... 9-10R
Steele, Chester K.
See Stratemeyer, Edward L.
Steele, Colin Robert 1944- ... 104
Steele, Curtis
See Davis, Frederick C(lyde)
Steele, Dale
See Glut, Donald F(rank)
Steele, Dirk
See Plawin, Paul
Steele, Elizabeth 1921- ... 45-48
Steele, Erskine
See Henderson, Archibald
Steele, Fletcher 1885-1971 ... CAP-1
Earlier sketch in CA 13-14
Steele, Frank 1935- ... 37-40R
Steele, Fred I(rving) 1938- ... CANR-17
Earlier sketches in CA 45-48, CANR-2
Steele, Fritz
See Steele, Fred I(rving)
Steele, George P(eabody II) 1924- ... 2R
Steele, Gordon (Charles) 1892-1981 ... 105
Obituary ... 102
Steele, Harwood R(obert) E(lmes) 1897- ... CAP-1
Earlier sketch in CA 15-16
Steele, Henry 1931- ... 41-44R
Steele, I(an) K(enneth) 1937- ... 45-48
Steele, Jack 1914-1980 ... 109
Obituary ... 102
Steele, James B(ruce, Jr.) 1943- ... 115
Brief entry ... 110
Steele, Mary Q(uintard Govan) 1922- ... CANR-22
Earlier sketches in CA 4R, CANR-6
See also SATA 3
Steele, (Henry) Max(well) 1922- ... 25-28R
See also SATA 10
See also DLBY 80
Steele, Michael Rhoads 1945- ... 111
Steele, Peter (R.) 1935- ... 108
Steele, Phillip W(ayne) 1934- ... 61-64
Steele, Richard W(illiam) 1934-
Brief entry ... 107
Steele, Robert (Scott) 1917- ... 49-52
Steele, Thomas J(oseph) 1933- ... 61-64
Steele, Timothy (Reid) 1948- ... CANR-16
Earlier sketch in CA 93-96
See also CLC 45
Steele, Wilbur Daniel 1886-1970 ... 109
Obituary ... 29-32R
Steele, William O(wen) 1917-1979 ... CANR-2
Earlier sketch in CA 2R
See also SATA 1, 27
Steelman, Robert J(ames) 1914- ... CANR-11
Earlier sketch in CA 69-72
Steely, John E(dward) 1922- ... 37-40R
Steen, Edwin B. 1901- ... 101
Steen, Frank
See Felstein, Ivor
Steen, John Warren, Jr. 1925- ... 15-16R
Steen, Malcolm Harold 1928- ... 29-32R
Steen, Marguerite 1894-1975 ... 97-100
Obituary ... 61-64
Steen, Mike
See Steen, Malcolm Harold
Steen, Sara Jayne 1949- ... 106
Steenberg, Sven 1905- ... 37-40R
Steene, Birgitta 1928- ... 85-88
Steensma, Robert Charles 1930- ... 41-44R
Steenson, Gary P(aul) 1944- ... 107
Steer, Alfred G(ilbert), Jr. 1913- ... 45-48
Steer, Charlotte
See Hunter, Maud L(ily)
Steere, Daniel C(onrad) 1938- ... 93-96
Steere, Douglas V(an) 1901- ... 13-14R
Steere, Richard 1643(?)-1721 ... DLB-24
Steers, J(ames) A(lfred) 1899-1987 ... 124
Steese, Edward 1902-1981 Obituary ... 105
Steese, Peter B(echler) 1933- ... 17-18R
Steeves, Frank Leslie 1921- ... 15-16R
Steeves, Harrison R(oss) 1881-1981
Obituary ... 104
Stefanelli, Vladimir Clain
See Clain-Stefanelli, Vladimir
Stefanics, Charlotte L(ouise) 1927- ... 116
Stefanile, Felix 1920- ... CANR-1
Earlier sketch in CA 45-48
Stefansson, Evelyn
See Nef, Evelyn Stefansson
Stefansson, Thorsteinn 1912- ... 77-80
Steffan, Alice Kennedy 1907- ... 5-6R
Steffan, Jack
See Steffan, Alice Kennedy
Steffan, Siobhan R.
See Goulart, Frances Sheridan
Steffan, Truman Guy 1910- ... 29-32R
Steffanson, Con
See Cassiday, Bruce (Bingham)
and Goulart, Ron(ald Joseph)
Steffek, Edwin F(rancis) 1912-1985 ... 89-92
Obituary ... 118
Steffen, Albert 1884-1963 Obituary ... 93-96
Steffen, Jerome O(rville) 1942- ... 112
Steffens, (Joseph) Lincoln 1866-1936
Brief entry ... 117
See also TCLC 20
Steffensmeier, Darrell J. 1942- ... 123
Stefferud, Alfred (Daniel) 1903- ... CAP-1
Earlier sketch in CA 15-16
Steffler, John 1947- ... 110
Stefflre, Buford 1916- ... 5-6R
Stegall, Carrie Coffey 1908- ... CAP-2
Earlier sketch in CA 25-28
Stegeman, Janet Allais 1923- ... SATA-49
Stegeman, John F(oster) 1918- ... 19-20R
Stegenga, James A. 1937- ... 25-28R
Steger, Shelby 1906- ... 49-52
Steglich, W(infred) G(eorge) 1921- ... 45-48

Stegman, Michael A(llen) 1940- ... 41-44R
Stegner, Page 1937- ... CANR-10
Earlier sketch in CA 21-22R
Stegner, Wallace (Earle) 1909- ... CANR-21
Earlier sketches in CA 3R, CANR-1
See also DLB 9
See also CLC 9
See also AITN 1
Stehling, Kurt R(ichard) 1919- Brief entry ... 110
Stehr, Hermann 1864-1940 ... DLB-66
Steible, Daniel J(oseph) 1912-1976 ... 45-48
Obituary ... 103
Steichen, Edward 1879-1973 Obituary ... 41-44R
Steichen, Paula 1943- ... 25-28R
Steig, Irwin 1901-1977 Obituary ... 73-76
Steig, William 1907- ... CANR-21
Earlier sketch in CA 77-80
See also SATA 18
See also DLB 61
See also CLR 2
See also AITN 1
Steiger, Andrew Jacob 1900- ... 5-6R
Steiger, Brad (E.) 1936- ... CANR-21
Earlier sketch in CA 33-36R
Steiger, Paul E(rnest) 1942- ... 77-80
Steigman, Benjamin 1889(?)-1974
Obituary ... 53-56
Steiman, Sidney 1922- ... 7-8R
Steimle, Edmund A(ugustus) 1907- ... 121
Stein, Aaron Marc 1906-1985 ... CANR-6
Obituary ... 117
Earlier sketch in CA 9-10R
Stein, Arnold (Sidney) 1915- Brief entry ... 114
Stein, Arthur (Benjamin) 1937- ... 29-32R
Stein, Ben
See Stein, Benjamin
Stein, Benjamin 1944- ... 106
Stein, Bob 1920- ... 37-40R
Stein, Bruno 1930- ... 37-40R
Stein, Calvert 1903- ... 29-32R
Stein, Charles
See Schwalberg, Carol(yn Ernestine Stein)
Stein, Charles S. 1940- ... 21-22R
Stein, Charles W(arner) 1918- ... 116
Stein, Dona ... 77-80
Stein, Edward V(incent) 1920- ... 15-16R
Stein, Emanuel 1908-1985 Obituary ... 114
Stein, George P(hilip) 1917- ... 65-68
Stein, Gertrude 1874-1946 Brief entry ... 104
See also DLB 4, 54
See also TCLC 1, 6
Stein, Harry 1938- ... 61-64
Stein, Harry 1948- Brief entry ... 120
Stein, Harve 1904- ... SATA-30
Stein, Herb 1928- ... 65-68
Stein, Herbert 1916- ... 106
Stein, Herman D(avid) 1917- ... 2R
Stein, Jack M(adison) 1914-1976 ... CANR-15
Obituary ... 103
Earlier sketch in CA 2R
Stein, Jan
See Hegeler, Sten
Stein, Jane Jacobson 1937- ... 97-100
Stein, Jerome L(eon) 1928- ... 81-84
Stein, Jess 1914-1984 Obituary ... 113
Stein, Joseph ... 15-16R
Stein, Leo Daniel 1872-1947 Brief entry ... 107
See also DLB 4
Stein, Leon 1910- ... 17-18R
Stein, Leon 1912- ... CANR-7
Earlier sketch in CA 19-20R
Stein, M(eyer) L(ewis) 1920- ... CANR-13
Earlier sketch in CA 17-18R
See also SATA 6
Stein, Mark (Avrum) 1951- ... 118
Stein, Martha L(inda) 1942- ... 53-56
Stein, Maurice Robert 1926- ... 49-52
Stein, Michael B. 1940- ... 45-48
Stein, Mini ... 29-32R
See also SATA 2
Stein, Morris I(saac) 1921- ... CANR-1
Earlier sketch in CA 3R
Stein, Peter (Gonville) 1926- ... 21-22R
Stein, Philip L(awrence) 1939- ... 61-64
Stein, R(ichard) Conrad 1937- ... CANR-22
Earlier sketch in CA 41-44R
See also SATA 31
Stein, Rita F. 1922- Brief entry ... 106
Stein, Robert 1924- ... 49-52
Stein, Robert H(arry) 1935- ... 101
Stein, Roger B(reed) 1932- ... CANR-2
Earlier sketch in CA 45-48
Stein, Sandra Kovacs 1939- ... 106
Stein, Sara Bonnett ... SATA-34
Stein, Sol 1926- ... CANR-2
Earlier sketch in CA 49-52
See also AITN 1
Stein, Stanley J. 1920- Brief entry ... 108
Stein, Susan M. 1942- ... CANR-14
Earlier sketch in CA 37-40R
Stein, Thomas A. 1924- ... 45-48
Stein, Toby 1935- ... 7-8R
Stein, Walter 1924- ... 25-28R
Stein, William B. 1915- ... 104
Stein, William W(arner) 1921- ... 2R
Steinbach, Alexander Alan 1894-1978 ... 85-88
Obituary ... 81-84
Steinbach, Meredith 1949- ... 107
Steinbeck, John (Ernst) 1902-1968 ... CANR-1
Obituary ... 25-28R
Earlier sketch in CA 2R
See also SATA 9
See also DLB 7, 9
See also DLBD 2
See also CLC 1, 5, 9, 13, 21, 34, 45
Steinberg, Aaron Zacharovich 1891-1975
Obituary ... 61-64
Steinberg, Alfred 1917- ... CANR-9
Earlier sketch in CA 5-6R
See also SATA 9
Steinberg, Charles S(ide) 1913-1978 ... CANR-4
Earlier sketch in CA 49-52
Steinberg, Danny D(avid Charles)
1931- ... CANR-14
Earlier sketch in CA 37-40R
Steinberg, David Joel 1937- ... 25-28R
Steinberg, Eleanor B(usick) 1936- ... 65-68
Steinberg, Erwin R(ay) 1920- ... CANR-12
Earlier sketch in CA 29-32R
Steinberg, Fannie 1899- ... 115
See also SATA 43
Steinberg, Fred J. 1933- ... 37-40R
See also SATA 4
Steinberg, Israel 1903(?)-1983 Obituary ... 109
Steinberg, J(ay) Leonard 1930- ... 57-60
Steinberg, Jeffrey 1947(?)-1981 Obituary ... 104
Steinberg, Jonathan 1934- ... 21-22R
Steinberg, Joseph L(awrence) 1928- ... 25-28R
Steinberg, Judah 1861-1908 Brief entry ... 106
Steinberg, Leo 1920- ... CANR-17
Earlier sketches in CA 45-48, CANR-1
Steinberg, Phillip Orso 1921- ... CANR-2
Earlier sketch in CA 5-6R
See also SATA 34
Steinberg, Rafael (Mark) 1927- ... CANR-9
Earlier sketch in CA 61-64
See also SATA 45
Steinberg, S(igrid) H(enry) 1899-1969 ... CAP-1
Earlier sketch in CA 9-10
Steinberg, Saul 1914- ... 89-92
Steinbergh, Judith W(olinsky) 1943- ... CANR-1
Earlier sketch in CA 45-48
Steinbicker, Paul G(eorge) 1906- ... CAP-2
Earlier sketch in CA 19-20
Steinbreder, Harry John, Jr. 1930-1985
Obituary ... 117
Steinbreder, Sandy
See Steinbreder, Harry John, Jr.
Steinbrueck, Victor 1911- ... 13-14R
Steinbruner, John David 1941- ... 77-80
Steinbrunner, (Peter) Chris(tian) 1933- ... CANR-1
Earlier sketch in CA 45-48
Steincrohn, Peter J(oseph) 1899-1986
Obituary ... 118
Brief entry ... 112
Steinem, Gloria 1934- ... 53-56
Steiner, Barbara A(nnette) 1934- ... CANR-13
Earlier sketch in CA 73-76
See also SATA 13
Steiner, Barry R(aymond) ... 115
Steiner, Charlotte 1900-1981 ... SATA-45
Steiner, Claude 1935- ... 97-100
Steiner, Frederick 1949- ... 116
Steiner, Gary A(lbert) 1931-1966 ... 11-12R
Obituary ... 103
Steiner, George 1929- ... 73-76
See also DLB 67
See also CLC 24
Steiner, George A(lbert) 1912- ... CANR-7
Earlier sketch in CA 13-14R
Steiner, Gerolf 1908- ... 29-32R
Steiner, Gilbert Y(ale) 1924- Brief entry ... 115
Steiner, H. Arthur 1905- ... 5-6R
Steiner, Irene Hunter 1920- ... 97-100
Steiner, Joerg 1930- ... 108
See also SATA 35
Steiner, Jorg
See Steiner, Joerg
Steiner, Kurt 1912- ... CANR-7
Earlier sketch in CA 17-18R
Steiner, Lee R. 1901- ... CAP-1
Earlier sketch in CA 13-14
Steiner, Paul ... CANR-4
Earlier sketch in CA 9-10R
Steiner, Peter O(tto) 1922- ... CANR-14
Earlier sketch in CA 37-40R
Steiner, Ralph 1899-1986 Obituary ... 119
Brief entry ... 113
Steiner, Roger J(acob) 1924- ... 45-48
Steiner, Rudolf 1861-1925 Brief entry ... 107
See also TCLC 13
Steiner, Shari 1941- ... 73-76
Steiner, Stan(ley) 1925-1987 ... CANR-16
Obituary ... 121
Earlier sketches in CA 45-48, CANR-1
See also SATA 14, 50
Steiner, Susan Clemmer 1947- ... 115
Steiner, Thomas R(obert) 1934- ... 45-48
Steiner, Vera P(olgar) John
See John-Steiner, Vera P(olgar)
Steiner, Wendy 1949- ... CANR-14
Earlier sketch in CA 81-84
Steiner-Prag, Hugo 1880-1945 ... SATA-32
Steinert, Marlis G(ertrud) ... 81-84
Steinfels, Peter (Francis) 1941- Brief entry ... 116
Steingold, Fred S(aul) 1936- ... 106
Steinhardt, Anne Elizabeth 1941- ... 104
Steinhardt, Herschel S. 1910- ... CAP-2
Earlier sketch in CA 23-24
Steinhardt, Milton 1909- ... 77-80
Steinhart, Carol E(lder) 1935- ... 57-60
Steinhauer, Harry 1905- ... CANR-1
Earlier sketch in CA 1R
Steinhaus, Arthur H. 1897-1970 ... CAP-1
Earlier sketch in CA 19-20
Steinheimer, Richard (V.) 1929- ... 123
Steinhoff, Dan 1911- ... 77-80
Steinhoff, William (Richard) 1914- ... 85-88
Steinitz, Kate T(rauman) 1889-1975 ... CAP-2
Earlier sketch in CA 23-24
Steinitz, Paul 1909- ... 104
Steinke, Ann (Elizabeth) 1948- ... 113
Steinke, Peter L(ouis) 1938- ... 29-32R
Steinkraus, Warren E(dward) 1922- ... 21-22R
Steinle, John G. 1916- ... 9-10R
Steinle, Paul (Michael) 1939- ... 77-80
Steinman, Lisa Malinowski 1950- ... 69-72
Steinmann, Anne G. 1906(?)-1987
Obituary ... 121
Steinmann, Martin, Jr. 1915- ... 3R
Steinmetz, Eulalie
See Ross, Eulalie Steinmetz
Steinmetz, Lawrence L(eo) 1938- ... CANR-11
Earlier sketch in CA 23-24R
Steinmetz, Rollin C. 1912(?)-1986
Obituary ... 121
Steinmetz, Urban G. 1920- ... CANR-10
Earlier sketch in CA 25-28R
Steintrager, James A(lvin) 1936- ... 93-96
Steinwedel, Louis William 1943- ... 37-40R
Steirman, Hy 1921- ... 29-32R
Steiss, Alan Walter 1937- ... CANR-12
Earlier sketch in CA 29-32R
Steitz, Edward S. 1920- ... 69-72
Stekert, Ellen J(ane) 1935- ... 33-36R
Stekler, Herman O. 1932- ... 19-20R
Stell, Aaron 1911- ... 57-60
Stell, Geoffrey (Percival) 1944- ... 124
Stellman, Jeanne M(ager) 1947- ... 102
Stellman, Steven D(ale) 1945- ... 85-88
Steltenkamp, Michael F(rancis) 1950- ... 112
Stelter, Gilbert Arthur 1933- ... CANR-15
Earlier sketch in CA 41-44R
Steltzer, Ulli 1923- ... 104
Stelzer, Dick 1950- ... 107
Stelzig, Eugene Louis 1943- ... 81-84
Stem, Thad(deus Garland), Jr.
1916-1980 ... 97-100
Obituary ... 101
Stember, Charles Herbert 1916- ... 21-22R
Stemp, Isay 1922- ... 29-32R
Stemp, Robin (Jenniver Pamela) 1944- ... 107
Stempel, Guido H(ermann) III 1928- ... 77-80
Stempel, John Dallas 1938- ... 110
Stempel, Thomas Ritter 1941- ... 110
Stempel, Tom
See Stempel, Thomas Ritter
Stenberger, Marten 1898- ... CANR-5
Earlier sketch in CA 7-8R
Stendahl, Krister 1921- ... CANR-12
Earlier sketch in CA 17-18R
Stene, Edwin O(tto) 1900- ... CAP-2
Earlier sketch in CA 21-22
Steneck, Nicholas H. 1940- ... 106
Steneman, Shep 1945- ... 107
Stenerson, Douglas C. 1920- ... 37-40R
Stenhouse, David 1932- ... 89-92
Stenius, George
See Seaton, George
Stensboel, Ottar 1930- ... 69-72
Stenson, Frederick 1951- ... 113
Stent, Gunther S(iegmund) 1924- ... 29-32R
Stenton, Doris Mary (Parsons) 1894-1971
Obituary ... 104
Stenus
See Huxley, Herbert H(enry)
Stenzel, Anne K(atherine) 1911- ... 57-60
Stenzel, George 1910- ... 45-48
Stepanchev, Stephen 1915- ... CANR-7
Earlier sketch in CA 17-18R
Stepanian, Michael 1939- ... 45-48
Stephan, John J(ason) 1941- ... 41-44R
Stephan, Leslie (Bates) 1933- ... CANR-24
Earlier sketches in CA 21-22R, CANR-9
Stephan, Ruth 1910- ... 5-6R
Stephen, David 1910- ... 106
Stephen, George 1926- ... 102
Stephen, Jan 1933- ... 3R
Stephen, Leslie 1832-1904 Brief entry ... 123
See also DLB 57
See also TCLC 23
Stephen, Parel Lukose 1898- ... CAP-1
Earlier sketch in CA 9-10
Stephen, R. J.
See Barrett, Norman (S.)
Stephen, Sid 1942- ... 105
Stephen, Sir Leslie
See Stephen, Leslie
Stephens, A. Ray 1932- ... CANR-13
Earlier sketch in CA 77-80
Stephens, Alan 1925- ... 19-20R
Stephens, Alexander H. 1812-1883 ... DLB-47
Stephens, Ann Sophia (Winterbotham)
1813-1886 ... DLB-3
Stephens, C(harles) Ralph 1943- ... 122
Stephens, Casey
See Wagner, Sharon B.
Stephens, Charles
See Goldin, Stephen
Stephens, Charles Asbury 1844(?)-1931 ... DLB-42
Stephens, Donald G. 1931- ... 21-22R
Stephens, Edna Buell 1903- ... CANR-14
Earlier sketch in CA 37-40R
Stephens, Edward Carl 1924- ... 23-24R
Stephens, Eve
See Ward-Thomas, Evelyn Bridget Patricia Stephens
Stephens, Frances
See Bentley, Margaret
Stephens, Henrietta Henkle 1909-1983 ... CANR-6
Obituary ... 109
Earlier sketch in CA 9-10R
Stephens, Ian Melville 1903-1984
Obituary ... 112
Stephens, J(ohn) M(ortimer) 1901- ... 13-14R
Stephens, James 1882(?)-1950
Brief entry ... 104
See also DLB 19
See also TCLC 4
Stephens, James Charles 1915- ... CANR-3
Earlier sketch in CA 7-8R
Stephens, Jeanne
See Hager, Jean
Stephens, Joyce 1941- ... 69-72
Stephens, Lester D(ow) 1933- ... 45-48
Stephens, M(ichael) G(regory) 1946- ... CANR-3
Earlier sketch in CA 49-52
Stephens, Martha (Thomas) 1937- ... 77-80
Stephens, Mary Jo 1935- ... 37-40R
See also SATA 8
Stephens, Meic 1938- ... 65-68
Stephens, Michael D(awson) 1936- ... CANR-22
Earlier sketches in CA 57-60, CANR-7
Stephens, Otis H(ammond), Jr. 1936- ... 65-68
Stephens, Reed
See Donaldson, Stephen R.
Stephens, Robert O(ren) 1928- ... 25-28R
Stephens, Rockwell R(ittenhouse) 1900- ... 53-56
Stephens, Rosemary 1924- ... 77-80
Stephens, Thomas M. 1931- ... 29-32R
Stephens, W(illiam) P(eter) 1934- ... CANR-12
Earlier sketch in CA 29-32R
Stephens, W(illiam) Richard 1932- ... 29-32R
Stephens, Wade C. 1932- ... 23-24R
Stephens, Will Beth 1918- ... 37-40R
Stephens, William M(cLain) 1925- ... 57-60
See also SATA 21
Stephens, William N(ewton) 1927- ... CANR-1
Earlier sketch in CA 2R
Stephenson, Alan M. G. ?-1984 Obituary ... 113
Stephenson, Andrew M(ichael) 1946- ... 124
Brief entry ... 118
Stephenson, David 1947- ... 118
Stephenson, Gilbert T(homas)
1884-1972 ... CAP-1
Obituary ... 37-40R
Earlier sketch in CA 17-18
Stephenson, Howard 1893-1978 ... 37-40R
Stephenson, Jean 1892-1979 Obituary ... 85-88
Stephenson, John B(ell) 1937- ... 61-64
Stephenson, John Edward Drayton 1928-
Brief entry ... 112
Stephenson, Matthew A(rnold) 1935- ... 45-48
Stephenson, Maureen 1927- ... CANR-16
Earlier sketch in CA 85-88
Stephenson, Neal 1959- ... 122
Stephenson, (William) Ralph (Ewing)
1910- ... 17-18R
Stephenson, Richard M(anning) 1918- ... 109
Stephenson, Wendell Holmes
1899-1970 ... CANR-3
Earlier sketch in CA 3R
Stepka, Milan
See Benes, Jan
Stepp, Ann 1935- ... 106
See also SATA 29
Stepto, Robert B(urns) 1945- ... 101
Steptoe, John (Lewis) 1950- ... CANR-3
Earlier sketch in CA 49-52
See also SATA 8
See also CLR 2, 12
Steptoe, Lydia
See Barnes, Djuna
Sterba, Gunther Hans Wenzel 1922- ... 7-8R
Sterba, Richard F(rancis) 1898- ... 124
Stercho, Peter George 1919- ... 49-52
Sterland, E(rnest) G(eorge) 1919- ... 65-68
Sterling, Anthony
See Caesar, (Eu)Gene (Lee)
Sterling, Brett
See Hamilton, Edmond
and Samachson, Joseph
Sterling, Bruce 1954- ... 119
Sterling, Chandler W(infield) 1911- ... 23-24R
Sterling, Claire 1919(?)- ... 123
Sterling, Donald J(ustus), Jr. 1927- ... 77-80
Sterling, Dorothy 1913- ... CANR-5
Earlier sketch in CA 9-10R
See also SATA 1
See also SAAS 2
See also CLR 1
Sterling, George 1869-1926 Brief entry ... 117
See also DLB 54
See also TCLC 20
Sterling, Helen
See Hoke, Helen L.
Sterling, James 1701-1763 ... DLB-24
Sterling, Maria Sandra
See Floren, Lee
Sterling, Philip 1907- ... 49-52
See also SATA 8
Sterling, Richard W(hitney) 1922- ... 45-48
Sterling, Robert R. 1931- ... 29-32R
Sterling, Sandra
See Floren, Lee
Sterling, Theodor D(avid) 1923- ... 25-28R
Stermer, Bill 1947- ... 110
Stern, Alfred 1899- ... 53-56
Stern, Barbara L.
See Lang, Barbara
Stern, Bill 1907-1971 Obituary ... 89-92
Stern, Boris 1892-1984 ... CAP-2
Obituary ... 113
Earlier sketch in CA 17-18
Stern, Carl 1937- ... 97-100
Stern, Catherine B(rieger) 1894-1973
Obituary ... 37-40R
Stern, Clarence A. 1913- ... 19-20R
Stern, Curt 1902-1981 Obituary ... 105
Stern, Daniel 1928- ... CANR-5
Earlier sketch in CA 5-6R
Stern, Donald A. 1928(?)-1975 Obituary ... 57-60
Stern, E. Mark 1929- ... 37-40R
Stern, Edith Mendel 1901-1975 Obituary ... 57-60
Stern, Edward Severin 1924- ... 53-56

Stern, Elizabeth
See Uhr, Elizabeth
Stern, Ellen Norman 1927- CANR-14
Earlier sketch in CA 37-40R
See also SATA 26
Stern, Frances Meritt 1938- 112
Stern, Frederick Curtis 1929- 108
Stern, Frederick M. 1890(?)-1977
Obituary 69-72
Stern, Fritz 1926- CANR-1
Earlier sketch in CA 2R
Stern, G(ladys) B(ertha) 1890-1973
Obituary 45-48
Stern, George G(ordon) 1923-1974 CAP-2
Earlier sketch in CA 29-32
Stern, Gerald 1925- 81-84
See also CLC 40
Stern, Gerald M(ann) 1937- 69-72
Stern, Geraldine 1907- 101
Stern, Gerd Jacob 1928- Brief entry 106
Stern, Guy 1922- 41-44R
Stern, Harold P. 1922-1977 Obituary 69-72
Stern, Harold S. 1923(?)-1976 Obituary 65-68
Stern, Harry Joshua 1897- 69-72
Stern, Henry L. 1899- 97-100
Stern, J(ulius) David 1886-1971 Obituary 104
Stern, J(oseph) P(eter Maria) 1920- CANR-10
Earlier sketch in CA 23-24R
Stern, James 1904- 23-24R
Stern, Jane 1946- CANR-10
Earlier sketch in CA 61-64
Stern, Jay B(enjamin) 1929- CANR-18
Earlier sketch in CA 25-28R
Stern, Jean Gordon 1904(?)-1985
Obituary 117
Stern, Karl 1906-1975 CANR-12
Obituary 61-64
Earlier sketch in CA 11-12R
Stern, Laurence (Marcus) 1929-1979 85-88
Obituary 89-92
Stern, Louis William 1935- CANR-18
Earlier sketch in CA 25-28R
Stern, Madeleine B(ettina) 1912- CANR-22
Earlier sketches in CA 17-18R, CANR-7
See also SATA 14
Stern, Malcolm H(enry) 1915- 73-76
Stern, Marie 1909- 45-48
Stern, Michael 1910- CAP-2
Earlier sketch in CA 23-24
Stern, Milton R(alph) 1928- CANR-15
Earlier sketch in CA 41-44R
Stern, Nancy B. 1944- 110
Stern, Paula 1945- 102
Stern, Philip M(aurice) 1926- 104
Stern, Philip Van Doren 1900-1984 CANR-6
Obituary 113
Earlier sketch in CA 7-8R
See also SATA 13, 39
Stern, Richard (Gustave) 1928- CANR-1
Earlier sketch in CA 1R
See also CLC 4, 39
Stern, Richard Martin 1915- CANR-18
Earlier sketches in CA 3R, CANR-2
Stern, Robert A. M. 1939- 29-32R
Stern, Robert M. 1927- CANR-10
Earlier sketch in CA 23-24R
Stern, Rudi 1936- Brief entry 115
Stern, S. M.
See Stern, Samuel Miklos
Stern, Samuel Miklos 1920-1969 Obituary 111
Stern, Simon 1943- 89-92
See also SATA 15
Stern, Stewart 1922- Brief entry 113
See also DLB 26
Stern, Stuart
See Rae, Hugh C(rauford)
Stern, Susan (Tanenbaum) 1943-1976
Obituary 65-68
Stern, William B(ernhard) 1910-1972 CAP-1
Earlier sketch in CA 15-16
Stern, Zelda 1949- 116
Sternberg, Cecilia 1908-1983 73-76
Obituary 111
Sternberg, Jacques 1923- Brief entry 111
Sternberg, Josef von 1894-1969 81-84
See also CLC 20
Sternberg, Martin L(eo) A(ltar) 1925- 107
Sternberg, Patricia 1930- 118
Sternberg, Robert J(effrey) 1949-
Brief entry 119
Sternberg, Vernon (Arthur) 1915-1979
Obituary 104
Sternberger, Dolf 1907- 104
Sterne, Emma Gelders 1894- CANR-5
Earlier sketch in CA 7-8R
See also SATA 6
Sterne, Laurence 1713-1768 DLB-39
Sterne, Richard S(tephen) 1921- 15-16R
Sterner, Lewis George 1894- 7-8R
Sterner, R. Eugene 1912- CANR-3
Earlier sketch in CA 11-12R
Sternfeld, Robert 1917- 81-84
Sternfield, Allen 1930- 53-56
Sternheim, (William Adolf) Carl
1878-1942 Brief entry 105
See also DLB 56
See also TCLC 8
Sternlicht, Sanford 1931- CANR-10
Earlier sketch in CA 25-28R
Sternlieb, George 1928- CANR-8
Earlier sketch in CA 23-24R
Sternsher, Bernard 1925- 11-12R
Sterry, Rick 1938- 25-28R
Stertz, Eda 1921- 104
Stessin, Lawrence 1911- 9-10R
Stetler, Charles E(dward) 1927- 65-68
Stetler, Russell (Dearnley, Jr.) 1945- 41-44R
Stetson, Damon 1915- 85-88
Stetson, Erlene 108
Stettler, Howard Frederic 1919- 5-6R
Stettner, Irving 1922- CANR-16
Earlier sketch in CA 77-80
Steurt, Marjorie Rankin 1888- 15-16R
See also SATA 10
Steven, Hugh 1931- CANR-14
Earlier sketch in CA 41-44R
Stevens, Anita 1911- Brief entry 110
Stevens, Anthony (George) 1933- 110
Stevens, Ardis 1921- 45-48
Stevens, Art 1935- 124
Stevens, (John) Austin 53-56
Stevens, Austin N(eil) 1930- 104
Stevens, Bernice A. 37-40R
Stevens, Blaine
See Whittington, Harry (Benjamin)
Stevens, Bryna
See Donaldson, Bryna Stevens
Stevens, Carl
See Obstfeld, Raymond
Stevens, Carla M(cBride) 1928- CANR-12
Earlier sketch in CA 69-72
See also SATA 13
Stevens, Cat
See Georgiou, Steven Demetre
Stevens, Christopher 1948- 119
Stevens, Christopher
See Tabori, Paul
Stevens, Clifford 1926- CANR-6
Earlier sketch in CA 11-12R
Stevens, Clysle
See Wade, John Stevens
Stevens, Dan J.
See Overholser, Wayne D.
Stevens, David Harrison 1884-1980 77-80
Obituary 93-96
Stevens, Denis William 1922- CANR-3
Earlier sketch in CA 9-10R
Stevens, Diane 1944- 65-68
Stevens, E. S.
See Drower, E(thel) S(tefana May)
Stevens, Edmund William 1910- 109
Stevens, Edward 1928- CANR-11
Earlier sketch in CA 29-32R
Stevens, Edwin L(ockwood) 1913-1987 23-24R
Obituary 122
Stevens, Eleanour V(irginia) 1926- 29-32R
Stevens, Elisabeth (Goss) 1929- 110
Stevens, Fae Hewston
See Stevens, Frances Isted
Stevens, Frances Isted 1907- CAP-1
Earlier sketch in CA 9-10
Stevens, Franklin 1933- 29-32R
See also SATA 6
Stevens, George 1904(?)-1985 Obituary 116
Stevens, George (Cooper), Jr. 1932-
Brief entry 118
Stevens, George Putnam 1918- 45-48
Stevens, Georgiana G(erlinger) 1904- CAP-1
Earlier sketch in CA 17-18
Stevens, Gerald 1909- 7-8R
Stevens, Graeme R(oy) 1932- 118
Stevens, Gwendolyn 1944- 104
See also SATA 33
Stevens, Halsey 1908- 25-28R
Stevens, Harold 1917- 89-92
Stevens, Harvey A(lonzo) 1913- 89-92
Stevens, Holly 1924- 25-28R
Stevens, J. D.
See Rowland, D(onald) S(ydney)
Stevens, James (Richard) 1940- CANR-16
Earlier sketch in CA 93-96
Stevens, James F. 1892-1971 Obituary 33-36R
Stevens, Jane Greengold 1945- 108
Stevens, Joan 1908- CANR-2
Earlier sketch in CA 7-8R
Stevens, John
See Tubb, E(dwin) C(harles)
Stevens, Joseph C(harles) 1929- 17-18R
Stevens, Kathleen 1936- 116
See also SATA 49
Stevens, L(ewell) Robert 1932- 111
Stevens, Lauren R(ogers) 1938- 5-6R
Stevens, Leonard A. 1920- CANR-12
Earlier sketch in CA 19-20R
Stevens, Lucile Vernon 1899- 61-64
Stevens, Mark 19(?)- CLC-34
Stevens, Mark 1951- 122
Stevens, Martin 1927- 13-14R
Stevens, Michael 1919- 53-56
Stevens, Norma Young 1927- 21-22R
Stevens, Pam
See Gilbert, George
Stevens, Patricia Bunning 1931- 53-56
See also SATA 27
Stevens, Paul 1946- 123
Stevens, Peter 1927- 93-96
Stevens, Peter
See Geis, Darlene Stern
Stevens, Peter S(mith) 1936- 53-56
Stevens, R(obert) B(ocking) 1933- CANR-9
Earlier sketch in CA 21-22R
Stevens, R. L.
See Hoch, Edward D(entinger)
Stevens, Richard P. 1931- CANR-10
Earlier sketch in CA 21-22R
Stevens, Robert D(avid) 1921- 112
Stevens, Robert Tyler
See Staples, Reginald Thomas
Stevens, Robert Warren 1918-1987 CANR-1
Obituary 122
Earlier sketch in CA 45-48
Stevens, Roger (Bentham) 1906-1980
Obituary 105
Stevens, Rolland E(lwell) 1915- 81-84
Stevens, Rosemary (Anne) 1935- 85-88
Stevens, S. P.
See Palestrant, Simon S.
Stevens, S(tanley) S(mith) 1906-1973
Obituary 116
Stevens, Serita (Deborah) 1949- 119
Stevens, Shane 1941- 21-22R
Stevens, Sharon 1949- 77-80
Stevens, Sylvester K(irby) 1904-1974 CAP-1
Obituary 45-48
Earlier sketch in CA 15-16
Stevens, Tricia
See Pearl, Jacques Bain
Stevens, Trisha
See Pearl, Jacques Bain
Stevens, Wallace 1879-1955 124
Brief entry 104
See also DLB 54
See also TCLC 3, 12
Stevens, William 1925- 21-22R
Stevens, William W(ilson) 1914- 37-40R
Stevens-Arroyo, Antonio M. 1941- 120
Stevenson, Adlai E(wing) 1900-1965 CAP-1
Earlier sketch in CA 15-16
Stevenson, Anna (M.) 1905- SATA-12
Stevenson, Anne (Katharine) 1933- CANR-9
Earlier sketch in CA 17-18R
See also DLB 40
See also CLC 7, 33
Stevenson, Augusta 1869(?)-1976 2R
Obituary 65-68
See also SATA 2, 26
Stevenson, (William) Bruce 1906- 49-52
Stevenson, Burton Egbert 1872-1962 102
Obituary 89-92
See also SATA 25
Stevenson, Carol Dornfeld 1931- 7-8R
Stevenson, Charles 1908(?)-1979
Obituary 85-88
Stevenson, Christopher Sinclair
See Sinclair-Stevenson, Christopher
Stevenson, David 1942- 109
Stevenson, David Lloyd 1910-1975 CAP-2
Obituary 57-60
Earlier sketch in CA 23-24
Stevenson, Dorothy E(mily) 1892-1973 CAP-1
Obituary 49-52
Earlier sketch in CA 15-16
Stevenson, Dwight E(shelman) 1906- CANR-1
Earlier sketch in CA 2R
Stevenson, Elizabeth 1919- 1R
Stevenson, Florence CANR-16
Earlier sketch in CA 97-100
Stevenson, George J(ames) 1924- 9-10R
Stevenson, Gloria 1945- 61-64
Stevenson, Grace Thomas 1900- 37-40R
Stevenson, Harold W(illiam) 1921- 25-28R
Stevenson, Henry M(iller) 1914- 77-80
Stevenson, Herbert Frederick 1906- CANR-2
Earlier sketch in CA 7-8R
Stevenson, Hugh A(lexander) 1935- 112
Stevenson, Ian (Pretyman) 1918-
Brief entry 115
Stevenson, Ian Ralph 1943- 102
Stevenson, J. P.
See Haldane-Stevenson, James Patrick
Stevenson, James 1929- 115
See also SATA 34, 42
Stevenson, James Patrick
See Haldane-Stevenson, James Patrick
Stevenson, Janet 1913- 13-14R
See also SATA 8
Stevenson, John Albert 1890(?)-1979
Obituary 89-92
Stevenson, John P.
See Grierson, Edward
Stevenson, L(eland) W(ells) 1916- 107
Stevenson, Laura Caroline 1946- 120
Stevenson, Leslie (Forster) 1943- 65-68
Stevenson, (Arthur) Lionel 1902-1973 103
Obituary 45-48
Stevenson, Michael Ian 1953- 103
Stevenson, Richard
See Lipez, Richard
Stevenson, Robert 1905-1986 Obituary 120
Stevenson, Robert (Murrell) 1916- CANR-1
Earlier sketch in CA 3R
Stevenson, Robert Louis (Balfour)
1850-1894 YABC-2
See also DLB 18, 57
See also CLR 10, 11
Stevenson, Suzanne Silvercruys
1898(?)-1973 Obituary 41-44R
Stevenson, T(homas) H(ulbert) 1919- 61-64
Stevenson, Tom 1899(?)-1982 Obituary 106
Stevenson, Vera Kemp 1920- 57-60
Stevenson, Victoria F. 1878(?)-1973
Obituary 41-44R
Stevenson, W(illiam) Taylor 1928- CANR-18
Earlier sketch in CA 25-28R
Stevenson, (Stanley) Warren 1933- 41-44R
Stevenson, William 1925- 13-14R
Steward, F(rederick) C(ampion) 1904- 41-44R
Steward, Hal D(avid) 1922- 69-72
Steward, Julian H. 1902-1972 Obituary 33-36R
Steward, Samuel M(orris) 1909- 112
Stewart, A(gnes) C(harlotte) 77-80
See also SATA 15
Stewart, A(nthony) T(erence) Q(uincey)
1929- 25-28R
Stewart, (John) Allan 1939- 4R
Stewart, Allegra 1899- 45-48
Stewart, Angus (J. M.) 1936- 106
Stewart, Bertie Ann Gardner 1912- 5-6R
Stewart, Bill 1942(?)-1979 Obituary 89-92
Stewart, Charles
See Zurhorst, Charles (Stewart, Jr.)
Stewart, Charles J(oseph) 1936- 41-44R
Stewart, Charles T(odd), Jr. 1922- 101
Stewart, Christina Duff 1926- 65-68
Stewart, Cochrane
See Stewart, Kenneth
Stewart, D(avid) H(ugh) 1926- 21-22R
Stewart, Daniel K(enneth) 1925- 29-32R
Stewart, David
See Politella, Dario
Stewart, Desmond (Stirling) 1924-1981 37-40R
Obituary 104
Stewart, Donald Charles 1930- 37-40R
Stewart, Donald H(enderson) 1911- 29-32R
Stewart, Donald Ogden 1894-1980 81-84
Obituary 101
See also DLB 4, 11, 26
Stewart, Dorothy Mary 1917-1965
Obituary 104
Stewart, Douglas (Alexander) 1913- 81-84
Stewart, Edgar I(rving) 1900- 7-8R
Stewart, Edith Hamilton 1883- CAP-1
Earlier sketch in CA 11-12
Stewart, Elbert Wilton 1916- 37-40R
Stewart, Eleanor
See Porter, Eleanor H(odgman)
Stewart, Elizabeth Grey
See Reed, Elizabeth Stewart
Stewart, Elizabeth Laing 1907- 49-52
See also SATA 6
Stewart, Ella Winter 1898-1980 Obituary 101
Stewart, Eve
See Napier, Priscilla
Stewart, Frank 1946- CANR-20
Earlier sketch in CA 104
Stewart, Fred Mustard 1936- 37-40R
Stewart, Garrett (Fitzgerald) 1945- 93-96
Stewart, George 1892-1972 Obituary 33-36R
Stewart, George Rippey 1895-1980 CANR-3
Obituary 101
Earlier sketch in CA 1R
See also SATA 3, 23
See also DLB 8
Stewart, Hal D(ouglas) 1899- CAP-1
Earlier sketch in CA 15-16
Stewart, Harold C. 1891(?)-1976
Obituary 69-72
Stewart, Harold Frederick 1916- 69-72
Stewart, Harris B(ates) Jr. 1922- 45-48
Stewart, Hilary 1924- CANR-16
Earlier sketch in CA 93-96
Stewart, Horace Floyd, Jr. 1928- 49-52
Stewart, J(ohn) I(nnes) M(ackintosh)
1906- 85-88
See also CAAS 3
See also CLC 7, 14, 32
Stewart, James Alexander 1948- 113
Stewart, James Brewer 1940- 29-32R
Stewart, James S(tuart) 1896- 9-10R
Stewart, Jean
See Newman, Mona Alice Jean
Stewart, Jim
See Stewart, James Alexander
Stewart, John 1904(?)-1985 Obituary 116
Stewart, John (William) 1920- 33-36R
See also SATA 14
Stewart, John 1933- CANR-16
Earlier sketch in CA 97-100
Stewart, John 1941- 97-100
Stewart, John B(enjamin) 1924- 9-10R
Stewart, John G(ilman) 1935- Brief entry 112
Stewart, Judith Anne
See Maciel, Jud(ith Anne)
Stewart, K(athleen) Alison Clarke
See Clarke-Stewart, K(athleen) Alison
Stewart, Katharine Jeanne (Dark) 1914- 9-10R
Stewart, Kaye
See Howe, Doris Kathleen
Stewart, Kenneth 1918-1985 Obituary 118
Stewart, Kenneth N. 1901-1978 Obituary 77-80
Stewart, Kerry
See Stewart, Linda
Stewart, Lawrence D(elbert) 1926- 89-92
Stewart, Lawrence H(oyle) 1922- 17-18R
Stewart, Linda 101
Stewart, Margaret 1912- CANR-18
Earlier sketch in CA 25-28R
Stewart, Marie M(cCaffery) 1899- 7-8R
Stewart, Mark Armstrong 1929- 89-92
Stewart, Mary (Florence Elinor) 1916- CANR-1
Earlier sketch in CA 2R
See also SATA 12
See also CLC 7, 35
Stewart, Mary Rainbow
See Stewart, Mary (Florence Elinor)
Stewart, (Robert) Michael (Maitland)
1906- CANR-22
Earlier sketch in CA 106
Stewart, Michael 1924(?)-1987 Obituary 123
Stewart, Michael 1933- 116
Stewart, Natacha
See Ullman, Natacha
Stewart, Oliver 1895-1980 CANR-5
Earlier sketch in CA 7-8R
Stewart, Pat(ricia) 1944- 97-100
Stewart, Paul D(ekker) 1918- 1R
Stewart, Philip Robert 1940- 29-32R
Stewart, Phyllis Langton 1933- Brief entry 106
Stewart, Ramona 1922- CANR-6
Earlier sketch in CA 1R
Stewart, Randall 1896-1964 CANR-1
Earlier sketch in CA 1R
Stewart, Rex William 1907-1967 Obituary 110
Stewart, Rhea Talley 1915- 41-44R
Stewart, Robert G(ordon) 1931- 65-68
Stewart, Robert Neil 1891- 11-12R
See also SATA 7

Stewart, Robert T. 1920(?)-1977
Obituary 73-76
Stewart, Robert Wilson 1935- 49-52
Stewart, Rosemary (Gordon) CANR-15
Earlier sketch in CA 37-40R
Stewart, Sam
See Stewart, Linda
Stewart, Scott
See Zaffo, George J.
Stewart, Seumas 1919- 61-64
Stewart, Shelia 1928- 21-22R
Stewart, Stanley N(ordahl) 1931- 17-18R
Stewart, Suzanne 61-64
Stewart, Vincent (Astor, Jr.) 1939- 29-32R
Stewart, W(illiam) A(lexander) Campbell
1915- 13-14R
Stewart, Walter Bingham 1913- CANR-16
Earlier sketch in CA 85-88
Stewart, Will
See Williamson, John Stewart
Stewart, William Stanley 1938- 89-92
Stewart, Wynn 1934-1985 Obituary 116
Stewart, Zeph 1921- 41-44R
Stewig, John Warren 1937- CANR-14
Earlier sketch in CA 81-84
See also SATA 26
Steyaert, Thomas A(dolph) 1930- 37-40R
Steyer, Wesley W. 1923- 29-32R
Steyermark, Julian A(lfred) 1909- CANR-17
Earlier sketches in CA 13-14, CAP-1
Stibbs, Alan M(arshall) 1901- CANR-2
Earlier sketch in CA 4R
Stich, Stephen P(eter) 1943- 41-44R
Stick, David 1919- CANR-17
Earlier sketch in CA 97-100
Stickells, Austin T. 1914- 41-44R
Stickgold, Bob 1945- 104
Stickney, Trumbull 1874-1904 DLB-54
Stieber, Jack 1919- CANR-6
Earlier sketch in CA 2R
Stiehm, Judith 1935- 61-64
Stierlin, Helm 1926- 29-32R
Stierwell, Jay
See Swicegood, Thomas L. P.
Stiffel, Frank 1916- 117
Stigger, Judith A. 1949- 111
Stigler, George Joseph 1911- 41-44R
Stigum, Marcia (Lee) 1934- CANR-8
Earlier sketch in CA 61-64
Stigwood, Robert C. 1934- 102
Stiles, Ezra 1727-1795 DLB-31
Stiles, John R. 1916(?)-1976 Obituary 65-68
Stiles, Joseph 1903- CAP-2
Earlier sketch in CA 17-18
Stiles, Lindley Joseph 1913- CANR-3
Earlier sketch in CA 7-8R
Stiles, Martha Bennett 37-40R
See also SATA 6
Stiles, Merritt N. 1899-1975 Obituary 57-60
Stiles, Ned B. 1932- 17-18R
Stiles, Norman B. 1942- 114
See also SATA 36
Stilgoe, John R. 109
Still, C. Henry 1920- 11-12R
Still, James 1906- CANR-10
Earlier sketch in CA 65-68
See also SATA 29
See also DLB 9
Still, Richard R(alph) 1921- CANR-1
Earlier sketch in CA 1R
Still, William N(orwood), Jr. 1932- CANR-18
Earlier sketch in CA 25-28R
Stiller, Brian C(arl) 1942- 117
Stillerman, Robbie 1947- SATA-12
Stilley, Frank 1918- 61-64
See also SATA 29
Stillinger, Jack 1931- CANR-1
Earlier sketch in CA 1R
Stillman, Damie 1933- 45-48
Stillman, Edmund O. 1924-1983 Obituary 111
Stillman, Frances (Jennings) 1910-1975 CAP-1
Obituary 57-60
Earlier sketch in CA 15-16
Stillman, Irwin M(axwell) 1895-1975 49-52
Obituary 61-64
Stillman, Myra Stephens 1915- CANR-6
Earlier sketch in CA 5-6R
Stillman, Nathan 1914- 5-6R
Stillman, Richard J. 1917- CANR-14
Earlier sketch in CA 37-40R
Stillwell, Margaret Bingham 1887-1984 41-44R
Obituary 112
Stillwell, Norma Jamieson 1894- CAP-1
Earlier sketch in CA 15-16
Stillwell, Richard 1899-1982 Obituary 111
Stilson, Max 1919- 11-12R
Stilwell, William E(arle) III 1936- 107
Stimmel, Barry 1939- CANR-11
Earlier sketch in CA 69-72
Stimpson, Catherine R(oslyn) 1936- 41-44R
Stimson, William 1946- 122
Stinchcombe, Arthur L. 1933- CANR-23
Earlier sketches in CA 15-16R, CANR-8
Stinchcombe, William 1937- 105
Stine, G(eorge) Harry 1928- CANR-9
Earlier sketch in CA 65-68
See also SATA 10
Stine, Jovial Bob
See Stine, R(obert) L(awrence)
Stine, R(obert) L(awrence) 1943- CANR-22
Earlier sketch in CA 105
See also SATA 31
Stine, Whitney Ward 1930- CANR-7
Earlier sketch in CA 57-60
See also AITN 1
Stineman, Esther F. 1947- CANR-17
Earlier sketch in CA 97-100
Stinetorf, Louise (Allender) 1900- 11-12R
See also SATA 10
Sting
See Sumner, Gordon Matthew
Stinger, Charles L(ewis) 1944- 77-80
Stini, William A(rthur) 1930- Brief entry 107
Stinnett, Caskie 1911- 7-8R
Stinnett, Nick 1942- 110
Stinnett, Ronald F. 1929- 23-24R
Stinnett, Tim Moore 1901-1985 CANR-13
Obituary 115
Earlier sketch in CA 17-18R
Stinnette, Charles R(oy), Jr. 1914- 77-80
Stinson, James Emerson, Jr. 1937- 119
Stinson, Jim
See Stinson, James Emerson, Jr.
Stinson, Kathy 1952- 113
Stinson, Robert William 1941- 111
Stinton, T(homas) C(harles) W(arren)
1925-1985 Obituary 117
Stipe, Robert Edwin 1928- 49-52
Stirling, Alfred (Thorpe) 1902-1981 110
Obituary 108
Stirling, Anna Maria Diana Wilhelmina
(Pickering) 1865-1965 CAP-1
Earlier sketch in CA 9-10
Stirling, Arthur
See Sinclair, Upton (Beall)
Stirling, Betty Rutledge 1923- 9-10R
Stirling, (Thomas) Brents 1904- CAP-2
Earlier sketch in CA 25-28
Stirling, Jessica
See Coghlan, Margaret M.
Stirling, Lilla (May Elderkin) 1902- 107
Stirling, Matthew Williams 1896-1975
Obituary 53-56
Stirling, Monica 1916-1983 81-84
Obituary 111
Stirling, Nora B(romley) 1900- CANR-3
Earlier sketch in CA 7-8R
See also SATA 3
Stirnweis, Shannon 1931- SATA-10
Stitelman, Leonard (Arnold) 1932- 41-44R
Stites, Francis N(oel) 1938- 41-44R
Stites, Raymond S(omers) 1899-1974 65-68
Obituary 53-56
Stith, John E(dward) 1947- 117
Stith, William 1707-1755 DLB-31
Stitskin, Leon D. 1910-1978 CANR-1
Earlier sketch in CA 3R
Stitt, Milan 1941- 69-72
See also CLC 29
Stitt, Peter 1940- 123
Stitzel, Thomas E(dward) 1936- 93-96
Stivens, Dal(las George) 1911- CANR-14
Earlier sketch in CA 69-72
Stiver, Mary Weeden 1909- CAP-1
Earlier sketch in CA 13-14
Stivers, Robert L(loyd) 1940- 69-72
Stjernberg, Lloyd A(rmand) 1937- 25-28R
Stoan, Stephen K(uzman) 1942- 111
Stob, Ralph 1894-1965 1R
Obituary 103
Stobart, Thomas Ralph 1914- 13-14R
Stobaugh, Robert B. (Jr.) 1927- 101
Stobbs, John L(ouis) N(ewcombe)
1921- 15-16R
Stobbs, William 1914- 81-84
See also SATA 17
Stock, Barbara R(uth) 1942- CANR-19
Earlier sketch in CA 112
Stock, Brian 1939- 41-44R
Stock, Catherine 1952- 119
Stock, Claudette 1934- 65-68
Stock, Ernest 1924- 23-24R
Stock, Guy 1933- 124
Stock, Irvin 1920- 25-28R
Stock, Phyllis H(artman) 1930- 85-88
Stock, R(obert) D(ouglas) 1941- CANR-14
Earlier sketch in CA 41-44R
Stockanes, Anthony E(dward) 1935- 109
Stockard, James Wright, Jr. 1935- 15-16R
Stockard, Jimmy
See Stockard, James Wright, Jr.
Stockdale, Eric 1929- 25-28R
Stocker, Margarita 1955- 121
Stockhammer, Morris 1904- 13-14R
Stocking, David M(ackenzie) 1919- 25-28R
Stocking, George W(ard), Jr. 1928- 73-76
Stocking, George Ward 1892-1975
Obituary 61-64
Stocking, Hobart E(bey) 1906- 101
Stocking, Marion Kingston 1922- 25-28R
Stocking, S(usan) Holly 1945- 117
Stockman, David A(llen) 1946- 123
Stocks, Mary (Danvers Brinton)
1891-1975 13-14R
Obituary 118
Stockton, Adrian James 1935- 29-32R
Stockton, Francis Richard 1834-1902
Brief entry 108
See also SATA 44
Stockton, Frank R.
See Stockton, Francis Richard
See also SATA 32
See also DLB 42
Stockton, J. Roy 1893(?)-1972
Obituary 37-40R
Stockton, Jim
See Stockton, Adrian James
Stockton, John R(obert) 1903- 13-14R
Stockton, Ronald R. 1940- 118
Stockwell, Edward G(rant) 1933- 23-24R
Stockwell, John R(obert) 1937- 104
Stockwell, Robert P(aul) 1925- 17-18R
Stockwin, (James) Arthur (Ainscow)
1935- 103
Stockwood, (Arthur) Mervyn 1913-
Brief entry 117
Stoddard, Charles
See Kuttner, Henry
Stoddard, Edward G. 1923- 11-12R
See also SATA 10
Stoddard, Ellwyn R(eed) 1927- CANR-17
Earlier sketches in CA 45-48, CANR-1
Stoddard, George Dinsmore 1897-1981
Obituary 106
Stoddard, Hope 1900- 49-52
See also SATA 6
Stoddard, Richard 1942- 102
Stoddard, Richard Henry 1825-1903
Brief entry 114
See also DLB 3, 64
Stoddard, Sandol 1927- CANR-8
Earlier sketch in CA 7-8R
Stoddard, Solomon 1643-1729 DLB-24
Stoddard, Tom 1933- 37-40R
Stoddard, Whitney Snow 1913- 109
Stoddart, Jack Elliott 1916-1988 Obituary 124
Stodelle, Ernestine 1912- 117
Stoehr, C(arl) Eric 1945- 65-68
Stoessinger, John G. 1927- CANR-9
Earlier sketch in CA 13-14R
Stoetzer, O(tto) Carlos 1921- 109
Stoff, Sheldon (Ptaschevitch) 1930- 23-24R
Stoffel, Albert Law 1909- 65-68
Stoffel, Betty W. 1922- 19-20R
Stoffel, Ernest Lee 1923- 114
Stoffel, Lester L(enneth, Jr.) 1920- 45-48
Stoffle, Carla J(oy) 1943- CANR-7
Earlier sketch in CA 61-64
Stogdill, Ralph M(elvin) 1904- CANR-1
Earlier sketch in CA 1R
Stohl, Michael (Steven) 1947- 107
Stohlman, Martha Lou Lemmon 1913- 65-68
Stoianovich, Trajan 1921- 21-22R
Stoiber, Rudolph M(aria) 1925- 1R
Stoiko, Michael 1919- 11-12R
See also SATA 14
Stoil, Michael Jon 1950- 53-56
Stojanovic, Svetozar 1931- Brief entry 112
Stokely, James R(orex), Jr. 1913-1977 9-10R
Obituary 69-72
Stoker, Abraham 1847-1912 Brief entry 105
See also SATA 29
Stoker, Alan 1930- CANR-24
Earlier sketches in CA 23-24R, CANR-9
Stoker, Bram
See Stoker, Abraham
See also DLB 36
See also TCLC 8
Stoker, H(oward) Stephen 1939- CANR-8
Earlier sketch in CA 61-64
Stokes, Adrian Durham 1902-1972 CANR-5
Obituary 89-92
Earlier sketch in CA 13-14R
Stokes, Bob
See Wilkening, Howard (Everett)
Stokes, Carl B(urton) 1927- 69-72
Stokes, Cedric
See Beardmore, George
Stokes, Charles (Herbert) 1932- 103
Stokes, Charles J(unius) 1922- CANR-10
Earlier sketch in CA 25-28R
Stokes, Daniel M. J. 1950- 57-60
Stokes, Donald (Hubert) 1913-1986
Obituary 119
Stokes, Donald Elkinton 1927- CANR-1
Earlier sketch in CA 1R
Stokes, Doris 1919-1987 Obituary 122
Brief entry 115
Stokes, Eric (Thomas) 1924-1981 107
Obituary 103
Stokes, Geoffrey 1940- 69-72
Stokes, Henry J.M. Scott
See Scott-Stokes, Henry J.M.
Stokes, Jack (Tilden) 1923- 29-32R
See also SATA 13
Stokes, Olivia Pearl 1916- 37-40R
See also SATA 32
Stokes, Peg (Lee Ewing) 3R
Stokes, Robert
See Wilkening, Howard (Everett)
Stokes, Roy 1915- 19-20R
Stokes, Simpson
See Fawcett, F(rank) Dubrez
Stokes, Thomas L. 1898-1958 DLB-29
Stokes, William Lee 1915- CANR-20
Earlier sketch in CA 41-44R
Stokesbury, James L(awton) 1934- CANR-17
Earlier sketch in CA 93-96
Stokesbury, Leon 1945- CANR-21
Earlier sketch in CA 69-72
Stokke, Baard Richard 1937- 25-28R
Stokoe, William C(larence), Jr. 1919- 41-44R
Stokstad, Marilyn 1929- CANR-15
Earlier sketch in CA 37-40R
Stoler, Ann Laura 1949- 119
Stoler, Peter (Robert) 1935- 97-100
Stoll, Clarice Stasz
See Stasz, Clarice
Stoll, Dennis G(ray) 1912-1987 13-14R
Obituary 124
Stoll, John E(dward) 1933- 49-52
Stoller, Robert J(esse) 1924- Brief entry 117
Stollnitz, Fred 1939- 45-48
Stoloff, Carolyn 1927- CANR-9
Earlier sketch in CA 65-68
Stolorow, Robert D(avid) 1942- 102
Stolper, Wolfgang F(riedrich) 1912- 23-24R
Stolten, Jane (Henry) 97-100
Stoltenberg, Donald Hugo 1927- 89-92
Stoltzfus, Ben Franklin 1927- 103
Stolz, Lois Meek 1891- CAP-2
Earlier sketch in CA 21-22
Stolz, Mary (Slattery) 1920- CANR-13
Earlier sketch in CA 5-6R
See also SATA 10
See also SAAS 3
See also CLC 12
See also AITN 1
Stolzenbach, Norma Frizzell 1904- 41-44R
Stolzenberg, Mark 1950- 102
Stonberg, Selma F(ranks) 69-72
Stone, Alan CAP-2
Earlier sketch in CA 19-20
See also SATA 1
Stone, Alan A(braham) 1929- 17-18R
Stone, Albert E(dward) 1924- CANR-8
Earlier sketch in CA 19-20R
Stone, Albert E., Jr.
See Stone, Albert E(dward)
Stone, Alfred R. 1926- 17-18R
Stone, Alma 1908- 77-80
Stone, Barbara Haskins 1924(?)-1979
Obituary 89-92
Stone, Betty E. 1926- 9-10R
Stone, Brian 1919- 15-16R
Stone, Charles Sumner, Jr. 1924- 77-80
Stone, Christopher D(avid) 1937- 53-56
Stone, Chuck
See Stone, Charles Sumner, Jr.
Stone, Clarence N. 1935- 112
Stone, Clifford A. 1951-1986 Obituary 118
Stone, David (Anthony) 1929- 5-6R
Stone, David K(arl) 1922- 85-88
See also SATA 9
Stone, David U. 1927- CANR-7
Earlier sketch in CA 19-20R
Stone, Deborah
See Navas, Deborah
Stone, Donald D(avid) 1942- 81-84
Stone, Donald (Adelbert), Jr. 1937- 29-32R
Stone, Doris (Zemurray) 1909- 105
Stone, Doris (Mary) 1918- 117
Stone, Edward 1913- 37-40R
Stone, Elaine Murray 1922- CANR-17
Earlier sketch in CA 89-92
Stone, Elizabeth W(enger) 1918- 107
Stone, Ellery W(heeler) 1894-1981
Obituary 105
Stone, Elna CANR-5
Earlier sketch in CA 15-16R
Stone, Eugenia 1879-1971 9-10R
See also SATA 7
Stone, Frank A(ndrews) 1929- CANR-8
Earlier sketch in CA 61-64
Stone, Gene
See Stone, Eugenia
Stone, George Winchester, Jr. 1907- CANR-6
Earlier sketch in CA 7-8R
Stone, Gerald (Charles) 1932- 104
Stone, Grace Zaring 1891- CAP-2
Earlier sketch in CA 25-28
Stone, Gregory P(rentice) 1921-1981 CANR-1
Obituary 116
Earlier sketch in CA 49-52
Stone, Hampton
See Stein, Aaron Marc
Stone, Harris B. 1934- 57-60
Stone, Harry 1928- 13-14R
Stone, Helen V(irginia) 25-28R
See also SATA 6
Stone, Howard W. 1942- 124
Stone, Hoyt E(dward) 1935- 101
Stone, I(sidor) F(einstein) 1907- 61-64
Stone, Idella Purnell
See Purnell, Idella
Stone, Ikey
See Purnell, Idella
Stone, Irving 1903- CANR-23
Earlier sketches in CA 1R, CANR-1
See also CAAS 3
See also SATA 3
See also CLC 7
See also AITN 1
Stone, James Champion 1916- 17-18R
Stone, James H(erbert) 1918- 41-44R
Stone, Jerry 1942(?)-1987 Obituary 124
Stone, Joan 1930- CANR-13
Earlier sketch in CA 77-80
Stone, John (Timothy, Jr.) 1933- 102
Stone, John H(enry) 1936- 89-92
Stone, Jon 1931- 107
See also SATA 39
Stone, Josephine Rector
See Dixon, Jeanne
Stone, Julius 1907-1985 CANR-5
Obituary 117
Earlier sketch in CA 53-56
Stone, Justin (Federman) 1916- 116
Stone, L(awrence) Joseph 1912-1975
Obituary 61-64
Stone, Lawrence 1919- 15-16R
Stone, Louis 1910(?)-1985 Obituary 115
Stone, Marvin Lawrence 1924- 69-72
Stone, Melville 1848-1929 DLB-25
Stone, Merlin 1931- CANR-17
Earlier sketch in CA 101
Stone, Mildred Fairbanks 1902- CAP-1
Earlier sketch in CA 11-12
Stone, Nancy (Young) 1925- 49-52
Stone, Natalie
See Goldenbaum, Sally
Staff, Adrienneand Stone, Oliver 1946- 110
Stone, Patti 1926- 5-6R
Stone, Peter 1930- CANR-7
Earlier sketch in CA 11-12R
Stone, Philip James III 1936- 23-24R
Stone, Ralph A. 1934- 37-40R

Stone, Raymond ... CAP-2
Earlier sketch in CA 19-20
See also SATA 1
Stone, Reynolds 1909-1979 Obituary ... 89-92
Stone, Richard
See Delaney, Jack J(ames)
Stone, Richard A.
See Stratemeyer, Edward L.
Stone, Robert (Anthony) 1937- ... CANR-23
Earlier sketch in CA 85-88
See also CLC 5, 23, 42
Stone, Robert B. 1916- ... 29-32R
Stone, Roger D. 1934- ... 119
Stone, Ronald H. 1939- ... CANR-16
Earlier sketch in CA 77-80
Stone, Rosetta
See Geisel, Theodor Seuss
Stone, Rufus
See Cowie, Donald
Stone, Ruth 1915- ... CANR-2
Earlier sketch in CA 45-48
Stone, Samuel 1602-1663 ... DLB-24
Stone, Scott C(linton) S(tuart) 1932- ... CANR-18
Earlier sketch in CA 25-28R
Stone, Shelley C(lyde, Jr.) 1928- ... 61-64
Stone, Susan Berch 1944- ... 61-64
Stone, Thomas H.
See Harknett, Terry
Stone, Vernon A(lfred) 1929- ... 65-68
Stone, Wilfred (Healey) 1917- ... 21-22R
Stone, William F(rank) 1931- ... 41-44R
Stone, William Sidney 1928- ... 13-14R
Stone, Zachary
See Follett, Ken(neth Martin)
Stoneburner, (Charles Joseph) Tony 1926- ... 41-44R
Stonehouse, Bernard 1926- ... CANR-19
Earlier sketches in CA 49-52, CANR-2
See also SATA 13
Stonehouse, John (Thomson) 1925- ... 112
Stonehouse, Merlin 1911- ... 15-16R
Stoneman, Elvyn Arthur 1919- ... 17-18R
Stoneman, Paul 1947- ... 115
Stoneman, William H(arlan) 1904-1987 Obituary ... 122
Stonequist, Everett Verner 1901-1979 Obituary ... 85-88
Stoner, Carol Hupping 1949- ... 53-56
Stones, E(dgar) 1922- ... CANR-15
Earlier sketch in CA 37-40R
Stones, E(dward) L(ionel) G(regory) 1914-1987 Obituary ... 121
Stonesifer, Richard James 1922- ... 15-16R
Stong, Clair L. 1902(?)-1975 Obituary ... 61-64
Stong, Phil(ip Duffield) 1899-1957 ... SATA-32
Stong, Red
See Stong, Clair L.
Stonier, Tom (Ted) 1927- ... 7-8R
Stonor, Oliver 1903- ... CAP-1
Earlier sketch in CA 15-16
Stonum, Gary Lee 1947- ... 89-92
Stoodley, Bartlett Hicks 1907-1978 ... 1R
Obituary ... 103
Stookey, Richard 1938- ... 93-96
Stookey, Robert W(ilson) 1917- ... CANR-14
Earlier sketch in CA 81-84
Stoop, David 1937- ... 119
Stoop, Norma McLain ... 65-68
Stoops, Emery 1902- ... CANR-17
Earlier sketches in CA 1R, CANR-1
Stoops, John A(lbert) 1925- ... 29-32R
Stopelman, Francis
See Stoppelman, Frans
Stopes, M. C.
See Stopes, Marie (Charlotte) Carmichael
Stopes, Marie C.
See Stopes, Marie (Charlotte) Carmichael
Stopes, Marie (Charlotte) Carmichael 1880-1958 Brief entry ... 115
Stopford, Robert Wright 1901- ... CAP-1
Earlier sketch in CA 13-14
Stopp, Elisabeth (Charlotte Vellar-Etscheit) 1911- ... 7-8R
Stoppard, Miriam 1937- ... 120
Stoppard, Tom 1937- ... 81-84
See also DLB 13
See also DLBY 85
See also CLC 1, 3, 4, 5, 8, 15, 29, 34
Stoppelman, Francis
See Stoppelman, Frans
Stoppelman, Frans 1921- ... CAP-1
Earlier sketch in CA 9-10
Storer, Doug(las) 1899-1985 ... 57-60
Obituary ... 118
Storer, J(ames) D(onald) 1928- ... CANR-23
Earlier sketch in CA 107
Storer, Norman W(illiam) 1930- ... 41-44R
Storer, Tracy I(rwin) 1889- ... 13-14R
Storey, Anthony 1928- ... CANR-2
Earlier sketch in CA 49-52
See also DLB 14
Storey, Arthur 1915- ... 45-48
Storey, David (Malcolm) 1933- ... 81-84
See also DLB 13, 14
See also CLC 2, 4, 5, 8
Storey, Edward 1930- ... 97-100
Storey, Edward J. 1901- ... 89-92
Storey, John W(oodrow) 1938- ... 121
Storey, Margaret 1926- ... CANR-1
Earlier sketch in CA 49-52
See also SATA 9
Storey, R(obin) L(indsay) 1927- ... CANR-11
Earlier sketch in CA 21-22R
Storey, Robert F(ranklin) 1945- ... 85-88
Storey, Victoria Carolyn 1945- ... 33-36R
See also SATA 16
Storey, W(illiam) George 1923- ... CANR-6
Earlier sketch in CA 7-8R
Storfer, Muriel (Rosoff) Silberstein
See Silberstein-Storfer, Muriel (Rosoff)
Storing, Herbert James 1928-1977 Obituary ... 73-76
Storke, Thomas More 1876-1971 Obituary ... 89-92
Storm, Christopher
See Olsen, T(heodore) V(ictor)
Storm, Hester G(lory) 1903- ... 11-12R
Storm, Hyemeyohsts 1935- ... 81-84
See also CLC 3
Storm, Lesley
See Clark, Mabel Margaret (Cowie)
Storm, Mallory
See Fairman, Paul W.
Storm, Marian 1892(?)-1975 Obituary ... 61-64
Storm, Russell
See Williams, Robert Moore
Storm, Virginia
See Swatridge, Irene Maude (Mossop)
Storme, Peter
See Stern, Philip Van Doren
Stormer, John A. 1928- ... 25-28R
Storni, Alfonsina 1892-1938 Brief entry ... 104
See also TCLC 5
Storr, Anthony 1920- ... CANR-17
Earlier sketch in CA 97-100
Storr, Catherine (Cole) 1913- ... CANR-23
Earlier sketch in CA 13-14R
See also SATA 9
Storrer, Carol Marchal 1949- ... 112
Storrow, H(ugh) A(lan) 1926- ... 21-22R
Storrow, James J., Jr. 1917-1984 Obituary ... 111
Storry, Richard 1914(?)-1982 Obituary ... 106
Storsve, LaVaughn (Ernestine Kipena) 1921- ... 3R
Story, E(ugenia) Macer
See Macer-Story, E(ugenia)
Story, Edward M. 1921- ... 29-32R
Story, G(eorge) M(orley) 1927- ... CANR-9
Earlier sketch in CA 23-24R
Story, Jack Trevor 1917- ... 29-32R
Story, Ronald (D.) 1946- ... CANR-11
Earlier sketch in CA 65-68
Story, Thomas 1670(?)-1742 ... DLB-31
Story, William Wetmore 1819-1895 ... DLB-1
Stotland, Ezra 1924- ... 17-18R
Stott, D(enis) H(erbert) 1909-1988 ... CANR-8
Obituary ... 124
Earlier sketch in CA 13-14R
Stott, Douglas W(ayne) 1948- ... 109
Stott, Jane 1940- ... 85-88
Stott, John R. W. 1921- ... CANR-18
Earlier sketches in CA 5-6R, CANR-2
Stott, Leland H. 1897- ... 25-28R
Stott, Mary 1907- ... 104
Stott, Mike 1944- ... 104
Stott, Raymond Toole
See Toole Stott, Raymond
Stott, William (Merrell) 1940- ... 61-64
Stotts, Herbert Edward 1916- ... CANR-1
Earlier sketch in CA 1R
Stotts, Jack L. 1932- ... 49-52
Stotz, Charles Morse 1898-1985 Obituary ... 115
Stouck, David (Hamilton) 1940- ... 61-64
Stoudemire, Sterling A(ubrey) 1902- ... 37-40R
Stoudt, John Joseph 1911- ... 49-52
Stough, Furman C(harles) 1928- Brief entry ... 107
Stoughton, Clarence Charles 1895-1975 Obituary ... 61-64
Stoughton, Gertrude K. 1901- ... CAP-2
Earlier sketch in CA 25-28
Stoughton, William 1631-1701 ... DLB-24
Stout, Alan Ker 1900-1983 Obituary ... 110
Stout, Gardner Dominick 1903-1984 Obituary ... 111
Stout, George L(eslie) 1897-1978 ... 81-84
Obituary ... 77-80
Stout, Irving Wright 1903-1972 ... CANR-3
Earlier sketch in CA 1R
Stout, James (Harvey) 1954- ... 119
Stout, Jeffrey Lee 1950- ... 106
Stout, Joseph A(llen), Jr. 1939- ... CANR-2
Earlier sketch in CA 45-48
Stout, Neil Ralph 1932- ... 97-100
Stout, Rex (Todhunter) 1886-1975 ... 61-64
See also CLC 3
See also AITN 2
Stout, Robert Joe 1936- ... 65-68
Stout, Russell, Jr. 1932- ... CANR-18
Earlier sketch in CA 101
Stout, Ruth 1884-1980 ... 33-36R
Obituary ... 120
Stout, Wesley Winans 1889-1971 Obituary ... 89-92
Stoutamire, Albert 1921- ... 41-44R
Stoutenburg, Adrien (Pearl) 1916- ... 7-8R
See also SATA 3
Stovall, Floyd 1896- ... 9-10R
Stover, Allan C(arl) 1938- ... CANR-12
Earlier sketch in CA 69-72
See also SATA 14
Stover, Bill
See Stover, W.H.M.
Stover, Jo Ann 1931- ... 37-40R
Stover, John F(ord) 1912- ... CANR-1
Earlier sketch in CA 2R
Stover, Leon E(ugene) 1929- ... CANR-2
Earlier sketch in CA 49-52
Stover, Marjorie Filley 1914- ... 45-48
See also SATA 9
Stover, W(illiam) H(arrison) M(owbray) 1898-1980 ... 103
Obituary ... 97-100
Stover, Webster 1902- ... 53-56
Stow, (Julian) Randolph 1935- ... 13-14R
See also CLC 23
Stowe, David M. 1919- ... 11-12R
Stowe, Harriet (Elizabeth) Beecher 1811-1896 ... YABC-1
See also DLB 1, 12, 42
Stowe, James L(ewis) 1950- ... 89-92
Stowe, Leland 1899- ... 77-80
See also DLB 29
Stowe, Noel James 1942- ... 106
Stowe, Richard S(cribner) 1925- ... 73-76
Stowe, Rosetta
See Ogan, George F.
and Ogan, Margaret E. (Nettles)
Stowe, William McFerrin 1913- ... 7-8R
Stowell, Joseph M(ishael) 1944- ... 119
Stowers, Carlton 1942- ... CANR-14
Earlier sketch in CA 81-84
Stoy, R(ichard) H(ugh) 1910- ... 57-60
Strabolgi, Bartolomeo
See Tucci, Niccolo
Strachan, Hew (Francis Anthony) 1949- ... 61-64
Strachan, J(ohn) George 1910- ... 107
Strachan, Margaret Pitcairn 1908- ... 7-8R
See also SATA 14
Strachan, T(ony) S(impson) 1920- ... 13-14R
Strachan, W. J.
See Strachan, Walter John
Strachan, Walter John 1903- ... 120
Strachan, Winona Peacock 1918- ... 5-6R
Strachey, Barbara
See Halpern, Barbara Strachey
Strachey, Isobel 1907-1987 Obituary ... 122
Strachey, James 1889(?)-1967 Brief entry ... 124
Strachey, (Evelyn) John (St. Loe) 1901-1963 Obituary ... 93-96
Strachey, (Giles) Lytton 1880-1932 Brief entry ... 110
See also TCLC 12
Strackbein, O(scar) R(obert) 1900- ... 21-22R
Straczynski, J(oseph) Michael 1954- ... 109
Strader, June (Sellers) 1925- ... 97-100
Stradley, Mark
See Smith, Richard Rein
Stradling, Leslie Edward 1908- ... 104
Strage, Mark 1927- ... 81-84
Strahl, Leonard E. 1926- ... 29-32R
Strahlem, Richard E(arl) 1909- ... 37-40R
Straight, Michael Whitney 1916- ... CANR-7
Earlier sketch in CA 5-6R
Strain, Dudley 1909- ... CAP-1
Earlier sketch in CA 11-12
Strain, Frances Bruce ?-1975 ... CAP-2
Earlier sketch in CA 29-32
Strain, Lucille Brewton ... 69-72
Strainchamps, Ethel (Reed) 1912- ... 53-56
Strait, Raymond 1924- ... CANR-4
Earlier sketch in CA 53-56
Strait, Treva Adams 1909- ... 97-100
See also SATA 35
Straiton, E(dward) C(ornock) 1917- ... CANR-19
Earlier sketches in CA 45-48, CANR-3
Straiton, Eddie
See Straiton, E(dward) C(ornock)
Straka, Gerald Milton 1931- ... CANR-2
Earlier sketch in CA 7-8R
Straker, J(ohn) F(oster) 1904- ... CANR-11
Earlier sketch in CA 13-14R
Strakosch, Avery
See Denham, Avery Strakosch
Straley, John A(lonzo) 1894-1966 ... 1R
Obituary ... 103
Strand, Kenneth A(lbert) 1927- ... CANR-3
Earlier sketch in CA 11-12R
Strand, Mark 1934- ... 21-22R
See also SATA 41
See also DLB 5
See also CLC 6, 18, 41
Strand, Paul 1890-1976 Obituary ... 65-68
Strand, Paul E.
See Palestrant, Simon S.
Strand, Thomas 1944- ... 65-68
Strand, William K. 1931- ... 29-32R
Strandberg, Victor H(ugo) 1935- ... CANR-16
Earlier sketch in CA 89-92
Strang, Barbara M(ary) H(ope) 1925-1982 ... 37-40R
Obituary ... 106
Strang, Gerald 1908- ... CAP-2
Earlier sketch in CA 25-28
Strang, Ruth May 1895-1971 ... CANR-2
Earlier sketch in CA 3R
Strange, Dillon
See Norwood, Victor G(eorge) C(harles)
Strange, Jack Roy 1921- ... 19-20R
Strange, James F(rancis) 1938- ... 117
Strange, K(athleen) H(aidee) 1904- ... 113
Strange, Maureen 1948- ... 89-92
Strange, N. Blair
See Sargent, Brian (Lawrence)
Strange, Nora K.
See Stanley, Nora Kathleen Begbie Strange
Strange, Philippa
See Coury, Louise Andree
Strange, Susan 1923- ... 49-52
Stranger, Joyce
See Wilson, Joyce M(uriel Judson)
Strankay, Sam J(ames) 1905- ... 57-60
Strasberg, Lee 1901-1982 ... 15-16R
Obituary ... 106
Strasberg, Susan (Elizabeth) 1938- Brief entry ... 120
Strasburger, Victor C. 1949- ... 112
Strassels, Paul N. ... 109
Strasser, Bernard Paul 1895- ... CAP-1
Earlier sketch in CA 9-10
Strasser, Marland K(eith) 1915- ... CANR-6
Earlier sketch in CA 5-6R
Strasser, Otto (Johann Maximilian) 1897-1974 Obituary ... 53-56
Strasser, Susan 1948- ... CANR-24
Earlier sketch in CA 107
Strasser, Todd 1950- ... 123
Brief entry ... 117
See also SATA 41, 45
See also CLR 11
Strassfeld, Michael J. 1950- ... 120
Strassfeld, Sharon M(arcia) 1950- ... 107
Strassmann, W(olfgang) Paul 1926- ... 41-44R
Strassova, Helena 1924- ... 49-52
Stratemeyer, Edward L. 1862-1930 ... CAP-2
Earlier sketch in CA 19-20
See also SATA 1
See also DLB 42
Stratford, H. Philip
See Bulmer, (Henry) Kenneth
Stratford, Philip 1927- ... CANR-5
Earlier sketch in CA 9-10R
See also SATA 47
Strathern, Andrew (Jamieson) 1939- ... CANR-19
Earlier sketches in CA 49-52, CANR-2
Strathern, Ann Marilyn 1941- ... CANR-3
Earlier sketch in CA 49-52
Strati, Saverio 1924- ... CANR-23
Earlier sketches in CA 19-20R, CANR-7
Stratman, Carl J(oseph) 1917-1972 ... CAP-2
Earlier sketch in CA 19-20
Straton, Hillyer H(awthorne) 1905- ... CAP-1
Earlier sketch in CA 9-10
Stratton, Arthur M. 1910(?)-1975 Obituary ... 61-64
Stratton, George Malcolm 1865-1957 Brief entry ... 112
Stratton, Henry
See Nelson, Michael Harrington
Stratton, J(ohn) T(hedore) ... 61-64
Stratton, John R(ay) 1935- ... 45-48
Stratton, Porter Andrew 1918- ... 37-40R
Stratton, Rebecca Brief entry ... 115
Stratton, Roy (Olin) ... CAP-2
Earlier sketch in CA 21-22
Stratton, Ted
See Stratton, J(ohn) T(heodore)
Stratton, Thomas
See Coulson, Robert S(tratton)
and DeWeese, Thomas Eugene
Stratton, William David 1896- ... CAP-1
Earlier sketch in CA 9-10
Stratton-Porter, Gene 1863-1924 ... SATA-15
Stratyner, Barbara Naomi Cohen
See Cohen-Stratyner, Barbara Naomi
Straub, Peter (Francis) 1943- ... 85-88
See also DLBY 84
See also CLC 28
Strauch, Carl F(erdinand) 1908- ... 41-44R
Strauch, Judith V(ivian) 1942- ... 107
Strauch, Katina (Parthemos) 1946- ... 105
Straughan, Robert P(aul) L(ouis) 1924- ... 49-52
Straughn, Charles (Thomas II) 1933- ... 117
Straumann, Heinrich 1902- ... 13-14R
Straus, Dennis ... CANR-23
Earlier sketch in CA 105
Straus, Dorothea 1916- ... 37-40R
Straus, Murray A(rnold) 1926- ... CANR-10
Earlier sketch in CA 23-24R
Straus, Nathan 1889-1961 Obituary ... 89-92
Straus, Richard 1925-1986 ... CANR-22
Earlier sketch in CA 4R
Straus, Robert 1923- ... CANR-6
Earlier sketch in CA 57-60
Straus, Roger A(ustin) 1948- ... 109
Strauss, Albrecht B(enno) 1921- ... 37-40R
Strauss, Anselm L(eonard) 1916- Brief entry ... 114
Strauss, Bert(ram) Wiley 1901- ... 15-16R
Strauss, Botho 1944- ... CLC-22
Strauss, David 1937- ... 89-92
Strauss, Elaine Mandle 1916(?)-1982 Obituary ... 107
Strauss, Erich 1911- ... 13-14R
Strauss, Frances 1904- ... CAP-2
Earlier sketch in CA 29-32
Strauss, Gerald 1922- ... 9-10R
Strauss, Hans 1898(?)-1977 Obituary ... 69-72
Strauss, Harold 1907-1975 Obituary ... 104
Strauss, Helen M(arion) 1904(?)-1987 Obituary ... 122
Strauss, Herbert A(rthur) 1918- Brief entry ... 121
Strauss, Joyce 1936- ... 93-96
Strauss, Leo 1899-1973 ... 101
Obituary ... 45-48
Strauss, Lewis Lichtenstein 1896-1974 Obituary ... 45-48
Strauss, (Mary) Lucille Jackson 1908- ... CAP-1
Earlier sketch in CA 11-12
Strauss, Maurice B(enjamin) 1904-1974 ... CAP-2
Earlier sketch in CA 25-28
Strauss, Patricia (Frances O'Flynn) 1909-1987 Obituary ... 123
Strauss, Richard (Georg) 1864-1949 Brief entry ... 118
Strauss, Richard L(ehman) 1933- ... CANR-16
Earlier sketches in CA 49-52, CANR-1
Strauss, Victor 1907(?)-1979 Obituary ... 89-92
Strauss, W(allace) Patrick 1923- ... 41-44R
Strauss, Walter A(dolf) 1923- ... 81-84
Strauss, Walter L(eopold) 1928-1988 ... 81-84
Obituary ... 124

Strauss, Werner 1930- 29-32R
Strauss, William Louis 1914- 61-64
Strausz-Hupe, Robert 1903- 9-10R
Stravinski, Igor Fedorovich
See Stravinsky, Igor Fedorovich
Stravinsky, Igor Fedorovich 1882-1971 107
Obituary 29-32R
Stravinsky, Vera 1888-1982 106
Obituary 107
Strawinsky, Igor Fedorovich
See Stravinsky, Igor Fedorovich
Strawson, John 1921- CANR-12
Earlier sketch in CA 29-32R
Strawson, P(eter) F(rederick) 1919- 25-28R
Strax, Philip 1909- 61-64
Strayer, Barry L. 1932- 29-32R
Strayer, E. Ward
See Stratemeyer, Edward L.
Strayer, Joseph Reese 1904-1987 103
Obituary 123
Strayer, Sara Barker 1896(?)-1986
Obituary 118
Strean, Herbert S(amuel) 1931- CANR-19
Earlier sketch in CA 103
Streano, Vince(nt Catello) 1945- 53-56
See also SATA 20
Streatfeild, (Mary) Noel 1895(?)-1986 81-84
Obituary 120
See also SATA 20, 48
See also CLC 21
Streebeck, Nancy 1934- 118
Street, Alicia (Kumpula) 1911- 7-8R
Street, Arthur George 1892-1966 .... CAP-1
Earlier sketch in CA 13-14
Street, Harry 1919-1984 Obituary 112
Street, James H(arry) 1915- CANR-4
Earlier sketch in CA 53-56
Street, Jay
See Slesar, Henry
Street, Julia Montgomery 1898- CANR-2
Earlier sketch in CA 5-6R
See also SATA 11
Street, Lee
See Hampton, Kathleen
Street, Leslie
See Freemantle, Brian Harry
Street, Lucie 13-14R
Street, Margaret M(ary) 1907- 65-68
Street, Mattie (Waters) 1896- CAP-1
Earlier sketch in CA 15-16
Street, Pamela 1921- 45-48
Street, Robert
See Thomas, Gordon
Streeten, Paul Patrick 1917- CANR-11
Earlier sketch in CA 25-28R
Streeter, Edward 1891-1976 .... CANR-2
Obituary 65-68
Earlier sketch in CA 4R
See also DLB 11
Streeter, Herbert Andrus 1918- 5-6R
Streeter, James (Jr.) 61-64
Strehlow, Theodor (George Heinrich)
1908- Brief entry 106
Strehlow, Theodor George Henry
See Strehlow, Theodor (George Heinrich)
Streib, Dan(iel Thomas) 1928- 106
Streib, Gordon F(ranklin) 1918- 112
Streiker, Lowell D(ean) 1939- 49-52
Streit, Clarence Kirshman 1896-1986 .... 2R
Obituary 119
Streithorst, Tom 1932(?)-1981 Obituary 103
Strelka, Joseph P(eter) 1927- CANR-8
Earlier sketch in CA 61-64
Strelsky, Katharine (Anderson) 108
Strempek, Carol Campbell 37-40R
Stren, Patti 1949- 124
Brief entry 117
See also SATA 41
See also CLR 5
Streng, Frederick J. 1933- 21-22R
Streng, William D(ietrich) 1909- CANR-1
Earlier sketch in CA 1R
Streng, William Paul 1937- Brief entry 108
Streshinsky, Shirley G. 1934- CANR-20
Earlier sketch in CA 85-88
Strete, Craig Kee 1950- 114
See also SATA 44
Stretton, Barbara (Humphrey) 1936- 116
See also SATA 35, 43
Stretton, Charles
See Dyer, Charles (Raymond)
Stretton, Hesba
See Smith, Sarah
Stretton, Hugh 1924- 104
Stretton, Renshaw
See Dyer, Charles (Raymond)
Stribling, T(homas) S(igismund)
1881-1965 Obituary 107
See also DLB 9
See also CLC 23
Strich, Christian 1930- 109
Strick, Ivy 1952- 85-88
Strick, Philip 1939- Brief entry 109
Stricker, George 1936- CANR-14
Earlier sketch in CA 37-40R
Strickland, Arvarh E(unice) 1930- 21-22R
Strickland, Charles E(verett) 1930- 77-80
Strickland, Cowles 1903(?)-1971
Obituary 33-36R
Strickland, D. A.
See Strickland, Donald A(llen)
Strickland, Donald A(llen) 1934-
Brief entry 109
Strickland, Dorothy S(alley) 1933- 108
Strickland, Glenn G. 1917- 97-100
Strickland, Joshua 1896- 81-84
Strickland, Margaret 1930- 116
Strickland, Margot 1927- CANR-10
Earlier sketch in CA 65-68
Strickland, Phil D. 1941- 29-32R
Strickland, Rennard (James) 1940- 21-22R
Strickland, Rex W(allace) 1897- 45-48
Strickland, Ron(ald Gibson) 1943- 122
Strickland, Ruth Gertrude 1898- CANR-5
Earlier sketch in CA 5-6R
Strickland, Stephen P(arks) 1933- CANR-3
Earlier sketch in CA 45-48
Strickler, Susan (Elizabeth) 1952- 124
Strickon, Arnold 1930- Brief entry 108
Strieber, Whitley 1945- CANR-12
Earlier sketch in CA 81-84
Strieby, Irene Macy 1894- CAP-1
Earlier sketch in CA 11-12
Strietelmeier, John (Henry) 1920- 25-28R
Stright, Hayden Leroy 1898-1975 ....37-40R
Strike, Jeremy
See Renn, Thomas E(dward)
Striker, Cecil Leopold 1932- 109
Strimple, Earl O. 1938- 97-100
Strindberg, (Johan) August 1849-1912
Brief entry 104
See also TCLC 1, 8, 21
Stringer, David
See Roberts, Keith (John Kingston)
Stringer, Lorene A(dair) 1908- 37-40R
Stringer, Ruth M(arjorie) Pearson 1905- 7-8R
Stringer, William Henry 1908-1976
Obituary 65-68
Stringfellow, (Frank) William
1928-1985 .... CANR-9
Obituary 115
Earlier sketch in CA 5-6R
Stringfield, Leonard H(arry) 1920- 85-88
Strobel, Margaret 1946- 124
Strober, Gerald S. 1935- 85-88
Strobos, Robert Julius 1921- 102
Strobridge, Truman R(ussell) 1927- 41-44R
Strodach, George Kleppinger 1905- 5-6R
Strode, Hudson 1892-1976 .... CANR-8
Obituary 69-72
Earlier sketch in CA 15-16R
Strodtbeck, Fred L(ouis) 1919- 5-6R
Stroeyer, Poul 1923- CANR-14
Earlier sketch in CA 77-80
See also SATA 13
Stroh, Guy W(eston) 1931- 49-52
Stroh, Thomas F. 1924- CANR-11
Earlier sketch in CA 21-22R
Strohm, John
See Strohm, John L(ouis)
Strohm, John L(ouis) 1912-1987 Obituary .. 124
Strohm, Deborah 1947- 123
Strom, Ingrid Mathilda 1912- 13-14R
Strom, Leslie Winter
See Winter, Leslie
Strom, Robert D(uane) 1935- CANR-10
Earlier sketch in CA 25-28R
Stroman, Duane F(rederick) 1934- 104
Stromberg, Gustaf (Benjamin) 1882-1962
Obituary 112
Stromberg, Roland N(elson) 1916- CANR-21
Earlier sketches in CA 5-6R, CANR-6
Strommen, Merton P. 1919- CANR-5
Earlier sketch in CA 11-12R
Strong, Anna Louise 1885-1970
Obituary 29-32R
Strong, Charles
See Epstein, Beryl (M. Williams)
and Epstein, Samuel
Strong, Charles Olen 1925- 7-8R
Strong, David
See McGuire, Leslie Sarah
Strong, Donald Stuart 1912- 41-44R
Strong, Douglas H(illman) 1935- 117
Strong, Douglas Hillman 1935- Brief entry ... 111
Strong, Eithne 1923- 97-100
Strong, Harrington
See McCulley, Johnston
Strong, J. J.
See Strong, Jeremy
Strong, Jeremy 1949- 108
See also SATA 36
Strong, John W. 1930- 37-40R
Strong, John William 1935- 37-40R
Strong, Jonathan 1944- 37-40R
Strong, Kenneth William Dobson
1900-1982 104
Obituary 105
Strong, Leah A(udrey) 1922- 23-24R
Strong, Lennox
See Grier, Barbara G(ene Damon)
Strong, Pat
See Hough, Richard (Alexander)
Strong, Philip Nigel Warrington
1899-1983 109
Obituary 110
Strong, Roy (Colin) 1935- CANR-21
Earlier sketches in CA 49-52, CANR-1
Strong, Rupert 1911- 15-16R
Strong, Solange
See Hertz, Solange (Strong)
Strong, Susan
See Rees, Joan
Strong, Tracy B(urr) 1943- 93-96
Strong, William S. 1951- 124
Strongblood, Casper
See Webster, David Endicott
Strongin, Lynn 1939- CANR-1
Earlier sketch in CA 49-52
Strongman, K(enneth) T(homas)
1940- CANR-10
Earlier sketch in CA 61-64
Stroop, Helen E.
See Witty, Helen E. S(troop)
Strother, David B(oyd) 1928- 25-28R
Strother, David Hunter 1816-1888 .... DLB-3
Strother, Elsie (Frances Warmoth Weitzel)
1912- CANR-11
Earlier sketch in CA 65-68
Strother, Horatio Theodore 1930- 5-6R
Strother, Pat Wallace 1929- CANR-9
Earlier sketch in CA 65-68
Stroube, Hal 1921(?)-1983 Obituary 110
Stroud, Joe H(inton) 1936- 103
Stroud, Kandy (Andrea) 108
Stroup, Herbert H(ewitt) 1916- 15-16R
Stroup, Thomas B(radley) 1903- 25-28R
Strouse, Jean 1945- 103
Strousse, Flora G. 1897(?)-1974
Obituary 49-52
Strout, (Sewall) Cushing (Jr.) 1923- 15-16R
Strout, Richard L(ee) 1898- 69-72
Strover, Dorothea 9-10R
Stroyen, William Basil 1925- 25-28R
Stroyer, Poul
See Stroeyer, Poul
Strozier, Charles B(urnett) 1944- CANR-24
Earlier sketch in CA 107
Struble, Mitch 1945- 93-96
Struble, Virginia
See Burlingame, Virginia (Struble)
Struever, Stuart McKee 1931- 104
Strugatskii, Arkadii (Natanovich) 1925- 106
See also CLC 27
Strugatskii, Boris (Natanovich) 1933- 106
See also CLC 27
Struglia, Erasmus Joseph 1915- 15-16R
Struik, Dirk Jan 1894- CANR-6
Earlier sketch in CA 7-8R
Struk, Danylo 1940- 57-60
Strum, Philippa 1938- 61-64
Strummer, Joe 1953(?)- CLC-30
Strumpen-Darrie, Robert L. 1912- 13-14R
Strung, Norman 1941- CANR-14
Earlier sketch in CA 41-44R
Strunk, (William) Oliver 1901-1980 105
Strunk, Oliver 1901-1980 Obituary 97-100
Strunk, Orlo, Jr. 1925- CANR-1
Earlier sketch in CA 1R
Strunk, William, Jr. 1869-1946
Brief entry 118
Strupp, Hans H(ermann) 1921- CANR-2
Earlier sketch in CA 1R
Strutt, Malcolm 1936- 115
Strutton, William Harold 1918- 77-80
Strutz, Henry 1932- CANR-24
Earlier sketches in CA 7-8R, CANR-7
Struve, Walter 1935- 49-52
Struyk, Raymond J(ay) 1944- Brief entry ... 107
Stryjkowski, Julian 1905- CANR-3
Earlier sketch in CA 49-52
Stryk, Dan 1951- 120
Stryk, Lucien 1924- CANR-10
Earlier sketch in CA 15-16R
Stryker, (Philip) David 1916- 45-48
Stryker, Perrin 1908- 7-8R
Stryker, Sheldon 1924- 9-10R
Stryker-Rodda, Harriet 1905- 81-84
Stryker-Rodda, Kenn 1903- 73-76
Stuart, Aimee 1886(?)-1981 Obituary 103
Stuart, Alex
See Stuart, (Violet) Vivian (Finlay)
Stuart, Alice V(andockum) 1899- 13-14R
Stuart, Anthony
See Hale, Julian A(nthony) S(tuart)
Stuart, Charles
See Mackinnon, Charles Roy
and Reid, Charles (Stuart)
Stuart, Clay
See Whittington, Harry (Benjamin)
Stuart, Colin 1910- 104
Stuart, Dabney 1937- CANR-8
Earlier sketch in CA 17-18R
Stuart, David
See Hoyt, Edwin P(almer), Jr.
Stuart, Don A.
See Campbell, John W(ood)
Stuart, Douglas (Keith) 1943- 115
Stuart, Forbes 1924- 69-72
See also SATA 13
Stuart, Francis 1902- 13-14R
Stuart, Graham H. 1887- CAP-1
Earlier sketch in CA 13-14
Stuart, Ian 1927- CANR-13
Earlier sketch in CA 73-76
Stuart, Ian
See MacLean, Alistair (Stuart)
Stuart, Irving R. 1916- CANR-14
Earlier sketch in CA 41-44R
Stuart, Jane 1942- 41-44R
Stuart, Jay Allison
See Tait, Dorothy
Stuart, Jesse (Hilton) 1907-1984 ....7-8R
Obituary 112
See also SATA 2, 36
See also DLB 9, 48
See also DLBY 84
See also CLC 1, 8, 11, 14, 34
Stuart, Kenneth
See Cox, P(atrick) Brian
See also DLB 9
Stuart, Leslie
See Marlowe, Kenneth
Stuart, Lyle 1922- 81-84
Stuart, Margaret
See Paine, Lauran (Bosworth)
Stuart, Monroe
See Shapiro, Max
Stuart, Reginald (Charles) 1943- 116
Stuart, Richard Bernard 1933- 41-44R
Stuart, Sheila
See Baker, Mary Gladys Steel
Stuart, Sidney
See Avallone, Michael (Angelo), Jr.
Stuart, Simon (Walter Erskine) 1930- 29-32R
Stuart, V. A.
See Stuart, (Violet) Vivian (Finlay)
Stuart, (Violet) Vivian (Finlay) 1914- ... CANR-12
Earlier sketch in CA 13-14R
Stuart, W. J.
See MacDonald, Philip
Stuart, Warren
See MacDonald, Philip
Stuart-Clark, Christopher (Anthony)
1940- CANR-24
Earlier sketch in CA 107
See also SATA 32
Stuart-Jones, Edwyn Henry 1895-19(?) ... CAP-1
Earlier sketch in CA 15-16
Stub, Holger R(ichard) 1922- 41-44R
Stubbings, Hilda Uren
See U'Ren-Stubbings, Hilda
Stubblebine, James H(arvey) 1920-1987 ..97-100
Obituary 121
Stubblefield, Harold W. 1934- 17-18R
Stubbs, Harry C(lement) 1922- CANR-7
Earlier sketch in CA 15-16R
Stubbs, Jean 1926- 7-8R
Stubbs, John C(aldwell) 1936- 29-32R
Stubbs, P(eter) C(harles) 1937- 117
Stuber, Florian (Cy) 1947- CANR-24
Earlier sketch in CA 106
Stuber, Stanley I(rving) 1903-1985 ...... CAP-1
Obituary 116
Earlier sketch in CA 13-14
Stubis, Talivaldis 1926- SATA-5
Stubley, Trevor (Hugh) 1932- SATA-22
Stuckenschmidt, H(ans) H(einz) 1901- . CANR-18
Earlier sketch in CA 25-28R
Stuckey, Gilbert B. 1912- 65-68
Stuckey, Sterling 1932- 101
Stuckey, William Joseph 1923- 41-44R
Stucki, Curtis W(illiam) 1928- 15-16R
Stucky, Solomon 1923- 117
Stucky, Steven 1949- 109
Stucley, Elizabeth
See Northmore, Elizabeth Florence
Studd, Stephen (Allen) 1946- 116
Studer, Gerald C. 1927- 65-68
Studlar, Donley T(rent) 1947- 120
Stueart, Robert D. 1935- 105
Stuebing, (Arthur) Douglas 1913- 25-28R
Stueck, William Whitney, Jr. 1945- 105
Stuempke, Harald
See Steiner, Gerolf
Stuermann, Walter E(arl) 1919-1965 ....5-6R
Stuermer, Nina Roberta 1933- 104
Stuerup, Georg Kristoffer 1905- 25-28R
Stuhlmann, Gunther 1927- 25-28R
Stuhlmueller, Carroll 1923- CANR-24
Earlier sketches in CA 15-16R, CANR-9
Stulman, Julius 1906- 118
Stultifer, Morton
See Curtis, Richard (Alan)
Stultz, Newell M(aynard) 1933- 29-32R
Stumpf, Samuel Enoch 1918- 41-44R
Stumpf, Stephen A(lan) 1949- 111
Stumpke, Harald
See Steiner, Gerolf
Stunkard, Albert J(ames) 1922- 117
Stuntz, Albert Edward 1902-1976
Obituary 65-68
Stuntz, Laurance F(itzhugh) 1908- 61-64
Stupak, Ronald J(oseph) 1934- 29-32R
Sturdivant, Frederick D(avid) 1937- 41-44R
Sturgeon, Foolbert
See Stack, Frank H(untington)
Sturgeon, Theodore Hamilton 1918-1985 ..81-84
Obituary 116
See also DLB 8
See also DLBY 85
See also CLC 22, 39
Sturgeon, Wina 85-88
Sturges, Patricia P(atterson) 1930- 69-72
Sturges, Preston 1898-1959 Brief entry 114
See also DLB 26
Sturgill, Claude C(arol) 1933- CANR-9
Earlier sketch in CA 15-16R
Sturgis, James L(averne) 1936- 37-40R
Sturm, Ernest 1932- 65-68
Sturm, John E. 1927- 37-40R
Sturm, Rudolf 1912- Brief entry 109
Sturm, Sara
See Sturm-Maddox, Sara Higgins
Sturmey, S(tanley) G(eorge) 1924- 9-10R
Sturm-Maddox, Sara Higgins 1938-
Brief entry 108
Sturmthal, Adolf F(ox) 1903-1986 ....11-12R
Obituary 119
Sturrock, Jeremy
See Healey, Ben (James)
Stursberg, Peter 1913- 101
Sturt, Mary 1896- CAP-2
Earlier sketch in CA 23-24
Sturtevant, Catherine ?-1970 Obituary 104
Sturtevant, David Reeves 1926- 104
Sturtevant, Peter M(ann), Jr. 1943- 69-72
Sturton, Hugh
See Johnston, H(ugh) A(nthony)
S(tephen)
Sturtzel, Howard A(llison) 1894- CANR-6
Earlier sketch in CA 2R
See also SATA 1
Sturtzel, Jane Levington 1903- CANR-6
Earlier sketch in CA 2R
See also SATA 1

Sturup, Georg Kristoffer
See Stuerup, Georg Kristoffer
Stutler, Boyd B. 1889-1970 ... CAP-2
Earlier sketch in CA 23-24
Stutz, Robert Michael 1941- Brief entry ... 110
Styan, J(ohn) L(ouis) 1923- ... CANR-6
Earlier sketch in CA 5-6R
Stycos, J(oseph) Mayone 1927- ... 13-14R
Styles, Jimmie C(arter) 1931- ... 41-44R
Styles, (Frank) Showell 1908- ... CANR-21
Earlier sketches in CA 4R, CANR-6
See also SATA 10
Stylla, Joanne
See Branden, Victoria (Fremlin)
Styron, Rose (Burgunder) 1928- ... 17-18R
Styron, William 1925- ... CANR-6
Earlier sketch in CA 5-6R
See also DLB 2
See also DLBY 80
See also CLC 1, 3, 5, 11, 15
Styx, Marguerite (Salzer) 1908(?)-1975
Obituary ... 53-56
Suares, Guy 1932- ... 103
Suarez Lynch, B.
See Bioy Casares, Adolfo
and Borges, Jorge Luis
Suba, Susanne ... 29-32R
See also SATA 4
Subak-Sharpe, Genell J(ackson) 1936- ... 112
Subbiah, B(ommireddi) V(enkata)
1917-1975 ... 41-44R
Subilia, Vittorio 1911- ... CANR-4
Earlier sketch in CA 9-10R
Sublette, Edith Blanche 1909- ... 17-18R
Sublette, Walter (Edwards) 1940- ... 124
Sublette, Walter Edwards 1940-
Brief entry ... 117
Subond, Valerie
See Grayland, Valerie (Merle Spanner)
Such, Peter 1939- ... DLB-60
Sucharitkul, Somtow 1952- ... 118
Sucher, Harry V(ictor) 1915- ... 89-92
Su Chien 1884-1918 Brief entry ... 123
Suchlicki, Jaime 1939- ... 29-32R
Suchman, Edward A(llen) 1915-197(?) ... CAP-1
Earlier sketch in CA 13-14
Suchocki, Marjorie Hewitt 1933- ... 109
Suchoff, Benjamin 1918- ... CANR-11
Earlier sketch in CA 69-72
Suckling, John 1609-1642 ... DLB-58
Suckow, Ruth 1892-1960 Obituary ... 113
See also DLB 9
Suda, Zdenek 1920- ... 29-32R
Sudbery, Rodie 1943- ... 104
See also SATA 42
Sudermann, Hermann 1857-1928
Brief entry ... 107
See also TCLC 15
Sudhalter, Richard M(errill) 1938- ... 101
Sudman, Seymour 1928- ... CANR-15
Earlier sketch in CA 41-44R
Sue, Judy
See Epstein, Judith Sue
Suedfeld, Peter 1935- ... 41-44R
Suelflow, August R(obert) 1922- ... 11-12R
Sueltz, Arthur Fay 1928- ... CANR-2
Earlier sketch in CA 49-52
Suenens, Leon Joseph 1904- ... 61-64
Suffling, Mark
See Rowland, D(onald) S(ydney)
Sufrin, Sidney Charles 1910- ... CANR-17
Earlier sketches in CA 5-6R, CANR-2
Sugano, Takuo 1931- ... 123
Sugar, Bert Randolph 1937- ... CANR-9
Earlier sketch in CA 65-68
Sugarman, Daniel A(rthur) 1931- ... 21-22R
Sugarman, Tracy 1921- ... 21-22R
See also SATA 37
Sugden, John 1947- ... 120
Sugden, Mark 1902- ... CAP-1
Earlier sketch in CA 13-14
Sugerman, Shirley 1919- ... 65-68
Sugg, Redding S(tancill), Jr. 1922- ... CANR-2
Earlier sketch in CA 45-48
Suggs, George G(raham), Jr. 1929- ... 41-44R
Suggs, M(arion) Jack 1924- ... CANR-3
Earlier sketch in CA 1R
Suggs, Robert Carl 1932- ... 9-10R
Suggs, Willie Kathryn 1950- ... 77-80
Sugita, Yutaka 1930- ... 115
See also SATA 36
Sugnet, Charles (Joseph) 1944- ... 109
Suh, Dae-Sook 1931- ... 21-22R
Suhl, Benjamin ... 49-52
Suhl, Yuri 1908-1986 ... CANR-2
Obituary ... 121
Earlier sketch in CA 45-48
See also SATA 8, 50
See also SAAS 1
See also CLR 2
Suhor, Charles 1935- ... CANR-10
Earlier sketch in CA 25-28R
Suhr, Elmer George 1902-1976 ... 11-12R
Obituary ... 65-68
Su Hsuan-ying
See Su Chien
Su Hsuean-ying
See Su Chien
Suid, Lawrence Howard 1938- ... 101
Suid, Murray 1942- ... 97-100
See also SATA 27
Suinn, Richard M(ichael) 1933- ... 29-32R
Suits, Daniel B(urbidge) 1918- ... 29-32R
Sujata, Anagarika 1948- ... 65-68
Suk, Julie ... 115
Sukarno, (Ahmed) 1901-1970 Obituary ... 113
Sukenick, Ronald 1932- ... 25-28R
See also DLBY 81
See also CLC 3, 4, 6
Sukhotin-Tolstoy, Tatyana
See Tolstoy, Tatyana (Sukhotin)
Sukhwal, Bheru Lal 1929- ... 57-60
Suknaski, Andrew 1942- ... 101
See also DLB 53
See also CLC 19
Suleiman, Ezra N. 1941- ... 85-88
Suleiman, Michael W(adie) 1934- ... CANR-9
Earlier sketch in CA 21-22R
Suleiman, Susan Rubin ... 109
Sulimirski, Tadeusz Joseph 1898-1983
Obituary ... 110
Sulitzer, Paul-Loup 1946- Brief entry ... 122
Sulkin, Sidney 1918- ... CANR-17
Earlier sketches in CA 5-6R, CANR-2
Sullens, Idelle 1921- ... 23-24R
Sullivan, A(loysius) M(ichael) 1896-1980 ... CAP-2
Obituary ... 97-100
Earlier sketch in CA 29-32
Sullivan, Alvin 1942- ... 29-32R
Sullivan, Anita T. 1942- ... 123
Sullivan, C(harles) Gardner 1886(?)-1965
Obituary ... 113
See also DLB 26
Sullivan, Chester L(amar) 1939- ... 53-56
Sullivan, Clara K(atherine) 1915- ... 23-24R
Sullivan, Colleen ... 117
Sullivan, D(ale) H(owill) 1936- ... 61-64
Sullivan, Denis G(artland) 1929- ... 103
Sullivan, Dulcie Turner 1895-1969 ... CAP-2
Earlier sketch in CA 25-28
Sullivan, Earl L. 1942- ... 124
Sullivan, Ed(ward Vincent) 1902(?)-1974
Obituary ... 89-92
Sullivan, Edmund V(incent) 1938- ... 61-64
Sullivan, Edward A(nthony) 1936- ... 115
Sullivan, Edward Daniel 1913- ... 7-8R
Sullivan, Eleanor (Regis) 1928- Brief entry ... 112
Sullivan, Elizabeth L. 1904(?)-1985
Obituary ... 115
Sullivan, Francis (Patrick) 1929- ... CANR-7
Earlier sketch in CA 57-60
Sullivan, Francis John 1892-1976 ... CAP-2
Obituary ... 65-68
Earlier sketch in CA 25-28
Sullivan, Frank 1912-1975 ... 65-68
Obituary ... 61-64
Sullivan, Frank
See Sullivan, Francis John
See also DLB 11
Sullivan, George Edward 1927- ... 13-14R
See also SATA 4
Sullivan, J(ohn) P(atrick) 1930- ... CANR-10
Earlier sketch in CA 25-28R
Sullivan, Jack 1946- ... 119
Sullivan, James L(enox) 1910- ... 29-32R
Sullivan, Jerry 1938- ... 115
Sullivan, John L. 1908- ... 21-22R
Sullivan, Judy 1936- ... 53-56
See also AITN 1
Sullivan, Kevin 1918(?)-1987 ... 1R
Obituary ... 122
Sullivan, Marion F. 1899- ... 37-40R
Sullivan, Mark W(ilbur) 1927- ... 25-28R
Sullivan, Martin (Gloster) 1910-1980 ... 107
Obituary ... 104
Sullivan, Martin (Richard Preece) 1934- ... 29-32R
Sullivan, Mary B(arrett) 1918- ... 15-16R
Sullivan, Mary W(ilson) 1907- ... CANR-12
Earlier sketch in CA 73-76
See also SATA 13
Sullivan, Maurice William 1925- ... CANR-2
Earlier sketch in CA 7-8R
Sullivan, (Donovan) Michael 1916- ... CANR-3
Earlier sketch in CA 5-6R
Sullivan, Michael B. 1938- ... 77-80
Sullivan, Nancy 1929- ... 17-18R
Sullivan, Navin 1929- ... 5-6R
Sullivan, Pat
See Messmer, Otto
Sullivan, Peggy (Anne) 1929- ... CANR-12
Earlier sketch in CA 29-32R
Sullivan, Prescott 1904(?)-1985 Obituary ... 116
Sullivan, Richard 1908-1981 ... 77-80
Obituary ... 104
Sullivan, Richard E(ugene) 1921-
Brief entry ... 115
Sullivan, Rosemary 1947- ... 97-100
Sullivan, Ruth Christ 1924- ... 57-60
Sullivan, Sean Mei
See Sohl, Jerry
Sullivan, Sheila 1927- ... CANR-14
Earlier sketch in CA 77-80
Sullivan, Sister Bede 1915- ... 25-28R
Sullivan, Thomas Joseph, Jr. 1947- ... 81-84
See also SATA 16
Sullivan, Tom
See Sullivan, Thomas Joseph, Jr.
Sullivan, Vernon
See Vian, Boris
Sullivan, Victoria 1943- ... 65-68
Sullivan, Vincent F. 1899- ... CAP-2
Earlier sketch in CA 29-32
Sullivan, Walter 1906- ... 15-16R
Sullivan, Walter (Laurence) 1924- ... 41-44R
Sullivan, Walter Seager 1918- ... CANR-2
Earlier sketch in CA 3R
Sullivan, William M. 1945- ... 109
Sullivant, Robert S(cott) 1925- ... 1R
Sulloway, Alison G. 1917- Brief entry ... 111
Sulloway, Frank J(ones) 1947- ... 124
Brief entry ... 118
Sully, (Lionel Henry) Francois 1927-1971 ... CAP-2
Obituary ... 29-32R
Earlier sketch in CA 25-28
Sully, Kathleen M. 1910- ... 15-16R
Sully, Nina (Rosemary) 1948- ... 110
Sultan, Arne 1925-1986 Obituary ... 118
Sultan, Stanley 1928- ... CANR-10
Earlier sketch in CA 15-16R
Sultana, Donald Edward 1924- ... 103
Sulzberger, Arthur Hays 1891-1968
Obituary ... 89-92
Sulzberger, C(yrus) L(eo II) 1912- ... CANR-23
Earlier sketches in CA 53-56, CANR-7
Sulzberger, Marina Tatiana 1919(?)-1976
Obituary ... 111
Su Man-shu
See Su Chien
See also TCLC 24
Sumichrast, Jozef 1948- ... SATA-29
Sumichrast, Michael M. 1921- ... CANR-21
Earlier sketch in CA 104
Sumida, Jon Tetsuro 1949- ... 124
Sumiko
See Davies, Sumiko
Summer, Brian
See Du Breuil, (Elizabeth) L(or)inda
Summer, Charles Edgar 1923- ... 81-84
Summerfield, Harry L. 1940- ... 37-40R
Summerfield, Jack
See Summerfield, John D(udley)
Summerfield, Joanne 1940- ... 117
Summerfield, John D(udley) 1927- ... 23-24R
Summerfield, Margie 1949- ... 89-92
Summerfield, Penny 1951- ... 119
Summerforest, Ivy B.
See Kirkup, James
Summerhayes, Victor Samuel
1897(?)-1974 Obituary ... 53-56
Summerhill, J. K.
See Schere, Monroe
Summerlin, Sam(uel A.) 1928- ... 45-48
Summers, Andrew James 1942- ... CLC-26
Summers, Andy
See Summers, Andrew James
Summers, Anthony (Bruce) 1942- ... CANR-23
Earlier sketch in CA 69-72
Summers, Clyde Wilson 1918- ... 109
Summers, Essie
See Summers, Ethel Snelson
Summers, Ethel Snelson 1912- Brief entry ... 116
Summers, Festus P(aul) 1895- ... CAP-1
Earlier sketch in CA 11-12
Summers, Gene F(ranklin) 1936- ... CANR-12
Earlier sketch in CA 29-32R
Summers, Gordon
See Hornby, John (Wilkinson)
Summers, Hal
See Summers, Henry Forbes
Summers, Harrison B(oyd) 1894- ... 13-14R
Summers, Harry G(lenn), Jr. 1932- ... 123
Summers, Henry Forbes 1911- ... 109
Summers, Hollis (Spurgeon, Jr.) 1916- ... CANR-3
Earlier sketch in CA 5-6R
See also DLB 6
See also CLC 10
Summers, Ian 1939- ... 105
Summers, James L(evingston) 1910- ... 15-16R
See also SATA 28
Summers, JoAn 1943- ... 106
Summers, John A.
See Lawson, H(orace) L(owe)
Summers, Joseph H(olmes) 1920- ... 41-44R
Summers, Lionel M(organ) 1905-1975 ... 45-48
Obituary ... 103
Summers, (Alphonsus Joseph-Mary
Augustus) Montague 1880-1948
Brief entry ... 118
See also TCLC 16
Summers, Ray 1910- ... 13-14R
Summers, Robert 1922- ... 77-80
Summers, Robert E. 1918- ... 25-28R
Summers, Robert S(amuel) 1933- ... CANR-11
Earlier sketch in CA 69-72
Summers, Rowena
See Saunders, Jean
Summerscales, William 1921- ... 29-32R
Summersell, Charles Grayson 1908- ... CANR-19
Earlier sketches in CA 2R, CANR-3
Summerskill, Edith 1901-1980 Obituary ... 93-96
Summerson, John (Newenham) 1904-
Brief entry ... 117
Summerson, Rachel (Elizabeth) 1944- ... 107
Summerville, James 1947- ... 119
Sumner, Cid Ricketts 1890-1970 ... 5-6R
Obituary ... 29-32R
Sumner, Colin 1949- ... 111
Sumner, David (W. K.) 1937- ... 57-60
Sumner, Eldon
See Bruno, James Edward
Sumner, Gordon Matthew 1951- ... CLC-26
Sumner, Lloyd Quinton 1943- ... 103
Sumner, Richard (William) 1949- ... 69-72
Sumwalt, Martha Murray 1924- ... 69-72
Sun, Ruth Q(uinlan) 1907- ... 57-60
Sunagel, Lois A(nn) 1926- ... 93-96
Sund, Robert B(ruce) 1926- ... 29-32R
Sundarananda
See Nakashima, George Katsutoshi
Sunday, Billy
See Sunday, William Ashley
Sunday, William Ashley 1862(?)-1935
Brief entry ... 120
Sundberg, Trudy James 1925- ... 17-18R
Sundell, Roger H(enry) 1936- ... 23-24R
Sunder, Shyam 1944- ... 118
Sunderland, Eric 1930- ... CANR-21
Earlier sketch in CA 103
Sunderland, Glenn W. 1925- ... 25-28R
Sunderland, Lane V(on) 1945- ... 97-100
Sunderlin, Sylvia 1911- ... 73-76
See also SATA 28
Sunderman, James F. 1919- ... 19-20R
Sunderman, Lloyd Frederick 1905-1983
Obituary ... 109
Sundgaard, Arnold (Olaf) 1909- ... CANR-2
Earlier sketch in CA 45-48
Sundman, Per Olof 1922- Brief entry ... 111
Sundquist, James L(loyd) 1915- ... 29-32R
Sundquist, Ralph Roger, Jr. 1922-
Brief entry ... 106
Sung, Betty Lee ... CANR-10
Earlier sketch in CA 25-28R
See also SATA 26
Sung, P. M.
See Chun, Jinsie K(yung) S(hein)
Sungolowsky, Joseph 1931- ... 41-44R
Sunners, William 1903- ... CAP-1
Earlier sketch in CA 9-10
Sunoo, Harold Hak-Won 1918- ... 41-44R
Sunseri, Alvin R(aymond) 1925- ... 93-96
Sunshine, John 1897(?)-1987 Obituary ... 123
Sunstein, Emily W(eisberg) 1924- ... 53-56
Suny, Ronald Grigor 1940- ... 111
Sun Yat-sen, Madame
See Soong Ching-ling
Sun Yefang 1908-1983 Obituary ... 109
Super, Donald E(dwin) 1910- ... CANR-3
Earlier sketch in CA 3R
Super, R(obert) H(enry) 1914- ... 15-16R
Super Santa
See Berman, Ed
Supervielle, Jules 1884-1960 Obituary ... 114
Suponev, Michael 1923- ... 65-68
Suppe, Frederick (Roy) 1940- ... 41-44R
Suppes, Patrick (Colonel) 1922- ... CANR-20
Earlier sketches in CA 2R, CANR-4
Supraner, Robyn 1930- ... 69-72
See also SATA 20
Supree, Burt(on) 1941- ... 65-68
Surace, Samuel J. 1919- ... 21-22R
Suran, Bernard G(regory) 1939- ... 81-84
Suransky, Valerie Polakow
See Polakow, Valerie (Suransky)
Suret-Canale, Jean 1921- ... CANR-1
Earlier sketch in CA 49-52
Surette, (Philip) Leon 1938- ... 110
Surface, Bill
See Surface, William E.
Surface, William E. 1935-1980(?) ... CANR-13
Earlier sketch in CA 7-8R
Surge, Frank 1931- ... 69-72
See also SATA 13
Surkin, Marvin 1938- ... 61-64
Surkov, Alexei Aleksandrovich 1899-1983
Obituary ... 110
Surles, Lynn 1917- ... 13-14R
Surman, Charles Edward 1901- ... 7-8R
Surmelian, Leon (Zaven) 1907- ... CAP-2
Earlier sketch in CA 25-28
Surplus, Robert W. 1923- ... 7-8R
Surrey, (Arthur) John 1933- ... 117
Surrey, Peter J. 1928- ... 106
Surrey, Stanley Sterling 1910-1984
Obituary ... 113
Surtees, Robert Smith 1803-1864 ... DLB-21
Surtz, Edward 1910(?)-1973 Obituary ... 41-44R
Susac, Andrew 1929- ... 49-52
See also SATA 5
Susan
See Graham, (Maude Fitzgerald) Susan
Susann, Jacqueline 1921-1974 ... 65-68
Obituary ... 53-56
See also CLC 3
See also AITN 1
Suskind, Patrick
See Sueskind, Patrick
Suskind, Richard 1925- ... CANR-9
Earlier sketch in CA 15-16R
Suslov, Alexander 1950- ... 105
Suslov, Mikhail Andreyevich 1902-1982
Obituary ... 105
Susman, Warren (Irving) 1927-1985
Obituary ... 116
Suss, Elaine ... 102
Susser, Mervyn (Wilfred) 1921- ... CANR-1
Earlier sketch in CA 45-48
Susser, Samuel S. 1910- ... 97-100
Susskind, Charles 1921- ... CANR-15
Earlier sketch in CA 85-88
Sussman, Aaron 1903- Brief entry ... 116
Sussman, Barry 1934- ... 53-56
Sussman, Cornelia Silver 1914- ... CANR-13
Earlier sketch in CA 7-8R
Sussman, Henry 1947- ... 111
Sussman, Herbert L. 1937- ... 25-28R
Sussman, Irving 1908- ... CANR-13
Earlier sketch in CA 77-80
Sussman, Leonard R(ichard) 1920- ... CANR-4
Earlier sketch in CA 53-56
Sussman, Marvin B(ernard) 1918- ... CANR-19
Earlier sketches in CA 11-12R, CANR-4
Sussman, Susan 1942- ... 111
See also SATA 48
Sutch, Richard C(harles) 1942- ... 107
Sutcliff, Rosemary 1920- ... 5-6R
See also SATA 6, 44
See also CLC 26
See also CLR 1
Sutcliffe, Anthony (Richard) 1942- ... 106
Suter, Ronald 1930- ... 41-44R
Sutermeister, Robert Arnold 1913- ... 5-6R
Suther, Marshall E(dward), Jr. 1918- ... 1R

Sutherland, Arthur Eugene, Jr. 1902-1973 CAP-1
Obituary 41-44R
Earlier sketch in CA 19-20
Sutherland, C(arol) Humphrey V(ivian) 1908- 13-14R
Sutherland, Daniel E(llyson) 1946- 109
Sutherland, Donald 1915- 37-40R
Sutherland, Donald W(ayne) 1931- 9-10R
Sutherland, Douglas 1919- 23-24R
Sutherland, Earl Wilbur 1915-1974 Obituary 49-52
Sutherland, Efua (Theodora Morgue) 1924- 105
See also SATA 25
Sutherland, Elizabeth 1926- 85-88
Sutherland, Elizabeth
See Martinez, Elizabeth Sutherland
Sutherland, Fraser 1946- 102
Sutherland, Gordon (Brims Black McIvor) 1907-1980 Obituary 108
Sutherland, H(erbert) W(arren) 1917- 13-14R
Sutherland, James (Edward) 1948- CANR-2
Earlier sketch in CA 49-52
Sutherland, John (Anthony) 1933- CANR-16
Earlier sketch in CA 93-96
Sutherland, John P. 1920- 21-22R
Sutherland, Jon Nicholas 1941- 41-44R
Sutherland, Lucy Stuart 1903-1980 CAP-1
Obituary 105
Earlier sketch in CA 13-14
Sutherland, Margaret 1941- CANR-14
Earlier sketch in CA 77-80
See also SATA 15
Sutherland, N(icola) M(ary) 1925- 49-52
Sutherland, R(ussell) Galbraith 1924- CAP-1
Earlier sketch in CA 9-10
Sutherland, Robert D(onald) 1937- 37-40R
Sutherland, Roger
See Hicks, Roger W(illiam)
Sutherland, Ronald 1933- 25-28R
Sutherland, (Norman) Stuart 1927- 65-68
Sutherland, (William) Temple (Gairdner) 1906- CAP-1
Earlier sketch in CA 9-10
Sutherland, Zena Bailey 1915- 102
See also SATA 37
Suthinee
See Ambhanwong, Suthilak
Suthren, Victor (James Henry) 1942- CANR-23
Earlier sketch in CA 107
Sutnar, Ladislav 1897-1976 Obituary 104
Sutphen, Dick
See Sutphen, Richard Charles
Sutphen, Richard Charles 1937- CANR-11
Earlier sketch in CA 25-28R
Sutro, Alfred 1863-1933 Brief entry 105
See also DLB 10
See also TCLC 6
Sutro, John 1903(?)-1985 Obituary 117
Sutryn, Barbara M(ay) 1927- 120
Sutter, Franz
See Strich, Christian
Sutter, Frederic Koehler 1938- 107
Sutter, Ruth E(laine) 1935- 45-48
Suttles, Gerald 1932- 85-88
Suttles, Shirley (Smith) 1922- 15-16R
See also SATA 21
Suttmeier, Richard Peter 1942- CANR-6
Earlier sketch in CA 57-60
Sutton, Ann (Livesay) 1923- CANR-10
Earlier sketch in CA 5-6R
See also SATA 31
Sutton, Antony C. 1925- 97-100
Sutton, Carol 1933-1985 Obituary 115
Sutton, Caroline 1953- 106
Sutton, Christine 1950- 120
Sutton, David (John) 1944- 116
Sutton, David 1947- 101
Sutton, Denys 1917- CANR-20
Earlier sketches in CA 53-56, CANR-5
Sutton, Eve(lyn Mary) 1906- CANR-10
Earlier sketch in CA 65-68
See also SATA 26
Sutton, Felix 1910(?)- 77-80
See also SATA 31
Sutton, George Miksch 1898-1982 107
Obituary 109
Sutton, Gordon 1910- 23-24R
Sutton, Henry
See Slavitt, David R.
Sutton, Horace (Ashley) 1919- CANR-10
Earlier sketch in CA 13-14R
Sutton, Howard 1930- 65-68
Sutton, Jane 1950- 89-92
See also SATA 43
Sutton, Jeff
See Sutton, Jefferson (Howard)
Sutton, Jefferson (Howard) 1913-1979 CANR-10
Earlier sketch in CA 23-24R
Sutton, John L(awrence) 1917- 105
Sutton, L(aurence) P(aul) Elwell
See Elwell-Sutton, L(aurence) P(aul)
Sutton, Larry M(atthew) 1931- CANR-14
Earlier sketch in CA 37-40R
See also SATA 29
Sutton, Margaret Beebe 1903- 1R
See also SATA 1
Sutton, Maurice Lewis 1927- 13-14R
Sutton, Max Keith 1937- 93-96
Sutton, Myron Daniel 1925- 107
See also SATA 31
Sutton, Penny
See Wood, Christopher (Hovelle)
Sutton, Robert M(ize) 1915- 77-80
Sutton, Roberta Briggs 1899- 7-8R
Sutton, S(tephanne) B(arry) 1940- 29-32R
Sutton, Stack
See Sutton, Maurice Lewis
Sutton, Tony C.
See Sutton, Antony C.
Sutton, Walter 1916- 85-88
Sutton, William A(lfred) 1915- 61-64
Sutton-Smith, Brian 1924- CANR-17
Earlier sketch in CA 29-32R
Sutton-Vane, Vane Hunt
See Vane, (Vane Hunt) Sutton
Suttor, T(imothy) L(achlan) 1926- 21-22R
Suvin, Darko (Ronald) 1930- CANR-16
Earlier sketch in CA 89-92
Suvorov, Viktor (a pseudonym) 116
Suyin, Han
See Han, Suyin
Su Yuan-ying
See Su Chien
Su Yuean-ying
See Su Chien
Suzuki, D. T.
See Suzuki, Daisetz Teitaro
Suzuki, Daisetz T.
See Suzuki, Daisetz Teitaro
Suzuki, Daisetz Teitaro 1870-1966 121
Obituary 111
Suzuki, Teitaro
See Suzuki, Daisetz Teitaro
Suzuki, Tessa Morris
See Morris-Suzuki, Tessa
Svajian, Stephen G. 1906(?)-1977 Obituary 73-76
Svareff, Count Vladimir
See Crowley, Edward Alexander
Svarlien, Oscar 1906- CAP-1
Earlier sketch in CA 15-16
Svartvik, Jan 1931- 23-24R
Svejda, George J. 1927- 41-44R
Svenson, Andrew E. 1910-1975 5-6R
Obituary 61-64
See also SATA 2, 26
Svensson, Arne 1929- 49-52
Svestka, Oldrich 1922-1983 Obituary 110
Svevo, Italo
See Schmitz, Aron Hector
See also TCLC 2
Svirsky, Grigori 1921- 69-72
Svoboda, Frederic Joseph 1949- 116
Swaan, Wim 1927- CANR-18
Earlier sketch in CA 25-28R
Swabey, Marie Collins 1890-1966 CANR-16
Earlier sketch in CA 1R
Swadesh, Frances Leon 1917- 120
Swadley, Elizabeth 1929- 21-22R
Swados, Elizabeth 1951- 97-100
See also CLC 12
Swados, Harvey 1920-1972 CANR-6
Obituary 37-40R
Earlier sketch in CA 7-8R
See also DLB 2
See also CLC 5
Swaffer, Hannen 1879-1962 Obituary 112
Swaim, Alice Mackenzie 1911- CANR-6
Earlier sketch in CA 9-10R
Swaim, Lawrence 1942- 69-72
Swain, Bruce M(cArthur) 1943- 101
Swain, Charles 1801-1874 DLB-32
Swain, Donald C(hristie) 1931- 29-32R
Swain, Dwight V(reeland) 1915- CANR-7
Earlier sketch in CA 17-18R
Swain, Frank G. 1893(?)-1975 Obituary 53-56
Swain, James E(dgar) 1897-1975 CAP-2
Earlier sketch in CA 25-28
Swain, Joseph Ward 1891-1971 CAP-2
Earlier sketch in CA 21-22
Swain, Margaret (Helen) 1909- 53-56
Swain, Marshall (William) 1940- 124
Brief entry 117
Swain, Martha H(elen) 1929- 85-88
Swain, Olive 1896- 7-8R
Swain, Raymond Charles 1912- 9-10R
Swain, Roger (Bartlett) 1949- 102
Swain, Su Zan (Noguchi) 1916- CANR-6
Earlier sketch in CA 7-8R
See also SATA 21
Swainson, Donald 1938- 109
Swainson, Eleanor Frances 111
Swale, Rose 1947- Brief entry 116
Swale, Rosie
See Swale, Rose
Swales, Martin 1940- 81-84
Swallow, Alan 1915-1966 CANR-16
Obituary 25-28R
Earlier sketch in CA 1R
Swallow, Norman 1921- 21-22R
Swami Rama 1925- 119
Swami Sivananda Radha
See Radha, Sivananda
Swamy, Subramanian 1939- 49-52
Swan, Berta W(aterhouse) 1928- 29-32R
Swan, Bradford Fuller 1908(?)-1976 Obituary 65-68
Swan, Carroll J. 1914-1984 Obituary 112
Swan, Christopher C(ushing) 1946- 103
Swan, Gladys 1934- CANR-17
Earlier sketch in CA 101
Swan, Jon 1929- 89-92
Swan, Marie
See Bartlett, Marie (Swan)
Swan, Susan 1944- SATA-22
Swanberg, W(illiam) A(ndrew) 1907- CANR-8
Earlier sketch in CA 7-8R
Swander, Mary 1950- 122
Swanger, David 1940- 49-52
Swann, Brian 1940- 37-40R
Swann, Donald (Ibrahim) 1923- CANR-16
Earlier sketch in CA 23-24R
Swann, Francis 1913- CANR-4
Earlier sketch in CA 11-12R
Swann, Ingo 1933- 57-60
Swann, Lois 1944- CANR-12
Earlier sketch in CA 65-68
Swann, Peggy
See Geis, Richard E(rwin)
Swann, Peter C(harles) 1921- 7-8R
Swann, Thomas Burnett, Jr. 1928-1976 CANR-4
Earlier sketch in CA 5-6R
Swansea, Charleen 1932- CANR-16
Earlier sketch in CA 103
Swansen, Vern 1916- 49-52
Swanson, Arlene Collyer 1913- 5-6R
Swanson, Austin D. 1930- 25-28R
Swanson, Bert E(lmer) 1924- 29-32R
Swanson, Carl P(ontius) 1911- 45-48
Swanson, Don R(ichard) 1924- 15-16R
Swanson, Donald Roland 1927- 41-44R
Swanson, Edward I. 1923- 29-32R
Swanson, Gloria 1899(?)-1983 Obituary 109
Swanson, Gloria Borseth 1927- 77-80
Swanson, Gustav A(dolph) 1910- CANR-14
Earlier sketch in CA 77-80
Swanson, Harold B(urdette) 1917- 37-40R
Swanson, Neil H(armon) 1896-1983 Obituary 109
Swanson, Roy Arthur 1925- 17-18R
Swanson, (Karl) Thor (Waldemar) 1922- CANR-22
Earlier sketch in CA 45-48
Swanson, Walter S. J. 1917- 29-32R
Swanton, Ernest William 1907- CANR-18
Earlier sketches in CA 7-8R, CANR-2
Swanwick, Michael 1950- 119
Swarbrick, Andrew 1955- 120
Sward, Robert (Stuart) 1933- CANR-23
Earlier sketches in CA 7-8R, CANR-5
Swardson, Harold Roland, Jr. 1925- 4R
Swarthout, Doris L(ouise) 1931- 77-80
Swarthout, Glendon (Fred) 1918- CANR-1
Earlier sketch in CA 3R
See also SATA 26
See also CLC 35
Swarthout, Kathryn 1919- 41-44R
See also SATA 7
Swartley, David Warren 1950- 102
Swartley, Willard M(yers) 1936- 117
Swartz, Harry (Felix) 1911- CANR-6
Earlier sketch in CA 57-60
Swartz, Jon D(avid) 1934- 69-72
Swartz, Marc J(erome) 1931- 21-22R
Swartz, Marvin 1941- 101
Swartz, Mary I(sabelle) 1942- 97-100
Swartz, Melvin Jay 1930- 97-100
Swartz, Paul 1927- 7-8R
Swartz, Robert D(avid) 1937- 41-44R
Swartz, Robert J(ason) 1936- 17-18R
Swartz, Willis George 1902-1965 1R
Swartzlow, Ruby Johnson 1903- CAP-1
Earlier sketch in CA 15-16
Swarzenski, Hanns (Peter Theophil) 1903-1985 Obituary 116
Swatridge, Charles (John) CANR-7
Earlier sketch in CA 15-16R
Swatridge, Irene Maude (Mossop) CANR-7
Earlier sketch in CA 29-32R
Swaybill, Roger E(lliot) 1943- 105
Swayne, Geoffrey
See Campion, Sidney R(onald)
Swayze, (Sarah) Beulah G(arland) 1907- 7-8R
Swayze, E(rnest) Harold 1930- 1R
Swayze, John Cameron 1906- 102
Swearengen, Thomas F. 1924- 19-20R
Swearer, Donald K(eeney) 1934- 37-40R
Swearingen, Arthur Rodger 1923- CANR-10
Earlier sketch in CA 5-6R
Sweazey, George E. 1905- CANR-4
Earlier sketch in CA 1R
Swedburg, Wilma Adeline 7-8R
Swede, George 1940- 113
Sweeney, Amin 1938- 105
Sweeney, Barry
See Hand, G(eoffrey) J(oseph Philip Macaulay)
Sweeney, (Roderick) Charles (Hinton) 1922- CANR-16
Earlier sketch in CA 23-24R
Sweeney, Earl M. 1937- 112
Sweeney, Francis 1916- 7-8R
Sweeney, Henry Whitcomb 1898-1967 CAP-2
Earlier sketch in CA 17-18
Sweeney, James B(artholomew) 1910- CANR-12
Earlier sketch in CA 29-32R
See also SATA 21
Sweeney, James Johnson 1900-1986 CANR-6
Obituary 119
Earlier sketch in CA 7-8R
Sweeney, Joyce (Kay) 1955- 116
Sweeney, Karen O'Connor 1938- 89-92
Sweeney, (Charles) Leo 1918- CANR-15
Earlier sketch in CA 37-40R
Sweeney, R. C. H.
See Sweeney, (Roderick) Charles (Hinton)
Sweeney, Robert Dale 1939- 45-48
Sweeney, Thomas J(ohn) 1936- 41-44R
Sweeney, William J(oseph), III 1922- 45-48
Sweet, Donald H(erbert) 1925- 112
Sweet, Franklyn Haley 1916- 9-10R
Sweet, Frederick A(rnold) 1903- CAP-2
Earlier sketch in CA 17-18
Sweet, George Elliott 1904- 45-48
Sweet, J(ohn) P(hilip) M(cMurdo) 1927- 119
Sweet, James Stouder 1918- 41-44R
Sweet, Jeffrey 1950- 81-84
Sweet, Leonard Ira 1947- 97-100
Sweet, Muriel W. 1888-1977 106
Sweet, Paul R(obinson) 1907- 77-80
Sweet, Robert Burdette 1930- 85-88
Sweet, Waldo Earle 1912- 1R
Sweeting, George 1924- CANR-11
Earlier sketch in CA 65-68
Sweetkind, Morris 1898- 13-14R
Sweetland, Nancy A(nn) 1934- SATA-48
Sweetland, Richard C. 1931- 119
Sweetman, Jack 1940- CANR-10
Earlier sketch in CA 25-28R
Sweetman, Rosita (Anne) 1948- 124
Brief entry 118
Sweets, John Frank 1945- 89-92
Sweetser, Mary (Chisholm) 1894- 41-44R
Sweetser, Ted
See Sweetser, Mary (Chisholm)
Sweetser, Thomas P(atrick) 1939- 112
Sweetser, Wesley D(uaine) 1919- 37-40R
Sweezy, Alan Richardson 1907- 41-44R
Sweezy, Paul M(arlor) 1910- CANR-5
Earlier sketch in CA 1R
Sweigard, Lulu E. ?-1974 Obituary 53-56
Swell, Lila 97-100
Sweney, Fredric 1912- 1R
Swenson, Allan A(rmstrong) 1933- 77-80
See also SATA 21
Swenson, Clifford H(enrik) Jr. 1926- 45-48
Swenson, Judy Harris 1947- 120
Swenson, Karen 1936- 53-56
Swenson, Loyd S(ylvan), Jr. 1932- CANR-15
Earlier sketch in CA 41-44R
Swenson, May 1919- 7-8R
See also SATA 15
See also DLB 5
See also CLC 4, 14
Swenson, Peggy
See Geis, Richard E(rwin)
Swenson, Peggye 1933- 73-76
Swensson, Paul S. 1907- 77-80
Swerdlow, Amy (Miriam) G(alstuck) 1923- 105
Swerling, Jo 1897- DLB-44
Swetman, Glenn R(obert) 1936- CANR-4
Earlier sketch in CA 53-56
Swetnam, Evelyn (Frances) 1919- 93-96
Swets, John A(rthur) 1928- CANR-9
Earlier sketch in CA 21-22R
Swezey, Kenneth M. 1905(?)-1972 Obituary 33-36R
Swicegood, Thomas L. P. 1930- 53-56
Swick, Clarence 1883(?)-1979 Obituary 89-92
Swick, Kevin J(ames) 1943- 111
Swidler, Arlene (Anderson) 1929- CANR-12
Earlier sketch in CA 61-64
Swidler, Leonard 1929- CANR-7
Earlier sketch in CA 17-18R
Swierenga, Robert P. 1935- 25-28R
Swift, Augustus
See Lovecraft, H(oward) P(hillips)
Swift, Benjamin
See McKimmey, James
Swift, Bryan
See Knott, William C(ecil, Jr.)
Swift, Carolyn Ruth 1928- 107
Swift, David
See Kaufmann, John
Swift, E(dward) M(cKelvy) 1951- 107
Swift, Edd
See Swift, Edward
Swift, Edward 1943- 37-40R
Swift, George B. 1902(?)-1983 Obituary 110
Swift, Graham 1949- 122
Brief entry 117
See also CLC 41
Swift, Helen C(ecilia) 1920- 117
Swift, Helen Miller 1914- 2R
Swift, Hildegarde Hoyt 1890(?)-1977 Obituary 69-72
See also SATA 20
Swift, Howard W. 1908- CAP-1
Earlier sketch in CA 9-10
Swift, Joan 1926- 115
Swift, Jonathan 1667-1745 SATA-19
See also DLB 39
Swift, Kate 1923- 69-72
Swift, Marshall S(tefan) 1936- 53-56
Swift, Mary Grace 1927- 29-32R
Swift, Merlin
See Leeming, Joseph
Swift, Patrick 1927-1983 Obituary 110
Swift, Richard N(ewton) 1924- 2R
Swift, W. Porter 1914- 29-32R
Swigart, Rob 1941- CANR-11
Earlier sketch in CA 69-72
Swiger, Elinor Porter 1927- 37-40R
See also SATA 8
Swigg, Richard 1938- 103
Swihart, Altman K 1903- 1R
Swihart, Thomas L(ee) 1929- 107
Swinburne, Algernon Charles 1837-1909 Brief entry 105
See also DLB 35, 57
See also TCLC 8
Swinburne, Laurence (Joseph) 1924- CANR-15
Earlier sketch in CA 61-64
See also SATA 9
Swinburne, Richard 1934- CANR-10
Earlier sketch in CA 25-28R
Swindell, Larry (Nolan) 1929- 25-28R
Swindells, Robert (Edward) 1939- CANR-21
Earlier sketch in CA 97-100
See also SATA 34, 50
Swinden, Patrick 1941- 49-52

Swindler, William F(inley) 1913-1984 ....13-14R
Obituary 112
Swindoll, Luci 1932- 112
Swineford, Ada 1917- 61-64
Swinfen, Ann CLC-34
Swinfen, D(avid) B(erridge) 1936- 37-40R
Swinford, Betty (June Wells) 1927- CANR-7
Earlier sketch in CA 7-8R
Swinford, Bob
See Swinford, Betty (June Wells)
Swing, Raymond Gram 1887-1968
Obituary 89-92
Swing, Thomas Kaehao 1930- 9-10R
Swingle, Paul G(eorge) 1937- 41-44R
Swinglehurst, Edmund 1917- CANR-8
Earlier sketch in CA 57-60
Swinnerton, A(rnold) R(eber) 1912- 106
Swinnerton, Frank Arthur 1884-1982
Obituary 108
See also DLB 34
See also CLC 31
Swinnerton, James Guilford 1875-1974
Obituary 93-96
Swinson, Arthur 1915-1970 .... CAP-2
Earlier sketch in CA 17-18
Swint, Henry L(ee) 1909- 37-40R
Swinton, George 1917- 85-88
Swinton, John 1939- 111
Swinton, Stanley M(itchell) 1919-1982
Obituary 107
Swinton, William E(lgin) 1900- 13-14R
Swinyard, Alfred W(ilbur) 1915- 11-12R
Swire, Otta F(lora Macdonald Lois)
1898-1973 .... CAP-1
Earlier sketch in CA 13-14
Swisher, Carl Brent 1897-1968 .... CANR-16
Obituary 103
Earlier sketch in CA 1R
Swisher, (Frank) Earl 1902- CAP-2
Earlier sketch in CA 29-32
Swisher, Robert K., Jr. 1947- 61-64
Swisshelm, Jane Grey 1815-1884 .... DLB-43
Switzer, David Karl 1925- 57-60
Switzer, Ellen 1923- CANR-2
Earlier sketch in CA 45-48
See also SATA 48
Switzer, (Perry) Richard 1925- CANR-18
Earlier sketch in CA 25-28R
Swivett, R. G. O.
See Trippett, Frank
Swomley, John M., Jr. 1915- 9-10R
Swope, George S(teel) 1915- 29-32R
Swope, Herbert Bayard 1882-1958 .... DLB-25
Swor, Chester E(ugene) 1907- 11-12R
Sword, Randall S(tanford) 1942- 114
Sword, Wiley 1937- 85-88
Swortzell, Lowell (Stanley) 1930- CANR-1
Earlier sketch in CA 49-52
Swycaffer, Jefferson P(utnam) 1956- 119
Swyhart, Barbara Ann DeMartino 1942- 61-64
Syberberg, Hans-Juergen 1935- 93-96
Syburg, Jane 1927- 29-32R
Sydenham, Michael J(ohn) 1923- 19-20R
Sydney, C.
See Tralins, S(andor) Robert
Sydney, Frank
See Warwick, Alan R(oss)
Sydnor, Charles W(right), Jr. 1943- 77-80
Sydnor, James Rawlings 1911- 5-6R
Sydnor, (Charles) William 1911- 112
Syed, Anwar H(ussain) 1926- 102
Syers, Ed
See Syers, William Edward
Syers, William Edward 1914- CANR-4
Earlier sketch in CA 1R
Sykes, (Richard) Adam 1940- 29-32R
Sykes, Alrene 77-80
Sykes, Christopher (Hugh) 1907-1986 ....29-32R
Obituary 121
Sykes, Gerald 1903-1984 Obituary 113
Sykes, Jay G(ilbert) 1922- 45-48
Sykes, John 1918- 17-18R
Sykes, Roosevelt 1906-1983 Obituary 110
Sylva, Carmen
See Elisabeth (Ottilie Luise), Queen (Pauline)
Sylvander, Carolyn W(edin) 1939- 117
Sylvester, A(lbert) J(ames) 1889- 101
Sylvester, Arline 1914- 65-68
Sylvester, Bob
See Sylvester, Robert (McPhierson)
Sylvester, Dorothy 1906- 29-32R
Sylvester, Edward J(oseph) 1942- 118
Sylvester, Janet Hart 1917-1987 Obituary ... 123
Sylvester, Kathryn F. 1901(?)-1983
Obituary 111
Sylvester, Natalie G(abry) 1922- 97-100
See also SATA 22
Sylvester, Richard Standish 1926-1978 .. CANR-2
Obituary 77-80
Earlier sketch in CA 1R
Sylvester, Robert (McPhierson)
1907-1975 61-64
Obituary 57-60
Sylvester, William 1918- 45-48
Sylvestre, (Joseph Jean) Guy 1918- 61-64
Sylvia
See Ashton-Warner, Sylvia (Constance)
Sylvin, Francis
See Seaman, Sylvia S.
Symanski, Richard 1941- 111
Symcox, Geoffrey Walter 1938- 112
Syme, (Neville) Ronald 1913- CANR-6
Earlier sketch in CA 9-10R
See also SATA 2
Symington, David 1904-1984 .... CAP-2
Obituary 113
Earlier sketch in CA 29-32
Symmes, Robert Edward
See Duncan, Robert (Edward)
Symmons-Symonolewicz, Konstantin
1909- 37-40R
Symonds, Helen Sanford 1899- 5-6R
Symonds, John 105
Symonds, John Addington 1840-1893 .. DLB-57
Symonds, (John) Richard (Charters)
1918- 21-22R
Symons, Allene 1944- 110
Symons, Arthur 1865-1945 Brief entry 107
See also DLB 19, 57
See also TCLC 11
Symons, (Dorothy) Geraldine 1909- 85-88
See also SATA 33
Symons, Julian (Gustave) 1912- CANR-3
Earlier sketch in CA 49-52
See also CAAS 3
See also CLC 2, 14, 32
Symons, Leslie John 1926- 109
Symons, R(obert) D(avid) 1898-1973 ....41-44R
Symons, (H. B.) Scott 1933- 77-80
See also DLB 53
Symser, H(amilton) M(artin) 1901- 15-16R
Synan, Edward A(loysius) 1918- 19-20R
Synan, (Harold) Vinson 1934- CANR-14
Earlier sketch in CA 37-40R
Synge, (Edmund) J(ohn) M(illington)
1871-1909 Brief entry 104
See also DLB 10, 19
See also TCLC 6
Synge, (Phyllis) Ursula 1930- CANR-1
Earlier sketch in CA 49-52
See also SATA 9
Synnestvedt, Sig(fried T.) 1924-1977 ....37-40R
Syntax, John
See Dennett, Herbert Victor
Sypher, Francis Jacques, Jr. 1941- CANR-10
Earlier sketch in CA 57-60
Sypher, Lucy Johnston 1907- CANR-2
Earlier sketch in CA 45-48
See also SATA 7
Sypher, Wylie 1905- CANR-3
Earlier sketch in CA 2R
Syracuse, Marcella Pfeiffer 1930- 23-24R
Syrdal, Rolf A(rthur) 1902- 25-28R
Syred, Celia 1911- CANR-12
Earlier sketch in CA 29-32R
Syrett, David 1939- Brief entry 106
Syrett, Harold Coffin 1913-1984 Obituary ... 113
Syrkin, Marie 1899- CANR-6
Earlier sketch in CA 9-10R
Syrop, Konrad 1914- CANR-5
Earlier sketch in CA 9-10R
Syruc, J.
See Milosz, Czeslaw
Syvertsen, Edythe 1921- 73-76
Syverud, Genevieve Wold 1914- 21-22R
Szabo, Denis 1929- CANR-20
Earlier sketch in CA 89-92
Szabolcsi, Bence 1899-1973 Obituary 116
Szajkowski, Zosa
See Frydman, Szajko
Szancer, Henryk ?-1976 Obituary 61-64
Szaniawski, Jerzy 1886-1970 Obituary 29-32R
Szanto, George H. 1940- 41-44R
Szanton, Peter L(oeb) 1930- CANR-11
Earlier sketch in CA 69-72
Szasz, Kathleen 1912- 25-28R
Szasz, Margaret Connell 1935- 97-100
Szasz, Suzanne (Shorr) 1915- CANR-18
Earlier sketches in CA 5-6R, CANR-3
See also SATA 13
Szasz, Thomas (Stephen) 1920- CANR-9
Earlier sketch in CA 17-18R
Szathmary, Louis (Istvan) II 1919- 81-84
Szaz, Zoltan Michael 1930- CANR-3
Earlier sketch in CA 3R
Szczesniak, Boleslaw (B.) 1908- 11-12R
Szechter, Szymon 1920(?)-1983 Obituary 110
Szekely, Endre 1922- 17-18R
Szekeres, Cyndy 1933- SATA-5
Szent-Gyoergyi, Albert (von Nagyrapolt)
1893-1986 Obituary 120
Brief entry 112
Szent-Gyorgyi, Albert (von Nagyrapolt)
See Szent-Gyoergyi, Albert (von Nagyrapolt)
Szep, Paul Michael 1941- Brief entry 110
Szeplaki, Joseph 1932- 73-76
Szerlip, Barbara 1949- CANR-3
Earlier sketch in CA 49-52
Szigeti, Joseph 1892-1973 .... CAP-1
Earlier sketch in CA 9-10
Szilard, Leo 1898-1964 Obituary 113
Szirtes, George 1948- 109
See also CLC 46
Szittya, Ruth Outland 1910- 112
Szoeverffy, Joseph 1920- CANR-17
Earlier sketch in CA 65-68
Szogyi, Alex 1929- 45-48
Szporluk, Roman 1933- CANR-1
Earlier sketch in CA 45-48
Szudek, Agnes S(usan) P(hilomena) SATA-49
Szulc, Tad 1926- CANR-23
Earlier sketches in CA 11-12R, CANR-4
See also SATA 26
Szumigalski, Anne 1922- CANR-16
Earlier sketches in CA 49-52, CANR-1
Szumski, Bonnie 1958- 122
Szwarc, Josef 1947- 118
Szydlow, Jarl
See Szydlowski, Mary Vigliante
Szydlowski, Mary Vigliante 1946- 104
Szydlowski, Roman 1918(?)-1983
Obituary 111
Szyliowicz, Joseph S. 1931- 41-44R
Szymanski, Albert (John) 1942(?)-1985
Obituary 115
Szymanski, Richard
See Symanski, Richard

T

T. B. D.
See James, William Milbourne
T. N. T.
See Thomas, Cornelius Dickinson
T.R.B.
See Strout, Richard L(ee)
T. V. Vet
See Straiton, E(dward) C(ornock)
Taaffe, Edward James 1921- 85-88
Taaffe, James G. 1932- 17-18R
Taaffe, Michael
See Maguire, R(obert) A(ugustine) J(oseph)
Taagepera, Rein 1933- 109
Tabachnik, Abraham B(er) 1902-1970
Obituary 29-32R
Taback, Simms 1932- Brief entry 115
See also SATA 36, 40
Tabak, Israel 1904- Brief entry 105
Tabard, Geoffrey
See McNelly, Willis E(verett)
Tabard, Peter
See Blake, L(eslie) J(ames)
Tabb, Jay Yanai 1907-1976 .... CAP-2
Earlier sketch in CA 29-32
Taber, Anthony Scott 1944- 105
Taber, George M(cCaffrey) 1942- 65-68
Taber, Gladys (Bagg) 1899-1980 .... CANR-4
Obituary 97-100
Earlier sketch in CA 5-6R
See also SATA 22
Taber, Julian Ingersoll 1929- Brief entry 106
Taber, Robert 17-18R
Taber, Robert W(illiam) 1921- 73-76
Tabler, Edward C. 1916- 7-8R
Tablet, Hilda
See Swann, Donald (Ibrahim)
Tabor, Paul
See Tabori, Paul
Tabori, George 1914- CANR-4
Earlier sketch in CA 49-52
See also CLC 19
Tabori, Paul 1908-1974 .... CANR-5
Obituary 53-56
Earlier sketch in CA 5-6R
Taborsky, Edward (Joseph) 1910- CANR-3
Earlier sketch in CA 1R
Tabouis, Genevieve 1892-1985 Obituary 117
Tabrah, Ruth Milander 1921- CANR-10
Earlier sketch in CA 15-16R
See also SATA 14
Tacey, William S(anford) 1904- 37-40R
Tachau, Frank 1929- Brief entry 111
Tachau, Mary K(atherine) Bonsteel 1926- ..85-88
Tacheron, Donald Glen 1928- 21-22R
Tack, Alfred 1906- 104
Tadlock, Max R. 1919- 19-20R
Tadrack, Moss
See Caryl, Warren
Taegel, William S(tephens) 1940- 45-48
Taetzsch, Lyn 1941- CANR-8
Earlier sketch in CA 57-60
Taeuber, Alma Ficks 1933- 17-18R
Taeuber, Conrad 1906- 45-48
Taeuber, Irene Barnes 1906-1974
Obituary 106
Taeuber, Karl E(rnst) 1936- 17-18R
Tae-yong, Ro
See Rutt, Richard
Tafel, Edgar Allen 1912- 89-92
Taffy
See Llewellyn, D(avid) W(illiam) Alun
Taft, Charles P(helps II) 1897-1983
Obituary 110
Brief entry 105
Taft, Pauline Dakin 1891- CAP-1
Earlier sketch in CA 15-16
Taft, Philip 1902-1976 Obituary 69-72
Taft, Ronald 1920- 21-22R
Taft, William H(oward) 1915- 15-16R
Tafti, H. B. Dehqani
See Dehqani-Tafti, H. B.
Tafuri, Manfredo 1935- 69-72
Tafuri, Nancy 1946- 118
See also SATA 39
Tager, Jack 1936- 118
Tageson, Carroll W(illiam) 1925- 53-56
Taggard, Genevieve 1894-1948 .... DLB-45
Taggart, Dorothy T(rekell) 1917- 102
Taggart, (Paul) John 1942- CANR-1
Earlier sketch in CA 45-48
Taggart, John Scott
See Scott-Taggart, John
Taggart, Joseph Herman 1902-1984
Obituary 112
Taggart, Robert (III) 1945- Brief entry 111
Tagiuri, Renato 1919- 77-80
Tagliabue, John 1923- 21-22R
Tagliaferri, Aldo 1931- 77-80
Tagliavia, Sheila 1936- 104
Tagore, Amitendranath 1922- 61-64
Tagore, Rabindranath 1861-1941 120
Brief entry 104
See also TCLC 3
Taha, Hamdy A(bdelaziz) 1937- 37-40R
Taha, Karen T(erry) 1942- 120
Tahara, Mildred Machiko 1941- 104
Tahir, Abe M(ahmoud), Jr. 1931- 69-72
Tahir, Kemal 1910(?)-1973 Obituary 45-48
Tahlaquah, David
See LeMond, Alan
Tahtinen, Dale R(udolph) 1945- 65-68
Tai, Hung-chao 1929- 73-76
Taichert, Louise C(ecile) 1925- 89-92
Taikeff, Stanley 1940- 109
Taines, Beatrice (Green) 1923- CANR-14
Earlier sketch in CA 73-76
Taira, Koji 1926- 41-44R
Taishoff, Sol J(oseph) 1904-1982 73-76
Obituary 107
Tait, Alan A(nderson) 1934- CANR-10
Earlier sketch in CA 23-24R
Tait, Dorothy 1902(?)-1972 Obituary 33-36R
Tait, Douglas 1944- SATA-12
Tait, George E(dward) 1910- 7-8R
Tait, Katharine 1923- 65-68
Tait, L(eslie) Gordon 1926- 45-48
Taitz, Emily 1937- 85-88
Takacs, Carol Addison 1926- 124
Takagi, Akimitsu 1920- Brief entry 108
Takahashi, Akira 1932- 29-32R
Takahashi, Yasundo 1912- CANR-14
Earlier sketch in CA 41-44R
Takaki, Ronald T(oshiyuki) 1939- 37-40R
Takakjian, Portia 1930- SATA-15
Takashima, Shizuye 1928- 45-48
See also SATA 13
Takayama, Akira 1932- CANR-2
Earlier sketch in CA 49-52
Takeshita, Thomas Kohachiro
1891(?)-1973 Obituary 45-48
Taktsis, Costas 1927- 23-24R
Talafous, Don (Francis) 1926- 113
Talamantes, Florence Williams 1931- CANR-6
Earlier sketch in CA 57-60
Talamini, John T(homas) 1940-
Brief entry 113
Talarico, Ross 1945- 73-76
Talbert, Ansel Edward (McLaurine)
1912-1987 Obituary 124
Talbert, Charles Gano 1912- 5-6R
Talbert, Charles H(arold) 1934- CANR-14
Earlier sketch in CA 41-44R
Talbot, Alice-Mary 1939- 112
Talbot, Allan R. 1934- CANR-10
Earlier sketch in CA 21-22R
Talbot, Carol Terry 1913- 15-16R
Talbot, Charlene Joy 1928- CANR-8
Earlier sketch in CA 19-20R
See also SATA 10
Talbot, Edward Hugh Frederick Chetwynd
See Chetwynd-Talbot, Edward Hugh Frederick
Talbot, Godfrey (Walker) 1908- 107
Talbot, Gordon (Gray) 1928- CANR-14
Earlier sketch in CA 69-72
Talbot, Hugh
See Chetwynd-Talbot, Edward Hugh Frederick
Talbot, Kay
See Rowland, D(onald) S(ydney)
Talbot, Lawrence
See Bryant, Edward (Winslow, Jr.)
Talbot, Michael 1953- 119
Talbot, Nathan B(ill) 1909- 104
Talbot, Norman (Clare) 1936- CANR-9
Earlier sketch in CA 21-22R
Talbot, Ross B. 1919- 17-18R
Talbot, Toby 1928- 21-22R
See also SATA 14
Talbot Rice, David
See Rice, David Talbot
Talbot Rice, Tamara (Abelson)
See Rice, Tamara (Abelson) Talbot
Talbott, Basil 1899-1985 Obituary 117
Talbott, John E(dwin) 1940- 25-28R
Talbott, Robert D(ean) 1928- 57-60
Talbott, Strobe 1946- 93-96
See also AITN 1
Talcott, Dudley Vaill 1899-1986 Obituary ... 119
Talese, Gay 1932- CANR-9
Earlier sketch in CA 4R
See also CLC 37
See also AITN 1
Talker, T.
See Rands, William Brighty
Talkin, Gil
See Rosenthal, Alan
Talkington, Virginia Savage
See McAlester, Virginia
Tall, Deborah 1951- CANR-22
Earlier sketch in CA 105
Tall, Stephen
See Crook, Compton Newby
Talland, George A(lexander) 1917-19(?) .. CAP-2
Earlier sketch in CA 25-28
Tallcott, Emogene 29-32R
See also SATA 10
Tallent, Elizabeth (Ann) 1954- 117
See also CLC 45
Tallent, Norman 1921- 17-18R
Talleur, Richard W(iley) 1931- 97-100
Talley-Morris, Neva B(ennett) 1909- 57-60
Tallman, Albert 1902- 53-56
Tallon, Robert 1939- CANR-8
Earlier sketch in CA 11-12R
See also SATA 28, 43
Tally, Ted 1952- 124
Brief entry 120
See also CLC 42
Talmadge, Marian SATA-14

Talmage, Anne
See Powell, Talmage
Talmage, Frank (Ephraim) 1938- 97-100
Talmey, Allene
See Plaut, Allene Talmey
Talmon, Jacob L(aib) 1916-1980 ..... 13-14R
Obituary 101
Talmon, Shemaryahu 1920- CANR-12
Earlier sketch in CA 29-32R
Talpalar, Morris 1900- 73-76
Talvi
See Robinson, Therese
Talvj
See Robinson, Therese
Tamarin, Alfred H. 1913-1980 ..... CANR-4
Obituary 102
Earlier sketch in CA 29-32R
See also SATA 13
Tamasi, Aron 1897-1966 Obituary 114
Tambasco, Anthony J(oseph) 1939- 117
Tambi
See Tambimuttu, Thurairajah
Tambiah, S. J.
See Tambiah, Stanley Jeyaraja
Tambiah, Stanley Jeyaraja 1929- 123
Tambimuttu, Thurairajah 1915(?)-1983
Obituary 110
Tambs, Lewis Arthur 1927- CANR-4
Earlier sketch in CA 53-56
Tamburine, Jean 1930- 9-10R
See also SATA 12
Tamedly, Elisabeth L. 1931- 29-32R
Tames, Richard (Lawrence) 1946- 103
Tamir, Max Mordecai 1912- 29-32R
Tamir, Vicki 1924- 29-32R
Tammaro, Thom(as Michael) 1951- 109
Tammsaare, A(nton) H(ansen)
1878-1940 ..... TCLC-27
Tammuz, Benjamin 1919- 85-88
Tamny, Martin 1941- 37-40R
Tampion, John 1937- 73-76
Tamsin
See Summers, Ethel Snelson
Tamulaitis, Vytas 1913- 19-20R
Tamuno, Tekena N. 1932- 23-24R
Tana, Tomoe (Hayashima) 1913- 21-22R
Tanahashi, Kazuaki 1933- 122
Tanaka, Beatrice 1932- 115
Tanaquil, Paul
See Le Clercq, Jacques Georges
Clemenceau
Tanay, Emanuel 1928- 93-96
Tanchuck, Nathaniel 1912- 15-16R
Tancock, John (Leon) 1942- 105
Tancredi, Laurence R(ichard) 1940- 116
Tandem, Felix
See Spitteler, Carl
Tandon, Prakash 1911- 93-96
Tandy, Clifford Ronald Vivien
1919(?)-1981 Obituary 104
Tanenbaum, Jan Karl 1936- 61-64
Tanenbaum, Robert Brief entry 116
Tang, Peter Shen-Hao 1919- 3R
Tangerman, Elmer John 1907- CANR-23
Earlier sketch in CA 106
Tangri, Shanti S. 1928- 25-28R
Tangye, Nigel (Trevithick) 1909-
Brief entry 117
Tanham, George K(ilpatrick) 1922- CANR-1
Earlier sketch in CA 1R
Tania B.
See Blixen, Karen (Christentze Dinesen)
Taniguchi, Kazuko 1946- 93-96
Taniguchi, Masaharu 1893-1985 Obituary 116
Tanikawa, Shuntaro 1931- 121
Tanis, James (Robert) 1928- 118
Tanis, Norman Earl 1929- 110
Tanizaki, Jun'ichiro 1886-1965 93-96
Obituary 25-28R
See also CLC 8, 14, 28
Tank, Herbert 1922(?)-1982 Obituary 108
Tank, Ronald W(arren) 1929- 49-52
Tankard, Alice (Doumanian) 1926- 117
Tankard, James William, Jr. 1941- 73-76
Tanksley, Perry 1928- 37-40R
Tann, Jennifer 1939- 103
Tannahill, Reay 1929- CANR-2
Earlier sketch in CA 49-52
Tannehill, Robert C(ooper) 1934- 45-48
Tannen, Deborah F(rances) 1945- 118
Tannen, Jack 1907- 114
Tannen, Mary 1943- 105
See also SATA 37
Tannenbaum, Arnold S(herwood) 1925- 17-18R
Tannenbaum, Arthur C. 1941- 123
Tannenbaum, Beulah Goldstein 1916- CANR-7
Earlier sketch in CA 5-6R
See also SATA 3
Tannenbaum, D(onald) Leb 1948- 115
See also SATA 42
Tannenbaum, Edward R(obert) 1921- 19-20R
Tannenbaum, Frank 1893-1969 ..... 9-10R
Tannenbaum, Harold E. 1914- 5-6R
Tannenbaum, Percy Hyman 1927-
Brief entry 106
Tannenbaum, Robert 1915- 23-24R
Tanner, C(harles) Kenneth 1938- 53-56
Tanner, Clara L(ee) 1905- 41-44R
Tanner, Daniel 1926- 17-18R
Tanner, Edward Everett III 1921-1976 73-76
Obituary 69-72
Tanner, Helen Hornbeck 1916- 61-64
Tanner, Henry 1918- 73-76
Tanner, James M(ourilyan) 1920- CANR-5
Earlier sketch in CA 13-14R
Tanner, James T(homas) F(ontenot)
1937- 41-44R
Tanner, John (Ian) 1927- 103
Tanner, John
See Matcha, Jack
Tanner, Louise S(tickney) 1922- 69-72
See also SATA 9
Tanner, Paul O(ra) W(arren) 1917- 61-64
Tanner, Roy L(ynn) 1947- 118
Tanner, Stephen L. 1938- 123
Tanner, Tony 1935- 85-88
Tanner-Rutherford, C.
See Winchester, Clarence
Tanobe, Miyuki 1937- 69-72
See also SATA 23
Tanous, Peter (Joseph) 1938- CANR-7
Earlier sketch in CA 61-64
Tanselle, G(eorge) Thomas 1934- CANR-11
Earlier sketch in CA 21-22R
Tansill, Charles Callan 1890-1964 ..... 1R
Tanter, Raymond 1938- 45-48
Tantrist
See Cox, P(atrick) Brian
Tanyzer, Harold Joseph 1929- 11-12R
Tanzer, Lester 1929- 19-20R
Tanzer, Michael David 1935- 57-60
Tanzi, Vito 1935- CANR-5
Earlier sketch in CA 53-56
Tao Mulian
See Totten, George Oakley III
Tapia, Ralph J(ohn) 1925- 41-44R
Tapio, Pat Decker
See Kines, Pat Decker
Tapley, Caroline 1934- 97-100
Taplin, Glen W(illiam) 1917- 107
Taplin, Oliver 1943- 102
Taplin, Walter 1910- CAP-1
Earlier sketch in CA 9-10
Taplinger, Cecily Lent 1943-1983 Obituary 110
Taplinger, Richard Jacques 1911-1973
Obituary 41-44R
Taplinger, Terry
See Taplinger, Cecily Lent
Tapp, Jack Thomas 1934- 49-52
Tapp, June Louin 1929- 41-44R
Tapp, Kathy Kennedy 1949- 116
See also SATA 50
Tapp, Robert B(erg) 1925- 41-44R
Tappan, Paul Wilbur 1911-1964 ..... 5-6R
Tappert, Theodore G(erhardt)
1904-1973 ..... CANR-2
Earlier sketch in CA 2R
Tapply, William G(eorge) 1940- 118
Tapply H(orace) G(ardner) 1910- 15-16R
Tapscott, Stephen (J.) 1948- CANR-17
Earlier sketch in CA 89-92
Tapsell, R(obert) F(rederick) 1936- 21-22R
Taradash, Daniel 1913- 101
See also DLB 44
Taranovsky, Kiril 1911- 114
Taranow, Gerda 37-40R
Tarascio, Vincent J(oseph) 1930- 45-48
Tarassoff, Lev
See Troyat, Henri
Tarazaga, Santiago Genoves
See Genoves Tarazaga, Santiago
Tarbell, Ida M(inerva) 1857-1944
Brief entry 122
See also DLB 47
Tarbert, Gary C(harles) 1937- 101
Tarcher, Martin 1921- 19-20R
Tardieu, Jean 1903- Brief entry 116
Tardiff, Olive 1916- 73-76
Tardy, Gaye 1929(?)-1982 Obituary 108
Targ, Harry R. 1940- 118
Targ, Russell 1934- 104
Targ, William 1907- 61-64
Targan, Barry 1932- CANR-17
Earlier sketch in CA 73-76
Target, G(eorge) W(illiam) 1924- CANR-7
Earlier sketch in CA 7-8R
Tarica, Ralph 1932- 113
Tarkenton, Fran(cis Asbury) 1940- 103
Tarkington, (Newton) Booth 1869-1946
Brief entry 110
See also SATA 17
See also DLB 9
See also TCLC 9
Tarling, (Peter) Nicholas 1931- 21-22R
Tarlock, A(nthony) Dan 1940- CANR-16
Earlier sketch in CA 97-100
Tarlov, I. M. 1905(?)-1977 Obituary 69-72
Tarlton, Gillian Leigh 1953- 119
Tarn, John Nelson 1934- 41-44R
Tarn, Nathaniel 1928- CANR-5
Earlier sketch in CA 11-12R
Tarnawsky, Ostap 1917- 73-76
Tarnopol, Lester 1913- 77-80
Tarnower, Herman 1910-1980 89-92
Obituary 97-100
Tarpey, Elizabeth (Pinscher) 1880-1979 ..... CANR-4
Earlier sketch in CA 7-8R
Tarpey, Lawrence Xavier 1928- 23-24R
Tarpley, Fred 1932- 41-44R
Tarpy, Roger M(aynard) 1941- 93-96
Tarr, Herbert 1929- 13-14R
Tarr, Joel A(rthur) 1934- CANR-14
Earlier sketch in CA 37-40R
Tarr, Judith 1955- 120
Tarr, Rodger L(eRoy) 1941- 110
Tarr, Yvonne Young 1929- CANR-8
Earlier sketch in CA 61-64
Tarrance, V(ernon) Lance, Jr. 1940- 37-40R
Tarrant, Desmond 1924- 23-24R
Tarrant, John
See Egleton, Clive (Frederick)
Tarrant, John J(oseph) 1924- CANR-19
Earlier sketches in CA 53-56, CANR-4
Tarrant, Wilma
See Sherman, Jory (Tecumseh)
Tarrok, Peer
See Zwerenz, Gerhard
Tarry, Ellen 1906- 73-76
See also SATA 16
Tarsaidze, Alexandre 1901-1978 ..... 37-40R
Obituary 77-80
Tarshis, Jerome 1936- 61-64
See also SATA 9
Tarsis, Valery Yakovlevich 1906-1983
Obituary 109
Tarski, Alfred 1901(?)-1983 Obituary 111
Tarsky, Sue 112
See also SATA 41
Tart, Charles T(heodore) 1937- 29-32R
Tarter, Donald E(dward) 1938- 112
Tartre, Raymond S. 1901-1975 ..... CAP-2
Earlier sketch in CA 21-22
Tarver, Ben 1927- 113
Tasca, Henry J. 1912-1979 Obituary 89-92
Tasca, Jules 1938- 109
See also AITN 1
Tasch, Peter A(nthony) 1933- 73-76
Taschdjian, Claire L(ouise) 1914- 73-76
Tashjian, Dickran (Levon) 1940- 61-64
Tashjian, Virginia A. 1921- 29-32R
See also SATA 3
Tashlin, Frank 1913-1972 113
Obituary 110
See also DLB 44
Tasker, James 1908- 49-52
See also SATA 9
Tasker, Joe 1948-1982 Obituary 108
Tassin, Myron Jude 1933- 61-64
Tassin, Ray(mond Jean) 1926- 53-56
Tatar, Maria M. 1945- 85-88
Tatarkiewicz, Wladyslaw 1886-1980 103
Obituary 97-100
Tate, (John Orley) Allen 1899-1979 ..... 5-6R
Obituary 85-88
See also DLB 4, 45, 63
See also CLC 2, 4, 6, 9, 11, 14, 24
Tate, B. H.
See Boyer, Bruce Hatton
Tate, Claudia C. 1946- 121
Tate, Edward
See Dransfield, Michael (John Pender)
Tate, Eleanora E(laine) 1948- 105
See also SATA 38
Tate, Ellalice
See Hibbert, Eleanor Burford
Tate, Gary 1930- 23-24R
Tate, George T(homas) 1931- 21-22R
Tate, Jackson R. 1899(?)-1978 Obituary 81-84
Tate, James 1943- 21-22R
See also DLB 5
See also CLC 2, 6, 25
Tate, Joan 1922- CANR-1
Earlier sketch in CA 49-52
See also SATA 9
Tate, Marilyn Freeman 1921- 13-14R
Tate, Mary Anne
See Hale, Arlene
Tate, Merle W(esley) 1903- CAP-1
Earlier sketch in CA 17-18
Tate, Merze 17-18R
Tate, Richard
See Masters, Anthony
Tate, Robin
See Fanthorpe, R(obert) Lionel
Tate, Velma 1913- 23-24R
Tatelbaum, Judith Ann 1938- 104
Tatelbaum, Judy
See Tatelbaum, Judith Ann
Tatford, Brian F(rederick) B(arrington)
1927- CAP-1
Earlier sketch in CA 9-10
Tatford, Frederick Albert 1901- CANR-10
Earlier sketch in CA 15-16R
Tatgenhorst, John 1938- 65-68
Tatham, C. Ernest 1905- CAP-1
Earlier sketch in CA 9-10
Tatham, Campbell
See Elting, Mary
Tatham, Laura (Esther) 1919- 13-14R
Tati, Jacques
See Tatischeff, Jacques
Tatischeff, Jacques 1908-1982 Obituary 108
Tatlow, Antony 1935- 122
Taton, Rene 1915- 9-10R
Tatray, Istvan
See Rupert, Raphael Rudolph
Tattersall, Ian (Michael) 1945- 115
Tattersall, (Honor) Jill 1931- CANR-10
Earlier sketch in CA 25-28R
Tattersall, Lawrence H(olmes) 1933- 29-32R
Tattersall, M(uriel Joyce) 1931- CAP-1
Earlier sketch in CA 9-10
Tatu, Michel 1933- 25-28R
Tatum, Arlo 1923- 25-28R
Tatum, Billy Joe 1933- 61-64
Tatum, Charles M(ichael) 1943- 111
Tatum, Edward Lawrie 1909-1975
Obituary 113
Tatum, Jack
See Tatum, John David
Tatum, John David 1948- 104
Taub, Harald (Jay) 1918- 110
Taube, Evert 1890-1976 Obituary 61-64
Taube, Lester S. 1920- 69-72
Taubenfeld, Howard J(ack) 1924- 13-14R
Tauber, Abraham 1915(?)-1977 Obituary 69-72
Tauber, Edward S(anford) 1908-1988
Obituary 124
Tauber, Gerald E(rich) 1922- 89-92
Tauber, Gilbert 1935- CANR-9
Earlier sketch in CA 21-22R
Tauber, Kurt P(hilip) 1922- 21-22R
Tauber, Maurice F(alcolm) 1908-1980 105
Obituary 102
Tauber, Peter 1947- 37-40R
Taubert, Sigfred 1914- 120
Taubert, William H(owland) 1934- 103
Taubes, Frederic 1900-1981 ..... CANR-9
Obituary 104
Earlier sketch in CA 17-18R
Taubes, Susan
See Feldmann, Susan Judith
Taubman, William 1941- 23-24R
Taubr, Paul Raymond 1937- 29-32R
Taunton, Eric
See Westcott-Jones, K(enneth)
Tauranac, John 1939- 124
Tavard, George H(enry) 1922- CANR-16
Earlier sketches in CA 1R, CANR-1
Tave, Stuart M(alcolm) 1923- 104
Tavel, Ronald 1940- 21-22R
See also CLC 6
Taverne, Dick 1928- 85-88
Tavernier, Bertrand 1941- 123
Taves, Ernest H(enry) 1916- 93-96
Taves, Isabella 1915- CANR-8
Earlier sketch in CA 23-24R
See also SATA 27
Taviss, Irene
See Thomson, Irene Taviss
Tavo, Gus
See Ivan, Martha Miller Pfaff
Tavuchis, Nicholas 1934- 57-60
Tavy, Peter
See Hemery, Eric
Tawney, R(ichard) H(enry) 1880-1962
Obituary 93-96
Tax, Sol 1907- 7-8R
Taydo
See McDonald, Erwin L(awrence)
Taylor, A(lan) J(ohn) P(ercivale) 1906- 7-8R
Taylor, Alan Carey 1905-1975 Obituary 114
Taylor, Alan R(os) 1926- 109
Taylor, Alastair M(acDonald) 1915- 17-18R
Taylor, Albert E(dward) 1908- 89-92
Taylor, Alfred 1896-1973 105
Taylor, Alice J. 1909-1969 ..... CAP-2
Earlier sketch in CA 25-28
Taylor, Alice L(ouise) 1911-1985 61-64
Obituary 116
Taylor, Alison 1927- 21-22R
Taylor, Alix 1921- 5-6R
Taylor, Andrew (McDonald) 1940- CANR-11
Earlier sketch in CA 69-72
Taylor, Andrew (John Robert) 1951- 110
Taylor, Anique 1946- 109
Taylor, Ann 1782-1866 ..... SATA-35, 41
Taylor, Ann
See Smith, Richard Rein
Taylor, Anna 1944- 25-28R
Taylor, Anne (Gary) Pannell 1910-1984
Obituary 112
Taylor, Archer 1890-1973 Obituary 107
Taylor, Arnold H. 1929- 33-36R
Taylor, Art
See Taylor, Arthur (Stephen)
Taylor, Arthur (Stephen) 1929- 122
Taylor, Arthur Samuel 1894-1963 ..... 2R
Obituary 103
Taylor, Barbara G. 1942- 25-28R
Taylor, Barbara J. 1927- 53-56
See also SATA 10
Taylor, Bayard 1825-1878 ..... DLB-3
Taylor, Benjamin J. 1934- 21-22R
Taylor, Bernard 1934- CANR-24
Earlier sketch in CA 69-72
Taylor, Bert Leston 1866-1921 Brief entry 117
See also DLB 25
Taylor, Betty Jo 1933- 15-16R
Taylor, Bob L(eslie) 1923- 33-36R
Taylor, Brad
See Smith, Richard Rein
Taylor, Carl 1937- 69-72
See also SATA 14
Taylor, Cecil Philip 1929-1981 ..... 25-28R
Obituary 105
See also CLC 27
Taylor, Charlene M(ae) 1938- 33-36R
Taylor, Charles 1931- CANR-11
Earlier sketch in CA 15-16R
Taylor, Charles Alfred 1922- 109
Taylor, Charles D(oonan) 1938- CANR-17
Earlier sketch in CA 101
Taylor, Charles H. 1846-1921 ..... DLB-25
Taylor, Charles Lewis 1935- CANR-13
Earlier sketch in CA 77-80
Taylor, Clyde R(ussell) 1931- 45-48
Taylor, Constance Lindsay 1907- 106
Taylor, Cora (Lorraine) 1936- 124
Taylor, Cora Sibal 1941(?)-1987 Obituary 123
Taylor, D. J. 1960- 122
Taylor, Dalmas A(rnold) 1933- 57-60
Taylor, David 1900-1965 ..... 3R
See also SATA 10
Taylor, David (Conrad) 1934- 105
Taylor, David Alan 1943- 108
Taylor, Dawson 1916- 13-14R
Taylor, Day
See Parkinson, Cornelia M.
and Salvato, Sharon
Taylor, Dayna
See Parkinson, Cornelia M.
Taylor, (Joseph) Deems 1885-1966
Obituary 89-92
Taylor, Demetria 1903-1977 Obituary 73-76
Taylor, (Edmund) Dennis 1940- 119

Taylor, Desmond 1930- 37-40R
Taylor, Don(ald) 1910- 13-14R
Taylor, Donald L(avor) 1916- 19-20R
Taylor, Donald Stewart 1924- Brief entry 106
Taylor, Donna June 1949- 37-40R
Taylor, Duncan (Burnett) 1912- 25-28R
Taylor, Duncan Norton
See Norton-Taylor, Duncan
Taylor, Dwight 1902-1986(?) Obituary 121
Taylor, Earl Aulick 1904-1965 .... CAP-1
Earlier sketch in CA 13-14
Taylor, Edith 1913- 45-48
Taylor, Edward 1642(?)-1729 .... DLB-24
Taylor, Eleanor Ross 1920- 81-84
See also CLC 5
Taylor, Elisabeth Russell
See Russell Taylor, Elisabeth
Taylor, Elizabeth 1912-1975 .... CANR-9
Earlier sketch in CA 13-14R
See also SATA 13
See also CLC 2, 4, 29
Taylor, Elizabeth Tebbetts 101
Taylor, Ethel Stoddard 1895(?)-1975
Obituary 57-60
Taylor, Eugene Jackson 1913-1978
Obituary 81-84
Taylor, Florance Walton 37-40R
See also SATA 9
Taylor, Florence M(arian Tompkins)
1892- 15-16R
See also SATA 9
Taylor, Frank J. 1894-1972 .... CAP-1
Obituary 37-40R
Earlier sketch in CA 13-14
Taylor, Fred James 1919- 107
Taylor, (George) Frederick 1928- 77-80
Taylor, G(eorge) Jeffrey 1944- 116
Taylor, George
See Parulski, George R(ichard), Jr.
Taylor, George A(lbert) 1942- 102
Taylor, George E(dward) 1905- CANR-22
Earlier sketch in CA 2R
Taylor, Gordon O(verton) 1938- 25-28R
Taylor, Gordon Rattray 1911-1981 85-88
Obituary 105
Taylor, (Frank Herbert) Griffin 1917- 65-68
Taylor, H. Baldwin
See Waugh, Hillary Baldwin
Taylor, H. Kerr 1891(?)-1977 Obituary 73-76
Taylor, Harold 1914- 25-28R
Taylor, Harold L(awrence) 1934- 110
Taylor, Harold McCarter 1907- 109
Taylor, Harold S. 1901(?)-1985 Obituary 116
Taylor, Harry
See Granick, Harry
Taylor, Harry H. 1926- 57-60
Taylor, Henry 1800-1886 .... DLB-32
Taylor, Henry (Splawn) 1942- 33-36R
See also DLB 5
See also CLC 44
Taylor, Henry J(unior) 1902-1984 .... CAP-2
Obituary 112
Earlier sketch in CA 23-24
Taylor, Herb(ert Norman, Jr.)
1942-1987 97-100
Obituary 123
See also SATA 22
Taylor, Howard F(rancis) 1939- 110
Taylor, Hugh 1917(?)-1987 Obituary 123
Taylor, Hugh A(lexander) 1920- 115
Taylor, Ian 1944- 77-80
Taylor, Ina (Margaret Kathleen) 1949- 119
Taylor, Irving A. 1925- 61-64
Taylor, J. Thomas 1930- 107
Taylor, Jack W(ilson) 1915- 11-12R
Taylor, James B(entley) 1930- 37-40R
Taylor, James C(hapman) 1937- 77-80
Taylor, James R(owe) 1907- CAP-2
Earlier sketch in CA 17-18
Taylor, James Spear 1897(?)-1979
Obituary 85-88
Taylor, James Stephen 1935- 121
Taylor, Jane 1783-1824 .... SATA-35, 41
Taylor, Janelle (Diane Williams) 1944- 124
Taylor, Janelle (Williams) 1944-
Brief entry 118
Taylor, (Samuel) Jared 1951- 122
Taylor, Jed H(arbottle) 1902- CAP-1
Earlier sketch in CA 15-16
Taylor, Jenny 1910- 105
Taylor, Jerome 1918- CANR-1
Earlier sketch in CA 3R
Taylor, Jerry D(uncan) 1938- 115
See also SATA 47
Taylor, Jesse
See Amidon, Bill (Vincent)
Taylor, Jim 1937- 119
Taylor, Joan du Plat ?-1983 Obituary 109
Taylor, Joe Gray 1920- CANR-6
Earlier sketch in CA 57-60
Taylor, John 1916- 93-96
Taylor, John 1921- CANR-16
Earlier sketch in CA 23-24R
Taylor, John 1925- 81-84
Taylor, John (Alfred) 1931- 61-64
Taylor, John 1955- 124
Taylor, John F(rank) A(dams) 1915- 19-20R
Taylor, John G(erald) 1931- 29-32R
Taylor, John Laverack 1937- CANR-1
Earlier sketch in CA 45-48
Taylor, John M(axwell) 1930- 25-28R
Taylor, John Randolph 1929- 1R
Taylor, John Russell 1935- 5-6R
Taylor, John Vernon 1914- CANR-21
Earlier sketches in CA 9-10R, CANR-5
Taylor, John W(illiam) R(ansom) 1922- 49-52
Taylor, Joshua Charles 1917-1981 104
Taylor, Judy
See Hough, Judy Taylor
Taylor, Kamala (Purnaiya) 1924- 77-80
Taylor, Karen Malpede 1945- 45-48
Taylor, Karl K. 1938- 41-44R
Taylor, Katharine Whiteside 1897- CAP-2
Earlier sketch in CA 25-28
Taylor, Keith Weller 1946- 111
Taylor, Ken 1922- 108
Taylor, Kenneth N(athaniel) 1917- CANR-8
Earlier sketch in CA 19-20R
See also SATA 26
See also AITN 2
Taylor, (Paul) Kent 1940- CANR-9
Earlier sketch in CA 17-18R
Taylor, L(aurie) A(ylma) 1939- 111
Taylor, L(ester) B(arbour), Jr. 1932- CANR-11
Earlier sketch in CA 57-60
See also SATA 27
Taylor, Laurie
See Taylor, L(aurie) A(ylma)
Taylor, Lawrence 1942- 105
Taylor, (M.) Lee 1930- 41-44R
Taylor, Lester D(ean) 1938- 17-18R
Taylor, Lloyd A(ndrew) 1921- 41-44R
Taylor, Lloyd C(hamberlain), Jr. 1923- 57-60
Taylor, Lois Dwight Cole
See Cole, Lois Dwight
Taylor, Lord
See Taylor, Stephen James Lake
Taylor, Louis 1900- CANR-2
Earlier sketch in CA 7-8R
Taylor, Louise Todd 1939- 115
See also SATA 47
Taylor, Malcolm Gordon 1915- 109
Taylor, Margaret
See Burroughs, Margaret Taylor
Taylor, Margaret Stewart 89-92
Taylor, Marion Ansel 1904- 13-14R
Taylor, Mark 1927- 108
See also SATA 28, 32
Taylor, Mary Ann 1912- 97-100
Taylor, Maxwell D(avenport) 1901-1987
Obituary 122
Brief entry 111
Taylor, Michael J. 1924- CANR-7
Earlier sketch in CA 19-20R
Taylor, Michael J. H. 1949- CANR-14
Earlier sketch in CA 77-80
Taylor, Michael M. 1944- 97-100
Taylor, Mildred D. 1943- 85-88
See also SATA 15
See also SAAS 5
See also DLB 52
See also CLC 21
See also CLR 9
Taylor, Morris F. 1915- 37-40R
Taylor, Norman 1883-1967 .... CAP-2
Earlier sketch in CA 23-24
Taylor, Owen Reece 1912(?)-1983
Obituary 111
Taylor, Pat Ellis 1941- 111
Taylor, Paul 1948- 121
Taylor, Paul B(eekman) 1930- 81-84
Taylor, Paul S(chuster) 1895-1984 81-84
Obituary 112
Taylor, Paul W(arren) 1923- CANR-21
Earlier sketch in CA 4R
Taylor, Paula (Wright) 1942- 122
Brief entry 111
See also SATA 33, 48
Taylor, Peggy 1946- 120
Taylor, Peter (Hillsman) 1917- CANR-9
Earlier sketch in CA 15-16R
See also DLBY 81
See also CLC 1, 4, 18, 37, 44
Taylor, Philip Elbert 1908-1975 Obituary 61-64
Taylor, Phoebe Atwood 1909-1976
Obituary 61-64
Taylor, Phoebe Jean 1921(?)-1979
Obituary 89-92
Taylor, Ransom Theodore 1913- 45-48
Taylor, Ray J. 1918(?)-1977 Obituary 69-72
Taylor, Ray Ward 1908- CAP-2
Earlier sketch in CA 19-20
Taylor, Rebe Prestwich 1911- 13-14R
Taylor, Rex 1921- 13-14R
Taylor, Richard 1919- 17-18R
Taylor, Richard K(night) 1933- CANR-18
Earlier sketch in CA 101
Taylor, Richard S(helley) 1912- 115
Taylor, Richard W(arren) 1924- CANR-19
Earlier sketches in CA 7-8R, CANR-3
Taylor, Robert 1925- 81-84
Taylor, Robert B(artley) 1926- 81-84
Taylor, Robert Brown 1936- CANR-12
Earlier sketch in CA 61-64
Taylor, Robert, Jr. 1941- 118
Taylor, Robert Lewis 1912- CANR-3
Earlier sketch in CA 3R
See also SATA 10
See also CLC 14
Taylor, Robert Martin 1909- CAP-2
Earlier sketch in CA 25-28
Taylor, Robert R(atcliffe) 1939- 53-56
Taylor, Roland 1907- CAP-1
Earlier sketch in CA 13-14
Taylor, Ron(ald) W(illiam) 1922- CAP-1
Earlier sketch in CA 11-12
Taylor, Ronald (Jack) 1924- 93-96
Taylor, Ronald L(ee) 1938- 77-80
Taylor, Ross McLaury 1909(?)-1977
Obituary 69-72
Taylor, Rupert (Maurice) 1946- 45-48
Taylor, Ruth Mattson 1922- 101
Taylor, Samuel (Wooley) 1907- 73-76
Taylor, Samuel (Albert) 1912- 25-28R
Taylor, Sandra C. 1936- 123
Taylor, Stephen
See Taylor, Stephen James Lake
Taylor, Stephen James Lake 1910-1988
Obituary 124
Taylor, Sybil (Renee) 1933- 122
Taylor, Sydney (Brenner) 1904(?)-1978 .... CANR-4
Obituary 77-80
Earlier sketch in CA 5-6R
See also SATA 1, 26, 28
Taylor, T. G.
See Taylor, T(homas) Geoffrey
Taylor, T(homas) Geoffrey 1918-1987
Obituary 123
Taylor, Telford 1908- CANR-16
Earlier sketch in CA 25-28R
Taylor, Theodore 1921- CANR-9
Earlier sketch in CA 21-22R
See also SATA 5
See also SAAS 4
Taylor, Theodore Brewster 1925- 102
Taylor, Theodore W(alter) 1913- 119
Taylor, Thomas 1934- 23-24R
Taylor, Tim 1920-1974 45-48
Obituary 53-56
Taylor, Tom
See Taylor, J. Thomas
Taylor, Valerie
See Tate, Velma
Taylor, Vernon L. 1922- 33-36R
Taylor, Verta 1948- 114
Taylor, W(illiam) H(odge) 1904-1984
Obituary 113
Taylor, Walter Fuller 1900-1966 .... 1R
Taylor, Walter W(illard) 1913- 61-64
Taylor, Warren 1903- 23-24R
Taylor, Weldon J. 1908- 4R
Taylor, Welford Dunaway 1938- 37-40R
Taylor, Wendell H(ertig) 1905- 102
Taylor, William 1930- CANR-15
Earlier sketch in CA 81-84
Taylor, William David, Jr. 1902-1975
Obituary 107
Taylor, William E(dwards) 1920- CANR-10
Earlier sketch in CA 25-28R
Taylor, William L. 1937- 29-32R
Taylor, Zack 1927- 65-68
Taylor-Gooby, Peter 1947- 118
Taylor-Olson, Clara Mae 1899(?)-1988
Obituary 124
Tazewell, Charles 1900-1972 Obituary 37-40R
Tazieff, Haroun 1914- Brief entry 113
Tchaadaieff
See Sorokin, Pitirim A(lexandrovitch)
Tchekhov, Anton
See Chekhov, Anton (Pavlovich)
Tchernichovski, Saul (Gutmanovich)
1875-1943 Brief entry 116
Tchividjian, Gigi Graham 1945- 108
Tchobanoglous, George 1935- 102
Tchudi, Stephen N. 1942- CANR-22
Earlier sketch in CA 89-92
Tead, Ordway 1891-1973 Obituary 45-48
Teaford, Jon C(hristian) 1946- CANR-10
Earlier sketch in CA 65-68
Teague, Bob
See Teague, Robert
Teague, Kathleen 1937- 97-100
Teague, Michael 1932- 109
Teague, Robert 1929- 106
See also SATA 31, 32
Teal, G. Donn 1932- 33-36R
Teal, John J(erome), Jr. 1921-1982
Obituary 110
Teal, Val(entine M.) 1903- 61-64
See also SATA 10
Teale, Edwin Way 1899-1980 .... CANR-2
Obituary 102
Earlier sketch in CA 2R
See also SATA 7, 25
Teasdale, Sara 1884-1933 Brief entry 104
See also SATA 32
See also DLB 45
See also TCLC 4
Tebbel, John (William) 1912- 85-88
See also SATA 26
Tebbel, Robert E(verett) 1924- 7-8R
Tebbetts-Taylor, Elizabeth
See Taylor, Elizabeth Tebbetts
Tebeau, Charlton Watson 1904- 110
Tebelak, John-Michael 1949(?)-1985
Obituary 115
Tec, Leon 1919- 97-100
Tec, Nechama 1931- CANR-23
Earlier sketch in CA 11-12R
Teck, Alan 1934- 25-28R
Tedder, Arthur William 1890-1967 .... CAP-2
Earlier sketch in CA 23-24
Tedder, Lord
See Tedder, Arthur William
Teddy, Paul
See Aldrich, Jonathan
Tedeschi, (Theodore) James, Jr. 1928- 41-44R
Tedlock, E(rnest) W(arnock), Jr. 1910- CAP-2
Earlier sketch in CA 17-18
Tedrow, R. L.
See Tedrow, Richard L(ove)
Tedrow, Richard L(ove) 1913(?)-1987
Obituary 121
Teegen, Otto John 1899-1983 Obituary 109
Teer, Frank 1934- 53-56
Teeter, Don E(l) 1934- 73-76
Teeter, Karl V(an Duyn) 1929- 19-20R
Teeters, Negley K(ing) 1896-1971 .... CAP-2
Obituary 33-36R
Earlier sketch in CA 23-24
Teetor, Paul R(aymond) 1919- 113
Teets, Bruce E. 1914- 37-40R
Tee-Van, Helen Damrosch 1893-1976 49-52
Obituary 65-68
See also SATA 10, 27
Teevan, Richard C(ollier) 1919- CANR-4
Earlier sketch in CA 1R
Teffeteller, Gordon Lamar 1931- 115
Tefft, Bess H(agaman) 1915(?)-1977
Obituary 110
Tega, Vasile 1921- CANR-18
Earlier sketch in CA 102
Tegenfeldt, Herman G(ustaf) 1913- 73-76
Tegner, Bruce 1928- CANR-8
Earlier sketch in CA 61-64
Tegner, Henry (Stuart) 1901- CANR-12
Earlier sketch in CA 13-14R
Teich, Albert H(arris) 1942- 45-48
Teicher, Morton I(rving) 1920- CANR-11
Earlier sketch in CA 69-72
Teichmann, Howard (Miles)
1916-1987 .... CANR-17
Obituary 123
Earlier sketch in CA 69-72
Teikmanis, Arthur L. 1914- 15-16R
Teilhard de Chardin, (Marie Joseph) Pierre
1881-1955 Brief entry 105
See also TCLC 9
Teiser, Ruth 1915- 109
Teissier du Cros, Janet 1906- CAP-2
Earlier sketch in CA 17-18
Teitelbaum, Harry 1930- 23-24R
Teitelbaum, Michael 1953- 121
Teitelbaum, Myron 1929- 15-16R
Teixeira, Bernardo 1926- 108
Teixeira da Mota, Avelino ?-1982 Obituary 106
Tekeyan, Charles 1927- 29-32R
Telander, Richard F(orster) 1948- 65-68
Teleki, Geza 1943- CANR-19
Earlier sketches in CA 49-52, CANR-3
See also SATA 45
Telemaque, Eleanor Wong 1934- 104
See also SATA 43
Telescope, Tom
See Newbery, John
Telfer, Dariel (Doris) 1905-1987 .... CAP-2
Obituary 122
Earlier sketch in CA 25-28
Telfer, R(oss) 1937- 106
Telfer, William 1886-1968 .... CAP-1
Earlier sketch in CA 13-14
Telford, Charles W(itt) 1903- 65-68
Tell, Jack 1909(?)-1979 Obituary 89-92
Teller, Edward 1908- CAP-1
Earlier sketch in CA 13-14
Teller, James D(avid) 1906- 41-44R
Teller, Judd L. 1912-1972 Obituary 33-36R
Teller, Neville 1931- CANR-23
Earlier sketch in CA 103
Teller, Walter (Magnes) 1910- CANR-2
Earlier sketch in CA 5-6R
Tello, Carlos 1938- 112
Telser, Lester G(reenspan) 1931- 33-36R
Temianka, Henri 1906- 45-48
Temin, Peter 1937- 15-16R
Temkin, Pauline B. 1919- 25-28R
Temkin, Sara Anne Schlossberg 1913- 3R
See also SATA 26
Temko, Florence CANR-17
Earlier sketches in CA 49-52, CANR-1
See also SATA 13
Temmer, Mark J. 1922- Brief entry 107
Temp, George (Edward) 1929- 45-48
Temperley, Howard 1932- 85-88
Temperley, Nicholas 1932- 107
Tempest, Jan
See Swatridge, Irene Maude (Mossop)
Tempest, Margaret Mary 1892-1982
Obituary 108
See also SATA 33
Tempest, Sarah
See Ponsonby, D(oris) A(lmon)
Tempest, Theresa
See Kent, Louise Andrews
Tempest, Victor
See Philipp, Elliot Elias
Templar, Maurice
See Groom, Arthur William
Temple, Ann
See Mortimer, Penelope (Ruth)
Temple, Arthur
See Northcott, (William) Cecil
Temple, Cliff 1947- 111
Temple, Dan
See Newton, D(wight) B(ennett)
Temple, Herbert 1919- SATA-45
Temple, Joe 1917- 97-100
Temple, Nigel (Hal Longdale) 1926- 29-32R
Temple, Paul
See Durbridge, Francis (Henry)
and McConnell, James Douglas
Rutherford
Temple, Philip (Robert) 1939- CANR-22
Earlier sketch in CA 104
Temple, Robert (Kyle Grenville) 1945- CANR-16
Earlier sketch in CA 89-92
Temple, Robert M(ickler), Jr. 1935-
Brief entry 107
Temple, Ruth Z(abriskie) 1908- 61-64
Temple, Wayne C(alhoun) 1924- CANR-17
Earlier sketches in CA 1R, CANR-1
Temple, Willard H. 1912- 1R
Temple, William 1881-1944 Brief entry 120
Templeton, Charles B. 1915- 101
Templeton, Edith 1916- 53-56
Templeton, Janet
See Hershman, Morris
Templeton, John J(oseph), Jr. 1928- 25-28R

Tenax
See Lean, Garth Dickinson
ten Boom, Corrie 1892-1983 ... 111
Obituary ... 109
Tendryakov, Vladimir Fyodorovich
1923-1984(?) ... 104
Obituary ... 113
Tenenbaum, Frances 1919- ... CANR-12
Earlier sketch in CA 73-76
Tenenbaum, Shea 1910- ... CANR-1
Earlier sketch in CA 49-52
Tener, Robert L(awrence) 1924- ... 110
Teng, S(su)-Y(u) 1906- ... CANR-22
Earlier sketch in CA 13-14R
Tengbom, Mildred 1921- ... CANR-17
Earlier sketch in CA 97-100
Tenggren, Gustaf 1896-1970 ... SATA-18, 26
Ten Harmsel, Henrietta 1921- ... 106
Ten Hoor, Elvie (Marie Mortensen)
1900-1984 ... 11-12R
Obituary ... 112
TenHouten, Warren David 1939-
Brief entry ... 108
Tenison, Marika Hanbury
See Hanbury-Tenison, Marika
Tenison, Robin Hanbury
See Hanbury-Tenison, (Airling) Robin
Tenn, Ada N(ina) 1915- ... CANR-11
Earlier sketch in CA 25-28R
Tenn, William 1919- ... DLB-8
Tennant, Alan 1943- ... 108
Tennant, Emma 1937- ... CANR-10
Earlier sketch in CA 65-68
See also DLB 14
See also CLC 13
Tennant, Kylie
See Rodd, Kathleen Tennant
See also SATA 6
Tennant, Nora Jackson 1915- ... CANR-4
Earlier sketch in CA 9-10R
Tennant, (Charles) Roger 1919- ... 106
Tennant, Stephen (James Napier)
1906-1987 Obituary ... 122
Tennant, Veronica 1947- ... 103
See also SATA 36
Tennenbaum, Silvia 1928- ... CANR-21
Earlier sketch in CA 77-80
Tenneshaw, S. M.
See Beaumont, Charles
and Silverberg, Robert
Tenness, George
See Delk, Robert Carlton
Tenney, H(orace) Kent 1892-1982
Obituary ... 107
Tenney, Merrill C(hapin) 1904-1985 ... CANR-4
Obituary ... 115
Earlier sketch in CA 1R
Tenney, Tabitha Gilman 1762-1837 ... DLB-37
Tenniel, John 1820-1914 Brief entry ... 111
See also SATA 27
Tennien, Mark A. 1900(?)-1983 Obituary ... 108
Tennies, Arthur C(ornelius) 1931- ... 53-56
Tennison, Patrick Joseph 1928- ... CANR-23
Earlier sketch in CA 106
Tennissen, Anthony C(ornelius)
1920-1982 ... 114
Tennov, Dorothy 1928- ... 41-44R
Tennyson, Alfred 1809-1892 ... DLB-32
Tennyson, Charles Bruce Locker
1879-1977 ... 81-84
Obituary ... 73-76
Tennyson, Frederick 1807-1898 ... DLB-32
Tennyson, G(eorg) B(ernhard) 1930- ... CANR-9
Earlier sketch in CA 21-22R
Tenpas, Margaret (Susan Lyon) 1923- ... 85-88
Tensen, Ruth M(arjorie) ... 7-8R
Tent, Ned
See Dennett, Herbert Victor
TePaske, John J(ay) 1929- ... 117
Teplitz, Paul V(ictor) 1940- ... 111
Tepper, Albert 1928- ... 25-28R
Tepper, Michael 1941- ... CANR-12
Earlier sketch in CA 73-76
Tepper, Terri P(atricia) 1942- ... 107
Teran, Lisa St. Aubin de
See St. Aubin de Teran, Lisa
See also CLC 36
Terayama, Shuji 1936-1983 Obituary ... 109
Terban, Marvin ... SATA-45
Terborgh, George (Willard) 1897- ... CAP-2
Earlier sketch in CA 23-24
Terbovich, John B. 1933-1969 ... CAP-2
Earlier sketch in CA 21-22
Terchek, Ronald John 1936- ... 49-52
Terdiman, Richard 1941- ... 73-76
Terenzio, Stephanie 1932- ... 118
Teresi, Judith M.
See Goldberger, Judith M.
ter Haar, Jaap 1922- ... 37-40R
See also SATA 6
terHorst, J(erald) F(ranklin) 1922- ... 107
See also AITN 1
ter Horst, Robert 1929- ... 116
Terhune, Albert Payson 1872-1942
Brief entry ... 111
See also SATA 15
See also DLB 9
Terhune, William B(arclay) 1893-1987 ... 61-64
Obituary ... 122
Terkel, Louis 1912- ... CANR-18
Earlier sketch in CA 57-60
Terkel, Studs
See Terkel, Louis
See also CLC 38
See also AITN 1
Terkel, Susan N(eiburg) 1948- ... 115
Terlouw, Jan (Cornelis) 1931- ... 108
See also SATA 30
Terman, Douglas 1933- Brief entry ... 112
Terman, Sibyl 1902(?)-1975 Obituary ... 57-60
Terme, Hilary
See Hay, Jacob
Terner, Janet 1938- ... 102
Terni-Cialente, Fausta 1900- ... CANR-5
Earlier sketch in CA 7-8R
Terpstra, Vern 1927- ... CANR-11
Earlier sketch in CA 21-22R
Terr, Leonard B(rian) 1946- ... 73-76
Terrace, Edward L. B. 1936(?)-1973
Obituary ... 45-48
Terrace, Herbert S(ydney) 1936- ... 102
Terrace, Vincent 1948- ... CANR-9
Earlier sketch in CA 65-68
Terraine, John (Alfred) 1921- ... CANR-13
Earlier sketch in CA 5-6R
Terrall, Robert 1914- ... 102
Terras, Victor 1921- Brief entry ... 113
Terrell, Carroll F(ranklin) 1917- ... CANR-20
Earlier sketch in CA 102
Terrell, Donna McManus 1908- ... 57-60
Terrell, John Upton 1900- ... 29-32R
Terrell, Robert L(ouis) 1943- ... CANR-17
Earlier sketch in CA 41-44R
Terres, John K(enneth) 1905- ... CANR-5
Earlier sketch in CA 5-6R
Terrien, Samuel Lucien 1911- ... 81-84
Terrill, Ross 1938- ... 25-28R
Terrill, Tom E(dward) 1935- ... 41-44R
Terris, Susan 1937- ... CANR-12
Earlier sketch in CA 29-32R
See also SATA 3
Terris, Virginia R(inaldy) 1917- ... 65-68
Terry, Arthur 1927- ... 85-88
Terry, Bill 1931- ... 118
Terry, C. V.
See Slaughter, Frank G(ill)
Terry, Carol
See Talbot, Carol Terry
Terry, Charles S. 1926(?)-1982 Obituary ... 107
Terry, Doug(las) 1950- ... 120
Terry, Edith (Buchanan) 1952- ... 120
Terry, Edward D(avis) 1927- ... 29-32R
Terry, Luther L(eonidas) 1911-1985 ... CAP-2
Obituary ... 115
Earlier sketch in CA 33-36
See also SATA 11, 42
Terry, Margaret
See Dunnahoo, Terry
Terry, Mark 1947- ... 37-40R
Terry, Marshall 1931- ... 2R
Terry, Megan 1932- ... 77-80
See also DLB 7
See also CLC 19
Terry, Michael 1899-1981 ... 104
Terry, Robert H(arold) 1935- ... 29-32R
Terry, Robert Meredith 1939- ... 41-44R
Terry, Robert W(illiam) 1937- ... 37-40R
Terry, Sarah Meiklejohn 1937- ... 111
Terry, Saralee
See Kaye, Marvin (Nathan)
Terry, Walter 1913-1982 ... CANR-10
Obituary ... 107
Earlier sketch in CA 23-24R
See also SATA 14
Terry, William
See Harknett, Terry
Terson, Peter 1932- ... 104
See also DLB 13
Terstegge, Mabel Alice 1905- ... 93-96
Tertis, Lionel 1876-1975 ... 93-96
Obituary ... 57-60
Tertz, Abram
See Sinyavsky, Andrei (Donatevich)
Terwilliger, Robert E(lwin) 1917- ... 65-68
Terzani, Tiziano 1938- ... CANR-14
Earlier sketch in CA 77-80
Terzian, James P. 1915- ... 15-16R
See also SATA 14
Terzian, Kathryn
See Cramer, Kathryn
TeSelle, Eugene (Arthur, Jr.) 1931- ... 37-40R
TeSelle, Sallie McFague
See McFague, Sallie
Tesich, Steve 1943(?)- ... 105
See also DLBY 83
See also CLC 40
Teslik, Kennan Lee 1952- ... 113
Tessier, (Ernst) M(aurice) 1885-1973 ... CANR-3
Earlier sketch in CA 7-8R
Tessler, Mark A(rnold) 1941- ... CANR-16
Earlier sketches in CA 45-48, CANR-1
Tessler, Stephanie Gordon 1940- ... 124
Tester, Sylvia Root 1939- ... CANR-8
Earlier sketch in CA 11-12R
See also SATA 37
Teta, Jon (Anthony) 1933- ... 25-28R
Tetel, Julie 1950- ... 118
Tetel, Marcel 1932- ... 23-24R
Tetens, Tete Harens 1899(?)-1976
Obituary ... 65-68
Teternikov, Fyodor Kuzmich 1863-1927
Brief entry ... 104
Tether, (Cynthia) Graham 1950- ... CANR-6
Earlier sketch in CA 57-60
See also SATA 36, 46
Tetlow, Edwin 1905- ... 17-18R
Tetreault, Wilfred F. 1927- ... 106
Teune, Henry 1936- ... CANR-3
Earlier sketch in CA 49-52
Teunissen, John James 1933- ... 112
Teuscher, Robert H(erman) 1934- ... 77-80
Teveth, Shabtai (Amotz) 1926(?)-
Brief entry ... 117
Tevis, Walter 1928-1984 ... 113
See also CLC 42
Tewkesbury, Joan 1936- ... 101
Texon, Meyer 1909- ... 124
Tey, Josephine
See Mackintosh, Elizabeth
See also TCLC 14
Teynac, Francoise (Dolores Dupuis) ... 123
Teyte, Maggie 1888-1976 Obituary ... 65-68
Tezla, Albert 1915- ... CANR-14
Earlier sketch in CA 37-40R
Thacher, Alida McKay 1951- ... CANR-11
Earlier sketch in CA 69-72
Thacher, James 1754-1844 ... DLB-37
Thacher, Mary McGrath 1933- ... SATA-9
Thacker, Eric (Lee) 1923- Brief entry ... 107
Thacker, Ernest W(ichman) 1914- ... 13-14R
Thacker, Thomas William 1911-1984
Obituary ... 113
Thackeray, Milton G. 1914- ... 15-16R
Thackeray, William Makepeace
1811-1863 ... SATA-23
See also DLB 21, 55
Thackray, Arnold 1939- ... 49-52
Thackray, Derek V(incent) 1926- ... 103
Thackrey, Russell I. 1904- ... 37-40R
Thaddeus, Janice Farrar 1933- ... 13-14R
Thaden, Edward Carl 1922- ... 19-20R
Thain, Donald H(ammond) 1928- ... 3R
Thakur, Shivesh Chandra 1936- ... 29-32R
Thakura, Ravindranatha
See Tagore, Rabindranath
Thalacker, Donald William 1939-
Brief entry ... 108
Thalberg, Irving (Grant, Jr.) 1930-1987 ... 41-44R
Obituary ... 123
Thale, Jerome 1927- ... 15-16R
Thaler, Alwin 1891- ... CAP-1
Earlier sketch in CA 11-12
Thaler, M. N.
See Kerner, Fred
Thaler, Michael C. 1936- ... 124
See also SATA 47
Thaler, Mike
See Thaler, Michael C.
Thaler, Susan 1939- ... 21-22R
Thalheimer, Ross 1905-1977 ... 41-44R
Thalia
See Bokum, Fanny Butcher
Thalmann, Rita Renee Line 1926- ... CANR-19
Earlier sketches in CA 53-56, CANR-4
Thamer, Katie 1955- ... SATA-42
Thames, C. H.
See Marlowe, Stephen
Thames, Jack
See Ryan, John Fergus
Thamm, Robert 1933- ... 89-92
Thampi, Parvathi (Menon) 1925- ... 5-6R
Thane, (Lillian) Adele 1904- ... 25-28R
Thane, Elswyth 1900- ... 5-6R
See also SATA 32
Thanet, Neil
See Fanthorpe, R(obert) Lionel
Thant, U 1909-1974 Obituary ... 108
Tharaud, Lucien Rostaing, Jr. 1953- ... 69-72
Tharaud, Ross
See Tharaud, Lucien Rostaing, Jr.
Tharp, Louise (Marshall) Hall 1898- ... 4R
See also SATA 3
Tharpe, Jac Lyndon 1928-1985 ... CANR-7
Obituary ... 117
Earlier sketch in CA 57-60
Thass-Thienemann, Theodore 1900- ... 25-28R
Thatcher, David 1922- ... 77-80
Thatcher, Dora (Fickling) 1912- ... 13-14R
Thatcher, Dorothy Southwell 1903- ... CAP-1
Earlier sketch in CA 13-14
Thatcher, Floyd W(ilson) 1917- ... 102
Thatcher, Joan (Claire) 1934- ... 106
Thatcher, Julia
See Bensen, Donald R.
Thaxton, Ralph 1944- ... 114
Thayer, Charles Wheeler 1910-1969 ... 2R
Obituary ... 103
Thayer, Emma R(edington) Lee
1874-1973 ... CAP-1
Obituary ... 45-48
Earlier sketch in CA 9-10
Thayer, Ernest Lawrence 1863-1940
Brief entry ... 119
Thayer, Frederick C(lifton), Jr. 1924- ... CANR-12
Earlier sketch in CA 73-76
Thayer, George (Chapman, Jr.)
1933-1973 ... CAP-2
Obituary ... 45-48
Earlier sketch in CA 25-28
Thayer, Geraldine
See Daniels, Dorothy
Thayer, H(orace) S(tandish) 1923- ... 45-48
Thayer, James Stewart 1949- ... 73-76
Thayer, Jane
See Woolley, Catherine
Thayer, Lee (Osborne) 1927- ... CANR-18
Earlier sketches in CA 49-52, CANR-3
Thayer, Lee
See Thayer, Emma R(edington) Lee
Thayer, Marjorie Brief entry ... 116
See also SATA 37
Thayer, Mary Van Rensselaer
1903(?)-1983 ... 97-100
Obituary ... 111
Thayer, Molly
See Thayer, Mary Van Rensselaer
Thayer, Nathaniel B(owman) 1929- ... 45-48
Thayer, Peter
See Wyler, Rose
Thayer, Theodore 1904-1981 Obituary ... 103
Thayer, V(ivian) T(row) 1886-1979 ... CAP-2
Obituary ... 89-92
Earlier sketch in CA 17-18
Thayler, Carl 1933- ... 37-40R
Thayne, Emma Lou 1924- ... 65-68
Thayne, Miria Greenwood 1907- ... 21-22R
Theall, Donald Francis 1928- ... 105
Thebaud, Jo 1914- ... 49-52
Theberge, James D.
See Theberge, James Daniel
Theberge, James Daniel 1930-1988 ... 25-28R
Obituary ... 124
Thede, Marion Draughon 1903- ... CAP-2
Earlier sketch in CA 25-28
Thee, Marek 1918- ... 101
The Ear
See McLellan, Diana
Theen, Rolf H(einz) W(ilhelm) 1937- ... 41-44R
The Fourth Brother
See Aung, (Maung) Htin
The Gallerite
See Bason, Frederick (Thomas)
The Great Comte
See Hawkesworth, Eric
The Great Merlini
See Rawson, Clayton
Theil, Henri 1924- ... CANR-22
Earlier sketches in CA 17-18R, CANR-7
Theiner, George 1927- ... 29-32R
Theis, John William 1911- Brief entry ... 109
Theis, Paul A(nthony) 1923- ... 41-44R
Theisen, Jerome Paul 1930- ... 113
Theissen, Gerd 1943- ... 117
Thekaekara, Matthew P(othen)
1914-1976 ... 77-80
Obituary ... 69-72
Thelen, David Paul 1939- Brief entry ... 110
Thelen, Gil 1938- ... 73-76
Thelen, Herbert Arnold 1913- ... 108
Thelin, John R(obert) 1947- ... CANR-11
Earlier sketch in CA 69-72
Thelwell, Michael Miles 1939- ... 101
See also CLC 22
Thelwell, Norman 1923- ... CANR-4
Earlier sketch in CA 7-8R
See also SATA 14
Themerson, Stefan 1910- ... CANR-9
Earlier sketch in CA 65-68
Theo, Ion
See Theodorescu, Ion N.
Theobald, Lewis, Jr.
See Lovecraft, H(oward) P(hillips)
Theobald, Robert 1929- ... 37-40R
Theocharis, Reghinos D(emetrios)
1929- ... CANR-11
Earlier sketch in CA 13-14R
Theodorakis, Michalis 1925- Brief entry ... 105
Theodorakis, Mikis
See Theodorakis, Michalis
Theodorakopoulos, Ioannis 1900-1981
Obituary ... 108
Theodoratus, Robert J(ames) 1928- ... 41-44R
Theodore, Athena 1919- ... 41-44R
Theodore, Chris A(thanasios) 1920- ... 15-16R
Theodore, Sister Mary 1907- ... 7-8R
Theodorescu, Ion N. 1880-1967 Obituary ... 116
Theodorson, George A. 1924- ... 29-32R
Theoharis, Athan G(eorge) 1936- ... CANR-12
Earlier sketch in CA 29-32R
The Old Settler
See Lyman, Albert Robison
Theriault, Albert A(ugustine), Jr. 1928- ... 53-56
Theriault, Yves 1915- ... 102
Therio, Adrien 1925- ... DLB-53
Thernstrom, Stephan (Albert) 1934- ... 15-16R
Theroux, Alexander (Louis) 1939- ... CANR-20
Earlier sketch in CA 85-88
See also CLC 2, 25
Theroux, Paul 1941- ... CANR-20
Earlier sketch in CA 33-36R
See also SATA 44
See also DLB 2
See also CLC 5, 8, 11, 15, 28, 46
Theroux, Phyllis 1939- ... 110
Thesen, Hjalmar Peter 1925- ... 107
Thesiger, Wilfred (Patrick) 1910- ... CAP-2
Earlier sketch in CA 17-18
Thesing, William B(arney) 1947- ... 113
Thevenin, Denis
See Duhamel, Georges
Thibaudeau, Colleen 1925- ... 113
Thibault, Jacques Anatole Francois
1844-1924 Brief entry ... 106
Thibault, John C(rowell) 1922- ... 77-80
Thiebaud, Wayne 1920- ... 45-48
Thiebaux, Marcelle 1931- ... 122
Brief entry ... 110
Thieda, Shirley Ann 1943- ... 69-72
See also SATA 13
Thiele, Colin (Milton) 1920- ... CANR-12
Earlier sketch in CA 29-32R
See also SATA 14
See also SAAS 2
See also CLC 17
Thiele, Edwin R(ichard) 1895- ... CAP-1
Earlier sketch in CA 19-20
Thiele, Margaret Rossiter 1901- ... 21-22R
Thielen, Thoraf Theodore 1921- ... 7-8R
Thielens, Wagner P., Jr. 1925- ... 1R
Thielicke, Helmut 1908-1986 ... CANR-11
Obituary ... 118
Earlier sketch in CA 69-72
Thiem, (Ezra) George 1897-1987 Obituary ... 123
Thien-An, Thich 1926- ... 57-60
Thier, Herbert D(avid) 1932- ... 29-32R
Thierauf, Robert J(ames) 1933- ... CANR-12
Earlier sketch in CA 29-32R

Thiesenhusen, William C. 1936- ... 21-22R
Thiessen, John (Jack) 1931- ... CANR-15
Earlier sketch in CA 41-44R
Thiessen, John C(aldwell) 1890- ... 7-8R
Thiher, Allen 1941- ... CANR-14
Earlier sketch in CA 41-44R
Thiman, Eric Harding 1900- ... CAP-1
Earlier sketch in CA 13-14
Thimblethorpe, June Sylvia 1926-
Brief entry ... 117
Thimm, Alfred L. 1923- ... CANR-8
Earlier sketch in CA 61-64
Thimmesch, Nicholas Palen 1927-1985 ... 15-16R
Obituary ... 116
Thimmesch, Nick
See Thimmesch, Nicholas Palen
Thiong'o, Ngugi wa
See Ngugi, James T(hiong'o)
Thirion, Andre 1907- ... 101
Thirkell, Angela (Margaret) 1890-1961
Obituary ... 93-96
Thirkell, John Henry 1913- ... CANR-10
Earlier sketch in CA 13-14R
Thirlwall, John C(onnop, Jr.) 1904- ... 69-72
Thirsk, (Irene) Joan 1922- ... 25-28R
Thiry, Joan (Marie) 1926- ... 121
See also SATA 45
Thisby
See Turner, Dona M.
Thistle, Mel(ville William) 1914- ... 53-56
Thistlethwaite, Miles 1945- ... SATA-12
Thoby-Marcelin, (Emile) Philippe
1904-1975 Obituary ... 61-64
Thody, Philip 1928- ... CANR-9
Earlier sketch in CA 7-8R
Thoene, Alma E(vans) 1903- ... 49-52
Thoene, Peter
See Bihalji-Merin, Oto
Thoger, Marie 1923- ... CANR-11
Earlier sketch in CA 25-28R
Tholfsen, Trygve R(ainone) 1924-
Brief entry ... 108
Thollander, Earl 1922- ... CANR-18
Earlier sketch in CA 101
See also SATA 22
Thom, James Alexander 1933- ... CANR-15
Earlier sketch in CA 77-80
Thom, Robert 1929-1979 ... 21-22R
Obituary ... 85-88
Thom, Robert Anderson 1915- ... 61-64
Thom, Valerie M(acLaren) 1929- ... 124
Thoma, Henry F. 1909(?)-1983 Obituary ... 110
Thoma, Ludwig 1867-1921 ... DLB-66
Thoma, Richard 1902- ... DLB-4
Thomae, Betty Kennedy 1920- ... 61-64
Thoman, Richard S(amuel) 1919- ... 65-68
Thomas, A(rthur) J(oshua), Jr.
1918-1982 ... CANR-10
Earlier sketch in CA 5-6R
Thomas, A(ndrew) R(owland) B(enedick)
1904- ... 65-68
Thomas, Abraham V(azhayil) 1934- ... 61-64
Thomas, Alan (Cedric) 1933- ... 81-84
Thomas, Alan G. 1911- ... 25-28R
Thomas, Alexander 1914- ... 103
Thomas, Andrea
See Hill, Margaret (Ohler)
Thomas, Ann Van Wynen 1919- ... CANR-10
Earlier sketch in CA 5-6R
Thomas, Anna (Irena) 1948- ... CANR-24
Earlier sketch in CA 41-44R
Thomas, Annabel 1929- ... 106
Thomas, Arline 1913- ... 49-52
Thomas, Armstrong 1909(?)-1975
Obituary ... 57-60
Thomas, Art(hur Lawrence) 1952- ... 105
See also SATA 38, 48
Thomas, Audrey (Callahan) 1935- ... 23-24R
See also DLB 60
See also CLC 7, 13, 37
See also AITN 2
Thomas, Ben Bowen 1899-1977 Obituary ... 108
Thomas, Bill 1934- ... CANR-8
Earlier sketch in CA 61-64
Thomas, Bob
See Thomas, Robert J(oseph)
Thomas, Carl H.
See Doerffler, Alfred
Thomas, (Antony) Charles 1928- ... 119
Thomas, Charles W. 1903-1973
Obituary ... 41-44R
Thomas, Charles W(ellington) 1943- ... 65-68
Thomas, Claire Sherman 1923- ... 108
Thomas, Clara (McCandless) 1919- ... 25-28R
Thomas, Conrad Ward 1914- ... 37-40R
Thomas, Cornelius Dickinson 1920-1972 ... CAP-1
Earlier sketch in CA 19-20
Thomas, Craig (David) 1942- ... 112
Brief entry ... 108
Thomas, Cullen
See Kimes, Beverly Rae
Thomas, D(onald) M(ichael) 1935- ... CANR-17
Earlier sketch in CA 61-64
See also DLB 40
See also CLC 13, 22, 31
Thomas, D(avid) O(swald) 1924- ... 117
Thomas, Dan
See Sanders, Leonard
Thomas, Daniel B.
See Bluestein, Daniel Thomas
Thomas, Daniel H(arrison) 1904- ... 15-16R
Thomas, Dante 1922- ... 53-56
Thomas, Dave 1949(?)- Brief entry ... 115
Thomas, David 1931- ... 103
Thomas, David A(rthur) 1925- ... 13-14R
Thomas, David H(urst) 1945- ... 108
Thomas, David St. John 1929- ... 112
Thomas, David Winton 1901-1970 ... CAP-1
Earlier sketch in CA 9-10
Thomas, Denis 1922- ... CANR-15
Earlier sketch in CA 77-80
Thomas, Dian 1945- ... CANR-10
Earlier sketch in CA 65-68
Thomas, Diane Renee 1946(?)-1985
Obituary ... 117
Thomas, Donald 1926- ... 49-52
Thomas, Donald F. 1913- ... 29-32R
Thomas, Donald Roff 1924-1979 Obituary ... 111
Thomas, Dorothy Swaine 1899-1977 ... CAP-2
Obituary ... 69-72
Earlier sketch in CA 17-18
Thomas, Dylan (Marlais) 1914-1953 ... 120
Brief entry ... 104
See also DLB 13, 20
See also TCLC 1, 8
Thomas, E(ric) H(ubert) Gwynne
See Gwynne-Thomas, E(ric) H(ubert)
Thomas, Earl W(esley) 1915- ... 53-56
Thomas, Edison H(ugh) 1912- ... 85-88
Thomas, (Philip) Edward 1878-1917
Brief entry ... 106
See also DLB 19
See also TCLC 10
Thomas, Edward Llewellyn
See Llewellyn-Thomas, Edward
Thomas, Edwin J(ohn) 1927- ... 21-22R
Thomas, Egbert S.
See Ellis, Edward S(ylvester)
Thomas, Elizabeth Ann 1952- ... 85-88
Thomas, Elizabeth Marshall 1931- ... 19-20R
Thomas, Emory M. 1939- ... 97-100
Thomas, Ernest Lewys 1904- ... CANR-1
Earlier sketch in CA 2R
Thomas, Estelle Webb 1899- ... 23-24R
See also SATA 26
Thomas, Evangeline 1904- ... 117
Thomas, F(ranklin) Richard 1940- ... CANR-13
Earlier sketch in CA 77-80
Thomas, Frank P(atrick) 1916- ... 119
Thomas, G. K.
See Davies, L(eslie) P(urnell)
Thomas, George Finger 1899-1977
Obituary ... 73-76
Thomas, George I. 1915- ... 25-28R
Thomas, George Leicester, Jr. 1907- ... CAP-1
Earlier sketch in CA 11-12
Thomas, Gilbert (Oliver) 1891- ... 7-8R
Thomas, Gordon 1933- ... 9-10R
Thomas, Gordon L. 1914- ... 37-40R
Thomas, Graham Stuart 1909- ... CANR-19
Earlier sketches in CA 9-10R, CANR-4
Thomas, Gwyn 1913-1981 ... CANR-9
Obituary ... 103
Earlier sketch in CA 65-68
See also DLB 15
Thomas, H. C.
See Keating, Lawrence A.
Thomas, Harold Becken 1888-1971
Obituary ... 104
Thomas, Heather Smith 1944- ... CANR-6
Earlier sketch in CA 57-60
Thomas, Helen A. 1920- ... 101
Thomas, Helen Shirley 1931-1968 ... 7-8R
Obituary ... 103
Thomas, Henri (Joseph Marie) 1912- ... CAP-1
Earlier sketch in CA 9-10
Thomas, Henry 1886-1970 Obituary ... 29-32R
Thomas, Hugh Swynnerton 1931- ... CANR-5
Earlier sketch in CA 9-10R
Thomas, I(saac) D(avid) E(llis) 1921- ... 65-68
Thomas, Ianthe 1951- ... SATA-42
See also CLR 8
Thomas, Isaiah 1750-1831 ... DLB-43
Thomas, Ivo Herbert Christopher 1912- ... 5-6R
Thomas, J(eremy) A(mbler) 1947- ... 118
Thomas, J. C. ... 57-60
Thomas, J(ames) D(avid) 1910- ... CANR-6
Earlier sketch in CA 57-60
Thomas, J. James 1933- ... 53-56
Thomas, J. W. 1917- ... 101
Thomas, Jack Ray 1931- ... 41-44R
Thomas, Jack W(illiam) 1930- ... CANR-16
Earlier sketches in CA 49-52, CANR-1
Thomas, James H(arold) 1943- ... 119
Thomas, Jane Resh 1936- ... CANR-24
Earlier sketch in CA 106
See also SATA 38
Thomas, Jeannette Grise 1935- ... 101
Thomas, Jim
See Reagan, Thomas (James) B(utler)
Thomas, Joan Gale
See Robinson, Joan (Mary) G(ale Thomas)
Thomas, John 1890- ... 49-52
Thomas, John Allen Miner 1900-1932
Brief entry ... 107
See also DLB 4
Thomas, John Hunter 1928- ... 57-60
Thomas, John Lawrence 1910- ... 5-6R
Thomas, Joyce Carol 1938- ... 116
Brief entry ... 113
See also SATA 40
See also DLB 33
See also CLC 35
Thomas, K. H.
See Kirk, T(homas) H(obson)
Thomas, Keith (Vivian) 1933- ... CANR-15
Earlier sketch in CA 37-40R
Thomas, Kenneth Bryn ?-1978 Obituary ... 81-84
Thomas, Kurt 1956- Brief entry ... 114
Thomas, Latta R(oosevelt) 1927- ... 65-68
Thomas, Lawrence L(eslie) 1924- ... 45-48
Thomas, Lee 1918- ... CANR-1
Earlier sketch in CA 1R
Thomas, Lee
See Floren, Lee
Thomas, Leslie (John) 1931- ... CANR-22
Earlier sketch in CA 15-16R
Thomas, Lewis 1913- ... 85-88
See also CLC 35
Thomas, Lewis H(erbert) 1917-1983 ... CANR-13
Earlier sketch in CA 73-76
Thomas, Lionel H(ugh) C(hristopher)
1922(?)-1978 Obituary ... 104
Thomas, Liz
See Thomas, Elizabeth Ann
Thomas, Lorenzo 1944- ... 73-76
See also DLB 41
Thomas, Lowell (Jackson) 1892-1981 ... CANR-3
Obituary ... 104
Earlier sketch in CA 45-48
See also AITN 1, 2
Thomas, Lowell Jackson, Jr. 1923- ... 85-88
See also SATA 15
Thomas, M(ilton) Halsey 1903-1977 ... 25-28R
Obituary ... 73-76
Thomas, Mack 1928- ... 11-12R
Thomas, Mary Martha Hosford 1927- ... 53-56
Thomas, Mason P(age), Jr. 1928- ... CANR-22
Earlier sketch in CA 25-28R
Thomas, Mervyn
See Curran, Mona (Elisa)
Thomas, Michael
See Wilks, Michael Thomas
Thomas, (William) Miles (Webster)
1897-1980 Obituary ... 105
Thomas, Neal
See Thomas, Cornelius Dickinson
Thomas, Norman (Mattoon) 1884-1968 ... 101
Obituary ... 25-28R
Thomas, Norman C(arl) 1932- ... 19-20R
Thomas, Norman L(ee) 1925- ... 41-44R
Thomas, Owen Clark 1922- ... 9-10R
Thomas, Patricia J. 1934- ... 37-40R
Thomas, Paul 1908- ... CANR-22
Earlier sketches in CA 9-10, CAP-1
Thomas, Peter 1928- ... 37-40R
Thomas, Peter Wynne
See Wynne-Thomas, Peter
Thomas, Phillip Drennon 1938- ... 124
Thomas, Phyllis 1935- ... 119
Thomas, Piri 1928- ... 73-76
See also CLC 17
Thomas, R(ichard) Hinton 1912-1983 ... CANR-5
Obituary ... 110
Earlier sketch in CA 7-8R
Thomas, R(obert) Murray 1921- ... CANR-22
Earlier sketches in CA 19-20R, CANR-7
Thomas, R(onald) S(tuart) 1913- ... 89-92
See also CAAS 4
See also DLB 27
See also CLC 6, 13
Thomas, Richard (Earl) 1951- ... 107
Thomas, Robert 1930- ... 25-28R
Thomas, Robert C(harles) 1925- ... 101
Thomas, Robert J(oseph) 1922- ... CANR-13
Earlier sketch in CA 77-80
Thomas, Rollin G. 1896-19(?) ... CAP-1
Earlier sketch in CA 15-16
Thomas, Ross (Elmore) 1926- ... CANR-22
Earlier sketch in CA 33-36R
See also CLC 39
Thomas, S(idney) Claudewell 1932- ... 19-20R
Thomas, Sara (Sally) 1911(?)-1982
Obituary ... 106
Thomas, Sewell 1884- ... CAP-1
Earlier sketch in CA 9-10
Thomas, Sherilyn 1948- ... CANR-13
Earlier sketch in CA 73-76
Thomas, Sherry
See Thomas, Sherilyn
Thomas, Shirley ... 7-8R
Thomas, Stanley 1933- ... 21-22R
Thomas, Stephen N(aylor) 1942- ... 89-92
Thomas, T. M(athai) 1933- ... 53-56
Thomas, Ted
See Thomas, Theodore L.
Thomas, Theodore L. 1920- ... 29-32R
Thomas, Thom 1940- ... 108
Thomas, Tony 1947- ... 61-64
Thomas, Vaughan 1934- ... 81-84
Thomas, Victoria
See DeWeese, Thomas Eugene
Thomas, Virginia Castleton
See Castleton, Virginia
Thomas, W(alter) Ian 1914- ... 19-20R
Thomas, William 1906- ... 73-76
Thomas, William E(dward) 1942- ... 111
Thomas, William F. 1924- ... 69-72
Thomas, William G(ordan) 1931- ... 93-96
Thomas, William L(eRoy, Jr.) 1920- ... 41-44R
Thomasma, David Charles 1939- ... CANR-21
Earlier sketch in CA 104
Thomason, A(lan) Mims 1910-1985
Obituary ... 117
Thomason, Burke C(urtis) 1943- ... 113
Thomason, Tommy 1949- ... 73-76
Thometz, Carol Estes 1938- ... 11-12R
Thomey, Tedd 1920- ... CANR-2
Earlier sketch in CA 5-6R
Thomis, Malcolm I(an) 1936- Brief entry ... 118
Thomison, Dennis 1937- ... 53-56
Thomlinson, Ralph 1925- ... 41-44R
Thommen, George S. 1896- ... CAP-1
Earlier sketch in CA 15-16
Thompson, A(lbert) Gray 1928- ... 41-44R
Thompson, A(rthur) L(eonard) B(ell)
1917-1975 ... CANR-5
Obituary ... 61-64
Earlier sketch in CA 53-56
Thompson, Alan Eric 1924- ... 109
Thompson, Anne Armstrong 1939- ... 85-88
Thompson, Anne Hall Whitt 1930- ... 119
Thompson, Arthur A., Jr. 1940- ... 85-88
Thompson, Arthur W(illiam) 1920-1966 ... 1R
Thompson, Bard 1925-1987 ... CANR-1
Obituary ... 123
Earlier sketch in CA 3R
Thompson, Betty A(nne) 1926- ... 111
Thompson, Blanche Jennings ... 5-6R
Thompson, Brenda 1935- ... 106
See also SATA 34
Thompson, Brian 1935- ... 109
Thompson, Buck
See Paine, Lauran (Bosworth)
Thompson, C(lara) Mildred 1881-1975
Obituary ... 57-60
Thompson, Caroline 1956- ... 110
Thompson, Charles Lowell 1937- ... CANR-3
Earlier sketch in CA 49-52
Thompson, Charles Waters, Jr.
See Thompson, Toby
Thompson, China
See Lewis, Mary (Christianna Milne)
Thompson, Claude Holmes 1908- ... CAP-1
Earlier sketch in CA 11-12
Thompson, Corrie 1887- ... 61-64
Thompson, Craig 1907-1986 Obituary ... 121
Thompson, Daniel (Calbert) 1916- ... 15-16R
Thompson, David (Bradford) 1938- ... 57-60
Thompson, David H(ugh) 1941- ... 81-84
See also SATA 17
Thompson, Dennis F(rank) 1940- ... 53-56
Thompson, Dennis L. 1935- ... 41-44R
Thompson, (Arthur) Denys (Halstead)
1907-1988 ... CANR-4
Obituary ... 124
Earlier sketch in CA 9-10R
Thompson, Don(ald Arthur) 1935- ... 53-56
Thompson, Donald Eugene 1913- ... 109
Thompson, Donald L(ambert) 1930- ... 49-52
Thompson, Donald Neil 1939- ... 37-40R
Thompson, Donnis Stark 1928- ... 21-22R
Thompson, Dorothy 1894-1961 Obituary ... 89-92
See also DLB 29
Thompson, Duane G(len) 1933- ... 73-76
Thompson, Earl 1931(?)-1978 ... 85-88
Obituary ... 81-84
Thompson, Edgar T(ristram) 1900- ... 17-18R
Thompson, Edward Thorwald 1928- ... CANR-21
Earlier sketch in CA 105
Thompson, Eileen
See Panowski, Eileen Thompson
Thompson, Elizabeth Allen 1914-1984 ... 119
Thompson, Era Bell 1905-1986 ... 89-92
Obituary ... 121
Thompson, Eric
See Thompson, J(ohn) Eric S(idney)
Thompson, (Richard) Ernest 1949- ... 123
Thompson, (Richard) Ernest 1950(?)-
Brief entry ... 115
Thompson, Ernest Trice 1894-1985 ... 3R
Obituary ... 115
Thompson, Eugene Allen 1924- ... 104
Thompson, Evelyn Wingo 1921- ... 21-22R
Thompson, Ewa M(ajewska) 1937- ... 49-52
Thompson, Flora (Jane Timms)
1877(?)-1947 Brief entry ... 123
Thompson, Frances C(lements) 1906- ... CAP-1
Earlier sketch in CA 9-10
Thompson, Francis George 1931- ... CANR-23
Earlier sketch in CA 106
Thompson, Francis Joseph 1859-1907
Brief entry ... 104
See also DLB 19
See also TCLC 4
Thompson, Frank H., Jr. 1926- ... 25-28R
Thompson, Fred 1900-1987 Obituary ... 121
Thompson, Fred Dalton 1942- ... 69-72
Thompson, Fred P(riestly), Jr. 1917- ... 89-92
Thompson, G(ary) R(ichard) 1937- ... CANR-2
Earlier sketch in CA 45-48
Thompson, Gene
See Thompson, Eugene Allen
Thompson, George Clifford 1920- ... 104
Thompson, George G(reene) 1914- ... 21-22R
Thompson, George H(yman) 1923-
Brief entry ... 117
Thompson, George Selden 1929- ... CANR-21
Earlier sketch in CA 5-6R
See also SATA 4
Thompson, Gerald E(verett) 1924- ... 53-56
Thompson, Gertrude Caton
See Caton-Thompson, Gertrude
Thompson, Grant P(helps) 1940- ... 111
Thompson, Harlan (Howard) 1894-1987 ... CAP-1
Obituary ... 123
Earlier sketch in CA 9-10
See also SATA 10
Thompson, Harry C. 1921(?)-1980
Obituary ... 97-100
Thompson, (Harry) Harwood 1894- ... 65-68
Thompson, Helen M. (Smith) 1903- ... CAP-1
Earlier sketch in CA 13-14
Thompson, Henry O(rrin) 1931- ... 45-48
Thompson, Hilary 1943- ... SATA-49
Thompson, Hildegard (Steerstedter)
1901- ... 19-20R
Thompson, Hunter S(tockton) 1939- ... CANR-23
Earlier sketch in CA 19-20R
See also CLC 9, 17, 40
Thompson, Ian B(entley) 1936- ... 37-40R
Thompson, Irene 1919- ... 110
Thompson, Isabel
See Kelsay, Isabel Thompson
Thompson, J(ohn) Eric S(idney)
1898-1975 ... 65-68
Obituary ... 61-64

Thompson, J(esse) J(ackson) 1919- 7-8R
Thompson, Jack Maynard 1924- 41-44R
Thompson, Jacqueline 1945- CANR-17
Earlier sketch in CA 97-100
Thompson, James 1902-1983 Obituary 109
Thompson, James 1932- 73-76
Thompson, James D(avid) 1920-1973 .... CAP-2
Earlier sketch in CA 21-22
Thompson, James H.
See Freeman, G(raydon) L(a Verne)
Thompson, James W. 1935- 105
Thompson, Joan 1943- 97-100
Thompson, Joan Berengild 1915- 17-18R
Thompson, Joanna Maxwell Pullein
See Pullein-Thompson, Joanna Maxwell
Thompson, Joe Allen 1936- 37-40R
Thompson, John (Anderson) 1918- 5-6R
Thompson, John 1938-1976 .... DLB-60
Thompson, John Leslie 1917- 7-8R
Thompson, John Reuben 1823-1873 ..... DLB-3
Thompson, Josiah 1935- 41-44R
Thompson, Judith CLC-39
Thompson, Julian F(rancis) 1927- 111
See also SATA 40
Thompson, Julius Eric 1946- 49-52
Thompson, Karl F. 1917- 37-40R
Thompson, Kay 1912(?)- 85-88
See also SATA 16
Thompson, Ken D(avid) 1926- 65-68
Thompson, Kenneth W(infred) 1921- CANR-5
Earlier sketch in CA 11-12R
Thompson, Kent 1936- 49-52
Thompson, Kristin 1950- 108
Thompson, Laura (Maud) 1905- 53-56
Thompson, Laurence C(assius) 1926- ... CANR-7
Earlier sketch in CA 5-6R
Thompson, Laurence G(raham) 1920- 37-40R
Thompson, Lawrance (Roger)
1906-1973 .... CANR-10
Obituary 41-44R
Earlier sketch in CA 5-6R
Thompson, Lawrence Sidney
1916-1986 .... CANR-5
Obituary 121
Earlier sketch in CA 9-10R
Thompson, Leonard Monteath 1916- ... CANR-16
Earlier sketches in CA 2R, CANR-1
Thompson, Lewis 1915(?)-1972
Obituary 37-40R
Thompson, Loring M(oore) 1918- 45-48
Thompson, Luther Joe 1918- 21-22R
Thompson, Marian Spitzer 1899(?)-1983
Obituary 110
Thompson, Mary Wolfe 1886- 107
Thompson, Mel(vin R.) 1929- 73-76
Thompson, Morris Mordecai 1912- 109
Thompson, Neil 1929- 108
Thompson, Neville 1938- 37-40R
Thompson, Noel W. 1951- 123
Thompson, Paul (Richard) 1935- CANR-16
Earlier sketch in CA 21-22R
Thompson, Paul 1943- CANR-14
Earlier sketch in CA 77-80
Thompson, Phyllis Hoge 1926- CANR-13
Earlier sketch in CA 29-32R
Thompson, Ralph 1904-1979 Obituary 89-92
Thompson, (William) Ralph 1910- 53-56
Thompson, Randall 1899-1984 Obituary 113
Thompson, Richard 1924- 9-10R
Thompson, Richard A(rlen) 1930- 61-64
Thompson, Robert (Grainger Ker) 1916- ...49-52
Thompson, Robert Elliott 1921- 77-80
See also AITN 2
Thompson, Robert Farris 1932- 103
Thompson, Robert Norman 1914- 106
Thompson, Robert Sidney 1918- 111
Thompson, Roger Francis 1933- CANR-13
Earlier sketch in CA 73-76
Thompson, Roy Anton 1897- CAP-2
Earlier sketch in CA 29-32
Thompson, Russ
See Paine, Lauran (Bosworth)
Thompson, Ruth Plumly 1891(?)-1976
Obituary 113
See also DLB 22
Thompson, Samuel M(artin) 1902-1983
Obituary 110
Thompson, Sandra (Jean) 1943- 121
Thompson, Stanbury Dugard 1905- CAP-1
Earlier sketch in CA 11-12
Thompson, Steven L(ynn) 1948- 114
Thompson, Stith 1885-1976 .... CANR-5
Obituary 61-64
Earlier sketch in CA 7-8R
See also SATA 20
Thompson, Susan L. 1945- 114
Thompson, Susan O(tis) 1931- 85-88
Thompson, Sylvia Vaughn (Sheekman)
1935- 7-8R
Thompson, Thomas 1933-1982 .... CANR-14
Obituary 108
Earlier sketch in CA 65-68
Thompson, Thomas Kirkland 1914- 15-16R
Thompson, Toby 1944- 65-68
Thompson, Travis I. 1937- 37-40R
Thompson, Victor A(lexander) 1912- 25-28R
Thompson, Virginia 1937- 108
Thompson, Vivian L(aubach) 1911- CANR-1
Earlier sketch in CA 1R
See also SATA 3
Thompson, W(illard) Scott 1942- CANR-12
Earlier sketch in CA 25-28R
Thompson, Wayne C(urtis) 1943- 109
Thompson, Wayne N. 1914- 21-22R
Thompson, Wilbur R(ichard) 1923- 15-16R
Thompson, Willa 1916- 9-10R
Thompson, Willard Mead 1913- 5-6R
Thompson, William A(ncker) 1931- 77-80
Thompson, William Bernard 1914- CAP-1
Earlier sketch in CA 9-10
Thompson, William C. L.
See Edwards, William B(ennett)
Thompson, William D. 1929- 19-20R
Thompson, William E(llison), Jr. 1923- ...13-14R
Thompson, William Fletcher, Jr. 1929- 1R
Thompson, William Irwin 1938- CANR-9
Earlier sketch in CA 23-24R
Thompson, William Tappan
1812-1882 .... DLB-3, 11
Thompson, Wolfe
See Thompson, Mary Wolfe
Thoms, Herbert 1885-1972 Obituary 110
Thomsen, Harry 1928- 7-8R
Thomsen, Moritz 1915- 29-32R
Thomsen, Robert 1915(?)-1983 Obituary ... 117
Thomsen, Russel J(ohn) 1941- 37-40R
Thomsett, Michael C. 1948- 119
Thomson, Arthur Alexander (Malcolm)
1894-1969 .... CAP-1
Earlier sketch in CA 11-12
Thomson, Basil (Home) 1861-1939
Brief entry 110
Thomson, Beatrix 1900-1986 Obituary 120
Thomson, Betty Flanders 1913- 9-10R
Thomson, C(harles) Leslie 1914- 9-10R
Thomson, Daisy H(icks) 1918- CANR-20
Earlier sketch in CA 103
Thomson, Dale C(airns) 1923- 25-28R
Thomson, David 1912-1970 .... CANR-2
Obituary 29-32R
Earlier sketch in CA 1R
Thomson, David (Robert Alexander)
1914-1988 .... CANR-24
Obituary 124
Earlier sketch in CA 107
See also SATA 40
Thomson, Derick S(mith) 1921- CANR-12
Earlier sketch in CA 25-28R
Thomson, Douglas Ferguson Scott
1919- 41-44R
Thomson, Edward
See Tubb, E(dwin) C(harles)
Thomson, F(rancis) P(aul) 1914- 23-24R
Thomson, Frank S(elee) 1881-1975 57-60
Thomson, Garry 1925- 109
Thomson, George Derwent 1903-1987
Obituary 121
Thomson, George H(enry) 1924- 23-24R
Thomson, George Malcolm 1899- 9-10R
Thomson, George Paget 1892-1975 .... CANR-4
Obituary 61-64
Earlier sketch in CA 7-8R
Thomson, (George) Ian F(alconer)
1912-1987 ....9-10R
Obituary 122
Thomson, Irene Taviss 1941- 29-32R
Thomson, James 1834-1882 .... DLB-35
Thomson, James C(utting) 1909- 61-64
Thomson, James C(laude), Jr. 1931- 29-32R
Thomson, James Miln 1921- 109
Thomson, Joan
See Charnock, Joan
Thomson, John (Edward Palmer) 1936- 109
Thomson, Jonathan H.
See Thomson, Daisy H(icks)
Thomson, June (Valerie) 1930- CANR-21
Earlier sketch in CA 81-84
Thomson, Keith 1912- 29-32R
Thomson, Mortimer 1831-1875 .... DLB-11
Thomson, Peggy 1922- 85-88
See also SATA 31
Thomson, Peter 1913- 7-8R
Thomson, Peter (William) 1938- 108
Thomson, Randall J(oseph) 1946- 109
Thomson, Robert 1921- 25-28R
Thomson, Robert 1943- 122
Thomson, Robert W(illiam) 1934- CANR-21
Earlier sketch in CA 104
Thomson, Ronald William 1908- 25-28R
Thomson, Roy Herbert 1894-1976
Obituary 69-72
Thomson, S(amuel) Harrison
1895-1975 ....41-44R
Obituary 61-64
Thomson, Virgil (Garnett) 1896- 41-44R
Thomson, William A. 1879-1971
Obituary 33-36R
Thomson, William A(rchibald) R(obson)
1906-1983 103
Obituary 111
Thomy, Al(fred Marshall) 69-72
Thonssen, Lester 1904- 5-6R
Thorat, Sudhakar S. 1935- 45-48
Thorburn, David 1940- CANR-7
Earlier sketch in CA 53-56
Thorburn, Hugh G(arnet) 1924- 13-14R
Thorburn, John
See Goldsmith, John Herman Thorburn
Thoreau, Henry David 1817-1862 .... DLB-1
See also CDALB 1640-1865
Thorelli, Hans B(irger) 1921- CANR-6
Earlier sketch in CA 15-16R
Thoren, Arne 1927- 69-72
Thorer, Konrad
See Greve, Felix Paul (Berthold Friedrich)
Thoresen, Carl E. 1933- 57-60
Thorez, Maurice 1900-1964 Obituary 113
Thorlby, Anthony K. 1928- 25-28R
Thorman, Donald J. 1924-1977 ....17-18R
Obituary 73-76
Thorman, Richard 1924- 105
Thorn, Barbara
See Paine, Lauran (Bosworth)
Thorn, John 1947- CANR-17
Earlier sketch in CA 97-100
Thorn, Richard S(emour) 1929- 19-20R
Thorn, Ronald Scott
See Wilkinson, Ronald
Thorn, William E. 1923- 9-10R
Thornber, Jean H(ewitt) 1919- 61-64
Thornbrough, Emma Lou 25-28R
Thornburg, Hershel D(ean) 1936-1987 . CANR-14
Obituary 121
Earlier sketch in CA 37-40R
Thornburg, Newton K(endall) 1930- CANR-9
Earlier sketch in CA 23-24R
Thorndike, A.
See Thorndike, A(nthony) E(dward)
Thorndike, A(nthony) E(dward) 1941- 117
Thorndike, E. L.
See Thorndike, Edward L(ee)
Thorndike, Edward L(ee) 1874-1949
Brief entry 121
Thorndike, Joseph J(acobs), Jr. 1913-
Brief entry 117
Thorndike, (Everett) Lynn 1882-1965
Obituary 111
Thorndike, Robert Ladd 1910- CANR-1
Earlier sketch in CA 1R
Thorndike, (Arthur) Russell 1885-1972
Obituary 37-40R
Thorndike, Susan 1944- 41-44R
Thorndike, Tony
See Thorndike, A(nthony) E(dward)
Thorndyke, Helen Louise CAP-2
Earlier sketch in CA 19-20
See also SATA 1
Thorne, Alice Dunn 1910-1973 Obituary ...45-48
Thorne, Bliss K(irby) 1916- 17-18R
Thorne, Bradley D.
See Glut, Donald F(rank)
Thorne, Christopher 1934- CANR-11
Earlier sketch in CA 21-22R
Thorne, Edouard
See Greve, Felix Paul (Berthold Friedrich)
Thorne, Florence Calvert 1878(?)-1973
Obituary 41-44R
Thorne, Hart
See Carhart, Arthur Hawthorne
Thorne, Ian
See May, Julian
Thorne, Jean Wright
See May, Julian
Thorne, Jim 1922- CANR-1
Earlier sketch in CA 3R
Thorne, Nicola
See Ellerbeck, Rosemary (Anne L'Estrange)
Thorne, Ramsay
See Cameron, Lou
Thorne, Sabina 1927- 106
Thorne, Sterling
See Fuller, Dorothy Mason
Thorne, William James 1898- 5-6R
Thorning, Joseph F(rancis) 1896-1985 ... CAP-1
Obituary 115
Earlier sketch in CA 9-10
Thornley, Richard 1950- 117
Thornton, Big Mama
See Thornton, Willie Mae
Thornton, Emma Shore 1908- 114
Thornton, Francis John 1938- 85-88
Thornton, Gene 93-96
Thornton, Hall
See Silverberg, Robert
Thornton, J(onathan) Mills III 1943- 77-80
Thornton, James W., Jr. 1908- CANR-1
Earlier sketch in CA 1R
Thornton, Jerry
See Thornton, Emma Shore
Thornton, John Leonard 1913- CANR-4
Earlier sketch in CA 9-10R
Thornton, John W(illiam) 1922- 106
Thornton, John W(illiam), Jr. 1948- 106
Thornton, Lee 1944- 73-76
Thornton, Martin (Stuart Farrin) 1915- 9-10R
Thornton, Michael 1941- 105
Thornton, Peter Kai 1925- CANR-20
Earlier sketch in CA 102
Thornton, R(obert) K(elsey) R(ought)
1938- 119
Thornton, Richard C. 1936- 81-84
Thornton, Thomas Perry 1931- 11-12R
Thornton, W. B.
See Burgess, Thornton Waldo
Thornton, Weldon 1934- 25-28R
Thornton, Willie Mae 1926-1984 Obituary .. 113
Thornton, Willis 1900- CAP-1
Earlier sketch in CA 15-16
Thorp, Duncan Roy 1914- 13-14R
Thorp, Edward O. 1932- 23-24R
Thorp, Margaret Farrand 1891-1970
Obituary 104
Thorp, Roderick Mayne, Jr. 1936- CANR-6
Earlier sketch in CA 2R
Thorp, Willard 1899- CANR-3
Earlier sketch in CA 7-8R
Thorp, Willard Long 1899- 1R
Thorpe, Donald W(illiam) 1928- 29-32R
Thorpe, E(ustace) G(eorge) 1916- 9-10R
See also SATA 21
Thorpe, Earl(ie) E(ndris) 1924- 61-64
Thorpe, Elliott R(aymond) 1897- 65-68
Thorpe, George P. 1913(?)-1983 Obituary .. 110
Thorpe, J. K.
See Nathanson, Laura Walther
Thorpe, James 1915- CANR-17
Earlier sketches in CA 5-6R, CANR-2
Thorpe, Lewis (Guy Melville)
1913-1977 .... CANR-10
Earlier sketch in CA 9-10R
Thorpe, Louis P(eter) 1893- CANR-20
Earlier sketch in CA 2R
Thorpe, Michael 1932- CANR-8
Earlier sketch in CA 23-24R
Thorpe, Peter 1932- 57-60
Thorpe, Sylvia
See Thimblethorpe, June Sylvia
Thorpe, Thomas Bangs 1815-1878 ... DLB-3, 11
Thorpe, Trebor
See Fanthorpe, R(obert) Lionel
Thorpe, Trevor
See Fanthorpe, R(obert) Lionel
Thorpe, William Homan 1902-1986 ..... CANR-2
Obituary 119
Earlier sketch in CA 7-8R
Thorsell, Richard Lawrence 1938- 89-92
Thorsley, Peter L(arsen), Jr. 1929- 5-6R
Thorson, Thomas Landon 1934- 17-18R
Thorstad, David 1941- 57-60
Thorstein, Eric
See Merril, Judith
Thorvall, Kerstin 1925- CANR-13
Earlier sketch in CA 17-18R
See also SATA 13
Thorvall-Falk, Kerstin
See Thorvall, Kerstin
Thorwald, Juergen 1916- CANR-21
Earlier sketches in CA 49-52, CANR-1
Thouless, Robert H(enry) 1894-1984 77-80
Obituary 114
Thrapp, Dan Lincoln 1913- CANR-4
Earlier sketch in CA 11-12R
Thrasher, Crystal (Faye) 1921- CANR-8
Earlier sketch in CA 61-64
See also SATA 27
Threlkeld, Richard 1937- 65-68
Thresher, B(rainard) Alden 1896-1984
Obituary 111
Throckmorton, Burton Hamilton, Jr.
1921- 5-6R
Throckmorton, Peter 1928- 19-20R
Throneberry, Jimmy B. 1933- 89-92
Throneburg, James 5-6R
Thrower, Norman J(oseph) W(illiam)
1919- 41-44R
Thrower, Percy John 1913- CANR-4
Earlier sketch in CA 9-10R
Thubron, Colin (Gerald Dryden) 1939- .. CANR-12
Earlier sketch in CA 25-28R
Thubten Sigme Norbu 1922- Brief entry 109
Thuesen, Gerald J(organ) 1938- 37-40R
Thuillier, Jacques 1928- CANR-7
Earlier sketch in CA 11-12R
Thulstrup, Niels 1924- CANR-10
Earlier sketch in CA 21-22R
Thum, Gladys 1920- 41-44R
See also SATA 26
Thum, Marcella CANR-21
Earlier sketches in CA 11-12R, CANR-6
See also SATA 3, 28
Thumm, Garold W(esley) 1915- 15-16R
Thuna, Lee
See Thuna, Leonora
Thuna, Leonora 1929- CANR-16
Earlier sketch in CA 23-24R
Thundercloud, Katherine
See Witt, Shirley Hill
Thundy, Zacharias Pontian 1936- 102
Thundyil, Zacharias Pontian
See Thundy, Zacharias Pontian
Thurber, Helen (Wismer) 1902(?)-1986
Obituary 121
Thurber, James (Grover) 1894-1961 ... CANR-17
Earlier sketch in CA 73-76
See also SATA 13
See also DLB 4, 11, 22
See also CLC 5, 11, 25
See also SSC 1
Thurber, Walter A(rthur) 1908- CANR-12
Earlier sketch in CA 21-22R
Thurkettle, James 1929- 69-72
Thurley, Geoffrey John 1936- CANR-13
Earlier sketch in CA 61-64
Thurley, Jon (Mark) 118
Thurman, Christa C(harlotte) Mayer
1934- CANR-2
Earlier sketch in CA 49-52
Thurman, Howard 1900-1981 97-100
Obituary 103
Thurman, Judith 1946- CANR-1
Earlier sketch in CA 49-52
See also SATA 33
Thurman, Kelly 1914- 57-60
Thurman, Wallace (Henry) 1902-1934 124
Brief entry 104
See also DLB 51
See also TCLC 6
Thurman, Wayne L(averne) 1923- 49-52
Thurmond, Nancy Moore 1946-
Brief entry 114
Thurmond, (J.) Strom 1902- 89-92
Thurow, Lester C(arl) 1938- 81-84
Thursby, Vincent Victor 1918- 41-44R
Thurstan, Violetta CAP-1
Earlier sketch in CA 15-16
Thurston, David B. 1918- CANR-6
Earlier sketch in CA 7-8R
Thurston, Elliott Ladd 1895-1975
Obituary 89-92
Thurston, Harry 1950- 113
Thurston, Hazel (Patricia) 1906- 57-60
Thurston, Jarvis 1914- 15-16R
Thurston, Lorrin P. 1900(?)-1984
Obituary 114

INDEX

Thurston, Robert (Donald) 1936- CANR-15
Earlier sketch in CA 85-88
Thut, I(saac) N(oah) CAP-1
Earlier sketch in CA 15-16
Thwaite, Ann (Barbara Harrop) 1932- 5-6R
See also SATA 14
Thwaite, Anthony (Simon) 1930- 7-8R
See also DLB 40
Thwaite, M(ary) F. (Austin) 21-22R
Thwaites, Michael 1915- 77-80
Thwaites, Reuben Gold 1853-1913 ..... DLB-47
Thwing, Leroy (L.) 1879- 7-8R
Thygerson, Alton L(uie) 1940- CANR-18
Earlier sketches in CA 45-48, CANR-1
Tiant, Luis 1940- 73-76
(al-)Tibawi, A(bdul-)L(atif) 1910-1981 .. CANR-24
Obituary 105
Earlier sketch in CA 25-28R
Tibber, Robert
See Friedman, (Eve) Rosemary (Tibber)
Tibber, Rosemary
See Friedman, (Eve) Rosemary (Tibber)
Tibbets, Albert B. 1888- 7-8R
Tibbetts, Arnold M(acLean) 1927- CANR-16
Earlier sketch in CA 93-96
Tibbetts, Charlene 1921- 93-96
Tibbetts, John C(arter) 1946- 89-92
Tibbetts, John W(esley) 1928- 25-28R
Tibbetts, Norris L. 1892(?)-1983 Obituary .. 108
Tibbetts, Orlando L(ailer), Jr. 1919- ... CANR-11
Earlier sketch in CA 29-32R
Tibbetts, William
See Brannon, William T.
Tibble, Anne 1912-1980 .... CANR-10
Obituary 102
Earlier sketch in CA 9-10R
Tibbs, Ben 1907- 61-64
Tibbs, Virginia M.
See Scott, Virginia M(uhleman)
Tice, George A(ndrew) 1938- CANR-12
Earlier sketch in CA 61-64
Ticheburn, Cheviot
See Ainsworth, William Harrison
Tichenor, Tom 1923- 29-32R
See also SATA 14
Tichi, Cecelia 1942- 104
Tichy, H(enrietta) J. 1912- 21-22R
Tichy, Susan (Elizabeth) 1952- 123
Tichy, William 1924- 107
See also SATA 31
Tickle, P(hyllis) A(lexander) 1934- CANR-24
Earlier sketches in CA 65-68, CANR-9
Tickner, Fred(erick James) 1902- CAP-1
Earlier sketch in CA 9-10
Ticknor, George 1791-1871 .... DLB-1, 59
Tidball, Derek J(ohn) 1948- 120
Tidy, Michael 1943- 113
Tidyman, Ernest 1928-1984 73-76
Obituary 113
Tiede, Tom (Robert) 1937- 25-28R
Tiedt, Iris M(cClellan) 1928- CANR-24
Earlier sketches in CA 13-14R, CANR-7
Tiedt, Sidney W(illis) 1927- CANR-24
Earlier sketch in CA 13-14R
Tiegreen, Alan F. 1935- SATA-36
Tiempo, Edith (Lopez) 1919- 104
Tien, H. Yuan 1926- 49-52
Tien, Hung-Mao 1938- 73-76
Tierney, Brian 1922- 103
Tierney, Gene 1920- Brief entry 116
Tierney, John Lawrence 1892-1972 ...... CAP-2
Earlier sketch in CA 21-22
Tierney, Kevin (Hugh) 1942- 29-32R
Tierney, M. Leo 1932(?)-1986 Obituary 118
Tierney, Michael 1894-1975 Obituary 114
Tierney, Paul Ambrose 1895(?)-1979
Obituary 85-88
Tierney, Richard L(ouis) 1936- 111
Tierney, Tom 1928- CANR-23
Earlier sketches in CA 57-60, CANR-8
Tiersky, Ronald S. 1944- 118
Tietjens, Eunice 1884-1944 .... DLB-54
Tietze, Andreas 1914- 49-52
Tietze, Christopher 1908-1984 Obituary 112
Tiffany, Donald Wayne 1930- Brief entry ... 108
Tiffany, E. A. 1911- 103
Tiffany, Phyllis G. 1932- 37-40R
Tiffany, William R(obert) 1920- 5-6R
Tiffin, Joseph 1905- 17-18R
Tifft, Ellen CANR-1
Earlier sketch in CA 49-52
Tifton, Leo
See Page, Gerald W(ilburn)
Tigar, Michael E(dward) 1941- 77-80
Tigay, Alan M(errill) 1947- 124
Tiger, Derry
See Ellison, Harlan
Tiger, Jack
See Puechner, Ray
Tiger, John
See Wager, Walter H(erman)
Tiger, Lionel 1937- CANR-14
Earlier sketch in CA 25-28R
Tiger, Virginia Marie 1940- Brief entry 106
Tigerman, Stanley 1930- 114
Tiger Of The Snows
See Norgay, Tenzing
Tighe, Donald J. 1928- 29-32R
Tighe, Thomas B. 1907(?)-1983 Obituary ... 109
Tignor, Robert L. 1933- Brief entry 109
Tigue, Ethel Erkkila 1918- 21-22R
Tikhonov, Nikolai Semyonovich
1896-1979 Obituary 85-88
Tikhonov, Valentin
See Payne, (Pierre Stephen) Robert
Tikku, Girdhari L(al) 1925- 45-48
Tiktin, Carl 1930- CANR-13
Earlier sketch in CA 73-76
Tilden, Freeman 1884(?)-1980 97-100
Tilghman, Benjamin R(oss) 1927-
Brief entry 107
Till, Barry 1923- 49-52
Tillard, Jean-M(arie) Roger 1927- 45-48
Tillema, Herbert K(endall) 1942- 45-48
Tilleman, William Arthur 1932- 53-56
Tiller, Carl W(illiam) 1915- 108
Tiller, Terence (Rogers) 1916-1987 101
Obituary 124
Tilles, Solomon 1932- Brief entry 108
Tillett, Bill G(lenn) 1942- 118
Tillett, Gregory J. 1950- 110
Tilley, Ethel 1894- CAP-1
Earlier sketch in CA 9-10
Tilley, Patrick 1928- 106
Tilley, (William) Roger (Montgomerie)
1905-1971 .... CAP-2
Earlier sketch in CA 25-28
Tillich, Hannah 1896- 73-76
Tillich, Paul (Johannes) 1886-1965 ....7-8R
Obituary 25-28R
Tillinghast, B(urette) S(tinson), Jr. 1930- .. 65-68
Tillinghast, Pardon E(lisha) 1920- 11-12R
Tillinghast, Richard 1940- 29-32R
See also CLC 29
Tillion, Diana (Rutzebeck) 1928-
Brief entry 110
Tillion, Germaine Marie Rosine 1907- 104
Tillman, Rollie, Jr. 1933- 23-24R
Tillman, Seth Phillip 1930- 3R
Tillman, Stephen Frederick 1900(?)-1977
Obituary 69-72
Tillotson, Geoffrey 1905-1969 .... CAP-1
Earlier sketch in CA 13-14
Tilly, Charles 1929- CANR-20
Earlier sketch in CA 103
Tilly, Louise A(udino) 1930- 120
Tilly, Nancy 1935- 120
Tilly, Richard H(ugh) 1932- 17-18R
Tillyard, E(ustace) M(andeville) W(etenhall)
1889-1962 Obituary 93-96
Tilman, Harold William 1898-1978 103
Tilman, Robert O(liver) 1929- CANR-1
Earlier sketch in CA 45-48
Tilson, Everett 1923- 41-44R
Tiltman, Hessell 1897(?)-1976 Obituary ... 69-72
Tiltman, Ronald Frank 1901- CAP-1
Earlier sketch in CA 9-10
Tilton, Alice
See Taylor, Phoebe Atwood
Tilton, Eleanor M(arguerite) 1913-
Brief entry 110
Tilton, John W(ightman) 1928-1983 122
Brief entry 118
Tilton, Madonna Elaine 1929- 114
See also SATA 41
Tilton, Rafael
See Tilton, Madonna Elaine
Tilton, Timothy Alan 1942- 61-64
Timasheff, Nicholas S. 1886-1970 .... 2R
Obituary 29-32R
Timberlake, Carolyn
See Dresang, Eliza
Timberlake, Charles E(dward) 1935- 41-44R
Timberlake, Richard Henry, Jr. 1922- ...21-22R
Timerman, Jacobo 1923- 120
Brief entry 109
Timko, Michael 1925- 19-20R
Timlett, Peter Valentine 1933- Brief entry 111
Timmen, Fritz 1918- 53-56
Timmerman, Joan 1938- 118
Timmerman, John H(ager) 1945- 111
Timmerman, John Johnson 1908- 111
Timmermans, Claire 1938- 104
Timmers, J(an) Joseph M(arie) 1907- CAP-1
Earlier sketch in CA 13-14
Timmins, Lois Fahs 1914- 45-48
Timmins, William F(rederick) SATA-10
Timmis, John Henry III 1934- 104
Timmons, Bascom N(olly) 1890-1987 104
Obituary 122
Timmons, Bonnie 1951- 120
Timmons, Jeffry A. 1941- 108
Timms, Arthur W(arren) 1940- 120
Timms, David 1946- 109
Timms, E(dward) V(ivian) 1895-1960
Brief entry 112
Timms, Kathleen 1943- 122
Timms, Noel 1927- CANR-16
Earlier sketch in CA 15-16R
Timoney, Francis 1938- 61-64
Timoshenko, Stephen P. 1878-1972
Obituary 33-36R
Timothy, Hamilton B(aird) 1913- 102
Timothy, Peter 1725(?)-1782 .... DLB-43
Timpe, Eugene Frank 1926- 77-80
Timperley, Rosemary Kenyon 1920- ... CANR-17
Earlier sketch in CA 97-100
Timrod, Henry 1828-1867 .... DLB-3
Tinbergen, Jan 1903- CANR-2
Earlier sketch in CA 5-6R
Tinbergen, Niko(laas) 1907- 108
Tindall, George Brown 1921- 85-88
Tindall, Gillian 1938- CANR-11
Earlier sketch in CA 23-24R
See also CLC 7
Tindall, Kenneth (Thomas) 1937- 29-32R
Tindall, P(eggy) E(leanor) N(ancy)
1927- 29-32R
Tindall, William York 1903-1981 ...... CANR-16
Obituary 104
Earlier sketch in CA 3R
Tiner, John Hudson 1944- CANR-18
Earlier sketch in CA 101
See also SATA 32
Tiner, Ralph W., Jr. 1948- 124
Ting, Jan C(hing-an) 1948- 37-40R
Ting, Walasse 1929- 21-22R
Tingay, Lance 1915- 101
Tingle, Dolli 1920- CANR-10
Earlier sketch in CA 25-28R
Tingley, Donald F(red) 1922- CANR-10
Earlier sketch in CA 25-28R
Tingley, Elizabeth 1955- 114
Tingsten, Herbert 1896-1973 Obituary 45-48
Tinic, Seha M(ehmet) 1941- 37-40R
Tinkelman, Murray 1933- SATA-12
Tinker, Beamish
See Jesse, F(ryniwyd) Tennyson
Tinker, Ben (Hill) 1903- 102
Tinker, Edward Larocque 1881-1968 ..... CAP-1
Earlier sketch in CA 13-14
Tinker, Hugh (Russell) 1921- CANR-3
Earlier sketch in CA 5-6R
Tinker, Miles Albert 1893-1977 .... CANR-4
Earlier sketch in CA 7-8R
Tinker, Spencer Wilkie 1909- 41-44R
Tinkle, (Julien) Lon 1906-1980 104
See also SATA 36
Tinne, Dorothea
See Strover, Dorothea
Tinne, E. D.
See Strover, Dorothea
Tinnin, David B(ruce) 1930- 49-52
Tinniswood, Peter 1936- 25-28R
Tinsley, Ernest John 1919- 5-6R
Tinsley, James Robert 1921- 15-16R
Tinsley, Jim Bob
See Tinsley, James Robert
Tinsley, (John) Russell 1932- 17-18R
Tinterow, Gary 1953- 109
Tintner, Adeline R. 1912- 123
Tiomkin, Dimitri 1899-1979 Obituary 93-96
Tippett, Michael (Kemp) 1905- 109
Tippette, Giles 1934- CANR-17
Earlier sketch in CA 65-68
Tipping, Marjorie Jean 1917- 122
Tippit, Sammy 1947- 104
Tipple, John Ord 1916- 11-12R
Tipton, Charles Leon 1932- 41-44R
Tipton, David 1934- Brief entry 111
Tipton, James 1942- CANR-8
Earlier sketch in CA 57-60
Tiptree, James, Jr.
See Sheldon, Alice Hastings Bradley
See also DLB 8
Tirbutt, Honoria CANR-22
Earlier sketch in CA 106
Tirro, Frank (Pascale) 1935- 81-84
Tiryakian, Edward A(shod) 1929- CANR-19
Earlier sketches in CA 5-6R, CANR-2
Tischler, Barbara L. 1949- 123
Tischler, Hans 1915- CANR-6
Earlier sketch in CA 3R
Tischler, Nancy Marie (Patterson) 1931- 5-6R
Tischner, Rudolf (E.) 1879-1961 Obituary .. 112
Tisdale, Celes 1941- 57-60
Tisdell, Clement Allan 1939- CANR-15
Earlier sketch in CA 25-28R
Tise, Larry Edward 1942- 102
Tish-Tash
See Tashlin, Frank
Tisserand, Jacques
See Barnes, Jim
Titchener, James Lampton 1922- 45-48
Titchener, Louise 1941- 122
Titcomb, Margaret 1891- CANR-5
Earlier sketch in CA 5-6R
Titler, Dale M(ilton) 1926- 81-84
See also SATA 28, 35
Titley, David Paul 1929- 110
Titley, Norah M(ary) 1920- 118
Titmarsh, Michael Angelo
See Thackeray, William Makepeace
Titmuss, Richard M(orris) 1907-1973 109
Obituary 107
Tito, Josip Broz 1892-1980 Obituary 97-100
Tito, Marshal
See Tito, Josip Broz
Titon, Jeff Todd 1943- CANR-16
Earlier sketch in CA 89-92
Titra, Stephen Andrew 1945- 97-100
Titterton, Ernest William 1916- 109
Tittle, Charles R(ay) 1939- CANR-15
Earlier sketch in CA 41-44R
Tittler, Jonathan (Paul) 1945- 119
Tittler, Robert 1942- CANR-15
Earlier sketch in CA 81-84
Tittmann, George Fabian 1915-1978 ....7-8R
Obituary 81-84
Titus, Barry J(oseph) 1938- 1R
Titus, Charles 1942- 45-48
Titus, David Anson 1934- 97-100
Titus, Edward William 1870-1952 .... DLB-4
Titus, Eve 1922- 29-32R
See also SATA 2
Titus, Harold H(opper) 1896- 5-6R
Titus, Warren Irving 1921- 17-18R
Tiusanen, Timo 1936-1985 85-88
Obituary 117
Tjader, Marguerite 1901- 17-18R
Tjepkema, Sandra L(ynn) 1953- 114
Tjernagel, Neelak S(erawlook) 1906- 17-18R
Tkacik, Arnold J(ohn) 1919- 81-84
Toan, Arthur B(enjamin), Jr. 1915- 25-28R
Tobach, Ethel 1921- 81-84
Toback, James 1944- 41-44R
Tobe, John Harold 1907-1979 .... CANR-1
Earlier sketch in CA 3R
Tobey, George B., Jr. 1917- 49-52
Tobey, Kathrene McLandress 1908- CAP-2
Earlier sketch in CA 29-32
Tobey, Mark 1890-1976 Obituary 65-68
Tobey, Ronald C(harles) 1942- 73-76
Tobias, Andrew P. 1947- CANR-14
Earlier sketch in CA 37-40R
Tobias, Henry J(ack) 1925- 41-44R
Tobias, J(ohn) J(acob) 1925- 53-56
Tobias, Katherine
See Gottfried, Theodore Mark
Tobias, Phillip V. 1925- CANR-15
Earlier sketch in CA 37-40R
Tobias, Richard C(lark) 1925- 29-32R
Tobias, Ronald B(enjamin) 1948- 111
Tobias, Sheila 1935- 93-96
Tobias, Tobi 1938- CANR-16
Earlier sketch in CA 29-32R
See also SATA 5
See also CLR 4
Tobin, James 1918- CANR-5
Earlier sketch in CA 53-56
Tobin, James Edward 1905-1968 .... CAP-2
Earlier sketch in CA 23-24
Tobin, Kay 1930- 37-40R
Tobin, Richard Lardner 1910- CANR-1
Earlier sketch in CA 2R
Tobin, Sheldon S(idney) 1931- Brief entry .. 110
Tobin, Terence 1938- 53-56
Toby, Liz
See Minsky, Betty Jane (Toebe)
Toby, Mark 1913(?)-1972 Obituary 37-40R
Toch, Hans (Herbert) 1930- CANR-23
Earlier sketches in CA 19-20R, CANR-7
Toch, Henry 1923- CANR-21
Earlier sketches in CA 9-10R, CANR-6
Toczek, Nick 1950- 106
Tod, Ian J. 1945- 103
Tod, Osma Gallinger 1898-1982(?) CAP-1
Obituary 108
Earlier sketch in CA 9-10
Todd, Alden 1918- CANR-6
Earlier sketch in CA 3R
Todd, Anne Ophelia
See Dowden, Anne Ophelia
Todd, Barbara Euphan 1890-1976 104
Todd, Barbara K(eith) 1917- 61-64
See also SATA 10
Todd, Clark 1945(?)-1983 Obituary 110
Todd, Edgeley W(oodman) 1914-
Brief entry 109
Todd, Edward N. 1931- 53-56
Todd, Frances 1910- 13-14R
Todd, Frederick Porter 1903-1977
Obituary 73-76
Todd, Galbraith Hall 1914- 3R
Todd, Herbert Eatton 1908- CANR-12
Earlier sketches in CA 9-10, CAP-1
See also SATA 11
Todd, Hollis N(elson) 1914- 57-60
Todd, Ian A(lexander) 1941- 112
Todd, Ian Menzies 1923- 69-72
Todd, Janet M(argaret) 1942- CANR-1
Earlier sketch in CA 49-52
Todd, Jerry D(ale) 1941- 53-56
Todd, John M(urray) 1918- 9-10R
Todd, Karen (Iris) Rohne (Pritchett) 1936-
Brief entry 111
Todd, Leonard 1940- 65-68
Todd, Loreto 1942- 107
See also SATA 30
Todd, Malcolm 1939- 101
Todd, Paul
See Posner, Richard
Todd, Ruth Van Dorn 1889(?)-1976
Obituary 65-68
Todd, Ruthven 1914- 81-84
Todd, Virgil H. 1921- Brief entry 106
Todd, Vivian Edmiston 1912- 17-18R
Todd, William Burton 1919- 41-44R
Todd, William Mills III 1944- 65-68
Todman, Bill
See Todman, William S.
Todman, William S. 1916-1979 Obituary ..89-92
Todorov, Tzvetan 1939- 73-76
Todrank, Gustave H(erman) 1924- 41-44R
Todrin, Boris 1915- 61-64
Todsicher, J(ohn) Edgar 1926- CANR-14
Earlier sketch in CA 29-32R
Toekes, Rudolf L(eslie) 1935- 23-24R
Toepfer, Ray Grant 1923- 21-22R
Toeplitz, Jerzy 1909- 65-68
Toernqvist, (Per) Egil 1932- 29-32R
Tofani, Loretta 1953- 116
Brief entry 113
Toffler, Alvin 1928- CANR-15
Earlier sketch in CA 15-16R
Toft, (Eric) John 1933- 103
Tofte, Arthur 1902-1980 73-76
Obituary 103
Togliatti, Palmiro 1893(?)-1964 Obituary ... 113
Tohata, Seiichi 1899-1983 Obituary 110
Toka, Salchak Kalbakkhoreviich
1901-1973 Obituary 41-44R
Tokayer, Marvin 1936- 102
Toker, Franklin K(arl) B(enedict) S(erchuk)
1944- CANR-15
Earlier sketch in CA 81-84
Tokes, Rudolf L(eslie) 1935- Brief entry 114
Toklas, Alice B(abette) 1877-1967 81-84
Obituary 25-28R
See also DLB 4
Tokmakoff, George 1928- 123
Tolan, Stephanie S. 1942- CANR-15
Earlier sketch in CA 77-80
See also SATA 38

Toland, John (Willard) 1912- CANR-23
  Earlier sketches in CA 2R, CANR-6
  See also SATA 38
Tolbert, E(lias) L(ake) 1915- CANR-3
  Earlier sketch in CA 3R
Tolbert, Francis Xavier 1912-1984 ..... CANR-16
  Obituary 111
  Earlier sketch in CA 3R
Tolbert, Frank X.
  See Tolbert, Francis Xavier
Tolbert, Malcolm O(liver) 1924- 65-68
Tolbert, Mary Ann 1947- 116
Tolby, Arthur
  See Infield, Glenn (Berton)
Tolchin, Martin 1928- 120
Toldson, Ivory L. 1943- 114
Toledano, Ralph de 1916- 11-12R
  See also AITN 1
Toledano, Roulhac (Bunkley) 1938- 101
Tolegian, Aram 1909- CANR-6
  Earlier sketch in CA 2R
Tolf, Robert W(alter) 1929- 73-76
Tolischus, Otto D(avid) 1890-1967
  Obituary 93-96
Toliver, George
  See Masselink, Ben
Toliver, Harold E(arl) 1932- 23-24R
Toliver, Raymond F. 1914- 17-18R
Tolkien, J(ohn) R(onald) R(euel)
  1892-1973 .... CAP-2
  Obituary 45-48
  Earlier sketch in CA 17-18
  See also SATA 2, 24, 32
  See also DLB 15
  See also CLC 1, 2, 3, 8, 12, 38
  See also AITN 1
Toll, Robert C(harles) 1938- 53-56
Toll, Seymour I. 1925- 29-32R
Toll, William 1941- 114
Toller, Ernst 1893-1939 Brief entry 107
  See also TCLC 10
Toller, Kate Caffrey
  See Caffrey, Kate
Tollers, Vincent L(ouis) 1939- 57-60
Tolles, Frederick B(arnes) 1915-1975 .... 5-6R
  Obituary 103
Tolles, Martha 1921- 49-52
  See also SATA 8
Tolley, A(rnold) T(revor) 1927- 123
Tolley, Howard B(oyd), Jr. 1943- 53-56
Tolley, Kemp 1908- 45-48
Tolley, William Pearson 1900- 93-96
Tolliver, Ruby C(hangos) 1922- 111
  See also SATA 41
Tolman, Newton F. 1908-1986 .... 1R
  Obituary 120
Tolmie, Kenneth Donald 1941- 69-72
  See also SATA 15
Tolnai, Karoly
  See De Tolnay, Charles Erich
Tolnai, Vagujhelyi Karoly
  See De Tolnay, Charles Erich
Tolson, M. B.
  See Tolson, Melvin B(eaunorus)
Tolson, Melvin B(eaunorus) 1898(?)-1966 .. 124
  Obituary 89-92
  See also DLB 48
  See also CLC 36
Tolstoi, Aleksei Nikolaevich
  See Tolstoy, Alexey Nikolaevich
Tolstoy, Alexandra L(vovna) 1884-1979 ... 65-68
  Obituary 89-92
Tolstoy, Alexey Nikolaevich 1882-1945
  Brief entry 107
  See also TCLC 18
Tolstoy, Count Leo
  See Tolstoy, Leo (Nikolaevich)
Tolstoy, Dimitry 1912- 29-32R
Tolstoy, Leo (Nikolaevich) 1828-1910 123
  Brief entry 104
  See also SATA 26
  See also TCLC 4, 11, 17
Tolstoy, Mary Koutouzov 1884(?)-1976
  Obituary 69-72
Tolstoy(-Miloslavsky), Nikolai (Dimitrievich)
  1935- 81-84
Tolstoy, Tatyana (Sukhotin) 1864-1950
  Brief entry 117
Tolzmann, Don Heinrich 1945- CANR-17
  Earlier sketches in CA 49-52, CANR-2
Toma, Dave
  See Toma, David
Toma, David 1933- 118
Tomalin, Claire 1933- 89-92
Tomalin, Nicholas 1931-1973 Obituary 45-48
Tomalin, Ruth CANR-13
  Earlier sketch in CA 15-16R
  See also SATA 29
Toman, Walter 1920- 5-6R
Tomas, Andrew Paul 73-76
Tomasek, Robert D(ennis) 1928- 17-18R
Tomasevic, Nebojsa 1929- 81-84
Tomasi, Silvano M(ario) 1940- 115
Tomasic, D(inko) A(nthony) 1902- CAP-1
  Earlier sketch in CA 19-20
Tomasi di Lampedusa, Giuseppe
  1896-1957 Brief entry 111
Tomasson, Katherine 1895- CAP-1
  Earlier sketch in CA 9-10
Tomasson, Richard F(inn) 1928- CANR-1
  Earlier sketch in CA 45-48
Tomb, David A(lan) 1944- 117
Tomek, Ivan 1939- 120
Tomes, Margot (Ladd) 1917- SATA-27, 36
Tomeski, Edward Alexander 1930- 37-40R
Tomfool
  See Farjeon, Eleanor
Tomikel, John 1928- CANR-4
  Earlier sketch in CA 53-56
Tomin, Zdena 1941- 123
Tomkiewicz, Mina 1917-1975 .... CAP-2
  Earlier sketch in CA 29-32
Tomkins, Calvin 1925- CANR-8
  Earlier sketch in CA 15-16R
Tomkins, Jasper
  See Batey, Tom
Tomkins, Mary E(ileen) 1914- 61-64
Tomkinson, Constance
  See Weeks, Constance Tomkinson
Tomkinson, Michael 1940- CANR-22
  Earlier sketch in CA 93-96
Tomlin, E(ric) W(alter) F(rederick)
  1913-1988(?) CANR-3
  Obituary 124
  Earlier sketch in CA 5-6R
Tomlin, Lily
  See Tomlin, Mary Jean
  See also CLC 17
Tomlin, Mary Jean 1939(?)- Brief entry 117
Tomlins, Jack E(dward) 1929- 25-28R
Tomlinson, (Alfred) Charles 1927- 5-6R
  See also DLB 40
  See also CLC 2, 4, 6, 13, 45
Tomlinson, Edward 1891(?)-1973
  Obituary 45-48
Tomlinson, Gerald (Arthur) 1933- 85-88
Tomlinson, H(enry) M(ajor) 1873-1958
  Brief entry 118
  See also DLB 36
Tomlinson, Jill 1931-1976 .... CAP-2
  Earlier sketch in CA 29-32
  See also SATA 3, 24
Tomlinson, Kenneth Y(oung) 1944- 65-68
Tomlinson, Reginald R(obert)
  1885-1979(?) Obituary 104
  See also SATA 27
Tomlinson, T(homas) B(rian) 1925- 11-12R
Tomlinson-Keasey, Carol 1942- 101
Tommeraasen, Miles 1923- 21-22R
Tompert, Ann 1918- CANR-11
  Earlier sketch in CA 69-72
  See also SATA 14
Tompkins, C(linton) David 1937- 41-44R
Tompkins, Dorothy (Campbell) 1908- 17-18R
Tompkins, E(dwin) Berkeley 1935- 29-32R
Tompkins, Everett Thomas 1931- 107
Tompkins, J(oyce) M(arjorie) S(anxter)
  1897-1986 Obituary 121
Tompkins, Jane P(arry) 1940- CANR-17
  Earlier sketch in CA 29-32R
Tompkins, Jerry R(obert) 1931- 17-18R
Tompkins, Julia (Marguerite Hunter
  Manchee) 1909- 29-32R
Tompkins, Kathleen Burns 1934- 93-96
Tompkins, Peter 1919- CANR-12
  Earlier sketch in CA 11-12R
Tompkins, Richard A. 1896(?)-1977
  Obituary 73-76
Tompkins, Stuart R(amsay) 1886-1977 ... 37-40R
Tompkins, Tom
  See Tompkins, Everett Thomas
Tompkins, Walker A. 1909- 7-8R
Tompson, Benjamin 1642-1714 .... DLB-24
Toms, Bernard 1931- 17-18R
Tomson, Bernard 1909-1978 Obituary 77-80
Ton, Mary Ellen 1933- 112
Tonashi
  See Harrington, Mark Raymond
Tone, Teona 1944- 112
Toner, Raymond John 1908- 5-6R
  See also SATA 10
Toney, Albert (Livingston, Jr.) 1933- 120
Toney, Anthony 1913- CANR-9
  Earlier sketch in CA 17-18R
Tong, Raymond 1922- CANR-2
  Earlier sketch in CA 7-8R
Tong, Te-kong 1920- CANR-8
  Earlier sketch in CA 11-12R
Tongren, Sally S(tetson) 1926- 118
Tonkin, Humphrey 1939- CANR-16
  Earlier sketch in CA 41-44R
Tonkin, Peter (Francis) 1950- 101
Tonkinson, Robert 1928- 77-80
Tonks, Rosemary (D. Boswell) 1932- 89-92
  See also DLB 14
Tonn, Martin H. 1921- 7-8R
Tonquedec, Joseph de 1868-1962
  Obituary 112
Tonson, Jacob
  See Bennett, (Enoch) Arnold
Tonsor, Stephen (John) 1923- Brief entry .. 114
Toobin, Jerome 1920(?)-1984 Obituary 111
Toohey, Catherine 1949- 109
Toohey, Robert E(ugene) 1935- 89-92
Took, Belladonna
  See Chapman, Vera
Tooke, Ann (Mary Margaret) Hales
  See Hales-Tooke, Ann (Mary Margaret)
Tooke, Louise Mathews 1950- 105
  See also SATA 38
Tooke, Thomas (Renshaw) 1947- 73-76
Tooker, Elisabeth (Jane) 1927- 49-52
Toole, John Kennedy 1937-1969 104
  See also DLBY 81
  See also CLC 19
Toole, K(enneth) Ross 1920- Brief entry 112
Toole, Rex
  See Tralins, S(andor) Robert
Toole, William Bell III 1930- 21-22R
Toole Stott, Raymond 1910-1982
  Obituary 105
Tooley, M. J.
  See Tooley, Michael J(ohn)
Tooley, Michael J(ohn) 1932- 106
Tooley, Michael J(ohn) 1942- CANR-24
Tooley, R(onald) Vere 1898-1986 .... 9-10R
  Obituary 120
Toomay, Patrick J(ay) 1948- 65-68
Toombs, John 1927- 106
Toombs, Lawrence Edmund 1919- CANR-8
  Earlier sketch in CA 5-6R
Toomer, Derek 1946- 65-68
Toomer, Jean 1894-1967 85-88
  See also DLB 45, 51
  See also CLC 1, 4, 13, 22
  See also SSC 1
Toon, Peter 1939- 112
Toona, Elin(-Kai) 1937- CANR-15
  Earlier sketch in CA 81-84
Toonder, Martin
  See Groom, Arthur William
Toothaker, Roy Eugene 1928- 65-68
  See also SATA 18
Tooze, Ruth (Anderson) 1892- 5-6R
  See also SATA 4
Topel, L(ouis) John 1934- 118
Toperoff, Sam 1933- 45-48
Topkins, Katharine 1927- 49-52
Topkins, Richard 1925- 25-28R
Toplin, Robert Brent 1940- CANR-15
  Earlier sketch in CA 77-80
Topol, Allan 1941- 93-96
Topolski, Daniel 1945- 110
Topolski, Feliks 1907- Brief entry 112
Topor, Tom 1938- 105
Toppin, Edgar A(llan) 1928- 21-22R
Topping, Anne Marie 25-28R
Topping, Audrey R(onning) 1928- 41-44R
  See also SATA 14
Topping, C(oral) W(esley) 1889- 41-44R
Topping, Donald M(edley) 1929- 53-56
Topping, Seymour 1921- 49-52
Topping, Wesley
  See Topping, C(oral) W(esley)
Topsfield, L(eslie) T(homas) 1920-1981 . CANR-9
  Obituary 105
  Earlier sketch in CA 61-64
Tor, Regina
  See Shekerjian, Regina Tor
Torack, Richard M(aurice) 1927- 106
Torberg, Friedrich
  See Kantor-Berg, Friedrich
Torbert, Floyd James 1922- 105
  See also SATA 22
Torbert, William Rockwell 1944- 41-44R
Torbet, Laura 1942- CANR-16
  Earlier sketch in CA 69-72
Torbet, Robert G(eorge) 1912- 11-12R
Torbett, Harvey Douglas Louis 1921- 9-10R
Torchiana, Donald T(hornhill) 1923- 19-20R
Torchio, Menico 1932- 61-64
Torday, Ursula 97-100
Tordoff, William 1925- 120
Toren, Heller 77-80
Torgersen, Don Arthur 1934- 111
  See also SATA 41
Torgersen, Eric 1943- 37-40R
Torgersen, Paul Ernest 1931- 81-84
Torgerson, Dial 1928- 53-56
Torgerson Shaw, Ellen 1929(?)-1983
  Obituary 109
Torgoff, Martin 1952- 109
Torgovnick, Marianna 1949- 115
Torley, Luke
  See Blish, James (Benjamin)
Torme, Mel(vin Howard) 1925- Brief entry .. 118
Tormey, John Connolly 1942- 61-64
Tornabene, Lyn 1930- 69-72
Torney, Judith V.
  See Torney-Purta, Judith V(ollmar)
Torney-Purta, Judith V(ollmar) 1937- .. CANR-10
  Earlier sketch in CA 65-68
Torok, Lou 1927- 49-52
Torr, Iain
  See Mackinnon, Charles Roy
Torrance, E. Paul 1915- CANR-18
  Earlier sketches in CA 3R, CANR-3
Torrance, Thomas F(orsyth) 1913- CANR-5
  Earlier sketch in CA 9-10R
Torre, Jose de la
  See de la Torre, Jose
Torre-Bueno, Lillian de la
  See McCue, Lillian Bueno
Torregian, Sotere 1941- CANR-3
  Earlier sketch in CA 45-48
Torrence, Ridgely 1874-1950 .... DLB-54
Torrens, Robert George ?-1981 Obituary ... 105
Torres, Andres Segovia
  See Segovia, Andres
Torres, Edwin 111
Torres, Emmanuel 1932- 97-100
Torres, Jose Acosta 1925- 57-60
Torres, Sergio
  See Torres Gonzalez, Sergio A(ntonio)
Torres, Tereska
  See Torres-Levin, Tereska (Szwarc)
Torres Bodet, Jaime 1902-1974 101
  Obituary 49-52
Torres Gonzalez, Sergio A(ntonio) 1929- 117
Torres-Levin, Tereska (Szwarc) CANR-15
  Earlier sketch in CA 7-8R
Torres-Rioseco, Arturo 1897-1971 .... CAP-1
  Earlier sketch in CA 9-10
Torrey, E(dwin) Fuller 1937- 119
  See also CLC 34
Torrey, Gordon H(oward) 1919- 11-12R
Torrey, Norman Lewis 1894-1980 .... 3R
  Obituary 102
Torrey, Therese von Hohoff 1898(?)-1974
  Obituary 45-48
Torrey, Volta (Wray) 1905- 69-72
Torrie, James H(iram) 1908- 73-76
Torrie, Malcolm
  See Mitchell, Gladys (Maude Winifred)
Torro, Pel
  See Fanthorpe, R(obert) Lionel
Tors, Ivan (Lawrence) 1916-1983 103
  Obituary 110
Torsvan, Ben Traven
  See Traven, B.
Torsvan, Benno Traven
  See Traven, B.
Torsvan, Berick Traven
  See Traven, B.
Torsvan, Berwick Traven
  See Traven, B.
Torsvan, Bruno Traven
  See Traven, B.
Torsvan, Traven
  See Traven, B.
Tortolano, William 1930- 77-80
Tortora, Daniel F(rancis) 1947- CANR-13
  Earlier sketch in CA 73-76
Toscano, Peter Ralph 1920- 45-48
Tosches, Nick 1949- 81-84
Toson, Shimazaki
  See Shimazaki, Haruki
Tosti, Donald Thomas 1935- 49-52
Toth, Charles W(illiam) 1919- CANR-10
  Earlier sketch in CA 65-68
Toth, Emily 1944- 101
Toth, Lazlo
  See Novello, Don
Toth, Robert Charles 1928- 102
Toth, Stephen, Jr. 1950- 69-72
Toth, Susan Erickson Allen 1940- 105
  See also DLBY 86
Totham, Mary
  See Breinburg, Petronella
Totman, Conrad 1934- CANR-17
  Earlier sketch in CA 101
Totten, George Oakley III 1922- CANR-21
  Earlier sketches in CA 11-12R, CANR-5
Totten, Martha Wescoat 1957- 118
Totten, Sam(uel) 1949- 118
Totten, W. Fred 1905- 37-40R
Tough, Allen (MacNeill) 1936- 108
Touliatos, John 1944- 93-96
Toulmin, Stephen Edelston 1922- CANR-20
  Earlier sketches in CA 9-10R, CANR-5
Toulouse-Lautrec, Marie-Pierre (Mapie) de
  1901-1972 Obituary 37-40R
Toulson, Shirley 1924- CANR-17
  Earlier sketch in CA 101
Touraine, Alain 1925- 85-88
Toure, Askia Muhammad 1938- DLB-41
Toure, Askia Muhammad
  See Toure, Askia Muhammad Abu Bakr el
Toure, Askia Muhammad Abu Bakr el
  1938- 124
Tourneur, Cyril 1580(?)-1626 .... DLB-58
Tourneur, Dina-Kathelijn 1934- 108
Tourney, Garfield 1927- 57-60
Tournier, Michel 1924- CANR-3
  Earlier sketch in CA 49-52
  See also SATA 23
  See also CLC 6, 23, 36
Tournier, Paul 1898-1986 81-84
  Obituary 120
Tournimparte, Alessandra
  See Ginzburg, Natalia
Tours, Hugh Berthold 1910- CAP-1
  Earlier sketch in CA 9-10
Tourtellot, Arthur Bernon 1913-1977 .... CANR-4
  Obituary 73-76
  Earlier sketch in CA 5-6R
Tourtellot, Jonathan B. 1946- 111
Tourville, Elsie A(lma) 1926- 57-60
Tousley, Clare M. 1889(?)-1985 Obituary 114
Toussaint, Stanley D. 1928- 115
Touster, Alison
  See Reed, Alison Touster
Touval, Saadia E. 1932- 45-48
Touw, Kathleen 1949- 109
Tovey, Doreen Evelyn 1918- 104
Tovo, Jerome 1936- 45-48
Towber, Chaim 1902(?)-1972 Obituary ... 33-36R
Towell, Julie E. 1953- 122
Tower, Diana
  See Smith, Richard Rein
Tower, Don
  See Bower, Donald E(dward)
Tower, John G(oodwin) 1925- Brief entry ... 106
Tower, Margene 1939- 37-40R
Towers, Ivar
  See Kornbluth, C(yril) M.
Towers, Maxwell 1909- 57-60
Towey, Cyprian 1912- 21-22R
Towle, Joseph W(alter) 1909- CAP-1
  Earlier sketch in CA 13-14
Towle, Philip 1945- 117
Towle, Tony 1939- 37-40R
Towler, Juby Earl 1913- 13-14R
Town, Glenn P(atrick) 1949- 118
Town, Harold (Barling) 1924- CANR-15
  Earlier sketch in CA 41-44R
Towne, Anthony 1928-1980 .... 25-28R
  Obituary 117
Towne, Benjamin 1740(?)-1793 .... DLB-43
Towne, Mary
  See Spelman, Mary
Towne, Peter
  See Nabokov, Peter (Francis)
Towne, Robert (Burton) 1936(?)- 108
  See also DLB 44
Towne, Stuart
  See Rawson, Clayton

INDEX

Towner, Donald (Chisholm) 1903-1985 ... CAP-1
Obituary ... 117
Earlier sketch in CA 19-20
Towner, Jason
See Smith, Harold Ivan
Towner, W. Sibley
See Towner, Wayne Sibley
Towner, Wayne Sibley 1933- Brief entry ... 118
Townley, Ralph 1923- ... 23-24R
Townley, Rod 1942- ... CANR-12
Earlier sketch in CA 57-60
Towns, Elmer L(eon) 1932- ... CANR-2
Earlier sketch in CA 45-48
Towns, James E(dward) 1942- ... CANR-23
Earlier sketches in CA 61-64, CANR-8, 21
Towns, Jim
See Towns, James E(dward)
Townsend, Charles Bud 1929- ... 53-56
Townsend, Charles E(dward) 1932- ... 41-44R
Townsend, Charles R(ay) 1929- ... 69-72
Townsend, Doris McFerran 1914- ... CANR-19
Earlier sketch in CA 103
Townsend, Elsie Doig 1908- ... 29-32R
Townsend, Harry 1925- ... 25-28R
Townsend, Irving 1920- ... 101
Townsend, J(ames) Benjamin 1918- ... 23-24R
Townsend, J(acob) David 1888- ... 5-6R
Townsend, James B(arclay) J(ermain) 1910- ... 49-52
Townsend, Janet (Elizabeth) 1925- ... 107
Townsend, John Rowe 1922- ... 37-40R
See also SATA 4
See also SAAS 2
See also CLR 2
Townsend, Mark
See Wallmann, Jeffrey M(iner)
Townsend, Peter (Wooldridge) 1914- ... 29-32R
Townsend, Ralph M. 1901(?)-1976
Obituary ... 65-68
Townsend, Reginald T. 1890-1977
Obituary ... 73-76
Townsend, Richard E. 1897(?)-1975
Obituary ... 61-64
Townsend, Robert 1920- ... 45-48
Townsend, Sue 1946- Brief entry ... 119
See also SATA 48
Townsend, William Cameron 1896-1982
Obituary ... 106
Townsend, William H(enry) 1890-1964
Obituary ... 111
Townshend, Peter (Dennis Blandford) 1945- ... 107
See also CLC 17, 42
Townshend, Richard
See Bickers, Richard Leslie Townshend
Townson, Hazel ... CANR-18
Earlier sketch in CA 97-100
Toy, Henry, Jr. 1915- ... 37-40R
Toye, Clive 1933(?)- ... SATA-30
Toye, John Francis 1883-1964 ... CAP-1
Earlier sketch in CA 9-10
Toye, William Eldred 1926- ... CANR-4
Earlier sketch in CA 4R
See also SATA 8
Toynbee, Arnold J(oseph) 1889-1975 ... 5-6R
Obituary ... 61-64
See also AITN 2
Toynbee, Jocelyn M(ary) C(atherine) 1897-1985 ... 37-40R
Obituary ... 118
Toynbee, (Theodore) Philip 1916-1981 .. CANR-4
Obituary ... 104
Earlier sketch in CA 4R
Toynbee, Polly (Mary Louisa) 1946- ... CANR-9
Earlier sketch in CA 21-22R
Tozer, Mary (Christine) 1947- ... 101
Trabasso, Tom 1935- ... CANR-11
Earlier sketch in CA 23-24R
Trace, Arther Storrey, Jr. 1922- ... CANR-20
Earlier sketch in CA 3R
Tracey, Hugh (Travers) 1903-1977 ... CAP-2
Obituary ... 77-80
Earlier sketch in CA 29-32
Tracey, Patricia Cleland 1932- ... 7-8R
Trachman, Muriel Karlin ... CANR-15
Earlier sketch in CA 85-88
Trachte, Don(ald) 1915- ... 89-92
Trachtenberg, Inge 1923- ... 77-80
Trachtenberg, Marvin (Lawrence) 1939- ... 65-68
Trachtenberg, Paul 1948- ... 112
Trachtenberg, Stanley ... 119
Traci, Philip (Joseph) 1934- ... 41-44R
Tracy, Aloise
See Shoenight, Aloise
Tracy, Ann B(laisdell) 1941- ... 107
Tracy, Clarence 1908- ... 11-12R
Tracy, David W. 1939- ... 101
Tracy, Don(ald Fiske) 1905-197(?) ... CANR-2
Earlier sketch in CA 4R
Tracy, Doris 1925- ... 61-64
Tracy, Honor (Lilbush Wingfield) 1913- ... CANR-24
Earlier sketches in CA 61-64, CANR-8
See also DLB 15
Tracy, Jack W. 1945- ... 105
Tracy, James D. 1938- ... 102
Tracy, John A(lvin) 1934- ... 53-56
Tracy, L(ee) Jack 1926- ... 9-10R
Tracy, Leland
See Tralins, S(andor) Robert
Tracy, Louise Treadwell 1896-1983
Obituary ... 114
Tracy, Michael 1932- ... 15-16R
Tracy, Powers
See Ward, Don(ald G.)
Tracy, Robert E. 1928- ... 89-92
Tracy, Susan
See Marino, Carolyn Fitch
Tracy, Theodore J(ames) 1916- ... 29-32R
Tracy, Thomas Henry 1900- ... CAP-2
Earlier sketch in CA 17-18
Tracz, Richard Francis 1944- ... CANR-17
Earlier sketch in CA 29-32R
Trader Vic
See Bergeron, Victor (Jules, Jr.)
Traer, James Frederick 1938- ... 102
Trafzer, Clifford Earl 1949- ... 109
Trager, Frank N(ewton) 1905-1984 ... CANR-9
Obituary ... 113
Earlier sketch in CA 19-20R
Trager, George L(eonard) 1906- ... 41-44R
Trager, Helen G. 1910- ... 69-72
Trager, James 1925- ... CANR-15
Earlier sketch in CA 37-40R
Tragle, Henry Irving 1914- ... 37-40R
Trahan, Ronald 1950- ... 106
Traherne, Michael
See Watkins-Pitchford, Denys James
Trahey, Jane 1923- ... CANR-17
Earlier sketch in CA 17-18R
See also SATA 36
Train, Arthur (Cheney) 1875-1945
Brief entry ... 112
Train, Arthur K(issam) 1902(?)-1981
Obituary ... 104
Train, John 1928- ... 106
Traina, Richard P(aul) 1937- ... 25-28R
Trainer, David 1947- ... CANR-20
Earlier sketch in CA 25-28R
Trainer, Jennifer 1956- ... 108
Trainer, Orvel 1925- ... 45-48
Trainor, Richard
See Tralins, S(andor) Robert
Traister, Aaron 1904(?)-1976 Obituary ... 65-68
Trakas, Pedro N(icholas) 1923- ... 104
Trakl, Georg 1887-1914 Brief entry ... 104
See also TCLC 5
Tralbaut, Mark-Edo 1902-1976 ... CAP-2
Earlier sketch in CA 29-32
Tralins, Bob
See Tralins, S(andor) Robert
Tralins, Robert S.
See Tralins, S(andor) Robert
Tralins, S(andor) Robert 1926- ... CANR-14
Earlier sketch in CA 21-22R
Trambley, Estela Portillo 1936- ... 77-80
Trani, Eugene Paul 1939- ... 25-28R
Transtroemer, Tomas Goesta 1931-
Brief entry ... 117
Transtromer, Tomas Gosta
See Transtroemer, Tomas Goesta
Transue, Jacob
See Matheson, Joan (Transue)
Transue, Joan
See Matheson, Joan (Transue)
Tranter, John Ernest 1943- ... 110
Tranter, Nigel (Godwin) 1909- ... CANR-20
Earlier sketches in CA 11-12R, CANR-5
Trantino, Tommy 1938- ... 65-68
Trapido, Barbara 1941- ... 123
Trapier, Elizabeth du Gue 1893(?)-1974
Obituary ... 53-56
Trapp, E(dward) Philip 1923- ... 45-48
Trapp, Frank Anderson 1922- ... 57-60
Trapp, Maria Augusta von
See von Trapp, Maria Augusta
See also SATA 16
Traschen, Isadore 1915- ... 25-28R
Trask, David F(rederic) 1929- ... CANR-17
Earlier sketches in CA 3R, CANR-1
Trask, John Jacquelin 1904(?)-1977
Obituary ... 69-72
Trask, Jonathan
See Levinson, Leonard
Trask, Margaret Pope 1907- ... 3R
Trask, Roger R(eed) 1930- ... 41-44R
Trask, Willard (Ropes) 1900(?)-1980
Obituary ... 101
Trasler, Gordon (Blair) 1929- ... CANR-3
Earlier sketch in CA 3R
Trattner, Walter I(rwin) 1936- ... CANR-13
Earlier sketch in CA 37-40R
Traube, Ruy
See Tralins, S(andor) Robert
Traube, Shepard 1907-1983 Obituary ... 111
Traubel, Horace
See Traubel, Horace L(ogo)
Traubel, Horace L(ogo) 1858-1919
Brief entry ... 123
Traudl
See Flaxman, Traudl
Trauger, Wilmer K(ohl) 1898- ... CAP-1
Earlier sketch in CA 9-10
Traugott, Elizabeth Closs 1939- ... 41-44R
Traupman, John C. 1923- ... 41-44R
Traut, Dennis 1953- ... 111
Trautman, Donald T. 1924- ... 37-40R
Trautman, Ray 1907- ... 45-48
Travell, Janet (Graeme) 1901- ... CAP-2
Earlier sketch in CA 29-32
Traven, B. ?-1969 ... CAP-2
Obituary ... 25-28R
Earlier sketch in CA 19-20
See also DLB 9, 56
See also CLC 8, 11
Traven, Beatrice
See Goldemberg, Rose Leiman
Traver, Robert
See Voelker, John D(onaldson)
Travers, Ben 1886-1980 Obituary ... 102
See also DLB 10
Travers, Kenneth
See Hutchin, Kenneth Charles
Travers, Louise Allderdice 1891- ... CAP-1
Earlier sketch in CA 9-10
Travers, P(amela) L(yndon) 1906- ... 33-36R
See also SATA 4
See also SAAS 2
See also CLR 2
Travers, Robert J. 1911(?)-1974
Obituary ... 49-52
Travers, Robert M(orris) W(illiam) 1913- ... CANR-2
Earlier sketch in CA 7-8R
Travers, Virginia
See Coigney, Virginia
Travers, Will
See Rowland, D(onald) S(ydney)
Traversi, Derek A(ntona) 1912- ... 77-80
Travis, Charles S. 1943- ... 37-40R
Travis, Dempsey J. 1920- ... CANR-15
Earlier sketch in CA 85-88
Travis, Gerry
See Trimble, Louis P(reston)
Travis, Gretchen A. ... 103
Travis, John T. 1935- ... 25-28R
Travis, Neal 1939(?)- ... 103
Travis, Stephen H(enry) 1944- ... 106
Travis, Walter Earl 1926- ... 23-24R
Travis, William 1924- ... 25-28R
Travlos, John 1908(?)-1985 Obituary ... 118
Trawick, Buckner Beasley 1914- ... 7-8R
Traxler, Arthur E(dwin) 1900- ... CAP-2
Earlier sketch in CA 21-22
Traylor, Ellen Gunderson 1946- ... 122
Taylor, W. L. 1929- ... 37-40R
Traynor, Alex
See Lagerwall, Edna
Treacy, William 1919- ... 61-64
Treadgold, Donald W(arren) 1922- ... 11-12R
Treadgold, Mary 1910- ... 13-14R
See also SATA 49
Treadway, Terry
See Treadway, Theresa
Treadway, Theresa 1941- ... 107
Treadwell, Sandy 1946- ... 124
Treahearne, Elizabeth
See Maxwell, Patricia
Treanor, John Holland 1903(?)-1978
Obituary ... 77-80
Trease, (Robert) Geoffrey 1909- ... CANR-22
Earlier sketches in CA 7-8R, CANR-7
See also SATA 2
Treasure, G(eoffrey) R(ussell) R(ichards) 1929- ... 77-80
Treat, Ida
See Bergeret, Ida Treat
Treat, Lawrence 1903- ... 49-52
Treat, Payson J(ackson) 1879-1972
Obituary ... 37-40R
Trebach, Arnold S. 1928- ... CANR-12
Earlier sketch in CA 11-12R
Trebing, Harry M(artin) 1926- ... 29-32R
Trecker, Harleigh B(radley) 1911- ... CANR-5
Earlier sketch in CA 5-6R
Trecker, Janice Law 1941- ... CANR-9
Earlier sketch in CA 65-68
Tredennick, (George) Hugh (Percival Phair) 1899-1981 ... 109
Obituary ... 105
Tredez, Alain 1926- ... 85-88
See also SATA 17
Tredez, Denise 1930- ... CANR-8
Earlier sketch in CA 5-6R
See also SATA 50
Tredgold, Nye
See Tranter, Nigel (Godwin)
Tredgold, Roger F(rancis) 1911-1975 ... CANR-5
Earlier sketch in CA 7-8R
Tree, Christina 1944- ... CANR-12
Earlier sketch in CA 73-76
Tree, Cornelia
See Nichols, Nina (Marianna) da Vinci
Tree, Gregory
See Bardin, John Franklin
Tree, Michael (John) 1926- ... 9-10R
Tree, Ronald 1897-1976 ... 69-72
Obituary ... 65-68
Treece, Henry 1912-1966 ... CANR-6
Obituary ... 25-28R
Earlier sketch in CA 1R
See also SATA 2
See also CLR 2
Treece, Patricia 1938- ... 110
Trefethen, Florence 1921- ... 29-32R
Trefethen, James B(yron, Jr.) 1916-1976 ... CANR-11
Obituary ... 69-72
Earlier sketch in CA 21-22R
Trefflich, Henry (Herbert Frederick) 1908-1978 ... CAP-2
Obituary ... 77-80
Earlier sketch in CA 23-24
Trefftzs, Kenneth Lewis 1911- ... 13-14R
Trefil, James 1938- ... 101
Trefor, Eirlys
See Williams, Eirlys O(lwen)
Trefousse, Hans Louis 1921- ... CANR-14
Earlier sketch in CA 37-40R
Tregarthen, Enys
See Sloggett, Nellie
Tregaskis, Hugh 1905(?)-1983 Obituary ... 110
Tregaskis, Richard 1916-1973 ... CANR-2
Obituary ... 45-48
Earlier sketch in CA 3R
See also SATA 3, 26
Tregear, Thomas R(efoy) 1897- ... 21-22R
Treger, Harvey 1924- ... 61-64
Treggiari, Susan (Mary) 1940- ... 61-64
Tregidgo, Philip Sillince 1926- ... 105
Treglown, Jeremy (Dickinson) 1946- ... 114
Brief entry ... 111
Tregonning, Kennedy Gordon 1923- ... 9-10R
Trehey, Harold F. 1902(?)-1978 Obituary .. 77-80
Treichler, Jessie C(ambron) 1906(?)-1972
Obituary ... 37-40R
Treister, Bernard W(illiam) 1932- ... 101
Trejo, Arnulfo D(uenes) 1922- ... 57-60
Trejos, Carlota 1920- ... 49-52
Trekell, Harold E(verett) 1910- ... 49-52
Trelease, Allen William 1928- ... 108
Trelease, James J(oseph) 1941- ... 112
Trelease, Jim
See Trelease, James J(oseph)
Trelford, Donald Gilchrist 1937- ... 111
Trell, Bluma L(ee) 1903- ... 77-80
Trell, Max 1900- ... 41-44R
See also SATA 14
Treloar, Dorothy 1920(?)-1983 Obituary ... 111
Treloar, James A(rthur) 1933- ... 45-48
Trelos, Tony
See Crechales, Anthony George
Tremain, Rose 1943- ... 97-100
See also DLB 14
See also CLC 42
Tremain, Ruthven 1922- ... 85-88
See also SATA 17
Tremaine, Jennie
See Chesney, Marion
Tremayne, Jonathan
See Forrest-Webb, Robert
Tremayne, Ken(neth Eugene, Jr.) 1933- .. 17-18R
Tremayne, Peter
See Ellis, Peter Berresford
Tremayne, Sydney (Durward) 1912- ... CANR-5
Earlier sketch in CA 7-8R
Tremblay, Bill
See Tremblay, William Andrew
Tremblay, Marc-Adelard 1922- ... 41-44R
Tremblay, Michel 1942- Brief entry ... 116
See also DLB 60
See also CLC 29
Tremblay, William Andrew 1940- ... 89-92
Tremble, Freda B. 1894- ... 73-76
Treml, Vladimir G(uy) 1929- ... 25-28R
Tremmel, William Calloley 1918- ... 97-100
Trench, (William Francis) Brinsley Le Poer
See Le Poer Trench, (William Francis) Brinsley
Trendall, Arthur Dale 1909- ... CANR-22
Earlier sketches in CA 53-56, CANR-5
Treneer, Anne 1891- ... CAP-1
Earlier sketch in CA 9-10
Trengove, Alan Thomas 1929- ... 108
Trenhaile, John (Stevens) 1949- ... 110
Trenholm, Virginia Cole 1902- ... 15-16R
Trennert, Robert A., Jr. 1937- ... 57-60
Trensky, Paul I. 1929- ... 93-96
Trent, James W(illiam) 1933- ... 23-24R
Trent, Jimmie Douglas 1933- ... 49-52
Trent, May Wong 1939- ... 57-60
Trent, Olaf
See Fanthorpe, R(obert) Lionel
Trent, Robbie 1894- ... CAP-1
Earlier sketch in CA 9-10
See also SATA 26
Trent, Timothy
See Malmberg, Carl
Trent, William 1919- ... CANR-3
Earlier sketch in CA 3R
Trent, William P(eterfield) 1862-1939
Brief entry ... 122
See also DLB 47
Trento, Joseph John 1947- ... 45-48
Trento, Salvatore Michael 1952- ... 101
Trepp, Leo 1913- ... CANR-18
Earlier sketches in CA 7-8R, CANR-2
Trepper, Leopold Leib 1904-1982(?)
Obituary ... 105
Tresch, John William, Jr. 1937-
Brief entry ... 106
Trescot, William Henry 1822-1898 ... DLB-30
Trescott, Paul B(arton) 1925- ... CANR-2
Earlier sketch in CA 3R
Trese, Leo J(ohn) 1902- ... 5-6R
Tresemer, David 1948- ... 108
Treshow, Michael 1926- ... 57-60
Tresidder, Argus John 1907- ... CANR-5
Earlier sketch in CA 7-8R
Tresilian, Liz 1940- ... 25-28R
Tresilian, (Cecil) Stuart 1891-19(?) ... SATA-40
Tress, Arthur 1940- ... 101
Tresselt, Alvin 1916- ... CANR-1
Earlier sketch in CA 49-52
See also SATA 7
Tressidy, Jim
See Norwood, Victor G(eorge) C(harles)
Tressilian, Charles
See Atcheson, Richard
Tressler, Donald K(iteley) 1894-1981 ... CANR-4
Obituary ... 103
Earlier sketch in CA 45-48
Trethowan, K(enneth) Illtyd 1907- ... CANR-3
Earlier sketch in CA 1R
Tretick, Stanley 1921- ... 103
Trettel, (Mario) Efrem 1921- ... 69-72
Treuenfels, Peter 1926- ... 37-40R
Treuer, Robert 1926- ... 69-72
Trevanian (a pseudonym) 1930(?)- ... 108
See also CLC 29
Trevaskis, John 1911-1968 ... CAP-1
Obituary ... 33-36R
Earlier sketch in CA 9-10
Trevathan, Robert E. 1925- ... CANR-6
Earlier sketch in CA 2R
Trevelyan, George Macaulay 1876-1962 ... 89-92

Trevelyan, Humphrey 1905-1985 ....37-40R
Obituary 115
Trevelyan, Julian O(tto) 1910- 11-12R
Trevelyan, Katharine 1908- CAP-1
Earlier sketch in CA 11-12
Trevelyan, Raleigh 1923- CANR-22
Earlier sketches in CA 13-14R, CANR-6
Trevelyan, Robert
See Forrest-Webb, Robert
Trever, John C(ecil) 1915- 17-18R
Treverton, Gregory F(rye) 1947- 118
Treves, Ralph 1906- 13-14R
Trevino, Elizabeth B(orton) de 1904- CANR-9
Earlier sketch in CA 17-18R
See also SATA 1, 29
See also SAAS 5
Trevino, Lee (Buck) 1939- 113
Trevor, Elleston 1920- 5-6R
See also SATA 28
Trevor, Glen
See Hilton, James
Trevor, (Lucy) Meriol 1919- CANR-16
Earlier sketches in CA 3R, CANR-1
See also SATA 10
Trevor, William
See Cox, William Trevor
See also DLB 14
See also CLC 7, 9, 14, 25
Trevor-Roper, H(ugh) R(edwald) 1914- 101
Trew, Antony (Francis) 1906- CANR-2
Earlier sketch in CA 45-48
Trewin, Ion (Courtenay Gill) 1943- 69-72
Trewin, J(ohn) C(ourtenay) 1908-
Brief entry 112
Trez, Alain
See Tredez, Alain
Trez, Denise
See Tredez, Denise
Trezise, Philip Harold 1912- 109
Trezza, Alphonse F(iore) 1920- 118
Triandis, Harry C(haralambos) 1926- 41-44R
Tribbe, Frank C(alvert) 1914- 117
Tribble, Edwin 1907-1986 Obituary 119
Tribble, Harold Wayland 1899-1986
Obituary 121
Tribe, David (Harold) 1931- 25-28R
Tribe, Ivan M(athews) 1940- 122
Tribich, Susan 1945(?)-1985 Obituary 115
Tribune
See Armstrong, Douglas Albert
Trice, Borough
See Allen, A(rthur) B(ruce)
Trice, Harrison M. 1920- 23-24R
Tricker, B(rian) J(ohn) K(ingsbury)
1937- 25-28R
Trickett, Joyce 1915- 105
Trickett, Mabel Rachel 1923- 101
Triegel, Linda (Jeanette) 1942- 117
Triem, Eve 1902- CANR-9
Earlier sketch in CA 19-20R
Triere, Lynette 1941- 108
Trieschman, Albert E(well) 1931-1984 ....29-32R
Obituary 113
Triffin, Robert 1911- CANR-3
Earlier sketch in CA 2R
Trifonov, Yuri Valentinovich 1925-1981
Obituary 103
See also CLC 45
Trigg, Harry Davis 1927- 61-64
Trigg, Joseph Wilson 1949- 118
Trigg, Roger (Hugh) 1941- 49-52
Trigg, Yolanda Lillian 1926- 61-64
Trigger, Bruce G(raham) 1937- CANR-9
Earlier sketch in CA 23-24R
Trigoboff, Joseph 1947- 81-84
Trillin, Calvin 1935- CANR-20
Earlier sketch in CA 85-88
See also AITN 1
Trilling, Diana (Rubin) 1905- CANR-10
Earlier sketch in CA 7-8R
Trilling, Lionel 1905-1975 .... CANR-10
Obituary 61-64
Earlier sketch in CA 11-12R
See also DLB 28, 63
See also CLC 9, 11, 24
Trimble, Jacquelyn W(hitney) 1927- 15-16R
Trimble, John F(elix) 1925- 97-100
Trimble, Louis P(reston) 1917- CANR-6
Earlier sketch in CA 15-16R
Trimble, Marshall I(ra) 1939- 77-80
Trimble, Martha Scott 1914- 29-32R
Trimble, Vance H(enry) 1913- 49-52
Trimble, William Raleigh 1913- 9-10R
Trimby, Elisa 1948- 122
See also SATA 40, 47
Trimingham, J(ohn) Spencer 1904- CANR-3
Earlier sketch in CA 3R
Trimmer, Ellen McKay 1915- 9-10R
Trimmer, Eric J. 1923- 9-10R
Trimmer, Joseph F(rancis) 1941- CANR-13
Earlier sketch in CA 77-80
Tring, A. Stephen
See Meynell, Laurence Walter
Trinidad, Corky
See Trinidad, Francisco D., Jr.
Trinidad, Francisco D., Jr. 1939- 69-72
Trinkaus, Charles (Edward) 1911- 29-32R
Trinklein, Frederick E(rnst) 1924- 41-44R
Trinkner, Charles L. 1920- 29-32R
Trinquier, Roger Paul 1908- CANR-5
Earlier sketch in CA 9-10R
Triola, Mario F(rank) 1944- 57-60
Triolet, Elsa 1896-1970 Obituary 25-28R
Triplett, Kenneth E(arl) 1926- 57-60
Triplett, Raymond (Francis) 1921- 117
Tripodi, Tony 1932- CANR-12
Earlier sketch in CA 29-32R
Tripp, C(larence) A(rthur) 1919- 73-76
Tripp, Eleanor B(aldwin) 1936- 29-32R
See also SATA 4
Tripp, John 1927- 97-100
See also DLB 40
Tripp, John
See Moore, John Travers
Tripp, Karen 1923- 53-56
Tripp, L(ouis) Reed 1913- 5-6R
Tripp, Miles (Barton) 1923- CANR-12
Earlier sketch in CA 13-14R
Tripp, Paul 1916- 21-22R
See also SATA 8
Tripp, Wallace (Whitney) 1940- CANR-23
Earlier sketch in CA 106
See also SATA 31
Tripp, Wendell, Jr. 1928- 114
Trippett, Frank 1926- 21-22R
Trisco, Robert Frederick 1929- 41-44R
Triska, Jan Francis 1922- CANR-7
Earlier sketch in CA 5-6R
Trisler, Hank 1937- 121
Triton, A. N.
See Barclay, Oliver R(ainsford)
Tritt, Robert E(arl) 1921- 23-24R
Trittschuh, Travis Edward 1920- 5-6R
Trivas, A(lexander) Victor 1894-1970 ..... CAP-1
Obituary 29-32R
Earlier sketch in CA 19-20
Trivelpiece, Laurel 1926- 123
See also SATA 46
Trivers, Howard 1909-1987 73-76
Obituary 122
Trivett, Daphne Harwood 1940- 97-100
See also SATA 22
Trnka, Jiri 1912-1969 Obituary 111
See also SATA 32, 43
Trobian, Helen R(eed) 1918- 5-6R
Trobisch, Ingrid 1926- 97-100
Trocchi, Alexander 1925-1984 ....11-12R
Obituary 112
See also DLB 15
Trocme, Etienne 1924- 49-52
Troeger, Thomas H(enry) 1945- CANR-15
Earlier sketch in CA 89-92
Troelstrup, Arch William 1901- 17-18R
Troen, Selwyn K. 1940- 104
Trofimenkoff, Susan Mann 1941- 73-76
Trogdon, William (Lewis) 1939- 119
Brief entry 115
Trohan, Walter (Joseph) 1903- 81-84
Troiden, Richard (Russell) 1946- 89-92
Troise, Joe 1942- 103
Troisgros, Jean (Georges) 1926-1983
Obituary 110
Trojanowicz, John M.
See Troyanovich, John M(ichael)
Trojanowicz, Robert (Chester) 1941- 45-48
Trojanski, John 1943- 45-48
Trolander, Judith Ann 1942- 61-64
Trollope, Anthony 1815-1882 .... SATA-22
See also DLB 21, 57
Trollope, Frances 1779-1863 .... DLB-21
Trollope, Joanna 1943- 101
Troman, Morley 1918- 13-14R
Tromanhauser, Edward (Downer) 1932- ..41-44R
Trombley, Charles C(yprian) 1928- 65-68
Tromp, S. W.
See Tromp, Solco Walle
Tromp, Solco W.
See Tromp, Solco Walle
Tromp, Solco Walle 1909-1983 Obituary ... 116
Tronchin-James, (Robert) Nevil 1916- CAP-1
Earlier sketch in CA 9-10
Trooboff, Peter D(ennis) 1942- 65-68
Troop, Elizabeth 1931- Brief entry 116
See also DLB 14
Troop, Miriam 1917- 15-16R
Tropp, Martin 1945- 65-68
Trost, Lucille W(ood) 1938- CANR-9
Earlier sketch in CA 61-64
See also SATA 12
Trotsky, Leon 1879-1940 Brief entry 118
See also TCLC 22
Trott, Susan 1937- 97-100
Trotta, John 1936- 45-48
Trotta, Maurice S. 1907-1976 Obituary 111
Trotter, Grace V(iolet) 1900- CANR-1
Earlier sketch in CA 1R
See also SATA 10
Trotter, Jesse McLane ?-1983 Obituary 110
Trotter, Robert J(oseph) 1943- 120
Trotter, Sallie (W. B.) 1915- 29-32R
Trotti, John H. 1936- 118
Trotti, Lamar 1898-1952 .... DLB-44
Trottier, Pierre 1925- DLB-60
Troughton, Joanna (Margaret) 1947- 109
See also SATA 37
Trouncer, Margaret (Lahey)
1903-1982 .... CANR-10
Obituary 108
Earlier sketch in CA 5-6R
Troup, Cornelius V. 1902- CAP-1
Earlier sketch in CA 9-10
Troupe, Quincy (Jr.) 1943- Brief entry 113
See also DLB 41
Troupe, Quincy (Thomas, Jr.) 1943- 124
Trout, Charles Hathaway 1935- 113
Trout, Kilgore
See Farmer, Philip Jose
Troutman, Charles (Henry) 1914- 69-72
Trouve, Roger 1882(?)-1984 Obituary 112
Trow, M(eirion) J(ames) 1949- 120
Trow, Martin A. 1926- 118
Trow, W(illiam) Clark 1894- CANR-6
Earlier sketch in CA 5-6R
Trowbridge, Clinton W(hiting) 1928- ... CANR-10
Earlier sketch in CA 65-68
Trowbridge, Keith W(ayne) 1937- 108
Trowbridge, Leslie Walter 1920- CANR-13
Earlier sketch in CA 77-80
Trowell, Kathleen Margaret 1904- 65-68
Troxell, Eugene A(nthony) 1937- 73-76
Troxell, Mary D(earborn) 1907- 37-40R
Troy, George F(rancis), Jr. 1909-1969 ...... 2R
Obituary 103
Troy, Katherine
See Buxton, Anne (Arundel)
Troy, Lawrence M. 1928- 23-24R
Troy, Nancy J. 1952- 115
Troy, Una 1913- CANR-3
Earlier sketch in CA 1R
Troy, William 1903-1961 Obituary 89-92
Troyanovich, John M(ichael) 1936- 49-52
Troyat, Henri 1911- CANR-2
Earlier sketch in CA 45-48
See also CLC 23
Troyer, Byron L(eRoy) 1909- 65-68
Troyer, Johannes 1902-1969 .... SATA-40
Troyer, Warner 1932- 101
Troyka, Lynn Quitman 1938- 37-40R
Troyna, Barry 1951- 117
Truax, Carol 1900- CANR-5
Earlier sketch in CA 7-8R
Truax, Charles B. 1933-197(?) CANR-13
Earlier sketches in CA 21-22, CAP-2
Truax, R. Hawley 1889(?)-1978 Obituary ..81-84
Trubitt, Allen R(oy) 1931- 77-80
Trubo, Richard 1946- CANR-11
Earlier sketch in CA 61-64
Trubowitz, Sidney 1926- 23-24R
Truby, J(ohn) David 1938- CANR-24
Earlier sketches in CA 53-56, CANR-4
Truch, Stephen 1947- 115
Trudeau, G(arretson) B(eekman) 1948- 81-84
See also SATA 35
Trudeau, Garry B.
See Trudeau, G(arretson) B(eekman)
See also CLC 12
See also AITN 2
Trudeau, Margaret (Joan) 1948- 93-96
Trudeau, (Joseph Philippe) Pierre (Yves)
Elliott 1919- CANR-3
Earlier sketch in CA 45-48
Trudel, Marcel 1917- 104
Trudix, Marty
See Truman, Ruth
True, Dan 1924- 117
True, Michael 1933- CANR-17
Earlier sketch in CA 41-44R
Trueblood, Alan Stubbs 1917- 103
Trueblood, D(avid) Elton 1900- 41-44R
Trueblood, Paul Graham 1905- CANR-12
Earlier sketches in CA 17-18, CAP-1
Trueblood, Ted Whitaker 1913-1982
Obituary 111
Trueheart, Charles 1951- 45-48
Truemper, David G(eorge) 1939- 112
Truesdale, C(alvin) W(illiam) 1929- 29-32R
Truesdell, Leon E. 1881(?)-1979
Obituary 85-88
Truesdell, Sue
See Truesdell, Susan G.
Truesdell, Susan G. SATA-45
Truett, Fred M(oore) 1899- CAP-2
Earlier sketch in CA 21-22
Truett, Joe C(lyde) 1941- 118
Truffaut, Francois 1932-1984 81-84
Obituary 113
See also CLC 20
Truitt, Deborah H(unsberger) 1945- 45-48
Truitt, Evelyn Mack 1931- 57-60
Truitt, Gloria A(nn) 1939- 111
Truitt, John O(liver) 1934- 117
Truitt, Willis H(arrison) 1936- 57-60
Truman, Harry S 1884-1972 106
Obituary 37-40R
Truman, (Mary) Margaret 1924- 105
Truman, Ruth 1931- 53-56
Trumbo, Dalton 1905-1976 .... CANR-10
Obituary 69-72
Earlier sketch in CA 21-22R
See also DLB 26
See also CLC 19
Trumbull, Benjamin 1735-1820 .... DLB-30
Trumbull, John 1750-1831 .... DLB-31
Trumbull, Robert 1912- CANR-5
Earlier sketch in CA 11-12R
Trump, Fred(erick Leonard) 1924- 15-16R
Trumpener, Ulrich 1930- 25-28R
Trumper, Hubert Bagster 1902- CAP-1
Earlier sketch in CA 9-10
Trundlett, Helen B.
See Eliot, T(homas) S(tearns)
Trungpa, Chogyam
See Chogyam Trungpa
Trunk, Isaiah Elezer 1905-1981 89-92
Obituary 108
Trupin, James E. 1940- 37-40R
Trupp, Beverly Ann 1937- 105
Truscott, Alan (Fraser) 1925- 25-28R
Truscott, Lucian K(ing) IV 1947- 89-92
Truscott, Robert Blake 1944- 77-80
Truse, Kenneth (Philip) 1946- 105
Truss, Jan 1925- 102
See also SATA 35
Truss, Seldon
See Seldon-Truss, Leslie
Trussell, C(harles) P(rescott) 1892-1968
Obituary 89-92
Trussler, Simon 1942- CANR-12
Earlier sketch in CA 25-28R
Trustman, Alan Robert 1930- Brief entry ... 111
Truumaa, Aare 1926- 49-52
Truzzi, Marcello 1935- 41-44R
Tryon, Darrell Trevor 1942- 111
Tryon, Georgiana Shick 1945- 116
Tryon, Ruth Wilson 1892(?)-1987
Obituary 123
Tryon, Thomas 1926- 29-32R
See also CLC 3, 11
See also AITN 1
Tryon, Tom
See Tryon, Thomas
Tryon, W(arren) S(tenson) 1901- CAP-1
Earlier sketch in CA 11-12
Trypanis, C(onstantine) A(thanasius)
1909- CANR-24
Earlier sketches in CA 7-8R, CANR-7
Trythall, Anthony John 1927- 77-80
Trythall, J(ohn) W(illiam) D(onald)
1944- 29-32R
Tsadick, Marta Gabre
See Gabre-Tsadick, Marta
Tsambassis, Alexander N(icholas) 1919- ..23-24R
Tsatsos, Jeanne 1909- CANR-13
Earlier sketch in CA 29-32R
Tschacbasov, Nahum 1899-1984 Obituary .. 112
Tschebotarioff, Gregory P. 1899- 15-16R
Tschichold, Jan 1902(?)-1974 Obituary ...53-56
Tschudy, James Jay 1925- 13-14R
Tschumi, Raymond Robert 1924- CANR-3
Earlier sketch in CA 7-8R
Tsegaye, Gabre-Medhin (Kawessa)
See Gabre-Medhin, Tsegaye (Kawessa)
Tseng Wen-Shing 1935- 114
Tshiamala, Kabasele ?-1983(?) Obituary 109
Tsien, Tsuen-hsuin 1909- CANR-23
Earlier sketches in CA 17-18R, CANR-7
Tsiolkovsky, Konstantin Eduardovich
1857-1935 Brief entry 119
Tsipis, Kosta 1934- 110
Tsongas, Paul Efthemios 1941- 108
Tsou, Tang 1918- CANR-8
Earlier sketch in CA 5-6R
Tso Yiu-kam 1918(?)-1983 Obituary 110
Tsukahira, Toshio George 1915- 21-22R
Tsukinabe, Isao
See Vermeule, Cornelius Clarkson III
Tsuneishi, Warren M(ichio) 1921- 19-20R
Tsurutani, Taketsugu 1935- 104
Tsushima, Shuji 1909-1948 Brief entry 107
Tsuzuki, Chushichi 1926- CANR-3
Earlier sketch in CA 3R
Tsvetaeva (Efron), Marina Ivanovna
1892-1941 Brief entry 104
See also TCLC 7
Tu, Wei-ming 1940- 65-68
Tuan, Yi-Fu 1930- CANR-16
Earlier sketch in CA 93-96
Tuann, Lucy H(siu-mei) C(hen) 1938- 85-88
Tubb, E(dwin) C(harles) 1919- CANR-21
Earlier sketch in CA 101
Tubb, Ernest (Dale) 1914-1984 Obituary 114
Tubbs, Stewart L(ee) 1943- CANR-6
Earlier sketch in CA 57-60
Tucci, Giuseppe 1894-1984 Obituary 112
Tucci, Niccolo 1908- 81-84
Tuccille, Jerome 1937- CANR-12
Earlier sketch in CA 29-32R
Tuchinsky, Joseph S. 1937- CANR-10
Earlier sketch in CA 25-28R
Tuchman, Barbara (Wertheim) 1912- ... CANR-24
Earlier sketches in CA 1R, CANR-3
Tuchman, Gaye 1943- 85-88
Tuchman, Maurice 1936- CANR-4
Earlier sketch in CA 49-52
Tuchman, Phyllis 1947- 114
Tuchock, Wanda 1898(?)-1985 Obituary 115
Tucholsky, Kurt 1890-1935 .... DLB-56
Tuck, (John) Anthony 1940- 124
Tuck, Dorothy
See McFarland, Dorothy Tuck
Tuck, James A(lexander) 1940- 37-40R
Tuck, Lon 1938(?)-1987 Obituary 122
Tuck, Susan H. 1947- 118
Tucker, Ann
See Giudici, Ann Couper
Tucker, Anne 1945- CANR-19
Earlier sketch in CA 102
Tucker, Anthony 1924- 104
Tucker, Archibald Norman 1904(?)-1980
Obituary 101
Tucker, Audrie Manley
See Manley-Tucker, Audrie
Tucker, Bob
See Tucker, (Arthur) Wilson
Tucker, Caroline
See Nolan, Jeannette Covert
Tucker, David M(ilton) 1937- 101
Tucker, Edward L(lewellyn) 1921- 19-20R
Tucker, Ernest E(dward) 1916-1969 61-64
Tucker, Eva 1929- 17-18R
Tucker, Frank H(ammond) 1923- CANR-10
Earlier sketch in CA 25-28R
Tucker, Gabe
See Tucker, Gaylord B(ob)
Tucker, Gaylord B(ob) 1915- 110
Tucker, Gene M(ilton) 1935- CANR-15
Earlier sketch in CA 37-40R
Tucker, George 1775-1861 .... DLB-3, 30
Tucker, Georgina P. 1911- 97-100
Tucker, Gina
See Tucker, Georgina P.
Tucker, Glenn (Irving) 1892-1976 ....5-6R
Obituary 69-72
Tucker, Graham Harold 1925- 113
Tucker, Harry, Jr. 1921- 41-44R
Tucker, Helen 1926- CANR-11
Earlier sketch in CA 29-32R

INDEX

Tucker, Irwin St. John 1886-1982
Obituary ... 105
Tucker, James 1929- ... CANR-9
Earlier sketch in CA 21-22R
Tucker, Jonathan B(rin) 1954- ... 109
Tucker, Lael
See Wertenbaker, Lael (Tucker)
Tucker, Link
See Bingley, David Ernest
Tucker, Marcia 1940- ... 65-68
Tucker, Martin 1928- ... 17-18R
Tucker, Melvin J(ay) 1931- ... 113
Tucker, Michael R(ay) 1941- ... CANR-12
Earlier sketch in CA 61-64
Tucker, Nathaniel Beverley 1784-1851 ... DLB-3
Tucker, Nicholas 1936- ... CANR-11
Earlier sketch in CA 65-68
Tucker, Patricia 1912- ... 65-68
Tucker, Paul Hayes 1950- ... 110
Tucker, Robert C(harles) 1918- ... CANR-3
Earlier sketch in CA 3R
Tucker, Robin 1950- ... 53-56
Tucker, Ruth A(nne) 1945- ... 117
Tucker, St. George 1752-1827 ... DLB-37
Tucker, Wallace H. 1939- ... 121
Tucker, William E(dward) 1932- ... CANR-3
Earlier sketch in CA 11-12R
Tucker, William R(ayburn) 1923- ... 61-64
Tucker, (Arthur) Wilson 1914- ... 17-18R
Tucker-Fettner, Ann
See Giudici, Ann Couper
Tuckerman, Henry Theodore 1813-1871 ... DLB-64
Tuckey, John S(utton) 1921- ... CANR-7
Earlier sketch in CA 7-8R
Tuckman, Bruce W(ayne) 1938- ... CANR-11
Earlier sketch in CA 25-28R
Tuckman, Howard P(aul) 1941- ... CANR-10
Earlier sketch in CA 57-60
Tuckner, Howard 1932(?)-1980 Obituary ... 101
Tudhope, Richard
See Rodda, Peter (Gordon)
Tudor, Andrew Frank 1942- ... 107
Tudor, Dean 1943- ... CANR-8
Earlier sketch in CA 61-64
Tudor, Nancy (Patricia Rice) 1943-
Brief entry ... 109
Tudor, Tasha 1915- ... 81-84
See also SATA 20
See also CLR 13
Tudor-Craig, Pamela 1928- ... 124
Tudyman, Al 1914- ... 21-22R
Tuell, Jack Marvin 1923- ... 29-32R
Tueni, Nadia (Hamade) 1935-1983
Obituary ... 110
Tuerck, David G(eorge) 1941- ... CANR-14
Earlier sketch in CA 21-22R
Tuerk, Hanne 1951- ... 118
Tufail, Muhammad 1921(?)-1984 Obituary ... 113
Tuffnell, Everett S(pencer) 1917- ... CANR-7
Earlier sketch in CA 5-6R
Tuffs, J(ack) Elsden 1922- ... 7-8R
Tufte, Edward R(olf) 1942- ... CANR-1
Earlier sketch in CA 49-52
Tufte, Virginia J(ames) 1918- Brief entry ... 106
Tufts, Eleanor ... 77-80
Tufty, Barbara 1923- ... 37-40R
Tufty, Esther Van Wagoner 1896-1986
Obituary ... 119
Tugay, Emine Foat
See Foat Tugay, Emine
Tugendhat, Christopher Samuel 1937- ... 89-92
Tuggy, Joy Turner 1922- ... 21-22R
Tugwell, Franklin 1942- ... 57-60
Tugwell, Rexford Guy 1891-1979 ... 85-88
Obituary ... 89-92
Tulasiewicz, J(an) B(runo) 1913- ... 41-44R
Tulchin, Joseph S(amuel) 1939- ... 37-40R
Tulchin, Lewis 1905-1971 ... CAP-1
Earlier sketch in CA 19-20
Tuleja, Tad
See Tuleja, Thaddeus F(rancis)
Tuleja, Thaddeus F(rancis) 1944- ... 108
Tulis, Jeffrey 1950- ... 111
Tull, Charles Joseph 1931- ... 17-18R
Tull, Donald S(tanley) 1924- ... 81-84
Tull, James E. 1913- ... CANR-13
Earlier sketch in CA 77-80
Tullett, James Stuart 1912- ... 106
Tullis, F. LaMond 1935- ... 81-84
Tulloch, G(ertrude) Janet 1924- ... 65-68
Tullock, Gordon 1922- ... CANR-3
Earlier sketch in CA 3R
Tully, Andrew (Frederick, Jr.) 1914- ... 19-20R
Tully, Gordon F(rederick) 1935- ... 106
Tully, Grace George 1900-1984 Obituary ... 113
Tully, John (Kimberley) 1923- ... CANR-12
Earlier sketch in CA 69-72
See also SATA 14
Tully, Mary Jo 1937- ... CANR-22
Earlier sketch in CA 105
Tuma, Elias H. 1928- Brief entry ... 115
Tumelty, James J. 1921(?)-1979(?)
Obituary ... 104
Tumin, Melvin M(arvin) 1919- ... 45-48
Tumpson, Helen ... AITN-1
Tung, Ling
See Tung, William L(ing)
Tung, Shih-tsin (Shih-chin) 1900- ... 5-6R
Tung, William L(ing) 1907- ... 85-88
Tunick, Irve 1912-1987 Obituary ... 123
Tunick, Stanley B(loch) 1900- ... CAP-1
Earlier sketch in CA 17-18
Tunink, Wilfrid Bernard 1920- ... 5-6R
Tunis, Edwin (Burdett) 1897-1973 ... CANR-7
Obituary ... 45-48
Earlier sketch in CA 7-8R
See also SATA 1, 24, 28
See also CLR 2
Tunis, John R(oberts) 1889-1975 ... 61-64
See also SATA 30, 37
See also DLB 22
See also CLC 12
Tunley, Roul 1912- ... 13-14R
Tunnard, Christopher 1910-1979 ... CANR-6
Obituary ... 85-88
Earlier sketch in CA 7-8R
Tunnell, Doug(las Alan) 1949- ... 97-100
Tunner, William H(enry) 1906-1983 ... CAP-1
Obituary ... 109
Earlier sketch in CA 15-16
Tunney, Gene
See Tunney, James Joseph
Tunney, James Joseph 1898(?)-1978
Obituary ... 111
Tunney, John V(arick) 1934- ... 61-64
Tunney, Kieran 1922- ... 117
Tunnicliffe, C(harles) F(rederick) 1901- ... 104
Tunstall, (Cuthbert) Jeremy 1934- ... CANR-20
Earlier sketches in CA 7-8R, CANR-4
Tunstall, Shana Barrett
See Tunstall, Velma
Tunstall, Velma 1914- ... 53-56
Tunyogi, Andrew C(sapo) 1907- ... CAP-2
Earlier sketch in CA 29-32
Tuohy, Frank
See Tuohy, John Francis
See also DLB 14
See also CLC 37
Tuohy, John Francis 1925- ... CANR-3
Earlier sketch in CA 5-6R
Tuohy, William 1941- ... 37-40R
Tuohy, William Klaus 1926- ... 104
Tuohy, William S. 1938- ... 41-44R
Tuplin, W(illiam) A(lfred) 1902-1975
Obituary ... 111
Tupper, Margo (Browne) 1919- ... 19-20R
Tupper, Martin F. 1810-1889 ... DLB-32
Turabian, Kate L(arimore) 1893-1987
Obituary ... 123
Turbayne, Colin Murray 1916- ... CANR-24
Earlier sketch in CA 3R
Turbyfill, Mark 1896- ... 108
See also DLB 45
Turchin, Valentin F(yodorovich) 1931- ... 101
Turco, Lewis (Putnam) 1934- ... CANR-24
Earlier sketch in CA 13-14R
See also DLBY 84
See also CLC 11
Turell, Saul J. 1921-1986 Obituary ... 120
Turetzky, Bertram Jay 1933- ... 57-60
Turgeon, Charlotte Snyder 1912- ... CANR-3
Earlier sketch in CA 7-8R
Turgeon, Lynn 1920- ... 7-8R
Turiel, Isaac 1941- ... 122
Turing, John (Ferrier) 1908- ... CAP-2
Earlier sketch in CA 25-28
Turk, Frances (Mary) 1915- ... CAP-1
Earlier sketch in CA 9-10
Turk, Hanne
See Tuerk, Hanne
Turk, Herman 1929- ... 45-48
Turk, Laurel H(erbert) 1903- ... 21-22R
Turk, Midge
See Richardson, Midge Turk
Turk, Rudy H(enry) 1927- ... 97-100
Turkel, Christopher 1955(?)-1983
Obituary ... 110
Turkel, Pauline
See K-Turkel, Judi
Turkel, Robin R. 1929(?)-1984 Obituary ... 113
Turkevich, Ludmilla Buketoff 1909- ... 5-6R
Turki, Fawaz 1940- ... 41-44R
Turkle, Brinton 1915- ... 25-28R
See also SATA 2
Turkle, Sherry 1948- ... 102
Turkus, Burton B. 1902-1982 Obituary ... 108
Turley, William S(tephen) 1943- ... CANR-21
Earlier sketch in CA 105
Turlington, Bayly 1919-1977 ... 29-32R
Obituary ... 122
See also SATA 5
Turlington, Catherine (Isabel) Hackett
1900(?)-1978 Obituary ... 77-80
Turlington, Henry E. 1918- ... 21-22R
Turnage, Anne Shaw 1927- ... 77-80
Turnage, Mac(lyn) N(eil) 1927- ... 77-80
Turnbaugh, William A(rthur) 1948- ... 112
Turnbull, Agnes Sligh 1888-1982 ... CANR-2
Obituary ... 105
Earlier sketch in CA 3R
See also SATA 14
Turnbull, Andrew Winchester
1921-1970 ... CANR-3
Obituary ... 25-28R
Earlier sketch in CA 3R
Turnbull, Ann (Christine) 1943- ... 65-68
See also SATA 18
Turnbull, Bob 1936- ... CANR-14
Earlier sketch in CA 37-40R
Turnbull, Colin M(acmillan) 1924- ... CANR-3
Earlier sketch in CA 2R
See also AITN 1
Turnbull, Gael Lundin 1928- ... CANR-10
Earlier sketch in CA 65-68
See also DLB 40
Turnbull, John G. 1913- ... 3R
Turnbull, Patrick Edward Xenophon
1908- ... CANR-6
Earlier sketch in CA 7-8R
Turnbull, Stephen (Richard) 1948- ... CANR-20
Earlier sketch in CA 104
Turnell, (George) Martin 1908-1979 ... 45-48
Obituary ... 103
Turner, A(lmon) Richard 1932- ... 19-20R
Turner, Alberta Tucker 1919- ... CANR-17
Earlier sketches in CA 49-52, CANR-1
Turner, Alice K. 1940- ... 53-56
See also SATA 10
Turner, Amedee E. 1929- ... 9-10R
Turner, Ann W(arren) 1945- ... CANR-14
Earlier sketch in CA 69-72
See also SATA 14
Turner, (Henry) Arlin 1909-1980 ... CANR-6
Obituary ... 97-100
Earlier sketch in CA 7-8R
Turner, Arthur C(ampbell) 1918- ... 17-18R
Turner, Bessye Tobias 1917- ... 53-56
Turner, Bill
See Turner, W(illiam) Price
Turner, Bryan S(tanley) 1945- ... 115
Turner, Charles (Tennyson) 1808-1879 ... DLB-32
Turner, Charles W(ilson) 1916- ... CANR-13
Earlier sketch in CA 37-40R
Turner, Clair (Elsmere) 1890- ... CAP-1
Earlier sketch in CA 9-10
Turner, Clay
See Ballard, (Willis) Todhunter
Turner, D(avid) Harold 1912- ... 117
Turner, Daniel F(rank) 1947- ... 97-100
Turner, Darwin T(heodore) 1931- ... CANR-11
Earlier sketch in CA 21-22R
Turner, David R(euben) 1915- ... 57-60
Turner, Dean (Edson) 1927- ... 29-32R
Turner, Dennis C(lair) 1948- ... 61-64
Turner, Dona M. 1951- ... 103
Turner, E(rnest) S(ackville) 1909- ... 113
Turner, Edward R(euben) A(rthur) 1924- ... 81-84
Turner, Elizabeth 1774-1846 ... YABC-2
Turner, Eloise Fain 1906- ... 5-6R
Turner, Eric Gardner 1911-1983 Obituary ... 109
Turner, Ethel (Sybil) 1872-1958
Brief entry ... 111
Turner, Francis Joseph (Michael)
1929- ... CANR-22
Earlier sketch in CA 69-72
Turner, Frederick (William III) 1937- ... CANR-15
Earlier sketch in CA 37-40R
Turner, Frederick 1943- ... CANR-12
Earlier sketch in CA 73-76
See also DLB 40
Turner, Frederick C(lair) 1938- ... 25-28R
Turner, Frederick Jackson 1861-1932
Brief entry ... 113
See also DLB 17
Turner, George (Reginald) 1916- ... CANR-21
Earlier sketch in CA 103
Turner, George Allen 1908- ... CANR-10
Earlier sketch in CA 13-14R
Turner, George E(ugene) 1925- ... CANR-5
Earlier sketch in CA 53-56
Turner, George W(illiam) 1921- ... CANR-24
Earlier sketch in CA 104
Turner, Gladys T(ressia) 1935- ... CANR-13
Earlier sketch in CA 77-80
Turner, Graham 1932- ... CANR-14
Earlier sketch in CA 23-24R
Turner, Gwenda 1947- ... 118
Turner, H(arold) W(alter) 1911- ... CANR-10
Earlier sketch in CA 23-24R
Turner, Henry Andrew, Jr. 1919- ... 11-12R
Turner, Henry Ashby, Jr. 1932- ... 49-52
Turner, Henry Dicken 1919- ... 61-64
Turner, Henry Ernest William 1907- ... CAP-1
Earlier sketch in CA 9-10
Turner, Herbert Snipes 1891-1976 ... 41-44R
Turner, Howard M(oore), Jr. 1918- ... 15-16R
Turner, John Elliot 1917- ... CANR-3
Earlier sketch in CA 5-6R
Turner, John F(reeland) 1942- ... 97-100
Turner, John Frayn 1923- ... CANR-3
Earlier sketch in CA 9-10R
Turner, John H(enry) 1938- ... 77-80
Turner, Jonathan H. 1942- ... CANR-14
Earlier sketch in CA 37-40R
Turner, Josie
See Crawford, Phyllis
Turner, Judy
See Saxton, Judith
Turner, Justin George 1898-1976 ... 41-44R
Turner, Katharine Charlotte 1910- ... CAP-2
Earlier sketch in CA 23-24
Turner, Kay 1932- ... 69-72
Turner, Kermit 1936- ... 104
Turner, L(eonard) C(harles) F(rederick)
1914- ... 29-32R
Turner, Len
See Floren, Lee
Turner, Lloyd 1924- ... 103
Turner, Louis (Mark) 1942- ... CANR-15
Earlier sketch in CA 37-40R
Turner, Lynn Warren 1906- ... 7-8R
Turner, Martha Anne (Bonner) 1904-1985
Obituary ... 117
Turner, Mary
See Lambot, Isobel
Turner, Mason 1914- ... 123
Turner, Merfyn (Lloyd) 1915- ... 104
Turner, Morrie
See Turner, Morris
Turner, Morris 1923- ... CANR-15
Earlier sketch in CA 29-32R
Turner, Myron 1935- ... 112
Turner, Paul Digby Lowry 1917- ... 105
Turner, Paul R(aymond) 1929- ... 45-48
Turner, Peter Paul
See Jeffery, Grant
Turner, Philip 1925- ... CANR-11
Earlier sketch in CA 25-28R
See also SATA 11
Turner, Ralph 1936- Brief entry ... 107
Turner, Ralph H(erbert) 1919- ... 37-40R
Turner, Ralph Lilley 1888-1983 ... 7-8R
Obituary ... 109
Turner, Ralph V(ernon) 1939- ... 77-80
Turner, Richard E(ugene) 1920- ... 29-32R
Turner, Robert (Harry) 1915- ... CANR-1
Earlier sketch in CA 45-48
Turner, Robert C(lemens) 1908- ... 77-80
Turner, Robert Edward III 1938(?)- ... 120
Turner, Robert F(oster) 1944- ... CANR-13
Earlier sketch in CA 77-80
Turner, Robert Kean, Jr. 1926- ... 17-18R
Turner, Robert Y(ongue) 1927-
Brief entry ... 110
Turner, Roger (Humphrey George) 1943- ... 123
Turner, Roland 1943- ... 106
Turner, Ronald Cordell 1939- ... 41-44R
Turner, Sheila 1906- ... CAP-1
Earlier sketch in CA 13-14
Turner, Sheila
See Rowbotham, Sheila
Turner, Sheila R.
See Seed, Sheila Turner
Turner, Silvie 1946- ... 117
Turner, Stansfield 1923- ... 124
Brief entry ... 118
Turner, Stephen P. 1951- ... 122
Turner, Steve
See Turner, Stephen P.
Turner, (Clarence) Steven 1923- ... 29-32R
Turner, Susan 1952- ... 106
Turner, T. H. D. 1946- ... 122
Turner, Ted
See Turner, Robert Edward III
Turner, Thomas B(ourne) 1902- ... 41-44R
Turner, Thomas Coleman 1927- ... 7-8R
Turner, Thomas N(oel) 1940- ... 113
Turner, Tom
See Turner, T. H. D.
Turner, Victor Witter 1920-1983 ... CANR-3
Obituary ... 111
Earlier sketch in CA 7-8R
Turner, W(illiam) Price 1927- ... CANR-16
Earlier sketch in CA 23-24R
Turner, Wallace 1921- ... 19-20R
Turner, William O(liver) 1914- ... CANR-3
Earlier sketch in CA 2R
See also AITN 1
Turner, William W. 1927- ... CANR-12
Earlier sketch in CA 25-28R
Turney, Alfred (Walter) 1916- ... 73-76
Turney, Catherine 1906- ... 101
Turngren, Annette 1902(?)-1980 ... 11-12R
Obituary ... 101
See also SATA 23
Turngren, Ellen ?-1964 ... 7-8R
See also SATA 3
Turnill, Reginald 1915- ... CANR-15
Earlier sketch in CA 37-40R
Turnock, David 1938- ... 109
Turock, Betty J(ane) ... 110
Turow, Joseph G(regory) 1950- ... 111
Turow, Rita P(astron) 1919- ... 101
Turow, Scott 1949- ... 73-76
Turpin, James W(esley) 1927- ... 23-24R
Turpin, Lorna 1950- ... 107
Turpin, Waters Edward 1910-1968 ... DLB-51
Turska, Krystyna (Zofia) 1933- ... 106
See also SATA 27, 31
Tursun-Zade, Mirzo 1911-1977 Obituary ... 104
Turton, Godfrey (Edmund) 1901- ... 21-22R
Turton-Jones, Edith Constance (Bradshaw)
1904-1968 ... CAP-1
Earlier sketch in CA 9-10
Turville-Petre, Edward Oswald Gabriel
1908-1978 ... 9-10R
Obituary ... 77-80
Turyn, Alexander 1900-1981 Obituary ... 104
Tusan, Stan 1936- ... 105
See also CLC 22
Tushingham, A(rlotte) Douglas 1914- ... 41-44R
Tushnet, Leonard 1908-1973 ... CAP-1
Obituary ... 45-48
Earlier sketch in CA 15-16
Tusiani, Joseph 1924- ... CANR-20
Earlier sketches in CA 9-10R, CANR-5
See also SATA 45
Tuska, Jon 1942- ... CANR-13
Earlier sketch in CA 73-76
Tussing, A(ubrey) Dale 1935- ... 17-18R
Tutaev, David 1916- ... 23-24R
Tute, Warren (Stanley) 1914- ... CANR-1
Earlier sketch in CA 1R
Tuten, Frederic 1936- ... 37-40R
Tuthill, John Wills 1910- ... 108
Tutin, Thomas Gaskell 1908-1987
Obituary ... 123
Tutko, Thomas A(rthur) 1931- ... 69-72
Tutorow, Norman E. 1934- ... 25-28R
Tuttle, Alva M(aurice) 1900- ... 7-8R
Tuttle, Day
See Tuttle, (Frank) Day, Jr.
Tuttle, (Frank) Day, Jr. 1902- ... 116
Tuttle, Frank W(aldo) 1896- ... 61-64
Tuttle, Howard Nelson 1935- ... 41-44R
Tuttle, Russell (Howard) 1939- ... 77-80
Tuttle, W(ilbur) C(oleman) 1883-19(?) ... CAP-2
Earlier sketch in CA 21-22
Tuttle, William M., Jr. 1937- ... CANR-11
Earlier sketch in CA 29-32R
Tuttleton, James Welsey 1934- ... 41-44R
Tutuola, Amos 1920- ... 9-10R
See also CLC 5, 14, 29

Tuve, Merle Antony 1901-1982 Obituary 106
Tuve, Rosemond 1903-1964 .... CAP-1
Earlier sketch in CA 9-10
Tuveson, Ernest (Lee) 1915- 19-20R
Tuwhare, Hone 1922- 103
Tuzin, Donald F(rancis) 1945- 106
Tvardovsky, Alexandr Trifonovich
1910-1971 102
Obituary 33-36R
Twaddell, W(illiam) F(reeman) 1906- 81-84
Twaddle, Andrew C. 1938- 120
Twain, Mark
See Clemens, Samuel Langhorne
See also DLB 11, 12, 23, 64
See also TCLC 6, 12, 19
Twark, Allan J(oseph) 1931- 49-52
Twedt, Dik Warren 1920-1985 .... CANR-14
Obituary 115
Earlier sketch in CA 37-40R
Tweedale, J.
See Bickle, Judith Brundrett
Tweedale, Violet (Chambers) 1862-1936
Brief entry 116
Tweedie, Donald F(erguson), Jr. 1926- ...13-14R
Tweeten, Luther 1931- 89-92
Twelveponies, Mary
See Cleveland, Mary
20/1631
See Upward, Allen
Twersky, Isadore 1930- 120
Twersky, Jacob 1920- 49-52
Tweton, D. Jerome 1933- SATA-48
Twiggy
See Hornby, Leslie
Twin, Stephanie L. 1948- 101
Twiname, Eric 1942(?)-1980 Obituary 102
Twining, Nathan F(arragut) 1897-1982
Obituary 106
Twining, William (Lawrence) 1934- 123
Twisleton-Wykeham-Fiennes, Richard
Nathaniel 1909- CANR-11
Earlier sketch in CA 23-24R
Twiss, Sumner B(arnes), Jr. 1944-
Brief entry 114
Twist, Ananias
See Nunn, William Curtis
Twitchell, James B(uell) 1943- 118
Twitchell, Paul 1908(?)-1971 Obituary 111
Twitchett, Denis Crispin 1925- Brief entry .. 106
Twombly, Robert C(harles) 1940- 85-88
Twombly, Wells A. 1935-1977 ....41-44R
Obituary 69-72
Tworkov, Jack 1900-1982 Obituary 107
See also SATA 31, 47
Twyman, Gib
See Twyman, Gilbert Oscar III
Twyman, Gilbert Oscar III 1943- 109
Ty-Casper, Linda 1931- CANR-24
Earlier sketch in CA 107
Tydeman, William (Marcus) 1935- 119
Tydings, Joseph D(avies) 1928- 29-32R
Tyerman, Hugo 1880-1977 Obituary 77-80
Tyl, Noel 1936- 93-96
Tylden-Wright, David 1923- 25-28R
Tylecote, Mabel (Phythian) 1896-1987 ... CAP-1
Obituary 121
Earlier sketch in CA 13-14
Tyler, A. E.
See Armstrong, (Annette) Elizabeth
Tyler, Anne 1941- CANR-11
Earlier sketch in CA 9-10R
See also SATA 7
See also DLB 6
See also DLBY 82
See also CLC 7, 11, 18, 28, 44
Tyler, Converse 1903(?)-1978 Obituary ...81-84
Tyler, David B(udlong) 1899- 77-80
Tyler, Elias S. 1904(?)-1977 Obituary 73-76
Tyler, Hamilton A(lden) 1917- CANR-5
Earlier sketch in CA 11-12R
Tyler, J. Allen 1924- 101
Tyler, John Ecclesfield (?)-1966 .... CAP-1
Earlier sketch in CA 9-10
Tyler, Leona E(lizabeth) 1906- 17-18R
Tyler, Moses Coit 1835-1900 .... DLB-47, 64
Tyler, Parker 1907-1974 .... CANR-5
Obituary 49-52
Earlier sketch in CA 5-6R
Tyler, (John) Poyntz 1907-1971 .... 3R
Obituary 103
Tyler, Ralph Winfred 1902- 109
Tyler, Richard W(illis) 1917- CANR-24
Earlier sketch in CA 41-44R
Tyler, Robert L(awrence) 1922- 15-16R
Tyler, Ron(nie) C(urtis) 1941- CANR-12
Earlier sketch in CA 29-32R
Tyler, Royall 1757-1826 .... DLB-37
Tyler, S(amuel) Lyman 1920- 77-80
Tyler, Stephen A(lbert) 1932- 29-32R
Tyler, Varro Eugene 1926- 110
Tyler, Vicki 1952- 121
Tyler, W. T.
See Hamrick, Samuel J., Jr.
Tyler, William R(oyall) 1910- 37-40R
Tyler, Zeke
See Marshall, Mel(vin D.)
Tyler-Whittle, Michael Sidney 1927- CANR-4
Earlier sketch in CA 5-6R
Tylor, Edward Burnett 1832-1917
Brief entry 123
See also DLB 57
Tymchuk, Alexander J(ames) 1942- 57-60
Tymeson, Mildred McClary
See Petrie, Mildred McClary
Tymieniecka, Anna-Teresa CANR-9
Earlier sketch in CA 61-64
Tymms, Ralph Vincent 1913-1987
Obituary 123
Tymn, Marshall (Benton) 1937- 107
Tymon, Dorothy 85-88
Tynan, Katharine 1861-1931 Brief entry 104
See also TCLC 3
Tynan, Kathleen 97-100
Tynan, Kenneth (Peacock) 1927-1980 .. CANR-22
Obituary 101
Earlier sketch in CA 15-16R
Tyre, Nedra 104
Tyrell, Donald J(ohn) 1929- Brief entry 110
Tyrmand, Leopold 1920-1985 .... CANR-5
Obituary 115
Earlier sketch in CA 49-52
Tyrone, Paul
See Norwood, Victor G(eorge) C(harles)
Tyrrell, Bernard (James) 1933- 57-60
Tyrrell, Francis M(artin) 1916- Brief entry ... 107
Tyrrell, Joseph M(orten) 1927- 41-44R
Tyrrell, R(obert) Emmett, Jr. 1943- 85-88
Tyrrell, Robert 1929- 41-44R
Tyrwhitt, (Mary) Jacqueline 1905-1983(?)
Obituary 109
Tyrwhitt, Janice 1928- 97-100
Tysdahl, B(joern) J(ohan) 1933- 25-28R
Tysliava, Valerie 1914(?)-1984 Obituary 112
Tyson, Joseph B(lake) 1928- CANR-14
Earlier sketch in CA 37-40R
Tyson, Nancy Jane 1949- 117
Tyson, Richard 1944- 69-72
Tysse, Agnes N. 1904- 101
Tytell, John 1939- 29-32R
Tytler, Graeme (Douglas Colville) 1934- 117
Tzannes, Nicolaos S(tamatios) 1937- 57-60
Tzara, Tristan
See Codrescu, Andrei
and Rosenfeld, Samuel
See also CLC 47
Tzitsikas, Helene 1926- 45-48
Tzonis, Alexander 1937- 101

U

Ubbelohde, Carl (William, Jr.) 1924- CANR-6
Earlier sketch in CA 3R
Ubell, Earl 1926- 37-40R
See also SATA 4
Uble, T(homas) R(alph) O(bermeyer)
1931- CANR-13
Earlier sketch in CA 29-32R
Ucelay, Margarita 1916- 21-22R
Uchida, Tadao 1939- 65-68
Uchida, Yoshiko 1921- CANR-22
Earlier sketches in CA 13-14R, CANR-6
See also SATA 1
See also SAAS 1
See also CLR 6
Udall, Jan Beaney 1938- 65-68
See also SATA 10
Udall, Morris K(ing) 1922- CANR-1
Earlier sketch in CA 45-48
Udall, Nicholas 1504-1556 .... DLB-62
Udall, Stewart L(ee) 1920- 69-72
Ude, Wayne 1946- CANR-13
Earlier sketch in CA 77-80
Udell, Jon G(erald) 1935- CANR-16
Earlier sketches in CA 45-48, CANR-1
Uden, (Bernard Gilbert) Grant 1910- 102
See also SATA 26
Udo, Reuben Kenrick 1935- 77-80
Udoff, Yale M(aurice) 1935- CANR-12
Earlier sketch in CA 57-60
Udolf, Roy 1926- CANR-4
Earlier sketch in CA 53-56
Udovitch, Abraham Labe 1933-
Brief entry 105
Udry, J(oe) Richard 1928- 33-36R
Udry, Janice May 1928- CANR-6
Earlier sketch in CA 5-6R
See also SATA 4
Udy, Stanley Hart, Jr. 1928- Brief entry 106
Ueda, Makoto 1931- 21-22R
Uehling, Carl Theodore 1927- 29-32R
Uehling, Theodore Edward, Jr. 1935- .. CANR-20
Earlier sketch in CA 104
Ueno, Noriko
See Nakae, Noriko
Uffelman, F. C.
See Gehman, Richard (Boyd)
Uffenbeck, Lorin A(rthur) 1924- 61-64
Ugama, LeRoi
See Smith, LeRoi Tex
Ugarte, Francisco 1910-1969 .... CAP-1
Earlier sketch in CA 9-10
Ugarte, Michael 1949- 114
Ugboajah, (Francis) Okwu 1945- 93-96
Uhalley, Stephen, Jr. 1930- Brief entry 106
Uhl, Alexander H. 1899(?)-1976 Obituary ..69-72
Uhl, Melvin John 1915- 7-8R
Uhlfelder, Myra L. 1923- Brief entry 109
Uhlin, Donald M(acbeth) 1930- 49-52
Uhlinger, Susan J. 1942-1980 57-60
Obituary 120
Uhlman, Fred 1901-1985(?) 105
Obituary 116
Uhnak, Dorothy 1933- 81-84
See also AITN 1
Uhr, Carl George 1911- 81-84
Uhr, Elizabeth 1929- 25-28R
Uhr, Leonard (Merrick) 1927- CANR-7
Earlier sketch in CA 5-6R
Uitti, Karl David 1933- CANR-10
Earlier sketch in CA 17-18R
Ujfalussy, Jozsef 1920- Brief entry 114
Ulam, Adam B(runo) 1922- CANR-7
Earlier sketch in CA 13-14R
Ulam, S(tanislaw) M(arcin) 1909-1984 61-64
Obituary 112
Ulanoff, Stanley M(elvin) 1922- CANR-23
Earlier sketches in CA 17-18R, CANR-7
Ulanov, Ann Belford 1938- CANR-16
Earlier sketch in CA 49-52
Ulanov, Barry 1918- CANR-16
Earlier sketch in CA 4R
Ulbricht, Walter 1893-1973 Obituary 113
Ulc, Otto 1930- CANR-13
Earlier sketch in CA 77-80
Ulene, Art(hur Lawrence) 1936- 103
Ulett, George A(ndrew) 1918- 21-22R
Ulevich, Neal Hirsch 1946- 108
Ulibarri, Sabine Reyes 1919- Brief entry 105
Ulich, Robert 1890(?)-1977 Obituary 69-72
Ullah, Najib 1914- 13-14R
Ullah, Salamat 1913- 13-14R
Ulle, Robert F. 1948- 117
Ullendorff, Edward 1920- CANR-18
Earlier sketches in CA 3R, CANR-2
Ullian, Joseph S(ilbert) 1930- 41-44R
Ullman, Allan 1909(?)-1982 Obituary 106
Ullman, Barbara
See Schwalberg, Carol(yn Ernestine
Stein)
Ullman, Edward L(ouis) 1912- 45-48
Ullman, Elwood 1903(?)-1985 Obituary 117
Ullman, James Ramsey 1907-1971 ..... CANR-3
Obituary 29-32R
Earlier sketch in CA 3R
See also SATA 7
Ullman, Leslie 1947- 104
Ullman, Michael (Alan) 1945- 103
Ullman, Montague 1916- 41-44R
Ullman, Natacha 1929(?)-1986 Obituary 119
Ullman, Pierre L(ioni) 1929- 33-36R
Ullman, Richard Henry 1933- CANR-3
Earlier sketch in CA 3R
Ullmann, John E(manuel) 1923- 17-18R
Ullmann, Leonard P(aul) 1930- 17-18R
Ullmann, Liv 1939- 102
Ullmann, Stephen 1914-1976 .... CANR-4
Obituary 65-68
Earlier sketch in CA 7-8R
Ullmann, Walter 1910-1983 .... CANR-10
Obituary 108
Earlier sketch in CA 21-22R
Ullrich, Helen D(enning) 1922- 109
Ullstein, Hermann 1875(?)-1943
Brief entry 116
Ullyot, Joan 1940- 73-76
Ulm, Robert 1934-1977 .... SATA-17
Ulman, William A. 1908(?)-1979 103
Obituary 89-92
Ulmer, (Roland) Curtis 1923- 103
Ulmer, Diane K. 1943- 122
Ulmer, Louise 1943- 113
Ulmer, Melville J(ack) 1911- 21-22R
Ulmer, S(hirley) Sidney 1923- 41-44R
Ulrich, Betty Garton 1919- 29-32R
Ulrich, Carolyn F. 1881(?)-1970 Obituary ... 104
Ulrich, Heinz 1927(?)-1980 Obituary 97-100
Ulrich, (John) Homer 1906-1987 ...... CANR-2
Obituary 124
Earlier sketch in CA 7-8R
Ulrich, Louis E., Jr. 1918- 13-14R
Ulrich, Roger E(lwood) 1931- 41-44R
Ultan, Lloyd 1929- 117
Ultee, (J.) Maarten 1949- 109
Ulyanov, V. I.
See Lenin
Ulyanov-Lenin
See Lenin
Ulyatt, Kenneth 1920- CANR-8
Earlier sketch in CA 61-64
See also SATA 14
Umland, Craig (Owen) 1947- 61-64
Umphlett, Wiley Lee 1931- CANR-1
Earlier sketch in CA 49-52
Umstead, William Lee 1921- 81-84
Unada
See Gliewe, Unada (Grace)
Unamuno (y Jugo), Miguel de 1864-1936
Brief entry 104
See also TCLC 2, 9
Unbegaun, Boris Ottokar 1898-1973
Obituary 41-44R
Uncle Gordon
See Roe, F(rederic) Gordon
Uncle Gus
See Rey, H(ans) A(ugusto)
Uncle Mac
See McCulloch, Derek (Ivor Breashur)
Uncle Ray
See Coffman, Ramon Peyton
Uncle Shelby
See Silverstein, Shel(by)
Undercliffe, Errol
See Campbell, (John) Ramsey
Underdown, David (Edward) 1925- CANR-11
Earlier sketch in CA 7-8R
Underhill, Alice Mertie (Waterman)
1900-1971 .... 3R
Obituary 103
See also SATA 10
Underhill, Charles
See Hill, Reginald (Charles)
Underhill, Hal
See Underhill, Harold
Underhill, Harold 1926-1972 .... CAP-2
Earlier sketch in CA 25-28
Underhill, Liz 1948- 121
See also SATA 49
Underhill, Miriam E. 1898(?)-1976
Obituary 61-64
Underhill, Peter
See Soderberg, Percy Measday
Underhill, Ruth Murray 1884-1984 ..... CANR-3
Obituary 114
Earlier sketch in CA 3R
Underwood, Aggie
See Underwood, Agness May Wilson
Underwood, Agness May Wilson
1902-1984 Obituary 113
Underwood, Barbara 1952- 101
Underwood, Benton J. 1915- 101
Underwood, (Mary) Betty 1921- 37-40R
Underwood, Gary Neal 1940- Brief entry ... 113
Underwood, Jane H(ammons) 1931- 61-64
Underwood, John Weeden 1932- 19-20R
Underwood, Lewis Graham
See Wagner, C(harles) Peter
Underwood, Mavis Eileen 1916-
Brief entry 108
Underwood, Michael
See Evelyn, (John) Michael
Underwood, Miles
See Glassco, John
Underwood, Norman 1878(?)-1974
Obituary 53-56
Underwood, Paul S(taats) 1915-1985 77-80
Obituary 118
Underwood, Peter 1923- CANR-21
Earlier sketch in CA 104
Underwood, Sam J(esse) 1922- CANR-2
Earlier sketch in CA 45-48
Underwood, Ted Leroy 1935- 115
Underwood, Tim (Edward) 1948- CANR-24
Earlier sketch in CA 105
Undine, P. F.
See Paine, Lauran (Bosworth)
Undset, Sigrid 1882-1949 Brief entry 104
See also TCLC 3
Undy, R(oger) 1938- 115
Unett, John 13-14R
Ungar, Sanford J. 1945- CANR-13
Earlier sketch in CA 37-40R
Ungaretti, Giuseppe 1888-1970 .... CAP-2
Obituary 25-28R
Earlier sketch in CA 19-20
See also CLC 7, 11, 15
Ungaro, Harold R(aymond) Mancusi, Jr.
See Mancusi-Ungaro, Harold R(aymond),
Jr.
Ungaro, Susan Kelliher 1953- 103
Unger, Arthur 1924- 2R
Unger, Barbara 1932- CANR-13
Earlier sketch in CA 77-80
Unger, Douglas 1952- CLC-34
Unger, Hans 1915- 17-18R
Unger, Henry F. 1912- 13-14R
Unger, Irwin 1927- CANR-7
Earlier sketch in CA 11-12R
Unger, Jim 1937- CANR-13
Earlier sketch in CA 61-64
Unger, Len
See Unger, Leonard
Unger, Leonard 1916- 5-6R
Unger, Leonard 1934- 69-72
Unger, Marion
See Thede, Marion Draughon
Unger, Marvin H. 1936- 29-32R
Unger, Maurice Albert 1917- CANR-3
Earlier sketch in CA 9-10R
Unger, Merrill F. 1909- CANR-6
Earlier sketch in CA 2R
Unger, Peter K(enneth) 1942- Brief entry ... 109
Unger, Richard (Lawrence) 1939- CANR-15
Earlier sketch in CA 65-68
Unger, Richard W. 1942- 121
Unger, Walter P(eter) 1939- Brief entry 115
Ungerer, Jean Thomas 1931- 41-44R
See also SATA 5, 33
Ungerer, Miriam 1929- 117
Ungerer, Tomi
See Ungerer, Jean Thomas
See also CLR 3
Unger-Hamilton, Clive (Wolfgang)
1942- CANR-19
Earlier sketch in CA 101
Ungermann, Kenneth Armistead 1916- 9-10R
Ungs, Thomas D(ale) 1928- 81-84
Unkelbach, Kurt 1913- CANR-8
Earlier sketch in CA 23-24R
See also SATA 4
Unkovic, Charles M. 1922- 45-48
Unnerstad, Edith Totterman 1900- CANR-6
Earlier sketch in CA 5-6R
See also SATA 3
Unrau, Ruth 1922- 61-64
See also SATA 9
Unrau, William E. 1929- 37-40R
Unruh, Adolph 1908- 49-52
Unruh, Fritz von
See Von Unruh, Fritz
Unruh, Glenys Grace (Green) 1910- 29-32R
Unruh, John D., Jr. 1938(?)-1976
Obituary 105
Unser, Bobby
See Unser, Robert William
Unser, Robert William 1934- 97-100
Unstead, R(obert) J(ohn) 1915- CANR-23
Earlier sketches in CA 9-10R, CANR-7
See also SATA 12
Unsworth, Barry (Forster) 1930- 25-28R
Unsworth, Mair 1909- CANR-10
Earlier sketch in CA 25-28R
Unsworth, Walt(er) 1928- CANR-17
Earlier sketch in CA 29-32R
See also SATA 4

INDEX

Unterberger, Betty Miller 1923- 25-28R
Unterbrink, Mary 1937- 113
Unterecker, John 1922- 17-18R
Untereiner, Raymond Edward 1898-1983
Obituary 110
Unterman, Alan 1942- 97-100
Unterman, Issar Y(ehuda) 1886-1976
Obituary 61-64
Untermeyer, Bryna Ivens 1909- CANR-3
Earlier sketch in CA 7-8R
Untermeyer, Jean Starr 1886-1970
Obituary 29-32R
Untermeyer, Louis 1885-1977 ....5-6R
Obituary 73-76
See also SATA 2, 26, 37
Unthank, Luisa-Teresa 33-36R
Unthank, Tessa Brown
See Unthank, Luisa-Teresa
Unwalla, Darab B. 1928- 25-28R
Unwin, David S(torr) 1918- CANR-6
Earlier sketch in CA 9-10R
See also SATA 14
Unwin, Derick (James) 1931- 23-24R
Unwin, Nora S(picer) 1907-1982 ....21-22R
Obituary 120
See also SATA 3, 49
Unwin, Rayner S(tephens) 1925- 1R
Unwin, Stanley 1884-1968 ....7-8R
Upchurch, Boyd 1919- 25-28R
Updike, John (Hoyer) 1932- CANR-4
Earlier sketch in CA 4R
See also CABS 1
See also DLB 2, 5
See also DLBY 80, 82
See also DLBD 3
See also CLC 1, 2, 3, 5, 7, 9, 13, 15, 23, 34, 43
Updike, L(eRoy) Wayne 1916- 49-52
Updyke, James
See Burnett, W(illiam) R(iley)
Upfield, Arthur W(illiam) 1888-1964
Obituary 114
Upgren, Arthur P. 1897-1986 Obituary 120
Uphaus, Robert W(alter) 1942- 57-60
Uphaus, Willard Edwin 1890-1983 .... CAP-1
Obituary 111
Earlier sketch in CA 19-20
Uphoff, Norman T(homas) 1940- CANR-11
Earlier sketch in CA 29-32R
Uphoff, Walter H. 1913- CANR-14
Earlier sketch in CA 25-28R
Upits, Andrejs 1877-1970 Obituary 104
Upjohn, Everard M(iller) 1903-1978 ...... CAP-1
Obituary 81-84
Earlier sketch in CA 13-14
Uppal, Jogindar S. 1927- CANR-1
Earlier sketch in CA 45-48
Upright, Diane W(arner) 1947- 120
Upson, Norma 1919- CANR-8
Earlier sketch in CA 61-64
Upson, William Hazlett 1891-1975 ....5-6R
Obituary 57-60
Upton, Albert 1897- CAP-2
Earlier sketch in CA 23-24
Upton, Anthony F. 1929- 17-18R
Upton, Arvin 1914- 81-84
Upton, Bertha (Hudson) 1849-1912
Brief entry 121
Upton, Charles 1948- Brief entry 116
See also DLB 16
Upton, Dell 1949- 123
Upton, Joseph C(heshire) N(ash) 1946- ...81-84
Upton, L(eslie) F(rancis) S(tokes) 1931- ...61-64
Upton, Lee 1953- 123
Upton, Monroe 1898- CAP-2
Earlier sketch in CA 17-18
Upton, Robert CANR-13
Earlier sketch in CA 73-76
Upward, Allen 1863-1926 Brief entry 117
See also DLB 36
Upward, Edward (Falaise) 1903- 77-80
Urbach, Reinhard 1939- Brief entry 113
Urban, Michael E(dward) 1947- 111
Urban, Wilbur Marshall 1873-1952
Brief entry 119
Urban, William L(awrence) 1939- CANR-18
Earlier sketches in CA 45-48, CANR-2
Urbanek, Mae 1903- 77-80
Urbano, Victoria (Eugenia) 1926- CANR-2
Earlier sketch in CA 45-48
Urbanska, Wanda (Marie) 1956- 124
Urbanski, Edmund Stefan
See Urbanski, Edmund Stephen
Urbanski, Edmund Stephen 1909- CANR-23
Earlier sketch in CA 45-48
Urbanski, Marie M. Olesen 1922- 102
Urch, Elizabeth 1921- 103
Urda, Nicholas 1922- 21-22R
Urdang, Constance (Henriette) 1922- ... CANR-24
Earlier sketches in CA 21-22R, CANR-9
See also CLC 47
Urdang, Laurence 1927- CANR-17
Earlier sketch in CA 89-92
Ure, Jean SATA-48
Ure, Peter 1919-1969 .... CAP-1
Earlier sketch in CA 11-12
U'Ren, Hilda
See U'Ren-Stubbings, Hilda
Uren, Hilda
See U'Ren-Stubbings, Hilda
U'Ren-Stubbings, Hilda 1914- 29-32R
Uretsky, Myron 1940- 53-56
Urey, Harold C(layton) 1893-1981
Obituary 102
Uri, Pierre Emmanuel 1911- 97-100
Uriel, Henry
See Faust, Frederick (Shiller)
Uris, Auren 1913- CANR-22
Earlier sketch in CA 17-18R
Uris, Dorothy CANR-9
Earlier sketch in CA 61-64
Uris, Leon (Marcus) 1924- CANR-1
Earlier sketch in CA 1R
See also SATA 49
See also CLC 7, 32
See also AITN 1, 2
Urista, Alberto H. 1947- CANR-2
Earlier sketch in CA 45-48
Urkowitz, Steven 1941- 111
Urmson, J(ames) O(pie) 1915- 25-28R
Urmuz
See Codrescu, Andrei
Urness, Carol 1936- Brief entry 111
Uroff, Margaret Dickie 1935- 93-96
Urofsky, Melvin I. 1939- CANR-14
Earlier sketch in CA 37-40R
Urquhart, Alvin W. 1931- 13-14R
Urquhart, Brian Edward 1919- 105
Urquhart, Caroline 1940- 118
Urquhart, Colin 1940- 115
Urquhart, Fred(erick Burrows) 1912- ... CANR-21
Earlier sketches in CA 11-12R, CANR-6
Urquhart, Guy
See McAlmon, Robert (Menzies)
Urquhart, Jane 1949- 113
Urquhart, Judy 1942- 123
Urrutia Lleo, Manuel 1901-1981 Obituary ... 104
Urry, David (Laurence) 1931- 85-88
Urry, John 1946- 122
Urry, W(illiam) G(eorge) 1913-1981
Obituary 103
Ursini, James 1947- 61-64
Urvater, Michele 1946- 102
Urwick, Lyndall Fownes 1891-1983 ...... CAP-1
Obituary 111
Earlier sketch in CA 13-14
Urwin, Gregory J(ohn) W(illiam) 1955- 114
Ury, William Langer 1953- 109
Ury, Zalman F. 1924- CANR-17
Earlier sketch in CA 65-68
Urzidil, Johannes 1896-1970 Obituary ...29-32R
Us
See Deal, Borden
Usborne, Richard Alexander 1910- 104
Usco
See Stern, Gerd Jacob
Usdin, Gene (Leonard) 1922- 37-40R
Useem, Michael 1942- 61-64
Usher, Dan 1934- CANR-12
Earlier sketch in CA 29-32R
Usher, Frank (Hugh) 1909-1976 .... CANR-5
Earlier sketch in CA 7-8R
Usher, George 1930- 109
Usher, Margo Scegge
See McHargue, Georgess
Usher, Shaun 1937- 77-80
Usher, Stephen 1931- 29-32R
Usher-Wilson, Rodney N. 1908(?)-1983
Obituary 109
Usherwood, Elizabeth (Ada) 1923- 123
Usherwood, Stephen Dean 1907- CANR-19
Earlier sketches in CA 5-6R, CANR-3
Usikota
See Brinitzer, Carl
Uslaner, Eric M(ichael) 1947- 111
Usmiani, Renate 1931- 113
Usry, Milton F. 1931- 19-20R
Ussher, (Percival) Arland 1899-1980 ... CANR-10
Obituary 102
Earlier sketches in CA 13-14, CAP-1
Ussher, Percy Arland
See Ussher, (Percival) Arland
Ustinov, D(mitri) F(edorovich) 1908-1984
Obituary 114
Ustinov, Peter (Alexander) 1921- 13-14R
See also DLB 13
See also CLC 1
See also AITN 1
Uston, Ken(neth Senzo) 1935-1987 108
Obituary 123
Utechin, S(ergei) V(asilievich) 1921- 11-12R
Utgard, Russell O(liver) 1933- 49-52
Utke, Allen R(ay) 1936- 81-84
Utley, Francis Lee 1907-1974 .... CANR-2
Obituary 49-52
Earlier sketch in CA 3R
Utley, Freda 1898-1978 81-84
Obituary 77-80
Utley, (Clifton) Garrick 1939- 69-72
Utley, Ralph
See Cairns, Huntington
Utley, Robert M(arshall) 1929- CANR-2
Earlier sketch in CA 5-6R
Utt, Richard H. 1923- CANR-7
Earlier sketch in CA 9-10R
Utt, Walter C(harles) 1921- 21-22R
Uttley, Alice Jane (Taylor) 1884-1976 ... CANR-7
Obituary 65-68
Earlier sketch in CA 53-56
See also SATA 3, 26
Uttley, Alison
See Uttley, Alice Jane (Taylor)
Uttley, John 1914- 23-24R
Utton, Albert Edgar 1931- CANR-1
Earlier sketch in CA 45-48
Utz, Lois (Marie) 1932-1986 ....25-28R
Obituary 121
See also SATA 5, 50
Utz, Robert T(homas) 1934- 53-56
Uu, David
See Harris, David W.
Uveges, Joseph A(ndrew), Jr. 1938- 41-44R
Uvezian, Sonia CANR-9
Earlier sketch in CA 57-60
Uyl, Douglas J(ohn) Den
See Den Uyl, Douglas J(ohn)
Uzgiris, Ina Cepenas 1937- Brief entry 108
Uzzell, J(ohn) Douglas 1937- 93-96

V

v
See Chekhov, Anton (Pavlovich)
V., Nina
See Vickers, Antoinette L.
Vacca, Roberto 1927- CANR-1
Earlier sketch in CA 49-52
Vaccaro, Ernest B. 1905(?)-1979
Obituary 89-92
Vaccaro, Joseph P(ascal) 1935- 104
Vaccaro, Louis C(harles) 1930- CANR-1
Earlier sketch in CA 45-48
Vaccaro, Tony
See Vaccaro, Ernest B.
Vachell, Horace Annesley 1861-1955
Brief entry 120
Vachon, Brian 1941- 41-44R
Vachss, Andrew H(enry) 1942- 118
Vaculik, Ludvik 1926- 53-56
See also CLC 7
Vaczek, Louis 1913-1983 .... CANR-21
Obituary 111
Earlier sketch in CA 11-12R
Vadakin, James C(harles) 1924- 29-32R
Vadney, Thomas E(ugene) 1939- 45-48
Vaeth, J(oseph) Gordon 1921- 5-6R
See also SATA 17
Vago, Bela Adalbert 1922- 93-96
Vagts, Alfred (Hermann Friedrich) 1892- 5-6R
Vagts, Detlev F(rederick) 1929- 25-28R
Vagts, Miriam Beard 1901-1983 Obituary ... 110
Vahanian, Gabriel (Antoine) 1927- CANR-22
Earlier sketches in CA 3R, CANR-6
Vaid, Krishna Baldev 1927- CANR-8
Earlier sketch in CA 61-64
Vaidon, Lawdom
See Woolman, David S.
Vaihinger, Hans 1852-1933 Brief entry 116
Vail, (Marilyn) Elaine 1948- 109
Vail, Laurence 1891-1968 Obituary 112
See also DLB 4
Vail, Priscilla L. 1931- 101
Vail, Robert William 1921- CANR-12
Earlier sketch in CA 17-18R
Vaill, George D. 1911(?)-1986 Obituary 119
Vaillancourt, Jean-Guy 1937- CANR-21
Earlier sketch in CA 105
Vaillancourt, Pauline M(ariette) 104
Vailland, Roger (Francois) 1907-1965 103
Obituary 89-92
Vaillant, George E. 1934- CANR-13
Earlier sketch in CA 77-80
Vairo, Philip Dominic 1933- 102
Vaizey, John 1929-1984 .... CANR-4
Obituary 113
Earlier sketch in CA 7-8R
Vaizey, Marina 1938- 116
Vajda, Ernest 1887-1954 Brief entry 122
See also DLB 44
Vajda, Stephan 1926- 29-32R
Vajk, J(oseph) Peter 1942- 117
Vakar, N(icholas) P(latonovich)
1897-1970 .... CANR-20
Obituary 103
Earlier sketch in CA 3R
Valaskakis, Kimon Plato 1941- 89-92
Valbonne, Jean
See Leprohon, Pierre
Valbuena-Briones, Angel (Julian) 1928- .. CANR-3
Earlier sketch in CA 45-48
Valcoe, H. Felix
See Swartz, Harry (Felix)
Valdemi, Maria L. 1947- 114
Valdes, Donald M(anuel) 1922- 21-22R
Valdes, Ivy 1921- 105
Valdes, Joan 1931- 49-52
Valdes, Mario J. 1934- CANR-21
Earlier sketches in CA 13-14R, CANR-6
Valdes, Nelson P. 1945- 33-36R
Valdez, Luis 1940- 101
Valdez, Paul
See Yates, A(lan) G(eoffrey)
Valdman, Albert 1931- 103
Vale, C(orwyn) P(hilip) 1921- 49-52
Vale, (Henry) Edmund (Theodoric)
1888-1969 .... CAP-1
Earlier sketch in CA 9-10
Vale, Eugene 1916- CANR-12
Earlier sketch in CA 57-60
Vale, Lewis
See Oglesby, Joseph
Vale, Malcolm Graham Allan 1942-
Brief entry 109
Valen, Nanine 1950- 65-68
See also SATA 21
Valencak, Hannelore
See Mayer, Hannelore Valencak
See also SATA 42
Valency, Maurice 1903- CANR-10
Earlier sketch in CA 25-28R
Valens, E(vans) G., Jr. 1920- CANR-3
Earlier sketch in CA 5-6R
See also SATA 1
Valens, Evans G. CANR-14
Earlier sketch in CA 81-84
Valenstein, Suzanne G(ebhart) 1928- 77-80
Valente, Michael F(eeney) 57-60
Valenti, Jack 1921- 73-76
Valentin, Thomas 1922-1981 Obituary 103
Valentine, Alan (Chester) 1901-1980 .... CANR-2
Obituary 101
Earlier sketch in CA 5-6R
Valentine, Charles A. 1929- 25-28R
Valentine, Charles Wilfrid 1879-1964
Obituary 107
Valentine, D(onald) G(raham) 1929- 7-8R
Valentine, David
See Ludovici, Anthony M(ario)
Valentine, Douglas
See Williams, (George) Valentine
Valentine, Foy (Dan) 1923- CANR-10
Earlier sketch in CA 19-20R
Valentine, Helen (Lachman) 1893-1986
Obituary 121
Valentine, Helen
See Valentine, Sister Mary Hester
Valentine, Jean 1934- 65-68
Valentine, Jo
See Armstrong, Charlotte
Valentine, Lloyd Magnus 1922-
Brief entry 110
Valentine, Roger
See Duke, Donald Norman
Valentine, Sister Mary Hester 1909- CAP-2
Earlier sketch in CA 23-24
Valentine, Steven Richards 1956- 113
Valentine, Tom 1935- CANR-22
Earlier sketch in CA 45-48
Valentine, William Alexander 1905- 57-60
Valenzuela, Arturo A. 1944- 101
Valenzuela, Luisa 1938- 101
See also CLC 31
Valeo, Francis Ralph 1916- Brief entry 108
Valeran, A. B.
See Starr, S(tephen) Frederick
Valera y Alcala-Galiano, Juan 1824-1905
Brief entry 106
See also TCLC 10
Valeriani, Richard (Gerard) 1932- CANR-12
Earlier sketch in CA 65-68
Valeriano, Napoleon D(iestro)
1917(?)-1975 Obituary 53-56
Valery, Bernard 1913(?)-1984 Obituary 113
Valery, (Ambroise) Paul (Toussaint Jules)
1871-1945 122
Brief entry 104
See also TCLC 4, 15
Vales, Robert L(ee) 1933- 53-56
Valett, Robert E. 1927- CANR-22
Earlier sketches in CA 19-20R, CANR-7
Valette, Rebecca M(arianne Loose)
1938- CANR-8
Earlier sketch in CA 23-24R
Valgardson, W(illiam) D(empsey) 1939- ..41-44R
See also DLB 60
Valgemae, Mardi 1935- 41-44R
Vali, Ferenc Albert 1905-1984 .... CANR-3
Obituary 114
Earlier sketch in CA 1R
Valiani, Leo 1909- CANR-18
Earlier sketch in CA 101
Valin, Jonathan Louis 1948- 101
Valin, Martial (Henry) 1898-1980 Obituary .. 105
Valis, Noel M(aureen Ritter) 1945- 110
Valkenier, Elizabeth Kridl 1926- 119
Vall, Seymour 1925(?)-1987 Obituary 124
Vallance, Elizabeth (Mary) 1945- 102
Vallee, Hubert P(rior) 1901-1986 .... CANR-2
Obituary 119
Earlier sketch in CA 3R
Vallee, Jacques F. 1939- CANR-10
Earlier sketch in CA 17-18R
Vallee, Rudy
See Vallee, Hubert P(rior)
Valle-Inclan, Ramon (Maria) del
1866-1936 Brief entry 106
See also TCLC 5
Vallejo, Antonio Buero
See Buero Vallejo, Antonio
Vallejo, Cesar (Abraham) 1892-1938
Brief entry 105
See also TCLC 3
Vallen, Jerome J(ay) 1928- 93-96
Vallentine, John F(ranklin) 1931- CANR-19
Earlier sketches in CA 53-56, CANR-4
Valle Y Pena, Ramon del
See Valle-Inclan, Ramon (Maria) del
Valmaggia, Juan S. 1895-1980 Obituary ..97-100
Valsan, E. H. 1933- 29-32R
Valtz, Robert C. K. 1936- 13-14R
Value, Barbara Ann 1932-1986 Obituary 120
Vambe, Lawrence (Chinyani) 1917- 110
Vamos, Mara (Miriam) 1927- Brief entry 114
Vamplew, Wray 1943- CANR-20
Earlier sketch in CA 103
Van Abbe, Derek Maurice 1916- 57-60
Van Abbe, Salaman 1883-1955 .... SATA-18
Van Allsburg, Chris 1949- 117
Brief entry 113
See also SATA 37
See also DLB 61
See also CLR 5, 13
Van Alstyne, Richard W(arner) 1900- 11-12R
Van Anda, Carr 1864-1945 .... DLB-25
Van Anrooy, Francine 1924- 23-24R
See also SATA 2
Van Anrooy, Frans
See Van Anrooy, Francine
van Appledorn, Mary Jeanne 1927- CANR-10
Earlier sketch in CA 25-28R
Vanardy, Varick
See Dey, Frederic (Merrill) Van Rensselaer
Van Arsdel, Rosemary T(horstenson)
1926- 108
Van Ash, Cay 1918- CLC-34

Van Atta, Winfred 1910- CANR-1
Earlier sketch in CA 3R
Vanauken, Sheldon CANR-15
Earlier sketch in CA 85-88
van Beeck, Frans Jozef 1930- 115
Vanberg, Bent J(arl) 1915- 118
VanBibber, Max A(rnold) 1913(?)-1981
Obituary 103
Van Briggle, Margaret F(rances) Jessup
1917- 11-12R
Van Brocklin, Norm(an Mack) 1926-1983
Obituary 109
Van Brunt, H(owell) L(loyd) 1936- 49-52
Van Buitenen, J(ohannes) A(drian)
B(ernard) 1928(?)-1979 103
Obituary 89-92
Van Buren, Abigail
See Phillips, Pauline (Esther Friedman)
Van Buren, James G(eil) 1914- 57-60
van Buren, Paul (Matthews) 1924- CANR-11
Earlier sketch in CA 61-64
Van Buren, Raeburn 1891- 103
Van Caenegem, R(aoul) C(harles)
1927- CANR-23
Earlier sketch in CA 45-48
Van Campen, Karl
See Campbell, John W(ood)
Van Caspel, Venita 1922- 104
Vance, A. D.
See Vane-Wright, R(ichard) I(rwin)
Vance, Adrian 1936- 77-80
Vance, Barbara Jane 1934- 57-60
Vance, Bruce 1931- 33-36R
Vance, Cyrus R(oberts) 1917- 121
Vance, Edgar
See Ambrose, Eric (Samuel)
Vance, Eleanor Graham 1908- 9-10R
See also SATA 11
Vance, Ethel
See Stone, Grace Zaring
Vance, Gerald
See Silverberg, Robert
Vance, Jack
See Vance, John Holbrook
See also DLB 8
See also CLC 35
Vance, John Holbrook 1916- CANR-17
Earlier sketch in CA 29-32R
Vance, Lawrence L(ee) 1911- 49-52
Vance, Louis Joseph 1879-1933
Brief entry 112
Vance, Marguerite 1889-1965 Obituary 109
See also SATA 29
Vance, (Robert) Norman (Colbert) 1950- 122
Vance, Rupert B(ayless) 1899-1975
Obituary 61-64
Vance, Samuel 1939- 29-32R
Vance, Stanley 1915- CANR-3
Earlier sketch in CA 3R
Vance, William E. 1911-1986 105
Obituary 119
Vancil, Richard F(ranklin) 1931- CANR-8
Earlier sketch in CA 5-6R
Van Cise, Jerrold G(ordon) 1910- 114
Van Cleef, Eugene 1887-1973 Obituary 107
Van Cleve, John Walter 1950- 122
Van Cleve, Thomas Curtis 1888-1976 .... 41-44R
Obituary 65-68
Van Coevering, Jack
See Van Coevering, Jan Adrian
Van Coevering, Jan Adrian 1900- CAP-1
Earlier sketch in CA 9-10
van Corstanje, Auspicius
See van Corstanje, Charles
van Corstanje, Charles 1913- 107
van Croonenburg, Engelbert J(ohannes)
1909- 37-40R
Van Dahm, Thomas E(dward) 1924- 65-68
Van Dalen, Deobold B(ertrude) 1911- .. CANR-20
Earlier sketch in CA 3R
Van Dam, Ine 1947- 109
van Dam, J.
See Presser, (Gerrit) Jacob
Vande Kieft, Ruth Marguerite 1925- 17-18R
Van D'Elden, Karl H. 1923- 45-48
Vandeman, George E(dward) 1916-
Brief entry 114
Vandenberg, Arthur Hendrick 1884-1951
Brief entry 120
Vandenberg, Donald 1931- 29-32R
Vandenberg, Philipp 1941- CANR-23
Earlier sketches in CA 61-64, CANR-8
Vandenberg, T. F. 1941- 25-28R
van den Berghe, Pierre L. 1933- CANR-5
Earlier sketch in CA 11-12R
Van Den Bogarde, Derek Jules Gaspard
Ulric Niven 1921- 77-80
Vandenbosch, Amry 1894- 61-64
Vandenbosch, Robert 1922-1978 Obituary .. 107
Vandenburg, Mary Lou 1943- 73-76
See also SATA 17
Vandenburgh, Mildred 1898- 97-100
Vandenbusche, Duane (Lee) 1937- CANR-24
Earlier sketch in CA 45-48
van den Bussche, Henri O(mer) A(ntoine)
See Bussche, Henri O(mer) A(ntoine) van
den
van den Haag, Ernest 1914- CANR-6
Earlier sketch in CA 7-8R
van den Heuvel, Albert H(endrik) 1932- 19-20R
van den Heuvel, Cornelisz A. 1931- 13-14R
Van De Pitte, Frederick P. 1932- 45-48
Vander, Harry J(oseph) III 1913-19(?) CAP-2
Earlier sketch in CA 25-28
VanDerBeets, Richard 1932- 29-32R
Vanderbilt, Amy 1908-1974 .... CANR-3
Obituary 53-56
Earlier sketch in CA 4R
Vanderbilt, Arthur T. II 1950- 122
Vanderbilt, Cornelius, Jr. 1898-1974 .... CAP-1
Obituary 49-52
Earlier sketch in CA 9-10
See also AITN 1
Vanderbilt, Gloria (Laura Morgan)
1924- CANR-22
Earlier sketch in CA 89-92
Vander Boom, Mae M. SATA-14
Vanderburgh, R(osamond) M(oate) 1926- 105
Vander Goot, Mary 1947- 112
Vandergriff, (Lola) Aola 1920- CANR-18
Earlier sketch in CA 89-92
Vanderhaeghe, Guy 1951- 113
See also CLC 41
van der Heyden, A(ntonius) A(lphonsus)
M(aria) 1922- CANR-7
Earlier sketch in CA 57-60
Vander Hill, C(harles) Warren 1937- 33-36R
VanDerhoof, Jack W(arner) 1921- 53-56
Van der Horst, Brian 1944- 41-44R
Vander Kooi, Ronald C(harles) CANR-2
Earlier sketch in CA 45-48
van der Kroef, Justus M(aria) 1925- CANR-14
Earlier sketch in CA 41-44R
Vanderlip, D(odava) George 1926- CANR-15
Earlier sketch in CA 77-80
Vander Lugt, Herbert 1920- CANR-18
Earlier sketch in CA 101
van der Marck, Jan 1929- 119
van der Merwe, Nikolaas J(ohannes)
1940- 41-44R
van der Meulen, Daniel 1894- 117
VanderMolen, Robert 1947- 57-60
van der Ploeg, Johannes P(etrus) M(aria)
1909- CANR-15
Earlier sketches in CA 9-10, CAP-1
van der Poel, Cornelius J(ohannes)
1921- CANR-4
Earlier sketch in CA 53-56
Vanderpool, Harold Y(oung) 1936- 53-56
Vanderpool, James A(lbert) 1916-1983
Obituary 109
Van der Post, Laurens (Jan) 1906- 5-6R
See also CLC 5
Van Dersal, William R(ichard) 1907- 77-80
Vander-Schrier, Nettie 1922- 114
Vandersee, Charles (Andrew) 1938- 41-44R
Van Der Slik, Jack R(onald) 1936- 29-32R
van der Smissen, Betty
See van der Smissen, Margaret Elisabeth
van der Smissen, Margaret Elisabeth
1927- CANR-9
Earlier sketch in CA 19-20R
Van der Spiel, Luigi 1920- 102
van der Vat, Dan(iel Francis Jeroen) 1939- .. 109
Vanderveen, Bareld Harmannus 1932- 103
Vanderveen, Bart H.
See Vanderveen, Bareld Harmannus
Van der Veer, Judy 1912-1982 .... 33-36R
Obituary 108
See also SATA 4, 33
Vandervelde, Marjorie (Mills) 1908- CANR-10
Earlier sketch in CA 21-22R
Van der Veldt, James 1893(?)-1977
Obituary 73-76
Van der Veur, Paul W. 1921- 21-22R
Van Der Voort, Richard Lee 1936- 37-40R
Vanderwall, Francis W(illiam) 1946- 108
Vanderwerken, David L(eon) 1945- 119
Vanderwerth, W(illiam) C(onnor) 1904- 73-76
Vanderwood, Paul J. 29-32R
Vander Zanden, James Wilfrid 1930- CANR-19
Earlier sketches in CA 15-16R, CANR-5
van der Zee, Henri (Antony) 1934-
Brief entry 114
Van Der Zee, James (Augustus Joseph)
1886-1983 104
Obituary 109
van der Zee, John 1936- CANR-15
Earlier sketch in CA 21-22R
Vanderzell, John H. 1924- 45-48
VanderZwaag, Harold J. 1929- CANR-23
Earlier sketch in CA 45-48
van Deurs, George 1901- 25-28R
Van Deusen, Dayton G(roff) 1914- 11-12R
Van Deusen, Glyndon Garlock 1897- CANR-1
Earlier sketch in CA 1R
Van Deusen, L. Marshall 1922- 61-64
Van Deusen, Ruth B(rown) 1907- 5-6R
Van De Vall, Mark 1923- CANR-12
Earlier sketch in CA 29-32R
Van Devander, Charles W(ood) 1902-1986
Obituary 121
Van Devanter, Lynda (Margaret) 1947- 117
Van de Vate, Dwight, Jr. 1928- 61-64
Van Deventer, David E(arl) 1937-
Brief entry 115
Van Deventer, Fred 1903-1971 .... CAP-1
Earlier sketch in CA 15-16
VanDeventer, Robert 105
Van de Water, Frederic F(ranklyn)
1890-1968 Obituary 110
van de Wetering, Janwillem 1931- CANR-4
Earlier sketch in CA 49-52
See also CLC 47
Van Dine, S. S.
See Wright, Willard Huntington
See also TCLC 23
Vandiver, Edward P(inckney), Jr. 1902- .. CAP-1
Earlier sketch in CA 13-14
Vandiver, Frank E(verson) 1925- CANR-7
Earlier sketch in CA 7-8R
Vandivert, Rita (Andre) 1905- CANR-6
Earlier sketch in CA 5-6R
See also SATA 21
Van Dommelen, David B. 1929- 5-6R
van Dooren, Ingrid 1949- 114
Van Dooren, L(eonard) A(lfred) T(heophile)
1912- CANR-19
Earlier sketches in CA 7-8R, CANR-3
Van Doren, Carl (Clinton) 1885-1950
Brief entry 111
See also TCLC 18
Van Doren, Charles L. 1926- CANR-4
Earlier sketch in CA 5-6R
Van Doren, Dorothy Graffe 1896- 4R
Van Doren, Irita 1891-1966 Obituary 89-92
Van Doren, Mark 1894-1972 .... CANR-3
Obituary 37-40R
Earlier sketch in CA 3R
See also DLB 45
See also CLC 6, 10
Van Dorne, R.
See Wallmann, Jeffrey M(iner)
Vandour, Cyril
See Surmelian, Leon (Zaven)
Van Druten, John (William) 1901-1957
Brief entry 104
See also DLB 10
See also TCLC 2
Van Dusen, Albert E(dward) 1916- CANR-3
Earlier sketch in CA 5-6R
Van Dusen, Clarence Raymond 1907- 5-6R
Van Dusen, Henry P(itney) 1897-1975 .. CANR-3
Obituary 57-60
Earlier sketch in CA 3R
Van Dusen, Robert LaBranche 1929- 41-44R
Van Duyn, Janet 1910- 69-72
See also SATA 18
Van Duyn, Mona 1921- CANR-7
Earlier sketch in CA 9-10R
See also DLB 5
See also CLC 3, 7
Van Duzee, Mabel 1895- 7-8R
Van Dyke, Carolynn 1947- 116
Van Dyke, Dick 1925- Brief entry 112
Van Dyke, Henry 1928- 49-52
See also DLB 33
Van Dyke, Jon M. 1943- 29-32R
Van Dyke, Lauren A. 1906- 29-32R
Van Dyke, Vernon Brumbaugh 1912- CANR-23
Earlier sketch in CA 3R
Van Dyne, Edith
See Baum, L(yman) Frank
Vane, Brett
See Kent, Arthur William Charles
Vane, Michael
See Humphries, Sydney Vernon
Vane, Roland
See McKeag, Ernest L(ionel)
Vane, (Vane Hunt) Sutton 1888-1963
Obituary 113
See also DLB 10
Van Eerde, Katherine S(ommerlatte)
1920- 61-64
Van Egmond, Peter (George) 1937- 61-64
Vanek, Jaroslav 1930- 103
Van Engen, John H. 1947- 117
Van Ermengem, Frederic 1881-1972
Obituary 33-36R
Van Ess, Dorothy 1885(?)-1975 Obituary .. 61-64
Van Ettinger, Jan 1902- CANR-21
Earlier sketch in CA 2R
Van Every, Dale 1896-1976 .... CANR-3
Earlier sketch in CA 3R
Vane-Wright, R(ichard) I(rwin) 1942- 121
Van Fossen, Richard W(aight) 1927- CANR-6
Earlier sketch in CA 7-8R
van Fraassen, Bastiaan Cornelis CANR-14
Earlier sketch in CA 37-40R
Van Geil, Mercury E. C. L.
See McGilvery, Laurence
van Gelder, Dora 1904- Brief entry 116
Van Gelder, Lindsy 1944- 97-100
Van Gelder, Richard George 1928- 73-76
Vangelisti, Paul 1945- CANR-14
Earlier sketch in CA 77-80
Vangen, Roland Dean 1935- 105
Vanger, Milton Isadore 1925- 15-16R
Van Goethem, Larry 1934- 101
van Gulik, Robert Hans 1910-1967 .... CANR-3
Obituary 25-28R
Earlier sketch in CA 4R
VanGundy, Arthur B(oice), Jr. 1946- 110
Van Haaften, Julia 1946- 109
Van Hassen, Amy
See Wiles, Domini
Van Hattum, Rolland J(ames) 1924- CANR-21
Earlier sketch in CA 105
Van Hecke, B(resee) C(oleman) 1926- 29-32R
Van Heijenoort, Jean 1912-1986 Obituary 120
Van Herik, Judith 1947- 108
van Herk, Aritha 1954- 101
van het Reve, Karel 1921- 49-52
van Heyningen, Christina 1900- 19-20R
van Heyningen, William Edward 1911- 112
Van Hise, Della 1955- 121
Van Hoesen, Walter H. 1898(?)-1977
Obituary 69-72
Van Hook, Roger Eugene 1943- 29-32R
Van Hoose, William H. 1927- 89-92
Van Horn, Richard L. 1932- 53-56
Van Horn, William 1939- 115
See also SATA 43
Van Horne, Harriet 1920- Brief entry 113
Van Houten, Lois 1918- 77-80
Van Huss, Wayne D(aniel) 1917- 61-64
van Inwagen, Peter (Jan) 1942- 116
van Itallie, Jean-Claude 1936- CANR-1
Earlier sketch in CA 45-48
See also CAAS 2
See also DLB 7
See also CLC 3
Van Itallie, Philip H. 1899- CAP-1
Earlier sketch in CA 9-10
Van Iterson, S(iny) R(ose) 102
See also SATA 26
van Jaarsveld, Floris Albertus 1922- CANR-7
Earlier sketch in CA 5-6R
van Kaam, Adrian (L.) 1920- CANR-10
Earlier sketch in CA 19-20R
Van Kleek, Peter Eric 1929- 53-56
Van Krevelen, Alice 1914- 45-48
van Lawick, Hugo 1937- 85-88
van Lawick-Goodall, Jane
See Goodall, Jane
Van Leeuwen, Jean 1937- CANR-11
Earlier sketch in CA 25-28R
See also SATA 6
Van Lente, Charles R(obert) 1941- 65-68
van Lhin, Erik
See del Rey, Lester
Van Lierde, John 1907- CAP-1
Earlier sketch in CA 9-10
Van Lierde, Peter Canisius
See Van Lierde, John
van Lint, June 1928- 65-68
van Loon, Gerard Willem 1911- 45-48
Van Loon, Hendrik Willem 1882-1944
Brief entry 117
See also SATA 18
Van Meerhaeghe, M(arcel) A(lfons) G(ilbert)
1921- CANR-13
Earlier sketch in CA 77-80
Van Melsen, Andreas G(erardus) M(aria)
1912- CANR-4
Earlier sketch in CA 3R
Vann, J(erry) Don 1938- 29-32R
Vann, James Allen 1939- 110
Vann, Richard T(ilman) 1931- 21-22R
Vann, Robert L. 1879-1940 .... DLB-29
Van Ness, Peter 1933- 29-32R
Van Niel, Cornelius B(ernardus)
1897-1985 Obituary 115
Vannier, Maryhelen 1915- CANR-22
Earlier sketches in CA 3R, CANR-6
van Nieuwenhuijze, C(hristoffel) A(nthonie)
O(livier) 1920- 25-28R
Van Nooten, Barend A(drian) 1932- 45-48
Van Noppen, Ina (Faye) W(oestemeyer)
1906-1980 .... 5-6R
Obituary 103
Vannorsdall, John Warren 1924- 113
Van Nostrand, A(lbert) D(ouglass)
1922- CANR-16
Earlier sketch in CA 41-44R
Vannoy, Russell (Columbus) 1933- 119
Vano, Gerard S. 1943- 112
Vanocur, Edith C. 1924(?)-1975 Obituary .. 57-60
Vanocur, Sander 1928- 120
Brief entry 109
van Oort, Jan 1921- 29-32R
Van Orden, M(erton) D(ick) 1921- 37-40R
See also SATA 4
Van Orman, Bonny 1939(?)-1987
Obituary 122
Van Orman, Richard A(lbert) 1936- 21-22R
Van Osdol, William R(ay) 1927- 53-56
Van Over, Raymond 1934- Brief entry 112
van Overbeek, Johannes 1908- CAP-1
Earlier sketch in CA 13-14
Van Peebles, Melvin 1932- 85-88
See also CLC 2, 20
van Peursen, Cornelius Anthonie 1920- 53-56
Van Praagh, Margaret 1910- CAP-2
Earlier sketch in CA 17-18
Van Praagh, Peggy
See Van Praagh, Margaret
Van Proosdy, Cornelis 1919- CANR-5
Earlier sketch in CA 11-12R
van Ravenswaay, Charles 1911- 119
Van Rensselaer, Alexander (Taylor Mason)
1892-1962 73-76
See also SATA 14
Van Rensselaer, Mariana Griswold
1851-1934 .... DLB-47
Van Rensselaer, Mrs. Schuyler
See Van Rensselaer, Mariana Griswold
Van Rheenen, Gailyn 1946- 69-72
van Rijn, Ignatius
See Ingram, Forrest L(eo)
Van Riper, Francis A(lbert) 1946- CANR-11
Earlier sketch in CA 69-72
Van Riper, Frank
See Van Riper, Francis A(lbert)
Van Riper, Guernsey, Jr. 1909- CANR-6
Earlier sketch in CA 7-8R
See also SATA 3
Van Riper, Paul P(ritchard) 1916- 4R
Van Riper, Robert 1921- 37-40R
van Rjndt, Philippe 1950- CANR-14
Earlier sketch in CA 65-68
van Rooy, C(harles) A(ugust) 1923- 19-20R
Van Saher, Lilla 1912-1968 .... CAP-1
Earlier sketch in CA 11-12
Vansant, Carl 1938- 37-40R
Van Schaick, Frances L. 1912(?)-1979
Obituary 89-92
Van Scyoc, Sydney J(oyce) 1939- CANR-15
Earlier sketch in CA 89-92
Van Sertima, Ivan 1935- 104
Van Seters, John 1935- 115
Van Sickle, John V(alentine) 1892- 5-6R
Van Sickle, Neil D(avid) 1915- 41-44R

VanSickle, V. A.
See Carhart, Arthur Hawthorne
Vansina, Jan 1929- CANR-10
Earlier sketch in CA 65-68
Vansittart, Jane
See Moorhouse, Hilda Vansittart
Vansittart, Peter 1920- CANR-3
Earlier sketch in CA 1R
See also CLC 42
Van Slingerland, Peter 1929- 21-22R
Van Slooten, Henry 1916- 3R
Van Slyck, Philip 1920- 13-14R
Van Slyke, Donald Dexter 1883-1971
Obituary 104
Van Slyke, Helen (Lenore) 1919-1979 37-40R
Obituary 89-92
Van Slyke, Lyman P(age) 1929- 23-24R
Van Smith, Howard
See Smith, Howard Van
van Someren, Liesje
See Lichtenberg, Elisabeth Jacoba
Van Steenwyk, Elizabeth (Ann) 1928- CANR-18
Earlier sketch in CA 101
See also SATA 34
Van Stockum, Hilda 1908- CANR-5
Earlier sketch in CA 11-12R
See also SATA 5
van Straten, Florence W(ilhelmina)
1913- 19-20R
Van Tassel, Alfred J. 1910- 41-44R
Van Tassel, David Dirck 1928- 103
Van Tassel, Dennie L(ee) 1939- CANR-8
Earlier sketch in CA 57-60
Van Tassel, George W. 1910-1978
Obituary 112
Van Tassel, Roger (Carleton) 1924- 45-48
van Thal, Herbert (Maurice) 1904-1983 65-68
Obituary 111
Van Til, Cornelius 1895- CANR-3
Earlier sketch in CA 3R
Van Til, William 1911- CANR-10
Earlier sketch in CA 25-28R
Van Tine, Warren R(ussell) 1942- 53-56
Van Trump, James D(enholm) 1908- 41-44R
Van Tuyl, Barbara 1940- 53-56
See also SATA 11
Van Valkenburg, Samuel 1891-1976 5-6R
Obituary 103
Van Valkenburgh, Paul 1941- 89-92
Van Vechten, Benjamin D(avenport) 1935- 110
Van Vechten, Carl 1880-1964 Obituary 89-92
See also DLB 4, 9, 51
See also CLC 33
Van Vleck, David B. 1929- 101
Van Vleck, John Hasbrouck 1899-1980
Obituary 102
Van Vleck, L(loyd) Dale 1933- 53-56
Van Vleck, Sarita 1933- 13-14R
Van Vlissingen, Arthur 1894-1986
Obituary 120
Van Vogt, A(lfred) E(lton) 1912- 23-24R
See also SATA 14
See also DLB 8
See also CLC 1
Van Vooren, Monique 1933- 107
Van Voris, Jacqueline 1922- 57-60
van Vuuren, Nancy 1938- 49-52
Van Wagenen, Gertrude 1893-1978
Obituary 77-80
van Wageningen, J.
See Presser, (Gerrit) Jacob
Van Waters, Miriam 1887-1974 Obituary 45-48
Van Weddingen, Marthe 1924- CANR-14
Earlier sketch in CA 81-84
Van Wert, William F(rancis) 1945- 105
van Witsen, Leo 1912- 106
Van Woeart, Alpheus
See Halloway, Vance
Van Woerkom, Dorothy (O'Brien)
1924- CANR-11
Earlier sketch in CA 57-60
See also SATA 21
Van Wormer, Joe
See Van Wormer, Joseph Edward
Van Wormer, Joseph Edward 1913- CANR-5
Earlier sketch in CA 9-10R
See also SATA 35
Van Young, Eric (Julian) 1946- 122
Van Zandt, E. F.
See Cudlipp, Edythe
Van Zandt, Roland 1918- 19-20R
Van Zante, Helen Johnson 1906- 13-14R
Van Zanten, John W(illiam) 1913- 101
van Zeller, Claud 1905-1984 CANR-6
Obituary 113
Earlier sketch in CA 4R
van Zeller, Hubert
See van Zeller, Claud
Vanzi, Max (Bruno) 1934- 123
Van Zwienen, Ilse Charlotte Koehn 1929- 85-88
See also SATA 28, 34
van Zwoll, James A. 1909- CAP-1
Earlier sketch in CA 13-14
Vaqar, Nasrollah 1920- 41-44R
Vara, Albert C. 1931- 33-36R
Varah, Chad 1911- 57-60
Varandyan, Emmanuel P(aul) 1904- 65-68
Varas, Florencia
See Olea, Maria Florencia Varas
Varda, Agnes 1928- 122
Brief entry 116
See also CLC 16
Vardaman, E. Jerry 1927- 17-18R
Vardaman, George T(ruett) 1920- CANR-4
Earlier sketch in CA 3R
Vardaman, James M(oney) 1921- 104
Vardaman, Patricia B(lack) 1931- 37-40R
Vardamis, Alex A. 1934- 77-80
Vardre, Leslie
See Davies, L(eslie) P(urnell)
Vardy, Steven Bela 1936- CANR-19
Earlier sketches in CA 53-56, CANR-4
Vardys, V(ytautas) Stanley 1924- CANR-5
Earlier sketch in CA 15-16R
Vare, Daniele 1880-1956 Brief entry 119
Vare, Robert 1945- 103
Varenhorst, Barbara B(raden) 1928- 116
Varese, Louise 1890- 41-44R
Varg, Paul A(lbert) 1912- 118
Brief entry 113
Varga, Andrew Charles 1917- 113
Varga, Judy
See Stang, Judit
Vargas, Julie S. 1938- 57-60
Vargas Llosa, (Jorge) Mario (Pedro)
1936- CANR-18
Earlier sketch in CA 73-76
See also CLC 3, 6, 9, 10, 15, 31, 42
Vargish, Thomas 1939- CANR-14
Earlier sketch in CA 37-40R
Varlay, Rene G. 1927- 4R
Varley, Dimitry V. 1906- CAP-1
Earlier sketch in CA 17-18
See also SATA 10
Varley, Gloria 1932- 101
Varley, H(erbert) Paul 1931- 77-80
Varley, John (Herbert) 1947- 69-72
See also DLBY 81
Varley, John Philip
See Mitchell, Langdon (Elwyn)
Varma, Baidya Nath 1921- 41-44R
Varma, Devendra P. 1923- Brief entry 113
Varma, Monika 1916- 77-80
Varnac, d'Hugues
See Prevost, Alain
Varnado, Jewel Goodgame 1915- 9-10R
Varnalis, Costas 1884-1974 Obituary 53-56
Varner, John Grier 1905-1978 25-28R
Obituary 120
Varner, Velma V. 1916-1972 Obituary 37-40R
Varney, Carleton B(ates) 1937- CANR-16
Earlier sketch in CA 89-92
Vars, Gordon F(orrest) 1923- 23-24R
Vartan, Vartanig Garabed 1923- 61-64
Vartanian, Aram 1922- CANR-3
Earlier sketch in CA 3R
Vasconcelos (Calderon), Jose 1882-1959
Brief entry 118
Vas Dias, Robert (Leonard Michael)
1931- CANR-7
Earlier sketch in CA 19-20R
Vasey, Lloyd Roland 113
Vash, Carolyn L(ee) 1934- 121
Vash, Carolyn Lee 1934- Brief entry 116
Vasil, R(aj) K(umar) 1931- CANR-14
Earlier sketch in CA 37-40R
Vasiliu, Gheorghe 1881-1957 Brief entry 123
Vasiliu, Mircea 1920- 23-24R
See also SATA 2
Vaske, Martin O. 1915- CANR-2
Earlier sketch in CA 7-8R
Vasquez, John A(nthony) 1945- 108
Vass, George 1927- 37-40R
See also SATA 31
Vass, Winifred Kellersberger 1917- 57-60
Vassa, Gustavus
See Equiano, Olaudah
Vassi, Marco 1937- CANR-13
Earlier sketch in CA 61-64
Vassilikos, Vassilis 1933- 81-84
See also CLC 4, 8
Vassiliou, Yannis 1949- 117
Vasta, Edward 1928- 17-18R
Vasu, Nirmala-Kumara
See Bose, N(irmal) K(umar)
Vasvary, Edmund 1888-1977 Obituary 73-76
Vatikiotis, P(anayiotis) J(erasimos)
1928- CANR-6
Earlier sketch in CA 13-14R
Vatter, Harold Goodhue 1910- 5-6R
Vaudrin, Bill
See Vaudrin, William
Vaudrin, William 1943-1976 CAP-2
Earlier sketch in CA 29-32
Vaughan, Adrian 1941- 120
Vaughan, Agnes Carr 1887- CAP-1
Earlier sketch in CA 9-10
Vaughan, Alan 1936- 81-84
Vaughan, Alden T. 1929- CANR-7
Earlier sketch in CA 17-18R
Vaughan, Beatrice 1909(?)-1972
Obituary 37-40R
Vaughan, Bill
See Vaughan, William E(dward)
Vaughan, Carter A.
See Gerson, Noel Bertram
Vaughan, Clark (Alvord) 1924- 108
Vaughan, David 1924- 77-80
Vaughan, Denis 1920- 61-64
Vaughan, Donald S(hores) 1921- CANR-10
Earlier sketch in CA 17-18R
Vaughan, Frances E. 1935- Brief entry 107
Vaughan, Frederick 1935- 120
Vaughan, Harold Cecil 1923- 29-32R
See also SATA 14
Vaughan, Hilda
See Morgan, Hilda Campbell
Vaughan, James A(gnew) 1936- 49-52
Vaughan, John Edmund 1935- 61-64
Vaughan, Leo
See Lendon, Kenneth Harry
Vaughan, Paul 1925- 29-32R
Vaughan, Richard
See Thomas, Ernest Lewys
Vaughan, Richard Patrick 1919- 15-16R
Vaughan, Robert (Richard) 1937- 103
Vaughan, Roger 1937- 85-88
Vaughan, Sam(uel) 1928- 13-14R
See also SATA 14
Vaughan, Sheila Marie 1930- 23-24R
Vaughan, Virginia M(ason) 1947- 110
Vaughan, William E(dward) 1915-1977 5-6R
Obituary 69-72
Vaughan Williams, Ralph 1872-1958
Brief entry 115
Vaughan Williams, Ursula Wood
1911- CANR-24
Earlier sketches in CA 9-10R, CANR-6
Vaughn, Charles L(e Claire) 1911- 41-44R
Vaughn, Donald E(arl) 1932- 21-22R
Vaughn, Jack A(lfred) 1935- 85-88
Vaughn, Jesse Wendell 1903-1968 3R
Obituary 103
Vaughn, Lewis 1950- 111
Vaughn, Michael J(effery) 1943- 37-40R
Vaughn, Richard C(lements) 1925- CANR-9
Earlier sketch in CA 21-22R
Vaughn, Robert (Francis) 1932- 61-64
Vaughn, Ruth 1935- CANR-15
Earlier sketch in CA 41-44R
See also SATA 14
Vaughn, Sister Ann Carol 1922- 11-12R
Vaughn, Stephen L. 1947- 101
Vaughn, Toni
See Du Breuil, (Elizabeth) L(or)inda
Vaughn, William Preston 1933- 73-76
Vaupel, James W(alton) 1945- 111
Vaurie, Charles 1906-1975 CANR-4
Earlier sketch in CA 7-8R
Vaussard, Maurice (Rene Jean Arthur
Andre) 1888- 9-10R
Vautier, Ghislaine 1932- 112
Vavra, Robert James 1935- 25-28R
See also SATA 8
Vawter, F(rancis) Bruce 1921- CANR-4
Earlier sketch in CA 3R
Vayda, Andrew P. 1931- 19-20R
Vayhinger, John Monroe 1916- 73-76
Vayle, Valerie
See Brooks, Janice Young
Vaz, Edmund (Winston) 1924- 108
Vazakas, Byron 1905- CAP-2
Earlier sketch in CA 25-28
Vazov, Ivan (Minchov) 1850-1921
Brief entry 121
See also TCLC 25
Veach, William B. Templeton 1896- CAP-1
Earlier sketch in CA 9-10
Veaner, Allen B(arnet) 1929- 41-44R
Veatch, Henry Babcock 1911- CANR-6
Earlier sketch in CA 5-6R
Veatch, Robert M(arlin) 1939- CANR-11
Earlier sketch in CA 69-72
Veblen, Thorstein (Bunde) 1857-1929
Brief entry 115
Vecoli, Rudolph J(ohn) 1927- CANR-10
Earlier sketch in CA 19-20R
Vecsey, George S. 1909(?)-1984 Obituary 114
Vecsey, George Spencer 1939- CANR-10
Earlier sketch in CA 61-64
See also SATA 9
Vedder, James S(herman) 1912- 117
Vedder, John K.
See Gruber, Frank
Vedder, Richard K(ent) 1940- 115
Vedeler, Harold C. 1903- 122
Veder, Bob 1940- 104
Vedral, Joyce L(auretta) 1943- 117
Veeck, Bill
See Veeck, William Louis, Jr.
Veeck, William Louis, Jr. 1914-1986
Obituary 118
Veedam, Voldemar 1912-1983 Obituary 109
Veenendaal, Cornelia 1924- 117
Vega, Janine Pommy 1942- CANR-2
Earlier sketch in CA 49-52
See also DLB 16
Veglahn, Nancy (Crary) 1937- CANR-7
Earlier sketch in CA 19-20R
See also SATA 5
Veiga, Jose J(acinto da) 1915- CANR-15
Earlier sketch in CA 37-40R
Veiller, Anthony 1903-1965 DLB-44
Veillon, Lee 1942- 49-52
Veit, Fritz 1907- 111
Veit, Lawrence A. 1938- Brief entry 115
Veit, Stan(ley Stanford) 1929- 110
Vekemans, Roger 1921- 37-40R
Velasquez, Manuel G(onzales) 1942- 113
Veler, Richard P(aul) 1936- 49-52
Velez-Ibanez, Carlos G(uillermo) 1936- 118
Velie, Alan R. 1937- CANR-1
Earlier sketch in CA 45-48
Velie, Lester 1908- CAP-2
Earlier sketch in CA 17-18
Velikovsky, Immanuel 1895-1979 CANR-15
Obituary 89-92
Earlier sketch in CA 69-72
Veliz, Claudio 1930- 25-28R
Vella, Walter F(rancis) 1924- CANR-24
Earlier sketch in CA 45-48
Vellela, Tony 1945- 65-68
Velleman, Ruth A(nn) 1921- 110
Velthuijs, Max 1923- 89-92
Veltman, Vera
See Panova, Vera (Fedorovna)
Velvel, Lawrence R. 1939- 29-32R
Venable, Alan (Hudson) 1944- 45-48
See also SATA 8
Venable, Tom C(alvin) 1921- 29-32R
Venable, Vernon 1906- CAP-2
Earlier sketch in CA 21-22
Venafro, Mark
See Pizzat, Frank J(oseph)
Vendler, Helen (Hennessy) 1933- 41-44R
Vendler, Zeno 1921- Brief entry 105
Vendrovskii, David Efimovich 1879-1971
Obituary 33-36R
Vendrovsky, David
See Vendrovskii, David Efimovich
Veness, Molly 1900(?)-1985 Obituary 118
Veness, (Winifred) Thelma 1919-1971 5-6R
Obituary 122
Vengroff, Richard 1945- CANR-10
Earlier sketch in CA 65-68
Venison, Alfred
See Pound, Ezra (Loomis)
Veniste, Richard Ben
See Ben-Veniste, Richard
Venn, Grant 1919-1979 15-16R
Obituary 122
Vennard, Edwin 1902- CAP-2
Earlier sketch in CA 25-28
Vennema, Alje 1932- 101
Venner, J. G.
See Lewis, John (Noel Claude)
Venning, Corey 1924- 49-52
Venning, Hugh
See van Zeller, Claud
Venning, Michael
See Randolph, Georgiana Ann
Venter, Al(bertus) J(ohannes) 1938- 117
Venton, W. B. 1898-1976 CAP-2
Earlier sketch in CA 25-28
Ventura, Jeffrey
See Feinman, Jeffrey
Ventura, Piero Luigi 1937- 103
See also SATA 43
Venturi, Denise Scott Brown
See Brown, Denise Scott
Venturi, Marcello 1925- CANR-13
Earlier sketch in CA 29-32R
Venturi, Robert 1925- 61-64
Venuti, Lawrence (Michael) 1953- 120
Vequin, Capini
See Quinn, Elisabeth
Verba, Sidney 1932- CANR-3
Earlier sketch in CA 3R
Vercors
See Bruller, Jean (Marcel)
Vercors, J. Bruller
See Bruller, Jean (Marcel)
Verdenius, W(illem) J(acob) 1913- 25-28R
Verdery, John D(uane) 1917- 11-12R
Verdick, Mary (Peyton) 1923- CANR-4
Earlier sketch in CA 3R
Verdon, Dorothy
See Tralins, S(andor) Robert
Verdu, Matilde
See Cela, Camilo Jose
Verduin, John R(ichard), Jr. 1931- CANR-24
Earlier sketches in CA 23-24R, CANR-9
Verduin, Leonard 1897- 61-64
Verene, Donald Phillip 1937- CANR-15
Earlier sketch in CA 41-44R
Verey, David (Cecil Wynter)
1913-1984 CANR-15
Obituary 113
Earlier sketch in CA 65-68
Verga, Giovanni (Carmelo) 1840-1922 123
Brief entry 104
See also TCLC 3
Vergani, Luisa 1931- 23-24R
Vergara, Jose Manuel 1929- 97-100
Vergara, Joseph R. 1915- 29-32R
Vergara, Lisa 1948- 120
Vergara, William C(harles) 1923- 3R
Verghese, T. Paul
See Gregorios, Paulos Mar
Verhaeren, Emile (Adolphe Gustave)
1855-1916 Brief entry 109
See also TCLC 12
Verhalen, Philip A(ndrew) 1934- 69-72
Verhoeven, Cornelis 1928- CANR-23
Earlier sketches in CA 61-64, CANR-8
Verhoeven, Paul 1901-1975 Obituary 115
Verhonick, Phillis J. 1922(?)-1977
Obituary 73-76
Verhoogen, John 1912- 109
Verin, Velko
See Inkiow, (Janakiev) Dimiter
Verissimo, Erico (Lopes) 1905-1975
Obituary 115
Vermes, Geza 1924- 57-60
Vermes, Jean C(ampbell Pattison) 1907- 106
Vermes, Pamela 1918- 118
Vermeule, Cornelius Clarkson III 1925- 41-44R
Vermeule, E(mily) D. T. 1928- 17-18R
Vermillion, Robert 1915(?)-1987 Obituary 122
Vernadsky, George 1887-1973 Obituary 41-44R
Vernam, Glenn R. 1896-1980 CANR-10
Earlier sketch in CA 19-20R
Vernant, Jean-Pierre 1914- 109
Vernazza, Marcelle Wynn 1909- CANR-10
Earlier sketch in CA 19-20R
Verne, Jules 1828-1905 Brief entry 110
See also SATA 21
See also TCLC 6
Verner, Coolie 1917-1979 CANR-7
Earlier sketch in CA 53-56
Verner, Gerald 1897(?)-1980 Obituary 102
See also SATA 25
Verney, Douglas Vernon 1924- 13-14R
Verney, John 1913- 65-68
See also SATA 14
Verney, Michael P(almer) 1923- CANR-6
Earlier sketch in CA 13-14R

Verney, Peter (Vivian Lloyd) 1930- CANR-19
Earlier sketch in CA 81-84
Verney, Sarah
See Holloway, Brenda W(ilmar)
Verney, Stephen Edmund 1919- 104
Vernon, Eddie
See Stone, Hoyt E(dward)
Vernon, Edward
See Coleman, Vernon
Vernon, Frances 1963- 110
Vernon, Glenn M(orley) 1920- 49-52
Vernon, John 1943- 41-44R
Vernon, Judy 1945- 119
Vernon, Lee M.
See von Block, Bela W(illiam)
Vernon, Lorraine 1921- 113
Vernon, (Elda) Louise A(nderson) 1914- 53-56
See also SATA 14
Vernon, McCay 1928- 41-44R
Vernon, Philip Ewart 1905- CANR-12
Earlier sketch in CA 5-6R
Vernon, Raymond 1913- CANR-18
Earlier sketches in CA 5-6R, CANR-2
Vernon, Rosemary
See Smith, Susan Vernon
Vernon, Thomas Bowater 1939- 118
Vernon, Thomas S. 1914- 25-28R
Vernon, Tom
See Vernon, Thomas Bowater
Vernon, Walter N(ewton), Jr. 1907- CANR-12
Earlier sketch in CA 17-18R
Vernon-Jackson, Hugh (Owen Hardinge)
1925- 21-22R
Vernor, D.
See Casewit, Curtis W(erner)
Verny, Tom 1936- 73-76
Veronica, Sister Mary 1924- 19-20R
Verplanck, Gulian C. 1786-1870 .... DLB-59
Verral, Charles Spain 1904- CANR-16
Earlier sketches in CA 9-10, CAP-1
See also SATA 11
Verrette, Joyce
See Petratur, Joyce
Verrill, A(lpheus) Hyatt 1871-1954
Brief entry 111
Verrone, Robert J. 1935(?)-1984 Obituary 113
See also SATA 39
Versace, Marie Teresa Rios 1917- 19-20R
See also SATA 2
Ver Steeg, Clarence L(ester) 1922- 15-16R
Versteeg, Robert John 1930- 3R
Verval, Alain
See Lande, Lawrence (Montague)
Verwilghen, A(lbert-) Felix 1916- 25-28R
Verwoerdt, Adriaan 1927- 19-20R
Very, Alice (N.) 1894-1977 .... 21-22R
Obituary 120
Very, Jones 1813-1880 .... DLB-1
Veryan, Patricia
See Bannister, Patricia V.
Vesaas, Tarjei 1897-1970 Obituary 29-32R
Vesely, Erik 1905(?)-1970 Obituary 57-60
Vesenyi, Paul E. 1911- 53-56
Vesey, Godfrey (Norman Agmondisham)
1923- 89-92
Vesey, Paul
See Allen, Samuel
Vesey-FitzGerald, Brian Seymour
1900-1981 104
Obituary 105
Vesper, Karl H(ampton) 1932- 115
Vess, David M(arshall) 1925- 89-92
Vessel, Matthew F. 1912- Brief entry 108
Vesselo, I(saac) Reginald 1903- CAP-2
Earlier sketch in CA 17-18
Vestal, David 1924- 89-92
Vestal, Edith Ballard 1884-1970 .... CAP-2
Earlier sketch in CA 25-28
Vestdijk, Simon 1898-1971 Obituary 89-92
Vester, Frederic 1925- 120
Vester, Horatio 1906-1985 .... CAP-1
Obituary 117
Earlier sketch in CA 13-14
Vesterman, William 1942- 89-92
Vestly, Anne-Cath(arina) 1920- CANR-18
Earlier sketch in CA 85-88
See also SATA 14
Vet, T. V.
See Straiton, E(dward) C(ornock)
Vetere, Richard 1952- 104
Vetoe, Miklos 1936- 49-52
Vetter, Carole 1939- 25-28R
Vetter, Harold J. 1926- 29-32R
Vetterling-Braggin, Mary (Katherine) 1947- 124
Veverka, Frank B. 1923(?)-1985 Obituary 117
Vevers, (Henry) Gwynne 1916- 113
See also SATA 45
Vexillum
See Banner, Hubert Stewart
Veysey, Laurence R(uss) 1932- 21-22R
Vezhinov, Pavel
See Gouaov, Nikola Delchev
Vial, Fernand (Louis) 1905- CANR-21
Earlier sketch in CA 3R
Vialis, Gaston
See Simenon, Georges (Jacques Christian)
Vian, Boris 1920-1959 Brief entry 106
See also TCLC 9
Viano, Emilio C. 1942- 107
Viansson-Ponte, Pierre 1920-1979 101
Obituary 85-88
Viator, Vacuus
See Hughes, Thomas
Viaud, (Louis Marie) Julien 1850-1923
Brief entry 107
Vicar, Henry
See Felsen, Henry Gregor
Vicarion, Count Palmiro
See Logue, Christopher
Vicary, Dorothy
See Rice, Dorothy Mary
Vichas, Robert P. 1933- CANR-14
Earlier sketch in CA 29-32R
Vicker, Angus
See Felsen, Henry Gregor
Vicker, Ray 1917- 61-64
Vickers
See Kaufman, Wallace
Vickers, Antoinette L. 1942- 103
Vickers, Douglas 1924- CANR-11
Earlier sketch in CA 13-14R
Vickers, (Charles) Geoffrey 1894-1982 .... 41-44R
Obituary 106
Vickers, Hugo (Ralph) 1951- Brief entry 124
Vickers, John 1916- 9-10R
Vickery, Donald M(ichael) 1944- 101
Vickery, Florence E. 1906- 37-40R
Vickery, John B. 1925- 57-60
Vickery, Kate
See Kennedy, T(eresa) A.
Vickery, Olga W(estland) 1925-1970 .... CANR-3
Earlier sketch in CA 1R
Vickery, Robert L. (Jr.) 1932- 49-52
Vickery, Tom Rusk 1935- 53-56
Vickrey, William (Spencer) 1914- 41-44R
Victor, Charles B.
See Puechner, Ray
Victor, Edward 1914- CANR-3
Earlier sketch in CA 4R
See also SATA 3
Victor, Joan Berg 1942- 105
See also SATA 30
Victor, Sam
See Hershman, Morris
Victoria 1819-1901 .... DLB-55
Vida, Nina 1933- 117
Vidal, Gore 1925- CANR-13
Earlier sketch in CA 7-8R
See also DLB 6
See also CLC 2, 4, 6, 8, 10, 22, 33
See also AITN 1
Vidal, Nicole 1928- 25-28R
Vidaver, Doris 108
Vidger, Leonard P(erry) 1920- CANR-5
Earlier sketch in CA 9-10R
Vidich, Arthur J. 1922- 115
Vidler, Alec R.
See Vidler, Alexander Roper
Vidler, Alexander Roper 1899- CANR-5
Earlier sketch in CA 5-6R
Vidler, Virginia (Ellen) 1928-1986 69-72
Obituary 121
Vidor, King (Wallis) 1894(?)-1982
Obituary 108
Viebig, Clara 1860-1952 .... DLB-66
Vieg, John A.
See Vieg, John Albert
Vieg, John Albert 1904-1988 .... 3R
Obituary 124
Vier, Gene 1926- 105
Viereck, Ellen K. 1928- 53-56
See also SATA 14
Viereck, George Sylvester 1884-1962
Obituary 116
See also DLB 54
Viereck, Peter (Robert Edwin) 1916- CANR-1
Earlier sketch in CA 3R
See also DLB 5
See also CLC 4
Viereck, Phillip 1925- CANR-8
Earlier sketch in CA 7-8R
See also SATA 3
Viertel, Janet 1915- 53-56
See also SATA 10
Viertel, Joseph 1915- 15-16R
Viertel, Peter 1920- 15-16R
Viessman, Warren, Jr. 1930- 53-56
Vieth, David M(uench) 1925- 5-6R
Vieth von Golssenau, Arnold Friedrich
1889-1979 89-92
Vietor, John A(dolf) 1914-1982 Obituary 108
Viets, Wallace T(rowbridge) 1919- 17-18R
Vig, Norman Joseph 1939- 25-28R
Vigeland, Carl A. 1947- 122
Vigeveno, H(enk) S. 1925- 108
Vigfusson, Robin 1949- 106
Viggiani
See Viggiani, Guy
Viggiani, Guy 1932- 123
Vigil, Lawrence
See Finnin, (Olive) Mary
Vigliante, Mary
See Szydlowski, Mary Vigliante
Viglini, Janelle (Therese) 1933- 57-60
Vigna, Judith 1936- CANR-13
Earlier sketch in CA 77-80
See also SATA 15
Vigneault, Gilles 1928- DLB-60
Vigneras, Louis-Andre 1903- 65-68
Vigness, David M(artell) 1922- 15-16R
Vigness, Paul G. 1894- 41-44R
Vignone, Joseph A. 1939- 37-40R
Viguers, Ruth Hill 1903-1971 .... CAP-1
Obituary 29-32R
Earlier sketch in CA 15-16
See also SATA 6
Vikis-Freibergs, Vaira 1937- 53-56
Viksnins, George J(uris) 1937- 105
Viktoria Luise 1892-1980 Obituary 102
Vila, Bob
See Vila, Robert
Vila, Robert 1946- 106
Vilar, Esther 1935- CANR-8
Earlier sketch in CA 49-52
Vildrac, Charles
See Messager, Charles
Viljoen, Helen Gill 1899-1974 45-48
Obituary 103
Vilkitis, James R(ichard) 1941- 61-64
Villa, Jose Garcia 1914- CANR-12
Earlier sketch in CA 25-28R
Villa, Susie Hoogasian
See Hoogasian-Villa, Susie
Villada, Gene Harold Bell
See Bell-Villada, Gene Harold
Villa-Gilbert, Mariana 1937- 29-32R
Villanueva, Tino 1941- CANR-1
Earlier sketch in CA 45-48
Villard, Henry 1835-1900 .... DLB-23
Villard, Henry Hilgard 1911-1983 Obituary 111
Villard, Henry S(errano) 1900- 17-18R
Villard, Oswald Garrison 1872-1949
Brief entry 113
See also DLB 25
Villarejo, Mary (Holan) 1915- 11-12R
Villarejo, Oscar M(ilton) 1909- 19-20R
Villars, Elizabeth
See Feldman, Ellen (Bette)
Villas Boas, Claudio 1916- Brief entry 117
Villas Boas, Orlando 1914- Brief entry 117
Villasenor, David V. 1913- 13-14R
Villasenor, Victor Edmund 1940- 45-48
Villegas, Daniel Cosio 1898-1976
Obituary 65-68
Villemaire, Yolande 1949- DLB-60
Villere, Sidney Louis 1900- 69-72
Villers, Raymond 1911- CAP-2
Earlier sketch in CA 25-28
Villers, Robert 1921-1980 Obituary 93-96
Villet, Barbara 1931- 85-88
Villiard, Paul 1910-1974 .... CANR-10
Obituary 53-56
Earlier sketches in CA 25-28, CAP-2
See also SATA 20
Villiers, Alan (John) 1903- CANR-1
Earlier sketch in CA 4R
See also SATA 10
Villiers, Guy
See Goulding, Peter Geoffrey
Villiers, Marjorie 1903-1982 Obituary 107
Villoldo, Alberto Pedro 1949- 108
Vilmorin, Louise Leveque de 1902-1969
Obituary 104
Vilnay, Zev 1900-1988 Obituary 124
Vinacke, W(illiam) Edgar 1917- 5-6R
Vinal, Harold 1891-1965 Obituary 89-92
Vinaver, Eugene 1899- 13-14R
Vincent, Adrian 1917- 2R
Vincent, Charles 1945- 65-68
Vincent, Claire
See Allen, Charlotte Vale
Vincent, Clark E(dward) 1923- CANR-2
Earlier sketch in CA 4R
Vincent, E. Lee
See Vincent, Elizabeth Lee
Vincent, Elizabeth Lee 1897- CAP-2
Earlier sketch in CA 19-20
Vincent, Eric Douglas 1953- SATA-40
Vincent, Felix 1946- 118
See also SATA 41
Vincent, Gabrielle CLR-13
Vincent, Howard Paton 1904- 65-68
Vincent, Jack 1904- 29-32R
Vincent, Jack E(rnest) 1932- CANR-19
Earlier sketch in CA 102
Vincent, Joan 1920- 21-22R
Vincent, John Carter 1900-1972
Obituary 37-40R
Vincent, John J(ames) 1929- CANR-10
Earlier sketch in CA 57-60
Vincent, John R(ussell) 1937- 120
Vincent, Leona
See Vincent, Elizabeth Lee
Vincent, Mary Keith
See St. John, Wylly Folk
Vincent, Peter 1944- 37-40R
Vincent, R(aymond) J(ohn) 1943- 77-80
Vincent, Theodore G. 1936- CANR-13
Earlier sketch in CA 77-80
Vincent, William R.
See Heitzmann, William Ray
Vincent, William S(hafer) 1907- 41-44R
Vinciguerra, Mario 1887-1973 Obituary 104
Vincitorio, Gaetano L(eonard) 1921- 89-92
Vine, Louis L(loyd) 1922- CANR-3
Earlier sketch in CA 3R
Vine, Paul Ashley Laurence 1927- 23-24R
Vine, Sarah
See Rowland, D(onald) S(ydney)
Vineberg, Arthur 1903- 104
Vineberg, Ethel (Shane) 1902- 85-88
Vinegar, Tom
See Gregg, Andrew K.
Viner, George 1913(?)-1983 Obituary 109
Viner, Jacob 1892-1970 Obituary 104
Vines, Alice Gilmore 1923- 81-84
Vines, (Henry) Ellsworth (Jr.) 1911-
Brief entry 109
Vinest, Shaw
See Longyear, Barry Brookes
Viney, Wayne 1932- 103
Vineyard, Edwin Earle 1926- 5-6R
Vinge, Joan D(ennison) 1948- 93-96
See also SATA 36
See also CLC 30
Vinge, Vernor (Steffen) 1944- 101
Vining, Elizabeth Gray 1902- CANR-7
Earlier sketch in CA 7-8R
See also SATA 6
Vinogradov, Ivan M(atveyevich)
1891-1983 Obituary 109
Vinokur, Grigory
See Weinrauch, Herschel
Vinokurov, Yevgeny Mikhailovich 1925-
Brief entry 116
Vinson, Elaine
See Rowland, D(onald) S(ydney)
Vinson, J(ohn) Chal(mers) 1919- 11-12R
Vinson, J(ohn) William 1916-1979
Obituary 89-92
Vinson, James (Albert) 1933- 120
Brief entry 118
Vinson, Jane 1927- 77-80
Vinson, Kathryn 1911- 5-6R
See also SATA 21
Vinson, Rex Thomas 1935- 101
Vinton, Bobby
See Vinton, Stanley Robert, Jr.
Vinton, Eleanor W(inthrop) 1899-1977 61-64
Obituary 73-76
Vinton, Iris 1906(?)-1988 77-80
Obituary 124
See also SATA 24
Vinton, John 1937- 73-76
Vinton, Stanley Robert, Jr. 1935(?)-
Brief entry 120
Vinyard, C. Dale 1932- 25-28R
Vinz, Mark 1942- 93-96
Viola, Herman J(oseph) 1938- CANR-23
Earlier sketches in CA 61-64, CANR-8
Violett, Ellen 1925- 73-76
Violi, Paul 1944- CANR-24
Earlier sketch in CA 45-48
Violis, G.
See Simenon, Georges (Jacques Christian)
Viorst, Judith CANR-2
Earlier sketch in CA 49-52
See also SATA 7
See also DLB 52
See also CLR 3
Viorst, Milton 1930- 9-10R
Vip
See Partch, Virgil Franklin II
Vipond, Don (Harry) 1932- 65-68
Vipont, Charles
See Foulds, Elfrida Vipont
Vipont, Elfrida
See Foulds, Elfrida Vipont
Virga, Vincent 1942- 107
Virgines, George E. 1920- CANR-12
Earlier sketch in CA 25-28R
Virginius
See Connett, Eugene Virginius III
Virtanen, Reino 1910- CANR-4
Earlier sketch in CA 3R
Vis, William Ryerson 1886-1969 Obituary 110
Viscardi, Henry, Jr. 1912- CANR-5
Earlier sketch in CA 5-6R
Vischer, Helen (Cassin Lombard) Carusi
1905(?)-1986 Obituary 119
Visconti, Luchino 1906-1976 81-84
Obituary 65-68
See also CLC 16
Viscott, David S(teven) 1938- 29-32R
See also AITN 1
Visher, Emily B. 1918- 109
Visher, Halene Hatcher 1909- 45-48
Visher, John Sargent 1921- 109
Vishniak, Mark 1883-1976 Obituary 69-72
Vishny, Michele 1932- 69-72
Visocchi, Mark 1938- CANR-16
Earlier sketch in CA 93-96
Visscher, Maurice B(olks) 1901- 77-80
Visser, Margaret 1940- 123
Visser, W(illem) F(rederik) H(endrik)
1900-1968 .... CAP-2
Earlier sketch in CA 25-28
See also SATA 10
Visser 't Hooft, Willem Adolf 1900-1985 .... 9-10R
Obituary 116
Visson, Vladimir 1905(?)-1976 Obituary 69-72
Vita-Finzi, Claudio 1936- 89-92
Vital, David 1927- CANR-12
Earlier sketch in CA 29-32R
Vitale, Joseph T(homas) 1951- 107
Vitale, Philip H. 1913- 17-18R
Vitek, John D(ennis) 1942- 124
Vitelli, James R(obert) 1920- 29-32R
Vitezovic, Tomislav
See Kuehnelt-Leddihn, Erik (Maria) Ritter von
Vittengl, Morgan John 1928- 7-8R
Vittorini, Elio 1908-1966 Obituary 25-28R
See also CLC 6, 9, 14
Vitzthum, Richard Carleton 1936- 103
Vivante, Arturo 1923- CANR-10
Earlier sketch in CA 17-18R
Vivante, Paolo 1921- 29-32R
Vivas, Eliseo 1901- CANR-5
Earlier sketch in CA 7-8R
Viveash, Cherry Jacqueline Lee 1929- CAP-1
Earlier sketch in CA 9-10
Vivers, Eileen Elliott 1905- 41-44R
Vivian, Cordy Tindell 1924- 49-52
Vivian, Francis
See Ashley, (Arthur) Ernest
Viviano, Benedict T(homas) 1940- CANR-10
Earlier sketch in CA 23-24R
Vivienne
See Entwistle, Florence Vivienne
Vizard, Stephen
See James, (David) Burnett (Stephen)
Vizedom, Monika B(asch) 1929- 69-72
Vizenor, Gerald Robert 1934- CANR-21
Earlier sketches in CA 13-14R, CANR-5

Vizinczey, Stephen 1933- ... CLC-40
Vizzard, Jack
See Vizzard, John Anthony
Vizzard, John Anthony 1914- ... 29-32R
Vizzini, Salvatore 1926- ... 103
Vlach, John Michael 1948- ... 123
Vladeck, Bruce C. 1949- ... 101
Vladimirov, Leonid
See Finkelstein, Leonid Vladimirovitch
Vladimov, G.
See Vladimov, Georgii Nikolaevich
Vladimov, Georgii
See Vladimov, Georgii Nikolaevich
Vladimov, Georgii Nikolaevich 1931- ... 123
Vlahos, Olivia 1924- ... 21-22R
See also SATA 31
Vlasic, Bob
See Hirsch, Phil
Vlasic, Ivan Albert 1926- ... 9-10R
Vliet, R(ussell) G(ordon) 1929-1984 ... CANR-18
Obituary ... 112
Earlier sketch in CA 37-40R
See also CLC 22
Vlock, Laurel F(ox) ... 37-40R
Vloyantes, John P. 1918- ... 61-64
Voaden, Herman Arthur 1903- ... 103
Vo-Dinh, Mai 1933- ... CANR-13
Earlier sketch in CA 77-80
See also SATA 16
Vodola, Thomas M(ichael) 1925- ... CANR-19
Earlier sketches in CA 49-52, CANR-3
Voegeli, V(ictor) Jacque 1934- ... 21-22R
Voegelin, Eric 1901-1985 Obituary ... 114
Voehringer, Erich F(rederick)
1905-1973 ... CANR-2
Obituary ... 41-44R
Earlier sketch in CA 3R
Voeks, Virginia (Wilna) 1921- ... 15-16R
Voelcker, Hunce 1940- ... 77-80
Voelkel, Robert T(ownsend) 1933- ... 25-28R
Voelker, John D(onaldson) 1903- ... 4R
Voellner, Louada McCaughen
1888(?)-1986 Obituary ... 119
Vogau, Boris Andreyevich 1894-1937(?)
Brief entry ... 123
Vogel, Alfred T(ennyson) 1906- ... 104
Vogel, Arthur A(nton) 1924- ... CANR-10
Earlier sketch in CA 25-28R
Vogel, Dan 1927- ... 120
Vogel, David 1947- ... CANR-11
Earlier sketch in CA 65-68
Vogel, Ezra F. 1930- ... 13-14R
Vogel, Helen Wolff 1918- ... 19-20R
Vogel, Ilse-Margret 1918- ... CANR-7
Earlier sketch in CA 15-16R
See also SATA 14
Vogel, Irving L. 1918- ... 122
Vogel, Jerry 1896(?)-1980 Obituary ... 101
Vogel, John H., Jr. 1950- ... 77-80
See also SATA 18
Vogel, Linda Jane 1940- ... 61-64
Vogel, Lucy E(laine) ... 49-52
Vogel, Paula A(nne) 1951- ... 108
Vogel, Speed
See Vogel, Irving L.
Vogel, Stanley M(orton) 1921- ... 77-80
Vogel, Steven 1940- ... 53-56
Vogel, Victor H(ugh) 1905-1978 ... CANR-3
Earlier sketch in CA 4R
Vogel, Virgil (Howard) J(oseph) 1918- . CANR-10
Earlier sketch in CA 25-28R
Vogeler, Ingolf 1944- ... 107
Vogelgesang, Sandra Louise 1942- ... 57-60
Vogelgesang, Sandy
See Vogelgesang, Sandra Louise
Vogelman, Joyce 1936- ... 106
Vogelsang, Arthur 1942- ... 49-52
Vogelsinger, Hubert 1938- ... 25-28R
Vogenitz, David George 1930- ... 41-44R
Voget, Fred W. 1913- ... 61-64
Vogt, Bill
See Vogt, William McKinley
Vogt, Esther Loewen 1915- ... CANR-7
Earlier sketch in CA 17-18R
See also SATA 14
Vogt, Evon Zartman, Jr. 1918- ... 69-72
Vogt, Gregory ... SATA-45
Vogt, Joseph 1895- Brief entry ... 112
Vogt, Marie Bollinger 1921- ... 57-60
See also SATA 45
Vogt, William McKinley 1935- ... 89-92
Voight, Virginia Frances 1909- ... CANR-18
Earlier sketches in CA 7-8R, CANR-2
See also SATA 8
Voigt, Cynthia 1942- ... CANR-18
Earlier sketch in CA 106
See also SATA 33, 48
See also CLC 30
See also CLR 13
Voigt, David Quentin 1926- ... CANR-14
Earlier sketch in CA 41-44R
Voigt, Ellen Bryant 1943- ... CANR-11
Earlier sketch in CA 69-72
Voigt, Erna 1925- ... SATA-35
Voigt, Karsten D. 1941- ... 113
Voigt, Lieselotte E. Kurth
See Kurth-Voigt, Lieselotte E.
Voigt, Melvin J(ohn) 1911- ... CANR-5
Earlier sketch in CA 15-16R
Voigt, Milton 1924- ... 11-12R
Voigt, Robert J(oseph) 1916- ... 93-96
Voigt, William, Jr. 1902- ... 73-76
Voigt-Rother, Erna
See Voigt, Erna
Voils, Jessie Wiley ... CAP-2
Earlier sketch in CA 29-32
Voinovich, Vladimir (Nikolaevich) 1932- ... 81-84
See also CLC 10
Voitle, Robert (Brown, Jr.) 1919- ... 2R
Vojtech, Anna 1946- ... SATA-42
Volbach, Walther R(ichard) 1897- ... 29-32R
Volcker, Paul A(dolph) 1927- Brief entry ... 114
Volgyes, Ivan 1936- ... CANR-20
Earlier sketch in CA 104
Volin, Michael 1911- ... 101
Volk, Hannah Marie
See Wormington, H(annah) M(arie)
Volkan, Vamik D(jemal) 1932- ... CANR-19
Earlier sketch in CA 102
Volkart, Edmund H(owell) 1919- ... 21-22R
Volkening, Henry T. 1902-1972
Obituary ... 37-40R
Volker, Roger 1934- ... 53-56
Volker, Roy 1924- ... 57-60
Volkoff, Vladimir 1932- ... 73-76
Volkov, Leon 1920(?)-1974 Obituary ... 45-48
Vollert, Cyril (Oscar) 1901- ... 61-64
Vollmer, Howard M. 1928- ... CANR-13
Earlier sketch in CA 19-20R
Voloshinov, Vladimir
See Bakhtin, Mikhail (Mikhailovich)
Volpe, E(rminio) Peter 1927- ... CANR-15
Earlier sketch in CA 37-40R
Volpe, Edmond L(oris) 1922- ... CANR-1
Earlier sketch in CA 3R
Voltz, Jeanne Appleton 1920- ... CANR-21
Earlier sketch in CA 104
Volz, Carl (Andrew) 1933- ... 29-32R
Volz, Marlin M(ilton) 1917- ... 37-40R
von Abele, Rudolph (Radama) 1922- ... 104
von Baeyer, Hans C(hristian) 1938- ... 117
von Balthasar, Hans Urs 1905- Brief entry ... 106
von Berg, J(ohan) F(riedrich) ?-1983(?)
Obituary ... 108
von Bertalanffy, Ludwig 1901-1972 ... CAP-2
Earlier sketch in CA 25-28
von Block, Bela W(illiam) 1922- ... 104
von Block, Sylvia 1931- ... CANR-7
Earlier sketch in CA 53-56
von Bothmer, Dietrich Felix 1918- ... 106
von Brand, Theodor C. 1900(?)-1978
Obituary ... 81-84
von Braun, Wernher 1912-1977 ... CANR-9
Obituary ... 69-72
Earlier sketch in CA 7-8R
von Castlehun, Friedl
See Marion, Frieda
von Cube, Irmgard 1900(?)-1977
Obituary ... 73-76
von Daeniken, Erich 1935- ... CANR-17
Earlier sketch in CA 37-40R
See also CLC 30
See also AITN 1
von Daniken, Erich
See von Daeniken, Erich
See also CLC 30
von der Mehden, Fred R. 1927- ... 11-12R
von Doderer, Heimito 1896-1966
Obituary ... 25-28R
Vondra, Josef Gert 1941- ... 104
von Dreele, W(illiam) H(enry) 1924- ... 93-96
von Eckardt, Ursula M(aria) 1925- ... 13-14R
Von Eckardt, Wolf 1918- ... 7-8R
Von Elsner, Don Byron 1909- ... 3R
von Ende, Richard Chaffey 1907- ... 103
von Euler, Ulf (Svante) 1905-1983
Obituary ... 109
von Frank, Albert J(ames) 1945- ... 120
von Franz, Marie-Louise 1915- ... 85-88
von Frisch, Karl (Ritter)
See Frisch, Karl (Ritter) von
von Frisch, Otto 1929- ... 101
von Furstenberg, Egon (Edvard) 1946- ... 102
von Furstenberg, George Michael
1941- ... CANR-10
Earlier sketch in CA 65-68
von Glahn, Gerhard E(rnst) 1911- ... 15-16R
von Gronicka, Andre 1912- ... 25-28R
von Grunebaum, G(ustave) E(dmund)
1909-1972 ... CANR-3
Earlier sketch in CA 2R
Vo Nguyen Giap 1912(?)- Brief entry ... 115
von Habsburg-Lothringen, Geza Louis
Eusebius Gebhard Ralphael Albert Maria
1940- ... 105
Von Hagen, Victor Wolfgang 1908- ... 105
See also SATA 29
von Hayek, Friedrich A.
See Hayek, Friedrich August von
von Heidenstam, (Carl Gustaf) Verner
See Heidenstam, (Carl Gustaf) Verner
von
von Heller, Marcus
See Zachary, Hugh
von Hertzen, Heikki 1913- ... 37-40R
von Heyse, Paul (Johann Ludwig)
See Heyse, Paul (Johann Ludwig von)
von Hildebrand, Alice 1923- ... 21-22R
von Hildebrand, Dietrich 1889-1977 ... CANR-10
Obituary ... 69-72
Earlier sketch in CA 17-18R
Von Hilsheimer, George E(dwin III)
1934- ... 29-32R
von Hippel, Frank 1937- ... 93-96
von Hirsch, Andrew 1934- ... CANR-14
Earlier sketch in CA 81-84
von Hofe, Harold 1912- ... CANR-4
Earlier sketch in CA 3R
von Hoffman, Nicholas 1929- ... 81-84
von Hofmannsthal, Hugo
See Hofmannsthal, Hugo von
von Horn, Carl 1903- ... CAP-2
Earlier sketch in CA 21-22
von Horvath, Odon
See Horvath, Oedoen von
von Horvath, Oedoen
See Horvath, Oedoen von
von Kaschnitz-Weinberg, Marie Luise
1901-1974 Obituary ... 93-96
Von Klemperer, Klemens 1916- ... 23-24R
von Klopp, Vahrah
See Malvern, Gladys
von Koenigswald, (Gustav Heinrich) Ralph
1902-1982 Obituary ... 110
von Koerber, Hans Nordewin 1886- ... 41-44R
von Lang, Jochen
See von Lang-Piechocki, Joachim
von Lang-Piechocki, Joachim 1925- ... 101
von Laue, Max Theodor Felix
See Laue, Max Theodor Felix von
Von Laue, Theodore Herman 1916- ... 11-12R
von le Fort, Gertrud (Petrea)
See le Fort, Gertrud (Petrea) von
Von Leyden, Wolfgang Marius 1911- ... CANR-3
Earlier sketch in CA 5-6R
von Liliencron, (Friedrich Adolf Axel) Detlev
See Liliencron, (Friedrich Adolf Axel)
Detlev von
von Maltitz, Horst 1905- ... 77-80
Von Manstein, Erich 1887-1973 Obituary ... 45-48
von Meck, Galina 1891-1985 Obituary ... 116
von Mehren, Arthur T(aylor) 1922- ... 17-18R
von Mendelssohn, Felix 1918- ... 15-16R
Von Mering, Otto Oswald, Jr. 1922- ... 1R
von Miklos, Josephine Bogdan 1900-1972
Obituary ... 37-40R
von Mises, Ludwig (Edler)
See Mises, Ludwig (Edler) von
von Mises, Margit
See Mises, Margit von
Von Mohrenschildt, Dimitri Sergius 1902-
Brief entry ... 106
Von Molnar, Geza (Walter Elemer)
1932- ... 29-32R
von Moltke, Konrad 1941- ... CANR-19
Earlier sketch in CA 101
Von Moschzisker, Michael 1918- ... 37-40R
Vonnegut, Kurt, Jr. 1922- ... CANR-1
Earlier sketch in CA 3R
See also DLB 2, 8
See also DLBY 80
See also DLBD 3
See also CLC 1, 2, 3, 4, 5, 8, 12, 22,
40
See also AITN 1
Vonnegut, Mark 1947- ... 65-68
See also AITN 2
von Neumann, John 1903-1957
Brief entry ... 117
von Ost, Henry Lerner 1915- ... 101
Von Rachen, Kurt
See Hubbard, L(afayette) Ron(ald)
von Rad, Gerhard 1901-1971 Obituary ... 104
von Rago, Louis J(oseph)
See Rago, Louis J(oseph von)
Von Rauch, Georg 1904- ... 73-76
von Rezzori (d'Arezzo), Gregor
See Rezzori (d'Arezzo), Gregor von
von Rhein, John (Richard) 1945- ... 120
von Riekhoff, Harald 1937- ... 89-92
Von Rosenstiel, Helene 1944- ... 105
Von Salis, Jean-R. 1901- ... 21-22R
von Salomon, Ernst 1902-1972
Obituary ... 37-40R
von Schilcher, Florian 1944- ... 118
von Schlabrendorff, Fabian 1907-1980
Obituary ... 105
von Schmidt, Eric 1931- ... CANR-13
Earlier sketch in CA 17-18R
See also SATA 36, 50
Von Schmidt, Harold 1896(?)-1982
Obituary ... 107
von Schoenhoff, Ulrike
See Frank, Rudolf
von Schuschnigg, Kurt 1897-1977 ... 103
von Schwarzenfeld, Gertrude
See Cochrane de Alencar, Gertrude E. L.
von Staden, Heinrich 1939- ... 37-40R
von Staden, Wendelgard 1925- ... 110
von Sternberg, Josef
See Sternberg, Josef von
von Storch, Anne B. 1910- ... CAP-2
Earlier sketch in CA 29-32
See also SATA 1
von Trapp, Maria Augusta 1905-1987 ... 81-84
Obituary ... 122
Von Unruh, Fritz 1885-1970 Obituary ... 29-32R
See also DLB 56
von Wangenheim, Chris 1942-1981
Obituary ... 103
von Weizsaecker, Carl Friedrich 1912- ... 105
von Wiegand, Charmion 1898(?)-1983
Obituary ... 110
Von Wiren-Garczynski, Vera 1931- ... 41-44R
von Wodtke, Charlotte Buel Johnson
1918-1982 ... 112
von Wohl-Musciny, Ludwig
See de Wohl, Louis
von Wright, G(eorg) H(enrik)
See Wright, G(eorg) H(enrik) von
von Wuthenau, Alexander 1900- ... 65-68
von Zuehlsdorff, Volkmar J(ohannes)
1912- ... CANR-20
Earlier sketch in CA 7-8R
Vooren, Monique Van
See Van Vooren, Monique
Voorhees, Richard J(oseph) 1916- ... 5-6R
Voorhies, Barbara 1939- ... 104
Voorhis, Horace Jeremiah 1901-1984 ... CANR-6
Obituary ... 113
Earlier sketch in CA 3R
Voorhis, Jerry
See Voorhis, Horace Jeremiah
Voos, Henry 1928- ... 25-28R
Vorhees, Melvin B. 1904(?)-1977
Obituary ... 69-72
Vorobeva, Maria 1892-1984 Obituary ... 113
Vorpahl, Ben Merchant 1937- ... 41-44R
Vorspan, Albert 1924- ... CANR-13
Earlier sketch in CA 23-24R
Vorster, Gordon 1924- ... CLC-34
Vorzimmer, Peter J. 1937- ... 93-96
Vos, Clarence J(ohn) 1920- ... 45-48
Vos, Nelvin (LeRoy) 1932- ... 19-20R
Vosburgh, Leonard (W.) 1912- ... SATA-15
Vose, Clement E(llery) 1923-1985 ... 41-44R
Obituary ... 115
Vose, Ruth Hurst 1944- ... 109
Voskovec, George 1905-1981 Obituary ... 104
Voskuil, Dennis N(eal) 1944- ... 112
Voss, Carl Hermann 1910- ... CANR-10
Earlier sketch in CA 21-22R
Voss, E(rnst) Theodore 1928- ... 37-40R
Voss, Earl H. 1922- ... 9-10R
Voss, George L. 1922- ... 57-60
Voss, James F(rederick) 1930- ... 41-44R
Voss, Thomas M(ichael) 1945- ... 105
Votaw, Dow 1920- ... 19-20R
Voureka, Amalia
See Fleming, Amalia
Vournakis, John N(icholas) 1939- ... 57-60
Vowles, Richard B(eckman) 1917- ... 25-28R
Voyageur
See Allen, Cecil J(ohn)
Voyce, Arthur 1889- ... CAP-1
Earlier sketch in CA 13-14
Voyle, Mary
See Manning, Rosemary
Voynich, Ethel Lillian (Boole) 1864-1960
Obituary ... 104
Voysey, Margaret 1945- ... 108
Voysey, Michael 1920-1987 Obituary ... 123
Voznesensky, Andrei 1933- ... 89-92
See also CLC 1, 15
Vrba, Rudolf 1924- ... 21-22R
Vrbovska, Anca 1905- ... 81-84
Vredenburg, Harvey L. 1921- ... 25-28R
Vreeland, Diana Dalziel 1903(?)- ... 111
Vreeland, Jane D. 1915- ... 21-22R
Vrettos, Theodore 1919- ... 15-16R
Vreuls, Diane ... 57-60
Vries, Anne de
See de Vries, Anne
Vries, Leonard de 1919- ... 113
Vroman, Leo 1915- ... 49-52
Vroman, Mary Elizabeth (Gibson)
1923-1967 Obituary ... 109
See also DLB 33
Vroom, Victor H(arold) 1932- ... 11-12R
Vrooman, Jack Rochford 1929- ... 45-48
Vryonis, Speros (P.), Jr. 1928- ... 85-88
Vucinich, Alexander S. 1914- Brief entry ... 109
Vucinich, Wayne S. 1913- ... 13-14R
Vugteveen, Verna Aardema 1911- ... CANR-18
Earlier sketches in CA 7-8R, CANR-3
Vuilleumier, Marion 1918- ... 81-84
Vujica, Stanko M(irko) 1909-1976 ... 41-44R
Vulliamy, Colwyn Edward 1886-1971
Obituary ... 89-92
Vuong, Lynette Dyer 1938- ... 117
Vuong g(ia) Thuy 1938- ... 69-72
Vyn, Kathleen 1949- ... 89-92
Vyverberg, Henry (Sabin) 1921- ... 109
Vyvyan, C(lara) C(oltman Rogers) 1885- ... CAP-1
Earlier sketch in CA 9-10
Vyvyan, Nigel
See Nevill, Barry St-John

W

Waage, Frederick 1943- ... 104
Waagenaar, Sam 1908- ... 57-60
Waber, Bernard 1924- ... CANR-2
Earlier sketch in CA 3R
See also SATA 40, 47
Wabun
See James, Marlise Ann
Wacher, John Stewart 1927- Brief entry ... 105
Wachhorst, Wyn 1938- ... 106
Wachs, Mark Marshall 1933- ... 25-28R
Wachs, Saul P(hilip) 1931- ... 112
Wachsmann, Klaus Philipp 1907-
Brief entry ... 106
Wachtel, Albert 1939- ... 123
Wachtel, Howard M(artin) 1938- ... 49-52
Wachtel, Isidore H. 1909(?)-1979
Obituary ... 89-92
Wachtel, Paul L(awrence) 1940- ... 115
Wachter, Oralee (Roberts) 1935- ... 122
Wachter, Susan M. 1943- ... 120
Waciuma, Wanjohi 1938- ... 77-80
Wacker, Charles H(enry), Jr. 1925- ... 73-76
Wackerbarth, Marjorie ... CAP-1
Earlier sketch in CA 13-14
Wadbrook, William P. 1933- ... 45-48
Waddams, Herbert Montague 1911-1972
Obituary ... 107
Waddell, D(avid) A(lan) G(ilmour)
1927- ... CANR-23
Earlier sketch in CA 2R
Waddell, Eric (Wilson) 1939- ... 45-48
Waddell, Evelyn Margaret 1918- ... 53-56
See also SATA 10

Waddell, Helen (Jane) 1889-1965 102
Waddell, Jack O('Brien) 1933- 33-36R
Waddell, Martin 1941- 113
See also SATA 43
Waddington, C(onrad) H(al) 1905-1975 .. CANR-6
Obituary 61-64
Earlier sketch in CA 13-14R
Waddington, Miriam 1917- CANR-12
Earlier sketch in CA 21-22R
See also CLC 28
Waddington, Raymond B(ruce) 1935- 53-56
Waddy, Charis 1909- 69-72
Waddy, Lawrence H(eber) 1914- CANR-7
Earlier sketch in CA 13-14R
Wade, Alan
See Vance, John Holbrook
Wade, Bob
See Wade, Robert (Allison)
Wade, Carlson 1928- 29-32R
Wade, David 1929- 103
Wade, E(ileen) K(irkpatrick) 1892(?)-1985
Obituary 117
Wade, Francis C(larence) 1907- CAP-1
Earlier sketch in CA 13-14
Wade, Graham 1940- 107
Wade, Harry Vincent 1894-1973 Obituary .. 89-92
Wade, Henry
See Aubrey-Fletcher, Henry Lancelot
Wade, Henry William Rawson 1918- 109
Wade, Herbert
See Wales, Hugh Gregory
Wade, Hugh Mason 1913-1986 Obituary ... 118
Wade, Ira Owen 1896-1983 73-76
Obituary 109
Wade, Jennifer
See Wehen, Joy DeWeese
Wade, Jerry L(ee) 1941- 53-56
Wade, Jewel Millsap 1937- Brief entry 107
Wade, Joanna
See Berckman, Evelyn Domenica
Wade, John Stevens 1927- CANR-6
Earlier sketch in CA 13-14R
Wade, Kit
See Carson, Xanthus
Wade, L(arry) L(ee) 1935- 33-36R
Wade, Mason 1913- 11-12R
Wade, Nicholas (Michael Landon)
1942- CANR-16
Earlier sketch in CA 77-80
Wade, Rex A(rvin) 1936- 61-64
Wade, Richard Clement 1922- 17-18R
Wade, Robert (Allison) 1920- 108
Wade, Robert
See McIlwain, David
Wade, Rosalind Herschel 1909- CAP-1
Earlier sketch in CA 9-10
Wade, Theodore E., Jr. 1936- SATA-37
Wade, (Henry) William (Rawson) 1918- . CANR-4
Earlier sketch in CA 4R
Wade, Wyn Craig 1944- 103
Wadekin, Karl-Eugen
See Waedekin, Karl-Eugen
Wadepuhl, Walter 1895- 61-64
Wadia, Maneck S(orabji) 1931- CANR-13
Earlier sketch in CA 19-20R
Wadinasi, Sedeka
See Nall, Hiram Abiff
Wadley, Susan S(now) 1943- 77-80
Wadlington, Walter 1931- 33-36R
Wadlington, Warwick 1938- 73-76
Wadsworth, Barry James 1935- 37-40R
Wadsworth, Frank W(hittemore) 1919- ...11-12R
Wadsworth, James J(eremiah)
1905-1984 .... CAP-2
Obituary 112
Earlier sketch in CA 19-20
Wadsworth, Jerry
See Wadsworth, James J(eremiah)
Wadsworth, M(arshall) D. 1936- 45-48
Wadsworth, Michael E(dwin) J(ohn)
1942- 93-96
Wadsworth, Nelson B(ingham) 1930- 65-68
Waedekin, Karl-Eugen 1921- 73-76
Waehrer, Helen (Youngelson) 1938- 53-56
Waelder, Robert 1900-1967 .... CAP-1
Earlier sketch in CA 13-14
Waengler, Hans-Heinrich B. 1921- CANR-20
Earlier sketch in CA 41-44R
Waffle, Harvey W(illiam) 1904- 7-8R
Wagar, W(alter) Warren 1932- CANR-3
Earlier sketch in CA 5-6R
Wagatsuma, Hiroshi 1927- 21-22R
Wagemaker, Herbert, Jr. 1929- 93-96
Wagenaar, Theodore C(larence) 1948- 111
Wagener, Hans 1940- CANR-1
Earlier sketch in CA 45-48
Wagenheim, Kal 1935- 29-32R
See also SATA 21
Wagenknecht, Edward (Charles) 1900- . CANR-22
Earlier sketches in CA 2R, CANR-6
Wagenvoord, James 1937- 41-44R
Wager, Walter H(erman) 1924- CANR-8
Earlier sketch in CA 5-6R
Wager, Willis Joseph 1911- 37-40R
Waggaman, William Henry 1884(?)-1978
Obituary 77-80
Waggner, George 1894-1984 Obituary 114
Waggoner, Glen 1940- 121
Waggoner, Hyatt H(owe) 1913- CANR-9
Earlier sketch in CA 23-24R
Wagley, Charles (Walter) 1913- CANR-10
Earlier sketch in CA 13-14R
Waglow, Irving Frederick 1915- 4R
Wagman, Fredrica 1937- 97-100
See also CLC 7
Wagman, Naomi 1937- 57-60
Wagman, Robert John 1942- 93-96
Wagner, Anthony Richard 1908- CANR-20
Earlier sketches in CA 4R, CANR-5
Wagner, C(harles) Peter 1930- CANR-24
Earlier sketches in CA 21-22R, CANR-9
Wagner, Charles Abraham 1901- 7-8R
Wagner, David G(eorge) 1949- 114
Wagner, Denson
See Iannelli, Richard
Wagner, Doc
See Wagner, Edward J., Sr.
Wagner, Edward J., Sr. 1908(?)-1986
Obituary 118
Wagner, Edwin E(ric) 1930- 45-48
Wagner, Elaine 1939- 45-48
Wagner, Eliot 1917- 105
Wagner, Francis S(tephen) 1911- CANR-8
Earlier sketch in CA 61-64
Wagner, Frederick (Reese, Jr.) 1928- 7-8R
Wagner, Geoffrey (Atheling) 1927- CANR-2
Earlier sketch in CA 1R
Wagner, Gordon Parsons 1915-1987
Obituary 124
Wagner, Harvey M. 1931- CANR-6
Earlier sketch in CA 13-14R
Wagner, Helmut R(udolf) 1904- CANR-19
Earlier sketches in CA 53-56, CANR-4
Wagner, Jack Russell 1916- 49-52
Wagner, Jane 109
Wagner, Jean Pierre 1919- 23-24R
Wagner, Jon G(regory) 1944- 109
Wagner, Joseph Frederick 1900(?)-1974
Obituary 53-56
Wagner, Karl Edward 1945- CANR-3
Earlier sketch in CA 49-52
Wagner, Ken(neth) 1911- 37-40R
Wagner, Kenneth A. 1919- 53-56
Wagner, Lilya 1940- 112
Wagner, Linda Welshimer 1936- CANR-3
Earlier sketch in CA 11-12R
Wagner, Margaret D. 1949- 7-8R
Wagner, (Griegg) Marsden 1930- 69-72
Wagner, Nathaniel N(ed) 1930- 57-60
Wagner, Peggy
See Wagner, Margaret D.
Wagner, Philip L(aurence) 1921- 41-44R
Wagner, Philip Marshall 1904- 102
Wagner, Ray(mond) David 1924- CANR-19
Earlier sketches in CA 5-6R, CANR-3
Wagner, Ray Jay 1931- 77-80
Wagner, Richard Vansant 1935-
Brief entry 105
Wagner, Roy 1938- 41-44R
Wagner, Rudolph F(red) 1921- 37-40R
Wagner, Ruth H(ortense) 1909- 29-32R
Wagner, Sharon B. 1936- CANR-10
Earlier sketch in CA 25-28R
See also SATA 4
Wagner, Stanley P(aul) 1923- 29-32R
Wagner, Walter 1927(?)-1983(?) Obituary .. 109
Wagner, Walter F(rederick), Jr.
1926-1985 69-72
Obituary 116
Wagner, Wenceslas Joseph 1917- 37-40R
Wagoner, David (Russell) 1926- CANR-2
Earlier sketch in CA 2R
See also CAAS 3
See also SATA 14
See also DLB 5
See also CLC 3, 5, 15
Wagoner, Harless D. 1918- 29-32R
Wagoner, Jay J. 1923- 25-28R
Wagoner, John L(eonard) 1927-1984 69-72
Obituary 112
Wagoner, Walter D. 1918- 21-22R
Wagonseller, Bill R(oss) 1933- 107
Wagschal, Harry 1939- 108
Wagschal, Peter H(enry) 1944- CANR-19
Earlier sketch in CA 102
Wagstaff, (John) Malcolm 1940- 109
Wah, Fred(erick James) 1939- Brief entry ... 107
See also DLB 60
See also CLC 44
Wahking, Harold L(eroy) 1931- 29-32R
Wahl, Jan 1933- CANR-12
Earlier sketch in CA 25-28R
See also SATA 2, 34
See also SAAS 3
Wahl, Jean 1888-1974 Obituary 49-52
Wahl, Paul 1922- 11-12R
Wahl, Robert (Charles) 1948- CANR-1
Earlier sketch in CA 49-52
Wahl, Thomas (Peter) 1931- 9-10R
Wahlberg, Rachel Conrad 1922- 93-96
Wahler, Robert G(ordon) 1936-
Brief entry 109
Wahlke, John C(harles) 1917- CANR-11
Earlier sketch in CA 21-22R
Wahloo, Per 1926-1975 61-64
See also CLC 7
Wahloo, Peter
See Wahloo, Per
Wahlroos, Sven 1931- 57-60
Wahtera, John (Edward) 1929-1985 61-64
Obituary 117
Waide, Jan 1952- 105
See also SATA 29
Waidson, H(erbert) Morgan 1916- 7-8R
Waife, Marie
See Waife-Goldberg, Marie
Waife-Goldberg, Marie 1892-1985 .... CAP-2
Obituary 118
Earlier sketch in CA 25-28
Wain, Barry 1944- 122
Wain, John (Barrington) 1925- CANR-23
Earlier sketch in CA 7-8R
See also CAAS 4
See also DLB 15, 27
See also CLC 2, 11, 15, 46
Waine, Anthony 1946- 113
Wainer, Cord
See Dewey, Thomas B(lanchard)
Wainhouse, David Walter 1900-1976 .....17-18R
Obituary 65-68
Wainwright, Arthur William 1925- 114
Wainwright, Charles Anthony 1933- 37-40R
Wainwright, David
See Stansfield, Richard Habberton
Wainwright, Geoffrey 1939- CANR-15
Earlier sketch in CA 37-40R
Wainwright, Gordon Ray 1937- 113
Wainwright, J(oseph) Allan 1921- 13-14R
Wainwright, Jeffrey 1944- Brief entry 122
See also DLB 40
Wainwright, John 1921- 110
Brief entry 108
Wainwright, Nicholas Biddle 1914- 65-68
Wainwright, William J(udson) 1935- 120
Waisanen, F(rederick) B(rynolf) 1923- 45-48
Waite, A. E.
See Waite, Arthur Edward
Waite, Arthur Edward 1857-1942
Brief entry 121
Waite, Helen Elmira 1903- 3R
Waite, P(eter) B(usby) 1922- 11-12R
Waite, Robert G(eorge) L(eeson) 1919- ...11-12R
Waite, William W(iley) 1903- CAP-1
Earlier sketch in CA 15-16
Waith, Eugene M(ersereau) 1912- CANR-5
Earlier sketch in CA 5-6R
Waitley, Douglas 1927- CANR-9
Earlier sketch in CA 21-22R
See also SATA 30
Waitzmann, Dorothea 1915- 15-16R
Wajda, Andrzej 1926- 102
See also CLC 16
Wakefield, Connie LaVon 1948- 65-68
Wakefield, Dan 1932- 21-22R
See also CLC 7
Wakefield, Donam Hahn 1927- 37-40R
Wakefield, Herbert Russell 1888-1965 ......5-6R
Wakefield, Hubert George 1915-1984
Obituary 112
Wakefield, Hugh
See Wakefield, Hubert George
Wakefield, Jean L.
See Laird, Jean E(louise)
Wakefield, R. I.
See White, Gertrude M(ason)
Wakefield, Robert A. 1916- 15-16R
Wakefield, Sherman Day 1894-1971
Obituary 29-32R
Wakefield, Tom 1935- 101
Wakefield, Walter Leggett 1911- 81-84
Wakeford, John 1936- Brief entry 112
Wakeham, Irene 1912- 29-32R
Wakeley, John H(albert) 1932- 41-44R
Wakelin, Martyn Francis 1935- 65-68
Wakelyn, Jon L(ouis) 1938- CANR-1
Earlier sketch in CA 45-48
Wakeman, Frederic (Evans), Jr. 1937- .. CANR-1
Earlier sketch in CA 49-52
Wakeman, Geoffrey 1926- CANR-15
Earlier sketch in CA 37-40R
Wakeman, John 1928- 124
Wakeman, Robert Parker 1914(?)-1981
Obituary 104
Wakil, S(heikh) P(arvez) 1935- 85-88
Wakin, Edward 1927- CANR-17
Earlier sketches in CA 5-6R, CANR-2
See also SATA 37
Wako, Mdogo
See Nazareth, Peter
Wakoski, Diane 1937- CANR-9
Earlier sketch in CA 15-16R
See also CAAS 1
See also DLB 5
See also CLC 2, 4, 7, 9, 11, 40
Wakoski-Sherbell, Diane
See Wakoski, Diane
Waksman, Selman A(braham) 1888-1973 . CAP-1
Obituary 45-48
Earlier sketch in CA 15-16
Wakstein, Allen M. 1931- 29-32R
Walbank, F. W.
See Walbank, Frank William
Walbank, Frank William 1909- Brief entry ... 111
Walberg, Herbert J(ohn) 1937- 61-64
Walch, Timothy (George) 1947- CANR-21
Earlier sketch in CA 105
Walchars, John 1912- 81-84
Walck, Henry Z. 1908(?)-1984 Obituary 114
See also SATA 40
Walcott, Derek (Alton) 1930- 89-92
See also DLBY 81
See also CLC 2, 4, 9, 14, 25, 42
Walcott, Fred G. 1894- 37-40R
Walcott, Robert 1910- CAP-1
Earlier sketch in CA 13-14
Walcutt, Charles Child 1908- CANR-3
Earlier sketch in CA 2R
Wald, Carol 1935- 65-68
Wald, Malvin (Daniel) 1917- CANR-1
Earlier sketch in CA 45-48
Wald, Richard C(harles) 108
Walde, Ralph E(ldon) 1943- 53-56
Waldeck, Peter Bruce 1940- 41-44R
Walden, Amelia Elizabeth CANR-2
Earlier sketch in CA 1R
See also SATA 3
Walden, Daniel 1922- 25-28R
Walden, Howard T(albot) II 1897-1981 45-48
Obituary 103
Walden, John C(layton) 1928- 53-56
Walder, (Alan) David 1928-1978 ...... CANR-17
Obituary 81-84
Earlier sketch in CA 65-68
Walder, Dennis 1943- 117
Walders, Joe 1948- 85-88
Waldheim, Kurt 1918- 89-92
Waldhorn, Arthur 1918- CANR-3
Earlier sketch in CA 2R
Waldinger, Ernst 1896-1970 Obituary 104
Waldman, Anne 1945- 37-40R
See also DLB 16
See also CLC 7
Waldman, Bruce 1949- SATA-15
Waldman, Diane 1936- 33-36R
Waldman, Eric 1914- 19-20R
Waldman, Max 1919-1981 105
Obituary 103
Waldman, Milton 1895-1976 69-72
Obituary 65-68
Waldmeir, Joseph John 1923- 11-12R
Waldo, Anna Lee 1925- 85-88
Waldo, Dave
See Clarke, D(avid) Waldo
Waldo, E. Hunter
See Sturgeon, Theodore Hamilton
Waldo, Edward Hamilton
See Sturgeon, Theodore Hamilton
Waldo, Kay Cronkite 1938- 107
Waldo, Myra 93-96
Waldo, Ralph Emerson III 1944- 102
Waldo, Terry
See Waldo, Ralph Emerson III
Waldo, Willis H. 1920- 13-14R
Waldock, (Claud) Humphrey (Meredith)
1904-1981 Obituary 108
Waldorf, Paul D(ouglass) 1908- CAP-1
Earlier sketch in CA 15-16
Waldrip, Louise B. 1912- 37-40R
Waldron, Ann Wood 1924- CANR-7
Earlier sketch in CA 15-16R
See also SATA 16
Waldron, D'Lynn
See Waldron-Shah, Diane Lynn
Waldron, Eli 1916(?)-1980 Obituary 101
Waldron, Ingrid 1939- 53-56
Waldron, Martin O. 1925-1981 Obituary 103
Waldron-Shah, Diane Lynn 1936- 9-10R
Waldrop, Howard 1946- 118
Waldrop, Keith 1932- 117
Waldrop, Rosemarie 1935- CANR-18
Earlier sketch in CA 101
Waldrop, W. Earl 1910- 5-6R
Wale, Michael 81-84
Walen, Harry L(eonard) 1915- 41-44R
Wales, Hugh Gregory 1910- CANR-2
Earlier sketch in CA 5-6R
Wales, Nym
See Snow, Helen Foster
Wales, Robert 1923- 93-96
Wales, William
See Ambrose, David (Edwin)
Waley, Arthur (David) 1889-1966 85-88
Obituary 25-28R
Walford, Christian
See Dilcock, Noreen
Walford, Lionel Albert 1905-1979
Obituary 85-88
Walford, Roy L(ee, Jr.) 1924- 111
Walgenbach, Paul H(enry) 1923- 53-56
Walhout, Donald 1927- CANR-2
Earlier sketch in CA 5-6R
Walicki, Andrzej 1930- 101
Walinsky, Louis J(oseph) 1908- CAP-2
Earlier sketch in CA 17-18
Walinsky, Ossip J. 1887(?)-1973
Obituary 41-44R
Waliullah, Syed 1922- 23-24R
Walkden, (George) Brian 1923- CANR-10
Earlier sketch in CA 13-14R
Walkenstein, Eileen 1923- CANR-14
Earlier sketch in CA 69-72
Walker, Addison
See Walker, (Addison) Mort
Walker, Alan 1911- CANR-7
Earlier sketch in CA 13-14R
Walker, Albert L(yell) 1907- 41-44R
Walker, Alexander 1930- Brief entry 116
Walker, Alice 1944- CANR-9
Earlier sketch in CA 37-40R
See also SATA 31
See also DLB 6, 33
See also CLC 5, 6, 9, 19, 27, 46
Walker, Ardis Manly 1901- CANR-22
Earlier sketch in CA 37-40R
Walker, Augusta 1914- 21-22R
Walker, Barbara G(oodwin) 1930- 73-76
Walker, Barbara (Jeanne) K(erlin)
1921- CANR-16
Earlier sketch in CA 33-36R
See also SATA 4
Walker, Benjamin 1923- CANR-10
Earlier sketch in CA 25-28R
Walker, Bessie
See Henry, Bessie Walker
Walker, (James) Braz(elton) 1934-1983 ...69-72
See also SATA 45
Walker, Brooks R. 1935- 11-12R
Walker, Bruce (James) 1944- 85-88
Walker, Bryce S(tewart) 1934- 117
Walker, C(larence) Eugene 1939- CANR-10
Earlier sketch in CA 61-64
Walker, Charles 1911- 19-20R
Walker, Charles
See Gettings, Fred

Walker, Charles R(umford) 1893-1974 ... CAP-2
Obituary ... 53-56
Earlier sketch in CA 17-18
Walker, Cheryl 1947- ... 111
Walker, Claxton 1924- ... 101
Walker, Clive (Phillip) 1954- ... 124
Walker, D(aniel) P(ickering) 1914-1985 ... 85-88
Obituary ... 116
Walker, Dale L(ee) 1935- ... CANR-24
Earlier sketches in CA 57-60, CANR-8
Walker, Daniel Downing 1915- ... CANR-2
Earlier sketch in CA 2R
Walker, Danton (MacIntyre) 1899-1960
Obituary ... 93-96
Walker, David 1950- ... 104
Walker, David Clifton 1942- ... 69-72
Walker, David G(ordon) 1926- ... 110
Walker, David Harry 1911- ... CANR-1
Earlier sketch in CA 4R
See also SATA 8
See also CLC 14
Walker, David M(axwell) 1920- ... CANR-22
Earlier sketches in CA 11-12R, CANR-5
Walker, Deward E(dgar), Jr. 1935- ... CANR-19
Earlier sketch in CA 25-28R
Walker, Diana 1925- ... CANR-4
Earlier sketch in CA 49-52
See also SATA 9
Walker, Donald Smith 1918- ... 11-12R
Walker, Earl Thomas 1891- ... 105
Walker, Edward Joseph 1934- ... CANR-12
Earlier sketch in CA 21-22R
Walker, Edward L(ewis) 1914- ... CANR-11
Earlier sketch in CA 25-28R
Walker, Elinor 1911- ... 15-16R
Walker, Eric Anderson 1886-1976 ... CAP-2
Obituary ... 65-68
Earlier sketch in CA 13-14
Walker, Ethel Valerie 1944- ... 53-56
Walker, Evan 1933(?)-1982 Obituary ... 107
Walker, Everett 1906-1983 Obituary ... 109
Walker, Frank 1930- ... 69-72
See also SATA 36
Walker, Frank B. 1916(?)-1985 Obituary ... 117
Walker, Franklin (Dickerson) 1900-1979 ... 21-22R
Obituary ... 85-88
Walker, Geoffrey James 1936- ... 93-96
Walker, George F. 1947- ... CANR-21
Earlier sketch in CA 103
See also DLB 60
See also CLC 44
Walker, Gerald 1928- ... 11-12R
Walker, Gilbert James 1907-1982
Obituary ... 107
Walker, Glen 1937- ... 108
Walker, Graham S. 1956- ... 122
Walker, Gregory P(iers) M(ountford)
1942- ... 73-76
Walker, Greta 1927- ... 77-80
Walker, Harold Blake 1904- ... 17-18R
Walker, Harry
See Waugh, Hillary Baldwin
Walker, Helen M(ary) 1891-1983 Obituary ... 109
Walker, Hill M(ontague) 1939- ... 93-96
Walker, Holly Beth
See Bond, Gladys Baker
Walker, Ira
See Walker, Irma Ruth (Roden)
Walker, Irma Ruth (Roden) 1921- ... CANR-21
Earlier sketches in CA 7-8R, CANR-6
Walker, J.
See Crawford, John Richard
Walker, J(ohn) Ingram 1944- ... 112
Walker, Jack
See Thayer, Frederick C(lifton), Jr.
Walker, James Lynwood 1940- ... 37-40R
Walker, Janet A(nderson) 1942- ... 119
Walker, Jeanne 1924- ... 61-64
Walker, Jeanne Murray 1944- ... 111
Walker, Jeremy D(esmond) B(romhead)
1936- ... 21-22R
Walker, Joan ... 7-8R
Walker, John 1906- ... CANR-6
Earlier sketch in CA 7-8R
Walker, John 1933- ... 113
Walker, John (Bruce) 1938- ... 120
Walker, Joseph 1892-1985 Obituary ... 117
Walker, Joseph A. 1935- ... 89-92
See also DLB 38
See also CLC 19
Walker, Joseph E(rdman) 1911- ... 37-40R
Walker, Kathrine Sorley
See Sorley Walker, Kathrine
Walker, Keith 1934- ... 121
Walker, Kenneth Francis 1924- ... 33-36R
Walker, Kenneth Macfarlane 1882-1966 ... 7-8R
Walker, Kenneth R(oland) 1928- ... 37-40R
Walker, Kenneth Richard 1931- ... 17-18R
Walker, Laurence C(olton) 1924- ... 53-56
Walker, Lawrence David 1931- ... 53-56
Walker, Lenore E(lizabeth) 1942- ... 97-100
Walker, Leo ... 15-16R
Walker, Louise Jean 1891-1976 Obituary ... 110
See also SATA 35
Walker, Lucy
See Sanders, Dorothy Lucie
Walker, Mack 1929- ... 11-12R
Walker, Margaret Abigail 1915- ... 73-76
See also CLC 1, 6
Walker, Margaret Pope 1901(?)-1980
Obituary ... 101
Walker, Mark 1953- ... 117
Walker, Marshall (John) 1912- ... 17-18R
Walker, Martin 1947- ... 101
Walker, Mary Alexander 1927- ... 104
Walker, Matthew
See Mewhinney, Bruce
Walker, Mickey 1901-1981 Obituary ... 108
Walker, Mildred
See Schemm, Mildred Walker
Walker, (Addison) Mort 1923- ... CANR-3
Earlier sketch in CA 49-52
See also SATA 8
Walker, Morton 1929- ... CANR-22
Earlier sketch in CA 85-88
Walker, Nicolette (Daisy) Milnes 1943- ... 41-44R
Walker, Nigel (David) 1917- ... 61-64
Walker, Pamela 1948- ... 69-72
See also SATA 24
Walker, Peter F(ranklin) 1931- ... 13-14R
Walker, Peter N. 1936- ... CANR-14
Earlier sketch in CA 77-80
Walker, Philip Mitchell 1943- ... 29-32R
Walker, Raymond Myerscough
See Myerscough-Walker, Raymond
Walker, Richard L(ouis) 1922- ... CANR-7
Earlier sketch in CA 11-12R
Walker, Robert H(arris) 1924- ... CANR-23
Earlier sketches in CA 15-16R, CANR-7
Walker, Robert Newton 1911- ... 53-56
Walker, Robert W(ayne) 1948- ... CANR-23
Earlier sketch in CA 93-96
Walker, Roger W(illiams) 1931- ... 45-48
Walker, Ronald G(ary) 1945- ... CANR-16
Earlier sketch in CA 93-96
Walker, Ruth
See Walker, Irma Ruth (Roden)
Walker, Samuel 1942- ... 85-88
Walker, Scott 1950- ... 120
Walker, Shel
See Sheldon, Walter J.
Walker, Stanley 1898-1962 Obituary ... 93-96
Walker, Stella Archer 1907- ... 61-64
Walker, Stephen J. 1951- ... SATA-12
Walker, Stuart (Armstrong) 1880(?)-1941
Brief entry ... 120
Walker, Stuart H(odge) 1923- ... CANR-24
Earlier sketch in CA 45-48
Walker, Sydney III 1931- ... 23-24R
Walker, T. Michael 1937- ... 77-80
Walker, Ted
See Walker, Edward Joseph
See also DLB 40
See also CLC 13
Walker, Theodore J. 1922- ... 102
Walker, Walter (Colyear) 1912- ... 117
Walker, Walter (Herbert III) 1949- ... 117
Walker, Warren S(tanley) 1921- ... CANR-16
Earlier sketches in CA 11-12R, CANR-3
Walker, Willard (Brewer) 1926- ... CANR-23
Earlier sketch in CA 45-48
Walker, William Edward 1925- ... 11-12R
Walker, William G(eorge) 1928- ... 77-80
Walker, William H. 1913- ... 19-20R
Walker, William Otis 1896-1981 Obituary ... 105
Walkerley, Rodney Lewis (de Burgh)
1905- ... CAP-1
Earlier sketch in CA 9-10
Walkinshaw, Colin
See Reid, James Macarthur
Walkinshaw, Lawrence H(arvey) 1904- ... 45-48
Walkowitz, Daniel J(ay) 1942- ... 81-84
Wall, A(rthur) E(dward) P(atrick) 1925- ... 119
Wall, Barbara 1911- ... 97-100
Wall, Bennett H(arrison) 1914- ... 77-80
Wall, C. Edward 1942- ... 37-40R
Wall, Elizabeth S(pooner) 1924- ... 93-96
Wall, James M(cKendree) 1928-
Brief entry ... 113
Wall, John Nelson, Jr. 1945- ... 114
Wall, Joseph Barrye 1899(?)-1985
Obituary ... 117
Wall, Joseph Frazier 1920- ... CANR-13
Earlier sketch in CA 29-32R
Wall, Maggie 1937- ... 65-68
Wall, Margaret
See Wall, Maggie
Wall, Martha 1910- ... CAP-2
Earlier sketch in CA 25-28
Wall, Michael Morris 1942- ... 53-56
Wall, Mike
See Wall, Michael Morris
Wall, Patrick (Henry Bligh) 1916- ... 104
Wall, Patrick D(avid) 1925- ... 17-18R
Wall, Richard 1944- ... 41-44R
Wall, Robert Emmet, Jr. 1937- ... CANR-23
Earlier sketch in CA 45-48
Wall, T. D.
See Wall, Toby (Douglas)
Wall, Toby (Douglas) 1946- ... 119
Wall, Toby D.
See Wall, Toby (Douglas)
Wall, Wendy Somerville 1942- ... 49-52
Wallace, Alexander Fielding 1918- ... 33-36R
Wallace, Alexander Ross 1891-1982
Obituary ... 107
Wallace, Alfred Russel 1823-1913
Brief entry ... 123
Wallace, Amy 1955- ... 81-84
Wallace, Andrew 1930- ... 37-40R
Wallace, Anthony F(rancis) C(larke)
1923- ... CANR-13
Earlier sketch in CA 61-64
Wallace, Barbara Brooks ... CANR-11
Earlier sketch in CA 29-32R
See also SATA 4
Wallace, Ben J. 1937- ... 45-48
Wallace, Beverly Dobrin 1921- ... 101
See also SATA 19
Wallace, Bill 1947- ... SATA-47
Wallace, Bill
See Wallace, William Keith
Wallace, Bill
See Wallace, William N.
Wallace, Bronwen 1945- ... 112
Wallace, Bruce 1920- ... CANR-15
Earlier sketch in CA 85-88
Wallace, Daisy
See Cuyler, Margery S(tuyvesant)
Wallace, David H(arold) 1926- ... 25-28R
Wallace, David J. 1954- ... 124
Wallace, David Rains 1945- ... CANR-14
Earlier sketch in CA 81-84
Wallace, DeWitt 1889-1981 Obituary ... 103
Wallace, Dexter
See Masters, Edgar Lee
Wallace, Doreen
See Rash, Dora Eileen Agnew (Wallace)
Wallace, Ed(ward Tatum) 1906-1976
Obituary ... 69-72
Wallace, (Richard Horatio) Edgar
1875-1932 Brief entry ... 115
Wallace, Ernest 1906-1985 ... 13-14R
Wallace, Francis 1894(?)-1977 Obituary ... 73-76
Wallace, G(erald) L. 1938- ... 97-100
Wallace, George C(orley) 1919-
Brief entry ... 114
Wallace, Helen Kingsbury 1897- ... CAP-2
Earlier sketch in CA 25-28
Wallace, Helen M(argaret) 1913- ... CANR-12
Earlier sketch in CA 61-64
Wallace, Henry A(gard) 1888-1965 ... 105
Obituary ... 89-92
Wallace, Ian 1950- ... 107
Wallace, Ian
See Pritchard, John Wallace
Wallace, Irving 1916- ... CANR-1
Earlier sketch in CA 1R
See also CAAS 1
See also CLC 7, 13
See also AITN 1
Wallace, James Donald 1937- ... 108
Wallace, Joanne (M.) 1938- ... 117
Wallace, John A(dam) 1915- ... 5-6R
See also SATA 3
Wallace, John Malcolm 1928- ... 25-28R
Wallace, K(ay) K. 1949- ... 111
Wallace, Karl R(ichards) 1906-1973 ... 101
Wallace, Lew(is) 1827(?)-1905 Brief entry ... 120
Wallace, Lewis Grant 1910- ... CAP-2
Earlier sketch in CA 23-24
Wallace, Lila Bell Acheson 1889-1984
Obituary ... 112
Brief entry ... 105
Wallace, Lillian Parker 1890-1971 ... 2R
Obituary ... 103
Wallace, Luther T(ompkins) 1928- ... 15-16R
Wallace, Marc J., Jr. 1944- ... 114
Wallace, Marjorie ... 101
Wallace, Michael David 1943- ... 77-80
Wallace, Michele Faith 1952- ... 108
Wallace, Mike 1918- ... 65-68
Wallace, Myron Leon
See Wallace, Mike
Wallace, Nigel
See Hamilton, Charles Harold St. John
Wallace, Pamela 1949- ... 105
Wallace, Pat
See Strother, Pat Wallace
Wallace, Paul 1931- ... 61-64
Wallace, Paul A(nthony) W(ilson) 1891- ... CAP-1
Earlier sketch in CA 15-16
Wallace, Philip (Adrian) Hope
See Hope-Wallace, Philip (Adrian)
Wallace, Phyllis Ann ... 105
Wallace, Richard
See Ind, Allison
Wallace, Robert 1932- ... CANR-10
Earlier sketch in CA 15-16R
See also SATA 37, 47
Wallace, Robert Ash 1921- ... 2R
Wallace, Robert Kimball 1944- ... 69-72
Wallace, Ronald (William) 1945- ... CANR-20
Earlier sketches in CA 57-60, CANR-6
Wallace, Ronald S(tewart) 1911- ... CANR-5
Earlier sketch in CA 11-12R
Wallace, Ruby Ann 1923(?)- ... 112
Wallace, Samuel E(ugene) 1935- ... 41-44R
Wallace, Sarah Leslie 1914- ... 11-12R
Wallace, Sister M. Jean
See Paxton, Mary Jean Wallace
Wallace, Sylvia ... 73-76
Wallace, Tom 1874-1961 Obituary ... 93-96
Wallace, Walter L. 1927- ... 81-84
Wallace, Willard M(osher) 1911- ... 13-14R
Wallace, William A(ugustine) 1918- ... 41-44R
Wallace, William A(lan) 1935- ... 49-52
Wallace, William Keith 1947- ... 124
Wallace, William N. 1924- ... 15-16R
Wallace, William Stewart 1884-1970
Obituary ... 116
Wallace-Brodeur, Ruth 1941- ... 107
See also SATA 41
Wallace-Clarke, George 1916- ... 117
Wallace-Crabbe, Chris(topher Keith)
1934- ... CANR-14
Earlier sketch in CA 77-80
Wallace-Hadrill, Andrew (Frederic) 1951- ... 117
Wallace-Hadrill, D(avid) S(utherland)
1920- ... 29-32R
Wallace-Hadrill, John Michael 1916-1985 ... 7-8R
Obituary ... 118
Wallach, Erica 1922- ... 21-22R
Wallach, Ira 1913- ... 11-12R
Wallach, Janet 1942- ... 106
Wallach, Mark I(rwin) 1949- ... 69-72
Wallach, Michael A(rthur) 1933- ... CANR-11
Earlier sketch in CA 15-16R
Wallach, Paul I. 1927- ... CANR-8
Earlier sketch in CA 17-18R
Wallach, Robert Charles 1935- ... 107
Wallach, Sidney 1905-1979 ... 103
Obituary ... 89-92
Wallance, Gregory Joseph 1948- ... 109
Wallant, Edward Lewis 1926-1962 ... CANR-22
Earlier sketch in CA 4R
See also DLB 2, 28
See also CLC 5, 10
Wallechinsky, David 1948- ... 61-64
Wallek, Lee
See Johnson, Curt(is Lee)
Wallen, Carl J(oseph) 1931- ... 93-96
Wallenstein, Barry J(ay) 1940- ... CANR-11
Earlier sketch in CA 45-48
Wallenstein, Meir 1903- ... CAP-1
Earlier sketch in CA 15-16
Waller, Altina L(aura) 1940- ... 112
Waller, Brown
See Fraser, W(aller) B(rown)
Waller, Charles T(homas) 1934- ... 61-64
Waller, G(ary) F(redric) 1944- ... 112
Waller, Gary
See Waller, G(ary) F(redric)
Waller, George Macgregor 1919- ... 11-12R
Waller, Irene Ellen 1928- ... 109
Waller, J(ames) Irvin 1944- ... CANR-14
Earlier sketch in CA 61-64
Waller, John Stanier 1917- ... 45-48
Waller, Leslie 1923- ... CANR-2
Earlier sketch in CA 4R
See also SATA 20
Waller, Peter Louis 1935- ... 106
Waller, Robert J(ames) 1955- ... 117
Wallerstein, Immanuel 1930- ... CANR-24
Earlier sketches in CA 23-24R, CANR-9
Wallerstein, Judith Hannah Saretsky 1921-
Brief entry ... 105
Wallerstein, Judith (Hannah) S(aretsky)
1921- ... 124
Wallerstein, Mitchel B(ruce) 1949- ... 105
Wallerstein, Robert S(olomon) 1921- ... CANR-12
Earlier sketch in CA 33-36R
Walley, David 1945- ... 41-44R
Wallhauser, Henry T. 1930- ... 29-32R
Wallich, Henry C(hristopher) 1914- ... CANR-6
Earlier sketch in CA 2R
Wallich-Clifford, Anton 1923- ... 61-64
Wallig, Gaird (Elizabeth) 1942- ... 106
Walling, William (Herbert) 1926- ... 103
Wallis, Charles L(angworthy) ... CANR-8
Earlier sketch in CA 7-8R
Wallis, G. McDonald
See Campbell, Hope
Wallis, George A. 1892- ... 17-18R
Wallis, Hal B.
See Wallis, Harold Brent
Wallis, Harold Brent 1898(?)-1986
Obituary ... 120
Wallis, Jim 1948- ... 102
Wallis, Keith 1930- ... 25-28R
Wallis, Kenneth F(rank) 1938- ... CANR-24
Earlier sketch in CA 45-48
Wallis, R(ichard) T(yrrell) 1941- ... 45-48
Wallis, Redmond Frankton 1933- ... 7-8R
Wallis, Robert 1900- ... CAP-2
Earlier sketch in CA 29-32
Wallis, Roy 1945- ... CANR-17
Earlier sketch in CA 97-100
Wallis, Ruth O(tis) S(awtell) 1895-1978
Obituary ... 73-76
Wallis, W(ilson) Allen 1912- ... 41-44R
Wallmann, Jeffrey M(iner) 1941- ... CANR-14
Earlier sketch in CA 77-80
Wallner, Alexandra 1946- ... CANR-13
Earlier sketch in CA 73-76
See also SATA 41
Wallner, John C. 1945- ... SATA-10
Wallop, (John) Douglass III
1920-1985 ... CANR-13
Obituary ... 115
Earlier sketch in CA 73-76
Wallop, Lucille Fletcher 1912- ... 13-14R
Wallower, Lucille ... CANR-9
Earlier sketch in CA 21-22R
See also SATA 11
Wallraff, Charles Fredric 1909- ... 2R
Walls, David Stuart 1941- ... CANR-14
Earlier sketch in CA 37-40R
Walls, Dwayne E(stes) 1932- ... CANR-14
Earlier sketch in CA 41-44R
Walls, H(enry) J(ames) 1907- ... 11-12R
Walls, Ian G(ascoigne) 1922- ... 104
Walls, Ronald 1920- ... 103
Walls, William J(acob) 1885-1975 ... 81-84
Wallsten, Robert 1912- ... 101
Wallwork, Ernest (Edward) 1937- ... 41-44R
Walmsley, Arnold Robert 1912- ... 41-44R
Walmsley, Buck
See Walmsley, Haines
Walmsley, (Ronald) Charles 1910-1983
Obituary ... 110
Walmsley, Haines 1930(?)-1983 Obituary ... 111
Walmsley, Leo 1892-1966 ... CAP-1
Earlier sketch in CA 11-12
Walmsley, Lewis C(alvin) 1897- ... 61-64
Walmsley, Robert 1905-1976 ... CAP-2
Earlier sketch in CA 29-32
Waln, Nora 1895-1964 Obituary ... 89-92
Walpole, Horace 1717-1797 ... DLB-39
Walpole, Hugh (Seymour) 1884-1941
Brief entry ... 104
See also DLB 34
See also TCLC 5
Walpole, Ronald Noel 1903- ... 106
Walrath, Douglas Alan 1933- ... 120
Walrath, Jane Dwyer 1939- ... 97-100
Walrond, Eric 1898-1966 ... DLB-51
Walschap, Gerard 1898- ... 103

Walsdorf, John J(oseph) 1941- 115
Walser, Martin 1927- CANR-8
Earlier sketch in CA 57-60
See also CLC 27
Walser, Richard (Gaither) 1908- CANR-2
Earlier sketch in CA 5-6R
Walser, Robert 1878-1956 Brief entry 118
See also DLB 66
See also TCLC 18
Walsh, Annmarie Hauck 1938- 25-28R
Walsh, Bren(dan) 1921- 121
Walsh, Chad 1914- CANR-6
Earlier sketch in CA 3R
Walsh, Clune J(oseph), Jr. 1928- 114
Walsh, Des 1954- 116
Walsh, Donald Devenish 1903-1980 CANR-3
Obituary 97-100
Earlier sketch in CA 49-52
Walsh, Edward J(oseph) 1937- 37-40R
Walsh, Edward Warren 1930(?)-1986
Obituary 118
Walsh, Elizabeth M(iller) 1937- 120
Walsh, Ellen Stoll 1942- 104
See also SATA 49
Walsh, Ernest 1895-1926 Brief entry 109
See also DLB 4, 45
Walsh, George (Vincent) 1923- 109
Walsh, George (William) 1931- 118
Brief entry 114
Walsh, Gillian Paton 1939- 37-40R
See also SATA 4
Walsh, Jack 1919(?)-1984 Obituary 114
Walsh, James 1920-1986(?) Obituary 119
Walsh, James
See Robinson, Frank M(alcolm)
Walsh, James Edward 1891-1981
Obituary 104
Walsh, James J(erome) 1924- 11-12R
Walsh, James P(atrick) 1937- 111
Walsh, Jill Paton
See Walsh, Gillian Paton
See also SAAS 3
See also CLC 35
See also CLR 2
Walsh, John (Dixon) 1927- 17-18R
Walsh, John Evangelist 1927- 85-88
Walsh, Justin E(arl) 1933- CANR-10
Earlier sketch in CA 25-28R
Walsh, M.M.B. 101
Walsh, Marcus 1947- 118
Walsh, Marnie
See Walsh, M.M.B.
Walsh, Maurice 1879-1964 Brief entry 124
Walsh, Michael J. 1937- 106
Walsh, Myles E(ugene) 1937- 109
Walsh, P(atrick) G(erard) 1923- 25-28R
Walsh, Patricia L(ouise) 1942- 109
Walsh, Raoul 1887-1980 Obituary 102
Walsh, (Walter) Richard 1923- 25-28R
Walsh, Richard 1941- 120
Walsh, Robert 1784-1859 DLB-59
Walsh, Sheila 1928- 115
Walsh, (Michael) Stephen 1942- 37-40R
Walsh, (Richard) Taylor 1947- 73-76
Walsh, Thomas (Francis Morgan)
1908-1984 Obituary 114
Walsh, Timothy J(ames) 1927- 41-44R
Walsh, W(alter) Bruce 1936- 93-96
Walsh, Warren Bartlett 1909- CAP-2
Earlier sketch in CA 15-16
Walsh, William 1916- CANR-11
Earlier sketch in CA 65-68
Walsh, William B(ertalan) 1920- CANR-4
Earlier sketch in CA 49-52
Walsh, William Henry 1913-1986 Obituary 119
Walshe, M(aurice) O'C(onnell) 1911- 7-8R
Walshe, R(obert) D(aniel) 1923- CANR-21
Earlier sketch in CA 104
Walster, Elaine
See Hatfield, Elaine (Catherine)
Walster, Elaine Hatfield
See Hatfield, Elaine (Catherine)
Walster, G. William 1941- 85-88
Walston, Joseph
See Walston, Marie
Walston, Marie 1925- 41-44R
Walt, Lewis W(illiam) 1913- 33-36R
Waltari, Mika (Toimi) 1908-1979 11-12R
Obituary 89-92
Walter, Bruno
See Schlesinger, Bruno Walter
Walter, Claire 1943- 81-84
Walter, Dorothy Blake 1908- CAP-1
Earlier sketch in CA 11-12
Walter, Elizabeth CANR-17
Earlier sketch in CA 97-100
Walter, Eugene 1927- 11-12R
Walter, Eugene Victor 1925- 25-28R
Walter, Gladys Mae 1901-1973 41-44R
Walter, Hartmut 1940- 89-92
Walter, Ingo 1940- CANR-22
Earlier sketches in CA 17-18R, CANR-7
Walter, J(ulian) A(nthony) 1948- 120
Walter, Mildred Pitts SATA-45
Walter, Nancy
See Holmgren, Norah
Walter, Nina Willis 1900- 7-8R
Walter, Otis M. 1921- 5-6R
Walter, Robert H(enry) K(eamer, Jr.)
1922- 7-8R
Walter, Samuel 1916- 5-6R
Walter, Tony
See Walter, J(ulian) A(nthony)
Walter, Villiam Christian
See Andersen, Hans Christian
Walter, William Grey 1910-1977 103
Walters, A(lan) A(rthur) 1926- 29-32R
Walters, Anna L. 1946- 73-76
Walters, Audrey 1929- SATA-18
Walters, Barbara 1931- 65-68
See also AITN 2
Walters, Basil L(eon) 1896-1975
Obituary 89-92
Walters, C(harles) Glenn 1929- 81-84
Walters, Chad
See Smith, Richard Rein
Walters, Dorothy 1928- 65-68
Walters, Dorothy Mae Wells 1924- CANR-2
Earlier sketch in CA 7-8R
Walters, Dottie
See Walters, Dorothy Mae Wells
Walters, Eleanor 1955- 108
Walters, Helen B. ?-1987 Obituary 121
See also SATA 50
Walters, Hugh
See Hughes, Walter (Llewellyn)
Walters, Jack Edward 1896- 5-6R
Walters, Janet Lane 1936- 49-52
Walters, John Beauchamp 1906- CANR-6
Earlier sketch in CA 7-8R
Walters, John Bennett, Jr. 1912- 105
Walters, LeRoy (B., Jr.) 1940- 108
Walters, Nell
See Muse, Patricia (Alice)
Walters, Richard P(aul) 1935- 107
Walters, Rick
See Rowland, D(onald) S(ydney)
Walters, Robert Mark 1938- 69-72
Walters, Robert S(tephen) 1941- 29-32R
Walters, Ronald G(ordon) 1942- 85-88
Walters, Roy W(ashington) 1918- 93-96
Walters, Shelly
See Sheldon, Walter J.
Walters, Sister Annette 1910- 37-40R
Walters, Stanley D(avid) 1931- 53-56
Walters, Thomas N(oble) 1935- 65-68
Walters, Vernon A(nthony) 1917- 122
Waltham, Antony Clive 1942- CANR-10
Earlier sketch in CA 65-68
Walther, R(ichard) E(rnest) 1921- 41-44R
Walther, Regis (Hills) 1917-1983 CANR-8
Obituary 111
Earlier sketch in CA 19-20R
Walther, Thomas A. 1950- 107
See also SATA 31
Walther, Tom
See Walther, Thomas A.
Waltman, Jerold (Lloyd) 1945- 117
Waltman, John L. 1946- 120
Waltner, Elma 1912- 17-18R
See also SATA 40
Waltner, Willard H. 1909- SATA-40
Walton, Alfred Grant 1887-1970 CAP-1
Earlier sketch in CA 13-14
Walton, Bryce 1918- 21-22R
Walton, Clarence C. 1915- CANR-3
Earlier sketch in CA 1-4R
Walton, Clyde C(ameron) 1925- 29-32R
Walton, Craig 1934- 41-44R
Walton, Donald William 1917- 112
Walton, Douglas N(eil) 1942- 117
Walton, Ed(ward Hazen) 1931- CANR-22
Earlier sketch in CA 105
Walton, Elizabeth Cheatham 5-6R
Walton, Evangeline
See Ensley, Evangeline
Walton, George (H.) 1904- 19-20R
Walton, H(enry) J(ohn) 1924- 53-56
Walton, Hanes, Jr. 1942- 41-44R
Walton, J(ohn) Michael 1939- 117
Walton, John 1910- CANR-5
Earlier sketch in CA 2R
Walton, John 1937- 89-92
Walton, John K(immons) 1948- 124
Walton, Luke
See Henderson, Bill
Walton, Ortiz Montaigne 1933- 45-48
Walton, Richard Eugene 1931- 81-84
Walton, Richard J. 1928- 25-28R
See also SATA 4
Walton, Robert Cutler 1932- 73-76
Walton, Ronald (Gordon) 1936- 65-68
Walton, Su 1944- 25-28R
Walton, Vicki (Elizabeth) 1949- 65-68
Walton, W. Robert 1902- 69-72
Waltrip, Lela (Kingston) 1904- 5-6R
See also SATA 9
Waltrip, Mildred 1911- SATA-37
Waltrip, Robert
See Short, Robert Waltrip
Waltrip, Rufus (Charles) 1898- 5-6R
See also SATA 9
Waltz, Jon R(ichard) 1929- 17-18R
Waltz, Kenneth N(eal) 1924- 37-40R
Waltzer, Herbert 1930- 41-44R
Walvin, James 1942- CANR-17
Earlier sketches in CA 49-52, CANR-1
Walvoord, John F(lipse) 1910- CANR-6
Earlier sketch in CA 11-12R
Walwik, Theodore J. 1937- 25-28R
Walworth, Alice
See Graham, Alice Walworth
Walworth, Arthur 1903- 23-24R
Walworth, Nancy Zinsser 1917- CANR-3
Earlier sketch in CA 5-6R
See also SATA 14
Walz, Audrey Boyers 1907(?)-1983
Obituary 109
Walz, Edgar 1914- 29-32R
Walz, Jay 1907- 49-52
Walzer, Michael 1935- CANR-15
Earlier sketch in CA 37-40R
Walzer, Norman 1943- 111
Wambaugh, Joseph (Aloysius, Jr.)
1937- 33-36R
See also DLB 6
See also DLBY 83
See also CLC 3, 18
See also AITN 1
Wamble, Gaston Hugh 1923- 7-8R
Wamble, Thelma 1916- Brief entry 106
Wamsley, Gary L(ee) 1935- CANR-3
Earlier sketch in CA 49-52
Wanamaker, A(llison) Temple 1918- 17-18R
Wand, (John) William (Charles) 1885-? 103
Wandel, Joseph 1918- 93-96
Wanderer, Zev W(illiam) 1932- 105
Wandesforde-Smith, Geoffrey Albert
1943- 29-32R
Wandro, Mark 1948- 106
Wandycz, Piotr Stefan 1923- CANR-2
Earlier sketch in CA 2R
Wang, C(hing) H(sien) 1940- CANR-8
Earlier sketch in CA 61-64
Wang, (Fred) Fang Yu 1913- 37-40R
Wang, Hao 1921- 65-68
Wang, Hui-Ming 1922- 33-36R
Wang, J(en) Y(u) 1918- 45-48
Wang, John Ching-yu 1934- 41-44R
Wang, Julie C(aroline) 1947- 114
Wang, Leonard J(udah) 1926- 33-36R
Wang, Sabine E(isenberg) 1925- 37-40R
Wang, Yi Chu 1916- 61-64
Wangenheim, Chris von
See von Wangenheim, Chris
Wangensteen, Owen Harding 1898-1981 103
Wangensteen, Sarah (Anne) D(avidson)
1908- 120
Wangerin, Theodora Scharffenberg 1888- 5-6R
Wangerin, Walter, Jr. 1944- 108
See also SATA 37, 45
Wangermann, Ernst 1925- 103
Wang Gungwu 1930- CANR-10
Earlier sketch in CA 65-68
Wangyal, Geshe 1901(?)-1983 Obituary 108
Wang Zhongshu 1925- 117
Waniek, Marilyn Nelson 1946- CANR-15
Earlier sketch in CA 89-92
Wankowicz, Melchoir 1892(?)-1974
Obituary 53-56
Wanlass, Stanley G(len) 1941- 61-64
Wann, Kenneth D(ouglass) 1915- 7-8R
Wannamaker, Bruce
See Moncure, Jane Belk
Wannan, Bill
See Wannan, William Fielding
Wannan, William Fielding 1915- CANR-10
Earlier sketch in CA 21-22R
Wanrooy, Willem F(rederik) 1925- 118
Wanshel, Jeff(rey Mark) 1947- CANR-13
Earlier sketch in CA 57-60
Wantland, William C(harles) 1934- 111
Wantling, William 1933-1974 105
Obituary 89-92
Waples, Douglas 1893-1978 Obituary 77-80
Warbler, J. M.
See Cocagnac, Augustin Maurice(-Jean)
Warbridge, C. W.
See Woods, Clee
Warburg, Fredric (John) 1898-1981 105
Warburg, James Paul 1896-1969 CAP-2
Obituary 25-28R
Earlier sketch in CA 21-22
Warburg, Sandol Stoddard
See Stoddard, Sandol
See also SATA 14
Warburton, Amber Arthun 1898(?)-1976
Obituary 61-64
Warburton, Clark (Abram) 1896-1979 73-76
Obituary 89-92
Warburton, Minnie 1949- 101
Warch, Richard 1939- 105
Warcollier, Rene 1881-1962 Obituary 112
Ward, Aileen 1919- 7-8R
Ward, Alan Joseph 1936- 73-76
Ward, Allen M(ason) 1942- 89-92
Ward, Andrew (Spencer) 1946- 81-84
Ward, Anne G. 1932- 77-80
Ward, Artemus
See Browne, Charles Farrar
Ward, Arthur Henry Sarsfield 1883-1959
Brief entry 108
Ward, Barbara
See Jackson, Barbara (Ward)
Ward, Benedicta 1933- CANR-12
Earlier sketch in CA 65-68
Ward, Charles D(uane) 1935- 33-36R
Ward, Charles Dexter
See Taylor, John (Alfred)
Ward, Charlotte
See Chesney, Marion
Ward, Chester 1907-1977 Obituary 69-72
Ward, Colin 1924- 57-60
Ward, Craig 1892-1979 Obituary 85-88
Ward, David 1938- 29-32R
Ward, Dennis 1924- 13-14R
Ward, Don(ald G.) 1911- 19-20R
Ward, Donald 1909- 109
Ward, Donald 1930- 37-40R
Ward, Douglas Turner 1930- 81-84
See also DLB 7, 38
See also CLC 19
Ward, Ed(mund O.) 1948- 114
Ward, Elizabeth 1952- 110
Ward, Elizabeth Campbell 1936- 45-48
Ward, Elizabeth Honor (Shedden) 1926- 9-10R
Ward, Eric
See Ebon, Martin
Ward, Evelyn
See Everett-Green, Evelyn
Ward, Fred 1935- 85-88
Ward, Harry Merrill 1929- CANR-2
Earlier sketch in CA 2R
Ward, Herman Matthew 1914- CANR-18
Earlier sketches in CA 7-8R, CANR-2
Ward, Hiley Henry 1929- CANR-2
Earlier sketch in CA 2R
Ward, J. Alan 1937- 114
Ward, J(oseph) Neville 1915- 77-80
Ward, J(ohn) P(owell) 1937- 109
Ward, J(ohn) T(owers) 1930- CANR-7
Earlier sketch in CA 7-8R
Ward, James A(rthur) 1941- 49-52
Ward, James Myron 1919-1984 Obituary 112
Ward, John (Stanton) 1917- SATA-42
Ward, John M(anning) 1919- 23-24R
Ward, John Owen 1919- 13-14R
Ward, John Stephen Keith 1938- 109
Ward, John Towers 1930-1987 109
Obituary 122
Ward, John William 1922-1985 5-6R
Obituary 116
Ward, Jonas
See Ard, William (Thomas)
and Cox, William (Robert)
and Garfield, Brian (Wynne)
Ward, Jonathon
See Stine, Whitney Ward
Ward, Joseph A(nthony, Jr.) 1931- 2R
Ward, Justine Bayard Cutting 1879-1975
Obituary 61-64
Ward, (John Stephen) Keith 1938- CANR-16
Earlier sketch in CA 29-32R
Ward, Lynd (Kendall) 1905-1985 17-18R
Obituary 116
See also SATA 2, 36, 42
See also DLB 22
Ward, Maisie 1889-1975 69-72
Obituary 53-56
Ward, Martha (Eads) 17-18R
See also SATA 5
Ward, Mary Josephine
See Ward, Maisie
Ward, Melanie
See Curtis, Richard (Alan)
and Lynch, Marilyn
Ward, Michael 1939- 37-40R
Ward, Mrs. Humphry 1851-1920 DLB-18
Ward, Nathaniel 1578(?)-1652 DLB-24
Ward, Norman 1918- 41-44R
Ward, Olivia Tucker 1927- 57-60
Ward, Patricia A(nn) 1940- 57-60
Ward, Paul W. 1905-1976 Obituary 69-72
Ward, Pearl L(ewis) 1920- 107
Ward, Peter
See Faust, Frederick (Shiller)
Ward, Philip 1938- CANR-12
Earlier sketch in CA 25-28R
Ward, Philip C. 1932- 21-22R
Ward, R(ichard) H(eron) 1910-1969 CAP-1
Earlier sketch in CA 11-12
Ward, R. Patrick
See Holzapfel, Rudolf Patrick
Ward, Ralph Gerard 1933- 107
Ward, Ralph T(homas) 1927- 49-52
Ward, Richard J(oseph) 1921- 41-44R
Ward, Ritchie R(unyan) 1906- 29-32R
Ward, Robert 1943- 104
Ward, Robert E(rnest) 1927- 49-52
Ward, Robert Elmer 1937- 49-52
Ward, Ronald A(rthur) 1908- 53-56
Ward, Russel (Braddock) 1914- CANR-22
Earlier sketch in CA 103
Ward, Russell A(very) 1947- 110
Ward, Stephen R(alph) 1938- 65-68
Ward, Ted (Warren) 1930- CANR-16
Earlier sketch in CA 97-100
Ward, Theodora 1890-1974 CAP-2
Obituary 53-56
Earlier sketch in CA 33-36
Ward, Theodore (James) 1902-1983
Obituary 109
Ward, Virgil S(cott) 1916- 2R
Ward, Waylon O. 1942- 114
Ward, William Alan Heaton
See Heaton-Ward, William Alan
Ward, William Arthur 1921- 29-32R
Ward, William B(ethea) 1912- 5-6R
Ward, William Ernest Frank 1900- CANR-19
Earlier sketches in CA 11-12R, CANR-4
Ward, William G. 1929- 21-22R
Ward, William R(eed) 1918- 61-64
Ward, Winfred O'(Neil) 1933- 106
Warddel, Nora Helen
See Heron-Allen, Edward
Warde, Alan 1949- 112
Warde, William F.
See Novack, George (Edward)
Wardell, Dean
See Prince, J(ack) H(arvey)
Wardell, Phyl(lis Robinson) 1909- CAP-1
Earlier sketch in CA 11-12
Warden, G(erard) B(ryce) 1939- 29-32R
Warden, John 1936- 41-44R
Warden, Lewis (Christopher) 1913- 15-16R
Wardhaugh, Ronald 1932- 37-40R
Wardle, David 1930- 69-72
Wardle, (John) Irving 1929- 77-80
Wardle, Lynn D(ennis) 1947- 109
Wardle, Ralph Martin 1909- CANR-5
Earlier sketch in CA 2R
Wardman, Alan (Edgar) 1926-1986 77-80
Obituary 120
Ward-Perkins, John Bryan 1912-1981 93-96
Obituary 108
Wardroper, John (Edmund) 1923- 29-32R
Wardropper, Bruce W(ear) 1919- 15-16R

Ward-Thomas, Evelyn Bridget Patricia
Stephens 1928- ... CANR-5
Earlier sketch in CA 9-10R
Ware, Ciji 1942- ... 103
Ware, Clyde 1932- ... 33-36R
Ware, Emma 1896(?)-1975 Obituary ... 57-60
Ware, George W(hitaker) 1902- ... 13-14R
Ware, Gilbert 1933- ... 65-68
Ware, Jean (Jones) 1914- ... CAP-1
Earlier sketch in CA 11-12
Ware, John
See Mabley, Edward (Howe)
Ware, Kallistos (Timothy Richard)
1934- ... CANR-24
Earlier sketches in CA 11-12R, CANR-7
Ware, Leon (Vernon) 1909-1976 ... CANR-2
Earlier sketch in CA 2R
See also SATA 4
Ware, Leonard 1900(?)-1976 Obituary ... 69-72
Ware, Runa Erwin ... CAP-2
Earlier sketch in CA 29-32
Ware, Timothy
See Ware, Kallistos (Timothy Richard)
Ware, W. Porter 1904- ... 105
Ware, Wallace
See Karp, David
Ware, William 1797-1852 ... DLB-1
Wareham, John 1940- ... 101
Warenski, Marilyn L(iston) 1931- ... 117
Warfel, Harry R(edcay) 1899-1971 ... CAP-1
Earlier sketch in CA 13-14
Warfield, Gerald (Alexander) 1940- ... 117
Warford, Jeremy J(ames) 1938- ... 37-40R
Wargo, Dan M. 1920- ... 21-22R
Warhaft, Sidney 1921- ... 61-64
Warhol, Andy 1927(?)-1987 ... 89-92
Obituary ... 121
See also CLC 20
Wark, David M(ayer) 1934- ... 33-36R
Wark, Ian W(illiam) 1899- ... CAP-2
Earlier sketch in CA 29-32
Wark, Robert R(odger) 1924- ... CANR-8
Earlier sketch in CA 61-64
Wark, Wesley K. 1952- ... 123
Warkentin, Germaine (Therese) 1933- ... 109
Warkentin, John 1928- ... 11-12R
Warland, John
See Buchanan-Brown, John
Warlimont, Walter 1894- ... CAP-1
Earlier sketch in CA 15-16
Warlum, Michael Frank 1940- ... 37-40R
Warman, (William) Eric 1904- ... CAP-1
Earlier sketch in CA 13-14
Warman, Henry J(ohn) 1907- ... 41-44R
Warmbrand, Max 1896(?)-1976 Obituary ... 65-68
Warmbrunn, Werner 1920- ... 23-24R
Warmington, Brian Herbert 1924- ... 65-68
Warmington, E(ric) H(erbert) 1898-1987 ... 124
Warmington, William Allan 1922- ... 7-8R
Warmke, Roman F. 1929- ... CANR-9
Earlier sketch in CA 19-20R
Warnath, Charles F. 1925- ... 37-40R
Warne, Clinton L. 1921- ... 13-14R
Warne, Colston Estey 1900-1987 Obituary ... 122
Warne, William E(lmo) 1905- ... 41-44R
Warner, Alan 1912- ... 104
Warner, B. F.
See Bowers, Warner Fremont
Warner, Bob
See Warner, Robert
Warner, Charles Dudley 1829-1900 ... DLB-64
Warner, Daniel S(umner) 1906-1983 ... CANR-16
Earlier sketch in CA 3R
Warner, Deborah Jean 1941- ... 108
Warner, Denis Ashton 1917- ... CANR-3
Earlier sketch in CA 5-6R
Warner, Edythe Records 1916- ... 5-6R
Warner, Emily S(mith) 1902(?)-1980
Obituary ... 97-100
Warner, Esther S.
See Dendel, Esther (Sietmann Warner)
Warner, Francis (Robert le Plastrier)
1937- ... CANR-11
Earlier sketch in CA 53-56
See also CLC 14
Warner, Frank
See Richardson, Gladwell
Warner, Frank A. ... CAP-2
Earlier sketch in CA 19-20
See also SATA 1
Warner, Gary 1936- ... 23-24R
Warner, (George) Geoffrey John 1923- ... 3R
Warner, Gertrude Chandler 1890-1979 ... CANR-3
Earlier sketch in CA 4R
See also SATA 9
Warner, Glen 1947- ... 121
Warner, H(oyt) Landon 1911- ... 15-16R
Warner, Harry, Jr. 1922- ... 29-32R
Warner, Jack 1896-1981 Obituary ... 108
Warner, Jack L(eonard) 1892-1978
Obituary ... 108
Warner, James A(loysius) 1918- ... CANR-24
Earlier sketch in CA 45-48
Warner, Ken(neth Wilson, Jr.) 1928- ... CANR-10
Earlier sketch in CA 65-68
Warner, Kenneth (Lewis) 1915- ... CAP-1
Earlier sketch in CA 9-10
Warner, Langdon 1881-1955 Brief entry ... 112
Warner, Lucien (Hynes) 1900-1963
Obituary ... 112
Warner, Lucille Schulberg ... CANR-11
Earlier sketch in CA 69-72
See also SATA 30
Warner, Marina 1946- ... CANR-21
Earlier sketch in CA 65-68
Warner, Matt
See Fichter, George S.
Warner, Oliver (Martin Wilson)
1903-1976 ... CANR-3
Obituary ... 69-72
Earlier sketch in CA 3R
See also SATA 29
Warner, Philip 1914- ... CANR-18
Earlier sketch in CA 101
Warner, Rex (Ernest) 1905-1986 ... 89-92
Obituary ... 119
See also DLB 15
See also CLC 45
Warner, Richard 1943- ... 120
Warner, Robert 1905- ... 53-56
Warner, Robert M(ark) 1927- ... CANR-7
Earlier sketch in CA 11-12R
Warner, Sam Bass, Jr. 1928- ... CANR-17
Earlier sketches in CA 5-6R, CANR-2
Warner, Seth 1927- ... 53-56
Warner, Susan (Bogert) 1819-1885 ... DLB-3, 42
Warner, Sylvia (Constance) Ashton
See Ashton-Warner, Sylvia (Constance)
Warner, Sylvia Townsend 1893-1978 ... CANR-16
Obituary ... 77-80
Earlier sketch in CA 61-64
See also DLB 34
See also CLC 7, 19
Warner, Val 1946- ... CANR-23
Earlier sketch in CA 49-52
Warner, Virginia
See Brodine, Virginia Warner
Warner, W(illiam) Lloyd 1898-1970 ... CANR-2
Obituary ... 29-32R
Earlier sketch in CA 2R
Warner, Wayne E(arl) 1933- ... CANR-3
Earlier sketch in CA 49-52
Warner, William W(hitesides) 1920-
Brief entry ... 114
Warner-Crozetti, R(uth G.) 1913- ... 101
Warnick, Barbara 1946- ... 120
Warnock, G(eoffrey) J(ames) 1923- ... 21-22R
Warnock, Mary (Wilson) 1924- ... CANR-8
Earlier sketch in CA 5-6R
Warr, Peter B(ryan) 1937- ... 25-28R
Warrack, Graeme Matthew 1913-1985
Obituary ... 115
Warrack, John 1928- ... CANR-5
Earlier sketch in CA 15-16R
Warre, Michael 1922-1987 Obituary ... 121
Warren, Andrew
See Tute, Warren (Stanley)
Warren, Austin 1899-1986 ... 19-20R
Obituary ... 120
Warren, Betsy
See Warren, Elizabeth Avery
Warren, Bill 1943- ... 118
Warren, Billy
See Warren, William Stephen
Warren, Cathy ... SATA-46
Warren, Dave
See Wiersbe, Warren W(endell)
Warren, David 1943- ... 77-80
Warren, Donald Irwin 1935- ... CANR-1
Earlier sketch in CA 45-48
Warren, Donald R. 1933- ... 111
Warren, Doug(las) 1935- ... 61-64
Warren, E(ugene) H(oward), Jr. 1943- ... 111
Warren, Earl 1891-1974 ... 123
Obituary ... 49-52
Warren, Elizabeth
See Supraner, Robyn
Warren, Elizabeth Avery 1916- ... CANR-8
Earlier sketch in CA 7-8R
See also SATA 38, 46
Warren, (Francis) Eugene 1941- ... CANR-1
Earlier sketch in CA 49-52
Warren, Frank A. III 1933- Brief entry ... 115
Warren, Gordon Harris 1944- ... 114
Warren, Harold Ostrander, Jr. 1910-1985
Obituary ... 116
Warren, Harris G(aylord) 1906- ... CANR-5
Earlier sketch in CA 2R
Warren, Harry
See Guaragna, Salvatore
Warren, James E(dward), Jr. 1908- ... CANR-24
Earlier sketch in CA 23-24R
Warren, James Hugo, Jr. 1928(?)-1983
Obituary ... 110
Warren, Jefferson T(rowbridge) 1912- ... 41-44R
Warren, John Byrne Leicester
See De Tabley, Lord
Warren, Joyce W(illiams) 1935- ... 77-80
See also SATA 18
Warren, Kenneth 1931- ... 109
Warren, Lansing 1894-1987 Obituary ... 124
Warren, Lella 1899-1982 Obituary ... 113
See also DLBY 83
Warren, Louis Austin 1885-1983 ... CANR-21
Obituary ... 110
Earlier sketch in CA 5-6R
Warren, Louise 1909(?)-1981 Obituary ... 104
Warren, Lucian (Crissey) 1913- ... 101
Warren, Mary Bondurant 1930- ... CANR-12
Earlier sketch in CA 73-76
Warren, Mary Douglas
See Greig, Maysie
Warren, Mary Phraner 1929- ... CANR-5
Earlier sketch in CA 53-56
See also SATA 10
Warren, Matthew Madison 1907-1986
Obituary ... 119
Warren, Mercy Otis 1728-1814 ... DLB-31
Warren, Michael 1935- ... 112
Warren, Patricia Nell 1936- ... CANR-1
Earlier sketch in CA 45-48
Warren, Peter Whitson 1941- ... CANR-5
Earlier sketch in CA 53-56
Warren, Richard M. 1925- ... 112
Warren, Robert Penn 1905- ... CANR-10
Earlier sketch in CA 13-14R
See also SATA 46
See also DLB 2, 48
See also DLBY 80
See also CLC 1, 4, 6, 8, 10, 13, 18, 39
See also AITN 1
Warren, Roland L(eslie) 1915- ... CANR-10
Earlier sketch in CA 57-60
Warren, Sidney 1916- ... 25-28R
Warren, Thomas (Bratton) 1920- ... 103
Warren, Thomas L(eo) 1937- ... 111
Warren, Vernon
See Chapman, G(eorge) W(arren) Vernon
Warren, Virginia Burgess 1913- ... 15-16R
Warren, W(ilfred) Lewis 1929- ... CANR-21
Earlier sketch in CA 3R
Warren, W(illiam) Preston 1901- ... 37-40R
Warren, William Stephen 1882-1968 ... CAP-2
Earlier sketch in CA 21-22
See also SATA 9
Warrender, James Howard 1922-1985
Obituary ... 116
Warrick, Patricia Scott 1925- ... CANR-8
Earlier sketch in CA 61-64
See also SATA 35
Warriner, Charles K(ing) 1920- ... 41-44R
Warriner, John 1907(?)-1987 Obituary ... 123
Warrner, Thomas W(endell) 1955- ... 118
Warry, J(ohn) G(ibson) 1916- ... 7-8R
Warsaw, Irene ... CAP-1
Earlier sketch in CA 15-16
Warsh
See Warshaw, Jerry
Warsh, David (Lewis) 1944- ... 118
Warsh, Lewis 1944- ... CANR-24
Earlier sketches in CA 61-64, CANR-9
Warshaw, Jerry 1929- ... CANR-14
Earlier sketch in CA 37-40R
See also SATA 30
Warshaw, Leon J(oseph) 1917- ... 107
Warshofsky, Fred 1931- ... 11-12R
See also SATA 24
Warshofsky, Isaac
See Singer, Isaac Bashevis
Warth, Robert D(ouglas) 1921- ... 11-12R
Wartofsky, Marx W(illiam) 1928- ... 41-44R
Wartofsky, (William) Victor 1931- ... 29-32R
Wartski, Maureen (Ann Crane) 1940- ... 89-92
See also SATA 37, 50
Warwick, Alan R(oss) 1900-1973 ... 112
See also SATA 42
Warwick, Christopher 1949- ... 110
Warwick, Dennis 1930- ... 73-76
Warwick, Dolores
See Frese, Dolores Warwick
Warwick, Donald P(hillip) 1934- ... 118
Warwick, Jack 1930- ... 29-32R
Warwick, James 1894(?)-1983 Obituary ... 110
Warwick, Jarvis
See Garner, Hugh
Warwick, Ray 1911(?)-1983 Obituary ... 109
Warwick, Roger 1912- ... 109
Warzeski, Walter C. 1929- ... 37-40R
Wa-Sha-Quon-Asin
See Belaney, Archibald Stansfeld
Wa-sha-quon-asin
See Belaney, Archibald Stansfeld
Washburn, (Henry) Bradford (Jr.)
1910- ... CANR-3
Earlier sketch in CA 49-52
See also SATA 38
Washburn, Charles 1890(?)-1972
Obituary ... 104
Washburn, Dorothy K(oster) 1945- ... CANR-24
Earlier sketch in CA 106
Washburn, Jan(ice) 1926- ... 93-96
Washburn, Mark 1948- ... 77-80
Washburn, O(swell) A(aron) 1914- ... 57-60
Washburn, Sherwood L(arned) 1911-
Brief entry ... 105
Washburn, Wilcomb Edward 1925- ... 41-44R
Washburne, Carleton W(olsey) 1889- ... CAP-1
Earlier sketch in CA 15-16
Washburne, Heluiz Chandler 1892-1970 ... CAP-1
Obituary ... 104
Earlier sketch in CA 11-12
See also SATA 10, 26
Washington, Alex
See Harris, Mark
Washington, Booker T(aliaferro)
1858(?)-1915 Brief entry ... 114
See also SATA 28
See also TCLC 10
Washington, C.
See Pharr, Robert D(eane)
Washington, Chester Lloyd 1902-1983
Obituary ... 110
Washington, George 1732-1799 ... DLB-31
Washington, Gladys J(oseph) 1931- ... 29-32R
Washington, Harold R(obert) 1935- ... 112
Washington, Ida Harrison 1924- ... 107
Washington, Joseph R(eed), Jr. 1930- ... 11-12R
Washington, (Catherine) Marguerite
Beauchamp 1892-1972 ... CAP-1
Earlier sketch in CA 9-10
Washington, Mary Helen 1941- ... 65-68
Washington, Pat Beauchamp
See Washington, (Catherine) Marguerite
Beauchamp
Washton, Nathan S(eymour) 1916- ... 53-56
Wasiolek, Edward 1924- ... CANR-6
Earlier sketch in CA 2R
Waskin, Yvonne 1923- ... 23-24R
Waskow, Arthur I(rwin) 1933- ... CANR-4
Earlier sketch in CA 7-8R
Wasley, Robert S(echrist) 1918- ... 17-18R
Wasmuth, William J. 1925- ... CANR-24
Earlier sketch in CA 45-48
Wason, Betty
See Wason, Elizabeth
Wason, Elizabeth 1912- ... CANR-2
Earlier sketch in CA 4R
Wason, P(eter) C(athcart) 1924- ... 45-48
Wasow, Mona 1933- ... 110
Wassenbergh, Henri Abraham 1924- ... 21-22R
Wasser, Henry H. 1919- ... CANR-8
Earlier sketch in CA 21-22R
Wasserfall, Adel 1918- ... CANR-6
Earlier sketch in CA 3R
Wasserman, Aaron O(sias) 1927- ... 53-56
Wasserman, Burton 1929- ... 53-56
Wasserman, Dale 1917- ... 49-52
Wasserman, Earl R(eeves) 1913-1973 ... CAP-2
Earlier sketch in CA 17-18
Wasserman, Gary 1944- ... 69-72
Wasserman, Harvey 1945- ... 45-48
Wasserman, Jack 1921- ... 61-64
Wasserman, John L. 1938- ... 77-80
Wasserman, Max Judd 1895-1977 ... CANR-4
Earlier sketch in CA 5-6R
Wasserman, Paul 1924- ... CANR-1
Earlier sketch in CA 1R
Wasserman, Pauline 1943- ... CANR-24
Earlier sketch in CA 110
Wasserman, Selma (Ginsberg) 1929- ... 5-6R
Wasserman, Sheldon 1940- ... CANR-24
Earlier sketches in CA 65-68, CANR-9
Wassermann, (Karl) Jakob 1873-1934
Brief entry ... 104
See also DLB 66
See also TCLC 6
Wasserstein, Abraham 1921- ... 109
Wasserstein, Bruce 1947- ... 37-40R
Wasserstein, Susan 1952- ... 107
Wasserstein, Wendy 1950- Brief entry ... 121
See also CLC 32
Wasserstrom, Richard Alan 1936- ... CANR-6
Earlier sketch in CA 3R
Wasserstrom, (Jacob) William
1922-1985 ... 11-12R
Obituary ... 115
Wassersug, Joseph D. 1912- ... 19-20R
Wassil, Aly 1930- ... 19-20R
Wassmer, Arthur C(harles) 1947- ... 103
Wassner, Selig O. 1923- ... 25-28R
Wasson, Ben 1899(?)-1982 Obituary ... 114
Wasson, Chester R(eynolds) 1906- ... CANR-10
Earlier sketch in CA 15-16R
Wasson, David Atwood 1823-1887 ... DLB-1
Wasson, Donald 1914(?)-1976 Obituary ... 69-72
Wasson, John M. 1928- ... 45-48
Wasson, R(obert) Gordon 1898-
Brief entry ... 116
Wasti, Syed R(azi) 1929- ... CANR-7
Earlier sketch in CA 15-16R
Waswo, Richard 1939- ... 53-56
Watanabe, Hitoshi 1919- ... 73-76
Watanabe, Ruth T(aiko) 1916- ... 37-40R
Watanabe, Shigeo 1928- ... 112
See also SATA 32, 39
See also CLR 8
Waten, Judah Leon 1911- ... 101
Water, Silas
See Loomis, Noel (Miller)
Waterfield, Gordon 1903-1987 ... 61-64
Obituary ... 124
Waterfield, Robin (Everard) 1914- ... 49-52
Waterford, Van
See Wanrooy, Willem F(rederik)
Waterhouse, Charles 1924- ... 29-32R
Waterhouse, Ellis K(irkham) 1905-1985 ... 65-68
Obituary ... 117
Waterhouse, Keith (Spencer) 1929- ... 7-8R
See also DLB 13, 15
See also CLC 47
Waterhouse, Larry G(ene) 1944- ... 37-40R
Waterlow, Charlotte 1915- ... 25-28R
Waterman, Andrew (John) 1940- ... 109
See also DLB 40
Waterman, Arthur E. 1926- ... 17-18R
Waterman, Bic
See Joseph, Stephen M.
Waterman, Cary (Martha) 1942- ... 103
Waterman, Charles F(rederick) 1913- ... 49-52
Waterman, Guy 1932- ... 97-100
Waterman, John Thomas 1918- ... CANR-8
Earlier sketch in CA 5-6R
Waterman, Laura 1939- ... 97-100
Waterman, Leroy 1875-1972 ... CAP-1
Obituary ... 33-36R
Earlier sketch in CA 19-20
Waterman, Margaret 1909- ... 37-40R
Waterman, Richard Alan 1914-1971
Obituary ... 111
Watermeier, Daniel J(ude) 1940- ... 73-76
Water Rat
See Jones, Stephen (Phillip)
Waters, Bob 1921(?)-1987 Obituary ... 122
Waters, Brian Power
See Power-Waters, Brian
Waters, Chocolate 1949- ... 77-80
Waters, Chris
See Waters, Harold A(rthur)
Waters, D(avid) W(atkin) 1911- ... 25-28R
Waters, Enoch P. 1910(?)-1987 Obituary ... 122
Waters, Ethel 1896-1977 ... 81-84
Obituary ... 73-76
Waters, Frank (Joseph) 1902- ... CANR-18
Earlier sketches in CA 5-6R, CANR-3
See also DLBY 86
Waters, Harold A(rthur) 1926- ... 53-56

Waters, John F(rederick) 1930- ... CANR-23
Earlier sketch in CA 37-40R
See also SATA 4
Waters, K(enneth) H(ugh) 1912- ... 120
Waters, Marianne
See Waters, Chocolate
Waters, Mary-Alice 1942- ... CANR-9
Earlier sketch in CA 61-64
Waters, Michael 1949- ... CANR-10
Earlier sketch in CA 65-68
Waters, Roger 1944- ... CLC-35
Waters, Thomas F(rank) 1926- ... 81-84
Waters, William R(oland) 1920- ... 49-52
Waterston, Albert 1907- ... CAP-1
Earlier sketch in CA 13-14
Waterston, Barbara Johns 1940- ... 25-28R
Waterston, (Margaret) Elizabeth (Hillman) 1922- ... 69-72
Waterton, Betty (Marie) 1923- ... 111
See also SATA 34, 37
Wathen, Richard B. 1917- ... 37-40R
Wathern, Peter 1947- ... 105
wa Thiong'O, Ngugi
See Ngugi, James T(hiong'o)
Watjen, Carolyn L. T. ... 85-88
Watkin, David (John) 1941- ... 29-32R
Watkin, Edward Ingram 1888-1981 Obituary ... 103
Watkin, Lawrence Edward 1901- ... 81-84
Watkins, A(rthur) M(artin) 1924- ... CANR-7
Earlier sketch in CA 11-12R
Watkins, Alan (Rhun) 1933- ... 104
Watkins, Arthur Rich 1916- ... 41-44R
Watkins, Arthur Thomas Levi 1907-1965 ... 7-8R
Watkins, Arthur V(ivian) 1886-1973 Obituary ... 111
Watkins, Evan Paul 1946- ... 104
Watkins, Floyd C. 1920- ... CANR-18
Earlier sketches in CA 2R, CANR-2
Watkins, Frances Ellen
See Harper, Frances Ellen Watkins
Watkins, Gerrold
See Malzberg, Barry N(athaniel)
Watkins, Glenn (Elson) 1927- Brief entry ... 117
Watkins, Gordon R(onald) 1930- ... 37-40R
Watkins, Grace F. 1927- ... 23-24R
Watkins, Gwen(doline Mary) 1923- ... 116
Watkins, J(ohn) W(illiam) N(evill) 1924- ... 21-22R
Watkins, Jane 1929- ... 77-80
Watkins, Joan C.
See Casale, Joan T(herese)
Watkins, John C(umming), Jr. 1935- ... 113
Watkins, John G(oodrich) 1913- ... CANR-17
Earlier sketches in CA 2R, CANR-1
Watkins, Keith 1931- ... 106
Watkins, Mark Hanna 1903-1976 Obituary ... 65-68
Watkins, Mary M. 1950- ... CANR-20
Earlier sketch in CA 104
Watkins, Mel 1940- ... 89-92
Watkins, Peter 1934- ... 109
Watkins, Ralph J(ames) 1896-1984 ... 45-48
Obituary ... 113
Watkins, (Arthur) Ronald (Dare) 1904- ... 53-56
Watkins, T(homas) H(enry) 1936- ... CANR-14
Earlier sketch in CA 37-40R
Watkins, Vernon Phillips 1906-1967 ... CAP-1
Obituary ... 25-28R
Earlier sketch in CA 9-10
See also DLB 20
See also CLC 43
Watkins, William Jon 1942- ... 41-44R
Watkinson, Valerie
See Elliston, Valerie Mae (Watkinson)
Watkins-Pitchford, Denys James 1905- ... CANR-4
Earlier sketch in CA 9-10R
See also SATA 6
See also SAAS 4
Watkyn, Arthur
See Watkins, Arthur Thomas Levi
Watland, Charles D(unton) 1913-1972 ... CAP-2
Earlier sketch in CA 25-28
Watlington, Patricia (Sue) 1933- ... 37-40R
Watmough, David 1926- ... CANR-15
Earlier sketch in CA 85-88
See also DLB 53
Watney, John B(asil) 1915- ... CANR-5
Earlier sketch in CA 9-10R
Watney, Sanders ?-1983 Obituary ... 109
Watson, (John Hugh) Adam 1914- ... CANR-17
Earlier sketch in CA 25-28R
Watson, Alan
See Watson, William Alexander Jardine
Watson, Alan D(ouglas) 1942- ... CANR-6
Earlier sketch in CA 57-60
Watson, Aldren A(uld) 1917- ... CANR-4
Earlier sketch in CA 81-84
See also SATA 36, 42
Watson, Andrew Samuel 1920- ... 45-48
Watson, B. S.
See Teitelbaum, Michael
Watson, Barbara Bellow ... 77-80
Watson, Bernard B(ennett) 1911-1977 Obituary ... 69-72
Watson, Billy 1938- ... 77-80
Watson, Burton (DeWitt) 1925- ... CANR-18
Earlier sketches in CA 7-8R, CANR-3
Watson, Charles N(elles, Jr.) 1939- ... 113
Watson, Charles S(t. Denis), Jr. 1934- ... 61-64
Watson, Clarissa ... 69-72
Watson, Clyde 1947- ... CANR-4
Earlier sketch in CA 49-52
See also SATA 5
See also CLR 3
Watson, Colin 1920-1983 ... CANR-2
Obituary ... 108
Earlier sketch in CA 3R
Watson, David 1934- ... CANR-24
Earlier sketch in CA 45-48
Watson, David Christopher Knight 1934(?)-1984 Obituary ... 112
Watson, David Robin 1935- ... 109
Watson, Donald Stevenson 1909- ... CAP-1
Earlier sketch in CA 13-14
Watson, E(lliot) L(ovegood) Grant 1885-1970 ... CAP-1
Earlier sketch in CA 11-12
Watson, Elaine 1921- ... 115
Watson, Ernest W(illiam) 1884- ... 7-8R
Watson, Eunice L. 1932- ... 65-68
Watson, F. J. B.
See Watson, Francis John Bagott
Watson, Fletcher Guard (Jr.) 1912- ... 5-6R
Watson, Francis John Bagott 1907- Brief entry ... 116
Watson, Francis M(arion) 1921- ... 105
Watson, Frank
See Ames, Francis H.
Watson, Gayle Hudgens
See Hudgens, A(lice) Gayle
Watson, George (Grimes) 1927- ... CANR-20
Earlier sketches in CA 13-14R, CANR-5
Watson, George (Henry) 1936- ... 77-80
Watson, Goodwin 1899(?)-1976 Obituary ... 69-72
Watson, Graham (Angus) 1913- ... 104
Watson, Harold M. 1924- ... 37-40R
Watson, Harry Legare 1949- ... 111
Watson, Helen Orr 1892-1978 ... 7-8R
Obituary ... 77-80
See also SATA 24
Watson, (George) Hugh (Nicholas) Seton
See Seton-Watson, (George) Hugh (Nicholas)
Watson, Ian 1943- ... CANR-24
Earlier sketch in CA 61-64
Watson, J. R. 1934- ... CANR-18
Earlier sketch in CA 97-100
Watson, J(ohn) Steven 1916- ... 5-6R
Watson, J(ames) Wreford 1915- ... CANR-19
Earlier sketch in CA 25-28R
Watson, Jack Brierley 1927- ... 104
Watson, James 1936- ... CANR-4
Earlier sketch in CA 53-56
See also SATA 10
Watson, James B(ennett) 1918- ... 41-44R
Watson, James D(ewey) 1928- ... 25-28R
Watson, James Gray 1939- ... 29-32R
Watson, Jane Werner 1915- ... CANR-8
Earlier sketch in CA 7-8R
See also SATA 3
Watson, Janet Lynch
See Lynch-Watson, Janet
Watson, Jean 1936- ... CANR-16
Earlier sketch in CA 89-92
Watson, John A(rthur) F(ergus) 1903- ... 65-68
Watson, John H.
See Farmer, Philip Jose
Watson, Julia 1943- ... CANR-15
Earlier sketch in CA 41-44R
Watson, Ken 1925(?)-1984 Obituary ... 114
Watson, Lyall 1939- ... CANR-24
Earlier sketches in CA 57-60, CANR-8
Watson, Margaret Goodrich 1913- ... 15-16R
Watson, Mark Skinner 1887-1966 Obituary ... 89-92
Watson, Mary Gordon
See Gordon-Watson, Mary
Watson, Nan Marriott
See Marriott-Watson, Nan
Watson, Nancy Dingman ... CANR-4
Earlier sketch in CA 49-52
See also SATA 32
Watson, O(scar) Michael 1936- ... 33-36R
Watson, Patricia Seets 1930- ... 121
Watson, Patrick 1929- ... 97-100
Watson, Patty Jo (Andersen) 1932- ... CANR-13
Earlier sketch in CA 77-80
Watson, Pauline 1925- ... CANR-11
Earlier sketch in CA 69-72
See also SATA 14
Watson, Peter L(eslie) 1944- ... 53-56
Watson, Philip S(aville) 1909- ... 104
Watson, Richard A(bernethy) 1923- ... 45-48
Watson, Richard A(llan) 1931- ... 77-80
Watson, Richard F.
See Silverberg, Robert
Watson, Richard L(yness), Jr. 1914- ... 17-18R
Watson, Robert (Winthrop) 1925- ... CANR-4
Earlier sketch in CA 2R
Watson, Robert I(rving) 1909-1980 Obituary ... 111
Watson, Robert N(athaniel) 1953- ... 118
Watson, Roderick (Bruce) 1943- ... 102
Watson, Russell 1939- ... 77-80
Watson, Sally (Lou) 1924- ... CANR-3
Earlier sketch in CA 5-6R
See also SATA 3
Watson, Sara Ruth 1907- ... 37-40R
Watson, Sheila 1909- ... DLB-60
See also AITN 2
Watson, Thomas J(oel) 1948- ... 109
Watson, Tom, Jr. 1918- ... 21-22R
Watson, Wendy (McLeod) 1942- ... CANR-4
Earlier sketch in CA 49-52
See also SATA 5
Watson, Wilfred 1911- ... DLB-60
Watson, Will
See Floren, Lee
Watson, William 1917- ... 11-12R
Watson, William Alexander Jardine 1933- ... CANR-12
Earlier sketch in CA 13-14R
Watson Taylor, Elizabeth 1915- ... SATA-41
Watson-Watt, Robert A(lexander) 1892-1973 ... CAP-1
Obituary ... 45-48
Earlier sketch in CA 13-14
Watstein, Esther 1928- ... 57-60
Watt, (John) David (Henry) 1932-1987 Obituary ... 122
Watt, Donald 1938- ... 41-44R
Watt, Donald Beates 1893-1977 Obituary ... 73-76
Watt, Donald Cameron
See Cameron Watt, Donald
Watt, Douglas (Benjamin) 1914- ... 69-72
Watt, Frank Hedden 1889-1981 Obituary ... 105
Watt, George Steven Harvie
See Harvie-Watt, George Steven
Watt, (Raymond Egerton) Harry 1906-1987 Obituary ... 122
Watt, Ian 1917- ... 13-14R
Watt, John Robertson 1934- ... 37-40R
Watt, Kenneth E(dmund) F(erguson) 1929- ... 61-64
Watt, Richard M(artin) 1930- ... 5-6R
Watt, Ruth M. 1919- ... CANR-10
Earlier sketch in CA 57-60
Watt, Thomas 1935- ... 37-40R
See also SATA 4
Watt, W(illiam) Montgomery 1909- ... CANR-21
Earlier sketches in CA 2R, CANR-6
Wattenbarger, James L(orenzo) 1922- ... 106
Wattenberg, Ben J. 1933- ... 57-60
Wattenberg, William W(olff) 1911- ... 23-24R
Wattenmaker, Richard J. 1941- ... 104
Watters, Barbara H(unt) 1907-1984 ... CANR-3
Obituary ... 111
Earlier sketch in CA 7-8R
Watters, (Walter) Pat(terson) 1927- ... CANR-8
Earlier sketch in CA 23-24R
Watters, R(eginald) E(yre) 1912- ... 25-28R
Watterson, Henry 1840-1921 ... DLB-25
Watterson, Joseph 1900-1972 ... CAP-2
Obituary ... 33-36R
Earlier sketch in CA 25-28
Watt-Evans, Lawrence
See Evans, Lawrence Watt
Wattie, Margaret
See 'Espinasse, Margaret
Wattles, Santha Rama Rau 1923- ... CANR-1
Earlier sketch in CA 1R
Watts, A. J.
See Watts, Anthony J(ohn)
Watts, Al(bert) L. 1934- ... 85-88
Watts, Alan (James) 1925- ... 108
Watts, Alan Wilson 1915-1973 ... 41-44R
Obituary ... 45-48
See also DLB 16
Watts, Ann Chalmers 1938- ... 53-56
Watts, Anthony J(ohn) 1942- ... CANR-11
Earlier sketch in CA 25-28R
Watts, (Anna) Bernadette 1942- ... 29-32R
See also SATA 4
Watts, Charles Edwin 1929- ... CANR-2
Earlier sketch in CA 5-6R
Watts, David 1935- ... 53-56
Watts, Elizabeth (Bailey) Smithgall 1941- ... CANR-12
Earlier sketch in CA 73-76
Watts, Emily Stipes 1936- ... 81-84
Watts, Ephraim
See Horne, Richard Henry
Watts, Franklin (Mowry) 1904-1978 ... CANR-9
Obituary ... 89-92
Earlier sketches in CA 25-28, CAP-2
See also SATA 21, 46
Watts, Harold H(olliday) 1906- ... CAP-2
Earlier sketch in CA 13-14
Watts, Harriet M(ayor) 1933- ... 45-48
Watts, J(ames) Wash(ington) 1896-197(?) ... CANR-20
Earlier sketch in CA 2R
Watts, John (Francis) 1926- ... CANR-21
Earlier sketch in CA 25-28R
Watts, John D. W. 1921- ... 21-22R
Watts, Lew 1922- ... 41-44R
Watts, Mabel Pizzey 1906- ... CANR-3
Earlier sketch in CA 4R
See also SATA 11
Watts, May Theilgaard 1893-1975 ... 41-44R
Watts, Meredith W(ayne, Jr.) 1941- ... CANR-24
Earlier sketch in CA 45-48
Watts, Michael J(ohn) 1951- ... 122
Watts, Peter Christopher 1919- ... CANR-12
Earlier sketch in CA 69-72
Watts, Reginald John 1931- ... 29-32R
Watts, Richard (Jr.) 1898-1981 Obituary ... 102
Watts, Ronald L(ampman) 1929- ... 23-24R
Watts, Sarah Miles 1934- ... 65-68
Watts, Stephen 1910- ... 7-8R
Watts, Thomas D(ale) 1941- ... 117
Watts, William 1930- ... CANR-1
Earlier sketch in CA 45-48
Watzlawick, Paul 1921- ... CANR-4
Earlier sketch in CA 11-12R
Waud, Elizabeth
See Tattersall, M(uriel Joyce)
Waugh, Albert E(dmund) 1902-1985 ... 37-40R
Obituary ... 115
Waugh, Alec
See Waugh, Alexander Raban
Waugh, Alexander Raban 1898-1981 ... CANR-22
Obituary ... 104
Earlier sketch in CA 17-18R
Waugh, Auberon (Alexander) 1939- ... CANR-22
Earlier sketches in CA 45-48, CANR-6
See also DLB 14
See also CLC 7
Waugh, C. C. Roessel
See Waugh, Carol-Lynn Roessel and Waugh, Charles G(ordon)
Waugh, Carol-Lynn Roessel 1947- ... 107
See also SATA 41
Waugh, Charles
See Waugh, Charles G(ordon)
Waugh, Charles G(ordon) 1943- ... 123
Brief entry ... 118
Waugh, Coulton 1896(?)-1973 Obituary ... 41-44R
Waugh, Dorothy ... CANR-1
Earlier sketch in CA 2R
See also SATA 11
Waugh, Evelyn (Arthur St. John) 1903-1966 ... CANR-22
Obituary ... 25-28R
Earlier sketch in CA 85-88
See also DLB 15
See also CLC 1, 3, 8, 13, 19, 27, 44
Waugh, Harriet 1944- ... CANR-22
Earlier sketch in CA 85-88
See also CLC 6
Waugh, Harry 1904- ... 21-22R
Waugh, Hillary Baldwin 1920- ... CANR-2
Earlier sketch in CA 1R
Waugh, Linda R(uth) 1942- ... CANR-16
Earlier sketch in CA 89-92
Waugh, Nancy Collier 1930- ... 45-48
Waugh, Virginia
See Sorenson, Virginia
Waughburton, Richard
See Sykes, Christopher (Hugh)
Wauthier, Claude Rene 1923- ... 73-76
Wavell, Stewart Brooke 1921- ... 13-14R
Wax, Emmanuel 1911-1983 Obituary ... 109
Wax, Jimmy
See Wax, Emmanuel
Wax, Judith 1932(?)-1979 ... 101
Obituary ... 85-88
Wax, Murray L(ionel) 1922- ... 37-40R
Wax, Rosalie (Amelia) H. 1911- ... 45-48
Wax, Sheldon 1928(?)-1979 Obituary ... 85-88
Waxberg, Joseph David 1922- ... 108
Waxman, Chaim I(saac) 1941- ... CANR-19
Earlier sketch in CA 103
Waxman, Ruth B(ilgray) 1916- ... 93-96
Way, Irene 1924- ... 93-96
Way, Peter (Howard) 1936- Brief entry ... 115
Way, Robert E(dward) 1912- ... 57-60
Way, Walter L. 1931- ... 57-60
Way, Wayne
See Humphries, Adelaide M.
Wayburn, Peggy 1921- ... CANR-24
Earlier sketch in CA 45-48
Waylan, Mildred
See Harrell, Irene B(urk)
Wayland, Patrick
See O'Connor, Richard
Waymack, W(illiam) W(esley) 1888-1960 Obituary ... 93-96
Wayman, Alex 1921- ... 104
Wayman, Dorothy G. 1893-1975 ... 65-68
Obituary ... 61-64
Wayman, Norbury Lansing 1912- ... 41-44R
Wayman, Thomas Ethan 1945- ... 101
Wayman, Tom
See Wayman, Thomas Ethan
See also DLB 53
Wayman, Tony Russell 1929- ... 25-28R
Wayne, Alice
See Ressler, Alice
Wayne, Anderson
See Dresser, Davis
Wayne, David
See Balsiger, David W(ayne)
Wayne, Donald
See Dodd, Wayne (Donald)
Wayne, Doreen ... 29-32R
Wayne, Frances
See Wedge, Florence
Wayne, Jane Ellen 1936- ... CANR-20
Earlier sketches in CA 49-52, CANR-4
Wayne, (Anne) Jenifer 1917-1982 ... 105
Obituary ... 108
See also SATA 32
Wayne, Jerry 1919- ... 29-32R
Wayne, John 1907-1979 ... 85-88
Wayne, Joseph
See Overholser, Wayne D.
Wayne, Kyra Petrovskaya 1918- ... CANR-4
Earlier sketch in CA 4R
See also SATA 8
Wayne, Mary Collier 1913- ... 57-60
Wayne, Michael 1947- ... 112
Wayne, Philip
See Powell, Philip Wayne
Wayne, Richard
See Decker, Duane
Wayne, Stephen J(ay) 1939- ... CANR-20
Earlier sketches in CA 53-56, CANR-5
Wayre, Philip 1921- ... 89-92
Ways, C. R.
See Blount, Roy (Alton), Jr.
Ways, Max 1905-1985 Obituary ... 116
Waystaff, Simon
See Swift, Jonathan
Wazyk, Adam 1905-1982 Obituary ... 114
Wead, R(oy) Douglas 1946- ... CANR-20
Earlier sketch in CA 69-72
Weal, Michele 1936- ... 61-64
Weales, Gerald (Clifford) 1925- ... CANR-3
Earlier sketch in CA 5-6R
See also SATA 11
Wear, Ted Graham
See Wear, Theodore G(raham)
Wear, Theodore G(raham) 1902- ... CAP-1
Earlier sketch in CA 9-10

Weare, Ralston B.
See La Barre, Weston
Weare, Walter B(urdette) 1938- 73-76
Wearin, Otha Donner 1903- CANR-5
Earlier sketch in CA 15-16R
Wearing, J. P. CANR-19
Earlier sketch in CA 102
Weart, Edith L. 1898(?)-1977 Obituary 69-72
Weart, Spencer R(ichard) 1942- 25-28R
Weary, Ogdred
See Gorey, Edward (St. John)
Weatherall, Norman Leigh 1902- CAP-1
Earlier sketch in CA 11-12
Weatherby, Harold L(erow), Jr. 1934- 45-48
Weatherby, W(illiam) J(ohn) CANR-12
Earlier sketch in CA 19-20R
Weathercock, The
See Romaine, Lawrence B.
Weatherford, J(ack) McIver 1946- 111
Weatherford, Richard M(orris) 1939- 53-56
Weatherford, Willis Duke, Jr. 1916- 5-6R
Weatherhead, A(ndrew) Kingsley 1923- .. CANR-3
Earlier sketch in CA 5-6R
Weatherhead, Leslie D(ixon) 1893-1976 . CANR-4
Obituary 61-64
Earlier sketch in CA 5-6R
Weatherly, Edward H(owell) 1905- 7-8R
Weatherly, (John) Max 1921- 15-16R
Weatherly, Owen M. 1915- 5-6R
Weatherly, Tom 1942- 45-48
See also DLB 41
Weathers, Wesley Wayne 1942- 111
Weathers, Winston 1926- CANR-8
Earlier sketch in CA 23-24R
Weatherwax, Rudd (B.) 1908(?)-1985
Obituary 115
Weatherwise, Abe
See Sagendorph, Robb Hansell
Weaver, Anthony Frederick 1913- 15-16R
Weaver, Bertrand 1908-1973 .... CAP-1
Obituary 45-48
Earlier sketch in CA 15-16
Weaver, Carl H(arold) 1910- 73-76
Weaver, Charley
See Arquette, Cliff(ord)
Weaver, David H(ugh) 1946- 111
Weaver, Denis 1906-1984 Obituary 114
Weaver, Earl S(idney) 1930- 116
Weaver, Earle
See Willets, Walter E.
Weaver, Frank Parks 1904- 104
Weaver, Gordon (Allison) 1937- CANR-10
Earlier sketch in CA 25-28R
Weaver, Harriett E. 1908- CANR-20
Earlier sketches in CA 7-8R, CANR-5
Weaver, Herbert 1905- 61-64
Weaver, Horace R. 1915- 15-16R
Weaver, James H. 1933- 19-20R
Weaver, Jerry L(ee) 1939- 69-72
Weaver, John D(owning) 1912- CANR-4
Earlier sketch in CA 11-12R
Weaver, John L. 1949- 112
See also SATA 42
Weaver, Katherine Grey Dunlap 1910- 37-40R
Weaver, Kitty
See Weaver, Katherine Grey Dunlap
Weaver, Leon Hiram 1913- 7-8R
Weaver, Mateman
See Greene, A(lvin) C(arl)
Weaver, Peter 1925- CANR-15
Earlier sketch in CA 85-88
Weaver, Peter Malcolm 1927- 15-16R
Weaver, Richard L. II 1941- CANR-23
Earlier sketch in CA 106
Weaver, Robert C(lifton) 1907- 11-12R
Weaver, Thomas 1929- CANR-13
Earlier sketch in CA 61-64
Weaver, Ward
See Mason, F(rancis) van Wyck
Weaver, Warren 1894-1978 89-92
Obituary 81-84
Weaver, Warren, Jr. 1923- 41-44R
Weaver, William 1923- 116
Brief entry 112
Weaver, William Woys 1947- 123
Webb, Anthony
See Wilson, N(orman) Scarlyn
Webb, Barbara (Helen) 1929- 103
Webb, (Martha) Beatrice (Potter)
1858-1943 Brief entry 117
See also TCLC 22
Webb, Bernice Larson CANR-15
Earlier sketch in CA 37-40R
Webb, Bob
See Forrest-Webb, Robert
Webb, C(harles) R(ichard), Jr. 1919- 5-6R
Webb, Charles (Richard) 1939- 25-28R
See also CLC 7
Webb, Christopher
See Wibberley, Leonard (Patrick O'Connor)
Webb, Clifford (Cyril) 1895-1972 105
Webb, Eugene 1938- 29-32R
Webb, Forrest
See Forrest-Webb, Robert
Webb, Francis Charles 1925-1973 101
Webb, Frank J. DLB-50
Webb, George Ernest 1952- 113
Webb, Harri 1920- 104
Webb, Harry 1887-1984 Obituary 113
Webb, Henry J(ameson) 1915- 17-18R
Webb, Herschel (F.) 1924-1983 .... 7-8R
Obituary 109
Webb, Holmes 1904- CAP-2
Earlier sketch in CA 25-28
Webb, Igor 1941- 109
Webb, Jack (Randolph) 1920-1982
Obituary 108
Brief entry 106
Webb, James (C. N.) 1946-1980 103
Webb, James H(enry), Jr. 1946- 81-84
See also CLC 22
Webb, James Watson 1802-1884 .... DLB-43
Webb, Jean Francis 1910- CANR-21
Earlier sketches in CA 5-6R, CANR-6
See also SATA 35
Webb, Jon (Edgar) 1905(?)-1971
Obituary 104
Webb, Karl (Eugene) 1938- 105
Webb, Kempton E. 1931- 13-14R
Webb, Kenneth B(eals) 1902- 97-100
Webb, Lance 1909- CANR-10
Earlier sketch in CA 15-16R
Webb, Lionel
See Hershman, Morris
Webb, Lucas
See Burgess, M(ichael) R(oy)
Webb, Margot S. 1914- 77-80
Webb, Martha G.
See Wingate, (Martha) Anne (Guice)
Webb, Mary (Gladys Meredith)
1881-1927 .... DLB-34
See also TCLC 24
Webb, Mary (Gladys Meredith) 1881-1927
Brief entry 123
Webb, Mary Haydn
See Ross, Leah
Webb, Michael (Dennis Puzey) 1937- 124
Webb, Michael Gordon 1940- 109
Webb, Mrs. Sidney
See Webb, (Martha) Beatrice (Potter)
Webb, Muriel S(chlosberg) 1913- 17-18R
Webb, Nancy (Bukeley) 1915- CANR-21
Earlier sketch in CA 4R
Webb, Neil
See Rowland, D(onald) S(ydney)
Webb, Pauline M(ary) 1927- CANR-24
Earlier sketches in CA 61-64, CANR-8
Webb, Peggy (Elaine Hussey) 1942- 123
Webb, Peter B(randram) 1941- CANR-24
Earlier sketch in CA 106
Webb, Phyllis 1927- CANR-23
Earlier sketch in CA 104
See also DLB 53
See also CLC 18
Webb, R(obert) K(iefer) 1922- 25-28R
Webb, Richard 37-40R
Webb, Robert 1947- 118
Webb, Robert Forrest-
See Forrest-Webb, Robert
Webb, Rodman B. 1941- 110
Webb, Ross A. 1923- 37-40R
Webb, Rozana 1908- 29-32R
Webb, Ruth Enid Borlase Morris 1926- 9-10R
Webb, Samuel C(lement) 1934- 69-72
Webb, Sharon 1936- 113
See also SATA 41
Webb, Sidney (James) 1859-1947
Brief entry 117
See also TCLC 22
Webb, Spider
See Gohman, Fred Joseph
Webb, Stephen S(aunders) 1937- 104
Webb, Walter Prescott 1888-1963
Obituary 113
See also DLB 17
Webb, Willard 1903-1978 Obituary 77-80
Webb, William (Griffin) 1919- 25-28R
Webb, Wilse B(ernard) 1920- CANR-3
Earlier sketch in CA 3R
Webbe, Gale D(udley) 1909- 5-6R
Webber, Andrew Lloyd
See Lloyd Webber, Andrew
See also CLC 21
Webber, Bert
See Webber, Ebbert T(rue)
Webber, Ebbert T(rue) 1921- CANR-17
Earlier sketches in CA 45-48, CANR-2
Webber, George J(ulius) 1899-1982(?)
Obituary 108
Webber, Gordon 1912-1986 89-92
Obituary 120
Webber, Irma E(leanor Schmidt) 1904- 69-72
See also SATA 14
Webber, Joan Malory 1930-1978 .... CANR-7
Earlier sketch in CA 5-6R
Webber, Robert (Eugene) 1933- CANR-16
Earlier sketch in CA 89-92
Webber, (Edwin) Ronald 1915- CANR-4
Earlier sketch in CA 53-56
Webber, Ross A. 1934- 29-32R
Webber, Thomas L(ane) 1947- 85-88
Weber, Alfons 1921- 29-32R
See also SATA 8
Weber, Brom 1917- 15-16R
Weber, Bruce 1942- CANR-21
Earlier sketch in CA 97-100
Weber, Burton Jasper 1934- 103
Weber, Carl J(efferson) 1894-1966 .... CANR-3
Earlier sketch in CA 7-8R
Weber, Clarence A. 1903- CANR-13
Earlier sketch in CA 37-40R
Weber, David J. 1940- CANR-14
Earlier sketch in CA 37-40R
Weber, David R(yder) 1943- 89-92
Weber, Eric 1942- CANR-15
Earlier sketch in CA 101
Weber, Eugen 1925- CANR-2
Earlier sketch in CA 5-6R
Weber, Eugene 1939- 41-44R
Weber, Francis J. 1933- CANR-4
Earlier sketch in CA 11-12R
Weber, Frank George 1932- 45-48
Weber, Gerard Peter 1918- 11-12R
Weber, Hans H. 1935- 61-64
Weber, Hans-Ruedi 1923- CANR-2
Earlier sketch in CA 7-8R
Weber, J(ohn) Sherwood 1918-1978 .... 37-40R
Obituary 77-80
Weber, James A(mbrose) 1932- 102
Weber, Janice 121
Weber, Jean-Paul 1917- 45-48
Weber, Jerome C(harles) 1938- 73-76
Weber, Ken(neth J.) 1940- 116
Weber, Lenora Mattingly 1895-1971 .... CAP-1
Obituary 29-32R
Earlier sketch in CA 19-20
See also SATA 2, 26
See also CLC 12
Weber, Marc 1950- CANR-1
Earlier sketch in CA 49-52
Weber, Max 1864-1920 Brief entry 109
Weber, Nancy 1942- 101
Weber, Nathan 1942- 111
Weber, Nicholas F(ox) 1947- 120
Weber, Ralph Edward 1926- CANR-2
Earlier sketch in CA 5-6R
Weber, Robert L(emmerman) 1913- 53-56
Weber, Ronald 1934- 115
Weber, Rubin
See Rubinstein, S(amuel) Leonard
Weber, Sarah Appleton
See Appleton, Sarah
Weber, Simon 1910(?)-1987 Obituary 124
Weber, William A(lfred) 1918- 77-80
Weber, William J(ohn) 1927- 69-72
See also SATA 14
Weberman, Ben(jamin) 1923- 77-80
Webster, Alice Jane Chandler 1876-1916
Brief entry 116
See also SATA 17
Webster, Anthony 1923(?)-1987 Obituary ... 123
Webster, Augusta 1837-1894 .... DLB-35
Webster, Brenda S. 1936- 53-56
Webster, C(onstance) Muriel 1906- 49-52
Webster, Cyril Charles 1909- CAP-2
Earlier sketch in CA 25-28
Webster, David 1930- 29-32R
See also SATA 11
Webster, David Endicott 1929- 25-28R
Webster, Donald 1926- 118
Webster, Donald Blake, Jr. 1933- 37-40R
Webster, Douglas 1920-1986 .... 13-14R
Obituary 118
Webster, Edna Robb 1896- 69-72
Webster, Elizabeth 1918- 117
Webster, Frank V. CAP-2
Earlier sketch in CA 19-20
See also SATA 1
Webster, Frederick E., Jr. 1937- CANR-14
Earlier sketch in CA 37-40R
Webster, Gary
See Garrison, Webb B(lack)
Webster, Graham 1915- 49-52
Webster, Grant T. 1933- 104
Webster, Harvey (Curtis) 1906- 41-44R
Webster, J(ames) Carson 1905- 45-48
Webster, James 1925-1981 73-76
Obituary 104
See also SATA 17, 27
Webster, Jan 1924- CANR-14
Earlier sketch in CA 77-80
Webster, Jean
See Webster, Alice Jane Chandler
Webster, John 1579(?)-1634(?) DLB-58
Webster, Josh (Lew) 1949- 113
Webster, Margaret 1905-1972 Obituary .. 37-40R
Webster, Noah 1758-1843 ... DLB-1, 37, 42, 43
Webster, Noah
See Knox, William
Webster, Norman William 1920- 104
Webster, Paul 1916- 41-44R
Webster, Paul Francis 1907-1984
Obituary 112
Webster, Randolph Wyatt 1900- CAP-1
Earlier sketch in CA 19-20
Webster, Richard A. 1928- 21-22R
Webster, S(tanley) Eric 1919-1971 .... CAP-1
Earlier sketch in CA 17-18
Webster, Staten Wentford 1928- 23-24R
Webster, Thomas Bertram Lonsdale
1905-1974 105
Obituary 107
Webster, Tony
See Webster, Anthony
Wechman, Robert Joseph 1939- CANR-24
Earlier sketch in CA 45-48
Wechsberg, Joseph 1907-1983 105
Obituary 109
Wechsler, David 1896-1981 Obituary 103
Wechsler, Harold S(tuart) 1946- 110
Wechsler, Henry 1932- CANR-7
Earlier sketch in CA 17-18R
Wechsler, Herbert 1909- CANR-24
Earlier sketch in CA 2R
Wechsler, Herman J. 1904-1976 65-68
Obituary 61-64
See also SATA 20
Wechsler, James A(rthur) 1915-1983 101
Obituary 110
Wechsler, Judith Glatzer 1940- CANR-8
Earlier sketch in CA 57-60
Wechsler, Louis K. 1905- 65-68
Wechter, Nell Wise 1913- 57-60
Weckstein, Richard (Selig) 1924- 49-52
Wedberg, Anders 1913-1978 Obituary 77-80
Wedda, John A. 1911- 17-18R
Wedde, Ian 1946- 104
Wedderburn, Dorothy (Enid Cole) 1925-
Brief entry 113
Wedderburn, K(enneth) W(illiam) 1927- ... 77-80
Wedding, Dan 1949- 93-96
Wedding, Donald Keith 1934- 41-44R
Weddle, Ethel Harshbarger 1897- CANR-4
Earlier sketch in CA 11-12R
See also SATA 11
Weddle, Ferris 1922- 17-18R
Weddle, Robert S(amuel) 1921- 11-12R
Wedeck, Harry E(zekiel) 1894- CANR-4
Earlier sketch in CA 3R
Wedeen, Shirley Ullman 1926- 19-20R
Wedekind, (Benjamin) Frank(lin)
1864-1918 Brief entry 104
See also TCLC 7
Wedel, Alfred R(aphael) 1934- 117
Wedel, Alton F. 21-22R
Wedel, Cynthia Clark 1908-1986 Obituary ... 120
Wedel, Leonard E. 1909- 21-22R
Wedel, Theodore Otto 1892-1970 .... CANR-4
Earlier sketch in CA 5-6R
Wedel, Waldo Rudolph 1908- Brief entry ... 105
Wedell, Eberhard (Arthur Otto) George
1927- 104
Wedge, Bryant (Miner) 1921- CANR-10
Earlier sketch in CA 15-16R
Wedge, Florence 1919- 5-6R
Wedgwood, C(icely) V(eronica) 1910- .. CANR-21
Earlier sketch in CA 105
Wedgwood, Pamela
See Tudor-Craig, Pamela
Weed, Florence C(ollins) 1897(?)-1983
Obituary 109
Weed, Joseph J(ohn) 1901- 25-28R
Weeden, Robert B(arton) 1933- 85-88
Weedon, Chris 1952- 121
Weekes, Mark Kinkead
See Kinkead-Weekes, Mark
Weekes, Richard V. 1924- 15-16R
Weekley, Ian George 1933- 113
Weekly, William G(eorge) 1890(?)-1983
Obituary 111
Weeks, Albert L. 1923- 13-14R
Weeks, Christopher 1930- 23-24R
Weeks, Constance Tomkinson 1915- 17-18R
Weeks, (Norman) Donald 45-48
Weeks, Edward (Augustus) 1898- 85-88
Weeks, Edward J(oseph) 1902- CAP-1
Earlier sketch in CA 13-14
Weeks, Francis W(illiam) 1916-
Brief entry 111
Weeks, Grace E(zell) 1923- 49-52
Weeks, H(erbert) Ashley 1903- 45-48
Weeks, Jeffrey 1945- 108
Weeks, John (Stafford) 1928- 77-80
Weeks, Kent M(cCuskey) 1937-
Brief entry 112
Weeks, Lewis G(eorge) 1893-1977
Obituary 69-72
Weeks, Philip 1949- 110
Weeks, Robert Lewis 1924- 13-14R
Weeks, Robert P(ercy) 1915- 15-16R
Weeks, Sheldon G. 1931- CANR-13
Earlier sketch in CA 23-24R
Weeks, Thelma E(vans) 1921- 57-60
Weems, J. Eddie, Jr.
See Weems, John Edward
Weems, John Edward 1924- CANR-19
Earlier sketches in CA 3R, CANR-4
Weems, Mason Locke
1759-1825 .... DLB-30, 37, 42
Weenolsen, Hebe 111
Weer, William
See Kaufman, I(sadore)
Weerts, Richard Kenneth 1928- 49-52
Wees, Frances Shelley 1902- CANR-3
Earlier sketch in CA 5-6R
Wees, W(ilfred) R(usk) 1899- 61-64
Weesner, Theodore 105
Wegelin, Christof 1911- 45-48
Wegen, Ron(ald) SATA-44
Weglyn, Michi(ko Nishiura) 1926- 85-88
Wegner, Fritz 1924- SATA-20
Wegner, Robert E. 1929- 17-18R
Wehen, Joy DeWeese CANR-3
Earlier sketch in CA 5-6R
Wehlitz, (Annie) Lou(ise) Rogers 1906- 5-6R
Wehmeyer, Lillian (Mabel) Biermann
1933- CANR-8
Earlier sketch in CA 61-64
Wehringer, Cameron K(ingsley) 1924- 25-28R
Wehrle, Edmund S(heridan) 1930- 65-68
Wehrli, Eugene S(tanley) 1923- 45-48
Wehrwein, Austin C(arl) 1916- 77-80
Wei, Yung 1937- 49-52
Weichel, Kim 1951- 107
Weideger, Paula 1939- 65-68
Weidenbaum, Murray L(ew) 1927- CANR-14
Earlier sketch in CA 37-40R
Weidenfeld, Sheila Rabb 1943- 89-92
Weider, Ben 1923- 108
Weidhorn, Manfred 1931- 53-56
Weidlein, Edward R(ay) 1887-1983
Obituary 110
Weidman, Jerome 1913- CANR-1
Earlier sketch in CA 1R
See also DLB 28
See also CLC 7
See also AITN 2
Weidman, John 1946- 109
Weidman, Judith L(ynne) 1941- 107
Weidner, Edward William 1921- 15-16R
Weiers, Ronald M. 1941- CANR-19
Earlier sketch in CA 25-28R
Weigand, George R(obert) J(oseph)
1917- 15-16R

Weigand, Hermann J(ohn) 1892-1985 .... CAP-1
Obituary 117
Earlier sketch in CA 13-14
Weigel, Gustave 1906-1964 Obituary 107
Weigel, John A(rthur) 1912- 57-60
Weiger, John George 1933- CANR-20
Earlier sketch in CA 104
Weigert, Andrew J(oseph) 1934- 109
Weigert, Edith 1894- CAP-2
Earlier sketch in CA 29-32
Weigert, Hans Werner 1902(?)-1983
Obituary 111
Weightman, Gavin 1945- 120
Weightman, J(ohn) G(eorge) 1915- CANR-5
Earlier sketch in CA 9-10R
Weigl, Bruce 1949- 110
Weigle, Luther Allan 1880-1976 77-80
Obituary 69-72
Weigle, Marta 1944- CANR-11
Earlier sketch in CA 69-72
Weigley, Russell F(rank) 1930- CANR-19
Earlier sketches in CA 5-6R, CANR-2
Weihofen, Henry 1904- 37-40R
Weihs, Erika 1917- 93-96
See also SATA 15
Weik, Mary Hays 1898(?)-1979 .... 23-24R
Obituary 93-96
See also SATA 3, 23
Weil, Andrew (Thomas) 1942- CANR-20
Earlier sketch in CA 73-76
Weil, Ann Yezner 1908-1969 .... 7-8R
Obituary 103
See also SATA 9
Weil, Dorothy 1929- 93-96
Weil, Gordon L(ee) 1937- CANR-12
Earlier sketch in CA 73-76
Weil, Herbert S., Jr. 1933- 21-22R
Weil, Irwin 1928- 21-22R
Weil, James L(ehman) 1929- CANR-16
Earlier sketch in CA 93-96
Weil, Jerry 1928- 3R
Weil, Joseph 1875-1976 Obituary 65-68
Weil, Lisl 1910- CANR-2
Earlier sketch in CA 49-52
See also SATA 7
Weil, Mildred 45-48
Weil, Roman L(ee) 1940- CANR-14
Earlier sketch in CA 37-40R
Weil, Simone (Adolphine) 1909-1943
Brief entry 117
See also TCLC 23
Weil, Ulric Henry 113
Weilbacher, William Manning 1928- 108
Weilerstein, Sadie Rose 1894- 5-6R
See also SATA 3
Weill, Gus 1933- CANR-7
Earlier sketch in CA 53-56
Weiman, Eiveen 1925- 108
Weimann, Jeanne Madeline 1943- 108
Weimar, Karl S(iegfried) 1916- 5-6R
Weimer, Arthur M(artin) 1909-1987 .... 2R
Obituary 122
Wein, Jacqueline 1938- 93-96
Weinbaum, Stanley Grauman
1902(?)-1935 Brief entry 110
See also DLB 8
Weinberg, Arthur 1915- CANR-15
Earlier sketch in CA 25-28R
Weinberg, Bernard 1909-1973 Obituary 106
Weinberg, Daniel H. 1949- 120
Weinberg, Daniela 1936- 104
Weinberg, David Henry 1945- 89-92
Weinberg, Edgar 1917-1985 Obituary 117
Weinberg, Florence M(ay) 1933- 37-40R
Weinberg, Gerald M(arvin) 1933- CANR-18
Earlier sketch in CA 89-92
Weinberg, Gerhard L(udwig) 1928- CANR-3
Earlier sketch in CA 11-12R
Weinberg, Helen A(rnstein) 1927- 73-76
Weinberg, Herman G(ershon) 1908-1983 .. 45-48
Obituary 111
Weinberg, Ian 1938-1969 .... CAP-2
Earlier sketch in CA 21-22
Weinberg, Janet Hopson
See Hopson, Janet L(ouise)
Weinberg, Julius 1922- 37-40R
Weinberg, Julius R(udolph) 1908-1971 ... CAP-1
Earlier sketch in CA 17-18
Weinberg, Kenneth G. 1920- 41-44R
Weinberg, Kerry 29-32R
Weinberg, Kurt 1912- 41-44R
Weinberg, Larry
See Weinberg, Lawrence (E.)
Weinberg, Lawrence (E.) SATA-48
Weinberg, Lila (Shaffer) 25-28R
Weinberg, Martin S(tephen) 1939- CANR-15
Earlier sketch in CA 41-44R
Weinberg, Meyer 1920- CANR-4
Earlier sketch in CA 3R
Weinberg, Nathan Gerald 1945- 104
Weinberg, Robert Charles 1901-1974
Obituary 45-48
Weinberg, Robert E(dward) 1946- 97-100
Weinberg, Samuel Kirson 1912- CANR-1
Earlier sketch in CA 2R
Weinberg, Sanford Bruce 1950- 109
Weinberg, Steven 1933- CANR-5
Earlier sketch in CA 53-56
Weinberg, Werner 1915- CANR-16
Earlier sketch in CA 41-44R
Weinberger, Betty Kiralfy 1932- 65-68
Weinberger, Eliot 1949- 117
Weinberger, Leon J. 1926- 77-80
Weinberger, Marvin I(rvin) 1954- 113
Weinberger, Paul E. 1931- 29-32R
Weinbrot, Howard D. 1936- Brief entry 107
Weiner, Andrew D(avid) 1943- Brief entry .. 111
Weiner, Annette B. 1933- 93-96
Weiner, Bernard 1935- 57-60
Weiner, Charles 1931- Brief entry 109
Weiner, Dora B(ierer) 1924- 25-28R
Weiner, Egon 1906-1987 97-100
Obituary 123
Weiner, Elliot 1943- 122
Weiner, Florence 1931- 25-28R
Weiner, Henri
See Longstreet, Stephen
Weiner, Herbert 7-8R
Weiner, Hyman J(oseph) 1926- 49-52
Weiner, Irving B(ernard) 1933- 29-32R
Weiner, J(oseph) S(idney) 1915-1982 114
Weiner, Jonathan (David) 1953- 123
Weiner, Leonard 1927- 23-24R
Weiner, Linda 1943- 114
Weiner, Marcella Bakur 1925- Brief entry ... 105
Weiner, Myron 1931- CANR-4
Earlier sketch in CA 2R
Weiner, Neal (Orlove) 1942- 118
Weiner, Neil S(herman) 1936- 119
Weiner, Richard 1927- 89-92
Weiner, Sandra 1922- 49-52
See also SATA 14
Weiner, Skip
See Weiner, Stewart
Weiner, Stewart 1945- CANR-16
Earlier sketch in CA 89-92
Weinfield, Henry 1949- 37-40R
Weingand, Darlene E. 1937- 115
Weingart, L(aurence) O. 1931- 19-20R
Weingarten, Henry 57-60
Weingarten, Roger 1945- CANR-10
Earlier sketch in CA 61-64
Weingarten, Violet (Brown) 1915-1976 .. CANR-7
Obituary 65-68
Earlier sketch in CA 11-12R
See also SATA 3, 27
Weingartner, Charles 1922- 49-52
See also SATA 5
Weingartner, James J(oseph) 1940- 93-96
Weingartner, Rudolph H(erbert) 1927- 15-16R
Weingast, David E(lliott) 1912- 5-6R
Weinig, Jean Maria 1920- CANR-12
Earlier sketch in CA 29-32R
Weinig, Sister Mary Anthony
See Weinig, Jean Maria
Weininger, Richard 1887(?)-1979
Obituary 89-92
Weinland, James D(avid) 1894- 57-60
Weinman, Benzion 1897-1987 Obituary 121
Weinman, Irving 1937- 122
Weinman, Paul 1940- CANR-13
Earlier sketch in CA 77-80
Weinrauch, Herschel 1905- CAP-1
Earlier sketch in CA 15-16
Weinreb, Lloyd L(obell) 1936- 69-72
Weinrich, A(nna) K(atharina) H(ildegard)
1933- CANR-16
Earlier sketch in CA 37-40R
Weinryb, Bernard D(ov) 1905- 45-48
Weinstein, Allen 1937- 41-44R
Weinstein, Arnold 1927- 9-10R
Weinstein, Bernard L(ee) 1942- 111
Weinstein, Bob 1941- 120
Weinstein, Brian 1937- 21-22R
Weinstein, Donald 1926- 15-16R
Weinstein, Fred 1931- 65-68
Weinstein, Gerald 1930- 25-28R
Weinstein, Grace W(ohlner) 1935- CANR-10
Earlier sketch in CA 61-64
Weinstein, Howard 1954- CANR-23
Earlier sketch in CA 107
Weinstein, Jacob Joseph 1902-1974 110
Obituary 108
Weinstein, James 1926- 23-24R
Weinstein, Leo 1921- Brief entry 110
Weinstein, Mark A. 1937- 25-28R
Weinstein, Marlene 1946- 45-48
Weinstein, Martin E. 1934- 85-88
Weinstein, Michael 1898- CAP-1
Earlier sketch in CA 13-14
Weinstein, Nathan Wallenstein
1903(?)-1940 Brief entry 104
Weinstein, Norman Charles 1948- 37-40R
Weinstein, Robert A. 1914- 29-32R
Weinstein, Sol 1928- 15-16R
Weinstein, Warren 1941- 93-96
Weinstock, Herbert 1905-1971 .... CANR-2
Obituary 33-36R
Earlier sketch in CA 4R
Weinstock, John M(artin) 1936- 81-84
Weinstone, William W. 1898(?)-1985
Obituary 117
Weinswig, Melvin H. 1935- Brief entry 107
Weintal, Edward 1901-1973 Obituary 41-44R
Weintraub, Dov 1926- 109
Weintraub, Karl Joachim 1924- 25-28R
Weintraub, Robert E. 1925-1983 Obituary .. 110
Weintraub, Rodelle (Selma) 1933- 97-100
Weintraub, Sidney 1914-1983 .... CANR-6
Obituary 110
Earlier sketch in CA 2R
Weintraub, Sidney 1922- 108
Weintraub, Stanley 1929- CANR-22
Earlier sketches in CA 1R, CANR-2
Weintraub, Wiktor 1908- CANR-3
Earlier sketch in CA 7-8R
Weintraub, William 1926- 2R
Weinwurm, George F(elix) 1935- 33-36R
Weinzweig, Helen 1915- 106
Weir, Alice M.
See McLaughlin, Emma Maude
Weir, J(ohn) E(dward) 1935- 118
Weir, Joan 1928- 112
Weir, John
See Cross, Colin (John)
Weir, LaVada CANR-9
Earlier sketch in CA 23-24R
See also SATA 2
Weir, Molly 1920- CANR-12
Earlier sketch in CA 29-32R
Weir, Nancie MacCullough 1933- 65-68
Weir, Peter (Lindsay) 1944- 123
Brief entry 113
See also CLC 20
Weir, Robert M(cColloch) 1933- 93-96
Weir, Rosemary (Green) 1905- CANR-10
Earlier sketch in CA 13-14R
See also SATA 21
Weir, Thomas R(obert) 1912- 41-44R
Weir, Walter 1909- 5-6R
Weis, Elisabeth 1944- 112
Weis, Jack 1932- 105
Weis, Margaret (Edith) 1948- 111
See also SATA 38
Weis, Norman D(wight) 1923- 61-64
Weisberg, Barry 33-36R
Weisberg, Gabriel P(aul) 1942- 73-76
Weisberg, Harold 1913- 41-44R
Weisberg, Joseph Gotland 1911-1984
Obituary 112
Weisberg, Joseph S(impson) 1937- 107
Weisberger, Bernard A(llen) 1922- CANR-7
Earlier sketch in CA 5-6R
See also SATA 21
Weisberger, Eleanor (Burt) 1920- 97-100
Weisbord, Albert 1900(?)-1977 Obituary .. 69-72
Weisbord, Marvin R(oss) 1931- CANR-9
Earlier sketch in CA 65-68
Weisbord, Robert G. 1933- Brief entry 109
Weisbord, Vera Buch 1895-1987 73-76
Obituary 123
Weisbrod, Burton Allen 1931- CANR-21
Earlier sketches in CA 45-48, CANR-1
Weisbuch, Robert 1946- 104
Weisburd, Martin Harold 1940(?)-1978
Obituary 77-80
Weise, R. Eric 1933- 41-44R
Weisenborn, Guenther 1902-1969
Obituary 114
Weisenborn, Gunther
See Weisenborn, Guenther
Weisenburger, Francis Phelps 1900- CAP-1
Earlier sketch in CA 17-18
Weisenfeld, Murray 1923- 104
Weiser, Eric 1907- 17-18R
Weiser, Marjorie P(hillis) K(atz) 1934- 103
See also SATA 33
Weisgal, Meyer W(olf) 1894-1977
Obituary 89-92
Weisgard, Leonard Joseph 1916- 11-12R
See also SATA 2, 30
Weisgerber, Charles A(ugust)
1912-1977 .... 41-44R
Weisgerber, Jean 1924- 65-68
Weisgerber, Robert A(rthur) 1929- 49-52
Weisheipl, James A(thanasius) 1923- .. CANR-15
Earlier sketch in CA 41-44R
Weisheit, Eldon 1933- CANR-14
Earlier sketch in CA 29-32R
Weisinger, Mort 1915- 11-12R
Weiskopf, Bob
See Weiskopf, Robert J.
Weiskopf, Robert J. Brief entry 118
Weiskopf, Robert J. 1914- 123
Weisman, Herman M. 1916- 11-12R
Weisman, John 1942- CANR-1
Earlier sketch in CA 45-48
Weisman, Marilee 1939- 65-68
Weisman, Mary-Lou 1937- 109
Weismann, Donald L(eroy) 1914- 33-36R
Weismiller, Edward Ronald 1915- CANR-1
Earlier sketch in CA 3R
Weiss, Abraham 1895-1971 Obituary 104
Weiss, Adelle 1920- 81-84
See also SATA 18
Weiss, Allen 1918- 109
Weiss, Ann E(dwards) 1943- CANR-11
Earlier sketches in CA 45-48, CANR-1
See also SATA 30
Weiss, Arthur 1912- 25-28R
Weiss, Bennet A., Jr. 1926(?)-1983
Obituary 109
Weiss, Beno 1933- 123
Weiss, Bernard J(acob) 1936- 109
Weiss, Dale Eugene 1947- 114
Weiss, David 1909- CANR-12
Earlier sketch in CA 15-16R
Weiss, David 1928- 121
Weiss, Edna
See Barth, Edna
Weiss, Edna Smith 1916- 5-6R
Weiss, Elizabeth S(chwartz) 1944- CANR-11
Earlier sketch in CA 61-64
Weiss, Ellen 1953- 113
See also SATA 44
Weiss, Francis Joseph 1899(?)-1975
Obituary 53-56
Weiss, G(ustav) A(dolf) M(ichael) 1922- .. 41-44R
Weiss, Gaea (Laughingbird) 1941- 119
Weiss, Harry B(ischoff) 1883-1972 45-48
Weiss, Harvey 1922- CANR-6
Earlier sketch in CA 5-6R
See also SATA 1, 27
See also CLR 4
Weiss, Herbert F. 1930- 21-22R
Weiss, Irving J. 1921- CANR-10
Earlier sketch in CA 19-20R
Weiss, Jaqueline Shachter 1926- 119
Weiss, Jess E(dward) 1926- 49-52
Weiss, Joan Talmage 1928- CANR-2
Earlier sketch in CA 7-8R
Weiss, John 1818-1879 .... DLB-1
Weiss, John 1927- 19-20R
Weiss, Jonathan A(rthur) 1939- 93-96
Weiss, Kenneth M(onrad) 1941- 101
Weiss, Leatie 1928- 65-68
See also SATA 50
Weiss, Leonard W(inchell) 1925- CANR-6
Earlier sketch in CA 7-8R
Weiss, Lillian ?-1972 Obituary 104
Weiss, Louise 1893-1983 Obituary 109
Weiss, M(orton) Jerome 1926- CANR-9
Earlier sketch in CA 19-20R
Weiss, M. Jerry
See Weiss, M(orton) Jerome
Weiss, Malcolm E. 1928- CANR-11
Earlier sketch in CA 25-28R
See also SATA 3
Weiss, Margaret R. 57-60
Weiss, Melford Stephen 1937- 53-56
Weiss, Miriam (Strauss) 1905- CAP-2
Earlier sketch in CA 29-32
Weiss, Miriam
See Schlein, Miriam
Weiss, Morris S(amuel) 1915- 89-92
Weiss, Nancy J(oan) 1944- CANR-13
Earlier sketch in CA 77-80
Weiss, Nicki 1954- 108
See also SATA 33
Weiss, Paul 1901- CANR-3
Earlier sketch in CA 7-8R
Weiss, Peter (Ulrich) 1916-1982 .... CANR-3
Obituary 106
Earlier sketch in CA 45-48
See also CLC 3, 15
Weiss, Renee Karol 1923- 41-44R
See also SATA 5
Weiss, Robert M. 1929- 37-40R
Weiss, Robert S(tuart) 1925- 25-28R
Weiss, Roger W(illiam) 1930- 45-48
weiss, ruth 1928- 122
Weiss, Samuel A(bba) 1922- 41-44R
Weiss, Sanford 1927- 25-28R
Weiss, (Paul) Shandor 1954- 120
Weiss, Theodore (Russell) 1916- 9-10R
See also CAAS 2
See also DLB 5
See also CLC 3, 8, 14
Weiss, Thomas J(oseph) 1942- 105
Weiss, Winfried (Ferdinand) 1937- 117
Weissberger, L. Arnold 1907-1981
Obituary 103
Weissbort, Daniel 1935- CANR-2
Earlier sketch in CA 45-48
Weissenborn, Hellmuth 1898-1982
Obituary 107
See also SATA 31
Weisskopf, Kurt 1907- 25-28R
Weisskopf, Victor Frederick 1908- 107
Weisskopf, Walter A(lbert) 1904- 37-40R
Weissman, Benjamin M(urry) 1917- 73-76
Weissman, Dick
See Weissman, Richard
Weissman, Jack 1921- 13-14R
Weissman, Paul 1932- 45-48
Weissman, Philip 1911(?)-1972
Obituary 33-36R
Weissman, Richard 1935- 81-84
Weissman, Rozanne 1942- 101
Weissman, Stephen R(ichard) 1941- ... CANR-11
Earlier sketch in CA 57-60
Weissman, Steve
See Weissman, Stephen R(ichard)
Weissmuller, Johnny
See Weissmuller, Peter John
Weissmuller, Peter John 1904-1984
Obituary 111
Weisstein, Ulrich W(erner) 1925- 21-22R
Weisstub, D(avid) N(orman) 1944- 29-32R
Weith, Warren 1926- 114
Weithorn, Stanley S(tephen) 1924- 15-16R
Weitz, Henry 1911- 41-44R
Weitz, John 1923- 29-32R
Weitz, Martin Mishli 1909- CANR-13
Earlier sketches in CA 17-18, CAP-2
Weitz, Morris 1916-1981 .... CANR-7
Obituary 102
Earlier sketch in CA 5-6R
Weitz, Raanan 1913- CANR-1
Earlier sketch in CA 45-48
Weitzel, Eugene Joseph 1927- 5-6R
Weitzenhoffer, Andre M(uller) 1921- 7-8R
Weitzman, Alan 1933- 29-32R
Weitzman, Arthur J(oshua) 1933- 53-56
Weitzman, Elliot D. 1929-1983 Obituary 110
Weitzman, Martin L(awrence) 1942- 117
Weitzmann, Kurt 1904- 41-44R
Weixlmann, Joe
See Weixlmann, Joseph Norman
Weixlmann, Joseph Norman 1946- 109
Weizenbaum, Joseph 1923- Brief entry 113
Weizman, Ezer 1924- 111
Weizsaecker, Carl Friedrich von
See von Weizsaecker, Carl Friedrich
Welber, Robert 104
See also SATA 26
Welbourn, F(rederick) B(urkewood)
1912- 21-22R
Welburn, Ron(ald Garfield) 1944- CANR-17
Earlier sketches in CA 45-48, CANR-1
Welch, Ann Courtenay (Edmonds)
1917- CANR-18
Earlier sketches in CA 11-12R, CANR-3
Welch, Bob
See Welch, Robert Lynn

Welch, Charles Scott
See Smith, LeRoi Tex
Welch, Claude E(merson), Jr. 1939- ... CANR-14
Earlier sketch in CA 41-44R
Welch, Cyril 1939- ... 118
Welch, D'Alte Aldridge 1907-1970
Obituary ... 104
See also SATA 27
Welch, (Maurice) Denton 1915-1948
Brief entry ... 121
See also TCLC 22
Welch, Don(ovan LeRoy) 1932- ... CANR-20
Earlier sketch in CA 104
Welch, Finis R. 1938- ... 118
Welch, George Patrick 1901-1976 ... CAP-1
Obituary ... 65-68
Earlier sketch in CA 13-14
Welch, Herbert 1862-1969 ... CAP-1
Earlier sketch in CA 15-16
Welch, Holmes (Hinkley) 1921- ... 23-24R
Welch, J(oseph) Edmund 1922- ... 57-60
Welch, James 1940- ... 85-88
See also CLC 6, 14
Welch, Jean-Louise
See Kempton, Jean Welch
Welch, Jerome A. 1933- ... 65-68
Welch, June Rayfield 1927- ... 41-44R
Welch, Kenneth Frederick 1917- ... 105
Welch, Lew(is Barrett, Jr.) 1926-1971(?)
Obituary ... 113
See also DLB 16
Welch, Liliane 1937- ... 110
Welch, Martha McKeen 1914- Brief entry ... 114
See also SATA 45
Welch, Mary Ross 1918- ... 53-56
Welch, Mary-Scott (Stewart) 1914- ... 104
Welch, Michael Irene 1940- ... 97-100
Welch, Patrick
See Welch, George Patrick
Welch, Pauline
See Bodenham, Hilda Morris
Welch, Richard Edwin, Jr. 1924- ... 85-88
Welch, Robert H(enry) W(inborne), Jr.
1899-1985 Obituary ... 114
Welch, Robert Lynn 1956- ... 112
Welch, Ronald
See Felton, Ronald Oliver
Welch, Rowland
See Davies, L(eslie) P(urnell)
Welch, Stuart Cary 1928- ... 103
Welch, Timothy L. 1935- ... 85-88
Welch, William 1917- Brief entry ... 115
Welch, William A. 1915(?)-1976
Obituary ... 65-68
Welcher, Jeanne K. 1922- Brief entry ... 116
Welcher, Rosalind 1922- ... 45-48
Welchman, Gordon 1906(?)-1985
Obituary ... 117
Welcome, John
See Brennan, John N(eedham) H(uggard)
Weld, Philip S(altonstall, Sr.) 1914-1984
Obituary ... 114
Welding, Patsy Ruth 1924- ... 61-64
Weldon, Fay 1933- ... CANR-16
Earlier sketch in CA 23-24R
See also DLB 14
See also CLC 6, 9, 11, 19, 36
Weldon, John 1890(?)-1963 Obituary ... 115
Weldon, John F(rederick Stover) 1948- ... 113
Weldon, Lynn Leroy 1930- ... 97-100
Weldon, Michael J(ames) 1952- ... 117
Weldon, Rex
See Rimel, Duane (Weldon)
Weldon, (Nathaniel) Warren (Jr.) 1919- ... 29-32R
Welfare, Humphrey 1950- ... 124
Welfle, Richard A. 1901- ... CAP-1
Earlier sketch in CA 13-14
Welfling, Weldon 1912-1978 Obituary ... 111
Welford, A(lan) T(raviss) 1914- ... CANR-5
Earlier sketch in CA 13-14R
Welk, Lawrence 1903- Brief entry ... 105
Welke, Elton 1941- ... 65-68
Welker, David 1917- ... 57-60
Welker, Robert Henry 1917- ... 89-92
Welker, Robert L(ouis) 1924- ... 11-12R
Welkowitz, Joan 1929- ... 53-56
Well, Alan Stewart
See Sewart, Alan
Welland, Colin
See Williams, Colin
Welland, Dennis (Sydney Reginald)
1919- ... CANR-2
Earlier sketch in CA 5-6R
Wellard, James (Howard) 1909-1987 ... CANR-3
Obituary ... 122
Earlier sketch in CA 5-6R
Wellborn, Charles 1923- ... 29-32R
Wellborn, Fred W(ilmot) 1894- ... 11-12R
Wellborn, Grace Pleasant 1906-19(?) ... CAP-2
Earlier sketch in CA 17-18
Wellek, Rene 1903- ... CANR-8
Earlier sketch in CA 7-8R
See also DLB 63
See also CLC 28
Wellen, Edward (Paul) 1919- ... 85-88
Weller, Allen Stuart 1907- ... CANR-24
Earlier sketch in CA 3R
Weller, Charles 1911- ... 21-22R
Weller, George (Anthony) 1907- ... 65-68
See also SATA 31
Weller, Michael 1942- ... 85-88
See also CLC 10
Weller, Paul 1958- ... CLC-26
Weller, Robert P(aul) 1953- ... 118
Weller, Sheila 1945- ... 77-80
Wellershoff, Dieter 1925- ... CANR-16
Earlier sketch in CA 89-92
See also CLC 46
Welles, Margery Miller 1923-1985
Obituary ... 115
Welles, (George) Orson 1915-1985 ... 93-96
Obituary ... 117
See also CLC 20
Welles, Samuel Gardner 1913(?)-1981
Obituary ... 105
Welles, Winifred 1893-1939 Brief entry ... 112
See also SATA 27
Wellesbourne, Peter
See Williams, P(eter) F(airney)
Wellesley, Gerald 1885-1972 Obituary ... 104
Wellesley, Kenneth 1911- ... 106
Wellesz, Egon Joseph 1885-1974
Obituary ... 53-56
Wellford, Harrison 1940- Brief entry ... 111
Welling, William 1924- ... 81-84
Wellington, C(harles) Burleigh 1920- ... 2R
Wellington, Harry H(illel) 1926- ... 25-28R
Wellington, Jean Willett 1922- ... 2R
Wellington, John H. 1892- ... CAP-2
Earlier sketch in CA 25-28
Wellington, Kate
See Schulze, Hertha
Wellington, R(ichard) A(nthony) 1919- ... 61-64
Wellisch, Hans H(anan) 1920- ... 102
Wellisz, Leopold T. 1882-1972
Obituary ... 37-40R
Wellman, Alice 1900- ... 89-92
See also SATA 36
Wellman, Carl (Pierce) 1926- ... 37-40R
Wellman, Frederick L(ovejoy) 1897- ... 77-80
Wellman, Henry Q. 1945- ... 37-40R
Wellman, Manly Wade 1903-1986 ... CANR-16
Obituary ... 118
Earlier sketches in CA 3R, CANR-6
See also SATA 6, 47
Wellman, Paul I(selin) 1898-1966 ... CANR-16
Obituary ... 25-28R
Earlier sketch in CA 2R
See also SATA 3
Wellman, William A(ugustus) 1896-1975
Obituary ... 61-64
Wells, Anna Mary 1906- ... CANR-2
Earlier sketch in CA 5-6R
Wells, Arvin Robert 1927- ... 2R
Wells, Bella Fromm 1901(?)-1972
Obituary ... 104
Wells, C(olin) M(ichael) 1933- ... 41-44R
Wells, Carolyn 1869(?)-1942 Brief entry ... 113
See also DLB 11
Wells, Charles Jeremiah 1800-1879 ... DLB-32
Wells, David Franklin 1928- Brief entry ... 108
Wells, Dee (Alberta) 1925- ... 85-88
See also AITN 1
Wells, (William) Dicky 1910- ... 61-64
Wells, Donald A(rthur) 1917- ... 23-24R
Wells, Ellen B(aker) 1934- ... 103
Wells, Evelyn ... 53-56
Wells, George A(lbert) 1926- ... CANR-15
Earlier sketch in CA 81-84
Wells, George Philip 1901-1985 Obituary ... 117
Wells, H(erbert) G(eorge) 1866-1946 ... 121
Brief entry ... 110
See also SATA 20
See also DLB 34
See also TCLC 6, 12, 19
Wells, Harold P(hilmore) 1925- ... CANR-10
Earlier sketch in CA 65-68
Wells, Harry Kohlsaat 1911-1976 ... 5-6R
Obituary ... 65-68
Wells, Helen 1910-1986 ... 29-32R
See also SATA 2, 49
Wells, Helen
See Campbell, Hope
Wells, Henry W(illis) 1895-1978 ... 81-84
Obituary ... 77-80
Wells, Hondo
See Whittington, Harry (Benjamin)
Wells, J. Wellington
See de Camp, L(yon) Sprague
Wells, James B(uchanan) 1909- ... 45-48
Wells, James M. 1917- ... 19-20R
Wells, Jerome C(ovell) 1936- ... 41-44R
Wells, Jessica
See Buckland, Raymond
Wells, Joel F(reeman) 1930- ... CANR-23
Earlier sketch in CA 15-16R
Wells, John Campbell 1936- ... 104
Wells, John Jay
See Bradley, Marion Zimmer
Coulson, Juanita (Ruth)and Wells, John
Warren 1938- ... CANR-4
Earlier sketch in CA 49-52
Wells, June
See Swinford, Betty (June Wells)
Wells, Kenneth McNeill 1905- ... CAP-1
Earlier sketch in CA 13-14
Wells, Lawrence 1941- ... 120
Wells, Leon W. 1925- ... 17-18R
Wells, Linton 1893-1976 ... 97-100
Obituary ... 61-64
Wells, Lisa
See Racina, Thom
Wells, Louis T(ruitt), Jr. 1937- ... 65-68
Wells, M. Gawain 1942- ... 101
Wells, Marian (Louise Bradfield) 1931- ... 113
Wells, Merle William 1918- ... CANR-16
Earlier sketch in CA 85-88
Wells, Nigel 1944- ... 118
Wells, Peter D. 1936- ... 25-28R
Wells, (Frank Charles) Robert 1929- ... 97-100
Wells, Robert 1947- ... DLB-40
Wells, Robert
See Welsch, Roger L(ee)
Wells, Robert Vale 1943- ... CANR-12
Earlier sketch in CA 73-76
Wells, Robert W(ayne) 1918- ... CANR-2
Earlier sketch in CA 49-52
Wells, Ronald Vale 1913- ... CANR-14
Earlier sketch in CA 37-40R
Wells, Rosemary 1943- ... 85-88
See also SATA 18
See also SAAS 1
See also CLC 12
Wells, Samuel F(ogle, Jr.) 1935- ... 104
Wells, Samuel J(ames III) 1936- ... 123
Wells, Stanley W(illiam) 1930- ... CANR-10
Earlier sketch in CA 23-24R
Wells, Theodora (Westmont) 1926-
Brief entry ... 113
Wells, Tobias
See Forbes, DeLoris (Florine) Stanton
Wells, Tom H. 1917- ... 23-24R
Wells, Walter 1937- ... 25-28R
Wells, William D(eWitt) 1926- ... CANR-13
Earlier sketch in CA 61-64
Wells-Barnett, Ida B. 1862-1931 ... DLB-23
Wellstone, Paul David 1944- ... 107
Wellwarth, George E(manuel) 1932- ... CANR-3
Earlier sketch in CA 11-12R
Welmers, William Evert 1916- ... 104
Wels, Alena 1938(?)-1985 Obituary ... 115
Wels, Byron G(erald) 1924- ... CANR-8
Earlier sketch in CA 61-64
See also SATA 9
Welsch, Erwin Kurt 1935- ... 17-18R
Welsch, Glenn Albert 1915- ... CANR-10
Earlier sketch in CA 13-14R
Welsch, Roger L(ee) 1936- ... CANR-9
Earlier sketch in CA 21-22R
Welsh, Alexander 1933- ... CANR-6
Earlier sketch in CA 7-8R
Welsh, Andrew 1937- ... 110
Welsh, Anne 1922- ... 101
Welsh, David
See Hills, C(harles) A(lbert) R(eis)
Welsh, David J(ohn) 1920- ... 17-18R
Welsh, George Schlager 1918- ... 19-20R
Welsh, James Michael 1938- ... CANR-20
Earlier sketches in CA 53-56, CANR-4
Welsh, John R(ushing) 1916-1974 ... 37-40R
Welsh, Ken 1941- ... CANR-13
Earlier sketch in CA 77-80
Welsh, Marion E. 1910- ... 118
Welsh, Mary
See Hemingway, Mary Welsh
Welsh, Mary Flynn 1910(?)-1984 Obituary ... 112
See also SATA 38
Welsh, Paul 1911- ... 104
Welsh, Peter C(orbett) 1926- ... 25-28R
Welsh, Stanley L. 1928- ... 103
Welsh, Susan
See Collins, Margaret (Brandon James)
Welsh, William A(llen) 1940- ... 45-48
Welsman, Ernest 1912- ... 7-8R
Welt, Louis G(ordon) 1913-1974
Obituary ... 45-48
Welter, Erich 1900-1982 Obituary ... 107
Welter, Paul (R.) 1928- ... 121
Welter, Rush (Eastman) 1923- ... CANR-2
Earlier sketch in CA 5-6R
Weltge, Ralph (William) 1930- ... 23-24R
Welthy, Soni Halstead 1933- ... 15-16R
Weltmann, Lutz 1901- ... CAP-1
Earlier sketch in CA 11-12
Weltner, Linda R(iverly) 1938- ... 105
See also SATA 38
Weltsch, Robert 1891-1982 Obituary ... 108
Welty, Eudora 1909- ... 11-12R
See also CABS 1
See also DLB 2
See also CDALB 1941-1968
See also CLC 1, 2, 5, 14, 22, 33
See also SSC 1
Welty, Joel Carl 1901- ... CANR-2
Earlier sketch in CA 5-6R
Welty, S. F.
See Welty, Susan F.
Welty, Susan F. 1905- ... CAP-2
Earlier sketch in CA 17-18
See also SATA 9
Welwood, John 1943- ... 120
Welzenbach, Lanora F.
See Miller, Lanora
Wemple, Suzanne Fonay 1927- ... 106
Wenar, Charles 1922- ... 93-96
Wende, Philip 1939- ... 29-32R
Wendel, Francois Jean 1905-19(?) ... CAP-1
Earlier sketch in CA 13-14
Wendel, Natalja Rose 1900- ... 61-64
Wendel, Thomas H(arold) 1924- ... 53-56
Wendel, Tim 1956- ... 105
Wendelin, Rudolph 1910- ... SATA-23
Wender, Dorothea 1934- ... CANR-24
Earlier sketch in CA 45-48
Wender, Paul H. 1934- ... 109
Wenders, Wim 1945- ... 93-96
Wendland, Michael F(letcher) 1946- ... CANR-9
Earlier sketch in CA 65-68
Wendland, Mike
See Wendland, Michael F(letcher)
Wendorf, Patricia 1928- ... 113
Wendorf, Richard (Harold) 1948- ... 114
Wendroff, Zalman
See Vendrovskii, David Efimovich
Wendrowsky, Zalman
See Vendrovskii, David Efimovich
Wendt, Albert 1939- ... 57-60
Wendt, Gerald L(ouis) 1891-1973
Obituary ... 45-48
Wendt, Ingrid 1944- ... 117
Wendt, Jo Ann 1935- ... 109
Wendt, Lloyd 1908- ... 102
Wendt, Viola (Sophia) 1907- ... 104
Wendzel, Robert L. 1938- ... 112
Weng, Byron S. J. 1934- ... CANR-16
Earlier sketch in CA 41-44R
Weng, Hsing Ching
See Weng, Wan-go
Weng, Wan-go 1918- ... 97-100
Wengenroth, Edith Flack Ackley
1887-1970 Obituary ... 104
Wengenroth, Stow 1906-1978 Obituary ... 104
Wenger, (Anna) Grace 1919- ... 13-14R
Wenger, J(ohn) C(hristian) 1910- ... CANR-21
Earlier sketches in CA 3R, CANR-6
Wengert, Norman Irving 1916- ... 85-88
Wengrov, Charles 1925- ... CANR-7
Earlier sketch in CA 5-6R
Wenham, John W(illiam) 1913- ... 57-60
Wenhe, Mary B. 1910- ... 65-68
Wenk, Edward, Jr. 1920- ... 53-56
Wenkam, Robert 1920- ... CANR-4
Earlier sketch in CA 53-56
Wenkart, Heni
See Wenkart, Henny
Wenkart, Henny 1928- ... 11-12R
Wennblom, Ralph D. 1922(?)-1986
Obituary ... 121
Wenner, Jann S(imon) 1946- ... 101
Wenner, Kate 1947- ... 77-80
Wenner, Lettie McSpadden 1937- ... 65-68
Wenner, Manfred W. 1936- ... 29-32R
Wenner, Sim 1922- ... 2R
Wennerstrom, Mary H(annah) 1939-
Brief entry ... 110
Wensing, Michael G. 1950- ... 118
Wensinger, Arthur S(tevens) 1926- ... CANR-15
Earlier sketch in CA 37-40R
Wentink, Andrew Mark 1948- ... 105
Wentworth, Barbara
See Pitcher, Gladys
Wentworth, Elise H(ughes) 1931- ... 77-80
Wentworth, Harold 1904- ... CAP-1
Earlier sketch in CA 13-14
Wentworth, Michael J(ustin) 1938- ... 118
Wentworth, Robert
See Hamilton, Edmond
Wentz, Frederick K(uhlman) 1921- ... 11-12R
Wentz, Walter B. 1929- ... CANR-10
Earlier sketch in CA 25-28R
Wenzel, Siegfried 1928- ... 21-22R
Wepman, Dennis 1933- ... 120
Wepman, Joseph M. 1907- ... 45-48
Weppner, Robert S. 1936- ... 121
Werblow, Dorothy N. 1908-1972
Obituary ... 37-40R
Were, Gideon S(aulo) 1934- ... CANR-11
Earlier sketch in CA 65-68
Werfel, Franz (V.) 1890-1945 Brief entry ... 104
See also TCLC 8
Werich, Jan 1905(?)-1980 Obituary ... 102
Werking, Richard Hume 1943- Brief entry ... 113
Werkley, Caroline E(lsea) ... 29-32R
Werkman, Sidney L(ee) 1927- ... 49-52
Werkmeister, Lucyle (Thomas) 1908- ... 5-6R
Werkmeister, W(illiam) H(enry) 1901- ... 23-24R
Werlich, David P(atrick) 1941- ... 81-84
Werlich, Robert 1924- ... 11-12R
Werlin, Herbert Holland 1932- ... 61-64
Wermuth, Paul C(harles Joseph) 1925- ... 13-14R
Werne, Benjamin 1904-1978 Obituary ... 77-80
Wernecke, Herbert Henry 1895- ... 5-6R
Werner, Alfred 1911-1979 Obituary ... 89-92
Werner, D. Michael 1950- ... 120
Werner, Elsa Jane
See Watson, Jane Werner
Werner, Emmy Elizabeth 1929- ... 57-60
Werner, Eric 1901- ... 15-16R
Werner, Hazen G. 1895- ... 17-18R
Werner, Herma 1926- ... CANR-15
Earlier sketch in CA 85-88
See also SATA 41, 47
Werner, Jane
See Watson, Jane Werner
Werner, Jayne S(usan) 1944- ... 112
Werner, John R(oland) 1930- ... 41-44R
Werner, K.
See Casewit, Curtis W(erner)
Werner, M(orris) R(obert) 1897-1981 ... 107
Obituary ... 104
Werner, Peter Howard 1944- ... CANR-4
Earlier sketch in CA 53-56
Werner, Victor (Emile) 1894-1980 ... 29-32R
Obituary ... 93-96
Werner, Vivian 1921- ... 105
Wernette, J(ohn) Philip 1903- ... 5-6R
Wernick, Robert 1918- ... 97-100
Wernick, Saul 1921- ... 81-84
Werning, Waldo J. 1921- ... CANR-10
Earlier sketch in CA 13-14R
Wernstedt, Frederick L(age) 1921- ... 23-24R
Werr, Donald F. 1920- ... 21-22R
Werry, Richard R. 1916- ... 9-10R
Wersba, Barbara 1932- ... CANR-16
Earlier sketch in CA 29-32R
See also SATA 1
See also SAAS 2
See also DLB 52
See also CLC 30
See also CLR 3
Wershoven, Carol Jean 1947- ... 112
Werstein, Irving 1914(?)-1971 ... 73-76
Obituary ... 29-32R
See also SATA 14

Wert, Lynette L(emon) 1938- ... 106
Wertenbaker, Lael (Tucker) 1909- ... CANR-18
Earlier sketches in CA 5-6R, CANR-3
Wertenbaker, Thomas Jefferson
1879-1966 ... 7-8R
Wertenbaker, William 1938- ... 97-100
Werth, Alexander 1901-1969 ... CAP-1
Obituary ... 25-28R
Earlier sketch in CA 15-16
Werth, Kurt 1896- ... 81-84
See also SATA 20
Wertham, Fredric 1895-1981 ... 7-8R
Obituary ... 105
Wertheim, Arthur Frank 1935- ... 97-100
Wertheim, Bill 1944- ... 37-40R
Wertheim, Stanley 1930- ... 41-44R
Wertheimer, Barbara M(ayer)
1926(?)-1983 Obituary ... 110
Wertheimer, Leonard 1914- ... 116
Wertheimer, Linda Brief entry ... 123
Wertheimer, Marilyn L(ou) 1928- ... 102
Wertheimer, Max 1880-1943 Brief entry ... 123
Wertheimer, Michael (Matthew) 1927- ... CANR-2
Earlier sketch in CA 2R
Wertheimer, Richard F(rederick) II
1943- ... 29-32R
Wertheimer, Roger 1942- ... 37-40R
Werther, William B(lanchfield), Jr.
1947- ... CANR-21
Earlier sketch in CA 105
Werthman, Michael S(cott) 1939- ... 89-92
Wertime, Theodore A(llen) 1919-1982 ... 109
Obituary ... 106
Wertmuller, Lina 1928- ... 97-100
See also CLC 16
Werts, Margaret F. 1915- ... 102
Wertsman, Vladimir (F.) 1929- ... CANR-20
Earlier sketches in CA 61-64, CANR-8
Wertz, Richard W(ayne) 1933- ... 45-48
Wesander, Bioern Kenneth
See Cox, P(atrick) Brian
Wesberry, James Pickett 1906- ... 85-88
Weschcke, Carl L(ouis) 1930- ... 61-64
Wesche, L(ilburn) E(dgar) 1929- ... 93-96
Wesche, Percival A. 1912- ... 49-52
Weschler, Louis F(redrick) 1933- ... 41-44R
Wescott, Glenway 1901-1987 ... CANR-23
Obituary ... 121
Earlier sketch in CA 13-14R
See also DLB 4, 9
See also CLC 13
Wescott, Roger W. 1925- ... 25-28R
Wesencraft, Charles Frederick 1928- ... 61-64
Wesker, Arnold 1932- ... CANR-1
Earlier sketch in CA 4R
See also DLB 13
See also CLC 3, 5, 42
Weslager, C(linton) A(lfred) 1909- ... CANR-24
Earlier sketches in CA 21-22R, CANR-9
Wesley, Charles H(arris) 1891-1987 ... 101
Obituary ... 123
Wesley, Elizabeth
See McElfresh, (Elizabeth) Adeline
Wesley, George R(andolph) 1931- ... 41-44R
Wesley, James
See Rigoni, Orlando (Joseph)
Wesley, Mary 1912- ... 49-52
Wesley, Richard (Errol) 1945- ... 57-60
See also DLB 38
See also CLC 7
Wesling, Donald 1939- ... 101
Wesner, Maralene 1935- ... 112
Wesner, Miles 1933- ... 112
Wess, Martin 1906(?)-1975 Obituary ... 104
Wessel, Andrew E(rnest) 1925- ... 73-76
Wessel, Carl John 1911-1984 Obituary ... 113
Wessel, Helen (Strain) 1924- ... CANR-11
Earlier sketch in CA 13-14R
Wessel, Milton R(alph) 1923- ... 89-92
Wessel, Robert H. 1921- ... 2R
Wesselmann, Tom 1931- ... 108
Wessels, William L. 1889- ... 7-8R
Wesser, Robert F. 1933- ... 23-24R
Wessler, Ruth Ann 1938- ... 29-32R
Wessman, Alden E(benhart) 1930- ... 23-24R
Wesson, Joan
See Pittock, Joan (Hornby)
Wesson, Robert G(ale) 1920- ... CANR-18
Earlier sketches in CA 11-12R, CANR-3
West, Allan M(orrell) 1910- ... 109
West, Anna 1938- ... 106
See also SATA 40
West, Anthony (Panther) 1914-1987 ... CANR-19
Obituary ... 124
Earlier sketches in CA 45-48, CANR-3
See also DLB 15
West, Anthony C. 1910- ... 69-72
West, Barbara
See Price, Olive
West, Betty 1921- ... CANR-7
Earlier sketch in CA 7-8R
See also SATA 11
West, Beverly Henderson 1939- ... 119
West, Bill
See West, William G.
West, Bonnie 1946- ... 114
West, C. P.
See Wodehouse, P(elham) G(renville)
West, Charles Converse 1921- ... 81-84
West, D(onald) J(ames) 1924- ... CANR-20
Earlier sketches in CA 13-14R, CANR-5
West, David (Alexander) 1926- ... 23-24R
West, Delno C(loyde), Jr. 1936- ... 57-60
West, Don 1928- ... 57-60
West, E(dwin) G(eorge) ... 25-28R
West, Earle H(uddleston) 1925- ... 53-56
West, Edward Nason 1909- ... CAP-2
Earlier sketch in CA 19-20
West, Elliot 1924- ... 19-20R
West, Elmer D. 1907- ... CAP-1
Earlier sketch in CA 13-14
West, Emily Govan 1919- ... 109
See also SATA 38
West, Emmy
See West, Emily Govan
West, Eugenia Lovett ... 85-88
West, Francis (James) 1927- ... CANR-3
Earlier sketch in CA 7-8R
West, Francis Horner 1909- ... 118
West, Frank H.
See West, Francis Horner
West, Fred 1918- ... 7-8R
West, G(eorge) Allen, Jr. 1915- ... 19-20R
West, George Algernon 1893-1980
Obituary ... 97-100
West, Gertrude ... 110
West, Gordon 1896- ... CAP-1
Earlier sketch in CA 13-14
West, Henry Woolliscroft 1925- ... 41-44R
West, Herbert B(uell) 1916- ... 53-56
West, Herbert Faulkner 1898-1974 ... CAP-2
Obituary ... 53-56
Earlier sketch in CA 19-20
West, J. B.
See West, J. Bernard
West, J. Bernard 1913(?)-1983 ... 120
Obituary ... 110
West, James
See Withers, Carl A.
West, James King 1930- ... 45-48
West, (Mary) Jane 1939(?)-1981 Obituary ... 104
West, Jerry
See Svenson, Andrew E.
and Stratemeyer, Edward L.
West, (Mary) Jessamyn 1902(?)-1984 ... 11-12R
Obituary ... 112
See also SATA 37
See also DLB 6
See also DLBY 84
See also CLC 7, 17
West, John Anthony 1932- ... 81-84
West, John Foster 1918- ... 15-16R
West, John Frederick 1929- ... 103
West, Joyce (Tarlton) ... 106
West, Kirkpatrick
See Harris, F(rank) Brayton
West, Leonard J(ordan) 1921- ... 41-44R
West, Lindsay
See Weber, Nancy
West, Mae 1893-1980 ... 89-92
Obituary ... 102
See also DLB 44
West, Marion B(ond) 1936- ... 101
West, Mark
See Runyon, Charles W.
West, Morris L(anglo) 1916- ... CANR-24
Earlier sketch in CA 5-6R
See also CLC 6, 33
West, Muriel (Leitzell) 1903-19(?) ... CAP-1
Earlier sketch in CA 15-16
West, Nancy Richard
See Westphal, Wilma Ross
West, Nathanael
See Weinstein, Nathan Wallenstein
See also DLB 4, 9, 28
See also TCLC 1, 14
West, Owen
See Koontz, Dean R(ay)
West, Paul 1930- ... CANR-22
Earlier sketch in CA 15-16R
See also DLB 14
See also CLC 7, 14
West, Ray B(enedict), Jr. 1908- ... CANR-3
Earlier sketch in CA 2R
West, Rebecca 1892-1983 ... CANR-19
Obituary ... 109
Earlier sketch in CA 7-8R
See also DLB 36
See also DLBY 83
See also CLC 7, 9, 31
West, Richard S(edgewick), Jr.
1902-1968 ... CAP-1
Earlier sketch in CA 15-16
West, Robert C(raig) 1947- ... 89-92
West, Robert Frederick 1916- ... 5-6R
West, Robert H(unter) 1907- ... 37-40R
West, Thomas R(eed) 1936- ... 124
Brief entry ... 118
West, Token
See Humphries, Adelaide M.
West, Trudy
See West, Gertrude
West, Uta 1928- ... 85-88
West, V(ictoria Mary) Sackville
See Sackville-West, V(ictoria Mary)
West, Ward
See Borland, Harold Glen
West, William G. 1930- ... CANR-14
Earlier sketch in CA 37-40R
Westall, Robert (Atkinson) 1929- ... CANR-18
Earlier sketch in CA 69-72
See also SATA 23
See also SAAS 2
See also CLC 17
See also CLR 13
Westberg, Granger E(llsworth) 1913- ... CANR-6
Earlier sketch in CA 2R
Westbie, Constance 1910- ... 85-88
Westbrook, Adele ... 41-44R
Westbrook, Max (Roger) 1927- ... 37-40R
Westbrook, Perry D(ickie) 1916- ... CANR-21
Earlier sketches in CA 2R, CANR-6
Westbrook, Robert 1945- ... 25-28R
Westbrook, Wayne W(illiam) 1939- ... 97-100
Westbury, Ian Douglas 1939- Brief entry ... 106
Westby, David L. 1929- ... 45-48
Westby-Gibson, Dorothy Pauline 1920- ... 17-18R
Westcott, Cynthia 1898-1983 ... 7-8R
Obituary ... 109
Westcott, Jan Vlachos 1912- ... CANR-2
Earlier sketch in CA 4R
Westcott, Kathleen
See Abrahamsen, Christine Elizabeth
Westcott, W(illiam) F(ranklin) 1949- ... 113
Westcott-Jones, K(enneth) 1921- ... CANR-4
Earlier sketch in CA 53-56
Westebbe, Richard (Manning) 1925- ... 45-48
Westell, Anthony 1926- ... 101
Westerberg, Christine 1950- ... 61-64
See also SATA 29
Westergaard, John (Harald) 1927- ... CANR-11
Earlier sketch in CA 69-72
Westerhoff, John H(enry) III 1933- ... CANR-17
Earlier sketches in CA 45-48, CANR-1
Westerink, Leendert Gerrit 1913- ... 93-96
Westerman, Percy F(rancis) 1876-1959
Brief entry ... 110
Westermann, Claus 1909- ... CANR-15
Earlier sketch in CA 81-84
Westermeier, Clifford P(eter) 1910- ... 45-48
Westermeyer, Joseph John 1937- ... 109
Western, J(ohn) R(andle) 1928-1971 ... CAP-2
Earlier sketch in CA 21-22
Western, John (Charles) 1947- ... 105
Western, Mark
See Crisp, Anthony Thomas
(The) Western Spy
See Dillon, John M(yles)
Westervelt, Virginia Veeder 1914- ... CANR-10
Earlier sketch in CA 61-64
See also SATA 10
Westfall, David 1927- ... 117
Westfall, Don C. 1928-1973 ... CAP-2
Earlier sketch in CA 17-18
Westfall, Ralph (Libby) 1917- ... 5-6R
Westfall, Richard S(amuel) 1924- ... 23-24R
Westfeldt, Lulie 1896- ... CAP-1
Earlier sketch in CA 13-14
Westheimer, David 1917- ... CANR-2
Earlier sketch in CA 4R
See also SATA 14
Westhues, Kenneth 1944- ... CANR-11
Earlier sketch in CA 25-28R
Westin, Alan F(urman) 1929- ... CANR-10
Earlier sketch in CA 15-16R
Westin, Av(ram) 1929- ... 77-80
Westin, Jeane Eddy 1931- ... 85-88
Westin, Richard A(xel) 1945- ... 115
Westing, Arthur H(erbert) 1928- ... CANR-17
Earlier sketch in CA 41-44R
Westing, John Howard 1911- ... 11-12R
Westlake, Aubrey Thomas 1893-1985
Obituary ... 119
Westlake, Donald E(dwin) 1933- ... CANR-16
Earlier sketch in CA 19-20R
See also CLC 7, 33
Westlake, Helen Gum 1927- ... 41-44R
Westland, Lynn
See Joscelyn, Archie L.
Westley, Bruce H(utchinson) 1915- ... CANR-2
Earlier sketch in CA 2R
Westley, Dick
See Westley, Richard John
Westley, Richard John 1928- ... 112
Westley, William A. 1920- ... 37-40R
Westlund, Joseph 1936- ... 118
Westmacott, Mary
See Christie, Agatha (Mary Clarissa)
Westman, Barbara ... 105
Westman, Jack C(onrad) 1927- ... 93-96
Westman, Paul (Wendell) 1956- ... 106
See also SATA 39
Westman, Wesley C(harles) 1936- ... 29-32R
Westminster, Aynn
See Mundis, Hester
Westmore, Ann 1953- ... 109
Westmore, Frank 1923(?)-1985 Obituary ... 116
Westmoreland, Reg(inald Conway)
1926- ... 29-32R
Westmoreland, William C(hilds) 1914- ... 101
Westoff, Charles Francis 1927- ... 81-84
Westoff, Leslie Aldridge 1928- ... 77-80
Weston, Alan J(ay) 1940- ... 73-76
Weston, Allen
See Hogarth, Grace (Weston Allen)
and Norton, Alice Mary
Weston, Ann
See Pitcher, Gladys
Weston, Burns H. 1933- ... 29-32R
Weston, Carolyn 1921- ... 107
Weston, Corinne Comstock 1919- ... CANR-21
Earlier sketch in CA 2R
Weston, Glen E(arl) 1922- ... 49-52
Weston, Helen Gray
See Daniels, Dorothy
Weston, J(ohn) Fred(erick) 1916- ... CANR-1
Earlier sketch in CA 2R
Weston, John (Harrison) 1932- ... 17-18R
See also SATA 21
Weston, John
See Davies, John Evan Weston
Weston, Joseph H(arry) 1911(?)-1983
Obituary ... 111
Weston, Paul B(rendan) 1910- ... 15-16R
Weston, Rubin Francis 1921- ... 104
Weston, Susan B(rown) 1943- ... 81-84
Weston-Smith, M. 1956- ... 93-96
Westphal, Barbara Osborne 1907- ... CAP-1
Earlier sketch in CA 11-12
Westphal, Clarence 1904- ... CAP-2
Earlier sketch in CA 17-18
Westphal, Siegfried 1902-1982 Obituary ... 107
Westphal, Wilma Ross 1907- ... 21-22R
Westphall, Victor 1913- ... 119
Westrup, J(ack) A(llan) 1904-1975
Obituary ... 115
Westsmith, Kim 1945- ... 57-60
Westwater, Sister Agnes Martha 1929- ... 21-22R
Westwood, Gordon
See Schofield, Michael
Westwood, Gwen 1915- ... CANR-19
Earlier sketch in CA 25-28R
Westwood, J(ohn) N(orton) 1931- ... CANR-20
Earlier sketches in CA 13-14R, CANR-5
Westwood, Jennifer
See Chandler, Jennifer (Westwood)
See also SATA 10
Wetcheek, J. L.
See Feuchtwanger, Lion
Wetering, Janwillem van de
See van de Wetering, Janwillem
Wetherbee, Winthrop (III) 1938- ... CANR-12
Earlier sketch in CA 73-76
Wetherby, Terry (Lynne) 1943- ... 102
Wetherell, Elizabeth
See Warner, Susan (Bogert)
Wetherell-Pepper, Joan Alexander 1920- ... 9-10R
Wetherill, Peter Michael 1932- ... CANR-12
Earlier sketch in CA 61-64
Wethey, Harold E(dwin) 1902-1984 ... CANR-2
Obituary ... 113
Earlier sketch in CA 4R
Wetmore, Alexander 1886-1978 ... 85-88
Obituary ... 81-84
Wetmore, Ruth Y. 1934- ... 57-60
Wetmore, Thomas Hall 1915- ... 25-28R
Wetmore, William T. 1930- ... 9-10R
Wettenhall, Roger (Llewellyn) 1931- ... 109
Wetter, Gustav A(ndreas) 1911- ... 11-12R
Wettlaufer, George 1935- ... 57-60
Wettlaufer, Nancy 1939- ... 57-60
Wettstein, Howard K(enneth) 1943- ... 105
Wetzel, (Earl) Donald 1921- ... 25-28R
Wetzel, Elizabeth 1930- ... 114
Wetzel, Richard D(ean) 1935- ... 85-88
Weverka, Robert 1926- ... CANR-2
Earlier sketch in CA 49-52
Wevers, Richard Franklin 1933-
Brief entry ... 106
Wevill, David 1937- ... 13-14R
Wexler, Jean Stewart 1921- ... 65-68
Wexler, Jerome (LeRoy) 1923- ... 73-76
See also SATA 14
Wexler, Joyce Piell 1947- ... 97-100
Wexler, Norman 1926- Brief entry ... 116
Wexley, John 1907-1985 Obituary ... 115
Wexley, Kenneth N. ... 93-96
Weyand, Alexander Mathias 1892- ... 5-6R
Weybright, Victor 1903-1978 Obituary ... 89-92
Weygant, Noemi ... CANR-2
Earlier sketch in CA 45-48
Weyl, Joachim 1915-1977 Obituary ... 73-76
Weyl, Nathaniel 1910- ... CANR-5
Earlier sketch in CA 11-12R
Weyl, Woldemar A. 1901(?)-1975
Obituary ... 61-64
Weyler, Rex 1947- ... 110
Weyrauch, Walter O(tto) 1919- ... CANR-10
Earlier sketch in CA 13-14R
Weyrich, Paul M(ichael) 1942- ... 118
Wezeman, Frederick Hartog 1915-1981 ... CANR-6
Obituary ... 106
Earlier sketch in CA 11-12R
Whale, John (Hilary) 1931- ... 101
Whalen, Barbara G. 1928- ... 120
Whalen, Charles William, Jr. 1920- ... 105
Whalen, George J. 1939- ... CANR-16
Earlier sketch in CA 89-92
Whalen, Philip 1923- ... CANR-5
Earlier sketch in CA 9-10R
See also DLB 16
See also CLC 6, 29
Whalen, Richard J(ames) 1935- ... 15-16R
Whalen, William Joseph 1926- ... CANR-4
Earlier sketch in CA 2R
Whaley, Barton Stewart 1928- ... 41-44R
Whaley, Donald L. 1934- ... 33-36R
Whaley, Russell Francis 1934- ... 57-60
Whaling, Frank 1934- ... 113
Whalley, Dorothy 1911- ... CAP-1
Earlier sketch in CA 9-10
Whalley, George 1915- ... 101
Whalley, Janet 1945- ... 117
Whalley, Joyce Irene ... 103
Whalon, Marion K(elley) 1913- ... 119
Wharf, Michael
See Weller, George (Anthony)
Wharmby, Margot ... CANR-24
Earlier sketches in CA 17-18R, CANR-8
Wharton, Annabel Jane ... 123
Wharton, Anthony
See McAllister, Alister
Wharton, Anthony P.
See McAllister, Alister
Wharton, Clifton R(eginald), Jr. 1926- ... 41-44R
Wharton, David B(ailey) 1914- ... 73-76
Wharton, Edith (Newbold Jones)
1862-1937 Brief entry ... 104
See also DLB 4, 9, 12
See also TCLC 3, 9, 27
Wharton, Elizabeth Austin 1920-1985
Obituary ... 116
Wharton, Gary C(harles) 1940- ... 45-48
Wharton, George Frederick III 1952- ... 109
Wharton, John Franklin 1894-1977 ... 81-84
Obituary ... 73-76

Wharton, William (a pseudonym) ... 93-96
See also DLBY 80
See also CLC 18, 37
Whateley, Leslie Violet Lucy Evelyn Mary
1899-1987 Obituary ... 123
Whatmore, Leonard Elliott 1912- ... 13-14R
Whatmough, Joshua 1897- ... 5-6R
Wheat, Cathleen Hayhurst 1904- ... CAP-1
Earlier sketch in CA 17-18
Wheat, (Marcus) Ed(ward, Jr.) 1926- ... 118
Wheat, Gilbert Collins, Jr. 1927- ... 4R
Wheat, Joe Ben 1916- ... 41-44R
Wheat, Leonard F. 1931- ... 29-32R
Wheat, Patte 1935- ... CANR-19
Earlier sketch in CA 101
Wheatcroft, Andrew (Jonathan Maclean)
1944- ... 110
Wheatcroft, Geoffrey 1945- ... 124
Wheatcroft, John 1925- ... CANR-14
Earlier sketch in CA 37-40R
Wheatcroft, Stephen F(rederick) 1921- ... 7-8R
Wheatley, Arabelle 1921- ... SATA-16
Wheatley, Dennis (Yeats) 1897-1977 ... CANR-9
Obituary ... 73-76
Earlier sketch in CA 7-8R
Wheatley, Jon 1931- ... 29-32R
Wheatley, Phillis 1754(?)-1784 ... DLB-31, 50
See also CDALB 1640-1865
Wheatley, Richard C(harles) 1904- ... CAP-1
Earlier sketch in CA 11-12
Wheatley, Ronald 1923(?)-1985 Obituary ... 115
Wheatley, Vera (Semple) ... CAP-1
Earlier sketch in CA 15-16
Wheat-Lieber, Patte
See Wheat, Patte
Wheaton, Anne (Williams) 1892-1977
Obituary ... 69-72
Wheaton, Bruce R. 1944- ... CANR-22
Earlier sketch in CA 104
Wheaton, Philip D(amon) 1916- ... 104
Wheaton, William L. C. 1913-1978 ... CANR-3
Earlier sketch in CA 3R
Whedon, Julia
See Schickel, Julia Whedon
Whedon, Margaret B(runssen) 1926- ... 105
Whedon, Peggy
See Whedon, Margaret B(runssen)
Wheeler, Allen 1903-1984 Obituary ... 111
Wheeler, Bayard O. 1905- ... 41-44R
Wheeler, Bonnie G(rant) 1943- ... 109
Wheeler, Burton K(endall) 1882-1975
Obituary ... 53-56
Wheeler, Charles (Thomas) 1892-1974 ... CAP-2
Obituary ... 53-56
Earlier sketch in CA 29-32
Wheeler, Charles Stearns 1816-1843 ... DLB-1
Wheeler, Cindy 1955- ... 110
See also SATA 40, 49
Wheeler, David L. 1934- ... 37-40R
Wheeler, David Raymond 1942- ... 73-76
Wheeler, Douglas L. 1937- ... 29-32R
Wheeler, (Charles) Gidley 1938- ... CANR-24
Earlier sketch in CA 107
Wheeler, (John) Harvey 1918- ... CANR-17
Earlier sketches in CA 45-48, CANR-1
Wheeler, Helen Rippier ... CANR-14
Earlier sketch in CA 17-18R
Wheeler, Hugh (Callingham) 1912-1987 ... 89-92
Obituary ... 123
Wheeler, J(oseph) Clyde 1910- ... 2R
Wheeler, Janet D. ... CAP-2
Earlier sketch in CA 19-20
See also SATA 1
Wheeler, Jesse H(arrison), Jr. 1918- ... 45-48
Wheeler, John Archibald 1911- ... 57-60
Wheeler, Keith 1911- ... CANR-7
Earlier sketch in CA 7-8R
Wheeler, Leslie A. 1945- ... CANR-11
Earlier sketch in CA 65-68
Wheeler, Lora Jeanne 1923- ... 33-36R
Wheeler, Margaret 1916- ... CAP-2
Earlier sketch in CA 25-28
Wheeler, Mary Jane ... 29-32R
Wheeler, Michael 1943- ... CANR-9
Earlier sketch in CA 65-68
Wheeler, Molly 1920- ... 29-32R
Wheeler, Monroe 1900- ... DLB-4
Wheeler, (Robert Eric) Mortimer
1890-1976 ... 77-80
Obituary ... 65-68
Wheeler, Opal 1898- ... SATA-23
Wheeler, Paul 1934- ... 25-28R
Wheeler, Penny Estes 1943- ... 33-36R
Wheeler, Raymond Milner 1919-1982
Obituary ... 106
Wheeler, Richard 1922- ... CANR-8
Earlier sketch in CA 17-18R
Wheeler, Richard Paul 1943- ... 108
Wheeler, Richard S(eabrook) 1928- ... 45-48
Wheeler, Robert C(ordell) 1913- ... 61-64
Wheeler, Ruth Carr 1899- ... 5-6R
Wheeler, Sessions S(amuel) 1911- ... 17-18R
Wheeler, Thomas C. 1927- ... 104
Wheeler, Thomas H(utchin) 1947- ... 93-96
Wheeler, Tom
See Wheeler, Thomas H(utchin)
Wheeler, W(illiam) Lawrence 1925- ... 13-14R
Wheeler-Bennett, John 1902-1975 ... 65-68
Obituary ... 61-64
Wheelis, Allen B. 1915- ... 17-18R
Wheelock, Arthur Kingsland, Jr. 1943- ... 107
Wheelock, (Kinch) Carter 1924- ... 61-64
Wheelock, Frederic M(elvin) 1902-1987 ... 97-100
Obituary ... 124
Wheelock, John Hall 1886-1978 ... CANR-14
Obituary ... 77-80
Earlier sketch in CA 15-16R
See also DLB 45
See also CLC 14
Wheelock, Martha E. 1941- ... 25-28R
Wheelwright, Edward Lawrence 1921- ... CANR-21
Earlier sketch in CA 103
Wheelwright, John 1592(?)-1679 ... DLB-24
Wheelwright, John 1897-1940 ... DLB-45
Wheelwright, Philip (Ellis) 1901-1970 ... CAP-2
Earlier sketch in CA 23-24
Wheelwright, Richard 1936- ... 33-36R
Wheelwright, Steven C. 1943- ... 119
Whelan, Elizabeth M(urphy) 1943- ... CANR-24
Earlier sketches in CA 57-60, CANR-8
See also SATA 14
Whelan, Gloria (Ann) 1923- ... 101
Whelan, James Robert 1933- ... 102
Whelan, Joseph P(aul) 1932- ... 41-44R
Wheldon, Huw (Pyrs) 1916-1986 ... 107
Obituary ... 118
Whelpton, (George) Eric 1894-1981 ... CANR-5
Obituary ... 103
Earlier sketch in CA 9-10R
Whelpton, Pascal K(idder) 1893-1964 ... CANR-16
Earlier sketch in CA 2R
Whelton, Clark 1937- ... 69-72
Whetstone, Colonel Pete
See Noland, C. F. M.
Whetten, Lawrence L. 1932- ... CANR-11
Earlier sketch in CA 61-64
Whetten, Nathan Laselle 1900- ... 2R
Whicher, John F. 1919- ... 17-18R
Whiffen, Marcus 1916- ... CANR-12
Earlier sketch in CA 61-64
Whigham, Peter (George) 1925-1987 ... 25-28R
Obituary ... 123
Whinney, Margaret Dickens 1897-1975
Obituary ... 61-64
Whinnom, Keith 1927-1986 Obituary ... 118
Whipkey, Kenneth Lee 1932- ... CANR-4
Earlier sketch in CA 53-56
Whipple, Beverly 1941- ... 109
Whipple, Chandler (Henry) 1905- ... 25-28R
Whipple, Dorothy 1893- ... CAP-1
Earlier sketch in CA 13-14
Whipple, Edwin Percy 1819-1886 ... DLB-1, 64
Whipple, Fred Lawrence 1906- ... CAP-1
Earlier sketch in CA 11-12
Whipple, George 1927- ... 119
Whipple, James B. 1913- ... 29-32R
Whipple, Maurine 1910- ... 7-8R
Whisenand, Paul M. 1935- ... CANR-22
Earlier sketch in CA 69-72
Whisenhunt, Donald W(ayne) 1938- ... CANR-9
Earlier sketch in CA 57-60
Whisler, John A(lbert) 1951- ... 109
Whisler, Thomas Lee 1920- Brief entry ... 115
Whisnant, Charleen
See Swansea, Charleen
Whisnant, David E(ugene) 1938- ... 41-44R
Whistler, Laurence 1912- ... CANR-19
Earlier sketches in CA 9-10R, CANR-3
Whistler, Reginald John 1905-1944 ... SATA-30
Whistler, Rex
See Whistler, Reginald John
Whiston, Lionel (Abney) 1895- ... 69-72
Whitacre, Donald (DuMont) 1920- ... 69-72
Whitaker, Alexander 1585-1617 ... DLB-24
Whitaker, Arthur Preston 1895-1979
Obituary ... 112
Whitaker, Ben(jamin Charles George)
1934- ... 53-56
Whitaker, C(leophaus) S(ylvester), Jr.
1935- ... 29-32R
Whitaker, Carl A. 1912- Brief entry ... 114
Whitaker, David 1930- ... 21-22R
Whitaker, Dorothy Stock 1925- ... 13-14R
Whitaker, Frederic 1891-1980 ... CANR-4
Obituary ... 97-100
Earlier sketch in CA 7-8R
Whitaker, Gilbert R(iley), Jr. 1931- ... 11-12R
Whitaker, Haddon 1908(?)-1982 Obituary ... 105
Whitaker, James W. 1936- ... 102
Whitaker, John O(gden), Jr. 1935- ... 105
Whitaker, Malachi Taylor 1895-1976
Obituary ... 104
Whitaker, Mary 1896(?)-1976 Obituary ... 65-68
Whitaker, Peter 1952- ... 124
Whitaker, Rod 1931- ... 29-32R
Whitaker, Rogers E(rnest) M(alcolm)
1899-1981 Obituary ... 103
Whitaker, T(ommy) J(ames) 1949- ... 53-56
Whitaker, Thomas R(ussell) 1925- ... 25-28R
Whitaker, Urban George, Jr. 1924- ... 11-12R
Whitbeck, George W(alter) 1932- ... 73-76
Whitbread, Jane
See Levin, Jane Whitbread
Whitbread, Leslie George 1917- ... 37-40R
Whitbread, Thomas (Bacon) 1931- ... 13-14R
Whitburn, Joel Carver 1939- ... CANR-15
Earlier sketch in CA 33-36R
Whitby, Henry Augustus Morton
1898-1969 ... CAP-1
Earlier sketch in CA 11-12
Whitby, Sharon
See Peters, Maureen
Whitcher, Frances Miriam 1814-1852 ... DLB-11
Whitcomb, Edgar D(oud) 1918- ... 23-24R
Whitcomb, Hale C(hristy) 1907- ... CAP-2
Earlier sketch in CA 29-32
Whitcomb, Helen Hafemann ... CANR-6
Earlier sketch in CA 13-14R
Whitcomb, Ian 1941- ... CANR-8
Earlier sketch in CA 57-60
Whitcomb, John C(lement) 1924- ... CANR-4
Earlier sketch in CA 2R
Whitcomb, Jon 1906- ... CAP-1
Earlier sketch in CA 15-16
See also SATA 10
Whitcomb, Meg W. 1930- ... 123
Whitcomb, Philip W(right) 1891- ... 73-76
White, A(drian) N(icholas) Sherwin
See Sherwin-White, A(drian) N(icholas)
White, Alan ... CANR-3
Earlier sketch in CA 45-48
White, Alan R(ichard) 1922- ... 25-28R
White, Alex Sandri 1916(?)-1983(?)
Obituary ... 108
White, Alice Violet 1922- ... CANR-13
Earlier sketch in CA 61-64
White, Alicen ... 77-80
White, Amber Blanco
See Blanco White, Amber
White, Andrew 1579-1656 ... DLB-24
White, Andrew Dickson 1832-1918 ... DLB-47
White, Anne Hitchcock 1902-1970
Obituary ... 108
See also SATA 33
White, Anne S(hanklin) ... 93-96
White, Anne Terry 1896- ... 9-10R
See also SATA 2
White, Anthony Gene 1946- ... CANR-12
Earlier sketch in CA 73-76
White, Antonia 1899-1980 ... 104
Obituary ... 97-100
White, Babington
See Braddon, Mary Elizabeth
White, Barbara A(nne) 1942- ... 109
White, Beatrice (Mary Irene) 1902-1986
Obituary ... 119
White, Benjamin V(room) 1908- ... 101
White, Benton R. 1949- ... 124
White, Bessie (Felstiner) 1892(?)-1986
Obituary ... 121
See also SATA 50
White, Betty 1917- ... 7-8R
White, Brian Terence 1927- ... 105
White, Burton L(eonard) 1929- ... CANR-4
Earlier sketch in CA 45-48
White, Carl M(ilton) 1903-1983 ... 13-14R
Obituary ... 111
White, Carol 1946- ... 111
White, Carol Hellings 1939- ... 81-84
White, (Edwin) Chappell 1920- ... 25-28R
White, Claire Nicolas 1925- ... 108
White, Curtis 1951- ... 110
White, Cynthia L(eslie) 1940- ... 37-40R
White, Dale
See Place, Marian T(empleton)
White, Dan S(eligsberger) 1939- ... 97-100
White, David Manning 1917- ... CANR-4
Earlier sketch in CA 3R
White, David Omar 1927- ... 17-18R
White, Dori 1919- ... 37-40R
See also SATA 10
White, Dorothy Shipley ... CAP-1
Earlier sketch in CA 13-14
White, Douglas M(alcolm) 1909- ... CANR-4
Earlier sketch in CA 2R
White, E(lwyn) B(rooks) 1899-1985 ... CANR-16
Obituary ... 116
Earlier sketch in CA 13-14R
See also SATA 2, 29, 44
See also DLB 11, 22
See also CLC 10, 34, 39
See also CLR 1
See also AITN 2
White, Edgar B. 1947- ... 61-64
See also DLB 38
White, Edmund (Valentine III) 1940- ... CANR-19
Earlier sketches in CA 45-48, CANR-3
See also CLC 27
White, Edward M. 1933- ... 37-40R
White, Elijah (Brockenborough III) 1938- ... 69-72
White, Eliza Orne 1856-1947 ... YABC-2
White, Elizabeth H(erzog) 1901(?)-1972
Obituary ... 37-40R
White, Elizabeth Wade 1906- ... 97-100
White, Elmer G. 1926- ... 23-24R
White, Emmons E(aton) 1891- ... 73-76
White, Eric Walter 1905-1985 ... CAP-1
Obituary ... 117
Earlier sketch in CA 11-12
White, Ethel Lina 1887-1944 Brief entry ... 108
White, Eugene E. 1919- ... 13-14R
White, F(rederick) Clifton 1918- ... 113
White, Florence M(eiman) 1910- ... 41-44R
See also SATA 14
White, G(eorge) Edward 1941- ... CANR-12
Earlier sketch in CA 69-72
White, Gerald Taylor 1913- ... CANR-2
Earlier sketch in CA 5-6R
White, Gertrude M(ason) 1915- ... 81-84
White, Gillian Mary 1936- ... 19-20R
White, Glenn M. 1918(?)-1978 ... 93-96
Obituary ... 81-84
White, Gordon Eliot 1933- ... 101
White, H. T.
See Engh, Rohn
White, Harrison C(olyar) 1930- ... 45-48
White, Harry
See Whittington, Harry (Benjamin)
White, Helen Constance 1896- ... 7-8R
White, Hilda Crystal 1917- ... 5-6R
White, Horace 1834-1916 Brief entry ... 119
See also DLB 23
White, Howard Ashley 1913- ... 29-32R
White, Howard B. 1912(?)-1974 Obituary ... 53-56
White, Hugh Clayton 1936- ... 45-48
White, Hugh Vernon 1889- ... 7-8R
White, Irvin L(inwood) 1932- ... CANR-8
Earlier sketch in CA 57-60
White, James 1913- ... 109
White, James 1928- ... CANR-4
Earlier sketch in CA 53-56
White, James Boyd 1938- ... 111
White, James Dillon
See White, Stanley
White, James F(loyd) 1932- ... CANR-24
Earlier sketch in CA 107
White, James L. ?-1981 Obituary ... 115
White, James P(atrick) 1940- ... CANR-11
Earlier sketch in CA 69-72
White, Jane
See Brady, Jane
White, Jane Neal 1918- ... 110
White, John 1924- ... CANR-20
White, John Albert 1910- ... CAP-2
Earlier sketch in CA 23-24
White, John Baker
See Baker White, John
White, John H(enry) 1945- ... 124
Brief entry ... 117
White, John Hoxland, Jr. 1933- ... 25-28R
White, John K(enneth) 1952- ... 116
White, John W. 1939- ... CANR-13
Earlier sketch in CA 37-40R
White, John Wesley 1928- ... 29-32R
White, Jon (Ewbank) Manchip 1924- ... CANR-15
Earlier sketch in CA 13-14R
See also CAAS 4
White, Joyce C(arol) 1952- ... 112
White, Jude Gilliam 1947- ... CANR-23
Earlier sketch in CA 106
White, K(enneth) D(ouglas) 1908- ... CANR-12
Earlier sketch in CA 69-72
White, K(enneth) Owen 1902- ... CAP-2
Earlier sketch in CA 17-18
White, Karol Koenigsberg 1938- ... 5-6R
White, Katharine Sergeant 1892-1977
Obituary ... 104
White, Kenneth 1936- ... 25-28R
White, Kenneth Steele 1922- ... 93-96
White, Laurence B(arton), Jr. 1935- ... CANR-24
Earlier sketches in CA 65-68, CANR-9
See also SATA 10
White, Lawrence 1942- ... 115
White, Lawrence H(enry) 1954- ... 118
White, Lawrence J. 1943- ... CANR-14
Earlier sketch in CA 37-40R
White, Lee A. 1886-1971 Obituary ... 115
White, Leslie A(lvin) 1900-1975 ... CANR-3
Obituary ... 57-60
Earlier sketch in CA 2R
White, Leslie Turner 1903-19(?) ... CAP-1
Earlier sketch in CA 13-14
White, Lionel 1905- ... 103
White, Lonnie J(oe) 1931- ... 15-16R
White, Lucia ... 123
White, Lynn (Townsend), Jr.
1907-1987 ... CANR-2
Obituary ... 122
Earlier sketch in CA 5-6R
White, M(ary) E(llen) 1938- ... 21-22R
White, Margaret B(lackburn) 1936- ... 115
White, Mary Alice 1920- ... 11-12R
White, Maurine
See Miller (Riis), Maurine
White, Maury 1919- ... 77-80
White, Melvin R(obert) 1911- ... CANR-18
Earlier sketch in CA 23-24R
White, Minor (Martin) 1908-1976 ... CANR-10
Obituary ... 65-68
Earlier sketch in CA 19-20R
White, Morton Gabriel 1917- ... CANR-7
Earlier sketch in CA 5-6R
White, Nancy Bean 1922- ... 15-16R
White, Nicholas P. 1942- ... 73-76
White, Norval (Crawford) 1926- ... 77-80
White, Orion F(orrest) 1938- ... 53-56
White, Osmar Egmont Dorkin 1909-
Brief entry ... 105
White, Owen R(oberts) 1945- ... 41-44R
White, Patricia (Ann) 1937- ... 117
White, Patrick (Victor Martindale) 1912- ... 81-84
See also CLC 3, 4, 5, 7, 9, 18
White, Patrick C. T. 1924- ... 85-88
White, Paul Dudley 1886-1973 Obituary ... 45-48
White, Paul Hamilton Hume 1910- ... CANR-23
Earlier sketches in CA 5-6R, CANR-7
White, Paulette Childress 1948- ... 111
White, Percival 1887-1970 ... CANR-2
Earlier sketch in CA 1R
White, Philip L(loyd) 1923- ... 81-84
White, Phyllis Dorothy James 1920- ... CANR-17
Earlier sketch in CA 21-22R
White, Poppy Cannon 1906(?)-1975 ... 65-68
Obituary ... 57-60
White, Ramy Allison ... CAP-2
Earlier sketch in CA 19-20
See also SATA 1
White, Randall 1945- ... 121
White, Ray Lewis 1941- ... CANR-9
Earlier sketch in CA 21-22R
White, Reginald E(rnest) O(scar)
1914- ... CANR-21
Earlier sketches in CA 5-6R, CANR-5
White, Reginald James 1905-1971 ... 108
Obituary ... 104
White, Rhea A(melia) 1931- ... 77-80
White, Richard 1931- ... 110
White, Richard Alan 1944- ... 97-100
White, Richard C(lark) 1926- ... 45-48
White, Richard Grant 1821-1885 ... DLB-64

White, Robb 1909- CANR-1
Earlier sketch in CA 2R
See also SATA 1
See also SAAS 1
See also CLR 3
White, Robert B(enjamin), Jr. 1930-
Brief entry 118
White, Robert I. 1908- 3R
White, Robert Lee 1928- 19-20R
White, Robert Mitchell II 1915- 73-76
White, Robert R(ankin) 1942- 123
White, (William) Robin(son) 1928- CANR-20
Earlier sketches in CA 11-12R, CANR-4
White, Ronald C(edric), Jr. 1939- 93-96
White, Ruth C. 1942- 111
See also SATA 39
White, Ruth M(argaret) 1914- 17-18R
White, Ruth Morris 1902(?)-1978
Obituary 81-84
White, Sarah Harriman 1929- 11-12R
White, Sheldon Harold 1928- 105
White, Stanhope 1913- 23-24R
White, Stanley 1913- CANR-6
Earlier sketch in CA 9-10R
White, Stephanie F(rances) T(hirkell)
1942- 19-20R
White, Stephen D(aniel) 1945- 93-96
White, Steve
See McGarvey, Robert
White, Steven F(orsythe) 1955- 112
White, Suzanne 1938- 77-80
White, T(erence) H(anbury) 1906-1964 73-76
See also SATA 12
See also CLC 30
White, Ted
See White, Theodore Edwin
White, Terence de Vere 1912- CANR-3
Earlier sketch in CA 49-52
White, Theo Ballou 1903-1978 Obituary 111
White, Theodore Edwin 1938- CANR-12
Earlier sketch in CA 21-22R
White, Theodore H(arold) 1915-1986 ... CANR-3
Obituary 118
Earlier sketch in CA 2R
White, Thomas Justin, Jr. 1919-1987
Obituary 122
White, W. D. 1926- 37-40R
White, W(illiam) J(ohn) 1920-1980 ......13-14R
Obituary 97-100
White, Walter
See White, Walter F(rancis)
White, Walter F(rancis) 1893-1955 124
Brief entry 115
See also DLB 51
See also TCLC 15
White, William 1910- 23-24R
White, William A(nthony) P(arker)
1911-1968 .... CAP-1
Obituary 25-28R
Earlier sketch in CA 11-12
White, William Allen 1868-1944
Brief entry 108
See also DLB 9, 25
White, William F(rancis) 1928- CANR-1
Earlier sketch in CA 45-48
White, William Hale 1831-1913
Brief entry 121
White, William J(oseph) 1926- 97-100
White, William, Jr. 1934- CANR-14
Earlier sketch in CA 37-40R
See also SATA 16
White, William L(indsay) 1900-1973 101
Obituary 41-44R
White, William L. 1937-1985 Obituary 114
White, William Luther 1931- 29-32R
White, William S(mith) 1907- 5-6R
White, Zita
See Denholm, Theresa Mary Zita White
Whitebird, J(oanie) 1951- 69-72
White-Bowden, Susan 1939- 120
Whitechurch, Victor L(orenzo) 1868-1933
Brief entry 116
White Elk, Michael
See Walker, T. Michael
Whitefield, Ann
See Stone, Susan Berch
Whiteford, Andrew H(unter) 1913- 45-48
Whitefriar
See Hiscock, Eric
Whitehall, Harold 1905-1986 .... CAP-2
Obituary 118
Earlier sketch in CA 21-22
Whitehead, Alfred North 1861-1947
Brief entry 117
Whitehead, Barbara (Maude) 1930- 97-100
Whitehead, Don(ald) F. 1908-1981 ......11-12R
Obituary 102
See also SATA 4
Whitehead, E(dward) A(nthony) 1933- 65-68
See also CLC 5
Whitehead, (Walter) Edward 1908-1978 ...81-84
Obituary 77-80
Whitehead, Evelyn Annette Eaton 1938- 104
Whitehead, Frank S. 1916- 37-40R
Whitehead, G(eorge) Kenneth 1913- CANR-8
Earlier sketch in CA 61-64
Whitehead, James 1936- 77-80
See also DLBY 81
Whitehead, James D(ouglas) 1939- 105
Whitehead, John (Randolph) 1924- 120
Whitehead, John W. 1946- 117
Whitehead, Raymond Leslie 1933- 77-80
Whitehead, Robert J(ohn) 1928- CANR-13
Earlier sketch in CA 37-40R
Whitehead, William Grant 1943-1987
Obituary 124
Whitehill, Arthur M(urray, Jr.) 1919- ... CANR-13
Earlier sketch in CA 77-80
Whitehill, Walter Muir 1905-1978 ...... CANR-6
Obituary 77-80
Earlier sketch in CA 15-16R
Whitehorn, Katharine
See Lyall, Katharine Elizabeth
Whitehouse, Arch
See Whitehouse, Arthur George Joseph
Whitehouse, Arthur George Joseph
1895-1979 .... CANR-4
Obituary 89-92
Earlier sketch in CA 5-6R
See also SATA 14, 23
Whitehouse, Elizabeth S(cott) 1893-1968 . CAP-1
Earlier sketch in CA 13-14
See also SATA 35
Whitehouse, Franklin S., Jr. 1934-1985
Obituary 117
Whitehouse, Jack E(dward) 1933- 111
Whitehouse, Jeanne 1939- 103
See also SATA 29
Whitehouse, Roger 1939- 57-60
Whitehouse, Ruth D(elamain) 1942- 118
Whitehouse, W(alter) A(lexander)
1915- CANR-3
Earlier sketch in CA 2R
Whitelaw, William Menzies 1890(?)-1974
Obituary 45-48
Whiteley, Denys Edward Hugh 1914-1987
Obituary 123
Whitelock, Dorothy 1901-1982 Obituary 107
Whiteman, Maxwell 1914- CANR-10
Earlier sketch in CA 23-24R
Whiteman, Paul 1890(?)-1967 Obituary 113
Whitemore, Hugh 1936- CLC-37
Whitesell, (James) Edwin 1909- 41-44R
Whitesell, Faris Daniel 1895- 7-8R
Whiteside, Lynn W. 1908- 25-28R
Whiteside, Robert L(eo) 1907- 53-56
Whiteside, Thomas 1918(?)- Brief entry 109
Whiteson, Leon 1930- CANR-16
Earlier sketch in CA 23-24R
Whitfield, George J(oshua) N(ewbold)
1909- CAP-1
Earlier sketch in CA 11-12
Whitfield, James Monroe 1822-1871 .... DLB-50
Whitfield, John Humphreys 1906- 9-10R
Whitfield, Phil(ip John) 1944- 97-100
Whitfield, Raoul 1897(?)-1945 Brief entry .. 109
Whitfield, Shelby 1935- 49-52
Whitfield, Stephen J(ack) 1942- 61-64
Whitford, Bessie 1885(?)-1977 Obituary ...69-72
Whitford, Frank 1941- 97-100
Whitin, Thomson McLintock 1923- CANR-3
Earlier sketch in CA 2R
Whiting, Allen S. 1926- Brief entry 105
Whiting, Beatrice Blyth 1914- 7-8R
Whiting, Charles E. 1914(?)-1980
Obituary 97-100
Whiting, Frank M. 1907- 101
Whiting, John (Robert) 1917-1963 102
Obituary 89-92
See also DLB 13
Whiting, Kenneth R. 1913- CANR-5
Earlier sketch in CA 5-6R
Whiting, Nathan 1946- 41-44R
Whiting, Percy H(ollister) 1880- CAP-1
Earlier sketch in CA 15-16
Whiting, Robert 1942- 102
Whiting, Robert L(ouis) 1918- 17-18R
Whiting, Samuel 1597-1679 .... DLB-24
Whiting, Thomas A. 1917- CANR-3
Earlier sketch in CA 2R
Whitinger, R. D.
See Place, Marian T(empleton)
Whitington, R(ichard) S. 1912- 77-80
Whitlam, (Edward) Gough 1916- 109
Whitley, George
See Chandler, A(rthur) Bertram
Whitley, Mary Ann
See Sebrey, Mary Ann
Whitley, Oliver R. 1918- 77-80
Whitlock, Baird W(oodruff) 1924- 112
Whitlock, Brand 1869-1934 Brief entry 110
See also DLB 12
Whitlock, Glenn E(verett) 1917- 23-24R
Whitlock, Pamela 1921(?)-1982 Obituary ... 107
See also SATA 31
Whitlock, Quentin A(rthur) 1937- 109
Whitlock, Ralph 1914- CANR-20
Earlier sketch in CA 101
See also SATA 35
Whitlock, Virginia Bennett ?-1972
Obituary 37-40R
Whitlow, Roger 1940- 41-44R
Whitman, Albery Allson 1851-1901 ..... DLB-50
Whitman, Alden 1913- 17-18R
Whitman, (Evelyn) Ardis 11-12R
Whitman, Bertha Yerex 1892-1984
Obituary 114
Whitman, Cedric H(ubbell) 1916-1979 ....19-20R
Obituary 120
Whitman, David (deFreudiger) 1955- 113
Whitman, Edmund Spurr 1900- 17-18R
Whitman, Howard 1915(?)-1975
Obituary 53-56
Whitman, John 1944- CANR-11
Earlier sketch in CA 61-64
Whitman, Marina von Neumann 1935- ...17-18R
Whitman, Martin J. 1924- 104
Whitman, Robert Freeman 1925- 81-84
Whitman, Ruth (Bashein) 1922- CANR-12
Earlier sketch in CA 23-24R
Whitman, Sarah Helen (Power)
1803-1878 .... DLB-1
Whitman, Virginia Bruner 1901- CANR-4
Earlier sketch in CA 7-8R
Whitman, W(illiam) Tate 1909- CAP-1
Earlier sketch in CA 11-12
Whitman, Walt(er) 1819-1892 .... SATA-20
See also DLB 3, 64
See also CDALB 1640-1865
Whitman, Wanda ?-1976 Obituary 65-68
Whitmarsh, Anne (Mary Gordon) 1933- 106
Whitmont, Edward C. 1912- 115
Whitmore, Charles (Stanleigh) 1949- 117
Whitmore, Cilla
See Gladstone, Arthur M.
Whitmore, Eugene 1895- 7-8R
Whitmore, George 1945- 102
Whitnah, Donald R(obert) 1925- 11-12R
Whitnah, Dorothy L. 1926- CANR-16
Earlier sketch in CA 93-96
Whitnell, Barbara
See Hutton, Ann
Whitney, Alec
See White, Alan
Whitney, Alex(andra) 1922- 53-56
See also SATA 14
Whitney, Byrl A(lbert) 1901- CAP-1
Earlier sketch in CA 13-14
Whitney, Charles Allen 1929- 81-84
Whitney, Cornelius Vanderbilt 1899- 85-88
Whitney, Dallas (Cole) 1952- 117
Whitney, David
See Malick, Terrence
Whitney, David C(harles) 1921- CANR-5
Earlier sketch in CA 11-12R
See also SATA 29, 48
Whitney, Eleanor Noss 1938- CANR-6
Earlier sketch in CA 15-16R
Whitney, Elizabeth Dalton 1906- 21-22R
Whitney, George D(ana) 1918- 93-96
Whitney, Hallam
See Whittington, Harry (Benjamin)
Whitney, J(ohn) D(enison) 1940- CANR-3
Earlier sketch in CA 49-52
Whitney, J. L. H.
See Trimble, Jacquelyn W(hitney)
Whitney, John Hay 1904-1982 Obituary 106
Whitney, John Raymond 1920- 105
Whitney, Leon F(radley) 1894-1973 ..... CANR-5
Earlier sketch in CA 7-8R
Whitney, Marie Louise (Schroeder) Hosford
1925(?)- Brief entry 113
Whitney, Marylou
See Whitney, Marie Louise (Schroeder)
Hosford
Whitney, Peter Dwight 1915- 11-12R
Whitney, Phyllis A(yame) 1903- CANR-3
Earlier sketch in CA 4R
See also SATA 1, 30
See also CLC 42
See also AITN 2
Whitney, Robert Frost 1906(?)-1986
Obituary 119
Whitney, Steve(n) 1946- 81-84
Whitney, Thomas P(orter) 1917- 104
See also SATA 25
Whiton, James Nelson 1932- 13-14R
Whitridge, Arnold 1891- 11-12R
Whitrow, Gerald James 1912- CANR-3
Earlier sketch in CA 5-6R
Whitson
See Warren, Peter Whitson
Whitson, Skip 1944- 118
Whitt, Anne Hall
See Thompson, Anne Hall Whitt
Whitt, Richard 1944- 81-84
Whittaker, Kathryn Putnam 1931- 13-14R
Whittaker, Otto (Jr.) 1916- 25-28R
Whittaker, Robert Harding 1920- 105
Whittemore, Charles P(ark) 1921- 11-12R
Whittemore, Don 69-72
Whittemore, L(ouis) H(enry) 1941- 45-48
Whittemore, Mildred 1946- 11-12R
Whittemore, (Edward) Reed (Jr.) 1919- . CANR-4
Earlier sketch in CA 9-10R
See also DLB 5
See also CLC 4
Whittemore, Robert Clifton 1921- 11-12R
Whitten, Jamie L(loyd) 1910- CAP-2
Earlier sketch in CA 23-24
Whitten, Leslie H(unter) 1928- 17-18R
Whitten, Mary Evelyn 1922- 17-18R
Whitten, Norman E(arl), Jr. 1937- 17-18R
Whittet, G(eorge) S(orley) 1918- 23-24R
Whittet, T. D.
See Whittet, Thomas Douglas
Whittet, Thomas Douglas 1915-1987
Obituary 122
Whittick, Arnold 1898- CAP-1
Earlier sketch in CA 11-12
Whittier, John Greenleaf 1807-1892 ..... DLB-1
See also CDALB 1640-1865
Whitting, Philip (David) 1903- 97-100
Whittingham, Harry E(dward), Jr. 1918- 7-8R
Whittingham, Jack 1910-1972 Obituary ..37-40R
Whittingham, Richard 1939- 37-40R
Whittington, Geoffrey 1938- CANR-20
Earlier sketch in CA 104
Whittington, H(orace) G(reeley) 1929- 21-22R
Whittington, Harry (Benjamin) 1915- CANR-5
Earlier sketch in CA 23-24R
Whittington, Peter
See Mackay, James (Alexander)
Whittington-Egan, Richard 1924- CANR-20
Earlier sketches in CA 11-12R, CANR-5
Whittle, Amberys R(ayvon) 1935- 45-48
Whittle, Tyler
See Tyler-Whittle, Michael Sidney
Whittlebot, Hernia
See Coward, Noel (Pierce)
Whittlesey, E(unice) S. 1907- 93-96
Whittlesey, Susan 1938- 29-32R
Whitton, Charlotte (Elizabeth) 1896-1975
Obituary 89-92
Whitton, John Boardman 1892- CAP-2
Earlier sketch in CA 23-24
Whittow, J. B.
See Whittow, John B(yron)
Whittow, John B(yron) 1929- 120
Whitworth, John McKelvie 1942- 77-80
Whitworth, Reginald Henry 1910- 109
Whitworth, William 1937- 37-40R
Whiz, Walter
See Johnson, Curt(is Lee)
Whone, Herbert 1925- CANR-24
Earlier sketch in CA 108
Whorton, James C(lifton) 1942- 77-80
Whorton, M. Donald 1946- 117
Whritner, John Alden 1935- 45-48
Whyatt, Frances
See Boyd, Shylah
Whybray, Roger Norman 1923- 89-92
Whyte, Fredrica (Harriman) 1905- CAP-1
Earlier sketch in CA 11-12
Whyte, Henry Malcolm 1920- CANR-3
Earlier sketch in CA 7-8R
Whyte, James Huntington 1909- 7-8R
Whyte, Lancelot Law 1896-1972 .... CAP-1
Earlier sketch in CA 15-16
Whyte, Lewis (Gilmour) 1906-1986
Obituary 121
Whyte, Mal(colm Kenneth, Jr.) 1933- 106
Whyte, Martin King 1942- 81-84
Whyte, (Harry Archibald) Maxwell 1908- 105
Whyte, Robert Orr 1903- Brief entry 106
Whyte, William Foote 1914- CANR-18
Earlier sketches in CA 4R, CANR-3
Whyte, William H(ollingsworth) 1917- 9-10R
Wiarda, Howard J(ohn) 1939- CANR-21
Earlier sketches in CA 53-56, CANR-4
Wiat, Philippa
See Ferridge, Philippa
Wibberley, Leonard (Patrick O'Connor)
1915-1983 .... CANR-3
Obituary 111
Earlier sketch in CA 7-8R
See also SATA 2, 36, 45
See also CLR 3
Wiberg, Harald (Albin) 1908- SATA-40
Wice, Aubrey (Agnew) 1913(?)-1985
Obituary 119
Wice, Paul B(ernard) 1942- 57-60
Wick, Carter
See Wilcox, Collin
Wick, John W(illiam) 1935- CANR-15
Earlier sketch in CA 41-44R
Wick, Stuart Mary
See Freeman, Kathleen
Wick, Wendy
See Reaves, Wendy Wick
Wicke, Charles R(obinson) 1928- 37-40R
Wicke, Edith Schreiber
See Schreiber-Wicke, Edith
Wickenden, Elizabeth 1909- 2R
Wickens, Delos D(onald) 1909- CAP-1
Earlier sketch in CA 15-16
Wickens, James F. 1933- 57-60
Wicker, Brian 1929- 17-18R
Wicker, Ireene 1905(?)-1987 69-72
Obituary 124
Wicker, Randolfe Hayden 1938- 45-48
Wicker, Thomas Grey 1926- CANR-21
Earlier sketch in CA 65-68
Wicker, Tom
See Wicker, Thomas Grey
See also CLC 7
Wickers, David 1944- 77-80
Wickersham, Edward Dean 1927-1966 .....5-6R
Wickersham, Joan Barrett 1957- 105
Wickert, Frederic R(obinson) 1912- 23-24R
Wickes, George 1923- 9-10R
Wickes, Kim 1947- 109
Wickett, Ann 1942- 122
Wickett, William Harold, Jr. 1919- 108
Wickey, Gould 1891- 25-28R
Wickham, Edward Ralph 1911- 7-8R
Wickham, Glynne (William Gladstone)
1922- CANR-7
Earlier sketch in CA 7-8R
Wickham, Jean 1903- 69-72
Wickham, Mary Fanning
See Bond, Mary Fanning Wickham
Wickham, Thomas Frederick 1926- 13-14R
Wicklein, John (Frederick) 1924- 106
Wickremasinghe, Esmond 1920(?)-1985
Obituary 117
Wickremasinghe, S(ugiswara)
A(beywardena) 1901-1981 Obituary 108
Wicks, Ben 1926- 73-76
Wicks, Harold Vernon, Jr. 1931- 102
Wicks, Harry
See Wicks, Harold Vernon, Jr.
Wicks, Jared 1929- CANR-21
Earlier sketch in CA 25-28R
Wicks, John H. 1936- 17-18R
Wicks, Robert J(ohn) 1946- 113
Wicks, Robert Stewart 1923- 17-18R
Wickstrom, Lois 1948- 106
Wickwar, (William) Hardy 1903- 57-60
Wickwire, Franklin B(acon) 1931- 23-24R
Wickwire, Mary Botts 1935- 104
Widdemer, Mabel Cleland 1902-1964 ......5-6R
See also SATA 5

Widdemer, Margaret 18(?)-1978 ... CANR-4
Obituary ... 77-80
Earlier sketch in CA 5-6R
Widder, (John) Arthur, (Jr.) 1928- ... 5-6R
Widder, Milton 1907(?)-1985 Obituary ... 118
Widell, Helene 1912- ... 37-40R
Wideman, John Edgar 1941- ... CANR-14
Earlier sketch in CA 85-88
See also DLB 33
See also CLC 5, 34, 36
Widener, Alice 1905(?)-1985 Obituary ... 114
Widener, Don(ald) 1930- ... 37-40R
Widenor, William C(ramer) 1937- ... 102
Widerberg, Siv 1931- ... 53-56
See also SATA 10
Widgery, Alban G(regory) 1887- ... 5-6R
Widgery, David 1947- ... 69-72
Widgery, Jan 1920- ... 19-20R
Widick, B. J. 1910- ... 9-10R
Widicus, Wilbur W(ilson), Jr. 1932- ... 53-56
Widman, F. Lisle 1919(?)-1983 Obituary ... 111
Widmer, Eleanor (Rackow) 1925- ... 17-18R
Widmer, Emmy Louise 1925- ... 29-32R
Widmer, Kingsley 1925- ... CANR-3
Earlier sketch in CA 2R
Wiebe, M(elvin) G(eorge) 1939- ... 114
Wiebe, Robert H(uddleston) 1930- ... 5-6R
Wiebe, Rudy (H.) 1934- ... 37-40R
See also DLB 60
See also CLC 6, 11, 14
Wiebenson, Dora (Louise) 1926- ... 37-40R
Wiecek, William Michael 1938- ... 37-40R
Wiechert, Ernst 1887-1950 ... DLB-56
Wieck, Fred D(ernburg) 1910-1973
Obituary ... 104
Wieckert, Jeanne E. (Lentz) 1939- ... 89-92
Wiecking, Anna M. 1887-1973 ... CAP-1
Earlier sketch in CA 13-14
Wieczynski, Joseph L. 1934- ... 37-40R
Wieder, Laurance 1946- ... CANR-8
Earlier sketch in CA 57-60
Wieder, Robert S(hannon) 1944- ... 85-88
Wiederumb, Trotzhard
See Steiner, Gerolf
Wiedner, Donald L(awrence) 1930- ... 15-16R
Wiegand, Charmion von
See von Wiegand, Charmion
Wiegand, G(uenther) Carl 1906- ... 23-24R
Wiegand, William G(eorge) 1928- ... 11-12R
Wieghart, James G. 1933- ... 77-80
Wiegner, Kathleen K(napp) 1938- ... 93-96
Wiehl, Andrew (M.) 1904- ... 89-92
Wieland, George F(red) 1936- ... 89-92
Wieman, Harold F(rancis) 1917- ... 61-64
Wieman, Henry N(elson) 1884-1975 ... 61-64
Obituary ... 57-60
Wiemer, Rudolf Otto 1905- ... CANR-9
Earlier sketch in CA 23-24R
Wienandt, Elwyn A(rthur) 1917- ... 41-44R
Wiener, Daniel N(orman) 1921- ... 37-40R
Wiener, Harvey Shelby 1940- ... 102
Wiener, Joan
See Bordow, Joan (Wiener)
Wiener, Joel H. 1937- ... CANR-14
Earlier sketch in CA 37-40R
Wiener, Jon
See Wiener, Jonathan M.
Wiener, Jonathan M. 1944- ... 115
Wiener, Leigh Auston 1929- ... 108
Wiener, M. Jean 1896-1982 Obituary ... 107
Wiener, Martin J. 1941- ... 85-88
Wiener, Norbert 1894-1964 Obituary ... 107
Wiener, Philip P(aul) 1905- ... CAP-1
Earlier sketch in CA 9-10
Wiener, Sally Dixon 1926- ... 101
Wiener, Sam
See Dolgoff, Sam
Wiener, Solomon 1915- ... CANR-7
Earlier sketch in CA 19-20R
Wieners, John 1934- ... 15-16R
See also DLB 16
See also CLC 7
Wieniewska, Celina
See Janson-Smith, Celina
Wienpahl, Paul D(e Velin) 1916- ... 11-12R
Wier, Allen 1946- ... 77-80
Wier, Dara 1949- ... 77-80
Wier, Ester (Alberti) 1910- ... 11-12R
See also SATA 3
See also DLB 52
Wiersbe, Warren W(endell) 1929- ... CANR-23
Earlier sketches in CA 5-6R, CANR-7
Wiersma, Stanley M(arvin) 1930- ... CANR-11
Earlier sketch in CA 29-32R
Wiersma, William, Jr. 1931- ... CANR-1
Earlier sketch in CA 45-48
Wierwille, Victor Paul 1916-1985 ... CANR-2
Obituary ... 116
Earlier sketch in CA 7-8R
Wierzynski, Gregory H(ieronim) 1939- ... 73-76
Wierzynski, Kazimierz 1894-1969 Obituary ... 115
Wiese, Arthur E(dward) 1946- ... 73-76
Wiese, Kurt 1887-1974 ... 11-12R
Obituary ... 49-52
See also SATA 3, 24, 36
Wiesel, Elie(zer) 1928- ... CANR-8
Earlier sketch in CA 7-8R
See also CAAS 4
See also CLC 3, 5, 11, 37
See also AITN 1
Wiesen, Allen E. 1939- ... 29-32R
Wiesenfarth, Joseph (John) 1933- ... CANR-8
Earlier sketch in CA 5-6R
Wiesenthal, Simon 1908- ... CANR-13
Earlier sketch in CA 23-24R
Wiesner, Jerome B(ert) 1915- ... 15-16R
Wiesner, Portia
See Takakjian, Portia
Wiesner, William 1899- ... 41-44R
See also SATA 5
Wiest, Claire (Johnson) 1930- ... 113
Wigal, Donald 1933- ... CANR-14
Earlier sketch in CA 81-84
Wigan, Anthony ?-1983 Obituary ... 110
Wigan, Bernard (John) 1918- ... 15-16R
Wigan, Christopher
See Bingley, David Ernest
Wigan, Tony
See Wigan, Anthony
Wigforss, Ernst 1882(?)-1977 Obituary ... 69-72
Wigg, George (Edward Cecil) 1900-1983
Obituary ... 115
Wiggin, Kate Douglas 1856-1923
Brief entry ... 111
See also YABC 1
See also DLB 42
Wiggin, Maurice (Samuel) 1912- ... CANR-5
Earlier sketch in CA 11-12R
Wiggin, Paul 1934- ... 25-28R
Wiggins, Arthur W. 1938- ... 53-56
Wiggins, Charles W(illiam) 1937- ... 41-44R
Wiggins, David 1933- ... 118
Wiggins, Jack G(illmore) 1926- ... 41-44R
Wiggins, James B(ryan) 1935- ... 37-40R
Wiggins, James Russell ... AITN-2
Wiggins, James Wilhelm 1914- ... 17-18R
Wiggins, Robert A. 1921- ... 15-16R
Wiggins, Sam P. 1919- ... 21-22R
Wigginton, Eliot 1942- ... 101
See also AITN 1
Wigglesworth, Michael 1631-1705 ... DLB-24
Wigham, Eric Leonard 1904- ... 109
Wight, Frederick S.
See Wight, Frederick Stallknecht
Wight, Frederick Stallknecht (Van Buren)
1902-1986 Obituary ... 120
Wight, James Alfred 1916- ... 77-80
See also SATA 44
Wight, (Robert James) Martin
1913-1972 ... CAP-2
Earlier sketch in CA 21-22
Wightman, Edith Mary 1939(?)-1983(?)
Obituary ... 111
Wightman, George Brian Hamilton 1933- ... 107
Wighton, Charles Ernest 1913- ... 7-8R
Wighton, Rosemary Neville 1925- ... 11-12R
Wigmore
See Fabricius, Johan (Johannes)
Wignall, Anne 1912- ... 97-100
Wigner, Eugene Paul 1902- ... CAP-2
Earlier sketch in CA 25-28
Wigoder, Geoffrey Bernard 1922- ... 105
Wihl, Gary ... 120
Wiig, Howard (Calvert) 1940- ... 61-64
Wijasuriya, D(onald) E(arlian) K(ingsley)
1934- ... 81-84
Wik, Reynold M. 1910- ... CANR-14
Earlier sketch in CA 81-84
Wike, Edward L. 1922- ... 37-40R
Wikland, Ilon 1930- Brief entry ... 111
See also SATA 32
Wikler, Madeline 1943- ... 117
Wikramanayake, Marina 1938- ... 45-48
Wiksell, Milton J. 1910- ... 7-8R
Wiksell, Wesley 1906- ... CAP-1
Earlier sketch in CA 17-18
Wilber, Charles G(rady) 1916- ... CANR-21
Earlier sketch in CA 41-44R
Wilber, Charles K. 1935- Brief entry ... 113
Wilber, Donald N(ewton) 1907- ... CANR-2
Earlier sketch in CA 5-6R
See also SATA 35
Wilbers, Stephen 1949- ... 106
Wilbert, Johannes 1927- ... 124
Brief entry ... 118
Wilbourn, Carole C(ecile) 1940- ... CANR-14
Earlier sketch in CA 81-84
Wilbur, C. Keith 1923- ... CANR-11
Earlier sketch in CA 25-28R
See also SATA 27
Wilbur, C(larence) Martin 1908- ... 85-88
Wilbur, Crane 1887(?)-1973 Obituary ... 45-48
Wilbur, James B(enjamin) III 1924- ... CANR-14
Earlier sketch in CA 37-40R
Wilbur, Marguerite Eyer 1889- ... CAP-1
Earlier sketch in CA 11-12
Wilbur, Richard (Purdy) 1921- ... CANR-2
Earlier sketch in CA 2R
See also CABS 2
See also SATA 9
See also DLB 5
See also CLC 3, 6, 9, 14
Wilbur, William H(ale) 1888- ... CAP-1
Earlier sketch in CA 13-14
Wilburn, Jean Alexander 1915- ... 21-22R
Wilburn, Ralph G(lenn) 1909- ... CAP-1
Earlier sketch in CA 17-18
Wilby, Basil Leslie 1930- ... CANR-19
Earlier sketch in CA 103
Wilcher, Robert 1942- ... 121
Wilckens, Ulrich 1928- Brief entry ... 114
Wilcock, John 1927- ... CANR-2
Earlier sketch in CA 2R
Wilcocks, Julie 1943- ... 110
Wilcox, Clair 1898-1970 ... CANR-4
Earlier sketch in CA 5-6R
Wilcox, Collin 1924- ... CANR-14
Earlier sketch in CA 21-22R
Wilcox, Daniel 1941- ... 53-56
Wilcox, Dennis L. 1941- ... CANR-14
Earlier sketch in CA 37-40R
Wilcox, Desmond (John) 1931- ... CANR-21
Earlier sketch in CA 69-72
Wilcox, Donald J(ames) 1938- ... 109
Wilcox, Earl J(unior) 1933- ... 111
Wilcox, Francis (Orlando) 1908-1985 ... 37-40R
Obituary ... 115
Wilcox, Herbert 1891-1977 ... 57-60
Obituary ... 118
Wilcox, Howard 1913(?)-1987 Obituary ... 122
Wilcox, Jess
See Hershman, Morris
Wilcox, John T(homas) 1933- ... 45-48
Wilcox, Michael (Denys) 1943- ... 77-80
Wilcox, Paul L(orentus) 1899- ... 69-72
Wilcox, R(uth) Turner 1888-1970 ... 7-8R
Obituary ... 29-32R
See also SATA 36
Wilcox, Richard L. 1918-1978 Obituary ... 77-80
Wilcox, Robert K(alleen) 1943- ... CANR-24
Earlier sketch in CA 77-80
Wilcox, Roger P. 1916- ... 21-22R
Wilcox, Tamara 1940- ... CANR-19
Earlier sketch in CA 97-100
Wilcox, Virginia Lee 1911- ... 37-40R
Wilcox, Walter 1920-1983 Obituary ... 110
Wilcox, Wayne Ayres 1932-1974 ... CANR-4
Obituary ... 49-52
Earlier sketch in CA 7-8R
Wilcoxon, George Dent, Jr. 1913- ... 93-96
Wild, Jocelyn 1941- ... 116
See also SATA 46
Wild, John D(aniel) 1902-1972
Obituary ... 37-40R
Wild, Peter 1940- ... 37-40R
See also DLB 5
See also CLC 14
Wild, Robert A(nthony) 1940- ... 111
Wild, Robin (Evans) 1936- ... 116
See also SATA 46
Wild, Rolf H(einrich) 1927- ... 81-84
Wildavsky, Aaron 1930- ... CANR-2
Earlier sketch in CA 2R
Wilde, Alan 1929- ... 110
Wilde, D. Gunther
See Hurwood, Bernhardt J.
Wilde, Daniel U(nderwood) 1937- ... 57-60
Wilde, Jean T(oeplitz) 1898-1973
Obituary ... 45-48
Wilde, Jennifer
See Huff, T(om) E.
Wilde, Jocelyn
See Toombs, John
Wilde, Kathey
See King, Patricia
Wilde, Larry 1928- ... CANR-10
Earlier sketch in CA 25-28R
Wilde, Meta Carpenter (Doherty) 1907- ... 81-84
Wilde, Oscar (Fingal O'Flahertie Wills)
1854(?)-1900 ... 119
Brief entry ... 104
See also SATA 24
See also DLB 10, 19, 34, 57
See also TCLC 1, 8, 23
Wilde, Richard Henry 1789-1847 ... DLB-3, 59
Wilde, W(illiam) H(enry) 1923- ... CANR-11
Earlier sketch in CA 69-72
Wildeblood, Peter 1923- ... 65-68
Wilden, Anthony 1935- ... 37-40R
Wildenhain, Marguerite 1896- ... 77-80
Wilder, Alec
See Wilder, Alexander Lafayette Chew
Wilder, Alexander Lafayette Chew
1907-1980 ... 104
Obituary ... 102
Wilder, Amos Niven 1895- ... 81-84
Wilder, Billy
See Wilder, Samuel
See also DLB 26
See also CLC 20
Wilder, Charlotte Elizabeth 1898(?)-1980
Obituary ... 97-100
Wilder, Cherry
See Grimm, Cherry Barbara
Wilder, Gene
See Silberman, Jerome
Wilder, John Bunyan 1914- ... 5-6R
Wilder, Joseph 1895-1976 Obituary ... 116
Wilder, Laura Ingalls 1867-1957
Brief entry ... 111
See also SATA 15, 29
See also DLB 22
See also CLR 2
Wilder, Robert (Ingersoll) 1901-1974 ... CAP-2
Obituary ... 53-56
Earlier sketch in CA 13-14
Wilder, Robert D. 1916- ... 41-44R
Wilder, Roy (E.), Jr. 1914- ... 121
Wilder, Samuel 1906- ... 89-92
Wilder, Stephen
See Marlowe, Stephen
Wilder, Thornton (Niven) 1897-1975 ... 15-16R
Obituary ... 61-64
See also DLB 4, 7, 9
See also CLC 1, 5, 6, 10, 15, 35
See also AITN 2
Wilders, John (Simpson) 1927- ... 23-24R
Wilder-Smith, A(rthur) E(rnest) 1915- ... CANR-11
Earlier sketch in CA 57-60
Wildes, Harry Emerson 1890- ... 57-60
Wild Horse Annie
See Johnston, Velma B.
Wilding, Ann
See Budd, Mavis
Wilding, Michael 1942- ... CANR-24
Earlier sketch in CA 104
Wildman, Allan K. 1927- ... 105
Wildman, Eugene 1938- ... 25-28R
Wildman, John Hazard 1911- ... 37-40R
Wildman, Louis Robert 1941- ... CANR-5
Earlier sketch in CA 15-16R
Wildmon, Donald E(llis) 1938- ... CANR-13
Earlier sketch in CA 61-64
Wildrick, Stanley B. 1894-1984 Obituary ... 112
Wilds, Nancy Alexander 1926- ... 15-16R
Wildsmith, Alan 1937- ... 97-100
Wildsmith, Brian 1930- ... 85-88
See also SATA 16
See also SAAS 5
See also CLR 2
Wilenski, Peter Stephen 1939- ... 109
Wilenski, R(eginald) H(oward) 1887-1975 ... 61-64
Obituary ... 57-60
Wilensky, Harold L. 1923- ... CANR-15
Earlier sketch in CA 41-44R
Wilentz, Joan Steen 1930- ... 25-28R
Wilentz, Ted
See Wilentz, Theodore
Wilentz, Theodore 1915- ... 29-32R
Wiles, David K(imball) 1942- ... CANR-7
Earlier sketch in CA 53-56
Wiles, Domini 1942- ... 102
Wiles, Gordon Pitts 1909- ... 108
Wiles, John 1924- ... 11-12R
Wiles, Kimball 1913-1969 ... CANR-4
Earlier sketch in CA 5-6R
Wiles, Maurice Frank 1923- ... 108
Wiles, Peter John de la Fosse 1919- ... 5-6R
Wiles, Roy McKeen 1903-19(?) ... CAP-1
Earlier sketch in CA 19-20
Wiley, Bell
See Strauss, Frances
Wiley, Bell I(rvin) 1906-1980 ... CANR-4
Obituary ... 97-100
Earlier sketch in CA 7-8R
See also DLB 17
Wiley, David Sherman 1935- ... CANR-12
Earlier sketch in CA 61-64
Wiley, Farida A(nna) 1887(?)-1986
Obituary ... 121
Wiley, Jack 1936- ... CANR-8
Earlier sketch in CA 61-64
Wiley, Jay Wilson 1913- ... 5-6R
Wiley, John P., Jr. 1936- ... 89-92
Wiley, Karla H(ummel) 1918- ... 61-64
Wiley, Margaret L.
See Marshall, Margaret Wiley
Wiley, Paul L(uzon) 1914-1979 ... CANR-10
Earlier sketch in CA 5-6R
Wiley, Raymond A(loysius) 1923- ... 37-40R
Wiley, Richard 1944- Brief entry ... 121
See also CLC 44
Wiley, Stan
See Hill, John S(tanley)
Wiley, Tom 1906- ... 25-28R
Wiley, William Leon 1903- ... 111
Wilf, Alexander 1905(?)-1981 Obituary ... 103
Wilford, John Noble 1933- ... CANR-15
Earlier sketch in CA 29-32R
Wilford, Walton T. 1937- ... 49-52
Wilgus, A(lva) Curtis 1897- ... CANR-3
Earlier sketch in CA 7-8R
Wilgus, D. K. 1918- ... 37-40R
Wilhelm, Hans 1945- ... 119
Wilhelm, Hellmut 1905- ... 7-8R
Wilhelm, James Jerome 1932- ... 19-20R
Wilhelm, John R(emsen) 1916- ... 7-8R
Wilhelm, Kate
See Wilhelm, Katie Gertrude
See also CAAS 5
See also DLB 8
See also CLC 7
Wilhelm, Kathryn Stephenson 1915- ... 13-14R
Wilhelm, Katie Gertrude 1928- ... CANR-17
Earlier sketch in CA 37-40R
Wilhelm, Paul A. 1916- ... 61-64
Wilhelm, Walt 1893- ... 29-32R
Wilhelm II
See Hohenzollern, Friedrich Wilhelm
(Victor Albert)
Wilhelmina
See Cooper, Wilhelmina (Behmenburg)
Wilhelmsen, Frederick D(aniel) 1923- ... CANR-3
Earlier sketch in CA 2R
Wilhoit, Francis M(arion) 1920-
Brief entry ... 109
Wilk, David 1951- ... CANR-4
Earlier sketch in CA 53-56
Wilk, Gerard H(ermann) 1902- ... 69-72
Wilk, Max 1920- ... CANR-16
Earlier sketches in CA 3R, CANR-1
Wilk, Richard R(alph) 1953- ... 120
Wilke, Ekkehard-Teja 1941- ... 65-68
Wilke, Ulfert (Stephan) 1907- ... CAP-1
Earlier sketch in CA 15-16
Wilken, Robert L(ouis) 1936- ... CANR-16
Earlier sketch in CA 29-32R
Wilkening, Howard (Everett) 1909- ... 89-92
Wilkens, Emily 1917- ... 103
Wilkerson, Cynthia
See Levinson, Leonard
Wilkerson, David R(ay) 1931- ... 41-44R
Wilkerson, Hugh 1939- ... 104
Wilkerson, Loree A. R(andleman) 1923- ... 17-18R
Wilkerson, Rich(ard Preston) 1952- ... 123
Wilkes, Edward T. 1889-1983 Obituary ... 111
Wilkes, Glenn Newton 1928- ... CANR-17
Earlier sketch in CA 2R
Wilkes, Ian (Henry) 1932- ... 41-44R
Wilkes, John W(illiam) 1924- ... 25-28R
Wilkes, Paul 1938- ... CANR-15
Earlier sketch in CA 81-84
Wilkes, William Alfred 1910- ... 45-48
Wilkes-Hunter, R(ichard) ... 15-16R
Wilkie, Brian 1929- ... 15-16R
Wilkie, James W. 1936- ... 21-22R

Wilkie, Jane 1917- 102
Wilkie, Katharine E(lliott) 1904-1980 21-22R
See also SATA 31
Wilkie, Kenneth 1942- 85-88
Wilkin, Eloise (Burns) 1904-1987 124
See also SATA 49
Wilkins, Beatrice (Brunson) 1928- 61-64
Wilkins, Burleigh Taylor 1932- 105
Wilkins, Ernest J. 1918- 53-56
Wilkins, Frances 1923- 73-76
See also SATA 14
Wilkins, H. Ford 1901(?)-1983 Obituary 111
Wilkins, Kathleen Sonia 1941- 104
Wilkins, Kay S.
See Wilkins, Kathleen Sonia
Wilkins, Leslie T. 1915- CANR-22
Earlier sketches in CA 19-20R, CANR-7
Wilkins, Marilyn (Ruth) 1926- 105
See also SATA 30
Wilkins, Marne
See Wilkins, Marilyn (Ruth)
Wilkins, Mary
See Freeman, Mary Eleanor Wilkins
Wilkins, Mary Huiskamp 1926- CANR-18
Earlier sketches in CA 5-6R, CANR-2
Wilkins, Mesannie 1891- CAP-2
Earlier sketch in CA 25-28
Wilkins, Mira 1931- Brief entry 112
Wilkins, Roger (Wood) 1932- 117
Brief entry 109
Wilkins, Ronald J(ohn) 1916- CANR-16
Earlier sketch in CA 93-96
Wilkins, Roy 1901-1981 104
Wilkins, Thurman 1915- 7-8R
Wilkins, William R(ichard) 1933- 61-64
Wilkinson, Alec 1952- 109
Wilkinson, (Thomas) Barry 1923- SATA-32, 50
Wilkinson, Bertie 1898- 11-12R
Wilkinson, Bonaro
See Overstreet, Bonaro (Wilkinson)
Wilkinson, Brenda 1946- 69-72
See also SATA 14
Wilkinson, Bud
See Wilkinson, Charles B(urnham)
Wilkinson, (John) Burke 1913- 11-12R
See also SATA 4
Wilkinson, C. E. 1948- 109
Wilkinson, Charles B(urnham) 1916- 105
Wilkinson, Charlotte Jefferson 69-72
Wilkinson, Clyde Winfield 1910- 2R
Wilkinson, David 93-96
Wilkinson, Doris Yvonne 1936- 29-32R
Wilkinson, Elizabeth C. 1926- 123
Wilkinson, Ernest Leroy 1899-1978 CANR-3
Earlier sketch in CA 49-52
Wilkinson, G(eoffrey) K(edington) 1907- 3R
Wilkinson, J(oseph) F. 1925- 105
Wilkinson, James Hardy 1919-1986
Obituary 120
Wilkinson, James Harvie III 1944- 101
Wilkinson, John (Donald) 1929- 9-10R
Wilkinson, John Thomas 1893-1980 107
Obituary 104
Wilkinson, L(ancelot) P(atrick)
1907-1985 CANR-20
Obituary 116
Earlier sketches in CA 5-6R, CANR-3
Wilkinson, Lorna Hilda Kathleen 1909- CAP-1
Earlier sketch in CA 13-14
Wilkinson, Louis (Umfreville) 1881-1966
Obituary 116
Wilkinson, Maxwell Penrose 1905(?)-1985
Obituary 116
Wilkinson, Norman Beaumont 1910- 37-40R
Wilkinson, Patrick
See Wilkinson, L(ancelot) P(atrick)
Wilkinson, Paul 1937- CANR-14
Earlier sketch in CA 77-80
Wilkinson, Richard Gerald 1943- 45-48
Wilkinson, (William) Roderick 1917- 13-14R
Wilkinson, Ronald 1920- 7-8R
Wilkinson, Rosemary C(halloner)
1924- CANR-17
Earlier sketches in CA 49-52, CANR-1
Wilkinson, Rupert Hugh 1936- 11-12R
Wilkinson, Sylvia 1940- 17-18R
See also SATA 39
See also DLBY 86
See also AITN 1
Wilkinson, Walter 1888-1970 Obituary 104
Wilkinson, Winifred
See Hausmann, Winifred
Wilkon, Jozef 1930- 107
See also SATA 31
Wilks, Brian 1933- 69-72
Wilks, Ed 1928(?)-1984 Obituary 114
Wilks, John 1922- 73-76
Wilks, Michael Thomas 1947- 110
See also SATA 44
Wilks, Mike
See Wilks, Michael Thomas
Wilks, Yorick 1939- 73-76
Will
See Lipkind, William
Will, Frederic 1928- CANR-16
Earlier sketches in CA 49-52, CANR-1
Will, Frederick L(udwig) 1909- 13-14R
Will, George F. 1941- 77-80
Will, Lawrence Elmer 1893- CAP-2
Earlier sketch in CA 17-18
Will, Lester J. 1908(?)-1984 Obituary 111
Will, Robert E(rwin) 1928- 17-18R
Will, W(ilbur) Marvin 1937- 118
Willan, Anne 1938- CANR-6
Earlier sketch in CA 57-60
Willan, Thomas Stuart 1910- 11-12R
Willans, Jean Stone 1924- 65-68
Willard, Barbara (Mary) 1909- CANR-15
Earlier sketch in CA 81-84
See also SATA 17
See also SAAS 5
See also CLR 2
Willard, Beatrice E(lizabeth) 1925- 41-44R
Willard, Charles
See Armstrong, John Byron
Willard, Charlotte 1914-1977 81-84
Obituary 73-76
Willard, Dallas (Albert) 1935- 116
Willard, Mildred Wilds 1911- 23-24R
See also SATA 14
Willard, Nancy 1936- CANR-10
Earlier sketch in CA 89-92
See also SATA 30, 37
See also DLB 5, 52
See also CLC 7, 37
See also CLR 5
Willard, Portman
See Norwood, Victor G(eorge) C(harles)
Willard, Samuel 1640-1707 DLB-24
Willcock, M(alcolm) M(aurice) 1925- 65-68
Willcox, A(lexander) R(obert) 1911- 118
Willcox, Donald J. 1933- 49-52
Willcox, Isobel 1907- 111
See also SATA 42
Willcox, Sheila 1936- 73-76
Willcox, William Bradford 1907-1985 CANR-3
Obituary 117
Earlier sketch in CA 5-6R
Wille, Janet Neipris 1936- 109
Willee, Albert William 1916-1982 109
Willeford, Charles (Ray III) 1919- CANR-15
Earlier sketch in CA 33-36R
Willeford, William 1929- 25-28R
Willem, John M. 1909-1979 CAP-1
Obituary 93-96
Earlier sketch in CA 17-18
Willems, Emilio 1905- 105
Willems, J. Rutherford 1944- CANR-23
Earlier sketch in CA 45-48
Willen, Diane 1943- 117
Willensky, Elliot 1933- 29-32R
Willenson, Kim Jeremy 1937- 103
Willenz, June A. 1924- 121
Willerding, Margaret F(rances) 1919- 57-60
Willes, Mary (Janette) 1927- 120
Willets, F(rederick) W(illiam) 1930- 23-24R
Willets, Walter E. 1924- 25-28R
Willett, Brother Franciscus 1922- 15-16R
Willett, Edward R(ice) 1923- CANR-21
Earlier sketches in CA 5-6R, CANR-2
Willett, Frank 1925- 25-28R
Willett, John (William Mills) 1917- CANR-4
Earlier sketch in CA 9-10R
Willett, T(erence) C(harles) 1918- 37-40R
Willett, Thomas D(unaway) 1942- 108
Willetts, R(onald) F(rederick) 1915- CANR-2
Earlier sketch in CA 7-8R
Willey, Basil 1897- 9-10R
Willey, Darrell S. 1925- 41-44R
Willey, F. T.
See Willey, Frederick Thomas
Willey, Fred
See Willey, Frederick Thomas
Willey, Frederick Thomas 1910-1987
Obituary 124
Willey, Gordon R(andolph) 1913- CANR-2
Earlier sketch in CA 7-8R
Willey, Keith (Greville) 1930- CANR-9
Earlier sketch in CA 21-22R
Willey, Margaret 1950- 117
Willey, Peter (Robert Everard) 1922- 13-14R
Willey, R(oy) DeVerl 1910-197(?) CAP-2
Earlier sketch in CA 19-20
Willey, Richard J(ames) 1934- 41-44R
Willey, Robert
See Ley, Willy
Willgoose, Carl E(dward) 1916- CANR-6
Earlier sketch in CA 13-14R
Wilhelm, Sidney M(clarty) 1934- 11-12R
William, Maurice 1882(?)-1973 Obituary 45-48
William II
See Hohenzollern, Friedrich Wilhelm
(Victor Albert)
Williams, Alan F. 1933- 49-52
Williams, (Timothy) Alden 1932- 41-44R
Williams, Alice Cary 1892-1983 65-68
Obituary 111
Williams, Alice Davis 1901- 113
Williams, Ann, Jr. 1951-1985 Obituary 117
Williams, Anne
See Steinke, Ann (Elizabeth)
Williams, Aston R. 1912- 21-22R
Williams, Aubrey L(ake) 1922- CANR-6
Earlier sketch in CA 2R
Williams, Barbara 1925- CANR-17
Earlier sketches in CA 49-52, CANR-1
See also SATA 11
Williams, Barry 1932- 29-32R
Williams, Ben A(mes), Jr. 1915- 116
Williams, Benjamin Buford 1923- 113
Williams, Benjamin H(arrison)
1889-1974 37-40R
Williams, Bernard (Arthur Owen) 1929-
Brief entry 112
Williams, Bert Nolan 1930- 103
Williams, Beryl
See Epstein, Beryl (M. Williams)
Williams, Bill
See Crawford, William (Elbert)
Williams, Brad 1918- CANR-1
Earlier sketch in CA 2R
Williams, Bruce R(odda) 1919- 13-14R
Williams, Burton John 1927- 41-44R
Williams, Byron (Leigh) 1934- 29-32R
Williams, C(hester) Arthur, Jr. 1924- CANR-2
Earlier sketch in CA 2R
Williams, C(lifford) Glyn 1928- 29-32R
Williams, C(hristopher) J(ohn) F(ardo)
1930- 103
Williams, C(harles) K(enneth) 1936- 37-40R
See also DLB 5
See also CLC 33
Williams, Carl C(arnelius) 1903- 45-48
Williams, Carol M. 1917- 65-68
Williams, Carol T(raynor) 1935- 112
Williams, Catharine M(elissa) 1903- 37-40R
Williams, Cecil B(rown) 1901-1966 CAP-1
Earlier sketch in CA 11-12
Williams, Charles (Walter Stansby)
1886-1945 Brief entry 104
See also TCLC 1, 11
Williams, Charles
See Collier, James L(incoln)
Williams, Chester
See Schechter, William
Williams, Cicely 1907-1985 57-60
Obituary 117
Williams, Claerwen 1938- 102
Williams, Clyde C. 1881-1974 CAP-2
Earlier sketch in CA 23-24
See also SATA 8, 27
Williams, Coe
See Harrison, C. William
Williams, Colin 1934- 109
Williams, Colin W(ilbur) 1921- CANR-19
Earlier sketch in CA 25-28R
Williams, Cris
See De Cristoforo, R. J.
Williams, Cyril Glyndwr 1921- CANR-15
Earlier sketch in CA 37-40R
Williams, D.
See Ronald, David William
Williams, (Walter) Dakin 1919- Brief entry 116
Williams, Daniel Day 1910-1973 CANR-1
Obituary 45-48
Earlier sketch in CA 4R
Williams, David (Frank) 1909-1983
Obituary 109
Williams, David 1926- 122
Williams, David 1939- 73-76
Williams, David (Eliot) 1939- 123
Williams, David 1945- 97-100
Williams, David A. 1922- 29-32R
Williams, David Glenwood 1918- 7-8R
Williams, David L. 1940- CANR-10
Earlier sketch in CA 25-28R
Williams, David Rhys 1890- 7-8R
Williams, David Ricardo 1923- 101
Williams, Denis (Joseph Ivan) 1923- CANR-17
Earlier sketch in CA 93-96
Williams, Dorian 1914- CANR-3
Earlier sketch in CA 11-12R
Williams, Duncan 1927- 41-44R
Williams, E(ric) C(yril) 1918- 97-100
Williams, E(rnest) N(eville) 1917- 11-12R
Williams, Edward Ainsworth 1907-1976
Obituary 65-68
Williams, Edward Bennett 1920- 3R
Williams, Edward Francis 1903-1970
Obituary 29-32R
Williams, Edward G. 1929- 29-32R
Williams, Edward J(erome) 1935- CANR-10
Earlier sketch in CA 21-22R
Williams, Edward K. 1923-1966 CAP-1
Earlier sketch in CA 15-16
Williams, Edward V(inson) 1935- 121
Williams, Edwin B(ucher) 1891-1975 7-8R
Obituary 57-60
Williams, Edwin E(veritt) 1913- 45-48
Williams, Edwina Dakin 1885(?)-1980
Obituary 97-100
Williams, Eirlys O(lwen) CAP-1
Earlier sketch in CA 9-10
Williams, Elizabeth
See Dohen, Dorothy M.
Williams, (George) Emlyn 1905-1987 104
Obituary 123
See also DLB 10
See also CLC 15
Williams, Emmett 1925- CANR-2
Earlier sketch in CA 45-48
Williams, Eric (Ernest) 1911-1983 11-12R
Obituary 111
See also SATA 14, 38
Williams, Eric Eustace 1911-1981
Obituary 103
Williams, Ernest Wells 1896(?)-1980
Obituary 97-100
Williams, Estelle S. 1908- 123
Williams, Ethel L. 37-40R
Williams, F(rederick) Winston 1935- 103
Williams, Ferelith Eccles
See Eccles Williams, Ferelith
See also SATA 22
Williams, Frances 1935- 25-28R
Williams, Frances B.
See Browin, Frances Williams
Williams, Frances Leigh 1909- 13-14R
Williams, Frances Marion 1919- 57-60
Williams, Francis 1903-1970 Obituary 104
Williams, Francis Stewart 1921-1974 37-40R
Williams, Frank B(royles), Jr. 1913- 118
Williams, Frederick D(eForrest) 1918- 65-68
Williams, G(erhard) Mennen 1911-1988
Obituary 124
Williams, G. Robert 1948- 108
Williams, Garth (Montgomery) 1912- SATA-18
See also DLB 22
Williams, Geoffrey (John) 1943- 29-32R
Williams, Geoffrey J(ames) 1936- 118
Williams, George (Guion) 1902- 15-16R
Williams, George C(hristopher) 1926- 73-76
Williams, George Huntston 1914- CANR-16
Earlier sketches in CA 2R, CANR-1
Williams, George M(ason, Jr.) 1940- 61-64
Williams, George W(alton) 1922- 9-10R
Williams, George Washington
1849-1891 DLB-47
Williams, Geraint 1942- 124
Williams, Gertrude 1897-1983 Obituary 109
Williams, Gilbert M. 1917- 61-64
Williams, Glanmor 1920- 7-8R
Williams, Glanville Llewelyn 1911- 106
Williams, Gluyas 1888-1982 Obituary 108
See also AITN 2
Williams, Gordon (Maclean) 1934(?)-
Brief entry 116
Williams, Gordon Leslie 1933- 110
Williams, Greer 1909- CANR-10
Earlier sketch in CA 13-14R
Williams, Gregory 1952- 109
Williams, Griffith Wynne 1897-1972 CAP-2
Earlier sketch in CA 25-28
Williams, Gurney III 1941- 69-72
Williams, Guy Neal 1953- 77-80
Williams, Guy R. 1920- 13-14R
See also SATA 11
Williams, (David) Gwyn 1904- 103
Williams, Hank, Jr. 1949- Brief entry 117
Williams, Harold A(nthony) 1916- 37-40R
Williams, Harold R(oger) 1935- 53-56
Williams, Harold S(tannett) 1898- CANR-20
Earlier sketches in CA 11-12R, CANR-5
Williams, Harold Workman
See Wilson, Halsey William
Williams, Hawley
See Heyliger, William
Williams, Hazel Pearson 1914- 57-60
Williams, Heathcote 1941- 21-22R
See also DLB 13
Williams, Henry
See Manville, W(illiam) H(enry)
Williams, Henry Lionel 1895-1974
Obituary 45-48
Williams, Herbert (Lloyd) 1932- CANR-12
Earlier sketch in CA 29-32R
Williams, Herbert Lee 1918- 2R
Williams, Hermann Warner, Jr.
1908-1974 7-8R
Obituary 53-56
Williams, Hiram D. 1917- 13-14R
Williams, Hosea L(orenzo) 1926- 49-52
Williams, Howard L(loyd) 1950- 117
Williams, Howard Russell 1915- 15-16R
Williams, Hugh (Anthony Glanmor)
1904-1969 CAP-2
Earlier sketch in CA 25-28
Williams, Hugo 1942- 19-20R
See also DLB 40
See also CLC 42
Williams, Ioan Miles 1941- CANR-11
Earlier sketch in CA 25-28R
Williams, Ira E., Jr. 1926- 53-56
Williams, Irving G(regory) 1915- 41-44R
Williams, Isaac 1802-1865 DLB-32
Williams, J(ames) David Lewis
See Lewis-Williams, J(ames) David
Williams, J(ames) Earl 1922- 41-44R
Williams, J(ohn) H(argreaves) Harley 11-12R
Williams, J. R.
See Williams, Jeanne
Williams, J(ohn) Rodman 1918- 81-84
Williams, J. Walker
See Wodehouse, P(elham) G(renville)
Williams, J. X.
See Ludwig, Myles Eric
and Offutt, Andrew J(efferson V)
Williams, Jay 1914-1978 CANR-2
Obituary 81-84
Earlier sketch in CA 2R
See also SATA 3, 24, 41
See also CLR 8
Williams, Jay G(omer) 1932- 41-44R
Williams, Jeanne 1930- 25-28R
See also SATA 5
Williams, Jenny 1939- 112
Williams, Jeremy (Napier) Howard
See Howard-Williams, Jeremy (Napier)
Williams, Jerome 1926- CANR-1
Earlier sketch in CA 49-52
Williams, Joan 1928- 2R
See also DLB 6
Williams, Joel
See Jennings, John (Edward, Jr.)
Williams, John (Herbert) 1908-1976 CANR-10
Earlier sketch in CA 15-16R
Williams, John (Edward) 1922- CANR-2
Earlier sketch in CA 2R
See also DLB 6
Williams, John A(lfred) 1925- CANR-6
Earlier sketch in CA 53-56
See also CAAS 3
See also DLB 2, 33
See also CLC 5, 13
Williams, John Alden 1928- CANR-2
Earlier sketch in CA 3R
Williams, John B. 1919- 93-96
Williams, John D(elane) 1938- 57-60
Williams, John Edwin 1928- 93-96
Williams, John G(ordon) 1906- CAP-2
Earlier sketch in CA 23-24
Williams, John G. 1915- 120
Williams, John Henry 1887-1980 Obituary 105
Williams, John R(yan) 1919- 37-40R
Williams, John Stanley 1925- CAP-1
Earlier sketch in CA 9-10
Williams, John Stuart 1920- 65-68

INDEX

Williams, Jonathan (Chamberlain)
1929- CANR-8
Earlier sketch in CA 9-10R
See also DLB 5
See also CLC 13
Williams, Joy 1944- CANR-22
Earlier sketch in CA 41-44R
See also CLC 31
Williams, Joyce E(layne) 1937- 104
Williams, Juanita da Lomba Jones
1925- 37-40R
Williams, Justin, Sr. 1906- 101
Williams, Kate
See Flynn, Donald R(obert)
Williams, Kim 1924(?)-1986 Obituary 120
Williams, Kit 1946(?)- 107
See also SATA 44
See also CLR 4
Williams, L(aurence) F(rederic) Rushbrook
See Rushbrook Williams, L(aurence)
F(rederic)
Williams, L(eslie) Pearce 1927- 65-68
Williams, Lady
See Williams, Gertrude
Williams, Lawrence 1916(?)-1983
Obituary 108
Williams, Lawrence K(enneth) 1930- 29-32R
Williams, Lee E(rskine) II 1946- 41-44R
Williams, LeRoy T. 1944- 120
Williams, Leslie 1941- 107
See also SATA 42
Williams, Linda 1946- 110
Williams, Liza 1928- 102
Williams, Loring G. 1924-1974 CAP-2
Earlier sketch in CA 29-32
Williams, Louise Bonino 1904(?)-1984
Obituary 114
See also SATA 39
Williams, Lovett E(dward), Jr. 1935- 109
Williams, Lynn
See Hale, Arlene
Williams, Marcia 1932- 123
Williams, Margaret (Anne) 1902- 23-24R
Williams, Margaret (Vyner) 1914- 25-28R
Williams, Martin 1924- 49-52
Williams, Mary Alice 1949- Brief entry 123
Williams, Mary C(ameron) 1923- 57-60
Williams, Mary Elizabeth 1909-1976
Obituary 65-68
Williams, Mary McGee 1925- 25-28R
Williams, Mary Pat 1946- 112
Williams, Mason 1938- 25-28R
Williams, Maureen 1951- 85-88
See also SATA 12
Williams, Melvin D(onald) 1933- 73-76
Williams, Merryn 1944- CANR-15
Earlier sketch in CA 41-44R
Williams, Michael
See St. John, Wylly Folk
Williams, Miller 1930- 15-16R
Williams, Mona (Goodwyn) 1916- 81-84
Williams, Nancy M(argaret) 1929- 122
Williams, Ned 1909- 13-14R
Williams, Neville (John) 1924-1977
Obituary 111
Williams, Noel Trevor St. John 1918- 41-44R
Williams, Norman 1952- 118
See also CLC 39
Williams, Oliver F(ranklin) 1939- 114
Williams, Oliver P(erry) 1925- 37-40R
Williams, Ora (Ruby) 1926- 73-76
Williams, Oscar 1900-1964 CANR-6
Earlier sketch in CA 1R
Williams, P(eter) F(airney) 1931- 121
Williams, Patrick J.
See Butterworth, W(illiam) E(dmund III)
Williams, Patti 1936- 73-76
Williams, Paul (Revere) 1894-1980
Obituary 93-96
Williams, Paul (Hamilton) 1940- 121
Williams, Paul (Steven) 1948- 81-84
Williams, Paul O(sborne) 1935- CANR-24
Earlier sketch in CA 106
Williams, Pete
See Faulknor, Cliff(ord Vernon)
Williams, Peter W(illiam) 1944- 112
Williams, Philip Maynard 1920-1984
Obituary 114
Williams, Philip W(alter) 1941- CANR-11
Earlier sketch in CA 69-72
Williams, Phyllis S(awyer) 1931- 65-68
Williams, Ralph Mehlin 1911- 7-8R
Williams, Ralph Vaughan
See Vaughan Williams, Ralph
Williams, Randall Herbert Monier
See Monier-Williams, Randall Herbert
Williams, Raymond (Henry) 1921-1988 21-22R
Obituary 124
See also DLB 14
Williams, Rebecca (Yancy) 1899-1976
Obituary 65-68
Williams, Richard Hays 1912- CANR-2
Earlier sketch in CA 2R
Williams, Richard Lippincott 1910- 101
Williams, Robert C. 1938- CANR-14
Earlier sketch in CA 37-40R
Williams, Robert Coleman 1940- 23-24R
Williams, Robert Deryck 1917-1986 103
Obituary 120
Williams, Robert Hugh 1907(?)-1983
Obituary 109
Williams, Robert L(ewis) 1903- CANR-10
Earlier sketch in CA 15-16R
Williams, Robert Moore 1907-1977
Obituary 102
Williams, Robert P. 1906(?)-1977
Obituary 69-72
Williams, Robin M(urphy), Jr. 1914- 13-14R
Williams, Roger 1603(?)-1683 DLB-24
Williams, Roger J(ohn) 1893-1988 CANR-7
Obituary 124
Earlier sketch in CA 17-18R
Williams, Roger L(awrence) 1923-
Brief entry 112
Williams, Roger M(iller) 1934- 37-40R
Williams, Roger Neville 1943- 37-40R
Williams, Ronald Ralph 1906-1979 CANR-7
Earlier sketch in CA 15-16R
Williams, Rosalind
See Fergusson, Rosalind (Joyce)
Williams, Rosalind H. 1944- 109
Williams, Rose
See Ross, W(illiam) E(dward) D(aniel)
Williams, Russell J(ohn) 1944- 104
Williams, Samm-Art
See Williams, Samuel Arthur
See also DLB 38
Williams, Samuel Arthur 1946- 123
Brief entry 117
Williams, Selma R(uth) 1925- CANR-1
Earlier sketch in CA 49-52
See also SATA 14
Williams, Sherley Anne 1944- 73-76
See also DLB 41
Williams, Shirley
See Williams, Sherley Anne
Williams, Slim
See Williams, Clyde C.
Williams, Stanley W. 1917- 17-18R
Williams, Stephen 1926- Brief entry 114
Williams, Stirling B(acot), Jr. 1943- 29-32R
Williams, Strephon Kaplan 1934- CANR-20
Earlier sketch in CA 102
Williams, T(erence) C(harles) 1925- 29-32R
Williams, T(homas) David 1929- 123
Williams, T(homas) Harry 1909-1979 CANR-3
Earlier sketch in CA 4R
See also DLB 17
Williams, Tennessee 1911(?)-1983 7-8R
Obituary 108
See also DLB 7
See also DLBY 83
See also DLBD 4
See also CDALB 1941-1968
See also CLC 1, 2, 5, 7, 8, 11, 15, 19,
30, 39, 45
See also AITN 1, 2
Williams, Theodore C(urtis) 1930- 69-72
Williams, Thomas (Alonzo) 1926- CANR-2
Earlier sketch in CA 2R
See also CLC 14
Williams, Thomas (Andrew) 1931- 49-52
Williams, Thomas Howard 1935- 15-16R
Williams, Tina
See Wiles, Domini
Williams, Trevor Illtyd 1921- 109
Williams, Ursula Moray
See Moray Williams, Ursula
See also SATA 3
Williams, (George) Valentine 1883-1946
Brief entry 111
Williams, Vera B. 1927- 123
See also SATA 33
See also CLR 9
Williams, Vergil L(ewis) 1935- CANR-9
Earlier sketch in CA 57-60
Williams, Wallace Edward 1926-
Brief entry 105
Williams, Walter
See Williams, Walter E(dward)
Williams, Walter E(dward) 1936-
Brief entry 123
Williams, Walter G(eorge) 1903- CAP-1
Earlier sketch in CA 15-16
Williams, (Margaret) Wetherby CANR-3
Earlier sketch in CA 45-48
Williams, Willard F(orest) 1921- 15-16R
Williams, William Appleman 1921- CANR-3
Earlier sketch in CA 3R
See also DLB 17
Williams, William Carlos 1883-1963 89-92
See also DLB 4, 16, 54
See also CLC 1, 2, 5, 9, 13, 22, 42
Williams, William David 1917- 7-8R
Williams, William H(enry) 1936- 69-72
Williams, William P(roctor) 1939- CANR-23
Earlier sketch in CA 45-48
Williams, Wirt (Alfred, Jr.) 1921-1986 9-10R
Obituary 119
See also DLB 6
Williams-Ellis, (Mary) Amabel (Nassau
Strachey) 1894-1984 105
Obituary 114
See also SATA 29, 41
Williams-Ellis, Clough 1883- 13-14R
Williamson, Alan (Bacher) 1944- 57-60
Williamson, Anthony George 1932- 101
Williamson, Audrey (May)
1913-1986(?) CANR-3
Obituary 118
Earlier sketch in CA 49-52
Williamson, Bruce 1893-1984 Obituary 111
Williamson, Bruce 1930- 101
Williamson, Chilton 1916- 15-16R
Williamson, Chilton, Jr. 1947- 102
Williamson, Claude C(harles) H. 1891-? CAP-1
Earlier sketch in CA 17-18
Williamson, Craig (Burke) 1943- CANR-16
Earlier sketch in CA 29-32R
Williamson, David Keith 1942- 103
Williamson, David L(ouis) 1937- 111
Williamson, Duncan 1928- 123
Williamson, Edward 1908-1984 Obituary 113
Williamson, Ellen Douglas 1905-1984 17-18R
Obituary 114
Williamson, Eugene L. (Jr.) 1930- 11-12R
Williamson, Geoffrey 1897- 9-10R
Williamson, Gerald Neal 1932- 112
Williamson, Glen 1909- CANR-9
Earlier sketch in CA 57-60
Williamson, H(enry) D(arvall) 1907- 65-68
Williamson, Harold Francis 1901- 7-8R
Williamson, Henry 1895-1977 81-84
Obituary 73-76
See also SATA 30, 37
Williamson, J. N.
See Williamson, Gerald Neal
Williamson, J. Peter 1929- CANR-6
Earlier sketch in CA 1R
Williamson, Jack
See Williamson, John Stewart
See also DLB 8
See also CLC 29
Williamson, Jeffrey G(ale) 1935- CANR-18
Earlier sketch in CA 85-88
Williamson, Joanne Small 1926- 13-14R
See also SATA 3
Williamson, John Butler 1943- 89-92
Williamson, John G(rant) 1933- 45-48
Williamson, John Stewart 1908- CANR-23
Earlier sketch in CA 17-18R
Williamson, Joseph 1895- CAP-1
Earlier sketch in CA 11-12
Williamson, Juanita V. 1917- 37-40R
Williamson, Lamar, Jr. 1926- 89-92
Williamson, Moncrieff 1915- 102
Williamson, Norma (Goff) 1934- 65-68
Williamson, Oliver E(aton) 1932- 81-84
Williamson, Porter B(eyers) 1916- 110
Williamson, Rene de Visme 1908- CANR-13
Earlier sketches in CA 17-18, CAP-1
Williamson, Richard 1930- 37-40R
Williamson, Richard 1935- 109
Williamson, Robert C(lifford) 1916- 23-24R
Williamson, Robin (Martin Eyre) 1938- 29-32R
Williamson, Robin (Duncan Harry) 1943- 102
Williamson, Stanford Winfield 1916- 7-8R
Williamson, Tony
See Williamson, Anthony George
Williamson, William Bedford 1918- CANR-6
Earlier sketch in CA 3R
Williamson, William Landram 1920- 11-12R
Willie, Charles V(ert) 1927- CANR-14
Earlier sketch in CA 41-44R
Willie, Frederick
See Lovecraft, H(oward) P(hillips)
Willig, George 1949- 102
Willig, John M. 1913-1982 Obituary 107
Willig, Rosette F. 1950- 114
Willimon, William H(enry) 1946- 106
Willing, Jules Z. 1914-1981 108
Willing, Martha Kent 1920- 37-40R
Willingham, Calder (Baynard, Jr.)
1922- CANR-3
Earlier sketch in CA 5-6R
See also DLB 2, 44
See also CLC 5
Willingham, John J. 1935- 37-40R
Willingham, John R(obert) 1919- 17-18R
Willings, David 1932- 111
Willis, (George) Anthony Armstrong
1897-1976 69-72
Willis, Arthur J(ames) 1895-1983 CANR-5
Obituary 111
Earlier sketch in CA 7-8R
Willis, Charles
See Clarke, Arthur C(harles)
Willis, Cleve E(dward) 1942- 123
Willis, Cleve E. 1942- Brief entry 118
Willis, Connie 1945- 114
Willis, Corinne Denneny 21-22R
Willis, Donald C(halmers) 1947- CANR-15
Earlier sketch in CA 41-44R
Willis, E(dward) David 1932- 37-40R
Willis, Edgar E(rnest) 1913- 5-6R
Willis, Edward Henry
See Willis, Ted
Willis, Ellen Jane 1941- 106
Willis, F(rank) Roy 1930- 15-16R
Willis, Irene 1929- CANR-10
Earlier sketch in CA 65-68
Willis, James 1928- 109
Willis, Jerry W. 1943- 85-88
Willis, John A(lvin) 1916- 19-20R
Willis, John H(oward), Jr. 1929- 37-40R
Willis, John Ralph 1938- 121
Willis, Margaret 1899- CANR-19
Earlier sketches in CA 5-6R, CANR-3
Willis, Maud
See Lottman, Eileen
Willis, Meredith Sue 1946- CANR-16
Earlier sketch in CA 85-88
Willis, Nathaniel Parker 1806-1867 DLB-3, 59
Willis, Roy (Geoffrey) 1927- CANR-17
Earlier sketch in CA 77-80
Willis, Samuel
See Parker, Hershel
Willis, Sharon O(zell) 1938- 37-40R
Willis, Stanley E. II 1923- 23-24R
Willis, Ted 1918- CANR-23
Earlier sketches in CA 11-12R, CANR-7
Willis, Wayne 1942- 29-32R
Willison, George F(indlay) 1896-1972 CAP-1
Obituary 37-40R
Earlier sketch in CA 13-14
Willison, Marilyn Murray 1948- 105
Willke, John Charles 1925- CANR-24
Earlier sketches in CA 65-68, CANR-9
Willkens, William H(enry) R(obert)
1919- 23-24R
Wilmington, Harold L. 1932- 49-52
Willmott, Peter 1923- 23-24R
Willmott, Phyllis 117
Willner, Ann Ruth 1924- 23-24R
Willner, Dorothy 1927- 53-56
Willnow, Ronald D. 1933- 77-80
Willock, Colin 1919- CANR-10
Earlier sketch in CA 13-14R
Willock, Ruth 15-16R
Willoughby, Cass
See Olsen, T(heodore) V(ictor)
Willoughby, Charles Andrew 1892-1972
Obituary 104
Willoughby, David P(atrick) 1901- 37-40R
Willoughby, Elaine Macmann 1926- 101
Willoughby, Glynn
See Allentuck, Andrew
Willoughby, Hugh
See Harvey, Nigel
Willoughby, Lee Davis
See Brandner, Gary
and DeAndrea, William L(ouis)
and Toombs, John
and Webb, Jean Francis
Willoughby, William Reid 1910- 2R
Willrich, Mason 1933- 77-80
Willrich, Ted L. 1924- 29-32R
Wills, A(lfred) J(ohn) 1927- 21-22R
Wills, David Hilary 1904-1985 Obituary 117
Wills, Garry 1934- CANR-1
Earlier sketch in CA 3R
Wills, Geoffrey
See Staal, Cyril
Wills, Jean 1929- CANR-22
Earlier sketch in CA 105
Wills, John E(lliot), Jr. 1936- 45-48
Wills, Jonathan 1947- 69-72
Wills, Maurice Morning 1932- Brief entry 105
Wills, Maury
See Wills, Maurice Morning
Wills, Philip Aubrey 1907-1978 81-84
Wills, Thomas
See Ard, William (Thomas)
Willson, A(mos) Leslie, Jr. 1923- 11-12R
Willson, Meredith 1902-1984 49-52
Obituary 113
Willson, Robina Beckles
See Beckles Willson, Robina (Elizabeth)
See also SATA 27
Willwerth, James 1943- 57-60
Willy
See Colette, (Sidonie-Gabrielle)
Willy, Colette
See Colette, (Sidonie-Gabrielle)
Willy, Margaret (Elizabeth) 1919- 9-10R
Wilma, Dana
See Faralla, Dana
Wilmer, Clive 1945- Brief entry 122
See also DLB 40
Wilmer, Dale
See Miller, (H.) Bill(y)
and Wade, Robert (Allison)
Wilmer, Valerie (Sybil) 1941- 85-88
Wilmerding, John 1938- 111
Wilmeth, Don B(urton) 1939- CANR-19
Earlier sketch in CA 102
Wilmore, Gayraud S(tephen, Jr.) 1921-
Brief entry 114
Wilmore, Sylvia (Joan) Bruce 1914- 89-92
Wilmot, Anthony 1933- 77-80
Wilmot, William (Wallace) 1943- CANR-7
Earlier sketch in CA 57-60
Wilms, Barbara 1941- 57-60
Wilmut, Roger (Francis) 1942- CANR-19
Earlier sketch in CA 102
Wilner, Eleanor 1937- CANR-16
Earlier sketch in CA 93-96
Wilner, Herbert 1925-1977 CANR-3
Earlier sketch in CA 45-48
Wilroy, Mary Edith (Farr) 1910-1987
Obituary 122
Wilshire, Bruce W(ithington) 1932- 77-80
Wilson, A(lfred) Jeyaratnam 1928- CANR-12
Earlier sketch in CA 61-64
Wilson, A(ndrew) N(orman) 1950- 122
Brief entry 112
See also DLB 14
See also CLC 33
Wilson, Abraham 1899(?)-1983 Obituary 110
Wilson, Alison M. 1932- 120
Wilson, Alton H(orace) 1925- 61-64
Wilson, Andrew 1923- 29-32R
Wilson, Angus (Frank Johnstone)
1913- CANR-21
Earlier sketch in CA 7-8R
See also DLB 15
See also CLC 2, 3, 5, 25, 34
Wilson, Arthur 1595-1652 DLB-58
Wilson, Arthur M(cCandless) 1902-1979 61-64
Obituary 89-92
Wilson, August 1945- 122
Brief entry 115
See also CLC 39
Wilson, Augusta Jane Evans 1835-1909 DLB-42
Wilson, Barbara
See Janifer, Laurence M(ark)
Wilson, Barbara Ker
See Ker Wilson, Barbara
Wilson, Beth P(ierre) CANR-1
Earlier sketch in CA 49-52
See also SATA 8
Wilson, Betty 1923- 97-100
Wilson, Brian 1942- CLC-12
Wilson, Bryan R(onald) 1926- CANR-19
Earlier sketches in CA 5-6R, CANR-3
Wilson, Budge 1927- 121
Wilson, Callie C(oe) 1917- 124

Wilson, Camilla Jeanne 1945- 61-64
Wilson, Cammy
See Wilson, Camilla Jeanne
Wilson, Carlos 1941- 61-64
Wilson, Carole
See Wallmann, Jeffrey M(iner)
Wilson, Carolyn 1938- 21-22R
Wilson, Carroll L(ouis) 1910-1983 89-92
Obituary 109
Wilson, Carter 1941- 17-18R
See also SATA 6
Wilson, (Lindsay) Charles 1932- 65-68
Wilson, Charles McMoran 1882-1977 .... CAP-2
Obituary 69-72
Earlier sketch in CA 21-22
Wilson, Charles Morrow 1905-1977 .... CANR-4
Earlier sketch in CA 5-6R
See also SATA 30
Wilson, Charles Reagan 1948- 105
Wilson, Christine
See Geach, Christine
Wilson, Christopher B. 1910(?)-1985
Obituary 117
See also SATA 46
Wilson, Clifford (Allan) 1923- 93-96
Wilson, Clifton E. 1919- 23-24R
Wilson, Clyde N(orman, Jr.) 1941- 116
Wilson, Colin 1931- CANR-22
Earlier sketches in CA 2R, CANR-1
See also CAAS 5
See also DLB 14
See also CLC 3, 14
Wilson, Craig R. 1947- 57-60
Wilson, Crane
See O'Brien, Cyril C(ornelius)
Wilson, D. A.
See Wilson, Derek (Alan)
Wilson, D(udley) B(utler) 1923- 23-24R
Wilson, Dagmar 1916- SATA-31
Wilson, Dale 1894-1987 .... CAP-1
Obituary 121
Earlier sketch in CA 13-14
Wilson, Daniel J(oseph) 1949- 117
Wilson, Dave
See Floren, Lee
Wilson, (Anthony) David 1927- 97-100
Wilson, David 1942- CANR-16
Earlier sketch in CA 93-96
Wilson, David
See MacArthur, D(avid) Wilson
Wilson, David Allen 1926- CANR-7
Earlier sketch in CA 5-6R
Wilson, David Henry 1937- 113
Wilson, David L(ee) 1943- 112
Wilson, David Scofield 1931- 106
Wilson, Deirdre (Susan Moir) 1941- 97-100
Wilson, Derek (Alan) 1935- 123
Brief entry 115
Wilson, Derek A.
See Wilson, Derek (Alan)
Wilson, Dick
See Wilson, Richard Garratt
Wilson, Dirk
See Pohl, Frederik
Wilson, Don(ald) 1932- 81-84
Wilson, Don W(hitman) 1942- 61-64
Wilson, Dorothy Clarke 1904- CANR-6
Earlier sketch in CA 4R
See also SATA 16
Wilson, Douglas L. 1935- 37-40R
Wilson, (Archibald) Duncan 1911- 103
Wilson, E(dward) Raymond 1896-1987 61-64
Obituary 122
Wilson, (Harvey) Earl 1907-1987 69-72
Obituary 121
Wilson, Earl (Dean) 1939- 118
Wilson, Edmund 1895-1972 .... CANR-1
Obituary 37-40R
Earlier sketch in CA 3R
See also DLB 63
See also CLC 1, 2, 3, 8, 24
Wilson, Edward A(rthur) 1886-1970
Obituary 116
See also SATA 38
Wilson, Edward M(eryon) 1906-1977
Obituary 114
Wilson, Edward O(sborne) 1929- CANR-16
Earlier sketch in CA 61-64
Wilson, Elena 1907(?)-1979 Obituary 89-92
Wilson, Elizabeth Z. 1951- 123
Wilson, Ellen (Janet Cameron) ?-1976 49-52
Obituary 103
See also SATA 9, 26
Wilson, Eric (H.) 1940- CANR-20
Earlier sketch in CA 101
See also SATA 32, 34
Wilson, Erica CANR-23
Earlier sketches in CA 53-56, CANR-7
Wilson, Erle (Alexander Mann) 1898- 7-8R
Wilson, Ernest Charles 1896- 29-32R
Wilson, Ethel Davis (Bryant) 1888-1980 102
See also CLC 13
Wilson, Eugene E. 1887(?)-1974
Obituary 49-52
Wilson, Eugene Smith 1905-1981
Obituary 103
Wilson, Evan M(orris) 1910-1984
Obituary 112
Wilson, Everett K(eith) 1913- 93-96
Wilson, F(rank) P(ercy) 1889-1963 ..... CANR-1
Earlier sketch in CA 4R
Wilson, Forbes (Kingsbury) 1910-
Brief entry 112
Wilson, Forrest 1918- CANR-7
Earlier sketch in CA 53-56
See also SATA 27
Wilson, Francesca Mary 1888-1981
Obituary 103
Wilson, Francis Graham 1901-1976
Obituary 65-68
Wilson, Frank (Avray) 1914- CAP-1
Earlier sketch in CA 11-12
Wilson, Frank J. 1887-1970 .... CAP-1
Earlier sketch in CA 15-16
Wilson, Frank L(eondus) 1941- 57-60
Wilson, Fred 1937- 37-40R
Wilson, G(eorge) B(ulkeley) L(aird)
1908-1984 111
Obituary 114
Wilson, Gahan 1930- CANR-19
Earlier sketch in CA 25-28R
See also SATA 27, 35
Wilson, Garff B(ell) 1909- 45-48
Wilson, George C. 1927- 124
Wilson, George M(acklin) 1937- 25-28R
Wilson, George W(ilton) 1928- CANR-7
Earlier sketch in CA 19-20R
Wilson, Gina 1943- 106
See also SATA 34, 36
Wilson, Glenn Daniel 1942- CANR-21
Earlier sketch in CA 104
Wilson, (Leslie) Granville 1912- CANR-11
Earlier sketch in CA 69-72
See also SATA 14
Wilson, Gregory
See DeLamotte, Roy Carroll
Wilson, H. W.
See Wilson, Halsey William
Wilson, Halsey William 1868-1954
Brief entry 118
Wilson, (James) Harold 1916- CANR-16
Earlier sketch in CA 53-56
Wilson, Harold Stacy 1935- 41-44R
Wilson, Harriet E. Adams
1828(?)-1863(?) DLB-50
Wilson, Harriett (Charlotte) 1916- CANR-16
Earlier sketch in CA 2R
Wilson, Harris W(ard) 1919- 23-24R
Wilson, Harry Leon 1867-1939 Brief entry .. 108
See also DLB 9
Wilson, Hazel (Hutchins) 1898- CANR-6
Earlier sketch in CA 4R
See also SATA 3
Wilson, Helen Helga (Mayne) CANR-4
Earlier sketch in CA 11-12R
Wilson, Helen Van Pelt 1901- 105
Wilson, Howard Allan 1927- Brief entry 106
Wilson, Howard Hazen 1908-1978
Obituary 77-80
Wilson, Ian (William) 1941- 85-88
Wilson, Iris Higbie
See Engstrand, Iris (H.) Wilson
Wilson, Ivor (Arthur) 1924- CAP-1
Earlier sketch in CA 11-12
Wilson, J(anice) J. 1936- 97-100
Wilson, J(ohn) Tuzo 1908- 45-48
Wilson, Jack 1937- 23-24R
Wilson, Jacqueline 1945- CANR-17
Earlier sketches in CA 45-48, CANR-1
Wilson, Jacques M(arcel) P(atrick) 1920- .. 49-52
Wilson, James C(lyde) 1948- 111
Wilson, James Orville 1895- CAP-1
Earlier sketch in CA 11-12
Wilson, James Q(uinn) 1931- Brief entry ... 116
Wilson, James Robert 1917- 2R
Wilson, James Vernon 1881- CAP-1
Earlier sketch in CA 9-10
Wilson, Jaye 1938- 104
Wilson, Jeanne (Patricia Pauline)
1920- CANR-12
Earlier sketch in CA 69-72
Wilson, Jerry V(ernon) 1928- CANR-7
Earlier sketch in CA 57-60
Wilson, Jim
See Wilson, James Vernon
Wilson, Joan Hoff 1937- Brief entry 105
Wilson, Joe
See Wilson, Joseph T(homas)
Wilson, John 1588-1667 .... DLB-24
Wilson, John 1922- SATA-22
Wilson, (Richard) John (McMoran) 1924- ... 117
Wilson, John A. 1900(?)-1976 Obituary ... 69-72
Wilson, John A(braham) R(oss) 1911- ... 41-44R
Wilson, John Boyd 1928- CANR-5
Earlier sketch in CA 11-12R
Wilson, John (Anthony) Burgess 1917- .. CANR-2
Earlier sketch in CA 3R
See also CLC 8, 10, 13
Wilson, John C.
See Morrow, Felix
Wilson, John Dover 1881-1969 102
Obituary 93-96
Wilson, John F(rederick) 1933- Brief entry .. 117
Wilson, John Foster 1919- 109
Wilson, John Harold 1900-1982 Obituary ... 107
Wilson, John R. M. 1944- 69-72
Wilson, John Stuart Gladstone 1916- .. CANR-11
Earlier sketch in CA 13-14R
Wilson, Joseph T(homas) 1936- 117
Wilson, Joyce M(uriel Judson) CANR-12
Earlier sketch in CA 19-20R
See also SATA 21
Wilson, Julia 1927- 21-22R
Wilson, Jussem
See Wilson, Nelly
Wilson, Justin 116
Wilson, Katharine M(argaret) 1895- 89-92
Wilson, Keith 1927- CANR-9
Earlier sketch in CA 23-24R
See also CAAS 5
Wilson, Keith 1929- 121
Wilson, Kenneth G(eorge) 1923- 7-8R
Wilson, Kenneth L. 1897(?)-1979
Obituary 85-88
Wilson, Kenneth L(ee) 1916- 29-32R
Wilson, L(eland) Craig 1925- 37-40R
Wilson, Lanford 1937- 19-20R
See also DLB 7
See also CLC 7, 14, 36
Wilson, Larman C. 1930- CANR-14
Earlier sketch in CA 37-40R
Wilson, Leigh Allison 1957- 117
Wilson, Leonard G(ilchrist) 1928- CANR-7
Earlier sketch in CA 57-60
Wilson, Libby
See Wilson, Elizabeth Z.
Wilson, Lionel 1924- 105
See also SATA 31, 33
Wilson, Logan 1907- 45-48
Wilson, Louis D(oull) 1917- 93-96
Wilson, Louis Round 1876-1980
Obituary 93-96
Wilson, M(orris) Emett 1894- 5-6R
Wilson, Major L(oyce) 1926- 57-60
Wilson, Margaret (Wilhemina) 1882-1973
Obituary 113
See also DLB 9
Wilson, Margaret Gibbons 1943- 101
Wilson, Margery
See Strayer, Sara Barker
Wilson, Margo 1942- 110
Wilson, Marie B(eatrice) 1922- 53-56
Wilson, Marjorie
See Wilson, Budge
Wilson, Mary
See Roby, Mary Linn
Wilson, Maurice (Charles John) 1914- . SATA-46
Wilson, (Daphne) Merna 1930- 109
Wilson, Michael 1914-1978 85-88
Obituary 77-80
See also DLB 44
Wilson, Mitchell 1913-1973 .... CANR-3
Obituary 41-44R
Earlier sketch in CA 3R
Wilson, Monica Hunter 1908-1982 ..... CANR-6
Obituary 108
Earlier sketch in CA 2R
Wilson, N(orman) Scarlyn 1901- CANR-5
Earlier sketch in CA 7-8R
Wilson, Neill C(ompton) 1889- 7-8R
Wilson, Nelly 1930- 106
Wilson, Nick
See Ellis, Edward S(ylvester)
Wilson, Noel Avon 1914- 73-76
Wilson, Pat 1910- CANR-12
Earlier sketch in CA 29-32R
Wilson, Paul C(arroll) 1944- 77-80
Wilson, Paul R(ichard) 1942- Brief entry ... 109
Wilson, Penelope Coker
See Hall, Penelope C(oker)
Wilson, Peter (Cecil) 1913-1984 Obituary ... 113
Wilson, Peter N. 1928- 25-28R
Wilson, Phillip (John) 1922- 57-60
Wilson, Phoebe Rous 1924(?)-1980
Obituary 101
Wilson, Phyllis Starr 1928- 69-72
Wilson, R(oger) H(arris) L(ebus) 1920- .. 13-14R
Wilson, Raymond 1925- CANR-17
Earlier sketch in CA 97-100
Wilson, Richard Garratt 1928- 106
Wilson, Richard Guy 1940- CANR-21
Earlier sketch in CA 93-96
Wilson, Richard Lawson 1905-1981
Obituary 102
Wilson, Richard Trevor 1938- 118
Wilson, Richard W(hittingham) 1933- 73-76
Wilson, Robert (Edward) 1951- 124
Wilson, Robert Anton 1932- CANR-18
Earlier sketch in CA 65-68
Wilson, Robert L. 1925- CANR-9
Earlier sketch in CA 57-60
Wilson, Robert M(ills) 1929- CANR-9
Earlier sketch in CA 23-24R
Wilson, Robert M. 1944- CANR-2
Earlier sketch in CA 49-52
See also CLC 7, 9
Wilson, Robert McLachlan 1916- 109
Wilson, Robert N(eal) 1924- 17-18R
Wilson, Robert Renbert 1898-1975 .... CANR-23
Earlier sketch in CA 45-48
Wilson, Robin Scott 1928- 101
Wilson, Robley (Conant), Jr. 1930- CANR-14
Earlier sketch in CA 77-80
Wilson, Rodney N. Usher
See Usher-Wilson, Rodney N.
Wilson, Roger Burdett 1919- 45-48
Wilson, Ron(ald William) 1941- 112
See also SATA 38
Wilson, Ronald E(merson) 1932- 105
Wilson, (Edward) Ross (Armitage) 1914- ... 7-8R
Wilson, Samuel, Jr. 1911- CANR-6
Earlier sketch in CA 53-56
Wilson, Sandra 1944- 102
Wilson, Sarah 1934- SATA-50
Wilson, Sloan 1920- CANR-1
Earlier sketch in CA 1R
See also CLC 32
Wilson, Snoo 1948- 69-72
See also CLC 33
Wilson, Steve 1943- 73-76
Wilson, Theodore A(llen) 1940- 37-40R
Wilson, Thomas C(ave) 1907-1984
Obituary 112
Wilson, Thomas Williams, Jr. 1912- CANR-3
Earlier sketch in CA 7-8R
Wilson, Tom 1931- 106
See also SATA 30, 33
Wilson, Trevor (Gordon) 1928- 53-56
Wilson, W(illiam) Harmon 1905- 37-40R
Wilson, Walt(er N.) 1939- 69-72
See also SATA 14
Wilson, Wesley M. 1927- 11-12R
Wilson, Wilfrid George 1910- CAP-2
Earlier sketch in CA 21-22
Wilson, William A(lbert) 1933- 105
Wilson, William E(dward) 1906- CANR-2
Earlier sketch in CA 5-6R
Wilson, William H(enry) 1935- 15-16R
Wilson, William J. 1935- CANR-1
Earlier sketch in CA 45-48
Wilson, William P. 1922- 124
Wilson, William Ritchie 1911- 41-44R
Wilson, William S(mith) 1932- 81-84
Wilson, Woodrow 1856-1924 .... DLB-47
Wilson, Z. Vance 1950- 120
Wilt, Fred(erick Loren) 1920- CANR-9
Earlier sketch in CA 57-60
Wilt, Judith 1941- CANR-12
Earlier sketch in CA 57-60
Wiltgen, Ralph M(ichael) 1921- CANR-11
Earlier sketch in CA 25-28R
Wilton, (James) Andrew (Rutley) 1942- .. 97-100
Wilton, Elizabeth 1937- 69-72
See also SATA 14
Wiltse, Charles M(aurice) 1907- CANR-3
Earlier sketch in CA 3R
Wiltse, David 1940- CANR-22
Earlier sketch in CA 105
Wiltsee, Joseph L. 1920- 110
Wiltz, Chris(tine) 1948- CANR-24
Earlier sketch in CA 106
Wiltz, John Edward 1930- 11-12R
Wilwerding, Walter Joseph 1891-1966 ... CAP-1
Earlier sketch in CA 15-16
See also SATA 9
Wimmer, Larry T(urley) 1935- 101
Wimsatt, James I(rving) 1927- CANR-13
Earlier sketch in CA 61-64
Wimsatt, W(illiam) K(urtz), Jr.
1907-1975 .... CANR-3
Obituary 61-64
Earlier sketch in CA 1R
See also DLB 63
Winans, A(llan) D(avis, Jr.) 1936- CANR-12
Earlier sketch in CA 57-60
Winans, Edgar Vincent 1930- 5-6R
Winant, Fran 1943- 53-56
Winawer, Bonnie P. (Josephs) 1938- 17-18R
Wincelberg, Shimon 1924- 45-48
Winch, D(avid) M(onk) 1933- 45-48
Winch, Donald N. 1935- 123
Winch, John
See Campbell, (Gabrielle) Margaret (Vere)
Winch, Michael Bluett 1907- CAP-1
Earlier sketch in CA 11-12
Winch, Peter G(uy) 1926- 29-32R
Winch, Robert F(rancis) 1911-1977 .... CANR-24
Earlier sketch in CA 25-28R
Winch, Terence 1945- 93-96
Winchell, Carol Ann 1936- CANR-7
Earlier sketch in CA 61-64
Winchell, Constance M(abel) 1896-1983 .. CAP-1
Obituary 109
Earlier sketch in CA 9-10
Winchell, Wallace 1914- 53-56
Winchell, Walter 1897-1972 101
Obituary 33-36R
See also DLB 29
Winchester, A(lbert) M(cCombs) 1908- ... 41-44R
Winchester, Clarence 1895-1981 Obituary .. 104
Winchester, James H(ugh) 1917-1985 ... 17-18R
Obituary 117
See also SATA 30, 45
Winchester, Otis 1933- 21-22R
Winchester, Simon 1944- 107
Winckler, Paul A(lbert) 1926- 102
Wind, Edgar 1900-1971 Obituary 104
Wind, Herbert Warren 1916- CANR-6
Earlier sketch in CA 2R
Windal, Floyd, W(esley) 1930- 11-12R
Windchy, Eugene G. 1930- 41-44R
Windeler, Robert 1944- 102
Winder, Alvin E. 1923- 93-96
Winder, George Herbert 1895- CAP-1
Earlier sketch in CA 11-12
Winder, Mavis Areta 1907- 21-22R
Winder, R(ichard) Bayly 1920- 17-18R
Winders, Gertrude Hecker CANR-6
Earlier sketch in CA 4R
See also SATA 3
Windham, Basil
See Wodehouse, P(elham) G(renville)
Windham, Donald 1920- CANR-6
Earlier sketch in CA 2R
See also DLB 6
Windham, Douglas M(acArthur) 1943- ... 29-32R
Windham, Joan 1904- 21-22R
Windham, Kathryn T(ucker) 1918- CANR-11
Earlier sketch in CA 69-72
See also SATA 14
Windle, William Frederick 1898-1985 108
Obituary 115
Windley, Charles Ellis 1942- 65-68
Windmiller, Marshall 1924- 21-22R
Windmuller, John P. 1923- CANR-10
Earlier sketch in CA 25-28R
Windolph, F(rancis) Lyman 1889-1978 ... 41-44R
Windrow, Martin (Clive) 1944- Brief entry .. 110
Windsor, Annie
See Shull, Margaret Anne Wyse
Windsor, Claire
See Hamerstrom, Frances
Windsor, Duane 1947- 111
Windsor, Duke of
See Edward VIII
Windsor, Gerard (Charles) 1944- 124

INDEX

Windsor, Merrill C(ranston, Jr.) 1924- ... 113
Windsor, Patricia (Frances) 1938- ... CANR-19
Earlier sketches in CA 49-52, CANR-4
See also SATA 30
Windsor, Philip 1935- ... CANR-8
Earlier sketch in CA 5-6R
Windsor, Rex
See Armstrong, Douglas Albert
Windsor, Rudolph R. 1935- Brief entry ... 107
Windsor, (Bessie) Wallis Warfield (Spencer)
Simpson 1896-1986 Obituary ... 119
Windsor-Richards, Arthur (Bedlington)
1904- ... CAP-1
Earlier sketch in CA 11-12
Wine, Dick
See Posner, Richard
Wine, Sherwin T. 1928- ... 93-96
Winearls, Jane 1908- ... 103
Wineberg, Henry J. 1905(?)-1983
Obituary ... 109
Winebrenner, D(aniel) Kenneth 1908- ... CAP-1
Earlier sketch in CA 9-10
Winegarten, Renee 1922- ... 65-68
Winehouse, Irwin 1922- ... 11-12R
Winek, Charles L(eone) 1936- ... 65-68
Winer, Elihu 1914- Brief entry ... 111
Winer, Richard 1929- ... CANR-12
Earlier sketch in CA 73-76
Wines, Roger (Andrew) 1933- ... 23-24R
Winetrout, Kenneth 1912- ... 23-24R
Winfield, Arthur M.
See Stratemeyer, Edward L.
Winfield, Edna
See Stratemeyer, Edward L.
Winfield, Fairlee E(lizabeth) 1929- ... 118
Winfield, Gerald Freeman 1908-1984
Obituary ... 113
Winfield, Leigh
See Youngberg, Norma Ione (Rhoads)
Winfrey, Dorman H(ayward) 1924- ... 17-18R
Winfrey, John Crawford 1935- ... 57-60
Winfrey, Lee 1932- ... 69-72
Wing, Cliff W(aldron), Jr. 1922- ... 49-52
Wing, Donald G(oddard) 1904-1972
Obituary ... 37-40R
Wing, Frances (Scott) 1907- ... CAP-1
Earlier sketch in CA 17-18
Wing, George Douglas 1921- ... 17-18R
Wing, J. K. 1923- ... 29-32R
Wing, Jennifer Patai 1942- ... 57-60
Wing, R. L.
See Aero, Rita
Wing, Willis Kingsley 1899-1985 Obituary ... 116
Wingate, (Martha) Anne (Guice) 1943- ... 116
Wingate, Gifford W(endel) 1925- ... 65-68
Wingate, Isabel B(arnum) 1901-1987 ... 23-24R
Obituary ... 122
Wingate, John (Allan) 1920- ... CANR-24
Earlier sketch in CA 77-80
Wingate, John Williams 1899- ... 11-12R
Wingenbach, Charles E.
See Wingenbach, Gregory C(harles)
Wingenbach, Gregory C(harles) 1938- ... 13-14R
Winger, Fred E. 1912- ... 15-16R
Winger, Howard W(oodrow) 1914- ... CANR-7
Earlier sketch in CA 19-20R
Wingert, Paul S. 1900(?)-1974 Obituary ... 53-56
Wingfield, Sheila Claude 1906- Brief entry ... 108
Wingfield Digby, George Frederick 1911- . CAP-1
Earlier sketch in CA 11-12
Wingler, Hans M(aria) 1920- ... CANR-14
Earlier sketch in CA 29-32R
Wingo, E(lvis) Otha 1934- ... 37-40R
Wingo, Glenn Max 1913- ... 5-6R
Wingo, T(ullius) Lowdon, Jr. 1923- ... 23-24R
Wingo, Walter (Scott) 1931- ... 81-84
Wingren, Gustaf F(redrik) 1910- ... 15-16R
Winick, Charles 1922- Brief entry ... 109
Winick, Myron 1929- ... 107
Winick, Steven 1944- ... 61-64
Wink, Richard L(ee) 1930- ... 93-96
Wink, Walter Philip 1935- ... CANR-15
Earlier sketch in CA 37-40R
Winkelman, Donald M. 1934- ... 41-44R
Winkler, Allan M(ichael) 1945- ... 81-84
Winkler, Anthony C. 1942- ... 123
Winkler, Bee (Finkelberg) 1919- ... 15-16R
Winkler, Erhard M(ario) 1921- ... 89-92
Winkler, Franz E. 1907- ... 7-8R
Winkler, Henry R(alph) 1916- ... CANR-10
Earlier sketch in CA 17-18R
Winkler, Paul 1898-1982 Obituary ... 107
Winkler, Win Ann 1935- ... 73-76
Winkless, Nels(on Brock) III 1934- ... 57-60
Winks, Donald 1928- ... 25-28R
Winks, Robin William 1930- ... CANR-3
Earlier sketch in CA 5-6R
Winn, Albert Curry 1921- ... 106
Winn, Alison
See Wharmby, Margot
Winn, Charles S. 1932- ... CANR-23
Earlier sketch in CA 69-72
Winn, Chris 1952- ... 117
See also SATA 42
Winn, Ira Jay 1929- ... 57-60
Winn, James Anderson 1947- ... 120
Winn, Janet Bruce 1928- ... 105
See also SATA 43
Winn, Laura Rocke 1902- ... CAP-1
Earlier sketch in CA 13-14
Winn, Marie 1936(?)- ... 111
See also SATA 38
Winn, Ralph Bubrich 1895- ... 5-6R
Winn, Rowland (Denys Guy) 1916-1984
Obituary ... 114
Winn, Wilkins B(owdre) 1928- ... 49-52
Winnegrad, Mark Harris 1948- ... 77-80
Winner, Anna K(ennedy) 1900- ... 29-32R
Winner, Irene P(ortis) 1923- ... CANR-14
Earlier sketch in CA 41-44R
Winner, Percy 1899-1974 Obituary ... 45-48
Winner, Thomas G(ustav) 1917- ... CANR-15
Earlier sketch in CA 37-40R
Winner, Viola Hopkins 1928- ... CANR-4
Earlier sketch in CA 53-56
Winnett, Fred Victor 1903- ... 37-40R
Winnett, Thomas 1921- ... CANR-22
Earlier sketches in CA 61-64, CANR-7
Winnick, Karen B(eth) B(inkoff) 1946- ... 73-76
Winnicott, Donald (Woods) 1896-1971 ... CAP-1
Earlier sketch in CA 13-14
Winnifrith, Thomas John 1938- ... 108
Winnikoff, Albert 1930- ... 29-32R
Winnington, Alan 1910(?)-1983 Obituary ... 111
Winokur, Joan Gelman 1935- ... 41-44R
Winokur, Stephen 1941- ... 89-92
Winold, Allen 1929- ... 17-18R
Winsberg, Morton D. 1930- ... 15-16R
Winsborough, Hal (Liman) H. 1932- ... 11-12R
Winsett, Marvin Davis 1902- ... 3R
Winship, Elizabeth 1921- ... 41-44R
Winship, Laurence Leathe 1890-1975
Obituary ... 104
Winslade, William J(oseph) 1941- ... 118
Winslow, Dean Hendricks, Jr.
1934-1972 ... 37-40R
Obituary ... 41-44R
Winslow, Donald
See Zoll, Donald Atwell
Winslow, Gerald A. ... 109
Winslow, John Hathaway 1932- ... 37-40R
Winslow, Martha
See Rickett, Frances
Winslow, Ola Elizabeth 1885(?)-1977 ... CANR-3
Obituary ... 73-76
Earlier sketch in CA 2R
Winslow, Pauline Glen ... CANR-18
Earlier sketch in CA 101
Winslow, Pete
See Winslow, Dean Hendricks, Jr.
Winslow, Robert W(allace) 1940-
Brief entry ... 108
Winslow, Ron(ald A.) 1949- ... 103
Winslow, Thyra Samter 1893-1961
Obituary ... 89-92
Winslowe, John
See Richardson, Gladwell
Winslowe, John R.
See Richardson, Gladwell
Winsor, Justin 1831-1897 ... DLB-47
Winsor, Kathleen 1919- ... 97-100
Winsor, Mary P(ickard) 1943- ... 69-72
Winsor, Roy (William) 1912-1987 ... 65-68
Obituary ... 122
Winspear, Alban Dewes 1899- ... 45-48
Winspear, Violet 1928- ... 122
Winston, Alexander 1909- ... CAP-2
Earlier sketch in CA 25-28
Winston, Carl H. ... 2R
Winston, Clara 1921-1983 ... 25-28R
Obituary ... 113
See also SATA 39
Winston, Daoma 1922- ... CANR-1
Earlier sketch in CA 45-48
Winston, Douglas Garrett ... 41-44R
Winston, Eric V(on) A(rthur) 1942- ... 29-32R
Winston, Henry 1911-1986 Obituary ... 121
Winston, Kenneth I(rwin) 1940- ... 117
Winston, Krishna 1944- ... 104
Winston, Martin Bradley 1948- ... 118
Winston, Michael R(ussell) 1941- ... 113
Winston, Mike
See King, Florence
Winston, R(obert) A(lexander)
1907-1974 ... CAP-2
Obituary ... 49-52
Earlier sketch in CA 25-28
Winston, Richard 1917-1979 ... 25-28R
Obituary ... 93-96
Winston, Sarah 1912- ... 29-32R
Winstone, H(arry) V(ictor) F(rederick)
1926- ... CANR-21
Earlier sketch in CA 104
Wint, Guy 1910-1969 ... CANR-3
Earlier sketch in CA 2R
Winter, Abigail
See Schere, Monroe
Winter, Alice 1919- ... 15-16R
Winter, Bevis (Peter) 1918- ... CANR-8
Earlier sketch in CA 7-8R
Winter, Caryl 1944- ... 117
Winter, Colin O'Brien 1928-1981 Obituary ... 105
Winter, David Brian 1929- ... CANR-20
Earlier sketch in CA 103
Winter, David G(arrett) 1939- ... 57-60
Winter, Denis 1940- ... 118
Winter, Douglas E. 1950- ... 118
Winter, Edward H(enry) 1923- ... 1R
Winter, Elmer L(ouis) 1912- ... 13-14R
Winter, Gibson 1916- ... 49-52
Winter, Ginny Linville 1925- ... CANR-1
Earlier sketch in CA 4R
Winter, Gordon 1912- ... CANR-14
Earlier sketch in CA 77-80
Winter, Herbert R(einhold) 1928- ... 45-48
Winter, J(erry) Alan 1937- ... 41-44R
Winter, J. M. 1945- ... 73-76
Winter, John F. 1913- ... 104
Winter, Keith 1906-1983 Obituary ... 109
Winter, Klaus 1928- ... 29-32R
Winter, Leslie 1940- ... CANR-6
Earlier sketch in CA 1R
Winter, Michael Morgan 1930- ... CAP-1
Earlier sketch in CA 11-12
Winter, Milo (Kendall) 1888-1956 ... SATA-21
Winter, Nathan H. 1926- ... 21-22R
Winter, Paula Cecelia 1929- ... 107
See also SATA 48
Winter, R. R.
See Winterbotham, R(ussell) R(obert)
Winter, Ralph K(arl, Jr.) 1935- ... 122
Brief entry ... 118
Winter, Roger 1931- ... 37-40R
Winter, Ruth (Nancy G.) 1930- ... 37-40R
Winter, William D(avid) 1927- ... 25-28R
Winter, William O(rville) 1918- ... 49-52
Winterbotham, F(rederick) W(illiam)
1897- ... 57-60
Winterbotham, R(ussell) R(obert)
1904-1971 ... 3R
Obituary ... 103
See also SATA 10
Winterbotham, Russ
See Winterbotham, R(ussell) R(obert)
Winterfeld, Henry 1901- ... 77-80
Wintergreen, John P.
See Ryskind, Morrie
Wintergreen, Warren
See Adamson, Joseph III
Winterich, John 1891-1970 Obituary ... 29-32R
Winternitz, Emanuel 1898-1983 ... CANR-20
Obituary ... 110
Earlier sketch in CA 25-28R
Winterowd, W. Ross 1930- ... 17-18R
Winters, Anne 1939- ... 122
Winters, Bayla 1921- ... 21-22R
Winters, Bernice
See Winters, Bayla
Winters, Catherine (Mary) 1951- ... 118
Winters, Donald L(ee) 1935- ... 29-32R
Winters, Francis Xavier 1933- ... 61-64
Winters, Janet Lewis 1899- ... CAP-1
Earlier sketch in CA 9-10
Winters, John D(avid) 1917- ... 11-12R
Winters, Jon
See Cross, Gilbert B.
Winters, Marian 1924-1978 ... 101
Obituary ... 81-84
Winters, Marjorie
See Henri, Florette
Winters, Mike 1930- ... 119
Winters, Rosemary
See Breckler, Rosemary
Winters, Shelley
See Schrift, Shirley
Winters, (Arthur) Yvor 1900-1968 ... CAP-1
Obituary ... 25-28R
Earlier sketch in CA 11-12
See also DLB 48
See also CLC 4, 8, 32
Winterton, Gayle
See Adams, William Taylor
Winterton, Paul 1908- ... CANR-6
Earlier sketch in CA 5-6R
Winther, Barbara 1926- ... CANR-17
Earlier sketch in CA 97-100
Winther, Oscar Osburn 1903-1970 ... CANR-2
Earlier sketch in CA 3R
Winther, Sophus Keith 1893- ... 5-6R
Winthrop, Elizabeth
See Mahony, Elizabeth Winthrop
Winthrop, Henry 1910- ... 73-76
Winthrop, John 1588-1649 ... DLB-24, 30
Winthrop, John, Jr. 1606-1676 ... DLB-24
Wintle, Anne ... 29-32R
Wintle, Justin (Beecham) 1949- ... CANR-13
Earlier sketch in CA 77-80
Winton, Calhoun 1927- ... 11-12R
Winton, Chester Allen 1941- ... 89-92
Winton, Harry N(athaniel) M(cQuillian)
1907- ... 41-44R
Winton, John
See Pratt, John
Winton, Kate Barber 1882(?)-1974
Obituary ... 53-56
Wintrobe, Maxwell M(yer) 1901-1986
Obituary ... 121
Wintterle, John F(rancis) 1927- ... 29-32R
Wintz, Jack 1936- ... 109
Winwar, Frances 1900- ... 89-92
Winward, Stephen Frederick 1911- ... 11-12R
Winward, (Richard) Walter 1938- ... 105
Wippel, John Francis 1933- ... 114
Wippler, Migene Gonzalez
See Gonzalez-Wippler, Migene
Wirkus, Tom E(dward) 1933- ... 37-40R
Wirsing, Marie E(milia) 1931- ... 45-48
Wirt, Frederick Marshall 1924- ... 112
Wirt, Sherwood Eliot 1911- ... CANR-15
Earlier sketch in CA 41-44R
Wirt, William 1772-1834 ... DLB-37
Wirt, Winola Wells 1905(?)-1986 ... 93-96
Obituary ... 120
Wirtenberg, Patricia Z(arrella) 1932- ... 61-64
See also SATA 10
Wirth, Arthur G. 1919- ... CANR-10
Earlier sketch in CA 21-22R
Wirth, Beverly 1938- ... 118
Wirth, John D(avis) 1936- ... 29-32R
Wirth, Niklaus 1934- ... CANR-21
Earlier sketch in CA 105
Wirth, Thomas 1941- ... 117
Wirtz, (William) Willard 1912- ... 101
Wisberg, Aubrey ... 97-100
Wisberg, Marian Aline 1923- ... 109
Wisbeski, Dorothy (Gross) 1929- ... 11-12R
Wisbey, Herbert Andrew, Jr. 1919- ... 13-14R
Wisdom, (Arthur) John (Terence Dibben)
1904- ... 25-28R
Wisdom, Kenny
See Grogan, Emmett
Wisdome, Thomas
See Dunbar, Charles Stuart
Wise, Arthur 1923- ... 9-10R
Wise, Charles C(onrad), Jr. 1913- ... CANR-9
Earlier sketch in CA 21-22R
Wise, David 1930- ... CANR-2
Earlier sketch in CA 2R
Wise, Gene 1936- ... 93-96
Wise, Helen Dickerson 1928- Brief entry ... 106
Wise, Herbert H(erschel) 1928- ... 108
Wise, James Waterman 1901-1983
Obituary ... 111
Wise, John 1652-1725 ... DLB-24
Wise, John E(dward) 1905-1974 ... CAP-1
Obituary ... 49-52
Earlier sketch in CA 15-16
Wise, Leonard ... 77-80
Wise, Raymond L. 1895- ... 21-22R
Wise, S(ydney) F(rancis) 1924- ... CANR-16
Earlier sketch in CA 21-22R
Wise, Stephen S(amuel) 1874-1949
Brief entry ... 117
Wise, Terence 1935- ... 89-92
Wise, William 1923- ... CANR-6
Earlier sketch in CA 15-16R
See also SATA 4
Wise, Winifred E. ... 25-28R
See also SATA 2
Wisely, Rae 1938- ... 106
Wiseman, Adele 1928- ... 77-80
Wiseman, Ann (Sayre) 1926- ... CANR-9
Earlier sketch in CA 65-68
See also SATA 31
Wiseman, Anne Marie (Murray) 1932- ... 5-6R
Wiseman, B(ernard) 1922- ... CANR-24
Earlier sketches in CA 5-6R, CANR-8
See also SATA 4
Wiseman, Christopher S(tephen) 1936- ... 113
Wiseman, David 1916- ... 109
See also SATA 40, 43
Wiseman, Donald John 1918- ... 89-92
Wiseman, Francis Jowett 1905- ... CAP-1
Earlier sketch in CA 13-14
Wiseman, Frederick 1930- ... CLC-20
Wiseman, James R(ichard) 1934- ... CANR-1
Earlier sketch in CA 45-48
Wiseman, Robert F(rederick) 1935- ... 77-80
Wiseman, T(imothy) P(eter) 1940- ... CANR-18
Earlier sketches in CA 45-48, CANR-1
Wiseman, Thomas 1931- ... 25-28R
Wiser, William ... 37-40R
Wish, Harvey 1909-1968 ... CANR-3
Earlier sketch in CA 2R
Wishard, Armin 1941- ... 37-40R
Wishart, David J(ohn) 1946- ... 124
Brief entry ... 118
Wishart, E(rnest) E(dward) 1902-1987
Obituary ... 123
Wishart, Henry
See Shepherd, Robert Henry Wishart
Wiskemann, Elizabeth ?-1971 Obituary ... 111
Wisler, G(ary) Clifton 1950- ... SATA-46
Wisler, Gene C(harles) 1920- ... 11-12R
Wisloff, Carl Johan Fredrik 1908- ... CAP-1
Earlier sketch in CA 13-14
Wismer, Donald (Richard) 1946- ... 109
Wisner, Bill
See Wisner, William L.
Wisner, George 1812-1849 ... DLB-43
Wisner, William L. 1914(?)-1983 ... 111
Obituary ... 110
See also SATA 42
Wisneski, Henry 1940- ... 57-60
Wisse, Ruth R(oskies) 1936- ... 37-40R
Wissmann, Ruth Leslie ... CANR-2
Earlier sketch in CA 7-8R
Wister, John C(aspar) 1887-1982
Obituary ... 109
Wister, Owen 1860-1938 Brief entry ... 108
See also DLB 9
See also TCLC 21
Wistrich, Robert Solomon 1945- ... 107
Wiswall, F(rank) L(awrence), Jr. 1939- ... 29-32R
Wiswell, Ella Lury 1909- ... 111
Wiswell, Thomas George 1910- ... CANR-2
Earlier sketch in CA 7-8R
Wiswell, Tom
See Wiswell, Thomas George
Witchel, Dinah B(rown) 1936- ... 105
Witcover, Jules 1927- ... 25-28R
Witcutt, William Purcell 1907- ... CAP-1
Earlier sketch in CA 11-12
Witemeyer, Hugh 1939- ... 25-28R
Witham, (Phillip) Ross 1917- ... 105
See also SATA 37
Witham, W(illiam) Tasker 1914- ... 15-16R
Witheford, Hubert 1921- ... 102
Witheridge, Elizabeth P(lumb) 1907- ... 97-100
Withers, Carl A. 1900-1970 ... 73-76
See also SATA 14
Withers, E. L.
See Potter, G(eorge) W(illiam) (Jr.)
Withers, Josephine 1938- ... 101
Withers, Sara Cook 1924- ... 17-18R
Withers, William 1905-1987 ... 13-14R
Obituary ... 121
Witherspoon, Frances 1887(?)-1973
Obituary ... 45-48
Witherspoon, Irene Murray 1913- ... CANR-1
Earlier sketch in CA 4R
Witherspoon, John 1723-1794 ... DLB-31
Witherspoon, Mary Elizabeth 1919- ... 77-80
Witherspoon, Naomi Long
See Madgett, Naomi Long
Witherspoon, Thomas E. 1934- ... 81-84
Withey, J(oseph) A(nthony) 1918- ... 25-28R
Withim, Gloria 1929- ... 112

Withington, William Adriance 1924- CANR-14
Earlier sketch in CA 41-44R
Withrow, Dorothy E. 1910- 21-22R
Witkacy
See Witkiewicz, Stanislaw Ignacy
Witke, Roxane 1938- 69-72
Witker, Kristi 77-80
Witkiewicz, Stanislaw Ignacy 1885-1939
Brief entry 105
See also TCLC 8
Witkin, Erwin 1926- 37-40R
Witkin, Herman A. 1916-1979 .... CANR-1
Earlier sketch in CA 2R
Witkin, Lee D(aniel) 1935-1984 Obituary ... 114
Witkin-Lanoil, Georgia Hope 1943- 120
Witmer, Helen L(eland) 1898-1979 ...... CAP-2
Obituary 89-92
Earlier sketch in CA 25-28
Witt, Harold (Vernon) 1923- CANR-17
Earlier sketches in CA 3R, CANR-1
Witt, Howell Arthur John 1920- 109
Witt, Hubert 1935- CANR-12
Earlier sketch in CA 65-68
Witt, James F. 1937- 89-92
Witt, John (Clermont) 1907-1982
Obituary 106
Witt, Reginald Eldred 1907-1980 ....37-40R
Obituary 97-100
Witt, Shirley Hill 1934- CANR-5
Earlier sketch in CA 53-56
See also SATA 17
Witte, Ann Dryden 1942- 107
Witte, Glenna Finley 1925- CANR-10
Earlier sketch in CA 15-16R
See also AITN 1
Witte, John 1948- 93-96
Wittels, Harriet Joan 1938- 107
See also SATA 31
Witten, Herbert F. 1920- 5-6R
Witten, Ian H(ugh) 1947- 111
Wittenberg, Judith Bryant 1938- 102
Wittenberg, Philip 1895-1987 .... CAP-2
Obituary 122
Earlier sketch in CA 23-24
Wittenberg, Rudolph M. 1906-1986 ... CANR-22
Earlier sketch in CA 69-72
Wittermans, Elizabeth (Pino) 17-18R
Witters, Weldon L. 1929- 93-96
Wittgenstein, Ludwig (Josef Johann)
1889-1951 Brief entry 113
Wittich, Claus 1932- 113
Wittich, Walter A(rno) 1910- 49-52
Wittig, Alice J(osephine) 1929- 101
Wittig, Monique 1935- Brief entry 116
See also CLC 22
Witting, Clifford 1907- 4R
Wittke, Carl (Frederick) 1892-1971
Obituary 29-32R
Wittkofski, Joseph Nicholas 1912- 9-10R
Wittkower, Rudolf 1901-1971 Obituary ...33-36R
Wittkowski, Wolfgang 1925- CANR-24
Earlier sketches in CA 61-64, CANR-8
Wittliff, William D. 1940- 123
Wittlin, Alma S(tephanie) 45-48
Wittlin, Jozef 1896-1976 .... CANR-3
Obituary 65-68
Earlier sketch in CA 49-52
See also CLC 25
Wittlin, Thaddeus (Andrew) 1909- CANR-2
Earlier sketch in CA 45-48
Wittman, Sally (Anne Christensen) 1941- ... 107
See also SATA 30
Wittmer, Joe 1937- 45-48
Wittner, Lawrence S(tephen) 1941- 25-28R
Witton, Dorothy 73-76
Witton-Davies, Carl(yle) 1913- 9-10R
Wittreich, Joseph Anthony, Jr. 1939- .. CANR-12
Earlier sketch in CA 29-32R
Wittrock, M(erlin) C(arl) 1931- CANR-2
Earlier sketch in CA 49-52
Wittwer, Sylvan Harold 1917- 114
Witty, Helen E. S(troop) 1921- 105
Witty, Paul 1898-1976 73-76
Obituary 65-68
See also SATA 30, 50
Witty, Robert G(ee) 1906- CAP-2
Earlier sketch in CA 23-24
Witucke, Virginia 1937- 37-40R
Witze, Claude 1909(?)-1977 Obituary 73-76
Wixman, Ronald 1947- 122
Wixom, Hartt 1933- 120
Wizard, Mariann G(arner) 1946- 37-40R
Wobbe, R(oland) A(rthur) 1938- 102
Woddis, Hillel Chayim Keith 1914-
Brief entry 114
Woddis, Jack
See Woddis, Hillel Chayim Keith
Wodehouse, Lawrence 1934- CANR-19
Earlier sketches in CA 53-56, CANR-4
Wodehouse, P(elham) G(renville)
1881-1975 .... CANR-3
Obituary 57-60
Earlier sketch in CA 45-48
See also SATA 22
See also DLB 34
See also CLC 1, 2, 5, 10, 22
See also AITN 2
Woden, George
See Slaney, George Wilson
Wodge, Dreary
See Gorey, Edward (St. John)
Wodhams, (Herbert) Jack 1931- 115
Woebcke, Mary-Jane 1933- 25-28R
Woehr, Richard (Arthur) 1942- 57-60
Woehrlin, William F(rederick) 1928- 45-48
Woelfel, James W(arren) 1937- 41-44R
Woelfl, Paul A(loysius) 1913- 17-18R
Woerner, Karl Heinrich 1910-1969
Obituary 110
Woessner, Nina C. 1933- 29-32R
Woessner, Warren (Dexter) 1944- CANR-14
Earlier sketch in CA 37-40R
Woestemeyer, Ina Faye
See Van Noppen, Ina (Faye)
W(oestemeyer)
Woetzel, Robert K(urt) 1930- CANR-6
Earlier sketch in CA 5-6R
Wofford, Azile (May) 1896- 5-6R
Wofsey, Marvin M(ilton) 1913- 105
Wogaman, J(ohn) Philip 1932- CANR-20
Earlier sketch in CA 25-28R
Wogaman, Philip
See Wogaman, J(ohn) Philip
Wohl, Gerald 1934- 19-20R
Wohl, James P(aul) 1937- 77-80
Wohl, Paul 1901(?)-1985 Obituary 115
Wohl, Robert 1936- 104
Wohlberg, Meg 1905- SATA-41
Wohlgelernter, Maurice 1921- CANR-6
Earlier sketch in CA 15-16R
Wohl-Musciny, Ludwig von
See de Wohl, Louis
Wohlmuth, Ed 1935- 124
Wohlrabe, Raymond A. 1900-1977 ..... CANR-3
Earlier sketch in CA 4R
See also SATA 4
Woititz, Janet G. CANR-19
Earlier sketch in CA 101
Woito, Robert (Severin) 1937- 120
Woiwode, L.
See Woiwode, Larry (Alfred)
Woiwode, Larry (Alfred) 1941- CANR-16
Earlier sketch in CA 73-76
See also DLB 6
See also CLC 6, 10
Wojciechowska, Maia (Teresa) 1927- CANR-4
Earlier sketch in CA 11-12R
See also SATA 1, 28
See also SAAS 1
See also CLC 26
See also CLR 1
Wojtyla, Karol
See John Paul II, Pope
Wolberg, Lewis Robert 1905-1988 .... CANR-19
Obituary 124
Earlier sketches in CA 45-48, CANR-2
Wolcott, Harry F(letcher) 1929- 65-68
Wolcott, Leonard Thompson CANR-11
Earlier sketch in CA 13-14R
Wolcott, Patty 1929- 57-60
See also SATA 14
Wolcott, Roger 1679-1767 .... DLB-24
Wold, Allen L. 1943- CANR-22
Earlier sketch in CA 105
Wold, Jo Anne 1938- 61-64
See also SATA 30
Wold, Marguerite Hurrey 1914- 53-56
Wold, Ruth 1923- 37-40R
Woldendorp, R(ichard) 1927- CANR-12
Earlier sketch in CA 29-32R
Woldin, Beth Weiner 1955- 102
See also SATA 34
Woldin, Judd 1925- Brief entry 122
Wolf, Adolf Hungry
See Hungry Wolf, Adolf
Wolf, Arnold Jacob 1924- 29-32R
Wolf, Arnold Veryl 1916-1975 Obituary 104
Wolf, Barbara Herrman 1932- 57-60
Wolf, Bernard 1930- Brief entry 115
See also SATA 37
Wolf, Charlotte (Elizabeth) 1926- 29-32R
Wolf, Christa 1929- 85-88
See also CLC 14, 29
Wolf, Deborah Goleman 1938- 97-100
Wolf, Donald J(oseph) 1929- 13-14R
Wolf, Edwin II 1911- CANR-4
Earlier sketch in CA 2R
Wolf, Eric R(obert) 1923- 19-20R
Wolf, Frank 1940- 57-60
Wolf, Frank L(ouis) 1924- 57-60
Wolf, Fred Alan 1934- 115
Wolf, Frederick
See Dempewolff, Richard F(rederic)
Wolf, George 1890(?)-1980 Obituary 97-100
Wolf, George D(ugan) 1923- 29-32R
Wolf, Harold A. 1923- 15-16R
Wolf, Harvey 1935- 57-60
Wolf, Hazel Catharine 1907- 7-8R
Wolf, Herbert C(hristian) 1923- 15-16R
Wolf, Jack C(lifford) 1922- 57-60
Wolf, Jacqueline 1928- 109
Wolf, John B(aptist) 1907- 11-12R
Wolf, Karl E(verett) 1921- 17-18R
Wolf, Leonard 1923- CANR-3
Earlier sketch in CA 49-52
Wolf, Marguerite Hurrey 1914- 53-56
Wolf, Marvin J(ules) 1941- 117
Wolf, Michael D(avid) 1953- 121
Wolf, Miriam Bredow 1895- CAP-1
Earlier sketch in CA 9-10
Wolf, Peter (Michael) 1935- 53-56
Wolf, Ray 1948- 107
Wolf, Robert Charles 1955- 109
Wolf, Thomas H(oward) 1916- 69-72
Wolf, William 103
Wolf, William B. 1920- CANR-10
Earlier sketch in CA 19-20R
Wolf, William C(harles), Jr. 1933- 41-44R
Wolf, William J(ohn) 1918- 111
Wolfbein, Seymour L(ouis) 1915- CANR-6
Earlier sketch in CA 13-14R
Wolfe, Alan 1942- 108
Wolfe, Alvin William 1928- 2R
Wolfe, Bernard 1915-1985 .... CANR-3
Obituary 117
Earlier sketch in CA 3R
Wolfe, Bertram D(avid) 1896-1977 ....7-8R
Obituary 69-72
Wolfe, Burton H. 1932- 25-28R
See also SATA 5
Wolfe, Charles Keith 1943- CANR-15
Earlier sketch in CA 77-80
Wolfe, Christopher (F.) 1949- 123
Wolfe, Don Marion 1902-1976 Obituary ...65-68
Wolfe, (George) Edgar 1906- CAP-2
Earlier sketch in CA 25-28
Wolfe, Elizabeth
See Lederer, Paul Joseph
Wolfe, Gene (Rodman) 1931- CANR-6
Earlier sketch in CA 57-60
See also DLB 8
See also CLC 25
Wolfe, George Willoughby (Hooper)
1894(?)-1983 Obituary 111
Wolfe, Gerard R(aymond) 1926- CANR-11
Earlier sketch in CA 69-72
Wolfe, Harry Deane 1901-1975 ....41-44R
Wolfe, Harvey 1938- 45-48
Wolfe, Henry C. 1898(?)-1976 Obituary ...69-72
Wolfe, Herbert S(now) 1898- CAP-1
Earlier sketch in CA 15-16
Wolfe, J(ames) N(athan) 1927-1988
Obituary 124
Wolfe, James H(astings) 1934- 93-96
Wolfe, John N. 1910(?)-1974 Obituary 53-56
Wolfe, Josephine Brace 1917- 7-8R
Wolfe, Louis 1905- CANR-3
Earlier sketch in CA 5-6R
See also SATA 8
Wolfe, Martin 1920- 37-40R
Wolfe, Michael 1945- 123
Wolfe, Michael
See Williams, Gilbert M.
Wolfe, Peter (Bernard) 1929-1986
Obituary 121
Wolfe, Peter 1933- CANR-8
Earlier sketch in CA 21-22R
Wolfe, Randolph 1946- CANR-20
Earlier sketch in CA 104
Wolfe, Richard J(ames) 1928- 110
Wolfe, Rinna (Evelyn) 1925- 105
See also SATA 38
Wolfe, Ron 1945- 109
Wolfe, Roy I. 1917- 13-14R
Wolfe, Thomas (Clayton) 1900-1938
Brief entry 104
See also DLB 9
See also DLBY 85
See also DLBD 2
See also TCLC 4, 13
Wolfe, Thomas Kennerly, Jr. 1931- CANR-9
Earlier sketch in CA 15-16R
Wolfe, Thomas W. 1914- 93-96
Wolfe, Tom
See Wolfe, Thomas Kennerly, Jr.
See also CLC 1, 2, 9, 15, 35
See also AITN 2
Wolfe, (William) Willard 1936- 93-96
Wolfe, Winifred 1929-1981 .... CANR-10
Obituary 105
Earlier sketch in CA 17-18R
Wolfenden, George
See Beardmore, George
Wolfenden, John Frederick 1906-1985 106
Obituary 114
Wolfenstein, E. Victor 1940- 21-22R
Wolfenstein, Martha 1911(?)-1976
Obituary 69-72
Wolfert, Helen 1904- CAP-2
Earlier sketch in CA 17-18
Wolff, Anthony 1938- 49-52
Wolff, (Jenifer) Ashley 1956- 118
See also SATA 50
Wolff, Charlotte 1904-1986 .... CANR-15
Obituary 120
Earlier sketch in CA 37-40R
Wolff, Cynthia Griffin 1936- 49-52
Wolff, David
See Maddow, Ben
Wolff, Diane 1945- 77-80
See also SATA 27
Wolff, Ernst, 1910- 73-76
Wolff, Geoffrey (Ansell) 1937- 29-32R
See also CLC 41
Wolff, Helen 1906- 117
Brief entry 113
Wolff, Janet 1943- 77-80
Wolff, Janet L(oeb) 1924- 5-6R
Wolff, John U(lrich) 1932- CANR-18
Earlier sketch in CA 102
Wolff, Jurgen M(ichael) 1948- 57-60
Wolff, Konrad (Martin) 1907- 37-40R
Wolff, Kurt H(einrich) 1912- CANR-17
Earlier sketches in CA 49-52, CANR-1
Wolff, Maritta 1918- 17-18R
Wolff, Mary Evaline 1887-1964 Obituary 116
Wolff, Michael 1930- CANR-19
Earlier sketch in CA 25-28R
Wolff, Miles 1945- CANR-14
Earlier sketch in CA 73-76
Wolff, Richard D(avid) 1942- 73-76
Wolff, Robert Jay 1905-1977 ....25-28R
Obituary 73-76
See also SATA 10
Wolff, Robert Lee 1915-1980 Obituary 102
Wolff, Robert Paul 1933- 103
Wolff, Ruth 1909(?)-1972 Obituary 37-40R
Wolff, Sonia
See Levitin, Sonia (Wolff)
Wolff, Tobias (Jonathan Ansell) 1945- 117
Brief entry 114
See also CLC 39
Wolff, Victoria 1910- 111
Wolff, Virginia Euwer 1937- 107
Wolffe, B. P.
See Wolffe, Bertram (Percy)
Wolffe, Bertram (Percy) 1923(?)-1988
Obituary 124
Wolff-Salin, Mary 1932- 122
Wolfgang, Marvin E(ugene) 1924- 7-8R
Wolfinger, Raymond E(dwin) 1931-
Brief entry 112
Wolfle, Dael (Lee) 1906- 49-52
Wolfman, Augustus 1908(?)-1974
Obituary 53-56
Wolfman, Bernard 1924- 41-44R
Wolf-Phillips, Leslie 1929- 23-24R
Wolfram, Walter A. 1941- 29-32R
Wolfskill, George 1921- CANR-1
Earlier sketch in CA 2R
Wolfson, Harry Austryn 1887-1974 ...... CAP-2
Obituary 53-56
Earlier sketch in CA 19-20
Wolfson, Murray 1927- 17-18R
Wolfson, P(incus) J. 1903- 7-8R
Wolfson, Randy M(eyers) 1952- 120
Wolfson, Robert J(oseph) 1925- 93-96
Wolfson, Susan 1947- 120
Wolfson, Victor 1910- 33-36R
Wolgast, Elizabeth H(ankins) 1929- 113
Wolgensinger, Bernard 1935- 37-40R
Wolins, Leroy 1927- 107
Wolitzer, Hilma 1930- CANR-18
Earlier sketch in CA 65-68
See also SATA 31
See also CLC 17
Wolitzer, Meg 1959- CANR-18
Earlier sketch in CA 107
Wolk, Allan 1936- 77-80
Wolkers, Jan (Hendrik) 1925- Brief entry ... 116
Wolkoff, Judie (Edwards) Brief entry 115
See also SATA 37
Wolkstein, Diane 1942- CANR-14
Earlier sketch in CA 37-40R
See also SATA 7
Woll, Peter 1933- 15-16R
Wollaston, Nicholas 1926- 25-28R
Wolle, Muriel Sibell 1898- CAP-1
Earlier sketch in CA 13-14
Wollheim, Donald A(llen) 1914- CANR-19
Earlier sketches in CA 4R, CANR-1
Wollheim, Richard Arthur 1923- 101
Wollman, Nathaniel 1915- Brief entry 106
Wollstonecraft, Mary 1759-1797 .... DLB-39
Wolman, Benjamin B. 1908- CANR-11
Earlier sketch in CA 15-16R
Wolman, Harold L. 1942- 37-40R
Wolman, William 1927- 2R
Wolny, P.
See Janeczko, Paul B(ryan)
Woloch, Isser 1937- CANR-12
Earlier sketch in CA 29-32R
Woloszynowski, Julian 1898-1978
Obituary 85-88
Wolozin, Harold 1920- 37-40R
Wolpe, Joseph 1915- 17-18R
Wolpert, Stanley A(lbert) 1927- CANR-15
Earlier sketch in CA 23-24R
Wolrige Gordon, Anne 1936- 103
Wolsch, Robert Allen 1925- 57-60
Wolseley, Roland E. 1904- CANR-17
Earlier sketches in CA 2R, CANR-1
Wolsk, David 1930- 23-24R
Wolstein, Benjamin 1922- 11-12R
Wolter, Allan B(ernard) 1913- 106
Wolters, O(liver) W(illiam) 1915- 21-22R
Wolters, Raymond 1938- 29-32R
Wolters, Richard A. 1920- CANR-18
Earlier sketches in CA 7-8R, CANR-3
See also SATA 35
Wolterstorff, Nicholas Paul 1932- 69-72
Woltman, Frederick (Enos) 1905-1970
Obituary 89-92
Wolverton, Robert E(arl) 1925- 37-40R
Wolz, Henry G(eorge) 1905- 106
Womack, Brantly 1947- 114
Womack, David A(lfred) 1933- CANR-7
Earlier sketch in CA 53-56
Womack, Don (L.) 1922- 25-28R
Womack, John, Jr. 1937- 45-48
Womble, Vernon G. 1942(?)-1979
Obituary 89-92
Womer, Frank B(urton) 1921- 45-48
Womersley, Peter (John Walter) 1941- 118
Won, Ko
See Ko, Won
Wonder, Alvin
See Lourie, Dick
Wonder, Stevie
See Morris, Steveland Judkins
See also CLC 12
Wonders, Anne
See Passel, Anne W(onders)
Wonders, William C(lare) 1924- 41-44R
Wondriska, William 1931- CANR-4
Earlier sketch in CA 4R
See also SATA 6
Wong, Bing W. 1922- 73-76
Wong, Jade Snow 1922- 109
See also CLC 17
Wong, Lin Ken 1931- 13-14R
Wong, May 1944- 25-28R
Wong, Molly 1920- 93-96
Wong, Roderick 1932- 65-68
Wonnacott, Paul 1933- 21-22R

Wonnacott, Ronald J(ohnston) 1930- ... CANR-14
Earlier sketch in CA 29-32R
Wonnacott, Thomas H(erbert) 1935- ... CANR-14
Earlier sketch in CA 45-48
Wood, A(rthur) Skevington 1916- ... CANR-18
Earlier sketches in CA 11-12R, CANR-3
Wood, Abigail
See Marks, Jane (A. Steinberg)
Wood, Allen Tate 1947- ... 97-100
Wood, Allen W(illiam) 1942- ... CANR-17
Earlier sketch in CA 29-32R
Wood, Audrey ... SATA-44, 50
Wood, Audrey 1905-1985 Obituary ... 118
Wood, Barbara 1947- ... CANR-15
Earlier sketch in CA 85-88
Wood, Bari 1936- ... CANR-13
Earlier sketch in CA 81-84
Wood, Barry 1940- ... 29-32R
Wood, Benjamin 1820-1900 Brief entry ... 120
See also DLB 23
Wood, Bruce 1943- ... 57-60
Wood, Bryce 1909-1985(?) ... CANR-19
Earlier sketch in CA 2R
Wood, Catherine
See Etchison, Birdie L(ee)
Wood, Charles Gerald 1932- ... 106
See also DLB 13
Wood, Charles Osgood III 1933- ... 109
Wood, Charles T(uttle) 1933- ... 17-18R
Wood, Chauncey 1935- ... 37-40R
Wood, Christopher (Hovelle) 1935- ... 29-32R
Wood, Christopher 1941- ... 103
Wood, Clement Biddle 1925- ... 21-22R
Wood, David 1944- ... 97-100
Wood, David (Bowne) 1945- ... 93-96
Wood, David M(ichael) 1934- Brief entry ... 109
Wood, Derek Harold 1930- ... CANR-16
Earlier sketch in CA 93-96
Wood, Don 1945- ... SATA-44, 50
Wood, Donald 1926- ... 45-48
Wood, Donna (Marie) 1949- ... CANR-18
Earlier sketch in CA 97-100
Wood, Dorothy Adkins 1912-1975 ... CANR-6
Earlier sketch in CA 13-14R
Wood, E(dward) Rudolf 1907- ... CANR-3
Earlier sketch in CA 11-12R
Wood, Edgar A(llardyce) 1907- ... 77-80
See also SATA 14
Wood, Elizabeth A(rmstrong) 1912- ... 25-28R
Wood, Esther
See Brady, Esther Wood
Wood, Forrest G(len) 1931- ... 25-28R
Wood, Frances Elizabeth ... 107
See also SATA 34
Wood, Fred M. 1921- ... CANR-10
Earlier sketch in CA 15-16R
Wood, Frederic C(onger), Jr. 1932-1970 ... CAP-2
Earlier sketch in CA 25-28
Wood, Frederick Thomas 1905- ... CANR-5
Earlier sketch in CA 7-8R
Wood, G(eorge) R(obert) Harding
1878-1968 ... CAP-1
Earlier sketch in CA 9-10
Wood, Gordon R(eid) 1913- ... 77-80
Wood, Gordon S(tewart) 1933- ... 25-28R
Wood, Harley Weston 1911- ... 109
Wood, Harold A(rthur) 1921- ... 19-20R
Wood, (Elizabeth) Harriet Harvey
See Harvey Wood, (Elizabeth) Harriet
Wood, Herbert Fairlie 1914-1967 ... 110
Obituary ... 108
Wood, James 1889(?)-1975 Obituary ... 57-60
Wood, James (Alexander Fraser)
1918-1984 ... CANR-16
Earlier sketches in CA 2R, CANR-1
Wood, James E(dward), Jr. 1922- ... CANR-12
Earlier sketch in CA 29-32R
Wood, James L(eslie) 1941- ... CANR-8
Earlier sketch in CA 57-60
Wood, James Playsted 1905- ... CANR-3
Earlier sketch in CA 9-10R
See also SATA 1
Wood, Janet L(ouise) Sims
See Sims-Wood, Janet L(ouise)
Wood, John Armstead, Jr. 1932-
Brief entry ... 108
Wood, John Thomas 1939- ... 77-80
Wood, Joyce 1928- ... 25-28R
Wood, June S(mallwood) 1931- ... 61-64
Wood, Kenneth 1922- ... CANR-11
Earlier sketch in CA 69-72
Wood, Kerry
See Wood, Edgar A(llardyce)
Wood, Kirk
See Stahl, Le Roy
Wood, Larry
See Wood, Marylaird
Wood, Laura N.
See Roper, Laura Wood
Wood, Lee Blair 1893-1982 Obituary ... 106
Wood, Leland Foster 1885- ... 2R
Wood, Leon J(ames) 1918-1976 ... 29-32R
Wood, Leonard C(lair) 1923- ... 37-40R
Wood, Leslie A(lfred) 1930- ... 29-32R
Wood, (James) Lew(is) 1928- ... 65-68
Wood, Linda C(arol) 1945- ... 110
Wood, Lorna 1913- ... 69-72
Wood, Margaret (L. E.) 1910- ... 13-14R
Wood, Margaret I(sabel) 1926- ... 97-100
Wood, Marion N(ewman) 1909- ... 61-64
Wood, Mary 1915- ... 23-24R
Wood, Marylaird ... CANR-21
Earlier sketch in CA 81-84
Wood, Maurice Arthur Ponsonby 1916- ... 109
Wood, Michael 1936- ... 37-40R
Wood, Mrs. Henry 1814-1887 ... DLB-18
Wood, Nancy 1936- ... CANR-9
Earlier sketch in CA 21-22R
See also SATA 6
Wood, Neal (Norman) 1922- ... 2R
Wood, Pat
See Baxter, Patricia E. W.
Wood, Paul W(inthrop) 1922- ... 61-64
Wood, Peggy 1892-1978 Obituary ... 77-80
Wood, Peter 1930- ... 93-96
Wood, Phyllis Anderson 1923- ... CANR-14
Earlier sketch in CA 37-40R
See also SATA 30, 33
Wood, R(ichard) Coke 1905-1979 ... CANR-7
Earlier sketch in CA 53-56
Wood, Ramsay 1943- ... 103
Wood, Raymund F(rancis) 1911- ... 61-64
Wood, Robert Coldwell 1923- ... 3R
Wood, Robert L. 1925- ... 23-24R
Wood, Robert Paul 1931- ... CANR-5
Earlier sketch in CA 53-56
Wood, Robert S(tephen) 1938- ... CANR-7
Earlier sketch in CA 57-60
Wood, Robin
See Wood, Robert Paul
Wood, Ruth C. ... 37-40R
Wood, Sara
See Bowen-Judd, Sara (Hutton)
Wood, Serry
See Freeman, G(raydon) L(a Verne)
Wood, Susan 1946- ... 108
Wood, Sydney (Herbert) 1935- ... 112
Wood, Thomas W(esley), Jr. 1920- ... 81-84
Wood, Ursula
See Vaughan Williams, Ursula Wood
Wood, Wallace 1927-1981 Obituary ... 108
See also SATA 33
Wood, Walter Hunt, Sr. 1916(?)-1987
Obituary ... 124
Wood, William ... DLB-24
Wood, William P(reston) 1951- ... 118
Woodall, Corbet 1929(?)-1982 Obituary ... 106
Woodall, Ronald 1935- ... 73-76
Woodard, Bronte 1941(?)-1980 Obituary ... 101
Woodard, Carol 1929- ... 73-76
See also SATA 14
Woodard, Christopher R. 1913- ... 13-14R
Woodard, Gloria (Jean) H(iner) 1937- ... 45-48
Woodberry, Joan (Merle) 1921- ... CANR-6
Earlier sketch in CA 11-12R
Woodbridge, Benjamin 1622-1684 ... DLB-24
Woodbridge, Hensley Charles 1923- ... CANR-3
Earlier sketch in CA 9-10R
Woodbridge, Linda 1945- ... 118
Woodburn, Arthur 1890-1978 Obituary ... 108
Woodburn, John Henry 1914- ... CANR-4
Earlier sketch in CA 4R
See also SATA 11
Woodbury, Frank
See Chapman, Frank M(onroe)
Woodbury, Lael J(ay) 1927- ... 81-84
Woodbury, Marda 1925- ... CANR-17
Earlier sketch in CA 97-100
Woodbury, Mildred Fairchild 1894-1975
Obituary ... 57-60
Woodbury, Richard B(enjamin) 1917-
Brief entry ... 109
Woodcock, Bruce 1948- ... 119
Woodcock, George 1912- ... CANR-1
Earlier sketch in CA 3R
See also CAAS 6
Woodcott, Keith
See Brunner, John (Kilian Houston)
Wooden, Kenneth 1935- ... 81-84
Wooden, Wayne S(tanley) 1943- ... 109
Woodfield, William Read 1928- ... 9-10R
Woodford, Arthur M(acKinnon) 1940- ... CANR-7
Earlier sketch in CA 53-56
Woodford, Bruce P(owers) 1919- ... 57-60
Woodford, Frank B(ury) 1903-1967 ... CAP-1
Earlier sketch in CA 15-16
Woodford, Jack
See Woolfolk, Josiah Pitts
Woodford, Peggy 1937- ... 104
See also SATA 25
Woodforde, John 1925- ... CANR-10
Earlier sketch in CA 25-28R
Woodgate, Mildred Violet ... 11-12R
Woodham-Smith, Cecil (Blanche Fitzgerald)
1896-1977 ... 77-80
Obituary ... 69-72
Woodhead, Peter 1944- ... 124
Woodhouse, Barbara (Blackburn)
1910- ... CANR-13
Earlier sketch in CA 7-8R
Woodhouse, C(hristopher) M(ontague)
1917- Brief entry ... 108
Woodhouse, Charles Platten 1915- ... 105
Woodhouse, Edward J(ames) 1946- ... 117
Woodhouse, Martin (Charlton) 1932- ... CANR-16
Earlier sketch in CA 21-22R
Woodin, Ann Snow 1926- ... 13-14R
Woodin, Noel 1929- ... 4R
Wooding, Dan 1940- ... 102
Woodiwiss, Kathleen E(rin) 1939- ... CANR-23
Earlier sketch in CA 89-92
Wood-Legh, Kathleen Louise 1901-1981
Obituary ... 105
Woodley, Winifred
See Hedden, Worth Tuttle
Woodman, Anthony John 1945- ... CANR-23
Earlier sketches in CA 61-64, CANR-8
Woodman, Harold D. 1928- ... CANR-9
Earlier sketch in CA 23-24R
Woodman, James Monroe 1931- ... 17-18R
Woodman, Jim
See Woodman, James Monroe
Woodman, John E. 1932(?)-1983
Obituary ... 109
Woodman, Loring 1942- ... 45-48
Woodmason, Charles 1720(?)-? ... DLB-31
Woodrell, Daniel 1953- ... 121
Woodress, James (Leslie, Jr.) 1916- ... CANR-3
Earlier sketch in CA 5-6R
Woodrew, Greta 1930- ... 106
Woodrich, Mary Neville 1915- ... 25-28R
See also SATA 2
Woodring, Carl (Ray) 1919- ... 5-6R
Woodring, Paul (Dean) 1907- ... 17-18R
Woodrock, R. A.
See Cowlishaw, Ranson
Woodroffe, John
See Woodroffe, John George
Woodroffe, John George 1865-1936
Brief entry ... 121
Woodroof, Horace M(alcolm) 1906- ... CAP-2
Earlier sketch in CA 29-32
Woodruff, Archibald Mulford, Jr.
1912-1984 ... 105
Obituary ... 113
Woodruff, Asahel D(avis) 1904- ... 2R
Woodruff, J(ohn) Douglas 1897-1978 ... 107
Woodruff, John Douglas 1897-1978
Obituary ... 104
Woodruff, Judy (Carline) 1946- ... CANR-13
Earlier sketch in CA 73-76
Woodruff, Philip
See Mason, Philip
Woodruff, Sue (Carolyn) 1943- ... 117
Woodruff, William 1916- ... 101
Woodrum, Lon 1901- ... 104
Woods, B(obby) W(illiam) 1930- ... CANR-19
Earlier sketch in CA 25-28R
Woods, Clee 1893- ... 108
Woods, Constance
See McComb, K(atherine Woods)
Woods, Donald 1933- ... 121
Brief entry ... 114
Woods, Donald H. 1933- ... 25-28R
Woods, Elizabeth 1940- ... 101
Woods, Frederick 1932- ... CANR-7
Earlier sketch in CA 17-18R
Woods, George A(llan) 1926- ... 29-32R
See also SATA 30
Woods, Geraldine 1948- ... 97-100
See also SATA 42
Woods, Harold 1945- ... 97-100
See also SATA 42
Woods, Joan (LeSueur) 1932- ... 11-12R
Woods, John 1926- ... CANR-23
Earlier sketch in CA 13-14R
Woods, John (Hayden) 1937- ... CANR-11
Earlier sketch in CA 57-60
Woods, John A(ubin) 1927- ... 13-14R
Woods, John B(arrie) 1933- Brief entry ... 107
Woods, John David 1939- ... 37-40R
Woods, John E(dmund) 1938- ... 104
Woods, Kenneth F. 1930- ... 15-16R
Woods, L. B. 1938- ... 112
Woods, Lawrence
See Lowndes, Robert A(ugustine) W(ard)
Woods, Margaret 1921- ... 23-24R
See also SATA 2
Woods, Margaret S(taeger) 1911- ... 81-84
Woods, Nat
See Stratemeyer, Edward L.
Woods, Oliver (Frederick John Bradley)
1911-1972 Obituary ... 114
Woods, P. F.
See Bayley, Barrington J(ohn)
Woods, Pamela 1938- ... 106
Woods, Ralph L(ouis) 1904- ... CANR-2
Earlier sketch in CA 7-8R
Woods, Randall Bennett 1944- Brief entry ... 106
Woods, Richard (John) 1941- ... CANR-4
Earlier sketch in CA 53-56
Woods, Richard G(lenn) 1933- ... 109
Woods, Samuel H(ubert), Jr. 1926- ... 25-28R
Woods, Sara
See Bowen-Judd, Sara (Hutton)
Woods, Shadrach 1923-1973 Obituary ... 45-48
Woods, Sherryl 1944- ... 120
Woods, Shirley E(dwards), Jr. 1934- ... 119
Woods, Sister Frances Jerome 1913- ... 21-22R
Woods, Stockton
See Forrest, Richard S(tockton)
Woods, Stuart 1938- ... 93-96
Woods, William ... 77-80
Woods, William Crawford 1944- ... 29-32R
Woodside, Alexander Barton 1938- ... 123
Woodson, Carter G. 1875-1950 ... DLB-17
Woodson, Jack
See Woodson, John Waddie Jr.
Woodson, Jeff
See Oglesby, Joseph
Woodson, John Waddie Jr. 1913- ... SATA-10
Woodson, Leslie H(arold) 1929- ... 41-44R
Woodson, Meg
See Baker, Elsie
Woodson, Thomas (Miller) 1931- ... 104
Woodson, Wesley E(dward) 1918- ... 37-40R
Woodstone, Arthur ... 69-72
Woodward, Bob
See Woodward, Robert Upshur
Woodward, C(omer) Vann 1908- ... CANR-17
Earlier sketches in CA 5-6R, CANR-2
See also DLB 17
Woodward, Carl Raymond 1890-1974 ... 41-44R
Woodward, (Landon) Cleveland
1900-1986 ... SATA-10, 48
Woodward, Daniel Holt 1931- ... 37-40R
Woodward, David 1909-1986 Obituary ... 120
Woodward, David B(rainerd) 1918- ... 65-68
Woodward, David Reid 1939- ... 114
Woodward, E. L.
See Woodward, Ernest Llewellyn
Woodward, Ernest Llewellyn 1890-1971
Obituary ... 111
Woodward, G(eorge) W(illiam) O(tway)
1924- ... CANR-3
Earlier sketch in CA 7-8R
Woodward, Grace Steele 1899- ... CAP-1
Earlier sketch in CA 9-10
Woodward, Helen Beal 1914(?)-1982
Obituary ... 108
Woodward, Helen Rosen 1882- ... 7-8R
Woodward, Herbert N(orton) 1911- ... 65-68
Woodward, Hildegard 1898- ... 5-6R
Woodward, James B(rian) 1935- ... CANR-2
Earlier sketch in CA 49-52
Woodward, John (William) 1920- ... 21-22R
Woodward, John 1945- ... 113
Woodward, Lilian
See Marsh, John
Woodward, Llewellyn
See Woodward, Ernest Llewellyn
Woodward, Ralph Lee, Jr. 1934- ... 23-24R
Woodward, Robert H(anson) 1925- ... 17-18R
Woodward, Robert Upshur 1943- ... 69-72
Woodward, Stanley (Wingate) 1890- ... 5-6R
Woodward, Thomas B. 1937- ... 114
Woodward, W. Mary 1921- ... 45-48
Woodworth, Constance 1911-1983
Obituary ... 109
Woodworth, David (Perrin) 1932- ... 37-40R
Woodworth, G(eorge) Wallace
1902-1969 ... CAP-1
Earlier sketch in CA 15-16
Woodworth, G(eorge) Walter 1903- ... CAP-1
Earlier sketch in CA 19-20
Woodworth, Hugh (MacCallum)
1906-1978 Obituary ... 107
Woody, Regina Jones 1894- ... CANR-3
Earlier sketch in CA 5-6R
See also SATA 3
Woody, Robert H(enley) 1936- ... 93-96
Woody, Russell O(wen), Jr. 1934- ... 17-18R
Woodyard, David O. 1932- ... 23-24R
Woodyard, George 1934- ... 81-84
Woolard, Edgar 1899(?)-1978 Obituary ... 77-80
Wooldridge, Rhoda 1906- ... 77-80
See also SATA 22
Wooldridge, William C(harles) 1943- ... 45-48
Woolery, George W(illiam) 1931- ... 122
Wooley, John (Steven) 1949- ... 109
Woolf, Daniel J(ames) 1916- ... 7-8R
Woolf, Douglas 1922- ... CANR-2
Earlier sketch in CA 4R
Woolf, Harry 1923- ... CANR-1
Earlier sketch in CA 2R
Woolf, James Dudley 1914- ... 37-40R
Woolf, Leonard S(idney) 1880-1969 ... 7-8R
Obituary ... 25-28R
Woolf, Robert G(ary) 1928- ... 73-76
Woolf, S. J.
See Woolf, Stuart (Joseph)
Woolf, Stuart (Joseph) 1936- Brief entry ... 118
Woolf, (Adeline) Virginia 1882-1941
Brief entry ... 104
See also DLB 36
See also TCLC 1, 5, 20
Woolfe, H(arold) Geoffrey 1902- ... CAP-1
Earlier sketch in CA 11-12
Woolfenden, John R(ichards) 1904- ... 113
Woolfolk, Joanna Martine 1940- ... 110
Woolfolk, Josiah Pitts 1894-1971
Obituary ... 29-32R
Woolfolk, Robert L(ee IV) 1947-
Brief entry ... 112
Woolfolk, William 1917- ... 113
Woolgar, (George) Jack 1894- ... 17-18R
Woollam, William Gifford 1921- ... 11-12R
Woollcott, Alexander (Humphreys)
1887-1943 Brief entry ... 105
See also DLB 29
See also TCLC 5
Woolley, A(lban) E(dward, Jr.) 1926- ... CANR-14
Earlier sketch in CA 41-44R
Woolley, (Lowell) Bryan 1937- ... CANR-4
Earlier sketch in CA 49-52
Woolley, Catherine 1904- ... CANR-6
Earlier sketch in CA 2R
See also SATA 3
Woolley, Davis Collier 1908-1971
Obituary ... 116
Woolley, Geoffrey Harold 1892-1968 ... CAP-1
Earlier sketch in CA 11-12
Woolley, Herbert B(allantyne) 1917-1978
Obituary ... 81-84
Woolley, Richard van der Riet 1906-1986
Obituary ... 121
Woolley, (Alfred) Russell 1899- ... 7-8R
Woolman, David S. 1916- ... 29-32R
Woolman, John 1720-1772 ... DLB-31
Woolner, Frank 1916- ... 53-56
Woolner, Thomas 1825-1892 ... DLB-35
Woolrich, Cornell
See Hopley-Woolrich, Cornell George
Woolrych, Austin (Herbert) 1918- ... 2R
Woolsey, Arthur (Wallace) 1906- ... 45-48
Woolsey, Janette 1904- ... CANR-2
Earlier sketch in CA 4R
See also SATA 3
Woolsey, Sarah Chauncy 1835(?)-1905
Brief entry ... 115
See also DLB 42
Woolson, Constance Fenimore
1840-1894 ... DLB-12
Woolson, Roland S., Jr. 1930(?)-1977
Obituary ... 104
Woon, Basil 1894(?)-1974 Obituary ... 49-52

Wooster, Claire 1942- 101
Wooster, Ralph A(ncil) 1928- CANR-2
 Earlier sketch in CA 5-6R
Wooster, Robert 1956- 124
Wooten, James (Terrell) 1937- Brief entry .. 112
Wootten, Morgan 1931- 101
Wootters, John (Henry, Jr.) 1928- 113
Wootton, (Devere) Gareth 1937- 117
Wootton, (John) Graham (George)
 1917- CANR-10
 Earlier sketch in CA 7-8R
Worblefister, Petunia
 See Gribbin, Lenore S.
Worboys, Anne(tte Isobel) Eyre CANR-9
 Earlier sketch in CA 65-68
Worcester, Dean A(mory), Jr. 1918- 23-24R
Worcester, Donald E(mmet) 1915- CANR-19
 Earlier sketches in CA 2R, CANR-4
 See also SATA 18
Worcester, Gurdon Saltonstall 1897- CAP-1
 Earlier sketch in CA 11-12
Worcester, Joseph Emerson 1784-1865 .. DLB-1
Worchel, Stephen 1946- CANR-16
 Earlier sketch in CA 89-92
Worden, Alfred M(errill) 1932- 101
Worden, William L. 1910- CAP-1
 Earlier sketch in CA 15-16
Wordsworth, Jonathan 1932- CANR-20
 Earlier sketch in CA 29-32R
Worell, Judith 1928- CANR-7
 Earlier sketch in CA 57-60
Work, Robert E. 1928(?)-1986 Obituary 121
Work, Virginia 1946- 113
 See also SATA 45
Working, Russell (Craig) 1959- 124
Workman, Samuel K(linger) 1907- CAP-2
 Earlier sketch in CA 23-24
Workman, William D(ouglas), Jr. 1914- 5-6R
Works, John 1949- 123
Worland, Stephen T. 1923- 23-24R
Worley, Robert Cromwell 1929-
 Brief entry 108
Worline, Bonnie Bess 1914- 69-72
 See also SATA 14
Worlock, Derek John Harford 1920- 103
Worm, Piet 1909- 81-84
Wormald, Francis 1904(?)-1972 Obituary 104
Wormald, Jenny 1942- 112
Worman, Charles G(ordon) 1933- 119
Worman, Eli
 See Weil, Roman L(ee)
Wormell, Deborah 1946-1979 Obituary 114
Wormington, H(annah) M(arie) 1914- ... CANR-3
 Earlier sketch in CA 45-48
Wormley, Cinda
 See Kornblum, Cinda
Wormley, Stanton Lawrence 1909- CANR-12
 Earlier sketch in CA 73-76
Wormser, Baron Chesley 1948- 110
Wormser, Rene A(lbert) 1896-1981 .... CANR-11
 Obituary 104
 Earlier sketch in CA 15-16R
Wormser, Sophie 1897- 65-68
 See also SATA 22
Worner, Karl Heinrich
 See Woerner, Karl Heinrich
Woroniak, Alexander 1920- 41-44R
Woronoff, Jon 1938- CANR-11
 Earlier sketch in CA 29-32R
Worrall, Ambrose A(lexander) 1899-1972 . CAP-2
 Earlier sketch in CA 29-32
Worrall, Olga (Nathalie) 1906- 29-32R
Worrell, Albert C(adwallader) 1913- 37-40R
Worrell, Eric 1924-1987 Obituary 123
Worsley, Dale 1948- 104
Worsley, Gump
 See Worsley, Lorne (John)
Worsley, Lorne (John) 1929- Brief entry ... 111
Worster, Donald E(ugene) 1941- CANR-12
 Earlier sketch in CA 57-60
Worsthorne, Peregrine 1923- 45-48
Worswick, Clark 1940- 104
Worth, C. Brooke 1908- 101
Worth, Dean S(toddard) 1927- Brief entry .. 112
Worth, Douglas 1940- CANR-9
 Earlier sketch in CA 65-68
Worth, Fred L. 1943- 97-100
Worth, Helen 1913- 15-16R
Worth, Margaret
 See Strickland, Margot
Worth, Richard SATA-46
Worth, Sol 1922(?)-1977 81-84
 Obituary 73-76
Worth, Valerie
 See Bahlke, Valerie Worth
 See also SATA 8
Wortham, John David 1941- 37-40R
Worthen, Blaine Richard 1936- CANR-15
 Earlier sketch in CA 85-88
Worthington, Edgar Barton 1905- 109
Worthington, Janet Evans 1942- 115
Worthington, Marjorie (Muir)
 1898(?)-1976 .... CANR-2
 Obituary 65-68
 Earlier sketch in CA 1R
Worthington, Robin (Ann) 1932- 114
Worthley, Jean Reese 1925- 77-80
Worthy, James C(arson) 1910- 117
Worthy, Morgan 1936- 65-68
Worthylake, Mary Moore 1904- CANR-4
 Earlier sketch in CA 3R
Wortis, Avi 1937- CANR-12
 Earlier sketch in CA 69-72
 See also SATA 14
Wortley, Ben Atkinson 1907- 57-60
Wortman, Marlene Stein 1937- 112
Wortman, Max S(idones), Jr. 1932- ... CANR-16
 Earlier sketch in CA 23-24R
Wortman, Richard 1938- CANR-9
 Earlier sketch in CA 23-24R
Wortman, (Leo) Sterling 1923-1981
 Obituary 108
Worton, Stanley N(elson) 1923- 57-60
Woshinsky, Oliver Hanson 1939-
 Brief entry 109
Wosmek, Frances 1917- CANR-11
 Earlier sketch in CA 29-32R
 See also SATA 29
Woudenberg, Paul Richard 1927- 69-72
Woudhuysen, Jan Frank 1942- 107
Woudstra, Marten H. 1922- CANR-19
 Earlier sketch in CA 25-28R
Wouil, George
 See Slaney, George Wilson
Wouk, Herman 1915- CANR-6
 Earlier sketch in CA 5-6R
 See also DLBY 82
 See also CLC 1, 9, 38
Woy, James Bayly 1927- 15-16R
Woychuk, N(icholas) A(rthur) 1915- 13-14R
Woytinsky, Emma S(hadkhan)
 1893-1969 .... CAP-1
 Earlier sketch in CA 17-18
Woznicki, Andrew N(icholas) 1931- CANR-24
 Earlier sketch in CA 45-48
Wrage, Ernest J. 1911-1965 .... 2R
Wragg, David William 1946- CANR-4
 Earlier sketch in CA 53-56
Wragg, E(dward) C(onrad) 1938- CANR-23
 Earlier sketches in CA 57-60, CANR-8
Wraight, A(aron) Joseph 1913- 21-22R
Wreen, Michael 1950- 117
Wreford, James
 See Watson, J(ames) Wreford
Wren, Chris ?-1982 Obituary 108
Wren, Christopher S. 1936- 21-22R
Wren, Daniel Alan 1932- 41-44R
Wren, Ellaruth
 See Elkins, Ella Ruth
Wren, M. K.
 See Renfroe, Martha Kay
Wren, Melvin C(larence) 1910- 37-40R
Wren, Percival Christopher 1885-1941
 Brief entry 123
Wren, Robert Meriwether 1928- 106
Wren, Thomas Edward 1938- 77-80
Wren, Wilfrid John 1930- 109
Wrench, David F(razer) 1932- 41-44R
Wrench, (John) Evelyn (Leslie) 1882-1966 ..7-8R
Wrenn, John H(aughton) 1920- 2R
Wrenn, Robert L. 1933- 29-32R
Wrenn, Tony P(entecost) 1938- 89-92
Wrenn, Winnie Holden 1886(?)-1979
 Obituary 89-92
Wriggins, Sally Hovey 1922- 97-100
 See also SATA 17
Wriggins, W(illiam) Howard 1918- 61-64
Wright, A(nthony) Colin 1938- 120
Wright, A(mos) J(asper) 1952- 93-96
Wright, Alice E(dwards) 1905-1980 104
Wright, Andrew (Howell) 1923- 17-18R
Wright, Anna (Maria Louisa Perrott) Rose
 1890-1968 Obituary 109
 See also SATA 35
Wright, Arthur Frederick 1913-1976 77-80
 Obituary 69-72
Wright, Austin 1904- 61-64
Wright, Austin McGiffert 1922- CANR-4
 Earlier sketch in CA 3R
Wright, Barton A(llen) 1920- CANR-8
 Earlier sketch in CA 61-64
Wright, Basil Charles 1907-1987 105
 Obituary 123
Wright, Beatrice A(nn) 1917- CANR-12
 Earlier sketch in CA 21-22R
Wright, Benjamin Fletcher 1900-1976 77-80
 Obituary 69-72
Wright, Betty Ren SATA-48
Wright, Brooks 1922- 25-28R
Wright, Bruce S(tanley) 1912-1975 ...... CAP-2
 Earlier sketch in CA 19-20
Wright, Burton 1917- 81-84
Wright, Carolyne L(ee) 1949- 111
Wright, (Julia) Celeste Turner 1906- CAP-1
 Earlier sketch in CA 9-10
Wright, Charles (Penzel, Jr.) 1935- CANR-23
 Earlier sketch in CA 29-32R
 See also DLBY 82
 See also CLC 6, 13, 28
Wright, Charles Alan 1927- CANR-16
 Earlier sketches in CA 45-48, CANR-1
Wright, Charles David 1932-1978 104
Wright, Charles H(oward) 1918- 61-64
Wright, Charles R(obert) 1927- CANR-1
 Earlier sketch in CA 45-48
Wright, Charles Stevenson 1932- 11-12R
 See also DLB 33
Wright, Christopher 1926- 11-12R
Wright, Cobina ?-1970 Obituary 115
Wright, (Charles) Conrad 1917- 21-22R
Wright, Constance Choate 1897-1987 ....15-16R
 Obituary 121
Wright, Cynthia Challed 1953- 77-80
Wright, D(avid) G(ordon) 1937- 65-68
Wright, D(onald) I(an) 1934- CANR-3
 Earlier sketch in CA 49-52
Wright, Dare 1926(?)- 93-96
 See also SATA 21
Wright, David (John Murray) 1920- CANR-3
 Earlier sketch in CA 9-10R
 See also CAAS 5
Wright, David McCord 1909-1968 .... CAP-2
 Earlier sketch in CA 17-18
Wright, Deil S(pencer) 1930- 13-14R
Wright, Denis (Arthur Hepworth) 1911- 81-84
Wright, Don(ald Conway) 1934- CANR-20
 Earlier sketch in CA 104
Wright, Dorothy 1910- 13-14R
Wright, Edward A(rlington) 1906- 29-32R
Wright, Elizabeth Atwell 1919-1976
 Obituary 65-68
Wright, Enid Meadowcroft (LaMonte)
 1898-1966 .... CAP-2
 Earlier sketch in CA 17-18
 See also SATA 3
Wright, Esmond 1915- CANR-6
 Earlier sketch in CA 2R
 See also SATA 10
Wright, F(rank) J(oseph) 1905- 11-12R
Wright, Frances Fitzpatrick 1897- CAP-1
 Earlier sketch in CA 13-14
 See also SATA 10
Wright, Frances J.
 See Crothers, J(essie) Frances
Wright, Francesca
 See Robins, Denise (Naomi)
Wright, Frank Cookman, Jr. 1904-1982
 Obituary 107
Wright, G(eorge) Ernest 1909-1974 ..... CANR-2
 Obituary 53-56
 Earlier sketch in CA 2R
Wright, G(eorg) H(enrik) von 1916-
 Brief entry 112
Wright, Gavin Peter 1943- CANR-15
 Earlier sketch in CA 89-92
Wright, George B(urton) 1912- 23-24R
Wright, George Nelson 1921- CANR-1
 Earlier sketch in CA 45-48
Wright, George T(haddeus, Jr.) 1925- 7-8R
Wright, Gordon 1912- 11-12R
Wright, Grahame 1947-1977 103
Wright, H(arold) Bunker 1907- 5-6R
Wright, H(ugh) Elliott 1937- CANR-14
 Earlier sketch in CA 37-40R
Wright, H(arry) Norman 1937- CANR-8
 Earlier sketch in CA 57-60
Wright, Harold Bell 1872-1944 Brief entry .. 110
 See also DLB 9
Wright, Harrison M(orris) 1928- 41-44R
Wright, Helen 1914- 11-12R
Wright, Helen L(ouise) 1932- 116
Wright, Helena (Rosa Lowenfeld)
 1887-1982 Obituary 110
Wright, Herbert Curtis 1928- 105
Wright, Howard Wilson 1915- CANR-3
 Earlier sketch in CA 5-6R
Wright, Ione Stuessy 1905- CAP-1
 Earlier sketch in CA 13-14
Wright, Irene Aloha 1879-1972
 Obituary 33-36R
Wright, J(ames) Leitch, Jr. 1929- 23-24R
Wright, J(oseph) Patrick (Jr.) 1941- 103
Wright, J(ohn) Robert 1936- 111
Wright, J(ohn) Stafford 1905- CANR-11
 Earlier sketch in CA 57-60
Wright, Jack R.
 See Harris, Mark
Wright, James (Arlington) 1927-1980 ... CANR-4
 Obituary 97-100
 Earlier sketch in CA 49-52
 See also DLB 5
 See also CLC 3, 5, 10, 28
 See also AITN 2
Wright, James C(laud), Jr. 1922- 49-52
Wright, Jay 1935- 73-76
 See also DLB 41
Wright, Jim
 See Wright, James C(laud), Jr.
Wright, John D(ean), Jr. 1920- 117
Wright, John Eugene, Jr. 1931- 112
Wright, John J(oseph) 1909-1979 ...... CANR-2
 Earlier sketch in CA 4R
Wright, John S(hup) 1910- 37-40R
Wright, John S(herman) 1920- CANR-6
 Earlier sketch in CA 5-6R
Wright, Judith 1915- 15-16R
 See also SATA 14
 See also CLC 11
Wright, Katrina
 See Gater, Dilys
Wright, Kenneth
 See del Rey, Lester
Wright, L(aurali) R. CLC-44
Wright, Lafayette Hart 1917-1983 ....41-44R
 Obituary 109
Wright, Larry 1940- Brief entry 122
Wright, Lawrence 1947- 93-96
Wright, Leigh Richard 1925- 93-96
Wright, Leonard M(arshall), Jr. 1923- .. CANR-13
 Earlier sketch in CA 61-64
Wright, Linda Raney 1945- CANR-11
 Earlier sketch in CA 69-72
Wright, Louis Booker 1899-1984 .... CANR-1
 Obituary 112
 Earlier sketch in CA 4R
 See also DLB 17
Wright, Mary Clabaugh 1917-1970
 Obituary 109
Wright, Mary Pamela Godwin 1917- CAP-1
 Earlier sketch in CA 9-10
Wright, Michael R(obert) 1901- CAP-1
 Earlier sketch in CA 15-16
Wright, Monte Duane 1930- 41-44R
Wright, Muriel H(azel) 1889-1975
 Obituary 57-60
Wright, Nancy Means 104
 See also SATA 38
Wright, Nathalia 1913- 120
Wright, Nathan, Jr. 1923- 37-40R
Wright, Nathaniel, Jr.
 See Wright, Nathan, Jr.
Wright, Norman Edgar 1927- 101
Wright, Olgivanna Lloyd 1900(?)-1985
 Obituary 115
Wright, (Mary) Patricia 1932- CANR-10
 Earlier sketch in CA 65-68
Wright, Philip Arthur 1908- CAP-1
 Earlier sketch in CA 11-12
Wright, (Philip) Quincy 1890-1970 ..... CANR-5
 Obituary 29-32R
 Earlier sketch in CA 5-6R
Wright, R(obert) Glenn 1932- 111
Wright, R(obert) H(amilton) 1906- CANR-7
 Earlier sketch in CA 19-20R
 See also SATA 6
Wright, R(ichard) I(rwin) Vane
 See Vane-Wright, R(ichard) I(rwin)
Wright, Rebecca 1942- 105
Wright, Richard (Nathaniel) 1908-1960 108
 See also DLBD 2
 See also CLC 1, 3, 4, 9, 14, 21
Wright, Richard B(ruce) 1937- 85-88
 See also DLB 53
 See also CLC 6
Wright, Richard J. 1935- 89-92
Wright, Rick 1945- CLC-35
Wright, Robert Lee 1920- CANR-13
 Earlier sketch in CA 17-18R
Wright, Robert Roy 1917- 11-12R
Wright, Robin (B.) 1948- Brief entry 119
Wright, Ronald (William Vernon) Selby
 1908- CANR-6
 Earlier sketch in CA 2R
Wright, Rosalie Muller 1942- 77-80
Wright, Rosalind 1952- 61-64
Wright, Rowland
 See Wells, Carolyn
Wright, Russel 1904-1976 Obituary 69-72
Wright, Sarah E. 37-40R
 See also DLB 33
Wright, Stephen 1922- CANR-1
 Earlier sketch in CA 49-52
Wright, Stephen 1946- CLC-33
Wright, Sylvia 1917-1981 ....29-32R
 Obituary 104
Wright, T. M. 1947- 120
Wright, Theodore P(aul), Jr. 1926- CANR-9
 Earlier sketch in CA 15-16R
Wright, Theon 1904- Brief entry 109
Wright, Walter Francis 1912- 5-6R
Wright, Willard Hull 1894-1982 Obituary ... 107
Wright, Willard Huntington 1888-1939
 Brief entry 115
Wright, William 1930- CANR-23
 Earlier sketches in CA 53-56, CANR-7
 See also CLC 44
Wright, William C(ook) 1939- 41-44R
Wright, William E(dward) 1926- 23-24R
Wrightsman, Lawrence S(amuel), Jr.
 1931- CANR-11
 Earlier sketch in CA 23-24R
Wrightson, Patricia 1921- CANR-19
 Earlier sketches in CA 45-48, CANR-3
 See also SATA 8
 See also SAAS 4
 See also CLR 4, 14
Wrigley, Elizabeth S(pringer) 1915- 41-44R
Wriston, Henry M(erritt) 1889-1978 ..... CAP-1
 Obituary 77-80
 Earlier sketch in CA 11-12
Wrobel, Sylvia (Burroughs) 1941- 65-68
Wroblewski, Sergius C(harles) 1918- CANR-8
 Earlier sketch in CA 7-8R
Wrone, David R(ogers) 1933- CANR-6
 Earlier sketch in CA 57-60
Wrong, Dennis H(ume) 1923- 81-84
Wronker, Lili
 See Wronker, Lili Cassel
Wronker, Lili Cassel 1924- SATA-10
Wronski, Stanley P(aul) 1919- 15-16R
Wroth, Lawrence Counselman 1884-1970
 Obituary 29-32R
Wrottesley, A(rthur) J(ohn) F(rancis)
 1908- 45-48
Wryde, Dogear
 See Gorey, Edward (St. John)
Wrzos, Joseph Henry 1929- 49-52
Wu, Hsiu-Kwang 1935- 17-18R
Wu, John C(hing) H(siung) 1899-1986 104
 Obituary 118
Wu, Joseph S. 1934- 97-100
Wu, K(uo) C(heng) 1903-1984 .... 3R
 Obituary 113
Wu, Nelson I(kon) 1919- 11-12R
Wu, Silas H. L. 1929- 37-40R
Wu, William F(ranking) 1951- 109
Wu, Yuan-li CANR-12
 Earlier sketch in CA 17-18R
Wubben, Hubert H(ollensteiner) 1928- 102
Wubben, John 1938- 65-68
Wucherer, Ruth Marie 1948- CANR-8
 Earlier sketch in CA 61-64
Wu Ching-hsiung
 See Wu, John C(hing) H(siung)
Wuellner, Flora Slosson 1928- 53-56
Wuerpel, Charles E(dward) 1906- 105
Wul, Stefan
 See Pairault, Pierre
Wulf, Helen Harlan 1913- 53-56
Wulfekoetter, Gertrude 1895- 2R
Wulff, Lee 1905- 61-64
Wulff, Robert M. 1926- 49-52
Wulffson, Don L. 1943- CANR-19
 Earlier sketch in CA 102
 See also SATA 32

INDEX

Wuliger, Betty 1921- ... 65-68
Wullstein, L(eroy) H(ughes) 1931- ... 29-32R
Wunder, John Remley 1945- ... 107
Wunderlich, Ray C., Jr. 1929- ... 37-40R
Wundt, Wilhelm (Max) 1832-1920
Brief entry ... 121
Wundt, Wilhelm
See de Mille, Richard
Wunnakyawhtin U Ohn Ghine
See Maurice, David (John Kerr)
Wunsch, Josephine (McLean) 1914- ... CANR-15
Earlier sketch in CA 3R
Wuorinen, John H(enry) 1897-1969
Obituary ... 111
Wuorio, Eva-Lis 1918- ... 77-80
See also SATA 28, 34
Wurdemann, Audrey
See Auslander, Audrey (May) Wurdemann
Wurfel, Seymour W(alter) 1907- ... 73-76
Wurlitzer, Rudolph 1938(?)- ... 85-88
See also CLC 2, 4, 15
Wurmbrand, Richard 1909- ... 61-64
Wurmser, Leon 1931- ... 106
Wurtman, Judith J(oy) 1937- ... 113
Wuthnow, Robert 1946- ... CANR-15
Earlier sketch in CA 65-68
Wu Tien-wei 1922- ... 118
Wyandotte, Steve
See Thomas, Stanley
Wyant, William K(eblinger) 1913- ... 108
Wyatt, Arthur R(amer) 1927- ... 2R
Wyatt, B. D.
See Robinson, Spider
Wyatt, David K(ent) 1937- ... 29-32R
Wyatt, Dorothea E(dith) 1909- ... CAP-2
Earlier sketch in CA 23-24
Wyatt, James
See Robinson, Louie, Jr.
Wyatt, Joan 1934- ... 97-100
Wyatt, John 1925- ... CANR-22
Earlier sketch in CA 105
Wyatt, Rachel 1929- ... 101
Wyatt, Richard Jed 1939- ... 115
Wyatt, Robert John 1931- ... 73-76
Wyatt, Stanley P(orter, Jr.) 1921-1980 ... 11-12R
Obituary ... 120
Wyatt, Stephen (John) 1948- ... CANR-15
Earlier sketch in CA 81-84
Wyatt, Wesley Butler
See Torme, Mel(vin Howard)
Wyatt, (Alan) Will 1942- ... 101
Wyatt, William F., Jr. 1932- ... 37-40R
Wyatt, Woodrow Lyle 1918- ... 103
Wyatt-Brown, Bertram 1932- ... CANR-21
Earlier sketch in CA 25-28R
Wycherley, R(ichard) E(rnest) 1909- ... 77-80
Wyckoff, Charlotte Chandler 1893-1966 .. CAP-2
Earlier sketch in CA 17-18
Wyckoff, D(onald) Daryl 1936-1985 ... CANR-7
Obituary ... 114
Earlier sketch in CA 57-60
Wyckoff, Edith Hay 1916- ... 107
Wyckoff, James M. 1918- ... 19-20R
Wyckoff, (Gregory) Jerome 1911- ... 11-12R
Wyckoff, Peter (Gerritsen) 1914- ... 41-44R
Wyckoff, Ralph W(alter) G(raystone) 1897- ... 73-76
Wyckoff, Russell L. 1916(?)-1984
Obituary ... 112
Wycoff, Mary Elizabeth Jordon 1932- ... 15-16R
Wyden, Peter H. 1923- ... 105
Wyeth, Betsy James 1921- ... 89-92
See also SATA 41
Wyeth, N(ewell) C(onvers) 1882-1945 .. SATA-17
Wyeth, Paul James Logan 1920-1982
Obituary ... 107
Wykes, Alan 1914- ... CANR-2
Earlier sketch in CA 1R
Wykstra, Ronald A. 1935- Brief entry ... 106
Wyld, Lionel D(arcy) 1925- ... CANR-4
Earlier sketch in CA 3R
Wylder, Delbert E(ugene) 1923- ... CANR-12
Earlier sketch in CA 29-32R
Wylder, Edith (Perry) 1925- ... 29-32R
Wylder, Robert C. 1921- ... 11-12R
Wyler, Brenda (Florence) 1951- ... CANR-19
Earlier sketch in CA 89-92
Wyler, Rose 1909- ... 93-96
See also SATA 18
Wyler, William 1902-1981 Obituary ... 108
Wylie, Betty Jane ... CANR-21
Earlier sketch in CA 105
See also SATA 48
Wylie, C(larence) R(aymond), Jr. 1911- ... 45-48
Wylie, Craig 1908-1976 Obituary ... 69-72
Wylie, Elinor (Morton Hoyt) 1885-1928
Brief entry ... 105
See also DLB 9, 45
See also TCLC 8
Wylie, Francis E(rnest) 1905- ... 73-76
Wylie, Jeff
See Wylie, Francis E(rnest)
Wylie, Joanne 1928- ... 118
Wylie, John Anthony Hamilton 1919-1987
Obituary ... 123
Wylie, Jonathan 1945- ... 120
Wylie, Laurence William 1909- ... 21-22R
Wylie, Laurie
See Matthews, Patricia (Anne)
Wylie, Max (Melville) 1904-1975 ... 97-100
Obituary ... 61-64
Wylie, Philip (Gordon) 1902-1971 ... CAP-2
Obituary ... 33-36R
Earlier sketch in CA 21-22
See also DLB 9
See also CLC 43
Wylie, Ruth C(arol) 1920- ... 89-92
Wylie, Turrell V(erl) 1927- ... 41-44R
Wylie, William P(ercy) 1898- ... 7-8R
Wyllie, Eugene D(onald) 1929- ... 123
Brief entry ... 118
Wyllie, John (Vectis Carew) 1914- ... CANR-5
Earlier sketch in CA 11-12R
Wyllie, Peter J(ohn) 1930- ... CANR-5
Earlier sketch in CA 53-56
Wyly, Rachel Lumpkin 1892- ... CAP-2
Earlier sketch in CA 25-28
Wyman, David S. 1929- ... 25-28R
Wyman, Donald 1903- ... CANR-2
Earlier sketch in CA 5-6R
Wyman, Leland C(lifton) 1897-1988
Obituary ... 124
Wyman, Marc
See Howith, Harry
Wyman, Mark 1938- ... 101
Wyman, Mary Alice 1889(?)-1976
Obituary ... 61-64
Wyman, Oliver
See Holmes, Olive
Wyman, Walker D(eMarquis) 1907- ... 17-18R
Wymark, Olwen Margaret 1932- ... 104
Wymer, Norman (George) 1911- ... 104
See also SATA 25
Wymer, Thomas L(ee) 1938- ... 105
Wynand, Derk 1944- ... CANR-17
Earlier sketch in CA 77-80
Wynants, Miche 1934- ... SATA-31
Wynar, Bohdan S(tephen) 1926- ... CANR-10
Earlier sketch in CA 19-20R
Wynar, Christine L(oraine) 1933- ... 73-76
Wynar, Lubomyr R(oman) 1932- ... CANR-14
Earlier sketch in CA 73-76
Wynd, Oswald Morris 1913- ... CANR-1
Earlier sketch in CA 2R
Wynder, Mavis Areta
See Winder, Mavis Areta
Wyndham, Esther
See Lutyens, Mary
Wyndham, Everard Humphrey 1888- ... CAP-1
Earlier sketch in CA 13-14
Wyndham, John
See Harris, John (Wyndham Parkes Lucas) Beynon
Wyndham, Lee
See Hyndman, Jane Andrews Lee
Wyndham, Robert
See Hyndman, Robert Utley
Wynes, Charles E. 1929- ... 11-12R
Wyness, (James) Fenton 1903- ... CAP-1
Earlier sketch in CA 11-12
Wynette, Tammy
See Pugh, Wynette
Wynkoop, Mildred Bangs 1905- ... 57-60
Wynkoop, Sally 1944- ... 41-44R
Wynkoop, William M. 1916- ... 21-22R
Wynn, Alfred
See Brewer, Fredric (Aldwyn)
Wynn, Allan 1920-1987 Obituary ... 123
Wynn, D(ale) Richard 1918- ... CANR-4
Earlier sketch in CA 2R
Wynn, Daniel Webster 1919- ... 25-28R
Wynn, John Charles 1920- ... CANR-2
Earlier sketch in CA 3R
Wynn, (Francis Xavier Aloysius James Jeremiah) Keenan 1916-1986 Obituary ... 120
Wynn, Neil A(lan) 1947- ... 113
Wynne, Brian
See Garfield, Brian (Wynne)
Wynne, Frank
See Garfield, Brian (Wynne)
Wynne, May
See Knowles, Mabel Winifred
Wynne, Nancy Blue 1931- ... 85-88
Wynne, Ronald D(avid) 1934- ... 102
Wynne, Thorne D. 1908- ... 7-8R
Wynne-Jones, Tim(othy) 1948- ... 105
Wynne-Thomas, Peter 1934- ... 118
Wynne-Tyson, Esme 1898- ... 23-24R
Wynne-Tyson, (Timothy) Jon (Lyden) 1924- ... 19-20R
Wynn-Jones, Michael 1941- ... CANR-14
Earlier sketch in CA 69-72
Wynot, Edward D(avis), Jr. 1943- ... 105
Wynter, Edward (John) 1914- ... 69-72
See also SATA 14
Wynyard, Talbot
See Hamilton, Charles Harold St. John
Wyon, Olive 1890-19(?) ... CAP-1
Earlier sketch in CA 11-12
Wyrick, V(ictor) Neil, Jr. 1928- ... 15-16R
Wyschogrod, Edith 1930- Brief entry ... 111
Wyschogrod, Michael 1928- ... 89-92
Wyse, Lois (Helene) 1926- ... 108
Wyse, Marion 1952- ... 123
Wysor, Bettie 1928- ... CANR-13
Earlier sketch in CA 77-80
Wyss, Johann David Von 1743-1818 ... SATA-27, 29
Wyss, Max Albert 1908-1977 ... 106
Wyss, Thelma Hatch 1934- ... 29-32R
See also SATA 10
Wyss, Wallace A(lfred) 1944- ... 124
Brief entry ... 107
Wyszynski, Stefan 1901-1981 Obituary ... 108
Wyvis, Ben
See Munro, (Macfarlane) Hugh
Wyzanski, Charles E(dward), Jr. 1906-1986 ... CAP-1
Obituary ... 120
Earlier sketch in CA 17-18

X

Xaveria, M. Barton
See Barton, M. Xaveria
Xaveria, Sister
See Barton, M. Xaveria
Xeno
See Lake, Kenneth R(obert)
Ximenes, Ben Cuellar, Jr. 1911- ... 5-6R
Xixx, Jezebel Q.
See Borgmann, Dmitri A(lfred)

Y

Yaari, Ehud 1945- ... 37-40R
Yabes, Leopoldo Y(abes) 1912- ... 101
Yablokoff, Herman 1903-1981 Obituary ... 108
Yablonsky, Lewis 1924- ... 23-24R
Yabsley, Suzanne 1949- ... 124
Yacine, Kateb 1929- ... 11-12R
Yacorzynski, George Kassimer 1907- ... 2R
Yacowar, Maurice 1942- ... 41-44R
Yadin, (Rav-Aloof) Yigael 1917-1984 ... CANR-6
Obituary ... 113
Earlier sketch in CA 11-12R
Yaeger, Bart
See Strung, Norman
Yafa, Stephen H. 1941- ... 23-24R
Yaffe, Alan
See Yorinks, Arthur
Yaffe, Barbara 1953- ... 85-88
Yaffe, James 1927- ... CANR-12
Earlier sketch in CA 7-8R
Yaffe, Richard 1903- ... 69-72
Yager, Rosemary 1909- ... 3R
Yaggy, Duncan 1938- ... 116
Yaggy, Elinor 1907- ... 89-92
Yahil, Leni ... 29-32R
Yahraes, Herbert 1905- ... 81-84
Yahuda, Joseph 1900- ... CAP-1
Earlier sketch in CA 11-12
Yaker, Henri (Marc) 1922- Brief entry ... 109
Yakobson, Helen B(ates) 1913- ... 19-20R
Yakobson, Sergius O. 1901-1979
Obituary ... 89-92
Yakovenko, L.
See Kopelev, Lev (Zinovievich)
Yakumo Koizumi
See Hearn, (Patricio) Lafcadio (Tessima Carlos)
Yalden, Derek William 1940- ... 69-72
Yale, Wesley W(oodworth) 1900- ... CAP-2
Earlier sketch in CA 29-32
Yale, William 1888(?)-1975 Obituary ... 57-60
Yalem, Ronald J(oseph) 1926- ... 19-20R
Yalman, Ahmet Emin 1888-1972
Obituary ... 37-40R
Yalom, Marilyn K. 1932- ... 117
Yamada, Mitsuye (May) 1923- ... 77-80
Yamaguchi, J(ohn) Tohr 1932- ... 19-20R
Yamaguchi, Marianne (Illenberger) 1936- ... 29-32R
See also SATA 7
Yamamoto, J(erry) Isamu 1947- ... 77-80
Yamamoto, Kaoru 1932- ... CANR-12
Earlier sketch in CA 25-28R
Yamanouchi, Hisaaki 1934- ... 93-96
Yamasaki, Minoru 1912-1986 Obituary ... 118
Yamauchi, Edwin M(asao) 1937- ... CANR-19
Earlier sketches in CA 45-48, CANR-3
Yan, Chiou-Shuang Jou 1934- Brief entry ... 105
Yanaga, Chitoshi 1903- ... CAP-2
Earlier sketch in CA 25-28
Yanagimura, Shimpu
See Verwilghen, A(lbert-) Felix
Yancey, Philip D(avid) 1949- ... CANR-18
Earlier sketch in CA 101
Yancey, William L(ayton) 1938- ... 21-22R
Yancy, Robert J(ames) 1944- ... 57-60
Yandell, Keith E. 1938- ... 37-40R
Yanev, Peter (Ivanov) 1946- ... 77-80
Yaney, George L(evings) 1930- ... 104
Yaney, Joseph P(aul) 1939- ... CANR-9
Earlier sketch in CA 65-68
Yang, C(hing) K(un) 1911- ... 7-8R
Yang, Jay 1941- ... SATA-12
Yang, Linda (Gureasko) 1937- ... 57-60
Yang, Richard F. S. 1918- ... CANR-10
Earlier sketch in CA 25-28R
Yang, Sung Chul 1939- ... 117
Yang-Jen
See Shu, Austin Chi-wei
Yanikian, Gourgen Migirdic 1895-1984
Obituary ... 112
Yankelovich, Daniel 1924- ... 105
Yanker, Gary 1947- ... 37-40R
Yankowitz, Susan 1941- ... CANR-17
Earlier sketches in CA 45-48, CANR-1
Yannarella, Philip A(nthony) 1942- ... 73-76
Yannatos, James 1929- ... 102
Yannella, Donald 1934- ... CANR-8
Earlier sketch in CA 57-60
Yanoff, Morris 1907- ... 108
Yanouzas, John N(icholas) 1928- ... 41-44R
Yanovsky, Basile S.
See Yanovsky, V(assily) S(emenovich)
Yanovsky, V(assily) S(emenovich) 1906- .. 97-100
See also CLC 2, 18
Yans-McLaughlin, Virginia 1943- ... 89-92
Yao, Esther Lee 1944- ... 111
Yarber, Robert Earl 1929- ... 49-52
Yarborough, Betty Hathaway 1927- ... 45-48
Yarbro, Chelsea Quinn 1942- ... CANR-9
Earlier sketch in CA 65-68
Yarbrough, Camille Brief entry ... 105
Yarbrough, Ira 1910(?)-1983 Obituary ... 110
See also SATA 35
Yarbrough, Tinsley E(ugene) 1941- ... 109
Yarde, Jeanne Betty Frances 1925- ... CANR-23
Earlier sketch in CA 105
Yardley, Alice 1913- Brief entry ... 106
Yardley, Herbert O(sborn) 1889-1958
Brief entry ... 121
Yardley, Jonathan 1939- ... 73-76
Yardley, Richard Q(uincy) 1903-1979
Obituary ... 89-92
Yaremko, Michael 1914-1970 ... CAP-2
Earlier sketch in CA 25-28
Yarmey, A(lexander) Daniel 1938- ... CANR-17
Earlier sketch in CA 101
Yarmolinsky, Adam 1922- ... 37-40R
Yarmolinsky, Avrahm (Abraham) 1890-1975 ... CANR-7
Obituary ... 61-64
Earlier sketch in CA 5-6R
Yarmon, Morton 1916- ... 11-12R
Yarn, David H(omer), Jr. 1920- ... 19-20R
Yarnall, Sophia
See Jacobs, Sophia Yarnall
Yarnell, Allen 1942- ... 101
Yaroslava
See Mills, Yaroslava Surmach
Yarrow, Arnold 1920- ... 106
Yarrow, Marian J(eanette Radke) 1918-
Brief entry ... 105
Yarrow, P(hilip) J(ohn) 1917- ... 13-14R
Yarry, Mark Robert 1940- ... 110
Yar-Shater, Ehsan O(llah) 1920- ... 37-40R
Yartz, Frank Joseph ... 65-68
Yarwood, Doreen 1918- ... CANR-18
Earlier sketch in CA 101
Yashima, Taro
See Iwamatsu, Jun Atsushi
See also CLR 4
Yastrzemski, Carl (Michael, Jr.) 1939- ... 104
Yates, A(lan) G(eoffrey) 1923-1985 ... CANR-3
Obituary ... 116
Earlier sketch in CA 4R
Yates, Alan
See Yates, A(lan) G(eoffrey)
Yates, Alayne 1929- ... 81-84
Yates, Alfred 1917- ... 21-22R
Yates, Aubrey J(ames) 1925- ... 11-12R
Yates, Brock W(endel) 1933- ... 11-12R
Yates, David O.
See Womack, David A(lfred)
Yates, Donald A(lfred) 1930- ... 41-44R
Yates, Dornford
See Mercer, Cecil William
Yates, Elizabeth 1905- ... CANR-21
Earlier sketches in CA 2R, CANR-6
See also SATA 4
Yates, Frances A(melia) 1899-1981 ... 57-60
Obituary ... 105
Yates, Gerard Francis 1907-1979
Obituary ... 89-92
Yates, J. Michael 1938- ... 21-22R
See also DLB 60
Yates, Madeleine 1937- ... 109
Yates, Norris W(ilson) 1923- ... 11-12R
Yates, Paul 1954- Brief entry ... 117
Yates, Peter Bertram 1909-1976 Obituary .. 65-68
Yates, Raymond F(rancis) 1895-1966
Obituary ... 110
See also SATA 31
Yates, Richard 1926- ... CANR-10
Earlier sketch in CA 7-8R
See also DLB 2
See also DLBY 81
See also CLC 7, 8, 23
Yates, W(illiam) E(dgar) 1938- ... 49-52
Yatron, Michael 1921- ... 37-40R
Yauch, Wilbur Alden 1904-1982 Obituary ... 106
Yaukey, David (William) 1927- ... 61-64
Yaukey, Grace S(ydenstricker) 1899- ... CANR-1
Earlier sketch in CA 3R
See also SATA 5
Yavetz, Zvi 1925- ... CANR-16
Earlier sketch in CA 29-32R
Yavitz, Boris 1923- ... 114
Yaw, Yvonne 1936- ... 65-68
Yawetz, Zwy
See Yavetz, Zvi
Yazijian, Harvey Z. 1948- ... 107
Yeadon, David 1942- ... 104
Yeager, Allan Edward 1943- ... 101
Yeager, Robert Cushing 1942- ... 102
Yeager, W(illard) Hayes 1897- ... CAP-2
Earlier sketch in CA 19-20
Yeakley, Marjory Hall 1908- ... CANR-2
Earlier sketch in CA 3R
See also SATA 21
Yearley, Clifton K(rebs), Jr. 1925- ... 15-16R
Yearwood, Richard M(eek) 1934- ... 37-40R
Yeates, Mabel
See Pereira, Harold Bertram
Yeates, Maurice 1938- ... CANR-14
Earlier sketch in CA 41-44R
Yeatman, Linda 1938- ... 117
See also SATA 42
Yeats, William Butler 1865-1939
Brief entry ... 104
See also DLB 10, 19
See also TCLC 1, 11, 18
Yeats-Brown, F(rancis Charles Claypon) 1886-1944 Brief entry ... 119
Yeazell, Ruth Bernard 1947- ... 102
Yeck, John D(avid) 1912- ... 15-16R
Yee, Albert H(oy) 1929- ... CANR-1
Earlier sketch in CA 49-52

Yee, Chiang
See Chiang, Yee
Yee, Min S. 1938- ... 101
Yeganeh, Mohammed 1923- ... 5-6R
Yeh, George K(ung)-C(hao) 1904-1981
Obituary ... 108
Yeh, Wei-lien
See Yip, Wai-lim
Yehiya, Eliezer Don
See Don-Yehiya, Eleizer
Yehoshua, Abraham B. 1936- ... 33-36R
See also CLC 13, 31
Yelin, Shulamis S. ... 121
Yellen, Samuel 1906- ... 1R
Yellen, Sherman 1932- ... 29-32R
Yellin, Carol Lynn (Gilmer) 1920- ... 19-20R
Yellin, David G(ilmer) 1916- Brief entry ... 115
Yellin, Jean Fagan 1930- ... 41-44R
Yellowitz, Irwin 1933- ... CANR-4
Earlier sketch in CA 45-48
Yelton, Donald Charles 1915- ... 106
Yelverton, Eric Esskildsen 1888-1964 ... CAP-1
Earlier sketch in CA 9-10
Yen-Ping, Shen 1896(?)-1981 Obituary ... 103
Yenser, Stephen 1941- ... 114
Yensid, Retlaw
See Disney, Walt(er Elias)
Yeo, Cedric Arnold 1905- ... CAP-1
Earlier sketch in CA 17-18
Yeo, Wilma (Lethem) 1918- ... 25-28R
See also SATA 24
Yeoman, John 1934- ... 106
See also SATA 28
Yeomans, Patricia Henry 1917- ... 97-100
Yep, Laurence Michael 1948- ... CANR-1
Earlier sketch in CA 49-52
See also SATA 7
See also DLB 52
See also CLC 35
See also CLR 3
Yepsen, Roger B(ennet), Jr. 1947- ... 114
Yerbury, Grace D. 1899- ... 37-40R
Yerby, Frank G(arvin) 1916- ... CANR-16
Earlier sketch in CA 11-12R
See also CLC 1, 7, 22
Yergin, Daniel H. ... 103
Yerian, Cameron John ... 73-76
See also SATA 21
Yerian, Margaret A. ... 73-76
See also SATA 21
Yermakov, Nicholas 1951- ... 118
Yerushalmi, Yosef Hayim 1932-
Brief entry ... 112
Yeselson, Abraham 1921-1978 Obituary ... 77-80
Yesenin, Sergei Alexandrovich
See Esenin, Sergei (Alexandrovich)
Yeshayahu, Yisrael 1910-1979 Obituary ... 89-92
Yessian, Mark R(obert) 1942- ... CANR-10
Earlier sketch in CA 25-28R
Yetman, Norman R(oger) 1938- ... 29-32R
Yette, Samuel F(rederick) 1929- ... 102
Yeung Yue-man 1938- ... 110
Yevtushenko, Yevgeny (Alexandrovich)
1933- ... 81-84
See also CLC 1, 3, 13, 26
Yezierska, Anzia 1885-1970 Obituary ... 89-92
See also DLB 28
See also CLC 46
Yezzo, Dominick 1947- ... 53-56
Yglesias, Helen 1915- ... CANR-15
Earlier sketch in CA 37-40R
See also CLC 7, 22
Yglesias, Jose 1919- ... 41-44R
Yglesias, Rafael 1954- ... 37-40R
Yiannopoulos, Athanassios Nikolaos 1928- ... 2R
Yim, Kwan Ha 1929- ... 101
Yin, Robert K(uo-zuir) 1941- ... CANR-1
Earlier sketch in CA 49-52
Yinger, J(ohn) Milton 1916- ... 89-92
Yip, Wai-lim 1937- ... 33-36R
Yllo, Kersti 1953- ... 119
Ylvisaker, Paul 1921- ... CANR-16
Earlier sketches in CA 3R, CANR-1
Yngve, Victor H(use) 1920- ... 57-60
Yntema, Theodore O(tte) 1900-1985
Obituary ... 117
Yoakum, Robert 1922- ... 77-80
Yochelson, Samuel 1906(?)-1976
Obituary ... 69-72
Yochim, Louise Dunn 1909- ... 37-40R
Yocom, Charles Frederick 1914- ... CANR-7
Earlier sketch in CA 17-18R
Yoder, Dale 1901- ... CANR-2
Earlier sketch in CA 2R
Yoder, Don 1921- ... 85-88
Yoder, Glee 1916- ... CANR-9
Earlier sketch in CA 21-22R
Yoder, J(ames) Willard 1902- ... 37-40R
Yoder, Janice D(ana) 1952- ... 114
Yoder, Jess 1922- ... 45-48
Yoder, John H(oward) 1927- ... 15-16R
Yoder, Marie Angeline 1914- ... 7-8R
Yoder, Norman M. 1915- ... 21-22R
Yoder, Paton 1912- ... 93-96
Yoder, Sanford Calvin 1879- ... CAP-1
Earlier sketch in CA 15-16
Yogiji, Harbhajan Singh Khalsa 1929- ... 93-96
Yohe, W(illiam) Frederick 1943- ... 49-52
Yohn, David Waite 1933- ... 41-44R
Yohn, Rick 1937- ... CANR-8
Earlier sketch in CA 61-64
Yoingco, Angel Q. 1921- ... CANR-11
Earlier sketch in CA 25-28R
Yoken, Melvin B(arton) 1939- ... 65-68
Yola, Yerima
See Kirk-Greene, Anthony (Hamilton
Millard)
Yolen, Jane (Hyatt) 1939- ... CANR-11
Earlier sketch in CA 15-16R
See also SATA 4, 40
See also SAAS 1
See also DLB 52
See also CLR 4
Yolen, Steven H. 1942- ... 73-76
Yolen, Will (Hyatt) 1908-1985 ... CANR-5
Obituary ... 118
Earlier sketch in CA 5-6R
Yolton, John W(illiam) 1921- ... CANR-14
Earlier sketch in CA 37-40R
Yone, Edward Michael Law
See Law Yone, Edward Michael
Yonemura, Margaret V. S. 1928- ... 29-32R
Yonge, Charlotte (Mary) 1823-1901
Brief entry ... 109
See also SATA 17
See also DLB 18
Yonge, (Charles) Maurice 1899-1986
Obituary ... 118
Yonker, Nicholas J(unior) 1927- ... 117
Yoo, Grace S.
See Yoo, Young H(yun)
Yoo, Young H(yun) 1927- ... 41-44R
Yoo, Yushin 1940- ... CANR-2
Earlier sketch in CA 45-48
Yooll, Andrew M(ichael) Graham
See Graham-Yooll, Andrew M(ichael)
Yoors, Jan 1922(?)-1977 ... 81-84
Obituary ... 73-76
Yora, Shandrin M(arion) 1937- ... 120
Yorburg, Betty 1926- ... CANR-16
Earlier sketch in CA 29-32R
Yorck, Ruth (Landshoff) 1909-1966
Obituary ... 25-28R
Yordan, Philip 1913(?)- Brief entry ... 116
Yorick, A. P.
See Tindall, William York
Yorinks, Arthur 1953- ... 106
See also SATA 33, 49
York, Amanda
See Dial, Joan
York, Andrew
See Nicole, Christopher Robin
York, Carol Beach 1928- ... CANR-6
Earlier sketch in CA 3R
See also SATA 6
York, Elizabeth
See York, Margaret Elizabeth
York, Georgia
See Hoffman, Lee
York, Helen 1918- ... CANR-4
Earlier sketch in CA 53-56
York, Herbert (Frank) 1921- ... 29-32R
York, Jeremy
See Creasey, John
York, Margaret Elizabeth 1927- ... 103
York, Pauline
See Howl, Marcia (Yvonne Hurt)
York, Rebecca
See Buckholtz, Eileen (Garber)
and Glick, Ruth (Burtnick)
York, Reginald O(scar) 1942- ... 117
York, Simon
See Heinlein, Robert A(nson)
York, Thomas (Lee) 1940- ... 73-76
York, William 1950- ... 107
Yorke, Henry Vincent 1905-1974 ... 85-88
Obituary ... 49-52
See also CLC 13
Yorke, Katherine
See Ellerbeck, Rosemary (Anne
L'Estrange)
Yorke, Margaret
See Larminie, Margaret Beda
Yorke, Ritchie 1944- ... 77-80
Yorke, Roger
See Bingley, David Ernest
Yorke, Susan 1915- ... CANR-1
Earlier sketch in CA 3R
Yorkist
See Morrah, Dermot (Michael Macgregor)
Yoseloff, Martin 1919- ... 45-48
Yoseloff, Thomas 1913- ... 77-80
Yoshida, (Katsumi) Jim 1921- ... 41-44R
Yoshida, Shigeru 1878-1967 Obituary ... 113
Yost, Charles W(oodruff) 1907-1981 ... CANR-3
Obituary ... 104
Earlier sketch in CA 11-12R
Yost, Edna 1889-1971 ... 2R
Obituary ... 103
See also SATA 26
Yost, F(rank) Donald 1927- ... 29-32R
Yost, Nellie Snyder 1905- ... CANR-16
Earlier sketch in CA 29-32R
Yost, Stanley K. 1924- ... 11-12R
Youcha, Geraldine 1925- ... 93-96
Youd, Samuel 1922- ... 77-80
See also SATA 30, 47
Youdale, Peter J. 1928- ... 45-48
Youman, Roger J(acob) 1932- ... 65-68
Youmans, E(lmer) Grant 1907- ... CAP-2
Earlier sketch in CA 23-24
Youmans, Marlene 1953- ... 77-80
Young, Agatha
See Young, Agnes Brooks
Young, Agnes Brooks 1898-1974
Obituary ... 109
Young, Ahdele Carrine 1923- ... 107
Young, Al 1939- ... 29-32R
See also DLB 33
See also CLC 19
Young, Alan 1930- ... CANR-6
Earlier sketch in CA 57-60
Young, Alan R(oger) 1941- ... 89-92
Young, Alison 1922- ... 53-56
Young, Allen 1941- ... CANR-18
Earlier sketch in CA 101
Young, Andrew 1885-1971 ... CANR-7
Earlier sketch in CA 7-8R
See also CLC 5
Young, Angela
See Yardley, Alice
Young, Anne P(atricia) 1921- ... 65-68
Young, Arthur C(lements) 1923- ... 25-28R
Young, Arthur N(ichols) 1890-1984 ... 11-12R
Obituary ... 113
Young, Bernice Elizabeth 1931- ... 37-40R
Young, Bertram Alfred 1912- ... 105
Young, Billie 1936- ... 53-56
Young, Bob
See Young, James Robert
and Young, Robert W(illiam)
Young, Brittany
See Young, Sandra
Young, Carrie
See Young, Ahdele Carrine
Young, Carter Travis
See Charbonneau, Louis (Henry)
Young, Catherine
See Olds, Helen Diehl
Young, Charles M(atthew) 1951- ... 93-96
Young, Charles R(obert) 1927- ... 15-16R
Young, Chesley Virginia 1919- ... 33-36R
Young, Chic
See Young, Murat Bernard (Chic)
Young, Clarence ... CAP-2
Earlier sketch in CA 19-20
See also SATA 1
Young, Collier 1908(?)-1980 Obituary ... 103
Young, Collier
See Bloch, Robert (Albert)
Young, Dallas M. 1914- ... 19-20R
Young, David C(harles) 1937- ... 41-44R
Young, David P(ollock) 1936- ... CANR-24
Earlier sketches in CA 21-22R, CANR-9
Young, David S(amuel D'arcy) 1946- ... 113
Young, Delbert Alton 1907-1975 ... 105
Young, Dennis R(alph) 1943- Brief entry ... 107
Young, Dick 1918(?)-1987 Obituary ... 123
Young, Donald (Richard) 1933- ... CANR-12
Earlier sketch in CA 15-16R
Young, Donald Ramsey 1898-1977
Obituary ... 69-72
Young, Dorothea Bennett 1924- ... CANR-13
Earlier sketch in CA 13-14R
See also SATA 31
Young, Douglas (Cuthbert Colquhoun)
1913-1973 ... CAP-1
Obituary ... 45-48
Earlier sketch in CA 17-18
Young, Ed 1931- ... SATA-10
Young, Ed (Tse-chun) 1931- Brief entry ... 116
Young, Edgar Berryhill 1908- ... 104
Young, Edith ... 49-52
Young, Edward
See Reinfeld, Fred
Young, Edward J(oseph) 1907-1968 ... CAP-1
Earlier sketch in CA 11-12
Young, (Cecil) Edwyn 1913-1988 Obituary ... 124
Young, Elaine L.
See Schulte, Elaine L(ouise)
Young, Eleanor R. 1918- ... 37-40R
Young, Elisabeth Larsh 1910- ... 81-84
Young, Elizabeth ... 108
Young, Ellin Dodge 1932- ... 106
Young, Everett
See Cosby, Yvonne Shepard
Young, Ezra P(orter) 1902- ... 113
Young, Francis Brett 1884-1954
Brief entry ... 122
Young, Frank Carl 1907- ... CAP-1
Earlier sketch in CA 13-14
Young, Frank Wilbur 1928- Brief entry ... 108
Young, Fred(erick) L(ee) 1922- ... 25-28R
Young, G(eorge) M(alcolm) 1882-1959
Brief entry ... 120
Young, Gary 1951- ... 117
Young, George Berkeley 1913-1988
Obituary ... 124
Young, George F(rederick) W(illiam)
1937- ... 57-60
Young, Gregory G. 1929- Brief entry ... 110
Young, Harold Chester 1932- Brief entry ... 109
Young, Harold H(erbert) 1903- ... CAP-2
Earlier sketch in CA 19-20
Young, Howard Thomas 1926- ... 11-12R
Young, Hugo 1938- ... 25-28R
Young, I(sador) S. 1902- ... 102
Young, Ian (George) 1945- ... CANR-11
Earlier sketch in CA 29-32R
Young, J(ames) Harvey 1915- ... CANR-6
Earlier sketch in CA 2R
Young, J(ohn) Z(achary) 1907- ... CANR-19
Earlier sketch in CA 101
Young, James Allan 1934- ... 116
Young, James D(ean) 1925- Brief entry ... 111
Young, James Douglas 1921- ... 25-28R
Young, James J(oseph) 1940- ... CANR-16
Earlier sketch in CA 93-96
Young, James O(wen) 1943- ... 49-52
Young, James Robert 1921- ... 93-96
Young, James V(an) 1936- ... 69-72
Young, Jan
See Young, Janet Randall
Young, Janet Randall 1919- ... CANR-5
Earlier sketch in CA 5-6R
See also SATA 3
Young, Jessica (Hankinson) Brett
See Brett-Young, Jessica (Hankinson)
Young, Jim 1930- ... 109
Young, Jock 1942- ... 104
Young, John 1920- ... CANR-1
Earlier sketch in CA 45-48
Young, John Orr 1886-1976 Obituary ... 65-68
Young, John Parke 1895- ... 7-8R
Young, John V. 1909- ... 121
Young, John Wray 1907- ... 45-48
Young, Jordan Marten 1920- ... 21-22R
Young, Kenneth 1916-1985 ... CANR-3
Obituary ... 118
Earlier sketch in CA 9-10R
Young, Kenneth T(odd) 1916-1972
Obituary ... 37-40R
Young, Leontine R. 1910- ... CAP-1
Earlier sketch in CA 11-12
Young, Lesley 1949- ... 110
Young, Lois Horton 1911-1981 ... 11-12R
See also SATA 26
Young, Louise B. 1919- ... CANR-10
Earlier sketch in CA 25-28R
Young, Louise Merwin 1903- ... CAP-1
Earlier sketch in CA 11-12
Young, M(erwin) Crawford 1931- ... 15-16R
Young, Mahonri 1911- ... 81-84
Young, Margaret B(uckner) 1922- ... 23-24R
See also SATA 2
Young, Margaret Labash 1926-
Brief entry ... 110
Young, Marguerite ... CAP-1
Earlier sketch in CA 15-16
Young, Marjorie W(illis) ... 85-88
Young, Mary Elizabeth 1929- ... 37-40R
Young, Mary Elizabeth Reardon
1901(?)-1981 Obituary ... 105
Young, Michael (Dunlop) 1915- ... 101
Young, Miriam 1913-1974 ... 37-40R
Obituary ... 53-56
See also SATA 7
Young, Morris N. 1909- ... 33-36R
Young, Murat Bernard (Chic) 1901-1973
Obituary ... 41-44R
Young, Nacella
See Tate, Velma
Young, Neil 1945- ... 110
See also CLC 17
Young, Noel 1922- ... 57-60
Young, Norman J(ames) 1930- ... 77-80
Young, Oran R(eed) 1941- ... 112
Brief entry ... 109
Young, Otis E., Jr. 1925- ... 53-56
Young, Pam 1943- ... 109
Young, (Rodney Lee) Patrick (Jr.) 1937- ... 69-72
See also SATA 22
Young, Paul Thomas 1892-1978 ... CANR-3
Earlier sketch in CA 2R
Young, Pauline Vislick 1896- ... 7-8R
Young, Percy M(arshall) 1912- ... 15-16R
See also SATA 31
Young, Perry Deane 1941- ... 57-60
Young, Peter 1915- ... 13-14R
Young, Peter Alan 1934- ... 107
Young, Philip 1918- ... CANR-6
Earlier sketch in CA 11-12R
Young, Philip
See Steward, Samuel M(orris)
Young, Ralph Aubrey 1902(?)-1980
Obituary ... 97-100
Young, Richard E(merson) 1932- ... 29-32R
Young, Richard Knox 1913- ... 13-14R
Young, Richard Phillip 1940- ... 29-32R
Young, Robert 1944- ... 123
Young, Robert
See Payne, (Pierre Stephen) Robert
Young, Robert Doran 1928- ... CANR-17
Earlier sketch in CA 29-32R
Young, Robert J(ohn) 1942- ... 101
Young, Robert W(illiam) 1916-1969 ... CANR-5
Earlier sketch in CA 5-6R
See also SATA 3
Young, Rose
See Harris, Marion Rose (Young)
Young, Ruth 1884-1983 Obituary ... 111
Young, Sandra 1952- ... 124
Young, Scott A(lexander) 1918- ... CANR-20
Earlier sketches in CA 11-12R, CANR-5
See also SATA 5
Young, Seymour Dilworth 1897- ... CAP-2
Earlier sketch in CA 29-32
Young, Stanley (Preston) 1906-1975
Obituary ... 57-60
Young, Stark 1881-1963 ... 105
Obituary ... 89-92
See also DLB 9
Young, Stephen M(arvin) 1889(?)-1984
Obituary ... 114
Young, Thomas
See Yoseloff, Thomas
Young, Thomas Daniel 1919- ... CANR-14
Earlier sketch in CA 37-40R
Young, Vernon 1912-1986 ... 45-48
Obituary ... 120
Young, Virginia Brady 1921- ... 61-64
Young, Virginia G(arton) 1919- ... 15-16R
Young, Vivien
See Gater, Dilys
Young, Waldemar 1880-1938 ... DLB-26
Young, Warren C(ameron) 1913- ... 13-14R
Young, Warren R(ichard) 1926- ... 21-22R
Young, Wayland 1923- ... 13-14R
Young, Whitney M(oore), Jr. 1921-1971 ... CAP-1
Earlier sketch in CA 13-14
Young, William 1918- ... 45-48
Young, William C(urtis) 1928- ... 45-48
Young, William H(enry) 1912- ... 23-24R
Young, William J. 1938- ... 109
Youngberg, Norma Ione (Rhoads)
1896- ... 11-12R
Youngberg, Ruth Tanis 1915- ... 107

Youngblood, Ronald F. 1931- CANR-14
Earlier sketch in CA 37-40R
Youngdahl, Benjamin E(manuel)
1897-1970 .... CAP-2
Earlier sketch in CA 21-22
Youngdahl, Reuben K(enneth Nathaniel)
1911-1968 ....5-6R
Obituary 103
Younge, Sheila 1945(?)-1977 Obituary 73-76
Younger, Edward Eugene 1909-1979
Obituary 89-92
Younger, Paul 1935- 101
Younger, R(onald) M(ichel) 1917- CANR-10
Earlier sketch in CA 17-18R
Younger, Richard D(avis) 1921- 11-12R
Younghusband, Eileen (Louise)
1902-1981 Obituary 108
Younghusband, Francis (Edward)
1863-1942 Brief entry 113
Youngman, Henny Brief entry 107
Youngquist, Walter 1921- 61-64
Youngren, J(ohn) Alan 1937- 108
Youngs, Betty 1934-1985 117
See also SATA 42
Youngs, Betty F(errell) 1928- 33-36R
Youngs, Frederic A., Jr. 1936- Brief entry .. 112
Youngs, J. William T., Jr. 1941- CANR-10
Earlier sketch in CA 65-68
Youngs, Robert W(ells) 1913- 15-16R
Younie, William John 1932- 21-22R
Younin, Wolf 1908(?)-1984 Obituary 112
Younker, Lucas 1942- 65-68
Yount, John A(lonzo) 1935- CANR-5
Earlier sketch in CA 45-48
Yourcenar, Marguerite 1903-1987 ..... CANR-23
Earlier sketch in CA 69-72
See also CLC 19, 38
Youree, Gary 1931- CANR-2
Earlier sketch in CA 49-52
Yousuf, Ahmed
See Essop, Ahmed
Youtie, Herbert Chayyim 1904-1980
Obituary 97-100
Yowa
See McMurray, Nancy A(rmistead)
Yoxall, Harry W(aldo) 1896-1984 ....13-14R
Obituary 113
Yoxen, Edward (John) 1950- 123
Yu, Anthony C. 1938- Brief entry 110
Yu, Beongcheon 1925- Brief entry 108
Yu, Charles
See Targ, William
Yu, David C. 1918- 37-40R
Yu, Elena S. H. 1947- Brief entry 109
Yu, Frederick T. C. 1921- 11-12R
Yu, George T(zuchiao) 1931- 19-20R
Yu, Pauline (Ruth) 1949- 122
Brief entry 118
Yu, Ying-shih 1930- 25-28R
Yuan, Lei Chen
See De Jaegher, Raymond-Joseph
Yuan, T'ung-li 1895-1965 .... CAP-1
Earlier sketch in CA 9-10
Yudell, Lynn D. 1943- 29-32R
Yudewitz, Hyman 1906- 93-96
Yudkin, John 1910- 13-14R
Yudkin, Leon Israel 1939- CANR-12
Earlier sketch in CA 29-32R
Yudkin, Michael D(avid) 1938- 29-32R
Yudof, Mark G(eorge) 1944- 109
Yu-ho, Tseng
See Ecke, Betty Tseng Yu-ho
Yuill, P. B.
See Williams, Gordon (Maclean)
Yuill, Phyllis Jean (Marquart) 1941- 65-68
Yuill, William Edward 1921- CANR-2
Earlier sketch in CA 3R
Yukawa, Hideki 1907-1981 Obituary 108
Yuki
See Inoue, Yukitoshi
Yuma, Dan
See Dunham, Robert
Yun, Tan
See Lin, Adet J(usu)
Yunck, John A(dam) III 1917- 11-12R
Yungblut, John R(ichard) 1913- 41-44R
Yunkel, Ramar
See Martin, Jose L(uis)
Yurchenco, Henrietta 1916- 37-40R
Yurick, Sol 1925- 15-16R
See also CLC 6
Yurieff, Zoya I(osifovna) 1922- Brief entry .. 109
Yurka, Blanche 1887-1974 ....11-12R
Obituary 120
Yusko, A(aron) A(llen) 1935- 65-68
Yuzyk, Paul 1913- CANR-18
Earlier sketch in CA 101
Yzermans, Vincent Arthur 1925- 15-16R

Z

Zabaneh, Natalia (Shefka) 1946- 105
Zabeeh, Farhana 1919- 41-44R
Zabih, Sepehr 1925- CANR-9
Earlier sketch in CA 23-24R
Zabilka, Gladys M. 1917- 7-8R
Zablocki, Benjamin 1941- 37-40R
Zablocki, Clement J(ohn) 1912-1983
Obituary 111
Zabolotskii, Nikolai Alekseevich 1903-1958
Brief entry 116
Zacek, Jane Shapiro 1938- 109
Zacek, Joseph Frederick 1930- 37-40R
Zach, Cheryl (Byrd) 1947- 124
Zach, Nathan 1930- Brief entry 105
Zacharias, Lee
See Zacharias, Lela Ann
Zacharias, Lela Ann 1944- 85-88
Zacharis, John C. 1936- 73-76
Zachary, Elizabeth 1928- 109
Zachary, Hugh 1928- CANR-13
Earlier sketch in CA 23-24R
Zacher, Christian Keeler 1941- 105
Zacher, Mark W. 1938- 85-88
Zacher, Robert Vincent 1917- 2R
Zack, Arnold M(arshall) 1931- CANR-19
Earlier sketches in CA 11-12R, CANR-3
Zade, Mirzo Tursun
See Tursun-Zade, Mirzo
Zadeh, Norman 1950- 61-64
Zaehner, Robert Charles 1913-1974
Obituary 109
Zaffo, George J. (?)-1984 .... SATA-42
Zaffuto, Anthony A(ngelo) 1926- 101
Zafren, Herbert C(ecil) 1925- 45-48
Zagar, J. Janko 1921- 121
Zagarell, Sandra A(belson) 1943- 118
Zagat, Arthur Leo 1895(?)-1949
Brief entry 110
Zagona, Salvatore Vincent 1920-
Brief entry 108
Zagoren, Ruby 1922-1974 .... CAP-1
Earlier sketch in CA 17-18
Zagoria, Donald S. 1928- CANR-16
Earlier sketch in CA 23-24R
Zagorin, Perez 1920- 53-56
Zagst, Michael (Sidney) 1950- 121
Zaharias, Babe Didrikson
See Zaharias, Mildred Ella Didrikson
Zaharias, Mildred Ella Didrikson
1914(?)-1956 Brief entry 117
Zaharopoulos, George K. 1933- 41-44R
Zahava, Irene 1951- 57-60
Zahl, Paul Arthur 1910-1985 Obituary 117
Zahler, Helene S. 1911-1981 Obituary 104
Zahn, Curtis 1912- CANR-5
Earlier sketch in CA 7-8R
Zahn, Frank 1936- 97-100
Zahn, Gordon C(harles) 1918- 11-12R
Zahn, Muriel 1894- 5-6R
Zahn, Timothy 1951- 123
Zahniser, Marvin R(alph) 1934- 21-22R
Zahorchak, Michael G(eorge) 1929- CANR-15
Earlier sketch in CA 41-44R
Zahorski, Kenneth J. 1939- 123
Zaidenberg, Arthur 1908(?)- 108
See also SATA 34
Zaidi, S(yed) M(ohammad) Hafeez 1929- ..45-48
Zainu'ddin, Ailsa
See Zainu'ddin, Ailsa G(wennyth)
Thomson
Zainu'ddin, Ailsa G(wennyth) Thomson
1927- CANR-12
Earlier sketch in CA 29-32R
Zajonc, Robert Boleslaw 1923- Brief entry .. 106
Zakarian, Richard H(achadoor) 1925- 41-44R
Zakia, Richard D(onald) 1925- CANR-9
Earlier sketch in CA 65-68
Zakon, Alan J. 1935- 17-18R
Zakuta, Leo 1925- 17-18R
Zalamea, Luis 1921- 19-20R
Zalan, Magda 1936- 112
Zalben, Jane Breskin 1950- CANR-4
Earlier sketch in CA 49-52
See also SATA 7
Zald, Mayer N(athan) 1931- CANR-8
Earlier sketch in CA 19-20R
Zaldivar, Fulgencio Batista y
See Batista y Zaldivar, Fulgencio
Zaleski, Eugene 1918- 77-80
Zaleznik, Abraham 1924- 73-76
Zali, Paul M. 1922- Brief entry 110
Zalkind, Sheldon S(tanley) 1922- 65-68
Zall, Paul M. 1922- CANR-20
Earlier sketches in CA 2R, CANR-6
Zaller, Angelika Bita CANR-13
Earlier sketch in CA 77-80
Zaller, Robert 1940- CANR-13
Earlier sketch in CA 77-80
Zallinger, Jean (Day) 1918- SATA-14
Zallinger, Peter Franz 1943- 108
See also SATA 49
Zalon, Jean E(ugenia) 1919- 102
Zaltkovich, Charles T(heodore) 1917- 7-8R
Zaltman, Gerald 1938- CANR-7
Earlier sketch in CA 17-18R
Zalzanick, Sheldon 1928- 77-80
Zamble, Edward 1942- Brief entry 108
Zamiatin, Yevgenii
See Zamyatin, Evgeny Ivanovich
Zamonski, Stanley W. 1919- 11-12R
Zamoyski, Adam (Stefan Jan Maria Sariusz)
1949- 103
Zamoyta, Vincent C. 1921- 23-24R
Zampaglione, Gerardo 1917- CANR-14
Earlier sketch in CA 77-80
Zamyatin, Evgeny Ivanovich 1884-1937
Brief entry 105
See also TCLC 8
Zand, Dale Ezra 1926- 111
Zander, Alvin Frederick 1913- CANR-19
Earlier sketch in CA 2R
Zanderbergen, George
See May, Julian
Zaner, Richard M(orris) 1933- CANR-16
Earlier sketch in CA 29-32R
Zanetti, J(oaquin) Enrique 1885-1974
Obituary 45-48
Zangrando, Robert L. 1932- 25-28R
Zangwill, Israel 1864-1926 Brief entry 109
See also DLB 10
See also TCLC 16
Zangwill, Oliver Louis 1913- 109
Zanjani, Sally Springmeyer 120
Zants, Emily 1937- 37-40R
Zanuck, Daryl F(rancis) 1902-1979
Obituary 93-96
Zappa, Francis Vincent, Jr. 1940- 108
Zappa, Frank
See Zappa, Francis Vincent, Jr.
See also CLC 17
Zappler, Lisbeth 1930- CANR-4
Earlier sketch in CA 49-52
See also SATA 10
Zar, Rose 1923- 117
Zara, Louis 1910- CAP-2
Earlier sketch in CA 13-14
Zarchy, Harry 1912- CANR-2
Earlier sketch in CA 4R
See also SATA 34
Zarcone, Vincent P(eter), Jr. 1937- 61-64
Zarefsky, David (Harris) 1946- Brief entry ... 109
Zaremba, Joseph 1923- Brief entry 112
Zaretsky, Eli 1940- 85-88
Zaring, Jane (Thomas) 1936- 108
See also SATA 40
Zariski, Raphael 1925- 49-52
Zarnecki, George 1915- CANR-10
Earlier sketch in CA 57-60
Zarnecki, Jerzy
See Zarnecki, George
Zarnowitz, Victor 1919- 21-22R
Zarro, Richard A(llen) 1946- 33-36R
Zartman, I(ra) William 1932- CANR-5
Earlier sketch in CA 11-12R
Zaslavsky, Claudia 1917- CANR-1
Earlier sketch in CA 49-52
See also SATA 36
Zasloff, Joseph J(ermiah) 1925-
Brief entry 116
Zaslow, Morris 1918- CANR-24
Earlier sketch in CA 45-48
Zassenhaus, Hiltgunt 1916- 49-52
See also AITN 1
Zastrow, Erika
See Massey, Erika
Zatlin, Phyllis 1938- CANR-15
Earlier sketch in CA 41-44R
Zatlin Boring, Phyllis
See Zatlin, Phyllis
Zatlin-Boring, Phyllis
See Zatlin, Phyllis
Zatuchni, Gerald I. 1935- 37-40R
Zaturenska, Marya 1902-1982 .... CANR-22
Obituary 105
Earlier sketch in CA 13-14R
See also CLC 6, 11
Zauberman, Alfred 1903-1984 Obituary 112
Zavala, Albert 1930- Brief entry 117
Zavala, Iris M(ilagros) 1936- CANR-1
Earlier sketch in CA 45-48
Zavarzadeh, Mas'ud 1938- 106
Zavatsky, Bill
See Zavatsky, William Alexander
Zavatsky, William Alexander 1943- CANR-1
Earlier sketch in CA 49-52
Zavin, Benjamin B. 1920(?)-1981
Obituary 103
Zavin, Theodora 1922- 53-56
Zavrian, Suzanne (Ostro) 1928- 113
Zawadsky, Patience 1927- CANR-24
Earlier sketches in CA 23-24R, CANR-9
Zawadzki, Edward S. 1914-1967 .... CAP-2
Earlier sketch in CA 17-18
Zawodny, J(anusz) K(azimierz) 1921- .. CANR-11
Earlier sketch in CA 15-16R
Zax, Melvin 1928- 37-40R
Zayas-Bazan, Eduardo 1935- 53-56
Zdenek, Marilee 1934- 102
Zea, Leopoldo 1912- CANR-16
Earlier sketch in CA 29-32R
Zebel, Sydney H. 1914- 2R
Zebouni, Selma A(ssir) 1930- 17-18R
Zebrowski, George 1945- 41-44R
See also DLB 8
Zec, Philip 1910(?)-1983 Obituary 110
Zech, Paul 1881-1946 .... DLB-56
Zeck, Gerald Anthony 1939- 114
See also SATA 40
Zeck, Gerry
See Zeck, Gerald Anthony
Zeckendorf, William 1905- 73-76
Zedler, Beatrice H(ope) 1916- 41-44R
Zedler, Empress Young 1908- 41-44R
Zeeveld, W(illiam) Gordon 1902-1975 ....41-44R
Zeff, Stephen A(ddam) 1933- CANR-19
Earlier sketches in CA 11-12R, CANR-3
Zegger, Robert Elie 1932- 41-44R
Zehna, Peter W(illiam) 1925- CANR-1
Earlier sketch in CA 2R
Zehnle, Richard F(rederick) 1933- 29-32R
Zehnpfennig, Gladys Burandt 1910- CANR-5
Earlier sketch in CA 7-8R
Zehring, John William 1947- 117
Zei, Alki 77-80
See also SATA 24
See also CLR 6
Zeidenstein, Harvey 1932- 57-60
Zeidman, Irving 1908- CAP-2
Earlier sketch in CA 21-22
Zeidner, Lisa 1955- 110
Zeiger, Henry A(nthony) 1930- 11-12R
Zeiger, Larry
See King, Larry
Zeigerman, Gerald 1939- 21-22R
Zeigfreid, Karl
See Fanthorpe, R(obert) Lionel
Zeigler, L(uther) Harmon 1936- CANR-10
Earlier sketch in CA 15-16R
Zeilik, Michael 1946- 65-68
Zeisel, Hans 1905- CANR-6
Earlier sketch in CA 2R
Zeit, Calvin
See Barasch, Marc Ian
Zeitlin, Irving M. 1928- 21-22R
Zeitlin, Jonathan (Hart) 1955- 121
Zeitlin, Joseph 1906- 49-52
Zeitlin, Maurice 1935- CANR-10
Earlier sketch in CA 13-14R
Zeitlin, Patty 1936- CANR-12
Earlier sketch in CA 25-28R
Zeitlin, Solomon 1888(?)-1976 77-80
Obituary 69-72
Zeitz, James (Victor) 1940- 110
Zeka, Valentin
See Sokolov, Valentin
Zekman, Pamela (Lois) 1944- 106
Zekowski, Arlene 1922- CANR-1
Earlier sketch in CA 45-48
Zelazny, Roger 1937- 23-24R
See also SATA 39
See also DLB 8
See also CLC 21
Zeldin, Jesse 1923- 49-52
Zeldis, Chayym 1927- CANR-6
Earlier sketch in CA 3R
Zelditch, Morris, Jr. 1928- 53-56
Zeldner, Max 1907- CAP-1
Earlier sketch in CA 13-14
Zeldovich, Ia(kov) B(orisovich) 1914-1987
Obituary 124
Zeleny, Lawrence 1904- 61-64
Zeleny, Leslie D(ay) 1898- 45-48
Zelermyer, William 1914- 2R
Zeligs, Meyer A(aron) 1909-1978 .... CAP-2
Obituary 77-80
Earlier sketch in CA 23-24
Zeligs, Rose 57-60
Zelinka, Sydney 1906(?)-1981 Obituary 102
Zelinsky, Paul O. 1953- 121
See also SATA 33, 49
Zelinsky, Wilbur 1921- 15-16R
Zelk, Zoltan 1906-1981 Obituary 103
Zelko, Harold Philip 1908- CANR-1
Earlier sketch in CA 2R
Zell, Hans M(artin) 1940- 113
Zellan, Audrey Penn
See Penn, Audrey
See also SATA 22
Zeller, Belle 1903- 57-60
Zeller, Frederick A. 1931- 21-22R
Zellerbach, Merla 1930- 3R
Zellers, Parker 1927- 37-40R
Zellmann-Finkbeiner, Peter 1942- 49-52
Zellner, Arnold 1927- 41-44R
Zelman, Aaron S(hepard) 1946- 101
Zelman, Anita 1924- 101
Zelmer, A(dam) C(harles) Lynn 1943- .. CANR-16
Earlier sketch in CA 89-92
Zelomek, A. Wilbert 1900-1980
Obituary 97-100
Zelver, Patricia (Farrell) 1923- 29-32R
Zemach, Harve
See Fischtrom, Harvey
See also SATA 3
Zemach, Kaethe 1958- CANR-8
Earlier sketch in CA 57-60
See also SATA 39, 49
Zemach, Margot 1931- 97-100
See also SATA 21
Zeman, Jarold Knox 1926- 101
Zeman, Zbynek Anthony Bohuslav 1928- ...69-72
Zemansky, Mark W(aldo) 1900-1981
Obituary 105
Zend, Robert 1929- 115
Zender, Karl F(rancis) 1937- 110
Zenger, John Peter 1697-1746 .... DLB-24, 43
Zenkovsky, Serge A. 1907- CANR-2
Earlier sketch in CA 2R
Zens, Patricia Martin 1926-1972 ....7-8R
Obituary 120
See also SATA 50
Zentner, Carola 1927- 65-68
Zentner, Peter 1932- 29-32R
Zepeda, Ofelia 1954- 114
Zephir, Jacques J(oseph) 1925- 45-48
Zepke, Brent Eric 1943- CANR-13
Earlier sketch in CA 69-72
Zepp, Ira G(ilbert), Jr. 1929- Brief entry 114
Zerafa, Judy 1941- 113
Zerbe, Jerome 1904- 17-18R
Zerby, Lewis Kenneth 1916- 49-52
Zerden, Sheldon 1924- CANR-10
Earlier sketch in CA 25-28R
Zerin, Edward 1920- 7-8R
Zerman, Melvyn Bernard 1930- CANR-14
Earlier sketch in CA 77-80
See also SATA 46
Zernov, Nicolas (Michael) 1898-1980 ... CANR-6
Earlier sketch in CA 11-12R
Zerof, Herbert G. 1934- 85-88
Zesmer, David M(ordecai) 1924- 65-68
Zeta
See Cope, (Vincent) Zachary
Zetford, Tully
See Bulmer, (Henry) Kenneth
Zetler, Robert L. 1908- 2R
Zetterling, Mai (Elisabeth) 1925-
Brief entry 111
Zettl, Herbert (Lorenz) 1929- 41-44R
Zettler, Howard G. 1926- Brief entry 113
Zeuner, Frederick E(verard) 1905-1963 ......7-8R
Zevi, Bruno 1918- CANR-18
Earlier sketch in CA 101
Zevin, Ben David 1896(?)-1984 Obituary ... 114
Zevin, Jack 1940- 93-96

Zevin, Robert B(rooke) 1936- 117
Zeydel, Edwin H(ermann) 1893-1973 7-8R
Obituary 103
Zeyher, Lewis R. 1906- 25-28R
Zgusta, Ladislav 1924- 41-44R
Zhdanov, Andrei A(lexandrovich)
1896-1948 Brief entry 117
See also TCLC 18
Zheludkov, Sergei 1909(?)-1984 Obituary 111
Zhivkova, Lyudmila (Todorova) 1942-1981
Obituary 108
Zhukov, Georgi K(onstantinovich)
1896(?)-1974 Obituary 110
Ziadeh, Farhat Jacob 1917- CANR-14
Earlier sketch in CA 25-28R
Ziadeh, Nicola A(bdo) 1907- 29-32R
Ziavras, Charles E.
See Jarvis, Charles E(fthemios)
Zibart, Carl F. 1907- 73-76
Zidek, Anthony 1936- 17-18R
Zidek, Tony
See Zidek, Anthony
Ziedonis, Arvids, Jr. 1931- 57-60
Zieg, Joan (Gallina) 116
Ziegel, Vic 1938(?)- Brief entry 122
Ziegelmueller, George (William) 1930- 45-48
Ziegenhagen, Eduard A(rthur) 1935- 45-48
Zieger, Robert H. 1938- 29-32R
Ziegfeld, Edwin Henry 1905-1987
Obituary 123
Ziegfeld, Richard E(van) 1948- 109
Ziegler, Alan 1947- CANR-3
Earlier sketch in CA 49-52
Ziegler, Arthur P(aul), Jr. 1937- 57-60
Ziegler, Bette 1940- 81-84
Ziegler, Donald J(enks) 1924- 25-28R
Ziegler, Edward K(rusen) 1903- 57-60
Ziegler, Elsie Reif 1910- 3R
Ziegler, Isabelle 1904- 25-28R
Ziegler, Jack (Denmore) 1942- 109
Ziegler, Jean 1934- 97-100
Ziegler, Jesse H(unsberger) 1913- CANR-19
Earlier sketch in CA 25-28R
Ziegler, Philip (Sandeman) 1929- 49-52
Ziegler, Raymond J. 1922- 15-16R
Ziegler, Richard S. 1931- 101
Ziegler, Ronald M(elvin) 1935- 102
Ziegler, (Karl Reinhart Ludwig) Theobald
1846-1918 Brief entry 119
Ziel, Ron 1939- 23-24R
Ziemer, Gregor (Athalwin) 1899-198(?) CAP-1
Earlier sketch in CA 13-14
Ziemer, Paul 1921(?)-1985 Obituary 117
Ziemian, Joseph 1922-1971 65-68
Ziemienski, Dennis (Theodore) 1947- SATA-10
Ziemke, Donald C(harles) 1929- 7-8R
Ziemke, Earl F(rederick) 1922- 37-40R
Zierold, Norman (John) 1927- 19-20R
Zieroth, Dale 1946- 117
See also DLB 60
Ziesler, J(ohn) A(nthony) 1930- CANR-1
Earlier sketch in CA 45-48
Zietlow, E(dward) R. 1932- CANR-7
Earlier sketch in CA 19-20R
Zietlow, Paul Nathan 1935- 93-96
Zif, Jay Jehiel 1936- 37-40R
Ziff, Gil 1938- 106
Ziff, Larzer 1927- CANR-7
Earlier sketch in CA 15-16R
Zigler, Edward F(rank) 1930- CANR-15
Earlier sketch in CA 41-44R
Zigrosser, Carl 1891-1975 Obituary 111
Zijderveld, Anton C(ornelis) 1937- CANR-12
Earlier sketch in CA 29-32R
Zikmund, Barbara Brown 1939- 117
Zikmund, Joseph II 1937- CANR-15
Earlier sketch in CA 65-68
Zilahy, Lajos 1891(?)-1974 Obituary 53-56
Zilbergeld, Bernie 1939- 112
Zilbert, Edward R(udolph) 1925- 118
Zilg, Gerard Colby 1945- 57-60
Ziliox, Marc
See Fichter, George S.
Zillah
See Macdonald, Zillah K(atherine)
Zilmer, Bertram G. 1899(?)-1976
Obituary 65-68
Zilversmit, Arthur 1932- 25-28R
Zim, Herbert S(pencer) 1909- CANR-17
Earlier sketch in CA 15-16R
See also SATA 1, 30
See also SAAS 2
See also CLR 2
Zim, Sonia Bleeker 1909-1971 CANR-3
Obituary 33-36R
Earlier sketch in CA 4R
Ziman, H(erbert) D(avid) 1902-1983
Obituary 110
Ziman, J(ohn) M(ichael) 1925- 25-28R
Zimbardo, Philip G(eorge) 1933- 85-88
Zimbardo, Rose (Abdelnour) 1932- 17-18R
Zimelman, Nathan SATA-37
Zimet, Melvin 1913- 73-76
Zimet, Sara (Florence) Goodman 1929- 25-28R
Zimiles, Martha Rogers 1946- 41-44R
Zimiles, Murray 1941- 41-44R
Zimin, Alexander 1920-1980 Obituary 97-100
Zimmer, A(rno) B. 1945- 105
Zimmer, Anne Y(oung) 1920- 85-88
Zimmer, Basil G(eorge) 1920- 13-14R
Zimmer, Eric 1932- 61-64
Zimmer, Herbert 1924- 2R
Zimmer, Jill Schary
See Robinson, Jill
Zimmer, Maude Files 1905- 25-28R
Zimmer, Paul J. 1934- 21-22R
See also DLB 5
Zimmer, Timothy W. L. 1947- 29-32R
Zimmerli, Walther Theodor 1907-1983
Obituary 111
Zimmerman, Bill 1940- 69-72
Zimmerman, Bill
See Zimmerman, William
Zimmerman, Carle C(lark) 1897-1983 CANR-21
Earlier sketch in CA 25-28R
Zimmerman, Dale A. 1928- 124
Zimmerman, David R(adoff) 1934- 57-60
Zimmerman, Deirdre A. 1959- 120
Zimmerman, Ed 1933(?)-1972 Obituary 37-40R
Zimmerman, Eleanor (Goedeke) 1916- 61-64
Zimmerman, Everett (Lee) 1936- 110
Zimmerman, Franklin B(ershir) 1923- CANR-12
Earlier sketch in CA 13-14R
Zimmerman, Fred W(esley) 1921- CANR-2
Earlier sketch in CA 2R
Zimmerman, Gary 1951- 107
Zimmerman, Gordon G(lenn) 1922- 15-16R
Zimmerman, Irene 1907- 37-40R
Zimmerman, Irla Lee 1923- 57-60
Zimmerman, Isidore 1917(?)-1983
Obituary 111
Zimmerman, Joseph Francis 1928- CANR-17
Earlier sketches in CA 7-8R, CANR-2
Zimmerman, Mary K. 1945- 81-84
Zimmerman, Michael E(dward) 1946- 108
Zimmerman, Naoma 1914- 3R
See also SATA 10
Zimmerman, Paul A(lbert) 1918-
Brief entry 109
Zimmerman, Paul D. 115
Zimmerman, Paul Lionel 1932- CANR-10
Earlier sketch in CA 25-28R
Zimmerman, Robert
See Dylan, Bob
Zimmerman, Toni
See Ortner-Zimmerman, Toni
Zimmerman, Velma E. 1902- 29-32R
Zimmerman, William 1936- 53-56
Zimmerman, William 1940- 69-72
Zimmermann, Arnold E. 1909- 101
Zimmermann, Caroline A(nna) 1944- 102
Zimmermann, Ethel Agnes 1909-1984
Obituary 112
Zimmermann, Jon E(mil) 1933- 101
Zimmeth, Mary
See Schomaker, Mary Zimmeth
Zimnik, Reiner 1930- 77-80
See also SATA 36
See also CLR 3
Zimpel, Lloyd 1929- 37-40R
Zimring, Franklin E(ster) 1942- 93-96
Zimroth, Evan 1943- 93-96
Zimroth, Peter L. 1943- 93-96
Zinbarg, Edward D(onald) 1934- 21-22R
Zinberg, Norman E(arl) 1921- CANR-16
Earlier sketch in CA 85-88
Zindel, Bonnie 1943- 105
See also SATA 34
Zindel, Paul 1936- 73-76
See also SATA 16
See also DLB 7, 52
See also CLC 6, 26
See also CLR 3
Ziner, Feenie
See Ziner, Florence
Ziner, Florence 1921- CANR-1
Earlier sketch in CA 3R
See also SATA 5
Zingara, Professor
See Leeming, Joseph
Zink, David D(aniel) 1927- CANR-3
Earlier sketch in CA 45-48
Zink, Lubor Jan 1920- CANR-9
Earlier sketch in CA 65-68
Zinke, George William 1904- 7-8R
Zinkin, Taya (Nathalie) Ettinger 1918- CANR-2
Earlier sketch in CA 4R
Zinn, Howard 1922- CANR-2
Earlier sketch in CA 2R
Zinner, Paul E(rnest) 1922- 2R
Zinner, Stephen H. 1939- 119
Zinnes, Harriet CANR-21
Earlier sketches in CA 45-48, CANR-1
Zinoviev, Alexander 1922- Brief entry 116
See also CLC 19
Zinsser, William (Knowlton) 1922- CANR-12
Earlier sketch in CA 19-20R
Zintz, Miles V(ernon) 1918- 29-32R
Ziolkowski, Theodore (Joseph) 1932- CANR-12
Earlier sketch in CA 15-16R
Ziomek, Henryk 1922- CANR-1
Earlier sketch in CA 45-48
Zion, Eugene 1913-1975 81-84
Obituary 61-64
See also SATA 18
Zion, Gene
See Zion, Eugene
Zionts, Stanley 1937- 49-52
Zipes, Jack (David) 1937- CANR-9
Earlier sketch in CA 65-68
Zipser, Arthur 1909- 113
Ziring, Lawrence 1928- CANR-13
Earlier sketch in CA 73-76
Zisfein, Melvin Bernard 1926- 108
Zisk, Betty H(ershberger) 1930- 45-48
Ziskind, Sylvia 1906- 29-32R
Zistel, Era CANR-19
Earlier sketch in CA 25-28R
Zito, George V(incent) 1923- 113
Zitta, Victor 1926- 21-22R
Zivkovic, Peter D(ragi) 1929- 53-56
Zjawin, Dorothy 1945- 111
Zmijewsky, Boris 1946- CANR-20
Earlier sketch in CA 69-72
Zneimer, John (Nicolas) 1925- 29-32R
Zobel, Hiller B(ellin) 1932- 23-24R
Zobel, Louise Purwin 1922- 110
Zober, Martin 1918- 37-40R
Zochert, Donald (Paul, Jr.) 1938- 81-84
Zodhiates, Spiros 1922- CANR-10
Earlier sketch in CA 21-22R
Zodikoff, David H(yman) 1933- 37-40R
Zodrow, John 1944- 77-80
Zoellner, Robert 1926- 57-60
Zoffer, Gerald R. 1926(?)-1982 Obituary 107
Zohar, Danah 1944- 124
Brief entry 118
Zohn, Arnold 1924-1985 Obituary 116
Zohn, Harry 1923- CANR-10
Earlier sketch in CA 25-28R
Zoilus
See Lovecraft, H(oward) P(hillips)
Zola, Emile 1840-1902 Brief entry 104
See also TCLC 1, 6, 21
Zola, Irving Kenneth 1935- 107
Zola, Marion (Joy) 1945- 108
Zolar
See King, Bruce
Zolberg, Aristide R(odolphe) 1931- 21-22R
Zolbrod, Leon M(ax) 1930- 57-60
Zolbrod, Paul G(eyer) 1932- CANR-10
Earlier sketch in CA 21-22R
Zolf, Larry 1934- 101
Zoll, Donald Atwell 1927- 5-6R
Zolla, Elemire 1926- CANR-6
Earlier sketch in CA 11-12R
Zollinger, Gulielma 1856-1917 Brief entry 109
See also SATA 27
Zollinger, Norman 1921- 81-84
Zollitsch, Herbert G(eorge) 1916- 13-14R
Zollschan, George K(arl) 1930- 15-16R
Zolotow, Charlotte S. 1915- CANR-18
Earlier sketches in CA 5-6R, CANR-3
See also SATA 1, 35
See also DLB 52
See also CLR 2
Zolotow, Maurice 1913- CANR-1
Earlier sketch in CA 3R
Zolynas, Al(girdas Richard) 1945- 105
Zonia, Dhimitri 1921- SATA-20
Zonik, Eleanor Dorothy 1918- 15-16R
Zonis, Marvin 1936- 37-40R
Zonker, Patricia 85-88
Zook, David H(artzler), Jr. 1930-? 2R
Obituary 103
Zook, Deborah
See Green, Deborah
Zook, Paul D(avid) 1912- 7-8R
Zopf, Paul E(dward), Jr. 1931- 37-40R
Zophy, Jonathan Walter 1945- 104
Zorach, William 1887-1966 CAP-1
Earlier sketch in CA 15-16
Zorn, Robert L. 1938- 115
Zornes, Jeanne Doering 1947- 113
Zornow, William Frank 1920- 41-44R
Zoshchenko, Mikhail (Mikhailovich)
1895-1958 Brief entry 115
See also TCLC 15
Zosky, Brenda 1942- 89-92
Zotos, Stephanos 23-24R
Zsoldos, Laszlo 1925- 37-40R
Zubek, John P(eter) 1925- 37-40R
Zubin, Joseph 1900- 17-18R
Zubly, John Joachim 1724-1781 DLB-31
Zu-Bolton, Ahmos II 1935- DLB-41
Zubrow, Ezra B. W. 1945- CANR-10
Earlier sketch in CA 65-68
Zubrowski, Bernard 1939- 104
See also SATA 35
Zubrzycki, Jerzy (George) 1920- CANR-10
Earlier sketch in CA 21-22R
Zuck, Lowell H(ubert) 1926- 65-68
Zucker, Adolf Eduard 1890-1971 Obituary 116
Zucker, David Hard 1938- 37-40R
Zucker, Dolores Mae Bolton CANR-7
Earlier sketch in CA 17-18R
Zucker, Jack 1935- 29-32R
Zucker, Martin 1937- 112
Zucker, Moses 1902-1987 Obituary 123
Zucker, Norman L(ivingston) 1933- 19-20R
Zucker, Paul 1888-1971 CAP-2
Obituary 29-32R
Earlier sketch in CA 23-24
Zuckerman, Alan S(aul) 1945- CANR-22
Earlier sketch in CA 105
Zuckerman, Arthur J(acob) 1907- 41-44R
Zuckerman, Edward (Ben) 1948- 123
Zuckerman, Michael 1939- 37-40R
Zuckerman, Seth (Abram) 1961- 124
Zuckerman, Solly 1904- 65-68
Zuckerman, Yitzhak 1917-1981 Obituary 108
Zuckermann, George 1916- 53-56
Zuckmayer, Carl 1896-1977 69-72
See also DLB 56
See also CLC 18
Zuelke, Ruth E. 1924- 15-16R
Zuelzer, Wolf(gang) W(illiam) 1909-1987 110
Obituary 122
Zuesse, Evan M. 1940- 105
Zug, Margaret Philbrook 1945(?)-1976 69-72
Zugsmith, Leane 1903-1969 Obituary 115
Zukerman, Eugenia 1944- 110
Zukofsky, Louis 1904-1978 9-10R
Obituary 77-80
See also DLB 5
See also CLC 1, 2, 4, 7, 11, 18
Zulauf, Sander W(illiam) 1946- 101
Zulawski, Marek 1908-1985 Obituary 116
Zulli, Floyd (Jr.) 1922-1980 37-40R
Obituary 108
Zumbo, Jim 1940- 109
Zumwalt, Elmo Russell, Jr. 1920- 85-88
Zumwalt, Eva 1936- CANR-9
Earlier sketch in CA 65-68
Zundel, Veronica (Elsa) 1953- 120
Zunder, William (Limbery) 1938- 117
Zunkel, Charles Edward 1905- 57-60
Zunkel, Cleda 1903- 57-60
Zunser, Jesse 1898-1985 Obituary 118
Zunz, Olivier J. 1946- 110
Zupa, G. Anthony
See Zeck, Gerald Anthony
Zupko, Ronald Edward 1938- CANR-13
Earlier sketch in CA 37-40R
Zupnick, I(rving) L(awrence) 1920- 45-48
Zurcher, Arnold John 1903(?)-1974
Obituary 49-52
Zurcher, Louis A(nthony), Jr. 1936- CANR-15
Earlier sketch in CA 41-44R
Zurhorst, Charles (Stewart, Jr.) 1913- CANR-1
Earlier sketch in CA 45-48
See also SATA 12
Zuriff, G(erald) E(ugene) 1943- 123
zur Muehlen, Hermynia 1883-1951 DLB-56
zur Muhlen, Hermynia
See zur Muehlen, Hermynia
See also DLB 56
Zuromskis, Diane
See Stanley, Diane
Zuromskis, Diane Stanley
See Stanley, Diane
Zusne, Leonard 1924- 81-84
Zuwaylif, Fadil H. 1932- 45-48
Zuwiyya, Jalal (Zakariya) 1932- 77-80
Zwaanstra, Henry 1936- Brief entry 105
Zwar, Desmond L(aurence) G(audin)
1931- 107
Zwarensteyn, Hendrik 1913-1976 7-8R
Obituary 103
Zwart, Pieter (Hendrik) 1938- 53-56
Zweifel, Frances W. 1931- CANR-12
Earlier sketch in CA 73-76
See also SATA 14
Zweig, Arnold 1887-1968 Obituary 115
See also DLB 66
Zweig, Friderike M(aria Burger Winternitz)
1882-1971 Obituary 114
Zweig, Paul 1935-1984 85-88
Obituary 113
See also CLC 34, 42
Zweig, Ronald W. 1949- 124
Zweig, Stefan 1881-1942 Brief entry 112
See also TCLC 17
Zwerdling, Alex 1932- 57-60
Zwerenz, Gerhard 1925- 33-36R
Zwerling, L. Steven 1938- 61-64
Zwibak, Jacques 1902- 77-80
Zwick, Peter Ronald 1942- 116
Zwicky, Fritz 1898-1974 Obituary 49-52
Zwiebach, Burton 1933- 57-60
Zwinger, Ann 1925- CANR-13
Earlier sketch in CA 33-36R
See also SATA 46
Zwirn, Jerrold 1943- 109
Zworykin, Vladimir Kosma 1889-1982
Obituary 107
Zyla, Wolodymyr T(aras) 1919- CANR-2
Earlier sketch in CA 45-48
Zylberberg, Michael 1907-1971 CAP-2
Earlier sketch in CA 29-32
Zylbercweig, Zalman 1894-1972
Obituary 37-40R
Zyskind, Harold 1917- 57-60
Zytaruk, George John 1927- 110
Zytowski, Donald G(lenn) 1929- 29-32R

Contemporary Authors and *Contemporary Authors New Revision Series* Encompass Authors in Every Field—From Established Writers to Individuals Best Known for Their Non-literary Activities:

Novelists

(continued from front endsheets)

Hermann Hesse
Bohumil Hrabel
Aldous Leonard Huxley
LeRoi Jones
Yasunari Kawabata
Yashar Kemal
Thomas Keneally
Jack Kerouac
Jerzy Kosinski
Milan Kundera
Oliver La Farge
Margaret Wemyss Laurence
Doris Lessing
Jack London
Alison Lurie
Norman Mailer
Bernard Malamud
Andre Malraux
Vladimir Maximov
Mary McCarthy
Carson McCullers
N. Scott Momady
Brian Moore
Iris Murdoch
Vladimir Nabokov
Shiva Naipaul
V. S. Naipaul
Anais Nin
Joyce Carol Oates
Flannery O'Connor
Juan Carlos Onetti
Walker Percy
Katherine Anne Porter
Chaim Potok
Marcel Proust
Barbara Pym
Thomas Pynchon
Ayn Rand
Erich Maria Remarque
Jean Rhys
Alain Robbe-Grillet
Philip Roth
Gabrielle Roy
Juan Rulfo
Salman Rushdie
Ernesto Sabato
V. Sackville-West
J. D. Salinger
Irwin Shaw
Naoya Shiga
Mikhail Sholokhov
Claude Simon
Upton Sinclair
Isaac Bashevis Singer
Josef Skvorecky
Aleksandr I. Solzhenitsyn
Muriel Spark
John Steinbeck
William Styron
Jean Toomer
Anne Tyler
John Updike
Mario Vargas Llosa
Gore Vidal
Kurt Vonnegut, Jr.
Alice Walker
Evelyn Waugh
Fay Weldon
Eudora Welty
Elie Wiesel
P. G. Wodehouse
Herman Wouk
Richard Wright
Marguerite Yourcenar
. . . and more

Philosophers

Mortimer J. Adler
Theodor W. Adorno
William Barrett
Ernst Bloch
C. D. Broad
Albert Camus
Etienne Henry Gilson
Martin Heidegger
Sidney Hook
Claude Levi-Strauss
Gyorgy Lucas
Gabriel Honore Marcel
Karl R. Popper
Jean-Paul Sartre
. . . and more

Photographers

Berenice Abbott
Ansel Adams
Antony Armstrong-Jones
Eve Arnold
David Bailey
Margaret Bourke-White
Howard Dearstyn
Alfred Eisenstaedt
Ron Galella
Peter Jenkins
David Hume Kennerly
Francesco Scavullo
. . . and more

Physicians

Virginia Apgar
Christiaan Barnard
Beatrice Bishop Berle
T. Berry Brazelton
Mary S. Calderone
Michael E. DeBakey
Nawal El Saadawi
Henry Jay Heimlich
Milton Helpern
John H. Knowles
Frederick Leboyer
Robert B. Livingston
Elizabeth Miller
Jonathan Miller
William A. Nolen
Ray H. Rosenman
Richard Selzer
Andrew Weil
. . . and more

Playwrights

Marcel Achard
Edward Albee
Jean Anouilh
Samuel Beckett
Brendan Behan
Andre Brink
Abe Burrows
Paddy Chayefsky
Marc Connelly
Noel Coward
Friedrich Duerrenmatt
Christopher Durang
Lonne Elder III
Max Frisch
Athol Fugard
Charles Fuller
Tsegaye Gabre-Medhin
Frank D. Gilroy
John Guare
Wilson John Haire
Lorraine Hansberry
Moss Hart
Vaclav Havel
Lillian Hellman
Beth Henley
William Motler Inge
Eugene Ionesco
George S. Kaufman
Raymond Evenor Lawler
David Mamet
Mark Medoff
Arthur Miller
Jason Miller
Thomas Murphy
Sean O'Casey
Clifford Odets
Harold Pinter
David Rabe
Elmer Rice
Ntozake Shange
Sam Shepard
Neil Simon
Tom Stoppard
John Whiting
Oscar Wilde
Tennessee Williams
. . . and more

Poets

Ai
Anna Akhmatova
Rafael Alberti
Yehuda Amichai
Jean Arp
John Ashbery
W. H. Auden
John Berryman
Elizabeth Bishop
Paul Blackburn
Robert Bly
Gwendolyn Brooks
Paul Celan
Rene Char
John Ciardi
Cid Corman
e.e. cummings
James Dickey
Diane di Prima
Hilda Doolittle
Alan Dugan
Henry L. Dumas
Robert Duncan
Guenter Eich
T. S. Eliot
Odysseus Elytis
Hans Magnus Enzensberger
Lawrence Ferlinghetti
Carolyn Forche
Robert Frost
Allen Ginsberg
Nikki Giovanni
Louise Gluck
Robert Graves
Seamus Heaney
Ralph Hodgson
David Holbrook
Langston Hughes
Ted Hughes
Gyula Illyes
Robinson Jeffers
Galway Kinnell
Thomas Kinsella
Carolyn Kizer
Maxine Kumin
Stanley Kunitz
Philip Lamantia
Philip Larkin
Denise Levertov
Philip Levine
Audre Lorde
Robert Lowell
Hugh MacDiarmid
Archibald MacLeish
Louis MacNeice
Rod McKuen
Samuel Menashe
W. S. Merwin
Czeslaw Milosz
Marco Antonio Montes De Oca
Marianne Moore
Pablo Neruda
Christopher Okigbo
Nicanor Parra

Poets
(continued)

Octavio Paz
Lucio Piccolo
Sylvia Plath
Ezra Pound
Pierre Reverdy
Kenneth Rexroth
Adrienne Rich
Theodore Roethke
Muriel Rukeyser
Carl Sandburg
Delmore Schwartz
Giorgos Stylianou Seferiades
Anne Sexton
Dame Edith Sitwell
Sydney Goodsir Smith
Gary Snyder
Stephen Spender
Rabindranath Tagore
Dylan Thomas
Mona Van Duyn
Diane Wakoski
Derek Walcott
Robert Penn Warren
Richard Wilbur
William Carlos Williams
Yevgeny Yevtushenko
. . . and more

Political and Social Activists

Jane Alpert
Daniel Berrigan
Philip Berrigan
Romulo Betancourt
Stokely Carmichael
Eldridge Cleaver
William Sloan Coffin
Angela Davis
Vine Deloria, Jr.
Bernadette Devlin
W. E. B. DuBois
Dick Gregory
Thomas E. Hayden
Julius W. Hobson
Abbie Hoffman
Martin Luther King, Jr.
Adam Clayton Powell, Jr.
Charles Alan Reich
Jerry Rubin
Bobby Seale
Roy Wilkins
. . . and more

Politicians and World Leaders

David Ben-Gurion
Willy Brandt
Zbigniew K. Brzezinski
Jimmy Carter
Winston Churchill
Anthony Eden
Millicent Hammond Fenwick
Gerald R. Ford
Dag Hammarskjoeld
Jack Kemp
Edward Moore Kennedy
Ruhollah Khomeini
Nikita Sergeyevich Khrushchev
Henry A. Kissinger
Edward I. Koch
Mao Tse-tung
George S. McGovern
Golda Meir
Jawaharlal Nehru
Richard M. Nixon
Shimon Peres
Ronald Reagan
Anwar Sadat
Margaret Chase Smith
Strom Thurmond
Kurt Waldheim
Harold Wilson
. . . and more

Print Journalists

Jack Anderson
Russell Baker
Carl Bernstein
Jimmy Breslin
William F. Buckley, Jr.
Herb Caen
Maxine Cheshire
Oriana Fallaci
Sheilah Graham
Bob Greene
Seymour M. Hersh
Haynes Bonner Johnson
Anthony Lewis
A. J. Liebling
Walter Lippmann
Sylvia F. Porter
Mike Royko
William Safire
Susan Sheehan
Hedrick Smith
George Will
Gary Wills
Bob Woodward
. . . and more

Psychologists

Ernest Becker
Bruno Bettelheim
Joyce Brothers
Erik H. Erikson
Anna Freud
Erich Fromm
Howard E. Gruber
Joan Halifax
Thomas A. Harris
Arthur Janov
Carl Jung
Irene Chamie Kassorla
R. D. Laing
Timothy Leary
John E. Mack
Abraham H. Maslow
Rollo May
Stanley Milgram
Fritz Perls
Jean Piaget
Theodore Isaac Rubin
Lee Salk
Anne Seifert
June Singer
B. F. Skinner
. . . and more

Publishers

Sylvia Beach
William Maxwell Aitken Beaverbrook
Barry Bingham, Jr.
Hedley Donovan
Robert Giroux
Katharine Graham
Richard L. Grossman
William Jovanovich
Howard Kaminsky
Stefan Kanfer
Alfred A. Knopf
James Laughlin
Joseph W. Lippincott
William Loeb
Henry R. Luce
Scott Meredith
Henry Regnery
Barney Rosset
Maisie Ward
Helen Wolff
. . . and more

Radio Personalities

Bob Edwards
Garrison Keillor
Larry King
Gary Owens
Susan Stamberg
Studs Terkel
Lowell Thomas
. . . and more

Religious Figures

William Barclay
Harvey Cox
Henry Dumery
Mircea Eliade
Jerry Falwell
Billy Graham
Andrew M. Greeley
Pope John Paul I
Hans Kueng
Harold S. Kushner
Bernard J. F. Lonergan
Jacques Maritain
Malcolm Muggeridge
William J. Murray III
Reinhold Niebuhr
Norman Vincent Peale
Karl Rahner
Oral Roberts
Robert Schuller
Fulton J. Sheen
Lawrence Joseph Shehan
Ruth Carter Stapleton
Paul Tillich
. . . and more

Romance and Gothic Writers

Iris Bancroft
Barbara Cartland
Barbara P. Conklin
Janet Dailey
Daphne du Maurier
Anne Eliot
Anne Hampson
Constance Heaven
Georgette Heyer
Victoria Holt
Fannie Hurst
Johanna Lindsey
Norah Lofts
Laurie McBain
Natasha Peters
Paula Schwartz
Kathleen Winsor
Kathleen E. Woodiwiss
. . . and more

Scholars

Hannah Arendt
Jacob Bronowski
Norman O. Brown
Michel Foucault
Ivan Illich
R. W. B. Lewis
Lewis Mumford
Robert A. Nisbet
Susan Sontag
. . . and more

Science Fiction Writers

Poul Anderson
Isaac Asimov
Alfred Bester
James Blish
Ben Bova
Ray Bradbury
C. J. Cherryh
Arthur C. Clarke
Philip K. Dick
Gordon R. Dickson
Harlan Ellison
Joe Haldeman
Robert A. Heinlein
Frank Herbert
Ursula K. Le Guin
Fritz Leiber
Stanislaw Lem
Frank Belknap Long
Anne McCaffrey
Vonda N. McIntyre
Patricia A. McKillip
Michael Moorcock
C. L. Moore
Larry Niven
Andre Norton
Frederik Pohl
Jerry Pournelle
Joanna Russ
Robert Silverberg
Theodore Hamilton Sturgeon